THE ENCYCLOPEDIA OF NEW ENGLAND

THE ENCYCLOPEDIA OF

New England

The Culture and History of an American Region

Edited by Burt Feintuch and David H. Watters

Foreword by Donald Hall

A project of the Center for the Humanities at the University of New Hampshire

YALE UNIVERSITY PRESS / NEW HAVEN & LONDON

Frontispiece: Fishermen, Gloucester, Mass., 1987

Map on page xxiv by Deborah Reade.

Set in Adobe Caslon type by The Composing Room of Michigan, Inc. Printed in the United States of America by R. R. Donnelley and Sons.

Library of Congress Cataloging-in-Publication Data
The encyclopedia of New England / edited by Burt Feintuch and David H. Watters ; foreword by Donald Hall.
p. cm.
"A project of the Center for the Humanities at the University of New Hampshire."
Includes bibliographical references and index.
ISBN 0-300-10027-2 (alk. paper)
1. New England—Civilization—Encyclopedias. 2. New England—History—Encyclopedias. 3. New England—Encyclopedias. I. Feintuch, Burt, 1949– . II. Watters, David H. III. University of New Hampshire. Center for the Humanities.
F4.E53 2005
974′.003—dc22   2005010353

A catalogue record for this book is available from the British Library.

10 9 8 7 6 5 4 3 2 1

Major Support for *The Encyclopedia of New England* was provided by

The National Endowment for the Humanities
The University of New Hampshire Center for the Humanities:
    The Benjamin and Zelma Dorson Endowment for the Humanities
    The James H. Hayes and Claire Short Hayes Chair in the Humanities
The University of New Hampshire Parents Association
Office of the President, University of New Hampshire
Office of the Provost and Vice President for Academic Affairs, University of New
    Hampshire
Vice President for Research, Discretionary Research Fund, University of New
    Hampshire
The University of New Hampshire Foundation
The College of Liberal Arts, University of New Hampshire
Barbara and Felix McGuigan
Rouger Bougie
United Technologies
Neil and Winifred Cates
Caroline Hicks
Nancy Weil

Additional support was provided by
The Boston Globe
Salt Institute for Documentary Studies
Osher Map Library and Smith Center for Cartographic Education, University of
    Southern Maine

SECTION EDITORS AND CONSULTING EDITORS

Agriculture
Section editor: J. Ritchie Garrison, University of Delaware
Consulting editor: Hal S. Barron, Harvey Mudd College

Architecture
Section editor: Keith N. Morgan, Boston University
Consulting editor: Richard M. Candee, Boston University

Art
Section editor: Donna M. Cassidy, University of Southern Maine

Cities and Suburbs
Section editor: Robert L. Macieski, University of New Hampshire
Consulting editor: Bruce M. Stave, University of Connecticut

Education
Section editor: Joyce Antler, Brandeis University

Ethnic and Racial Identity
Section editors: Marilyn Halter, Boston University, with Robert L. Hall, Northeastern University
Consulting editors: Elliott R. Barkan, California State University, San Bernardino; Joanne Pope Melish, University of Kentucky; and William D. Piersen, Fisk University*

Folklife
Section editors: Horace P. Beck, Middlebury College,* and Jane C. Beck, Vermont Folklife Center
Consulting editor: Michael Hoberman, Fitchburg State College

Gender
Section editor: Barbara A. White, University of New Hampshire**

Geography and Environment
Section editor (Geography): Victor A. Konrad, Carleton University
Section editor (Environment): Theodore L. Steinberg, Case Western Reserve University
Consulting editor (Environment): John E. Carroll, University of New Hampshire

History
Section editor: Charles E. Clark, University of New Hampshire

Images and Ideas
Section editor: David H. Watters, University of New Hampshire

Industry, Technology, and Labor
Section editor: Gary Kulik, Winterthur Museum, Garden and Library

Law
Section editor: Alfred L. Brophy, University of Alabama School of Law
Consulting editors: Katherine Hermes, Central Connecticut State University; Alexandra Maravel, Central Connecticut State University; and James Walsh, Central Connecticut State University

Literature
Section editors: Paul Lauter, Trinity College, and Sandra A. Zagarell, Oberlin College
Consulting editor: David H. Watters, University of New Hampshire

Maritime New England
Section editor: W. Jeffrey Bolster, University of New Hampshire

Media
Section editor: Susan Smulyan, Brown University
Consulting editor: Mark Herlihy, Endicott College

Music and the Performing Arts
Section editor: Barbara L. Tischler, Horace Mann School

Politics
Section editor: Maureen F. Moakley, University of Rhode Island
Consulting editor: William E. Hudson, Providence College

Religion
Section editor: Louise A. Breen, Kansas State University
Consulting editor: Elizabeth C. Nordbeck, Andover Newton Theological School

Science and Medicine
Section editor (Science): Russell M. Lawson, Bacone College
Section editor (Medicine): Richard A. Meckel, Brown University

Sports and Recreation
Section editor: Warren Goldstein, University of Hartford

Tourism
Section editor: Dona Brown, University of Vermont

*deceased
**retired

PROJECT STAFF

For Hannah and Sophie, my mother, Janice, and to the memory of my father, Stanley Feintuch, none of whom came over on the *Mayflower*—BF

For Jan and Harper, my mother, Helen H. Bennett, and my father, Franklin B. Watters—DHW

CONTENTS

For 30 years, I have lived in the New Hampshire house, white clapboard and green shutters, where my grandmother was born in 1878, my mother in 1903. Great-grandparents had bought the farmhouse in 1865. By adding rooms for their numerous children, they turned it into the familiar New England extended farm. The original Cape had been built on the Grafton Turnpike, which became New Hampshire Highway Number Four and devolved into U.S. Route 4. Shortly after I moved in, I had the old chimneys replaced—they were pretty well burned out—and found on a brick from the eldest chimney the date of its fabrication: 1803. I keep this brick, as my ancestors kept everything that ever entered this house. In the attic, or in an unfinished loft the family called the Back Chamber, there remain dozens of broken rockers and knocked-down beds, highchairs, oil lamps, chamber pots, pretty boxes, tools, catalogues, postcards, toys, sofas, butter churns, yellow newspapers, lasts, spinning wheels for wool and flax, books, rusty stoves, cranks for machines of inscrutable purpose, broken dolls and dolls' furniture, bundles of letters, and chests of dead peoples' clothing. The house is an encyclopedia of New England. Only in the rural South, and in rural New England, do American houses willfully contain the history of a family.

Most of my life I have lived in various New Englands. I grew up in suburban Connecticut, a suburb of New Haven called Hamden, an area called Spring Glen where six-room houses squared out the tidy blocks. The homes looked alike; fathers drove the same cars; boys walked to Spring Glen School wearing the corduroy knickers that their mothers had bought at Malley's and Shartenberg's. There were other centuries in the neighborhood, but we paid little attention to them. Just down the road was the New Haven Reservoir that my great-grandfather Hall had worked to construct. A day laborer, one noon in 1861 he walked off his job into the city to enlist for a year in the Civil War. (After his 12 months, he returned and was drafted and hired a substitute.) Not far from the reservoir were the remains of Eli Whitney's factory, where he attempted the mass-production of firearms in 1798.

In the summer, taking the train, I left the middle-middle-class precinct of Spring Glen to visit this farm, where there were no cars or tractors or modern conveniences like money or electric iceboxes. For refrigeration, my mother's father stored the summer's ice under sawdust beside the cow barn, great transparent oblongs that he had sawed from Eagle Pond in February. At the Boston and Maine depot, my grandfather waited with Riley the horse, who pulled a buggy that bumped us a mile to the house. Weekday summer mornings Riley hauled the mowing machine, afternoons the rake and a hayrack, as my grandfather and I collaborated to gather hay for the winter cattle, sheep, and horse. There were no blocks here—only old farmhouses needing paint, cellar holes where houses had fallen in, and the shacks of the shack people. Of course I preferred the domain of want to schooltime's suburb. A disappearing land and culture became the garden of poetry.

My New England altered to Harvard, to Cambridge and Boston—urban and academic and fierce, dominated by wealth, class, and intelligence. After that I flitted about, as Americans are supposed to do: two years at Oxford, a year at Stanford, back to Harvard on a fellowship. Stanford was the farthest from New Hampshire; England was closer because I lived in the daily presence of history layered in the earth, solid in architecture. When I taught in Michigan for a decade and a half, its environment felt as far from New England as California's. Michigan's past was Henry Ford and the battle of the overpass, only 20 years ago. Ann Arbor was lively, gregarious, and agreeable. When I lived there I accepted its assumptions; I did not look wistfully eastward. But the soil was thin: not enough corpses. When I returned, I lived fully in New England as if for the first time and cherished the qualities and sensibilities that I had acquired without acknowledgment.

The difference in this sensibility is historical. In New England there are malls and franchise highways and tracts and office highrises and Wal-Marts and cloverleaves and condos that could be lifted intact and translated to California or Texas or Indiana without seeming out of place. Yet within miles of these monuments of the moment we find an old barn still standing incongruous in the city, or a mummified granite Victorian edifice still in municipal use, or a patch of stone wall that embodies the energy, hope, and fatigue of 18th-century farmers clearing their land, avid for the liberty of the one-family farm. Or we find a country town complete with village green, white wooden church, and Civil War monument—a town that rich mill owners and retired executives have populated and preserved. History is the New England earth. It is a layered history, not so many levels as Troy but present enough to keep us aware that we are not the first inhabitants here, that we come, we go, and others will follow us. An ox track becomes U.S. Route 4. Canals become straight and weedy streams interrupted by ruined locks. Railroad lines become paths for skiing or biking or hiking or snowmachines. A few remain railway lines. A track not far from my house runs one passenger train a day, each way, and you can travel north from D.C. to Pennsylvania Station to Hartford to Brattleboro to my depot in Claremont; or north from Claremont to White River Junction to Montreal. Even some rituals persist. In country towns, a few elementary schools still hold Prize Speaking Day, when pupils recite "Little Boy Blue" and the Gettysburg Address.

In my neighborhood there are families bearing names familiar from the lists of revolutionary and Civil War dead. There are also names that recall the migrations—descendents of Canadian French who came to chop trees, Italians who labored in the quarries, Poles who worked in the mills. History is present in newcomers from Vietnam and Cambodia. I met my first Kurd last year in Boston.

It seems only half a life to live without connection to the past. When we visit England there are Roman roads and the ruins of villas and fortifications. Italy and Greece take us further and more grandly back, Mesopotamia, India, and China even further. New England is to the rest of the United States what Europe is to New England. For me, as I push toward 80, there is comfort in these connections. Through literature and thought, through Egyptian pyramid and Greek Parthenon, we find links to our ancestors who imagined these monuments or—most of our predecessors—slaved to build them. Perhaps the most intimate connections are more domestic than monumental: the wooden bowl, the ornamental bead, the rusted apple peeler, the glass bracelet that a Roman infant wore. In New England the fragments of centuries neatly stitch us together, not so many years as Italy's, not so few as Ann Arbor's. New England is empty mills, new inventions, wooden scythes, a Mother Hubbard wrapped in paper and stored in a chest, a snowmachine, biotechnology, and contrails from Logan and Pease Air Force Base streaking the blue air above the cellar hole of a farmer who came north after the Revolution to build his land.

INTRODUCTION

From the earliest days of European settlement, New England has claimed a
central role in American culture. From poetry to politics, industry to medicine, architecture to education, New England has long seemed a primary
source of American civic, literary, and religious culture and values. At a time of competing claims from Americans of other regions, the novelist and historian Bernard
DeVoto described New England as "something fixed and permanent in the flux of
change and drift." It is, he claimed, "the first old civilization, the first permanent civilization in America." The perception that American history began in New England
is pervasive, enduring, and in many ways inaccurate, but the region has capitalized
on that perception for a long time. If many Americans consider that the signing of
the Declaration of Independence signaled the birth of the nation, even more of us
imagine that the Pilgrims' landing at Plymouth was the nation's moment of conception. The idealized image of the New England village, complete with white steepled
church on the green and surrounded by colonial houses, has become a familiar
American icon, representing American community, domesticity, faith, and individualism.

Much of this sense of New England's centrality in American culture is, at the
least, open to reinterpretation. Contemporary scholars are reconsidering what was
once considered a given in studies of history, culture, and place, while globalization is
forcing us to reinterpret relations among people, places, and institutions. But New
Englanders have long asserted their claim to centrality, a claim that is at the core of a
regional identity developed over four centuries. And New England's centrality persists as a primary American idea, even though many would argue that the region's influence was never as great as was claimed and that, furthermore, what influence it did
have ebbed long ago.

Although cultural boundaries between New England and the nation have sometimes been hard to define, its geographical and political boundaries are more clearly
fixed than those of any other American region. Connecticut, Massachusetts, Rhode
Island, New Hampshire, Vermont, and Maine: New England comprises six states in
the northeasternmost portion of the United States. The name itself is considerably
older than the nation. Arriving at a place that had been populated for approximately
11,000 years by diverse peoples, Captain John Smith named it New England in 1614.
Since that time a host of familiar icons—Yankees, Boston Brahmins, brick mill
complexes, Winslow Homer seascapes, L. L. Bean, the Kennedy family, Harvard,
Yale—have joined with New England's geography to offer a profound sense of regional identity.

Of course, the South and the West are also considered durable, recognizable, and culturally resonant American regions. But unlike New England, the South and the West are often regarded as distinct from the nation as an entity. Literary critics, often Harvard educated or employed, tend to describe early southern and western authors as regional writers, while early New England writers, such as Nathaniel Hawthorne and Emily Dickinson, are identified as the creators of America's national literature. The "otherness" often associated with the South may explain its long tradition of regionalization. But until recently much of the huge and varied body of research chronicling individual aspects of New England ignored New England's regional distinctiveness.

The tension between New England as metaphor for the nation and New England as a particular place is further complicated by history and demographics. The general narrative of New England's history begins with discovery and progress and goes on to chronicle the development of patterns of settlement, governance, religion, literary creativity, industrialization, and commerce that influenced the nation. In most accounts, though, the story begins late, with the arrival of the English Separatists at Plymouth, and ends prematurely, with images of abandoned farms and industrial decline and decay. Much of the scholarship and literature of New England embodies one or the other of these two models: New England as the inspiration for a national civic, literary, and religious culture or, more recently, New England as the ruined empire: bleak, cold, decayed, and dispirited. In "The Oven Bird," Robert Frost asks, "What to make of a diminished thing?" and much of the scholarship on New England stops at the midpoint of the 20th century.

This familiar idea of New England generally ignores the many different voices that have contributed to the region's development from the beginning. The idea that the stereotypical New England settlement contained the seed of a great nation acknowledges neither the degree to which Indian populations had already formed the land to their own purposes nor the degree to which they contributed to the infinitely nuanced history of cross-cultural assimilation. Neither does the essentialist idea of New England as the home of the "Yankee" recognize the region's broader cultural diversity. By 1830 migration had dramatically changed New England's population, and today fewer than 20 percent of New Englanders claim British ancestry. Ethnic communities ranging from Haitians to Soviet Jews, newly recovered histories of African Americans, efforts at Franco-American cultural renewal, restoration of historic synagogues, the establishment of Native American reservations and casinos, the efflorescence of Irish pubs, and the growth of the second-largest Cambodian community in the United States all testify to New England's complex cultural fabric. As a consequence, examining New England requires a pluralist vision.

One of the most intriguing qualities of New England, then, is that it has long harbored a fundamental contradiction. In popular consciousness, New England receives disproportionate credit for the "national culture" while simultaneously standing on its own as one of America's most distinctive regions. It is both a prototypically American place and a unique place within America. Contemporary scholarship demands that we reevaluate New England's claims to be either central or distinctive. But even today the idea that New England is somehow unique remains.

The relation between the perennial idea of New England's fixed regional identity and the fact that life in the six states is constantly changing motivated us to create *The Encyclopedia of New England*. The abiding idea of New England is powerful, we believe, thanks to the region's ability to absorb change and refashion itself, even as it maintains a sense of continuity and historical significance through reliance upon familiar, resilient symbols. We may live in an increasingly globalized world, but for many people place is a significant component of identity. Along with exploring and documenting New England's well-known symbols—from Robert Frost to lobsters—the *Encyclopedia* features articles on recently recovered aspects of cultural history, such as the African American mariner population. Similarly, it explores emerging cultural forms and practices, as exemplified in changing ways of doing business, from tourism to biotechnology to tribal casinos.

The Encyclopedia of New England takes today's New England as its primary subject; it does not focus comprehensively on history, although New England's deep historical tradition and remarkably strong preservationist ethos are discussed. Nor is it a gazetteer, filled with the latest statistics, although these appear in various entries. We began with the goal of understanding lived realities in this distinctive place, viewing the region as the product of social, economic, and historic interactions among diverse people, communities, and institutions, not as a single, easily characterized place.

Culture is the underlying order of social life. It is the way people make useful sense of their world. *The Encyclopedia of New England* attempts to examine what is meaningful, distinctive, or characteristic about life in this region, recognizing that culture maintains significant continuities and precedents while at the same time constantly changing. What strikes us as we think about New England is that the idea of "New England" is powerful enough to have endured vast transformations. Echoes of the past are strong in New England, so though the *Encyclopedia* features many entries on historical subjects, these deal with topics that are significant in present-day life. At the same time, we emphasize that new social formations appear, thrive, and re-create themselves constantly. For that reason, the *Encyclopedia* addresses many features of contemporary life in New England that at first glance may seem surprising: the region with the second most densely populated state in the union has areas with fewer people per square mile than Utah; the land of the Pilgrim Fathers is now predominantly Catholic; its inhabitants have not been primarily of English descent since the Civil War. Descendents of the original Pequot inhabitants now run the largest casino in the country, and Ella Grasso, Malcolm X, and John Preston, author of *Winter's Light: Reflections of a Yankee Queer,* have all called New England home.

In the *Encyclopedia* we distinguish between the idea and the realities of the region, examining how the two contribute to the state of mind that is regional identity. We depict today's New England as lived experience, historically rooted. Thus we seek to convey both the common ground and the local variations of a regional identity shared by citizens from Calais, Maine, to Boston's Chinatown, from the Northeast Kingdom to "Cheever country," from Harvard Square to Federal Hill to the White Mountains. Region, we maintain, is a state of mind, not simply a geographical formation or a historical fact.

But if this is true, we must go beyond the concrete in our examination of New England, linking images and ideas of the region to the "things" of life here. We not only consider each subject as a symbol of the region or in relation to common regional images and ideas, we also examine prevailing or influential images and ideas of New England as a whole. And because change, like New England's weather, is a constant factor, we consider transformations of the subjects—and of the region itself—over time. We want the *Encyclopedia* to tell the stories of all the people who live in New England. New arrivals and oldest inhabitants should find themselves in this book.

The Encyclopedia of New England is thus the first comprehensive reference work of its kind. Its hundreds of thematically organized entries were written by academics, journalists, independent scholars, and experts based in museums and other institutions. Each is a specialist, and in many cases the entries represent new scholarship, particularly because we encouraged authors to write about their subject as it exists in the region's contemporary life.

Place matters. Region is one way people ground themselves, relate to others, and, ideally, develop an ethic of stewardship for the things they care about. For all its variety, New England has coherence as well, in its history, in its political boundaries, in its images and symbols. *The Encyclopedia of New England* first and foremost identifies the key elements of this singular place. At the same time, in an era when some cite the speed at which information and capital fly around the globe barely tethered to anything of substance to argue that regional identity has no significance, we hope that *The Encyclopedia of New England* will provide ample evidence to the contrary.

We had two goals when we created *The Encyclopedia of New England*. The first, consonant with any reference work, was that readers would find it convenient to locate the information they seek. The second, perhaps less common among reference works, was that readers would be able to explore broad subjects by reading entries grouped topically. We have therefore organized the book thematically in 22 sections, ranging from Agriculture to Tourism. Each section has an introduction that discusses the topic from precolonial or (where appropriate) colonial times to the present. Some sections also contain shorter overviews, which focus in greater depth on particular periods that are significant in the history of the subject. In the Industry, Technology, and Labor section, for example, overview essays cover the Industrial Revolution, New England's industrial decline, and the post-industrial New England of today. Following the introduction and overview essays, entries covering various aspects of the subject (for example, specific industries) appear in alphabetical order. A table of contents at the beginning of each section lists the entries in the section and provides cross references to related articles elsewhere in the volume. Thus, in the Industry section, readers will be directed to the Maritime New England section for fishing, shipbuilding, and the slave trade; to the Images and Ideas section for an entry on candy that includes PEZ, NECCO, and Peter Paul Candy; and to the Gender, Media, Music and the Performing Arts, and Science and Medicine sections for various aspects of the publishing industry.

Throughout the development process, the most difficult decisions involved where to place entries within the *Encyclopedia*. Should Father Robert F. Drinan, a Jesuit priest, a law professor, a former law-school dean, and a former U.S. congressman, appear in the Religion, the Law, the Education, or the Politics section? In some cases, general principles applied: politicians who were living at the time the *Encyclopedia* went to press appear in Politics; others whose significance is more historical may be located in the History section. As polymaths, Father Drinan and Charles Eliot Norton (president of Harvard, historian, and belletrist) were placed in the Images and Ideas section, in testimony to the range of their achievements. Some subjects for which no separate section exists fall in different sections according to emphasis: food crops such as blueberries and maple syrup appear in Agriculture, whereas food traditions such as those surrounding clambakes and apples, cider, and applejack are in Folklife, and regional foods such as tollhouse cookies, hermits, and seafood appear in Images and Ideas.

In other instances, we made judgments on the basis of the subject's enduring cultural significance: Jonathan Edwards was a fine literary stylist, but most would agree that his primary significance today lies in his role in the transformation of religion in New England, and he appears in the Religion section. Cotton Mather, on the other hand, though an important religious figure, is studied more today as a literary figure, and he appears in Literature. (Like his father, Increase, and other members of his family, Mather was prominent in a number of realms, so he can also be found in the History section in an entry on the Mather family.)

In a book of this scope, it was impossible to give separate entries to every significant person, event, or location, and many important figures and events are discussed in the contexts of broader issues. Thus, readers looking for William Lloyd Garrison will find him discussed in a number of entries including those on abolition, African American press, Boston's Freedom Trail, and the sculptor Edmonia Lewis, of whom he was a patron. The comprehensive index will locate not only persons, places, or events that are mentioned only once, such as Robert McCloskey, who is discussed in the entry on children's literature, but also those that appear many times, for instance Lowell, Mass., which is significant in a number of realms—early industrialization, labor relations, ethnic diversity—and is therefore discussed in a number of entries, as well as in a separate entry on the city.

Similar problems confronted us when choosing where to place the illustrations: should John Singleton Copley's famous portrait of the patriot and silversmith Paul Revere, for example, be used to illustrate the entry on Copley (Art), Revere (History), or silver (Industry, Technology, and Labor)? We chose to place it with the Copley entry. Readers wishing to find an illustration of a particular subject should consult the index, where illustration pages are given in italic type.

This encyclopedia of the region is intended to illuminate everyday life in today's New England. Subjects were deemed appropriate for inclusion when they either constituted a distinctive component of regional culture or were characteristic of the ways of life that constitute the region. In a region with such a powerful historical consciousness, we were challenged to evaluate which historical topics merited inclusion; our working principle throughout was to include subjects that remain significant in the contemporary culture of the region. Readers will therefore find information on presettlement Indian cultures as well as on contemporary cultural issues in those communities. But though the book ranges from before European contact to the early 21st century, the first principle has been to present information on the lived experience of the region.

Most entries end with suggestions for further reading. These are not intended to be comprehensive. Instead, our goal is to direct readers to the most useful and accessible sources of additional information, usually secondary sources rather than primary documents. Thus the *Encyclopedia* invites further exploration, leading outward from its entries to many other sources. We hope that readers will enjoy this book in many ways: as a reference to answer questions on a variety of topics; as a source of multifaceted information on individual subjects; and as a reader in which browsers and scholars alike can immerse themselves in a single thematic section or a collection of sections as they experience the richness and complexity that make up New England.

ACKNOWLEDGMENTS

We would especially like to thank two academic administrators at the University of New Hampshire who were wonderfully supportive of *The Encyclopedia of New England*: Walter Eggers, former provost and vice president for academic affairs, whose enthusiasm, leadership, and financial support made the project possible in its earliest days, and then-president Dale Nitzschke, who joined Walter in his keenness for the project, and whose support was invaluable. This project has outlasted a number of other academic officers at the university; we wish also to thank Joan Leitzel, who succeeded Dale Nitzschke to the presidency; executive assistant to the president Gregg Sanborn; and Donald Sundberg, vice president for research and public service. Thanks also to Marilyn Hoskin and Ted Kirkpatrick, dean and associate dean, respectively, for funding from the UNH College of Liberal Arts, and to the University of New Hampshire Foundation, and its director, Young P. Dawkins, for financial support. At the foundation, staff member Barbara McGuigan has been a staunch advocate, and her research has led to financial rewards for the project; she and her husband, Felix, have even made individual gifts to the project. We would also like to offer a special note of gratitude to the University of New Hampshire Parents Association, which has been a major benefactor over the years. Two gifts to the UNH Center for the Humanities were invaluable in the resources they made available for this project; we gratefully acknowledge the Benjamin and Zelma Dorson Endowment for the Humanities and the James H. Hayes and Claire Short Hayes Chair in the Humanities. Current UNH president Ann Weaver Hart, provost Bruce Mallory, and vice president for research and public service John D. Aber have all been supportive. We thank them all.

Many others at the university contributed their expertise. Joanne Adams taught us to use the database that tracked the work. Staff photographers Gary Samson, Doug Prince, Ron Bergeron, and Lisa Nugent were always willing to help us out. We had the pleasure of a student volunteer, Amanda Grappone, whose work with the photographic resources of the university was much appreciated. College of Liberal Arts technogeeks (their term, not ours) Dee-Ann Dumas and Stormy Gleason kept our computers running and handled the networking. The Dimond Library reference staff—Debbie Watson, Louise Buckley, Peter Crosby, Valerie Harper, David Severn, and Deanna Wood—were invaluable when we came to them with reference requests and challenged them in the process of fact-checking. The same is true for the library's Department of Special Collections, where we thank William Ross, Valerie Cunningham, Rebecca Ernest, Roland Goodbody, Nancy Mason, Richard Maxfield, Elizabeth Slomba, and Mylinda Woodward.

University of New Hampshire grants administrators Jennifer Price, Amy Philbrick, Angele Cook, and Nicole Runde made the financial work surprisingly pleasant. Maryann Mrozcka produced a wonderful promotional video for the project, and staff at UNH Publications designed a beautiful brochure in the early years of the project.

Many people at the University of New Hampshire Center for the Humanities worked hard on this project. Thanks go to them all, with particular appreciation for the contributions of Joanne Sacco, Jennifer Beard, Suzanne Guiod, and Joan Howard.

We were inspired to produce this encyclopedia by *The Encyclopedia of Southern Culture,* whose editors, Charles Reagan Wilson and William Ferris, were generous with their support and experience. Funds from the National Endowment for the Humanities were essential for this project, and we wish to acknowledge the NEH's significant role in our project and, more broadly, in the intellectual life of the nation. We were grateful for the interest and support of William Ferris, who chaired the NEH during a critical time in our project's development. And our NEH program officer, Joe Herring, was always helpful in the sometimes arduous process of raising funds for this long-running project.

The Boston Globe generously opened its massive photo library to us; thanks are due to *Globe* librarian Lisa Tuite for facilitating our research there, as did Richard P. Gulla, at that time the paper's public relations director. And Alan Waugh, at the Boston Globe Store, made the work of rights and permissions much easier than anyone might reasonably have expected.

Most of the *Encyclopedia*'s maps come from the Osher Map Library and Smith Center for Cartographic Education at the University of Southern Maine. Faculty Scholar Matthew H. Edney contributed his considerable expertise there, joined by staffers Yolanda I. Theunissen, George S. Carhart, and Roberta L. Ransley-Matteau.

Many others went out of their way to help with this project. We thank Kathryn Chisholm of the Tuttle Library in Antrim, N.H.; Mary DeLashmit, director of the Holderness (N.H.) Free Library; John Faro of the Heritage State Park Visitors' Center in Lawrence, Mass.; Donna Gilbreth of the New Hampshire State Library; Barbara Levine, textual editor at Southern Illinois University's Center for Dewey Studies; Maria Melo, assistant to the director of the New Bedford (Mass.) Free Public Library; William Putnam of the Lowell Observatory in Flagstaff, Ariz.; and Nancy J. White of the Statistical Information Office at the U.S. Bureau of the Census.

At Yale University Press, Executive Editor Lauren Shapiro and Managing Editor Susan Laity were as good as it gets. Their careful stewardship and enthusiastic support, not to mention their cool competence when it came to managing countless small details, had a great deal to do with the quality of this book. We are deeply appreciative of their work. Two other editors at the press were especially helpful over the course of the project; because they have moved on to other careers, we want to highlight their contributions. We valued the reference experience of project editor

Fred Kameny, who brought the *Encyclopedia* to Yale. Richard Miller was an advocate and guide whose intelligence and experience had considerable impact on the shape and nature of this book. And to the many talented people at the press who are listed on the project staff page, we offer our deep appreciation for their excellent and careful work.

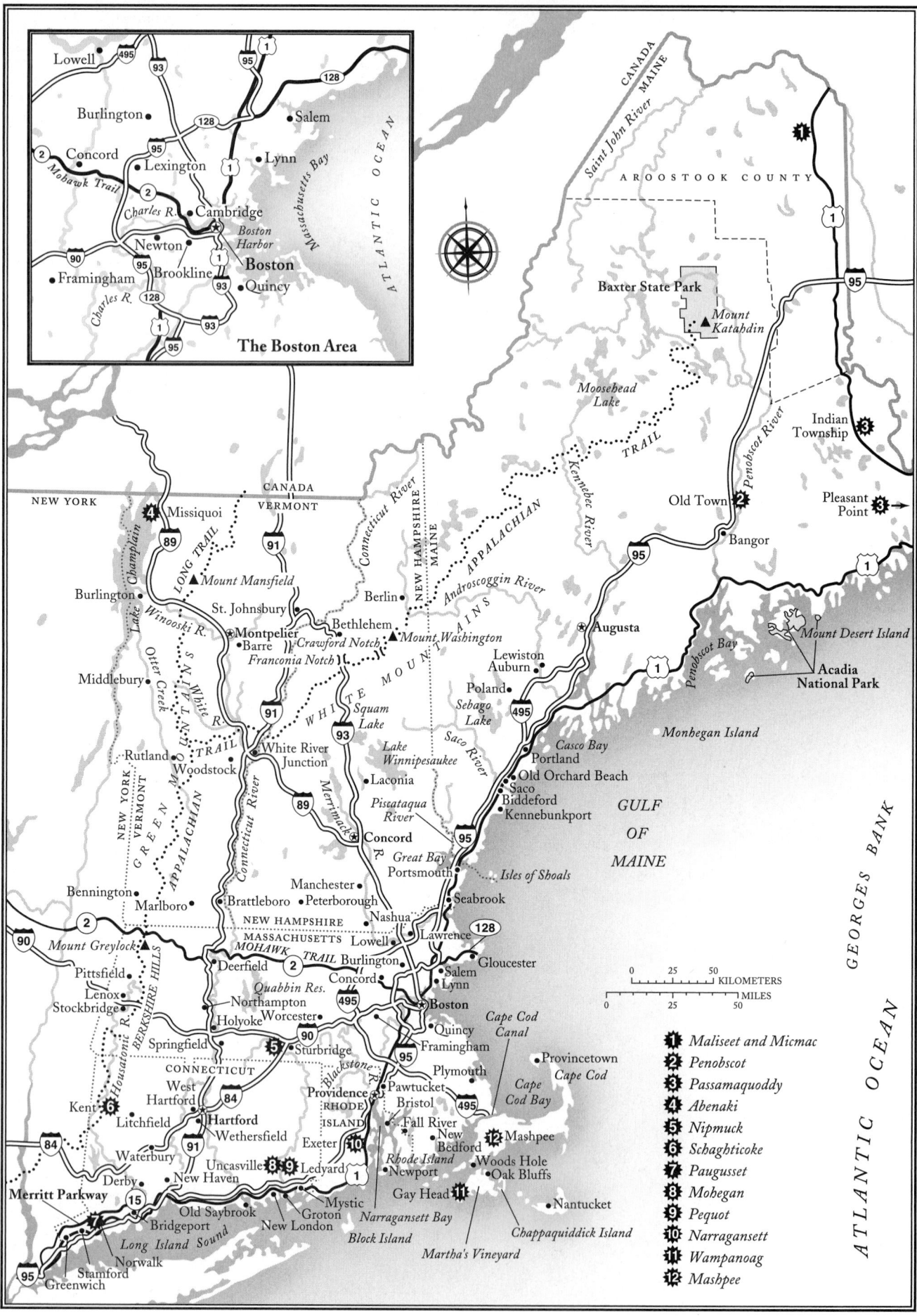

The Boston Area

Lowell
Burlington
Concord
Lexington
Salem
Lynn
Mohawk Trail
Charles R.
Cambridge
Boston Harbor
Newton
Boston
Framingham
Brookline
Quincy
Charles R.

ATLANTIC OCEAN

Massachusetts Bay

CANADA MAINE
Saint John River
AROOSTOOK COUNTY

Baxter State Park
Mount Katahdin
Moosehead Lake
TRAIL
Kennebec River
Penobscot River
Old Town
Bangor
Indian Township
Pleasant Point

NEW YORK
CANADA
VERMONT
Missiquoi
LONG TRAIL
Mount Mansfield
Burlington
Lake Champlain
Winooski R.
St. Johnsbury
Montpelier
Barre
Berlin
Bethlehem
Crawford Notch
Franconia Notch
Mount Washington
Augusta
APPALACHIAN
Androscoggin River
Lewiston
Auburn
Poland
Sebago Lake
Penobscot Bay
Mount Desert Island
Acadia National Park
Monhegan Island

GULF OF MAINE

NEW HAMPSHIRE MAINE
WHITE MOUNTAINS
Middlebury
Otter Creek
GREEN MOUNTAINS
Rutland
Woodstock
White River Junction
Squam Lake
Lake Winnipesaukee
Laconia
Saco River
Portland
Old Orchard Beach
Saco
Biddeford
Kennebunkport
Casco Bay

NEW YORK VERMONT
APPALACHIAN TRAIL
Connecticut River
Merrimack R.
Concord
Piscataqua River
Great Bay
Portsmouth
Isles of Shoals
Manchester
Peterborough
Bennington
Marlboro
Brattleboro
Nashua
Seabrook

GEORGES BANK

Mount Greylock
BERKSHIRE HILLS
Pittsfield
Lenox
Stockbridge
Housatonic R.
Deerfield
MOHAWK TRAIL
Burlington
Concord
Lowell
Lawrence
Salem
Lynn
Gloucester
NEW HAMPSHIRE
MASSACHUSETTS

Quabbin Res.
Northampton
Holyoke
Worcester
Springfield
Sturbridge
CONNECTICUT
Boston
Quincy
Framingham
Plymouth
Cape Cod Canal
Provincetown
Cape Cod
Cape Cod Bay

West Hartford
Kent
Litchfield
Hartford
Wethersfield
Waterbury
Blackstone R.
Providence
RHODE ISLAND
Pawtucket
Bristol
Fall River
New Bedford
Mashpee
Woods Hole
Oak Bluffs

Derby
New Haven
Uncasville
Ledyard
Exeter
Newport
Gay Head
Nantucket

Merritt Parkway
Old Saybrook
Mystic
New London
Groton
Rhode Island
Narragansett Bay
Block Island
Chappaquiddick Island
Martha's Vineyard

Bridgeport
Norwalk
Stamford
Greenwich
Long Island Sound

0   25   50 KILOMETERS
0   25   50 MILES

1 *Maliseet and Micmac*
2 *Penobscot*
3 *Passamaquoddy*
4 *Abenaki*
5 *Nipmuck*
6 *Schaghticoke*
7 *Paugusset*
8 *Mohegan*
9 *Pequot*
10 *Narragansett*
11 *Wampanoag*
12 *Mashpee*

ATLANTIC OCEAN

New England

THE ENCYCLOPEDIA OF NEW ENGLAND

Agriculture

J. Ritchie Garrison, *Section Editor*

Hal S. Barron, *Consulting Editor*

Section-opening image: Mucking out at the Rancourt Dairy Farm, Vassalboro, Maine, 1987

INTRODUCTION

The Pilgrims' first effort to plant a crop is a familiar grade-school tale. Half the company, having arrived in November 1620, were dead by the early spring of 1621. The *Mayflower* was still anchored in Plymouth Harbor, its crew awaiting the return of fair weather, better health, and the trip back to England. Many of the adults, including William Bradford, were still sick, but if the plantation were to survive, it was essential to get in a crop. Bradford remembered that "they (as many as were able) began to plant their corn, in which service Squanto served them in good stead, showing them both the manner how to set it, and after how to dress and tend it. Also he told them, except they got fish and set with it in these old grounds it would come to nothing." The settlers also planted English crops such as wheat and peas, "but it came not to good, either by the badness of the seed or the lateness of the season or both, or some other defect." This is a useful story. It embodies national myths of persistence in the face of hardship, adaptation to new ways of understanding and doing things, and contact with native groups who had much to teach Europeans. But it also tells about agriculture in New England, about efforts to grow things on a landscape that is often perceived as marginal or hostile to productive farming, and about a way of life that now seems quaint and vaguely romantic, but persists.

The visible remains of the agricultural past—the artificial lines of stone walls in the woods, the barns behind old farmhouses, and the few remaining pastures that extend up the slopes of the region's uplands—remind us of how important farming was for most who lived there. Yet those same cultural relics reinforce the public perception that farming was unprofitable and hard, that people abandoned agriculture as soon as better alternatives became available, and that industry and technology rapidly reordered an older way of life. These perceptions often oversimplify complex events and trends that varied by subregion and over time. Scholars have debated about when New England's economic changes became visible and are divided over the degree and extent to which New England's early agricultural production was driven by commercial motivations and the basic need to provide subsistence for family and community. The result is a lively interest in New England farming.

These debates are understandable given the nature of the evidence. Commercial and subsistence motives were entwined in New England from the early 17th century. Bradford's history, *Of Plymouth Plantation, 1620–1647* (1630–50), reminds us of the dualism. If the more religious of the first Pilgrim settlers had risked their lives to establish a place for their families to worship God as they saw fit, the realities of moving to and living in a non-European world required certain compromises. The survival and prosperity of the colony's households depended on building shelter and growing food. The colony's existence also depended on the willingness of London merchant "adventurers" to pay the freight for carrying settlers across the Atlantic in exchange for profits on marketable products. Thus, Bradford's remarks on planting the first crop of Indian corn responded to urgent needs of the colonists and their initial dependence on Native Americans, while the letters that he often copied into his history of Plymouth captured his sponsors' impatience with the rate of return on their investment.

This return was slow in coming, for the kinds of agricultural products the New England environment was best suited to produce largely duplicated those available from English farms. The cost of freighting livestock and grain across the Atlantic to Europe rarely rendered such cargos profitable in the 17th century. Merchants could successfully export forest products, fish, and some manufactured items (such as ships) in various ports around the Atlantic world, but except for livestock and some specialty items such as cranberries, blueberries, and maple syrup, the agricultural market for New England foodstuffs would remain largely local throughout its history.

Once established, New England farms did produce abundantly despite the land's reputation for thin, rocky soils. The region sustained a very high rate of population growth and enjoyed one of the best longevity rates in the world during the colonial period. This growth rate alone would have required modest surpluses as the region expanded. Nevertheless, it is clear that 17th-century New England showed signs of specialized development, partly because the New England environment differed from one section to another, and partly because settlement proceeded at uneven rates. Even a preliminary study of the dates of incorporation for New England towns shows wide variation. Not surprisingly, the earliest settlement occurred along the coast, where land was accessible from the sea or by river, but within a few years of the landings at Plymouth and Boston, farmers and their families moved inland in search of high-quality soil.

Wethersfield, Conn., and Springfield, Mass., were among the earliest inland destination points in the Connecticut River valley during the mid-1630s and were far removed from coastal contact. That the settlers in these communities bypassed the upland terrain of inland Massachusetts and Connecticut to claim land on New England's most fertile soils suggests that their choices were influenced by future prospects, not just short-term expediency. Moreover, these valley landscapes and those on the other major New England river valleys yielded better crops and more animal fodder than farms on thinner soils or steeper slopes. This selective settling of the region's agricultural landscape contributed in important ways to the rapid growth rates of the region as well as to its general health, as people moved first onto the lands best able to support agricultural yields. That growth also contributed to growing conflicts with Native Americans who did not share European views on private property ownership or the proper means of farming.

Europeans were puzzled by native husbandry. For one thing, planting and tending crops was largely the responsibility of native women rather than men. For another, their fields seemed messy to Englishmen trained in traditions of monocropping, in which a wheat field was a wheat field and everything else was a weed. Picture their astonishment when they confronted Native American fields in which corn, beans, pumpkins, and squashes intermingled, the beans climbing up cornstalks in search of sunlight, the squashes and pumpkins smothering competing plants below. Modern scientists have come to appreciate these planting strategies as ecologically sound; 17th-century Englishmen, unacquainted with the subject of ecology, saw slovenly fields and lazy men who let their women do the work. The Englishmen made over the riotous fields into proper English tillage and mowing as soon as they had the chance, but they valued indigenous foodstuffs. New Englanders have incorporated "Indian" pudding, pumpkin muffins, baked beans, squash, and maple sugar into a regional cuisine, but their borrowing from native culture was selective and occurred over time.

Settlers arrived as English men and women; they soon learned to adapt to an alien world that was hotter in the summer and colder in the winter than the one they had left. They shared the land with people who spoke in strange languages, wore improper clothing, and knew how to survive in a place that had trees as far as anyone could see. This curious new world was an inversion of familiar patterns. In England, there was an abundance of labor and cleared fields; land and woods were largely controlled by elites. In New England, land and trees were initially abundant and cheap, but the labor to clear and prepare fields was expensive or unavailable. Most of the work was done by family members who labored over one or two generations to improve their farms. The labor shortage and external conditions contributed to the early patterns of settlement formation.

For much of the 17th century, settlers established towns on old fields cleared by Native Americans. The cleared fields were used for tillage and were enclosed by fences to keep free-ranging livestock out. Just as Squanto had demonstrated, native crops such as corn, squash, and beans grew well in the area, but the colonists quickly established European grains including wheat, rye, and barley; fruits such as apples, pears, and peaches; and garden crops to provide the principal ingredients for European diets. Most of the Native American plants and garden crops were adapted for hoe cultivation, but European grains were best sown in enclosed, cleared fields and required animal power and plowing equipment for efficient production.

The best soils and climate for this type of grain-based agriculture in southern New England were located on river plains where the land was relatively level, free of stones, and silty. Growing seasons differed from year to year and by elevation and proximity to the coast, but most families could expect about 150 days between killing frosts, with more along the southern coastline, Cape Cod, and the islands. Outside of riverain areas or low-lying sections of the coast, much of New England's topography was uneven. Parts of it were swampy or sandy, and rocks were almost everywhere, ranging in size from cobbles to boulders. Even after they removed trees and stumps, farm families would spend years carting rocks away from their hill-farm tillage fields. Small wonder, then, that early settlers took advantage of clearings made by Native Americans, and moved quickly inland along the region's riverways, the

Connecticut, Housatonic, and Merrimack Rivers being the most important. By 1710, most of the best farmland in southern New England was taken up, and families had to begin settling more marginal agricultural land or move north, where the growing season was shorter and native peoples controlled by the French were closer.

The northern New England uplands range from gently rolling hills to steeply sloped rills, some of which reach above timberline. Growing seasons could be as short as 95 frost-free days in some of the more northern or higher elevations. Most New England soils were acidic, and portions of the landscape were poorly drained. The area's best soils were limestone-based in Aroostook County, Maine, far to the north, where winter came early and transportation was difficult until the railroad arrived in the second half of the 19th century. Soils generally varied so much from town to town and farm to farm that it is difficult to accurately characterize typical growing conditions in New England outside of a few favored locations such as the Connecticut River valley. Some soils were well drained; others were damp and boggy. Corn grew fairly well in these conditions, but the traditional English grains—wheat, rye, barley, and, later, oats—usually did not yield very abundantly, especially on land that was inadequately fertilized or limed. Nevertheless, rainfall was abundant, and trees and grasses grew well even on steeper slopes. New England's most important crops, corn and hay, performed consistently in this environment. Both were crucial to the maintenance of people and animals.

Animals, especially cattle, were critical components in this agricultural landscape. Although New Englanders did produce most of the grains they needed to survive, it is now apparent that once European grasses crowded out the native types, the region was well suited to hay production. More so than many New Englanders have realized, the region's early agricultural surpluses came in the form of beef that could be driven to market. Cattle needed pastures but could eat their way around rocks and stumps, could defend themselves against predators, and moved to market on their own power. Although few families sent more than one or two animals to market in a year, the abundance of beef cattle was visible in the region's foodways. Unlike most of the rest of colonial America, New Englanders preferred beef to pork.

These characteristics promoted an intensive and controlled mode of agricultural production and a considerable investment in agricultural infrastructure such as fences and barns. Who would build this infrastructure? With so much available land, there was little incentive to work as an agricultural laborer, even for high wages. Although traction and plowing equipment—never common in the 17th century—might be rented or shared, most families had to look to their own resources to prepare land and maintain animals. They might change work with other members of the community in times of acute need, such as during haying or reaping seasons, but for the most part, farms operated independently. Livestock fitted neatly into a labor-short production strategy, as cattle and hogs required relatively little supervision.

In spite of nostalgic traditions to the contrary, New England farms were not self-sufficient operations. The most prosperous farms were generally owned by middle-aged men; they and their families had already worked for 20 to 30 years to build a farmstead. Younger families simply had not had time to make or accumulate much, and older families often had given property away to married children. By the end of the 17th century, then, first-generation New England towns had become more stratified by wealth and age. Only the richest families could afford the range of resources to produce their own food and clothing. Few of them attempted to, either because they lacked adequate labor or because imported European goods made by trained artisans were generally better than what ordinary households could produce. Throughout the colonial period, then, all New England families exchanged goods or services to balance out what they could not make or did not wish to do themselves. Such trading also earned credit for imported items—things as basic as salt for preserving food and as extravagant as imported silks and calicoes. Much of this exchange was handled locally, but not all of it could be. The tradition of general, mixed agricultural production made sense given the area's weather, soils, and population, but it was flexible enough to accommodate early frosts, excessive rains, and disrupted markets.

There were a number of reasons why New England farm families began to shift productive strategies during the 18th century. Some were push factors. As the population expanded, it became impossible to set up offspring on their own farms except with great expense or by having siblings share the same land. Some children would benefit from moving to new towns and establishing their own farms on inexpensive land, but doing so meant breaking up the family unit and embarking on the immense labor of building a new farm. Moreover, the best land was already distributed by the 1780s. What was left was hillier, swampier, or farther north or west where the growing season was shorter. Alternatively, children could stay in their natal towns but would have to make a living as artisans or merchants. Population pressure was only one factor in shifting production strategies; critical crops like wheat were suffering from fungal and insect attacks. By the mid-1700s, New Englanders had become net importers of flour, much of it shipped from New York and Pennsylvania. Buying land for children or paying for imported flour required money, either in cash or in credits recorded on some merchant's ledgers. Either way, there were incentives to engage in profit-making activities, even if profit was only the means to an end.

The pull factors seem more nebulous at first. There were simply more opportunities to generate and use surpluses. By the early 18th century, the farms in New England's earliest towns were nearly three generations old. Land was cleared, fences were up, barns were finished, and more surplus labor was available. Markets were different in 1730 from those in 1630. England had become a major maritime and colonial power. Sugar production in the Caribbean had expanded to a point where islands such as Barbados had shifted production almost entirely to the commercial crop and were importing foodstuffs and livestock. At least some of this demand seems to have prompted an expansion of livestock production in New England, with the surplus funneled through port towns. Simultaneously, Boston had become the largest city in the British colonial mainland by 1690, and its merchants then dominated the coastal maritime trade. An enterprising group, long accustomed to the vagaries of New England's agricultural surpluses, these merchants specialized in patterns of circular trading in which they moved up and down the coast and through the Caribbean, picking up and selling cargos where it was advantageous. If a cargo of corn would sell in coastal North Carolina for pine tar, the tar might be sold in Jamaica for molasses, which New England distilleries could convert to rum. The rum would buy New England beef, and so on. Estimating this trade is notoriously difficult, because merchants had a vested interest in disguising their activities to minimize customs duties and local farm accounts were just that, local. Clearly, larger economic changes affected farmers' productive strategies.

Although the number of potential markets for New England's farm products grew as new colonies were settled and as England gained control over greater portions of the Caribbean, actual production in New England waxed and waned according to a variety of factors: weather conditions, war, inflation, and government regulation. Markets were not the only factor prompting more specialized agricultural production. Standards of living changed, and some of the improvements penetrated into the hinterlands. By the 1730s, rural people were importing greater quantities of European textiles and foodstuffs, notably rum, sugar, molasses, tea, and citrus fruits. The quantity and variety of these goods would increase as the century passed. There were now more items to buy if the money could be found. Although most agricultural production remained focused on the household level, with local exchanges among community members to balance out inequalities, there were signs that families were increasing selected types of agricultural production for market.

Whether this preindustrial agrarian economy was essentially capitalist in its outlook has been an important topic of scholarly debate. The evidence is mixed. Most farm accounts from this period are with neighbors and local merchants. Most involve exchanges of goods and services to balance the needs of the household. Production appears to be focused on the preservation and nurturing of the family unit, not on maximizing profits. This profile is generally referred to as the household mode of production. The problem is that farm accounts predictably record local exchanges rather than long-distance ones and do not by themselves prove or disprove market involvement. The market-focused interpretation emphasizes behavior that transcends a local or household need. Production might take forms that exceed local or regional need, or that move in the same cycles as urban production or prices.

To put it another way, why would the price of any commodity vary in rural New England in the same way as it would in a seaport city if the hinterlands were not tied to wider markets? Of course, New England farmers did not care about the theoretical merits of these interpretations. Most simply produced things for the survival of their families and for purchasing necessities and luxuries at local stores. If they could satisfy most of their needs via their own production, they did that, but if they could do better by selling goods in the market, they produced what would sell. The point to remember is that both demand and production were dynamic and that important changes occurred in the 18th century. Not all New England farm families benefited or lost equally as these changes took place.

A few changes were clear by the time of the Revolution. By then, important sections of New England's agrarian economy were becoming specialized. Agricultural surpluses were centered on the Connecticut River valley, portions of coastal Connecticut, Narragansett Bay, and the best agricultural lands of Essex County in Massachusetts. Much of this specialized production was related to convenient trans-portation and the quality of arable land. Although some crops were exported based on their reputation for quality—onions from Wethersfield, to cite one example—other products involved a labor-intensive process of local exchanges that yielded a marketable commodity—such as stall-fed steers from Hatfield and Deerfield, Mass. Parts of Rhode Island specialized in raising mutton and horses for the Caribbean, and some southern sections of that colony based their production on slavery. It is im-portant not to overstate the commercial scale of this production or to forget that many sections of New England were still wilderness at the time of the Revolution. This unsettled land included much of far western Connecticut and Massachusetts, portions of Worcester County, Mass., and western Rhode Island, nearly all of what would become Vermont, most of New Hampshire outside of the greater Merrimack River valley, and nearly all of inland Maine. What is impressive about these unsettled or sparsely settled areas is how quickly they developed in the postrevolutionary era.

The Revolution itself retarded the development of the New England economy. Trade with England was cut off and society was disrupted for nearly 10 years, start-ing with the close of Boston in 1774 to the rebuilding of the merchant fleet in 1783–84. Independence ended local British control, but it also cut off important markets in the British West Indies that had long purchased New England and American agri-cultural products. Crushing state taxes in 1785 and 1786 caught many farm families in the newly settled regions of Massachusetts in a web of indebtedness and foreclosure, and brought about armed political insurgency. Then, in the last decade of the 18th century, the New England economy went through a sustained expansion that af-fected most communities in the region. It is in this period that we can clearly see a commercial nexus beginning to take hold. The prices for labor and commodities in farmers' accounts began to resonate to the same rises and falls as those in New En-gland cities. The volume of consumer goods expanded along with the need to pro-duce income to pay for these goods. The demand for agricultural products also in-creased, both regionally, as cities grew, and internationally, as trade expanded after war broke out between Britain and France in 1793.

Although the market for New England's agricultural goods was generally favor-able in the 1790s, changes were subtle, and different New England states varied in their response. Some sections of New England, notably Rhode Island and sections of eastern Massachusetts, were becoming more urban (see table). By the time of the first federal census in 1790, only 81 percent of Rhode Island residents and 86.5 percent of Massachusetts residents were classified as rural compared to 100 percent in Maine and Vermont and about 97 percent in Connecticut and New Hampshire. Although these urban populations were still small, the trend away from farming was already apparent before industrialization took hold in southeastern New England. Most of the region's families, however, continued to produce for home consumption, and most continued to raise a mix of crops and animals.

What was new was the intensification of work as farm families sought gains in productivity. Probate inventories show a marked improvement in the number of tools farm families owned. Not everyone owned a plow, but by 1800, the majority of

Percentage of Rural Population to Total Population, 1790–2000

	Connecticut	Maine	Massachusetts	New Hampshire	Rhode Island	Vermont
1790	97.0	100.0	86.5	96.7	81.0	100.0
1800	94.9	97.6	84.6	97.1	79.2	100.0
1810	93.9	96.9	78.7	96.8	76.6	100.0
1820	92.4	97.1	77.2	97.0	77.0	100.0
1830	90.6	96.8	68.9	95.0	68.8	100.0
1840	87.4	92.2	62.1	90.0	56.2	100.0
1850	84.0	86.5	49.3	82.9	44.4	98.1
1860	73.5	83.4	40.4	77.9	36.7	98.0
1870	67.0	79.0	33.3	73.8	25.4	93.1
1880	58.1	77.4	25.3	70.0	18.0	90.0
1890	49.1	71.9	18.0	60.7	14.7	84.8
1900	40.1	66.5	14.0	53.3	11.7	77.9
1910	34.4	64.7	11.0	48.2	9.0	72.2
1920	32.2	61.0	10.0	43.5	8.1	68.8
1930	29.6	59.7	9.8	41.3	7.6	67.0
1940	32.2	59.5	10.6	42.4	8.4	65.7
1950	30.7	59.0	13.3	41.4	13.0	63.6
1960	31.0	60.1	13.2	40.2	10.1	63.0
1970	22.6*	49.2*	15.4*	43.6*	12.9*	67.8*
1980	21.2*	52.5*	16.2*	47.8*	13.0*	66.2*
1990	20.9*	55.4*	15.7*	49.0*	14.0*	67.8*
2000	12.3*	59.8*	8.6*	40.8*	9.1*	61.8*

Note: In general, *urban* was defined as territory, persons, and housing units in urbanized areas and as all places, incorporated or unincorporated, outside of urbanized areas that had 2,500 or more persons
*Figures affected by new definitions of *urban*
Source: U.S. Census Bureau

well-established farm households did. There were also signs that political disruption had prompted changes in husbandry. Although flocks of sheep had expanded in the 1760s during boycotts of British woolens and manufactured goods following the Stamp and Townsend Acts, New England women participated in a noticeable expansion of home textile production between 1770 and 1820. Flocks of sheep listed on town tax valuations grew in size, and more families owned them. The records for flax production are not systematic, but anecdotal evidence indicates that more people planted the crop and invested in equipment like hatchels and breaks for processing it into linen. Many of these contributions to household economy reflected the efforts of women and coincided with a significant rebuilding of the region's agricultural out-buildings and support structures.

Historians have taken for granted the common use of barns and outbuildings on the New England landscape. Recent efforts to systematically study different regions of the country via the Federal Direct Tax assessment of 1798 have demonstrated how unusual New England's patterns were. In much of rural New England, more than 90 percent of households owned barns, the majority of which were larger than 1,000 square feet. In southern states, fewer than 40 percent of householders seem to have owned barns; in Pennsylvania about 50 to 80 percent of the households owned barns, even in areas where the winters are as long and as cold as in New England. Clearly, barns were not necessary components for subsistence in the rest of the United States, where quite a number of families lived in rural areas without any agricultural out-buildings.

It appears that New Englanders systematically built barns as flexible structures that could shelter varied agricultural activities. The evidence for extensive barn-building for storage of fodder and animals emphasizes the significance of meat and wool production to the greater New England economy. Barns improved the chances for stock to survive harsh winters, facilitated winter work under shelter, and improved the management of farm resources. The mean barn size in many of New England's rural communities by 1800 was a 30-by-40-foot building. Some were much larger and would have accommodated much larger herds than were necessary for household use. Rather than thinking of New England's barns as normal investments in a subsistence economy, then, we must think of them as remarkably common elements in progressive farming. They were designed to increase productivity by minimizing loss and by facilitating yearlong work routines.

Efforts to improve productivity were also visible in better breeding, the importation of livestock with desirable characteristics, and the formation of agricultural societies and fairs. Some elements of these changes were put in place in the 1790s and early 1800s, but most of them occurred after the 1810s. Although various promoters advertised the lineage of their horses and cattle, the animal that spurred the greatest popular frenzy in the early 19th century was the merino sheep. Imported from Spain and famous for their soft, superior woolen fleeces, the rams and ewes set off the merino craze in which some investors spent as much as $1,500 to buy a prize ram. The long-term impact was less dazzling than such record prices would indicate, for the merinos proved a bit delicate for the New England climate and disease environment, but, mixed with the region's common sheep, the breed improved both the quality and, to a lesser extent, the yield of New England sheep at a time when woolen manufacturing was beginning to grow. Vermont would become the center of New England's wool production—its uplands were well adapted for pasturing sheep and other animals—but other sections of New England also raised sheep for wool and mutton. The interest in sheep also spawned the New England agricultural fair and contributed to a growing interest in agricultural reform.

Elkanah Watson of Pittsfield, Mass., created the first such fair in 1807, during the early phases of merino enthusiasm, by proposing to exhibit two merinos in a public celebration of progressive agriculture. He went on to help found the Berkshire Agricultural Society in 1811 and, by 1819, had persuaded the Massachusetts General Court to pass general legislation for the incorporation of agricultural societies. During the next three decades nearly 100 agricultural societies were established in New England. Meanwhile, the agricultural fair had caught on at the county level as a means of encouraging agricultural improvement.

By 1840 New England agriculture was adjusting to the challenges produced by urbanization, improved transportation, and western production. More than a third of Massachusetts and Rhode Island residents were living in urban settings, and railroads were under construction. By contrast, northern New England remained rural. Census takers classified Vermont as 100 percent, Maine as 92.2 percent, and New Hampshire as 90 percent rural. Although most farmers continued to plant and harvest corn, wheat production declined even further. Population figures in many up-

Southern view of Orange, (central part.)

Woodcut of Orange, Mass., by John Warner Barber, 1839

land communities stabilized or declined, and those who stayed in farming generally had to balance a broad range of subsistence activities with specialized market production. Conversely, the rapid growth of cities and manufacturing districts increased the local market for produce. In consequence, New England's agriculture became increasingly fragmented as different communities focused on producing commodities that grew well locally or had a ready market. Connecticut River valley farmers continued to raise foodstuffs but also sought profitable niche products. They turned first to broomcorn and later to tobacco. A few tried to cultivate silkworms or raised teasels for the textile industry. Shaker communities specialized in and became well known for their seeds. Many upland farmers expanded their dairy herds, especially after the railroad network improved in the 1840s. They made and marketed butter and cheese in New England's growing urban centers. Others near urban areas raised vegetables and fruits, trying to capitalize on the market for fresh groceries.

There is evidence that efforts to improve soil quality intensified. Many farmers imported Peruvian guano in the 1850s, and farms near cities added stable and street litter to their soil as a topdressing. In general, farms established on good soils continued to provide a living for the families that owned them, but the rapid development of commerce and manufacturing provided jobs for thousands of men and women who once would have remained on the farm.

During the 1850s, cautious reformers were speaking pessimistically in the agricultural press about the competition from larger and more fertile western farms, the seductions of city and business life that lured promising young people out of rural areas, and the get-rich-quick mentality that made people so impatient with the slow process of building wealth from farming. They had reason for concern, but their fears were misplaced. In southern New England, urban populations expanded rapidly both from natural increase and from immigration. Although the number of farming families declined relative to the whole population, the number of farms actually increased in every New England state as families continued to partition holdings equally among heirs, and new farms were built on underused land. Average farm size declined slightly in southern New England states but expanded in the north as more land was put into production (see tables). There the absence of large-scale manufacturing may have encouraged New Englanders' efforts to increase income through farming since there were few other options.

The Civil War complicated these trends. Thousands lost their lives in battle or through disease. Others had a chance to see portions of the country they never would have without military service. Death cut an uneven swath because most young men in the first three years of the war enlisted with friends, relatives, and neighbors in the same regiment. If that regiment ended up on the front lines at Fredericksburg or Gettysburg, an entire generation of a town's young men might be wiped out. It appears that the pool of marriage-aged men declined in some portions of New England, and women inherited numerous farms in the 1870s and 1880s. Not all farms suffered equally, and over time these changes even brought some benefits. Poor agricultural land went out of production and returned to forest. For those farms that remained in business, swelling numbers of immigrants made hired labor more affordable beginning in the 1850s. More workers made possible the expansion of certain types of labor-intensive agriculture, such as tobacco production in the Connecticut River valley. Many of these immigrants eventually sought to acquire land and run their own farms.

The process by which new immigrant groups increased their role in New England farming in the second half of the 19th century is still poorly understood. The evidence suggests that the reformers who decried the state of agriculture in the 19th century were actually more concerned about the flight of old Yankee families to western states or out of farming altogether than by any actual decline in the number of farms. The agricultural high-water mark occurred in 1880, when every New England state recorded the highest number of farms ever reported to the Bureau of

Number of Farms by State, 1850–2003

	Connecticut	Maine	Massachusetts	New Hampshire	Rhode Island	Vermont
1850	22,445	46,760	34,069	29,229	5,385	29,763
1860	25,180	55,698	35,601	30,501	5,406	31,556
1870	25,508	59,804	26,500	29,642	5,368	33,827
1880	30,598	64,309	38,406	32,181	6,216	35,522
1890	26,350	62,013	34,374	29,151	5,500	32,573
1900	26,948	59,299	37,715	29,324	5,498	33,104
1910	26,815	60,016	36,917	27,053	5,292	32,709
1920	22,655	48,227	32,001	20,523	4,083	29,075
1930	17,195	39,006	25,598	14,906	3,322	24,898
1940	21,163	38,980	31,897	16,554	3,014	23,582
1950	15,615	30,358	22,220	13,391	2,598	19,043
1960	8,292	17,360	11,179	6,542	1,395	12,099
1970	4,490	7,971	5,703	2,902	700	6,874
1982	3,754	7,003	5,401	2,757	728	6,315
1990	3,900	7,300	6,900	3,000	770	7,000
2003	4,200	7,200	6,100	3,400	850	6,500

Average Acreage per Farm by State, 1850–2000

	Connecticut	Maine	Massachusetts	New Hampshire	Rhode Island	Vermont
1850	106.2	97.4	98.5	116.1	102.9	138.6
1860	99.5	102.8	93.8	122.8	96.4	135.5
1870	92.7	97.6	103.0	121.7	93.6	133.9
1880	80.2	101.9	87.5	115.6	82.8	137.5
1890	85.5	99.7	87.2	118.7	85.3	134.9
1900	85.5	106.2	83.4	123.1	82.9	142.7
1910	81.5	104.9	77.9	120.1	83.8	142.6
1920	83.8	112.5	77.9	126.9	81.2	145.7
1930	87.4	119.0	78.3	131.5	84.1	156.5
1940	71.5	108.3	60.8	109.3	73.6	155.5
1950	81.5	137.7	74.7	128.0	73.5	185.2
1960	106.7	177.5	102.2	171.9	98.9	243.4
1970	121.0	221.0	123.0	211.0	98.0	279.0
1982	118.0	210.0	113.0	170.0	86.0	249.0
1990	110.0	199.0	99.0	159.0	95.0	214.0
2000	92.0	187.0	93.0	135.0	86.0	197.0

Census. The consequence was that average acreage per farm declined noticeably in southern New England between 1870 and 1900, and grew only marginally in northern New England (see tables).

Meanwhile, New England's agricultural production remained steady in some areas, grew in new ways, and declined in others. The value of livestock fluctuated according to economic conditions but remained roughly the same between 1860 and 1900. Hay production generally went up during this period, reflecting the expansion of pasture and mowing lands to accommodate the growing quality of herds (see tables). Dairying and egg production became important sources of income for farm families advantageously located near rail transportation and urban markets. Some families continued to process butter, cheese, cream, and milk on the farm, but increasingly factories were established to process raw milk into commercial products with identifiable brand names. Egg and poultry production also grew in places such as southern New Hampshire and Maine, catering to New Englanders' preference for brown eggs. Similarly, Maine farmers in Aroostook County expanded production of potatoes during the later part of the century as improved rail connections, good soil conditions, a frost-resistant crop, and an influx of French Canadians to work the fields coincided with increased demand for inexpensive starches to feed growing numbers of European immigrants who had long included potatoes in their diets.

Bulk grains fared less well. Corn production generally declined after 1860, in some states precipitously. Massachusetts farmers had raised 2.3 million bushels of corn in 1850, and Maine families had harvested 1.7 million. Fifty years later, the figures were 1.5 million and 645,040, respectively. In 2001 the amount of corn harvested in New England was so low as to be statistically insignificant (see table). The other New England states followed similar trajectories. Evidence indicates that, over time, most of the region's farmers avoided direct competition with midwestern farms that had natural advantages in the production of bulk grains and meat. To survive, New England farmers emphasized the production of perishables for which there was a con-

Value of Livestock by State, 1850–2002 (in dollars)

	Connecticut	Maine	Massachusetts	New Hampshire	Rhode Island	Vermont
1850	7,467,490	9,705,726	9,647,710	8,871,901	1,532,637	12,643,228
1860	11,311,079	15,437,533	12,737,744	10,924,627	2,042,044	16,241,989
1870	14,036,030	18,685,703	13,639,383	12,197,236	2,508,106	19,111,068
1880	10,959,296	16,499,376	12,957,004	9,812,064	2,254,142	16,586,195
1890	9,974,618	18,280,140	14,200,178	10,450,125	2,364,970	16,644,320
1900	10,932,212	17,106,034	15,798,464	10,554,646	2,593,659	17,841,317
1910	14,163,902	25,161,839	20,741,366	11,910,478	3,276,472	22,642,766
1920	23,472,693	39,780,102	33,524,157	19,160,923	4,840,279	42,385,331
1930	20,443,530	25,988,049	23,842,014	13,314,025	3,878,364	36,071,729
1940	15,673,608	16,870,129	19,721,839	9,534,049	2,603,499	28,065,322
1950	32,153,005	30,392,754	40,028,165	18,004,115	5,323,344	58,492,869
1960	37,860,241	37,638,175	41,342,112	20,201,800	6,058,484	75,171,592
1982	183,266,000	256,578,000	142,008,000	76,312,000	12,237,000	349,348,000
1990	195,833,000	219,895,000	115,937,000	63,172,000	12,524,000	–
2002	143,110,000	241,247,000	107,244,000	61,686,000	8,408,000	401,482,000

Source: David B. Dodd, *Historical Statistics of the United States: Two Centuries of the Census, 1790–1990* (Westport, Conn.: Greenwood, 1993); USDA Census of Agriculture (2002)

tinuous market. Dairying, poultry production, orchards, potatoes, market gardening, and horticulture fit these criteria.

Despite the substantial number of farms through 1900, local shifts in the agricultural landscape were noticeable. Although the greatest amount of cleared acreage was attained in the 20 years after the Civil War, farms in the higher elevations began to revert to woodland after 1880. Those located near such cities as Boston, Hartford, Worcester, Mass., and New Haven, Conn., were sometimes sold for suburban home-lots as the value of the land eclipsed any immediate profit from agriculture. Well-managed farms on good soils continued to provide a living for many families in the post–Civil War period, however, and a few profited handsomely. By contrast,

Production of Hay by State, 1850–2002 (tons of hay)

	Connecticut	Maine	Massachusetts	New Hampshire	Rhode Island	Vermont
1850	516,131	755,889	651,807	598,854	74,818	866,153
1860	562,425	975,803	665,331	642,741	82,722	940,178
1870	563,328	1,053,415	597,455	612,648	89,045	1,020,669
1880	564,079	1,107,788	684,679	588,170	82,646	1,052,183
1890	612,906	1,192,228	793,167	659,368	101,392	1,205,953
1900	535,336	1,133,932	848,950	653,265	75,410	1,329,972
1910	549,487	1,113,390	832,727	582,579	80,309	1,502,780
1920	627,787	1,303,472	820,905	587,958	82,725	1,696,508
1930	326,189	884,740	421,070	362,899	43,311	1,141,206
1940	341,646	746,225	410,845	354,257	41,609	1,137,876
1950	349,082	619,969	398,522	301,556	34,664	977,639
1960	326,505	563,121	365,857	253,249	37,236	1,042,246
1970	203,000	408,000	239,000	204,000	25,000	904,000
1982	190,034	414,555	241,584	165,999	17,708	886,084
1990	171,000	420,000	237,000	167,000	17,000	754,000
2002	170,199	446,171	209,771	159,579	15,900	1,017,408

Note: Figures for 1990 and 2002 are the sum of categories identified as "alfalfa," "alfalfa mixtures," and "hay, all other"

Production of Corn by State, 1850–2001 (in thousands of bushels)

	Connecticut	Maine	Massachusetts	New Hampshire	Rhode Island	Vermont
1850	1,935	1,750	2,345	1,574	539	2,032
1860	2,060	1,546	2,157	1,415	461	1,525
1870	1,570	1,090	1,398	1,278	312	1,700
1880	1,880	961	1,798	1,350	373	2,014
1890	1,472	381	1,330	989	254	1,701
1900	1,932	645	1,540	1,081	288	2,322
1910	2,531	649	2,029	916	398	1,715
1920	2,062	288	1,516	483	311	937
1930	576	63	349	112	76	259
1940	363	207	311	147	47	278
1950	231	54	214	66	36	102
1960	2,132	451	1,728	564	264	3,172
1982	628	648	592	146	11	1,173
2001	0	0	0	0	0	0

farms on marginal soils seldom yielded more than a hardscrabble existence, much of it associated with selling forest products. Without additional sources of income, many families in the more remote uplands gave up farming or began to use their old properties as summer places. After 1900 the number of farms in New England began to decline in every state except Maine. That trend accelerated in the next two decades. By then, even Maine had experienced a decline in the number of farms.

The decline in the number of farms had benefits. Reforestation was better for the ecology of steep upland slopes, brooks, and streams. Those families who left farming enabled those who remained to begin the process of consolidating land into larger, more productive farm units, either by buying out marginal farmers or by leasing land from the owners. Consolidation prepared the way for some forms of mechanization, which had already included a small number of horse-drawn mowing machines just before the Civil War, and horse rakes and gangplows by the end of the century. Hay balers and corn harvesters were available after 1900. As farming became less profitable than other forms of employment, the ethnic makeup of farm families also shifted. Descendants of original settlers had controlled the rural property of New England for several generations. As these families changed occupations, they often sold or rented farmland to whoever could pay for it. One common path was for farm laborers to become tenants, save money, and eventually buy the farms they worked. Many Polish families who moved into the Connecticut River valley in the 1880s and 1890s to work as agricultural laborers became tenants in the 1910s and 1920s, and bought farms cheaply during the Great Depression, when farm values were depressed all over the region.

Many trends visible in the late 19th century continued into the 20th century. Most farmers continued to raise a significant portion of their own food and specialized in a product that earned cash. These specialty crops varied according to location, markets, and soil characteristics. Farmers in southeastern Massachusetts often raised cranberries in bogs that were unsuitable for raising much else. Blueberry production was centered on the rocky, acidic soils of Washington County, Maine. Farms in the

Strawberry picking at Ward's Berry Farm, Sharon, Mass., 1987

early 1980s, providing a newly invigorated market for firewood. On farms not devoted to livestock, dairy, and poultry production, farm woodlots grew in importance and provided some income in winter months when labor was otherwise underused. A small but visible back-to-the-land movement renewed or invigorated interest in farming, open-space management, alternative energy, renewable resources, and ecology. A broad range of people from former hippies to burned-out executives sought to renew their contacts with nature and growing things. Some tried growing alfalfa sprouts and soybeans; others set out evergreen trees for the Christmas season, grew herbs and flowers, or planted market vegetables for sale on roadside stands. Most of these "farms" were small. Many were sustained by a spouse employed elsewhere. Quite a few were managed by or co-partnered by women. These farms represented a continuation of New England's tradition for agricultural diversity, its flexibility in responding to personal interests and market opportunities, and a love of the New England landscape.

For more traditional commercial farmers, the period was often trying. Although the number of farms continued to slide during the 1970s and 1980s, inflation and population growth sent land values soaring at a time when government tax rates were seldom indexed for inflation (see table). The values of farms in tiny Rhode Island had risen from $44.3 million in 1950 to $50 million in 1970 during a period when the number of farms actually declined from 2,598 to 700. Twelve years later, farm values had ballooned to $173 million and by 1990 had hit $481 million. Figures were even higher in Massachusetts and Connecticut, where values more than doubled in the eight years between 1982 and 1990, passing the $2 billion mark in both states. Farm families who lived modestly suddenly found that their landholdings subjected them to crushing estate taxes because they owned farms that appeared valuable on paper owing to inflation. Most gentleman's farms went out of existence or were put into

…f Farms by State, 1950–1990 (in thousands of dollars)

	Connecticut	Maine	Massachusetts	New Hampshire	Rhode Island	Vermont
1950	315,251	226,518	314,710	124,845	44,328	196,405
1960	392,810	256,157	354,285	118,058	52,411	240,003
1970	499,000	283,000	396,000	146,000	50,000	429,000
1982	1,188,000	1,053,000	1,111,000	555,000	173,000	1,305,000
1990	2,313,000	1,984,000	2,571,000	1,133,000	481,000	2,273,000

Note: In 1997, Congress shifted control of the census of agriculture from the Department of Commerce, Bureau of Census, to the Department of Agriculture, National Agricultural Statistics Service. At that time some of the statistical categories, including farm valuation, changed.

trusts. Simultaneously, the higher property valuations increased property tax liability. By the late 1970s, hard-pressed dairy farmers in southern New England virtually stopped building taxable structures like silos and put their ensilage in large piles covered by tarpaulins, weighted down with old tires. The piles were not pretty, but they carried no tax liability. Soaring property values on farms near suburban developments also encouraged a number of families to cash in their assets. Middle-aged farmers could become instantly wealthy by selling their land for development and retiring early. Aware of the problem, local and state governments began to debate the merits of altering zoning codes, reducing property tax burdens on farmers, and buying up development rights with public tax dollars in order to keep some of the landscape open and to preserve the region's agricultural aesthetic and environment.

For many families, agriculture remained a way of life, but to stay in business they had to manage their assets by forecasting profits and tracking costs with care. By the 1980s many of the larger operations were controlling bookkeeping and some building operations with computers. Many of these farms concentrated on high-volume or high-profit commodities and planned strategies that gave the farm some income year-round. As efforts to run these farms as businesses grew and as the scale of operations increased, many farm families maintained management control of the operation but got the work done with help from hired labor. These full-time farm families often sent their children to college to learn management, marketing, and computer skills while simultaneously maintaining general knowledge in fields as esoteric as integrated pest management, crop genetics, and tractor maintenance. Depending on what commodities the farm produced, hired labor came from local schoolchildren free for the summer, hired laborers who worked all year on a full- or part-time basis, and migrant workers who labored seasonally, picking crops. Many of these migrant workers were recent immigrants from Central American or Caribbean nations. A number of farms specializing in market crops such as strawberries or blueberries now also maintain pick-your-own plans in which the consumer provides the labor. These arrangements benefit the farmer by reducing exposure to high labor costs and complex labor regulations. A percentage of the savings is passed on to consumers. For many urban and suburban families, these pick-your-own operations and local roadside stands represent their only direct contact with New England agriculture.

Much recent history of New England agriculture suggests that the region's division into two basic groups will continue. Agriculture remains relatively vigorous in Vermont, sections of the Connecticut River valley, and portions of Maine. For the most part, farms in these areas remain family owned and operated. They are commercially oriented and are presently either remote or profitable enough to stave off development—at least until market conditions change. Elsewhere, sometimes in the interstices of suburban neighborhoods, New Englanders continue to farm specialty products and to supplement their incomes from nonfarm sources. These families have maintained some farm activities because they gain economic advantages and personal satisfaction from smaller, limited operations on a few acres. The product mix has changed, but this regional diversity reflects a long tradition. For centuries before Europeans came, Squanto's ancestors planted. In Bradford's time, farming provided families and communities with nourishment and some surpluses. In our own, full-time farmers still raise portions of their own food but depend on selling what they raise in a regional and national market. Most New Englanders, including its farmers, now live in a world of business and manufacturing, but the region's traditions are deeply rooted in an agrarian past. We delight in pumpkins on frosty October evenings, we still eat more beef than pork, and there are few treats as delicious as fresh corn on the cob. Typically, we purchase these items from supermarkets, for not many of us want to get up to pick corn in the early light of some dewy August dawn. Thankfully, some still do.

David Grayson Allen, *In English Ways: The Movement of Societies and the Transferal of English Local Law and Custom to Massachusetts Bay in the 17th Century* (1981); John Warner Barber, *Historical Collections, Being a General Collection of Interesting Facts, Traditions, Biographical Sketches, Anecdotes, Etc., Relating to the History and Antiquities of Every Town in Massachusetts* (1839); William R. Baron and Anne E. Bridges, "Making Hay in Northern New England: Maine as a Case Study, 1800–1850," *Agricultural History* 57 (1983); Hal S. Barron, *Those Who Stayed Behind: Rural Society in 19th-Century New England* (1984); Peter Benes, ed., *The Farm* (1988); Percy W. Bidwell, "The Agricultural Revolution in New England," *American Historical Review* 26 (1921); Bidwell, *Rural Economy in New England at the Beginning of the 19th Century* (1972 [1916]); Percy W. Bidwell and John I. Falconer, *History of Agriculture in the Northern United States, 1620–1860* (1973 [1925]); William Bradford, *Of Plymouth Plantation, 1620–1647: The Complete Text, with Notes and an Introduction by Samuel Eliot Morison* (1952); Christopher Clark, *The Roots of Rural Capitalism: Western Massachusetts, 1780–1860* (1990); William Cronon, *Changes in the Land: Indians, Colonists, and the Ecology of New England* (1983); James Deetz, *In Small Things Forgotten: The Archaeology of Early American Life* (1977); J. Ritchie Garrison, *Landscape and Material Life in Franklin County, Massachusetts, 1770–1860* (1991); Paul W. Gates, "Two Hundred Years of Farming in Gilsum," *Historical New Hampshire* 33 (1978); Steven Hahn and Jonathan Prude, eds., *The Countryside in the Age of Capitalist Transformation: Essays in the Social History of Rural America* (1985); Thomas C. Hubka, *Big House, Little House, Back House, Barn: The Connected Farm Buildings of New England* (1984); Stephen Innes, *Labor in a New Land: Economy and Society in 17th-Century Springfield* (1983); Sydney V. James, *The Colonial Metamorphoses in Rhode Island: A Study of Institutions in Change* (2000); Sylvester Judd, *History of Hadley: Including the Early History of Hatfield, South Hadley, Amherst, and Granby, Massachusetts* (1976 [1905]); Mark A. Mastromarino, "Fair-Weather Friend: Merino Sheep and the Origins of the Modern American Agricultural Fair," in Dublin Seminar for New England Folklife, *Annual Proceedings* (1993); David Meyer, *The Roots of American Industrialization* (2003); Margaret Richards Pabst, *Agricultural Trends in the Connecticut Valley Region of Massachusetts, 1800–1900* (1941); Jonathan Prude, *The Coming of Industrial Order: Town and Factory Life in Rural Massachusetts, 1810–1860* (1999); Randolph A. Roth, *The Democratic Dilemma: Religion, Reform, and the Social Order in the Connecticut River Valley of Vermont, 1791–1850* (1987); Winifred Barr Rothenberg, *From Market-Places to a Market Economy: The Transformation of Rural Massachusetts, 1750–1850* (1992); Howard S. Russell, *A Long, Deep Furrow: Three Centuries of Farming in New England* (1976); John T. Schlebecker, *Whereby We Thrive: A*

History of American Farming, 1607–1972 (1975); Amy D. Schwartz, "Colonial New England Agriculture: Old Visions, New Directions," *Agricultural History* 69 (1995); David C. Smith, William R. Baron, Anne E. Bridges, Janet TeBrake, and Harold W. Borns, Jr., "Climate Fluctuations and Agricultural Change in Southern and Central New England, 1765–1880," *Maine Historical Society Quarterly* 21 (1982); David C. Smith and Anne E. Bridges, "The Brighton Market: Feeding 19th-Century Boston," *Agricultural History* 56 (1982); Robert Blair St. George, *Conversing by Signs: Poetics of Implication in Colonial New England Culture* (1998); Myron Stachiw and Nora Pat Small, "Tradition and Transformation: Rural Architectural Change in 19th-Century Central Massachusetts," in *Perspectives in Vernacular Architecture,* vol. 3, ed. Thomas Carter and Bernard L. Herman (1989); Daniel Vickers, *Farmers and Fishermen: Two Centuries of Work in Essex County, Massachusetts, 1630–1850* (1994); Thomas Durant Visser, *Field Guide to New England Barns and Farm Buildings* (1997); Harold F. Wilson, *The Hill Country of Northern New England: Its Social and Economic History, 1790–1930* (1936); Joseph Sutherland Wood, *The New England Village* (1997).

J. Ritchie Garrison

Agriculture in the Precolonial and Colonial Eras

Agriculture in the Precolonial and Colonial Eras Despite the existence of such important cities as Boston, Salem, Mass., Newport, R.I., and Portsmouth, N.H., New England's economy and society between 1620 and 1775 were essentially rural and rooted in agriculture. Agriculture was one of the earliest points of contact between English settlers and Native Americans. It gave the colonies a source of capital with which to develop an economic system in their new home. Not only farmers but magistrates, merchants, ministers, soldiers, artisans, lumbermen, and fishermen engaged directly or indirectly in agriculture. It gave women the means with which to participate in the production, manufacture, and marketing of goods. As settlers pushed the frontiers farther inland from the coast, they depended on agriculture to support their efforts.

Discussions of New England agriculture usually begin with Plymouth Plantation's first meager grain crops; colonists did not introduce farming to New England, however. For centuries, except for those living most northeasterly, the Algonquian tribes of New England had derived up to half their livings from farming. Using extensive, long-fallow agriculture, the tribes raised beans, squash, pumpkins, and, most important, maize, which the English called Indian corn. Though crop combinations and the use of alewives as fertilizer helped maintain soil productivity, the planting grounds eventually ran out, and new ones had to be cleared. Native American land-clearing methods included the use of fire. In addition to providing planting grounds, burned areas grew up to grass that attracted deer, thereby facilitating the hunt. Furthermore, strawberries, raspberries, and other wild fruits thrived on the burned lands and, along with wild nuts, provided an important segment of the annual diet. Although the native inhabitants of New England farmed, their dependence on hunting, fishing, and gathering required mobility, and therein lay the most critical difference between their use of the land and the sedentary farming of the English colonists.

The colonists, too, employed extensive, long-fallow agriculture, and they integrated Native American crops, cultivation practices, and land-clearing methods with their own. Although plows and harrows were still scarce, early colonial farmers were able to rely on hoe husbandry because they settled on land previously cultivated by Indians. More than 60 towns settled before 1650 were established where Native Americans had either cleared the undergrowth or planted crops. The settlers were determined to replicate the agriculture they knew in England and imported plows and oxen as rapidly as possible. The introduction of foreign livestock and English farming methods created great hardships for the Indians. In fact, problems caused by English livestock contributed to the outbreak of King Philip's War in 1675.

Colonial governments used the English agricultural concept of "improvement" as a rationale for appropriating lands from the Native Americans and allotting it to settlers. Improvement included building houses, barns, and fences; manuring, plowing, planting, and mowing the land; and using the land to pasture livestock. Under English law Indians had clear legal claim only to their planting grounds. Colonial magistrates allotted unoccupied land to settlers according to their ability to improve it. Although many early town proprietors expected inhabitants to live on home lots clustered close to a community's church and plant their fields on great lots located outside of town, many families moved to their large parcels and set up farmsteads. Towns retained common land for pasture, wood, stone, and other natural resources to be made available to all inhabitants. Planting and haying fields were fenced against intrusion by grazing livestock, which farmers turned loose to forage freely. Undivided land in unsettled areas of southeastern new England usually became privately owned by 1690, but northern and western areas took longer to settle. Between 1725 and 1760, Massachusetts, Connecticut, and New Hampshire sold whole townships in Maine and Vermont to land speculators. However, the northern frontier remained sparsely settled until the end of the French and Indian War in 1763.

Farmers typically owned anywhere from 30 to 250 acres, but the percentage used for agriculture varied according to the quality and type of land as well as the farmer's resources. Estate inventories from the 1640s, which do not include pasturage, suggest that even though they probably owned more, ordinary farming families managed between 10 and 40 acres of arable and mowing land. By 1750 farms in the hinterlands generally ranged from 50 to 200 acres, including pasturage, with a few exceptions such as the Narragansett region and portions of New Hampshire and Maine, where private landholders still held vast farming estates. Farms in the older towns tended to be smaller. Although families converted more acreage to cropland and pastures, the original farms decreased in size as families divided their land among succeeding generations.

Men were primarily responsible for livestock management, for clearing and plowing, and for sowing, cultivating, and harvesting field crops. Women were generally responsible for the home gardens and orchards and for the barnyard animals. Dairying was among the first colonial market ventures, and it was women who manufactured butter and cheese. They participated in other types of agricultural production, manufacture, and marketing as well. Some went door to door selling their cider, beer, spun wool and linen, vegetables, and fruit products. Although they were often shrewd traders, they usually lacked the literacy and accounting skills to operate independently beyond local exchange markets. Nonetheless, women played vital, though scarcely recorded, roles in New England's colonial agricultural economy.

Agricultural production was diverse. Many farmers fished, trapped furs, and timbered because the seasonal nature of each occupation allowed them to work productively at different times of the year. The landless found seasonal work on farms, while gentleman farmers, which included governors, selectmen, judges, and ministers, leased out their land and livestock to tenants. Merchants took country pay in the form of livestock or farm products or traded merchandise for labor on their own farms. Farming households were linked to one another and to the towns by cultivated fields, trails, and roads. Neighboring farm families had systems of reciprocity that allowed them to exchange labor, equipment and livestock, crops, and manufactured goods. Family members did most of the work on farms, supplemented in some instances by indentured workers, slaves, or seasonal wage laborers. Some families produced only enough for themselves and local or regional barter. Others produced surpluses that found markets outside New England.

The linchpin of colonial New England's agricultural economy, and one of the region's earliest industries, was grazing livestock, the most useful of which were cattle. Oxen were the preferred beasts of burden for all farming, freight, and logging operations. Horses were used for riding and for carrying small loads. Clearing land and raising crops were labor-intensive tasks, but the abundant meadows and marshes along the coastline and inland rivers provided immediate pasture and hay. English grasses and clovers spread rapidly and by the beginning of the 18th century were the preferred sources of hay. Some sheep, dairy cows, working oxen, and breeding bulls were placed under the watch of keepers and herded on town commons. Other cattle, along with hogs, goats, and horses, were branded or earmarked and turned loose to fend for themselves.

Although field and orchard crops did not prove as profitable as livestock production, harvests often yielded surpluses for market.

The English grains included barley, oats, rye, and wheat, and common field crops included flax, tobacco, and peas. Wheat yields were hampered by depleted soils and by the wheat blast (identified today as black stem rust) that struck in the 1670s. The most important grain crop was Indian corn. It became New England's staple grain, feeding both the settlers and their animals. Like wheat and cattle, it was legal tender in all the colonies. Fruit trees did not require cleared land for planting, and orchards therefore became a regular feature of New England's landscape. Apples in particular did well, and by the 18th century, cider had replaced beer as the mainstay farm beverage. Other field and garden crops included cabbage, carrots, onions, parsnips, turnips, and a variety of herbs for culinary and medicinal uses. By the second decade of the 18th century, horticultural imports and exports, and domestic nursery and seed industries, were prosperous undertakings for some families.

Regions that produced surpluses of livestock or crops for internal markets were usually flanked by centers that processed the animals or plants. For example, Lynn, Mass., famous for its shoe industry, had a plentiful supply of hides from the cattle herds in the nearby Merrimack River valley as well as southern New Hampshire and Maine. The rich pastures of Narragansett Bay supported herds of dairy cattle, and Rhode Island became famous throughout the Atlantic colonies for its cheese. The Connecticut River valley, between northern Massachusetts and southern Connecticut, was New England's breadbasket, producing abundant wheat, corn, and other grains; farmers also raised market crops of potatoes, onions, tobacco, flax, and hay on the valley's fertile alluvial soil. Regions near seaports such as Boston, New London, Conn., Salem, Mass., and Providence raised cattle and hogs for salt beef and pork along with grains used to make bread for ship provisioning.

Farm produce became part of the triangular Atlantic trade network. New England ships left with diverse cargoes of potatoes, cabbage, grain, flax, corn, apples and other fruits, horses, cattle, sheep, hogs, geese, ducks, turkeys, and hens. Processed or manufactured agricultural goods included wool, cider, eggs, barreled beef and pork, leather, shoes, flour, bread, tallow, beeswax, soap, candles, cheese, butter, and flaxseed. These goods were traded with Virginia and Maryland, the Carolinas, the West Indies, the Wine Islands, southern Europe, and England. Horses were in such demand for the West Indies sugar industries that Massachusetts and Connecticut passed legislation to protect their breeding stock and to curtail the shipment of stolen animals, but

Rhode Island sold its Narragansett Pacers to extinction.

Land management habits varied among families and communities. Most farmers concentrated their efforts on clearing, tilling, and fencing. Hay meadows were often left on their own to regenerate year after year. Farmers manured some fields with dung, lime, marl, gypsum (called land plaster or plaster of Paris), ashes, seaweed, seashells, and various types of barnyard and household wastes. They also rotated grain, corn, and grass crops. With land readily available and labor and manure in short supply, however, many farmers tended to clear new plots for planting rather than improve old plots. By the mid-1700s, soils in some heavily farmed areas of Massachusetts, Connecticut, and Rhode Island showed signs of exhaustion.

Colonial agriculture was not as backward and inefficient as period reformers sometimes claimed. Colonists were seeding pastures and hayfields with clover and English grasses as early as the 1640s and possibly earlier. Nurseries and seed companies made countless fruits, nuts, garden vegetables, and herbs available for home and market production as early as 1719. Contemporary records indicate that by 1750 gentleman farmers were shifting to intensive farming and increasing the productivity of their farms by means of improved tools, more fertilizing, and better livestock-breeding practices. Yeomen farmers often imitated their more prosperous neighbors, and gradually the ideas spread. Regardless of how conservative farmers were, they wanted their efforts to yield a surplus.

During the second half of the 18th century, agriculture became more commercialized and specialized, particularly in Massachusetts and Connecticut. Changing and expanding markets affected farm labor and farm people. With the increased population in the older settlements and cities, some people migrated west. Some left the farm for employment in artisans' shops, warehouses, docks, stores, and garrets. With the growth of urban populations, farmers found larger local markets for their goods. Nevertheless, even though New England had begun the shift from an agrarian to a commercial economy, rural life and agricultural interests were never far from city and town dwellers in the colonial and Revolutionary periods.

Percy Wells Bidwell and John I. Falconer, *History of Agriculture in the Northern United States, 1620–1860* (1973 [1925]); William Cronon, *Changes in the Land: Indians, Colonists, and the Ecology of New England* (1983); Stephen Innes, *Creating the Commonwealth: The Economic Culture of Puritan New England* (1995); Howard S. Russell, *A Long, Deep Furrow: Three Centuries of Farming in New England* (1976); Laurel Thatcher Ulrich, *Good Wives: Image and Reality in the Lives of Women in Northern New England, 1650–1750* (1982).

Pamela Snow

Agricultural Settlements, 1750–1850

In the mid-1700s, New England as a whole was still an underpopulated region. A quarter of a million people hugged the coastline between the Kennebec River in Maine and the boundary with New York Colony to the south. However, the population distribution in the region was uneven. In Massachusetts continuous settlement extended only halfway through the colony; the western half was almost empty except for the Connecticut River valley. Vermont, vulnerable to French and Indian attacks from the north, remained unsettled. Most New Englanders resided in the southeastern region: Rhode Island and Connecticut were almost entirely occupied, and three-quarters of the area's population lived in Massachusetts.

During the 17th and 18th centuries, the overwhelming majority of New Englanders were farmers. Laborers for hire were scarce in a region where land was still plentiful for one and all; farmers therefore relied on their sons, and to a lesser extent their daughters, to assist them. The children in return expected as adults to be "established," preferably on a farm of their own. Farming couples also relied on their children for support in old age, which required that they settle nearby. By the mid-1700s, this practice had become increasingly difficult on the seaboard, where population pressure was a growing problem. The last unimproved land, which was at any rate poor, had been taken. Farming couples faced a limited range of possibilities. One option was to buy nearby improved land for their children, but demographic pressure was driving prices up. Another was to divide the family holding, but farmers were reluctant to create uneconomical units. Some divisions nonetheless took place, leading to a drop in the average farm size, yet still there was not enough land for everyone. Placing one's children as apprentices or sending them to college to train for a profession was another possibility, but there was a limit to the number of artisans, lawyers, and ministers New England society could absorb. In any case farming was usually the preferred option. Many felt that only a freehold guaranteed economic independence and a sure food supply. Parents could sell their land and use the proceeds to finance resettlement on the frontier, where land was cheap and abundant. Alternatively, they could provide their children with capital, usually a part of their inheritance, which would allow them to migrate. The money could be used to purchase cleared land, stock, and equipment. Parents could also attempt to secure a grant from the general court and, if they were lucky, use it to establish some of their children. Genuinely poor people were unlikely to become farmers unless they first took a tenancy allowing them to accumulate a minimum of capital: one needed tools, stock, seeds, provisions, building material, and store credit to start farms.

The population outflow took several directions. In the 1760s, New Hampshire, western Massachusetts, the Hudson River valley, and Pennsylvania were destinations of choice. The Royal Proclamation of 1763, which forbade settlement west of the Alleghenies, and the end of the Seven Years' War redirected at least some of the flow toward Vermont, New Hampshire, Maine, and Nova Scotia (which then included New Brunswick). Speculative ventures such as the huge tracts that New Hampshire's governor Benning Wentworth had been selling to friends and relatives since 1749 also attracted settlers, as buyers tried to turn a quick profit by reselling the land. By the time the U.S. census of 1790 was taken, all of New England, with the exception of mountainous regions and the district of Maine, was settled. Since 1750 the population had quadrupled to slightly more than 1 million, with most of the region still overwhelmingly rural. In Rhode Island, the most urbanized state, city dwellers accounted for just 19 percent of the population. Massachusetts, now home to only one-third of the region's inhabitants, was 87 percent rural. Maine and Vermont, still sparsely populated, could not even boast a single city.

After the Revolution, demographic growth resulted in increased population density in rural areas, in movements to nearby towns and cities, and in migrations toward Maine and the West. Consequently, by the mid-1800s, the profile of the region had changed significantly. The population had almost tripled, but the number of those living in cities had increased tenfold. By 1850 the majority of the population of Rhode Island and Massachusetts lived in urban areas, that is, towns with 2,500 or more people. Nonetheless, the rest of New England remained as rural as ever: the proportion of the population residing in rural areas ranged from 98 percent in Vermont to 84 percent in Connecticut. There were now two New Englands: an urban-industrial region along portions of the coast and major river valleys and the broad rural expanse that surrounded them. The two developed a symbiotic relationship, with the former buying the products of the latter and hiring some rural sons and daughters to work in urban businesses.

The great majority of New England farmers were freeholders. The various New England governments, both before and after the Revolution, had generally preferred land policies that favored quick settlement. Great proprietors were found only on the fringes of the region. Part of southern Maine was claimed by individuals holding letters patent issued by the king in the 17th century. After the Revolution their claims led to conflicts with would-be settlers. Those conflicts were resolved in the 1820s, when a compromise was reached allowing most squatters to purchase their holdings at a relatively reasonable rate. Contested titles also led to conflicts in Vermont in the late 1760s, when New York challenged the validity of the Wentworth grants. The settlers, gathering behind Ethan Allen and the Green Mountain Boys, resolved the matter to their advantage during the Revolution.

Farmers fought states and proprietors not only out of self-interest but also for ideological reasons. They wanted the republic to be a country of freeholders all striving to achieve a standard of living that would cover their present needs, allow them to establish a "competency" for their children, and provide for security in old age. They greatly feared dependency in the form of lifelong tenancy and disdained wage-earning occupations. Cheap if not free, land was perceived as a prerequisite for achieving this cherished independence. Farming was only one of the strategies freeholders used to make a living, however. The versatility of 18th- and early-19th-century farming couples, especially on the frontier, enabled them to exploit a multiplicity of resources. Their economic activities ranged from subsistence and market farming to the production of lumber, cordwood, potash, and maple sugar to fur trapping to trading with Indians to household manufacturing. Young unmarried males also engaged in stints of seasonal wage labor; females spent their winters spinning, weaving, and, later, plaiting straw.

Combining field crops, stock raising, and dairying, farming itself was usually unspecialized until well into the 19th century. Several reasons explained this state of affairs. First, farm communities could not have purchased the items they did not produce themselves, even if individuals could and did swap beans for eggs and apples for chickens. Second, diversification minimized the consequences of crop failures: not everything would fail at the same time. It also facilitated crop rotations and delayed soil exhaustion. Third, markets were limited and could not absorb large quantities of a given product until cities had expanded. Even commercially inclined farmers were forced to diversify until well into the 19th century.

Most prerevolutionary changes in farming practices can be traced to demographic pressure. Farmers were obliged first to intensify cultivation and then to shift their crops. They practiced "extensive" farming, cropping the same fields for several years in a row and then leaving them fallow. At the beginning of the 18th century, the fallow period lasted up to 15 years. By the time of the Revolution the shortage of land had forced farmers to reduce the fallow period to one or two years along the seaboard. Continuous cropping and limited crop rotations also facilitated the spread of bugs and diseases, which made some crops uncertain. Black stem rust had devastated wheat crops at the end of the 17th century and led to the abandonment of that staple everywhere except on the frontier. Western Connecticut and northern Vermont produced wheat into the 18th century, and Maine continued growing the crop until the 19th. It was cultivated in those regions by pioneer farmers in acute need of cash to stock and equip their farms. Elsewhere farmers fell back on corn and other grains. Bugs ravaged the field-pea crops in the 18th century, leading to their replacement by beans. Gardening expanded and by the late 18th century was supplying many families with a year-round supply of vegetables. "Irish" potatoes, introduced in mid-18th-century gardens, moved to the fields after the Revolution.

After the war the extension of farming to less fertile areas, growing demand from local industries and expanding urban markets, and improved communications with the West—where grain could be grown cheaply on new soil—encouraged other shifts in production as well as greater regional diversification. From the beginning of the century onward, farmers tried their hands at specialty crops. Crops with industrial applications, such as hops, broomcorn, Fuller's teasels (used to raise the nap of woolen fabrics), or mulberry bushes, were usually short-lived. Tobacco, fruit, and vegetables, by contrast, gained a secure foothold and soon were cultivated near cities by specialized farmers.

Animal husbandry followed the same general trend as crop growing. Eighteenth-century stock was made up of all-purpose animals raised for their meat, milk, hide, fleece, and labor power, left to forage for most of their food, and allowed to breed unselectively. In the beginning of the 19th century the first attempts were made at improving breeding stock with the importation of pedigreed animals that were bred for specific markets. The "merino craze" of the 1810s, which incited local farmers to raise large flocks of improved sheep to supply the nascent textile industry, was a good example of the process. The craze quickly died out but was not the last attempt at specialization in the area of animal husbandry. Some regions were successful in their efforts: the Champlain Valley, for example, became a center for horse and sheep breeding.

The arrival of cheap western grains, especially wheat, in the 1820s also encouraged farmers to switch to products for which they enjoyed a comparative advantage: fodder, meat, dairy products, and perishable crops. Maine and Vermont, for instance, became important producers of potatoes. Farmers in upland regions that were unfit for tillage focused their efforts on stock raising, butter and cheese making, and forest products.

Specialization was seldom complete, though. Most farmers who grew commercial crops did so in addition to a wide range of subsistence crops, which served as insurance against market downturns. By the mid-1800s, New England farming was still a mixture of market and subsistence production; the proportion of each varied with the accessibility of markets and ecological constraints.

Andrew H. Baker and Holly Izard Patterson, "Farmers, Adaptations to Markets in Early 19th-Century Massachusetts," in *The Farm*, ed. Peter Benes (1988); Percy Wells Bidwell and John I. Falconer, *History of Agriculture in the Northern United States, 1620–1860* (1973 [1925]); Christopher Clark, *The Roots of Rural Capitalism: Western Massachusetts, 1780–1860* (1990); Toby Ditz, *Property and Kinship: Inheritance in Early Connecticut, 1750–1820* (1986); Donald B. Dodd, *Historical Statistics of the States of the United States: Two Centuries of the Census, 1790–1990* (1993); J. Ritchie Garrison, *Landscape and Material Life in Franklin County, Massachusetts, 1770–1860* (1991); Bettye Hobbs-Pruitt, "Self-Sufficiency and the Agricultural Economy of 18th-Century Massachusetts," *William and Mary Quarterly*, 3d ser., 41 (1984); Alan Taylor, *Liberty Men and Great Proprietors: The Revolutionary Settlement on the Maine Frontier, 1760–1820* (1990).

Béatrice Craig

Decline of Agriculture, 1920–50

When World War I came to an end, agriculture in New England seemed, at least on the surface, to be in fairly stable condition. Although there had been a general and gradual population decline in Maine, New Hampshire, and Vermont, the area Harold Wilson described as "the Hill Country," that trend seemed to have slowed or even stopped. Some consolidation of small farms into large production units had taken place, and subsistence agriculture had diminished, at least on the poorer, glaciated soils. The main crops were prosperous—hay was grown nearly everywhere; potatoes were cultivated in the far north; buckwheat, barley, and the heavier grains were raised in many locations; and the growth of the Boston milk shed through extension of the railroads meant profits for some and a fair living for others.

Growth of truck crops increased considerably near the larger cities, where farms frequently were worked by recently immigrated laborers. In some areas, farmers still enhanced their incomes by cutting fuelwood for the urban market and providing pulpwood to the paper mills. Some farmers continued to function near the shore in the saltwater farm custom, but this practice, never widespread, was of limited consequence. Farmers in general raised fewer animals, although some country beef, pork, and mutton found their way to city butcher shops. In many places, poultry was significant both for meat and for eggs. The region was increasingly dependent on railroad transport from other areas for its food supply.

Within a decade several trends that had just begun by 1920 intensified rapidly. The amount of hay and oats dropped precipitously as trucks and automobiles replaced animal power everywhere. In the cities, trams and trolleys replaced the ubiquitous horse. The Haymarket squares in virtually every city were empty and only the name survived to indicate the amount of hay sold in earlier times.

Machinery both on the farm and elsewhere, often driven by electrical power, meant that the amount of heavy work also diminished greatly, and this trend continued throughout the period. Machinery hauled by tractors on the farm, such as mowing machines, hay balers, milking machines, and cream separators, and even pumped running water made life on the farm much easier. These machines increased the acreage usable by an individual, and that increase, coupled with high initial costs and smaller fields in New England, meant that large farms in the Midwest were able to produce more, and New England farmers found themselves with increased competition. By the end of this period electricity was available everywhere (though very costly in some areas), with the Rural Electrification Agency completing the electrical grid and subsidizing cooperatives among consumers in more remote locations.

With the diminution of hard physical work caused by the introduction of machinery came a corresponding decline in caloric intake. Although data are incomplete, the amount of calories consumed by humans probably dropped by about 50 percent from 1900 to 1930. This trend, although more slowly thereafter, continued, leading to a heightened interest in nutrition, fostered in part by the increased availability of more exotic foods such as citrus fruits, peaches, nuts, and salad materials. Prohibition meant that less barley and hops were grown as the malt and fermenting agents used in beer essentially disappeared from 1920 to 1933. Buckwheat and rye, which were cold- and wet-tolerant crops useful on smaller farms, also diminished as white bread replaced the dark loaves that had been the norm on most tables.

New England benefited to a certain degree from the establishment of large marketing cooperatives that became an important force in U.S. agriculture after the passage of the Agricultural Marketing Act of 1928. Sales of dairy products, citrus fruit, and, particularly in New England, cranberries, were increased substantially by these cooperative ventures. Important examples include Cabot Creamery, Ocean Spray, and West Lynn Creameries. Although this development was a boon for Cape Cod cranberry growers, it was a mixed blessing elsewhere, where prices went down and availability increased. There was a small backlash against oleomargarine as this spread replaced butter in many homes. Occasionally, state and federal taxes were levied on similar "artificial" products. In Vermont, for example, New York milk had to be dyed crimson before it could be sold.

Research into breeding better plants and animals improved farm production throughout the region; new federal funding was mandated for research by state experiment stations, where new disciplines were also funded. Such specialties as agricultural economics, rural sociology, agricultural engineering, plant pathology, and home economics became commonplace not only in the curricula of agricultural universities but also on farms themselves. Federal funding supported soil erosion studies, pastureland research, and better farm accounting. The Purnell Act (1925) and Bankhead Jones Act (1935) changed farm life significantly as funds flowed down to the practicing farmer. By the end of the 1920s, rural radio stations with their emphasis on weather, prices, crop predictions, and market conditions also had a significant impact on farming in New England. Farming had become a sophisticated art.

During the Depression years of the 1930s, as unemployment increased, the amount of food grown for local farm use increased. Extension agents provided much-needed home demonstrations of canning, preserving, and cooking techniques. A White House conference on children's health and nutrition held in 1929 was followed by state conferences and a stepped-up program concentrating on health and nutrition in schools throughout the region. More and more children ate school lunches prepared using high-standard diets developed by food researchers.

After 1940, New England crop production diminished or was static, but crops were grown on less acreage, and more chemicals were used both to enhance growth and to inhibit plant and insect pests. Soon the availability of good-paying jobs in war work and in military service itself meant that subsistence farming continued to decline, and many small farms were abandoned after 1940. The cost of modern farming with its attendant machinery helped this slide.

During the war this decline was partially masked by the widespread use from 1942 to 1947 of part-time labor. The Victory Volunteers and the extraordinarily successful Women's Land Army used casual labor, vacation help, and other part-time labor sources to plant, cultivate, and harvest about 30 percent of the nation's crops during the war years. Maine, Vermont, and Connecticut all sponsored such ventures before the creation of federal programs.

By 1950 New England agriculture was increasingly dominated by monocultures grown using large amounts of fertilizer, pesticides, and herbicides. These crops were sold to urban consumers who depended initially on railroads and later increasingly on highway vehicles to transport high-quality foods to them in fresh condition. Several large distributors grew substantially in size and began investing in grocery stores. This development would be a major factor in agriculture after 1950.

Connecticut continued to produce a niche crop of shade tobacco used mainly in cigar wrappers, but this demand diminished somewhat as many adults gave up smoking. Salt hay grown since the 1630s in Massachusetts continued to be a niche crop; florists used the hay for bedding soils in greenhouses. Two mainstay crops—barley and potatoes—diminished somewhat in importance. The immense growth in the consumption of frozen french fries affected New England potato growers, since the potatoes grown for this purpose needed water application at two or three crucial times during their life cycle, which elsewhere was done by irrigation. The specific gravity of the potential frozen tuber controlled its taste, shape, and firmness. The most competitive areas in frozen french-fry production, such as Idaho, used land where irrigation supplied almost all the water. In New England's climate, the precipitation came at the wrong time. In addition, New England's soil was generally too acidic, so sugar beets, which were tried as an alternative crop, were also ineffective.

The poultry and broiler industry had short-lived success after World War II, but the need to import grain from long distances and the location of poultry breeders far from the major markets of New York City eventually ended this initially profitable agrarian venture. Among the legacies of the broiler period are the large silos and poultry houses that appear to be part of the traditional New England landscape. Vermont and New Hampshire

continued to maintain a small general agrarian industry, but the tourist trade replaced the farmer family, in a life often mythologized by urbanites who wished to experience "farm life" during vacation periods. Parts of Rhode Island, Connecticut, and eastern Massachusetts became bedroom communities for the region's large cities. Agricultural sales there were steadily reduced to birdseed, flowers, and lawn materials in what had been hay and feed emporia. Market gardens survived and grew in importance in these locales, whereas items such as Maine baking potatoes found themselves supplanted by imports from Florida, Virginia, and Long Island.

By 1950 the internal combustion engine dominated rural life, altering agriculture completely. Major crops had disappeared or become specialty items. Food intake changed almost completely. Rail and truck traffic created national competition. Nostalgia for rural life and ethics was increasingly seen in tradition-laden aspects such as Thanksgiving menus, patio-grown tomatoes, and the pleasures of mowing a lawn amid one's flowers purchased in local greenhouses. Few actual full-time farmers remained by the 1950s, as even the great potato, dairy, and beef farms of 1920 had nearly disappeared. State universities remained tied to agriculture, though fewer and fewer students took these courses. In a sense, rural New England was transformed not because of population failures but because it adapted to the realities of a world in which regional agriculture had become increasingly less important.

Clarence Albert Day, *Farming in Maine, 1860–1940* (1963); Thomas C. Hubka, *Big House, Little House, Back House, Barn: The Connected Farm Buildings of New England* (1984); Howard S. Russell, *A Long, Deep Furrow: Three Centuries of Farming in New England* (1976); Charles Morrow Wilson, *Aroostook, Our Last Frontier: Maine's Picturesque Potato Empire* (1937); Harold F. Wilson, *The Hill Country of Northern New England: Its Social and Economic History, 1790–1930* (1936).

David C. Smith

Contemporary Agriculture In New England physical geography and market forces have shaped an agricultural system that is constantly subjected to changing technology and economic conditions. Driving through the countryside, one encounters evidence of both past and present farm activities and a few hints of future patterns: one-ton bales of hay neatly wrapped in white plastic next to an old barn, now obsolete for housing livestock and storing feed, that is being dismantled; a herd of 200 dairy cows on a summer day looking across a valley from their free-stall shed while their owner cuts and hauls fresh grass to them; or the construction of a

new tobacco barn in response to the growing popularity of cigars.

Although New England agriculture is present in many rural areas and small towns, and occasionally in cities, it plays a minor role within the national farm economy. Approximately 28,250 farms (1.2 percent of the U.S. total) are located in the region. Cash receipts for products from these operations totaled $1.96 billion dollars in 2003. A typical New England farm contains 142 acres, far fewer than the national average of 436. However, the region's net farm income per acre of farmland of $77 indicates intensive agriculture with strong commodity prices (see table). Intensive farming involves big inputs of labor per unit of land and usually yields large economic returns per acre. Fruits and vegetables for fresh-produce markets and nursery crops are some of the more labor-intensive farm products. Extensive operations entail less labor per acre but more area per farm. Large-scale potato production for both processed and unprocessed markets is extensive agriculture. Connecticut ($317) and Rhode Island ($93) are the two leading U.S. states in income per acre. Rhode Island, Connecticut, and Massachusetts rank second, third, and fourth nationally in value of farmland per acre. Little Rhode Island also is fourth in the country in net income per farm operation. These numbers are only half the story, for in northern New England farms are larger and tend to produce crops with lower yields per acre; extensive agriculture is the norm as opposed to the intensive farming practiced in the three southern New England states. New Hampshire is a bit of an anomaly with its high tax on farmland—fifth in the nation in 1995—while farmers are not generating large returns per acre.

Contemporary New England agriculture is a composite of major sectors such as dairy, egg, and nursery enterprises; a variety of niche markets have also been developed and maintained. A large urban demand for milk products combined with a cool, wet climate and soils conducive to forage production has resulted in widespread dairy farming. Approximately 236,000 milk cows inhabit New England, with 146,000 of them (62 percent) in Vermont. Milk represents 29 percent of all New England agricultural receipts. This farm sector benefits from a well-developed collection, processing, and marketing infrastructure that has resulted from stability made possible by federal and state regulation of production and sales within geographic regions. New England milk flows into both the New England and New York Federal Order Districts (milk supply and pricing zones established by the U.S. government).

Vermont has been especially successful in

Barn frame and wrapped hay, 1997

promoting a positive image for its dairy industry. Black-and-white Holsteins (the most common dairy breed found in the region) in a green pasture are a big part of the state's rural appearance. Cabot Creamery, with its international cheese market, and Ben and Jerry's upscale ice cream take advantage of and reinforce this long tradition. However, farms are confronted with challenges posed by economies of scale that lead to handicaps for small operations and increase the size of those that stay in business. With large herds being managed to augment production per cow, a variety of environmental concerns have led to a growing number of regulations that add to farmers' responsibilities. How much milk-enhancing drug should be permitted in cattle, and what kind should be used? How can massive piles of manure be handled without damage to the water quality in nearby brooks and ponds?

Eggs are the second most important livestock product, generating about 6 percent of all receipts. Maine accounts for 56 percent of the value, much of it associated with the world's largest brown egg producer, DeCoster, in Turner. This business is representative of an agriculture trend in its factorylike atmosphere and large permanent workforce of immigrants. Although the brown egg is traditionally preferred by New Englanders, it does enjoy an international market as well. Hens are confined to small cages and fed a diet to maximize production. Working and living conditions of the largely Mexican employees are problematic, with health and wage issues resulting in frequent and prolonged legal actions against owners and management.

With its high-value fruits (apples, berries, and others) and vegetables (such as tomatoes and sweet corn) and occasional factory farms,

New England Agriculture

	New England	Connecticut	Maine	Massachusetts	New Hampshire	Rhode Island	Vermont
Number of farms	28,250	4,200	7,200	6,100	3,400	850	6,500
Average size (acres)	142	83	190	85	132	71	192
Cash receipts (thousands of dollars)	1,961,568	484,534	498,764	384,746	150,057	57,225	402,722
Average income per acre (dollars)	77	317	34	63	12	93	84
Farmland value per acre (dollars)	3,779	9,500	1,750	9,300	3,100	9,300	2,050
All cattle (thousands)	522	54	91	48	39	5	285
Dairy cows (thousands)	236	21	34	18	16	1	146
Milk, cash receipts (thousands of dollars)	571,625	55,760	87,898	43,269	41,072	2,869	340,730
Chickens (thousands)*	9,916	3,745	5,473	280	219	—	199
Eggs, cash receipts (thousands of dollars)*	126,406	44,123	70,530	4,879	3,261	—	3,613
Greenhouse and nursery cash receipts (thousands of dollars)	495,699	207,834	25,000	148,865	56,000	38,000	23,000
Potatoes, cash receipts (thousands of dollars)**	115,217	—	108,498	5,804	—	915	—
Aquaculture, cash receipts (thousands of dollars)	61,963	15,200	38,220	6,527	1,350	556	110

*Excluding Rhode Island
**Tabulation for Maine, Massachusetts, and Rhode Island only
Source: New England Agriculture Statistics (2003)

New England States among U. S. Leaders (Ranking in Top Five)

	Item	Rank
Connecticut	Farmland value per acre	3
	Net farm income per acre	2
	Real estate tax per acre of farmland	3
Maine	Maple syrup production	3
	Wild blueberry production	1
Massachusetts	Cranberry production	2
	Farmland value per acre	4
	Net farm income per acre	4
	Real estate tax per acre of farmland	4
New Hampshire	Real estate tax per acre of farmland	5*
Rhode Island	Farmland value per acre	2
	Net farm income per acre	1
	Net farm income per operation	4
	Real estate tax per acre of farmland	1
Vermont	Maple syrup production	1

*This figure, exceptionally, comes from the New England Agriculture Statistical Sources publication "Agricultural Summary and Commodity Ranking by State, 1995" (Concord, N.H.)
Source: New England Agricultural Statistics (1997)

New England is not immune from the issues associated with employing foreign nationals in jobs that pay such low wages or involve such poor working conditions that they deter potential local applicants. The impact of immigrant labor is widespread in some rural communities, as schools provide an increasing number of Spanish-language classes and local stores stock Latin American food items.

Crops account for nearly half of all farm income, with potatoes the most important commodity. Most (94 percent) of the region's potatoes are grown in Maine, and nine-tenths of those are harvested in Aroostook County (aka "the County"). Because the growing season is just long enough and the limestone bedrock along the New Brunswick border modifies soil acidity, farmers can produce spuds suitable for the markets of northeastern United States.

Potatoes grown in this area are similar in quality to those from nearby Canada and compete in the same markets. Canadian interests, such as McCain, whose french-fry plant in northern Maine is the world's largest, control much of the state's processing capacity, and most potatoes imported into the United States from Canada pass through ports of entry along the Maine-Canada boundary. The international dimension, when combined with great fluctuations in year-to-year quality, quantity, and prices, has resulted in an atmosphere of uncertainty leading to a decline in acreage planted.

There is no need to travel to rural areas to see farmers. Greenhouse and nursery goods are leading sources of farm earnings in the three southern New England states. These are linked to urban environments and the pace of development. Shrubs, turf, and ornamental trees are part of landscape design in almost every new residential or commercial project. Their production requires much labor and relatively little space. However, these enterprises are usually found close to consumers on high-value city or suburban land. White Flower Farm, in Litchfield, Conn., and Garden in the Woods, located in Framingham, Mass., and operated by the New England Wildflower Society, are examples of success in the horticulture sector. Fruits and vegetables such as strawberries, sweet corn, and tomatoes for the fresh market are also situated close to buyers, and these operations often face the same problems that greenhouses and nurseries confront. Many producers have their own roadside stands or pick-your-own options, but public markets such as the one located next to Monument Square in Portland, Maine, are important outlets for produce. Urban congestion, pressure from development, and high real estate taxes are constant concerns.

Agricultural supply companies have shifted much of their focus toward urban and suburban farmers. Some traditional agricultural equipment dealerships are now largely lawn and garden shops. New England seed firms, such as Johnny's Selected Seeds in Albion, Maine; Vermont Bean Seed Company of Fairhaven, Vt.; and Shepherd's Garden Seeds in Litchfield, Conn., have been especially successful in recognizing and responding to the expanding demand for their products. Connecticut and Rhode Island are classic urban agricultural environments. Sixty-six percent of farm receipts in Rhode Island are from greenhouse and nursery sales, and 12 percent are from the mix of minor crops that the U.S. Department of Agriculture refers to as "all other crops" for statistical purposes. Mushrooms, herbs, and the like would be included in the latter category. After one accounts for all major crops, the livestock contribution to Rhode Island's receipts is only 15 percent. Land in the smallest state is too valuable for many farm animals. Connecticut exhibits much the same pattern, with no single crop representing more than 4 percent of farm receipts. The mix of greenhouse and nursery products is 43 percent. Animal products, especially milk, continue to play a big role in the state's farm economy, generating 12 percent of receipts.

New England states rank in the top three nationally in the production of three crops: maple syrup (Vermont is first, Maine third), wild blueberries (Maine ranks first), and cranberries (Massachusetts comes in second) (see table). These are small-market products that have strong regional identities. Maple syrup under a Vermont label sets the tone for many pancake meals and is a popular gift for tourists to take back home to friends and relatives. The Green Mountain State produces 51 percent of the region's volume. Wild blueberry farming is largely a Maine enterprise, with its operations concentrated in Washington County. Jasper Wyman and Son is one of the largest processors. This crop does well on the thin, sandy, acid soil that is plentiful in that part of the state. Wild blueberries thrive under physical conditions that would lead to failure for most other commercial farming enterprises. Much of the crop is harvested by migrant workers and processed for the national and international markets. Management of this product entails significant integration with the Canadian wild blueberry business in nearby New Brunswick. Because the Maine crop ripens first, the same labor pool and processing capacity that accommodates U.S. producers can be made available to Canadians later in the season.

Massachusetts cranberries have a fine reputation in the national market and are associated with the southeastern part of that state, which also happens to include Plymouth and the origins of that great American meal-centered holiday, Thanksgiving. Not a bad promotional tool for a food! Although a lack of additional land suitable for the crop limits expansion in Massachusetts, new cranberry bogs are being developed in Maine. Ocean Spray continues to be a major marketer of this crop.

Most agricultural regions have one or two

Abandoned farmhouse near Lancaster, N.H., 1976

products that come as a surprise to the uninitiated traveler. Connecticut River valley tobacco may fall into this classification. Rich land in western Massachusetts and central Connecticut has a long history of producing excellent shade tobacco widely used for cigar wrappers, a high-value market. Although the industry is of modest scale and has suffered general decline during the past half century, recent growth in the popularity of cigars has resulted in an expansion of acreage and the construction of new tobacco barns by a few farmers. Tobacco politics will probably play a role in the future of this trend.

Aquaculture is a relatively new dimension of agriculture in the region, and the U.S. Department of Agriculture began including information on these operations as part of *New England Agricultural Statistics* in 1990. Today aquaculture accounts for 3 percent of farm receipts. Fish farming is concentrated in Connecticut and Maine. This activity may not fit the traditional image of agrarian New England, but it is a growing aspect of small coastal communities.

New England's agriculture is a significant component of the region's landscape, and the continued success of many operations is a testament to the ability of the region's farmers to adjust to changing technological and economic forces. Many of New England's physical limitations are offset by its large urban markets, diverse ecology, and capacity to take advantage of niche opportunities. The future is likely to produce fewer red barns and more fiberglass greenhouses.

Greg Cox, "Grower Surrounded by 100,000 People: An Excellent Location for a Massachusetts Grower," *Farming: The Journal of Northeast Agriculture* 1, no. 7 (1998); Susan Harlow, "Is Big Bad? The Answer New England States Arrive at May Well Determine the Future Face of Farming in the Region," *New England Farmer* 22 (1998); John F. Hart, *The Land That Feeds Us* (1991); Don Hurlbert and Eleanor Jacobs, "Catch the Wave: Maine's Cranberry Production Climbs as the Taste for This Tart Fruit Grows," *New England Farmer* 22 (1998).

Paul B. Frederic

Abandoned Farms During the late 19th century, both the image and the reality of the abandoned farm exemplified New Englanders' concerns about the general decay of an idealized rural life. Although there was continuous debate among journalists and politicians about the veracity of reports of New Englanders abandoning their hilly farms, out-migration from rural New England certainly heightened during the mid-1800s. After 1870 families abandoned northern New England farms in significant numbers, a trend that continued well into the 20th century. Between 1930 and 1990 the decline accelerated; by the late 1970s, only 12 percent of New England's acreage was committed to agriculture, compared to nearly 50 percent in 1900.

Public alarm over the rising number of abandoned or unoccupied farms in New England surfaced during the last quarter of the 19th century, receiving considerable coverage in the popular press. By the 1890s, several state governments had created agencies to investigate this phenomenon. Observers argued that many farms were never tenable in the first place and pointed out that emigrants secured a better life by leaving the region and establishing themselves in urban areas. But many commentators believed that abandoned farms portended a bleak future for the region and worried about the enervation of community life in rural areas as youths departed and left farming to their aging parents.

Abandoned farms became a metaphor through which elite New Englanders expressed their dissatisfaction with industrialization, urbanization, immigration, rampant materialism, and change. Articles published in popular magazines—*The Nation* and *Atlantic Monthly* among them—grappled with the factors that caused abandonment. A recurring theme in many pieces was a strident nativism. Concerned with the disappearance of the allegedly pure, intelligent, hardworking Yankee yeomanry (and perhaps the eclipse of their social dominance), writers charged that as rural New England industrialized, its old Anglo-Saxon stock left the countryside and were replaced by Irish Catholic immigrants and other "defectives and degenerates." With peculiar power, the evidence of abandoned farms called forth conflicting emotions of nostalgic pastoral memories and fears about what people in the region were losing to modernization.

The effort to understand farm abandonment shaped the region's literature, art, and social policy. Many people chose to stay in rural towns and sought to revitalize their communities. They searched for new kinds of crops or economic opportunities, established Old Home Week, and encouraged rural tourism during the summer. Authors captured a variety of perspectives on rural communities. Edith Wharton's novel *Ethan Frome* offered a bleak picture of the old Yankee stock that tenaciously held onto farms, portraying an environment that crushed its characters' spirits and imagination. Other authors, such as local-color fiction writers Sarah Orne Jewett and Mary Wilkins Freeman, poets Robert Frost and Edwin Arlington Robinson, and the photographer, author, and antiquarian Wallace Nutting appropriated the image of the abandoned farm and captured in their work the nostalgia of city dwellers for a simple, rural life that seemed to be slipping away. Their treatments helped shape a public impression that lingers into the 21st century. Although they sometimes portrayed rural residents as desperate and disappointed, even degenerate, all evoked images of stone walls, barns, houses, orchards, and gardens falling into decay until the forest eventually engulfed them.

Liberty Hyde Bailey, ed., *Cyclopedia of American Agriculture IV*, s.v. "Abandoned Farms" (1907–11); Hal S. Barron, *Those Who Stayed Behind: Rural Society in 19th-Century New England* (1984); Michael Bell, "Did New England Go Downhill?" *Geographical Review* 79 (1989); Sally McMurry, *Families and Farmhouses in 19th-Century America: Vernacular Design and Social Change* (1988); Harold F. Wilson, *The Hill Country of Northern New England* (1936).

Sally McMurry

Agricultural Press High levels of literacy, the need to respond to changing markets, and a progressive scientific spirit set the stage for a thriving agricultural press in New England in the late 18th century. Publications flourished in the 19th century but declined as agriculture became less significant to the region in the early years of the 20th century.

New England's first agricultural publications were almanacs. The earliest of these were issued in the 17th century and often included fragments of practical farming advice. Robert B. Thomas's *Farmers' Almanac*, first published in 1792, was the first almanac to become an ambitious annual journal. Two early farming manuals written by New Englanders are Jared Eliot's *Essay on Field Husbandry* (1760) and the Reverend Samuel Deane's *New England Farmer or Georgical Dictionary* (1790). The new Massachusetts Society for Promoting Agriculture began publishing pamphlets and annual volumes of papers—largely reprints from English sources—in the 1790s. Beginning in 1813, the society offered the *Massachusetts Agricultural Repository and Journal*, which was edited and largely written by John Lowell, the society's most active officer from 1813 to 1832. A semi-annual at the beginning (1813–15) and end (1826–32) of its life, and a quarterly through its middle years, it presented articles on scientific farming methods and experimental crops to an elite audience.

In 1822, Thomas Green Fessenden, a New Hampshire minister's son who had farmed as a boy, began publishing the *New England Farmer* as a weekly. This popular journal applauded technical innovations, covered the period's various agricultural societies and their fairs, and exhorted farmers to practice frugality and temperance. In its several incarnations, the *New England Farmer,* published from 1822 to 1846, 1848 to 1871, and 1868 to 1913, was one of the most enduring of the region's agricultural journals.

During the 1830s and 1840s, a spate of magazines emerged in New England and throughout the nation in response to the demand for information on scientific farming methods. Most, such as the *Northern Farmer,* published in Newport, N.H., from 1832 to 1834, and the *Connecticut Valley Farmer,* edited by the Reverend John Adams Nash, which merged with the *New England Farmer* in 1856, survived for a few years only. Others, such as the *Kennebec Farmer,* founded in 1833 and quickly renamed the *Maine Farmer,* lasted for several decades. The *Maine Farmer* became one of the most influential agricultural journals in New England. Published until 1924, it featured articles on every facet of the region's agriculture. The *Maine Farmer* was reborn in 1924 as a supplement to the *Portland Press Herald*'s Sunday edition. The *Massachusetts Ploughman* was first published in 1840 and lasted until 1906. The New Hampshire State Agricultural Society published a journal from 1850 to 1863 under three titles: the *Granite Farmer* (1850–53), the *Granite Farmer and Visitor* (1854–58), and the *New Hampshire Journal of Agriculture* (1858–63). In 1863, the *New Hampshire Journal of Agriculture* merged with another journal, the *Dollar Weekly Mirror,* to become the *Mirror and Farmer,* of Manchester, N.H., which was published until 1908. Other enduring journals include the *Connecticut Farmer,* published in Hartford and New Haven from 1875 to 1927, and the *New England Homestead,* a Springfield, Mass., publication that lasted from 1868 to 1969.

New England had no important agricultural journal after the *New England Homestead* ceased publication. Country-life essayists analyzed the decline of agriculture and celebrated the joys of rural life, but their audience consisted of urban and suburban dwellers, not working farmers. In 1977, Rural Press USA of Raleigh, N.C., began a fourth iteration of the *New England Farmer* as a monthly tabloid. The present *Farmer* provides about 5,400 paid subscribers, an audience of roughly the same size that Fessenden served, with news of

maple sugaring, dairying, and other traditional farm concerns.

Albert Lowther Demaree, *The American Agricultural Press, 1819–1860* (1941); Paul W. Gates, *The Farmer's Age: Agriculture, 1815–1860* (1960); Nathaniel Hawthorne, "Thomas Green Fessenden," *American Monthly Magazine* 11 (1838); Donald B. Marti, *To Improve the Soil and the Mind: Agricultural Societies, Journals, and Schools in the Northeastern States, 1791–1865* (1979).

Donald B. Marti and David H. Watters

Apples

Apples Apples have dominated New England agriculture since the colonial era. The subject of myth and legend since antiquity, and symbols of health, youthfulness, and prosperity in literature and art, apples are considered the fruit of paradise and were a staple of colonial diets. Edward Johnson noted in 1654 in his *Wonderworking Providence of Sion's Saviour in New England* that Massachusetts abounded with "orchards filled with goodly fruit trees" and that apples were the "prime article of culture" in New England.

According to legend, William Blaxton planted the first colonial orchard in the Massachusetts Bay Colony in 1625 on Boston's Beacon Hill. Blaxton later moved to Rhode Island, where he established a new apple variety named Blaxton's Yellow Sweeting. Colonial governors, including John Winthrop, planted orchards on their land, trading trees and acreage as valuable property. Early settlers also showed Native Americans how to plant orchards in exchange for agricultural advice about indigenous crops. Colonists grafted and cultivated apples for particular uses. The first recorded American variety created through grafting, the Roxbury Russet (named for the

Apple harvest, Harvard, Mass., 1975

Massachusetts town), was grown specifically for making cider.

Many New England families owned and tended apple orchards for their own use. Apples could be stored for long periods in home cellars and had myriad applications; they were eaten raw or cooked, pressed for juice, or baked in pies. A popular dish made of spiced apples sweetened with molasses and topped with pastry was called apple slump (Louisa May Alcott, who chronicled October apple picking in *Little Women,* would give this name to her family's orchard house in Concord, Mass.). Lesser apples were fed to livestock, and apple-tree wood was useful for whittling and firewood; apple blossoms decorated houses, and dried applehead dolls amused children. Apple cider was often considered safer to drink than water, and fermented applejack was used as a preservative and medicine.

John Chapman, a colonial resident of Leominister, Mass., distributed apple seeds from northeastern cider presses throughout the Midwest; he would later become known as the legendary Johnny Appleseed. These seeds, however, did not produce trees similar to their New England source. Apple growers were able to grow genetically identical trees only by grafting a bud stick onto rootstock. Occasionally, unique seedlings appeared, which growers then propagated to develop new varieties. New England varieties of apples now include Cortland, New England Red Delicious, Macoun, Empire, Rome, Crispin, Gala, and Golden Delicious. Antique varieties include Baldwin, Northern Spy, and Pippin. Discovered as a chance seedling in 1870, the popular Macintosh apple accounts for nearly two-thirds of a total New England apple harvest of approximately 6 million bushels annually.

The apple industry remains a vital part of New England's agricultural economy. Since 1912 laws have been passed to regulate the quality of apples sold. Today, growers cultivate apples to be more pest and disease resistant, using fungicides to prevent blemishing from flyspeck and to avoid cedar apple rust, which causes lesions, spotting, and defoliation. Scientists have developed better grafting methods and have introduced mechanisms such as the apple-tree shaker to harvest fruit. Picking machines have displaced many migrant workers in the orchards. Devices have been patented to pare, core, and slice apples. Even orchard management has become computerized; the University of Vermont maintains a "virtual orchard" on the Internet with a Listserv discussion group to connect researchers and growers. The important role of apples in New England's agricultural history is still celebrated annually at apple festivals and fairs, and New Englanders continue to enjoy the autumn tradition of apple picking at orchards throughout the region.

R. F. Carlson et al., *North American Apples: Varieties, Rootstocks, Outlook* (1970); Elizabeth S. Helfman, *Apples, Apples, Apples* (1977); Warren Manhart, *Apples for the 21st Century* (1995); Joan Morgan and Alison Richards, *The Book of Apples* (1993).

Elizabeth D. Schafer

Aquaculture

Aquaculture is the general term for the production of aquatic organisms through human intervention in the rearing process. Mariculture (the controlled rearing of marine species) and shellfish culture (the production of mollusks and crustaceans) are specific forms of aquaculture.

Early evidence suggests that aquaculture, in some form, has been practiced in what is New England since well before the first Europeans landed. The first colonists would have encountered great mounds of mollusk shells discarded on the shores of the region's bays, estuaries, and inland rivers by indigenous tribes.

Historically New England has been known for its bountiful harvesting and consumption of fishery resources. During the rapid expansion of the 1800s, however, as in recent times, the region experienced widespread depletion of many fish species. By the mid-1800s, citizens' groups and legislators were calling on state governments to address the restoration of fish stock. The political commitment that followed, coupled with federal initiatives, resulted in modern aquaculture practices in the form of publicly funded fish hatcheries and rearing stations. After having limited success with propagating major food species, regional hatchery programs soon began to focus on recreational and game species, as they do today.

Commercial aquaculture in the private sector was a direct result of the success of public fish hatcheries. Scientific research in water control, predation, parasitic diseases, and hatchery design has enabled private parties to operate fish hatcheries and rearing facilities in their own backyards. Most aquaculturists in New England began as operators of small-scale facilities located on or near their properties. These mom-and-pop operations were initially conceived as part-time activities that would eventually realize enough profit to cover costs and perhaps supplement income. In recent years, however, the industry has become more competitive in the hopes of increasing profits and moving beyond the economic breakeven point. Many firms now operate as full-time enterprises. Nonetheless, the industry remains characterized by a small number of operators closely connected by friendships, mutual interests, and long-term relationships with their customers.

Freshwater production in the region generally consists of coldwater game and food species such as brook and rainbow trout. Geographically these operations are distributed relatively equally throughout New England. These fish are typically sold as stock for locally owned ponds and, to a lesser degree, as food for retail outlets. Current industry techniques involve rearing fish at high density in a small number of raceways, circular pools, or rearing ponds. Such facilities can produce between 50,000 and 100,000 fish annually.

Commercial mariculture occurs chiefly in the coastal bays of Connecticut and Massachusetts, where efforts have centered on the cultivation of shellfish, primarily oysters, for local and regional markets. More recently, attention has shifted to the growing number of high-intensity Norwegian-style salmon farms operating in the coastal waters of Maine. The technology used by these operations, which raise salmon for the domestic and international market in stationary net pens anchored in bays and lagoons, has proven successful, and further expansion can be expected domestically as other production obstacles are overcome and demand for the product increases.

Although opposition to aquaculture development does exist in New England, it is usually limited to proposed operations in commonly owned coastal waters. Competing users of these waters have, at times, become fierce and vocal in their opposition, as evidenced in Maine in the 1980s, when net-pen salmon farming was introduced. As a result of this and other conflicts, individual states have begun to play a more active role in regulating what has traditionally been a virtually unregulated, obscure New England industry.

John Bardach, "Aquaculture Moving from Craft to Industry," *Environment* 2 (1988); Elisabeth Mann Borgese, *Seafarm: The Story of Aquaculture* (1980); Art Tiddens, *Aquaculture in America: The Role of Science, Government, and the Entrepreneur* (1990).

Jeffrey T. Royal

Blueberries

One of the few edible fruits native to New England, the lowbush wild blueberry (*Vaccinium angustifolium*) grows primarily in northern Maine, where it prefers moist, well-drained, acidic soils. Before Europeans settled the region, Native Americans harvested the wild berries, which they found both delicious and helpful in combating fever. Colonists ate them fresh from the bush and used them in breads, cakes, puddings, and soups. Wild blueberries were also used to dye cloth navy blue, and during the Civil War, wild blueberries were crushed into a nutritious drink.

The blueberry industry expanded quickly during the 1940s and 1950s, displacing many cranberry bogs. By the 1960s, the blueberry in-

Harvesting blueberries with rake, West Jonesport, Maine, 1974

dustry had become a commercialized, multi-million-dollar business. Between 1980 and 1985 alone, blueberry consumption in the United States increased by 50 percent, and the majority of these berries were grown in New England. In the 1990s some 80,000 acres of land yielded annual harvests of up to 70 million pounds of wild blueberries; one half of wild blueberry acreage is burned and left fallow every year to stimulate alternate-year berry production. Growers typically enjoy a particularly exceptional crop every six or so years. In 2003 wild blueberry growers in Maine, the region's key producer, reported a yield of 80.2 million pounds.

Wild blueberries were traditionally harvested using handheld berry rakes. As demand increased, blueberry growers adopted new management techniques and such technological advances as overhead irrigation systems to prevent frost. Harvesting methods changed from hand picking to mechanized shakers, and although workers continued to examine berries for defects, machines such as tilt belts separated soft and firm berries, water tanks revealed ripe berries, and destemmers and blowers removed debris. Larger companies used electronic sorters, and freeze-drying methods were improved.

Today, wild blueberries are often still harvested using traditional handheld berry rakes, then quickly sorted, cleaned, and processed to preserve their freshness and flavor. They are generally shipped to markets in cellophane-wrapped pint and quart containers but are also sold in the field to consumers willing to pick their own produce. This cottage industry has proved profitable to smaller blueberry producers. Individual quick-freezing technology now allows berries to be frozen and kept fresh for up to two years; 90 percent of the region's annual wild blueberry crop is sold frozen. Growers also sell blueberry branches to florists for ornamental uses.

Maine produces more than half of the wild blueberries consumed globally. The Wild Blueberry Association of North America was formed in 1981 to promote the fruit to markets worldwide and is headquartered in Bar Harbor, Maine. The wild blueberry industry currently supports some 2,000 employees in Maine's Washington, Hancock, and Knox Counties. High-profile brands such as Betty Crocker, Post, and Hood have included wild blueberries from Maine in their baking products, cereals, and beverages. Recent studies rank blueberries first in anti-oxidant activity when compared with 40 other fruits and vegetables, making wild Maine blueberries a popular choice for their ability to neutralize free radicals associated with cancer, heart disease, and age-related health risks.

Frank L. Caruso and Donald C. Ramsdell, eds., *Compendium of Blueberry and Cranberry Diseases* (1995); Paul Eck, *Blueberry Science* (1988); Eck and Norman F. Childers, eds., *Blueberry Culture* (1966); Katie Letcher Lyle, *The Wild Berry Book: Romance, Recipes, and Remedies* (1994).

Elizabeth D. Schafer

Brighton Market The Brighton Market, located 6 miles west of Boston, was the center of livestock sales and meat processing for the New England retail food trade from the time of the Revolution through 1967. Before refrigeration, surplus farm animals were driven to Boston for sale and slaughter as early as 1647. Such animals became a source of salt beef for local and military use. During the Revolutionary War, farmer Jonathan Winship began to manage this meat trade and was contracted to supply colonial troops. He continued this work sporadically until the Massachusetts Society for Promoting Agriculture held its first annual cattle show at Winship's Brighton farm on October 8, 1816. Over the next decade, an auction hall, a hotel, and stock pens were erected on the site. These buildings soon proved too modest for the burgeoning trade, however, and in 1850 new quarters—hotels, slaughterhouses, auction rooms, and exhibition halls—were constructed, and the Brighton Market was established.

The livestock trade was most active in the autumn, when drovers brought animals to market from Maine, Vermont, and western Massachusetts. In the early days of the Brighton Market, animals were made available for inspection all week, though auctions were held only on Mondays. The auction was moved to Wednesday at midcentury; Tuesdays

and Fridays were later added to the auction schedule, and by 1860, livestock sales occurred every day of the week except Sunday. In 1825, the Brighton Market became the show and auction site for the famed merino sheep imported from Spain. This enterprise brought the market recognition as a major northeastern trade center for animals and animal products.

By 1865, as many as 34 slaughterhouses were in operation at Brighton, and the processing and sale of blood, bones, hooves, manure, hides, and entrails became a lucrative side business. In 1872, a new abattoir, capable of processing 300 beef cattle each working day, was built. This facility, which used ice as a coolant, remained in use until chemical refrigeration replaced it in the 1880s.

With the advent of the railroad, "drover specials," with stock cars for animals and passenger cars for their drovers, became a standard feature on all rail lines serving Boston. By 1873, Texas and western cattle trains ran on a regular basis, and with them, large numbers of animals began arriving in Boston. In the 1860s and 1870s, 135,000 to 150,000 cattle and more than 400,000 sheep arrived each year, while the number of swine arriving at Brighton Market often surpassed half a million annually. As the railroad network extended out from Boston, the catchment area for the animals became larger. A grand union stockyard was built in nearby Watertown in 1870 to accommodate animals railed in from the West.

The Watertown yard site continued to serve the Brighton Market until 1923, though the last major overland drives to Brighton ended about 1910. The market itself remained the central location in northern New England for the sale of beef, oxen, dairy cows, sheep, swine, and poultry well into the 20th century. As time went on, fewer oxen were auctioned, but the poultry and veal trade grew steadily. Auction prices and the number of animals sold were reported weekly in the agricultural press, and farmers used these data to determine when to sell. The market's high standards of operation and controlled pricing made it a significant economic force in New England for more than a century. The Brighton Market closed in 1967.

Isaac C. Libby, "Cattle Drovers Life," *Maine Farmer*, September 24, 1863, November 14, 1867; David C. Smith and Anne E. Bridges, "The Brighton Market: Feeding Boston in the 19th Century," *Agricultural History* 56 (January 1982); U.S. Commissioner of Agriculture, *Annual Report*, 1870.

David C. Smith

Commercialization Early in the 20th century, the pioneering scholar Percy Wells Bidwell divided the history of New England

into two parts, a "period of self-sufficient economy," lasting until about 1800, and a subsequent "period of transition to commercial agriculture." Bidwell's interpretation, contrasting a distant, noncommercial past with the later emergence of an urban, industrialized immigrant society, reflected a significant strand in New Englanders' understanding of their history. It neatly captured modernism's paradoxical pair: faith in progress and nostalgia for a purer, uncorrupted way of life. All subsequent historians of rural New England have had to grapple with the same polarities. Recent studies have largely confirmed Bidwell's perception of discontinuity while rejecting the notion of a single transition from one way of life to another. Most scholars identify a set of subtler, though powerful, changes that commercialized agriculture in several stages and took different forms across the region.

The first critical change occurred in the 17th century, as white settlers occupied southern New England, replacing Native Americans' communal fields with permanent, fenced farms that were privately owned. Colonial farming was neither purely commercial nor self-sufficient. New England farmers did not produce one staple export crop. Those in fertile areas accessible by water sold farm products for export, those near towns provided market supplies, and inlanders traded some crops or the products of land clearance for distant sale. But most farmers were not primarily guided by these commercial links. Instead, using mostly family labor, they evolved patterns of household-based production that achieved a measure of local, rather than individual, self-sufficiency through networks of exchange between neighbors and kin. Farm families' main concern was to secure their livelihoods and pass on resources and property to their children; diversified production and the division of land were more prominent means to this end than profits from trade. Prosperous families who anticipated running short of land for their children often moved to frontier regions, where they could preserve their way of life. Even in areas like Essex County, Mass., which had expanding urban centers, 18th-century farmers did little to meet rising market demand for produce.

The expansion of Atlantic trade and disruptions caused by the American Revolution steered the New England countryside toward commercialization. But these external influences only supplemented more powerful internal pressures from population growth, land shortage, and migration. Changes during the half century after independence were largely structured by the household economy itself; agriculture was not transformed, but intensified effort turned it outward in new ways.

Farmers expanded herds, improved land, modified their crop regimes, and tried new crops. In cases such as sheep raising and the Connecticut River valley stall-fed cattle trade, they directed activities to specific markets. Local self-sufficiency was still valued, however. Heavy reliance continued to be placed on family labor, home manufactures, and intermittent local exchange. Larger farmers sought to diversify, not specialize, their output. The dynamic expansion and diversification of rural New England in the early 19th century was driven by an effort to intensify and preserve the elements of household-based production.

By the 1820s there were signs, first noticeable in southern New England, that this effort was leading to greater commercial dependence. To meet some of their basic needs, farm households were substituting store-bought imported goods for local products. Many farmers ceased to produce grain for their own food, purchasing flour brought in from outside New England and concentrating on corn and hay crops for livestock feed. The heavy workload borne by farm women and the availability of factory-produced cloth induced families to abandon home textile manufacture. Many families increased livestock production and took up butter or cheese making to pay for these purchases, a reorganization that increased their reliance on commerce. The expansion of road, canal, and railroad networks reinforced this shift, easing many New England farmers' access to markets but also exposing the region to fiercer western competition. Commercialization could both expand and restrict opportunities for farmers: in some cases local soil conditions, topography, demography, and transport helped determine what balance was struck.

Many farmers adopted new types of iron plow, many of them made by local blacksmiths, and simple devices such as hay rakes; by midcentury a few were also investing in mowing machines and other labor-saving devices. Overall, New England farmers were slower to adopt new equipment than those in other parts of the North, and the value per farm of their implements and machinery was below the national average in 1860. This regional average, however, concealed a marked disparity between relatively high values for farm equipment in the parts of eastern Massachusetts, Rhode Island, and Connecticut that lay close to large urban markets and much lower investment in more distant or upland areas of New England.

To some extent patterns of household production and family labor still determined farmers' adaptation to new circumstances. Changes in farm architecture and design, traced by Thomas C. Hubka in a study of mid-century southern Maine and New Hampshire, reflected the continued importance of farmhouses as centers of production. But competition pressed farmers toward new crops and levels of output that older patterns of family labor and local exchange could not sustain. Especially in fertile districts near cities, where market gardening expanded, or in other regions that became centers of fruit, broomcorn, or tobacco production, demand for hired labor—long an intermittent feature of New England farming—became greater and more permanent. From the 1830s through the Civil War, the number of farm laborers in these regions, an ever larger proportion of them French Canadian and Irish immigrants, increased. Though the bases of family farming changed little, the growth of wage work brought with it an increasing shift toward social stratification.

The expansion of specialized crop production by means of hired labor was but one of three broad patterns of farming apparent by the mid-1800s. Although wage labor and market sale permitted increased incomes and unprecedented prosperity, this trend was not universal. More modest farms on pockets of good land throughout New England continued dairy, hay, and crop production using mainly family labor as before. In the uplands, where soils were poorer or quickly worn out, prosperity and continuity were more elusive, and population stagnated or declined. Farmers supplemented their livings by felling timber and selling it for lumber or fuel, often with detrimental medium-term effects on the environment. Many upland farmers remained tied to such activities as sheep raising, even when markets were unfavorable, because the shortage of labor prevented them from switching to more lucrative but labor-intensive enterprises. People in all parts of rural New England migrated to the West, to towns, or to factory employment, but those from poorer, upland regions contributed disproportionately to this movement.

In the second half of the 19th century, the spread of railroads and the growth of cities fostered further changes even in fertile farm districts. Western competition eclipsed New England livestock. Railroads led to significant transformations in dairying: except in Vermont, rail transport displaced local cheese and butter with products shipped from New York State and the Midwest; but it also extended the distance over which fresh milk could be delivered to urban areas. Between 1860 and 1900 dairying in Connecticut changed over almost entirely from cheese to milk production. Many farmers, especially those near towns, concentrated increasingly on growing vegetables or fruits; a few became horticultural specialists, supplying grafts and seeds to other growers. Late in the century, as poultry diseases were brought under control, egg and broiler production also became more commercialized. Large flocks began to supplant the minimum of barnyard poultry that had been kept on many farms; concurrently, keeping poultry shifted from women's work to a male occupation.

Since early in the century a sense of moral crisis had been apparent in discussions of rural New England; this theme would enter the literary discourse of authors ranging from Henry David Thoreau to Edith Wharton. Commentators such as the Reverend Henry Colman, who compiled reports on Massachusetts agriculture in the 1840s, warned of the threat to New England's moral integrity as farmers became more dependent on other regions to supply their foodstuffs and other needs. Out-migration to the frontier, competition from western farms, and the stagnation of upland populations created a persistent apprehension of rural collapse, a frequent theme of discussion in the farming press and at county and local agricultural and horticultural fairs. Only recently have social and economic historians demonstrated that this fear was exaggerated, that relatively few farms were abandoned in the 19th century, and that most New England agriculture remained viable, even profitable. Indeed, from the Civil War on, farmers throughout New England had increased their investment in plows, seeders, mowing and reaping machinery, and dairying equipment. The U.S. agricultural census of 1900 revealed the region to have the highest values of farm implements per improved acre of any in the nation; all six New England states stood among the top 10 by this criterion, with Massachusetts heading the list. But the sense of crisis was exacerbated by urbanization and mass immigration, nativist anxieties about the decline of Yankee predominance, and suspicions of commerce itself.

The general belief in the existence of a crisis engendered nostalgia for a mythical self-sufficient past and was rooted in the actual experiences of farm families, who from the 18th century on had faced the prospect of dwindling local resources and widening distant opportunities. Even though few farms were abandoned, all families had members who migrated to towns, cities, or the frontier. In many parts of New England the political influence of farmers was weakened by the growth of urban populations. State-sponsored agricultural colleges, experiment stations, and extension services tended to accelerate the process of rural adaptation to new commercial and social conditions. Huge numbers of young people pursued literacy, formal education, and practical skills—so prominent a part of New England culture—as a means of breaking their ties to the land on which they had grown up. Nostalgia could serve as a salve for the emotional upheaval that migration involved and for the wider social anxieties that became attached to it. These themes helped shape Bidwell's analysis of New England's rural history.

In light of 19th-century fears, the present-day condition of rural New England seems doubly paradoxical. On one hand, commercial pressures on traditional farming have finally become unendurable. Dairying, for instance, has virtually disappeared from much of southern New England, as overproduction, competition, and suburbanization drive all but the most heavily capitalized farms out of business. On the other hand, middle-class prosperity, the counterculture's return to the land since the 1960s, and various manifestations of the environmental movement have combined to repopulate rural areas and give fresh impetus to truck farms, dairies, and other producers geared to specialty production for niche markets. From the perspective of the 21st century, the shift from corn and beans to organic vegetables and goat cheese could well appear to be the biggest transformation since the dispossession of New England's native inhabitants—once more underlining the subtler character of 18th- and 19th-century change.

Percy W. Bidwell, "The Agricultural Revolution in New England," *American Historical Review* 26 (1921); Christopher Clark, *The Roots of Rural Capitalism: Western Massachusetts, 1780–1860* (1990); Clarence H. Danhof, *Change in Agriculture: The Northern United States, 1820–1870* (1969); Thomas C. Hubka, *Big House, Little House, Back House, Barn: The Connected Farm Buildings of New England* (1984); Paul Glenn Munyon, *A Reassessment of New England Agriculture in the Last 30 Years of the 19th Century* (1978); Winifred Barr Rothenberg, *From Market-Places to a Market Economy: The Transformation of Rural Massachusetts, 1750–1850* (1992); Howard S. Russell, *A Long, Deep Furrow: Three Centuries of Farming in New England* (1976); Daniel Vickers, *Farmers and Fishermen: Two Centuries of Work in Essex County, Massachusetts, 1630–1850* (1994).

Christopher Clark

Corn The history of corn in New England encapsulates the history of Native American–European encounter. According to William Bradford's *Of Plymouth Plantation, 1620–1647* (1630–50), the Pilgrims first saw maize (*Zea mays*), which he called *corn* (the word used for any grain), in mid-November 1620 near present-day Truro, Mass., while searching for a place to settle. A company of men set out from the ship to explore the area and discovered cleared fields, a house, and several mounds of sand. Digging into the mounds they "found in them divers fair Indian baskets filled with corn, and some in ears, fair and good, of divers colours, which seemed to them a very goodly sight (having never seen any such before)." Thus began an important episode in the transformation of world culture—the introduction of North American plants and Native American culture to western Europeans. Native Americans, who had depended upon corn for millennia, taught the English how to raise, harvest, and store it, and the settlers quickly discovered that corn gave better yields on New England soils than any grain they had brought from home. It remains the most important grain in the region's history.

For much of the early history of New England, people distinguished maize from European grains by calling it "Indian corn," although they noted variations—Bradford described the different colors of the kernels found in Indian corn. By the mid-19th century, most Americans, including New Englanders, referred to maize as "corn" and had introduced new cultivars through careful seed selection. Timothy Dwight catalogued Canada, Flint, Nantucket, Chicken, Sweet, Long-Island, Guinea, Virginia, Carolina, and Missouri varieties in the 1820s.

Early settlers found that, unlike European grains, corn required few tools or elaborate field preparation. They could plant in hills on newly cleared fields amid stumps and rocks with little more than a hoe. Although Native Americans efficiently planted beans, squash, and pumpkins alongside their corn—the vegetables growing around the hills of corn reduced weeds, helped retain moisture, and increased yields—Europeans thought such fields looked unkempt. They preferred to separate the corn from other plants, thereby facilitating the growth of weeds in the spaces between the hills. The English kept down the weeds by hoeing, typically three times a summer before harvest.

As settlers improved their fields by removing stumps and rocks, they began to cross plow cornfields into grids, spacing furrows 3 to 4 feet apart and planting corn in hills at the intersections. As the corn grew they hoed the earth around the stalks to a height of about 6 inches. This practice continued until the widespread use of seed drills in the second half of the 19th century encouraged farmers to plant in rows spaced closer together. Modern farmers using tractors, sophisticated planters, and improved seeds have dramatically increased yields per acre, catering to New England's current market for sweet and feed corn (see the table on corn production in the Introduction). Today, much of the corn grown in New England is sold at roadside stands and supermarkets for family suppers. When New Englanders eat corn on the cob, Indian pudding, or corn-and-molasses (anadama) bread, they continue traditions of Native American and English exchange that began with the first settlers.

Percy W. Bidwell and John I. Falconer, *History of Agriculture in the Northern United States, 1620–1860* (1925); William Cronon, *Changes in the Land: Indians, Colonists, and the Ecology of New England* (1983); Timothy Dwight, *Travels in New England and New York* (1969); Howard S. Russell, *A Long, Deep Furrow: Three Centuries of Farming in New England* (1976).

J. Ritchie Garrison

Country Life Essayists Part of the back-to-nature movement that captured the interest of the American middle class at the turn of the 20th century, country life essayists in New England owed their success more to the residents of cities than to the rural farmers whose land they helped to transform into suburbs. Beginning in the 1890s and continuing through World War I, these essayists extolled the virtues of simple country living in hundreds of books, newspapers, and magazines targeted at the residents of an increasingly urban and industrialized culture.

Practitioners of a species of nature writing, country life essayists worked in a tradition exemplified by *Walden* (1854), the chronicle of Henry David Thoreau's two years in the woods near Concord, Mass. Like Thoreau, these essayists explored nearby nature, describing the fields and forests in and around New England's cities and towns. Unlike Thoreau, however, they sought to soothe and comfort their readers with visions of rural gentility, not remind them that "the mass of men lead lives of quiet desperation."

Central among these essayists was Liberty Hyde Bailey (1858–1954), dean of the College of Agriculture at Cornell University and the most prominent philosopher of the Country Life Movement. Appointed chairman of the Commission on Country Life by Theodore Roosevelt in 1908, Bailey was also the founding editor of *Country Life in America*, the most popular suburban periodical in the nation. An ardent conservationist and active supporter of nature study, Bailey wrote several eloquent books in support of rural ideals, including *The Holy Earth* (1915), his most important work. Even better known than Bailey was John Burroughs (1837–1921), whose prose idylls in praise of nature were read by several generations of New Englanders, many of whom came to visit Burroughs at Slabsides, his woodland retreat on the banks of the Hudson River.

Other popular country life essayists include Dallas Lore Sharp (1870–1929), a Boston University professor and former Methodist minister whose books *A Watcher in the Woods*

(1903) and *Beyond the Pasture Bars* (1914) sold more than 100,000 copies each; Walter Prichard Eaton (1878–1929), a drama critic and Princeton University professor who wrote nearly a dozen books of rural essays from his farmhouse near Sheffield, Mass.; Ray Stannard Baker (1870–1946), the muckraking journalist who, under the pen name David Grayson, wrote nine volumes of semi-autobiographical essays that sold more than 2 million copies; Bradford Torrey (1843–1912), a Massachusetts native whose many nature books reflect his lifelong interest in ornithology; Mabel Osgood Wright (1859–1934), a Connecticut resident whose *Friendship of Nature* (1894) was reprinted seven times during her life; Frank Bolles (1856–1894), secretary of Harvard University, whose rambles in Massachusetts and New Hampshire appear in *Land of the Lingering Snow* (1891) and *From Blomidon to Smoky* (1894); Winthrop Packard (1862–1943), a columnist for the *Boston Transcript* and author of *Wild Pastures* (1909), *Wildwood Ways* (1909), and *Wood Wanderings* (1910); and Rowland Evans Robinson (1833–1900), a Vermont native and author of *In New England Fields and Woods* (1896), among other works. These writers created a distinctive New England rural literature that continues today through such writers as Donald Hall and Maxine Kumin, as well as in the pages of *Yankee* magazine and *Vermont Life.*

William L. Bowers, *The Country Life Movement in America, 1900–1920* (1974); Paul Brooks, *Speaking for Nature* (1980); Thomas J. Lyon, *This Incomperable Lande: A Book of American Nature Writing* (1989); Howard S. Russell, *A Long, Deep Furrow: Three Centuries of Farming in New England* (1982); Peter J. Schmitt, *Back to Nature: The Arcadian Myth in Urban America* (1969).

Daniel J. Philippon

Country Life Movement The Country Life Movement, which thrived in the first two decades of the 20th century, had as its aims the revitalization of rural society and the strengthening of the country's agricultural economy. The educators, government officials, clergy, and social and agricultural scientists involved in the movement were concerned with the relative decline of the rural population—especially in the Northeast—as the United States became increasingly urban and industrial. They feared that the nation might lose its vitality if the rural population that had historically replenished American cities continued to dwindle. Country Life reformers were also concerned by the exodus of the most promising individuals from the countryside, presenting the specter of a backward rural America and a woefully inefficient agricultural base.

The concerns of Country Life reformers came to national attention in 1908, when President Theodore Roosevelt created the Country Life Commission and charged it with the investigation and solution of rural problems. Led by the horticulturist Liberty Hyde Bailey, of Cornell University, and Kenyon Butterfield, president of the Massachusetts Agricultural College, the commission declared in a 1909 report to Congress that rural America needed "better farming, better living, and better business."

Members of the Country Life Movement believed that "better living" required many changes in rural homes and institutions. Reasoning that a more satisfactory education would keep more rural youth in the countryside, they chose schools as their primary focus. Reformers proposed that country school curricula be broadened and enriched by adding such courses as nature study, practical agriculture, home economics, physical education, music, and art. In addition, reformers advocated that children of different grade levels be separated instead of being taught together, as they were in one-room schools, and that the virtually universal recitation method be abandoned. Such sweeping redirection demanded substantial reorganization, specifically through the consolidation of several one-room schools into a centralized, graded school. Massachusetts, which had consolidated some rural schools as early as the 1860s, became a model for this endeavor.

Those interested primarily in "better farming" and "better business" focused their efforts on adult education through agricultural extensions. The placement of extension agents in rural counties began in 1903 in Texas; the system spread rapidly because of its perceived efficacy in carrying improved practices and methods from agricultural scientists to farmers, reaching the Northeast by 1910. In 1914 Congress passed the Smith-Lever Act, which provided federal matching funds to states and counties participating in the extension program.

Country Life reformers succeeded in creating a number of organizations, including the Department of Church and Country Life of the Presbyterian Church and the American Country Life Association, but by the 1920s public interest in the problems of rural America had clearly begun to wane. The glut of farm products after 1920 indicated that there were too many, not too few, people in the countryside. In addition, rural groups had been generally unreceptive to proposed reforms, and the spirit of social and economic innovation that had in general characterized the Progressive Era had died.

David Danbom

Cranberries The wild cranberry (*Vaccinium macrocarpon*), one of the few fruits indigenous to New England, was used by Native Americans for food, medicine, and dyes long before the first Thanksgiving. When the Pilgrims arrived in 1620, they named the fruit "crane-berries" because the berries' white flowers reminded them of the heads of cranes. The settlers continued to use the tart red berries for medicinal purposes, as well as to dye rugs, blankets, and clothing. Rich in various vitamins, cranberries were brought on long sea voyages to prevent scurvy; they eventually became so valuable that regulations were passed to protect vines on public lands.

Henry Hall of Dennis, Mass., was the first New Englander to cultivate wild cranberries. In 1810 he began transplanting vines to a humanmade bog and was the first person taxed for earning income from cranberries. Other ambitious agriculturists soon duplicated his efforts, and the commercial production of "red gold" boosted the New England economy as fishing and shipbuilding declined.

Cape Cod and Plymouth County, Mass., became the center of the 19th-century cranberry industry and, along with Bristol County, Mass., remain so today. The Massachusetts Department of Agriculture enumerated the first cranberry census in the mid-1850s, noting that 197 acres on Cape Cod were growing cultivated cranberries. By 1865 more than 1,000 acres supported cranberries. In 1888 the Cape Cod Cranberry Growers' Association was formed, and by the end of the century, hundreds of thousands of barrels of cranberries were being sold.

In 1898 the first commercial cranberry cannery opened at Wareham, Mass., making syrup and jam until 1901. Realizing that the number of berries overwhelmed the markets, Marcus L. Urann, president of the United Cape Cod Cranberry Company, proposed that the fruit be canned as cranberry sauce and sold under the name Ocean Spray. Cranberry growers soon merged into a cooperative known as the Cranberry Canners in 1930; later the cooperative would be renamed Ocean Spray Cranberries. Eighty-five percent of cranberry growers in the Northeast were affiliated with this group. Although New England settlers first made cranberry juice in 1683, Ocean Spray introduced the first commercially available cranberry juice cocktail in 1930. The company has continued to expand its line of sauces, juices, and other cranberry products.

The cranberry growing season lasts from April through November; harvest typically begins shortly after Labor Day. The cranberry vine, a native wetland plant, thrives in a unique environment: it must grow in an acid peat soil and requires adequate fresh water and

Cranberry harvest, Carver, Mass., 1991

sand coverage to prosper. Under the best conditions, cranberry vines will last indefinitely. In fact, Cape Cod boasts some vines that have survived for more than 150 years and continue to bear fruit. Growers once used wooden harvest scoops to comb vines before mechanical pickers were devised during World War II. Today, many cranberry growers make use of modern technological methods including lasers to level sand and computers to map bogs. Helicopters are used to inspect crops, apply fertilizer, and remove crated cranberries, preventing damage to the bogs. In dry harvesting, berries are picked and delivered to processing plants to be sold fresh or frozen. Wet harvesting cranberries for juice and sauce involves flooding bogs so that the berries float and are pumped into trucks. At the packing plant, cranberries are examined, processed, and shipped to markets.

Massachusetts remains the region's leading cranberry producer, averaging 105 barrels per acre. Bay State cranberry growers maintain roughly 14,200 acres of bogs and produced approximately 1.45 million barrels of the fruit in 2002. The Massachusetts-based Ocean Spray, North America's leading producer of cranberry-based products, reported revenues of $1 billion in 2003. Maine's commercial cranberry industry disappeared in the early 1900s but experienced a rebirth in the 1990s with the establishment of commercial plantations. Maine cranberry growers maintain 200 acres of bogs and produced more than 2,000 barrels of the fruit in 1997. Cherryfield Foods has planned a 900-acre operation, and Maine's governor Angus King publicly announced support for the state's cranberry industry in October 1996. Whereas Maine is home to approximately 38 cranberry growers, more than 500 Massachusetts families make their living growing cranberries.

The Cape Cod National Seashore protects wild cranberries and maintains the Cranberry Bog Trail, and Ocean Spray's Cranberry World Visitor's Center at Lakeville-Middleboro, Mass., documents the role of cranberries in New England's history. While cranberry growers continue to contribute to the region's economy, cranberry bogs provide shelter to hundreds of species of wetland plants and animals. Their rich crimson color enhances the unique natural beauty of the New England landscape.

Paul Eck, *The American Cranberry* (1990); William Jaspersohn, *Cranberries* (1991); Charles W. Johnson, *Bogs of the Northeast* (1985); Katie Letcher Lyle, *The Wild Berry Book: Romance, Recipes, and Remedies* (1994).

Elizabeth D. Schafer

Dairying English colonists brought the first dairy cattle to New England during the 17th and 18th centuries. The production of milk, cheese, and butter, so integral to the English agricultural tradition, was replicated in early colonial settlements. Demand for milk and cheese in the colonies was not great, however, nor did colonists have sufficient hay to over-winter large numbers of cattle, so dairy herds were often small. Milk cows were merely one facet of a system of mixed general agriculture that provided colonial farmers with a living.

In the 19th century, surplus milk beyond the needs of farm families was converted into cheese and butter, then sold or bartered for goods. The home production of cheese in New England peaked at 27 million pounds at midcentury and later was eclipsed by butter. An extensive rail transportation network coupled with the rapid increase of Boston's population opened a major market for dairy products later in the century. Farmers near Boston shipped milk, while those at greater distances shipped butter. The iced butter car and later mechanical refrigeration brought still more farmers into the market. Because of their perishability, dairy products were secure from western competition and became an important source of cash income for farmers throughout New England during the 1870s and 1880s.

The resultant dairy market expansion was reflected in widespread farm operation reorganization. Farmers added more dairy cattle and built barns specifically designed to accommodate larger milking herds and hay storage. New breeds from Europe were introduced and breed associations were established to register animals. Farmers extended milking through the winter months and experimented with corn ensilage as year-round feed. With the advent of a test to measure butterfat, herd improvement associations were established as early as 1908 at the urging of public officials, and farmers began keeping production records for individual cows. State governments, in turn, began to regulate dairy farming in the interest of public health, particularly in an effort to control the spread of tuberculosis. In the final decades of the 19th century, the adoption of pasteurization and the appointment of milk inspectors in Massachusetts and New York gradually improved the quality of the region's milk supply. As milk became safer to drink, more people began drinking more of it. And farmers, confronted by a situation in which large Boston milk dealers could set both retail and wholesale milk prices at will, organized to secure fair prices for production.

During the 20th century, most New England farmers specialized in dairy production. Dairy farming became capital-intensive—bulk milk tanks in the 1950s and 1960s were an important watershed—and small producers were often forced out of business. In 1910 there were 190,000 farms in New England, but by the late 1990s that number had fallen to 26,500. As the number of dairy farms declined, remaining farms increased in size, often absorbing neighboring operations. Through mechanization, selective breeding, and herd management, milk production consistently increased: fewer, larger farms produced more milk. Thus, in 1940, 11,300 Vermont farms produced just over 1 billion pounds of milk. By

1998 only 1,815 farms produced 2.6 billion pounds of milk.

Historically, the core workforce on a dairy farm was the family: parents, grandparents, and children worked side by side in roles often prescribed by age and sex. In the 20th century, women often were responsible for bookkeeping, washing the milking equipment, and, when necessary, haying in the field. For affluent male farmers it was a matter of pride that their wives and daughters never learn to milk. In the late 20th and early 21st centuries, both by economic necessity and personal interest, women have become actively involved in all aspects of farm operation.

Because dairy farms nationwide have outproduced their market, the price farmers receive for milk, which is set by the federal government, has remained low, with the intent that inefficient producers would be forced out of business. In the 1980s two programs administered by the U.S. Department of Agriculture were established to address this problem: the Dairy Diversion Program (1984) attempted to reduce overproduction by paying a premium to farmers who capped their production, and the Whole Herd Buyout Program (1986–87) offered farmers an economic incentive to leave farming. In the late 1990s the Northeast Dairy Compact was created to augment farm income whenever fluid milk prices fall below a minimum set by the compact. Nevertheless, low milk prices continue to force still more farmers out of business, and some suggest that the future of agriculture in New England lies with such alternatives to dairy as fallow deer or specialty food products.

Thomas C. Hubka, *Big House, Little House, Back House, Barn: The Connected Farm Buildings of New England* (1984); Howard S. Russell, *A Long, Deep Furrow: Three Centuries of Farming in New England* (1976); Gregory Sharrow, ed. *Families on the Land: Profiles of Vermont Farm Families* (1995); Harold F. Wilson, *The Hill Country of Northern New England: Its Social and Economic History, 1790–1930* (1967).

Gregory L. Sharrow

Eastern States Exposition (Big E)

The Eastern States Exposition in West Springfield, Mass., is a major agricultural fair, attracting 1.1 million visitors in 2004. The exposition was founded by New England businessmen who believed that the region was overindustrialized and sought to restore balance by promoting agribusiness and celebrating traditional ideals. The leaders of the Eastern States movement, including Joshua Loring Brooks, a wealthy Springfield printer, and Horace A. Moses, owner of the Strathmore Paper Company, envisioned the exposition as a forum for encouraging cooperation between agriculture and industry.

Brooks conceived of a regional, agricultural, and industrial exposition that would provide demonstrations of new farming methods, inspire farm families by holding annual competitions, and entertain and educate rural and urban visitors. In May 1914, 63 local businessmen, leading farmers, and agricultural administrators incorporated the Eastern States Agricultural and Industrial Exposition with $200,000 in capital stock. It was reorganized and reincorporated as the Eastern States Exposition in 1923 as a tax-exempt nonprofit educational institution. Land was purchased on the Agawam River near the junction of three New England railroads and, later, two major highways.

Having persuaded the National Dairy Show to hold its 10th annual event there in October 1916, the trustees constructed dikes and erected a coliseum, a half-mile racetrack, and modern fairgrounds in just 10 months. In January 1917 John C. Simpson was hired as general manager. Simpson had formerly managed the Minnesota and Iowa state fairs. The first annual exposition, held over October 12–20, 1917, attracted 138,000 fairgoers with its horse show, national vegetable show, and entertainment, including nightly concerts, hippodrome and circus acts, children's rides, and horse and auto racing. The fairgrounds were taken over by the U.S. Ordnance Department after America's entry into World War I.

The exposition expanded with the return of peace. In the 1920s came the advent of Governors' Day; its pageantry and pyrotechnic spectaculars had doubled annual attendance at the fair by the time of the Great Depression and helped finance new construction projects. The new Industrial Arts Building was constructed in 1924, and ice facilities were installed in the Coliseum the following year. The fairgrounds suffered serious damage from floods in 1927 and 1936, and the fair was closed in 1938 by a hurricane that caused $200,000 in damage. In 1942, the U.S. Army Quartermaster Corps took over the property for the duration of World War II (retaining control until 1947), and Brooks retired as president.

One of Brooks's dreams was to create the Avenue of States, the only place a person could, within minutes, stand in all six New England states. His idea was to erect a replica of each state's original state house on lots conveyed by warrantee deeds. Brooks persuaded Massachusetts (in 1919), Maine (in 1925), Vermont (in 1929), New Hampshire (in 1930), and Connecticut (in 1938) to construct the buildings on property perpetually freed from taxation by Massachusetts law. The Avenue of States was not completed, however, until Rhode Island erected its exhibition building in 1957.

Storrowton Village is another unique feature of the exposition. Trustee Helen Osborn Storrow was dissatisfied with the cottages that housed the Home Department, which she chaired. In 1927 she purchased the circa 1794 Gilbert Farmstead in West Brookfield, Mass., dismantled it, and had it reconstructed on the fairgrounds as a permanent exhibition building. By 1930 two more period houses, a store, tavern, town hall, meetinghouse, schoolhouse, blacksmith's shop, and law office joined it, creating a nostalgic rendition of an early-19th-century New England village. Staffed by costumed interpreters, today's Storrowton provides an oasis from the frenetic bustle of the 17 fair days and symbolizes year-round the exposition's original mission.

Post–World War II crowds appreciated such patriotic displays, and opening day of the fair in 1947 broke the record for attendance with 83,402 fairgoers. In the 1950s and 1960s, the fair attracted national attention. President Dwight D. Eisenhower visited the fair in 1952, and the fair appeared in *National Geographic* magazine in 1954. J. C. Penney, an exposition trustee since 1926, declared it "one of the greatest institutions in America."

After the city of Springfield announced plans to build a civic center and sports complex, the exposition's 165-member board of trustees considered, but overwhelmingly rejected, a relocation offer made by the state of Connecticut in 1972. In 1978 fair attendance broke the 1 million mark for the first time. In the 1990s the old racetrack was leveled and ice-skating and hockey were ended in the Coliseum when maintenance and repair costs proved prohibitive. Celebrating its 75th anniversary, the trustees wished to make the Big E "the Disney of the fair industry." A two-phase, $10-million capital improvement plan, the largest in its history, has made a state-of-the-art food court, permanent midway area, new minipark, and enlarged agricultural complex a reality at the Eastern States Exposition.

J. Loring Brooks, Jr., *"J.L.": A Biography* (1952); Frances M. Gagnon, *Eastern States Exposition, 1916–1996: An Illustrated History at 75 Years* (1997); Donald B. Marti, *Historical Directory of American Agricultural Fairs* (1986).

Mark A. Mastromarino

Extension Agencies

Historically, agricultural extension agencies were established to serve a dual education and action purpose: first, to "extend," communicate, or diffuse new agricultural information and innovations; and second, to organize partnerships and initiatives aimed at addressing agricultural issues and problems. Various public and private agencies and organizations carry an agricultural extension function; the largest and most visible of these is the national Cooperative State Research, Education, and Extension Service (CSREES). CSREES is a partnership between the U.S. Department of Agriculture, state and county governments, and land-grant colleges and universities. It carries the broad mission of advancing "a global system of research, extension, and higher education in the food and agricultural sciences and related environmental and human sciences to benefit people, communities, and the Nation." CSREES-affiliated offices are located at land-grant universities in all New England states. A New England Cooperative Extension Consortium was established in 1990 to strengthen public access, quality, and collaborative activity among the region's six-state cooperative extension systems.

Although a national system of extension agencies was not created until the passage of the Smith-Lever Act of 1914, the roots of agricultural extension reach back to the early years of the republic. In New England, the first extension agencies were agricultural societies founded in the late 18th century by wealthy men interested in advancing agricultural methods and knowledge, primarily for economic reasons. Examples include the Kennebec Agricultural Society, founded in Maine in 1787, and the Massachusetts Society for Promoting Agriculture, founded in 1792. Modeled after similar societies in England, their purpose was to spread new ideas and knowledge among their aristocratic members and to encourage them to experiment with new methods. These so-called learned societies did not include or involve many ordinary farmers, although they did make attempts to reach and influence them.

In 1811 Elkanah Watson, a wealthy businessman who owned a farm in Pittsfield, Mass., founded the Berkshire Agricultural Society, which pioneered another early extension agency: the county fair. County fairs gave ordinary farmers the opportunity to see and learn about new developments in agricultural technologies, methods, and products. They also served important political and social functions, offering a way for rural people to share their experiences and opinions about the issues of the day. Fairs proved popular and influential, spreading rapidly to nearly every county in New England by 1820.

In addition to the county fair, the agricultural press was one of the most effective of the early extension agencies. Important examples include the *New England Farmer,* established in 1822, and the *Maine Farmer,* established in 1833. Such publications achieved much success by midcentury, reaching a growing and increasingly receptive audience with their promotion of scientific and technical improve-

ments and their celebration of the dignity and value of farming and rural life.

The development and spread of county agricultural fairs, the flowering of an agricultural press, and the growth of a movement for self-education in "useful knowledge" through such associations as the Lyceum (established in 1826 in Connecticut) helped stimulate the creation of popular local agricultural societies and clubs throughout New England. These societies encouraged experimentation and debate and spread news of innovations and methodological improvements throughout the region. By 1858 there were approximately 900 such societies and clubs in the United States, with at least 95 in New England alone.

Public support for extension agencies grew significantly during the mid-1800s. In the 1830s federal appropriations were granted to the U.S. Patent Office to address concerns over crop failures and "soil exhaustion" in the Northeast. Beginning in the 1850s, state agricultural societies, departments, and boards were established. Advances in education, the budding growth of the agricultural sciences, and new developments in transportation and communication combined to spur interest in improvement through agricultural extension work. New England states played a key role in the evolution of extension work to address those issues especially important to the region during the second half of the 19th century: growing urbanization and industrialization, the need for specialization to meet new markets, and concerns over declining fertility and productivity coupled with rising competition from the fertile farmlands of the Midwest. With leadership provided by the Massachusetts State Board of Agriculture, the U.S. Agricultural Society was formed in 1852 and led the call for the creation of a federal department of agriculture. In the same decade, Justin Smith Morrill, a senator from Vermont, sponsored legislation calling for the use of federal land grants to establish a national system of colleges devoted to the "liberal and practical education of the industrial classes," with a special focus on agriculture and the mechanical arts. Success was achieved on both fronts in 1862 with the establishment of the U.S. Department of Agriculture (USDA) and the passage of the Morrill, or Land-Grant, Act.

In 1859 the Massachusetts State Board of Agriculture led the way in pioneering "farmers' institutes," one of the most important innovations in extension work of this period. After modest beginnings, the idea grew into a national movement. Held over a few days in rural communities throughout the nation, farmers' institutes were devoted to the dual purpose of disseminating scientific and practical agricultural knowledge and methods and

developing a "community sense" that would be useful in engaging people in addressing local issues and problems.

At the turn of the 20th century, land-grant colleges and their agricultural experiment stations developed a broad program of extension work that included reading and correspondence courses, short courses, itinerant schools, cooperative experiments, demonstration farms, home economics programs, farm trains, institutes, bulletins and surveys, nature study, and boys' and girls' clubs. Official departments of extension were created at most land-grant colleges during this period, inspired in part by the national leadership of Kenyon Butterfield, who served as president of the Rhode Island Agricultural College from 1903 to 1906 and the Massachusetts Agricultural College from 1906 to 1924.

The Smith-Lever Act, signed into law in 1914 by President Woodrow Wilson, brought a national extension system into being that featured a cooperative partnership between the USDA, land-grant colleges, and state and county governments. The purpose of the system, in the words of the act, was to "aid in diffusing among the people of the United States useful and practical information on subjects relating to agriculture and home economics, and to encourage the application of the same." The new extension agencies developed three focal points for their work: the farm, the home, and the neighborhood or community. The agencies created "4-H" (head, hands, heart, health) programs that aimed to engage youth in making positive contributions to the farm, home, and community.

The story of the development and accomplishments of the cooperative extension agencies in New England mirrors those from other regions of the nation. Through the 1950s cooperative extension in New England focused its work on the farm, the home, and the rural community, pursuing economic, civic, and cultural ends. The post–World War II era, however, brought a dramatic reduction in the number of farms in the region and a major shift in rural economic and cultural life. Reflecting these changes, New England's cooperative extension agencies began to broaden the focus of their work in the 1960s by, for example, developing the national Expanded Food and Nutrition Education Program (EFNEP), which provides nutrition education programs to low-income families in both urban and rural areas. The broadly cast mission of the University of Maine Cooperative Extension is "to help Maine people improve their lives through an educational process that uses research-based knowledge focused on issues and needs." Areas of work in the New England states that flow from such broad mission statements include youth and families; nutrition, food safety, and health; economic and community development; environment and natural resources; and agriculture.

As challenges in all of these areas continue to grow, and as communities struggle to find creative and effective solutions to tough public problems in an environment of deregulation and devolution, extension agencies in New England are shaping a new role for their dual functions of education and action. The University of New Hampshire Cooperative Extension system's current statewide initiative, "Strengthening New Hampshire Communities," is positioning extension in that state as a key force for community development and civic capacity building aimed at addressing an array of economic, social, and environmental issues and challenges. Other extension agencies in New England are also shifting in this direction, in part due to the renewal of land-grant universities' commitment to their outreach and public service missions. The future of extension agencies is thus becoming closely tied to their ability to contribute something of value to the public work of civic renewal.

Harry C. Boyte and Nancy N. Kari, *Building America: The Democratic Promise of Public Work* (1996); David B. Danbom, *The Resisted Revolution: Urban America and the Industrialization of Agriculture, 1900–1930* (1979); Joseph F. Kett, *The Pursuit of Knowledge under Difficulties: From Self-Improvement to Adult Education in America, 1750–1990* (1994); Wayne D. Rasmussen, *Taking the University to the People: 75 Years of Cooperative Extension* (1989); Howard S. Russell, *A Long, Deep Furrow: Three Centuries of Farming in New England* (1976); Roy V. Scott, *The Reluctant Farmer: The Rise of Agricultural Extension to 1914* (1970); Tamara Plakins Thornton, *Cultivating Gentlemen: The Meaning of Country Life among the Boston Elite, 1785–1860* (1989).

Scott J. Peters

Farmland Preservation Agricultural land use has been a primary influence in shaping the character of New England's cultural landscape. During the past century, a decline in the number of farms and amount of farmland in the region has been driven by changing technology, a transportation system that gave other regions of the United States an increased share of New England's food and fiber market, and expansion of urban and recreational land needs. Between 1880 and 2003, land in farms decreased from 21.5 million to 4.0 million acres, a loss of 81 percent (see table).

Since the 1960s suburban growth in southern New England, including the southern portions of Maine and New Hampshire, has been the major factor in the loss of farmland. Improved roads made it possible for suburban and rural residents to commute into city employment centers, accelerating urban sprawl. The better transportation network encouraged the decentralization of both industry and services that also compete for land. In New England, an area with limited productive soils, much of the best space for development is also the most desirable for farming. In an unregulated land market, development interests always win out over agriculture, though not all the land acquired through this process is paved over or built upon. Rather, a farm taken out of production may have only a modest amount of its acreage used for construction. What remains is allowed to revert to forest. For example, in Rhode Island (the most densely populated of the New England states), of the 60,000 acres lost between 1960 and 1974, only about 1,000 acres of high-quality farmland were actually developed. Northern New England has experienced modest pressure from the growth of population clusters as well as from an expanding demand for

recreational space related to summer and winter activities. In the past century, declining agricultural profits from marginal farmland have been another important factor in the loss of open acreage. Reforestation is one of the most visible aspects of farmland loss as the land near roads and towns is built on and much of the rest is allowed to return to trees. Old stone walls running straight as an arrow through both forested residential developments and woodland attest to this process.

These trends in New England have generated concern for maintaining the capability of meeting food needs as well as protecting visual images of the agrarian environment, an important tourist resource. As a result, the region has become a leader in formulating farmland preservation policies. With the emergence of the environmental awareness political agenda during the 1970s, protection of farmland became a national issue. Because the federal government chose not to take a lead in the debate, states have been the primary force behind preservation efforts. State and local government programs that reduce the rate of farmland conversion fall into four classes: reduced real estate taxes, including current-use assessment and circuit breaker credits (circuit breaker programs trigger tax relief when obligations reach a predetermined level; for example, once real estate taxes exceed a set percentage of farm income, a farmer would be excused from additional taxes); reduced estate taxes; regulation of land through the zoning, purchase or transfer of development rights, right to-farm laws, and land banking; and incentives to encourage continued production of specific commodities. Although all New England states have enacted farmland protection programs, some are more active than others. Most notable, in 1970 Vermont passed Act 250

Loss of New England Farmland, 1880–2003

	1880		2003		1880–2003	
	Land in farms (thousands of acres)	Percentage of state's land in farmland	Land in farms (thousands of acres)	Percentage of state's land in farmland	Farmland lost (thousands of acres)	Percentage of farmland lost
Connecticut	2,454	78	360	12	2,094	−85
Maine	6,553	33	1,370	7	5,183	−79
Massachusetts	3,359	67	520	10	2,839	−85
New Hampshire	3,721	65	450	8	3,271	−88
Rhode Island	515	77	60	9	455	−88
Vermont	4,883	82	1,250	21	3,633	−74
Total	21,484	53	4,010	10	17,474	−81

Note: The U.S. Department of Agriculture revised the definition of a farm several times between 1880 and 2003. Some farmland may have been lost or added with each change.

Source: U.S. Census (1880) and New England Agriculture Statistics (2003)

to regulate land use throughout the state. Agricultural zoning has been introduced in the region, but for political reasons this approach has remained weak. A few municipalities, such as Auburn, Maine, have adopted local plans to establish agricultural districts.

Every New England state has passed enabling legislation permitting state or local governments to purchase development rights. These programs involve great public expense, and only the three southern states have allocated significant resources to support this approach. By the early 1990s, Connecticut had spent $43 million to purchase development rights on about 18,000 acres of farmland. All New England states have right-to-farm laws that protect basic agricultural activities that may irritate neighbors not involved in farming. Programs to support individual products are costly and often subject to legal challenges. Maine's milk subsidy tax was disallowed in 2001; advocates are fighting to reintroduce it.

In addition to government programs, private organizations play a role in farmland preservation. For example, the Vermont Land Trust has been involved in efforts to buy farmland that is under intense pressure from developers and then to resell the land with certain restrictions for its use.

In spite of these attempts to stem the loss of farmland, acreage continues to decline. The political cost of land regulation and the public expense of tax incentives and acquiring development rights constrain the impact of preservation agendas. In addition, all programs other than the outright purchase of rights appear to delay conversion rather than stop it. The amount of land in agriculture shrinks as New England farmers adjust to ever-changing economic conditions and cultural values concerning images of open space, spotted cows, and local produce.

Mark B. Lapping, Thomas L. Daniels, and John W. Keller, *Rural Planning and Development in the United States* (1989); Timothy J. Rickard, "Problems in Implementing Farmland Preservation Policies in Connecticut," *Journal of Rural Studies* 2 (1986); Frank Schnidman, Michael Smiley, and Eric G. Woodbury, *Retention of Land for Agriculture: Policy, Practice and Potential in New England* (1990).

Paul B. Frederic

Field Patterns Seventeenth-century New Englanders re-created the two field patterns they were familiar with in England—nucleated villages surrounded by open fields, and isolated farmsteads with contiguous fields. Both patterns were in place during the first generation of settlement. Many early communities created blocks of land known as divisions, from which town officials periodically granted plots to the town's inhabitants. As

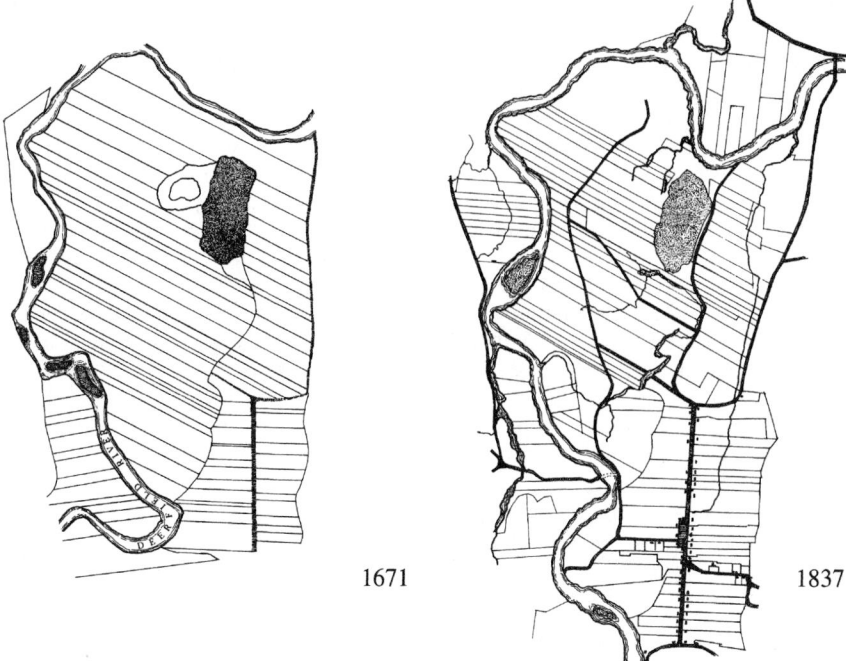

Field patterns, North Meadows, Deerfield, Mass., 1671 and 1837. Diagonal lines represent the boundaries of individual tillage and mowing fields.

families acquired land in this fashion, they came to own small fields scattered about the town. In fertile areas, such as the Connecticut and Merrimack River valleys, some communities created open fields, large sections of land in which each family might own one or two lots suitable for tillage. Although individual farmers made decisions about what to plant on their own lots, they had to cooperate to maintain the open-field fence, for only the outer perimeter of the open field was protected from the depredations of hungry livestock. By the Civil War, most farmers considered these open-field systems inconvenient, but individual lots were seldom fenced until the 20th century.

Instead of creating open fields, most surveyors laying out new towns in the 18th century set aside large lots for separate farmsteads, and families became distributed over most of the landscape. In towns where these isolated farmsteads were common, settlers were more likely to own contiguous fields of tillage, mowing, pasture, and woodlot. Even in these communities, many families owned parcels in different parts of the town because natural resources were never distributed equally. Tillage and mowing fields were usually located in level bottomlands or on gentle slopes, and pasture and woodlots were on top of hills and ridges. Surveyors frequently laid out tillage fields in long strips to facilitate plowing. By contrast, fields for mowing and pasture were approximately square or set out in broad rectangles because it was easier to

manage livestock or haying within those configurations.

Field boundaries were marked by fences and by tree lines. Trees growing along the boundaries of tillage fields were cut down because the foliage shaded the crops growing there. Trees were more common on the borders of mowing fields and were often allowed to grow in various sections of pasture to provide shade for grazing cattle.

Farmers generally kept unimproved fields for future use or as woodlots; some were so swampy or rugged that few farmers bothered to improve them. Marsh areas, however, were valuable sources of hay and were prized in some coastal areas of Connecticut, Rhode Island, and Massachusetts. Similarly, woodlots provided most families with a source of fuel and building materials, and many upland sections of New England marketed forest products ranging from lumber to pine tar.

In the decades after 1880, farmers in more poorly situated towns stopped using their fields for pasture or crops, and the land returned to forest cover. In some cases old fields were more valuable as forest than as cleared land. During the Great Depression, families who continued to farm fertile valley lands or owned favorably located hill farms bought out their neighbors and consolidated a number of small fields into larger holdings. These larger fields were better suited to mechanized types of farming and permitted economies of scale as agricultural strategies changed.

After World War II, the rapid expansion of the interstate highway network, the growth of suburbs, and the huge escalation of property values led developers to build homes and businesses on former agricultural land within convenient commuting distance of urban or industrial centers. In these areas, only the most profitable forms of agriculture or small farms owned by families of means have persisted. Tillage fields on good bottomland and level uplands still yield crops, and mowing fields and pastureland in some parts of the region support dairying. For the most part, older field patterns persist only on the periphery of the suburbs, sometimes as fence lines in the woods, sometimes as open fields still under production.

David Grayson Allen, *In English Ways: The Movement of Societies and the Transferal of English Law, Local Law, and Custom to Massachusetts Bay in the 17th Century* (1981); Hal S. Barron, *Those Who Stayed Behind: Rural Society in 19th-Century New England* (1984); J. Ritchie Garrison, *Landscape and Material Life in Franklin County, Massachusetts, 1770–1860* (1991); Stewart G. McHenry, "Eighteenth-Century Field Patterns as Vernacular Art," *Old Time New England* 69 (1978).

J. Ritchie Garrison

Gentleman Farmers Although in many respects a British cultural practice, gentleman farming as it existed in 18th- and 19th-century New England emerged from different social conditions and served different cultural functions. British gentry and aristocrats practiced gentleman farming as an extension of their status as landholders and landlords. In New England, however, there was no hereditary elite; land ownership was broadly distributed, and agricultural rents did not form the primary basis of wealth. When the practice of gentleman farming emerged in New England in the 18th century, it did so according to the needs of a developing mercantile elite. Boston's merchants built country seats to go along with their town houses, hoping to partake of the power and prestige of the British landed classes by imitating their way of life.

Following the Revolutionary War, the new practice of experimental agriculture transformed both the public functions and private meanings of gentleman farming. From the 1780s to the Civil War, many of the region's leading merchants and industrialists, along with their relatives in politics and the professions, experimented with new crops, livestock, tools, and techniques on their farms. In addition, patrician Yankees encouraged agricultural innovation and improvement by founding and participating in agricultural societies. The first and most important of these societies, the Massachusetts Society for Promoting Agriculture (established in 1792), awarded

premiums, published a journal, and sponsored agricultural fairs. In their private and public efforts, gentleman farmers claimed no other motive than a civic-minded concern for the welfare of New England's yeomanry and the well-being of the region as a whole, but their rural pursuits undoubtedly served their class interests. As it had in the colonial period, the country seat attested to its owner's personal refinement, and in the wake of the Revolution, the public benevolence represented by efforts to improve agriculture offered a far better justification for political leadership than inherited status and wealth.

By midcentury, more anxious to establish themselves as well bred than public spirited, New England gentleman farmers turned from such practical matters as crop diseases and milk cows to ornamental concerns such as horticulture and fancy livestock. The shift away from the utilitarian intensified in the Gilded Age, when prominent New Yorkers took up gentleman farming in New England. On his Berkshire estate, the sculptor Daniel Chester French oversaw farm operations but focused far more attention on creating lavish formal gardens. On their massive estate in Shelburne, Vt., William Seward Webb and Lila Vanderbilt Webb retained something of the older spirit of experimental agriculture, but the scale and nature of their operations, the centerpiece of which was a château-like barn occupying almost 2 acres, partook far more of aristocratic display than republican philanthropy.

It is notable that these new gentleman farmers, unlike their predecessors, settled in remote areas of New England where agricultural decline and rural depopulation made old farmland cheap and readily available and where railroad lines made travel from New York City fast and convenient. More recently, appealing images of rural simplicity and the Yankee past—and the tax shelters provided by farm operations—have motivated the purchase of older farms, but gentleman farming in New England no longer functions as an expression of class identity.

Alan Emmet, *So Fine a Prospect: Historic New England Gardens* (1996); Tamara Plakins Thornton, *Cultivating Gentlemen: The Meaning of Country Life among the Boston Elite, 1785–1860* (1989).

Tamara Plakins Thornton

The Grange In 1867 Oliver Hudson Kelley, a Boston-born Minnesota farmer and employee of the U.S. Department of Agriculture, began organizing the Patrons of Husbandry, better known as the Grange. The Grange was a fraternal organization of farmers whose activities included secret rituals, educational programs, and social activities intended as an

antidote to the isolation experienced in many rural communities. The organization swept through the Midwest, West, and South in the early 1870s as farmer cooperatives bought and sold goods, and antimonopoly farmers successfully passed "granger laws" to regulate railroads. Grange membership approached 1 million by 1875 but plummeted when the organization was later beset by conflict between members who advocated political activism and those who preferred a more moderate approach.

In 1871 Jonathan Lawrence of St. Johnsbury, Vt., organized Green Mountain 1, the first Grange in New England. Because New England farmers did not participate significantly in the first burst of Grange strength, the organization spread slowly throughout the region. Growth was steady after 1880, however, and eastern states were largely responsible for a resurgence in Grange membership. Led by Maine and New Hampshire, New England became a significant force in the Grange by 1890.

Most Grangers sought similar educational, social, and financial benefits from their membership. New England Grange meetings featured literary and musical programs, debates on agricultural practices, social dinners (and sometimes dances), and nonpartisan discussions of the major issues of the day. The Grange also promoted literacy, for all Grange leaders insisted that members be encouraged to read. During the 19th century, agricultural lectures and discussions at New England Grange meetings focused on such topics as crop rotation, plant diseases, fertilizers, sheep raising, and the best rations for dairy cows. Grangers also debated social issues like the newest clothing styles and whether rural people should strive to be fashionable. The Grange may also have been the first secret order to admit women. New England members valued the importance of Grange ritual and its goal of expressing and reinforcing the beauty and value of rural life.

New England members also sought the economic benefits of membership by organizing cooperatively to buy and sell their crops as early as the 1870s. Grange business agents combined member orders to secure bulk discounts, saving New England Grangers thousands of dollars. Although they were not involved in the early railroad fight waged in the mid-1870s by midwestern members, New England Grangers fought their own railroad battles in the 1880s. Like their midwestern counterparts, New Englanders were victimized by discriminatory rates for short hauls, and they campaigned vigorously for state and federal legislative relief. New England Grangers heartily supported the establishment of the Interstate Commerce Commission in 1887.

By the end of the 19th century, New England Grangers formed a formidable block of voters, and used their influence to encourage progressive state and national legislation. New England members helped formulate the Grange platform supporting women's suffrage, prohibition, rural free delivery of mail, direct election of senators, and primary elections. In the early 20th century, the Grange continued to support progressive legislation such as antitrust measures, parcel post delivery, national aid for highway construction, and the Pure Food and Drug Act of 1906.

The Grange continues to be an important part of rural life for thousands of New Englanders, particularly through its emphasis on community service. Current New England membership in the Grange exceeds 15,000 and includes many young people, who can become full members at age 14. The National Grange sponsors youth conferences and state camps, and young Grange members are often active in groups such as 4-H. The Grange motto, "In essentials, unity. In non-essentials, liberty. In all things, charity," emphasizes the organization's mission of cooperation and service among rural dwellers.

Guy B. Horton, *History of the Grange in Vermont* (1926); David H. Howard, *People, Pride and Progress: 125 Years of the Grange in America* (1992); D. Sven Nordin, *Rich Harvest: A History of the Grange, 1867–1900* (1974); Thomas A. Woods, *Knights of the Plow: Oliver H. Kelley and the Origins of the Grange in Republican Ideology* (1991).

Thomas A. Woods

Hay Today, as in the 18th and early 19th centuries when New England's was largely an agrarian culture, "getting in the hay" remains an essential part of the region's agricultural cycle. From the beginning of settlement, farmers depended on cattle for both meat and dairy products, and the principal fodder for cattle was hay.

Early English settlers had problems locating adequate forage for their animals. Because nearly all indigenous New England grasses contained a high percentage of roughage, cattle did not get sufficient nutrition over the long winters, so farmers had to plant English grasses to sustain them. In coastal areas, families found that salt-marsh grasses made good fodder. Hay from these lands was highly prized, and the production of salt-marsh hay continued well into the 20th century.

Although many early farmers simply cut hay for household use on fields known as mowing land, hay was a marketable crop, generally sold by the ton. After the mid-1700s, some farmers experimented with improved grasses such as timothy and clover, and conscientiously plowed and manured their fields to increase yields. During the 19th century, more farmers planted improved grasses as part of crop-rotation strategies. More recently, farmers have turned to alfalfa, soybeans, and other legumes to help maintain fertility, but many still plant traditional grasses or simply mow whatever comes up in the spring.

Before the 20th century, haying was generally done two or three times a year, depending on the amount of rainfall during the growing season. Before the 1840s, much of the work was done on a cooperative basis as neighbors rotated from one farm to the next. A line of men worked their way across the field, cutting the hay with razor-sharp scythes. This work was physically demanding, requiring upper-body strength, stamina, rhythm, and coordination. Most men carried a whetstone and a small jug of oil into the fields—they had to stop and sharpen the scythe blades frequently.

Cutting hay, American Farmers' Almanac, 1837

Although the number of workers on a haying crew could vary greatly, many tasks were apportioned according to size and age. In addition to the scythemen, haying usually required rakers to rake the newly cut hay into windrows for drying. After the hay had dried sufficiently, men pitched it onto a wagon as boys treaded it down to consolidate the mass and then drew it to the barn, where they forked it into the haymows.

Timing was important; it was dangerous, for instance, to put green or wet hay into barns because it might ferment and spontaneously combust. Drying it sufficiently might require turning over the windrows in the fields once or more, and an ill-timed rainstorm might delay the task of putting it up in the barn. Moreover, haying was generally done in June after planting was finished and before the corn crop needed hoeing. Delays in putting up the hay

Bringing in hay, Stark, N.H., 1972

affected the sequence of other farm tasks. If the hay grew well after the first cutting, farmers might cut it again in August or September, and some even got in a third cutting before frost ended the growing season. The amount and quality of hay was influenced by the soil, varieties of grasses, attention to fertilizing, and the care taken while putting it up in the barn. If the season was poor and yields were down, many farmers might not be able to keep all their cattle through the winter; if hay was abundant, families might keep cattle longer until market conditions seemed best. Either way, the hay crop directly affected the household's economy.

Mechanization proceeded slowly. A few progressive farmers purchased mowing machinery before the Civil War, but many farmers did not adopt mowing machinery and hay rakes until the late 19th or early 20th centuries. Mechanized hay baling was not common until the 20th century, when gasoline-powered tractors became widely available.

Production has been affected by markets for livestock and dairy products in the 20th and 21st centuries (see the table on hay production in the Introduction). In general, the region's production has declined as the number of farms has decreased and as farmers have supplemented hay with other fodder crops. As more farmers turned to alfalfa and silage, they became less dependent on hay. Vermont, with its active dairy business, remains the leader in hay production. Today, hay bales and, more recently, large rolls or bundles of hay are still a common sight on New England's farm fields; they remind us that hay remains one of the region's most important farm products.

J. Ritchie Garrison, *Landscape and Material Life in Franklin County, Massachusetts, 1770–1860* (1991); Thomas C. Hubka, *Big House, Little House, Back House, Barn: The Connected Farm Buildings of New England* (1984); Mark Kramer, *Three Farms: Making Milk, Meat and Money from the American Soil* (1980); John R. Stilgoe, *Common Landscape of America, 1580 to 1845* (1982).

J. Ritchie Garrison

Horticulture

New England horticulture had its roots in the practices of Native Americans, who cleared the coastal areas of southern New England. Here, and in inland areas of rich intervale soils, such as in Deerfield, Mass., natives grew beans, corn, tobacco, pumpkins, and other squash long before European colonists arrived. With planting sticks and implements made of stone, bone, and clamshells, they broke up the land and used herring and other fish to fertilize it. Methodically, they planted corn on small hillocks, and then beans, which climbed the cornstalks. Among the hills of corn grew the squash, whose low-growing leaves made effective mulch. Although Native Americans did not maintain orchards, they harvested native berries and nuts. Far from inferior, New England soil favored a tremendous selection of vegetables, fruits, nuts, and flowers.

The New England colonies began as experiments in horticulture, varying from region to region as soil quality changed. Colonial households often had a garden and later an orchard, with grains, corn, and hay raised on larger fields adjacent to the house lot, in nearby fields, or as part of common lands. The colonists needed to trade in order to survive, and horticulture became an important economic activity, with the produce of farms either used by the colonists themselves or shipped overseas—especially to the Caribbean—becoming part of the world market. New England apples made their way to Calcutta. The colonists differed from Native Americans in that they not only grew vegetables for personal use but began to grow them commercially. Commerce has affected horticultural practice for three centuries.

Native Americans taught colonists to burn fields, break them up quickly, and fertilize them with fish. The English noticed that the vegetable seeds they brought from home—cucumbers, onions, and turnips—produced crops that were much larger than they had been in the Kent or Surrey countryside. Gardeners grew root vegetables in great quantities. Garden plots needed to be enclosed, first with fencing and later with stone walls, to keep out foraging pigs, wild animals, and sheep.

Colonists began to modify Indian practices with strict property divisions and the use of hand tools to break up and seed the land. Finding many native grasses low in nutrients, they quickly planted English grasses for pasturage and fodder. They began to fertilize their plots (with seaweed if they lived along the coast) and by the mid-1700s could raise green vegetables, cauliflowers, and melons under glass hotbeds. The Boston merchant Peter Faneuil developed one of the first greenhouses in New England. As manufacturers improved greenhouses with heat and better glass during the 19th century to meet rising demand from urban populations, horticulturists were able to extend the growing season. Greenhouses eventually became more affordable for the middle class. By the end of the 19th century, growers were able to irrigate their fields with hoses, steam pumps, and even windmills. The extension of rail lines, the development of refrigerated cars, the perfection of canning, and the invention of techniques to produce frozen foods by Clarence Birdseye expanded markets, even as they laid the groundwork for other regions to provide food to New England.

Other early Americans contributed to plant culture by discovering new seeds or hybridizing old standbys. Benjamin Franklin sent the first rhubarb seeds to his friend Jared Eliot in Saybrook, Conn., where it quickly became popular. The mainstay of the expanding vegetable garden came from Peru via Ireland: the potato. With the arrival of the Scotch Irish in New England in large numbers in 1719, the potato became a regional staple. Gentleman and ministers grew several varieties, eventually in such abundance that they became part of the export trade. Greenwich, Conn., grew wealthy through the potato trade. Only when blight attacked wheat did potato growing in Maine catch on.

Hybridization helped to increase trade and offered disease-resistant strains of plants. New varieties of potato and winter squash quickly developed; Albert Bresee of Hubbardton, Vt., propagated the Early Rose potato, an American favorite, and J. J. H. Gregory of Marblehead, Mass., developed the Hubbard squash. Hybridization affected corn, too. Onions and wheat, which did well in the Connecticut River valley, were also exported. Harvests in vegetables were so rich that produce merchants rented stalls in market towns, frequently named after those in England. There they sold their lettuces, celery, horseradish, and snap beans. The livelihood was not without problems: the turnip fly and pea weevil attacked vegetable plots; caterpillars consumed fruit trees; the Hessian fly and wheat midge attacked the wheat.

Shakers were among the most successful horticulturists, eventually marketing native-grown seeds. Most Shaker villages in the 19th century marketed seeds and culinary and medicinal herbs, with their settlements at Harvard, Mass., and Canterbury, N.H., prominent among New England villages. The New Lebanon, N.Y., Shaker village, however, just across the Massachusetts border, set the standard for Shaker seed distribution. The seed industry in New England has continued to this day, with several companies, such as Johnny's Selected Seeds of Albion, Maine, specializing in hybrids developed for northern growing conditions and in heritage varieties. The Eastern Native Seed Conservancy of Great Barrington, Mass., supports the collection and distribution of heritage seeds and sponsors an heirloom tomato project.

During the 18th and 19th centuries, flax, broomcorn, and hops became important plants for the region. Scotch Irish immigrants centered in Derry, N.H., grew flax for the fibers used to create the linens for which they were famed, and many English families grew flax to provide family linens. The trade in seed and oil became profitable in southern Connecticut. Levi Dickinson, a Massachusetts farmer, experimented with varieties of broomcorn and eventually manufactured his own brooms. Broom making also became a significant industry for the Shakers. Planted at greater intervals, broomcorn was more labor intensive than field corn. If its seed matured, it was used for livestock feed. Hops were grown for beer, but since the crop needed a good deal of manure, its production peaked and then declined.

Like the Native Americans, colonists had vast cornfields, but they also planted barley, pease, rye, and other English grains. Grown for beer, barley did not take well to New England soil, so the colonists turned to apples for cider and vinegar. New Englanders grew apples along stone walls and highways, even among clumps of rocks. John Chapman of Leominster, Mass., was reported to scatter apple seeds wherever he traveled, earning him the name Johnny Appleseed.

With the spread of orchards, cider quickly replaced beer as the chief New England beverage. The Reverend William Blaxton planted the first orchard on the Shawmut peninsula, later Boston, in the 1620s, and within a generation, orchards grew from Massachusetts through the Connecticut River valley. New England was an important area for fruit propagation as the early Americans improved European fruits. The Roxbury Russett apple, created in 1647, was named for the Massachusetts town and is still considered the finest cider apple. The Westfield Seek-No-Further, Baldwin, and Rhode Island Greening were all developed in this region and are still available today from nurseries that sell heirloom varieties. Pears and peaches did well with gentleman cultivators; the Bartlett pear was born in Roxbury in 1770. John Kenrick opened a nursery in Newton, Mass., in 1832 and introduced the Beurre Bosc pear, originally developed in Belgium or France. Native nut trees such as the cherry, black walnut, and chestnut provided food as well as timber.

New Englanders also began cultivating wild strawberries, propagating new varieties such as Hautboy, Early Hudson, and Early Scarlet. Cultivated berries were forced in greenhouses, and the demand for them was so great that by midcentury the first strawberry festivals were held. Other wild berries were also domesticated. Cranberries, initially harvested from bogs in Massachusetts, were transplanted and cultivated. Henry Hall of Cape Cod contributed to their cultivation by enriching the soil with sand, producing juicier berries. New varieties were propagated with such speed that local communities passed ordinances to preserve wild shrubs. Horticulturists also discovered that asparagus roots liked sandy soil, and a market developed for this

vegetable. Ephraim Bull of Concord, Mass., propagated the Concord grape, whose wide use includes desserts and drinks.

More important for the future of horticulture was the arrival of livestock. Domesticated animals, cattle, sheep, and pigs became part of the Massachusetts Bay Colony and created the need for fences to keep the animals away from the vegetable plots. Their manure introduced English grasses and weeds to the New England countryside, crowding out native grasses. The ox changed horticultural practice even more as the plow he pulled dug deeply into the soil and contributed to its erosion and loss of native plants. English horticulture warmed the land and dried the soil, creating seasonal extremes.

Even as early settlers concentrated on food crops, they began to grow flowers, relying on seeds and cuttings from home. Flowers and herbs were grown for medicinal, culinary, and ornamental purposes. Lady Fenwick in Saybrook, Conn., is believed to have started the first ornamental garden. At the Moffatt-Ladd house in Portsmouth, N.H., one of the few remaining colonial gardens—created by the Whipple family—is maintained on its original location. Few colonists took the time to learn native wildflowers. When economic prosperity allowed for greater flower gardening in the early years of the republic and the Victorian age, New Englanders looked the world over for new and exotic plant species. Especially popular were plants from the Far East. Commercial flower growing of hybridized foreign plants increased substantially. By the mid-1800s, New Englanders, often inspired as much by Romanticism's nature religion as by scientific discovery, identified and collected native species in herbariums. Emily Dickinson's collection is preserved at Harvard University. The Shaker sister Cora Helena Sarle recorded in watercolors all the native flowers and herbs found at her Canterbury Shaker Village. By the turn of the 20th century, New Englanders influenced by the Colonial Revival movement lamented the loss of native plants and sought to preserve them. Amateur and professional botanists scoured the countryside, as did Robert Frost, who sought rare orchids at his Derry farm. Today, the New England garden is filled with hybrids, many with origins far beyond the borders of the United States.

In the 20th century, horticulture expanded in the region as other kinds of farming declined; today it ranks at or near the top of farm income in the New England states. In eastern Connecticut, mushroom growing is a profitable business, and specialty crops marketed to the burgeoning ethnic populations are grown by long-time farm families as well as

new immigrants who make up a large portion of newer farm families. Immigrants have also revitalized the ornamental horticulture business, especially in southern New England. Ornamental horticulture is booming in the region. The passage of the North American Free Trade Act in 1993, however, has placed New England commercial growers of cut flowers and plants at a disadvantage, with the importation of less expensive products from Latin America. White Flower Farm in Litchfield, Conn., has developed a significant market for its annuals and perennials through its catalog sales. The Massachusetts Horticultural Society sponsors a huge annual flower show in Boston, and smaller lawn and garden shows and rose festivals, such as that at Hartford's Elizabeth Park, ensure that New Englanders will know the latest varieties suited for the region and can purchase the tried and true traditional ones. In recent years, heritage varieties of lilacs have become popular, and the Wentworth Coolidge Mansion of Portsmouth has sponsored the propagation of lilacs from the first lilacs imported to America by John Wentworth in the 18th century. Even wildflowers have become a garden staple, and visitors can see an extraordinary collection at the Garden in the Woods, in Framingham, Mass.

Until 50 years ago, most New Englanders derived some of their sustenance from their own land. Most homes had an orchard or vegetable garden, many with such New England natives as the elderberry, dewberry, gooseberry, or currant. They also had fruit trees, some grown from grafts cultivated for hundreds of years. The expansion of suburbs and the increase in numbers of people who commute to work caused a decline in raising vegetables and fruits, and even flowers. People no longer had the time to maintain a plot, and with convenience shopping, many lacked the inclination. With the desire for farm-fresh produce and specialty ethnic foods, however, farmers' markets have made a comeback in many New England towns.

Land development has confronted citizens with the loss of native ecology, creating an interest in planting native flora. Efforts by associations such as the New England Wildflower Society in Framingham have helped to conserve native plants. Concerned gardeners have reintroduced once common natives such as the jack-in-the-pulpit to their plots and have added others, such as monarda, to attract native birds and butterflies. Environmental associations encourage today's New Englanders to set aside part of their yard for a backyard habitat.

Galen Beale and Mary Rose Boswell, *The Earth Shall Blossom: Shaker Herbs and Gardening* (1991); William

Cronon, *Changes in the Land: Indians, Colonists, and the Ecology of New England* (1983); Howard S. Russell, *A Long, Deep Furrow: Three Centuries of Farming in New England* (1976); Tamara Plakins Thornton, *Cultivating Gentlemen: The Meaning of Country Life among the Boston Elite, 1785–1860* (1989).

Suzanna Nyberg

H. P. Hood and Sons

In 1846 Harvey Perley Hood began a one-man milk delivery route in Charlestown, Mass., laying the foundation for the family business that would become the region's leading dairy. In 1856 Hood bought a dairy farm in Derry, N.H., and began his wholesale milk business. Thanks to the advent of the railroad and rapid urban population increase, Hood was able to contract with the Concord and Manchester, N.H., and Lawrence, Mass., railroads to send milk to Boston markets via train. Hood conducted business even on Sundays, something most New England business owners did not do at the time.

In 1880 Charles Harvey Hood, H. P. Hood's oldest son, began working for his father. Like Harvey, Charles H. Hood learned the business from the ground up—milking cows, cleaning barns, and riding the milk train. Gilbert Henry Hood, H. P. Hood's youngest son, also worked in the business, and H. P. Hood and Sons was incorporated in 1890. A company plant and central offices were established in Charlestown in 1892.

H. P. Hood and Sons was the first dairy in the Northeast to use sanitary methods to produce and sell milk. In 1895 pasteurization was introduced, and C. H. Hood hired the first bacteriologist to test milk daily and to prepare special milk for babies; shortly thereafter the company introduced its trademark sterilized-glass milk bottles for delivery. Hood was also the first to adopt an incubation technique to detect bacteria in dairy farms; this technique was later adopted nationally. H. P. Hood and Sons organized local retail peddlers who covered some 2,000 milk routes to deliver Hood's high-quality pasteurized milk to households throughout New England.

When H. P. Hood died in 1900, Charles H. Hood became the company's second president. That year Hood introduced its creamery ice cream to retail stores. In 1947 the company hired its first female driver, and by 1954 women filled major roles in the corporations' upper management. H. P. Hood and Sons was one of the first major American employers to offer workmen's compensation and a comprehensive major medical plan to employees. The corporation sold stock only to its employees and even printed a newsletter, "Spotlight," that promoted Hood's image as a New England tradition.

H. P. Hood and Sons promotional character, 1990

Beginning in the 1950s, H. P. Hood and Sons expanded its product line to include margarine, instant nonfat dry milk, orange juice, and frozen pizza. Hood has persistently catered to health-conscious consumers, introducing Nuform lowfat milk, the first major branded lowfat milk in the East, in 1969; and super-premium ice milk, Hood Light, in 1986. Hood's Nuform brand became the most extensive line of lowfat dairy products in New England. The company also pioneered ultra-high-temperature pasteurization, enabling extended-shelf-life dairy products to be sold nationally and internationally.

The corporation underwent key changes in the late 20th century; in 1972 it celebrated its 125th anniversary, its name changed from H. P. Hood and Sons to H. P. Hood, Inc., and the first woman was elected to the board of directors. In 1980 the Agway Corporation bought H. P. Hood, Inc., continuing to sell dairy products under the Hood name. By 1985 the corporation consisted of the Dairy Company, the Citrus Company, and the Empire (State) Cheese Groups, and employed some 1,800 people. The Hoodsie Cup, with its famous wooden spoon, celebrated its 50th anniversary in 1997. This popular ice cream novelty, which originally sold for five cents, featured famous movie stars, sports figures, and American warplanes on the lids in the 1940s and 1950s; the lids are now collectors' items.

In 1995 H. P. Hood, Inc., was purchased by Jon Kaneb, the corporation's third owner, and in 2004 it became H. P. Hood LLC when it acquired the New York–based Crowley Foods and the Minneapolis-based Kemps. Annual sales in 2004 were approximately $2.2 billion, and the firm employed about 5,000 workers.

H. P. Hood's corporate offices are now based in Chelsea, Mass. The corporation is the largest producer of dairy products in New England and has a national reputation for such brands as Lactaid, Nesquick, and Coffeemate.

Benjamin King

Intervales

Interval (or interval) land is the term commonly used in New England for bottomland—low-lying land along a watercourse. One of New England's treasured agricultural resources, intervales have supported farming in the region for thousands of years. Native Americans used these broad, level, stone-free, fertile floodplains for corn and other crops long before Europeans arrived, while the rich soil, natural grass, and convenient access to water drew European colonists. Often referred to as meadows (or fresh meadows) intervales were a source of wild hay, offering excellent grazing for livestock. With the advent of agricultural mechanization, intervales became the most productive and easily worked part of the farm. In fact, since the late 1800s New England's agricultural decline has largely come in upland environments, while intervale acreage continues to be farmed.

Intervales range in size from an acre or less near brooks to hundreds of acres along major waterways such as the lower Connecticut River. Most are old lakebeds, the result of the natural drainage of post-glacial lakes, or alluvial plains created by rivers depositing sediment when overtopping their banks. The repeated flooding and associated sediment drop of the latter ensures that the soil remains rich in nutrients washed in from upstream. Stones left by the retreating glacier have been buried by the alluvium deeply enough to allow farming.

The soils that dominate intervales are among the most productive in New England, based on U. S. national standards, and are considered prime class I agricultural land. Intervale soils common to New England include Hadley and Fryeburg, the two most desirable for crop farming. These are nearly level, well drained, deep, and easy to work. The two are similar, although Hadley, located in southern New England, is warmer and thus a bit more productive than the cooler Fryeburg associated with the valleys of northern New England. These soils are somewhat higher than the wetter, more flood-prone soils like Rumney and Podunk. Because of their good drainage, the Hadley and Fryeburg lands are among the first cultivated in the spring. Flooding is the only significant concern with these soils, but it usually occurs during the spring before planting or in the fall after harvest. Stream-bank erosion can also be a problem, but this can often be managed through the use of riprap (a layer of stones shoring up the embankment) or plantings of woody vegetation. Cold-air drainage can cause a late frost in the spring or an early frost in the fall, resulting in crop damage that may be avoided on higher ground.

Today most of New England's intervales are devoted to row crops or forage production. Tobacco is grown in Massachusetts and Connecticut on the large intervales along the Connecticut River, and in northern New England intervales promote extensive corn, potato, and hay raising. Unlike other types of farmland in New England, intervale land is not threatened by development. The periodic flooding discourages developers, while zoning regulations exclude most construction.

As New England continues to lose farmland to development, intervales are likely to become the last sites of crop production, holding the region's agricultural landscape together.

William Cronon, *Changes in the Land: Indians, Colonists and the Ecology of New England* (1983); John Gerrard, ed., *Alluvial Soils* (1987); U.S. Department of Agriculture, *Soil Survey of Hampshire County, Massachusetts—Central Part* (1981); Joseph Wood, *The New England Village* (1997).

Paul B. Frederic

Labor

Labor During his spring work in 1844, an exhausted New England farmer named Henry Dana Ward wrote to his brother, "Labor is the *great* thing in farming." His letter, preserved in a manuscript collection at the American Antiquarian Society in Worcester, Mass., continues: "Labor saving machines do the work of many mechanisms—for the farmers none have been invented." Indeed, machines suitable for the region's small, rocky fields and uneven terrain were long in coming; until the late 19th century, securing sufficient labor each season remained the central challenge for the region's farmers. Even after mechanization, affordable and reliable labor remained a paramount concern. What changed over time was not the need but rather the source of available labor.

Traditionally, farm labor was a mix of family, live-in, and day help. For practical reasons, farm families relied as much as possible on their children to assist with the endless rounds of farm tasks. The need for paid help fluctuated according to family structure: it was greatest when the internal labor force was either too young or had grown and departed, and least during children's teenage and young adult years. Middling farmers without working-age sons "changed works" with neighbors,

Apple pickers, Fairview Orchards, Ayer, Mass., 1978

obtaining day help in exchange for goods or reciprocal labor, or hired local youths to work for room and board and modest wages. Large-scale farmers hired adult live-in and day laborers to complement the family labor pool. Similarly, middling farm wives assisted one another and recruited paid help as needed for particular tasks or seasons, while women whose husbands employed many hands relied on a combination of live-in and day help to supplement their own and their daughters' efforts. Until the early 19th century, hired laborers and domestic help were men and women of similar culture from the community or towns nearby.

In the 17th and 18th centuries, young men worked for others with the expectation that they would become propertied farmers themselves. This prospect began to erode in the next century, as options for securing viable farmland diminished and regional agriculture was undermined by western competition. By the 1830s, many Yankees were finding that farm labor compared unfavorably with new opportunities in the diversified regional economy. Henry Colman, editor of the *New England Farmer,* lamented in 1840 that the country was being swept "almost clean of young men" by the lure of new mechanical employment and professions. Yankee women, too, increasingly found emerging alternative employment in factories or in outwork networks more attractive than live-in service. As native-born men and women left fields, plows, and hearths in hopes of making a better living, Irish and French Canadian laborers (and, later, other immigrant groups) took their places. And as Yankees left their farms, immigrants bought them and continued New England's traditional livelihood.

Farm labor was, and has remained, mostly seasonal, low-paying work. Most live-in laborers could expect to be offered a contract from April to November, leaving them to fend for themselves during the harshest time of year. A December-to-March agreement, if offered, was at drastically lower wages. Day la-

borers were more autonomous, for they lived independently of their employers, but their employment was more precarious; they were hired only when family or contract labor could not meet the demands of the moment.

New England farmers still rely on laborers to tend crops and cattle, orchards, and market gardens. Much of the most labor-intensive work today is undertaken by seasonal young employees and migrant workers, the least costly help available. There are still some old-time farmhands, for whom working on the land is simply a way of life. In each generation, farmers' children, the internal labor force, continue to face the difficult choice of staking their livelihoods in New England's rocky soil or following easier paths. Ironically, New England's agricultural landscape and its tillers of the soil are at the heart of Yankee culture, if not its workaday reality.

Andrew H. Baker and Holly V. Izard, "New England Farmers and the Marketplace, 1780–1865: A Case Study," *Agricultural History* 75 (1991); Hal S. Barron, *Those Who Stayed Behind: Rural Society in 19th-Century New England* (1984); Clarence H. Danhof, *Change in Agriculture: The Northern United States, 1820–1870* (1969); Stephen Innes, ed., *Work and Labor in Early America* (1988).

Holly V. Izard

Maple Syrup "Maple: It's the flavor of Vermont!" shouts an advertisement in *Vermont Life,* reinforcing one of the most endearing and enduring images of New England. From the colonial period onward, maple sugar and syrup production has flourished in the region. Although New York, Ohio, Pennsylvania, Wisconsin, Michigan, and eastern Canada all produce maple goods in substantial quantities, northern and western New England seem to most Americans to have dominated the trade. Capitalizing on this association, restaurants charge extra for "real" maple syrup, particularly if it's from Vermont, the leading producer in New England.

Many northeastern woodlands indigenous peoples, such as the Abenaki of northern New England and Quebec, relied on saps and gums of spruce, birch, and maple trees for food and gum products. Maple trees, in particular, supplied the tribes with a sweet syrupy substance for mixing with corn, rice, and other foodstuffs. In addition, they boiled down the sweet-water sap into sugar to be used by the tribe or traded for other goods. Abenakis cut a slanting gash into a tree, inserted an elderberry twig spile with its pith hollowed out, and collected the drips in birch-bark containers. Later they used iron or tin spiles that the European Americans devised. Some historians and anthropologists dispute the sugar-making capacities of the indigenous people, arguing

Syruping off the maple sap on a family farm, Waitsfield, Vt., 1940

they had to await the arrival of the more reliable European American iron pots and noting the absence of any description of the practice in travelers' accounts of the day. Other scholars believe that sugar making definitely predated Indian-European contact, perhaps by centuries.

Early European American settlers eagerly exploited the sap-producing maple groves. Many French colonists and British New Englanders depended on maple sugar for a nip of sweetness because it was more plentiful and cheaper than sugarcane products. Although no broad market existed for the maple sugar, colonial farmers harvested the sap for many domestic uses. By the late 1700s, Thomas Jefferson was espousing the virtues of maple sugar and attempted to introduce the tree to his Virginia estate, Monticello, after procuring maple seeds from Bennington, Vt. Abolitionists, such as Benjamin Rush (who wrote a treatise on the healthful properties of maple sugar) and the Vermont Quaker Henry Miles, called for the expansion of maple sugar production to undercut the Caribbean sugarcane market, which used slave labor for the production of sugar. By 1860, American sugar producers had made the equivalent of 6.6 million gallons. Following the Civil War, however, improvements in transportation made cane sugar more widely available, and as the demand for maple sugar decreased, farmers began to produce and market maple as syrup. By the 1890s, the first organizations of maple syrup producers were formed, with the goal of sharing common production problems and solutions with one another.

Over the past century or so, the maple industry has had to counter maple syrup imitations, road-salt damage to the trees, a decline in small farm operations, and, in the 1980s, an attack of pear thrips that riddled leaves and hurt sap volume. In the early 20th century, maple production continued as an adjunct of the family farm enterprise. Syrup was sold locally or to a list of repeat customers. After World War II, technological advances brought energy savings and efficiency into the sugarhouse, including new reverse-osmosis systems and evaporators. Although wood was still the primary source of heat, evaporator systems fueled by oil, gas, and steam also became available. With these advances came higher standards for syrup production and the institution of the grading system that identified types of syrups for the consumer: U.S. Grade A in light, medium, and dark varieties; U.S. Grade B, which tends to be darker and is called "utility" grade; and U.S. Grade C, which is unclassified.

Today New Englanders blend modern technology with traditional methods. Larger, more sophisticated producers dominate the industry, but some local farmers also continue to produce syrup as a hobby or for supplemental income. Many producers tap their trees with a network of plastic tubing and boil sap in improved evaporators; others continue to gather sap in pails using the traditional methods of horse and sled.

Production levels have varied, depending largely on weather conditions. From 1989 to 1997, production in the four northern New England states totaled about 6,082,000 gallons, or about 675,000 gallons per year. In 1992, a bumper-crop year throughout New England, Vermont alone accounted for an estimated 570,000 gallons, valued at more than $12 million. Four years later, Vermonters tapped and processed another 550,000 gallons. In 1997, however, the region experienced a 17 percent production decline because of erratic weather. In spite of these ups and downs, the industry remains vibrant, lucrative, and a lasting part of New England culture into the 21st century.

Charles M. Barbeau, "Maple Sugar: Its Native Origins," *Transactions and Proceedings of the Royal Society of Canada* 40 (1946); James M. Lawrence and Rux Martin, *Sweet Maple: Life, Lore and Recipes from the Sugarbush* (1993); Helen Nearing, *The Maple Sugar Book* (1950); Noel Perrin, *Amateur Sugar Maker* (1972).

Thomas L. Altherr

Massachusetts Horticultural Society Founded in Boston in 1829, the Massachusetts Horticultural Society (MHS) quickly established itself as the leading institution of its kind in the United States. It sponsored the publication of horticultural information in its periodical, *Transactions,* maintained a horticultural library, distributed foreign plants, and awarded premiums at weekly, seasonal, and annual exhibitions. In addition, the MHS in 1831 established the Mount Auburn Cemetery in Cambridge, the first garden cemetery in the United States, although it relinquished management of that institution three years later.

In these early decades, the society attracted a mixed membership of professional and amateur horticulturists. The professionals contributed the bulk of exhibition offerings, but the amateurs, members of the Boston elite, set the tone of the MHS and dominated its affairs. Elite Bostonians were drawn to horticulture for ideological reasons tied to their upper-class status. As MHS members, they applied the horticultural concept of "cultivation" to human beings, as a way to legitimize the ranking of one "variety" over another, and they presented their pursuit of horticulture both as proof that they could appreciate what had no market value—the beauty and perfection of nature—and as an antidote to materialism.

Between the Civil War and World War I, the MHS lost its status as a central institution of the Brahmin class but retained some of its upper-crust overtones. Exhibitions and awards reflected MHS members' major interest, the cultivation of flowers and the design of ornamental gardens on suburban estates. As long as it had served as a counterweight to greed and materialism, the society had admitted only men, but by 1864, the MHS accepted its first female member. Thereafter, the society concerned itself with female leisure and charity work, offering botany instruction to young ladies, sponsoring window-box projects in low-income neighborhoods, supporting school and community gardens, and encouraging beautification projects.

After World War I, the society consciously strove to transform itself into a national institution with a broad membership. In 1923, it dropped its initiation fee and assumed publication of *Horticulture,* reworking a trade periodical that served the flower industry into a popular magazine devoted to the home gardener. By the end of World War II, membership had skyrocketed from about 1,000 mainly local members to 9,000 members from 46 states. The annual spring flower show, featuring displays by amateurs, professionals, and local garden clubs, attracted huge crowds. Prizes and medals recognized a wide range of horticultural accomplishments nationwide from scientific research to landscape design.

The society continues to maintain a spectacular horticultural library and to sponsor horticultural exhibitions, but its origins in the class concerns of the antebellum Boston elite have long been obscured. Today the MHS, with more than 12,000 members, offers adult education, horticultural internship opportunities, a telephone hotline for gardening questions, and a "plantmobile" that presents science workshops in area schools. For tens of thousands of horticultural enthusiasts from New England and beyond, its spring flower show in Boston is a fixture on the gardening calendar. Society publications no longer reach a mass audience—the MHS severed its connection with *Horticulture* in 1981—but its library is the largest and best of its type in the nation, reflecting the depth and decades of collecting. Amateur gardeners and professional historians alike make use of its more than 100,000 books, periodicals, botanical prints, and seed catalogs.

Albert Emerson Benson, *History of the Massachusetts Horticultural Society* (1929); Edward I. Farrington, *Twenty-five Historic Years: How an Exhibition, a Magazine, and a Library Brought New Life to a Famous Institution: The History of the Massachusetts Horticultural Society from March, 1929* (1955); Robert Manning, *History of the Massachusetts Horticultural Society, 1829–1878* (1990); Tamara Plakins Thornton, *Cultivating Gentlemen: The Meaning of Country Life among the Boston Elite, 1785–1860* (1989).

Tamara Plakins Thornton

Migrant Labor New England growers have used migrant farm labor for at least a century. Traditionally they were able to rely on neighboring farm families, artisans, shoe and textile workers laid off during seasonal lulls, and the "strolling poor" of less workable or more crowded farm areas to assist during harvest. Labor shortages emerged in agricultural areas, however, as growing industrial and urban opportunities lured rural dwellers to cities and as the opening of vast, more fertile lands in the West attracted emigrants.

After the Civil War, as railroad systems crossed the continent and as "bonanza" farms in the West sent vast quantities of inexpensive grain into eastern markets, New England farmers were compelled either to abandon farming altogether or to convert from staple agriculture to producing highly perishable foods—milk, butter, eggs, vegetables, and fruit—for trade, or "truck," in the region's cities and resort areas. The production of wheat in the region fell from 1 million bushels in 1860 to 137,000 bushels in 1899 while the yields of specialty crops rose across the board. Cranberry production climbed from 13,333 barrels in 1872 to 208,333 in 1899; the onion crop of the Connecticut River valley increased from 32,611 bushels in 1875 to 342,259 in 1899;

and by 1890 Maine's Aroostook County, rapidly establishing itself as the nation's prime potato area, produced 5 million bushels compared to the 86,500 it had raised in 1860.

Yet these increased yields took place as the migration of New Englanders to industrial cities accelerated. Mechanization had enhanced production by automating some front-end processes, but tree fruits and crops grown in soft or sandy soils resisted mechanical harvesting; some, such as apples, still do. Moreover, these larger, highly perishable crops had to be harvested in a perilously short time. As growers' need for harvest labor grew extreme, they began to hire new immigrants; by the 1890s Polish immigrants were harvesting onions and tobacco in the Connecticut River valley, Finns and Cape Verdeans were moving seasonally for the cranberry harvest in southeastern Massachusetts, and French Canadians were picking fruit in northern Maine and Vermont. As immigrants sought steadier, more lucrative work, growers near urban centers turned to the labor of foreign-born women, children, and men; growers in more remote sections of the region turned largely to Native Americans and African Americans. By 1917, when men had entered munitions factories and European immigration was suspended, 3,000 southern African Americans were harvesting tobacco in Connecticut.

The use of migrant farm labor has always swelled in times of real or perceived labor scarcity. The Great Depression caused a labor surplus in many agricultural areas, but as the 1930s drew to a close and war in Europe loomed, growers recruited African Americans and others more assiduously. Micmac laborers from Canada entered the Maine potato harvest at this time. By 1943, as the war absorbed the male population, farmers prevailed upon the federal government to recruit foreign harvest labor. In the fall of 1942 the War Food Administration began the Labor Importation Program by recruiting thousands of Mexican workers for western harvests; by 1944 the program had also placed West Indians, Puerto Ricans, and German and Italian prisoners of war in harvest and processing jobs in the Northeast. Southern growers, worried that northern wages would deplete their traditional pools of harvest labor, requested that migrant workers secure permission from county officials before moving; wartime tire and gas rationing also kept them near home. As a result, Jamaican and Puerto Rican workers, through contracts between governments, displaced African Americans in New England harvests.

Today, as an increasing number of Puerto Rican immigrants have found permanent jobs and homes, some New England growers have turned to Mexicans and Mexican Americans.

Of crop workers interviewed in New England in 2000–2002, 75 percent were foreign born and 45 percent were migrants. In 1997, according to the New England Apple Council, about 3,250 Jamaicans harvested New England crops, apples and tobacco in particular.

Understanding of the relation between migrants and their native places has changed significantly in the last decades of the 20th century and the first decade of the 21st. Migrant farmworkers are no longer viewed as rootless people; indeed, their relation to their homes is critical to explaining why they travel such long distances for such short-term, poorly compensated employment. The vast majority of migrant laborers have probably been sojourners, taking temporary farm jobs that pay substantially better than work (if available at all) at home in order to buy land, build a home, or support or enhance an existing household. In 2000–2002, 42 percent of all seasonal farmworkers in New England were living away from their families while doing farmwork.

Data from the National Agricultural Workers Survey for 2000–2002 show that the family incomes of 34 percent of seasonal farm workers in New England were below the poverty line, compared to 33 percent nationwide. Historians attribute this poverty partly to the fact that federal law has long treated the farm as different from the factory, a place where labor relations were face to face and virtually familial. Thus until the 1960s farmworkers were exempted from nearly all legislation designed to protect workers, such as the rights to bargain collectively and to receive minimum wage, workmen's compensation, unemployment insurance, and health insurance. Since then some legislation, particularly the Migrant and Seasonal Agricultural Worker Protection Act of 1983, has extended coverage long guaranteed industrial workers to farmworkers, but many laws are inadequately enforced or exclude the large numbers working on very small farms. Although agricultural New England remains reliant upon this labor source, the quality of life of migrant workers remains substandard.

David Griffith, Ed Kissam, and Jeronimo Camposeco, *Working Poor: Farmworkers in the United States* (1995); Cindy Hahamovitch, *The Fruits of Their Labor: Atlantic Coast Farmworkers and the Making of Migrant Poverty, 1870–1945* (1997); Marilyn Halter, "Working the Bogs," in *Between Race and Ethnicity: Cape Verdean American Immigrants, 1860–1965* (1993); Harald E. L. Prins, "Tribal Network and Migrant Labor: Mi'kmaq Indians as Seasonal Workers in Aroostook's Potato Fields, 1870–1980," in *After King Philip's War: Presence and Persistence in Indian New England*, ed. Colin G. Calloway (1997).

Kathryn Grover

Morgan Horse New England is the birthplace of the Morgan, the first American breed of light horse. Known for their beauty, spirit, and strength, Morgans can be found throughout the United States and in approximately 20 other countries. The first Morgan, known as Figure, was born in West Springfield, Mass., the offspring of an imported English thoroughbred named True Briton and an unnamed mare believed to have Arabian blood. According to legend, in 1791 Figure was given as payment for a debt to the schoolmaster Justin Morgan, who brought the horse to his home in Randolph Center, Vt. Morgan, who traveled around the New England frontier giving singing lessons, often rode his young stallion, whom people admired for his versatility and strength. Figure could pull more weight, clear more land, travel greater distances, and race faster than other workhorses. Local residents soon took notice of the abilities of "the Justin Morgan horse."

New England horse breeders eventually expressed great demand for Figure's stud services, and the little Morgan prolifically produced progeny. Thrifty New Englanders valued his offspring as gentle and hardy workhorses. Advertisements for his services were published in New England newspapers, and a new breed of American horses was classified as Morgans. Figure died of an infection at age 31; longevity is among the fortunate genetic traits he transmitted to his progeny. Known for their versatility and adaptability, Morgans were considered highly useful by New England farmers because they could drag logs and pull stumps, yet still drive the family to church on Sunday. Morgans excelled at harness racing, which prevailed in parts of New England where residents considered flat racing immoral. Several thousand Morgans carried Vermont troops during the Civil War.

Aware that no rules regulated breeding, Colonel Joseph Battell of Middlebury, Vt., worried that the breed might be ruined. He printed the first volume of the *American Morgan Horse Register* in 1894, and owners registering Morgans were required to prove their horse's descent from Figure. Battell also donated a herd of broodmares and acreage near Middlebury to the Vermont Experiment Station to establish the United States Morgan Horse Farm, which was eventually transferred to the University of Vermont. By 1948 the Morgan Horse Club closed its registry, permitting only the offspring of registered parents. As automobiles replaced horses for utilitarian tasks, the breeding of Morgans has become a leisure activity as well as a commercial venture. The association has regulated recent scientific advancements such as use of frozen semen and embryo transplants to preserve the registry's integrity.

Today, all registered Morgans are descendants of Figure. Morgans share similar conformation characteristics, standing from 14.1 to 15.1 hands with strong haunches, sloping shoulders, a short back, crested neck, tapered head, and full mane and tail. Most are chestnut or bay in color. Morgan bloodlines helped establish such popular breeds as the Standardbred, the American Saddlebred, the American Quarter Horse, and the Tennessee Walking Horse. Morgans participate in national horse shows and endurance rides and are used as workhorses, as pleasure mounts, and in therapeutic riding programs. In tribute to their heritage, Morgans compete in the Justin Morgan Performance Class, racing under harness and on the flat, pulling a 1,000-pound stoneboat, and exhibiting under saddle. The National Museum of the Morgan Horse is located at the American Morgan Horse Association headquarters at Shelburne, Vt.

Betty Bandel, *Sing the Lord's Song in a Strange Land: The Life of Justin Morgan* (1981); Janet Wilder Dakin, *Jeffy's Journal: Raising a Morgan Horse* (1990); Jeanne Mellin, *The Morgan Horse* (1961); Peggy Jett Pittenger, *Morgan Horses* (1974).

Elizabeth D. Schafer

Morrill Act The Morrill Act was introduced by Vermont congressman Justin Smith Morrill in 1857 and passed into law in 1862. Under the provisions of the act, states were granted 30,000 acres of federal land for each of their congressmen. Funds from the sale of that land were used for the establishment of at least one college that would emphasize agriculture and the mechanical arts. Institutions established under the Morrill Act became known as land-grant colleges.

The Morrill Act was designed with the intent of training technicians and mechanics in response to the country's growing industrialization, but also clearly specified that scientific and classical studies should not be excluded. It was an important benchmark for New England farmers: the federal government had adopted a policy in support of agricultural education and scientific study to improve farm practices. A second Morrill Act, passed in 1890, provided annual federal financial support that enabled these institutions to develop responsible agricultural programs. Soon these schools offered comprehensive agricultural curricula that included model working farms and extension services, as well as traditional liberal arts education and intercollegiate sports.

The Morrill Act fostered several colleges in New England that are now state universities. The Massachusetts Agricultural College (now the University of Massachusetts) was chartered in 1863; the Maine State College of Agriculture and the Mechanical Arts (now the University of Maine) was founded in 1865; the New Hampshire State College of Agriculture and Mechanical Arts (now the University of New Hampshire) was established as a division of Dartmouth College in 1866 and relocated to Durham in 1893; and the Storrs Agricultural School (now the University of Connecticut) was founded in 1881. The Vermont Agricultural College, also founded under the Morrill Act, was absorbed in 1865 by the University of Vermont, the founding of which considerably predated the act. Perhaps the best-known of the land-grant colleges in New England is the prestigious Massachusetts Institute of Technology.

In the popular mind today, many of these institutions are associated far more with affordable higher education and spectacular sports teams than with agricultural research and vocational instruction. In fact, in addition to greatly broadening the scope of educational programs offered, they have expanded upon their original goals. The motivation, however, has changed. New England's 19th-century advocates for the scientific study of agriculture had hoped to preserve farming's central place in the region's diversifying economy; today the goal is worldwide agricultural and environmental improvement. This historical piece of legislation written by the Vermont congressman is also significant for democratizing higher education. Open admissions policies made college and graduate education more readily available to women, minorities, and people of modest means. Sons and daughters of New England farmers, along with many others, benefited greatly.

Committee on the Future of the Colleges of Agriculture in the Land Grant University System, Board of Agriculture, National Research Council, *Colleges of Agriculture at the Land Grant Universities: A Profile* (1995); Paul W. Gates, *The Farmer's Age: Agriculture, 1815–1860*, vol. 3 of *The Economic History of the United States* (1960); Alan I. Marcus, *Agricultural Science and the Quest for Legitimacy: Farmers, Agricultural Colleges, and Experiment Stations, 1870–1890* (1985); Fred A. Shannon, *The Farmer's Last Frontier: Agriculture, 1860–1897*, vol. 5 of *The Economic History of the United States* (1968).

Holly V. Izard

Out-migration and Rural Depopulation Out-migration and rural population loss are long-standing themes in the history of New England. The trend began in some of the region's older towns during the 1700s but reached its peak during the early to mid-1800s, as New England's country dwellers pursued new opportunities in the city and on the western frontier. In Vermont and New Hampshire, for example, many townships not only stopped growing but declined by more than 25 percent over the course of the century.

This population drop came at a time when the nation as a whole was experiencing rapid economic and demographic growth and American culture was celebrating expansion. During the mid-1800s, editorialists in the New England agricultural press regularly worried about their neighbors who had succumbed to the "Western craze" or the "Genesee fever" and ignored the virtues of staying put. They had choice words, too, for young men who traded the independence and wholesomeness of life on the farm for more dubious careers in the city. By the end of the century, popular writers such as Josiah Strong and Rollin Lynde Hartt were likening isolated, depopulated towns in the region to rural areas in the South occupied by supposedly depraved poor mountain whites. The only thing growing in a rural New England village, they said, was the graveyard.

Such remarks are less an accurate description of conditions in the New England countryside than a reflection of their authors' anxieties about larger changes in American society as it became increasingly urban, secular, and culturally diverse. Still, historians have subsequently used comments like these to paint a picture of exceptional decline: Harold F. Wilson spoke, for instance, of the "winter" of northern New England's history. Population loss came to be seen as a broad indictment of rural New England society, a wide-ranging expression of discontent with everything from economic competition intensified by newer western agricultural methods to the region's stony soil and harsh climate.

In fact, population decline in the New England countryside is more accurately characterized as the culmination of predictable processes of settlement and maturation in rural communities and not as an aberrant condition. Out-migration from urban as well as rural areas was commonplace throughout 19th-century American society. In growing cities, however, more than enough new people were moving in to take the place of those who left. Rural New England communities, by contrast, were fully settled by the mid-1800s, and local opportunities to attract newcomers were few. Residents who had a stake in the area stayed, but there were not enough niches for all their children or for substantial numbers of new settlers. Rates of migration from rural New England, then, were not exceptionally high; rather, rural locales decreased in population primarily because few new people

moved in. Such conditions were not confined to New England but came to characterize newer rural communities in other regions as they, in turn, matured after the settlement period.

Since the 19th century, rural depopulation has continued to be an issue of concern in New England as well as other agrarian regions of the country. This has become especially pronounced in more recent years as the combination of newer forms of agricultural technology and methods of production and expanding suburban and exurban settlements have sharply reduced the number of family farms operating in the countryside.

Hal S. Barron, *Those Who Stayed Behind: Rural Society in 19th-Century New England* (1984); Paul Glenn Munyon, *A Reassessment of New England Agriculture in the Last 30 Years of the 19th Century: New Hampshire, a Case Study*, rev. ed. (1978); Lewis D. Stilwell, *Migration from Vermont* (1948); Harold F. Wilson, *The Hill Country of Northern New England: Its Social and Economic History, 1790–1930* (1967 [1936]).

Hal S. Barron

Oxen Oxen—castrated bulls or steer of any breed that are trained to work—were the critical draft animals in New England's early agricultural development. Their importance is often overlooked because their early use and significance are not well documented. Throughout colonial history oxen toiled under the yoke, ready for any task demanded of them. By the late 17th century, they could be found in every New England community where soil had to be tilled and materials moved on land. And though they were not the fastest mode of transportation, they were dependable, cost effective, and readily available.

Teams of well-trained oxen provided the much-needed power to tame a new land and begin agricultural endeavors. In New England this meant that oxen were used for a variety of tasks including logging, moving stones, pulling stumps, plowing and harrowing fields, making roads, and hauling carts in summer and sleds in winter filled with everything the early colonists purchased, sold, or moved.

A team of oxen competes in the 4-H "Best Trained Team" class, 1986

Oxen pulled covered bridges into place, moved large buildings, and hauled anything from wood products to pots and pans. They were preferred over horses and mules because they could survive on coarse roughage and were cheaper and easier to put to work. At the end of their working lives, families could slaughter them or sell them to market.

Oxen also worked best in cool weather; the hotter, more humid climate to the south and the drier climates to the west decreased their pace and efficiency. Oxen had no fear of water and were comfortable in the wet soils and swamps common to the region. In addition, their slow pace and patient manner made them much less likely to break the farm implements they pulled through the rocky hillside fields.

Settlers in all parts of the country used oxen as draft animals at one time or another, but New England is the only region that boasts numerous oxen today. Hundreds of ox teamsters can still be found throughout the region. They are most often seen at country fairs and in parades or historic events in rural communities and range in age and ability from small children driving calf teams in 4-H events to adults competing in log-skidding competitions, plowing matches, and pulling. People from around the nation and the world attend such events to glean from these teamsters and their animals skills that have long been lost in other regions.

Oxen can be found in every New England state and their numbers are holding steady at approximately 5,000 oxen throughout the region. Teams still wear the simple wooden yoke and are driven with a small stick or whip; the training techniques and commands used to control oxen have remained unchanged for centuries. Teams of oxen found in New England today are a stark reminder of the challenges faced by the early settlers of this nation. The tradition of working cattle, a distinctive part of New England's cultural past, has been preserved and will probably remain for generations to come.

Drew Conroy, *Oxen, A Teamster's Guide* (1999); Robert Pike, *Tall Trees, Tough Men* (1967); Howard S. Russell, *A Long, Deep Furrow: Three Centuries of Farming in New England* (1976); Asa Sheldon, *Yankee Drover* (1988 [1862]).

Drew Conroy

Potatoes The potato, a tuberous vegetable first domesticated in Peru as early as the sixth century, was introduced to Europe after the Columbian Exchange, in the second half of the 16th century. By the end of the 18th century, potatoes were a staple food in Europe and England, and the Irish economy de-

Sorting potatoes at the LaBrie potato farm, Saint Agatha, Maine, 1994

pended heavily on the crop. Potatoes were introduced to New England by the Scotch Irish, who planted them in Londonderry (now Derry), N.H., in 1719, and were kept as a delicacy to be served with roast meat. First planted in beds with beets and carrots resulting in small yields, potatoes became a more common and plentiful crop after the American Revolution. Potatoes fed the crews of men who constructed the new transportation links throughout the United States during the Industrial Revolution, were used in animal feed, and provided a source of starch for the growing textile industry after 1840. Now one of New England's best-known commercial crops, potatoes are easily cultivated both for family use and in large quantities for commercial sale.

The Great Irish Famine of 1845–49 was caused by a late-season blight that led to the failure of potato crops over subsequent years, the death of more than a million Irish, and the influx of as many Irish immigrants to North America, primarily to Boston. The late blight also reduced potato production throughout the United States; in fact, by 1850, potato production was reduced by half, while prices more than doubled. Efforts to combat the blight, which continued to appear sporadically, led New England potato growers to adopt early maturing varieties, such as the Early Rose. Hardier varieties, such as the Green Mountain and Katahdin, used primarily for baking, were also introduced.

Many growers believed that potatoes fared better in harsher climates, and at the turn of the century, Aroostook County and northern Penobscot County in Maine—areas with extensive limestone soils that are both productive and easily tilled—had become the center of commercial potato cultivation. Commonly grown as a first- or second-year rotation crop, Maine potatoes were often planted in burned-over, unplowed land. While some growers harvested with plows, many did so by hand. The Bangor and Aroostook Railroad, which opened in 1894, was developed largely as a result of the demanding market needs of potato production. Potatoes cooked in various ways became a staple in the diet of most New Englanders, and the crop grew steadily in importance until after World War II.

In the early 1920s researchers discovered that many potato diseases were plant viruses transmitted by aphids, a hardy insect that wintered in shrubs adjacent to cultivated fields. Experimental work has since focused on disease prevention through methods such as certified seed stocks and controlled use of insecticides. State government agencies have played a strong role in supporting potato research, as well as in providing extensive marketing information for farmers. Since World War I, the University of Maine at Presque Isle has maintained an experimental farm devoted to potato research and marketing.

Growing competition caused by national dietary shifts and increased cultivation in other regions has diminished the New England potato crop in recent years. The profit margin has also narrowed. Extensive use of frozen potato products has led to significant potato cultivation in the semi-arid West, where the specific gravity of the tuber can be controlled through irrigation. In New England, land has been consolidated into the hands of fewer potato producers. The increased use of harvesting machinery has diminished the need for manual labor, while the cost of cultivation has increased. Potatoes nevertheless remain a significant agricultural product; more than 68,000 acres of New England farmland are still dedicated to potato production.

Percy Wells Bidwell and John I. Falconer, *History of Agriculture in the Northern United States, 1620–1860* (1973 [1925]); Howard S. Russell, *A Long, Deep Furrow: Three Centuries of Farming in New England* (1976); Redcliffe N. Salaman, *The History and Social Influence of the Potato* (1985 [1949]); David C. Smith, *History of the Maine Agricultural Experiment Station* (1980).

David C. Smith

Poultry Poultry has been a source of sustenance for New Englanders since before colonial times. The annual Thanksgiving celebration commemorating the Pilgrims' place in regional and national history played a crucial role in securing the turkey's significance in America. Benjamin Franklin, in fact, once proposed adopting the native bird as the country's national emblem. Flocks of ducks kept on small family farms provided early settlers with meat, eggs, and feathers for down pillows and blankets. Daniel Webster reportedly kept Chinese geese—bred and prized in New England for their egg production and valued for their use as noisy alarm systems—on his farm in Marshfield, Mass.

In the 18th and 19th centuries, surplus poultry from ships arriving in New England harbors interbred arbitrarily with breeds introduced by original colonists, resulting in new breeds, while other distinctive New England breeds came about by design. Among the first superior breed of chicken to emerge in the early 19th century was the Rhode Island Red, a large red bird commonly found in Rhode Island and southern Massachusetts. Other famous breeds such as the New Hampshire, Plymouth Rock, and Light Brahma were also developed in New England. Little Compton, R.I., was generally considered the center of goose raising in the United States through the early 20th century; geese were popular for their ease of upkeep, for medicinal uses of their fat and oil, and as the traditional Christmas dinner.

The first agricultural exhibition dedicated exclusively to poultry was held in 1849 at the Public Garden in Boston, where the turnout was exceptional. Hundreds of breeders and fanciers showed more than 1,400 domestic fowls to over 10,000 attendees. Daniel Webster was said to be among the exhibitors, presenting wild geese and java fowls. The New

Candling eggs at Bernier Egg Farm, Sanford, Maine, 1987

England Society for the Improvement of Domestic Poultry, formed in Boston in 1850, was one of the nation's first organized poultry societies. A meeting of poultrymen in 1873 in Boston to discuss standards of excellence in poultry breeding led to the formation of the American Poultry Association. *Production of Capons,* the first college bulletin dedicated exclusively to poultry, was published in Rhode Island in 1892.

In the early 19th century, New England poultry breeders typically kept small flocks on family farms. Ira Hubbard, whose family had farmed in Walpole, N.H., since the late 1700s, began actively breeding poultry in 1914. His son Oliver Hubbard, one of the first students to major in poultry at the New Hampshire Agriculture College (now the University of New Hampshire), founded Hubbard Farms. During the 1920s and 1930s, the spread of a deadly bacterial disease called pullorum could quickly wipe out an entire infected flock. The Hubbards, with the help of poultry specialist A. W. "Red" Richardson, the first poultry professor at the New Hampshire Agriculture College, developed a pullorum-free breed so distinctly different from the Rhode Island Red that it came to be called the New Hampshire Red. The demand for this breed became so great that Hubbard Farms quickly grew into a national, then international, operation and is now considered a leader in poultry genetics. Its research is supported by Merck Research Laboratories.

The poultry industry flourished throughout the region into the early 20th century. Whereas some regional breeders concentrated on breeding meat or dual-purpose birds, others focused solely on raising the New Hampshire Red, which produced the brown-shelled eggs preferred by New Englanders. Many shrewd Yankee breeders, however, looked beyond regional borders to the major live poultry market in New York City. This market preferred the Barred Plymouth Rock breed, so clever New Hampshire breeders crossed a Barred Rock male with the New Hampshire female, producing offspring that not only had barred feathers but grew faster and had hybrid vigor. This new market outlet led to a rapid expansion of the industry, and large poultry houses were constructed while feed companies, hatcheries, and processing plants all flourished. Breeders in Delaware, Maryland, and Virginia, however, competed with New England breeders for the rich New York market. Factors such as proximity to market, lower feed costs, and milder climates requiring less expensive housing gave the Middle Atlantic states a decided advantage over New England breeders.

When World War II created a meat shortage for New Englanders, broilers became a popular alternative to red meat as a protein source. The broiler industry expanded and the hatching egg industry also flourished. New Hampshire breeders and poultrymen quickly recognized the demand for fertile hatching eggs to supply the broiler industry; this was the golden opportunity they had been seeking. Once again, however, breeders in other areas of the country discovered that their lower feed costs enabled them to produce both broilers and hatching eggs, and soon the New England hatching egg industry could not survive the competition.

New England consumers continue to prefer fresh, local, brown-shelled eggs, and New Hampshire poultrymen continue to provide these eggs in response to market demand. Although New England's poultry industry is no longer a major economic or agricultural force, regional poultrymen and breeders and the region's long tradition of poultry fancying, breeding, and education have contributed significantly to the development of the modern domestic poultry industry.

American Poultry Historical Society, *American Poultry History, 1823–1973: An Anthology Overview of 150 Years, People—Places—Progress* (1974); Edmund Saul Dixon, *A Treatise on the History and Management of Ornamental and Domestic Poultry* (1857); U.S. Department of Agriculture, *People on the Farm: Broiler Growers* (1977).

Winthrop C. Skoglund

Rural Communities Rural communities grew distinctive in New England only in the 1750s, as the region's economy emerged from decades of economic stagnation. Until then, nearly every community in New England had been "rural," that is—apart from seaside towns whose residents made their livings from fishing or shipping—predominantly agricultural. Market towns were scarce. Low demand for New England's grain, livestock, cloth, and timber left its countryside the poorest in British America, unable to support many merchants or manufacturers. Neither could the region's economy prosper from territorial expansion. The dangers of New England's northern frontier, occupied by the French and Abenaki, made it difficult to establish new farms.

These forces gave New England's rural communities their unique character. The demand for slaves and indentured servants was low, as was the chance of accumulating wealth through agriculture. New England farmers did not have a staple crop, such as rice, sugar, or tobacco, that could justify the cost of bound labor. Nor were the region's merchants and manufacturers numerous or powerful enough to overshadow its farmers or rural artisans. Communities and countryside alike were thus relatively egalitarian.

New England's rural communities were also more homogeneous than other British American communities. Descendants of the original Anglo-Saxon settlers took up nearly every opportunity, discouraging immigrants from Scotland, Ireland, and Germany. Indeed, the native Anglo-Saxon population had grown so rapidly that by 1750 landlessness had increased and young couples found it harder to establish independent households. Still, rural New Englanders were more likely to own land than other British Americans. They lived longer, were more apt to marry, and had larger families. The regional economy might not have generated wealth, but it provided the means for basic survival.

The rural economy centered on household production. Few households were self-sufficient, but most met their needs within their local communities. Families produced much of their household's food, clothing, and manufactures, trading goods and services with neighbors to secure what they could not provide for themselves. Not everyone was happy with this spare material existence or interdependent way of life. For the most part, however, rural New Englanders were content to have their own shops or farms, good prospects for their children, a modest surplus to sell, and fruitful, cooperative marriages.

Rural New England's social order supported a distinctive spiritual order. Except in Rhode Island, which had a substantial Quaker minority and a spiritually fractious population, nearly all denizens of the countryside in the colonial era embraced Reformed (or Calvinist) theology, which demanded that they live by God's "covenants." Covenant theology confirmed a way of life that emphasized the need for forbearance and unity.

New England's rural communities were unsettled between 1750 and 1820 by the rising ambitions of their inhabitants, the quickening pace of the economy, and the growing influence of the cities and market towns. Increased demand in the West Indies for New England's beef intensified the use of land and labor. Farmers converted woodlots to pasture, deforesting the countryside as they went. Systematic use of family and exchange labor increased the production of manufactured goods, from shoes to textiles.

Meanwhile, Britain's victory in the French and Indian War in 1763 opened northern New England to settlement. Demographic pressure pushed thousands of rural New Englanders into Vermont, New Hampshire, and Maine, where they cleared new towns and met the continued demand for livestock, timber, potash, and barrel staves.

The American Revolution encouraged the rising aspirations of rural New Englanders. Young people, to improve their prospects, more often moved and married away from home. Young women spent more time in school, making literacy and accounting skills nearly universal by 1800. Premarital pregnancy and family size dropped as couples focused on achieving economic independence and establishing fewer children in better circumstances. Life was not uniformly easy, but the average wealth of rural New Englanders rose.

Economic growth increased inequality, however, as some profited more than others from competition or government policies. The power of merchants, financiers, and land speculators also grew as farmers and rural artisans relied more on nonlocal markets and credit. Farmers sometimes blamed government and entrepreneurs for their problems and occasionally used violent means to protect their farms: witness the Green Mountain Boys' resistance to New York speculators claiming title to land in Vermont and Shays's Rebellion against foreclosures in central Massachusetts.

Economic development and the Revolution unsettled the spiritual life of the countryside as well. Rural New Englanders rejected Calvinism in large numbers to become Methodists, Freewill Baptists, and Universalists. These egalitarian faiths rejected the idea that God had granted grace to a predetermined elect. They also harbored a certain animosity toward the world's temporal elite. These beliefs made sense in a world that was growing less egalitarian in fact as it grew more so in conviction.

After the Revolution rural New Englanders opted for a less strictly ordered way of life. Their embrace of religious dissent was part of that movement. Family, neighborhood, and community remained powerful forces in people's lives, but rural New Englanders grew more ready than they had been in earlier times to defend autonomy and privacy.

Rural communities were further unsettled between 1815 and 1850 by widespread industrialization. New roads and canals tied the region to the rest of the country. New England's land was too poor or expensive and its growing season too short to compete with western meat and grain. Farmers turned to sheep, which produced wool for the region's textile mills, and to dairy and truck farming, which supplied New England's cities with perishables.

Rural manufacturing declined as factories monopolized textile production and as blacksmithing, furniture making, and carpentry moved to towns, where artisans could serve more customers. Rural communities were wedded more narrowly to agriculture and to "outwork" provided by town-based merchants and manufacturers, who commissioned farm families to fashion shoes, clothes, and other labor-intensive commodities. Some textile, paper, and machine-tool factories located in rural communities to take advantage of waterpower sites. But many rural residents migrated to cities to take up factory jobs.

As the wealth of New England's rural communities grew, so did inequality. The capital costs of owning a farm or shop had increased. Population growth had exhausted the supply of new land in northern New England. Underpaid women and children performed most outwork, while underpaid Irish or French Canadian immigrants did much labor on commercial farms. New Englanders were generally not pleased to see equality and self-employment decline or their young people move to cities or the West for higher wages. But for those who operated their own farms, it was an era of unprecedented prosperity.

Political power passed from countryside to city and from farmer to manufacturer. By 1850 only one-fourth of all employed males worked in agriculture in southern New England, and only half the population lived in towns of fewer than 2,500 people. In northern New England four-fifths of the population still lived in rural communities, but only half of all employed males worked in agriculture. Farmers and rural manufacturers had to forge links with more distant customers, suppliers, and creditors if they were to prosper.

These changes transformed rural communities socially and spiritually. Revivals and temperance crusades shook New England's countryside, which by midcentury was the most churchgoing and teetotaling region in rural America. The new order was quicker to abandon people whose reputations had sunk because of drink, adultery, or neglect of church. Rural people had less need of churches and temperance societies to enforce moral discipline, however, because they still lived in small communities consisting of relatives and neighbors. But the divide between the respectable and the unrespectable was well known, as important as the distinction colonial communities had drawn between the elect and the damned.

Between 1850 and 1900 midwestern wool and mutton production overwhelmed New England's sheep farmers. The consequences were dramatic in hill towns: depopulation, reforestation, and slow economic growth. Schools consolidated and neighborhood churches closed. Rural communities had fewer institutions to bind them together. But as young people left, the distribution of wealth became more equal, leaving hill towns with a more mature, propertied population.

Farmers on better land prospered by concentrating on fruits, vegetables, and dairy products for urban markets or on specialty products like shade tobacco, which provided the wrappers for cigars. Farm incomes in New England were among the highest in the nation, and farms covered half of all acreage in the region from 1850 through 1910. Increasingly, however, immigrants from Ireland and French Canada made up the agricultural labor force.

In the 20th century, rural communities experienced more dramatic changes. As Americans turned to the automobile for transportation, the demand for hay and horses collapsed, and rural communities became more accessible to suburban development. Many farmers went out of business. Vermont remained rural, with one-third of its male workforce employed in agriculture and two-thirds of its population living in towns of fewer than 2,500 people. In southern New England, by contrast, only 5 percent of employed males worked in agriculture, and less than 20 percent of the population lived in small towns. Rural communities were no longer the bedrock of New England society. They persisted, however, though their links with the nonrural world were stronger than ever. Rural New Englanders resisted school consolidation and at first opposed expensive road-building programs, but automobiles and improved roads eventually strengthened schools and other rural institutions. Farmers defended their economic interests by forming marketing cooperatives and creating agricultural lobbying organizations. Rural people made more and more of their purchases through mail-order catalogs or from town merchants, but their acquisitions remained for the most part practical. Many continued to produce some clothing, foodstuffs, and other goods at home. They listened to radio and embraced the translocal rural culture that it promulgated—becoming less distinctive as New Englanders in the process—but they did not abandon older forms of entertainment.

Traditional rural communities have nearly disappeared since World War II. By 2000 only 2 percent of New England's population lived in towns of fewer than 2,500 people, and less than one-tenth of the land remained in farms. Suburbanization, urban sprawl, interstate highways, and the growth of the recreation and pulpwood industries have left their mark on the countryside. These changes may lead, however, to the development of a new kind of rural community in which open space, scenic vistas, large lots, privacy, and a leisurely pace of life are as important as farming, industry, and strong bonds among neighbors. By that enlarged definition, the 2000 census classified one-tenth of southern New England's population and half of northern New England's population as rural.

Hal S. Barron, *Those Who Stayed Behind: Rural Society in 19th-Century New England* (1984); Barron, *Mixed Harvest: The Second Great Transformation in the Rural North, 1870–1930* (1997); Christopher Clark, *The Roots of Rural Capitalism: Western Massachusetts, 1780–1860* (1990); Robert A. Gross, *The Minutemen and Their World* (1976); Daniel P. Jones, *The Economic and Social Transformation of Rural Rhode Island, 1780–1850* (1992); John J. McCusker and Russell R. Menard, *The Economy of British America, 1607–1789* (1985); Randolph A. Roth, *The Democratic Dilemma: Religion, Reform, and the Social Order in the Connecticut River Valley of Vermont, 1791–1850* (1987); Laurel Thatcher Ulrich, *A Midwife's Tale: The Life of Martha Ballard, Based on Her Diary, 1785–1812* (1990).

Randolph Roth

Sheep Of all the domestic animals brought by English settlers to New England, sheep were the hardest to raise. Preferring smooth pastures to rough grazing land, they did poorly on the region's wild meadows. These docile animals also fell prey to wolves and other predators more easily than did aggressive livestock such as swine and goats. As conditions improved, sheep farming became a significant, though economically unstable, part of New England husbandry, reaching its peak in the 19th century.

The first sheep arrived in New England from England, France, and Holland in the 1630s. Colonial assemblies, eager to replace expensive imported cloth with homegrown woolens, offered tax incentives to sheep farmers and paid bounties for the elimination of wolves. These measures had little effect, however, and farmers were forced to specialize in sheep only where environmental conditions were suitable. Thousands of sheep grazed on Nantucket and Martha's Vineyard, for example, as well as on smaller islands cleared of predators. Other centers of sheep production included coastal Essex County, Mass., the Connecticut River valley, and Rhode Island's Narragansett county. Where sheep numbers

were substantial, townspeople often hired shepherds to graze the animals on common or undivided lands.

Although weavers in Rowley, Mass., produced the first bolt of cloth from New England wool in 1643, their achievement scarcely marked the birth of a local industry. Colonial producers could not compete with more efficient English manufacturers of wool and cloth. Nor did an export market develop in mutton, because it was hard to preserve the meat by salting or smoking. Merchants sold live sheep to the West Indies, but this was a minor part of New England's extensive commerce with the islands. Sheep contributed more to family subsistence than to regional economic development; many New Englanders kept just a few animals to provide wool for homespun.

Sheep raising flourished in the late 18th and early 19th centuries only because of an artificial stimulus to domestic demand for wool. The Revolutionary War and the Embargo Act of 1807, in conjunction with trade restrictions and, eventually, the War of 1812, stopped the flow of English woolens and created a protected market for New England producers. To provide local mills with a finer grade of wool, farmers improved their stock by selective breeding and began to import merino sheep from Spain, the fleeces of which fetched higher prices than the coarser domestic wool. The merino craze of 1812–15, encouraged by agricultural improvement societies, halted abruptly in 1816, when peace with Britain brought renewed foreign competition.

The profitability of sheep raising fluctuated during succeeding decades. Farmers turned to mutton breeds, such as New Leicesters, in the late 1820s when wool prices declined. During the 1830s, when prices rose again and textile mills flourished under tariff protection, wool growing enjoyed its greatest prosperity, particularly in Vermont and western Massachusetts. This short-lived economic resurgence ended as wool prices dropped after 1837 and western sheep raisers began to compete directly with New Englanders. Many farmers turned to dairying, which promised steadier profits, although some Vermonters continued to raise sheep as a means of dealing with the labor shortage created by emigration.

Wool prices dropped further in the 1890s, and as the 20th century opened, New England sheep farming continued to decline. Sheep population in the region shrank from over a million animals in the post–Civil War decades to fewer than 100,000 a century later—reflecting a nationwide trend, especially after World War II. Sheep raising in New England today continues mainly in Vermont, providing lamb for a regional market (especially for

kosher consumers in New York City), wool for local weavers, and some purebred stock for breeders in other parts of the country.

Hal S. Barron, *Those Who Stayed Behind: Rural Society in 19th-Century New England* (1984); Percy Wells Bidwell and John I. Falconer, *History of Agriculture in the Northern United States, 1620–1860* (1973 [1925]); Howard S. Russell, *A Long, Deep Furrow: Three Centuries of Farming in New England* (1976); Harold F. Wilson, *The Hill Country of Northern New England: Its Social and Economic History, 1790–1930* (1936).

Virginia DeJohn Anderson

Societies and Fairs New England's first agricultural organizations, founded in the late 18th century by the commercial and political elite of its cities and central towns, were modeled after British institutions. But it was a Yankee innovator, Elkanah Watson of Plymouth, Mass., who created the modern societies that began to sponsor annual countywide fairs. One of the earliest American societies, the Massachusetts Society for Promoting Agriculture (MSPA), was incorporated in Boston in 1792; its aim was to acquire and disseminate agricultural intelligence by awarding premiums for specific improvements, publishing agricultural experiments, and establishing an agricultural library. Membership was self-selective, and lifetime dues were set at five dollars. By 1800 similar agricultural societies had been organized on a local level in Maine and in Worcester and Middlesex Counties in Massachusetts.

In 1809 Elkanah Watson was elected a member of the MSPA. Two years earlier, the retired businessman had moved from Albany, N.Y., to Berkshire County, Mass., intending to raise fine-fleeced Spanish merino sheep and establish woolen factories. Dissatisfied with the MSPA's efforts to promote the breed, Watson experimented with exhibiting his own sheep. In 1810 he convinced local leaders to stage a grand livestock exhibition in Pittsfield. Its success inspired the founding in 1811 of the Berkshire Society for Promoting Agriculture and Manufactures, which strove to bring agricultural improvements to working farmers by infusing the annual fair with a sense of excitement and a spirit of emulation. Membership, at first elective, was soon opened to any man who paid the one-dollar annual dues, which supported prizes given to members who exhibited the best livestock and domestic manufactures at the society's autumn fairs. Watson actively promoted the formation of similar fair-based societies over the next decade, lobbying legislatures for state support and writing pamphlets and newspaper essays. By 1825 dozens of county societies across New England and New York held annual fairs. From

Poster for Worcester (Mass.) South Agricultural Society Fair, ca. 1870

1816 to 1835, the MSPA sponsored a cattle show and fair at Brighton, the region's major livestock market.

Watson and his colleagues were typical antebellum reformers interested as much in moral as in agricultural improvement. Tapping into the era's urge to associate, these organizers adapted somewhat disreputable traditions—Old World market fairs and harvest-home feasts (often marked by festive abandon)—as well as the elite Anglo-American sheepshearings of later years, transforming them into progressive farmers' holidays of innocent recreation and rational amusement. The agricultural fair became a prominent social event on the rural calendar, as farm families traveled to town commons, and later fairgrounds, to visit with distant neighbors; buy and sell farm animals and produce; watch plowing matches, trials of oxen, or horse races; and attend society programs, dinners, and dances.

The traditional New England fair survived beyond its "golden age," from the 1850s through the 1870s, because of its multifunctional purpose and its appeal to human nature. The institution soon expanded well beyond its communal roots, as a growing agricultural press, government experiment stations, and land-grant colleges assumed the fair's educational functions. In keeping with a trend toward commercialization and recreation, agricultural societies purchased land for fairgrounds and began to consider fairs a source of revenue to pay off mortgages. Because members usually enjoyed free admission, trustees increasingly focused on attracting greater numbers of paying customers, usually those not engaged in agriculture. The dwindling farm population of New England accelerated this transition in the 1900s.

Rail transportation and greater state involvement contributed to a trend toward bigness. State fairs were first held before the Civil War, although New England did not hold a large fair until 1916, when the Eastern States Exposition opened in West Springfield, Mass.

Chicago's Columbian Exposition of 1893 spawned even greater spectacle and imitative midways at agricultural fairs across the nation. By then, however, fairs had become big business and were under the management of professionals.

Today, the agricultural fair remains a vibrant institution of rural education, commerce, and recreation. More than 2,000 fairs continue to draw approximately 125 million American fairgoers each year. Although they are now chiefly a midwestern phenomenon, nearly 100 major agricultural fairs are still held in New England. The best known are the Eastern States Exposition (Big E), Common Ground and Fryeburg fairs in Maine; the Deerfield and Sandwich fairs in New Hampshire; the Topsfield fair in Massachusetts; the Durham fair in Connecticut; and the Rutland and Tunbridge fairs in Vermont.

Donald B. Marti, *Historical Directory of American Agricultural Fairs* (1986); Wayne Caldwell Neely, *The Agricultural Fair* (1935); Tamara Plakins Thornton, *Cultivating Gentlemen: The Meaning of Country Life among the Boston Elite, 1785–1860* (1989); Elkanah Watson, *History of the Rise, Progress, and Existing State of the Berkshire Agricultural Societies, in Massachusetts* (1819).

Mark A. Mastromarino

Stone Walls In his poem "Mending Wall," Robert Frost recalled the annual drudgery of walking the fence line with his neighbor to mend the stone walls separating their properties. Where frost heaves had toppled the stones or hunters had pulled down the wall in search of small game, the two men laboriously set the rocks back in place. When the poet asked his neighbor why they should bother, pointing out that his apple trees would never cross over to his neighbor's pine forest, the man replied tersely, "Good fences make good neighbors."

Like other forms of fencing, stone walls were originally built to protect valuable crops and meadowland from foraging animals, which in the early years of colonial settlement were allowed to wander freely on undivided and unused land. As settlement progressed, families increasingly used walls to pen in animals. Although stone walls are associated with almost all of New England, they are actually most common in the uplands, where stones were plentiful and frequently inhibited tilling and mowing. In fertile river valleys, such as the Connecticut River valley, and in flatter, sandier soils, such as those of Cape Cod, one finds relatively few stone walls.

Some stone walls marked social boundaries. In rural New England, the most elaborate were found near houses and yards; these walls were sometimes as high as four feet and were

Stone wall construction at New Hampshire exhibit, Smithsonian Folklife Festival, 1999

usually carefully laid. The most skilled builders selected specific stones for the face of the wall and set them to create an even surface. Often the tops of these walls were left nearly flat, emphasizing both the expertise of the builder and the artificiality of the wall's geometry.

Other stone walls were purely functional. On stony upland landscapes, many farmers created walls as part of the arduous process of clearing their fields of unwanted rocks. The greatest efforts went into fencing lands that were tilled and mowed—fields that roaming livestock would have damaged and that families would have had to clear before plowing. In pasture areas, many farmers simply tossed stones on field boundaries or heaped them in piles, allowing animals to graze around the rocks. Walls such as these were assembled with varying degrees of precision, the quality of work depending in part on the nature of the stones. Rounded stones, which were common in most parts of the glacially scoured uplands, were hard to keep in place because they rolled easily. "And some are loaves and some so nearly balls," Frost observed, adding, "We have to use a spell to make them balance." Some field enclosures were hardly more than bands of rubble 9 or 10 feet across and rarely more than 3 feet high.

The openings in stone walls were almost always protected by gates hung from wooden posts. In the 19th century, however, many farmers began using stone posts, which were strong and impervious to rot. Elsewhere, fence openings were simply closed off with bars that farmers and travelers could remove for passage.

Although many stone walls in southern New England date to the 18th century, the greatest era of stone-wall building was between 1790 and 1860, when settlement spread throughout the area and forest cover was cleared. After the Civil War, fewer families farmed, and numerous fields began to revert to woods. Many stone walls survive today, marking the efforts of those who first cleared the land—and those who considered themselves good neighbors. They have become, in popular perception, quintessential features of the New England landscape.

Susan Allport, *Sermons in Stone: The Stone Walls of New England and New York* (1990); J. Ritchie Garrison, *Landscape and Material Life in Franklin County, Massachusetts, 1770–1860* (1991); Henry H. Glassie, *Pattern in the Material Folk Culture of the Eastern United States* (1968); John R. Stilgoe, *Common Landscape of America, 1580 to 1845* (1982).

J. Ritchie Garrison

Tobacco The leading cash crop of the Connecticut River valley, New England's most fertile agricultural region, has historically been shade tobacco. Grown in tents to protect their leaves from the damaging effects of the sun, shade tobacco plants reach heights of 8 to 10 feet and can take up to 15 weeks to mature. The plants ripen from the bottom up, and the leaves are picked and sown onto laths; they then cure in tobacco sheds for six to eight weeks. The leaves will shrink during this long process, and their dark green color will change to light brown.

The commercial cultivation of tobacco began in 1801, when Mrs. Prout of East Windsor, Conn., made the first New England cigars. Tobacco growing took hold in the Connecticut River valley area between Hartford, Conn., and Deerfield, Mass., where conditions were ideal. The light sandy loam of the valley produced superb wrapper leaves, the best of which were known as the Connecticut Broadleaf. By the 1830s New England tobacco farmers specialized in growing leaves for wrappers and binders, while filler was grown in other parts of the country and the Caribbean.

In 1901 the Connecticut Agricultural Experiment Station discovered that the shade of cheesecloth tents replicated the cloud cover of Sumatra, the leading competitor in tobacco leaf cultivation. The Connecticut River valley's hot, humid summer climate combined with the shade of the tents replicated a tropical environment and abetted the growth of shade tobacco. Between 1910 and 1923, the annual yield of shade-grown tobacco increased from 1.8 million pounds to 8.6 million pounds. Hartford County became known as "Tobacco Valley," and the fields of white netting and picturesque red tobacco sheds used for air curing the tobacco covered the landscape. In the meantime, farmers continued to cultivate nearly equal amounts of outdoor, or broadleaf, tobacco.

Examining tobacco leaves, Connecticut River valley, 1956

The production and sale of tobacco generated millions of dollars for the region. Tobacco growing also provided jobs for thousands of young people and children. Young workers also came from other eastern states, and hundreds of immigrant agricultural laborers—particularly from Puerto Rico and Jamaica—began moving to Hartford and Springfield. Many of these workers made the valley their permanent home, contributing to the region's ethnically rich and diverse population. Shade tobacco farming in Connecticut was central to Mildred Savage's novel *Parrish* (1959), which was made into a feature film starring Troy Donahue.

Beginning in the mid-1950s, tobacco production diminished as cigar smoking lost popularity, manufactured tobacco composite began to replace leaf wrappers, and commercial and residential development became a more profitable use of agricultural land. According to the U.S. Department of Agriculture, shade tobacco acreage in Connecticut declined from 8,300 to 720 between 1948 and 1992. The most significant reduction occurred between 1976 and 1982, when tobacco acreage declined from 3,200 to 870. Acreage in Massachusetts peaked at 2,500 in 1965 and reached a low in 1983 at 170 acres.

By the mid-1990s, however, tobacco cultivation in the Connecticut River valley enjoyed modest increases in tandem with the revival of interest in smoking fine cigars. Connecticut acreage increased from 720 acres in 1992 to 970 acres in 1995, while Massachusetts acreage rose from 230 to 270 acres between 1993 and 1995. In 2002 tobacco acreage in the Connecticut River valley was approximately 3,000.

Some of the shade tobacco farms in this region continue to be owned and operated by the same families who began cultivating this important cash crop early in the 19th century.

Eleanor Charles, "With Cigars in Vogue, Farmers Return to Tobacco," *New York Times,* January 7, 1996; James F. O'Gorman, *Connecticut Valley Vernacular: The Vanishing Landscape and Architecture of the New England Tobacco Fields* (2002); Margaret R. Pabst, *Agricultural Trends in the Connecticut Valley of Massachusetts, 1800–1900* (1941); Elizabeth Ramsey, *The History of Tobacco Production in the Connecticut Valley* (1930); Howard S. Russell, *A Long, Deep Furrow: Three Centuries of Farming in New England* (1976).

James C. O'Connell

Women's Farmwork In New England, farm women's work was shaped by rural households' early and intense involvement in capitalist markets. The popular image of "self-sufficient" farms was a reality only briefly, if ever. Until the late 18th century, most families lacked the tools and time for home production. Between the Revolution and the Civil War, many farm women sold surplus butter and cheese, chickens and eggs, and textiles. But the transition to wage labor was swift in New England. Spinning and weaving were soon centralized in factories, while merchant capitalists "put out" work in boot- and shoemaking and palm-leaf hatmaking to rural households. Some farmers' daughters migrated to factory villages; others earned money working "by the piece" at home.

The commercialization of market gardening and dairying did not expand women's income potential in New England as it did in other regions, for there capitalist expansion was accompanied by a shift from female to male control. Traditional women's duties included care of the garden, the dairy, and the poultry yard, but with the advent of large-scale, market-oriented production, these became male responsibilities. It is possible that New England women preferred the independent, if modest, earnings that piecework yielded. The U.S. commissioner of agriculture reported in 1871: "In New England very little regular labor in the fields is performed by women. . . . The wives and daughters of farmers sometimes aid in spreading and raking hay . . . [and] in 'dropping' corn or other seeds. Women sometimes assist in milking, but not so generally as in former generations. . . . [One] correspondent writes that 'female outdoor labor is unknown—incompatible with New England institutions.'"

The exemption (or exclusion) of farmers' daughters from field and barn labor did not extend to immigrants, however. "Canadian women, and occasionally Irish, hire out or work on shares in different parts of New England, though the number employed is not large, and they will undertake nearly all kinds of farm work," the report of 1871 continued. African American women labored in the tobacco fields of the Connecticut River valley. Irish, French Canadian, Polish, and Scandinavian women all milked, hayed, and planted, first for low wages on Yankee-owned farms and then on their families' holdings.

By the early 20th century, farm women had few opportunities to earn money, for outwork had disappeared as industry centralized. The disproportionate exodus of young women from rural areas alarmed residents; even sons who were to inherit family farms had difficulty in finding wives. At a conference on extension work in 1916, E. Merritt suggested that "if it is considered advisable to keep a larger proportion of women on our farms, it will be necessary to make farming as economically attractive as the nearby towns. . . . A new industry may be required to give her employment, but care should be taken that the farm woman retain absolute control over the products of her labor." But off-farm employment, rather than agricultural operations or home-based handicrafts, increasingly occupied rural women. New England women traveled the path from home production to waged employment more swiftly and completely than rural women in other regions of the country.

Christopher Clark, *The Roots of Rural Capitalism: Western Massachusetts, 1780–1860* (1990); Nancy F. Cott, *The Bonds of Womanhood: "Woman's Sphere" in New England, 1780–1835* (1977); Sally McMurry, *Transforming Rural Life: Dairying Families and Agricultural Change, 1820–1885* (1995).

Nancy Grey Osterud

Architecture

Keith N. Morgan, Section Editor

Richard M. Candee, Consulting Editor

INTRODUCTION

New England projects a distinct physical identity through its architecture even for those who have never visited the area. New Englanders have defined themselves through the character of the places where they live and work—the buildings, the towns, and the larger landscape. A large part of the New England myth depends on the concept of self-reliance and individualism. Not surprisingly, therefore, the image of the region's architecture begins with the New England house—the original colonial structure and its present-day progeny. Of course, architectural history has both truthful and deceptive (perhaps self-deceptive) strains. But the New England house calls forth a firm, if flexible, image that is an appropriate introduction to the architecture of the area. It is a site of specific regional materials and building technology and a house type that can be explored in terms of structure, plan, design, and use.

NATIVE DWELLINGS

The wigwam was the earliest and longest-lasting form of shelter in the New England region. In a letter of 1524 to his patron, King Francis I of France, the explorer Giovanni da Verrazano provided the first European description of a wigwam. The hemispherical form accommodated the nomadic needs of the Niantic, Narragansett, Penobscot, and other Native American groups who hunted and fished the New England woodlands and seacoasts for many centuries before the arrival of Europeans. Massachusetts colonists learned the term *wigwam* from the Algonquians and soon applied it to all Indian dwellings. A flexible framework of saplings lashed together and covered with bark or woven reed matting, the wigwam could be easily assembled or reused as groups moved about to seasonal hunting grounds.

In 1761 Ezra Stiles, president of Yale College, recorded in words and drawing the structural and spatial configuration of a wigwam on a visit to an Indian village at Niantic, Conn. Today reconstructions of this ubiquitous precontact New England house can be found at Plimoth Plantation in Plymouth, Mass., or at the Mashantucket Pequot Museum and Research Center in Ledyard, Conn. The environmental determinants of the wigwam form provide a natural segue to the houses of the English and other settlers who nearly obliterated Native Americans in New England.

COLONIAL HOUSES

The first homes of the English immigrants to New England included wigwams and hovels built into the earth. Soon, however, colonists began to construct more substantial dwellings, symbols of their desire to dominate the land. Indeed, the early New England colonists built larger and more permanent houses—and did so sooner—than did their contemporaries in the Middle Atlantic and southern colonies. The early buildings were naturally derived from postmedieval house forms of middle-class English farmers that the colonists had known before immigration. English colonists arrived from a country where the timber supply had been badly depleted by the British navy and by extensive rebuilding during the reign of Queen Elizabeth I and after. In contrast, New England abounded in pine, oak, and chestnut, making possible extensive house building.

Like the wigwam, the colonial house can be understood in structural and spatial terms. A series of prototypes (with many variants) emerged, some serving as the foundation for more substantial later buildings, others continuing to serve, especially in rural areas, throughout the entire colonial era and into the 19th century. Initially, carpenters who emigrated from around East Anglia generally raised stud-framed houses with chimney bays and lobby-entry plans, especially in the Massachusetts Bay Colony and early settlements of Connecticut. Artisans from western and northern counties of England used plank construction for open-plan houses in the Plymouth Colony and sections of Rhode Island; settlers in Maine and New Hampshire also commonly used plank construction.

The earliest permanent houses were generally single-room structures one to two stories high. With the passage of time and the increasing wealth of settlers, subsequent generations often added to early buildings or completely replaced them with more substantial dwellings. A stone foundation and cellar were common, but the chimney and its placement remained defining characteristics. Hall-and-parlor houses, with a central chimney mass dividing the two rooms on each floor and a tightly winding staircase located in front of the chimney, became a prevalent model. Two-story houses often incorporated a lean-to along the rear of the house as well, either as an integral element or as a later addition. The gable of such houses could be symmetrical or in the form of a saltbox (a dwelling with two stories in front, one in back, and a long sloping roof in the rear); both forms became symbolic of New England architecture. Despite the potential for a third fireplace in these rear spaces, this luxury was rarely incorporated until the Revolution.

In Rhode Island another model emerged in the late 17th century, one characterized by a stone wall at the end of one gable and one or two fireplaces. A Rhode Island stonender, as these houses were called, might have the chimney mass exposed or concealed by wooden clapboarding. During the first half of the 18th century, a house similar in structure and shape to the Rhode Island stonender emerged in the Narragansett Basin: it had a square plan and frame of one to two stories. Four principal corner posts supported an interior space, often of three rooms, all heated by the interior chimney. The square-plan house was a New England invention, not an adaptation of English forms.

For a century after the 1650s New Englanders also used a form of sawn or hewn logs, squared and tightly fit together (sometimes with protective features such as loopholes for guns), for defensive dwellings and other purposes. The squared logs

The Cooper-Frost-Austin House (ca. 1690), Cambridge, Mass., an example of a saltbox

could either be rabbited into corner posts or joined at the corners by dovetails. A product of the first waterpowered sawmills on the upper Connecticut, Maine, and New Hampshire frontiers, log cabins evolved after the end of the conflicts with Native Americans into hand-hewn military garrisons for blockhouses and forts.

Claims in Harold Shurtleff's *Log Cabin Myth* (1939) to the contrary notwithstanding, by the second quarter of the 18th century there were also log cabins of traditional pole construction in New England, with the wide insterstices between the round logs chinked with stones, daub, mud, and other materials. As late as the 1798 Direct Tax assessment, the majority of homes in some rural towns of Maine, in particular, were of this type of log. They were quickly replaced by framed buildings, although a few survive in Vermont.

An alternative French log-building tradition, *en columbage,* with hewn logs fitted into corner posts, came to the Madawaska Territory along the Saint John River valley of northwestern Maine with the displacement of the Acadians in the 18th century. Culturally isolated, the French-speaking population continued to build in squared log (which were up to 6 inches thick, chinked with flax and lime) throughout the 19th century.

A more substantial double-pile house (two rooms deep) with a central stairway was seen first in cities in the late 17th century and became gradually more common elsewhere by the second half of the 18th century. Either two interior chimneys or four exterior chimneys heated the four principal rooms on each floor. These impressive, balanced structures represented the top of the market and have survived in large numbers. The New England house, however, did not evolve chronologically from the simplest to the most elaborate. All these housing models continued to be built throughout the colonial period, and some well into the 19th century. Indeed, by the time of the Direct Tax assessment of 1798, the dominant house form remained a single-story unit of modest size. Most of New England proved a challenging environment for those who sought to prosper as farmers (one need only attempt to dig a garden in New England today to experience the frustration of trying to cultivate the rock-filled soil). The substantial colonial mansions that survive, often in coastal areas, in fact give a false impression of how New Englanders lived.

Beyond the important structural and spatial patterns, the colonial New England house evolved in characteristic phases. The first-period (1620–1725) dwelling facades showed asymmetrical planning, with off-center or side entrances. As the 17th century progressed, projecting entrance pavilions, called porches, and jetties or overhangs on the front or gable-end elevations at the second or third levels joined the pattern. Brackets or pendants provided minor ornamentation on an otherwise utilitarian exterior. Chamfered (molded) posts and beams and painted or sponged decoration relieved the severity of the interior architecture.

At the end of the 17th century, the first indications of a more urbane architectural formula, derived from Renaissance forms, appeared in colonial Boston. With the imposition of a new royal charter in 1691, London merchants immigrated to the city, bringing with them a desire for urban architectural pretension. By the second quarter of the 18th century, these new ideals of symmetry and classical ornamentation began to alter subtly the first-period models. Although decoration derived from builders' guides modified the general appearance of buildings, the plan and structure of the first-period house still influenced New England architecture. In the second half of the 18th century, builders experimented with increased exterior symmetry, concealment of the interior frame within the wall or decorated corner boards, and greater elaboration of window and door openings and of paneling and fireplaces. The sash window, introduced at the end of the 17th century, became a hallmark of these new forms. Joiners produced molded panels for walls and doors and elaborate ornamentation for chimneypieces.

NEW ENGLAND ARCHITECTURE
AFTER THE REVOLUTION

Builders during the postrevolutionary period continued these classical forms but used them in a tighter and more attenuated or vertical manner. Reliance on English builders' guides diminished, as New England produced the first book on architecture written by an American: Asher Benjamin's *The Country Builder's Assistant,* published in Greenfield, Mass., in 1797. Benjamin continued to write books for American carpenters and builders, often popularizing the designs of his contemporaries, such as the Boston architect Charles Bulfinch. Indeed, Bulfinch became a regional phenomenon, not only radically changing the character of architecture in Boston but also de-

The Mitchell House (1790), a typical Nantucket, Mass., Quaker house, featuring a roof walk

signing state capitols for Massachusetts, Connecticut, and Maine; in 1817 he was chosen as the architect of the U.S. Capitol.

Bulfinch and Benjamin's designs for meetinghouses changed the image of Congregational churches throughout the region, just as disestablishment was altering the relation between church and state in New England. David Hoadly in New Haven, Conn., John Holden Greene in Providence, Samuel McIntire in Salem, Mass., and Alexander Parris in Portland, Maine, all contributed to a consistent but varied regional interpretation of neoclassical forms. Seacoast towns experienced the greatest innovation in architectural forms owing to the success of the shipping economy. Because these guidebooks offered new models primarily for ornamentation, traditional patterns of planning and framing persisted. An important new addition to the spectrum of plan models was the popularity in the early 19th century of the end house, a building whose gable faced the street or road. Builders placed the entrance on one side of the gable facade and provided a hallway with a series of rooms opening off it. Probably derived from urban town-house forms, the end house became one of the dominant plans of 19th-century architecture throughout New England.

The sixth edition of another Benjamin guide, *American Builder's Companion* (1827), introduced heavier, Greek-derived decorative forms. Again, these European ornamental traditions were drafted onto traditional plans and building patterns. The gabled roof was increasingly turned to face the road or street, in imitation of a Greek temple. Through these builders' guides, the three-bay, side-entrance end-house plan became a dominant form in both city and country.

Although wood remained plentiful, brick gained popularity during the rebuilding of New England that accompanied the prosperous Federal period. Boston had been legislating the use of masonry construction from the mid-17th century onward, but only in 1803 did an ordinance receive strict enforcement. The brick house, both in the rapidly expanding coastal towns and throughout the hinterland, became common during the early 19th century, especially in areas rich in clay. Stone construction emerged as a significant option as well; marble was used in Vermont and the Berkshires, and granite in New Hampshire and at many coastal sites. Indeed, the urban variant of the Greek Revival style of New England architecture expressed geometric severity in part because of the difficulty of working the hard granite of the region. As the 19th century progressed, New England became less distinctive in its building forms, more tied to expanding national patterns. Nevertheless, the 20th and 21st centuries have perpetuated many of these forms; detached housing, the romantic Cape Cod cottage, and colonial imagery and wood construction remain regionally dominant.

COMMUNAL PATTERNS

If the New England detached house is the region's stereotype, communal spaces also marked the regional landscape significantly. The counterthrust to traditionally self-sufficient New England individualism perhaps emerged first in the mid-18th-century religious revival. In the late 18th and the early 19th centuries, a sense of community over individual evolved as the Industrial Revolution took hold. Religious, utopian, and corporate models encouraged congregation in distinctive spaces.

New England towns adopted clear patterns of settlement and spatial organization. Raising a meetinghouse and defining a common were, theoretically, the recommended steps in establishing a new settlement. Yet many early farmers claimed dispersed house sites on the most desirable agricultural lands, often river bottoms that provided pastures for cattle. The mythological image of the nuclear village with the colonial meetinghouse and prosperous houses surrounding a pastoral town common rarely existed in the colonial period, although certain early towns set aside a town common for agricultural use and military training. New Haven was laid out as an orthogonal grid, with the town common at the center, the location of the most prominent churches and the colony house (and later state capitol). Boston established its large common in 1634 on land on the western side of the Shawmut Peninsula, away from the busy port and harbor. Hatfield, Mass., and Windsor, Conn., created rectilinear town greens. In the 19th century, the town common became a landscaped park with the houses of prosperous citizens lining its edges. The Village Improvement Society movement of the late 19th century transformed places such as Litchfield, Conn., and Stockbridge, Mass., into the picture-perfect villages of New England myth.

From the late 18th century on, different types of communal settlements emerged in New England. One could look, for example, to the important role of the "Shaking Quakers," a radical millennialist group led by Mother Ann Lee, who claimed to embody the promise of a second coming of Christ. Lee and her few British followers gathered in nearby New York State in 1787 and spread their gospel through nine new communities founded in Massachusetts, New Hampshire, and Maine during the early 1790s. Separating individuals from their family connections, isolating the sexes, and developing innovative agricultural and light industrial sites allowed the Shakers to expand and prosper for half a century (a small number survived vestigially into the true new millennium). The Shakers' New England settlements such as those at Hancock, Mass., Canterbury, N.H., and Sabbathday Lake, Maine, document their unique practices of worship, work, and communal living.

Similarly, the more traditional Protestant denominations also adopted communal forms, to which they gave a distinctive New England stamp. Following on the popular outdoor camp-meeting revivals that began on the Kentucky frontier in 1800, New England Methodists used these vacation tent communities to rapidly expand the faithful. The ultimate example of the revival camp meeting is the Wesleyan Grove site on Martha's Vineyard, Mass., developed from 1835 onward. Around a central open space, to which a cast-iron tabernacle was later added for the revival meetings, arose a tightly packed village, first of tents, and then of miniature wooden cottages, often ornamented with Gothic Revival openings and trim. These cottages line the serpentine streets of the meeting grounds, providing a model for the emerging American suburb. Indeed, adjacent to Wesleyan Grove is Oak Bluffs, a planned suburban community laid out by the landscape gardener Robert Morris Copeland in 1867. As the largest Protestant denomination of the 19th century, the Methodists influenced other camp meetings in New England and well beyond. Less dominant Christian sects and even the Spiritualists seeking communion with their departed loved ones sought the cool shade of a lakeside retreat for revival and refreshment in the heat of the summer.

THE INDUSTRIAL LANDSCAPE

The pastoral image of New England contradicts the region's significance as the heartland of the Industrial Revolution in America. The architectural expression of American industry derives from New England experiments. The earliest efforts to harness waterpower for machine production of textiles occurred in the Blackstone Valley of Rhode Island in the 1790s and rapidly expanded to the stream and river valleys of much of New England. Rhode Island speculators built first wooden and then stone mills along the waterways, expanding into villages for workers who were originally housed in family cottages.

The Boston Associates launched larger capitalist enterprises at Waltham, Mass., in the 1810s and Lowell, Mass., in the 1820s. Ever larger brick mills consolidated all the stages of textile production into a single corporate campus of long, tall, narrow brick monsters. More paternalistic than their Rhode Island predecessors, these investors expanded their control into the entire environment of their workers, providing housing, stores, churches, schools, and civic buildings, all under company control. The Lowell model inspired many midcentury imitators; Lawrence, Mass., and

Manchester, N.H., were two of the largest. Smaller water sources occasionally produced conglomerates of the Rhode Island and Massachusetts architectural patterns, such as the intact hill town of Harrisville, N.H.

These industrial zones worked in concert with the surrounding agricultural landscape, providing jobs for farmers' daughters and a market for their products. A trip through any area of New England today still reveals this surprising mix of farms and factories as unlikely neighbors. Certain mill-owning families sought to create model communities, such as the Cheney silk mill village in Manchester, Conn., or the utopian experiments of Hopedale, Mass. Samuel D. Warren ornamented the workers' residences of his Cumberland Mills in Westbrook, Maine, with distinctive streets of detached houses, from Downing-inspired cottages of the 1850s to Cottage Place, a street designed by the Portland architect John Calvin Stevens in 1886.

RESORT LIFE

Through the wealth of the Industrial Revolution, New England became the home of the summer vacation and its architectural counterpart. As early as the 1820s, city dwellers traveled by steamship to hotels on Nahant, a peninsula north of Boston extending into the Atlantic Ocean, for fresh air, exercise, and escape from the city heat. By the 1840s sites such as Newport and Bar Harbor, Maine, had become summer playgrounds for easterners of means. Eventually, most of the Maine seacoast, from York Harbor in the south to Grindstone Neck in the north, became a continuous string of summer colonies. The mountains and lakes of northern New England likewise hosted middle- and upper-class tourists at hotels and mineral spas of constantly expanding scale. Often a colonial tavern evolved into a modest hostelry and then a wooden extravaganza.

At a less permanent level, another type of city in the woods emerged, the New England summer campground, designed to invigorate urbanites by giving them several weeks or months in tents or wooden shanties along the shores of mountain lakes. While family camps became common in New England in the 1870s, camps for boys and girls also became a commonplace of the regional summer landscape. As early as the 1840s, poor boys from the cities traveled to island or mountain sites to escape summer in the slums. School-based campgrounds, such as the one organized by the Gunnery School in Connecticut in the 1870s, preceded the widespread development of both YMCA and private campgrounds throughout the region. The New Hampshire lakes were especially important in these developments, with Squam and Newfound Lakes attracting the earliest experiments.

For those who sought greater comfort on holiday, resort housing followed distinctive regional patterns. Wood was the material of choice, with stick-work ornament, patterns in shingles, and proper clapboards modulating over time. The same resorts that first built major hotels often became laboratories for experimentation in private vacation architecture. The two dominant modes coalesced: the so-called Shingle Style, picturesque compositions in flexible envelopes of cedar shingles starting in the late 1870s, and the dominant Colonial Revival, derived from the earlier forms of the

1880s but quickly becoming more proper and archaeologically dependent on actual colonial buildings. These forms have never lost their appeal. A train trip from New York to Portland or a drive along Route 1A will reveal the predominance of these mixed summer idioms.

Community buildings, such as the Narragansett Pier or Newport casinos in Rhode Island, both designed by McKim, Mead and White in the 1880s, further reinforced the cachet of this image. In the western hills of Connecticut or the Berkshires of Massachusetts and on to the Green Mountains of Vermont and the White Mountains of New Hampshire, the Colonial Revival resort or country house settled easily into the regional landscape. Summer colonies of artists or writers, from Old Lyme on the Connecticut shore to Dublin and Cornish in the hills of New Hampshire, chose the colonial ideal, often with an overlay of Italian Renaissance urbanity, as the expression of summer idylls. Even in the 21st century, the vitality of this architectural mode remains unchallenged.

THE NEW ENGLAND LANDSCAPED SUBURB

New England also played a role in the formulation of suburban planning. Developments such as Cottage Farm in Brookline, Mass., at first a short carriage ride and soon a railroad commute from the central city, grew in the late 1840s as an alternative to urban living for the middle and upper classes. House forms and plans followed the freedom of the landscape, extending into nature through porches, bay windows, and verandahs. The picturesque paradigm of the idealized suburb with its winding, tree-lined streets emerged even earlier in the Rural Cemetery Movement, introduced to the United States at Mount Auburn Cemetery (dedicated 1831) in Cambridge, Mass., and copied in multiple early examples throughout New England. At Mount Auburn the cemetery initially collaborated with the newly founded Massachusetts Horticultural Society to create a planned landscape of exceptional beauty and variety.

The role of New England as a nursery for professional landscape designers cannot be overemphasized. The Boston area came to dominate the country. Mid-19th-century civil engineers and landscape gardeners such as Robert Morris Copeland, Ernest Bowditch, and others prepared the ground for Frederick Law Olmsted, who moved from New York to Brookline in 1883. From Fairsted, his home and studio, Olmsted designed public parks, rural cemeteries, suburban developments, and private estates throughout the region and the nation. City and regional planning emerged as a national model in the work of Charles Eliot and Sylvester Baxter in envisioning and realizing the Boston Metropolitan Park System in the 1890s and in the designs of Arthur Shurcliff and John Nolen in the early 20th century.

ARCHITECTURAL PROFESSIONALISM

The Civil War fanned the fires of New England industries, and the region emerged from the conflict with a booming economy. Despite the interruptions of recessions in 1873 and 1893, New Englanders continued to build voraciously in city and country.

The founding of the country's first collegiate program in architecture at the Massachusetts Institute of Technology in 1867 made Boston briefly the epicenter of American architectural progress. The move of Henry Hobson Richardson from New York to Boston in 1874 reinforced Boston's dominance through his influential commissions and the many apprentices he trained. The publication of *American Architect and Building News,* the nation's first architectural periodical, began in Boston in 1876.

Although academic programs and publications tied New England firmly to European trends in architecture, at the same time a desire to invoke a regional architectural identity emerged in the recording and reworking of the colonial tradition. Arthur Gilman, Ware and Van Brunt, Peabody and Stearns, and Arthur Little in Boston; Stone, Carpenter and Wilson in Providence; John Calvin Stevens in Portland; and a range of architects working in Newport all contributed to an exploration of the usable colonial past. Between 1870 and 1930 the Colonial Revival reset the image of New England for the region and the nation. From the pens of the finest designers to the brochures of the lumberyards, Colonial Revival buildings were ubiquitous.

Over time the designs became less imaginative and more archaeological, but the preponderance of these forms is undeniable. Every building type—with the exception of the tall office building, not an important New England form—succumbed to a regional celebration of the past. But the housing market was the strongest candidate for this image making, with firms such as Boston's Royal Barry Wills setting the pace in the shelter magazines of the first half of the century. Today in the exurban zones of housing sprawl, the colonial house remains the market leader and theoretically a connection to New England roots.

One of the support systems for the maturing of the Colonial Revival in New England emerged from the mutually helpful relationships of architects and various artisans through the Arts and Crafts movement. New England gave birth to the American form of this English-inspired design philosophy when the Society of Arts and Crafts was founded in Boston in 1897. The architects who subscribed to this style worked predominantly in two modes, Colonial Revival, especially for domestic architecture, and Gothic Revival, seen in the construction of churches and schools. New England spawned a renewed use of Gothic as an ecclesiastical architectural formula, especially through the work of Ralph Adams Cram and Bertram Grosvenor Goodhue for Protestant churches and of Maginnis and Walsh for Roman

First Parish Church (Richard Upjohn, 1846), Brunswick, Maine, an example of Gothic Revival

Catholic church architecture. Both firms and their contemporaries commissioned fine wood carving, stained glass, and metalwork for churches and collegiate buildings in the Gothic mode throughout the United States from the 1890s through World War II.

REGIONAL TYPES

Certain building forms that emerged in New England became both characteristic of the region and influential beyond its bounds. The Puritan meetinghouse, the principal civic and religious building for the Massachusetts Bay Colony, evolved as a highly adaptable space. Rectangular or foursquare in plan, deemphasizing the liturgical axis of Catholic or Anglican worship, the meetinghouse provided an auditorium space that centralized the public life of the colonial community. As the major counterpoint to the private dwelling, the meetinghouse became the base for a series of logical extensions. One of the most common was the adaptation of the form for town houses, the first purpose-built structures that announced the gradual separation of church and state in New England. The square-plan town house with hip roof (in which four planes tapered to the ridge line) and crowning bell tower marched west from New England into the upper Midwest as one symbol of the migration of individuals and institutions from the New England hearth.

Education, another regional institution that influenced the nation, also produced an architectural form in New England. Home to the nation's first public school (Boston Latin School), oldest private academy (Roxbury Latin School), and first college (Harvard), New England generated a vocabulary of academic architecture in the 17th century and has continued to influence this field ever since. Mid-19th-century experiments in standardizing public schoolhouse design emerged from the innovations of Horace Mann in Massachusetts and Henry Barnard in Connecticut. New England disseminated the image of the elm-treed pastoral campus as the ideal of academic architecture at both the collegiate and boarding school level.

As an outgrowth of its emphasis on education, New England also inaugurated the small public library as a building type. New Hampshire (1849) and Massachusetts (1851) introduced the earliest enabling legislation for public libraries, and New England led the nation in the number of libraries built in the late 19th century. Large cities, suburban towns, and small villages saw the library as a symbol of democracy and knowledge; wealthy individuals saw the institution as an opportunity for family memorialization. A leading form giver, the architect H. H. Richardson built five libraries in towns surrounding Boston from the late 1870s through the mid-1880s. Debates over the proper form of library organization and the role of professional librarians took place throughout New England.

Among the clients for public libraries were immigrants who poured into New England's industrial cities after the Civil War. In Worcester, Mass., Providence, Boston, and elsewhere, a distinctive regional worker-housing form emerged. Called the three-decker, these wooden three-story, three-family units, extended with front and rear porches, represented the response of the private sector to the need for industrial housing. The earliest examples date to the 1870s, but the greatest proliferation occurred from the turn of the 20th century into the 1920s. Street after street of these ubiquitous structures arose near factories and extended into the suburbs. Their role was challenged during the early 20th century by the construction of more low-scale, often colonial-inspired housing by specific industries for their workers and then by the federal government to house its workforce during World War I.

Another response to the needs of industrial workers and a surprising area for New England experimentation, the night lunch wagon and its descendant, the modern diner, came into being in the late 19th century. Providence and Worcester share the honor for gestation of this mobile architectural form. Observing the problems of workers on the late shift in finding places to eat, enterprising individuals in the 1880s converted street trolleys into restaurants and kitchens on wheels. Having identified a lucrative niche, these innovators added scale, ornamentation, and culinary range, as the wagon gradually became a stationary object with a more industrial, streamlined appearance by the 1920s.

New England's seacoast generated a range of architectural responses. Lighthouses from Maine to Connecticut set the pattern for seafaring assistance throughout the nation. The Boston Light at the entrance to Boston Harbor marks the site of the first (1713–16) lighthouse in North America and the second oldest (1783) surviving tower. Maine retains the largest number of historic lighthouses (64 of 66 originally built), romantically perched on rocky promontories and harbor islands. Indeed, Maine boasts more lighthouses than the rest of the Atlantic or all of the Pacific coastlines. In the 1840s the architect and engineer Alexander Parris designed a particularly fine group of granite lighthouses there.

New England also witnessed the birth of the marine lifesaving service in the United States. The Massachusetts Humane Society, founded in 1785, began construction of seacoast huts to shelter shipwrecked mariners in 1787. Until the mid-19th century, Massachusetts remained the only state with a comprehensive network of lifesavers and stations. In 1878 Congress chartered the United States Life Saving Service, which erected 57 stations along the New England coast from Maine to Rhode Island.

Coastal fortifications also marked the federal presence in New England. Fort Adams, overlooking Newport Harbor, and Fort Warren, on Georges Island in Boston Harbor, represent the military defense system that Congress inaugurated following the War of 1812; they continued as important parts of the federal landscape through the Civil War. Poured concrete observation buildings, ranging from a modern tower in Nahant, Mass., to an imitation Shingle Style summerhouse in Little Compton, R.I., provided surveillance for enemy submarines or aircraft. Another New England military contribution to architectural history, the Quonset hut, that ubiquitous arched metal movable building, first appeared during World War II at the Quonset Naval Air Station in Rhode Island.

Specific agricultural, occupational, or ethnic communities generated localized and fascinating architectural forms. One of the most common is the connected New England farmhouse, the composite of home, shed, and barn joined as a single unit.

More localized are distinctive forms such as the houses of oyster gatherers in New Haven on Long Island Sound or the whalers' houses of Stonington, Conn., the life of the sea inspiring distinctive land-based buildings. The Madwaska twin barns and potato storage houses of the Saint John River valley of northern Maine record the contributions of Acadian immigrants from Canada to the New England landscape.

MODERN NEW ENGLAND

Contrary to its image as the guardian of the past, the region also served as a laboratory for experiments in modernism from the 1920s onward. When Harvard University invited Walter Gropius, former director of Germany's Bauhaus, to accept a teaching position in the school of architecture in 1937, it institutionalized a pattern that had been developing for a decade. In 1929–30 George Sanderson designed a studio in Lenox, Mass., for the painters Suzy Frelinghuysen and George L. K. Morris directly modeled on Le Corbusier's studio for the French sculptor Amédée Ozenfant (1922). Architects such as Eleanor Raymond, Carl Koch, and Ned Goodell launched modernist experiments in the suburbs of Boston throughout the early 1930s. Beyond the geography of Greater Boston, but not the influence of Harvard, A. Everett "Chick" Austin directed Hartford's Wadsworth Atheneum into an early advocacy of International Modernism. Austin's own house (Leigh French, Jr., 1930) and the Avery Memorial addition (Morris and O'Connor, 1934) to the Atheneum gave the stamp of high culture to this international, minimalist formula.

Beyond his influential teaching at Harvard, Gropius organized in 1939 The Architects Collaborative (TAC), the firm that became synonymous with modernism and New England throughout the country. TAC's suburban housing developments in Lincoln and Lexington, Mass., and elsewhere gave legitimacy to modernism, often in communities best known for colonial resources. As the century progressed, Connecticut also hosted key modernist buildings—Philip Johnson's Glass House (1949) in New Canaan or a substantial group of houses by Gropius's former collaborator Marcel Breuer in the 1950s and by Peter Eisenman in the 1970s in the Berkshire Hills near colonial Litchfield.

As the largest city in the region and the engine of New England's economy, Boston sponsored the most significant architectural developments in the second half of the 20th century. Greater Boston's colleges and universities, especially Harvard and MIT, commissioned internationally recognized architects to design influential, innovative additions to their campuses. Following the oil embargo of the early 1970s, Boston entered a period of unprecedented growth, generating a vertical skyline almost overnight. The largest public works project, the notorious Big Dig, suppressed the central highway through the core of the city.

Directly paralleling new construction in Boston and other major urban centers of New England, however, the historic preservation movement entered an equally strong period of growth beginning in the 1970s. New legislation at the state and municipal levels created commissions to oversee the preservation of existing resources and to modify the impact of new construction. The museumlike approach of sites

Frelinghuysen-Morris House (George K. Morris and John Butler Swann, 1935–40) and Studio (George Sanderson, 1930), Lenox, Mass.; the studio is the earliest modern building in New England

like Strawbery Banke in Portsmouth, N.H., or Old Sturbridge Village in Sturbridge, Mass., contrasted with the adaptive reuse of mill complexes for housing or the designation of large and powerful urban historic districts. The creative tension between innovation and conservation that has characterized New England throughout much of its history has therefore returned to stasis; what is old is new, and always will be.

Kenneth A. Breisch, *Henry Hobson Richardson and the Small Public Library in America* (1997); Bainbridge Bunting, *The Houses of Boston's Back Bay: An Architectural History, 1840–1917* (1967); Richard M. Candee, ed., *Building Portsmouth: The Neighborhoods and Architecture of New Hampshire's Oldest City* (1992); Herbert Wheaton Congdon, *Old Vermont Houses, 1763–1850* (1973 [1946]); Abbott Lowell Cummings, *The Framed Houses of Massachusetts Bay: 1625–1725* (1979); Janice P. Cunningham, John Herzan, Geoffrey Rossano, and Linda Spencer, *Historic Preservation in Connecticut*, 6 vols. (1991–97); Donald Cyr, "Acadian Architecture Evident in Restored Family Home," *St. John's Valley Times*, July 22, 1981; Marian C. Donnelly, *The New England Meeting Houses of the Seventeenth Century* (1968); Antoinette Forrester Downing, *Early Homes of Rhode Island* (1937); John S. Garner, *The Model Company Town: Urban Design Through Private Enterprise in Nineteenth-Century New England* (1984); Anthony N. B. Garvan, *Architecture and Town Planning in Colonial Connecticut* (1951); James L. Garvin, *A Building History of Northern New England* (2001); James L. Garvin and Bryant Tolles, *Buildings of New Hampshire* (forthcoming); Richard W. Hale, Jr., "The French Side of the Log Cabin Myth," *Proceedings of the Massachusetts Historical Society* 72 (1957–60): 118–20; Kingston W. Heath, *The Patina of Place: A Cultural Weathering of a New England Landscape* (2001); Historic American Buildings Survey, *Maine Catalogue: A List of Measured Drawings, Photographs, and Written Documentation in the Survey, 1974* (1974); Michael Holleran, *Boston's "Changeful Times": Origins of Preservation and Planning in America* (1998); Thomas C. Hubka, *Big House, Little House, Back House, Barn: The Connected Farm Buildings of New England* (1984); William H. Jordy, ed., *Buildings of Rhode Island* (2004); Harold Kirker, *The Architecture of Charles Bulfinch* (1969); Arthur Krim, *The Three-Deckers of Dorchester: An Architectural Historical Survey* (1977); James Lindgren, *Preserving Historic New England: Preservation, Progressivism, and the Remaking of Memory* (1995); W. Barksdale Maynard, "'An Ideal Life in the Woods for Boys': Architecture and Culture in the Earliest Summer Camps," *Winterthur Portfolio* 34 (1999); Naomi Miller and Keith Morgan, *Boston Architecture, 1975–1990* (1990); Peter Nabokov and Robert Easton, *Native American Architecture* (1989); Julie Nicoletta, *The Architecture of the Shakers* (1995); Robert Blair St. George, *Conversing by Signs: Poetics of Implication in Colonial New England Culture* (1998); Douglass Shand-Tucci, *Built in Boston: City and Suburb, 1800–2000*

(1999); Ralph Shanks and Wick York, *The U.S. Life-Saving Service: Heroes, Rescues, and Architecture of the Early Coast Guard* (1996); Earle G. Shettleworth Jr., ed., *A Biographical Dictionary of Architects in Maine,* 7 vols. (1984–); Myron O. Stachiw, ed., *The Early Architecture and Landscapes of the Narragansett Basin,* 3 vols. (2001); Bryant F. Tolles, Jr., and Carolyn K. Tolles, *New Hampshire Architecture: An Illustrated Guide* (1979); Vermont Division of Historic Preservation, *A Guide to Vermont Architecture* (1996); Ellen Weiss, *City in the Woods: The Life and Design of an American Camp Meeting on Martha's Vineyard* (1987); Joseph S. Wood, *The New England Village* (1997); Cynthia Zaitzevsky, *Frederick Law Olmsted and the Boston Park System* (1982).

Keith N. Morgan

Architecture, 1620–1725 Seventeenth-century New England architecture was both traditionally English and, in certain respects, relatively new. Most of the region's European settlers were English and carried with them a variety of localized building practices from East Anglia, the West Country, and other areas. The newness came not so much from the new environment but from a revolution in housing that had swept the English countryside, particularly in the Southeast, in the late 1500s and early 1600s. Migrating housewrights, carpenters, and joiners replicated these postmedieval innovations as well as older traditions in the colonies. At the same time, the abundance of wood, particularly stands of large white pine, influenced the exterior covering and, to a degree, the framing of houses. Once these building practices took hold, they persisted into the first quarter of the 18th century. For this reason architectural historians usually date the first period of New England architecture from 1620 to 1725. In fact, some aspects of 17th-century architecture endured unchanged throughout the colonial period.

Most 17th-century New England houses were built of wood. Brick houses were rare before 1700 and remained so outside of Boston until after 1800; stone houses were even rarer. Building in wood, colonial housewrights and carpenters drew upon centuries-old traditions of house framing. These English practices varied somewhat from region to region, and evidence of the variations can be seen in New England houses throughout the first period. Despite these regional differences, the core of medieval and postmedieval English houses consisted of an oak frame of vertical posts secured to horizontal beams by mortise-and-tenon joints (interlocking heavy timbers secured by wooden pegs).

The roof of this sturdy yet flexible box frame was supported by large principal rafters or smaller common rafters that were usually tied to purlins—beams that ran horizontally between the rafters to prevent the roof from racking or shifting sideways. To keep the frame square, diagonal braces ran between beams and posts and between rafters and beams. Spaced between the heavy load-bearing posts were slenderer studs that ran vertically between beams and provided places for attaching exterior and interior walls. In England walls were made of interwoven sticks—known as wattles—covered over with clay daubing.

Within established traditions of English house framing, significant innovations took place in the late 1550s and early 1600s. These changes produced the postmedieval houses that would be built in 17th-century England. Refinements in carpentry and the positioning of structural members enhanced the mechanical efficiency of frames. The most notable change that transformed the houses of middling farmers and craftsmen in rural England was the incorporation of chimneys. This addition necessitated or facilitated the erection of partitions to subdivide the interior space that had traditionally consisted of a single hall with an open hearth. In the southeast of England this innovation produced a dwelling with a central chimney flanked on one side by a hall for cooking and eating and on the other by a more formal parlor. At the same time, service rooms such as dairies and butteries were moved to the rear of the house. By the early 1600s, windows of houses in the southeast of England were being glazed. Domestic interiors in some regions thus became cleaner and, to a degree, lighter. Changes occurred more slowly in other parts of England, particularly in upland regions, but over the course of the 17th century these innovations spread throughout the realm and were transplanted to New England.

Nearly all the dwellings built in New England before 1660 have vanished. The first houses were temporary structures described by a contemporary as "wigwams, huts and hovels." Although some of these dwellings did incorporate elements of Native American architecture, others drew upon English traditions of sod houses or pallisado houses, whose walls consisted entirely of driven posts. One pallisado house is known to have lasted 150 years, though most were probably replaced within a few years or a generation. During this period, colonists also erected more substantial earthfast structures that employed post-and-beam frames but placed the posts directly into the ground instead of seating them in sills resting on stone foundations. It is currently impossible to determine how common earthfast framed houses were or to estimate how long they lasted, but they formed part of the first generation's housing stock.

Of the fully framed houses with foundations built before 1660, only six or seven survive within the original boundaries of the Massachusetts Bay Colony. Among these is the Fairbanks House of around 1637 in Dedham, Mass., the oldest wood-frame structure in North America. No frame houses predating 1660 remain standing in Maine, New Hampshire, Connecticut, Rhode Island, or the old Plymouth Colony. There may be 80 to 90 extant houses dating from the period 1661 to 1700, when the second and third generations came of age: three in New Hampshire and neighboring Maine; approximately 64 within the original boundaries of the Massachusetts Bay Colony; between five and nine within the former boundaries of the Plymouth Colony; possibly six in Rhode Island; and perhaps six to 10 in Connecticut. Another 230 to 250 houses probably date from the quarter century after 1700. Substantial English settlement did not occur in Vermont during the first period.

Even though these dwellings were built primarily by New England–trained housewrights, they often contain evidence of localized English carpentry practices in their framing and joinery. In spite of these minor variations, the surviving dwellings usually have such English features as post-and-beam frames, massive chimneys, and relatively steeply pitched gabled roofs. Originally, they would have had casement windows with leaded, diamond-shaped panes of glass. Interior finishes might include plastered walls, horizontal and vertical sheathing, and carved or incised decoration of exposed framing elements.

The size and layout of these surviving first-period houses are somewhat misleading. Overwhelmingly, the surviving houses are larger, two-story structures, even though most of New England's 17th-century colonists would have lived in one- or two-room single-story houses or what we refer to today as half houses, two-story dwellings with a single room on each floor and a smaller end bay containing a chimney and entry. The late 17th-century Peak House in Medfield, Mass., is a rare survivor. Many others were probably replaced or enlarged. A study of 144 surviving pre-1725 Massachusetts houses revealed that 82 began as one-story single-room houses or half houses.

Over time, occupants expanded their homes by adding lean-tos to the ends or, more commonly, to the backs of houses. Relatively few of the houses that survive have the complex, asymmetrical massing produced by these additions, though rear lean-tos containing service rooms became integral to some houses constructed after 1680, producing the classic New England saltbox. There are also few extant examples of the larger, complex houses of 10 or more rooms built by members of the elite. The Turner House of around 1668 (popularly known as the House of the Seven Gables) in Salem, Mass., is a notable example. The more common extant houses are relatively symmetrical hall-and-parlor houses, with a central chimney mass dividing the two rooms on each floor and a tightly winding staircase located in front of the chimney, to which a rear lean-to may have been added. These houses proved large enough and adaptable to the needs of later owners.

Many of these houses reveal adaptations to the challenges and opportunities provided by New England's weather. Cellars became a

The Richard Jackson House (ca. 1664), Portsmouth, N.H.

standard feature, replacing dairies and butteries as places to keep provisions cool, but not frozen, during the frigid winters. The ready availability of oak, cedar, and pine determined exterior coverings. Overlapping clapboards, approximately four feet long, covered the outside of most structures, as they proved to be more durable than walls of exposed wattle and daub. By the 1660s shingles of cedar and pine replaced thatch as the preferred roofing material, though thatched roofs may have persisted longer in some areas. This shift to wood shingles led to the erection of lighter roof frames of the principal rafters and common purlins in eastern Massachusetts and coastal Connecticut. The increased use of sawmills in the last quarter of the 17th century aided in the production of building elements such as common rafters, studs, collars, and floor joists of smaller size, continuing a process of refinement that was well established in England.

The region's stands of pines and the erection of sawmills produced other innovations. In New Hampshire and Maine, colonists began to erect one- and two-story houses made entirely of square mill-sawn logs or planks that interlocked at the corners. In southeastern and northeastern New England, builders also used mill-sawn pine planks to replace wall studs and horizontal sheathing. Instead of cutting and laboriously joining to the frame studs and sheathing, carpenters clad the outside of the frame with mill-sawn, vertical planks that ran from the sills to the plate. Clapboards were nailed directly to the outside of the planks. This process reduced the number of structural components and joints and, by doing so, reduced costs. During the 1700s,

plank framing spread to Connecticut and western Massachusetts.

Not all architectural changes during the 17th century were innovative, however. During the late 1600s and early 1700s, a dramatic revival of projecting porches, facade gables, and framed jetties or overhangs took place. Several of the houses that are popularly regarded as stereotypically 17th century date from this period: the Appleton-Taylor-Mansfield House of around 1680 (the so-called Ironworks House) in Saugus, Mass.; the Parson Capen House of around 1683 in Topsfield, Mass.; the Ward House of around 1683 in Salem, Mass.; and the Stanley-Whitman House of around 1707–20 in Farmington, Conn. These houses were all exceptional in their size, decorative elaboration, and cost and were undoubtedly intended to showcase their occupants' wealth and status. Even frontier towns such as Deerfield, Mass., acquired one or two such houses, which stood out amid the numerous one-story dwellings and the less ambitious two-story hall-and-parlor houses.

Each New England town also had a meetinghouse that served as both a place of worship and the seat of local government. This duality of purpose was the defining characteristic of these public buildings. Nonetheless, it is wrong to view them as either religiously meaningless or inspired by secular precedents such as English market houses, for it is here, and not in their homes, that English colonists gave expression to their Puritanism. Meetinghouses were original architectural expressions of strongly held religious principles that de-emphasized traditional aspects of religious architecture. Regardless of their dimensions, roof

lines, and shape—rectangular or square—17th-century New England meetinghouses lacked towers and steeples, rounded or pointed windows, stained-glass windows, and other obvious references to traditional ecclesiastical architecture. On the interior, the absence of an altar and of long aisles for processions and the presence of a high pulpit clearly distinguished these meetinghouses from medieval parish churches, denying any place special sanctity within the auditory. Pulpits, pews, and other finish work found inside such meetinghouses could be finely wrought examples of joinery that were hardly plain, but iconographically the meetinghouse style was self-consciously plain. In its spirit and in many particulars, this style would persist throughout the 18th century.

Richard Candee, "A Documentary History of Plymouth Colony Architecture, 1620–1700," *Old Time New England* 59:3 (Jan.–March 1969), 59:4 (Apr.–June 1969), and 60:2 (Oct.–Dec. 1969).; Candee, "First Period Architecture in Maine and New Hampshire: The Evidence of Probate Inventories," in *Early American Probate Inventories: The Dublin Seminar for New England Folklife Annual Proceedings, 1987* (1989), ed. Peter Benes; Abbott Lowell Cummings, "Connecticut and Its Building Traditions" *Connecticut History* 35:1 (Spring 1994); Cummings, *The Framed Houses of Massachusetts Bay, 1625–1725* (1979); Cummings, *Early New England Architecture* (1984); Claire W. Dempsey, Laura B. Driemeyer, Richard B. Greenwood, Myron Stachiw, and William McKenzie Woodward, *The Early Architecture and Landscape of the Narragansett Basin* (2001); Marian Card Donnelly, *The New England Meeting Houses of the Seventeenth Century* (1968); Robert B. St. George, "'Set Thine House in Order': The Domestication of the Yeomanry in Seventeenth-Century New England," in *New England Begins: The Seventeenth Century* (1982).

Kevin M. Sweeney

Architecture, 1725–80

Continuity rather than dramatic change characterized New England architecture from 1725 to 1780. Housewrights continued to hew, join, and raise post-and-beam frames primarily of oak in southern New England or of pine in northern and western New England. Gabled roofs remained the norm, though the pitch of these roofs became less angled over the course of the century. Oak, pine, or cedar shingles covered roofs, and oak or pine clapboards clothed most exterior walls. A single chimney usually stood at or near the center of the house. Well into the second quarter of the 18th century, interior finishes continued to focus on decorating the exposed building frame. The only widespread change was the gradual replacement of casement windows by sash windows with large panes of glass, introduced in Boston just after 1700.

Despite the traditional features of most

houses, the region's 18th-century housing stock exhibited variations in size and plan that reflected significant economic stratification. We should be skeptical of comments like the observation of the Englishman Thomas Anburey in 1778 that "these houses are all after the same plan." Surviving examples and other documentary sources indicate that he was wrong. The historian Lee Soltow has demonstrated that the 1798 Federal Direct Tax—the so-called window tax—documented a very broad spectrum of house size in prerevolutionary New England.

The vast majority of dwellings that dotted the countryside were isolated single-story, one- to three-room farmhouses. Some of these were single-room cottages measuring only 10 by 14 feet. Others were one-story, two-room, hall-and-parlor houses, which had a central chimney and small entry into which the front door opened. More common may have been the 800- to 900-square-foot New England square-frame house of three rooms—hall, parlor, and kitchen—with a massive off-center chimney and corner staircase to the garret above. Like the single-room house, this was a socially open dwelling in which the front door provided direct entry into the hall. Windows would have been at a premium in all of these houses, and paint uncommon on interior or exterior surfaces.

Some of these single-story dwellings would have been log houses. Since the late 1600s, New Englanders had built houses by interlocking squared logs or round tree boles. By the 1760s and 1770s, log houses or huts represented one-half to two-thirds of the new housing in recently settled towns in northern and western New England. Conceived of as temporary structures, they were replaced as a family's economic situation improved and towns matured. Only a few examples remain of the hundreds that once stood.

The two-story 18th-century houses that today misleadingly outnumber their more humble contemporaries have survived in disproportionate numbers. Only in urban areas and wealthier farming regions such as northeastern Massachusetts and the Connecticut River valley would they have formed a majority of the housing stock on the eve of the Revolution. Most of these two-story houses would have been fairly traditional in their plans and architectural ornament, though their interior finish made greater use, after midcentury, of plaster, paint, and raised paneling. Throughout the period, a few were still built with hewn jetties or overhangs between the first and second stories and on the gable ends above the second story. Half houses, two-story houses with a single room on each floor and a smaller end bay containing a chimney and entry, could

The Wentworth-Gardner House (1760), Portsmouth, N.H.

be found in urban areas and some country towns in the Connecticut River valley. A few two-story versions of New England square-frame houses also survive from the mid-18th century. Probably more common were hall-and-parlor houses, which had two rooms on each floor flanking a center chimney. The classic New England saltbox with its integral lean-to and sweeping rear roof continued to be built in most areas of the region. They usually had three to five rooms below and three chambers above.

During the third quarter of the century, an enlarged version of the classic saltbox plan grew in popularity. In this form, which first appeared around 1700, the back half of the house rose to a full two-story height contained under a centered roofline, destroying the distinctive shape of the saltbox house but preserving its characteristic floor plan. Referred to by geographers and architectural historians as the New England Large, these center-chimney houses, which had up to 10 rooms of varying size, stood out on the landscape and were not, as was once believed, commonplace. They were often the homes of local notables and well-to-do farmers. Like saltboxes, these structures contained 2,000 square feet or more; some exteriors may have been painted in earth tones of red or yellow ocher.

Yet another plan, a two-story, central-hallway house with two chimney stacks, heralded a new architectural style. Rare at the time, these houses with their symmetrical facades, square four-room plans, and classically inspired architectural details gave expression to

a style known today as Georgian. Rooted in a Renaissance architectural vocabulary, the style was introduced from England in masonry houses built in Boston: the 1690–91 Foster-Hutchinson House, 1711 Clark-Frankland House, and the 1737–40 mansion of Thomas Hancock, none of which is extant. Beginning around midcentury, the central-hallway plan and other elements of this style were incorporated into more modest versions constructed in the countryside by the rural gentry and clergy.

Even though they were usually built of wood, these rural mansions were distinguished from the two-story, center-chimney houses by their two chimneys, elaborate doorways, and such architectural embellishments as corner quoins and cornices (small scroll brackets under the projecting crown molding). As a rule they were between 2,800 and 3,200 square feet in area. The impact of these houses was often heightened by the use of either a large gambrel roof, with its double slope, or a hip roof, in which four planes tapered to the ridgeline. The exteriors of these mansion houses might have been painted in shades of tan or gray, known as stone colors in the period, and the trim picked out in white, suggesting a solidity of masonry that belied their wooden clapboarding.

Innovations in interior finish could be found in such mansions as well as in some of the more ambitious dwellings with traditional plans. A hallmark of the Georgian style was molding and paneling made of white pine boards that hid the building's frame. Important rooms such as the parlor and parlor chamber often had raised paneling, molded fireplace surrounds, encased beams, and interior cornices with crown moldings. Central hallways had impressive stairways with turned balusters. These wooden surfaces might be painted yellow ocher, verdigris, or Prussian blue or given a faux finish called graining to suggest more exotic materials such as cedar or marble. Ceilings in these mansions tended to be higher and were plastered, and windows became larger and more plentiful, resulting in brighter, more colorful decors. Such interiors were considered more refined and thus better suited to entertainments such as receiving visitors for tea. But even in these houses, secondary rooms upstairs and in the back were sometimes still finished with vertical or horizontal pine sheathing that recalled 17th-century interiors.

As the century progressed, housewrights, joiners, and carpenters made increasing use of English pattern books as sources for plans, interior paneling, and exterior ornamentation. William Salmon's *Palladio Londinensis* (1734) was in use in eastern Massachusetts in the decade in which it was printed. Peter Harrison, the gentleman architect from Newport, R.I., used James Gibbs's *Book of Architecture* (1728) when he designed Boston's King's Chapel in the late 1740s. Abraham Swan's *British Architect* (1745) provided sources for paneling in Marblehead's Lee Mansion of 1768. The resulting houses were as expressive of their occupants as were the more traditional one- and two-story center-chimney houses.

The design and embellishment of public buildings also bore the mark of the new Georgian style. Here, too, wood remained the material of choice, though there were notable exceptions, such as the Newport Province House of 1739–41 and the 1761 Wethersfield, Conn., meetinghouse, both of which were built of brick. Meetinghouses as a rule retained their dual purpose as places of worship and seats of local government, though a growing number of these structures in larger towns were devoted solely to public worship. The buildings as a rule were larger than their predecessors and assumed a fairly standard plan, with the main entrance on the long side facing the pulpit. Stair towers were added to the ends of some meetinghouses, and in a few instances the tower was topped with a steeple, providing clear evidence of the growing influence of English fashions and pattern books. The exteriors were painted in a range of colors in addition to white, such as yellow, blue, or orange. The windows, doors, and sometimes the trim were often highlighted in contrasting hues.

State houses and courthouses also adopted Georgian architectural embellishments such as elaborate baroque doorways topped with triangular or scroll pediments. Some had imposing gambrel or hip roofs. Yet in their scale and architectural ornament all these buildings remained domestic, resembling to a large degree contemporary Georgian mansion houses. Only after the Revolution, with the creation of republican governments and the availability of architects with engineering skills, did the scale and character of public buildings change fundamentally.

Abbott Lowell Cummings, *Architecture in Early New England* (1984); Claire W. Dempsey, Laura B. Driemeyer, Richard B. Greenwood, Myron Stachiw, and William McKenzie Woodward, *The Early Architecture and Landscape of the Narragansett Basin* (2001); James L. Garvin, *A Building History of Northern New England* (2001); J. Frederick Kelly, *Early Domestic Architecture of Connecticut* (1963); Michael Steinitz, "Rethinking Geographical Approaches to the Common House: The Evidence from Eighteenth-Century Massachusetts," in *Perspectives in Vernacular Architecture, III*, ed. Thomas Carter and Bernard L. Herman (1989); Kevin M. Sweeney, "Mansion People: Kinship, Class and Architecture in Western Massachusetts in the Mid-Eighteenth Century," *Winterthur Portfolio* 13 (Winter 1984); Sweeney, "Meetinghouses, Town Houses, and Churches: Changing Perceptions of Sacred and Secular Space in Southern New England, 1720–1850," *Winterthur Portfolio* 28 (Winter 1994).

Kevin M. Sweeney

Architecture, 1780–1830

In most parts of New England, the oldest buildings identifiable today were constructed in the half century after the American Revolution. Even cities and towns that can count two centuries of earlier settlement rarely boast more than a handful of buildings from the colonial period, most of which have undergone significant expansion and remodeling. One possible reason for this pattern is the widespread prosperity that characterized the early national period. Across the region populations grew, communities became more densely settled, and the economy diversified with expanding opportunities for trade and manufacturing to complement the well-established livelihoods of farming, fishing, and forestry. Within this context, more durable homes, grander public buildings, and larger workplaces were constructed, increasing the likelihood of their survival and significantly contributing to New England's historic landscape.

New Englanders continued to favor wood-frame construction in their buildings, and the general trend of simplifying building techniques continued during this period. Frames were composed of lighter members and linked with simpler joints, and plank walls replaced stud walls in many areas. Both bay framing and square framing remained popular, and the latter spread through the region, while log building continued on the northern and western frontiers. Numerous widespread technological improvements—particularly in contrast to the colonial period—led to more labor-saving materials and methods, including machine-cut nails. The construction of larger, more durable dwellings continued the trend that had long distinguished the region, where a high percentage of more moderate-sized houses predominated.

The expanding and diversifying economy encouraged construction, and greater numbers of buildings were dressed up with classical ornamentation: entablatures, pediments, and fanlights were added to doors, moldings and cornices to windows and eaves, and, occasionally, ambitious treatments to facades. At the same time, however, many buildings remained unpainted and largely unornamented. Covered in weatherboards, clapboards, or shingles, many of the dwellings, barns, workplaces, and public buildings of the countryside received little interior finish, had few secure openings, and were only nominally heated.

Many domestic plans from the colonial era remained popular throughout this period. A beginner's house could still consist of nothing more than a single room and a garret; an average house might comprise two or three rooms. The central chimney remained critical, ensuring the persistence of the hall-and-parlor plan (in which two rooms on each floor flanked the central chimney) and a variety of double-pile (two rooms deep) plans. Plans commonly included a workspace—the kitchen—and a more public space that might be called the hall, the best room, or the parlor. Many houses, whether of one or two stories, continued to include first-floor sleeping rooms. Larger and more ambitious houses added more specialized public rooms—for example, a family sitting room or a dining room as well as a formal parlor. Whereas the center-passage plan, with its wide, deep entry and stair hall, was widely accepted in other regions of the young country, in New England this choice was usually attractive only to the wealthy and fashionable. Most New Englanders preferred the lobby entrance provided by the chimney bay, and some even clung to the old-fashioned choice of a direct entrance into one of the main rooms.

Across the region, buildings of this period are commonly found in the center villages of rural communities. The emergence of these villages was particularly important in the early national period, accomplished through the construction of new public buildings, residences, and stores and shops. The regional preference for an established church and public education meant that public buildings were common features in each town, becoming more numerous as denominations multiplied and communities became more willing to erect special-purpose buildings. For many small towns and dissenting congregations, 18th-century meetinghouses—small, plain, nearly square buildings under gabled roofs— remained useful and affordable. Wealthier congregations in larger communities continued to move away from this model, however, seeking to distinguish their buildings from others in the landscape and signaling them, often for the first time, as uniquely religious. Schools and town houses were constructed in many communities; they were often small, one-room buildings under gabled roofs but occasionally borrowed the high-hipped roofs (in which four planes tapered to the ridgeline) of early meetinghouses. Private groups and individuals also added significantly to the polish of the center villages by constructing academies, Masonic lodges, and inns and taverns that were often among the most elaborately finished in the community.

Shire and market towns also experienced significant growth and change with the addition of large, ambitious courthouses and increasing numbers of retail stores, which complemented the public buildings and residences of the villages. Former commons, the town's public fields and pastures, were transformed into parks that provided cultivated, genteel settings for these buildings and their patrons.

With the rise in mechanized manufacturing, beginning in the 1790s, a new settlement form appeared in the New England landscape: the mill communities that grew up along the waterways. Up until that time, small-scale processing plants could be found throughout the region, but the textile industry in particular was dependent on waterpowered multistory factories to house spinning and weaving. Although many companies continued to build these in wood, brick and stone became the preferred materials. Some followed the model of Rhode Island's small villages, others the larger urban model exemplified by the Boston Associates at Lowell, Mass. Together these new communities helped transform the settlement pattern of the region during the 19th century.

New England's cities were also growing in number and size, continuing to provide the region's most refined landscapes. Boston remained the core community; there professional architects and real estate developers joined the urban elite to create a distinctive landscape of order, uniformity, and elegance. Through increasingly ambitious projects, this coalition laid out wider, straighter streets in newly regular grids and lined them with brick residences, shops, banks, offices, and stores. Smaller cities followed suit, exemplified by the

exceptional period landscapes that survive in Portsmouth, N.H., Newburyport, Mass., and Bristol and Providence, R.I. As in the villages, churches and schools in the region's cities were built and rebuilt and the civic landscape was decorated with new state houses, courthouses, and markets. These important public buildings were joined by academies and hotels, creating genteel districts that contrasted with the hectic, often dirty waterfront zones of trade, processing, and manufacturing. Elite builders and homeowners followed these institutions to newly opened residential districts that encircled cities, contributing to the development of neighborhoods that were increasingly segregated by class and function.

More frequently than in the countryside, the largest and most impressive houses in cities were three- or four-story brick structures. The rising price of land in urban areas encouraged for the first time maximizing lot development and minimizing lot frontage. As a result, the facades were usually narrow and based on one of two plans: either the traditional wide front was turned 90 degrees from the street, thereby positioning the entry on the side and deep into the lot; or rooms were laid out from front to rear rather than side by side, with entry through a side passage or directly into the front room. The side-hall plan became the most popular one in Boston, used repeatedly for single-family houses as well as in paired and row houses. Rendered in wood as a freestanding dwelling under an end-gabled roof, the plan eventually became the region's most popular 19th-century house type.

The availability of consumer goods and participation in the fashion trends of the Atlantic rim were also signs of the times. After decades of reticence, New England's elite rushed to embrace the neoclassical forms and ornament that had been popularized by English builders and architects since the mid-18th century. Building proportions became more vertical and designs emphasized the taut surface of the wall. Ornamental vocabulary remained that of ancient Rome and the Renaissance, as the classical forms were taken apart and recombined to enrich entire buildings, especially entries and other openings and specific features like fireplaces. Particularly lavish public buildings and mansions often had a screen of pilasters rising from the first floor pedestal to support the cornice and the roof. An overlay of decorative features enhanced this familiar formula, including elliptical fans, delicate chains of flowers and leaves, and accents of ovals, urns, shields, and swags. Later in the period, avant-garde designers turned to the precedents of Greece and to the simpler, more geometrical compositions of pure neoclassicism.

U.S. Custom House (attrib. Perley Putnam, 1818–19), Salem, Mass.

This surge of activity led to the emergence of self-proclaimed architects and market-savvy craftsmen whose identities and careers are far better known than those of their colonial predecessors. The most ambitious would-be architects found their greatest opportunities in Boston: Charles Bulfinch, Asher Benjamin, Alexander Parris, and Peter Banner all launched successful careers there after winning important commissions. In the smaller cities and even in the countryside, notable craftsmen and designers also made names for themselves through the patronage of the elite and by winning important public building contracts, including the carver-turned-designer Samuel McIntire of Salem, Mass.; accomplished meetinghouse builders such as Connecticut's Lavius Fillmore and David Hoadley; and New Hampshire's Bradbury Johnson. Across the region, artisans, whether well known or unknown, undertook the challenging task of construction that created the emblematic built landscape of New England.

Richard Bushman, *The Refinement of America: Persons, Houses, Cities* (1992); Richard Candee, *Building Portsmouth: The Neighborhoods and Architecture of New Hampshire's Oldest City* (1992); Claire W. Dempsey, Laura B. Driemeyer, Richard B. Greenwood, Myron Stachiw, and William McKenzie Woodward, *The Early Architecture and Landscape of the Narragansett Basin* (2001); James L. Garvin, *A Building History of Northern New England* (2001); Thomas C. Hubka, *Big House, Little House, Back House, Barn: The Connected Farm Buildings of New England* (1984); Jack Larkin, *The Reshaping of Everyday Life, 1790–1840* (1988); Walter Muir Whitehill,

Boston: A Topographical History (1968); Joseph S. Wood and Michael P. Steinitz, *The New England Village* (1997).

Claire W. Dempsey

Architecture, 1830–80

Improved building technologies and growth within the architectural profession brought dramatic changes to New England's built environment during the period 1830–80. These advancements enabled architects and clients to erect structures in a wider variety of historical styles, ranging in inspiration from Greek temples to Italian Renaissance palaces to Swiss chalets. The end of this period coincided with the beginnings of the Colonial Revival, a style whose popularity began in New England and swept the country. These factors, along with the new industrialized economy that inspired the construction of great mill complexes, set the foundation for the region's architectural development well into the early 20th century.

Greek Revival became a prominent style in the 1820s and remained so for the next two decades. New England's conservative building tradition produced many instances in which traditional Federal-period houses, churches, and commercial blocks were simply dressed in architecture derived from ancient Greece; the differences, however, were not merely superficial. Improvements in woodworking technology meant that ornamental trim could be produced on a larger scale, more affordably, and in greater quantity, eliminating the need for expensive artisans. Dimensionally sawn lumber for house frames led to the development of a braced-frame construction using iron nails, an economical alternative to heavy timber frames assembled with wooden joinery. Improvements in transportation meant that granite from various New England quarries—and later, sandstone from quarries in western Massachusetts, Connecticut, Nova Scotia, and New Jersey—became more affordable for masonry construction.

New England's architectural conservatism was expressed in the persistence of traditional house forms well into the mid-19th century. The urban row house that was three bays wide remained standard, and the one-and-a-half- and two-story central-hall plan became popular. In each case a typical Greek Revival–style house might feature a doorway with pilasters and a frieze that framed sidelights and transoms with Greek moldings, updating the Federal-style arched doorway. Even in small towns it was not uncommon to find Doric columns flanking the doors or a full portico supported on columns. These embellishments, not restricted to large houses, provided even common mechanics with a sense of domestic grandeur. Accelerating a trend begun in the Federal period, chimneys became a less important architectural feature as bake ovens began to be replaced by stoves.

The most significant change in floor plans was the popularization of the side-hall plan for freestanding houses. In this departure from the central-hall tradition, an entrance to one side of the gabled end led into a stairway hall. Flanking the hall were two rooms, often joined by double doors that opened to create one larger space. If the gabled end was parallel to the street, the entrance would be oriented toward the side yard and driveway. Frequently a verandah ran the length of the facade opposite the hall—the beginning of the traditional American front porch. A later variation of this, probably dictated by small building lots in New England towns, featured a single parlor in the gable-end room overlooking the street. On one side was a porch with the main entrance facing either the street or the side yard.

The growth of the architectural profession brought forward an active group of designers who would bring change to traditional building patterns. Foremost among them was Richard Upjohn, who practiced in Boston from 1834 to 1839 but who, from his New York office, continued to have a major impact on New England in the 1840s and 1850s. Upjohn's design for the (now demolished) Lyman House in Brookline, Mass., in 1842 made it the first suburban Italianate villa in the Boston area. His Gothic Revival churches in several New England towns were also highly influential in popularizing that style for ecclesiastical work. Upjohn influenced a generation of young architects, including Arthur Gilman, Gridley J. F. Bryant, Alexander R. Esty, and Edward Cabot in Boston; Thomas Tefft and Alpheus Morse in Providence; Henry Austin in New Haven, Conn.; and Charles A. Alexander in Portland, Maine. The leading architects offered wealthy clients new historical styles to replace Greek Revival. The Italian Renaissance, derived mostly from English interpretations, became the style of choice from the mid-1840s into the 1850s for houses, public buildings, and commercial structures. Even large granite warehouses featured stone brackets and rusticated stone facing in the manner of an urban palazzo.

Both Italianate villas and Gothic Revival–style cottages were popular among the middle class, especially in semirural suburban communities. Given the availability of mass-produced ornamentation, it was common to find small, one-and-a-half-story houses with a gable end facing the street; they might boast Gothic vergeboard (carved or cut ornamentation along the sloping roof end) and pointed-arch windows or Italianate brackets under roof and porch eaves, often combined with Greek Revival–style detailing. In 1841 Catherine Beecher joined her male colleagues offering advice on domestic architecture with her *Treatise on Domestic Economy*.

The interest in these picturesque Romantic styles had a different impact on church design. The influence of Richard Upjohn's stone Gothic Revival churches for wealthier congregations, or wood board-and-batten construction for others, was significant throughout the region. Important also was the North Italian,

Mark Twain House (Edward T. Potter, 1874), Hartford, Conn., a Queen Anne, Stick Style house

or Rundboginstil (round arched style). In part, this may have been a reaction by various Protestant groups to the prevalence of the Gothic Revival for Episcopal and Catholic churches. Regional architects like Thomas W. Silloway, George F. Meacham, John Stevens, and John D. Towle of Boston were particularly adept at translating Italian Romanesque details into wood or brick.

By the late 1850s the pervasiveness of the mansard roof (two slopes on all sides, with the lower slope steeper than the upper) in New England distinguished its architecture from the rest of the country's. The first house with a mansard roof was the Deacon House in Boston, erected in 1846 under the direction of the French architect Jean Lemoulnier. Demolished long ago, this house marked the inception of a wave of popularity for contemporary French architecture. By the late 1850s the mansard roof became the dominant feature for almost all types of buildings, including commercial blocks, schools, and public buildings. Even large mill complexes were built with what was called at the time a "French roof." Early examples were more directly based on French precedents in which the lower pitch of the mansard was relatively shallow and less prominent, with small dormer windows. The picturesque possibilities of this roof quickly became apparent to architects, who began making the pitch of the mansard almost vertical, with elaborately ornamented dormer windows, often combined with a cupola on the peak of the roof. The city halls in Boston (Arthur Gilman and Gridley J. F. Bryant, 1862–65) and Providence (S. J. F. Thayer, 1874–78) are two of the most superb surviving representations of the influence of France's Second Empire. The layout of Boston's Back Bay streets and many of that neighborhood's earliest houses reflected the strong influence of French fashion.

Prosperous manufacturers—particularly those in the textile and shoe industries—were significant in transforming New England's architectural landscape. New towns such as Lowell and Lawrence, Mass., and Lewiston, Maine, were founded to support the mills. Many older communities were transformed into major manufacturing centers with large mill buildings and worker housing. For a brief period the first mill towns were attractively landscaped and contained industrial architecture that reflected the elegant simplicity of Greek Revival. In the years following the Civil War, however, mill design became more functional in appearance, while worker housing began to resemble congested tenements.

Although the popularity of the mansard style continued throughout the 1870s, countervailing stylistic influences were introduced by a new generation of architects, many of whom had traveled abroad and been educated in Europe. Others were educated in the country's first school of architecture, established at the Massachusetts Institute of Technology in 1865. Led by Boston firms such as Ware and Van Brunt, Cummings and Sears, and Peabody and Stearns, Venetian Gothic architecture had a brief period of popularity. Harvard's Memorial Hall (Ware and Van Brunt, 1866–78) is the most spectacular surviving representation of this influence. Also in vogue was what has been called the Stick Style, an American adaptation of European picturesque architecture introduced into Newport, R.I., by the New York architect Richard Morris Hunt. Unlike the Venetian Gothic, which was essentially a masonry style, technology made possible the replication of picturesque Stick Style ornament for the middle class. Examples of machine-cut ornament proliferated for suburban homes and summer cottages—the camp meeting colony on Martha's Vineyard being the most famous example.

Boston led the dissemination of architectural ideas in the first enduring design journal, *The American Architect and Building News* (1876), in which many of the earliest designs that led to the Colonial Revival were published. New Englanders were among the first to develop an appreciation of colonial architectural heritage, in part because so much of it survived. The region's conservatism again played a role. Because the traditional two-story, central-hall plan had never entirely lost favor, it became easier to adapt and revive both the form and style of 18th-century precedents.

Bainbridge Bunting, *Houses of Boston's Back Bay* (1967); James L. Garvin, *A Building History of Northern New England* (2001); Sarah Bradford Landau, "Richard Morris Hunt, the Continental Picturesque, and the Stick Style," *Journal of the Society of Architectural Historians* (October 1983); Douglass Shand-Tucci, *Built in Boston City and Suburb, 1800–1950* (1998); Everard M. Upjohn, *Richard Upjohn Architect and Churchman* (1968).

Roger G. Reed

Architecture, 1880–1930

Many of this era's leading architects (some of whom constructed buildings of national importance) worked in New England, sampling from a wide range of architectural styles. Local contractors from Maine to Connecticut ignored academic architectural fashions to put up houses and public buildings in every imaginable style. Still, the conservative nature of designers and clients ensured that architectural motifs alluding to the area's colonial past would endure. For the most part, New England's builders lacked interest in skyscrapers and the nascent modernism favored by Europe's leading architects and America's few progressive designers. Building in New England through the 1930s was largely dominated by the Colonial Revival.

By 1880, Henry Hobson Richardson, trained at the Ecole des Beaux-Arts, had become America's most respected architect, largely on the strength of his acclaimed Trinity Church in Boston (1877). In the years preceding his untimely death in 1886, Richardson designed a number of highly regarded libraries and university buildings in Massachusetts and Vermont in his signature Romanesque style. Countless Richardsonian Romanesque churches, town halls, YMCAs, firehouses, railroad stations, and village libraries were built in New England through the close of the century. Two of Richardson's draftsmen, Charles McKim and Stanford White (the two designing partners of the New York firm McKim, Mead and White), established their reputation with a series of public buildings adapted from Roman and Renaissance models, perhaps none more influential than the Boston Public Library (1887–95). Other notable firms that worked in New England in the classical mode include Richard Morris Hunt, Carrère and Hastings, Peabody and Stearns, and George B. Post. John Russell Pope's unexecuted master plan for Dartmouth College (1922) featured strong symmetries and powerful buildings rendered in a restrained classical vocabulary. Ralph Adams Cram sought to redirect architectural practice with his reinvigorated Gothic style, erecting robust Collegiate Gothic designs at Williams College and Boston University. James Gamble Rogers returned to his alma mater, Yale University, in the 1920s to create several of that campus's landmark Collegiate Gothic buildings. The English-inspired Arts and Crafts style also had a small presence, mostly in urban settings, the Fleur-de-Lis Studios in Providence (1885–86) being the region's most extraordinary example.

Those who built houses drew from an even broader stylistic repertoire. Along the rough Atlantic coast, architects built scores of handsome Shingle Style dwellings. America's corporate millionaires who summered in Newport called on designers to construct their grand "cottages" in the style of French châteaus, English country houses, and Italian villas. In new suburbs throughout New England, houses built in the Queen Anne, Tudor Revival, and Swiss chalet styles frequently mixed architectural details to produce hybrid designs thought to express their individuality. None of these styles ever challenged the regionwide popularity of the Colonial Revival, however, the symbolic associations and scale of which made it appropriate for both domestic and institutional use.

This determined preference for the colonial era and its architectural models spurred New Englanders to recover or rebuild parts of the colonial landscape they had so energetically destroyed through the first half of the 19th century. The region's cultural elites in particular fashioned scores of houses, even entire villages, to correspond with a largely idealized image of a preindustrial, uncomplicated colonial past. Their architectural efforts formed part of a national movement celebrating that past known as the Colonial Revival (popularly defined as the nation's pre-1840 history), a movement that was reinforced in literature, art, and revived handicraft traditions.

Interest in America's colonial past emerged just before the Civil War, but New Englanders, amateurs and professionals alike, set out in the 20 years following the conflict to survey the region's historic landscape. They searched for authentic architectural survivals to restore and protect, and for sites they could rebuild. By virtue of their histories or association with colonial events, entire villages seemed worthy of restoration, including Old Lyme and Litchfield, Conn.; Gloucester, Stockbridge, and Deerfield, Mass.; Dublin and Cornish, N.H.; and the small communities of Kittery, York, and South Berwick, Maine, that bordered the Piscataqua River. Existing houses were restored (often imaginatively, if firm evidence was lacking) for summer or year-round use.

Such luminaries as William Dean Howells, Wallace Nutting, Maxfield Parrish, and Sarah Orne Jewett endorsed the movement through the colonial-style houses they commissioned or through well-publicized restorations of colonial-era dwellings. Most builders liberally interpreted the colonial style to describe a symmetrical, one- or two-story structure detailed with as many 18th-century architectural features as budgets permitted, including Palladian windows, pedimented porticoes, six-over-six double-hung sash windows with wavy glass panes, classical moldings, and hipped roofs (in which four planes tapered to the ridgeline). Dark exterior shutters stood out against a stark white paint mistakenly believed to be an authentic colonial-era color. Elaborate masonry versions of the Colonial Revival went up, but it was the ordinary frame interpretations that best suited the New England disposition for thrifty simplicity.

Few designers used the style more effectively than the New York architect Charles A. Platt. Around 1900 Platt created a new American country-house type for fellow members of the Cornish Art Colony in Cornish and Plainfield, N.H. His modestly scaled dwellings were derived from 18th-century New England vernacular designs (sometimes enriched

with Italian Renaissance details) and were meant to contrast with the grand mansions of America's nouveaux riches going up at the same time in Newport. While Newport's moneyed industrialists sought comparison to European nobles and royalty, Colonial Revival builders like Platt emphasized their clients' links to American history and the cultural authority of ancestral ties and traditional values. The demand for colonial-inflected designs was so strong that McKim and White's firm turned out Colonial Revival houses in Boston's Back Bay for the elite. Even Cram was briefly compelled to put aside the Gothic in his Fourth Academy Building at Phillips Exeter Academy, Exeter, N.H. (1915), whose Georgian features mirrored the school's central buildings.

With the exception of a few surviving historic houses, by 1900 the colonial character of New England's cities had been nearly erased by a thriving commercial culture. Since the 1830s mills had been the prominent feature of New England's urban landscape, growing throughout the 19th century to extensive complexes made up of factory buildings, boardinghouses, canals and races, warehouses, and power plants. New England mills made what would be one last great expansion in the early 20th century. The Amoskeag Mill Company in Manchester, N.H., then the world's largest textile mill, framed the banks of the Merrimack River for more than a mile on both sides. Manufacturing prosperity spilled into cities and provided the capital for libraries, museums, opera houses, and civic structures throughout the six-state area.

Political leaders and wealthy patrons favored the elaborate Beaux-Arts style that conveyed a cultivated, European image. With their classical detailing and expensive materials, buildings such as McKim, Mead and White's Rhode Island State House (1892–1904) and Christopher Grant La Farge and Benjamin Wistar Morris's Morgan Memorial at the Wadsworth Atheneum (1910) in Hartford, Conn., stood in pointed contrast to nearby industrial structures. But it was understood that the wealth and architectural embellishments of New England's cities flowed from the prosperity of their factories and the largesse of the men who owned them.

Because of the rapid expansion of mills, corporations could no longer house all their workforce—now composed of Irish, Italian, German, East European, and French Canadian immigrants—who were increasingly segregated into crowded, unsanitary surroundings. Middle-class row houses and clusters of tenements that provided homes for immigrant families and the poorest of the cities' population made up the bulk of urban domestic ar-

chitecture at the turn of the 20th century. The affluent increasingly gave up their elegant urban dwellings for expansive estates just beyond the reach of the city. And by the 1910s, white, middle-class citizens followed suit, leaving cities for the new neighborhoods strung along trolley and rail lines. But their suburban dwellings came from lumberyards, mail-order catalogs, and developers' plan books rather than from architects' drafting tables. The need to house the ever-increasing populations who remained behind in densely packed circumstances inspired new urban house types such as the three-decker (one apartment on each of three floors), found mainly in Boston and the region's southern cities, and Hartford's "perfect six" apartment buildings (two identical units on each of three floors). Urban reformers refused to give up on the cities and worked to improve the lives of those left behind by providing better housing, schools, and health care. Others, inspired by Frederick Law Olmsted's Emerald Necklace in Boston and the City Beautiful Movement, focused their labors on urban design, including the establishment of important park systems.

While architects elsewhere in America experimented with tall buildings, Art Deco motifs, Early Modern styles, and advanced construction technologies in the opening decades of the 20th century, such possibilities went mostly unexplored in New England. Certainly, the continued strength of the Colonial Revival blunted efforts to introduce recently imported architectural styles. At the very moment New York and Philadelphia corporations commissioned International Style skyscrapers as markers of their modern aspirations, the Aetna Life and Casualty Company in Hartford hired James Gamble Rogers to create a monumentally scaled Colonial Revival headquarters. And while much of the nation prospered in the decade before the Depression, the New England economy weakened as production in the great mills slowed, then ended. By the mid-1930s, many mills had closed. In spite of the efforts of the Harvard Society for Contemporary Art, a socially prominent young Harvard-educated group who championed modern art and the works of European architects, New England remained resolutely "colonial." Modernism finally reached New England in the late 1930s with the arrival of the Bauhaus exiles, who established Harvard's Graduate School of Design as the nation's authoritative center of modern architecture.

Alan Axelrod, ed., *The Colonial Revival in America* (1985); Doreen Bolger Burke, *In Pursuit of Beauty: Americans and the Aesthetic Movement* (1986); Sarah L. Giffen and Kevin D. Murphy, eds., *"A Noble and*

Three-decker housing (ca. 1910), Portsmouth, N.H.

Dignified Stream": The Piscataqua Region in the Colonial Revival, 1860–1930 (1992); Kenneth T. Jackson, *Crabgrass Frontier: The Suburbanization of America* (1985); T. J. Jackson Lears, *No Place of Grace: Antimodernism and the Transformation of American Culture, 1880–1920* (1981); Karal Ann Marling, *George Washington Slept Here: Colonial Revivals and American Culture, 1876–1986* (1988); Bridget A. May, "Progressivism and the Colonial Revival: The Modern Colonial House, 1900–1920," *Winterthur Portfolio* (Summer–Autumn 1991); Maureen Meister, ed., *H. H. Richardson: The Architect, His Peers, and Their Era* (1999).

Marlene Elizabeth Heck

Architecture, 1930 to the Present

Boston, bastion of tradition, is the undisputed center of contemporary architecture in New England. Seeking notable modern buildings and complexes in the six states, one is struck by the concentration in Boston, whereas much of the region maintains an older cultural identity. Preservation is the watchword for much of the area, evident in the restoration of Strawbery Banke in Portsmouth, N.H., the revitalization of mill towns such as Manchester and Harrisville, N.H., widespread adaptive reuse in Lowell, Mass., and the development of such historic enclaves as Salem, Mass. Buildings of the 19th-century Sprague Electric Company factory in North Adams, Mass., were converted into the Massachusetts Museum of Contemporary Art, creating the largest gallery in the United States.

Only with the end of World War II did modernism encroach upon the region's architecture. One example, in which elements of modernity are organized according to classical principles, is the B. B. Chemical Building in Cambridge, Mass. (Shepley, Bulfinch, Coolidge, Abbott, 1937). Long horizontal window bands, glass bricks, and a clear linear articulation enhance the fine proportions of this prewar structure. Acting as catalysts for the introduction of the new style, technology-related industries and universities led the way, soon to be followed by corporations. Largely through the ubiquity of academic institutions, New England became a major force in the dissemination of the modern movement.

Few architects and educators have had a greater impact on the rise and diffusion of modernism than Walter Gropius (1883–1969). Arriving at Harvard in 1937, he served as head of the Graduate School of Design from 1938 to 1952 and founded The Architects Collaborative. Gropius's own house in Lincoln, Mass., along with that of his collaborator, Marcel Breuer, remain exemplars of the International Style. They inspired tech-built houses by Carl Koch and those designed by Gropius's firm The Architects Collaborative (TAC) on Six-Moon Hill in Lexington, Mass., which, in a time of McCarthyism, were condemned as Communist-derived. At the invitation of Gropius, the Swiss art historian Sigfried Giedion delivered the Norton lectures at Harvard that resulted in the publication of *Space, Time, and Architecture* (1941), the canonical text promoting modernism. Under Gropius's influence, popular neo-Georgian historicism was banished from the campus. His own Graduate Student Complex (1949) is an embodiment of ideas gleaned from the Bauhaus school in Dessau, Germany.

Postwar growth in the university population created demands for new facilities and dormitories. Because of the presence of European-trained architects at leading schools of architecture, modernism flourished on New England soil. In 1949 the Finnish architect Alvar Aalto designed Baker House at the Massachusetts Institute of Technology. Its serpentine brick wall provides students with views up and down the Charles River—the whole focused on a central dining hall—while the entry staircase on the campus facade functions as a fluid meeting place. Shortly thereafter, Eero Saarinen devised a master plan (unexecuted) for a plaza at MIT opposite the imposing classical main building on Massachusetts Avenue. Two structures remain as tributes to his genius. The interdenominational cylindrical brick chapel (1955) rises from a curvilinear moat, the shifting-light reflections of which bounce across Harry Bertoia's metal altar screen, contributing to the meditative spirituality of an almost mystical space. In contrast, the concrete dome of Kresge Auditorium (1954–55), balanced on three points, stands as a triumph of innovative form.

Yale University was a prime force in modern architecture in the early 1950s. No building contributed more to the cause than Louis Kahn's extension to the Yale Art Gallery (1950–54). An aesthetic best exemplified by Mies van der Rohe's architecture in Chicago, the museum's interior is dominated by a concrete tetrahedral space frame. Architectural expressionism culminated at Yale with Paul Rudolph's Art and Architecture building (1958–62), noted for its striated concrete revetment throughout. Admired at the outset, then vilified, but always influential, Yale's School of Art and Architecture has served as a mirror of attitudes toward modernism.

Rudolph's ideology favoring megastructures led to his design of the ensemble of buildings forming the campus of Southeastern Massachusetts University at Dartmouth (1970s). At Yale, noteworthy examples of modernism's variety are seen in Saarinen's Morse and Stiles Colleges, dormitories sympathetic both to students and to the university context. In the Ingalls Hockey Rink (1957), Saarinen daringly defined the building's function, its parabolic curves and overall rhythm simulating the game. Gordon Bunshaft's Beinecke Library (1961) also spoke of contents, the rare marbles and elegant sunken court with sculpture by Isamu Noguchi hinting at the rare books and manuscripts within.

In nearby New Canaan, Conn., Philip Johnson, coauthor of *The International Style* and organizer of the first architectural exhibit at New York's Museum of Modern Art in 1932, erected his Glass House (1949), the essence of industrial modernity, though guided by classical tenets, as dictated by Mies.

In the same year, Frank Lloyd Wright built a Usonian house for Dr. Zimmerman and his wife in Manchester, N.H. Of moderate cost, it incorporates his design philosophy, based on organic principles. The Zimmerman house is an integral part of the surrounding landscape, as compared to the Johnson house, which is a veritable "machine in the garden."

In architecture, as in politics, the 1960s constitute a watershed. The glass-curtain wall, symbolic of the corporate economy, transformed the profile of cities large and small. A glance at the skyline of any downtown area, be it Stamford, Conn., or Worcester, Mass., reveals clusters of undistinguished high-rise buildings. Once symbols of aspiration and power, the postwar skyscrapers created a monotonous townscape, reinforced by the bleak housing projects that developed largely on the urban periphery. Exceptions include Constitution Plaza in Hartford, Conn. (1960s). The glass surface of Phoenix Mutual Life's elliptical tower (Harrison and Abramowitz), however, could not prevent the subsequent decline of the city.

Boston's relative resistance to modernism was shattered by the master plan that I. M. Pei drew for Government Center, which would determine the future prospect of the city and reverse the fortune of the central business district. Under the guise of urban renewal, the Boston Redevelopment Authority sponsored the demolition of 85 percent of the building on the 60-acre site of the West End and old Scollay Square. Centering on the enormous brick plaza, the plan's fulcrum was the new City Hall (1962–69), designed by Kallmann, McKinnell, and Knowles. A product of 1960s mentality, the goal was a "celebration of government," to encourage interaction between the citizens and the machinery of the legislative bodies, visually as well as physically. Even more monolithic, Rudolph's State Services Building (1970), combining the Health, Education, and Welfare Departments, presents an amalgam of ridged concrete, labyrinthine passageways, and theatrical spaces, originally designed to converge on a central tower (unexecuted).

Across the river in Cambridge, concrete was poured in abundance when José Luis Sert became dean of Harvard's Graduate School of Design and constructed a series of buildings that hardly betray his Mediterranean roots. Holyoke Center (1965), harboring information services, the enormous Science Center (1972), and the three dormitory towers of Peabody Terrace (1964) incorporate vocabulary used in Le Corbusier's Unité d'Habitation outside Marseilles. Boston University's amorphous campus was given visibility by the tower of its law school (1964), fronting on the

Charles River, designed by Sert's firm. But the momentous event was the building of Le Corbusier's Carpenter Center for the Visual Arts at Harvard (1960–63), a giant sculptural mass hedged between the neo-Georgian Fogg Art Museum and the Faculty Club. Kevin Roche also built arts centers during this period at the University of Massachusetts (Amherst campus), and at Wesleyan University in Middletown, Conn.

Renewal of Boston's Back Bay began with the multiuse Prudential Center complex (Charles Luckman, 1960s), since enlarged and restructured, featuring a large-scale shopping mall. I. M. Pei's rebuilding and expansion of the Christian Science Center (1973) transformed the southwest border of the Back Bay, providing linkage to the South End and Massachusetts Avenue. A masterful site plan creates open spaces between the Mother Church, the Sunday School, and the administrative tower. In 2000–2002, Ann Beha Associates was in charge of a renovation program for the complex, featuring the Mary Baker Eddy Library for the Betterment of Humanity.

As the financial, commercial, and banking center of New England, Boston underwent a building boom from the mid-1970s until 1990. No structure has been more prominent than the John Hancock building (I. M. Pei, 1970–75), the history of which has been marred by severe engineering problems, extending to the weakening of infrastructure surrounding Copley Square landmarks. The Hancock today is the quintessential ornament to the city, a fulfillment of Pei's paper plans, a paean to the art of the skyscraper.

An increase in adaptive reuse followed the unrest of the 1960s, the Arab oil crisis, the passage of the National Historic Preservation Act of 1966, the Boston Landmarks legislation of 1976, and disenchantment with many post–World War II buildings. To commemorate the nation's Bicentennial, the city, together with the Rouse Corporation, undertook a massive renovation of the Quincy Market area, a pioneering project in entertainment marketplaces. More important, this renovation stimulated the rehabilitation of the entire waterfront area and gave birth to new glass towers, along with their postmodern descendants. Among the skyscrapers, the Federal Reserve Building (Hugh Stubbins, 1977–78) is conspicuous by virtue of its high-tech aspects embodied in the powerful formal stance of its aluminum-sheathed tower, reflecting changing atmospheric states.

Additions to the academic landscape continued, few more notable than Louis Kahn's library at Exeter, N.H. (1970). Its brick exterior bows to the older buildings of the academy, while the interior dramatically bespeaks

Phoenix Mutual Life Building (Harrison and Abramowitz, 1963), Hartford

the functions of a library—to provide a place to read and store books. Its geometric components, intimate spaces, and luxurious details are engulfed in a poetic play of light. Philip Johnson's addition to the Beaux-Arts Boston Public Library (1973) adheres to the older building's scale and materials, but the interior is austere, the lobby overbearing.

A transformation in the modern aesthetic occurred with the proliferation of high-rise commercial buildings in the 1980s in every New England urban center. Adhering to the historicist, postmodern style, these structures are characterized by the surface ornaments of classicism—namely, pedimental cornices, Palladian windows, interior atria, exotic greenery—in addition to being touched by some of the whimsy and streamlined decor that marked the architecture of the 1920s and 1930s. Testimony is found in a glance at the business districts of Providence, New Haven and Stamford, Conn., and Springfield, Mass., as well as in the domestic architecture throughout the region.

The era also featured the promotion of contextual architecture, apparent with varying degrees of success in museum additions in Portland, Maine (Henry Cobb of I. M. Pei, 1983), the Hood Art Museum in Hanover, N.H., and the Williams College Museum, Williamstown, Mass. (both by Charles Moore, 1985, 1983–86), the Arthur M. Sackler Museum (James Stirling, 1984) and later the Busch-Reisinger Museum (Gwathmey Siegel, 1990), both at Harvard, and, not least, the Yale Center for British Art (1974–77), Kahn's swan song at Yale, which faces his earlier art museum. Changing times called for a new language, and the Center for British Art shows concern with the streetscape in form and usage: the ground story accommodates both town and gown, and the entry simulates a British hall therefore serving as the appropriate home for the museum's contents.

Respect for the past, hardly surprising in New England, was perpetuated in the region's buildings in the 1990s, as evident in Ozawa Hall, the Music Shed at Tanglewood in Lenox, Mass. (William Rawn, 1994). Urbanistic interventions include the conversion of a warehouse to Tower Records (Frank Gehry, 1987) on a site fronting the Massachusetts Turnpike and the formation of open spaces in Post Office Square Park (Harry Ellenzweig, 1989–90) in downtown Boston. Glimpses of a revival in the rail network are visible along the northeast corridor in rehabilitated stations in New Haven, Providence, Worcester, Mass., and Boston, as well as in the subway system of Boston. Still, the victory is for the private rather than the public domain—for the automobile rather than mass transit—in the form of the largest federal project in the country: the depression of the central artery in downtown Boston ("the Big Dig"), constituting a window on the past and a refusal to come to grips with the future.

Back in the mid-1960s, Christopher Rand dubbed Cambridge the hub of a "new universe" because of the high-tech areas concentrated there and around Route 128. Currently, the immediate area around MIT is the East Coast equivalent to Silicon Valley; the newly converted buildings along the Charles are occupied by computer-related industries, vital to the current strong economy of the region. Perhaps the most outstanding single structure of the 1990s is the Federal Court House (Pei Cobb Fried, 1998) on Fan Pier in Boston. No longer a center of American town life, this enormous structure may stimulate growth in the harbor area. The restoration of the Bulfinch Court House in Cambridge (Graham Gund, 1986) attempts to revive the symbolic import of this once dominant building type, as does the new Suffolk County Courthouse on New Chardon Street in Boston (Kallmann, McKinnell, Wood, 2000).

Like the country at large, the region participated on a grand scale in the malling of America. Indeed, one of the first malls was Shopper's World in Framingham, Mass., which opened on October 4, 1951. More copious on the outskirts, these huge shopping complexes, catering largely to suburbanites, have also penetrated the inner city, as marked by Copley Place and the Prudential Center in Back Bay, Boston, and by Providence Place in Providence. Characteristic, too, of major cities, is the proliferation of medical buildings—the

enlargement of Massachusetts General and the Longwood Hospital areas in Boston and the facilities in the Dartmouth-Hitchcock Medical Center in Lebanon, N.H. (1990s), cited as a New England medical village.

Nevertheless, although New England harbors prime examples of modern architecture, its general architectural fabric—spired white churches, village greens, authentic works of Federal and Georgian architecture—remains unique to the region. (Tracy Kidder's best-selling *House* [1985] chronicled the construction of a Massachusetts house, a postmodern updating of the Greek Revival style that is iconic of New England villages.) Old fishing towns and industrial cities have decayed, but there are intermittent signs of renewal. Excellent examples of community, commercial, and domestic architecture exist throughout the region, evident in the works of such Boston firms as Andrea Leers-Jane Weinzapel, Schwartz-Silver, and out-of-state architects like Robert Venturi and Denise Scott Brown Venturi.

Environmentally, Vermont is the most intact of all New England states. There, modern architecture is dominated by the vacation industry, as seen in the building of ski resorts, modest domestic homes, and campus architecture, all with respect to the local New England vernacular. New England's general prosperity in the 1990s led to renewed building by high-tech corporations and major universities. "Celebrity" architects have been commissioned to design highly visible buildings such as the Stata Center at MIT (Frank Gehry, 2004) and the postmodern Norman Rockwell Museum in Stockbridge, Mass. (Robert A. M. Stern, 1993).

Most significant, however, is the attempt to revitalize downtown areas of major New England capitals, namely Providence and Hartford. Thus far Providence has had remarkable success, whereas Hartford continues its downward course. As the one major city in Rhode Island, Providence was ready for a revival for several reasons: it is a railroad hub between Boston and New York, boasts two major universities, and possesses a significant sampling of pre–Civil War architecture. The opening of Waterplace Park and Riverwalk (William D. Warner, 1994), the rebuilding of the Amtrak station (SOM, 1986), and the addition of hotels, malls, and office buildings in the vicinity of the state house led to a cultural, as well as an urban, revival.

Underplaying the social tenets of modernism, New England has always maintained ties to its European ancestry. In the global economy at the beginning of the 21st century, the region enlists new technologies while at the same time guarding its heritage.

William J. R. Curtis, *Boston: Forty Years of Modern Architecture* (1980); Eva Jacob, *New Architecture in New England* (1974); Donlyn Lyndon, *Boston: The City Observed* (1982); Naomi Miller and Keith Morgan, *Boston Architecture, 1975–1990* (1990); Susan and Michael Southworth, *AIA Guide to Boston* (1992).

Naomi Miller

Appleton, William Sumner, Jr.

(1874–1947) Antiquarian, preservationist. The founder and first manager of the Society for the Preservation of New England Antiquities (SPNEA), the region's preeminent preservation agency (now Historic New England), William Sumner Appleton, Jr., significantly influenced not only the shaping of New England's architectural heritage but also the development of the modern preservation movement in the United States.

Appleton was born in Boston, descended from one of the city's most prominent families; his grandfather Nathan helped establish the textile industry at nearby Lowell. Reared on Beacon Hill and educated at Saint Paul's School in New Hampshire, Appleton attended Harvard (1892–1896), where he studied under the historians Edward Channing and Albert B. Hart, the literary critic Barrett Wendell and, most influential to his budding interest in architecture, the fine arts professors Charles Eliot Norton and Denman Ross. Young Appleton's inability to establish a career, however, together with family pressures, led to a nervous collapse in 1904.

Meanwhile, New England's physical and cultural landscapes were dramatically changing. With increasing urbanization, older homes and neighborhoods were giving way to apartment houses, office buildings, and tenements. With increased immigration and the rise of nativism, Boston's Yankees perceived themselves as a pressed minority. Under the mantle of progressivism and simultaneous with the Colonial Revival movement, many strove to remake their cultural identity and restore the social leadership of their group through an affirmation of values associated with colonial life and its architecture.

Recovering from his ill health, Appleton immersed himself in the activities of the Sons of the Revolution. In 1905 he organized a campaign to preserve Boston's Paul Revere House. In addition to remaking Revere's memory and architectural legacy, that drive defined historic preservation as a means to boost tourism, Americanize immigrants, and define appropriate Yankee values. Pledging to focus full time on the preservation of historic buildings and to accent scientific method, business-minded management, and architectural aesthetics, SPNEA (founded 1910) helped professionalize and masculinize the preservation movement. The unmarried Appleton invested his life and wealth in SPNEA. Besides writing the society's *Bulletin* for its first decade and regularly contributing to SPNEA's journal, *Old-Time New England*, thereafter, he occasionally wrote for the Boston and New York metropolitan newspapers.

By the time of Appleton's death in Lawrence, SPNEA had acquired not only an extensive archive but almost 50 properties, mostly 17th- and early 18th-century homes scattered throughout eastern Massachusetts, coastal Maine, and New Hampshire. These buildings typically reflected Appleton's cultural interests: his medievalist enchantment with Anglo-Saxonism; his antimodernist identification with rough-hewn, timber-frame carpentry; and his love for the small towns and countryside. He continually urged New Englanders of diverse backgrounds to preserve and respect that heritage. Influenced by the architects Norman M. Isham and Joseph E. Chandler, Appleton accepted the contemporary practice of remaking early structures in the name of restoring them to their ostensibly original appearance. Nonetheless, he generally based his restorations on the findings of historical archaeology and made his scientific methodology a standard for the field throughout New England and the nation.

Charles B. Hosmer, Jr., *Presence of the Past: A History of the Preservation Movement in the United States before Williamsburg* (1965); James M. Lindgren, *Preserving Historic New England: Preservation, Progressivism, and the Remaking of Memory* (1995); "William Sumner Appleton, 1874–1947," *Old-Time New England* 38 (April 1948).

James M. Lindgren

Barns and Farm Buildings

Perhaps the key distinguishing characteristic of New England agricultural architecture in all periods is the quantity and variety of buildings on a typical farm. English farm builders brought with them an ancient tradition of constructing separate agricultural buildings for separate operations, so that a prosperous farm in 1800 might have included a major English barn, granary, stable, pig house, wood house or woodshed, and numerous other specialized sheds for crop and animal shelter and craft activities. These various agricultural structures are still apparent on surviving farms that have preserved complete records of their farm buildings.

The architectural style of most early farm buildings was English; the varying forms depended on the era of construction and the function of the building. Although some, such as the principal barn, are recognizable by their size and shape, many are not, in that the distinction between barns and other farm build-

Barn frame during dismantling, Chichester, N.H.

ings in New England is subtle. Sheds and other outbuildings, for example, were often constructed in the same manner as small barns. Moreover, farm buildings were often used for nonfarm practices such as home industries and crafts, further complicating the identification of New England's many and disparate farm buildings.

English traditions gave a unique quality to New England's architecture. Despite the basic ethnic homogeneity of the region during colonial times, English farmers were exposed to new architectural ideas through farm journals. The successes of colonial German barn builders in Pennsylvania, for example, were widely publicized throughout New England and influenced the design and development of 19th-century New England barns.

New England barns and farm buildings have historically been used for processing, sheltering, and storing agricultural products, animals, and implements. Although today's metal barns differ slightly from one another, early barns could be classified according to their design, structural system, and functional characteristics. By 1810 or so, English building traditions had essentially been abandoned in New England, and new practices—reinforcing greater unity and standardization in barn construction and usage—were adopted, resulting in the ubiquitous all-American, double-sloped, gambrel-roof barn.

The basic unit of agricultural building brought by English settlers was the three-bay English barn with the major door in the center of the eave side. In England this barn was for

hay threshing and storage, but because of New England's severe climate, this style was enlarged and adapted for animals. For nearly 200 years, the English barn, with its medieval, heavy-timber, mortise-and-tenon construction system, was the choice of New England farmers. After 1800, the all-important entrance changed from the eave side to the gable end. The new barn type was simpler to build and easy to expand, by the addition of multiple bays along a central service drive. By the 1850s, it was the dominant barn style in New England.

The development of this new, larger barn was associated with the expansion of dairy farming, which meant allowing more room for animals and feed. At that time, some extraordinarily large barns were constructed, including those at Canterbury Shaker Village, the largest in the state of New Hampshire. New Englanders also experimented with other forms, such as round barns, with notable survivors in Vermont (at Westview Farm in Waterford and Round Barn Farm in Waitsfield), and the great classic stone barn at Hancock Shaker Village in Massachusetts.

There are two major wood structural systems of the New England barn: the medieval, hand-hewn, heavy-timber, mortise-and-tenon system; and the modern, machine-tooled, balloon-frame, stud-and-nail system. Between 1850 and 1950, these two fundamentally different modes of construction vied with and overlapped each other. In the 1850s the medieval system dominated, but by the 1920s only the major structural frame remained from the older system, while the rest of the barn followed newer technological systems.

During the last quarter of the 19th century, farmers began to adopt the double-sloped roof or gambrel barn, but this style never became as popular in New England as it was in other areas of the country. Because of the many declines in New England's agricultural economy during the 20th century, most surviving farm buildings originate from the 19th and early 20th centuries. The farms that have survived into the late 20th and early 21st centuries generally have additional one-story, metal-clad buildings with concrete floors and industrial, wood-truss construction. Although lamented by rural preservationists, these new buildings reflect the spirit of change and experimentation characteristic of the New England farm since the early 19th century.

Because of the long history of mixed farming and home industry in New England, little distinction in either exterior form or construction exists between agricultural and nonagricultural buildings. In fact, on a typical New England farm, agricultural buildings may stretch from the principal barn to the house in a smooth or jagged line, connecting many building types and incorporating changes in usage over time. So popular was this tradition that the linking of diverse agricultural buildings became a distinct regional style in New England during the 19th century.

As agriculture declined in the 20th century, the New England barn entered the region's symbolic landscape through the work of such artists and illustrators as Maxfield Parrish, Eric Sloane, and Andrew and Jamie Wyeth. The rapid loss of barns to development, neglect, and fire has led to preservation movements in several states; many historic barns are now preserved at farm museums or have been moved for preservation and display to such sites as the Shelburne Museum and Old Sturbridge Village. Some post-and-beam construction companies specialize in traditional barn construction, thereby keeping traditional skills alive, albeit for wealthy clients.

Henry Glassie, *Pattern in the Material Folk Culture of the Eastern United States* (1969); Thomas C. Hubka, *Big House, Little House, Back House, Barn* (1984); Allen G. Noble, *Wood, Brick, and Stone: The North American Settlement Landscape* (1984); Thomas D. Visser, *Field Guide to New England Barns and Farm Buildings* (1997).

Thomas C. Hubka

Benjamin, Asher (ca. 1773–1845) Architect and author. Asher Benjamin, one of the most influential architectural writers in America during the first half of the 19th century, was born in Greenfield, Mass. Although no apprenticeship document survives, it is

likely that he served as an apprentice to a housewright in the vicinity of Suffield, Conn., where he began to receive payments for specialized architectural ornaments, such as Ionic capitals, in 1794. That he was employed to design and install the circular staircases in Charles Bulfinch's Connecticut State Capitol in Hartford in 1794 is further testimony to his precocious talent. Between 1796 and 1801 Benjamin practiced as a housewright in such Connecticut River valley towns as Deerfield and Greenfield, Mass., and Windsor, Vt.

In 1797 Benjamin published *The Country Builder's Assistant*, a modest carpenters' guide derived from, but intended to undercut, similar English guides by William Pain, William Halfpenny, and other writers. It was the first such book by an American. In 1799 he advertised a school of architecture, one of the first in America, in the *Windsor* (Vt.) *Gazette* but soon thereafter moved to Boston. After several years of obscurity, he established an architectural practice and designed a substantial number of handsome Federal-style churches, town houses, and detached houses, including the Charles Street Meetinghouse (1806–07), the Old West Church (1806), the Chauncey Street Church (1808), and houses for James Colburn (1808), William Minot (1807), and Edward Everett (c. 1808). The Exchange Coffee House (1809), one of the first multifunctional hotel buildings in America, was also a Benjamin commission. Approximately 50 buildings can be identified as Benjamin's designs, with a high concentration in the Boston area and additional commissions scattered throughout New England. It is likely that he designed many more than are documented.

Benjamin's principal means of supporting his family and his chief claim to prominence in the history of American architecture, however, were his builders' guides, which he wrote, revised, and published at the rate of one every two or three years, from 1797 until his death. Altogether he wrote seven books that appeared in more than 50 editions. The impact of these books in New England and throughout the eastern United States was extensive; to a degree, they defined the Federal and Greek Revival styles for the average American during the first half of the 19th century. With the advent of the Greek Revival style in the 1820s Benjamin avoided any commitment to temple imagery and cannily developed a simple decorative vocabulary derived from the Greek fret. The *Practical House Carpenter* (1830) became his most successful book; its influence is visible today in hundreds of fretted frontispieces throughout New England. Indeed, the restrained nature of Benjamin's work in both the Federal and Greek Revival styles seems to be an unconscious expression of the New En-

gland ethos. Benjamin died in Springfield, Mass.

Kenneth Hafertepe and James F. O'Gorman, *American Architects and Their Books to 1848* (2001); Florence Thompson Howe, "Asher Benjamin, Country Builder's Assistant," *Antiques* 40 (1941); Jack Quinan, "Asher Benjamin and American Architecture," *Journal of the Society of Architectural Historians* 38 (October 1979); Juliette Tomlinson, "Asher Benjamin, Connecticut Architect," *The Connecticut Antiquarian* 6 (1954).

Jack Quinan

Building Materials When the German immigrant Walter Gropius designed an American house for himself in 1936–37, it naturally showcased the principles of the "New Architecture" he had come to Harvard to teach. But in carrying through the project in the Boston suburb of Lincoln, Gropius made a concession he would not have made in Germany: he built his house of wood and allowed it to be framed—and rather heavily so—in the idiom of the local carpenters. Was he displaying a newcomer's sensitivity to regional custom or merely recognizing that in New England this was the easiest way of translating design into substance? Probably both. And despite his subsequent efforts—and those of the Bostonian R. Buckminster Fuller—New England never abandoned its attachment to wood and brick assembled into rather traditional forms.

New England's early settlers found the land more heavily wooded than England and laced with waterways that made moving softwood timber relatively easy. Initially imitating the Indians' wigwams, frameworks of saplings covered with birch bark or animal skins, the settlers quickly turned to more substantial wooden structures. But the strong local relation with lumber was shaped by more than nature. Beginning in the 17th century, the West Indian trade and the region's singular demographic growth spurred a production, commodification, and even standardization of light building lumber unusual by either American or English standards. The riving of clapboards, shingles, and laths for domestic use and export became an important source of rural employment; boards and planks were produced in sawmills, a technology virtually unknown in England. By 1700 New England was exporting boards and other lumber to the equally wooded southern colonies, which lacked the waterpower and mill infrastructure to compete with the North.

New England's marriage of English carpentry with continental sawmill technology is a process about which we know little. But the region's vernacular architecture came to be more thoroughly wooden than that of England, characterized by a complex layering of light lumber around the basic English frame, a development that extended carpentry's traditional domain. Building with brick, by contrast, began relatively late and was never as prevalent as in parts of the Middle Atlantic and southern states, contemporary imagery notwithstanding. John Winthrop's early attempts to build with brick were frustrated by poor sources of clay. After a series of devastating fires throughout the late 17th and 18th centuries in Boston, Portsmouth, N.H., and other seaports, brick and slate replaced wood-sheathed and shingled buildings. With the rise of industrial cities in the 19th century, large-scale brick making and granite quarrying provided needed materials. New England buildings that appeared to be constructed of brick were usually masonry shells with wooden infill. Influenced by the difficulty of working granite (a plentiful local resource), carpenters also became adept at imitating stone architecture in their own medium. Only by uniting significant capital, political influence, and immigrant workers in the late 19th century was New England granite fully exploited.

Granite quarried in Quincy, Mass., for the Bunker Hill Monument was transported to Charlestown by America's first railroad. Granite quarrying was so extensive in Concord, N.H., by the time of General Lafayette's visit in 1825, that he nicknamed New Hampshire "the Granite State." Large public structures made of granite, such as Quincy Market in Boston (1825) and the Vermont Capitol Building in Montpelier (1832), helped turn it into a popular building material. In Vermont, the Granite Hills, especially the highest—Millstone Hill in Barre—offered a limitless supply; stone from this quarry is still used in buildings today. Granite quarries on islands along the Maine coast were used in the 19th and 20th centuries. In smaller cities and towns in northern New England, a distinctive combination of brick with a first-story granite facade became a signature style for commercial buildings. By the 1830s commercial quarrying of marble was under way in Vermont, providing stone for urban buildings, especially decorative blocks carved by Italian artisans who arrived throughout the 19th century. Rutland, Vt., was also a source for builder's slate. Brownstone from quarries in Middletown, Conn., was used in buildings locally and exported to Boston as early as the 17th century; quarries along the Connecticut River into Massachusetts supplied brownstone for architectural styles popularized by Henry Hobson Richardson and others working in the Romanesque and other revival styles.

The lumber industry also contributed to the early division of New England into producer and consumer regions. Densely forested Maine ("the Pine Tree State")—and to a lesser extent New Hampshire—long functioned primarily as lumber reserves for southern New England and only secondarily as agricultural land. With granite, slate, lime, and brick added to their list of exportable commodities in the 19th century, both states came to define themselves as suppliers of building materials. This geography of production and consumption would be replicated in the upper Midwest and on the Pacific coast in the 19th century, largely at the impetus of New England settlers. Today, many New England builders and architects retain a preference for wood, brick, granite, and other local materials.

Charles Carroll, *The Timber Economy of Puritan New England* (1973); Abbott Lowell Cummings, *The Framed Houses of Massachusetts Bay, 1625–1725* (1979); Mark Erlich, *With Our Hands: The Story of Carpenters in Massachusetts* (1986); Gilbert Herbert, *The Dream of the Factory-Made House: Walter Gropius and Conrad Wachsmann* (1984).

Gregory Clancey

Bulfinch, Charles (1763–1844) Architect. Perhaps the region's best-known designer, Charles Bulfinch is often claimed among the nation's first professional architects. Born into Boston's wealthy and educated elite, Bulfinch was educated at Harvard, toured Europe as a young man, and showed a lifelong interest in architecture. He provided "gratuitous advice in Architecture" to his family and associates and developed a wide reputation for his designs. The critical event of his professional career was the financial failure of his most ambitious project, the complex of buildings at Franklin Place in Boston that included the Tontine Crescent. Having lost his own and several family members' fortunes, Bulfinch was required to take paid employment to augment his fees for architectural designs. He served as chair of Boston's board of selectmen for 19 years; his parallel post as superintendent of police provided him a regular income. In 1817 he was appointed architect of the U.S. Capitol and spent the next 13 years in Washington. On his return to Boston in 1830 he led a retired and quiet life until his death at age 80.

Bulfinch's architectural output was large and diverse, with as many as 75 projects to his credit during the 30 years that constituted the core of his New England career. He won commissions for the period's most prestigious projects, including state houses for three states in the region, four Massachusetts county courthouses, and many of the public buildings constructed or remodeled in Boston. The architect's personal accounting listed eight churches and meetinghouses, six banks, four insurance buildings, five school and college buildings, two hospitals, a theater, a concert hall, a market, a prison, a jail, and an almshouse. Spread throughout the region and beyond through their publication in pattern books and periodicals, Bulfinch's buildings were well known and widely imitated.

Bulfinch's designs include a number of exceptional works, executed in both the richly ornamented early neoclassical style and its later, more purely geometric phases. His notable early works include the first Boston Theater (1793–94), the Massachusetts State House (1795–97), and the United States Bank in Boston (1798). Later examples, more commonly executed in stone, include the Suffolk County Courthouse (1810–12) and the octagonal New South Church (1814). His domestic commissions for both city and country houses provided sophisticated plans for genteel living, seen in the Joseph Barrell house (1792–93) and the Beacon Street house of Harrison Gray Otis (1805–08).

As city planner and architect, Bulfinch played a critical role in Boston's shift from a mixed array of freestanding wood buildings toward a more uniform landscape of brick; Franklin Place (1793–95), Park Row (1803–05), and the Colonnade (1810–12) attest to the importance he attributed to this aspect of his work. In a rapidly growing city, Bulfinch oversaw a broad range of improvements and new construction at an unprecedented scale. Bulfinch's use of ornament and innovative domestic planning and his ambitious goal of regularizing the urban landscape placed him among the most accomplished designers of the period. His contribution to the reshaping of the region's landscape remains underappreciated.

Kenneth Hafertepe and James F. O'Gorman, *American Architects and Their Books to 1848* (2001); Harold Kirker, *The Architecture of Charles Bulfinch* (1969).

Claire W. Dempsey

Camp Meeting Cottages The camp meeting cottage is a unique building type invented circa 1860 at Wesleyan Grove, the Methodist camp meeting place in the historic core of Oak Bluffs on Martha's Vineyard, Mass. This cottage form spread to other camp meetings and religious resorts throughout New England and the nation. Transmitted, perhaps, by pattern books, where they appear as "Martha's Vineyard Cottages," but more likely through stereopticon photographs, cottage versions can be found in Yarmouth, Sterling, Framingham, and Hamilton, Mass.; Old Orchard Beach and Ocean Park, Maine; and Plainville and Willimantic, Conn. Similar cottages stand or once stood at Methodist revival grounds in Ocean Grove, N.J.; Round

Wesleyan Grove Camp Meeting cottages, Oak Bluffs, Martha's Vineyard, Mass.

much material display for a once poor people, their defenders could respond that they proved that Christians did as well as "heathens" because the camp meeting worked for them as an "engine of progress." The cottages both enabled and celebrated a middle-class communitarianism.

Kenneth O. Brown, *Holy Ground: A Study of the American Camp Meeting* (1992); Stanford E. Demars, "Worship By-the-Sea: Camp Meetings and Seaside Resorts in 19th-Century America," *Focus* 38, no. 4 (Winter 1988); Ellen Weiss, *City in the Woods: The Life and Design of an American Camp Meeting on Martha's Vineyard* (1987).

Ellen Weiss

Catholic Churches Historically, Catholic culture and values in New England have been expressed by ecclesiastical architecture. Spanning nearly 400 years of service to an ethnically pluralistic constituency, Catholic churches in New England are diverse in architectural styles and liturgical arts. At present, there are about 1,500 parishes in New England, serving approximately 5 million Catholics, nearly 40 percent of the region's population. Catholic life revolves around the church edifice and the parish, the defining unit and institution by which new immigrants are integrated into American society.

French Jesuit missionaries arrived to minister to Native Americans in northern Maine and built the first documented chapel in 1604 on the island of Sainte-Croix in Passamaquoddy Bay. The 17th- and 18th-century missionary outposts along the Atlantic seaboard contained chapels that are believed to have been small rectangular timber-framed structures with gabled roofs.

Acadian French in Aroostook County, Maine, built distinctive wood churches in the Saint John River valley by translating the Christian basilica form from stone into simple vernacular with few academic details. A rare remaining example of colonial-era style is Our Lady of Mount Carmel (1909, Madawaska, Maine), built by Theophile Daoust. The basic elements are a tall central nave with a high-pitched gabled roof and clerestory flanked by distinct aisles. Each aisle has a series of six elongated arched windows surrounded by simple wooden molding. The clear glass has an intricate mullion design of double arches topped by a circular motif.

The Acadian tradition of the harvest mass is preserved at nearby Saint David's parish in Grand Isle, Maine, where the concept of sacred space extends beyond a church building. The annual mass is held inside a dirt-floor building used for storing potatoes, decorated for the event with lavish displays of fruits, vegetables, and foliage in celebration of God's

Lake and Shelter Island, N.Y.; Lakeside, Ohio; Des Plaines, Ill.; Bay View, Mich.; and Pacific Grove, Calif., as well as at meetings of other denominations or of Chautauquas, camp meeting outgrowths.

The Wesleyan Grove camp meeting cottage is a one-and-a-half story rectangular cabin, some 11 to 16 feet wide and about twice as deep, with its short, or gable end to the front containing a fixed arrangement of doors and windows. Because the buildings are placed closely together, limiting side views, all architectural ornament is restricted to this facade. The ornamentation can include two different patterns of sawn board or "gingerbread" dropped from the eaves and from a balcony that is cantilevered over the central entry. Double doors—typically in a round-headed Romanesque style, or a pointed Gothic style—open from the second floor onto a cantilevered balcony, a useful arrangement for hauling furniture up to the bedrooms. In the lower level, two lancet windows with matching round or pointed tops bracket central double doors. The doors, exceptionally wide for the building's size, allude both to the tents which previously stood on the site and to churches, which for Methodists of southern New England could be either Romanesque or Gothic. The cottage facades layered church and tent references onto the form of a house to make a new building type.

The cottages were also unusual structurally. They were built of vertical pine planks laid over a light frame of six 4-by-4 posts without any intermediary bracing. The planking must have acted as lateral support. Doors and windows were cut out of the plank wall, the remaindered pieces fixed with battens to be used as shutters during the winter. The wide double doors, when open, reveal almost the entire interior, making for a remarkable lack of privacy. Family life was on display with what seemed to outside observers a studied indifference to scrutiny, in that inhabitants went about their domestic routines in full view of strangers. This was, in some sense, part of the program. Methodist revivalists wanted to forge their families into a tribe similar to the ancient Israelites, to breed a community of feeling that would compensate for the long year when they were isolated by rural distances or, most often, by urban tensions because of what they saw as the greed and selfishness of a competitive, materialistic age.

At Oak Bluffs, the cottages, about 500 of them, opened onto tent platforms that met the public paths and parks directly without spatial mediation. They sat packed together in concentric circles around the tabernacle, on radial lanes, or around smaller tangential circles that served as extra preaching spaces for Big Sunday. The cottages and their community arrangement thus became a critique of the physical, social, and moral isolation their inhabitants had fled. And if tourists, attracted by the fame of the intensely dramatic revival week, found that the cottages evoked too

The Cathedral of the Immaculate Conception (Patrick Keely, 1869), Portland, Maine

bounty. French Canadians eventually settled throughout New England and the spread of Catholicism influenced church architecture throughout the region.

The stabilization of the Catholic Church in New England through a vigorous building program was the legacy of two French priests: Francis Anthony Matignon (1753–1818) and John Cheverus (1768–1836). During the episcopacy of Bishop Cheverus (1810–23), five new churches were erected throughout the region to serve a growing Catholic constituency.

In 1800 a few hundred Irish Catholics who had been renting a Huguenot meetinghouse for Catholic services commissioned Charles Bulfinch to build Boston's first Catholic church—Holy Cross on Devonshire Street (1803). Bulfinch created a Renaissance tripartite facade separated by Ionic pilasters; a cupola graces the entrance, flanked by baroque consoles.

The oldest extant Catholic church in New England is Saint Patrick's (1807), a Federal-style structure of native brick on a hill overlooking the Damariscotta River in Damariscotta Mills, Maine, built by Nicholas Codd, an Irish housewright who built homes for the wealthy parish founders whose lumber mills provided materials for Boston churches. The interior panels of Saint Patrick's include shallow relief carvings of a harp surmounting an olive branch, a reminder of the congregation's Irish roots. The pews are backless plank benches, and according to the custom, women sat on the Epistle side (right) and men on the Gospel side.

The period of greatest Catholic immigration (mostly Irish) took place between 1820 and 1860; 85 percent of Catholics settled in urban areas. The resultant need for churches created a building boom that was subsidized by loyal parishioners and energetic clergy known affectionately as the "brick and mortar" priests. Saint Mary's (1823), the oldest church in New Hampshire, was built in Claremont with funds from French Catholics in Maine. The Sacred Heart parish (1878) in Hallowell, Maine, was built by parishioners who, after a full day's work in the quarries, came to the hillside site in the evening with lanterns to build the Gothic clapboard structure. Saint Denis's in Fort Fairfield, Maine, which began in 1842 as a small wood-frame structure with a gabled roof on a stone foundation, was replaced in 1872 by a larger wooden Gothic building with short twin towers and a clapboard exterior. The congregation continued to grow and prosper, and in 1930 the modest building was again replaced, by an eclectic stone church with a tall asymmetrical tower. The extravagantly ornate coffering and sculpture and neoclassical interior of the equally eclectic brick Saint Anne's (1899) in Berlin, N.H., designed by M. H. Roy of Lewiston, Maine, belie the economic modesty of this paper-producing mill town.

From the Civil War through the 1950s the Catholic Church continued to grow in New England through an influx of Irish, French Canadian, Italian, German, Portuguese, and eastern European immigrants. Many urban churches from the 1960s onward were revitalized by the reconstituted congregations made up of Hispanic, Asian, and African immigrants. Ukrainian Catholics of the Eastern Rite often built Byzantine churches such as Saints Peter and Paul (1915) in Ansonia, Conn., to reflect the architecture of their native country. Lithuanian artists, fleeing from communism, devoted their talents to ecclesiastical arts; Vytautas Jonynas designed the interior of the Saint Anthony shrine (1965) in Kennebunkport, Maine, a fine example of an expressionist sculptural ensemble.

The dominant style of the 19th and early 20th centuries was Gothic Revival in stone, brick, or wood, with occasional Romanesque, Baroque, or Renaissance elements. An excellent example of the Arts and Crafts style is the Church of the Blessed Sacrament (1888) by Heins and LaFarge in Providence. Parish churches became the epicenters of Catholic complexes, offering facilities for multiple services.

The rapid expansion of the church created a market for an ever-increasing cadre of architects who were beginning to penetrate the mainstream of the architectural profession. Patrick C. Keely was the first architect to build monumental Roman Catholic structures, including cathedrals for the seven archdioceses of New England and scores of parish churches, and his prestige helped soften regional prejudice against Catholics. The recently restored Cathedral of the Holy Cross (1866–75) in Boston is built of Roxbury pudding stone and covers one acre. The largest Catholic church in New England, it seats 3,500 people. The overall design of Saint John's (1856) in Bangor, Maine, is characteristic of Keely's French Gothicism. In the interior of the Cathedral of Saints Peter and Paul (1838), in Providence, exotic marbles and colored hardwoods contribute to the polychromatic effect so frequent in Gothic Revival architecture.

The majestic gray stone Church of Saints Peter and Paul (1928–38) in Lewiston, Maine, was designed by Timothy G. O'Connell on the scale of a Gothic cathedral, complete with Chartres-style stained-glass windows. Its tapered twin square towers and multiple spires rise dramatically from a steep rocky ledge overlooking the town. In the spirit of medieval craftsmanship, O'Connell rejected the convenience of cast stone, opting instead for intricate stone carvings like those found at Saint Mary's (1928) in Stamford, Conn.

Religiously inspired architecture had a forceful spokesman in the prolific writer and lecturer Charles D. Maginnis (1867–1955). The firm of Maginnis and Walsh invigorated Catholic architecture by successfully reinterpreting a wide range of historical styles. Maginnis's seminal design for Saint Catherine of Genoa (1907–21) in Somerville, Mass., influenced numerous architects who imitated its Lombardian style. Holy Family (1923) in Dorchester, Mass., established the firm as leaders in Gothic Revival. The interiors of the Chapel at Emmanuel College in Boston, Sacred Heart Church in Portland, Maine, Christ the King in Rutland, Vt., and the chancel of H. H. Richardson's Trinity Church, Boston, reveal Maginnis's subtle geometry, rhythmic patterns, and hierarchy of enrichment that focus attention on the altar, the theological heart of sacred space. In 1948 Maginnis was awarded the American Institute of Architect's Gold Medal for Achievement.

Following World War II, the urban drain forced the relocation of 80 percent of parishes to the suburbs, a move that sometimes resulted in prefabricated structures of poor quality. In a parallel development, the Catholic Church engaged in a building program of distinguished modernist examples. The Benedictine Order commissioned Pietro Belluschi to design the Portsmouth Priory Chapel (1961) in Rhode Island. Belluschi used an exposed free-standing structural system of radiating laminated wood arches, enclosed by a solid octagon of redwood and fieldstone, on which is superimposed a smaller octagonal nave of vertical wood and stained glass. Richard Lippold created a gold-and-silver filigree sculpture above the altar, which catches the light and radiates it throughout the interior.

Richard Koehler and Nicholas Isaak used contiguous circles to accommodate private meditation spaces and congregational prayer for the Benedictine Abbey Church (1967) at Saint Anselm College in Manchester, N.H. The Cathedral of Saint Joseph (1962) in Hartford, by Otto R. Eggers and Daniel T. Higgins, successors to the firm of John Russell Pope, is U-shaped in plan and contains 26 faceted glass windows nearly 70 feet high and set in reinforced concrete. Its decorative program includes contributions by the International Institute of Liturgical Art in Rome. Three rising metallic planes define the windowless geometry of the Cathedral of the Immaculate Conception (1977) in Burlington, Vt., designed by Edward Larrabee Barnes. The interior is lit by a skylight that runs the length of the nave, throwing immense shadow patterns above a ring of light formed by splayed lunettes. The surrounding grove of locust trees provides additional processional space.

The liturgical changes adopted by the Second Vatican Council (1962–65) emphasized a less hierarchical ordering of interior space, recalling the prayer services of the early church. Recent architecture has responded to contemporary liturgical principles: Saint Anthony's (deCastro Nelson Associates, 1979), Cambridge, Mass.; Saint Raphael's (Keefe Associates, 1993), Medford, Mass.; and Holy Trinity (William E. Whited, 1999), Lisbon Falls, Maine. These design concepts provide welcoming community spaces, often with enclosed courtyards, while the interior ritual spaces flow gracefully to encourage an enhanced level of participation by congregants, a priority of the Vatican reforms.

Marilyn J. Chiat, *America's Religious Architecture* (1997); Dolores Liptak, *Immigrants and Their Church* (1989); Wilfrid H. Paradis, *Upon This Granite: The History of Catholicism in New Hampshire, 1647–1997* (1998); Virginia Chieffo Raguin and Mary Ann Powers, eds., *Sacred Spaces: Building and Remembering Sites of Worship in the 19th Century* (2002); Peter W. Williams, *Houses of God: Region, Religion, and Architecture in the United States* (1997).

Milda B. Richardson

Civic Architecture Civic architecture declares a region's official presence. Buildings dedicated to government offices, community services, and social rituals define the realms of government action (and inaction), of political, economic, and social order, and of public gathering and celebration. Although civic architecture incorporates elements of national authority, it is also firmly rooted in local institutions and traditions. Until the late 19th and early 20th centuries, therefore, New England's civic architecture was closely tied to the most prominent civic institution: the New England town. The earliest civic buildings—meetinghouses and town houses—served New Englanders as places of worship, government halls, marketing centers, and judicial chambers. Beginning in the 18th century and accelerating through the 19th, civic functions for New England towns began to split off from these multipurpose buildings and find homes in an array of purpose-built structures: courthouses, market halls, town halls, armories, fire stations, and auditoriums. At the same time, structures for state government went up in state capitals, and federal architecture began to appear in the form of customhouses, courthouses, and post offices. In the 20th century, as efficiency gained in importance, federal and state office buildings lost distinctiveness as civic architecture began to emulate commercial office design.

Seventeenth-century New England public culture revolved around the meetinghouse. This building provided a place for religious worship, town meetings, and a variety of other functions. Underscoring its use for both sacred and secular purposes, 17th-century documents often describe the meetinghouse as the "town house" or "town's house." In the most prominent and active port towns, however, New Englanders built separate town houses for secular business. New England's first town house was built in Boston in 1657: a three-story wooden structure set on pillars and closely following English town halls and market halls of the period in design and function. The open ground-floor space, initially intended for use as a market, ultimately served the merchants of Boston as an exchange: a place to meet, gather news, and transact business. The upper stories of the Boston Town House provided space for the colonial government and judicial proceedings. A wooden town house known as the Colony House was erected in Newport, R.I., in 1687; similar structures were built in the Massachusetts towns of Salem, Plymouth, and Barnstable.

In the 18th century town houses in New England began to proliferate beyond the seaport centers, spurred in part by the economic prosperity of the period. Spreading notions of gentility also caused New Englanders to rethink their townscapes and advocate new types of public and social buildings. In addition, a shift in the symbolic function of the meetinghouse led to a desire for structures reserved exclusively for sacred activities, and townspeople often moved secular business to the newly built town houses. Towns like Newtown and Lebanon, Conn.; East Greenwich, R.I.; Falmouth, Hadley, and Westfield, Mass.; Exeter, N.H.; and York, Maine, also built town houses in a bid to retain the county court sessions and their attendant economic prosperity. In these cases, a building committee comprising county justices and town select-

Boston City Hall (Kallman, McKinnell, and Knowles, 1968) and Faneuil Hall (John Smibert, 1740–42; enlarged by Charles Bulfinch, 1805–6)

men made design and location decisions, and the town and county shared the cost, ownership, and maintenance of the building.

Although town houses accommodated town meetings and, in some county seats, judicial proceedings, the New England colonies began to house their legislatures in more substantial brick buildings, often modeled after the latest English designs. A new town house was built in Boston in 1711–13 when the original 1657 structure burned to the ground. The newer building burned in 1747, was rebuilt, and survives today as the Old State House. The wooden Newport Colony House was enlarged in 1711 and finally replaced in 1739 with a brick building designed by Richard Munday. A state house was built of wood in Portsmouth, N.H., to occupy the "parade" at the center of town. These buildings largely followed the earlier town house form of an undivided, unheated room on the ground floor above which were the government chambers. Freestanding market buildings also first appeared in the 18th century. Boston's Faneuil Hall, built 1740–42 and later enlarged, typified the plan of these buildings: market stalls on the ground floor and chambers for public meetings above. Peter Harrison used a similar design for the Brick Market in Newport in 1762.

Purpose-built courthouses were the last new civic building type to appear in New England in the 18th century. As the legal profession began to grow in numbers and influence toward the end of the century, and economic prosperity quickened the pace of commercial litigation, New Englanders began to construct buildings to serve only the courts. In the early 18th century some county seats like Worcester and Lenox, Mass., lacking the economic activity to support new town houses, built small one-story courthouses, but it was not until the late 18th century that large, specialized courthouses began to appear in the major urban centers. The first of these buildings, the Suffolk County Courthouse, went up in Boston in 1769. This brick three-story building with cupola retained a portion of the undivided first-floor space typical of early town houses but also shared the space with offices for probate records and a registry of deeds. The inclusion of jury rooms and special courtroom furnishings for lawyers and justices further differentiated this new building type from earlier town houses.

The 19th century ushered in a rebuilding of civic structures in New England. Each of the New England states built a new state house in the postrevolutionary period, most of which were designed by a new breed of builder: the professional architect. Charles Bulfinch built three of New England's new state houses: the Connecticut State House in Hartford (1793–

96); the Massachusetts State House in Boston (1795–97), and the Maine State House in Augusta (1829–32). Stuart Park designed a new state house in Concord, N.H., which was built in 1816–19, and Vermont's state house, designed by Ammi Young, was constructed in 1833–38. The single exception to this building campaign was the state of Rhode Island, whose legislature traveled on a circuit to each of the county seats until the members established a single state capitol in Providence in the 1890s and authorized construction of a new state house designed by the architecture firm of McKim, Mead and White, built in 1895.

The 19th century was also a period of growth in New England's city governments, and city halls sprang up to house proliferating municipal functions. The first wave of city hall construction occurred just before midcentury and resulted in new municipal structures made of brick with brownstone trim in the Italianate style. Typical of these buildings are the Exeter Town Hall in New Hampshire, built by Arthur Gilman (1855), and the Newburyport City Hall in Massachusetts, built by local architect F. C. Coffin (1851). Many other towns and cities built government structures at midcentury in the Second Empire style, including Boston's city hall built by Gridley J. F. Bryant (1862–65), and Providence City Hall, built by Samuel J. F. Thayer (1874–78). Buildings constructed later in the century adopted the Romanesque style, most notably Cambridge City Hall, Massachusetts, designed by Longfellow, Alden, and Harlow (1889), and the Lowell City Hall, also in Massachusetts, built by Merrill and Cutler (1890–93).

After about 1850 the federal government began to assert its presence architecturally in New England towns through the construction of customhouses, courthouses and post offices. The responsibility for design and construction of these buildings came under the Office of Construction, a division of the Treasury Department. Setting a pattern that would continue into the 20th century, the Office of Construction often combined federal services into one building, as in the Italianate style courthouse and post office built in Windsor, Vt. (1857–58) and the federal building constructed in Providence (1904–08).

In the early years of the 20th century, architects and their clients turned to the Colonial Revival as the most appropriate style for such civic buildings as town halls and courthouses. This trend is most clearly visible in the seven town and city halls built between 1900 and 1930 by the architectural firm of Kilham, Hopkins, and Greeley. Their designs for the Tewksbury, Mass., Town Hall (1919) and the Lexington, Mass., Town Offices (1927–28)

typify New Englanders' penchant for redbrick structures echoing well-known colonial-era buildings. Other examples of the surge in popularity of this style for civic buildings include the Lebanon, N.H., Town Hall by Larson and Wells (1923–24) and the Kennebunk, Maine, Town Hall by J. D. Leland and Company (1922). Courthouse architecture also began to reflect the Colonial Revival style, most notably in the Providence County Courthouse (1924–33), designed by Jackson, Robertson, and Adams.

In the second half of the 20th century large-scale civic projects began to be constructed in New England, most notably Boston's Government Center. In the 1960s, following a master plan laid out by I. M. Pei and designed to revitalize the Scollay Square neighborhood, a new city hall designed by Kallman, McKinnell, and Knowles was built, flanked by the John Fitzgerald Kennedy Federal Office Building designed by The Architects Collaborative (TAC). These buildings, arranged around a brick plaza, epitomize the changing meaning of civic architecture in New England. Although they, like their predecessors, occupy prominent public spaces and rely on a monumental scale for effect, civic buildings in New England can no longer be distinguished easily from contemporary commercial office buildings, underscoring, perhaps, the changed nature of the business of government.

Lois Craig and the Staff of the Federal Architecture Project, *The Federal Presence: Architecture, Politics, and Symbols in United States Government Building* (1978); Henry-Russell Hitchcock, *Temples of Democracy: The State Capitols of the USA* (1976); William L. Lebovich, *America's City Halls* (1984); Martha J. McNamara, *From Tavern to Courthouse: Architecture and Ritual in American Law, 1658–1860* (2004).

Martha J. McNamara

Colleges and Campuses Evoking images of expansive green spaces, ordered, stylized buildings, and self-contained social and learning environments, New England college campuses have undergone a steady evolution in philosophy and form over a period of nearly 400 years. New England collegiate architecture, and its derivative preparatory school architecture, has been characterized by great diversity in function and style. Campuses and buildings often evoke the authority and tradition of British colleges and universities, where early generations of leading settlers were educated. Elite institutions patronized prominent architects to create signature buildings, and the foremost landscape architects were selected to design campuses. As a result, the New England landscape is identified with education, and New England campuses have, in turn, influenced the design of colleges across the nation. Many of the region's campuses present a gallery of architectural styles reflecting evolving philosophies about education and its place in American society.

The first main buildings at the region's colonial colleges—Harvard, Yale, the College of Rhode Island (later Brown University), and Dartmouth—were freestanding, multipurpose structures situated on open tracts of land in settled communities. The region's first main college structures—Old College (1638–42) and old Harvard Hall (1674–82) in the first-period style at Harvard and Henry Caner's early Georgian College House (1717–18) at Yale—incorporated religious, academic, residential, and administrative functions. More specialized, rectangular-plan brick buildings in the Georgian style included the first Stoughton Hall (1697–99), Massachusetts Hall (1719–20), Thomas Dawes's Hollis Hall (1763), and Francis Bernard's new Harvard Hall (1764) at Harvard; and Connecticut Hall (1750) and the Athenaeum (First Chapel, 1761) at Yale. The supreme example of the Georgian vernacular is Joseph Brown's University Hall (1770–71), erected for the College of Rhode Island and modeled after Nassau Hall (1755–56) at Princeton. Evidence of concerted campus planning occurred initially at Harvard, where, borrowing from the traditional enclosed courtyard of the English colleges, the modified open-ended or three-sided quadrangle (formed by Harvard, first Stoughton, and Massachusetts Halls) was constructed between 1674 and 1718. This pioneering campus layout was employed in early building arrangements at Dartmouth but otherwise had little impact on higher educational planning until the early to mid-19th century.

Between 1780 and 1830, the Federal style registered a marked impact on New England collegiate architecture, producing an array of general and single-function buildings arranged in rows or around open quadrangles. Most notable were Dartmouth Hall (1784–91) at Dartmouth; University Hall (1813) by Charles Bulfinch at Harvard; Hope College (1822) at Brown; Griffin Hall (ca. 1828) at Williams; and the College Edifice (1801–07) and the Old Mill (1825–29), both designed and built by John Johnson, at the University of Vermont. Other outstanding Federal structures, largely serving dormitory purposes, were erected at Waterville College (later Colby College, in Maine), Yale, Harvard, Bowdoin (Brunswick, Maine), Middlebury (Vermont), Washington College (later Trinity, in Hartford), and the American Literary, Scientific, and Military Academy campuses at Norwich, Vt. (later Norwich University) and Middletown, Conn. (later Wesleyan University).

Exercising great influence on New England and American campus planning to the Civil War was the extroverted, tripartite row plan developed at Yale by Thomas Clap and subsequently enlarged by the painter and amateur architect Jonathan Trumbull. Between 1750 and 1793, a three-building scheme (Connecticut Hall, First Chapel, and South College) evolved, later to be expanded into a seven-building grouping known as the Old Brick Row. The collegiate row, customarily consisting of three or five separate buildings (with a central building set at right angles to the main longitudinal axis), came to dominate campus planning in New England for more than half a century. It was subsequently adopted at Middlebury College, the University of Vermont, the American Literary, Scientific, and Military Academy (Norwich), Dartmouth, Bowdoin, Waterville, the Maine State Seminary (later Bates College), Amherst College (Massachusetts), Washington College, Wesleyan University, and Brown. The exceptions to this standard were Tufts, with its mall-like hilltop plan, and Williams College, whose buildings were positioned randomly in relation to the rolling, rural landscape. Since 1865 a majority of these academic groupings (the Yale, Norwich, Colby, and Trinity rows no longer exist) have been incorporated into larger, more ambitious campus plans.

The row idea provided a foundation for buildings in a variety of early and mid-Victorian Romantic styles. Embodying the principles of the picturesque, these styles were based on a harmonious interplay of nature and culture, a theme that made its mark on educational philosophy and on the region's collegiate architecture during the four decades preceding the Civil War. The most common style, highly suited to the academic community, was Greek Revival, best represented by Ammi Burnham Young's templelike buildings (1828–40) at Dartmouth; Thomas U. Walter's Recitation (Champlin) Hall (1836–37) at Colby; Isaac Damon's Johnson Chapel (1826) at Amherst; Old Chapel (1835–36) at Middlebury; and Russell Warren's Manning Hall (1834–35) at Brown. Fine Gothic Revival structures were also to be seen; at Harvard, Richard Bond designed Gore Hall (1838–41), and at Yale, Henry Austin designed the College Library (1842) and Alexander J. Davis the Graduates Hall (1851–53). The impact of the Italianate Revival is evident in Gridley J. F. Bryant's Ballou Hall (1852–54) for Tufts; Bryant's Hathorn Hall (1856–57) at the Maine State Seminary; and Francis H. Fassett's Seth Adams Hall (1861) for the Medical School of Maine at Bowdoin. Although less popular, the Romanesque Revival was employed by Richard Upjohn in the imposing Bowdoin College Chapel (1844–55) and by Paul Schultze in the Appleton Chapel (1856) and Boylston Hall (1857) at Harvard.

In the years following the Civil War, the row idea was largely supplanted by revived forms of the enclosed and open quadrangle and by more complicated, systemically organized, and outwardly focused campus-planning patterns. The advent of the professional architect and landscape designer produced major changes in planning practices. The grandiose collegiate master plan became the norm rather than the exception. A singular example was Wellesley College's hilltop complex (1875; it burned in 1914) by Hammatt and Joseph E. Billings, whose Italianate and Gothic Revival styles combined all institutional functions in one great linear masonry block. The renowned landscape architect Frederick Law Olmsted prepared sweeping master plans for the Massachusetts Agricultural College (1866; later the University of Massachusetts) and the Maine State College of Agriculture and Mechanic Arts (1867; later the University of Maine), both characterized by random building placement and parklike settings. In 1875 the English architect William Burges produced a highly significant but only partially realized master plan for Trinity College, consisting of four connected quadrangles.

During this period, the burgeoning American university system accommodated in enlarged preplanned campuses a wide spectrum of late Victorian eclectic and more recent styles common to institutional architecture. The High Victorian Gothic won particular favor in Ware and Van Brunt's Memorial Hall (1866–78) at Harvard; William Appleton Potter's Stearns Chapel (1870–73) at Amherst; Samuel D. Backus and William D. Preston's Memorial Hall (1867–82) at Bowdoin; and the three dormitories and Battell Chapel (1869–86) by Russell Sturgis, Jr., on the Old Campus at Yale. At Dartmouth the late Romanesque Revival style was chosen for Wilson Hall (Old Library; 1884–85) by Samuel J. F. Thayer, and at the University of New Hampshire for Thompson Hall (1891–93) by Dow and Rand-

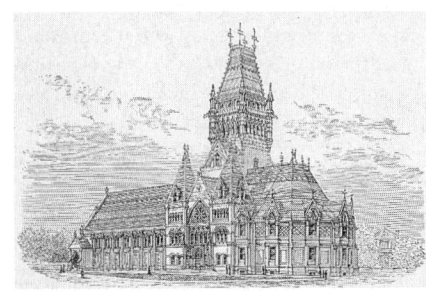

Memorial Hall (Ware and Van Brunt, 1866–78) Cambridge, Mass.

lett of Concord. Landmark structures in the so-called Richardsonian Romanesque exist in Rollins Chapel (1884–85) at Dartmouth by John Lyman Faxon; the Billings Library (1883–85) at the University of Vermont by H. H. Richardson; and Sever (1878) and Austin (1881–84) Halls by Richardson at Harvard. An especially notable example of landscape design providing a setting for a variety of architectural styles is found in the campus of Smith College, in Northampton, Mass. Through such designs at Smith, Wellesley, Mount Holyoke, and other women's colleges, New England institutions made a visible statement about the significance of women's education in the region.

With the creation of the modern American university in the late 1800s came the Beaux-Arts mode of campus planning. Following such magnificent and expansive planning examples as Stanford University, the University of Chicago, and Columbia University, William Welles Bosworth was inspired to do a monumental Classical Revival design (1913–37) for the Massachusetts Institute of Technology in Cambridge. The Classical Revival is perhaps most impressively illustrated in the Walker Art Building (1894) by McKim, Mead and White at Bowdoin, Horace Trumbauer's monumental Widener Library (1912–13) and the still imposing Harvard Stadium (1899–1903) by McKim, Mead and White, both at Harvard; and the Bicentennial Buildings (1901–02) by Carrère and Hastings at Yale. Superb examples of the early Collegiate Gothic Revival can still be observed in the Searles Science Building (1894) and Hubbard Hall (1903), both by Henry Vaughan, at Bowdoin; and Thompson Memorial Chapel (1903–05) at Williams by Allen and Collens.

During the 1920s and 1930s, many New England higher educational institutions financed and constructed ambitious new complexes accommodating a broad spectrum of specialized functions. Under the enlightened guidance of the New York architect James Gamble Rogers, Yale underwent a massive transformation in the form of seven new residential colleges (1929–33) in the Collegiate Gothic and Georgian Revival modes, as well as the Collegiate Gothic Hall of Graduate Studies (1926–32), Sterling Law School (1927–31), and Sterling Memorial Library (1927–31). Yale's massive Collegiate Gothic Payne Whitney Gymnasium by John Russell Pope followed in 1930–32. A lovely, soaring monument to the Collegiate Gothic is Trinity College Chapel (1932), designed by Frohman, Robb and Little. Other superlative examples of the Georgian Revival are evident in the residential houses (1913–30) at Harvard by Coolidge, Shepley, Bulfinch and Abbott; the residential complex at Smith by Ames and Dodge (ca. 1928); and a collection of academic buildings (1927–58) at Bowdoin and the Harvard Business School complex (1923–24) by McKim, Mead and White.

The post–World War II New England colleges and universities constitute a living museum of contemporary institutional architecture, with numerous major architects and firms represented. Among the most important buildings of the 1950s are Eero Saarinen's David S. Ingalls Hockey Rink (1953–59) at Yale; Paul Rudolph's Jewett Arts Center (1955–58) at Wellesley; Harrison and Abramovitz's "Three Chapels" (1953–54) at Brandeis; Saarinen's Kresge Auditorium and Chapel (1950–55), at MIT; and the Graduate Center (1948–52) by The Architects Collaborative (TAC) at Harvard. A period of unusually extensive construction, the 1960s was distinguished by Harrison and Abramovitz's Hilles Library (1964–65) at Radcliffe College, Cambridge; William E. Pereira's New England Center (1968–69) at the University of New Hampshire; Harrison and Abramovitz's Hopkins Center (1960–62) and Pier Luigi Nervi's Leverone Field House (1961–63) at Dartmouth; Saarinen's Stiles and Morse Colleges (1960–62), Gordon Bunshaft's Beinecke Library (1961–63), and Philip Johnson's Kline Science Laboratories (1962–66) at Yale; and LeCorbusier's Carpenter Center for the Visual Arts (1960–61) and Minoru Yamasaki's William James Hall (1963) at Harvard. More recently, excellent, pace-setting designs were commissioned for the University of Massachusetts Library (1971–73) by Edward Durrell Stone; the Southeastern Massachusetts University master plan (1962–72) by Paul Rudolph; the Yale Center for British Art (1972–77) by Louis I. Kahn; the Bates College Library (1972–73) by TAC; the Bowdoin Visual Arts Center (1973–75) by Edward Larrabee Barnes; the Arthur M. Sackler Museum of Art (1981–82) at Harvard by James Stirling; and Simmons Hall (2002) by Steven Holl and the Stata Center (2004) by Frank Gehry, both at MIT.

Reflecting the same design tradition as the collegiate architecture of New England are the campus plans and buildings of the region's preparatory schools. Phillips Academy in Andover, Mass., features two brick Federal structures by Charles Bulfinch, one of which once stood at the center of the former Andover Theological Seminary three-unit row. These buildings remain today as the core of the Andover campus, reorganized and substantially expanded between 1921 and 1932 by the New York architect Charles A. Platt in collaboration with Guy Lowell and Olmsted Brothers. Between 1929 and 1932, Platt also designed three Georgian Revival buildings similar to those at Andover for Deerfield Academy in Massachusetts. The Taft School in Watertown, Conn., is accommodated largely in a single Collegiate Gothic complex, with portions by Bertram Goodhue Grosvenor (1908–13) and James Gamble Rogers (1927–29). At Groton School in Massachusetts Vaughan's Saint John's Chapel (1899–1900) reflects the

Fairbanks House (ca. 1637), with later additions, Dedham, Mass.

Late Gothic Revival; adjacent buildings are by Peabody and Stearns of Boston. Vaughan's Gothic masterpiece, the Chapel of Saint Peter and Saint Paul (1886–94), is the focal point of the campus of Saint Paul's School, Concord, N.H., which includes other buildings designed by Vaughan, Rogers, Goodhue, Ralph Adams Cram, R. Clipston Sturgis, Ernest Flagg, George Snell, and Charles Z. Klauder. The Loomis Chaffee School in Windsor, Conn., originated with a collection of Georgian Revival buildings (1913–23) organized around a rectangular quadrangle, planned by the New York City firm of Murphy and Dana. One of the finest preparatory school structures is Cram's Saint George's School Chapel (1923–24) in Middletown, R.I. Exceptional modern buildings exist in Louis I. Kahn's library (1971–73) and Kallman McKinnell and Wood's gymnasium (1970–71) at Phillips Exeter Academy; Edward Larrabee Barnes's Kittredge Dormitory (1969–70) at Saint Paul's; and I. M. Pei's Paul Mellon Art Center (1970–71) at Choate Rosemary Hall, in Wallingford, Conn.

Given the continuing prestige of New England's educational institutions, the strong identification of the image of a college campus with those in such profusion in New England, and the prevalence of ever larger capital campaigns among wealthy alumni, New England is likely to continue a tradition of distinguished college architecture and campuses.

Patricia McGraw Anderson, *The Architecture of Bowdoin College* (1988); Bainbridge Bunting and Margaret Henderson Floyd, *Harvard: An Architectural History* (1985); Peter J. Ferguson, James F. O'Gorman, and John Rhodes, *The Landscapes and Architecture of Wellesley College* (2001); Reuben A. Holden, *Yale: A Pictorial History* (1967); Helen Lefkowitz Horowitz, *Alma Mater: Design and Experience in the Women's Colleges from Their Nineteenth Century Beginnings to the 1930s* (1993); Charles Z. Klauder and Herbert C. Wise, *College Architecture in America and Its Part in the Development of the Campus* (1929); Keith Morgan, *Charles A. Platt: The Artist as Architect* (1985); Douglass Shand-Tucci, *Harvard University: An Architectural Tour* (2001); Bryant F. Tolles, Jr., "The Evolution of a Campus: Dartmouth College Architecture Before 1860," *Historical New Hampshire* 42 (1987); Paul Venable Turner, *Campus: An American Planning Tradition* (1984).

Bryant F. Tolles, Jr.

Colonial Houses

The term *colonial house* within the context of the 13 original colonies defines a structure for dwelling, whether high style or vernacular, built from the time of the earliest 17th-century settlements until the signing of the Declaration of Independence in 1776, when the area ceased, politically, to have colony status.

New England colonial houses reflect one of two basic styles. The earlier form derived from English postmedieval prototypes, and scholars refer to these houses with much of their structure forthrightly exposed as 17th century or first period. The later style, known as Georgian or second period, came into use about 1725 (though with progressive manifestations in Boston in the 1690s) and was prominent throughout the final half century of the colonial period. Replacing or modifying the postmedieval, this style relied on Renaissance principles emanating ultimately from continental Europe but deriving for the most part from English models. By this change in fashion the house frame was largely concealed through an application of classically inspired finish trim. The relatively small number of buildings that survive from the first period are located primarily in the broad coastal areas of New England. For the second period there is a much greater body of extant structures, and for both groups architectural historians recognize developmental gradations of style that result in early, middle, and late phases.

Complicating the matter of classification, the widespread resumption of building activity following the Revolution entailed little or no alteration in building styles—certainly in outward appearances—before the pervasive and rapid adoption of neoclassical ideas that coincided more or less with the establishment of the republic in 1789. Thus one encounters such interesting anomalies as the Governor John Langdon House in Portsmouth, N.H., for which documents reveal a construction campaign extending from 1783 to the late 1780s. Historical circumstances notwithstanding, the governor, an ardent patriot, erected a structure that varies little from those built before the Revolution by his Tory predecessors. Scholars throughout the 20th century have increasingly referred, with good reason, to the dwellings built during this brief period between the Revolution and 1790 as postcolonial houses.

The term *colonial house* (or variants thereof) appears before the end of the 19th century in the wake of the new historical self-consciousness generated in America by the Philadelphia Centennial Exhibition of 1876. Scholarly writings before 1900 on the subject of Early American architecture reveal that the term denoted no firm chronological boundary. In those writings, "colonial architecture" as a generic period in American architectural history extended with some vagueness into the early years of the 19th century, some time after the newly established United States had ceased to be colonies. Once this imprecision had been sanctioned in formal publications of the Colonial Revival, it became strongly rooted in the popular mind, and one frequently finds that houses of the early 19th century are still referred to indiscriminately at the local level as colonial houses.

Scholars have shown that a wide variety of domestic buildings were present in early New England, but surviving examples dominate the popular and scholarly perception of the period. The so-called saltbox was a two-story, gabled-roofed structure with a one-story element at the rear (often containing the kitchen and storage rooms) that lengthened the double-sloped roofline over the back of the house. This is a popular revival form. The 18th century's Georgian-style colonial home, with its elegant doorways and distinctive white trim, was often the residential preference of New England elites. Fine examples of the style can be found, among other locations, in the Connecticut River valley. First-period homes with sharp gables and projecting second stories, as in Salem's famous House of the Seven Gables, find continued expression in contemporary revival forms. Post-and-beam construction has enjoyed renewed popularity since the 1970s, recalling the materials and techniques used in colonial homes. Indeed, colonial houses are distinguished as much for their construction materials and techniques as for their design, since English wood construction technology flourished with the plentiful supply of oak, pine, and other timber in New England.

Abbott Lowell Cummings, *The Framed Houses of Massachusetts Bay, 1625–1725* (1979); Antoinette F. Downing, *Early Homes of Rhode Island* (1937); J. Frederick Kelly, *Early Domestic Architecture of Connecticut* (1924); Frederick Koeper and Marcus Whiffen, *American Architecture, 1607–1976* (1981).

Abbott Lowell Cummings

Colonial Revival

The Colonial Revival was a multifaceted cultural phenomenon that profoundly shaped the way we perceive and manipulate our natural and built environments up to the present moment. Emerging at the middle of the 19th century, and stimulated by the nation's Centennial celebration in 1876 with the international exhibition in Philadelphia, the Colonial Revival signaled a renewed interest in all things associated with the American past. Allusions to early America could be found especially in literature, painting, sculpture, and architecture. The Colonial Revival in architecture took three forms: the publication of studies on 17th-, 18th-, and early 19th-century architecture; the restoration of surviving buildings judged to be representative of lost or threatened building traditions; and the design of new buildings based on earlier styles. In all three contexts the term *colonial* was applied broadly to denote any artifacts that were thought to date from the preindustrial period.

During the 19th and early 20th centuries,

colonial buildings were thought to have been produced by builders and carpenters who lacked formal education but possessed innate and refined aesthetic sensibilities. To late 19th-century nostalgics, colonial buildings were considered as simple and harmonious (characteristics lacking in the modern age) as the society that had produced them.

New England possessed a wealth of historic buildings that were publicized in books and magazines by Boston architects. The architectural firm of Robert Swain Peabody and John Goddard Stearns became a center for the production of Colonial Revival imagery in Boston. In a series of influential articles published in the Boston journal *American Architect and Building News,* Peabody recommended that New England architects follow the example of their British contemporaries in reviving earlier building traditions. At the time the English were rediscovering their medieval vernacular buildings and, led by the architect Richard Norman Shaw and others, incorporating salient elements of earlier buildings, such as irregular massings and combinations of traditional materials like brick and stone, into new designs. Peabody cautioned, however, that it was not adequate simply to imitate the British Queen Anne; instead he urged that the Georgian houses of New England serve as the basis of a uniquely American revival style.

Peabody singled out for emulation picturesque vernacular houses such as the 17th-century Fairbanks House in Dedham, Mass., which typified what he imagined to have been the untutored aesthetic of colonial builders. At the same time, Peabody admitted that many New England carpenters of the 18th and early 19th centuries had absorbed the lessons of classicism through the popular handbooks for builders published by Asher Benjamin. However, in his article "The Georgian Houses of New England," published in *American Architect and Building News,* Peabody suggested that classicism had been absorbed into the vernacular tradition: "The use of classical detail was universally agreed to, and the orders were naturally used by every carpenter." Naturalizing the application of classicism in colonial New England, Peabody could maintain his image of the unschooled builder, although we now understand Early American artisans and clients to have been better educated and more stylistically ambitious than Peabody imagined. Peabody's image of the colonial builder also implied an opposition to many mid-19th-century architects who were preoccupied with the revival of foreign styles and whose work was often characterized by decorative excess.

As early as 1863, the Boston architect John Hubbard Sturgis had made measured drawings of John Hancock's famed house, which was demolished amid public outcry that year. Peabody had been a student at the Ecole des Beaux-Arts in Paris, where architectural training since the 18th century had emphasized drawing and culminated in the graphic reconstruction of a classical ruin. In 1873 he published the drawings he had made in Europe under the title *Notebook Sketches.* In the 1870s and 1880s the draftsmen whom Peabody employed followed his example: William E. Barry published his *Pen Sketches of Old Houses* in 1874, Arthur Little's *Early New England Interiors* appeared in 1878, and in 1886 Frank E. Wallis published in *American Architect* sketches of New England architecture he had made earlier in the company of Arthur Little. These early publications stimulated the increasingly widespread dissemination of images of New England's earlier architecture into the 20th century, most notably in the series of approximately 450 plates that were brought out by the editor of *American Architect,* William Rotch Ware, under the title *The Georgian Period,* between 1898 and 1902.

Publications of New England architecture encouraged practitioners from other regions to travel to the region to see for themselves surviving buildings of the colonial period. Among them, architects from the New York firm of McKim, Mead and Bigelow and their friend Stanford White made a sketching tour of New England in 1877. Both New England architects and their counterparts from other areas used earlier buildings as models for their new designs. The John Hancock house was frequently used as a model for Colonial Revival buildings; the firm of Sturgis and Brigham, for example, produced two domestic designs in Cambridge, Mass., based on the Hancock house: the E. W. Hooper house (1872) and the Arthur Astor Carey house (1882). Robert Peabody used the Hancock house as a model for the Massachusetts State Building at the World's Columbian Exposition in Chicago in 1893.

In the *Report of the Massachusetts Board of World's Fair Managers* (1894), Peabody suggested that "the valuable quality in the design of the original Hancock house was the air of aristocratic distinction and reserve and dignity that it bore, without losing a homelike and comfortable appearance." Here Peabody summarized the two characteristics that drew architects and patrons to colonial architecture: its quality of understatement, which contrasted with the florid colors, textures, and decoration of much 19th-century architecture; and its association with a comfortable domesticity that was perceived to be in jeopardy from 19th-century industrialization. The unprecedented growth of factories and cities as a consequence of mechanized production was often blamed for having brought an end to small-scale family and community life as they were imagined to have existed during the colonial period. In fact, families and communities had never been as trouble-free as Colonial Revivalists liked to think.

Domestic life in the colonial period was also a central focus of the many historic house museums that were founded in New England between 1900 and 1930. Since the 1870s, architects and others interested in colonial domestic buildings had been able to gain access to

Colonial Revival Cape Cod house (Royal Barry Wills, 1941), Providence

well-known houses that were opened by their owners to the public on a paying basis.

As the movement grew to preserve historic houses as museums, women took increasingly important roles in the process. At the local level, women saved buildings such as the Old Gaol in York, Maine, which had served as both a jail and a residence since the early 18th century. National women's organizations, including the National Society of the Colonial Dames of America and the Daughters of the American Revolution, also participated in the preservation movement. For example, the Colonial Dames of Connecticut published some of their research on historic houses in that state in 1923, while their counterparts in New Hampshire opened the Moffatt-Ladd house (1764) in Portsmouth to the public in 1912. Just two years earlier, in 1910, William Sumner Appleton had founded the first regionwide preservation organization, the Society for the Preservation of New England Antiquities (SPNEA). Mostly middle or upper class, preservationists were motivated by an antipathy for aspects of industrial America. Like their contemporaries who published studies of colonial buildings or designed new houses in the colonial style, preservationists gave physical form to a desire to revisit a romanticized colonial New England.

Subdivisions of the post–World War II era have perpetuated the stereotypes of colonial architecture first conceived in the 1870s. The Boston architect Royal Barry Wills populated the suburbs with single-family houses based on early New England architecture but updated with many conveniences of the modern home. In Wills's houses, overscaled chimneys, leaded-glass casement windows, and hand-wrought details proliferate as signs of colonial domestic life that appeal to middle-class buyers. The house types known to Wills and other architects of his generation as the saltbox, Cape Cod, and garrison colonial have also inspired developers, contractors, and builders within New England and beyond. These domestic types, now constructed with such modern materials as plywood, wallboard, and aluminum siding, continue to evoke nostalgic sentiments of colonial New England and to provide practical house plans for builders. Spread across the landscape of the United States, they represent the legacy both of building traditions that stretch back to the 17th century and of the Colonial Revival, which first invested this architecture with symbolic meaning.

Alan Axelrod, ed., *The Colonial Revival in America* (1985); Margaret Henderson Floyd, "Measured Drawings of the Hancock House by John Hubbard Sturgis: A Legacy to the Colonial Revival," in *Architecture in Colonial Massachusetts*, ed. A. L. Cummings (1979); Sarah L. Giffen and Kevin D. Murphy, eds.,

"A Noble and Dignified Stream": The Piscataqua Region in the Colonial Revival, 1860–1930 (1992); Charles B. Hosmer, Jr., *Presence of the Past: A History of the Preservation Movement in the United States before Williamsburg* (1965); Elisabeth Blair MacDougal, ed., *The Architectural Historian in America* (1990); Pauline C. Metcalf, ed., *Ogden Codman and the Decoration of Houses* (1988); Kevin D. Murphy, *Colonial Revival Maine* (2004); William B. Rhoads, *The Colonial Revival* (1977); Geoffrey L. Rossano, *Creating a Dignified Past: Museums and the Colonial Revival* (1991); Richard Guy Wilson, *The Colonial Revival House* (2004).

Kevin D. Murphy

Congregational Churches Congregational churches, called meetinghouses until the middle of the 19th century, dominated early New England townscapes. Erected in town centers, these unconsecrated buildings combined civic and religious functions. As with the early New England experiment in theocratic government, 17th-century meetinghouses derived generally from English practices but had no dominant prototypes and varied greatly in their design. By 1700 most new buildings were square in plan, two stories high, and typically hip-roofed (having four planes tapering to the ridge line). The familiar form of colonial meetinghouses—rectangular in plan, with the main door centered on a long side and often with attached entry porches and bell towers—appeared by the 1720s. These houses of worship, sometimes ridiculed by Anglicans as barnlike, continued to be built throughout New England in strikingly similar fashion until the 1790s.

The architecture expressed New England ambitions based in the Reformation Protestant theology advocated by the Puritans to simplify settings, demystify religious ritual, and give teaching a primary role in worship. Architecturally appointed interiors were brightly colored and marbleized but had no iconographic symbolism or other evidence of so-called popery. The pulpit occupied the center of the long wall opposite the main entrance. It placed the minister within easy hearing of those worshipers who sat in ground-floor box pews as well as those in benches in the second- (and sometimes third-) tier galleries. This arrangement contrasted sharply with the gable-end orientation of European Anglican and Roman Catholic churches whose interiors were divided into progressively more sacred spaces of nave, choir, and sanctuary. Purposely replacing the mysterious with the familiar, Congregationalists used a communion table rather than an altar. The tables were often hinged to the deacons' pew, located immediately in front of the pulpit, so that they could disappear when not in use.

New England Congregational doctrine held that all church members, or saints, were equal in the eyes of God, and the architecture of their meetinghouses accordingly undermined class distinction and privilege. In contrast to Anglican practices, for instance, wealthy parishioners were not buried under the church floor with elaborate monuments, and the burying ground itself, often separated from the meetinghouse, was under the control of civil authorities. Nevertheless, social dis-

The Rockingham Meetinghouse (1787), in Rockingham, Vt., typifies 17th- and 18th-century Congregational meetinghouses, used for both worship and town meetings

tinctions were evident in seating arrangements, as high-priced pews nearest the pulpit were sold to wealthier parishioners, while people of low social class, servants, and slaves were relegated to the gallery or pews at the rear of the building.

The Congregational meetinghouse and its role in the town changed dramatically in the years following the Revolutionary War. New and renovated structures were turned 90 degrees to become more churchlike in appearance. Main entrances were moved to the gable end under the steeple, bench pews replaced box pews, and the pulpit stood at the far end across the long axis.

At least two circumstances may have contributed to these changes. First, in many towns de facto separation of church and state, which predated legal disestablishment in the early decades of the 19th century by many years, had effectively raised the status of other denominations. Beginning with the Great Awakening of the 1740s, many churches splintered, and new denominations, whose members resented paying a minister's tax to the town while supporting their own church, were formed. They successfully competed with Congregational churches for members, financial support, and community leadership and replaced a dominant Congregational meetinghouse with rival places of worship. Second, increasing numbers of court and town houses built expressly to serve civic needs also challenged traditional habits and beliefs and probably contributed to widespread perceptions that houses of worship should look more churchly.

In the 1820s and 1830s, in apparent reaction to Anglicized designs, some rural congregations reversed the interior plan by placing the pulpit against the front vestibule wall. This innovation probably expressed opposition to Anglican notions of progressive spaces. By mid-19th century, Congregational churches again assumed uniform design but on a church plan, often incorporating many churchly features so ardently rejected before. During the Colonial Revival of the late 19th and early 20th centuries, the image of the white-clapboard meetinghouse became a New England icon, contributing to an architectural tradition of new churches and civic buildings modeled on such forms.

Peter Benes and Philip D. Zimmerman, *New England Meeting House and Church, 1630–1850* (1979); Marian Card Donnelly, *The New England Meeting Houses of the Seventeenth Century* (1968); Edmund W. Sinnott, *Meetinghouse and Church in Early New England* (1963); Kevin M. Sweeney, "Meetinghouses, Town Houses, and Churches: Changing Perceptions of Sacred and Secular Space in Southern New England, 1720–1850," *Winterthur Portfolio* 28:1 (Spring 1993).

Philip D. Zimmerman

Connected Farm Buildings

In a typical arrangement of connected farm buildings, which are unique to New England, the farmhouse and barn are attached by a string of support structures to form a single complex. This distinctive architectural plan is largely confined to northern New England, with some examples in Connecticut and Rhode Island. The typical connected farmstead is composed of four types of buildings: the big house, or front house, which contains the major living rooms; the little house, or kitchen and food-preparation rooms; the back house, for farmwork and storage; and the barn, for sheltering animals and storing crops. This architectural organization was captured in the 19th-century children's refrain "Big house, little house, back house, barn."

The origin of this unique building type has long been attributed to the harsh New England winters and the desirability of a covered passage from house to barn—an assumption that is only partially correct. Most connected farms were built in the second half of the 19th century, after nearly 200 years of settlement in which the connected farm building plan was not used. Furthermore, winters were far more severe in other parts of America heavily settled by New England farmers, but neither they nor any other farmers elected to build in the connected style.

The connected farm building became popular in New England primarily because it was a symbol of progressive farm improvement for the common farmer after the first quarter of the 19th century. The style represented the most modern and efficient arrangement for

many farmers, handily accommodating the multiple tasks of the typical mixed farming and home-industry production system that by the mid-19th century had become the only viable means of survival for most New England farmers. Farm journals, publications by state boards of agriculture and by horticultural societies, and even almanacs advised New Englanders to diversify activities, from raising silkworms to dairying, and connected buildings provided interior spaces and yards for such work. In other areas of the country, connected buildings were not useful because larger and increasingly specialized farming practices dictated more dispersed plans.

A secondary factor was the influence of wealthy New England merchants who, at the beginning of the 19th century, followed European precedent and connected their residences to their carriage houses in neoclassical, Palladian styles. This arrangement appealed to New England farmers because it extended many of their previous English farm-building traditions, such as the common practice of adding to existing structures. Most farmers selected the new plan after the mid-19th century, when it came to represent a progressive model of well-ordered efficiency for the New England farm.

From about 1850 to 1930 farmers over a wide area of northern New England chose connected farm buildings. In many farming districts, 50 to 75 percent of farms were built or remodeled in that style, which was both practical and affordable; to achieve this architectural plan, some farmers simply had to move, realign, and connect existing buildings. Ex-

The Jones Farm (1780–1900), Milton, home of the New Hampshire Farm Museum

tended farm buildings, however, might also require a considerable financial investment because of increased labor demands, which were met by hired help, family members, and often neighbors. An extra strain was often placed on farm women, who had to cook meals for hired men while taking on new dairy, poultry, and canning responsibilities and caring for the attractive parlors and front yards that signified the domesticity of the progressive farm family.

Owing to the gradual decline of New England farming in the 20th century, the connected farm plan has acquired a romantic and antiquated appearance. Yet during the 19th century, for many it symbolized the most progressive ideas of farm improvement.

Thomas C. Hubka, *Big House, Little House, Back House, Barn: The Connected Farm Buildings of New England* (1984); Anthony N. B Garvan, *Architecture and Town Planning in Colonial Connecticut* (1951); Howard S. Russell, *A Long, Deep Furrow: Three Centuries of Farming in New England* (1976); Thomas D. Visser, *Field Guide to New England Barns and Farm Buildings* (1997).

Thomas C. Hubka

Cram, Ralph Adams (1863–1942)

Architect, writer. America's preeminent Gothicist, Ralph Adams Cram was born in Hampton Falls, N.H. Among the most distinguished American church architects of the 20th century, Cram was also a religious figure of national importance whose work transformed the visual image of American Christianity and influenced the dawning of the post–World War II ecumenical movement. In conjunction with a succession of designing partners, most notably Bertram Grosvenor Goodhue, Cram designed churches for nearly every Christian tradition; Anglicans, Roman Catholics, Presbyterians, Lutherans, Congregationalists, Methodists, Unitarians, Baptists, and Swedenborgians all sought him out. His work, moreover, is found from Honolulu (the Central Union Church, 1924) and Los Angeles (the chancel of Saint Vincent's, 1930) to Florida (the Rollins College Chapel, Winter Park, 1931) and Maine (the chancel of Portland's Saint Luke's Cathedral, 1900) and is conceived in a wide variety of classical, Byzantine, and medieval styles. Despite their diversity of style and initial planning, Cram's churches are immediately identifiable by their imaginative Gothic forms, their skillful mass and scale, and their exquisite detail (which was the work of Cram's partners).

All this Ralph Adams Cram did, as it were, with his right hand; with his left he did much more. A *Washington Star* article once protested that Cram's genius was "beyond the reach of ordinary powers of analysis." Cram

was an architectural writer, an essayist, a poet, a playwright, a short story writer (most admired today for his horror stories, some of which are still in print), and, before founding his architectural firm (originally Cram and Wentworth) in 1889, art critic for the *Boston Transcript*. A polymath, Cram matched his architectural achievement by writing 24 books and hundreds of scholarly and polemical articles in several fields. A leader in the 1890s of Boston's Bohemia, a group of mostly homosexual artists, musicians, writers, and social theorists, Cram never lost his wide-ranging, interdisciplinary edge. In 1914 he became head of the School of Architecture at the Massachusetts Institute of Technology and was named the first chair of the Boston City Planning Board; during the 1920s and 1930s his writings earned him respect as a social theorist. Cram wrote the preface to Henry Adams's *Mont-Saint-Michel and Chartres* (1933), was a founder of the Medieval Academy of America, and published the first full drawings of the Cathedral of Palma. A leading interpreter of Japanese art and architecture in the West, Cram was also the leading ecclesiologist of the Anglican Communion, and his best-known nonfiction books today reflect his role in these two disparate fields: *Church Building* (1899) remains a classic text, and *Impressions of Japanese Architecture and the Allied Arts* (1907) is still in print.

Cram's magnificent series of parish churches and collegiate structures remains his principal claim to fame and rank. In New England they include All Saints, Ashmont, near Boston (1892); All Saints, Peterborough, N.H. (1916); Saint George's School Chapel, Middletown, R.I. (1928); Saint Stephen's in Cohasset (1899) and Our Savior's Church in Middleborough (1897), both near Boston; and Emmanuel Church in Newport (designed with Goodhue, 1900). Cram was also supervising architect of Wellesley College, as he was of Princeton University.

Masterful residential work by Cram in New England includes the House-on-the-Moors (1918) north of Boston in Gloucester; the Ide House (1889) in Williamstown, Mass.; and the Whittemore House (1889) in York Harbor, Maine. Although Cram remains best known for his work at Princeton and West Point and for two New York City masterworks—Saint Thomas Church on Fifth Avenue (with Goodhue, 1914), and the nave of Saint John the Divine (1911), which the Harvard medievalist A. Kingsley Porter called "a tenth symphony"—he designed a series of small, austere chapels in New England, mostly Norman in feeling, including Saint Elizabeth's in Sudbury (1918); Saint Anne's in Arlington (1919); and Englewood Chapel, Nahant (1921),

all in Massachusetts. Each a modest masterpiece, this line culminated in Cram's superb Conventual Church of Saint Mary (1889) for the Cowley Fathers on the banks of the Charles River near Harvard University. This church, along with Boston's Federal Building (1933), an immense Art Deco skyscraper, is a splendid example of his last work in New England. Cram also influenced a number of artists and architects: he was the chief patron of the sculptor Johannes Kirchmayer and discovered the stained-glass designer Charles Connick, two Bostonians who were preeminent in their fields. Cram died in Boston.

Ralph Adams Cram, *My Life in Architecture* (1936); Douglass Shand-Tucci, *Boston Bohemia, 1881–1900: Ralph Adams Cram: Life and Architecture* (1995).

Douglass Shand-Tucci

Education of Architects

Before the 19th century, New England offered little in the way of formal education to aspiring architects. Housewrights and carpenters passed on traditional English construction techniques, responding slowly to the changing styles desired by elite New Englanders who had seen new buildings in London or in English design books. It was not until 1867 that the first American academic program in architecture opened at the Massachusetts Institute of Technology, led by William Robert Ware. The region's leading architects were traditionally trained as engineers, but Ware opted for the educational system of the Ecole des Beaux-Arts, inviting Eugène Létang from Paris to lead MIT's design studio. Students at MIT sketched the landscape of the region, picturesque English buildings from colonial times, and, after 1876, the classical and medieval casts at the Museum of Fine Arts in Boston's Copley Square. The Rhode Island School of Design in Providence was organized in 1878 to offer training in industrial design, including architectural drafting and mechanical drawing courses; it created a separate department of architecture in 1901, modeled on MIT's program.

In 1889 the Boston Architectural Club (now the Boston Architectural Center) established an enduring educational program for draftsmen financially unable to attend MIT, hiring leading architects as instructors. In 1894 Harvard's architectural program was founded by Paris-trained Arthur Rotch and directed by English-born H. Langford Warren, who had attended MIT and served as a senior draftsman for H. H. Richardson. By 1894, therefore, a unique combination of French and English influences distinguished New England architectural education. In the early 20th century, MIT and the Cambridge School of Architecture and Landscape Architecture (established in 1915) both played pivotal roles in the training of women.

Other influences were less formal. In 1910 William Sumner Appleton formed the Society for the Preservation of New England Antiquities (SPNEA) to preserve colonial buildings. At around the same time, Harvard's Georgian building program, the domestic designs of Royal Barry Wills, and the restoration of Colonial Williamsburg by Boston's Perry, Shaw and Hepburn in the 1930s helped create a recognizable Colonial Revival style with a New England signature. Architectural training in New England evolved radically when the German-born architect Walter Gropius joined the Harvard faculty in 1936 and introduced international modernism to the curriculum. Harvard assumed national leadership in education but stood apart from the architectural traditions of the region, producing a bifurcation between the cultural landscape of New England and the mechanistic, anticontextual bent of architectural education.

In the 1950s MIT's more environmentally sensitive program incorporated the ideas of the Scandinavian architect Alvar Aalto with those of the planner Kevin Lynch, author of *The Image of the City* (1960), thereby emphasizing the importance of integrating historic buildings into modern urban design. Stimulated by this theory and by destructive urban renewal in the 1950s and 1960s, academic historic-preservation programs, such as the one at Boston University, further influenced architects in training to incorporate historic, regional styles from the colonial period, as well as 19th-century urban, commercial, and industrial architectural forms.

Yale provided a counterpoint to the Boston programs. In the 1920s and 1930s, Beaux-Arts pedagogy was the cornerstone of Yale's national reputation. In 1950 George Howe was appointed the chair and introduced a nonpolemical modernism to Yale, valuing both domestic and international ideals. Vincent Scully's *The Shingle Style* (1955) and his courses in architectural history at Yale influenced architects and landscape architects alike over four decades. The appointments of Paul Rudolph in 1958 and Charles Moore in 1965 as chairs brought an increasing commitment to the relations among buildings, place, and society.

The region continues to be a national center for architectural education with new schools of architecture accredited at Roger Williams University (1985) in Bristol, R.I., and at Northeastern University (2002) in Boston.

Margaret Henderson Floyd, *Architectural Education and Boston: Centennial Publication of the Boston Architectural Center* (1989); Caroline Shillaber, *Massachusetts Institute of Technology School of Architecture and Planning, 1861–1961: A Hundred Year Chronicle* (1963); Robert Stern, "Yale, 1950–1965," *Oppositions* 4 (October 1974); William Robert Ware, "An Outline of a Course of Architectural Instruction," *Society of Arts of the Massachusetts Institute of Technology* (1866).
Margaret Henderson Floyd

Gropius, Walter (1883–1969)

Architect and educator. Walter Gropius was born in Berlin, Germany, on May 18, 1883. After a successful early career as an architectural designer and educator, Gropius immigrated to the United States, where he accepted a teaching position at the Harvard University Graduate School of Design. Convinced that modern architecture should express the social and economic conditions of the industrial era, Gropius revolutionized architectural training in the United States and provided inspiration to future architects through both the buildings he designed and his innovative architectural practice.

In his native Germany, Gropius trained at the Institutes of Technology in both Munich and Berlin, then completed a three-year apprenticeship with Peter Behrens, an influential early modern architect. After serving in World War I, Gropius became director of two schools in Weimar, an arts academy and a school of applied arts, which he combined into a single school known as the Bauhaus ("architecture house"). There Gropius began to develop the innovative teaching methods he brought to Harvard, centering on the interdependence of different forms of design and the need for practical training. Architects, according to Gropius, should learn not only the techniques of building design but also practical crafts, so they could familiarize themselves with various materials and processes. Gropius's progressive political views and teaching methods caused him to fall into disfavor in conservative Weimar, and in 1925 he moved his school to Dessau. The new Bauhaus building in Dessau is one of his best-known works. Gropius resigned as director of the Bauhaus in 1928, continuing his practice in Germany until 1934, when he left in reaction to the rise of Nazi power.

After living in England for three years, Gropius moved to Harvard, where he remained for the rest of his academic career. Gropius brought to Harvard, and to architectural education in the United States more generally, an emphasis on geometric design, interdisciplinary artistic training, and pragmatic assignments focusing on present-day social and economic circumstances. Gropius also put his theories of artistic collaboration into practice. Until 1943 he worked with Marcel Breuer, who had also come from the Bauhaus to Harvard, and in 1946 Gropius formed The Architects Collaborative (TAC), a firm based in Cambridge with founding partners Norman Fletcher, John Harkness, Sarah Harkness, Robert McMillan, Louis McMillen, and Benjamin Thompson.

In the realm of domestic architecture Gropius is remembered for his own residence, Gropius House (1937–38), in Lincoln, Mass., which he designed with Breuer. For it Gropius and Breuer combined geometric design and modern materials with New England vernacular traditions: the house incorporates familiar white clapboards, for example, but they run

Walter Gropius in front of his 1937–38 house in Lincoln, Mass.

vertically rather than horizontally. Working as part of TAC, Gropius designed the Harvard Graduate Center (1949–50) in Cambridge and the John F. Kennedy Federal Office Building (1961–66) in Boston. Perhaps his best-known project is the Pan American building (1958–63) in New York City. Gropius's career-long interest in machines and prefabricated parts is evident in these structures, which are modular designs constructed around cast concrete and steel frames. Gropius died in Boston.

Ise Gropius, *Walter Gropius: Buildings, Plans, Projects, 1906–1969* (1972); Klaus Herdeg, *The Decorated Diagram: Harvard Architecture and the Failure of the Bauhaus Legacy* (1983); Reginald Isaacs, *Gropius: An Illustrated Biography of the Creator of the Bauhaus* (1991).

Marina Moskowitz

Landscape New England was the launching ground for the profession of landscape architecture in the United States. Building on a tradition of progressive agriculture and transcendental philosophy, New England emerged in the early 19th century as a center for landscape gardening. During the second half of the century and the first decades of the 20th, New England landscape architects dominated the national practice. The first academic programs in landscape architecture were established at the turn of the 20th century in New England, and landscape architectural firms of international standing are still based in the region.

In an age of self-improvement following the American Revolution, organizations such as the Massachusetts Society for the Promotion of Agriculture, founded in 1792, encouraged citizens to create model farms and gardens. The wealthy began to build ideal country estates, such as the Vale (1793), shipping merchant Theodore Lyman's estate and the site of the earliest surviving greenhouses in New England, and Governor Christopher Gore's Gore Place (1805–6), both in Waltham, Mass. Later the Transcendentalist writings of Concord-based Henry David Thoreau and Ralph Waldo Emerson focused New England intellectuals on the centrality of nature as a guide to spiritual growth.

The origins of the American public park can be traced to the rural cemetery movement, especially to Mount Auburn Cemetery (1831) in Cambridge, Mass. Initially a collaborative effort of the cemetery company and the Massachusetts Horticultural Society (founded 1827), Mount Auburn, laid out by civil engineer Alexander Wadsworth with horticultural direction from Henry A. S. Dearborn, became a national model for landscape cemeteries. Many New England cities and towns sought to replicate this example. Sleepy Hollow Cemetery (1855) in Concord, Mass., was designed by Robert Morris Copeland and H. W. S. Cleveland in response to the writings of Emerson. Swan Point Cemetery (1846) in Providence was later embellished with a landscape plan by Cleveland (1886).

Responding to the popular success of rural cemeteries as public landscaped spaces, New England cities and towns were eager to create parks where residents could find release from urban pressure, a place to contemplate nature, and, eventually, a site for recreation. From the mid-19th century on, America's premier planner of public parks was the Connecticut-born Frederick Law Olmsted, who emerged as a landscape architect with his plans for Central Park in New York City (1857–58). When his native Hartford authorized funding to create a municipal park in 1853, Olmsted, preoccupied with Central Park, recommended the Swiss émigré Jacob Weidenmann for the commission. Weidenmann's design for Bushnell Park (1861) and his scheme for Hartford's Cedar Hill Cemetery (1865) established his reputation as a landscape designer, reinforced by his popular book *Beautifying Country Homes* (1870).

After he began receiving important commissions in the Boston area, especially for the Boston municipal park system, Olmsted moved in 1883 to Brookline, Mass., where he continued his national practice designing public parks, residential subdivisions, institutional projects, and private estates. The development of Harvard's Arnold Arboretum (founded 1873), on which Olmsted was a consultant, was a further inducement for the move. His Brookline office became the training site for the leaders of the next generation of landscape architects, including Charles Eliot, creator of the Trustees of Public Reservations (1891), the nation's first private-sector landscape conservation organization, and the Boston Metropolitan Park System (1893), the model for public regional landscape planning; the great plantsman and country-estate designer Warren Manning; Arthur Shurcliff, city planner and landscape architect for Colonial Williamsburg; and John Charles Olmsted and Frederick Law Olmsted, Jr., who continued the leadership of the firm until 1950.

Massachusetts was also the pioneer in the education of landscape architects. Both the Massachusetts Institute of Technology and Harvard established curricula in landscape architecture in 1900, although the program at MIT was discontinued in 1909. But the Harvard program, under the direction of Frederick Law Olmsted, Jr., and Arthur Shurcliff, quickly became nationally dominant. Because women were excluded from the Harvard program until World War II, two important training alternatives arose—the Lowthorpe School of Landscape Architecture, Gardening, and Horticulture for Women, established in 1901 at Groton, and the Cambridge School of Architecture and Landscape Architecture, founded in 1915 by faculty from the Harvard program. New England–trained female architects like Beatrix Jones Farrand, the only female founding member of the American Society of Landscape Architects (1899), and Marian Coffin, an influential designer for wealthy private clients and institutions, became national leaders in the field.

Private estate design became a major component of landscape architecture in the early 20th century. For the American country house, a formal landscape revival based on the Italian tradition emerged from the summer art colony of Cornish, N.H. From 1890 on Cornish landscape architects and writers like Charles A. Platt, Rose Standish Nichols, and Ellen Biddle Shipman were tastemakers in private estate design. Platt's Italian-inspired, architectonic country-house landscapes, such as Faulkner Farm (1897–98) in Brookline and Maxwell Court (1901–3) in Rockville, Conn., frequently appeared in publications and were widely emulated. In the Berkshire hills of western Massachusetts, the novelist Edith Wharton designed geometric Italianate gardens for her estate the Mount (1902) in Lenox, as did the sculptor Daniel Chester French (whose works include the *Minute Man* in Concord and the seated Lincoln in the Washington, D.C., Lincoln Memorial) for his summer house Chesterwood (1920s) in Stockbridge.

One of the most inventive members of the country-house movement was the Cambridge-based landscape architect Fletcher Steele, whose elegant gardens, both historically derived and modernist, of the 1920s and 1930s exerted a powerful influence on the next generation of landscape architects. The series of garden rooms Steele created between 1922 and 1955 for Mabel Choate at her summer house Naumkeag in Stockbridge are among his finest works. Parallel to these domestic projects was the emergence of city planning as a domain for landscape architects, particularly represented by the work of Cambridge-based John Nolen from 1904 until his death in 1937.

During the Depression public commissions predominated, especially municipal and regional parks. Following World War II more functional corporate and public commissions offered natural opportunities for the emergence of modernism in landscape design. Harvard-trained Dan Kiley, one of the leaders in this movement, maintained an international practice from the 1940s until his death in 2004, designing austerely beautiful landscapes for institutions, for example, the U.S. Air Force Academy (1959), and museums, such as the East Building of the National Gallery of Art (1978), with his small staff in northern Vermont. In contrast, the practice of Hideo Sasaki, established at Watertown, Mass., in 1953, evolved into a large collaborative model for landscape architecture offices, paralleling the clients it served. Today well-established networks of educational institutions and professional practices help maintain New England's leadership in the field of landscape architecture.

Karl Haglund, *Inventing the Charles River* (2003); Robin Karson, *Fletcher Steele, Landscape Architect: An Account of the Gardenmaker's Life, 1885–1971* (1989); Blanche Linden-Ward, *Silent City on a Hill: Landscapes of Memory and Boston's Mount Auburn Cemetery* (1989); Keith Morgan, ed., *Shaping an American Landscape: The Art and Architecture of Charles A. Platt* (1995); Peter Walker and Melanie Simo, *Invisible Gardens: The Search for Modernism in the American Landscape* (1996).

Keith N. Morgan

Libraries

Many early innovations in library design and planning have their origin in New England, and the public library building, along with the meetinghouse and village green, has become synonymous with the region's landscape and character. Although a handful of exceptional monuments, such as Peter Harrison's Redwood Library in Newport, R.I. (1750), and the Providence Athenaeum (William Strickland, 1839) were built before the mid-19th century, few book collections were large enough to warrant the erection of a building. The largest library of this period was Gore Hall at Harvard (Richard Bond, 1837–41), a Gothic Revival building designed to accommodate 100,000 volumes in two-story alcoves flanking a monumental hall. A similar arrangement was employed at Yale by Henry Austin (1842–46) and for the Boston Athenaeum (Edward C. Cabot and George M. Dexter, 1847–59).

During the quarter century immediately following the nation's first legislation authorizing the establishment of free, tax-supported libraries in New Hampshire and Massachusetts in 1849 and 1851, more than 450 public libraries were founded in the United States. Although about half of these were located in New England, fewer than three dozen of these institutions were housed in their own, purpose-built structures. An early example, the first Boston Public Library on Boylston Street (1855–59), was designed by Charles Kirk Kirby to accommodate an unprecedented 240,000 books. Like Gore Hall and the Boston Athenaeum, its reference collection was shelved in alcoves in an impressive multistory hall. The ground floor was arranged as a public lending library with its own storage, delivery, and reading rooms; this was the first such plan to appear anywhere in the United States.

Although many libraries followed the example of Boston's great book hall, its lending library became an even more significant paradigm for the American public library as larger town libraries in New England, such as those in Concord (Snell and Gregorson, 1873) or Pittsfield (William Potter, 1874–75), Mass., began experimenting with combinations of the two arrangements. In 1877 the capacity of Gore Hall was increased through the addition of the country's first freestanding metal book stacks, which were devised by the librarian Justin Winsor in collaboration with the architectural firm of Ware and Van Brunt.

Also in 1877 construction began in Woburn, Mass., on the first of Henry Hobson Richardson's well-known libraries. Here and in his other libraries in North Easton (1877–83), Quincy (1879–81), and Malden (1883–85), Mass., and in Billings Memorial Library at the University of Vermont (1883–86), Richardson constructed an alcove system like the one at Harvard but set it within a monumental Romanesque Revival shell. Heavily criticized by contemporary librarians, Richardson's exterior imagery and shelving arrangement nonetheless strongly influenced American libraries throughout the country.

The Richardsonian idiom was superseded only at the turn of the century by a renewed interest in Classicism of the type exhibited best in McKim, Mead and White's palatial Boston Public Library on Copley Square (1887–98) as well as in the Blackstone Memorial Library in Branford, Conn. (Solon S. Beman, 1893–96), and the Ives Memorial Library in New Haven (Cass Gilbert, 1906–11), Conn. Concurrently, alcove book rooms gave way to single-story freestanding shelves and metal book stacks. This trend was further encouraged in the early 20th century through the introduction of "open stacks" and by guidelines established in connection with Andrew Carnegie's extensive library philanthropy. Between 1899 and 1917 more than 1,600 public library buildings (including some 85 in New England) were erected in the United States through the Carnegie program. Carnegie's new corporate philanthropy partially eclipsed the earlier tradition of local architectural patronage in New England and ultimately dispersed the focus of library design and construction throughout the country.

As both publishing and collections expanded during the 20th century, monumental structures capable of holding several million volumes replaced earlier libraries. At Harvard, the Widener Library (Horace Trumbauer, 1908–13) supplanted Gore Hall, while at Yale, James Gamble Rogers designed an impressive 14-story book stack for Sterling Memorial Library (1927–31). Later in the century Philip Johnson's addition to the Boston Public Library (1971) more than doubled its size. The Beinecke Rare Book and Manuscript Library at Yale (Gordon Bunshaft of Skidmore, Owings and Merrill, 1960–63) and the Phillips Exeter Library (Louis Kahn, 1965–72) exemplify the best in recent academic design. And a renaissance in small public library building, restoration, and enlargement has served to reassert the prominence of this uniquely democratic institution as the cultural and architectural heart of many New England communities, where the public library continues to flourish as one of the region's greatest contributions to the American landscape.

George Bobinski, *Carnegie Libraries: Their History and Impact on American Public Library Development* (1969); Kenneth A. Breisch, *Henry Hobson Richardson and the Small Public Library in America: A Study in Typology* (1997); Sidney Ditzion, *Arsenals of a Democratic Culture: A Social History of the American Public Library Movement in New England and the Middle States, 1850–1900* (1947); Haynes McMullen, "Prevalence of Libraries in the Northeastern States before 1876," *Journal of Library History* 22 (1987); Jesse H. Shera, *Foundations of the Public Library* (1949); Abigail A. Van Slyck, *Free To All: Carnegie Libraries and American Culture, 1890–1920* (1995).

Kenneth A. Breisch

Newport Cottages

During the 19th and early 20th centuries, America's leading architects built summer "cottages" for the nation's social and financial elite in Newport, R.I. In reality mansions, these houses reflect the evolution of American domestic architecture by its finest theorists and designers. Along Bellevue Avenue and Ocean Drive, Newport's cottages served as backdrops for a society centered on sport, fashion, and parties in settings of spectacular natural beauty.

During the first half of the 19th century, southern planters, China trade merchants, and a circle of artists and writers built Gothic Revival and Italianate villas, popular for the romantic effect of their towers, bay windows, and porches that harmonized with the landscape. Kingscote (1839–41), designed by the English architect Richard Upjohn for the Georgia planter George Noble Jones, and Malbone (1848–49), designed by Alexander Jackson Davis, are examples of Gothic Revival cottages by the leading proponents of the style in America. Upjohn also built the Italianate Edward King House (1845–47), which was featured in the widely read *The Architecture of Country Houses* (1852) by Andrew Jackson Downing, the influential theorist and promoter of picturesque cottage architecture.

Between 1860 and 1890 a new generation of architects, well traveled and formally trained

The Breakers (Richard Morris Hunt, 1893–95), Newport, R.I.

in Europe, transformed the Newport cottage. Richard Morris Hunt, the first American to attend the Ecole des Beaux-Arts in Paris, designed the J. N. A. Griswold House (1861–62) in the Stick Style with wood cross sections reminiscent of medieval French building. Henry Hobson Richardson, another Ecole des Beaux-Arts graduate, created the William Watts Sherman House (1874). The half-timbered house was an American version of the Olde English style covered in a New England material—the wood shingle. Charles Follen McKim and Stanford White were apprentices to Richardson on the Watts Sherman House. In 1879 they formed their own firm and created several Shingle Style villas in Newport, such as the Samuel Tilton (1881–82) and Isaac Bell (1881–83) houses. Contemporaries referred to the new style as "modernized colonial." These cottages combined the shingled walls and high gables of colonial American buildings, which the architects sketched and photographed in Newport and other New England coastal towns, with English, European, and Japanese motifs.

The Newport cottage became a palace in the years 1890–1914. Richard Morris Hunt introduced Beaux-Arts classicism and Parisian opulence to Newport with Ochre Court (1888–91), a French Renaissance château for the Ogden Goelets; Marble House (1888–92), a Louis XIV–style showpiece for the William K. Vanderbilts; and the Breakers (1893–95), an Italian Renaissance palazzo for the Cornelius Vanderbilts. Newport's millionaires were the merchant princes of an American Renais-

sance, commanding commercial empires, collecting art, and sponsoring great buildings in the manner of modern Medici. Edith Wharton was a critical observer of this scene; Newport's cottages were described in minute detail as the settings for the psychological development of her characters in *The House of Mirth* and *The Age of Innocence*. Henry James predicted the demise of Newport's cottages in *The American Scene* (1907), calling the houses "white elephants."

Changing social and economic conditions after World War I ended Newport's century-long cottage boom. The remains are nonetheless remarkable. The Preservation Society of Newport County currently owns and maintains the Isaac Bell House, Marble House, and the Breakers. The J. N. A. Griswold House is home to the Newport Art Museum; the William Watts Sherman House and Ochre Court are owned by Salve Regina University; the Edward King House is a city-owned senior center; and the Samuel Tilton House is privately owned. All but the Samuel Tilton House are open to the public for tours. The Newport cottage remains today a social and an architectural legacy of the American search for the dream house.

Antoinette F. Downing and Vincent J. Scully, *The Architectural Heritage of Newport, R.I., 1640–1915* (1967); Mark Alan Hewitt, *The Architect and the American Country House, 1890–1940* (1990); Vincent J. Scully, *The Shingle Style and the Stick Style* (1971); Richard Guy Wilson, *McKim, Mead and White, Architects* (1983).

John R. Tschirch

Olmsted Landscape Architecture Firm The most prolific, influential American landscape architectural firm in the history of the country was the 150-year practice of Frederick Law Olmsted, his associates, and his successors. In fact, it was Frederick Law Olmsted, Sr. (1822–1903), who invented the term "landscape architecture" to define the broad land-planning principles that underlay his multiple designs for parks, subdivisions, and private estates. Born in Connecticut, he emerged as a landscape architect with his designs for Central Park in New York City (1857–58) and continued to dominate his profession until his retirement in the 1890s. He moved his office from New York to Brookline, Mass., in 1883, where the successor firms continued to be based until 1980, when the Olmsted home and office, called Fairsted, were purchased by the National Park Service to create the Olmsted National Historic Site. Over this period the firm prepared plans for approximately 3,500 commissions in nearly every state in the union and several foreign countries. Using both the pastoral and naturalistic traditions of 18th-century England, the Olmsted firm sought to create unified designs that would encourage social interaction and provide an antidote to the pressures of urban life. Among the firm's best-known public projects in New England are the Boston Park system (1878–1900), the Hartford Parks (1870–1900), and the Eastern and Western Promenades in Portland, Maine (1904–05).

In the years before the establishment of academic programs, the Olmsted office was the training ground for future generations of landscape architects. John Charles Olmsted (1852–1920), the stepson and nephew of the founder, joined the firm in 1875 and became a partner in 1884. A number of other gifted designers were trained in the Olmsted office in these years, including Henry Sargent Codman (1864–93) and Charles Eliot (1859–97), both of whom died early in their careers. Eliot formed a partnership with Frederick Law Olmsted, Sr., and John Charles Olmsted from 1893 until 1897 under the name Olmsted, Olmsted, and Eliot and was responsible for the early development of the Boston Metropolitan Park System and the establishment of the Trustees of Public Reservations. After Eliot's death, John Charles and Frederick Law Olmsted, Jr. (1870–1957), formed the partnership Olmsted Brothers.

Other key practitioners who worked for the firm in the years around the turn of the 20th century included Warren Manning (1860–1938), a horticulturist and the designer of scores of private estates, public parks, and city plans. Arthur Shurcliff (1870–1957) worked with the Olmsteds from 1896 to 1904 before embarking on a career as a city and regional planner and later as supervisor of the landscape development of Colonial Williamsburg, Va., in the 1920s–1940s.

In addition to several other leading landscape architects who began their careers in the Olmsted office, the firm was instrumental in establishing the first four-year curriculum in landscape architecture at Harvard in 1900 under the direction of Frederick Law Olmsted, Jr., and Arthur Shurcliff. The younger Olmsted continued his father's tradition as an important public figure in the profession, serving as an adviser to the development of public spaces in Washington, D.C., from 1900 until his death and as a founder and later the president of the American Society of Landscape Architects. After 1980 the successor firm took the name Olmsted Office and moved to Freemont, N.H., closing in 1999.

Charles E. Beveridge and Paul Rocheleau, *Frederick Law Olmsted: Designing the American Landscape* (1995); [Charles W. Eliot], *Charles Eliot, Landscape Architect* (1902); Albert Fein, *Frederick Law Olmsted and the American Environmental Tradition* (1972); Cynthia Zaitzevsky, *Frederick Law Olmsted and the Boston Park System* (1982).

Keith N. Morgan

Parris, Alexander (1780–1852)

Architect and engineer. Born in Halifax, Mass., and raised in nearby Pembroke, Alexander Parris was Boston's leading architect in the 1820s; Quincy Market (1824–26) is his most renowned project. Parris also produced significant buildings in Portland, Maine, and Richmond, Va., and, later, major engineering projects throughout coastal New England.

His early training consisted of a three-year apprenticeship to a housewright, close study of English architectural handbooks, and a keen eye for Charles Bulfinch's buildings in Boston. In 1801 Parris moved to booming Portland to design and build large houses for the mercantile elite. In eight years he constructed at least six houses and commercial buildings, and designed two churches—most now demolished or altered. Saint John's Episcopal Church in Portsmouth, N.H. (1807), the best extant example of his early work, is derived from English handbooks and Bulfinch's Boston churches.

The Embargo of 1807 crippled Portland's economy, but the international tensions introduced Parris to military engineering, and he built fortifications for Portland Harbor. In 1809 he left Maine and traveled the eastern seaboard in search of work, gaining commissions for three large houses in Richmond, including the Virginia governor's mansion and John Wickham House (both 1811–13). Wickham House demonstrates the profound influence on Parris of English-born architect B. Henry Latrobe, whom he met in Washington, D.C. Wickham House is bolder in scale and simpler in ornament than Parris's earlier work, and shows Latrobe's manner of reflecting interior spaces in exterior forms. Henceforth, Parris's work owed more to Latrobe than to Bulfinch.

Parris commanded a corps of builders and craftsmen during the War of 1812, after which he settled in Boston, opening the city's first professional architectural office. Benefiting from Bulfinch's relocation to Washington in 1817, Parris led the profession in Boston for the next decade. Through the 1840s his office trained a generation of architects and engineers, including Isaiah Rogers, Richard Upjohn, and Gridley J. F. Bryant. By 1828 Parris had completed two dozen diverse projects in the Boston area. Many of these survive with Parris's design still recognizable, including the Parker-Appleton Houses (1817–19), the David Sears House (1819–21, now the Somerset Club), Saint Paul's Church (1819–20), and Quincy Market (1824–26) in Boston, and Stone Temple in Quincy, Mass. (1827–28).

Quincy Market and Stone Temple secured his architectural reputation for their bold neoclassical design and skillful use of granite. The market, which demonstrates Parris's ability to organize an effective urban place, was renovated and adapted in the 1970s as part of the Faneuil Hall Marketplace complex to house restaurants, shops, and offices. The Stone

Quincy Market (Alexander Parris, 1824–26), Boston

Temple is the centerpiece of its community, built of the finest Quincy granite at the congregation's specific direction, combining simple, large-scale exterior geometry with a bright interior beneath a huge domed ceiling.

Despite these architectural successes, Parris struggled financially. From the late 1820s, he shifted toward engineering. Between 1827 and 1832 he superintended the construction of granite drydocks for the navy at Charlestown, Mass., and Norfolk, Va. Other utilitarian buildings at Charlestown, including the quarter-mile-long granite Ropewalk (1835–37), occupied Parris through the 1830s. The most notable projects of his late years were a half dozen granite lighthouses for which Parris was both designer and onsite supervisor of construction. His Maine lighthouses still stand at Saddleback Ledge (1839–40), Mount Desert Rock (1847), and Monhegan Island (1849–51). Parris returned to Pembroke in 1845, but maintained an office in Boston through 1850. He continued to travel and practice until his death in Pembroke in 1852.

Arthur J. Gerrier, "Alexander Parris, 1780–1852," *A Biographical Dictionary of Architects in Maine* 4, no. 1 (1987); Pamela J. Scott and Edward F. Zimmer, "Alexander Parris, B. Henry Latrobe, and the John Wickham House," *Journal of the Society of Architectural Historians* 61, no. 3 (October 1982); E. F. Zimmer, "Parris, Alexander," *Dictionary of Art* (1996).

Edward F. Zimmer

Philanthropy and Housing Reform

American 19th-century reformers identified

unsafe and inadequate housing as one of the greatest challenges facing the country. Focusing primarily on urban areas, they sought to improve or supplement existing housing. Before the government-sponsored emergency housing initiatives of World War I, employer-built workers' housing—constructed largely for mill and factory operatives—and philanthropic model housing constituted the only alternatives to the speculative market. Beginning in the mid-19th century, Boston became one of the principal centers of philanthropic housing reform. Spanning more than a half century, New England reform efforts relied on the philosophy and architectural solutions of British housing reformers; a conviction that philanthropy should not be equated with charity; the presupposition that model housing could reform but not replace the private market; and a growing belief in the necessity of expanding the scope of reform as well as professionalizing its participants. Like their American and European counterparts, philanthropic reformers in New England promoted various notions of the ideal living community, ranging from the well-designed model tenement to the unified urban neighborhood to the self-contained garden suburb.

Philanthropic building organizations led by prominent local citizens introduced model housing to the Boston area beginning in the 1850s, dividing their efforts between established urban centers and the newly accessible suburbs. Following British precedents, these limited-dividend corporations, including the Model Lodging House Association (1854) led by future Harvard professor Charles Eliot Norton and the Boston Cooperative Building Company (1871), initiated by physician Henry Ingersoll Bowditch, offered a modest return on capital investments. Whether renovating existing structures or constructing new tenement buildings and single-family houses, building companies worked with local architects to incorporate the latest advances in planning, ventilation, and sanitation.

Settlement houses in Boston supplemented the small-scale efforts of building companies beginning in the 1890s. Boston's first settlement house, the Andover House (later the South End House), modeled itself on the original British settlement, Toynbee Hall in London. The South End House's longtime director Robert A. Woods identified inadequate housing as only one in a host of interconnected urban problems, becoming a leading national advocate of municipal-wide reform that would originate in local neighborhoods. To this end, the South End House built a clubhouse in 1901 that provided room for its programs while also standing as a symbol of neighborhood unity. The building was

designed in the Colonial Revival style, emphasizing its ties to newly recovered regional building traditions and linking the growing immigrant population of the district with the American past.

During the early 20th century, reform housing planned for suburban locations drew upon the traditions of urban philanthropic housing, American industrial experiments in workers' housing, and the garden city movement originating in Great Britain. Following the influential lead of Forest Hills Gardens in New York City (1909–12), the Boston architectural firm of Kilham and Hopkins designed several model suburban projects in New England, including a portion of Forest Hills Cottages (Woodbourne) in Boston, for the Boston Dwelling House Company (1911). Intended for lower-income workers, these comprehensively planned communities would influence the firm's own proposals for government-sponsored World War I housing, as well as subsequent postwar development.

Alan Axelrod, ed., *The Colonial Revival in America* (1985); David P. Handlin, *The American Home: Architecture and Society, 1815–1915* (1979); Lawrence J. Vale, *From the Puritans to the Projects: Public Housing and Public Neighbors* (2000); Sam Bass Warner, Jr., *Streetcar Suburbs: The Process of Growth in Boston (1870–1900)* (1962); Robert A. Woods, *The Neighborhood in Nation-Building: The Running Comment of Thirty Years at the South End House* (1923).

Maura Lyons

Railroad Stations   More than 4,000 railroad stations have been built in New England since 1835. Regrettably, most of these once ubiquitous civic structures have been demolished. Lost in the wake of evolving transportation needs and prevailing economic trends, the railroad station was at one time considered the single most important building in town. Of the few hundred or so remaining depots throughout the region, some are still used for passenger rail while many others have been converted to alternative uses. These remaining structures include some of New England's most notable architectural and vernacular examples.

Between 1881 and 1886, the renowned architect Henry Hobson Richardson executed 12 railroad station designs. Of the nine he designed and built for the Boston and Albany Railroad, four remain today, at Palmer, South Framingham, Wellesley Hills, and Woodland (Newton), Mass. The other commissions at North Easton and Holyoke, Mass., and New London, Conn., all survive intact and are distinguished in their synthesis of his mature style.

Boston's South Station, designed by Shepley, Rutan and Coolidge (1899), was at the time of its completion the single busiest depot in America. The track layout and interiors have all been altered significantly over the years, but its austere granite facade with classical references has survived and been preserved. In Worcester, Mass., the commodious BeauxArts second Union Station (1911), designed by Watson and Huckel, has been renovated for reuse as a passenger station and is protected as a historic structure. The wooden station building in Lexington, Mass. (ca.

Union Station (Watson and Huckle, 1911), Worcester, Mass.

1850), is a fine example of the early railroad porte-cochere style of depot. Earlier still is the wooden Gothic Revival depot at West Brookfield, Mass. (ca. 1847), which may be one of the oldest remaining station buildings in the United States. This structure ceased operations as a passenger station in 1884.

Though demolished, the brownstone and brick Providence Union Depot (1848) designed by Rhode Island native Thomas Alexander Tefft was commissioned by three separate railroad companies and had the distinction of being the first union station (uniting multiple railroad lines) in the United States. Its design was an eclectic pre-Richardsonian mix of Romanesque and Italianate styling, and it was instantly recognizable for its two clock towers and articulated building form. In 1885 *American Architect* magazine included Tefft's depot as one of the 20 best buildings in the United States. The sprawling, five-building second Union Station (1899), designed by Stone, Carpenter and Wilson, survives as a mixed-use structure, having been superseded by the nearby stainless steel domed and limestone-faced Amtrak station by Skidmore, Owings and Merrill (1986).

In addition to Richardson's New London station, Connecticut has several other railroad stations worthy of mention. Waterbury station, built in 1909, was designed by McKim, Mead and White, and features a 245-foot-high brick clock tower with Italianate references. The restored New Haven station designed by Cass Gilbert (1920) once featured a separate waiting room for ladies and a gentlemen's smoking room, both common in most early depot layouts. In Stamford, the new station dating from 1986 was designed by Skidmore, Owings and Merrill and is remarkable for its load-bearing exposed truss work. Also notable is the eclectic wooden towered depot at Canaan (1872), Cornwall Bridge Station (1886), and Hartford's Union Station (1889), designed by Shepley, Rutan and Coolidge.

In Vermont, the red brick White River Junction station (1937) is still served by daily passenger trains from New York and Montreal. Bennington's granite station (1898), designed by William C. Bull, has served a series of mixed uses since passenger service ended in 1933. The preserved brick Union Station in Burlington (1916), designed by Fellheimer and Long (designers of Cincinnati's famous Art Deco station), now houses several community organizations along the waterfront.

The large wooden North Conway, N.H., depot (1874), designed by Nathaniel J. Bradlee, is notable for its dramatic and exaggerated Victorian roof features. The rural Potter Place Depot in Andover, N.H., also dating from 1874, is characteristic of the modified Stick

Trinity Church (Henry Hobson Richardson, 1872–77), Copley Square, Boston

Style common in so many regional examples. Other New Hampshire stations of note include Laconia (1892) and New Boston Stations (1895), designed by Bradford Lee Gilbert, and Durham station (1896).

Of Maine's few remaining depots, both Rockland station (1918), designed by Coolidge and Shattuck, and Gardiner station (1911), designed by George Burnham, exist mostly intact despite the long absence of train service. Other notable surviving structures in Maine include those at Freeport (1912), Bucksport (1874), and Yarmouth (1906).

Ronald Dale Karr, *The Rail Lines of Southern New England* (1995); Steven Parissien, *Station to Station* (1997); Janet Greenstein Potter, *Great American Railroad Stations* (1996); Jeffrey Richards and John M. MacKenzie, *The Railway Station* (1986).

Marc F. Mazzarelli

Richardson, Henry Hobson (1838–86) Architect. Widely recognized as the leading architect of his time, Henry Hobson Richardson played a central role in the development of American architecture in the second half of the 19th century. By the number and influence of his buildings, he left his mark on the architecture of New England.

Born in Louisiana, Richardson came north to enter Harvard College, graduating in 1859. A student at the Ecole des Beaux-Arts in Paris during the Civil War, he opened his own office in New York in 1866, where his practice was based until 1878. Richardson's early works reflect the influence of the contemporary Gothic Revival and Second Empire styles. By 1870, however, Richardson began to explore his own design approach, drawing on Romanesque precedents, as exemplified by his Brattle Square Church, Boston (1869–73); New York State Hospital, Buffalo (1869–80); and Hampden County Court House, Springfield, Mass. (1871–74, altered). In 1872 Richardson won the competition for Trinity Church, Boston (1872–77), with a Romanesque Revival design. This granite and brownstone structure includes a sanctuary with a Greek cross plan and an attached parish house. The pyramidlike massing disciplines the building's picturesque tendencies and unifies the asymmetrical composition to create a central focus for Copley Square. This project brought Richardson national recognition and shaped his ensuing career.

In 1874 Richardson moved to Brookline, Mass., to maintain direct involvement in the construction phase of the Trinity Church project; four years later he brought his office to Brookline as well. In the years that followed, Richardson's career blossomed. As his fame grew, Richardson was called on to design buildings in Washington, Pittsburgh, Cincinnati, Chicago, and Saint Louis; his monument to the Ames family of transcontinental railroad financiers (1879–82), a pyramid, was erected in Albany County, Wyo. Still, over his 20-year career, the majority of his buildings were located in New England.

The works of Richardson's mature years moved away from references to historic precedents and details. Instead, they came to depend on the simplification of form and the qualities of their materials to create a strong sense of gravity and repose. At the same time, Richardson was creating new responses to a series of emergent building types: between 1876 and 1885 he created small public library buildings for the Boston suburbs of Woburn, North Easton, Quincy, and Malden; he also designed a series of railroad stations, including nine for the Boston and Albany Railroad. His best-known institutional buildings are Sever Hall (1878–80) and Austin Hall (1881–84) at Harvard University and the Allegheny County Court House and Jail, Pittsburgh (1883–88). He designed urban commercial buildings in Hartford and Boston, but his Marshall Field Wholesale Store in Chicago (1885–87, destroyed) was his best work of this type.

In addition Richardson was responsible for a significant number of residential projects, contributing to the development of the Shingle Style and of a more open, "living hall" approach to interior planning. His Sherman House, Newport, R.I. (1874–76), is a representative early work, while the Stoughton House, Cambridge, Mass. (1882–83), is a mature Shingle Style structure.

Although he was in deteriorating health in his last years, Richardson practiced his profession at a hectic pace until his death in Brookline, on April 27, 1886. His leading apprentices kept his practice going under the name Shepley, Rutan and Coolidge, supervising the completion of his unfinished buildings.

Margaret Henderson Floyd, *Henry Hobson Richardson: A Genius for Architecture* (1998); Jeffrey Karl Ochsner, *H. H. Richardson: Complete Architectural Works* (1982); James F. O'Gorman, *Living Architecture: A Biography of H. H. Richardson* (1997); Marianna Griswold Van Rensselaer, *Henry Hobson Richardson and His Works* (1969 [1888]).

Jeffrey Karl Ochsner

Summer Camps As early as a century ago, summer camps for boys and girls were recognized as a uniquely American contribution to education. It is fitting, therefore, that the summer camp movement should have originated in New England, where education has always been highly prized. Most of the hundreds of camps founded in the region proved ephemeral, but a handful of early camps survive today with some original architecture intact. Although summer camps have changed in focus several times since the movement's inception—from vacation spots where wealthy children could learn woodcraft and rugged survival skills to places where poor children from the city could enjoy a few weeks of fresh air to centers for concentrated study of everything from music to chess, the architecture of the camps has retained certain core elements and ideas. Living in the woods in rustic wooden buildings, children experience nature close up, in a manner far removed from their wintertime lives.

Organized camping emerged gradually after the Civil War, which first popularized "camping out," a fad by the 1870s. The earliest campgrounds, used by schools and groups organized by the Young Men's Christian Association (YMCA) had no permanent structures; the campers slept in tents. The oldest surviving YMCA camp, Camp Dudley in Westport, N.Y., was founded in 1885 as a tent camp; it moved to its current location 23 years later. Another early camp, Keewaydin Dunmore in Salisbury, Vt., descended from a canoe expeditionary tenting camp of 1894 in Maine.

The first summer-long boys' camp built on a fixed site with frame buildings for sleeping and dining was Camp Chocorua, on Church Island, Squam Lake, N.H. (extant 1881–89). Its originator, Ernest B. Balch, was the son of a founder of nearby Holderness School, where some early campers were students. The architecture—well documented in period photographs—was improvised and shantylike, offering a kind of Robinson Crusoe fantasy for eight- to 15-year-olds whose parents were summering at the newly opened Asquam House Hotel on the lake shore. All that survives today of Chocorua is the outdoor chapel; its white birch cross was a much-imitated feature of the camp. Vacationing educators and journalists reported extensively on Chocorua and its more famous offshoot, Camp Asquam, also on Squam Lake (extant 1887–1909). Even more than Chocorua, Asquam set the pattern for modern summer camps, with a "director," "council," and sturdy wooden buildings. Asquam was copied in turn by Pasquaney, on Newfound Lake near Hebron, N.H. (founded 1895). Both catered to the sons of wealthy Bostonians and New Yorkers whose parents were busy touring.

The architecture of Asquam and Pasquaney was identical: board-and-batten construction faced with slabs, wide verandas with rustic hornbeam posts, hipped roofs, and casement, or "camp"-style, windows. At Pasquaney, dormitories flowed together with picturesque ramps and porches, and campers covered every surface with pencil and penknife initials. Architecturally, these elite camps were "semi-aboriginal," aiming to promote masculinity among the boys, and toeing a careful line between too much roughness (intolerable to doting Victorian mothers) and too little (which implied effeminizing luxury). Architectural borrowings can be detected from sources as crude as board-and-batten hunters' camps in the north woods of Maine, to a tasteful cottage illustrated in *Shoppell's Modern Houses* (1895). Asquam went bankrupt, but a few of its buildings survive as part of modern Camp Deerwood, including the former Aristocracy Hall dormitory, now Ritz (1889), the oldest surviving summer camp building in America. Pasquaney still operates today and offers a unique living laboratory of 19th-century camping, with many original structures intact, including the first dormitory, Dana Hall (1894–95).

Asquam's director, Dr. Winthrop T. Talbot, proved an effective promoter of the summer camp idea, and by 1900 new camps were appearing at an explosive rate throughout New England and beyond. Some of the earliest camps still in operation in New England are Hale, Center Sandwich, N.H. (1900; oldest extant building, 1902); Awosting, Morris, Conn. (1900; located in New York until 1933); Abnaki, North Hero, Vt. (1901; moved to current site, 1916); Jewell, Colebrook, Conn. (1901; located in New Hampshire until 1955); Pine Island, Belgrade Lakes, Maine (1902; still has an original building); Cobbossee, Winthrop, Maine (1902; oldest building, 1923); Tecumseh, Center Harbor, N.H. (1903; several early buildings); Mowglis, Hebron, N.H. (1903; several early buildings); Belknap, Tuftonboro, N.H. (1903; moved to current site, 1907); Becket, Becket, Mass. (1903; oldest buildings, ca. 1906–17); Moosilauke, Orford, N.H. (1904; parts of some buildings, pre-1908); Brantwood, Peterborough, N.H. (1904; oldest buildings, 1920s); O-AT-KA, Sebago, Maine (1906; several early buildings); Kohut, Oxford, Maine (1907, moved to current site ca. 1911); Androscoggin, Wayne, Maine (1907; moved to current site, 1937); Lawrence, Bear Island, N.H. (1907); Winona, Bridgton, Maine (1908; a ca. 1898 building from the earlier North End Union Benevolent Society Camp burned in 1995); and Pemigewassett, Wentworth, N.H. (1908; oldest building, 1909). Several of these are YMCA camps.

Girls' camps quickly followed. Virtually nothing is known of how the earliest girls'

Birch Lodge and Dana Hall dormitories (1894–96), Camp Pasquaney, near Hebron, N.H.

camps differed from boys' in programming or architecture. Camp Onaway, in Hebron, N.H. (1911), still uses some buildings once occupied by the first girls' camp, Redcroft (1900). Kehonka, in Wolfeboro, N.H. (1902), lasted until 1985. Other pioneering girls' camps that still operate include Wyonegonic, Denmark, Maine (1902; oldest building, 1916); Aloha, Fairlee, Vt. (1905); Farwell, Newbury, Vt. (1906); Runoia, Belgrade Lakes, Maine (1907; oldest building transported to current site, 1914); Alford Lake, Hope, Maine (1907); and Wohelo, Raymond, Maine (1907; oldest building, 1910s). No systematic architectural survey has been done of early camps, and only recently, with the rise of vernacular architecture studies, have camps' rustic structures received any serious attention from historians. Despite their crudeness and generally poor rate of survival, these buildings bring to life the back-to-nature educational philosophies of a bygone era.

W. Barksdale Maynard, "An Ideal Life in the Woods for Boys: Architecture and Culture in the Earliest Summer Camps," *Winterthur Portfolio* (Spring 1999); Maynard, "Chocorua, Asquam, Pasquaney: Where Summer Camps Began," University of Delaware master's thesis (1994); Porter Sargent, *A Handbook of Summer Camps* (1935); Abigail A. van Slyck, "Kitchen Technologies and Mealtime Rituals: Interpreting the Food Axis at American Summer Camps, 1890–1950," *Technology and Culture* (October 2002)

W. Barksdale Maynard

Summer Houses The seacoast, mountains, and lakes of New England have long been associated with summer vacations and the desire for leisure, recreation, privacy, independence, and escape from the rigors of urban and suburban life. The resultant architectural form—the summer house or cottage—originated in New England as early as the second half of the 18th century. New Hampshire governor John Wentworth is credited with erecting one of New England's first summer houses around 1768–71 at Lake Wentworth near

Wolfeboro, N.H. During the early- to mid-1800s, affluent Boston families seeking rural settings and a cooler, healthier alternative to city life built summer homes or developed large estates in adjacent towns to the west of the city or along the North or South Shores of Massachusetts.

The summer house movement, however, did not peak until the late 19th and early 20th centuries. Largely an outgrowth of burgeoning tourism and the development of the resort hotel industry, specialized single-season residences appeared in New England communities endowed with agreeable climate, scenic landscape, convenient transportation access (by roadway, water, and rail) and, in some cases, an architectural legacy with roots deep in regional history. Houses of the immediate post–Civil War era were built in conjunction with resort hotel complexes as well as by individual families along the New England coast and at desirable interior locations. Inspired primarily by the Gothic Revival style, many of these relatively small, modestly adorned cottages were conceived in the Stick and Swiss Chalet variants.

A direct product of America's economic ascendancy from the 1880s to World War I, the concept of the summer house became attractive to those benefiting from increased purchasing power and more available time for leisure and material pursuits. The largest and most ornate of these structures were constructed at major resort communities such as Newport, R.I.; Bar Harbor, Maine; the Berkshire Hills in western Massachusetts; and along the coast north of Boston. Designed largely by well-known, city-based architects and architectural firms, these lavish, often ostentatious residences and their dependent outbuildings were planned in a variety of eclectic styles and building materials reflecting the influence of American, English, and continental European cultural tastes. Initially popular were the Second Empire, Italianate, and English Queen Anne styles, later followed by the Beaux-Arts Classical, the French Châteauesque, and the second Renaissance, Neoclassical, late Gothic, and Spanish Renaissance Revival styles. More indigenous American styles such as the versatile Shingle, the Colonial Revival, and the Craftsman also were embraced by architects and their clients.

Executed in many of these same picturesque styles, particularly the Shingle and the Colonial Revival, and appearing in far greater numbers, were the less extravagant, more practical summer cottages of the Connecticut and Rhode Island shorelines, Cape Cod and the Islands, the New Hampshire and Maine coasts, the White Mountains, and the Lake Champlain basin of Vermont. Notably outstanding collections of such buildings can be seen today at Tamworth (Chocorua), Jackson, Bethlehem, and Rye, N.H.; Watch Hill and Weekapaug, R.I.; Harwichport, Chatham, and Marblehead, Mass.; Old Saybrook, Old Lyme, and Stonington, Conn.; and York, Kennebunkport, Camden, and the Penobscot Bay islands of Islesboro, Vinalhaven, and North Haven in Maine. Since World War I, the phenomenon of the summer house or cottage has continued in a broad array of architectural and lifestyle forms, and is still much in evidence in contemporary New England life.

Carole Owens, *The Berkshire Cottages: A Vanishing Era* (1984); Roger G. Reed, *A Delight to All Who Know It: The Maine Summer Architecture of William R. Emerson* (1990); Vincent J. Scully, Jr., *The Architecture of the American Summer: The Flowering of the Shingle Style* (1989); Bryant F. Tolles, Jr., *Summer Cottages in the White Mountains: The Architecture of Leisure and Recreation, 1870 to 1930* (2000).

Bryant F. Tolles, Jr.

Textile Mills By the mid-1820s two forms of purpose-built structure for the manufacture of woven textiles had emerged in New England. These mills became a distinctive feature of the region's industrial landscape, and today, whether transformed for contemporary purposes (housing, high-tech corporations, shopping malls, and colleges) or empty reminders of a prosperous past, they remain a defining presence on the landscape.

Commonly set at right angles to a river, with doors opening directly into two or three stories at one end, the early mills served small firms in Rhode Island and other New England states with modest waterpower sources from the 1790s through the mid-19th century. From the beginning, bell cupolas (to call the family labor force to work) tended to be placed above the gable end of the building or over a separate stairway tower. Each factory housed either cotton pickers or wool cards and spinning, weaving, and other machines on separate floors where women and children worked under the supervision of a male foreman. Several mills might be erected by a single company over decades of successful operation.

Along the Merrimack River and other extensive power sites, the Boston Associates built factories modeled on a standard developed at Waltham, Mass., by the Boston Manufacturing Company between 1813 and 1822. In the early years of industrial textile production, handlooms had been used for weaving in waterpowered spinning mills, but by 1815 a fully integrated powered factory had evolved at Waltham. The Waltham model called for mills to be built of brick over a partially exposed granite foundation; they were five to seven stories high, roughly 150 feet long, and some 45 feet wide. By the time Lowell was ready to operate in 1822, these corporate mills also had a projecting brick stairway tower at the central bay of the long wall. The Lowell mills were directly adjacent to huge power canals that fed massive waterwheels (later turbines) like those of Waltham's second factory, where this design was first fully articulated. For fire protection, pickers were located in small buildings in front of the mill and connected to the first story by covered wooden bridges. Cupolas in the Waltham-Lowell system were always placed in the middle of the main ridge over the first mill. Until the 1840s a clerestory, or "double roof," provided a fully lit, open-span attic, and in these early decades corporate expansion simply repeated this factory form. By the 1850s, however, two mills might be joined by a projecting brick pavilion (with a central cupola) into a single long factory.

Structural flooring was universally of wooden posts and beams in all periods. Initially, the frame was joisted and covered with thin floorboards. But as leather belts and high-speed shafting came into wider use, production speed increased, and a new structural system was adopted, featuring large, closely spaced wooden beams in place of small floor joists and thick flooring to reinforce internal stability and limit vibration. This modified design became known as "slow burning" mill construction as mutual insurance companies recognized its merits in reducing or slowing the spread of fire. Lower insurance premiums made the design the standard for floors and roofs by the 1880s.

Shared materials and design vocabularies unified the region's textile factories into identifiable icons of industrial progress. The double roof and a less expensive "false," or narrow "eyebrow," roof served as models for other industrial buildings. In the 1820s and 1830s neoclassical detailing and plain brick walls re-

The Boott Cotton Mills, ca. 1870, in Lowell, Mass.

flected the region's urban vernacular style; by the 1840s and 1850s brick piers between large windows were combined with simple, milled Greek Revival woodwork. Although some factories adopted the skylights first used in 1825 in Dover, N.H. (based on those of the ship houses at the Charlestown Navy Yard outside Boston), by 1850 many factories had reverted to pitched and dormered roofs, with later buildings adopting the mansard style. All textile mills are long and narrow because the need for windows limited factory depth until the introduction of gas lighting in the 1850s.

After the Civil War, expansion tended to be by alteration and accretion rather than new construction. While vast new factories made of stone were powered by steam at Fall River, Mass., most textile mills used water as their main source of power until the introduction of electricity. Though abandoned when textile companies moved south in the 20th century, many standing mills continue to bear architectural witness to America's industrialization, immigration, and labor history.

Efforts by the nonprofit Society for Industrial Archaeology and creation of the Historic American Engineering Record in the National Park Service during the early 1970s encouraged conversion of a wide range of factories and mills throughout the industrial Northeast. Rehabilitation into commercial and residential uses was further fostered by new federal tax policies for certified rehabilitation of commercial properties eligible for the National Register of Historic Places from the late 1970s and by tax credits for the creation of affordable housing that help provide market funding.

Betsey Hunter Bradley, *The Works: The Industrial Architecture of the United States* (1999); John Coolidge, *Mill and Mansion: A Study of Architecture and Society in Lowell, Massachusetts, 1820–1865* (1967); Robert F. Dalzell Jr., *Enterprising Elite: The Boston Associates and the World They Made* (1993); Laurence Gross and Richard M. Candee, *Industrial Heritage '84, New England: Guidebook, North Coast Massachusetts, New Hampshire, and Maine Excursion* (1984).

Richard M. Candee

Three-Deckers A "three-decker" is a three-story, three-family dwelling in which the three apartments are stacked, like decks, to house one family on each floor. Although the form is found elsewhere, the extraordinary popularity of three-deckers in New England cities strengthens its identification with the region. New England's three-deckers have two distinct regional characteristics: wooden construction and three porches ("piazzas") stacked at the rear of the building. Other common traits are the use of mortise-and-tenon joints for the main frame of the building, the placement of the narrow end of the building facing the street, and the incorporation of three separate landings and entrances off the shared front and rear stairways. Most three-deckers were built as detached structures, although many were paired to make double three-deckers with mirror-image plans around a brick party wall.

Three-deckers were predominantly built in New England between the 1880s and 1930s. Large concentrations are found in the Greater Boston metropolitan area, Worcester and Fall River, Mass.; Woonsocket, R.I; and Hartford and Waterbury, Conn. After the Civil War, rising land costs and the need for easy access to work sites in many of New England's growing urban industrial centers created a demand for affordable housing. Multifamily housing emerged to combat the housing shortage. Tenement houses were built for the poor and apartment houses for the wealthy. Three-deckers were a popular regional solution because they combined the economics of multiple family housing (on a smaller scale) with the ideal of the detached house, which provided light and air on all four sides. While three-deckers were built in a range of sizes, prices, and luxuriousness, they predominantly housed the working class.

Three-deckers were an improvement over tenement houses—attached, multistory buildings that often had poor lighting and ventilation. Each apartment in the average three-decker had four to six rooms as well as a private bathroom (or water closet). In contrast, the units in a tenement house generally consisted of three or four rooms and common water closets or perhaps outhouses. Three-deckers were usually built in less crowded neighborhoods, often in nearby suburbs. With the potential for two rent-generating apartments, three-deckers also opened the possibility of home ownership to many who would not otherwise have been able to afford it.

Three-deckers had several links to immigrants. Many of the designers and speculative builders of three-deckers were immigrants who were part of the same community as the owners and tenants of the building. Often the three families in a building were further connected by family, ethnic, or occupational ties. For some French Canadians, this shared ethnic heritage had architectural manifestations: French Canadian builders in places like Manchester, N.H., and Southbridge and Fitchburg, Mass., added exterior stairs and large wraparound porches to give the three-deckers a distinctly French Canadian style.

The 1930s marked the end of the era of three-deckers. With access to cheaper land brought by the automobile, the collapse of the housing market during the Depression, and postwar developments in cheap tract housing, three-deckers lost their economic advantage.

The preference for single-family homes also contributed to the decline of three-deckers. But the most significant factor was the concerted opposition of housing reformers. The National Housing Association, a New York–based organization founded in 1910, spearheaded the campaign against three-deckers by censuring them as tenement houses. In addition to the stated antipathy to multifamily housing in general, a less-freqently voiced objection was to the people who lived in three-deckers: suburbanites did not want immigrants in their neighborhoods.

Charged with being fire hazards and bringing down property values, three-deckers were banned in many parts of New England beginning in the 1910s. Construction all but ceased in the 1930s until the late 1980s when some three-deckers have again been built to provide low-cost housing. Despite their lack of prestige, three-deckers are an important presence in the urban landscape of New England.

Arthur J. Krim, *The Three-Deckers of Dorchester: An Architectural Historical Survey* (1977); Marilyn W. Spear, *Worcester's Three-deckers* (1977); Sam Bass Warner, Jr., *Streetcar Suburbs: The Process of Growth in Boston, 1870–1900* (1978); Robert A. Woods and Albert J. Kennedy, *The Zone of Emergence: Observations of the Lower Middle and Upper Working Class Communities of Boston, 1905–1914* (1969).

Diane Jacobsohn

Art

Donna M. Cassidy, Section Editor

INTRODUCTION

Over the past four centuries the visual arts, especially painting, prints, and photography, have played a key role in shaping New England's cultural identity. Using selective lenses, artists have framed visions of the people and landscape that have come to stand for the region—the stern Puritan, the frugal, hardworking New Englander, the skilled crafts worker, the Yankee, a rural and community-focused locale, the picturesque village with white-steepled church, the harsh, rugged environment. They have pictured a place of contrasts, one that possessed pastoral and wilderness landscapes and seascapes, and was inhabited by both the elite New Englanders of colonial portraits and Boston School paintings, and the working-class rural folk in itinerant portraits and genre scenes. Crucial historical moments and agencies have contributed to the formation of regional identity and the circulation of images of New England in the larger national culture—the Colonial Revival, the growth of art museums, the rise of the mass media, the power of New York and Boston as art centers, and the intersection of tourism and art colonies.

Region as a category of analysis in the visual arts has typically centered on style—a method particularly useful in studying the decorative arts. In the 18th century, for example, distinctive forms and visual qualities marked furniture from New England: Newport, R.I., was the sole producer of block and shell case furniture, whereas the bombé desk was found exclusively in Boston manufactured furniture. Local craft training, wood types, and patron desires, among other factors, accounted for these characteristic features. Looking for a regional style in painting or photography is more problematic because New England artists, like American artists generally, were connected to an international art network, and from the 18th century on, many studied in Europe and brought manners indebted to this training to the United States. Multiple styles can be identified in New England art both over time and at the same time, with art in small-town rural New England often differing from that in urban centers like Boston. Artists and scholars alike have argued for a regional art style, however, as Marsden Hartley did in the 1930s when he claimed that mysticism defined the region's painting tradition. Although such traditions are often invented to serve the needs of a particular historical moment, we can still examine why, and how, artists working in New England adapted imported styles to a regional context and patronage.

Art historians have also turned their attention to iconography, its treatment, and its cultural context in exploring region. Common subjects in New England art (like those listed above) do not simply reflect preexisting realities; they are selected by artists to create a particular image of place. Scholars have examined how constructs of New England have functioned historically and ideologically—how, for instance, the mid-19th-century image of the Yankee expressed anxiety about contemporary social changes for New York viewers and patrons, and how the image of an ideal old New England responded to post–Civil War urbanization, industrialization, and tourism. Such representations of New England were often manufactured by outsiders, especially New York artists. Although numerous professional artists have lived and worked in New England from the 17th century onward, and museums and historical societies throughout the region exhibit their work, New York artists played a significant role in defining New England identity, as their work was often mass-produced in prints, photography, and advertising.

Upper-class Boston artists joined the ranks of these New York artists. The image of New England as a rural locale, ethnically and racially homogeneous, with wilderness and seashore reserves, was the vision of these urban artists who saw in the region what they themselves needed and desired, particularly with the advance of modernization. These same representations in turn shaped New Englanders' sense of self and place. New England art, then, is not exclusively the product of the region's inhabitants or natives or bound by its geographic borders; it is constituted of those visual representations and works by artists who have helped to define, or at times to challenge, prevailing images of region. These images were not fixed or singular but were made and re-made to fit the needs and interests of the time, and the visual arts participated in this ever-changing process of giving meaning and form to New England.

Native Americans produced the first art and images of the region. In the 17th century, several traditions existed that were related to sacred practices and daily life, including sculpture in stone and wood, pottery, copper ornaments, quillwork, beadwork, wampum belts, basketry, and birch-bark art. Pictographs have been found in several petroglyph sites (as in the Narragansett Bay region and Solon and Machias, Maine) and in quillwork and wampum. Responding to early European travelers and traders, Native Americans quickly incorporated new materials (beads, silver) and European decorative devices (floral imagery) into their work. The artistic exchange between the colonizers and colonized was reciprocal. European settlers adopted Native American crafts but refused to recognize native arts as art because they did not fit into European definitions of fine art; doing so would recognize a level of civilization and humanity that would disrupt the categorization of native people as the primitive "other."

Even art objects produced by the first European settlers—portraits—ranked low in the hierarchy of the fine arts according to academic standards. Portraits, however, had an important social function: they helped the New England elite assert their position and power in colonial society. Modeled after English styles—neo-medieval and Baroque in the 17th century, Georgian and rococo in the 18th—colonial portraits worked to characterize the region as a "new" England. In form, style, and presentation of the sitter, John Foster's *Reverend Richard Mather* (1670, Massachusetts Historical Society, Boston), an anonymous artist's *John Freake* (ca. 1674, Worcester [Mass.] Art Museum), and Thomas Smith's *Self Portrait* (1690, Worcester Art Museum) defined 17th-century culture and values—Puritanism, mercantilism, and the tensions between spirituality and materialism. During the following century John Smibert, Joseph Blackburn, Robert Feke, and John Singleton Copley continued to paint colonial merchants and their wives, portraying them as genteel, industrious, and materially successful. Copley's *John Hancock* (1765, Museum of Fine Arts, Boston) shows the sitter dressed in plain wool attire and modest bob wig attending to a ledger at his desk—a sedate setting for this wealthy man known for sporting velvet suits, driving around Boston in a yellow carriage, and neglecting the family business. In its time, such work responded to attacks on upper-class entitlements and extravagances and singled out the reserved New Englander diligently at work as an archetype for region—a type repeated in Copley's *Paul Revere* (ca. 1768, Museum of Fine Arts, Boston) and *Samuel Adams* (1770–72, Museum of Fine Arts, Boston). Copley's style, with its brilliant colors, crisp edges, and detailed textures, conveyed these same qualities to viewers and offered a distinct contrast to the 18th-century painterly English style. A similar reserve is pictured in the many images of colonial matrons—elderly, prayerful women seated in a chair and holding a book, as in Joseph Badger's *Mrs. John Edwards (Abigail Fowle)* (ca. 1750–60, Museum of Fine Arts, Boston) and Copley's *Mrs. Michael Gill (Relief Dowie)* (1770–71, Tate, London). Through such portraits, elite white culture came to stand for the region.

Native Americans occasionally appear but are either represented as English gentlemen and gentlewomen or made to conform to notions of Indianness, as in the murals in the McPhaedris-Warner House in Portsmouth (ca. 1720), which copy John Verelst's portraits of four Iroquois from the Mohawk Valley (1710). African Americans, too, are presented in terms of their relation to the elite culture. In *Flora* (1796, Stratford [Conn.] Historical Society), the 19-year-old slave sold to Asa Benjamin in New Haven County, Conn., is depicted as a flat silhouette without the substance or presence of wealthy white sitters, signifying the position of blacks in colonial New England.

Considered craft workers during the colonial period, Copley and his painter colleagues would have undoubtedly identified with the sitter in *Paul Revere*—an artisan at work displaying the teapot as the expression of his skill. This portrait, along with the many others filled with furniture, silver, and assorted artifacts, identified New England with high-quality craft. Colonial New England in fact witnessed the development of distinctive decorative arts, produced both for local patrons and for a wider international market. The region, especially Boston, was a major production center of simply decorated, utilitarian redware in the 17th and 18th centuries. Furniture and silverware, like contemporary portraits, were based on English styles yet evolved regional characteristics.

Trained in England, 17th-century craft workers brought with them the neo-medieval manner—blocky, heavy proportions, geometric and floral designs—along with some knowledge of Renaissance and mannerist trends, as was the case with Thomas Dennis and William Searle, who both worked in Ipswich, Mass. These artisans revised English antecedents to fit native materials, economics, and patron desires, resulting in new regional forms, such as the Brewster chair with its lathe-turned parts (Plymouth, Mass.), the Hartford sunflower chest, and the Hadley chest

Joseph Tapping stone (ca. 1678, King's Chapel Burial Ground, Boston)

with its low-relief strap work, simple structural form, and tulip-and-leaf motif, popularized in the Connecticut River valley in the late 17th and early 18th centuries. Silversmiths like John Hull and Robert Sanderson—and later Jeremiah Dummer and John Coney—and gravestone carvers followed a similar pattern. Gravestone carving was based in a Puritan emblematic tradition and European decorative arts practices. Gravestones like that of Joseph Tapping (ca. 1678, King's Chapel Burial Ground, Boston) included symbols and motifs derived from European emblem books and the winged death's head that typified these New England markers into the 18th century.

A new affluence and the expansion of consumer capitalism in the 18th century resulted in a profusion of specialized furniture forms and high-style furniture shops in Boston, Newport, Salem, Mass., and Portsmouth. The Townsend-Goddard shop in Newport epitomized the high point of 18th-century New England craft. Furniture makers and silversmiths worked in such styles as Queen Anne and Chippendale, based again on English models and marked by classical details, orientalizing features, s-curves, cabriole legs, and claw-and-ball feet. Furniture makers preferred fine-grained mahogany from Central America and the West Indies—a clear indication of New England's involvement with international trade—and produced regional forms (Boston bombé bureaus and block front tables, Newport block and shell case furniture) and a Chippendale style devoid of the lavish decoration typical of Philadelphia chairs by contrast. Silversmiths like Jacob Hurd and Paul Revere designed globular teapots characteristic of New England manufacture.

After the Revolution, Boston exerted increasing power as the cultural center of the region through institutions like the Boston Athenaeum. As aspiring young artists traveled to European art academies for instruction, the taste of wealthy Boston patrons turned in the same direction and favored the new proto-Romantic styles popular in British and French art as evidenced in Gilbert Stuart's *Colonel James Swan* (1795, Museum of Fine Arts, Boston) and Washington Allston's *William Ellery Channing* (1809, Museum of Fine Arts, Boston). A group of elite Bostonians supported Allston so that he could complete his grand history painting *Belshazzar's Feast* (1817–43, Detroit Institute of Arts)—a painting type heralded as the highest form of expression according to European art standards. In the new republic, paintings also advanced and reinforced emerging social values. Stuart's portrait *Mrs. Richard Yates* (1793–94, National Gallery of Art, Washington, D.C.) and Prudence

Punderson Rossiter's silk-on-silk embroidery picture *The First, Second and Last Scene of Mortality* (1783, Connecticut Historical Society, Hartford) pictured women sewing and embroidering, activities that marked the sitter's leisure class and the high value placed on domesticity for the New England republican woman. These women created thousands of samplers, often under the direction of professional instructors at dame schools, academies, and female seminaries, and produced schools of work in Boston, Salem, and Newport in the last decades of the 18th century.

The same turn toward European and especially British taste also marked the decorative arts from the late 18th to the early 19th century. The Federal style popular at this time was part of a larger neoclassical art movement and especially drew from the work of British architect Robert Adam. The Salem architect and carver Samuel McIntire best exemplified this style in his interior designs and furniture with straight, slender tapering legs, delicate inlay, subtle curves, and classical details like draped urns produced for Salem's prosperous merchants. The elegant classical details of this style also characterized the silver work of Paul Revere, in particular the oval teapots with fluted sides and swag and ribbon designs. Neoclassical clean lines and direct forms fit the designs of the Shakers, who produced a regional vernacular neoclassicism at this same time; the order, harmony, and efficiency that constituted the Federal style concurrently defined Shaker aesthetic principles. During this period artifact-related industries expanded, further identifying the region with craft production—for example, the various Bennington, Vt., potteries from the small Norton potteries in 1794 to the United States Pottery in 1853, and the Boston and Sandwich Glass Company, founded in 1825.

Boston's Europeanized taste was countered in subregions within New England. Ralph Earl tempered the British aristocratic portrait in his paintings of the leading families of Connecticut's northwest country towns such as *Elijah Boardman* (1789, Metropolitan Museum of Art, New York), who stands well dressed yet at work in his dry goods store, and *Roger Sherman* (1775–76, Yale University Art Gallery, New Haven, Conn.), who wears an old suit with a patch on one leg. Both portraits emulate Copley's style, and both reassert notions of New England regional identity as frugal, stern, and industrious, as did the so-called folk or plain portraits by late-18th- and early-19th-century itinerant artists. Exemplifying the latter, Matthew Prior's *Jesse and Lucy A. Hartshorn* (1836, Old Sturbridge Village, Mass.) and Erastus Salisbury Field's *Joseph Moore and His Family* (1839, Museum of Fine Arts, Boston) exhibit what the art historian Ellen Grayson calls the artisan aesthetic in contrast to the cosmopolitan style: the artisan aesthetic, with its invisible brushstroke and multiple layers of pigment, implied practice and painstaking labor and was associated with industry; the cosmopolitan style, with its visible strokes, implied technical virtuosity and innate genius. The artisan style helped identify the rural New Englander as industrious, simple, and plain—characteristics also singled out by Timothy Dwight and reinforced in daguerreian portraits of the 1840s. With these folk portraits, we see the shift of regional identity away from the urban elite to the inhabitants of the rural countryside—a shift that occurred simultaneously in landscape and genre painting.

The New England elite emulated not only the portraits of their British counterparts but their taste for landscape painting. Ralph Earl, in *Landscape from Denny Hill* (1790s, Worcester Art Museum) and many other works, regionalized the European landscape formulas of the Picturesque and the Beautiful, and framed the regional landscape as a pastoral countryside in which New Englanders—with their neat white houses and steepled villages—lived in harmony with nature. This image would be repeated throughout much of the 19th century in the art of the Hudson River School. Foremost in this group was Thomas Cole, whose 1835 lecture "Essay on American Scenery" (published in 1836) defined the landscape of the American Northeast, including New England, as characteristic of the nation. For him, this region possessed natural resources and features—wilderness, mountains, bountiful waterways, dazzling autumn scenery—that distinguished it from European scenery, as well as markers like the white steepled church, which carried associations in the same manner as classical ruins in European landscape paintings. In *New England Scenery* (1839, Art Institute of Chicago) Cole combined features that made up the archetypal regional landscape and defined New England as an ideal preindustrial locale where culture was in balance with nature—an image constructed by other anti-industrialist New Englanders like Timothy Dwight and broadened by Cole's student Frederic Edwin Church in his own *New England Scenery* (1851, George Walter Vincent Smith Art Museum, Springfield, Mass.).

The pastoral middle landscape was not the only New England pictured by the Hudson River School. Cole represented the White Mountains as a wilderness that overwhelmed small human settlements in *The Notch of the White Mountains* (1839, National Gallery of Art). The wilderness remained a common image of New England well into the 19th century in such works as Sanford Gifford's *Mount Mansfield* (ca. 1858, George Walter Vincent Smith Art Museum) and Church's *Twilight in the Wilderness* (1860, Cleveland Museum of Art). By midcentury, however, the White Mountains and other New England sites assumed a more civilized look. Picturesque views like John Frederick Kensett's *Mount Washington* (1851, Corcoran Gallery of Art, Washington, D.C.), with figures standing in a cleared foreground plane and the mountain wilderness far off in the distance, became the norm; such scenes of an accessible and domesticated nature were replicated by the White Mountain School in the later part of the century. These landscapes typically erased the presence of tourism's transformation of nature, excising, for example, railways from view. Only in the photographs of Samuel Bemis and the Kilburn Brothers do we see the presence of such elements of the tourist industry. The stereopticons of the Kilburn Brothers, oil paintings of the Hudson River School, and prints in guidebooks and circulated by the American Art-Union also served to attract the middle class, merchants, and professionals from Boston, New York, and other northeastern cities in need of an escape to nature. These images shaped how other Americans perceived the region and distinguished New England as a cultivated locale at the same time that the West, with its immeasurable spaces, was being represented as the new American wilderness.

Similarly, paintings, photographs, lithographs, and panoramas of the coast pictured New England as alternately pastoral and wild. While scholars have often associated these seascapes, especially such so-called luminist works as Fitz Hugh Lane's *Brace's Rock, Brace's Cove* (1864, Terra Museum of American Art, Chicago), with Transcendentalism, these paintings also identified the region with 19th-century commercial developments—shipbuilding, whaling, tourism. Lane's *Three Master on the Gloucester Railway* (1857, Cape Ann Historical Association, Gloucester, Mass.) and *Boston Harbor at Sunset* (1850–55, Museum of Fine Arts, Boston) detail the well-ordered working wharves of the New England coast—an image of region rein-scribed in photographs like the Bierstadt Brothers' *Whale Ship Hove Down for Repairs* (1862, New Bedford [Mass.] Whaling Museum) and John P. Soule's *Boston Harbor and East Boston from State Street Block* (1863, Boston Athenaeum). Martin Johnson Heade's paintings of the salt marshes in Newburyport, Mass., and Newport, like those of the Hudson River School painters, defined the regional landscape as a pastoral, well-ordered realm controlled by yeomen. But New England seascapes also described a world where nature was out of control and threatening, as in Church's *Coast Scene, Mount Desert (Storm off Mount Desert)* (1863, Wadsworth Atheneum, Hartford) and Heade's *Thunder Storm on Narragansett Bay* (1868, Amon Carter Museum, Fort Worth, Tex.).

Antebellum landscapes and seascapes depicted an overwhelmingly rural, preindustrial New England and celebrated the harsh life of the natives by inference. Genre paintings defined New Englanders in a similar way. Along with theater and popular literature, paintings such as William Sidney Mount's *The Long Story* (1837, Corcoran Gallery of Art) played a key role in inventing the Yankee as farmer-philosopher: rustic, clownish provincial, unaffected, trickster-trader, independent, innocent, direct, clever. This character, performing in such works as Mount's *Bargaining for a Horse* (1835, New-York Historical Society), critiqued Jacksonian democracy and expressed anxieties regarding economic speculation. In the 1840s and 1850s genre painters continued to see the region as a rural preserve in opposition to the increasingly complex world of the city (read: New York). Representations of New England by Tompkins Matteson, Jerome Thompson, Arthur Fitzwilliam Tait, John W. Ehninger, and Winslow Homer focused on scenes of carefree work, the charms of rural life, and harmonious community in the maple sugaring camps and harvest rituals. These artists, like contemporary landscape painters, were based in New York, where they exhibited and sold their art. Receiving wide circulation in prints reproduced by *Ballou's Pictorial* and *Harper's Weekly,* their images helped make the construct of rural New England common among middle-class viewers and readers.

Nineteenth-century sculpture in New England, often designed by native sons and daughters, built a sense of regional identity that did not depend on outsiders' conceptions. Richard Greenough's *Benjamin Franklin* (1856), the first outdoor public sculpture in Boston, was followed by numerous monuments to the region's political and cultural leaders. Thomas Ball's mass-produced statuette of Daniel Webster (1853), and Hiram Powers's sculpture of the same man for the Massachusetts State House (1859), established Webster as the region's hero. Each state memorialized its own leaders in sculpture (Nathan Hale in Connecticut, for example). Other monuments were dedicated to writers, clerics, and educators such as Henry Wadsworth

Longfellow, Nathaniel Hawthorne, William Ellery Channing, and John Harvard, thus identifying New England as a realm of the politically and intellectually powerful.

The politics of abolitionism and the Civil War further influenced the region's cultural identity. During and immediately after the war, genre paintings and sculpture equated New England with abolition and free labor. Eastman Johnson's maple sugaring paintings (1860–66) describe a community of laborers from Fryeburg, Maine, producing a type of sugar not associated with slave labor. John Rogers's popular mass-produced sculpture *The Fugitive's Story* (1869, Yale University Art Gallery) identified the region with abolition through its representation of Henry Ward Beecher, William Lloyd Garrison, and John Greenleaf Whittier. Public sculptures lining Boston's Commonwealth Avenue and Public Garden created an image of the city as an abolitionist stronghold, as did Edmonia Lewis's portraits of John Brown and Robert Gould Shaw. Augustus Saint-Gaudens's *Memorial to Robert Gould Shaw and the Massachusetts Fifty-fourth Regiment* (1884–96, dedicated 1897) at Boston Common (later identified with the region in Charles Ives's musical composition *Three Places in New England* [1903–14]) presented the achievement of the first all-black regiment in the Civil War, in Massachusetts.

Declines in regional agricultural markets and in whaling, shipping, and textile manufacturing marked the postwar period and created a need to preserve and mythologize the region. As in the local-color literature of Sarah Orne Jewett and her contemporaries, late-19th-century genre painting idealized a rural New England that was quickly fading and recast early-19th-century themes that celebrated rural life. William Morris Hunt, George Fuller, and other tonalists emulated the Romantic realism of the French painter Jean-François Millet (whose works were collected by Bostonians) by painting rural women in the countryside bathed in a hazy, indistinct light. The country girls, barefoot boys, and rural folk frolicking in New England farmlands and along the seashore pictured by Winslow Homer and Eastman Johnson along with cozy scenes of country life in Rogers's sculptures like *Checkers up at the Farm* (1875, New-York Historical Society) defined the region as a locale where innocence and contact with nature still ruled the day. The New England countryside was packaged as therapeutic and restorative for the leisured classes just as it was in contemporary tourist literature.

Accompanying the rise of tourism in the late 19th century was an increase in art colonies across the region. Tourist locales and art colonies emerged largely in areas economically in decline and, as such, seemed frozen in time. Artists visiting these sites tended to see and paint a premodern New England. Their works looked back nostalgically to preindustrial, antebellum times when the region and nation were imagined as uniform and uncontentious, and when life was simple and without large-scale factories, agricultural depression, and a permanent working class. Even industrial scenes evoke this earlier time. When Homer represented factories in *The Morning Bell (Old Mill/The Mill)* (1871, Yale University Art Gallery), he, too, looked back to the small mills and mill girls of 1830s New England.

Nostalgia, escapism, and a turn toward the past shaped the tone of much turn-of-the-century art in, and of, the region. Puritans and Pilgrims became common themes, as in George Boughton's *Pilgrims Going to Church* (1867, New-York Historical Society); Rogers's sculpture *"Why Don't You Speak for Yourself, John?"* (1885, Smithsonian American Art Museum, Washington, D.C.), inspired by Henry Wadsworth Longfellow's "The Courtship of Miles Standish" (1853); and Saint-Gaudens's *Puritan* (1883–86, Metropolitan Museum of Art). Public sculpture such as Hammat Billings's *National Monument to the Forefathers* (Plymouth, 1889) and Daniel Chester French's *Minute Man* (1874, Concord, Mass.) hailed the colonial period and the Revolutionary War as central to regional identity.

Painters and photographers engaged in escapism by turning from modern culture toward the past and the tourist present. The Ten, a group of American impressionist painters who exhibited together from 1898 to 1919, captured on canvas transient moments of light outdoors and focused on middle-class leisure activities like their impressionist counterparts in Europe. They were attracted to such tourist meccas as the Isles of Shoals, Cape Cod, Nantucket, Martha's Vineyard, Cape Ann, and Newburyport in Massachusetts, as well as to Colonial Revival colonies in Old Lyme, Greenwich, and Cos Cob in Connecticut. Willard Metcalf's *October* (1909, Museum of Fine Arts, Springfield) defined the colonial home as a marker of regional identity, while Childe Hassam's *Church at Old Lyme, Connecticut* (1905, Albright-Knox Art Gallery, Buffalo, N.Y.) revived the earlier 19th-century image of the white steepled New England village. Anxious about modernization and immigration, older families in the region, who often lived in or near such buildings, looked to such paintings to assert their identity as the "real" New Englanders. Impressionist paintings, along with photographs like Wallace Nutting's *Nuttinghame Blossoms* (1908, private collection), were part of a larger Colonial Revival movement that equated regional and national identity with the colonial past, with its rural culture, handcrafted goods, and (perceived) homogeneous population of English settlers sharply contrasted with modern culture, with its urban growth, mass-produced goods, and new immigrants from southern and eastern Europe.

Crafts, furniture, and other decorative arts objects played a key role in the Colonial Revival. For makers and consumers, colonial decorative arts and artifacts, from hooked rugs to needlework, possessed the moral superiority associated with colonial life and architecture and had great appeal as many yearned for the handcrafted at a time when these objects were being mass-produced more frequently. Antiques collecting came into vogue, as did the business of reproducing colonial objects. Reaching back to its colonial past, Deerfield, Mass., invented a new civic identity as a craft center through such organizations as the Society of Blue and White Needlework, the Pocumtuck Basket Makers, and the Deerfield Society of Arts and Crafts. Needlework designers emulated those in local collections, and furniture makers replicated the 17th-century Hadley chests common to the region. Artisans belonging to the Society of Arts and Crafts, Boston, drew from New England craft traditions as inspirations, thereby identifying these objects as regional, as in silversmith George Christian Gebelein's work, which depended heavily on Paul Revere's. Along with his books and hand-colored photographs of colonial life and homes, Wallace Nutting (a former Congregational minister) began manufacturing reproduction colonial furniture in 1918, eventually setting up factories in Saugus and Framingham, Mass. Colonial crafts also served to Americanize immigrants, as in one settlement house workshop for vocational training for Italian and Jewish immigrants called "Paul Revere Pottery."

The domestic interior filled with colonial antiques, from pewter plates and gateleg tables to oriental artifacts associated with the China trade, prevailed in the paintings of the Boston School and impressionists—for example, Edmund Tarbell's *New England Interior* (1906, Museum of Fine Arts, Boston) and William Paxton's *Portrait of Elizabeth Blaney* (1916, private collection)—and the photographs of Nutting, Frances and Mary Allen, Emma Coleman, Chansonetta Stanley Emmons, and Emma Sewall. Such works identified the region not only with the colonial past but also with the feminine and largely upper class; they dramatically contrasted New England with the gritty masculinity of Frederic Remington's western cowboys and George Bellows's working-class New York immigrants. New England art conflated domesticity and the "proper" sphere for women with the colonial past as women sat next to four-poster beds or tended spinning wheels, as in Cecelia Beaux's *New England Woman* (1895, Pennsylvania Academy of the Fine Arts, Philadelphia), Lucia Fairchild's *The Women of Plymouth* (ca. 1893, Blow-Me-Down Grange, Plainfield, N.H.), Nutting's *The Quilting Kitchen* (ca. 1915, Library of Congress, Washington, D.C.), and Edmund Tarbell's *My Family* (1914, private collection).

The conservative gender identity that characterized Boston School paintings was pictured in an equally conservative style. Despite the promotion of oriental art by such critics and collectors as Arthur Wesley Dow and Ernest Fenollosa, Boston art patrons like Isabella Stewart Gardner and educational institutions like the School of the Museum of Fine Arts remained traditional in taste in comparison to those in New York. The Armory Show of 1913 (the International Exhibition of Modern Art) received a cool reception in Boston, where artistic taste still demanded the genteel refinement typified by John Singer Sargent's portraits. Throughout the 19th century, Boston patrons embraced art in the European idealizing and moralizing manner, as in Allston's paintings and in neoclassical sculpture like Thomas Crawford's *Orpheus and Cerebus* (1843, Museum of Fine Arts, Boston)—a manner continued in Sargent's public murals at the Museum of Fine Arts and Boston Public Library. Fine art remained the province of social privilege, although popular arts began to reach beyond class boundaries. The Drawing Act of 1870, which required Massachusetts public schools to teach art, brought art—but primarily industrial arts—to a wider spectrum of society. The Museum of Fine Arts and organizations like the Boston Art Club, the St. Botolph Club, and even the Society of Arts and Crafts helped members of the elite assert their identity and position. Such institutions defined "fine" art and distinguished it from the popular and industrial arts that were the domain of the lower classes.

Outside Boston another New England contested the image of a feminine region embodied in the Boston School's languid, enervated women in interiors, the impressionists' domesticated landscape, the Puritans and Pilgrims, Sargent's genteel

Bostonians, and the aging region of Eastman Johnson's *The Nantucket School of Philosophy* (1887, Walters Art Gallery, Baltimore). Winslow Homer pictured a wild, expansive nature, a masculine region. Rural, working-class New Englanders (including women) in *Fog Warning* (1885, Museum of Fine Arts, Boston) and *A Summer Night* (1897, Musée d'Orsay, Paris) possessed a vitality and physical power absent in the Boston School's domestic interiors, while *Northeaster* (1895, Metropolitan Museum of Art) and other coastal views represented the region as a new frontier and wilderness, not the settled landscape of the contemporary impressionists and tonalists. Homer's art addressed a male audience—businessmen who went hunting and fishing in search of "authentic" adventures away from the city—and was praised for its healthy, rejuvenating qualities. His masculine Maine and "strenuous life regionalism" (as the art historian Sarah Burns has labeled his work) paralleled the rise of Maine as a summer resort in the 1880s and 1890s. He represented a New England that outsiders desired to see, just as the earlier Hudson River paintings of the White Mountains had for their generation.

Other representations challenged the image of an antimodern, ethnically homogeneous New England constructed by the Colonial Revival, the impressionists, and Homer. The photographers Herbert Collins and Margaret Sutermeister documented Boston's African American communities, while Lewis Hine delineated a New England ethnically diverse and subject to the problems associated with industrialization in his photographs of workers in Maine's sardine canneries and New Hampshire's textile industry for the National Child Labor Committee (1910). These photographs contested the predominant image of the region as a refuge and therapeutic retreat from industrialization and immigration. Despite such challenges, the New England pictured in turn-of-the-century art largely reiterated that defined by early-19th-century image makers—rural, preindustrial, Yankee, white, and supported by the tourist industry, the Colonial Revival movement, and elite artists and patrons.

Like these artists, Native American artists turned to the past and past traditions to fashion a regional and racial identity. Various tribal traditions were sources for 19th-century art: the turn-of-the-century figurative birch-bark items of Passamaquoddy Joseph Tomah; the multicolored Gay Head clay pottery of the Wampanoag; and the Victorian fancy basketry of the Penobscot, Passamaquoddy, and Micmac. These traditional art forms were transformed by new social and economic realities and interaction with white culture. With the development of tourism at sites like Bar Harbor, Maine, Campobello Island, New Brunswick, just off the Maine Coast, and Martha's Vineyard, Native American artists had a new market for their artifacts and set up shops both in their own reservations and at tourist sites. The style and form of the artifacts changed in this context. Ceremonial clubs, for instance, which were originally undecorated combat weapons in the 17th century and status symbols with spirit carvings in the 18th and 19th centuries, became colorful carvings with human faces beginning in the mid-19th century in response to tourism.

Indeed, tourism continued to shape New England art well into the 20th century. Many early-20th-century modernists made New England central to their art. The

Ash Can painters, or the New York realists, as well as the avant-garde, summered at Monhegan Island and Ogunquit, Maine, and Gloucester and Provincetown, Mass.; some bought property and spent half the year in New York and half in New England. A few of these artists pictured the region abstractly, as Stuart Davis did in his Gloucester harbor view *Swing Landscape* (1938, Indiana University Art Museum, Bloomington); others like Marsden Hartley in *The Dark Mountain No. 1* (1909, Metropolitan Museum of Art) depicted the desolate declining northern farmlands. Robert Henri, George Bellows, and John Sloan were attracted to wilder places like Monhegan Island, where they represented the region as Homer did in his Prout's Neck painting—directly confronting a rugged nature and romanticizing working-class fisherfolk as the primitive "other." For this group, the Maine coast and folk possessed the energy, power, and genuine ruggedness that had been lost in modern life.

Pastoral New England also figured into the modernists' work. Inspired by the contemplative writers Ralph Waldo Emerson and Henry David Thoreau, John Marin and Marguerite Zorach, among others, sought spirituality and a lost paradise where people could peacefully coexist with nature; they produced works in which the New England landscape became increasingly abstracted but stood for this edenic world. The female nude was often used to signify this lost paradise as well as the sense of liberation that nature, and New England in particular, held for painters like Marin and sculptors like Gaston Lachaise and William Zorach. The New England folk held special meaning for these artists, too. In Ogunquit, Hamilton Easter Field and Robert Laurent collected folk art and colonial portraits from the locals in the 1910s and marketed this art in New York. Modernist painters and sculptors adopted the simple forms and surface design characteristic of folk art in their work and revived glass painting, embroidery, and rug making. New England folk art was lauded as the predecessor of the authentic, abstract, and emotional style of the modernists, just as non-Western art had been regarded in relation to the European avant-garde.

The folk continued to play an important role in New England art of the 1920s and 1930s, when region became highly valued in American art and culture. At this time the regionalist movement emerged in response to modernization, consumerism, and the instability surrounding the Great Depression. Several themes mark this movement: a search for an essential America in the natural landscape and its folk, a longing for the imagined intimacy and stability of rural communities, and a reverence for the past as an antidote to the chaotic present. These themes are evident in New England art of the period: Paul Sample's *Beaver Meadow* (1939, Hood Museum of Art, Dartmouth College, Hanover, N.H.), Molly Luce's *Reading from Robert Frost* (1932, Childs Gallery, Boston), Andrew Wyeth's *Charlie Ervine* (1937, collection of Mr. and Mrs. Andrew Wyeth), and Marsden Hartley's *Down East Young Blades* (ca. 1940, Wadsworth Atheneum). Post office murals funded by the Treasury Department's Section of Painting and Sculpture (1934–43) like Sample's *Apponaug Fishermen* (1942, Apponaug, R.I.) and Lewis Rubinstein's *Cranberry Pickers* (1940, Wareham, Mass.) highlighted the working folk—a subject also celebrated in such sculptures as George Aaron's scene of fishing, shipping, and manual labor at the Old Harbor Village Housing Project in South Boston (ca. 1930s) and Victor Kahill's *Maine Lobster-*

Marguerite Zorach, Land and Development of New England *(ca. 1935, Farnsworth Art Museum, Rockland, Maine)*

man (exhibited at the 1939 World's Fair, New York). These works constructed an image of a steadfast, productive region to counter the unstable, declining industries and farms of the Depression era.

With secure funding from the federal government for paintings on canvas, artists challenged the stereotype of the region as rural, white, and static, as Allan Rohan Crite did in his paintings documenting black community life in Boston's South End in the 1930s. But the image of small-town New England took on new relevancy during the Depression, especially in Farm Security Administration (FSA) photographs. Roy Stryker, director of the FSA, sent photographers to New England as part of his small-town project, which produced such works as Marion Post Wolcott's photographs of white-steepled town centers, Yankee peddlers, and maple sugaring in New Hampshire and Vermont, and Jack Delano's pictures of small-town rituals like the Presque Isle, Maine, potato festival. Many FSA photographs depicted non-Anglo groups, but those circulated in mass-produced magazines, journals, and exhibitions relied on a familiar cast of regional stereotypes: Yankee farmers at the plow, autumn scenery, the general store, the town meeting. These photographs not only served the needs of the Depression by defining shared cultural values but were reproduced in popular national magazines and picture books depicting American life during World War II. For Stryker, images of small-town America battled fascism and represented what Americans were fighting for. The same icons—the town meeting, Thanksgiving dinner, regional architecture—served as markers of national identity in Norman Rockwell's *Freedom of Speech* and *Freedom from Want* (both 1943, Norman Rockwell Museum, Stockbridge, Mass.) and survived in Paul Strand and Nancy Newhall's book *Time in New England* (1950).

In the post–World War II years and into the early 21st century, New England art has evolved from past traditions and images and simultaneously has challenged them. The stoic yet mystical workers in N. C. Wyeth's *Dark Harbor Fishermen* (1945, Portland [Maine] Museum of Art), the deserted, isolated spaces of New England farmhouses in Andrew Wyeth's *Christina's World* (1948, Museum of Modern Art, New York), and the sunlit coastal views in Fairfield Porter's *Island Farmhouse* (1969, private collection) recall earlier regional images. Contemporary western Massachusetts realist painters work in a precise descriptive style recalling that of John Singleton Copley and Ralph Earl, while landscapes—from Neil Welliver's to Eliot Porter's—remain a dominant subject in regional art. These artists' styles and subjects appeal to a popular audience, one served by the numerous commercial art galleries that sell sunny and nostalgic New England scenes drawn from 19th-century models.

Tourism and popular audiences have continued to shape contemporary Native American art, which depends both on traditional forms and on modern consumer capitalism. Artists work with traditional forms revised to fit tourist expectations, as in Stanley Neptune's ceremonial clubs, William Altvater's splint baskets, and Gladys Widdiss's Gay Head souvenir pottery. The status of these artifacts as art is still debated. Native American artists have received wide recognition as artists: the Sweetser family member and Abenaki elder basket maker Newt Washburn was named a National Endowment for the Arts National Heritage Fellow, for example. Although important collections of Native American art can be found in the Haffenreffer Museum of Anthropology, in Bristol, R.I.; the Peabody Essex Museum in Salem; and Harvard's Peabody Museum of Archaeology and Ethnology in Cambridge, Mass., the region's major art museums do not include this art in their collections.

Joyce Kozloff's mural *New England Decorative Arts* (1979–85), done for the Harvard Square subway station in Cambridge, also draws from the region's past. It visualizes New England history and identity through the culture's art and artifacts: gravestones, weather vanes, quilts, an 18th-century engraving of sailing ships, a folk landscape, ship figureheads, stencils, and silhouettes. Kozloff uses these familiar emblems and icons to communicate to a wide audience and works in a medium—painted and glazed ceramic tiles—that refers to a long-standing regional craft tradition that has taken on new life in recent decades. Post–World War II ceramics show a shift from pottery for function to ceramics as sculpture, as a fine art. This shift is demonstrated in recent works that draw from Bauhaus design and non-Western craft traditions to those that evidence painterly concerns, and subjects like the primitive, myth, and politics. Studio furniture, pottery, and glass are major regional presences, with the program at the Rhode Island School of Design as center. Organizations such as the New Hampshire League of Craftsmen work to support and advocate contemporary regional crafts, which, like the visual images of New England, now function as part of regional tourism, while schools like Haystack Mountain School of Crafts in Deer Isle, Maine, work to teach fine craftsmanship in black-smithing, ceramics, glass, metal, and wood to both professionals and amateurs through its summer programs.

Carl Andre's *Stone Field Sculpture* (1977, Hartford), with its 36 glacial boulders organized near a burial ground, both refers to past grave markers and distinctive regional geography and relies on avant-garde styles. The avant-garde has assumed a stronger presence in the region since World War II. Expressionism has been a favored style in the region since 1940, distinguishing Boston art from that of New York. German expressionism shaped collecting taste among Boston patrons and art institutions as well as the work of the Boston expressionists (Hyman Bloom, Jack Levine, Karl Zerbe) and the gestural expressionists (Katherine Porter, Philip Guston). Other artists, such as Maud Morgan and Bob Thompson, worked in abstraction. The region has continued to serve as summer art colony and summer school for the New York avant-garde (for example, Skowhegan School of Painting and Sculpture and the Artists' Equity Program in the Berkshires), bringing innovative modes into the region. While the figurative drawing and realism of Boston University's School of Fine Arts continues the conservative Museum School tradition, numerous art institutions, most prominently the Institute of Contemporary Art in Boston and the Massachusetts Institute of Technology's List Visual Arts Center in Cambridge, have emerged committed to contemporary, cutting-edge art. Such institutions have sought to combat the notion of New England, and Boston more specifically, as a bastion of conservative artistic taste.

Experimental and traditional artists have contested other long-held images of the region. The performance artist Marilyn Arsem, who is a member of Mobius, Boston's artist-run center for experimental art, explored three traditional New England images in *Stirring, Spinning, Sweeping* (first performed in 1992)—the woman at the spinning wheel, the woman over the cauldron, and the woman with the broom. Her work not only meditates on forgotten women and their work but also subverts regional stereotypes, showing, for example, the spinster tied up with rope and gauze, not idealized as in the Boston School interiors. Berenice Abbott's photographs of Route 1 in Maine with its roadside architecture and signage of the automobile culture signifies a dynamic, commercial region and counters the image of the pastoral New England village. Dynamics of class and race are offered in the work from the Salt Institute for Documentary Studies in Portland, while Richard Yarde foregrounds African American history, culture, and literature as well as the experience growing up black in the Boston area in his work. Industrialization and its history has been placed into the visual iconography of New England in Ralph Fasanella's paintings and in public art like Mico Kaufman's sculpture of female textile workers in Lowell, Mass.

Over the past four centuries, powerful and influential artists, patrons, and institutions have codified their representation of New England, and their sense of regional identity, in the visual arts. They have created multiple New Englands, but certain images of the region—particularly that of a premodern New England—have dominated. The history of tourism is intricately tied to this popular image of the region, an image that has not gone unchallenged or uncontested and that will undoubtedly be formed and re-formed in the future.

Alan Axelrod, ed., *The Colonial Revival in America* (1985); Pamela Belanger, *Inventing Acadia: Artists and Tourists at Mount Desert* (1999); Peter Benes, ed., *Painting and Portrait Making in the American Northeast* (1995); David Bjelajac, *Millennial Desire and the Apocalyptic Vision of Washington Allston* (1988); Sarah Burns, *Inventing the Modern Artist: Art and Culture in Gilded Age America* (1996); Burns, *Pastoral Inventions: Rural Life in 19th-Century American Art and Culture* (1989); Burns, "Revitalizing the 'Painted-Out' North: Winslow Homer, Manly Health, and New England Regionalism in Turn-of-the-Century America," *American Art* 9 (Summer 1995); Catherine H. Campbell et al., *The White Mountains: Place and Perceptions* (1980); Wendy A. Cooper, *In Praise of America: American Decorative Arts, 1650–1830* (1980); Wayne Craven, *Colonial American Portraiture* (1986); DeCordova and Dana Museum and Park, *New England Now: Contemporary Art from Six States* (1988); Thomas Andrew Denenberg, *Wallace Nutting and the Invention of Old America* (2003); Trevor Fairbrother, with contributions by Theodore E. Stebbins, Jr., William L. Vance, and Erica E. Hirshler, *The Bostonians: Painters of an Elegant Age* (1986); William Gerdts, *Art across America: Two Centuries of Regional Painting, 1710–1920*, vol. 1 (1990); Sarah L. Giffen and Kevin D. Murphy, *A Noble and Dignified Stream: The Piscataqua Region in the Colonial Revival, 1860–1930* (1992); Erica E. Hirshler, *A Studio of Her Own: Women Artists in Boston, 1870–1940* (2001); William Newell Hosley, *The Great River: Art and Society in the Connecticut Valley, 1635–1820* (1985); Michael A. Jehle, ed., *Picturing Nantucket: An Art History of the Island with Paintings from the Collection of the Nantucket Historical Association* (2000); Elizabeth Johns, *American Genre Painting: The Politics of Everyday Life* (1991); Johns, *Winslow Homer: The Nature of Observation* (2002); Patricia Johnston, *Joyce Kozloff: Visionary Ornament* (1986); Elizabeth Mankin Kornhauser, with Richard L. Bushman, Stephen H. Kornhauser, and Aileen Ribeiro, *Ralph Earl: The Face of the Young Republic* (1991); Joan A. Lester, *We're Still Here: Art of Indian New England* (1987); William C. Lipke and Philip N. Grime, eds., *Vermont Landscape Images, 1776–1976* (1976); Lucy R. Lippard, *The Lure of the Local: Sense of Place in a Multicentered Society* (1997); Robert McGrath, *Gods in Granite: The Art of the White Mountains of New Hampshire* (2001); Marilee Boyd Meyer, consulting curator, *Inspiring Reform: Boston's Arts and Crafts Movement* (1997); Angela Miller, *Empire of the Eye: Landscape Representation and American Cultural Politics, 1825–1875* (1993); David C. Miller, ed., *American Iconology: New Approaches to 19th-Century Art and Literature* (1993); Museum of Fine Arts, Boston, *New England Begins: The 17th Century* (1982); Marlene Park and Gerald E. Markowitz, *Democratic Vistas: Post Offices and Public Art in the New Deal* (1984); Priscilla Paton, *Abandoned New England: Landscape in the Work of Homer, Frost, Hopper, Wyeth, and Bishop* (2003); Lisa N. Peters, *Visions of Home: American Impressionist Images of Suburban Leisure and Country Comfort* (1997); Sally M. Promey, *Painting Religion in Public: John Singer Sargent's Triumph of Religion at the Boston Public Library* (1999); Susan Rather, "Carpenter, Tailor, Shoemaker, Artist: Copley and Portrait Painting around 1770," *Art Bulletin* 79 (June 1997); Carrie Rebora, ed., *John Singleton Copley in America* (1995); Bruce Robertson, *Reckoning with Winslow Homer: His Late Paintings and Their Influence* (1990); William F. Robinson, *A Certain Slant of Light: The First 100 Years of New England Photography* (1980); Caroline F. Sloat, ed., *Meet Your Neighbors: New England Portraits, Painters, and Society, 1790–1850* (1992); Theodore E. Stebbins, Jr., and Judith Hoos Fox, *Boston Collects: Contemporary Painting and Sculpture* (1986); Roger B. Stein, *Seascape and the American Imagination* (1975); Carol Troyen, *The Boston Tradition: American Paintings from the Museum of Fine Arts, Boston* (1980); William H. Truettner and Roger B. Stein, eds., *Picturing Old New England: Image and Memory* (1999); John Michael Vlach, *Plain Painters: Making Sense of American Folk Art* (1988); H. Barbara Weinberg, Doreen Bolger, and David Park Curry, *American Impressionism and Realism: The Painting of Modern Life, 1885–1915* (1994); John Wilmerding, *American Marine Painting* (1987); Wilmerding, *The Artists' Mount Desert: American Painters of the Maine Coast* (1994); Marianne B. Woods, "Viewing Colonial America through the Lens of Wallace Nutting," *American Art* 8 (Spring 1994); Robert G. Workman, *The Eden of America: Rhode Island Landscapes, 1820–1920* (1986).

Donna M. Cassidy

Abbott, Berenice (1898–1991) Photographer. Berenice Abbott, a native of Springfield, Ohio, moved to Greenwich Village in 1918, immersing herself in the flourishing post–World War I bohemian life. In 1921 Abbott relocated to Paris, where she learned photographic portraiture from the renowned surrealist Man Ray. From 1925 to 1929 she worked in her own studio, photographing the era's leading figures in art and literature, among them James Joyce and Djuna Barnes. In 1966 she moved to Monson, Maine, where she spent the rest of her long life.

Returning to New York in 1929, Abbott found monumental changes taking place and began to document the city's built environment photographically. *Changing New York,* with a text by leading art critic Elizabeth McCausland, was eventually funded by the Federal Art Project of the Works Project Administration and published in 1939.

Abbott's next project was equally ambitious and took twice as long to accomplish. In 1939 she embarked on a two-decade effort to use photography as a means of illustrating scientific principles. Throughout the 1940s Abbott designed and patented a number of photographic inventions, such as the distortion easel, which enabled the photographer to distort images as if in a funhouse mirror, and her Supersight process, an image-projection system that produced superior tonal definition. In 1941, with McCausland's editorial assistance, she published the commercially suc-

cessful *Guide to Better Photography,* which provided a succinct statement of Abbott's belief in realistic, straightforward photography with the print unmanipulated by the artist; *The View Camera Made Simple* followed it in 1948. Finally, in 1958, the MIT-based Physical Science Study Committee of Cambridge, Mass., hired Abbott to illustrate a high school physics textbook. The project, which lasted three years, resulted in technically sophisticated yet hauntingly beautiful images describing the physical properties of light, waveforms, and motion.

In 1954 Abbott embarked on the project that brought her to New England, a photographic series on the automobile culture of U.S. Route 1, which stretches from Fort Kent, Maine, to Key West, Fla. Seeking to capture aspects of small-town life and its relation to growing commercialism, Abbott made nearly 400 8-by-10-inch photographs, as well as 2,000 small-format Rolleiflex images. Her last book, *A Portrait of Maine,* with a text by artist and writer Chenoweth Hall, was published in 1968.

Abbott's Maine images for the most part move beyond the stereotypical views characteristic of the region's tourist-based iconography in favor of a detailed depiction of Maine work, town life, leisure, and nature. Unlike previously published image-text combinations—as varied as Paul Strand and Nancy Newhall's *Time in New England* (1950) and Jim Moore's *Maine Coastal Portrait* (1959)—

the Abbott-Hall collaboration offers a vivid presentation of working-class life on the coast with minimal sentimentalism. "A Young Lobsterman of Stonington" revisits a familiar theme, but in contrast to the romantic portraits of "old salts" familiar to readers of *Yankee* magazine, this young lobsterman strides purposefully toward the task at hand. Abbott captures not only the wooden traps but also, significantly, the oil and gasoline essential to the modern fishing industry, thereby dismantling nostalgic constructions of coastal fishing life as a phenomenon outside the modern.

Abbott is unusual among 20th-century photographers for the astonishing breadth of her photographic accomplishments. Her keen vision was based on photography's realist promise as a communications medium capable of both recording and interpreting history. Her belief in the camera's ability to document culture's time-specific lineaments as seen through the eyes of an artist led her to chronicle—unforgettably—some of the major developments of the 20th century.

Berenice Abbott, *Berenice Abbott, Photographer: A Modern Vision,* ed. Julia Van Haaften (1989); Berenice Abbott and David Prince, *Berenice Abbott's Portrait of Maine* (2000); Hank O'Neal, *Berenice Abbott: American Photographer* (1982); Bonnie Yochelson, *Berenice Abbott: Changing New York* (1997).

Elspeth Brown

Allston, Washington (1779–1843) Painter. Washington Allston was America's first great Romantic painter. Until his death in 1843, his history paintings fed an American appetite for narrative art, while his mastery of Venetian glazing convinced admirers that he could transcend the material world to imbue his work with spirituality.

Born at Brook Green Domain on the Waccamaw River in South Carolina, Allston was the son of Rachel Moore Allston and William Allston, a Revolutionary War hero who served under Francis Marion. After William Allston's death in 1781, Rachel Allston married Henry Collins Flagg, an army medical officer and son of a Rhode Island shipping merchant. Dr. Flagg's influence helped the nine-year-old Washington Allston to travel north to the Newport, R.I., home of Robert Rogers, where he first displayed a talent for painting. While in Newport he met his lifelong friends miniaturist Edward Green Malbone and writer William Ellery Channing, as well as Channing's sister, Ann, later to become Allston's first wife.

While in New England, Allston studied at Harvard and graduated with honors in 1800. Later that year he returned to South Carolina and converted his inheritance to cash to fund his study of painting in Europe. In 1801 he and

Berenice Abbott, U.S. 1 Rubenstein's Antiques, Rockland, Maine *(1954, New York Public Library)*

Malbone sailed for London, and within months Allston was admitted to the school of the Royal Academy. While in London, Allston visited the studio of Benjamin West, began a series of landscapes, and held his first public exhibition. There he also learned to apply glaze over paint in such a way as to enliven colors and suggest depth. It was a technique that, combined with his fascination with mystical subjects, would later persuade admirers of his deep spirituality. In 1803, he and painter John Vanderlyn traveled to France for further study, and in 1804 he set out for Italy alone. Allston spent the next four years in Italy, where he formed an enduring friendship with Samuel Taylor Coleridge.

In 1808 Allston returned to Boston, where he married Ann Channing. He threw himself into portrait work, primarily of his new Channing relations, although he was particularly pleased with his portrait of his own mother (1809). Still drawn to Europe, Allston sailed for England in 1811 with Ann and his new pupil, Samuel F. B. Morse.

During this second stay in England—from 1811 to 1818—Allston emerged as an accomplished painter. Sir George Beaumont commissioned *The Angel Releasing St. Peter from Prison* (1814–16, Museum of Fine Arts, Boston). *The Dead Man Restored to Life by Touching the Bones of the Prophet Elisha* (1811–14) won a prize of 200 guineas when exhibited at the British Institution. Thomas Sully spearheaded a subscription to buy the painting for the Pennsylvania Academy of the Fine Arts, where it remains today. Allston's time in London was marred, however, by war between England and America, his own serious illness, and, in 1815, Ann Channing Allston's sudden death. In 1818 Allston returned to Massachusetts for good, bringing with him a legendary reputation, very little money, and the furled canvas of his unfinished masterpiece, *Belshazzar's Feast* (1817–43, Detroit Institute of Arts).

Settling first in Boston and finally in Cambridgeport, Mass., Allston lived from painting to painting. In 1820, a consortium of 10 Boston benefactors pledged $1,000 each to a fund from which Allston could draw while finishing *Belshazzar's Feast*. In 1830 Allston married Martha Remington Dana, the sister of his close friend Richard Henry Dana, but neither her support nor his friends' generosity could elicit a completed masterpiece. In 1843, Washington Allston was found dead in his studio, his unfinished painting before him.

After his death, *Belshazzar's Feast* was exhibited as a monument to thwarted genius, confirming Allston as a suitably romantic hero of an age in which the spiritual and the mystical held a particular fascination. Allston's biblical themes, Italian landscapes, and Romantic

sensibility appealed to a new generation of Boston writers, thinkers, artists, and patrons. In the 1830s, such writers as Nathaniel Hawthorne, William Channing, and Ralph Waldo Emerson found both inspiration and warning in Allston as an example of a romantic, brooding genius in a pragmatic, Yankee culture. Allston's reputation today stands firmly on his portraits of women in reverie and on his paintings of biblical subjects, including *Elijah in the Desert* (1817–18, Museum of Fine Arts, Boston), in which a tiny figure of Elijah prays in the foreground, dwarfed by a blasted tree and towering clouds.

David Bjelajac, *Millennial Desire and the Apocalyptic Vision of Washington Allston* (1988); Jared Bradley Flagg, *The Life and Letters of Washington Allston* (1892); William H. Gerdts and Theodore E. Stebbins, Jr., *"A Man of Genius": The Art of Washington Allston (1779–1843)* (1979); Edgar Preston Richardson, *Washington Allston: A Study of the Romantic Artist in America* (1948).

Elizabeth Otterson Wiley

American Neoclassic Sculptors and Patrons

The first international style to have an impact on American sculpture was neoclassicism, which is characterized by an interest in Greco-Roman subject matter and a reinterpretation of classical form. Although American neoclassic sculptors came from various parts of the eastern United States and found patronage in cities from Portland, Maine, to Cincinnati, Ohio, they had an unusually devoted following in New England, especially in Boston. The preponderance of patrons there was the result of a number of factors. Many of these patrons had been educated at Harvard, following which they took the Grand Tour of Europe. These two experiences predisposed them to understand and prefer art in the neoclassical style. Most were wealthy and felt a responsibility to use their money to promote social and cultural development in the United States; many were related by blood or marriage, creating a network of shared taste and interest.

One of the earliest sculptors to benefit from this devotion was Horatio Greenough (1805–52), who, after graduating from Harvard in 1825, traveled to Italy to study and work as a sculptor. Over the ensuing decades, Italy became the destination for most aspiring American sculptors, notably Thomas Crawford (ca. 1815–57), who arrived there in 1835, and Hiram Powers (1805–73), who expatriated to Florence in 1837. Indeed, Nathaniel Hawthorne set his novel *The Marble Faun* (1859) in Rome and based several of its characters on American School sculptors, including Powers. Although Crawford came from New York and Powers from Ohio, they, like Greenough, benefited

from the attention of New England patrons. Other American sculptors of the next generation to do so included Harriet Hosmer (1830–1908), William Wetmore Story (1819–95), William Henry Rinehart (1825–74), and Randolph Rogers (1825–92).

The most important of their patrons were the politician and educator Edward Everett and the U.S. senator Charles Sumner. Everett's support for Greenough began when the younger man was still at Harvard and continued through the period when Greenough was completing his most important work, a commission he received from Congress in 1832 to sculpt a colossal figure of George Washington for the rotunda of the Capitol building in Washington, D.C. Everett was even more closely involved in the career of Powers. As he did with Greenough, Everett sent potential clients to Powers, advised him on subject matter, and gave him moral support. When Powers's famous *The Greek Slave* (Corcoran Gallery of Art, Washington, D.C.) was exhibited in London in 1845, Everett, who was then serving as American ambassador to Britain, helped promote it.

Charles Sumner admired and praised the work of both Greenough and Powers, but the sculptors who benefited most from his support were William Wetmore Story (of Massachusetts) and Thomas Crawford. As an early admirer of Story's talent, Sumner advised him to pursue a career in art, and the two remained close during Story's formative years in Boston and then in Italy. Sumner was even closer to Crawford and was almost solely responsible for the exhibition of Crawford's important *Orpheus and Cerebus* (1843, Museum of Fine Arts, Boston) at the Boston Athenaeum in 1843, an event that made Crawford famous.

Among the other New Englanders who were instrumental in promoting American neoclassic sculptors was the wealthy merchant Thomas Handasyd Perkins, who was especially attentive to Greenough and even secured him passage to Europe on one of his ships. Members of Perkins's extended family, including John Perkins Cushing and Samuel Cabot, also supported American sculptors. Other important patrons in Boston included David Sears, Francis Calley Grey, George Hillard, George Ticknor, and Hannah Lee.

Large collections of American sculpture from this period are held at the Museum of Fine Arts, Boston, the Wadsworth Atheneum, Hartford, and the Chrysler Museum, Norfolk, Va.

Wayne Craven, *Sculpture in America*, 2d ed. (1984); William H. Gerdts, *American Neo-Classic Sculpture: The Marble Resurrection* (1973); Gerdts, intro. to Nicolai Cikovsky, Jr., Marie H. Morrison, and Carol Ockman, *The White Marmorean Flock: 19th-Century*

Women Neoclassical Sculptors (1972); Joy Kasson, *Marble Queens and Captives: Women in 19th-Century Sculpture* (1990).

David B. Dearinger

Art Colonies

Art Colonies From the mid-19th century to the present more art colonies have been established in New England than in any other part of the United States. This is due, in part, to the proximity of mountains, farms, and seacoast to the region's large urban art centers. The earliest artists' colony in America was founded at the village of North Conway in the White Mountains of New Hampshire, in 1851, when Benjamin Champney and John Frederick Kensett summered at the Intervale for a full season. That same year Kensett exhibited a large and celebrated canvas entitled *The White Mountains from North Conway* at the American Art-Union in New York (now in the Wellesley [Mass.] College Art Museum). In Champney's account of the founding of the "American Barbizon"—adopted from the French Barbizon painters who emphasized the study of objects in open air—he remarked that the famous painting served as an "advertisement" for the region "so much so that next season many artists followed in our wake."

Within a few years a rival colony of Boston and New York painters emerged, centered on the village of West Campton, N.H., in the neighboring Pemigewasset Valley. Led by Asher Durand and Daniel Huntington, this group of highly partisan painters engaged in a friendly and amusing verbal exchange with the North Conway artists in the pages of *The Crayon*, the leading art journal of the period, as to the relative merits of the two locales for food, lodging, and scenery. Similarly, other New Yorkers and Bostonians, among them Thomas Doughty and Thomas Cole, began to flock to Mount Desert Island in Acadia National Park, Maine, as early as the 1830s.

In the decades following the Civil War, New Hampshire remained the preferred site for artists seeking summer retreat on the East Coast. While midcentury artists were generally in search of wilderness, or a serviceable proximity to it, postwar painters were more often seeking a pastoral refuge from the pressures of urban life. The colony at Cornish, N.H., was founded by the New York sculptor Augustus Saint-Gaudens in 1895, followed shortly thereafter by the establishment of a community in Dublin in 1898, founded by the painter Abbott Thayer. In these instances New Yorkers tended to congregate at Cornish in the Upper Connecticut River valley, while Bostonians generally chose Dublin, N.H. Childe Hassam's perennial visits from 1889 to 1894 to the poet Celia Thaxter's Isles of Shoals retreat, off the coast of Portsmouth, provided the impetus for yet another New Hampshire summer colony, composed largely of Boston painters, musicians, and writers. Perkins Cove, in Ogunquit, Maine, had become a well-established art colony by the 1890s, eventually attracting the likes of Hamilton Easter Field, Henry Strater, Peggy Bacon, and Walt Kuhn. In 1899 three major art colonies were formed at Provincetown on Cape Cod, at Gloucester, Mass., and at Old Lyme, Conn. These communities, unlike the inland New Hampshire retreats, offered a pleasing combination of seacoast and water, together with the allurements of New England rural life.

At present several colonies founded in New England during the early 20th century continue to flourish, foremost among them the MacDowell Colony in Peterborough, N.H., the Rockport Art Association on Boston's North Shore, and the summer school at Eastport, Maine. Unlike the 19th-century colonies, these communities feature art schools as well as serving as summer retreats from the city. The MacDowell Colony, for example, hosts musicians, painters, sculptors, poets, playwrights, and novelists year-round for stays up to two months at a time. The most recent additions to the New England art colony movement are Skowhegan, Maine, and the Vermont Studio Art School in Johnson. In both locations nationally celebrated artists offer instruction to aspiring painters and sculptors in rural, communal settings.

Pamela Belanger, *Inventing Acadia: Artists and Tourists at Mount Desert* (1999); Jane Curtis, Will Curtis, and Frank Lieberman, *Monhegan, The Artists' Colony* (1995); Robert L. McGrath and Barbara J. MacAdam, *"A Sweet Foretaste of Heaven": Artists in the White Mountains, 1830–1930* (1988); Louise Tragard, *A Century of Color, 1886–1986: Ogunquit, Maine's Art Colony* (1988); John Wilmerding, *The Artists' Mount Desert: American Painters on the Maine Coast* (1994).

Robert L. McGrath

Art Pottery

Art Pottery New England, with its long tradition of vernacular pottery, has been home to famous potteries that linked functional ware with aesthetic movements of the late 19th and early 20th centuries, setting the stage for development of the vital "art pottery" movement centered around studios and universities. *Art pottery* is a somewhat vague term used in part to designate any work produced by an individual artist-potter, but it may more accurately describe the revolt against commercial and industrial attitudes, and particularly in response to the art nouveau movement of the 1890s and early 1900s originating in France and England. In New England, a vigorous community of craftspeople and artists making hand-thrown and hand-decorated pottery reflects not only the continuity of a 200-year-

Edwin O. Scheier and Mary Scheier, vase with female figure design (1992, University of New Hampshire Library)

old heritage but assurance of continued future growth and value to the arts in America.

Native American pottery existed before and during colonial times, but the roots of contemporary forms are deeply embedded in European culture, transferred here by immigrants to the New World. As settlers moved west from the coast, redware potteries were established to provide utilitarian ware for an expanding frontier. William Drinker arrived in Massachusetts from England in 1635 to begin work as a potter in Charlestown. Captain John Norton manufactured pots in Bennington, Vt., later famous for its Bennington Stone Ware Factory. Peter Clark, a Revolutionary War hero, raised four sons in New Hampshire, each of whom went into the potter's trade.

Pottery in New England moved from this functional base to an aesthetic one. In the late 19th century, prominent companies produced richly decorated pottery in art nouveau styles. The Grueby Faience Co. of Boston (1897–1919) developed a line of art pottery and architectural tiles in matte glazes that are still highly prized by collectors. The famed Dedham Pottery produced celebrated crackleware in Massachusetts from 1896 to 1943; reproduction Dedham Pottery continues to be made in Concord, Mass. The Low Art Tile Works of Chelsea, Mass., manufactured relief-scene tiles from 1883 to 1902. The Hampshire Pottery in Keene, N.H., offered a diversified line of redware and stoneware products from 1871 through 1923. Most of these potteries ultimately failed because of increased competition and changing technologies.

After World War II pottery in New England underwent a profound change. Returning servicemen brought with them new aesthetics from Europe and, particularly, from Asia. Ceramic design shifted from concerns for function to those of self-expression. The vessel became metaphor, and metaphor became sculpture. Universities became the centers of intellectual training and galleries the means of marketing. During the 1960s and 1970s ceramic artists embarked on robust aesthetic adventures as they entered the mainstream of American art.

Such diverse currents enriched contemporary ceramics. Bauhaus design appeared in the work of Karen Karnes of Vermont, Michael Cohen of Massachusetts, and Vivika and Otto Heino, formerly of New Hampshire. Dorothy and Lyle Perkins and Harriet Brisson of Rhode Island approached form as industrial design. Japanese folk craft aesthetics strongly influenced many potters, including Malcolm Wright of Vermont, Rick Hirsch, formerly of Massachusetts, Todd Piker and Joy Brown of Connecticut, and John Baymore of New Hampshire. Islamic architectural influences appeared in the work of Mary Kring Risley of Connecticut. Painterly concerns dominated the work of Ann Gabhart of Massachusetts, Jay LaCouture of Rhode Island, and Wally Mason of Maine. Primitivism and myth motivated Edwin and Mary Scheier of New Hampshire (during the 1950s and 1960s) and William Wyman of Massachusetts. Romanticism has infused the work of Chris Gustin of Massachusetts and Hayne Bayless of Connecticut. Political satire has been a vehicle of expression for Gerry Williams of New Hampshire. During the 1960s and 1970s, New Hampshire potters were influenced by mainstream art movements, particularly abstract expressionism coming from the West Coast.

The rising role of the academy in the ceramic arts has encouraged a new generation of artists to explore clay as a medium of expression. The University of New Hampshire (Maryse Searls McConnell), Colby College (Jon Keenan), Keene State College (Sam Azzaro), Dartmouth College (Karen Williamson), the New Hampshire Institute of Art (Al Jaeger), and Plymouth State College (Susan Tucker) are among those institutions and teachers emphasizing clay as an artistic medium in curricula.

The legacy of colonial pottery in New England lives on, through the dedication of many young people to clay as a means of self-expression. A leading journal published in New Hampshire, the *Studio Potter*, founded in 1972 by and for potters, portrays the scope and brilliance of American ceramics and publishes archival first-person interviews with American ceramic artists, defining the past while illuminating the future. Through services offered to craftspeople and ceramic artists by the League of New Hampshire Craftsmen, the New Hampshire Potters' Guild, and the New Hampshire Art Association, there continue to be markets and galleries for functional vessels as well as for sculptural objects.

Harold F. Guilland, *Early American Folk Pottery* (1971); Elaine Levin, *History of American Ceramics, 1607 to the Present: From Pipkins and Bean Pots to Contemporary Forms* (1988); Lura Woodside Watkins, *Early New England Potters and Their Wares* (1950); Gerry Williams, ed., *Studio Potter* 1, no. 1 (1972).

Gerry Williams

Boston School The term "Boston School" refers not to an organization or an academy but to a distinctive artistic aesthetic shared by many of Boston's leading painters during the 1890s and the first half of the 20th century. Distinguished by their traditional technique and their resistance to the increasing role of abstraction in modern art, such artists as Edmund Tarbell, Frank Benson, Philip Hale and Lilian Westcott Hale, William Paxton, and Joseph DeCamp developed a pictorial strategy that combined careful academic figure painting with an impressionist interest in light and color. Their work falls into three basic categories: dark and graceful portraits, bright outdoor figural compositions, and elegantly appointed interiors populated by fashionably dressed young women.

Art in Boston had developed a distinctive character early in the 19th century; by midcentury, local collectors widely admired the moody, atmospheric paintings of the Barbizon School. William Morris Hunt, the city's aesthetic tastemaker, nurtured this interest in French art throughout the 1860s and 1870s. Thus Bostonians were predisposed to favor impressionism, the new French style that developed in the 1870s and 1880s, and Boston artists were among the first Americans to adapt its bright colors and broken brushwork to their own work. As early as 1894, the French critic S. C. de Soissons, in *Boston Artists: A Parisian Critic's Notes*, remarked upon "the new school" of Boston painters, including Tarbell and Benson, whose landscapes and outdoor figural compositions "are painted in lively and sunny colors, so that one might say that the light of the sun penetrated every corner of their pictures."

A French aesthetic also permeated Boston portraits. Here the model was not impressionism but the Academy. Most Boston painters had studied either at the Académie Julian or at the Ecole des Beaux-Arts in Paris, and they valued traditional craftsmanship and the strong foundation in anatomical rendering

Edmund C. Tarbell, New England Interior *(ca. 1906, Museum of Fine Arts, Boston)*

they had mastered during their early training. In their commissioned portraits, the palette is generally dark, the mood sober, and the figure carefully rendered. Reserving impressionism for their outdoor summer work, Boston artists used both styles simultaneously, perhaps following the example set by John Singer Sargent, a frequent visitor and one of the city's favorite painters.

In the early years of the 20th century, Edmund Tarbell, then acknowledged as the leader of the Boston artists, developed a new manner of painting inspired by his discovery of the work of the 17th-century Dutch artist Johannes Vermeer (the subject of historical research by Tarbell's colleague Philip Hale). In such works as *Girl Crocheting* (1904, Canajoharie [N.Y.] Library and Art Gallery) and *New England Interior* (ca. 1906, Museum of Fine Arts, Boston), Tarbell combined academic studies of figures indoors with an impressionist interest in light effects. His interiors, inhabited by young women surrounded by New England antiques, oriental porcelains evoking the China trade, and copies of old master paintings, quickly became identified with the Boston School. Some scholars have found these images deliberately antifeminist for depicting women and the fine objects around them in the same manner, but other historians feel they are artistically (rather than politically) charged as statements that uphold conservative aesthetic values in the face of modern art. Most of the Boston painters were influential teachers; their style and predilection for traditional representation has been passed to a third and even fourth generation of like-minded artists.

Trevor J. Fairbrother, *The Bostonians: Painters of an Elegant Age, 1870–1930* (1986); R. H. Ives Gammell, *Boston Painters, 1900–1930* (1986); Erica E. Hirshler, *A Studio of Her Own: Women Artists in Boston, 1870–1940* (2001); Bernice Kramer Leader, "The Boston School and Vermeer," *Arts Magazine* 55 (November 1980).

Erica E. Hirshler

Church, Frederic Edwin (1826–1900)

Painter. America's leading landscapist of the 1850s and 1860s, Frederic Edwin Church did more than any other painter of the mid-19th century to establish New England as the source of national identity. Although his career was spent largely in New York, Church traveled widely—to South America, Jamaica, Labrador, and the Middle East—painting brilliantly detailed, scientifically observant panoramic landscapes. The extent of his travels and the nature of his output have somewhat obscured Church's New England roots. Born into a prominent Hartford family, Church focused extensively on New England

Frederic Edwin Church, New England Scenery *(1851, George Walter Vincent Smith Art Museum, Springfield, Mass.)*

subjects from the late 1840s to the early 1860s, when he solidified his central place in American art.

At an early age Church determined to become a landscape painter. His family supported this decision, and the young artist studied from 1844 to 1846 in Catskill, N.Y., under the tutelage of Thomas Cole. Cole's only pupil of note, Church absorbed his teacher's preference for landscapes with allegorical or biblical content. He often made topical references to contemporaneous national events in his history and landscape paintings, and during the period between the Mexican War and the Civil War he used natural events to symbolize national conflicts and historical dilemmas.

Between 1846 and 1854, Church painted a series of landscapes exploring the symbolic identity of New England as the seedbed of national values. His *Hooker and Company Journeying through the Wilderness from Plymouth to Hartford, in 1636* (1846, Wadsworth Atheneum, Hartford), a topic most likely suggested to him by Cole, implied a trajectory directly connecting 17th-century migration with 19th-century expansion across the continent. Church made associations between New England's colonial struggles and the evolution of New World liberties in several paintings including *West Rock, New Haven* (1849, New Britain [Conn.] Museum of American Art), which depicts the site where the English regicides of Charles I took refuge from the Crown's avenging agents. *New England Scenery* (1853, George Walter Vincent Smith Art Museum, Springfield, Mass.), engraved for

distribution to American Art-Union members, is Church's most explicit portrayal of New England as model agrarian republic. This ideal landscape, with a covered wagon in the foreground suggesting the spread of New England values to the West, implicitly rebukes the slaveholding South and defends New England's moral preeminence in the history of the nation. This model of the fruits of free labor was shared by such New England luminaries as Harriet Beecher Stowe and Calvin Stowe, Henry David Thoreau, and Theodore Parker.

In the mid- to late 1850s, Church's interests centered increasingly on remote areas as he expanded his New World rhetoric to encompass the Western Hemisphere, from the ice fields of Labrador to the Andes of South America. During this decade he also traveled repeatedly to Maine, first to coastal regions and then to the inland wilderness around Mount Katahdin. Church's growing attraction to unsettled nature is evident in his Maine paintings. *Twilight in the Wilderness* (1860, Cleveland Museum of Art), a synthesis of Maine landscapes, is perhaps his greatest work. Painted on the eve of the Civil War, *Twilight*, with crimsonstreaked sky fading into a luminous distance, uses a dramatic moment in nature to suggest the gathering energies of war. The culmination of Church's decade-long exploration of national mission, *Twilight*'s final blaze of light suggests an end and a new beginning, apocalypse and millennium, leaving open the resolution.

After the Civil War, Church concentrated much of his effort on designing and building

Olana, his great house—now open to the public—in Hudson, N.Y. In his final years Church frequently visited his camp near Mount Katahdin; his last dated canvas was painted there in 1895. He died in New York City.

Gerald L. Carr, *In Search of the Promised Land: Paintings by Frederic Edwin Church* (2000); Franklin Kelly, *Frederic Edwin Church* (1989); Kelly, *Frederic Edwin Church and the National Landscape* (1988); Kelly and Gerald L. Carr, *The Early Landscapes of Frederic Edwin Church, 1845–1854* (1987); Angela L. Miller, *The Empire of the Eye: Landscape Representation and American Cultural Politics, 1825–1875* (1993).

Angela Miller

Cole, Thomas (1801–48) Painter. America's leading landscape painter during the second quarter of the 19th century and founder of the Hudson River School, Thomas Cole was born in Bolton-le-Moors, England. Trained as an engraver, he immigrated to the United States in 1818 and worked as an itinerant portrait painter in Ohio before his family moved to Pittsburgh, Pa., in 1823. Cole moved to Philadelphia, where he studied landscape paintings on exhibit at the Pennsylvania Academy of the Fine Arts, and then to New York City, where, in the fall of 1825, his paintings of Hudson Valley scenery brought him almost instant success. During his brief career he painted European and American scenes as well as history paintings and allegories, of which his five-part series, *The Course of Empire* (1836, New-York Historical Society), and the four-part *Voyage of Life* (begun 1839, Munson-Williams-Proctor Arts Institute, Utica, N.Y.; second version, National Gallery of Art, Washington, D.C.), are best known.

The painter Col. John Trumbull, president of the American Academy of Fine Arts and a highly influential figure among patrons and collectors, played a crucial role in Cole's early career. In the fall of 1825 Trumbull arranged for the exhibition of Cole's work and exposed him to an extensive network of aristocratic patrons and collectors, among them Daniel Wadsworth. The son of a great Hartford financier and the future founder of the Wadsworth Atheneum, Wadsworth commissioned five works from the artist and helped Cole to receive commissions from a number of New England patrons, including Hartford lawyer Henry Barnard and the writer S. G. Goodrich (pseudonym Peter Parley).

In the summer of 1827, Wadsworth, an amateur landscapist and ardent landscape tourist, urged Cole to visit the White Mountains. Cole revisited the White Mountains in 1828 and 1839; among the works that resulted were views of Mount Washington, Lake Winni-pesaukee, Mount Chocorua, and Crawford Notch. In 1845, Cole traveled with the Boston artist Henry Cheever Pratt to Mount Desert Island, Maine, where he made drawings he later used for two views of Frenchman's Bay.

Cole's *View from Mount Holyoke, Northampton, Massachusetts, after a Thunderstorm*, popularly known as *The Oxbow* (1836, Metropolitan Museum of Art, New York), established the panoramic mode of composition that would characterize the Hudson River School. Working from sketches made at the site (by the 1830s a popular tourist attraction), Cole juxtaposed contradictory perspectives along with other visual and symbolic oppositions—storm and sunshine, wilderness and pastorale—to produce a spectacular panorama of Connecticut River valley scenery. A smaller work, *New England Scenery* (1839, Art Institute of Chicago), shows an idealized view of the New England countryside complete with rolling farmland, a village church nestled among trees, and distant mountains.

Almost from the beginning of Cole's career, his work was well known in New England. In 1828, Wadsworth sent Cole's *St. John in the Wilderness* (1827, Wadsworth Atheneum) to the Boston Athenaeum's second annual exhibition. Cole himself staged showings in Boston of *The Garden of Eden* (1828, now lost) and *Expulsion from the Garden of Eden* (1828, Museum of Fine Arts, Boston) and the enormous *Angel Appearing to the Shepherds* (1834, Chrysler Museum, Norfolk, Va.). In 1843 and 1844 he exhibited his *Voyage of Life* and *Angels Ministering to Christ* (1843, Worcester [Mass.] Art Museum) at the Boston Artists' Association's annual exhibitions. In 1844, the Wadsworth Atheneum purchased Cole's 10-foot-wide *Mount Etna from Taormina, Sicily* (1843).

Cole died in Catskill, N.Y., at the height of his fame. During the next two decades, his work exerted a powerful influence on Hudson River School artists—among them his pupil Frederic Edwin Church—who often recalled in their works the themes and imagery of Cole's panoramic landscapes and moralizing allegories.

J. Bard McNulty, ed., *The Correspondence of Thomas Cole and Daniel Wadsworth* (1983); Ellwood C. Parry III, *The Art of Thomas Cole* (1988); Richard Saunders, *Daniel Wadsworth, Patron of the Arts* (1981); Earl A. Powell, *Thomas Cole* (2000); William H. Truettner and Alan Wallach, eds., *Thomas Cole: Landscape into History* (1994).

Alan Wallach

Contemporary Art and Artists The hub of artistic energy in New England is Boston. Its museums, galleries, and institutions of higher education have contributed to the city's development and growth, as has its particular responsiveness to art trends in Europe, New York, and, more recently, Asia. Historically, the cultural climate in Boston has been conservative. The Armory Show of 1913, which introduced avant-garde art to New York, Chicago, and Boston, met with its coolest reception in Boston. The Museum of Fine Arts (MFA), Boston, long resisted collecting the work of contemporary American artists. It did collect French impressionists, but when the fledgling Museum of Modern Art (MoMA) in New York allied itself with the School of Paris painters, the Boston branch of MoMA, under the leadership of James Plaut, adopted a preference for Italian and northern European contemporary art and, in 1948, changed its name to the Institute of Contemporary Art (ICA).

During and after World War II, many artists who immigrated to the United States—and particularly to Boston—brought with them strong admiration for the work of northern European artists, especially the German expressionists (whose work was displayed at Harvard's Busch-Reisinger Museum and the Institute of Contemporary Art). This manifested itself in the development of a strong figurative style known as Boston expressionism, which became the prevailing trend from 1940 to 1985. Between 1940 and 1955, figurative expressionism emerged in the work of Hyman Bloom (a Lithuanian immigrant), Jack Levine (born in Boston of Lithuanian descent), and Karl Zerbe (from Germany), all of whom admired the masters Rembrandt, El Greco, and Goya, the German expressionists, and Georges Rouault, Chaim Soutine, Marc Chagall, and Amedeo Modigliani.

These artists were profoundly affected by the war, the aftermath of the Holocaust, and social injustice in any form, and their work challenged universal ideals and expressed hope in religious affirmation. Hyman Bloom created a rich and complex body of work, integrating respect for leading European artists of the past and an appreciation of a mystical Eastern aesthetic into a psychologically charged, visionary style, as seen in *The Medium* (1951, Hirshhorn Museum and Sculpture Garden, Washington, D.C.). Bloom's early paintings and drawings exhibited a high level of draftsmanship and skilled composition; his work became looser and more abstract in his later years.

Jack Levine invested his artistic energies in satirically addressing social concerns. Drawing from Rembrandt's group and individual portraits, he challenged contemporary political institutions such as the legislature in *Gangster Funeral* (1952–53, Whitney Museum of

American Art, New York) and *The Senator* (1958, private collection).

Karl Zerbe, moved by Max Beckmann's bold, figurative canvases, often presented a cropped figure that dominates the canvas, as in the colorful, cynical *Harlequin* (1943, Whitney Museum of American Art, New York), or *Job* (1949, Museum of Fine Arts, Boston), depicting a distraught figure who, kneeling with clenched fists, confronts the viewer with a searing intensity. Zerbe played a significant role at the School of the Museum of Fine Arts, Boston (also known as the Museum School); as a dynamic director of painting and drawing, he introduced his students to important art developments throughout the world and demanded proficiency in basic skills while encouraging them to develop an individual style. He was a galvanizing force in the Boston art community, organizing gallery shows, promoting Artists Equity, inviting renowned artists to teach in summer programs in the Berkshires (including Hyman Bloom, Oskar Kokoschka, and Ben Shahn), and securing fellowships for students to study in Europe. Most significant, Bloom, Zerbe, and Levine helped set a standard of dedication to the craft of drawing, a competency in rendering the human figure, and a profound respect for artistic tradition.

Many of Zerbe's students who remained in New England instructed the next generation of artists. Jason Berger, for example, taught at the School of Practical Art, renamed the Art Institute of Boston; Bernard Chaet at Yale University; Calvin Burnett at Massachusetts College of Art; John Wilson, Henry Schwartz, and Barnet Rubenstein at the Museum School; and David Aronson and Arthur Polonsky at Boston University. David Aronson was profoundly influenced by Zerbe's probing introspection, both in painting and in sculpting mystical Judeo-Christian themes. Zerbe also shaped Arthur Polonsky, whose deft draftsmanship captures the psychological drama between the freedoms of youth and the tugs of advanced age. Zerbe's student Henry Schwartz developed a strong visionary style with jarring spatial perspectives; Barbara Swan, another of his students, evolved a thoughtful figurative style, creating portraits with reflective surfaces.

During the 1950s, New York became the center of the American art world with the advent of abstract expressionism. Although Boston was responsive to the New York School of abstract expressionism, holding exhibitions of Jackson Pollock, Franz Kline, Willem de Kooning, and Mark Rothko, it was entrenched in figurative expressionism so that artists who were eager to embrace abstract expressionism—such as Ellsworth Kelly and Larry Poons (of the Museum School)—moved to New York.

In the late 1960s and early 1970s, the Museum School underwent internal changes, becoming less structured and focusing on mixed media and site works. Many of its faculty (Joseph Ablow, David Aronson, Reed Kay, Arthur Polonsky) moved to the visual arts department at Boston University, where figurative drawing and realism continued to dominate. During the same period, faculty at the Massachusetts College of Art, including Lawrence Kupferman and Calvin Burnett, were divided in their teaching philosophies between Clement Greenberg's unabashed embrace of formalist aesthetics and abstract expressionism, and painting from observation, with emphasis on formal values.

Boston's traditional academic community has enriched the arts. At the Massachusetts Institute of Technology in 1950, Gyorgy Kepes, painter, photographer, and philosopher, invigorated the art department and promoted exhibitions at Hayden Gallery. The gallery was renamed the List Visual Arts Center in 1985, and it gained a prestigious reputation under the leadership of Katy Kline by showing an international roster of artists and by promoting cutting-edge, contemporary themes that bridge technology and ideology.

At Harvard, Paul J. Sachs, who trained Alfred Barr (the first director of MoMA), helped launch the Harvard Society for Modern Art and inspired nephew James Plaut, first director of the Institute of Contemporary Art. Le Corbusier's Carpenter Center for the Visual Arts introduced design concepts from the Bauhaus movement. These innovators attracted luminaries to Cambridge for the Charles Eliot Norton Lectures, extending invitations to Ben Shahn, John Cage, Richard Estes, Frank Stella, and others. In 1965, graduate students Michael Fried, Charles Millard, Kenworth Moffett, and Rosalind Kraus organized the exhibition *Three American Painters: Kenneth Noland, Jules Olitski, Frank Stella* to support their argument that these artists evolved from Edouard Manet and synthetic cubism to a new modernism of color field and abstract painting. In 1971 Moffett became the first curator of 20th-century art at the MFA, and for a brief period the showing of color field painting (ribbons of color applied directly to the canvas) brought attention to Boston. Brandeis University's Rose Art Museum, founded in 1961, made an early commitment to showing and collecting contemporary art under the inspired mentorship of Sam Hunter, and continues to be a supporter under current director Joseph D. Ketner.

In the mid-1960s, Boston painters formed their own style of gestural expressionism. Examples include Museum School student Katherine Porter, whose grid-based paintings became more loosely constructed but maintained a dynamic tension, and whose palette and approach reflected admiration for Philip Guston; and Gregory Amenoff, inspired by Max Ernst and French symbolists. Natalie Alper, John McNamara, and Jo Ann Rothschild each used varied, broad strokes of rhythmic cadences over large canvases.

The political instability of the Vietnam War years encouraged protest art in many forms, and the proliferation of art magazines and journals brought artists together internationally. In 1968, artists in Boston organized Artists Against Racism and War and promoted integration of minority artists in ACT Now workshops. In 1970, at the urging of artist Dana Chandler, whose powerful angry images deal directly with the frustrations of racism, the exhibition *Afro-American Artists: New York and Boston* was organized by Edmund Barry Gaither and Benny Andrews and held at the MFA. In 1971, the Boston Visual Artists Union, founded as a forum for artists to meet and discuss issues, became a national model.

Following the Vietnam War, a return to conservatism in art prevailed, along with a renewed emphasis in teaching form and value. Beginning in 1975 neo-expressionism emerged in the work of Gerry Bergstein, a student of Jan Cox, the Belgian surrealist painter who succeeded Zerbe at the Museum School. Bergstein, in the spirit of René Magritte, constructed witty and probing trompe l'oeil tableaux; his style soon became three-dimensional in layering. Todd McKie, with an economy of line, mined the subconscious vein of surrealism, with biomorphic shapes that establish relationships both humorous and poignant.

From 1973 to 1978 the charismatic New York painter Philip Guston was invited to Boston University as guest instructor when his own work evidenced a return to figuration. He had a powerful impact on many students, particularly Jon Imber, whose roughly delineated figurative style is both naive and profound. In this vein, Morgan Buckley's jigsawlike compositions are animated, brightly colored, and tightly designed stage sets that probe sociopolitical issues. Aaron Fink, also influenced by Guston and a strong German expressionist heritage, gives monumental presence to icons of contemporary culture.

Western Massachusetts, removed from the tensions of urban activity, has nurtured several realist painters, including Gregory Gillespie,

Scott Prior, Jane Lund, and Frances Gillespie, whose precise studies have quiet intensity and drama, recalling the tradition of John Singleton Copley's intimate portraiture. The tableau still life became an expressive vehicle for Barnet Rubenstein, James Aponovich, and Emily Eveleth, who used daily objects to investigate formal relationships in a symbolic way.

Landscape has always been an important artistic theme in New England. During the interwar years Marsden Hartley, Milton Avery, and Fairfield Porter remained quiet forces through New England museum shows with their expressionist and realist canvases. The Maine terrain as interpreted by Neil Welliver was translated into a rich, densely overlaid tapestry of vegetation; Dennis Pinette depicted quiet, agrarian scenes. Wolf Kahn and Conley Harris explored natural light in the presence of nature. Landscape, real and imaginary, became an expressive vehicle for Michael Mazur, Lois Tarlow, and younger artists Sarah Supplee, Elaine Spatz-Rabinowitz, Joel Janowitz, and Anne Neely. Cityscapes of George Nick, Richard Sheehan, and Joel Babb record the place and time of a particular region.

Abstract, nonobjective minimalism, influenced by Agnes Martin, is intellectually explored by Bill Thompson, whose titles give a clue to his spare canvases, like *Question and Answer* (1996, private collection). David Moore's thinly painted vertical and horizontal bands of color vibrate optically but are frozen by a glossy finish, as in *Mystery Ride 1* (1995, Gallery NAGA, Boston). Ellen Gallagher, a graduate of the Museum School and participant in the Whitney Museum's biennial of 1995 in New York, builds her canvas with small pod shapes or eyes that are played off against open spaces to create a hypnotic intensity, as in *Bling Bling* (2001, Gagosian Gallery, New York).

Maggi Brown, who also studied at the Museum School, adds and subtracts elements to explore opposite experiences: *Leaves with Non-Leaves* (1996, private collection) presents a grid of ginkgo leaf forms, real and painted; *Ginkgo White* (1995, private collection) is a completely abstract interpretation that captures the essence of serenity. Alfred DeCredico, who teaches at the Rhode Island School of Design, layers a painting with ordered, historical references that take on a new identity, as in *Poliuto, a Field of Stones* (1991, private collection). Deborah Muirhead, teaching at the University of Connecticut at Storrs, creates in *Soldier* (1995) a dialogue between abstraction and historical narrative with the application of textual references to African Americans whose lives are suspended between fact and fiction. Maud Morgan, the "grande dame" of Boston art, rode the wave of abstraction with silkscreen, collage, and painting, always re-

turning to the expressive self-portrait, even in her nineties.

From the 1970s on, area museums have featured exhibitions of new work by New England artists in all media. Participants include the combined ICA and MFA exhibitions; the Triennial at the Fuller Museum of Art in Brockton, Mass.; the Danforth Museum of Art in Framingham, Mass.; the Fitchburg (Mass.) Museum of Art; the Currier Museum of Art in Manchester, N.H.; the Rhode Island School of Design in Providence, and the Portland (Maine) Museum of Art Biennials instituted in 1998. The DeCordova Museum and Sculpture Park, in Lincoln, Mass., has featured a yearly selection in *The DeCordova Annual Exhibition* (formerly the *Artists/Visions* series) since 1989, and now collects exclusively the work of contemporary New England artists. The Wadsworth Atheneum, in Hartford, home to one of the earliest collections of modern art in New England, supports contemporary art and artists through its MATRIX series and with the Tremaine Lectures in Contemporary Art. Significantly, the exhibition *New England Now* (1987), organized and curated by a museum member from each New England state, revealed "no unifying theme, no attitude, no *look* that could be called *New English.*" The eclecticism of the exhibition mirrored the diversity of the contemporary visual arts in the region. New England artists have responded to all possibilities; thus, "pluralism" is the most appropriate designation, with continuing interest in realism and figuration.

Pamela Edwards Allara, "The Humanist Vision: Expressionist Art in Boston, 1945–1985," in *Expressionism in Boston, 1945–1985: DeCordova Museum, Lincoln, Massachusetts* (1986); Bill Bagnall and Sherry Lang, *The DeCordova/Three Decades (1950–1980)* (1980); Serge Guilbaut, "The Frightening Freedom of the Brush: The Boston Institute of Contemporary Art and Modern Art," and Reinhold Heller, "The Expressionist Challenge: James Plaut and the Institute of Contemporary Art," both in *Dissent: The Issue of Modern Art in Boston,* Institute of Contemporary Art, Boston (1985); Patricia Hills, ed., *Social Concern in the '80s: A New England Perspective* (1984); Andrew C. Hyde, *Boston Collects Boston* (1973); Wendy Tarlow Kaplan, *The Eighth Triennial,* Fuller Museum of Art, Brockton, Mass. (1997); Theodore E. Stebbins, Jr., and Judith Hoos Fox, *Boston Collects: Contemporary Painting and Sculpture* (1986); Steven T. Zevitas, *New American Paintings 2* (1996).

Wendy Tarlow Kaplan

Contemporary Art Institutions New England's cultural environment is enhanced by a number of institutions that focus exclusively or primarily on the presentation of contemporary art. These institutions were founded in response to the perception that the region's major art museums were not collect-

ing or showing contemporary art, a trend that was particularly apparent when contrasted with the contemporary emphasis at institutions in New York such as the Solomon R. Guggenheim Museum and the Museum of Modern Art.

The Institute of Contemporary Art (ICA) in Boston, founded in 1936, is the oldest noncollecting contemporary art institution in the region. The DeCordova Museum and Sculpture Park in Lincoln, Mass. (founded 1948; opened 1950), concentrates on art of the postwar era but is unique in its focus on art produced within New England. The DeCordova holds the region's largest permanent collection of New England contemporary art. The Massachusetts Institute of Technology's List Visual Arts Center in Cambridge, Mass., like the ICA, has established its reputation through exhibitions that have international as well as national import. Since 1964 the Aldrich Museum of Contemporary Art in Ridgefield, Conn., has promoted emerging artists and trends in contemporary art.

Despite some regional advantages, contemporary art institutions in New England face special challenges. Building a wider audience for the art of our time—which can often seem remote and inaccessible—requires creative and extensive educational programming that places the works within a meaningful context in a changing world. Of note are the Docent-Teens program at the ICA and the Student Docent Program at the Aldrich Museum of Contemporary Art. Both programs engage precollege youth in the public interpretation of contemporary art.

In the wake of reduced federal and state support for the arts, lack of funding is a major impediment for institutions specializing in contemporary art. It is not surprising that, among New England institutions that concentrate primarily on contemporary art, many are associated with academic institutions—the MIT List Visual Arts Center, the Rose Art Museum at Brandeis University, Boston University Art Gallery, the University Gallery at the University of Massachusetts in Amherst, the Institute of Contemporary Art at the Maine College of Art in Portland, the David Winton Bell Art Gallery at Brown University, and the Fine Arts Center Galleries at the University of Rhode Island in Kingston. Although only partially funded by their parent institutions, these museums do have relatively stable support, often in the areas of staff salaries and facilities.

A positive indicator of the continued interest in contemporary art in the region is the development, since 1986, of the Massachusetts Museum of Contemporary Art (MASS MoCA) in North Adams. With support announced by the legislature in 1988, the museum opened in May 1999. The 13-acre, 27-building historic mill complex was renovated with both private and public funds (the state of Massachusetts provided $35 million in matching funds). MASS MoCA provides a venue for large-scale visual and performance art with an emphasis on work that incorporates new technology.

Charles Giuliano, "Inside the ICA," *Art New England* 15 (1993/94); Giuliano, "Started on a Whim," *ARTnews* 86 (1987); Daniel Ranalli, "Forum: A New DeCordova," *Art New England* 16 (1995); Christine Temin, "Hard Hats and Talking Heads: A MASS MoCA Progress Report," *Boston Globe,* June 15, 1997.

Vicki C. Wright

Copley, John Singleton (1738–1815)

Portrait and history painter. John Singleton Copley, the premier 18th-century portrait painter, was born to Irish immigrants who ran a tobacco shop on Boston's hurly-burly Long Wharf. Copley was largely self-taught, learning the engraver's trade from his stepfather, Peter Pelham, and the conventions of British portraiture from artistic treatises, prints, and the work of Joseph Blackburn, Robert Feke, and other artists in Boston. Toward the end of his extraordinarily successful 20-year career from 1753 to 1774 in the American colonies as a portrait painter, Copley was able to afford a grand house on Beacon Hill. At the height of his second career, in London, he was acclaimed as one of England's most innovative history painters.

Although Copley's first clients were middle-class, his brilliant technique, talent for capturing a likeness, and keen awareness of English fashion soon made him the favorite portraitist of New England's elite. For many of his early portraits, he borrowed costumes, poses, and settings from English mezzotints. By the mid-1760s this dependence on such sources lessened, although he occasionally incorporated a telling detail (such as the English pier table in his portrait of Marblehead merchant Jeremiah Lee [1769, Wadsworth Atheneum, Hartford]) to underscore his subject's social aspirations. Copley's portraits were not just flattering likenesses; they gratified his sitters' fantasies of status and power.

In an era of mounting political tensions Copley remained neutral (despite his marriage into a prominent Tory family in 1769), painting both loyalists such as Thomas Hutchinson and Benjamin Hallowell, and patriots such as Paul Revere and John Hancock. By the mid-1760s Copley was earning more than £300 a year; nevertheless, his frustration with Boston's provincialism ("Was it not for preserving the resemblance of particular persons, painting would not be known in the place," he

John Singleton Copley, Paul Revere (1768, Museum of Fine Arts, Boston)

wrote) motivated him to test his talents in a more sophisticated climate. In 1766 he exhibited *Henry Pelham (The Boy with a Squirrel)* (1765, Museum of Fine Arts, Boston) in London, where Sir Joshua Reynolds and Benjamin West praised it and encouraged Copley to come to England to study.

Copley first tried his skills in New York, spending seven months and painting some 32 portraits there in 1771. His paintings of the 1770s contain fewer showy objects and are darker and more dramatically lit than those of the 1760s. The sobriety of these portraits (for example, *Samuel Adams,* ca. 1770, Museum of Fine Arts, Boston) may reflect the darkening political climate, a climate that also affected the market for Copley's portraits. In June 1774 he left Boston to make his career abroad.

Copley spent several months in Paris and Rome, settling in London by June 1775. The two works exhibited in 1777 at the Royal Academy—*Mr. and Mrs. Ralph Izard* (1775, Museum of Fine Arts, Boston) and *The Copley Family* (1776–77, National Gallery of Art, Washington, D.C.)—established his reputation as a portraitist.

But it was as a history painter that Copley hoped to make his mark. In 1778 he exhibited *Watson and the Shark* (National Gallery of Art), a dramatic composition that elevated an ordinary boy's attack by a shark to an exalted

level normally reserved for religious martyrs or military heroes. The painting caused a sensation; Copley's election to the Royal Academy followed. His English history painting *The Death of Major Peirson* (1782–84, Tate, London) immortalized a young British officer killed in battle with the French. Its epic grandeur and intense realism appealed to British nationalism and placed Copley at the center of new contemporary history painter in Europe.

After the mid-1780s, however, Copley's career declined. His history paintings proved financially disappointing; his portraits were often derided in the press. Diminishing commissions, monetary difficulties, and deteriorating health marked the next two decades. Copley suffered a stroke in August 1815 and died a month later.

Guernsey Jones, ed., *Letters and Papers of John Singleton Copley and Henry Pelham, 1739–1776* (1914); Emily Ballew Neff, *John Singleton Copley in England* (1995); Jules David Prown, *John Singleton Copley,* 2 vols. (1966); Carrie Rebora, Paul Staiti, Erica E. Hirshler, Theodore E. Stebbins, Jr., and Carol Troyen, *John Singleton Copley in America* (1995).

Carol Troyen

Corporate Art Patronage

A region rich in both business and cultural resources, New England has a long tradition of corporate art patronage. Where once only a handful of large companies supported the arts, today many small and midsize businesses are patrons. A study conducted by the New England Foundation for the Arts, published as *Arts, Cultural, and Humanities Organizations in the New England Economy* (1997), showed that the nonprofit arts and culture industry not only depends on corporate and private philanthropy to survive but in 1996 gave back an estimated $3.9 billion to the economy of the region.

The most highly visible form of corporate arts sponsorship is direct support for exhibitions and performance events such as Bell Atlantic's underwriting of *Picasso: The Early Years, 1892–1906* and Fleet Financial Group's sponsorship of *Monet in the 20th Century* at Boston's Museum of Fine Arts in 1997 and 1998. United Technologies has similarly funded shows at Hartford's Wadsworth Atheneum, most notably *Marsden Hartley* (2003) and *Pieter de Hooch, 1629–1684* (1998–99). Significant support for the performing arts is evident in Bank of America's Celebrity Series and the Xerox Corporation's sponsorship of the national Pianists' Program in conjunction with the National Endowment for the Arts.

Corporate patronage takes many forms. In addition to cash, businesses throughout New England also donate equipment, materials, services, and even property to arts organizations. Many also loan their skilled executives to serve on boards or provide pro bono assistance. Partnerships such as Business Volunteers for the Arts and Volunteer Lawyers for the Arts recruit volunteers and match their specific skills with the needs of cultural groups. The Greater Hartford Arts Council conducts unified programming and fund-raising, tapping companies ranging from giants like Aetna to those with fewer than 20 employees. Recognizing the importance of public relations in philanthropy, the New Hampshire Business Committee for the Arts honors outstanding corporate leaders through a highly publicized awards program. Since 1985 winners have included Fleet Bank, Continental Cablevision of New England, and Chubb Life America, among many others. A few New England corporations have created distinguished collections of regional art that are open to the public. State Street Bank is known for its collection of early New England maritime artifacts, and Hartford Steam Boiler's collection of American art and furniture, donated to the Florence Griswold Museum, Old Lyme, Conn., in 2001, is widely renowned. Polaroid Corporation organizes traveling exhibitions culled from its extraordinary photography collection, begun in the 1940s with early assistance from Ansel Adams. FleetBoston and Fidelity Investments have both

collected extensively in diverse media and maintain collections overseen by full-time curators. Xerox, a major regional and national supporter of the arts, opens exhibitions at its headquarters in Stamford, Conn., to the public and has developed a corporate collection of more than 1,100 artworks.

Corporate leaders generally agree that a flourishing cultural climate is good for business. They view supporting the arts as a way to be good community citizens, enhance the quality of life for their clients and employees, and build positive visibility. Although corporate support for the arts in New England steadily increased in the last two decades of the 20th century, contributions everywhere inevitably rise and fall with economic cycles and competition for philanthropic dollars. When government support for health and social services declines, as in the late 1990s, cultural groups fear a shift away from giving to the arts. New England corporate patrons, like those in other parts of the United States, then must struggle to balance requests from the social, educational, and cultural sectors.

American Association of Fund-Raising Counsel, *Giving USA* (2000); Debra E. Blum and Susan Gray, "Big Business Means Big Philanthropy," *Chronicle of Philanthropy*, July 16, 1998; David Finn and Judith A. Jedlicka, *The Art of Leadership: Building Business-Art Alliances* (1998); Margaret Jane Wyszomirski and Pat Clubb, eds., *The Cost of Culture: Patterns and Prospects of Private Arts Patronage* (1989).

Joyce Cohen

Crite, Allan Rohan

Crite, Allan Rohan (1910–) Painter, printmaker, author, and historian. Allan Rohan Crite, an internationally recognized artist, is known regionally for his social commentaries, his promotion of cultural heritage education, and his encouragement of young Boston artists. A vital member of the New England art community, Crite is perhaps best known for the scenes of black life in Boston he painted during the 1930s. Throughout his career and through various means, Crite has worked to critique negative stereotypes and dispel false assumptions about African Americans. His artwork falls loosely into three categories: his illustrations of black spirituals; his artistic interpretations of the Bible from an Afro-Asian perspective; and his "neighborhood paintings," which focus on black life in the city.

Born in North Plainfield, N.J., Crite moved to Boston with his parents, Annamae and Oscar William Crite, when he was an infant and still resides there. Crite credits his mother and an elementary school teacher with encouraging his artistic talent and enrolling him in art classes at the Children's Art Center of Boston's Museum of Fine Arts. A member of the

Allan Rohan Crite, 1991

city's growing African American community, which numbered 120,000 by 1940, Crite attended the Boston Latin School and graduated from English High School in 1929. He received a scholarship to study art at the School of the Museum of Fine Arts, Boston, which he attended from 1929 to 1936. Crite received his bachelor of arts degree from Harvard University Extension School in 1968. An Episcopalian, he has also studied Roman Catholicism, and he lectures on the subject of liturgical art. Crite holds several honorary doctorates, including one in divinity from the General Theological Seminary of the Episcopal Church in New York.

Crite worked for the Works Project Administration from 1934 to 1937. While participating in the Federal Arts project in 1934, he produced many oil paintings of Boston, Cambridge, Roxbury, and South End neighborhoods. Crite sought to represent human aspects of African American culture, recording traditions and values through scenes of ordinary black people at work and play. Documents of a life that disappeared with urban renewal, Crite's paintings such as *Parade on Hammond Street, 1935* (Phillips Collection, Washington, D.C.), in which black spectators watch a brightly uniformed Elks marching band, depict typical neighborhood street scenes of pushcarts and street vendors, conversations and celebrations, churches and schools.

Regarding distortions of Africa as the "dark continent" both damaging and disturbing, Crite has also created religious art that recognizes the Afro-Asian geography of the Bible and returns black figures to biblical imagery through his influential illustrated books *Were*

You There When They Crucified My Lord? (1944), which includes a black Christ; *All Glory: Brush Drawing Meditations on the Prayer of Consecration* (1947); and *Book of Revelation* (1994). Crite's illustrated interpretation of Negro spirituals, *Three Spirituals from Earth to Heaven* (1948), integrates his knowledge of African American history and religious life to eradicate negative minstrel stereotypes.

Crite's work is far-ranging. He has written historical pictorial essays on such diverse subjects as Boston's African Meeting House and its role in the abolitionist movement, and the story of the black 54th Massachusetts Regiment in the Civil War. In 1977 he wrote "An Artist's Sketchbook of the South End—A Walking Tour about Black People," a booklet illustrated with color lithographs that traces black migratory patterns and the development of the South End. His work has also appeared in national Episcopal Church publications.

In addition to his writings, Crite has fulfilled major church commissions for the chapel at the Massachusetts Institute of Technology, Grace Church on Martha's Vineyard, and Holy Cross Church in Morrisville, Vt. His work is also represented in numerous permanent museum collections, including the Museum of Fine Arts, Boston, the Museum of Modern Art in New York, and the Smithsonian American Art Museum, Washington, D.C. Crite lives with his wife, Jackie Cox-Crite, in Boston's South End, where they maintain the Allan Rohan Crite Research Institute, a museum that houses an impressive collection of Crite's artwork in various media and includes a library of rare art books, recorded lectures, slides of major exhibitions, and hundreds of published and unpublished manuscripts recording 60 years of research and scholarly writing.

Julie Levin Caro, Allan Rohan Crite, and Barbara Earl Thomas, *Allan Rohan Crite: Artist-Reporter of the African-American Community* (2001); Theresza D. Cederholm, *Afro-American Artists: A Bio Bibliographical Directory* (1973); DeCordova Museum, *By the People, for the People: New England* (1977); Cedric Dover, *American Negro Art* (1960).

Diane D. Turner

Earl, Ralph (1751–1801) Portrait and landscape painter. Ralph Earl was born in Shrewsbury, Mass., moving shortly thereafter with his family to Leicester, Mass. He began his painting career in New Haven, Conn., in 1774. Between 1774 and 1778 Earl painted a number of leading patriots, including Roger Sherman (1775–76, Yale University Art Gallery, New Haven), capturing in the full-length portrait the Yankee virtues of honesty, frugality, piousness, and industry that the sitter embodied. With New Haven engraver Amos Doolittle,

Earl created a series of four engravings of the Battles of Lexington and Concord of 1775, now in the Connecticut Historical Society in Hartford, that are among America's first historical prints. In spite of the patriotic nature of these endeavors, Earl declared himself a loyalist and in 1778 fled to England. He spent his early years in England painting the Norwich gentry. By 1783 he was studying in London under American expatriate Benjamin West, absorbing the techniques and conventions of the British portrait tradition so well that he exhibited several pictures at the Royal Academy in 1784 and 1785.

Returning to America in 1785, Earl established himself as an artist in New York City. A small debt he had incurred while on board ship landed Earl in prison, where, while confined, he fell prey to alcoholism. Nonetheless, he was able to earn money painting wealthy members of the Society for the Relief of Distressed Debtors and was released from prison in January 1788. Earl's release marked a turning point in his career. His court-appointed guardian, Dr. Mason Fitch Cogswell, convinced Earl to move to Connecticut and provided him with numerous portrait commissions. Modifying his artistic ambitions, Earl plied his trade as an itinerant artist for the next 10 years.

During this time, Earl furthered the formation of a national image by portraying a segment of American society that had never before received the attention of a trained and gifted artist. He created a style appropriate to the aesthetic sensibilities of his rural sitters by rejecting the British aristocratic manner and using broad brushstrokes to create realistic likenesses of his subjects, as in *Elijah Boardman* (1789, Metropolitan Museum of Art, New York) and *Oliver Ellsworth and Abigail Wolcott Ellsworth* (1792, Wadsworth Atheneum, Hartford). Favoring primary colors made from pigments readily available in remote areas, Earl surrounded his sitters with emblems of the new nation and faithfully reproduced his subjects' attire, locally made furnishings, and newly built houses against a backdrop of regional landscape features. By including landscape features in his portraits, Earl created a taste for landscape painting among his rural patrons. In England, landscape painting was just emerging as a mode of high artistic expression. In America, however, Earl was one of only a few artists receiving commissions for pure landscapes.

In 1798 Earl traveled north in search of new commissions, possibly because of increasing competition from his imitators. The following year he became the first American artist to travel to Niagara Falls, where he took sketches of the "stupendous cataract" for a large-scale

panorama. The panorama opened to great fanfare in Northampton, Mass., and later traveled to New Haven, Philadelphia, and London.

Toward the end of his life Earl painted a panoramic landscape of his hometown, entitled *Looking East from Denny Hill* (1796, Worcester [Mass.] Art Museum), that captures, in fertile farmlands and prosperous town centers, the prevailing belief in the promise of America. In 1801, while on a trip to Bolton, Conn., Ralph Earl died of "intemperance." Earl was widely regarded as the initiator of the so-called Connecticut School of portrait painters, and his distinctive style has come to exemplify early New England portraiture.

Laurence B. Goodrich, *Ralph Earl: Recorder for an Era* (1967); Elizabeth Mankin Kornhauser, "Ralph Earl as an Itinerant Artist: Pattern of Patronage," in *Itinerancy in New England and New York,* ed. Peter Benes (1986); Kornhauser, with Richard L. Bushman, Stephen H. Kornhauser, and Aileen Ribeiro, *Ralph Earl: The Face of the Young Republic* (1991); Robert Blair St. George, *Conversing by Signs: Poetics of Implication in Colonial New England Culture* (1998).

Elizabeth Mankin Kornhauser

Education "Like many artists, [Winslow] Homer had strong New England roots," observed the brochure for an exhibition at Boston's Museum of Fine Arts in 1996. Why should so many artists have come from this region? Certainly, at least in part, because for centuries New Englanders have taken art education seriously. With shifting emphasis, they planned for art education to refine and morally improve those exposed to it; to celebrate local views—of Boston harbor and Cape Ann, Mass., Maine's rocky coast, and the White Mountains—increasing tourism; and to create a new class of workers, "art labor," from whose appealing mass-produced designs local corporations could reap vast profits.

All three artistic ambitions—moral refinement, celebration of the local landscape, and utilitarian art skills—can be traced back to colonial pedagogy. Around the 1740s, affluent youth were refined and taught useful skills of painting on glass and needlework at the classes of Peter Pelham, stepfather of John Singleton Copley. They also enrolled in the Boston classes of Mrs. Condy, who drew patterns of all sorts for pocketbooks, screens, pictures, and chimneypieces and sold hers for less than those from London. Boston also boasted Mrs. Hiller, who taught waxwork, filigree, painting on glass, Japanning, quillwork, feather work, and embroidering with gold and silver. In 1754 the London school keeper John Leach came to Boston's North End and offered classes in drawing, a skill useful to sea artists who took prospects of land and surveyed harbors.

Soon after the Revolution, new elite private academies offered girls art instruction. Students' samplers, silk paintings, and drawings survive from, among others, Mary Balch's school, opened in Providence, in 1785; Sarah Pierce's Litchfield (Conn.) Academy, opened in 1792; Mrs. Rowson's, opened in Boston in 1797; the Dorchester, Mass., school co-directed by Mrs. Judith Foster Saunders and Miss Clementina Beach, opened in 1803; and Miss Eloise Payne's, opened in Newport, R.I., in 1811.

In the first years of the 19th century, art education was under no governmental authority and was subject to no overall plan. Any artistically oriented women and men could invent their own teaching methods and use them not only in academies but in print and publishing shops, at exhibitions, and in the common schools. Around this same time distinctions were constructed that separated professional and nonprofessional artists, usually along class and gender lines. But debates were emerging over who should receive art education and what they should be taught. Although women in Boston petitioned London-trained John Rubens Smith to open his drawing school, this teacher charged that the city's too numerous women artists needed to be replaced by a class of professional male artists. Women of means came to disdain their old-fashioned art instruction focusing on needlework, and by the late 1830s republican motherhood and feminism began attracting them to a more modern, less art-based, and more literary education—a curriculum usually limited to men. Commercial galleries such as Doggett's Repository in Boston and the Boston Athenaeum's art gallery, both opened in 1827, became promoters of male professional artists.

Nonprofessional art education also flourished, for art fascinated general educators. The esteemed Round Hill School in Northampton, Mass., co-founded in 1823 by the Harvard mineralogy professor Joseph Green Cogswell and historian George Bancroft, hired German artist-teacher Francis Graeter two years later to help the boys learn to draw what they saw in the Connecticut River valley landscape. By the mid-1830s Graeter had moved to teach at Bronson Alcott's Boston experiment, the Temple School. Universal art education found one of its best advocates in Elizabeth Palmer Peabody, who ran her own schools, documented Alcott's in her work *Record of a School* (1835), and later published various essays on art.

Schools never exist in a vacuum. With increasingly inexpensive image reproduction prospering in Boston and Hartford, teachers and writers generated hundreds of products: art books, magazines, prints, and drawing cards. In 1825 the first of many editions of *The Eye and the Hand,* William Bentley Fowle's adaptation of Napoleon's national drawing curriculum, was illustrated with wood and steel engravings. In the 1830s lithography, the print process that best emulated chalk and pencil marks, was exploited for landscape lessons. Hartford lithographers Kellogg and Kellogg invited Benjamin Coe, Frederic Edwin Church's childhood art teacher, to draw landscapes on lithographic stones for prints, drawing books, and drawing cards. Small magazines also shared this mission. In "Essay on American Scenery," which appeared in the *American Monthly* in January 1836, painter Thomas Cole urged readers to find in rural nature, such as New Hampshire's White Mountains, an "exhaustless mine from which the poet and the painter have brought such wondrous treasures." Through the 1850s publishers commissioned artists to design exercises for beginners in drawing books and drawing cards. Pages of lines straight and curved prepared students to draw trees, houses, fences, and landscapes in the spirit of Cole's landscapes. Copying from drawing books with New England views established the region as a source of pride and destination to visit.

Despite the encouragement to study and create art in America, many believed that true art was found only in Europe, that only the European tour could provide a legitimate art education. In the 1850s Harvard-educated Charles Callahan Perkins devoted himself to researching art in Italy for two texts on sculpture. But upon his return in the 1860s, new agricultural and technical colleges, the fruits of the federal government's Morrill Land Grant Act of 1862, gave him fresh ideas. Perkins committed 10 years of his life to creating a unique Massachusetts counterpart to this legislation: industrial art education for children and evening classes for working adults.

Perkins and Boston business leaders succeeded when a law called the Drawing Act was passed in 1870. This act required Massachusetts to offer free art classes in public schools and in evening drawing classes—private schools usually charged a fee—to nurture new female and male workers whose design skills would upgrade New England's textile, shoe, and hat manufacture. These efforts led to the importation from England of Walter Smith, a renowned art teacher trained in South Kensington and committed to the use of art in industry. Smith's charge was to invent the new curriculum for an art labor class, to form a traveling art museum for schools, and, after three years, to found and direct a state-supported art school. Coincidentally, for a more affluent class of citizens, Boston was establishing its own Museum of Fine Arts and associated school, which was under more of an industrial influence than is generally appreciated today, particularly in the area of textile surface design. The Massachusetts law, coupled with the promotion of art for jobs by land-grant colleges, converted art education from an independent entrepreneurial enterprise to an instrument of the state government, and from an elite concern to one intended to improve the masses and to promote regional prosperity. The new art education was to be open to all.

This shift created fierce rivalries. Although industrial, technical systems were far narrower than the earlier approaches to art, Walter Smith became Boston's darling. The Vermont landscape artist and Boston teacher William Bartholemew, who before the war had built his reputation lithographing Vermont scenery, fell out of favor. Smith enhanced his celebrity at the Philadelphia Centennial Exposition of 1876, where his students' creations proved that his art curriculum was a product exportable to out-of-state, even international markets. Although Winslow Homer demonstrated his distrust of industrially oriented art education in his watercolor *The Blackboard* (1877, National Gallery of Art, Washington, D.C.), which depicted an industrial art lesson, the movement kept gaining momentum. By the late 1880s and early 1890s, the U.S. Senate was reflecting on its legislative success in its massive four-volume report *Art and Industry;* the Massachusetts industrial art idea had become an official federal symbol and hope for the American economy.

By the end of the 19th century the "art labor" idea had exhausted itself. The Museum of Fine Arts, Boston, was acquiring the finest collection of Japanese art outside Japan. Art education in the 20th century was to be radically transformed under its influence. The Ipswich, Mass., artist Arthur Wesley Dow saw in the Japanese aesthetic the opportunity to rethink populist art education. Now students would use line to express feelings, to create a visual music. Schools would give students Japanese ink brushes to explore line and "notan," the balancing of dark and light spaces. Dow's pedagogy, published as *Composition* in 14 editions beginning in 1899, made him and Ipswich famous. His inspiring summer art classes (1890–1907) cultivated more New England artists and teachers and prepared them to welcome to Boston the so-called Armory Show (or International Exhibition of Modern Art), much of it from Europe, first displayed in New York City in 1913.

In the 20th century, travel, leisure, and disposable wealth continued to attract summer students, many of them teachers to the region. Teaching artists such as Dow, Albert Munsell, Charles Woodbury and Elizabeth Perkins, Charles Hawthorne, and Hans Hofmann lent an aura to studying art in the New England landscape. But their successes had little to do with what was taught the rest of the year in schools. American law delegates curriculum control to individual town or city school committees. Their judgments of art's benefit tended to reflect the needs of local businesses, labor conditions, and families' ambitions. Idiosyncratic practices are the result. Equity seems less important than local independence. So it is, too, in fine arts education at the college level in New England, whether at private, independent art schools, state-supported independent art schools, or universities.

When one considers the two-century-long history of New England art education, the notion of a unified system seems something of a fiction. Although the early motives for investing in art education remain current today, ultimately each institution that teaches art is on its own. The 21st century's emphasis on technical art education—interactive computer graphics—will challenge and suggest new aesthetics to artists with pencil, camera, paint, textiles, video, and film. And art programs at New England schools, as in the rest of the nation, will be as magnetic as the personalities of those who direct and teach at them.

Georgia Brady Barnhill, Diana Korzenik, and Caroline F. Sloat, *The Cultivation of Artists in 19th-Century America* (1997); Maurice Brown and Diana Korzenik, *Art Making and Education* (1993); Isaac Edwards Clarke, *Art and Industry: Education in the Industrial and Fine Arts in the United States*, 4 vols. (1884–98); Diana Korzenik, *Drawn to Art: A 19th-Century American Dream* (1985); Peter C. Marzio, *The Art Crusade: An Analysis of American Drawing Manuals, 1820–1860* (1976); Betty Ring, *Girlhood Embroidery: American Samplers and Pictorial Needlework, 1650–1850*, 2 vols. (1993); Foster Wygant, *Art in American Schools in the 19th Century* (1983); Wygant, *School Art in American Culture, 1820–1970* (1993).

Diana Korzenik

Fasanella, Ralph

Fasanella, Ralph (1914–97) Painter. Ralph Fasanella was a self-taught artist who created an important series of works depicting New England's labor history. Fasanella was born to Italian immigrants in New York City, where his father was an ice deliveryman and his mother was a garment worker. The most formative influences on Fasanella's life were his parents: his father introduced him to the physical rigors of working-class life, while his socially conscious mother taught him about the workers' struggle and the value of self-education. The Great Depression radicalized Fasa-

Senator Ted Kennedy and Ralph Fasanella at Lawrence Heritage State Park, Mass., with the artist's painting Lawrence 1912, The Bread and Roses Strike *(1977, New York Historical Society), 1988*

nella's political beliefs, and he became active in antifascist and trade union causes. His antifascist zeal led him to volunteer for the Abraham Lincoln Brigade, which fought Francisco Franco in the Spanish Civil War. On his return to New York in 1938, Fasanella became a union organizer.

In 1944, disillusioned by the labor movement and plagued by a painful sensation in his fingers, Fasanella started to draw. The result was an immediate outpouring of creative energy. Fasanella left organizing and began to paint full time. He painted obsessively, capturing the vibrant moods of his native city and the tumult of American politics. In 1950 he married Eva Lazorek, a schoolteacher who supported the couple through the more than two decades of her husband's artistic obscurity and blacklisting by the Federal Bureau of Investigation. In 1972 Fasanella was featured in *New York* magazine, and Patrick Watson's illustrated coffee-table book *Fasanella's City* came out in 1973. Critics and the public acclaimed his large-scale, intricate paintings of urban life and political subjects, but Fasanella's sudden fame caused a creative block that lasted until the mid-1970s, when author Bill Kahn suggested that he travel to Lawrence, Mass., for inspiration.

Fasanella spent more than two years in Lawrence researching the Bread and Roses strike of textile workers there in 1912. The result was a series of 18 canvases, ranging in size from 3 to more than 10 feet wide, that depict the life of the mill town's diverse immigrant population and the events of the strike. The most important work, *Lawrence 1912: The Bread and Roses Strike* (1977), portrays the height of the conflict, in which national

guardsmen marched into Lawrence to break up the demonstration. The painting shows a child being trampled by a guardsman's horse, protesters destroying mill equipment, a group of strike leaders addressing a large crowd of workers, and another group of leaders standing trial. The Lawrence series represents one of the largest and most significant bodies of historical painting by any self-taught American artist, and for the most part it is freely accessible to the viewing public. Paintings from the series can be seen at the Heritage State Park Visitors' Center in Lawrence, Mass., the Hirshhorn Museum and Sculpture Garden in Washington, D.C., and Lewiston-Auburn College at the University of Southern Maine. The 5-by-10-foot *Great Strike: Lawrence 1912* (1978) hung in the hearing room of the U.S. House Committee on Education and Labor on Capitol Hill in Washington until the new Republican majority elected to the House of Representatives in 1994, apparently unhappy with the painting's prolabor message, had it removed.

In the mid-1980s Fasanella made a similar but much briefer journey to New Bedford, Mass., where he spent months acquainting himself with workers and fishermen. That trip resulted in a series of paintings on the New Bedford working class, including a large canvas entitled *Labor Education: New Bedford Union Hall* (1986), which the city of New Bedford acquired and now displays at the New Bedford City Hall. Fasanella's work is distinct from that of such regional artists as Winslow Homer whose paintings offer a primarily nostalgic view of rural New England. Fasanella focused rather on urban and labor history at a time when these issues were being revived in the popular consciousness. His images of industrial New England emerged concurrently with the rediscovery, revitalization, and celebration of New England's immigrant and industrial past and related events such as the founding of the Lowell National Historical Park. Ralph Fasanella, called the best American primitive artist since Grandma Moses, died at age 83.

Paul S. D'Ambrosio, *Ralph Fasanella's America* (2001); D'Ambrosio, "Ralph Fasanella: The Making of a Working-Class Artist," *Folk Art* (1995); Herbert F. Johnson Museum of Art, *Urban Visions: The Paintings of Ralph Fasanella* (1985); Patrick Watson, *Fasanella's City* (1973).

Paul S. D'Ambrosio

Field, Erastus Salisbury (1805–1900)

Artist. Between 1825 and 1850 many middle-class New Englanders wanted portraits of themselves and their families to document their prosperity. Numerous artists of varying ability set out to satisfy this demand, painting in rural areas and towns throughout the region. Among them was Erastus Salisbury Field, who, judging by the number of his surviving works, was among the more prolific and successful itinerant regional portraitists of the period.

Field was born in Leverett, Mass., where his forebears had worked as farmers for several generations. Recognizing their son's artistic talent, Field's parents sent 19-year-old Erastus to New York City in late 1824 to study with Samuel F. B. Morse. Morse had been commissioned to paint General Lafayette's portrait during his American tour; Field would always remember meeting Lafayette and observing Morse painting the portrait. His apprenticeship was cut short, however, by the premature death of Morse's wife in February 1825, after which Field returned to Leverett. Although his painting style was little influenced by his brief association with Morse, Field's New York experience provided him with a glimpse of the life and work a respected professional painter. This, perhaps more than any technical lessons he may have learned in Morse's studio, inspired Field to work as an artist for the next 60 years.

Field developed an efficient and distinctive painting style during his travels throughout western Massachusetts and Connecticut, southern New Hampshire, and eastern New York. Typically depicting adults in half-length and children standing on patterned carpets in full-length poses, Field employed assured drawing and brushwork, bright, clear colors, and minimal modeling to create attractive and decorative likenesses. His most ambitious work, a nearly life-size portrait of the hatmaker and dentist Joseph B. Moore and his family, painted in 1839, represents the distillation of his previous 15 years of painting experience.

The same year that Field painted the Moore family, Morse introduced Louis Daguerre's photographic process to America. Like numerous other itinerant portraitists, Field soon found his works competing with cheap daguerreotypes that had begun to encroach upon his portrait business. In 1841 Field returned to New York City, where he lived until 1848; when he was no longer able to support himself there by painting, he moved back to Leverett. By the middle of the 1850s Field had acquired a camera and worked as a photographer in addition to painting individual and group portraits based on photographs he made. Field spent the remainder of his life in Leverett, living frugally and continuing to paint well into his eighties. His later subjects included biblical events, exotic foreign locales, and visionary historical scenes that lined the walls of his makeshift studio. Field died in Leverett at age 95, the oldest man in Franklin County, Mass.

In his flat, linear portraits of middle-class individuals posed with characteristic objects such as books, quill pens, and musical instruments, Field emphasized patterns in clothes and furnishings and bold colors. His imaginative historical and biblical works also appealed to New England sensibilities. For example, *The Garden of Eden* (ca. 1865, Shelburne Museum, Vt.)—familiar from innumerable editions of *The New-England Primer,* needlework samplers, and gravestones—sets the scene of Eve's temptation in a semitropical garden with mountains receding into the background. Field also capitalized on current events, such as President Ulysses S. Grant's trip to India. In *The Historical Monument of the American Republic* (ca. 1876, photoengraving by Edward Bierstadt after Field's painting, Museum of Fine Arts, Springfield, Mass.), Field captured the confidence and optimism of the post–Civil War years, which culminated in the Centennial of 1876.

From the time of landmark exhibits in the 1930s, Field's work has become emblematic of a "folk," "naive," or "limner" style identified with both New England and America of the 19th century, and his paintings are found in numerous public and private collections.

Mary Black, *Erastus Salisbury Field: 1805–1900* (1984); Deborah Chotner, *American Naive Painting* (1992).

Richard Miller

Furniture

"New England furniture," with rare exception, served as a synonym for "American furniture" for most of the 20th century. Turn-of-the-century collectors and antiquarians, imbued with the regional chauvinism of their generation, gathered, restored, and published New England styles and types to the exclusion of furniture forms from other parts of the original American colonies. Subsequent scholarship built on these antiquarian efforts and extended this northeastern bias for much of the 20th century. With rare exception, such as the highly developed rococo forms of 18th-century Philadelphia, the furniture of colonial New England remains vastly overdetermined in popular understanding of American material culture.

Little attention was paid to American furniture before the Civil War. Indeed, collecting furniture in the antebellum period was often considered to be a harmless eccentricity within literary or artistic circles. Objects were saved and displayed primarily for their historical associations rather than their aesthetic qualities. In Plymouth, Mass., the 17th-century turned armchairs of Governor Carver and Elder Brewster were placed on exhibit in the 1830s to serve as reminders of that community's glorious past. In a similar vein, Daniel Wadsworth, an antiquarian and patron of the arts in Hartford, purchased an early-18th-century cane chair in 1827 from the family on whose land stood the "Charter Oak," the focus of an important local myth. Wadsworth compounded his unusual act by commissioning Smith Ely, a New York City chair maker, to produce a series of reproductions and placed these chairs in the Wadsworth Atheneum to serve as object lessons for a growing population unfamiliar with the founding legend of the Charter Oak.

Wadsworth's actions, though exceptional, were not singular. It raised eyebrows in Cambridge, Mass., for example, when Harvard professor Henry Wadsworth Longfellow accepted "Castle Craigie," a hoary pre-Revolutionary mansion from his father-in-law as a wedding present in the 1830s. When Longfellow began to collect Queen Anne furniture for the venerable house, a visiting English critic chided him for filling his home with "trumpery antiques." The very word "antique" still referred to the classical past in popular usage and was only humorously applied to American decorative arts in such communities as Plymouth, Hartford, and Cambridge.

After the Civil War influential tastemakers like Clarence Cook began to recommend furnishing the well-appointed home with antiques as a sign of breeding and taste. "Everybody can't have a grandfather, nor things that came over on the Mayflower," he wrote in 1881. Everyone could, however, include a venerable turned chair, gateleg table, or spinning wheel in the parlor, according to Cook. Such thinking not only cultivated the demand for affordable antiques but also led to the development of hybrid furniture forms such as the spinning wheel chair. Constructed from the parts of obsolete spinning wheels, such objects placed an icon of traditional female domestic labor in the middle-class parlor just as textile production made the final move to the factory. Such sentimental forms provided reminders of idealized "good old days" and served to cover the traces of New England's now preeminent industrial culture.

Industrialization produced far more than mere novelty seating furniture. Indeed, the economic engines that fueled the construction of highly organized mill cities for the textile business also propelled a boom in the furniture industry. Small communities such as Gardner, Mass., became major centers of chair production, and larger cities such as Boston hosted such imposing concerns as A. H. Davenport and J. S. Paine's furniture companies. Machine-made, often by immigrant labor, the furniture produced in New England in the last quarter of the 19th century covered a wide spectrum of quality and price point. From inexpensive grain-painted pine "cottage suites" to elegant custom pieces in the latest revival style and specialty forms such as the rattan furniture of the Heywood Wakefield Company, New England firms serviced a broad market and reinforced the national appetite for goods in the Victorian era.

Responses to this Victorian world of goods varied. Although photographic evidence points to the persistence of "overstuffed" upholstered furniture well into the 20th century, especially among Italian and eastern European immigrant populations for whom textiles carried important meaning, a reform style took hold as well in the shape of the Arts and Crafts movement. Initially organized by the Boston-based Society of Arts and Crafts, this return to craft found countless followers in New England on the eve of the turn of the century. Based on the mid-19th-century writings of John Ruskin and William Morris, the Arts and Crafts movement sought to provide an antidote to the vicissitudes of modern life by promoting handicraft at all levels of society. Woodworking, metalsmithing, jewelry making, and the textile arts all enjoyed a renaissance under the auspices of the Society of Arts and Crafts, Boston. Led by Harvard professor Charles Eliot Norton, the first professor of fine arts at an American university, the society sought a social purpose beyond simple aesthetic reform. It advocated nothing less than the realignment of designers and workers into "mutually helpful relations," as claimed in its mission statement in 1897. Handicraft, according to Norton and his followers, would renew the relation between art and labor—an age-old union torn asunder by the machine, according to their idealized notions.

The rapidly advancing culture of consumption, however, proved to be the end of the Arts and Crafts ideology, for as soon as the movement became a style it was co-opted by the furniture industry. The ideal of handicraft went by the wayside as factories were tooled up to produce "mission oak" furniture for an ever-widening middle-class audience. The reification of handiwork inherent in Arts and Crafts, however, fed the antiquarian impulse in New England. Indeed, the furniture produced by members of the Society of Arts and Crafts, Boston, and the host of smaller organizations throughout the region, such as the Deerfield Society of Arts and Crafts, looked to vernacular forms of historic furniture for inspiration rather than the idealized English prototypes often found in such cities as Chicago. An oak chest produced shortly after the turn of the century by Dr. Edwin Thorn, Caleb Allen, and Cornelius Kelly of Deerfield, Mass., illustrates the close relationship between past and present in the early 20th century. Assembled by Allen of Dr. Thorn's carved panels and Kelly's wrought iron hardware, the chest is a close interpretation of the 17th-century Hadley chests on view in the museum of the local Pocumtuck Valley Memorial Association.

Acolytes of Arts and Crafts and students of the decorative arts in New England not only visited the material remains of the colonial era at museums such as Memorial Hall but increasingly relied upon such groundbreaking studies as those of Irving W. Lyon and Luke Vincent Lockwood. Lyon, a Hartford physician, can be named as the founding father of American furniture history. A prominent collector, Lyon trained his scientific mind on his avocation and produced *The Colonial Furniture of New England: A Study of the Domestic Furniture in Use in the 17th and 18th Centuries* in 1891. Well ahead of his time, Lyon pioneered the genre of the illustrated furniture survey and employed primary documents to assist in the identification of schools of furniture making as well as specific cabinetmakers. For his part, Lockwood clearly announced his preferences in the preface to his volume *Colonial Furniture in America* (1901). "New England," he noted "is particularly rich in examples of the earliest" period, while "the South is woefully lacking." In this way the material culture of New England aided in the construction of a regionally specific past for the United States.

Americana exhibitions in major urban museums built on this scholarship and reinforced the New England agenda. R. T. H. Halsey, an author and collector, acted as curator for several early landmark displays of American furniture and related decorative arts. In 1909, Halsey assisted in the organization of the Hudson-Fulton Celebration at the Metropolitan Museum of Art, New York. The aftereffects of this project had a profound impact on the future of American decorative arts and helped legitimize this area of study. The Hudson-Fulton project led to the Metropolitan's acquisition of the Boston-based collection of H. Eugene Bolles, the founding of a highly influential group of Americana collectors known as the Walpole Society, and the eventual establishment of the American Wing in 1924. The catalog of the American Wing, first published in 1925, belies a regional slant in the very title, *The Homes of Our Ancestors as Shown in the American Wing of the Metropolitan Museum of Art of New York from the Beginnings of New England through the Early Days of the Republic.* With the installation of the American Wing in New York, the New England bias in furniture making and related decorative arts became institutionalized.

The hegemony of New England forms, aided by the earlier publishing efforts of the region's antiquarians and display schemes of large museums, ironically achieved dominance through the market. Individual entrepreneurs, such as Harvard-educated Congregational-minister-turned-furniture-scholar Wallace Nutting, developed sophisticated methods to sell reproduction furniture by linking their products to the original prototypes (now in museums) and a glorious narrative of New England history. Nutting acquired a collection of 17th- and early-18th-century furniture to use as props in his highly popular hand-tinted photographs and as objects in a chain of five museum houses that he organized in three New England states. He then wrote two texts based on his collection, *Furniture of the Pilgrim Century* (1922) and the three-volume *Furniture Treasury* (1928–33). In print for the balance of the 20th century, these books became the standard reference works on American furniture.

Nutting was as much businessman as antiquarian, however. He established a factory to manufacture reproductions of his period furniture. These "antiques of the future" were then sold at department stores throughout the country. In conjunction with his highly popular writings and photographs, Nutting's furniture placed physical history lessons in countless American homes. Singular perhaps for the heterogeneous, yet interconnected, nature of his Colonial Revival empire, Nutting endured many competitors in his lifetime.

The market for furniture in the "colonial style" supported large corporations as well as individual craftsmen. The Erskine-Danforth Company is a prime example of a furniture maker that took advantage of the post–World War I economic boom to expand its operation. With roots in Connecticut, it was perhaps natural for Danersk, as the company was known, to interpret traditional forms such as the well-known "Sunflower" chests of Wethersfield, Conn. What is remarkable, however, is the market demand for such products as Danersk eventually moved production to large furniture factories in North Carolina. On the local level, most cities supported a custom cabinetmaker such as Nathan Margolis of Hartford. Trained in eastern Europe, Margolis quickly established a reputation for restoring period furniture as well as constructing accurate reproductions.

The 1920s market for New England–style Colonial Revival furniture served to establish a common language and set of assumptions about the past in the same way that modern furniture would hold out the promise of a future after World War II. Periodicals such as the magazine *Antiques*, founded in 1922, offered in-depth scholarly articles by such authorities as Nutting as well as myriad advertisements for both reproduction and original furniture. This convergence of culture and commerce led to a remarkable organization of the Americana market in the period. Certain forms and local traditions became aestheticized and prized by connoisseurs. The Hadley chest of the Connecticut River valley became the subject of numerous articles and more than one monograph. Furniture from the mid-18th-century Newport, R.I., shops of Christopher Townsend and John Goddard were regarded as first among equals. The 19th-century Salem, Mass., carver Samuel McIntire became a modest household name again in the 20th century.

Little progress can be traced in furniture scholarship from the 1920s through the 1970s. For some 50 years, a pattern emerges of refinement and microregional identification rather than any attempt at synthesis. Numerous modest studies identified individual cabinetmakers and added to the growing list of desirable names. Despite this expansion of the canon, such lines of inquiry fundamentally served the overall organization of the American market. In the 1950s the well-known Boston and New York antiques dealer Israel Sack published a best-selling volume dedicated to educating the consumer. Although Sack grouped American furniture into three categories "Good, Better, and Best," it was not until the 1970s that new perspectives on furniture history emerged.

Another strain of New England furniture developed in the postwar period, a modern take on domestic furnishings that looked to the past while remaining in the present. Following a wartime resurgence in popular faith in the therapeutic nature of craft, craft ideology and the practical goal of educating the returning servicemen led to the establishment of programs in furniture making throughout the region. This studio furniture movement is typified by the department organized at the Rhode Island School of Design and the Program in Artisanry at Boston University, as well as the show *The Maker's Hand* (2003–4) at the Museum of Fine Arts, Boston. Ironically, the resulting emphasis on handcraftsmanship owes as much to Progressive Era notions of social reform through manual labor as any historic movement in New England furniture making.

Regionalism has clearly served as a fundamental organizational principle for furniture study since the turn of the 20th century. An often-missed point, however, is the fact that the politics of region formation—the very way in which New England's history became the nation's past—have played an equal role in shaping popular understanding of American furniture. That the material remains of colonial New England domestic life have been collected, cataloged, bought, sold, and given pride of place in museums from coast to coast has far less to do with any period historical logic than with the need for an idealized "old" New England in the modern era.

Richard Bushman, *The Refinement of America: Persons, Houses, Cities* (1992); Jonathan Fairbanks, *New England Begins* (1982); Thomas Andrew Denenberg, *Wallace Nutting and the Invention of Old America* (2003); John T. Kirk, *American Furniture in the British Tradition* (1982); William H. Truettner and Roger B. Stein, eds., *Picturing Old New England: Image and Memory* (1999).

Thomas Andrew Denenberg

Gardner, Isabella Stewart (1840–1924)

Art collector and museum founder. Isabella Stewart Gardner was an art collector, connoisseur, designer, mentor, and patron to a wide circle of late-19th- and early-20th-century artists and literary figures. Founder and architect of the famous Gardner Museum in Boston, she was a pioneer in both American art collecting and the field of interior design in the early 20th century. A millionaire in her own right and married to the even wealthier John L. Gardner, a Boston banker, Gardner was a brilliant woman, often compared to the political writer and intellectual Madame de Staël and the ruler and art patron Isabelle d'Este.

Gardner suffered great personal loss in her early years, most notably the death of her only child in infancy. She struck out boldly thereafter, seeking to develop her intellectual and artistic interests in the face of Victorian Boston's still puritanical society. Because she achieved in her roles as muse, mentor, patron, and designer the success that eluded her in her roles as wife, mother, and matron, it may be argued that the former roles better suited her formidable—indeed, domineering—personality.

Her social circle included her lifelong mentors Julia Ward Howe and Charles Eliot Norton, novelist F. Marion Crawford, philosophers George Santayana and William James, composer Martin Loeffler, painters Dennis Bunker and Dodge MacKnight, interior designers Elsie de Wolfe and Henry Sleeper, Pulitzer Prize–winning biographer Maud Howe Elliot, opera star Nellie Melba, Orientalist Okakuro Kakuzo, historian Henry Adams, playwright Lady Gregory, Henry James, who immortalized Gardner in print, and John Singer Sargent, who did so on canvas.

Gardner exerted considerable influence on them all. She figured in James's *Portrait of a Lady* (1881) and *The Golden Bowl* (1904), and probably secured for Sargent what he arguably considered the great commission of his life: his Boston Public Library murals (1895–1919). She likewise facilitated the publication of Loeffler's music. Other artists and literary figures, including architects Harold Peto and Ralph Adams Cram and poet T. S. Eliot, spoke of the significance of her influence. Most notable was her patronage of the art historian Bernard Berenson; she played a key role in launching his career, which had a revolutionary effect on the study of Italian Renaissance art and on connoisseurship in general.

Sympathetic to Boston's increasing ethnic diversity in the late 19th century and to the emerging feminist, Jewish, gay, Irish Catholic, and African American populations (Berenson, for example, was Jewish, Julia Ward Howe a leading American feminist), Gardner found in those nascent communities an acceptance withheld by most of Back Bay's Brahmin society. This acceptance shaped and enabled her most characteristic achievements, including the establishment of America's first great art collection, which she began to assemble in the 1890s with Berenson's help. Gardner brought the first Raphael to America, while her Matisse was the first to enter an American museum. Also important was her design of Fenway Court—the Isabella Stewart Gardner Museum—a remarkable work intended as a protest against conventional museum design and based on the premise that "joy, not education" is a museum's chief function. Fenway Court, a 15th-century Venetian-style palazzo turned outside-in, is very much an "architec-

ture of fragments," a collage that reflects, for all its traditional elements, a modern sensibility. The design of Fenway Court centers around perhaps the first sculpture court in America (filled with abundant horticulture, another of Gardner's interests) and features a series of fascinating interiors that profoundly influenced the pioneering American interior decorators Elsie de Wolfe and Henry Sleeper.

Gardner was one of 12 honorary sponsoring vice presidents of the Armory Show of 1913, which was largely responsible for introducing modern art to Americans. A forceful cultural maverick and one of the most formidable figures of America's Gilded Age, Gardner will chiefly be remembered for her museum, the only institution in the Western world founded by, designed by, and named after a woman. Fenway Court and its historic collection, installed by Gardner, continue to play a role in the Boston art scene. In fall 2004 the Gardner Museum announced that Renzo Piano and the Renzo Piano Building Workshop would design a new building to accommodate exhibitions, public programs, and offices, thereby preserving the museum's historic structure and furthering its educational mission.

Morris Carter, *Isabella Stewart Gardner and Fenway Court* (1925); Linda J. Docherty, "Collection as Creation: Isabella Stewart Gardner's Fenway Court," in *Memory and Oblivion: Proceedings of the 29th International Congress of the History of Art* (1999); Hilliard T. Goldfarb, *The Isabella Stewart Gardner Museum: A Companion Guide and History* (1995); Rollin Van N. Hadley, ed., *The Letters of Bernard Berenson and Isabella Stewart Gardner, 1887–1924* (1987); Douglass Shand-Tucci, *The Art of Scandal: The Life and Times of Isabella Stewart Gardner* (1997).

Douglass Shand-Tucci

Genre Painting

From its earliest formulations, the painting of daily life in New England selectively portrayed the rituals and folkways of a never-changing countryside for the amusement or instruction of an overwhelmingly urban audience. Haying scenes, husking bees, maple sugaring, and berry picking were frequently on display in metropolitan galleries, with a cast of characters featuring shrewd Yankee farmers, laughable bumpkins, wholesome country girls, and frolicking children. Over the course of the 19th century, however, the rhetoric of New England genre painting shifted from its earlier moralizing and occasionally satirical tone to an increasingly sentimental, nostalgic, and escapist one that prevailed after the Civil War. Although the New England of the genre painters was largely an invention, it played a vigorous part in shaping concepts of region and even nationhood while creating an image of archaic simplicity and quaintness that continued to color 20th-century representations of life and landscape in the old Northeast.

The Long Island painter William Sidney Mount (1807–68) played the most important part in formulating the conventions that would come to be identified with the representation of daily life in New England. His images of whittling Yankee farmers, barn dances, and village life were combinations of painstaking local observation and invention. Mount drew on a range of popular types and stories already in circulation and recast them as moralizing pictorial narratives strongly indebted to 17th-century Dutch and early-19th-century British paintings of rustic life. Operating on several levels of meaning, Mount's paintings could be read in different ways. In *Dance of the Haymakers* (1845, Museums at Stony Brook, New York), for example, the open barn serves as a stage for two farmhands performing a jig to the tune of a country fiddle, while outside the door a young black boy keeps time with a pair of sticks. The painting celebrates the seasonal joys, as well as the abundance and naturalness, of country life. At the same time, it comments on young America's political and social hierarchy, dominated by white males and marginalizing both blacks and women, here relegated to the hayloft. For Mount's New York audience and patrons, the painting cast country folk in the role of entertainers whose clownish capers and carefree indolence helped affirm and bolster a sense of urban superiority at a time of active and unstable social mobility. Finally, by representing supposedly genuine rural types, *Dance of the Haymakers* and its like contributed to the construction of regional and national identity, a vital social and political enterprise in the era of Jacksonian democracy and after. Although Mount's Long Island settings and characters were not, strictly speaking, of New England, contemporaries read them as authentic images of Yankee life, and they gained a large audience by reproduction in mass-marketed gift book annuals in the 1830s and 1840s.

In the 1840s and 1850s, increasing nativism, sectional division, expansionism, and bitter political strife over the issue of slavery created a climate favorable to representations of New England country life as preeminently all-American, in reaction to competing claims of southern slave states and uncontained western territories. While the message was more often implicit than not, it is clear that the constant reiteration of wholesome, regional themes in painting, popular prints (especially those of Currier and Ives), and illustrated magazines was part of a cultural and political campaign affirming the value, authenticity, and authority of northern—and specifically New England—ideology and regional life. T. H. Matteson (1813–84) and Arthur Fitzwilliam Tait (1819–1905) both produced romantic, harmonious scenes of maple sugaring in Vermont. John Whetten Ehninger (1827–89) cre-

Eastman Johnson, Husking Bee, Island of Nantucket *(1876, Art Institute of Chicago)*

ated popular paintings and illustrations of New England harvest scenes, and Winslow Homer (1836–1910) in his early career as a graphic artist drew a series of comic scenes based on New England folklore, including husking parties and apple-peeling bees, for the magazines *Ballou's Pictorial* and *Harper's Weekly.* Jerome Thompson (1814–86), a native of Massachusetts, specialized in idyllic Maine and Vermont landscapes celebrating the charms of rural New England, where free labor gathered the fruits of land freely owned. Thompson's *Apple Gathering* (1856, Brooklyn [N.Y.] Museum of Art), for example, represents a new, snake-free American Garden of Eden. Cheerful young men and women flirt wholesomely while harvesting an abundant crop on a hill overlooking an ancestral homestead framed by rugged New England mountains.

It is significant that Thompson, Ehninger, Homer, and their peers were all based in New York. Members of the National Academy of Design, they exhibited in New York and sold much of their output to collectors there and in other eastern cities. Alluding to the idea of an America deeply rooted in the traditions and values of Puritan ancestors, paintings that mythologized New England as a wholesome Eden reminded audiences of America's godly origins and exalted the act of purchasing such paintings to the status of a patriotic gesture at a time when the future of America as a nation was in grave doubt.

Eastman Johnson (1824–1906) tapped into this market with resounding success. Born in Maine and trained in Düsseldorf, Paris, and The Hague, Johnson settled in New York in 1858. In the 1860s Johnson produced critically acclaimed scenes of slave life in the South concurrently with paintings that hymned the virtues of traditional New England customs. *Corn Husking* (1860, Everson Museum of Art,

Syracuse, N.Y.), recast Mount's *Dance of the Haymakers* as a scene of family unity and harmony in which a sturdy Yankee farmer, a courting couple, and a grandfather and granddaughter affirm the continuity of families and the value of productive, communal work on the untainted New England soil. During the Civil War, Johnson worked on a series of paintings and studies celebrating the work and play of maple sugaring in Fryeburg, Maine— an emphatically northern theme. In the late 1860s, Johnson visited Nantucket Island off Massachusetts, and for the next decade he drew much of his subject matter from island life.

As minutely descriptive as Mount's, Johnson's work was more dexterous, suave, and painterly, in the more up-to-date, European vein that appealed to the generation of businessmen and industrialists whose war profits fueled their collecting enterprise. Johnson's patrons came from a small circle of Republican businessmen, members (along with the artist himself) of the Union League and the Century Clubs in New York. During the war years, Johnson's New England idylls appealed to the enthusiasm for the Union cause, for which these patrons worked ardently. After the war, his Nantucket scenes, which portrayed a serene world untouched by progress, answered a growing demand and need for nostalgic images to function as antidote to the social and political upheavals of the Reconstruction years. Johnson's *Husking Bee, Island of Nantucket* (1876, Art Institute of Chicago) was one of his most highly acclaimed. Created the year of the American Centennial, which sparked a growing interest in early Americana, *Husking Bee* represents the Nantucket community as an extended family of hardy, rural folk, gathered in happy and festive labor. Behind their ranks, the rooflines of a barn and a quaint old homestead allude to ancestral roots

and venerable tradition. Johnson's other Nantucket scenes, which feature cranberry picking, rustic interiors, and old salts reminiscing around a Franklin stove, catered to the same appetite for picturesque, antimodern subjects that denied the reality of progress and tumultuous social fragmentation in metropolitan America.

The shift to nostalgic New England themes occurred concurrently with the development of New England tourism, which capitalized on the idea of the countryside as a therapeutic resource for the health and sanity of the modern middle and leisured classes. During the time of Johnson's tenure there, Nantucket itself, long languishing in the decay of the once-flourishing whaling industry, embarked on the development of tourism to rejuvenate the island's economy. Paradoxically, this most modern of leisure enterprises had the greatest stake in preserving quaintness and archaism to attract business. Indelibly identified with Nantucket, Johnson, too, functioned as a pictorial historic preservationist whose income depended on his ability to produce scenes of quaint and picturesque charm in which all evidence of modernization was carefully concealed. Elsewhere in New England, Winslow Homer painted the beaches and dunes of Gloucester, Mass., in much the same spirit, depicting children wading, sailing, and picking berries, while Thomas Waterman Wood (1823–1903) produced a series of works featuring ancient Yankee farmers in the rustic village of Montpelier, Vt.

The painters' New England was largely a region innocent of textile mills, cities, immigrants, economic depressions, and machines. Increasingly detached from historical circumstance and change, images of New England life constituted a museum of authentic Americanness, evoking the idea of the old home, the simple life, and a homogeneity long gone from culture and society. By the late 19th century, rustic genre painting had been displaced by more cosmopolitan, urban styles, but its conventions and formulas migrated to the pages and covers of popular magazines. They flourished anew in the art of Norman Rockwell (1894–1978), who kept the myth of the New England village alive through much of the 20th century.

Dona Brown, *Inventing New England: Regional Tourism in the 19th Century* (1995); Sarah Burns, *Pastoral Inventions: Rural Life in 19th-Century American Art and Culture* (1989); Teresa Carbone and Patricia Hills, *Eastman Johnson: Painting America* (1999); Patricia Hills, *Eastman Johnson* (1972); Hills, *The Painters' America: Rural and Urban Life, 1810–1910* (1974); Elizabeth Johns, *American Genre Painting: The Politics of Everyday Life* (1991); Marc Simpson, Sally Mills, and Patricia Hills, *Eastman Johnson: The Cran-*

berry Harvest, Island of Nantucket (1990); Roger B. Stein, "After the War: Constructing a World Past," in *Picturing Old New England: Image and Memory,* ed. William H. Truettner and Stein (1999).

Sarah Burns

Glass Glass, from the utilitarian products of short-lived 18th-century glasshouses to the highly decorative works of 19th-century manufacturers and the modern efforts of studio artists, has long been a favorite subject of students and collectors. Glassmaking, in contrast, has had a fitful history in New England. Indeed, it took almost two centuries for a glass manufacturer to achieve long-term financial viability in the region.

Although documentary evidence exists for a glasshouse in Salem, Mass., as early as the 1630s, most glass used in 17th-century New England was imported from England. These objects ranged from fine decanters, goblets, and wineglasses to utilitarian bowls, "squat" bottles of colored glass, and windowpanes. Such imported goods played an important role in the transfer of English culture to the colonies by allowing for familiar foodways and fashionable architecture in the New World. These early forms had an afterlife, too; even simple objects, such as cylinders and crown glass windowpanes, became aestheticized in the late 19th century for their "old-fashioned" character, and as "bull's-eye" lights over traditional Georgian doorways.

Modest glasshouses began to dot the New England landscape in the course of the 18th century. Works were established in communities from East Hartford, Conn., to Temple, N.H. The Germantown Glassworks of Braintree, Mass., is an example of a successful pre-Revolutionary War firm that employed skilled German artisans—a pattern of labor common in the more successful (and better-known) mid-Atlantic glasshouses of Caspar Wistar, Henry Stiegel, and John Frederick Amelung. Although most of these local manufacturers produced simple blown bottles in colored glass, distinctive forms developed in this period, including the ribbed flask or pocket bottle of the Pitkin Glassworks of East Hartford, Connecticut, the Nutmeg State, became known for flask and bottle making in the early years of the 19th century as full-size molds came into use to produce highly figured containers that often depicted famous persons such as George Washington and General Lafayette or historic events. The variety of forms produced in this period has made such flasks prized collectibles in later generations.

The New England glass industry came of age in the 19th century with the rise of large companies dedicated to the manufacture of flint glass. Flint glass used lead to produce a clear color suited to new fashions of taste. Advances in technology allowed glass to be pressed into distinctive patterns and blown into molds as well as free-blown in the time-honored practice. At the high end of the market, glass compotes, pitchers, plates, and tumblers were engraved or "cut" on a wheel to produce brilliant designs. Although much attention has been paid to the well-known New England Glass Company in East Cambridge and the Boston and Sandwich Glass Company on Cape Cod, numerous manufacturers found the economic climate of the region conducive to business, and flourished in the decades before the Civil War. The work of lesser-known shops, such as the South Boston Flint Glass Works, often remains misidentified as generic "Sandwich glass," even though they often outproduced the larger and better-known company.

Glassmaking enjoyed a renaissance after World War II as a new generation rediscovered traditional hot glassblowing and sought to raise the status of the craft to that of a fine art. A watershed moment occurred in 1967 when Dale Chihuly came to the Rhode Island School of Design (RISD), initially to earn a master's degree in fine arts, and then to establish the glass department there in 1969. Chihuly taught at RISD for 15 years, garnered numerous international awards, and influenced countless students who developed glass as a respected artistic medium.

Raymond E. Barlow and Joan E. Kaiser, *The Glass Industry in Sandwich,* 4 vols. (1993); Donald Kuspit, *Chihuly* (1998); Arlene Palmer, *Glass in Early America* (1993); Kenneth M. Wilson, *New England Glass and Glassmaking* (1972).

Thomas Andrew Denenberg

Goddards and Townsends Furniture makers. Between them, the members of the large Quaker family of the Townsends and the Goddards in Newport, R.I., made some of the finest furniture in colonial America. Most of the furniture is not signed, so it is often difficult to assign credit to the correct family member, but it is usually agreed that John Goddard was the finest craftsman among them.

The founders of the dynasty were Job Townsend (1699–1765) and his brother Christopher (1701–73). Job's sons, Job E., Jr. (1726–1818), and Edmund (1736–1811), and Christopher's sons, John (1732–1809) and Jonathan (1745–72), eclipsed their fathers. In turn, some of their sons followed in the same profession, but by then the heyday of Newport furniture making was past. John Goddard (1723–85) apprenticed to Job Townsend and married his daughter Hannah. Of their 16 children, six became cabinetmakers, but too late to be as important as their father and their uncles. Three of them were loyalists and established a partnership in Nova Scotia after the Revolutionary War.

A key moment in the careers of John Goddard and the second-generation Townsends was the arrival in Newport in the 1740s of the architect Peter Harrison (1716–75), as many of the most distinctive features of their furniture may be ascribed to his suggestions. Goddard and his colleagues worked chiefly in Santo Domingo mahogany (imported along with smuggled Haitian molasses for Newport's rum industry), but also in other woods. Thanks in part to lucrative patronage from merchants in the rum industry, they were able to perfect their characteristic block-front case pieces with stylized carved shells and molded bracket feet, and one of these, a six-shell secretary-desk, was sold at auction in 1989 for more than $12 million, a world record price. The Goddards and Townsends were usually sparing with ornament, aspiring instead to perfection in design and proportion. Their best pieces were in a simple Baroque style that would have been considered out of date in other furniture-making centers. Like the Goddards and Townsends, many of Newport's wealthy elite were Quakers who probably preferred understated elegance in their furniture as in their expensive but plain clothing, although the same furniture was made for wealthy Anglicans, Baptists, and Jews, as well as for export. John Goddard also made several unusual pieces reminiscent of the French style, and John Townsend uniquely incorporated "stop-fluting" on the legs of some of his pieces. Much of their output was exported to other American colonies and the Caribbean. Like most 18th-century furnishings, Goddard-Townsend furniture lost favor in the 19th century, but, thanks to the activities of such dealers as Wallace Nutting and Israel Sack, the Goddard style has come to be seen as the epitome of taste and value.

The Goddards and Townsends appear to have had little or no influence on furniture makers in Boston and Salem, such as Benjamin Frothingham (1734–1809), John Cogswell (1738–1819), Job Coit I and II (1692–1742 and 1717–45), Nathaniel Gould (1734–82), and John Chipman (ca. 1746–1819), but they greatly influenced Grindal Rawson of Providence (1719–1803) and a few furniture makers in eastern Connecticut, including Benjamin Burnham (1729–99) and Samuel Loomis (1748–1814).

The public can see fine examples of Goddard-Townsend furniture at the Museum of Fine Arts, Boston; the Rhode Island Historical Society and the Rhode Island School of Design Museum, Providence; the Newport

Historical Society, the Newport Restoration Foundation, and the Preservation Society of Newport County, Newport; the Garvan Collection at Yale University, New Haven, Conn.; the Metropolitan Museum of Art, New York City; the H. Francis du Pont Winterthur Museum, Del.; and the Diplomatic Reception Rooms of the United States Department of State, Washington, D.C.

Ethel Hall Bjerkoe, *The Cabinetmakers of America* (1957); Ralph E. Carpenter, Jr., *The Arts and Crafts of Newport, Rhode Island, 1640–1820* (1954); Margaretta M. Lovell, "Such Furniture as Will Be the Most Profitable: The Business of Cabinetmaking in 18th-Century Newport," *Winterthur Portfolio* 26 (Spring 1991); Michael Moses, *Master Craftsmen of Newport: The Townsends and the Goddards* (1984); Joseph K. Ott, *The John Brown House Loan Exhibition of Rhode Island Furniture* (1965).

John F. Millar

Hartley, Marsden (1877–1943)

Painter and poet. Throughout his career, Marsden Hartley created paintings and poems that contributed to such icons of New England identity as crashing wave coastal views, rural folk, the French-Canadian bather and strongman, and lobsters. In response to turn-of-the-century outmigration, his early images defined the region's northern climes as desolate and deteriorating. After the 1930s, however, his work reimagined this locale as vital, joining in the larger cultural turn toward region as the source of national identity.

Born in Lewiston, Maine, Hartley moved to Ohio to be with his family in 1893 and studied painting at the Cleveland School of Art, the Chase School, and the National Academy of Design in New York. He returned to his native state almost every summer between 1900 and 1911, painting both brilliantly colored scenes such as *Carnival of Autumn* (1908, Museum of Fine Arts, Boston) and somber-toned views of deserted farms and bare trees such as *The Dark Mountain No. 1* (1909, Metropolitan Museum of Art, New York). Influenced by Albert Pinkham Ryder's moonlit romantic scenes, the darker works convey Hartley's sorrowful memories of Maine—his mother's death and father's departure—as well as his view of a northern New England in decline.

After 1912 Hartley opted to spend more time among avant-garde art circles in New York and Europe. He still visited New England occasionally and in 1924, while living in France, painted his memories of Maine in dark *paysages* that recall his earlier works. In other New England images of the 1910s and 1920s, including his abstract Provincetown Harbor views and his Cézannesque White Mountain paintings, however, Hartley's painting became increasingly experimental and abstract as he

Marsden Hartley, Abundance *(1939–40, Currier Museum of Art, Manchester, N.H.)*

came under the influence of modernist styles like cubism and German expressionism.

In the 1930s economic problems, critical condemnation of his "foreign-inspired" art, and conflicts with his patron, the New York photographer and art dealer Alfred Stieglitz, set the stage for Hartley's nativist rebirth. Recognizing that he had to market himself as American to succeed as an artist, Hartley resettled in his native state and worked toward constructing a national identity rooted in New England. In essays such as "On the Subject of Nativeness—A Tribute to Maine" and "The Six Greatest New England Painters," both written in 1937, Hartley defined an American tradition that matched his own mystical realism with the works of such New England artists as Ryder and Winslow Homer. In his later paintings such as *Down East Young Blades* (ca. 1940, Wadsworth Atheneum, Hartford), broad-chested folk function as embodiments of a new New England, allowing Hartley an acceptable form in which to express the homoerotic. Hartley also produced visions of prosperity; in his *Abundance* (1939, Currier Museum of Art, Manchester, N.H.), logs cut from the northern woods fill the canvas. These robust images stand in sharp contrast to his earlier dark landscapes and to the spinsters and Brahmin scholars whom he identified with a feeble New England in his poems of 1923.

As a modernist, Hartley represented New England's landscape and people as primitive, choosing subjects for his paintings and writings—like the wild coast and Mount Katahdin in Maine—that satisfied his viewers' longing for a sense of place. Hartley's personal expressionist approach to regional landscape has had a lasting impact on New England art,

providing inspiration to later-20th-century artists such as Howard Rackliffe.

Donna M. Cassidy, *Marsden Hartley: Region, Race, and Nation* (2005); Elizabeth Mankin Kornhauser, ed., *Marsden Hartley* (2003); Townsend Ludington, *Marsden Hartley: The Biography of an American Artist* (1992); Gail R. Scott, ed., *The Collected Poems of Marsden Hartley, 1904–1943* (1987); Scott, *Marsden Hartley* (1988).

Donna M. Cassidy

Heade, Martin Johnson (1819–1904)

Landscape and seascape painter. Martin Johnson Heade is best known for his incandescent renderings of New England's coastal marshes and for his startlingly original views of approaching storms. He is also recognized for the paintings of lush tropical scenery and hummingbirds that he painted after three journeys to South America (1863, 1866, and 1870) as well as for his depictions of Florida's swamplands.

Born in Lumberville, Pa., Heade learned to paint from the Quaker artist and craftsman Edward Hicks (of *Peaceable Kingdom* fame). He then embarked on years of travel, first to Europe between 1837 and 1840, and then throughout New York, New Jersey, and the midwestern United States during the 1840s and early 1850s. By 1857 he had established himself as a painter of landscapes and seascapes in Rhode Island, but within two years he relocated to New York City's famous Tenth Street Studio Building, where he worked alongside many of America's most famous landscape painters. He continued to travel widely, making numerous trips to New England, before marrying in 1883 and settling permanently in Saint Augustine, Fla.

Critics in Heade's day, including the influential Henry T. Tuckerman, characterized the artist as a natural-history painter. Heade exemplified the trend in American landscape painting—beginning in the 1850s—away from the allegorizing of the Hudson River School and toward the Ruskinian ideal of "truth to nature." His marsh scenes, in particular, demonstrate an extraordinary fidelity to the subtle details of regional flora and fauna along with attentiveness to changing light and atmospheric conditions. Yet Heade's most memorable canvases, such as *Approaching Storm: Beach near Newport* (1860–63, Museum of Fine Arts, Boston), are often characterized today as "eerie" or "surreal." Here the livid light generated by storm clouds evokes a mood of foreboding, and Heade's use of strong contrasts and exquisite details creates a tension between the static and dynamic qualities of the scene.

Heade forsook the conventional categories of American landscape painting—above all, the sublime and the picturesque—and dissented from the prevailing tradition in which visual images were mediated by literary frames of reference. Unlike many painters of his day who used "New World" nature to certify America's progress toward millennial perfection, Heade's view of nature was closely observed but at times elusive, unsettling, and ominous. *The Stranded Boat* (1863, Museum of Fine Arts, Boston), for instance, may suggest the uncertain future of the American ship of state in the midst of the Civil War. Whereas the dominant Romantic iconography was both optimistic and theologically driven, Heade's images are of a natural world whose moral implications are at best ambiguous.

Heade, a self-conscious skeptic who adopted the pen name "Didymus," or Doubting Thomas, had an independence of spirit in keeping with the curiously obsessive nature of his work. An ardent sportsman who wrote numerous articles on hunting for *Forest and Stream* magazine, Heade (from a retrospective viewpoint) helped to give aesthetic shape to the new tough-minded ethic of the "strenuous life" popularized in the wake of the Civil War. Yet, at their most intense, his paintings invite speculations and interpretations that go well beyond conventional notions of realism.

Sarah Cash, *Ominous Hush: The Thunderstorm Paintings of Martin Johnson Heade* (1994); David C. Miller, "'Kindred Sprits': Martin Johnson Heade, Painter; Frederick Goddard Tuckerman, Poet; and the Identification with Desert Places," *American Quarterly* 32 (1980); Theodore E. Stebbins, Jr., *The Life and Work of Martin Johnson Heade: A Critical Analysis and Catalogue Raisonné* (2000); Stebbins, with contributions by Janet L. Comey, Karen E. Quinn, and Jim Wright, *Martin Johnson Heade* (1999).

David C. Miller

Homer, Winslow (1836–1910)

Painter, illustrator, and graphic artist. By the end of the 19th century Winslow Homer was America's most famous native-born painter. He initially made his reputation depicting Civil War events for popular publications, but his lasting fame has been built largely on his depictions of coastal Maine as a virile landscape still true to the founding vision of the nation.

Born in Boston, Homer grew up in Cambridge and was apprenticed to the Boston lithographer J. H. Bufford at 19. Determined to be independent, Homer left lithography (and Boston) in 1859 for New York, where he spent the next 20 years working as an illustrator and painter. Aside from a brief period at the National Academy of Design, where he learned to use oil paint, Homer was self-trained. Until the 1890s he was generally thought of as a painter of the Civil War and its aftermath; his illustrations of wartime and paintings of black life in the

South made a great impression on the public. After the war, however, he painted subjects of middle-class leisure found at resorts from the shores of New Jersey to the White Mountains of New Hampshire, such as *Mount Washington* (1869, Art Institute of Chicago), as well as rustic scenes of both farms and seaports. His many rural Yankee views of the 1870s, including *Crossing the Pasture* (1872, Amon Carter Museum, Forth Worth, Tex.), were seldom set in New England but nonetheless offered a generalized northeastern image of innocence and simplicity. Homer did not create a distinctive vision of New England until he moved from New York City to Prout's Neck, Maine, a few miles south of Portland, in 1883.

Maine was becoming a favorite tourist destination at this time, and Homer and his brothers actually bought up most of Prout's Neck with the intention of developing it as an exclusive summer resort where their parents could retire. Even though Homer derived a large portion of his income from this resort (which still exists today), he barricaded his studio against summer visitors. Homer's image of Maine must be understood in this context: as completing the work of predecessors such as Frederic Edwin Church, and as rebuking the work of contemporaries such as Childe Hassam who catered to tourists and their desire for genteel views of warm, beautiful scenery.

In contrast, Homer's Maine paintings are year-round landscapes. His first works after moving to Maine reflected the lifesaving techniques he had studied in New Jersey and the fishermen he observed on a trip to the North Banks off the coast of Nova Scotia. Beginning in 1890 he transferred these "northern" characteristics specifically to the Maine landscape, painting views that focused on men of the sea and projected a distinctive image of northern hardiness and vigor. Whereas earlier paintings of the shores of Maine were topographically (and touristically) descriptive, Homer reduced his view to a rocky shoreline with a few lonely figures (or none at all) threatened by an overwhelming sea. When not hostile to civilization, Homer's paintings are indifferent to it. *Northeaster* (1895, Metropolitan Museum of Art, New York), lacking any trace of human figures, is the quintessential version, balancing provocatively on the edge of abstraction.

During the harshest winter months Homer traveled south, either to Florida for fly-fishing or to Bermuda or the Bahamas as a tourist. On these visits he produced colorful watercolors, including one of his most powerful studies of the violence of nature against humankind, *The Gulf Stream* (1899, Metropolitan Museum of Art). He also painted many hunting subjects, most of which were based on his trips to hunt-

ing camps in the Adirondacks and to Quebec. The most famous of these, however, was actually done on Prout's Neck. *Fox Hunt* (1893, Pennsylvania Academy of the Fine Arts, Philadelphia) inverts the usual order of hunter and hunted as a fox, slowed by deep snow, is attacked by a flock of crows.

At the time of his death at Prout's Neck in 1910, Homer was best known for his views of coastal Maine. In their simplicity, his Maine paintings became a tabula rasa onto which painters of the next generation, whatever their aesthetic allegiance, projected their needs for an authentic, forceful American art. After his death, even postcards began to reflect Winslow Homer's perspective of the region, one that still lingers in the popular imagination.

Nicolai Cikovsky, Jr., and Franklin Kelly, *Winslow Homer* (1995); Helen A. Cooper, *Winslow Homer Watercolors* (1986); Elizabeth Johns, *Winslow Homer: The Nature of Observation* (2002); Bruce Robertson, *Reckoning with Winslow Homer: His Late Paintings and Their Influence* (1990); William H. Truettner and Roger B. Stein, eds., *Picturing Old New England: Image and Memory* (1999).

E. Bruce Robertson

Itinerant Artists

The first decades of the 19th century found a steadily growing number of itinerant artists traveling through New England's countryside. These artists both stimulated and satisfied a demand for painted portraits, offering inexpensive works done in the sitter's home or in temporary studios set up in village taverns. The rise of itinerant artists was related to the transformation of New England's economy by increases in agricultural productivity, improvements in transportation and communications, the emergence of rural industrialization, and the commercialization of farming and artisanal enterprise. With these changes came a new landscape of commercial and manufacturing villages and a population of professionals, merchants, manufacturers, and artisans with disposable income and an interest in emulating the ways of the elite. This emerging middle class took up the commissioning and ownership of portraits, a traditional expression of status, democratizing the genre in the process.

A few itinerant artists received formal academic training in Europe. One such was Ralph Earl (1751–1801), who spent the years after the Revolution working as a traveling portraitist. Others with academic training, such as Charles Bird King (1785–1862), went on the road early in their careers to establish reputations that enabled them to set up permanent studios in urban centers. The majority of New England's itinerant artists either were self-taught or had served apprenticeships with commercial painters. The latter group's training was in the art of decorative painting, which could range from lettering signs and banners to embellishing tin tea trays. Thus the portraits by itinerant artists often reflect their training as ornamental painters, with an emphasis on line, decorative patterning, the use of a relatively unmixed palette, and an arbitrary sense of perspective.

The commercial background of many itinerant artists also influenced their business practice. Most offered a range of services with portrait painting at one end of the spectrum and house and sign painting at the other. Some adjusted the style of their portraits to suit the means of their clientele. William Matthew Prior (1806–73), for example, offered "cheap and flat" likenesses executed in quick-drying tempera paint on inexpensive cardboard to his less wealthy patrons and portraits "with shade and shadow," painted during several sittings, to those of greater means. Similarly, Rufus Porter (1792–1884) courted a wide clientele by offering four styles of portraits, ranging from paper silhouettes cut in pairs for 20 cents to miniature portraits painted on ivory for eight dollars. Strategies like these expanded the market for portraits.

In early-19th-century New England a career as an itinerant artist offered occupational and social mobility, primarily to socially ambitious, entrepreneurial young men. For most, itinerancy was the prelude to a more settled professional existence; many became urban-based artists, while others left behind their artistic ambitions to become merchants, lawyers, and so on. These were opportunities enjoyed by only a few generations of New Englanders. The rise of itinerant artists began with the social upheaval that followed the Revolution and continued until the commercial introduction of photography in 1839 gradually began to erode their market. Many of New England's itinerant painters continued to find patronage into the mid-19th century, but by the start of the Civil War, the tradition of itinerant portraiture was redefined by the daguerreian artist.

Peter Benes and Jane Montague Benes, eds., *Itinerancy in New England and New York* (1986); David Jaffee, "One of the Primitive Sort: Portrait Makers of the Rural North, 1760–1860," in *The Countryside in the Age of Capitalist Transformation: Essays in the Social History of Rural America*, ed. Steven Hahn and Jonathan Prude (1985); Caroline F. Sloat, ed., *Meet Your Neighbors: New England Portraits, Painters, and Society, 1790–1850* (1992); John Michael Vlach and Simon J. Bronner, eds., *Folk Art and Art Worlds: Essays Drawn from the Washington Meeting on Folk Art* (1986).

Jessica F. Nicoll

Landscape Painting According to traditional accounts, the birthplace of American landscape painting was the Hudson River valley and adjacent Catskill wilderness. Once the urban taste for American scenery had taken root beginning in the 1820s, however, New England's river valleys, mountain ranges, and rocky coastline offered rival attractions. While its proximity to New York City, which after the 1820s dominated both publishing and art training nationally, influenced the Hudson River valley's status as representative national landscape, metropolitan institutions such as the National Academy of Design and the American Art-Union contributed to the commodification of American scenery through exhibition and print distribution, and scenic subject matter expanded to include the less settled reaches of New England.

In the early 19th century the White Mountains hosted increasing numbers of tourists in search of the picturesque. Tourism and the taste for landscape—wilderness and pastoral, painted and real—flourished side by side; each encouraged the other. Daniel Wadsworth, one of Thomas Cole's earliest patrons, cultivated a taste for New England scenery at Monte Video, his estate above the Farmington River valley near Hartford. In 1826 Wadsworth was among the first wave of tourists seeking the picturesque in the White Mountains; at his prompting, Cole traveled there in 1827 and 1828 and produced some of the earliest landscape portraits of New England's partially settled hinterlands. For Wadsworth, Cole painted the *View in the White Mountains* (1827, Fine Arts Museums of San Francisco) and the *View on Lake Winnipiseogee* (1828, Wadsworth Atheneum, Hartford); for James Hillhouse of New Haven, Conn., he painted *Corroway [Chocorua] Peak, N.H.—After Sunset* (1827–28, present location unknown). White Mountain–inspired works commissioned by Robert Gilmor of Baltimore and Stephen Van Rensselaer of New York indicate a wider patronage for New England scenes.

In addition to the spread of tourism, a number of factors contributed to the growing popularity of New Hampshire's White Mountain region. The 1826 "Willey tragedy," a rockslide in Crawford Notch that killed a family of early settlers, became the stuff of legend, both verbal and visual. Cole memorialized the event years later in his painting *Notch of the White Mountains* (1839, National Gallery of Art, Washington, D.C.), as did William Bartlett and Nathaniel Parker Willis in "The Willey House," in *American Scenery; or, Land, Lake, and River: Illustrations of Transatlantic Nature* (2 vols., 1838–39). In an era dominated by the aesthetics of association, such dramatic events helped travelers form meaningful ties to the region. In addition, the naming of mountain ranges such as the Presidential in New Hampshire, and of geologic formations such as Pulpit Rock in Crawford Notch and the Old Man of the Mountain in Franconia Notch inscribed natural features with sensationalistic, patriotic, or religious import.

The urban attraction to wilderness eventually gave way to a preference for more domesticated or pastoralized scenery in which mountain forms were seen across vales and atmospheric distances. Such qualities won the White Mountain region its sobriquet "the Switzerland of America" and were later conventionalized by artists of the so-called White Mountain School, centered in and around North Conway, N.H.

The popularity of New England scenery prepared the way for—and followed—the pattern of travel and the infrastructure of tourism. Travel commentaries such as Theodore Dwight's *Northern Traveller* (1825) and his *Sketches of Scenery and Manners in the United States* (1829), guidebooks such as Thomas Starr King's popular *The White Hills: Their Legends, Landscape, and Poetry* (1860), widely circulated albums of prints with accompanying text such as Bartlett's and Willis's *American Scenery* (1840), and the jointly written *Home Book of the Picturesque; or, American Scenery, Art, and Literature* (1852) encouraged the economic, social, and artistic exploitation of New England for its historic interest, as well as its value as therapeutic retreat and as nationalist landscape. By 1851 the American Art-Union chose New York artist John Frederick Kensett's *The White Mountains: Mount Washington* (1851, Wellesley College Museum, Mass.) as one of five paintings to be engraved for national distribution to its members. This painting recalled the country's patriarch and linked the political and social heritage of the nation to the geography of New England. Numerous other New York painters, including Albert Bierstadt, Asher B. Durand, and Jasper Cropsey, made the summer journey to New England in search of scenic fare during the 1850s and 1860s. The Green Mountains in Vermont, particularly Mount Mansfield, offered a second destination for tourists in the later 19th century. Photography also played an important role in popularizing such tourist havens in northern New England; indeed, among the earliest landscape daguerreotypes made in America were pictures of Crawford Notch (1840).

Travel literature, with its conventionalized categories of picturesque, beautiful, and sublime, contributed vitally to the touristic packaging of New England scenery. Visitors found aesthetic qualities in the isolated hamlets of agrarian New England, where rural poverty was presented as picturesque reverie. For those in search of the "middle landscape" that balanced American commercial and industrial development with the desire for continuity between past and present, the "arcadian vales" of the lower Connecticut River valley offered evidence of economic growth, powerful links to history, and an aesthetically and socially settled landscape. In 1836, when Cole painted his famous *View from Mount Holyoke, Northampton, Massachusetts, after a Thunderstorm (The Oxbow)* (Metropolitan Museum of Art, New York), the singular feature of a river doubled back on itself had become a tourist mecca. Cole, however, took pains to eliminate all signs of tourism, using the subject to explore the transition from the wild mountaintop to the settled agrarian landscape of the valley. Popularized in prints such as William Bartlett's *View from Mount Holyoke* in *American Scenery*, the oxbow river took its place within the emergent landscape of picturesque travel and tourism.

While urban tourists and artists sought out an aesthetically domesticated nature, others turned to a revived interest in sublime wilderness, in tandem with a therapeutic quest for new experiences. Those in search of unsettled nature—including the painter Frederic Edwin Church and his companion Theodore Winthrop (*Life in the Open Air*, 1871)—were drawn to the interior of Maine. Yet by the 1830s lumbering had become a leading source of wealth for Maine. The cultivated illusion of a wilderness experience, brought to life in Church's Maine landscapes such as *Mount Ktaadn* (1853, Yale University Art Gallery, New Haven) and his epic *Twilight in the Wilderness* (1860, Cleveland Museum of Art), coexisted with this extractive industry.

With growing sectional tensions between the North and the South in the 1850s, writers and artists came to associate the rugged qualities of New England scenery and its pronounced seasonal cycles with moral rectitude, thrift, industry, and other Yankee virtues rhetorically denied southerners. Currier and Ives, a New York City–based firm, marketed prints by George Henry Durrie, the antebellum artist of seasonal rural life in New England. Some artwork reflected belief in the connection between the physical landscape of New England and its moral character, as in Church's *New England Scenery* (1851, George Walter Vincent Smith Museum, Springfield, Mass.), a composite of the region's scenic variety that combined specific regional qualities with a symbolic narrative of New England's central importance to the formation and dissemination of national values.

Throughout much of the 19th century New England experienced an agrarian decline as well as the migration of many of its leading artists and writers to New York City. As key features of its historical and regional identity

eroded, the region acquired a second, mythic life in visual and verbal images. The 17th-century history of Edward Whalley and William Goffe, the two English regicides who sought protection from the Crown in the wilderness above New Haven, acquired symbolic resonance in the ongoing creation of New World liberty (see Church's *West Rock, New Haven*, 1849, New Britain [Conn.] Museum of Art). By the time of the lavish two-volume *Picturesque America* (1874), chapters on New England downplayed industry while canonizing the historic landscape of the region and its ties to national origins in such episodes as the migration of the Hooker party to Connecticut, the "Charter Oak" of Hartford, and the Whalley and Goffe episode.

New England's mythic existence has been remarkably long-lived, persisting in 20th- and 21st-century calendar images of the region. Ironically, this image has been largely the creation of exiled New Englanders and outsiders. Those who never left, like the artist Fitz Hugh Lane, preferred a more intimate exploration of place resistant to nationalist rhetoric or regional self-promotion. By contrast, popular lithographs, illustrations, and urban views emphasized the development and industry excised by most painted images.

Dona Brown, *Inventing New England: Regional Tourism in the 19th Century* (1995); Thomas Cole, "Sketch of My Tour to the White Mountains with Mr. Pratt," *Bulletin of the Detroit Institute of Arts* 66 (1990); Martha J. Hoppin, ed., *Arcadian Vales: Views of the Connecticut River Valley* (1981); Donald Keyes, Catherine Campbell, Robert McGrath, and R. Stuart Wallace, *The White Mountains: Place and Perceptions* (1980); Angela Miller, *The Empire of the Eye: Landscape Representation and American Cultural Politics, 1825–1875* (1993); J. Bard McNulty, ed., *The Correspondence of Thomas Cole and Daniel Wadsworth* (1983); John Wilmerding, *Paintings by Fitz Hugh Lane* (1988); John Sears, *Sacred Places: American Tourist Attractions in the 19th Century* (1989).

Angela Miller

Lane, Fitz Hugh (1804–65) Marine

painter. Fitz Hugh Lane was born and died in Gloucester, Mass., where he spent most of his life. Trained as a lithographer with the William S. Pendleton firm from 1832 to 1837, he worked with several other Boston lithographers before 1847. Under the influence of the British-trained marine painter Robert Salmon, Lane established himself as a painter of marine subjects. During the mid-1840s he published a three-lithograph series of descriptive views of Gloucester, New Bedford, and Newburyport, Mass. In 1848 he took up permanent residence in Gloucester, cultivating, from then on, a largely local clientele. Lane was active in town affairs, and frequently helped organize Fourth of July celebrations

for which he painted banners and signs. Although Lane's legs were partially paralyzed from infantile polio, he made numerous sailing and sketching trips between 1848 and 1863. In addition to his images of Boston and Gloucester harbors completed during the mid-1850s, his signature work includes views of the Owl's Head, Camden Hills, Blue Hill, and Mount Desert areas of Maine.

Lane's art gradually transcended the literal and somewhat awkward renditions of New England locales that catered to popular taste in the 1840s. His highly geometric and light-suffused visions of marine, harbor, and shoreline prospects began to take on a new tonality in the late 1840s, developing beyond the essentially topographic renderings of commercial life that characterized his earlier work. While art historians associate Lane's art with an Emersonian fusion of God and nature, this view should be balanced by an account of the artist's career from the standpoint of the social and cultural history of New England. During the 1850s Gloucester's fishing industry was transformed by the advent of the railroad, making it possible to ship fish to distant markets; the concurrent growth of tourism in the region brought considerable change as well. The subtle poetry of Lane's pictorial images in these years reflects—and quite possibly helped to shape—the concerns and desires of his patrons during this transformation of the city's social and economic life; his work also reflects a nostalgia for the passing of an earlier way of life.

Lane's paintings at the height of his career, such as *Boston Harbor at Sunset* (1850–55, Museum of Fine Arts, Boston), are characterized by a mathematical precision, quiescent mood, crystalline light reflecting off polished surfaces, and close attention to varied atmospheric effects. In contrast to his works of the 1840s in which busy productive labor is the norm, little happens in these works. Instead, the artist stresses the interplay of color and light and the meticulous patterning of forms, whether human-made or natural. These hallmarks of what historians of American art have called luminism may or may not attest to Lane's putative Transcendental faith, but the artist's numerous images of stranded and decaying boats, especially his *Dream Painting* (1862, private collection) are more than meditations on mortality. These paintings—in which the boat represents America—suggest that Lane, whose primary loyalties were to his region, resisted the nationalistic rhetoric of the day and had profound apprehensions about the outcome of the Civil War.

Barbara Novak, *American Painting of the 19th Century: Realism, Idealism, and the American Experience* (1979); Roger B. Stein, *Seascape and the American*

Imagination (1975); John Wilmerding, *Fitz Hugh Lane, 1804–1865, American Marine Painter* (1964); Wilmerding, *Paintings by Fitz Hugh Lane* (1988).

David C. Miller

Levine, Jack (1915–) Artist.

Born in Boston's crowded South End, one of eight children of an immigrant shoemaker, the artist Jack Levine remained attached to the urban world of pushcarts, street people, and horse-drawn wagons. The painting *Homage to Boston* (1949, Hirshhorn Museum and Sculpture Garden, Washington, D.C.) suggests Levine's complex appreciation of the city where he grew up, a city whose slums and poor residents often served as the subjects of his work. He boasted that he was the last surviving social realist painter, claiming as well to be the first American-born artist to paint Judaic themes. Although he often insisted that he was not religious, Levine managed to define a strong Jewish identity in a dazzling archive of small paintings of Bible stories: Adam and Eve, Cain and Abel, and Saul and David, among others. And he painted a number of Hebrew teachers and kings, such as Maimonides, Hillel, Nehemiah, and Asa.

An artistic prodigy, Levine crayoned sketches of the Boston police strike at the age of four. Harold Zimmerman nurtured Levine's obvious teenage talent in classes at the Roxbury Settlement House. Along with Hyman Bloom, another of Zimmerman's promising pupils, the young artist studied Renaissance and Baroque art at the Museum of Fine Arts and went on to learn classical techniques with Denman Ross at Harvard University. Ross extended Levine's appreciation of color and craft. He also gave both Levine and Bloom twelve dollars a week to paint whatever they wanted. Later, Ross bought a number of Levine's works from this period; they are now in the collection of the Fogg Art Museum at Harvard.

During the Depression Jack Levine was one of more than 3,600 artists subsidized by the Federal Arts Project. Grateful for that brief period when artists could be assured of materials, a place to work, and $23 a week, he produced two paintings by age 22 that were distinguished enough to be put on permanent loan at the Museum of Modern Art in New York City. *The Feast of Pure Reason* (1937, Museum of Modern Art, New York), a dark political satire, would remain one of his most famous works. More affirmative was *String Quartet* (1934–37), a creation suggestive of how human beings could together produce beauty. The Metropolitan Museum of Art bought this painting in 1942 and reproduced it for public appreciation in New York subway cars.

After his tour in the army, Levine married the artist Ruth Gikow and moved to New York City, where the couple had a daughter in 1949. Subsequent years brought many honors. In Boston the Institute of Contemporary Art organized his first retrospective show, which traveled to five other cities from 1952 to 1955. In 1957 Colby College in Waterville, Maine, awarded him an honorary doctor of fine arts degree.

Always an individualist, Levine never spoke of himself as a member of any school. Yet in the 1950s he joined with such realist painters as Edward Hopper to protest the art world's total absorption in abstract expressionism. Levine's social realist paintings—such as *Witches Sabbath* (1963, Benton Foundation, Chicago), about the McCarthy hearings—leave viewers as stunned by the power of his designs, images, colors, and glazes as they are by his ideas. The lasting solidity of his work reflects the quality of the artists from the past Levine studied so rigorously.

Stephen Robert Frankel, comp. and ed., *Jack Levine* (1989); Frank Getlein, text of *Jack Levine*, by Jack Levine (1966); Selden Rodman, *Conversations with Artists* (1961); Barbara Rose, *American Art since 1900: A Critical History* (1967).

Eugenia Kaledin

Lewis, (Mary) Edmonia (ca. 1844–after 1909) Sculptor.

Edmonia Lewis was born near Albany, N.Y., between 1843 and 1845, to an African American father and a mother of African and Ojibwa descent. After her parents' early death, her mother's Native American family raised her. Called Wildfire in her youth, she took the name Mary Edmonia Lewis on her admission to Oberlin College in 1856. Lewis was one of about 10 American women sculptors, described by Henry James somewhat condescendingly as "the White Marmorean Flock," who spent significant portions of their careers in Italy. Like these other women (including Harriet Hosmer and Anne Whitney), Lewis worked in a style that can best be described as neoclassicism, though she expanded on the style's traditional themes.

Lewis's education at Oberlin, where she first studied art as part of a college preparatory course, was financed by her brother Sunrise, a California gold miner. The school was a logical choice, because it had recently enacted an enrollment policy encouraging women and "minorities" to apply. Nonetheless, Lewis's stay at Oberlin was not unmarred by bigotry and intolerance; she was accused and then acquitted of poisoning her roommates—both of whom survived—and was physically assaulted by a mob.

After graduation Lewis moved to Boston to study sculpture. Attracted to the city because it was a center of abolitionist activity—she had obtained a letter of introduction to William Lloyd Garrison—Lewis stayed in Boston from 1863 until 1865. Through Garrison she was introduced to the neoclassical sculptor Edward Brackett, with whom she studied informally. Anne Whitney had a studio in the same building as Lewis and offered her some critiques. The Boston-area writer and abolitionist Lydia Marie Child was also supportive of Lewis's career. An important Boston patron was Anna Quincy Waterston, of whom Lewis made a small portrait bust. The most important work of this period, and perhaps Lewis's most significant early piece, was her portrait bust of Colonel Robert Gould Shaw. Lewis made close to a hundred plaster copies of this sculpture, which helped finance her trip to Rome; the marble version was created in 1867. The Shaw bust had particular significance to Lewis, because Shaw had been the leader of the first all-black regiment to fight in the Civil War.

In 1865 Lewis left for Italy, the center of neoclassical sculpture. She set up a studio in Rome and frequented members of the expatriate community there, including Charlotte Cushman, Robert and Elizabeth Barrett Browning, and Harriet Hosmer, who arranged for Lewis to study with her own former teacher, John Gibson. For the first decade of Lewis's stay in Rome, the young sculptor executed her works in marble personally, without the aid of Roman workers.

Like many of her peers, Lewis produced "fancy pieces"—that is, decorative works to adorn the gardens of the wealthy, such as the putti *Awake* (1871) and *Asleep* (1872), now in the San Jose (Calif.) Public Library; but she excelled in her use of neoclassical form as a vehicle for expressing her ethnic experiences. *Forever Free* (1867, Howard University Gallery of Art, Washington, D.C.) shows a man and woman of African descent, the man raising his arm to display his broken manacles in a direct reference to the recent abolition of slavery. *The Old Arrow Maker and His Daughter* (1872, Smithsonian American Art Museum, Washington, D.C.) is based on Henry Wadsworth Longfellow's poem *The Song of Hiawatha* (like Lewis's mother, Hiawatha was an Ojibwa). The piece depicts Minnehaha plaiting rushes before her wedding, an event linked by Longfellow's poem to tribal reconciliation. Lewis dedicated *Hagar* (1875, Smithsonian American Art Museum) "to all women who have suffered." Based on the Old Testament story of Abraham fathering a child with the servant of his wife, Sarah, the work relates directly to the experiences of many slave women taken as concubines by their masters.

The Death of Cleopatra, Lewis's last surviving major work, was created for the Philadelphia Centennial Exposition (1876, Smithsonian American Art Museum). The sculpture shows Cleopatra, a traditional symbol of Africa, in the throes of death in what may be a reference to the disappointments of the Reconstruction era. Although widely viewed as an important work at the time of its creation, the sculpture disappeared after the centennial exhibition only to surface again, severely damaged and initially unrecognized, in 1987 a storage warehouse in Forest Park, Ill. The location of several other works, like the exact date of Lewis's death, remains unknown.

Melissa Dabakis, "'Ain't I a Woman?': Anne Whitney, Edmonia Lewis, and the Iconography of Emancipation," in *Seeing High and Low: Representing Social Conflict in American Visual Culture*, ed. Patricia Johnston (2005); Elsa Honig Fine, *Women and Art* (1978); William Gerdts, intro. to Nicolai Cikovsky, Jr., Marie H. Morrison, and Carol Ockman, *The White Marmorean Flock: 19th-Century American Women Neoclassical Sculptors* (1972); Samella Lewis, *African American Art and Artists* (2003); Charlotte Streifer Rubinstein, *American Women Sculptors: A History of Women Working in Three Dimensions* (1990); Rinna Wolfe, *Edmonia Lewis: Wildfire in Marble* (1998).

Mara R. Witzling

Luce, Molly (1896–1986)

Painter. Molly Luce was born Marian C. Luce on December 18, 1896, in Pittsburgh, Pa., the daughter of Artemas Barrett Luce and Celia (Clark) Luce. She became one of the most significant painters of the American Scene—a group of artists who sought to create a distinctly American style by depicting quintessential American subjects engaged in everyday life—and was arguably the most important New England regionalist painter. She died in Little Compton, R.I., on April 16, 1986.

Although Luce was born in Pittsburgh, her grandparents lived in the farmlands of the Western Reserve, that region of Ohio originally reserved as a western territory of colonial Connecticut and settled by many Connecticut residents in the 19th century. Here Luce observed a landscape that bore some resemblance to what she would later paint in New England. Luce graduated from Wheaton College in Norton, Mass., in 1916, and then attended the Art Students' League in New York, where she met fellow artists Peggy Bacon, Alexander Brook, Yasuo Kuniyoshi, Reginald Marsh, Lloyd Goodrich, Betty Burroughs, and Alan Burroughs. The group often visited the Goodrich family summerhouse in Little Compton, where they were exposed to small-town New England. Ultimately, many of the group summered or purchased year-round homes in Little Compton.

In 1922 Luce made her first trip to Europe, where she studied the paintings, architecture,

Molly Luce, Reading from Robert Frost *(1932, Childs Gallery, Boston)*

and people of Italy, France, and England. On her return in 1923, she joined the Whitney Studio Club (the predecessor of the Whitney Museum of American Art) in New York, where Alexander Brook—by then assistant director of the Whitney—nominated her for a one-woman exhibition in 1924. Luce's canvases were of American church suppers, factories, village streets and libraries, country kitchens, and roadside stands. The show was a great success and led to Luce's being represented by several of New York's best galleries showing young "modern" artists, including the Artists' Gallery, Montross, Walker, and Macbeth.

In 1926 Luce married Alan Burroughs, who, though trained as a painter, had chosen to follow in the footsteps of his father, Bryson Burroughs, curator of painting at the Metropolitan Museum of New York from 1909 to 1934. The couple first lived in Minneapolis, where Burroughs had been appointed curator of painting at the Minneapolis Institute of Art, then moved back to New England when Burroughs began work at the Fogg Art Museum at Harvard University. From Boston, Luce began to exhibit widely in juried and invitational museum exhibitions across the country. Her subjects were increasingly of small-town New England, although she would return to northeast Ohio for summers and create what she had termed "the obligatory Kingsville painting." In 1929 they moved to Belmont, Mass., and two years later purchased "Threeways," a summerhouse in Little Compton, where the couple moved permanently in 1942, on Alan's retirement from Harvard. Burroughs died in 1965.

Although Molly Luce may have been the most active female regionalist painter, the most committed painter of the American Scene in New England, and the originator of

"American Brueghelism," she, like most of her contemporaries, went into a critical eclipse in the early 1950s. The regionalists, American Scene, and social realist painters all experienced the same withdrawal of critical acclaim when abstract expressionism and other, newer forms of modernism pushed them aside. Luce's paintings had joined the permanent collections of the Whitney Museum in the 1920s and the Metropolitan Museum in the 1930s and 1940s, but by the late 1950s she had been nearly forgotten in the inner circles of the New York art world. Nevertheless, she continued to paint with authority and vigor, never losing her own belief in the value of her work. Her later paintings depicted the seasons and moods of the natural world in New England, replacing the people and human activities of her earlier work.

As the revival scholarship and collecting of regionalist, social realist, and American Scene painting began in the 1970s and 1980s, Luce's reputation returned along with others of her era. Moreover, as criticism and collecting have changed, art by women has become one of the most vigorous new areas of scholarship and collecting. Luce lived to see a revival of interest in her work and the beginnings of interest in woman artists as an area for study and acquisition.

D. Roger Howlett, *Molly Luce: Eight Decades of the American Scene* (1980); Robert L. McGrath, *Paul Sample: Painter of the American Scene* (1988); Eleanor Tufts, *American Women Artists, 1830–1930* (1987).

D. Roger Howlett

Modernism

New England has been dissociated from modernism and modern art because of the way the region and New York were viewed by both early-20th-century and subsequent commentators. Historical narratives of American modernism locate this art in New York in the first decades of the 20th century among avant-garde artists and patrons like Robert Henri and Alfred Stieglitz, while scholars analyzing modernist subject matter have focused on urban themes like John Marin's New York watercolors of 1911–12. New York was pictured as a modern city, and its art was equally new. Boston, as New England's art capital, had a different reputation. Entrenched in the Colonial Revival, the city and its art were linked with the past. The hostility of Boston audiences to modern art apparent during the Armory Show's run from April 28 to May 19, 1913, reaffirmed this identity: only five works were sold (compared to 115 in New York), and no art critic defended this exhibition. Bostonians like Desmond Fitzgerald and Denman Waldo Ross were interested in the new experimental art, and some critics hailed the postimpressionist manner of Boston painters Charles Hopkinson and Dodge MacKnight as modern. These artists, however, had little or no national prominence. Boston School paintings like Edmund Tarbell's *New England Interior* (1906, Museum of Fine Arts, Boston) represented the aesthetic conservatism of Boston and the region by association. Despite this image, modernism would find its place in the history of New England art.

As an art movement, modernism rebelled against academic art like that of the Boston School. Wanting to bring authentic emotion and a sense of "real" life to their work, modernists rejected standardized academic art—both the classicism typified by Abbott Thayer's mural at Bowdoin College Museum of Art, Brunswick, Maine (1894), and the descriptive realism exemplified by William Paxton's *Tea Leaves* (1909, Metropolitan Museum of Art, New York). The New York realists, or the Ash Can School, staged the first revolt against this art. Henri, John Sloan, George Bellows, and others were interested in gritty subjects painted with slapdash brushwork, and turned to cataloging working-class life in New York, its emotional, physical, and sexual freedom, and its rugged masculinity. Modernists in the Stieglitz circle like Marin and Marsden Hartley found escape from what they perceived to be a repressive, materialist culture in expressive, nonrepresentational styles like fauvism, expressionism, and cubism, and in so-called primitive art and societies.

In search of these values, modernists of various persuasions colonized New England—the suburban outposts of New York like Westport, Conn., distant sites like Ogunquit and Monhegan, Maine, and Provincetown and Gloucester, Mass., and long-established haunts like the White Mountains of New Hampshire. They were attracted to, and established, art colonies in the region because of their European experiences. Hamilton Easter Field drew from his knowledge of the Breton art colony in setting up his Ogunquit art school, while Provincetown became a magnet for the avant-garde because it possessed a bohemian milieu with which many artists had become familiar in Paris.

These American painters, many fresh from Europe, applied lessons learned there to their painting of New England. Both Hartley and Stuart Davis reworked synthetic cubism: Hartley interpreted Provincetown harbor as a series of flat geometric shapes in *Provincetown Abstraction* (1916, Amon Carter Museum, Fort Worth, Tex.), and Davis transformed the busy Gloucester waterfront into a panorama of abstract patterns and vibrant colors in *Swing Landscape* (1938, Indiana Museum of Art, Bloomington). Charles Demuth used cubist fragmentation and futurist force lines in painting the classical proportions and tower of the Provincetown Methodist church in *After Sir Christopher Wren* (1920, Metropolitan Museum of Art). The geometric structure and purist forms favored by these cubist-inspired modernists found an ideal theme in New England architecture, and works like Demuth's *Early Houses, Provincetown* (1918, Museum of Modern Art, New York), Niles Spencer's *New England Landscape* (1924, Albright-Knox Gallery, Buffalo, N.Y.), and George Ault's *The Green Fish House* (1921, Coe Kerr Gallery, New York) identified the rural and colonial, and simple forms and values, with the region—albeit in a modern style. This turn to the past and tradition shaped other representations of New England. While some artists focused on modern scenes, as in Marguerite Zorach's *Brunswick Mills* (1930, private collection) and Charles Sheeler's *Amoskeag Canal* (1948, Currier Museum of Art, Manchester, N.H.), most modernists pictured New England, especially Maine, as a primitive place where escape from the city and modern culture was possible.

The New York realists and avant-garde envisioned the New England landscape as an ideal antimodern locale. In the 1910s, artists associated with Robert Henri spent time in Monhegan, a remote, sparsely populated island with a small fishing village. Looking to Winslow Homer's late paintings at Prout's Neck, Maine, they painted elemental nature with all its force and power as in the crashing waves and pounding surf in George Bellows's *From Rock Top, Monhegan* (1913, private collection) and George Luks's *Great Waves (Coast of Maine)* (1922, Hirshhorn Museum and Sculpture Garden, Washington, D.C.). Hartley depicted other primitive terrains—the boulder-strewn glacial moraine of Dogtown Common in Gloucester (early 1930s) and the rocky profile of Mount Katahdin (1939–42). He compared Dogtown Common to Stonehenge and Easter Island, thereby connecting this place to non-Western religious monuments. By painting Katahdin, a sacred Native American site, he turned to a premodern culture—one imagined as natural, primitive, and religious.

New England offered other types of escape from modern culture. For many modernists, the region's landscape promised contact with the spiritual. In *Maine Landscape* (1919, Farnsworth Art Museum, Rockland, Maine), Marin transformed trees into a religious icon: flat, hazy forms seem to float and their insubstantiality defines them as ethereal, even mystical. This construct of nature as spiritual had a long history in American and New England art—a history not lost on the painter and his Stieglitz circle colleagues who often wrote of their indebtedness to Ralph Waldo Emerson and Henry David Thoreau. These painters also packaged New England as a paradise where people could be in tune with nature. In Marguerite Zorach's *Farm in the Hills* (1915, private collection), the edenic world envisioned earlier in the century in Henri Matisse's *Joie de Vivre* (1905–6, Barnes Collection, Philadelphia) is restaged with a New Hampshire farm as setting. In similar fashion, Marin pictured the female nude as natural and unencumbered by society, dancing along the Maine shore and floating on the sea in *Dance by the Sea* (1942, Richard York Gallery, New York).

While some artists pictured these idealized nudes as embodiments of antimodernity, others defined the New England folk and their cultural products in this way. Early-20th-century critics, collectors, and writers viewed folk art as the product of an earlier, rural society; makers of objects from weather vanes to portraits were considered proto-modernists, concerned with personal expression not standardized formula. In Ogunquit, Hamilton Easter Field and Robert Laurent began collecting folk art and colonial portraits from local people in the 1910s. Collectors associated with Field, like Edith Halpert (who opened a folk art gallery in New York in 1931) and Abby Aldrich Rockefeller, followed, and artists working at Field's Summer School of Graphic Arts (founded 1911) in Ogunquit began adopting folk mannerisms in their own work. Field's and Laurent's collections of paintings on glass and mirrors influenced Hartley's *Tinseled Flower* (1917, Museum of Fine Arts, Boston), for example. Marguerite Zorach's *City of Bath* (1927, Farnsworth Art Museum) evidences the simple forms and surface design characteristic of folk art, while the decorative animal patterns of the mural in her Georgetown, Maine, farmhouse is strikingly similar to the painting of a deer in the Rockefeller collection.

Field encouraged his students to look as much to the folk as to their art, to get the "local tang" and to get "in touch with the native Ogunquit life." In Maine, modernist artists identified with the local inhabitants—the fisherfolk, woodsmen, shipbuilders, hunters—and saw them and their way of life as an alternative to modern, standardized, middle-class life. These artists romanticized the premodern way of life of the New England folk. Hartley viewed the Maine and Nova Scotia fisherfolk through the lens of the primitive: he compared them to the Native Americans of the Southwest, seeing them as simple, and shaped their forms with an eye to non-Western art, as in *Down East Young Blades* (ca. 1940, Wadsworth Atheneum, Hartford). As a socialist, Rockwell Kent was attracted to Monhegan because he considered it an ideal human community based on hard physical labor.

The New England folk were moreover identified with traditional concepts of the masculine and feminine in modernist representations. In the early 20th century, changes from the sexual revolution to the feminization of service jobs challenged established notions of male and female roles. Middle-class businessmen sought to reconstruct their masculinity by exercising in New York sports clubs or testing their mettle hunting in the Maine woods. The Maine folk embodied this vigorous, physical masculinity in paintings like Bellows's *The Big Dory* (1913–15, New Britain [Conn.] Museum of Art), Kent's *Toilers of the Sea* (1907, New Britain Museum of Art), Carl Sprinchorn's *Lumberjacks—Shin Pond, Maine* (1941, private collection), Hartley's *Canuck Yankee Lumberjack at Old Orchard Beach, Maine* (1940–41, Hirshhorn Museum and Sculpture Garden), and Marguerite Zorach's *Land and Development of New England* (ca. 1935, Farnsworth Art Museum). Zorach's painting not only presents the region's settlement as a masculine activity but visualizes family relations that show no signs of changing 20th-century gender roles: the hunter-father dominates both the family and landscape; the mother, in contrast, sits in the lower part of the canvas, acting the part of nurturer.

The New England that these modernists painted was ethnically diverse. Bellows's *The Big Dory* and Hartley's *Down East Young Blades* celebrate the Anglo fishermen, reinscribing the Yankee's long domination of the region. Yet these artists also represented the new immigrant groups that had transformed the region. For them, New England working-class immigrants, like those in New York, signified the antimodern, the "real." In 1915, Henri discovered a band of gypsies in Ogunquit and commented on one young girl whom he painted: "No regular Methodist-born Maine

child can laugh with such freedom." Hartley's *Canuck Yankee Lumberjack at Old Orchard Beach* and *Finnish-Yankee Sauna* (1938–39, Frederick R. Weisman Art Museum, Minneapolis) showed the mixing of ethnicities. For him, the fusion of the declining Yankee with these new immigrants produced a new type—one in which Yankee features and behaviors dominated, and one that would serve as the source of the region's rebirth.

Early-20th-century modernists represented New England to serve their own needs and those of a quickly changing culture. They constructed the region as an antimodern, primitive locale—in opposition to the urban and commercial—embodied in the folk and the landscape. They formed an image of an ideal, premodern New England—an image that continues to shape 21st-century culture and notions of regional identity.

Doreen Bolger, "Hamilton Easter Field and His Contribution to American Modernism," *American Art Journal* 20 (1988); Milton Brown, *The Story of the Armory Show* (1963); Jessica F. Nicoll, *The Allure of the Maine Coast* (1995); Nicoll, *Hamilton Easter Field (1873–1922): Pioneering American Modernism* (1994); Nicoll, *Marguerite and William Zorach: Harmonies and Contrasts* (2001); Bennard B. Perlman, *Robert Henri: His Life and Art* (1991); Bruce Robertson, "Perils of the Sea" and "Yankee Modernism," in *Picturing Old New England: Image and Memory,* ed. William H. Truettner and Roger B. Stein (1999); Robert K. Tarbell, *Marguerite Zorach: The Early Years, 1908–1920* (1973); Louise Tragard, *A Century of Color: Ogunquit, Maine's Art Colony* (1987).

Donna M. Cassidy

Morgan, Maud (1903–99) Painter and printmaker. Through both teaching and example, Maud (Cabot) Morgan was an important figure in the New England art scene. Maud Cabot was born in New York City to Francis Higginson Cabot, a merchant related to the Cabots of Boston, and Maud Bonner of Canada. She graduated from Barnard College in 1925 after spending a year at the Sorbonne. Fascinated by cultural politics, Cabot traveled extensively, visiting Russia, China, and India.

In the early 1930s Maud Cabot returned to Paris, where she met James Joyce, Ernest Hemingway, and her future husband, the artist Patrick Morgan. Although she had previously studied drawing, it was Patrick Morgan who urged her to begin painting. She pursued art studies first in Paris and then in New York with her most important mentor, the abstract expressionist Hans Hofmann. Although few women artists received critical attention at this time, Maud Morgan enjoyed early success. In 1938 the Metropolitan Museum of Art and the Whitney Museum of American Art each purchased still-life paintings from her first solo exhibition.

Maud Morgan and Frank Stella, 1991

During the 1940s and 1950s Maud and Patrick Morgan taught studio art—Maud at Abbott Academy, and Patrick at Phillips Academy, both in Andover, Mass. The Morgans' house on the Phillips Andover campus became a haven for students seeking intellectual stimulation and exposure to the latest trends in art, film, music, and literature.

Although Maud Morgan began her career working in a realistic mode, she soon embraced abstraction. From 1940, when she first heard the musical experiments of composer John Cage, she strove to translate individual tones and their reverberations into vibrant color patterns. Her work gained recognition through shows at the Yale University Art Gallery, in New Haven, Conn., alongside the work of Jackson Pollock, Mark Rothko, and Barnett Newman, and at sales galleries in New York and Boston. Nonetheless, Morgan deferred to her husband's career and the needs of her family, which included her son, Alexis, and daughter, Victoria, until 1957, when she and her husband separated.

Establishing her own studio first in Boston and then in Cambridge, Morgan soon became known as a supporter of liberal political causes and an advocate for artists' rights. During this period she created abstract serigraphs and paintings that convey anger, pain, joy, and hope through dramatic color combinations. Morgan consistently documented her life's challenges in candid self-portraits. Attacked and bruised while traveling alone in Sicily, the artist managed a stoic smile in *At Mount Etna after the Palermo Mugging* (1985, private collection). Finally divorced at age 78, Morgan embarked on a six-month journey to remote areas of Africa, subsequently incorporating pure color patterning into her paintings.

Always eager to experiment, Morgan at age 80 produced a series of large-scale handmade paper pieces at Rugg Road Papers and Prints in Somerville, Mass. In her ninetieth year, following a tribute to her at the Addison Gallery of American Art in Andover, Mass., Morgan met photographer Michael Silver; together they produced a sequence of unique photographic prints. At age 93 Morgan designed a series of boldly colored abstract paper collages.

Her autobiography, *Maud's Journey: A Life from Art* (1995), displays the same penetrating frankness evident in her expressive self-portrait *The Knitted Cap* (1993, private collection). In recognition of her stature as grande dame of the Boston art scene, the Museum of Fine Arts, Boston, now annually awards the Maud Morgan Prize to an outstanding midcareer female artist. Maud Morgan died in Cambridge at age 96.

Addison Gallery of Art, *Maud Morgan: A Retrospective Exhibition, 1927–1977* (1977); Wendy Tarlow Kaplan, *Maud in the '90s: Paintings by Maud Morgan and Collaborative Prints with Michael Silver*, Art Complex Museum, Duxbury, Mass. (1995); Lois Tarlow, "Profile: Maud Morgan," *Art New England* (October–November 1991); Christine Temin, "Feting Maud Morgan, Art Adventurer," *Boston Globe*, March 2, 1993.

Wendy Tarlow Kaplan

Museum of Fine Arts, Boston

The Museum of Fine Arts (MFA), Boston, was America's first major art museum and today is among the world's great encyclopedic museums. The museum was founded on February 4, 1870, when the Massachusetts state legislature approved the incorporation of a new museum for "the preservation and exhibition of works of art," with the goal of "making, maintaining, and establishing collections of such works, and of affording instruction in the Fine Arts." One original purpose of the new museum's founding was to instruct manufacturers in the arts of design, as reflected in its seal's motto: "Art, Industry, Education"; here one can see the influence of the Victoria and Albert Museum in London. Another impetus behind the museum's founding was to make available to a wider public the paintings and sculptures crowded into the Boston Athenaeum, as well as engravings belonging to Harvard College and architectural casts housed at the Massachusetts Institute of Technology.

The original museum building (a Victorian gothic structure of striped red brick and terracotta, designed by the firm of Sturgis and Brigham) opened on July 4, 1876, in what by the end of the century had become Copley Square—the cultural, intellectual, and religious center of Boston. By 1900, however, the museum and its school (opened in 1877) had outgrown the original building. In 1909 the museum moved out of the city center to 12 acres on Huntington Avenue and a handsome, classical revival building, designed by Guy Lowell in 1907, that has undergone significant expansion in subsequent decades to accommodate ever-increasing numbers of objects and visitors. I. M. Pei designed the major west wing addition, which opened in 1981.

The museum's collections include approximately 750,000 works of art from throughout the world and from early civilization to the present day. Many of the strengths of the collections reflect the museum's identity and long history as a major New England institution. For example, in 1905 the museum joined Harvard University in a 40-year archaeological expedition based at the Great Pyramids of Giza. The museum's share of the antiquities excavated during this expedition brought to Boston a group of Old Kingdom Egyptian sculpture equaled only in Cairo. Similarly, several adventurous Bostonians traveled to Japan in the late 19th century; the museum's preeminent collection of Japanese art was substantially formed by these pioneering connoisseurs at a time (pre-1900) when acquisitions of American and European art had only begun. Boston collectors were also fundamental in assembling the museum's world-famous holdings of French impressionist and postimpressionist painting as well as in shaping its American collections, which are especially rich in the arts of early New England, including quantities of superb Paul Revere silver and more than 100 portraits by John Singleton Copley and Gilbert Stuart.

The museum has long been known for its scholarship and research, for its collections of art of the classical world, Asia, and Europe, and for its collections of musical instruments, textiles, and fashion. Through acquisitions and gifts it has broadened its connections to new audiences of contemporary and African art. In 1969 the MFA formed a partnership with the National Center of Afro-American Artists. In many respects, the MFA is the defining art museum for New England, especially as some of its collections of furniture, painting, and decorative arts helped shape the image of the region through such exhibits as "New England Begins" in 1982. Maxim and Martha Karolik donated their extraordinary collection of 18th-century American furniture, paintings, watercolors, and folk art in 1949, and this collection has also played a role in developing ideas of New England.

In 1999 director Malcolm Rogers initiated a major restructuring of curatorial departments. In 2002 Rogers unveiled Foster and Partners' plan for renovation and expansion of the facility over five years, funded by a $425-million capital campaign, which moved into its public phase in fall 2004. Groundbreaking for a new wing for the MFA's Art of the Americas collection is set for 2005. Several conservation laboratories continue to care for objects that are documented and interpreted through the MFA's exhibitions, programs, research, and publications.

Walter Muir Whitehill, *Museum of Fine Arts, Boston: A Centennial History*, 2 vols. (1970).

Gilian Ford Shallcross

Museums

New England is home to one of the greatest repositories of art in the United States. Until recently the region's collections, both public and private, rivaled or excelled in extent and variety those of many European countries. Although a few museums were founded in the late 18th and early 19th centuries, it was the vast wealth of New England after the Civil War that made large-scale collecting possible—and New England collectors, believing that the arts were an essential element in the life of the community, formed their collections to suit public needs. New England's museums—in particular, its university art museums—grew from these collections, becoming the models for future American museums and the training grounds for museum leaders. For beyond collection and exhibition, New England's museums are exemplary in their commitment to education, community, and innovation (see table).

In 1807 a group of leading Boston citizens founded the Boston Athenaeum to serve as a "Reading Room, a Library, a Museum, and a Laboratory," combining in this earliest manifestation museum exhibition, education, and experimentation, a mixture that was propagated in New England museums thereafter. In Brunswick, Maine, James Bowdoin III made a bequest of paintings and drawings in 1811 to the college bearing his father's name, beginning both the first college art collection and a New England philanthropic tradition.

University art museums flourished in New England, exerting a profound influence on museum culture in America. The Yale University Art Gallery, founded in 1832 by the patriot-artist and collector John Trumbull as a way of enriching the lives of undergraduates, has since grown into a large and impressive collection. The museum seeks to engage students in the study of original works of art and introduce them to all aspects of museum work, from research to exhibition. The museum's current building, designed by the distinguished architect Louis I. Kahn, is a national landmark that pointed the way toward a new direction in museum architecture. In 1977 Yale alumnus Paul Mellon donated the collection that founded the Yale Center for British Art. The Center surveys the development of British art, life, and thought from the Elizabethan period on with a permanent collection dedicated to teaching and research.

From their inception, Harvard University's art museums have shaped America's museum

Art Museums in New England (visitors of 10,000 or more yearly)

Museum	Location	Established	Visitors per Year
Connecticut			
New England Center for Contemporary Art	Brooklyn	1975	12,000
Thomas J. Walsh Art Gallery, Quick Center for the Arts	Fairfield University, Fairfield	1990	10,000
Hill-Stead Museum	Farmington	1946	40,000
Bruce Museum of Arts and Science	Greenwich	1912	103,000
Wadsworth Atheneum	Hartford	1842	220,000
Mystic Art Association	Mystic	1914	10,000
New Britain Museum of American Art	New Britain	1903	45,000
Silvermine Guild Art Center	New Canaan	1922	11,000
Yale Center for British Art	Yale University, New Haven	1977	110,000
Yale University Art Gallery	New Haven	1832	146,000
Lyman Allyn Art Museum	New London	1930	37,144
Slater Memorial Museum	Norwich	1888	12,000
Florence Griswold Museum	Old Lyme	1936	54,661
Aldrich Contemporary Art Museum	Ridgefield	1964	21,259
William Benton Museum of Art	University of Connecticut, Storrs	1966	35,704
Mattatuck Museum	Waterbury	1877	40,000
Joseloff Gallery	University of Hartford, West Hartford	1970	10,000
Museum of Art and History at Weston	Weston	ca. 1980	15,000
Maine			
University of Maine Museum of Art	Bangor	1946	25,000
Bowdoin College Museum of Art	Brunswick	1811	20,969
Bates College Museum of Art	Lewiston	1986	16,559
Ogunquit Museum of American Art	Ogunquit	1952	10,000
Institute of Contemporary Art at Maine College of Art	Portland	1983	20,000
Portland Museum of Art	Portland	1882	160,000
The Farnsworth Art Museum and Wyeth Center	Rockland	1948	70,000
Center for Maine Contemporary Art	Rockport	1952	15,000
Wendell Gilley Museum	Southwest Harbor	1979	24,420
Colby College Museum of Art	Waterville	1959	27,060
Massachusetts			
Mead Art Museum	Amherst College, Amherst	1821	35,000
University Gallery	University of Massachusetts, Amherst	1975	10,000
Addison Gallery of American Art	Phillips Academy, Andover	1931	21,902
Attleboro Museum, Center for the Arts	Attleboro	1929	15,000
Institute of Contemporary Art	Boston	1936	27,105
Isabella Stewart Gardner Museum	Boston	1903	160,000
Museum of Fine Arts	Boston	1870	1,000,000
Photographic Resource Center	Boston University, Boston	1976	10,000
Fuller Museum of Art	Brockton	1969	44,000
Harvard University Art Museums	Cambridge	1895	137,309
List Visual Arts Center	Massachusetts Institute of Technology, Cambridge	1950	14,000
McMullen Museum of Art	Boston College, Chestnut Hill	1976	75,000
Cape Museum of Fine Arts	Dennis	1981	25,000
Art Complex Museum	Duxbury	1967	10,000
Fitchburg Art Museum	Fitchburg	1925	20,000
Danforth Museum of Art	Framingham	1975	37,306
DeCordova Museum and Sculpture Park	Lincoln	1948	120,000
Tufts University Gallery	Medford	1955	16,398
MASS MoCA	North Adams	1988	105,000
Smith College Museum of Art	Northampton	1920	(not avail.)
Berkshire Artisans/Lichtenstein Center for the Arts	Pittsfield	1975	50,000
Berkshire Museum	Pittsfield	1903	85,000
Provincetown Art Association and Museum	Provincetown	1914	25,000
Rockport Art Association	Rockport	1921	50,000

(continued)

Art Museums in New England (visitors of 10,000 or more yearly) (continued)

Museum	Location	Established	Visitors per Year
Peabody Essex Museum	Salem	1799	109,500
George Walter Vincent Smith Art Museum	Springfield	1896	87,083
Museum of Fine Arts	Springfield	1933	103,541
Norman Rockwell Museum at Stockbridge	Stockbridge	1967	179,919
Davis Museum and Cultural Center	Wellesley College, Wellesley	1889	30,000
Sterling and Francine Clark Art Institute	Williamstown	1950	219,092
Williams College Museum of Art	Williamstown	1926	65,243
Worcester Art Museum	Worcester	1896	129,381
New Hampshire			
Museum of New Hampshire History	Concord	1823	44,201
Saint-Gaudens National Historic Site	Cornish	1926	40,000
Hood Museum of Art	Dartmouth College, Hanover	1772	38,352
Belknap Mill Society	Laconia	1970	40,000
Currier Museum of Art	Manchester	1929	67,908
New Hampshire Institute of Art	Manchester	1896	27,500
Sharon Arts Center	Sharon	1947	36,000
Rhode Island			
Fine Arts Center Galleries	University of Rhode Island, Kingston	1968	25,000
Newport Art Museum	Newport	1912	41,434
Annmary Brown Memorial	Brown University, Providence	1905	(not avail.)
David Winton Bell Gallery	Brown University, Providence	1971	10,000
RISD Museum	Rhode Island School of Design, Providence	1877	95,532
Vermont			
Bennington Museum	Bennington	1875	51,000
Brattleboro Museum and Art Center	Brattleboro	1972	20,551
Robert Hull Fleming Museum	University of Vermont, Burlington	1931	(not avail.)
Southern Vermont Arts Center	Manchester	1929	35,000
Middlebury College Museum of Art	Middlebury	1968	18,446
Shelburne Museum	Shelburne	1947	119,558

Source: The Official Museum Directory: 2004, 34th ed. (National Register Publishing, 2004).

culture through their collections, exhibition practices, and teaching. The Fogg Art Museum opened to the public in 1895 as a collection of prints and casts. Under the directorship of Edward W. Forbes it grew into a renowned collection with particular strengths in drawings and 19th-century French art. Its Georgian-style building, opened in 1927, was intended as a laboratory and training center for museum directors, curators, and art historians. In the Fogg's famed museum course, founded and taught by associate director Paul J. Sachs, graduate students studied all aspects of museum leadership, becoming the first generation of American museum professionals. As directors and curators of many of America's art museums in the midcentury period, Sachs's "museum men" put an indelible stamp of connoisseurship and quality on American museum practice. In the 1970s, Harvard's collections of ancient, Asian, Islamic, and Indian art were relocated next door, to the Arthur M.

Sackler Museum, whose building, designed by James Stirling, is another example of innovative museum architecture. The Busch-Reisinger Museum, founded as the Germanic Museum in 1903, is also part of the Harvard complex. It houses the country's first outstanding collection of European modern art, acquired from German-speaking countries in the period between the world wars by director Charles L. Kuhn, who rescued many works of art banned by the Nazis.

Harvard and Yale were not the only educational institutions to produce museum leaders and leading art historians. In the expansionist years of the 1920s schools and universities throughout the region, benefiting from alumni bequests, built college art museums intended to draw students toward the study of art history and museum practice. The Williams College Museum of Art in Williamstown, Mass., founded in 1926, has rivaled Harvard in training America's museum directors

and curators. At Williams, the art historians S. Laine Faison, Whitney Stoddard, and William H. Pierson, Jr., inspired graduates to enter the museum field. Known as the Williams "Mafia," these students include the current directors of the Guggenheim and the Museum of Modern Art in New York and of the National Gallery in Washington, D.C. Other colleges, including Smith, Dartmouth, Wellesley, Colby, Bates, Middlebury, and the Rhode Island School of Design, developed distinguished collections that became teaching tools for undergraduates as well as rich resources for scholars and visitors.

Building community was also integral to New England's philanthropic museum culture. Thanks to the largesse of local collectors, every New England city of note may claim as part of its cultural patrimony the founding of a public or private art museum. Social ambition combined with generosity of spirit prompted wealthy New Englanders to support city and private museums that would become homes for their collections. Boston has been the hub of such endeavors. Founded by the Massachusetts state legislature in 1870, the Museum of Fine Arts (MFA) opened its doors in Copley Square in 1876 with a collection of paintings, casts, and copies intended to improve the character of the working classes and instruct artisans in good design. The move to the Fenway in 1909 coincided with the acquisition of original works of art from around the world that appealed to the aesthetics of middle-class audiences. Nearby, Isabella Stewart Gardner opened Fenway Court in 1903 with acquisitions of Titian and Rembrandt paintings that were unrivaled in quality and rarity. Her patronage of American artists and her unique house museum offered a bold alternative to the MFA, from whose Brahmin circles she was excluded. The Museum of the National Center of Afro-American Artists has provided the region with a unique venue for exploring African American heritage since its founding in 1969. Under the continuous leadership of Edmund Barry Gaither, it has forged an unbroken record of public service in celebration of the world heritage of black people through changing exhibitions of contemporary and historical African, African American, and Caribbean art.

New England museums, both public and private, have shaped the identities of their communities. Worcester, Mass., Hartford, and smaller cities such as Portland, Maine; Manchester, N.H.; and Fitchburg, Mass., looked to their museums as sources of civic pride and cultural enrichment. The Worcester Art Museum (founded 1896; opened 1898) became a pioneer in museum education in the 1920s and continues to be a vital member of its community through employment and internship programs connected with its fine collection. The artist Eleanor Norcross endowed the Fitchburg Art Museum as a gift to her city in 1925. Using its collection as a teaching tool, the museum has developed a middle school within the museum in one of the most innovative museum–public school partnership programs in the country—breaking new ground in the area of community outreach. In Williamstown, the Sterling and Francine Clark Art Institute (founded 1950; opened 1955), a well-endowed private museum, houses a distinguished private collection while reaching out beyond its walls to create education programs and maintain a nationally recognized research institute.

New England has also been a pioneer in the development of museums of modern and contemporary art. Under the leadership of A. Everett "Chick" Austin, who became director of Hartford's Wadsworth Atheneum in 1927, the museum became a leading center for modern art, dance, and music in America. In 1928 three Harvard College sophomores founded the Harvard Society for Contemporary Art in Harvard Square; it was the first gallery to be designed as a model for a modern art museum and served as an inspiration to Alfred H. Barr, Jr., founding director of the Museum of Modern Art in New York. The Boston Museum of Modern Art (now the Institute of Contemporary Art; ICA) was established in 1936. Relocated several times over the decades, the ICA has remained Boston's center for contemporary mid-career artists and has provided the region with groundbreaking exhibits. In the western Massachusetts town of North Adams the Massachusetts Museum of Contemporary Art (MASS MoCA) was created in a vast renovated factory building; it opened in 1999. In an unusual partnership between city and state, the museum has provided a unique setting for cutting-edge installation art and become a source of economic renewal to the North Adams community.

Far beyond their particular missions, New England's museums have provided the nation with a wellspring of talent through training opportunities for museum professionals. Their community-oriented programs and innovative new art venues have made New England's museums a cultural mecca and placed the region at the forefront of America's evolving art museum world.

Kathryn Brush, *Vastly More Than Bricks and Mortar: Reinventing the Fogg Art Museum in the 1920s* (2004); James Cuno, Marjorie B. Cohn, Ivan Gaskell, Deborah Martin Kao, David Gordon Mitten, Robert D. Mowry, Peter Nisbett, William W. Robertson, and Stuart Cary Welch, *Harvard's Art Museums: 100 Years of Collecting* (1996); *Dissent: The Issue of Modern Art in Boston* (1985); S. Lane Faison, *Williams College Museum of Art: Handbook of the Collection* (1979); Edmund B. Gaither, *Massachusetts Masters: Afro-American Artists* (1985); Eugene R. Gaddis, *Magician of the Modern: Chick Austin and the Transformation of the Arts in America* (2000); Hilliard T. Goldfarb, *The Isabella Stewart Gardner Museum: A Companion Guide and History* (1995); Martha Hoppin, *Eleanor Norcross: Character Is Everything* (2000); Susan Matheson, *Art for Yale: A History of the Yale University Art Gallery* (2001); Craig Hugh Smyth and Peter M. Lukehart, *The Early Years of Art History in the United States* (1993); Jennifer Trainer Thompson, Nicholas Whitman, and Joseph Thompson, *MASS MoCA: From Mill to Museum* (2000); Nicholas Fox Weber, *Patron Saints: Five Rebels Who Opened America to a New Art, 1928–1943* (1992); Walter Muir Whitehill, *The Museum of Fine Arts: A Centennial History*, 2 vols. (1970).

Sally Anne Duncan

Native American Art Native American art in New England is deeply entwined with issues of tradition, economics, politics, and identity and is the product of a postcolonial legacy that reaches back to the 17th century. Significant differences in the development of native art forms between northern and southern New England resulted from differing cultural histories. Throughout the past four centuries, Native American artists have maintained a balance between internal and external influences on materials, styles, and forms. The ultimate goal, however, has largely been cultural and economic survival, a struggle that continues today.

Contemporary Native American art in New England stems from the adaptation of precontact art forms to meet changing 19th-century economic needs. During this period, Native American peoples faced dwindling economic reserves as the fur trade and other sources of income dwindled. In response, Native American artists, especially women, modified traditional skills such as porcupine quillwork, birch-bark work, beadwork, wood carving, and basketry to manufacture articles for sale as souvenirs to tourists and other non-Indian markets. This was especially true in northern New England, where to a lesser degree this practice continues to the present. The transformation of these centuries-old forms and techniques allowed Native American artists to survive in a changing world while maintaining strong ties to important cultural traditions.

Basketry was, and continues to be, one of the most important of the contemporary arts. It is also one of the oldest continuously practiced art forms in New England, with precontact roots. By the early 1800s, Native American women had begun to sell their traditional ash-splint baskets to local farmers and merchants. They often would walk long distances carrying these baskets on their backs from house to house. Gradually, as the century progressed, Native American artists incorporated European designs and decorations into these baskets to make them appealing to a wider consumer base. In northern New England, this included the use of commercial aniline dyes and sweet grass. During the late 19th century, European production of work baskets became more and more mechanized, pushing many of the small craftsworkers out of business. This was especially true in southern New England, where the majority of basket makers ceased commercial production by the early 1900s. In northern New England, the beginning of widespread tourism and the creation of resorts softened this trend. Native artists began to focus on the production of fancy baskets that were made exclusively to meet the needs of this new market.

The establishment of large resort areas in northern New England also contributed to the transformation and continuity of other art forms. Native artists in this area had used

Molly Molasses
(ca. 1980; private collection), by the Penobscot artist Ssipsis, is made of birchbark, sweetgrass, felt, and sequins

birch bark for thousands of years to make various containers and utensils. During the 17th century, they began to trade these items with European fishermen and explorers. This trade expanded greatly with the arrival of tourists, and new forms such as laundry baskets were created to meet this growing market. Elaborately carved birch root clubs were another traditional art form that was adapted to the tourist economy. Originally carved by Penobscot men as badges of a warrior's status, they became popular symbols of Native American identity for thousands of Victorian souvenir hunters.

During the first half of the 20th century, Native American art in New England began to take on a much deeper meaning. Throughout the region, native groups began to organize both tribal and regional councils, with the goal of protecting their land base, culture, and tribal identity from local and state authorities. Native art became a way of visually expressing an individual's Native American background. Native artists in New England began to adopt designs, clothing, and materials from Native American tribes of the Plains, as native identity superseded tribal identity. Plains-style feather bonnets, moccasins, vests, and beadwork were most prevalent in southern New England, where pressure from nonnative neighbors and authorities was the greatest.

A significant shift in Native American arts has occurred in the past two decades. Strong interest in federal recognition as well as a growing appreciation by the general public has meant significant expansion. Native artists are increasingly interested in revitalizing traditional tribal styles while at the same time maintaining a contemporary perspective. In

northern New England, traditional arts that had been adapted to the tourist trade continue to flourish. Many of the region's basket makers have joined together to form a cooperative marketing organization. A new generation of root club carvers has emerged, building on the works of the past, but with a renewed sense of their importance as carriers of tribal identity. Across New England, museums have begun to recognize the important contributions made by contemporary Native American artists working in traditional forms and materials or in modern and postmodern forms. In recent years many regional exhibitions have been held at the Boston Children's Museum, the Abbe Museum in Bar Harbor, Maine, the University of Maine's Hudson Museum, the Peabody Essex Museum in Salem, Mass., and the Mashantucket Pequot Museum and Research Center in Connecticut, featuring both contemporary and historic Native American art from New England. Many Native American artists in New England have taken to the fine arts as an avenue of cultural and personal expression, combining Western painting or sculpture with indigenous inspiration and meaning.

Joan Lester, *We're Still Here: Art of Indian New England* (1987); Ann McMullen and Russel Handsman, eds., *A Key into the Language of Woodsplint Basketry* (1987); Dan L. Monroe, foreword, *Gifts of the Spirit: Works by 19th-Century and Contemporary Native American Artists* (1996); Ruth B. Phillips, *Trading Identities: The Souvenir in Native North American Art from the Northeast, 1700–1900* (1998).

Stephen Cook

New York Realists in New England

During the first decade of the 20th century,

New England became a vacation spot for New York realist painters associated with the painter Robert Henri, including the Ash Can School. For the most part, these New York artists—Henri, Rockwell Kent, George Luks, William Glackens, John Sloan, Randall Davey, Edward Hopper, and George Bellows—were interested in the texture of modern, industrialized life, and especially concerned with portraying the lives of the poor and working classes and the entertainment and culture of the urban masses. Urban dramas of power and class captured their attention in the city; on their summer sojourns they turned to older scenes of rural labor or wild nature, often modeling their work after the paintings of Winslow Homer. Most arrived in New England after May and left in October, like other tourists, and visited the same resorts that other, more traditional artists visited.

Robert Henri became the leader of New York's realist painters shortly after 1900. Although the group closest to him was known as the Ash Can School (after the derisive comments of a critic who likened their work to ash cans), there are no clear divisions between the larger group of realists and the Ash Can artists. In fact, Henri first visited Maine at the suggestion of the Philadelphia artist Edward Redfield, who was, if anything, an impressionist. Although many of the New England subjects the realists painted were no different than those depicted by other artists, their visits to the region seem to have reintroduced traditional American themes into the realists' art. While only one young New Yorker attempted to beard Homer in his den at Prout's Neck, Maine (Leon Kroll, only peripherally a member of the Henri circle), all were inspired to emulate the hardy, virile realism of Homer's work.

Henri first visited Monhegan, Maine, an island well known for its dramatic scenery, in 1903. He depicted the island in paintings such as *Storm Tide* (1904, Whitney Museum of American Art, New York). His positive experience led his prize pupil, Rockwell Kent, to visit in 1905 and spend nearly six years there, producing paintings such as *Toilers of the Sea* (1907, New Britain [Conn.] Museum of American Art) that gained him his first success. Kent's scenes of laboring fishermen cast in the piercing light of winter were compared favorably, and inevitably, with the work of Winslow Homer. Henri returned to Monhegan bringing with him his pupils Randall Davey, Edward Hopper, and George Bellows. Of these, only Bellows regularly returned. During World War I fear of enemy warships drove Henri and his colleagues to explore the Southwest. The desire to emulate the work of Homer, weakened by the advent of experimental avant-garde art and war, began to diminish.

Rugged Monhegan was not the only site in New England explored by Henri's circle; George Luks and William Glackens vacationed often along the New England coast, and most members of the group visited Gloucester, Mass. Their response to these landscapes, mediated by the paintings produced for decades by earlier painters, was less unified. Only John Sloan produced a significant body of work in Gloucester, adjusting his journalist's eye for urban bustle to the calmer setting of small-town life in such paintings as *Gloucester Trolley* (1917, Canajoharie [N.Y.] Library and Art Gallery). But as Grant Holcomb noted in *John Sloan: The Gloucester Years* (1980), even Sloan complained that "there was an artist's shadow beside every cow in Gloucester, and the cows themselves are dying from eating paint rags."

Bruce Robertson, *Reckoning with Winslow Homer: His Late Paintings and Their Influence* (1991); H. Barbara Weinberg, Doreen Bolger, and David Park Curry, *American Impressionism and Realism: The Painting of Modern Life, 1885–1915* (1994); Richard West, *"An Enkindled Eye": The Paintings of Rockwell Kent* (1985).

E. Bruce Robertson

Parrish, Maxfield (1870–1966) Artist and illustrator.

The most popular American illustrator of the early 20th century, Maxfield Parrish produced advertisements, magazine covers, calendar art, children's book illustrations, and art prints. A key figure in the Cornish, N.H., art colony whose aesthetic was largely informed by classical and Renaissance influences, Parrish's work posits an unspoiled, pastoral, slightly fantastic interpretation of New England's scenic landscape.

Born Frederick Parrish in Philadelphia, the artist adopted the family name Maxfield as a middle name, and ultimately dropped his given name altogether. His father was Stephen Parrish, a successful artist known for his etchings. His mother, Elizabeth Bancroft Parrish, came from a family of inventors and toolmakers, and gave her son a love of things mechanical and a sharp eye for the advantageous business deal.

After studying architecture at Haverford College, Parrish attended classes at the Pennsylvania Academy of the Fine Arts and at the Drexel Institute in Philadelphia. At the Pennsylvania Academy he met a painting instructor named Lydia Austin, whom he married in 1895. That year Parrish executed his first cover design for a national publication, the *Harper's* Easter issue. In 1898 Parrish moved from Philadelphia to Plainfield, N.H., where he became an active member of the Cornish art colony. He maintained his home there for the rest of his life.

Parrish had traveled extensively throughout Europe in his youth, studying classical and Renaissance art and architecture. He was also strongly influenced by the mountainscapes of the American West, where he traveled in 1902 and again in 1920. Combining Greek vases, Renaissance gardens, trees from New Hampshire, mountains from Colorado, and costumes reminiscent of the Roman toga, Parrish created a dreamy, vaguely recognizable world in his paintings. He then illuminated this world with dramatic, low-glancing light and suffused the entire image with iridescent color. By 1920 Parrish had also studied the writings of Jay Hambidge, whose theory of "dynamic symmetry" drew on the forms of the Greek vase.

Parrish's most famous painting contains all of these features. In *Daybreak* (1922, private collection), the classical columns, the distant mountains, and the two nymphlike figures are all arranged according to the dynamic triangles of Hambidge's theory. The brilliant blue was so characteristic of his work that "Parrish blue" became, in the 1920s and 1930s, a household term. *Daybreak*, published as an art print by the House of Art, created a national sensation. It was hung in private living rooms and public spaces across the nation.

In 1932 Parrish announced, "I'm done with girls on rocks." Thereafter, he would devote himself to landscapes. Most of the "girls on rocks" had been produced either as magazine covers or as illustrations for Edison Mazda calendars; the new landscapes appeared on calendars and greeting cards published by Brown and Bigelow, a national calendar and greeting card company. These later paintings still featured brilliant colors and dramatic lighting effects, but the subject matter was more literally based on the New England landscape. The farms and churches depicted in his landscapes represent actual—not imagined—places, while evidence of the modern world is notably absent.

While Parrish's early work had placed a classical, ideal world before a mass audience, his later work brought images of rural New England to that same national audience. His combination of nostalgia and photographic realism strongly influenced another great New England illustrator—Norman Rockwell. Parrish continued to work until the age of 91. He died at "The Oaks" in Plainfield.

Laurence Cutler, Judy Goffman, and the American Illustrators Gallery, *Maxfield Parrish* (1993); Alma Gilbert, *Maxfield Parrish: The Masterworks* (1992); Coy Ludwig, *Maxfield Parrish* (1973); Sylvia Yount, *Maxfield Parrish* (1999).

Carrie Brown

Photography

New England's visual identity has been shaped and expressed strongly by photography. Although portraiture played the leading role in mid-19th-century photography, landscape and townscape views predominated by late century. Despite New England's extensive industrial history, however, the region's photographic representation has been marked by an idealized "middle landscape" of settled villages and rural folkways, with a more recent emphasis on the regenerative virtues of untrammeled nature. New England's symbolic power as a national landscape of agrarian, Jeffersonian ideals has dramatically shaped the region's photographic image, so successfully defining the region's visual representation that alternative interpretations of New England regional identity remain a largely unwritten chapter of photographic history.

Soon after the French scenic artist Louis Daguerre announced his success with his daguerreotype process in 1839, enthusiasts on both sides of the Atlantic set to work improving the process and establishing their own daguerreian studios. The new process meant that, for the first time, middle-class (and some working-class) sitters could have their portraits made for as little as 50 cents, often taken in urban parlors or by traveling itinerant daguerreotypists, whose covered wagons doubled as studios. The most famous urban studio is Boston's Southworth and Hawes (1844–61), whose photographers advertised themselves as artists to distinguish their work from the cheap "picture factories." Although Southworth and Hawes patented the Grand Parlor Stereoscope and made several unusual outdoor views, the studio is mostly remembered for its outstanding portraiture. The Tremont Street studio was an important magnet for Boston's elite: eminent Bostonians such as Chief Justice Lemuel Shaw and John Quincy Adams came to the studio to have their portraits taken and to see the numerous portraits and views on display. Contemporaries found that, unlike most daguerreotype portraits, Southworth and Hawes's work surpassed a mere surface "likeness," and instead gave expression to the sitter's inner character and individuality. The images are distinctive for their dramatic lighting, inventive posing, and the crisp expressiveness of their sitters. These publicly displayed images provided antebellum Americans with the iconography of character and virtue, a visual amulet against the era's hypocrites and confidence men; to the extent that the portraits revealed such national ideals as virtue and sincerity, they visually imbricated New England identity with American nationalist ideals.

As photographic representation became

widespread in the 19th century through the innovations of the ambrotype, tintype, and *cartes-de-visite*, New England entrepreneurs began to develop markets for inexpensive views of tourist destinations. One of the most popular new formats was the stereograph, a double photograph that, when viewed with a stereoscope, appears as a three-dimensional image. The stereograph "craze" of the late 19th century contributed to the development of New England's tourist and resort industry; as a result, many of the industry's innovators featured stereograph view sets of the White Mountains and other popular destinations. The views depicted tourist attractions, such as New Hampshire's Flume and Tip Top House; popular hotels; and favored landscapes, such as Profile Lake and Franconia Notch, N.H. New England was also home to some of the largest manufacturers of stereoscopic views. In the 1870s, for example, the Kilburn Brothers of Littleton, N.H. (1865–1909), erected a partially mechanized three-story factory where they produced, on average, 3,000 finished stereographs each day; in later years, the firm's several hundred itinerant canvassers sold these views door to door.

The popularity of New England imagery continued throughout the late 19th century, when the pressures of industrialization and immigration gave rise to the Colonial Revival movement. The many books and lectures, reproduction furniture, restored homes, and, especially, popular hand-tinted photographs of colonial scenes and interiors by Wallace Nutting (1861–1941) celebrated a mythic New England past where sturdy yeomen worked the farm and industrious womenfolk guarded the hearth. In *The Quilting Kitchen* (1915, Library of Congress, Washington, D.C.), for example, a woman dressed in "colonial" garb serenely works her quilt beside an expansive brick hearth, her maternal figure one of several colonial objects artfully arranged within the sparse yet alluring interior. Along with other genre photographers such as Emma Sewall (1836–1919) and Chansonetta Stanley Emmons (1858–1937), Nutting elaborated on a visual tradition that portrayed the rural New England home as the domestic haven in a heartless commercial world, the anchor of "traditional" (Yankee) family values under siege by modernization. At the same time, Nutting's photographic production mirrored these developments: at the height of this aspect of his business in 1911, he had more than 100 colorists in his employ, young women who lived and worked in his Framingham, Mass., barn and studio for a weekly wage of five dollars.

Since the 1840s, regional photography has privileged the Anglo-American subject, whether the cultural elite or Yankee "folk."

Through this subject, Anglo-American "whiteness" has been constructed and maintained as an integral component of New England regional identity. This visual tradition has not gone uncontested, however. In turn-of-the-century Boston, photographers such as Herbert Collins (1882–1966) and Margaret Sutermeister (1875–1950) quietly articulated a competing definition of regional identity through their documentation of that city's African American communities; more recent projects have documented rural New England's Jamaican migrant workers.

The widely circulated Colonial Revival photographs, however, have shaped an image of New England that is both Anglo-American and pastoral. Nonetheless, 19th-century New England was transformed by the Industrial Revolution. Lewis Hine (1874–1940), a reform photographer who documented the conditions of industrial labor for such Progressive organizations as the National Child Labor Committee (NCLC), photographed the workers of Maine's sardine canneries and New Hampshire's textile industry as part of the NCLC work. In an Eastport, Maine, cannery image, barefoot boys flecked with scales and sardine parts hunch over a slimy worktable, cutting and cleaning the fish for canning. As an explicit rebuttal to the gritty documentary realism of Hine and other Progressive reform photographers, New England corporations hired photographers to produce publicity photographs celebrating the accomplishments of American capital. In Providence and other New England industrial cities during the 1910s, industrial efficiency consultants Frank and Lillian Gilbreth pioneered the use of photography in rationalizing the work process.

Despite this urban, industrial photographic tradition, however, New England's 20th-century regional identity continued to be shaped through a persistent trio of visual tableaux: the crusty Yankee "folk" toiling with their traps, nets, and teams; the covenanted community of the agrarian small town; or, increasingly, the pristine beauty of northern New England's seemingly unpopulated wilderness. Many of these photographic conventions were further refined through the work of individual state tourism bureaus, beginning in the early years of the century. In Maine, for example, state tourism photographer George W. French (1882–1970) helped sell the state as a "vacationland" for weary city dwellers throughout the 1930s and 1940s.

At this same time, Roy Stryker, director of the Farm Security Administration's photography section, began sending more photographers to document New England. Jack Delano (1914–97) covered the fall 1940 harvest;

John Collier, Jr. (1913–92), photographed the Maine potato harvest; and Marion Post Wolcott (1910–90) documented rural New England in winter. Stryker had developed photographic "shooting scripts" that directed the photographers to produce images conforming to preconceived ideas of rural and small town life. Many of the FSA New England images echo the unabashed boosterism of corporate publicity photographs: happy, normal families sit down to dinner; little girls learn sewing skills at their mother's knee. Even though many of the farm families were non-Anglo immigrants (Polish tobacco farmers, French-Canadian potato growers, for example), these photographs smooth over ethnic or religious difference through their reliance on traditional gender and family narratives, epitomized in New England community life. Reproduced in national magazines and in popular American life picture books during World War II, these photographic tableaux reminded Americans of what they were fighting for while demonstrating the patriotic virtues of Armenians, Russians, and other immigrants. Some of Post Wolcott's work, however, suggests a more complex regional portrait. Keenly aware of the dynamics of class, she sympathetically photographed paper mill workers on their way home, their gray figures wearily marking their route across an ice-white New Hampshire townscape.

The FSA project dramatically shaped the photographic representations of the region after World War II. Verner Reed (1923–), the main *Life* magazine freelancer in New England from 1953 through 1957, photographed not only the region's prominent politicians like John Fitzgerald Kennedy but scenes of small-town life, as in *Evening Chores* (Webster, N.H., 1953), *Taffy Pull* (Massachusetts, 1955) and *Fish on Scales* (Cape Cod, 1957), particularly reminiscent of the earlier work of Delano and Wolcott. Reed's photographs also received wide circulation in *Time, Fortune,* and *Vermont Life*. At this same time, the New England photographic work of Paul Strand (1890–1976) and Berenice Abbott (1898–1991), both of whom had previously photographed modernism in its abstract and realist forms, relied on the symbolic power of New England's "middle landscape." Strand began collaboration with Nancy Newhall (1908–74), the Museum of Modern Art's interim curator of photography, resulting in the publication *Time in New England* (1950). This project, a product of the 1930s antifascist politics and the pervasive celebration of American folk traditions, featured Strand's solemn photographic tributes to New England architecture, landscapes, and folk, accompanied by New England writings from the 17th century to the present. New England's villages and farms symbolized, for Strand as well as others, a model society for those seeking to discover a "usable past" in the aftermath of the Depression and war. Abbott began photographing New England in 1954 when she traveled the length of U.S. Route 1, from Maine to Florida, documenting vanishing small-town life. Although many of these images work within the settled visual tradition of the New England village, Abbott also documented the new roadside architecture and signage of a flourishing automobile culture. These Route 1 images, some of which were published in *A Portrait of Maine* (1968), present a new conceptualization of New England: one that is mobile and commercial rather than static and preindustrial.

Since Strand made his first organic closeups of plants and trees while summering in Georgetown, Maine, in 1927–28, photographers have been increasingly drawn to New England's natural landscape. Eliot Porter's (1901–90) crisp portraits of northern Maine ferns, mosses, and landscapes suggest a natural world as yet untouched by urban life; the dye-transfer color process he has pioneered allows him to interpret nature's verdant greens and lush browns. The natural landscape is Paul Caponigro's (1932–) favored subject as well, infused with a personal resonance influenced by the work of Minor White (1908–76), whose black-and-white images of rock formations and swirling water function as visual metaphors for inner experience.

Many contemporary New England photographs engage the themes made popular in earlier images, but others have produced new ways of seeing the region. Work from the Salt Institute for Documentary Studies in Portland, Maine, shies away from an idealized New England landscape, instead presenting a complex portrait in which dynamics of class and race help define a new regional identity. Much of contemporary New England photography, however, does not lend itself easily to a regional interpretation. More recent projects by such New England–based photographers as Lotte Jacobi (1896–1990), Rose Marasco (1948–), Abe Morell (1948–), and Nicholas Nixon (1947–) elude the regional imprimatur; their work may have been made "in" New England, but with some exceptions—such as the recent project by Frank Gohlke (1942–) on the Sudbury (Mass.) River—cannot be said to be "about" New England. At the same time, however, these more nuanced distinctions are often overshadowed in the public imagination, as tourist publications and popular magazines continue to promote an idealized New England of folk, fun, and foliage.

Berenice Abbott, *Berenice Abbott, Photographer: A Modern Vision*, ed. Julia Van Haaften (1989); Donna M. Cassidy, "'On the Subject of Nativeness': Marsden Hartley and New England Regionalism," *Winterthur Portfolio* 29 (Winter 1994); James C. Curtis, "Salt, the FSA, and the Documentary Tradition," in *Maine, a Peopled Landscape: Salt Documentary Photography, 1978–1995*, ed. Hugh T. French (1995); Beaumont Newhall, *The History of Photography, from 1839 to the Present* (1988); *Photographing Maine, 1840–2000* (2000); William F. Robinson, *A Certain Slant of Light: The First 100 Years of New England Photography* (1980); Kim Sichel, *Black Boston: Documentary Photography and the African American Experience* (1994); Robert A. Sobieszek, *The Spirit of Fact: The Daguerreotypes of Southworth and Hawes, 1843–1862* (1976); Historic New England, Boston, Library and Archives (photograph collection); Marianne Berger Woods, "Viewing Colonial America through the Lens of Wallace Nutting," *American Art* 8 (Spring 1994).

Elspeth Brown

Pilgrims and Puritans

During the 19th and 20th centuries powerful artistic images were created of New England's Pilgrims and Puritans. Those images evoked a simpler, agrarian society and became symbols of faith, perseverance, and unity of purpose in the face of adversity. The earliest depictions captured important historical moments such as the landing at Plymouth or the signing of the Mayflower Compact and memorialized specific individuals; later ones portrayed general scenes of everyday life and anonymous people.

Initially, interest in such works came from the descendants of the original settlers, who formed elite societies and research organizations such as the Massachusetts Historical (1791) and the New England Historic Genealogical (1843) Societies. One of the earliest pictorial representations of the Pilgrims' arrival in the New World dates from 1800, when Boston artist Samuel Hill engraved an invitation for the Sons of the Pilgrims celebrating the 180th anniversary of the landing. Using Hill's basic design in different media, the artist Michele Felice Corné in Newport, R.I., painted the scene on a fireboard (ca. 1809), and Enoch Wood and Sons of Burslem, England, made Staffordshire earthenware plates between 1818 and 1846 featuring "The Landing of the Fathers at Plymouth Dec 22 1620." By the 1830s well-trained academic artists such as Robert Weir were creating large, complex historical paintings like the *Embarkation of the Pilgrims at Delft Haven, Holland, July 22nd, 1620* (1836–43), a mural commissioned for the U.S. Capitol Rotunda.

Three works from the later 19th century demonstrate how the Pilgrim and Puritan themes can serve contemporary ideological ends. George Henry Boughton's *Pilgrims Going to Church* (1867, New-York Historical Society) depicts unnamed Plymouth families walking through the wilderness protected only by their Bibles and a few soldiers in armor. Displayed at the Centennial Exhibition in Philadelphia in 1876, this image has served since then as a major representation of America's New England beginnings in late-19th- and 20th-century history textbooks. By the 1920s A. S. Burbank was printing postcards based on Boughton's Pilgrim paintings for his Pilgrim Book and Art Shop to promote tourism in historic Plymouth, Mass.

The Centennial and the Colonial Revival that followed it prompted other representations of Pilgrims and Puritans. The prominent sculptor Augustus Saint-Gaudens unveiled his anything-but-defenseless *The Puritan* (1883–86, Metropolitan Museum of Art, New York) in Springfield, Mass., on Thanksgiving Day in 1887. A heroic public statue depicting Deacon Samuel Chapin, one of Springfield's founders, the sculpture is more idea than portrait. A tall, commanding figure strides resolutely toward the viewer, carrying a massive Bible and a staff. The large statue conveys the unmistakable image of austerity, masculinity, and elite religious and political power as enduring principles of the founding Puritan fathers. Other important commemorative sculptures of Puritans can be found in Salem, Mass., and Boston.

Meaning and memory shift in a later depiction of the early colonists. Lucia Fairchild Fuller, a well-known miniaturist and portrait artist, painted *The Women of Plymouth*, one of six murals for the Hall of Honor in the Women's Building at the Chicago World's Columbian Exposition in 1893. Fuller's work shows the feminine side of colonization. The female figures it depicts, grouped in circles, are relatively passive; unlike Saint-Gaudens's *Puritan*, they do not stride aggressively forward into the viewer's space. Instead they create the impression of a quiet, stable haven appropriate more to Victorian ideals of womanhood than to the realities of 17th-century Plymouth.

In the early 20th century the first Thanksgiving became a popular theme. Jennie A. Brownscombe emphasized the role of women as mothers in her *First Thanksgiving at Plymouth* (1914, Pilgrim Hall Museum, Plymouth). Though Pilgrim fathers and their families dominate the foreground of Brownscombe's painting, Native Americans are finally depicted as participants in the feast.

Images of Pilgrims and Puritans have also found a place in the world of commerce. The illustrator-artist N. C. Wyeth took pride in his early New England heritage. Born in Needham, Mass., Wyeth often visited Plymouth as a child. He drew on that childhood experience in fulfilling his last mural commission (1940–

45), for the Metropolitan Life Insurance Company in New York City. Located in the building's Madison Avenue lobby, the large-scale *Coming of the Mayflower* and six other kindred works nostalgically portray an idyllic world of peace and plenty. At this time, with the Depression wearing on at home and the threat of German militancy abroad, these heroic images evoked a simpler past and the promise of America's beginnings. By linking Pilgrim themes with the world of business, Wyeth's generalized storybook scenes positioned Metropolitan Life as a pillar of America's earliest values.

Today these and other artworks continue to uphold New England's primary position in American history and promote cultural tourism. But as the racial and ethnic demographics of our own times change, they raise new questions about our nation's Anglo-Saxon ascendance. While it remains to be seen how those questions will be answered as the 21st century unfolds, a new generation of artists may provide us with different, more inclusive perceptions of America's beginnings.

Carl L. Crossman and Charles R. Strickland, "Early Depictions of the Landing of the Pilgrims," *Antiques* (November 1970); Charlene G. Garfinkle, "Lucia Fairchild Fuller's 'Lost' Woman's Building Mural," *American Art* 7, no. 1 (1993); Kathryn Greenthal, *Augustus Saint-Gaudens: Master Sculptor* (1985); Robert D. San Souci, *N. C. Wyeth's Pilgrims* (1991); Roger B. Stein, "Gilded Age Pilgrims," in *Picturing Old New England: Image and Memory,* ed. William H. Truettner and Stein (1999).

Sara C. Junkin

Porter, Eliot (1901–90) Photographer. Eliot Porter, a color photographer known for closely observed nature studies, was raised in Winnetka, Ill. In 1910 his father bought Great Spruce Head Island in Maine's Penobscot Bay, where Porter (and later his family) summered nearly every year for the remainder of his life. Porter entered Harvard College in 1920, graduating cum laude with a major in chemical engineering. After his graduation from Harvard Medical School in 1929, Porter taught (bacteriology), tutored (biophysics), and worked as a medical researcher. Precise observation of nature's microscopic formations sensitized him to the value of the close-up, a way of seeing that directly influenced his later photographic work.

During these years Porter resurrected an earlier interest in nature and photography, taking pictures of birds in their natural environments. Around 1936 his brother, the American landscape painter Fairfield Porter, introduced him to Alfred Stieglitz. It was Stieglitz's exhibition of Porter's work in 1938–39 that sparked Porter's decision to devote his full energies to nature photography.

In 1939 Porter began using Kodak's newly introduced Kodachrome film. The complex dye-transfer print process, which Porter used for the remainder of his life, enabled him to highlight the unusual colors produced by ambient light that most observers, trained to collapse unrecognizable colors into narrow categories, ignore. As a result Porter's color photographs, in which marsh grass might be blue-violet as well as brown, teach us, as he hoped, "to see beyond what [we] have been conditioned to see."

Porter's first monograph, *"In Wildness Is the Preservation of the World,"* from Henry David Thoreau (1962), culminated a 12-year effort to interpret, through photographs, key passages from Thoreau. Porter was captivated by Thoreau's conception of nature as a continuum of cycles, patterns, and scale. A lush close-up of verdant, glistening leaves is paired, for example, with Thoreau's journal entry of June 4, 1854: "Now is the time [to] observe the leaves, so fair in color and so perfect on form." Eliot's images illustrate and interpret Thoreau's texts; we see the landscape not only through Thoreau's eyes but through Eliot's as well.

Porter published more than 20 books during his lifetime, several of them with the Sierra Club. His projects concentrated on natural environments, featuring places such as Baja California (1967), the Colorado River (1969), Iceland (1972), New England, and Santa Fe, N.Mex., where he moved with his family in 1946. In 1966, inspired by the landscape of his Maine summers, Porter published *Summer Island: Penobscot Country.* Porter's autobiographical narrative is punctuated by black-and-white landscapes describing childhood memories, while the second half of *Summer Island* features the lush color of Porter's maturity. The color studies for which Porter became increasingly known provided the material for the first solo exhibition of color photographs ever presented at New York's Metropolitan Museum of Art in 1979.

Throughout his work Porter explores the intricate biological and aesthetic relationships that endow nature's abstract patterns with their lyrical beauty. His close studies often portray the interaction between organic material and the physical environment—the overlapping orbits formed by lichens on rock, for example, or a tumultuous sea of tangled branches—from which emerge emotionally powerful, sometimes placeless abstractions. Often, as in *Ruffed Grouse's Nest, Silver Lake, New Hampshire, June 13, 1953* (Amon Carter Museum, Fort Worth, Tex.), nature's brilliant beauty acts as a metaphor for both the persistence of form and the cycle of death, decay, and rebirth.

Porter's New England photographs depict the beauty of an unpeopled natural landscape that has escaped the ravages of industrialization, urbanization, or tourism. The artist aimed to translate into photographic terms his own emotional response to the natural environment, sparking in turn the viewer's aesthetic and spiritual awakening (in the Transcendentalist sense of that term). By inspiring an appreciation of the intrinsic beauty of the natural landscape, Porter hoped to ensure its preservation.

James M. Carpenter, *Fairfield Porter, Paintings; Eliot Porter, Photographs* (1969); Eliot Porter, *Eliot Porter* (1987); Porter, *Intimate Landscapes: Photographs* (1979); John Rohrbach, Rebecca Solnit, and Jonathan Porter, *Eliot Porter: The Color of Wildness* (2001).

Elspeth Brown

Portraiture New England's earliest European settlers, the English, brought with them the ideas, customs, and artistic traditions of the mother country, including portraiture. Nowhere in the Western art tradition was the art of portraiture more popular than in England, where an acute sense of one's position both in society and among one's forebears led to an almost obsessive interest in preserving the likenesses of family members and friends. The rise of Puritan sensibility, with its condemnation of religious and classical subject matter, likewise left portraiture as almost the only genre that artists could practice freely. These attitudes inevitably took root in New England and indeed in all of Britain's North American colonies.

The story of portraiture in New England may be said almost to predate New England itself, for one leading settler had his likeness committed to canvas before setting foot in the New World. John Winthrop, soon to be governor of the Massachusetts Bay Colony, sat for an unidentified artist in London around the year 1629. The only known image of a *Mayflower* passenger is that of Edward Winslow, who was portrayed by an unidentified artist in London in 1651. The earliest portrait known to have been executed in New England is that of eight-year-old Elizabeth Eggington, painted in 1664 by an artist who dated but unfortunately did not sign the picture; no clue to the artist's identity exists. Also in 1664 Dr. John Clark sat for another unknown artist. A few years later a third unidentified artist painted several portraits in Boston. The best known of this group is *Elizabeth Freake and Baby Mary* (ca. 1671–74, Worcester [Mass.] Art Museum). The earliest identified painter who worked in New England was Captain Thomas Smith (d. ca. 1691), a mariner-turned-portraitist who settled in Boston in 1650 but whose known work dates from the late 1680s.

His best (and best-known) painting is his self-portrait (ca. 1690). It was also in New England that the earliest portrait print in America was published, a woodcut of the Reverend Richard Mather, engraved in 1670 by John Foster. Such portraits emulated late mannerist, Baroque, and neo-medieval styles popular in 17th-century Europe. They moreover contained emblems and objects, from skulls to elite furnishings, that identified both 17th-century culture and the sitter's place in that culture.

An unidentified artist known as the Pollard Limner after his frank, straightforward likeness of the 100-year-old Mrs. Anne Pollard (1721) painted about a dozen portraits in Massachusetts around 1720; the stark directness of his portrayals has caused some to conjecture that he was native-born. The engraver Peter Pelham (1695–1751) arrived in Boston from London in 1727. Although he could and did paint an occasional portrait—most notably, that of the Reverend Cotton Mather (1728)—he contributed more importantly to art as an engraver of handsome mezzotint portraits (including one based on his portrait of Mather) and as the first teacher of his stepson, John Singleton Copley.

Most of Pelham's engravings were after portraits by the most significant artist to work in New England (or the American colonies) up to that time, John Smibert (1688–1751). A native of Scotland, Smibert studied in Italy from 1719 to 1722 and subsequently became a moderately successful portraitist in London. Competition there was fierce, however, and when Smibert was invited to teach drawing at a school to be established in Bermuda, he readily accepted, leaving England in January 1729. Funding for the school never materialized, however, and Smibert settled in Boston. By the time he retired in 1746, Smibert had painted more than 250 portraits, most in a style deriving from the Baroque tradition of Godfrey Kneller. Smibert's depictions are more matter-of-fact than Kneller's, however, as the New England merchants who made up the majority of his sitters preferred realism to idealism. His most ambitious painting, *The Bermuda Group* (1729–31, Yale University Art Gallery, New Haven, Conn.), depicted eight subjects, including Smibert, and was the first group portrait to be executed and exhibited in America. The other significant artist working in New England during the second quarter of the 18th century was Robert Feke (ca. 1707–ca. 1752). Born on Long Island, he was in Boston in 1741, the year he painted a group portrait of Isaac Royall and his family, a work clearly indebted to Smibert's *Bermuda Group*. Nothing is known of Feke's training, if any; an acquaintance reported in 1744 that he had "never had any teaching." He had settled in Newport, R.I.,

by 1742 and painted portraits there throughout the 1740s.

Joseph Blackburn (fl. 1754–78) arrived in Newport from Bermuda in 1754, bringing with him the new Georgian rococo style in which paint is manipulated more fluidly, with more attention being paid to the sitter's clothing than to his or her face. He spent the next nine years painting mainly in Boston and Portsmouth, N.H. By no means a first-rate artist, Blackburn nonetheless produced for a time the most stylish portraits in New England.

More important was Blackburn's influence on John Singleton Copley (1738–1815). Having been introduced to art by his stepfather, Copley began drawing as a child; his earliest surviving works date from 1753. Copley's first portraits, of Mr. and Mrs. Joseph Mann (1753–54), are painted in a naive style; but by studying mezzotint engravings, the paintings still on view in John Smibert's studio, and the portraits that Blackburn was then painting in Boston, Copley became an accomplished artist in a short time. He quickly surpassed Blackburn, who, with potential sitters flocking to the younger painter, was forced to move to Portsmouth and in 1763 to quit America altogether.

Combining the Georgian rococo style with the artist's strong powers of observation, Copley's portraits are amazingly lifelike and visualize the sitter's status and position in society. Copley depicted most of the leading families of Massachusetts and made trips to Portsmouth, New York, and Philadelphia. Among his many fine portraits are those of Epes Sargent (ca. 1760), John Hancock (1765), Paul Revere (1768), Samuel Adams (1770–72), and Frances Deering Atkinson (1765). He also drew portraits in pastel and painted miniatures. In 1774, with the political situation in America increasingly unsettled, Copley undertook a long-planned visit to Italy and England. He never returned to America, spending the rest of his lengthy career in London as a history painter and portraitist.

Another New England portrait painter who departed for England around this time was Ralph Earl (1751–1801). Earl was a loyalist, but he eventually returned to America to ply his craft in Connecticut, Massachusetts, Vermont, and New York City. Throughout his career he painted in an attractive, direct provincial style. Other important provincial portraitists active in New England in the years just before and just after the Revolution include John Durand (d. 1782), who divided his time among New York City, Connecticut, and Virginia; Benjamin Blyth (1746–1811), who worked in Salem, Mass., in the 1760s and 1770s before moving to Virginia in the early 1780s; Winthrop Chandler (1747–90), who worked in northern Connecticut and central

Massachusetts; Samuel King (ca. 1748–1819), active throughout his life in Newport; Richard Jennys (ca. 1734–after 1809) and his son William (1774–1859), who worked in Connecticut and Massachusetts; Edward Savage (1761–1817), a Massachusetts native who spent the last part of his career in that state; and the anonymous artist known as the Beardsley Limner, who was active in Massachusetts and Connecticut between 1785 and 1805. John Trumbull (1756–1843), a native of Lebanon, Conn., and a member of a prominent Connecticut family, painted portraits in his home state early and late in his career but spent most of his life outside New England.

When Gilbert Stuart (1755–1828) settled in Boston in July 1805, he was the first top-notch artist to reside in New England since Copley's departure a generation earlier. And, like Copley, he redefined the regional portrait tradition. Born in Rhode Island, Stuart began his career in Newport, went to London in 1775, and became one of Britain's leading portraitists. After painting in Dublin from 1787 to 1792, he returned to America, where he quickly established his reputation as the new nation's best portrait painter. After working in New York, Philadelphia, and Washington, D.C., he moved to Boston, where he spent the rest of his life. Stuart is noted for a fluid brushstroke mannered after late-18th-century British art and was particularly adept at capturing both the appearance and personality of his sitters. Among the most noteworthy of his Boston portraits are those of Commodore Thomas Macdonough (ca. 1815–18), Josiah Quincy (1825), and John Adams (1824).

Boston's leading portraitist after Stuart's death was Chester Harding (1792–1866), a native of Conway, Mass., who worked in several cities outside New England before returning east. Like Stuart, he was skilled at capturing both likeness and personality; his best work, though in a more rugged style, shows the influence of Stuart in its painterly handling. Samuel F. B. Morse (1791–1872), born in Charlestown, Mass., painted portraits in New England early in his career; he abandoned the art altogether when he invented the telegraph.

Edward Greene Malbone (1779–1807) was the leading miniaturist in America at the beginning of the 19th century. He was born in Newport and spent much of his short career working in Boston. Other important miniaturists who worked in New England include Anson Dickinson (1779–1852), a Connecticut native who worked extensively in New England and along the eastern seaboard, and Sarah Goodridge (1788–1853), who spent virtually her entire career working in Boston.

Among the prominent folk artists who practiced portraiture in 19th-century New

Erastus Salisbury Field, Joseph Moore and His Family *(1839, Museum of Fine Arts, Boston)*

England were Erastus Salisbury Field (1805–1900), active in western and central Massachusetts and in Vermont; William Matthew Prior (1806–73), a native of Maine who traveled throughout New England from his base in Boston; and Horace Bundy (1814–83), a Vermonter who painted portraits primarily in northern New England.

By the end of the 19th century, each New England state could boast of numerous portraitists who were constantly employed in painting public officials and other worthies. The best of these continued to be based in Boston; they included Edmund C. Tarbell (1862–1938), Joseph R. DeCamp (1858–1923), Frank Weston Benson (1862–1951), and Charles S. Hopkinson (1869–1962). More recently, Gardner Cox (1906–88) created portraits quite unlike the conventional images characteristic of official portraiture; muted in color and often unflattering (although always accurate), Cox's arresting portraits are among the most distinctive produced in the United States. His subjects include Earl Warren (1963) and Robert F. Kennedy (1968).

The best portrait sculptors in America at the beginning of the 20th century, Augustus Saint-Gaudens (1848–1907) and Daniel Chester French (1850–1931), maintained studios in New York City, but both had close ties to New

England: Saint-Gaudens kept a second home and studio in Cornish, N.H., while French—a native of Concord, Mass.—had a home and studio in Stockbridge, Mass. The leading American realist sculptor in the latter part of the 20th century was Walter Hancock (1901–98), who from 1931 had a home and studio in Cape Ann, Mass. Among his notable portrait busts is one of Robert Frost (1950).

The first artist to sculpt portraits in New England was J. B. Binon, a French émigré who worked in Boston from 1818 to around 1820. He executed a few busts, the best known of which is a larger-than-life-size marble of John Adams (1818). Binon permitted a young Bostonian, Horatio Greenough (1805–52), to observe the carving of that piece. Twenty years later Greenough rose to become America's leading sculptor. Early in his career Greenough produced a number of notable portrait busts; his sitters included John Quincy Adams (1828). He subsequently left Boston for Italy, where he spent the rest of his career. Hiram Powers (1805–73), a native of Woodstock, Vt., is generally considered to be Greenough's successor as America's leading sculptor; though he spent most of his career in Italy and never worked in New England, he did execute a number of portrait busts of prominent New Englanders. Two portrait sculptors who re-

mained in New England were Henry Dexter (1806–76) and Edward Augustus Brackett (1818–1908), both based in Boston.

Two leading portrait-photography firms have been based in Boston. From 1844 to 1861 Albert Sands Southworth and Josiah Johnson Hawes produced thousands of distinctive daguerreotype and other photographic portraits of such well-known figures as Daniel Webster, Francis Parkman, and Lola Montez. Bachrach Photographers, the leading U.S. portrait-photography chain, opened a studio in Boston in 1911, taking pictures of prominent Americans from every field—among them, Eleanor Roosevelt—and of visitors from abroad. The firm is best known for having made portraits of all the U.S. presidents since Andrew Johnson.

Peter Benes, ed., *Painting and Portrait Making in the American Northeast* (1995); Wayne Craven, *Colonial American Portraiture: The Economic, Religious, Social, Cultural, Philosophical, Scientific, and Aesthetic Foundations* (1986); Frank H. Goodyear, Jr., *American Paintings in the Rhode Island Historical Society* (1974); Leah Lipton, *Charles Hopkinson: Pictures from a New England Past* (1988); Lipton, *A Truthfull Likeness: Chester Harding and His Portraits* (1985); Nina Fletcher Little, *Paintings by New England Provincial Artists, 1775–1800* (1976); Ellen Miles, *The Portrait in 18th-Century America* (1993); Museum of Fine Arts, *New England Begins: The 17th Century* (1982); Andre Oliver, Ann Millspaugh Huff, and Edward W. Hanson, *Portraits in the Massachusetts Historical Society* (1988); Michael Quirk, Marvin Sadik, and William Gerdts, *American Portraiture in the Grand Manner, 1720–1920* (1981).

David Meschutt

Public Sculpture

Throughout the 19th century New Englanders celebrated their heroes in portrait statues. The prevailing convention for these slightly larger-than-life figures was established in 1826, when Sir Francis Chantrey's *George Washington* was placed in a "Doric Temple" in the Massachusetts State House. Although the English sculptor had never seen the first president, he produced a convincing likeness, thereby fulfilling the primary aesthetic criterion for 19th-century audiences. Subsequent sculptors chafed at the limitations of verisimilitude and the perceived ugliness of 19th-century apparel, and preferred unblemished marble for their creations. The committees responsible for commissioning monuments in New England, however, were generally composed of statesmen, businessmen, and merchants who wanted their didactic commemorations outdoors, where they were most accessible. Thus, in 1846 Robert Ball Hughes first attempted to cast his *Nathaniel Bowditch* in bronze (recast ca. 1880, Mount Auburn Cemetery, Mass.), but the concrete-filled portrait of the seated astronomer quickly

Carl Andre, Stone Field Sculpture *(1977, Hartford)*

deteriorated. American founding techniques vastly improved within the decade, and the Ames Manufacturing Company in Chicopee, Mass., successfully cast Richard Greenough's *Benjamin Franklin* in 1855.

Although many aspiring American sculptors traveled to Europe for training and materials, a sculptor's ties to New England were often important in obtaining commissions. Greenough received the *Franklin* commission—Boston's first outdoor monument—partly because he resided in the city. Individual states consistently championed their native sons: Maine favored Franklin Simmons; Vermont supported Larkin Mead. Besides Greenough, Thomas Ball, Martin Milmore, and William Wetmore Story were among the Massachusetts natives who received commissions from their home state. Women were not excluded: Emma Stebbins's portrait of educator *Horace Mann* was dedicated at the Massachusetts State House (1864); Anne Whitney won the competition for a monument to commemorate the abolitionist Charles Sumner planned for the Boston Public Garden in 1875. Ultimately, however, Whitney received only a $500 prize, and the Sumner Memorial Committee awarded the commission to Ball. Whitney finally erected her *Sumner* in Cambridge, Mass. (1902).

The region's hero was the "godlike" Daniel Webster. Ball's enormously popular statuette (1853) was mass-produced and appeared in parades and shop windows, while Hiram Powers's heavily criticized statue (ultimately funded at $19,000) was dedicated at the Massachusetts State House (1858). With the exception of Webster and Washington, commemoration was generally divided along state lines. The Connecticut Revolutionary martyr Nathan Hale was memorialized in Hartford by Karl Gerhard (1886) and Enoch Woods (1889), and by Frederick MacMonnies in New London (1890, cast 1934). A son of New Hampshire,

Webster was honored at the State Capitol (Ball, 1886), where he was paired with the Revolutionary hero John Stark (Carl Conrads, 1894) and the abolitionist senator John Hale (artist unknown, 1892). This pantheon of great men expanded to include Henry Augustus Lukeman's portrait of President Franklin Pierce (1913). Local communities celebrated their writers, clerics, and educators: Henry Wadsworth Longfellow was memorialized in Portland, Maine (Simmons, 1888); Nathaniel Hawthorne's image was raised in Salem, Mass. (Bela Lyon Pratt, 1916); Edna St. Vincent Millay's portrait was erected in Camden, Maine (Robert Willis, 1989); William Ellery Channing was honored by his native city of Newport, R.I. (W. Clark Noble, 1892), and his adopted city of Boston (Herbert Adams, 1902). Daniel Chester French fabricated a handsome seated portrait of John Harvard for Harvard University in 1884.

The Civil War created a tragic new market for monuments. Both public and private agencies commissioned the works that line Boston's Commonwealth Avenue and Public Garden, shaping the city's image as an abolitionist bastion. The Commonwealth sponsored the Sumner commission; the city honored Wendell Phillips with a portrait by French (1915); a public subscription funded Olin Levi Warner's portrait of the abolitionist editor of the *Liberator*, William Lloyd Garrison (1886). After viewing Ball's *Emancipation Group* in Washington, D.C., local politician and museum entrepreneur Moses Kimball ordered a replica for Boston's Park Square (1877). Ball's now-controversial motif of a seminude slave whose features derived from one-time fugitive Archibald Alexander, kneeling in gratitude beneath Abraham Lincoln's outstretched hand, originated in abolitionist imagery.

The sheer scale of the carnage of the Civil War also inspired a new nonportrait monument. Milmore's poignant Union soldier at

parade rest, introspective and withdrawn, was conceived for Forest Hills Cemetery in Roxbury, Mass. (1869), and was copied in bronze, granite, and zinc for cemeteries and town squares throughout New England. A more complex monument type, fusing figures of servicemen with such allegorical figures as Peace, History, and America was introduced by Randolph Rogers in his design of 1866 for *Soldiers' and Sailors' Monument* in Providence (1870), a format he repeated in Worcester, Mass. (1874). This flexible composite of images proved popular, and it was employed by Simmons in Portland (1890), Mead in St. Johnsbury, Vt. (1868), Milmore at the Boston Common (1877), and numerous monument manufacturing companies.

In his *Memorial to Robert Gould Shaw and the Massachusetts Fifty-fourth Regiment* (1897), Augustus Saint-Gaudens transcended the conventions of Civil War monuments. In an unusually deep relief, the equestrian colonel proceeds along Boston's Beacon Street, flanked by his troops. The state's first black regiment demonstrated its discipline and courage in battle at Fort Wagner, S.C., where many died. Saint-Gaudens carefully individuated his figures, who march with a rhythmic, purposeful cadence. He replaced the traditional Victory with an ethereal female floating overhead, bearing an olive branch and poppies. Set into a massive frame designed by the architect Charles Follen McKim, the monument faces the Boston Common and the State House.

Revolutionary valor was also recalled in nonportrait images commissioned after the Civil War, as New Englanders began to search their past. Raymond Porter's *Green Mountain Boy* in Rutland, Vt. (1915), celebrates Vermont's colonial resistance to land claims made by New York and New Hampshire. Concord, Mass., proclaimed its role in the Revolution by commissioning *The Minute Man* (1874) from French. His alert sentinel clutches a musket and guards the contested bridge where British and colonists engaged a century before. Lexington belatedly celebrated its preeminent status in the Revolution by acquiring its *Minute Man* (1900) from Henry Kitson.

With considerable foresight, architect and sculptor Hammatt Billings designed colossal monuments to Daniel Webster (1852) and a minuteman (1859). Although these were never realized, his *National Monument to the Forefathers* was finally dedicated at Plymouth in 1889. This 81-foot granite ensemble includes a towering Faith hovering over personifications of Law, Liberty, Morality, and Education. Reliefs depict the Pilgrims' history. As a symbol of New England, this rather astonishing assemblage was undermined by Saint-Gaudens's "portrait" of Deacon Samuel Chapin, a founder of Springfield, Mass. Commissioned by his descendant Chester Chapin, and popularly known as *The Puritan* (1883–86, Metropolitan Museum of Art, New York), this powerful figure is rendered even more monumental because of his billowing cape and mighty stride. Like Ball's *Webster*, the *Puritan* was popularized through copies and reductions.

While most 19th-century public sculpture was didactic, Frederick MacMonnies's *Bacchante with an Infant Faun* (1893–94) sparked a furor in Boston. The dancing nude woman, clutching an infant Bacchus and a bunch of grapes, was presented by the sculptor to McKim, the principal architect of the Public Library. He, in turn, planned to site the sculpture in the courtyard of his masterful creation. The exuberant abandon of the *Bacchante* provoked opposition between library officials (among them Harvard professor Charles Eliot Norton) and artists (among them Saint-Gaudens and French). Following a hotly debated Boston exhibition, McKim donated the *Bacchante* to New York's Metropolitan Museum. Today a new bronze, cast in 1993 for the fountain, is displayed in an alcove in the Public Library. Pratt's draped females, *Art and Science* (1911), guard the entrance to McKim's library.

Monuments to civic heroes continued to appear in the 20th century, along with new images dedicated to New England's industry, such as Mico Kaufman's commemoration of Lowell's female textile workers (1984). The region's older maritime commerce was celebrated more frequently. Leonard Craske's *Gloucester Fisherman* (1925) portrays a sturdy New Englander braving a squall, and Victor Kahill's plaster *Maine Lobsterman*, which was initially exhibited at the 1939 World's Fair, proved so popular that it was cast in 1970 (Harpswell, Maine). For his *Spirit of the Sea* (1962), a gift to his adopted town of Bath, Maine, William Zorach celebrated the state's maritime history with a lyrical female fountain figure. More recently, Susumu Shingu reiterated the region's connection with the sea in his *Echo of the Waves* (1983), a graceful kinetic abstraction that is appropriately sited at the New England Aquarium in Boston.

Few of these commissions provoked the public, but a number of recent projects have generated intermittent controversy. In the charged climate of the 1960s, Claes Oldenburg's phallic *Lipstick (Ascending) on Caterpillar Tracks* (1969–70, Yale University, New Haven, Conn.) criticized the Vietnam War as well as the university's architecture. Carl Andre's *Stone Field Sculpture* (1977), an installation of 36 boulders, was lampooned as a waste

of taxpayers' money. A native of New England, Andre arranged his giant "markers" in eight orderly rows that increased in number and diminished in size, echoing the nearby headstones in an old burying ground and evoking the unique glacial geology of the New England region through his materials. In Boston, after a prolonged public debate reminiscent of colonial town meetings, the *New England Holocaust Memorial* was dedicated in 1995. Designed by Stanley Saitowitz, its six giant glass towers are etched with the numbers of the Holocaust dead. Lava rocks in subterranean pits glow faintly, and biographical excerpts line the visitor's path beneath the towers. Both sensory and cerebral, the *Holocaust Memorial* nonetheless continues to elicit criticism because of its busy location between Faneuil Hall and Boston's City Hall.

John Beardsley, *Art in Public Places* (1981); Marty Carlock, *A Guide to Public Art in Greater Boston: From Newburyport to Plymouth* (1993); Wayne Craven, *Sculpture in America* (1984); Janet A. Headley, "Anne Whitney's Leif Erikson: A Brahmin Response to Christopher Columbus," *American Art* 17 (Summer 2003); Museum of Fine Arts, Boston, *American Figurative Sculpture in the Museum of Fine Arts, Boston* (1986); Martha Norkunas, *Monuments and Memory: History and Representation in Lowell, Massachusetts* (2002); Julia Rosenbaum, "Displaying Civic Culture: The Controversy over Frederick MacMonnies' *Bacchante*," *American Art* 14 (Fall 2000); James E. Young, *The Texture of Memory: Holocaust Memorials and Meaning* (1993).

Janet A. Headley

Reproductions In the 19th century self-appointed moralists of the middle class, such as New Englanders Catherine Beecher and Harriet Beecher Stowe in *The American Woman's Home* (1869), proclaimed that the reproduction of paintings would encourage aesthetic refinement and moral uprightness among members of the public aspiring to middle-class status. Those who could not afford original paintings could purchase inexpensive engravings and lithographs to hang in their parlors and dining rooms. These art reproductions, *The American Woman's Home* suggested, would augment the power of the home to shape the family and the nation.

Imagined as the quintessential rural region, New England was one of the subjects that provided moral lessons. Although city dwellers were their target audience, artists and entrepreneurs who reproduced paintings as engravings and lithographs rarely depicted urban scenes. Their New England did not include factory precincts or ethnic neighborhoods. The paintings they chose for reproduction typically showed thriving farms and rural villages where New Englanders of English stock sustained values of hard work,

family loyalty, religious piety, and democratic fraternity.

In paintings entitled *New England Scenery*, Thomas Cole in 1839 and Frederic Edwin Church in 1851 depicted pastoral landscapes. The painters led the viewer's eye to a rural village in the middle distance, whose civilizing force was symbolized by a prominent church steeple. These essential elements appeared in an engraving by James Smillie based on John Frederick Kensett's painting *The White Mountains: Mount Washington* (1851, Wellesley College Museum, Mass.), which was distributed to more than 8,000 members of the American Art-Union. Other artists, such as Eastman Johnson and George Henry Durrie, elaborated the pastoral vision of New England, especially its celebration of the rural village, and entrepreneurs eagerly reproduced their paintings as engravings and lithographs for mass sale.

The lithographic firm Currier and Ives favored New England paintings that portrayed rural simplicity and forms of cooperative activity, equivalents of the New England town meeting. Reproductions such as the Currier and Ives lithographs of Johnson's *Corn Husking* (1861, Everson Museum of Art, Syracuse, N.Y.) and Durrie's *Autumn in New England, Cider Making* (1863, New York Historical Association) were published in large lots, some of which numbered in the hundreds of thousands. Increasingly, however, scenes that idealized New England rural life were generalized to the nation as a whole and associated with a quaint, receding past. The best-selling Currier and Ives lithograph of Durrie's *Home to Thanksgiving* (1867), based on Durrie's *Farmyard Winter* (1862, New-York Historical Society), emphasized the theme of travelers returning home. This theme became prominent as economic decline and out-migration transformed New England farms and villages. By 1874 the image of the rural village with its steeple evoked a vanishing world. In that year F. Gleason offered a chromolithograph of Durrie's painting *Going to Church* (1853, White House Collection), giving it the nostalgic title *Winter Sunday in Olden Times*.

In the late 19th century Louis Prang's chromolithographic firm expanded the idealized vision of New England to maritime scenes, reproducing Louis K. Harlow's watercolors of rustic fishing villages. Prang also tested the market with a chromo of Winslow Homer's watercolor *The Watch, Eastern Shore* (1894, private collection). But that venture proved a commercial failure. The market for art reproductions suitable for framing was on the decline.

By the 1890s moralists no longer saw art reproductions as a means of reaching a broad public. The image of New England found in engravings and lithographs had always competed with comparable representations put to other purposes in magazine, calendar, and advertising illustration. Until the 1960s Norman Rockwell's cover artwork for the *Saturday Evening Post* occasionally offered, if in disposable form, the moralizing imagery once associated with rural New England. Moralists were finally superseded by promoters of tourism, who detached images of New England farms and villages from their didactic meanings and used them to portray New England as a place of escape and respite for busy urbanites.

Sarah Burns, *Pastoral Inventions: Rural Life in 19th-Century American Art and Culture* (1989); Bryan Le Beau, *Currier and Ives: America Imagined* (2001); Peter C. Marzio, *The Democratic Art: Pictures for a 19th-Century America; Chromolithography, 1840–1900* (1979); Angela Miller, *The Empire of the Eye: Landscape Representation and American Cultural Politics, 1825–1875* (1993); William H. Truettner and Roger B. Stein, eds., *Picturing Old New England: Image and Memory* (1999).

Rodney D. Olsen

Rockwell, Norman (1894–1978) Illustrator. Norman Rockwell was born in New York City and grew up in a tough neighborhood on Manhattan's Amsterdam Avenue. He studied at the National Academy of Design and at the Art Students League with artists George Bridgeman and Thomas Fogarty, and published his first illustrations in 1912. Rockwell's early idealized renderings of New England were direct responses to the grittiness of his city upbringing. A quintessentially urban mode of escapism—summer boarding in the country with his family in Orange County, N.Y.—proved particularly influential to his work. In *My Adventures as an Illustrator* Rockwell reminisced, "Those summers seemed blissful. I guess I have a bad case of the American nostalgia for the clean, simple country life as opposed to the complicated world of the city." The vision of a pure, old-fashioned America, packaged and heavily marketed by promoters of New England tourism, became integral to the work of the nation's most popular illustrator. Reproduced on magazine covers and in advertisements, Rockwell's pictures made their way into the homes of millions of Americans. Even today, Rockwell's New England images continue to proliferate in the media: in magazines, on telephone calling cards, on the World Wide Web, and in films such as George Roy Hill's comedy *Funny Farm* (1988).

Rockwell's early depictions of New Englanders expressed attitudes now identified with the Colonial Revival movement of the 1920s. Reminiscent of simpler, seemingly more honest times, these images mediated between past and present. *Saturday Evening Post*

Norman Rockwell in his studio, 1966

(*SEP*) covers *Pipe and Bowl Sign Painter* (February 6, 1926) and *Silhouette of a Colonial Lady* (September 24, 1927), along with advertisements for such products as Interwoven Socks—depicting turkeys and a befuddled Pilgrim dodging Indian arrows (*SEP*, November 18, 1922) and a colonial father "socking" his son (*SEP*, February 11, 1928)—portrayed icons of the past behaving like ordinary contemporary Americans. An elderly grandmother with her colonial house furnishings pictured on the cover of the 1925 Montgomery Ward catalog and the picturesque Colonial Revival–style main street of an Overland Motors advertisement (*SEP*, March 17, 1923) used associations with New England frugality, honesty, tradition, and handicraft to sell modern, national, standardized products.

Rockwell lived near New York City during his early career, but in 1938 he moved to Arlington, Vt., first as a summer resident and then as a year-rounder; when his studio there burned in 1943, Rockwell relocated to West Arlington. Once he became a New Englander himself, Rockwell began to root his representations more explicitly in locale. Although still seeking to suggest a universality of experience, Rockwell highlighted specific aspects of regional character, community, and topography. One of the paintings in his famous *Four Freedoms* series (*SEP*, February 20, 27, March 6, 13, 1943; subsequently sent on national tour and reproduced as war-bond posters), *Freedom of Speech*, evoked the ideal of participatory politics in its depiction of a New England town

meeting. Here and elsewhere Rockwell used his Vermont neighbors as models to lend authenticity to his work. In *Shuffleton's Barbershop* (*SEP*, April 29, 1950), Rockwell rendered a modest local barbershop as a place where the spaces of work and leisure (commercial and noncommercial) literally merged. Photographs, combined with rough on-site sketches, helped Rockwell to convey a sense of a particular New England place as both unique and typical.

Rockwell left Vermont in 1953 and moved to Stockbridge, Mass. In *Home for Christmas (Stockbridge Mainstreet at Christmas)* (*McCall's*, December 1967), Rockwell introduced Americans to this picturesque Berkshire town where he died in 1978. The formation of the Norman Rockwell Museum in 1969, the opening of Rockwell's studio to the public on the new museum site in 1986, and the inauguration of the museum's new exhibition building in 1993 have helped Stockbridge become the cultural and tourist mecca of western Massachusetts.

Michele H. Bogart, *Artists, Advertising, and the Borders of Art* (1995); Maureen Hart Hennessey and Anne Knutson, *Norman Rockwell: Pictures for the American People* (1999); Karal Ann Marling, *Norman Rockwell* (1997); Laurie Norton Moffatt, *Norman Rockwell: A Definitive Catalogue* (1986); Norman Rockwell (as told to Tom Rockwell), *Norman Rockwell: My Adventures as an Illustrator* (1960).

Michele H. Bogart

Rogers Groups Thanks to the extensive distribution of the popular anecdotal genre pieces known as Rogers Groups, John Rogers (1829–1904) became the most widely known American sculptor of the 19th century. Many of his sculptures were inspired by themes and subjects drawn from New England history and literature. In such works as *The Fugitive's Story* (1869) and *"Why Don't You Speak for Yourself, John?"* (1885), Rogers helped shape the rich visual and literary imagery of New England that became a national middle-class commodity during the second half of the 19th century.

Born into a distinguished family in Salem, Mass., Rogers initially pursued a career as a mechanic and draftsman while using his leisure time to model small figures in clay for the amusement of family and friends. When he lost his job in the Panic of 1857, he decided to attempt a career as a professional sculptor. He spent nearly a year in Europe seeking instruction and encouragement but found the prevailing neoclassical taste in sculpture at odds with his own naturalistic style. Discouraged, he returned home and took a job in the office of the city surveyor in Chicago.

The turning point for Rogers came in 1859, when he sent one of his groups, *Checker Players,* to a local fair in Chicago, where it attracted many admirers. Greatly encouraged, Rogers moved to New York City, where he quickly learned how to reproduce and market his statuettes. Within a few years demand for the pieces led to the construction of a factory, where upwards of 20 assistants helped the sculptor turn out thousands of plaster copies finished with a coat of gray or tan paint. Promoted by catalogs and stereopticon cards, Rogers Groups were sold in stores across the country for an average price of $14.

Rogers perfected a straightforward realistic style, modeling figures that usually stood between 12 and 14 inches high. Using expressive gestures and facial features with carefully selected accessories, he depicted simple events and themes that were easily understood by an emerging middle class eager to bring art into nicely decorated parlors. His best works, including several proabolitionist pieces and a series celebrating the Union soldier, captured the popular sentiments and emotions surrounding the Civil War. His *Union Refugees* won Rogers election to the National Academy of Design in 1863. In *Taking the Oath and Drawing Rations* (1865), perhaps his finest work, a dignified southern woman takes an oath of loyalty from a conquering though sympathetic Union officer. The underlying message of reconciliation toward the South won the sculptor much praise. Rogers also excelled at portrait sculpture, producing one of the best contemporary images of Abraham Lincoln in *The Council of War* (1868).

During the last two decades of his career Rogers turned more to the amusing, often overtly sentimental scenes of everyday life for which he is most famous. His anecdotal *Coming to the Parson* (1870) sold 8,000 copies. He also illustrated historical subjects, popular legends, and scenes from Shakespeare, whose staginess and excessive use of detail often made them less successful than works based on more ordinary subjects. Rogers attempted several large-scale works as well. His seated figure of Lincoln, one-third larger than lifesize, won him a gold medal at the World's Colombian Exposition in Chicago in 1893. In 1910 a bronze replica of the original plaster piece was cast and placed at the entrance to the present-day Central High School in Manchester, N.H.

By 1893 declining sales and poor health forced Rogers to sell his business and retire to his home in New Canaan, Conn., where he died in 1904. Between 1860 and 1893 Rogers's firm produced an estimated 80,000 copies of some 80 sculptures, an unrivaled accomplishment within the American realist tradition and a unique achievement.

Rogers's Connecticut studio, built in 1878, became a National Historic Landmark in 1966. The New Canaan Historical Society now runs the studio as a museum, where visitors may view a large collection of Rogers's famous statues, many of them sculpted on-site.

Paul and Meta Bleier, *John Rogers' Groups of Statuary: A Pictorial and Annotated Guide for the Collector* (1971); Walter A. Dyer, "The Sculptures of John Rogers," *Antiques* 9 (1926); Chetwood Smith and Mary Chapin Smith, *Rogers Groups, Thought and Wrought* (1934); David H. Wallace, *John Rogers: The People's Sculptor* (1967).

Dean Lahikainen

Saint-Gaudens, Augustus (1848–1907)

Sculptor. Augustus Saint-Gaudens was the best known and most influential American sculptor of the last quarter of the 19th century and a major force in changing artistic taste in the United States. In sculpture, this change was manifested in a shift from neoclassicism, which had been the dominant style of the antebellum period, to the freer, more realistic concerns being expressed by the leading sculptors of Europe, most notably the French. Although Saint-Gaudens was born in Ireland and spent the early years of his professional career in New York and Europe, he became as affiliated with New England as with any of those places.

Saint-Gaudens began his formal art training in 1863 at New York's National Academy of Design while gaining practical experience as a cameo cutter. In 1867 he went to Paris, where he studied in the atelier of François Jouffroy and at the Petit Ecole and the Ecole des Beaux-Arts. He spent the early 1870s in Rome, where he met his first major patrons. On his return to the United States, he took an active role in the New York art world. He joined the Tile Club, began participating in the annual exhibitions of the National Academy, and in 1877 was one of the founders of the innovative Society of American Artists.

The sculptor's connection to New England began while he was studying and working in Europe in the 1870s. There, in 1873, he met his future wife, Augusta Homer, a member of an old Boston family. Among the other New Englanders he befriended during these years were Henry Adams, John La Farge, John Singer Sargent, and William Dean Howells.

Saint-Gaudens's first artistic success was a life-size bronze monument to Admiral David Farragut, which was unveiled in Madison Square Park, New York, in 1881. Other major commissions soon followed, including a figure of the goddess Diana for the top of Madison Square Garden; the large relief monument to Robert Gould Shaw in Boston Common; the gilded bronze equestrian statue of William Tecumseh Sherman at the corner of Central Park in New York; and the allegorical figure for the Washington, D.C., grave of Marion Hooper, Henry Adams's wife.

In 1885 Saint-Gaudens and his wife rented an old inn for the summer at Cornish, N.H.; the sculptor used its barn for his studio. They continued to rent the property each summer until 1891, when they bought the inn, remodeled it, and named it Aspet after the small French village where the sculptor's father was born. In subsequent years they added several studios to the grounds, and Aspet became the year-round center of an active and influential art colony. Kenyon Cox, Thomas Dewing, Paul Manship, Willard Metcalf, Charles Adams Platt, and Abbott Thayer were among their neighbors. In 1904 a fire in one of the studios destroyed a number of Saint-Gaudens's models, casts, drawings, and tools. Following the sculptor's death in 1907, Aspet and the surrounding property were transferred to the Saint-Gaudens Memorial, a corporation founded by Augusta and her son, Homer, to preserve the memory of her husband. Today Saint-Gaudens's home is a designated National Historic Site and is maintained by the National Park Service.

John Dryfhout, *The Work of Augustus Saint-Gaudens* (1982); Kathryn Greenthal, *Augustus Saint-Gaudens, Master Sculptor* (1985); Homer Saint-Gaudens, *The Reminiscences of Augustus Saint-Gaudens* (1913); University Art Galleries, University of New Hampshire, and Thorne-Sagendorph Art Gallery, Keene State

College, *A Circle of Friends: Art Colonies of Cornish and Dublin* (1985).

David B. Dearinger

Sample, Paul Starrett (1896–1974)

Painter. Among the best-known New England painters of the 1930s, Paul Starrett Sample enjoyed national prominence until the demise of the regionalist movement at the close of World War II. Born in Louisville, Ky., Sample graduated from Dartmouth College in 1920. He returned to his alma mater as artist-in-residence in 1938 and remained in this position until 1962, living in nearby Norwich, Vt. While in residence at Dartmouth, Sample joined John Steuart Curry (University of Wisconsin) and Grant Wood (University of Iowa) in a triumvirate of American Scene painters in academe. Generally hostile to European modernism, they helped to shape the conservative art curriculum of many colleges and universities during the period. In depicting primarily rural activities and historic events, these and other American Scene painters of the regionalist movement created images that embodied American democratic and religious traditions—traditions they felt could form a bulwark against communism and fascism. Their work also reflected a critique of urbanism and unregulated capitalism.

Sample's first major regionalist work, *Church Supper* (1933, Museum of Fine Arts, Springfield, Mass.), reveals the influence of Grant Wood in its use of rounded pneumatic figures, bulbous hills, and ribbon roads. The rotund Vermonters seated at diagonally aligned tables also recall the robust peasants in the work of the Flemish master Pieter Brueghel the Elder (1525/30–69) and reveal Sample's lifelong affection for Brueghel's paintings. A second celebrated canvas, *Janitor's Holiday,* acquired by the Metropolitan Museum of Art in New York in 1937, was largely responsible for securing Sample's national reputation. Equally indebted to Brueghel's rural genre scenes, this painting is among the foremost examples of the work of the "Brueghel Revival" group, a subset of regionalist artists that also included Wood, Molly Luce, and Thomas Hart Benton.

Sample's last nationally celebrated work of art, *Beaver Meadow* (1939, Hood Museum of Art, Dartmouth College, Hanover, N.H.), was painted on the eve of World War II. This elegiac canvas celebrated Vermont as a rural Eden, free of the gritty realities of modern industry and urbanism. Its nostalgic view of small-town New England influenced many artists including Norman Rockwell, whose wartime series *The Four Freedoms* was set in Arlington, Vt. Sample's *Maple Sugaring* (1944,

private collection), a scene depicting a figure carrying sap buckets to a sugarhouse, has been used as the logo for a Vermont maple syrup producer for more than 50 years. Affirming the ideal of rural self-sufficiency, the image has also become a major icon of Vermont's enduring pastoral mythology.

During the war years, Sample toured the Atlantic and Pacific theaters of combat as an artist and correspondent for Time-Life; many of his reportorial images were published in *Life* magazine during the 1940s. By this time, however, the regionalist movement had been eclipsed by the emergence of the New York school of abstract expressionism. Sample, together with his rural cohort, largely disappeared from the national scene. The artist's late works, partially derived from the postimpressionist aesthetic system of the French artist Paul Cézanne, focused on pastoral sentiment at the expense of rural narrative, striving to integrate small figures with broadly conceived, geometrically abstracted elements of landscape. Sample died at his home in Norwich, Vt.

John Haletsky, *Paul Sample: Ivy League Regionalist* (1984); Robert L. McGrath, *Paul Sample: Painter of the American Scene* (1988).

Robert L. McGrath

Sculpture, 1900 to the Present

During the 20th century and into the 21st, numerous sculptors have spent major parts of their careers in New England, where they often have found natural settings conducive to creative endeavor, studio spaces to accommodate their work, natural resources suitable as artistic mediums, commissions, and teaching positions. Their sculptures reflect diverse styles from traditional realism to modern and contemporary trends. Within this diversity, New England sculptors traditionally have produced at least three general types of works: the public monument, figurative sculpture, and sculpture inspired by the natural environment.

The public monument is often inspired by the region's rich history; its moral spirit and tradition of patriotism; and its impressive number of war heroes, important statesmen, and learned men and women. Public sculpture also serves to reinscribe the region's traditional values. Examples of early-20th-century works include Daniel Chester French's *Melvin Memorial* (1906–8), located in Concord, N.H., honoring three brothers who died in the Civil War. Richard Recchia's equestrian statue of the Revolutionary War hero General John Stark was erected in 1948 in Manchester, N.H. In Boston, more recent public monuments include Lloyd Lillie's work depicting Mayor James Curley (1980, Copley Place); Penelope Jencks's sculpture representing the historian Samuel Eliot Morison (1982, Commonwealth Avenue); and Isabel McIlvain's statue of John Fitzgerald Kennedy (1989, State House).

Figurative sculpture in New England shares with public monuments a strongly humanistic approach, specifically, an emphasis on human dignity, depth of character, and the spirit of the individual. An abiding interest in classical values within many New England artistic and educational circles has in some cases been an important stimulus. George Demetrios pro-

Tom Doyle, Dolmen *(ca. 1997, Roxbury, Conn.)*

duced many character heads using people of Cape Ann, Mass., as models. Marianna Pineda depicted women as oracles in a series on the female figure. Leonard Baskin has conveyed tragic dignity in his carved wood figures, often in mammoth proportions. Harold Tovish has concentrated on the human head throughout his career, often evoking the endurance of the human spirit.

Many sculptors of the region have also frequently produced works influenced by the natural environment, whether in the use of local stone or wood, or in the choice of subjects or abstract forms. Wood and stone carvers such as Robert Laurent and his artistic successors worked and taught at the Ogunquit School of Painting and Sculpture in Ogunquit, Maine. Nick Edmonds has carved many wood landscape sculptures containing tree and rock motifs. Elliot Offner has depicted birds and other wildlife, with an accent on motion and feeling. Gilbert Franklin has sculpted a series of figurative works with forms inspired by rocks and shells, while Richard Rosenblum has composed large figures out of tree roots. Using blocks of stone, Dimitri Hadzi has produced large abstract sculptures, including one in Boston at Copley Place featuring a waterfall (1982–83). For a private memorial (1997), Tom Doyle has worked with local stone to create a dolmen-like form on outcropping rocks in a field in Roxbury, Conn.

New England has several influential venues for the display of sculpture by artists from this region and beyond, including the DeCordova Museum and Sculpture Park in Lincoln, Mass.; Chesterwood, the Stockbridge, Mass., home and studio of Daniel Chester French, which features an annual outdoor show; and the Massachusetts Museum of Contemporary Art (MASS MoCA) in North Adams, which opened to the public in 1999.

Wayne V. Andersen, *American Sculpture in Process: 1930–1970* (1975); John H. Dryfhout, *The Work of Augustus Saint-Gaudens* (1982); Margaret A. Robinette, *Outdoor Sculpture: Object and Environment* (1976).

Trudie Grace

Seascapes A seascape is an artwork depicting a marine landscape. Some of the most important products of American art were created in this genre, which typically reflects the historical and artistic developments of the 19th century and artists' sentiments about life, nature, and cultural identity. The cultural and social historians Raymond Williams and Eric Hobsbawm first proposed that 19th-century Europeans "invented" traditions, developed cultural symbols, and produced images to support the establishment of national and regional identities. A prime example of the invention of culture and place in New England, and particularly of its seascape, is the discovery by landscape painters of Mount Desert Island, Maine, and its subsequent transformation into a tourist destination and a national symbol of New England's coastal wilderness.

Seascapes had been created by earlier New England artists, including the overmantel paintings, ship paintings, and harbor scenes of Michele Felice Corné, as well as early Romantic works by Washington Allston. New Englanders also favored vernacular images of the working waterfront, lighthouse scenes, and popular whaling panoramas, but the signature seascape tradition involved a group of painters who were drawn to the rugged Maine coast. In 1845 the Hudson River School painter Thomas Cole introduced the impressive scenery of Mount Desert Island to New Yorkers and potential tourists, and during the 1850s and 1860s Frederic Edwin Church, Cole's talented student, promoted the island's wild beauty. Church's paintings enjoyed impressive critical success in the Northeast and generated enthusiasm among metropolitan audiences for this increasingly accessible coastal wilderness. In his works, the bold, sculptured coast of Mount Desert Island appeared to be the work of a divine creator; this mountainous wilderness soon became a symbol of the northeastern landscape, the bedrock of the nation.

At first glance, Church's *Beacon, off Mount Desert Island* (1851, private collection) depicts simply a stone mariner's beacon, a broad expanse of empty sea, and a radiant, cloud-filled sky. Yet the image contains multiple layers of meaning: literal and symbolic associations that promoted elite attitudes about the Maine seacoast as a symbol of America's national identity and provided a visual meditation on Protestant ideas of salvation. The beacon is an emblem of safety, perhaps even of salvation, because of its grounding on rock. Beacons, like ships, were understood as metaphors for the human condition. A day marker directs vessels to safe channels and harbors, and a beacon offers assurance of safe passage; at an emblematic and symbolic level, the beacon could offer guidance to salvation, both personal and national. Distant ships and sea birds hovering near the beacon are the only signs of life. Church's contemporaries could read these as emblems of a divine presence that reinforced Protestant symbolism of personal transcendence and salvation. At its most commercial level of meaning the painting appealed to those for whom it was a vicarious substitute for travel. To this audience *Beacon* was a visual novelty for city dwellers seeking to escape the heat of summer.

Similarly, Church's *The Wreck* (1852, The Parthenon, Nashville, Tenn.) is a painting of dramatic sky, clouds, and the sea, intermingled with powerful associations of personal religious transcendence. The storm-tossed or wrecked ship was a popular subject in the 19th century. The sea and New England's coastline were essential for transportation, commerce, and military power. Simultaneously beautiful and dangerous, the rocky coastline was both the route to business opportunity and a continuing peril for travelers. Several elements in *The Wreck* suggest a hopeful outcome in a Puritan world of predestination. Natural signs abound: most obvious is the cruciform formed by the wrecked schooner's mast and spars, signifying Protestant notions of personal deliverance. Just beyond the mast, seabirds circle—visual conventions suggesting salvation, ministered by natural spirits. The sky opens in a halo of light, the sun casts light through clouds to the sea, and the ship's bow points at and pierces this light. The cross of light is a celestial reflection of the cruciform shape of the spars on the wrecked schooner. Moreover, the ratlines on the mast create a triangular shape, subtly reinforcing the rays of the light cross. To mid-19th-century audiences, this light was the "most essential element of sublimity."

In 1863 Church produced one of his most powerful paintings, *Coast Scene, Mount Desert* (Wadsworth Atheneum, Hartford), an image of light breaking through sunrise mist over a rocky New England coast that held important associations for Americans during the Civil War. In the image Church represented associations of struggle and triumph with issues of national importance and personal loss. Great waves crash against an unyielding rocky shore. At the center foreground a prominent rock functions as a microcosm of the vast, sublime crags that tower beyond. The water and rock in the foreground are suggestively repeated many times in the craggy peninsula in the middle distance and the great headland. At the right, passages of rock appear as suggestive profiles, impassive, unmoving, rock heads—silent witness to the unceasing tumult of wave and water. Church's primeval wilderness is a New England vision of America much as his ancestors in the Massachusetts Bay Colony and Connecticut might have imagined it. Paintings such as *Coast Scene* accomplish in visual terms what the "Battle Hymn of the Republic" and the Gettysburg Address accomplish in speech.

Other painters followed Church to Mount Desert, including Fitz Hugh Lane, whose seascapes are more contemplative. Lane is also well known for his luminous scenes of Massachusetts's North Shore and his Boston harbor paintings. Martin Johnson Heade created dramatic canvases of thunderstorms on Rhode Island's Narragansett Bay, while John Frederick

Kensett pictured empty beaches and antediluvian rock formations. American seascapes were transformed from the Romantic mode to the modern by Winslow Homer, especially in his late impressionist paintings of rock and surf done at his Prout's Neck studio in Maine. In the 20th century, Maine's coast was rediscovered by another generation of artists whose seascapes took many forms, from the images of hardy fisherman by N. C. Wyeth to the abstract works of John Marin and Marsden Hartley. As in the earlier case of Church, these artists were linked by aesthetics and the marketplace to the New York art world but found a refuge and personal inspiration in the elements of the Maine coast.

Pamela J. Belanger, *Inventing Acadia: Artists and Tourists at Mount Desert* (1999); Dona Brown, *Inventing New England: Regional Tourism in the 19th Century* (1995); Eric Hobsbawm and Terence Ranger, *The Invention of Tradition* (1983); David Lowenthal, *The Path Is a Foreign Country* (1985); John F. Sears, *Sacred Places: American Tourist Attractions in the 19th Century* (1989); Roger B. Stein, *Seascape and the American Imagination* (1975); John Wilmerding, *American Marine Painting* (1987).

Pamela J. Belanger

Shaker Design

Shaker design is the tangible aesthetic expression of the Christian, communitarian Shaker movement founded in the late 18th century by the English-born Ann Lee. The radical religion of the Shakers developed and flourished in New York and New England between 1780 and 1800 before spreading westward to Ohio and Kentucky in the early 19th century. Its growth was part of a larger religious revival in the northeastern United States known as the Second Great Awakening.

Shaker leaders of the years 1780–1815 created a new social order to fulfill their religious objectives. This creation involved the rejection of the old order of Christian belief and practice and of prevailing American social, economic, and political relationships. The Shaker way required appropriate substitutions and alternatives to the old order in belief, behavior, and material culture. The ultimate expression of the new Shaker way was the concept of planned communities, called Shaker villages, of which 19 were established, nine in New England.

Shaker design is a collective visual expression of the community rather than an individual aesthetic preference. Developing out of a particular time and place, it is essentially a New England vernacular interpretation of neoclassicism. However, the Shakers generated highly original and creative applications of the neoclassical style, which rejected many aspects of the prevailing fashion system of

Trustees' House, hallway, Canterbury Shaker Village, N.H.

Anglo-American culture. Shaker material culture, from architecture to oval boxes, responded more to internal Shaker purpose than to traditional market forces. Ornamentation was subordinated to form and function. Color, though intense, was subject to collective intent and used within the communities to distinguish specific functions. Variation in form and decoration was permitted among their communities but only within a relatively narrow definition of Shaker propriety.

The resulting design system is unmistakably Shaker, within the broader context of Anglo-American neoclassicism. It is also surprisingly industrial in character for a system originally created to serve religious ends. Classic Shaker design calls for replication and standardization. The Shakers did not invent peg rail, which features turned wooden pegs projected from a horizontal molded rail, but they elevated a minor native architectural feature to the status of a Shaker signature. Shaker peg rail appearing on all sides of every room in every building exemplifies the role of replication and standardization in Shaker design. In their use of peg rail, the Shakers employed an early concept of industrial design to enhance the originality of Shaker interiors and maintain the quality of indoor woodworking.

Shaker design expresses the Shaker community ideals of order, harmony, integrity, efficiency, and functionality. These principles, as commonly interpreted from a 20th-century perspective, mark the Shakers as exponents of the credo that form follows function and as precursors of American modernism. This interpretation is partly legitimate, but it distorts the original intent of Shaker design.

In the early 19th century, Shaker design involved process as well as product. It was a way

of translating complex ideas into physical forms ranging from buildings to household furnishings to woodenware. The goal of the process was to produce not one-of-a-kind, original designs but practical, appropriate ones that met the tests of utility, quality, and "good fit" and could be replicated. The practical result of this process is that "Shaker made" represents a continuum of products, some of which are obvious bearers of the Shaker style, and some of which veer toward the prevailing style systems of the wider society. For example, Shaker peg rail could immediately "Shakerize" any interior space. Such rails maintained their essential Shaker character even when the wooden pegs were replaced with iron hooks. Similarly, the Shaker oval box still expresses Shaker efficiency and minimalism whether made entirely by hand or with the aid of machinery.

The Shakers created their distinctive oval boxes by adapting a common 19th-century bentwood storage container or measure. These round boxes with fitted lids were fastened with a straight seam riveted with metal tacks and were used for storing dry goods and cheeses. The Shakers improved the design, durability, and strength of these boxes by selecting superior quartersawed hardwoods, quartersawing the single side piece of wood, refining the shape to an oval, and inventing elongated finger-lap joints that were fastened with copper tacks. The result was a virtually indestructible "Shaker style" box.

Shaker furniture makers followed a similar adaptive path, transforming such vernacular forms as the ladder-back chair into a Shaker design. The signature Shaker chair pares fine hardwood stock to minimal dimensions to maximize strength, durability, lightness, and practicality. On straight ladder-back chairs the Shakers embedded a replaceable wooden button, or tilter, into the feet of the chair's rear stiles to permit the user to lean back and tilt the chair with ease. On these same chairs, vernacular splint or rush seats, which became dirty and brittle with wear, were replaced with narrow strips of Shaker handwoven fabric tape. This cloth tape was in turn interwoven into a colorful, flexible, and long-lasting chair seat.

Shaker case furniture, whether freestanding or built into Shaker interior architecture, also exhibited features of the Shakers' design aesthetic. Stressing pure geometry, these furniture forms achieved freshness through the creative application and interplay of bilateral symmetry, asymmetry, graduation in drawer sizes, and surface refinement. Built-in storage cupboards and cases of drawers are as integral to Shaker interior design as peg rail. Always crafted primarily to serve a mundane storage function, Shaker case furniture elevated the storage of material goods to an art form.

By the late 19th century, the Shakers were successfully marketing their own design concept to the larger world, especially in the form of "production" chairs made in the New Lebanon, N.Y., community. Non-Shaker furniture makers in the northeastern and midwestern United States also traded on the Shaker name and design tradition. Gustav Stickley played a lead role in incorporating Shaker design into the broader design tradition of Anglo-American arts and crafts. Modern designers and architects worldwide have found inspiration in Shaker minimalism and functionality, which has particular resonance in Scandinavia, with its historic traditions of creative woodworking, and among custom handcrafted furniture makers in New England.

Within the late-18th- and early-19th-century Shaker mentality, there existed a desire for control and precision that led the Shakers to seek ways to substitute unfailing modes of workmanship for risky ones. This attitude opened the door for technological innovation (new tools and machines) and ongoing refinement. Universal Shaker designs—in ladder-back chairs and case furniture, for instance—were standardized over time, but village-by-village refinement led to distinctive regional features, affecting such characteristics as the numbers, size, and distribution of cupboard doors and drawers on case furniture as well as the overall proportion and manipulation of symmetry on built-in cabinetry and freestanding case furniture.

Although Shaker material culture bears the imprint of specific times and places, Shaker design is rarely bound by context. It is universal in nature, that is, outside the normal boundaries of time and space, and immediately recognized as a "good fit" and as useful by non-Shakers. Although influenced by the world's fashion system and consumer-market forces, and although originally built to give form to sectarian ideals, Shaker design transcends its origins and retains a universal appeal.

John T. Kirk, *The Shaker World: Art, Life, Belief* (1997); Timothy D. Rieman and Jean M. Burks, *The Complete Book of Shaker Furniture* (1993); June Sprigg, *Shaker Design* (1986); Scott T. Swank, *Hands to Work, Hearts to God: Shaker Life, Art, and Architecture* (1999).

Scott T. Swank

Stuart, Gilbert (1755–1828)

Painter. Gilbert Stuart was born in North Kingstown, R.I., and grew up in that state's colonial capital of Newport, to which his Scottish family had moved after the failure of their snuff mill.

He brought a distinctive sense of taste to early American artistic circles as a leading portrait painter. Stuart's ability to secure the patronage of wealthy and politically important clients, in addition to his technical skill, caused other artists to view his success as a benchmark of accomplishment.

Stuart created numerous works for the rising merchant class in post-Revolutionary New England, but he is best known for his portraits of George Washington, including the Vaughan portrait (1795, National Gallery of Art, Washington, D.C.), the Landsdowne portrait (1796, National Portrait Gallery, Washington, D.C.), and the unfinished Athenaeum portrait (1796, National Portrait Gallery). In fact, the image found on the one-dollar bill is a reverse engraving of Washington's head from Stuart's Athenaeum portrait, an unfinished canvas. The absence of pigment in this work speaks to the trouble Stuart often had completing projects and remaining financially solvent. Stuart also painted an image of the first U.S. president in a New England Revolutionary War context, his *Washington at Dorchester Heights* (1806, Museum of Fine Arts, Boston).

Other portraits exemplify Stuart's wide range of talent and his ability to mimic the various artistic styles he studied while traveling in Europe. Stuart went to London in 1775 to work with the great teacher of numerous American painters Benjamin West. At West's studio he learned to loosen his brushwork and create imagery evoking a sense of movement. The canvases he painted after studying with West stand in sharp contrast to the stiff compositions that Stuart created in the limner style while he was still a young man in New England. In paintings such as *The Skater (Portrait of William Grant)* (1782, National Gallery of Art), the subject appears to be gliding through space, and the background of the visual field is marked with soft colors and loosely defined details. When the Royal Academy exhibited *The Skater* in 1878, many thought that this canvas was the work of the canonized British artist Thomas Gainsborough.

Stuart may have left New England at an early age to find his own artistic voice, but in 1793 he returned to the newly formed United States and lived in several of its cities until his death following a stroke in 1828. Stuart's fame was such in post-Revolutionary America that having a portrait by him on one's wall was a clear symbol of status. His refinement and skill helped his clients construct a sense of their identity, wealth, and good taste. Stuart thus found several affluent patrons while living in Boston. Colonel James Swan, for exam-

ple, who had become a well-known merchant, commissioned Stuart to paint a bust-length portrait of himself in 1795. In that work, as in *The Skater,* Stuart used vivid colors, loose brushwork, and carefully modeled flesh tones to create a confident image of his subject. During his lifetime contemporaries celebrated Stuart's style; it was often emulated after his death.

James Thomas Flexner, *America's Old Masters,* rev. ed. (1980); Richard McLanathan, *Gilbert Stuart* (1986); Charles Merrill Mount, *Gilbert Stuart: A Biography* (1964); Carol Troyen, *The Boston Tradition: American Paintings from the Museum of Fine Arts, Boston* (1980).

David Brody

The Ten (Impressionism)

The Ten American Painters was a group of Boston and New York impressionists who withdrew from the once-progressive Society of American Artists in 1898 in order to exhibit their work in smaller, more personalized shows. Led by Childe Hassam, John H. Twachtman, and J. Alden Weir, The Ten included Frank W. Benson, Joseph De Camp, Thomas W. Dewing, Willard L. Metcalf, Robert Reid, Edward E. Simmons, and Edmund Tarbell. Winslow Homer and Abbott H. Thayer were invited to join but declined. When Twachtman died in 1902, William Merritt Chase replaced him.

Trained primarily at the School of the Museum of Fine Arts, Boston, and the Académie Julian in Paris, The Ten were linked (with the exception of Chase) by birth, residence, or subject matter to New England and shared a commitment to diverse impressionist styles. Constituting a loosely organized academy of impressionism, they exhibited together with great success for two decades, earning respect and recognition for American art.

Perhaps America's best-known and most beloved impressionist, Childe Hassam (1859–1935) began painting Boston cityscapes and later sunny evocations of fashionable New England retreats, notably the rocky landscape and colorful beauty of poet Celia Thaxter's garden on Appledore Island, off the coast of Maine and New Hampshire. Sojourns in Gloucester and Provincetown, Mass., Newport, R.I., and Cos Cob and Old Lyme, Conn., produced similarly appealing, sun-drenched images, including the gleaming facade of Old Lyme's stately Congregational church, and the busy, colorful *County Fair, New England* (1890, Manoogian Collection, Detroit).

Ensconced on Round Hill Road in Greenwich, Conn., Twachtman (1853–1902) captured the subtle poetry of nature's evanescent moods in evocative, impressionistic paintings of the brook, pool, waterfall, and woods on his property. *Winter Harmony* (1900, National Gallery of Art, Washington, D.C.) conveys the cool dampness of wintry New England. In *Gloucester Harbor* (1900, Canajoharie Library and Art Gallery, New York), Twachtman employed bolder, looser brushwork to depict the scenic fishing village in his final years.

Benson (1862–1951) and Tarbell (1862–1938), Massachusetts natives and long-time teachers at the School of the Museum of Fine Arts, both painted interior scenes of fashionable ladies, such as Tarbell's *Breakfast Room* (1903, Pennsylvania Academy of the Fine Arts, Philadelphia). Later, Benson executed sparkling outdoor depictions of his wife and daughters in white dresses on Maine's North Haven island, as in *Summer* [or *Summer Afternoon*] (1909, Museum of Art, Rhode Island School of Design, Providence).

Dewing (1851–1938), born in Boston, spent his career in New York, but summered at the art colony in Cornish, N.H. He painted ethereal young women in long gowns seated in tranquil rooms or gliding through soft green landscapes.

Born in Lowell, Mass., Metcalf (1858–1925) recorded the changing moods and seasons of the New England countryside in colorful, meticulous canvases. His *May Night* (1906, Corcoran Gallery of Art, Washington, D.C.), immortalizing Florence Griswold's artists' hostelry in Old Lyme, and *Gloucester Harbor* (1895, Mead Art Museum, Amherst College, Mass.), are other standouts.

From his farm in Branchville, Conn. (now a National Historic Site), Weir (1852–1919) created luminous landscapes of his property and cheerful views of mill towns around the state.

Boston-based De Camp (1858–1923) employed dynamic brushwork and bold colors in portraits, mostly of genteel women. Both Massachusetts natives, Reid (1862–1929) and Simmons (1852–1931) were best known for murals for the Boston State House and elsewhere, but also created bright, decorative portraits and landscapes.

By the time they disbanded in 1918, The Ten had become conservatives in an art world shaken by the realism of The Eight and the modernism of the Armory Show of 1913. Their depictions of New England's elegant interiors and busy cityscapes, rolling countrysides and peaceful farms, sun-splashed gardens and busy harbors endure as some of the most beautiful and evocative images of the region.

William H. Gerdts, *American Impressionism* (1984); Ulrich W. Hiesinger, *Impressionism in America: The Ten American Painters* (1991); Susan G. Larkin, *The Cos Cob Art Colony: Impressionists on the Connecticut Shore* (2001); Patricia Jobe Pierce, *The Ten* (1976); Spanierman Gallery, *The Ten American Painters* (1990); Susan Strickler, *Impressionism Transformed: The Paintings of Edmund Tarbell* (2001).

Stephen May

Tonalism Tonalism refers to an approach in painting that lasted from roughly 1880 to 1920. It employed a prevailing color or depicted forms through a softening and blurring haze, a "colored atmosphere," as one scholar has put it. The term derives from discussions among turn-of-the-century artists about achieving what they identified as a "tonal" quality. This quality involved both mood and technique. Artists working in a "tonal" mode spoke of conveying to viewers the spirit and emotive valences of the scenes before them; they were interested less in transcribing a scene than in evoking its poetic qualities. Technically they achieved the desired effect largely by applying glazes and by blending tints on the canvas. In this, they were distinct from French impressionists, who tended to juxtapose colors starkly on the canvas, and from other painters, who used the palette to mix colors before applying them to the canvas.

In their attempt to capture affect, tonal artists gravitated toward landscape scenes. Like many critics and writers of the period, they found in the natural world a connection to the spiritual. Tonal works of art are characterized by intimate, bucolic images of nature. With its wooded glens and gently rolling hills and pastures, the New England countryside, and Connecticut in particular, proved attractive to many artists, including Homer Dodge Martin, Leonard Ochtman, Dwight William Tryon, and John Twachtman. Aspects of the seasons as well as nature's subtle transitions—twilight, sunset, and dawn—appear as recurrent motifs.

The emergence of tonal ideals and their history in New England is closely linked to William Morris Hunt, an artist schooled in the Barbizon style, who not only taught in Boston in the 1870s but also backed the work of Barbizon artists among collectors and dealers. The Barbizon School's focus on pastoral landscapes and the poetic in nature prefigured the work of many tonal artists. George Inness, a well-known landscapist whose later works rely on veils of muted colors, increasingly spoke of art's role in arousing a subjective, emotional response. His influence and the earlier efforts of Hunt helped to outline a direction for tonal art. In 1899 Henry Ward Ranger, a Barbizon-inspired painter, founded an art colony in Old Lyme, Conn. Drawing a range of artists, the colony under Ranger's stewardship advanced tonal principles and helped associate them with the kinds of landscape found in the Northeast.

While the intellectual and technical underpinnings of tonal works suggest a general coherency, one would be hard-pressed to call tonalism a movement. A wide variety of artists working in different media and to different ends employed what could be called tonal qualities in their work; artists as distinct as painters James McNeill Whistler and Childe Hassam and photographer Edward Steichen have been associated by scholars with tonal practices. Tonalism is perhaps best thought of as an affinity on the part of artists for certain types of aesthetic values, among which the most important were the predominance of a single color or hue, an interest in the evocation of mood, and an attention to craftsmanship and finish.

Wanda M. Corn, *The Color of Mood: American Tonalism, 1880–1910* (1972); William H. Gerdts, Diana Dimodica Sweet, and Robert R. Preato, *Tonalism: An American Experience* (1982); Clara Ruge, "The Tonal School in America," *International Studio* 27 (1906).

Julia Rosenbaum

Trumbull, John (1756–1843) Painter and patriot. In the course of his life John Trumbull served as a soldier and a diplomat, but his lasting fame derives from his career as an artist. In several important paintings, Trumbull created a pictorial record of the American Revolution and the beginning of an American national art.

Trumbull was born in Lebanon, Conn., the youngest child of the merchant Jonathan Trumbull, Sr., who later served as governor of Connecticut during the Revolution. He graduated from Harvard College in 1773. At the outbreak of the Revolution, Trumbull, who like his family was a patriot, took a post in the First Regiment of Connecticut, where he came to the notice of George Washington. He became the general's aide, using his artistic talent to draw accurate maps of enemy positions, and was later promoted to the rank of colonel.

On finishing his military service, Trumbull returned to his first love, art. Seeking to become a professional artist, Trumbull traveled to London in 1780 to study with Benjamin West, an American who had risen to the top of the British art world and whose history paintings would influence the course of Trumbull's own artistic career. But not long after his arrival, Trumbull was imprisoned in retaliation for the Americans' execution of Major André.

After the war ended, Trumbull resumed his studies in 1784, planning several history paintings to commemorate events of the Revolution. He eventually painted six. The subjects included the Battle of Bunker Hill, the surrender at Yorktown, and the signing of the

Declaration of Independence (suggested by Thomas Jefferson). Trumbull persuaded the participants to pose for these works, increasing their value as historical records.

In 1794 Chief Justice John Jay chose Trumbull to be his secretary during the negotiation of what became known as Jay's Treaty, which settled border, trade, and commerce disputes with Great Britain. Afterward, Trumbull remained in Europe for several years on diplomatic assignments and married an Englishwoman, Sarah Harvey, in 1800.

After his return to America, Trumbull was an active participant in the emergent national art scene. He received a government commission to exhibit his Revolutionary War paintings permanently in the Capitol Rotunda. Four large canvases were hung in 1826 and remain there today. He also served as president of the American Academy of the Fine Arts from 1817 until 1836.

Late in life, Trumbull helped create two important art institutions in his native state of Connecticut. In 1832 he donated about 100 of his masterworks to Yale College in New Haven, designing a neoclassical building to house them. The Trumbull Gallery, now part of the Yale University Art Gallery, was the first college art collection in the nation. Trumbull also inspired his nephew-in-law Daniel Wadsworth to found the Wadsworth Atheneum in Hartford in 1842; several of Trumbull's paintings are at the core of the museum's collection.

John Trumbull died on November 10, 1843, and was interred with his wife beneath the Trumbull Gallery, where their remains still lie.

Helen A. Cooper, ed., *John Trumbull: The Hand and Spirit of a Painter* (1982); Daniel C. Faviata, ed., *John Trumbull: A Founding Father of American Art* (2001); Irma B. Jaffe, *John Trumbull: Patriot-Artist of the American Revolution* (1975).

Holly Heinzer

Wabanaki Root Clubs

The root clubs made in Maine by Penobscot and other Wabanaki peoples are a distinct and ongoing native New England tradition. Also referred to as war or ceremonial clubs, they are most often formed from the root burl, root tips, and trunk of the birch tree. Faces and animal images may be carved into the burl and protruding root stocks, while leaf patterns and symbolic eastern woodlands designs are chip-carved into the handle.

Root clubs have been carved and used for centuries and continue to be valued by the Penobscot people as part of their cultural identity. Old root clubs have been found throughout New England in basements and under floorboards and have been passed down

Stan Neptune, Penobscot carver, and a collection of Wabanaki root clubs, 2002

as family heirlooms. The earliest known documented root club dates from the late 1700s. Its root tips were carved into animal shapes.

Although this traditional art form flourishes today, a review of the history of root clubs reveals that their usage and style have changed over time. The earliest examples were used as weapons in hand-to-hand combat. Most of these clubs did not feature decoration. The root tips were sharpened to a point, there were no carvings within the burl, and the handle was plain. Chief Madockawando of the Penobscot Nation may have used a club of this type in raids on English settlements in York and Wells, Maine, in 1691 and 1692.

From the mid-18th to the mid-19th century, carvings on root clubs seem to have represented spirit beings, their faces just barely emerging from the burl. Such clubs could have been carried as status symbols, possibly representing spirit protectors, and may have been used in healing ceremonies and other, related native rituals. For the Penobscot, these clubs expressed the life and spirit of the tree from which they came.

By the mid-19th century Penobscot carvers had begun to sell "souvenir clubs" to nonnative tourists. Carvings on the burl changed from spirit to human faces, and artists began to add color. In the late 19th or early 20th century, feathers, braids, headbands, and even the Plains Indian headdress were added to conform to the tourist's stereotypical view of an American Indian, making the clubs even more salable. These tourist items were and are still

very much a part of the root club tradition. Identified carvers from the turn of the century include Louis Nicola, John Susep, and Frank Loring ("Big Thunder").

The Wabanaki root club tradition has continued throughout the 20th century with work being done by Penobscot artists Claude Dennis; Russell Joe; and Jerry, Leo, Clarence, and Ronald Francis (or "Senabeh" in the case of the latter Francis) and Passamaquoddy carver John Francis, all now deceased. Today, Penobscot artists such as Stan Neptune, his son Joe ("Petagasis"), Calvin Francis, and Frank Loring; Passamaquoddy carver Richard Keezer; and Maliseet artists Mark Flewelling and Dominic Polchies create and sell finely carved clubs. Like their forebears, these contemporary root clubs express Wabanaki identity and the continuity of native New England culture.

Joyce Butler, *Spirits in the Wood* (1997); Lee-Ann Conrad, with Christine Nicholas, *Artists of the Dawn: Christine Nicholas and Senabeh* (1987); Joan Lester, *We're Still Here: Art of Indian New England* (1986).

Joan Lester and Stan Neptune

Wadsworth Atheneum

The Wadsworth Atheneum in Hartford is the nation's oldest continuously operated public art museum. Established in 1842, its collections have grown over the decades to incorporate nearly 50,000 works of art. The Wadsworth's diverse holdings include Mediterranean antiquities, Renaissance and Baroque paintings, Meissen and Sèvres porcelain, early American furniture and decorative arts, costumes and textiles, African American art, 19th-century American landscapes, European and American impressionist paintings, modern masterpieces, and contemporary works of art.

The Wadsworth Atheneum began as the vision of Daniel Wadsworth (1771–1848), a patron of the arts with deep familial ties to New England. The descendant of influential political, military, and social leaders, Wadsworth witnessed the transformation of the American colonies into a bustling new republic with expanding commercial and industrial enterprises. He came of age at a time when Americans sought to shape and define a national identity, when leading cities like Boston, Providence, and Pittsfield, Mass., began to establish cultural centers or "atheneums" (named after the Athenaeum in ancient Rome) to display works of art, historical objects, and natural specimens. Such organizations were generally private institutions, but Wadsworth sought to establish a permanent public center. His initiative, a two-story Gothic Revival building designed to hold his collection, also sheltered other Hartford cultural institutions, including the Connecticut Historical Society, the Young Men's Institute (a prominent literary society later known as the Hartford Library Association), and the Natural History Society. Appropriately named after its founder, the Wadsworth Atheneum opened to the public on July 31, 1844.

The passing of time brought change. An addition to the Atheneum in 1857 housed the newly established Watkinson Library and reflected Hartford's growing literary culture. Throughout the 19th century, the city evolved into an important center of publishing and drew such literary figures as Harriet Beecher Stowe, Charles Dudley Warner, and Mark Twain. Nevertheless, attendance remained low and the Atheneum declined, reaching a low point in the mid-1880s, when it closed for more than a year.

At this turning point the Reverend Francis Goodwin initiated efforts to revive the institution. The son of James Goodwin, one of the community leaders who had helped Daniel Wadsworth found the Atheneum, Goodwin embodied Gilded Age ideals of moral reform and civic improvement. In collaboration with his first cousin and boyhood friend J. Pierpont Morgan, Goodwin opened a newly renovated Atheneum to the public in 1893. Renovation led to expansion. In 1905 Elizabeth Hart Jarvis Colt, the wife of Hartford's renowned firearms manufacturer Samuel Colt, died and bequeathed to the Atheneum funds for the construction of a new building. Two years later Morgan announced plans to donate a new building to the Atheneum. The Tudor Revival Colt Memorial and the Renaissance Revival Morgan Memorial opened to the public in 1910 and 1915, respectively, giving the museum new space to display its collection.

Growth and expansion continued in the 1930s and 1940s under the directorship of A. Everett "Chick" Austin, Jr. From his arrival in October 1927 until his resignation in early 1945, Austin led the museum into modern times and established the venerable institution as a national leader of the arts. Under his tenure, the Wadsworth was the first American museum to hold a surrealist exhibition, the first to purchase works by Salvador Dalí and Piet Mondrian, and the first to organize a major retrospective of Pablo Picasso. Austin also designed and oversaw the construction of the Avery Memorial (1934), the first museum building in the United States with an International Style interior.

The Wadsworth Atheneum has continued the tradition of artistic leadership. The museum's influential MATRIX program, established in 1975, is an active, rapidly changing exhibition series dedicated to contemporary artists, including Sol LeWitt, Jasper Johns, Andy Warhol, and Keith Haring. MATRIX draws today's most creative, cutting-edge works of art to New England and has served as a model for programs in museums across the nation.

Linda Ayres, ed., *"The Spirit of Genius": Art at the Wadsworth Atheneum* (1992); Eugene R. Gaddis, *Magician of the Modern: Chick Austin and the Transformation of the Arts in America* (2000); Elizabeth Mankin Kornhauser, *American Paintings before 1945 in the Wadsworth Atheneum* (1996); Richard Saunders, *Daniel Wadsworth: Patron of the Arts* (1981).

Trina Evarts Bowman

White Mountain School The earliest formulation of a White Mountain School occurs in Samuel Isham's *History of American Painting,* published at New York in 1910. In this broad study of American painting from colonial times to the turn of the century, Isham makes a vague distinction between a "White Mountain School" and the better-known "Hudson River School." At most he intimates that the former can be associated with Boston and the latter with New York. This mild confusion has been taken up from time to time in the art historical literature and in art exhibitions, where the notion of a discrete White Mountain School has gained favor in some quarters. More recently, the art historian Angela Miller, in an important publication on 19th-century landscape painting, has reopened the question by arguing that the "so-called White Mountain school of artists focused friendly rivalries between New York and Boston, and had at least an equal claim to being a national school."

The difficulty with this regional paradigm (that is, Boston versus New York) is that artists from both cities painted in the White Mountains during the same season (often cheek by jowl), were good friends, and practiced aesthetics that were so closely allied as to appear virtually indistinguishable at times. The friendly association between Benjamin Champney of Boston and John Frederick Kensett of New York, for example, was centered on the creation of the artists' colony at North Conway, N.H., rather than any putative urban rivalry between schools of art.

Whatever claims can be made for a distinctive art of the White Mountains, interest in the region as an artistic subject began with the artist Thomas Cole, a founder of the Hudson River School of painters who explored America's wilderness in the Northeast. Widespread publicity about the destruction in 1826 of the Willey family home by a landslide and flood in Crawford Notch, N.H., led Cole to the region in 1827, and his paintings and description of the mountains made the region a destination for other artists and for tourists. Frederick Edwin Church, Asher B. Durand, and Albert Bierstadt, among others, established thematic associations for viewing the mountains as a place of sublime manifestations of God's spirit and the spirit of American freedom. Many artists, such as Benjamin Champney, took up residence in hotels and provided paintings for wealthy tourists to take home to Boston, New York, and Philadelphia—images of natural wonders that, by the closing decades of the 19th century, belied the rapid development and deforestation of the region. Popular prints, guidebooks, and especially the stereoscopic photographs of the Kilburn Brothers of Littleton, N.H., promulgated images of the White Mountains as a defining component of regional identity.

In this writer's view the only evidence for a White Mountain School lies not with urban artists (who mostly visited the region during summer months and shared a common idealizing penchant) but with such native New Hampshire painters as Edward Hill (1843–1923) and Frank H. Shapleigh (1842–1905). For much of their careers Hill and Shapleigh were resident artists at one or more of the grand hotels during the season and produced numerous inexpensive canvases for tourists as souvenirs. Unlike the better-known New York and Boston painters, they seldom produced for urban art galleries and did not command comparable prices or critical esteem. As a consequence of these commercial connections, their work is often characterized by a rapid and loosely painted facture that placed emphasis on the broader configuration of the landscape rather than the more detailed conceptual approach of the academically trained city artists. Another distinctive feature of their respective styles lies in the choice of subject matter. Where the urban artists tended to paint the grand vista of unspoiled wilderness, Hill and Shapleigh focused on well-known tourist sites such as Crawford Notch and the Old Man of the Mountain. Moreover, they were not averse to representing the activities, accessories, and logistics of tourism. Included in their canvases are scenes of boating and fishing as well as such contemporaneous features as hotels, stagecoaches, and railroads, aspects of the tourist experience generally repressed in paintings of the academically trained artists. In sum, the expedient "tourist touch" of the hotel artists' rapidly painted canvases, together with the unselective nature of their subjects, comes closest to defining a nativist style constituting a White Mountain School.

Catherine H. Campbell, *The White Mountains: Place and Perception* (1980); Robert L. McGrath, *Gods in Granite: The Art of the White Mountains of New Hampshire* (2001); McGrath and Barbara J. Mac-Adam, *"A Sweet Foretaste of Heaven": Artists in the White Mountains, 1830–1930* (1988).

Robert L. McGrath

Women and Art Women have historically been associated with art in New England in three capacities: as producers, as subjects, and as patrons. As makers of art, their media have covered a wide range, from the needle arts to the more academic areas of painting and sculpture. As subject, the "New England Woman" has been employed by both male and female artists as a symbol of sturdiness, frugality, and simplicity, characteristics that are often attributed to the region. New England women have also been important patrons of the arts, through their financial support of specific artists, by opening their homes as congregating places for groups of artists, or in helping to establish collections of art.

The notable New England women artists of the 18th and 19th centuries were not trained in the academic tradition. Women received instruction in the arts of sewing and painting at young ladies' academies; they produced quilts, samplers, mourning pictures, and theorem paintings. Particularly in their samplers, girls depicted a pastoral vision of home, hearth, and abundance. Prudence Punderson Rossiter (1735–1822) of Preston, Conn., was an especially accomplished needle artist. In *The First, Second and Last Scene of Mortality* (1783, Connecticut Historical Society, Hartford), an elaborate needle-picture with an eschatological message, she depicts a young woman at her embroidery in a domestic interior, flanked by a baby in a cradle and a coffin inscribed with the artist's initials. Eunice Pinney (1770–1849), a Groton, Conn., matron, sent watercolors to her daughter, a painting instructor in Virginia. Some were based on engravings, but many others depicted the daily life of women in her community, the most striking of which is an image of two women at the tea table, a robust matron proudly holding a baby and a somewhat slumping childless companion, a vivid illustration of a woman's pride in achieving the status of wife.

Ruth Henshaw Miles Bascom (1771–1848), born in Leicester, Mass., lived in several towns in Massachusetts and New Hampshire with each of her two husbands and recorded her daily activities in a diary for more than 50 years. At about age 40 she began to make profile portraits of her friends and neighbors, achieved by taking a silhouette on a piece of paper, which she then traced and embellished with pastel and pieces of fabric, ribbons, and

other adornments. In addition to these amateurs, women artists offered their services for hire. Among the earliest portrait "limners" were Sarah Perkins (1771–1831), from Plainfield, Conn., and Ruth Shute (active 1828–35), a New Hampshire native who worked alongside her husband, Samuel, as an itinerant portraitist in New Hampshire, Vermont, Massachusetts, and upper New York State.

A remarkable group of professional American women sculptors, later described by Henry James as the "White Marmorean Flock," lived in Rome during the mid-19th century. Most of these expatriates, who excelled in the neoclassical style, had connections to New England. Harriet Hosmer (1830–1908), the daughter of a physician from Watertown, Mass., was the most famous member of the group, which constellated around the actress Charlotte Cushman. Hosmer had met Cushman in Boston during the early 1850s and, soon after, following her advice, pursued her study of neoclassical sculpture in Rome with the British sculptor John Gibson. Hosmer belonged to a distinguished group of English-speaking expatriates including Elizabeth Barrett and Robert Browning and Frederick, Lord Leighton. She was soon joined in Rome by New England natives Louise Lander (1826–1923), whose story Nathaniel Hawthorne fictionalized in his novel *The Marble Faun;* Anne Whitney (1821–1915); and Margaret Foley (ca. 1827–77). Two other members of the group, Edmonia Lewis (ca. 1845–1909) and Emma Stebbins (1815–82), also had connections to New England.

Another New England woman abroad during the 19th century was the painter Elizabeth Gardner Bouguereau (1837–1922) from Exeter, N.H., who took up residence in Paris, where she married her teacher William Bouguereau. His intervention on her behalf allegedly caused the Académie Julian in Paris to admit women students, which later played an important role in the education of many other women artists during the late 19th and early 20th centuries. In 1866, Gardner Bouguereau was the first American woman to exhibit at the Paris Salon, where she won a gold medal 11 years later.

At the turn of the 20th century two other important women sculptors were associated with New England. Anna Hyatt Huntington (1876–1973) was born in Cambridge, received her early education in Boston, and retired to an estate in Connecticut. Meta Vaux Warrick Fuller (1877–1968), an African American born in Philadelphia, studied in France, and settled in Framingham, Mass., with her husband, Dr. Solomon Fuller.

Several noteworthy New England women painters in the later 19th and early 20th centuries are associated with the Boston School. Lydia Field Emmet, who worked with William Merritt Chase and painted a mural for the Women's Building in the World's Columbian Exhibition of 1893, and her younger cousin Ellen Emmet Rand (1875–1940), a portrait painter, are among this group. Ellen Day Hale (1855–1940), who was related to Nathan and Everett Hale, studied at the newly accessible Académie Julian and exhibited at the Paris Salon. Hale returned to Cape Ann, Mass., where she became an important figure in the etching revival movement. Her younger sister-in-law Lilian Westcott Hale (1880–1963) was born in Connecticut, studied with Chase in New York and in Boston with Edmund Tarbell and her future husband, Philip Hale, Ellen Day Hale's brother.

From the late 19th century onward, several venues around New England became popular summer refuges for artists from metropolitan centers. Numerous women artists who initially pursued the dream of escaping the city's heat and hustle through the peace and tranquillity offered by New England art colonies established more permanent attachments to the region. Maria Oakey Dewing (1845–1927) was a native New Yorker who studied with William Morris Hunt in Boston and with Thomas Couture in Paris. She became part of a vital group of New York artists and writers, and married one of them, Thomas Dewing. The Dewings spent summers at the art colony in Cornish, N.H., along with Abbott Thayer and Augustus Saint-Gaudens. Although Oakey Dewing gave up figure painting after her daughter's birth, she continued to paint still lifes, many of them derived from her garden in Cornish. She is also noted for her understanding of botany.

Cecilia Beaux (1855–1942) provides a good example of a "New England Woman artist," in both her geographic locus and her choice of subject. Although she was born and bred in Philadelphia, where she pursued her early career, and then made her career as a mature artist in New York City, her mother's family had roots in Connecticut. In 1905, she began to spend her summers at Green Alley, her home in Gloucester, Mass., retiring there after a fall in which she broke her hip in 1924. Beaux's portrait *New England Woman* (1895, Pennsylvania Academy of the Fine Arts, Philadelphia), depicting her aunt Mrs. Jedediah H. Richards seated in a light-suffused domestic interior, is a poignant image of New England womanhood. The seated figure, observed as if from over her shoulder, is caught looking up from a sheaf of paper (perhaps a newspaper) open on her lap, to gaze out a curtained window. A pile of books on a side table further emphasizes her contemplative wisdom. A color harmony in white, accented with lavender and ocher, the work is imbued with an aura of order and peace, the cloistered refuge of contained domesticity.

Winslow Homer made women the subject of many of his works; his depictions of New England women are especially distinguished in that they are shown as agents rather than as passive objects of the gaze. Homer, who ultimately made his home in Prout's Neck on the Maine coast, presented images of women engaged in the varied activities of a productive life. In *The Morning Bell (Old Mill/The Mill)* (1871, Yale University Art Gallery, New Haven, Conn.), a young woman mill-worker crosses a bridge on her way to work; in *Noon Recess* (1873, private collection), a schoolteacher takes a hurried break in her classroom; in *Bridle Path* (1868, Sterling and Francine Clark Art Institute, Williamstown, Mass.), women ride horses through the White Mountains; and in *A Summer Night* (1890, Musée d'Orsay, Paris), depicting "a party of Homer's Prout's Neck neighbors," two women dance together by a moonlit sea.

Isabella Stewart Gardner (1840–1924) and Celia Thaxter (1835–94) represent two contrasting means by which New England women fostered and patronized the arts. Gardner, a wealthy Boston-based matron, was an avid collector of European Renaissance and Baroque art. With the guidance of the connoisseur Bernard Berenson, she filled her Venetian-styled Fenway mansion with an idiosyncratic accumulation of drawings, paintings, and sculpture, the majority of which expressed her love of old masters. She began collecting art on receiving her father's inheritance in 1891, and in 1903, she opened her house and its contents to the public as the Isabella Stewart Gardner Museum. Gardner was not the only woman from Boston whose appreciation of art ultimately benefited the cultural life of the city; other important women collectors whose acquisitions continue to enhance Boston collections included Maria Antoinette Evans, Sarah Choate Sears, and Susan Cornelia Warren, the latter two of whom supported contemporary artists.

Celia Thaxter's support of contemporary art was intellectual rather than financial. The keystone of a community of artists and writers on Appledore Island in the Isles of Shoals, off the coast of Portsmouth, N.H., and Kittery, Maine, Celia Laighton moved to the Isles from Portsmouth when she was four. Her family established and ran the Appledore Hotel. There she met Levi Thaxter, her father's business partner, marrying him at the age of 16. A poet, artist, and skilled gardener, Thaxter spent most of her winters in Newtonville, Mass., returning to her family's enclave on Appledore only during the summer, until the winter of 1870, when her husband began to winter in Florida and she took up year-round residence on the island. Many artistic luminaries of the last decades of the 19th century were attracted to the conversation, poetry, and music of her flower-filled salon, immortalized by American impressionist Childe Hassam in his painting *Room of Flowers* (1894, private collection), depicting a young woman reading among abundant flowers. Hassam commemorated Thaxter's garden in many works, including his illustrations for her book of poems *An Island Garden* (1894). The landscape around the Isles of Shoals was the subject of works by Hassam, J. Appleton Brown, and Ross Turner, among others. Thaxter has been recognized as an artist in her own right for her watercolors of flora on the Isles of Shoals and for her delicate painting on china.

Lilla Cabot Perry (1848–1933), a descendant of two notable Boston families, the Lowells and the Cabots, was distinguished as both an artist and a patron. After her marriage to literature professor Thomas Perry, her home became a meeting place for artists and intellectuals. In her thirties, she began to study painting, first in Boston and later in Paris. For the remainder of her life, she used her friends and acquaintances in domestic interiors as her subjects; she also painted numerous works when she accompanied her husband during an eight-year teaching stay in Japan. As a patron, Cabot Perry was distinguished as a founder of the Guild of Boston Artists in 1914. Perry was particularly impressed with the works of Claude Monet and spent 10 summers in residence at his estate in Giverny. She also wrote several magazine articles detailing Monet's painting method and was instrumental in introducing his work to Boston. New England women collectors and patrons supported and cultivated a taste for impressionism in the region, resulting in the presence of major museum collections of European and American impressionist painters.

Two 20th-century women who established particularly strong New England connections through their summering habits were Marguerite Zorach (1887–1968) and Peggy Bacon (1895–1987). Marguerite Thompson, born in California, went to Paris in 1908 to study, became influenced by fauvism and modernism, and met her future husband, William Zorach, there. Both Zorachs lived in New York, where they were part of the avant-garde scene, but early on they began to spend their summers in various New England locales, among them Provincetown, Mass., Peterborough, N.H., and Georgetown, Maine, where they established a permanent residence. Although before her marriage Thompson Zorach was primarily a painter, the exigencies of family life led her to make original experiments that involved the application of modernist pictorial principles to tapestries, rugs, and other needlework media.

Peggy Bacon, the daughter of two painters, received her initial artistic inspiration in the Cornish, N.H., art colony that she had visited as a girl with her parents. Primarily a graphic artist, Bacon lived and studied in Provincetown between 1915 and 1917, where she came under the influence of the Ash Can School. In the 1920s and 1930s she was associated with a group of radical artists in the Woodstock, N.Y., art colony, including her husband, Alexander Brook. Later in life she became a central figure in the summer art colony in Ogunquit, ultimately establishing year-round residency in Cape Porpoise, Maine. Bacon depicted a range of human interactions in her work. Whereas her earlier works are characterized by a somewhat acerbic edge, her later ones present a more indulgent and generous view of the human condition, often featuring sympathetic views of daily life in New England.

Conversely, a number of distinguished 20th-century women artists who were born in New England ultimately left the region to make their careers elsewhere. Lois Mailou Jones (1905–), born in Boston, studied at the School of the Museum of Fine Arts, Boston, and began a 40-year teaching career at Howard University in Washington, D.C., shortly after graduation. As a young woman, Jones participated in the Harlem Renaissance and in her thirties studied painting in Paris at the Académie Julian. Louise (Berliawsky) Nevelson (1899–1994) immigrated as a young girl with her Russian Jewish family to Rockland, Maine, where her father ran a lumber business. Acutely aware of her outsider status, she left Maine at 20, married, had a child, and traveled alone to Europe, returning to pursue her career in New York. May Stevens (1924–) was born into a working-class family in Quincy, Mass. After receiving her bachelor of arts degree from the Massachusetts College of Art, she left to study at the Arts Student League in New York, where she has lived ever since. Some contemporary women artists who stayed to make their careers in New England are Dahlov Ipcar, the daughter of Marguerite and William Zorach, painter and collagist Maud Morgan, and Boston sculptors Mags Harries, Penelope Jencks, and Marianna Pineda.

Mirra Bank, *Anonymous Was a Woman* (1979); C. Kurt Dewhurst, Betty MacDowell, and Marsha MacDowell, *Artists in Aprons: Folk Art by American Women* (1979); Alicia Faxon and Sylvia Moore, eds., *Pilgrims and Pioneers: New England Women in the Arts*

(1987); Charlotte Streifer Rubinstein, *American Women Artists* (1982).

Mara R. Witzling

WPA Art and Artists

During the Depression of the 1930s the federal government funded several programs to support art and artists throughout the nation. Although the most obvious productions of this period are the large-scale murals and sculptural works from the Treasury Department's Section of Painting and Sculpture, and the Treasury Relief Art Project (TRAP), it was the Federal Art Project (FAP) of the Works Progress Administration (WPA) that had the greatest long-term influence on the development and appreciation of the visual arts in New England and the rest of the country.

Unlike most of the Treasury Department's programs, which focused on projects for specific locations and were highly selective and controlled directly from Washington, D.C., the WPA/FAP program, under the direction of Holger Cahill, distributed funds to each state to set up local programs, often locally supervised, including paying artists to produce individual works of art in their own studios. This structure created a potential for artistic freedom and experiment that was unparalleled in any other government art program of the period.

Cahill appointed Richard Morrison as regional director for New England. Although each state had its own FAP director, Morrison's specific concern for the survival of individual artists, combined with his direct connection to Washington, enabled him to develop and coordinate strong and diverse artist-oriented programs throughout New England. State directors had considerable autonomy, however, and could mold the character of their local projects without breaking national regulations. Wayland W. Williams, director of the Connecticut FAP, and Pierre Zwick, in Vermont, strongly emphasized community acceptance and sponsorship of artwork, while Harley Perkins in Massachusetts, Samuel Green in Rhode Island, and Omer Lassonde in New Hampshire focused on keeping artists employed even if it meant allowing them to work on their own projects. Maine's director, Dorothy Hay Jensen, assigned most of her 14 artists to poster projects and had only two participants in what was categorized as the creative arts.

Beyond the difference in emphasis among state projects, artists could participate in diverse media within each state. The categories included Creative Arts (painting, drawing, fine prints, sculpture, and murals); the Poster, Crafts, and Teaching Divisions; and the Community Art Center projects. Furthermore, there was an innovative silkscreen workshop in western Massachusetts and the specialized documentary work of the Index of American Design. The index was developed to create a visual record of significant objects produced before 1900 in the United States. It prospered in New England not only because of the plentiful early American design materials in the region but also because an essential technique for the meticulous rendering of images in watercolor was developed and taught by Suzanne Chapman, who was borrowed for the WPA/FAP from the Museum of Fine Arts, Boston. Index artists, for example, carefully portrayed Shaker objects and architecture, contributing to the growing interest in Shaker design as the religion's membership declined and villages closed. A distinctive body of photographic work was produced in Vermont, creating images of independent farm families whose self-sufficiency preserved traditional New England values. These photographs were created, in part, as a response to Walker Evans's compelling images of Depression-era poverty in the South.

The numbers of WPA artists fluctuated constantly, from a high of 375 in 1935 in Massachusetts to fewer than 20 on a regular basis in Maine and New Hampshire. Cahill and Morrison were proud of the diversity on the project. Jack Levine, one of the struggling Boston expressionists, and Allan Rohan Crite, a young African American urban realist, were given their starts on the project, including having their work shown at the Museum of Modern Art in New York. Karl Zerbe, a veteran German immigrant painter, John Steuart Curry, a Midwest regionalist living in Connecticut, and Blanche Lazzell, a New York– and Paris-trained artist, were all given new audiences for their work that would have been impossible in the limited art market of that time.

By 1942, Federal Art Project activities had been shifted to the War Services Program, and were completely liquidated by July 1943. The WPA/FAP had employed more than 5,000 artists nationally, and more than 500 artists in New England. Perhaps the greatest accomplishment of the project in New England was the public's exposure to the work of local and national artists through hundreds of traveling exhibitions and thousands of individual art works hung in public schools, libraries, and museums. The project's mission had been twofold: the employment of artists to preserve their skills, and a commitment to giving the community the cultural benefits of their work. Although these two parts were sometimes in conflict, the combination ultimately contributed to the blossoming of American art and its appreciation in the postwar years.

Federal Art Project, *Federal Art in New England* (1937); Richard D. McKinzie, *The New Deal for Artists* (1973); Edith A. Tonelli, *By the People, for the People: New England* (1977).

Edith A. Tonelli

Wyeth, Andrew

(1917–) Painter. Andrew Newell Wyeth, perhaps the best-known American painter of the late 20th century, divides his time between Maine and Pennsylvania and has made the people and land of Maine central elements in his art. His understated, penetrating portraits and landscapes, have proved popular with the American public.

Born in Chadds Ford, Pa., in 1917, the youngest child of the famed illustrator N. C. Wyeth, Andrew Wyeth spent childhood summers at the family summer home in Port Clyde, Maine. A sickly child, Wyeth was tutored at home and trained by his father. When he was only 20 years old, his first one-man watercolor show sold out in New York City. In 1940 Wyeth married Maine summer resident Betsy James. Following the tragic death of his father in 1945, Wyeth's work took on greater depth, maturity, precision, and detail.

Over the years Wyeth has chronicled the resilient people, rocky fields, scrubby woods, battered dories, tidal inlets, and weathered houses of coastal Maine in muted, autumnal tones and egg tempera and dry-brush watercolor. To Wyeth, simple objects such as ragged lace curtains blowing in a breeze or the worn metal on an oarlock convey the gritty qualities of Mainers and of the Maine life he admires. Austere, intimate, and introspective, his ostensibly appealing, tranquil pictures communicate a sense of isolation and nostalgia, with undercurrents of anxiety or potential menace.

Wyeth's long familiarity with his Maine neighbors enhances the psychological intensity of portraits of his friends, such as the fisherman Walt Anderson in *Adrift* (1982, Collection of Andrew and Betsy Wyeth); the proud army veteran Ralph Cline in *The Patriot* (1964, Collection of Andrew and Betsy Wyeth); the insatiably curious Forrest Wall in *Man from Maine* (1951, private collection); and the teenager Siri Erickson, who posed for early nude pictures such as *Siri* (1968, Brandywine River Museum, Chadds Ford).

For nearly three decades beginning in 1939, Wyeth created a memorable series of drawings, watercolors, and tempera paintings of his Cushing neighbors Alvaro and Christina Olson and their isolated saltwater farmhouse that represent New England and Maine for the artist. Most famous is *Christina's World* (1948, Museum of Modern Art, New York), which has become an icon of American art; it depicts an indomitable, crippled woman

(Christina Olson) in a faded pink dress looking yearningly up a deserted hillside toward her house.

Bucking the abstract and conceptual currents of 20th-century art, Wyeth is regularly dismissed by establishment critics as reactionary and out of step with contemporary trends. Nevertheless, his evocative images that transform everyday sights into enduring visions of New England life have earned him a secure place in the history of American art. His works hang in major museums, his exhibitions consistently break museum attendance records, and his art commands high prices on the market. A recipient of the Presidential Medal of Freedom (1963) and congressional Gold Medal (1990), Wyeth is a member of the American Academy of Arts and Letters, the Académie des Beaux-Arts, and an Honorary Citizen of Maine.

The Brandywine River Museum in Chadds Ford, the Portland (Maine) Museum of Art, and the Farnsworth Art Museum in Rockland, Maine, have important collections of Wyeth's Maine art. The Farnsworth also houses the Center for the Wyeth Family in Maine, a gallery and archive devoted to the study of three generations of Wyeth artists, and it maintains the Olson House in nearby Cushing. Now in his eighties, with his hold on the public's affection unabated, Wyeth lives quietly and paints with vitality. His son Jamie, an acclaimed artist in his own right, carries on the family tradition with compelling paintings of Maine's people, wildlife, and islands.

James H. Duff, Andrew Wyeth, Thomas Hoving, and Lincoln Kirstein, *An American Vision: Three Generations of Wyeth Art: N. C. Wyeth, Andrew Wyeth, James Wyeth* (1987); Richard Meryman, *Andrew Wyeth: A Secret Life* (1996); Betsy James Wyeth, *Christina's World* (1982); Andrew Wyeth (introduction, with commentaries by Andrew Wyeth as told to Thomas Hoving), *Andrew Wyeth: Autobiography* (1995).

Stephen May

Wyeth, N. C. (1882–1945) Artist and illustrator. One of America's most aesthetically and commercially successful 20th-century illustrators, Newell Convers Wyeth was born in Needham, Mass., to Andrew Newell Wyeth and Henriette Zirngiebel. In his book illustrations and murals Wyeth dramatized New England's past in terms of masculine endeavors. In his late illustrations and paintings he depicted his Maine neighbors with an almost mystical dignity that would become a family tradition.

The colonial history of the Wyeth family, with its stories of action and daring dating back to Nicholas Wyeth's arrival in Cambridge, Mass., in 1645, thrilled and inspired the young N. C. Wyeth. The Zirngiebels, particularly his grandfather John Denys Zirngiebel, director of the Harvard Botanical Gardens, encouraged the artist's "strange love for things remote." Wyeth's desire to be an artist alarmed his father; his mother, however, sent him to the Mechanic Arts School in Boston to learn drafting, the Massachusetts Normal Arts School, and the Eric Pape School of Art, also in Boston. After studying with the artist George L. Noyes in Annisquam, Mass., in 1901, he followed three fellow students to the Howard Pyle School of Art in Wilmington, Del. Wyeth thrived under Pyle, who shared his sense of drama and history and who—particularly important in light of Wyeth's father's skepticism about his choice of career—had found status, honor, and financial security as an illustrator. In February 1903 Wyeth's illustration of a rider on a bucking bronco was published as the cover of the *Saturday Evening Post*. Magazine work, both illustrations and advertising art, formed the foundation of his career.

Eager to capture the active, manly, and rugged version of the American spirit, Wyeth traveled west, but by 1910 he was based in Chadds Ford, Pa., summer home of the Pyle School. In 1906 he married Carolyn Bockius

and eventually had five children, three of whom, Henriette, Carolyn, and Andrew, would become artists. By all accounts, he was an outstanding father: imaginative, playful, devoted, fearless; he doted on his children and they worshiped him. After noting Andrew's artistic talent and distaste for school, Wyeth became his son's teacher; traces of the father's style are evident in the son's work.

Commissions to illustrate the Charles Scribner's Sons editions of Robert Louis Stevenson's *Treasure Island* (1911) and *Kidnapped* (1913)—novels perfectly suited to Wyeth's swashbuckling, romantic style—assured his family's security and remain among the most popular images in the history of American illustration. Yet in a world that drew strong distinctions between illustrations and art, Wyeth longed for recognition as a fine artist. The short brushstrokes and sunlit pastels of *Mrs. N. C. Wyeth in a Rocking Chair* (1910, private collection) and *Summer Days* (1909, private collection) reflect his admiration for Childe Hassam and impressionism. His ongoing mural work, including *In the Dark Days of the Civil War* (1922, Federal Reserve Bank, Boston) and *An Apotheosis of Franklin* (1925, Franklin Savings Bank of New York), however, confirmed his reputation for depicting an idealized national past. His final mural commission, a series representing the spirit of New England for the Metropolitan Life Insurance Company (1940–45, New York), focused on the Pilgrims, a subject that allowed him to make a statement based on his own New England heritage. The series, unfinished at the time of his death, was later completed by his son Andrew Wyeth and his son-in-law John McCoy.

By the 1930s the focus of Wyeth's work had shifted, both in Chadds Ford and at the family's summer home in Port Clyde, Maine, to painting country people in moments of reflection. While *Springhouse* (1944, Delaware Art Museum, Wilmington), and *Nightfall* (1945, private collection) have some narrative properties, their subject is human dignity and stoicism. In *Dark Harbor Fishermen* (1945, Portland [Maine] Museum of Art), a figure in the foreground stands in a dory, awash to his knees in herring, shoveling fish into the bait basket of the first of a group of waiting fisherman. Herring is prime lobster bait, but these herring glow with a silvery light that illuminates the scene, while the somber fishermen involved in a timeless magical ritual reflect the rugged dignity that marks the painter's best work.

On October 19, 1945, in Chadds Ford, the artist and his three-year-old grandson, Newell, were killed when a train hit their stalled car. N. C. Wyeth's studio, with the painting he was working on at the time of his death still on its easel, is now open to the public as part of the Brandywine River Museum in Chadds Ford.

Douglas Allen and Douglas Allen, Jr., *N. C. Wyeth: The Collected Paintings, Illustrations and Murals* (1972); David Michaelis, *N. C. Wyeth: A Biography* (1998); Betsy James Wyeth, ed., *The Wyeths: The Letters of N. C. Wyeth, 1901–1945* (1971).

Elizabeth Otterson Wiley

Yarde, Richard (1939–) Painter. Richard Yarde is a painter best known for his work (often monumental in scale) in watercolor. His subjects are most often figurative, and his images emphasize lively patterns, color, and semi-abstracted forms. Yarde has played a central role in defining the possibilities of watercolor in the late 20th century and in elevating the medium to the status of painting in acrylic or oil. He received his bachelor of arts degree (1962) and master of fine arts degree (1964) from Boston University and an honorary doctorate from the Massachusetts College of Art in 1998. Yarde cites his Boston University professors Walter Murch, Conger Metcalf, and Reed Kay among those who influenced his work. Boston subjects formed his early important work, such as an autobiographical series of neighborhood street scenes, and *The Apartment* series, chronicling his family life. His portrait series during the 1970s featured important New England figures such as "Sweet Daddy" Grace. His work has both documented African American life in New England and served as an inspiration to other artists.

A dedicated teacher, Yarde has been a professor of art in Massachusetts for more than 35 years and has won numerous grants and awards. His work is found in major collections, including the Museum of Fine Arts, Boston; the Museum of the National Center of Afro-American Artists, Boston; the Smithsonian American Art Museum, Washington, D.C.; and the Metropolitan Museum of Art, New York. He lives in Northampton and works in Amherst, Mass.

Before 1991, Yarde was best known for his watercolors of African American history and cultural experience. Subjects range from architectural forms (doors, gates, apartment interiors) to local Christmas pageants, family and neighbors (inspired by his early years growing up in Boston), and portraits of prize-fighter Jack Johnson, Malcolm X, and Paul Robeson, among others. His most ambitious project during this time was the installation *Savoy* (1982), in which he re-created the famous Harlem ballroom environment complete with freestanding painted silhouettes of dancing figures, a band, and singers. (The installation began at Mount Holyoke College and traveled to San Diego, Baltimore, and New York.) Despite realistic aspects of his figurative imagery, Yarde is interested more in the pictorial relationship of his subject and its surroundings filtered through his own memory and experience rather than in presenting an objective, literal description.

In 1991 Yarde suffered a life-threatening kidney failure, was virtually immobilized, and was unable to paint for a year. The debilitating illness and the complications he encountered in seeking successful treatment through mainstream channels (for both body and mind) had a profound effect on his art. His work of the 1990s took on dramatically new autobiographical and soul-searching themes as he explored himself from the inside out. Wooden portrayals of hands (alluding to his own, initially stiffened by strokelike symptoms associated with his illness) gave way to hands with open palms symbolizing human touch, prayer, and healing. He painted abstracted maplike images based on his medical X-rays and codelike patterns drawn from the plethora of medical data that physicians used to map his body. He arranged these marks into various configurations that reference acupuncture and Tibetan blood-letting charts, Braille texts, and other coded formulas, embracing a full range of cross-cultural spiritual and ritual healing techniques.

Yarde's monumental *Mojo Hand* (1996) epitomizes much of his new iconography and his personal triumph over death: two rows of open-palmed handprints frame an X-ray view of a horizontally placed human torso with abstract DNA patterns placed to the left and configurations of hundreds of white dots form the 23d Psalm ("Yea, though I walk through the valley of the shadow of death, I will fear no evil") in a Braille pattern to the right. Consistent with his earlier work, Yarde's signature approach to watercolor prevails: his virtuoso control over pooling pigment is revealed as he constructs forms and lays in backgrounds with irregular and variously sized patches or squares and dots and skillfully leaves select areas of white paper in reserve, imbuing his images with a luminosity, vibrance, and vitality. References to African American quilting traditions (in which fragments are stitched together to create a whole), the spontaneity of jazz improvisation, and the rhythmic patterns of African fabrics and art are all evident in his work.

In watercolors such as *Mojo Hand*, Yarde's work has become both more specific and more universal. The handprints appear individualized yet allude more generally to prayer, to human touch (both the artist's creative hand and the rejuvenating hands of the masseuse, doctors, and nurses who healed him). The framing placement of the hands also suggests the protection of a spiritual or human healer. The X-ray and DNA imagery reduces the human figure to its most basic elements, revealing the underlying vulnerability of the body and the artist's heightened awareness of his physical and psychological self as he was poked and prodded for tests during his illness. The flat, painted Braille code is not raised and thus inscrutable to the blind but equally confounding to the sighted, who lack the knowledge to decipher it (the DNA code offers a similar lack of legibility for the nonscientist). This element of mystery, the unknowable, or knowledge just beyond our grasp, connects to the idea of the *Mojo*—the healing charm or amulet that can work for good or evil, based on the charmer's intent. The fundamental aspect of the *Mojo* is not the physical object itself but rather the spiritual belief that invests the *Mojo* with its power. For Yarde, painting was the *Mojo* through which he was able to repair his spirit while healing his body. Yarde continues to manipulate his building blocks of watercolor wash to explore how humans define our place in the world: the relationship between the self and our surroundings; the secular and the spiritual, the realistic and the abstract—seemingly endless topics in his now revitalized, creative hands. His work has had a profound impact on generations of students.

Courtney Callender and Edmund Barry Gaither, *Richard Yarde: Recent Works* (1976); Michael S. Harper and Sally Yard, *Savoy: An Installation by Richard Yarde* (1982); Jeffrey Keough and Richard Mühlberger, *Mojo Hand: Recent Work by Richard Yarde* (1996).

Shelley R. Langdale

Cities and Suburbs

Robert L. Macieski, Section Editor

Bruce M. Stave, Consulting Editor

INTRODUCTION

Euuropean settlement of New England began with an urban metaphor. John Winthrop delivered his famous sermon aboard the *Arbella* en route to Massachusetts Bay, declaring, "We must consider that we shall be as a city upon a hill, the eyes of all people are upon us." Though Winthrop was speaking of the Puritans' opportunity, or obligation, to work out their salvation and return God's favor by committing their hearts to the common good, Winthrop framed many of the values that shaped New England cities and suburbs for generations. Without defining the "due form of government . . . civil and ecclesiastical" necessary for the creation of a spiritually thriving community, Winthrop nonetheless used urban imagery to express the culmination of the Puritans' covenant with God. If settlers held to their obligations, then God "shall make us a praise and glory that men shall say of succeeding plantations, 'the Lord make it like that of New England.'"

Yet the quintessential New England scene is not a bustling city or a sprawling suburb but a quaint village: a church spire paying homage to heaven, carefully arranged white clapboard houses, the elm-lined public green, a few shops tucked nearby, and perhaps a small mill anchoring a turn in a gently flowing river, all nestled together in a clearing in the woods. With its false and true elements, the notion of the New England village persists in our imagination. In many respects this ideal is an inspiration in the siring of new settlements and a constant reference point in the region's urban maturation.

Puritans began to turn metaphor to place in Boston. In 1630 the Reverend William Blackstone, a Church of England clergyman who had settled on the Shawmut Peninsula near what would later become the Boston Common, invited Governor Winthrop and his band to settle across the river in Charlestown to avail themselves of the abundant fresh water on the peninsula. Winthrop accepted Blackstone's invitation and negotiated the purchase of land for their settlement. Blackstone, no doubt, soon regretted his hospitality as more and more Puritans arrived in Boston. His privacy irreparably disrupted, Blackstone left Boston to retreat to the solitude of Cumberland, R.I. Winthrop and his followers remained.

Puritans organized the town to promote social and moral conditions they believed favorable to God. Many initial settlements in New England were tightly knit communities clustered around the church or meetinghouse. Clergy and prominent laymen of the Congregational Church had established a theocracy in the Massachusetts Bay Colony by 1634, and before 1647 only "freemen" had a voice in town meetings and in the election of representatives to the Massachusetts General Court. Early land grants in the region required that a minister reside or a church be established in the new settlements, and anyone who strayed from the group was viewed with suspicion. The General Court even decreed in 1635 that no dwelling could be built more than half a mile from the meetinghouse (a ruling rescinded five years later). Ejection from the community was a severe punishment for transgression of community values, for many settlers shared William Bradford's earlier assessment as the *Mayflower* stood off Cape Cod in November 1620 that before him lay a "hideous and desolate wilderness, full of wild beasts and wild men," the devil's haunt. It is not incidental that in Nathaniel Hawthorne's *Scarlet Letter* (1850), the adulterer Hester Prynne lived at the edge of town. Over the centuries, the meaning assigned to nature shifted dramatically, but the commitment to community remained.

In Boston, as elsewhere in the early New England settlements, land had both public and private purposes. Property was divided among those inhabitants admitted to the town, the most and best land going to those with greater wealth and status. House lots were grouped along the principal roads close to the meetinghouse, and farm lots were distributed according to a similar social hierarchy. Many towns also set aside land for the community as a whole, often for pasturage. In 1634, for instance, Winthrop purchased 45 acres from Blackstone for the "Common use," and the community clarified this in a law of 1640 that stated: "There shall be no land granted either for house plot or garden out of ye open ground or Common field." Bostonians used the Common to exercise horses, graze cattle, conduct militia exercises, and occasionally engage in duels. It also became a popular spot for public executions, such as the hanging of Quakers Marmaduke Stevenson and William Robinson in 1659 and Mary Dyer in 1660.

Bostonians, like their counterparts elsewhere, set aside land for burying grounds. King's Chapel Burying Ground was the first, laid out in 1630, where Winthrop, Thomas Dudley, John Endicott, William Saltonstall, and the Reverend John Cotton, among other prominent early settlers, are buried. The Old Granary Burying Ground, Copp's Hill Burying Ground, and the Central Burying Ground were additional colonial-era cemeteries located on dedicated public lands.

Puritans in Boston also laid the foundation of New England's reputation as a center for education in these early years by allocating public land and resources for the establishment of schools to "advance learning and perpetuate it to posterity," reproducing Puritan clergymen when the present ones "shall lie in the dust." John Cotton was a particularly effective advocate for the creation of a school in America. In 1635 he persuaded the town of Boston to establish the Boston Latin School, now the oldest public school in the nation. The following year the General Court of the Massachusetts Bay Colony voted funds to establish a college that would provide classical instruction offered by such institutions as Cambridge University in England. The college, located across the Charles River in Newetowne, was later named to honor the Reverend John Harvard, a Presbyterian minister who arrived in 1637 and who, upon his death, left a 400-volume library and £780 to the institution. Newetowne was soon renamed Cambridge after John Harvard's alma mater in England.

Dispersion began almost immediately upon settlement as the spiritual imperatives of the Congregational faith to cluster around the church or meetinghouse and the limited availability of arable land led to the rapid establishment of new towns. Not only did a ring of towns emerge around Boston, including Cambridge, Charlestown, Roxbury, Dorchester, and Watertown, but between 1634 and 1636, Massachusetts Bay settlers also founded several towns in Connecticut. Small lots of poor quality led Bay Colony newcomers to petition the General Court for a grant of land in the Connecticut River valley, establishing the towns of Windsor, Wethersfield, and Hartford. The "fruitfulness and commodiousness of Connecticut," as Winthrop stated, was a powerful lure to settlers whose "cattle and towns were so near one another." In 1636 Thomas Hooker led the largest congregation to emigrate, driving 160 head of cattle and large numbers of sheep, swine, and fowl from Cambridge to Hartford.

Other communities were established in the course of the 17th century. Saybrook, while initially less successful as a settlement, became an important military post. New Haven, with its deep harbor and navigable rivers running to a fertile backcountry, promised to serve as a major mercantile center between Boston and New Amsterdam. New Haven's nine-square layout embodied the biblical commonwealth ideal of founder John Davenport.

Disputes within Congregationalism contributed to colonial dispersion in New England while conscientious dissent gave rise to less cohesive patterns of settlement. Roger Williams, an ordained clergyman in the Church of England, arrived in Boston in 1631 but soon found himself in trouble with authorities for heretical positions that ranged from questioning whether people should have to pay taxes to support ministers to denying scriptural justification for an established church. Banished for his "divers new and dangerous opinions," Williams escaped efforts to send him back to England and set out alone through snow-filled woods until he reached Mount Hope, where his friend Ousamequin (Massasoit), chief of the Wampanoags, had his winter camp. Despite nagging conflicts with Plymouth Colony over land claims, Williams made friends with the Wampanoag sachem and local Narragansett leaders who offered him land. Exploring the area in a dugout canoe, Williams found a good spring where the Moshassuck River enters the Providence River. There he replanted his settlement, "a shelter for persons distressed of conscience," and "having made covenantes of peaceable neighborhood with all the sachems and natives round about us, and having in a sense of God's merciful providence unto me in my distress, called the place Providence."

The "otherwise minded" gravitated to Rhode Island and the Providence Plantations, where religious liberty as we might understand it today was planted, even if it had not yet fully bloomed. In Rhode Island, settlements were not structured as tightly around a single church center and diversity of belief was given significant reign. Williams wrote no constitution for his settlement but did secure the agreement of his friends "that no man should be molested for his conscience," and all signed a simple statement promising to work for the "public good of the body in an orderly way by the major consent," but "only in civil things." Religious liberty and the diversity of accepted beliefs often made town governance difficult. It is little wonder that Cotton Mather called Rhode Island "the fag end of creation" and the "sewer of New England."

The Antinomian Controversy within the Congregational Church also contributed to the founding of several towns. Arriving in Boston in 1634, Anne Hutchinson argued for antinomianism and was banished from the Massachusetts Bay colony, settling in what became Portsmouth, R.I.; some of her followers and sympathizers, such as William Coddington, founded the town of Newport, R.I. A site of urban diversity, Newport allowed Quakers to settle in 1657 and, in 1658, Jews, who formed the second synagogue in the American colonies. It soon became one of the most important commercial centers in the colonies. The founders of Exeter and Dover, N.H., flirted with antinomianism, but both drew back into the Massachusetts Bay fold and took advantage of the emerging maritime economy.

The pursuit of wealth posed a greater threat than religious dissent to Puritan ideals of social unity. By the end of the 17th century, settlement patterns became more diffuse, home lots gravitated toward outlying farming plots, and the community focal point shifted from the meetinghouse to the market. Church membership declined as commercial opportunities multiplied. In the port cities of Portland, Maine, Portsmouth, N.H., Salem and Boston, Mass., Newport, R.I., and New London and New Haven, Conn., all roads led not to the church, but to the wharf and warehouse. In agricultural villages dispersed throughout the New England hinterland, such as Hartford and Concord, Mass., settlers scraped out a living from the land, while Boston at century's end pushed most agricultural pursuits off the peninsula. Farm and city met, however, at the waterfront as an urban market took shape. In Boston the town dock expanded into a series of wharves that ringed much of the city, and ship masts vied with church spires for preeminence over the city's skyline. Shipbuilding and the carrying trade in Salem and Newport competed directly with Boston, but none rivaled Boston's commercial dominance in the region. As the early East Boston settler Samuel Maverick expressed it, Boston was "the center town and metropolis of this wilderness work."

The Atlantic trade enriched New England's port cities and transformed them into entrepôts in the British mercantile system. In theory these port cities secured marketable commodities in exchange for manufactured goods from England. Urban merchants in New England were resourceful. When the early fur trade was exhausted, fishing from Gloucester and New Bedford, Mass., and the timber trade out of Portland and Portsmouth took over. More significant, cities from Portland to Newport turned to shipbuilding, the carrying trade, and illicit trade with the Dutch, French, and others to generate profits. British authorities saw the shipping practices emanating from these ports as endemic violations of the Navigation Acts. Fines and forfeiture failed to halt the illicit trade but did contribute to mounting tensions between colonists and colonial authorities. Merchants in vibrant shipbuilding centers like Salem, Boston, and Newport became important middlemen for other ports. As seaports prospered, so too did inland towns, such as Hartford, which grew to the status of a small city by the late 18th century. Merchants on waterfronts established extensive international connections in the West Indies and triangle trade. For the capable merchants of New England's port cities, profit was a common calling.

Colonial merchants funneled their commercial rewards into modest manufacturing enterprises that diversified local economies. Artisans fared well with their weak guilds and shortened periods of traditional apprenticeship. Coopers, sail- and rope makers, carpenters, smiths, and bakers were among the craftspeople who practiced in cities. Increasing specialization accompanied urbanization so that within carpentry, for instance, which began as a general craft, by 1750 joiners, housewrights, cabinetmakers, carvers, and chainmakers could be found. Professional soap boilers and tallow chandlers increasingly took up common household tasks like candle making. At the end of the 18th century, small-scale industry emerged, turning local minerals to iron, constructing carriages, and gathering home textile production into manufactories. Bankers, insurance brokers, printers and publishers filled the ranks at the upper end of the social ladder. The thousands of common laborers toiling along the docks, wharves, and streets of urban New England sustained mercantile activity at the lower end.

Although New England colonies persisted as predominantly English Protestant settlements, trade brought inevitable social, ethnic, and religious diversity. The centrality of New England port cities in the slave trade, for instance, particularly Newport, contributed to the influx of a small but significant population of Africans. Slavery was less extensive in New England than in Virginia and Maryland or Georgia and the Carolinas, but it was also proportionately more urban than in the South. By 1700 Africans made up one-sixth of Boston's population, one-third of Africans in New Hampshire lived in Portsmouth, and half of those in Rhode Island lived in Newport. As wealth in the port cities increased, and as European wars diminished the flow of indentured servants, Africans increasingly served the urban elite as domestics and in the maritime trades. Irish immigrants, largely Presbyterians from Ulster, also contributed to the growing diversity of New England cities.

Urban society became more socially stratified as trade expanded. By the time of the Revolution, New England's seaport cities possessed a highly stratified social structure with the "better sort," including lawyers, physicians, and merchants, at the top; the "middling sort," composed of shopkeepers, artisans, and mechanics, among others; and a "lower" or "inferior sort," made up of unskilled laborers, indentured servants, and slaves. The gap between rich and poor widened as cities matured. In Boston, for instance, taxable wealth grew ever more concentrated, with 15 percent of the city's property owners accounting for 66 percent of Boston's taxable wealth in 1771, and the top 5 percent controlling more than 44 percent of this taxable wealth. The ranks of Boston's propertyless residents stood at 29 percent. Similar concentrations of wealth developed elsewhere: 10 percent of the population of Portsmouth held half the city's taxable assets, and 10 percent of the population of Newburyport, Mass., controlled 57 percent of the taxable wealth in 1770. Social differences did not disrupt Winthrop's vision of a highly stratified community, but they could threaten social harmony.

Community order was maintained, however, in part through city government. Although the urban elite were not descendants of aristocrats, their hold on government offices was persistent. Greater success in the commercial economy led to a greater concentration of political power in New England cities. In the frontier towns and villages of the region there seemed to have been little concentration of economic and political power and higher degrees of political participation. In medium-sized cities and secondary market towns, greater concentrations of wealth signaled lower levels of political participation. In the largest cities, Boston in particular, wealth and political power were highly concentrated. Provincial officials and decision makers could be found in greater numbers in Boston as well.

Although merchant princes replaced the Puritan aristocracy of saints in New England cities, residents in Boston and other towns in the region did not abandon their commitment to the common good, though their motivation may have changed. With growth, urban society manifested poverty, crime, violence, moral transgression, and social disorder. Cities appointed constables, who labored to keep theft and violence to a minimum and assumed other civic responsibilities such as public firefighting. Severe fires struck Boston in 1676, 1679, 1711, and 1760. Early on, Bostonians voted that all families equip themselves with leather buckets to fight fires and that all adult males join the bucket brigade when the alarm sounded. Following the disastrous conflagration in 1711, Boston purchased three new suction engines and organized a public fire department in 10 fire wards. After a serious fire in Newport in 1730, the town purchased the latest pumping engine, constructed a building to house it, and established its first engine companies.

City officials in New England also assumed responsibility for public sanitation and the public welfare. Early on, Bostonians quarantined ships from plague-ridden ports and forbade the dumping of household slop on city streets or garbage on highways or the waterfront. Zoning may have been some years off, but government officials established regulations governing the appropriate depth for privy vaults. Bostonians restricted the width and weight of carts on the meandering streets and forbade shopkeepers to pile merchandise in ways that obstructed public passage. Overseers of the poor provided for the town's aged, disabled, and indigent populations, and Boston and Newport far surpassed other colonial cities in providing for public derelicts and the needy. The growing popularity of urban taverns for communication, entertainment, social contact, and political bargaining led government officials in many port cities to strive to control or prohibit gambling, prostitution, brawls, and vice of various sorts to ensure the public order.

With prosperity from the Atlantic trade, New England cities began to emerge as cultural centers. Boston, which had two bookstores by 1647, could boast of 34 by 1711. Sowing the seeds of future literary flowering, Bostonians purchased books for the Boston Public Library, initially founded in the Town House where town meetings took place. Following the fire in 1711, they used public funds to replace lost volumes and provided for new accessions. The first regular newspaper, the *Boston News Letter*, began publication in 1704, followed by the *Boston Gazette* in 1719. News, information, and learning were vital to the commercial economy, and all New England cities, particularly the port cities, committed themselves to these objectives in varying degrees. Freedom of thought and practice prevailing in Newport by the mid-18th century made it a "receptacle for people of severall Sorts and Opinions," according to one European observer, conditions that fostered a remarkable level of sophistication.

City space became increasingly differentiated as urban economies moved beyond subsistence. Distinct shopping areas emerged, such as Washington Street in Newport or State Street in Portsmouth, where the urban elite could purchase fine and rare furniture and other household goods, made in Europe or by the talented craftsmen drawn to urban markets. Fine clothing, handsome coaches, and splendid residences in distinct enclaves surfaced in the cityscape. In settings of decorum and dignity, learning and arts occupied the leisure of the urban elite.

Elite residential enclaves began surfacing in some cities, and the growing social and economic differences in New England contributed to the appearance of suburbs. As early as 1718, real estate entrepreneurs advertised a new development at Boston's Barton's Point, claiming the neighborhood was "laid out in House Lotts with two Streets Cross, that have a very fine prospect upon the River and Charlestown and a great part of Boston." In the region around Boston nonfarm, low-density residential housing emerged for the middle and upper classes who journeyed from home to work each day using private forms of transportation. According to the historian Carl Bridenbaugh, by 1760 "the country encircling Boston from Danvers to Medford to Middleborough was dotted with gentlemen's seats laid out and built to display the elegance of a rising aristocracy." Irresolvable conflicts within Britain's colonial empire, however, threatened this prosperity and recast the relation between seaport cities and the hinterland.

New England cities played a pivotal role in the war with Great Britain. As tensions with England mounted following the Seven Years' War over the cost of empire, Atlantic seaboard ports were the first to feel the brunt of new colonial policies aimed at tightening the collection of customs duties and restricting a rampant illegal trade. British officials ceased Boston's issuance of its own currency and the Sugar Act increased duties on non-British goods and prohibited trade in many commodities. Boston merchants took the lead in protesting British policies by mounting a nonimportation movement that spread dissatisfaction to other colonies. The ire of powerful urban groups—printers, lawyers, merchants, shipowners, tavern keepers, and real estate developers—was further roused by the first direct tax on the colonies, the Stamp Act. The "Democratic Thermometer" rose "some Degrees above the Boiling Heat" with this new tax on legal documents, newspapers and broadsides, licenses, insurance policies, playing cards, and other materials. The Stamp Act, the seizure of ship crews by British press-gangs, and the actions of overzealous customs inspectors ignited open popular resistance.

In Boston, the "Metropolis of Sedition," merchants and masses earned the city lasting fame as the "cradle of liberty." Residents expressed their discontent with action: reasoned and impassioned appeals, popular demonstrations and symbolic gestures, and rescue riots and other unruly actions from the "lower sorts." The prosperity of the commercial economy unraveled. Resistance led to repeal of the Stamp Act, emboldening further challenge to imperial authority and incurring further determination by Parliament to bring the colonies into line, to pay and obey.

In 1768 British troops were sent to Boston and quartered in homes and in makeshift barracks set up on the Commons. Conflict was inevitable, and the eyes of the colonial world turned to the Massachusetts capital as a series of events sparked the outbreak of revolution. First came the Boston Massacre, when a group of boys and men threw snowballs at British soldiers, who dispersed their attackers by gunfire, killing five. In 1773, in America's best-known act of protest, the Boston Tea Party, organized colonists dramatically moved against trade restrictions and the English monopoly over a single commodity by dumping 342 chests of tea into the harbor. The British retaliated by closing the Boston port. New hardships sent the city reeling.

Resistance was not limited to Boston. Urban newspapers had fanned the flames of dissent. In port cities along the New England coast, where tax policies struck first and hardest, discontent surfaced in acts of similar protest, such as the burning of the *Gaspee* by Providence merchants and artisans in 1772 in Narragansett Harbor, and symbolic gatherings at the liberty tree in Newport. In Portsmouth the Sons of Liberty pressured for repeal of the Stamp Act, supported demonstrations, and forced the local tax collector to resign. From Connecticut to Maine the "political iniquities were encouraged" with passage of the Townsend duties, and the Congregational minister of Dover, N.H., Jeremy Belknap, later wrote, "the eyes of the people were opened."

When war erupted and British troops clamped down on New England ports, interior towns and cities seized the initiative. The shots of revolution fired in Lexington signaled the shifting terrain of struggle against the British, with interior towns assuming the mantle of resistance. The victory of patriots from Vermont, New Hampshire, and Massachusetts at the Battle of Bennington, Vt., was a prelude to the surrender of British General John Burgoyne at Saratoga, N.Y., leading to the colonists' success.

Eight years of war took a toll on the region's cities. Most rebounded, but not all. Boston's population dropped from 16,000 to 3,500 between 1775 and 1776 and Newport's from 11,000 to 5,300. Years of British occupation, the cessation of trade, the destruction of the urban fabric, the exodus of many families, and the loss of many men and addition of many widows and orphans to the tax rolls seemed at first an insurmountable strain. But Boston soon recovered, renewing old trade routes, and initiating new trade with China and the Far East. Newport was less fortunate, suffering not only population loss but also the emergence of Providence as Rhode Island's capital. The demise of the international slave trade in 1810 doomed Newport to secondary status.

Boston suburbs returned to health with the city's revitalization. Newly settled towns in the northern frontier such as Bennington, Montpelier, and Brattleboro, Vt., and Auburn, Lewiston, and Augusta, Maine, all attracted settlers, but it was commerce, not religion, that determined their growth. The cities of New England benefited from new state constitutions, internal improvements, the U.S. Bank charter, the opening of western settlements, and the renewal of trade and fishing. By 1790 Boston, Salem, Newport, Providence, Gloucester, Newburyport, Portsmouth, New Haven, New Bedford, and Taunton and Beverly, Mass., were among America's 20 largest urban centers.

Revival of trade returned prosperity to New England cities following the Revolution, but industrialization remade the region. The war heightened awareness of industry's crucial role in the new nation. Initial efforts to establish textile manufacturing in New England failed but furthered the quest. The Quaker merchant Moses Brown gathered many of the machine prototypes together in a small wool processing or fulling mill in Pawtucket, R.I., and recruited a young English immigrant, Samuel Slater, to make them workable. In 1790, with the help of local metalworkers, carpenters, and other artisans, Slater started America spinning, successfully introducing waterpowered cotton-spinning technology to the new nation. Nine children between the ages of 7 and 12 composed the nation's first industrial workforce and spun cotton thread, while Slater put out other tasks, from willowing to weaving, to local households. Partners Moses Brown and William Almy used their extensive commercial networks and Quaker associations to market their thread. With characteristic New England paternalism, Slater also opened a Sunday school to foster the appropriate industrial morality. At mills from Pomfret, Conn., to New Ipswich, N.H., entrepreneurs copied Slater's methods. As Slater told a visiting President Andrew Jackson some years later, "I suppose I gave out the psalm and they've been singing the tune ever since."

If the New England textile industry was born on the Blackstone River, it came of age on the Merrimack River in an industrial version of Winthrop's vision of a city upon the hill: Lowell, Mass. By the early 1820s, Francis Cabot Lowell had resolved some of the textile industry's technical deficiencies by introducing the power loom, structuring an integrated production process that eliminated outwork, and establishing the financial and administrative systems necessary for modern industry. New Englanders, however, who had "heard with pain of the corrupt and profligate state of society in the manufacturing towns of the old world . . . looked upon the establishment of an exclusively manufacturing community . . . as an act fraught with consequences dangerous to our moral and social character." Lowell, along with his Boston Associates (a group of Boston industrialists drawn from the Brahmin set), hoped to allay such fears by designing an industrial center that was not terribly distant from Winthrop's vision, replete not only with factories worked by young women drawn from the New England countryside but also with churches, schools, and a strict system of moral oversight.

Few cities attracted the national and international attention that Lowell did in its early years. John Greenleaf Whittier grew poetic about this "city springing up, like the enchanted palaces of the Arabian tales," a place that made him feel that he had been "thrust forward into a new century." Visitors from Davy Crockett to Charles Dickens, Henry Clay to the Hungarian statesman Lajos Kossuth, marveled at its productive achievements, its social and moral order, and its cultural vitality. Lucy Larcom, perhaps the best known of the "mill girls," found in the city of Lowell a "widening of life." Many joined in praise of this industrial experiment, but it did not maintain its reputation for long. Constant competitive pressures, immigration, persistent urban growth, and all the social and industrial unrest characteristic of modern factories soon broke the spell.

Throughout New England, however, entrepreneurs followed the calling to "let the rivers be the seats of your creative industry," and put "nature's capital," the region's waterfalls, to work. The Boston Associates endeavored to replicate their Lowell success by laying plans and investing capital in new textile centers like Chicopee, Holyoke, and Lawrence in Massachusetts, and Manchester, Dover, and Nashua in New Hampshire. Smaller mill villages also surfaced along the region's rivers, following more closely the Rhode Island textile system of family-based labor pioneered by Slater.

Elsewhere, industries of all sorts emerged more haphazardly: brass buttons in Waterbury, Conn., barbed wire in Worcester, Mass., shoes in Lynn, Mass., carriages in Concord, N.H., clocks and watches in Waltham, Mass., machine tools in Providence, firearms in Hartford, and so on, establishing a regionally diverse industrial base. Some cities, such as Danbury, Conn., were noted for a single product (hats), while others, like Bridgeport, Conn., were celebrated for variety of manufacturing. Subregions also emerged, such as Brass Valley in Connecticut's Naugatuck Valley. The 30 miles around Fall River, Mass., contained the nation's highest concentration of textile manufacturing.

Railroads accelerated commercial exchange and industrial growth. A web of railroads knit the region together, furthering connections within New England and to markets beyond. The New York and New Haven line extending to Boston served as a major New England thoroughfare and an important corridor to New York City and national and international markets. The Blackstone Canal built between Providence and Worcester was redundant upon its completion because the newly constructed Providence and Worcester Railroad line was more efficient. The Boston and Albany and Boston and Maine lines helped to tie northern and southern sections of the region, while contributing to making Boston a major hub in this network. Together these lines transformed the region, reshaped the relation between urban centers and what Ralph Waldo Emerson referred to as the "suburbs and outskirts of things." Other forms of transportation—the steam ferry, omnibus, horsecar, and trolley—further altered both the internal dynamics of cities and their relation to suburbs.

Industry became a magnet drawing labor from home and abroad, expanding and diversifying New England cities. Slater and his compatriots scoured the countryside for poor families from the abundant hardscrabble farms. The Boston Associates sent agents throughout northern New England to recruit young women whose labor held greater value in Lowell or Manchester than it did at home. They were soon joined in the 1840s and 1850s by Irish immigrants so devastated by famine that they crossed the Atlantic in huge numbers, considered mere cargo to provide ballast in "coffin ships." Those who could muster the energy to make it away from the Boston wharves might find themselves gathered in new industrial cities such as Holyoke. The overworked, unproductive lands in Quebec also began their yield of families that ultimately drained a quarter of the province's population. Throughout New England, many little Canadas emerged in the last decades of the 19th century, making cities like Woonsocket, R.I., distinctly French.

As industry expanded, so too did the range of cultures, customs, and languages

Covered railroad bridge, Ticonic Fall, Waterville and Winslow, Maine, 1869

that immigrants brought to New England. Swedes, Germans, and English came, and places like Fall River became known as little Lancashire. By century's end, immigrants from eastern and southern Europe journeyed to particular cities and specific neighborhoods, Bridgeport's West End for Hungarian migrants, for instance, Providence's Smith Hill for Jews, New Bedford for Cape Verdeans. Italians not only settled in large numbers in Boston's North End; individual blocks became noted for their concentrations of Sicilians, Neapolitans, or Calabrese. Although immigrants were a boon to industry, by the early 20th century many old-stock New Englanders wearied and worried about the consequences to the republic of such an ethnic and racial onslaught. One of the most homogenous regions of the country had become one of the most diverse, particularly the southern half.

Commercial life in New England cities became more specialized, and distinct spaces known as downtown surfaced in the urban landscape. One new downtown institution was the department store, for example Jordan Marsh and Filene's in Boston. As elsewhere, streets were paved, lights installed, and amenities catered to a distinctly female constituency. In such cities as Providence and Bridgeport, entrepreneurs constructed arcades, some domed with glass and metal, that brought the commercial street indoors. Shoppers enjoyed not only safe passage through a corridor of shops displaying an abundance of goods but also protection from inclement weather. Financial institutions and business districts also occupied downtown space, along with cultural institutions, the offices of city government, and large, often elegant railroad stations that served as nodes in regional transportation networks. Unlike New York or Chicago, where commercial and financial buildings reached ever closer to heaven thanks to steel, concrete, elevators, and other technologies, New England cities retained a relatively low skyline until the mid-20th century.

Residential areas also became highly specialized. Race, ethnicity, and particularly economic status determined residence in New England cities. With few exceptions, such as Beacon Hill in Boston and Benefit Street in Providence, wealthy residents were often the first to leave cities for the suburbs. Distinct middle- and working-class neighborhoods with identifying institutions such as churches, mutual aid societies, schools, and saloons carved the urban landscape into definable territories. By the end of the 19th century, African Americans were the most residentially concentrated group in urban New England. Two of the most noted black neighborhoods were Boston's New Guinea, along the wharves, and another community near downtown, which one historian described as a "mixture of combustible houses, bars, sailor dance halls, and low boarding houses." Again, African Americans made the best of these circumstances by developing their own network of associations and their own institutions of aid, solace, and uplift.

Growth often magnified urban dangers, real and perceived, but municipal institutions continued their commitment to the public good, public health, and public safety. The threat of urban epidemics paralleled urban expansion and challenged municipal governments to secure a supply of fresh water, attend to the removal of animal waste from city streets, and construct sewers to carry human waste. Municipal governments assumed responsibility for constructing and maintaining reservoirs, aqueducts, and waterworks.

The persistent threat of fire required city governments to use professional forces. Early 19th-century volunteer fire brigades might continue to vie for the honor of extinguishing conflagrations and proudly displayed their abilities at firemen's musters, but as cities grew, property values increased, and neighborhoods became ever more congested, volunteer fire brigades were turned into fire departments. Fires continued to threaten to engulf cities, but paid firefighters using modern equipment now battled the blazes. In the aftermath of the great Boston fire of 1872, for instance, Mayor P. C. Cheney thought it time to update equipment and purchased an Amoskeag steam fire engine. Able to shoot a steady stream of water more than 270 feet, such equipment changed urban firefighting and required a more professional force to tend it.

The need for expanded police protection became evident early in the 19th century. As the number of poor in cities multiplied, so did the demand for greater police authority. The threat of crime, petty and grand, grew beyond the ability of local constables to control. Maintaining order among a diverse populace posed many challenges. Mob outbursts could threaten social peace. Conflicts between Protestants and Catholics, such as the Broad Street riot and the burning of the Ursuline Convent in Boston, and between white and black workers, such as the Hard-Scrabble and Snow Hill riots in Providence, posed dangers requiring enhanced police power. Following the Snow Hill riot in 1831, Providence's mayor appealed for incorporation as a city in order to attain such authority. Police were also increasingly called upon to protect property in industrial conflicts, such as early strikes in Pawtucket, Dover, and Manchester. Day and evening patrols were expanded and police were trained and equipped into professional forces. Despite these advances, the state militia or National Guard was required to quell unrest because the loyalty of law enforcement, policing their own, remained uncertain.

New Englanders' faith and commitment to public education remained strong. Antebellum reformers like Horace Mann led the crusade for free schools for children. Labor organizers like the Providence carpenter Seth Luther also campaigned vigorously to enhance educational opportunities for all citizens. In most cities there were informal opportunities to better oneself, such as attending lectures or participating in discussions at the lyceums. Citizens created institutions to meet the demand for improvement, such as athenaeums in Boston, Providence, Worcester, and other cities. In some instances, residents seeking educational opportunities had to create their own institutions—for example, founding African Meeting Houses in Boston, Newport, and Providence or constructing parochial schools for Irish, French Canadians, and Italians throughout the region.

New England's urban elite also created their own institutions. A vibrant literary culture surfaced in Boston in the mid-19th century. Following the Civil War, Bostonians who lamented that they were no longer the Hub of the Universe tried to reassert themselves culturally by founding the Museum of Fine Arts and the Boston Symphony. In Worcester, it was the Worcester Art Museum, in Hartford, the Wadsworth Atheneum, and in Manchester, the Currier Gallery (now the Currier Museum of Art). By the early 20th century, many native-born urban dwellers believed that culture and education were more important than ever for they could Americanize the foreign born, introducing them to the requisite principles of citizenship.

Poverty, of course, persisted even as New England prospered and its cities grew. Edward Bellamy in his best-selling novel *Looking Backward, 2000–1887* (1888), provides this account of a Boston neighborhood: "As I passed I had glimpses within of pale babies gasping out their lives amid sultry stenches, of hopeless-faced women deformed by hardship, retaining of womanhood no trait save weakness, while from the windows leered girls with brows of brass. Like the starving bands of mongrel curs that infect the streets of Moslem towns, swarms of half-clad brutalized children filled the air with shrieks and curses as they fought and tumbled among the garbage that littered the court-yards." By the end of the century, New England reformers gradually shifted their explanation for social distress from deficiencies in the individual to environmental conditions. Carroll Wright, chief of the Massachusetts Bureau of Labor, observed after touring northern cities for the federal government in the 1890s that "bad housing is a terribly expensive thing to any community. . . . It explains much that is mysterious in relation to drunkenness, poverty, crime, and all forms of social decline."

Such conditions, however, provided opportunities for politicians and reformers alike. After the Civil War, workers for political machines and ward bosses challenged the "better sort" for political power. The increasing concentration of working-class residents, particularly immigrants, coupled with the steady growth of cities and the accompanying demand for both municipal services and public utilities, opened the door for enterprising politicians. Ward bosses marshaled support to win control of neighborhoods and ultimately city governments by exchanging patronage for votes. Despite the disdain of traditional political elites who saw only corruption and self-aggrandizement, political machines met the needs of urban residents. Jobs, relief, or just sympathy in troubled times could all be had in return for loyalty. Boston's Martin Lomasney put it thus: "I think that there's got to be in every ward somebody that any bloke can come to—no matter what he's done—to get help. Help, you understand, none of your law and justice, but help." Mayor James Michael Curley, immortalized in Edwin O'Connor's novel *The Last Hurrah* (1956), bypassed Democratic Party channels and mobilized pent-up resentment against the Yankee establishment, "chowder heads," and Good Government Association "Goo Goos" to become one of Boston's most effective and beloved politicians.

While urban bosses tried to meet the needs of their constituents through patronage, middle- and upper-middle-class professionals sought other means. Settling in immigrant working-class neighborhoods was one way, they believed, to address and alleviate social distress. Settlement houses were but one approach in the Progressive reform arsenal that built on New England's long tradition of reform and gave new meaning to Winthrop's ideal of a city upon a hill. In cities throughout New England, reformers, often women, followed the model of Jane Addams's Hull House in Chicago, settling among the poor, learning of their needs, and seeking to address them. The Sprague and Hope Street settlements in Providence, the Walnut Street settlement in Manchester, and the Denison House, Robert Gould Shaw House, and South End House in Boston were all efforts to bridge the gap between the classes. The settlement workers applied emerging techniques of social work and tended to the social, health, and cultural needs of the diverse urban populace. The houses often served as magnets drawing together diverse strains of reform. Boston became one of the centers of the settlement house movement and drew into its orbit a diverse range of talented and energetic reformers. Through settlements and other acts of municipal housekeeping, women in New England transformed city government and their "place" in the public sphere.

For some, industry, immigrants, and urban corruption proved too much, and they responded by withdrawing from the promise and problems of urban life and heading for the suburbs. New transportation—first the omnibus, followed by the commuter railroad—enabled the flight from the city. In 1834 the Boston and Worcester line provided rail service for suburbanites traveling from Brookline to Boston. A decade later seven companies provided such service, offering special commuter and family fares and free weekend round trips for Bostonians who might be tempted to purchase land in outlying areas. Railroad and omnibus companies joined realtors in promoting suburban living. An advertisement for the Boston and Lowell line read: "Somerville, Medford, and Woburn present many delightful and healthy locations for residence, not only for gentlemen of leisure, but the man of business in the city, as the cars pass through these towns often during the day and evening affording excellent facilities for communication with Boston." Suburban developers reciprocated by including railroad timetables in the advertisements and reminding potential purchasers that every lot was "within a few minutes' walk of the station." Competition between commuter rail companies brought prices down, expanding the movement to the suburbs and in turn increasing service to the city. Even Henry David Thoreau noted enthusiastically in his journal, "Five times a day I can be whirled to Boston within an hour."

The appeal of the suburbs was never merely a negative response to the city; suburbs possessed virtues that seemed to magnify with time and change. Most significant, suburbs harbored a place called home. Since the 18th century the home was considered a bastion against society, a place of refuge, a place free from outside control and the negative influences of the city. Over time, the home attained an ennobling function, with spiritual potential born of architectural design. The Hartford theologian Horace Bushnell argued in *Christian Nurture* (1847) that home and family life could foster "virtuous habits," helping to assure the blessed "eternal peace of 'home comforts' in heaven." John Howard Paynes, the New England–born and educated lyricist of "Home Sweet Home," comforted the footloose Americans yearning for their childhood home. The symbolic value of the home translated readily into physical form, as the Yale theologian Timothy Dwight contended, for "the habitation has not a little influence on the mode of living, and the mode of living sensibly affects the taste, manners, and even the morals, of the inhabitants." The suburban home may have held special appeal in New England, where notions of home easily conflated with the romantic ideal of the New England village.

To be sure, the appeal of the suburb in New England did contain a positive remedy for what were seen as the ills of the city. "A man's health," Thoreau wrote in 1862, "requires as many acres of meadow to his prospect as his farm does loads of muck." Emerson noted in his journal in 1865, "There is no police so effective as a good hill and wide pasture in the neighborhood of a village, where the boys can run and play and dispose of their superfluous strength and spirits." The suburbs not only provided health and safety unattainable in the city; adherents of the suburb believed they could provide equal, if not better, public services as well. Education, so valued in New England culture, was among the most important of such services, and Emerson could proudly boast by mid-19th century that Concord was "the one town in which the best system of education can be secured."

New England urbanites reacted to the challenges before them by importing suburban characteristics such as the omnibus, creating streetcar suburbs within city boundaries. Urban transportation systems enabled dispersion of residential settlement and facilitated the expansion of the urban perimeter. Starting in 1868 aggressive annexation of Roxbury, Dorchester, Charlestown, West Roxbury, and Brighton doubled the area of Boston and would no doubt have continued until Brookline voted against union and brought the movement to a halt. Sam Bass Warner in his classic study of Boston's streetcar suburbs noted that improved street railways allowed the city to grow by one-half to one-and-a-half miles per decade. Real estate companies, lumber firms, and trolley companies thrived, and ward bosses had a steady stream of patronage positions as electric wires and gas and water pipes needed to be constructed.

Boundaries between city and suburbs blurred, but class distinctions were sharply drawn in vernacular architecture. The streetcar suburbs were most dense near the inner city, where multifamily homes, situated on narrow lots, were most common. The quintessential New England working-class multiple-family house was the three-decker, and in some cities, like Worcester, variations on the three-decker style were profuse. As one approached the periphery of the streetcar suburbs, the lots gradually became larger and single-family Shingle Style houses more the norm. Neighborhoods of three-deckers and larger single-family homes transformed New England cities, helping to make the region, at least the southern part, one of the most urbanized sections of the country. By World War I, for instance, Massachusetts and Rhode Island were the most urban areas in the country, with more than 90 percent of their populations living in cities.

New England urbanites also followed the lead of the suburbs by importing "nature" to the city, which was no longer that hideous and desolate place of William Bradford. City dwellers shared with their suburban counterparts a faith in the uplifting influence of nature. The creation of pastoral cemeteries, boulevards, public parks, and recreational attractions introduced "nature" into cities with the intention of diminishing the denigrating effects of urban life. In Cambridge, Jacob Bigelow of Boston designed Mount Auburn Cemetery (1831), the first rural cemetery, introducing pastoral elements into urban life. The cemetery stood in striking contrast to urban congestion and the encroaching grid of Boston. Bigelow designed the landscape to shut out the city, and many viewed it as an "improvement" upon nature. Other landscaped cemeteries followed, such as Swan Point in Providence and Valley Street Cemetery in Manchester. Zoos—for example, the Franklin Park Zoo in Boston, Roger Williams Park Zoo in Providence, and Beardsley Park Zoo in Bridgeport— served a similar function, domesticating nature for the benefit of city dwellers. Wide, tree-lined boulevards, such as Elm Street in New Haven and Beacon Street in Brookline, also brought open space and linear strips of nature into cities. As the park movement developed, boulevards also served as an effective passageway between open spaces, and tree planting became something of a civic responsibility.

As urbanites recognized the need for open land, city beautification was often conceived as a form of social uplift, and no space was more important than parks. The Hartford native and, after 1883, Brookline resident Frederick Law Olmsted inspired the modern park movement and established some of the leading principles in landscape architecture. Following his success in creating New York's Central Park with Calvert Vaux, Olmsted shaped similar "breathing spaces" that were designed to promote "social discourse" between the classes in increasingly congested New England cities. Their most ambitious project was a complex series of parks, parkways, zoos, and gardens that were linked throughout Boston. Although never completed as planned, the Emerald Necklace, as they called it, did improve drainage in the city and contribute to the civilizing of New England's premier city. Also notable among Olmsted's parks were Bridgeport's Seaside Park, the largest urban waterfront park in the nation, situated on land donated to the city by Bridgeport's former mayor and showman, P. T. Barnum.

The park movement was a vital part of the urban planning movement that emerged in the late 19th century as one of the most effective means of structuring New England ideals in the New England landscape. Since the early colonial period, there were efforts to prohibit or control certain types of behavior and land uses. Lowell and Manchester were also entirely planned to promote industrial harmony and order. Elsewhere, subdivisions such as Brookline's Linden Place included specific provisions governing use, such as a required setback of 30 feet for dwellings, and deeds that forbade sales to "any Negro or native of Ireland." By the end of the 19th century, urban planning was professionalized, and New England cities and suburbs were subject to the planner's design. Chestnut Hill, on the outskirts of Boston, offers an excellent example of the City Beautiful movement inspired by the Chicago Exposition of 1893. The Massachusetts architect John Nolen introduced the City Efficient planning movement in cities such as Bridgeport, where efficiency of function was claimed to achieve its own beauty. Planning enabled the creation and transplantation of the New England village ideal virtually anywhere. During World War I, for instance, the U.S. government built homes for workers, erecting what they called "urban villages" within the densely settled cities of Portsmouth and Bridgeport. By the 1920s planning efforts were bolstered by zoning practices. Zoning insured homogeneity of land use and reinforced the rigidly segregated patterns that had taken hold of New England cities and suburbs.

By 1920 urban growth virtually came to a halt, and metropolitan expansion took over in New England as cities flowed into suburbs that consumed acre upon acre of countryside. If trolleys contributed to decentralization, the automobile ensured it, making suburban ideals not only more attractive but possible for greater numbers of people as well. Parkways such as Connecticut's Merritt Parkway, constructed with Works Progress Administration money in the 1930s, continued the boulevard ideal. Mass-production techniques applied to home construction brought the purchase of a Cape Cod cottage within the means of more and more people. After World War II the Colonial style and its modified version, the ranch, gave millions of families across the country access to a piece of New England heritage. Suburban growth crept outward from New England's city centers at a ferocious pace, and more and more people commuted to work. In 1923, *National Geographic* did a special issue on the auto industry in which it noted, "Cities are spreading out. . . . Connecticut, as far as Stamford, Greenwich, and New Canaan, is peopled with those who work in Gotham by day and sleep in the country by night."

Public policy fully encouraged urban decentralization and suburban dispersion in New England. The Federal Highway Act of 1916 and Interstate Highway Act of 1956 subsidized the road, the truck, and private automobile over urban mass transportation. Construction of Interstate 95 along the coast also brought mixed results, benefiting the movement between cities and suburbs but eviscerating whole sections of cities like Bridgeport, New Haven, Providence, and Pawtucket, mainly where the working-class and immigrant populations lived. Depression-era housing policies, particularly those of the Home Owners Loan Corporation and Federal Housing Authority, were based on anti-urban ideals. The policies did lasting harm to inner-city housing markets composed of low-income and minority residents while supporting the movement of the middle class and the sons and daughters of immigrants to suburbs that were sharply segregated by race and income.

Federal policies encouraged the unrestricted spread of suburbs and the metropolis, to the detriment of New England cities and the people who lived in them. Capital became increasingly scarce in the region's cities. Federal military contracts tended to be awarded to plants that relocated to the South and Southwest, where land needs, taxes, and political conditions were much more favorable. Industrial jobs left the cities, but little moved in to replace them. Subdivisions, those "little boxes on the hillside" that Malvina Reynolds sang about, devoured mile after mile of countryside. Urban commercial areas suffered from competition from shopping malls sprouting up on the outskirts of cities. Some urban centers, like Pawtucket and Bridgeport, responded by constructing malls in the center city, but shoppers preferred the apparent safety and convenience of suburban consumption. Services in urban areas declined with the flight of the tax base. By the late 1950s, New England cities were suffering in the shadow of the prosperous suburbs.

At the same time that industry was departing the region for warmer climes and suburbs were filling with blue-collar workers moving "up" by moving out, cities increasingly became harbors of the poor, of immigrants, and of minorities. Federal policies promoted racial polarization by locking blacks out of the suburbs, and local practice in the cities encouraged segregation of housing, schooling, and access to jobs and public services. Federal low-income housing concentrated the poor, often minority, in islands of despair within decaying cities. African Americans, enticed north during World War II, found themselves struggling to hang on to jobs that seemed intent upon heading south. Between 1900 and 1970, African Americans went from 2.1 to 16.3 percent of Boston's population, 2.7 to 8.9 percent of Providence's, and 2.7 to 26.3 percent of New Haven's.

Efforts to break down de facto segregation in housing, schools, and the workplace brought measured change to New England cities, but their very successes tended to propel "white flight." Too little substantive change occurred, however, to forestall the riots of the late 1960s that swept Bridgeport, Hartford, New Haven, Providence, and Boston as they did elsewhere in the nation. The bitterly contested busing crisis in Boston, arising from efforts to integrate schools and housing in the mid-1970s, seriously tarnished the image of that city as the cradle of liberty.

By the 1970s most New England cities had suffered population losses, and urban recovery seemed doubtful. As early as the 1940s there were concerted efforts at urban renewal but not until the late 1980s and 1990s could some New England cities declare victory. When John B. Hynes defeated James Michael Curley in Boston's 1949 mayoral race, he set out to create a "New Boston." Hynes inaugurated a campaign to revive the city, remove "blighted" areas, and restore it to financial preeminence. Among the most controversial aspects was the Boston Housing Authority's demolition of the congested West End neighborhood to replace it with a complex of high-rise luxury apartments, modern shopping centers, and sprawling parking lots, documented eloquently by Herbert Gans in *The Urban Villagers* (1962). Public hostility to throwing poor people out of their homes without adequate provision for relocation threatened to put a halt to urban renewal, but it did not.

Planning proceeded, but with greater caution. The Prudential Center, constructed on a massive site of old railroad yards, aimed to restore the financial economy. Government Center took some 60 acres of land previously occupied by Scollay Square, Haymarket Square, and Bowdoin Square, providing additional office space and room for new state and federal office buildings. The War Memorial Auditorium (now John B. Hynes Auditorium) helped to fortify the service economy, attracting tourists, visitors, and conventioneers. Renovation of Quincy Market and Faneuil Hall as tourist attractions, construction of Tufts Medical Center, and the new wing of the Boston Public Library were but a few of the components aiding renewal. Today's Central Artery/Ted Williams Tunnel Project in Boston (the Big Dig), the

New England Cities of Population 25,000 or More

Connecticut		Maine		Massachusetts		New Hampshire		Rhode Island		Vermont	
Branford	28,683	Bangor	31,473	Agawam	28,144	Concord	40,684	Coventry	33,668	Burlington	38,889
Bridgeport	139,529	Lewiston	35,690	Amherst	34,874	Derry	34,021	Cranston	79,269		
Bristol	60,062	Portland	64,249	Andover	31,247	Dover	26,884	Cumberland	31,840		
Cheshire	28,543			Arlington	42,389	Manchester	107,006	East			
Danbury	74,848			Attleboro	42,068	Merrimack	25,119	Providence	48,668		
East Hartford	49,575			Barnstable	47,821	Nashua	86,605	Johnston	28,195		
East Haven	28,189			Beverly	39,862	Rochester	28,461	Newport	26,475		
Enfield	45,212			Billerica	38,981	Salem	28,112	North			
Fairfield	57,340			Boston	589,141			Kingston	26,326		
Glastonbury	31,876			Braintree	33,828			North			
Greenwich	61,101			Bridgewater	25,285			Providence	32,411		
Groton	39,907			Brockton	94,304			Pawtucket	72,958		
Hamden	56,913			Brookline	57,107			Providence	173,618		
Hartford	121,578			Cambridge	101,355			South			
Manchester	54,740			Chelmsford	33,858			Kingston	27,921		
Meriden	58,224			Chelsea	35,080			Warwick	85,808		
Middletown	43,167			Chicopee	54,653			West Warwick	29,581		
Milford	52,305			Danvers	25,212			Woonsocket	43,224		
Naugatuck	30,989			Dartmouth	30,666						
New Britain	71,538			Dracut	28,562						
New Haven	123,626			Everett	38,037						
Newington	29,306			Fall River	91,938						
New London	25,671			Falmouth	32,660						
New Milford	27,121			Fitchburg	39,102						
Newtown	25,031			Framingham	66,910						
Norwalk	82,951			Franklin	39,560						
Norwich	36,117			Gloucester	30,273						
Shelton	38,101			Haverhill	58,969						
Southington	39,728			Holyoke	39,838						
Stamford	117,083			Lawrence	72,043						
Stratford	49,976			Leominster	41,303						
Torrington	35,202			Lexington	30,355						
Trumbull	34,243			Lowell	105,167						
Vernon	28,063			Lynn	89,050						
Wallingford	43,026			Malden	56,340						
Waterbury	107,271			Marlborough	36,255						
West Hartford	63,589			Medford	55,765						
West Haven	52,360			Melrose	27,134						
Westport	25,749			Metheun	43,789						
Wethersfield	26,271			Milford	26,799						
Windsor	28,237			Milton	26,062						
				Natick	32,170						
				Needham	28,911						
				New Bedford	93,768						
				Newton	83,829						
				Northampton	28,978						
				North Andover	27,202						
				North Attleboro	27,143						
				Norwood	28,587						
				Peabody	48,129						
				Pittsfield	45,793						
				Plymouth	51,701						
				Quincy	88,025						
				Randolph	30,963						
				Revere	47,283						
				Salem	40,407						

(continued)

New England Cities of Population 25,000 or More (Continued)

Connecticut	Maine	Massachusetts		New Hampshire	Rhode Island	Vermont
		Saugus	26,078			
		Shrewsbury	31,640			
		Somerville	77,478			
		Springfield	152,082			
		Stoughton	27,149			
		Taunton	55,976			
		Tewksbury	28,851			
		Waltham	59,226			
		Watertown	32,986			
		Wellesley	26,613			
		Westfield	40,072			
		West Springfield	27,889			
		Weymouth	53,998			
		Worcester	172,648			

Source: U.S. Census (2000).

largest engineering project of urban renewal of its kind, endeavors to straighten out some of the consequences of short-sighted efforts of the past.

Many of the old industrial centers were harder to revive. Providence probably represents the most successful urban comeback. Preservationists, led by Antoinette Downing, succeeded in halting the destruction of the dilapidated neighborhood along Benefit Street. As in many cities, the area improved but the poor, in this case African Americans, were driven from their homes. Gentrification helped the city to retain and exploit its historic appeal, a pattern followed throughout the nation with varying success. By the 1980s, arts groups were moving into empty buildings in run-

Suburban housing outside Boston, 1969

down sections of the downtown, bringing life to previously deserted areas. Mayor "Buddy" Cianci leveraged federal funds to aid in these efforts, creating Providence River Walk and Water Place Park, complete with gondola rides. Controversy surrounded the construction of a convention center, posh hotels, and a high-end shopping mall, but few would now deny their contribution to the resuscitation of the city.

Elsewhere the results have been mixed. Bridgeport, the first New England city to declare bankruptcy, still struggles, with some success, toward revival. Captain's Cove, a new minor-league baseball stadium, and a hockey rink have helped develop service industries capable of drawing suburbanites back to the city, if only for an evening. Gentrification has remade seaport cities like Portsmouth and Portland into fashionable destinations to visit, but more costly places to live. Manchester, with its new convention center and renovated mill yard, is also on the rebound. The fate of other cities, such as Woonsocket, Pawtucket, Lawrence, Lynn, and Brockton, is less certain. On the whole, New England cities have regained some of their former luster and again are seen as valuable repositories for culture, education, and health. By the late 1990s several New England cities even registered their first population growth since World War II.

New England's suburbs show no sign of slowing their march across the region, though the luster of suburban life has been tarnished. Despite the promise of escaping the crime, poverty, drugs, and delinquency often associated with cities, suburbanites have found that although you can take the family out of the city, you can't always leave the social ills there. The appeal of life in a single-family dwelling situated in Edenic nature has not faded, but it has helped to generate one of the most pressing problems in many states: sprawl. The rampant spread of suburbs now seen in many states, such as New Hampshire, threatens to undermine the ideal that spurred this growth. The absence of planning in suburban developments has generated longer commutes and excessive traffic, a failure to recognize limits to the natural resource base, and the construction of numerous strip malls that make life more convenient but purge it of individuality and beauty—all endangering the virtues once sought in suburban existence.

New England cities and suburbs are dynamic places whose destinies will never be conclusively written. They are and will be the harbors of hope and promise, of civility and strife, of our successes and failures as a people. If we have not yet attained John Winthrop's ideal of a city upon a hill, we can at least say that the influence of the region's cities and suburbs has been profound, often shaping the growth and development patterns of cities nationwide.

Domenica M. Barbuto, *American Settlement Houses and Progressive Social Reform: An Encyclopedia of the American Settlement Movement* (1999); Thomas Bender, *Toward an Urban Vision: Ideas and Institutions in 19th-Century America* (1975); Carl Bridenbaugh, *Cities in Revolt: Urban Life in America, 1743–1776* (1955); Van Wyck Brooks, *The Flowering of New England, 1815–1865* (1936); Lawrence Buell, *New England Literary Culture: From Revolution through Renaissance* (1984); Richard M. Candee, *Atlantic Heights: A World War I Shipbuilder's Community* (1985); Charles E. Clark, *The Eastern Frontier: The Settlement of Northern New England, 1610–1763* (1983); William Corbett, *Literary New England: A History and Guide* (1993); Bruce C. Daniels, *The Connecticut Town: Growth and Development, 1635–1790* (1979); Herbert J. Gans, *The Urban Villagers: Group and Class in the Life of Italian-Americans* (1962); David R.

Goldfield and Blaine A. Brownell, *Urban America: From Downtown to No Town* (1979); Constance McLaughlin Green, *The Rise of Urban America* (1965); William F. Hartford, *Working People of Holyoke: Class and Ethnicity in a Massachusetts Mill Town, 1850–1960* (1990); Michael Holleran, *Boston's "Changeful Times": Origins of Preservation and Planning in America* (1998); Kenneth T. Jackson, *Crabgrass Suburbs: The Suburbanization of the United States* (1985); J. Anthony Lukas, *Common Ground: A Turbulent Decade in the Lives of Three American Families* (1985); Leo Marx, *The Machine in the Garden: Technology and the Pastoral Ideal in America* (1964); Thomas H. O'Connor, *Boston A to Z* (2000); Douglas W. Rae, *City: Urbanism and Its End* (2003); Sam Bass Warner, Jr., *Streetcar Suburbs: The Process of Growth in Boston, 1870–1900* (1969); Perry D. Westbrook, *A Literary History of New England* (1988).

Robert L. Macieski

Augusta, Maine Home to 18,560 people according to the 2000 census (down from 21,325 in 1990), Maine's capital city encompasses 55 square miles of urban, suburban, and rural landscape on both sides of the historic Kennebec River. In many ways resembling other small cities in the region, Augusta at the same time remains in search of its New England identity.

The area was first inhabited by a succession of native peoples, now called the Wabanaki, who used and derived their cultural character in part from the Kennebec River. What would become Augusta first attracted Europeans in the form of Pilgrim fur traders from Massachusetts, who established a trading post on the river in 1628. Though the post succeeded economically, the Pilgrims made no attempt to settle or to establish civic or religious institutions in the region as they did in Plymouth.

When the Kennebec Proprietors took up Pilgrim claims beginning in 1749, with the goal of attracting permanent residents to the Kennebec, they built a fortified storehouse (today's Old Fort Western), then laid out lots for settlers. Guided more by possible profits than by civic or religious doctrine, they made no provision for the common lands and church lots that so often characterize early New England towns. Instead, a more secular village of small house lots and stores grew up along the river, as retail trade based on Kennebec timber defined the community. In 1799 Augusta became the shire town of Kennebec County.

Augusta's sense of place changed again during the 19th century. Maine became the 23d state in 1820, and in 1827 the state legislature, seeking to relocate the capital from Portland to a more geographically central yet accessible location, chose the city as the new seat of government. In a granite statehouse designed, like that of Massachusetts, by Charles Bulfinch, its dome graced by South Gardiner native W. Clark Noble's sculpture *Lady Wisdom*, the legislature convened for the first time in January 1832. Five years later, a dam was built across the Kennebec River, turning the capital into a New England mill town. These developments brought new identities and new faces to the city—the Irish, among others, came to help build the dam; French Canadians followed to work in the mills; and state workers swelled the daytime population—but left in place local cultural attitudes and values.

Though this mix of people, resources, and institutions continues to dominate the life of the city, change is knocking once again at Augusta's door. Growing numbers of African, Hispanic, and Asian Americans, while still a small percentage of the overall population, now call the city home. The old cotton mill burned in 1989, and the Edwards Dam across the Kennebec River, once the source of its power, was breached in 1999, ending century-old ways of life and opening the way for a proposed new Franco-American cultural center and a river economy based on fish, not lumber.

The University of Maine at Augusta, founded in 1965 as a two-year community college, has grown into a four-year school offering a variety of degrees. With branch campuses in Bangor and Lewiston, the university serves nearly 6,000 students, most of them adult learners. Maine's capitol complex, overlooking a park designed in 1911 by the Olmsted Brothers of Boston, was substantially renovated at the turn of the 21st century and houses among its several buildings the Maine State Museum. New retail development near Interstate 95 (today's river) has altered the role of the traditional downtown, but local business leaders, serving on the Heart of Augusta team and working with government officials as part of the Capital Riverfront Improvement District, are redefining the community on the basis of its original primary assets: the river and a diverse group of citizens willing to work together in the sometimes independent-minded New England way to make Augusta a city of both tradition and transformation.

Charles E. Clark, *Maine: A Bicentennial History* (1977); Robert P. Tristram Coffin, *Kennebec, Cradle of Americans* (1937); Leon E. Cranmer, *Cushnoc: The History and Archaeology of the Plymouth Traders along the Kennebec* (1990); Richard W. Judd, Edwin A. Churchill, and Joel W. Eastman, eds., *Maine: The Pine Tree State from Prehistory to the Present* (1995).

Jay Adams

Bangor, Maine Bangor stands on the banks of the Penobscot River at the head of tide, 24 miles upriver from Penobscot Bay. It serves as a merchandising center and distribution hub for northern and eastern Maine. Located in the center of the state, it is Maine's third largest city after Portland and Lewiston, with a population in 2001 of roughly 31,000.

In 1525, Estevan Gomez, a Portuguese navigator in the service of Spain, set foot on the site of Bangor, followed by the French explorer Samuel de Champlain in 1604. It was another century before a town began to grow. Bangor was a trading post from the outset and eventually became the gateway to the vast timberland of the interior. Millions of acres of pine trees yielded masts, logs, and sawed lumber for the needs of the growing cities of young America.

Incorporated as a town in 1791, Bangor is believed to have been named after the Reverend Seth Noble's favorite Welsh hymn of the same name, meaning "high choir" in Welsh and "the white choir" in Celtic. It became the seat of Penobscot County in 1816. Drawing upon the vast forests of Maine, Bangor was home to a thriving lumber business and expanding ship-building industry, making it one of the busiest ports in New England. By 1872 Bangor was known as the lumber capital of the world. One could walk across the Penobscot River, stepping from deck to deck on the ships that thronged the harbor to deliver this bounty. Immense fortunes were made not only from owning and trading land but also from supplying the industries that harvested and shipped forest products. Waves of Irish immigrants contributed to the manpower required. Rivaling their counterparts in Boston, the wealthy cultivated sophisticated tastes in architecture, clothing, and entertainment. This era came to an end with the panic of 1873. Sawmills and shipyards eventually gave way to the pulp and paper industries.

The next boom occurred during World War II, when the U.S. Air Force turned the local airfield into a major staging area. Fighter, bombardment, and reconnaissance groups, as well as a refueling wing, all operated from Dow Air Force Base. During the course of the war nearly 100,000 combat crew members passed through Dow on military aircraft, either en route to or returning from the war. This time it was service personnel and their

Augusta, Maine, 1854

dependents who poured into the area, as the population of the base rose as high as 7,000. One bonus to the city was the number of men and women who found they liked Bangor's quality of life and returned to settle there after the war.

The culture of Bangor combines the fruits of the past and the achievements of the present. Splendid houses built by lumber money still grace the city's streets. One of the oldest continuously performing symphony orchestras in the nation resides in Bangor and reached the 100-year mark in 1997. Bangor International Airport now occupies the site of the former Dow Air Force Base. The oldest of the city's colleges is Bangor Theological Seminary (1814), followed by Beal College (1891, a school of business and accounting), Husson College (1898, providing business and health education), the University College of Bangor (1946, since 1995 a branch of the University of Maine at Augusta), and Eastern Maine Technical College (1966). Bangor's medical facilities include Saint Joseph Hospital, Eastern Maine Medical Center, and the Acadia Hospital (for mental illness and chemical dependency), as well as the Bangor Mental Health Institute. The Bangor Public Library claims the highest circulation per capita in the nation for a city of its size. A marina, a municipal golf course, a ballpark, and three museums are also within city limits and contribute to the vitality of the new service industry. The best-selling novelist Stephen King makes his home in Bangor, and William Cohen, secretary of defense in the Clinton administration, is a native son.

David C. Smith, *A History of Lumbering in Maine, 1861–1960* (1972); Deborah Thompson, *Bangor, Maine, 1794–1916: An Architectural History* (1988); James B. Vickery, ed., *Bangor, Maine: An Illustrated History, 1769–1776* (1976); Abigail Ewing Zelz and Marilyn Zoidis, *Woodsmen and Whigs: Historic Images of Bangor, Maine* (1991).

Elizabeth Trowbridge

Boston Boston, the capital of Massachusetts since 1632, was founded in 1630 on the Shawmut Peninsula near the mouths of the Charles and Mystic Rivers. Boston never submitted to the hard facts of its geography, isolation in the New World, and circumscription by water. In the 17th century, bold feats of the Puritans' imagination elevated the scraggly seashore village to a "city upon a hill," a model community to the world; in the more pragmatic 19th century, astounding feats of urban engineering created a new landmass that obliterated the old peninsular topography and allowed the city to expand.

Boston remained a city of modest size, annexing as it grew in the 1860s and 1870s small communities in the north, west, and south.

Until 1700 Boston never had more than 7,000 inhabitants. In 1790 Boston counted 18,230 souls; but by 1890, after substantial immigration, particularly from Ireland, Italy, Russia, and the Canadian Maritime Provinces, the population had risen to 448,477. After declining following World War II, the population of Boston has again begun to rise, reaching 589,141 in the 2000 census. The modest increase can be explained partly by the flight to the suburbs of well-heeled Bostonians and the expanding ranks of the postwar middle class composed of children of Boston's immigrants. An extensive subway system, an excellent commuter railway system, access to the Amtrak rail line from South Station, and two major circumferential highways encouraged the growth of the Boston metropolitan area, an amorphous group of independent communities that is home to almost 4 million people, half the population of Massachusetts.

Boston is a city in which boundaries of any kind are not easily erased. Old topographic outlines assert themselves in the popular perception that Boston is the old peninsula plus the Back Bay. Historic periods, reflected in the city's Federal, Victorian, and modern architecture, do not fuse but coexist, as does Boston's multi-ethnic population. The largest groups have distinct enclaves. The old Brahmin class settled on the south slope of Beacon Hill and in the Back Bay; the hill's north slope was home to half the city's black population. Middle-class Yankees settled in the West End, Irish immigrants in South Boston, and Jews and Italians in the North End. Jewish residents eventually moved to Roxbury, Dorchester, and Mattapan, which became solidly black communities during the 1960s as the Jews prospered and moved even farther west to Brookline, Newton, and beyond. Chinese immigrants settled near the old Leather District. Their community of 19,000 is today the fifth-largest Chinatown in the United States. The ethnic composition of Boston in 2000 was 54 percent white, 25 percent black, 14 percent Hispanic, and over 7 percent Asian; 2,365 persons identified as American Indians.

Although ethnic segregation is gradually eroding as immigrants prosper and disperse into the middle-class suburbs, the impression of Boston as a collection of disparate and distrusting ethnic neighborhoods persists, reinforced by the city's pervasive sense of history that is cultivated by residents and city officials alike. That sense of history coexists with an equally strong dedication to the future, represented not only by the numerous high technology companies found along Route 128, but also by the world-class hospitals and medical research centers (among them the Massachusetts General Hospital, Brigham and Wom-

en's Hospital, and Children's Hospital), and the more than 30 universities and colleges in Boston and its vicinity, including Harvard University and the Massachusetts Institute of Technology (MIT), which, though located on the other side of the Charles River in Cambridge, extend their long tentacles into Boston. Boston's diversity is further unified by its residents' perennial loyalty to its sports teams, including the Celtics and Bruins, who formerly shared space in the Boston Garden, now in the city's new Fleet Center, and the Boston Red Sox, who play in historic Fenway Park. Though the question of building a new stadium arises perennially, Fenway Park is one of only two old-time major league stadiums left, and Bostonians want to keep it that way.

A number of firsts occurred in Boston. The city had the first public Latin School (1635), the first labor union (1648), the first newspaper (1704), the first public reading of the Declaration of Independence (July 18, 1776), the first school for the blind (1832), the first surgical operation under ether (1846), the first transmission of sound over wire (1875), and the first subway (1897). It was home to the first Catholic president of the United States (John F. Kennedy, 1961–63); and it sent the first black senator to Washington since Reconstruction (Edward W. Brooke, 1966).

The first eminent Bostonians were the shrewd and inspired intellectuals of the original Puritan community, including John Winthrop (governor of the Massachusetts Bay Company), John Cotton, Richard Mather, Samuel Danforth, and Increase Mather, who established a short-lived theocracy with strict religious, moral, and social laws. They bequeathed to Boston what Martin Burgess Green called "a tradition of personality-style in which powerful forces of will and intellect were harnessed to firmly moral purposes." They also laid the foundations for its commerce, when in 1631 Winthrop launched the ship *Blessing of the Bay* and Boston's history of maritime trading began. Shipbuilding, fishing, whaling, and trading soon made Boston an important outpost of imperial Britain, and a royal governor was sent there in 1691. The social life of 18th-century Boston imitated that of London. The city had a miniature court around the governor, and Bostonians then began to crave large fortunes and elegant manners as intensely as they had once aspired to intellectual and moral distinction.

Disenchantment with England grew throughout the 18th century as the mother country tried both to check the colonies' rise to power and to squeeze them for money by passing laws that restricted free trade, levied import duties, and imposed taxes. England's answer to colonial protest was to send troops.

On March 5, 1770, a first clash, which became known as the Boston Massacre, left five colonists dead. The first to fall was a black man, Crispus Attucks. Three years later a largely symbolic tax on tea provoked the Boston Tea Party. Ninety Bostonians disguised as Indians stormed three ships of the East India Company and dumped 342 chests of tea into the harbor.

The depression years following the Revolution eclipsed Boston commerce until trade with China and the exploitation of the American West restored Boston's preeminence. In 1807 Boston shipping totaled 310,309 tons, one-third of the cargo carried by the mercantile marine of the United States. The 19th century was a time of astounding physical and economic growth for Boston. By 1830 Boston was second only to New York as a banking city. The new prosperity financed an enormous construction project. Beginning in 1824 the Boston peninsula was enlarged from 783 acres to 1,801 acres by cutting down the hills and using the excavated earth to fill in the coves. In 1856 the draining of the mud flats in the Back Bay began. Irish laborers filled them in with gravel brought by railway from Needham, 9 miles away. The new landmass around the peninsula and in the Back Bay and the destruction of 770 houses in the great fire of 1872 created an opportunity to rebuild Boston on a grand, metropolitan scale.

During the first half of the 19th century, Boston emerged as the "Athens of America," where the power of money was kept in check by the authority of intellect. In Boston the life of the mind was accorded an important and dignified place. Responsibility was a key word for Boston's elite, a small group of families that provided the city with intellectual, political, and financial leaders. They tied art to social purposes, applied moral criteria to the operations of culture, and considered education an

ethical obligation. A concrete expression of their philosophy was the founding of 30 benevolent institutions between 1810 and 1840, including hospitals, schools, savings banks, insurance companies, lyceums, and libraries. The abolition of slavery became an important Boston cause, fueled by the passionate speeches of William Lloyd Garrison, Wendell Phillips, William Ellery Channing, and Theodore Parker, and by the literary works of James Russell Lowell, Henry Wadsworth Longfellow, and Richard H. Dana.

Passage of the Fugitive Slave Law in 1850 motivated Harriet Beecher Stowe to write her novel *Uncle Tom's Cabin,* published in Boston in 1852. It also spawned several efforts by Bostonians to make the law a dead letter by making it unenforceable. The most notable instance was the Boston riot in 1854 to rescue the fugitive Anthony Burns, which left one U.S. marshal dead. The subsequent trial and verdict that demanded his return to slavery turned out the city in protest against the "death of liberty." Urban conflict was not new to Boston. Two notable antebellum riots reflected the intense anti-Irish, anti-Catholic sentiment in the city: the burning of the Ursuline convent and school (1834) and the Broad Street riot (1837) when a Protestant fire brigade collided with an Irish funeral. Tensions between the native-born and immigrant populations persisted into the 20th century. Perhaps the most notorious involved the trial and execution of Italian immigrant anarchists Nicola Sacco and Bartolomeo Vanzetti in 1927.

During the Gilded Age, as Yankees were being replaced by Irish in the city government, they intensified their efforts to organize Boston's high-cultural life. They founded the Public Library (1852), the Museum of Fine Arts (1870), the Boston Symphony Orchestra (1881) and the Boston Opera (1908). By 1900 the Yankees and their culture were in retreat. Of Boston's inhabitants, 35 percent were foreign-born and 70 percent were of foreign parentage. Immigration caused a shift in the city's commerce. Cheap labor nurtured shoe and textile industries, and shipping became an adjunct to manufacturing. In the 1930s Boston's main industries were printing and publishing, clothing manufacture, sugar refining, boots and shoes, bread and pastries, confections, cutlery, foundry, and machine shop products, malt liquors, and wholesale meat-packing. Some 70 years later Boston's most dynamic industries are high technology and biotechnology companies that benefit from the proximity of several major research universities.

In the early 21st century, Boston is still an eminently habitable and walkable city, because the large-scale topographic structures created

in the early and mid-19th century have withstood considerable economic, social, and cultural changes, from mass immigration to mass flight into the suburbs. The old peninsula, site of the colonial settlement, serves today as the city's financial center where glass skyscrapers jostle with classicist and Art Deco limestone and granite buildings. Abutting to the west is Beacon Hill, the Brahmins' first residential area, created adjacent to the Back Bay when the draining of the Charles River mud flats yielded land for fancy townhouses. Both areas have retained their upscale residential character. Beacon Hill is separated from Washington Street—once the busy thoroughfare atop the long neck connecting the peninsula to the main land—by the Boston Common (1634), the oldest publicly owned land in the United States. Along the Common's western border is the Public Garden (1837), America's first botanical garden, a formal parkscape around an artificial lake. The two parks are the beginning of the Emerald Necklace (1878–95), a system of parks, parkways, and tree-lined malls designed by Frederick Law Olmsted that encircles Boston to the north, west, and south. From the Public Garden it continues through Commonwealth Avenue and into the Muddy River Improvements, Jamaica Pond, and the Arnold Arboretum, ending at Franklin Park.

At the end of the 19th century, as the city grew in commerce and population, space on the peninsula and even on the recently claimed lands west of it grew tight. As the newly wealthy wished to endow charitable institutions, the city and its philanthropists began eyeing the undeveloped lands to the south of the Back Bay. Imposing temples to the arts, intellect, and leisure, among them Massachusetts Horticultural Hall (1900), Symphony Hall (1900), the New England Conservatory's Jordan Hall (1902–3), Simmons College (1902), the Isabella Stewart Gardner Museum (1903), and Harvard Medical School (1906), were erected helter-skelter along Huntington Avenue and the Fenway without concern for their aesthetic or functional relationship to their environment or to the city they were to serve.

It was not until the third quarter of the 20th century, when significant parts of Boston were being rethought by urban planners, that some of the mishaps were corrected. The first step in connecting the area between Copley Square and Symphony Hall to Boston's 19th-century core was the construction of Prudential Center (1965) as an office, residential, and shopping complex on the vast, dismal lot of the Boston and Albany Railway yard that had also always been a physical and psychological barrier between the Brahmin Back Bay and the

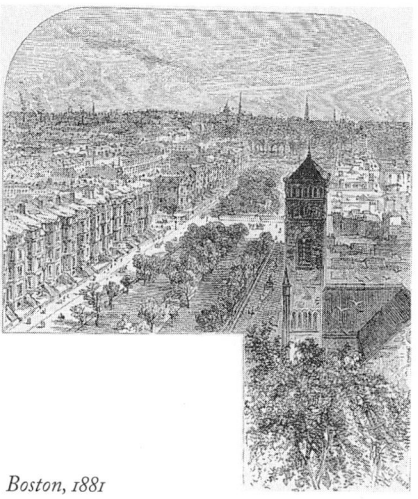

Boston, 1881

Irish South End. The second step was the execution of a master plan by I. M. Pei and Partners for the 30-acre lot between the Prudential Center and Symphony Hall belonging to the First Church of Christ, Scientist. Pei's finely balanced arrangement of clean rectangles, circles, half- and quarter-rounds along a 700-foot reflecting pool and an 80-foot fountain mitigates the monumental scale of the buildings. The neo-Romanesque Mother Church (1895) and its massive neo-Baroque extension (1904–6) find their counterpoint in Pei's 26-story upright rectangle of exposed concrete that houses the church's administration and the editorial offices of its newspaper, the *Christian Science Monitor.*

The key element in integrating this newly designed area between Boylston Street and Huntington Avenue was to create easy access from Copley Square. Since the late 1940s, when the Insurance District established itself to the east, the square began to emerge as Boston's new center. In the 1880s, it had already aspired to being an intellectual and religious hub, since it was flanked on the east by Henry Hobson Richardson's neo-Romanesque Trinity Church (1877), on the south by the striped red brick and terra cotta edifice of the Museum of Fine Arts (1876, no longer standing) and on the west by McKim, Mead and White's handsome neo-Renaissance Boston Public Library (1895, on land granted in 1880). Harvard Medical School (1883) was one block to the west, and MIT (1872) and the Boston Society of Natural History (1864) had settled one block to the east of Copley Square.

As long as Copley Square was split into two triangular lots by Huntington Avenue, however, it remained difficult for pedestrians to navigate and was unattractive as an urban space. In 1969 traffic was rerouted, uniting the triangular lots to form a square that in 1990 was transformed into a pleasant city park. In 1967 the John Hancock Mutual Life Insurance Company commissioned Henry N. Cobb of I. M. Pei and Partners to design a 790-foot, 60-story office building on the lot south of Trinity Church. From an eight-story base that visually relates the building to its immediate neighbors rises a 52-story tower in the shape of a rhomboid, sheathed in anodized aluminum and 10,344 units of half-inch-thick tempered glass. It reflects the sky and the city and at a certain angle appears as a sliver. Cobb's beautiful Hancock Tower (1975) has become a signature feature of the Boston skyline.

Architectural completion of Copley Square and its integration with the Prudential Center and Symphony Hall area was achieved in 1984, when private developers constructed Copley Place, a 9.5-acre, $500 million office and upscale shopping complex, on the air rights above the Massachusetts Turnpike, and connected it via a glassed-in footbridge across Stuart Street to the Westin Hotel at the once vacant southwest corner of Copley Square. When in 1993 Copley Place was linked by another footbridge across Huntington Avenue to the new Prudential Mall, private enterprise had accomplished what decades of city planning had been unable to bring about—the extension of the city's core to Symphony Hall and the eradication of the physical and psychological barrier between the Back Bay and the South End.

Other urban redevelopment projects were less successful. The complete demolition of the West End in 1958, which spared only the West Church, the Harrison Gray Otis House, Saint Joseph's Church, Massachusetts General Hospital, and the Charles Street Jail, leveled a lower-middle-class, largely Jewish neighborhood and replaced it with apartment towers, a poorly laid-out shopping mall, and municipal and federal office buildings. Although most of the Jewish West Enders could not afford to move back, the city built an attractive modern synagogue on Martha Road. The Boston Synagogue remains the only operating Jewish house of worship in downtown Boston.

The poor redevelopment experience in the West End taught the city to secure a master plan before proceeding with the equally radical destruction of Scollay Square, "where Sailors and their Valentines/Now skip it, trip it, fancy free" (H. Daland Chandler). In 1960, I. M. Pei was hired to propose a plan for Government Center that would set modern office buildings in relation to nearby Faneuil Hall (1805) and Quincy Market (1826), Boston's most important ensemble of early-19th-century architecture. As in his later plan for the Christian Science complex, Pei used large geometric structures that balance each other across an immense open space. The extensive brick plaza surrounding the cubic City Hall by Kallman, McKinnell, and Knowles, however, has always alienated Bostonians rushing through its red-hot or icy, windswept vastness.

Fortunately, one of Pei's rectangular buildings, screening City Hall from Faneuil Hall, was not erected. On the narrow grass strip between the two structures, the city unveiled in 1995 a modest memorial to the Jews murdered in Nazi Germany. The six slender glass columns of the New England Holocaust Memorial work well as a quiet, sculptured space of reflection where pedestrians may pause between two very busy and visually demanding urban areas.

For four centuries Bostonians have looked westward and neglected their waterfront property. Since the 1960s, half-hearted efforts have been made to revitalize it. When the New England Aquarium opened on the once decrepit Central Wharf in 1969, the waterfront gained a new lease on life. Hotels, office buildings, and luxury condominiums went up between Long Wharf and Rowes Wharf. The area will not come into its own, however, until the Central Artery has been removed. This elevated highway system has ringed Boston since the 1950s, effectively separating the Financial District from the waterfront and isolating the North End. Although the presence of the expressway helped preserve the integrity of the North End as a middle-class, largely Italian American neighborhood built around an 18th-century core, the separation of the Financial District from the waterfront has prevented the former's prosperity from revitalizing the latter. This is changing; the Central Artery Project, popularly called the Big Dig, the largest urban construction project in the United States, replaced the elevated highway with an underground roadway system at the cost of $12 billion. The 2.7 million cubic yards of excavated dirt will cap Spectacle Island, converting the former garbage dump into a 105-acre park. The relocation of the expressway will restore a historic aspect of Boston by reconnecting the North End and the waterfront to the core of the Shawmut Peninsula and invite Bostonians to rediscover their city as a seaport.

Cleveland Amory, *The Proper Bostonians* (1947); Robert Campbell and Peter Vanderwarker, *Cityscapes of Boston: An American City through Time* (1992); Samuel Adams Drake, *Old Landmarks and Historic Personages of Boston* (1900); Martin Burgess Green, *The Problem of Boston: Some Readings in Cultural History* (1966); Oscar Handlin, *Boston's Immigrants: A Study in Acculturation* (1979); Howard Mumford Jones and Bessie Zaban Jones, eds., *The Many Voices of Boston: A Historical Anthology, 1630–1975* (1975); Thomas H. O'Connor, *The Boston Irish: A Political History* (1995); Anthony M. Sammarco, *Boston's West End* (1998); Cynthia Zaitzevsky, *Frederick Law Olmsted and the Boston Park System* (1982).

Susanne Klingenstein

Boston Common No landmark is more evocative of Boston than the 48-acre park that lies immediately to the west of downtown. For more than 350 years the Boston Common has served as training ground, pasture, public gathering site, promenade, and, finally, park and playground. That an expanse of priceless urban real estate remains undeveloped is one of the wonders of Boston's history.

When the Reverend William Blaxton (Blackstone), the first English settler of Shawmut Peninsula, departed in 1634, he sold most of his land to the town of Boston. In 1640 the town voted that henceforth "there shall be no land granted either for house plot or garden out of ye open ground or Common field." In the 17th century the Common was largely

Boston Common, 1984

treeless, which fit with its primary function as a militia mustering ground and pasture for cattle and sheep. The Common also became the scene of civic ceremonies, such as the shooting of a Wampanoag sagamore in 1656 and the hanging of Quakers in 1659. As early as 1675 "the Gallants a little before sunset" took strolls here with their consorts.

The first steps in transforming the Common into an urban park were taken in the 1720s and 1730s, when rows of trees were planted along Tremont Street, forming a walkway long known as the Mall. But the basic function of the Common remained pastoral and military: the Common was the primary Boston base of the British army for eight years until the evacuation of the town in 1776.

As late as the end of the Revolution the Common was a country pasture on the outer edge of Boston. The relocation of the state capitol to Beacon Hill, on the north edge of the Common, in 1798 soon brought development—at first residential, later commercial—to its borders. The Common began to change. Tree-lined malls went up on Beacon (1816), Charles (1823–24), Park (1826), and Boylston Streets (1836), and by 1860 much of the Common was shaded by trees. Public executions on the Common ended in 1812, and the cows were evicted in 1830.

Although the Common preserved open space, it limited expansion of the city's business district, which contributed to the congestion that threatened to strangle Boston at the end of the 19th century. Boston's upper class beat back schemes to bisect the common with

roads or streetcar lines; instead the nation's first subway opened in 1897 beneath part of the Common. Some of the bordering streets were widened at its expense, and in the 20th century an underground parking garage was constructed. Nonetheless, the Common has survived largely intact.

Throughout Boston's history the Common has served as a public gathering place. Here Bostonians celebrated military victories from Louisburg (1745) to World War II. Here George Whitefield preached the Great Revival; Liberty Trees proclaimed Revolution; the city welcomed Lafayette, Andrew Jackson, and Pope John Paul II; and activists protested the war in Vietnam. Numerous monuments remind visitors of the city's past, none more striking than that commemorating Colonel Robert Gould Shaw and the 54th Massachusetts Regiment, erected on the highest point of the Common on Beacon Street opposite the statehouse. Designed by Augustus Saint-Gaudens and dedicated in 1897, this grand bronze relief honors the first black regiment to fight in the Civil War. Today the Common hosts annual events such as the Walk for Hunger and open-air productions of Shakespeare, while thousands use it every day for strolling and play.

The adjacent Public Garden, with its landmark swan boats, and the Central Burying-ground (1756), although never part of the Common, function as extensions. The site of the Garden, lowland on the edge of the Back Bay, was given away by the town to private ropewalk operators in 1794. The town repur-

chased the land in 1824 and in 1839 leased it to a private group that converted it into a European-style botanic garden. The formality of the Public Garden, with its manicured lawns on which walking is prohibited, contrasts with the casualness of the Common.

Samuel Adams Drake, *Old Landmarks and Historic Personages of Boston* (1900); Walter Firey, *Land Use in Central Boston* (1947); M. A. DeWolfe Howe, *Boston Common: Scenes from Four Centuries* (1921); Thomas H. O'Connor, *Boston A to Z* (2001); Walter Muir Whitehill, *Boston: A Topographic History* (1959; 2d ed., enl., 1968).

Ronald Dale Karr

Brattleboro, Vt. Founded around Fort Dummer in 1724 on low hills above the nearby Connecticut River, and with the Green Mountains bordering to the west, Brattleboro was the first permanent English settlement in Vermont. The town, chartered in 1753, thrived early as a crossroads for traders and travelers moving between Boston and Canada, and in later years as the first important stop for those coming into Vermont from the southeast. River-based mills and commerce provided the basis for an economy that notably included printing establishments and manufacturers of paper. In 1845 Dr. Robert Wesselhoeft opened his Brattleboro Hydropathic Institution, exploiting the area's plentiful mineral springs by offering a "water cure" for various physical and psychic ailments. Wesselhoeft's establishment, which also doubled as a resort, made Brattleboro famous by attracting wealthy patients and boarders from throughout the United States and Canada, including Henry Wadsworth Longfellow, James Russell Lowell, Harriet Beecher Stowe, and William Dean Howells. The arrival of the railroad in the 1850s further boosted the mineral springs' attraction and the town's growth.

After the Civil War, despite the decline in popularity of hydropathy, the town continued to prosper. J. Estey and Company, a maker of parlor organs, provided the main economic stimulus, employing a workforce of 500 at its peak. Many of these workers were newly arrived immigrants: by the turn of the 20th century almost one-third of the community's 7,000 residents were foreign-born or the children of foreign-born parents, primarily from Ireland, French Canada, Sweden, and Germany.

The organ company's success nourished Brattleboro's identity as a center of culture in an agricultural backcountry, an impression that had been fostered initially by the resort visits of Longfellow and his contemporaries. The presence in town of Larkin G. Mead, Jr., a leading Gilded Age sculptor, and the residency of Rudyard Kipling in nearby Dummerston in the 1890s further burnished that image, as did local printing establishments that published several of the nation's most widely regarded literary magazines.

In the 20th century Brattleboro maintained its economic base in the lumber and paper industries and as an important printing center. That base broadened following the arrival of Interstate 91 in the 1960s, which led to the expansion of area tourism and summer home ownership and the growth of the ski industry at nearby Stratton and Mount Snow.

Brattleboro, with a population of approximately 12,000, continues to occupy a position of cultural leadership in the state. Its citizens cherish their reputation as a "college community without a college," earned through support for an unusually large number of local cultural and arts institutions that include the New England Bach Festival Orchestra and Chorus, the Brattleboro Music Center, two resident theater companies, a museum and arts center, the School for International Training and World Learning, and the annual Marlboro Music Festival, held in the neighboring town, at Marlboro College. Located in Brattleboro also are the Brattleboro Retreat, one of the nation's oldest private psychiatric hospitals, and the Austine School for the Deaf.

Harold A. Barry, Richard E. Michelman, Richard M. Mitchell, and Richard H. Wellman, *Before Our Time: A Pictorial Memoir of Brattleboro, Vermont, from 1830 to 1930* (1974); Mary R. Cabot, ed., *Annals of Brattleboro, 1681–1895*, 2 vols. (1921–1922); Stuart Murray, *Rudyard Kipling in Vermont: Birthplace of the Jungle Books* (1997).

Gene Sessions

Bridgeport, Conn. "When you're not on Broadway, everything is Bridgeport," quipped the New York syndicated columnist Arthur "Bugs" Baer in 1915, evoking the ordinariness and practicality of Bridgeport from the vantage point of a nearby glittery entertainment world. For most of the 20th century, Bridgeport, population 139,529 in 2000, has been the economic hub of Fairfield County and the most important industrial city in the state. Incorporated in 1836 from the colonial towns of Stratford and Fairfield, Bridgeport (population 4,570 in 1840) quickly became a commercial port, transportation hub, and new manufacturing center. A Yankee city, it soon gave way to immigrants—first Irish, then Germans and Scandinavians—all attracted by jobs in the burgeoning metal industries. The circus impresario P. T. Barnum was involved in drawing industry to the young city in the 1850s and 1860, and served as its mayor in 1875. The Barnums and original Yankee families such as the Wheelers and Beardsleys donated hun-

dreds of acres of park land to the city in the late 19th century, earning Bridgeport its sobriquet, "the Park City."

The industrial city grew modestly to 48,866 in 1890, when it was poised for explosive expansion. Aided by Connecticut and New York capital investments, varied industries making munitions, machine-tools, sewing machines, typewriters, brass-casting, automobiles, graphophones, and corsets were established or expanded. Another wave of immigrants, from eastern and southern Europe, became the city's workforce. Many industrial inventions were perfected in Bridgeport, while Gustave Whitehead's first flight in an airplane in 1901 (two years before the Wright Brothers) remains part of local lore. The city also claims the origins of the popular Frisbee toy, designed from Frisbie Pie Company tins that workers used to toss on their lunch breaks.

World War I made Bridgeport a key center of Allied munitions production, with Remington Arms and other companies producing an estimated two-thirds of Allied ammunition. The city's population swelled to roughly 170,000 for the duration. Wartime strikes by machinists and others in the munitions industries turned national attention to the city, raising the specter of radical immigrants and unbridled labor discontent.

The 1920s and 1930s were a golden age of immigrant communities. With the Immigration Restriction Acts of 1921 and 1924, new European arrivals chose to settle in Bridgeport and extend their ethnic fraternal clubs, singing societies, sports teams, and houses of worship to new areas of the city. Italians composed the largest group, followed by Russians, Poles, Slovaks, and others scattered throughout neighborhoods in the South End and East Side. Only the Hungarians clustered in one section, the West End, where they built powerful organizations; two of the largest Hungarian American fraternal groups located their national headquarters in Bridgeport. Skilled German and British craftsmen continued to be attracted to the city. The Bridgeport Socialist Party emerged from this labor and ethnic mix, rising to political power during the economic and political crisis of the Great Depression. The socialist Jasper McLevy, a slate roofer by trade, remained mayor from 1933 until 1957, though his reformist politics had faded considerably by the end of his tenure.

World War II brought another economic boom, adding airplanes and helicopters to the munitions industry. It brought demographic changes as well. African Americans began moving from the South and Puerto Ricans from the island and from New York City into Bridgeport during the war boom, a trend that

continued after the war. In the postwar readjustment, city boosters established the Barnum Festival, a month-long celebration and carnival with a massive Fourth of July parade, which tapped into the Barnumesque historical and cultural legacy. The city has provided a nurturing environment for entertainers of all sorts: in the 19th century, Barnum's Jenny Lind, "the Swedish Nightingale," and the midget Tom Thumb; in the 20th century, the popular cartoonists Al Capp, creator of the comic strip "Li'l Abner," and Walt Kelly, whose characters in his strip "Pogo" commented on national politics and the foibles of P. T. Bridgeport, the strip's pompous local politician.

The city still retains its profile as an ethnic city. Postwar prosperity led some of Bridgeport's European immigrants to move to the city's suburbs, expanding the populations of Fairfield, Stratford, Trumbull, and Monroe. New ethnic groups, including Puerto Ricans, Cubans, West Indians, other Caribbean and Latin Americans, Portuguese, and, most recently, Asians, expand Bridgeport's ethnic cultures and cuisines.

The city's dependence on metal industries and defense contracts spelled disaster when the process of deindustrialization hit most American industries and contraction in defense spending raised unemployment rates in the 1980s. The city declared bankruptcy in 1991, the largest U.S. city ever to do so. Its newer black and Hispanic populations bore the brunt of these economic changes. At the beginning of the 21st century the city has shown strong recovery; it continues to search for the key to economic prosperity, refurbishing infrastructure and revitalizing downtown with projects like the new site of Housatonic Community-Technical College and the Harbor Yard Ballpark, home of the Bridgeport Bluefish minor league baseball team. The Barnum Museum (est. 1893), a gift to the city from P. T. Barnum, remains a major attraction.

Cecelia Bucki, *Bridgeport's Socialist New Deal, 1915–1936* (2000); Elsie Nicholas Danenberg, *The Story of Bridgeport* (1936); David W. Palmquist, *Bridgeport: A Pictorial History* (1981); George C. Waldo, Jr., *History of Bridgeport and Vicinity* (1917).

Cecelia Bucki

Brookline, Mass. Three miles west of downtown Boston, the town of Brookline has been one of the nation's best-known elite suburbs since the mid-19th century. Set off from Boston in 1705, it retained its municipal independence while the city grew around it. Selectmen and town meeting still govern a community of 57,061 persons (2000). Despite considerable wealth (in 2000 its median family income was $92,993 and median house value $599,500), the town does not lack diver-

sity: significant numbers of college students, elderly people, and professionals of many ethnic and religious groups live there. In addition to being the boyhood home of President John F. Kennedy, Brookline also claims the former Massachusetts governor and presidential candidate Michael S. Dukakis as a lifelong resident. The Kennedy birthplace at 83 Beals Street was designated a national historic site in 1969.

A small farming community well into the 19th century, Brookline had only 484 residents in 1790. After the Boston and Worcester Railroad opened a branch to Brookline Village in 1848, suburbanization came quickly. Hundreds of commuting businessmen and professionals moved into the area, along with many poor Irish Catholic immigrants. The population jumped from 1,682 to 5,164 between 1844 and 1860.

Brookline's public services, such as its excellent schools, public library, paid police force, gas lighting, and playgrounds, gave its citizens the confidence to reject annexation by Boston in 1873. The gracious estates of famous Boston families like the Cabots, Lowells, Lawrences, and Amorys gave the town a fashionable reputation, although 48 percent of households were headed by blue-collar workers. The lower middle classes that dominated nearby streetcar suburbs such as Dorchester and Somerville were nonetheless largely absent from Brookline. Formal and informal controls isolated the predominately Irish working class within the town.

In the late 1880s the reconstruction of Brookline's Beacon Street as a Parisian-style boulevard by Henry M. Whitney and Frederick Law Olmsted, both Brookline residents, launched a building boom in the northern part of town. By 1890 12,103 persons lived in Brookline, and by 1900 that figure had risen to 19,935. In addition to Olmsted, 19th-century Brookline was home to many prominent individuals, including the financial publisher Henry V. Poor, the art collector Isabella Stewart Gardner, and the architect Henry H. Richardson. Brookline's schools and town government were nationally recognized.

In the 20th century Brookline continued to grow while remaining among Boston's most prestigious suburbs. It became one of the first Massachusetts communities to adopt zoning and subdivision control bylaws. After 1915 Brookline gained a significant middle-class Jewish population. Older working-class neighborhoods did not expand, and some were removed by urban renewal projects after World War II. Residential development in the form of expensive single-family homes and apartments pushed the population to 57,589 by 1950. Limited new construction has occurred since then; in 1990, 67 percent of the housing units

had been built before 1950. Although there are local shopping districts in Brookline Village and Coolidge Corner, most of Brookline remains residential. Brookline is home to three colleges, Hebrew College (1921), Hellenic College (1937), a Greek Orthodox institution, and Newbury College (1962).

Even after a century and a half of intensive development Brookline retains significant open space, especially in the southern part of the town. Though located less than 5 miles from downtown Boston, Brookline still boasts the shaded lawns and fine old country homes that built its reputation as the home of the wealthy. Though these showpieces continue to impress, only 17 percent of Brookline's population lives in detached single-family homes.

John Gould Curtis, *History of the Town of Brookline, Massachusetts* (1933); Ronald Dale Karr, "Brookline and the Making of an Elite Suburb," *Chicago History* 13, no. 2 (1984); Karr, *New England at a Glance: Profiles from the 1990 Census* (1993).

Ronald Dale Karr

Burlington, Mass. Burlington, 12 miles northwest of Boston, is one of the few post–World War II boom towns in New England. As late as 1950 it was a sleepy rural community of 3,250 inhabitants; by 1970 it was home to 21,980. Today, with its malls and office complexes, Burlington is a scaled-down version of the suburban "edge cities" that have developed around many American metropolitan areas.

First settled by Europeans around 1642 as part of the new town of Woburn, Burlington was set aside as Woburn's Second Parish in 1730. Incorporation as the town of Burlington occurred in 1799. A year later the census counted 534 inhabitants. Nineteenth-century Burlington was almost exclusively a farming community, and although the Middlesex Turnpike passed through town in 1811, the railroads subsequently bypassed it. The population peaked at 711 in 1880 but declined to 593 by 1900, remaining virtually the same as it had been 100 years earlier.

Burlington did not begin to grow until after 1910. The population rose to 885 in 1920, then nearly doubled in the following decade. A number of subdivisions were promoted to Boston residents as sites for summer homes or one-acre "chicken farms," and some buyers discovered that their automobiles made it possible to live in this rural town year round. Even during the 1930s, when the population of many other suburbs stagnated, Burlington grew from 2,275 to 3,250 inhabitants.

At the end of World War II, Burlington was poised for rapid growth. The establishment of the Burlington Water District in 1949 ensured an ample supply of water, and Boston's circumferential highway, Route 128, was

built through the town between 1949 and 1951. Developers quickly turned Burlington's farms into house lots. Factories and office parks sprang up around the town's four Route 128 interchanges and along the Middlesex Turnpike, which paralleled the limited-access Route 3. Burlington became one of the fastest-growing towns in Massachusetts if not in all New England.

As late as 1938 the town had only one church and no high school. In 1973 it completed its third high school building, having outgrown the other two, and counted eight churches and a synagogue. The Burlington Mall, which opened in 1968, quickly became the region's most important shopping destination. By the 1970s only a few old farmhouses recalled rural Burlington. Even the attractive town common is a product of the 20th century.

Burlington today is one of the Boston region's most important commercial and office districts, yet it remains an agreeable residential suburb. Nearly all nonresidential development is in the far southern part of the town along Route 128 (now congruent with Interstate 95) and Route 3, while most of the population lives in single-family homes on short streets in post–World War II subdivisions. By 1980 relatively little open space remained, and only about 100 new housing units, many of them apartments, were built per year in the 1980s. With construction slowed and family size decreasing, Burlington's population in 2000 was 22,876. The census showed that more than two-thirds of employed resident adults held white-collar jobs. Burlington is a solid middle-class community, convenient to employment opportunities, and with a secure tax base that other towns envy.

John E. Fogelburg, *Burlington: Part of a Greater Chronicle* (1976).

Ronald Dale Karr

Burlington, Vt. Burlington, population 38,889 in 2000, is Vermont's largest city and the seat of Chittenden County. Originally chartered by New Hampshire governor Benning Wentworth in 1763, Burlington later became a part of New York. Recognizing Burlington's potential as a Lake Champlain port, Ira Allen, youngest brother of Ethan Allen, organized the Onion River Land Company, an association of Allen family members, to purchase New Hampshire titles in the region. The company sold land and supplies to settlers and speculators, while Ethan Allen and the Green Mountain Boys thwarted New York efforts to evict New Hampshire titleholders. In 1791, when Vermont was admitted to the union as the 14th state, Burlington's population numbered 330. That same year Ira Allen convinced the state legislature to establish the University of Vermont in Burlington.

Burlington at first grew slowly, but the opening of the Erie and Champlain-Hudson Canals, connecting Burlington to New York City and the West, enhanced its value as an entrepôt for shipments to Montreal. Lumber traffic from Quebec established Burlington as one of the nation's leading inland ports. When the railroads arrived in 1849, the town was already Vermont's leading commercial center and the state's largest and most diverse manufacturing center. Employment opportunities attracted a good number of French Canadian and Irish immigrants. By 1850 Burlington's population of 7,500 was the most heterogeneous in the state. Burlington village was incorporated as a city, and its agricultural hinterlands were reconstituted as South Burlington in 1864.

By 1890 Quebec's depleted forests and new tariff schedules devastated the lumber industry, while lake traffic, except for ferrying activities, succumbed to railroad competition. Burlington acquired some new industry and retained remnants of its old manufacturing, particularly textile mills, but its greatest economic strengths were in trade, finance, and banking. With a population of 14,590, it ranked as Vermont's largest city.

Burlington's waterfront traditionally was dominated by businesses dependent on lake traffic, but in recent years these have been replaced by recreational facilities overlooking Lake Champlain. The central business district is situated on a plateau above and east of the waterfront, with the University of Vermont

sitting further east on the crest of the hill. Residential neighborhoods lie to the north and south.

Although the city's population leveled off at approximately 37,000 in the latter half of the 20th century, growth in the areas adjacent to Burlington has been rapid. A major contributor to this growth has been IBM, which in 1957 located its principal Vermont facility in the area. In the 1980s IBM employed more than 8,000 workers. Despite reduction in its workforce since that time, it remains the largest private employer in the state. With incomes exceeding those of most Vermonters, IBM employees, along with the area's medical, legal, financial, and academic professionals and area students, provide the core of the constituency for the upscale shopping and restaurants that now dominate Burlington's commercial landscape.

Although Burlington has voted Democratic in state and presidential elections since early in the 20th century, in 1981 it elected Bernard Sanders, a self-styled socialist, as mayor and with one two-year exception has since elected independents. Despite recent efforts by some local institutions to attract racial minorities into the workforce, blacks, Asian Americans, and Native Americans constitute less than 4 percent of the population, a larger percentage than for the state at large. In addition to the University of Vermont (1791), the city is home to Champlain College (1878), Trinity College (1925), and Burlington College (1962). The Shelburne Museum, with a world-renowned collection of folk art, is 11 miles south of Burlington.

David J. Blow, *Historic Guide to Burlington Neighborhoods*, 2 vols. (1991–97); Historic Preservation Program of the University of Vermont, *The Burlington Book: Agriculture, History, Future* (1980); Robert B. Michaud, *Salute to Burlington: An Informal History of Burlington, Vermont* (1991); David E. Robinson, *Burlington* (1997).

Samuel B. Hand

Cambridge, Mass. Home to two of the country's greatest universities, Cambridge, as much as Boston, is the cultural heart of New England. Beyond Harvard University, founded as Harvard College in 1636, and the Massachusetts Institute of Technology, founded in Boston in 1861 and relocated to Cambridge in 1916, however, lies a vibrant, diverse, sometimes gritty city of 101,355 persons (2000).

Founded in 1631 as Newetowne across the Charles River from Boston, the settlement lost many of its inhabitants when the Reverend Thomas Hooker led his Puritan followers to Connecticut in 1636. Renamed Cambridge after the English university that spawned many a Puritan divine, the town originally stretched west to Newton and north to Billerica, but as the outlying sections attracted residents, they were set off from Cambridge proper. With the incorporation of Brighton and West Cambridge (Arlington) in 1807, Cambridge was reduced to the 6-square-mile area that, with minor adjustments, it still occupies.

As late as 1790 most of present-day Cambridge, aside from the village of Old Cambridge near Harvard College, consisted of farms and mudflats. The census that year found only 2,115 inhabitants for a community encompassing what are now Brighton and Arlington. The opening of the West Boston Bridge in 1793 and the Canal Bridge in 1809 reduced the road distance between Boston and Old Cambridge from 8 to 3 miles and put the town directly in the path of commerce between Boston and the hinterland.

Cambridge exploited its proximity to Boston. Commercial farming, tanneries, stockyards, and factories employed a growing workforce, and by 1830 the town was attracting residents who commuted to jobs in Boston. In 1846, when the population had reached roughly 13,000, the town was incorporated as a city. In 1890 it counted 70,028 inhabitants.

By the beginning of the 20th century Cambridge had developed into an industrial city, but one with a difference. Harvard and MIT cast long shadows over the Old Cambridge and Cambridgeport sections of the city. Harvard Square, with its bookstores, boutiques, restaurants, and street performers, is the heart of the former Old Cambridge, its once rural mansions stretching northwest along Brattle Street.

Burlington, Vt., with Lake Champlain and northern New York in the distance, 1988

Harvard Square, Cambridge, Mass., 1990

Cambridgeport encompasses a poor black neighborhood, high-tech office complexes in Kendall Square, and crowded student apartment buildings near Central Square. Residents tend to be young, well educated, and cosmopolitan. Away from Harvard and MIT, in East and North Cambridge, are the city's lower-middle- and working-class neighborhoods, whose mostly Roman Catholic residents are often at odds with the other Cambridge. Predominantly of Irish, Italian, and Portuguese descent, these inhabitants have more in common with neighbors in Somerville and Charlestown than with fellow Cambridge residents who are oriented toward the city's universities.

The population of Cambridge peaked in 1950 at 120,740 then declined to 95,322 by 1980, as household size shrank and relatively little new housing was built (nearly two-thirds of the existing housing units in 1990 had been constructed before 1940). Most of the small factories that once characterized the city have closed. In addition to Harvard and MIT, Cambridge is home to Radcliffe College of Harvard University (1867), Lesley College (1909), and the Episcopal Divinity School (1867). The Smithsonian Institution's Astrophysical Observatory moved to Cambridge from Washington, D.C., in 1955. The city has many museums, most associated with Harvard, including the Museum of Cultural and Natural History, the Fogg Art Museum, the Busch Reisinger Museum, and the Arthur M. Sackler Museum. Mount Auburn Cemetery (1831) contains the graves of many of the city's famous 19th-century inhabitants, including

Henry Wadsworth Longfellow and Mary Baker Eddy. The Craigie-Longfellow House (built 1759) on Brattle Street is a national historic site.

Henry C. Binford, *The First Suburbs: Residential Communities on the Boston Periphery, 1815–1860* (1985); Lucius R. Paige, *History of Cambridge, Massachusetts, 1630–1877* (1877); Robert Bell Rettig, *Guide to Cambridge Architecture: Ten Walking Tours* (1969); S. B. Sutton, *Cambridge Reconsidered: Three and a Half Centuries on the Charles* (1976).

Ronald Dale Karr

Cemeteries New England historically has influenced cultural patterns throughout the United States, so it is not surprising that it likewise shaped the country's deathways. The assumptions that underlie the choice of a loved one's burial place and the appearance of the modern cemetery derive from changes in custom initiated in New England. A family may have special wishes such as an ethnic or religious burial, but they also look for a quiet atmosphere and a carefully maintained landscape. Many more historical New England graveyards are at the same time art museums and arboretums worth visiting.

Researchers have discovered extensive evidence of red ochre used in Native American burial and crematory ceremonies in southern New England, much like those of the so-called Red Paint of eastern Maine, whose burial practices were noted for their long duration and ceremonial complexity. For the first two centuries of European settlement, burials took place in the corners of fields, in town burial grounds, or in church graveyards, where land-

scape was of no concern. With increasing urbanization, however, city land became too valuable for burial of the dead. Churchyards became crowded, and the unhygienic practice of multiple burials in one grave caused concern. Sometimes buildings were erected right over a burial ground. Other times remains were moved again and again as a city continued to grow.

In 1796 a group of men in New Haven, Conn., attempted to solve this problem when they bought 6 acres of flat land at the edge of town and established the New Burial Ground, now known as the Grove Street Cemetery. The state legislature granted the nonprofit private cemetery a charter guaranteeing burial rights in perpetuity and its owners the right to tax its users for the cost of maintenance. The guarantee of perpetuity, the provision for upkeep, and the practice of allowing a family to buy a large lot were all valuable innovations, but when avenues had been neatly laid out in straight lines and grass and trees planted, few people purchased lots. Consequently, few towns followed New Haven's example of establishing an "ornamental ground," as this model came to be called.

In 1831 a group of Bostonians, in cooperation with the Massachusetts Horticultural Society, purchased 37 bucolic acres across the Charles River from Boston to establish Mount Auburn Cemetery. The roads and paths were laid out to follow the contours of the land and to provide picturesque views of the woods, the river, and Boston itself. The founders had in mind the landscape model of Capability Brown's great 18th-century English estates, picturesquely natural yet controlled by man. Although many scenic New England graveyards already existed, the Mount Auburn founders were the first to deliberately plan such a landscape. When changes in religious attitudes caused people to wish to bury their dead where nature might offer solace and encouragement, Mount Auburn became immediately popular, as its beauty offered comfort to mourners and spiritual uplift to visitors. A. J. Downing, America's first native landscape architect, cited the popularity of Mount Auburn in his campaign for cities to establish public parks that would bring the benefits and lessons of nature to city dwellers. The effort to bring nature into the city also contributed to the development of modern urban planning.

Additional responses to the expansion of urban immigrant New England led to heightened interest in the colonial past as the touchstone of democracy and American character and encouraged further recognition and commemoration of the fallen forefathers. In 1927 Harriette Merrifield Forbes of Worcester, Mass., published the first serious study of regional cemetery monuments, *Gravestones of Early New England*. Others soon followed suit, and the old graveyards of New England became tourist attractions. Visitors to Portsmouth, N.H., or Salem, Mass., commonly seek out old graveyards in the course of their sightseeing. Dedicated organizations throughout New England record and preserve old graveyards, and historical societies take great pride in their early stones. Boston early had to forbid gravestone rubbing in the three graveyards featured along the popular Freedom Trail: the Granary Burial Ground, the King's Chapel Burying Ground, and Copp's Hill Burying Ground. More recently Boston has become the first city to invest large sums of money to restore and arrange long-term maintenance not only for those three conspicuous yards but also for the many neglected, forgotten burial sites. The Historic Burying Ground Initiative, with city resources and financing from private foundations, organizes neighborhood groups concerned for their nearby burial grounds.

Puritan belief in simplicity and dislike of ornamentation has persisted in the New England character through the centuries. Cemeteries devoted to specific ethnic or religious groups are austere, with none of the color and flamboyance found, for instance, in Chicago's Assyrian, Bohemian, Czech, and Slavic cemeteries. Traditionally Protestant cemeteries such as Mount Auburn or Swan Point in Providence have few of the elaborate monuments and elegant mausolea that Woodlawn in New York and Bellefontaine in Saint Louis display in every section.

Despite their Spartan tastes, New Englanders never wanted for competent monument carvers. Soon after the beginning of the 19th century, marble—for centuries the medium of sculptors—became popular for gravestones. The work of Boston's Alpheus Cary, whose modest stones show his artistry in panels with small relief carvings, spread throughout Massachusetts. After midcentury, John Evans of Boston carved gravestones from limestone. By the end of the century, power tools were available and sturdy granite became the stone of choice. Barre, Vt., with its vast granite quarries and immigrant Italian masons, became an important source of gravestones. The Italian carvers' memorials for their own dead make Hope Cemetery in Barre a mecca for anyone interested in gravestones.

Arthur J. Krim, "Diffusion of Garden Cemeteries in New England," *Proceedings, New England–St. Lawrence Valley Geographical Society* 13 (1983); Blanche Linden-Ward, *Silent City on a Hill: Landscapes of Memory and Boston's Mount Auburn Cemetery* (1989); Barbara Rotundo, "The Rural Cemetery Movement," *Essex Institute Historical Collections* 109 (July 1973); David Schuyler, *The New Urban Landscape: The Redefinition of City Form in 19th-Century America* (1986).

Barbara Rotundo

The new Charles River Crossing of the Central Artery/Ted Williams Tunnel Project, Boston, 2003: traffic on I-93 flows on the Leonard P. Zakim Bunker Hill Bridge (left), the Leverett Circle Connector Bridge, and their connecting loop ramps to Route 1

Central Artery/Ted Williams Tunnel Project, Boston (Big Dig)

The largest urban infrastructure project in the nation's history, Boston's Central Artery/Ted Williams Tunnel Project has taken nearly 20 years and an estimated $14.6 billion (2003 estimate) to plan, permit, and construct. A highway disappearing act of sorts, the 7.5 miles of new urban roadway, half of which is in tunnels, was dreamed up in the 1970s. This megaproject combined two efforts. The first was the Ted Williams Tunnel from South Boston to Logan Airport, which has relieved congestion on the Interstate 93 Central Artery through downtown Boston since it opened on December 15, 1995. The second effort is an eight- to 10-lane Central Artery tunnel that replaces the elevated highway viaduct's six lanes (the most heavily traveled in the country), thereby turning nearly 27 acres of highway area into parks, housing, offices, and cultural destinations upon its anticipated completion in 2005.

The Central Artery viaduct had sliced through the city, isolating neighborhoods and generally blighting all in its path. Persuaded in 1970 by contractor Bill Reynolds that the structure could be removed without shutting down Boston, Fred Salvucci led the campaign to remove it and, while working for Mayor Kevin White and then for Governor Michael Dukakis, built a uniquely effective political coalition of business, labor, environmentalists, neighborhoods, Republicans, and Democrats around a vision of a rebuilt city in the viaduct's empty corridor.

The new tunnel is being built under the old city by reinforcing the existing viaduct and then digging the new tunnel underneath it, while traffic safely travels overhead and pedestrians and motorists continue to use city streets above the growing tunnel. Careful engineering fit the new tunnel walls almost up against the foundations of centuries-old historic buildings that could not be relocated or damaged, and moved all utilities for sewers, electricity, phones, and water from beneath the street to new sites where they would not interfere with the tunnel. The cross-harbor tunnel was constructed quite differently, with steel tubes floated in, sunk to the harbor floor, and sealed together.

Architecture, urban design, and public art also played important roles in fitting this new tunnel and its access ramps comfortably into a busy city. Architects considered the visual impact of the five warehouse-sized tunnel ventilation buildings and the look of the highway itself. Urban designers influenced the placement of highway ramps in order to create the most attractive and safe environments for pedestrians, residents of adjacent neighborhoods, and drivers. Three new "gateways" to Boston were carefully landscaped to shape and control approaching motorists' views of the skyline. The first public arts program for a highway project of this scale was created to humanize the environments created by the new highway and tunnel structures, adding elements ranging from art over the harbor tunnel portals celebrating its namesake, Red Sox slugger Ted Williams, to local schoolchildren's art on construction fencing, to the creation of pedestrian bridges and bridge lighting.

Building this federally funded state project in city territory involved these three levels of government in many negotiations regarding their relative authority and responsibilities. Often at loggerheads, these bureaucracies were able to work out arrangements for land ownership, environmental mitigation, land use and traffic authority, costs and funding, and exactly what would be funded through the approximately 85 percent federal share.

The project has also mandated close cooperation of public and private sectors. A private firm, Bechtel/Parsons Brinckerhoff, was hired for preliminary design and construction management; meanwhile, the Artery Business Committee (ABC) was created to act as advocate and watchdog of the extensive information, access, and "housekeeping" programs as well as to oversee design and construction matters.

Community participation has also played a major role in shaping the project. A massive effort by residents of Boston's North End, Charlestown, and Cambridge resulted in plans for a beautiful cable-stayed bridge across the Charles River (Leonard P. Zakim Bunker Hill Bridge; Christian Menn, 2002), replacing one that would have added 17 piers as obstacles to river traffic. Chinatown residents and business owners resisted traffic routing that would have created additional hazards for the neighborhood's intense pedestrian activity. Move Massachusetts 2000, WalkBoston, and ABC joined forces with the city of Boston to redesign the Central Artery surface streets, to create a more pedestrian-friendly environment, and to advocate a special management and funding program for developing the new land above the tunnel.

Dan McNichol and Andy Ryan, *The Big Dig* (2000); Peter Vanderwarker, *The Big Dig: Reshaping an American City* (2001).

Rebecca Barnes

Chinatown, Boston The earliest Chinese to settle in Boston probably arrived as trade relations between the United States and China grew more active after the founding of the American republic. The Boston merchant Major Samuel Shaw's appointment as the first consul general to China in 1786 increased contact between the city and China, bringing a small number of Chinese merchants to the area. It was not until the 1870s, however, that the first sizable group of Chinese settled in

Tyler Street in Boston's Chinatown, 1998

Boston. In 1870 Calvin Sampson brought 75 Chinese laborers from California to break a strike at his shoe factory in North Adams, Mass. After their three-year contract expired, a number of these Chinese migrated to Boston to work on the construction of the Pearl Street Telegraph Exchange. Eventually the Chinese occupied the area between Boylston Street and Kneeland Street currently known as Chinatown, a neighborhood that had previously been settled by successive waves of Irish, Jewish, Iranian, and Syrian immigrants. By 1900 approximately 850 Chinese, many of whom were recent migrants from the western United States, lived in Boston; approximately 250 resided in Chinatown.

The Geary Act of 1898 required Chinese living in the United States to carry identification papers with them at all times. Persons found without such papers were subject to imprisonment and deportation. During a raid of Boston's Chinatown on October 11, 1903, local police and Immigration Bureau investigators entered homes, restaurants, and other establishments without warrants and arrested 234 Chinese for failing to produce their ID papers on demand. Only after being taken into custody and crowded into small holding cells were these people permitted to contact friends for assistance in procuring their papers. In the end 50 arrestees were found to be illegal immigrants. This raid stands as one of the most celebrated cases of police harassment of the Chinese American community.

With the repeal of the Chinese Exclusion Acts in 1943, the passage of the War Brides Act after World War II, and the Immigration Act of 1965, the Chinese population of Boston has

grown steadily. The 2000 census reports more than 75,000 Chinese living in the Greater Boston area. Of the 5,500 living in Chinatown many are new immigrants. Thirty-nine percent speak a dialect of Chinese at home, and almost 35 percent live below the federal government's poverty line. Lack of fluency in English limits employment opportunities for many residents, and certain problems therefore continue to plague the community. The economy, based largely on the tourist and restaurant trades, cannot support that part of the immigrant population whose job and English-language skills are minimal. Joblessness has contributed to a rise in the numbers of disaffected youths and an increase in gang violence.

The most pressing issue for Chinatown, however, is the poor quality of its housing. The situation has been exacerbated as the Fitzgerald Expressway, Tufts University Medical School, and New England Medical Center have encroached on the neighborhood, thereby decreasing available space for housing. As leases have come up for renewal, some Chinese businesses have moved into bordering areas, most notably replacing adult bookstores and movie theaters in the section of Boston known as the Combat Zone. Housing needs continue to be pressing, however. Fortunately, a number of community organizations have formed over the years to take on the challenges of health care, housing, employment, child care, and care for the elderly.

Doris C. J. Chu, *Chinese in Massachusetts: Their Experiences and Contributions* (1987); Gene Koo, *Representing Chinatown: Power and Legitimacy in Boston's Chinese Community* (1997); K. Scott Wong, "'The Eagle Seeks a Helpless Quarry': Chinatown, the Police, and the Press, the 1903 Boston Chinatown Raid Revisited," *Amerasia Journal* 22 (1996).

K. Scott Wong

Cityscapes To a casual observer driving along its highways, New England cities appear to be little different from their counterparts elsewhere in the nation. Sleek, modern office towers dominate the downtown skyline in Boston, Providence, and Hartford as in Kansas City, Omaha, and Cincinnati. Superhighways rip through decaying residential neighborhoods and skirt grim, abandoned factories. In New England as throughout much of the United States, one is struck by the sharp contrast between glittering high rises and shabby, gray neighborhoods, between the physical landmarks of wealth and the concrete reminders of poverty. Yet a closer examination reveals certain distinctive features of the New England cityscape. Though Boston and the lesser hubs are recognizably American cities, they also bear the distinguishing marks of their New England heritage.

This regional distinctiveness is evident in the pattern of the streets. Although 17th-century New Haven, Conn., was laid out in a strict grid pattern of rectangular blocks surrounding a rectangular green, elsewhere in New England the first settlers eschewed such geometric precision. In Boston a complex web of narrow, crooked streets developed, and this pattern survives, making driving in the downtown and the North End a nightmare for the uninitiated. The earliest streets of Hartford conformed to the natural terrain, resulting in a disorderly pattern of thoroughfares in the central business district. Similarly, 18th-century Portland, Maine, consisted of Fore, Middle, and Back streets, none of which was laid out with a ruler, and the consequent irregular street pattern in the heart of Maine's largest city might well confuse midwesterners accustomed to a neat grid of numbered avenues. Church steeples might better serve to orient newcomers to early New England cities and towns.

Nineteenth-century residential areas were often laid out in a grid pattern, but the main thoroughfares of expanding New England cities were roads dating from the colonial era. These roads radiated from the old town centers and followed the natural terrain. Thus a neat pattern of straight streets perpendicular to one another characterized many 19th-century tracts such as Boston's Back Bay, yet the overall street pattern of Boston, Hartford, New Haven, and Providence never resembled the uniform grid of Manhattan, Philadelphia, Chicago, and Minneapolis. West of the Appalachians, federal government surveyors divided the land into square townships and sections, and rural roads followed the township and section lines straight across the countryside. As urban areas expanded, this existing rural grid encouraged the perpetuation of a rectangular street pattern. In New England, however, topography and a legacy of meandering colonial byways determined that cities would not expand in an endless succession of straight, numbered thoroughfares, with 39th Street predictably following 38th Street.

The urban housing patterns of late-19th- and early-20th-century New England also resulted in a distinctive cityscape. In New England cities, the two- and three-family dwelling prevailed to a degree unknown in other American urban areas. The three-decker, a three-story, three-unit structure, was a housing type associated almost exclusively with New England. In Worcester, Mass., 6,000 such structures were built between 1880 and 1930, and they constituted almost half of all the buildings constructed from 1890 to 1910, earning Worcester the nickname "City of Three-Deckers." But other New England cities could challenge Worcester for the title. Throughout the region the single-family dwelling was less prevalent than in other American cities. By 1930 one-family homes constituted 80 percent of the dwelling structures in all American cities with 100,000 or more people, whereas the figure for the 13 New England cities in this population category was only 57 percent. Boston and Providence were more densely populated than Detroit or Indianapolis, with more residents sharing a structure and fewer single-family homes dotting the landscape.

Although New Englanders were willing to live stacked on top of one another, they were not among the earliest devotees of the skyscraper. The steel-framed high rise was a product of Chicago and migrated eastward, transforming lower and midtown Manhattan during the first three decades of the 20th century. In 1891 the Massachusetts legislature, however, imposed a maximum height limit of 125 feet on buildings in downtown Boston, and before the late 1920s the only office structure that exceeded this limit was the 32-story Customs House Tower. In 1928 the legislature discarded the height restriction, allowing the construction of additional skyscrapers such as the United Shoe Machinery Building. Yet by the 1930s Boston was still a relatively low-rise city that had not succumbed to skyscraper mania. Likewise, other New England cities had few high-rise giants. The 527-foot Travelers Tower had no rivals in Hartford, and the Industrial Trust Building dominated the Providence skyline, soaring far above the less lofty buildings lining the downtown streets of Rhode Island's capital.

New Englanders expressed their uneasiness with the import from the Midwest via Manhattan when they tried to mask their new office structures with an architectural vocabulary more appropriate to the region. Thus New Haven's 13-story Union Trust Company headquarters built in 1927 was a Colonial Revival structure, its architects referring to it as a tower "of pure Colonial design." Similarly, in 1920 Hartford's 17-story Connecticut Trust Building with its red brick, white trim, and classical details was designed to be a compatible neighbor to the city's Federal period Old State House.

After World War II, however, the homogenizing effects of urban renewal, public housing, and highway construction threatened much of the existing cityscape. Highway planners seemed dedicated to transforming Boston into Los Angeles, with freeways radiating in every direction from the city center and inner and outer beltways linking the multilane spokes of asphalt. The elevated Central Artery cut through the historic heart of Boston, isolating the North End and the waterfront from the central business district. Likewise, in Providence and New Haven new freeways cut off the downtown from the waterfront that had once been the source of the cities' commercial prosperity.

Eager to Manhattanize the New England metropolis, urban renewal planners and commercial developers added scores of new office towers to the skyline. Boston's Prudential Center and Hartford's Constitution Plaza, both constructed in the early 1960s, owed more to the ideas of Le Corbusier than to the regional urban traditions of New England. These multipurpose developments of high rises in open plazas were being proposed in cities throughout the nation. During the 1960s, 1970s, and 1980s, one high rise after another appeared in central Boston, including that ultimate glass behemoth, the 61-story John Hancock Tower. In the early 1980s Hartford's City Place robbed the venerable Travelers Tower of its distinction as the city's tallest structure, and in Worcester the sleek Worcester County National Bank Building and the high-rise Mechanics Bank Building opened in the early 1970s, symbols of that city's unwillingness to be left behind in the race for commercial prominence.

Meanwhile, the drab public housing projects of New England were indistinguishable from those in a score of older metropolitan areas elsewhere in the nation. The bleak brick towers of Boston's Columbia Point project epitomized the worst in public housing design, and by the last decades of the 20th century Providence's Codding Court and Roger Williams Homes were painful reminders of good intentions gone awry.

In the last three decades of the 20th century, however, some local groups sought to battle the homogenization of the cityscape and preserve or restore distinguishing features of the New England city. In 1955 the Massachusetts legislature established Beacon Hill as a historic district, and 11 years later Massachusetts lawmakers created the Back Bay Architectural Commission to ensure that new construction in the Back Bay district was compatible with the existing late-19th-century structures. Beginning in 1956 the Providence Preservation Society sought to safeguard the traditional urban fabric of Rhode Island's capital. Similarly, Greater Portland Landmarks, formed in the early 1960s, and the Hartford Architecture Conservancy, founded in 1973, fought to preserve the best from the past.

As New Englanders mobilized in defense of their urban heritage, they also became enamored once more with the waterfront. During the 1970s and 1980s Boston's old wharves were transformed into luxury apartments and new multi-use waterfront projects such as

Rowes Wharf appeared in the city's once shabby dock district. Providence likewise promoted waterfront revitalization; shops and restaurants moved into rehabilitated structures and thousands of visitors flocked to the annual waterfront festival.

Thus at the turn of the 21st century the process of homogenization was tempered by a healthy respect for the distinguishing features of the indigenous cityscape. Beacon Hill and Back Bay survived as distinctive Boston neighborhoods, unlike anything in Cleveland, Milwaukee, or Los Angeles. In the 1980s Worcester still boasted 4,500 three-deckers, constituting one-fifth of the city's housing stock and marking Worcester as unquestionably a New England city. And the street pattern inherited from the colonial era continued to distinguish the cityscape of New England.

Elizabeth Mills Brown, *New Haven: A Guide to Architecture and Urban Design* (1976); Robert Campbell, *Cityscapes of Boston: An American City Through Time* (1992); Michael P. Conzen and George K. Lewis, *Boston: A Geographical Portrait* (1976); Michael Holleran, "Boston's 'Sacred Sky Line': From Prohibiting to Sculpting Skyscrapers, 1891–1928," *Journal of Urban History* 22 (1996); Elliott B. Knowlton, ed., *Worcester's Best: A Guide to the City's Architectural Heritage* (1984); Naomi Miller and Keith Morgan, *Boston Architecture, 1975–1990* (1990); Douglas W. Rae, *City: Urbanism and Its End* (2003); Walter Muir Whitehill, *Boston: A Topographical History* (1968).

Jon C. Teaford

Commuting Just about half of all New Englanders are engaged in a regular commute between home and work, according to the U.S. census of 1990. In a sense, this trip gets more attention than it deserves. After all, half the population does not commute to work, and the Nationwide Personal Transportation Survey of 1990 reports that even among those who do, commuting accounts for less than 20 percent of all trips taken.

Yet there are reasons for viewing the commute as more important than these numbers suggest. First, unlike trips taken to visit friends or stores, commuting takes place at certain concentrated times (rush hours) and in specific locations (the routes to business districts). It creates peak levels of traffic congestion and intense pressure for improvements to the transportation system. Second, the constraints of the commute often affect where people live and work. Throughout New England the time spent commuting has continued to grow.

Commuting in New England got a big boost in 1843. Before then, the distance between home and regular place of work could be no farther than a person could travel in an hour on foot or on horseback. In 1843, however, the rail line that for almost a decade had

carried goods between Boston and Newton introduced the region's first rail car intended for regular daily commuting service. It immediately attracted passengers to Boston, and the suburban land boom began.

By the late 1800s regular steam rail service had transformed small villages for 30 miles around Boston into commuter suburbs and had enabled workers from some Connecticut towns to commute to New York City. By 1920 electric streetcar and trolley lines had created higher density commuter corridors within and around Boston, Hartford, Bridgeport, Conn., and many smaller cities throughout New England. These lines lost riders, converted to buses, or simply terminated service altogether as commuters turned to automobiles, but their influence on land-development patterns in New England remains evident today.

The shift to private cars had a great impact on commuting. Previous transportation improvements had spurred residential development far from central cities; the pervasiveness of automobiles and the development of suburban highways promoted a similar dispersal of work sites. Office parks sprouted at major intersections on Route 128, Boston's circumferential highway, as soon as that road opened in the late 1950s. This initially gave employees who had moved to nearby suburbs an easy drive to work, but massive growth in suburban jobs and the inability of public transit to serve these widely scattered workplaces spawned commutes to the suburbs that in many cases were worse than those to the old downtowns.

There is increasingly a difference between New Englanders who commute to the old downtowns and those who do not. Engineers and workers in high-technology firms are almost exclusively commuting to suburban locations. Employees in finance, law, insurance, and real estate are a growing share of commuters to the downtowns. In Boston, for example, only one major high-tech firm (Teradyne) remains in the center city. Those who commute to jobs in New England downtowns also tend to be higher paid than their suburban-job counterparts. About 97 percent of commuters on Metro-North Commuter Railroad's service from Connecticut travel to New York's Grand Central Terminal, and the average household income on the line is well over $100,000. This is undoubtedly the wealthiest group of public transportation patrons anywhere in the country. They are also the only ones who enjoy the luxury of a rolling bar car. The state of Connecticut insists that the publicly subsidized railroad maintain the bar cars, even though converting them to regular passenger coaches would provide much-needed additional seats.

A shortage of seats is a constraint on commuter trains to both New York and Boston. Limited parking space at suburban rail stations is an even more serious problem. Village centers grew around the New England commuter rail stations built in the 1800s, and few towns are willing to mar the old village green with a parking garage in order to accommodate increasing out-of-town commuter traffic. The Massachusetts Bay Transportation Authority, which governs rail travel throughout the Boston area, has in some cases built new commuter rail stations with huge commuter parking lots (some with more than 1,000 parking spaces) outside the old village centers.

Meanwhile, more and more commuters are driving to work by themselves. In 2000, 77

Rush hour, Route 128, Waltham, Mass., 1974

percent of New Englanders made the trip to work alone, up from 64 percent in 1980. To accommodate this growth, transportation agencies have proposed constructing new circumferential highways around cities such as Nashua and Portsmouth, N.H., projects that often elicit opposition from residents of nearby areas or fail to meet federal environmental standards. Boston-area projects have met with somewhat more success. In 1991 construction began on Boston's new Central Artery and third harbor tunnel. The most expensive (per mile) transportation project in the country, the "Big Dig" is slated for completion in 2005. Transit officials also restored the Old Colony rail line in 1997 as an alternative to the automobile for commuters on the South Shore.

Jeffrey P. Brown, *Who Works in Boston: Commuting Patterns in the Boston Metropolitan Area* (1984); Stephen M. Falbel, *The Demographics of Commuting in Greater Boston,* 2d rev. ed. (1998); Toni Marzotto, Vicky Moshier Burnor, and Gordon Scott Bonham, *The Evolution of Public Policy: Cars and the Environment* (2000); New Hampshire Department of Employment Security, *New Hampshire Commuting Patterns: 1990 U.S. Census* (1994).

Marc Warner

Concord, N.H.

Concord (population 40,687 in 2000) is in the south central portion of the state, about 15 miles north of Manchester and 64 miles northwest of Boston. Originally named Rumford, the city took its present name in 1765 after the peaceful settlement of a boundary dispute with Massachusetts. Concord has served as the state capital since 1808, is also the seat of Merrimack County, and hosts the state library and the Museum of New Hampshire History, which connects the modern state capital to its historic roots.

Since the 1803 opening of the first New Hampshire Turnpike, which connected Concord and Portsmouth, the capital has been important to trade and transportation. Before 1860, the largest stagecoach factory in the United States turned out Concord coaches, a vital mode of transportation that was especially popular in the American West. Granite quarrying and carving also became a vibrant industry, and Marquis de Lafayette's 1825 visit to these quarries led a young lawyer, Philip Carrigain, to pen a seven-stanza song entitled "Lafayette's Return" for the occasion, including the line, "He comes, by fond entreaties moved, The Granite State to see," thus creating the popular New Hampshire nickname, "the Granite State." Concord granite was used to build Boston's Quincy Market and the Library of Congress in the nation's capital.

The arrival of the railroad in 1842 guaranteed that the city would be a major transportation hub throughout the 19th century and into

Capitol Center for the Arts, Concord, N.H., 2004

the 20th. At the height of the rail era, 25 passenger trains daily departed Concord, which had become the largest and most important rail center north of Boston; the Boston and Maine Railroad became the city's largest employer. Even after rail's decline in the 1920s, the city remained a shopping and commercial center. Additionally, Concord has become a center for health care in northern New England, and that industry employs more than 5,000 workers.

Concord also serves as an important center of finance. The printing industry, together with electronic equipment, leather, wood, and metal products, and dairy processing and distribution are the economic mainstays of the city. Downtown Concord has remained vital and alive despite the development of malls and discount merchandisers on the city's periphery. Some specialty retailers have relocated from malls to the attractive downtown, which retains its active trade thanks in part to the daily presence of government, finance, and legal office workers. The neoclassical golden-domed statehouse, completed in 1819, is a landmark and a historical anchor for Concord's downtown. The cultural life of the city has been reinvigorated by the 1992–95 restoration of the classical Capitol Theater as the Capitol Center for the Arts, which draws significant crowds to the Victorian-era downtown. The Capitol Theater was refurbished from its vaudeville and movie house days to become the largest theater in the state and home to theatrical, dance, musical, and cultural events.

Notwithstanding the importance of government, finance, and shopping for Concord, tourism and recreation have assumed a prominent role in the life and economy of the city, the region, and, indeed, the entire state. Since

the decline of the textile industry after World War II, New Hampshire has capitalized on its lakes, mountains, forests, and seacoast to build a year-round vacation and tourist economy that supplements the newer electronics, plastics, and research and design segments. Concord benefits as the urban gateway to New Hampshire's Lakes Region, which draws summer vacationers and winter sports enthusiasts. Concord is home to Saint Paul's School, the Christa McAuliffe Planetarium, and the Franklin Pierce Manse, home site of the only U.S. president from New Hampshire.

Leon W. Anderson, *Concord's Trials and Tribulations, 1725–1977* (1977); Committee for a New England Bibliography, *New Hampshire: A Bibliography of Its History* (1979); Ralph N. Hill, *Yankee Kingdom: Vermont and New Hampshire* (1984); William L. Taylor, ed., *Readings in New Hampshire and New England History* (1971).

James P. Hanlan

Cultural Institutions

Observers of American public life have informally agreed that the influence of New England's cultural institutions has been disproportionate to the region's economic, political, and population resources. As Alexis de Tocqueville put it in the early 19th century, "The civilization of New England has been like a beacon lit upon a hill, which, after it has diffused its warmth immediately around it, also tinges the distant horizon with its glow."

New England's cultural institutions, public and private, have set the pace for the rest of the nation. In higher education Harvard (1636), in Cambridge, Mass., was the first college to be established in the colonies. In the 19th century it was the first to transform itself into a university along modern lines. Today Harvard retains its preeminence in wealth, productivity, and influence. Known to historians of education as the "mother of colleges," Yale (1701), in New Haven, Conn., took the lead in propagating higher education. Yale alumni played a decisive role in founding some 41 colleges and universities throughout the country during the 19th century.

Free public education in the United States began when Massachusetts passed the Old Seducer Satan Act in 1647, requiring every town of 50 or more households to establish a tax-supported school. Connecticut's Common School Fund (1784), which used the proceeds of the sale of western lands to support public education, broke new ground in education financing. Building on these foundations, the 19th-century education reformer Horace Mann created a statewide system of public schools and teacher training in Massachusetts that became the model for the rest of the nation. The Hartford native Noah Webster, believing that "America must be as independent in literature as she is in politics . . . as famous for arts as for arms," made New England the national center for the production of spelling and reading books.

New England also led the way in the popularization and democratization of culture. The nation's first public library was founded on the 1665 bequest of the Boston merchant Robert Keayne. In the 18th century New England became the center for the establishment of social libraries, private clubs that purchased and lent books to members. In the 19th century, using proceeds from the state's Literary Fund, New Hampshire established the first tax-supported libraries. Relying on both public and private funds, the Boston Public Library (1854) became a paradigm for modern urban library systems throughout the country. Lyceums—associations sponsoring popular series of lectures, debates, and scientific demonstrations—began with the efforts of Josiah Holbrook and Lyman Beecher in the mid-1820s. Within a decade thousands of lyceums had been established throughout the country, bringing to towns and villages the talents of leading scientists, writers, and social critics like Benjamin Silliman and Ralph Waldo Emerson. The Lowell Institute, founded in 1839 to support public lectures, provided the initial funding for public broadcasting in the region, with its support for the WGBH radio station in 1950.

New England's art institutions have set an example for other U.S. regions. Contributions from private collectors and collections donated by Harvard, the Massachusetts Institute of Technology, and the Boston Athenaeum became the basis for the Boston Museum of Fine Arts (1870). Closely tied to Harvard, the museum became more than a venue for the exhibition of objets d'art, serving as the nursery of American art historical scholarship. Yale established the nation's first university art gallery in 1832 and its first art school in 1864. Hartford's Wadsworth Atheneum and Providence's Rhode Island School of Design are examples of two superb smaller-scale museums in the region.

Musical culture flourished in New England following the Revolution in the form of commercial enterprises publishing music and psalm books, launched by entrepreneurial composer-hymnodists like William Billings and Daniel Read in the late 18th and early 19th centuries. In the early 19th century the composer, publisher, and musical educator Lowell Mason transformed Americans' appreciation for serious music, and periodicals such as John Dwight's *Journal of Music* sought to set national standards of musical taste. The Boston Symphony Orchestra (1881), under the patronage of financier Henry Lee Higginson,

became the model for the modern nonprofit musical organization in the United States.

As industrial decline and the loss of population to suburbs weakened urban society in the 20th century, many cities responded by emphasizing cultural institutions such as museums, music halls, and civic centers to draw suburban and urban residents, as well as tourists, to downtown areas. Although New York became the nation's financial center and Washington its political hub, New England's universities—particularly Harvard and Yale—continued to set the American standard for educational excellence. New England's cultural beacon shows no signs of dimming.

Bernard Bailyn, *Education in the Forming of American Society* (1960); Carl Bode, *The American Lyceum: Town Meeting of the Mind* (1968 [1956]); Paul J. DiMaggio, "Cultural Entrepreneurship in 19th-Century Boston," in *Nonprofit Enterprise in the Arts: Studies in Mission and Constraint*, ed. Paul J. DiMaggio (1986); Jesse H. Shera, *Foundations of the Public Library: The Origins of the Public Library Movement in New England, 1629–1855* (1965).

Peter Dobkin Hall

Elm Street   For more than a century, "Elm Street" was America's greatest example of vernacular urbanism. Few cities across the nation lacked a version of this Yankee innovation, even as far away as Honolulu and Anchorage. Today, long after the trees have succumbed to Dutch elm disease, Elm Street remains a presence in the collective memory.

The ornamental planting of American elms began in Connecticut and Massachusetts as early as the 1750s. The tree was chosen for its rapid growth, tenacity, and graceful form. A century later, "village improvement societies" made elm-planting a regional practice. Driving this was a new interest in spatial beauty but also the need to reverse economic decline as agricultural production moved westward. Beautiful or "improved" towns could compete for a new source of revenue—vacationers seeking the "old New England" made famous by the engravings of Currier and Ives and by countless penny novelists.

Elm Street was more than the sum of its trees. The interlocking limbs evoked a Gothic cathedral—an image that underscored the popular belief that America was "nature's nation." The abolitionist Henry Ward Beecher invoked a classical reference instead; the elms of New England were "as much a part of her beauty as the columns of the Parthenon were the glory of its architecture."

Long before most American cities had parks, curbside elms infused the urban scene with natural beauty and rural values. This urban pastoralism was perhaps best expressed by Charles Dickens after an 1842 visit to New

Haven, known as the "City of Elms." Its trees seemed to "bring about a kind of compromise between town and country," he wrote; "as if each had met the other half-way, and shaken hands upon it."

In the late 19th century, Elm Street was as vital to New England's identity as the white steeple or town common. But not everyone was convinced of its glories. In *The American Scene* (1907), Henry James sensed more than a little subterfuge. To him the verdant columns were so seductive that the visitor hardly noticed the poverty all about. In winter, however, the leafy shroud was removed, revealing "the poor dear old white paint—immemorial, ubiquitous, save as venturing into brown or yellow."

As Yankee pioneers struck out for the West, they took along a memory of elm-lined lanes, if not sapling elms. Elm Street followed manifest destiny all the way to the Pacific, evolving into a national institution as universal as baseball and apple pie. By 1937 more than 25 million American elms shaded the streets and parks of America. Less than a generation later, the trees were under siege. Efforts to combat Dutch elm disease were successful at first, but failed as labor and resources were diverted to fight World War II.

By the time the GIs returned, New England's cherished elms were dying by the thousands. The loss of the elm changed the face of New England. But the trees did not die in vain. Today, the importance of species diversity is well understood by urban foresters. Elm Street was a monoculture, inherently unstable. Planting the tree in such vast numbers helped bring about the very contagion that spelled its doom.

Thomas J. Campanella, *Republic of Shade: New England and the American Elm* (2003).

Thomas J. Campanella

Fall River, Mass.   The southeastern Massachusetts city of Fall River, known as Troy from 1804 until 1834, sits on the east shore of Mount Hope Bay at the mouth of the Taunton River. Originally the southern part of the agricultural community of Freetown (settled in 1686), the site attracted attention because of its proximity to an abundant waterpower source (initially used to run saw- and gristmills) and was set off as a separate town in 1803 named Fall River. The following year its name changed to Troy, only to return to its original name in 1834. The rapidly flowing Quequechan River spills out of Watuppa Pond and falls 127 feet in less than half a mile before emptying into the Taunton River at Mount Hope Bay. Local families—the Bordens, Durfees, and Bowens—and the entrepreneurs Dexter Wheeler and David Anthony built mills along the river. Among the first were the Fall River Manufactory, the Troy Cotton and Woolen Manufactory, the Fall River Iron Works, and the Pocasset Manufacturing Company. By 1825 the town had 2,000 inhabitants, 700 of whom worked in cotton mills.

By the 1870s Fall River had eclipsed New England's other textile communities. The huge granite mills that still dominate the city's topography attracted thousands of immigrants. These workers found housing in company tenements clustered around the mills. Factory owners built spacious homes overlooking the Taunton River on the city's northern highlands, giving that section a reputation for gracious living.

In 1890 Fall River had more than 74,000 inhabitants, 48 percent of whom were foreignborn, one of the highest percentages in the nation. Most were from England, Ireland, or French Canada, with French Canadians being the dominant group. By 1900 new arrivals from the Azores contributed to a Portuguese community that constituted almost 20 percent of the city's population. Smaller communities of Poles and Russians contributed to Fall River's ethnic diversity.

Fall River's population, which peaked in 1925 at just under 130,000, declined as southern competition and a lack of investment drove the city to bankruptcy in the 1930s. Garment factories slowly filled the void. By the second half of the 20th century the city produced more garments than cotton cloth, and its remaining mills were switching to synthetic fibers. In the 1960s, however, foreign competition began to squeeze the city's garment shops. The population fell below 100,000 and unemployment rose.

In the last decade of the 20th century Fall River's 10 percent unemployment rate—one of the highest in the region—improved to 4 percent, 14 percent of the city's inhabitants still lived in poverty. In 2000 the population was 91,938, 20 percent of whom were foreignborn, most of them elderly. Although 91 percent of the city's residents were white according to the 2000 census, there was a small black and Hispanic population and a growing but still small Asian community. Even with the arrival of new immigrants, the Portuguese and French Canadians who established themselves at the turn of the 20th century still dominate the city's ethnic landscape.

Fall River remains a city of laborers. Many of the city's workers find jobs in manufacturing, many in the remaining garment factories located in the granite buildings that once housed a majority of the nation's spindles. But increasing numbers of workers find employment in the city's growing factory-outlet retail sector.

Fall River achieved notoriety in 1892 when Lizzie Borden was tried for the ax murder of her father and stepmother. Although Borden was acquitted, the murder is still attached to her name, and the local historical society maintains a room dedicated to the case. Agnes de Mille's classic *Fall River Legend* (1948) and Jack Beeson's opera *Lizzie Borden* (1965) are based on the murder. Fall River is home to Bristol Community College (1966) and the Marine Museum. As a tourist attraction and war memorial the city maintains several naval vessels in Mount Hope Bay's Battleship Cove.

John T. Cumbler, *Working-Class Community in Industrial America: Work, Leisure, and Struggle in Two Industrial Cities, 1880–1930* (1979); Thomas Russell Smith, *The Cotton Textile Industry of Fall River, Massachusetts: A Study of Industrial Localization* (1944); Donald R. Taft, *Two Portuguese Communities in New England* (1967 [1923]); Richard W. Wilkie and Jack Tager, eds., *Historical Atlas of Massachusetts* (1991).

John T. Cumbler

Fire and Firefighting

New Englanders harnessed fire to cook food, heat their homes, and relieve the darkness of night. From the time of the Native Americans, they hunted game and cleared the land with fire. Fire energized most New Englanders' activities, both at home and at work. The day started and ended at the hearth, and much of the intervening hours' work revolved around the open flame. From earliest settlement, fire was at the center of a New England family's life; the hearth was constructed in the middle of the house where it could provide the most heat (as opposed to fireplaces in the South, which were built into external walls). Nathaniel Hawthorne makes a major character of the huge central chimney in *The House of the Seven Gables* (1851). Housewives oversaw what the historian Margaret Hindle called the home's "power plant and the household's bustling workplace."

When fire was the source of all fuel and heat, a typical New England household burned 30 to 40 cords of wood (more than an acre of trees) each year. "Here is good living for those that love good Fires," wrote Francis Higginson, an English colonist arriving in 1630. Accustomed to fuel shortages at home, Higginson now contemplated the seemingly endless forests of New England. "Nay, all *Europe* is not able to afford so great Fires as *NewEngland*." Farmers often maintained their own wood lots for this purpose and chopped away as needed, but even town dwellers who bought their wood from dealers had their work cut out for them. The lighting of a wood fire on an open hearth required many manipulations, and women and men in New England shared the various tasks associated with everyday chores of chopping, splitting, and hauling wood, cooking over a flame, and disposing of ashes and waste. In fact, to Connecticut's Harriet Beecher Stowe, an orderly procession of wood from the forest to the family hearthside was a symbol of domestic tranquility. Until World War I, many women thought of women's liberation in terms of an equitable distribution of responsibilities in homesteading and fire building.

By the turn of the 20th century, the industrialization of New England had suggested to Henry Adams a different symbol. Adams saw the region's factory fires transforming the rural American landscape into a gritty world where "tall chimneys reeked smoke on every horizon, and dirty suburbs filled with scrap-iron, scrap-paper, and cinders formed the setting of every town." At the end of the 20th century, New England's industrial fires had gone out, although the region continues to suffer from the acid rain produced by fires of Midwestern factories. Although gas and oil are now the most common domestic fuels, the traditional wood stove has made a limited comeback, particularly among New Englanders concerned about renewable resources, and because of the aesthetic appeal of a bright, warm fire.

The fundamental problem with fire has been that the same form of energy that could build a town could destroy it. As a popular proverb phrased it, "Fire is a good servant, but a bad master." For much of New England's history, fire prevention and protection were considered a civic duty. Paul Revere was a firefighter. John Hancock was a fire warden, and he bought the city of Boston a fire engine. Samuel Adams was on Boston's force for nine years. Ralph Waldo Emerson was a member of the fire brigade in Concord, Mass.

Of all the cities in the American colonies, early Boston, with its densely packed wooden homes and buildings jammed into crowded streets on the narrow peninsula, was particularly vulnerable to uncontrollable fires. One fire after another began in blacksmith's shops or bakeries sitting cheek-by-jowl with houses. On January 14, 1653, Boston suffered the first "great fire" on record, prompting some of the first legislation for fire prevention, depending mainly on the coordination of citizens' individual efforts. Each household was required, for example, to keep a ladder long enough to reach the ridge pole supporting the roof so that owners and firefighters could reach roof fires in time to prevent their spreading. Boston's fire defenses equaled those of any late 17th- or early 18th-century European city, but they did not prevent a series of blazes culminating in a 1711 fire, by far the most extensive to strike colonial America. Cotton Mather looked back on the city's first 70 years and lamented, "ten times has the fire made notable ruins among us."

Firefighters at Kerr Mills fire, Fall River, Mass., 1987

The ease with which fires were touched off, and the danger of their spreading through the tightly packed city, created an atmosphere of high anxiety. Citizens' groups patrolled the streets every night. Open fires were banned near any structure and in ships anchored at the city's wharves. Despite rigorous prevention efforts, fires were kindled by "a Taylour Boy who fell asleep," or from "careless and negligent performance of the worke of Chimney sweeping," or "by reason of drunkenness." Negligence was severely punished, and arson became a capital crime. After the Boston fire of 1679, a farmhand in Lynn, Mass., was sentenced to work 21 years for the man whose barn he burned to the ground. A woman's act of arson resulted in the death of a young boy trapped in his home, for which she was publicly burned at the stake. When the Roxbury, Mass., home of Joshua Lamb was destroyed by fire in midsummer 1681, his black servant, Maria, was charged, convicted, and "burnt to Ashes" on the Boston Common.

Other New England towns had fire problems as well, although none as serious as Boston. Newport, R.I., was one of the five most populous towns in the colonies during the 17th century and periodically lost a house to fire. In 1705 a blaze in a smithy extended to a nearby dwelling, but the flames were soon extinguished. In general, the rural character of much of New England allowed households to confine fires to a single dwelling or structure. Many small towns went without organized fire protection for centuries. Stratford, Conn., founded in 1639, did not establish a formal fire department until 1875.

By the 1760s Bostonians and New Yorkers were comparing their fire services, apparatus, frequency of alarms, and the effectiveness of their companies with those of London, Bristol, and other British cities. In spite of its efforts and innovation, Boston suffered a series of fires culminating in a conflagration in 1760, the damage from which contributed to the growing anti-British sentiment when Parliament refused to offer any help in rebuilding. Instead, donations poured in from the colonial governments of Connecticut, Maryland, New Hampshire, New York, and Pennsylvania. While the British alienated their colonists in time of tragedy, the colonies wisely strengthened their mutual ties.

Fire prevention in the 19th century was largely an elaboration of earlier practices, although the era's most successful inventions created fire hazards that had no precedent in the colonial period. Local officials responded with widely varying laws and regulations concerning all kinds of potential hazards. In Farmington, Conn., for example, the use of portable stoves was prohibited, and homeowners were required to store their matches in iron boxes.

Fire companies throughout the cities and towns of New England began to vie with each other to be the first on the scene of a fire, and firefighters became popular figures in their neighborhoods. Fire companies developed strong camaraderie, active political involvement, and colorful leaders. The fireman became a community hero, invested with a kind of glamour that they would later share with cowboys, explorers, and even later with aviators and athletes. Nineteenth-century parades and musters became carnivals offering companionship to men of kindred responsibilities and shared danger. By the end of the 1800s it would have been unthinkable for a town event to be held without a parade of firemen in their elaborate and colorful uniforms, with their bright red steam engines. Firefighters' public appearances were often grand theater. In 1869 the bandleader Patrick Gilmore conducted a monumental National Peace Jubilee in Boston. He gathered 100 red-shirted firemen from the Boston department, provided each with a hammer and anvil, and conducted them in a rousing performance of Verdi's "Anvil Chorus."

Boston's great fire of 1872, though largely confined to the commercial district, destroyed almost 800 buildings across 65 acres at a loss of $75 million. The great fires in Chicago, Boston, and Baltimore prompted tightening of fire codes. The requirements Boston instituted in response were as advanced as any: brick barriers between floors; fireproofed boiler rooms, stairs, and elevators; and elimination of wooden roofing and trim. But New England's (if not the nation's) most tragic fire occurred there in the early days of World War II. The Cocoanut Grove nightclub was engulfed in flames on November 28, 1942, sparked by an electrical short that ignited a highly combustible artificial palm tree. Because the only two exits to the overcrowded club were revolving doors, 492 people, almost half of those trapped inside, were killed and others seriously injured, many of them servicemen ready to leave for Europe and the Pacific. The disaster prompted many of the fire prevention standards for public buildings that are used today. Two years later, the Great Hartford Circus Fire killed 169 people, many of them children, when the Big Top, waterproofed with a mixture of gasoline and paraffin, ignited. A 2003 fire started by a pyrotechnic mishap at the Station Club in West Warwick, R.I., when 100 people died, most struggling to make it through a door piled with bodies, was reminiscent of the Cocoanut Grove blaze.

The heroism of New England firefighters is legendary, as in the January 28, 1966, Paramount Hotel Fire in Boston when a gas explosion on a bitterly cold night set ablaze this crowded 11-floor structure in Boston's Combat Zone. Eleven died that night, but if not for the "magnificent courage" of Boston firefighters the number would have been much higher. New England firefighters have also suffered devastating tragedy. The worst loss of firefighters was the Vendome Hotel fire of June 17, 1972, in Boston, in which nine firefighters were killed when a wall collapsed. On December 3, 1999, six Worcester, Mass., firefighters lost their lives in a fire at the Worcester Cold Storage and Warehouse Company. The brotherhood of firefighters extends deep into the New England community, owing, in part, to the family and ethnic, often Irish, ties of the men and women in service.

Throughout New England's towns and villages, the firemen's muster remains an enduring American tradition. In the age of professionalized and scientific fire services, the color and camaraderie of the region's firefighting traditions continued through the course of the 20th century. In 1999 a muster of volunteer fire crews from Conway and North Conway, N.H., along with a traditional barn-raising, were held near the Washington Monument on the National Mall, as representative of New England community purpose in the annual Smithsonian Folklife Festival.

Fires have often struck at the New England sense of identity, when a historic church, house, or mill complex burns. When the Malden Mills complex in Lawrence, Mass., burned on December 11, 1995, 3,000 employees were put out of work, and most assumed this was yet another death knell to what was once one of New England's premier industries. The owner, Aaron Feuerstein, however, vowed to keep workers on payroll and to rebuild the mills, becoming a symbol of ethical leadership and New England resilience.

The region has several museums dedicated to the history of firefighting, including the Connecticut Fire Museum on the grounds of the Connecticut Trolley Museum in East Windsor, Conn., and the New England Fire and History Museum in Brewster, Mass., which houses 30 pieces of antique fire apparatus and Arthur Fiedler's fire helmet collection.

Arthur Wellington Brayley, *A Complete History of the Boston Fire Department from 1630 to 1888* (1889); Donald J. Cannon, ed., *Heritage of Flames: The Illustrated History of Early American Firefighting* (1977); Margaret Hindle and Robert M. Hazen, *Keepers of the Flame: The Role of Fire in American Culture, 1775–1925* (1992).

Louis Mazzari

Framingham, Mass. The town of Framingham, with a population of 66,910 in 2000, is located 17 miles west of Boston. It is the core community of a loosely defined area of about 15 towns now identified as MetroWest, with a regional population of about 200,000 people. In 1660–62, Thomas Danforth of Framlingham, England, received a land grant designating the area as "Mr. Danforth's Farms." In 1700 Framingham (the English spelling altered) was incorporated as a town with 350 people and a town meeting system of government, still in effect today. In 1790 the U.S. census population of Framingham was 1,598; by 1890 it had grown to 9,239.

Transportation has from the beginning played a major role in Framingham's development. In 1806 a 40-mile private toll road for stagecoach traffic (today's Route 9) was developed as a link between Boston and Worcester,

Mass. Framingham Center was the midway point, making it a major horse-changing stop; this stimulated local business. A railroad line from Boston to Albany, N.Y., first proposed in 1827, was supposed to follow the "Worcester Turnpike" but was perceived by the Turnpike Proprietors as a threat to the continued collection of tolls. The resulting pressure caused the railroad bed to be moved to its present location, 3 miles to the south. Hotels, banks, and other businesses soon centered around the railroad station, causing a division in the town that is still evident today: The area north of Route 9 remains suburban and quasi-rural, while the southern part of town is more urban and diverse. Framingham's architectural gem, Henry Hobson Richardson's 1885 railroad station, is now a restaurant, but still provides a platform for the commuter rail line to Boston. Route 9 itself is a heavily traveled strip of malls, restaurants, and businesses.

At the end of the 20th century, Framingham's population was 82 percent white or non-Hispanic; the comparable figure for Metro West is 89.2 percent. Framingham's Hispanic population, now approaching 6,000, has been growing steadily since 1990. The median household income in Framingham was $57,000 in 1997, and in MetroWest, $65,000. Services (31 percent), retail trade (23.5 percent), and manufacturing (16 percent) account for more than half of MetroWest's employment.

Framingham voters repeatedly reject efforts to abandon their traditional New England town meeting form of government, making Framingham the largest "town" in Massachusetts, if not in America. It is also the home of the Danforth Museum of Art, a regional and community museum and art school founded in 1975, and of Framingham State College (1839), the first Normal School (teachers college) in America, now a liberal arts college with 4,300 undergraduates and an equal number of graduate and continuing education students. The Framingham Heart Study, which began in 1948 with more than 5,000 Framingham residents and continues today with their children, has contributed to the understanding, prevention, and treatment of cardiovascular disease.

Danforth Museum of Art, *Around the Station: The Town and the Train* (1978); MetroWest Economic Research Center, *Approaching the Millennium: Income, Jobs and the New MetroWest Economy* (1998); Josiah H. Temple, *History of Framingham, Massachusetts, 1640–1885* (1997 [1887]).

Leah Lipton

Government According to popular mythology, New England has been a region of both autocratic big-city bosses and pure democracy in the form of the hallowed town

meeting. It has supposedly nurtured the best and the worst of American local government. The fact is, however, that urban and suburban governments in New England have deviated notably from the myth. The towns have not been so unsullied or the cities so decadent. Instead, a distinctive pattern of urban and suburban government has developed in New England that defies stereotypes and distinguishes the region from the South, Midwest, and West.

The New England town meeting developed during the colonial era, and New Englanders throughout history have proven reluctant to abandon it in favor of the mayor and council that, along with state incorporation, distinguish the city from the town. During the 17th and 18th centuries, proposals that Boston obtain a city charter suffered repeated defeat. Though 14 communities in the 13 colonies acquired charters and operated under the city form of government, there were no city governments in New England before the American Revolution. In 1784, however, five Connecticut communities and Newport, R.I., opted for a mayor and council and became cities. Bostonians clung to the traditional town meeting, not accepting city government until 1822, by which time the community's population had reached 43,000.

During the following century 41 additional Massachusetts communities chose to become cities, but none has opted for that status since Gardner abandoned town government in 1923. By the mid-1990s, highly urbanized Massachusetts had only 39 cities, in contrast to 312 towns, with Rhode Island claiming only eight cities and 31 towns. Moreover, some of the communities clinging to town status were good-sized population centers. Three towns in Massachusetts and six in Connecticut had more than 50,000 residents. In other parts of the country every ambitious village opted for municipal incorporation and city status, but in New England the notion of city government often struck a dissonant chord. City government remained an alien import from states to the south and west that was incompatible with the political predilections of many New Englanders.

Though vivid tales of corrupt urban politicians have long circulated in New England, those city governments that did exist were not necessarily incompetent. During the late 19th century Boston was probably the best-governed city in the United States. A superb park system designed by the renowned Frederick Law Olmsted, the finest public library in the nation, and an innovative intercepting sewer system were all monuments to the success of city government in New England's hub.

These services, however, increased the local

tax burden, a subject of chronic complaint throughout the late 19th and 20th centuries. Elsewhere in the nation, cities diversified their tax structure and adopted sales or income taxes during the half century after World War II, but New England cities remained unusually dependent on the property tax. In 1991–92, 52.5 percent of all city taxes in the United States derived from property levies, whereas in Boston the property tax accounted for 93.5 percent of city tax revenues. The figures for Hartford, Providence, Manchester, N.H., and Portland, Maine, were even higher, above 98 percent. Even Burlington, Vt., which profited from selective sales taxes, reaped more than 80 percent of its taxes from property levies. In the late 20th century New England's municipal tax structure was as antiquated as its venerable town meetings.

Another abiding feature of New England city government in the late 19th and 20th centuries was ethnic politics. In 1885 Hugh O'Brien became the first Irish Catholic mayor of Boston; in 1896 Irish Catholic Edwin McGuinness likewise broke the Yankee monopoly on power by assuming Providence's highest office; and three years later New Haven, Conn., inducted its first Irish-born mayor, Cornelius Driscoll. Throughout the 20th century Irish Catholic politicians dominated Boston city government and ensured that others of their religion and national ancestry secured city jobs. The same thing happened in other New England cities, though in the second half of the 20th century Italian Americans rebelled against Irish hegemony, especially in Connecticut and Rhode Island.

As early as 1945 New Haven voters placed Italian American William Celantano in the mayor's office, ousting the Irish incumbent, John Murphy. In 1953 Dominick DeLucco became mayor of Hartford, and 14 years later Antonina Uccello was elected chief executive of Connecticut's capital. Then in 1974 Providence elected its first Italian American mayor, Vincent "Buddy" Cianci, Jr., who won repeated reelection, despite a variety of criminal charges leveled against him over the years. Though a Republican in a heavily Democratic city, Cianci benefited from Italian American dissatisfaction with Irish domination, and this ethnic factor contributed to his victories.

Ethnic bitterness was to become one of the uglier features of government in New England's largest city. During the first half of the 20th century, Mayor James Michael Curley exploited his humble Irish origins, securing a loyal following among have-not Irish Catholics resentful of the Yankee elite. Curley played on ethnic and social divisions to win four terms as mayor of Boston. In the late 1960s and early 1970s mayoral hopeful Louise

Day Hicks likewise exploited the antagonism between Irish and African Americans. Hicks suffered defeat, but her campaigns and the concurrent clash over busing to achieve racial balance in the schools demonstrated that ethnic tension was as much a factor in Boston's city politics in the late 20th century as it had been 100 years earlier.

Boston's Irish Catholics, however, never established a powerful citywide machine similar to New York City's Tammany Hall. From the 1890s onward Boston's dominant Democratic Party was deeply divided, with ward leaders jealously guarding their patches of turf and prominent figures such as Curley and Mayor John "Honey Fitz" Fitzgerald leading personal factions. Some may have viewed Curley as a boss, but he bossed only his personal following. He was neither the dictatorial commander of a unified Democratic Party nor the unchallenged leader of city government.

Even as the suburbs became increasingly populous, they remained devoted to town government. Yet by the early 20th century some suburbanites had recognized the shortcomings of the much-vaunted town meeting. Far from being model forums for direct democracy, town meetings were ill attended. In 1915, for example, the Boston suburb of Brookline had almost 34,000 residents, but only about 150 to 250 persons attended most town meetings. Moreover, rumor had it that unscrupulous interests eager to influence local decisions were importing Boston barflies to vote at Brookline's town gatherings. Realizing that the traditional town meeting was not suited to a heavily populated commuter suburb—yet unwilling to adopt city government—Brookline voters in 1915 opted for an innovative compromise, the representative town meeting. Under this new form of government, all residents would be able to attend and speak at the town meeting, but only elected representatives could vote. Preserving the semblance of broad participation, New England's representative town meetings usually had more than 200 voting representatives elected by precinct.

By the mid-1990s, 40 Massachusetts towns had adopted representative town meetings. Especially commonplace in the Boston suburbs, this modification of traditional town government exists in Dedham, Framingham, Milton, Natick, Needham, Wellesley, and Weymouth. In Connecticut's Fairfield County, the suburban commuter towns of Darien, Fairfield, Greenwich, and Westport also operate under this form of government.

During the last decades of the 20th century a number of suburban New England towns turned to another alternative, the town council. Under this scheme a small body, compara-

ble to a city council, governed the community, with administrative authority usually vested in a town manager. In 1945 Bloomfield became the first Connecticut town to adopt the plan, but after the adoption of home rule in 1957 additional Connecticut towns were able to tailor the system to their needs. Some retained the town meeting along with a town council, and others created the position of mayor. In 1966 Massachusetts voters approved a home-rule amendment to their constitution, allowing towns to experiment with new forms of government, and five years later the rapidly growing Springfield suburb of Agawam became the first Massachusetts town to accept the council plan. By the mid-1990s, 29 Massachusetts towns were governed by councils, including the Boston suburbs of Arlington, Lexington, and Watertown.

Thus New England suburbs have clung to the name "town" and eschewed the imported institution of city government, yet the distinction between towns and cities has grown increasingly blurred. Town councils and managers differ little from city councils and managers, but the persistent devotion to town government reflects a deep-seated New England reluctance to abandon past institutions, no matter how outmoded.

Constance K. Burns and Ronald P. Formisano, eds., *Boston, 1700–1980: The Evolution of Urban Politics* (1984); Robert A. Dahl, *Who Governs? Democracy and Power in an American City* (1961); Edwin A. Gere, Jr., *Modernizing Local Government in Massachusetts: The Quest for Professionalism and Reform* (1984); Charles Phillips Huse, *The Financial History of Boston* (1916); John Fairfield Sly, *Town Government in Massachusetts (1620–1930)* (1930); Joseph F. Zimmerman, *The Massachusetts Town Meeting: A Tenacious Institution* (1967).

Jon C. Teaford

Hartford Connecticut's capital and third largest city, Hartford is located on the Connecticut River about 40 miles north of Long Island Sound. In 2000 the city's population was 121,578. Hartford was founded by Dutch traders in 1633 and first attracted English settlers in 1635, when Thomas Hooker and 60 persons disaffected with Massachusetts theocracy left Newetowne (now Cambridge) and settled near the Dutch fort. Those newcomers created the Fundamental Orders (1639), the first colonial government with a written constitution. In 1662 the Hartford colony was united with that of New Haven under a royal charter that would be supplanted by a popular constitution in 1818. In 1687 Captain Joseph Wadsworth is believed to have hidden the charter in an oak tree when British governor Sir Edmund Andros was dispatched to Hartford to seize it, an event commemorated by a monument on the city's Charter

State Capitol Building, Hartford, 2002

Oak Avenue. In 1875 Hartford became the sole capital of Connecticut, a role it had shared with New Haven since 1701. The original statehouse in Hartford, completed in 1796, became a cultural center in 1996, after a new, gold-domed structure was built to take its place.

An early center of publishing, Hartford boasts the oldest continuously issued newspaper in America, the *Hartford Courant* (1764). During the revolutionary era a group of religious and political conservatives known as the Connecticut Wits gained prominence by satirizing egalitarianism and what they deemed the excesses of Jeffersonian democracy. With the decline of federalism after 1820, a more romantic and humanitarian spirit found expression in Lydia Sigourney, whose literary circle included Samuel G. Goodrich (Peter Parley), John Greenleaf Whittier, and the *Hartford Times* editor Gideon Welles, who served as secretary of the navy during the Civil War. Two contemporaries made significant contributions in theology or religion, the African American abolitionist J. W. C. Pennington and Horace Bushnell, author of *Christian Nurture* (1847). Bushnell Park, designed by Frederick Law Olmsted, and the residential Bushnell Towers, designed by I. M. Pei, honor their namesake in the city's bustling downtown district. During the post–Civil War era, *Courant* editor Charles Dudley Warner, Harriet Beecher Stowe, and Mark Twain established a literary community at Nook Farm, where Twain wrote *Tom Sawyer* (1876) and *Huckleberry Finn* (1884).

The Stowe and Twain homes are now museums housing original manuscripts and published works. Other significant collections of New England cultural history are held by the Connecticut Historical Society, the Connecticut State Library and Archives, and the Watkinson Library at Trinity College. The American decorative arts collection of the Wadsworth Atheneum includes paintings by the Hartford-born artist Frederic Edwin Church and members of the Hudson River School.

In the 19th century Hartford emerged as a financial and precision manufacturing center. It still retains its distinction as "the insurance capital of the world," but many businesses long associated with Hartford relocated elsewhere in the late 20th century. Coupled with the flight of the affluent to the suburbs, Hartford's industrial exodus has deprived the city of much of its traditional economic and cultural base. A few cultural organizations—notably the Hartford Stage, the Wadsworth Atheneum, and the Hartford Symphony—cling to downtown locations, but their clientele comes chiefly from the suburbs. Downtown redevelopment efforts in the 1960s and 1970s succeeded only in expanding office space for nonresident business personnel and shifting slums to Frog Hollow and the North End. With abundant money to demolish and rebuild, contemporary Hartford has fallen victim to its own affluence: little remains of the city that once charmed Clemens and Stowe.

With nearly equal numbers of black (54,338) and white (55,869) residents, along with 44,137 Hispanic city dwellers, Hartford has experienced its share of racial and ethnic tensions. In 1966, attempting to provide equal educational opportunities to inner-city children, Hartford launched a voluntary school-busing program that by the late 1970s was busing some 1,500 mostly black and ethnic students to suburban schools in the Hartford area. That program enjoyed moderate success but by the early 1990s had lost much of its effectiveness. In July 1996 the Connecticut Supreme Court ruled in *Sheff v. O'Neill* that Hartford's public schools were racially and ethnically isolated. It ordered the legislature and executive branch to search immediately for remedies to that isolation. Governor John Rowland's multiracial Education Improvement Panel issued recommendations five months later. Although progress toward desegregation has been made in the intervening years, *Sheff* plaintiffs maintain that it has gone neither fast nor far enough.

Hartford was nonetheless the first major northeastern city to elect an African American woman, Carrie Saxon Perry, as mayor in 1987. Agencies such as the Charter Oak Cultural Center have begun to showcase the rich cultural heritage of Hartford's ethnic communities. Trinity College has launched an ambitious project to revitalize Frog Hollow, once a site of gang violence, while the people of Asylum Hill and the West End are showing renewed interest in these still attractive residential neighborhoods. Like many urban centers at the beginning of the 21st century, Hartford faces both the challenge and the opportunity of forging a new cultural identity that will integrate historic traditions with those of its more recent residents.

Ellsworth S. Grant and Marion H. Grant, *The City of Hartford, 1784–1984: An Illustrated History* (1986); Glenn Weaver, *Hartford: An Illustrated History of Connecticut's Capital* (1982).

Gary E. Wait

Holyoke, Mass. One of New England's largest planned industrial cities, Holyoke lies in west central Massachusetts on the Connecticut River. Founded by the Boston Associates, a group of Boston-area entrepreneurs who decided to create a textile manufacturing center at Hadley Falls, the original development consisted of factories connected by 4.5 miles of canals to a dam at the 60-foot-high falls. The newly incorporated town (1850), which had been the Ireland parish section of West Springfield, was rebaptized Holyoke, a respectable Yankee moniker, so as not to advertise its growing number of Irish workers.

During the 1850s Holyoke grew slowly, but the Civil War spurred industrial activity, and New England's textile and paper mills flourished. Holyoke's population grew from 3,245 in 1860 to 10,733 in 1870. Holyoke was incorporated as a city in 1873 and became known as the Paper City, as 11 paper mills were built to utilize the inexpensive power and chemically pure water provided by the Connecticut River. In 1890 Holyoke produced 80 percent of fine writing paper made in the United States. The industry declined after 1899, when a national paper trust, the American Writing Paper Company, took over the city's paper factories and slowly ran them into the ground. The paper mills, which made expensive paper mainly from rags, lost their edge to mills located closer to wood-pulp supplies, whose product was cheaper.

Holyoke's deindustrialization began in the 1920s and continued through the 1960s, as textile mills closed and shifted operations to the South. Holyoke has maintained a specialty-paper industry, however, as well as factories that make silk, cotton, woolen, and alpaca products. The city still has well over 100 manufacturing concerns. Approximately half of Holyoke's manufacturing jobs are in paper products, printing, and publishing.

In the 19th century thousands of immigrants—first Irish Catholics, later French Canadians and Poles—were attracted to work in the mills. Toward the end of the century Holyoke had one of the country's highest percentages of foreign-born residents. Its population peaked at 60,203 in 1920. Industrialization created a large impoverished working class living in tenements. The city's social ills were exacerbated by the neglect of absentee factory owners.

Holyoke in the 20th and early 21st centuries provides a classic example of the immigrant struggle. In 1948 Mary Doyle Curran described the assimilation difficulties encountered by three generations of Holyoke's Irish in her semi-autobiographical novel *The Parish and the Hill*. Since the 1950s the city's Saint Patrick's Day Parade, one of the largest in America, has strongly marked the Irish presence in Holyoke. Tracy Kidder's *Among Schoolchildren* (1989), based on the author's observations of a fifth-grade class in a Holyoke public school, explains the problems experienced by Puerto Ricans attempting to assimilate into American society as well as the tensions between the Puerto Ricans and the Irish. Holyoke's population, 39,838 in 2000, is now more than 41 percent Hispanic.

Holyoke rises steeply from the Connecticut River in a topographical reflection of its social stratification. The Flats is a working-class neighborhood located near the mills. High Street, above the factories, is the city's main commercial district. Beyond High Street stretches the middle-class residential area, culminating in the Highlands, the city's most prestigious neighborhood. Mount Tom towers over all. Since 1979 the Holyoke Mall at the

junction of Interstate 91 and the Massachusetts Turnpike has drawn commercial activity away from the downtown. Holyoke Community College was established in 1946, and Mount Holyoke College (1837) is in nearby South Hadley.

Constance McLaughlin Green, *Holyoke, Massachusetts: A Case Study of the Industrial Revolution in America* (1939); William F. Hartford, *Working People of Holyoke: Class and Ethnicity in a Massachusetts Mill Town, 1850–1960* (1990).

James C. O'Connell

Homelessness The homeless in New England have had many names, from the "strolling poor" of the colonial era to the "town poor" of the 19th century to the "tramps" of the 20th. In New England's early years towns were responsible for their own homeless citizens but could "warn out" indigent newcomers. Part of the Puritan ethic inherent in New England culture held that work and economic success were signs of God's favor. As a result, people who were destitute or had no place to live were regarded as not just a financial burden to the community but also of lesser moral character. Yesterday's homeless might have been transient laborers, widows, unemployed seamen, or disabled individuals; today they often are people who cannot meet their bills as the result of a job loss or failure to find affordable housing.

The contemporary term *homelessness,* referring to the lack of a stable, secure place to live, takes the focus off individuals and emphasizes the phenomenon as a social condition. Homelessness throughout New England, as in the rest of the nation, typically increases and declines in accordance with prevailing economic conditions. The sustained period of U.S. economic growth that began in 1991 was not, however, accompanied by a significant drop in the number of homeless New Englanders. Both urban and rural homelessness in the United States have increased for 20 straight years. Homelessness no longer affects just impoverished, single adults; when available housing costs more than individuals or families can afford, it also affects members of the middle class. Stereotypically, homelessness is chronic, but in New England it is usually short-term or intermittent if social services can help individuals find housing. But when those services are cut as demand for them increases, the amount and severity of homelessness inevitably rise.

It is hard to determine exactly how many homeless people there are in New England. Most of them—especially those in rural areas—are never identified by the agencies that compile official figures. Thus most surveys underestimate the full extent of homelessness.

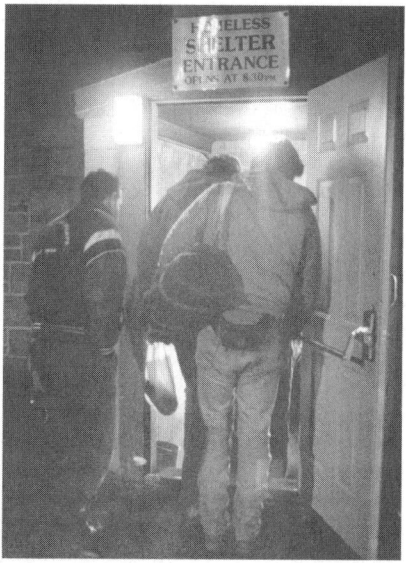

Homeless shelter at Grace Church, Framingham, Mass., 1992

Family homelessness increased markedly over the last decade of the 20th century, with families making up 75 percent of Massachusetts's homeless population (18,000 parents and children). Of the remaining 25 percent of that state's homeless people, one-third are veterans and one-tenth are elderly. Increasing numbers of youth are also homeless, living independently and struggling to get by. Ten percent of high school students in New Hampshire and Maine report having had no place to stay sometime during the preceding year.

Fire and other residential disasters can suddenly put people on the street. Most homelessness is caused by a lack of available or affordable housing, a lack felt especially by low-wage earners. An improving economy often leads to higher rents, effectively pricing low-wage earners out of the market. Policies at the state and federal levels also influence the ability of people to secure housing. The New England economy has experienced declining conditions over the past two decades, forcing more working people into homelessness. Almost 200,000 manufacturing jobs were lost between 1984 and 1996. The fishing industry experienced significant declines as a result of economic and environmental pressures. Unemployment, downsizing, and the loss of wages, retirement benefits, and health insurance make it difficult for people to pay escalating housing costs and meet other basic needs. When jobs open up, they are often poorly compensated in high-cost urban areas. At least a third of all people who are homeless hold down paying jobs while living on the streets and in shelters.

Domestic violence is another major cause of homelessness in New England. In Massachusetts alone more than 2,000 women take refuge in shelters each year, but twice that number are turned away because the shelters are full. While shelter clients are often mistakenly believed to be street people, former prisoners, and the mentally ill, the fact is that by far the majority of clients (73 percent in Rhode Island) come to shelters directly from their own homes or from the homes of family or friends. Less than 8 percent come from institutions. Over half of the homeless report that they have at least a high school education.

In sum, homeless New Englanders vary widely. Some find a way to live on the streets even in the coldest winter months. Only a few turn to shelters such as Boston's Pine Street Inn or Rosie's Place. Families may double up in one apartment or home or live in campgrounds during the summer and move into cheap seasonal rentals during the cold months. Wherever they are found, the number of New Englanders that are officially recognized as homeless is but the tip of a very large iceberg.

Fannie Mae Foundation, *Understanding Homelessness: New Policy and Research Perspectives* (1997); McCormick Institute for Public Policy, "Homelessness in New England," *New England Journal of Public Policy* 18, no. 1 (1992); Yvonne Vissing, *Out of Sight, Out of Mind: Homeless Children and Families in Small-Town America* (1996).

Yvonne Vissing

Housing and Housing Policy

From hillside to seacoast, New England is full of beautiful homes. Houses dating back to the 1600s and 1700s impart a sense of history and charm to a region increasingly dominated by growth and high technology. The grand mansions overlooking the ocean at Newport, R.I., the fashionable brownstones of Boston's Back Bay, the homes of Cape Cod clad in simple weathered shingles, the rolling rural estates of Connecticut, New Hampshire's simple clapboard dwellings, and the fishermen's homes that dot the coast of Maine demonstrate the varied taste and culture of the region. New Englanders attempt to preserve the integrity of historical housing and often recapture its styles in new construction.

Mass-housing efforts were made early on in New England by industrialists eager to keep workers near at hand, notably by the owners of large factories that developed along rivers throughout New England. Multistory textile mills, such as those of Lawrence, Mass., or Manchester, N.H., spread for miles in virtually self-contained communities. The proximity of employees helped the industry grow. Three-decker houses were a common working-class housing type throughout New England. Many lumberyards sold plans for several distinct styles of three-deckers, and

different ethnic groups also put their unique stamp upon them. As immigration increased in the 1880s and 1890s, more three-deckers were built. They were exceptionally flexible. Families often rented out units until they became self-sufficient. Until then sharing, particularly taking in boarders, was commonplace.

During World War I, the federal government first experimented with publicly funded housing. In Bridgeport, Conn., and Portsmouth, N.H., the U.S. Housing Corporation primarily constructed high-quality brick single-family detached housing aimed at attracting and retaining well-paid skilled war workers. This initiative was short lived, but the housing continues to be highly desirable as rental and owner-occupied properties. Following passage of a low-income act in 1938, the federal government again entered the housing business in select New England cities. In Bridgeport, Conn., in 1939 a large area of dilapidated housing was cleared and a low-density community, Yellow Mill Village, later renamed Father Panik Village, was constructed for low-income families. It was the largest such type in New England and sixth largest housing project in the United States. By the 1960s this neighborhood, like other public housing projects in the region, had been transformed into slums where poor people were concentrated and segregated. Condemned in 1982 by federal housing authorities as "deplorable," Father Panik Village residents began relocating in 1988 and the project was finally torn down in the late 1990s.

By the 1920s suburban developments became more popular for those who sought a home of their own or to flee the mix of racial, class, and ethnic diversity that was typical of urban areas. Beginning in the late 1930s federal policy promoted this exodus from cities. The lending policies of the Federal Housing Administration, for instance, color coding neighborhoods according to income and racial profiles, contributed to urban flight and the concentration of poor and minorities in urban centers. Federal highway acts subsidized suburbanization, providing the infrastructure for urban flight and the creation of bedroom communities. As the expanding middle class and established elites rushed to build homes at a comfortable remove from growing urban populations and their concomitant problems, many New England cities found their tax bases crumbling. Urban decline led to the large-scale development of public housing in the 1960s, especially in connection with urban renewal.

Massachusetts, Rhode Island, and Connecticut were the primary, if dubious, beneficiaries of urban renewal, although the more

northern New England states were also affected. Housing and other problems in places such as Boston's South End triggered racial strife during the Civil Rights movement. Individual homes and small apartment buildings were replaced by large public housing complexes, such as the Bunker Hill and Harbor Point projects in Boston. Neighborhoods were methodically destroyed throughout New England, from Constitution Plaza in Hartford to Fox Point in Providence to the largely Greek and Italian North End in Portsmouth, N.H., to the Concourse in Waterville, Maine. In a few cases, high-density high-rise housing projects were so isolated from public amenities such as supermarkets, and so dehumanizing in scale, that structures built became uninhabitable within a decade of their construction. Since the 1980s there have been considerable efforts to humanize or tear down high-rise projects in the region and replace them with lower density, more suburban-style dwellings.

The preservation of historical housing, often owned by New England elites, continues today. Federal and state policies that influence housing for the bulk of the region's population have gone through considerable changes in recent years. In general, no system coordinates New England's regional housing policy. There is no right to housing, and regulations and standards vary widely from place to place. A historic New England tenet encourages the region's residents to be their brothers' keepers, but the degree to which this philosophy is put into practice is highly variable. Some smaller New England communities were known to ship people lacking housing to urban areas, where they thought more resources would be available.

Most housing policies that influence people who need housing assistance are determined at the federal level. Yet most of the practical, day-to-day decisions that affect housing policies within an individual community are implemented and monitored locally through town zoning and planning offices. The most pervasive housing policies are municipal zoning ordinances, which regulate housing types, dictate where residential and other types of buildings may be located, and set criteria for building codes. Housing is in many ways the most local of all social policies. Some New England states do more with their housing programs than others; Vermont, for example, has instituted an effective residential planning system whose goal is to promote and expand the supply of affordable rental and home-ownership opportunities within the state. Yet all of the New England states are grappling with complex changes in housing needs, resources, and policies.

Federal housing policy set in the National Housing Act of 1949 made an explicit declaration that every family should have a decent home and a suitable living environment—a position that has been reaffirmed at different times since then by Congress. But in the 1990s Congress began undermining this position. According to the New England Housing Network (formed in 1995), unprecedented federal budget cuts aimed primarily at low-income people, combined with a dramatic shift of responsibilities to state and local government, will present enormous challenges for communities across the region. Many New England communities work with housing-finance authorities to develop their own consolidated plans to deliver housing assistance—which is almost always federal.

Each year every state must submit a comprehensive affordable housing strategy to the U.S. Department of Housing and Urban Development (HUD) in order to qualify for community block, shelter, or home grants. Every state's plan can be accessed through HUD's Web site on the Internet or often by visiting individual state Web sites. Although public housing in New England has generally appeared to be workable and beneficial for the residents of the region, that may change in the future. As the federal government cuts programs and places more responsibility for housing policy in the hands of individual states, the housing options for New Englanders of very low, low, and even moderate income may become increasingly uncertain.

Throughout New England the median price for a house has tripled since 1980, rising twice as fast as incomes. Although costs in different areas vary, in 2000 the average home in New England sold for $229,772. That price is prohibitive for most people who live in the region, and few homes are available, particularly in urban or coastal areas, below that price. Cambridge, Mass., in fact, had the highest proportion of houses in the nation valued at $1 million or more (12 percent). Once one owns a house, insurance, property taxes, repairs, and general maintenance push the monthly cost upward. When people experience economic problems, monthly housing expenses often eat up too large a chunk of monthly income. In the late 1980s and early 1990s foreclosure rates skyrocketed in many parts of New England.

Renting is less expensive than buying a home, and the number of renters in the region has increased. Although in the past people rented until they could afford to buy, today at least 42 percent of the region's renters cannot afford a down payment, and only 5 percent of New Hampshire renters can afford to buy a median-priced home (which cost $133,000 in 2000). Even larger numbers of low- and mod-

erate-income households are struggling to survive in the private housing market and are paying more than 50 percent of their income for rent. In New England the median rents are $600 a month. More than half (55 percent) the renters in Massachusetts cannot afford the average fair-market rent for a two-bedroom apartment ($736/month). Tenants must earn $2,453 a month (three times the minimum wage) to afford that Massachusetts two-bedroom. In Vermont, where the same apartment costs $640 per month, one would have to earn an annual salary of $25,600. In many areas, the few jobs that pay that well are difficult to find.

More than 1 million low-income people in New England, including the elderly, the disabled, and families, live in federally subsidized housing. Most of these households have annual incomes of less than $8,000 and are at serious risk of displacement and homelessness.

There are some 363,000 units of HUD-assisted housing in New England, which are home to about 900,000 low-income residents. Public housing units, administered by state or local authorities and often federally subsidized, number 89,971 in the region, and 218,000 individuals or families receive rental subsidies from the Section 8 program. To be eligible for either type of assistance, tenants must meet income guidelines and usually pay about 30 percent of their income in rent. Nearly 200,000 households are on HUD subsidies waiting lists, where they often remain for three years or more.

Congress made drastic cuts in federal housing programs in the mid- to late 1990s that had a negative impact throughout New England. Clinton administration changes in the Section 502 direct-loan home-ownership program sponsored by the Department of Agriculture's Rural Development division (formerly the Farmers' Home Administration) have made it difficult for New England states to use this initiative to create low- and moderate-income housing. Rural Development programs are important to the region; Vermont, for example, has historically received 50 percent more funds from Rural Development programs than from HUD. The Rural Development program provides interest subsidies and guarantees mortgages for low-income families, enabling them to qualify for ownership. The program was once so successful that nearly all New England states exceeded their Section 502 allocations. But in the late 1990s most New England states used less than 40 percent of their allocation because of underwriting regulations. By now requiring that principal, interest, taxes, and insurance amount to less than 38 percent of household income, the program has made it extremely difficult for most moderate- to low-income families to

qualify in light of New England's lofty housing costs.

Many federal subsidies for housing have been reduced or eliminated altogether, which often puts the neediest people at the most severe risk of housing loss. The personal, social, and economic impacts of these cuts and program changes began to be felt in the mid-1990s, but their full force took effect in 1997, causing acute and extensive distress for families and communities. Modified eligibility standards along with funding cuts have drastically reduced the access of low-income families to much-needed housing assistance. With housing subsidies and emergency assistance lowered, rent controls eliminated, and eviction laws loosened, fewer families have been able to avoid homelessness or make the transition from homelessness to permanent housing. Increasing numbers of people have also found themselves living in substandard and overcrowded housing.

Fannie Mae Foundation, *Understanding Homelessness: New Policy and Research Perspectives* (1997); McCormick Institute for Public Policy, *Homelessness in New England,* special issue of *New England Journal of Public Policy* 18, no. 1 (1992); Yvonne Vissing, *Out of Sight, Out of Mind: Homeless Children and Families in Small-Town America* (1996).

Yvonne Vissing

Lewiston-Auburn, Maine

Often called the Twin Cities, Lewiston and Auburn face each other on the banks of the Androscoggin River in southwestern Maine. The population of Lewiston was 35,690 in 2000, down from 39,757 in 1990. Auburn had 23,203 residents in 2000, down from 24,209 in the previous census. Together, the two cities make up Maine's second-largest urban area.

The site of Auburn was home to Anasagunticook (Androscoggin) Indians until their village was destroyed in 1690. Auburn was settled by Europeans in the mid-1780s, and the lowlands that are now its center were flooded for the planting of wheat and rye and later apples and potatoes. Auburn was incorporated in 1842 after separating from the town of Minot. When Androscoggin County was created in 1854, Auburn was named the county seat. In 1869 Auburn became a city, having annexed neighboring Danville two years earlier. Lewiston was settled in 1770 and incorporated as Maine's 95th town in 1795 with a population of 532. In the 19th century it grew from a farming village to a multi-ethnic mill and factory town. In 1863 Lewiston became a city.

The agricultural and industrial developments of the early 19th century influenced the development of both Lewiston and Auburn. Sawmills, grist mills, and tanning and pulling mills were the first to draw on the river's wa-

Village of Lewiston Falls, later part of Lewiston-Auburn, Maine, 1869

terpower. The first shoe factory in Maine was established in 1835 in West Auburn by settlers from Massachusetts. In 1836 the Minot Shoe Company, later known as James Monroe and Company, moved the shoemaking district from the west to the north. Innovations and demand generated by the Civil War increased shoe production, and by 1871, 25 shoe companies were making 2 million shoes yearly. Peak production came in 1922. The industrial decline of the 1930s led to mill and factory closings. World War II brought only modest recovery in this manufacturing sector.

Lewiston's industries have included printing, poultry hatching, and the manufacture of electrical equipment, but cotton mills fueled the town's growth. The first cotton mill, established in 1845, was the base for a broad development of mills, dams, and canals by the Lewiston Falls Cotton Mill Company, later called the Franklin Water Power Company. Bates Manufacturing, once Maine's largest employer, was founded by the Boston industrialist Benjamin Bates in 1850. Five years later Bates donated funds to transform the Maine State Seminary of Lewiston into New England's first coeducational college, incorporated in 1855 and reincorporated as Bates College in 1863. Between 1852 and 1866, eight huge cotton mills were built, and by the end of the Civil War these mills employed more than 3,500 women and 1,500 men, producing more than 30 million yards of cotton annually. By the 1920s, competition from southern textile mills gradually displaced the textile industry in the city. Lewiston's last remaining textile-producing facility, the bedspread division of Bates Manufacturing, closed in 2001.

Several factors contributed to the growth of Lewiston and Auburn: the establishment of the first railroad in central Maine in 1848, with connections to Portland; the reconstruction of the North Bridge in 1871 and construction of the South Bridge in 1872 connecting Lewiston and Auburn; the completion of a dam on the Little Androscoggin River in 1874; and the expansion of a horse-drawn street railway in the

1880s and 1890s. In the early 20th century, the changeover from steam to electric power, helped by the construction of the Deer Rips Dam in 1905, spurred new industrial growth until the Depression. A steady stream of immigrant workers—mostly Irish in the 1840s, French Canadian in the 1860s, and German in the 1880s—kept the Lewiston cotton mills and the Auburn shoe factories humming. While Auburn's business and city leaders crafted a more genteel New England image for their community, Lewiston has always been seen as an immigrant city, although an influx of 2,000 Somalis in 2001 created tension.

The decisive influence of the Franco-American community can be seen in Lewiston's distinctive architecture, from the tenement housing of "Frenchville" to the magnificent Saints Peter and Paul Church, built during the early decades of the 20th century with money donated by mill workers. The extension of the Maine Turnpike to Auburn in 1955 and the building of the Auburn-Lewiston Airpark (Airport) in the 1970s gave the cities new accessibility and are reshaping their economic contours. Lewiston-Auburn College houses branches of the University of Maine at Augusta and the University of Southern Maine. The Lewiston-Auburn branch of the latter is home to the Franco-American Heritage Collection. Bates College is home to the Edmund S. Muskie Archives.

Richard W. Judd, Edwin A. Churchill, and Joel W. Eastman, eds., *Maine: The Pine Tree State from Prehistory to the Present* (1995); Lewiston Historical Commission, *Historic Lewiston: Its Architectural Heritage* (1997); Maine Arts Commission, *Cultural Mosaic: Lewiston-Auburn* (1998).

Melanie Gustafson

Lowell, Mass. Lowell, a city of 15 square miles located 25 miles northwest of Boston at the junction of the Concord and Merrimack Rivers, was the nation's leading industrial city in the first half of the 19th century. In 1823 a group of Boston investors, known collectively as the Boston Associates, began manufactur-

ing cotton textiles in East Chelmsford at the Pawtucket Falls of the Merrimack River. The success of the Merrimack Manufacturing Company led to expansion of water-powered mills at the site, and a new town, named after the industrialist Francis Cabot Lowell, was founded in 1826 with a population of 2,500. By 1836, when Lowell was incorporated as a city, it had grown to 16,000, with its eight major mills employing 6,000 people.

Lowell's mills, which housed all the equipment for turning raw cotton into finished cloth, set the pace for textile manufacturing in the United States. Combining a system of corporate paternalism with monthly cash wages, Lowell's firms sought to industrialize without perpetuating the overcrowding and class antagonisms associated with English factory towns of this era. To avoid creating a permanent working class, the companies hired the unmarried daughters of Yankee farmers to work in the mills and built red-brick boardinghouses where the young women could live under the watchful eye of company matrons. Visitors came from throughout the world to marvel at the success of the Lowell experiment, and mill towns patterned after the Waltham-Lowell system, named for the two towns in which it originated, emerged throughout New England.

Lowell's ethnic composition changed dramatically, as successive waves of Irish, French Canadian, Greek, Portuguese, and Polish immigrants were attracted to the city's mills. Lowell's population grew from 33,000 in 1850 to more than 77,000 in 1890; its workforce increased from 10,000 to 15,000 over the same period. The population continued to rise dur-

The Makredes Ensemble plays in front of Boott Cotton Mills at the Lowell (Mass.) Folk Festival, 1992

ing World War I, reaching almost 113,000 at its peak in 1920.

Nonetheless, Lowell had been losing business to other cities since the 1880s. Steam power gradually supplanted waterpower as the most efficient industrial energy source, and by 1890 Fall River had surpassed Lowell as New England's preeminent industrial center. Many Lowell firms had established branch plants in the South by 1910, and with the outbreak of World War I several closed their northern operations entirely. Decline set in after the war, and only three of Lowell's textile mills—the Merrimack, Lawrence, and Boott—continued sporadic operations during the Great Depression.

By 1980 the city's population had fallen to 92,000, with limited textile production persisting only in small specialty firms scattered around the city. Urban renewal gutted most of the city's brick factories and boardinghouses, replacing them with nondescript public housing, parking lots, and highways. Unemployment far exceeded national levels, and the city's housing stock deteriorated.

Since the mid-1970s high-tech industry and tourism have breathed new life into the famed City of Spindles. Wang and Raytheon moved to Lowell during the "Massachusetts miracle" of the 1980s, creating thousands of new jobs, and Lowell's population rebounded to 105,167 by 2000. The establishment of the Lowell National Historical Park (1978), celebrating Lowell's role as the birthplace of America's Industrial Revolution, revitalized the city's downtown. The American Textile History Museum relocated to Lowell in 1997, enhancing cultural offerings that include the New England Quilt Museum (1976), the Whistler House Museum of Art (in the James Abbott McNeill Whistler birthplace, 1908), and the University of Massachusetts at Lowell (1894).

Lowell's economic upturn has attracted a new wave of immigrants. In 2000, 22 percent of the population was foreign-born, with Cambodians, Laotians, and Colombians predominating among the recent arrivals. Of the earlier waves of immigrants the Portuguese, French Canadian, and Greek communities remain noteworthy. Since 1987 Lowell has celebrated its diversity every July with the Lowell Folk Festival, the largest event of its kind in New England. Today Lowell is a postindustrial pioneer, once again serving as an example of urban possibilities in a new era.

Mary H. Blewett, *The Last Generation: Work and Life in the Textile Mills of Lowell, Massachusetts, 1910–1960* (1990); Robert F. Dalzell, Jr., *Enterprising Elite: The Boston Associates and the World They Made* (1987); Thomas Dublin, *Women at Work: The Transformation of Work and Community in Lowell, Massachusetts, 1826–1860*, 2d ed. (1993); Laurence F. Gross, *The Course of Industrial Decline: The Boott Cotton Mills of Lowell, Massachusetts, 1835–1955* (1993).

Thomas Dublin

Lynn, Mass.

Lynn (population 89,050 in 2000), located north of Boston, is a seaside city of old brick buildings and three-deckers, of the *Lynn Evening Item* and urban renewal, and video stores with titles in Cambodian. Founded in 1629, Lynn was the nation's largest manufacturer of shoes throughout the 19th century and became a magnet for immigrants, first from Great Britain and Ireland; later from southern and eastern Europe; and currently from Southeast Asia and Russia. Lynn was a prosperous city until the Great Depression when its shoe industry, like New England's textile industry, largely abandoned the region. Now, Lynn is struggling to redefine itself in a high-tech age.

Because its shallow harbor precludes a thriving sea trade, Lynn's early European residents quickly established a variety of mills, and shoemaking was practiced on a small scale as early as 1635. By the middle of the 18th century John Adam Dagyr, a Welsh immigrant, set up shop in Lynn, producing high-quality shoes and boots. Dagyr was largely responsible for Lynn's prominence as a center for shoemaking. When George Washington passed through Lynn in 1788, he noted that the city produced 175,000 pairs of shoes annually.

By 1830, artisan shoemaking had become industrial manufacturing, and the arrival of the railroad in 1838 advanced Lynn's national position as a shoemaking power. In the 1880s, Jan Matzeliger, a young African American inventor, developed a mechanical lasting device that sewed the upper part of the shoe to the sole. Earlier in the century, an artisan could complete 10 pairs of shoes a day; Matzeliger's process allowed for production of 700 pairs a day.

Mary Baker Eddy, who organized the first meeting of Christian Scientists in 1875, also wrote *Science and Health with a Key to the Scriptures* (1906) while living in Lynn. In 1889 a devastating fire nearly ruined Lynn's industry, but the city quickly rebuilt, and eight years later it was the premier manufacturer in a region that produced more than 60 percent of the nation's shoes. The city's shoeworkers produced 15 million pairs of shoes a year.

In the 1890s Lynn's other major industry, electrical machinery, was developed by the recently established General Electric company. Lynn became a showcase for G.E.'s electric street lighting, and for decades afterward, municipal officials from across the country would visit "the best lighted city in the world." For many decades, Lynn residents referred affectionately to General Electric's West Lynn Works as "the Lights." In 1942 G.E. developed the first turbojet at its Lynn facility.

Lynn experienced growing prosperity through the 1920s, which in turn created a population explosion that remade the city. Between 1885 and 1915 the number of immigrants rose from 9,800 to 29,500. By 1915 one of every three residents was foreign-born. Immigrants arriving after the turn of the century came mostly from southern and eastern Europe.

By the end of World War II, the shoe industry had largely left Lynn, although the city was still mostly industrial. As recently as the early 1980s, more than a third of Lynn's workers were still employed in manufacturing. At the same time, G.E. built its Factory of the Future in Lynn, seeking to provide a model for the future of heavy industry. Between 1982 and 1985, however, the company led the state in number of jobs lost, and the Factory of the Future closed in 1996.

With the growth of the high-tech industry in suburban Massachusetts, Lynn, like other Northeast cities, lost both jobs and population. And in 1981, another devastating fire hit the downtown. By 1990 nearly 16 percent of Lynn families were living near the poverty level. Per capita income was three-fourths that of the state average, and both the dropout and crime rates were higher than state averages.

Lynn has benefited from the establishment of North Shore Community College, built on the site of the 1981 fire. In 1993, the city formed a strategy for improving public safety and developing programs for young people. In recent years, Lynn has seen a new influx of immigration, largely from the Caribbean, Southeast Asia, and Russia. In 1995, 37 percent of schoolchildren lived in homes where English was not the primary language, and Lynn's school system offered bilingual programs in Spanish, Cambodian, Russian, Greek, and Vietnamese.

Elizabeth Hope Cushing, *The Lynn Album: A Pictorial History* (1990); Alan Dawley, *Class and Community: The Industrial Revolution in Lynn* (1976); Joanne S. Foley, *Lynn* (1995); Alonzo Lewis and James Newhall, *History of Lynn* (1989 [1890]).

Louis Mazzari

Manchester, N.H.

Located 58 miles northwest of Boston in south central New Hampshire's Hillsborough County, Manchester is the state's largest city, with a population of 107,066 at the time of the 2000 census. Slightly more than 13 percent of the state's residents (147,809) lived in the Manchester metropolitan area in 1990. Incorporated as Derryfield in 1751, the town was renamed Manchester, after the English industrial city, in 1810.

Manchester's industrialization began with a

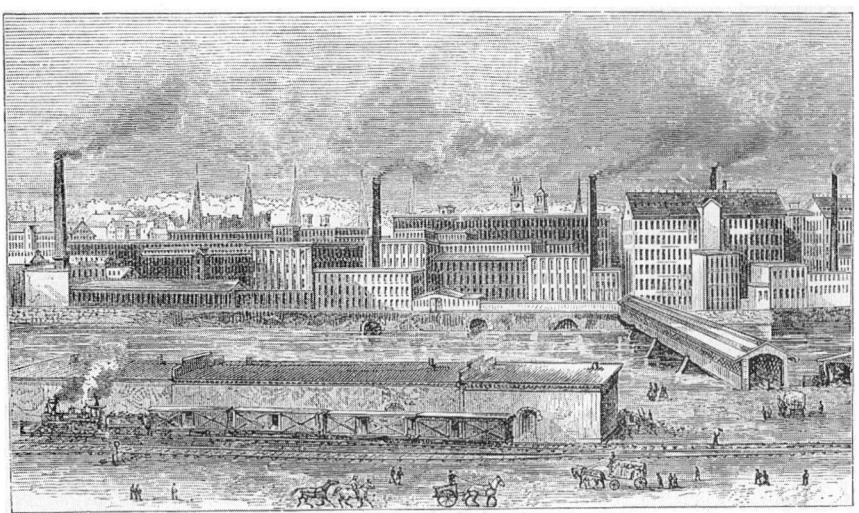

Manchester, N.H., 1881

Grace Holbrook Blood, *Manchester on the Merrimack: The Story of a City*, rev. ed. (1975); James P. Hanlan, *The Working Population of Manchester, New Hampshire, 1840–1886* (1981); Tamara K. Hareven and Randolph Langenbach, *Amoskeag: Life and Work in an American Factory City* (1978); C. E. Potter, *The History of Manchester, Formerly Derryfield, in New Hampshire* (1856).

James P. Hanlan

Massachusetts Bay Transportation Authority

The Massachusetts Bay Transportation Authority, or MBTA, is the public transit agency serving metropolitan Boston. Although the MBTA itself was created in 1964, it is the direct successor to companies that date back to 1856. The MBTA's nickname, the "T," derives from its logo, the letter T in a circle.

Boston's unique geography—originally a hilly peninsula linked to surrounding towns by bridges—has caused the city to be a pioneer in many aspects of public transportation. Long travel distances and narrow, crooked streets forced Bostonians to develop new techniques for moving people throughout the 19th and early 20th centuries.

The horse-drawn omnibus first appeared in Boston in 1826. Similar to a large stagecoach, with one door at the rear, the omnibus was slow, crowded, and uncomfortable. Steam railroads arrived in 1834, but steam power was expensive and impractical for routes with frequent stops. A one-day tally of persons entering the city in 1851 showed that approximately one-third traveled by horse-drawn conveyance (private carriage, cart, or omnibus), one-third by steam railroad, and just less than one-third on foot.

Boston was the world's fifth city to develop a horse-drawn street railway system, after New York, New Orleans, Paris, and Brooklyn. Parallel efforts by two groups of investors led to construction of horse railway lines from Boston to Cambridge and Roxbury in the mid-1850s; first to open was the Cambridge Rail Road, on March 26, 1856. Other lines quickly followed. The horse railway had a mechanical efficiency three to four times greater than that of the omnibus. The faster travel speed and lower fare allowed many families to settle in formerly rural areas of Boston's suburbs. But by the mid-1880s, the city's horsecar system had reached the practical limit of equine power. Demands for longer routes and faster speeds could not be met. Mechanical (cable) propulsion was successful in other cities, and experiments with electrically powered transit were conducted elsewhere; but the owners of Boston's street railways were reluctant to modernize.

In 1886 Henry M. Whitney sought to build

small textile mill in 1805. The first canal around the Amoskeag Falls of the Merrimack River opened direct water transportation to Boston in 1807. By 1838 what would become the world's largest cotton mill, the Amoskeag Manufacturing Company, was under construction. In 1846 Manchester became New Hampshire's first incorporated city, with a population of 10,125.

Owned by Boston-based investors but locally managed, the Amoskeag Company established policies designed to win the loyalty of workers and town residents alike. To ensure a stable community and a quiescent labor force, the Amoskeag supported community services, gave generously to local churches, and provided workers with excellent benefits. The company determined the layout of the city and controlled business growth by placing deed restrictions on prime industrial land. About 15 percent of its workers lived in low-rent company tenements; the rest lived in privately owned housing clustered around churches in ethnic neighborhoods. With their nearly 8 million square feet of floor space, the Amoskeag mills stretched along the river for more than a mile and by 1906 produced 4 million yards of cloth per week.

Manchester's first factory workers were native-born New England women. Gradually they were replaced by immigrant laborers—first the Irish, then, after 1870, French Canadians, Greeks, Poles, and other ethnic groups. By 1910 Franco-Americans, originally attracted to Manchester because of its location on a major rail line to Quebec, composed 38 percent of the city's population and 35 percent of the Amoskeag's labor force. The Association Canado-Américaine is still an active cultural and social institution within the city.

By 1890, 44,126 people lived in Manchester.

Although after 1900 some residents worked in shoe manufacturing or at the famous 70-20-4 cigar factory, up to two-thirds of the city's workers were dependent on the Amoskeag or its subsidiaries. The Amoskeag flourished through World War I but declined in the 1920s because of shrinking markets, foreign and southern competition, the advent of silk and rayon, and management's decision not to invest in new technologies. By 1935 the Amoskeag was bankrupt. Local civic, banking, and business leaders rallied to form Amoskeag Industries of Manchester, purchased the failed company's buildings, and rehabilitated them for the manufacture of textiles, leather and rubber goods, automobile accessories, electrical instruments, confectioneries, beverages, and dairy products. This effort brought economic recovery and gave Manchester the reputation of being "the city that would not die."

The famous bell tower of the old Amoskeag Company now rises above a retail complex in which outlet stores flourish. Manchester is the state's financial capital and a major transportation and distribution center for northern New England. It is home to electronic firms such as Osram Sylvania and textile manufacturers such as Velcro USA, as well as several institutions of higher learning: Saint Anselm College, Southern New Hampshire University, Notre Dame College, and the University of New Hampshire at Manchester. The New Hampshire Performing Arts Center in the restored Palace Theater, the Verizon Wireless Arena (northern New England's largest indoor venue), the Currier Museum of Art, the Manchester Institute of Arts and Sciences, and the Manchester Historic Association Museum and Library all contribute to the cultural life of the city.

a mechanized railway to serve land that he and other investors owned in Brookline. When the existing street railway companies resisted his efforts, Whitney and his associates quietly purchased a majority of the stock in those companies and consolidated them into his own West End Street Railway in 1887. The West End became the world's largest street railway company, and Boston was the first major city to unify its transit lines under one corporate management.

A visit to Richmond, Va., to observe an electric streetcar line built by Frank J. Sprague prompted Whitney to build his new Beacon Street line as an electric rather than cable operation. The line, which opened in January 1889, was the first successful electric car line in a large city. It spurred a rapid conversion of horse railways to electric propulsion, as well as the expansion of street railways into more distant areas. Ninety percent of the West End's track was electrified by 1895, although some horsecar lines continued until 1900.

Growing congestion on downtown Boston streets prompted construction of the first subway in America (and the fourth in the world), which opened on September 1, 1897. The Tremont Street Subway was modeled after a line in Budapest that had opened the previous year. An electrically powered elevated railroad, similar to one in Chicago, was opened in 1901, and the first underwater rail tunnel in the United States was built between Boston and East Boston in 1904. Expansion of this subway and rapid transit system has continued to the present day.

The Boston Elevated Railway Company took over operations of the West End Street Railway at the end of 1897. The "Elevated," or "El," operated Boston's transit system for almost 50 years. Inflation and other factors caused the company to cease being profitable during World War I. Under the Public Control Act of 1918, the Massachusetts governor appointed trustees to manage the system, while taxpayer subsidies assured the continued payment of dividends to stockholders. Buses were introduced in 1922, beginning a 60-year process of conversion from streetcars to rubber-tired vehicles.

The Metropolitan Transit Authority, a public agency, was created in 1947 to assume the assets and operations of the Elevated. Two years after its inception, the MTA raised fares and eliminated free transfers. This action inspired members of the Progressive Party to write the campaign song "MTA," better known as "Charlie on the MTA," for Walter A. O'Brien, a candidate in Boston's 1949 mayoral election. Written by Jacqueline (Berman) Steiner and Beth Lomax Hawes in 1949, "Charlie on the MTA" is a song about a mythical Charlie—"the man who never returned" because he didn't have the extra nickel needed to get off a trolley car. The song was re-recorded by the Kingston Trio 10 years later, but because of Walter O'Brien's leftist politics, the candidate's name was changed to George in the Kingston Trio's version.

The MBTA, which took over the operations of the MTA in 1964, was established to widen the transit system's geographical service area and to allow it to operate additional services. Later it acquired bus companies in outlying towns, as well as the region's commuter rail lines. During major renovations of its facilities in the 1970s and 1980s, the MBTA acquired its impressive public art collection, the first of its kind in the country, with the help of federal funding. The MBTA holds more than 70 pieces of public art displayed in or near its facilities, including sculptures, monuments, stained glass, ceramic tiles, murals, and student art.

Today the MBTA operates subways and rapid transit lines as well as bus, streetcar, and trackless trolley lines throughout the metropolitan area. The authority also contracts for the operation of commuter trains and ferries. The MBTA service map is characterized by its distinctive Green, Red, Orange, and Blue Lines. Approximately 1 million passengers per day board the subway, bus, and ferry systems of the MBTA, while roughly 127,000 suburban passengers use its commuter lines daily.

Charles W. Cheape, *Moving the Masses: Urban Public Transit in New York, Boston, and Philadelphia, 1880–1912* (1980); Frank Cheney and Anthony M. Sammarco, *Trolleys under the Hub* (1997); Bradley H. Clarke and O. R. Cummings, *Tremont Street Subway: A Century of Public Service* (1997); Brian J. Cudahy, *Change at Park Street Under: The Story of Boston's Subways* (1972).

Charles Bahne

Montpelier, Vt. Montpelier, located in central Vermont in a narrow valley at the convergence of the Winooski and North Branch Rivers, is the nation's smallest capital city and the seat of Washington County. With a population of 8,035 according to the 2000 census, this compact, bustling community of government and commerce with its well-kept homes perched on surrounding hills in no way resembles the modest settlement that for 19th-century Vermonters had the reputation of being "the loneliest village in New England," and that was once described as a "pothole on a foggy river bank."

Chartered in 1781 as a grant to several individuals from Massachusetts, the township acquired its first settler in 1787 when Colonel Jacob Davis built a house there and gave the town its name. Its location in the upper watershed of the Winooski River contributed, in subsequent years, to more than two dozen episodes of significant flooding, two of the most destructive occurring in 1927 and 1992. *Winooski* means "wild onion land" in the language of the Abenaki Indian groups who lived

Montpelier, Vt., statehouse, 1923

in the area for centuries prior to European contact, and during the early years of the 19th century the town was occasionally described, to the annoyance of its residents, as Montpelier-on-the-Onion.

A diverse economy emerged early, reliant initially on saw, grist, woolen, flour, and paper mills based on the riverways. In 1805 legislators designated the town as the state capital. In the 1820s and 1840s enterprising merchants founded promising insurance companies, enabling Montpelier to become known as an "insurance town." The arrival of the Vermont Central Railroad in 1849 put into place the last of the city's early principal economic components.

Growth nevertheless remained slow until the 1880s when construction of a railroad spur line to granite quarries in nearby Barre, Vt., led to the establishment of approximately 30 granite finishing plants, most of them located along the Winooski River. This economic expansion caused Montpelier's population—and its community of foreign-born residents, primarily from Ireland, French Canada, Scotland, Italy, and Spain—to almost double in size between 1890 and 1915.

In the last half of the 20th century the city's size remained stable at around 8,500 residents. Following World War II the granite industry and small manufacturing gradually were replaced as vital economic elements by a white-collar administrative and managerial service sector composed largely of highly educated professional workers. The expansion of state government, other public employment, associated services, and the continued growth of the insurance industry spurred this trend, as Montpelier became "a city of clerks." This white-collar economy, in turn, influenced a substantial suburban development in the rural communities peripheral to Montpelier, a growth pattern accelerated by the arrival in 1970 of Interstate 89. The interstate also hastened the emergence of tourism as an additional robust element in the local economy.

In the 2000s Montpelier claims a growing reputation within the state as a center for the arts. Its citizens support a philharmonic orchestra, an art museum, a regional arts organization, and a community theater. Montpelier is home to a number of educational institutions, including Vermont College, the New England Culinary Institute, Woodbury College, and the Vermont Institute of Natural Science.

A. M. Hemenway, *The History of the Town of Montpelier for the First 102 Years* (1882); Ralph Nading Hill, *The Winooski: Heartway of Vermont* (1949); Perry H. Merrill, *Montpelier: The Capital City's History* (1977); Daniel Pierce Thompson, *History of the Town of Montpelier to the Year 1860* (1995 [1860]).

Gene Sessions

Nashua, N.H. Nashua, with approximately 86,605 residents in the city and 180,557 in the metropolitan area according to the 2000 census, is the seat of Hillsborough County. It is located 40 miles northwest of Boston, and about 35 miles south-southeast of Concord, N.H., at the confluence of the Merrimack and Nashua Rivers. Nashua is the state's second largest city and is known as "the gate city of New Hampshire." It is the southernmost of the three Merrimack Valley cities that, together, make up the southern tier of New Hampshire. This region is the economic and social center and home to about one-third of the population of this otherwise largely rural state. The three Merrimack Valley cities (Nashua, Manchester, and Concord) are within easy driving distance of one another and of the Massachusetts border. Politically, the three cities help to provide some partisan balance to an otherwise largely Republican state, as most of the state's Democratic voters reside in the Merrimack Valley urban communities. The valley is the industrial heartland of New Hampshire.

Originally part of Dunstable, Mass., the community retained the name of Dunstable after settlement of a boundary dispute with Massachusetts made it part of New Hampshire in 1741. In 1836 the name was changed to Nashua. Nashua's development was tied to that of the Merrimack River for navigation and as a source of power for textile mills in the 19th century. With the opening of the Middlesex Canal in 1804, the town became the head of navigation on the Merrimack. In the wake of investments in the textile industry throughout the Merrimack Valley by absentee investors, Nashua grew into a center of cotton textile manufacturing. It attracted immigrants from Ireland, Canada, and European countries to work in the mills.

The textile industry declined after the Great Depression, but thanks to the efforts of the Nashua, New Hampshire Foundation, the city reshaped itself as an important industrial center for shoes, paper products, electronics, plastics, avionics, and electronic equipment, particularly for the defense industry, with an increasing emphasis on research and development. The city and its suburbs contribute to the cultural life of the region by hosting an impressive choral society and an equity theater company.

The interdependence of the southern New Hampshire economy with that of Massachusetts is most evident in Nashua. Heavy commuting traffic along Interstate 93 and Route 3 testifies daily to the close ties between the two states. While the greater Nashua region serves as a major regional employment center, it also provides commuting refuge from heavily in-dustrial older Massachusetts cities such as Lowell and, via daily commuter rail connections, Boston. Nashua has attracted solidly comfortable middle-class residents and entices shoppers across the state line to its sales-tax-free retailers, traditionally fueling the resentment of merchants in neighboring Massachusetts communities. Voted one of the "best places to live in America" by *Money* magazine in 1997, Nashua is home to Daniel Webster College and Rivier College.

Committee for a New England Bibliography, *New Hampshire: A Bibliography of Its History* (1979); Elizabeth F. Morison, *New Hampshire: A Bicentennial History* (1976); Nashua History Committee, *The Nashua Experience* (1978); E. E. Parker, *History of the City of Nashua* (1897).

James P. Hanlan

New Bedford, Mass. New Bedford lies along the coast of southeastern Massachusetts at the mouth of the Acushnet River 56 miles south of Boston. The New Bedford area was originally home to the Wampanoag Indians. Settled by colonists from Plymouth, it was set apart from its parent town of Dartmouth in 1787. New Bedford's fine harbor made the site ideal for shipbuilding and whaling, and it grew from a small fishing village to a town of 3,313 by 1790. The eastern shore was incorporated as the town of Fairhaven in 1812.

During the colonial era immigrants to the region were primarily of English descent. Members of the Society of Friends (Quakers) were particularly attracted to the area and gradually came to dominate the town's religious and political life. Active abolitionists, the Quakers made New Bedford a safe home for people of color. Descendants of local black slaves were joined by free persons and fugitive slaves from the South until they numbered more than 1,500 and constituted approximately 6 percent of the population in 1860. Paul Cuffe, the son of a local slave, became a wealthy merchant by the time he died in 1817. The owner of several ships, he took part in the settlement of free blacks in Sierra Leone in Africa. Frederick Douglass also lived in New Bedford after his escape from slavery, drawn to the town by the availability of jobs and the prosperous black community.

The whaling industry made New Bedford one of the richest towns in the United States by the time it became a city in 1847. It was the fourth busiest port in the country, with more than 300 whaling vessels. Whaling opportunities brought in Portuguese from the Azores and Madeira and from the Cape Verde Islands off the western coast of Africa. These men settled in New Bedford in the mid-19th century and were followed by the migration of women and children. The whaling industry declined steadily after the Civil War; the last successful voyage, by the schooner *John R. Manta,* took place in 1925.

During the final quarter of the 19th century the town's economic base came to rest increasingly on the manufacture of cotton textiles. The work available in the mills attracted a large migration of French Canadians, and New Bedford's population rose to 40,733 by 1890. Textile prosperity lasted only until the 1920s, however, when the mills began moving to the South. Commercial fishing has remained critical to the city's livelihood, with New Bedford ranking as the largest fishing port in the United States during part of the 1980s. Overharvesting of the banks off the New England coast has severely weakened that industry, however. Having peaked at 121,217 in 1920, New Bedford's population has fallen considerably, with each successive census showing a decline. This trend reversed itself in 1990, when figures rose slightly over 1980 totals, to 99,922, possibly in response to the creation of jobs related to tourism and gambling. By the 2000 census, the population had fallen again to 93,768. In 1996 the Wampanoag shifted the focus of their effort to introduce casino gambling in the area from New Bedford to nearby Fall River, where it was eventually defeated in a referendum vote.

New Bedford is currently a diverse city with major Latino, Portuguese, and Cape Verdean communities. Proud of its heritage as the Whaling City, it is home to the New Bedford Whaling Museum, Fort Rodman, and the Seaman's Bethel, immortalized by Herman Melville as the "Whaleman's Chapel." The Northeast Maritime Institute, founded in 1981, trains students for careers in the Coast Guard and merchant marine.

Everett S. Allen, *Children of the Light: The Rise and Fall of New Bedford Whaling and the Death of the Arctic Fleet* (1973); Stephen L. Cabral, *Tradition and Transformation: Portuguese Feasting in New Bedford* (1989); Leonard Bolles Ellis, *History of New Bedford and Its Vicinity, 1620–1892* (1892); Marilyn Halter, *Between Race and Ethnicity: Cape Verdean American Immigrants, 1860–1965* (1993).

Paul Albert Cyr

New Haven, Conn. Founded in 1638 by Reverend John Davenport and Theophilus Eaton, New Haven was a separate colony until it was unwillingly absorbed by Connecticut under its 1662 charter. New Haven was co-capital of Connecticut (with Hartford) from 1701 to 1875. The founders laid out the city around nine central squares, making it the first planned city in the New World. The planning is still evident in the New Haven Green, which dominates the city center. New Haven assumed its current boundaries when a munic-

ipal government was established and neighboring towns were pared off in 1784. With a population of 7,000 in the first federal census of 1790, the city boasted a population of 20,345 by the middle of the 19th century and 108,000 by 1900. The population of the city peaked in 1950 at 164,443, before urban renewal and increased suburbanization. The 2000 census figure was 123,626.

While the city's founders were of English extraction, African Americans were a notable presence from earliest settlement. In 1800 there were approximately 200 blacks in the city, 85 of them slaves. Large numbers of Irish settled in New Haven by the 1850s, and they were joined at the end of the century by large numbers of Italians and eastern European Jews. Along with Germans, Poles, Lithuanians, Greeks, Puerto Ricans, and other immigrant groups, they have made New Haven an ethnically diverse city far removed from its Yankee origins. The immigrant influence is evident in the ethnic churches and synagogues, summer festivals, community and fraternal organizations, and pizza, a part of its culture in which New Haven takes particular pride.

Situated on Long Island Sound, New Haven based its early economy on the sea. New Haven ships were extensively involved in the coastal and West Indies trade as well as the oyster trade. Manufacturing received a notable start in 1798 when Eli Whitney established an armory on the principle of interchangeable parts just across the city line in Hamden. Whitney's concern was later absorbed by the city's Winchester Repeating Arms. Before the Civil War, New Haven was noted for its carriage manufacturers. By the 20th century, the city was home to J. B. Sargent and Company (hardware), A. C. Gilbert (Erector Sets and American Flyer trains), and numerous small manufactories. This industrial heritage has now largely been replaced by the service sector, telecommunications, and biotechnology research.

Yale University has been central to life in New Haven since it consolidated its Wethersfield, Saybrook, and New Haven campuses in 1716. Its art gallery, along with the Yale Center for British Art and Yale Repertory Theater, its libraries, and its lectures, add immeasurably to the cultural vibrancy of New Haven. During recent periods of economic hardship, however, town-gown tensions have been evident given the proximity of the wealthy university to some impoverished areas of the city. Also important are the New Haven Symphony, Long Wharf Theater, and Shubert Theater, the latter the site of many world premieres, including *Oklahoma!* and *South Pacific.* In 1996 the International Festival of Arts and Ideas was

established, an annual offering of the best and most original world arts and ideas. The wealth of artistic and cultural offerings in the city is the reason New Haven is widely considered the arts capital of Connecticut. New Haven also boasts a rich architectural heritage, from the Greek Revival and neo-Gothic architecture of the churches on the Green to modern structures designed by the architects Louis Kahn, Eero Saarinen, and I. M. Pei.

During the 1950s, New Haven was beset by the host of urban ills that characterized many Connecticut cities. High unemployment and poverty rates, poor public health, and a deteriorating infrastructure and housing stock led to urban renewal attempts as early as 1957, with the razing of parts of the downtown area to create Church Street Center. Mayor Richard Lee, elected to eight terms starting in 1954, led these efforts at revitalization. The construction of Interstates 95 and 91 cut a swath through the city, as well. Mayor John DeStefano, Jr., has continued renewal efforts since his election in 1994, and the city was named an All-American City in 1998. A huge Ikea department store opened in the Long Wharf area in 2004.

Robert A. Dahl, *Who Governs? Democracy and Power in an American City* (1961); Rollin G. Osterweis, *Three Centuries of New Haven, 1638–1938* (1953); Douglas W. Rae, *City: Urbanism and Its End* (2003); Floyd Shumway and Richard Hegel, eds., *New Haven: An Illustrated History* (1981).

Robert J. Imholt

Newport, R.I. Newport (population 26,476 in 2000) is Rhode Island's leading tourist destination. As in Rhode Island generally, the city's population is overwhelmingly white (84.1 percent in 2000, compared to the state average of 85 percent), whereas in the 1750s it was more than 19 percent African American, reflecting Newport's prominence in the African slave trade. By the end of the 20th century, the black population was 7.8 percent, above the state proportion of 4.5 percent, evidence of the enduring presence of Newport's colonial legacy. The other substantial minority population in Newport in 2000 was Hispanics, who numbered 1,467 or 5.5 percent of the city's people. Beginning with an influx of Irish laborers in 1824 to build Fort Adams, Irish have made up a large part of the majority white population. Rhode Island's first Catholic parish, Saint Mary's Roman Catholic Church, was established in 1828; Senator John Kennedy and Jacqueline Bouvier were married there on September 12, 1953.

The city was founded in 1639 when the antinomians William Coddington and friends seceded from the fractious town of Pocasset (Portsmouth). Originally refugees from the

Massachusetts Bay Colony, Coddington's group had gone into exile the previous year and established a settlement on the northern end of Aquidneck Island. Coddington, who held the deed to the island, was made the "judge" of the town, but his authority was constantly disputed. As a result, he and most of the wealthy members of the Pocasset community removed themselves to a protected harbor site on the southern end of the island, where they established the city of Newport.

Newport's harbor became the leading port in Rhode Island in the 17th and 18th centuries. On the strength of its ocean commerce Newport became the fifth largest town in colonial British America and boasted a sophisticated culture. Bishop George Berkeley resided there in 1729–31, and the Townsend-Goddard families crafted what is arguably the finest furniture made in America in the 18th century. Peter Harrison, one of colonial America's leading architects, designed several of Newport's principal structures, including the Redwood Library (1748), Brick Market (1762), and Touro Synagogue (1763), the oldest extant synagogue in the United States. Gilbert Stuart, who later became one of America's most accomplished portrait artists (his picture of George Washington appears on the dollar bill), grew up in Newport.

On the eve of the American Revolution, Newport, with a population of 9,209, had twice as many people as Providence and was the principal capital (with Providence) of Rhode Island. But after the Revolution, Newport's power and influence sharply declined. Ravaged by war—Newport was occupied by the British for three and a half years, causing almost half the residents to flee—by radical changes in commerce, and by bad weather, Newport soon fell far behind Providence. In 1790 Newport counted 6,716 people; by 1890 it had only 19,457 to Providence's 145,472. In recognition of this size differential, Providence became the sole capital of the state in 1900.

Newport regained a measure of glory in the 19th century as it became the "Queen of Resorts" for America's Gilded Age aristocracy. Already regarded as a holiday destination by southern planters fleeing the heat and fevers of the South in the 18th century (when its nickname was the "Carolina hospital"), its fame increased in the 19th. Concurrently with the rise of tourism was the increase in the naval presence, with the establishment of the Naval War College in 1884 and the development of the Atlantic Fleet in Narragansett Bay after 1900. During World War II, Newport was a training base for thousands of naval personnel and home to a portion of the Atlantic Fleet. Newport's split personality, symbolized by "Blood Alley" with its sailor bars

and brothels along West Pelham Street and Bellevue Avenue with its elegant Gilded Age mansions, ended when the navy withdrew most of its operations in 1973. Tourism became Newport's main industry.

The industry is now year-round, and the mansions, the beaches, indeed the whole thrust of the city's economic development, are geared to cater to it. In the summer, the city is alive with the Newport Music Festival (classical music performed in the mansions), the Newport Jazz Festival, the Newport Folk Festival, the Newport Waterfront Festival, the Newport Film Festival, the International Tennis Hall of Fame Tournament, yachting regattas, visits by the "Tall Ships," and innumerable other attractions. Weekend traffic jams are common on America's Cup Boulevard and Thames Street. The Vanderbilt mansion "The Breakers"—the jewel of the Newport County Preservation Society—receives 400,000 visitors a year. The society owns 11 properties and boasts of being the largest outdoor museum in the country. In addition, Newport has a large number of restored homes dating from the colonial era, thanks in part to the Newport Restoration Foundation. Queen Anne's Square in the heart of the city is one of the most beautiful plazas, with Trinity Church (1726) dominating a space that sweeps down to the harbor. Even the loss of the America's Cup yacht races in 1983 did not stop the tourism juggernaut. A host of other racing events are staged each year, and the Museum of Yachting flourishes as part of Fort Adams State Park. Salve Regina, once a small Catholic women's college, is now a university occupying a campus that encompasses many of the former mansions of the Gilded Age aristocracy.

In the 1980s and 1990s intense real estate development around the harbor and on Ocean Drive displaced most of the commercial buildings in favor of condominiums, "dockominiums," pleasure craft, and harbor cruise boats. Thames Street has been refurbished with boutiques, antiques shops, and eateries for all tastes. In recent decades, Goat Island, the site of the Naval Torpedo Station during World War II, has been completely redeveloped with luxury condominiums, a luxury hotel, and marinas. Newport's tourist reputation, which began in the 18th century, continues strong in the 20th and 21st centuries.

Judith A. Boss, *Newport: A Pictorial History* (1981); Elaine F. Crane, *A Dependent People: Newport, Rhode Island, in the Revolutionary Era* (1985); Antoinette E. Downing and Vincent J. Scully, Jr., *The Architectural Heritage of Newport, Rhode Island, 1640–1915,* 2d ed. (1977); J. C. P. Jeffreys, *Newport, 1639–1976: An Historical Sketch* (1976); George H. Kellner and J. Stanley Lemons, *Rhode Island: The Ocean State* (2004).

J. Stanley Lemons

Newton, Mass. Settled in 1639 as Cambridgetown and legally established as New Towne in 1688, Newton acquired its present name in 1691. Its dozen original villages were incorporated by city charter in 1874. Newton lies along the Charles River 7 miles west of Boston, Mass. Bordered on the east by Brookline, on the south by Dedham, on the north by Watertown and Waltham, and on the west by Wellesley, Newton had 83,829 residents at the time of the 2000 census. The city is connected to Boston by two venerable thoroughfares, Commonwealth Avenue and Beacon Street. Like most New England towns and cities, Newton prizes its identity and culture.

Two public monuments signify the changing and diversifying character of Newton's peoples over time. One honors the earliest settlers—Jackson, Hyde, Hammond, Fuller, Prentice—Anglo Yankees all. The other honors Newton men killed in Vietnam—Pagnano, Esposito, Charnock, O'Neill, Morocco—none of English descent. Newton's African American community dates back to the free slave population of the 18th and 19th centuries. Indeed, Newton's cultural diversity reflects both colonial settlement and later U.S. immigration patterns that brought first Catholics and then, in the early 1950s, Jews to the city in large numbers, with both groups quickly coming to outnumber Protestants. The city's numerous churches and synagogues attest to these successive waves of immigrants.

Historically, Newton has adhered to a rather traditional business culture, especially in land use and financial planning. Yet the Garden City has also embodied striking unorthodoxies, from abolitionism and the Underground Railroad in the 19th century to an outspoken antiwar movement during the Vietnam years. In the latter period Newton became the central community in a congressional district that elected the first Catholic priest, Robert Drinan, to the U.S. Congress; later it elected an acknowledged homosexual, Barney Frank, to the same seat. Another claim to fame is the Fig Newton, an iconic American edible, which the Nabisco Company named after the city in the 1920s.

Newton's relation to education has always been significant. Located within the Boston metropolitan area with its 50-plus colleges and universities, Newton houses two major institutions, Boston College (1863) and Andover Newton Theological School (1807). Public education became especially important when Newton began to grow more cosmopolitan after World War II, significantly altering its social profile and characteristic lifestyles. In 1962 the Massachusetts Turnpike was extended from Route 128 east through Newton's northern edge, providing a connection to Boston and points north and south of the Hub. In response to the area's developing technological, electronic, and research industries, especially along Route 128, Newton became home to many young salaried technical professionals. Also moving in were newly minted academics, who joined expanding college faculties in the post-Sputnik era of the late 1950s, and people in the "helping professions," teaching, social work, clinical psychology, public advocacy. These highly educated and credentialed newcomers fashioned a public school system reflecting their standards of high achievement and a willingness to utilize updated educational methods for their children. By the 1960s Newton had become well known locally and nationally for the excellence of its public schools. It soon acquired such amenities as take-out gourmet food establishments and a 10-screen cinema complex showing only foreign and "art" films.

As in 1874, contemporary Newton still consists of several villages, though their number and their names may have changed over time: Auburndale, Chestnut Hill, Lower Falls, Newton Centre, Newton Corner, Newton Highlands, Newtonville, Nonantum, Oak Hill, Thompsonville, Upper Falls, Waban, and West Newton. They are as much a state of mind as they are geographic locations, and they lack formal borders for the most part. Each one has its own specific character, however, and Newtonians all know in which village they live.

Francis Jackson, *History of the Early Settlement of Newton County of Middlesex, Massachusetts, from 1639 to 1800: With a Genealogical Register of Its Inhabitants, Prior to 1800* (1909 [1854]); Newton Tercentenary Corporation, *Newton, Massachusetts, 1688–1988: A Celebration of 300 Years* (1988); Newton Times, *The Village of Newton* (1977); Henry K. Rowe, *Tercentenary History of Newton* (1930).

Seymour Leventman

Northampton, Mass. This small city (population 28,978 in 2000), situated on the Connecticut River in west-central Massachusetts, is now known as a vibrant and progressive cultural center. Home to many renowned artists and writers and host to a number of arts and music festivals, Northampton is enlivened by a street youth culture and a strong lesbian and gay presence. Its once prosperous postwar downtown, a victim of shopping malls, has been reborn as a mélange of shops, galleries, performance venues, and restaurants. If tourism is the boom industry, Smith College, founded in 1871 and now the city's largest employer, is an important cultural resource. A loose network of social and political reform groups has drawn many to settle in the city's changing neighborhoods. Some see a tale of

two cities: "Noho," for Northampton's progressive turn-of-the-21st-century cultural scene, and "Hamp," an early-20th-century moniker for an industrial, commercial, and legal center with deep Yankee roots nourished by generations of Irish, French Canadian, Polish, German, 19th-century English, Jewish, and Italian immigrants. Northampton is also the site of the nearly 200-year-old Three County Fair, sponsored by the Hampshire, Franklin, and Hampden Agricultural Society.

This complex identity signals but the latest twist in a long and rich history. Purchased from Algonquian Indians, "Nonotuck" was settled by English colonists in 1654 as an extension of agriculture and the fur trade up the "Great River." Prominent ministers Solomon Stoddard and his grandson Jonathan Edwards addressed colonial tensions between religious and worldly life. In 1786 Daniel Shays led armed farmers in a tax revolt to the county courthouse in Northampton. Days later, the town's first newspaper, the *Hampshire Gazette,* was established as a voice of law and order. By the 1820s, downtown Northampton was beginning to take on its modern shape.

Liberalism in commerce was joined by Unitarianism in religious life. Other sects soon followed. Plans to make Northampton the New York City of New England yielded the Northampton–New Haven Canal. Railroads and industry proved dominant. The abolitionists of the utopian Northampton Association of Education and Industry took over a Mill River site, manufacturing silk and advocating equality for women and African Americans. Members, including Sojourner Truth, stayed on to form the industrial village of Florence.

Health- and education-related entities included water cures, the diet reformer Sylvester Graham (inventor of the graham cracker), Clarke School for the Deaf, and Smith College. The "Swedish Nightingale" Jenny Lind appeared under the auspices of P. T. Barnum and returned for her honeymoon, dubbing Northampton the "paradise of America." Indeed, the town had become a tourist resort, drawing southern whites as well as reform-minded orators and writers.

In 1883 the town became a city. Silk moths ringing its seal showed that industry's centrality. By the turn of the 20th century, Northampton was one-quarter foreign-born (population 14,990 in 1890). Diversity was the new norm. Looking backward to a more rural past, Northampton marketed itself as the Meadow City. Yet Catholics, once eyed suspiciously, moved to center stage. French and Polish were spoken in churches and neighborhoods. The Irish came to dominance in politics. A Vermont Yankee, Calvin Coolidge, crossed the river from Amherst College, rose to be mayor, and returned after his U.S. presidency (1923–29). By then immigration had declined and the silk industry faded.

The Northampton State Hospital, founded as the Northampton Lunatic Hospital in 1858, was a landmark facility whose history reflects the changing treatment of the mentally ill in Massachusetts. Its population peaked at about 2,500 in the 1950s, and conditions deteriorated. Following a class-action suit and the deinstitutionalization of the mentally ill, the hospital closed in 1993.

With the rapid growth of the University of Massachusetts at nearby Amherst in the

Main Street, Northampton, Mass., 1992

1960s, Northampton became the social and commercial center of the Five Colleges consortium, which also includes Amherst, Hampshire, Mount Holyoke, and Smith. A robust women's movement proved fertile ground for progressive politics and the lesbian community. Hispanics and Asians became the new ethnics. The *Daily Hampshire Gazette* now covers animated political debates and the region's many cultural riches alongside school news, lesbian wedding announcements, Wal-Mart's local plans, and Barnum-like New Age ads.

Christopher Clark, *The Communitarian Moment: The Radical Challenge of the Northampton Association* (1995); Helen Lefkowitz Horowitz and Kathy Peiss, eds., *Love across the Color Line: The Letters of Alice Hanley to Channing Lewis* (1996); Tracy Kidder, *Home Town* (1999); Peter A. Thomas, *In the Maelstrom of Change: The Indian Trade and Cultural Process in the Middle Connecticut River Valley, 1635–1665* (1990).

Paul Gaffney

Pittsfield, Mass.

Nestled in the rough, mountainous terrain of the Berkshire Hills of western Massachusetts, Pittsfield was founded relatively late in the history of the commonwealth. The hardships of passing the "Berkshire Barrier" discouraged early migration from the east, so the first settlers came north from the Connecticut River valley in 1734. The settlement was founded at the fork of two branches of the Housatonic River, an area known by the native Mohegan name of Pontoosuc, or "the hunting ground for winter deer." Although sparsely populated, the village was incorporated in 1761, and by 1800 it boasted 3,000 inhabitants.

In 1801, when imported textiles were scarce and expensive, the Berkshire Woolen Mills were built to take advantage of the untapped power of the Housatonic River. In 1806 Elkanah Watson, a prominent local farmer, imported the country's first two merino sheep from Spain as part of a plan to establish Pittsfield as a major milling center. Watson founded a society for the promotion of agriculture and manufacturing, the first such society to include average farmers and women among its members, and in September 1811 it sponsored one of the nation's first agricultural fairs in Pittsfield's Park Square.

Pittsfield quickly became one of the main industrial centers of the region, leading the state in woolen and paper manufacturing until the Civil War. The town was home to a number of celebrated authors during this period, most notably, Oliver Wendell Holmes, Sr., and Herman Melville. Portions of *Moby-Dick* (1851), *Pierre* (1852), and *The Piazza Tales* (1856) were written at Arrowhead, Melville's farm

(now the home of the Berkshire Historical Society), each reflecting the local landscape—indeed, Melville claimed to have imagined his giant whale by looking at the humpbacked Mount Greylock, the highest peak in Massachusetts, from his study window.

Named after the British prime minister William Pitt, Pittsfield became the Berkshire County seat in 1868 and was incorporated as a city in 1889. According to the 1890 census, the population stood at 17,281. The character of the city was and remains that of an urban industrial area in rural isolation. Agriculture and the textile industries were in decline by the end of the 19th century, but the city rebounded in 1901 when General Electric bought the local Stanley Electric plant. Two years later G.E. moved its primary operations to Pittsfield, transforming the city into a company town during World War II and its aftermath, when the manufacturer became one of the leaders of the nation's military-industrial complex. Immigrants from Italy and eastern Europe migrated to work in "Tank Town," and the population reached more than 60,000 at its peak in the mid-1960s. Berkshire Community College was founded in the city in 1960.

As the military and heavy industrial economic sectors shrank in the late 20th century, G.E. began to pull out of Pittsfield, sending the city into a steep decline. The town's population was 45,793 according to the 2000 census. In a regional economy now based on tourism and the arts, Pittsfield's renewal is delayed by current battles among G.E., the Environmental Protection Agency, and the city

to negotiate the cleanup of decades of dangerous industrial waste.

June C. Nash, *From Tank Town to High Tech: The Clash of Community and Industrial Cycles* (1989); J. E. A. Smith, *The History of Pittsfield, Berkshire County, Massachusetts*, 2 vols. (1869, 1876).

Deborah Applegate

Portland, Maine

With a 2000 population of 64,249, Portland, seat of Cumberland County, is Maine's largest city. Machigonne ("knee" or "bad clay") was the Native American name for the area. Originally just a 3-mile peninsula, the city now occupies more than 20 square miles of land on the southern Maine coast. The Neck, as the peninsula was called, and several of the surrounding towns were once a part of neighboring Falmouth. Portland was incorporated and took its name in 1786 but did not become a city until 1832. From 1820 until 1831 it served as the capital of Maine.

The deep, sheltered harbor of Casco Bay has enabled Portland to develop lucrative maritime pursuits. The early mast trade took Maine's white pine to England for the king's ships, and the growth of shipping and shipbuilding made Portland one of the most important harbors in America. Ships designed, built, or repaired in Portland have traveled the world, and fish caught and packed on the waterfront have long been sold in markets worldwide. The Portland Head Light, built in 1791, is one of the oldest lighthouses in the United States.

The history and landscape of the area have also shaped many of Portland's influential sons

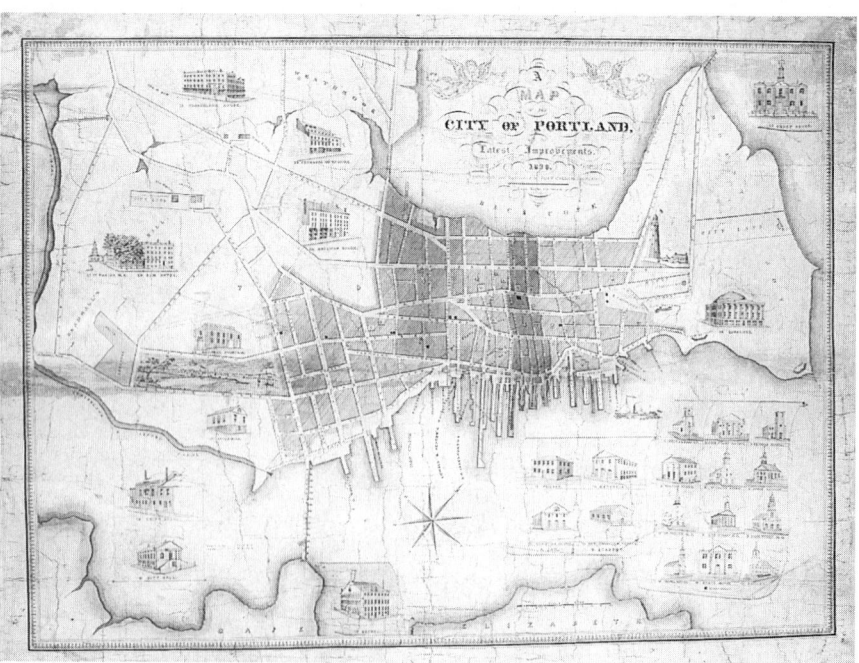

Map of Portland, Maine, 1836

and daughters. The poet Henry Wadsworth Longfellow, former Speaker of the House Thomas B. Reed, and early Seventh-Day Adventist leader Ellen White all grew up in Portland.

Once the winter port for Canada, Portland began receiving goods and visitors from Europe early on. Today's residents are largely of white European descent, with Franco-Americans, Irish, Italians, and Jews making up the city's largest ethnic populations. Portland's African American community has been centered historically on Munjoy Hill, site of the Green Memorial Church. Late 20th-century waves of immigration from African and Asian countries have diversified Portland's ethnic makeup and are still changing the face of the city.

European settlers built the first house in Portland in 1632 following earlier exploration. Abenaki Indians had long used the area as a summer retreat, but there was no permanent settlement until George Cleeves and Richard Tucker received their grant from England in 1637. The city's history is marked by periods of settlement and desertion. The Neck was twice attacked and burned by Indians, and in 1775 it was destroyed by the British Navy. After each calamity the town was abandoned until villagers slowly returned to the area to rebuild. On the Fourth of July in 1866 a devastating fire was ignited by a firecracker carelessly tossed into a pile of hay. Damage amounting to $5 million–10 million left 12,000 people homeless, making this the largest urban fire the United States had known. Refashioned in grand Victorian style, the city was rebuilt in two years and adopted the phoenix as the symbol of its resurrection.

The 1866 fire, the decline of marine shipping, and the dominance of larger metropolitan areas later diminished Portland's national importance. The city never regained its former status but maintained light industries such as oil and grain distribution. World War II brought a shipbuilding boom and the Portland-Montreal oil pipeline to the harbor. Subsequent economic shifts, along with the growth of malls and suburbia, brought further change to Portland. Tourism, boutiques, and arts organizations have now claimed much of the downtown and waterfront and are reshaping the economic and cultural base of the city.

Portland is home to the Westbrook College (1831) campus of the University of New England, the University of Southern Maine (1878), the Maine Historical Society museum and library, and the Portland Museum of Art, which houses a distinguished collection of paintings and glass. The city also hosts the Cumberland County Civic Center, a prime cultural and entertainment venue.

William David Barry, *A Vignetted History of Portland Business, 1632–1982* (1982); Irwin T. Sanders and Joseph H. Helfgot, *Portland, Maine: Upbeat Downeast, a Community Social Profile* (1977); William Willis, *The History of Portland* (1865); Writers' Program of the Works Projects Administration, *Portland City Guide* (1940).

Stephanie Philbrick

Portsmouth, N.H.

Portsmouth (population 20,784 in 2000) is marketed and widely perceived as a colonial seaport town. It is in reality a microcosm of northern New England's typical patterns of history, commerce, and cultural identity. First settled by Europeans in 1623, Portsmouth lies 2 miles from the Atlantic Ocean on a tidal estuary called the Piscataqua River, which separates New Hampshire from Maine. New Hampshire's principal seaport, the city supports commercial fishing, light industries, and a growing number of technology firms. In the last quarter of the 20th century Portsmouth emerged as New Hampshire's cultural capital.

Portsmouth consists of a small, dense harbor district with abutting commercial, waterfront-industrial, and residential areas. Scattered residential suburbs and outlying commercial and light-industrial zones interspersed with salt creeks and bogs surround this core. The organization of the landscape reflects the layering of several centuries.

In accepting the regional Yankee myth of a homogeneous population, Portsmouth's citizens have often overlooked local ethnic diversity. Irish, Italian, and Jewish neighborhoods had already established themselves in the city by the turn of the 20th century, when modest numbers of Central European, French Canadian, Greek, and other immigrants were coming to town. The ethnic composition of the population diversified further during World War II and the Cold War, with influxes of workers for the Portsmouth Navy Yard (now the Portsmouth Naval Shipyard) and Pease Air Force Base. Since the 1970s Asian and Hispanic residents have added to the mix. Africans and African Americans have lived in Portsmouth since 1645. Since the eve of the Revolution black residents have constituted 2–4 percent of the city's population, giving Portsmouth the largest proportion of black inhabitants of any city in New Hampshire. Adding to the cultural mix are the gays and lesbians who have made Portsmouth their home.

Portsmouth's colonial reputation notwithstanding, the city's built environment dates mostly from the 19th and 20th centuries. The foundations of the myth that locks Portsmouth in perpetual longing for its colonial past were laid in 1823 during the bicentennial celebration of settlement in New Hampshire, which followed close on the heels of the exhaustion of the area's accessible timberlands, the permanent loss of the West Indies trade in the War of 1812, and a fire that swept away 15 acres of 18th-century structures in 1813. New sources of prosperity were found in banking, steam-powered industry, beer brewing, and an expanded navy yard; Market Square was rebuilt in primarily Victorian styles; and large West End neighborhoods sprang up in a single generation. But old families cultivated a notion of loss and memory that they expressed in a reverent exhibit of ancestral portraits displayed

Portsmouth, N.H., 1989

for the bicentennial. Historical preservation efforts began with the renovation of the Moffat-Ladd mansion in 1862, culminating in resistance to 1960s urban renewal and in the establishment of the Strawbery Banke Museum, originally envisioned as a northerly Williamsburg. As urban renewal swept away real colonial buildings in the North End, Portsmouth citizens refurbished their 19th-century buildings in such a way as to endow them with an imaginary 18th-century appearance, transfiguring even the Victorian North Church (1854) and high school (1855). Since the 1960s a few subdivisions have been built, favoring colonial ornament on ranch-style houses.

Portsmouth's gritty downtown began to be transformed in the 1970s. Groups concerned with cultural amenities sprang up by the dozen, and the town gained an active visual- and performing-arts population. A block grant funded a pedestrian-friendly reconfiguration of Market Square. As businesses abandoned the downtown for outlying commercial strips, Portsmouth carved out a new economic niche and identity by commodifying waterfront ambiance, a walkable historic environment, cultural activities, and the natural splendor of its seaside location and nearby mountains. These charms attracted tourists, new residents, and high-tech businesses. Portsmouth's traditional blue-collar population has viewed the revitalization and "colonialization" of Portsmouth's mostly Federal era and Victorian downtown with reactions ranging from pride to hostility to indifference.

Another far-reaching transformation occurred in early 1991, when Pease Air Force Base closed after 40 years of service as a Strategic Air Command. Some 1,200 civilian jobs were lost, and more than 3,000 military personnel and their families left the area. A model for the economic development of former military bases, the facility has now been transformed into an industrial-business park known as the Pease International Tradeport. By March 1999 the booming Tradeport boasted three jobs in private industry for every civilian job that had been lost when the air force base closed. The Portsmouth Naval Shipyard managed to stay off the short list of base closings throughout the 1990s, but its February 1999 workforce of 3,400 was less than half that of 1989. Even at that level, however, the shipyard was the second-largest employer north of Boston at the time, after Maine's Bath Iron Works.

Raymond A. Brighton, *They Came to Fish: A Brief Look at Portsmouth's 350 Years of History, Its Local and World-wide Involvements, and the People Concerned, through the Eyes of a Reporter*, rev. ed. (1979); Richard M. Candee, *Building Portsmouth: The Neighborhoods and Architecture of New Hampshire's Oldest City* (1992); Peter E. Randall, *Portsmouth and the Piscataqua* (1982); Mark J. Sammons and Valerie Cunningham, *Black Portsmouth: Three Centuries of African-American Heritage* (2004).

Mark J. Sammons

Poverty At the beginning of the 21st century, New England had a comparatively low poverty rate. But this was not always the case; the history of poverty in New England is marked both by sizable shifts in economic welfare and inequality and by important responses to poverty and pauperism.

During the late 1700s and early 1800s poverty increased rapidly, and New England was among the first areas in the nation to recognize the growing numbers of poor. The early transition to manufacturing and the growth of cities in New England were accompanied by economic disruption and instability in the labor market. By 1850 a relatively high proportion of New England's population was classified as paupers. In response, early New Englanders adopted poor relief measures that included a mixture of public and private efforts.

Volunteer benevolent societies sprang up throughout New England in both urban and rural areas. The Female Benevolent Society was founded in the manufacturing city of Lynn, Mass., in 1814. The Cambridge Female Humane Society was also founded in 1814 in the semirural village of Cambridge, Mass. Rural Hopkinton, N.H., had its own society as well: the Chesterfield Female Benevolent Society. Many private charitable organizations were organized by women, and served women and children in the community who had fallen on hard times. Private charity, however, was never sufficient to meet the needs of all the poor, and public assistance was rendered as well.

Public assistance for the poor was also a local responsibility. Settlement laws identified residents whom the town was legally required to support, as opposed to drifters who were not their responsibility. "Warning out" was a common practice that involved telling nonresident poor people to leave before they could establish residence and make a claim for poor relief on the town. As public welfare budgets grew and the administrative work of deciding residency claims and disputes became burdensome, towns began searching for streamlined procedures and cheaper methods of delivering poor relief. The citizenry began to differentiate between the "worthy" poor—the sick, very old, very young, insane, disabled, and widowed—and the "unworthy" poor—able-bodied needy people who were regarded as lazy, intemperate, shiftless, or spendthrifts.

Reformers saw the poorhouse as the answer to managing the latter group; a trip to the poorhouse, where the individual was expected to labor in return for minimal sustenance, would take away the luxury of staying at home and receiving cash assistance. Between 1820 and 1870, the poorhouse movement was in full swing in New England.

Although laws provided for constructing workhouses and poor farms, most small agricultural towns relied on less costly and more efficient means of poor relief. The practice of auctioning off paupers, often referred to disparagingly as the "New England method," was commonly used. Individuals, families, and sometimes whole groups were put on the block to be "sold" to the lowest bidder—the person who agreed to keep, feed, and clothe them for the year at the lowest expense to the town. In return, the poor were expected to provide labor to the bidder. This practice was common in farming communities where unskilled labor was in demand and food and lodging were cheap. By the early to mid-1800s larger towns and cities had turned to holding the "unworthy" poor in poorhouses. By the late 1800s, however, poorhouses had become little more than warehouses where all classes of poor were held together and the emphasis on work had fallen away. Reformers worked for centralization and rationalization of public poor relief, organizing state boards of charity and advocating for county and state administration. Massachusetts was the first state to organize a state board of charities in 1863, and was among the first states to establish state-run poor farms in the 1850s.

As the early history of poor relief in New England demonstrates, attitudes about poverty and the poor have drawn on religious and moral doctrines that prescribed work, thrift, temperance, and marriage. The poor have been categorized as either "ours" or "not ours" and as either "worthy" or "unworthy," with assistance given less grudgingly to "our worthy" poor. Even the working poor were stigmatized if they were seen as strangers. For example, Stephan Thernstrom's *Poverty and Progress* (1964) recounted the hard lot of working poor immigrants in Newburyport during the mid-1800s, when Irish with little education and skills were treated as outcasts by the local elite, whose own class status was assumed to reflect superior morals. These early attitudes, and the charity and programs that resulted, reflect ambivalence about the nature of poverty and a moral commitment to work that continues to the present.

For the past few decades, poverty has been a less pressing issue for New England politicians and reformers. Since the middle of the

20th century, the region's large middle class, diversified economic base, high educational levels, and low inequality have meant that the incidence of overall poverty has not been as severe as in other parts of the nation (9.1 percent in 2000, versus 11.6 percent nationally). Still, the region is not immune to potentially negative economic turns that affect the larger national, restructured economy. Further, internal variations exist between the southern three states and the northern three, and between the urban and rural areas of the region.

The level of educational attainment in New England is among the reasons for its lower poverty rate. Industrial restructuring and the global economy have created a two-tiered job market in the United States. For those in the upper tier, wages and benefits are good. Those in the lower tier have lower wages and less generous benefits, frequently in jobs that are temporary or part-time. A college education has become a prerequisite for obtaining a job in the upper tier. Regions with a greater proportion of college graduates therefore have relatively greater proportions of workers in more secure and higher-paying jobs. New England has a high percentage of bachelor's degree recipients (30.8 percent in 2000, versus 25.6 percent nationally).

Economic restructuring and corporate downsizing negatively affected the region in the late 1980s and early 1990s, and poverty rates went up as a result. But the region has shown resilience in response to these economic changes. During the American industrial era, manufacturing jobs provided a vehicle for upward mobility and fueled the growth of urban centers in New England and elsewhere. Lowell, Mass., was the first industrial city in the nation, and other New England cities grew with the textile industry. While occupational disruption and higher levels of poverty and inequality accompanied the early period of industrialization, as the industrial economy matured, it created an avenue for mobility and the ultimate growth of the middle class. When manufacturing jobs disappeared in the last half of the 20th century, parts of New England were able to recover economically through growth in information technology and white-collar services. Such diversification is a buffer against poverty, provided that the population has the necessary training for the jobs available. In the aggregate, the skills of New England's highly educated workforce match the skills required in the new economy better than residents of other regions, particularly urban areas.

The geographical distribution of poverty also helps to explain New England's relatively low poverty rate. At the beginning of the Great Society era, the poor were found disproportionately in rural areas. Since 1960, poverty has declined, but the geographic distribution has shifted. Since 1976 the poverty rate has been higher in central cities than in nonmetropolitan areas, reversing a historical trend. Since 1990, the gap has widened even further. New England is unique compared to other regions that dominated the industrial era in that it has relatively few large cities and metropolitan areas. This implies that the region's poverty rate has not been affected as much as some other regions by the shift in the geographic distribution of poverty from rural to central city areas.

Single-parent families headed by women historically have a high incidence of poverty. Because the growth of single-mother families in New England has been the same as that nationwide, the region's poverty level has not increased relative to the rest of the country as a consequence of a disproportionate increase in single-parent families. Women's labor force participation in New England, however, is higher than in other regions (62 percent in 2000, compared to 60 percent nationally). The additional family income from working women further contributes to the region's relatively low poverty rate.

The strength of its middle class is another factor contributing to New England's relatively low incidence of poverty rate. As measured by the Gini Index of Income Concentration in 1999, New England had a comparatively low level of income inequality, measuring .445, compared to .463 for the nation as a whole. The greater the extent of income inequality, the greater the poverty level. New England is simultaneously low on both of these, and is unique in this regard.

The overall generalizations described so far do not apply uniformly across the region, however. Several rural, remote counties in the northern three states and the inner cities of the largest urban centers have significant pockets of poverty and unemployment. The three northern states are much more rural than the southern three, and have fewer urban centers or suburban areas. Maine and northern Vermont and New Hampshire have always had high poverty rates and lower educational attainment. Their economies are less diversified and more dependent on single industries, creating vulnerability in the economy of the late 1990s. Some of these remote areas have faced significant economic decline.

The communities in rural down east Maine that depend primarily on fishing have been devastated by the collapse of the fishing industry on Georges Bank and by global competition in the fishing, fish processing, and fish farming industries. Small towns like Millinocket, Maine, and Berlin, N.H., that are dependent on the lumber and paper industries have been affected negatively by global changes in these industries. There is some optimism that recreation and tourism will help these remote areas adapt to a changing economic reality. Some accounts suggest that the combination of early paternalism and self-reliance in these small northern communities provided a supportive civic culture that buffered citizens against hard times. Still, New England's overall resilience is being challenged, and its claim as the region with the lowest poverty rate will be at stake as economic restructuring continues to affect the region and the nation.

Josiah H. Benton, *Warning Out in New England* (1911); Cynthia M. Duncan, "Understanding Persistent Poverty: Social Class Context in Rural Communities," *Rural Sociology* 61 (1996); Duncan, *Worlds Apart: Why Poverty Persists in Rural America* (1999); Benjamin J. Klebaner, "Pauper Auctions: The 'New England Method' of Poor Relief," *Essex Institute Historical Collection* (1955); A. E. Luloff and Mark Nord, "The Forgotten of Northern New England," in *On Their Own: The Poor in Modern America*, ed. David J. Rothman and Sheila M. Rothman (1972); Stephan Thernstrom, *Poverty and Progress: Social Mobility in a 19th-Century City* (1964); Walter I. Trattner, *From Poor Law to Welfare State: A History of Social Welfare in America* (1984).

Sally K. Ward, Cynthia Duncan,
and Jody Grimes

Providence Providence, the sole capital of Rhode Island since 1900 (it was originally co-capital with Newport), is located at the head of Narragansett Bay just 40 miles southwest of Boston. The town was established in 1636 when Roger Williams, banished from the Massachusetts Bay Colony for his religious ideas, settled on land he had purchased from the Narragansett. Williams's radical adherence to the principles of religious freedom and separation of church and state brought religious dissidents and ornery individualists to Providence from all over New England.

A farming and fishing village through most of the 17th century, Providence by the mid-18th rivaled its more prosperous neighbor Newport in oceangoing commerce and manufacturing. The Revolution gravely injured Newport, and after the war the new state's political and cultural center shifted to Providence. Providence's leaders responded aggressively to postwar economic realities by finding trade opportunities in China, South America, and Europe; John Brown was the second New England merchant to send one of his ships, the *General Washington,* to China. His brother Moses Brown brought the Industrial Revolu-

Providence skyline, 2004

tion to the United States when he engaged the English-born Samuel Slater to build America's first waterpower-driven spinning machine. The success of Slater Mill made Providence, and Rhode Island, a center for the manufacture of textiles and textile machinery. The giant B. B. and R. Knight Company, makers of Fruit of the Loom, owned 19 mill villages in southern New England and in 1893 boasted of being the world's largest textile manufacturer.

Providence's leaders developed some of the nation's first banks and insurance companies; built turnpikes, canals, and railroads; and opened the door for invention and ingenuity. In the 1790s local jewelers and silversmiths developed new ways to fabricate costume jewelry, and at the turn of the 21st century Providence remained the center of the nation's jewelry industry. At the time of the Civil War the city's machine tool industry was so advanced that the Corliss Steam Engine Works was the only plant in the nation with the capacity to mill the giant washer needed for the revolving turret of the ironclad *Monitor.* By the 1890s Providence boasted "five industrial wonders of the world": Brown and Sharpe (precision machine tools), Gorham Manufacturing Company (silverware and monuments), American Screw Company, Corliss Steam Engine Company, and the Nicholson File Company. The finest American automobile built before World War I, the ALCO, was manufactured in Providence. Rhode Island became the nation's first urban industrial state; until the 1970s it was the most densely populated state in the nation.

Providence began to fade as an industrial powerhouse in the early 20th century. Automobile manufacturing left after 1913, and the textile industry declined after World War I. Providence and Rhode Island entered an economic depression that lasted, excepting the frantic period of World War II, until the mid-1950s. The town of Providence had 6,380 people in 1790; the city of Providence boasted 132,146 in 1890. Providence's population peaked at 267,918 in 1925 but then began to fall. The decline was particularly severe during the 1950s, as a return to prosperity and the completion of Interstate 95 encouraged an exodus to the suburbs— Providence's population fell by 40 percent that decade. However, Providence remains New England's second largest city. The 2000 census recorded a city population of 173,618, with a metropolitan-area figure of 1,174,548.

By the late 1950s and early 1960s Providence was suffering from general urban decay. Urban-renewal plans called for razing whole sections of the downtown. Fortunately, the city and state were too poor to carry out the wholesale demolitions, and most of the city's historical architecture survived to be redeveloped. The Providence Preservation Society sprang into existence in the mid-1950s, and the College Hill Preservation District (1960) saved fine old structures and converted a dilapidated section of town into a showcase, but at the cost of displacing many African Americans who lived there. The East Side, a section immediately adjacent to the business district, remains a stable and affluent area. Massive revitalization in the 1980s and 1990s involved constructing new buildings, moving railroad tracks and the railroad station, relocating rivers, and opening up new river walkways and Waterplace Park. The downtown district has been dramatically transformed, and the frequent celebration of "WaterFire" during the summer draws thousands. By 2003 Providence had 30 historic districts, including most of the downtown commercial area. It is no wonder that Providence has been dubbed the "Renaissance City."

The city has long been home to a diverse blend of ethnicities, with Africans arriving during the era of the Atlantic slave trade, then Irish and French Canadians joining the urban population in the 19th century. That mixture became ever richer as waves of immigrants from all over Europe, especially Italy, and the Cape Verde Islands were drawn to booming factories in the 19th and early 20th centuries. By 1920 two-thirds of the city's people were foreign-born or the children of foreign-born parents. Providence developed distinct ethnic neighborhoods, but these continue to change as new arrivals displace older immigrant groups. For example, the Federal Hill section, an Irish enclave in the mid-1800s, became predominantly Italian in the early 1900s and was evolving into a Hispanic neighborhood at the turn of the 21st century. In spite of considerable deindustrialization, a substantial segment of Providence's population (25.3 percent in 2000) remains foreign-born, with new immigrants from Africa, Asia, and South America joining those from Russia, Ireland, Italy, and Portugal. By 2000 the city had a majority "minority" population totaling 54.2 percent.

Providence is home to numerous academic institutions, including Brown University (1764), Rhode Island College (1854), the Rhode Island School of Design (1877), Johnson and Wales University (1914), and Providence College (1917). Few cities of Providence's size support as many major cultural institutions; the Rhode Island Historical Society, the Providence Athenaeum, the Museum of Art at the Rhode Island School of Design, the Rhode Island Philharmonic, Rhode Island Ballet, Trinity Square Repertory Theater, the Rhode Island Civic Chorale, and the Providence Singers are all flourishing organizations. The First Baptist Church, one of America's finest examples of colonial architecture, lies at the foot of College Hill, and the State House, an impressive Beaux Arts structure (1895–1901), has been restored to its original appearance.

John Hutchins Cady, *The Civic and Architectural Development of Providence, 1636–1950* (1957); Patrick T. Conley and Paul R. Campbell, *Providence: A Pictorial History* (1982); George H. Kellner and J. Stanley Lemons, *Rhode Island: The Ocean State* (2004); William G. McLoughlin, *Rhode Island: A Bicentennial History* (1978).

J. Stanley Lemons

Quincy, Mass. Quincy was settled in 1625 in the northern section of Braintree, Mass. Initially named Mount Wollaston, the town gained a reputation in the 17th century when Thomas Morton built Merrymount there, a settlement where he traded with Native Americans, gave them liquor and guns, and ultimately was exiled for setting up a maypole and lampooning the newly settled Pilgrims at Plymouth. When John Adams and his son John Quincy Adams achieved national prominence, residents pressed to separate from Braintree; Quincy was incorporated in 1792 and declared a city in 1888. To this day, Quincy, like Cambridge, has retained a cultural identity distinct from Boston.

Hometown of the Adams family, Quincy was so named in honor of Colonel Josiah Quincy, a country gentleman who had prospered in shipbuilding. The Quincy family supplied Boston with leaders and were allies of the Adamses. Josiah Quincy's son, Josiah, Jr., with John Adams defended the British soldiers in the Boston Massacre trial. Josiah III, a Boston mayor, congressman, and president of Harvard, inherited the Quincy farmhouse.

Notable town buildings include the 1730 farmhouse that John Adams purchased in 1787. Known as the "Old House," the Adams mansion doubled in size according to the wishes of Abigail Adams. In 1946 the family made a gift of it and its furnishings to the country; today only 5 of its 40 acres remain. The house contains a remarkable library, rare 18th- and 19th-century porcelain, and historic documents. Noteworthy also is Thomas Crane Public Library, designed by the architect H. H.

Richardson with opalescent windows created by the artist John LaFarge, and the United First Parish Church, considered the finest Greek Revival church in the United States. The Dorothy Quincy mansion was the birthplace and home of the woman who became John Hancock's wife.

Until 1830 Quincy was a farming community, but after incorporation it grew rapidly, becoming an important manufacturing city. As one of the commercial centers of Massachusetts, it is known for its granite quarries, shipbuilding machinery, and radio transmitters. Immigrants from many countries worked in Quincy's quarries and shipyards. Industry initially grew through the expansion of the shoe trade as tanneries developed on the town's borders. The facilities to quarry granite improved with the use of iron rather than wooden wedges to split rock. In 1825 the Bunker Hill Monument and King's Chapel in Boston were built with Quincy granite. Horse-drawn wagons conveyed granite from the quarry to the Neponset River wharf, and the Quincy granite trade expanded and became famous throughout the world.

During World War I, 36 destroyers were built in the Quincy shipyards, where all manner of vessels, from the seven-masted schooner *Thomas W. Lawson* to the aircraft carrier *Lexington*, were built. Although the shipyards closed in 1986, Quincy remains a town of diversified manufacturing. Its 2000 population was 88,025, with Asians the largest ethnic minority group. The town is home to Quincy Junior College and Eastern Nazarene College.

S. Allen Chambers, ed., *Discovering Historical America* (1982); Federal Writers' Project, *Massachusetts: A Guide to Its Places and People* (1937); Reader's Digest Association, *America's Historic Places: An Illustrated Guide to Our Country's Past* (1988).

Suzanna Nyberg

Rutland, Vt. Rutland, the seat of Rutland County, is located in south central Vermont between the Green and Taconic Mountains. In 1769 farmers from Massachusetts became the first settlers at a location near Otter Creek that had once been a disputed territory for hunting and fishing by Iroquois and Abenaki, and that later served as a crossing point of two main routes through the early Vermont wilderness. During the Revolutionary War a fort was constructed there as part of a northern defense line against British invasion from Canada. By the 1830s the town had emerged as a manufacturing center, primarily for small-scale production of woolens and agricultural implements.

The Green Mountains and waterways that were difficult to navigate limited development until the railroad's arrival in 1849. Within a

Rutland, Vt., 1980

decade several rail lines connected Rutland to eastern cities and Canada, opening a period of vigorous economic expansion that established the town as one of the state's leading industrial centers. Important in the transformation was the decision by local entrepreneurs to begin exploiting intensively the area's vast marble deposits. Quarrying had started as early as 1795, but "marble fever" did not set in until several railroads competed to carry and deliver the heavy stone. By the 1890s the Vermont Marble Company, headed by former governor Redfield Proctor, employed 1,800 workers and had become the largest marble company in the world.

Rutland, in turn, became for a few years not only the most populous city in the state but the most ethnically diverse, with workers from at least 23 countries claiming jobs in the area's sheds, mills, and factories. This enlarged workforce attracted to Vermont, for the first time, the organizing efforts of a major national labor union, the Knights of Labor, which established an energetic chapter in Rutland in 1886. In 1904 and 1935 Vermont Marble workers conducted strikes in bitter labor disputes.

After World War II Rutland entered a new period of economic difficulty. The marble industry and the railroads declined, and a long-desired interstate highway through the city failed to materialize. The hard times were offset somewhat, however, by ski industry expansion in nearby Killington and Pico, and related condominium and vacation home construction. In 2000, despite its economic troubles, Rutland, with 17,292 residents, remained Vermont's second largest city after Burlington.

In the 2000s Rutland continues to be a working-class community with a small-town sensibility and a strong ethnic heritage. Situated in a section of New England defined by Yankee traditionalism, Rutland projects the marks of its distinctiveness: a blend of Italian, Irish, and French-Canadian ways, pragmatic blue-collar spirit, and a record of populist political activism that regularly moved against the state's dominating currents. Its local newspaper, the *Rutland Herald,* published continuously since 1794, was acknowledged to be one of the finest small-city dailies in the nation. Rutland is home to a regional medical center and the College of Saint Joseph, and hosts the Vermont State Fair each fall.

Dawn D. Hance, *The History of Rutland, Vermont, 1761–1861* (1991); Curtis B. Johnson, ed., *The Historic Architecture of Rutland County* (1988); Tyler Resch, *The Rutland Herald History* (1995); Jim Shaughnessy, *The Rutland Road* (1964).

Gene Sessions

School Busing in Boston and Hartford Busing—the practice of transporting schoolchildren by bus to schools outside of their neighborhoods as a means of achieving racial integration—had profound effects on the cities of Hartford and Boston in the 1970s and beyond. In both cases, voluntary programs failed to address underlying inequalities in schools, and the resulting legal cases and social and political conflicts (against a backdrop of declining white enrollment and persistent funding gaps) challenged New England's image of educational quality and equality.

Hartford schoolchildren were first bused out of their districts in 1966. This was the first response to a 1964 Harvard report suggesting that Hartford was no longer able to solve its own educational problems and should seek metropolitan cooperation to enable its children to receive a quality education. The program was called Project Concern. At its peak in the late 1970s, 1,500 Hartford students traveled to the 13 surrounding suburban communities and six nonpublic schools participating in this voluntary integration effort. Hartford students were to benefit from enhanced educational opportunities made possible by more generous suburban school funding, while suburban systems were able to provide their students with a multiracial and multicultural environment. No suburban students traveled into the city.

The program was deemed a success primarily because urban students demonstrated significant reading growth and urban and suburban students formed friendships within the school setting. Changing demographics and slimmer school budgets, however, resulted in a reduction of participants by half by the early 1990s. The 1989 *Sheff v. O'Neill* school desegregation case was settled on appeal in 1996 when the Connecticut Supreme Court ruled

William Bulger (with microphone) and antibusing protesters at Bunker Hill Monument, Charlestown, Mass., mid-1970s

that segregation in the Hartford schools violated the state constitution. In the intervening years, the number of white students in Hartford schools had declined, and with the reluctance of courts in Hartford, as in Boston, to include predominantly white suburban schools, in-district busing could not truly integrate schools. Moreover, Hartford schools were beset with enormous funding and administrative problems that complicated desegregation efforts and compromised other attempts to improve school quality. The court decision did not mandate judicial remedies but called on the government to develop plans to address the imbalance. In response, Governor John Rowland established the Education Improvement Panel, which recommended legislative action to improve school quality, facilitate school choice, and increase parental involvement.

School desegregation and busing in Boston were far from a voluntary occurrence, aside from a small program, METCO (Metropolitan Council for Educational Opportunity), that permitted some Boston students to attend schools outside the district in the 1960s. African American families organized to seek school improvements, facing a school board dominated by members with deep political roots in Irish and other white ethnic communities who wanted to preserve neighborhood schools. By 1971 Boston was significantly in violation of the Massachusetts Racial Imbalance Act of 1965, legislation that defined any school with a nonwhite enrollment of more than 50 percent as imbalanced, giving the state

commissioner of education the right to refuse state aid to districts that failed to correct such an imbalance. The Massachusetts State Board of Education withheld $21 million from the Boston public schools in 1971. In June 1974, Judge W. Arthur Garrity, Jr., in response to a suit brought by the National Association for the Advancement of Colored People against the Boston School Committee in U.S. District Court, concluded that the school committee had deliberately promoted segregation within the district schools.

The U.S. Circuit Court of Appeals and the U.S. Supreme Court upheld Judge Garrity's decision during the following year and busing was implemented, primarily among Irish South Boston and Charlestown and black Roxbury and Dorchester, all low-income communities. Initially, fear and insufficient planning spawned harassment and violence; buses were stoned and other property damaged. Resistance was quickly organized through groups such as ROAR (Restore Our Alienated Rights) and through the leadership of local politicians, including Louise Day Hicks, Albert "Dapper" O'Neill, and William Bulger. Both sides appealed to traditions of New England freedom, with Charlestown white residents echoing Paul Revere with the chant, "The buses are coming!" While African Americans and many whites saw the busing controversy in terms of racism, some whites, particularly the Irish, saw the case in terms of class, with a government and prominent institutions dominated by liberal and Brahmin elements violating principles of local control.

The crisis produced indelible images of buses and students being attacked at South Boston and at Charlestown High Schools, of mothers in a prayer march facing the state police near the Bunker Hill Monument, and of a black attorney, Ted Landsmark, being attacked outside Boston City Hall on April 5, 1976, by a white student wielding an American flag. Garrity's court supervised the Boston schools until 1985, when authority was returned to the Boston School Committee. By that time, public school enrollment had declined to 57,000, and white enrollment dropped to 28 percent, as white families moved to the suburbs or enrolled their children in private or parochial schools. Subsequent busing programs included more choice and input from parents and students, under a "controlled choice" plan adopted by the Boston School Committee.

By the late 1990s, the nonwhite population of Boston schools was so high that schools could no longer be effectively desegregated no matter how many students were moved. Emphasis once again was directed toward the question of improving Boston's troubled schools, the same question that led to desegregation in the first place.

Ronald P. Formisano, *Boston against Busing: Race, Class, and Ethnicity in the 1960s and 1970s* (1991); J. Anthony Lukas, *Common Ground: A Turbulent Decade in the Lives of Three American Families* (1985); Michael Patrick MacDonald, *All Souls: A Family Story from Southie* (1999); Sondra Astor Stave, *Achieving Racial Balance: Case Studies of Contemporary School Desegregation* (1995).

Sondra Astor Stave

Settlement Houses In the late 19th century New England became a national leader in the development of settlement houses, also known as social settlements, which were established to improve social welfare in the neighborhoods where they were located. The authoritative *Handbook of Settlements,* compiled by Robert A. Woods and Albert J. Kennedy in 1911, listed 58 settlement houses in New England. Only the New York state area had more. Forty-seven settlements were located in Massachusetts, four in Connecticut, four in Rhode Island, two in Maine, and one in New Hampshire. Boston hosted 35 settlements, far more than any other city in the region. Among other New England cities, Cambridge, Mass., was home to five settlements; Hartford to three; and Providence to two. Other cities with a settlement house were Lynn, Newton, Salem, Springfield, Waltham, and Worcester, Mass.; New Haven, Conn.; East Greenwich and Peace Dale, R.I.; Danbury, N.H.; and Lewiston and Portland, Maine.

Boston became the primary laboratory for settlements in New England. As the region's center of industrial and urban development, it was subject to all the social problems that reformers sought to solve. By the late 19th century the large majority of Boston's residents were immigrants and their children, who faced cultural, social, and economic adjustments to the difficult conditions of urban life and work. The city also was heir to a tradition of middle-class reform based in religious revivalism and social advocacy. That legacy helped generate the idealistic cadres who established social settlements.

The American settlement house was originally an English import. First introduced in the poor neighborhoods of London, the settlement house was a place where public-spirited college graduates supplied education, cultural programs, and social activities to improve the "mental" and "moral" life of neighborhood people. Stanton Coit, Jane Addams, and Robert A. Woods saw these English institutions as a possible means of addressing urban problems in the United States. After traveling to England, Woods led the settlement movement in Boston. In 1891 he established Andover House, later known as the South End House, with the aim of recreating the "healthy corporate vitality" characteristic of a "well-ordered village." The philanthropist and activist Caroline Emmerton was the driving force behind another noteworthy Massachusetts settlement house, founded in Salem in 1907–8 and supported by revenues from the House of the Seven Gables historic site.

Settlement services were devised to ameliorate the dehumanizing and deracinating conditions of urban life and help keep immigrant and working-class families off the path to serious decline. Education was central to settlement programs, with classes being offered in domestic economy, hygiene, civics, and English among other subjects. Settlement workers saw their job as building citizenship and involvement in public life. They organized clubs for young people and children to pursue athletic, artistic, literary, and social interests that would lead to positive civic attitudes. They encouraged the foreign-born to become active in public affairs and to gain a voice in neighborhood self-government.

Settlement houses also served young reformers as a school of life experience, where they could learn about the practical problems of the industrial-urban world. Settlement workers undertook organized studies of neighborhood schools, playgrounds, housing, labor conditions, and street maintenance. Volunteers from middle-class and Protestant backgrounds gained a mutual social relationship with the poor and foreign-born. As a result,

they developed a partnership with immigrant and working-class communities that furthered broad-based social reform.

The settlement movement reached a crest at the time Woods and Kennedy compiled their handbook of settlements in 1911. The expansion of public school programs and the rise of the mass high school eventually lessened the need for settlement houses. The social services provided to needy families and communities by the New Deal also undercut social settlements. More than any other factor, however, the social mobility and successful acculturation of second- and third-generation descendants of immigrants substantially reduced the need for settlement houses. By the end of the Great Depression, the settlement movement was in irreversible decline.

Domenica M. Barbuto, *American Settlement Houses and Progressive Social Reform: An Encyclopedia of the American Settlement Movement* (1999); Mina Carson, *Settlement Folk: Social Thought and the American Settlement Movement, 1885–1930* (1990); Rivka Shpak Lissak, *Pluralism and Progressives: Hull House and the New Immigrants, 1890–1919* (1989); Arthur Mann, *Yankee Reformers in the Urban Age: Social Reform in Boston, 1880–1900* (1954); Robert A. Woods, *Americans in Process: A Settlement Study* (1902).

Reed Ueda

Shopping Malls

The architectural idea of combining different merchants within one building is as old as New England's colonial cities. The Arcade in downtown Providence, built in 1826, is the best surviving example of these types of marketplaces. Modern shopping centers, or malls, first came into widespread use with the construction of the vast post–World War II suburbs and of the state and interstate highways that made their development possible. The proliferation of malls transformed not only retail practices but also the daily routines of New Englanders, as the regional economic importance of cities rapidly declined and suburbs gained in economic and political power.

The first large shopping center in New England was Shopper's World of Framingham, Mass., which opened in October 1951 off Routes 9 and 30. Built on a 70-acre site and boasting 44 retail outlets, a 250,000-square-foot Jordan Marsh department store, and parking for 6,000 automobiles, Shopper's World was one of the first large regional shopping centers in the country. The New York architects Ketchum, Gina, and Sharp designed the complex as a U-shaped group of nine buildings surrounding a large open-air courtyard. Jordan Marsh, crowned by a dome, hovered over the mall from its central location between the two arms of the U. The *Boston Globe* called the complex "an enormous, spreading monument to democratic free enterprise." Two years

after Shopper's World opened, the developers, Suburban Centers Trust of Boston, filed for bankruptcy; they had been unable to lure a second large department store into the mall, and the suburban population in the area had grown more slowly than projected.

Nevertheless, other New England shopping centers soon followed the Shopper's World example, moving retail outlets to the suburbs en masse. Allied Stores Corporation of New York hired architect John Graham of Seattle to design the Northshore Shopping Center on Route 128 in Peabody, Mass., in 1958. The South Shore Plaza, designed by Los Angeles architect Victor Gruen, opened in 1961 in Braintree, Mass. The Westgate Mall in Brockton, Mass., built in 1963, was the first fully enclosed shopping center in New England. In 1964 the Trumbull Shopping Park opened on 75 acres outside Bridgeport, becoming the first enclosed mall in Connecticut.

As suburban shopping centers captured what had traditionally been downtown's retail dollar, so downtowns looked to suburban shopping centers as a model for their own redevelopment. Providence (1965); Stamford (1965) and Bridgeport (1967), Conn.; Lebanon, N.H. (1968); Portland, Maine (1975); and New Bedford (1974), Newburyport (1975), and Salem (1977), Mass., all created downtown malls to compete with suburbia's retail success. Cities created downtown pedestrian malls by prohibiting traffic on a main street; installing plantings, benches, or fountains; and providing plenty of parking. The Chapel Square Mall in downtown New Haven, Conn., which opened in 1967, was the largest and most expensive of these efforts. Developed by Roger Stevens, the enclosed mall contained Macy's and Malley's department stores; a parking garage designed by architect Paul Rudolph in unadorned concrete; a hotel, an office building, and 36 retail stores.

Quincy Market, which opened at Boston's Faneuil Hall Marketplace in 1976, was a highly touted attempt to lure retail dollars back downtown. Developed by James Rouse, a banker turned shopping-center developer, along with architects Benjamin and Jane Thompson, the project transformed three 1826 granite warehouses into an urban retail facility. The developers rented space to gourmet food stores, local-craft shops, street performers, and numerous street vendors to create a popular festival marketplace. Most significant, the developers did not rely on a department store to anchor the project. The market's success exceeded all predictions, and soon a number of cities would discover that they, too, could compete with the suburbs by selling history to suburbanites.

In the 1980s and 1990s shopping centers

took a new turn with the proliferation of outlet malls, clusters of strip shopping centers no longer housed in a single building or along a pedestrian walkway. The fastest growing segment of retail marketing today, outlet malls bring together numerous factory stores to offer lower-priced or damaged goods to consumers. New England's largest concentration of outlet malls is located in Kittery, Maine, which has 15 centers with more than 120 stores catering to tourists. Freeport, Maine, turned its entire downtown into an outlet mall with the flagship store of L. L. Bean at its center. Clinton, Conn., also has a popular outlet mall directly off Interstate 95.

Jane Algmin, *Boston's Downtown Crossing: Its Effects on Downtown Retailing* (1980); Lizbeth Cohen, "From Town Center to Shopping Center: The Reconfiguration of Community Marketplaces in Postwar America," *American Historical Review* 101 (1996); Kenneth T. Jackson, *The Crabgrass Frontier: The Suburbanization of the United States* (1985); Thomas Muller, *The Economic and Fiscal Effects of Regional Shopping Malls: The Vermont Experience* (1980).

M. Jeffrey Hardwick

Springfield, Mass.

Located in southwestern Massachusetts on the east bank of the Connecticut River, Springfield was founded as a trading settlement by the Puritan merchant William Pynchon in 1636. Pynchon established an autocratic government in Springfield that allowed him to completely control the community's affairs until his return to England in 1652. Springfield grew into a major industrial city early in the 19th century and still has a diversified manufacturing base.

During the American Revolution the Continental Army stored armaments at Springfield because of its remoteness from the sea, and in 1794 President George Washington established the Springfield Armory to manufacture small arms for the new federal government. By the 1820s the armory's mass-production techniques, including the use of interchangeable parts, helped to establish new standards of industrial organization.

The Western Railroad connected Springfield to Boston and Albany in 1839, and five years later a line reached the city from New York. As the "crossroads of New England," Springfield became an increasingly attractive manufacturing center. The demands of the Union Army during the Civil War spawned a boom at the armory as well as other local factories producing military supplies, and the city grew rapidly. After the war Springfield produced railroad cars, machine tools, and bicycles, and in 1893 native sons Charles E. and J. Frank Duryea built America's first automobile. The population increased from 44,179 in 1890 to 129,338 in 1930.

Horton Court, Dr. Seuss National Memorial Sculpture Garden, the Quadrangle, Springfield, Mass., 2004

In the early 20th century Springfield's middle-class home ownership and attractive neighborhoods earned it the epithet City of Homes. The neoclassical architecture of the Municipal Group (1913) and the museum-library complex called the Quadrangle symbolized the city's civic progressivism in the 1910s. Springfield was noted for the quality of its public education and particularly for the Springfield Plan of the 1940s, which promoted democratic values and ethnic harmony.

After World War II Springfield grappled with the same urban decline and suburban flight that plagued most northeastern cities. Urban renewal and highway construction transformed much of downtown and the North End during the 1960s. The 1980s were a time of further downtown construction, extensive preservation of historic buildings, and the opening of a new Basketball Hall of Fame, commemorating James Naismith's invention of basketball in Springfield in 1891.

Springfield has been a multiethnic community since the arrival of large numbers of Irish Catholics in the early decades of the 19th century. Since then Germans, Italians, French Canadians, Eastern European Jews, Poles, Greeks, and Lebanese have made their home there. The city has had a significant African American community since the antebellum era, when Frederick Douglass made a public appearance in Springfield. Antislavery activist John Brown also resided there for a period of time. Puerto Ricans began coming to Springfield during the 1950s to work on nearby Connecticut Valley tobacco farms. In 1990 Springfield's population of 156,983 was 19 percent African American, 17 percent Hispanic, and 1 percent Asian.

The recession of the 1990s undermined Springfield's manufacturing base, and the city lost further population to its suburbs. In 2000 the population had dropped to approximately 152,082, while that of the metropolitan area reached more than 584,000. Springfield shares television stations, airport, and economic base with Hartford, 28 miles to the south, and maintains a self-conscious distinctness from Boston. The city is home to Springfield College (1885), American International College (1885), Western New England College (1919), and Springfield Technical Community College (1964). The Quadrangle complex houses three museums, a library, a planetarium, and an art gallery. Every September the Eastern States Exposition (the Big E) is held in West Springfield.

Richard D. Brown, *Urbanization in Springfield, Massachusetts, 1790–1830* (1962); Michael H. Frisch, *Town into City: Springfield, Massachusetts and the Meaning of Community, 1840–1880* (1972); Stephen Innes, *Labor in a New Land: Economy and Society in 17th-Century Springfield* (1983); James C. O'Connell and Michael F. Konig, *Shaping an Urban Image: The History of Downtown Planning in Springfield, Massachusetts* (1990).

James C. O'Connell

Stamford, Conn.

Established in 1641, Stamford, Conn., evolved from a Puritan village into an industrial town and has since become a research, corporate, and financial center. Covering an area of almost 40 square miles, it is located 36 miles from New York City on the northern shore of Long Island Sound. Stamford was founded by dissident Puritans from Wethersfield, Conn. By 1790 its population, almost all descended from English Protestants, had increased to approximately 4,000. Three principal waves of immigrants have arrived since the early 19th century. In the late 1840s came the Irish, fleeing famine at home. They were followed at the turn of the 20th century by an outpouring of newcomers from Italy, Russia, Greece, Germany, and elsewhere in Europe. The Stamford population grew from 15,700 in 1890 to 28,836 in 1910, an increase of nearly 85 percent in 20 years. Beginning in the 1830s African Americans from the South and the West Indies and, beginning in the 1970s, Hispanics from Latin America have constituted what can be considered a third, albeit extended, wave of immigration. The census of 2000 put Stamford's total population at 117,083, of whom 69.8 percent were classified as white, 15.4 percent as black, and 16.8 percent as Hispanic.

Stamford has adapted well to major shifts in the American economy. For 200 years agriculture was the mainstay. After 1840 commerce and industry played increasingly significant roles. In 1848 the New York, New Haven, and Hartford Railroad radically improved Stamford's accessibility when it made the town a permanent and frequent stop. In 1869 Henry R. Towne opened a shop with 30 employees to produce the Yale pin-tumbler lock. By 1890 the "lock works" had spread over 21 acres and employed 1,000 people. The Yale example was followed by other light-manufacturing firms producing goods that ranged from wallpaper to typewriters. After World War I innovative and research-oriented corporations such as Pitney Bowes, American Cyanamid, and CBS established facilities in Stamford. Champion International and the Xerox Corporation were Fortune 500 companies that followed suit. In 1998 the Swiss Bank Corporation, soon to merge with the Union Bank of Switzerland, established its regional headquarters, the SBC Warburg Center, in downtown Stamford.

The founding Puritans brought with them the town meeting, which remained the principal organ of government for 250 years. In 1850 the Borough of Stamford, less than a mile square, was chartered to serve the needs of the core area. In the post–Civil War era, with increased population, the need for further structural reform became apparent. A new charter in 1893 established the City of Stamford within the Town of Stamford. The city covered about one-fifth of the town area but was home to four-fifths of the population. The new municipal government consisted of a mayor with limited powers and a common council based on four wards. The adoption of another charter, for the city only, in 1933 gave the mayor veto, appointive, and operational powers but did not solve the problem of divided government. Consolidation was strongly opposed in some neighborhoods. A majority of voters finally approved a merger in 1947. A large Board of Representatives, based on 20 districts, was created to reassure "country" residents that their voices would be heard, and the city and town were consolidated in 1949. In 1998 new provisions strengthened the mayor's powers and increased the terms of both mayor and representatives from two to four years.

Stamford is a blend of urban and suburban. Multistory office buildings and a large indoor mall have given the downtown a skyline for the first time, while private homes, gracious gardens, and wooded areas flourish in North Stamford. The number of commuters to New York City jumped significantly after World War II, when veterans used the G.I. Bill of Rights to purchase homes.

Private, public, and nonprofit institutions provide both essential services and amenities. Key civic functions are supplied by one of the busiest public libraries in the state; a hospital and clinic network; public, private, and parochial schools; and about 90 churches and synagogues. The University of Connecticut began offering extension courses in 1952 at Stamford High School. The program grew into the Stamford branch of the state university and moved to its own campus in North Stamford ten years later. In 1998 it moved downtown into a state-of-the-art facility with a focus on information technology.

Amenities are many, including public parks and playgrounds, beaches, and marinas. A renovated Palace Theater and a Center for the Arts are among the venues for plays, operas, ballets, and concerts performed by both touring and local companies. A branch of the Whitney Museum, the Stamford Museum, and private galleries all offer opportunities for viewing art. Stamford remains a small city loyal to its own urban-suburban cultural mix.

Robert Atwan, Kenneth H. Brief, and Barry Hoffman, eds., *Stamford: 350 Years, 1641–1991* (1991); Estelle F. Feinstein, *Stamford from Puritan to Patriot: The Shaping of a Connecticut Community, 1641–1744* (1976); Feinstein, *Stamford in the Gilded Age: The Political Life of a Connecticut Town, 1868–1893* (1973); Estelle F. Feinstein and Joyce S. Pendery, *Stamford: An Illustrated History* (1984).

Estelle F. Feinstein

Streetcar Suburbs The term *streetcar suburbs* was coined by Sam Bass Warner in his 1962 book of that title to describe Boston neighborhoods developed after they became accessible by public transportation in the late 19th century. The term has since been extended to include virtually any residential area that was developed during the street railway era—roughly from 1860 to 1915—and that was not immediately adjacent to an employment center. Boston's streetcar suburbs include the Dorchester, Jamaica Plain, and Roslindale districts, plus nearby cities such as Somerville and Everett. Among early streetcar suburbs in other cities are Rhode Island's South Providence neighborhood and the Fair Haven district of New Haven, Conn. Later examples are Springfield's Forest Park and adjacent sections of Longmeadow, along with Worcester's Vernon Hill, all in Massachusetts, and the West End in Hartford, Conn.

The horse-drawn street railway, with its affordable fare, allowed the majority of workers to live farther than walking distance away from their employment for the first time. Introduced in Boston in 1856, street railways served most areas within 5 miles of that city's downtown by 1865. By 1875 horsecars operated in more than a dozen cities throughout New England. The street railway network was electrified in the decade after 1889, more than doubling the streetcar's rate of travel. New lines were rapidly extended farther away from central cities into formerly rural areas.

The development of the streetcar suburb had a profound impact on the city of Boston, whose population quadrupled in the last half of the 19th century. A desire for better municipal services in the outlying areas led to the city's annexation of five adjacent towns between 1868 and 1874.

Warner's research showed that the development of Boston's streetcar suburbs resulted from a series of decentralized decisions. Residents demanded improved transportation, and private transit companies built it. The new accessibility in turn brought the subdivision of large lots and farms to house new arrivals. Other services, such as utilities, schools, and churches, soon followed. A growing population led to still better transit service, and new houses were often squeezed in between older ones.

A similar process occurred in and around medium-sized New England cities such as Portland, Maine; Worcester and Springfield, Mass.; Providence, R.I.; and Hartford and New Haven, Conn., but that process has not been as well studied or documented in these communities as it has been in Boston. In general, streetcar suburbanization in these cities took place later and on a smaller scale than in the Massachusetts capital.

Annexation, for example, played a lesser role in other New England cities than in Boston. Providence and Portland did annex large areas of adjacent communities in the late 19th century, but most New England cities were unable to significantly expand their limits during the streetcar suburb era, even as residential development crossed municipal boundaries.

Most streetcar suburbs are heterogeneous neighborhoods whose housing stock ranges from apartment buildings to single-family homes. The prototypical streetcar suburb, however, consists primarily of detached two- and three-family houses. In many New England cities, the dominant dwelling type of the era was the three-decker: a detached three-family, three-story house of simple frame construction whose architectural decoration (or lack of it) reflected the financial means of the owner. The adoption of this building type could offer a step into homeownership, with one family subsidizing its mortgage with the rent of two others. The detached structures, unlike row houses and urban tenements, also offered ventilation and private yards. The three-decker's peak in popularity coincided with that of the electric streetcar, from about 1890 until 1915.

The simplicity of the three-decker's construction made it easy for small entrepreneurs to become real estate developers. As Warner notes in his work, many developers in Boston's streetcar suburbs built just one or two dwellings during their career: one to live in and perhaps another to rent or sell. Many of these small developers were construction tradesmen who relied on the labor of family members and friends.

Real estate professionals were also active in erecting homes for speculation; in some streetcar suburbs entire streets were lined with identical houses. Often these tract homes were two- instead of three-family dwellings.

Streetcar suburb residents typically belonged to the lower and middle classes. They included recent arrivals from rural New England and Eastern Canada, as well as established immigrants from Ireland and other European countries.

The era of the streetcar suburb came to an end with the increased popularity of the private automobile after 1910.

Alexander von Hoffman, *Local Attachments: The Making of an American Urban Neighborhood, 1850 to 1920* (1994); Douglass Shand-Tucci, *Built in Boston: City and Suburb, 1800–2000* (1999); John R. Stilgoe, *Borderland: Origins of the American Suburb, 1820–1939* (1988); Sam Bass Warner, Jr., *Streetcar Suburbs: The Process of Growth in Boston, 1870–1900* (1962).

Charles Bahne

Street Railways

Street railways provided essential transportation in cities and many small towns throughout New England from approximately 1860 until after 1920. Boston's earliest horse-drawn street railways, which opened in 1856, proved a model for other cities. Within four years, more than 20 horsecar lines had been chartered around Boston; by 1874 horse railways were operating in every New England state. The next two decades were a period of modest expansion of the industry within urban areas. In an era when few city residents could afford a horse, many people found the street railway to be the first and only transportation alternative to walking.

During the 1880s street railway managers sought replacements for horse propulsion, which was slow, unreliable, and expensive. Several kinds of mechanical power were considered. New England's only cablecar line opened on January 1, 1890, over College Hill in Providence, but experiments in electric traction showed the most promise. The region's first electric streetcar line opened in Derby, Conn., on May 1, 1888.

Again, Boston led the way. The Beacon Street line to suburban Brookline, which opened in January 1889, was widely recognized as the first successful electric railway in a major city. It spurred the rapid electrification and expansion of street railways throughout New England. The horse as a motive force was virtually extinct by 1895, while the track network continued to grow until the advent of World War I. Lines reached out from the cities, encouraging development in rural areas.

Eventually streetcar lines from nearby cities touched each other, and through-car routes were established. New England had few true interurbans built on private rights-of-way, but it had many intercity lines operating on public roads. Most of southern New England and parts of New Hampshire and Maine were crisscrossed by trolley tracks; Massachusetts had the densest street railway network in the nation. By making enough connections, one could ride by trolley from Fairfield, Maine, to New York City and beyond. Trolley lines also operated in scattered cities throughout northern New England.

Rural street railways often served as feeder lines to the steam railroads. Many companies carried freight, milk, mail, and express, as well as passengers. In some cities, post office cars plied the streets on designated routes. Even funerals could be conducted by trolley, with special cars built for the purpose.

Street railways also offered inexpensive recreation opportunities. Streetcar companies built and operated picnic groves and amusement parks to attract off-peak ridership; some of these used excess electricity generated by the railway. Pleasure rides aboard open cars provided welcome respite from summer heat, and many railways had elegant parlor cars that could be chartered. Maps and guidebooks promoted sightseeing by trolley, often over long distances.

The industry's peak year was 1918, and the decline that followed was swift. Rapid inflation, failure of regulatory agencies to approve needed fare increases, and, above all, competition from private automobiles caused the abandonment of New England's street railway lines. Many were replaced by buses. By 1930 half of the Massachusetts network was out of service. As the nation entered World War II only five New England cities—Boston, Worcester, New Bedford, Providence, and New Haven—still had streetcar service, along with an interurban line between Sanford and Springvale, Maine. Service in all cities but Boston was discontinued by the fall of 1948.

Streetcars and related artifacts from several New England cities have been preserved in the region's three trolley museums: the Seashore Trolley Museum in Kennebunkport, Maine; the Connecticut Trolley Museum in East Windsor, Conn.; and the Shore Line Trolley Museum in East Haven, Conn. Canobie Lake Park in Salem, N.H., initially developed for the purpose of generating leisure excursions for the Massachusetts Northeast Street Railway Company, is one of the few such amusement parks remaining.

Stephen P. Carlson with Thomas W. Harding, *From Boston to the Berkshires: A Pictorial Review of Electric Transportation in Massachusetts* (1990); Frederick A. Kramer with Ed Wadhams, *Connecticut Company's Streetcars* (1993); Edward S. Mason, *The Street Railway in Massachusetts: The Rise and Decline of an Industry* (1932); William D. Middleton, *The Time of the Trolley* (1967).

Charles Bahne

Urban Renewal

Urban renewal in New England started with the rebuilding of New Haven, Conn., called "A Model City" in the

The international headquarters of the Knights of Columbus in New Haven, Conn., was part of Mayor Richard Lee's ambitious Oak Street renewal project, which also included the Oak Street Connector and the New Haven Coliseum. Almost 900 households and 250 businesses were relocated or displaced to make way for the new construction, which was completed in 1969. Only 1 mile of the proposed 10-mile, eight-lane Connector was built; the Coliseum shut down in 2002. Displaced residents continue to hold an annual "Oak Street Alumni" reunion.

early 1950s, when Mayor Richard E. Lee renovated the downtown with federal funds and became almost unbeatable at the polls. It was a somewhat different story when John Collins, Boston's mayor in 1960, staked his own career on a massive urban renewal program and hired Lee's top administrator, Edward J. Logue, to drive it. By the end of the 1960s, Boston had become arguably the nation's most striking example of the failure of urban planning.

Many Bostonians celebrated the success of the "New Boston," in Mayor John B. Hynes's phrase from the 1950s. To them, New Boston was the much-needed modernization of a city in serious decline. Just as many, however, saw urban renewal as a program for an antiseptic downtown, a measure that replaced close-knit neighborhoods with housing projects that fostered racism and violence. To critics in those neighborhoods, urban renewal lent itself to concern with real estate values and investment profits at the expense of working-class neighborhoods and people of color.

Boston had suffered the fate of most big northern cities during the 1930s: urban decay, a declining population, and a withering tax base. But by the mid-1950s, Hynes's aggressive modernization had pegged Boston, along with Cleveland, as the American cities most ambitious about physical renewal. I. M. Pei developed master plans for both. In Boston, he designed a mix of skyscrapers, open spaces, and low-rise structures for the 61-acre Government Center on the site of Scollay Square, the city's long-time center for vaudeville and nightlife, which had turned into a district of honky-tonk bars and tattoo parlors. The plan was to draw 50,000 people a day to new state and federal office buildings, reviving the city's core. To complement the development, developers constructed a 48-acre West End project, clearing an old Italian neighborhood and replacing it with 2,400 high-rise apartment units. Displaced residents, however, felt that special interests were conspiring with public officials to steal their homes. In his well-documented critique of the West End experience, *The Urban Villagers* (1962), the sociologist Herbert Gans pointed out that Boston's West End, although officially categorized a "slum," was more accurately described as "a stable, low-rent area." Many residents displaced from their lifelong neighborhood found that their new housing was more expensive. As Jon Teaford writes in *The Rough Road to Renaissance* (1990), "By 1963, to many commentators the West End was a symbol of all that was wrong with urban renewal."

Spurred by the backlash against the redevelopment of the West End, Collins's plans for Boston included proposals to address the human element in city planning as well as its

bricks and mortar, because the uprooting of families caused by urban renewal was seen as aggravating the city's social problems. Even with an unparalleled level of funding and staffing, though, Boston's urban planners failed to stem the deterioration of the city, providing a cautionary tale for the rest of the nation. As elsewhere, the Boston situation raised questions about just how scientific and effective top-down urban planning could be.

The West End experience had also left Boston with active local community organizations throughout its low-income neighborhoods. Many of these groups came to feel that their own neighborhoods were being threatened by the federal government in the form of urban renewal and by the Boston Redevelopment Authority. In 1970, following years of neighborhood activism, Mayor Kevin White allied himself with community advocates and told the city council that "for too long urban renewal in Boston has emphasized rebirth of the downtown area at the expense of the neighborhoods," signaling the end of Great Society efforts at federally funded urban renewal in Boston. By then, even Richard Lee had retreated before the difficulties of top-down urban planning after New Haven emptied its downtown during the course of the 1960s and was unable to stem its own racial disturbances.

In the 1950s, the automobile had been a major factor in Boston's plans for revitalization. In 1959, *Architectural Forum* criticized the city's John F. Fitzgerald Expressway as cutting "a rude gash" through downtown Boston, and Frederick Law Olmsted's Emerald Necklace was trimmed through the Fens to make way for the new expressways. But nowhere were highway foes more active and successful than in Boston. Mayor Kevin White and governors Daniel Walker and Francis Sargent repudiated highway construction, and neighborhood opposition eventually shelved plans for finishing the Southeast Expressway and an Inner Belt that would complete Interstate 95 from Maine to Florida. Federal highway money was shifted to mass transit projects.

In the 1970s, funding was directed toward preservation. Working with local citizens, the federal government created the first urban national park in Lowell, Mass., expanding opportunities for private business investment rather than relying solely on federal funding. Since then, renewal efforts throughout the region have been tied most often to private efforts. By the late 1970s and into the 1980s, long after the Prudential Center and Government Center, among a number of other results of urban renewal, first showed the profitability of downtown construction and development, Boston found itself in a tremendous building boom.

In Hartford, urban renewal focused on a 12-block area bordering the Connecticut River. This multi-ethnic neighborhood with a strong African American community was replaced by a cluster of modern buildings set atop a parking garage; the signature building was the curved, two-sided Aetna Insurance Company building. The project did little, however, to revitalize downtown life.

In Portsmouth, N.H., a campaign led by local librarian and preservationist Dorothy Vaughan in the 1950s stopped developers from destroying the historic Puddle Dock area, although residents were relocated when Strawbery Banke, a museum, was established on the site. Urban renewal in the early 1970s caused the destruction of the historic North End, but after the collapse of other large-scale urban renewal projects, efforts turned to mixed-use revitalization projects, such as the one that has transformed downtown Providence.

During the 1980s, Boston probably suffered the nation's greatest housing shortage, owing to gentrification occasioned by a large influx of young professionals. Conversion of rental properties to condominiums for the affluent made affordable housing a leading political issue. Into the 2000s, Boston's urban development continued to be shaped by its attractiveness as an investment site for banks and financial companies and high-tech firms and as a medical and educational center.

Elise M. Bright, *Reviving America's Forgotten Neighborhoods: An Investigation of Inner City Revitalization Efforts* (2000); Jane Jacobs, "The Death and Life of Great American Cities," in Jewel Bellush and Murray Mausknecht, eds., *Urban Renewal: People, Politics, and Planning* (1967); Thomas H. O'Connor, *Building a New Boston: Politics and Urban Renewal, 1950–1970* (1993); Fred Powledge, *Model City: A Test of American Liberalism: One Town's Efforts to Rebuild Itself* (1970); Alan R. Talbot, *The Mayor's Game: Richard Lee of New Haven and the Politics of Change* (1967); Jon C. Teaford, *The Rough Road to Renaissance: Urban Revitalization in America, 1940–1985* (1990); Stephan Thernstrom, *Poverty, Planning, and Politics in the New Boston: The Origins of ABCD* (1969).

Louis Mazzari

Urban Transportation New England has long been a center of innovative urban transport development. Transportation modes have expanded from local city centers to form a dense network of suburban communities that continues to define the region. The early emergence of colonial town centers in Boston, Newport, R.I., New Haven, Conn., and Portsmouth, N.H., promoted a suburban estate culture in the surrounding countryside. By the mid-18th century these large seaport towns had a system of elite London-style carriage coaches and shallops—small private

"The T," 1981

ships—that could reach plantation estates on Rhode Island's Narragansett Bay, or on Tory Row along the Charles River in Cambridge, Mass.

After the Revolutionary War, during the prosperous 1790s, a series of bridges were built to carry private stagecoach lines hourly from Boston to outlying centers in Cambridge, Roxbury, and South Boston, promoting real estate development in New England's first suburban districts. The Boston bridges also served as links in a regional hub of radial turnpikes built to access rural districts. A complementary set of ferry crossings in Boston Harbor was established by the early 19th century; similar systems soon appeared in Portland, Maine, and Providence. The innovation of steamboat service from Boston to the rural peninsula of Nahant, Mass., in 1818, supported the first summer cottage colony of Massachusetts's North Shore. Similar steamboat ferry lines to the South Shore followed by the 1820s.

Boston's suburbs continued to expand with the introduction of steam railroad lines from the city; routes expanded to Providence and to Worcester and Lowell, Mass., in 1835, resulting in the most advanced urban transport network of its time. These railroad lines sponsored the first "commutation tickets" to the Boston suburbs of Brookline and Newton in 1846 with a series of branch lines to other nearby towns such as Medford, Dedham, and Watertown, Mass. Hourly stages were replaced by large capacity omnibus lines to Dorchester, Charlestown, and Jamaica Plain, Mass., by the 1830s. Boston's outlying resorts, such as the Wyeth Hotel at Fresh Pond in

Cambridge, and Cambridge's landscaped Mount Auburn Cemetery (1831), which served as a park for weekend excursions, promoted further omnibus service and suburban development during the 1840s. By the 1850s Providence, Portland, and Hartford, Conn., each had hourly omnibus service from the city center to picturesque outlying destinations, resulting in similar suburban development.

In 1856 the first New York–style horse-drawn streetcars in New England brought passengers from Boston to Cambridge. These high-capacity streetcars had developed, by the Civil War, into a regional network of suburban lines that spread to Waltham, Quincy, and Lynn, Mass., creating an interurban transit service that was among the most extensive in the United States. The region's smaller cities of Providence, Portland, Hartford, and Worcester; coastal Connecticut cities of Bridgeport and Norwalk; and Merrimack Valley textile towns of Lowell and Lawrence also established street railroads in the 1860s. The Panic of 1873 forestalled further rail installation, but the return of urban prosperity in the 1880s resulted in the rapid adoption of horsecar transit in most of New England's small cities, including Burlington, Vt., and Newport.

The problems of suburban horsecar operation led to the innovation of mechanical propulsion. A San Francisco–style cable railway was adopted on College Hill in Providence in 1890. Elsewhere electric trolleys proved to be the most effective mode of urban street transit. In 1889 Boston was among the first cities to adopt electric trolley cars; its Beacon Street line to Brookline resulted in the first streetcar suburb for working-class residents. Such trolley routes inspired the classic streetscape of wooden three-decker apartment rows reproduced in many New England industrial cities such as Worcester and Fall River, Mass., and Waterbury, Conn. By 1895, electric trolleys had replaced horsecars in most New England cities, and even small towns such as Calais, Maine, and St. Albans, Vt., adopted the new technology. The electric railway also allowed suburban service to be extended between the newly prosperous industrial centers of southern New England and coastal Maine. By World War I, a dense network of interurban trolley lines webbed the rural highways from Waterville, Maine, to Waterbury, Conn., permitting working-class families to reach seashore resorts such as Old Orchard Beach, Maine, and Nantasket, Mass.

Electric railway technology encouraged the innovation of the first American subway system in Boston in 1897 from the Public Garden to Park Street Station with a right turn at Boylston Street, circumscribing the sacred space of Boston Common. Boston soon built a

network of overhead elevated lines that stretched to neighboring Charlestown and Roxbury and reached Cambridge in 1912 over the Charles River Bridge. These lines created a transit system that defined downtown Boston at the Winter and Summer Street intersection—today known as Downtown Crossing—with its landmark Filene's and Jordan Marsh department stores. In Providence a short subway tunnel was built under College Hill in 1914, and a number of high-speed electric lines linked the city to the East Providence suburbs.

By 1910 the suburban expansion of New York City had reached into southern Connecticut with the electrification of commuter railroad lines extending service to New Haven and Danbury. Elsewhere, suburban railroad service operated with steam engines from Boston to Framingham, Concord, and North Easton, Mass., with rustic depots designed by the Boston architect H. H. Richardson. Commuter trains reached Essex County estates through the Salem tunnel (1839) with its Gothic-style depot. Numerous trolley lines provided affordable service for middle-class passengers, linking Hartford, Portland, Manchester, and Bridgeport to shoreline or lakeside amusement parks such as Canobie Lake Park in Salem, N.H., and Whalom Park in Fitchburg, Mass.

The motorcar, introduced by the Duryea brothers in Springfield in 1893, was first limited to use by the affluent for pleasure drives along the suburban parkways of Newport and Boston. The introduction of mass-produced automobiles after 1910 transformed suburban travel patterns. Much of the interurban trolley network was abandoned, and construction of state highway systems was promoted through the Federal Highway Act of 1921. Regional bus companies were chartered, such as Vermont Transit from Burlington in 1921, and Peter Pan Lines in 1933, which connected Springfield and Worcester to Boston over the highways built as public works projects during the Depression. Beginning in 1930 a series of express roads were extended from Boston, including Route 9 to Worcester and Route 1 to Providence. Most innovative was the circumferential artery around Boston—Route 128, which extended from the Blue Hills to the Middlesex Falls. In 1938 the Merritt Parkway, with its distinctive Art Deco bridges, was opened to carry motor traffic from New York through the estate district of southern Connecticut. Springfield, Hartford, and Portland also improved auto parkways before the outbreak of the World War II.

Postwar prosperity permitted expansion of regional highways that transformed the bounds of suburban commuting. State toll roads, first in Maine (1947) and New Hampshire (1954), opened resort travel from Boston. The Massachusetts Turnpike (1956) and Connecticut Turnpike (1958), with their orange-roofed Howard Johnson's rest stops, permitted long distance commuting from Boston and New York to music festivals at Tanglewood in the Berkshires and Newport. The completion of circumferential Route 128 in 1950, then Interstate 495 and the construction of Route 3, extended the Boston suburban district to southern New Hampshire and Cape Cod by the 1960s. The new suburban highway culture eventually brought about the downfall of local streetcar systems, with the exception of Boston's trolley subway, immortalized by the postwar campaign anthem "Charlie on the MTA," written in 1949 by Jacqueline (Berman) Steiner and Beth Lomax Hawes for Walter A. O'Brien, the Progressive Party candidate in Boston's mayoral election.

Since 1980 the outer limits of Boston commuting have extended north beyond Portsmouth to outlet malls in Kittery and Freeport, Maine and south to the Foxwoods and Mohegan Sun casino resorts in Connecticut. New York suburban sprawl extended into Connecticut along Interstate 91 from New Haven up the Connecticut River valley to the college towns of Amherst and Northampton, Mass., and farther north to Vermont's ski resorts. Beyond the remote reaches of northern New England, the overlap of suburban beltways around Providence, Hartford, and Portland has created a nearly continuous roadside culture of national franchise shopping centers from Boston to New York.

Nevertheless, within the older industrial cities such as Lowell, Manchester, and Bridgeport, local bus routes serve immigrant working communities, while commuter train service still operates from Boston to bedroom communities in Cape Ann, and from New York City to southern Connecticut. Traditional transport modes are also maintained in Boston and Portland, with ferry service to outlying suburbs on the South Shore and Casco Bay, respectively, and bicycle paths permit daily commuters access to the congested centers of Providence and Cambridge. In Boston, urban transport innovation continues with the Central Artery/Ted Williams Tunnel Project, which aims to place the city's major urban throughways underground, creating the first American auto-subway system, by 2005.

John Hutchins Cady, *The Civic and Architectural Development of Providence* (1957); Brian J. Cudahy, *Change at Park Street Under* (1972); Martin Dibner, ed., *Portland* (1972); Ellsworth S. Grant, *The City of Hartford* (1986); George W. Hilton and John F. Due, *Electric Interurban Railways in America* (1960); Arthur J. Krim, *Northwest Cambridge* (1977); John R. Stilgoe, *Metropolitan Corridor* (1983); Walter Muir Whitehill, *Boston: A Topographical History* (1976).

Arthur Krim

Waterbury, Conn. Named "Matetacoke" by the Tunxis Indians before a small group of families from Farmington, Conn., purchased the land, Mattatuck Plantation was founded in 1674 and incorporated as the town of Waterbury in 1686. The city of Waterbury was incorporated in 1853, and the city and township were consolidated in 1902. By the time of the 2000 census, its population was 107,271. Located approximately 90 miles northeast of New York City at the junction of the Naugatuck and Mad Rivers in western Connecticut's New Haven County, Waterbury became a regional industrial center for brass and timepiece manufacturing. The city prospered throughout the 19th and early 20th centuries due to the acumen of local craftspeople and entrepreneurs who transformed domestic production of buttons and clocks into centralized factory systems that produced a host of brass products and timepieces. Waterbury's factories flourished with the labor of immigrant and native-born workers. Post–World War II technology, however, made its facilities obsolete and decimated the industries that once fortified the city's economy.

Because its rocky soil made farming unprofitable, Waterbury initially developed into a busy town where cottage industries thrived. Button making first spurred Waterbury's economy as New England's textile industry grew during an embargo against British goods before the War of 1812. By the 1850s, area craftspeople began mass producing clocks made with Waterbury brass workings. As the demand for clocks, watches, and brass products grew, so did the factories and the need for workers. In the 19th century Waterbury became an ethnically diverse city where Irish, French Canadian, Lithuanian, German, and Italian neighborhoods developed. As the 20th century approached, blacks from the South began migrating to Waterbury, but labor unions prohibited them from working in the brass industry until World War I.

In 1880 Waterbury Watch Company issued the first series of affordable pocket watches—what later became known as Ingersoll's Yankee "dollar watches"—that democratized timekeeping and brought fame to Waterbury. Waterbury Watch Company became New England Watch in 1898, and the company was purchased by Robert H. Ingersoll and Brothers Company in 1914. New England Watch Company and Waterbury Clock Company manufactured the dollar watches, which continued to be marketed under the Ingersoll name. Many of these watches were made to commemorate people and events such as the Chicago World's Columbian Exposition (1893), the Paris Exposition (1900), the Pan American Exposition in Buffalo (1901), and the Saint Louis World's Fair (1904). In 1922 Waterbury Clock Company bought out Ingersoll's company, which was experiencing financial trouble. Waterbury Clock later became U.S. Time, then the Timex Corporation.

Industry continued to support the city until after World War II, when cheaper plastics and aluminum replaced the more costly brass as basic industrial materials. When brass factories began to close in the postwar period, Waterbury, like many small New England cities, suffered from high unemployment rates and economic depression.

Industry still defines Waterbury by the communities it attracted, built, and maintained. These communities remain strong and pride in Waterbury is evident from the diverse denizens who populate this city of more than 100,000 residents. Waterbury is home to several educational institutions, including Teikyo Post University, Naugatuck Valley Community-Technical College, and a branch of the University of Connecticut. Notable Waterbury museums include the Timexpo Museum and the Mattatuck Museum.

Sando Bologna, *The Italians of Waterbury: Experiences of Immigrants and Their Families* (1993); Brass Workers History Project, *Brass Valley: The Story of Working People's Lives and Struggles in an American Industrial Region* (1982); Frank W. Chesson, *Images of America: Waterbury* (1996); Charles Monagan, *Greater Waterbury, A Region Reborn: A Contemporary Portrait* (1989).

Sheila A. Brennan

West Hartford, Conn. Founded in 1679, West Hartford was part of Hartford until its incorporation in 1854. As in many Connecticut towns, the settlers' initial impetus for separation was the desire to have their own parish in order to avoid spending a good part of "God's time" traveling on the Sabbath. Originally called the West Division, the town was named West Hartford in 1806.

After the first settler, Thomas Hosmer, built a dam and sawmill on Trout Brook in 1679, the population grew slowly. Fewer than 1,000 inhabitants were listed in the census of 1790, almost all of Anglo-Saxon origin and the Congregational faith. At least 20 families had owned black servants, but by 1791 most of them had been freed, reflecting the antislavery writings of Noah Webster, the West Division's most famous son.

For 200 years farming was the chief occupation in the town. Cattle, merino sheep, and thoroughbred horses were the main sources of wealth. Farmers made weekly trips to the

Hartford market in their wagons, carrying grain, meat, and milk. The town was not destined to become a manufacturing center like Hartford. The first real industry, taking advantage of the fine clay deposits in the south end, was pottery making.

During the last decade of the 19th century the population began a 70-year period of rapid growth, jumping from 1,930 to almost 3,200. By then agriculture was giving way to real estate development. In 1895, for instance, the former Stanley farm was being promoted as "Hartford's new and handsome suburb," with more than 200 lots for sale. Spurring development was the new electric trolley line running from Hartford west to Unionville. Between 1910 and 1970 the town burgeoned, growing in population from 4,800 to more than 68,000; in 2000 there were 63,589 West Hartford residents, a figure that attests to Connecticut's depressed economy in the mid-1990s.

For much of its history West Hartford has remained predominantly a suburb of white Anglo-Saxon and European descent. It is one of the wealthiest communities in Connecticut and has the largest elderly population of any suburban town in the state. Aside from the small number of African Americans who have lived there since the earliest days, the first non-Anglo immigrants, in the mid-19th century, were Irish laborers. Several black residents served in the 29th and 30th Union regiments during the Civil War. Not until the 1920s did the 20th century's tide of immigration reach the town. Hartford's numerous Jews established their own community in the North End. By 1930 more than 1,300 Swedes had settled in the city's midsection. After World War II, stimulated by the G.I. Bill of Rights, a large number of second-generation Irish and Italians moved from Hartford to West Hartford and other suburbs. The census figures of 2000 highlighted the influx of minorities, who accounted for 16 percent of the total population of 63,589, including 3,990 Hispanics and Latinos, 3,053 Asians, and 3,053 African Americans.

The largest enterprise to make West Hartford its home was Pratt and Whitney Machine Tool. Founded in 1860, it established Hartford's reputation as a major machine-tool center and made enormous contributions to the metalworking technology of the world, especially in the perfection of standard lengths and precision gauges essential to mass production. In 1940 the company moved its 2,600 employees to Hartford's 20-acre Charter Oak Park, a former racetrack.

Even better known worldwide than Pratt and Whitney was Colt's Manufacturing, founded in 1847 by the inventor of the revolver, Samuel Colt. In 1965 Colt's began moving its operations

to West Hartford and eventually abandoned the landmark Colt Armory in Hartford.

Despite an invasion of malls, discount stores, and national chains, West Hartford features five vibrant shopping areas. The oldest and most attractive is the Center, acclaimed, according to historian Nelson R. Burr as "an upscale, cosmopolitan shopping and dining destination for the region." Protected by the cluster of town buildings and the zoning limitation on business expansion into adjacent residential areas, the Center remains the heart of local commerce.

Noah Webster, author of the first American dictionary, is not the town's only claim to cultural excellence. Its public school system, including two high schools, has been called the best in Connecticut. In addition, West Hartford is the home of the American School for the Deaf (1817), the first institution for the handicapped in North America; Saint Joseph College (1932), a branch of the University of Connecticut (1940); and the University of Hartford (1957). It has produced a variety of well-known artists and authors, such as the 19th-century writer Rose Terry Cooke, the longtime *New Yorker* contributor Brendan Gill, the children's author Oliver Butterworth, the historian Bernard Bailyn, and the popular history writer Larry Collins.

Richard N. Boulton and Bice Clemow, *The West Hartford Story* (1954); Nelson R. Burr, *From Colonial Parish to Modern Suburb: A Brief Appreciation of West Hartford* (1976); Ellsworth S. Grant, Miriam Butterworth, and Richard Woodworth, *Celebrate! West Hartford, an Illustrated History* (2001); William H. Hall, *West Hartford* (1930).

Ellsworth S. Grant

Worcester, Mass.

Worcester, situated on the Blackstone River approximately 40 miles west of Boston, is the third largest city in New England, with a population of 172,647 (2000) and a metropolitan population of 429,882. Known as the Heart of the Commonwealth because of its central location, Worcester had a difficult time of it early on. Strife with the Indians in the late 17th century delayed Worcester's permanent settlement until 1713; the town was incorporated in 1722. Although it was the county seat, Worcester grew slowly and in 1775 was still a small farming community with fewer than 2,000 residents. After the Revolution, Worcester was plagued by falling farm prices and rising taxes. In September 1786, during Shays's Rebellion, rebels seized the courthouse to prevent the courts from foreclosing on area farms. The rebels were not dispersed until the Massachusetts militia arrived in December.

Worcester remained a farming community; in the first federal census in 1790 the popula-

tion was only 2,095. Because the town had limited waterpower resources, only minor manufacturing had entered the area by the 1820s. With the opening of the Blackstone Canal connecting Worcester and Providence in 1828 and the completion of the Boston and Worcester Railroad in 1835, Worcester became a more attractive industrial site. Using steam for power, Stephen Salisbury II and William T. Merrifield built the Court and Merrifield Mills in the 1830s and 1840s and rented space in these complexes to numerous artisans. The Union and Washburn Mills and the Junction and Stone Shops contributed to a diversified industrial takeoff that included the manufacturing of textile machinery, boots and shoes, agricultural implements, skates, and musical instruments. The population grew from 7,500 in 1840 to 17,000 in 1850; Worcester was incorporated as a city in 1848. The Blackstone Canal closed in 1848, but the Providence and Worcester Railroad began operation in 1847, and its connections soon earned Worcester the moniker Junction City.

After the Civil War companies such as Washburn and Moen, the largest producer of barbed wire in the world; Crompton and Knowles, the loom maker; Wyman-Gordon, the bicycle and later auto-crankshaft manufacturer; Graton and Knight, the producer of leather belts; and Norton Company, the manufacturer of emery wheels, along with numerous foundries and firms making machine tools, knives, guns, corsets, railroad lunch cars, shoes, carriages, carpets, and envelopes flourished in Worcester. By 1900 the metal trades accounted for more than 40 percent of the city's manufacturing and Worcester's population had grown from 85,000 in 1890 to almost 120,000 in 1900. While many of the city's industrial workers lived close to their places of employment in neighborhoods such as Bell Hill, Greendale, and Quinsigamond Village, after 1890 the electric trolley made it possible for workers to commute to the city from the inner suburbs.

At the turn of the 20th century the largest ethnic groups in Worcester were the Irish, French Canadians, and Swedes, but immigrants from southern and eastern Europe were beginning to flow into the city. While many of the new immigrants retained their ethnic and religious identity, corporate paternalism and control also shaped their lives. This corporate social control led to labor strife during and after World War I. The decline of the city's metal trades and the boot and shoe industry in the 1920s and 1930s reflected the general deindustrialization of New England. World War II stimulated Worcester's industrial economy, however, and the city's population peaked at 203,000 in 1950.

As far back as the 1850s the city developed public amenities, including the first public park in the United States (Elm Park, 1854) and a fine building for cultural and social events (Mechanics Hall, 1857). It is known for its many academic institutions, among them the College of the Holy Cross (1843), Worcester Polytechnic Institute (1865), Worcester State College (1874), Becker College (1887), Clark University (1887), and Assumption College (1904); for the outstanding collection of the Worcester Art Museum; and for the historical research library of the American Antiquarian Society.

Although manufacturing still accounts for almost 25 percent of total employment in the city, service industries, such as education, biotechnology, health care, banking, insurance, recreation, and tourism, have increasingly dominated Worcester since 1955. In the mid-1990s Worcester's downtown landscape underwent a dramatic transformation. A convention center (1997) was added to the Worcester Centrum (1982), a successful all-purpose arena; Union Station (2000) was converted to a shopping and transportation center; and the new Worcester Medical Center was completed in 2000. The city's future depends on the success of its efforts to rejuvenate downtown; to replace or renovate its housing stock, including its three-deckers; and to educate and find work for its newest immigrants.

Charles W. Cheape, *Family Firm to Modern Multinational: Norton Company, a New England Enterprise* (1985); Charles A. Nutt, *History of Worcester and Its People*, 4 vols. (1919); Roy Rosenzweig, *Eight Hours for What We Will: Workers and Leisure in an Industrial City, 1870–1920* (1983); Charles G. Washburn, *Industrial Worcester* (1917).

Bruce Cohen

Zoning Long before legislators wrote the first zoning laws, New Englanders possessed a distinct sense of society and place that shaped the lay of the land. When English settlers began forming townships on land purchased or purloined from earlier inhabitants, they sought to create well-ordered Christian communities. They organized the family farm as the basic social unit of production and the town as the fundamental unit of settlement to support a congregational church and create their divine, yet worldly, city upon a hill. John Winthrop, in his famous sermon "A Modell of Christian Charity" (1630), preached that God "shall make us a praise and glory that men shall say of succeeding plantations, 'the Lord make it like that of New England.'"

In New England, as elsewhere, growth was the stimulus to the passage of zoning laws. By the 18th century, individual freedom that rooted land use in private hands replaced the community determination of land use characteristic of the initial village system. While land management concentrated on the rights of the individual in the 19th century, the cities of New England grew into complex systems of interdependent public services, private utilities, and individual property holdings. Excessive individualism and land speculation often led to crowded, unsafe, and unhealthy conditions in New England cities.

Municipalities slowly redefined old public duties of landholders and expanded traditional nuisance laws directed against noxious trades, dangerous construction, and disorderly houses, to support fire, health, and building codes. Strictures on construction in cities like Boston provided precedent and impetus for passage of the New York Zoning Law of 1916, the prototype statute in the nation. New England communities rapidly followed suit. Within five years, there were 62 zoned communities in Massachusetts. Cities like Providence developed zoning ordinances in conjunction with the establishment of building codes. Other cities such as Portland, Maine, subsequently harmonized existing building codes to match new zoning strictures.

Zoning law in New England emerged under the guise of preserving traditional values within the context of growth. These restrictions on private property are justified by recalling the traditional exercise of police power intended to protect the health, safety, morals, and general welfare of citizens.

Zoning emerged simultaneously with the practice of city planning during the Progressive Era. Where zoning regulated growth, planning endeavored to create building programs for the orderly development of cities, suburbs, and metropolitan areas. The legality of zoning hinged upon planning. The Supreme Court's *Euclid Village* decision (1926), for instance, declared zoning constitutional when based on comprehensive planning. Planning failures, however, have frequently hindered zoning. Proximity to debt limit in Bridgeport, Conn., during the 1920s made it impossible to implement city planning and undermined zoning restrictions. Hartford and Springfield, Mass., in the same period, developed "pay-as-you-go" city plans that were more supportive of zoning ordinances.

Zoning did not necessarily contravene patterns of expansion, but it did provide protection against speculation and encourage uniform development. In suburbs, zoning promised to protect homeowners by preserving neighborhood homogeneity. Realtors developed vacant land with confidence that adjoining lots would be improved according to existing zoning ordinances. Newton, Mass., for instance, developed one of the most impressive zoning records by continually strengthening the town's single-family dwelling zone.

Zoning has also facilitated economic development. The Providence Chamber of Commerce reported in the late 1920s that zoning attracted manufacturers who knew precisely where to locate plants and workers. Former manufacturing communities, like Manchester, N.H., today use mixed-use zoning to revitalize abandoned manufacturing districts.

Increasingly, New Englanders use zoning to retain traditional qualities of rural life. To protect its rural character against rampant ski resort and second home development, Vermont enacted landmark legislation in 1970 known as Act 250. The measure, hailed by conservationists, established strict land-use guidelines that restricted rapid growth and banned billboards. Subsequent legislation strengthened efforts to preserve endangered farm lands, punish land speculation, and retain the traditional rural character of the state. Nonetheless, in 2004 the National Trust for Historic Preservation declared the entire state "endangered" because of the proliferation of "big box" stores.

Zoning has often given urban and suburban dwellers a defense against "undesirable" activities and people. Throughout the region, communities use zoning to restrict adult book and movie stores and inhibit "red-light" districts. Interacting with real estate prices, zoning law has often reinforced segregation of New Englanders by income, ethnicity, and race. Land and structure limitations priced certain groups out of particular urban areas or suburbs. Although a 1948 Supreme Court decision outlawed racial or ethnic covenants designed to exclude "non-Caucasians," market forces and banking practices, sustained by zoning practice in New England, nevertheless produced roughly the same result—class, ethnic, and racial segregation.

Theodora Kimball Hubbard and Henry Vincent Hubbard, *Our Cities To-Day and To-Morrow: A Survey of Planning and Zoning Progress in the United States* (1929); Maria Newman, "Endangered: Quaint Towns. Green Hills. Vermont!" *New York Times*, May 24, 2004; Seymour I. Toll, *Zoned America* (1969); Sam Bass Warner, *The Urban Wilderness: A History of the American City* (1972).

Robert L. Macieski

Zoos Before the advent of zoological gardens, traveling showmen brought animals from distant parts of the world to New England. In the 18th century menageries exhibited lions, camels, elephants, bears, sea lions, tigers, zebras, buffaloes, and monkeys throughout urban and rural New England. The first elephant displayed in the region arrived in Salem, Mass., in 1796, having developed a taste for strong beer on the sea voyage to Amer-

Roger Williams Park Zoo, Providence, 1993

ica. Its exhibition career lasted until 1816, when it was shot by a farmer in Alfred, Maine.

Traveling menageries reached their greatest heights of popularity between 1820 and 1850, with quite extensive inventories of animals. One of the more famous was the for-profit Zoological Institute of New York, which merged nine menageries and traveled through New England from 1834 to 1854. By 1850 the menageries began to join with circuses, orienting themselves more toward entertainment and the display of exotic animals.

Zoos in New England have never quite captured the public's imagination or entertainment dollar as they have in other parts of America. Perhaps the reliance on and fascination with the Atlantic Ocean, which has given the region the excellent New England Aquarium in Boston and the Mystic Aquarium Institute for Exploration in Connecticut, explains the relatively weak zoological tradition in New England. Cold winters also make it extremely expensive to house tropical animals in the Northeast. Today four New England zoos are accredited by the American Zoo and Aquarium Association: Beardsley Zoological Gardens in Bridgeport, Conn.; Capron Park Zoo in Attleboro, Mass.; Franklin Park Zoo in Boston; and Roger Williams Park in Providence. Two smaller municipal parks are the Buttonwood Zoo in New Bedford, Mass., and the Forest Park Zoo in Springfield, Mass.

The oldest zoological garden in New England is Roger Williams Park. Providence had planned for a zoo before the Civil War, but the idea took shape only after 1865. A descendant of Rhode Island's founder, Roger Williams, Betsy Williams bequeathed her 103-acre farm to the city for a park; the zoo officially opened on June 9, 1872. Now located on 430 acres directly off Interstate 95, the park features more than 150 species housed in naturalistic settings arranged geographically into the Plains of Africa, Australasia, Madagascar, the Marco Polo Trail, Tropical America, and Habitat Rhode Island.

The largest zoological garden in New England, the Franklin Park Zoo of Dorchester, was founded in 1911. Named after Ben Franklin, it is located in the 527-acre Franklin Park at the end of Boston's 7-mile Emerald Necklace park system. The original plans for the zoo, drafted by the landscape architect Frederick Law Olmsted in 1884–85, included a small parcel of land for the Boston Zoological Society. Over the course of the 20th century Franklin Park gradually acquired new land and animals, expanding its operations. In 1991 Massachusetts governor William Weld signed legislation to create Zoo New England, a quasi-private nonprofit organization, to oversee the finances and management of the two Boston-area zoos, Franklin Park and Stone Memorial.

The Stone Memorial Zoo, founded in 1905, began its life as the Middlesex Falls Zoo. Charles Price, superintendent of the Metropolitan District Commission's Middlesex Falls Reservation, launched the enterprise as an addition to the Boston suburb's park system. In 1969 the zoo was renamed in honor of the late director Walter D. Stone.

New England also has many privately run animal parks and petting zoos. These include the Wild Kingdom of York, Maine; the Friendly Farm of Dublin, N.H.; and McCray's Farm and Country Creamery of South Hadley, Mass.

Robert J. Goldsack, *Remembering Benson's Wild Animal Farm, Hudson, New Hampshire* (1998); R. J. Hoage and William A. Deiss, *New World, New Animals: From Menagerie to Zoological Park in the 19th Century* (1996); Linda Koebner, *Zoo Book: The Evolution of Wildlife Conservation Centers* (1994).

M. Jeffrey Hardwick

Education

Joyce Antler, Section Editor

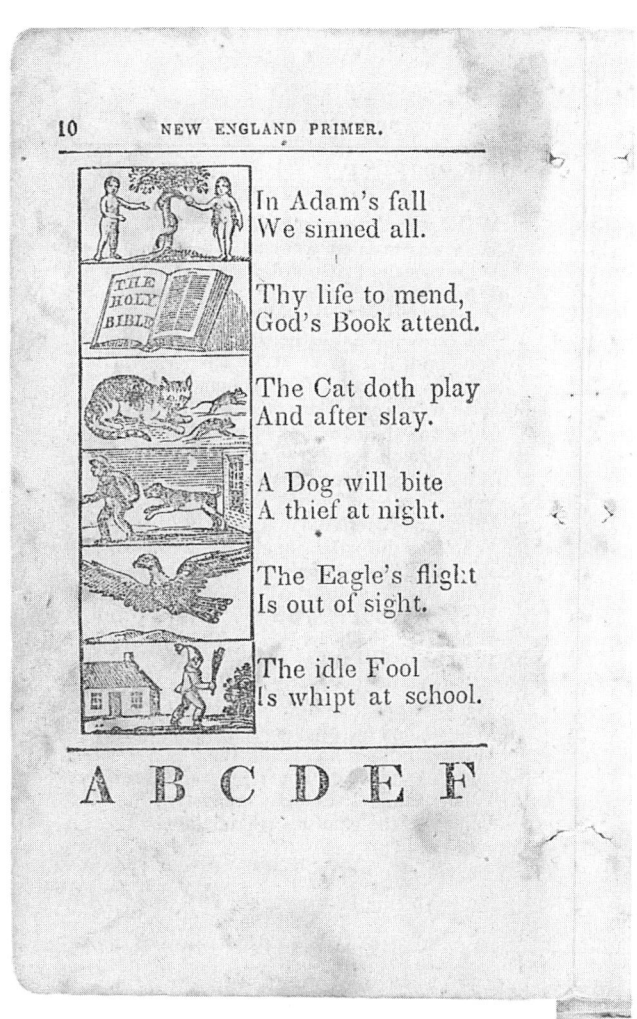

In Adam's fall
We sinned all.

Thy life to mend,
God's Book attend.

The Cat doth play
And after slay.

A Dog will bite
A thief at night.

The Eagle's flight
Is out of sight.

The idle Fool
Is whipt at school.

A B C D E F

INTRODUCTION

From the colonial period to the present, New England has been a seedbed of ideas and practices that have shaped and influenced education throughout the United States. Through its landmark education acts and innovative pedagogical approaches, the region established a powerful tradition of leadership at every educational level. The prominence of New England educational institutions fostered the region's unparalleled influence on education throughout the nation; at the same time, its institutions maintained and celebrated distinctive regional and local identities.

The culture of reform and innovation that characterized more than three and a half centuries of education in New England made its schools a model for the nation. Particularly important in promoting public education was the principle that the twin goals of moral education and the achievement of literacy were community responsibilities. From the 17th century onward, New England's ministers, teachers, legislators, reformers, and administrators struggled to create schools that would carry out the educational mandate shared by the community at large. The extension of schooling to progressively wider groups of citizens—with respect to religious denomination, race, economic level, and gender—has marked much of the region's educational history.

The importance that New Englanders placed on education led to the continued expansion of the very nature of schooling. From the colonial period's dame schools and grammar schools to 19th-century academies, common schools, and high schools, educational leaders created new institutions that responded to the needs of a rapidly changing society. The most optimistic among them were convinced that improved schools would foster new kinds of learning that would enhance individual potential and at the same time sustain democratic values and ensure social and political stability. New schools meant new curricula: New Englanders were at the forefront of nearly every curriculum reform of the 19th century—among them, the introduction of music and art; manual, industrial, and vocational training; and athletics and physical education into the public schools. New England reformers, nurturing a vision of free public education appropriate for children with disabilities, also pioneered the development of "special" schools as extensions of common schools.

New Englanders' firm belief in education as the mainspring of an ideal society applied to almost the entire life span, from infancy through elementary school, high school, and postsecondary school education to education for mature adults. Building on the Puritans' abiding interest in the religious education of even the youngest children, most New England towns established infant schools—and societies to promote them—by the early 19th century. New England also pioneered the American kindergarten movement in the 1850s and the nursery-school movement 75 years later as well as other developments in preschool and children's education, including children's museums. At the other end of the generational spectrum, educators in the region established the lyceum movement in the 19th century and created athenaeums, libraries, historical museums and societies, religious and outdoor education, and other forms of both formal and informal adult education. The emergence of Elderhostel in the mid-20th century was just one of the latest manifestations of the region's interest in transmitting culture across the generations.

Perhaps nothing was more characteristic of New England education than its wide variety of institutions of higher learning. From Harvard and Yale Universities, founded to train ministers in the 17th and early 18th centuries; to Brown and Dartmouth, founded at the time of the American Revolution; to a half dozen liberal arts colleges founded in the early 19th century; to the region's pioneering women's colleges founded before and after the Civil War; to a growing number of specialized institutes, colleges, and universities of specialized purpose, New England's institutions of higher learning educated an increasingly diverse student body. Added to the mix of liberal arts colleges and universities that dotted New England's landscape of higher education were growing numbers of state-chartered, public-supported institutions; those that catered to Catholic students; and, by the mid-20th century, Brandeis University, the nation's first Jewish-sponsored, nonsectarian institution of higher learning.

The purposes of New England's earliest colleges, established to train ministers and others of the educational elite, gave way to a broader focus in the 19th century in terms of both enrollment and curricula. As the century drew to a close, the goals and objectives of higher education at the region's colleges and universities remained diverse and at varied stages of development: some were oriented toward character training, others toward a more or less "classical" curriculum, still others toward scientific or academic research or skills training. In each of these directions, New England institutions continued to suggest new approaches while harnessing the traditions and structures of the past.

In addition to their curricula, pedagogies, and faculties, New England's colleges and universities have been distinguished by their extracurricular life. Many of the first intercollegiate sports events—including meets in crew, baseball, cricket, and track and field—took place in New England; the Head of the Charles regatta, held annually in October, remains a distinctive ritual for crew teams from all over the nation and the world. New England undergraduates have also participated in campus-specific class days and festivals; in musical and dramatic performances; and in the social rituals of fraternities, sororities, and other student clubs and organizations. Many New England students joined the reform causes of their time—whether the settlement movement of the 1890s; the pacifist causes of the 1930s and 1940s; the Civil Rights, antiwar, and feminist movements of the 1960s and 1970s; or the environmental movement today. The energy and commitment of these young men and women on behalf of sports, student government, social justice organizations, and other aspects of school life helped define a unique campus culture at each school.

Today the region is home to some 280 colleges and universities, which enroll a diverse student body of approximately 800,000 students (see table). The concentration of such student enrollments, as well as endowments, library holdings, think tanks and institutes, and research and development capital, has contributed enormously to the region's growth and prosperity. Through their partnerships with schools and businesses, their affiliated museums and arts and humanities institutes, their faculty experts and research programs, New England's institutions of higher education have been a major influence on the region's culture, lifestyles, and public policies. Their impact has been felt at all levels of the New England educational system.

In the contemporary period, as in earlier eras, New England's schools and colleges have shaped the region. They have provided dominant images of New England in the mind of the nation: from the traditional one-room schoolhouse and the New England "schoolmarm" teaching the basics to children of all ages; to the academies and prep schools of the New England countryside, which catered largely to the needs of elite students; to the more imposing common or public schools, which gathered a broader-based, largely urban clientele. Together, these images have reflected and molded the changing face of American schooling. Traditional liberal arts colleges, which have emphasized moral values and liberal culture, and research universities, offering specialized training and opportunities for research excellence, have both played leading roles in forming American ideas about teaching and learning, about schools and democracy, and about the role of culture itself as a part of the national purpose. Horace Mann's vision of schools as intrinsic in developing educated citizens was expressed in different ways in these varied institutions and in the myriad forms of learning that grew around them as part of New England's cultural landscape. Often, the reality was far different—sometimes much darker and usually far more diverse—from the harmonious, hopeful visions of New England educators and their representations in the culture at large. But the struggle to improve institutions and continually shape opportunities for meaningful learning, often in the face of contested ideas and bitter disputes over resources and approaches, became itself part of the New England tradition.

EDUCATION IN COLONIAL NEW ENGLAND

Colonial schools set roots that profoundly influenced the subsequent development of schooling in all regions. For the Puritans who settled in New England, education became a critical means of building and sustaining the well-ordered religious commonwealth. Critical to this goal, schools were established early in the colonies' history, their mission seen as congruent to those of family and church. Intertwined in purpose and often in structure, these institutions provided the Protestant underpinnings for New England's foundational educational achievements.

Education became a matter of "public concernment" almost from the beginning

Colleges and Universities with Enrollments of over 1,000

Connecticut

Albertus Magnus College
New Haven

Enrollment: 1,500
Established: 1925

University of Bridgeport
Bridgeport

Enrollment: 2,200
Established: 1927

Central Connecticut State University
New Britain

Enrollment: 11,540
Established: 1849

Charter Oak State College
Newington

Enrollment: 1,252
Established: 1973

Connecticut College
New London

Enrollment: 1,800
Established: 1911

University of Connecticut
Storrs

Enrollment: 24,051
Established: 1881

Eastern Connecticut State University
Willimantic

Enrollment: 4,994
Established: 1889

Fairfield University
Fairfield

Enrollment: 5,154
Established: 1942

University of Hartford
West Hartford

Enrollment: 6,844
Established: 1877

University of New Haven
West Haven

Enrollment: 5,113
Established: 1920

Quinnipiac College
Hamden

Enrollment: 6,500
Established: 1929

Sacred Heart University
Fairfield

Enrollment: 5,569
Established: 1963

Saint Joseph College
West Hartford

Enrollment: 2,022
Established: 1932

Southern Connecticut State University
New Haven

Enrollment: 12,127
Established: 1893

Teikyo Post College
Waterbury

Enrollment: 1,400
Established: 1890

Trinity College
Hartford

Enrollment: 2,333
Established: 1823

Wesleyan University
Middletown

Enrollment: 2,850
Established: 1831

Western Connecticut State University
Danbury

Enrollment: 5,806
Established: 1903

Yale University
New Haven

Enrollment: 11,126
Established: 1701

Maine

Bates College
Lewiston

Enrollment: 1,694
Established: 1855

Bowdoin College
Brunswick

Enrollment: 1,609
Established: 1794

Colby College
Waterville

Enrollment: 1,814
Established: 1813

(continued)

Colleges and Universities with Enrollments of over 1,000 (continued)

Husson College
Bangor

Enrollment: 1,892
Established: 1898

University of Maine at Augusta
Augusta

Enrollment: 5,571
Established: 1965

University of Maine at Farmington
Farmington

Enrollment: 2,413
Established: 1863

University of Maine at Orono
Orono

Enrollment: 9,945
Established: 1865

University of Maine at Presque Isle
Presque Isle

Enrollment: 1,427
Established: 1903

University of New England
Biddeford

Enrollment: 2,200
Established: 1953

University of Southern Maine
Gorham

Enrollment: 10,700
Established: 1878

Massachusetts

American International College
Springfield

Enrollment: 1,084
Established: 1885

Amherst College
Amherst

Enrollment: 1,682
Established: 1821

Anna Maria College
Paxton

Enrollment: 1,255
Established: 1946

Assumption College
Worcester

Enrollment: 2,455
Established: 1904

Babson College
Wellesley

Enrollment: 3,397
Established: 1919

Bentley College
Waltham

Enrollment: 5,728
Established: 1917

Berklee College of Music
Boston

Enrollment: 3,400
Established: 1945

Boston College
Chestnut Hill

Enrollment: 13,551
Established: 1863

Boston University
Boston

Enrollment: 28,318
Established: 1839

Brandeis University
Waltham

Enrollment: 4,753
Established: 1948

Bridgewater State College
Bridgewater

Enrollment: 8,839
Established: 1840

Clark University
Worcester

Enrollment: 2,910
Established: 1887

College of the Holy Cross
Worcester

Enrollment: 2,826
Established: 1843

Curry College
Milton

Enrollment: 2,330
Established: 1879

Eastern Nazarene College
Quincy

Enrollment: 1,387
Established: 1918

Emerson College
Boston

Enrollment: 4,071
Established: 1880

(continued)

Colleges and Universities with Enrollments of over 1,000 (*continued*)

Emmanuel College
Boston

Enrollment: 1,524
Established: 1919

Endicott College
Beverly

Enrollment: 1,958
Established: 1939

Fitchburg State College
Fitchburg

Enrollment: 5,575
Established: 1894

Framingham State College
Framingham

Enrollment: 6,626
Established: 1839

Gordon College
Wenham

Enrollment: 1,617
Established: 1889

Hampshire College
Amherst

Enrollment: 1,172
Established: 1965

Harvard University
Cambridge

Enrollment: 19,539
Established: 1636

Harvard (1636) and Radcliffe (1876) colleges merged in the early 1970s.

Lesley College
Cambridge

Enrollment: 5,630
Established: 1909

Massachusetts College of Art
Boston

Enrollment: 2,315
Established: 1873

Massachusetts College of Liberal Arts
North Adams

Enrollment: 1,745
Established: 1894

**Massachusetts College of Pharmacy and
    Health Sciences**
Boston

Enrollment: 1,632

Established: 1823

Massachusetts Institute of Technology
Cambridge

Enrollment: 10,204
Established: 1861

Merrimack College
North Andover

Enrollment: 2,587
Established: 1947

Mount Holyoke College
South Hadley

Enrollment: 2,089
Established: 1837

Mount Ida College
Newton Centre

Enrollment: 2,009
Established: 1899

Nichols College
Dudley

Enrollment: 1,363
Established: 1815

Northeastern University
Boston

Enrollment: 22,599
Established: 1898

Regis College
Weston

Enrollment: 1,138
Established: 1927

Salem State College
Salem

Enrollment: 13,417
Established: 1854

Simmons College
Boston

Enrollment: 3,340
Established: 1899

Smith College
Northampton

Enrollment: 3,112
Established: 1871

Springfield College
Springfield

Enrollment: 5,000
Established: 1885

Stonehill College
North Easton

Enrollment: 2,649
Established: 1948

(*continued*)

Colleges and Universities with Enrollments of over 1,000 (continued)

Suffolk University Boston	Enrollment: 5,254 Established: 1906
Tufts University Medford	Enrollment: 8,933 Established: 1852
University of Massachusetts Amherst Amherst	Enrollment: 24,416 Established: 1863
University of Massachusetts Boston Boston	Enrollment: 13,346 Established: 1964
University of Massachusetts Dartmouth North Dartmouth	Enrollment: 7,122 Established: 1969
University of Massachusetts Lowell Lowell	Enrollment: 12,485 Established: 1975
Wellesley College Wellesley	Enrollment: 2,267 Established: 1870
Wentworth Institute of Technology Boston	Enrollment: 3,152 Established: 1904
Western New England College Springfield	Enrollment: 4,600 Established: 1919
Westfield State College Westfield	Enrollment: 5,008 Established: 1838
Wheaton College Norton	Enrollment: 1,474 Established: 1834
Wheelock College Boston	Enrollment: 1,077 Established: 1888
Williams College Williamstown	Enrollment: 2,066 Established: 1793
Worcester Polytechnic Institute Worcester	Enrollment: 3,874 Established: 1865
Worcester State College Worcester	Enrollment: 5,646 Established: 1874

New Hampshire

Daniel Webster College Nashua	Enrollment: 1,099 Established: 1965
Dartmouth College Hanover	Enrollment: 5,386 Established: 1769
Franklin Pierce College Rindge	Enrollment: 4,500 Established: 1962
Hesser College Manchester	Enrollment: 2,766 Established: 1900
Keene State College Keene	Enrollment: 4,573 Established: 1909
College for Lifelong Learning Concord	Enrollment: 2,039 Established: 1972
Plymouth State College Plymouth	Enrollment: 4,041 Established: 1871
Rivier College Nashua	Enrollment: 2,200 Established: 1933

(continued)

Colleges and Universities with Enrollments of over 1,000 (*continued*)

Saint Anselm College
Manchester

Enrollment: 1,985
Established: 1889

Southern New Hampshire University
Manchester

Enrollment: 5,363
Established: 1932

University of New Hampshire
Durham

Enrollment: 13,426
Established: 1866

University of New Hampshire at Manchester
Manchester

Enrollment: 1,086
Established: 1967

Rhode Island

Brown University
Providence

Enrollment: 7,723
Established: 1764

Bryant College
Smithfield

Enrollment: 3,373
Established: 1863

Johnson and Wales University
Providence

Enrollment: 9,172
Established: 1914

New England Institute of Technology
Warwick

Enrollment: 2,603
Established: 1940

Providence College
Providence

Enrollment: 5,336
Established: 1917

Rhode Island College
Providence

Enrollment: 8,513
Established: 1854

Rhode Island School of Design
Providence

Enrollment: 2,086
Established: 1877

University of Rhode Island
Kingston

Enrollment: 14,362
Established: 1892

Roger Williams College
Bristol

Enrollment: 4,115
Established: 1956

Salve Regina University
Newport

Enrollment: 2,246
Established: 1934

Vermont

Castleton State College
Castleton

Enrollment: 1,622
Established: 1787

Champlain College
Burlington

Enrollment: 2,876
Established: 1878

Johnson State College
Johnson

Enrollment: 1,450
Established: 1828

Lyndon State College
Lyndonville

Enrollment: 1,150
Established: 1911

Middlebury College
Middlebury

Enrollment: 2,284
Established: 1800

Norwich University
Northfield

Enrollment: 2,703
Established: 1819

Saint Michael's College
Colchester

Enrollment: 2,687
Established: 1904

University of Vermont
Burlington

Enrollment: 10,118
Established: 1791

Source: Peterson's Guide to Four-Year Colleges, 32d ed. (Princeton: Peterson's, 2002); college and university Web sites.

of the colonial period. Compulsory education first occurred in Massachusetts in 1642, when selectmen enjoined parents to teach children themselves or to procure teaching for them. By that time, grammar schools had been established in Massachusetts, Rhode Island, and Connecticut. In 1647 the General Court of Massachusetts passed its famous Old Deluder Satan law, which required towns of 50 families or householders to establish reading (primary) schools, and towns of 100 or more families to establish grammar (secondary) schools. This was the first attempt of any American government to shape the public good through education.

The Massachusetts statute was quickly adopted by other New England colonies. As a consequence, the number of children taught in formal schoolrooms was significantly higher in New England than elsewhere in the colonies. Grammar schools instructed older students (usually boys) in the ancient languages, especially Latin, although instruction in reading and writing English was sometimes offered to younger children. Most of the younger children, and most girls, learned English reading and writing in "petty" or "dame" schools, where instruction was usually provided by women, often in their own homes or in churches, meetinghouses, shops, and fields. Seventeenth-century missionary efforts by John Eliot and Thomas Mayhew included literacy instruction in native languages; Eliot created a primer, a catechism, and his great Indian Bible (1663). In the 18th century, Eleazar Wheelock educated Native Americans at his Moor's Indian Charity School in Lebanon, Conn., which was absorbed into Dartmouth College. Wheelock's student Samson Occom raised substantial funding for Dartmouth. In recent years, Native Americans have asserted control over education for their children in tribal schools and in curriculum development.

Through these varied means, nearly 90 percent of adult white New England males were literate by the end of the 18th century. That this number included farmers, workers, and rural artisans as well as the urban gentry signaled the universality of white male literacy—and the wide availability of education—in New England, especially in comparison to literacy rates in the mid-Atlantic and southern states at this time. Until the middle of the 19th century, however, female literacy lagged well behind male literacy, as did that of African Americans. By the time of the American Revolution, the Puritan tradition of classical grammar-school education had largely given way to a more utilitarian emphasis; town-supported writing schools and private vocational schools teaching mathematics, science, and other vocational subjects now far outnumbered grammar schools. In this manner, New England's schools, created from European models, demonstrated the first of many transformations. In the faster-paced world of 18th-century mercantilism, schools had to train a new commercial elite requiring vocational and writing skills, not those taught in the ancient curriculum. Changes in the purpose of schooling were gradual and nondisruptive yet profound.

Harvard, the first New England college, was founded in 1636 with the express purpose of training ministers to serve the needs of the Puritan community. Established less than 10 years after the creation of the Massachusetts Bay Colony, this university, named after benefactor John Harvard, was remarkable by any standard. Its Puritan founders, desiring to replicate the advanced learning that had been characteristic of the Puritan experience in England, moved immediately to institutionalize higher education in the colonies based on the English academic model. Most of the college's early students came from New England's professional and landed families, yet some students came from more diverse backgrounds. During its first 50 years, approximately half of Harvard alumni became ministers; others entered business, teaching, and public service. Yale, founded in 1701, intended to train men for service in the church and "civil" society. By the time of the American Revolution, Brown and Dartmouth had been created, making New England home to four of nine colonial colleges. Five more colleges (Williams, Bowdoin, Middlebury, Waterville [Colby], and Amherst) and one state university (Vermont) all established between 1791 and 1831, were also affiliated with particular Protestant denominations. While religion was paramount in the founding of these institutions, in each instance local issues determined the reasons and circumstances of their establishment.

EDUCATION AND NATION BUILDING

New England shared in the national consensus that education was the key to the maintenance of the republic. After the American Revolution, each New England state provided tax support for the public education of its citizens. In the next half century, the region instituted major educational changes, including the expansion and broadening of public-school curricula and support; the development of new modes of teacher training, including the establishment of normal schools; the widening of the teacher base to include women; and the founding of infant schools, kindergartens, and programs for adults.

The manner in which local experience shaped ideas and politics that became national in content and scope is illustrated by the contributions of Connecticut-born country schoolmaster Noah Webster. While teaching in the 1770s, Webster developed a spelling book and, later, a grammar and reader, both of which became popular throughout the country, helping to create a unified national system of instruction. In the early 19th century, Webster served in the Massachusetts legislature and was an active promoter of the common-school idea. With strong regional roots and allegiance, Webster led the way in showing how diverse patterns of language could be standardized, thus providing the means for creating and disseminating a national culture. Most of the other writers of the first American schoolbooks were also New Englanders; despite their emphasis on national standards, they, too, advanced the virtues of New England in their works.

In the 40 years after the American Revolution, a particularly American kind of academy schooling became the most rapidly developing form of education in the new nation. The various New England academies were especially influential. The Phillips Academy in Andover, Mass., established in 1778, and Phillips Exeter, established three years later in New Hampshire, offered both classical and practical subjects and served as college preparatory schools, although students boarded with local

Science laboratory, Phillips Exeter Academy, ca. 1960

families. In the 19th century, these and other preparatory schools became boarding schools that catered largely to elite families who could afford them. Girls were educated in separate academies. New England was a leader in establishing female preparatory schools, like Sarah Pierce's Litchfield Female Academy (established 1792) in Connecticut. Stressing academic subjects, girls' schools helped to train a new generation of leaders and provided a new occupational role for women as teachers.

NEW ENGLAND EDUCATIONAL REFORM

The New England tradition of educational reform flourished in the 19th century. Among the most important educational reformers were Bronson Alcott and Elizabeth Peabody, who were active participants in the New England–centered Transcendentalist movement. Together with Ralph Waldo Emerson, Henry David Thoreau, Margaret Fuller, and other prominent New England Transcendentalists, these reformers challenged the principles of religious and educational orthodoxy in a way that gave preference to ideas of self-culture (individual transformation rather than collective action) and spiritual awakening. Peabody had started a school in Boston before she became Alcott's assistant at the Temple School, a private school in Boston that Alcott established in 1834 to give expression to his belief in the perfection of children, based on the assumption that they were born with intuitive truth. Margaret Fuller, a teacher for several years before she briefly joined Alcott and Peabody at the Temple School, also shared the Transcendentalist belief in individual perfection and spiritual awakening. Fuller began her famous conversations for women after leaving the Temple School and before the publication of her book

Woman in the Nineteenth Century (1845), in which she espoused greater rights for women. In 1860 Peabody, a close colleague and friend of the reformer Horace Mann, established the first English-speaking kindergarten in the United States. With her sister Mary, who married Horace Mann, Peabody wrote a book advocating the adoption of kindergartens throughout the nation to help children realize their individual potential and to introduce them to the world of learning. Her reforms, like those of Fuller, drew heavily on her teaching background and her involvement with Transcendentalist ideas.

Closely associated with the reform currents sweeping New England in the early 19th century were new ideas about providing special instruction for children with disabilities. The American School for the Deaf, founded in Hartford in 1817 by the Reverend Thomas Hopkins Gallaudet and others, was the nation's first facility for children with special needs; teachers from the school helped establish schools for the deaf in other localities. In 1832 the well-known reformer Dr. Samuel Gridley Howe opened the New England Asylum for the Blind (now Perkins School for the Blind). The first facilities for children with mental retardation opened in New England as well. Physical education and school athletics also got their start in New England: concerned about the adverse effects of industrial conditions on student health and academic performance, the Round Hill School in Northampton and Harvard and Amherst Colleges were the first institutions in the nation to establish physical education programs for youth.

From New England reformers, too, came progressive new ideas about active learning; in particular, the educational philosophy of Francis Wayland Parker and John Dewey deeply influenced the practice of education in schools throughout the nation. Born in New Hampshire, Parker became a teacher and principal in that state before studying in Germany in the 1870s, where he became familiar with the innovations of Friedrich Froebel, Johann H. Pestalozzi, and others. As superintendent of schools in Quincy, Mass., supervisor of the Boston school system, and principal of the Cook County Normal School in Chicago, Parker developed new approaches to the education of children. His ideas about active learning, individualized curricula, and child-centered instruction greatly influenced Dewey, who considered Parker the father of progressive education. While the mature formulations of each man's educational philosophy were elaborated at the Cook County Normal School and at Dewey's Laboratory Schools in Chicago, both reformers spent formative years in New England—Parker in New Hampshire and Dewey in Burlington, Vt., where he attended public schools and the University of Vermont and taught school.

Dewey's great theme—that school as a whole must be related to "life as a whole"—sprang in part from his childhood experiences and the nature of the community he found in New England. His ideas became the touchstone of a movement for progressive, experimental education not only in the United States but also throughout the world, influencing the open- and free-school movements of the 1960s and 1970s and such contemporary approaches as community-based curricula, cooperative teaching, environmentalism, global teaching, and many others. Even during times of conservative reaction, Dewey's educational thought continued to influence debate.

THE COMMON-SCHOOL MOVEMENT

Although the effort to develop tax-supported universal public education took place throughout the nation, Massachusetts was more closely associated with the common-school movement than any other state. Horace Mann, first secretary of the Massachusetts Board of Education, is widely recognized as the movement's most important leader. A lawyer who had been active in a wide variety of reform causes, including abolition, temperance, prison reform, and the improved treatment of the mentally ill, Mann came to believe that the reform of schooling was the "preventive" that could bring about needed change in every other arena. Concerned about the poor quality of facilities, irregular enrollments, and the substandard, haphazard instruction that characterized most 19th-century district schooling, Mann believed that a national system of graded, coordinated public schools could create an educated citizenry and assure the future of democracy. Henry Barnard, who was secretary to Connecticut's and then Rhode Island's Board of Commissioners before becoming the first U.S. commissioner of education, shared Mann's concern about children of the "manufacturing population" who were replacing the families from the "country homes of New England." Both men believed that common schools offered the opportunity to educate the two populations alongside each other, instilling the discipline, skills, and values needed by the new society.

The establishment of classes that were not divided by grade level and of intermediate schools intended primarily for immigrant youth indicated the contradiction between the rhetoric of common schools and their reality. By the end of the century, classrooms designated specifically for immigrant youth, the poor, and African Americans (who did not go to school with whites) routinely separated urban students—deemed "different" by means of class, racial, or linguistic background and social behavior—from wealthier, usually native-born, children. Catholics, especially Irish immigrants, often rejected the nonsectarian but clearly Protestant-based common schools, preferring parochial schools. Moreover, the bureaucratization of urban school systems, developing piecemeal in different areas but nearly complete by the third quarter of the century, resulted in rigid, largely inflexible administrations that left little room for students' individual development. Although it thus fell short of its goal of inclusion and opportunity for all, the common-school ideal of free public education remained a beacon for generations of reformers.

The establishment of public high schools became a critical component of the common-school crusade. Here, too, New England led the nation. English High School, the first American high school, was established in Boston in 1821 as a complement to its Latin school. While publicly supported Latin schools were presumed to prepare students for college, the new high school offered more advanced training to boys entering the practical trades. It was also an alternative to the many tuition-based private academies that flourished at the time. In 1827 Massachusetts passed a law requiring towns of 500 persons to establish high schools teaching U.S. history, surveying, algebra, bookkeeping, and geometry; towns of 4,000 or more had to add classics. Although the law was often ignored, for more than half a century Massachusetts remained the only state to require towns to establish high schools. By 1865, 70 percent of the state's population lived in towns with public high schools.

Fewer girls than boys attended common schools, especially high schools, although the number of female students increased substantially over the course of the 19th century. The employment of women as teachers also increased. By the mid-19th century, the movement of women teachers from colonial dame schools and early academies to public schools had greatly expanded opportunities for women. Massachusetts was the first state to promote the employment of women as public school teachers, a pattern that soon would become dominant in the region. In Massachusetts, slightly more than 50 percent of teachers were female in the early 1830s, but by 1860, women constituted almost 80 percent of the state's teachers. Over the course of the 19th century, it is estimated that perhaps 25 percent of all Massachusetts women taught at some time in their lives.

Teaching had become women's work ideologically as well as statistically, with educators arguing that the best teachers exhibited so-called female qualities. The first prominent advocate for the feminization of teaching was Catharine Beecher, daughter of prominent Congregationalist minister Lyman Beecher. Catharine Beecher, who was the first to envision teaching as a respectable and influential "profession" belonging exclusively to women, attended Sarah Pierce's Litchfield school. In 1823 she and her sister Mary established the Hartford Female Seminary. One of the few institutions that educated women beyond the elementary level, the seminary offered a curriculum parallel to that of men's colleges.

Other women teachers from New England founded institutions to educate female students. Most significant was the achievement of two teachers from the hill country of western Massachusetts, Zilpah Grant and Mary Lyon, who raised sufficient funding to charter the first fully endowed institution of higher education for young women, Mount Holyoke Seminary, which opened in 1837. For these founders, Mount Holyoke embodied a national rather than a local cause, and indeed, its success in educating young women at the collegiate level would inspire the creation of colleges for women after the Civil War. Mount Holyoke graduates founded 10 "daughter" schools and colleges, including Mills College in California, as well as seminaries in Africa and Asia. Many of the students who came to Mount Holyoke represented a newer class of students who sought higher education for vocational reasons, rather than for character training or for education in the humanities. This extension of advanced schooling to young women in lower-income brackets offers one example of the expansion of access and opportunity that would come to characterize New England education. As a consequence of the rapid expansion of women into the teaching profession and the growth of the profession as a whole, states created academies to standardize and professionalize teacher training. Massachusetts established the first government-funded normal school in 1839 in Lexington, Mass.

VOCATIONAL, ADULT, AND INFORMAL EDUCATION

Several mechanics' institutes were established in New England in the 19th century. Worcester Polytechnic Institute was opened in 1865; a number of high schools added manual and vocational courses by 1890. Agriculture and the mechanic arts were given collegiate status with the establishment of the region's land-grant colleges promoted by the Morrill Act of 1862. In 1906 Massachusetts became the first state to establish a Commission for Industrial Education.

Institutions other than schools began to play increasingly important roles in educating Americans during the early 19th century. Given the abundance of educational-reform ideas in New England, it is not surprising that the region pioneered in developing education outside the classroom. Lyceums and libraries were two of the most important forms of popular education directed to non-school-going adults. Founded by Yale graduate Josiah Holbrook, the lyceum movement encouraged the public discussion of ideas and, in Holbrook's words, furthered "useful knowledge" among adults through the sponsorship of lectures, debates, demonstrations, entertainments, and performances. Holbrook established the first lyceum in Massachusetts in 1826 and traveled tirelessly to promote his idea; in less than a decade, the movement had spread to more than 3,000 communities across the nation. It was widely reported, for example, that the "mill girls" of Lowell, Mass., flocked to hear lyceum lecturers and other speakers. (So enthusiastic were these working women about "self-improvement" that owners had to post signs along the lines of "No reading in the mills.") In addition to promulgating lectures and other events, lyceums established circulating libraries, collected historical and scientific materials, and participated in educational reform of the common schools. With many of the movement's most popular speakers—including Ralph Waldo Emerson and Henry Ward Beecher—coming from New England, lyceums were instrumental in establishing a national culture that recognized regional distinction.

The rapid proliferation of public libraries in the early 19th century paralleled the lyceum movement. Here, too, New England was at the forefront in advancing popular education for adults. The Boston Apprentice's Library was formed in 1820, and in 1849 New Hampshire passed the first law establishing libraries on a statewide basis. The first national library organization was established a quarter of a century later, when Melvil Dewey, the librarian at Amherst College in Massachusetts and creator of the Dewey decimal system, organized a meeting of librarians as part of the Centennial Exhibition of 1876. The meeting resulted in the creation of the American Library Association, headed by Justin Winsor, a Boston librarian.

The American Antiquarian Society, both a learned society and an independent research library, was founded in 1812 in Worcester, Mass. The society houses the largest collection of printed materials on early U.S. history, with an emphasis on New England.

HIGHER EDUCATION

Patterns of education in New England affected the development of higher education in other regions. Graduates of these colleges founded many new institutions in the West and South; Yale, for example, became known as the "mother of colleges" because of the proliferation of colleges its graduates created. This influence extended to governance as well as curriculum. The Dartmouth case was particularly important in the early part of the 19th century. As state governments increasingly sought control over private collegiate institutions, Dartmouth College took to the courts to prevent New Hampshire's legislature from transforming the college into a state institution. Dartmouth lost in the state courts, but with Daniel Webster defending the rights of the college in *Dartmouth College v. Woodward* (1819), the Supreme Court ruled in Dartmouth's favor. Putting into place the principle that higher education was outside governmental control, the Dartmouth College decision was crucial in the development of higher education in the United States, leading to the founding of many private and denominational colleges throughout the country and guaranteeing the perpetuity of private endowments. Since states could no longer change charters and transform old establishments, the decision also fostered the creation of new state universities.

Curricular developments at New England's major universities set trends throughout the nation. The Yale Report of 1828, which declared that a collegiate education should "lay the foundation for a superior education" through the traditional classical curriculum based on Latin and Greek, established the pattern for much liberal arts education until the end of the century. By 1850, Brown University had developed a more "practical" model, including industrial and business courses and an elective system. Another major challenge to the traditional curriculum came in 1869 from the newly installed president of Harvard, Charles Eliot. Eliot, the Beacon Hill–born son of a Boston mayor and congressman, had taught at Harvard and the Massachusetts Institute of Technology (MIT). His model of "New Education" championed an elective system based on specialized useful knowledge that was grounded in studies of pure and applied science, mathematics, and living European (rather than classical) languages. Under Eliot's 40-year tenure, Harvard's courses of instruction and faculty increased more than fivefold and each student was allowed to develop a personal program. Although his more conservative successor, A. Lawrence Lowell, replaced Eliot's open elective system with a system of concentration and distribution, his reforms had a lasting impact on American higher education.

The platform that Eliot enjoyed as president of the nation's most prestigious university allowed him to influence education at all levels throughout the country: as chair of the National Education Association's Committee of Ten, Harvard's president helped redirect the curricula and policies of the nation's secondary schools. In this position, Eliot also helped create the College Entrance Examination Board, which established a national system of entrance exams for the nation's colleges.

Other significant developments in the region's landscape of higher education came in response to the changing needs of an increasingly industrialized society. Founded in 1861 to prepare students for careers in engineering and the natural sciences, MIT quickly occupied the scientific and technological vanguard in research as well as teaching endeavors. Embracing rather than shunning industry, the institution's earliest academic and administrative leaders encouraged an entrepreneurial model that tacitly approved of faculty and staff involvement with industry; by the 1920s, an unusually close relationship between the university and industrial groups had arisen. Interactions among MIT, the industrial sector, and the government grew more complex during World War II as the university pioneered major technological efforts directed toward securing an Allied victory—such as computer research, defense systems, and systems analysis. By the end of the war, MIT was firmly established as a leading national resource for the creation of scientific knowledge and problem solving.

That MIT has bridged the boundary between university and industry has had a major impact on the culture and economy of the region. Collaboration between MIT classrooms and laboratories, on one hand, and local industrial firms (many of them founded by alumni, faculty, or students), on the other, have led to exchanges of ideas, resource sharing, and the building of networks that have contributed to the region's economic and cultural leadership. The close connection between MIT and industry helped to spawn "America's technology highway," Route 128 in Massachusetts. While MIT set the pattern of industrial-academic partnerships that promoted the technology industry in the Greater Boston area, other local institutions—including Northeastern University, Wentworth Institute, Boston University, Tufts University, Harvard University, and Brandeis University—also formed productive relationships with industrial and biotechnical firms, furnishing industry with scientists, technicians, and engineers, and a constant stream of new scientific and technological ideas. Because of the close connection between the intellectual power of its universities and the development of leading-edge technology, Boston is considered one of several "cities of intellect" or "science regions" in the nation.

While New England's research universities played a vital role in shaping the region's intellectual climate and molding its wide social influence, other collegiate institutions contributed to New England's distinctive cultural climate. In Massachusetts, for example, Northeastern University emphasized the complementary relationship between classroom study and out-of-school experience. Growing out of the Boston YMCA, which sponsored an Evening Institute, Evening Law School, and other programs to serve nontraditional students, Northeastern was chartered as a college connected to the Boston YMCA before becoming an independent institution in 1948. Other institutions of higher education for nontraditional or special students include the Berklee College of Music, the Massachusetts College of Art (both in Boston), and the Rhode Island School of Design in Providence.

Though historically overshadowed by the vigorous and well-supported tradition of private education in New England, public institutions of higher education, including six land-grant colleges and more than 80 junior colleges, teachers colleges, mechanics' institutes, and other types of state institutions, have educated a variety of distinct nonelite populations. The University of Vermont, chartered in 1791, was one of the nation's first state institutions; the others were founded in the late 19th century as a consequence of the Morrill Act, which established funding for land-grant colleges (the idea was developed by Vermont storekeeper Justin Morrill). The breadth and sophistication of public institutions' offerings have steadily increased, yet the politics of funding research and teaching in the region has been complicated by the status, influence, networks, and traditions of private colleges and universities; in New England, private institutions educate almost half of all postsecondary students, compared to little more than one-fifth elsewhere.

Opportunities for women in higher education expanded in new directions with the founding of Wellesley (1870) and Smith (1871) Colleges, the chartering of Mount Holyoke as a college (1888), and the opening of the Radcliffe Annex (1894). With these four of the "Seven Sister" colleges located in New England, the region's commitment to the highest-quality liberal arts education for women was clear; each of these institutions promoted excellence in education and became a national institution. In addition to their advanced curricula, the women's colleges provided a community of women professors and support for women students. Other women's institutions would follow, among them Catholic colleges for women, but most of the growth in women's education came through coeducation. In 1873 Boston University became the first university in New England to grant degrees to women. From their founding in the late 19th century, all of the state universities admitted women on an equal basis with men. Pembroke, affiliated with Brown University, was, like Radcliffe, a coordinate institution, as was Tufts's Jackson College and another coordinate female college at Clark. All of these eventually merged with their male affiliates, leaving the liberal arts women's colleges and a few remaining Catholic colleges as the sole women-only schools in the region. The trend toward coeducation accelerated in the late 1960s and early 1970s when Yale and Dartmouth joined other Ivy League universities in admitting women. In the 1970s and 1980s, several of the remaining women's schools in the region, including Wheaton and Emmanuel, opened their doors to men, a trend that continues: Leslie University in Cambridge will admit men starting in 2005.

New England's traditional liberal arts colleges continued to thrive in the 20th and 21st centuries. Relatively small, highly selective residential schools like Amherst, Bates, Bowdoin, Colby, Connecticut College, Middlebury, Mount Holyoke, Smith, Trinity, Wellesley, Wesleyan, and Williams remain dedicated to liberal culture and undergraduate life, encouraging individuality and self-discovery. Yet these institutions, whose bucolic image historically framed and modeled national ideals of undergraduate education, have adapted to and helped to establish new currents of academic life. Many offer innovative curricula—including opportunities for interdisciplinary studies, research, and internships in government, industry, the arts, and the sciences—as well as a lively, increasingly networked and connected undergraduate campus life. The region also boasts other, newer colleges that have been pioneers in less structured, more experimental collegiate education, including Bennington, Hampshire, the College of the Atlantic, and Simon's Rock College of Bard.

Throughout their history, New Englanders have grappled in a variety of ways with issues of racial, religious, sex, and class-based exclusion at all levels of schooling.

Only after the Civil War, for example, did the first of a small number of African Americans graduate from Harvard College and several of its graduate and professional divisions. The numbers of African Americans at Harvard, Yale, and other elite northeastern schools expanded slowly over the next century. While these students acknowledged that many positive advantages accrued from their Ivy League educations, many encountered Ivy League racism as well. Since the Civil Rights era, African Americans, Hispanic Americans, Asian Americans, and members of other racial minorities have been welcomed at these and most other area institutions. Problems of equity for students and faculty nonetheless remain.

The increasing access of minority students to New England schools follows the pattern of diversification that has characterized the region's colleges and professional schools. Students of different religious faiths found places in New England schools as well. By the turn of the century, immigrant Catholics and Jews increasingly came to challenge the kind of "academic nativism" that had been reflected in several centuries of admissions policies practiced by Harvard, Yale, and the other elite schools. Nonetheless, both Harvard and Yale instituted quotas for Jews (and perhaps Catholics as well) from the 1920s through the late 1940s. The selective admissions policies practiced by school officials (also reflected in the very small number of racial minorities admitted) found ready congruence in the exclusionary social practices of many campus student groups. The breaking down of formal and informal barriers to admission of Jews and other minorities after World War II pointed to a major shift in enrollment priorities and to a much more diversified student body, trends that would heighten in the last decades of the 20th century and the beginning of the 21st century as a consequence of the Civil Rights movement. Today, elite colleges and many other New England institutions actively recruit men and women of different races, religions, sexual orientations, and political and cultural backgrounds.

THE PROBLEM OF PLURALISM IN NEW ENGLAND PUBLIC SCHOOLS

Conflicts over racial segregation in Boston schools became bitter in the 1970s when Judge Arthur Garrity, to counteract the city's "dual" system of schooling for blacks and whites, put into effect a plan to desegregate Boston's public schools. Led by the Boston School Committee and supported by local antibusing groups, the opposition to the court-ordered plan was so intense that Boston became known in some quarters as the "Little Rock of the North." Protests against the plan sprang in good part from political considerations that were local and particular and which represented clashes over ethnic and communitarian values in the city. Other cities in New England took vastly differently approaches to the problem of desegregation (inner-city schools in Connecticut, for example, relied on voluntary efforts), but Boston captured nationwide attention both because of the strength of its initial resistance to the "forced-busing" plan imposed by the court, and because the city's complex reactions to the issue reflected those of many other communities. Although the goals of integration were never fully achieved, Boston did make substantial progress in providing

Elementary school children, Boston, 1992

equal educational opportunities to students of different races. Like other New England communities, it continues to struggle with questions of equal opportunity, parental choice, and race.

The predominance of the Puritan heritage within New England culture had several consequences for religious education in the region. The establishment of both Catholic and Jewish schools came relatively late: the first Catholic school was founded in Boston only in 1844, a response of Irish immigrants to the Protestant character of public schools. The number of parochial schools rose slowly, although each school enrolled an ever-larger number of students; eventually each parish was required to have its own school. Catholics' struggles to maintain their own schools often affected political life, as when, in the late 19th century, the Massachusetts Republican Party sponsored legislation to ban private schools that did not instruct in English. The anti-Catholic, nativist sentiment that drove such legislation was aimed at Catholic schools started by French Canadians who taught in their native tongue. The resulting school wars brought many immigrant New Englanders solidly into the Democratic camp. Tensions concerning Catholic-only enrollment policies, coupled with the increasing size of the Catholic population in the United States (largely because of immigration), led to the establishment of a sizable number of Catholic colleges by the mid-19th century. Among the most important were Holy Cross and Boston College in Massachusetts and Saint Anselm College in New Hampshire. Today New England is home to numerous other Catholic institutions, including Emmanuel and Regis Colleges.

The history of Jewish education in New England is also comparatively short but took place in a variety of settings, including individual homes, storefront classrooms, synagogues, and schools of diverse nature. The arrival of large numbers of immigrant

Jews at the end of the 19th century led to the establishment of many *cheders* (one-room Jewish schoolhouses) and Talmud Torahs (more highly organized schools). Second-generation Jews often attended synagogue-based Sunday schools and supplementary Hebrew schools. Immigrant children were also trained in manual and technical skills at Hebrew industrial schools, like those created by reform-minded teachers in Boston's North and West Ends for Jewish girls and boys, respectively. Founded in 1937, the Maimonides School in Brookline, Mass., became the first independent Jewish day school in New England; today there are more than a dozen such schools. The communal nature of Jewish education in the region is suggested by the development in the early 20th century of such organizations as the Associated Boston Hebrew Schools, the Hebrew Teachers Training School, and the Bureau of Jewish Education, a central agency of Jewish education in the Boston metropolitan region which has counterparts in Providence and several other New England cities. Hebrew College, founded in Massachusetts in 1921 to offer education in Hebrew literature, laws, and education, trained many Hebrew educators who set up schools and institutions throughout Boston, New England, and the nation. The nonsectarian Jewish-sponsored Brandeis University, founded in 1948, established one of the nation's first and most distinguished departments of Near Eastern and Judaic studies, which has also trained secular and rabbinic educators whose influence is felt across the country.

New England has continued to be a center of reform and innovation where ideas of educational change and improvement are tested, elaborated, and revised. Throughout the 20th century, following the tradition of Alcott, Peabody, Howe, Parker, Dewey, and Mann, New Englanders pioneered reforms that influenced schooling in other parts of the country. In the 1980s, for example, Theodore Sizer, one of the most influential school reformers of the contemporary period, established the Coalition of Essential Schools, a high school and university partnership headquartered at Brown University, which developed a variety of dynamic strategies to revitalize teaching and learning through collaborations among students, teachers, parents, and administrators.

Today, New England's schools, colleges, and universities are among its most important assets. Stewards of culture and at the same time agents of social transformation, New England's educational institutions continue to preserve the best and most workable traditions of the past while they attempt to accommodate changing circumstances. At the start of the 21st century, the landscape of education remains dotted with controversies about the best ways of making schools and teachers accountable, diversifying student and teacher populations, and constructing effective approaches to teach children, youth, and nontraditional students of all ages. As other regions have begun to attract growing proportions of postsecondary students as well as significant research and development support, concerns about the erosion of the region's historical leadership in higher education have begun to be heard. Yet new opportunities have also emerged, as in, for example, the steadily increasing number of foreign students who study at New England's colleges and universities, and the related phenomenon represented by the internationalization of many aspects of higher education. The challenge for New England is to continue to adapt to the new global responsibilities of America's leadership role and to the needs of the region's ever-changing populations. While building on the region's distinctive legacies, educational leaders, allied with citizens and students, must also offer fresh perspectives on learning and teaching at all levels. The kaleidoscope of educational programs and institutions in the region, coupled with their powerful presence in the cultural life of the region as a whole, suggests that New England will remain a major source of educational innovation and influence.

David F. Allmendinger, Jr., "Mount Holyoke Students Encounter the Need for Life-Planning, 1837–1850," *History of Education Quarterly* 19 (1979); Allmendinger, Jr., *Paupers and Scholars: The Transformation of Student Life in 19th-Century New England* (1975); Bernard Bailyn, *Education in the Forming of American Society: Needs and Opportunities for Study* (1960); Robert L. Church and Michael W. Sedlak, *Education in the United States: An Interpretive History* (1976); Lawrence A. Cremin, *American Education: The Colonial Experience, 1607–1783* (1970); Cremin, *American Education: The National Experience, 1783–1876* (1980); Ronald P. Formisano, *Boston against Busing: Race, Class, and Ethnicity in the 1960s and 1970s* (1991); Roger L. Geiger, *To Advance Knowledge: The Growth of American Research Universities, 1900–1940* (1986); David D. Hall, *Worlds of Wonder, Days of Judgment: Popular Religious Belief in Early New England* (1989); Helen Lefkowitz Horowitz, *Alma Mater: Design and Experience in the Women's Colleges from Their 19th-Century Beginnings to the 1930s,* 2d ed. (1993); Carl F. Kaestle, *Pillars of the Republic: Common Schools and American Society, 1780–1860* (1983); Michael B. Katz, *Class, Bureaucracy and Schools: The Illusion of Educational Change in America* (1975); Katz, *The Irony of Early School Reform: Educational Innovation in Mid-19th-Century Massachusetts* (2001); Marvin Lazerson, *Origins of the Urban School: Public Education in Massachusetts, 1870–1915* (1971); Kenneth A. Lockridge, *Literacy in Colonial New England: An Enquiry into the Social Context of Literacy in the Early Modern West* (1974); Rebecca S. Lowen, *Creating the Cold War University: The Transformation of Stanford* (1997); Robert Middlekauff, *Ancients and Axioms: Secondary Education in 18th-Century New England* (1963); Dan A. Oren, *Joining the Club: A History of Jews and Yale,* 2d ed. (2001); Robert L. Osgood, "Undermining the Common School Ideal: Intermediate Schools and Ungraded Classes in Boston, 1838–1900," *History of Education Quarterly* 37 (1997); Joel Perlmann, Silvana R. Siddali, and Keith Whitescarver, "Literacy, Schooling, and Teaching among New England Women," *History of Education Quarterly* 37 (1997); Joseph Reimer, "Passionate Visions in Contest: On the History of Jewish Education in Boston," in *The Jews of Boston: Essays on the Occasion of the Centenary (1895–1995) of the Combined Jewish Philanthropies of Greater Boston,* ed. Jonathan D. Sarna and Ellen Smith (1995); Walter Herbert Small, *Early New England Schools* (1969 [1914]); Werner Sollors, Caldwell Titcomb, and Thomas A. Underwood, eds., *Blacks at Harvard: A Documentary History of African-American Experience at Harvard and Radcliffe* (1993); Barbara Miller Solomon, *In the Company of Educated Women: A History of Women and Higher Education in America* (1985); Marcia Graham Synott, *The Half-Opened Door: Discrimination and Admissions at Harvard, Yale, and Princeton, 1900–1970* (1979); Jon Teaford, "The Transformation of Massachusetts Education, 1670–1780," *History of Education Quarterly* 10 (1970); David Tyack and Elisabeth Hansot, *Managers of Virtue: Public School Leadership in America, 1820–1980* (1982); Maris A. Vinovskis, "Trends in Massachusetts Education, 1826–1860," *History of Education Quarterly* 12 (1972).

Joyce Antler

American Antiquarian Society

The American Antiquarian Society (AAS), both a learned society and an independent research library located in Worcester, Mass., is widely considered to be one of the preeminent repositories for all aspects of American history and culture through 1876 (and, for some aspects of New England history, a bit beyond). Although its membership, constituency, and reputation are national—even international —in scope, the society remains closely connected with the region in which it was established. Its library provides extraordinary resources for research on New England history (and the history of the New England diaspora into the Old Northwest and beyond) within the society's collecting period. With holdings numbering close to 3 million books, pamphlets, broadsides, manuscripts, prints, maps, and newspapers, the society preserves the largest single collection of printed source material relating to the history, literature, and culture of the United States from 1620 to 1870. The availability of this material signifies the importance of print culture in New England from the earliest times and contributes to an emphasis on New England within scholarship on American life to 1870.

Founded in 1812 by the patriot printer-publisher Isaiah Thomas (1749–1831), AAS was the third historical organization in the country (after the Massachusetts Historical Society, 1791, and the New-York Historical Society, 1804) but the first to assume collecting responsibilities continentally. The printed collections are focused on print materials produced before 1877 anywhere in the present-day United States and other former British possessions of the Americas, in addition to modern secondary and reference works (including local histories and genealogies). The manuscript collections are more regional in focus. They are particularly strong in papers of Puritan divines, personal correspondence and diaries of individuals and families in central New England, and materials documenting the history of the book trades, nationally as well as regionally. The strength of the collections lies in their comprehensiveness. AAS has collected not only fine first editions of canonical authors and the papers of the most distinguished individuals of the past, but also print material and manuscripts reflective of all levels of society and forms of cultural production. Accordingly, the society's collections have helped fuel scholarly trends in social and cultural history toward telling, for example, the stories of women, not just men; of blacks, not just whites; of laborers, not just bosses; of readers, not just authors and publishers.

More than 400 scholars supported by a visiting research fellowship program established in 1972 have produced hundreds of important books and articles, many of them, not surprisingly, on aspects of New England's history. The society's publications and public programs have also helped enrich the study of the region. Membership in AAS is elective; the ranks include distinguished scholars, collectors, and civic and historically minded people, including business and professional leaders. The library is not just for members, but is open, free of charge, to experienced researchers working on specific projects that require use of the collections.

The society's dual role as a regional and a national institution brings both tensions and opportunities. While proud of the strength of its holdings of New England material in all genres, the society reminds potential constituents that it is also rich in collections relating to the rest of the country. Of all members since 1812, just about half were New Englanders; the present proportion is about 46 percent (the rest are scattered throughout the country and abroad). Members residing in the region have contributed more than their share in helping govern AAS and in supporting the society financially.

The AAS collections cannot document what New England has become in the 20th century. Limiting coverage to the period before 1876, however, has added strength to strength, fostering collections that are uncommonly useful to researchers, containing vast materials to document the experience of such groups as Native Americans, African Americans, Irish, and French Canadians, along with the "Yankees," in building New England.

American Antiquarian Society, *A Society's Chief Joys* (1969); Nancy H. Burkett and John B. Hench, eds., *Under Its Generous Dome: The Collections and Programs of the American Antiquarian Society* (1992); John B. Hench, ed., "Serendipity and Synergy: Collection Development, Access, and Research Opportunities at the American Antiquarian Society in the McCorison Era," *Proceedings of the American Antiquarian Society* 102, pt. 2 (1992); Walter Muir Whitehill, chap. 3, *Independent Historical Societies* (1962).

John B. Hench

American School for the Deaf

The first permanent educational institution for deaf pupils in the United States, the Connecticut Asylum for the Education and Instruction of Deaf and Dumb Persons opened in Hartford in 1817; it was renamed the American School for the Deaf (ASD) in 1822 when it expanded to add vocational training. ASD established patterns that distinguished American deaf pedagogy for half a century, including use of sign language for instruction, residential placement of deaf children, acceptance of indigent pupils, government financial support, vocational training, and employment of deaf teachers. American Sign Language evolved at ASD from the French Sign Language introduced by deaf Frenchman Laurent Clerc, one of the school's founders. In 1847 ASD's instructors initiated the *American Annals of the Deaf,* the oldest surviving American educational journal. ASD's alumni created the first organization of deaf Americans, the New England Gallaudet Association of Deaf-Mutes; in 1854 this group established the principle that deaf organizations in the United States would be led by deaf people.

Parental concern and evangelical millenarianism provided the impetus for ASD's establishment. Mason Fitch Cogswell, father of a deaf child and a prominent Hartford physician, drew together a group of politicians, merchants, and ministers to incorporate the school in 1816. Influenced by the Second Great Awakening, Hartford's elite accepted the arguments of the Reverend Thomas Hopkins Gallaudet, Cogswell's neighbor and ASD's first principal, that New England's upper class bore a responsibility to enlighten deaf people with religious truth and thus prepare them for the millennium: "Every charitable effort, conducted upon Christian principles," Gallaudet said at the school's opening, "forms a part of the great system of doing good, and looks forward to that delightful day when the earth shall be filled with righteousness, and peace, and joy in the Holy Ghost."

Gallaudet, Cogswell, and ASD's directors intended the school to be a regional, if not national, institution. Fundraising and recruiting efforts by Gallaudet and Clerc in 1816 and 1817 took them throughout New England, New York, and New Jersey; they received private donations from all these areas. Connecticut awarded its first annual grant to the school in 1819, and Congress awarded the school the first federal land grant in 1820. By 1845 all New England states had authorized support for their indigent deaf children at ASD. In return, commissioners from each state served as ex officio directors of the institution. By 1822 ASD had enrolled pupils from every New England state.

ASD's regional character began to decline when its monopoly on publicly supported deaf education in New England ended. In 1867 Massachusetts decided to fund deaf pupils at either ASD or the newly opened Clarke School for the Deaf in Northampton. Clarke based its instruction on speech and lipreading rather than sign language, thus challenging the system that ASD had pioneered and which had been copied by all American schools for deaf pupils before 1867. Other New England states soon followed Massachusetts's example, either authorizing their deaf stu-

American School for the Deaf, West Hartford, Conn., 2002

dents to attend private in-state schools or building their own publicly supported institutions. As the popularity of speech and lipreading spread and more options became available to New England's deaf students in the late 19th century, ASD's regional influence and importance waned. ASD nevertheless bequeathed an educational and cultural heritage that has made America's deaf community the most independent and powerful in the world. Today, ASD is located in West Hartford and enrolls more than 200 day and residential deaf students.

Jack R. Gannon, *Deaf Heritage: A Narrative History of Deaf America* (1981); Harlan L. Lane, *When the Mind Hears: A History of the Deaf* (1984); John Vickrey Van Cleve and Barry A. Crouch, *A Place of Their Own: Creating the Deaf Community in America* (1989).
John Vickrey Van Cleve

Athletics and Physical Education

In the 1800s Boston thought of itself as "the Athens of America." An early leader in education, it spread its influence across New England, then across the growing nation. The region likewise became the birthplace of physical education and organized school sports in the United States. The Round Hill School in Northampton, Mass., introduced the first significant physical education program in 1823, and the first intercollegiate sports event was a rowing match between Harvard and Yale in 1852.

The development of physical education programs was an outgrowth of the region's—and the nation's—urbanization. As cities grew, becoming crowded and unsanitary, people worked long hours in dimly lit, poorly ventilated factories and offices. Public health suffered. City children were noticeably less healthy than rural children and as a result were poorer students. Physical activity programs were initially designed to improve student health and thereby improve academic performance. This movement took hold before the Civil War, during a period of rising interest in public health.

Early school exercise programs were based on similar programs in European schools. The most popular athletic activity of the early 1800s was German gymnastics, based on the teachings of Friedrich Jahn. Three German immigrants—Charles Beck, who taught at the Round Hill School, and Charles Follen and Francis Lieber, who taught at Harvard—brought the activity to Massachusetts in the 1820s and soon made Boston the focal point for gymnastics in America.

The Round Hill School recognized the importance of physical activity in the curriculum and became the first American school to hire a teacher specifically for physical education. The program included dancing, gymnastics, baseball, wrestling, long hikes, riding, and running. Beck, who taught Latin and gymnastics at Round Hill from 1825 to 1830, developed the first outdoor school gymnasium as well as the nation's first school gymnastics program. By 1833 Boston's public schools required daily exercise of all students.

Follen, assisted by Beck, opened the first college gymnasium, furnished with equipment for German gymnastics, at Harvard in 1826, followed by an outdoor public gymna-sium in Boston the same year. In 1827 Lieber opened the first public swimming pool under the control of the Boston gymnasium. In 1832 John Warren, a Harvard professor of anatomy, published *The Importance of Physical Education*, the first American work on the topic. Colleges began to provide gymnasiums and other facilities for physical activity, primarily in response to student demand rather than administrative interest in the value of exercise. In short, athletic facilities were tools for student recruitment. Many New England schools imitated Harvard's German gymnasium model and generally demonstrated a growing interest in physical activity and health.

In 1861 Amherst became the first college to recognize the full value of physical education in the curriculum. The college hired Dr. Edward Hitchcock, a graduate of Harvard's medical school, as a professor of hygiene and physical education, the first such recognized position in the United States. Hitchcock's program began as German gymnastics but was later modified to light gymnastics, employing lightweight hand apparatus and exercising to music. Hitchcock also started one of the nation's first intramural school sports programs.

The region's first women's colleges included physical activity as an important part of their programs. At Hartford Female Seminary, founded in 1823 by Catharine Beecher, 30 minutes of daily exercise was required, and other physical activities were encouraged. The Female Monitorial School in Boston required exercise starting in 1825, while after 1837 Mount Holyoke Seminary required daily calisthenics. These programs had to deal with public concern about the "female" image—particularly whether such physical activity was appropriate for ladies.

Two early influential teacher-training programs for physical education began in New England. Dio Lewis started the Normal Institute for Physical Education in Boston in 1861; this 10-week course was the first of its kind in the United States. In 1881 Dudley Sargent of Harvard University founded the Sanatory Gymnasium, later the Sargent School for Physical Education, which eventually merged with Boston University. In 1887 Sargent began the influential Harvard Summer Session to train physical-education teachers.

In 1889 Mary Hemenway, assisted by Amy Morris Homans, organized the Boston Conference to discuss gymnastics systems. Many prominent leaders of physical education spoke on the German, Swedish, and Sargent systems. Although there was little interest in sports and games other than gymnastics, this conference was the first to bring experts together to discuss which system of physical education might be best for Americans.

In 1892 George Fitz, a doctor who taught in Harvard's short-lived baccalaureate program in physical education (1891–99), founded the first American physical-education research laboratory. Harvard's program awarded the first degree in physical education, earned by James F. Jones in 1893.

Although the dominant early influence on American physical education was German, the English universities of Oxford and Cambridge were the models for organized school sports. Sporting activity was present at every level from the earliest years at New England colleges; students used games to vent their energy and break up the monotony of the academic routine. The earliest teams were organized and directed by students; school officials usually ignored these activities, occasionally banning any game that was considered dangerous or that interfered with academics.

Yale introduced rowing to the region in 1843, followed by Harvard in 1844. Other schools followed suit, then ventured into other sports. The first intercollegiate baseball game took place in 1859 between Amherst and Williams Colleges. The 1864 Yale crew was the first to hire a professional coach. By 1875 intercollegiate contests were held in baseball, cricket, football, and track and field as well as rowing. New England continued its leadership in sports when basketball was invented in 1891 at the YMCA Training School (now Springfield College). Women adopted the new game so enthusiastically that in some parts of the country basketball was considered exclusively a women's sport until World War I.

During the second half of the 19th century, secondary schools developed teams in imitation of college sports, often competing against college teams. Eventually athletic associations and conferences were formed at both the collegiate and secondary-school levels to organize and regulate competition. By the 1920s most high school and college sports were regulated by national sports organizations.

Although fewer than two dozen colleges had teams in 1875, the popularity of collegiate sports increased rapidly, in part because they reflected the interests and values of leading businessmen who often gave financial support as alumni. Many of the problems common to college sports—such as professionalism and excessive outside influence, especially by alumni—date from this era, when school authorities avoided any official role in sports. By the late 19th century football was the most popular school sport and was so influential that the problems associated with the game led colleges to regulate athletics and eliminate harmful outside influences.

In the early 21st century, only minor regional differences in physical education and school athletics remain. Every school sport follows a national rulebook, and regional differences in the popularity of various sports result primarily from differences in climate. The current homogeneity notwithstanding, the tradition of physical education and school athletics in the United States has its roots in 19th-century New England.

John Rickards Betts, *America's Sporting Heritage, 1850–1950* (1974); Ellen Gerber, *Innovators and Institutions in Physical Education* (1971); Stephen Hardy, *How Boston Played: Sport, Recreation, and Community, 1865–1915* (1982); John Krout, *Annals of American Sport* (1929); Benjamin G. Rader, *American Sports: From the Age of Folk Games to the Age of Televised Sports* (1996); Ronald A. Smith, *Sports and Freedom: The Rise of Big-Time College Athletics* (1988); Richard Swanson and Betty Spears, *History of Sport and Physical Education in the United States* (1995).

William H. Freeman

Barnard, Henry (1811–1900) Education reformer and author. Henry Barnard was born in Hartford, where he spent his formative years and resided for most of his life. As a reformer and the country's first commissioner of education, he devoted his professional energies to establishing common schools open to both male and female students from all societal classes.

Barnard attended Hartford schools and the Monson Academy in Massachusetts, and was graduated from Yale College (now Yale University) in 1830. He taught school briefly before studying law; he was admitted to the bar in Connecticut but never practiced. In his early twenties he traveled extensively—to Washington, D.C., where he met many prominent political figures, and throughout the American South. As a delegate to the International Peace Conference in London in 1831–32, Barnard met prominent English social reformers who influenced his ideas for universal public education in the United States.

Barnard emerged as a rising star of the reformist Whig Party and was elected to the Connecticut legislature in 1837, becoming an outspoken advocate of prison reform. He was also instrumental in the passage of the 1838 law that established a permanent Board of Commissioners of the Common Schools, a step similar to that taken by Massachusetts in the previous year.

Like his friend and mentor Horace Mann, Barnard was appointed secretary of the Board of Commissioners; he used this position, as well as his allies among the Whig reformers, to advance the cause of common schools. Improved schoolhouses, a longer school year, gradation of classes, systematic record keeping, centralization, teacher professionalism, and taxation for the support of schools were among the main planks of his reform agenda. One of his most important contributions as secretary was surveying the state and compiling the first comprehensive report on the condition of Connecticut's schools. His principal goal was the creation of schools that were "good enough for the rich and cheap enough for the poor."

The Board of Commissioners was abolished in 1842 (Massachusetts's had barely survived), a victim of partisan wrangling between the Whigs and the Democrats. Barnard was called to assume a comparable position in Rhode Island, where he remained until 1849. There he strengthened the state's role in education, sponsored successful teachers' institutes (which were often evangelical in nature), edited the *Journal of the Rhode Island Institute of Instruction,* and published his first significant book, *School-house Architecture* (1842). His heart remained in Connecticut, however, and in 1850 he returned to become head of the newly established Normal School and the state superintendent of common schools, position he held until 1855.

During this period Barnard was active in the American Institute of Instruction, the national (but predominantly New England) reform organization. In 1854 he founded the massive *American Journal of Education,* which he edited until 1882. By 1858 national prominence led to his appointment as the chancellor of the University of Wisconsin and agent for Wisconsin's normal schools. He developed a comprehensive design for a state educational system, topped by a well-articulated plan for higher education, but remained in this post a brief 18 months. Barnard returned to Hartford and occupied himself with scholarly work until 1866, when he became president of the newly reopened Saint John's College in Annapolis, Md., a position he occupied for one year.

Like his fellow Whigs, Barnard had long advocated a more significant federal role in education. A highly visible national reformer with friends in high places, he was appointed in 1867 as the nation's first commissioner of education, in charge of the new Department of Education. Barnard was a weak administrator, however, and his ineffectiveness, coupled with his concentration on scholarly work and the nation's political turmoil, led to his dismissal and the demotion of the department to the status of a bureau.

For the remainder of his life Barnard lived in Hartford, traveling occasionally and reading and corresponding extensively. Until his death in 1900 he was revered as the "Nestor of American education."

Henry Barnard, *Henry Barnard: American Educator,* ed. Vincent P. Lannie (1974); Robert B. Downs,

Henry Barnard (1977); Ralph C. Jenkins and Gertrude Chandler Warner, *Henry Barnard: An Introduction* (1937); Edith Nye MacMullen, *In the Cause of True Education: Henry Barnard and 19th-Century School Reform* (1991).

Edith Nye MacMullen

Boston University Boston University is an independent, coeducational, nonsectarian institution on the banks of the Charles River in Boston. The school is the fourth largest independent university in the United States, with more than 29,000 students from each of the 50 states and 135 other countries. Boston University traces its foundations to 1839, when Methodist clergy and laity decided that the denomination needed a seminary to train its ministers. They founded the Newbury Biblical Institute in Newbury, Vt.; the institute's rapid growth led to its relocation in 1847 to Concord, N.H., where it received a new name, the Methodist General Biblical Institute. In 1867 the institute moved again to Brookline, Mass., and was renamed the Boston Theological School.

The acting president of the Boston Theological School was William Fairfield Warren, who soon envisioned the growth of a university around the school. Three wealthy Boston businessmen—Jacob Sleeper, Lee Claflin, and Isaac Rich—shared Warren's vision. In 1869 the legislature of Massachusetts granted their petition to charter Boston University. Warren became the university's first president, serving until 1903. His Methodist roots helped shape the university from its beginning as an institution open to all people regardless of race, sex, class, or creed.

In 1872 the Great Fire of Boston destroyed most of Isaac Rich's property, which had been bequeathed to Boston University and was a key financial resource for the school. This and other fiscal difficulties led President Warren and the university trustees to sell some of the Brookline properties and move the school to more affordable properties in the Beacon Hill neighborhood of Boston. At this time, the university comprised its founding School of Theology, the School of Medicine, the School of Law, the College of Music, the School of Oratory, and the College of Liberal Arts; the Graduate School would soon be added. Among the many achievements of Boston University's schools and colleges, there are a number of notable "firsts." Boston University was the first university in the world to open all its departments to women; the first female student to graduate from the School of Law, Lelia Josephine Robinson (1881), was also the first woman to be admitted to the Massachusetts Bar (1882). The first black student to graduate from the School of Medicine, Solomon Carter Fuller (1897), became the first black psychiatrist in the United States. (Boston University's Solomon Carter Fuller Mental Health Center is named after this distinguished pioneer in Alzheimer's Disease.) And a young professor at the now-defunct School of Oratory named Alexander Graham Bell invented the telephone in 1876.

In the early 20th century, the search began for a permanent setting for the university's schools and colleges, which were scattered throughout the city. By 1928 Boston University had purchased 15 acres nestled between Commonwealth Avenue and the Charles River. With a more unified campus, the university began to focus on the promotion and development of extracurricular student activities. At the same time, it continued to purchase properties near the center of its campus, thus adding to its size and resources. The presence of people such as Howard Thurman, who was appointed dean of Marsh Chapel in 1953, and Martin Luther King, Jr., who received a doctorate in Systematic Theology in 1955, led to the university's central position in the national debate over racial injustice. Almost half of all doctoral degrees in religion and philosophy awarded to black students in the United States between 1952 and 1967 were given by Boston University. Other social issues became prominent topics of discussion and stimuli for action among Boston University's students in the following years, including the war in Vietnam, the draft, and equal rights for women and minorities. Such social consciousness and activism gave the university its occasional nickname of "Berkeley East."

In the last quarter of the 20th century and the beginning of the 21st, Boston University has continued to expand its buildings, programs, and recruiting areas. Boston University currently boasts 14 schools and colleges on its Charles River campus, along with three schools at its Medical Campus in Boston's South End. The university attracts world-famous scholars—Elie Wiesel, Saul Bellow, Sheldon Glashow, Robert Pinsky, and Derek Walcott, to name just a few—to teach students in both its undergraduate and graduate programs. Boston University's ongoing commitment to the community is evident in its current contract with the town of Chelsea, Mass., to manage its troubled public school system and through the merger of the Boston University Medical Center Hospital with Boston City Hospital, a move that saved jobs and allowed for the continued care of Boston's citizens. Boston University has earned a reputation as one of the leading research universities in the United States while simultaneously maintaining its commitment to serve the community and the city in which it finds its home.

Kathleen Kilgore, *Transformations: A History of Boston University* (1991); Sally Ann Kydd, *Boston University* (2002).

Niki Johnson

Boston University, 1998

Brandeis University Brandeis University, founded in 1948, is the nation's first Jewish-sponsored nonsectarian university. Following the early American tradition of denominationally inspired colleges, such as Yale (founded by Congregationalists) and Brown (founded by Baptists), Brandeis's earliest advocates—most prominently Rabbi Israel Gold-

Statue of Louis Brandeis (Robert Berks, 1956) on Brandeis University campus, Waltham, Mass.

stein and Albert Einstein—aimed to create the new university as both the Jewish gift to the nation and a rebuke to the many prominent institutions which at that time discriminated against Jews. The opportunity came when the charter of Middlesex University, a struggling medical and veterinary school in Waltham, Mass., became available. Established as a model meritocracy, open to all men and women "without reference to race, religion, ethnicity, or national origin," the new university was named in honor of the first Jewish Supreme Court Justice, Louis D. Brandeis.

Abram Sachar became the university's first president and served for the next 20 years, building the school into a major research university in a history of rapid, substantive growth unparalleled in the annals of higher education in America. Sachar attracted many distinguished scholars who were then living in retirement, among them the novelist and critic Ludwig Lewisohn and the anthropologist Paul Radin. He offered a home to several pre- and post-Holocaust emigrants of world eminence—including Herbert Marcuse, Nahum Glazer, and Alexander Altmann—and assembled a corps of young scholar-teachers who were persuaded to invest their early careers in an unproven experiment by the energy and ideals of the new university. Many became luminaries in their fields: Leonard Levy (legal studies), Abraham Maslow and Richard Held (psychology), Lawrence Fuchs (immigration), Merrill Peterson, Frank Manual, and Walter Laqueur (history), Saul Cohen (chemistry), and Eugene Gross (physics). Sachar also invited nonacademics with international experi-

ence such as Eleanor Roosevelt and the political journalist Max Lerner to join the faculty. Other notables in the early faculty included Irving Howe and Lewis Coser, founders of the democratic-socialist magazine *Dissent;* Philip Rahv, a founder of *Partisan Review;* and the composers Leonard Bernstein, Arthur Berger, and Harold Shapiro, the first in a long line of eminent resident composers. Sachar also brought playwrights, actors, and directors to the Theater Arts program; artists and sculptors to join the art historians on the fine arts faculty; and poets, novelists, critics, and historians to the literature department. In order to assemble a library sufficient for the young university as quickly as possible, Sachar created the National Women's Committee to raise money. The organization, composed not of alumnae but of women dedicated to the aims of the university, soon numbered some 70,000 members in 250 chapters.

From its beginnings, Brandeis has been distinguished by an atmosphere of intellectual ferment, academic seriousness, and scholarly productivity, as well as by a passion for social justice. The sixties cultural and political icons Abbie Hoffman and Angela Davis were graduates; in May 1970 students and faculty at helped spearhead strikes and protests at hundreds of American colleges following the reescalation of the Vietnam War. The Heller School of Social Policy and Management is one of the nation's premier graduate schools in the area of social welfare, and the International Center for Ethics, Justice and Public Life, established in 1998, offers an array of programs dealing with conflict resolution, human rights, and public ethics.

While it is among the smallest of America's 61 research universities—326 full-time and 139 part-time faculty members teaching 3,100 undergraduate and 1,300 graduate students— Brandeis has earned national and global renown for its faculty and graduates. It is particularly strong in the sciences: 15 members of its science faculties have been elected to the National Academy of Science. In the early 1970s life scientists at the university were pioneers in interdisciplinary research, an approach that can be found today in the Rosenstiel Medical Sciences Research Center and the recently established Volen Center for Complex Systems. In addition, 35 faculty members have been named to the American Academy of Arts and Sciences and four have won MacArthur Foundation "genius" awards. The Department of Near Eastern and Judaic Studies is considered the major center of Jewish studies outside of Israel.

Abram L. Sachar, *Brandeis University: A Host at Last* (1976).

Jacob Cohen

Brown University Brown University is a private, nonsectarian, coeducational university in Providence. The third-oldest university in New England and the seventh-oldest in the United States, it is part of the elite northeastern group of colleges known as the Ivy League.

The school was founded in 1764 in Warren, R.I., and was originally named Rhode Island College. Established by the Baptist Church in order to create a more educated ministry, it was, however, governed from the beginning by a board of directors that also included Congregationalists, Quakers, and Anglicans. The college graduated its first class of seven men in 1769. The following year, after a vigorous debate between representatives of Newport, R.I., and Providence, the college moved to the latter city. The relocation, engineered by members of Providence's merchant-industrialist Brown family, added significantly to the city's growing preeminence in Rhode Island. In 1804, in recognition of the family's contributions, the college was renamed Brown University. The first campus buildings were built on family property on what would become known as College Hill in the city's elite East Side.

During the 19th century Brown emerged as one of the principal universities in New England. In the 1830s it was a leader, for better or worse, in moving university education away from sole emphasis on the classics to a "practical" set of courses that included business and industrial pursuits. In 1891 it admitted women for all degrees, albeit in a cautious manner, by establishing Pembroke College, a separate women's institution on campus. This internal differentiation ended in 1972, when Brown became fully coeducational. Pembroke College was abolished, to be reincarnated in 1981 as the Pembroke Center for Teaching and Research on Women.

Brown enrolls approximately 7,500 students. It pioneered a liberal grading system that allows students to choose to receive a grade (A, B, C, or no credit—no Ds or Fs) or to opt for a simpler pass-fail formula (satisfactory/no credit). The politically and socially active student body has influenced the university to enforce strict harassment codes, promote equal support for female and male athletes, and introduce theme dormitories to the campus. Brown has a number of endowed programs, including the famous Annenberg Institute for School Reform, established by Theodore R. Sizer, professor of education emeritus and founder of the Coalition of Essential Schools, which advocates greater teacher and student autonomy.

Architecturally, Brown possesses a classic Ivy League ambience that fits well into the

*College green and
Sayles Hall, Brown
University, Provi-
dence, 1981*

Benefit Street area of Old Providence. Surrounded by historic heritage homes, the cam-
pus features an eclectic mix of Colonial and
Greek Revival styles as well as the Beaux Arts
John Carter Brown Library, an independently
funded and administered institution for the
study of advanced research in history and the
humanities. The oldest building at Brown is
University Hall, built in 1770 and used as a
barracks for troops during the Revolutionary
War. Also significant is the home of the John
Nicholas Brown Center for the Study of
American Civilization, the recently restored
Nightingale-Brown House, which was built
in 1792 and is one of the largest 18th-century
frame houses still in existence in the United
States.

Brown University represents many traditional aspects of New England culture. Its
founding was rooted in the climate of religious
diversity that was most notable in early Rhode
Island. Its support came from the region's
philanthropic, community-minded business
elite who wanted to leave their names for posterity while raising the level of cultural sophistication in their home city. And it is also a visible symbol of the legacy of quality higher
education for which New England is famous.

Peter J. Coleman, *The Transformation of Rhode Island,
1790–1860* (1963); William G. McLoughlin, *Rhode
Island: A Bicentennial History* (1978); Mack Thompson, *Moses Brown: Reluctant Reformer* (1962).

Eric Jarvis

Catholic Colleges and Universities

The 1789 chartering of Jesuit-founded Georgetown College in Washington, D.C., marked
the beginnings of Catholic higher education
in the United States. It was a former president
of Georgetown, Benedict Fenwick, S.J., the
second bishop of Boston, who brought the Jesuit tradition of a classical education rooted in
an intellectually rigorous Catholicism to New
England, founding the College of the Holy
Cross in Worcester, Mass., in 1843 (chartered
1865). As waves of immigrants from Ireland
arrived during the mid-19th century, it became
imperative to provide a Catholic education for
the new population, and in 1847 John McElroy, S.J., began the long process of founding a
Catholic college in Boston. Navigating the
virulent anti-Catholicism of Protestant Massachusetts, he succeeded in gaining a state
charter for Boston College in 1863, but it specified that religion could not be a condition of
admission. Father McElroy's college, which

would "educate the sons of the Irish poor" who
were unwelcome at Harvard, admitted its first
students in 1867.

This founding narrative was repeated with
several variations into the 20th century, during
the first of what the historian David O'Brien
defines as three phases of Catholic higher
education in America. Across New England
orders of religious men and women founded
academies and colleges to meet the educational needs of the Catholic immigrant communities, for if the communities were to prosper, they would need, in addition to priests
—as the Boston diocesan paper pointed out in
1864—"thoroughly educated lawyers, doctors,
merchants." When "Catholic lads" were educated together they would not only support
one another but also advance the "whole
Catholic body." By 1917 five religious orders
were staffing colleges across New England:
Benedictines at the College of Saint Anselm
in Manchester, N.H. (1889); Edmundite
Fathers at Saint Michael's College in Burlington, Vt. (1904); Assumptionists at Assumption College in Worcester (1904); and Dominicans at Providence College in Rhode
Island (1917). Saint Joseph's College in Standish, Maine, also opened in 1917, the culmination of long-held plans of the Portland Community of the Sisters of Mercy.

As higher education for women gained acceptance in the latter half of the 19th century,
orders of religious women sought to make
such education available to the daughters—
and future mothers and teachers—of a growing Catholic middle class. Although Catholic
resistance to modernity and anxiety over the
proper role of women complicated this effort,
women's schools proliferated: 12 were founded
in Massachusetts by the mid-20th century,
three each in Connecticut and Vermont, four
in New Hampshire, one in Rhode Island.
Some, like Our Lady of the Elms (Chicopee,
Mass.) followed a common pattern of evolution, beginning as an academy for girls (1899),
developing into a normal school (1908), and
then becoming a college (1928). Others, such
as Emmanuel College (1919), founded in
Boston by the Sisters of Notre Dame de Namur, and Regis College (1927), established by
diocesan Sisters of Saint Joseph in staunchly
Protestant Weston, Mass., offered women a
bachelor's degree from the outset. In New England as elsewhere, however, a number of
women's institutions—challenged particularly by the shift to coeducation in formerly
all-male institutions—later closed or merged:
in 1974 Newton College, founded in 1950 by
the Religious of the Sacred Heart, merged
with Boston College, which had become fully
coeducational in 1972. Others sought to maintain enrollment by establishing graduate pro-

grams—coeducational by federal law—and developing adult and preprofessional education.

The third Jesuit-founded New England institution, Fairfield University in Connecticut (1945) belongs to the second phase of Catholic higher education. Supported by mounting applications from World War II veterans benefiting from the G.I. Bill but also by the increased prosperity and desire for higher education of an assimilating Catholic population, existing institutions grew and new schools appeared. In 1947 the archbishop of Boston, Richard Cardinal Cushing—an avid builder of Catholic institutions—invited Augustinian priests to found Merrimack College north of the city to respond to the "needs and aspirations" of returning soldiers. In Easton, Mass., the Congregation of the Holy Cross opened Stonehill College in 1948. In Bridgeport, Conn., diocesan leaders struck a new note, specifying fully lay governance when they founded Sacred Heart University in 1963.

Most Catholic institutions retain a historical commitment to the educational philosophy of the founding order. But since the 1960s an increasing percentage of faculty members and administrators are laypersons, and shifts have occurred in the traditional relations between colleges and their founding congregations. Socioeconomic factors, combined with changes in the church following the Second Vatican Council (1962–65)—especially the decreasing numbers of priests and nuns—influenced academic and student life in New England Catholic institutions. Instructional costs increased as lay faculty replaced religious. To be fully competitive, Catholic institutions in this third phase developed more diverse curricula, a wider international outlook, and, in several institutions, a significant range of graduate programs. Catholic institutions have also sought to recruit more broadly and to reach beyond traditional sources of support, while seeking to honor their founding traditions. An ongoing discussion focuses on the challenge of balancing a strong Catholic identity with the imperative to compete in a complex academic environment.

Alice Gallin, ed., *American Catholic Higher Education: Essential Documents, 1967–1990* (1992); Philip Gleason, *Contending with Modernity: Catholic Higher Education in the 20th Century* (1995); David J. O'Brien, *From the Heart of the American Church: Catholic Higher Education and American Culture* (1994); O'Brien, "Catholic Higher Education at the Crossroads: Prospects and Projects," *Santa Clara Lectures* (1995); Tracy Schier and Cynthia Russett, eds., *Catholic Women's Colleges in America* (2002).

Carol Hurd Green

Children's Museums

Children's museums in New England are an extension of the

The Science Center of Connecticut, West Hartford, Conn., 2002

region's interest in children's education, dating back to the colonial era. The idea of the children's museum evolved in the early 1900s, supported by Swiss psychologist Jean Piaget's theory that "to know an object is to act upon it." New England's children's museums have introduced several innovations, most notably the discovery room, featuring the hands-on concept of learning through touching.

The Children's Museum in Boston, the oldest children's museum in New England and one of the pathfinders for children's programs and activities, was founded in 1913 in a city-owned park building in Jamaica Plain, Mass. It exhibited aquariums and terrariums and in 1916 began offering classes for children who were blind or deaf. A branch museum, the Barnard Memorial, opened on Warrenton Street in Boston in 1919.

In 1962 Michael Spock, son of the famed baby doctor Benjamin Spock, became director and infused the museum, which had changed little since 1913, with a new vitality. The following year, Spock introduced the hands-on participatory exhibit *What's Inside*, the first of many pioneering installations that developed into the discovery-room concept. The museum's *Playspace*, aimed at infants and very small children, has served as a model for other institutions. The Children's Museum briefly merged with the Computer Museum (now part of Boston's Museum of Science), another wonderful learning space for children with an emphasis on hands-on technology.

Since the 1960s the impact of the Children's Museum, with its themes and installations, has been far-reaching; it has influenced many types of museums throughout the country and abroad. Additionally, it has become a center for training museum professionals. Among the hands-on children's museums and programs established in its wake are the Discovery Center of the Museum of Science, Boston; opened in 1978, the Discovery Center encourages children's interest in science through participatory activities for all ages. The New England Aquarium, Central Wharf, Boston—originally the Children's Tidepool—opened in June 1969 as the first of several participatory aquatic environments built to revitalize urban waterfronts. The Children's Museum of Southeastern Connecticut, in Niantic, opened in 1992, features participatory exhibits such as the Health Discovery Center, a research submarine, and the CAN-STRUCT building exhibit.

Many children's museums were started by communities intent on furthering their children's extracurricular educational experience. The Children's Museum in South Dartmouth, Mass., was opened in 1952 by a group of local women who wanted to stimulate children's interest in the arts, natural sciences, and humanities. The Discovery Museum in Essex Junction, Vt., was founded in 1974 by a group of local citizens who perceived a need for supplemental educational opportunities for area children. The Science Center of Connecticut in West Hartford was established as the Children's Museum of Hartford in 1927; it opened as a nature center exhibiting donated or loaned natural history materials and items illustrating life in foreign countries. The Children's Museum of Portsmouth, N.H., opened in July 1983 thanks to community interest in developing an educational resource for schools, groups, and families. These institutions infuse fun and a spirit of discovery and wonder into the education of the region's children.

Joanne Cleaver, *Doing Children's Museums: A Guide to 265 Hands-On Museums* (1992); Barbara F. Zucker, *Children's Museums, Zoos, and Discovery Rooms: An International Reference Guide* (1987).

Martin J. Manning

Coeducation

Historically, coeducation has taken various forms, from combining boys and girls within a classroom to seating them on opposite sides of the room to offering sex-differentiated curricula within the same school. Mixed schooling, as coeducation was called, has been a long-standing feature in America's lower schools but has provoked controversy at the college level. While such New England states as Massachusetts, Connecticut, and Rhode Island led the way to coeducation at the secondary level, many New England colleges, like those in the South, remained resistant to its practice, supporting single-sex higher education more firmly than the Midwest and West.

With younger children coeducation was neither the first nor the most obvious way to organize schooling. Eighteenth-century New Englanders valued basic literacy for both boys and girls and routinely sent male and female youngsters to single-sex rudimentary dame schools run by women in their homes. Securing advanced education for girls took longer. Early public district schools primarily served boys, allowing girls to attend during less-popular summer sessions. As the common-school movement took hold in the mid-1800s, advocates Horace Mann in Massachusetts and Henry Barnard in Connecticut successfully supported age-graded, organized elementary schools open to children of all backgrounds. Advanced vocationally oriented education usually occurred in private academies, some of which practiced coeducation.

Objections to coeducation arose from presumed gender differences in intellect, behavior, and vocational destination. The belief that women were intellectually inferior to men was not dispelled until expanded post-Revolutionary educational options demonstrated women's achievements. As for behavior, coeducation's opponents worried that girls would distract boys; advocates countered that girls would temper boys' rowdiness. Expectations for different gender-based vocational futures proved the most tenacious block to coeducation in high school and college.

In 1900 high schools were small institutions without clear vocational missions. When the comprehensive high school took hold around the 1920s, however, greater gender differentiation appeared within coeducational schools. Girls headed to commercial education, home economics, and liberal arts, while boys pursued varied vocational training. At the postsecondary level, narrow views of women's vocational options promoted the proliferation of female-oriented teachers colleges.

The country's oldest and most prestigious colleges began in New England as institutions for men. When Ohio's Oberlin became the first coeducational college in 1833, Harvard had been educating men for 200 years. In 1873 Boston University became the first fully coeducational college in New England, opening its full range of undergraduate and graduate programs to both sexes.

Widespread national acceptance of collegiate coeducation followed the federal Morrill Land-Grant Act of 1862. Around the country, land-grant money created new, coeducational institutions. But in New England funds were frequently divided among existing schools, few of which were advocates of coeducation. Tradition, coupled with the development of strong women's colleges, made New England a holdout in single-sex collegiate education. Final resistance to coeducation eased in the late 1960s and early 1970s, when such Ivy League schools as Yale University and Dartmouth College began admitting women. Women's colleges proceeded more slowly, but in the 1970s and 1980s most opened their doors to men, established coordinate-educational arrangements with nearby male colleges, or both. The trend continues: at the beginning of the 21st century Smith College in Northampton and Mount Holyoke College in South Hadley, Mass., remained women-only at the undergraduate level, though admitting males to their graduate programs.

Lynn D. Gordon, *Gender and Higher Education in the Progressive Era* (1990); Carol Lasser, ed., *Educating Men and Women Together: Coeducation in a Changing World* (1987); Barbara Miller Solomon, *In the Company of Educated Women: A History of Women and Higher Education in America* (1985); David Tyack and Elisabeth Hansot, *Learning Together: A History of Coeducation in American Public Schools* (1990).

Linda Eisenmann

Colonial Education

Every society educates its young. Everywhere in early America, elders modeled for youth the ways of the culture that those youngsters would one day inherit. But in New England, far more than in other areas of English America, elders of European descent preached as well as practiced. They preached in churches and families and, more important, in books and schools. Their children absorbed the manners and morals of their communities less by living and more by formal learning than children anywhere else in the colonies.

In England, Puritans put a premium on literacy that their compatriots did not. They fought for the publication of the Bible in English and for instruction of children to read it—and other texts—for themselves. In New England, "dame" schools and elementary schools were quickly established to achieve these ends. And the distinctive reliance of New Englanders on reading, writing, and abstract instruction exposed them, despite themselves, to disturbing experiences of discontinuity and enticing intimations of self-awareness and innovation. Early educators sought neither self-consciousness for their pupils nor change for their society. But their reliance on formal institutions to socialize the young tacitly conceded that the past could not provide children with an adequate preparation for the future and that the ways of the parents would not offer adequate guidance to their offspring.

The schools of colonial New England struggled to deny these dark implications. They strove to impart orthodoxy in religion and manners alike. The preeminent texts on which teachers relied—the shorter catechism of the Westminster Assembly and, by the 1680s, *The New-England Primer*—aimed to avert an unwanted individualism by demanding obedience, stasis, and self-denial. The *Primer* spoke incessantly of service and sin, of the obligations of "the dutiful child," and of the punishments that awaited all who failed to fulfill those obligations. In every lesson it inveighed against self-interest and asserted submission to authority. And its injunctions to social conformity were reinforced by the technique of rote memorization used in classes.

These schools achieved their ends in remarkable measure. In 1647 Massachusetts mandated that each town establish a school, lest the "old deluder," Satan, wrest the settlement from the saints. (A decade before it demanded elementary schools in every town, the colony established a college in the wilderness.) Towns often defied the mandate of the central government in Boston, and those that complied with it sometimes did so erratically, but by the eve of the American Revolution New England was among the few societies in the world to achieve virtually universal male literacy. It was also among the few societies in the world with widespread female literacy and with a few female academies for the daughters of its elite.

But the schools—and the college, called Harvard after its first patron—diverged from their English exemplars in decisive ways. Schools could not be supported in the New

World as they had been in the Old, by private benefaction. New England had neither sufficient supply of benefactors nor prospect of surplus wealth for that. Educational institutions at every level had to turn to their communities for financial contributions, and their communities inevitably claimed the right to control those institutions. The independence of public opinion and popular prejudice that English pedagogues took for granted was never a prerogative of New England teachers or, for that matter, of Harvard professors. (In the 18th century, when evening schools proliferated to teach young apprentices and tradesmen, those schools were as sensitive to the preferences of the marketplace as town schools were to the sentiments of the taxpayers in their communities.)

The subordination of schooling to public purposes assured a degree of conservatism in early New England education. The reliance on schools and on learning from formal texts, however, precluded that very conservatism. It fractured the continuity between generations that prevailed in other precincts of colonial America, where children still came of age through immersion in the community. It entailed dilemmas of self-conscious transmission of culture that did not confront others elsewhere—at least not to the same degree. It subjected successive groups of youth to new ideals and expectations based on the inculcation of abstract ideals. And it drove some of those New England students to a tortured inner life that their schoolmasters never taught and to a conflict of generations—a rhythm of deterioration and revival—that their communities never sought.

James Axtell, *The School upon a Hill: Education and Society in Colonial New England* (1974); Bernard Bailyn, *Education in the Forming of American Society* (1960); Lawrence Cremin, *American Education: The Colonial Experience, 1607–1783* (1970).

Michael Zuckerman

Common Schools

The movement to create public ("common") schools in New England began in 1647, when the Massachusetts Bay Colony ordered communities of more than 50 families to provide instruction in reading to their children or to pay a neighboring town to do it, it "being one of the chief projects of that old deluder Satan," so the ordinance ran, "to keep men from the knowledge of the scriptures." The Old Deluder Satan Act, as it came to be known, was quickly replicated in other colonies before the end of the 18th century. Despite models put forward by Thomas Jefferson and others, however, no system of public, compulsory, and nonsectarian education was formally instituted until after the Massachusetts reformer Horace Mann began

McGuffey reader (1840)

a nationwide campaign for common schools in 1837. Mann was one of a group of 19th-century reformers including Henry Barnard, James Carter, and Calvin Stowe, to name a few, who were committed to common-school improvement.

Before the development of public-school systems, education was haphazard even in New England, which prided itself on its commitment to literacy. Reading lessons typically began in "dame" schools run by women in their homes. Families who sought and could afford further education for their children sent them to privately supported schools, which often admitted only boys. Until Mann's reforms, the only truly public institutions for children in New England were orphanages, asylums, and reform schools. Common schools, in the early phases of their development, were aimed at those whose need for reform was perceived as greatest.

With massive waves of immigration, largely from Catholic Ireland, turning commercial and waterfront districts into Irish ghettos, other social dislocations—industrialization, urbanization, the decline of family farms and independent artisans—further changed the character of work and workplaces. The impulse to avoid class stratification at a time of industrialization stemmed from fears that American society would begin to resemble that of industrialized England. Common schools, proponents alleged, would function as a blanket social-insurance policy by maintaining public order, enlarging the pool of trustworthy labor, and protecting the institutions most at risk from the unschooled. Public

education, moreover, was occasionally seen as an "antidote" to the religious and cultural foreignness of new immigrant populations.

Middle-class opponents of the common-school movement appealed to the rights of property: in their view, compulsory taxation—particularly of the elderly or childless—was theft. Poor parents occasionally resented public schools as camouflaged charity. Compulsory schooling did no good, moreover, for families who relied on their children's labor. Particularly in Massachusetts, the Irish rebelled against compulsory Protestant schooling. The texts used in common schools—primers, geographies, histories, and the ubiquitous McGuffey readers—tended to exalt Protestant American Anglo-Saxons and to ignore or disparage others. The curriculum and instructional methods were pervasively religious; "nonsectarian" simply meant broadly Protestant rather than narrowly denominational. While parents of other faiths (or no faith) rightly suspected the professed religious neutrality of a curriculum that openly taught Protestant values as founded on the King James Bible, conservative Protestant parents charged the schools with promoting atheism, infidelity, and Universalism for accommodating religious plurality to the degree that they did. The so-called Lowell Experiment, which created public schools in Lowell, Mass., specifically for Irish children and purged texts of anti-Catholic propaganda, was resisted by reformers who refused to surrender the common schools' Protestantizing mission.

In other respects common schools fell short as havens of democracy. While wealthy pupils, it was alleged, would learn "compassion" for their less fortunate classmates as the needy in turn learned to emulate the decorum and ambition of their "betters," the arrival of large numbers of poor immigrant children made it difficult for public schools to attract children whose parents could afford private ones. New England classrooms were racially segregated; black families in New England, moreover, were disproportionately poor and less able to do without their children's labor. Poor children, and girls in greater numbers across races and classes, managed more often to elude compulsory education laws. As religious conflicts prompted the gradual if uneven secularization of common schools by the end of the 19th century, however, so other obstacles to making them truly "common," democratic, and accessible spurred a culture of consistent improvement and innovation in public education.

The image of New England as a place of educational excellence, with its well-built and well-equipped schoolhouses run by trained male and female teachers, derived from the common-school movement and was encouraged by such artists as Winslow Homer and such writers as Harriet Beecher Stowe. The belief in common schools continued to inspire reformers in New England during educational reform movements from the 1960s until today, as seen in the writings of Robert Coles and the activities of Theodore Sizer and his Coalition of Essential Schools, making New England schools models for the nation.

Vincent P. Lannie, "Alienation in America: The Immigrant Catholic and Public Education in Pre–Civil War America," *Review of Politics* 32 (1970); David Nasaw, *Schooled to Order: A Social History of Public Schooling in the United States* (1979); Stanley K. Schultz, *The Culture Factory: Boston Public Schools, 1789–1860* (1973); Lee Soltow and Edward Stevens, *The Rise of Literacy and the Common School in the United States: A Socioeconomic Analysis to 1870* (1981).

Tracy Fessenden

Dartmouth College

Dartmouth College was granted a charter by King George III on December 13, 1769, the ninth and last college established in the English colonies before the American Revolution. An outgrowth of Moor's Indian Charity School of Lebanon, Conn., the college was founded by Eleazar Wheelock, a graduate of Yale and a Congregational minister strongly influenced by the Great Awakening. One of his first pupils was Samson Occom, a Mohegan who helped him raise money in England for the college, including a large gift from William Legge, second earl of Dartmouth, for whom the school is named. But few Native Americans came to the school, so Wheelock broadened its mission and moved it to Hanover, N.H., to land granted to him by Governor Benning Wentworth.

The college struggled in the early years with few students, primitive conditions, and limited resources, but unlike many other colleges it stayed open throughout the Revolutionary War years and graduated more students in the last decade of the 18th century than any college except Harvard. One source of support in the early years came from across the Connecticut River; six years before it became a state and six years before the founding of the University of Vermont, the Vermont legislature granted 23,000 acres to support Dartmouth. As late as 1840 one-third of the college's income came from rents in Wheelock, Vt.

When Eleazar Wheelock died in 1779, he willed the college to his son, John Wheelock. The younger Wheelock was controversial from the beginning in part because he thought he owned the college, and the trustees finally removed him from the presidency in 1815. His removal was part of a larger controversy over

Baker Library, Dartmouth College, Hanover, N.H.

control; one faction (mostly Republicans) wanted the state to take over the college, while another (mostly Federalists) opted for the status quo. The state legislature created Dartmouth University, which for a time existed side by side with Dartmouth College. The state court upheld the action of the legislature, but the United States Supreme Court reversed the ruling (*Dartmouth College v. Woodward*) in 1819. Daniel Webster (class of 1801) argued the college's case against state intervention. Chief Justice John Marshall, for the majority, argued that Dartmouth's charter was a contract within the meaning of the Constitution and could not be altered by legislation. This landmark decision not only preserved Dartmouth as a private college but also protected other American private colleges and corporations from legislative interference.

Dartmouth remained a provincial college through most of the 19th century. It did have a medical school (founded in 1797, the fourth in the nation), and the Thayer School of Engineering, the first professional engineering school in the nation, was established in 1867, but no modern languages were taught before 1859 and the first professor of history was appointed in 1893. At the time of the Civil War, 85 percent of Dartmouth's students came from New Hampshire and Vermont. An alumnus who later taught there described it as "a college of pinched and grinding frugality almost without aesthetic adornment." But that could have been said of most American colleges in the 19th century.

Dartmouth became a modern college during the administrations of presidents William Jewett Tucker (1893–1909) and Ernest Hopkins (1916–45). Tucker was a Social Gospel minister who had been dismissed from Andover Theological Seminary because of his liberal views, while Hopkins, only the second president who was not a clergyman, had been a businessman and secretary of the college. They each improved the faculty, expanded the student body and made it more selective, built a modern physical plant, and greatly increased business and alumni support. In 1900 the world's first graduate school of management, the Amos Tuck School of Business Administration, was established. Hopkins even defended the creation of a controversial mural painted on the walls of the basement of Baker Library (built in 1928) by Mexican artist José Clemente Orozco. The mural, which angered many alumni, was critical of both American capitalism and American higher education.

The alumni were more pleased with the undefeated football teams in 1924 and 1925. Dartmouth fielded its first football team in 1881 with uniforms borrowed from Princeton, but for years the college could not compete with the big three—Harvard, Yale, and Princeton. An exception occurred in 1903 when Dartmouth defeated Harvard in the inaugural game in the new Harvard stadium. The team that year was led by Matthew Bullard, one of the few African Americans to attend Dartmouth in the early 20th century. If Dartmouth could not compete in football, it virtually invented winter sports. Fred Harris (class of 1911), from Brattleboro, Vt., not only introduced skiing to the campus but also founded the Dartmouth Outing Club and organized the first winter carnival his senior year.

Only a few Native Americans attended Dartmouth in the first 200 years of its history, but Dartmouth sports teams were known as the Indians. When more Native Americans began to attend Dartmouth in the 1970s and a Native American studies program was established in 1972, many questioned the use of the Indian symbol. After much controversy it was abandoned. An even greater change came in the fall of 1972 when women were admitted as regular students.

Dartmouth now has a major library, 3 professional schools, 18 graduate programs in the arts and sciences, more than 900 faculty members, and state-of-the-art facilities including the Rockefeller Center for the Social Sciences and the Hood Museum of Art. Now an Ivy League institution, it is a university in all but name. Perhaps because of Daniel Webster's famous plea, "It is a small college, but there are those who love it," it remains Dartmouth College to this day.

Ralph Nading Hill, *The College on the Hill: A Dartmouth Chronicle* (1964); Leon Burr Richardson, *History of Dartmouth College* (1932).

Allen F. Davis

Desegregation Cities in New England, as in most other northern states, have been faced with the problem of schools that are racially imbalanced because of segregated housing patterns. A number of strategies for desegregation have been tested: the state of Connecticut attempted voluntary busing from its predominantly black cities to the suburbs; Lowell, Mass., tried to draw all races to its innovative magnet schools; Cambridge, Mass., initiated a plan of controlled choice that mixed students by both race and household income. Boston has employed similar approaches in its own attempts at desegregation. As the largest and most influential New England city and the place where desegregation orders have been most dramatically resisted, Boston is the cynosure. Its successes and failures reflect those of other New England cities and constitute a microcosm of the national effort.

School segregation was an issue in Boston as early as the mid-19th century, when black schoolchildren were compelled to attend a segregated school on Beacon Hill. One of the school's graduates, William C. Nell, denounced segregation in the pages of the abolitionist newspaper the *Liberator,* petitioned the school committee for change, and, when unsuccessful, led boycotts of the school between 1844 and 1849. In 1849 a black parent, Benjamin Roberts, filed a lawsuit against the policy on behalf of his child, but in *Roberts v. Boston* Justice Lemuel Shaw found for the defendant, declaring that separate but equal facilities were legal. Roberts and his allies continued their fight at the State House and in 1855 prevailed, when the Massachusetts legislature at last outlawed segregation.

This law proved to be no permanent remedy. A hundred years later, under the guidance of a school committee versed principally in patronage, the system both condoned and encouraged segregation. Inequity was the result: in Dorchester's dilapidated Christopher Gibson School, the overwhelmingly black student body was subjected to racial slurs and forced to attend classes in the basement. In 1965 the Kiernan Report found that 45 out of 55 Boston schools were racially imbalanced, but the Boston School Committee, led by South Boston's Louise Day Hicks, refused to acknowledge that even a state of de facto segregation existed. In the face of this conflict, the state legislature passed the Racial Imbalance Act of 1965, which prohibited nonwhite enrollment of more than 50 percent in any given school. The act demanded only partial integration ef-

forts: although all-black schools would be considered racially imbalanced and subject to desegregation, all-white schools would not.

In the meantime the committee's intransigence helped inspire an alternative, voluntary effort: in 1966 the Metropolitan Council for Educational Opportunity (METCO) was founded to bus minority children to white suburbs. This limited program could not, however, solve the problem—compulsion was needed to bring the system into compliance with the law. The necessary precedents for federal action were provided by the 1954 Supreme Court decision *Brown v. the Board of Education,* in which "separate but equal" schools were found "inherently unequal," and in the 1971 decision *Swann v. Charlotte-Mecklenberg,* which permitted busing as a remedy for governmentally sponsored segregation. In 1972 the National Association for the Advancement of Colored Persons (NAACP) filed *Morgan v. Hennigan,* a federal case alleging that the Boston School Committee had intentionally maintained segregated schools. On June 21, 1974, Judge Arthur Garrity found in favor of the plaintiffs, declaring that the defendants had "knowingly carried out a systematic program of segregation" through districting, open enrollment, and transfers. As a remedy, Garrity ordered, in what became known as Phase I of the desegregation plan, increased minority hiring, the redrawing of districts, and a busing system that included the pairing of schools in Roxbury and South Boston.

The first day of school in September 1974, which passed without incident at 150 of 165 schools, was chaos in South Boston. In a pattern that continued for 10 days, school buses transporting black children from Roxbury were attacked by onlookers throwing rocks and bottles and yelling, "Niggers, go home!" At South Boston High School, racial slurs and scuffles became common, and in October a full-scale fight broke out in the cafeteria. In December black students had to be led to safety out the back door as hundreds of angry residents, reacting to the stabbing of a white student, surrounded the school. By the end of the year South Boston High was heading toward court receivership, and 6,000 students had dropped out of the Boston school system.

In September 1975 Judge Garrity implemented Phase II of the desegregation plan, dividing the city into nine districts with 22 citywide magnet schools designed to attract students of all races. Busing was increased to 25,000 students from the previous year's 15,000, and the policy now affected the entire city except East Boston. Working-class Charlestown's reaction mirrored South Boston's: whites fought blacks in high school, clashed with the police, and rallied behind Louise Day Hicks's organi-

zation Restore Our Alienated Rights (ROAR). In April 1976, their outrage, rooted in a desire to be free of government interference, culminated in the memorable image of a protester spearing a black passerby with an American flag.

By the opening of the next school year, however, the fury had begun to subside. In 1977 John O'Bryant became the first black representative elected to the school committee since 1895; school committee members were replaced with more reform-minded individuals as a new districting and at-large voting system was introduced. In 1983 the mayoral race between black activist Mel King and South Boston's antibusing advocate Ray Flynn, a campaign marked by civility rather than rancor, set the stage for a populist Flynn administration that stressed new opportunities for all.

These events, plus an increasing biracial desire for parental choice, led to the "controlled-choice" plan of 1989. Three geographic zones were set up for elementary and middle schools: parents could list, in order of preference, the schools they wanted their children to attend. By 1995, 95 percent of Boston students attended a school of choice, and 80 percent of parents supported the new plan. By contrast, in 1975 only 25 percent of students had attended their school of choice.

Controlled choice introduced a period of relative stability, but just as a series of court decisions in favor of desegregation had encouraged the filing of *Morgan v. Hennigan* in 1972, by the late 1990s a series of federal decisions striking down desegregation and affirmative action initiatives had encouraged disgruntled parents to file suit against the racial status quo. In two separate cases, the courts found that white applicants had been illegally bypassed for admission to the prestigious Boston Latin High School in favor of lower-scoring minority applicants. By 1999 these decisions had led the school to change its admission policy, abandoning minority set-asides in favor of a system in which students were admitted solely on the basis of grades and test scores. The impact was immediate: whereas in 1998 Boston Latin's population was 21 percent black and 10 percent Hispanic; by December 2003 the groups' percentages had dipped to 11.8 and 5.5, respectively.

In 1999 the advocacy group Children First filed a lawsuit seeking to overthrow the controlled-choice plan in favor of one that would eliminate race as a factor in student assignment. Fearing a loss in court and perceiving that a race-neutral policy would have little immediate impact on the schools' racial composition (then 50 percent black, 26 percent Hispanic, 14 percent white, and 10 percent Asian), the school board approved a policy that provided for limited neighborhood choice with no consideration of race. Half the places in a given school would go to local children who could walk to the school; the other half would go to children within the school's geographic zone who had requested that school. The plan was immediately opposed by Children First, which wanted all seats to go to neighborhood children, as well as by civil rights activists who feared the plan would promote segregation. To date the plan has withstood legal challenge, and Superintendent Donald Payzant is promoting it as the best way to simultaneously maximize school choice, promote neighborhood schools, and prevent pockets of segregation.

Boston has not been alone in confronting the demands of desegregation. In 1989 Milo Sheff, a student in the Hartford school system, filed a class action suit against the state of Connecticut alleging that the concentration of minority students in 16 urban school districts constituted illegal discrimination. Unlike the city of Boston, the state of Connecticut was not accused of being actively responsible for this segregation; rather, the plaintiffs claimed that the state had not done enough to remedy a situation caused by outside factors. In 1996 the State Supreme Court upheld Sheff on appeal and found that minority children had been denied equal educational opportunities. In remediation, the state committed $500 million to a five-year plan that would reduce class sizes, expand regional school choice through magnet schools, renovate inner-city schools, and institute a voluntary busing program in the cities of Hartford, Bridgeport, and New Haven that connected inner-city schools to the suburbs. By 2004 five urban magnet schools had opened, and the state was considering ways to persuade both white students and students in general to enroll. (Only 900 of 2,400 places were filled, and the state remained 10 percent shy of its 28 percent nonminority goal.)

Although both Boston and the state of Connecticut have achieved some success in mixing white and minority students, the hope for integration envisioned in the early 1970s has not become a reality. In part, demographics have intervened: between 1950 and 1970, 36 percent of Boston's white population left the city while the black population rose by 312 percent. This trend, accelerated by a forced-busing policy that resulted in many white parents either moving from the city or enrolling their children in private schools, continued unabated over the next 20 years. The white population in Boston schools diminished steadily from 60 percent in 1972 to 35 percent in 1980 before plummeting to 15 percent in the late 1990s. Overall enrollment, down from 90,000 in 1972 to 62,000 in the early 1990s, consisted of increasingly needy children: by 1985, 93 per-

cent qualified for the free-lunch program, a sure index of poverty.

Belief in the value of racial integration also changed. By the 1990s, 80 percent of the American people favored integration, but as Ronald Formisano points out, most whites endorsed only voluntary integration involving middle-class blacks. Support for forced busing waned, fueled by court losses and White House administrations that failed to prosecute desegregation cases. Although desegregation has increased opportunities for minority students and enhanced racial tolerance, the future of school integration remains unclear. Deliberate segregation of students remains illegal, but the type of voluntary plans developed by the city of Lynn, Mass., that both guarantee children placement in their neighborhood school and employ race as a primary factor in granting transfers, continue to be struck down. Color-blind policies that indirectly promote integration, even policies that consider race as one among many factors, may be permissible. But voluntary plans that aim to *keep* schools integrated through racial quotas seem defunct. The result, may be, as Gary Orfield of Harvard's Civil Rights Project maintains, a segregation more profound than any that existed before busing.

Some hope remains. In New England, the Manchester, Conn., and Cambridge school systems, noting the fact that low-income children learn best when placed with more affluent peers, have developed assignment plans that emphasize economic integration. There has been resistance: even in politically liberal Cambridge, parents protest that it is not their child's responsibility to uplift others and fear that their children will be isolated and their education diluted. Proponents hope that physically upgrading facilities, improving teaching and curriculum, and limiting the number of low-income students who attend a given school will make all schools attractive places to learn. This approach, which has also been adopted in places like Charlotte-Mecklenburg, N.C., and San Francisco, shows promise, demonstrating that innovative ways to attain integration may yet succeed where involuntary busing has faltered.

Emmett H. Buell, Jr., and Richard Brisbin, Jr., *School Desegregation and Defended Neighborhoods* (1982); Muriel Cohen, "A Long Road Traveled and a Long Road Ahead," *Boston Globe*, June 21, 1984; Brian L. Fife, *Desegregation in American Schools: Comparative Intervention Strategies* (1992); Ronald P. Formisano, *Boston against Busing: Race, Class, and Ethnicity in the 1960s and 1970s* (1991); J. Anthony Lukas, *Common Ground: A Turbulent Decade in the Lives of Three American Families* (1985); Charles V. Willie and Susan L. Greenblatt, *Community Politics and Educational Change: Ten School Systems under Court Order* (1981).

Christopher A. Fahy

Dewey, John (1859–1952) Philosopher and educator. John Dewey was the preeminent American public intellectual during the first half of the 20th century. His work was rooted in a theory of knowing that was variously called pragmatism, instrumentalism, and (Dewey's choice) experimentalism. This theory had a strong New England imprint through the works of Harvard's William James. According to experimentalism, "truth" was not a static property that certain ideas possessed; rather, propositions, ideas, and beliefs were to be counted as "true" only to the extent that they fulfilled human needs when put to some experiential test. Consequently, philosophy became a form of "intelligent" engaged action, not a cloistered academic discipline involved in what Dewey saw as a futile attempt to mirror unchanging essences. The key term for Dewey was *experience,* a disciplined and purposeful activity, which, he argued, should be the central aim of education.

Dewey was born in Burlington, Vt., on the eve of the Civil War. His father, Archibald Sprague Dewey, served as a quartermaster during the war, then returned to Burlington and opened a cigar store, gaining a reputation for his punning advertisements ("Hams and cigars, smoked and unsmoked"). John's mother, Lucina Dewey, was a devout Congregationalist who tried, unsuccessfully, to inculcate this piety in her son. His schooling in Burlington consisted of traditional recitation and rote learning; in high school he endured the "classical" education that he would so vigorously oppose when he began to write about education. Yet the educational experiences he would promote in his Laboratory Schools bore strong traces of small-town work in the crafts.

In 1894 Dewey joined the University of Chicago faculty and sought an opportunity to put his theories of learning to the test. He founded the university's Laboratory Schools, one of the major themes of which was to break down the divisions between school-based "learning" and social activity (including occupations). In his widely popular *School and Society,* a book based on his work in the Laboratory Schools, he tells the story of a young student in Moline, Iowa, who did not connect the Missouri River in his textbook with the body of water flowing through his town.

Dewey's educational influence was strongest in the Midwest. At Ohio State University, one of his most astute disciples, Boyd Bode, would lecture to classes of 500. The Illinois-based National Council of Teachers of English developed *An Experience Curriculum in English,* which was strongly influenced by Dewey's ideas. After his move to Columbia University in 1904 he had a profound influence on some of the country's leading educators, including Lucy Sprague Mitchell, William Kilpatrick, and Louise Rosenblatt. While there was no comparable figure in New England, his influence was evident in the *Journal of Education,* which was published in Boston and regularly examined how to integrate education into the wider activity of the community. His influence can be seen in the emergence of the "writing-process movement" of the late 1970s and the curricular work—and Dewey-like experimental school—of Nancie Atwell in Maine.

In the 1930s Dewey became critical of the ways his ideas were used in some strands of the progressive education movement. In his last major pedagogical work, *Experience and Education,* he attacked those who failed to understand the rigor implicit in his concept of "experience" and who instead fostered student-chosen activity with little planning or direction from the teacher. He also criticized those who turned his interest in occupations into narrowly focused vocational training programs that served to maintain socioeconomic distinctions.

Lawrence Cremin, *The Transformation of the American School* (1961); John Dewey, *"The School and Society" and "The Child and the Curriculum"* (1990); Alan Ryan, *John Dewey and the High Tide of American Liberalism* (1995); Robert Westbrook, *John Dewey and American Democracy* (1991).

Thomas Newkirk

Elderhostel Elderhostel is a worldwide educational organization offering programs for adults 55 years of age and older. Founded in 1975 on the campus of the University of New Hampshire by social theorist and activist Martin P. Knowlton and university administrator David Bianco, Elderhostel features not-for-credit learning experiences for active adults who are interested in remaining engaged in a rapidly changing world. Groups of 30 to 50 participants live together in college dormitories, conference centers, hotels, or other retreats and, for fun and edification, take liberal arts and science classes and a wide variety of special-interest classes and activities that range from folk dancing to bird watching.

Elderhostel programs are created on site and coordinated through state or regional directors and the international headquarters in Boston. They are usually one to three weeks in duration, and many involve substantial domestic or international travel. Elderhostel also offers service programs that provide an opportunity to learn while volunteering for public-interest projects, and it supports a network of independent, community-based institutes for learning during retirement years. Elderhostel programs are offered in every state and in more than 90 countries. A sister organization, Elderhostel Canada, offers programs in all provinces. Each year close to 200,000 indi-

Camp Calumet Elderhostel group bird-watching in Freedom, N.H., 1993

viduals participate in Elderhostel programs throughout the world.

The Elderhostel idea incorporates some of the venturesome spirit found in the youth-hostel movements in Europe. The organization began by reaching out to a growing population that was no longer satisfied with existing opportunities but was eager to learn and try new experiences. Created on a land-grant university campus with a tradition of public service, and immediately offered as an opportunity at small neighboring institutions (Franklin Pierce College, Keene State College, New England College, and Franconia College), the program flourished as an experiment in adult, nontraditional learning.

A small academic organization that soon developed the dynamic characteristics of a movement, Elderhostel was founded the same year that Robert N. Butler published his landmark book *Why Survive? Being Old in America* (1975). Both the movement and the book focused national attention on an undervalued and underserved population. Around this time, colleges and universities began to increase academic and research opportunities in gerontology. Indeed, representatives of the New England Gerontology Center were present at the preliminary discussions concerning the creation of "an American Elders Hostel Association." In the years since the establishment of Elderhostel as a modest initiative in northern New England, there has been a remarkable transformation in the attitudes and policies that affect older Americans. While far too many live uncertain and marginal lives, the country is moving from merely assessing the needs of a vulnerable and dependent population to enabling older Americans to play a

more creative and highly valued role. Evaluations by more than a million participants reveal that Elderhostel programs have, indeed, made their lives richer.

Robert N. Butler, *Why Survive? Being Old in America* (1975); Eugene S. Mills, *The Story of Elderhostel* (1993); Harry R. Moody, *Abundance of Life: Human Development Policies for an Aging Society* (1988).

Eugene S. Mills

Extracurricular Activities in Colleges and Universities Undergraduate life at New England's colleges and universities is characterized by extracurricular activity as well as academic effort. Intercollegiate sports, fraternal and sororal organizations, local traditions, and even shared social-protest movements have contributed to the distinctive identity of New England's institutions of higher education. Each fall, for instance, colleges from across New England send representatives to Boston for what has become a ritual of collegiate experience: the Head of the Charles regatta. Dozens of sculls race on the Charles River in one of the oldest intercollegiate competitions in the country; the race exemplifies how undergraduates at institutions across the region experience college life fully. Indeed, for many students, what is extracurricular is in fact cocurricular—avenues for personal growth are at least as important as their formal learning. These avenues comprise what historian Frederick Rudolph has called the "Collegiate Way." No American college or university has ever been able to escape this awesome task of meeting the social needs of students, balancing their formal learning with a proper dose of extracurricular opportunities.

The breadth and depth of extracurricular

May Day hoop rolling at Wellesley College, Wellesley, Mass., 1973

activities at New England's colleges today belie their modest beginnings. By the early 19th
century, students had begun to grow restless
with the one-dimensional nature of college
life. Neither the classroom nor compulsory
chapel services provided the kind of social interaction that students at New England's colleges desired; as a result they developed their
own practices and customs outside the prescribed collegiate routine. Many such customs
grew into traditions. Students at Bowdoin, for
example, participated in Class Tree Day, where
members of each class were freed from
the day's lectures and recitations to scour the
countryside in search of a suitable tree to be
planted on the college grounds as a gift from
their class. Students regularly looked for a tree
as far away from the campus as possible so that
the day might also be one filled with drink.

The Fourth of July was another anticipated
yearly event. Although colleges did not officially recognize the day as a holiday in the
early national and antebellum period, students
at New England's colleges frequently celebrated the day by cutting classes. Moreover,
they did so in large enough numbers to undermine the daily routine. In 1846 well over three-
fourths of students at Waterville (now Colby)
College not only refused to go to class but also
insisted on marching across campus with
horns and bells, thereby disturbing the few
students who chose to attend their recitations.
At Williams College in the 1830s and 1840s,
Fourth of July celebrations were often violent,
as students broke windows, fired guns, and
threw fireballs across campus.

Commencement also provided ample opportunities for the development of annual
customs among students. On Class Day at
Amherst, held before graduation, seniors gathered in the morning to hear mock recitations
complete with impersonations of faculty members. The afternoon was filled with speeches
and songs, and a class dinner followed in the
evening. The seniors kept vigil throughout the
night, completing the day's events with an
oration to the rising sun delivered from the
college bell tower. And at 19th-century Williams, students who delivered addresses on
commencement eve were expected to entertain their classmates with generous amounts
of wine beforehand. Matriculation had its traditions, too. At nearly all men's colleges, each
new freshman could count on some form of
hazing, perhaps in the form of being "smoked
out" of his room or tied to the top of a pine tree
in minimal clothing.

While practices such as these were predicated partly on casting aside college laws, certain other extracurricular elements that
emerged during the 19th century complemented the curriculum. Students formed literary societies not only in order to cultivate
their intellect and verbal skills, but also to
share their goals and values in an attempt to
mold themselves into respectable gentlemen.
Colleges cautiously embraced the extracurriculum, and in so doing, the president and
faculty of the schools became guardians over
more than just the intellectual growth of these
students; they became instruments in the social transition from boyhood to manhood.

The fraternal organizations that followed
were the logical fruits of both literary societies
and the array of emerging student traditions.
Unlike the literary societies, however, the new
fraternal organizations did not have cultivation of the intellect at their base. On the contrary, these organizations sought to embrace
and promote social practices and values simply
for their own good, not as a complement to intellectual pursuits.

The women's colleges that emerged in the
late 19th and early 20th centuries also encouraged gendered behavior and social interaction.
Where the men had alcohol, tobacco, and card
playing, women enjoyed tea parties, drama,
and all-female dances. Social activities and involvement, however, appear to have been
more important at women's schools than at
men's. Dress and behavior became crucial to
attaining social acceptance. And, as at men's
colleges, women's colleges witnessed a class
stratification based upon refinement, popularity, and interests that had important impacts
on their day-to-day lives. Social and academic
ceremonies were widespread. Tree Day at
Wellesley and Ivy Day at Smith and Mount
Holyoke did more than connect classes to
their campuses. They also became public performances where social presentation and performance were judged. Differences notwithstanding, by the end of the 19th century the
extracurriculum at both men's and women's
colleges had become a central part of the undergraduate experience.

The various social organizations and opportunities that emerged in the 19th century
facilitated the rise of what is probably the most
distinguishing characteristic of extracurricular
life: college athletics. What began as a means
of promoting fitness rapidly developed into
organized competition among students in
baseball, football, and other physical activities.
By the beginning of the 20th century, athletics
had become the preferred means of bolstering
community among students and feeding their
desire for competition. New England colleges
and universities, like those in other parts of the
country, scrambled to lay claim to school colors. Athletics provided new opportunities for
colleges to connect with each other, heighten-
ing old rivalries and establishing new ones.
Football, more than any other sport, came to
exemplify this competitive spirit. As the rivalry that developed between Bowdoin College and the University of Maine suggests,
students experienced exhilaration at defeating
a dreaded foe or shame at being beaten.
Alumni emerged amid this competition to demand institutional support for football programs, believing that victory on the field of
play was a sign of institutional superiority.

In the Progressive Era, football served as a
metaphor for the harshness and competition

of life outside the colleges, but it also came under scrutiny for its brutality and unfairness. For reformers like Harvard graduate Theodore Roosevelt, football embodied his "strenuous life," but it also violated the commitment to free and fair competition that was at the heart of Progressive reform. It was a sport in need of regulation, if for no other reason than to protect the lives of its participants. In 1905, for instance, at least one Harvard player suffered a concussion in all but two games. Thus, as with early-20th-century business practices, football and college athletics as a whole responded to intense pressure to regulate activities by establishing common rules of conduct for all games and teams. Regulated athletics became an icon of Progressivism, glorifying human abilities over those of machines and fostering a rugged yet contained individualism that was a hallmark of the era.

Athletics flowered in a time when American higher education became more egalitarian. In the wake of World War II, more and more individuals decided to go to college. The increase in enrollments that began with the G.I. Bill created an even greater need for a comprehensive extracurriculum at colleges and universities. This expansion of higher education to include greater numbers of the middle class reached a watershed in the 1960s, when student culture took center stage in antiwar protests and the Civil Rights movement. Indeed, the student culture of the 1960s enjoyed an unprecedented and as-yet-unmatched prominence. American students joined with their counterparts in other parts of the globe in the most significant generation-based challenge to established authority of the modern era. At Bowdoin in 1970, students went so far as to launch a strike in protest of both the war in Vietnam and the shootings at Kent State University. Faculty and administrators, including the college's president, sided with the students in their protest, much to the consternation of town leaders and more conservative alumni.

Although many of their geopolitical goals proved unattainable, students of the 1960s succeeded in planting the seeds of a more tolerant, inclusive student body at colleges across the country. Their work in bringing the issue of civil rights to the forefront of national consciousness also served to highlight inequities for minority and female students within higher education. In the decades that followed, colleges made significant efforts to redress imbalances of ethnicity and gender among the student population. As a result, colleges expanded extracurricular opportunities to meet the needs of the changing student body. What became known as multiculturalism thus emerged alongside a growth of student services, as colleges and universities accepted more and more responsibility for providing nonacademic opportunities to an increasingly diverse student body.

Undergraduate life at New England colleges and universities stands apart from that of other parts of the country; the very geography, climate, and culture of New England promote activities that are singularly its own. The seasons appear in their most extreme forms in New England, encouraging a variety of outdoor activities. The region's rich immigrant past also influences student culture, as schools have adopted various ethnic and religious traditions. Moreover, New England colleges and universities are infused with a sense of history that grows directly from New Englanders' own close connection with their past. College students in New England are continually reminded of the legacy of great deeds and great individuals that they inherit, often influencing the formation of their contemporary culture.

The importance of the extracurriculum in the history of New England undergraduate life cannot be overstated. Fraternities and sororities, athletic teams and competition, student advocacy groups, and organizations that promote student interest and culture all work to encourage collegiality and community, while providing opportunities for competition and debate. Along with the residential experience of college, extracurricular activities constitute laboratories where ideas and values can be tested and shared.

David F. Allmendinger, *Paupers and Scholars: The Transformation of Student Life in 19th-Century New England* (1975); Helen Lefkowitz Horowitz, *Alma Mater: Design and Experience in Women's Colleges from Their 19th-Century Beginnings to the 1930s,* 2d ed. (1993); Horowitz, *Campus Life: Undergraduate Cultures from the 18th Century to the Present* (1987); David O. Levine, *The American College and the Culture of Aspiration, 1915–1940* (1986); James McLachlan, "The Choice of Hercules: American Student Societies in the Early 19th Century," in *The University in Society, Volume 2: Europe, Scotland, and the United States from the 16th to the 20th Century,* ed. Lawrence Stone (1974); Frederick Rudolph, *The American College and University: A History* (1962); Wilson Smith, "Apologia pro Alma Mater: The College as Community in Ante-Bellum America," in *The Hofstadter Aegis: A Memorial,* ed. Stanley Elkins and Eric McKitrick (1974); John R. Thelin, *Games Colleges Play: Scandal and Reform in Intercollegiate Athletics* (1994).

Kenneth Nivison

Harvard University On October 28, 1636, the Great and General Court of the Massachusetts Bay Colony provided funds for the construction of a "schoale or colledge" in what is now Cambridge, Mass. Two years later John Harvard, a young minister in Charlestown with financial resources of his own, died, bequeathing to the new college half his estate and all his impressive library. In total, John Harvard's gifts exceeded the initial grant of the colony, which quickly renamed its new institution Harvard College.

Harvard was a small, financially precarious New England college throughout its first 170 years. An "Indian College" was erected in about 1655, but the effort failed a decade later. More impressive in these early years were the college's graduates: the great 17th-century divines Increase Mather, his son Cotton Mather, and Solomon Stoddard; governors of all the New England states a number of others; eight signers of the Declaration of Independence; two U.S. presidents (John Adams and his son John Quincy Adams); generals, merchants, and manufacturers; artists, architects, and writers such as John Trumbull, Charles Bulfinch, and Washington Allston; as well as many clergymen, judges, senators and members of Congress, scholars, and presidents of Harvard and other colleges.

The curriculum, based on old medieval divisions of learning, changed little over this period. Students were asked to recite passage from texts, rather than write essays or take written examinations. Early in the 19th century, pressure for reform began to build, largely from outside the newly designated university. New subjects (such as modern languages) demanded attention, and the old system of recitations provided little intellectual stimulus for either teacher or student. New faculty, often trained in Europe, and new students from New York and farther South, were attracted to this now energetic institution. Reform came only in fits and starts, however, and even after the Civil War Harvard had more in common with its 17th-century heritage than with the modern university of today.

In 1869 Charles W. Eliot, a young chemistry professor at the Massachusetts Institute of Technology with a somewhat forbidding personality (stemming from a disfiguring birthmark covering almost half his face), was elected president. After a forceful inaugural address of an hour and 45 minutes, it was obvious that change was in store for Harvard. In his first year in office Eliot unleashed a storm of new initiatives, proposing new admissions requirements, appointing new faculty members from outside the academic community, introducing the concept of student choice in a new course-based curriculum, requiring written exercises and exams, and challenging the old rules about compulsory chapel. Criticism and resistance arose, but Eliot, who had long steeled himself against what others might say, pressed on. He served as president for 40 years, until 1909, and the university he left had become the standard-bearer for American higher education. Its faculty had been recruited from throughout the scholarly world, and students came from every state and scores

Harvard Yard, Harvard University, Cambridge, Mass.

of counties overseas. The university's libraries, laboratories, and museums were unparalleled. And, to back it all up, the university now had a substantial endowment, enabling it to offer financial aid. Undergraduates were free to study whatever they wished. The Graduate School and the professional schools—Divinity, Engineering, Law, Medicine, and the newest, Business—set the pace for the nation. Eliot himself had become the nation's schoolteacher, issuing his "five-foot shelf" of books for the self-education of all citizens.

Eliot had little interest in students' social lives, however, and he had provided little guidance for students seeking their way through the now untrammeled curriculum. His successor, A. Lawrence Lowell, remedied these omissions, providing a structured residence system of freshman dormitories and living clusters for upperclassmen called "houses," each with its own dining room, library, common rooms, and other amenities, watched over by a "master" and other faculty members and graduate students. On the curricular side Lowell introduced the now standard concepts of concentration ("majors" at most other colleges) and distribution. A new kind of university began to emerge during the presidency of James Conant, another chemist (1933–53). Harvard's resources, scientific and otherwise, were organized for the national defense during World War II. Like many other universities, it worked closely with federal and state agencies to provide for the security of country. Substantial funding began to flow to promote these efforts, and Harvard grew commensurably in scholarly capacity and in public service activities.

Harvard today is a complex institution,

which includes Harvard College and the university's distinguished professional schools—the School of Dental Medicine, School of Design, School of Education, John F. Kennedy School of Government, and School of Public Health were added to the existing schools—as well as the Radcliffe Institute for Advanced Study, formed in 1999 after a merger with Radcliffe College, which had been founded in 1879 to provide women with access to Harvard teaching. The university is also affiliated with some 150 research and academic centers. There are almost 20,000 degree candidates enrolled at any one time and more than 2,000 full-time faculty members. The university provides about $250 million annually in direct financial aid, with further support provided through loans and employment opportunities—sufficient financial aid so that all needy students can complete their programs of study.

John T. Bethell, *Harvard Observed* (1998); Harvard University, *Fact Book 2003–2004* (2004); Samuel Eliot Morison, *Three Centuries of Harvard* (1936).

John B. Fox, Jr.

Jewish Education The presence and availability of Jewish educational resources in New England reflect both the history and the current situation of New England Jewry. Despite New England's long and rich tradition of education, the history of Jewish education in New England is comparatively short. This can be attributed in part to New England's Puritan heritage, which did not encourage toleration of religious minorities. With the exception of the celebrated Newport, R.I., community, significant Jewish settlement dates back only to the mid-19th century.

The first Hebrew school in New England

was established in 1838 as part of Congregation Mishkan Israel in New Haven, Conn. The Mishkan Israel Hebrew School, moreover, remains the oldest continuing Jewish religious school in New England. Ohabei Shalom in Boston, the first synagogue in the Boston area, was founded in 1843 and also housed one of the first Jewish religious schools in New England.

Today, Jewish educational resources may be found in major New England cities and university towns. In Boston, which boasts the largest Jewish community in New England, the Bureau of Jewish Education, sponsored by the oldest federated charity in North America, supports more than 135 Jewish educational programs ranging from nursery school to adult education. Over 15,000 students are enrolled in nursery-, elementary-, and secondary-school programs that cover the spectrum of American Judaism and are taught by more than 2,000 professional Jewish educators.

The vibrant Jewish community integrated into the university town of New Haven boasts a wide variety of educational programs at all levels, including the Makom Hebrew High School, an after-school program with more than 350 students that serves as a national model for Hebrew high-school programs. Even the smaller, more sparsely populated Jewish communities in New England maintain pluralistic Jewish educational programming. The Portland, Maine, area, for example, hosts a nondenominational community Hebrew day school for preschool through second grade, in addition to several synagogue-affiliated religious schools; adult education courses ranging from Hebrew to Talmud are available through the synagogues and the Jewish community center.

New England is most renowned for Jewish higher education. The Hebrew College in Brookline, Mass., is devoted to graduate and undergraduate training in Jewish studies and Jewish education, and it boasts a library containing more than 100,000 volumes of Hebraica and Judaica. Jewish studies have become a fully recognized part of the curriculum of several major New England universities, including Harvard, Yale, and Brown as well as the Jewish-founded, nonsectarian Brandeis University. Beyond formal courses, various educational and social activities are a significant part of the Hillel organizations on many New England university and college campuses.

Dan Oren, *Joining the Club: A History of Jews and Yale* (1985); Nitza Rosovsky, Pearl K. Bell, and Ronald Steel, *The Jewish Experience at Harvard and Radcliffe* (1986); Howard Morley Sacher, *A History of the Jews in America* (1992); Mervin F. Verbit, ed., *World Register of University Studies of Jewish Civilization: Inventory of Holdings* (1985).

Susan Roth Breitzer

Students at transitional kindergarten class, Carousel School, Waltham, Mass., 1990

Kindergarten and Nursery School

New England has long been a center for innovation, advocacy, writing, training, and research related to the education of young children. The Puritans were passionately concerned with education as a prerequisite for salvation and believed that children as young as 12 or 18 months could begin to learn Scripture and catechisms. The teaching of children aged four and under, originally the responsibility of fathers, became the province of mothers and dame school teachers—often poor widows—who were paid a pittance to teach and care for young children in their homes.

In the early 19th century, when male evangelical Sunday-school advocates began promoting common schools, female evangelical reform groups started infant-school societies to educate young children of the poor. By 1830 infant-school societies had been established in most New England cities, including Boston, Hartford, and Providence, and a petition was submitted to the Boston school committee to make infant schools part of the public system. Early childhood education was also a key interest for American followers of European Romanticism, which emphasized the innocence and pliability of the infant soul. Bronson Alcott, who founded the Temple School in Boston, wrote about communing with children as a redeeming personal experience and about education as a liberating process. These new ideas about learning and a new conception of women as gentle, maternal home educators, along with questions about whether it was healthy for young children to receive early intellectual stimulation, figured prominently in the American child-rearing literature that appeared in the 1830s, much of it written by New Englanders and published in Boston. In-

fant schools died out, but many young children in antebellum New England attended school informally by accompanying their older brothers and sisters.

The American kindergarten movement began in New England in the late 1850s. Connecticut educator Henry Barnard wrote about kindergartens he had seen abroad, established in Germany beginning in 1837 under the influence of Friedrich Froebel, who advocated play in the classroom and work with such materials as clay. Transcendentalist writer and educator Elizabeth Peabody opened the first English-speaking kindergarten in the United States in Boston in 1860 and began energetically promoting kindergarten as a new form of child-centered education and a career option for women. Private kindergartens and training schools were started in most New England cities in the 1870s and 1880s, and charity or free kindergartens for poor and immigrant children were opened in Boston and elsewhere. Pauline Agassiz Shaw, daughter of noted Harvard professor Louis Agassiz and wife of wealthy industrialist Quincy Adams Shaw, sponsored a network of charity kindergartens in Boston, some of which were located in public-school buildings. In 1888 the Boston public schools assumed responsibility for these classes, and public kindergartens were opened thereafter in other New England cities and large towns. Today, New Hampshire is the only state that doesn't offer universal kindergarten.

In the 1920s New England led the way again when Abigail Adams Eliot started the first nursery school in America on Ruggles Street in the Roxbury section of Boston. African American and white children attended this nursery school together, and Eliot

ran integrated parent education programs as well. Under Eliot's direction, Massachusetts had the largest federally sponsored Works Progress Administration emergency nursery-school program in the country during the Depression. Nursery schools were also started on such college campuses as Wellesley, and the Smith College Nursery School in Northampton, Mass., was part of the Institute for the Coordination of Women's Interests, a novel project designed to help educated mothers of young children pursue careers.

Research on preschool education and on young children was a focus at many colleges and universities in New England, such as Wheelock College in Boston and the Department of Child Study at Tufts University in Medford, Mass. Influential psychologist Arnold Gesell did extensive research on young children's development and started an experimental clinical nursery school at Yale University in New Haven, Conn., where the Bush Center in Child Development and Social Policy is one of the premier institutions for research and advocacy on child welfare issues today. Although the availability and quality of preschool programs for poor and rural children have always been concerns, New England is a region that continues to regard early childhood education as a central issue.

Barbara Beatty, *Preschool Education in America: The Culture of Young Children from the Colonial Era to the Present* (1995); Marvin Lazerson, "Urban Reform and the Schools: Kindergartens in Massachusetts, 1870–1915," *History of Education Quarterly* (1971); Dean May and Maris Vinovskis, "A Ray of Millennial Light: Early Education and Social Reform in the Infant School Movement in Massachusetts, 1826–1840," in *Family and Kin in Urban Communities, 1700–1930*, ed. Tamara Hareven (1977); Michael Steven Shapiro, *Child's Garden: The Kindergarten Movement from Froebel to Dewey* (1983).

Barbara Beatty

Liberal Arts Colleges

Like the white wooden chapel, the bucolic liberal-arts college campus has been a distinguishing characteristic of New England's landscape since the colonial period. One can hardly conjure an image of New England without summoning a picture of the Gothic buildings of Yale, the brick and mortar of Bowdoin, or the college green at Dartmouth. Such images as these have inspired liberal arts colleges in other parts of the country to emulate those in New England. In this way, the New England college has been, to many observers, the essence of New England.

This idyllic image is not, however, the historical reality. Since the founding of Harvard in 1636, New England's liberal arts colleges have been engaged in continual struggles, both internal and external, to define what they represent, defend their form of higher education, and engage in the business of turning out graduates who are trained not as technicians but as thinkers. Their responses to the pressures of a modernizing, commercial society have been numerous and varied. Their common desire to survive and to enhance their prestige has united them over time and place.

The region's liberal arts colleges also share the goal of preparing future leaders for public life. Since Harvard began training clergy to guide new settlers, New England's colleges have always contributed to the leadership of the region and nation. They have been concerned with providing students with as broad an educational experience as possible. The desire to inculcate values, to build character, and to open and prepare the mind to receive new and different truths has long been a defining characteristic of the New England liberal arts college.

While such colleges as Harvard and Yale (1701) were founded with the express intent of training clergy, that purpose changed in the wake of the American Revolution. Colleges had to educate citizens of the new republic who would guard the legacy of the Revolution. Newly christened Americans in New England engaged in a process of college building to meet the evolving needs of the region. Whereas from 1636 to 1769 only four colleges were founded in New England, six colleges and one state university were established between the years 1791 and 1831.

The creation of these colleges was partially due to economic changes wrought by the Revolution. Many young men in New England saw such colleges as Williams (1793) in Massachusetts, Bowdoin (1794) in Maine, Middlebury (1800) in Vermont, Waterville (Colby, 1813) in Maine, and Amherst (1821) in Massachusetts as places that could help them escape the farm life their fathers had led. Religion continued to be a critical element of the colleges' identities. In New England, the bastion of Congregationalism and Federalism, Congregationalists boasted the strongest showing in the field of higher education. Colleges maintained at least a moderate amount of autonomy, in part because of the decentralized organizational structure of Congregationalism and in part because of the colleges' reliance on support from outside the dominant religious sect. In their foundations, governance, and administration, the colleges were driven more by local needs and concerns than denominational interests.

As this proliferation of colleges opened educational doors for increasing numbers of young men, the portrait of the typical college student changed notably. No longer were college students solely the sons of wealthy families or professionals. Indeed, many benevolent organizations, such as the American Education Society (1815), arose to help young men of limited means pay for a college education. The influx of middle-class students made colleges increasingly tumultuous arenas. As a result, New England colleges became both participants in and targets of the many crusades for moral reform that dominated the social landscape of the 19th century.

During the early 19th century, slavery, war, and commercial capitalism were frequent topics of campus discussion, energizing students and instilling in them a public consciousness that would direct their thoughts and actions throughout the century's turmoil. While students at Bowdoin witnessed the creation of Harriet Beecher Stowe's *Uncle Tom's Cabin* (1852), their counterparts at Dartmouth in Hanover, N.H., saw their president, Nathan Lord, jettison his antislavery views for proslavery ones. The Civil War brought unique challenges. Enrollments declined as students enlisted, and professors likewise answered President Lincoln's call for troops. Both the Union and Confederate armies constituted proof that New England's colleges had been producing leaders, as many graduates were placed in command over other men.

During the late 19th century, a period of industrialization and modernization, New England's colleges faced a serious threat, as many began to question the utility of the old liberal arts college. The age of the American university followed the Civil War, as educational reformers of the Gilded Age and Progressive Era sought to replace colleges with modern, progressive universities modeled after the institutions of Germany. These new colleges placed an emphasis on science, modern languages, and professional training. Above all else, university reformers wanted their colleges to be practical. Moreover, instructors at these colleges were to be professionals, experts in a particular field. The liberal-arts college professor was discredited for his inability to delve deeply enough into one subject so as to master it. Many colleges engaged in self-reform to adopt and adapt some of the innovations embodied in the new universities. For example, Joshua Lawrence Chamberlain, alumnus of Bowdoin College and its president from 1871 to 1883, attempted to modify the curriculum by placing more emphasis on science and modern languages. Despite the pressure for reform, New England colleges generally remained committed to producing well-rounded individuals of good character and leaders of society.

The university moment, as it might be called, also fostered an egalitarian attitude toward higher education. Educational opportunities for women in New England increased with the expansion of Mount Holyoke (1837) and the founding of Wellesley (1870) and Smith (1871), all in Massachusetts. While the founders intended these colleges to reinforce traditional domestic and deferential roles for women, the students instead used the experience to redefine cultural notions of womanhood. Catholics would also find higher education friendlier in post–Civil War New England. Holy Cross (1843) in Worcester, Mass., Boston College (1863), and Saint Anselm (1889) in Manchester, N.H., despite heavy nativist opposition, gained a foothold in the New England educational landscape, thanks in large measure to the influx of Catholic immigrants.

Since the founding of the world's first alumni association at Williams College in 1821, graduates have made their collective presence part of colleges' broader identity. Alumni provided critical support as New England's colleges weathered the often tumultuous years of the late 19th and early 20th centuries. Meanwhile, the elective system that emerged in new universities, allowing students to choose which courses they would take and enabling them to focus in depth on one subject, challenged the traditional liberal arts curriculum. Such an innovation, while initially a threat, ultimately encouraged liberal arts colleges to adopt a philosophical outlook that has since become a defining characteristic. Colleges embraced the elective system on their own terms; students would be allowed to sample a variety of courses, but a standard core curriculum would reinforce the need for a well-rounded education. Thus liberal arts colleges became what they are today—places where a student learns a good deal about one subject and at least something about many others.

The mid-20th century brought new challenges to New England's colleges. They supported the war effort during World War II, but in the immediate postwar period, as the G.I. Bill enabled hundreds of veterans to attend college in New England, their enrollments and finances became strained. A few decades after the war, however, a significant shift occurred. In the 1960s, the same colleges that had been so instrumental in support of the Civil War and the world wars became territory hostile to America's involvement in the Vietnam War. Exemptions from the draft given to young men who attended college, combined with the ideological convictions of students, professors, and administrators who opposed the war effort, created a charged atmosphere at campuses in New England and across the nation. The same colleges that had fostered participation and patriotism in previous wars became havens for dissenters, places of vocal and heated opposition to the federal government and its policies.

The second half of the 20th century forced many colleges to address the issue of finance in ways they had never considered, as they bore an increasingly heavy burden to provide students more than just a classroom education and a place to live. Partly the result of changes in the home and partly because of efforts to attract students who more accurately reflected the nation's ethnic diversity, professional support services emerged and grew at New England's colleges. The movement for a diverse student body pitted many colleges against one another as they bid for the most qualified minority students. Tuition and donations from alumni that had built modest endowments in the past were no longer seen as sufficient sources of capital for future growth. Thus New England's colleges continue to make endowment building a top institutional priority at the beginning of the 21st century.

Although residue from the 1960s and 1970s, such as grade inflation, still plague many institutions, the colleges of New England seem to have moved away from the polemics, and concomitant ideological battles among faculty members over the merits of Marxism, that marked the Vietnam era. Such disputes have given way to what many consider new crises for New England's liberal arts colleges, including renewed debates over what constitutes a "canon" of liberal education. Many colleges attempt to alter their overall educational and institutional identity in order to improve their ranking in the *U.S. News and World Report* annual listing of the nation's best colleges. This effort has served to dull many of the differences between New England colleges and those of other regions, as well as the distinctions among New England colleges. The result has been a cultural diffusion among liberal arts colleges in New England and the nation.

In spite of all they have weathered since 1636, New England's liberal arts colleges have never been in decline. New Englanders, like most Americans, have not only demonstrated unswerving faith in education as a means of bettering society, they have continuously sought to improve higher education. This process of constant refinement, combined with the steady commitment to the basic goals of a liberal arts education and the belief that such an education is useful in all times, has endowed New England's colleges with their most distinguishing characteristics.

David F. Allmendinger, *Paupers and Scholars: The Transformation of Student Life in 19th-Century New England* (1975); Richard M. Freeland, *Academia's Golden Age: Universities in Massachusetts, 1945–1970* (1992); Helen Lefkowitz Horowitz, *Alma Mater: Design and Experience in Women's Colleges from Their 19th-Century Beginnings to the 1930s*, 2d ed. (1993); Daniel Walker Howe, *The Unitarian Conscience: Harvard Moral Philosophy, 1805–1861* (1970); George E. Peterson, *The New England College in the Age of the University* (1964); Frederick Rudolph, *The American College and University: A History* (1962); Rudolph, *Mark Hopkins and the Log: Williams College, 1836–1872* (1956); Marilyn Tobias, *Old Dartmouth on Trial: The Transformation of the Academic Community in 19th-Century America* (1982).

Kenneth Nivison

Literacy to 1800 The New England region, and Massachusetts in particular, figures prominently in the history of literacy in the United States. In the 17th century, English Calvinists carried to the New World a firm belief in the value of basic literacy in ensuring a godly life, and New England developed a reputation as a place associated with literary activities as diverse as the development of the common-school movement; the flowering of such New England writers as Ralph Waldo Emerson, Nathaniel Hawthorne, and Henry David Thoreau; and the establishment in the colonial era of two of the world's most prominent universities, Harvard and Yale. The early emphasis on literacy led to the creation of the first presses in the English colonies and, later, an influential publishing industry that contributed to New England's prominence in American history and literature.

The influx of English Calvinists into New England in the so-called Great Migration of the 1630s indelibly shaped regional attitudes toward both basic and advanced literacy. These early immigrants imagined a "Bible commonwealth" that relied on biblical principles to guide it. Leaders of Puritanism, with its unrelenting insistence on the all-encompassing role of God's will in human life as revealed in the Bible, expected individuals to read God's word, sermons, and devotional literature. New England churches were primary arbiters of the literacy that was so essential to the promulgation of the faith of the New World. New England families were encouraged to teach basic literacy by means of primers and catechisms. The Puritan vision promoted the small community, with the church as its hub, as the ideal place to foster and replicate the faith and keep a close eye on followers. This vision supported the efforts of civil authorities to create a literate populace for the sake of social order and economic development. For the Puritans, then, literacy was a form of social control and conditioning. The Sunday service was seen as a mode of education for believers, and reading was centered on the Bible and the sermons at the heart of Protestant culture.

The Calvinist perspective insisted on the centrality of the Bible in the lives of the faithful. As Adolphe Meyer has noted, the Puritans viewed the Bible as "God's sacred blueprint" for their mission. Although the Puritan vision of the shape of the state was essentially an elitist one, advocating rule by a small, well-educated group of male elect, it did promote universal basic literacy for all followers. All Puritans were expected to be able to read a short biblical passage and answer questions about it in order to open their minds and souls to salvation, which was often manifested to believers through read or spoken texts.

Because of the link between biblical knowledge and salvation, the Puritans promoted schooling in various ways, both formal and informal. Nonetheless, the quality of education was uneven at best in the 17th and 18th centuries. Many children learned their letters in the home setting, at "dame" schools run by women in the community. The most popular textbook in 17th-century New England, other than the Bible, was the *New-England Primer*, a small, inexpensive book featuring familiar hymns and picture alphabets accompanied by short verses designed to reinforce Puritan tenets ("A. In Adam's Fall/We Sinned All"; "I will fear GOD, and honour the KING"). The *Primer* remained popular well into the 19th century. Another popular text used to teach reading was Michael Wigglesworth's popular poem *The Day of Doom* (1662), which many children memorized.

In 1642 Massachusetts passed a law mandating the teaching of basic literacy skills to all children. The law had a dual purpose: to provide for poor children by establishing an apprenticeship system, and to promote universal literacy. Similar laws followed in other New England states. Despite the legislative imprimatur, the law left the means of education up to parents and individual towns. In 1647, the General Court of Massachusetts passed a measure mandating the establishment of town schools in communities of 50 households or larger; this law met with resistance on the part of many settlers whose children were needed to work the farm. Moreover, many towns did not provide public education for girls. In general, Puritans were not necessarily interested in building a more formal educational system to ensure a literate population, and literacy rates during the colonial period rose and fell. Nevertheless, New England had a very high literacy rate compared to other areas of the colonies and to most of Europe. By the time of the American Revolution, New England's larger towns and cities supported female academies. Such missionaries as John Eliot in the 17th century, and Samson Occom and Eleazar Wheelock in the 18th, made sporadic efforts to instruct Native Americans. As evidenced by letters, petitions, and the poetry of Phillis

Wheatley, slaves and free people of color in New England also gained literary skills, though generally at much lower rates than the white population.

In 1783 Noah Webster published *The American Spelling Book*, which gradually replaced the *New-England Primer* as the primary literacy textbook. Webster's book, popularly known as the "Blue-Backed Speller" because of its binding, was a tremendous cultural force. Not only did it aid in standardizing American spelling, but it also contributed to the establishment of a unique American national identity.

By the late 18th and early 19th centuries, significant cultural and economic forces were radically transforming the agrarian New England landscape and, in turn, altering attitudes toward literacy and education in general. The most significant of these changes was the emergence of the "Republican Motherhood" credo. In the aftermath of the American Revolution, growing national disquiet over the future of democracy translated into public recognition of the important role that women, mothers in particular, played in transmitting patriotic values to future generations. This valorization of motherhood and mothers-as-teachers became more prevalent as the Industrial Revolution took hold in New England, dramatically changing home life for many. A new genre of texts called "fireside literature" developed specifically to educate readers, primarily female, about their social roles and responsibilities. These texts satisfied to some extent the demand for additional education and training for mothers. Instead of serving the soul, literacy skills were now seen as serving the future of the American democratic project.

Warren Button and Eugene F. Provenzo, Jr., *History of Education and Culture in America*, 2d ed. (1989); William J. Gilmore, *Reading Becomes a Way of Life: Material and Cultural Life in Rural New England, 1780–1835* (1989); Adolphe E. Meyer, *An Educational History of the American People* (1957).

Lisa Stepanski

Lyceums

"A town lyceum," wrote Josiah Holbrook, founder of the lyceum movement, "is a voluntary association of individuals disposed to improve each other in useful knowledge, and to advance the interests of their schools." Holbrook organized the first lyceum in Millbury, Mass. (near Worcester), in 1826, and subsequently traveled throughout New England to promote his plan. By 1830, Massachusetts alone had 78 lyceums; by 1834, lyceums had spread to 3,000 towns nationally, remaining prominent in American cultural life through the 1860s. Though best remembered for sponsoring lecture series (and pro-

moting such "star" speakers as Ralph Waldo Emerson and Henry Ward Beecher), lyceums also organized debates, dramatic and musical performances, scientific demonstrations, and other entertainment; they also frequently encouraged educational reform, established circulating libraries, and collected natural-history materials. In so doing, lyceums participated in a broad cultural imperative during the antebellum period to diffuse "practical" knowledge to the public.

Lyceums underwent a transformation during the 1830s and 1840s, possibly as a result of changes in their perceived audience. At first, they had a fundamentally local focus, drawing lecturers—usually unpaid—primarily from the community. Scientific inquiry played a particularly prominent role in the early years, owing to a desire to educate young men in practical subjects. Rapidly, however, organizers found humanistic topics more popular than scientific information, and they increasingly sought well-known, talented lecturers to speak on history, biography, travel, literature, self-culture (individual transformation rather than collective action), and the American character in order to appeal to a wider adult audience of both men and women. Gradually, certain speakers became known both regionally and nationally and came to command salaries as high as $100 per lecture in the 1850s; such generous rates allowed some traveling speakers to make careers of lyceum lecturing. Thomas Starr King, for example, explained that he lectured for "FAME—Fifty [dollars] and My Expenses." From the 1840s on, then, lyceums abandoned many of their earlier functions, such as holding debates, lending books, and displaying natural history collections, in favor of sponsoring popular lectures.

The lyceum's birth in New England influenced the tenor of the movement throughout its life, especially because of the high number of New England–based traveling lecturers. Ralph Waldo Emerson, one of the most famous, became a nationally known symbol of wisdom and culture. Historians have suggested that the lyceum thus helped foster a sense of New England as a national leader in education and culture. More significantly, scholars Donald Scott and Mary Kupiec Cayton have argued that Americans gained a sense of belonging to a national public by attending popular talks. Lyceums can thus be said to have linked national identity to the education of adult citizens by helping to define both regional difference and national unity in the context of promoting knowledge.

Although the number of lyceums declined during the 1860s, popular lectures continued to be sponsored by various institutions, in-

cluding young men's societies, mercantile libraries, and Chautauquas, facilitated by the establishment of such central booking offices as the Boston Lyceum Bureau.

Carl Bode, *The American Lyceum: Town Meeting of the Mind* (1956); Mary Kupiec Cayton, "The Making of an American Prophet: Emerson, His Audiences, and the Rise of the Culture Industry in 19th-Century America," *American Historical Review* 92 (1987); Donald M. Scott, "The Popular Lecture and the Creation of a Public in Mid-19th-Century America," *Journal of American History* 66 (1980).

Carolyn Eastman

Lyon, Mary (1797–1849)

Educator, founder of Mount Holyoke. By founding Mount Holyoke Seminary (today called Mount Holyoke College), the first permanently endowed women's institution of higher learning, Mary Lyon set the future direction of higher education for women. Like other seminaries, Mount Holyoke prepared young women to be teachers. But the South Hadley, Mass., school was distinguished by its combination of an advanced program and a sizable endowment. Mount Holyoke offered a curriculum based on the nonclassical portion of the standard college course. Its mission was to train teachers "possessing so much of a missionary spirit that they would labor faithfully and cheerfully, receiving only a moderate salary." Its financial underpinnings gave it the stability needed for institutional permanence and raised women's education to a level of importance previously reserved for men. Mount Holyoke's influence on education was widely felt. Its graduates went forth to serve as educators throughout the nation. Daughter seminaries were formed, and after the Civil War, endowed women's colleges were envisioned and created.

Mary Lyon was born and raised in the hill town of Buckland in western Massachusetts. Following the death of her father and her mother's later remarriage, Lyon became self-

Mary Lyon, ca. 1840

supporting in 1810. She was educated in district schools, and after beginning her teaching career in 1814, engaged in further study at Sanderson Academy in Ashfield, Mass.; Amherst Academy; and Rev. Joseph Emerson's seminary in Byfield, Mass. During the summer of 1823, Lyon studied with Rev. Edward Hitchcock, future Amherst College professor and president, who became a lifelong supporter of Lyon and her cause.

In 1824 Lyon and educator Zilpah Grant entered a 10-year partnership. With Grant in the leading position of principal, they worked together, first at Adams Academy in Derry, N.H., from 1824 to 1828, and then at Ipswich Seminary in Massachusetts from 1828 to 1834. This arrangement contributed to Lyon's growth as an educator and provided her with valuable administrative experience. Lyon's own work at winter schools in Buckland and Ashfield from 1824 to 1830 gave her additional opportunity for professional development. Lyon and Grant's joint effort to establish a permanently endowed seminary in the early 1830s failed, owing to public indifference, inactivity on the part of trustees, and prejudice against educating women.

In 1834 Mary Lyon left Ipswich with a determination to alter the course of women's higher education by demonstrating the viability of a suitably endowed, properly administered educational institution for women. In an amazing display of organizational skill and endurance, Lyon planned, networked, and fundraised. Her search for financial support extended to the ordinary citizen. She printed circulars and enlisted the service of dedicated men in promoting her cause.

On November 8, 1837, Mount Holyoke Seminary opened to 80 students in a nearly completed building. Until her death in 1849, Lyon, as Mount Holyoke's principal, worked continually to raise its academic standards. In 1893, the institution's name was formally changed to Mount Holyoke College, and the school founded by Mary Lyon became a prototype for women's colleges throughout the region and the country.

Beth B. Gilchrist, *The Life of Mary Lyon* (1910); Elizabeth A. Green, *Mary Lyon and Mount Holyoke: Opening the Gates* (1979); Helen Lefkowitz Horowitz, *Alma Mater: Design and Experience in the Women's Colleges from Their 19th-Century Beginnings to the 1930s*, 2d ed. (1993); Sydney R. MacLean, *Notable American Women*, vol. 2, s.v. "Mary Lyon" (1971).
Susan Williamson

Mann, Horace (1796–1859) Educator and U.S. representative. Known as the "father of American public education," Horace Mann was an educational pioneer whose reforms generated a common-school revival in the United States and produced a system of education that ultimately spread throughout the world. Mann's theories coincided with the philosophy of political and social democracy that emerged during the Jacksonian era and awakened in people a faith that universal education was the harbinger of an improved life in a republic.

Horace Mann, born in Franklin, Mass., overcame frail health, poverty, and an unhappy childhood to graduate with honors from Brown University in 1819 and from law school in Litchfield, Conn., in 1823. He practiced law in Dedham, Mass., and Boston for 14 years before serving in the Massachusetts House of Representatives from 1827 to 1833. He was a state senator from 1833 to 1837 and during his last two years in office held the position of Senate president. A crusader for his beliefs, Mann championed moralistic legislation (including temperance laws and laws against lotteries), favored the establishment of state hospitals for the mentally impaired, encouraged commercial and industrial expansion, and supported railroad development. He was one of the signers of the epoch-making Education Bill of 1837, which established the Massachusetts State Board of Education. Abandoning his successful legal practice and promising political future, Mann accepted the secretaryship of the board at an annual salary of $1,500.

During the next dozen years Mann transformed the Massachusetts school system into a national model. He had faith in the power of education to solve society's shortcomings, and he used the lyceum movement to mobilize opinion in favor of public schooling. The 12 annual reports that he wrote during his tenure as secretary were disseminated throughout the nation. These reports incorporated his ideas for progressive educational change and expressed his hope that public schools, by providing a common experience for all children without regard to their social, ethnic, religious, or economic status, would help the next generation to develop a sense of community in an increasingly heterogeneous environment. His aggressive efforts won praise but also provoked controversy. Some church leaders charged that his programs removed religion from the schools. They demanded the restoration of the sectarian instruction that had been excluded from common schools since 1827. Mann, however, promoted nonsectarian moral education and emphasized the need for improved instruction, high professional standards, and a revised curriculum. He believed in an inductive teaching method rather than a dogmatic textbook approach and maintained that kindness was more effective in motivating students than repression and fear. The reforms he instituted—such as mandatory school attendance, longer school years, and a neutralized school environment free from sectarian or political bias and propaganda—permanently influenced American education.

In 1848 Mann resigned from the board of education when he was chosen as an antislavery Whig to fill the seat of former president John Quincy Adams in the U.S. House of Representatives. While in Congress he supported the restriction of liquor traffic, protective tariffs, and federal funding for internal improvements. In 1852 he ran for governor of Massachusetts on the Free Soil ticket but was defeated. The following year Mann was appointed first president of Antioch College, a nonsectarian institution in Yellow Springs, Ohio, that admitted students without regard to race or sex. He retained that position until his death.

Robert B. Downs, *Horace Mann: Champion of Public Schools* (1974); Jonathan Messerli, *Horace Mann: A Biography* (1972); Louise Hall Tharp, *Until Victory: Horace Mann and Mary Peabody* (1953); E. I. F. Williams, *Horace Mann: Educational Statesman* (1937).
Leonard Schlup

Massachusetts Institute of Technology The Massachusetts Institute of Technology (MIT), a coeducational land-grant institution of higher learning, sprawls for more than a mile beside the Charles River Basin in Cambridge, Mass. Its 4,100 undergraduates and 6,200 graduate students are offered a full range of courses, but the school is known primarily for its preeminence in science and engineering; the Nobel Prize has been awarded 57 times to MIT researchers in fields ranging from physics to economics. The school is also noted for its interdisciplinary approaches and for integrating classroom teaching and practical experience, reflected by its motto, "Mens et Manus" (Mind and Hand). The beaver, a symbol of industrious behavior and often referred to as the engineer of the animal kingdom, is the school's mascot.

Spurred by the vision of its founder, William Barton Rogers, for a school that would offer in-depth training in science and technology to aid development of the rapidly expanding and increasingly industrialized United States, the Massachusetts legislature in 1861 established MIT by charter; the first 15 students enrolled in 1865 in temporary quarters. The school's early decades were marked by the construction of buildings at Copley Square in Boston, increased numbers of students, and a burgeoning curriculum, as well as several unsuccessful attempts by Harvard University to absorb the fledgling institute. By 1916 MIT (known colloquially as "Boston Tech") had outgrown the confines of Copley Square

In a typical MIT student hack, a police car is placed atop the MIT dome, Cambridge, Mass., 1994

and moved to a cluster of stately connected buildings designed by Welles Bosworth in Cambridge. The corridors linking academic departments symbolized the benefits of interdisciplinary communication.

In the 1930s then-president Karl Taylor Compton reorganized MIT into schools, bolstered research in basic sciences, created a division of humanities, and paved the way for the transformation of the institute into a world-class university. Vannevar Bush, a former dean of engineering, coordinated the nation's war-related research during World War II, bringing to campus the "Rad Lab," which engineered critical advances in radar technology and produced systems for spotting enemy aircraft and submarines. MIT also provided much of the expertise for development of the atomic bomb at the University of Chicago and Los Alamos, N.Mex. After the war, Rad Lab facilities, equipment, and know-how were successfully diverted to peacetime research, and many labs received continued federal funding. In 1952 MIT established Lincoln Laboratory in Lexington, Mass., a facility where government-funded research, primarily defense-related, could be conducted under secure conditions.

The MIT faculty has included many prominent and colorful figures. Ellen Swallow Richards, the first woman to be a regular student, graduated in 1873, joined the faculty, and founded the home economics movement. In the 1930s Harold Edgerton developed techniques for "seeing the unseen" through stroboscopic flash photography of extremely rapid events. Norbert Wiener, a child prodigy and the quintessential absent-minded professor, was a seminal thinker in many areas, and gave birth to cybernetics in the 1940s. Jay Forrester's magnetic core memory (1953) paved the way for vastly improved electronic digital computers. In the 1950s Noam Chomsky sparked a revolutionary approach to linguistics, transformational grammar, which looks for the basis of language in innate structures in the mind.

An abundant workload and less-than-generous grading have always characterized student life at MIT, causing frustration but also engendering pride, evident in favorite adages like "Tech is Hell" and "Getting an education at MIT is like taking a drink from a fire hose." A perennial tradition is the student "hack," an irreverent, benign prank, often involving surprising and clever applications of technology. The 1982 Harvard-Yale football game, for example, was interrupted when a remote-controlled weather balloon buried beneath the turf at Harvard Stadium suddenly inflated, displaying the message "MIT."

Recent decades at MIT have featured less government funding and an increase in partnerships with business. New construction has given the campus a facelift as well as additional space for new programs. The Stata Center for Computer, Information, and Intelligence Services (a radical Frank Gehry de-

sign, supplanting the venerable Building 20, which housed the Rad Lab) will allow the university to continue time-honored traditions of random meetings and cross-disciplinary collaboration. Several initiatives suggest that MIT's research in the opening years of the 21st century will be in areas concerning electronic sharing of information. "DSpace," for example, is a digital repository for preserving and sharing the intellectual output of MIT's faculty, including work in progress, and the "Open Course Ware" initiative gives free online access to a wide spectrum of educational materials, making them available for curriculum development around the world.

Robert Buderi, *The Invention That Changed the World: How a Small Group of Radar Pioneers Won the Second World War and Launched a Technological Revolution* (1996); Julius A. Stratton and Loretta H. Mannix, *Mind and Hand: The Birth of MIT* (2005); Francis Wylie, *M.I.T. in Perspective* (1976).

Jeffrey Mifflin

One-Room Schoolhouses New England's long association with educational leadership began with a series of School Acts passed by the New England colonial legislatures of the 17th century. The most influential of these were the Massachusetts School Acts of the 1640s, which required townships with a population greater than 50 people to build and staff a school. The intent was to teach all children the basics skills of reading, writing, and arithmetic. In the years after the Revolution, each of the New England states followed through with laws providing tax support for the public education of its citizenry. The wording of Vermont's 1791 constitution was typical: "A school or schools shall be established in each town by the legislature, for the convenient instruction of youth."

The logistics of these "common schools" were simple. Towns were divided into a number of districts. Within each district a one-room schoolhouse was constructed. Built at a crossroads or along a main road, most schools were simple wooden structures approximately 20 by 30 feet in area. Interiors were sparsely furnished with desks of varying sizes to fit students who ranged in age from 5 to 18. Educational equipment and materials were minimal. Some schools had a blackboard or a globe, while many others had no educational materials besides those brought by the pupils, or "scholars." This educational model was widely replicated along the frontier in the United States as settlers from the East moved westward.

During the mid-19th century common schools were frequently criticized. Many schoolhouses were in terrible condition and lacked such basic requirements as privies for use by the teachers and scholars. Pedagogical

North School, a one-room school-house that served Kensington, N.H., for 100 years (1842–1943)

problems abounded. Most teachers lacked professional training. There were no standard schoolbooks or learning materials. Before the passage of compulsory attendance laws, teachers never knew how many students would attend on a given day and were expected to teach whoever walked in the door. Male teachers received a miserly pay averaging about five dollars per week in the 1850s; female teachers earned about half that amount. Oversight of the schools was left to school boards consisting of townspeople, generally with no training in education, who were willing to examine teachers and make regular inspection visits to the district schools.

Educators like Horace Mann, the pioneering secretary of the first state board of education in Massachusetts, promoted a number of reforms in the 19th century to improve education. The first teacher-training colleges, known as "normal schools," opened in Massachusetts in 1839 to instruct teachers in the latest effective educational strategies. Beginning in 1852 the state required student attendance a minimum of three months per year and provided for some state support of schooling costs.

The rural consolidation movement, begun as part of the progressive movement in the 1890s, accelerated the decline of one-room schools in New England. As it became more efficient to transport students from outlying areas to centrally located town schools in the early part of the 20th century, many one-room schoolhouses were closed. Today only a handful of one-room schoolhouses remain in northern New England and Massachusetts, primarily in isolated communities and on islands along the seacoast.

Lawrence A. Cremin, *American Education: The National Experience, 1783–1876* (1980); Andrew Gulliford, *America's Country Schools* (1996); Carl F. Kaestle, *Pillars of the Republic: Common Schools and American Society, 1780–1860* (1983); Ruth Zinar, "Educational Problems in Rural Vermont, 1875–1900: A Not So Distant Mirror," *Vermont History* 4 (1983).

Garet D. Livermore

Palmer, Alice Freeman (1855–1902)

Educator. Alice Elvira Freeman Palmer, the second president of Wellesley College and a powerful advocate of higher education for women, was born in Colesville, N.Y. Her studies at the coeducational Windsor Academy in New York whetted her ambitions to attend college. Promising her uneasy parents that she would not marry until she had repaid them for her college expenses and provided for the education of her siblings, she applied to the University of Michigan, which had started to admit female students in 1870 and was considered the best institution available to women at the time. Freeman delivered a commencement address when she graduated from Michigan, one of 11 women in the class of 1876. She taught for a year at a girls' seminary in Lake Geneva, Wisc., then returned to the University of Michigan to begin graduate work in history. Although she never completed a Ph.D. degree, Michigan awarded her an honorary doctorate in 1882.

In 1877 Alice Freeman accepted the post of preceptress at a high school in Saginaw, Mich. She received three successive offers to join the faculty at newly founded Wellesley College; finally, in 1878, she accepted the invitation to head the history department there. Four years later Freeman became vice-president and acting president of the college. In 1882 she was appointed Wellesley's second president. The death of the college's founder, Henry F. Durant, enabled her to be a far more active and independent president than her predecessor, Ada L. Howard, had been. In her highly successful six-year administration, Freeman established a network of Wellesley preparatory schools throughout the country (15 of them by 1887) and significantly raised the college's admission standards. She also established a pattern of direct faculty participation in the college's administrative structure. She became a founder of the Association of Collegiate Alumnae (later renamed the American Association of University Women) in

1882 and served as president of that body in 1885–86.

In 1887, to the chagrin of the college community, Freeman married Harvard professor George Herbert Palmer (1842–1933) and resigned as Wellesley's president. Though as a wife she willingly limited herself to a more domestic sphere, she remained professionally active in higher education. She continued to serve Wellesley as a trustee and a member of the college's executive committee. Assured that she need be in residence only 12 weeks per year, she agreed to be the first dean of women at the nascent University of Chicago and held that post from 1892 to 1895. Back in New England, Palmer worked toward the transformation of the Harvard Annex into Radcliffe College and, as a member of the Massachusetts State Board of Education, led the campaign to improve the state's normal schools in the 1890s. An influential voice in education throughout her life, Palmer was a role model and symbol who bridged traditional and emerging views of women.

Ruth Bordin, *Alice Freeman Palmer: The Evolution of a New Woman* (1993); George Herbert Palmer, *The Life of Alice Freeman Palmer* (1908); Patricia Ann Palmieri, *In Adamless Eden: The Community of Women Faculty at Wellesley* (1995); Barbara Miller Solomon, *In the Company of Educated Women: A History of Women and Higher Education in America* (1985).

Laura Prieto

Parker, Francis Wayland (1837–1902)

Educator and education reformer. Francis Wayland Parker, often called the father of progressive education, is remembered for improving schooling through child-centered instruction and enhanced teacher preparation. Part of a long New England tradition of educational innovation that included the reformers Bronson Alcott and Horace Mann, Parker in turn influenced John Dewey and other educators of the Progressive Era.

Parker was born to a farming family in Piscatauquog (Bedford Township), N.H., and when his father died the boy was apprenticed to a local farmer. Parker longed to attend school, however, and eventually managed to fund his own tuition at an academy in nearby Mont Vernon. In 1854 he assumed the first of several teaching positions in his home state, and in 1859 he became a school principal in Carrollton, Ill. Returning to New Hampshire in 1861, he enlisted in the Union Army and rose to the rank of lieutenant colonel, a title he used throughout his life. After the war Parker became a grammar-school principal in Manchester, N.H.

Considered one of the best educators in New England, Parker moved to Dayton, Ohio, to become principal of the First District

School in 1868. He soon also took charge of the Dayton school district's normal school, which trained teachers, and developed a reputation as an educational reformer.

From 1872 to 1875 Parker furthered his education at the University of Berlin, where he was influenced by Friedrich Froebel's work with kindergartners and by Johann F. Herbart's pedagogical methods. While in Germany Parker developed ideas about the link between education and democracy. He came to believe that schools should teach students of all economic classes and both genders together and that self-control should replace extrinsic rewards and punishments.

Parker was able to put some of his ideas into practice when he returned to the United States in 1875 and became superintendent of the schools in Quincy, Mass. Visitors from throughout the nation and around the world came to Quincy to observe Parker's new educational approaches. The "Quincy system" was significant because, compared with traditional methods, it offered students the benefit of less formality and more individualization in curriculum and instruction.

From 1880 to 1883 Parker served as a supervisor of the Boston school system. In 1883 he became head of the Cook County Normal School (later the Chicago Normal School) in Illinois. In 1900 Parker founded the Chicago Institute, an innovative practice school in which students from kindergarten through twelfth grade were taught by teacher trainees. With Parker as its head, the institute in 1901 became part of the University of Chicago, where John Dewey directed the Department of Education. Soon after the institute opened, Parker died while on a trip to Pass Christian, Miss.

Parker won wide recognition for the emphasis he placed on active learning. He favored discarding rote memorization and building education instead around the knowledge and experiences of the individual child. He added science and geography to the traditional course of studies and recommended that reading and writing be taught through a correlated curriculum. In 1894 Parker published his ideas in *Talks on Pedagogics: An Outline of the Theory of Concentration.* Despite his many contributions to educational reform Parker claimed no originality of thought or method. Rather, he wrote, "The rule is that whatever any teacher *effectively* applies, he must discover for himself."

Jack K. Campbell, *Colonel Francis W. Parker, the Children's Crusader* (1967); David E. Kapel, Charles S. Gifford, and Marilyn B. Kapel, eds., *American Educators' Encyclopedia*, rev. ed. (1991); John F. Ohles, ed., *Biographical Dictionary of American Educators*, vol. 2 (1978).

Susan Anderson Wunder

Parochial Schools Since the Middle Ages, the term *parochial schools* has literally meant "parish schools" in a variety of Christian denominations. In general American usage it has come to refer to all elementary and secondary schools, parish-supported or diocesan, under Roman Catholic auspices. The American bishops who gathered at the First Plenary Council of Baltimore in 1852 recommended such schools as a way of dealing with the growing number of Irish immigrants. Despite this urging, Catholic clergy tended to yield to the public system, regardless of curricula that took a negative view of the Catholic Church and of linguistic stocks other than English. Only after 1866, with the influx of German immigrants accustomed to a system of religious schools, did widespread establishment of such schools and their systematic organization and administration begin to take place, a process greatly accelerated by the mandate of the third Baltimore Council in 1884 that Catholic parents send their children to Catholic schools. The period from 1919 to 1958 saw the expansion of parochial schools into the largest private school system in the world, enrolling 12 percent of all school-age children in the United States. After 1965, the number of such schools declined somewhat as a more assimilated and less triumphalist Catholic population made greater use of public schools, a crisis in vocations eroded the number of teachers, and diocesan fiscal crises mandated increasing tuition.

In 1829, the Diocese of Boston comprised the entirety of the New England states. It attempted to follow the council's recommendation by establishing "pay schools"—day schools that charged tuition under the direction of a single master—but such schools tended to be precarious and short-lived. Not until 1844 was the first parochial school founded, at Holy Trinity Parish in Boston, a German parish. By the time the Roman Congregation de Propaganda Fide urged in 1875 that Catholic schools be founded in every locality in America, the Archdiocese of Boston only had 16 parochial schools. By 1900 it had 61 schools, the smallest number of schools in the nine largest dioceses, but a total school population of 39,000, the third-largest number of students. The local tradition, then, was one of fewer but larger schools. Elsewhere in New England, new dioceses were continually being created, assuming control of schools already in existence, and developing new ones. In 2000, the Catholic population of New England was organized into three archdioceses and seven dioceses, which supported 100 high schools with a total enrollment of 45,500 and 345 elementary schools with a total population of 90,000.

Harold J. Buetow, *Of Singular Benefit: The Story of Catholic Education in the United States* (1970); Mary A. Grant and Thomas C. Hunt, *Catholic School Education in the United States* (1992); Robert H. Lord, John Sexton, and Edward Harrington, *History of the Archdiocese of Boston*, 3 vols. (1945); Timothy Walch, *Parish School: Parochial Education from Colonial Times to the Present* (1996).

Joseph M. McCarthy

Peabody, Elizabeth Palmer (1804–94) Educator, educational reformer, historian, memoirist, and translator. Elizabeth Palmer Peabody's career touched on many of the literary, reformist, and educational movements of the 19th century. Best known as an educational reformer and kindergarten advocate, Peabody blended her belief in New England's cultural primacy with a shrewd sense of the cultural limits placed on single women and a widening involvement in national reforms.

Born in Billerica, Mass., to Nathaniel Peabody and Elizabeth Palmer, both of whom were teachers, Elizabeth Palmer Peabody felt "pre-natally educated for the profession which has been the passionate pursuit of my life." Educated at her mother's school in Salem, where the family moved in 1808, Peabody learned that culture was the particular province of women. Her mother taught her and her sisters that the schools founded by their New England ancestors—mishearing this as "Ann Sisters," Peabody imagined sturdy white-robed women building schools in the wilderness—had ensured American literacy and liberty.

During the 1820s Elizabeth Peabody taught at her own school in Lancaster, Mass., spent two years as a tutor in Hallowell, Maine (1823–25), and taught privately in Boston with her sister Mary (who would marry the educator Horace Mann in 1843). She published several guides to the history of ancient Israel and Greece for use by women studying at home. In all her teaching Peabody combined rigorous training in grammar, history, languages, and literatures with emphasis on moral development.

In the mid-1820s Peabody renewed her earlier acquaintance with the Unitarian clergyman William Ellery Channing and under his tutelage tempered her philosophical rationalism with a new appreciation for the place of emotion in religion and in life. In 1834 Peabody became assistant at Bronson Alcott's Temple School in Boston, a private institution whose curriculum was based on Alcott's belief that education could give form to the intuitive truth that children already possessed. Peabody held a similar view but resigned in 1836 when she feared that Alcott's conversations with his pupils about childbirth would cause a scandal. Returning to her family home in Salem,

Peabody encountered Nathaniel Hawthorne, whose career she encouraged; Hawthorne married her sister Sophia in 1842.

In 1839 Peabody opened a bookshop, lending library, and press on West Street in Boston. The shop became the site for several of Margaret Fuller's "conversations," classes for women on a variety of topics. It also hosted discussions of the formation of Brook Farm, an experimental utopian community, and meetings of the Transcendental Club. Peabody contributed several essays to the Transcendentalist *Dial,* which she also published for a year (1842–43), and her press issued works by Hawthorne and translations by Fuller.

In 1860, influenced by the work of German educator Friedrich Froebel, Peabody established, in Boston, the first English-speaking kindergarten in the United States. She traveled to Europe in 1867–68 to see the kindergarten on its home ground and upon her return launched a vigorous campaign to establish Froebelian kindergartens in American public schools. In her view Froebel's pedagogy gave Channing's and Ralph Waldo Emerson's insights a firm scientific foundation, providing a structure whereby children's play would lead gently to more rigorous intellectual study.

Peabody became interested in Native American education in 1880 and crusaded for the Nevada Paiute people, who had suffered treaty violations and other injustices at the hands of white settlers. In the final years of her life she devoted her time to writing essays and letters of reminiscence, providing insightful portraits of Emerson, Hawthorne, and the poet Jones Very. Peabody died in Jamaica Plain, Mass., and is buried in the Sleepy Hollow Cemetery in Concord, Mass.

Ruth M. Baylor, *Elizabeth Palmer Peabody: Kindergarten Pioneer* (1965); Bruce A. Ronda, *Elizabeth Palmer Peabody: A Reformer on Her Own Terms* (1999); Bruce A. Ronda, ed., *Letters of Elizabeth Palmer Peabody, American Renaissance Woman* (1984); Louise Hall Tharp, *The Peabody Sisters of Salem* (1950).

Bruce A. Ronda

Perkins School for the Blind Founded in 1829, the New England Asylum for the Blind—today the Perkins School for the Blind—was the first facility in North America intended expressly for the instruction of blind students. Located in Watertown, Mass., the Perkins School represents a distinctly New England form of what the school's first director, Samuel Gridley Howe, called "practical benevolence."

Motivated by successful efforts to educate the blind in France, and by an 1830 census esti-

mate of some 1,500 blind persons in New England (not counting those who languished with other "unfortunates" in almshouses), a board of prominent Bostonians headed by physician John Dix Fisher and visually impaired historian William H. Prescott decided to establish a school in Boston. Though inexperienced, Howe was appointed director by the board and became 19th-century America's most effective advocate for blind persons, and indeed for all who historically had been considered societal burdens.

Beginning modestly in 1832 in his father's home with two teachers from Europe and two pupils, Howe soon relocated the school to the Pearl Street home of trustee Thomas H. Perkins. When in 1839 enrollment reached 65, Perkins donated $25,000, with the condition that a matching $25,000 be raised to support the school, which was subsequently renamed the Perkins Institution and Massachusetts Asylum for the Blind. Howe, however, rejected the implications of the word *asylum.* Under his leadership the institution became the preeminent facility of its kind and a world center for innovation. The school was moved to its present location in Watertown in 1912.

Among the school's notable students was Laura Bridgman, who had been rendered deaf, blind, and without the sense of smell by scarlet fever. She entered the school in 1837 at the age of seven and was taught by Howe; later she became an instructor at the school. Bridgman's education was an achievement that brought international acclaim to the school. Charles Dickens's account of this feat in *American Notes* (1842) later influenced Helen Keller's parents to enroll her in the school; Keller's "Teacher" and lifelong companion, Anne Sullivan, was Perkins's 1886 class valedictorian.

Throughout his tenure Howe never wavered from his conviction that people with disabilities could lead productive lives; successive directors and generations of instructors

endeavored to make his mission a reality through research and teacher training. Perkins's faculty and staff have led the campaign for blind literacy by lobbying for federal legislation (1837); expanding the scope of materials available to a growing blind literati; and inventing such key materials as Boston Line Type, the dominant American system until supplanted by Braille, and David Abraham's Perkins Brailler. The school is a leader in the development and dissemination of literacy and instructional materials and assistive and adaptive technology for people with visual impairments. In 1982 the school's charter was amended to allow for educating and training persons with handicaps other than visual.

One of the region's myriad private schools, accredited by the New England Association of Schools and Colleges and the National Association of Independent Schools, Perkins offers day or residential services to 180 blind, visually impaired, multihandicapped blind, and deaf-blind students and clients, ranging from infants to elderly. In addition to academics, also emphasized are daily living skills, mobility training, physical education, vocational training, and work experiences. While students from the six New England states account for three-quarters of its enrollment—nearly all in the preschool and lower school—older students and those with severe impairments come from throughout the United States and from many other countries. The Perkins campus overlooking the Charles River has four gymnasiums, a swimming pool, four athletic fields, a library, and a chapel, and is home to the Howe Press, the Braille and Talking Book Library, and the New England Center for Deafblind Children. The myriad services and facilities of the Perkins School attest to its founders' prescience and a commitment to making education and independence possible for all students.

Joseph P. Lash, *Helen and Teacher: The Story of Helen Keller and Anne Sullivan Macy* (1980); Perkins School for the Blind, *The Lantern Magazine* (published biannually); Philip L. Safford and Elizabeth J. Safford, *A History of Childhood and Disability* (1996); Harold Schwartz, *Samuel Gridley Howe, Social Reformer, 1801–1876* (1956).

Philip L. Safford

Preparatory Schools The stereotypical prep school image—well-heeled boys in blazers ushered across green quadrangles by obligatory chapel bells—is inextricably linked to New England. This image, however, is an oversimplification, amplified by popular fiction and films. The image of the New England prep school has been developed since the 19th century, with Louisa May Alcott's *Jo's Boys* (1886), for example, depicting a school with a homelike setting. In addition, J. D. Salinger's *The Catcher in the Rye* (1951), John Knowles's *A Separate Peace* (1959), John Irving's *The World According to Garp* (1978), and Lorene Cary's *Black Ice* (1991) all chronicled life at these schools in fiction. John McPhee's *The Headmaster: Frank L. Boyden of Deerfield* (1966) provides insight into one of the legendary headmasters who shaped a school in his image.

Today, the typical image of a New England boarding school persists—exemplified by Saint Paul's, Andover, Exeter, Groton, Kent, Deerfield, and Choate—with genteel buildings of brick and stone supported by white colonial columns, rising inseparably from the rural landscapes of Massachusetts, Connecticut, and New Hampshire. But the definition of "private school" rests on only six shared characteristics: self-governance, self-support, self-defined curriculum, self-selected students, self-selected faculty, and small size. In New England, both day schools and boarding schools, either religiously affiliated or unaffiliated, single-sex or coeducational, military or not, all fit into a regional mosaic of independent education (see table). Almost all have adopted college preparation as their main educational mission, even the so-called second-chance schools for students who have not succeeded in public schools.

In the late 1700s, both the American and French Revolutions had greatly disturbed the fabric of education in the nation. Citing a superficially educated mercantile class and the new republic's purposeful lack of gentry, America's intellectuals claimed the nation was at a crossroads between a progressive society and barbarism. These Federalists, the supporters of a strong national government as framed by the newly written Constitution, believed that the path to salvation lay in the refinement of civilized Christian gentlemen who, as John Adams explained, were "not the rich or the poor, the high-born or the low-born," but "all who received a liberal education."

In 19th-century New England, the distinction between public and private education was a question of semantics rather than funding: "public" referred to schooling in groups, while "private" referred to tutoring at home. Several different modes of public education were geared toward college preparation in the late 18th and early 19th centuries: day schools, town-supported Latin Grammar schools, preparatory departments within colleges, and academies. Private day schools were often haphazard affairs founded by recent college graduates and lasting only a few years. They offered two educational tracks: "academical," which was classical in nature, and "useful," which was typically vocational. Town-supported Latin Grammar schools dated back to the 17th century and were solely dedicated to preparing classically educated religious and civil leaders. Ironically, these schools were seen as aristocratic, anathema to the new republic, and by the early 19th century most had lost both popular and economic support. Academic preparatory departments within colleges were prevalent in most institutions, with the exception of Harvard and Yale. Those universities' reliance on outside institutions to prepare prospective students had a direct impact on the development of the New England prep school, which ultimately evolved from the private academy.

The first two academies of significance in the region grew out of the piety and philanthropy of the Phillips family, who created and endowed both the Phillips Academy in Andover, Mass., in 1778 and the Phillips Exeter Academy in Exeter, N.H., in 1781. Loosely based on the writings of Benjamin Franklin, the schools' curriculum sought to incorporate the building of character with a humanistic education. Although these two schools established the framework for most of the academies in the region, they were somewhat different from their modern boarding-school incarnations. Most notably, the academy boarded students with local families rather than housing them on campus. The Federalists objected to this practice and suggested that the lessons of the day were promptly lost when the students left the school and "dissipated" in town. They argued that this disconnection from their schoolmasters was not conducive to educating scholars and Christian gentleman and began a search for new educational methods.

The Federalists found their model in the theories and practices of the Swiss, most notably Johann Heinrich Pestalozzi and his successor, Phillip Emanuel von Fellenberg. Pestalozzi, inspired by Jean-Jacques Rousseau, suggested that the school should be directly modeled on the home. Fellenberg later developed these ideas into an academy at Hofwyl, Switzerland, in which one can see the earliest evolution of the New England boarding school. Here was the first attempt at a curriculum that integrated the intellectual and the spiritual; a school in which students lived, studied, and played with their masters. Classical studies were well integrated with scientific and aesthetic pursuits, as well as the new system of German gymnastics. The Federalist patricians felt this indeed was a system that would develop Christian scholars and gentleman.

A 1960 reconstruction of the original 1660 schoolhouse of Hopkins Grammar School (now the Hopkins School), New Haven, Conn., a prep school for day students and the country's fifth-oldest educational institution

New England Preparatory Boarding Schools with Enrollments of over 300

Connecticut

Avon Old Farms School Boys (Grade 9–postgraduate) Boarders and day students
Avon Established: 1927 Enrollment: 369
Students help run the school through campus jobs.

Hotchkiss School Coed (Grade 9–postgraduate) Boarders and day students
Avon Established: 1891 Enrollment: 562
Originally a boys' school; became coeducational in 1974.

Pomfret School Coed (Grade 9–postgraduate) Boarders and day students
Avon Established: 1894 Enrollment: 347
Originally a boys' school; became coeducational in 1968.

Cheshire Academy Coed (Kindergarten–postgraduate) Boarders and day students
Cheshire Established: 1794 Enrollment: 353
Established as the coeducational Episcopal Academy. In the mid-1800s the academy became a boys' boarding school with a military program and remained so until the early 1900s, when it gave up its military affiliation, became a preparatory school for Yale University, and was renamed the Roxbury School. In 1937 the academy adopted its present name. In 1969 girls were readmitted as day students and in 1975 as boarders.

Miss Porter's School Girls (Grades 9–12) Boarders and day students
Farmington Established: 1843 Enrollment: 323
Students may apply to study through the Chewonki Foundation, an environmental education center located on the Maine coast.

Kent School Coed (Grade 9–postgraduate) Boarders and day students
Kent Established: 1906 Enrollment: 550
Episcopalian; originally a boys' school; became coeducational in 1960 but did not merge its two campuses until 1992.

Canterbury School Coed (Grade 9–postgraduate) Boarders and day students
New Milford Established: 1915 Enrollment: 358
Roman Catholic; originally a boys' school; admitted girls as day students in 1970 and as boarders in 1972.

Westminister School Coed (Grade 9–postgraduate) Boarders and day students
Simsbury Established: 1888 Enrollment: 372
Originally a boys' school; admitted girls as day students in 1971 and as boarders in 1977.

Suffield Academy Coed (Grade 9–postgraduate) Boarders and day students
Suffield Established: 1833 Enrollment: 402
Established as the Connecticut Literary Institution to prepare men for the ministry. In 1843 it was renamed Suffield Academy and became coeducational. After World War II the school became nondenominational and became a boys' school again; it became coeducational again in 1974.

Choate Rosemary Hall Coed (Grade 9–postgraduate) Boarders and day students
Wallingford Established: 1890 Enrollment: 852
Rosemary Hall for Girls was established in 1890; Choate School for Boys was established in 1896; the two merged in 1974 as Choate Rosemary Hall, but it did not become a single coeducational institution until 1977. Students are offered the opportunity to study abroad.

Taft School Coed (Grade 9–postgraduate) Boarders and day students
Watertown Established: 1890 Enrollment: 572
Originally a boys' school; became coeducational in 1971.

Loomis Chaffee School Coed (Grade 9–postgraduate) Boarders and day students
Windsor Established: 1914 Enrollment: 762
Established as the coeducational Loomis Institute; split in 1926 into the Chaffee School, for girls, and the Loomis School, for boys; reunited under the current name in 1972. Students must work on campus to help run the school. Students are offered the opportunity to study abroad.

Maine

Fryeburg Academy Coed (Grade 9–postgraduate) Boarders and day students
Fryeburg Established: 1792 Enrollment: 673
A school program allows students to prepare for skiing competitions.

(continued)

New England Preparatory Boarding Schools with Enrollments of over 300 (continued)

Maine Central Institute	Coed	(Grade 9–postgraduate)	Boarders and day students
Pittsfield	Established: 1866	Enrollment: 513	

Massachusetts

Brooks School Coed (Grades 9–12) Boarders and day students
North Andover Established: 1926 Enrollment: 355
Although the school has strong ties to the Episcopal Church it is a nonsectarian establishment.

Phillips Academy Coed (Grade 9–postgraduate) Boarders and day students
Andover Established: 1778 Enrollment: 1,087
Originally a boys' school; became coeducational in 1973 when it joined with the Abbot Academy for Girls, established in 1829. Students are offered the opportunity to study abroad. The Bread Loaf Writing Workshop is offered to help South African teachers and inner-city high school students refine their writing skills.

Cushing Academy Coed (Grade 9–postgraduate) Boarders and day students
Ashburnham Established: 1865 Enrollment: 425
Students may spend terms studying in France and Spain.

Belmont Hill School Boys (Grades 7–12) Boarders (5 day) and day students
Belmont Established: 1923 Enrollment: 420
Students may participate in exchange programs with schools in France and Spain.

Governor Dummer Academy Coed (Grades 9–12) Boarders and day students
Byfield Established: 1763 Enrollment: 371
Originally a boys' school; admitted girls as day students in 1971 and as boarders in 1973.

Concord Academy Coed (Grades 9–12) Boarders and day students
Concord Established: 1922 Enrollment: 348
Originally a girls' school; now coeducational. Students have the opportunity to study abroad, to attend a term at the Mountain School in Vermont, and to attend a city term in New York City.

Middlesex School Coed (Grades 9–12) Boarders and day students
Concord Established: 1901 Enrollment: 334
Originally a boys' school; became coeducational in 1974.

Noble and Greenough School Coed (Grades 7–12) Boarders (5 day) and day students
Dedham Established: 1866 Enrollment: 543
Established on Beacon Hill, Boston, as Noble School, a private day school; changed its name to Noble and Greenough School in 1892. In 1917 the school absorbed Volkmann School, and in 1922 it moved to Dedham, adding its boarding facilities. Students may choose to study abroad or through the Maine Coast Semester Program.

Deerfield Academy Coed (Grade 9–postgraduate) Boarders and day students
Deerfield Established: 1797 Enrollment: 598
Originally a boys' school; became coeducational in 1989. Students may choose to participate in volunteer or congressional programs. They may also study abroad, attend the Mountain School of Milton Academy, or participate in the Maine Coast Semester Program.

Williston Northampton School Coed (Grade 7–postgraduate) Boarders and day students
Easthampton Established: 1841 Enrollment: 540
Established as Williston Seminary; in 1971 merged with Northampton School for Girls, which was established 1924, and changed its name. Students have the opportunity to study in France and Spain.

Groton School Coed (Grades 8–12) Boarders and day students
Groton Established: 1884 Enrollment: 354
Established with close ties to the Episcopal Church, it draws its student population from many different religious backgrounds. Students have the opportunity to study abroad.

Lawrence Academy Coed (Grades 9–12) Boarders and day students
Groton Established: 1793 Enrollment: 386
Established as the coeducational Groton Academy, it adopted the name Lawrence Academy in 1846 in honor of Amos and William Lawrence, who endowed the school.

(continued)

New England Preparatory Boarding Schools with Enrollments of over 300 (continued)

Tabor Academy   Coed   (Grades 9–12)   Boarders and day students
Marion   Established: 1876   Enrollment: 485
Students have the opportunity to study celestial navigation, piloting, and seamanship on the academy's schooner. It is also a Naval Honor School that can nominate students to the U.S. service academies.

Milton Academy   Coed   (Kindergarten–grade 12)   Boarders and day students
Milton   Established: 1798   Enrollment: 995
Established as a coeducational institution; split in 1901 into two separate schools, Milton Academy Boys' School and Milton Academy Girls' School; reunited in 1973. In 1983 Milton Academy purchased the Mountain School in Vershire, Vt. Students have the opportunity to study abroad.

Northfield Mount Hermon School   Coed   (Grade 9–postgraduate)   Boarders and day students
Northfield   Established: 1879   Enrollment: 1,025
The Northfield Seminary for Girls, established 1879, and the Mount Hermon School for boys, established 1881, joined in 1971 as a coeducational institution with boarding on both campuses. Students may choose to study abroad or to serve in apprenticeships with local businesses. Students must help run the school through participation in a work program.

Berkshire School   Coed   (Grade 9–postgraduate)   Boarders and day students
Sheffield   Established: 1907   Enrollment: 383
Originally a boys' school; became coeducational in 1969.

Saint Mark's School   Coed   (Grades 9–12)   Boarders and day students
Southborough   Established: 1865   Enrollment: 330
Episcopal; originally a boys' school; became coeducational in 1977 when it merged with Southborough School for Girls.

Dana Hall School   Girls   (Grades 6–12)   Boarders and day students
Wellesley   Established: 1881   Enrollment: 450

Wilbraham and Monson Academy   Coed   (Grade 6–postgraduate)   Boarders and day students
Wilbraham   Established: 1804   Enrollment: 345
In 1971 Monson Academy, established in 1804, merged with Wesleyan Wilbraham Academy, established in 1817, and took the new name.

Worcester Academy   Coed   (Grade 6–postgraduate)   Boarders and day students
Worcester   Established: 1834   Enrollment: 640
Established as coeducational Worcester County Manual Labor High School; became Worcester Academy in 1846; reorganized as a boys' school; became coeducational again in 1974 after a gap of several decades.

New Hampshire

Proctor Academy   Coed   (Grades 9–12)   Boarders and day students
Andover   Established: 1848   Enrollment: 336
Affiliated with the Unitarian Church but nondenominational in practice; established as Andover Academy; renamed in 1879 in honor of a local benefactor; admitted girls as boarders in 1971. Curriculum has an extensive arts program. Students have the opportunity to study in the desert Southwest and abroad. A sailing program allows students to sail from New England to the Caribbean.

Saint Paul's School   Coed   (Grades 9–12)   Boarders and day students
Concord   Established: 1856   Enrollment: 525
Episcopal; students have the opportunity to study abroad.

Phillips Exeter Academy   Coed   (Grade 9–postgraduate)   Boarders and day students
Exeter   Established: 1781   Enrollment: 1,048
Originally a boys' school, Phillips Exeter admitted girls to the day school in 1970 and to the boarding school in 1971. Students have the opportunity to do a term as a congressional intern in Washington, D.C., to do half a year at the Mountain School of Milton Academy in Vershire, Vt., and to study abroad.

Kimball Union Academy   Coed   (Grade 9–postgraduate)   Boarders and day students
Meriden   Established: 1813   Enrollment: 313
Established to prepare both boys and girls for the ministry; became a boys' school in 1935; became coeducational again in 1974. Students help run the school by participating in a work program.

(continued)

New England Preparatory Boarding Schools with Enrollments of over 300 (continued)

Brewster Academy	Coed	(Grade 9–postgraduate)	Boarders and day students
Wolfeboro	Established: 1820	Enrollment: 349	

Established as Wolfeborough and Tuftonborough Academy; changed its name in 1887.

Rhode Island

Saint George's School	Coed	(Grades 9–12)	Boarders and day students
Newport	Established: 1896	Enrollment: 340	

Originally a boys' school; became coeducational in 1972. The school has close ties with the Episcopal Church but is open to students of all religions. Students have the opportunity to participate in work and study internships, year-round research cruises, and summer sessions in France.

Portsmouth Abbey School	Coed	(Grades 9–12)	Boarders and day students
Portsmouth	Established: 1926	Enrollment: 340	

Established as Portsmouth Priory School; changed its name in 1969. Originally a boys' school; girls admitted as day students in 1991 and as boarders in 1992.

Vermont

Lyndon Institute	Coed	(Grades 9–12)	Boarders and day students
Lyndon Center	Established: 1867	Enrollment: 617	

Primarily a day school; in 1994 it began enrolling as boarders international students and students in the fine arts program.

St. Johnsbury Academy	Coed	(Grade 9–postgraduate)	Boarders and day students
St. Johnsbury	Established: 1842	Enrollment: 1,029	

Reincorporated in 1873 and broadened its scope to serve a wide range of students, not just those bound for liberal arts colleges. Serves most students in the area through a voucher system.

Source: Handbook of Private Schools: 1997, 78th ed., and 2004, 85th ed. (Boston: Porter Sargent, 1997, 2004); Peterson's Private Secondary Schools, 1997–98, 18th ed. (Princeton: Peterson's, 1997); National Association of Independent Schools Web site.

The seminal New England boarding school was founded in 1823 by George Bancroft and Joseph Cogswell. Based on the Swiss model, Round Hill, near Northampton, Mass., provided a thorough education and trained the physical and moral faculties of the students in its charge. Round Hill was highly structured but revolutionary in that education was now a round-the-clock affair, with students living under the same roof as their teachers. Student-teacher ratios were always low (around 12:1), and the heads of school set uniformly high standards that all boys were expected to meet; the school routinely graduated students who entered Harvard in the junior class. But though Round Hill seemed to be an unqualified educational success, the school was poorly administered and closed its doors in 1834.

Gone but not forgotten, Round Hill evoked intense loyalty in its alumni, who would attempt to re-create the educational experience for their sons. The result was Saint Paul's School in Concord, N.H. Founded in 1856 by Dr. George Shattuck, the school embraced the Federalist tradition of raising Christian gentleman, and to this day maintains strong ties to the Episcopal Church. Saint Paul's also reflected the emerging Victorian ideal of education, which took great pains to isolate its young charges from the perceived evils of adult society. In the peace of rural New Hampshire, Saint Paul's was able to create an ordered familial existence with the singular mission of developing the mind, body, and character of its students.

This all-encompassing mission of the New England boarding school changed little during the 19th century. Despite generous endowments, these schools required both economic and human capital to maintain their familial quality and high standards. The emphasis on developing moral character presupposed that all who enroll in the school were in agreement as to the form and shape of this morality. For Saint Paul's, and the rest of the New England boarding prep schools, this assumption resulted in an influx of students from across the Northeast who shared three characteristics: parental desire to remove their children from the urban influences of the Industrial Revolution, a common morality, and the financial resources to support relatively expensive tu-

itions. This commingling of wealthy scions connected families heretofore geographically removed from one another and may have incubated the notion of an elite class in American society—a wholly unintended by-product of a boarding school education.

As America marched toward the 20th century, society, and the demands placed on secondary education became larger. Such progressive educators as Horace Mann and Thomas Dewey began searching for a way to educate not just a handful of college-bound students but the population at large. At roughly the same time, the colleges founded in the 18th century were modernizing their curriculums and raising the standards of preparation needed to gain admission.

The future of the New England preparatory school was shaped by both these trends. Around 1900, the boarding-school ideal of family schools inspired the development of country day schools with similar missions situated in suburban areas. As urban centers expanded, many of these schools redefined themselves as independent day schools rather than country schools. At the same time, the academies of New England were being absorbed into the burgeoning public-education system. Several, like Phillips Exeter and Andover, followed St. Paul's example and became private boarding schools. Such universities as Princeton, Harvard, and Yale exerted influence to create "feeder" preparatory schools, among them Lawrenceville in New Jersey and Groton in Connecticut. Much of this trend was a reaction to the rise of neighborhood common schools and to uncertainty about the quality of popular education. In Boston and other cities throughout New England urban public education was often thought to be too heterogeneous and bureaucratic. Much like their Victorian counterparts, some of the wealthy and well educated opted out of the public system and enrolled their sons in schools far removed from the city.

New England also boasts a long tradition of preparatory schools for girls. By the late 18th century, female academies, originally offering training in needlework and other domestic arts for the merchant elites of New England's towns, evolved into academies with broad curricula. In the antebellum era, such women reformers as Catharine Beecher, who established a school in Hartford, wrote works advocating female academies as true preparatory schools once women's colleges, such as Mount Holyoke, were founded. Such distinguished preparatory schools as Miss Porter's School in Farmington, Conn., and Dana Hall School in Wellesley, Mass., contribute to the reputation of New England's elite schools.

Education in the 20th century became increasingly political. The mercantile class had evolved into a large middle class, and schools, once considered a private good, were fast becoming a public one. State support of basic education was extended to include the secondary level, and by the 1930s public high schools were the rule. This was by no means an easy transition. The Catholic church, deeply suspicious of "Protestant" public education, set up a network of Catholic schools throughout America, while some common-school advocates, citing inequity, sought to absorb private education into the public system. Ironically, many advocates for public education were the wealthy graduates of private schools who viewed education as a road to social reform but still opted to send their own sons to boarding schools. Ultimately, the tension between private education and the common-school movement was framed in the 1925 United States Supreme Court case *Pierce v. Society of Sisters*, which recognized private education as fulfilling the requirements of compulsory education.

For the bulk of the 20th century, New England preparatory schools existed within this framework, with minimal modifications. In the 1960s and 1970s, social mores forced boarding schools to shift from all-boys schools to coeducational institutions. Around the same time, the colleges that preparatory schools served began to shift their admissions requirements from an emphasis on classical rigor to considerations of equity and diversity. Public schools began to surpass preparatory schools in numbers of elite college-bound graduates. Shaken from isolation, many of the New England preparatory schools began to adopt the advancements of public education, including the commitment to a more diverse student population and a multicultural curriculum. Today, many prep schools are more racially diverse than suburban public schools, most of which reflect the relatively homogeneous group of students who live in the immediate geographic locality. At the same time, prep schools continue to occupy a place of distinction within the fabric of education in New England.

Pearl Rock Kane, ed., *Independent Schools, Independent Thinkers* (1992); James McLachlan, *American Boarding Schools: A Historical Study* (1970); Arthur G. Powell, *Lessons from Privilege: The American Prep School Tradition* (1996).

Pearl Rock Kane and Christopher Lauricella

Public Higher Education

New England is home to six land-grant, flagship state universities, 83 other public two- and four-year institutions, and three military academies. Public institutions of higher education claim 51 percent of total student enrollment in New England. Yet the region's public higher education system is often described as beleaguered. In part because of the dominance of the independent sector, public higher education remains underappreciated and, as a consequence, underfunded and undersupported. But the preponderance of independent higher education within New England is indeed an artifact of the region's history.

Public higher education was profoundly expanded by the Morrill Land-Grant Act of 1862, which called for federal money to support agricultural and mechanical education. The largess of federal funds prompted many states to establish or reinvigorate public institutions of higher education. Before the century's end, land-grant universities were founded in five New England states—Massachusetts (1863), Maine (1865), New Hampshire (1866), Connecticut (1881), and Rhode Island (1892)—while Vermont applied Morrill funds to its existing university.

Most state universities had few resources during their early years, but by 1900 state institutions in the Midwest and West, and to a lesser degree in the South, developed into sound research universities, often the pinnacle of higher education in their state. The universities of Michigan, California, and Wisconsin are prime examples. The pattern in New England was different, however, because private institutions were firmly entrenched and powerful. The history of the University of Massachusetts (UMass), originally the Massachusetts Agricultural College (MAC), is revealing. MAC remained an agricultural college until well into the 20th century, its efforts to transform itself into a major university thwarted by the extraordinary political clout of the independent institutions. For example, Charles Eliot, the president of Harvard from 1869 to 1909, actively lobbied the state legislature to continue its pattern of strong support for the independent sector at the expense of various public institutions. As a result, the development of UMass into a major research institution was delayed until after World War II.

During the second half of the 19th century and the first part of the 20th other kinds of public institutions grew up in New England. Teachers colleges and agricultural or mechanical schools slowly developed into four-year state colleges. In addition, the public junior college was born. World War II exerted a profound impact on higher education. Enrollments swelled with students entering under the provisions of the G.I. Bill. The first wave of baby boomers was born, forcing a second great swell in enrollments one generation later. The number of institutions, particularly those that are now called community colleges, proliferated.

Themes in postwar public higher education included systemization and coordination. With the exception of Rhode Island, each New England state created a system connecting the various branch campuses of its land-grant university, linking the smaller state colleges or universities to one another, connecting the community colleges, or some combination of the three. Examples include the Connecticut State University system of four-year institutions or the University of Maine system for the branch campuses of the land-grant institution. The goal of each system, governed by a lay board of trustees, is to enhance planning and governance for the efficient use of resources.

A statewide coordinating board or other agency is typically responsible for all public higher education within each state. Variously called commissions, coordinating councils, or boards of governors, their goals are to improve quality and access through broad oversight. Coordinating bodies also centralize governance and planning, and they assist lay boards of trustees with decision making and placing recommendations before senior state officials.

Coordinating boards everywhere have been the subject of much criticism. Institutions claim that such bodies interfere with campus autonomy, while state legislatures regularly assert that they do not provide enough coordination. Both the general public and state officials demand increased accountability, including public examinations of the curriculum, and studies of faculty workloads. A criticism that is unique in New England, however, is that the various coordinating bodies have not been effective lobbyists to governors and legislators on behalf of the public sector. As a result, independent institutions maintain the lion's share of both public and private resources.

Evidence of the dominance of the independent sector is plentiful. In 2000, independent institutions across the country enrolled only 22 percent of all students, but that figure was 49 percent in New England. Harvard, Yale, and MIT together enroll 5 percent of New England's students but represent an astounding 66 percent of the endowment wealth of the region. According to the 2001 Endowment Study by the National Association of College and University Business Officers, the average endowment assets at independent institutions in the region was $69,000 per student; it was only $6,682 per student in the public sector, rendering public colleges and universities dependent on state allocations. In 2002, the average state per capita appropriation in New England, however, was only $168.32 compared to the national average of $216.17. Prestige often influences grants and donations received, as well as the caliber of both students and faculty, which in turn affects allocations and gifts in a troubling cycle. In the shadow of the Ivy League, state universities find it difficult to garner the regard they deserve.

In an effort to fortify the system of public higher education and reinforce its connection to regional economy and industry, the New England Board of Higher Education (NEBHE) was established in 1955, when the six state governors signed the New England Higher Education Compact. The NEBHE produces reports and initiates research projects that illustrate the role of higher education in the region's continued development. Although the NEBHE encompasses all aspects of higher education, the contributions and needs of public institutions are well voiced, particularly through the NEBHE quarterly publication, *Connection.*

Individual public institutions of higher education respond to the lack of financial resources by increasing the role that development and voluntary giving play in their fiscal futures, raising tuition, and attempting to do more with less. But the most exacting cost of

the problem is diminished access for potential students. As public institutions raise tuition to compensate for unallocated state funds, the cost of higher education, even at community colleges, has become prohibitive to an increasing number of students.

Connection: New England's Journal of Higher Education and Economic Development, various issues including "Trends and Indicators in Higher Education 2002" (2002); Patricia H. Crosson, "Where All Politics Is Local: Massachusetts," in Terrence J. MacTaggart and associates, *Restructuring Higher Education: What Works and What Doesn't in Reorganizing Governing Systems* (1996); Edward R. Hines, *Higher Education and State Governments: Renewed Partnership, Cooperation, or Competition?* (1988); Frederick Rudolph, *The American College and University: A History* (1990 [1962]); Edgar B. Shick, Richard J. Novak, James A. Norton, and Houston G. Elam, *Shared Visions of Public Higher Education Governance: Structures and Leadership Styles That Work* (1992).

Jana Nidiffer

Reform Movements

New England has served as the wellhead for the creation and reform of public education. In New England was born the concept of a publicly supported American educational system intended to serve the needs of society. For example, in 1630 the Puritan leader John Winthrop told his fellow colonists, "We must consider that we shall be as a city upon a hill the eyes of all people upon us." The goal of the Puritans was the creation of the good society that would serve as a beacon for the rest of the world. Education was essential in achieving and maintaining this ideal society. Lawrence Cremin, in a lecture at the Harvard Graduate School of Education in 1989, asserted that Americans have a long-standing tendency to involve education in the most fundamental aspirations concerning its society. Similarly, in *Tinkering toward Utopia,* David Tyack and Larry Cuban wrote, "Conversation about schools is one way that Americans make sense of their lives." New England's colonists had a strong influence on the role that public education now plays in the lives of citizens and the goals of government.

New England's involvement with public education began with the Puritans' goal of creating a well-ordered religious society that could serve as a model for the rest of the world. They used education as the means for both sustaining the current society and creating a more ideal society. The Puritans first passed the Massachusetts Bay Colony law of 1642, which called for the investigation of the ability of children in the colony "to read and understand the principles of religion and the capital laws of this country." Five years later the Old Deluder Satan Act was enacted. This law required any community of at least 50 households to appoint a teacher to provide in-

struction in reading and writing and communities of 100 or more households to establish a grammar school. These laws were the government's first attempts, but by no means the last, to use education to achieve a preferred outcome. The Massachusetts Bay Colony had faith in education as a tool for maintaining social stability and attaining social reform, and such faith ultimately led to the development of a universal public-school system even as government moved from sectarian to secular.

From 1642 to the present, New England has played a major role in the development and reform of public education. It was the site of the first American institution of higher education, Harvard College, in 1636. In addition to the grammar schools that proliferated in New England, the academy movement championed by Benjamin Franklin had an important beginning in Boston. In 1821 the English Classical School was founded. A few years later the school was renamed English High School and became the first high school in the United States.

The next major reform of education occurred during the nationalist period with the push to the West in pursuit of the nation's manifest destiny and with the influx of large immigrant populations. In 1837 Horace Mann, the first secretary of the Massachusetts Board of Education, became a major force in the common-school movement. The common-school movement emphasized professional autonomy over community control. It also used schools as an instrument of public policy to achieve a desired end, much as the Puritans used education to build a city upon the hill. In the case of the common-school movement, the reformers sought to build a system of common-school experiences in order to socialize the children of immigrants, rid the growing urban centers of poverty and crime through education, and establish a professional elite that would direct the education of citizens for the new social order of democratic participation in a republic form of government. For both the Puritans and the common-school reformers, education was a favored means of improving not just education but society as well. Education adeptly supported a theocracy in one period and a democracy in another, reformed in the second case to meet the new goal.

During the 19th century New Englanders led the way in educational reform in several other areas, such as education for the deaf (the American School for the Deaf was founded in 1817) and for the blind (the Perkins School was established in 1829), and in the movements for kindergarten and arts education. During the Progressive Era of the late 19th and early 20th centuries, many New Englanders responded to Thomas Dewey's program of reform, which called for a child-centered education and also envisioned schools functioning to socialize students and, by extension, to assimilate immigrant children into American life. This progressive impulse in the 1930s led to efforts to enlist schools in the restructuring of American society in response to the Depression.

In *Public Education,* Lawrence Cremin asserted that the important questions that education raises go "to the heart of the kind of society we want to live in and the kind of society we want our children to live in." As education had been the means in earlier centuries to achieve the desired or good society, in the middle part of the 20th century education was called upon to change—to emphasize excellence so that the United States could be more competitive with the Russians, who were first in space. Less than a decade after Sputnik, the nation shifted gears once again, and the fundamental value moved from excellence to equity with the dawning of the Civil Rights movement. In 1983 it was proclaimed that as a nation we were at risk because our "mediocre" schools meant that we could not compete in the global marketplace. Over the past few decades Theodore Sizer of Brown University has been a leader in educational reform through the Coalition of Essential Schools, founded in 1984. From the 1970s on, Yale University's James P. Comer has addressed the needs of inner-city students with plans for schools to provide basic health as well as academic services to children while Donald Graves at the University of New Hampshire has advocated new methods of writing instruction at all levels of education.

Business leaders have pushed schools to raise academic standards in order to produce their vision of the educated worker; high-stakes testing resulting from state and national accountability mechanisms was the impetus for the formulation of a unique New England interstate testing compact; plaintiffs in Connecticut, New Hampshire, and Vermont have challenged their state's scheme for financing public education; and Massachusetts has legislated a plan according to which parents can send their children to a school other than their neighborhood school. Each of these reforms was backed by a group that sought to use the schools to attain a goal—an "educated" workforce, a model citizen, equitable distribution of and access to state resources for education, and parental choice in the upbringing of their children. Another example of educational reform with New England flair is the rise of charter schools in 1991. Massachusetts, in its omnibus Education Reform Act of 1993, was one of the first states to adopt the concept of competition among public schools as a cure

for the problems of the nation's schools, followed by Rhode Island, New Hampshire, and Connecticut. Maine may join their ranks in 2005.

From colonial New England to the present, public education has often been the contested ground for competing visions of the good society. As long as public education is seen as a tool to reshape society, opposing groups will struggle to control it. As a result, it is likely that public education will walk the path of reform again and again, in New England and throughout the nation.

Lawrence A. Cremin, *Public Education* (1976); Cremin, *Popular Education and Its Discontents* (1989); David Tyack and Larry Cuban, *Tinkering toward Utopia: A Century of Education Reform* (1995).

Todd A. DeMitchell

Rural Schools Many years ago, rural schools dominated the American educational landscape, but today only 26 percent of public schools are located in the nation's rural areas. Certain regions still operate a substantial number of rural schools: in the Central Plains, for example, 46 percent of public schools are located in towns of fewer than 2,500 people. New England's rural schools represent only 22 percent of its public schools, but in the region's most rural states—Maine, New Hampshire, and Vermont—rural schools constitute 43 percent, 34 percent, and 52 percent, respectively. In Connecticut, Massachusetts, and Rhode Island, less than 6 percent of public schools are in rural areas.

New England's rural schools have changed

over the years, but certain features and conditions have persisted. Because of small enrollments, many classrooms combine in one room several grades taught by one teacher, and a small number of one-room schoolhouses still operate. Across the nation, rural teachers, administrators, and students are still largely Caucasian. In New England, 97 percent of rural students are white. There is, however, significant ethnic diversity in rural New England, notably a large Franco-American population in Maine, New Hampshire, and Vermont.

Rural schools in New England are supported by communities that continue to regard themselves as agricultural, even though only 5 to 15 percent of New England's rural people live or work on farms today. Well into the 20th century, the school year was scheduled around agricultural activities, and rural education prepared students for a role in an agricultural economy. In the larger agricultural areas of New England, schools still suspend classes to allow students to participate in the harvest, but today most rural students are educated within local economies that are much more diverse, oriented toward small manufacturing, trade, services, and the recreation industry.

Improved transportation and the spread of telecommunications have improved educational opportunities in rural areas, but costs continue to be high because of geographic isolation, and school funding continues to be low because of weak tax bases. For the past 100 years, policymakers have addressed these

School on Cliff Island, Maine, 1971

problems largely through school consolidation, arguing that fewer but larger schools allow for more diverse course offerings, more support services, and savings based on economies of scale. Rural people in New England and elsewhere have resisted this trend for various reasons. The small schools typical of rural areas allow for more individualized instruction, more personal relationships, and a stronger tie between school and community. Students in some of New England's rural states have high-school completion rates above the national average, lead the nation in average proficiency in both reading and mathematics, and score at a rate above the national average in college entrance exams.

Rural schools have advantages for communities as well as for students. They contribute significantly to the local economy and may be the area's largest employer. They provide social activities that range from athletic events to community suppers. They contribute to the public life of the community as polling places and sites for other public services. In short, they are a vehicle for and symbol of community. Many rural people perceive school consolidation (as well as statewide standards and curricula) as a threat to their communities, diminishing local authority and teaching children to value urban society more highly than rural styles of life. Rural schools continue to play a central role in the lives of many rural New England communities and to function as vital educational institutions.

Robert V. Carlson, "A Case Study of the Impact of a State-Level Policy Designed to Improve Rural Schools in the State of Vermont," Appalachia Educational Laboratory (1994); Alan J. DeYoung and Barbara Kent Lawrence, "On Hoosiers, Yankees, and Mountaineers," *Phi Delta Kappan* 77 (1995); Cynthia M. Duncan and Nita Lamborghini, "Poverty and Social Context in Remote Rural Communities," *Rural Sociology* 59 (1994); Clifton Johnson, *The Country School in New England* (1893).

Susan K. Woodward and Walter G. McIntire

Schoolmarms

Beginning in the early 1800s, in response to economic change and new beliefs about the necessity of female education, hundreds of young New England women became teachers. These women and their successors played a defining role in American education during the 19th century and in the development of intellectual culture within New England and far beyond.

As the economy of New England began to shift toward industrialization, the economic importance of the home, and the work that women did in the home, began to decline. Women became less occupied with spinning cloth and making soap and candles, but unlike men, they lacked the freedom to travel to cities

Teacher and pupils at North Sutton School, Sutton, N.H., 1905

in search of work or to move west in search of new farmland. As a result, women in their late teens and early twenties often became economic burdens on their families. The shift in economic production, coupled with the phenomena of low male population and delayed marriage, created a need among young women for meaningful employment. Many turned to teaching.

Although formal education in New England had previously been designed for boys and men, by the early 1800s educational opportunities for girls and young women expanded dramatically. Advocates of female education often justified advances in female literacy and higher learning by invoking women's maternal responsibilities to the young nation. If America was to retain its vitality and grow in strength through the coming generations, these advocates believed, women must be educated in order to instill principles of good citizenship in their sons. As laws mandating public support for education gradually came into effect, girls' education improved.

Advances in public education stimulated an increased demand for teachers qualified to instruct girls. This new demand, together with an increasing supply of young women eager to be educated as teachers, led to unprecedented opportunities for women. By 1810 many town and district schools had opened their doors to girls and begun to employ women teachers. At first, some of the new classes for girls were taught only during special summer sessions,

but even so, girls began to enjoy academic equality with boys. And even though the pay the women teachers received was often a fraction of what men received for similar work, these "schoolmarms," as they were called, enjoyed a new kind of social status and intellectual influence.

This development in women's roles coincided with widespread religious belief that female education would be central in world redemption. New England schoolmarms, armed with a commitment to enable women to play the part that God had ordained for them, fostered female learning not only in New England but also in the western territories and southern states, where New England women founded many schools. New England schoolmarms were active in other parts of the world as well, and in many cases were the first missionaries to introduce American Protestant culture to women outside North America.

Although *schoolmarm* has fallen into disrepute as a term, the influence and occasional bravery of pioneering schoolmarms from New England who went South during Reconstruction, or even earlier, has left a lasting legacy, evident in the example of Charlotte L. Forten Grimké (1837–1914), an African American teacher trained in Salem, Mass., who accompanied occupying troops to the South Carolina Sea Islands to teach liberated slaves. Images of schoolmarms were popularized by the paintings and illustrations of Winslow Homer in the late 19th century. Literary representations of schoolmarms were likewise common: Frances Harper's *Iola Leroy; or, Shadows Uplifted* (1892) depicts the destruction of a school run by New England women during the Reconstruction. Louisa May Alcott's novels *Little Men* (1871) and *Jo's Boys* (1886) presented an image of educational reform and leadership for women teachers.

David Allmendinger, "Mount Holyoke Students Encounter the Need for Life Planning, 1837–1850," *History of Education Quarterly* 19 (1979); Mary Kelley, "'Vindicating the Equality of Female Intellect': Women and Authority in the Early Republic," *Prospects* 17 (1992); Linda K. Kerber, *Women of the Republic: Intellect and Ideology in Revolutionary America* (1980); Amanda Porterfield, *Mary Lyon and the Mount Holyoke Missionaries* (1997).

Amanda Porterfield

Service Colleges and Academies

New England has a rich history of military and maritime colleges and service academies. The region's oldest, Norwich University in Northfield, Vt., is also the oldest private military college in the United States. Of the region's four maritime institutions, two—the U.S. Coast Guard Academy and the Naval War College—are federally supported, while the Maine Maritime Academy and the Massachusetts Maritime Academy are state institutions. Maritime institutions reflect and support New England's long tradition of reliance on the sea for its commerce and trade.

Norwich University was founded in 1819 in Norwich, Vt., as the American Literary, Scientific and Military Academy by U.S. Army captain Alden Partridge, who had previously been the superintendent of the U.S. Military Academy at West Point. Partridge wanted every state to have a private military college with a curriculum built around his belief that every male citizen should know how to fight to defend his country. Norwich is therefore considered the birthplace of the Reserve Officer Training Corps (ROTC) and the first private institution to grant degrees in civil engineering. The university currently enrolls 3,000 students, and all four ROTC programs are represented. In 1972 Norwich merged with the all-female Vermont College and in 1974 became one of the first military colleges to admit women into the Corps of Cadets.

The Massachusetts Maritime Academy was founded in 1891 by the state legislature as the Massachusetts Nautical Training School. The institution began as a floating trade school aboard the school ship *Nantucket*, berthed next to the USS *Constitution* in Boston. Since its founding, the academy has grown from a school of 40 cadets to a four-year coeducational college granting baccalaureate degrees, with an annual enrollment of 750 in five distinct majors. It is located at the state pier in Buzzards Bay.

The Maine Maritime Academy was established in 1941, with a class of 29 students studying at the campus of the Eastern State Normal School in Castine, Maine. The *Mattie*, a coastal schooner out of Camden, Maine, served as its first training ship. The academy grew greatly during World War II in response to the rapid buildup of the U.S. merchant marine. The Maine Maritime Academy grants three degrees, including an associate degree in science, a bachelor of science, and a master of science in 10 academic majors. It annually enrolls approximately 650 students.

The oldest federal service academy in New England is the U.S. Coast Guard Academy, founded in 1876. The academy was originally established aboard the cutter *Dobbin*, which served as both classroom and training vessel. Having been relocated several times during its history, the academy is now in New London, Conn., and is the home port of the three-masted barque *Eagle*, the only square-rigger training ship under an American flag. The academy educates men and women to be commissioned officers in the U.S. Coast Guard. It offers a bachelor of science degree in eight dis-

ciplines and has an enrollment of more than 800 cadets; one quarter are women.

The U.S. Naval War College was founded in 1884 by Secretary of the Navy William E. Chandler. He issued General Order No. 325, establishing "a college for an advanced course of professional study for Naval officers, to be known as the Naval War College." Founded in Newport, R.I., the Naval War College is the oldest war college in the nation and the oldest institution of its kind in continuous existence in the world. Attendance at the Naval War College is considered essential for senior officers. The college has evolved into four resident colleges, with more than 500 students graduating annually. The student body consists of U.S. military officers from all branches of the armed forces, career civilians from a variety of federal government agencies, and international naval officers. Qualified graduates from the College of Naval Warfare and the College of Naval Command and Staff (both part of the larger Naval War College) receive a master of arts degree in National Security and Strategic Studies. The Naval War College also hosts off-campus instruction through its College of Continuing Education via correspondence courses worldwide.

James M. Aldrich, *Fair Winds, Stormy Seas: Fifty Years of Maine Maritime Academy* (1991); Irving Crump, *Our United States Coast Guard Academy* (1975); William Ellis, *Norwich University, 1819–1911: Her History, Her Graduates, Her Roll of Honor* (1911); John B. Hattendorf, B. Mitchell Simpson, III, and John R. Wadleigh, *Sailors and Scholars: The Centennial History of The U.S. Naval War College* (1984).

Richard W. Schneider

Sizer, Theodore R. (1932–) Education

reformer. Born in New Haven, Conn., Theodore Sizer was educated at Yale and at Harvard, where he joined the education faculty in 1961. As a historian of secondary education, he embraced the action-oriented "progressive" pedagogical theories of John Dewey but stressed their conflict with the emphasis on

process and structure that was the institutional legacy of the Progressive Era. This combination of views made him a heterodox figure within the education establishment through successive cycles of reform.

Becoming dean of Harvard's Graduate School of Education in 1964, he used rising federal funding to greatly expand its programs, particularly in social policy. He developed a controversial proposal for market-based school choice for poor urban students. During his tenure, the school's student body became increasingly diverse, as, to a lesser extent, did its faculty.

As funding declines undermined many of his innovations at Harvard, Sizer resigned in 1972 and became headmaster of Phillips Academy in Andover, Mass.; there he oversaw the school's transition to coeducation and accelerated its evolution beyond "preppy" traditionalism while reinforcing its reputation for excellence.

Sizer began the most influential phase of his career in 1981, when he left Andover to head *A Study of High Schools,* an inquiry into American secondary education sponsored by the National Association of Secondary School Principals and the National Association of Independent Schools. Whereas contemporary reports reviewed quantitative inputs and results, Sizer's group examined qualitative experience in the schools and found unfocused curricula, overworked teachers, and disengaged students not respected as learners or individuals. His resulting book, *Horace's Compromise* (1984), considered how school structures and practices prevent teachers from giving students the individual attention necessary to bring forth their best efforts. Instead of more centralized authority to enforce standards, the study pointed toward reform of basic school structure and encouraged a "less is more" curricular philosophy.

The study's recommendations are promoted by the Coalition of Essential Schools, a partnership between high school and univer-

Theodore R. Sizer, 1982

sity led by Sizer and based at Brown University, where he was professor (1984–96) and director of the Annenberg Institute for School Reform. The Coalition of Essential Schools is guided by a set of principles designed to develop students' "habits of mind" by focusing on mastery of core skills and knowledge, as demonstrated by interdisciplinary projects ("exhibitions") described by Sizer in *Horace's School* (1992); to free educators to offer personalized teaching that treats the student as a "worker" in learning rather than as a passive recipient; and to foster high expectations, trust, and decency among students, teachers, and administrators.

This program was denounced both as elitist and as a continuation of the progressivism that cultural conservatives blamed for poorly performing schools. Sizer countered that only more engaged, effective teaching and learning could improve schools. He opposed externally imposed standards, particularly national or statewide testing: the state could not set "proper standards for Americans," he insisted, "but should limit its requirements to literacy, numeracy, and the foundations of citizenship."

This libertarian bent—combined with institutional resistance to change—led Sizer to a growing skepticism about the possibility of reform within public-school systems, evident in the third volume of his trilogy, *Horace's Hope* (1996). After retiring from Brown, he became codirector, with his wife, Nancy F. Sizer, of the Francis W. Parker Charter School (in Devens, Mass.), which is quasi-public but outside any system.

Sizer is the best-known school reformer of his time but increasingly stands outside the mainstream of reform. His program, influential among educators, is grounded in the responsibilities of citizenship, the professionalism of teachers, and the essential dignity of students.

Theodore R. Sizer, *Horace's Compromise: The Dilemma of the American High School* (1985); Sizer, *Horace's Hope: What Works for the American High School* (1996); Sizer, *Horace's School: Redesigning the American High School* (1992); Sizer, *Places for Learning, Places for Joy: Speculations on American School Reform* (1972); Sizer, *The Red Pencil: Convictions from Experience in Education* (2004); Theodore R. Sizer and Nancy Faust Sizer, *The Students Are Watching: Schools and the Moral Contract* (1999).

André Mayer

Special Education Preceding the emergence of the quintessentially American idea of the common school, the even more radical notion that children with significant disabilities could lead productive lives took root in New England. In fact, Horace Mann and his 19th-century collaborators in reform viewed special schools as "extensions" of the common school. As in Europe, impairments in hearing and vision were first addressed as educational challenges, the model of convenience, if not of choice, being the residential school, or "asylum."

Founded by Dr. Mason Fitch Caldwell (whose daughter was deaf), Rev. Thomas Hopkins Gallaudet, and Laurent Clerc, a deaf instructor from Paris, the Connecticut Asylum for the Education and Instruction of Deaf and Dumb Persons (American School for the Deaf) opened in 1817 in Hartford. Like those that followed, this first facility for specialized instruction reflected the spirit of reform stirring in New England, personified by a young Boston physician, abolitionist, and sometime revolutionary, Samuel Gridley Howe. Named in 1832 to lead the newly chartered New England Asylum for the Blind (Perkins School), Howe joined with Dorothea Dix in campaigning for humane treatment of persons with mental illness. In 1848, having gained a seat in the Massachusetts legislature, he convinced that body of its moral duty to provide instruction for persons with mental retardation.

As a consequence of an 1867 legislative victory in Massachusetts led by Gardiner Greene Hubbard (whose daughter Mabel was deaf), Harriet Rogers, a former teacher at the school for the deaf financed by Hubbard, founded the Clarke School for the Deaf at Northampton, Mass. At Clarke, Rogers introduced speech instruction, aided by a young "instructor of vocal physiology"—and Mabel's future husband—Alexander Graham Bell. That legislation also established day classes at the Boston School for Deaf-Mutes, whose pupils could have specialized instruction yet live at home with their families. In 1877 the school was renamed the Horace Mann School to acknowledge Mann's advocacy in that cause, consistent with his broader vision that the common school should serve all.

That vision, culminating in the 1975 enactment of federal legislation assuring all children with disabilities a free appropriate public education (amended in 1990 as the Individuals with Disabilities Education Act), was nurtured in New England through successive "firsts." In 1851 Massachusetts's compulsory school-attendance law explicitly included "crippled children," while the Providence system was among the first to serve pupils with health impairments. In 1896 Providence became one of the nation's first cities to form special classes for children with mental retardation, a trend accelerated in Massachusetts by Walter Fernald and in Connecticut by Arnold Gesell, the first official school psychologist. Publications of the Yale Child Study Center and the Gesell Institute of Human Development stressed early identification of children's needs for medical or educational intervention.

Clearly, children with disabilities have not always been beneficiaries of enlightened service in New England or elsewhere; the eugenics movement, pernicious myths, and misuse of mental testing fostered stereotypes, segregation in institutions, and exclusion from schooling. But today the core beliefs of early reformers—that exceptional children have a *right* to an education appropriate to their unique needs, with the goal of maximum independence as productive citizens in an inclusive society—are reflected in schools throughout New England, for example in Vermont's statewide resource-consultant system as well as in the region's culturally diverse urban centers.

Harlan Lane, *When the Mind Hears: A History of the Deaf* (1984); Philip L. Safford and Elizabeth J. Safford, *A History of Childhood and Disability* (1996); Margaret A. Winzer, *The History of Special Education: From Isolation to Integration* (1993).

Philip L. Safford

State Policy and Public Education Since the mid-1960s New England state departments of education have gradually shifted their focus from individual student rights to student and school achievement. At first, New England state legislators passed laws that protected the rights of individual children, and state departments of education played important roles in implementing such legislation. Recently, although these departments have varied significantly in their approaches, they appear increasingly to have moved from moral suasion and incentives to policy mandates and regulation for K–12 schools, thus challenging the New England tradition of strong autonomy for local school districts. At the same time, state departments of education have begun to encourage more local choice through the creation of charter schools.

In 1972 the Massachusetts legislature passed Chapter 766, which guaranteed that students with disabilities would receive appropriate education, and it was the job of the state department of education to implement this legislation. (Chapter 766 later became an important model for P.L. 94-142, the federal law that guarantees a free and appropriate education for children with disabilities.) Greg Anrig, Massachusetts Commissioner of Education from 1973 to 1981, also provided moral leadership in addressing the fact that students of color were receiving unequal, segregated education. Drawing upon the Racial Imbalance Act of 1956, Anrig used state magnet funds to offer incentives for districts to desegregate their schools. When these failed to persuade the Boston public schools to desegregate, the federal court mandated a desegregation plan in 1974. (Later, Connecticut also struggled with desegregation issues that led to the 1989 *Sheff v. O'Neill* case pertaining to the Hartford school district.)

Throughout this period, state departments of education continued to certify teachers and teacher education programs, distribute state educational aid, collaborate with regional school accreditation organizations, and serve as a pass-through for federal funds. New England state departments focused on different initiatives: Connecticut sought innovative ways to improve teaching standards and mentoring for new teachers; Vermont implemented school reviews that focused on teaching and learning. State departments also worked to provide support to urban school districts that were struggling.

In more recent decades, however, the focus of the governors and legislators has shifted from advocating for the rights of individual students to monitoring and mandating student achievement. The states have concentrated on two areas: school and district accountability and school choice. Most states developed comprehensive curriculum standards that laid out in detail what schools were expected to teach from year to year. The states also increased the number and distribution of courses that high school students needed to graduate and began to create assessments to measure student achievement. Although there was a great deal of variety in state responses, ranging from the high-stakes standardized Massachusetts Comprehensive Assessment System (MCAS) tests in Massachusetts to the Portfolio Assessment in Vermont, in 2004 New Hampshire, Rhode Island, and Vermont began collaborating to produce reading and mathematics tests for grades 3–8.

Some state leaders believe that the more aggressive stance of the states has been necessary to address the lack of achievement among different students in both urban and suburban districts. Nonetheless, especially after the federal "No Child Left Behind" Act of 2001 began to take effect, many local school districts and teachers have resented the intrusive federal and state roles that increasingly limit teacher autonomy in the classroom. Some applaud the fact that the federal requirement that all subgroups (such as children with disabilities, English-language learners, and those who receive free lunches) make "adequate yearly progress" toward proficiency on standardized tests has motivated school districts to focus resources on individuals and groups of children who often have not previously per-

formed well on standardized tests. On the other hand, many observers note that "teaching to the test" has had a significant reductionist impact on teaching and learning. They decry the fact that many elementary schools no longer offer arts, science, or social studies instruction because these curricular areas are not being tested.

Ironically, while state departments of education were becoming more regulatory, they were also supporting charter schools and school choice as ways of improving teaching and learning. Charter schools—public schools that are free of the constraints of unions and school bureaucracies—were originally touted by conservatives as an answer to the public school "monopoly." Parents impatient with the lack of good options in urban school districts often were eager to enroll their children in charter schools, which attracted both educational reformers and private companies eager to make a profit. Students' academic results in charter schools varied widely, but the number of charter schools has continued to increase in the first decade of the 21st century.

The equity and adequacy of state funding formulas for schools have become contentious topics debated in legislatures and courtrooms as issues of financial capacity and resources have been raised. New England states vary in their methods and amounts of state financial support for local schools, which are dependent on local property taxes. Vermont made the controversial decision to reallocate funds from more affluent districts in order to support needier districts. Massachusetts, on the other hand, tied financial reform that gave more resources to all districts (and significantly more resources to poorer districts) to state standards as measured by MCAS. Following economic downturns, however, education aid in Massachusetts was reduced, and the state aid formula is again being challenged in court. At the same time, funding has often been reduced for the state departments of education where fewer people are being expected to do more work.

During a period of educational change, it is difficult to have a clear picture of what is occurring. At this time we can conclude that top-down academic mandates combined with underfunding are creating significant dilemmas for urban and many rural school districts—and thus for state departments of education. The continued need to eliminate the academic gap between haves and have-nots gives educators, parents, policymakers, and researchers much to observe, debate, and address in the coming decades.

Marya R. Levenson

Webster, Noah (1758–1843) Educator and lexicographer. America's foremost lexicogra-

pher, Noah Webster, was born in West Hartford, Conn. After preparatory tutoring under Nathan Perkins, a local minister, and military service in the Revolutionary War, Webster graduated from Yale College in 1778. He then did clerical work while reading law. Admitted to the bar in 1781, he was unable to earn an adequate income during those turbulent times and practiced only briefly. While teaching school in 1782 at Goshen, N.Y., Webster became interested in compiling textbooks, based on the American experience, to replace British books on grammar, spelling, and reading and to help standardize spelling and pronunciation in the new nation. Patriotism as well as scholarship motivated him to write the three-volume *A Grammatical Institute of the English Language* (1783), which included his famous "Blue-Backed Speller," with its nationalistic preface and widespread influence on primary education.

In 1787 Webster urged the adoption of the Constitution to supplant the Articles of Confederation and in the process formed associations with George Washington, Alexander Hamilton, John Adams, James Madison, Benjamin Franklin, and John Jay. Advocating a strong federal government, he belonged to the Federalist party and wrote political pamphlets promoting the Federalist cause. While living in New York City, he edited two Federalist newspapers, the *American Minerva* and the *Herald* (later the *Commercial Advertiser* and the *Spectator*, respectively). Webster also supported state and federal copyright laws,

Janusz Korczak, Noah Webster *(1942–42), West Hartford, Conn.*

and he traveled extensively to lecture on the English language. In 1798 he moved to New Haven, Conn., where he represented his district in the Connecticut legislature, contributed articles to journals, continued his philological pursuits, and wrote books and essays on history, epidemics, climatology, physical science, and other topics.

A writer, journalist, pamphleteer, teacher, and lecturer, Webster concentrated primarily on lexicographical activities after 1800. He published his first dictionary, the *Compendious Dictionary of the English Language,* in 1806. In 1812 he relocated to Amherst, Mass., where he helped to establish Amherst Academy and Amherst College, and also served in the Massachusetts legislature. In 1822 Webster returned to New Haven, where he lived for the rest of his life except for brief intervals in France, England, and Washington, D.C.

Webster's crowning achievement came in 1828 with the publication of his two-volume, 70,000-word *An American Dictionary of the English Language,* a scholarly work of high distinction. His definitions of words were remarkable for their discrimination and succinctness. In justifying the production of a new dictionary, Webster carefully illustrated the deficiencies in the work of Dr. Samuel Johnson, including inaccurate etymologies. In proposing a norm of simple diacritical marking that reflected speech patterns in his native New England, he created standards that could accommodate regional variations in pronunciation nationwide. Webster's dictionary continues to be published today, and remains the standard for American English spelling and pronunciation.

Webster, a person of encyclopedic knowledge and diverse interests, emerged as America's schoolmaster, a unifying figure for the entire nation. His nationalistic views and sense of cultural independence were intertwined with his works. Certainly his most important contribution was as a lexicographer, for his dictionary, and the revised and enlarged versions since his time, profoundly affected American culture. Webster's birthplace, the Noah Webster House, is home to the Museum of West Hartford History and the Noah Webster Foundation, which contains collections of Webster's papers, dictionaries, and artifacts.

John S. Morgan, *Noah Webster* (1975); Richard J. Moss, *Noah Webster* (1984); Richard M. Rollins, ed., *The Autobiographies of Noah Webster* (1989); Ervin C. Shoemaker, *Noah Webster: Pioneer of Learning* (1936).

Leonard Schlup

Women's Colleges Although united by an early dedication to education in the liberal arts and teacher preparation, the women's colleges of New England are varied in their origins, structure, and specific educational missions. Established over the six New England states between 1870 and 1960, the schools for women arose alongside a system of men's institutions that denied them admission. Their founders were educators, wealthy benefactors, communities of religious women, and others dedicated to women's higher education. Their campus locations have ranged from the distinctly rural to the more cosmopolitan settings of the coordinate women's colleges affiliated with universities. Between the extremes of vocational training and pure liberal arts, the women's colleges have devised a variety of ways to accommodate students' career goals. Differences in their financial strength are indicated by reported endowment figures showing book values from zero to almost $55 million in the early 1960s. Financial considerations, together with the social changes of that decade, affected the stability of women's colleges and led those that endured to develop varying degrees of connection to coeducational schools.

Four prestigious Massachusetts colleges for women were among the first in New England. Mount Holyoke, Wellesley, Smith, and Radcliffe, alongside the three Seven Sister schools outside New England—Barnard, Bryn Mawr, and Vassar—developed into national institutions and set standards for other women's colleges to adopt or modify. Each was fully committed to the liberal arts and sought to provide for women the best education then possible according to the standards set by schools for men. Their founders, although dedicated to educational reform, subscribed to the 19th-century notion that women were properly confined to the realms of teaching and domesticity. Nevertheless, the colleges they created served to expand women's legitimate domain. Following in the tradition established by Mount Holyoke, substantial endowments enabled these four schools to prevail.

Mount Holyoke, Wellesley, and Smith began as residential schools with structured, protective environments variously connected to evangelical Christianity. Mount Holyoke Female Seminary was founded in 1837 by educator Mary Lyon. It offered a three-year course for the preparation of teachers on a campus with a single main building, where a resident faculty supervised the students' highly regulated lives. Mount Holyoke did not achieve full college standing until 1888. But in an era of instability for women's schools, its success as a financially secure institution of higher learning paved the way for endowed women's colleges later in the century.

Wellesley College was chartered in 1870, with Mount Holyoke trustee Henry Fowle Durant as its benefactor and founder. Despite its collegiate status, Wellesley adopted many features of a seminary, including a campus with a single main building, luxurious and imposing, that housed both faculty and students. Durant appointed a Mount Holyoke graduate as Wellesley's first president, and like Lyon before him, he envisioned an all-female faculty.

After the death of benefactor Sophia Smith, a group of men connected to Amherst College established Smith College in 1871. To distinguish the new school, located in Northampton, Mass., from a seminary, they set high admissions standards, requiring a classical secondary-school background, and they rejected the discipline of the seminary in favor of the kind of order provided by a residential system of cottages under the presidency of a man.

Unlike Mount Holyoke, Wellesley, and Smith, Radcliffe College began as an experimental outgrowth of a university. In 1879 an early incarnation of Radcliffe, commonly called the Harvard Annex, provided an alternative to the type of education provided by women's colleges. In a nonresidential program free from seminary associations, the Annex offered courses in the liberal arts taught by members of the Harvard faculty. After an unsuccessful attempt by its founders to make it part of Harvard, the Annex was renamed Radcliffe College and chartered separately in 1894.

From their beginnings through the first two decades of the 20th century, the Seven Sisters moved toward a shared, mature concept of a women's college characterized by a scholarly and professional faculty, a residential collegiate campus formed by quadrangles, and a student life that flourished free from faculty control.

Coordinate education provided a way for men's colleges to address women's requests for admission without becoming coeducational. Radcliffe has been credited with providing a model for the coordinate relationship between Pembroke College and Brown University in Providence, a partnership formed in 1891. Tufts University of Medford, Mass., became coeducational in 1892 but subsequently moved to separate the sexes and establish a coordinate institution for women, Jackson College, in 1910. Clark University of Worcester, Mass., founded a coordinate women's college in 1942, and Radcliffe's coordinate arrangement with Harvard was strengthened by their joint-education agreement of 1947.

In 1919 the Sisters of Notre Dame de Namur established Boston's Emmanuel College, making it the first Catholic institution of higher education for women in New England. Dedicated to "the liberal and useful arts and sciences," Emmanuel addressed women's vocational goals within the curriculum. Other

Catholic women's schools subsequently opened throughout New England, including three in the Boston area: Regis College in 1927, Newton College of the Sacred Heart in 1946, and Cardinal Cushing College in 1956. Both Newton and Cushing closed in the 1970s as a result of financial problems.

Bennington College in Vermont was designed to offer an alternative to the traditional approach of the Seven Sister schools. President William Neilson of Smith participated in its lengthy planning process. An experimental college for women, Bennington opened in 1932 with a curriculum emphasizing the arts and a social life unconstrained by imposed rules. Programs of study were fashioned to meet the interests of individual students, and fieldwork brought together the vocational and the academic.

From the 1930s through the 1950s, American culture placed a singular emphasis on women's domestic role; women's place in the labor force therefore became problematic both for society and for individual women wishing to work. In response to this situation many women's colleges since 1960 have developed continuing-education programs that provide an educational base for the careers of adult women. The Radcliffe Institute for Independent Study was established in 1960 to offer women with family duties the opportunity to work on artistic and scholarly projects on a part-time basis. Restructured as the Bunting Institute, the research center promoted women's achievement in the professions, the arts, and business.

A survey of women's colleges in New England in the early 1960s shows 27 accredited four-year schools distributed over the region's six states: 16 in Massachusetts; 4 in Connecticut; 2 each in New Hampshire, Rhode Island, and Vermont; and 1 in Maine. In addition to the Seven Sisters and coordinate schools, they include 13 Catholic women's colleges, 1 state-supported institution, 2 private teachers colleges, and several private independent schools.

Driven by financial concerns as well as student preference, most single-sex schools of both genders were considering coeducation in the 1960s. By 1975 most men's colleges admitted women, including such bastions of male education as Amherst, Dartmouth, and Yale. Only about one-fourth of the women's colleges in New England became coeducational between 1960 and 1975, however, among them Bennington in Vermont; Anna Maria, Wheelock, and Framingham State in Massachusetts; Connecticut College in New London; Salve Regina in Newport, R.I.; and Saint Joseph's in Standish, Maine. Pembroke merged with Brown in 1971.

The women's colleges that remained single-sex generally chose to enter relationships with coeducational schools through cross-registration and exchange programs, consortium arrangements, and dual-degree plans. Wellesley's cross-registration agreement with MIT, begun in 1967, became official in 1968–69. The informal association of Mount Holyoke and Smith Colleges with Amherst, dating back to the founding of these schools, was formalized in the late 1960s when the three institutions joined with Hampshire College and the University of Massachusetts to form Five Colleges, Inc., a consortium whose benefits include faculty as well as student interchange. By 1970 the opportunity for a residential coeducational experience was available to the women of Mount Holyoke, Smith, and Wellesley through the Twelve College Exchange. Radcliffe further strengthened its ties to Harvard while retaining its separate identity in their "nonmerger merger" agreement of 1971. On October 1, 1999, the two schools officially merged in a move that created the Radcliffe Institute for Advanced Study.

By the early 1990s cross-registration agreements had become common, and several women's colleges were offering dual-degree programs with coeducational institutions. Through affiliations such as these, women's colleges are able to offer a diversity of academic offerings and educational experience, including coeducation. Such arrangements serve women's professional goals by providing them with opportunities to study architecture, engineering, and other subjects not taught at the women's schools. The extent to which these interinstitutional relationships have been implemented varies. Nevertheless, they have altered the concept of the women's college by diminishing its distinctly female identity.

The women's movement, by contrast, has served to strengthen the notion of the women's college by asserting the importance of a separate place for women dedicated to their own concerns. The movement contributed to the decision of women's institutions to remain single-sex, and also to the recognition of women's studies as a legitimate part of the college curriculum. Several women's colleges in the New England area offer major programs in women's studies. Against the backdrop of the women's movement, with its emphasis on women's leadership roles, Smith College inaugurated its first woman president in 1975.

As of 2002, there were about a quarter as many women's colleges in New England as there had been in the early 1960s. The exclusion that motivated their original founding no longer applies, and virtually no women's college has been created for several decades. Those that endure do so in self-conscious awareness of their redefinition.

Allan M. Cartter, ed., *American Universities and Colleges,* 9th ed. (1964); Elizabeth Alden Green, *Mary Lyon and Mount Holyoke: Opening the Gates* (1979); Helen Lefkowitz Horowitz, *Alma Mater: Design and Experience in the Women's Colleges from Their 19th-Century Beginnings to the 1930s,* 2d ed. (1993); Mabel Newcomer, *A Century of Higher Education for American Women* (1975 [1959]); Patricia A. Palmieri, *In Adamless Eden: The Community of Women Faculty at Wellesley* (1995); L. Clark Seelye, *The Early History of Smith College, 1871–1910* (1923); Barbara Miller Solomon, *In the Company of Educated Women: A History of Women and Higher Education in America* (1985).
Susan Williamson

Women's Studies Women's studies is both the interdisciplinary study of all aspects of women's lives and the reexamination of all existing disciplines from the starting point that gender is important. Because New England is particularly rich in institutions of higher learning, the region hosts a wealth of women's studies programs and departments. The first such programs were not founded on the East Coast, however, and the conservatism of many schools in the Northeast may have slowed their growth in the region. Harvard University, for example, started its program later than most schools and has kept it small. It remains to be seen how the 1999 merger of Radcliffe College with Harvard University will affect women's studies at Harvard.

Students have now come to expect at least some course offerings in women's studies in almost all institutions of higher learning, both public and private. This interest is not confined to liberal arts colleges but extends to schools with a heavy emphasis on engineering and the sciences, such as MIT in Cambridge, Mass., and to schools concentrating on business, such as Bentley College in Waltham, Mass. Women's studies courses and programs also exist at church-affiliated institutions, such as the Catholic Boston College in Chestnut Hill, Mass., and Regis College in Weston, Mass. The National Association for Women in Catholic Higher Education was founded in 1992 by Sharlene Hess-Biber, former head of the Boston College women's studies program.

In some schools the women's studies program or department is supplemented by a research center on women, whose purpose is not primarily to teach but rather to produce studies of various kinds. One example is Wellesley College, which has not only a Department of Women's Studies but also a Center for Research on Women. Various universities and colleges have research arms linked to women's studies; they include the Simmons Center for Women and Leadership, the Schlesinger Library at Radcliffe, and Brown University's Pembroke Center. In some universities the women's studies program is supplemented by research institutes with a more specialized focus, such as the Hadassah Research Institute on Jewish Women at Brandeis University. Other schools provide a women's studies or gender-based specialization within a field. For example, Northeastern University's Law School and the Harvard Divinity School allow students to specialize in gender studies.

Women's studies programs offer courses primarily on the undergraduate level, although some offer graduate courses and even graduate degrees. The vast majority of women's studies courses are cross-listed with other departments. Clark University in Worcester, Mass., is the only school in New England that offers a Ph.D. in women's studies. Brandeis University offers nine different joint master's degrees that pair women's studies with anthropology, American history, English and American literature, comparative history, Near Eastern and Judaic studies, music, psychology, social policy, and sociology. The Graduate Consortium in Women's Studies, established at Radcliffe College in 1992, is open to graduate students from Boston College, Brandeis, Harvard, MIT, Northeastern, Simmons, and Tufts and offers interdisciplinary courses team-taught by faculty from these Boston-area schools.

The ties between women's studies and other disciplines are especially strong in the social sciences, the humanities, and the arts, although efforts are usually made to build connections with the natural sciences as well. Women's studies programs strenuously attempt to teach in ways that take race, ethnicity, religion, and sexual orientation into account and that are not ethnocentrically focused on the United States. Most women's studies programs welcome men, although the rate of male college students' participation in women's studies courses is not great. Male participation is higher on the graduate student and faculty levels.

Women's studies programs sometimes engage in off-campus action projects; certain branches of the University of Maine, for example, provide student support to shelters for battered women. Most programs, however, focus on academic matters and leave issues pertaining to affirmative action, rape counseling, and sexuality services to other departments of a college or university. A few offer special internships to give students useful experience in the community, such as Brandeis University's Internship in the Prevention of Violence against Women and Children.

Although women's studies courses are as rigorous as those in any other area, the field is still stereotyped by some as overly political or ideological. In some colleges and universities,

therefore, students in such programs may feel isolated. As a relatively new field (the first programs were started in the 1970s), women's studies usually has far fewer resources than other disciplines. Nevertheless, enrollments in women's studies courses are usually strong, and most programs are able to mount conferences and lecture series that bring great excitement to their campuses.

Shulamit Reinharz

Yale University Yale was founded in 1701 by a group of Congregational ministers who persuaded the Connecticut General Court to issue a charter for the "Collegiate School." The fledgling college rotated among a number of towns—Killingworth, Wethersfield, and (Old) Saybrook—until it settled permanently at New Haven in 1716. As local funds proved inadequate for its support, the trustees sought outside benefactors. In response to the substantial gift by the English nabob Elihu Yale, the trustees named the first collegiate building Yale College in 1718, a change officially confirmed by a new charter in 1745. During the 18th century Yale served as the provincial college for Connecticut with the purpose of educating young men for service "both in Church and Civil State." After the American Revolution, President Ezra Stiles (1778–95) brought Yale and the state closer together in terms of financial support and governance with an aspiration to university status.

During the first half of the 19th century Yale attracted a geographically diverse student body drawn from the southern states and the Ohio Valley, where many New Englanders had migrated. Graduates founded many new

colleges in the West and South modeled after their alma mater, which became known as the "mother of colleges." The increasing industrialization of New England led to public demands that the old classical curriculum be dropped in favor of more practical studies. Led by President Jeremiah Day (1817–46), the faculty prepared the Yale Report of 1828, which defended the classical curriculum and asserted that a collegiate education should "lay the foundation for a superior education," setting the pattern for liberal arts education throughout the nation. While defending the college, Yale moved toward its goal of becoming a university by establishing schools of medicine (1810), theology (1822), law (1843), and a separate undergraduate science and engineering school (1854). Yale awarded the first three Ph.D. degrees in the United States in 1861, and in 1887 it officially changed its name to Yale University.

As Yale looked increasingly beyond New England after the Civil War, the historic link with the state of Connecticut withered. In 1872 state-appointed members on Yale's governing body were replaced with alumni trustees. In the last quarter of the 19th century both Yale's student body and its graduates became more closely connected with New York City. The fortunes made by some of these graduates, particularly the corporation lawyer John Sterling, provided the base for Yale's growth in the 20th century. During the first half of the century Yale's leaders feared that this growth had weakened the undergraduate community; a large gift from the Harkness family of New York made it possible to create a system of residential colleges that recaptured the atmo-

Branford College courtyard, Yale University, New Haven, Conn.

sphere of the small New England college within a larger urban university.

After World War II Yale came under increasing criticism that its undergraduate student body was too elite and exclusively male. Under President Kingman Brewster (1963–76), Yale College admitted a majority of public school graduates, as well as larger numbers of Jews, African Americans, and ethnic minorities. In 1969 Yale College admitted women for the first time; the graduate and professional schools had done so since the late 19th century. Yale was also forced to devote more attention to the well-being of New Haven as the city entered a period of economic decline. In the last decades of the 20th century and the beginning of the 21st, the university made new commitments to revitalize the city's commercial core and encourage residential development.

Yale University's influence on New England and national culture is manifold. Presidents William Howard Taft, Gerald Ford, George H. W. Bush, Bill Clinton, and George W. Bush are graduates of either the college or the Law School, as are innumerable other political, business, educational, and cultural leaders. Yale's libraries and museums are among the nation's leading institutions for research and exhibitions, including the Beinecke Rare Book and Manuscript Library (designed by Gordon Bunshaft), the Yale University Art Gallery and the Yale Center for British Art (both designed by Louis Kahn), and the Peabody Museum of Natural History. Aside from signature buildings designed by leading architects, Yale's campus plan, with its Gothic Revival residential colleges, has defined the look of American university education in the eyes of many in the region and across the country.

Yale celebrated its tercentenary in 2001 and is today acknowledged as a leading international university with approximately 11,000 students in Yale College, the Graduate School of Arts and Sciences, and professional schools of Architecture, Art, Divinity, Drama, Engineering, Forestry and Environmental Studies, Law, Management, Medicine, Music, and Nursing. It continues to face the challenge of reconciling its international standing and student body with its New England collegiate roots and the well-being of the city that has been its home for the past three centuries.

Jurgen Herbst, *From Crisis to Crisis: American College Government, 1683–1819* (1999); Brooks Mather Kelley, *Yale: A History* (1974); Dan A. Oren, *Joining the Club: A History of Jews at Yale* (1985); George W. Pierson, *The Founding of Yale* (1988); John S. Whitehead, *The Separation of College and State: Columbia, Dartmouth, Harvard and Yale, 1776–1876* (1973).

John S. Whitehead

Ethnic and Racial Identity

Marilyn Halter, Section Editor, with Robert L. Hall

Elliott R. Barkan, Joanne Pope Melish, and William D. Piersen, Consulting Editors

INTRODUCTION

In 1614 Captain John Smith dubbed a part of North America *New* England, an expression connoting a fresh and innovative alternative to the Old World mother country. In the realm of racial and ethnic identities, however, both popular and traditional scholarly notions of the region have typically conveyed nothing new at all. To this day most view the region as a fixed and homogeneous society whose culture is fundamentally English, whose racial complexion is white, and whose sensibilities are Yankee. Yet from the beginning New England has been far more diverse than this uniform image suggests, with the Native American, English, African American, French, Jewish, and other resident populations of the colonial era engaging in complex and varied relations. By the 19th century successive waves of more and more diverse immigrants had made New England the most multiethnic region in the country. Still, the true extent of its diversity remained largely invisible. Over the past few decades newcomers to the region hail from an even wider range of cultural and racial backgrounds. These primarily non-European and often nonwhite settlers pose a formidable challenge to any persistent conception of Anglo-Saxon homogeneity. Moreover, rediscovery of racial, ethnic, and working-class history in the 20th century has fundamentally altered our understanding of the context within which New England's icons and images were created. One need only examine the racial and ethnic composition of the region over time to demonstrate that there has always been something new about New England after all.

Although social scientists sometimes disagree on the precise definition of *ethnicity*, the term usually refers to the cultural characteristics perceived as shared by groups of real or putative common ancestry. Since it came into widespread use, the word *ethnic* has generally been reserved for the descendants of European immigrants. Those of non-European extraction were given racial designations or subsumed under the broader category of *minorities*. If ethnicity has been on the map at all in New England, it has been linked to social-class standing and basically considered a working-class phenomenon. The simple assumption is that working-class people are more genuinely ethnic. And this view is consistent with a good deal of sociological scholarship associating strong ethnic identities with lower-class ways of life, no matter what the geographic setting.

Other New England inhabitants—for example, Native Americans, African Americans, and Chinese Americans—have historically been perceived in racial terms. But even this level of distinction has often collapsed into a dualistic vision of a black-and-white society where whites are European, blacks are African, and Native Americans, Asians, and Latinos disappear altogether. Furthermore, the peculiar idea persists in both the region and the nation as a whole that if your race is white, you are defined by an ethnicity—whether Irish, French Canadian, or Italian—but if your race is black or mixed, you are defined by skin color alone. Because Americans of African descent are often seen solely in racial terms, their distinctive cultural identities go unrecognized. Yet with the number of multiracial immigrants on the increase, the nonwhite populations of New England hail from multiple homelands, bringing with them a wealth of ethnocultural traditions. Black New Englanders, for instance, may be Cape Verdean, Haitian, or West Indian. Even the umbrella terms *Asian, Hispanic,* or *Latino* obscure more than they explain. Asian populations in the region—among them Chinese, Vietnamese, Cambodians, Koreans, and South Asians—come from extremely diverse ethnic backgrounds and have arrived under quite distinctive circumstances. Latinos include Puerto Ricans, Brazilians, and Dominicans, groups that have their own individual histories, demographic profiles, and patterns of integration and adaptation.

Like their counterparts of European extraction, New Englanders of non-European descent have widely varying ethnicities, speak different languages, practice numerous religions, observe diverse customs, maintain distinctive cuisines, and engage in their own forms of music, literature, art, and material culture. Thus racial designations are becoming less and less useful to our understanding of the social dynamics of diversity. Most of the immigrants arriving in New England in the past several decades do not readily fit the rigid binary system of racial classification. Ethnicity as a social category is more versatile than race and can be used for all nationalities, no matter what their racial composition.

One way of discussing the development of New England's contemporary racial and ethnic makeup is to look at the region's successive *new*comers over the very long term. Once upon a time the human ancestors of all present-day residents of New England, including the peoples we now call Native Americans, migrated to the region from somewhere else. In that sense the story begins with Asian newcomers whose ancestors formed what might be called the Native American baseline. The Native Americans who lived in New England on the eve of European colonization were descendants of nomadic hunters who some 12,000 years earlier had themselves been newcomers to the region. Although agriculture had become their main means of subsistence before the Europeans arrived in the early 17th century, their way of life combined hunting and fishing with cultivating in a regular annual cycle. Among the most numerous of the Algonquian-speaking peoples who inhabited the region were the Abenaki, Narragansett, Pequot, and Wampanoag nations.

After Virginia, New England was the setting for the second major cultural contact between the English and native North Americans in the 17th century. Although most accounts of European settlement in New England begin with the arrival of 102 English Pilgrims at Plymouth Rock in 1620, these religious dissenters were not the first Europeans to touch New England's shores. Since at least the late 1500s, fishers from several European states had dried their catches on the shores of Cape Cod and Maine after harvesting the Grand Banks. And the first English attempt to colonize the region was made as early as 1607 with the ill-fated Popham Colony in Maine. It was apparently disease more than brute force and overwhelming numbers that cleared a path for European settlement, after English fishermen stopping on the coast in 1616 set off what is now known as a "virgin soil epidemic." During the period of European colonization, densely settled Algonquian-speaking peoples encountered the full force of epidemics, massacre, and forced assimilation. On the eve of the 1620s an estimated 126,000 to 144,000 natives inhabited southern New England; during the initial contact period some 90 percent of them died off or were killed. The Pilgrims who arrived at Plymouth Rock were peacefully greeted by the Wampanoag leader Massasoit. Fifty-five years later, in 1675, relations between the native peoples and the newcomers had deteriorated so badly that Massasoit's son Metacom, known to the colonists as King Philip, would lead the Algonquian Indians in a war to drive the English settlers out of the region. It was a war that the natives nearly won.

The first voluntary arrivals, usually referred to as "settlers" rather than "immigrants," came from England to an essentially colonial, agrarian society. Although a sprinkling of newcomers from other nationalities, including Irish Protestants, Germans, and Sephardic Jews, immigrated to the region during colonial times, the English overwhelmingly dominated the settler population through the 1840s. Not long after the Puritans embarked on the Great Migration of the 1630s, the forced transfer of Africans to the region began; the captives, most of them young adult males, were transported in the bowels of slave ships on a trade route from the West Indies to Boston. Although frequently overlooked, slavery certainly existed in the region during colonial times, and some New England merchants actively engaged in the transatlantic slave trade. The region was part of a web of economic interdependence that included Africa and the Caribbean as well as continental Europe and the British Isles. Although specialists disagree, the importation of Africans into what is now Massachusetts dates to at least 1638, when the Salem ship *Desire,* commanded by Captain William Pierce of Boston, imported several Africans into the colony.

Although it is difficult to estimate the numbers of black newcomers imported as slaves, it is clear that Massachusetts (including the port of Boston) had long been involved in the Atlantic slave trade. In 1680 Africans in New England probably numbered fewer than 1,000, constituting less than 1 percent of the region's population. Before Rhode Island entered into the slave trade in the 1720s, Massachusetts was the principal colonial carrier of slaves. By 1770, however, Rhode Island was running about 70 percent of the American trade in African slaves and went on to control as much as 90 percent later in the 18th century. The commercial significance of large-scale agriculture around Narragansett Bay, the success of the rum-distilling industry, and the sustaining role of slaving voyages out of Newport before the American Revolution and out of Bristol afterward all contributed to the long-term social and economic importance of the slave trade in Rhode Island until 1787, when the state legislature passed an act forbidding its citizens from participating in it.

Although the number of slaves imported directly was insignificant in the larger hemispheric context, direct importation was not the only link between Boston, other New England port towns, and the overseas slave trade. New England colonies surpassed those of the South in the volume of slave-carrying trade, though most of the

Africans they transported went to places other than New England. A typical pattern in the middle of the 18th century, as in the middle of the previous one, was for Boston-based vessels to set sail for Africa, collect African captives, and deliver them to Barbados and other West Indian islands or to southern mainland colonies such as Virginia. After exchanging the Africans in the islands, such vessels could and did return to Boston with cargoes of wine, salt, sugar, and tobacco.

According to a census conducted in 1754, there were more than 900 slaves over age 16 in Boston. By 1755 blacks made up about 2 percent of the population of the Massachusetts Bay Colony and about 8 percent of the population of Boston. As in much of the rest of New England, a high proportion of the black new arrivals in Massachusetts during the legal slave trade had been shipped there from the West Indies rather than directly from Africa.

Colonial African Americans pursued both agricultural and mechanical forms of employment, engaging in the production of foodstuffs and livestock in rural areas and in cities and becoming bakers, carpenters, sawyers, cabinetmakers, blacksmiths, printers, tailors, and coopers, among other occupations. During the late 18th and early 19th centuries, a number of black New Englanders, particularly women, were engaged in domestic service for private households, but many others were agricultural workers, stockmen, or dairy hands. In addition to the major deployment of slave labor in dairying and cattle raising, slaves tended sheep and horses and cultivated vegetables and tobacco.

Though in smaller numbers, slaves also labored in northern New England. In 1895 the African American historian W. E. B. Du Bois stated that "the statistics of slavery in New Hampshire show how weak an institution it always was in that colony." Du Bois estimated that the number of slaves in New Hampshire between 1730 and 1790 ranged from a high of 681 in 1773 to a low of 158 in 1790. Slavery in Maine, though relatively short-lived in comparison with the institution of the southern states, lasted about 120 years. During that time the number of slaves never went above 600. Throughout much of the period, until it was admitted to the union as a state in 1820, present-day Maine was administratively part of Massachusetts. After 1680 Maine's small slave population was concentrated in the towns that were secure from conflict with the Native Americans and wealthier than the norm—Kittery, Wells, York, and Falmouth—and they were held by a few very wealthy families.

Blacks fought in the American Revolution, some on the American side but many more in support of the British armies, for practical as well as abstract reasons, since military service was one way to make ends meet. A number of the black Revolutionary War veterans, like Prince Hall and Lemuel Haynes, would gain prominence in the postrevolutionary era. Many others, exercising their recently gained freedom of movement, gravitated toward the bustling coastal towns, especially Boston, as a way to solve the problem of how to make a living once the war was over.

By 1780 the number of African Americans in New England had risen to about 14,000, roughly 2 percent of the region's population. They were clustered in coastal areas and along river systems. In some townships in the Narragansett region of Rhode Island, blacks made up one-sixth to one-third of the inhabitants. Their pres-

Frontispiece, Lydia Maria Child, An Appeal in Favor of That Class of Americans Called Africans *(Boston, 1833)*

ence in such areas was largely due to the greater availability of jobs in the maritime industries—such as whaling, the cargo trade, shipbuilding, and coopering—which in the 18th and 19th centuries were among the most racially diverse in New England. By the 1790 census the overwhelming majority of the 17,000 blacks in New England were nominally free. Nevertheless, 3,763 African Americans were enumerated as slaves in that same census. Vermont abolished slavery in its state constitution of 1777; Massachusetts did so by judicial decision in 1783; Rhode Island and Connecticut both passed gradual abolition acts in 1784, with Connecticut passing a second in 1797.

Within 50 years of the American Revolution most African Americans in the North had made the transition from slavery to freedom. The timing and smoothness of that transition varied according to local economic conditions. Ironically, the emancipation of the region's enslaved people may have intensified rather than diminished racial hostility. Earning a living was almost always a mortal struggle for black New Englanders and would continue to be one well beyond the end of the Civil War, as successive waves of new immigrants created stiff competition for jobs. Many African Americans moved to coastal cities where the maritime industries offered work and recently established black churches, lodges, societies, and schools offered an organized social life. This network of institutions enabled some to find jobs, friends, and places to live while providing a base from which to resist both racial discrimination and the persistent horror of slavery farther south. Out of this milieu, several of New England's African American abolitionists became key figures in the antislavery movement.

For two centuries, not only did the English constitute the overwhelming majority of the region's population but the Anglo-Saxon Protestant heritage that was transplanted with them became normative, dominating New England's cultural identity. Triumphantly emerging from the American Revolution, English Americans had overthrown British rule, nearly obliterated the Native American population, and relegated African Americans to a separate, lower caste. Beginning in the 1830s, however, several waves of newcomers representing other ethnic backgrounds started to arrive in larger numbers, complicating and challenging the firm grip that the long-standing Yankee residents had over the region's religious, political, and socioeconomic life.

Although a sprinkling of Irish and Scotch Irish settlers were among the first voluntary immigrants to come to colonial New England—with Protestant Irish continuing to arrive in small numbers, especially to less populated areas of northern New England, throughout the 17th and 18th centuries—the migration of Irish Catholics did not begin in earnest until the 1830s. Pushed out by the interlocking factors of overpopulation, the mechanization of agriculture, and exploitative practices that made it difficult for Ireland's peasants to eke out a living off British-owned land, many more began to see emigration as a means to improve their economic lot. The men could often find work as day laborers on the construction projects springing up as the towns of New England grew into cities. The Irish Catholic influx escalated to a flood, however, in the mid-1840s when a catastrophic potato blight hit Ireland's single-crop agricultural economy, causing a famine so severe that a million people died from starvation, malnutrition, typhus, and other diseases and another 1.5 million fled, two-thirds of them to the United States.

The vast majority of famine-stricken survivors came to the cities of the northeastern seaboard, including Boston. Between 1850 and 1870, the foreign-born population of Massachusetts more than doubled, and Irish newcomers made up much of that increase. By 1870 Irish-born immigrants in New England's largest cities greatly outnumbered those born in either Germany or England (see table). At the height of the devastation wrought by the famine, for example, the city of Boston, which had been receiving immigrants at a rate of between 4,000 and 5,000 annually, recorded some 37,000 arrivals in the year 1847. The transatlantic journey was so perilous, and the passengers who lived through the crossing arrived so weakened, that the vessels they came in were dubbed "coffin ships." Unlike their able-bodied compatriots who migrated in earlier decades, the "famine Irish" had trouble obtaining employment. Traumatized and largely unskilled in a city with a labor market that could not absorb such a glut of new residents, women often fared better than men, since they were able to fulfill a growing demand for domestic help in Yankee households.

The Irish immigrants to Boston encountered an Anglo-Saxon cultural and political dominance 200 years in the making, an entrenched Yankee population openly hostile to them, and often the expression of virulent hatred and suspicion of anything associated with Roman Catholicism. Episodes of anti-Irish sentiment had erupted even before the mass migration of the famine Irish; the most notorious case was the burning in 1834 of an Ursuline convent in Charlestown (now Somerville), Mass., by an angry Yankee mob. As the numbers of Irish Catholic settlers grew, so did the volume of organized anti-immigrant and anti-Catholic initiatives, culminating in the 1850s with the formation of the nativist Know-Nothing political party, many of whose leading members were from Massachusetts. Discrimination in employment was widespread, and signs reading "No Irish Need Apply" were a common sight in storefront windows. Yet in spite of this antagonistic environment, the Irish began to adjust to their new civic culture, becoming citizens at high rates, using their new-found voting rights, and mobilizing the compatriot community, so that by the closing decades of the 19th century and well into the 20th, they had become a dominating political force of their own within traditionally Yankee strongholds.

Although the Irish bore the brunt of nativist sentiment, they were not the only mid-19th-century influx of Catholic newcomers with whom the Anglo-Saxon majority had to contend. Spurred by overpopulation and the repeated subdivision of plots of land in Quebec, French Canadians—those who stayed would not be dubbed Franco-Americans until the early 20th century—began to migrate across a land border to the United States in significant numbers during the 1830s, with roughly 275,000 coming over the span between 1830 and 1900. Including their American-born offspring, the census of 1900 lists approximately 570,000 New Englanders of "French-Canadian stock."

Moving to both urban and rural areas, they had established small communities in Winooski, Vt., and Woonsocket, R.I., as early as 1814 and 1815. Before 1850 Franco-American enclaves had also been established in Madawaska, Maine, and Burlington, Vt. Other prominent centers of French Canadian settlement and so-called Little Canadas were Fall River, Southbridge, Springfield, and Lowell, Mass.; Manchester, N.H.; and Lewiston and Biddeford-Saco, Maine. Often those who came to labor in New England's mill towns and apparel manufacturing cities represented the first large group of non-English-speaking settlers. The 12th annual report of the Massachusetts Bureau of Statistics and Labor, published in 1881, dubbed French Canadians "the Chinese of the East," a designation viewed by some Franco-Americans as a hostile epithet deserving of protest.

Gradual improvement in the economic conditions of New England's French Canadians, particularly among members of the second and third generations, freed a growing number from the daily grind of subsistence, enabling them to devote more energy and money to the survival of ethnic traditions and institutions. Geographic

Urban Immigrant Populations in 1870, Selected Nationalities

	Total	Irish	Germans	English
Boston	250,526	59,900	5,606	6,000
Providence	68,904	12,085	596	2,426
New Haven, Conn.	50,840	9,601	2,423	1,087
Worcester, Mass.	41,105	8,389	325	893
Lowell, Mass.	40,928	9,103	34	1,697
Cambridge, Mass.	39,634	7,180	482	1,043
Hartford	37,180	7,438	1,458	787
Portland, Maine	31,413	3,900	82	557
Lawrence, Mass.	28,921	7,457	467	2,456
Charlestown, Mass.	28,323	4,803	216	488
Lynn, Mass.	28,233	3,232	17	330
Fall River, Mass.	26,766	5,572	37	4,042

proximity to the Quebec homeland, coupled with their improving economic status, facilitated the growth and vitality of ethnic mutual-aid societies and the Franco-American press, enabling many Franco-American New Englanders to remain apart from public schools and churches and other organizations that were not French. Although the notion of a transnational identity is most often associated with contemporary migration flows, the Franco-American experience in New England, characterized by frequent movement back and forth across the Canadian border and by the maintenance of strong cultural and religious ties to Quebec, was an early example of the type of transnational network that is common among international migrants today.

During the 1880s and 1890s, as Italians, Portuguese, and Poles began to occupy the lowest rungs on the occupational and social ladder, the image of the French Canadians, who were moving up a rung or two, began to improve. Within the Franco-American community, tensions have long existed between the energetic movement to preserve the culture and language, known as *survivance,* and the forces of assimilation. The Franco-American presence in New England can be seen most strongly today in areas of northern Maine and western Vermont. Indeed, population figures show that right up through the mid-1980s, Canadians were the most prevalent foreign population in the northern New England states.

The Irish and Franco-American influx of the 19th century brought religious diversity to New England, but the Chinese were the first voluntary migrants who were not of European descent. As a result of the China trade, after the American Revolution, a small number of Chinese sailors, merchants, and household servants arrived in the region, representing the earliest presence of nonwhite voluntary settlers. The first sizable group of Chinese to migrate to New England came by way of California in 1870 to work in North Adams, Mass., the bustling center of the nation's boot and shoe industry. When the laborers at the large C. T. Sampson shoe factory went out on strike, the owner fired them all and devised a bold plan to bring in 75 Chinese replacement workers. The day they arrived and were met by a hostile, stone-throwing crowd generated much interest throughout the region. The experiment proved successful for the company, as within three months the migrants were producing at a faster rate than the previous workers. Fifty more Chinese laborers were hired, triggering strong anti-Chinese sentiment in the press and dividing the local labor force.

Ineligible for U.S. citizenship according to the naturalization law of 1790 and prohibited from bringing their wives and children with them, these immigrants were not able to follow the same course of adaptation to New England society as had their European counterparts. After their contract expired, some stayed on in North Adams, but most relocated, many to the Boston area, to become the pioneer settlers of Boston's Chinatown. Because of their differing racial ancestry, the Chinese immigrants were viewed by the native-born in this period as impossible to assimilate, and racial discrimination was so strong that the newcomers had no choice but to congregate in isolated areas and rely on coethnic support to survive. Boston's Chinatown, like its counterparts in other major cities at the time, was an insular enclave where

Chinese traditions were maintained and where the boundaries between that ethnic community and the larger society were rigidly drawn.

Although once viewed in popular imagery as a region of quaint Yankee villages surrounded by pastoral countryside, New England was already highly urbanized and highly industrialized by the last quarter of the 19th century. The workings of the global economy in conjunction with local circumstances brought immigrants from all over Europe seeking employment in the mills and factories that sustained the region's expanding industrial base. Between 1880 and 1920, the nation as a whole received the largest wave of immigrants in its history, more than 23 million, and a good share of those newcomers came streaming into New England. By 1910, at 33 percent, Rhode Island held the largest proportion of foreign-born residents of any state in the country. Massachusetts ranked second with 31.2 percent. Also in 1910, eight of the 50 U.S. cities having 100,000 or more inhabitants were located in New England, and all eight were among the top 15 cities nationwide in the percentage of foreign-born white residents: in New Haven and Bridgeport, Conn.; Boston, Cambridge, Worcester, Lowell, and Fall River, Mass.; and Providence, R.I., the percentage of the total populations that was foreign-born white ranged from 32 percent in New Haven to 42.6 percent in Fall River.

Unlike the bulk of newcomers from earlier waves of immigration, who came primarily from northwestern Europe, this surge was dominated by arrivals from countries in southern and eastern Europe and included sizable numbers of Italians, Portuguese, Poles, Lithuanians, Jews, and Greeks. By 1915 these groups had been joined by Armenians fleeing their homeland in the wake of the genocidal horrors perpetrated on them by the Turkish army.

Although the majority of Italians landing in America during this period settled in New York City, significant numbers made their way to southern New England. They were labeled "birds of passage," because the typical pattern was for working-age males to stay only as long as it took to earn enough cash to purchase land in their native Italy. These sojourners had high rates of return migration, with approximately one-third of them going back home. Others did settle more permanently, especially after 1900, and Italian Americans remain the largest ethnic group in Connecticut and the second-largest in Rhode Island today. Early on, they created employment niches as market gardeners in Rhode Island, stone quarry workers in Vermont, shoemakers in New Haven, fruit growers in Glastonbury, Conn., and laborers in the cotton and woolen mills of Lawrence. The more entrepreneurial opened small businesses, especially food-related enterprises, within Italian neighborhoods in cities of all sizes throughout southern New England.

Studies of Italian American communities in the region stress the strength and persistence of Old World loyalties and traditions in the New World setting, emphasizing alliances within the enclave based on common village, provincial, or regional origins, a phenomenon that has been called *campanilismo.* Such levels of insularity were probably in part an adaptive response to persistent Anglo suspicion and negative stereotyping. More residentially aggregated than other newcomers to the region, immigrants primarily from Naples and Sicily established a Little Italy in the North End of Boston that still maintains its ethnic character today. The enclave is especially known for its religious festivals celebrating the various patron saints of the Catholic Church.

The earliest Portuguese presence dates to the mid-17th century, when Portuguese Sephardic Jews made their way via Brazil to New England, especially Newport, R.I., where a century later, in 1759, the congregation started building Touro Synagogue, the oldest synagogue in America, still holding services today and designated a national historic site. During the mid-19th century, whaling ships began to bring Portuguese Catholics from the Azores to U.S. shores in more substantial numbers. Whaling vessels made regular stops in the Azores and Madeira, recruiting able bodies to fill out their crews; many of these single men stayed on in New England, particularly around the ports of New Bedford and Edgartown, Mass. Thousands more, including women and children, began to leave their impoverished islands after 1880 to populate cities and towns throughout Massachusetts and Rhode Island, lured by the need for unskilled laborers in the cotton mills and needle trades in places like Fall River, New Bedford, and Lowell, and Pawtucket, R.I. Already in 1910 Portuguese immigrants made up 40 percent of the labor force in the textile mills of New Bedford and Fall River. Others made their living off the sea, especially in the fishing community of Provincetown and the villages of Nantucket and Martha's Vineyard, also in Massachusetts.

The Portuguese newcomers established communities in which the Catholic Church and various folk-religious festivals were at the center of community life. At the same time, like the Italians, they exhibited high rates of return migration, especially during the years of the Great Depression. As with the other populations from southern and eastern Europe, the mass migration of Portuguese newcomers was drastically reduced by the immigration acts of the 1920s. But when the Azorean island of Faial was devastated by volcanic eruptions and earthquakes in 1957, the U.S. government passed the Azorean Refugee Act (1958), circumventing the quota system to allow some 4,800 islanders into the country. Many came to New England, where family and occupational networks were already in place to assist the refugees. Though Portuguese Americans established vibrant ethnic enclaves in New England, a longing for their island homelands and a sense of being torn between two worlds continued to permeate their music and literature. Since 1981, however, they have been able to hold dual citizenship in the United States and Portugal, a change that has made way for a more workable transnational identity.

The late-19th-century demand for unskilled labor also pulled a sizable number of Poles to the region; by 1930 more than 10 percent of the U.S. Polish population had settled in western and central New England. They were largely rural peasants with a sprinkling of political exiles. Some gravitated to the manufacturing towns of Massachusetts and Connecticut. Others used their agricultural skills to become successful farmers along the Connecticut River valley, a region where Polish construction workers had been employed on the railroads until they were laid off amid the recession of 1887. During the second half of the 20th century, smaller waves of World

War II refugees, and in the 1980s Solidarity-era asylum seekers, joined the post-1965 economic migrants from Poland to New England. Suzanne Strempek Shea's novels *Selling the Lite of Heaven* (1994) and *Hoopi Shoopi Donna* (1996), set in contemporary western Massachusetts, provide a window onto the dynamics of blue-collar Polish American communities in the region. As depicted in Shea's writings, life in these enclaves revolved around church, school, labor unions, voluntary organizations, and the polka. Indeed, Pulaski Park, an open-air dance hall in Three Rivers, Mass., is known as the polka capital of New England. Immigrants from Lithuania, who also relocated to the region in this period, tended to follow settlement and occupational patterns similar to those of the Poles, although they were more concentrated in Boston than their Polish counterparts.

Although most of the newcomers from Europe were Catholic, this wave also brought significant numbers of Greeks, who belonged to the Greek Orthodox Church, and people of the Jewish faith. The Jewish population, fleeing political oppression, initially came from areas of Poland and Lithuania as well, but by the 1880s and 1890s, the majority were refugees of the anti-Semitic attacks of tsarist Russia. Both the Greek and Jewish immigrants found opportunities for employment as unskilled and semiskilled workers in the textile and shoe industries. On average, however, both groups were also more entrepreneurial than the other populations emigrating at this time, with Greeks more concentrated in food-service enterprises, while Russian Jews started out as peddlers in dry goods and then gained a foothold in businesses related to the clothing industry.

But it was not solely immigrants from southern and eastern Europe who were settling in the region in such large numbers at the turn of the 20th century. Arrivals from the Cape Verde Islands, an archipelago located off the coast of West Africa under Portuguese colonial rule since the mid-15th century, were also making New England their home. These newcomers of mixed African and Portuguese heritage were the first in U.S. history to make the transatlantic journey from Africa of their own volition. Like the Azoreans, Cape Verdeans initially came to southeastern New England as crew on whaling vessels and subsequently brought their families to join them in their new country, settling primarily in New Bedford and on upper Cape Cod in Massachusetts and in Providence. Their adaptation and employment patterns differed from those of the Azoreans, owing largely to the dynamics of socially constructed notions of race. For the most part, the Cape Verdean migrants considered themselves to be white ethnic Portuguese and therefore European, but from the moment they disembarked at the piers, they were treated as nonwhite and African. Racial discrimination meant that they were rarely hired in the region's factories, except as janitorial help, while the Azorean Portuguese kept them out of the fishing industry. Instead, Cape Verdeans labored in dockside occupations, as domestics, and especially as cranberry workers on southeastern New England's productive bogs.

In spite of attempts to close off the primary avenues of employment to these Afro-Portuguese settlers and the efforts of the other Portuguese immigrants to keep them from joining compatriot churches and communal organizations, the Cape Verdeans developed their own parallel associational life, were able to maintain their distinctive

Crioulo culture, and have sustained close ties to the Cape Verde Islands. They are unique among migrants to the region, indeed to the whole country, not only because of their particular ethnoracial composition but because, unlike any other immigrants, the Cape Verdeans were able to take control of their own passage to the United States. By the end of the 19th century, they were buying up old whaling vessels and converting them into passenger ships that transported immigrants directly from the Cape Verdes to the ports of New Bedford and Providence. Perhaps more than any other group to reach New England's shores, the Cape Verdeans confounded the idea of a monolithic European whiteness in the region. The challenges they faced as a foreign-born population of color adapting to New England society bear more than a passing resemblance to what the majority of recent arrivals representing a variety of nationalities confront today.

The gender distribution of foreign migration to New England in this period was more balanced than in the nation as a whole. Before the 1930s immigrants to America were much more likely to be men than women, but in New England the ratio was far less skewed. In 1910, for example, there were 129 men for every 100 women among the foreign-born in the United States overall, while in New England men outnumbered women by only 105 to 100. Part of the reason for the difference is that at the time of the 1910 census, though male arrivals from southern and eastern Europe strongly outnumbered females, the foreign-born populations in the region were still heavily weighted toward Irish, Canadian, and English immigrants, groups whose numbers have historically included more female arrivals. The dire conditions in Ireland during the famine years, combined with domestic employment opportunities for women in this country, evened the ratio early on. That pattern continued throughout the 19th century, while among Canadian newcomers—not only the French but also English speakers—women were in demand as workers in the booming apparel industries.

The second-wave immigrants continued to swell the Catholic ranks and added significant numbers of Jews and Greek Orthodox to the mix, further unsettling the Protestant majority in New England. Nativist sentiments reared up again, this time buoyed by the new pseudoscience of social Darwinism, which posited the superiority of Anglo-Saxons over the peoples of southern and eastern Europe, populations that were then referred to as inferior "races." This variation of supposedly scientific racism, with its blatant prejudice and ethnic stereotyping, fueled a national movement to restrict immigration, especially from the geographic regions of Europe in which these unwanted groups originated. Migration from Asia had already been virtually eliminated by passage, in 1882, of the Chinese Exclusion Act and, in 1907, of the Gentlemen's Agreement with Japan.

New England politicians, activists, and intellectuals were key players in the effort to curb the flow of immigration in this period. The Immigration Restriction League, founded in 1894 by several Harvard graduates and based in Boston, advocated literacy tests for incoming migrants as a way of stemming the tide. They succeeded in their efforts when Congress passed the Immigration Act of 1917, requiring that new arrivals be able to read and write (in any recognized language). Part of the reason for the league's success was the support its members received from Massachusetts senator Henry Cabot Lodge, the descendant of a long-established Yankee family, who lobbied vociferously for its passage. The 1917 law was the predecessor to the even more restrictive National Origins Act of 1924, which featured a quota system that sharply reduced immigration from countries in southern and eastern Europe. Again Lodge was one of the leading figures in guiding the bill through Congress.

Owing to the vicissitudes of American immigration policy as well as the needs of the economy, particularly when labor was in short supply during the two world wars, the other major group of immigrants of color to settle in New England before the contemporary flow came from the English-speaking Caribbean (primarily Jamaica, Trinidad, and Barbados). Although most were bound for New York City, Boston was the destination for significant numbers, who were mainly transported there by United Fruit Company steamers. Later, by the start of World War II, severe shortages of agricultural labor, especially in the Connecticut River valley, brought additional West Indian settlers to the Nutmeg State. Never large enough to constitute a separate ethnic enclave, the British West Indian immigrants were dispersed throughout African American neighborhoods and held the same menial, unskilled, and low-paying jobs as the rest of the black population. The women almost all worked as domestics, replacing the earlier Irish help and competing with native-born black women as white employers increasingly showed a preference for hiring foreign-born people of color.

As an adaptation strategy, West Indian newcomers attempted to assert their British ethnic identity. West Indian community institutions celebrated Empire and Coronation Day, for example, and held cricket matches in Boston's Franklin Park. But no matter how much they tried to emphasize their foreignness, their self-definition ultimately conflicted with how others defined them. For the most part Boston's white majority did not differentiate them from the larger black population.

During World War II, farmers and growers in Connecticut were able to play on white racial prejudice and use black workers, both Jamaican and African American, as a lever to control the demands of their white agricultural hands. The presence of these workers caused tension, much as Chinese shoemakers had in Massachusetts almost a century earlier, with Connecticut growers exacerbating conflicts based on racial identities among members of the laboring classes. West Indian New Englanders today, however, particularly women, have carved out their own economic niche within the health-care sector as nurses, nurse's aides, and hospital workers, establishing networks to maintain and expand that entry into the region's economy.

New England labor needs during World War II also brought the first significant numbers of Puerto Ricans to the region. The inhabitants of Puerto Rico, a U.S. territory, were granted American citizenship in 1917 and thus are not classified as immigrants. Their citizenship status allowed them to migrate freely from the island to New England, where they worked as both factory operatives and agricultural hands in Connecticut and Massachusetts during the war. Many stayed on after the war ended, and others arrived from the island to join them. By the 1960s there were established Puerto Rican communities in the cities of Bridgeport, Hartford, Spring-

Watching the annual Puerto Rico Day parade, Boston, July 1992

field, and Boston. The flow of Puerto Rican settlers to southern New England continues strong to this day. The U.S. Census Bureau considers members of this group international migrants despite their American citizenship, and as such they constitute the largest share of the overall "foreign-born" population of both Connecticut and Massachusetts. The ease of movement between Puerto Rico and the mainland has led to a pattern of circular migration. It is also not unusual for Puerto Ricans to spend their working years in New England and then return to Puerto Rico to retire.

An examination of the current state of New England ethnicity reveals how thoroughly the demographics of the region have changed over the past several decades. As in other parts of the nation, shifts in New England's ethnic and racial populations have resulted from the 1965 liberalization of immigration policy and from administrative actions regarding refugee populations. These changes have opened the doors to a steady stream of newcomers, particularly after 1980. Unlike the primarily European voluntary migrants of the past, most recent arrivals come from Asia and Latin America. They are also more likely to be women. Today there is no difference between the gender ratios of the native-born and foreign-born populations: both are 51 percent female. These non-European and often nonwhite settlers possess multicultural identities that cannot easily be made to fit the immutable bipolar racial structure of American society as a whole. Nor can they be readily subsumed by the tripartite classification of Native American, European, and African American ancestries that has traditionally served as a catchall for the composite New England population. At the same time, the proportion of native-born African Americans has remained small. At the start of the 20th century, the group constituted less than 1 percent of the U.S. black population; by 2000 that number stood at only 2 percent of the national total. Nonetheless, race relations in the region came under a national microscope with the Boston busing crisis of the mid-1970s.

Recent immigrants to New England are much more ethnically and racially diverse than they used to be. They come from a wider array of countries and continents than ever before in the region's history. Until 1960, 98 percent of immigrants to the region were non-Hispanic whites—even as late as 1970, close to 80 percent of the region's immigrants came from Canada or Europe. By the end of the 20th century, the percentage of white immigrants had plummeted—in Massachusetts it had dropped below 50 percent, making the nonwhite immigrant population the majority. Instead of Canadians, Portuguese, British, Irish, and Italian arrivals, newcomers are streaming into New England from such countries as Cambodia, China, Vietnam, Haiti, the Dominican Republic, and Jamaica.

Yet even within the large umbrella categories of Europeans, Latin Americans, and Asians, immigration patterns are extremely changeable. In the 1980s, for example, after Puerto Ricans, the largest numbers of immigrants to Massachusetts were from Cambodia, Haiti, Portugal, and Vietnam. Now they come from Brazil, El Salvador, Russia, India, and China. Thus not only has the recent influx changed the face of older ethnic neighborhoods, it has also reshaped the composition of existing Asian and Hispanic communities. The Roxbury section of Boston, for instance, historically home to Irish, Jewish, and Italian immigrants, was later settled by African American and Cape Verdean families, who constitute more than three-quarters of the current residents. Now large numbers of Latinos are moving into the neighborhood. The Spanish-speaking population is composed primarily of long-standing Puerto Ricans and more recent Dominican arrivals, with the result that you are as likely today to hear the harmonies of salsa and merengue on Roxbury street corners as you are rhythm and blues. Thus it is no longer possible to define the community's issues in terms of black and white alone. In Roxbury, as in much of the region, the ethnic and racial mix is so variegated, fluid, and complex that it wipes out any notion of New England homogeneity.

Pronounced racial and ethnic differences do exist, however, between northern and southern New England. Massachusetts and its two southern neighbors, Rhode Island and Connecticut, are now home to considerably larger absolute and relative numbers of immigrants than their northern neighbors. In 1998, for example, of the nearly 1.3 million foreign-born persons living in New England, only about 100,000 resided in northern New England, with the remaining 1.2 million spread throughout Massachusetts, Connecticut, and Rhode Island. According to the 2000 census, Maine, Vermont, and New Hampshire, respectively, were once again the three whitest states in the nation. The countries of immigrant origin also differ markedly between northern- and southern-tier states. In southern New England, for instance, the largest percentage of the foreign-born, at 16.8 percent, are Puerto Rican, whereas Puerto Ricans make up less than 3 percent of the corresponding population of northern New England. Conversely, the highest percentage in the northern tier, at 31.3 percent, totaling almost a third of the foreign-born, are Canadians. In southern New England, Canadians make up only 5.1 percent of the population. Important shifts are taking place, too, in Massachusetts. Although immigrants to that state continue to be more highly concentrated in the larger metropolitan areas—Boston first and foremost, but also New Bedford, Springfield, Worcester, Lowell, and Fall River—they no longer live primarily in the central cities, as did their predecessors: a majority of Massachusetts's foreign-born inhabitants reside in the suburbs.

Another significant trend of the two decades leading up to and beginning the 21st century has been New England's increasing reliance, especially in the southern tier, on foreign workers. Newcomers from abroad and U.S. territories such as Puerto Rico have provided growth not only in the labor force but in the overall population. Only the mid-Atlantic region surpasses New England in its share of immigrants within the labor force. Indeed, in the absence of this new wave of immigrants, the region's civilian labor force would have lost nearly 200,000 of its members.

The huge economic expansion of the 1980s, dubbed the Massachusetts Miracle though it occurred throughout New England, was what first attracted so many new immigrants to the area from both the high and low ends of the economic scale. The region's banking, financial, and real estate sectors flourished, requiring a well-educated labor force; at the same time, because growth was experienced throughout the economy, unskilled workers could also find employment in low-paying jobs shunned by others. In addition to purely economic incentives, Massachusetts has been the first choice for significant numbers of political refugees, and the state has also seen a net gain in secondary refugee settlement since the Refugee Act became law in 1980. The commonwealth has a long history of providing refuge to people seeking freedom from religious and political persecution and continues to represent that tradition well.

New immigrants also play an important role in the small-business sector of the region's economy. It was more than 170 years ago that American society reached its zenith in levels of self-employment. During the 1820s and 1830s great religious upheavals coincided with a wide-ranging flurry of small-business activity to create what has been called a shopkeeper's millennium, particularly in the Northeast, including New England. As the early-19th-century market economy expanded, the proportion of free white Americans running their own businesses soared to 80 percent. Since that time entrepreneurship of this type has been in steady decline except among immigrants. The entrepreneurial spirit has shown itself to be surprisingly resilient in New England's postindustrial economy, particularly in the case of ethnic-based businesses.

Some ethnic groups have laid claim to their own distinctive economic niche—the many Greek-owned pizza places in Connecticut and Massachusetts come to mind. Others prosper in retail stores clustered within an immigrant neighborhood and supported by coethnic clientele—the business sectors of Cambodian refugees in Lowell, Revere, and Fall River, Mass., provide a case in point. Here one finds the startup ventures typical of new immigrant communities, such as small grocery stores, restaurants, beauty parlors and barbershops, travel agencies, and photo and money-transfer services. Finally, some recent immigrant populations, such as Jews from the former Soviet Union, have been able to go beyond the enclave economy to establish businesses that cater to both compatriot and other customers. New immigrants and their ventures have already been credited with revitalizing depopulated and decaying neighborhoods in New England's cities and older suburbs, rejuvenating business districts overrun with vacant storefronts, restoring dilapidated residences, and expanding the tax base of metropolitan areas fallen prey to deindustrialization and the failures of urban renewal.

At times defying stereotypical notions of the poor and huddled masses, the most recent newcomers to New England not only come from widely varying ethnic and racial backgrounds but in some instances are as likely to get off a jumbo jet carrying designer luggage as they are to disembark from the steerage section of an overcrowded boat with tattered bundles hoisted over their shoulders. They arrive with a range of educational attainments and skills—and from a number of countries—unprecedented in the history of migration to the region. Adding to the mix is a substantial population of foreign students who attend New England colleges and universities, particularly in Massachusetts. The signs of diversity are everywhere, from the number of fans that wave Dominican flags in the stands at Fenway Park to the proliferation of bilingual ads and announcements on public buses and subway trains to the multiethnic smorgasbord of restaurant choices available to adventurous eaters in cities and towns throughout the region.

As contemporary immigration patterns in New England continue to evolve, the frameworks we use to understand the adaptation process are also changing. Recent immigrants, such as Dominicans and Brazilians, increasingly engage in global movement and circular migration, adopting transnational identities that challenge earlier rubrics concerning assimilation and incorporation. Despite predictions that homeland country ties will weaken as immigrants assimilate, ease of travel, enhanced technology, and sending-state policies to encourage emigrants' continued participation in the life of their homeland have meant that increasing numbers stay connected to the communities they leave behind. Such long-term transnational ties complicate conventional notions about straight-line assimilation of immigrants into New England society and culture, just as they challenge the impact of migration on sending-country life. Thus, for new arrivals, the process of becoming a New Englander may be only one facet of an evolving dual or multiple global identity.

The contemporary flowering of cultural expression from the multiple communities that make up New England's ethnic and racial mosaic is not without precedent. In the mid-1960s, as U.S. immigration policy was being liberalized, long-oppressed groups of Americans began vying for recognition and self-determination within the wider culture. Black nationalists, spearheading these efforts, were quickly followed by the stirrings of a new Chicano militancy and the American Indian movement. These largely political initiatives were accompanied by a new interest in unearthing buried cultural roots and unveiling occluded histories as well as celebrating distinctive heritages. By 1983 such activities had resulted in the U.S. Congress publicly acknowledging that the Mashantucket Pequot were the surviving descendants of an American Indian nation almost destroyed by New England settlers and their Indian allies in 1637. Today tribes such as the Pequot and the Gay Head Wampanoag have won precedent-setting legal battles and have reemerged as players in the game of cultural survival. The business enterprises of the Pequot include casinos and sand and granite mining. Other Native Americans in the region, among them Maine's Penobscot and Passamaquoddy, are reasserting their presence by means of successful tribal land claims.

By the mid-1970s, white ethnic groups had begun to assert their own brand of cultural pride. Initially part of a backlash against racial minority movements, they were the descendants of second-wave immigrants who had arrived primarily from southern and eastern Europe in the late 19th and early 20th centuries and who had faced discrimination from the native population at the time. The ethnic revival that has propelled so many to reconnect actively with their ancestral cultures continues to gain intensity in the 21st century as New Englanders of all stripes rediscover and research their roots. The region's contemporary cultural florescence and its celebration of hyphenated identities are clearly evidenced by a proliferation of ethnic festivals, a renewed zeal for genealogy, and heightened interest in ethnic artifacts, cuisine, music, literature, film, and language.

Two striking examples of this trend are the recent establishment of major centers for the fostering of Yiddish and of Irish culture, respectively. In 1997 the Yiddish Book Center, an organization founded in 1980 and dedicated to the preservation and revitalization of Yiddish writing and culture, opened an impressive multimillion-dollar facility in Amherst, Mass. The 37,000-square-foot complex has been designed to look like a 19th-century eastern European shtetl and houses a book repository and processing center, exhibit galleries, an auditorium, an outdoor amphitheater, a sound studio, a kosher kitchen, a storytelling courtyard, and more. In 1999 the Irish Cultural Centre, founded in 1989, held a grand-opening celebration to mark the first phase of a similar facility promoting all things Irish. Located on 47 acres in Canton, Mass., the center offers extensive playing fields for Gaelic sporting events.

Perhaps the most common public display of interest in cultural diversity, however, resides in the widespread popularity of ethnic festivals such as Saint Stephen's Church Bazaar, the Armenian celebration held yearly in Watertown, Mass.; West Indian Week in Hartford; the Franco-American Festival de Joie in Lewiston, Maine; and the Portuguese Feast in New Bedford. Typically sponsored by a combination of commercial, civic, and cultural organizations, these gatherings offer ethnic food, music, craft displays, performances, and exhibits for young and old alike. Indeed, the new Irish Cultural Centre has been funded by proceeds from the annual Irish Festival, a three-day extravaganza held in Easton, Mass., that features more than 30 bands, a street marketplace with vendors of Irish goods, a parade, horse and dog shows, a step-dancing *feis,* and an agricultural fair among its panoply of activities.

Clearly, New Englanders are intent on finding ways to give expression to their ethnic identities. But ethnic festivals also raise public awareness of the particular sponsoring group, giving outsiders who participate an opportunity to learn more about the heritage of a culture different from their own and raising multiethnic consciousness. Whether newly arrived or descendants of those who migrated 150 years ago, ethnics reshape their own cultural identification as they internalize the symbols and values of the civic culture. Ethnic solidarity and diversity are maintained to a certain degree even as the new-

Passamaquoddy Youth Confederacy drumming circle, Indian Township, Princeton, Maine, 1995

comers embrace national and local cultures. At the same time, changing contemporary communities inspire new perspectives on New England's past.

Gerard J. Brault, *The French-Canadian Heritage in New England* (1986); Colin G. Calloway, comp. and ed., *Dawnland Encounters: Indians and Europeans in Northern New England* (1991); Doris C. J. Chu, *Chinese in Massachusetts: Their Experiences and Contributions* (1987); Jay Coughtry, *The Notorious Triangle: Rhode Island and the African Slave Trade, 1700–1807* (1981); Adelaide M. Cromwell, *The Other Brahmins: Boston's Black Upper Class, 1750–1950* (1994); W. E. B. Du Bois, *The Suppression of the African Slave-Trade to the United States of America, 1638–1870* (1970 [1896]); Herbert J. Gans, *The Urban Villagers: Group and Class in the Life of Italian-Americans* (1982); Marilyn Halter, *Between Race and Ethnicity: Cape Verdean American Immigrants, 1860–1965* (1993); Halter, ed., *New Migrants in the Marketplace: Boston's Ethnic Entrepreneurs* (1995); Oscar Handlin, *Boston's Immigrants* (1979 [1941]); L. M. Hauptmann and J. D. Wherry, eds., *The Pequots of Southern New England: The Fall and Rise of an American Indian Nation* (1990); James Horton and Lois Horton, *Black Bostonians: Family Life and Community Struggle in the Antebellum North* (1999 [1979]); Louise Lamphere, *From Working Daughters to Working Mothers: Immigrant Women in a New England Industrial Community* (1987); Marsha McCabe and Joseph D. Thomas, eds., *Portuguese Spinner, an American Story: Stories of History, Culture, and Life from Portuguese Americans in Southeastern New England* (1998); Thomas O'Connor, *The Boston Irish: A Political History* (1995); William Dillon Piersen, *Black Yankees: The Development of an Afro-American Subculture in 18th-Century New England* (1988); Elizabeth Hafkin Pleck, *Black Migration and Poverty: Boston, 1865–1900* (1979); Neal Salisbury, *Manitou and Providence: Indians, Europeans, and the Making of New England, 1500–1643* (1982); Jonathan D. Sarna and Ellen Smith, eds., *The Jews of Boston: Essays on the Occasion of the Centenary (1895–1995) of the Combined Jewish Philanthropies of Greater Boston* (1995); Mark R. Schneider, *Boston Confronts Jim Crow, 1890–1920* (1997); Judith E. Smith, *Family Connections: A History of Italian and Jewish Immigrant Lives in Providence, Rhode Island, 1900–1940* (1985); Barbara Miller Solomon, *Ancestors and Immigrants: A Changing New England Tradition* (1965 [1956]); Stephan Thernstrom, ed., *Harvard Encyclopedia of American Ethnic Groups* (1980).

Marilyn Halter with Robert L. Hall

Abenaki The Abenaki are the indigenous peoples of northern New England, the "people of the Dawnland." At first contact with Europeans, they occupied a region that stretched from the Atlantic to Lake Champlain and from northern Massachusetts to the Saint Lawrence River valley. Abenaki peoples included the Penobscot, Norridgewock, and Kennebec in eastern Maine, the Androscoggin in western Maine, the Pennacook and Pigwacket of New Hampshire's Merrimack Valley and White Mountains, the Sokoki and Cowasuck in the Connecticut River valley, and the Missisquoi, Winooski, and other groups on the shores of Lake Champlain.

The French called them Abenaqui or Oubenaqui; the English dubbed those with whom they dealt in Maine Eastern Indians. English expansion after King Philip's War in 1675–76 and recurrent conflicts drove many Abenaki to seek refuge at French mission villages like Saint Francis (Odanak) and Bécancour (Wôlinak) on the Saint Lawrence. The English and Americans often applied the name Saint Francis Indians to all Western Abenaki. Abenaki people called themselves Wabanaki, although the Wabanaki Confederacy also includes the Passamaquoddy, Maliseet, and Micmac of northern Maine and the Maritime Provinces. Anthropologists have tended to separate the Abenaki into Eastern (Maine) and Western (Vermont) divisions on the basis of linguistic differences.

Most Abenaki sided with France in the Anglo-French imperial wars between 1689 and 1763. Many embraced Catholicism, and all shared an interest in curbing English expansion. Abenaki warriors burned settlements, carried off captives, and waged guerrilla warfare to keep their country free of English invaders; the English put bounties on Abenaki scalps, burned the village of Norridgewock in Maine in 1724, and, in a famous raid by Major Robert Rogers and his New Hampshire Rangers, burned Odanak in 1759. The British victory in the Seven Years' War (1756–63) deprived the Abenaki of their French allies and opened their country to English settlement. Many Abenaki who remained in New England supported their colonial neighbors during the American Revolution, but white encroachment on Abenaki lands continued after the war.

Primarily hunters, Abenaki peoples practiced a diversified economy that included fishing, gathering, and corn agriculture. After European diseases, the fur trade, and the invasion of Abenaki lands by English soldiers and settlers disrupted their subsistence patterns in the 17th and 18th centuries, many Abenaki maintained traditional ways of living in the more remote reaches of their homelands.

Others participated in the developing regional economy as farm laborers, basket makers, trappers, loggers, and mill workers. Some worked as guides for travelers and tourists: Penobscots Joe Polis and Joseph Attean, for example, accompanied Henry David Thoreau on his treks through the Maine woods.

Like other New England Native Americans, the Abenaki were assumed by white Americans to be dying out in the 19th century. Many married non-Indians; most lived in poverty. Remaining inconspicuous was a way for Abenaki people to avoid racism; it was easy and convenient for European American New Englanders to ignore them or assume that they had disappeared. In their view of New England's future, there was no place for Abenaki.

But Abenaki persisted amid persecution, "resurfacing" in the 20th century. The Penobscot and Passamaquoddy won a dramatic victory when President Jimmy Carter signed the Maine Indian Land Claims Settlement Act in 1980, granting them $81.5 million in compensation for lands taken by Maine and Massachusetts in treaties found to be in violation of the Indian Trade and Intercourse Act of 1790. Vermont's Western Abenaki have promoted awareness of Native American issues and culture and, under the aggressive and often controversial leadership of Homer St. Francis, have challenged the state on issues of sovereignty. They have campaigned for federal recognition as the Saint Francis–Sokoki Band of the Abenaki Nation of Vermont; they have developed social-service programs, such as the Abenaki Self-Help Association and the Dawnland Center; they have made efforts to preserve and promote the teaching of the Abenaki language; they have kept traditional dances alive and revived the art of basket making; and they have established an Abenaki heritage center in Swanton, Vt., under the direction of Dr. Frederick Wiseman. At the same time, other groups identifying themselves as Abenaki have stepped forward in Vermont, New Hampshire, and Massachusetts. Supposedly invisible at the end of the 19th century, Abenaki are very much in evidence in the 21st century.

Colin G. Calloway, *The Western Abenaki of Vermont, 1600–1800: War, Migration, and the Survival of an Indian People* (1990); William A. Haviland and Marjory W. Power, *The Original Vermonters: Native Inhabitants, Past and Present*, rev. ed. (1994); Maine Indian Program, *The Wabanakis of Maine and the Maritimes: A Resource Book about Penobscot, Passamaquoddy, Maliseet, Micmac, and Abenaki Indians* (1989); Frederick M. Wiseman, *The Voice of the Dawn: An Autohistory of the Abenaki Nation* (2001).

Colin G. Calloway

Acadians Not all French-speaking New Englanders came from Quebec. Some, known as Acadians, trace their origins to areas in the Canadian Maritime Provinces that were settled by colonists from Poitou, Brittany, Normandy, and other provinces of France. New England's Acadians fall into two groups, each with a distinct history. The Acadians of northern Maine, a mixed Acadian and French Canadian population, did not immigrate to the United States but found themselves there in 1842 at the conclusion of a boundary dispute. The other group began leaving Canada voluntarily in the 1880s. Northern Maine Acadians live in rural communities and have succeeded at preserving their language and culture. They do not identify with French-speaking groups elsewhere in the United States. The late-19th-century Acadian immigrants headed for Boston or for various New England mill towns, where they often joined already established French Canadian communities.

New England's first Acadian residents came from southern New Brunswick. They relocated to the Upper Saint John Valley, now the boundary between Maine and New Brunswick, when loyalist refugees flooded the area they occupied in 1783. They applied for and received provincial government grants upriver and were immediately joined by French Canadian immigrants attracted by the region's good soil. The two populations intermarried. French Canadian immigration to the area continued until the Great Depression. Anglophone immigrants were few, and they were often assimilated into the French population. The Acadian first arrivals and their Canadian spouses, established on the best land, quickly constituted a tightly knit, endogamous group. They rapidly dominated local social, political, and economic life.

The Madawaska Territory, as the region was called, was at the heart of the area claimed by both Britain and the United States during the northeastern boundary dispute. The Webster-Ashburton Treaty, signed in 1842, split the 4,000-member community lengthwise along the river: Maine had acquired some 2,000 Acadians. But the river was the local highway, and settlers paid little attention to the boundary, continuing to marry and transact all manner of business with their cross-border counterparts. By 1900 the Acadian population on the Maine side numbered 13,850, 90 percent of whom used French as their first language. By 1950 there were 26,294 of them. Their number has since slowly declined as a result of rural-to-urban migration.

The people of the Madawaska Territory worked in agriculture (first producing wheat, then lumber-camp supplies, and finally potatoes), the lumber industry, and in the 20th century the pulp and paper industry. Fraser Papers, which owns a pulp mill on the New Brunswick side of the Saint John and a paper mill across the river in Maine, is the largest regional employer and draws its labor force from both sides of the international boundary.

In the early 19th century the Madawaska French were sufficiently isolated from the rest of the United States to be largely protected from its influence. But as time passed, public schools and railroads, roads and cars, radios, movies, and television, and extended schooling gradually drew the region into the American cultural orbit. Nativist hostility toward non-Anglo-Saxon cultures and languages in the late 19th and early 20th centuries was also felt, and by the 1950s local French culture was on the defensive. The wind shifted in the 1960s, though, and Saint John Valley residents began to view their culture as an object not of embarrassment or even shame but of pride. They introduced bilingual education in area schools, launched a yearly Acadian festival, and founded a number of historical societies dedicated to preserving the region's heritage. Measures then were taken to safeguard the local architectural tradition and, with particular vigor, to maintain French as a language of communication. In 1990 the U.S. Congress crowned these efforts by passing the Maine Acadian Culture Preservation Act, whose purpose is to preserve and interpret sites associated with Acadian culture in the state of Maine.

Canadian residents of the Saint John Valley view the preservation of their culture somewhat differently. On the New Brunswick side of the river people call themselves "Madawaskayens" and stress that they are neither Acadian nor French Canadian but a blend of the two. Their American counterparts, by contrast, tend to downplay, or even ignore, their Canadian ancestry. No one has yet properly studied what accounts for these differing perceptions of cultural identity. But one can note that until recently New Brunswickers associated being Acadian with poverty. Acadians were poor fishermen and lumbermen, eking a living on the inhospitable eastern shore. In Anglo New England, French Canadians were second-class citizens derisively called "frogs," and their children were punished for speaking French on school playgrounds. Acadians, in contrast, had been romanticized since Henry Wadsworth Longfellow's poem *Evangeline* (1847) about two lovers separated when the British drove French-speaking colonists out of Nova Scotia in 1755. It is therefore not surprising that Saint John Valley Mainers prefer to identify with the heroes rather than the frogs. Currently, the term *Maine Acadian* as used in the implementation of the 1990 act, refers to the Saint John Valley French and their descendants.

The other Acadian New Englanders, late-19th-century immigrants, reside outside the Saint John Valley. Often their place of origin determined where they resettled. In Massachusetts, Fitchburg Acadians came from southeastern New Brunswick and Nova Scotia; Leominster attracted people from Kent County, N.B.; the Gardner and Shirley groups hailed from northern New Brunswick; Waltham Acadians came from southern Nova Scotia and Cape Breton Island. Prince Edward Island's Acadians went to Old Town and Rumford, Maine.

In most instances the Acadians usually found French Canadians already established when they reached their destinations and soon blended with them: they attended the same church, sent their children to the same parochial school, and intermarried. Most Acadians thus became Franco-Americans, many of whom subsequently became anglicized. In Rumford, Maine, however, Acadians were on their own. They continued to identify themselves as Acadians and developed their own specific institutions.

In the latter decades of the 20th century, a few attempts were made at recapturing the Acadian heritage outside the Saint John Valley. In the 1970s the Rumford group established an Acadian society, which fostered social and cultural events, such as a fiddle festival. It did not stand the test of time, however. In Massachusetts amateur genealogical researchers renewed interest in Acadian culture and history, creating Fitchburg's Acadian Cultural Society in 1985; that organization still exists, publishing a quarterly newsletter, *Le Réveil acadien*. In Massachusetts as in Rumford the French language has largely died out, and interest in one's Acadian heritage has become mostly the preserve of a small number of genealogists and amateur historians.

Raymond Breton and Pierre Savard, eds., *The Quebec and Acadian Diaspora in North America* (1982); Béatrice Craig, "Cultural Face-Off: Yankees, British, and the St. John Valley French," *Revue Rivière/River Review* 3 (1997); Craig, "Early French Migrations to Northern Maine, 1785–1850," *Maine Historical Society Quarterly* 25 (1986); New England–Atlantic Provinces–Quebec Center, *The French in New England, Acadia, and Quebec* [1973].

Béatrice Craig

African American Abolitionists

In New England as elsewhere, African Americans steadily resisted slavery from the outset of their enslavement until the outbreak of the Civil War. Their tactics changed as their own legal status was slowly transformed at the end of the 18th century. Before that time most people of African descent in New England were slaves, as they were elsewhere, and their earliest resistance focused on the slave trade and on slavery itself as it was practiced locally. By around 1790, after the passage of gradual emancipation laws in some states and the adoption of new constitutions in others had severely reduced the number of people of color still enslaved in the North, free African American leaders turned their attention toward abolishing southern slavery. At the same time, they also saw their own widespread unemployment, poverty, and illiteracy as significant obstacles to the abolition of slavery in the South and engaged in a host of self-improvement efforts that were closely related to their antislavery activities.

Some of the first African American abolitionists were slaves who seized on revolutionary rhetoric to petition their provincial governments for freedom in the 1770s. A good example is the petition of Peter Bestes, Sambo Freeman, Felix Holbrook, and Chester Joie to the Massachusetts General Assembly in 1773 seeking civil and religious liberty and noting ironically, "We expect great things from men who have made such a noble stand against the designs of their *fellow-men* [the British government] to enslave them." In the postrevolutionary period, prominent free people of color also attacked slavery. For example, between 1776 and 1820 Lemuel Haynes, a black minister to a white congregation in Vermont who was also a Revolutionary War veteran, wrote a series of essays and sermons that opposed slavery and demanded equal rights for African Americans in the context of republican ideology. Haynes argued that slavery threatened republican liberty for whites as well as blacks, since it undermined the virtue required to sustain a free republic. The establishment of societies to promote black solidarity and self-help also must be included in the catalog of Federal era antislavery efforts of free African Americans, for an important goal of these organizations was to promote abolition by demonstrating the capacity of former slaves for responsible citizenship. Some of the earliest of these organizations were founded in New England: the African Union Society of Newport, R.I., in 1780, the African Society of Providence in 1793, and the African Society of Boston in 1796.

In the 1820s antislavery agitation by African Americans in New England and other regions became more militant in response to a number of factors. The American Colonization Society's proposals to colonize freed slaves in Africa, popular among whites, aroused nearly universal opposition among blacks. A newly aggressive rationalization of slavery put forth by southern leaders coincided with increasing racial hostility in the northern states. Escaped slaves and free blacks from the South drawn to Boston, Hartford, and other northern cities served as fresh witnesses to the horrors of slavery. Increasing antislavery agitation on the part of white evangelicals mirrored escalating sectional hostility.

One of the first and most powerful antebellum black voices to attack slavery in New England was that of David Walker, a freeborn North Carolina native who had emigrated to Boston as a young man and worked as a clothing dealer. Walker's *Appeal . . . to the Coloured Citizens of the World*, published in Boston in 1829, called for black unity, militant resistance to slavery and exploitation, and ultimate self-government for all African Americans. Published shortly before the appearance of the first issue of William Lloyd Garrison's *Liberator*, Walker's *Appeal* shocked even white abolitionists and prompted the passage of laws against the circulation of incendiary publications in Georgia and North Carolina. Walker died in 1830 under mysterious circumstances.

Maria W. Stewart was another pioneer black abolitionist, one whose public lectures in Boston challenged not only the tyranny of slavery and racism but also conventional notions of appropriate behavior for women. The first American-born woman, black or white, to lecture publicly on political issues before an audience of both men and women, Stewart understood resistance to slavery and oppression as a religious imperative. Like David Walker, Stewart believed that black liberation would inevitably be achieved, by violent means if necessary. She was also a powerful advocate for equal education and full participation in business and politics for black women.

Although separate black antislavery organizations such as the Massachusetts General Colored Association and the Female Anti-Slavery Society of Salem (Mass.) had been established in the late 1820s and early 1830s, blacks as well as whites were attracted to William Lloyd Garrison's call for immediate abolition in 1831. Many blacks became agents for the *Liberator* when it appeared in January of that year, and their efforts caused African Americans to constitute three-quarters of the paper's subscription list in its early years. Blacks also provided a quarter of the signatures on the constitution of the New England Anti-Slavery Society at its inception in 1832. When the American Anti-Slavery Society was founded in Philadelphia in December

1833, James Barbadoes, a Boston barber, was one of three African American delegates, and he was also elected to the board of counselors of the Massachusetts Anti-Slavery Society. Jehiel C. Beman, a *Liberator* agent in Connecticut, also served as one of the managers of the Middletown Anti-Slavery Society. Frederick Douglass served as president of the New England Anti-Slavery Society in 1847, and Charles Lenox Remond was president of the Essex (Mass.) Anti-Slavery Society from 1845 to 1850.

Women's auxiliaries also made an important contribution to the new abolitionism, especially in the years before 1840. Susan Paul, an African American woman, was one of the counselors of the Boston Female Anti-Slavery Society, founded in 1833. She later became a vice president of the Second Anti-Slavery Convention of American Women, held in Philadelphia in 1838. Such national conventions were held annually from 1832 through 1839, until women were admitted to the previously all-male societies.

African American children, too, participated in the abolitionist crusade. In 1833 black youth of both sexes in Boston formed the Juvenile Garrison Independent Society, and children in other cities followed suit. These societies initiated black youth into activism; for example, William Cooper Nell, an original member of the Boston Juvenile Garrison Independent Society, later became a leader in the struggle to integrate Boston's public schools and to protect and support fugitive slaves.

By the 1840s the lecture circuit had become a principal tool for recruiting new supporters of abolishing slavery. Foremost among African American lecturers was Frederick Douglass, who first addressed a local antislavery convention on Nantucket Island in 1841 and was subsequently hired as an agent for the Massachusetts Anti-Slavery Society. Another notable lecturer was Charles Lenox Remond, a barber from Salem, who lectured throughout New England and in 1840 went to London as a delegate to the World Anti-Slavery Convention. (His expenses were supported largely by women's auxiliaries in Maine and Rhode Island, and he refused to participate in the proceedings when he discovered that the women delegates from the United States were not allowed to take part.) His sister, Sarah Parker Remond of Salem, who delivered antislavery lectures in the United States and Great Britain, was the most popular of a number of African American female lecturers.

The publication of pamphlets and narratives by African Americans, especially former or escaped slaves, was another powerful weapon in the antislavery struggle. Many lecturers who had been fugitives published popular narratives, including Douglass, William Wells Brown of Boston, and James W. C. Pennington of Hartford. In 1853 Brown also published an antislavery novel, *Clotel; or, The President's Daughter*, considered the first novel written by an African American.

The split that took place in the abolitionist movement in 1840 between Boston-centered Garrisonians, who embraced a range of reforms including women's rights, and New York–based abolitionists, who resisted such activities, also divided African American abolitionists. Most significant, the split heightened blacks' awareness of the persistent prejudice within the ranks of white abolitionists and encouraged them to reinvigorate their own convention movement and to emphasize a variety of self-improvement strategies—temperance, education, suffrage, mutual aid—that were seen as inseparable from emancipation. As a resolution passed at the 1855 Colored National Convention put it, "In our elevation lies the freedom of our enslaved brethren."

After 1840 the tone of African American abolitionist protest also became increasingly militant. Henry Highland Garnet's 1843 "Address to the Slaves of the United States" called for a slave uprising, and the passage of the 1850 Fugitive Slave Act convinced many blacks that a sectional war over slavery was inevitable. The 1857 Dred Scott decision, denying any citizenship rights to African Americans, inspired black abolitionists in Boston to hold the first annual Crispus Attucks Day on March 5, 1858, pointedly commemorating the black man who was the first to die in the Boston Massacre on that date in 1770. In several New England states African Americans lobbied local legislatures for state support for black military companies; only in Rhode Island were they successful. Once the Union Army began recruiting African American men in 1863, blacks eagerly joined the 54th Massachusetts and other black regiments to fight to end slavery.

R. J. M. Blackett, *Building an Antislavery Wall: Black Americans in the Atlantic Abolitionist Movement, 1830–1860* (1983); Peter P. Hinks, *To Awaken Our Afflicted Brethren: David Walker and the Problem of Antebellum Slave Resistance* (1997); James Oliver Horton and Lois E. Horton, *In Hope of Liberty: Culture, Community, and Protest among Northern Free Blacks, 1700–1860* (1997); Joanne Pope Melish, *Disowning Slavery: Gradual Emancipation and "Race" in New England, 1780–1860* (1998); Jane H. Pease and William H. Pease, *They Who Would Be Free: Blacks' Search for Freedom, 1830–1861* (1974); Benjamin Quarles, *Black Abolitionists* (1969); Patrick Rael, *Black Identity and Black Protest in the Antebellum North* (2002); Marilyn Richardson, ed., *Maria W. Stewart, America's First Black Woman Political Writer: Essays and Speeches* (1987); Shirley J. Yee, *Black Women Abolitionists: A Study in Activism, 1828–1860* (1992).

Joanne Pope Melish

African American Press The African American press, defined as newspapers and magazines owned, managed, and aimed at African Americans, provides a voice to and for black communities. In the 19th century New England produced a rich literature promoting temperance, abolition, prison reform, and the end of child labor. The African American press, relying on the persuasive power of the printed word, developed amid this spirit of reform. Numerous African American newspapers opposed slavery in antebellum New England; in the years since the Civil War, black periodicals in the region have promoted racial pride, ethnic and national identity, and black advancement and equality. With a reputation for resistance and self-sufficiency going back to the first European settlers, New England has afforded an environment conducive to black protest against white racism.

Antebellum black newspapers were aimed not at slaves but at ex-bondsmen and free blacks. Along with slave narratives and lecture tours, the African American newspaper was a way for abolitionists to advance their ideas. Not surprisingly, cities with large black communities sustained more newspapers. In total, since the first issues printed, Massachusetts has published more than 50 black newspapers; Connecticut, 35; Rhode Island, 20; and Maine and New Hampshire, one each. There is no record of a black newspaper ever being published in Vermont.

The church was the cultural, social, and political center of the New England black community, and ministers often were publishers or editors of early black periodicals. The Reverend Samuel Ringgold Ward, for example, edited the Boston *Impartial Citizen* before the Civil War.

From 1831 to 1865 the white abolitionist William Lloyd Garrison published the *Liberator*, which elicited support from both white and black Bostonians. Although the *Liberator* had a circulation of only 3,000 paid subscribers, many more read its message of immediate emancipation. The *Liberator* became the most successful antebellum abolitionist periodical, and Garrison founded the New England Anti-Slavery Society in 1832. Ironically, the success of the *Liberator* in nurturing a forceful abolitionist movement in Boston hampered attempts to start an African American newspaper. The *Anti-Slavery Herald*, founded in 1838 by the black printer Benjamin Roberts, failed right away because the city could not support two abolitionist newspapers. In 1853 Roberts tried again, this time launching the *Self-Elevator*, but that publication met the same fate as its predecessor.

Two newspapers, the *Negro* and the *Negro-American*, were launched in Boston after the Civil War, but each printed only a few issues, in 1886 and 1887, before collapsing. In 1894 the black journalist Charles Alexander briefly ran the unsuccessful Boston *Monthly Review*. With modest wage earners unable to subscribe, black businesses constituting a meager advertising base, and editorial antagonisms often unavoidable, there was no scarcity of reasons why the black press got off to a rocky start.

The situation improved, however, in time. To protest Booker T. Washington's assimilationist philosophy, William Monroe Trotter and George Forbes established the *Boston Guardian* in 1901. Subscribers supported that publication until 1957. In 1904 Alexander took over Boston's *Colored Citizen*, launched by Washington to compete with Trotter's radical *Guardian*. That venture failed, and Alexander began publishing his own monthly in 1905; *Alexander's Magazine* lasted for four years. Alexander later moved to Los Angeles and became the western correspondent for *New Era* magazine, founded in Boston in 1916 by Pauline Hopkins and Walter Wallace.

Inspired by Boston's history as a wellspring of radical politics, Hopkins thought that the right magazine could resuscitate the city's resistance politics. In 1900 she launched the *Colored American* magazine to counter Jim Crow laws, lynching in the South, black disenfranchisement, and northern political apathy. After four years and acrimonious fighting among its editors, the monthly closed its Boston headquarters and moved to New York City.

Nor is Boston the only New England city to have published black newspapers. The *Bay State Banner* has appeared weekly in Dorchester, Mass., since 1965. Thirteen cities in Connecticut have or once had black presses. Hartford has been home to 11, all now defunct except for the weekly *Hartford Inquirer* and *North End Agents*. New Haven has had 20, most of which have not lasted. In New Hampshire only one black newspaper has been published, the Concord biweekly *Herald of Freedom*, which circulated from 1835 until 1846. Rhode Island boasts two titles: *Hantu: The New England Regional Conference Newsletter*, founded in 1980, and the biweekly *Providence American*, launched in 1986. Maine has hosted only the *Advocate of Freedom*, a weekly published by the Maine Anti-Slavery Society in Hallowell between 1838 and 1841. That publication was superseded by the *Liberty Standard*, which remained in business from 1841 until 1848.

African American women have played an important role in supporting the black press through difficult times. Women's social groups have raised money through such activities as sewing circles, fairs, and church events to keep black presses rolling. In addition, many talented female writers wrote for newspapers and magazines. The *Woman's Era*, an illustrated monthly started in Boston in 1894 by Josephine St. Pierre Ruffin, voiced the concerns of the local Woman's Era Club and became the official journal for the National Federation of Afro-American women.

James P. Danky, ed., *African-American Newspapers and Periodicals: A National Bibliography* (1998); Martin E. Dann, *The Black Press, 1827–1890: The Quest for National Identity* (1971); I. Garland Penn, *The Afro-American Press and Its Editors* (1969 [1891]); Roland E. Wolseley, *The Black Press, U.S.A.* (1971).
                                    Debra J. Rosenthal

African Americans to 1900 African Americans arrived in New England shortly after the great migration of white Puritans in the 1630s. By the latter 1640s a slave-trade route between Boston and the West Indies had been established. The prominence of slavery in New England history and trade was inevitably a central, shaping force in the lives of African American New Englanders both before and long after slavery was abolished nationally.

The abolition of slavery in New England was ambiguous and protracted. Vermont's constitution of 1777 declared all men to be born equally free and is usually described as having abolished slavery, but in fact the first chapter of its bill of rights stipulated that no person should be held as a "servant slave or apprentice" after reaching the age of 21 if male and 18 if female—a conditional abolition; in 1786 the clause was eliminated. In the 1783 case of *Commonwealth v. Jennison*, the Massachusetts State Constitution of 1780 was interpreted as granting rights incompatible with slavery; however, the wording of the decision was so ambiguous that slaves continued to be sold there for several years. No legal cases testing a similar clause in the New Hampshire constitution of 1783 are recorded, but slaves there were taxed as property until 1789, and the first federal census (1790) reported 158 slaves in the state. In 1857 the New Hampshire legislature passed an act interpreted as finally abolishing slavery. Rhode Island and Connecticut passed *post-nati* statutes that freed children born to slaves after March 1, 1784, upon reaching their majority—18 years for women and 21 for men in Rhode Island, 25 years (reduced to 21 in 1797) for all children in Connecticut. While these acts freed no one for many years, they served to discourage slaveholding. Still, the Federal Census of 1790 reported nearly 1,000 slaves in Rhode Island and more than 2,600 in Connecticut. Final abolition bills did not end slavery in the two states until 1842 and 1848, respectively.

Statehood for Maine, formerly a part of Massachusetts, was part of the Missouri Compromise (1820), and Boston was an important center for abolitionist activity throughout the first half of the 19th century, as well as the site of such famous fugitive slave cases as those of George Latimer in 1842 and Anthony Burns in 1854. However, Boston, like most other towns and cities throughout New England, was also the scene of intense, persistent prejudice against African Americans, and violent riots by whites against African American communities erupted repeatedly there, as well as in Hartford and Providence, during the antebellum period.

In spite of such obstacles, African Americans were able to sustain a distinctive culture and build strong community institutions. Many were able to achieve financial success and make an important contribution to New England's economic life and technological progress, as demonstrated most prominently by their high visibility in the maritime industries and the work of the inventor and scientist Lewis H. Latimer in electricity and the inventor Jan Matzeliger in manufacturing and mass production. New England was a stage on which were mounted the dramas of both white America's racism and support for a national system of slavery and its antislavery efforts, as well as black America's fight for abolition and struggle for the authority of citizenship and self-definition in various cultural realms from economics to education and politics to art.

African American New Englanders were deeply involved in colonial and later national political life. This involvement manifested itself on at least two levels. African Americans contributed in the important ways to the creation and development of the new nation; at the same time, they were working for a collective self-definition that ran against the grain of that nation's ruling ideology. Crispus Attucks, the son of African and Native American parents who is often honored as the first martyr of the American Revolution, was one of several men shot down in the Boston Massacre on March 5, 1770. African Americans would continue to play a significant role in the American Revolution—some fighting for the colonies, some for the British, but on either side hoping for liberty. African Americans Peter Salem and Salem Poor, among others, played noteworthy roles in the battles of Bunker Hill, Lexington, and Concord.

Inspired in part by the ideals set forth by white Americans to justify the American Revolution, African American New Englanders fought for liberty on other fronts as well. They filed petitions against enslavement with the colonial government, and after the Revolu-

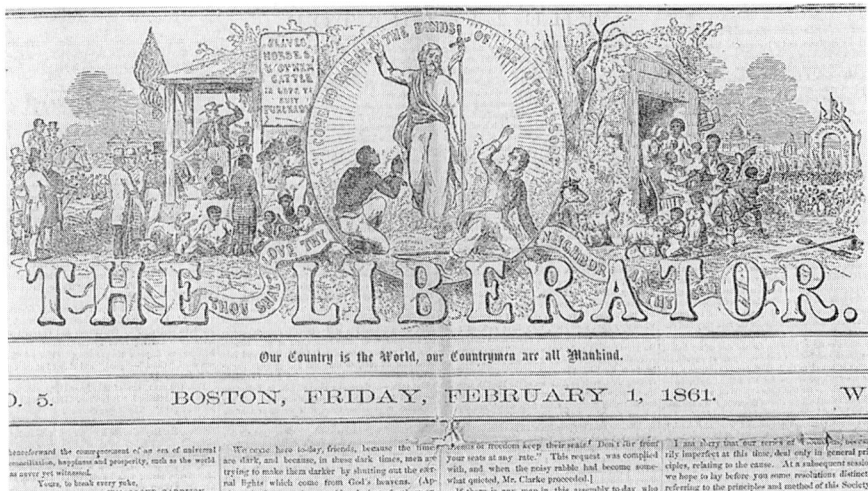

Masthead, The Liberator *(Boston), February 1, 1861*

tion, armed with the ideals professed by the white framers of the new government, they continued to petition for their liberty and for recognition of their rights. In a case argued in 1781 by the white lawyer Theodore Sedgwick, Elizabeth Freeman of Massachusetts based her claim to freedom on the Massachusetts constitution. At about the same time, Captain Paul Cuffe—the great seaman, businessman, and advocate of African colonization—protested the taxation without representation of African Americans in Massachusetts. Although the Massachusetts Constitution did not abolish slavery explicitly, as did Vermont's, and although the state government did not immediately address the issue of African American representation, Freeman's and Cuffe's cases effectively established legal precedent for the recognition of African American freedom and rights in Massachusetts. African Americans were active in other important protests as well, participating, for example, in Shays's Rebellion in 1786 and challenging state and federal laws by various means in their opposition to the system of slavery. New England was also the site of the first *Amistad* trial (1840), in which the rights of 53 Africans who had seized control of the slave ship by that name were upheld by a federal district court judge in Hartford before being confirmed by the U.S. Supreme Court, in a case that helped ignite antislavery sympathy among northerners and emphasize growing sectional divisions nationally.

The list of New England black abolitionists is a virtual who's who of the antislavery movement, including such important activists as David Walker, Maria W. Stewart, Frederick Douglass (who later relocated his efforts to Rochester, N.Y.), William C. Nell, Frances E. W. Harper (who became one of the first

women to be a professional public speaker when she accepted a position with the Maine Anti-Slavery Society), and William Wells Brown, among many others. When debates over slavery and African American rights were transferred to the battlefield during the Civil War, African Americans again struggled for recognition while placing themselves on the front lines—as demonstrated perhaps most famously by the Massachusetts 54th Infantry's charge on South Carolina's Fort Wagner in 1863.

African American communal self-organization played a significant role in the struggle against a social and political environment shaped by the dominant population's assumption and practice of white supremacy. As James Oliver Horton and Lois E. Horton have written, the African Society, founded in Boston in 1796, worked as "both an instrument of socialization and a reflection of community values." The same can be said of many of its African American counterparts. Perhaps one of the most important of these organizations was black Freemasonry. In 1787 Prince Hall obtained a charter for a black Masonic lodge in Boston that would eventually include some of the most influential African American male leaders in New England, among them David Walker and W. E. B. Du Bois. While the Freemasons focused the efforts of black men, women also organized. For example, the Afric-American Female Intelligence Society was formed in Boston in 1832 to provide a cultural and literary forum for free black women. Other organizations indicate both the extent of African American communal activism and the complexity of the political and philosophical issues they were founded to address. In 1780, for example, free African Americans in Rhode Island formed the African Union Society to promote emigration to Africa, a move opposed by the Philadelphia Free African Society. The African Society in Boston was a vehicle for mutual aid and charity, promoting the principles of morality, temperance, and self-improvement that were prominent in the writings of social and political activists such as Stewart and Walker.

Religion was a central presence for African Americans in New England as elsewhere, and black churches served multiple but deeply related purposes—social, political, economic, and spiritual. In Boston, for example, the African Meeting House, dedicated in 1806, was the birthplace of the New England Abolitionist Society, a school (until 1834), and a gathering place for the Boston black community. Now a museum, this building continues to confirm the importance to African Americans of a dynamic, communal religion based in many spiritual and cultural traditions and exerting its influence on all areas of social life. The dominant form of religious practice was Christian, but as William D. Piersen, among many others, has noted, the various forms of African American Christianity were often rich combinations of African religious practices and folkways and European American Christian frameworks. From these varied roots grew many important New England institutions that gave rise to distinguished African American leaders.

John Marrant, whose remarkable career eventually took him to New England, became chaplain of the African Lodge of the Freemasons in Boston in the late 18th century. The Reverend Thomas Paul of New Hampshire organized the founding of the African Baptist Church, also in Boston, in 1805. Lemuel Haynes, born in Connecticut, became one of Vermont's best-known and well-respected ministers in the late 18th and early 19th centuries, often leading a primarily white congregation. In Connecticut, Jehiel C. Beman and his yet more influential son Amos Gerry Beman worked to make the church's presence felt in all areas of life. The younger Beman coordinated the formation of the New Haven Literary and Debating Society, cofounded the Connecticut State Temperance Society of Colored People, helped organize the American and Foreign Anti-Slavery Society, presided over an 1843 national convention of African Americans in Buffalo, N.Y., and contributed his efforts to the first national African American association, the National Council of Colored People, founded in 1853. The Reverend Beman provides an excellent illustration of African American religious leadership in 18th-and 19th-century New England.

In all African American institutions education was a constant, vital theme, inseparable from larger political and economic struggles. From Phillis Wheatley's poem "To the University of Cambridge, in New-England" of 1767 to W. E. B. Du Bois's doctorate from Harvard in 1895, African Americans participated in, contributed to, critiqued, and transformed education in New England at all levels. Two early New England African American leaders and successful businessmen, Amos Fortune and Wentworth Cheswill, both of New Hampshire, promoted education in substantial ways—Cheswill by contributing to the Newmarket Social Library, in which he was a shareholder, and Fortune by founding the Jaffrey Social Library and by donating money for a town school.

But education, like all else, was clouded by racial prejudice. In 1835 Noyes Academy in Canaan, N.H., was literally removed from its foundation by angry white area residents for accepting such students as Henry Highland Garnet and Alexander Crummell, who would become two of the most extraordinary leaders of their age. Other versions of this incident occurred throughout New England. Students admitted to Wesleyan University in Connecticut in 1832 and to Harvard Medical School in 1850 were asked to leave. The Quaker schoolmistress Prudence Crandall met with resistance in Connecticut when she enrolled African Americans into her girls' boarding school. White parents protested and withdrew their children, and when Crandall, with the help of William Lloyd Garrison and others, made plans for an exclusively African American school, the Connecticut legislature passed a law prohibiting the establishment of a school for African Americans who were not Connecticut residents. Eventually Crandall was arrested, and her court case led to the ruling that African Americans were not citizens. In virtually all states, poor buildings and inadequate resources characterized segregated schools for African Americans, and African Americans continued to work for open educational opportunities.

In Massachusetts the efforts of Benjamin Roberts, William C. Nell, and many others led to the desegregation of Boston schools in 1855. Alexander Lucius Twilight of Vermont became the first African American to graduate from an American college when he received his A.B. from Vermont's Middlebury College in 1823 (he was later the first black man elected to a state legislature, also in Vermont). Other graduates followed, marking at least symbolic progress: Edward Jones from Massachusetts's Amherst College (1826), John Russwurm from Maine's Bowdoin College (1826), and Edward Mitchell from New Hampshire's Dartmouth College (1828). Harvard followed much later, when Edwin C. J. T.

Howard, George L. Ruffin, and Robert T. Freeman received their degrees from Harvard Medical School, Law School, and Dental School, respectively, in 1869. In 1870 Richard T. Greener became the first graduate of Harvard College; Alberta V. Scott did not become Radcliffe's first black recipient of an A.B. until 1898. In time, however, Harvard became an important educational center for African Americans, producing many of the leaders of a rising generation of black male leaders toward the turn of the 19th century, including Robert H. Terrell (A.B. in 1884), W. Monroe Trotter (A.B. in 1895), and W. E. B. Du Bois (A.B. in 1890, A.M. in 1891, and Ph.D. in 1895).

In the fine arts, landscape painter Edward Mitchell Bannister of Rhode Island was the first black artist to earn national recognition, exhibiting at the National Academy of Design in 1879.

Writing and publication were essential to African American communal self-definition in the 18th and 19th centuries, and many of the most important African American writers worked in New England. The institutions founded by African Americans, as well as antislavery organizations founded by whites, became significant centers of writing and publishing. In numerical terms the major publications were autobiographies and memoirs, many of them slave narratives published both before and after the Civil War, including the stories of Venture Smith (Connecticut), Elleanor Eldridge (Rhode Island), and the first of Douglass's autobiographies (Massachusetts), to name only a few. But African Americans published in virtually every genre, including journalism, essays, sermons, travel narratives, histories, poetry, fiction, and drama. Robert Roberts's *The House Servant's Directory; or, A Monitor for Private Families* (1827) was one of the first books published by an African American. William Wells Brown alone published in each of these genres before the end of the Civil War, and such works as the *Productions of Mrs. Maria W. Stewart* (1835) and Ann Plato's *Essays including Biographies and Miscellaneous Pieces in Prose and Poetry* (published in Hartford in 1841) suggest the important and early presence of female writers long before the Civil War.

In the pre–Civil War years came such historical publications as *Light and Truth* (1844) by Robert Benjamin Lewis, once of Maine, and William Cooper Nell's *Colored Patriots of the American Revolution*, published in Boston in 1855. In the realm of poetry and fiction, from the early poems of Wheatley and Lucy Terry in the 18th century to the work of James M. Whitfield in the 19th and from Harriet Wilson's pioneering fictional critique of northern white racism in the autobiographical novel

Our Nig; or, Sketches from the Life of a Free Black, in a Two-Story White House, North, Showing That Slavery's Shadows Fall Even There (1859) to Pauline Hopkins's summation of the effects of the racist past in her *Contending Forces* (1900), African American New Englanders have worked to challenge dominant assumptions about U.S. history. In the process they have demonstrated the vitality, complexity, and depth of the African American presence in New England.

Lorenzo Johnston Greene, *The Negro in Colonial New England, 1620–1776* (1942); James Oliver Horton and Lois E. Horton, *Black Bostonians: Family Life and Community Struggle in the Antebellum North* (1979); Horton and Horton, *In Hope of Liberty: Culture, Community, and Protest among Northern Free Blacks, 1700–1860* (1997); Sidney Kaplan and Emma Nogrady Kaplan, *The Black Presence in the Era of the American Revolution* (1989); Leon F. Litwack, *North of Slavery: The Negro in the Free States, 1790–1860* (1961); William D. Piersen, *Black Yankees: The Development of an Afro-American Subculture in 18th-Century New England* (1988); Benjamin Quarles, *Black Abolitionists* (1969).

John Ernest

African Americans, 1900 to the Present

New England has historically been home to a relatively small number of African Americans. With a stagnant industrial base during the first great black migration to the north in 1915–29, the region attracted fewer blacks than did the West and Midwest. After World War II the African American population began to expand, and new communities developed.

Because African Americans have never constituted more than 1 percent of the population of Maine, New Hampshire, and Vermont, southern New England is the focus here. Yet even in the three northern states, black Americans have risen to prominence, challenging segregated public accommodations and employment from the 1940s through the 1960s. In New Hampshire, Juanita Bell and Lionel Johnson have served in the legislature, and Valerie Cunningham has led the effort to record the history of African Americans in Portsmouth and to establish that coastal city's Black Heritage Trail. In Maine, Gerald Talbot founded the Portland chapter of the National Association for the Advancement of Colored People (NAACP), was the first black Mainer to serve in the state legislature, and donated the substantial collection of documents and memorabilia that established the Gerald Talbot African American Archive at the University of Southern Maine in Portland. In Vermont the folklorist Jane Beck brought to the public the remarkable story of Daisy Turner, the centenarian daughter of a slave, and writer Howard Frank Mosher re-

NAACP Youth Council dancers, Lynn, Mass., 1992

counted in his novel *A Stranger in the Kingdom* (1989) a complex tale of bigotry and misunderstanding based on a 1950s court case.

At the start of the 20th century only 59,099 African Americans lived in New England, constituting about 1 percent of the region's population and less than 1 percent of the black population nationwide. The migration of 1915–29 did not change matters much: by 1930 New England's 94,086 blacks made up about the same percentage of the population as in 1900. After World War II, however, there was another migration: Connecticut in 1970 was 5.9 percent African American; Massachusetts, 3 percent; and Rhode Island, 2.6 percent. By 2000 those figures had risen to 9.1 percent for Connecticut (309,843 African Americans), 5.4 percent for Massachusetts (343,454), and 4.5 percent for Rhode Island (46,908). The population of each of the northern New England states was less than 1 percent African American (Maine, 6,760; New Hampshire, 9,035; Vermont, 3,063), and the three ranked among the bottom 10 states for percentage of black residents. Only 2 percent of African Americans (719,063 people) in the United States lived in the six state region. The 2000 census also gave respondents a chance to identify themselves as belonging to "two or more races"; when the numbers in this category are added to those in the "Black or African American" category the totals rise: Connecticut, 339,078; Maine, 9,553; Massachusetts, 398,479; New Hampshire, 12,218; Rhode Island, 58,051; Vermont, 4,492.

The low numbers of blacks in New England contributed to peaceful race relations in the first half of the century, and African Americans and whites lived in proximity with

one another. But when the black communities expanded geographically after World War II, they became more segregated. Most black New Englanders clustered in urban areas. In Massachusetts, the cities (not metropolitan areas) with the most African Americans are Boston (149,202), Springfield (31,960), Brockton (16,811), Cambridge (12,079), Worcester (11,892), and Lynn (9,394). Thus, about two-thirds of African American Bay Staters lived in just six cities in 2000. The Boston public schools, especially the high schools, remain overwhelmingly nonwhite; little progress has been made in desegregation. A similar picture emerges in Connecticut, where about two-thirds of the state's black residents live in eight cities and towns: Hartford, New Haven, and Bridgeport all have more than 40,000 African Americans, while Stamford, Waterbury, Norwalk, Bloomfield, and East Hartford all have about 10,000–20,000 black residents. In Rhode Island, Providence ranks sixth in the region, with 25,243 black residents in 2000.

Until the civil rights movement of the 1960s, most black workers occupied the lowest rungs of the economic ladder, with some important exceptions. Early in the century black entrepreneurs had carved out a niche in such fields as food service and barbering, but new immigrants drove out these small business owners by various means, including appeals to supposedly white solidarity.

After the migration of the 1950s and 1960s, New England's African Americans had to fight their way into better-paying jobs in manufacturing, construction, transportation, and education. In Boston and other cities black workers picketed construction sites to enforce fair hiring ratios, and by the 1970s the black working class and middle class had made progress. The decline of industry throughout the region in the 1980s contributed to worsening conditions in the inner cities. Many black communities suffered a plague of violence; in Hartford's largely African American North End, unemployment had risen beyond 30 percent by 1990; that year in Massachusetts, where African Americans made up only 4.6 percent of the population, 31 percent of prisoners were black.

Black New Englanders were particularly active in the early civil rights movement. Late-19th- and early-20th-century New England was largely free of overt racial violence, while the rest of the country experienced an epidemic. A 1919 study listed 3,224 American lynchings in the previous 30 years, only one of which occurred in New England. Black New Englanders voted freely, and segregation was legally banned in most states. New England's African Americans defended their own rights and protested the worsening national conditions. William Monroe Trotter, Boston publisher of the militant *Guardian* newspaper, won supporters throughout the region. For a decade the NAACP's largest branch—albeit also its whitest—was in Boston, and black Bostonians joined in large numbers after World War I. Mary Evans Wilson traveled throughout the region, helping new NAACP branches in Springfield and New Bedford, Mass., and Providence. Marcus Garvey's black nationalist movement had some supporters among New England's small West Indian population, and the region's black railroad men responded to the organizing efforts of A. Philip Randolph and joined the newly formed Brotherhood of Sleeping Car Porters. In 1915 activists rallied on the Boston Common against the movie *The Birth of a Nation;* two years later Providence African Americans staged a silent parade to protest racial violence throughout the country.

As black communities grew in the latter part of the century, they confronted de facto segregation. Boston NAACP leaders Ruth Batson, Melnea Cass, and Tom Atkins joined other community leaders, such as Mel King, Paul Parks, and Ellen Jackson, to challenge segregation in schools. They advocated a simple reassignment plan, but the school committee remained intransigent. When a federal court ruled in favor of integration through school busing, Boston's black students were subjected to three years (1974–77) of stone throwing, epithets, and screaming mobs; the busing crisis in Boston was probably the longest-lasting antiblack mobilization in American urban history. A milder version of the same story unfolded during the 1960s in New Haven. There a more liberal school board approved a revamped feeder plan to alleviate segregation in the 91 percent black Bassett Junior High. When white parents challenged the plan, board members relented. Later (1970–71) New Haven was the scene of the highly charged murder trial of Black Panther Party leader Bobby Seale, who was released when the jury failed to reach a unanimous verdict. Whites in Hartford also blocked integration plans. Providence probably had the smoothest experience with desegregation, although black parents boycotted schools there for six weeks. In southwestern New England, from New London to Cape Cod, significant Cape Verdean, Native American, and Latino populations complicated but also blurred the artificial black and white categories that characterize American race relations. No New England city experienced an urban rebellion approximating those of Newark, N.J., Detroit, Mich., and the Watts section of Los Angeles, in the 1960s, but smaller uprisings occurred in nine Connecticut cities, Providence, and Boston.

Once this period of turbulence had ended, African American New Englanders began to make their numbers felt in politics. The election of Tom Atkins to the Boston City Council in 1966 broke a decades-long white monopoly; Bruce Bolling, Charles Yancey, and other blacks have served on that body ever since. African Americans have won election to most urban New England city councils and school boards. Hartford, New London, and New Haven have elected black mayors, the most prominent among them being two-term winner John Daniels of New Haven. Blacks have also served in the Maine, Rhode Island, Connecticut, and Massachusetts legislatures in the 20th and 21st centuries and in the Vermont legislature in the 19th century. Conservative Republican Gary Franks of Waterbury, Conn., won three terms in the U.S. House of Representatives (1990–96), and Edward Brooke of Massachusetts was elected to the Senate in 1966; so far they are the only black New Englanders to serve in those legislative bodies.

The site of several leading universities, New England was also home to many African American writers and intellectuals during the 20th century. Fiction writers include the Bostonians Pauline Hopkins, who wrote short stories and serialized novels for the *Colored American* magazine from 1900 to 1904, and Dorothy West, whose novel *The Living Is Easy* (1948), portrayed upper-class black Bostonians of the 1920s. Walter J. Stevens's autobiographical memoir depicted the same milieu. The poets Samuel Allen, William Stanley Braithwaite, and Derek Walcott all lived in Boston at various times during the century. Ann Petry of Old Saybrook, Conn., wrote African American novels, short stories, and fiction for young adults.

Many African American intellectuals have studied and taught in the region's universities. Historians who have lived and worked in the region include John W. Blassingame (Yale), Nathan Irvin Huggins (Harvard), and C. Eric Lincoln (Clark); other leaders in the historical profession, such as Benjamin Quarles (Boston public schools), John Hope Franklin (Harvard), and Rayford Logan (Harvard) studied there. A prolific chronicler of Massachusetts African Americans is Robert C. Hayden of New Bedford and Boston. The sociologist Adelaide Cromwell and economist Glenn Loury have both taught at Boston University. In the 1990s Harvard University's W. E. B. Du Bois Institute assembled a faculty of nationally prominent scholars that included the literary critic Henry Louis Gates, Jr., the theologian and social critic Cornel West (now at Princeton University), and the sociologist William Julius Wilson. The poet Michael Harper is at Brown University in Providence, with dramatist Ed Bullins at Boston's Northeastern University and writers Samuel R. Delany, John Edgar Wideman, and Julius Lester at the University of Massachusetts in Amherst. Ruth Simmons is president of Brown University.

Black New Englanders have also contributed significantly in music and art. The painter Allan Rohan Crite depicted street scenes of African American life in Boston and illustrated many books. The New Bedford statue of Lewis Temple, who invented the iron-toggle harpoon tip, was designed by local sculptor Jim Toatley. Boston tenor Roland Hayes was the first African American to sing with a major symphonic orchestra. In 1950 Boston's Elma Lewis opened a nationally acclaimed school of the arts that thrived for 40 years. The region has produced such outstanding artists as the pianist Horace Silver, born in Norwalk, Conn.; Boston drummers Roy Haynes, Alan Dawson, and Tony Williams; and Massachusetts saxophonists Johnny Hodges and Paul Gonsalves, who anchored Duke Ellington's reed section.

African American New Englanders have made nationally significant contributions to the liberal professions as well. In education Maria Baldwin of Cambridge, Mass., was principal of a largely white school for the first 20 years of the century, where she subverted the dominant paradigm of white educational leadership. Elizabeth Carter Brooks was a prominent educator in New Bedford and, like Baldwin, helped lead the National Association of Colored Women's Clubs (NACW). Josephine St. Pierre Ruffin, though not a teacher, helped found the NACW and attempted to integrate the white women's club movement.

Black New Englanders have made a name for themselves also in law, science, and medicine. In the early 20th century William Henry Lewis of Cambridge served as assistant U.S. attorney general; he held the highest appointment of any African American until the Franklin Delano Roosevelt administration and after leaving government service became a noted trial lawyer. Early NAACP leaders Butler Wilson (Boston), Clement Morgan (Cambridge), and George W. Crawford (New Haven) were also locally prominent. New Haven's Constance Baker Motley was another NAACP leader and the first African American woman to attain a federal judgeship. In 1907 Ernest Everett Just was the only student to graduate magna cum laude from Dartmouth College in Hanover, N.H.; he went on to become an eminent zoologist, biologist, physiologist, and research scientist. In the 1980s and 1990s the law schools at Yale and Harvard boasted such prominent legal scholars as Stephen Carter (Yale) and Christopher Edley, Randall Kennedy, A. Leon Higginbotham, and Charles Ogletree (Harvard). In 1997 Springfield's Roderick Ireland became the first black justice of the Massachusetts Supreme Judicial Court. America's pioneering black psychiatrist was Solomon Carter Fuller of Boston, who was succeeded in the latter half of the century by writers and practitioners James P. Comer (Yale) and Alvin Poussaint (Harvard).

The black nationalist leader Malcolm X, whose father had been murdered for propounding notions of racial equality, spent his teenage years living with his sister in Roxbury, Mass., on the outskirts of Boston. Louis Farrakhan, head of the separatist Nation of Islam, grew up in Roxbury, assisted Malcolm X at his Boston mosque, and replaced him as minister there when Malcolm moved to New York City. Martin Luther King, Jr., met Coretta Scott, the woman he would marry, in Boston, where Scott was working on a degree in voice at the New England Conservatory of Music. King was earning his doctorate in theology at Boston University, where since 1969 the King Center has addressed the personal, educational, and career-development needs of Boston University students. The Martin Luther King Papers, some 83,000 documents, are also housed at the civil rights leader's Boston alma mater.

Robert C. Hayden, *African-Americans in Boston: More Than 350 Years* (1991); William Lee Miller, *The 15th Ward and the Great Society: An Encounter with a Modern City* (1966); U.S. Bureau of the Census, *Negroes in the United States, 1920–1932* (1935); Robert Austin Warner, *New Haven Negroes: A Social History* (1940).

Mark R. Schneider

African Meetinghouses   In colonial New England meetinghouses were located at the center of town, both physically and psychologically. Distances were measured from them, and as William Root Bliss wrote, meetinghouses "stood for certain customs, principles, and opinions which were believed to be as immutable as a divine decree." The region's African meetinghouses, though few in number, were equally critical institutions in the lives of black New Englanders.

New England's African meetinghouses were located in seaports with substantial black communities. They included the Abyssinian Church of Portland, Maine, and the African Meeting House on Nantucket Island, as well as Boston's First African Baptist Church.

The First African Baptist Church was officially formed in 1805 in Boston with a congregation of 20. Thomas Paul, an African American preacher from New Hampshire, obtained funding for the church. Located at 8 Smith Court, it is the oldest African meetinghouse still standing in the United States. In 1832 the famed abolitionist William Lloyd Garrison founded the New England Anti-Slavery Society at the church, and over the course of the 19th century, the First African Baptist played host to the most distinguished figures in the nation's abolitionist movement, including Frederick Douglass, Wendell Phillips, and Charles Sumner. In addition to its use as a place of worship and center of abolitionist activism, the meetinghouse also served as a school for black children for 150 years—from 1808 until school desegregation in 1955. Over the years the First African Baptist was also known as the Abolition Church, the Black Faneuil Hall, Belknap Street Church, and Joy Street Church.

In 1840 the congregation split and a second African meetinghouse, the Twelfth Baptist Church, was established in Roxbury. Purchased by a Jewish congregation in 1898, the original meetinghouse was converted to a synagogue; it was sold in 1972 to Sue Bailey and Howard Thurman and two years later was designated a National Historic Landmark.

Built in 1828, Portland's Abyssinian Church is Maine's oldest African American meetinghouse and the third oldest African American meetinghouse in the United States. Before the Civil War it operated a school for black children and hosted antislavery rallies. Its members actively participated in the work of the Underground Railroad, often hiding runaway slaves in their homes or at the church. The church closed in 1918, and subsequent owners left the building to deteriorate. In the 1990s the building was restored for use as a cultural center and museum of African American life in Maine. *Anchor of the Soul: A Documentary*

about Black History in Maine, a video produced in 1994 by Shoshana Hoose and Karine Odlin, examines the history of Portland's black community, the Abyssinian Church, and its successor, the Green Memorial AME Zion Church.

In the early 1800s Nantucket's lucrative whaling industry and tolerant Quaker culture lured African Americans from the North and the South. In 1825 the black community, which numbered approximately 300 among Nantucket's 7,000 residents, built a one-room meetinghouse on the south end of town. The meetinghouse was a center of education and political activity, spearheading one of the first equal-education bills in the country. Boston's Museum of Afro-American History purchased the building in 1989 and began restoring it. The meetinghouse is architecturally unique. Like the hull of an overturned ship, its walls curve to a vaulted ceiling. African American shipwrights likely constructed the building.

The meetinghouse in Farmington, Conn., the First Church of Christ, built in 1771, also played an important role in the history of African Americans in New England. In 1841, 32 African captives, freed by the U.S. Supreme Court following their mutiny aboard the Spanish slave ship *Amistad,* were sponsored by Farmington abolitionists and attended the First Church of Christ for several months while awaiting passage back to Africa.

William Root Bliss, *Side Glimpses from the Colonial Meeting-House* (1970 [1894]); Robert C. Hayden, *The African Meeting House in Boston: A Celebration of History* (1987); Carl Seaburg, *Boston Observed* (1971).

Louis Mazzari

Amistad Case   In 1839 Sierra Leonean captives were illegally transported from the African island of Lombokor to the Spanish colony of Cuba in a Portuguese slaver. Once smuggled into Havana, 53 of the Africans were sold to José Ruiz and Pedro Montes, who shipped them along the Cuban coast aboard the schooner *La Amistad.* On July 1–2, 1839, shortly after the *Amistad*'s departure, the Africans, led by Singbe Pieh (Joseph Cinque), revolted, killing the ship's captain and cook but sparing Ruiz and Montes; one African also died. When ordered to sail to Africa, the Spaniards maintained a meandering course that by August 25 brought them near the coast of New York's Long Island. Shortly after being captured by the USS *Washington*, the mutineers were jailed in New Haven, Conn., to await a hearing. So began a lengthy ordeal for the Mende tribesmen (many of the detainees spoke the Mende language) that focused widespread attention on New England. Ruiz and Montes insisted that the Africans were slaves in Cuba at the time of purchase and thus could be tried for piracy and murder. As Spanish authorities demanded the return of the ship and its human cargo, abolitionists mobilized in behalf of the mutineers.

The *Amistad* Committee—organized by the prominent New York businessman and lawyer Lewis Tappan; the Reverend Joshua Leavitt, editor of the abolitionist newspaper the *Emancipator;* and the Reverend Simeon Jocelyn, the white minister of a black Congregational church in New Haven—raised funds and garnered public sympathy for the captives. Two African-born seamen, James Covey and Charles Partt, translated for the prisoners. The U.S. Circuit Court of Hartford, convening in September 1839 before thousands of onlookers, refused to release the captives and remanded the case to the district court. In January 1840 Judge Andrew T. Judson, ruling that the Africans had been illegally kidnapped and that their rebellion had been legitimate, ordered all captives to be returned to Africa except Antonio, slave of the slain *Amistad* captain, who would be sent back to Cuba.

The Van Buren administration, believing the Africans should be returned to Spain under Pinckney's Treaty (1795), had a naval vessel waiting to transport them back to Cuba before abolitionists could appeal the anticipated verdict. But with the unexpected ruling, it was the government that filed an appeal to a U.S. Supreme Court stacked with southern former slaveowners, including Chief Justice Roger B. Taney. The *Amistad* Committee secured John Quincy Adams, former president of the United States, to argue the case before the Court, which in March 1841 affirmed the original ruling on a vote of eight to one. The mutineers were free, but private funds had to be raised to return them to Africa. Antonio was whisked to Canada via the Underground Railroad.

On November 17, 1841, the 35 surviving Africans (others having died in prison), James Covey, and five white missionaries left New York for Sierra Leone, where they arrived in mid-January 1842. Little is known of what happened to Cinque after his repatriation, but he remains a leading symbol of resistance to the Atlantic slave trade. Although the Spanish government demanded reparations, sectional divisions within the U.S. Congress hampered that effort, and the coming of the Civil War brought it to a permanent end.

The *Amistad* saga remained little known among members of the American public until the release in 1997 of Steven Spielberg's Hollywood film *Amistad,* much of it shot in Newport, R.I. The movie drew attention to abolitionism in Connecticut, whose Freedom Trail features several stops related to the case, and gave rise to exhibits, tours, and, in Hartford, courtroom reenactments of the trial. On March 25, 2000, a replica of the *Amistad,* whose name in Spanish means friendship, was christened at Connecticut's Mystic Seaport. It docked there for half the year and now spends its time sailing the American coast, a floating classroom and promoter of interracial harmony.

John Warner Barber, *A History of the "Amistad" Captives* (1840); Mary Cable, *Black Odyssey: The Case of the Slave Ship "Amistad"* (1971); Howard Jones, *Mutiny on the "Amistad": The Saga of a Slave Revolt and Its Impact on American Abolition, Law, and Diplomacy* (1987); R. Earl McClendon, "The *Amistad* Claims: Inconsistencies of Policy," *Political Science Quarterly* 48 (1933).

Robert L. Hall

Arabs Home to more than 300,000 Arab Americans, New England has long been a popular site for immigration from the Arab world. Exact population figures are hard to come by, in part because the term *Arab American* includes immigrants and their descendants from a wide geographic region. The 2000 census reported 86,272 citizens of Arab and mixed descent (Egyptian, Iraqi, Jordanian, Lebanese, Palestinian, Syrian, Arab/Arabic, and "other Arab") in New England, approximately 12,000 more than were reported in the 1990 census. Even this number, contend Arab American community leaders, reflects only about 25 percent of the actual number of Arab New Englanders. According to some estimates, by the early 1990s there were 150,000 Arab Americans residing in Massachusetts alone, with progressively smaller populations located throughout Connecticut, Maine, Rhode Island, New Hampshire, and Vermont.

Individual Arabs arrived in Boston in the 1880s, but the first significant wave of Arab immigration occurred between the early 1900s and World War I. Originating from lands then under Ottoman rule, especially Lebanon and Syria, the immigrants were predominantly Christian and initially male, escaping famine, war, and poverty, and attracted by the prospect of of earning enough to send money home to their families. These early immigrants settled largely in urban areas around New England and made their living mainly as peddlers in dry goods and as textile workers. Their descendants, however, are represented in all occupations and have largely assimilated into American life.

New waves of Arab immigrants arrived after World War II, following Israel's occupation of the West Bank and Gaza Strip in June 1967, and in the wake of the Lebanese civil war of the mid-1970s. Many came as students or professionals from newly independent Arab states. These immigrants tended to be highly educated and were more likely to be Muslim than previous immigrants. Carrying with them a heightened sense of their political and social identity as Arabs at a time when pluralist ethnic identities were receiving more attention within the United States, they adopted the name Arab American. Most of today's Arab Americans were born in New England, and fewer than 25 percent speak Arabic at home.

New England has been home to several prominent Arab Americans, notably the author and poet Kahlil Gibran, who settled in Massachusetts in 1912; the former U.S. Senate majority leader from Maine George Mitchell; and the former White House chief of staff and governor of New Hampshire John Sununu. New England boasts renowned centers of Middle Eastern scholarship; Harvard University in Cambridge, Mass., for example, attracts Arab and Arab American scholars from around the world. Arab and Arab American student associations are active at area colleges such as the Massachusetts Institute of Technology in Cambridge and Brown University in Providence.

Cultural activities in New England include the *Arabic Hour,* broadcast weekly on cable television in Boston and parts of Rhode Island. New England is a center for literary innovations in Arab American poetry and works by women writers. Arab influences are visible as well in architectural and religious structures around the region. Arab-inspired domes and arches are found on historical buildings in Cambridge and on dozens of mosques and Eastern Orthodox churches across the region.

Arab Americans in New England share with their counterparts around the country a deep devotion to their families and ethnic communities. But they face racial ignorance, stereotyping, and discrimination from the community at large. Following the terrorist attacks in New York and Washington, D.C., on September 11, 2001, discrimination increased against Arabs and Arab Americans (and Muslims generally) in the workplace, at educational institutions, and elsewhere. The passage of the USA Patriot Act later that year, despite a provision "condemning discrimination against Arab and Muslim Americans," raised concerns about government-sanctioned singling out of this community for special scrutiny. Facing the backlash emanating from these acts and from the federal government's Middle Eastern policy, Arabs and Arab Americans work to counter negative portrayals of their community by joining organizations such as the Association of Arab-American University Graduates and the American-Arab Anti-Discrimination Committee and by publishing extensive studies on Arab Americans.

Elizabeth Boohsahda, *Arab-American Faces and Voices: The Origins of an Immigrant Community* (2003); Hussein Ibish, ed., *Report on Hate Crimes and Discrimination against Arab-Americans: The Post–September 11 Backlash, September 11, 2001–October 11, 2002.* Arab-American Anti-Discrimination Committee (2003); Joanna Kadi, ed., *Food for Our Grandmothers: Writings by Arab-American and Arab-Canadian Feminists* (1994); Ernest McCarus, ed., *The Development of Arab-American Identity* (1994); Najib E. Saliba, *Emigration from Syria and the Syrian-Lebanese Community of Worcester, MA* (1992); John Zogby, *Arab America Today: A Demographic Profile of Arab Americans* (1990).

Souad Dajani

Armenians History-minded Armenians trace their origins to the Anatolian plateau in Asia Minor more than two and a half millennia ago. The Armenian people first appear in the royal inscriptions of Darius I, king of Persia (522–486 B.C.), and in the histories of Herodotus as Armenioi, Armina, or Armenians. By the second century B.C. Armenians had established trade outposts on the shores of the Mediterranean and Black Seas, later adding stops along the Silk Road to the Far East, where they served as middlemen in world commerce. When Armenia espoused Christianity in A.D. 301, it became the first Christian nation. The Armenians' distinctive Indo-European language features a 38-character alphabet invented to record religious texts in the Armenian Apostolic Church; both written and spoken Armenian would become distinguishing features of Armenian national culture in the diaspora.

Immigration to New England from the Armenian homelands in Asia Minor began around 1867. The first recorded Armenian visitor to the region, known only as Garo, arrived in Worcester, Mass., as the domestic servant of an American Protestant missionary on leave from his post in the Near East. Like other immigrants, Garo quickly learned that he could earn more money working in Worcester's wire mills. His enthusiastic letters home encouraged a stream of Armenian immigrants who hoped to escape poverty and improve their quality of life. Although there are no statistics for ethnic groups entering the United States before 1899, categories such as Turkey in Asia, Asiatic Turkey, and Turkey in Europe are believed to include Armenian newcomers.

This confusion about the provenance of immigrants was compounded by general ignorance of the region and by American bigotry. At the time, Armenians were mistakenly labeled Asians because they came from Asia Minor, and they were considered part of the so-called Yellow Peril. They were routinely discriminated against until a landmark ruling

"Armenian Night" in New England, 1930

in 1909 by the U.S. Circuit Court of Massachusetts in Boston declared that Armenians belonged to the white or Caucasian race. This ruling gave Armenians the right to citizenship (and the ownership of property) as white persons.

By 1915 Massachusetts had received the largest number of Armenian immigrants entering New England. Of these 4,239 foreign-born workers, two-thirds were employed in manufacturing and machine industries as unskilled or semiskilled laborers. Armenians also lived and worked in the mill towns and industrial cities of Rhode Island, Connecticut, New Hampshire, and Maine. Although they earned significantly higher wages than they might have in Turkey, many immigrants, exhausted and worn out by factory work, chose to go back home.

But in April 1915 the Ottoman Empire's Armenian minority suffered what has been called the first genocide of the 20th century. During World War I the Turkish army forced the relocation of hundreds of thousands of surviving Armenians. The bloody campaign to eliminate the non-Turkic-speaking peoples of Anatolia continued through 1922 and took the lives of an estimated 1.2 million Armenians. Those who had kin overseas eventually sought refuge with them. There would be little or no possibility of returning to the devastated home territories, a state of affairs that irredentist groups based in the Middle East refused to accept.

By 1933 almost 16,000 adults were listed in an *Armenian Directory* for New England. More than 11,000 of those had settled in Massachusetts, nearly 7,000 of them in metropolitan Boston, with Worcester and Providence

claiming close to 2,000 each. Watertown, Mass., has been favored by Armenians since 1890, when a few immigrants went to work at the Hood Rubber factory there. It has remained an important commercial and cultural center for New England's Armenians since this early settlement. In 1990 Watertown was home to an estimated 7,000 Armenian residents, one-fifth of the town's population. In the 2000 census, 45,206 New Englanders reported single or mixed Armenian ancestry. Reliable figures are generally unavailable for post–World War II Armenian immigrants, many of them genocide survivors who entered the United States from other lands. Twice diasporans, they brought with them languages and skills acquired as sojourners elsewhere. Accomplished craftspeople (jewelers, photographers, engravers, tailors), small shopkeepers, and trained professionals, these new immigrants adjusted more readily to American life than their earlier compatriots, who had to battle prejudice and ignorance in schools and in the workplace.

Entering communities with established Armenian churches representing the Armenian Apostolic, Catholic, and Protestant faiths, newcomers became the immediate beneficiaries of earlier settlers. They discovered active political parties associated with men's coffeehouses, Armenian- and English-language presses, Armenian schools, hometown associations, philanthropic organizations (largely organized and directed by women), and fraternal societies already in place. Their contribution to community life would take the form of invigorating these institutions at a time when they were losing the interest of an older population further along in the assimilation process. Immigrant support of the churches, once the religious and administrative centers of Armenian communities in the Near and Middle East, has been crucial to the continuing importance of these congregations.

New England's Little Armenias have grown since World War II as a direct result of a series of political disturbances in the Middle East; the 1967 war in Lebanon in particular devastated Beirut's old and prosperous Armenian community. In the 1980s and 1990s profound dissatisfactions with life in the former Soviet Socialist Republic of Armenia fueled new migrations. The hardships suffered in the Caucasus from the effects of the earthquake of 1988 and the long war with Azerbaijan over the region of Mountainous Karabagh stirred sympathies in the diaspora. Volunteering financial aid, medical supplies, and trained personnel, New England's Armenians joined their compatriots in providing much-needed relief.

Some Armenians, however, continued to long for a return of their historic homeland.

In the 1970s and early 1980s members of Armenian terrorist organizations struck Turkish targets around the world. In Somerville, Mass., on May 4, 1982, the honorary Turkish consul Orhan R. Gunduz was shot to death in his car while he stopped at a red light. New England Armenians, jolted from their complacency and political quiescence, were divided in their reactions to these events. The Armenian Tashnagtsutiun (Armenian Revolutionary Federation) Party, founded in 1890, raised funds for the legal aid of imprisoned Armenian "freedom fighters." The other two political parties, the moderate Ramgavars and the Social Democratic Hunchags, along with most Armenian Americans, would not condone terrorism.

The recognition of an independent Republic of Armenia in 1991 has clearly captured the hearts and opened the purses of diasporans, although few Armenian Americans have sought to relocate there. New England's flourishing communities continue to find themselves strengthened by the influx of new immigrants whose strong attachments to the Armenian language, culture, and religion serve not only as reminders of what the older generation is in danger of losing through assimilation but also as encouragement to successive generations born in the United States. The accomplishments of Armenians with ties to New England such as the abstract expressionist painter Arshile Gorky, who immigrated to Watertown in 1920, and the Somerville-born composer Alan Hovhaness, as well as those of doctors, lawyers, engineers, educators, and financiers are a continuing source of communal pride.

The new generation, now largely responsible for maintaining the intellectual, cultural, and spiritual heritage of Armenia, is committed to supporting a variety of local organizations and national institutions that subsidize the instruction of the young and reinforce the connection with a struggling Republic of Armenia. In the 1960s and 1970s the numbers of students attending Armenian Saturday, Sunday, and day schools increased, as did enthusiasm for Armenian athletics, summer camps, internships, and college-based Armenian clubs.

Armenian New Englanders have made efforts to preserve both their collective past and a culture that risks being lost to assimilation. In 1977 Providence erected the Armenian Martyrs' Memorial Monument in the North Burial Ground to commemorate the genocide of 1915. Massachusetts is home to many Armenian cultural organizations, among them the Armenian Cultural Foundation of Arlington, the Armenian Library and Museum of America and Project SAVE Armenian Photograph Archives of Watertown, and the acclaimed Sayat Nova Dance Company (sponsored by the international Armenian General Benevolent Union) of Boston. The National Association of Armenian Studies and Research in nearby Belmont and the Zoryan Institute for Contemporary Armenian Research and Documentation of Cambridge make impressive use of the financial resources of local Armenian American elites. Funds raised to establish university chairs in Armenian studies at Harvard, Tufts, and Boston Universities place strong emphasis on education, which should come as no surprise for a people who have produced more doctorates per capita than any other ethnic group in the United States, a record of which Armenian Americans are justly proud.

Anny Bakalian, *Armenian-Americans: From Being to Feeling Armenian* (1993); Federal Writers' Project of the Works Progress Administration of Massachusetts, *The Armenians in Massachusetts* (1937); Richard G. Hovannisian, ed., *The Armenian People from Ancient to Modern Times*, vol. 2 (1997); Robert Mirak, *Torn between Two Lands: Armenians in America, 1890 to World War I* (1983); Jenny K. Phillips, *Symbol, Myth, and Rhetoric: The Politics of Culture in an Armenian-American Population* (1989).

Joan Bamberger

Attucks, Crispus

Attucks, Crispus (ca. 1723–70) Patriot. Crispus Attucks was the first person to die at the Boston Massacre on March 5, 1770. Most of his life is undocumented. He was born around 1723 and was probably a slave owned by Deacon William Brown of Framingham, Mass., until November 1750, when he escaped. Not much is known of his ancestry, but he is believed to have been a tall, muscular man of mixed Natick Indian and African heritage. While a free man, Attucks served on whaling ships operating out of several New England ports.

Attucks's fame stems from his becoming a martyr for the colonial cause against the British Empire. For several months American colonists and two British regiments unpopularly quartered in Boston had jeered at and harassed one another. On March 5, tensions heated up as several boys in the town pelted the soldiers with snowballs and ice, causing other soldiers to come to their comrades' aid. While dining at Thomas Simmons's "victualing-house," Attucks answered the call of the fire bell and led 20 to 30 laborers and sailors to the Custom House on King Street. Carrying a large stick, he and the others joined a growing crowd who were taunting and exchanging words with the British soldiers. Attucks struck a grenadier with his stick and was quickly gunned down by a British soldier. He was the first of five to die in the massacre.

Although all five men were given a public funeral, attended by some 10,000 people, Crispus Attucks received the most attention. During the trial that ensued, Attucks's death was the focus of both the defense and the prosecution. Defending the actions of the British soldiers, John Adams placed the entire blame on Attucks for organizing a raucous part of the crowd and striking a soldier in a fit of "mad behavior." The prosecution, in contrast, described Attucks as an innocent martyr who was maliciously killed.

Though the soldiers were acquitted, Attucks's name and legacy lived on. During the Civil War, African American companies used the name "Attucks Guards." From 1858 to 1870 Boston blacks observed a Crispus Attucks Day, and in 1888 the city erected a monument on Boston Common to the patriot's legacy. One hundred years later, in 1998, the U.S. Mint authorized the issuance of 500,000 commemorative silver coins bearing Attucks's likeness, which were unveiled at the Old State House in Boston on the 228th anniversary of the massacre. Having led the fight for liberty and freedom, Crispus Attucks is an important symbol of African American patriotism.

Philip S. Foner, *Blacks in the American Revolution* (1976); Benjamin Quarles, *The Negro in the American Revolution* (1961); Hiller B. Zobel, *The Boston Massacre* (1970).

Leslee K. Gilbert

Brazilians

Brazilians Brazilian migration to New England increased substantially in the mid-1980s, owing to the Brazilian political and economic crisis of that era. The initial contact networks that supported the migratory movement had been formed during World War II, when Boston engineers and technicians went to work in mineral prospecting in Brazil's Vale do Rio Doce, especially in Governador Valadares, Minas Gerais. After the war other networks formed when a Boston company built a railway in the Vale do Aço in Minas Gerais.

During the 1980s most Brazilian immigrants to New England originated from these two areas. In the 1990s, however, immigrants started to come from other states in Brazil. These states are socioeconomically diverse, suggesting that the migratory movement is related not to pockets of poverty but to the loss of social mobility that occurred in the 1980s and to the large contingent of foreign workers inside Brazil. Other factors contributing to Brazilian migration include unemployment, low salaries, the failure of government efforts to stabilize the Brazilian currency vis-à-vis the U.S. dollar, and the unsuitability of the Brazilian educational system to the country's labor market.

In 2000 there were a reported 212,428 foreign-born Brazilians in the United States. Because Brazilians are not categorized, however, accurate quantification is impossible. The Brazilian consulate in Boston estimated 180,000–200,000 in Massachusetts in 2001; a 2003 estimate is 231,000. Sizable immigration has recently focused on Boston, Framingham, and Somerville, Mass., and on Danbury, Conn. According to the consulate, Massachusetts has the second-largest Brazilian population in the United States, after New York.

Brazilian New Englanders tend to be target-earner immigrants, working for up to four years, saving a set amount of money, and returning to start small businesses or buy property in their homeland. Despite the absence of official data, the return rate is visibly high. Brazilians earn on average five times as much in New England as they do in Brazil, even though they may be performing less-qualified work, such as cleaning, gardening, and catering, than they did in Brazil.

In the early stages of the migratory movement, Brazilian immigrants were mostly single men between the ages of 20 and 35. During the 1990s the migrant population aged, displayed a more balanced male-female ratio, and showed increasing numbers of nuclear families. Massachusetts is home to New England's largest Brazilian population, who live mainly in Somerville, Cambridge, East Boston, Allston-Brighton, Framingham, Marlboro, and Lowell as well as on Cape Cod. Substantial numbers have also settled in Connecticut, New Hampshire, and Rhode Island.

As speakers of Portuguese, Brazilians refuse the designation "Hispanic." Although they take part in some Portuguese-speaking communities, they tend to form their own organizations: the Brazilian Immigrant Center (Allston), for example; soccer leagues; and centers for the practice of *capoeira*, a martial art created by African slaves in Brazil. They also tend to have their own ethnic churches. The number of Brazilian evangelical (Presbyterian, Baptist) and Pentecostal (Assembly of God, Universal Church of the Kingdom of God) churches is increasing, although Brazil is traditionally a Catholic country. A Massachusetts Brazilian Web site, many new businesses, and carnival, music, and dance celebrations attest to the vitality of the community in 2005.

Franklin Goza, "Brazilian Immigration to North America," *International Migration Review* 28, no. 1 (1994); Maxine Margólis, *Little Brazil* (1993).

Ana Cristina Braga Martes

Cambodians
In the years following the U.S. war in Indochina, some 152,000 Cambodians left their homeland to settle in the United States. Most fled after the Vietnamese overthrew the brutal Pol Pot regime in January 1979. Escaping starvation and mass murder at the hands of the Khmer Rouge, many made their way to holding camps on Cambodia's western border with Thailand, where they often spent years waiting for permission to enter a third country.

Resettlement policy in the United States at first emphasized the dispersal of small numbers of refugees over the entire 50 states. This policy was quickly undermined, however, by the large numbers of Cambodian newcomers who simply decided to move on to communities of their own choosing. These secondary migrants came to New England to reunite with friends and relatives and to seek employment opportunities in electronics, computers, and medical assembly plants. As the population grew, others were attracted to what was perceived as a thriving Cambodian American community. The U.S. government eventually modified its approach to relocation, identifying a select number of so-called cluster communities for Khmer (Cambodian) resettlement in which jobs, social services, and housing were available. Boston was one of these cluster communities.

Today New England is home to the second-largest Cambodian population in the United States, numbering approximately 10,000 and located an hour north of Boston in Lowell, Mass. Significant Khmer populations also have settled in the Massachusetts cities of Lynn, Revere, Fall River, Amherst, and Boston as well as in Providence, R.I. Khmer culture has been featured at the annual Folk Festival in Lowell. Cambodian needlework, especially the story cloths that recount in images the war at home and the journey to America, is included in exhibits of New England folk art. In August 1997 Lowell's Cambodian and Laotian communities staged the first annual Southeast Asian Water Festival, inspired by the boat races held yearly in their countries of origin, on the Merrimack River in Lowell Heritage State Park. The celebration offers thanks for water and protective nature spirits and features boats built by hand in Cambodia. Although a small number of Cambodians have converted to Christianity, the overwhelming majority remain Theravada Buddhist. In New England alone, Cambodians have established 12 temples staffed by some 50 resident monks.

Unlike their counterparts in a few North American cities, most Cambodians in New England came from rural backgrounds and had little formal education. (Educated members of the Khmer middle class were executed in large numbers during the Pol Pot era.) The Cambodians population is also quite young, with large numbers of school-age children. The gap between rural and uneducated Cam-

bodian parents and their American-educated children has been a source of tension in Cambodian families and the community as a whole. Though American educators regard Cambodian children as quiet and respectful, dropout rates are high. A number of researchers have noted an increasing bifurcation within the community between the small number of Khmer who came to the United States with social and educational resources and a much larger group who lack these advantages. Whereas the better-off Cambodian immigrants have been able to pull themselves into the American middle class, the less-advantaged majority seems to be falling further behind. This pattern of educational and economic bifurcation will probably remain a serious challenge to the efforts of Cambodian Americans to adapt to their new homeland in coming years.

David P. Chandler, *The Tragedy of Cambodian History: Politics, War, and Revolution since 1945* (1991); Sucheng Chang, ed., *Not Just for Victims: Conversations with Cambodian Community Leaders in the United States* (2003); May M. Ebihara, Carol A. Mortland, and Judy Ledgerwood, eds., *Cambodian Culture since 1975: Homeland and Exile* (1994); Dith Pran, comp., and Kim DePaul, ed., *Children of Cambodia's Killing Fields: Memoirs by Survivors* (1997); Nancy J. Smith-Hefner, *Khmer American: Identity and Moral Education in a Diasporic Community* (1999).

Nancy Smith-Hefner

Canadian Maritimers
Maritime Canada comprises three Canadian provinces: New Brunswick, Nova Scotia, and Prince Edward Island. The first major immigrant group to arrive in Atlantic Canada, the French, traded with the native Micmac and Maliseet peoples, who in turn helped the French establish settlements, including the first successful agricultural settlement in Canada at Port-Royal in Nova Scotia in 1605. Nova Scotia and parts of Quebec, New Brunswick, and Maine, all largely settled by the French, were known as Acadia until 1713; thereafter, the name applied only to Nova Scotia.

The Canadian Maritimes are known for their rich and culturally diverse ethnic population and have long welcomed immigrant groups from various backgrounds. Acadian French, Scottish Gaels, Yorkshire settlers, United Empire loyalists, Irish, and the original inhabitants—the Micmac and Maliseet—have all left an indelible imprint on the landscape and culture of the area. For the past 200 years and in the present, economic instability has been a constant problem; as a result, outmigration has historically been an unfortunate but inherently accepted part of life in Maritime Canada.

Strong ties have always existed between Maritime Canada and the New England states. Coal from the island of Cape Breton was traded to New England businesses, while New England fishing fleets have plied the waters off the coasts of New Brunswick, Prince Edward Island, and Nova Scotia for more than two centuries. Treaty rights designate that the Micmac may cross the Canadian-American border at will. Maine's potato and blueberry fields and many other opportunities for work in New England led to a circular migration pattern after 1900 among the Micmac between the Canadian Maritimes and the New England states. Largely due to this circular migration, the Micmac are Boston's most plentiful Indian group, outnumbering historically local tribes like the Wampanoag. Although the strong ties between New England and Maritime Canada have many sources, geographic proximity is the most obvious and most important connection.

Large-scale migration to New England from the Canadian Maritimes began during the later 1800s and continued steadily until the outbreak of World War II. Changes in American immigration laws in the 1920s coupled with booming western Canadian industry caused migrating Maritimers to move toward the Canadian West. Strong ties between the fishing industries in Nova Scotia and New England likely made passage an easy proposition before mass transit was available. By 1865, regular steamship service ran between Halifax, N.S., and Boston, and less than 15 years later easily accessible rail service to New England could be had from virtually anywhere in the Canadian Maritimes.

Although several developments in the late 19th and early 20th centuries influenced migration patterns, the Maritimes' floundering economy was unable to sustain rapid population growth; New England's economy, meanwhile, was booming. Maine had a flourishing pulp and paper industry, and Massachusetts's textile mills and shoe factories thrived. In the late 1800s, steamers full of young job seekers regularly left Halifax harbor. And by 1921, an estimated 325,000 former Maritimers had emigrated to other parts of the world, about 75 percent of them to the United States. In their headlines and editorials, Maritime newspapers expressed concern over the loss of so many young, able-bodied workers to the United States.

Although all New England states welcomed Maritime Canadians, most settled in the urban areas in and around Boston, with large concentrations in outlying Roxbury, Waltham, and Watertown. Boston's urban occupations offered relatively easy work compared to the arduous life of a farmer or fisher-

man. Stories throughout the Maritimes about wealth and affluence in Boston were so plentiful that Maritimers coined the expression, still used today, that names the contiguous 48 states "The Boston States." Immigrating Maritimers not only benefited from New England's boom but also helped to keep its growth steady. In the early 20th century, a new wave of emigrating Canadians took jobs as laborers, plumbers, and machinists in the burgeoning construction industry. Many Maritimers spoke English, but those landing from some areas, especially Cape Breton, were monoglot Gaelic speakers with minimal knowledge of English. Other Maritimers, especially those from New Brunswick, spoke French. Gaelic remained part of the lives of many Maritimers through regular church services held in Gaelic at Boston's Scotch Presbyterian Church.

One enduring sign of the strong relationship between New England and Nova Scotia is an event in Boston that has occurred each year since 1917. On December 6, 1917, the ships *Imo* and *Mont Blanc* collided in Halifax harbor. When the *Mont Blanc* exploded two hours later with a force of more than 2 kilotons, the blast and ensuing fire killed 2,000 people and decimated much of the city. Although relief came from many places, it came most rapidly and substantially from Boston. In remembrance of that fateful event and to honor Boston's quick response, each year the citizens of Halifax present a special Christmas tree to the people of Boston. The symbolic gesture illustrates that although immigration between Maritime Canada and New England may have slowed in recent years, ties to "The Boston States" remain strong.

Gary Burrill, *Away: Maritimers in Massachusetts, Ontario, and Alberta; An Oral History of Leaving Home* (1992); Charles W. Dunn, *Highland Settler: A Portrait of the Scottish Gael in Cape Breton and Eastern Nova Scotia* (1991); Errol Sharpe, *A People's History of Prince Edward Island* (1976).

Cliff McGann

Cape Verdeans

The first voluntary mass migration of a population of African descent to the United States began in the latter half of the 19th century, when Cape Verdeans left their drought-stricken archipelago, located approximately 375 miles off the west coast of Senegal and first colonized by Portugal in the second half of the 15th century, to make southeastern New England their new home. Although they are little known outside the region, these Afro-Portuguese settlers are of significance as the only major group of Americans to have made the voyage from Africa to the United States on their own initiative.

The ill effects of the dry climate in the Cape

Verde Islands, always plagued by scanty and erratic rainfall, were exacerbated by colonial mismanagement of the land. By the end of the 18th century, islanders were experiencing severe and recurrent drought, famine, and high mortality. Unable to escape overland to more favorable conditions, young Cape Verdeans seized the chance to leave home in search of a better life as crew members aboard the New England whaling ships that were beginning to visit the archipelago's protected harbors, particularly on the island of Brava.

When Yankee seamen began to lose interest in whaling because of decreasing profits in the industry, ship captains looked to the Cape Verde Islands for hands they could recruit for less money than their American counterparts. Subject to impoverished conditions at home, the men of the archipelago were eager for berths on a whaler, no matter what the pay, as a way of escaping constant suffering. Cape Verdean seamen earned a reputation as skilled, disciplined, and able whalers. Nonetheless, they were routinely allotted the lowest rates in the division of profits and were often subject to harsh, discriminatory treatment in the mariners' hierarchy because of their race and ethnicity. This exploitation at sea foreshadowed what Cape Verdeans would face once they began to settle more permanently in New England.

By the late 19th century, with the advent of steamship travel and the decline of whaling and sealing, old sailing vessels had become obsolete and were available for sale at low cost. Some early Cape Verdean migrants seized this opportunity to buy up these old, Essex-built Gloucester fishermen. Pooling their resources, they converted the vessels into packet boats that regularly plied the waters between the Cape Verdes and the ports of New Bedford, Mass., and Providence, R.I., carrying cargo and passengers. Thus, unlike most other immigrant groups, black or white, the Cape Verdeans came to have control over their own means of passage to the United States. Not since the *Mayflower* had the transatlantic voyage to the shores of New England been made so directly.

During this same period cheap sources of labor were needed for expanding textile mills, on the cranberry bogs, and in the maritime-related occupations of southern coastal New England. Increasing numbers of Cape Verdeans, including women and children, were arriving to fulfill the demand, fleeing their land of continual hunger. Contrary to the popular image of local Yankee families picking cranberries on a Sunday afternoon, the cranberry industry began to require a large and intensive agricultural workforce early on, particularly during the autumn harvest. Italians,

Poles, and Finns all provided the necessary labor in turn, but by 1910 Cape Verdean immigrants completely dominated the harvest. Although most remained as seasonal pickers, a few were able to purchase land in the cranberry district and turn their property into productive bogs. Brought up as peasants on the islands, Cape Verdeans' connection to the land has endured. At the same time, with the cranberry industry still viable today, they have been able to achieve economic security and upward mobility. Their children may not choose to remain in the cranberry business, but they typically go on to college and middle-class occupations. This is no small feat in a society where people of color who have worked the land have traditionally done so only as slaves, tenants, or sharecroppers, not as proprietors, and have otherwise been ghettoized into the larger cities.

The Cape Verdean settlers brought with them a distinctive cultural identity with its own customs, folklore, cuisine, music, literature, and language, Cape Verdean Creole. They migrated freely to New England as Portuguese colonials and hence defined themselves in terms of ethnicity. Yet their mixed African and European ancestry caused them to be looked on and treated as an inferior racial group. Although Cape Verdean New Englanders sought recognition as Portuguese Americans, white society, including other Portuguese immigrants in the region, excluded them from their social and religious associations. They suffered similar discrimination in housing and employment. At the same time, Cape Verdeans chose not to identify with New England's black population. Their Catholicism already set them apart from the primarily Protestant African Americans; but, more important, they quickly perceived the adverse effects of racism on the upward mobility of anyone considered nonwhite in the United States.

As a by-product of a society that is organized on the basis of a rigid binary racial structure, official U.S. census or immigration records have been hopelessly deficient where such multiracial populations as the Cape Verdeans are concerned. Entrenched definitions of black and white formed the basis of classification when Cape Verdeans began arriving in New England in large numbers. Routinely grouped under other broader categories, those who looked phenotypically most European or white were listed as Portuguese, whereas others were labeled black Portuguese, African Portuguese, or Atlantic Islanders.

As is the case for other immigrants who cannot be neatly categorized within a dualistic system of racial classification, official population records have not provided accurate demographic data on Cape Verdean New Englanders. Packet ship passenger lists allow us, however, to generate reliable population estimates. Between 1820 and 1975 some 35,000 to 45,000 Cape Verdeans immigrated to the shores of New England. In the nearly 30 years since the islands became an independent nation, approximately 60,000 Cape Verdeans have arrived in the United States, owing to its liberal immigration policy. In 2000, the estimated number of Cape Verdeans and their descendants living in the United States stood at 400,000, slightly more than the total population of the home country itself.

The racial branding that Cape Verdeans were subject to from the moment they arrived in the United States was the beginning of a pattern to which the Afro-Portuguese newcomers would have to adjust repeatedly as they settled in their new homeland. As early as 1924 the leaders of the Cape Verdean community in New Bedford began to prefer the designation Cape Verdean to Portuguese and certainly to black Portuguese. This marked the beginning of the long-standing attempt by various members of the Cape Verdean American community to be recognized by the wider society as a distinct ethnic group with a specific cultural heritage. Not until many years later, on the 1980 federal census forms, was it even possible for Cape Verdean Americans to identify themselves officially as such.

As is characteristic of other mixed-race immigrants to the region, issues of identity among Cape Verdeans are an ever-evolving and complex matter. Identity confusion crops up often in the literature about and by Cape Verdeans. Neither black nor white but sometimes white, sometimes black, sometimes African, Portuguese, and brown (one reporter who took literally the translation of Cape Verde even labeled them "green") this is a population continually in the process of redefining itself. And it is not simply a matter of exchanging one self-definition for another. Economic and social adaptation often has more to do with how people are defined by others than with how they see themselves.

The vast majority of today's Cape Verdean Americans still reside in southeastern New England (87 percent in the 2000 census). Although New Bedford remains the historical hub of the Cape Verdean American community, Brockton, Mass.; metropolitan Boston, especially the Dorchester neighborhood; and Pawtucket, R.I., are drawing much larger numbers of new immigrants. These communities support burgeoning commercial districts of Cape Verdean-owned restaurants and other small businesses as well as social services geared to meeting the needs of the newcomers.

Shortly after gaining independence from Portugal in 1975, the Republic of Cape Verde made a gift to the United States of the historic schooner *Ernestina*, the last Cape Verdean packet boat in existence. The *Ernestina* sailed ceremoniously into its new home port of New Bedford in 1982. In 1986 at the tall ships celebration of the Statue of Liberty's centennial, the vessel took its place at the front of the flotilla, in recognition of its unique status as the only surviving ship in the parade that had actually carried immigrants to the United States.

Briton Cooper Busch, "Cape Verdeans in the American Whaling and Sealing Industry, 1850–1900," *American Neptune* 45 (1985); Marilyn Halter, *Between Race and Ethnicity: Cape Verdean American Immigrants, 1860–1965* (1993); Robert Hayden, *African Americans and Cape Verdean Americans in New Bedford: A History of Achievement* (1993); Maria Luisa Nunes, *A Portuguese Colonial in America, Belmira Nunes Lopes: The Autobiography of a Cape Verdean American* (1982).

Marilyn Halter

Chinese By 2000 there were 115,978 Chinese and Chinese Americans living in New England, with the majority living in Massachusetts (84,392) and most of them concentrated in the Boston area (75,615). Although the Chinese population of New England is small compared with that of other U.S. regions, especially the West Coast and Hawaii, Chinese actually appeared in New England well before they went to California to participate in the Gold Rush of 1848. The reason for their early arrival on the East Coast is directly related to the region's wider history.

During the colonial period there existed a brisk trade between China and British America, focusing primarily on tea and porcelains. The Boston area, especially the port city of Salem, Mass., was a major center of that trade. After the American Revolution trade relations between China and the United States became a major source of revenue for those involved. The first American trade ship, the *Empress of China,* reached China in 1784. On board was a Boston merchant, Major Samuel Shaw, who became the first American consul general to China in 1786. From that point on there was steady contact between the Chinese and sailors, merchants, diplomats, and missionaries from New England. It is now generally acknowledged that trade between China and the United States brought the first Chinese to New England, as Chinese were recruited to serve on American trading vessels and other Chinese came to serve on the household staffs of wealthy New England families.

In addition to commercial trade, American missionary activity in Asia brought Chinese to New England to study in the region's well-

cause of poor health, and Wong Foon graduated from Monson Academy, attended the University of Edinburgh, and returned to China in 1857 as China's first Western-trained physician. Yung Wing remained in New England, however, and became the first Chinese to graduate from an American university, Yale, in 1854. During this period Yung converted to Christianity and became an American citizen (1852). He was convinced that American schooling was the answer to China's sociopolitical problems. On his return to China after graduation, Yung encouraged the Chinese government to send Chinese youths to the United States to get a Western education.

Yung's plans for the Chinese Educational Commission were put into effect in 1872. The mission was to send 30 students to the United States each year for four years. These 120 young people would study in America for 15 years and then go back home to aid in China's modernization. A low-ranking official, Chin Lan Pin, was in charge of their Chinese education, while Yung was responsible for their Western curriculum. Originally housed in Springfield, Mass., the mission soon moved to Hartford, Conn., where it stayed until 1882, when it was recalled because of conflicts over its operation.

While heading the mission, Chin and Yung were also involved in Chinese diplomatic negotiations with Spain and Peru. Their efforts enabled China to put an end to the infamous "coolie trade," conducted by Western merchants, to Cuba and Peru. Afterward Chin and Yung became the first Chinese ministers to the United States, Spain, and Peru. In 1875 a permanent Chinese legation was established in Washington, D.C.

While residing in New England, Yung demonstrated a profound commitment to life in the United States. He became a naturalized citizen and married Mary Louise Kellogg, daughter of a prominent New England family, in 1875. After his wife's death in 1886, Yung raised the couple's two sons and occasionally traveled to China in the service of the Chinese government. Although the U.S. ban on Chinese naturalization cost Yung his American citizenship in 1898, he spent his final years in retirement in Hartford, writing his memoirs and corresponding with friends and family.

The tradition of Chinese attending New England schools continued into the 20th century. One of the best-known graduates of Wellesley College is Soong Mei-ling. Soong, daughter of a prominent and wealthy Chinese entrepreneur, graduated from Wellesley in 1916 and later married Chiang Kai-shek, who eventually became president of the Republic of China. Better known as Madame Chiang Kai-shek, she toured the United States in 1943

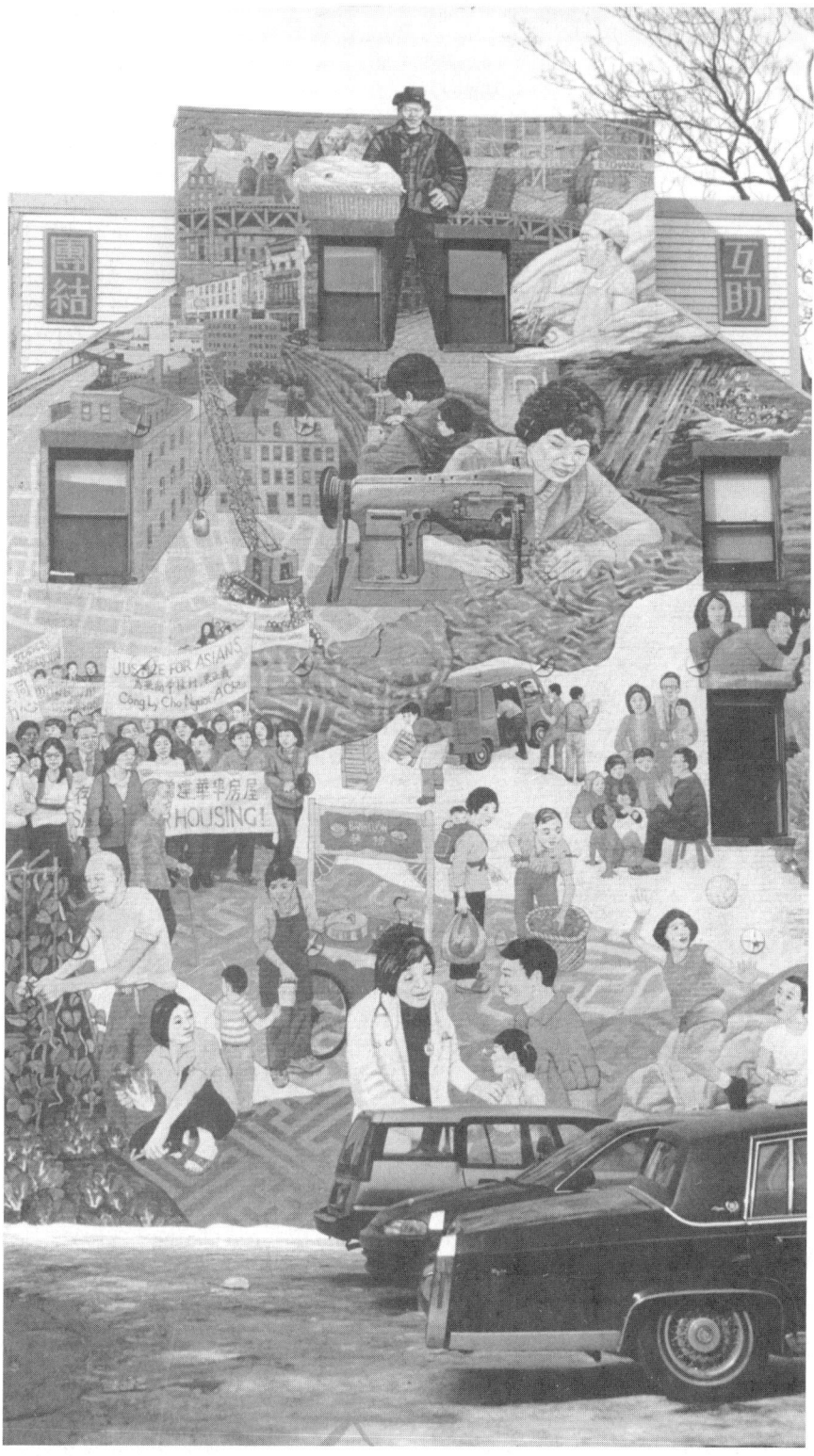

History of Chinatown mural on Asian American Resource Workshop building, Boston, 1993

known educational institutions. One of the most famous to do so was Yung Wing, a young Chinese student at missionary schools in Macao and Hong Kong. In 1846 Yung and two other Chinese students, Wong Shing and

Wong Foon, accompanied the Reverend Samuel Brown, a graduate of Yale University in 1832, to New England, where they attended the Monson Academy in Massachusetts. Wong Shing returned to China in 1849 be-to gather support for China's war effort against the Japanese.

In more recent decades New England colleges and universities have perhaps become even more important to the fate of China. A great number of Chinese nationals have attended institutions such as MIT, Harvard, and Yale, with hopes of improving the quality of life in their homeland. Chinese students who had spent time in America were among the most active participants in China's student-inspired democracy movement during the 1980s and 1990s.

The Chinese in New England have also played important roles in American labor history. In 1870 about 75 Chinese workers, mostly under the age of 18, were recruited by Calvin T. Sampson to break a strike in his shoe factory in North Adams, Mass., led by the Secret Order of the Knights of Saint Crispin. Those workers signed three-year contracts and lived in quarters connected to Sampson's shoe factory. For this brief period, the tiny town of North Adams had one of the largest Chinese populations east of the Mississippi River. Although little is known of the everyday lives of the Chinese who were brought to North Adams, they may have been a more visible element in the community than is generally believed.

Newspaper and magazine accounts reveal that many of them attended local churches and Sunday schools, where they took English lessons. A few developed relationships with their teachers, at least one of which led to marriage, and one Chinese worker was adopted by a North Adams family. Another member of the group is known to have married a local woman and opened a store on Main Street in North Adams. At least two of the immigrants purchased burial plots in North Adams, an indication that they probably did not expect to return to China.

Records on the Chinese in North Adams are scarce after 1873. Some workers likely stayed in the area for a while, though most left for other cities, such as Boston. The Chinese left no obvious marks of their stay in North Adams, but their experience there is a noteworthy chapter in the history of both American labor and Chinese immigration to New England.

Boston Chinatown is the site of one of the most infamous police raids on an American immigrant community. In 1903, in the wake of a murder there, the Boston police and the U.S. Immigration Bureau conducted a raid on the Chinese enclave in search of illegal immigrants. Although 234 Chinese were arrested, only 50 were found to be in the country illegally. This harassment of Boston's Chinese residents was one of a number of events that prompted a boycott of American goods in China in 1905. One of the most interesting facts to emerge from the raid, however, was evidence of a number of marriages between Chinese males and Irish American women. These marriages and other examples of cooperation between Chinese, white ethnics, and American blacks indicate that, contrary to the strict segregation typical of Chinatowns on the West Coast, the Chinese immigrant and Chinese American population in New England, though small, has perhaps been integrated into the larger society to a greater degree than elsewhere.

Since the end of World War II, and especially after the passage of the Immigration Act of 1965, the Chinese population of New England has increased. The end of the war brought an end to the federal legislation prohibiting most Chinese immigration, especially that of women. And the Immigration Act of 1965 provided for a number of preferences that favored family reunification. As a result, the Chinese American birthrate has risen, and the number of new immigrants settling in the region has steadily increased. Although many Chinese newcomers are of the professional class, many others are restricted to low-paying jobs with little opportunity for social mobility. Among newer immigrants, the lack of English-language proficiency can pose a major obstacle to economic advancement. Non-English-speaking Chinese New Englanders often face limited employment opportunities, the effects of which can be poverty, poor housing, inadequate health care, disaffected youth, and gang violence. These issues are not unique to Chinese immigrant and Chinese American communities, however; they are part of larger social dilemmas confronting American society. Chinese New Englanders have contributed to efforts to solve these problems by forming organizations to improve conditions within their own communities and by joining broader-based efforts to meet the challenges of modern American life.

Doris C. J. Chu, *Chinese in Massachusetts: Their Experiences and Contributions* (1987); Thomas E. La Fargue, *China's First 100: Educational Mission Students in the United States, 1872–1881* (1987 [1942]); Y. C. Wang, *Chinese Intellectuals and the West, 1872–1949* (1966); Yung Wing, *My Life in China and America* (1909).

K. Scott Wong

Dominicans   Large-scale out-migration from the Dominican Republic, a Caribbean nation occupying two-thirds of the island of Hispaniola, is relatively recent, dating back only to the early 1960s. The 2000 census reported 631,897 Dominicans in the United States aged 16 and older; unofficial counts put that figure somewhere between 900,000 and 1.1 million. An estimated 10 to 15 percent of the Dominican Republic's population is said to live in the United States. Though most early migrants left the island for political reasons, primarily economic motives have driven migration since the early 1980s. Most migrants settle in New York. In 1990, 70 percent of all persons of Dominican ancestry in the United States resided in New York State, 65 percent of them in New York City.

In the last two decades of the 20th century, an increasing number of Dominicans were nonetheless settling in New England. In fact, Latinos are the fastest-growing minority in the region, and Dominicans are the fastest-growing Latino immigrant group. The majority of Dominican New Englanders live in Massachusetts (30,177), with a large population residing in Boston (7,938). Many of these individuals come from Baní, a city of approximately 100,000 located 40 miles from the Dominican capital, Santo Domingo. There are also Dominican communities in smaller Massachusetts cities, such as Lawrence, Lynn, and Haverhill, as well as concentrations in New Hampshire, Rhode Island, and Maine.

Studies of Dominican migrants to the United States indicate a heterogeneous community profile. Whereas early migrants, arriving during the 1960s and 1970s, came primarily from the middle sectors of Dominican society, during the 1980s and 1990s many less skilled workers and highly skilled professionals also began arriving. Nonetheless, the poorest segment of the Dominican population is still underrepresented.

In eastern Massachusetts, where most Dominicans living in the state reside, the 2000 census reported slightly more women than men (53 percent). The overwhelming majority were foreign born (67 percent), though 27 percent had become naturalized U.S. citizens. Forty-six percent came during the 1990s. Twenty-six percent had completed only grade school, 24 percent had completed high school, and another 14 percent had some college. Thirty-two percent reported speaking English "not well" or "not at all." When asked about their racial identity, 23 percent classified themselves as white, 8 percent classified themselves as black, and 58 percent chose the "Other" race category, signaling their identification with a third, Hispanic race option.

Limited education and English-language skills put Dominicans at a disadvantage in an economy with declining numbers of low-skilled manufacturing jobs and increasing growth in high-tech industries, construction, and business services. In 2000, just over 30 percent of Dominicans were living below the poverty line. Most found jobs in production, transportation, and material moving occupations (27 percent) or the service sector (27 percent). Still, many of the Latino small-business owners in Boston are Dominicans. Indicating both the community's passionate interest in politics and the gains that Latinos have made in the region, seven Dominicans ran for local or statewide political office in Lawrence, Mass., in the November 1999 elections, and three of them won.

The Dominican community is known for its transnational character. Many migrants maintain strong ties to their communities of origin. The flow of people, money, goods, and social remittances back and forth between New England and the island is steady. The three main Dominican political parties have organizations in the region. The archdiocese of Boston coordinates with the Dominican church hierarchy. Community-development organizations with chapters in Boston and Baní have arisen as well. There is some evidence that these ties persist among the second generation.

Emelio Betances and Hobart A. Spalding, Jr., eds., *The Dominican Republic Today: Realities and Perspectives; Essays in English and Spanish* (1996); P. Graham, "Imagining the Nation and Defining the District: Dominican Migration and Transnational Politics," in *Caribbean Circuits: New Directions in the Study of Caribbean Migration,* ed. Patricia Pessar (1997); Patricia Pessar, *A Visa for a Dream: Dominicans in the United States* (1996); Frank Moya Pons, *The Dominican Republic: A National History* (1995).

Peggy Levitt

Douglass, Frederick (ca. 1818–95) Abo-

litionist orator, writer, and newspaper editor. Although Frederick Douglass started his life as a slave in a remote cabin along the Tuckahoe Creek on Maryland's Eastern Shore, he transformed himself into a New Englander on the wharves of Baltimore, Md. Born Frederick Augustus Bailey, he spent his early years in the home of his remarkable grandmother Betsy Bailey, who was permitted by their master to raise her many children and grandchildren. When Frederick was eight, his owner sent him to live with Hugh Auld, a ship's carpenter whose home was behind the wharves of Baltimore's busy harbor. As a slave child Frederick could not attend school, but with help from Auld's wife, Sophia, he taught himself to read. From white playmates he heard of the *Columbian Orator,* a book of excerpts of speeches on freedom from which schoolboys were taught republican virtues. Frederick bought a copy and, behind the warehouses, declaimed the speeches and mastered the diction with which later, in New England, he would match the eloquence of the nation's greatest orators.

Frederick grew into a strong teenager, and the Aulds sent him back to the Eastern Shore

Lithograph of Frederick Douglass, ca. 1890

to work as a field hand. There he taught other slaves to read and persuaded them to join him in a plot to escape. The boy was caught, however, and returned by his owner to Baltimore, where he learned the skilled trade of caulking boats. Traveling dressed as a seaman, with false papers, he made good his escape. In New York City he was reunited with Anna Murray, a free black woman whom he had courted in Baltimore. The two were married and journeyed to New Bedford, Mass., a prosperous Quaker city where fugitive slaves were relatively safe and could find jobs. Once there he took the name he made famous, Frederick Douglass.

Douglass might have lived an obscure life if he had not heard William Lloyd Garrison deliver a fiery antislavery speech. Douglass soon raised his voice in the same cause. After his first great public speech at the 1841 annual meeting of the New England Anti-Slavery Society on Nantucket, he was sent out as an agent of the society. To be nearer Boston, Douglass moved with his family to Lynn, Mass. Traveling widely in New England and westward, he gave powerful speeches describing, from his own experiences, the horrors of slavery. He published these stories in the *Narrative of the Life of Frederick Douglass, an American Slave* (1845).

In 1847, after an extended trip to the British Isles during which he spoke to large crowds of antislavery proponents, he moved his family to Rochester, N.Y. There he edited the first of a series of antislavery newspapers, the *North Star* (later *Frederick Douglass's Paper*), and con-

tinued intensive lecture tours across the Northern states. Douglass abandoned Garrison's sole reliance on moral suasion as the way to combat slavery and embraced any form of attack on the institution, including political action. Though once close to the antislavery militant John Brown, Douglass did not abet Brown's 1859 raid on Harper's Ferry, an attempt to obtain arms that would be used to incite a slave revolt. A warrant was nonetheless issued for his arrest in connection with that attack. Douglass left Rochester for Canada and then England, returning to Rochester in 1860.

When the Civil War began, Douglass vigorously argued that the aim of the war should be the end of slavery and that black men should be allowed to fight for their freedom. After President Abraham Lincoln signed the Emancipation Proclamation on January 1, 1863, Douglass issued his famous injunction "Men of Color, to Arms!" and helped recruit African American soldiers for the famous 54th Massachusetts Regiment, in which his son Lewis served as sergeant major.

Always a champion of full civil rights for former slaves North and South, Douglass put too much faith after the war in gaining the vote for the freed people of the South. He was convinced that once they were full voting citizens, they could protect themselves. He failed to recognize the power of the often violent drive to restore white supremacy and underestimated the immensely debilitating problem of poverty that freed slaves faced.

In 1855 Douglass published *My Bondage and My Freedom,* a revision and expansion of his 1845 autobiography. In 1881 he brought the story up to date with the *Life and Times of Frederick Douglass.* In 1882 Anna Murray Douglass died, and in 1884 Frederick Douglass married Helen Pitts, a white woman. With great dignity the couple withstood criticism of their interracial marriage from both the black and white communities. Throughout the 1880s, in the face of increasing setbacks for African Americans, Douglass continued to speak out on behalf of his people's civil rights. Never accorded a government post commensurate with his talents, Douglass was finally appointed minister to Haiti in 1889. Having fended off expansionists eager to annex the republic, he resigned in 1891. His last great speech, "Lessons of the Hour" in 1894, attacked lynching as an evil means of social control. Douglass died a year later at his home in Washington, D.C., Cedar Hill, which is now a historic site visited yearly by thousands of admirers.

John W. Blassingame, ed., *The Frederick Douglass Papers, Series One: Speeches, Debates, and Interviews,* 5 vols. (1979–92), *Series Two: Autobiographical Writings,* 2 vols. to date (1999–); David W. Blight, *Frederick Douglass' Civil War: Keeping Faith in Jubilee* (1989);

Waldo E. Martin, *The Mind of Frederick Douglass* (1984); William S. McFeely, *Frederick Douglass* (1991).

William S. McFeely

Du Bois, W. E. B. (1868–1963)

Civil rights activist. William Edward Burghardt Du Bois, a prominent African American scholar and civil rights activist, was one of the most influential black leaders of his generation. Du Bois was born in 1868 and raised in the small town of Great Barrington, Mass. The son of Alfred Du Bois and Mary Burghardt, young William played and attended school with his predominantly white peers. Although his family was poor, Du Bois did not feel that he faced color barriers in elementary school, because he was an excellent student. At Great Barrington High School, he was the only black student in his class and the only person to attend college. He graduated in 1884 as the class valedictorian.

Du Bois attended Fisk University in Tennessee, where he became increasingly aware of political and social events of the time. He began writing persuasive editorials about the problems facing African Americans for the campus newspaper, of which he became the editor. Du Bois graduated from Fisk in 1888, again the class valedictorian, then accepted a scholarship to Harvard University. Studying under such luminaries as William James and George Santayana, Du Bois became the first African American to earn a Harvard doctorate, as a pioneer in the field of sociology. His dissertation, "The Suppression of the African Slave Trade," was published in 1896. Du Bois married Nina Gomer the same year. He then went on to teach history and economics at Atlanta University while conducting research for the school's program on the "Negro problem." His classic study, *The Souls of Black Folk*, came out in 1903.

Du Bois was a leader in the Niagara Movement, which demanded full civil rights for all blacks. He was particularly vocal in his opposition to Booker T. Washington, the African American spokesman for the notion that the races should be "separate but equal" and the founder of the Tuskegee Institute in Alabama. Du Bois regarded Washington as too conciliatory toward whites. A gifted orator, he gave speeches throughout the country denouncing Washington and other blacks who he thought were compromising too much with the whites.

Du Bois was a founding member of the National Association for the Advancement of Colored People (NAACP) in 1909 and served as an editor of its magazine, *Crisis*, for 25 years. The NAACP sought to empower African Americans through education, legal action, and organization. In December 1918 the NAACP sent Du Bois to the Versailles Peace Conference in France, in the hopes that he would have a chance to voice the concerns of African Americans to a larger audience. Du Bois was disappointed, however, with the apathetic response of major world powers to his pleas. He organized a Pan African Congress in Paris in 1919 and continued to lead similar events to highlight the status of black men in the world.

During his lifetime Du Bois published three volumes of autobiography: *Darkwater* (1920), *Dusk of Dawn* (1940), and *The Autobiography of W. E. B. Du Bois* (1968). His descriptions of his New England childhood present a complex mix of Edenic mythology and racial consciousness. Emphasizing his Negro, French, and Dutch but not Anglo-Saxon genealogical heritage, Du Bois carefully distances himself in his writings from white "Yankees," even as he embraces New England educational values. Among his other books are *Black Reconstruction* (1935) and *Black Folk, Then and Now* (1939).

After his wife's death in 1950, Du Bois married Shirley Graham. He died 13 years later in Accra, Ghana, while editing *The Encyclopedia Africana*.

Great Barrington, Mass., maintains historic markers at the church Du Bois attended, the location of his family farm, and the gravestone of his first wife and son. The site of the homestead Du Bois inhabited in his boyhood is now a National Historic Landmark.

David Levering Lewis, *W. E. B. Du Bois: Biography of a Race, 1868–1919* (1993); David Levering Lewis, ed., *W. E. B. Du Bois: A Reader* (1995); Jack B. Moore, *W. E. B. Du Bois* (1981); Arnold Rampersad, *The Art and Imagination of W. E. B. Du Bois* (1976).

Robin O'Sullivan

Eldridge, Elleanor (1785–1862)

Businesswoman. Elleanor Eldridge was born to former slaves in Warwick, R.I., in 1785. Her paternal grandfather was African born and her maternal grandmother was a Narragansett Indian. Elleanor's father, Robin, was freed after serving in Rhode Island's "black regiment" during the Revolutionary War, and the Eldridge family was considered part of the local black elite. Her brother George was elected African governor of Warwick from 1801 to 1804, following the custom of the New England slave community to elect local leaders to conduct rituals, settle disputes, and mediate relations with white civil authorities. Eldridge, then a teenager, acted as his consort. Throughout her life and personal struggles, Eldridge showed how free women of color could survive economically in a New England society unwilling to grant or recognize their civil rights.

At age 10, Eldridge was sent by her father to work for white families and became an accomplished weaver and dairywoman. Later she became a house painter and worked as a domestic servant in the cold months. She borrowed money and spent her meager savings to invest in real estate, buying a home in Providence. Eldridge used the legal system and the help of benevolent white women to protect her family and fight her creditors, struggles that were presented to her on numerous occasions throughout her life.

Her troubles began in 1831. While Eldridge was visiting relatives in Massachusetts, a rumor reached Providence that she had died. In response to the news, the mortgage holder started to sell one of her properties. She returned in time to cancel the sale, promising to continue paying the interest on the debt and to repay the principal when she could. Meanwhile, her brother was accused of stabbing a man. Eldridge hired a carriage and drove to the courthouse, posting his $500 bail. She acted as his lawyer, and he was acquitted for lack of evidence.

Soon after, Eldridge went to Connecticut as a nursemaid, since cholera had driven away many of her Providence customers. She was unable to repay her mortgage, and in her absence, her property was sold. Eldridge sued the mortgage owner for "trespass and ejectment," and accused the sheriff of selling the property without proper advertising. To support her claim, she hired private detectives, who failed to find evidence that the sale had been properly advertised. She sued the sheriff for perjury, but he swore in a "strangely agitated" way that he had conducted the sale correctly. The case was eventually settled out of court in 1837, and although Eldridge regained her property, she remained seriously in debt.

A group of white, middle-class women led by Frances Whipple Greene McDougall decided to help Eldridge by writing and selling her biography, *Memoirs of Elleanor Eldridge* (1838). The first biography of a free black woman, the memoirs were intended to illustrate the intersections of race, class, and gender in Jacksonian America. Ostensibly inspired by sisterhood, McDougall actually presented Eldridge as an object lesson to "the colored population . . . of industry and untiring perseverance." The biography is also filled with feminist indignation. McDougall wrote: "The subject of this wrong, or rather this accumulation of wrongs, was a woman, and therefore weak,—a *colored woman*—and therefore contemptible. No *man* would have been treated so; and if a *white woman* had ever been the subject of such wrongs, the whole town, nay the whole country, would have been indignant: and the actors would have been held up to the contempt they deserve!"

Eldridge traveled from Boston to Philadelphia to sell her biography, which helped pay her remaining debts. By the late 1840s Eldridge had amassed more property and was among the wealthiest "people of color" in Providence. She never married and died of consumption in Providence at age 76.

Jane Lancaster, "Encouraging Faithful Domestic Servants: Race, Deviance and Social Control in Providence," *Rhode Island History* 51, no. 3 (1993); Bert Loewenberg and Ruth Bogin, eds., *Black Women in American Life* (1976); Rayford W. Logan, "Eldridge, Elleanor," in *Dictionary of American Negro Biography*, ed. Rayford W. Logan and Michael R. Winston (1982); Sandra G. Shannon, "Elleanor Eldridge," in *Notable Black American Women*, ed. Jessie Carney Smith (1992).

Jane Lancaster

English The national origin of New England's settler population was overwhelmingly English between 1620 and about 1840. Though the region's character ceased to be essentially English soon thereafter, and its destiny now probably lies with other ethnic groups, the first five or six generations of English settlers and their descendants exercised such a dominant influence on the nation's constitutional, intellectual, and religious development that to a large degree the United States is an outgrowth of the cultural views of these people.

In 1690 about 90 percent of all Europeans in what would become the 13 colonies were of English birth or descent. In the first federal census (1790) about 72 percent of whites in the six states that now constitute New England were identified as having English surnames, and a further 14 percent were of "unassigned" origin. For the country these figures were 61 percent and 6.6 percent, respectively.

New England families before the Revolution had an average of six to 10 children and as a group enjoyed the longest life expectancy in Western society. By the mid-19th century a great many of their offspring had helped settle upper New York and the Old Northwest, to be replaced back home increasingly by non-English immigrants. As industrialization set in after 1865, the region's pull revived; by 1890 one in every six English-born Americans, or about 134,000, lived in the region—the highest figure ever. In Fall River, Lawrence, and New Bedford, Mass., and Providence and Pawtucket, R.I., they made up a quarter of all immigrants: 9 to 15 percent of these towns' populations. Though immigration restrictions after 1920 favored the English among others, they did not fill their quotas. Resurgence came with the arrival of 100,000 or so war brides—British wives of American soldiers stationed in Britain during World War II—an unknown number of whom settled in New England. This was the only instance of women outnumbering men among English immigrants. During the 1960s the postwar "brain drain" from Europe peaked when almost half Britain's science and engineering graduates left each year for the United States, many actively recruited by American firms.

In 2000, when the federal census for the third time asked respondents to state their own ethnicity (single or multiple), 10.9 percent of the 225 million Americans who responded (out of 281 million in all) chose "English," a group outnumbered by "German" and "Irish." An additional 1.1 million citizens claimed to be "British," and the same number placed themselves in other categories that may signify partial or entire English ethnicity. These categories were of decreasing value for sorting out actual national origins: 163 million Americans gave a single ancestry, which if true would mean that no ethnic intermarriage had occurred in about a century. Demographers have estimated German and English origins to be roughly equal in the nation's white population, with each accounting for roughly 35 percent of the total. That said, 13 percent of New Englanders labeled themselves "English," with another 1.2 percent choosing "British" or other possibly intersecting terms. These include the categories Canadian and Australian but not Welsh, European, Northern European, or Celtic, which nevertheless may also signify partial or entire English heritage. More verifiably, since 1961 about 10 percent of European immigrants to the United States have come from the United Kingdom. Though less than 3 percent of all immigrants, they are Europe's largest immigrant group—about 800,000 as of 2000—no New England city makes the top 10 of their intended destinations. Startlingly, between 1990 and 2000 the number of people claiming English ancestry fell 25 percent, with comparable declines for other European ancestries, even while those calling themselves Europeans more than tripled. Yet "English" remained the primary ethnic group claimed in Maine and Vermont.

Attraction to and repulsion from English ways have alternated over the decades in the New Englander's outlook. The Pilgrims of Plymouth hoped to found a separate Church of England cleansed of all pomp and ornament. At Massachusetts Bay the dual nature of the early settlers' motivations is seen in the New England Company's purpose (1628): "the propagation of the Gospel of Jesus Christ and the particular good of the several adventurers." Only after many years was the hope silently abandoned that the Church of England would ever model itself on New World congregationalism. Joannah Sill, an early Puritan settler, rued her physical and moral hardship; she "found no presence of God" as a result. During the American Revolution, one estimate pegged a third of the colonists as pro-British, a third as pro-independence, and a third as neutral. Indeed, 100,000 loyalists—one of every 25 colonists—fled to Canada to remain subjects of King George, though the loyalists tended to have arrived since 1763 and to have lived south of New England. A half century later New Hampshire native Daniel Webster could be publicly Anglophilic, taking pride in his father's having fought for the British against the French in Canada in 1759; and while secretary of state in the 1840s, Webster hung portraits of Queen Victoria, the duke of Wellington, and Prime Minister Lord Melbourne in the vestibule of his mansion in Washington, D.C. He nevertheless negotiated Maine's border with the British, employing a modicum of deception to win thousands of acres for the state. Nathaniel Hawthorne, while serving as U.S. consul in Liverpool in the 1850s, was more even-minded. He wrote of England, "It is our forefathers' land, our land, [and] I will not give up such a precious inheritance," at the same time observing that "the dirt of a poverty-stricken English street is a monstrosity unknown on our side of the Atlantic."

But English inventiveness and thrift were carried to New England, soon producing great industrial empires—and dirty streets. It is telling that an Englishman built the first New World watch, in Connecticut in 1773, and that another, Samuel Slater, built the first American textile mill, in Rhode Island in 1793, from plans memorized in England. It is more broadly significant that shipbuilding, beginning in 1631, could so well serve raw-material exports and then industrial exports beginning in Slater's time; many English continued to share with the mother country a maritime way of life. Taking an even broader view, some evidence suggests that U.S. capitalism was born in the stony soil of inland New England in the 1770s: agricultural production on the mostly small farms rose by a factor of two and a half in 30 years, and market integration began with the convergence of prices for labor and goods across the region. With surpluses finally at hand, exports to elsewhere in the British imperial world took off, for cash or credit and no longer for barter.

In a related trend, protection for New England–based manufacturers and shippers since 1790 has most often been directed against British goods—recompense perhaps for wrongs inflicted in earlier days. The War of 1812 ushered in three decades of intense anti-British animosity centering on trade, and in the Civil War the British need for cotton from the South nearly led the country to make war on the Union, souring relations for a decade.

British ownership of a disproportionate share of U.S. land, mines, factories, and railroads—as well as New Englanders' ownership of parts of the American West—has irritated many Americans, who at times saw "old American" finance in league with the former overlord; this animosity was displaced in the United States only around 1975 by wariness of Arab or Japanese influence.

Before the Revolution some New Englanders admired the British model of government for its representational nature, while others condemned its corruptibility and entrenched hierarchies. Indeed, though nationally homogeneous, English New Englanders were not culturally so, people from south and east England having mixed their folkways and beliefs with those from the north and west country, who tended to be more royalist. Most, however, considered Englishness and a free mode of government to be synonymous, and because they also viewed the nomadic French hunters and trappers across the mountains as less civilized than the family-minded, agricultural English, they felt qualified to improve, perhaps even perfect, their model of government. By the mid-18th century, the goal was classical republican life in North America. When Revolution stirred in the 1760s, New Englanders had the highest standard of living on average in the English-speaking world and so felt perhaps most acutely of all colonists their exclusion from direct political power in London. Anti-British sentiment was concentrated in the region, as is best shown in the person of Samuel Adams, "father of the Revolution," whose master's thesis at Harvard College in 1743 propounded the right of revolution. It seems that fear of attack by the French or the Indians or both had accounted for much of the attachment to Britain's rule; once this fear had been removed in 1763 by Anglo-American arms, the colonists felt less of a need for London's guardianship. Yet John Adams, cousin of Samuel, was unsure whether America would craft a constitution as well balanced as England's, and he later admitted to Thomas Jefferson that he had read the works of Lord Bolingbroke—in which social hierarchies are assumed—five times through.

More proximately, rejection of formal ties to the Crown came about to preserve the inborn and inalienable rights the colonists felt they held as English subjects. The *Lawes and Libertyes of Massachusetts* (1648) contained guarantees, soon copied in Connecticut, of due process of law. In 1791 these were embodied in the U.S. Bill of Rights; and, to cite another example, the Eighth Amendment to the Constitution, proscribing excessive bail and cruel and unusual punishment, is taken nearly verbatim from the English Bill of Rights of 1689. The concept of sending two senators from each state to the U.S. Congress mimics the 13th-century practice of sending two knights from every shire to meet the king in Parliament. Small shires, and small U.S. states, prize this system.

It is a paradox that a generation or two after 1776 the more conservative constitutional feeling coalesced around New England Federalists, who wanted close ties to Britain rather than France and briefly threatened to secede from the union in 1814 in order to preserve their influence in the Senate against Democrats from the new states. In the early Federal period, however, English newcomers, fewer though they were, included many artisans sympathetic to the French Revolution, and it is from this point that the region's sympathies began to settle firmly on republicanism.

With their connections to British shipping and commercial interests, the English profited from the slave trade, then through their church and other connections they—especially the Quakers—led the abolitionist movement, forming the first international pressure group. Methodist and Episcopal (Anglican) missionaries worked both sides of the ocean, and Mormonism returned the favor by founding a denomination that then reached back to England. Not so coordinated but nonetheless homogeneous was the fervid anti-Catholicism of 1850s England and New England. As the Irish poured out of Ireland, New England writers among others began using all three (English) names—Henry Wadsworth Longfellow, for one. Of course, no group puts up a uniform front indefinitely: the long history of denominational schisms and rivalries, begun with Anne Hutchinson's case in 1637, reveals an oft-repeated difficulty of people drawing away from their culture of origin. In another realm English woolen workers in Sanford, Maine, as in many towns, founded a short-lived political club in 1886 to influence city government and a cooperative to benefit themselves. This kind of ethnic-based social action was more rare among the English in industrial America than among other groups, though employers feared English workers for a time as more likely to unionize than others.

That New England, more so than other regions, was first settled mostly by families of middling economic circumstances and by people with skills is a crucial factor in American history. Overall the English have proved socially mobile. A society with roughly equal numbers of women and men was stable and readily transferable to other locations. Whether religious, economic, or political, the settlers' sense of mission drove them to educate themselves and to conquer. America soon transformed itself from republic to empire.

The enduring cultural traits of the English, even if not limited to those of that ethnic stock, resound today in the region's life. About a quarter of U.S. private schools, and even more boarding schools, are located in the region, continuing an old English custom not limited to the very wealthiest families. The Episcopal Church is twice as strong in New England on a per capita basis as it is nationally, most of all in Rhode Island and Vermont. Some other denominations with English roots are also disproportionately strong in New England, particularly the many current divisions of Congregationalism (most descended from the Puritan churches) and Unitarianism. Others, however, such as Methodism, have few adherents here, and in no denomination do adherents make up more than a small percentage of the region's population. If eaters of fish and drinkers of tea or ale are unusually numerous among New Englanders, it is certainly not because all are of British descent. Certain English traditions suffuse American culture without really claiming it. Still, if New Englanders do not collectively share any one foreign culture today and are competing to assert the traditions of other nations, languages, and creeds, the cultural descendants of the English have such a significant lead that they will not give it up soon, or willingly.

Bernard Bailyn, *The Peopling of British North America* (1986); Rowland Berthoff, *British Immigrants in Industrial America, 1790–1950* (1953); James M. Cornelius, *The English Americans* (1990); William Cronon, *Changes in the Land: Indians, Colonists, and the Ecology of New England* (1983); Charlotte Erickson, "English," in *Harvard Encyclopedia of American Ethnic Groups*, ed. Stephan Thernstrom (1980); David Hackett Fischer, *Albion's Seed: Four British Folkways in America* (1989); Winifred Barr Rothenberg, *From Market-Places to a Market Economy: The Transformation of Rural Massachusetts, 1750–1850* (1992).

James M. Cornelius

Farrakhan, Louis

Farrakhan, Louis (1933–) Black nationalist leader. Louis Farrakhan, controversial head of the Nation of Islam, was born Louis Eugene Walcott in New York City but grew up in the Boston suburb of Roxbury, Mass., already a site of racial tension during his youth. A dutiful Episcopalian, Louis distinguished himself as a first-rate student, a competitive athlete, and a promising classical violinist (at age 16 he performed on the *Ted Mack's Amateur Hour*). After attending the prestigious Boston Latin School, he went south to college in Winston-Salem, N.C., in 1950.

Taking the stage name "the Charmer," Louis left college to become a calypso singer. At the age of 22, after hearing a speech by Malcolm X, he converted to the Nation of Islam, a black nationalist organization founded

Minister Louis Farrakhan addressing an audience of women, Dorchester, Mass., 1994

by Wallace D. Fard (Fard Muhammad) whose members are sometimes known as the Black Muslims. He then abandoned calypso singing to become Louis X, Malcolm's protégé. Returning to Boston, he took over as minister of the fledgling Mosque No. 11.

A charismatic native son, Louis X swelled the ranks of temple membership. Making his way up the organizational ladder, he put his artistic abilities to work writing and recording the Black Muslim theme song, "A White Man's Heaven Is a Black Man's Hell." Louis also wrote two plays for the Nation of Islam, *Orgena* ("a Negro" spelled backward) and *The Trial,* both indictments of white America. The 1959 CBS television documentary that alarmingly brought Black Muslims to national attention, *The Hate That Hate Produced,* featured excerpts from *The Trial.*

After Malcolm X was assassinated in 1965, Louis X replaced him as the Nation of Islam's national spokesperson and as minister of New York's prestigious Harlem mosque, Temple No. 7. Elijah Muhammad, the leader of the Nation of Islam, then gave Louis the surname Farrakhan. When Elijah Muhammad died in 1975, his son Wallace Muhammad took over as leader of the Nation of Islam. Under Wallace, in a move toward orthodox Islam, the organization became the World Community of Islam in the West (WCIW). Contesting that change, Farrakhan seceded from the WCIW to revive the Nation of Islam in 1977.

Farrakhan is considered by many to be the most problematic of all African American leaders. Critics call him a racist demagogue and an anti-Semite. Certain scholars have raised questions that implicate Farrakhan in the murder of Malcolm X. Farrakhan nonetheless has retained a loyal constituency. He proved his wide-based influence on October 16, 1995, when he gave the keynote address at the Million Man March in Washington, D.C., the largest mass demonstration in U.S. history. In the aftermath of the march, Farrakhan went abroad to embrace Libyan president Moammar Khadafy and Iraqi president Saddam Hussein, which heightened the controversy surrounding him.

In early 2000, however, following a bout with prostate cancer, Farrakhan appeared to make tentative steps toward reconciling his organization with traditional Islam, expressing a desire to diversify the Nation of Islam and abandon the inflammatory rhetoric for which he had been known in the past.

Florence Hamlish Levinsohn, *Looking for Farrakhan* (1997); Arthur J. Magida, *Prophet of Rage: A Life of Louis Farrakhan and His Nation* (1996); Lawrence H. Mamiya, "Minister Louis Farrakhan and the Final Call: Schism in the Muslim Movement," in *The Muslim Community in North America,* ed. Earle H. Waugh, Baha Abu-Laban, and Regula B. Qureshi (1983).

Josiah Ulysses Young III

54th Massachusetts Regiment As the North's first African American regiment during the Civil War, the Massachusetts 54th Infantry contributed to New England's self-image as the vanguard of abolitionism. The heroism of the regiment on the battlefield also bolstered blacks' claim to the rights and responsibilities of citizenship. The 54th, along with its sister regiment, the Massachusetts 55th, symbolized the expansion of the war's purpose to include not only preserving the union but also ending slavery.

Once Abraham Lincoln's Emancipation Proclamation had authorized the enlistment of black soldiers in January 1863, Massachusetts governor John A. Andrew ordered the mustering of 1,000 volunteers. Virtually all were free blacks from the North, including two sons of the prominent abolitionist Frederick Douglass. Colonel Robert Gould Shaw, scion of an eminent white abolitionist family in Boston, was the regiment's first commander. The U.S. government initially allowed only white officers in so-called colored units. After persistent lobbying by Governor Andrew and his allies, the War Department promoted the 54th's black sergeant Stephen A. Swails to second lieutenant in January 1865. The 54th also had to fight for equal pay; the War Department paid white privates $13 per month, while black privates received only $10. The 54th refused any amount of compensation that was lower than what white soldiers earned, compelling Congress to equalize pay in June 1864.

The 54th's famous assault on Battery Wagner, a key Confederate fortress defending the harbor at Charleston, S.C., established the regiment's legendary martial prowess. On July 11, 1863, the 54th stormed the fort's parapet; Sergeant William H. Carney of New Bedford grabbed the national flag from the dying standard-bearer and planted it on the Confederate rampart. But the 54th was then driven back. Despite wounds to his chest, arm, and legs, Carney safeguarded the flag in retreat, which earned him the first Medal of Honor ever awarded to an African American. The flag he saved now hangs in the Massachusetts Hall of Flags. When this courageous though ill-conceived assault ended, 272 of the 54th's 600 men had been killed, wounded, or captured; among the dead was Colonel Shaw. This engagement and others like it persuaded many skeptical Americans that blacks fought with courage and skill equal to that of their white counterparts.

Late-19th-century Victorian New England granted the 54th a place in the region's cultural pantheon. The *New Englander and Yale Review* of 1889 contained an article by Joseph E. Roy entitled "Our Indebtedness to the Negro for Their Conduct during the War." Boston paid tribute to the 54th Regiment in 1897, when the renowned artist Augustus Saint-Gaudens unveiled his stunning bas-relief bronze memorial in its honor, located on the Beacon Street side of the Boston Common. The monument was originally conceived as depicting only Colonel Shaw, but his family demanded that the piece commemorate the entire regiment. Saint-Gaudens's work portrays a sea of grim-faced black warriors, rifles shouldered, marching to war with Shaw riding in their midst.

Despite this tangible reminder of the 54th's sacrifices, the memory of the regiment faded in the first half of the 20th century. The reconciliation of North and South, the advent of American imperialism, and the Great Depression all refocused Yankee minds. Only gradually did the 54th reenter popular consciousness. The Saint-Gaudens memorial figured in works by the poets John Berryman and Robert Lowell, who both lived on Beacon Hill's north slope during the 1940s. In 1965 Peter Burchard published *One Gallant Rush: Robert Gould Shaw and His Brave Black Regiment.* As Civil War reenactments multiplied, history buffs and descendants of the original 54th portrayed the regiment. In 1989 the resurgence of the regiment's prestige culminated with the acclaimed Hollywood film *Glory,* which reintroduced the heroism of the 54th to New England and the nation.

Russell Duncan, *Where Death and Glory Meet: Colonel Robert Gould Shaw and the 54th Massachusetts Infantry* (1999); Joseph T. Glatthaar, *Forged in Battle:*

The Civil War Alliance of Black Soldiers and White Officers (1990); James Henry Gooding, *On the Altar of Freedom: A Black Soldier's Civil War Letters from the Front*, ed. Virginia Matzke Adams (1991).

David A. Cecere

Franco-Americans The descendants of the French Canadians who settled in New England (and upper New York state), primarily in the second half of the 19th and first quarter of the 20th centuries, are customarily referred to as Franco-Americans. Though the name may not reveal that the migrants were originally Quebecois and, to a lesser extent, Acadians, it does underline the importance they attached to their mother tongue. For generations an astonishingly large number of Franco-Americans were also defined by a shared vision known as *survivance,* or loyalty to the French Canadian heritage. This ideal, zealously sustained by an large network of bilingual Catholic parishes, schools, and societies—French-language newspapers also played an important role—reached the height of its influence at the turn of the 20th century and in the years immediately following World War I. The group today is by no means as cohesive, distinct, or vigorous as it once was; yet to a remarkable degree, it still has a certain identity. A Franco-American presence continues to be strongly felt in the three northeastern population centers where French Canadians settled in significant numbers: northern Maine, especially the upper Saint John Valley; western Vermont and upper New York State; and central and southeastern New England, including southern Maine.

Nearly half of the area's Franco-Americans initially resided in Massachusetts, another quarter in southern Maine and New Hampshire, mostly in small and medium-sized cities and towns. Today's localities with the most Franco-American residents and the largest Franco-American percentage of the total population are Biddeford-Saco and Lewiston-Auburn, Maine; Manchester, N.H.; and Woonsocket, R.I. Next in importance are Central Falls, Fall River, Fitchburg, Holyoke, Lowell, New Bedford, Salem, and Southbridge, Mass.; Nashua, N.H.; and Warwick, R.I. As in the case of other ethnic groups, the relatively high density of the Franco-American population in certain cities tends to influence estimates of the overall size of the group. The most reliable finding is that Franco-Americans numbered 573,000 by 1900. It is difficult to estimate the current Franco-American population. According to the latest numbers available from the year 2000 census, 720,337 New Englanders reported their ancestry as French Canadian, with 2,138 claiming Acadian roots. It is likely, however, that a

Franco-American district of Manchester, N.H., with steeple of Saint Marie's Church, 1980

goodly number of those who called their background either Canadian (106,837) or French (1,499,472) should be included in the total. Census statistics relative to French-language use at home are also unreliable, as many individuals who regard themselves as Franco-Americans may not speak French at home—indeed, may never have heard it spoken there.

All things considered, one may conservatively fix the present-day Franco-American population of New England at about 1.5 million. Over time the group has evolved a good deal and, so far as education and employment are concerned, is indistinguishable today from the general New England population.

The slow but steady flow of immigrants from French Canada to the Northeast in the first half of the 19th century became a mass migration in the three or four decades following the Civil War. This exodus was prompted on one hand by harsh living conditions in Quebec and the Maritime Provinces, whose economies could not support a rapidly expanding population, and on the other by the relative attractiveness of wages, particularly in cotton mills, and of the cross-border standard of living. The textile boom of the later 19th century and a growing disenchantment with this kind of work among American-born employees and Irish immigrants created a great demand for mill operatives. Although French Canadians were initially represented in many trades and occupations throughout New England, their concentration in the textile industry was quite remarkable.

Several mill agents actively recruited French Canadian labor in the years before and after the Civil War, but the vast majority of immigrants came as the result of enthusiastic letters received and stories told by relatives and friends about living and working conditions in New England. Most Quebecois who came to the region simply took the train—a relatively easy and inexpensive way to travel—and fully intended to return home after having made their fortune.

Among the early published narratives, the best-known is Honoré de Beaugrand's part novel, part promotion *Jeanne la fileuse* (Joan, the spinner, 1878), which gives a highly favorable account of the immigration and settling-in process in Lowell, Mass. *Les Canadiens-français de la Nouvelle-Angleterre* (The French Canadians of New England, 1891), an account of the experiences of the Jesuit priest Edmond Hamon, who served 10 years in Franco-American parishes, says a bit more about the dark side of the immigration experience but is scarcely less enthusiastic. Father Hamon's exalted vision of future French Canadian immigrants working in mills and other occupations but living the rest of the time with their families in *citadelles,* enclaves replicating Quebec's manners and mores in virtual isolation from mainstream American culture, strikes most observers today as impractical at best.

Many influential Franco-American leaders—parish priests, doctors, lawyers, businessmen, newspaper editors, and heads of fraternal and social organizations—voiced similar opinions well into the 1930s, however, campaigning tirelessly to advance the cause of survivance as they saw it. Since most dedicated Franco-Americans subscribed to a more moderate view, one acknowledging the needs and aspirations of individuals living in American society, a clash seemed inevitable.

It occurred in the 1920s when Elphège Daignault, the crusading editor of *La Sentinelle*, Woonsocket's French-language newspaper, attacked the bishop of Providence for what he considered to be assimilationist policies. The struggle reached the boiling point when the powerful Union Saint-Jean Baptiste d'Amérique, a mutual society founded at Woonsocket in 1900, defended the bishop and was in turn assailed by the Association Canado-Américaine, a rival fraternal organization, established in 1896 and based in Manchester, N.H. In the end, 62 Sentinellistes were briefly excommunicated, sending shock waves throughout the entire Franco-American community.

During this and other crises the Franco-American parochial schools kept on an even keel. The remarkable thing about these bilingual educational establishments—in 1949, probably the system's peak, there were about 200 of them—was their uniform doctrine and pedagogy despite the absence of central control. Administered and taught mainly by French Canadian and Franco-American nuns belonging to 30-odd religious orders, the schools were very similar. Diocesan standards were maintained in the English-language part of the program by annual written examinations for all enrolled students, but each religious community trained its own teachers in French- and English-language subjects. Interestingly, a consensus was reached early on as to what constituted Franco-American survivance ideology. Perhaps the best summary of these principles in the wake of the *Sentinelle* affair is to be found in Josaphat T. Benoît's *L'Ame franco-américaine* (The Franco-American soul, 1935). Franco-American parochial schools provided an excellent education, often under difficult economic conditions, to thousands of children.

The rise and decline of this once thriving educational system follows closely that of other Catholic parochial schools in the United States. Parochial school closings beginning in the mid-1960s can be attributed to four main causes: a lower birthrate after the baby boom, rising costs brought on by inflation, a decreasing number of religious vocations, and the decline of Catholicism. Until 1947 Assumption High School and Assumption College of Worcester, Mass., founded in 1904, recruited their student bodies almost exclusively from the Franco-American milieu. These two bilingual schools graduated numerous individuals who later achieved distinction in various professions.

Some 330 French-language daily and weekly newspapers intended for Franco-Americans saw the light of day, beginning with *Le Protecteur canadien* (The Canadian protector), published at Saint Albans, Vt., from 1868 to 1871. The years between 1880 and 1900 were the golden age of Franco-American journalism, and Ferdinand Gagnon (1849–86), founder of the widely read *Le Travailleur* (The worker), published at Worcester from 1874 to 1886, is regarded as its patron saint. Although there were still 28 Franco-American newspapers in 1935, the last of these, *Le Travailleur*, founded anew in 1931 by Wilfrid Beaulieu, ceased publication in 1978.

Many Franco-American New Englanders have achieved celebrity status. They include the Massachusetts residents Louis Cyr (1863–1912), the "Strongest Man in the World"; Eva Tanguay (1878–1947), a singer-dancer known as the "I Don't Care Girl"; John C. Garand (1888–1974), inventor of the semi-automatic M1 rifle; Leo Durocher (1905–91), the contentious manager of the Brooklyn Dodgers and the New York Giants; Jack Kerouac (1922–69), novelist and cult figure of the Beat Generation; Robert Goulet (1933–), a star of Broadway and Hollywood; and Emeril Lagasse (1959–), TV personality and one of the country's best-known chefs; Joan Benoit Samuelson (1957–) of Maine, gold medalist in the first women's Olympic marathon in 1984; New Hampshire's René Gagnon (1925–79), one of the Iwo Jima flag raisers in 1945, and Grace Metalious (1924–64), author of the best-selling 1956 novel *Peyton Place*; Napoleon "Larry" Lajoie (1874–1959) of Rhode Island, elected to the Baseball Hall of Fame in 1937; and Vermont's Rudy Vallee (1901–86), radio, film, and Broadway performer.

Since the turn of the 20th century Franco-Americans have also had their share of mayors, state legislators, and judges. Except in Rhode Island, they have met with more modest success, electing one of their own to the governorship or to either house of Congress. Top elected officials include Governors Aram J. Pothier (1909–15, 1925–28), Emery J. San Souci (1921–23), and Philip W. Noel (1973–77); U.S. Representatives Louis Monast (1927–29), Aime J. Forand (1937–39, 1941–61), Fernand J. St. Germain (1961–89), and Jim Langevin (2000–); and U.S. Senator Felix Hebert (1929–35), all of Rhode Island, along with U.S. Representatives Alphonse Roy (1938–39) and Norman E. D'Amours (1975–85), both of New Hampshire.

Franco-Americans became keenly aware of the rapid and spectacular social transformation of Quebec known as the Quiet Revolution beginning in the 1960s, and, early on, most of them no doubt observed it sympathetically. Quebecois officials initially made numerous efforts to influence American public opinion in their favor—promoting the idea of possible independence—by actively supporting Franco-American cultural activities. Combined with U.S. government grants to improve foreign-language instruction and educational programs at the time of the American Bicentennial, this substantial aid stimulated a remarkable upsurge of interest in the group's heritage that lasted into the 1980s.

Since then, however, contacts have become less frequent, and individual and group manifestations of Franco-American connectedness with Quebec have fallen off, except among seniors. Above all, the sharp decline of fluency in French among the younger generations of Franco-Americans—a sore subject for the Quebecois—poses a serious threat to the strength of that bond.

The revival of interest in the Franco-American cultural heritage in the 1960s and 1970s coincided with a similar resurgence among other ethnic groups. It was marked by commemorations, fairs, and other public events, professional meetings, and the founding of new organizations. Academic involvement was an important part of this renaissance. Although enthusiasm for these activities may now have lost some of its intensity, there are still many signs of continued Franco-American vitality in New England, concentrated for the most part at the parish level and among older generations. Two bright beacons light the way in the 21st century: the French Institute of Assumption College in Worcester, founded by Claire Quintal in 1979, hosts annual meetings, sponsors major publications, and serves as a clearinghouse for Franco-American activities and manifestations of all sorts, and the Franco-American Resource Opportunity Group at the University of Maine in Orono, headed by the indefatigable Yvon Labbé, publishes a bilingual newspaper, *FAROG Forum*, that covers the Franco-American scene in its own inimitable way.

Gerard J. Brault, *The French-Canadian Heritage in New England* (1986); Armand B. Chartier, *The Franco-Americans of New England: A History* (1999); C. Stewart Doty, ed., *The First Franco-Americans: New England Life Histories from the Federal Writers' Project, 1938–1939* (1985); Doty, "'Monsieur Maurras est ici': French Fascism in Franco-American New England," *Journal of Contemporary History* 32 (1997); André Duval, *Québec-Boston: Celebrating New England–Nouvelle France, 350 Years of Partnership in Shaping North America* (1980); Olivier Maurault, *The French of Canada and New England* (1950); Robert B. Perreault, *One Piece in the Great American Mosaic: The Franco-Americans of New England* (1976); Claire

Quintal, ed., *Steeples and Smokestacks: A Collection of Essays on the Franco-American Experience in New England* (1996).

Gerard J. Brault

Germans Although not the region's largest immigrant group, Germans have settled in New England and influenced its culture from colonial times to the present. The heaviest immigration occurred from 1870 to 1910, when many German workers, seeking opportunities no longer available at home, settled in New England cities and established small but vibrant ethnic communities. Most came from southeastern Germany, especially Saxony.

In the 18th century New Englanders actively sought German Protestants as ideal settlers. Between 1740 and 1742 Germans were recruited to settle in Waldoboro, Maine, but few survived an Indian attack in 1746. In the early 1750s the Massachusetts Bay Colony approved land grants to provide buffers against Indian attacks and hired agents to settle Germans on its western frontier and along the Kennebec River in Dresden, Maine. At about the same time, Benjamin Franklin planned a German settlement and glass factory in Braintree (now Quincy), Mass. These efforts produced little in the way of lasting results, although a few descendants of Waldoboro's Germans became noted shipbuilders during the 19th century.

Several German émigrés played a prominent role in the educational and cultural life of 19th-century Massachusetts. Karl Beck established the first indoor gymnasium at the Round Hill School in Northampton and later taught at Harvard University. Karl Follen, also a Harvard professor, developed a long-used anthology of German literature, along with a guide to German grammar, and founded the first public gymnasium, the Tremont Gymnasium. Before going to Columbia University, Franz Lieber stopped in Boston to direct that gymnasium and establish a swimming school. Karl Douai, an 1848 republican revolutionary, moved to Boston and founded the first U.S. kindergarten. In 1815 Johann Gottlieb Graupner, a member of Joseph Haydn's orchestra, had founded Boston's Handel and Haydn Society, which still exists today. From 1881 until 1918 the conductors of the Boston Symphony Orchestra were all either German or Austrian.

Still, few Germans settled in New England until the last third of the 19th century. Economic depression in Germany in the late 1870s and early 1880s resulted in large-scale emigration (1882 brought the most Germans ever into the United States). Textile and related machine industries, which predominated in the kingdom of Saxony, suffered severely. Skilled workers from those industries settled in the textile cities of Massachusetts and New Hampshire. Saxons made up over 40 percent of the Germans who settled in Holyoke, Mass., for instance, to work in the Germania mill, founded by German emigrants. Likewise, more than 35 percent of the German immigrants to Lawrence, Mass., and Manchester, N.H., came from Saxony. Saxon weavers, machinists, and loom fixers found highskilled jobs in New England mills and later became supervisors.

By 1890 German newspapers existed in Boston, Clinton, Holyoke, Lawrence, Roxbury, and Springfield, Mass.; Manchester, N.H.; Bridgeport, Hartford, New Haven, and Waterbury, Conn.; and Providence, R.I. Germans also settled in the Massachusetts cities of Fitchburg, Worcester, and Cambridge and in Pawtucket, R.I. In each location they established small but thriving ethnic communities. In Boston, for instance, Germans preferred the Roxbury and Jamaica Plain sections. Given that Germans never constituted more than 4 percent of the foreign-born population, the strength and vibrancy of ethnic life in those districts was extraordinary. Each city had more than one German church. German grocery stores, restaurants, sausage manufactures, doctors and pharmacies, and often breweries flourished. German music tutors and language schools thrived, with Maximilian Berlitz founding what has since become a language-teaching empire in Providence in 1878. German clubs and mutual-aid societies, with their substantial meeting halls, became the keystones of ethnicity. *Sangerbunde* (singing societies) and *Turnvereine* (gymnastic clubs) conducted New England–wide competitions. Musical events often attracted audiences in the thousands, Germans and non-Germans alike.

To maintain contact with the more numerous German populations in other U.S. regions, German New Englanders formed chapters of the German-American National Alliance. In addition to fostering German language and culture, these groups lobbied until 1917 for American neutrality during World War I. In these efforts they found willing allies among local Irish Americans. The American entry into the war led to anti-German hysteria across the United States. The situation in New England was more mixed. Local politicians and English-language newspapers largely supported the Germans in Lawrence and Manchester. The *Providence Journal,* however, gained a national reputation for its attacks on Germans. The German conductor of the Boston Symphony Orchestra was removed, imprisoned, and later deported. Germans in New Haven, a center of munitions manufacturing, received the unwarranted attention of federal authorities. Across New England many German-language newspapers ceased to publish.

World War I did not drive German ethnics out of the region, however. German clubs remained active in many New England cities. New England–wide singing and gymnastic events revived in the 1920s, continuing into the 1940s and beyond. In 1985 branches of the Turners Society, a fellowship organization founded by midwestern Germans in 1851, still existed in Adams, Clinton, Fitchburg, Holyoke, and Springfield, Mass., as well as in Bridgeport and Providence. German-language newspapers published until 1942 in Hartford, Holyoke, and Lawrence.

Relatively few Germans immigrated to the United States or to New England between the two world wars. One of the most famous was Bauhaus founder Walter Gropius, who taught at Harvard from 1937 to 1952. From the 1930s to the 1950s, German émigrés contributed greatly to the development of alpine skiing in the region. During World War II German prisoners of war were put to work in the woods of Stark, N.H. Few Germans settled in New England after the war, and those who did were mostly educators, scientists, and spouses of returning military personnel.

For 40 years a branch of the Bruderhof community, a German utopian movement of families and single persons dedicated to nonviolence, mutual service, and brotherly love, occupied a 50-acre compound in Norfolk, Conn. Known also as the Hutterian Brethren, they supported themselves by manufacturing furniture, toys, and physical-therapy equipment. In 1999 the group sold the Norfolk property to the Mission of Tao Confucianism and left Connecticut.

German enclaves have also disappeared from New England cities. That they lasted as long as they did testifies to the tenacity of ethnic newspapers, clubs, and churches. German New Englanders put aside Old World religious and provincial animosities and united to preserve their native language and culture. Because many came from the same regions of southeastern Germany, they were more homogeneous than German immigrants generally, which helped strengthen ethnic ties.

In New England today, Germans make up a small proportion of the total population For the 2000 census, 42,885,165 Americans, or 15.2 percent of the U.S. population, listed their ancestry as German. In the six New England states, however, only 434,235 persons, or 1.55 percent of the region's population, listed their ancestry as German, of which the largest number (377,152, or 5.9 percent of the state's population) lived in Massachusetts. German Americans have virtually disappeared as a visible, united ethnic group in New England.

Kathleen Neils Conzen, "Germans," in *Harvard Encyclopedia of American Ethnic Groups*, ed. Stephan Thernstrom (1980); Goethe Society of New England, *Germans in Boston* (1981); Oscar Handlin, *Boston's Immigrants, 1790–1880: A Study in Acculturation*, 15th rev. ed. (1991); Robert P. McCaffery, *Islands of Deutschtum: German-Americans in Manchester, New Hampshire, and Lawrence, Massachusetts, 1870–1942* (1994).

Robert P. McCaffery

Grace, Charles "Sweet Daddy" Emmanuel (1881–1960) Minister. "Sweet Daddy" Grace was born Marceline Manoël de Graça in 1881 on the island of Brava, Cape Verde, located off the coast of West Africa. At age 10, he immigrated with his family to New Bedford, Mass. They were part of the significant flow of Afro-Portuguese Cape Verdeans to arrive in the region during the early decades of the 20th century. Although the vast majority of Cape Verdeans are of the Catholic faith, Grace grew up to become a charismatic evangelical leader, founding the United House of Prayer for All People and becoming perhaps the best-known Cape Verdean immigrant to New England. By the late 1930s he had an estimated following of 500,000, and by the time of his death in 1960 his church claimed some 3 million worshipers in 350 congregations around the nation.

As a young man, Grace worked as a cook and a peddler of patent medicines both on the streets of New Bedford and on Cape Cod. He also operated a small grocery store. Although his itinerant revivalist career began in the South, where he traveled in his "gospel car" preaching to primarily black followers at rural tent meetings, he erected his first church building in West Waltham, Mass., in 1919. By 1921 he had declared himself a bishop, but on finding that the Cape Cod community did not respond to his brand of enthusiasm, he returned to New Bedford, where he organized a House of Prayer for All People in a former Jewish synagogue. Bringing his unorthodox style of baptism and faith healing to all who would listen, Grace preached with such fervor that his congregants reached levels of religious ecstasy that were often audible throughout the neighborhood. For mass baptismal ceremonies, he brought his new converts out of the church to area beaches and coves.

Dressed in wide-brimmed hats and suits of bright purple, chartreuse, and yellow, with 4-inch-long manicured fingernails painted in similarly bold colors, this flamboyant figure rose to prominence almost overnight. "Sweet Daddy" Grace, as his parishioners liked to call him, became increasingly extravagant as his flock swelled and he began to amass hundreds of thousands of dollars. In a 1952 *Ebony* magazine article about him entitled "America's

Funeral procession of "Sweet Daddy" Grace, 1960

Richest Negro Minister," he declared, on the subject of race: "I am a colorless man. I am a colorless bishop. Sometimes I am black, sometimes white. I preach to all races." Among his many teachings was the singular claim that God came to America in 1900 when "Sweet Daddy" himself first reached the shores of southeastern New England. Although Grace shifted his headquarters to Harlem in the 1930s, he returned to New Bedford once more in 1951 to erect a new United House of Prayer that is still active today.

Arthur Huff Fauset, *Black Gods of the Metropolis: Negro Religious Cults of the Urban North* (1971 [1944]); Joseph R. Washington, Jr., *Black Sects and Cults* (1984 [1972]).

Marilyn Halter

Greeks The first great wave of Greek immigration to the United States took place between 1900 and 1924, with more than 400,000 arrivals. The European market for Greece's major export, currants, had declined, devastating the country's economy. The barren and arid Greek countryside could not yield a livelihood for many of its people. Departing initially from Sparta, Greeks came to America in search of new economic opportunities.

Some Greeks had arrived earlier. After the Greek War of Independence from Ottoman rule (1821–30), a few philhellene New Englanders adopted young Greek orphans and brought them to the United States. Jonathan Miller of Vermont adopted Lucas Miltiades, who in 1891 became the first American of Greek descent to be elected to Congress. An-

other adoptee was Evangelos Sophocles, who became a professor of Greek at Harvard University. Michael Anagnos, brought to the United States in 1861 by Samuel Gridley Howe, became director of the Perkins Institution in Boston, where he developed a program for the deaf and blind. His most famous student was Anne Sullivan, Helen Keller's gifted teacher. Some of the New England Perkinses, usually regarded as Anglo-Saxon, are believed to be descendants of a Greek merchant named Perkentzis who came to American shores via London in the 1780s and whose family later changed the name to Perkins.

The first Greek mass migrants were mainly unskilled young men with little education and no knowledge of English. After arriving at Ellis Island, they remained in urban centers working in restaurants and factories or as bootblacks and peddlers. Most headed for New York and Chicago, but many migrated to New England, where mill and factory owners welcomed unskilled workers. By 1894 about 125 Greeks were employed in Lowell, Mass.; by 1910 the city's Greek population had risen to 20,000. Lowell's Greek community was the first to build a Greek Orthodox church (1906) that conformed to Byzantine architecture. Greeks in Lowell, however, were regarded with suspicion; they posed an economic threat to the French Canadian and Irish factory workers who had preceded them. To avoid harassment or attack, Greeks often walked in groups. Unable to find, or afford, living quarters, they were forced to pool their resources and move into single-room tenements. Mill owners seemed to prefer Greek workers to those of other ethnicities, ostensibly because of their sobriety and general indifference to union organizations. Greek participation in labor conflicts varied by region; during the 1912 strike in Lowell, Greeks struck along with other workers but negotiated separately through their own organization.

Lynn, Mass., like its sister cities Lowell and Lawrence, drew many Greek immigrants to its leather and shoe factories as well as its General Electric plant. Greeks became part of the demographic landscape in Lynn, which was also home to Italian, Jewish, Polish, and Irish communities; Greeks, however, tended to interact only with other Greeks there and in neighboring Peabody. To be sure, ethnic insulation involves both voluntary and involuntary components, but the Greeks were clearly victims of exclusion and discrimination. In 1943, for example, Harry Agganis, a promising young athlete, had to call himself Ted Casey to play ball during his school years in Lynn. A few years later he became Boston University's most popular football player and New England's star athlete. In 1952 he signed a contract with the Boston Red Sox, but he died in June 1955. Harry Agganis was immortalized in 1994 by sculptor Armand LaMontagne at the Sports Museum of New England.

The Greek experience in New England was captured by Mary Vardoulakis's novel *Gold in the Streets* (1945). This was the first Greek American novel to describe the struggles of Greek immigrants transitioning from villagers to industrial workers in the mill town of Chicopee, Mass. A later novel written by H. L. Mountzoures, *The Bridge* (1972), details a Greek American family facing and resolving domestic problems in Connecticut. In his novels *Zeus Has Two Urns* (1976) and *The Tyrants* (1977), Charles E. Jarvis portrays the events that shaped one Greek community in Lowell.

A second influx of Greek newcomers after World War II not only added numbers to the population but reinvigorated ethnic and related organizations. The 2000 census reported 1,153,307 people of Greek ancestry in the United States. Of these, 135,255 resided in New England (Massachusetts, 78,172; Connecticut, 27,603; New Hampshire, 15,279; Rhode Island, 6,482; Maine, 5,423; Vermont, 2,296). The Greek cultural organization Paideia built a Hellenic Studies Center on the main campus of the University of Connecticut in Storrs dedicated to researching, preserving, and promoting Hellenic culture and history. This accomplishment was followed by the construction of an adjoining Byzantine Greek Orthodox chapel, Three Hierarchs, dedicated in 1995. Three Hierarchs is the first Greek Or-

thodox chapel at a major American state university.

An ethic of success and achievement was the Greeks' signature throughout the 20th century. Children were expected to exceed, not succeed, their parents. Both men and women strove to move from blue- to white-collar status in one generation. In 1949 Mary B. Treudley noted the upward mobility of Greeks in the *American Sociological Review.* She wrote that the formal community established by the Greeks in Boston not only provided a sense of belonging and cushioned cultural conflict but rewarded successful climbers. Building churches, recruiting and retaining members, raising funds, and disbursing monies were pragmatic skills that Greeks transferred to the larger community, skills that were sought after in America and facilitated assimilation. Complementing these talents were the independent spirit and entrepreneurial ethos that characterized the first and second waves of Greek immigration. If ethnic pride derives from occupational status and success, then the factory represented a dead end, while independence and mobility could be realized through proprietorship. It is not surprising, then, that when Greeks left their New England factory jobs, many established their own businesses, ranging from restaurants—the most popular commercial endeavor—to confectionery stores, florist shops, and dry-cleaning establishments. Greek-owned pizza parlors are common throughout New England. Americans of Greek descent tend to be concentrated in professional, managerial, and administrative occupations. The 2000 median income of Greek Americans was $63,240, exceeding the national average of $50,046. Thirty-five percent of Greek Americans hold a college or graduate degree, while the national average is 24.4 percent. The corresponding data for Greeks in New England reflect these national averages.

Greek Americans have been active participants in New England politics. In 1949, George Christopher Eliades, a 1925 graduate of Boston University Law School, became the first American of Greek descent to be elected mayor of Lowell. Greek Americans take pride in Paul Tsongas, who became a U.S. senator from Massachusetts in 1978; Matina Souretis Horner, who served as president of Radcliffe College; and Michael Dukakis, former Massachusetts governor and the 1988 Democratic Party nominee for president. Democrat George Athanson served as mayor of Hartford from 1971 to 1981, longer than any other mayor of that city since 1812. Maine Republican Olympia Bouchles Snowe was the youngest woman and the first Greek American woman to be elected to the House of Representatives in

1979; in 1994 she, too, became a U.S. senator. In the arts, Theodore Antoniou, award-winning professor of music at Boston University since 1978, has composed more than 100 pieces of contemporary symphonic, chamber, solo, choral, and electronic music. His works have been performed throughout Europe and at the Tanglewood Music Festival, where Antoniou has served as assistant director of contemporary activities at the Berkshire Music Center.

Although the Greek American community is not as homogeneous as it was in the past, it continues to derive its core identity from the Greek Orthodox Church. There are approximately 60 Greek Orthodox churches in New England, the majority in Massachusetts. Lowell's Holy Trinity Hellenic Orthodox Church celebrated its 100th anniversary as an incorporated parish in March 2000. The Hellenic College and the Holy Cross Greek Orthodox School of Theology in Brookline, Mass., prepare students from various Orthodox jurisdictions for ordination to the priesthood and church service. The two schools form one educational community, sharing the same campus and facilities, and enjoy a pan-Orthodox international presence that reflects the ecumenical and global vision of the church.

The Greek experience in America has been one of perseverance and accomplishment in diverse areas of life. The value placed on family life, independence, and hard work has been transmitted across generations and continues to facilitate Greek adaptation to the rigorous and competitive demands of American society.

Lawrence A. Lovell-Troy, *The Social Basis of Ethnic Enterprise: Greeks in the Pizza Business* (1990); Theodore Saloutos, *The Greeks in the United States* (1964); Alice Scourby, *The Greek Americans* (1984); Nick Tsiotos and Andy Dabilis, *Harry Agganis, the Golden Greek: An All-American Story* (1995).

Alice Scourby

Gypsies Several related ethnic groups, originally from India and referred to as Gypsies by outsiders, have lived in or passed through New England since they first began immigrating to North America in the middle of the 19th century. At least two Gypsy groups, the Romnichels from England and the Rom from eastern Europe, have had long-term associations with New England and become a significant part of the region's history. During the 19th century Gypsies attracted much more attention and comment than they do today. While now outwardly integrated into the majority society and generally invisible as groups, Romnichels and Rom in New England remain distinct ethnic communities.

The Romnichels, or English Gypsies, came to England in the 1500s and began immigrat-

Gypsy camp, Salem, Mass., 1924

ing to the United States in 1850. Their three centuries of association with England had a significant influence on Romnichel language and culture and has remained a source of pride and a focus for ethnic identity. The Romnichel ethnic language, referred to as Rom'nes, embeds words of Indic origin in English grammar. Kinship is reckoned bilaterally with a bias toward the male side. Groupings known as breeds are identified by surname and considered distinctive in dialect and custom.

The ethnic boundary between non-Gypsies (*gaujos*) and Romnichels is buttressed by an ideology of ritual purity expressed in the division of household items and tasks, such as dishes and laundry, into spheres of the clean and the polluted. The traditional form of marriage has been elopement, the wedding celebration being a recent development. There is no formal leadership; internal social control is based on peer pressure. Until recently Romnichels were associated with the Episcopal and other Protestant churches. The recent adoption of fundamentalist forms of Christianity has spurred the establishment of churches led by Romnichel pastors and the organization of revival meetings.

The arrival of Romnichels in New England coincided with an increased demand for draft horses in agriculture and urban transportation; for more than half a century trading in horses became the group's predominant occupation, one that played a significant ideological role in their ethnic identity. Shortly after the Civil War, Romnichel horse dealers began establishing sales stables in New England cities that remained in business through the 1920s. The number and longevity of the businesses and the social organization that grew up around them are unique to the area. Romnichel horse trade was integral to urban growth; the Romnichel stable in Worcester, Mass., for example, was said to have supplied half the horses bought by that city. In addition to the stable businesses Romnichels conducted seasonal fortune-telling at seaside resorts and in cities. Fortune-telling camps offered customers exotic diversion on summer excursions or a short streetcar ride from home. With the decline in the horse trade after World War I, many Romnichels relied on the formerly secondary trades of making and selling baskets and rustic furniture, fortune-telling, and the sale of whatever items they could sell at profit. Today driveway paving and roofing are major occupations; sales activities also remain prominent, but fortune-telling has diminished in importance. Whenever possible, economic activities continue as independent family enterprises.

Most of the ancestors of the two main divisions of American Rom, the Kalderash and Machwaya, immigrated between 1895 and 1914. They are the descendants of Gypsies who had spent several hundred years in areas influenced by Serbian and Romanian cultures. The Rom speak a Vlach dialect of Romani, an inflected Indic language containing loan words from Greek, Serbian, Romanian, and Russian, testifying to the areas that have contributed to Rom culture.

The Rom at first patronized Eastern Orthodox churches and later turned to the more accessible Roman Catholic churches. The rich complex of Rom religious practices includes the observance of Christmas, Easter, and a number of saints' days. The dead are commemorated in feasts celebrated at intervals up to a year after death and in household rituals. Since the 1970s many Rom have converted to the Pentecostal faith, attending churches organized by Rom pastors.

Rom kinship is organized in patrilineal groups called *vitsas.* Marriages are arranged on the initiation of the groom's family, which pays a bride-price to the family of the bride.

Married couples move in with the groom's parents and often grandparents, as the most common residential unit is the extended family. An ideology of purity and related ritual practices governs social relations, etiquette, and everyday life, regulating sex- and age-related tasks and distinguishing the Rom from non-Gypsies (*gazhe*). Business and social disputes and ritual infractions are adjudicated by the *kris,* an ad hoc court of respected elders. Other means of social control are peer pressure, the influence of older people, and charges brought in local courts of law. A Rom Baro, a "big man" whose connections are believed to be effective, often can wield influence beyond his own vitsa.

Most Rom men had in the past been skilled coppersmiths who repaired and retinned bakery, brewery, and dairy utensils, commercial food-preparation vats, and other industrial equipment, performing the work in camps outside New England cities. Horse-trading and fortune-telling were also Rom occupations. It was the Rom who most fully developed fortune-telling as an urban business, one that came to be predominant following the decline of the horse trade and the replacement of copper by stainless steel and aluminum. Driveway paving, auto-body work, and the buying and selling of automobiles or scrap metal are other present-day Rom occupations.

Through the late 1920s Rom periodically gathered in camps of up to 1,000 persons on the outskirts of New England cities to celebrate saints' day feasts, baptisms, and weddings. The camps also attracted customers for fortune-telling as well as spectators for mock weddings and other forms of entertainment. Conflicts with local authorities and internal quarrels drew negative attention to these camps. Newspapers often reported on alleged depredations or involvement in fortune-telling scams. Urban settlement and the establishment of fortune-telling businesses brought additional problems: Rom parents, for example, were frequently charged in connection with the truancy of their school-age children. In 1930 Providence responded by organizing a special class for Gypsy youngsters.

Old-country stereotyping and prejudices followed Gypsies to America. Whereas New England newspapers carried mostly positive stories about Gypsy shrewdness or enterprise, local populations did not always share these views. Present-day non-Gypsy New Englanders report that camping Gypsies were often feared and suspected of kidnapping or theft when children went missing or items of value were stolen. The more superstitious projected magical powers onto Gypsy women, an old theme that the novelist Stephen King, writing under the pseudonym Richard Bachman, worked into his 1984 mystery *Thinner.* Today both the Rom and the Romnichels have begun gradually drifting toward a more mainstream existence, as their children receive more education and increasing numbers enter conventional occupations.

Angus Fraser, *The Gypsies* (1992); William G. Lockwood and Sheila Salo, *Gypsies and Travelers in North America: An Annotated Bibliography* (1994); Matt T. Salo and Sheila Salo, "Romnichel Economic and Social Organization in Urban New England, 1850–1930," *Urban Anthropology* 11 (1982).

Matt T. Salo and Sheila M. Salo

Haitians Haitians are among the fastest-growing Caribbean immigrant populations in New England today. During the 1980s there was a dramatic increase in the number of Haitian arrivals, and their numbers swelled after the chaotic 1991 military coup that ousted President Jean-Bertrand Aristide. Although Haitians also reside in other urban centers, the largest and most fully developed Haitian community in New England is found in Greater Boston. Whereas fewer than 3,000 Haitians lived in Boston and its environs in 1970, neighborhood leaders estimate that the area is now home to about 70,000 Haitian immigrants. Only Miami and New York have larger Haitian American communities.

Some Haitians have come to Boston directly from their island homeland, but many more have relocated from other large Haitian immigrant communities. Constrained by residential congestion and troubled by rising crime rates in New York City, scores of middle- and working-class families were drawn to the area during the 1980s because of Boston's reputation for good schools and its booming economy. Haitians often saw the city as a haven for intellectuals that offered them economic advancement and their children educational opportunity. Highly educated Haitians are not the only ones to be attracted to the region, however. The influx includes migrants from a wide range of socioeconomic and educational backgrounds.

Haitian newcomers have had to struggle against many odds. Although most left Haiti to escape political persecution, the vast majority are categorized as economic migrants. Consequently, many have experienced the disruptions and disadvantages common to political refugees but have not been granted the benefit of resettlement services provided by the federal government to immigrants with refugee status. Furthermore, as a black immigrant population, they face racial discrimination. Thus far New England's Haitians have not established a strong economic niche for themselves, although they are well represented in health-care occupations. Despite

these drawbacks the population continues to grow and to organize.

Boston's Haitian community first began to coalesce in May 1974, when Haitian flag day was celebrated with a boisterous procession of honking cars and the waving of blue-and-red anti-Duvalier flags. The first Haitian bands, a dance club, and a cultural center were also created at that time. By the early 1980s both the Cambridge Haitian American Association and the Haitian Multi-Service Center in Dorchester, Mass., had opened their doors, offering a range of programs that included employment, housing, and legal assistance; Creole and English classes, document translation, and other interpreting services; and educational counseling.

Religious participation has been high among newcomers to the region. Although most Haitians are Catholic, increasing numbers are joining evangelical Protestant congregations, a legacy of the Protestantism brought to Haiti by hundreds of American missionaries in the 19th century. Some 40 churches in the Greater Boston area currently serve the Haitian community, with most offering services in Creole and some in French. Many Haitian immigrants have creatively combined their more institutionalized Christian practices with less formal traditional vodun beliefs and practices, such as ritual healing.

Coming from a highly class-stratified society, Haitians have often had difficulty adjusting to a cultural situation in which race predominates over both social class and ethnicity. Language, too, has been a significant factor in the development of Haitian social and settlement patterns. New England's first-generation Haitian immigrants are the most likely to exhibit a strong national identity, speak Haitian Creole (which is not simply a dialect of French but a separate language), and associate primarily with coethnics. Although they often settle in neighborhoods with a high concentration of English-speaking black residents, either African American or West Indian, most Haitians do not actively identify with either of these groups. Older Haitians view themselves as distinctive from other Afro-Caribbean migrants owing to linguistic and cultural differences and to Haiti's unique history of early self-rule. Second-generation immigrants, however, are beginning to reverse this pattern. Younger people appear more willing to shed their traditional culture, speak English exclusively, and attempt to fit into New England's increasingly multiracial mix.

Robert Lawless, "Haitian Migrants and Haitian-Americans: From Invisibility into the Spotlight," *Journal of Ethnic Studies* 14 (1986); Charles Rodin, "From Haiti to Boston," *Boston Globe Magazine* (December 15, 1996); Alex Stepick, *Pride against Preju-*

dice: Haitians in the United States (1998); Flore Zephir, *Haitian Immigrants in Black America: A Sociological and Sociolinguistic Portrait* (1996).

Marilyn Halter

Hall, Prince (ca. 1735–1807) Activist, founder of African American Freemasonry. Details of Prince Hall's life remain sketchy. Some biographers believe that Hall was born in Barbados, though firm documentation is absent. Several accounts place him in the Boston household of William Hall as a slave or indentured servant until his manumission in 1770. What is certain, however, is that Prince Hall was a leader in helping Boston's blacks achieve a sense of racial identity. A chef, leather dresser, and day laborer, he agitated for abolishing slavery and educating black children, published several addresses, and was a founder and leader of the African Lodge of Free and Accepted Masons, an enduring fraternal group important to middle-class blacks the world over.

Although information about his life is scant, Hall's ideas and values are accessible because he signed several petitions to the Massachusetts legislature in the 1770s, published Masonic "charges" in the 1790s, and petitioned Boston selectmen in favor of schooling for black children in the 1790s. The petitions of the 1770s refocus American revolutionary philosophy, pressing patriots to respect slaves' natural right to liberty. A supporter of migration to Africa, Hall nonetheless put his efforts into improving the situation for blacks in America. Hall and other free black Bostonians in 1775 founded the group that would become the Masonic African Lodge and in 1796 established the African Benevolent Society. He was also a prominent member of the School Street Congregational Church.

As master of the Masonic lodge, Hall wrote charges in which he advocated benevolence, charity, and avoidance of strife. He urged his fellow lodge members to be proud of their heritage but cautioned them to be circumspect in their dealings with whites, some of whom could turn violent. He also expressed his belief that virtue and decorum were essential if blacks were to achieve upward social mobility. A strong critic of racism, Hall protested the taxation of blacks, whose children could not attend publicly supported schools, and reproached Bostonians for providing fewer educational opportunities for black children than were available in Philadelphia.

Already a center of revolutionary thought, Boston became a crucible of black culture; knowledge from throughout the black Atlantic, free and enslaved, flowed into the city. Hall had black associates in other American cities, including Providence and Philadelphia, and maintained contacts with blacks throughout the Atlantic world. For the African Lodge he recruited black chaplains: first John Marrant, a Methodist and Mason who had preached in South Carolina, England, and the Maritimes, and then Absalom Jones, a renowned Philadelphia minister and Mason.

Although some whites protested Prince Hall's black Freemasonry, Martin Delany insisted in *The Origin and Objects of Ancient Freemasonry: Its Introduction into the United States, and Legitimacy among Colored Men* (1853) that "to deny to black men the privileges of Masonry, is to deny the child the lineage of its own parentage. From whence sprung Masonry but from Ethiopia, Egypt, and Assyria—all settled by the children of Ham?" Soon international, Prince Hall Freemasonry was established in Liberia by 1850. Today the order promotes charity, decorum, and upward mobility.

In his professional life Hall achieved fame as a chef and caterer for the quality of his food and the style of his service. The sea-turtle feasts he staged for Boston's commercial elite were spectacular displays featuring a carapace stuffed with turtle ragout carried on the shoulders of four black men and served tableside from the shell. Economic success and a solid reputation gave Hall the means to employ other African Americans. A model of respectability, he fostered his compatriots' emerging racial self-consciousness. Hall died in Boston in 1807; a headstone and a later monument mark his grave in Copp's Hill Burying Ground.

Thomas J. Davis, "Emancipation Rhetoric, Natural Rights, and Revolutionary New England: A Note on Four Black Petitions in Massachusetts, 1773–1777," *New England Quarterly* 62 (1989); Martin R. Delany, William A. Muraskin, *Middle-Class Blacks in a White Society: Prince Hall Freemasonry in America* (1975); Charles H. Wesley, *Prince Hall: Life and Legacy* (1977).

John Saillant

Hentoff, Nathan "Nat" Irving

(1925–) Writer and civil libertarian. A perceptive and eminent civil libertarian, newspaper columnist, and music critic, Nathan Irving Hentoff has examined modern cultural life in New England through his writings. The sociopolitical complexity of race relations between black and white Americans is the focus of Hentoff's book *The New Equality* (1964). *The Day They Came to Arrest the Book* (1982) depicts the suppression of civil rights that occurs during a high school censorship controversy over Mark Twain's *Huckleberry Finn*.

Hentoff was born in Boston, the only son of Simon and Lena Hentoff. He attended the Boston Latin School, received a bachelor's de-

Nat Hentoff tours Grove Hall neighborhood of Boston with community activist Sandy Hall, 1986

gree in 1945 from Northeastern University, and spent one year pursuing postgraduate studies at Harvard University. From 1944 to 1953 he worked as a writer for radio station WMEX in Boston. In 1950 he married, then divorced, Miriam Sargent and attended the Sorbonne in Paris on a Fulbright Fellowship. His second marriage, to Trudi Bernstein in 1954, produced two daughters, Jessica and Miranda. In 1959 that marriage ended and Hentoff wed essayist Margot Goodman. They have two sons, Nicholas and Thomas.

The insightful analysis of jazz by the writer George Frazier, who wrote for the jazz magazine *Down Beat*, the *Boston Herald*, and *Life* magazine, was one of several influences on Hentoff, who incorporated Frazier's discerning approach into his own musical criticism. During the 1950s Hentoff wrote introspective biographical profiles and social inquiry for *Down Beat*. During his years as associate editor of that magazine (1953–57), he focused on the artistic contributions of African Americans to the evolution of jazz. He collaborated with Nat Shapiro in 1955 to publish *Hear Me Talkin' to Ya*, the first history of jazz recounted by the musicians themselves. Hentoff was a cofounder and coeditor of the *Jazz Review* from 1958 to 1961 and coedited the anthology *Jazz* (1959). He contributed to the *New Yorker* as a staff writer from 1960 to 1993 and writes a nationally syndicated column for the *Village Voice*, where he has been on staff since 1957. *American Music Is* (2004) is a collection of Hentoff's music columns.

From the 1960s to the present, Hentoff has concentrated on social and political issues involving education, racism, and civil liberties, most recently in *the War on the Bill of Rights and The Gathering Resistance* (2003). The meticulous technique employed by journalists I. F. Stone and George Seldes shaped his writing style. In 1985 Northeastern University awarded Hentoff an honorary doctorate of laws in recognition of his literary achievements. Hentoff's first autobiography, *Boston Boy* (1986), offers a memorable portrayal of the cultural significance of ethnic and class relations in Boston. His second autobiographical work, *Speaking Freely: A Memoir* (1997), recounts his years as a social commentator for the *Village Voice*, *Washington Post*, and *New Yorker*.

Nst Hentoff, *The Nat Hentoff Reader* (2001); Nat Hentoff and Albert J. McCarthy, eds., *Jazz: New Perspectives on the History of Jazz by 12 of the World's Foremost Jazz Critics and Scholars* (1975 [1959]).

Kimberly Charmaine Welch

Irish

Irish men and women lived at Plymouth, and the records of all six New England states list Irish surnames among their earliest residents. Four signers of the Declaration of Independence were Irish born. During the 17th and 18th centuries, Irish immigration to North America was a primarily Protestant movement away from British Northern Ireland. Immigrants were Anglicans, Methodists, and Presbyterians. Catholics, facing intense prejudice, came in much smaller numbers, rarely moving further south than Newfoundland.

Many early Irish immigrants came to New England seeking better economic opportunities. English landlords began consolidating land they had once leased to farmers into more profitable large holdings, which left many small farmers homeless. Between 1730 and 1775 about 100,000 left Ulster for the Americas, many for New England. Some of these immigrants arrived as families with the education and financial means to support their ventures. They often assimilated smoothly into the new culture, achieving social and financial independence. Many more, however, among them small farmers expulsed from their land, came as indentured servants or redemptioners, who were auctioned as servants upon their arrival in America to pay for their passage. But poor and wealthy Irish alike fought for the independence of their new land, constituting between 35 and 40 percent of American forces in the Revolutionary War.

American society grew more tolerant after that war, which made it possible for Irish and French Catholics to organize New England's first Catholic parish, located in a former French Huguenot church in Boston. Claudius

The South Boston Irish American Society climbs Dorchester Heights to celebrate Evacuation Day (commemorating the end of the British occupation of Boston in 1776), March 17, which coincides with Saint Patrick's Day, 1994

Florent Bouchard de la Poterie celebrated the first official Mass there on November 2, 1788. In 1792 Bishop John Carroll of Maryland sent another French priest, François Matignon, to serve the Boston Catholics. Four years later Matignon was joined by Jean Lefebvre de Cheverus, who became Boston's first bishop in 1808. Both tended to be conciliatory toward and were accepted by Boston's Protestant community.

By 1799 Irish Catholics had decided to build their own church in the heart of the city, according to a design by Charles Bulfinch. Four years later, on September 29, 1803, Bishop Carroll dedicated the Church of the Holy Cross. Despite this auspicious beginning, limited funds prevented Catholics from doing much more building until the 20th century. Instead, they often took over vacated Protestant churches for their services, among them Saint Stephen's on Hanover Street in Boston's North End.

During the 1840s, potato-crop failures in Ireland and the indifference of the ruling British government resulted in thousands of deaths from starvation and a massive wave of emigration. Those Irish who were able fled to Canada, often settling in the Maritime Provinces, or the United States, where they usually stayed on the East Coast. From Canada—English territory and therefore anathema—Catholics gradually moved south into New England; Boston became the most Irish city in the United States.

The immigrants of the famine era were largely Catholic, illiterate, poor, and unskilled; many were ill when they arrived in their new home. In 1847 alone 37,000 came to Boston. Such numbers pushed New England cities be-

yond the limits of their housing and welfare capabilities, straining the native-born population's generosity and patience. Smoldering anti-Catholic sentiment burst into full flame. Protestants perceived Catholics as "papists" who were loyal above all to Rome, detrimental to morality and democracy, and an internal threat to the republic. Novels relating the sordid details of events that supposedly transpired behind convent walls fanned the fires of animosity. Believing the Catholic Church to be a cover for white slavery and prostitution, a mob burned down the Ursuline Convent in Charlestown, Mass., in 1834 to put an end to these horrific—and fictitious—practices.

Anti-Catholicism reached its political peak during the 1850s with the rise of the anti-Catholic, anti-immigrant Know-Nothing Party, which flourished throughout New England but had its greatest electoral success in Massachusetts. Although the Know-Nothing Party eventually dissolved, it was succeeded by the American Protection Agency after the Civil War in reaction to increased Catholic immigration from southern and eastern Europe.

Prejudice limited employment opportunities for Irish immigrants, particularly Catholic ones. Young single Irish women often traveled to New England alone and, like their married counterparts, frequently became domestics in middle- and upper-class homes. Irish men, whose knowledge of farming was outdated by American standards, had few skills. Unable to get jobs as laborers, thousands were forced to abandon their families to seek employment elsewhere. Irish families thus had more female-headed households than any of New England's other white ethnic groups. No matter what their occupation, Irish immigrants worked hard for very low wages and could rarely afford decent housing or sustenance for their families.

A number of Irish publications appeared to inform, entertain, and guide Irish immigrants in their new land. *The Pilot,* for example, contained news from Ireland and the United States. *Donahoe's Magazine* printed fiction for its Irish-immigrant readers and advice columns to help them negotiate American customs, asserting all the while that Irish Catholics would deliver Protestant America into the true—that is, Catholic—faith. Other popular Catholic magazines were the *Columbiad* and the *Republic.* Didactic works such as Father Bernard O'Reilly's *Mirror of True Womanhood* (1877), the Reverend George Deshon's *Guide for Catholic Young Women* (1893), the Reverend Francis Lasance's *Catholic Girl's Guide* (1906), and T. E. Shield's *Education of Our Girls* (1907) aimed to teach Catholic women proper behavior.

Irish Catholic schools helped ensure the survival of the immigrants' culture and faith. Returning from the third plenary council in Baltimore in 1884, Archbishop John Williams announced that he would establish a parochial school system in Boston. Many Irish Catholics saw public schools as places where their children were subject to thinly veiled Protestant proselytizing. Not all Irish took advantage of Catholic education, however, seeing more value in the social and business relationships their children could forge through public-school contact with Protestants.

William O'Connell succeeded Archbishop Williams and, as cardinal, was instrumental in building and modernizing educational institutions in the Boston archdiocese. During his tenure (1907–44) parochial elementary schools increased in number from 75 to 158, high schools from 22 to 67, private and preparatory schools from 10 to 24. The College of the Holy Cross (1843) in Worcester, Boston College (1863), and Saint John's (the former Boston Ecclesiastical) Seminary in Brighton (1883) expanded. Emmanuel College, the first Catholic women's college in New England, was established in 1919. Catholic architects and builders carried out much of this expansion, among them Charles D. McGinnis and his partner, Timothy Francis Walsh, who constructed the cardinal's residence and most of the buildings at Holy Cross in Worcester, along with nearly 300 other projects.

Catholic social clubs, including the Catholic Total Abstinence Union of America, Catholic Reading Circles, Friendly Sons of Saint Patrick, and the Society of Brendan, helped men and women make social or business connections. The Knights of Columbus, the largest of the benefit societies, began as an insurance agency for Catholics in Connecticut in 1882. The Catholic Union of Boston was primarily a social club whose activities included educational, religious, and charitable projects. Established in 1861, the Boston conference of the Society of Saint Vincent DePaul cared for abandoned children and eventually provided certain educational and employment services, along with a foster-home system. Women were encouraged to focus on the family but could join charities and devotional societies. In 1910 Archbishop O'Connell approved the establishment of the League of Catholic Women, which federated over 40 women's societies. Events like the contemporary Saint Patrick's Day parade, first organized in 1901, served as demonstrations of Irish ethnic pride and solidarity.

Gradually second-generation Irish moved away from Boston, often living in cheap two- and three-decker houses in Dorchester, Charlestown, East Boston, and South Boston.

Eventually they bought or rented homes in accessible streetcar suburbs such as Jamaica Plain, Brookline, and Newton. By the late 19th century some Irish Catholics had entered the middle class, forming an elite group of civil servants, businessmen, and professionals that included philanthropist Thomas Bernard Fitzpatrick; businessmen James Phelan and James M. Prendergast; and Charles A. De-Courcy, a state supreme court justice from 1911 until 1924. Irish women moved into better jobs as well, becoming teachers, nurses, or office workers.

As they succeeded in business, so, too, did the Irish excel in politics, as evidenced by a number of Boston mayors: Patrick Collins (1902–5), John F. "Honey Fitz" Fitzgerald (1906–8 and 1910–14), James M. Curley (1914–18), John Hynes (1950–60), and Ray Flynn (1984–92). The Irish American Thomas P. "Tip" O'Neill stood third in line to the U.S. presidency when he served as Speaker of the House from 1977 until 1987. John F. Fitzgerald's daughter Rose married Joseph P. Kennedy and established a political dynasty that produced a U.S. president, a U.S. attorney general, senators, and several congressmen and continues to cast a long shadow over American political and social life.

The Catholic Church continued to play a vital role in the Irish community throughout the 20th century. Like Cardinal O'Connell before him, Richard Cardinal Cushing encouraged Catholics to support parochial schools, establish Catholic social organizations, and take pride in their ethnic and religious heritage. From the 1940s through the 1960s Cardinal Cushing promoted tolerance and acceptance. Though he proved unable to halt violent Irish Catholic attacks on black schoolchildren during the busing crisis of the 1970s, Cardinal Cushing did help break down some of the barriers between Catholics and other ethnic and religious groups.

Irish Americans now constitute nearly 20 percent of New England's population (2,721,574 in 2000) and have achieved social acceptance and economic security. Irish immigration dropped off during most of the 20th century. It peaked again during the 1980s, when economic hard times in the Irish homeland drove as many as 100,000 young Irish to the United States, half of whom were estimated to be in Boston. The "new Irish" were a diverse group of urban and rural, high-school- and university-educated young people who often worked illegally. To assist these immigrants, the Irish Cultural Center was founded in October 1989; the center currently serves immigrants of all ethnic groups, fostering a sense of community among them.

By the mid-1990s the economic situation in Ireland had begun to improve, though competition was still fierce for a limited number of positions. While many recent young Irish immigrants awaited their chance to go back home, their presence strengthened ties between New England and Ireland. In June 1998 those ties were honored when the million-dollar Irish Famine Memorial, sculpted in bronze by Robert Shure, was unveiled at Washington and School Streets in downtown Boston.

Donald Harman Akenson, *The Irish Diaspora: A Primer* (1993); Hasia Diner, *Erin's Daughters in America: Irish Immigrant Women in the 19th Century* (1983); Michael Glazier, ed., *The Encyclopedia of the Irish in America* (1999); Kerby A. Miller, *Emigrants and Exiles: Ireland and the Irish Exodus to North America* (1985); Thomas O'Connor, *The Boston Irish: A Political History* (1995); Dennis P. Ryan, *Beyond the Ballot Box: A Social History of the Boston Irish, 1845–1917* (1983).

Regina M. Faden

Italians At the turn of the 20th century, the typical Italian immigrant to New England was a male peasant or laborer from Italy's impoverished south who came to the United States with the notion of making money and then returning home. Half of all immigrants probably returned to Italy, while many went back and forth before ultimately making their homes in the New World.

Italian immigrants settled primarily in the industrial cities of New England, such as Boston, Lawrence, and Worcester, Mass.; Providence, R.I.; and New Haven and Bridgeport, Conn. The largest wave began in the early 1900s, with mass industrialization, and lasted until the U.S. government imposed immigration quotas in the 1920s. But a new wave arrived between the end of World War II and the 1960s. Economic opportunities in southern Italy have improved since then, and Italians dissatisfied with conditions at home now typically seek employment within the European Union.

More residentially segregated than most immigrant groups, Italians formed ethnic enclaves in New England cities, often with other émigrés from their native villages. In Boston, where Italians became the second-largest immigrant population, newcomers from Naples and Sicily settled in the North End, while those from the small village of San Donato and nearby Atina gravitated to Boston's Brighton and Nonantum, a village of 4,000 in the bordering suburb of Newton. Multigenerational Italian immigrant families continued to live in their enclaves even when they were assimilated and able to afford better housing elsewhere. They stayed together in part to avoid the disdain of more established Americans but especially to enjoy family, compatriots, and ethnic-based institutional life.

The parish church was central to neighborhood life, the more so as Italians assimilated. The immigrants "Italianized" their parishes. They revered their saints and introduced *feste*, annual celebrations in the saints' honor. At the same time, New England churches acculturated Italians to Irish American Catholicism. Irish clergy dominated archdioceses in the region. They imposed their own interpretation of Catholicism, more authoritarian and impersonal than was customary for southern Europeans.

Feste unify communities and affirm ethnicity. They are not simply survivals of times past. Although the number of feste has dwindled over the years, with the growth of ethnic pride that occurred in the late 20th century, some communities created new celebrations and older ones became symbolically more ethnic. In Newton's Nonantum the society sponsoring the one remaining festa replaced the American red, white, and blue sashes previously worn by ones featuring Italy's national colors, red, white, and green. And in Brighton, Italians from the last significant wave of immigration introduced in the 1990s a festa for the eponymous saint of the village from which most of them had emigrated, San Donato.

Italians also have established a range of secular organizations. The first were mutual aid associations based on members' village of origin. They offered sickness and death benefits and assistance in citizenship. By the early 21st century remaining village-of-origin groups had assumed almost exclusively social functions, and their language of communication had shifted from village dialect to English. Italian Americans no longer needed the economic benefits the groups initially provided.

As immigrants assimilated, their conception of ethnicity broadened from village to nation. The foremost organization of Italian Americans in New England, the Sons of Italy, reflects this newly formed identity. Originally open only to males of Italian descent—though women could join the weak sister organization, Daughters of Italy—the Sons have responded to changing mores and lower rates of immigration by admitting female members as well as spouses of Italians and Italian Americans. The ethnic social base accordingly has come to be socially, not merely biologically, defined.

Not all ethnic neighborhoods have remained socially intact, however. The larger, more working-class, and more ethnically homogeneous the neighborhood, the less demographic turnover it tends to display. For these reasons the Italian presence remained stronger in the mill town of Lawrence, Mass., than in nearby Lowell. Lawrence had contained a larger working-class Italian population since the early 20th century. Middle-class Italian Americans, by contrast, like those in Bridgewater, Conn., and suburban Providence, are more inclined to move to ethnically mixed suburbs and to taper off ties to their old ethnic neighborhoods. They identify less with their ethnic heritage and are less influenced by it.

Geographic and economic mobility, plus involvement in non-Italian institutional life, have contributed to intermarriage. Yet intermarriage rates are lower among Italians than among other white ethnic groups (Irish, Polish, and German, for example), nationally as well as regionally, and Italian traditions often permeate multiethnic families.

Economic conditions in New England have influenced Italian American work experiences. When the region industrialized, Italian immigrants worked in the factories. Like their counterparts from other countries, they took jobs that few native-born Americans wanted. Thus Italians were employed in the shoe and hat industries of Newburyport, Mass., in the cotton and woolen mills of Lawrence, and in the shoemaking and shoe-repair businesses of New Haven. Their niche work typified ethnic labor-market segmentation at the time.

Immigrant Italians also worked in construction and landscaping, trades built on European skills. Many had been stonemasons, bricklayers, and the like or peasants before setting sail for the United States; their talents could be put to good use in the expanding New England economy. Many skilled Italian sculptors and quarrymen found work in Vermont's burgeoning granite industries.

Although immigrant and second-generation Italian Americans tended to engage in unskilled manual labor longer than most immigrant groups of their time, later generations did acquire white-collar and skilled blue-collar jobs. When the public sector expanded in the postwar period, Italian Americans were drawn to municipal positions that provided job security, health insurance, and pensions, benefits that many had never enjoyed. They often joined fire, police, and public works departments, where skill requirements at the time were minimal. Yet even when families found white-collar work, they—along with the Irish—experienced higher rates of "backward skidding" to blue-collar jobs than other immigrant groups.

Some Italian Americans went into business for themselves—in the trades, as peddlers, and as small shop owners in their own residential neighborhoods. They opened grocery stores that featured ethnic foods and became tailors and barbers, as well as landscapers and contractors. In Boston more than four times as many Italians as Irish worked in business (though twice as many Jews as Italians were so employed) in the early 1900s. Even when in business for themselves, though, shop owners often identified more closely with their working-class roots and working-class neighbors than with businessmen. Although a small proportion of Italians enriched themselves through organized crime, their children subsequently "made it," socially as well as economically, through legitimate lines of work.

On average, Italians experienced less economic mobility than other immigrant groups. First, they came from less entrepreneurial backgrounds than Jews, Greeks, Armenians, and other groups. Instead, they valued manual trades that were often passed down from father to son. Further, many thought of themselves as sojourners, planning to return to Italy one day, which also made them less willing to invest heavily in enterprises here. Jews were typically as residentially insular as Italians, but they placed a higher value on education and nonmanual work and experienced more economic mobility as a result.

Although successive generations of Italian New Englanders have experienced economic mobility, they have also been victims of deindustrialization, as factories shut down and relocated to the South and outside the United States in search of cheaper labor. Municipal employment options for Italian Americans also took a beating. When local governments sought to contain expenses, they outsourced some of the jobs traditionally held by Italian Americans. Emphasizing efficiency, private firms employed fewer workers and were less responsive to local ethnic pressures than public-sector employers had been.

Ethnic dynamics also influenced Italian New Englanders' political experiences. During the early period of mass immigration New England Italians were integrated into the American political system through Irish-dominated machine politics. Urban machines offered Italians, along with other poor immigrants, jobs, material assistance, and a friendly environment in exchange for votes. But the tensions between Italian and Irish New Englanders kept politics fragmented and friction-ridden, preventing political bosses from consolidating power as they had in New York City, for example, through Tammany Hall. Ethnic differences divided workers with common socioeconomic concerns. New England's Yankee-run Republican Party played on the ethnic divisions, wooing Italian American workers from the Democratic Party. In New Haven, for example, the GOP effectively competed for the Italian vote by offering positions both on party slates and in government. Democrats, too, offered Italians political spoils. By the late 1950s Italians in New Haven were thus being elected to political office in numbers disproportionate to their share of registered voters. Republicans in Providence courted Italian voters, too, and Italian representation was high, for instance, in Federal Hill, the city's Little Italy. Italians were the only major ethnic group whose loyalty the Democrats could not count on.

The shift from ward to at-large and nonpartisan municipal governance gave rise to coalition politics. In emerging coalitions Italians had some, but rarely dominant, influence. But by the 1990s coalition politics had enabled an Italian American, Thomas Menino, to be elected mayor of Boston for the first time; Menino has been reelected three times.

New England Republicans also courted Italians at the state level. They promoted "representatives of the Italians" as an electoral strategy long after Italian immigration had slowed. Nonetheless, the first Italian American governor (in 1946), who later became the first Italian American senator in the United States, was a Democrat, John O. Pastore, from Rhode Island.

Robert Dahl, *Who Governs? Democracy and Power in an American City* (1961); Herbert Gans, *The Urban Villagers: Group and Class in the Life of Italian-Americans* (1982); John Roche, "Suburban Ethnicity: Ethnic Attitudes and Behavior among Italian Americans in Two Suburban Communities," *Social Science Quarterly* 63, no. 1 (1982); Judith Smith, *Family Connections: A History of Italian and Jewish Immigrant Lives in Providence, Rhode Island, 1900–1940* (1985); Stephan Thernstrom, *The Other Bostonians: Poverty and Progress in the American Metropolis, 1880–1970* (1973).

Susan Eckstein

Jews Jews have been part of the region's cultural and social fabric reaching back to early colonial times and today constitute a highly visible minority presence in all six states, as they do in the United States at large. The current Jewish population of 425,000 (or slightly less than 3 percent of the total population of 14 million) is concentrated in the more densely developed urban and suburban areas of southern New England (Connecticut, Massachusetts, and Rhode Island claim all but 25,000 of the region's Jews).

Northern and rural sections, however, have long known an active Jewish life and presence. As a National Public Radio commentator from Vermont's Northeast Kingdom pointed out in a recent audio essay on the 2000 census results, "The most popular politician in the state is a Brooklyn Jew with an accent thick enough to *schmear* on a bagel" (Bernie Sanders, the House of Representatives' only declared Independent). Jews, from the secular to the occasionally observant to the Orthodox and marking all shades in between, have affected New England's dynamic cultural history, its varied economy, and its prominent role on the national political stage.

Longfellow's sympathetic poem "The Jewish Cemetery at Newport" serves as a eulogy on an early but apparently vanished Jewish presence in New England, yet the story it tells is essentially true. As a haven for religious dissenters (that is, non-Puritans), Roger Williams's Rhode Island attracted, in addition to Anabaptists, Quakers, and so forth, a contingent of Sephardic Jews who in 1650 founded Yeshuat Israel, the congregation that later was housed in what remains the nation's earliest Jewish house of worship, Touro Synagogue (1763). These Sephardic Jews, whose "very names," Longfellow says, suggest a "foreign accent" and "different climes," went on to become notable members of Newport's and Rhode Island's prosperous colonial merchant (and, often, slave-owning) class. Rhode Island posed an obvious exception to the prerevolutionary norm; while Jews—mostly peddlers—passed through the Puritan colonies, they made no permanent inroads or settlements until the war and its aftermath institutionalized American secularism. Harry Golden, in his series of humor-tinged essays entitled *Travels through Jewish America* (1974), notes that "the first Jew in Hartford, Connecticut was David the Peddlar, who was arrested in 1659 and charged with selling nutmeg to the mistress of the house when the head of the family was absent." The story seems typical. Until Puritans had thoroughly transformed themselves into Yankees—that is, until mercantilism had completely supplanted Christian piety as the region's defining social order—Jews would have been unwelcome guests in most communities, insufficiently rooted to make permanent homes or found congregations.

The revolutionary and constitutional period, however, ushered a gradual change. While New England remained less attractive to Jewish settlement than the Middle Atlantic and southern states, Jewish merchants made their way. "David" had a home of sorts: by 1777, Hartford had a "Jew's Street," a thoroughfare known for its sellers of used goods. Even rural areas knew an occasional Jewish deeded presence. The history of Montague, Mass., a village in the Connecticut River valley, tells of "Silas Lamson, a Jew," who took ownership in 1837 of a sawmill and began producing scythe snaths (handles) there. Jews knew a solitary, marginal existence, to be sure. As the historian Stephen J. Whitfield points out, "An American Jewish culture was unimaginable" as late as the mid-19th century in any region. In reality, the handful of New England Jews, whether of Sephardic or Ashkenazic origin, were all but invisible. In the imaginations of their neighbors, by contrast, they had conferred upon them a mythical status that bears a significant resemblance to the image of the "noble red man," whose precolonial cultural existence had been terminated and whose postencounter life was a perpetual disappointment to Yankee projections.

Indeed, the parallel is significant. If Jews knew any prominence in early- to mid-19th century New England, it was *as* Indians. The notion that Native Americans made up some part of the Ten Lost Tribes of Israel gained popularity during this period; evidence—often gathered by congregational ministers—poured in from all corners of North America, including the Berkshire town of Pittsfield, Mass., where, in 1815, a farmer plowing his field found a Jewish phylactery. As Rabbi I. Harold Scharfman points out in his 1976 book on Jewish American pioneers, the learned New England clergymen and historians who examined the artifact never considered the possibility that an actual Jew might have dropped the item while passing through. Perhaps in keeping with their self-consciously modernizing and republican sensibility, New Englanders of Puritan stock, as Longfellow's poem suggests, chose to see Jews as ghosts—ancient leavings of an ancient, pre-American world whose existence was incommensurate with the onrush of modernity. The view was largely sympathetic, though often patronizing as well. In a region of the nation whose English founders had habitually referred to it as the New English Canaan and whose descendants frequently took Old Testament names like Hepzibah and Jabez, the Jews of old played an important symbolic role.

New England's status as a home for Jews evolved to a new stage as numbers increased in the mid-1800s. German Jews followed their Sephardic predecessors in the wake of the European upheavals of the 1840s. Many of these immigrants were both educated and satisfactorily financed—sufficiently so, in any case, to found new congregations. Both Hartford and Boston saw the establishment, during this period, of substantial temples: Boston's Kadal Kodosh Obahei Shalom was founded in 1843 and Hartford's Temple Beth Israel in 1847. The history of these German Jews is well documented, in large part because they—along with their handful of Sephardic counterparts—constituted the nation's established Jewry when the much larger influx of eastern European Jews of the late 19th century began. A product of both Sephardic and German strains, the poet Emma Lazarus created something of a stir when she visited the Emersons of Concord, Mass., invited there by the eminent essayist's daughter, Ellen. "A real, unconverted Jew" like Lazarus was bound to bring some excitement to the staid atmosphere of Concord; the Transcendentalists, of course, were notably receptive not only to exoticism but, more particularly, to the products of German culture.

But a major distinction was to be drawn, naturally, between the unthreateningly scarce and charmingly cosmopolitan first- and second-wave Jews and the teeming masses of steerage-class eastern European Jews who began arriving by the boatload along the Eastern Seaboard in the 1880s. Lazarus's "huddled masses yearning to breathe free" were not so joyfully greeted by New England's Brahmin elite, by its other immigrant groups, or, for that matter, by some of the Jews who had preceded them. If the earliest Jewish arrivals had derived certain benefits from their relative wealth or from their hold on the Yankee imagination, those who followed in the third wave were subject, for several succeeding decades, to all manner of anti-Semitic acts and policies. Having come in large numbers (the Jewish population of Hartford, for example, grew from 1,500 in 1880 to 18,000 in 1920), without money or English, and having emerged not from a secularized, *kultured* western Europe but from an isolated, largely Orthodox shtetl background, these Jews disturbed the Yankee sensibility: "The Jew makes me creep," commented Henry Brooks Adams. The jazz critic and memoirist Nat Hentoff, whose father and mother had come to Boston from Russia, suggests that the Brahmins were not the only persecutors of the recent arrivals: "When the first Jews from Eastern Europe came, with their herrings and black bread, to Boston in 1882, they were told to go away . . . by the embarrassed German Jews . . . who were afraid that the Brahmins might make some connection between these greenhorns and the true Jewish gentlemen and ladies of Boston."

Though this particular contingent was turned away and sent south to New York, many boats similarly loaded followed in its wake, and the third-wave Jews found their way through the cities of New England. As in New York and the nation's other major cities, the shtetl Jews gravitated—with notable exceptions—to the textile industry, and tended to populate urban enclaves. They were well represented not only in Boston and in Hartford but in Worcester, Springfield, and Lawrence, Mass. (where they played a prominent role in the 1912 Bread and Roses strike), throughout the cities of southern Connecticut, including New Haven and Bridgeport, as well as in Providence and other urban areas of Rhode Island. To a lesser extent, they also settled in northern and rural areas, where, as they gradually accumulated capital, they became leading merchants. Jews could be found in places as far-flung as Portsmouth, N.H., where the Shapiro House has now evolved into one of four Jewish house museums in the United States; North Adams, Mass., where—according to the local memory—the Irish and Italian factory workers grew accustomed to getting all their shopping done before the Jewish *shabbos;* and some dozens of other communities besides. Bethlehem, N.H., became home to a summer (and now year-round) community of Hasidic Jews whose base was in Brooklyn.

Successive decades of New England Jews followed the national trend. Having survived the relative poverty and ghettoization of life in places like Boston's Roxbury, they went on to settle suburban communities. Increased prosperity was only one factor in the redistribution; another was the redlining and blockbusting practices employed by realtors in the 1950s and 1960s to transform Roxbury into an African American ghetto and to restrict Jews in the same act; the segregation of Boston's ethnic communities is described by J. Anthony Lukas in *Common Ground.* Jews faced other discriminatory policies, too, including the now well-known Ivy League quota system, which controlled Jews' access to some of New England's elite institutions of higher education throughout the first half of the 20th century. But the period brought triumphs as well, mostly in the form of personal success stories. Louis Brandeis, the Supreme Court justice and prominent American advocate of the Zionist movement, was a product of Boston's Jewish community. Lawrence, Mass., was the home of the composer and conductor Leonard Bernstein, who went on from his historic debut at Tanglewood in the 1940s to become assistant conductor of the New York Philharmonic and director of successive orchestras throughout the United States and the world. In politics, New England Jewry produced the nation's first Jewish senator, Abraham Ribicoff of Connecticut, as well as William Cohen of Maine—whose family retained its Jewish surname even after converting to Christianity. The first Jew to be nominated as a vice presidential candidate by a major party, Joseph Lieberman, represents Connecticut in the Senate. Current House members, in addition to Sanders of Vermont, include Barney Frank of southeastern Massachusetts.

Jewish life in New England has long been enhanced by its rural contingent. In the early 20th century, Jewish farming communities were established in various locations in western and southeastern Massachusetts, Aroostook County, Maine (where Jews once constituted the largest potato growers and

merchants), and throughout Connecticut, where Jews were once prime movers in both the dairy and poultry industries. The area surrounding Danielson, Conn., became home, in the aftermath of World War II, to more than 100 Jewish farming households, many of which included Holocaust survivors and their children. And though many of these Jewish farms have long since disbanded—following a region- and nationwide trend away from family farming in general—a newer generation of contemporary Jews, many of them products of the 1960s and 1970s back-to-the-land movement, have settled in rural sections of all six New England states. For the past decade or so, the Conference on Judaism in Rural New England (based in Montpelier, Vt.) has worked "to foster and enhance communication among communities, synagogues and individuals"— to bring together, in the words of its mission statement, "young people, parents, gays and lesbians, political activists, recovering alcoholics"—all of whom share in common both Judaism and a rural New England perspective.

In less isolated settings, New England Jews are served, represented, and highlighted not only by their religious affiliations but by such institutions as Brandeis University in Waltham, Mass., Hebrew College (which is also the home of the American Jewish Historical Society's Boston office), the Elie Wiesel Center for Judaic Studies at Boston University, and—in newly designed buildings on the campus of Hampshire College in Amherst, Mass.—the National Yiddish Book Center, which houses the world's largest collection of Yiddish books, manuscripts, and documents. Newly arrived immigrants, frequently Russian-speaking, continue to infuse the region with a diverse Jewish population.

In a world where overt and often violent acts of anti-Semitism are certifiably on the rise, New England has offered not only sanctuary but revival. Thus, the supreme irony afforded us as we revisit Longfellow's premature elegy; that "the dead nations never rise again" may be true, but what of a nation that has found fertile ground upon which it might induce the miracle of continual rebirth and reinvention?

Shifra R. Deykin, *Vignettes of the the Early Days in the Jewish Community of Great Barrington, Massachusetts* (1987); Harry Golden (with Bruce Goldhurst), *Travels through Jewish America* (1974); Nat Hentoff, *Boston Boy* (1986); Herman J. Levine and Benjamin Miller, *The Jewish Farmer in Changing Times* (1966); Rosie Rosenzweig, *Jewish Guide to Boston and New England* (1995); Jonathan D. Sarna, *American Judaism: A History* (2004); Jonathan D. Sarna and Ellen Smith, *The Jews of Boston* (1995); I. Harold Sharfman, *Jews on the Frontier* (1976).

Michael Hoberman

Koreans New England's Korean community has been characterized historically by its high percentage of students. In 1995 there were 7,500 students of Korean ancestry in the region, up from 750 in 1980. The overall Korean population in New England is relatively small, constituting less than 3 percent of Koreans living in the United States. According to the 2000 census, there were 29,337 Koreans in the region: 17,369 in Massachusetts, 7,064 in Connecticut, 1,800 in New Hampshire, 1,560 in Rhode Island, 875 in Maine, and 669 in Vermont. Korean families are residentially assimilated, tending to move to suburbs rather than concentrate in urban ethnic enclaves. The large number of students explains why the three main population centers for Koreans in New England are Cambridge, Boston, and Brookline, Mass. Most of the Korean residents of these three cities are students at nearby universities or young professionals.

The first reports of Koreans in New England date back to 1883, when a diplomatic group from Korea visited New England schools and farms in an effort to help modernize Korean education and farming technology. That same year also brought the first Korean students to the region's educational institutions. By 1919 approximately 25 Koreans were enrolled at Boston-area schools. Some of them had fled Korea before Japanese annexation in 1910 and arrived in New England via China or Europe. Others came directly from Japanese-occupied Korea with Japanese passports. Differences in political allegiance among these students were a divisive force in the community. Among these early arrivals was Syngman Rhee, a Korean nationalist who came in 1908 to pursue a master's degree in political science at Harvard University. Rhee later became the first president of South Korea, from 1948 to 1960.

The early Korean population in New England consisted primarily of students who would leave the area after graduation. The first permanent settlers came in the 1920s as secondary migrants from Hawaii. Between 1950 and 1964 the majority of Koreans who moved to New England came as wives of American servicemen, adoptees, and students. After the Immigration Act of 1965 more Koreans were able to immigrate to the United States, but students continued to dominate the New England Korean population.

Today's Koreans in New England fall into four major categories: immigrant families and descendants of immigrants, students from other parts of the United States or abroad, wives of American servicemen and their children, and children adopted by New England families. Many of the immigrants initially came to New England as students and opted to remain in the area. Others are relatives who followed them to the United States.

Despite their shared ethnicity, Korean New Englanders maintain separate voluntary associations. Immigrant Koreans have organized more than 15 associations based on social, political, religious, or professional interests. For example, the Korean-American Citizens' League of New England, established in 1990, encourages participation in U.S. politics. The Korean Society of New England sponsors social events and celebrations of Korean holidays as well as an annual dinner to honor American veterans of the Korean War. Students of Korean ancestry are organized around school-based Korean Student Associations that sponsor intercollegiate cultural and social events. The one possible exception to this separation within the Korean community is in the area of religion, where Korean war-brides mix with immigrant families, and English-speaking Korean Americans join the English ministries of ethnic Korean places of worship.

Because of the transient nature of the student population and the subsequent lack of a stable customer base, businesses catering to the Korean American community did not take root in New England until the 1980s. Today there are many Korean-owned establishments, the most numerous being the more than 250 Korean dry cleaners in the region. Among the Korean-owned businesses that cater mainly to local Korean and Asian American communities are more than 29 restaurants, three karaoke clubs, 13 Asian grocery stores, three Korean-language newspapers, six beauty salons, and two stores that rent videos from Asia. About 90 percent of these businesses are based in Massachusetts. For Koreans concerned about their children's education, there are 21 Korean schools that teach Korean language and culture and provide tutoring in math and SAT preparation for Korean American youth every Saturday.

As in other parts of the United States, Korean New Englanders have organized themselves largely around religion. The former Harvard librarian Rin Paik points out in a 1995 Korean-language article that the first Korean church in New England was established in 1953, with services held at Boston University's Marsh Chapel. Today the Korean Church of Boston, now located in Brookline, Mass., is one of more than 53 Korean Protestant churches in the region. In addition, there are three Korean Catholic churches and two Korean Buddhist temples. In recent years, with the coming of age of second-generation Korean Americans in the area, a number of English-language ministries to Korean American young adults in New England have been established within the Protestant tradition.

Bong-Youn Choy, *Koreans in America* (1979); Maureen Dezell, "Koreans Keep the Faith," *Boston Globe,* January 12, 1995; Won Moo Hurh, *The Korean Americans* (1998); Won Moo Hurh and Kwang Chung Kim, *Korean Immigrants in America: A Structural Analysis of Ethnic Confinement and Adhesive Adaptation* (1984); Franklin Ng, ed., *The Asian-American Encyclopedia* (1995).

Karen Chai Kim

Ku Klux Klan The history of New England and that of the Ku Klux Klan have always been inextricably intertwined. After the Civil War northern abolitionists, educators, and members of the American Missionary Association, many of whom had formerly run depots on the Underground Railroad, went south to teach newly freed slaves. Their presence stirred the wrath of southerners, some of whom formed the Klan to keep blacks in their place, by violence if necessary.

Federal investigations obliterated the Klan in the late 19th century, but in the 1920s the newly invigorated order swept the nation. The Baptist minister and novelist Thomas Dixon, who preached with evangelical southern fervor to large Boston audiences for a brief time and was a summer visitor to York, Maine, wrote *The Clansman* (1905), which became a best-seller and inspired D. W. Griffith's epic film *Birth of a Nation* (1915). Many New Englanders, such as Oswald Garrison Villard, the grandson of the Boston abolitionist William Lloyd Garrison, a founder of the NAACP, and the owner of the *New York Evening Post,* opposed the racist film. But many northerners, fearing black migration, flocked to see it. Patrons filled Boston's Tremont Theater daily, sparking a Ku Klux fever in the region.

Ku Klux Klan speaker, Scotland, Conn., 1980

Two public relations experts, Edward Young Clark and Elizabeth Tyler, worked with the Klan leader William Joseph Simmons in Georgia to attract and recruit members nationwide. They increased membership by advertising themselves as "100 percent American" and widening the net of enemies who threatened the nation to include Jews, communists, and Catholics. When Klan organizers divided the nation into nine domains, they stationed a Grand Goblin in Boston. Rural New England areas and eastern cities became breeding grounds for Klan activity. Nineteenth-century New England had had its own secret societies, the American Protective Association and the Whitecap movement, and their residual support helped to revive the Klan. Clergymen, particularly in Maine and Rhode Island, became important in the Klan's growth. In Portland, Maine, the Reverend C. H. Marvin determined that secret societies had a basis in Scripture.

Aligning itself with the Republican Party in the North, the Klan endorsed candidates and put Klansmen in office in Portland. So powerful was the Klan that the Massachusetts delegation at the Democratic National Convention in 1924 felt pressured to change its candidate. Klan members were active in Maine and New Hampshire gubernatorial races in the 1920s, holding rallies in both states. The Klan also invited the ire of northern blacks. When Calvin Coolidge won the presidency, moderate blacks in Boston asked him whether he relied on Klan support. Coolidge refused to respond.

The Klan's corruption and excesses, however, particularly a Grand Dragon's rape and murder of a young Indiana woman named Madge Oberholtzer in 1925, disgusted northerners, and in 1926, 600 New Haven, Conn., Klansmen resigned as a group. By 1928 the Klan had declined in power, disappearing in the North.

Yet the connection between New England and the Klan persisted. In the 1930s, when northeastern manufacturers abandoned textile mills and moved to the South, the Klan helped them keep labor unorganized and cheap, often brutalizing organizers. Samuel Green, Grand Dragon of Georgia, declared that Yankee organizers would not tell the South how to run its business. Klansmen resorted to terror to keep activists at bay. Vermont activist Joseph Shoemaker's attempt to organize for public ownership of utilities, a 30-hour work week, and unemployment insurance in Tampa, Fla., led in 1946 to his brutal murder, whose known perpetrators were never punished. Eventually the Dies Committee, a standing congressional committee that became the House Committee on Un-American Activities, promised to investigate the Klan thoroughly, but its own right-wing biases led the Massachusetts congressman Thomas Eliot to fear that the inquiry would amount to a whitewash, only making matters worse. The Klan hated President John F. Kennedy, rejoicing in his assassination, and fought the northern civil rights workers who came south in the 1960s. Klan recruiters were once again active in New England in the 1980s and 1990s, but with little success.

Fred J. Cook, *Ku Klux Klan: America's Recurring Nightmare* (1989); Wyn Craig Wade, *The Fiery Cross: The Ku Klux Klan in America* (1987).

Suzanna Nyberg

Latin Americans Latin Americans are a large and diverse group of people. In geographic terms, Latin America comprises the Caribbean islands of Cuba, Hispaniola, and Puerto Rico; Mexico; Central America; and the continent of South America from Venezuela to the southern tip of Patagonia. When Christopher Columbus found his way to these indigenously populated lands in 1492, he called them Las Indias, the Indies, and El Nuevo Mundo, the New World. Although the region gained its independence from Spain in 1821, Spanish has remained the dominant language in most countries; the exception is Portuguese-speaking Brazil, with its 160 million people. It was when Mexico became a European kingdom under the emperor Maximilian I (1870) that the region came to be known as Latin America, a term that differentiated it from the English-speaking nations of United States and Canada.

Latin Americans come to New England predominantly from Puerto Rico, the Dominican Republic, Cuba, El Salvador, and Colombia. Anglo-Americans have traditionally referred to these immigrant groups as Spanish-speaking, Hispanic, or Hispanic American. To many Anglos the word *Hispanic* denotes race as well as national origin, but today it is more widely understood as an ethnic, not a racial, category. Since the early 1980s the term *Latino* has been used more and more commonly by both Anglo and some Latin American constituencies. Often politically expeditious, *Latino* can have class or status connotations as well. At present it appears that Latin Americans residing in New England would rather be identified by their country of origin than by any ethnic designation.

During the second half of the 19th century New England attracted many Latin Americans to its colleges and universities. It was not until the early 1940s, however, that a sizable number of Puerto Ricans immigrated to the region, settling particularly in Connecticut and Massachusetts, states that still retain New England's highest concentrations of Latinos.

Latin American children in traditional Sunday dress, 1986

This migratory movement occurred as a result of World War II, when thousands of American military personnel were sent to fight in Europe. As part of the war effort many Puerto Ricans came to work in New England's factories. When Puerto Ricans were granted American citizenship in 1917, it became easier for them to travel and settle in the continental United States. Moreover, the Puerto Rican government began to encourage unemployed workers to relocate to the mainland in search of better working conditions. Once the war ended, the United States continued to expand its industrial base nationally as well as internationally. Many Puerto Ricans either settled permanently in New England or began a circular pattern of travel between their home island and the continent in which many continue to engage today. During the 1950s and 1960s hundreds of Puerto Ricans resettled in several New England cities: Bridgeport, Hartford, New Britain, and Waterbury, Conn., and Boston, Springfield, and Holyoke, Mass. Many workers came to toil in Connecticut's tobacco fields and to work in the expanding industries. Boston at the time had vibrant shoe and beer industries, and many Puerto Ricans found work there. Springfield had a heavily industrialized economic base and Holyoke a largely agricultural one. During the 1970s and 1980s New England received many immigrants from the Dominican Republic, Colombia, El Salvador, Guatemala, and Cuba, among other countries. The international changes affecting the world's economy during the early 1980s brought many skilled and professional Puerto Ricans to New England. Some moved from the cities to the suburbs as well as to states outside the region; others moved back to Puerto Rico after living many years in New England.

The 2000 census lists 320,323 persons of Latin American ancestry residing in Connecticut and 428,729 in Massachusetts, with a total of 875,225 making their homes in New England. Like other migratory groups, Latin Americans have had to adjust to the transition from an economy once dominated by agriculture and industry to one in which high-tech manufacturing and service-oriented jobs are primary.

Of all ethnic New Englanders, Puerto Ricans and other Latinos have the largest proportion of persons that live below the poverty level, including almost half the members of that group who are under age 18. In 1999 the per capita income for Latinos was $13,270, lower than the regional average for any of the five principal racial groups. Among Latino families, 35.7 percent have incomes below the poverty level. Most such families (68.5 percent) are headed by single females. Owing to the high cost of real estate in both Connecticut and Massachusetts, most Latin American families live in rented dwellings.

Overall, the educational attainment of New Englanders of Latin American descent has lagged behind that of other racial and ethnic groups. The number of high school or college graduates is comparatively low, while the number of school dropouts is very high. Many Puerto Rican and Dominican children attend federally mandated bilingual-education programs whose curricula are often perceived as substandard. The result is a second-class level of instruction and achievement within the larger system.

In 2000 Latinos 16 and older made up 4.8 percent of the New England labor force (employed plus unemployed). The workforce participation rate for Latino men, at 60.4 percent, was lower than that of all others in New England (66.9 percent). Their unemployment rate was an extremely high 10.5 percent versus 4.3 percent for all others. At 7.8 percent, the unemployment rate for Latino women was much higher than the 4.3 percent rate for all other New England women. The lack of formal education and work experience has forced many into low-paying, service-oriented jobs.

Discrimination against dark-skinned Latinos remains a critical problem throughout New England, and many families feel its negative impact. As in other ethnic groups, lighter-skinned Latinos tend to experience much less discrimination than their darker-skinned counterparts.

Although many Latinos define themselves as Roman Catholic, one of the outcomes of the migratory experience has been the establishment of local churches administered by local preachers. The most active churches throughout the region are the Pentecostal, Jehovah's Witnesses, the International Church of Christ, and other fundamentalist sects. Many Latinos also practice Santería, which has traditionally blended African and Christian religious rituals and practices into everyday life experiences.

Second- and third-generation Latinos are rapidly becoming more assimilated into the dominant culture, although their parents' heritage continues to be reflected in the art, music, foodways, and language of Latino communities. Latin Americans brought with them to New England a long-standing love of celebrations, as we see in the many cultural festivals that take place during the year. Every group celebrates its national holidays with music and dances (merengue; salsa; tango; *cumbia,* a couple dance of mixed Indian and Spanish origin; and *plena,* a particularly Puerto Rican form), parades, and artistic presentations. Social and political clubs have sprung up all over New England to safeguard and promote the interests of the various Latin American national groups. The Panamerican Society of New England (1941) and the Puerto Rican Festival of Massachusetts (1967) represent Latino culture at its best. Another significant medium of cultural expression can be found in local newspapers such as *El Mundo* of Boston. Radio and television programs such as *La Herencia Puertorriqueña* (Puerto Rican heritage) and *Con Salsa,* among others, have contributed to solidifying cultural tradition in the Boston area. In addition to local radio and television programming in Spanish, Latinos keep abreast of their culture by listening to TV Sud, an international network covering the entire hemisphere, as well as Spanish-language CNN, Univisión, and Telemundo. The urban landscape has been enriched by the establishment of restaurants, bodegas (grocery stores), *botánicas* (herbal medicine stores), music discos, fashion boutiques, travel agencies, and many other businesses that confer a distinct Latin American flavor on local districts.

The Puerto Rican Voter Registration Program and other state and local efforts of this kind have increased the political participation of Latinos, who lag behind other ethnic groups in terms of overall political effectiveness. Nelson Merced of Dorchester became the first Latin American to be elected to the Massachusetts legislature in November 1988. Several others have since followed in his footsteps. Latinos have also been elected to local city councils and school committees in the Bay State and in Connecticut; they will likely go on to gain influence statewide as economic conditions and educational opportunities improve.

Boston Persistent Poverty Project, *Latinos in Boston: Confronting Poverty, Building Community* (1993); Richard Chabran and Rafael Chabran, eds., *The Latino Encyclopedia,* 6 vols. (1995); Edwin Melendez, ed., *Latino Poverty and Economic Development in Massachusetts* (1993); Ralph Rivera and Sonia Nieto, *The Education of Latino Students in Massachusetts: Issues, Research, and Policy Implications* (1993); María E. Pérez y Gonzalez, *Puerto Ricans in the United States* (2000); Thomas M. Stephens, *Dictionary of Latin American Racial and Ethnic Terms* (1989); Barbara A. Tenenbaum, ed., *Encyclopedia of Latin American History and Culture* (1996).

Angel Amy-Moreno

Lewis, Elma

Lewis, Elma (1921–2004) Arts educator and administrator, community leader, activist. A native of Roxbury, Mass., Elma Lewis helped establish the reputation of Boston's African American arts community internationally while preaching a message of self-empowerment to generations of inner-city schoolchildren. Her lifelong crusade on behalf of cultural awareness and artistic achievement among all African Americans was often waged in a climate of racial polarization. Along with fear and respect from community leaders, however, came honors for Lewis from universities and arts organizations around the world.

Lewis was born September 16, 1921. Her parents had emigrated from the West Indies and were followers of black nationalist Marcus Garvey. As a child Lewis sang in local churches to help support her family, gaining early exposure to Boston's rich array of cultural resources. Upon graduating from Emerson College, she earned a master's degree in education from Boston University. She then taught speech, dance, and drama in various area institutions before opening the Elma Lewis School of Fine Arts in 1950.

The school was founded in a small apartment in Roxbury with "three hundred dollars and a secondhand piano," as Lewis recalled. More than 6,000 students studied under her over the next four decades. Many went on to distinguished careers in the performing arts. Gifted or not, though, Lewis's students always learned important lessons about themselves. Lewis was a stern taskmaster and demanded total dedication. "The point," she insisted in an interview in 1996, "was to make people, not artists."

Though the school struggled financially for years and finally closed in the mid-1980s, nothing, including chronic diabetes, held Lewis down for long. In 1969 she conducted a cleanup of Roxbury's Franklin Park. Duke Ellington and Boston Pops conductor Arthur Fiedler were among the stars who played there free. Bill Cosby, Ossie Davis, Harry Belafonte, and Muhammad Ali are a few of the many celebrities who have donated their time and talents to Lewis's programs. A *New York Times* profile in 1968 rightfully described Lewis as "Sol Hurok, Tyrone Guthrie and P. T. Barnum rolled into one."

In 1971 Lewis was the first to stage Langston Hughes's pageant *Black Nativity;* it remains one of Boston's treasured holiday traditions. Another dream of Lewis's was realized in 1980 when the Museum of the National Center of Afro-American Artists opened in Roxbury. Of the center she said, "It is where we, the blacks, are going to state our black heritage and share our culture and the beauty of our arts with all people, black and white alike."

Her critics notwithstanding, Lewis was a visionary arts administrator whose influence reached far beyond Boston's black community. In 1981 she received one of the first MacArthur Foundation's so-called genius grants honoring her achievements. In 1983 President Ronald Reagan awarded Lewis a special arts medal, and in 1988 the National Black Arts Conference made Lewis a Living Legend. An honorary degree bestowed on Lewis by Harvard University in 1972 cited her for having brought "fresh new impetus to an ancient strain within our total culture."

A 75th birthday celebration for Lewis drew hundreds of her former protégés and lifelong admirers, including the poet Maya Angelou and former United Nations ambassador Andrew Young. In an interview in 1996 Lewis commented that her former student Talley Beatty, the renowned choreographer, asked

Elma Lewis and children stage Langston Hughes's Black Nativity, *1991*

artists to "show me the body of your work" when evaluating them. Said Lewis, "When I leave here, the body of my work will be all these wonderful people out there in the world, doing great things."

Joseph P. Kahn, "The Lioness in Winter," *Boston Globe,* September 12, 1996; Sara Rimer, "An Arts Leader for Whom 'Anything Is Possible,'" *New York Times,* December 28, 1998; Carol Rivers, "Black America's Barnum, Hurok and Guthrie," *New York Times,* November 17, 1968.

Joseph P. Kahn

Lithuanians Lithuanians began to arrive and settle in New England in great numbers during the second half of the 19th century. Boston and most notably South Boston were the largest centers of Lithuanian settlement. By 1915 Boston's Lithuanians numbered more than 15,000. The first generation of Lithuanian immigrants were fleeing tsarist oppression in the Russian Empire or seeking an escape from poverty. Since many of them were not educated, they sought employment in sugar refineries or machine shops. Later they concentrated in garment factories. The first Lithuanian union, the United Garment Workers of America, Lithuanian Local 149, which had 700 members, was formed in Boston in 1909.

Other important centers of Lithuanian immigration were Lowell and Lawrence, Mass., where again the garment industry was the greatest employer. In Worcester, Mass., many worked in the steel, carpet, and paper indus-

tries. In Hudson, Mass., most were employed in tanneries, rubber factories, and sawmills. Lithuanians settled in Waterbury, Conn., as early as 1849, and there are still approximately 8,000–10,000 Lithuanians living there. Hartford was another important Lithuanian community. In Vermont, Lithuanians settled in places such as Bellows Falls, Graniteville, Rutland, and Winooski, where they worked in quarries or on farms. Maine Lithuanians worked in the forest and ice industries of Portland and Lewiston. In New Hampshire Lithuanians settled at Nashua.

Almost every Lithuanian ethnic community had its relief associations, which provided much-needed aid for their members in times of illness. These organizations also greatly contributed to the development of Lithuanian cultural life in New England. Lithuanians soon had their own newspapers, such as *Darbininkas* (The worker), an organ of the Lithuanian Roman Catholic Worker's Association that first saw publication in Boston in 1915. Another newspaper, *Keleivis* (The traveler), founded in Boston in 1905, was for decades the voice of the Lithuanian Socialist League of America. Lithuanians founded a number of Roman Catholic or Lutheran parishes and parochial schools, as well as choirs and other cultural groups. The American Lithuanian Cultural Archives were established in Putnam, Conn., in 1941. After World War II, when Lithuania was annexed by the Soviet Union, many educated, middle-class Lithuanians immigrated to the United States

and settled in New England. These new arrivals organized a number of Lithuanian scientific and academic associations. In 1953 the Lithuanian Encyclopedia Press was established in Boston; it has since published the 36-volume *Lietuviy enciklopedija* (Lithuanian encyclopedia, 1969) and the six-volume English-language *Encyclopedia Lituanica* (1970–78).

As economic conditions and security of employment improved, many relief associations disbanded, reorganizing as chapters of fraternal associations such as the Knights of Lithuania. By the 1950s it was not unusual to find entire city blocks of Lithuanian-owned stores, restaurants, taverns, funeral homes, real estate agencies, and other institutions. American-born Lithuanians now began to enter municipal, state, and federal government services and to work in most of the professions: as lawyers, doctors, pharmacists, architects, teachers, engineers, and so forth. Lithuanians have also always been active in the arts.

Some prominent Lithuanians of New England have been Senator Frank Monchum of Connecticut; Anna Kaskas, who sang with the New York Metropolitan Opera; and Vytautas Marijosius, music director of the Lithuanian State Opera, who periodically conducted the Hartford String Orchestra. Since Lithuania regained its independence from the Soviet Union in 1991, there has been no significant increase in Lithuanian immigration to the United States.

Simas Suziedelis, ed., *Encyclopedia Lituanica,* 6 vols. (1970–78); William L. Wolkovich, *From the Nemunas to the Assabet: A History of the Lithuanians and Lithuanian-Americans of Hudson, Mass., 1866–1966* (1966).

Andrius Valevicius

Malcolm X (El-Hajj Malik El-Shabazz) (1925–65) Pan-Africanist leader. Born Malcolm Little in 1925 in Omaha, Nebr., Malcolm X is known for his strong critiques of American racism. After a fatherless and virtually motherless early adolescence in Lansing, Mich., Malcolm left school in the eighth grade to move in with his half-sister, Ella Little Collins, in Boston. The three teenage years he spent living in the middle-class black and Jewish section of Roxbury, Mass., known as the Hill, and in the dance halls, nightclubs, and pool rooms of Boston's South End, left a deep imprint on the future civil rights leader. After a series of burglaries landed him in Massachusetts prisons before his 21st birthday, Malcolm became a disciple of Elijah Muhammad and a devotee of the Nation of Islam.

At the Norfolk (Mass.) Prison Colony, to which he was transferred in 1948, Malcolm studied theology and ancient history and got his first taste of public speaking. After his release, he became a minister in the Nation of

Malcolm X visits Intervale Street Nation of Islam headquarters, Roxbury, Mass., 1964

Islam, organizing temples such as Boston's Mosque No. 11. A clever orator, formidable intellect, and master debater, Malcolm rose through the ranks to become minister of the coveted Temple No. 7 in Harlem. Before long he became the Nation of Islam's national spokesman and leader. For many, Malcolm X *was* the Nation of Islam.

Elijah Muhammad suspended Malcolm X from the Nation of Islam, however, for his poorly timed and, in the view of many, disrespectful remarks about President John F. Kennedy's assassination in 1963. Malcolm described the murder as a case of "chickens coming home to roost," adding that "as an old farm boy," he was "glad" it had happened. What he meant, Malcolm later explained, was that the violence propagated by the United States abroad—in Vietnam, for instance—had finally taken the life of one of its beloved sons, revealing the truth about America to the world. Malcolm X scholars believe, though, that Nation of Islam officials suspended Malcolm less because of those ill-fated remarks than because of his widespread popularity, his unveiling of the Black Muslim prophet Elijah Muhammad's adultery, and his desire to move the Nation of Islam from its isolationist position. Malcolm soon realized that suspension meant banishment. He thus left the Nation of Islam in March 1964 to found two organizations, the Muslim Mosque, Inc., and the black nationalist, pan-Africanist Organization of Afro-American Unity (OAAU).

Malcolm adopted orthodox (Sunni) Islam; made a hajj, or pilgrimage to Mecca; and traveled in Africa, notably to Ghana. Abandoning what he now regarded as Elijah Muhammad's specious teachings and pouring his energies into the OAAU, Malcolm sought alliances with the civil rights movement, American socialists, and Third World revolutionaries. Assassinated while delivering a speech on February 21, 1965, in the Audubon Ballroom in New York City, Malcolm is more popular today than he was during his lifetime. The consensus is that he was struck down while making creative and progressive strides for human rights.

In 1998 the Boston Landmarks Commission voted unanimously to designate Malcolm X's boyhood home in Roxbury, built in 1874, a historic landmark. "Malcolm X learned a lot about himself and humanity when he lived here," said Rodnell Collins, Malcolm's half-nephew, at the dedication of his uncle's former Dale Street home. "That's what this house is all about."

George Breitman, *The Last Year of Malcolm X: The Evolution of a Revolutionary* (1980); James Cone, *Martin and Malcolm and America: A Dream or a Nightmare?* (1992); William W. Sales, Jr., *From Civil Rights to Black Liberation: Malcolm X and the Organization of Afro-American Unity* (1994); Malcolm X and Alex Haley, *The Autobiography of Malcolm X* (1965).

Josiah Ulysses Young III

Maliseet The Maliseet traditionally lived in the maritime area of northern Maine and southeastern New Brunswick, Canada. They are sometimes called Wolastoqiyik, "people of the Saint John River." Archaeological evidence of settlements dates back more than 10,000 years in the region. With the passage of time, extensive trade routes developed to the north and south, bringing cultural exchange between tribal groups.

European contact in the 16th and 17th centuries wrought the most dramatic changes to the culture of New England's native people, including the Maliseet. Religious missionaries and explorers changed trading patterns and brought devastating diseases to Native American communities in the Maritimes. Eager to benefit from the exchange of European goods, many Maliseet spent their winters deep in the woods in small hunting groups seeking the profits of the fur trade.

Maliseet communities spanned what today are the borders between the United States and Canada. In 1794 the Jay Treaty between Great Britain and the United States recognized the rights of native people to cross the borders freely. When the farming and logging industries encroached on their traditional hunting territory in the late 1800s, many Maliseet families moved to the Houlton area in northeastern Maine. With few employment opportunities there, Maliseet men and women earned their living making baskets, fishing, harvesting fiddleheads, and doing odd jobs.

In the 1970s this community incorporated as the Houlton Band of Maliseet Indians. The Maine Indian Land Claims Settlement Act of 1980 accorded the group federal recognition and created a $900,000 fund for the acquisition of land. It did not grant the Houlton Band the right to self-governance, however, as it did to the Penobscot and Passamaquoddy. Today the Houlton Band has approximately 80 acres held in trust in Houlton and Littleton, Maine. Much of this land is currently leased to area farmers. The settlement act also brought the Maliseet health and education services from the federal government.

The Houlton Band has an elected council and governor who oversee tribal resources and relations with state and federal governments. Since gaining federal recognition, the Maliseet have built a tribal center along the Meduxnekeag River near Houlton, erected a 50-unit housing development, and engaged in various business and infrastructure projects.

Canada today is home to seven recognized Maliseet bands. Together with the Houlton Band, they form the Maliseet Nation. Of that nation's more than 3,000 people, approximately 680 are members of the Houlton Band in Maine.

Vincent Erickson, "Maliseet-Passamaquoddy," in *Northeast*, ed. Bruce G. Trigger, vol. 15 of *Handbook of North American Indians*, gen. ed. William C. Sturtevant (1978); Robert M. Leavitt, *Maliseet and Micmac: First Nations of the Maritimes* (1995); Maine Indian Program, *The Wabanakis of Maine and the Maritimes: A Resource Book about Penobscot, Passamaquoddy, Maliseet, Micmac, and Abenaki Indians* (1989); Frederick John Pratson, *Land of the Four Directions* (1970).

Susie Husted

Mashpee The Mashpee are the largest of the five bands of the Wampanoag, the original Native American inhabitants of southeastern Massachusetts. The contemporary Mashpee community is centered in the town of Mashpee, Mass., where it has been a distinct presence since the 17th century.

The Wampanoag in Mashpee rose to prominence as the largest of a number of Indian reservations established by colonial authorities after King Philip's War (1675–76). An existing Wampanoag community in that location became the basis of a Christian Indian town, and English missionary Richard Bourne organized the Mashpee Indian Church in 1670. Having remained neutral during King Philip's War, the Mashpee were granted perpetual title to their land by the Plymouth Colony in 1685. For the next three centuries, however, the struggle to retain control of this land would be a central theme of Mashpee life.

The Mashpee were able to function as a

Displaying a new flag, Mashpee, Mass., 1970

self-governing community until 1746, when colonial authorities appointed a board of white overseers. The Mashpee strongly opposed this change, appealing to the courts and the king of England to remove the new administrators. Throughout the 1700s the Mashpee resisted the encroachment of neighboring white communities, frequently petitioning the courts to uphold their ownership of their land. After the Revolutionary War, in which many Mashpee men were killed, intermarriage with both black and white nonresidents increased, but the Mashpee continued to maintain an Indian cultural identity.

After decades of struggle the Mashpee were granted the right of self-governance in 1834. By 1859 a total of 371 Mashpee were residing on some 16,000 acres of land. In 1870 the state of Massachusetts incorporated Mashpee as a town and enacted provisions for the sale of land previously held by the Indians. Consequently, ownership of 86 percent of Mashpee land had passed to non-Indians by 1934.

The 20th century was a period of increased Mashpee commitment to maintaining Indian identity and traditions. The Wampanoag Nation was formed in 1928 to unite the various Wampanoag communities in Massachusetts and promote Wampanoag culture. After World War II the population of Mashpee swelled with new residents, and the Mashpee lost control of the town government. Non-Mashpee homeowners and developers increasingly restricted the Mashpees' access to the coast, and the Mashpee were no longer able to hunt and fish throughout the town. In response the Mashpee Tribal Council was in-

corporated in 1974 to protect and promote Mashpee interests.

In 1976 the council filed suit in federal court to recover lands lost in the 1870 decision incorporating the town. The trial focused on the issue of whether the Mashpee constituted a tribe, and a jury found against the Indians in 1977. Although subsequent appeals of the decision have proven unsuccessful, the Mashpee continue to pursue legal efforts to recover their land and achieve tribal recognition from the federal government. Today the cultural and social life of the approximately 2,200 Mashpee remains centered on traditional places and institutions, including the Old Indian Burial Ground and Indian Meeting House, the Mashpee Indian Museum, and the annual Fourth of July Mashpee powwow.

Kathleen J. Bragdon, *Native Peoples of Southern New England, 1500–1650* (1996); Paul Brodeur, *Restitution: The Land Claims of the Mashpee, Passamaquoddy, and Penobscot Indians of New England* (1985); Jack Campisi, *The Mashpee Indians: Tribe on Trial* (1991); Laurie Weinstein-Farson, *The Wampanoag* (1989).

Robert G. Goodby

Metacom (King Philip) (ca. 1630–76)

Algonquian sachem. The Algonquian sachem Metacom, also known as King Philip, was born in or near Mount Hope in what is now Rhode Island. In 1675 and 1676 Metacom led a coalition of Native American peoples in an effort to oust English settlers from New England. He nearly succeeded. In proportion to the population at the time, King Philip's War was the most fatal conflict in American history; its brutality has led New Englanders—indeed, all Americans—to wrestle with its legacy for centuries.

Metacom was the son of Massasoit, the Wampanoag sachem who in 1620 greeted the first Pilgrims in the land they named Plymouth. Although Massasoit initially welcomed the newcomers, he became increasingly aggrieved by the incursion into native territory of ever mounting numbers of English settlers and by the attempts of English missionaries to convert Indians to Christianity. Metacom, who was given the English name Philip, inherited his father's sachemship in 1662, by which time relations between native peoples and colonists had deteriorated still further. In June 1675 the execution of three of Metacom's men, accused of murdering a Christian Indian minister, sparked the war that to many seemed inevitable; within days, Wampanoag warriors were attacking English towns. Soon they were joined by the Narragansett, Pocumtuck, and Nipmuck, as well as by former Christian Indians and, eventually, by the Abenaki in the north. (The Mohegan and Pequot fought as allies of the English.) In

14 months of warfare the native fighters nearly forced the colonists to abandon New England entirely, destroying more than half of all English settlements in southeastern New England. The English had greater resources to withstand the long winter months, however, and in the spring of 1676 the tide of the war began to turn. On August 12, 1676, Philip was killed near his birthplace, Mount Hope; he was shot, quartered, and decapitated, and his head was affixed atop a stake in Plymouth, where for decades it remained, a grisly monument to a grisly war.

If King Philip's War proved devastating to English colonists, its effects on New England's native peoples were more devastating still. During the hostilities hundreds of Christian Indians were imprisoned on islands in Boston Harbor, where more than half died of starvation or exposure. At the war's end native adult male captives were shipped out of New England and sold into slavery in the West Indies; women and children were forced into domestic servitude. Those who escaped these fates fled north and west.

Metacom's death effectively marked the war's end, but his story captured the imagination of subsequent generations of European Americans, especially in the first half of the 19th century, when poets, playwrights, and novelists romanticized his plight. Today those Indians who remained in New England—and those who have since returned—view Metacom as a hero. In the 1980s and 1990s Native American activists protested Thanksgiving Day celebrations in the town of Plymouth "in the spirit of King Philip," declaring it a day of mourning. In 1997 they succeeded in securing a pledge from the town to allocate $15,000 for a King Philip memorial, a fitting counterpoint perhaps to the severed head that once stood over the town.

James D. Drake, *King Philip's War: Civil War in New England, 1675–1676* (1999); Douglas Leach, *Flintlock and Tomahawk: New England in King Philip's War* (1958); Jill Lepore, *The Name of War: King Philip's War and the Origins of American Identity* (1998); Eric B. Schultz and Michael J. Tougias, *King Philip's War: The History and Legacy of America's Forgotten Conflict* (1999).

Jill Lepore

Micmac

The Micmac traditionally occupied today's Canadian province of Nova Scotia and most of the eastern half of New Brunswick. Skilled in the use of the canoe, they relied heavily on hunting both land and sea mammals. Families moved each year from summer villages to winter camps. The Micmac were among the first Native Americans to have contact with Europeans, from the attempted Viking settlements in the 11th cen-

Micmac craftsman David Sanipass examining the crooked knife he is making, Presque Isle, Maine, 1994

tury to the recorded visit of John Cabot in 1497. Regular trade developed between the Micmac and the Europeans, particularly the French, English, and Dutch, and continued steadily thereafter.

The Micmac were among the first American Indians to suffer the effects of the epidemics that spread after the arrival of the European explorers and settlers. As early as 1565, with European fishing expeditions making regular visits to the coast of the Gaspé Peninsula in today's province of Quebec, plagues such as typhus affected the Micmac population. Again in 1617, one of the worst years for New England's native peoples, a devastating epidemic swept through many Micmac villages. Like their neighbors the Abenaki, the Micmac at this time were feeling the effects of European encroachment and British-French territorial battles in the area.

In 1713 the Micmac, along with other native groups, signed a treaty in Portsmouth, N.H., in which they agreed to stop fighting the British but refused to accept British rule in Acadia. Not until the Treaty of Boston in 1726 did they acknowledge British sovereignty over the core of their homeland, dubbed Nova Scotia by the British. Resistance continued, however. The British considered the Indian nations to be out of compliance with the treaties they had signed—that is, rebels rather than enemies. Thus, according to the British, the rules of warfare did not apply. High bounties were offered for Micmac scalps. The struggle for territory and trading and fishing rights, along with increasing pressure from settlers, resulted in continued raids on British settle-

ments by the tribes of northern New England. Some Acadian Micmacs sought refuge from increasing British pressure in New Brunswick.

It wasn't until 1760, when the Micmac, along with the Passamaquoddy and Maliseet, reluctantly signed treaties with the British, that peace began to settle in the area. During the American Revolution, in hopes of overthrowing British rule, many Micmacs sided with the Americans.

The 1800s brought the establishment of reserves in Canada. The sale of crafts and seasonal labor were the primary types of employment available on or near those enclaves. By the late 1800s many Micmacs moved south to Boston and New York, seeking jobs that could provide them greater economic security.

Until the late 20th century the Micmac, one of the largest Native American groups in New England, received no federal or state aid, because the U.S. government did not recognize them as a tribe. In 1973 the Aroostook Band of Micmacs, which now numbers 920, received state recognition in Maine, and in 1991, with the Aroostook Band of Micmacs Settlement Act, they gained federal recognition in the United States. The act gave the same status to the Micmac as had been given to the Maliseet under the Maine Indian Claims Settlement Act of 1980. The Aroostook Band received funds for land acquisition and property taxes, as well as access to federal aid programs.

Bruce J. Bourque, *Twelve Thousand Years: American Indians in Maine* (2001); Harald E. L. Prins, *The Mi'kmaq: Resistance, Accommodation, and Cultural Survival* (1996); Ruth Holmes Whitehead, *Elitekey: Micmac Material Culture from 1600 A.D. to the Present*

(1980); Whitehead, *The Old Man Told Us: Excerpts from Micmac History, 1500–1950* (1991).

Susie Husted

Mohegan Like the Pequot, the Mohegan originated in present-day upstate New York near Lake Champlain. Around 1500 the Mohegan and Pequot moved south to the Thames River valley in Connecticut. The Connecticut Mohegan have often been confused in history with the Mahican of New York's Hudson River valley. Although their homelands are only 100 miles apart, the two tribes are distinct.

The 17th century brought enormous change to the Mohegan, as it did to many of New England's native peoples. The smallpox epidemic of 1634–35 reduced the tribe's population by more than 50 percent. The English moved the remaining Mohegan onto reserves with the Pequot soon afterward. Other neighboring tribes, including the Nipmuck and Narragansett, were also incorporated into these communities, making specific population estimates difficult during this period.

Those families that survived into the 18th century saw their community's population reduced once again. In the decade following 1775 several hundred Mohegan left Connecticut with the Christian Brotherton Indians. First they moved to upstate New York to live with the Oneida and Stockbridge Indians, then some continued on to Wisconsin when their New York lands were sold after 1822. An important leader of the Brotherton movement was the Reverend Samson Occom (1723–92), a Mohegan who gained fame as a teacher, preacher, author of sermons and hymns, and advocate of Native American education. Born near Norwich, Conn., he assisted the missionary work of the Reverend Eleazar Wheelock, serving as the primary fund-raiser in England for what became Dartmouth College. The descendants of Connecticut's Mohegan still reside today in these Native American communities in Wisconsin.

Connecticut's native peoples traded extensively with the Dutch and, later, English colonists. The original Pequot and Mohegan community that had migrated from upstate New York split in two in 1631, after the death of their prime leader. Two young men, Sassacus and Uncas, rivaled to replace him. The tribal council chose Sassacus, but Uncas refused to accept his leadership. Uncas was allied with the English and eventually settled his own village away from the Pequot. Many people followed Uncas and came to adopt his clan name, Mohegan, meaning "wolf." Soon after this separation, another smallpox epidemic descended on both the Pequot and Mohegan villages. During the Pequot War of

1636–37 the Mohegan sided with the English colonists. Although some refused to fight against their cousins, many Mohegan, including their leader, Uncas, provided information and soldiers to the English in the attacks on Pequot communities. The Mohegan remained allied with the English, acting as scouts during King William's War (1689–97) and Queen Anne's War (1702–13) against the Abenaki in the upper Connecticut River valley.

The wars and epidemics that shrank the Mohegan population made it difficult for members of the tribe to pay the debts they owed to English traders. Many families sold their land in exchange. After the death of the Mohegan leader Ben Uncas in 1769, the remaining land was placed in trust to the family of the Englishman John Mason, Uncas's friend. Mason, under pressure from his fellow colonists, signed over the deed to the land to the government of Connecticut in 1774.

The Mohegan began to become politically active again within Connecticut in the early 1900s. In 1920 the Mohegan Indian Association was formed to revitalize traditional arts and language and to facilitate tribal councils. During the same decade, the Mohegan sent representatives to the meetings of the Algonquin Indian Council of New England. Then in 1931 tribal member Gladys Tantaquidgeon and her brother Harold opened the Tantaquidgeon Indian Museum, celebrating Mohegan culture. The Mohegan Tribal Nation, which now numbers more than 1,600, gained federal recognition in 1994, regaining a portion of their land in Connecticut at Uncasville. Today the Mohegan maintain numerous successful economic enterprises, including the Mohegan Sun Casino in Uncasville, to support their educational, social, and community efforts.

Martin Barker and Roger Sabin, *The Lasting of the Mohicans: History of an American Myth* (1995); Richard Carlson, *Rooted Like the Ash Trees: New England Indians and the Land* (1987); Melissa Fawcett, *Medicine Trail: The Life and Lessons of Gladys Tantaquidgeon* (2000); William S. Simmons, *Spirit of the New England Tribes: Indian History and Folklore, 1620–1984* (1986).

Susie Husted

Moses, Robert Parris (1935–) Educator, civil rights pioneer.

Robert Parris Moses came to New England to study metaphysical philosophy at Harvard University. He became a notable leader of the modern civil rights movement in the 1960s and still devotes himself to bettering the lives of underprivileged minorities.

Born in New York city, Moses was raised in Harlem and attended Manhattan's Stuyvesant High School, later graduating from Hamilton College in upstate New York in 1956. He earned a master's degree in philosophy from Harvard the following year and began teaching mathematics in New York.

In June 1960 Moses volunteered to work with the Southern Christian Leadership Conference in Atlanta, Ga., where he met Ella Baker, an organizer for the Student Nonviolent Coordinating Committee. It was through the SNCC that Moses first traveled to Mississippi. Convinced that voter registration was the key to breaking down racial oppression, Moses left his teaching job after the 1960–61 school year and spent four years in the South. When SNCC activists divided over the relative priorities of direct action against segregation and voter registration, Moses quietly returned to Mississippi to register voters in McComb, Ruleville, Greenwood, and other towns. He helped establish the Council of Federated Organizations to coordinate civil rights work with older organizations.

Moses and his colleagues had limited success against Mississippi's formidable repression, but SNCC activists did inspire African Americans to attempt to register to vote and changed race relations there fundamentally. Moses himself brought charges against local thugs after he was assaulted and in another case encouraged a black witness to a murder to testify against the killer. Three years later the witness was gunned down. These and subsequent murders, burnings, and beatings made Mississippi the most dangerous state in the union for civil rights workers.

Influenced by the French existentialist writer Albert Camus, Moses developed a deliberately noncharismatic style of leadership by example. A cerebral rather than emotional orator, he sought to empower local communities and develop new leaders. He could be pragmatic as well as idealistic, and, calculating difficult realities, he helped launch the Freedom Summer of 1964, which brought some 1,000 mostly white college students to Mississippi. During that year six activists were killed, 80 beaten, and 1,000 arrested; 68 buildings were burned. These sacrifices laid the groundwork for the Voting Rights Act of 1965, which ended African American disfranchisement nationally.

Also in 1964 Moses helped create the Mississippi Freedom Democratic Party. African Americans organized their own separate election and sent a delegation to the Democratic National Convention in Atlanta, demanding to be seated. The all-white Dixiecrat regulars attempted to force a bad compromise on the black delegates, and Moses successfully urged its rejection. For many 1960s activists this was a crucial turning point. Many gave up on the Democratic Party, and Moses himself became disillusioned. When he was drafted in 1966, he left the country to work in obscurity in Canada for two years. He then taught in Tanzania, returning to the United States only when draft resisters were pardoned in 1977.

Settling in Cambridge, Mass., with his wife and four children at that time, Moses returned to Harvard for further study. Dissatisfied with his daughter's math education at the Martin Luther King Jr. Elementary School, the former teacher created his own instructional methodology. By observing the way children learn, he developed a five-step program to help students draw abstract and generalizable conclusions from their concrete experience. For example, Cambridge children learned the concept of negative integers by riding in two directions on the Red Line subway. The MacArthur Foundation awarded Moses a so-called genius grant to advance the idea, and the Algebra Project's methodology is now used in more than 100 city schools. The technique is rooted in empowerment strategies similar to those employed by civil rights workers in Mississippi, and Moses returned there in the 1990s as a teacher trainer, coming full circle to the place where he began his career.

Taylor Branch, *Parting the Waters: America in the King Years, 1954–63* (1988); Eric Burner, *And Gently He Shall Lead Them: Robert Parris Moses and Civil Rights in Mississippi* (1994); Alexis Jetter, "Mississippi Learning," *New York Times Magazine* (February 21, 1993); Emily Stoper, *The Student Non-Violent Coordinating Committee: The Growth of Radicalism in a Civil Rights Organization* (1989).

Mark R. Schneider

Narragansett

The Narragansett are a federally recognized Indian tribe of about 2,400 people, most of whom live in Rhode Island. The tribe owns approximately 2,500 acres of land within the southwestern part of the state, 1,945 of which are held in federal trust. Residents of Narragansett Bay and southeastern New England for many centuries, the Narragansett maintain extensive relations with other native communities and tribes throughout New England.

In the 1600s the major native settlements were on the western side of Narragansett Bay. Here, at Cocumscussoc, the chief sachem Canonicus invited Roger Williams to establish a trading post in 1636. A brief period of cordial relations ended in 1637 with the Pequot War. In December 1675 colonial forces in present-day South Kingstown, R.I., brutally killed many Narragansett men, women, and children in a preemptive attack known as the Great Swamp Fight. That episode occurred during King Philip's War (1675–76), which ended open military native resistance to European penetration in the region. Since then the

Narragansett have in many ways made and remade their lives, culture, and identity apart from the non-Indians who occupy their lands.

Illegally stripped of tribal status by the state of Rhode Island in 1880, the Narragansett nevertheless maintained a separate tribal identity. After detribalization the tribal council brought land claims against Rhode Island that were dismissed by the state supreme court in 1898. Several unsuccessful appeals were then made to the U.S. Bureau of Indian Affairs, the last in 1937.

In the 1970s, led by the Narragansett ethnohistorian and medicine woman Ella Wilcox Sekatau and tribal coordinator Eric Thomas, the Narragansett filed suit against the state of Rhode Island, claiming that the general assembly had violated the Non-Intercourse Act of 1790 when it auctioned tribal lands in the 1880s. An out-of-court settlement in 1978, affirmed by the U.S. Congress with passage of the Rhode Island Indian Claims Settlement Act, returned more than 1,900 acres to the tribe. "This isn't the first time there was an attempt to get the land back," according to chief medicine man Lloyd Wilcox, "it started the day it was taken."

With federal recognition in 1983, the Narragansett established a government-to-government relationship with the United States. In 1980, before federal recognition, between $100,000 and $200,000 in federal grants were obtained by Narragansett leaders. By the 1990s the federal appropriation had increased to around $2 million, funding programs in education, housing, employment assistance, historic preservation, real estate, economic development, and natural resources. A new community center was opened in 1995, and a health center was dedicated in 1996.

Each summer tribal members convene at the meetinghouse church on reservation lands in Charlestown, R.I. They hold traditional Narragansett and nonsectarian Christian ceremonies, recount the history of the Narragansett, and celebrate their people's survival against what the tribal historian Lucille Dawson has called the European invasion. In 1997 Dr. Sekatau referred to the necessity of living with the newcomers as "coexistence," that is, maintaining a separate identity and culture while establishing relations with other non-Narragansett peoples when necessary or beneficial. The annual meeting signifies the Narragansetts' decision not to be assimilated by the larger, non-Indian society. It is a public statement of their long and continuous but separate presence in what is now called New England.

David J. Bernstein, *Prehistoric Subsistence on the Southern New England Coast: The Record from Narragansett Bay* (1993); Kathleen J. Bragdon, *Native People of Southern New England, 1500–1650* (1996); Ruth Wallis Herndon and Ella Wilcox Sekatau, "The Right to a Name: The Narragansett People and Rhode Island Officials in the Revolutionary Era," *Ethnohistory* 44 (1997); William S. Simmons, *The Narragansett* (1989).

Paul A. Robinson

National Yiddish Book Center

The National Yiddish Book Center in Amherst, Mass., was founded in 1980 by Aaron Lansky, a young scholar dedicated to saving Yiddish books from being discarded by a generation of Jews who could no longer read the language of their parents and grandparents. Lansky, a graduate of Hampshire College and a MacArthur Fellow, established the center after he discovered that thousands of priceless Yiddish books that had survived the ravages of Hitler and Stalin were being destroyed. As of 1997, the center and its worldwide network of nearly 300 *zamlers* (volunteer book collectors) had rescued 1.4 million Yiddish volumes that contain the culture and sensibility of the past thousand years of Jewish history. Books continue to arrive at the center at the rate of 500 to 1,000 per week. As the only comprehensive supplier of Yiddish books in the world, the center distributes these volumes to research libraries, colleges and universities, and readers who lack access to primary Yiddish texts. The center has helped to establish or strengthen Yiddish collections at 437 major libraries in 20 countries, including China, Japan, and Australia.

The center's irreplaceable Yiddish texts—novels, short stories, plays, poetry, history, philosophy, science, and children's books—represent the rich cultural heritage of more than 90 percent of America's Jews and more than 80 percent of the world's Jewish population. It is a heritage both universal and unique. While Yiddish literature accurately reflects the turbulent advent of modernism, it departs radically from other literatures of Europe because of the extreme historical conditions in which it briefly flowered and by which it was extinguished. In claiming permanence for Yiddish literature, in removing from Yiddish the label of a "dead language" and celebrating instead its relevance and vitality, the center has enlarged public understanding not only of Jewish culture but of modern Western history as well.

The center's activity has thrived at a time when a new generation of young Jews, fascinated by the world that the Holocaust sought to destroy, has avidly turned to Yiddish sources as a key to unlock the past. Historians and other scholars have redefined Jewish studies to include broad questions of social and cultural significance. Yiddish literature, music, theater, and film have gained recognition as a body of work of critical importance. As Isaac Bashevis Singer predicted when he accepted the Nobel Prize for Literature in 1978, "Yiddish has not spoken its last word. It contains treasures that have not been revealed to the eyes of the world."

The center opens its collection to the public through innovative educational conferences, publications, audiotapes, broadcasts, and special events. It publishes the *Pakn-Treger*, an English-language quarterly magazine featuring book reviews, fiction, essays, new translations, photographs, and other material related to the Jewish diaspora. With more than 30,000 members, the National Yiddish Book Center is one of the largest Jewish cultural organizations in the United States.

In 1997 the National Yiddish Book Center moved to its permanent home on a 10-acre site adjacent to the campus of Hampshire College and in the heart of the Five College community, composed of Amherst, Hampshire, Mount Holyoke, and Smith Colleges and the University of Massachusetts. Open to the public free of charge, the architecturally distinctive 37,000-square-foot building, designed to echo the lines of a traditional Eastern European shtetl, contains a book repository, a visitor's center with extensive exhibits about the history of Yiddish literature, a theater, the Yiddish Writers Garden, and many unique resources.

Daniel Benjamin, "Preserving the Printed Word," *Time* (January 15, 1990); Rick Lyman, "A Culture Preserved," *New York Times*, June 16, 1997; Elizabeth Mehren, "A Real Mensch," *Los Angeles Times*, July 28, 1997.

Nancy Sherman

Nation of Islam

The Nation of Islam, at once a preeminent black nationalist organization and a unique African American adaptation of Islam, is active in all six New England states. The organization took root in Detroit, Mich., in 1930, succeeding both the American-born Moorish Science Temple, a religionationalistic body, and the Harlem-based black nationalist movement led by Marcus Garvey. Its members are sometimes called Black Muslims.

In traditional Islam divinity does not take human form and Muhammad was the final prophet. The Nation of Islam departs from these beliefs, revering its founder, the enigmatic W. D. Fard (Fard Muhammad), as God. Fard's divinity was proclaimed by his chief apostle, Elijah Muhammad, born Elijah Poole in Sandersville, Ga., in 1897. Elijah Muhammad typified those who joined the Nation of Islam during the Great Depression and the southern migrations to northern industrial cities: early Black Muslims had little or no formal education, were blue-collar workers bitter about racial persecution, and, though reared in the black church, rejected Christianity as "the white man's religion."

According to Elijah Muhammad, Allah (God), incarnated in Fard Muhammad, created blacks alone; other so-called races are mutations of the "black seed." Blacks are thus the Original People, whose ancient and unimpeachable identity is Asian. Their nature is divine. Of special significance is the tribe of Shabazz, a primal, highly accomplished people who founded great civilizations in Egypt and Mecca. A misled segment of Shabazz migrated to "the jungles of Africa" (East Asia). Descendants of this splinter group, so-called American Negroes, are in reality the "Lost-Found Tribe of Shabazz." Elijah Muhammad's charge was to rescue Shabazz from its alienation and return community members to their former glory.

Politically, the Nation of Islam is separatist: its goal has been to establish a sovereign territory within the United States. Preferring isolation and capitalist enterprise, its cardinal ethic has been "do for self." The Nation of Islam has owned several impressive U.S. businesses, among them restaurants, farms, and a bank; it also publishes a national weekly newspaper, the *Final Call* (formerly *Muhammad Speaks*), promoting racial pride. Elijah Muhammad was reportedly a multimillionaire when he died in 1975, and many within the Nation of Islam, now home to well-educated, professional blacks, are members of the middle class. With Muhammad's death, leadership passed to his son, Wallace Muhammad, who steered the Nation of Islam to orthodox (Sunni) Islam. The Nation of Islam thus became the World Community of Islam in the West (WCIW). The change was contested by Louis Farrakhan, then known as Louis X. In 1977 Farrakhan broke from the WCIW to restore Elijah Muhammad's organization, the Nation of Islam.

Of special note in New England are Mosque No. 14 in Hartford, Mosque No. 13 in Springfield, Mass., and Boston's Mosque No. 11. Malcolm X founded the historic Mosque No. 11 in 1953 in Grove Hall on the Roxbury-Dorchester, Mass., line. Its first minister was Ulysses X; its most famous, Louis Farrakhan. Minister Don Muhammad heads the temple today. Under his leadership Mosque No. 11 has sponsored such community-service events as a forum on the HIV/AIDS crisis addressing HIV's connection to substance abuse and its effects on women and children. As the Nation of Islam began taking steps toward rapprochement with orthodox Islam early in the 21st century, Boston's Don Muhammad has

stressed the importance of his organization's role in addressing the unmet social, educational, and occupational needs of the African American community.

Claude Andrew Clegg III, *An Original Man: The Life and Times of Elijah Muhammad* (1997); E. U. Essien-Udom, *Black Nationalism: A Search for an Identity in America* (1971); C. Eric Lincoln, *The Black Muslims in America* (1973); Elijah Muhammad, *Message to the Blackman in America* (1965).

Josiah Ulysses Young III

Nativism and Anglo-Saxonism

Nativism, a movement by ruling elites to limit immigration to homogeneous racial types, and Anglo-Saxonism, the belief in a historic and superior Anglo-Saxon race, have influenced American history in profound ways. The two interrelated ideas have a long association with New England.

The myth of the Anglo-Saxon race goes back to Roman historian Tacitus. His little book *Germania* (A.D. 98) depicted robust barbarians practicing primitive democracy in the northern forests that bordered the Roman Empire, among them forebears of the Angles and Saxons who later invaded England. Hoping to shame the decadent Romans of his time, Tacitus held up this portrait as a counterexample, reminding Romans of their own similar beginnings.

The idea of a special Anglo-Saxon race that was naturally superior and yet also naturally democratic—at least where its own people were concerned—was a tenacious one. It was part of the cultural baggage that English and German immigrants brought to North America in the 17th and 18th centuries.

All so-called Anglo-Saxons in North America were originally immigrants. As such, they repeatedly came into conflict with the Native Americans whose property they proceeded to expropriate. During the colonial period, when native peoples often still outnumbered immigrants and labor was scarce, Anglo-Saxon colonists encouraged European immigration unreservedly and viewed immigrants in a positive light. By contrast, they stigmatized cohabitation with Native Americans. Having been schooled by Protestant England's brutal conquest of Catholic Ireland, British colonists distinguished themselves from their French and Spanish counterparts by their strong aversion to racial mixing.

After several generations of settlement, descendants of the early immigrants began to think of themselves as natives and looked more searchingly and judgmentally at new arrivals. By the end of the 18th century, Americans, now citizens of a new republic, were ready for the first of several outbreaks of nativism that have checkered U.S. history.

Anti-immigrant movements usually functioned according to patterns set during the colonial era. Many involved more than simple race prejudice, however. Interested parties often cloaked a mix of social, economic, and political motives in a guise of simple nativism, with the goal of achieving more complex ends. In this regard one of the earliest cases is also one of the most instructive.

The Alien Acts, written and pushed through Congress mainly by New England Federalists in 1798, were a response not so much to immigration as to the tendency of immigrants to support Thomas Jefferson's Republican Party. With a view to taking this strong voter base away from Jefferson, the Naturalization Act extended the time for naturalization from five years to a prohibitive 14 and added other debilitating restrictions that were designed to discourage those seeking American citizenship.

The Alien Acts enabled their backers to achieve short-term political success by attacking the group least able to defend itself: unnaturalized immigrants. Unlike citizens, members of this group could not claim constitutional protection and often lacked the political connections to organize effective protest. This defenseless enemy would prove an irresistible target for politicians throughout American history. Although the federal government ceased to enforce the Alien Acts when Jefferson came to power, an important precedent had been set. In future periods of anxiety and crisis, immigrants would often be the first to suffer attack.

For the better part of the 19th century nativism became strongly anti-Catholic—so much so that many have mistakenly assumed that nativism and anti-Catholicism were synonymous from the outset. Fear of Catholicism was firmly embedded in New England's Protestant past. Early New Englanders, fleeing religious persecution and what they saw as "popish" impurities in their own church and society, were Protestant in the true sense of the word. Their protest against Catholicism took deep root in the American collective memory. American politics has always been predominantly Protestant in the sense that it has usually proved easier to motivate citizens to political action opposing an external enemy than it is to get people to support a stated program. From America's first third party, the Anti-Masons, to the anti-immigrant legislation of the late 1990s, U.S. politicians have always felt more comfortable defining themselves in negative terms. Anti-Catholicism is an excellent and enduring illustration of this tendency.

In the mid-19th century, when poor Irish Catholics began to arrive in considerable numbers, the idea of America as a Protestant republic was severely challenged. During this period of increased democratization and economic transition that historians now call the market revolution, free-floating anxiety found a focus of sorts in what many Americans viewed as the alien practices and beliefs of a growing Roman Catholic Church.

This movement not only involved religious prejudice but brought back memories of the Irish as the first people to be colonized and subdued by the young British Empire. Now these former subjects were gaining American citizenship in record numbers. The Irish influx was seen as both a challenge to America's Protestantism and a threat to democratic government. The Irish, in part because of their hierarchical church, were seen as lacking the civic virtues needed by citizens of a republic.

These feelings expressed themselves in many ways, among them anti-Catholic violence. In 1834, to cite the most famous example, the Ursuline Convent school in what is now East Somerville, Mass., was assailed, looted, and set on fire by a mob of some 100 men who apparently believed they were liberating Protestant girls from Catholic imprisonment. Not all forms of anti-immigrant violence were overtly this disorderly, however.

A more organized response to these demographic changes was the creation of the American Party, known as the "Know-Nothings," dedicated to curbing Catholic influence in the United States. Claiming that descendants of the first Anglo-Saxons in America were now "native Americans," this group sought to limit Catholic immigration and further entrench the power of the superior and homogeneous racial stock to which they saw themselves as belonging. The Know-Nothings later split over the issue of abolition, with many of its members joining the new Republican Party. Soon the Civil War and slavery eclipsed fear of immigration as crucial political issues, and nativism waned.

The reasons for this eclipse were in large part economic. The industrialization of postbellum America once again made workers a scarce commodity. Industrial leaders turned to immigration to fill the labor gap. As in the early colonial period, immigrants were viewed favorably because they had a vital economic role to play. New industrial working conditions led to unprecedented labor radicalism, however, and soon the fires of nativism were burning brighter than ever. This time the threat was once again political rather than religious: communism had replaced Catholicism as the nativist bugbear of choice.

The nativism of the late 19th century, practiced against the new immigrants from eastern Europe, was different from previous outbreaks in one important way—it was now buttressed by pseudoscience. Renewed interest in Tacitus and the nation's supposed Anglo-Saxon heritage combined with the vulgar generalizations of social Darwinism to produce a form of racial prejudice bearing all the authoritative weight of a new science that for many elites had supplanted the Judeo-Christian philosophy of their forebears. Immigrants were now seen not just as belonging to an inferior group but almost as members of an entirely different species. In New England, supporters of the Colonial Revival movement such as Wallace Nutting and William Sumner Appleton invoked the "Anglo-Saxon values" of early Americans.

This new form of nativism found a champion in the scion of one of New England's most distinguished families, Henry Cabot Lodge. From his influential position in the U.S. Senate, Lodge persistently backed legislation limiting immigration. Supporting him was the Boston-based Immigration Restriction League. Founded by a group of lawyers in 1894, the league lobbied hard for a bill denying immigration visas to those who were not literate in some language. Since the majority of the new immigrants from eastern Europe could not read or write, the object of this legislative exercise was easy to discern. The bill was defeated in 1897, but it finally passed in 1917 shortly before the declaration of war and over the president's veto.

Although the league disbanded that year, its legacy was evident in the National Origins Act of 1924. This law specified exact quotas of immigrants from different lands. A guiding force behind passage of the bill was Albert Johnson (R-Wash.), chairman of the House Immigration Committee. As might be expected, the most generous quotas were allotted to America's Anglo-Saxon neighbor Great Britain (more than 65,000 immigrants per year). The lowest (usually 100 per country) were assigned to nations in Asia and ranged from 100 to 6,524 for eastern European nations. Canada and Latin American nations were not subject to quotas, and Japanese immigration was mostly banned. This race-based system remained in effect, with various modifications, until 1965.

For most of the 19th century the East Coast and particularly New England were centers of American nativism. During World War I, anti-German sentiment had engulfed both the East Coast and the Midwest. By midcentury, the focus had shifted to the West Coast and California in particular. In the mid-1990s, nativism was also a key issue nationally. Just as the New England Federalists scored political points by attacking the immigrant base of Jefferson's power, so did a Republican Congress, opposing President Bill Clinton, make denial of social services to unnaturalized immigrants a political shibboleth. In this most recent period of nativist activity, the overt racism of earlier days was gone, but the careful student of history could still detect many familiar parallels.

John Higham, *Strangers in the Land: Patterns of American Nativism, 1860–1925* (2002 [1955]); Desmond King, *Making Americans: Immigration, Race, and the Origins of the Diverse Democracy* (2000); Barbara Miller Solomon, *Ancestors and Immigrants: A Changing New England Tradition* (1956); Tacitus, *The "Agricola" and the "Germania,"* trans. H. Mattingly (1970).

Richard Bradley

Neighborhoods New England is home to an abundance of racial and ethnic neighborhoods formed by the northward migration of African Americans from the South and by steady streams of immigrants. The earliest neighborhoods in the 19th century included communities of freed slaves on Dixwell Avenue in New Haven, Conn., and Copp's Hill in Boston and enclaves of Irish and French-speaking Canadians throughout the region. The great wave of immigration that began in the 1880s brought concentrations of Germans, Italians, Jews, Portuguese, Poles, Swedes, and Chinese to the region's largest cities, especially Boston and Worcester, Mass.; Providence, R.I.; Portland, Maine; and Hartford, Conn. After 1910 two great migrations of African Americans from the South contributed to the diversity of New England cities. Changes in immigration trends in the 1960s led to an influx of newcomers from Asian countries, the Caribbean Islands, and Central and South America.

Drawn to employment opportunities in the region's urban and industrial centers, new waves of immigrants and migrants have repeatedly altered the character of inner-city neighborhoods. The studies of social mobility examined by Howard P. Chudacoff and Judith E. Smith in *The Evolution of American Urban Society* (5th ed., 2000) show a consistent trend throughout U.S. history. Historically, neighborhoods of first settlement turned over as much as half their population each year. Not only did immigrants and migrants move annually (or more often) from one neighborhood to another, but whole groups migrated from the inner city to the outer boroughs and eventually to the suburbs as their socioeconomic circumstances and level of assimilation evolved. This trend continues. Frog Hollow in Hartford long housed European immigrants who worked in bicycle and typewriter factories. Today, Puerto Rican and other Latin American residents have created a Latino cultural center, Guakía, in the neighborhood.

Likewise, in early-21st-century Boston, Vietnamese markets and restaurants dot the thoroughfares of Chinatown, making migration patterns evident there. At the same time, Chinese markets and Chinese Christian churches have appeared in Boston's western boroughs of Allston and Brighton. Jamaica Plain, long considered the bastion of Boston's poor African American community, became home to Latino Bostonians, particularly Puerto Ricans, in the 1990s.

Although inner-city working-class neighborhoods tend to be ethnically and racially diverse, one group may dominate a neighborhood's public identity. Fox Point in Providence has been called the cultural heart of Rhode Island's Portuguese and Cape Verdean communities, although these groups share the area with Irish, Syrian Lebanese, and African Americans. In Portland, Maine, Munjoy Hill was the home of the orthodox Jewish community throughout much of the 20th century, but Portland's Italian community also was concentrated there, especially along Newbury Street. The names "Chinatown" or "Little Italy" refer to the ethnic group whose cultural presence, if not its population, predominates in a given area.

The locations of racial and ethnic neighborhoods tend to be determined by external factors, not the decisions of newcomers. These neighborhoods are usually within walking distance of areas that once offered unskilled employment, harking back to a time before automobiles and accessible public transportation. They consist of both commercial and residential components. Older housing stock, particularly tenements and multifamily apartment buildings, is typical of inner-city residential areas. Because racial and ethnic neighborhoods exist in older parts of cities, they are often associated with crime and urban blight. With its bars and dance halls, Boston's North End was the city's red-light district throughout much of the 19th century. It was a magnet for crime, prostitution, and alcohol-related incidents until the mid-20th century, when an area across town known as the Combat Zone, abutting Chinatown, inherited these problems.

Other external forces have affected residential patterns, neighborhood boundaries, and socioeconomic, racial, and ethnic demographics, among them poverty, racism, xenophobia, government and civic needs, and commercial interests. Outsiders wielding derogatory labels such as slum, ghetto, and barrio have devalued the communities residing in the areas so designated, thereby paving the way for so-called urban renewal and other assaults on largely racial and ethnic urban districts. Efforts to rejuvenate crumbling inner-city

neighborhoods began in the 1950s. In practice they were little more than slum-clearance programs. In a now classic case, Boston's poor and multiethnic West End was razed to make way for new government buildings and upscale downtown housing. Socioeconomic, racial, and ethnic ghettoization was also promoted by federally funded housing projects such as the 1,504-unit Columbia Point in Dorchester, Mass., built in 1953.

In the 1960s two forms of "redlining" transformed urban neighborhoods and created ghettoes. In the traditional form of this practice, banks refused to offer mortgage loans, and insurers homeowners' policies, for houses in poor, inner-city neighborhoods. Low-income mortgage and insurance applicants were thus barred from the only homes they could afford. Before long, a second style of redlining came into vogue. Financial agencies chose certain areas in which to offer federally insured mortgages to black would-be homeowners, thereby creating new African American neighborhoods. Blacks were granted loans only in those districts. Boston Bank's Urban Renewal Group, to cite a notorious example, decided to promote minority home ownership through federally insured mortgage loans in Roxbury, Mattapan, and Dorchester, Mass. These were Boston's primary Jewish neighborhoods, where lenders could not make any money because most mortgages had been paid off. Real estate agents resorted to the tactic known as blockbusting: by playing on residents' fears and prejudices, they frightened homeowners into selling their properties fast at prices well below what they were worth. The homes were then sold for top dollar to African American buyers. The influx of blacks into targeted neighborhoods, and the migration of Jews to other suburbs, helped dismantle the area's traditional Jewish community.

Gentrification in the 1980s—the reclaiming of inner-city homes and neighborhoods by middle- and upper-class residents, most of them white—further transformed traditional racial and ethnic neighborhoods. Property values rose in tandem with the socioeconomic status of the new residents, placing homeownership and rentals beyond the means of long-time poor and minority residents.

Nonetheless, by the end of the 20th century, New England was seeing a resurgence in the number and diversity of its urban ethnic enclaves. New Asian and Latino immigrants have replicated the social and residential patterns established by their European predecessors, creating self-contained communities within larger neighborhoods or cities that attract the newly arrived. The title of sociologist Herbert J. Gans's book *The Urban Villagers: Group and Class in the Life of Italian-Americans*

(updated ed., 1982) suggests the complex social network that is typical of ethnic enclaves. In these communities immigrants find places to live, work, shop, play, and worship. Surrounded by compatriots, they are able to retain linguistic and cultural traditions.

Although racial and ethnic neighborhoods may be culturally heterogeneous, they are almost always homogeneous with regard to class—that is, working-class or poor. Within each neighborhood's ethnic area, however, and particularly within each individual ethnic group residing there, a distinct social structure exists. This structure includes established immigrants or descendants of immigrants who have achieved authority in the community as business owners or entrepreneurs and who often interact with mainstream society. New immigrants live and work within the enclave, where their linguistic, social, and cultural needs can be met. Continued immigration brings fresh newcomers, who renew the call for clergy, businesses, residences, and jobs for people who do not speak English. Enclaves allow immigrants to be isolated and protected from mainstream American society. They serve as a bridge between the old world and the new.

Though New England's racial and ethnic neighborhoods serve similar functions, each one has its own personality. The Boston historian Thomas O'Connor spoke in his work, for instance, of the differences between the Irish communities of South Boston, Charlestown, Worcester, Lowell, and Springfield, Mass. The character of an immigrant neighborhood can be shaped by the nature of the area in which it has developed or by its inhabitants' region of origin. Chain-migration networks often brought family members and old-country neighbors one after another to America, with the result that ethnic neighborhoods frequently contain concentrations of people from the same sending-country villages or regions. Thus Boston's Italian North End was divided into areas inhabited primarily by emigrants from the Abruzzi and Campania regions of the Italian mainland on the one hand and the island of Sicily on the other. Each subcommunity perpetuated its separateness in its own Catholic parish, the Saint Leonard of Port Maurice and the Sacred Heart churches.

Ethnic communities are conceptual as well as geographic. Not all members of Portland, Maine's Jewish community live on Munjoy Hill, for example. Patterns of residential mobility and assimilation that draw residents of ethnic enclaves out into heterogeneous neighborhoods and suburbs do not necessarily eliminate the role of the enclave as a cultural center that fosters a sense of community. Little Italys throughout the region retain their significance as bastions of Old World culture and connection for descendants of immigrants who live elsewhere.

Ethnic communities are geographically identifiable because of clusters of institutions like churches, businesses, and restaurants. These institutions define the geographic and cultural boundaries of the ethnic neighborhood. In the 1920s the markers of the Syrian enclave in Central Falls, R.I., included the Syrian American Club, Aleppian Aid Society, Saint Ephraim's Church, and at least a half dozen markets. Germans who came to Providence, R.I., in the latter decades of the 19th century to work in the area's textile mills established a neighborhood around Olneyville Square. Many also worked at nearby breweries. Their neighborhood markers included German halls, the Deutsch-Dramatischer Verein (German Dramatic Society), the Gesangverein Lassalle (Singing Society Lassalle), the Turnverein Vorwarts (the Providence Turners, or gymnasts), and specialty butchers, bakers, and grocers.

Public celebrations commemorate the transplantation of regional traditions, calling to mind the geographic heritage and local identity of racial and ethnic communities. Saint Patrick's Day parades, Chinese New Year festivities, and the Saints' Days celebrated by immigrants of traditionally Catholic countries serve dual purposes. They unify community members and transmit a public statement of group identity to outsiders. Feast days form the focal point of Catholic ethnic group celebrations, and the names of the commemorated saints also identify the origins of a community's mutual aid or benefit societies.

Some communities develop their public identity as ethnic enclaves in a bid for tourist dollars. Boston's North End and Providence's Federal Hill continue to be bastions of Italian culture whose specialty food markets and restaurants provide Italian Americans with traditional fare, but business owners know the importance of cultivating a non-coethnic clientele. The Italian identity of these communities, itself a postimmigration construction, has been transformed by publicity and tourism. In the early 21st century, for example, the culinary styles served by many of the newer restaurants in Boston's North End reflect contemporary tastes for northern Italian cuisine in a neighborhood traditionally inhabited by peoples from southern Italy.

Racial and ethnic neighborhoods have been shaped by such internal forces as patterns of migration and assimilation and by such external forces as city politics, commercial interests, and intolerance, as well as by the racial and ethnic "roots" phenomenon that began in the 1970s. High mobility rates, the ongoing search for employment opportunities, and immigration policies, among other factors, have kept racial and ethnic neighborhoods in a constant state of flux. Boston, notorious a few decades ago for illegal lending practices, has substantially increased the number of affordable mortgages provided to low- and moderate-income homebuyers of all races and ethnicities. Dorchester's Columbia Point, once a crime-ridden residential destination for poor and minority citizens, has been transformed into Harbor Point, a successful, racially integrated, mixed-income community. In Bridgeport, Conn., the sheet metal workers union launched a "family reunification program" in early 2000 to provide free job training to non-custodial black and Hispanic fathers of children who live in public housing. Migrants and immigrants have almost always had to struggle before they find their place in America's cities, but these are hopeful signs for New England's racial and ethnic communities old and new.

Mark Abrahamson, *Urban Enclaves: Identity and Place in America* (1996); George J. Borjas, *To Ghetto or Not to Ghetto: Ethnicity and Residential Segregation* (1997); Hsiang-Shui Chen, *Chinatown No More: Taiwan Immigrants in Contemporary New York* (1992); Kathleen Neils Conzen, "Immigrants, Immigrant Neighborhoods, and Ethnic Identity: Historical Issues," *Journal of American History* 66 (1979); Kenneth L. Kusmer, *A Ghetto Takes Shape: Black Cleveland, 1870–1930* (1976); Hillel Levine and Lawrence Harmon, *The Death of an American Jewish Community: A Tragedy of Good Intentions* (1992); J. Anthony Lukas, *Common Ground: A Turbulent Decade in the Lives of Three American Families* (1985); Judith E. Smith, *Family Connections: A History of Italian and Jewish Immigrant Lives in Providence, Rhode Island, 1900–1940* (1985).

Kristen A. Petersen

Nipmuck

The Nipmuck traditionally occupied present-day central Massachusetts and northern Connecticut and Rhode Island. They relied on an agricultural subsistence, supplemented by fishing and hunting. Their villages were predominantly located along the shores of small lakes and ponds. Some Nipmuck villages were subject to the Pequot Nation of Connecticut and were historically considered to belong to the Pequot Confederacy. It wasn't until the Pequot lost political power in the aftermath of the Pequot War of 1636–37 that the subject Nipmuck villages were regarded by many historians as possessing a separate identity.

With parts of their territory located less than 50 miles from Boston Harbor, the Nipmuck came into early contact with European settlers. Consequently, they were among the first to fall prey to the epidemics of the early 1600s.

Nipmuc chief Wise Owl praying in the medicine circle on Nipmuck tribal land, Thompson, Conn., 1995

Beginning in 1640, unregulated European squatting on Nipmuck lands and large sales of Nipmuck territory took a great toll on the Nipmuck land base. The English purchased three major tracts of land between 1643 and 1655. The loss of this land devastated the lifeways of the Nipmuck, who were still heavily reliant on agriculture. When King Philip's War wreaked further devastation in 1675 and 1676, many Nipmucks were forced to seek refuge with their northern neighbors, the Abenaki. Others turned west and to the Delaware Nation of New Jersey.

Like many of their Algonquian neighbors in southern New England, the remaining Nipmucks were confined to villages run by Puritan missionaries as the European colonists settled their land. By the eve of King Philip's war, most Nipmucks lived in one of seven praying villages. The Puritan praying villages encouraged Nipmucks to give their allegiance to the English and not join King Philip's uprising against the colonists in 1675.

Today two bands of Nipmuck people maintain land bases in southern New England. The Chaubunagungamaug Nipmucks have a privately owned 10-acre reservation in Connecticut. The Hassanamisco Nipmucs (their chosen spelling) currently own two acres in Grafton, Mass. Each band has filed separately for federal recognition. In 2001 the Nipmuc Nation at Hassanamisco received federal recognition from a political appointee of the Clinton administration. Later that same year the Bush administration put a hold on the decision, however, and ultimately reversed it. Both bands host annual powwows and festivals in Connecticut and Massachusetts that are open to the public.

Dennis A. Connole, *The Indians of the Nipmuck Country in Southern New England, 1630–1750: An Historical Geography* (2001); Thomas L. Doughton, "Unseen Neighbors: Native Americans of Central Massachusetts, a People Who Had 'Vanished,'" in *After King Philip's War: Presence and Persistence in Indian New England*, ed. Colin G. Calloway (1997); Stephen J. Reno with Zara Ciscoe Brough, *A History of the Nipmuc Indians of Central Massachusetts* (1984);

William S. Simmon, *Spirit of the New England Tribes: Indian History and Folklore, 1620–1984* (1986).

Susie Husted

Passamaquoddy Unlike many Native American groups today, the Passamaquoddy have continuously occupied some of their ancestral territory, located in eastern Maine, for at least the past 3,000 years. Many of the 2,400 Passamaquoddy today (per 2000 census) still speak their native language, a rarity for native peoples in the northeastern United States, and instruction in their elementary schools is provided in both Algonquian and English. Members of the Abenaki confederacy, the Passamaquoddy (from Pestumokadyik, "people who spear pollack") have a feeling of reverence for their land, even though their two reservations, Pleasant Point near Eastport and Indian Township near Princeton, are located in Maine's poorest county.

The Passamaquoddy way of life has changed dramatically since 1603, when the tribe encountered Europeans such as French explorer Samuel de Champlain. As traditional fishers, hunters, and gatherers, the Passamaquoddy relied heavily on maritime resources. They hunted seal and porpoise; speared bass, sturgeon, and salmon; fished for shad, salmon, and alewives; and gathered clams, lobsters, and seabird eggs. Women wove beads made of quahog shell into decorative items of ritual clothing. Men hunted moose and bear and trapped such smaller game as otter, beaver, and muskrat. Summer settlements in coastal areas disappeared in the fall, when smaller camps were set up further inland for the winter season. Women directed the task of moving a family's lodging. Contact with French and English settlers brought warfare and such epidemic diseases such as smallpox and influenza, which seriously affected the Passamaquoddy population.

The Passamaquoddy have given us a rich legacy of native verse and mythology that has been translated into English. Creation legends and songs portray their culture hero Kuloskap, born of a divine woman, as a benevolent god representing the principle of good. Although the French Jesuit missionaries converted the Passamaquoddy to Roman Catholicism in the 17th century, they retain some of their native beliefs and do not find the two belief systems conflictual. Each summer since 1965 the Passamaquoddy have celebrated native rituals at the Revival of Indian Ceremonial Days at the Pleasant Point Indian Reservation. The Sipayik Museum there displays many native artifacts, including a 17-foot traditional lightweight birch-bark canoe.

In the 1960s severe poverty and the realization that the state of Maine had sold or leased more than 6,000 acres of Passamaquoddy land led to a major native-rights struggle. Along with two other Maine peoples, the Penobscot and Maliseet, the Passamaquoddy finally agreed to the Maine Indian Claims Settlement Act of 1980, which, among other rights, earned the Indians an $81.5 million compensation payment from the state.

Although many Passamaquoddy still follow a migratory pattern for employment opportunities, leaving the reservation for economic reasons in the winter and returning in the spring and summer, economic prospects have improved since the settlement of 1980. The Passamaquoddy have purchased tens of thousands of acres of land, and they own the successful Northeast Blueberry Corporation, the third largest blueberry farm in the world. In 1985 they bought the Rockland, Maine, radio stations WRKD and WMCM, which became the first tribally owned broadcast outlets in the United States. They have patented and invested in developing a promising new method of burning coal that dramatically reduces smokestack emissions. They also have a high-stakes bingo operation and a cable television station that broadcasts on the reservation. Despite improving economic conditions, many serious health and social problems continue to plague the Passamaquoddy, as they do other Native American peoples.

Paul Brodeur, *Restitution: The Land Claims of the Mashpee, Passamaquoddy, and Penobscot Indians of New England* (1985); Vincent O. Erickson, "Maliseet-Passamaquoddy," in *Northeast*, ed. Bruce G. Trigger, vol. 15 of *Handbook of North American Indians*, gen. ed. William C. Sturtevant (1978); John Dyneley Prince, *Passamaquoddy Texts* (1921); Susan M. Stevens, "Passamaquoddy Economic Development in Cultural and Historical Perspective," *American Indian Economic Development* (1978).

Nancy Johnson Black

Paugussett The Paugussett were a small group of Algonquian-speaking Indians who once dominated the territory along both sides of the Housatonic River in present-day Connecticut. By the early 17th century the Paugussett controlled a strip of land that extended almost to the present-day boundary of Massachusetts. Their principal village, also known as Paugussett, was located along the eastern side of the Housatonic River and had more than 200 inhabitants in 1710. The Paugussett also established a fort about a half mile north of the mouth of the Naugatuck River and another fort near present-day Milford. In addition to their main village of Paugussett, the tribe had other settlements, at Turkey Hill in Derby; Pauguaunuch in Stratford Township (Fairfield County), where there were 25 families in 1710; Naugatuck; and Poodatook.

The Paugussett splintered in 1731 on the death of the sachem Konckapotanauh. According to the diary of Ezra Stiles, the second president of Yale College, a number of Paugussetts joined other Indian groups. Those who did not remained on three principal reservations: Turkey Hill, Coram Hill in Huntington, and Golden Hill in Bridgeport, which had been established in 1659 as Connecticut's first Indian reservation. In 1760 white settlers attempted to evict the Paugussett from all but 6 acres of their Golden Hill reservation. The tribe filed suit and won, but the victory was hollow. Settlers were forced to pay for the land they had taken, but the tribe still lost most of its reservation. By the mid-1860s the Paugussett had sold most of their land to white Americans.

At its peak the group is said to have numbered between 700 and 800 persons. By 1762, Paugussett numbers had thinned dramatically. It was reported that 127 members of the group had moved to Schaghticoke and only 60 individuals lived along the Housatonic. In 1842 the Paugussett sold all remaining land and resettled on a new reservation site (also named Golden Hill) in Trumbull, Conn. Surviving mixed-blood families continue to live at the Golden Hill reservation.

In 1996 the U.S. Bureau of Indian Affairs ruled that residents of Golden Hill failed to qualify for federal recognition as an Indian tribe, although Connecticut state government does recognize them. Hoping to establish a casino and sell tax-free cigarettes, the Paugussett appealed the decision. Their lawyer, Bernard Wishnia, argued that William Sherman

Bonnet maker James Neptune at Passamaquoddy Reservation, Pleasant Point, Maine, 1977

of Trumbull was a common ancestor and Paugussett tribal chief. But the Bureau of Indian Affairs remains unconvinced that Sherman—who is identified in various public records as being "white, black, colored, or Negro"—was of Indian descent or even had close associations with the Paugussett. Another issue is whether the Paugussett have existed continuously as a people since their initial contact with English colonists in the 1650s. Chief Quiet Hawk of the Golden Hill Paugussett threatened in late 2001 to file claims to more than 700,000 acres of land in Connecticut. Litigation continues.

Laura E. Conkey, Ethel Boissevain, and Ives Goddard, "Indians of Southern New England and Long Island: Late Period," in *Northeast*, ed. Bruce G. Trigger, vol. 15 of *Handbook of North American Indians*, gen. ed. William C. Sturtevant (1978); John William De Forest, *History of the Indians of Connecticut from the Earliest Known Period to 1850* (1970 [1850]); Frederick Webb Hodge, ed., *Handbook of American Indians North of Mexico* (1969 [1907]); Ezra Stiles, *The Literary Diary of Ezra Stiles (1769–1776)*, ed. Franklin Bowditch Dexter (1901).

Stephen D. Glazier

Pennington, James William Charles

(1807–70) Abolitionist, minister, and educator. As a minister and educator, James William Charles Pennington became an active participant in New England's abolitionist movement. He was born a slave on Maryland's Eastern Shore and at age four saw his family break up when his mother and an older brother were sold to his master's oldest son. As a young man, Pennington worked as a stonemason and blacksmith until he escaped from his master at age 21. A dangerous journey brought Pennington to the home of a sympathetic Pennsylvania Quaker, who taught the young man how to read and write. He continued his education at an evening school and under private tutoring on the western end of New York's Long Island until 1830.

During the early 1830s Pennington taught in segregated schools in the Long Island community of Newtown and in New Haven, Conn. He studied theology at Yale's School of Divinity, where he was permitted to attend lectures but could not participate in discussion, and held pastorates in Newtown's African Congregational churches from 1838 to 1840. In 1838 Pennington officiated at the wedding of the famous African American abolitionist Frederick Douglass and Anna Murray in New York. In Hartford, Pennington served twice as president of the otherwise all-white Hartford Central Association of Congregational Ministers. In 1841 he was named president of the Union Missionary Society, a precursor of the American Missionary Movement founded five years later by noted abolitionist Lewis Tappan. Pennington's history of African Americans, *A Text Book of the Origin and History of Colored People* (1841), ascribed African American social attributes to environmental rather than biological factors.

During the 1840s Pennington represented the New England abolitionist movement at international antislavery conferences. In 1843 the Connecticut State Anti-Slavery Society sent him to the World's Anti-Slavery Convention. From 1847 to 1855 Pennington was pastor of the First Shiloh Presbyterian Church in New York. In 1849 his commitment to abolitionism caused him to attend the World Peace Congress in Paris as part of a larger delegation. That same year Pennington published his autobiography, *The Fugitive Blacksmith* (1849), which denounced the evils of slavery and American racism. Pennington's abolitionist sentiments were influenced by Lewis Tappan, whose belief in nonviolence he shared until the Civil War.

With the passage of the Fugitive Slave Act (1850), Pennington traveled to Europe to avoid recapture. A $150 payment to his former master's estate secured his manumission in 1851. Having largely abandoned his commitment to pacifism, Pennington recruited African Americans for the Union Army during the Civil War. He spent his later years in the Third New York Presbytery as a member without a pastorate. In 1869 or 1870, weakened by alcoholism and hoping to improve his health, Pennington moved to Jacksonville, Fla., where he died in October 1870.

James William Charles Pennington, *The Fugitive Blacksmith; or, Events in the History of James W. C. Pennington* (1971 [1849]); Pennington, *A Text Book of the Origin and History of Colored People* (1969 [1841]); Herman E. Thomas, *James W. C. Pennington: African American Churchman and Abolitionist* (1995); Joseph R. Washington, Jr., *The First Fugitive Foreign and Domestic Doctor of Divinity: Rational Race Rules of Religion and Realism Revered and Reversed or Revised by the Reverend Doctor James William Charles Pennington* (1990).

Kimberly Charmaine Welch

Penobscot

In the 21st century, the Penobscot of eastern Maine are attempting to retain remnants of their traditional identity despite the sweeping sociocultural changes that have engulfed this Abenaki nation over the past 400 years. Few of the approximately 2,000 remaining members of the nation today speak their native Algonquian language, though efforts are now being made to preserve it, along with traditional Penobscot songs, dances, and crafts. Roman Catholicism imposed by French Jesuit missionaries in the 17th century has been the group's predominant religion, but native beliefs, spirituality, and shamanism have sparked renewed interest.

Before European exploration, the Penobscot (from Panawahpskek, "where the rocks spread out") lived in villages located throughout the Penobscot River watershed. This environment was well suited to trapping, hunting, fishing, and gathering. In this region of the United States many Native American peoples, including the Penobscot, were loosely organized groups with patrilineal tendencies that did not tend to develop well-defined territories outside family hunting lands. Large summer villages were replaced by dispersed settlements with the coming of winter. Beginning as early as 1615, European diseases, against which the Penobscot had little immunity, and warfare combined to wipe out well over 50 percent of the native inhabitants of the region. This devastating loss destroyed much of the social fabric of Penobscot life, as families and villages were annihilated.

With European incursions wreaking havoc on their traditional means of subsistence, the Penobscot managed to continue making handcrafted baskets, moccasins, and birch-bark canoes. Once the French and then the British were expelled from the Northeast, these items came to be designed primarily for use by Americans. Penobscots have also served as guides to sparsely inhabited woodland areas. In the mid-19th century Penobscot Joseph Attean accompanied Henry David Thoreau on the wilderness treks described in Thoreau's *Maine Woods* (1864).

Village organization was traditionally kin-based, and leadership was vested in a sagamore, or chief, usually the head of a large family. By 1866 lifetime appointments to such leadership positions were replaced by annual elections. Now Penobscot are governed by an elected tribal council whose 12 members serve staggered four-year terms.

The Penobscot gained U.S. citizenship in 1924 but lacked voting rights in Maine state elections until 1953. Every two years they elect a governor, a lieutenant governor, and a non-voting tribal representative to the Maine legislature. To qualify for listing on the tribal rolls, one must possess at least one-quarter Penobscot blood. Approximately 25 percent of the Penobscot live today on the federal reservation located near Old Town, Maine.

In 1972 the Penobscot joined with the Passamaquoddy to launch a legal battle against the state of Maine to recover their ancestral lands. The case was settled out of court in 1980, with the Penobscot receiving $40.3 million of an $81.5 million payment from the federal government. They used the money to regain more than 300,000 acres of land from lumber companies, provide new housing to tribe members, and start their own light industries. Until it closed, the Penobscot benefited from employment opportunities at their Indian Island audiocassette-tape-assembly plant, Olamon Industries. By 1996 Olamon had become the second-largest producer of audiocassettes in the United States and was diversifying into other product areas. Leasing land back to lumber companies generated revenues averaging more than $500,000 a year from 1983 to 1993 for tribal members. The Maine Indian Lands Claim Settlement (1980) has helped to ameliorate some of the worst conditions caused by the poverty endured by the Penobscot over the past few centuries, but in 2005 they continue their struggle for tribal sovereignty, particularly on environmental issues, with the state and federal government. Referendum efforts by the Penobscot to enter the gaming industry have been defeated by Maine voters in recent years.

Jim Adams, "Maine Kills Casino in Anti-Sovereignty Hangover," *Indian Country Today* (2003); Paul Brodeur, *Restitution: The Land Claims of the Mashpee, Passamaquoddy, and Penobscot Indians of New England* (1985); Eunice Nelson, *The Wabanaki: An Annotated Bibliography of Selected Books, Articles, Documents about Maliseet, Micmac, Passamaquoddy, Penobscot Indians in Maine Annotated by Native Americans* (1982); Dean Snow, "Eastern Abenaki," in *Northeast*, ed. Bruce G. Trigger, vol. 15 of *Handbook of North American Indians*, gen. ed. William C. Sturtevant (1978).

Nancy Johnson Black

Pequot The Pequot are an American Indian people whose homeland encompassed much of eastern Connecticut, with villages located on the coast and along the Thames and Mystic Rivers. The Pequot language, now extinct, was part of the Eastern Algonquian language family and closely related to the dialects of neighboring Indian peoples.

The origin of the Pequot has long been debated. Traditional Pequot belief claims descent from the Delaware peoples southwest of Connecticut. Early European American scholars also argued for a recent migration into Connecticut, but modern anthropological research supports a local version of Pequot origins, on the basis of their cultural similarity to adjacent peoples, ancient archaeological artifacts, and the absence of archaeological evidence for recent migration.

At the time of European contact, the Pequot were a loosely organized group led by a number of chiefs, or sachems. Their economy was based on horticulture, hunting, fishing, and gathering. In the early 1600s the Pequot assumed a central position in regional trade networks, both as producers of wampum and as a conduit for furs supplied by more northern Indian peoples.

By 1630 the Pequot were the dominant power in Connecticut, which was becoming a focus of English settlement. The killing of two English traders by allies of the Pequot led to a series of raids that culminated in the Pequot War of 1636–37, in which the English vowed to exterminate the tribe. An English army, joined by Mohegan and Narragansett warriors, attacked and burned the main Pequot village at Mystic on May 26, 1637. Some 400 Pequots—some sources place the number as high as 700—mostly women and children, were slaughtered during this attack, in which only two English soldiers died. Following the massacre, the remaining Pequots were actively pursued, killed outright, or sold into slavery. The tribe was declared dissolved, and the use of the name Pequot legally banned. The Pequot War is cited by many scholars as the first instance of genocide in North America; it has shaped Pequot identity ever since.

The few Pequot who survived the war were dispersed throughout southern New England, but by 1650 many had returned to their traditional homeland. English colonial authorities established a number of Indian towns for these refugees, which became the nucleus for the Pequot settlements that persisted into the 20th century: Paucatuck, in Stonington, and Mashantucket, in Ledyard, Conn. These communities maintained a continuous Pequot presence, and a sense of tribal identity, over the next 300 years despite declining population, the loss of land to legislative acts, and encroachment by neighboring European Americans. In the 19th century the name Pequot had become associated with the plight of Native Americans generally, and Herman Melville chose it as the name of the whaling ship in *Moby-Dick* (1851).

Pequot fortunes improved dramatically in the 1970s, when Elizabeth George Ploufe reunited dispersed tribe members and founded the modern Pequot Nation. During that decade the Pequot initiated legal action to regain lands it had lost during the 19th century. In 1983 the Mashantucket Pequot received tribal recognition from the U.S. government, which cleared the way for a $900,000 compensation payment, received in 1987, for lands seized in violation of federal law. This settlement was used to fund capital projects, tribal housing and health services, and the purchase of land to expand the reservation. With the establishment of the highly profitable Foxwoods Resort Casino, the Mashantucket Pequot have reemerged as a powerful economic and political force in eastern Connecticut. In 1998 profits from the nation's most successful gambling facility allowed the Pequot to open a $193 million museum, where tribal artifacts found near the casino itself are housed.

Kathleen J. Bragdon, *Native Peoples of Southern New England, 1500–1650* (1996); Laurence M. Hauptman and James D. Wherry, eds., *The Pequot in Southern New England: The Fall and Rise of an American Indian Nation* (1990); Neal Salisbury, *Manitou and Providence: Indians, Europeans, and the Making of New England, 1500–1643* (1982).

Robert G. Goodby

Poles Few Poles settled in New England before the 19th century. New Englanders, appreciative of the services of the Revolutionary War heroes Kazimierz Pulaski and Tadeusz Kosciuszko, feted political exiles from Polish insurrections (1830, 1846, 1848, and 1863) as democratic compatriots in the struggle against tyranny. Still, only 169 Poles resided in the region in 1860. By 1930 there were 362,285, 10 percent of all American Poles. In 2000, 747,290 New Englanders claimed Polish ancestry. Massachusetts claimed 323,210; Connecticut, 284,272; New Hampshire, 51,183; Rhode Island, 43,159; Maine, 24,982; and Vermont, 20,484.

The arrival of "Polanders" at Jamestown on October 1, 1608, opened the story of the Poles in North America. Few others came before the American Revolution. Only after Russia, Prussia, and Austria partitioned the Polish Lithuanian Commonwealth in 1795, and an independent Poland disappeared from the map of Europe until 1918, were exile and emigration woven into the fabric of Polish history. Pulaski and Kosciuszko, along with other exiles of the gentry class, were early political émigrés. Although Lithuanians, Ukrainians, and Jews also migrated from the lands of the former commonwealth, the ethnic Polish migration was predominantly Roman Catholic and spoke Polish.

Polish immigration declined after the U.S. Congress enacted quotas in 1921 and 1924 that discriminated against southern and eastern Europeans. The World War II diplomatic decisions that consigned Poland to Soviet control, however, brought large numbers of political émigrés, exiled soldiers, and displaced persons to New England and elsewhere in the United States between 1947 and 1956. The Immigration Act of 1965 brought new waves of Polish immigration, and the Solidarity era of the 1980s saw a goodly number of refugees seeking asylum.

In the 1880s rural peasants from Russian- and Austrian-controlled Poland made up the vast majority of Polish political exiles. They populated cities and manufacturing and mill towns, locating primarily in Massachusetts (187,063 by 1930) and Connecticut (133,813 by 1930). Rhode Island, New Hampshire, Vermont, and Maine attracted smaller but not insignificant numbers of Poles.

Immigrant settlements replicated Polish communities elsewhere. In New England,

Poles erected 82 Roman Catholic parishes (59 between 1900 and 1909) and 30 parishes of the schismatic Polish National Catholic Church. There were 35 parochial schools staffed by seven sisterhoods; an orphanage in New Britain, Conn.; and a hospital staffed by Felician sisters in Bangor, Maine. Local branches of the Polish national insurance fraternals exemplified Polish self-reliance and the commitment to preserving ethnic identity. By 1944 the Polish National Alliance had 27,951 members in New England; the Polish Roman Catholic Union, 16,929; and the Polish Women's Alliance, 4,685. Polish-language media included newspapers (*Wschod* [1905] in Providence; *Gazeta Bostonska* [1910–16] and *Kuryer Codzienny* [1917–63], both in Boston; *Gazeta Nowa Anglia* [1915–46] in Chicopee and *Gwiazda* [1923–53] in Holyoke, Mass.; and *Przewodnik Katolicki* [1907–66] in New Britain), radio programs from 1936, and cable television since the 1980s. In large communities, Polish societies often combined into "a united Polish society" (*centrala*) to coordinate activities and defend community interests.

Land hunger drove emigration from Poland. Rural peasants left to find work, accumulate investment capital, and return home to purchase land. These unskilled or skilled agrarian laborers accepted mill and factory jobs; many women worked in the textile mills. A unique contribution of New England Poles was their role in agriculture. Settling on both sides of the Connecticut River from Middletown, Conn., north to southern Vermont, Poles purchased abandoned farms and from 1885 revived the region's declining agrarian economy. By 1930, 66,734 Poles belonged to the region's rural farm and nonfarm population. Family solidarity enabled Poles to compete with American farmers. The peasant family was an economic unit, but the sight of men, women, and children toiling together in the fields provoked Yankee bias. The loss of land to Poles, Anglo-Saxon nativism, the pseudoscientific racism popular among New England intellectuals who deemed eastern and southern Europeans inferior groups, and the Immigration Restriction League of Boston all fostered prejudice and ethnic stereotyping. As the farmers prospered and their children assimilated, prejudices abated, although stereotyping persisted, resurfacing in the 1970s in the guise of "Polack" jokes.

Poles met prejudice and discrimination within the Roman Catholic Church as well. The elevation of a handful of immigrant pastors and second- and third-generation priests to the rank of monsignor acknowledged Polish contributions to New England Catholicism. No Pole, however, has been elevated to New England's episcopate.

The immigrants' rural background has made a mark on New England popular culture. Polka music is identified as Polish and has thrived under bandleaders Ray Henry, Walt Solek, Louis "Happy Louie" Dusseault, and Jas and Stas Przasnyski, known as "the Connecticut Twins." Polish American baseball Hall of Famer Carl "Yaz" Yastrzemski of the Boston Red Sox, the son of Long Island potato farmers, became a New England sports legend. The novels of Suzanne Strempek Shea, *Selling the Lite of Heaven* (1994) and *Hoopi Shoopi Donna* (1996), transport readers into contemporary Polish Catholic homes in western Massachusetts.

Education, and especially the G.I. Bill, has helped Polish Americans integrate themselves socially and advance economically. In 1998, 78.5 percent of Polish Americans over age 25 nationwide possessed a high school education, 23.1 percent a bachelor's degree, and 9 percent a doctorate or other postgraduate degree. These figures mark a dramatic change from the early days of immigration, when some children entered the labor force on making their first Holy Communion and few finished high school. Polish New Englanders are no longer primarily factory and mill workers: in 1990, 33 percent were in managerial and professional specialties; 32 percent in technical, sales, and administrative occupations; 11 percent in service jobs; and 11 percent in precision production, crafts, and repair; a further 11 percent worked as operators, fabricators, and laborers. A major change over time was the decline of employment in farming, forestry, and fishing to .01 percent. The median Polish American household income in 1990 was $45,827. Chairs of Polish studies at Harvard and Central Connecticut State Universities symbolize the value placed on higher education by the Polish community.

Poles have also been active in the realm of politics. There were once 40 branches of the Union of Polish Socialists in America in New England. Most Poles pursued political representation and patronage through Polish Democratic and Republican clubs. Nonpartisan Polish American Citizen clubs required members to become voting citizens. State federations of political clubs existed in Massachusetts, Connecticut, and Rhode Island in the 1920s and 1930s, when a New England Polish American Political Federation represented 110 member clubs. Political successes include the 1938 election of Boleslaus J. Monkiewicz, a New Britain Republican, who was the first New England Pole elected to Congress. The first Polish American governor was Maine's Edmund (Marciszewski) Muskie (1955–59), who later became a U.S. senator (1959–80) and then U.S. secretary of state (1980).

For the most part Poles have assimilated to American culture. In 2000 only 5.3 percent of those in New England spoke Polish at home. Nevertheless, an ongoing interest in homeland politics is an important component of ethnicity. During World War I more than 2,000 recruits from New England (10 percent of all recruits from the United States) enlisted in the Polish army in France to fight for independence. When the Polish American Congress was organized in 1944 to lobby for Poland's independence and the interests of Polish Americans, branches appeared in Connecticut, eastern and western Massachusetts, Rhode Island, and New Hampshire. Between 1981 and 1989 Solidarity support groups lobbied in Boston, Providence, and Hartford. Former president of Poland Lech Walesa's visit to Connecticut and Massachusetts in April 1996 and his address to the Connecticut General Assembly symbolize the continuing link between New England's Polish diaspora and Poland.

Stanislaus A. Blejwas, "The Local Ethnic Lobby: The Polish American Congress in Connecticut, 1944–1974," in *The Polish Presence in Canada and America*, ed. Frank Renkiewicz (1982); Blejwas, "The 'Polish Tradition' in Connecticut Politics," *Connecticut History* 33 (1992); Blejwas, "Puritans and Poles: The New England Literary Image of the Polish Peasant Immigrant," *Polish American Studies* 42 (1985); Blejwas, *A Rhode Island Ethnic Group: Polish Americans* (1995); Blejwas, *St. Stanislaus B. and M. Parish, Meriden, Connecticut: A Century of Connecticut Polonia, 1891–1991* (1991); John J. Bukowczyk, ed., *Polish Americans and Their History: Community, Culture, and Politics* (1996); Helena Znaniecka Lopata, *Polish Americans* (1994); James S. Pula, *Polish Americans: An Ethnic Community* (1995).

Stanislaus A. Blejwas

Portuguese The Portuguese communities of New England, spread throughout the southeastern part of the region, are among the largest immigrant groups in the area. The overwhelming majority comes from the Azores, an archipelago of the North Atlantic ocean that became an autonomous region of Portugal following that country's Revolution of the Flowers in 1974. Continental and Madeiran Portuguese have also come to New England, though in smaller numbers. Cape Verdeans were classified as Portuguese until 1975, when that chain of islands became an independent republic. Most of the Portuguese-speaking residents of Massachusetts reside in Fall River and New Bedford, although large concentrations are also found in Boston, Cambridge, and Somerville. Nearly 10 percent of Rhode Island's population is of Portuguese descent.

The Portuguese have maintained a connection with New England from the beginning of the European arrival in North America. The navigator Estevan Gomez, who came to Maine in 1525, is the first sure presence. Although there is no evidence to support the claim by some that Miguel Côrte-Real arrived in 1502, it is a fact that his brother Gaspar Côrte-Real reached Newfoundland, probably before 1500. It was during another trip, in 1501, that Gaspar declared the territory Land of the King of Portugal, as indicated on the anonymous Cantino map of the world drafted in 1502. Sending a ship to take the news back to the king, he stayed on to explore what he called Terra Nova (New Land) and was never heard from again. Miguel then got permission from the king to mount a search for his lost brother and left Lisbon with that objective. He, too, was never heard from again. The next recorded Portuguese-related presence was that of Portuguese Sephardic Jews who had migrated to Newport, R.I., soon after their arrival (from Brazil and Curaçao) in New Amsterdam in 1654. Among them was Abraham Lopez, who was instrumental in introducing the sperm-oil industry to North America.

But the real history of the Portuguese in New England begins in the last decades of the 18th century. About 1,000 miles west of mainland Portugal, the Azores became a key stopping point on whaler routes between the South Atlantic and the Pacific. Azoreans, the "hardy peasants of those rocky shores" that Herman Melville described in *Moby-Dick* (1851), were recruited in large numbers. In *Whaling and Fishing* (1855), Charles Nordhoff drew a lasting profile of these "Western Islands Portuguese," plentiful on almost every vessel from New Bedford: "They are quiet, peaceful, inoffensive people, sober and industrious, penurious almost to a fault, and I believe invariably excellent whalemen. They are held in great esteem by ship owners and captains." Azoreans had settled in Martha's Vineyard, Mass., as early as 1770, adopting American family names, and had soon intermarried with Americans. By 1780, 200 Azorean whalemen were enlisted as crew on American whalers, and many of these later settled in New England.

Though surrounded by water in the middle of the ocean, the Azoreans have traditionally turned their backs to the sea. Basically a farming people, only 3 percent of the Azorean population lives off the ocean. Whenever they had the opportunity, they left ship, opting for the developing cotton and manufacturing industries of Fall River and New Bedford or cranberry and strawberry cultivation in rural Massachusetts. By 1870 there were about 9,000 predominantly Azorean Portuguese in the United States, with more than one-third of

these living in Massachusetts, particularly in the cities of Fall River and New Bedford but with communities spreading to Cape Cod, Taunton, Lowell, Lawrence, and Gloucester. At the end of the 1800s most of the skippers in the Provincetown fleet, for example, were Azorean. During this period slightly half of the Portuguese in North America had settled in California, where open agricultural land attracted many Azoreans; by 1890, however, New England had become the main region of migration for the Portuguese. According to the 1900 census, 17,885 lived in Massachusetts, 2,865 in Rhode Island, and 865 in Connecticut, with a significant increase taking place from 1900 to 1930, when 188,875 Portuguese migrated to the United States (Fall River alone had 22,431 in 1920).

The first wave of Portuguese migration established a network that spread throughout southeastern Massachusetts and increasingly into Rhode Island. Bowing to the pressure to adapt to an anglicized culture that held the political and economic power, many Portuguese Americanized their names, changing Rodrigues and Rosa to Rogers, Ferreira to Smith, Pereira to Perry, Simas and Simoes to Simons, Martins to Martin, and Silva to Sylvia, to give a few examples.

After the Depression the number of incoming Portuguese dropped significantly (10,752 between 1931 and 1950); but the Azorean Refugee Acts of 1958 and 1960, passed by Congress after the 1957–58 Capelinhos volcanic eruption off the Azorean island of Faial, along with the Immigration Act of 1965, created a second wave of migration to the region. Between 1971 and 1980, 106,710 Portuguese entered the United States, and the 2000 census found 1,177,112 Portuguese and persons of Portuguese descent in the United States. In that year 436,352 New Englanders claimed single or mixed Portuguese ancestry, 279,722 of them in Massachusetts. The population of that state's Bristol County, which includes the cities of Fall River (43,253 Portuguese) and New Bedford (36,239), is 29 percent Portuguese. Neighboring Rhode Island was home to 91,445 persons of Portuguese extraction in 2000; of the other states Connecticut had the most (44,695), followed by New Hampshire (13,095), Maine (5,351), and Vermont (2,044).

The anthropologist Estellie Smith has called the Portuguese in the United States an "invisible minority," for in spite of their high numbers in New England, they go largely unnoticed outside certain parts of that region. The understated nature of their presence is rooted in an Azorean culture that evolved over 500 years of isolation on fragile islands far from any mainland, surrounded by frequently rough seas, subject to vicious storms, and

cyclically tormented by volcanoes and earthquakes. The Catholic faith offered the only hope of salvation from despair. The church and family are still the strongest factors in Azorean resistance to alien American values. The most common goal among Portuguese immigrants (which most reach within a few years of arrival) is to purchase a house, preferably in the suburbs and not too far from other family members, a goal met by working hard at whatever jobs they can find.

The adjective "invisible" does not apply to social and cultural life within the Portuguese community, however. Small businesses thrive, particularly construction companies, ethnic commercial enterprises (notably, restaurants), and industrial fishing (New Bedford's fleet is predominantly Portuguese), though Portuguese immigrants have played an important role as laborers in the textile mills and clothing manufactories of southeastern Massachusetts. Key to this workforce, they have also been active labor unionists. Public religious *festas*, along with a variety of social and cultural activities, enliven the year-round lives of New England's Portuguese communities. The Portuguese festa of the Blessed Sacrament, or Festa dos Madeiras, annually congregates some 100,000 people in New Bedford, and Fall River's Festa do Espírito Santo (Feast of the Holy Ghost) gathers similar numbers. The Day of Portugal (June 10) is celebrated throughout Massachusetts and Rhode Island communities, and the Blessing of the Fleet in Provincetown and New Bedford, Mass., and Stonington, Conn., once a largely Portuguese fishing village, has become a mainstream American event. Concessions at these festas, along with dozens of Portuguese restaurants, have introduced Portuguese kale soup, *massa sovada* (sweetbread), *papos-secos* (hard rolls), and *linguiça* and *chouriço* (sausages) to a wider American public. One of the predominant flowers in the gardens of southeastern New England, the *hortênsia* (hydrangea), was brought from the Azores.

New England's Portuguese mass media give voice to the Portuguese community, helping its members maintain a sense of connection: outlets include newspapers (particularly the *Portuguese Times* of New Bedford and *O Jornal* of Fall River, with the Portuguese daily *Diário de Notícias* having been published between 1922 and 1972), radio programs (WJFD in New Bedford), and cable television (local channels in New Bedford and Warren, Mass., and worldwide coverage from Portugal's RTP International broadcast throughout New England and the world). The story of the Portuguese community is also finding a literary audience through the work of Francis X. Gaspar, whose novel *Leaving Pico* (1999) chronicles life in Provincetown's Portuguese fishing community in the 1950s. The critically acclaimed Portuguese American poet John Medeiros (1901–95), a native of Fall River, will soon be honored by the erection of a monument in that city's State Heritage Park.

Azorean and Portuguese New Englanders maintain close ties with their family members on the other side of the Atlantic, often returning to the homeland for feasts and vacations or receiving summer visits from relatives in their American homes. Longing for the homeland is central to the musical and literary traditions of America's Portuguese diaspora, giving rise to a style known as "saudade" (nostalgic yearning or homesickness). Other contacts with the mother culture include performing artists, educators, scholars, writers, and speakers from the homeland, who offer a rich and diverse calendar of events throughout the year, as well as from the Portuguese American community, which has produced its own share of such figures. Individuals such as the literary giant John Dos Passos, of Portuguese descent and with New England connections, and the half-Portuguese composer John Philip Sousa are often cited as notable Portuguese in America, though there are numerous publicly recognized Portuguese Americans. Humberto Sousa Cardinal Medeiros, archbishop of Boston from 1970 until his death in 1983, was born in the Azores, and William Wood, the son of Azorean parents, was the entrepreneur behind the American Woolen Company of Lawrence, Mass., the world's largest textile conglomerate in the early 1900s. Portuguese American musicians include Joe Raposo, the first music director of *Sesame Street*, and the classical violinist Elmar Oliveira. The nationally renowned celebrity chef Emeril Lagasse got his first cooking lessons in the Fall River kitchen of his Azorean mother, Hilda. Though Portuguese Americans lack a strong national political presence (there has been only one Portuguese congressman, California's Tony Coelho, who managed Albert Gore's presidential campaign in 2000), the community has had its share of state and local politicians in Massachusetts and Rhode Island.

One of the most significant changes occurring in Portuguese families upon their arrival in the United States is the improved status of women in the household, even though the 1974 political revolution in Portugal had already brought about great changes in women's lives. In recent decades more young Portuguese women than men are attending college, and women are increasingly visible in all areas of public life. Laurinda de Andrade, who came from the Azores as young child in 1917, graduated from Pembroke College and Columbia University and wrote one of the best Portuguese American autobiographies, *The Open Door* (1968). Mary Fonseca was a Massachusetts state senator from 1953 to 1984 and an assistant to the majority whip. Portuguese American women continue to make strides in New England politics at various levels.

Portuguese American letters have blossomed in recent decades as the teaching and study of Portuguese language and culture has developed at the university level. Programs at Brown University, since 1975, and more recently at the University of Massachusetts and Dartmouth College are especially prominent. The Department of Portuguese and Brazilian Studies at Brown founded the first academic outlet for original works and cultural study of Portuguese America, the journal *Gávea-Brown*, published since 1980 in Providence.

Academic interest in Portuguese culture is part of a broader movement among Portuguese Americans to reaffirm their heritage. The economic and political realities of the past, which caused many to downplay their ethnicity, have given way to new, more favorable conditions. Members of the Portuguese community may now join in broader American social and cultural activities without having to deny their social and cultural backgrounds. More Portuguese New Englanders are now acquiring U.S. passports, perhaps because they are no longer required to abandon Portuguese citizenship when they do so. Despite hardships, the Portuguese have created a vibrant, multifaceted life for themselves in New England that promises to improve as a new century unfolds.

Onésimo T. Almeida, "A Profile of the Azorean," in *Issues in Portuguese Bilingual Education,* ed. Donaldo P. Macedo (1980); Marsha McCabe and Joseph D. Thomas, eds., *Portuguese Spinner, an American Story: Stories of History, Culture, and Life from Portuguese Americans in Southeastern New England* (1998); Miguel Moniz, comp., *Azores* (1999); Leo Pap, *The Portuguese-Americans* (1992 [1981]); Francis M. Rogers, *Americans of Portuguese Descent: A Lesson in Differentiation* (1974); M. Estellie Smith, "Portuguese Enclaves: The Invisible Minority," in *Social and Cultural Identity: Problems of Persistence and Change,* ed. Thomas K. Fitzgerald (1974); Donald R. Taft, *Two Portuguese Communities in New England* (1967 [1923]); Jerry R. Williams, *And Yet They Come: Portuguese Immigration from the Azores to the United States* (1982).

Onésimo T. Almeida

Puerto Ricans Puerto Ricans have a unique status among America's ethnic groups as a result of the historical relation between the United States and Puerto Rico. Acquired by the United States after the Spanish-American War in 1898, Puerto Rico was established as a protectorate in 1900 and became a commonwealth in 1952. Under the Jones Act of 1917, residents were granted U.S. citizenship and were thus free to travel, work, and settle on the mainland. The pace of immigration to New England, relatively slow through the 1930s, picked up rapidly during the 1940s and accelerated further in the 1950s and 1960s as a part of the great migration to the Northeast focused on New York City.

The push of migration was the absence of employment at home in the face of a fast growing population, and the pull, especially to New York and New England after World War II, was agricultural and industrial employment. As economic opportunities improved on the island, many immigrants traveled back and forth between New England and Puerto Rico, but in recent decades communities have put down roots and become an even more significant part of New England's population and culture. Moreover, Puerto Ricans have left New York City seeking better employment and living conditions in smaller cities such as Bridgeport, New Haven, and Hartford, Conn., and Fitchburg, Lowell, Lawrence, and Springfield, Mass. Puerto Rican populations grew dramatically in New Hampshire and Maine in the 1990s (see table).

In the 1990 census Massachusetts passed Connecticut as the New England state with the most Puerto Ricans. The census tells a story of continuing growth in the community, but it also reveals that Puerto Rican populations are a diminishing percentage of Latino New Englanders, owing to the large influx of Dominicans and other groups. In the 1970s, for example, Puerto Ricans constituted 75 percent of Massachusetts Latinos, but only 53 percent in 1990 and 49 percent in 2000.

New England's 428,936 Puerto Ricans in 2000 may be compared with the 1,050,293 members of that group found residing in New York State in the same year, and New York City remains the most significant cultural center for Puerto Ricans in the Northeast.

The history of Puerto Ricans in Connecticut is especially significant, given the rapid growth of the population there in the 1950s and 1960s and the emergence of the state as a center of Puerto Rican political, economic, and cultural influence. Early migration, in the so-called pioneer phase through the 1940s, centered on agricultural employment through contract labor. Some 20,000 Puerto Ricans a year arrived on the mainland in the late 1940s. This employment focused in part on Connecticut's shade tobacco industry, where Puerto Ricans joined Jamaicans to work in hard conditions. Other agricultural workers harvested fruit and vegetables, following the apple harvest, for example, in Massachusetts and northern New England. Some found em-

Puerto Rican Population in New England

	1980	1990	2000
Connecticut	88,361	146,842	194,443
Maine	714	1,250	2,275
Massachusetts	76,450	151,193	199,207
New Hampshire	1,316	3,299	6,215
Rhode Island	4,621	13,016	25,422
Vermont	324	659	1,374
Total	171,786	316,259	428,936

Source: U.S. Census, 1980, 1990, and 2000

ployment in the poultry industry. Abuses of migrant workers led to reforms in the late 1940s, and the Hartford area became a magnet for more permanent migration. With the advent of cheap air travel after World War II, migration and travel back and forth increased dramatically. In addition to Hartford, Bridgeport and New Haven also saw growth in their Puerto Rican populations, sometimes directly from the island but often by way of New York City.

In New England Puerto Ricans faced the same patterns of racial discrimination encountered elsewhere in the Northeast, and racism has been a persistent problem. The problems of racism were compounded by nomenclature, as government officials, and census records, recorded Puerto Ricans as Hispanics and designated individuals as black or white. Many Puerto Ricans prefer the designation Puertorriqueño or Borrinqueño to denote origins distinctive from those of other Hispanics or Latinos. Racism was compounded by a lack of educational opportunities in urban schools, especially in bilingual programs, and by economic decline in Hartford and other cities. Home ownership rates for Puerto Ricans lag behind those of many other ethnic groups in New England cities, and poverty rates remain high despite a rising middle class. Socioeconomic issues facing Puerto Ricans in New Haven were one focus of an early scholarly study, Lloyd H. Rogler's *Migrant in the City* (1972). As Joseph P. Fitzpatrick notes, New England's urban Puerto Rican communities in the 1970s were less established than those of other ethnicities and therefore more impoverished. In Boston in the 1970s, for example, menial labor was the only employment available to many, with the result that 40 percent of Puerto Ricans lived in poverty and high numbers dropped out of school. In many New England cities Puerto Ricans had to compete with other Hispanic immigrants for the few available jobs. In the past two decades, however, the communities have matured and economic conditions have improved. At the University of Massachusetts

in Boston, the Mauricio Gaston Institute for Latino Community Development and Public Policy sponsors speakers, conferences, and research to increase understanding of the experiences of Latinos in Massachusetts. National Puerto Rican organizations, such as Aspira and La Raza, have worked to improve educational, employment, and political opportunities through local affiliates and projects. Entrepreneurial activity is increasing in the Puerto Rican community, from neighborhood bodegas and restaurants to service industries and high-tech businesses.

The cultural presence of Puerto Ricans in New England is growing at many levels. The University of Connecticut established its Institute of Puerto Rican and Latino Studies in 1994, and Connecticut Public Television produced the first documentary on the Puerto Rican experience in the state, *Puerto Rican Passages*, the following year. Also in 1994, the Connecticut Cultural Heritage Arts Program honored Bernabela Quiñones, a *mundillo* (handwoven bobbin) lace maker, as one of that state's premier traditional artists. Hartford's Institute for Community Research has sponsored several exhibits and cultural events on the links between Puerto Rican traditional arts and communities in Connecticut. In 1999 it mounted *Mano a Mano: Puerto Rican Traditional Arts from Island to City*, which featured works by 15 artists. Hartford holds an annual Puerto Rican Day parade in June. In Massachusetts the Festival Puertorriqueño de Massachusetts, Inc., sponsors the Puerto Rican Day celebration.

The Catholic Church in New England has established many special ministries to Latinos, including Puerto Ricans. Bridgeport and Boston both had one by the 1960s, and the trend accelerated after 1976, when Latinos issued a forceful call for more Spanish-speaking parish priests. Catholics still constitute the majority religious group among Puerto Rican New Englanders despite declining numbers in recent decades. They give particular emphasis to celebrations of El Dia de los Innocentes (Day of the Holy Innocents) on December 27,

El Dia de los Tres Reyes (Three Kings' Day or Little Christmas) on January 6, and El Dia de las Candelarias (Candlemass) on February 2. El Dia de la Raza (Columbus Day) and El Fiesta de Santiago Apostol (Saint James's Day) are also the focus of local celebrations. Evangelical Protestantism is a growing force among Puerto Ricans. In New Haven the Star of Jacob Pentecostal Church draws more Puerto Ricans than do Catholic churches, a sign of the increasing strength of that and other Protestant denominations. New England's Puerto Ricans also practice Santería and Espiritismo. *Botanicos* in urban centers serve these religions and Catholics by offering for sale herbs, items for use in religious rituals, and prayers.

Puerto Rican musicians based on the island and in New York regularly tour New England, and local bands can be found in most cities. The region has not produced its own literary movement, but Nuyorican authors and artists find a large audience in the region.

Puerto Ricans have been underrepresented in New England's political life, but they are beginning to come into their own with the growth and increased stability of the community. In Hartford Eddie A. Perez became the city's first Latino mayor in 2001. He emigrated from Puerto Rico as a child and attended Trinity College. Hartford has the largest Puerto Rican community of any New England city, and Mayor Perez has built a coalition of many Latino and non-Latino groups to bring dynamic leadership to the city.

José E. Cruz, *Identity and Power: Puerto Rican Politics and the Challenge of Ethnicity* (1998); Joseph P. Fitzpatrick, *Puerto Rican Americans: The Meaning of Migration to the Mainland* (1987); Fitzpatrick, "Puerto Ricans," in *Harvard Encyclopedia of American Ethnic Groups*, ed. Stephan Thernstrom (1980); Derek Green, "Puerto Rican Americans," in *Gale Encyclopedia of Multicultural America*, ed. Jeffrey Lehman (2000); Oscar Handlin, *The Newcomers: Negroes and Puerto Ricans in a Changing Metropolis* (1959); Clara E. Rodriguez, *Puerto Ricans: Born in the U.S.A.* (1989); Arlene Torres, "Puerto Ricans," in *American Immigrant Cultures: Builders of a Nation*, ed. David Levinson and Melvin Ember (1997); Bonnie Urciuoli, *Exposing Prejudice: Puerto Rican Experiences of Language, Race, and Class* (1996).

David H. Watters

Ruffin, Josephine St. Pierre (1842–1924)

Social activist. With the exception of a few years early in her marriage, Josephine St. Pierre Ruffin lived her entire life in Boston. During her adult years Ruffin was an active and influential resident of the city.

Ruffin's father, John St. Pierre, was of African, French, and Indian descent. Her mother, Eliza Matilda St. Pierre, was English by birth. Josephine married George Lewis Ruffin in 1858, and the two then moved to England. When the Civil War erupted in the United States, however, the couple returned to Boston to participate in the abolitionist movement. George was the first African American graduate of Harvard Law School and subsequently became the first black municipal judge.

Abolitionism was only the first cause for which Ruffin labored. After the Civil War, Ruffin organized the Kansas Relief Association to help provide financial assistance for black migrants from the South as they moved west. Thereafter she organized, led, and participated in many clubs and associations devoted to a variety of causes. She belonged to African American organizations, woman suffrage groups, and community service clubs. In 1893 Ruffin founded the New Era Club with her daughter, Florida. The club's monthly publication, *Woman's Era,* was the first newspaper published by African American women in the United States. As editor of this newspaper, Ruffin joined the New England Women's Press Association. As a member of that organization and as president of the New Era Club, Ruffin was eligible to attend a biennial meeting of the General Federation of Women's Clubs in Milwaukee, Wis., in 1900. When the meeting convened, however, organizers allowed Ruffin to attend only as a delegate from the New England Women's Press Association. They would not recognize her as president of the New Era Club, because it was a club for African American women. Refusing to attend as anything but president of the New Era Club, Ruffin was barred from the meeting.

Ruffin is perhaps best known as the founder of the National Association of Colored Women, an organization that exists to this day. In 1895 she organized a convention of representatives from black women's clubs across the country to meet in Boston. The direct impetus of the meeting was an insulting, racist letter written and published by the president of the Missouri Press Association that defamed all African American women. Attendees at the Boston gathering composed a reply to the letter and then spent the rest of the convention laying the groundwork for a national association that would meet regularly to improve the status and protect the dignity of all African American women.

Paula Giddings, *When and Where I Enter: The Impact of Black Women on Race and Sex in America* (1984); Darlene Clark Hine, ed., *Black Women in America: An Historical Encyclopedia* (1993).

Suzanne L. Wones

Schaghticoke

Schaghticoke is both a place-name and the name of an American Indian group. Variously spelled Scatticook, Scaticook, Scattacook, Schaticook, Skachkook, Skatecook, Scaticoke, and so on, the term derives from the Algonquian word *pishgatikuk.* According to Eunice Mauwee, granddaughter of the first recorded Schaghticoke sachem at Kent, Conn., *pishgatikuk* meant "at the confluence of two rivers."

During the early historic period there were three geographically discrete communities of Schaghticoke in northeastern North America. Historians have tended to treat them as socially discrete as well, although this may not necessarily be so. One Schaghticoke community was located at the confluence of the Hudson and Hoosic Rivers in eastern New York. A second group resided in the Sheffield region of western Massachusetts between the Housatonic and Green Rivers. And a third made its home at the juncture of the Housatonic and Webatuck Rivers in northwestern Connecticut.

Scaticook along the Hudson River in New York was originally a Mahican village to which Governor Bellomont allowed the relocation of a number of New England Indians who were fleeing the wrath of English colonists during King Philip's War in 1676. As the surrounding lands were slowly sold off to white settlers and the natives began to feel the deleterious effects of contact-induced disease and debt, the community began to disband. By 1754 the last of its members supposedly left to join other Algonquian-speaking Indian communities in French Canada.

The Skatecook Indians of the southern Berkshire region were also part of the Mahican tribe. In 1734 they were visited by the Reverend John Sargent, a Calvinist minister from Yale College who preached the Christian doctrine and taught school to the Indian children. Soon afterward the Skatecook left their village in Sheffield and merged with another Mahican village under the sachemship of John Konkapot to form the Christian Indian town of Stockbridge, Mass. Indian Stockbridge thrived until the American Revolution. A good many Stockbridge Indians fought and died for the American cause. This loss of life, combined with continual white encroachment, caused increased economic and social discomfort for the Stockbridge community.

About this time the Oneida Indians of central New York invited Stockbridge and other Indian groups to settle among them. Many Stockbridge families accepted, and by 1785 much of the community had migrated west to New Stockbridge in Oneida country. Members eventually removed even further westward, ending up in Wisconsin. Their descendants are now known as the Stockbridge-Munsee Mohican.

Originally known as the Schaghticoke tribe, the Schaghticoke Tribal Nation of Kent, Conn., Inc., comprises descendants of Weantinock, Pootatuck, Mahican, and Pequot indigenous peoples. Recognized as an American Indian tribe by Connecticut from first contact, the Schaghticoke were officially recognized by the federal government in January 2004. The Schaghticoke Reservation at Kent consists of over 400 acres bounded by the Housatonic River on the east and the New York state line on the west in the Schaghticoke Mountains. The reserve was originally much larger, encompassing lands far outside the township of Kent. Three families presently live on the reservation, which is mainly undeveloped woodland; the majority have lived off-reservation since the late 1800s because the countryside provided few employment opportunities. Like the Stockbridge community with whom they had close ties, the Schaghticoke at Kent were also a mainly Christianized community. Moravian missionaries converted tribal members, including sachem Gideon Mauwee, in the 1740s. Mauwee invited the Moravians to build a mission and live at Schaghticoke, which they did until 1769. A stone structure still standing on aboriginal lands north of the present reservation is traditionally considered by tribal members to be the ruins of the chapel.

The tribe continues to practice cultural traditions and leadership strategies known since the 18th century, when the Kent Schaghticoke are first mentioned in colonial documents. These include native crafts, rattlesnake lore, herbal medicine, powwows, and name-giving ceremonies. Formal political leadership rests with a tribal council, which includes a chief, as well as an informal leadership consisting of culture keepers and other elders.

Shirley W. Dunn, *The Mohicans and Their Land, 1609–1730* (1994); Patrick Frazier, *The Mohicans of Stockbridge* (1992); E. M. Ruttenber, *Indian Tribes of Hudson's River: To 1700* (1992 [1872]).

Lucianne Lavin

South Asians

New England's South Asians trace their ancestry or place of birth to one of seven countries—India, Pakistan, Bangladesh, Sri Lanka, Nepal, Bhutan, and the Maldives. The 2000 U.S. Census does not provide figures for Nepalese, Bhutanese, or Maldivian Americans, so the numbers for those South Asian residents are at best approximations. The term *South Asia* is of relatively recent origin; much of the region so designated was once called the Indian subcontinent. South Asians speak more than 30 languages and practice seven primary religions: Hinduism, Islam, Jainism, Buddhism, Sikhism, Zoroastrianism, and Christianity.

The first recorded presence of a South Asian in the United States dates back to 1790, when an Indian from Madras is believed to have visited Massachusetts. Shortly thereafter many young Indians traveled to Salem, Mass., as part of that city's growing India trade and could be seen working on the India wharves. In 1851 six Indians marched in Salem's Independence Day parade. There is no record of what happened to these men, although they are believed to have married black women and thereby been absorbed into Salem's African American community.

Most of New England's South Asian residents arrived after 1965. The total U.S. population of South Asians stands at more than 2 million, a figure that includes approximately 60,000 U.S.-born offspring of immigrants and about 100,000 South Asians who arrived in the United States as young children. The population of South Asians in New England is approximately 85,000. Immigration and Naturalization Service data reveal that in 1998 there were about 60,000 immigrants from South Asia, some of whom will eventually make their homes in New England. Most immigrants come directly from countries in South Asia, but some are twice and sometimes thrice migrant. Indians whose ancestors were shipped by the British as indentured laborers to Africa may migrate from Kenya, Uganda, and South Africa, while still others may stop over for a brief sojourn in England en route from Africa to the United States. Many Bangladeshis, too, come from Africa, England, the Middle East, and Australia.

South Asians have established themselves firmly in the New England economy. Roughly 45 percent of them hold professional or managerial jobs, and about 50 percent work in technical, sales, and administrative positions. The preponderance of high-tech firms, universities, and hospitals has drawn South Asians with advanced degrees to the region. South Asian restaurants are also fast becoming popular in New England. Increasingly, however, there is noticeable socioeconomic diversity in South Asian communities. Many established immigrants sponsor extended-family members who may not be as professionally qualified as they, and these newer immigrants work in lower-paying service jobs as gas station attendants, convenience store clerks, and cab drivers.

South Asian students are a visible presence on many New England campuses. Yale, Harvard, Brown, and Boston Universities, along with the Massachusetts Institute of Technology, have active South Asian student associations. As with all immigrants, there is a difference in the pan–South Asian sensibility between first- and second-generation individuals. Members of the immigrant generation still use national and regional parameters to

define their identity. South Asian immigrants may call themselves Sri Lankans, Bangladeshis, and Pakistanis more readily than South Asians. Some even prefer to call themselves Gujarati, Bengali, Kannadiga, or Punjabi (specific regional ethnicities in India). National allegiances often intersect with religious, linguistic, and cultural allegiances. Bangladeshis, for example, may find themselves at Bengali art and musical festivals because of a shared language and culture, whereas religion may align them with Pakistanis during Muslim festivals. Second-generation South Asians are less concerned with regional or national distinctions, seeking instead to forge alliances not only among all South Asians but also with other Asian American subgroups and African and Hispanic Americans.

S. Chandrasekhar, ed., *From India to America: A Brief History of Immigration; Problems of Discrimination, Admission, and Assimilation* (1982); Naheed Islam, "Bengalis," in *American Immigrant Cultures: Builders of a Nation*, ed. David Levinson and Melvin Embers (1997); Joan M. Jensen, *Passage from India: Asian Indian Immigrants in North America* (1988); Sunaina Maira and Rajini Srikanth, eds., *Contours of the Heart: South Asians Map North America* (1996).

Rajini Srikanth

Temple, Lewis (1800–1854) Blacksmith, inventor.

The African American blacksmith Lewis Temple invented a type of harpoon in the mid-19th century that tremendously increased the efficiency of American whaling. In *The Yankee Whaler* (1926), Clifford Ashley proclaimed the so-called Temple's toggle "the single most important invention in the whole history of whaling."

Born a slave in Richmond, Va., Temple made his way to New Bedford, Mass., and married Mary Clark there in 1829. It is not known how he came to New Bedford, but the city was a station on the Underground Railroad and a place to which runaway slaves often fled. It was also a port town of international fame and significance in an industry dependent on skilled craftspeople. By 1836 Temple owned a smithy on Coffin's Wharf, and in 1841 he opened a larger shop at the Walnut Street Wharf. Though he was not a whaleman and had never been to sea, he specialized in whale craft.

Eighteenth-century American whalers had traditionally used a relatively small harpoon whose arrow-shaped head featured two barbs, or "flues." Somewhat later whalemen tried a single-flued device with a malleable iron shaft that was supposed to bend and lodge the single barb deeper into a whale's blubber. Neither style eliminated the tendency for the harpoon to "draw," or pull out, however, with the result that many more whales got away than were killed.

Temple's design incorporated a razor-sharp front barb and a pointed back barb as a single head that pivoted between the parallel sides of the end of the shaft. A small wooden dowel held the tip in place while the whale was being struck. This pin would break as the whale swam off, enabling the head to pivot open inside the blubber. The concept resembled one employed by Bering Sea Eskimos as early as the Norton period (ca. 700 B.C.–A.D. 400), though the Eskimo harpoon tips were designed to detach from the shaft with only the head remaining lodged at right angles in the whale. Given the historical, geographic, cultural, and economic scope of American whaling, Lewis Temple's ingenious adaptation of this ancient aboriginal technology had extraordinary significance. These tools were made by the tens of thousands and were used almost to the exclusion of any others until the end of the American whale fishery in the 1920s.

Temple never patented his toggle iron, and other blacksmith shops came out with a supposedly improved variation on the original. Temple, who never fully profited from his invention, was in dire financial straits when he died in May 1854, having been severely injured in a fall.

In the 1980s community members in New Bedford organized to bring long-overdue recognition to Temple's life and work. The African American sculptor Jim Toatley was commissioned to create a statue of the inventor. Dedicated in July 1987, the work stands today in front of the New Bedford Free Public Library opposite the sculpture of a harpooner standing in the bow of a whaleboat poised to dart his iron.

Robert C. Hayden, *African Americans and Cape Verdean Americans in New Bedford: A History of Community and Achievement* (1993); Hayden, *Eight Black American Inventors* (1972); Sidney Kaplan, "Lewis Temple and the Hunting of the Whale," *New England Quarterly* 26 (1953); Thomas G. Lytle, *Harpoons and Other Whalecraft* (1984).

Michael P. Dyer

Trotter, William Monroe (1872–1934)

Civil rights activist and journalist. William Monroe Trotter launched and edited Boston's *Guardian* newspaper in 1901 and published it weekly until his death in 1934. Through it he demanded civil rights for African Americans, counterposing this stance to the accommodationist policies of Booker T. Washington, then the leading spokesperson for black aspirations. Trotter argued that colored Americans (the term he preferred) should vote independently but in a bloc, casting their ballots for the candidate who promised most regardless of party. Trotter's militancy and dedication made him the foremost leader of Boston's

African American community in the early 20th century.

Trotter was born in Ohio but grew up in Hyde Park, now a section of Boston. He was the son of Virginia Isaacs and James Monroe Trotter, a soldier in the Massachusetts 55th Colored Infantry during the Civil War. A prosperous real estate broker, James Trotter shifted his political loyalties to the Democratic Party and was appointed recorder of deeds in Washington, D.C., then the highest office to which African Americans were appointed. The Trotters had three children. William Monroe, the eldest, attended an integrated public school and Harvard University, becoming the first African American Phi Beta Kappa when he graduated in 1895. Four years later he married Geraldine Pindell, who collaborated with him on the *Guardian* until her death in 1918.

At the turn of the 20th century Boston's African American community stood for civil rights but was divided over Booker T. Washington's national leadership. Trotter led a minority that saw the Tuskegee, Ala., principal as an obstacle to civil rights. In July 1903 he disrupted a speech Washington was giving and was arrested and briefly imprisoned. The so-called Boston Riot isolated Trotter at first, but as the white supremacy movement gained strength nationally, his arguments for civil rights earned more adherents. During his lifetime Trotter launched a series of short-lived national political organizations that campaigned for putatively pro–civil rights candidates who often proved disappointing. When President Theodore Roosevelt discharged African American soldiers from the army without due process after a trumped-up incident at Brownsville, Tex., in 1906, Trotter oriented his supporters toward anti-Roosevelt Republicans and, later, Democrats.

In 1905 he briefly joined W. E. B. Du Bois in launching the African American Niagara Movement. Trotter maneuvered for control of the Boston branch, damaging the organization. In 1909 the Niagaraites joined with white liberals to form the National Association for the Advancement of Colored People, but when Trotter remained aloof, his influence waned.

Trotter's courageous and outspoken manner earned him episodic attention for the remainder of his career, however. A supporter of Woodrow Wilson in the election of 1912, Trotter protested against the president's segregation of federal departments in Washington, D.C., during a private interview. President Wilson denounced him, but militant African Americans praised his courage and daring. In 1915 he mobilized the Boston African American community against D. W. Griffith's film *Birth of a Nation,* which presented racist organizations in a positive light. After World War I he traveled incognito to Paris to campaign for civil rights at the Paris Peace Conference, later testifying before the Senate Foreign Relations Committee against adoption of the Versailles Treaty.

Trotter condemned Marcus Garvey's black nationalist movement during the early 1920s for its rejection of civil rights issues. Although he respected such radicals as A. Philip Randolph who raised economic questions, he never argued for the rights of the working class irrespective of race as Randolph did. Trotter was an isolated figure in his last years. His body was discovered at the foot of a building in 1934, and although his death was reported as an accident, his biographer concludes that Trotter probably committed suicide.

Deeply rooted in the New England abolitionist tradition, Trotter never lost sight of the goal of full citizenship rights for African Americans. His political independence foreshadowed the African American shift from the Republican to the Democratic Party during the 1930s. Trotter's career formed a vital link in the chain between late-19th-century militants and the founders of the modern civil rights movement. In 1969 Boston's first desegregated public school was named after him, and seven years later his home at 97 Sawyer Avenue in Boston was named a National Historic Landmark.

Stephen R. Fox, *The Guardian of Boston: William Monroe Trotter* (1970); Mark R. Schneider, *Boston Confronts Jim Crow, 1890–1920* (1997).

Mark R. Schneider

Underground Railroad

The term *Underground Railroad* refers to a series of loosely associated regional efforts, at varying levels of organization, to help fugitive slaves escape to the northern United States and Canada before the Civil War. Those fugitives fortunate enough to reach its networks of "tracks," "conductors," and "stations" were provided food, shelter, protection, and guidance on their journey north. Activities linked to the Underground Railroad include everything from such individual efforts as those of African American sailors who brought information to black communities in the North to such group actions as those of the vigilance committees organized to resist enforcement of the 1850 Fugitive Slave Act. Little is known about the actual number of fugitives aided, with estimates ranging from roughly 30,000 to more than 100,000. Since those caught providing aid to fugitive slaves could lose their property, liberty, or even their lives, few people maintained reliable records of having done so, and many of the records that were maintained were destroyed, the great exception being those collected by African American abolitionist William Still in *The Underground Rail Road* (1872).

Underground Railroad routes crisscrossed New England, with lines stretching from the coastal cities of Providence, Boston, and Portland through Maine to Nova Scotia as well as through New Hampshire and Vermont to Montreal. Others passed by land through Norwich, Conn., and Pawtucket, R.I., to various Canadian destinations.

New England was important to the Underground Railroad not only because it offered access both to the coast and to Canada but also because it was the home of a great number of black and white antislavery activists, among them William Wells Brown, James W. C. Pennington, William Lloyd Garrison, and Theodore Parker. Boston, for example, was the home of the African Meeting House, at which the New England Anti-Slavery Society was founded in 1832, and the Prince Hall Masonic Lodge, an important center of support for political, social, and economic reform for African Americans. The antislavery activism, publicity, and propaganda of these individuals and organizations were as important a part of the Underground Railroad as the actual transportation of fugitive slaves. But organized activity included also physical resistance to federally protected slaveholding interests. When Anthony Burns, a fugitive slave from Virginia, was captured in Boston in 1854, for example, local opposition was so strong that more than 1,000 soldiers had to be brought in to escort Burns to the ship that would take him back to slavery. In Connecticut the Underground Railroad was associated particularly with the town of Farmington, which had served as home to the Africans awaiting U.S. Supreme Court judgment in the *Amistad* case. Such highly publicized trials helped to define and intensify debates over slavery and increase participation in antislavery activity.

Although the various regional lines were important in helping fugitives and in organizing antislavery sentiment, the Underground Railroad was not an established, nationwide institution, and it was not the only means by which escaped slaves fled to relative freedom. Many runaways did not discover organized help until they had made significant progress on their own; and many individuals who simply helped traveling fugitives have later been claimed as workers on the Underground Railroad. Nonetheless, the stories of slaves who escaped and the legend of a secret system for assisting them were important parts of the Underground Railroad's attempt to undermine the security of the system of slavery. In 1998 President Bill Clinton signed the National Underground Railroad Network to

Freedom Act, which charged the National Park Service with preserving and interpreting sites associated with the Underground Railroad.

Charles L. Blockson, *Hippocrene Guide to the Underground Railroad* (1994); Larry Gara, *The Liberty Line: The Legend of the Underground Railroad* (1996 [1961]); Wilbur Henry Siebert, *Vermont's Anti-Slavery and Underground Railroad Record, with a Map and Illustrations* (1937); Horatio T. Strother, *The Underground Railroad in Connecticut* (1962).

John Ernest

Vietnamese The end of the Vietnam War brought hundreds of thousands of Southeast Asian refugees to the United States. The 2000 census listed 46,452 Vietnamese Americans in New England, nearly three-fourths of whom lived in Massachusetts. In two decades Vietnamese Americans have built small businesses, parishes and temples, and cultural and political organizations that bolster a sense of community and create a new Asian presence in New England.

High-ranking military commanders, government officials, or businesspeople working with U.S. companies in South Vietnam headed many refugee families who arrived in the United States directly after the war. American resettlement agencies hoped to scatter the refugee population throughout the country in order to avoid concentrating the immigrants in one location. By the mid-1980s, however, many families had relocated to find better jobs, cheaper rents, or refugee services. A second wave of migration—who as a group were labeled "boat people"—added fishermen, farmers, and urbanites to the newly established enclaves. Through the late 1980s and early 1990s, a third wave brought hundreds of Amerasian children in search of their American fathers. In this same period a fourth group of immigrants consisted of detainees released from Vietnam's political reeducation camps. According to the 2000 census the total Vietnamese American population of New England is 46,452; almost three-quarters of these live in Massachusetts.

The Vietnamese American communities of New England hinge on a variety of institutions, organizations, and networks that address diverse cultural, political, religious, and economic concerns. The bulk of these are based in Boston. Older organizations such as the Vietnamese American Civic Association provide citizenship classes, English-language instruction, and job referrals. Catholic parishes and Buddhist temples also offer refugee services. Other organizations, such as the Vietnamese Community of Massachusetts and the Vietnamese Veterans Association, focus on political issues (U.S. foreign policy in Viet-

Vietnamese children waiting to perform the Lotus Dance at a New Year's celebration, Quincy School, Boston, 1990

nam, for example) and cultural events (among them Tet, the Lunar New Year celebration). In 1994 young professionals established the Vietnamese American Initiative for Development (Viet-AID) in order to address long-term community development. The New England Intercollegiate Student Association represents Vietnamese Americans on 18 campuses. Second-generation Vietnamese Americans also participate in existing Asian American institutions and organizations.

In Fields Corner, a neighborhood of Dorchester in the city of Boston, several dozen enterprises owned and run by Vietnamese Americans line Dorchester Avenue. They include gift shops, doctors' and dentists' offices, travel agencies, a bookshop, grocery stores, and restaurants. Established in the mid-1980s, this humble commercial district lends visibility to the community. Because of the successes of Vietnamese American entrepreneurs, Fields Corner often attracts the kudos—and sometimes the ire—of Boston's longtime residents.

Part of Vietnamese American community building involves modifying New Englanders' perceptions of history. Each year on April 30—the day Saigon surrendered to communist forces in 1975—Vietnamese veterans of the war in Vietnam visit Boston City Hall, the state house, and local war memorials. The Dorchester War Memorial, erected in 1981, lists the names of Dorchester's Vietnam veterans. By standing in front of that monument, former officials of the Army of the Republic of South Vietnam offer their own perspective on the war. In this way, the former members of the South Vietnamese military demand that passersby acknowledge not only their past in a war-torn homeland but their present, here and now, in New England today.

James M. Freeman, *Changing Identities: Vietnamese Americans, 1975–1995* (1995); Steven J. Gold, *Refugee Communities: A Comparative Field Study* (1992); Je-

remy Hein, *From Vietnam, Laos, and Cambodia: A Refugee Experience in the United States* (1995); Nazli Kibria, *Family Tightrope: The Changing Lives of Vietnamese Americans* (1993).

Karin Aguilar-San Juan

Wampanoag The Wampanoag are a Native American people whose traditional homeland encompassed present-day eastern Rhode Island and southeastern Massachusetts, including Cape Cod, Nantucket, and Martha's Vineyard.

Descendants of Indian peoples who had lived in southeastern New England for millennia, the Wampanoag spoke a number of closely related dialects of the Eastern Algonquian language family, all of which are now extinct. The Wampanoag were organized into a number of independent communities, each led by a sachem. Particular sachems might also have influence over neighboring groups, but no single leader held authority over all the Wampanoag. Their traditional economy was based on a mixture of horticulture, hunting, gathering, and fishing. Estimates of the Wampanoag population in 1600 range from 5,000 to 24,000.

The earliest recorded encounters between the Wampanoag and Europeans come from the voyages of Bartholomew Gosnold in 1602 and Samuel de Champlain in 1605. In 1614 the English captain Thomas Hunt kidnapped more than two dozen Wampanoags, including Squanto, who later escaped and returned to his homeland, where he translated for the Pilgrims and advised them on native agricultural practices. In 1616–18, diseases of European origin devastated the Wampanoag, producing a mortality rate as high as 95 percent and facilitating the subsequent establishment and expansion of English colonies.

In 1620 the Pilgrims settled on Wampanoag lands in Plymouth, where they were visited in 1621 by Massasoit, the sachem of an important Wampanoag village at Pokanoket (Bristol, R.I.). Massasoit's people, weakened by the epidemic, were being subjected to increasing encroachment from their Narragansett neighbors. The sachem quickly established an alliance with the colonists that lasted until his death in 1661.

In spite of their close ties to Plymouth Colony, the Wampanoag continued to assert control over their homelands in the face of expanding English settlements, and relations between the two peoples deteriorated throughout the 1660s. In King Philip's War (1675–76), Massasoit's son Metacom (King Philip) inspired an uprising against the English that spread throughout Indian New England. The war ended in August 1676, when Metacom was surrounded and killed at Mount Hope

Beverly M. Wright, chair of the Wampanoag Tribal Council, in her office, 1994

near Bristol, R.I. This event marked the loss of Wampanoag autonomy, a condition that would persist for the next three centuries.

After King Philip's War the Wampanoag continued to live in their traditional homeland. Many adopted Christianity and became economically integrated with the dominant English culture without losing their sense of Wampanoag identity. Distinct Wampanoag communities have been maintained to this day despite the steady loss of land to neighboring white populations and the loss of many aspects of traditional culture. Hobbamock's Homesite at Plimoth Plantation in Plymouth, Mass., is a reconstructed village where visitors can view a living exhibit of Wampanoag daily life in 17th-century New England.

In 1928 tribe members organized the Wampanoag Nation to safeguard Wampanoag identity and promote the tribe's political interests. The formation in the 1970s of a Wampanoag Tribal Council by the people of Acquinnah (Gay Head) marked the beginning of an effort to receive official recognition from the federal government that succeeded in 1987. This followed the unsuccessful 1977 effort of the Mashpee Wampanoag Tribal Council to receive recognition and regain title to thousands of acres of land lost during the 19th century. In 1983 Massachusetts gave back to the Wampanoag 238 acres of land on Martha's Vineyard, including the Gay Head cliffs, from whose multicolored clay tribal artisans are once again fashioning traditional pottery. Federal recognition of the Wampanoag led to efforts, now ongoing for years, to establish a site for tribe-

sponsored gaming in southeastern Massachusetts. Organized into five bands (Assonet, Gay Head, Herring Pond, Mashpee, and Namasket), the Wampanoag today are an increasingly visible presence in southeastern Massachusetts.

Kathleen J. Bragdon, *Native Peoples of Southern New England, 1500–1650* (1996); Jack Campisi, *The Mashpee Indians: Tribe on Trial* (1991); Neal Salisbury, *Manitou and Providence: Indians, Europeans, and the Making of New England, 1500–1643* (1982); Laurie Weinstein-Farson, *The Wampanoag* (1989).

Robert G. Goodby

West Indians At the beginning of the 21st century, people from the English-speaking Caribbean in New England numbered at least 118,000, with the largest concentrations residing in Massachusetts and Connecticut. Commonly referred to as West Indians, they consist of clearly distinct groups from several countries: Guyana (the former British Guiana) in South America; Belize (the former British Honduras) in Central America; and such Caribbean islands as Jamaica, Barbados, Trinidad and Tobago, Saint Vincent, Antigua, Montserrat, and Grenada.

Immigrants from the West Indies began to come to New England as early as the 1870s, although it was not until around World War I that a permanent, more visible West Indian presence began to form. Following the routes of United Fruit Company steamers, West Indian men and women arrived in Boston, from which city some dispersed to Plymouth, New Bedford, and Malden, Mass., and to Providence, R.I. By 1950 there were 6,570 West Indians in Massachusetts, constituting 9 percent of that state's black population. Although the growth of the West Indian community was stunted by the restrictive McCarran-Walter Immigration Act of 1954, it picked up again in the latter 1960s owing to the liberal provisions of the Hart-Cellar Immigration Act of 1965. The so-called Massachusetts Miracle of the 1980s lured still more West Indians both from other U.S. states and from the Caribbean. The 1990 census reported 51,304 West Indians in Massachusetts (excluding Hispanic groups), and by 2000 the number had increased to 81,451. Most of these immigrants and their children are spread out in black enclaves in Cambridge, Roxbury, Dorchester, Mattapan, and Brockton.

Connecticut's West Indian community got a much later start, in the World War II era, when farmers were recruited from the Caribbean to offset the labor shortage in the Connecticut River valley. As in Massachusetts, West Indian immigration to Connecticut stalled in the 1950s and early 1960s, picking up again in the late 1960s. By the mid-1990s the

estimated 58,000 West Indians in Connecticut had formed clusters in Stamford, Norwalk, Bridgeport, Danbury, and, especially, Greater Hartford.

In the early years many of the men were laborers and the women worked as domestics or nannies. The writer Jamaica Kincaid, who emigrated from Antigua in 1966 and now lives in Bennington, Vt., told the story of a poor West Indian girl who comes to New York City as an au pair in her novel *Lucy* (1990). After 1965 the changing demographics of immigration brought more middle-class and professional migrants. It was clear by the century's end that West Indians, aided by their proficiency in English and effective kinship network, had made significant inroads into New England's service-based economy, particularly in the health-care sector.

Similar successes have been registered in self-employment. The post-1965 influx spurred a phenomenal increase in West Indian entrepreneurship. Restaurants and other businesses, with their bright, tropical signs and decorations on Blue Hill Avenue through Roxbury, Dorchester, and Mattapan, Mass., and on Albany Avenue in Hartford's North End, underscore the progress West Indians have made in this area. In fact, as the Jamaican-born scholar Ransford Palmer points out, the West Indian business district on Albany Avenue is a nostalgic reminder of Spanish Town Road, a commercial thoroughfare leading into Jamaica's capital, Kingston.

Such features clearly affirm the existence of a distinct black immigrant subculture. Because West Indians traditionally settle in established black residential neighborhoods, they tend to be submerged into the larger African American community. Not content to be subsumed, West Indians have striven since the early 1900s to project their distinctive foreign identity. Before the mid-1960s, when all their homelands were colonies, that identity resided in their affiliation with Great Britain. In Massachusetts they demonstrated their link to British culture by openly celebrating such events as Coronation Day and Empire Day. Their connection to African Americans, by contrast, has been somewhat problematic. Tensions between the two black groups bred by misconceptions on both sides have been known to explode; in 1985, for example, a Jamaican high school student in Danbury, Conn., killed an African American schoolmate who was part of a group that regularly taunted the immigrant youth. An abundance of evidence nonetheless shows that West Indians, having developed race consciousness, have worked with their American-born counterparts in the struggle for black advancement. In the 1920s and 1930s Boston West Indians were in the vanguard of union activism on behalf of black workers. In the 1940s and 1950s journalists of the West Indian weekly *Boston Chronicle* played prominent roles in protest movements denouncing a host of injustices against the city's blacks. In the 1970s many of the activists during the busing crisis were black Bostonians of West Indian descent. Similar examples exist in Connecticut, where in 1990 West Indian community leaders, convinced that minority solidarity would constitute a formidable step toward economic and political empowerment, launched an effort to bring disparate West Indian groups, African Americans, and Hispanics together in a united front.

Coalitionist black activism notwithstanding, West Indian immigrants' distinctiveness continues to define itself by way of community churches and associations. Saint Cyprian's Episcopal Church in Roxbury, Greenwood Memorial Methodist Church in Dorchester, the Church of the Holy Spirit Episcopal Church in Mattapan, Mass., and Saint Monica's Episcopal Church in Hartford are among the region's most significantly West Indian parishes. Immigrant-community associations are numerous and varied, ranging from those based on island or national origin to pan–West Indian organizations and cricket sports clubs.

Perhaps nothing defines the West Indian subculture more vividly than the carnival. A pre-Lenten celebration in West Indian homelands, the carnival has been modified in New England to fit the specific context of immigrant life. Since the late 1970s the first and the third weeks of August have been reserved for celebrations of Caribbean culture in Hartford and Boston, respectively. They are marked by a variety of cultural events, among them performances of the Caribbean steel pan music that has become extremely popular in the United States, and culminate in a flamboyant parade of floats displaying aspects of Caribbean ethnicity. The carnival and its accompanying celebrations in Massachusetts and Connecticut were prompted by a strong determination to affirm the presence, the distinct identities, and the cultures of the Caribbean people and their descendants in New England. Having evolved over the years, the festivals now serve a twofold function. While asserting and projecting the foreignness of the Caribbean people are still important objectives, affirming the West Indians place and stake in American society has become pivotal. The exhibition of Caribbean culture, aimed at attaining social visibility, is now accompanied by efforts at political and economic empowerment within New England society. It is thus now common to see black activists and politicians in the parade or articulating their agendas at the postparade dispersal ceremony. At the dispersal venues literature and posters depicting life in the West Indies often share table or booth space with flyers, petitions, and proposals pertaining to regional or national political, economic, and social issues that have particular relevance to blacks.

Pleased as West Indians and their American-born children are about the official recognition evinced by such events as Caribbean Week, these festivities are still confined to the periphery and largely shunned by mainstream media. Pointing to their contributions to the ever-evolving character of Massachusetts and Connecticut in particular, many are demanding more mainstream recognition. So, despite their disappointment with the pace of change, West Indians are optimistic about their future place in New England. The words of Sebastian Joseph, one of the pioneer organizers of the carnival, best describe this hope: "One day the Caribbean Carnival will be recognized, like the regatta on the Charles, the Boston Marathon, and the Saint Patrick's Day Parade, as part of the true spirit of New England."

Roy Bryce-Laporte and Delores Mortimer, *Caribbean Immigration to the United States* (1976); Lance Carden, *Witness: An Oral History of Black Politics in Boston, 1920–1960* (1989); Robert Hayden, *African Americans in Boston: More than 350 Years* (1991); Ransford Palmer, *Pilgrims from the Sun: West Indian Migration to America* (1995); Ira Reid, *The Negro Immigrant: His Background, Characteristics, and Social Adjustment, 1889–1937* (1969 [1939]); Barry Werth, "A Different Shade of Black," *New England Monthly* (January 1987).

Violet M. Johnson

Folklife

Horace P. Beck and Jane C. Beck, Section Editors
Michael Hoberman, Consulting Editor

INTRODUCTION

"New England" still conjures images of farms, forests, and mountains running to a deeply indented coastline beset with islands, rocks, and shifting shoals and peopled by hardworking, frugal, self-reliant Yankees who keep to themselves and are known for understatement. The reality is quite different. One can still find rural landscapes in northern New England, but even here there are fewer farms, and the craggy coast is littered with houses; farther south, windswept dunes run into crowded beaches; and sprawling, urban metropolises like Boston, Hartford, and Providence are surrounded by small neighborhoods and ethnic communities. In these neighborhoods and communities, urban and rural alike, folklife—the traditions of everyday life passed down informally from one generation to the next through observation, example, and practice—flourishes. Families hold on to cherished beliefs and practices, celebrations, and foodways. Today more than ever, with technological advances and instant communication, no community is isolated, and although members may keep to their own, they also become a part of the larger New England scene.

One such community, of Wampanoag families, still lives in Mashpee, Mass. Their ancestors met the English Pilgrims who arrived on the *Mayflower*. Although few can speak their native tongue, stories are still passed down through the generations, and a subtle difference in worldview and way of life distinguishes them from their Cape Cod neighbors. Family traditions tell of five Virginians, sons of slave concubines and their masters, whose fathers told them that if they went north they would find a piece of land sticking out into the ocean that looked like an arm bent at the elbow. If they went to a little town (Mashpee) right where the muscle of the arm would be, they would find safety and people who would take them in. Families maintain tales of remarkable herbal cures, ritualistic apprenticeships, and spiritual encounters that nourish their descendants and provide them with a distinct identity.

While Native Americans like the Wampanoag are the oldest New England residents, the Hmong, a tribal people from the mountains of Laos, are among the most recent newcomers. The settlement in Providence, which began in the mid-1970s as the Hmong fled Laos, grew to a community of some 300 families by the year 2000. Their housing is not distinctive, and most of the refugees have taken factory jobs, but their way of life differs greatly from that of many other Rhode Island families. A communal garden allows them to maintain their own foodways, and neighborhood markets have grown up within the community to cater to their dietary needs. A number of the women still continue their traditional embroidery skills, creating colorful story cloths for themselves, for sale outside the community, and as keepsakes for their children, depicting their own family history.

Rituals and celebrations continue. Although a family might consult a doctor for a serious medical problem, members might also hold a traditional healing ceremony. Although a wedding might take place in a local church, traditional marriage negotiators might be included for both the bride's and groom's families. Old traditions frequently influence new ways of living. One man, who is a shaman, an elder, and a community leader, has three daughters who have become lawyers. They attribute their choice of career to their father's role as shaman and to observing him mediating disputes, negotiating, and problem solving within the Hmong community. This same parent, who could neither read nor write, often used Hmong folktales to influence his children and shape their lives. Every New Year he would tell the story of his and his wife's life together, how they met, and their ensuing traditional courtship, to encourage his children to select their mates wisely. He also made a point of recounting his family's escape from Laos every year so his children would not forget.

In addition to the Hmong, numerous waves of immigrants from many different lands have settled in New England. This immigration has occurred largely in the past 100 years, and each wave of new people changes the tenor of New England. It is no longer the sole domain of the stereotypical Yankee—and probably never was.

The English, French, and Spanish brought their ways to America, where they found a host of small but distinct linguistically and culturally related Indian peoples referred to as Algonquians: Micmac, Maliseet, Passamaquoddy, Penobscot, Abenaki, Wampanoag, Nipmuck, Narragansett, Pequot, Niantic, Mohegan, Montauk, Schaghticoke, and Mahican. The conflicts between the Europeans and the Indians were inevitable given their radically different cultures and the fact that the Euro-

Dragon dance, Vietnamese New Year, Dorchester, Mass., 1987

peans wanted the natives' land for themselves. Warfare and the devastating effects of disease eventually pushed the Indians into more remote areas—mountains, swamps, and forests—where they found an element of safety.

Because of constant fear of attack from hostile natives and other Europeans, the first settlements of the English colonists were established on islands in bays out of sight of European explorers and protected by water. Serious colonization began in the 17th century, mostly along the waterfront in small hamlets at the heads of harbors. The French came for the fur trade and as missionaries and tended to settle farther north. The English gradually moved northward as far as they could travel by river, which effectively stopped their progress. The northern parts were later settled by people moving up the Hudson River valley and the Connecticut River valley, with other groups coming in from what is now Canada.

The early English settlers were mostly urbanites and above all devout Protestant dissenters who came to America to be free to practice their religions. The Separatists settled Cape Cod, the Puritans the Massachusetts Bay Colony, and the Quakers Cape Cod and Nantucket. Only Roger Williams, a Baptist, founded a colony in Rhode Island that was nonsectarian, and as a result Jews fleeing the Portuguese Inquisition settled in Newport and established the first synagogue there.

First along the coast and later inland, towns were named mostly for the town or hamlet from which the settlers had come. Hence we have Boston in Massachusetts and New Boston in Connecticut; New London in both Connecticut and New Hampshire; and Bristol in each of the six New England states. As later immigrants came from other areas they named their towns accordingly. Irish Protestant and French immigrants to Maine named Belfast, Lubec, and Calais (pronounced *Ca'llis*). Old gravestones reveal surnames found in the old country and the new— Almeys and Chaces in Tiverton, R.I., and in Tiverton, England; Dodges in New Shoreham on Block Island, R.I., and in Shoreham, England; Lowells in Boston, Mass., and in Boston, England.

Because the British settlers came in groups from different areas of Britain, the dialect of each of the states maintained different speech rhythms and sounds from colonial days, later modified by immigrant groups—particularly the Irish, the French Canadians, and the Portuguese. Until recently, a sharp-eared person could not only identify the "New England twang" but could further distinguish accents from the individual states.

As the settlers spread out they described the characteristics of the countryside but did so in distinct ways. They named places for what they looked like, what could be found there, who lived there, and in some cases with biblical references in mind, such as Galilee and the Sin and Flesh Brook, R.I.; Canaan, N.H.; and Sodom, Vt. (now Adamant, Vt.). Some places were named for a folly or disaster, including Sachem's Head, Conn., where three Indian chiefs were decapitated; Bowen's Ledge, Maine, where Captain Bowen lost his ship; Bunker's Whore, Maine, where the lover of Captain Bunker drowned; Norman's Woe, Mass., the reef on which Captain Norman died; and Brandy Pond, Maine, where a supply of brandy broke through the ice.

The soil of New England was at best "bony" (full of rocks, gravel, and sand) and not good farmland. The forests were thick and had to be cleared once the natural savannas had been occupied. Timber was plentiful; that which was not cut into lumber and used to build houses was a nuisance and was burned, resulting in one of New England's earliest industries, the potash industry, where wood ashes are used in making soap and glass. Settlers dealt with the superabundance of stone by making stone fences.

If the land was not good for agriculture, the sea and the coast, with its shipping trade, and the rivers and streams, with a variety of mills, more than made up for it as a source of livelihood and income. Fish, clams, lobsters, mussels, scallops, and oysters were abundant. Even some of the seaweed was useful and tasty. Whales and waterfowl numbered into the millions. There were myriad good, deep-water harbors with ship timber growing down to the water's edge. And so from the beginning the sea and ships played a major role in European New England life. The people of Nantucket said to their children, pointing seaward, "Yonder lie the green pastures where you, your children, and your children's children shall go for their bread."

The fishing industry took hold first. Every cove and harbor had its fleet, and each harbor had its distinct type of boat that met the requirements of the particular area. Shipbuilding flourished. As fishing went farther offshore and vessels began going "foreign," larger ships were built, and larger ships required deep-water harbors. Moreover, each fishing enterprise called for different types of vessels, which eventually evolved into the likes of Gloucester fishing schooners and the sharp-lined clippers that went around the Horn to China and California, while the tubby whalers were designed to carry large cargoes of whale oil and big crews and to keep out at sea for long periods.

Life aboard ship was not only hazardous, it was isolated. Sailors could be at sea for months at a time or away from home six or seven years. There were few, if any, women aboard, and the crews devised their own forms of entertainment. In the watch below, they did knot work and made scrimshaw (carving on bone). They told stories, usually about wrecks and disasters and mighty men, like Bully Waterman, a Yankee clipper ship captain who was renowned for his fast sailing records. They sang songs called fo'c'sle songs made up from the maritime experience. Shanties were sung to keep a rhythm and help with tedious work such as hoisting a sail or bringing up the anchor. The men often added dance-hall ditties and scatological material. When it came to hiring during slack times, being a good entertainer often meant being hired, for "a good ship is a happy ship."

Early New Englanders were involved in the "triangle trade," where slaves were brought from Africa and traded in the West Indies for sugar, which was then brought to New England to be turned into rum. Slavery did not take hold in New England, not because of the Puritans' superior moral quality but because of the business-oriented realization that slavery in New England would not reap the immense profits possible in the South. Thus only small numbers of Africans were imported into the region. Slaves brought to New England remained concentrated in coastal urban centers, near rivers, and in the Narragansett Bay region. Although many African Americans maintained their work traditions, too few remained to have any major effect on backcountry Yankee folkways. Black workers from the South found their way to the lumber woods and quarries of northern New England after the Civil War, but climate and conditions were not always pleasant for people who had grown up in southern climes. Frequently in northern New England, away from the coast, blacks would live in isolation or perhaps in a cluster of two or three families. Within the family strong traditions were maintained, but these traditions seldom extended to the larger community.

Shipbuilding became a major industry. A precise business requiring great skill in joinery and architecture, shipbuilding in good times meant employment for many shipwrights. In slack times when there was no work, shipbuilders turned to house carpentry, building structures as they had built ships. Without the sea to contend with, these solid buildings have withstood the ravages of time for centuries.

Towns were laid out to facilitate shipping interests. The common was near the water, the roads were designed to allow supplies to be hauled to the water, and the turns were such that they could be negotiated by the huge masts that required as many as 30 span of oxen to draw them. Houses were sited with the cardinal points of the compass in mind and fronted the sea. On the roof was often a widow's walk and a cupola from whose height those at home could watch for incoming ships. A weathercock on the church signaled wind direction, and a clock in the belfry looked seaward. As people moved inland from the sea, they took these traditions with them, and cupolas still look out over woods and pastures, while weathercocks point the wind where no ship sails.

Because of the interest in seafaring, New England schools taught geography, mathematics, and navigation, among other things, and the language of the people became larded with seafaring lingo. They "swabbed" the floor, came in the "foredoor," and opened the "hatch" to the cellar. Clothes were "slatted" on the line. In a hurry New Englanders were "under full sail." An old man was "butt sprung" and "weak in the waterways," or his "top hamper" was shot away.

Above all else in New England religion permeated every aspect of life and dictated the attitudes of the dominant culture. If the religious sects of New England had a forename, it would be "austerity." Life to New Englanders was a serious business. They dressed plainly, they ate simple food, and *play* was not in their vocabulary. Work was a constant. So was sin, which preoccupied them at all times. They strove for perfection in all things, and anything less was attached to sin. "Good enough" would not do, and the comment "Nobody will notice or know" was always met with the rejoinder, "But you will and God will." Children were admonished to love work. Protestantism in general instilled in its followers a strain of guilt regarding individual and collective behavior and a desire to atone for past sins.

These forces combined to encourage the development of a way of life onshore as singular as that aboard ship. Some activities, though not strictly recreational, were more enjoyable than others, but all had a purpose. Hunting and fishing, while more pleasurable than plowing, were practical and important because they put food on the table. Venison, especially deer, was a frequent staple in northern New England.

Thanks to ineffective refrigeration and relatively slow transportation, New England foods until well into the 20th century depended on local foodstuffs. Much was seasonal and was prepared as the settlers had done in their homelands. Fish—fresh, salted, and brined—was often on New England tables. Shellfish were abundant. Apples in all forms, from pies to jelly to cider—sweet, hard, and applejack—were standard fare. Likewise, berries were gathered in season, made into pies, jams, and jellies, and canned. Many foods were so popular that they became associated with regional and local areas. Hence one finds New England clam chowder and boiled dinner, Rhode Island "journey" (which became "johnny") cakes, Boston baked beans and brown bread. One eats Block Island swordfish, Ipswich clams, and Maine lobster. Oyster stew, salt pork and milk gravy, and maple syrup or sugar, used as sweetening, were standard. Seasonal foods were common, such as scup and johnnycakes in the spring, green corn in the summer, and cranberry sauce in the fall. Meals often followed a weekly round, with beans and brown bread served on Saturday night. Special days had special foods: salmon and peas for Independence Day, turkey and cranberry sauce for Thanksgiving, and goose and applesauce for Christmas.

Although New England weather has never been greatly admired, along the coast the climate had the proper conditions for milling cloth, an industry that was not found in the South before the advent of air-conditioning. As early as the late 18th century, Slater's Mill, the region's first textile mill, was a going concern in Rhode Island and ushered in the Industrial Revolution. Other textile mills grew up beside major waterfalls such as those at Pawtucket, R.I.; Fall River and Lowell, Mass.; Manchester, N.H.; and Winooski, Vt. By the 1840s boatbuilding, fishing, shipping, logging, and milling along the region's many streams and rivers were the major industries. The effects of the Industrial Revolution began to be felt in outlying areas away from the urban centers.

After a time captains and mates of ships were New Englanders, but crews were picked up in various ports and included such nationalities as Irish, Portuguese, Cape Verdean, West Indian, Italian, Scandinavian, and Nova Scotian. Often these men settled in New England. The Portuguese made their way to the area around New Bedford, Mass., and went into fishing, cranberry farming on Cape Cod, various industries in southern New England, or shipbuilding. The ever-burgeoning rapid industrialization ashore soon required more workers than the settlers could provide, and industries were forced to accept immigrants from other cultures and religions than their own. The Yankees owned the mills, but immigrants made up an ever-larger part of the workforce.

As it had been from the beginning, America continued to be the land of opportunity for European immigrants fleeing political, social, or religious persecution. But with new possibilities came hardship and discrimination for the new Americans. Because of the economic prospects, urban areas were the first destinations. Thus after the Great Potato Famine in Ireland during the 1840s, many Irish found their way to Boston and from there to other New England states. As early as 1835, *Niles Register* reported sarcastically that the pope was setting up a new country in Maine (most immigrants were Roman Catholic), while later in Boston signs were posted, "No Irish need apply." Despite such measures, the Irish found work building railroads and canals and in the mills and factories, in the fisheries, and in the lumber woods as well as in domestic service.

Russian Jews, fleeing the pogroms and mandatory military service under the tsar, and other Russians, Poles, and Germans likewise escaping military service found their way to this country. Some of these immigrants moved north and inland into the lumber woods, quarries, and mills. The concentration of different immigrant groups was greatest in the cities, where they tended to hold on to their traditional ways. In the more rural areas of New England, there was a greater emphasis on becoming "American," learning the language, and fitting in. For this reason the dominant Yankee character of northern New England lingered into the mid-20th century.

Franco-Americans are northern New England's largest minority. They came from Quebec and Acadia: the Quebecois mostly to Vermont and to central and southeastern New England, and the Acadians mostly to the Saint John River valley (Aroostook County) in Maine and to Boston. As early as 1840 the French Canadians and the Prince Edward Islanders were crossing the Canadian border to work in the lumber woods. Although many came with their families in hopes of finding better land to farm and better economic conditions, it was the textile mills that attracted the bulk of French Canadian immigrants. Whole families worked in the mills, and neighborhoods of French Canadians known as "Little Canada" or "French Village" sprang up. Strong family ties existed between mill communities, with people moving frequently among them.

Although French Canadians lived in neighborhoods where French was spoken, the second generation became fluent in English, and by the third generation many were losing the French language altogether. But other traditions were maintained, particularly those related to the Catholic religion. On Easter morning before sunrise, children would gather running water, which they would keep through the year as holy water. New Year's was more significant than Christmas in the French Canadian calendar, and although Franco-Americans began to cut Christmas trees and celebrate Christmas, they also maintained their celebration of New Year's with large family gatherings and an array of French foods. The family would gather after midnight mass and the fun would begin—including French songs and music. Quebecois fiddling, with its double bowing, energetic rhythms, and repertoire of reels and waltzes, and French Acadian fiddling, which has a cleaner, more melodic style, have both contributed to the New England musical tradition and remain vital today.

The region's geography and landscape have contributed significantly to its folklife. Stone is not only plentiful in the fields of New England but beneath the surface as well, where granite, marble, slate, soapstone, talc, copper, and coal can be found. With the advent of the railroad and the introduction of new steam or compressed-air drills and carving tools, the quarrying of stone developed into a major industry. The Welsh came to work in the copper mines of Vermont and the slate quarries, settling in the Williamsburg area in Maine and the Poultney–Fair Haven region in Vermont. Some of the early Welsh were exceptional carvers, crafting slate fans, picture frames, and gravestones as well as specialty items like a Welsh Bible cover. Today, with the emphasis on roofing slate, these skills have been lost. The Welsh influence survives, however, within communities where Welsh choirs still sing in the church.

Skilled masters from the marble and granite area of northern Italy came to practice their craft and earn a decent wage in both Rhode Island and Vermont, particularly in Barre, Vt., which became known as "The Granite Center of the World." Between 1880 and 1910 its population soared from 2,700 to 12,800. While many of the region's Italians are third and fourth generation, and most have lost their language, they continue to celebrate saints' days and festivals, make grappa, collect mushrooms, and eat specialty foods.

The large paper companies in the woods of Maine, New Hampshire, and Vermont required workers for their logging camps. Frequently, sailors would pass the winter in the lumber camps where life was similar to that on the frosty Atlantic, but drier. Native Americans, French Canadians, Swedes, Russians, and other immigrants swelled their ranks. Life in lumber camps led to a corpus of occupational songs, many adapted from the sea and shaped by incidents in the lumber woods. Songs and stories filled long winter evenings in camp. The best singers and storytellers would hold sway as men gathered around the deacon's seat to listen. Others whittled as they listened, some carving "spruce gumbooks"—boxes fashioned to look like books and hollowed out to hold spruce gum as presents for wives or sweethearts. The men exchanged different carving techniques such as chip carving or a tradition known as the "crown of thorns," interlocking carved pieces of wood. Scandinavians introduced the challenge of carving a fan from a single piece of cedar, while others tried to whittle out a series of balls in cages from a single piece of wood.

In rural areas Yankee traditions dominated, and even ethnic outsiders might come to be accepted and celebrated on the basis of their adherence to them. While Alex Turner, a black farmer in Grafton, Vt., might carry three buckets of eggs to the store—one in each hand and one on his head—this was cause for only passing interest. He became renowned when he carried a barrel of flour home on a bet, 4 miles up hill, without ever setting it down. This feat of strength fit the New Englanders' admiration for the strong man, and henceforth it was retold over and over around the stove at the general store, and Turner's reputation was made.

The general store was at the heart of most small towns in New England. Not only was it the place to go for almost anything that was needed, it frequently served as the post office and as a gathering place—for men, at least. In the evening or on bad days, men would assemble around the stove and gossip and swap lies. Young boys would hover around the edges, listening and learning the art of telling a good story.

Although play was not part of the Puritans' way of life, strong music and dance traditions—as well as communal work activities such as corn-huskings, barn-raisings, apple-parings, and so forth—developed to ease the workload. Sunday was still God's day, but Saturday night might bring some sort of entertainment. In many small communities barn dances were held in the summer and "kitchen tunks" or "kitchen junkets" in the winter. People would gather in the kitchen, often putting the fiddler on the kitchen table. The Anglo-Scots-Irish repertoire consisted of reels, waltzes, jigs, and schottisches. New styles were sometimes introduced when a new family moved into the area from elsewhere. A family from Kansas moved into a mountain township in Vermont, for example, and introduced "singing calls," a square-dancing tradition that quickly became popular. A dinner would be brought out at midnight and then the party would disperse, returning home sometimes with little sleep before the early morning milking began.

As in the British Isles, there was a strong ballad tradition in New England, and in keeping with the Puritan ethic, some of the native ballads focused on sin. In one such ballad, fair Charlotte froze to death because she insisted on going to a dance clad only in silk, shunning warm clothing; in another ballad, the boy who broke the Sabbath by working on Sunday died of a snake bite for his efforts.

By the 1880s an active interest in the study of folklore had evolved. Francis James Child of Harvard was engaged in writing his life's work, *The English and Scottish Popular Ballads.* The English Folklore Society had been founded in 1878, and 10 years later a number of people assembled in Cambridge, Mass., and founded the American Folklore Society. Child was elected its first president. Because he was so busy with his ballad work, however, William Wells Newell was chiefly responsible for shaping the early development of the American Folklore Society. There were two different views of folklore: one was held by Child and the Cambridge group (literary scholars who regarded folklore as "the remnants of the unlettered portion of European literary tradition") and a second was forwarded by Franz Boas and his cohorts at Columbia, who considered folklore to be a reflection of a particular culture. This division continued until the 1950s and diminished only with the advent of the professional folklorist who began to emerge from academic folklore programs at that time. The idea of the public folklorist, people who today work with various state-level agencies and educational endeavors, evolved from these academic programs.

Child's monumental ballad work inspired a host of ballad hunters. George Lyman Kittredge, trained by Child, continued his legacy, as did Phillips Barry, who influenced collectors such as Helen Hartness Flanders, Mary Smyth, and Fannie Hardy Eckstorm, who began recording songs in the late 1920s and amassed a considerable collection.

Along with the interest in folklore and the ballad came an interest in the revival of handicrafts. By 1897 handicrafts were being exhibited at Copley Hall in Boston. With the Depression came an added stimulus to the handicraft movement, which became a panacea for the ills of industrial society. In 1931 the League of New Hampshire Arts and Crafts was founded, and many handicraft projects were developed throughout the region as successful work relief programs. By the 1940s Allen Eaton was working on his book *Handicrafts of New England,* which documented a number of traditional crafts and their makers.

With the Industrial Revolution, and as fortunes began to be made, recreational summer tourism began to develop. From the mid-19th century tourists from urban areas began to travel to the New England backcountry for a variety of reasons—such as to hunt, fish, and camp. Some came for a brief tour, and others built summer cottages, returning to them generation after generation. These "backcountry people" built small enclaves where their lives continued much as they did in Philadelphia or Boston, although under somewhat more rustic conditions, and they did not much intrude on the local population. Tourists and residents alike regarded backcountry people as social inferiors whom they treated with amusement, condescension, and sometimes a degree of contempt.

Summer visitors were an irritant to the locals and were referred to as "flatlanders" in Vermont and the "Summer Complaint" in Maine. They enjoyed what the locals endured. They played at what the locals worked at, and frequently they did not understand local mores. But they had money and did much to flesh out a dollar-starved economy. The locals used the money to assuage their irritation. When a female tourist said to the attendant in a filling station, "My, there are a lot of strange people in Maine," he responded, "Yes ma'am, but they all go home on Labor Day."

Tourists and summer residents provided a boon to the local economy through seasonal employment or as a market for local products. Families of Indians capitalized on the resort trade, serving as guides, particularly in the Maine woods, and selling baskets to summer people. By the turn of the century, Indian products were popular items for visitors to take home.

From 1630 until the close of the French and Indian War (1763) and even through the American Revolution, the English colonies were almost continuously at war with Indians. When the battling ceased because the settlers had gained the advantage, Native Americans were decimated and scattered; in many cases, they made a conscious effort to become invisible to the dominant society. A majority of tribal traditions and languages were lost. What was not lost, however, was a lifestyle of intimacy with the woods and a strong affinity for the land—attitudes and values that were subtly passed on to following generations.

Colonists kept Indian place-names to some degree. They identified some native species by Indian names: moose, quahog, and muskrat. They learned some skills, such as how to tap a maple tree, how to hunt whales (Gay Head Indians were in too short supply as harpooners aboard whaleships), and how to use snowshoes. They learned about growing American vegetables, about Native American edibles, and about medicinal roots and herbs.

Many rural New Englanders seldom saw a doctor before the turn of the century and therefore practiced a variety of home remedies, treating anything from asthma to boils to rheumatism. But it was the Native Americans who had the most extensive knowledge of roots and herbs. Molly Orcutt, an Abenaki medicinal woman known from Troy, Vt., to Bethel, Maine, was sought for her ability to cure dysentery—a remedy she steadfastly kept to herself. Most communities depended on "granny women"—women who traveled the neighborhood helping at births or in times of sickness. Sometimes these women would be half Indian, privy to knowledge of which plants to gather and how best to prepare them. A farm family who lived next to an Abenaki couple preserved a recipe given to them for poison ivy; they still claim that it is better than "any store-boughten medicine."

While the resort trade provided the natives with an opportunity to gain some extra income, it also gave them a reason to continue the tradition of woods craft as guides, as well as canoe building and the making of both brown ash and sweetgrass baskets. Today, basketry remains an important symbol of their traditional identity.

The advent of electricity, the radio, and the automobile and the building of navigable highways greatly affected New England folklife. Electricity provided new ways of entertainment, such as being able to read into the night or listen to the radio. Before electricity, there was little reason to go to town other than for supplies. Now the cinema and bright lights of the city were alluring, and many people went "to town" and never returned. Electricity also made some chores, such as drawing water by hand, easier, or eliminated them altogether. Before the automobile, people had stayed home because it was time-consuming or difficult to move long distances, but with its development, people could travel in a few minutes distances that had taken a horse a day to traverse. People who lived on islands had lived "by the side of the road" on once well-traveled waterways. Now, owing to the ease of automobile travel and the eclipse of the coastal sailing ship, they were isolated. At the same time, backcountry areas became more accessible.

If new ways eradicated many of the old ways, they also stirred up new folkways. The filling station became a new social center, assuming the role once played by the blacksmith's shop or the general store. People began to use electrical power as a means of reliably freezing food, and although canning traditions fell into oblivion, new recipes and methods were developed for frozen goods.

A 19th-century New Englander would have felt reasonably comfortable with the folklife of the region through World War II and for a time afterward. But by the 1950s some major changes were occurring. While the cities of Boston, Hartford, Providence, and New Haven, Conn., had become cosmopolitan in nature, with ethnic neighborhoods in various parts of the city, rural New England began to feel the trend toward suburbanization, certainly around the major urban areas but well beyond their sway as well. Shortly before World War II a few ski areas had been established, but their development in Maine, New Hampshire, Vermont, and the Berkshires of Massachusetts began to make an economic difference after the war. As the ski areas burgeoned, so did the houses and condominiums, public lodging, and restaurants around them. An influx of new people who were attracted to the rural beauty and to a different way of life and who were fed up with urban social problems or intent on reaping the monetary rewards of development settled in the small towns and became part of the fabric of life there. Whereas a short time before, living had been at a subsistence level and business had often been conducted on a barter-and-exchange basis, land values rose and cash flowed into the local economy. To property owners who viewed their land for its potential value to their livelihoods, the newcomers seemed to want worthless land. Who would covet a rocky point with no protective cove or a bony mountaintop with a view?

This was also the era of iconoclastic "back-to-landers" and hippies, many of whom seemed to revere poverty. Furthermore, they challenged authority, the nuclear age, the work ethic, and accepted norms of morality and "freedom" took on a very different meaning for them. They were a countercultural force battling for social and political issues: for civil rights, environmentalism, and the welfare state and against the

Janet Comeau with cashmere goats at her Meadow Mountain Farm, West Brownfield, Maine, 1993

Vietnam War. The movement resulted in a migration from urban to rural areas. Hippies came to rural New England to "find themselves," to get closer to basic elemental values, and to remove themselves from the world of capitalism. Some set up communes, much to the distrust of their more conservative neighbors. Thirty to 40 years later, many of these aging hippies have remained in rural New England, becoming successful and contributing participants in the local culture and often setting up their own businesses, which are a boon to the local economy. Although their views have been tempered over the years, their activism and concern for social and political issues are still important.

A number of back-to-landers were interested in the revival of both folk music and handicrafts. Many came bringing their instruments, and with their commitment to a simpler way of life, they tried to work with their hands. The astoundingly popular success of the Newport Folk Festival in 1965 was an indication of this interest and was not lost on Ralph Rinzler, whose association with the Newport Folk Festival shaped his development of the Smithsonian's Folklife Festival in 1967. This festival significantly influenced the development of public folklore on both the national and state levels during the 1970s and 1980s.

With better transportation and the advent of the personal computer, the most intricate and important business transactions could be carried out from remote places. As a result, there has been a new move away from urban areas. Many summer residents or children of those who went to the summer colonies now are permanent residents of the area. Since the 1950s the migration out of cities to the more rural areas of New England has been steady; in many cases, the population of small towns has doubled. This in turn has led to a clash between locals and "outlanders," and for the first time the locals are outnumbered.

Just as summer visitors had been irritants at the turn of the century, these new residents continue to be a thorn in the side of locals. Frequently, newcomers were unhappy with conditions as they existed. They wanted better roads, better schools, better police and fire protection, more services. They wanted an environment that suited their aesthetic values that had been shaped in an urban environment, and they wanted to protect those values. At the same time they wanted to maintain the facade of the "quaintness" of rural life they found so desirable. The Windham Foundation in Grafton, Vt., for example, originally from out of state, has bought up much of the town and is engaged in preserving its picture-postcard image.

Today, New England remains an integral geographic region; some of its landscape is still defined by steepled churches, town greens, and coastal waters, but the number of farms and the vast forests are declining. Global warming has not yet affected its climate demonstrably, and the weather is still harsh and unpredictable. Hurricanes and ice storms, bleak winters and short summers continue to inform a way of life. But the towns and villages are no longer well defined. Development has encouraged urban sprawl, and shopping plazas and fast-food restaurants add a touch of "Everywhere USA." The general store remains, but it is now more often called "The Country Store" and is devoted to selling knickknacks to tourists among its utilitarian objects. Trace chains and Lydia Pinkham pills are no longer part of the mix. The local diner generally has given way to a host of national franchises and fast-food restaurants where it is easier to get a croissant, a bagel, or a Danish than a johnnycake. Many people prefer Japanese sushi to a traditional New England boiled dinner or red flannel hash.

Despite the gradual dissolution of so many Yankee folk traditions, certain aspects of New England folklife remain as icons. Sugaring is still viewed as an important part of New England farm life, and products such as maple syrup and maple candy remain popular, both locally and with tourists. The lobster continues to bring people to Maine, not to a "lobster boil" but to a "lobsterfest," and the clambake continues to draw people to Massachusetts. The picture of the fisherman in his sou'wester is still a viable advertisement for New England products, and the Boston Market restaurant runs neck and neck with the likes of the Outback Steakhouse. Samuel Adams's name sells beer, "Minute Man" remains vital as a popular appellation, and "John Hancock" is still a major insurance company. But these are part of a myth, part of New England's past, and as such are nostalgic symbols.

At the same time this myth informs and influences the future. In recent years harvest figures (figures made with pumpkin heads, wire, and straw) have become increasingly popular, and many will tell you that this is an old New England tradition. Although this is not the case, it adds to the festive atmosphere of the fall tourist season and sells farm products. Newcomers view it as part of the harvest and therefore assume it to be a remnant of old New England.

A dominant culture no longer presides, but only an overarching myth of what New England is, still based on the Yankee stereotype. Today, New Englanders find themselves wrestling with that myth, and without necessarily understanding the historical values that feed it, they are superficially trying to conform to it. In this attempt they are establishing new directions and a new New England.

Ann Banks, ed., *First-Person America* (1980); Horace P. Beck, *The Folklore of Maine* (1957), *Folklore and the Sea* (1973); Jane C. Beck, ed., *Always in Season* (1982); Jane C. Beck, *The General Store in Vermont: An Oral History* (1980); Jane S. Becker and Barbara Franco, *Folk Roots, New Roots: Folklore in American Life* (1988); Benjamin A. Botkin, *A Treasury of New England Folklore: Stories, Ballads, and Traditions of the Yankee People* (1989 [1947]), rev. ed.; Sarah Boyer, *In Our Own Words: Stories of North Cambridge, Massachusetts, 1900–1960, as Told to Sarah Boyer* (1997); Jeremy Brecher, Jerry Lombardi, and Jan Stackhouse, eds., *Brass Valley: The Story of Working People's Lives and Struggles in an Industrial Region* (1982); Paul Brodear, *Restitution: The Land Claims of the Mashpee, Passamaquoddy, and Penobscot Indians of New England* (1985); Colin G. Calloway, *The Abenaki* (1989); Calloway, *The Western Abenakis of Vermont, 1600–1800: War, Migration, and the Survival of an Indian People* (1991); Joseph Conforti, *Imagining New*

England: Explorations of Regional Identity from the Pilgrims to the Mid-20th Century (2002); William Doerflinger, *Shantymen and Shantyboys: Songs of the Sailor and Lumberman* (1951); Paul T. Doherty, *Smoke from a Thousand Campfires* (1993); Richard M. Dorson, *Buying the Wind* (1964); Dorson, *Jonathan Draws the Long Bow* (1946); George Francis Dow and John Henry Edmonds, *The Pirates of the New England Coast, 1630–1730* (1923); Samuel Adams Drake, *A Book of New England Legends and Folk Lore in Prose and Poetry* (1901); Allen H. Eaton, *Handicrafts of New England* (1949); Fannie Hardy Eckstorm, *Indian Place-Names of the Penobscot Valley and the Maine Coast* (1941); Eckstorm, *Old John Neptune and Other Maine Indian Shamans* (1945); Eckstorm, *The Penobscot Man* (1970 [1904]); Fannie Hardy Eckstorm and Mary Winslow Smyth, *Minstrelsy of Maine: Folk Songs of the Woods and Coast* (1927); Fannie Hardy Eckstorm, Phillips Barry, and Mary Winslow Smyth, *British Ballads from Maine: The Development of Popular Songs with Texts and Airs* (1929); Helen Hartness Flanders, *Ancient Ballads Traditionally Sung in New England* (1960–1965); Flanders, *Ballads Migrant in New England* (1953); Flanders, *The New Green Mountain Songster: Traditional Folk Songs of Vermont* (1939); Helen Hartness Flanders and George Brown, *Vermont Folk-Songs and Ballads* (1968); Roland Palmer Gray, ed., *Songs and Ballads of the Maine Lumberjacks: With Other Songs from Maine* (1925); Lisa Weber Greenberg, *Stories to Tell: The Narrative Impulse in Contemporary New England Folk Art* (1988); Michael Hoberman, *Yankee Moderns: Folk Regional Identity in the Sawmill Valley of Western Massachusetts, 1890–1920* (2000); Thomas Hubka, *Big House, Little House, Back House, Barn* (1983); Gale Hunting, *Songs the Whalemen Sang* (1964); Edward Ives, *George Magoon and the Down East Game War: History, Folklore, and the Law* (1988); Ives, *Joe Scott, the Woodsman-Songmaker* (1978); Richard W. Judd, *Common Lands, Common People: The Origins of Conservation in Northern New England* (1997); Richard W. Judd, Edwin A. Churchill, and Joel W. Eastman, eds., *Maine: The Pine Tree State from Prehistory to the Present* (1995); Eloise Hubbard Linscott, ed., *Folk Songs of Old New England,* (1939); Jill Linzee and Michael P. Chaney, *Deeply Rooted: New Hampshire Traditions in Wood* (1997); Lucy R. Lippard, *The Lure of the Local: Senses of Place in a Multicentered Society* (1997); Bunny McBride, *Molly Spotted Elk: A Penobscot in Paris* (1995); John Moody, "The Native American Legacy," in *Always in Season: Folk Art and Traditional Culture in Vermont,* ed. Jane C. Beck (1982); Frank Oppel, ed., *Tales of the New England Coast* (1985); William D. Piersen, *Black Yankees: The Development of an Afro-American Subculture in 18th-Century New England* (1988); Jennifer Post Quinn, *An Index to the Field Recordings in the Flanders Ballad Collection at Middlebury College, Middlebury, Vermont* (1983); Franz Lee Rickaby, *Ballads and Songs of the Shanty-Boy* (1926); Howard S. Russell, *A Long Deep Furrow: Three Centuries of Farming in New England* (1976); Joe Sherman, *Fast Lane on a Dirt Road: Vermont Transformed, 1945–1990* (1991); "Sur Bois: Franco-American Woodcarvers of Northern New England." Exhibition brochure, Franco-American Centre, Manchester, N.H. (1996); Jean Patten Whitten, "Fannie Hardy Eckstorm: Descriptive Bibliography," *Northeast Folklore* 16 (1975); Howard Fisher Wilson, *The Hill Country of Northern New England: Its Social and Economic History, 1790–1930* (1967); George P. Winship, *Sailors' Narratives of Voyages along the New England Coast 1524–1624* (1905); Pamela Wood, *The SALT Book* (1977); Rosemary Levy Zumwalt, *American Folklore Scholarship: A Dialogue of Dissent* (1988).

Horace P. Beck and Jane C. Beck

African American Folklife Sold into a world whose climate and culture were alien, New England's first Africans concentrated initially on surviving. On the heels of survival came reconciliation and adaptation, followed by efforts to create a meaningful existence in an inhospitable new world. Those themes—adaptation, reconciliation, and creation—characterize much of African American folklife and culture. And while black New Englanders had much in common with other African Americans, the region left its imprint on certain aspects of their ways of life.

Blacks began to arrive in the region in the late 17th century. African-born, shipped either directly from Africa or via the West Indies, most New England slaves were young and had survived for months in harsh circumstances. Upon arrival they were typically placed not on plantations with other slaves but in homes. Despite their place at the bottom of the household hierarchy, the vast improvement in their living conditions relative to the experience of crossing the Atlantic or laboring in the West Indies often facilitated Africans' adaptation to enslavement. Living and working in close proximity to their owners, lacking private space and time, Africans were introduced to a Yankee work ethic and capitalist outlook. Though much of the European American lifestyle clashed with West African mores, many habits of thought and lifestyle easily aligned: Venture Smith, brought to Connecticut as a child in 1737, learned the value of thrift as a boy in West Africa and put the lesson to good use when he saved enough money to buy his own freedom as an adult in New England.

Yet enslaved black New Englanders did develop a distinct folklife. Despite their lack of communal space, most African Americans lived in river and port cities; one-third of 18th-century New Hampshire's black residents lived in Portsmouth. That type of population concentration, periodically infused with slaves from the West Indies, Africa, and the American South, ensured the retention of certain African cultural practices and strains of an African worldview.

Among the earliest public manifestations of African folklife were Negro Election Day festivals. When whites held elections, free and enslaved blacks organized their own weeklong election festivities, often drawing on the financial resources of slave owners for food and drink. These 18th- and early-19th-century events in New Hampshire, Massachusetts, Rhode Island, and Connecticut blended Yankee and African traditions of dance, dress, and drink, fostering a distinct African American identity. Each celebration crowned a black king or governor, along with lesser personages, and thus reinforced social hierarchy among slaves while

critiquing white society in various ways for the benefit of black, white, and Indian revelers. Unique to New England yet common to enslaved Africans, Negro festivals were an important part of pan-African folklife from New Hampshire to Barbados to Uruguay. Ironically, the American South, with the largest slave population in North America, rarely witnessed black festivals. New England's small number of slaves per household minimized the fear of rebellious conspiracies that stifled the custom in the South.

The cultural influence went both ways. Accounts of Portsmouth's black king Nero padding his slim calves to create an appearance of royal voluptuousness evince European American norms penetrating black culture; for whites, prominent calves signaled virility. Likewise, the African style of parading, with the king or governor preceded by a colorfully dressed band playing a wide variety of instruments, gave rise to similarly styled 19th-century American political parades. African Americans also formed burial societies that evolved after emancipation into social clubs and civic organizations. Most notable of these was the African Union Society of Newport, R.I., devoted to "improving the education and economic stature of Newport's African population," which included the black gravestone carver Pompe Stevens among its charter members.

Election Day festivals gradually disappeared over the course of the 19th century, in part because of new, post–Revolutionary War cultural forms that reconciled freedom with continued oppression by intertwining expressions of African American culture with a language of protest. One of the key sites for such expression was the black church. During the century that followed the Revolution African American churches sprouted from Maine to Connecticut, providing a place for a corporate expression of faith and sustaining a tradition of black spiritual music. The Green Memorial African Methodist Episcopal (AME) Zion Church in Portland, Maine, has a decades-old tradition of Thursday-night chicken suppers and an annual picnic that is still alive today. Churches also served as a base for mounting attacks on white oppression and training men and women as leaders in the fight for full citizenship rights.

Black New Englanders also organized parades and other celebrations commemorating significant events such as Britain's abolition of slavery in the West Indies in 1833. Performing a function similar to that of the churches, these gatherings celebrated community and culture while reminding white Americans of the unfulfilled promises of the Constitution. Public celebrations furthermore provided op-

portunities for free people of color to exhibit styles of dress, craftwork, and music born of African culture but with a distinctly American inflection. The quilt made by a black woman from Boston for an antislavery fair in 1835 likely combined an African style with the explicitly political poetry that was woven into the fabric.

After national emancipation was completed in 1865, a number of African descendants from the South and the West Indies arrived in New England. This migration was not without attendant tensions: West Indian immigrants imported their own ways of living, and relations between first- and second-generation West Indians and black New Englanders were not always amicable. Some West Indians established churches or associations in an attempt to ensure that their transplanted identity and culture would flourish; before the Great Depression, for instance, immigrants in New Haven, Conn., founded the Nevis Club in honor of their small home island in the Lesser Antilles.

Organized social gatherings proved one of many mechanisms for the continuation of black folklife in New England into the mid-20th century, although the lifestyles they reinforced could vary according to class as well as birthplace. Upper-class black Bostonians, who were usually American born, sponsored debutante balls and Saturday soirées; in New Haven middle- and upper-class folk gathered to listen to classical music and play bridge. At the lower end of the class spectrum "rent party" attendees paid a small fee (which went toward the host's monthly rent) to enjoy music and drink; the music—island sounds or southern blues—and drink—rum for West Indians, whiskey for southern migrants—likely varied somewhat depending on the host's origins. Although a diversity of culture and perspective remains, the broad common cultural ground and mutual experience of facing racism have bound most black Americans and black immigrants together—not necessarily in harmony but in worldview.

As a new century begins, the bonds between blacks will be tested. Black folklife has always possessed a didactic quality—whether expressed in festivals, the blues, the church, or gangsta rap—teaching future generations of black men and women how to live in a society that defines success and happiness by white norms and keeping black knowledge of racial injustice a visible theme in American culture. The educational function of black folklife, in New England and beyond, is imperiled by a powerful hybridized commercial culture that threatens to wipe away what is distinctive and valuable in black America. In the 1960s, African Americans in New Haven who could not afford to travel to New York or buy tickets to see black performing artists at the Apollo Theater would go hear local or lesser-known groups such as the Voices in the park. Popular black culture in the 1990s has been increasingly commercialized and diluted, and that kind of communal experience is a less frequent one. While it is important not to romanticize the burden of living on a tight income, it is equally important to recognize what might be lost as American culture—white and black—becomes increasingly homogenized.

The House of Blues in Cambridge, Mass., provided a good example of the challenges facing African American folk culture. The House of Blues built on a rich black musical heritage and could have provided a means of keeping black ties vibrant. But the Blues Brothers—two white guys—served as the club's logo in 1995, the patrons were predominantly white, and the venture was connected with large corporations that in many respects epitomize the market culture's drain on the vitality of black folklife. The point is not that white New Englanders should not participate in the blues or other dynamic aspects of black culture; cross-cultural interaction and influence have always been an important part of the story in the region. But any version of the blues that is homogenized to increase consumption is likely to be blues without a heart.

Some black New Englanders have responded by emphasizing certain aspects of black life and culture. In 1970 Elma Lewis and the Roxbury-based National Center of Afro-American Artists resurrected Langston Hughes's Black Nativity, a powerful annual celebration of the black gospel music that Hughes grew up with in the early 20th century. The growth of Afrocentric school programs may be another creative modern adaptation to the threat of cultural erosion. And some other, less obvious facets of black folklife will endure: styles of humor; particular mannerisms; preferences in food, music, or dress. But even these distinctions may wear away as upward mobility increases and black New Englanders spread out into suburbs and bedroom communities. Black culture will remain a site of tension as it seeks to accommodate the increasingly varied nature of black experience in New England while continuing to sustain the sense of mutuality and identity that gives coherence to the term "African American folklife."

Richard Balzer, *Street Time* (1972); Robert J. Cottrol, *The Afro-Yankees: Providence's Black Community in the Antebellum Era* (1982); Gina Dent, ed., *Black Popular Culture* (1992); Michael Eric Dyson, *Between God and Gangsta Rap: Bearing Witness to Black Culture* (1996); James Oliver Horton and Lois E. Horton, *In Hope of Liberty: Culture, Community, and Protest among Northern Free Blacks, 1700–1860* (1997); Daniel Lieberfeld, "Million-Dollar Juke Joint: Commodifying Blues Culture," *African American Review* 29 (1995); William D. Piersen, *Black Yankees: The Development of an Afro-American Subculture in 18th Century New England* (1988); Robert Austin Warner, *New Haven Negroes: A Social History* (1940).

Scott Hancock

Agriculture With a few notable exceptions, such as the lower Connecticut River valley of Massachusetts and Connecticut, farming in New England has always posed more challenges than rewards. The stalwart few who, for successive generations in some cases, have mustered up sufficient stick-to-it-iveness to build and maintain viable farms have

Walking home from the sugarhouse in Whitefield, Maine, Maple Sunday (the fourth sunday in March), 1993

done so by adapting effectively to ever-changing circumstances, both natural and socioeconomic. From dairy products, maple sugar, and apples to such regional specialties as cranberries, potatoes, and tobacco, agriculture in New England is a diverse enterprise, and it has changed dramatically over time. Sheep once dominated the landscape of northern New England, but as wool became unprofitable, farmers made the transition to dairy cattle. Dairy farming in turn evolved from the production of cheese and butter for consumption at home to that of whole milk in bulk for shipment to market. Indeed, most farming in New England was for subsistence first and foremost until well after World War I. Profitability has again become an issue, and 21st-century dairy farmers are experimenting with an array of alternatives from fallow deer to value-added specialty products.

Historically, neighborly relations have been a basic component of farm experience. Before World War II dairy farmers in particular depended on their immediate neighbors for help with such labor-intensive activities as threshing grain, filling silos, harvesting ice, and bucking cordwood. Known as "changing works," this system of mutuality also formed the foundation for rural sociability, as farm neighbors moved from house to house during the winter months eating, dancing, and visiting with one another. Kitchen "tunks" or junkets, as they were called, died out as changes in technology and farm operation made possible by the internal combustion engine and rural electrification enabled farmers to work alone.

Family-run farms have endured because the family as a work unit is well suited to seasonal variations in the demand for labor. On a farm "every hand has to do"—men, women, and children have specific sets of responsibilities on which the operation of the farm depends. Older male farmers often considered it a matter of pride that their wives did not work in the barn or the fields. Farm women today commonly play a direct role in farm operation or have off-farm jobs. Children grow up working with their parents and grandparents and often stay on as adults. Negotiating the transfer of responsibility—and of property—from one generation to the next can be a complex, slow-moving process. Despite late-20th-century threats to the economic viability of the family farm, it is not uncommon for a farm to be operated by a single family over a span of generations.

Each type of farming has its own distinctive occupational traditions. On dairy farms, for example, a vast array of knowledge centers on milking, and a farmer's day is bounded by barn chores in the morning and evening. There are also seasonal routines—fixing fences in the spring and butchering in the fall—and activities such as sugaring and haying that require a finely tuned relationship to the weather. Field patterns, farmstead layout, building types, and the organization of interior space are also shaped by regionally specific farm traditions.

Until recently farm culture distinguished itself by such common features as costume (men's overalls and women's aprons), foodways (hard cider and salt pork), and social rituals (kitchen dances and the Grange). Farm life was separate and in many instances isolated from life in urban areas. Today farm neighborhoods have become suburbanized, and although farmers are still set apart by time-consuming work responsibilities, outwardly their lives seem much like those of their nonfarm neighbors. Nevertheless, contemporary farmers insist that farming is a distinctive way of life. They are quick to point out, for example, that children who grow up on farms learn to accept responsibility early, which shapes their lives as adults.

Dublin Seminar for New England Folklife, *The Farm*, ed. Peter Benes, Jane Montague Benes, and Ross W. Beales, Jr. (1988); Charles Fish, *In Good Hands: The Keeping of a Family Farm* (1995); Scott E. Hastings, Jr. and Elsie R. Hastings, *Up in the Morning Early: Vermont Farm Families in the Thirties* (1992); Thomas Hubka, *Big House, Little House, Back House, Barn* (1983); Gregory Sharrow and Meg Ostrum, eds., *Families on the Land: Profiles of Vermont Farm Families* (1995).

Gregory L. Sharrow

American Folklore Society The American Folklore Society (AFS) is one of the older U.S. scholarly societies and the only nationwide organization of professional folklorists. The society's founding, on January 4, 1888, at Cambridge, Mass., marked a changeover from the study of literary relics and antiquities to the scientific pursuit of traditional lore, especially where balladry and the cultures of such groups as Native Americans, African Americans, Mexicans Americans, and Franco-Americans were concerned. The society quickly dedicated itself to the study of lore that was "living" or "in use" while moving away from the older, more anthropological European orientation. It attracted many well-known names—Samuel Clemens, Oliver Wendell Holmes, and James Russell Lowell, among others—and was one of the first scholarly groups to invite women into the fold.

At the start collectors and scholars feared that North American folklore was vanishing quickly in the face of rural out-migration, burgeoning mass media, and the rapid growth of metropolitan areas. We now know that while some forms of lore may disappear, others can adapt to modern environments, showing an amazing ability to reshape and renew themselves.

Harvard folklorist Francis James Child's discovery that certain English and Scottish ballads had survived more intact in the southern Appalachian Mountains than in their native lands gave a significant boost to the field of folklore study. Child's influential collection *The English and Scottish Popular Ballads* (1882–98) was a scholarly compendium of folk songs and folklore from previously oral traditions. His early findings inspired generations of researchers and fieldwork that still goes on today.

In 1988 the 1,100-member AFS, now based in Columbus, Ohio, celebrated its 100th anniversary with a five-day conference in the Massachusetts city of its birth. The study of folklore had changed considerably in the intervening century. No longer looking primarily toward the preservation of endangered folk crafts, artifacts, and practices, AFS members, according to the centennial issue of the society's *Journal of American Folklore,* saw their calling as "an ongoing examination of the present." The 1988 Cambridge conference featured topics ranging from the narratives of born-again Christians to the customs and traditions of prison inmates to women in American spa culture, along with demonstrations of Jewish paper cutting and Palestinian needlework. Then as now, music remained a major focus for many members of the folklore society, with traditional fiddlers and black gospel music among the most popular folk genres.

Originally, the AFS was run by and for college professors; in 2001, many of its 1,200 members worked for federal or state agencies, historical societies, and museums. AFS members who are held in the highest esteem receive the honor of being named Fellows. Once an esoteric discipline indulged in by a few, folklore is now widely respected and widely taught in American colleges and universities.

William M. Clements, ed., *100 Years of American Folklore Studies: A Conceptual History* (1988); Susan A. Dwyer-Shick, *The American Folklore Society and Folklore Research in America, 1888–1940* (1979); Catherine Foster, "That's Folklore," *Christian Science Monitor,* November 7, 1988; Carol Stocker, "Folklore: It's Mass. Culture," *Boston Globe,* October 29, 1988.

Tristram Potter Coffin

Anglo-American Folklife The early European settlement of New England was predominantly by people of English origin. To their ranks came the Irish and the Scots in the 18th century, and throughout the colonial and early national periods New England remained primarily a culture based on traditions of the British Isles, despite the arrival of people from France and northern Europe. It was not until after the Industrial Revolution that other sizable ethnic groups immigrated, most notably

Irish and French Canadian Catholics, and they were not readily accepted by those of English descent. As a result, traditions from the British Isles formed the basis of what was understood as "Yankee" New England culture until the 20th century and still inform regional identity, particularly in the northern three states.

The cultural traditions of Anglo-Americans included the usual elements: legends, tales, songs, superstitions, customs, beliefs, cures, art, architecture, ways and practices, and so on. Many of these traditions culminated in the New England "Yankee": a stereotypical character who was depicted as having considerable dry, sharp wit; a parsimonious, taciturn, stoic nature; a quiet manner of speaking; and quick business acumen. Yankees kept their own council inviolate, in both prosperity and adversity. They "prepared for ill and not for good" as the basis for a worldview that did not, on the surface, hold human nature in high esteem. In fact, a good deal of spare time was spent in contemplating whether people were spawned by the devil or a wingless angel, and the Yankees' opinions usually leaned toward the former. Despite misgivings, they maintained a regard for their fellows.

The scope of Anglo-American traditions has been, at least partially, preserved in sermons, letters, and diaries. Samuel Sewall, a Puritan merchant and judge in the Salem witch trials, produced an enormous diary that is a trove of folklore; Puritan minister Cotton Mather followed in the footsteps of his father, Increase Mather, as a collector of lore, legends, and cures in his *Curiosa Americana, Magnalia Christi Americana,* and *The Angel of Bethesda.* Widely disseminated Puritan broadside verse, colonial grave inscriptions, almanacs, proverbs, and dialects are also important sources for study by folklore scholars in recent times. Anglo-American folklore in New England, however, has not received the same attention that it has in other regions, in part because of the academic proclivities of early scholars and in part because of the perception that folk traditions were not as vital in a region so educated and "modern" as New England.

Folklore scholarship has been ongoing in the British Isles for centuries but did not begin in this country until the late 19th century with the studies of Harvard professor James Francis Child. Child was interested in English and Scottish ballads, but because many of the songs he studied were extant in New England, he was in fact making excursions into regional folklore. Unfortunately, Child and his disciple George Lyman Kittredge worked only from printed sources, never collecting from the New Englanders who sang the songs or variants of them. It was, in a sense, unfortunate

that Child chose to work only in balladry, for it was he who set the tone for the future scholarship that was to begin in the 20th century. Scholars such as Phillips Barry, Fannie Hardy Eckstorm, Mary Smyth, and Helen Hartness Flanders began, for the first time, to collect from oral tradition. Following Child's lead, however, they concentrated primarily on ballads, especially on those songs that comprised the 305 songs that Child had selected for his canon.

Little attention, therefore, was paid to other folk traditions and material culture abroad in the land. Even the broadside ballad was frequently overlooked as this research began, and much valuable material was therefore never retrieved. The few exceptions were Eckstorm's study of place-names; Lincoln and Joanna Colcord's research of the language and ways of seafarers; the Works Progress Administration's collection of folk materials in the 1930s; and the haphazard work of local historical societies.

Much folklore in New England was either adapted from the lore of the British Isles or was modeled after it. A popular song that originally began, "In London city where I did dwell," for example, became "In Boston city." Another, beginning, "As I walked out in Dublin City I spied a poor soldier" (dying of venereal disease) was changed to "in Boston City." A "black thorn winter" in an English song became a "blackberry winter," signifying a poor summer crop because a late New England frost had killed the blossoms.

Because of the morbid Puritan outlook on the world, Anglo-American folklore tended to be overly concerned with doom, disaster, and ways to avoid it or learn from it. Funerals, murders, and hangings were the subject of endless songs, usually ending in "Drinking and bad company has made a wretch of me," or "Prepare in death to follow me." Places were often named for the disaster that overtook someone there or the result of some folly committed by someone. Hence we have place-names such as Norman's Woe (on Massachusetts's Cape Ann), where a captain was drowned, or Great Eastern Rock (near Block Island), where a ship's bottom was ripped out.

With Irish immigration, the macabre overtones of the Puritan worldview were softened but by no means obliterated. Irish immigrants came in the 19th century to work on the canals, on the railroads, in the lumber woods, in fishing vessels, and in the factories. They introduced a good deal of balladry that can usually be identified by its "Come all Ye," or similar beginnings, and by a livelier tune. While the Irish continued the songs of disaster, they also stressed songs related to labor, often with more jovial themes, such as "Heenan and Say-

ers," about a prize fight, or "M'Cluskey and Bull Gordan," about an ox pulling contest.

Anglo-American traditions were not just a compendium of songs, legends, and tales gradually acquiring an American identity through localization. They touched all facets of life. Folk medicine was based on cures and charms used in the British Isles. The double cross on the door, witch hazel and lilac bushes in the yard, and witch balls on the roof were all Old World devices to keep out evil spirits. Many of our common weeds and plants, such as plantain, digitalis, primrose, hollyhock, and mullein, were imported for medicinal use. As colonists learned of local flora and fauna and their value from the natives, they accepted or rejected them as they conformed to the standards of home. Likewise they prepared and used them in traditional ways.

In England and Ireland people wore clothes that denoted their occupation. So it was at first in New England. As time wore on, however, new Americans adopted their own dress codes: a smock and straw boater for the butcher; the "slicker" and "sou'wester" for fishermen; plaid shirts, "stagged," or fringed, pants, and spiked boots for the logger. The same was true of foodways. As the colonists adopted new foods, they chose them first because they resembled the foods of home and then prepared them in traditional ways. As Puritan ways faded, food took on a livelier aspect. New inventions improved cookery, and meals changed; but old preferences and taboos, clearly influenced by sanitary and other practical concerns, died hard. A true Yankee would only eat oysters in months that have the letter *R* in them, for instance, and would never eat pork during the summer. The New England (really English) boiled dinner and boiled codfish are still gastronomically titillating to the New England palate.

Each New England state is said to have its own dialect, its own speech rhythms, and its own colloquialisms. A survey of New England town and city names reveals that many had their origin in the British Isles: Boston, Bristol, Tiverton, Belfast, Lymington, Padistow. A perusal of gravestones in these communities clearly shows the origins of the deceased. A further evaluation of immigration explains pronunciations, speech rhythms, and colloquialisms. In Maine, the use of "dear" or "dearie" is common regardless of the sex of the person addressed, reminiscent of the use among Northumbrians. In Vermont, a rabbit is still called a "kuney" (coney).

Legends and tales of Irish, English, Scottish, and Welsh heroes have been transported to New England with relatively little change. While original tales may have stressed the noble lineage of the hero—and sometimes his intelligence—in America strength, courage, and the intestinal fortitude to endure suffering and climatic conditions are stressed. When New Englanders began to develop native heroes, they performed similar deeds but in different ways and sometimes with different intent. Folk hero Barney Beal of Maine, for instance, lifted a dory full of fish out of the water and killed a horse with his fist. Fred Carver was said to have bit hunks out of oxen's backs when he lost his temper. And legend holds that Walter Carey, of western Massachusetts, routinely pulled Model T Fords out of ditches. Other folk heroes endured cold, starvation, and torture, but nowhere is their noble ancestry or intelligence stressed. Sometimes they are patriotic; often they befriend the poor (especially if they "donate" property that belongs to someone else); but in the main they are traditional folk characters with a twist.

Collectively, these influences have contributed to the image of New England and the New Englander. The white, Anglo-Saxon Yankee is still a cornerstone of New England folklife but is only one cultural tradition among many and has been subsumed largely by the cultures of more recently arrived ethnic groups, reflecting ongoing changes in the region's cultural makeup and traditions.

Horace P. Beck, *The Folklore of Maine* (1957); Jane C. Beck, *Always in Season: Folk Art and Traditional Culture in Vermont* (1982); Benjamin A. Botkin, *A Treasury of New England Folklore: Stories, Ballads, and Traditions of the Yankee People* (1947); Francis James Child, *English and Scottish Ballads*, 10 vols. (1882–98); Richard M. Dorson, *Jonathan Draws the Long Bow* (1946); Helen Hartness Flanders and George Brown, eds., *Vermont Folk-Songs and Ballads* (1931); Michael Hoberman, *Yankee Moderns: Folk Regional Identity in the Sawmill Valley of Western Massachusetts, 1890–1920* (2000); Clifton Johnson, *What They Say in New England, and Other American Folklore* (1963); George Lyman Kittredge, *The Old Farmer and His Almanac* (1924).

Horace P. Beck

Apples, Cider, and Applejack

Apples and sweet or hard cider have played an important role in New England life since the first settlers arrived. Only the crabapple tree had been known to Native Americans. New England's first colonists brought apple seeds and cuttings, which they carefully nurtured into orchards. In fact, some New England towns placed a bounty on transplanted apple trees to encourage their proliferation, and grafting, or crossing of varieties, was an important spring ritual. Almost every farm in the region had a small orchard of a dozen or so apple trees, frequently of different types. Winter apples such as Russetts and Fameuses stored well, whereas Wolf Rivers and Rhode Island Greenings made excellent pies; Alexanders were good for drying, Winesaps for applesauce; Tallman Sweets were well suited to baking; and Baldwins and Russetts made tasty cider.

Originally, the apple was most important as a source of cider and hard cider, known as cider brandy or applejack. Applejack is considered the more potent, as it is made by siphoning off the part of the barrel of hard cider that doesn't freeze. Many families had their own recipes for hard cider, and almost all put down a few barrels for their personal consumption, along with a couple of barrels for cider vinegar.

By the early 19th century almost every New England town had a cider mill. Johnny Appleseed (John Chapman), a native of Leominster, Mass., became an American legend for selling or giving away thousands of apple-tree seedlings to pioneer farmers from the Allegheny Mountains to Ohio and beyond. U.S. president John Adams, who lived to the age of 91, is reputed to have drunk a tankard of hard cider every morning before breakfast. The beverage was generally believed to be strengthening and healthful. Sometimes hard cider would be laced with pepper to help people stay warm in the cold of winter. It was a standard act of hospitality for a host to draw off a pitcher of hard cider as a way of welcoming guests. And farmers willing to part with a jug of hard cider are said to have been those who had their roads rolled first. By 1830, with the temperance movement gaining steam, distilleries began to go under, leaving farmers as the chief producers of hard cider.

Sweet cider was preserved by boiling it down to one-seventh of its volume. It was then used in cooking when a sweet syrup was needed, as for mincemeats, or was mixed with spring water and consumed as a version of sweet cider. If the cider was boiled down further, it became cider jelly.

Apple recipes continue to play a large part in a New Englander's diet. Many New Englanders continue to eat apple butter, apple crisp, apple dumplings, applesauce, apple pie, boiled cider pie, Indian pudding, applesauce cake, and baked apples, to mention a few. In the past, apples were strung up and dried for winter storage, a tiresome task that gave rise to apple-paring bees. Such social gatherings usually began at "early candle light." Apples were pared, sliced, and cored by older members of the community, while children were assigned the task of stringing them together with a steel knitting needle. People also dried apples on racks over the stove. Whole apples were peeled and dried as well for later use in apple-head dolls.

The apple has widely been held to possess certain supernatural qualities. According to the Bible, it was the fruit that led to Adam and Eve being driven from the Garden of Eden. In Celtic mythology an apple tree often served as the entrance to fairyland. In years gone by a forked piece of apple wood was considered an excellent divining rod. Some traditions held that a woman who sat before an applewood fire would become pregnant—and, what's more, that the smoke from the chimney would point in the direction of the child's father. If a single person peeled an apple and threw the peel over his or her right shoulder, the way the peel fell to the ground would reveal the initials of that person's future spouse. The apple was used, too, as a weather prognosticator. When apple skins were thick, New Englanders looked for a long, hard winter.

New England speech was full of apple sayings, such as "Every cider apple has a worm," "The rotten apple injures its neighbor," and "Many an applecart tips over." Proverbial comparisons such as "round as an apple," "no bigger than a pint of cider half drunk up," and "sweeter than apple cider" abound.

Apples and cider also played a central role in New England folk medicine. "An apple a day keeps the doctor away" is a well-known adage. A variant is "Eat an apple going to bed, make the doctor beg his bread." Two teaspoons of honey and two teaspoons of apple cider vinegar were considered good for everyone from expectant human mothers to heifers. The apple or its juice has been used as a cure for jaundice, gout, burns, coughs, stiff joints, and warts and as a means of bringing out, or exposing, the measles.

Apples and cider still play an important role in New England. Apple orchards function as a significant part of the economy, particularly in Vermont's Lake Champlain valley, where apple orchards are big business. Although only a very few people still make applejack, cider remains a popular drink, particularly in the fall and especially at Thanksgiving. And apples continue to be an extremely popular native fruit.

Vrest Orton, *The American Cider Book: The Story of America's Natural Beverage* (1973); Mark Rosenstein, *In Praise of Apples: A Harvest of History, Horticulture, and Recipes* (1996); George Albert Stilphen, *The Apples of Maine: A Compilation of the History, Physical, and Cultural Characteristics of All the Varieties of Apples Known to Have Been Grown in the State of Maine* (1993); David Scofield Wilson and Angus Kress Gillespie, eds., *Rooted in America: Foodlore of Popular Fruits and Vegetables* (1999).

Jane C. Beck

Arts and Crafts

Objects of artistic and utilitarian value created by self-taught or apprenticed artists reflecting the traditions, values, and aesthetics of ethnic, regional, occupational, community, or family groups fall under the art-and-craft rubric. The folk arts and crafts of New England consist of objects related to the region's history or folklore, from Native American baskets to ship's figureheads to Yankee hooked rugs, or made by folk artists and craftspeople who live in the region.

Native and European New Englanders had always produced objects that met utilitarian and aesthetic needs: split ash baskets, log cabin quilts, hooked rugs, wooden boats, duck decoys, fishing lures. These items were not regarded as art or much seen outside rural communities in the region, however, until formally trained professional artists of the modernist school took notice of them early in the 20th century and helped bring the artifacts, although not their creators, to a wider—and influential—audience. The modernists saw in folk art something they themselves wanted to achieve: vigor, simplicity, abstraction. As artists and wealthy patrons began to appreciate the aesthetic value of these objects, folk art and craft became the province of antique dealers and collectors, fine-art curators in museums, and interested philanthropists. To this day these three groups constitute the primary market for folk arts and crafts, just as artifacts more often than not are still deemed more important than their makers.

When Hamilton Easter Field established the Ogunquit School of Painting and Sculpture in 1913, a small group of artists began summering in this Maine seaside community. Returning to Ogunquit year after year well into the next decade, they saw many local objects—decoys, weather vanes, paintings, hooked rugs. As Beatrix T. Rumford notes in *Perspectives on American Folk Art* (1980), these modernists "recognized in the neglected carvings and portraits many of the same abstract qualities that were the essence of their own art and came to appreciate what America's unschooled eighteenth- and nineteenth-century craftsmen and amateurs, unshackled by aesthetic theories, had achieved." Several in the Ogunquit group amassed extensive collections of artifacts that became part of the first exhibit of American folk art in 1924 at the Whitney Studio Club in New York City. Individuals often hired by wealthy philanthropists scoured the New England countryside to gather folk artworks for their patrons' collections. The discoveries they made in New England's towns and villages became the basis of the renowned folk-art collections that were later donated to museums. Abby Aldrich Rockefeller's collection, for example, can be seen at Colonial Williamsburg in Virginia; Electra Havemeyer Webb's became the core of Vermont's Shelburne Museum; and Henry Francis du Pont's is now on display at his former Winterthur, Del., mansion.

With the dispersion of New England folk art to collections in other parts of the United States, the public came to regard New England folk art as American folk art. In the 1910s and 1920s, during the Colonial Revival movement, antiquarians such as Clara Endicott Sears and Wallace Nutting collected colonial objects as a means of harking back to America's Anglo-Saxon roots when the country was opening its doors to newcomers from southern and eastern Europe and anti-immigrant sentiment was running high. The Wallace Nutting collection of American furniture and decorative arts, one of the largest, can be viewed at the Wadsworth Atheneum in Hartford, Conn. The Shaker, Transcendentalist, Native American, and American artifacts and paintings collected by Clara Endicott Sears are housed at Fruitlands in Harvard, Mass., site of Bronson Alcott's utopian experiment in 1843 and of the museum Sears founded in 1914. Other collections of American folk art and decorative crafts on public display in the region include that of Bertram K. and Nina Fletcher Little, at the one-time summer retreat the couple named Cogswell's Grant in Essex, Mass., now operated by Historic New England, and the Flynt Center of Early New England Life of Historic Deerfield (Mass.), which displays more than 25,000 objects made or used in America between 1650 and 1850. The Museum of Fine Arts in Boston includes among its holdings the extensive Maxim Karolik collection of paintings and decorative arts. Local historical societies in towns throughout New England also house arts and crafts collections of varying quality and size.

In 1932 Holger Cahill, a leading American folk-art enthusiast, "staged the most comprehensive showing of American primitives yet assembled." In the now classic essay that appeared in the show's catalog, Cahill distinguished among primitive, provincial, and folk art. He called folk art "the expression of the common people, made by them and intended for their use and enjoyment. It is not the expression of professional artists made for a small, cultured class, and it had little to do with the fashionable art of its period. It does not come out of an academic tradition passed on by schools, but out of craft tradition plus the personal quality of the rare craftsman who is an artist." Cahill's description of folk arts (and crafts) remains definitive. In 1974 Jean Lippman and Alice Winchester curated *The Flowering of American Folk Art* at New York's Whitney Museum of American Art. Their landmark exhibit defined folk art and its artists as having these common denominators: "independence from cosmopolitan, academic traditions, lack of formal training—a simple and unpretentious rather than sophisticated approach, originally more typically in rural than urban places and from craft rather than folk-art traditions." In this definition we see how folk artists can be regarded as unschooled and the work they do as primitive. Both notions were related to the idea that folk arts came from the lower or so-called peasant classes of Europe and from countries that sent many emigrants to settle in New England. While Lippman and Winchester's landmark show made its mark on the elite art world, the terms *folk art* and *folk craft* can create controversy. Academic folklorists and art scholars may want to tie folk art and craft to a community, tradition, or single artist's body of work, whereas the collector may wish simply to accumulate items regardless of such considerations, and the art dealer may have more interest in evaluating pieces for their monetary value, as many sought-after items fetch high commissions. In fact, folklorists, art historians, art dealers, and museum curators—all of whom have a stake in the folk-art-and-craft world today—may each have their own definitions of what constitutes the genre.

New England's seafaring heritage has had a great influence on folk art and craft in the region. The gaff-rigged sailboats called Beetle Cats, first built between 1921 and 1941 by John Beetle of New Bedford, Mass., and now made by Charles York in the same city, and the model ships and ships in a bottle made by Erik Ronnberg, Sr., of Rockport, Mass., appeal to both collectors and tourists. Maritime folk crafts include the nets made by Portuguese Americans in Provincetown, Mass., and decoys such as those carved by Fred Dolan of Center Barnstead, N.H.

The region's long, dark winters have been the traditional time for hooking rugs such as those of Eileen Friedrich of Groton, Mass., and Cleland Selby of Essex Junction, Vt., or making quilts such as those of Sally Palmer Field of South Chelmsford, Mass. Often the designs of these folk artworks incorporate narrative themes drawn from rural or family life. Seasonal scenes have always been prominent in the paintings of Herman Arthur Haskins of North Adams, Mass.; Rose Labrie of Rye, N.H.; and African American folk artist Ellis Ruley of Norwich, Conn. Nantucket lightship baskets such as those made on wooden molds by Bobby Marks of Osterville, Mass., or Karol Linquist of Nantucket, Mass., are widely known for their high quality, although many baskets on the market today are poor, imported imitations.

Many professional artists, curators, and antiquarians still consider folk art and craft to be inferior to more formal artistic genres. This view has changed over the past 20 years, as professionally trained public-sector folklorists

Fred Dolan carving a decoy, 1999

throughout the region have mounted major exhibitions of locally produced objects. One such exhibit was organized by Jane C. Beck for the Vermont Arts Council in 1982. *Always in Season: Folk Art and Traditional Culture in Vermont* showed that "folk art is rooted in shared activities of the local community. These activities are not only shared by family and friends, but they help shape the individual's point of view, a viewpoint that is based on the reality of personal experience and communal activity rather than creation in isolation." In addition to identifying folk artists in Vermont, the show emphasized the narrative impulse in folk art and craft. The items featured in the exhibition—hooked rugs with country scenes, carved birdhouses, Native American baskets, fish and bird decoys—were presented as personal or collaborative expressions of art-and-craft styles common to New England.

Under the auspices of state and regional arts councils and historical societies mandated to reach new audiences, folk art and craft have come to be viewed in a new light. State folklorists have begun to work collaboratively on regional projects, such as traditions of the Appalachian Trail in New England and the narrative impulse in New England folk art. Meanwhile they still conduct surveys of traditional arts and crafts that are uniquely tied to their state's particular geographic environment: knot tying in Rhode Island and Maine, blacksmithing in New Hampshire, and boatbuilding on Vermont's Lake Champlain, for example. Folk-artists-in-the-classroom and apprenticeship programs, as well as cultural

exhibits at state folklife centers or museums, often emphasize the role of artists in the community or connect works to their natural and cultural environments. When a woodcarver visits a second-grade classroom to show children how decoys are carved, he or she both carries on and exemplifies that tradition.

Jane C. Beck, ed., *Always in Season: Folk Art and Traditional Culture in Vermont* (1982); DeCordova and Dana Museum and Park, *Stories to Tell: The Narrative Impulse in Contemporary New England Folk Art* (1988); Allen H. Eaton, *Handicrafts of New England* (1949); Eugene W. Metcalf, Jr., and Claudine Weatherford, "Modernism, Edith Halpert, Holger Cahill, and the Fine Art Meaning of Folk Art," in *Folk Roots, New Roots: Folklore in American Life*, ed. Jane S. Becker and Barbara Franco (1988); Beatrix T. Rumford, "Uncommon Art of the Common People: A Review of the Trends in the Collecting and Exhibiting of American Folk Art," in *Perspectives on American Folk Art*, ed. Ian M. G. Quimby and Scott T. Swank (1980); John Michael Vlach and Simon J. Bronner, eds., *Folk Art and Art Worlds* (1986).

Eleanor Wachs

Auctions According to the dictionary, an auction is a sale of goods or property to the highest bidder, but anyone who has ever attended a New England country auction knows it can be far more, at once social event, entertainment, and battle of wits. New England auctions take many forms: art auctions, fish auctions, estate auctions, farm and cattle auctions, country auctions, charity auctions, and other specialty auctions. Among the more unusual was the New Hampshire roadkill auction, at which the frozen carcasses of animals

killed on the road (excluding deer and moose) were auctioned off once a year by sealed bid. This auction, which drew bidders from all over the Northeast, ran for 14 years before it was called off owing to the spread of rabies in the mid-1990s. Today, though most New England auctions find their counterparts in other areas of the country, auctions remain deeply ingrained in New England culture as a first resort for disposing of unwanted goods and raising funds for individuals and organizations.

The New England country auction is usually a sale of personal belongings occasioned by an owner's death or relocation. Sometimes, the owner's real estate is auctioned off as well; many auctioneers are licensed realtors. Large auctions are generally held either on the property or at an "auction barn" and traditionally begin on Saturday mornings, sometimes running to Sunday. Often local charitable groups sell food and soft drinks on the auction site to raise money. Smaller auctions are usually held on Wednesday or Thursday evenings. Auction notices, which include short listings of items for sale, are generally posted in local store windows and on supermarket bulletin boards. Experienced auction-goers make a point of buying the local newspaper on Thursdays to check the listings. They arrive early, either to get good seats in the auction barn or to find a prime location for their folding chairs on the lawn or under the tent. Attendees usually park along the road or in an adjoining field.

In addition to the auctioneer, a typical auction crew includes several runners, who hold up goods, help scan the crowd for bids, and deliver the merchandise to buyers, and a bookkeeper, who records the names and addresses of bidders, assigns them auction numbers, and collects the payments at the end of the auction. Prospective buyers may frequently view the items to be auctioned before the bidding starts.

The auctioneer begins by briefly explaining the bidding and payment procedure and the rules that govern the removal of purchases, perhaps listing upcoming sales. When the first item goes on the block it is often a time of testing: there may be several minutes of psychological maneuvering between the auctioneer and the audience, particularly when the auctioneer is unknown or young. Good auctioneers strike a delicate balance, giving buyers hope of landing a bargain while emphasizing that the auctioneer is controlling the proceedings. The auctioneer suggests an opening bid, which is usually fairly close to the anticipated selling price. A buyer may make a counteroffer, or the auctioneer may lower the opening bid until someone in the audience accepts it. From this point, the price steadily rises.

Fast talk is the hallmark of the country auc-

Livestock auction, East Thetford, Vt., 1986

tioneer and the subject of many jokes about inexperienced auction-goers. Many, though not all, auctioneers chant in a formulaic, rhythmic, often musical way. The chant helps the auctioneer speak rapidly and move goods quickly. When bids are slow to materialize, a formulaic run of nonsense syllables can often fill the gap. Chants vary widely and can be distinctive—many modern auctioneers attend auction schools and practice using tape recordings. The late Bus Mars, a noted auctioneer from Pawlet, Vt., used to sing his chant, nodding his head to keep the beat. More than one auction-goer found her- or himself nodding in rhythm and almost hypnotically bidding on an item. Country auctioneers also have a reputation for teasing and cajoling the audience, particularly when bidding is slow. Many auctioneers live in the community and know their audiences well; they may make personal remarks that elicit laughter from the crowd and sometimes embarrass the butt of the joke. In *The Devil's Dictionary*, Ambrose Bierce defined an auctioneer as "the man who proclaims with a hammer that he has picked a pocket with his tongue."

Bidding takes some form of "I have X, who will give me Y?" The auctioneer usually pits two bidders against each other; when one drops out, another may jump in. As the price rises, the pace slows, and the increments may become smaller. Before "knocking down" the item, the auctioneer usually gives "fair warning"; "Going once, going twice, . . . sold" and "Are we all done?" are common formulas. The

auctioneer can hasten bidding when the crowd becomes inattentive or slow to bid by selling an item the second he receives a bid on it.

In rural areas, livestock auctions are weekly events and auctions of farms and farm equipment are frequent occurrences. Auctions have also become a popular way for service organizations such as the Rotary and Lions Clubs and for volunteer fire departments to raise money. "Tailgate" auctions—weekly affairs, usually held in parking lots, at which an auctioneer moves from car to car, selling items on consignment—are beginning to compete with garage sales as a way to dispose of unwanted goods. The Skinner gallery, with auctions in Boston and Bolton, Mass., is ranked in the top echelon of art and antique auction galleries. In 1997 the Boston gallery auctioned a previously unknown work by the Massachusetts painter Fitz Hugh Lane for $3.85 million, a world record for a painting sold at auction. One of New England's best-known and most successful commercial auctions, the Portland Fish Exchange, was founded by local fishermen on the waterfront in Portland, Maine. The fish exchange, which opened its daily display auction with an $8 a pound bid for haddock in May 1986, had a rough go of it initially and nearly folded two years later. But it survived, and in 1997, 23 million pounds of seafood from more than 400 fishing vessels were sold at the auction to buyers throughout the eastern seaboard. Modeled after European auctions, the Portland Fish Exchange was

once the only display auction of fish in the continental United States. Now it faces competition from imitators, among them a fish auction established in 1997 in Gloucester, Mass., and from World Wide Web–based fish- and seafood-auction sites backed by millions of dollars in venture capital.

Emma Bailey, *Sold to the Lady in the Green Hat* (1962); Ralph Cassady. Jr., *Auctions and Auctioneering* (1967); Koenraad Kuiper, "The Oral Tradition in Auction Speech," *American Speech* 67 (1992); Doug Stewart, "'Twenty-Five Dollar Bid an' Now 30 Now 30 . . . ,'" *Smithsonian* 25, no. 5 (1994).

Karen Rockow

Ballads A genre of both written and oral literature, the ballad can be minimally defined as a narrative poem or song in stanzas. The edition of traditional ballads compiled by Harvard professor Francis James Child, *The English and Scottish Popular Ballads*, has been the representative collection ever since it was published between 1882 and 1898.

The English ballad initially seems to have attracted scholarly attention in the early 18th century when the British literary critic Joseph Addison wrote enthusiastically in the *Spectator* (1711) of "Chevy Chase," a ballad celebrating the 1388 Battle of Otterburn, and "Babes in the Wood," a sentimental account of two lost children widely printed on broadsides. Addison took pains to draw structural parallels between the ballads and the Greek classics, thereby identifying the material as worthy of literary scrutiny and affirming its artistic merit. As Addison's early notice implicitly recognizes, the ballad may have both oral and written forms.

Pride of place, however, has come to be given to ballads that have circulated orally rather than in print and thus exhibit certain stylistic peculiarities: a spare, elliptical story that is often more spatial than linear, rendering more of a narrative's context than it does of its unfolding through time; a high proportion of dialogue to narrative; limited numbers of characters, about whom we learn only through their conversation and action; repetition both within texts and between texts of certain phrases or clauses, sometimes even verses; and a metrical irregularity that is regularized in singing by the force of the melody. Early enthusiasts saw the ballad as a spontaneous form of literature, close to the origins of language itself, that reflected a homogeneous, relatively classless, and undeveloped society. Ballads thus were seen as reflecting group thought rather than individual expression.

Such views on what he came to call the popular ballad were articulated by Harvard's Child. Child sought early manuscripts containing the remnants of this early form of lit-

Folksingers with Helen Hartness Flanders and Robert Frost (far right) at Bread Loaf School of English, Middlebury, Vt., ca. 1940

erature with the intent of recording all that was left. In the years following the publication of Child's canonical work, scholars continued to show interest in the kinds of texts to which he drew attention. The age for their creation and vital transmission having passed, students sought examples of these oral treasures in manuscripts and living memories. In the United States a lively competition developed between states, with collectors seeking to show how many so-called Child ballads they could find. New England did particularly well, as the works of Helen Hartness Flanders, Fannie Hardy Eckstorm, Mary Winslow Smyth, and Phillips Barry attest.

These scholars and those who followed in their footsteps have also recognized that many other musical exemplars deserve to be called ballads, that similar song stories exist in other languages, and that literary artists have made works of great beauty imitating aspects of the popular ballad. In fact, the earliest piece of New England literature is believed to be a ballad depicting the disappointments of the early settlers, "An Old Song, Wrote by One of Our First New-England Planters" (ca. 1630–40). New England's first best-seller was Michael Wigglesworth's *Day of Doom* (1662), a long poem in ballad form presenting a frightening description of the Last Judgment. And though neither composition has survived, the 12-year-old Benjamin Franklin wrote two ballads in 1718, one of them a sailor's song about Blackbeard the pirate. Notable collections have also been made of more contemporary

ballads displaying a literate sensibility: narrative, self-conscious, linear, and expansive texts that reflect particular cultural concerns and exhibit different stylistic features from the earlier ones. There are first-person accounts of occupational experiences such as "The Jam on Gerry's Rock," which records a lumberman's fatal accident. Edward Ives has been a leader in collecting occupational ballads and in tracing the lives, experiences, and poetic or musical productions of occupational poets. Collectors have also gathered lyric songs with only minimal narratives, such as "Black Is the Color of My True Love's Hair," a lament for lost love expressing hope for a future reunion. Many of the folk songs collected and still sung fall into this category and are at or outside the margins of the traditional ballad. Singers of songs, for their part, seldom distinguish narrative from lyric.

David Buchan, *The Ballad and the Folk* (1997 [1972]); Francis James Child, *The English and Scottish Popular Ballads* (1882–98); Edward D. Ives, *Joe Scott, the Woodsman-Songmaker* (1978); D. K. Wilgus, *Anglo-American Folksong Scholarship since 1898* (1982 [1959]).

Mary Ellen Brown

Basketry Basket making was practiced among Native American communities throughout New England long before the colonial period and continues to be a popular regional craft through the present day. Native Americans passed on the tradition to European settlers, who also brought some of their own basket-making traditions. During the 17th

century, every New England home had a few baskets of various sizes, from tiny baskets that held odds and ends to large laundry and storage baskets. Baskets were plentiful because of the availability of basket-making materials collected from the rich woodlands of the region. Some groups, such as the Shakers, made baskets a part of their economy. Three traditions—Native American, Shaker, and Nantucket lightship—exemplify some of the best of New England basketry, and their reputations extend well beyond the region's borders.

The basket maker uses natural materials and one of three techniques: plaiting, coiling, or weaving. In plaiting, the basket maker cross-weaves the wefts, which are horizontal threads, and the warps, which are threads that run lengthwise, creating a checkerboard effect. In coiling, strips or bundles of fibers are wrapped into a spiral and sewn together at various points. In weaving, the wefts and warps are interlaced. Baskets are classified according to materials: ash splint baskets, willow baskets, root or branch baskets, sturdy birch bark baskets. Shaker baskets are generally made from ash and poplar trees; lightship baskets from the island of Nantucket are made partly of native woods and partly of imported cane materials; other baskets are made of various materials, including reeds from China, raffia from Madagascar, and palm leaves from Cuba and Florida.

The most ubiquitous New England basket type is the ash splint basket produced by several Native American groups, particularly the Micmac, Passamaquoddy, and Penobscot of Maine. The popularity of this basket is due to the ash itself, which is extremely pliable. The trunk of the black ash tree is cut into logs, which are then pounded to separate the splints so they can easily be peeled. The splint's thickness depends on its annual growth; thicker splints make for sturdier baskets, such as those used for laundry. The basket maker first forms the ribs, or side pieces, and then begins to weave in smaller splints until the desired size and design are created. The basket is finished when its handles are made by threading splints into the rim so as not to show; no nails or metal are used. Some ash splint baskets are decorated with a simple pattern made by dipping a potato into dye and then stamping it onto the basket.

Some New England baskets were made by families in rural and ethnic communities and given to neighbors, sold at roadsides to tourists, or brought to market. For example, willow baskets and woven birch bark baskets, a Scandinavian tradition, could be found in places where immigrants from Finland settled in New England, particularly on Cape Ann in Massachusetts. Sweetser baskets of Vermont

Baskets made by Newt Washburn, ca. 1985

are also well known, as are Abbott baskets of Maine and Stevens baskets of Connecticut. Sweetser baskets were made by Arthur Sweetser of Waterbury, Vt., during the 1940s; he learned the tradition of making black ash splint baskets from his father, who learned it from his grandmother. Newt Washburn, a member of this family, learned basket making in 1923 when he was eight years old and continues the tradition today.

The Shakers, who established their communal societies in New England in the late 18th century, are well known for their excellent craftsmanship. In addition to making furniture and running successful seed businesses, the Shakers also made and sold baskets as well as other crafts. The Shakers made "fancy baskets" of white poplar that were woven on wooden forms. They also made black split ash baskets for home and farm use. Shaker baskets are characterized by their variety of patterns.

There has long been a tradition of basket making on Nantucket Island—possibly derived from Native American tradition—but the "faraway island" is best known for its lightship baskets. Originally designed for utilitarian rather than decorative purposes, these baskets are often made in graduated sizes to nest one inside the other. Lightship baskets are particularly distinctive because they are woven on a mold, have sturdy wooden bottoms, and are very tight. They are made from a variety of native and imported woods, including oak and rattan. The wooden molds were often passed down from one generation of basket makers to the next.

Lightship baskets were originally made by men stationed on the South Shoal lightship beginning in the 1850s. Mitchell "Mitchie" Ray and Jose Reyes were two of the best-known lightship basket makers. Reyes was known for putting a piece of decorative scrimshaw—at the suggestion of scrimshaw maker Charlie Sayle—on the basket's top and turning the baskets into expensive ladies' pocketbooks, called "friendship baskets," which are still made by hand on Nantucket today. Ray was known for the trademark rhyme on his baskets:

I was made on Nantucket
I'm strong and I'm stout.
Don't lose me or burn me,
And I'll never wear out.

The Nantucket basket-making tradition has continued on the island. Michael Kane and Judy and Bill Sayle (son of Charlie Sayle) are well-known basket makers who use wooden molds in the traditional way. Visitors can stop by their shops and watch the baskets being made in various stages. Bobby Marks, a sixth-generation Nantucketer (now of Osterville, Mass.), owns a successful shop called Oak and Ivory. While traditional basket shops, such as Micmac Images in Presque Isle, Maine, can be found throughout New England, many are poor imitations tailored to the demands of the tourist market. However, basket makers such as Helen Baller of Orleans, Mass., and Newt Washburn of Vermont, and organizations such as the Maine Arts Commission and the Maine Indian Basketmakers Alliance keep the basket-making tradition alive in New England.

Edward Deming Andrews and Faith Andrews, *Work and Worship among the Shakers: Their Craftsmanship and Economic Order* (1974); Allen H. Eaton, *Handicrafts of New England* (1949); Katherine Seeler and Edgar Seeler, *Nantucket Lightship Baskets* (1972); Martha Wetherbee and Nathan Taylor, *Shaker Baskets* (1993).

Eleanor Wachs

Cape Verdean Folklife The significant effect of Cape Verdean culture on southeastern New England since the 1830s is often overlooked. Cape Verdeans have nonetheless occupied a unique position in the development of cities such as Providence and Pawtucket, R.I.; Brockton and New Bedford, Mass.; and other areas in a triangle roughly bounded by Gloucester and Cape Cod in Massachusetts and the Connecticut city of Bridgeport. Early Cape Verdean immigrants to New England were often whalers, stevedores, or cranberry pickers, but many were attracted to factory jobs as New England grew increasingly industrialized late in the 19th century.

Owing to the islands' location off the African coast and their history of Portuguese colonization, the *Crioulo*, or Creole, culture of the Cape Verde Islands blends African and European elements. In New England seasonal celebrations in which Catholic saints' days have been overlaid on much older African and Portuguese rituals are a benchmark of Cape Verdean folklife. The *Canta ris* (kings' sing), for example, sends musicians strolling from house to house on New Year's Eve in emulation of the journey of the Magi. The collection of food and money, ritual toasts, and special songs for the occasion are all Cape Verdean in content. The tradition, often informally organized in New England by families and community members, has become less robust in recent years but still persists.

The *mastro* custom, in which a ritual ship's mast is festooned with a sail made of greenery, breads, fruits, and other treats, reflects the long-standing connection between Cape Verdeans and the sea. Active mastro rituals are observed in both Providence's Camp Street neighborhood and Mattapoisett, Mass., on Saint John's Day and on Saint Phillip's Day in Dorchester, Mass., where many elderly immigrants from the active volcanic island of Fogo arrived in the 1990s. The Dorchester celebration features *kola* dancing and *bandeira*, ceremonial banners that are dipped in the sea and blessed in church before being carried through the community.

The clubs of southeastern New England are home to an active music and dancing scene, in which both the older and the younger generations of Cape Verdean Americans take part. Hot spots include the Main Event and Verdean Veterans Hall in New Bedford, the Cape Verdean Progressive Center and the Tropical Ilhas in East Providence, and the Ilha Verde and the Cape Verdean American Community Development Center (CACD) in Pawtucket. Customary dances range from the *morna*, based on the stately, expressive national song form with its poetic lyrics, to the *koladera* or *funana*, both double-time shimmy steps similar to the Brazilian samba and Dominican merengue, respectively. Some popular older musical groups include the Ivo Pires Band, with the da Graca Brothers and Protazio "Tazinho" Brito; John Pina and the Sorrentoes; and Antone "Toi" Grace and the Verdatones. Younger audiences can be found enjoying the likes of Joao Cerilo and Tropical Power, the Mendes Brothers, and Netinhos de Vovo. The newer bands favor electric guitars, keyboards, and drum machines, whereas the earlier ensembles play older, traditional instruments such as the *cavaquinho* (ukulele); *viola*, an unusual 12-string guitar with double heart–shaped sound holes; the maracas; and other acoustic guitars.

Cape Verdean culture has twice been a focus at the Smithsonian Institution's Folklife Festival, most recently in 1995. This exposure has brought to light artisans in other areas, such as luthiers (people who make stringed instruments), shell sculptors, and weavers of *pano*, a strip cloth created on a backstrap loom that served as currency during the days of the slave trade and is considered today to be an icon of Cape Verde's African origins and mercantile heritage.

Occupational prospects have broadened considerably for Cape Verdeans since the whaling days. One constant has remained, however: the strong flow of goods, income, and goodwill from New England back to the North Atlantic archipelago. As Cape Verde has made the difficult transition from Portuguese colonial dependent to sovereign nation, Cape Verdean New Englanders, part of a worldwide emigrant population often referred to as the "tenth island," have been at the forefront of maintaining an active exchange with the homeland and with one another.

Ronald Barboza, *A Salute to Cape Verdean Musicians and Their Music* (1989); Sam Beck, *Manny Almeida's Ringside Lounge: The Cape Verdeans' Struggle for Their Neighborhood* (1992); Marilyn Halter, *Between Race and Ethnicity: Cape Verdean American Immigrants, 1860–1965* (1993); Belmira Nunes Lopes, *A Portuguese Colonial in America, Belmira Nunes Lopes: The Autobiography of a Cape Verdean-American* (1982).

Daniel L. Kahn

Child, Francis James (1825–96)

Educator, philologist, and scholar of ballads. Born in Boston, Francis James Child was the son of Mary (James) and Joseph Child, a Boston sailmaker. He was Harvard's Boylston professor of rhetoric, oratory, and elocution from 1851 to 1876, when he became professor of English. Today Child is remembered for his erudite collection *The English and Scottish Popular Ballads* (1882–98), which raised interest in folk songs and folklore, legitimating their study.

Child was educated at the Boston Latin School before matriculating at Harvard, a member of the class of 1846. Graduating at the top of his class, he was immediately given a post as tutor in mathematics. A year later he acquired a similar position in history and political economy while also serving as a tutor in rhetoric. Child spent parts of the years 1849–51 in Europe, focusing particularly on a study of German language and philology. These subjects had been made prominent by Jacob and Wilhelm Grimm, whose picture is said to have occupied a prominent place in his study.

A member of the Cambridge Unitarian Church and active in support of the Union during the Civil War, Child was also involved in various college endeavors. He was a central player in the development of the Harvard library, serving for most of his academic career as a member of the book- and manuscript-acquisition committee. Child's interest in the library was related to his own research, which depended on the availability of rare books and manuscripts on which to base accurate critical editions of literature. In 1855 or so Child agreed to become general editor of a new edition of British poets, which eventually expanded to 130 volumes. In it he failed to include Chaucer, because some of the relevant manuscript material had not been printed and was thus unavailable to him; he did, however, write a learned treatise dealing with Chaucer's language and the silent *e* in Middle English.

His 7-volume edition of anonymous early British poetry, *English and Scottish Ballads* (first published in 1857–58 and reissued in revised form in 1860), was inadequate, he quickly recognized, for similar reasons: Child had relied in part on published editions of works such as Bishop Thomas Percy's *Reliques of Ancient English Poetry*, first issued in 1765, rather than original manuscripts. Through his efforts the Early English Text Society was persuaded to print a facsimile edition of the Percy collection in 1867, which in part provided a more solid basis for an entirely different collection of ballads.

Involving an international network of scholars and correspondents who helped him gather manuscript materials gave him vital comparative information, and in some instances advised him specifically on the order and structure of the edition. *The English and Scottish Popular Ballads* contained 305 ballads in multiple versions arranged in roughly chronological fashion. Those chosen for inclusion represented for Child an early form of literature, originally transmitted orally among members of a relatively homogeneous and largely classless society. Child's work, the final volume of which was completed and published by his handpicked successor George

Lyman Kittredge after the older scholar's death, was quickly recognized as canonical. Having forever linked his name to the traditional English and Scottish ballad, Child shaped at least a generation of comparative folk-song scholarship, inspiring folklorists to engage in intensive fieldwork to recover ballads and other songs from singers across the nation.

Although Child viewed his texts as literary artifacts, scholars found more than 100 Child ballads, frequently in many versions, in the repertoires of traditional singers. New England was particularly fertile ground for such field research. The canonical nature of the Child collection has been challenged by a number of scholars, who question Child's implied theory of oral tradition. His legacy endures in the folk-song scholarship he inspired, in the library he helped develop, and in Harvard University's folklore and mythology program.

Michael J. Bell, "'No Borders to the Ballad Maker's Art': Francis James Child and the Politics of the People," *Western Folklore* 47 (1988); Sigurd Bernhard Hustvedt, *Ballad Books and Ballad Men: Raids and Rescues in Britain, America, and the Scandinavian North since 1800* (1930); James D. Reppert, "William Macmath and F. J. Child," *PMLA* 71 (1956); Sigrid Rieuwerts, "In Memoriam: Francis James Child (1825–1896)," in *Ballads into Books: The Legacies of Francis James Child*, ed. Tom Cheesman and Sigrid Rieuwerts (1997).

Mary Ellen Brown

Clambakes

Despite its reputation as the quintessential "Yankee" dining experience, the clambake, reportedly a firmly established Native American tradition, was slow to be adopted by European settlers, who eschewed Native American foods and methods for the more familiar and "civilized" foods of Europe. Gradually, however, the combination of steamed shellfish and vegetables became not only desirable but increasingly ritualized and symbolic. Today, virtually all New Englanders agree that in-shell clams, potatoes, onions, corn, and watermelon are essential ingredients to the clambake menu. In addition to this traditional fare, variations include lobster, clam chowder, crunchy Rhode Island–style frankfurters (otherwise known as "Saugy's"), Italian sausage, and linguica, or Portuguese sausage.

Preparation of the New England clambake is as much a matter of ritual and pride to the bakemaster as are its ingredients. The ultratraditionalist with access to an ocean beach will create a basic rock-lined sandpit that is heated by burning wood and then filled with just the right layering of food and seaweed covered by a wet canvas sheet that steams the meal to perfection. Family secrets, such as whether quahogs or cherrystone clams are the best vari-

Adding corn to a waterfront clambake, 1959

eties to use, or whether onions go inside or outside the pit (both issues of serious and prolonged debate), are often passed down through generations and jealously guarded. Whether the clambake is prepared in a rock-lined sandpit or in aluminum foil on a suburban grill, each bakemaster typically has a pre-scribed method of placement and materials, as well as exotic techniques for timing the cook-ing process that range from testing the tender-ness of onions and potatoes placed in wet cot-ton bags on top of the mound, to a simple reliance on "instinct."

Place is as important as menu at a clam-bake. More New Englanders have experi-enced the traditional clambake at organized events such as "Old Home Days"; at shore dinner halls like Rocky Point, R.I., which popularized them with tourists; or even heated on backyard grills in foil pans than have ever enjoyed one on the shoreline itself. Indeed, perhaps the only venue where one can find taciturn Yankees voluntarily sitting at table with strangers is at the shore dinner hall. The older the hall, the more dilapidated, the more inconvenient, the better. If it was in op-eration when they were children (or better yet, when grandfather was a child), they will go. Well-kept restaurants (and some would say well-prepared clambakes by newer restau-rants) are suspect and strictly for tourists—otherwise known as those "from away."

Although those from outside the region of-ten associate clambakes with the state of Maine, summer travelers find that every New England state with a coastline cheerfully touts the meal as being "the authentic (Rhode Is-land, Connecticut, Massachusetts, etc.) expe-rience!" In truth, it is a regional tradition that has come full circle; in 1997 the Wampanoags announced plans for the development of tribal land in Massachusetts—not for a casino but for a culture and history park whose main fea-ture would be the traditional Indian clambake.

Kathy Neustadt, *Clambake: A History and Celebration of an American Tradition* (1992); Russell M. Peters and John Madama (photographer), *Clambake: A Wampanoag Tradition* (1992).

Gretchen A. Adams

Collectors, Connoisseurs, and Schol-ars

In the late 19th century the study of folk-lore emerged on two major fronts: anthropo-logical and literary. Anthropologists regularly used fieldwork methods—that is, gathering information from living peoples—in their studies of North American Indian cultures, while literary folklorists sought to establish European American connections in the printed texts of beliefs, ballads, and children's lore.

In 1890 the anthropologist Jesse Walter Fewkes experimented with a cylinder phono-graph machine to record a few samples of Maine Passamaquoddy music for the Bureau of American Ethnology. In so doing, Fewkes ushered in a new era in which audio equip-ment was used to collect and preserve oral tra-ditions. Another anthropologist, Frank G. Speck, recorded cylinders of Abenaki, Penob-scot, Maliseet, and Passamaquoddy music in Maine between 1905 and 1910. Such record-ings were intended for laboratory study rather than home entertainment.

Literary folklorists were somewhat slower to take advantage of the new collecting tech-niques, since in the 1890s they were only just becoming aware that material relevant to their interests could still be gathered from living in-formants. The work done at Harvard by Fran-cis James Child from the 1870s through the 1890s placed magnificent texts of English and Scottish popular ballads before an American readership, but scholars believed that the oral musical tradition associated with those texts had died out at an earlier time. William Wells Newell argued in the 1880s that such songs were still being sung in New England com-munities and urged his colleagues to begin recording them. His *Games and Songs of Amer-ican Children* (1883), which drew heavily on material gathered from New England infor-mants, served as a clarion call to literary folk-lorists by demonstrating that European con-nections were still evident in American living traditions. Newell's energy and scholarship led ultimately to the 1888 founding in Cam-bridge, Mass., of the American Folklore Soci-ety, an organization of both anthropologists and folklorists.

Newell's work inspired other folklorists to undertake fieldwork, but it was largely the in-fluence of Harvard professor George Lyman Kittredge that sustained momentum in this area. A Shakespeare scholar, Kittredge had studied under Child and had edited a popular edition of Child's canon of ballads. Widely re-garded at the turn of the century as the highest authority in the land on matters pertaining to ballad scholarship, Kittredge lent his expertise and editorial advice to academic and amateur collectors in all parts of the country.

By 1903 Phillips Barry was writing down folk songs he encountered in Vermont, and during the next two decades he contributed numerous studies of ballads to the *Journal of American Folklore*. Barry focused his consider-able research talents on tracing the historical background of songs gathered in New En-gland and encouraged folklore colleagues to collect not only texts but tunes. In his writings Barry demonstrated how important melodies could be to the diffusion of songs from one place or time to another.

The first stand-alone regional collection of New England folk songs was *Songs from the Hills of Vermont*, compiled by Edith Sturgis and Robert Hughes in 1919. Although modest in format, it documented a local farm family's song repertoire (with melodies) and included scholarly notes compiled with assistance from George Lyman Kittredge. In 1924 Roland Palmer Gray published *Songs and Ballads of the Maine Lumberjacks*, which, although lacking tunes, continued to enhance public awareness of local song traditions.

While literary folklorists scoured New England fields and forests for remnants of old British ballads, other connoisseurs sought to record sea chanteys and songs from the days of sail, an oral tradition that by the 1920s was beginning to fade. Joanna Colcord's *Roll and Go: Songs of American Sailormen* (1924) was inspired by Colcord's earlier life in Searsport, Maine, and voyages with her sea-captain father in the early 1890s. Instead of tracing detailed individual song histories, Colcord emphasized in her descriptive notes the context in which the songs had been sung.

In the mid-1920s the work of two other Maine women set high standards for folksong collecting and research. An accomplished writer on Maine Indians and woods lore, Fannie Hardy Eckstorm was the daughter of a naturalist, guide, and fur trader. Wilderness trips with her father acquainted Eckstorm with the songs of woodsmen, and she combined this familiarity with solid historical research in *Minstrelsy of Maine* (1927). The book's coauthor, Mary Winslow Smyth of Connecticut, was a summer resident on the Maine coast and contributed material gathered around Mount Desert Island. In 1929 Eckstorm and Smyth were on the verge of publishing another book, *British Ballads from Maine*, when they met Phillips Barry and agreed to incorporate his contributions to notes on the songs. The book originally lacked notated music, but at Barry's urging the editors brought ethnomusicologist George Herzog to Maine from the Dakotas, where he was doing research on Native Americans. Herzog hastily visited a number of singers and wrote down the melodies of their ballads, which were then incorporated into the book.

Up to this time New England's few folksong collectors had not used sound-recording equipment. In 1930 Helen Hartness Flanders, a writer from Springfield, Vt., and George Brown, a trained musician from the Boston area, undertook to collect ballads and songs in Vermont's West River valley. Brown made the first field trip carrying a Dictaphone cylinder machine in his car. By following leads that Flanders had gathered ahead of time and inquiring at local stores and post offices, Brown was able to capture on cylinders samples of a rich singing tradition already on the wane in New England. Flanders and Brown's jointly edited *Vermont Folk Songs and Ballads* was published in 1931 and featured a wide range of local and imported songs. Barry and Eckstorm, following the example of Flanders and Brown, made extensive use of recording equipment in the early 1930s, generating some 180 cylinders. Although Barry died suddenly in 1937, his *Maine Woods Songster* was published posthumously in 1939. Meanwhile, Flanders took on an indefatigable assistant,

Marguerite Olney, and devoted the next three decades to collecting New England folk music. Together, Flanders and Olney recorded hundreds of ballads and songs from singers in all six New England states and published several volumes. Alan Lomax from the Library of Congress visited with Flanders in 1939 and obtained her help in recording numerous disks, including the first substantial collection of New England fiddle tunes, for the Archive of Folk Song in Washington, D.C.

The 1930s gave rise to a national recreational folk-dance movement, and folk festivals created new opportunities for the public presentation of folk music. In 1937 Ralph Page and Beth Tolman published *The Country Dance Book*. A New Hampshire dance caller, Page traveled widely in New England and beyond during the 1940s and 1950s, calling, teaching, and recording squares, quadrilles, and contra dances. Eloise Linscott's *Folk Songs of Old New England* appeared in 1939, containing songs, ballads, children's games, and dance tunes gathered in Massachusetts, Maine, and New Hampshire.

Beginning in the 1940s the increased availability of recording equipment and a growing interest in folklore caused the ranks of collectors to swell. Alan Lomax and Sidney Robertson Cowell made recordings of songs and fiddle tunes played by Carrie Grover of Gorham, Maine, in 1941. Eloise Linscott continued to collect material, making several trips in particular to northern New England. Folk performers Frank and Anne Warner gathered an impressive storehouse of songs from Lena Bourne Fish in New Hampshire. Horace Beck collected songs and lore in Maine during the late 1940s and later published some of his finds in *The Folklore of Maine* (1957). Gale Huntington's *Songs the Whalemen Sang* (1964) featured many New Bedford and Nantucket songs compiled from 19th-century manuscript sources. In 1978 Paul Wells produced an important documentary album, *New England Traditional Fiddling*, that featured various fiddling styles with extensive background notes. Dudley Laufman has remained a major figure as a dance caller and musician since the 1950s and has undertaken extensive research on 20th-century dance musicians in New Hampshire. Since the late 1950s Edward D. "Sandy" Ives has made a specialty of studying woods songs from Maine and the Canadian Maritime Provinces. In books such as *Larry Gorman: The Man Who Made the Songs* (1964) and *Joe Scott: The Woodsman-Songmaker* (1978), Ives has been able to show the considerable influence of individual song makers on a regional repertory. Margaret MacArthur has been an avid collector, researcher, and performer of the traditional songs of Vermont

since moving there in the late 1940s; her ongoing appearances in schools and concerts continue to increase public appreciation for New England's ballad-singing tradition. A list of additional musicians, collectors, and presenters deserving mention would fill many pages.

The intellectual and artistic climate of Boston and Cambridge, Mass., in the 1960s gave rise to a dynamic coffeehouse scene where folk-revival performers such as Joan Baez, Tom Rush, Patrick Sky, Eric Anderson, Jim Rooney, Maria Muldaur, and many others got their start as successful entertainers. During the 1980s a second revival occurred, making the Boston-Cambridge area a mecca for singer-songwriters. Rounder Records, which now features one of the country's largest catalogs of "roots" music recordings, is still based in Cambridge, Mass., where it was launched in the early 1970s. Predating Rounder is Folk Legacy Records, founded in Vermont in 1961 by Sandy and Caroline Paton and now well established in Connecticut.

Today, folklore societies, living-history museums, and state-sponsored arts organizations can be found throughout New England. New archival collections such as the Irish Music Archives at Boston College now complement older archives such as the Flanders Ballad Collection at Middlebury College and the Northeast Archives of Folklore and Oral History at the University of Maine. Folk arts coordinators at these centers are too numerous to name individually, but they have done a superb job of documenting, presenting, preserving, and encouraging participation in New England's various streams of folk music.

Roger D. Abrahams, "Rough Sincerities: William Wells Newell and the Discovery of Folklore in Late-19th Century America," in *Folk Roots, New Roots: Folklore in American Life*, ed. Jane S. Becker and Barbara Franco (1988); Benjamin A. Botkin, *A Treasury of New England Folklore: Stories, Ballads, and Traditions of the Yankee People* (1989 [1947]); *Brave Boys: New England Traditions in Folk Music* [sound recording] (1977); compact disc, 1995); William M. Doerflinger, *Songs of the Sailor and Lumberman*, rev. ed. (1990); Helen Hartness Flanders and Marguerite Olney, *Ballads Migrant in New England* (1953); Jennifer Post Quinn, *An Index to the Field Recordings in the Flanders Ballad Collection at Middlebury College, Middlebury, Vermont* (1983); Jeanne Patten Whitten, *Fannie Hardy Eckstorm: A Descriptive Bibliography*, special issue of *Northeast Folklore* 16 (1975).

Steve Green

Dolls In colonial New England, dolls were scarce. The labor-intensive economy, a rigid Puritanical doctrine, and the association of "poppets" with the supernatural restricted play among 17th-century New England children to handmade wood and corncob dolls made from materials native to the region. The doll population increased among children of the colonial elite over the course of the 18th century as the Enlightenment influenced child-rearing ideals and increased international trade and the declining influence of the church gave rise to manufacturers, merchandise, and markets. At the forefront of these changes were prosperous sea captains in Salem, Mass., who transported British and French "babies," adult-looking wooden dolls with peg joints, glass eyes, and flax or human-hair wigs, to the shores of New England.

By the early 19th century growing markets, the rise of the "new" middle class, and the doctrine of domesticity were fueling the international doll economy. The cult of true womanhood and the sanctioning of play by educational theorists led to a surge in dolls. Toy shops in New England sold elegantly dressed and wasp-waisted dolls with china, papier-mâché, or wax heads. Made from a costly combination of cloth, wax, kid leather, and wood, these fragile German, French, and English imports were often kept out of the hands of children. Fearing that refined dolls from abroad could promote political degeneracy at home, antebellum experts railed against them. In order to instill democratic values and domestic skills, some authors of household compendiums promoted doll *making*.

Changing notions of play, decreasing family size, and an expanding consumer culture gave rise to a golden age of dolls. Beginning in the 1860s, manufacturers in France and Germany flooded toy and department stores with hard "composition" dolls with breakable bisque, or unglazed porcelain, heads. Romanticized representations of Victorian women and idealized girls and babies were dressed in up-to-date continental fashions. Far less costly than these were palm-sized dolls made of unglazed white china. These stiff dolls were called Frozen Charlottes after Fair Charlotte from a Vermont ballad about a vain young woman who froze to death.

In rural New England manufacturers and machinists also produced dolls. In Springfield, Vt., Joel Addison Hartley Ellis (1830–98), an inventor and carriage manufacturer, used the region's abundant waterpower, timber (rock maple), and labor and adapted local whittling traditions to produce flexible, durable wooden dolls with metal hands and feet. Hit by the depression of 1873, however, Ellis's venture failed after one year. The hard and heavy wooden dolls Ellis and his successors made were just as unpopular as breakable bisques among many mothers toward the end of the 19th century. Drawing on the domestic values of her antebellum girlhood and Progressive Era concerns about children, Martha Jenks Wheaton Chase (1851–1925) invented

soft and safe "stockinet" dolls, which women workers produced at the M. J. Chase Company in Pawtucket, R.I., for girls *and* boys worldwide.

Chase was not unusual among inventors and manufacturers of dolls—Arnold Print Works is another example—many of whom drew on New England's textile tradition to produce dolls in the 20th century. Johnny Gruelle secured patents for Raggedy Ann (1915) and Raggedy Andy (1920), and his family manufactured the popular playthings in a shirt factory in Norwalk, Conn. During the Depression the Anamay Doll Company produced cloth dolls in Woburn, Mass., and Barbara Annalee Davis launched what became a highly successful doll-making business in Meredith, N.H. While these ventures sprang from New England soil, Coleco, the Connecticut Leather Company, purchased the rights to manufacture the Cabbage Patch Kids from a Georgian doll designer in the early 1980s. In 1984 women and children purchased 20 million of the baby dolls inspired by Martha Chase's creations and marketed to appeal to a maternalistic ethos.

Dorothy S. Coleman, Elizabeth A. Coleman, and Evelyn J. Coleman, *The Collector's Encyclopedia of Dolls*, 2 vols. (1968–86); Miriam Formanek-Brunell, *Made to Play House: Dolls and the Commercialization of American Girlhood, 1830–1930* (1993); Inez Bertail McClintock and Marshall McClintock, *Toys in America* (1961); Madeline Osborne Merrill and Richard Merrill, *Dolls and Toys at the Essex Institute* (1976).

Miriam Formanek-Brunell

Foodways Several major elements have helped shape the diet and the complex of activities known as foodways in New England: the geography and climate of the region, the cultivated foods and agricultural techniques of its indigenous peoples, British gastronomic preferences and recreational calendars, Puritan values and sensibilities, and the critical role New England played in American history, along with industrialization, urbanization, and immigration.

Certain foods are readily associated with New England: Boston baked beans served with brown bread, for example; Indian pudding; a boiled dinner of corned beef and cabbage; chowders of various kinds; and johnnycakes, a form of cornbread. Some foods are linked with specific states—Vermont maple syrup, Maine lobsters and blueberries, and Rhode Island shore dinners or clambakes on the beach—while others are connected to certain times of year, such as salmon dinners with peas on the Fourth of July. Thanksgiving—the closest thing that Americans have to a national meal—is the best-known example of

the latter category and inextricably interweaves turkey, cranberries, and pumpkin pie in the popular imagination with Pilgrims, Indians, the harvest season, and New England.

In sharp contrast to the usual images of Thanksgiving abundance, the British settlers, who generally lacked farming and fishing skills and failed in their first attempts to grow wheat, found life extremely hard in New England: nearly half the population of Plymouth Colony died during the first year of settlement. To survive, the colonists increasingly turned to their Native American neighbors, who introduced them to a host of previously unknown foodstuffs and to the agricultural techniques for their successful cultivation. The Indian triad of corn, beans, and squash, most important among these new foods, was quickly integrated into the colonists' culinary repertoire. Two hybrid results were "Rye-and-Indian," a coarse bread coupling the familiar British rye with the meal of the new grain, corn; and succotash, which called for corn to be stewed with beans and was consumed as a vegetable rather than a grain.

A wealth of aquatic resources was also near at hand. In 1602 the English explorer Bartholomew Gosnold had conferred the name Cape of Cod on the fish-hooked peninsula in southeastern Massachusetts because of the prevalence of that fish, which steadily became such a reliable source of prosperity for the Commonwealth that in the 1700s the "sacred cod" was identified as a symbol of Massachusetts; a carved wooden cod hangs in the statehouse in Boston to this day. The "abundance of Sea-Fish . . . almost beyond beleeving" that Francis Higginson reported at Salem, Mass., in 1630 affected not only the diet but also the culture of the region, shaping its occupational patterns, industrial development, economy, and symbolic systems.

As food supplies stabilized, English recreational patterns reasserted themselves—sporting activities, agrarian festivals, and tavern life prominent among them—joined by such new occasions as Election Day and Training Day, when the colonial militia drilled; each special day became associated with certain foods and feasting behaviors. Particularly prominent in the developing calendar of food events were the Puritan-sanctioned communal harvest sessions that merged work with play and eating, the so-called bees for apple paring, sugaring off, salt haying, and corn husking. Over time weekly menus also developed in the region, in which chowders appeared early in the week, boiled dinners in the middle, and leftovers toward the end. Saturday was fish day—which distinguished Puritans from members of the Church of England, who fasted on Friday—as well as baking day, with baked beans

Demonstrating Yankee cooking at the Smithsonian Folklife Festival, 1999

and brown bread the most common evening meal. Sunday, with its prohibitions against Sabbath work, usually featured leftover codfish and beans.

By the mid-1700s public dining had proliferated in New England, mixing marketing activities, fund-raising opportunities, and, increasingly, political rallies. In the years leading up to and following the American Revolution, ever increasing numbers of people took to celebrating the uniqueness of the indigenous American culture and its history with food, in Forefathers' Day banquets, "Indian-style" clambakes, and harvest-home feasts, heavily investing these meals with national symbolism. In 1796 Joel Barlow, a member of the group of young writers known as the Connecticut Wits whose aim was to create a national literature, offered up his mock epic poem *The Hasty Pudding* ("I sing the sweets I know,/the charms I feel,/My morning incense,/and my evening meal"), equating New England with cornmeal mush, as an act of literary patriotism. In that same year the new nation's first cookbook was also published, Amelia Simmons's *American Cookery*, which featured for the first time in print such novelties (and regional New England favorites) as slapjacks, Rye 'n' Injun, Election cake, "cramberry" sauce, and pumpkin pie.

New England's high rate of literacy, especially among its women—a by-product of the Puritan insistence on direct access to the Word of God—exerted a growing influence on the region's foodways and dictated to a large extent not only what New Englanders ate and felt they should eat but also what oth-

ers outside the region believed them to eat. During the early to mid-1800s New England's female authors and readers flooded the literary market, producing and consuming a literature largely defined by its domestic focus, from advice books on household management by Lydia Maria Child and Catharine Beecher to the novels of Harriet Beecher Stowe and, later, Sarah Orne Jewett. The women's magazines that emerged at midcentury carried the menus, recipes, and household philosophy of New England as regular features for their national readership, and newspapers, general periodicals, and even farm journals soon followed suit.

Since early Puritan times food in New England had been associated with moral issues; during the 19th century this affiliation took explicit forms. Sylvester Graham—whose health-food reform practices were adopted by some of New England's most radical intentional communities, such as Brook Farm, Fruitlands, and some of the Shaker settlements—was a vigorous advocate of wholegrain flours and touted New England's tradition of bread making as a sacred responsibility. The Boston Cooking School, which helped to further disseminate information about New England's cuisine across the country through its graduates and the widely popular cookbooks of its various directors—Mary Lincoln, Maria Parloa, and Fanny Farmer—was founded in 1879 on the principle that cooking could and should be made more scientific to promote greater social welfare.

A related project, the New England Kitchen, initiated in Boston in 1890, sought to

use "scientific eating" to feed the working poor. Although failing in this mission, it nonetheless established the nation's first school lunch program and led directly to the 1908 founding of the American Home Economics Association, whose goal was to bring proper nutrition to the entire nation. It is interesting to note that many of the same women who had helped found the American Folklore Society in 1888 were among those involved in these philanthropic food-reform activities.

By the second half of the 19th century the Industrial Revolution had affected every aspect of life in New England, and the greater quantities of and accessibility to foodstuffs required by the cities and factory towns helped spur scientific and technological advances in safer canning techniques, the development of refrigeration, and the improvement of transportation systems. At the same time a new concept of leisure was giving rise to summer resorts, popular amusements, sporting events, and commercial eating establishments throughout the region, all of which served to promote New England's food as a commercial and cultural commodity—the more "authentic," the better. By the late 19th century the once distinctive regional New England cuisine existed as much in the antimodernist, nostalgic local-color literature and tourist brochures as it did in Yankee kitchens.

The population of New England, which before the 1800s consisted almost exclusively of Native Americans, English immigrants, and African slaves, had by the middle of the 19th century expanded to include Irish immigrants and Acadians from French Canada, as well as Scandinavians, central European Jews, eastern Europeans, and Mediterraneans. By the turn of the century in the Yankee stronghold of Boston approximately one-third of the population was foreign-born. Diverse ethnic groups drawn by different occupational opportunities brought with them their own gastronomic traditions, foods, and distinctive foodways, with the result that transplanted Italians in Connecticut, Rhode Island, Massachusetts, and Vermont or Irish, French, and native populations in New Hampshire, Vermont, and Maine literally affected the flavor of the region.

Like the 17th-century colonists before them, to survive and thrive these new pilgrims have had to—and will continue to have to—adopt new foods and food customs at the same time as they preserve and adapt the old. Throughout the 20th century New England's foodways have reflected opposing trends toward the greater uniformity afforded by technology and conglomerate marketing on the one hand and an increasing diversity of ethnic populations and their resurgent desires to express cultural uniqueness on the other. It is an interesting twist that in this context the venerable and once-defining Yankee cuisine has become but one of many ethnic foodways in modern New England.

The American Heritage Cookbook and Illustrated History of American Eating and Drinking (1964); Catharine Beecher, *The American Woman's Home; or, Principles of Domestic Science* (1975 [1869]); Alice Morse Earle, *Customs and Fashions in Old New England* (1968 [1893]); Harvey Green, *Fit for America: Health, Fitness, Sport, and American Society* (1986); Harvey A. Levenstein, *Revolution at the Table: The Transformation of the American Diet* (1988); Kathy Neustadt, *Clambake: A History and Celebration of an American Tradition* (1992); Sandra L. Oliver, *Saltwater Foodways: New Englanders and Their Food, at Sea and Ashore, in the 19th Century* (1995); Laura Shapiro, *Perfection Salad: Women and Cooking at the Turn of the Century* (1986).

Kathy Neustadt

Franco-American Folklife

Contemporary Franco-American folklife in New England has its roots in the western provinces of 16th- and 17th-century France. Transplanted to the North American soil of New France and Acadie—the Micmac name that the French adopted for the region now including New Brunswick, Nova Scotia, and Prince Edward Island—it incorporated elements of Amerindian culture and, later, of other European traditions, particularly from the British Isles.

In 1839, after a failed rebellion against Canada's English majority and with dwindling resources of land to be shared by a swelling population, French Canadians began migrating en masse to the United States. They were attracted by California gold, midwestern mines, and, especially, the mill towns of New England. Through the early decades of the 20th century, textile factories, pulp and paper mills, and shoe shops drew more than a million French Canadians primarily to urban settings. Here folk culture shed much of its agrarian nature, although farming traditions have sometimes been maintained by rural families or North Woods lumbermen. In the 21st century folklife remains essential to an evolving Franco-American culture.

Music may be the form of folklife that has best survived the migrations of French-speaking Canadians to and around North America. Some of the tunes sung today in New England came to New France on the lips of explorers sent by Louis XIII. Others have more recent origins in Canada or the United States. Traditional instruments, whether native to Canada or borrowed from other traditions, include the fiddle, the button accordion, the harmonica, the jaw harp, and—for keeping time—spoons, bones, and wooden clogs.

Many a Franco-American mother has rocked her baby to sleep with favorite lullabies dating back hundreds of years, such as "A la claire fontaine" (By the clear stream). The Franco-American folk songs we know today come from two distinct but overlapping sources. The first group, though occasionally set down in handwritten notebooks, has remained primarily oral, which makes them difficult subjects of research. The others were codified in a widely disseminated series titled *La Bonne Chanson* (The good song), compiled by Charles-Emile Gadbois and first published in 1938. Not surprisingly, the first group tends to be more bawdy, with drinking songs and tales of clerical impropriety being among the favorites. The Saint John River valley of northern Maine in particular hosts a long but disappearing tradition of *complaintes,* rather monotone lamentations on the trials and tribulations of life sung in a minor key.

La Bonne Chanson, on the other hand, had the logo "A home where people sing is a happy home." These wholesome family songs of old bore the seal of approval of the Roman Catholic Church. The songbooks, more than 30 million of which were distributed, were generally mandated in Franco-American parochial schools throughout New England until the early 1970s. The most popular songs from the collection today celebrate nature ("Gai lon la, gai le rosier"), love ("Isabeau s'y promène"), faith ("Le Credo du paysan"), legends ("Il était un petit navire"), nonsense ("Boumbari-boum-boum-babari"), tradition ("La Bénédiction"), the old country ("En passant par la Lorraine"), and good times ("Chevaliers de la Table Ronde"). Despite its censored content, *La Bonne Chanson* remains to this day the most accessible source of French-Canadian folk music.

Where there was music, dancing was never far behind. For many years after the migration to New England, Saturday night meant moving all the furniture out of the kitchen for a dance. From jigs to reels to quadrilles, dance traditions flourished. They live on today in the soirée, which can be either a family-centered, relatively spontaneous affair or professionally organized.

The saying "Qui perd sa langue perd sa foi" (Lose your language and you lose your faith), promoted in particular by parish priests, was the watchword of earlier generations. The slogan encapsulates a once powerful force among Franco-American New Englanders, urging them to preserve their French as the mainstay of their culture and the Roman Catholic faith as it had been practiced in Canada. Their language, from an older continental tradition but universally understandable, evolved in North America in response to New World realities

and often in a tug-of-war with English. But traditional linguistic elements are still much in evidence today, whether in the realm of vocabulary—*échelle* (ladder), for example, is the word for stairs—or pronunciation.

Franco-American speech in New England, unlike the Cajun dialect of ethnic cousins isolated for many generations in the bayou country of Louisiana, benefited from parochial schools in which French was the language of instruction for half of every school day. Franco-American New Englanders also maintained closer contact with the French-speaking world because of the proximity of Canada and occasional migration from France, especially by religious communities brought in to teach in the schools.

Traditional tales and oral history have been prominent features of Franco-American folklife in New England. Raconteurs were accorded a special place in the agrarian and hunting society of French Canada. Their tradition, inexpensive entertainment, came with them to New England. Emile Lévesque of Augusta, Maine, whose family had migrated from Trois-Pistoles, Quebec, inherited his extensive repertoire of tales from his father. In 1968 and again in the mid-1990s the Northeast Archives of Folklore and Oral History at the University of Maine made recordings of Lévesque telling tales of fabulous creatures and events. Among the most popular was "La Chasse-galerie," in which a high-spirited—and well-lubricated—group of lumberjacks ask the devil to endow them with the power to fly home on New Year's Eve for an all-night celebration with their girlfriends and wives. When after an astonishing series of adventures the revelers are found in the depths of the forest at dawn, their companions strongly suspect that the previous evening's events had more to do with drink than with the devil. Lévesque has since passed away, as the venerable folk genre he practiced is itself in the process of doing. With it will be lost a tradition sometimes dating all the way back to 17th-century France.

Although storytelling in the classic manner is on the wane, oral history survives. Older Franco-Americans can still relate the story of migration, establishment in New England, and work in the mills. Those in their 50s and 60s can recall and speak of life in the heyday of Franco-American schools and groups. Genealogists are creating a whole new approach to storytelling based on civil and church records. Genealogical societies, found in most New England states, are among the most vibrant Franco-American organizations in existence today.

Along with food for the spirit must go food for the physical being. Recipes inherited from life in the mill towns and most often passed down from Canada continue to enjoy widespread popularity in the Franco-American community. The best-known and best-loved Franco-American dish is the *tourtière*, a meat pie, which may have as many recipes as cooks. Its common elements are pie crust (with its own variations), meat (most often pork, sometimes in combination with hamburger or veal), some type of binder (potatoes, crackers, or bread crumbs), diced onion, and various spices.

Fresh game was originally a main ingredient in many French Canadian dishes. This tradition continues in the Saint John River valley, where residents still make *sept-pâtes,* a concoction with seven crusts and seven different meats. Pork, although not as popular as it once was, remains a staple of many traditional dishes, whether the *pâté* known in different regions as *guerton, gorton,* or *creton,* among other spellings; the pork roast, whose congealed drippings are spread on toast; *pattes de cochon* (pigs' feet) and *boulettes* (meat balls); *boudin* (blood sausage); salt pork, used to flavor many dishes; or *tête à fromage* (head cheese), made with a pig's head. Estelle Gamache Ross, a specialist in Franco-American foods from Allenstown, N.H., says about the popularity of pork products in Franco-American cuisine: "The pig was cheap to keep; you fed it leftovers." Franco-American foods, unlike their French cousins, are hardy rather than fancy. They were sustenance for loggers and farmers, not dainty meals for city dwellers. Other traditional favorites include *fèves au lard* (beans baked with salt pork), pea soup, crêpes, and—for dessert—*pets-de-soeur* ("nun's farts," deep-fried pastry balls served in maple syrup), and berry, maple syrup, and sugar pies.

As Bernard Genest notes in *Sur bois: Franco-American Woodcarvers of Northern New England,* a 1996 exhibition catalog published by the Franco-American Centre of Manchester, N.H., "In Québec as in New England, winters are long and harsh and isolation can be difficult to bear." In the Canada of yesteryear, people wore knives on their belts, and wood was everywhere. Whittling was as common to the farmer, fisherman, lumberman, trapper, hunter, and explorer as trees. From utilitarian carving emerged an art form. Subjects were nature, life as it was lived, religious objects, and historical figures. This love of wood and the desire to "allow the form to emerge" was brought by French Canadians to the logging camps and textile mills of New England and passed on to their Franco-American descendants. It continues to thrive, albeit quietly and without fanfare.

Another such tradition, usually but not exclusively practiced by women in the Franco-American community, is textile art. The skills required to fashion clothing, sweaters, mittens, and caps were primarily survival techniques for families exposed to harsh Canadian winters. For most, store-bought clothes had been neither available nor affordable. Migration to New England mill towns meant that ready-made clothes became plentiful, if not within the financial reach of most. But with ample fabric near at hand, spinning and weaving were forsaken. Still, material was used over and over; pieces of cloth called *catalognes* were woven into drapes, bedcovers, or *tapis* (braided rugs). All the while, less functional textile art also flourished in both homes and convents. Cross-stitch, embroidery, crochet, and other forms of needlework decorated both the mundane and the sacred. Convents were often the chosen repository of such talents, while baptismal sets and liturgical items were the beneficiaries. Today's textile artists have often inherited both their ability and their patterns from parents who learned the crafts in Canada.

The sport most closely associated with Franco-Americans is snowshoeing. *Clubs de raquetteurs* (snowshoe clubs), first organized in Canada, were introduced in Franco-American cities throughout New England early in the 20th century. Although their numbers have dwindled, the clubs are still found in the northern states of the region. As snowshoeing becomes an Olympic sport, we should remember that New England's international competitions were forerunners of this winter activity and helped boost its popularity. The region had its share of medalists, some of whom, such as Armand Pinard of the Club Alpin of Manchester, can still tell the story of snowshoeing's heyday. Today's winter outdoor enthusiasts, however, are more likely to travel the wooded hills and valleys of New England into Canada on snowmobiles than snowshoes, Franco-Americans numerous among them.

Family and community customs are at the core of traditional culture. Franco-Americans tend to be very family- and church-centered. They also enjoy coming together in clubs and at social events, many of which stem from religious and seasonal festivities. As is often true for other Americans regardless of religion, Christmas is a high point in Franco-American family life. The Roman Catholic midnight mass is often followed by a traditional home-based celebration called a *réveillon.* At the summer solstice in June comes the Saint-Jean-Baptiste, the feast of John the Baptist, patron saint of French Canadians and Franco-Americans. Today Quebecois mark the day as something of a *fête nationale,* or national holiday. Less grandiose than in earlier generations, when parades with marching bands and floats, dances, and bonfires or fireworks were held in most Franco-American communities, celebrations of the day are still quite common. The elements of Saint John's Day—food, dance, and fire—date from a pre-Christian era. Franco-Americans in Manchester made the holiday an institution well over a century and a quarter ago. Among other locations, festivals of one kind or another can usually be found sometime in the summer in urban centers where the Franco-American presence is strong: Woonsocket, R.I.; Hartford; Lowell and Worcester, Mass.; Barre, Vt.; Manchester and Berlin, N.H.; and Biddeford, Lewiston, Augusta, and Madawaska, Maine.

Academic efforts to honor and preserve Franco-American culture in the region include the Franco-American Studies program of the University of Maine at Orono, which features courses in a broad range of subjects that pertain to the experience of Mainers and other New Englanders of French Canadian ancestry. The same campus also houses the Franco-American Centre, which aims to link the university and the Franco-American community. Among its many cultural offerings are *Le Forum,* a bilingual periodical published six times a year. The University of Maine at Augusta offers a course titled Franco-American Women, while the Fort Kent campus of that system is home to the Acadian Archives. The Franco-American Women's Institute, which aims to record and preserve the voices of Franco-American women in Maine and beyond, is affiliated with all campuses of the University of Maine. The Lowell (Mass.) Folklife Project of the American Folklife Center houses, among other things, artifacts related to the Franco-American experience in that textile city.

Traditional sayings and beliefs still pepper the speech of older Franco-Americans. But, as is generally the case among other ethnic groups, the wisdom they encapsulate rarely dictates the decisions of contemporary life. Franco-Americans are still a devoutly religious people. Particularly in the older generation, faith remains anchored in the liturgical practices of the Roman Catholic Church. Shrines such as Notre-Dame-de-Grâces in Colebrook, N.H., and Our Lady of La Salette in Enfield, N.H., and Attleboro, Mass., attract numerous worshipers. A younger generation, not always in agreement with church doctrine and teaching, nevertheless carries the tradition of a people with deeply spiritual roots.

Normand R. Beaupré, *L'Enclume et le couteau: The Life and Work of Adelard Coté, Folk Artist* (1982); Gerard J. Brault, *The French-Canadian Heritage in New England* (1986); Armand Chartier, *Histoire des Franco-Américains de la Nouvelle-Angleterre, 1775–*

1990 (1991); Dyke Hendrikson, *Quiet Presence* (1980); Betty A. Lausier Lindsay, *Nothing Went to Waste in Grandmother's Kitchen* (1981); Julien Olivier, *D'la boucane: Une Introduction au folklore Franco-American de la Nouvelle-Angleterre* (1979); Julien Olivier and Michael Parent, *Of Kings and Fools: Stories of the French Tradition in North America* (1996); Claire Quintal, ed., *Steeples and Smokestacks: A Collection of Essays on the Franco-American Experience in New En*gland (1996); Quintal, *Le Patrimoine folklorique des Franco-Américains* (1986).

Julien Olivier

Heroes and Villains

Heroes and villains incarnate or transgress a society's ideals in an out-of-the-ordinary way. Their biographies tend to be fluid, preserving what we wish to remember and eliminating what we do not. As this process goes on, such individuals attract anecdotes, tales, and motifs from similar figures of other times and places as if by centrifugal force. Indian Sam Hyde, for example, who allegedly hid behind trees to shoot deer in Danversport and Dedham, Mass., and by curving his rifle killed 60 pigeons on a branch with one shot, also lured to himself stories once told of the legendary Baron Munchausen and later of scouts in the American West.

Heroes and villains, along with the feats they accomplish, are larger than life; they are more skilled, more vigorous, more cunning, stronger, faster, or smarter than the rest of us. The African-born slave Venture Smith, who earned his freedom and widespread respect in late-18th-century Connecticut, was a towering man of huge physical strength and is said to have weighed 300 pounds. John Chapman of Leominster, Mass., better known as Johnny Appleseed, walked thousands of miles in the young American nation, planting countless fruit trees throughout the Midwest. The ever-anonymous Yankee Trader, like his British ancestor, hung about taverns, village stores, and fairs making slick deals, playing tricks, inventing contraptions, and outwitting local yokels. Phineas T. Barnum, a Connecticut Yankee who supposedly lived by the motto "There's a sucker born every minute," made and lost fabulous sums from frauds and performers as disparate as the midget Tom Thumb, the soprano Jenny Lind, and a circus that still survives today.

The fine line between heroes and villains is shown by Connecticut's Benedict Arnold, whose name has come to be a synonym for traitor. Having been a patriot officer for several years, Arnold made an aborted attempt in 1780 to turn the fort at West Point, N.Y., over to the British and then fled behind enemy lines, where he was given a Redcoat command. There were mitigating circumstances, however, and Americans might have been kinder to his name. Arguably the Americans'

best line general, crucial in the victory over Burgoyne at Saratoga, N.Y., Arnold had been unfairly passed over for promotion and, in 1779, had married the lovely, persuasive Peggy Shippen, an ardent loyalist. Many colonists, moreover, saw the armed struggle with the British as a rebellion against government abuses, not a war of independence. But Arnold had been our man, and he did us wrong. As the new nation emerged from its colonial past, Americans treated him mercilessly.

Paul Revere, by contrast, from the same historical era, might be seen as the quintessential folk hero, whose feats are often immortalized in musical ballads or narrative poems. Revere's "midnight ride" of April 18, 1775, to warn Boston-area residents—and Lexington minutemen—that British troops were on the way, was etched forever on the national memory, with less than scrupulous historical accuracy, by Henry Wadsworth Longfellow in 1863. A silversmith with some formal schooling when he made his famous ride, Revere manufactured gunpowder during the war. Once the Revolution ended, he expanded his industrial activities, thus becoming one of the first to take advantage of what the new nation would pride itself on being—a land of opportunity for all.

Often the New England hero—or heroine—has thrown off the shackles of oppression. For example, Elizabeth Freeman, an African American woman from Sheffield, Mass., known as Mum Bett, was the first slave in the United States to be legally set free from her masters. Her mistress, Mrs. John Ashley, struck Freeman one day with a hot kitchen shovel, and Freeman appealed to Stockbridge attorney Theodore Sedgwick. Thanks to Sedgwick and a 1780 Massachusetts law allowing slaves to sue their owners, a county court in 1783 granted Mum Bett her freedom. The precedent established by that case eventually led to the abolition of slavery throughout the Commonwealth. After working many years for the Sedgwicks and serving as a sought-after nurse midwife, Freeman died in 1829. Her remains lie in the old Stockbridge burial ground.

Ida Lewis, the daughter of a 19th-century Rhode Island lighthouse keeper, attained hero status after her father fell seriously ill, leaving Ida to take care of the lighthouse, her father, and several school-age siblings on her own. Every weekday Lewis rowed the children from the island lighthouse to the mainland in a heavy wooden boat that few women of the era would even have tried to operate. Her boating and swimming skills were such that over the course of the 39 years she spent tending the beacon at Lime Rock, Lewis saved no fewer than 18 lives, and possibly more—the

last one at age 63. The following year, she became a lifetime beneficiary of the Carnegie Hero Fund, which assured her a good monthly pension. A *Harper's Weekly* article on Lewis questioned whether rowing boats was an appropriate feminine activity but concluded that only a "donkey" would consider it unfeminine to pull drowning people from the drink. The night Lewis died, in 1911, all the ships in Newport Harbor tolled their bells in tribute.

These days, heroes are harder to find. The media explosion of the 20th century, and the advent of the Information Age, makes and breaks them with numbing regularity. A notable New England villain in the 1980s was the wealthy Newport, R.I., socialite Claus von Bülow, who was convicted, and then acquitted, of trying to murder his hypoglycemic wife with injections of insulin (she remains in a coma). His aristocratic lifestyle and personal arrogance made von Bülow an icon of 1980s excess.

Contemporary heroes tend to be sports figures, such as baseball greats Carl Yastrzemski and Ted Williams and Olympic figure skater Nancy Kerrigan. Or they may be politicians, such as Maine's Margaret Chase Smith, who spoke out boldly against McCarthyism during the early 1950s, and George Mitchell, the architect of peace in Northern Ireland during the late 1990s. But the relentless and unforgiving scrutiny to which figures in the public eye are subject leaves few reputations untarnished. Had John Fitzgerald Kennedy, a bona fide New England hero, occupied the White House in the 1990s instead of the 1960s, public perceptions of this charismatic leader with a roving eye would probably have been quite different from what they were during his shortened lifetime.

One thing is nonetheless certain: heroes and villains come and go, with few of them surviving over many generations. Today, many specialists don't even know the name and exploits of Sam Hyde or Venture Smith or Ida Lewis, and fewer and fewer of us remember revolutionary heroes like Nathan Hale or Ethan Allen. Perhaps that is Benedict Arnold's ultimate revenge: we still know who he was.

Horace P. Beck, *The Folklore of Maine* (1957); Benjamin A. Botkin, *A Treasury of New England Folklore: Stories, Ballads, and Traditions of the Yankee People* (1947); Mary Louise Clifford and Candace Clifford, *Women Who Kept the Lights: An Illustrated History of Female Lighthouse Keepers* (2001); Tristram Potter Coffin, *Uncertain Glory: Folklore and the American Revolution* (1971).

Tristram Potter Coffin

Hunting and Trapping

When the first permanent European settlers arrived in New England, they soon discovered that they

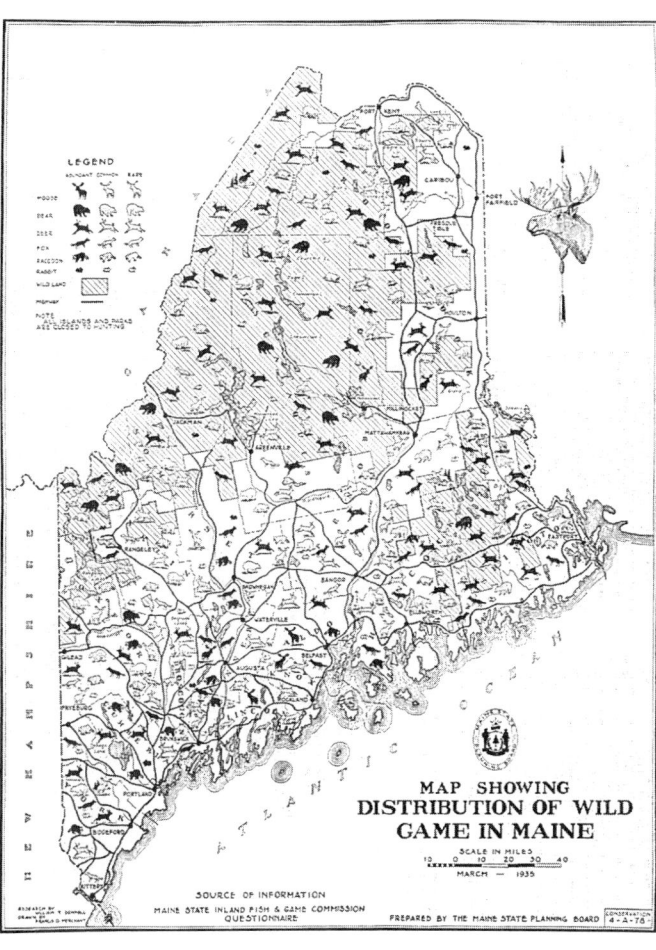

Map showing distribution of wild game in Maine, 1935

of the 18th century greatly expanded the number of traps trappers could set and the kinds of creatures they could catch. These devices varied in size, from the huge bear trap with its spiked jaws requiring a crank to open, to very small ones to catch weasels. Basic to these traps was the choice of a place to set them, the choice of bait, the erection of the "cubby" device to steer the animal over the trap, and, if possible, a way to ensure that it did not escape when the trapped leg went numb and the animal gnawed or twisted it off. This was accomplished by setting the trap in a place where the animal would fall into water and drown or be suspended in air.

Trapping season typically began after deer season. At one time, it was not uncommon for trappers to have a "territory," sometimes miles in length, that they considered their own. Trappers would go to their camps in the woods, usually alone, occasionally with another trapper, and tend their traps from there all winter. Nearly every trapper had personal secret devices or tricks they used to disguise their traps in order to eliminate human scent and tracks. The scents they used to lure animals were concocted from secret family recipes onto which they attached their own ideas and passed them to their children. Until recently, trapping was a common pastime for farm boys who might run a trapline in the winter as an escape from normal activities and as a means to raise a little money to buy things they otherwise could not have. In rural areas, farmers and loggers still often trap as a part-time occupation to increase their income; it is not unusual for a casual trapper to make an extra $2,000 to $3,000 a year with pelts. Today the professional trapper in New England is not a rarity.

A successful hunter had added status within a community. An early courting song began, "The first thing you say [is] I killed a deer." Nearly every town had a gunsmith, some of whom eventually became famous; Remington, Winchester, Colt, Smith and Wesson, and others such as Henry and A. Kendall from Vermont made valuable guns that still work today. The manufacture of fine hunting rifles and shotguns is still a specialty in New England, with such firms as O. F. Mossberg and Sons, Sturm, Ruger and Company, and the Marlin Firearms Company, as well as a host of smaller manufacturers and gunsmiths.

Hunting was divided into several categories: the hunting of big game such as deer, bear, moose, and caribou; "varmints," such as cougar, wolf, and fox; small game, such as rabbits and squirrels; and birds, which broke down into upland birds and waterfowl. One went "hunting" for big game; "birding" or "shooting" for woodcock, quail, partridge, and turkey; and "gunning" for waterfowl.

would have to know how to hunt and trap if they were to survive. Of course, hunting and trapping lifeways had already been established by the native peoples. The newcomers, unprepared for a frontier experience, were fortunate to be able to rely on such knowledge and skills, as hunting and trapping were essential not only to procure food, but also to protect them from predators and help them pursue their businesses, which included the exporting of fur.

The fur trade attracted European explorers and then settlers to New England. The trade in beavers, for instance, was especially lucrative because their fur produced high-quality felt for fashionable hats in the London market. But many of the animals in North America and the techniques needed to trap them were not familiar to the settlers. They therefore had to depend on the native population, first to bring in pelts and later to train them in trapping techniques. While trapping was basically to procure pelts for sale, it was also essential for survival. Skins, fur, and flesh were used for clothing and food. Also, settlers' flocks, fowl, and gardens were a source of food for a horde of "varmints": skunks, weasels, raccoons, porcupines, woodchucks, mink, foxes,

wolves, bear, bobcat, and cougar, to say nothing of the domestic supply of food. Even deer and rabbits posed a threat to a kitchen garden.

The earliest trapping devices were snares, deadfalls, box traps, monkey-puzzle traps, or spears launched by releasing a trigger. Snares were of two sorts, one set from a bent sapling that would spring tight when an animal stuck its head through to get the bait. The deadfall was simply a cul-de-sac with a heavy weight above it balanced on a baited trigger. When an animal took the bait, the trigger would dislodge and the creature would be pinned or crushed by the weight. The box trap was similar, except that a door would fall behind the victim and it could not escape. The monkey puzzle was made by placing bait inside a small hole in a log or a tree and driving two or three beaver teeth into the hole on an angle. The quarry would stick its head or paw in for the bait and would impale itself on the teeth when it tried to withdraw. Snares were strong enough to take deer, and one even caught Massachusetts's Governor Winthrop's horse. Deadfalls could be made with heavy logs or boulders forming the "cubby," and they often were permanent fixtures built to squash a bear.

The introduction of leghold traps at the end

In a puritanical society where play and sport were frowned upon, an individual could find a legitimate respite from daily cares by going afield with a gun. But hunting had added significance. In Europe, hunting had long been the sole property of the aristocracy. The king owned the deer and the swans, and it was a capital offense to take one. In New England anyone could hunt, and this gave the bourgeoisie a feeling of superiority not shared by those at home. The only contemporary equivalent to aristocratic hunting in New England is found at the Blue Mountain Forest Association, or Corbin Park, a 10,000-acre private preserve in New Hampshire stocked with big game. Most New England hunters support traditions of open lands for hunting in the forest commons.

Another aspect of hunting was that hunters learned to handle themselves in the wilderness: to know where they were, to survive bad weather, to recognize and track animals, to move about quietly, and to demonstrate courage and endurance. These traits proved invaluable to settlers when confronting hostile Native Americans, from whom such skills were originally learned, and later helped them defeat British forces. As dependence on game for food became less necessary, beginning around the turn of the 20th century, hunting developed into a recreational subculture. But some New Englanders living in rural areas still depend on game to supplement their stringent diets, harvesting it any way they can. In Maine hunters often donate game to food pantries and soup kitchens.

Hunting developed its own set of rituals, which could be practiced at hunting camps that were set up in rural areas or on marshes, sometimes less than a mile from home. Here a group of people would congregate every year to hunt. They "went into deer camps" or "to camp" for birds. In some rural areas of Maine, New Hampshire, and Vermont today, all but essential business stops for deer season; schools might be closed for "opening day"; and young and old hunters repair to camp, where youth learn how to conduct themselves in the woods, discover how to live in primitive conditions, and master woodcraft. They listen to stories of past hunts and of the archetypal deer that got away, to humorous tales about the mistakes both hunters and quarry make, to accounts about remarkable shots, and so on. They learn how to make and use lures to entice game and, for a short time at the beginning of winter, generally re-create a semblance of the way of life of their ancestors. In these camps horseplay and tradition intermix. In European traditions dating to the Middle Ages, hunters who missed the buck had their shirttails cut off; a youth who killed a first deer

was anointed with its blood and sometimes ate of the raw liver.

Similar traditions and rituals existed for fowling, especially water fowling. People traveled great distances to spend a week hunting grouse and woodcock in Vermont and New Hampshire and ducks and geese in Maine and the salt marshes along the entire New England coast—especially on Cape Cod and Merrymeeting Bay in Maine. Shooting birds was more complex than hunting big game because there were more varieties, each with singular characteristics. And whereas hunting deer, caribou, and moose primarily involved either stalking or waiting for the game to pass, bird shooting required various breeds of hunting dogs—including spaniels, pointers, setters, tollers, Chesapeake and Labrador retrievers—to find the quarry and retrieve it, plus scores of devices or calls to lure birds to the gun. For waterfowl there was the matter of bait, blinds, and decoys, both live and artificial: a sinkbox, a sneakbox, a pit blind, a stone blind, or a brush blind, to mention a few. Clothing for hunting birds varied more widely than that for hunting big game. Types of guns and boats also varied. The punt gun, for instance, was a small cannon capable of firing a pound or so of shot and killing a hundred birds at a time after it drifted down on a "raft" or a "bed" of birds, and was used primarily by "market hunters" who sold birds by the barrel to expensive restaurants and hotels in New York and Boston.

Live birds were used to decoy wild flocks and led to the breeding of "call duck" birds small enough to be carried in the coat pocket and the use of "fliers," young Canada geese marked by a leg strap that flew out to the wild flocks and brought them within range. Wooden decoys called blocks were made everywhere, artfully crafted to resemble a live bird and sold for about a dollar apiece during the 1930s. Some decoy makers such as Joe Lincoln and A. Elmer Crowell of Cape Cod or Shang Wheeler of Essex, Conn., produced exceptional blocks; indeed, a Crowell decoy has sold for more than $600,000. Some fowling pieces are presently valued at more than $40,000.

It is interesting to note that these ritualistic aspects of hunting bloomed during the late 19th and early 20th century, at the time that the vast supply of game had begun to become depleted, partly by hunting but considerably more so by other circumstances. Although the passenger pigeon that used to darken the skies was extinct a couple of years after its hunting began, the heath hen died of disease, and the turkey was nearly exterminated by the chestnut tree blight that decimated its habitat. Logging also changed habitats; deer en-

croached on moose, and moose died by disease carried by the deer. As a result, hunters banded together and helped institute laws to preserve game, specifying seasons, bag limits, and weaponry. Fish and game departments began to determine license fees and types of clothing, shot, and decoys to be used.

Hunting and trapping provide a way for some New Englanders to reenter their past and relive in some measure the lives of their ancestors. It allows parents to pass on to their children generations-old skills and secrets. It enables people to interact with nature in a special way that involves reading the wilderness while experiencing the camaraderie of years of shared experience. Whether and how much hunting and trapping will continue is in doubt. Today, most of New England's population is urban, with many people having roots that go back only 50 years or less. Older roots would probably include hunting and trapping as a necessary way of life and lead to an understanding and appreciation of their traditions and uses. Whereas some organizations lobby against traditional aspects of hunting and trapping, others seek to educate the public about the function they play in conserving wildlife species and the traditional lifeways of rural communities. State fish and game departments work to educate the public about the positive function of hunting for the maintenance of healthy herds, especially deer; and environmental writers present a vision—at once new and old—of an ecosystem that supports both communities and hunters and trappers, who consider themselves conservationists of New England's wild places.

William Cronon, *Changes in the Land: Indians, Colonists, and the Ecology of New England* (1983); Jan E. Dizard, *Going Wild: Hunting, Animal Rights, and the Contested Meaning of Nature* (1994); Heritage Plantation of Sandwich, *The Songless Aviary: The World of A. E. Crowell* (1992); Richard William Judd, *Common Lands, Common People: The Origins of Conservation in Northern New England* (1997); John M. Miller, *Deer Camp: Last Light in the Northeast Kingdom* (1992).

Horace P. Beck

Hunting Lore Hunting and trapping confirm several basic human desires, the origins of which are ancient: to provide, to protect, to learn, and to teach. Hunting and trapping, as they occur within the context of country life, entail a close relationship with and passion for the outdoors, the land, the seasons, and animals. Participants in this culture have developed stories and rituals to confirm and perpetuate its values.

In 1794 Samuel Williams described the value that Native Americans in Vermont placed on hunting: "The subsistence and safety of the tribe depended so much upon the hunter and warrior that these became the most necessary, useful, and honorable professions. . . . Eminence in these professions was the surest way to subsistence, to distinction, to honor, and renown." The honor and renown that Williams notes have been part of New England hunting folklore and associated folk arts for centuries. Whether contemporary hunting and trapping traditions are practiced within the remote, coniferous forests of interior northern New England or in more urbanized, less mountainous southern New England, one finds that they are imbued with specific patterns of storytelling and rituals. Within the material culture of those who trap, and particularly those who hunt, are numerous expressive devices based on personal experience. These include an iconography of folk art and crafts, such as paintings of deer and other indigenous wildlife, a hooked rug honoring a child's first deer, incised powder horns or fungi with illustrations of hunting camps; woodcarvings of beavers and bears, decoys, and gunstocks; snapshot albums that identify place, fraternity, family relationships, or animals hunted or trapped; narrative forms such as hunters' journals or logbooks; and poetry, including lyrical ballads portraying relationships between men and deer or men and women. In addition, hunting camp architecture and the interiors of home and camp are often culturally revealing.

Within hunting stories of Native American and European origin are incidents and character types exhibiting a close and respectful relationship among humans, animals, and the environment. These relationships require character traits such as honesty, patience, independence, self-assurance, endurance, inventiveness, and prowess as well as an understanding of the natural world. Because serious hunters and trappers maintain a close relationship with wildlife, many of these stories include human traits that are animal-like, and many contain similar, if not identical, morals.

Hero stories, those about daring and tenacious ridge runners, trackers, sharpshooters, or trappers, often include stereotypical characters with behaviors similar to those of animals. Legendary animal stories include those about the elusive white-tail deer; "Ole' Slew Foot," the deer with one injured leg; "The Whistler," who, when running through the woods emitted a shrill whistle through a bullet hole in his antler; and "The General," a deer of epic proportions in Vermont's fabled Northeast Kingdom.

Human competition stories are also common. A typical story line might involve a shrewd trapper who buys up trapping rights to a large section of watershed unbeknownst to other trappers in the vicinity. Or a competitor

might paint a deer hunter's camp with a salt solution, thus making it inviting to hungry porcupines. In *Deer Camp* (1992), a hunter outsmarts others camp members by lacing the evening's pot of chili with laxative; he quickly dispatches the trophy deer the next morning while other camp members are indisposed in the backhouse. Stories with morals about honesty often include lazy hunters or affluent "flatlanders" who steal another's deer, hunt deer at night using a jacklight, participate in illicit bear hunts, or merely procure their deer through purchase.

Hunting rituals often involve a contemporary form of initiation whereby a boy or girl, at approximately age 12, is taken to a hunting camp or to the woods to hunt for the first time. During this experience, and during hunting excursions, rural youths learn the ways of the outdoors through survival skills, cooperation with others, and the wisdom of elders. Storytelling often provides a context for the young person to understand the significance of this newly gained experience. Within the hunt are specific rituals that signal initiatory activity; for instance, after a young hunter's first kill, an elder (often an uncle or grandfather) will smear the animal's blood on the novitiate's face. In raccoon hunting, when the lead houndsman yells, "tree'd," a youth is expected to climb the tree to pinpoint and kill the raccoon, after which he or she must carry it from the field. With bear or upland and waterfowl hunting, coming of age is often celebrated with the gift of a hound—a setter or retriever puppy—and often a gun, and with it an education in responsibility, use, and care.

Deer hunting, the most popular form of hunting in New England, is often a group or family-related activity. Franco-Americans, for instance, often incorporate the entire family into the hunting ritual. Younger generations whose Franco-American parents and grandparents lived and worked in southern New England mills often return to northern New England, traveling long distances to hunt near the "home place." Future generations will perpetuate stories and lore that have grown around the ancestral hunting camp.

Alphonse H. Gilbert, *Vermont Hunters: Characteristics, Attitude, and Levels of Participation* (1977); Edward Hoagland, "The New England Wilderness," in *Walking the Dead Diamond River* (1970); John M. Miller, *Deer Camp: Last Light in the Northeast Kingdom* (1992); Samuel Williams, *Natural and Civil History of Vermont* (1794).

John M. Miller

Irish American Folklife The Irish can be found in every corner of New England. Nearly 3 million residents, or 20 percent of the region's population, claim Irish ancestry. More

than 26 percent of Massachusetts residents are Irish Americans, the highest state percentage in the nation, and many see Boston as the capital of Irish America.

During the colonial period a significant number of Irish Protestants settled in New England, as evidenced by Irish place-names such as Belfast and Limerick, Maine; Dublin and Londonderry, N.H.; and Orange County, Vt. In 1737 Boston merchants of Irish Protestant descent formed the Charitable Irish Society, the oldest Irish organization in America today.

The Great Potato Famine of 1845–49 brought a steady stream of Irish men and women to New England, most of them Catholic this time. These new Irish immigrants were not always welcome. Discouraged from pursuing certain forms of employment by the prevalent notice "No Irish Need Apply" during the late 19th century, they remained clannish, forming enclaves whose cornerstones were the town hall, the parish, and the pub. While famines, political persecution, and economic hardship drove the Irish to New England, music, dance, their native tongue, and shared sports traditions kept the Irish diaspora cohesive. Relying on a network of religious, political, cultural, and patriotic associations, they eventually forged an easily recognized and often formidable ethnic identity.

Robert Frost's inaugural advice to President John F. Kennedy to "be more Irish than Harvard" recognized the value of what the Irish brought to New England: an earthy, passionate, good-humored mindset that complemented but often competed with the cerebral, stoic outlook of New Englanders of British descent. As the region's first large ethnic minority, the Irish challenged and helped transform the singular Anglo-Saxon culture embedded in New England since the 1600s. They also supplied much of the manual labor, political leadership, and cultural creativity that contributed to the industrial and urban development of the region.

The 19th-century Irish immigrants worked as loggers, domestics, fishermen, canal and railroad builders, and masons, later taking jobs in New England's many shoe and textile factories or paper mills. As time passed and discrimination lessened, they became police officers, politicians, teachers, and lawyers.

Long regarded as a race of storytellers, Irish immigrants brought with them to New England the widely admired skill of conversation, with political rallies and wakes serving as arenas for the Irish gift of gab. Irish picnics during the early 1900s advertised "dancing, athletic events and oratory." Irish wakes often involved entire days of drinking, storytelling, and song. John Fitzgerald, grandfather of

John F. Kennedy, earned the nickname "Honey Fitz" for the mellifluous rendition of "Sweet Adeline" he sang at Irish funerals. Today, professional storytellers such as Jay O'Callaghan and Sharon Kennedy carry on an ancestral tradition, combining Irish American and Celtic themes in performances geared to mainstream audiences. A 24-hour continuous reading of James Joyce's *Ulysses* takes place in Boston every June to commemorate Bloomsday, the anniversary of the day (June 16, 1904) on which the action of the novel takes place. Novelists Edwin O'Connor, George V. Higgins, and James Carroll chronicled the Boston Irish in the 20th century, as Sarah Orne Jewett did in the 19th. Cork-born poet Greg Delanty, now living in Burlington, Vt., has offered an immigrant's insights on New England in the late 20th century in several volumes of poetry.

The popularity of certain aspects of Irish American folklife, the Irish language, for example, tends to ebb and flow. In the 1870s and 1880s Philo-Celtic societies dedicated to the use and preservation of the Irish language formed in New England, inspired by William Butler Yeats's Celtic revival in Ireland. Harvard University offered its first Celtic language course in 1896, and the *Irish Echo,* an Irish-language newspaper, flourished in Boston from 1886 to 1894. In the 1950s Irish oratorical competitions throughout New England drew enthusiastic response and injected vitality into the Irish-speaking community. In the 1980s Irish-language immersion weekends became popular. Today, Irish courses are taught in dozens of colleges and community centers throughout New England, and speakers of Gaelic can be found everywhere from Portland, Maine, to Providence. The lilting rhythm of Irish, superimposed upon American English, has shaped the distinctive speech patterns of Boston, New Hampshire, Maine, and Vermont.

Irish organizations have played an important role in sustaining Irish folklife. As an educated Irish American middle class emerged from earlier generations of impoverished refugees, cultural groups such as the Wild Geese Society in Greenwich, Conn., and the Eire Society in Boston focused the attention of their membership on art, literature, and theater. Fraternal organizations such as the Ancient Order of Hibernians, with a regional membership of 25,000 men and women, emphasized retaining an allegiance to Catholic principles and Ireland's reunification. Clubs representing Ireland's 32 counties, such as the Mayo Society (1905) and the Galway Men's Benevolent Society (1904), continue to flourish. The folk tradition of sending money back to Ireland, initiated during the famine years, has been formalized by philanthropic groups like the American Ireland Fund, the Irish American Partnership, and the John F. Kennedy Trust. The Boston Irish Famine Institute, an offshoot of the city's Irish Famine Memorial, sends food and supplies to famine-ravaged countries in Africa and Asia. Project Children in Connecticut, Between in New Hampshire, and the Cape Cod Irish Children's Program all work to bridge the gap between Catholic and Protestant youth in Northern Ireland.

Organizations such as The Irish Ancestral Research Association (TIARA), formed in Sudbury, Mass., in 1983, have tapped into the growing nationwide popularity of genealogy, stimulating a renewed interest in Irish roots. The Irish Cultural Centre, which opened new facilities in Canton, Mass., in 1999, provides a permanent setting in which Irish Americans may take classes, participate in sporting events, attend concerts, and study their heritage, complementing smaller Irish clubs from Glastonbury and New Haven, Conn., to Lawrence and Springfield, Mass., that keep Irish traditions alive. The 1990s Irish stage extravaganza *Riverdance* spawned a new generation of Irish step dancers, and traditional Irish music can often be heard in local films, commercials, coffeehouses, and concert halls. Irish folk music is a regular feature on radio stations in several of New England's major cities. The radio station WGBH-FM airs the popular Irish-music show *Celtic Sojourn* every weekend, and WROL-AM, also in Boston, broadcasts Irish music throughout the day and evening on Saturdays. Green Linnet Records of Danbury, Conn., has been one of the most important promoters and beneficiaries of North America's fascination with Irish music, often recording such traditional instruments as the fiddle; the tin whistle; the bodhran, a Celtic drum; and the uilleann pipes, or Irish bagpipes.

Sports have played a central role in Irish American folklife. New England has the largest of the 10 North American divisions of the Gaelic Athletic Association, a group formed in Ireland in 1884 to promote ancient sports such as Gaelic football, hurling, camogie, and curragh rowing. Boston was the first American city to hold a Gaelic match under GAA rules in 1886, and it continues to produce exceptional teams that compete nationally. Notable Irish American athletes include James Brendan Connolly of South Boston, who won the triple jump to become the first gold medalist in the first modern Olympics held in Athens in 1896. Nancy Kerrigan was a silver medalist in figure skating in the 1994 Winter Olympics. Beginning in 1929 the legendary runner Johnny Kelly competed in more than 60 Boston marathons, finally sitting out the race at the age of 91 in 1999.

The 150th anniversary of the Irish Potato Famine, commemorated worldwide, prompted many Irish New Englanders to reflect upon their ethnic history and reclaim a connection to it. Yet conflict remains at the core of Irish American identity. Like other European Americans, the Irish contend with Old World values, the urge to assimilate, and the often shallow perceptions of the marketplace and media. Irish Americans have been influenced by disparate strands: an authentic traditional culture replenished by successive generations of immigrants; a hybrid Irish American culture shaped by Hollywood and Broadway; and a pejorative, stereotyped image of the Irish that features fighting drunks and hapless leprechauns.

These strands are apparent in the annual Saint Patrick's Day parades, perhaps America's most public display of ethnic pride. While 19th-century celebrations often featured a show of political muscle and carried strong overtones of Irish nationalism, green-tinted shenanigans and rowdiness have characterized modern parades, as the perception of Irishness clashes with the reality. Saint Patrick's Day parades have historically been more political than religious, despite the connection with Ireland's patron saint. But both religion and politics were part of the mix when the issue of gay parade marchers was first raised in 1992, dividing older, more conservative Irish New Englanders and a younger generation that tends to be more tolerant.

Irish festivals, a less boisterous expression of Irish culture, have steadily gained in popularity since the 1980s and may ultimately replace parades as a more faithful representation of Irish folklife. They are held in cities such as Fairfield, Glastonbury, and New Haven, Conn.; Billerica, Easton, and Malden, Mass.; and Newport and Providence, R.I. A cross between tailgate parties and family picnics, they call to mind early vaudeville circuits of musicians and entertainers crisscrossing small-town America. Music and dancing, sporting events, lectures, and singsongs, along with carnival attractions and vendors of shamrock-green merchandise, produce an intimate setting in which Irish American culture is proudly displayed to young and old alike.

Studying Irish American culture has proved to be one of the best ways of preserving it. Harvard's Celtic Languages and Literatures Department is world renowned for its advanced offerings in Gaelic, while Boston College, the University of Massachusetts, and Stonehill College boast multidisciplinary Irish studies programs. Libraries at Harvard, Yale, Boston College, and Stonehill in Massachusetts and Colby College in Waterville, Maine, as well as the Boston Public Library, the John F. Kennedy Library, and the Archdiocese of Boston, contain important Irish scholarly collections.

Although Irish New Englanders may appear "more Irish than Harvard," they take great satisfaction in the contributions they have made to the cultural life of the region. Having helped to shape New England so pervasively, they proudly call it home.

Michael Coffey and Terry Golway, *The Irish in America* (1997); James B. Cullen, *The Story of the Irish in Boston* (1889); Oscar Handlin, *Boston's Immigrants, 1790–1865: A Study in Acculturation* (1941); Neil Hogan, *The Wearin' o' the Green: St. Patrick's Day in New Haven, Connecticut, 1842–1992* (1992); Thomas H. O'Connor, *The Boston Irish: A Political History* (1995); O'Connor, "The Irish in New England," *New England Historical and Genealogical Register* 139 (1985); Michael P. Quinlin and Colette M. Quinlin, *The Guide to the New England Irish* (1994); Dennis P. Ryan, *Beyond the Ballot Box: A Social History of the Boston Irish, 1845–1917* (1983).

Michael P. Quinlin

Italian American Saints' Feasts and Festivals

The saint's feast, a tradition brought to America by Italian immigrants, is an act of Christian devotion, civic identity, and community celebration. As Italians and Italian Americans settled in many cities throughout New England, including Providence; Barre and Proctor, Vt.; New Haven and Waterbury, Conn.; and many others, ethnic neighborhoods developed across the region. Boston's North End, for example, is home to a sizable Italian American community and is composed of perhaps eight or more smaller neighborhoods, each with residents hailing from a specific Italian town. As individual and social needs changed from those of a predominantly agrarian society to those of the urban neighborhood, many of these immigrant communities maintained their European traditions.

During the early decades of the 20th century, Italian men founded mutual aid and benefit societies in the name of their Italian town's patron saint. In Boston, the Madonna Della Grazie Society started in 1903, the Saint Agripina Society in 1908, and the Saint Anthony Society in 1910. These and similar societies shared several salient characteristics. Membership was restricted exclusively to men and was available only to those with a blood connection to a specific town. These societies existed to raise money for members and their families, as well as for charitable purposes. The primary focus of the society was, of course, the patron saint's feast, which was the sole revenue-generating event for the society and the greatest statement of a given community's ethnic pride and civic identity.

In New England, saints' feasts and festivals—which generally have an outdoor component such as a parade, music and dancing, and street vendors—are typically celebrated in the summer, regardless of their celebration dates in Italy. Traditional feasts share a common structure: typically beginning on a Friday, they tend to run for three or four days. The event opens when a statue of the saint first appears before the devotees, usually in association with a short procession. An evening dance follows, with music provided by a local band playing from an elaborate bandstand. Sunday is the feast's focal point, involving a mass and a lengthy procession. Society members carry the saint to a church service in the morning. About noon, a procession begins, lasting as long as eight hours. During the procession, teams of men carry the statue on litters, and a band might march in front of the saint, drawing the crowd's attention. Spectators donate money by pinning bills on long flowing ribbons draped over the statue.

Beginning in the 1950s, the traditional feast celebration slowly and permanently changed in Boston and throughout much of the region. Demographic shifts eroded the Italian community; societies built permanent chapels to house the saint, thereby raising their expenses; and the North End attracted new residents who no longer favored the traditional feasts. Feast-day entertainment has expanded greatly, and each festival competes to hire "name" acts instead of local bands. Food at the feasts now reflects both traditional Italian and contemporary fare.

Men of Saint Agripina's Chapel carry a figure of the saint, North End, Boston, 1978

One of New England's best-known Italian festivals takes place during the last full weekend in June in Gloucester, Mass., whose Italian community originated largely in Boston. By the 1920s, a festival in honor of Saint Peter had begun, featuring the blessing of the town's fishing fleet. In Gloucester, the festival is rooted not in a particular society from a particular place, but rather is more generally a pan-Italian event. In fact, many civic, ethnic, and social groups participate, including a Portuguese church, which carries a statue of Saint Fatima.

Frances M. Malpezzi and William M. Clements, *Italian-American Folklore* (1992); Stephen Wilson, ed., *Saints and Their Cults: Studies in Religious Sociology, Folklore, and History* (1983).

Stephen Matchak

Logging

The forest products industry in New England—and the folk culture it has influenced—is deeply rooted in the region's history. New England's land and the resources on it have driven its economic development, settlement patterns, and cultural identity for centuries. The region's virgin timber, ideal for shipbuilding, was one of its most attractive resources to early settlers. Since its founding in 1921 the Maine-based retailer L. L. Bean has created a worldwide market in clothing and other products derived from woods culture. The intensity and effect of logging and lumbering on New England's culture and natural environment have varied depending on the locations of excellent growth, bodies of water on which to float logs, and the accessibility of manufacturing equipment to produce the finished product.

During the 19th century, logging in New England's northern woods centered on such major rivers as the Penobscot, Kennebec, and Androscoggin in Maine; the Connecticut River between New Hampshire and Vermont; and the Champlain Canal. Beginning in the western region of New England, the Lake Champlain valley had its first timber boom during colonial settlement. By 1815, however, the trade in timber had declined considerably. The British market had slowed, an international boundary and tariffs had been established, and accessible timber had been depleted. This changed in 1823 with the opening of the Champlain Canal, which connected the region to the Hudson River valley and beyond. Moreover, in 1843 another canal opened at the Chambly Rapids on the Richelieu River, connecting Lake Champlain to the Saint Lawrence and enabling lumber from the Ottawa River valley and beyond to be brought into Burlington, Vt., for manufacture, establishing the small city as a lumber port producing Canadian lumber for shipment by rail to East Coast ports and markets.

As Richard Ober notes in *At What Cost? Shaping the Land We Call New Hampshire,* by 1885 some 680 timber companies were operating in New Hampshire's White Mountains. With seemingly reckless abandon, hillsides were stripped, streams were choked with runoff, and forest fires became common. At the turn of the century, visitors to the New Hampshire grand resort hotels saw the disastrous effects firsthand. Officials of the Connecticut-based New Hampshire Land Company purchased tracts of land to sell to timber companies while refusing to sell to local farmers or to the owners of the resort hotels. In response, Governor Frank West Rollins spearheaded the establishment of the Society for the Protection of New Hampshire Forests in 1900. Moreover, Congressman John Weeks of Massachusetts (a native of Lancaster, N.H.) sponsored legislation allowing the federal government to purchase privately owned land to protect the headwaters of navigable streams. More than a hundred mill owners joined other advocates to support the legislation that became the Weeks Act in 1911, ending a fierce debate by powerful interests—textile mill owners, railroad operators, and conservationists. Land acquisition began immediately for the White Mountain National Forest, and before long some 50 national forests had been established in the East. During this era of progressive reform and national land-use policy, New Hampshire had become the starting point for the national forest system.

The economic might of the burgeoning pulp and paper industry played itself out in Maine as in no other state. The pace of growth was astonishing. In 1885 there were 21 pulp and paper mills operating in Maine; by 1906, the number had grown to 109. Portland's Hugh Chisholm formed a conglomerate in 1897 with several financiers to create International Paper Company. The newspaper industry, along with Congress, became alarmed about the "paper trust" that had been established in International Paper, but a group of investors based in Bangor, Maine, formed a competitor that developed into Great Northern Paper Company. The group had purchased lands and controlled much of the area around the confluence of the east and west branches of the Penobscot River, where "Magic Millinocket" grew from a township of eight individuals in 1900 to an entire city. Indeed, the development and harnessing of water flows on the west branch of the Penobscot culminated in the construction of the Ripogenous Dam at Chesuncook Lake in 1917. In the 1990s nearly half of the state's total land area was owned by the pulp and paper industry. Great Northern Paper Company alone owns more than 2 million acres of forestland—close to 11 percent of the state. The Seven Islands Company, International Paper Company, and Champion International are among more than a dozen corporations with major landholdings in Maine.

The magnitude of the forest products industries in the northern woods of New England cannot be overstated. It is apparent in geographic, economic, and cultural terms. In fact, because of the sheer magnitude of capitalization and rapid development of the pulp and paper industry early in this century, a forceful regard for the importance of land conservation as well as the folklife attached to logging developed concurrently in both Maine and New Hampshire.

The University of Maine offered its first course in forestry in 1900 and now offers a significant degree program through the forestry school. Documentation of northern New England's heritage of work in the woods has been ongoing since the mid-1950s through the work of folklorist Edward D. Ives. First established as the Northeast Folklore Society and the Northeast Archives of Folklore and Oral History, the Maine Folklife Center now operates a research and publications program. The annual publication of *Northeast Folklore* has provided such works as "Argyle Boom" (an extensive oral history of the Penobscot River sorting booms north of Orono); "Suthin': An Oral History of Grover Morrison's Woods

Rolling logs down skids, West Swanzey, N.H., 1942

Operation at Little Musquash Lake, 1945–1947"; and "White Pine on the Saco River: An Oral History of River Driving in Southern Maine."

In an effort to preserve cultural artifacts, folklorists and enthusiasts throughout much of the 20th century were drawn to the region's logging industry, where they found a rich body of traditional songs associated with life in the logging camps. Helen Hartness Flanders, for instance, was asked by the Vermont Commission on Country Life to collect rural New England songs, starting in 1930. Over 30 years, she documented approximately 9,000 songs, now archived at Middlebury College in Vermont. "The Jam on Gerry's Rocks," a song widely known in the logging camps, is a chronicle of death among "shanty boys"— loggers, that is:

> Come all ye jovial shanty boys,
> Wherever you may be,
> I hope you pay attention,
> And listen unto me;
> Concerning six brave shanty boys
> With courage strong and brave,
> Who broke the jam on Gerry's rocks
> And met with a watery grave.

Like Flanders, William Doerflinger, educated at Princeton, conducted considerable field research, first in Nova Scotia and then in New England and New York. His book *Shantymen and Shantyboys* (1951) is an important chronicle of those songs. Folklorist Edward D. Ives is probably the most accomplished scholar of logging songs and, more generally, logging folklife. His book *Joe Scott, The Woodsman-Songmaker* (1978) reconstructs the life of an itinerant poet and song maker who composed and printed songs, selling them in logging camps. Decades after Scott's death, his songs continued to be popular among loggers, although in most cases they were no longer attributed to their author. Ives's book tells the story of entertainment in the logging camps, adding flesh and blood to the historical record.

Field researchers have also examined woodworking craft traditions among New England loggers, such as chain saw art and other forms of carving. The Rangeley Lakes Region Logging Museum, in one of Maine's historic logging centers, has exhibited a considerable amount of this work, including the chain saw carvings of artists such as Rodney Richard, fan towers and gumbooks by William Richard, and carved models of logging equipment by Carl Trafton. And headquartered both in Concord, N.H., and in Bethel, Maine, the Northern Forest Center has in recent years mounted significant research efforts in the traditional culture of the northern woodlands.

Stephen Ballew, Joan Brooks, Dona Brotz, and Edward Ives, "Suthin': An Oral History of Grover Morrison's Woods Operation at Little Musquash Lake, 1945–47," *Northeast Folklore* 18 (1977); Michael P. Chaney, "White Pine on the Saco River: An Oral History of River Driving in Southern Maine," *Northeast Folklore* 29 (1990); Edward D. Ives, "Argyle Boom," *Northeast Folklore* 17 (1976); Richard Judd, ed., *Maine: The Pine Tree State from Prehistory to the Present* (1995); Richard Ober, ed., *At What Cost? Shaping the Land We Call New Hampshire* (1992); Robert E. Pike, *Tall Trees, Tough Men* (1967); David C. Smith, *Lumbering in Maine, 1861–1960* (1972); Jennie Versteeg, ed., *Lake Champlain: Reflections on Our Past* (1987).

Michael P. Chaney

Maritime Lore There was a time when seafaring was so important to New England that Nantucket Islanders spoke for most of the region when they told their children, pointing to the sea, "Yonder lie the green pastures where you, your children, and your children's children shall go for their bread." In the 1940s Captain Archie Spurling of Little Cranberry Island, Maine, skipper of a fishing schooner, had this to say of those who went to sea: "They is three kinds. There are sailors, fishermen, and seafaring men. Sailors go 'long-shore in coasters, fishermen go to the Grand Banks. Them that goes foreign is seafarin' men, don't'cha know." This statement is not only accurate, it sums up an attitude.

Spurling's categorization can be further broken down. There were 'long-shore men who supplemented subsistence farming by fishing, and among those who went to the Banks were some who ventured to the ice for seals. Seafaring men—it was not considered a way of life for women—worked on large vessels with specialized functions. Some ships served the China trade, taking sailors away from their home ports for a year or maybe two; some were whalers that set off for as long as nine years (though the average was three or four). There were slavers taking part in the triangle trade between Europe, Africa, and America; ships that carried commercial goods to Europe; and high-flying clippers that tore up the seas setting speed records. In times of war privateers plied the seas.

Each of these activities had its own geographic center—fishing in Maine and Gloucester, Mass.; whaling in Nantucket, Mass., and southern New England; slaving in Rhode Island; the China trade in Boston and Salem, Mass.; privateering also in Salem and in Newport, R.I. Since crews rarely went from one type of ship to another, and since the occupations were all quite distinctive, each one tended to have its own separate folklore, which took its place in the general body of sea lore.

Marine art was as realistic and as representative as the artist could make it. For the most part it was done by old-timers who had "swallowed the anchor," or retired. By building model ships or painting scenes, usually violent, from their seafaring days, they were often trying to recapture the past.

Whalers were an exception to this generalization. Long away from home, often sailing in dangerous or unfamiliar waters, whalers experienced extended periods of inactivity while they waited for whales or lay becalmed that allowed art to flourish aboard ship. Captains often decorated their logs with pictures of whales taken or lost, of passing ships, of newfound islands—the latter to serve as aids to navigation during subsequent voyages. The crew spent idle moments scrimshawing and doing knot work. Mostly they made useful objects—busks, pie crimpers, marlinespikes, clothespins, swifts, walking sticks—out of whalebone or walrus ivory. These they decorated with scenes or sayings. Not infrequently they carved elaborate scenes on whale teeth and walrus tusks depicting an encounter with a whale, a ship, or a busty lass. Knot work consisted of satchels, bags, decorative trim, rings, and wristbands.

Singing was of two types, chanteys and "fo'c'sle" songs. The former were further divided into long- and short-haul chanteys, work songs designed to coordinate gang effort. Long-hauls, used for hard jobs that took a long time, such as bringing up the anchor or raising a spar aloft, were slow and mournful, while the short-hauls, used for quick work, such as trimming a sail, were usually bright and lively. Moreover, chanteys served other purposes, too. "Shenandoah," for example, was used to get the anchor when a vessel was swinging off for home, thus alerting other ships whose crew members might wish to send word to distant families. When a sailor heard a certain short-haul, he would know where to go and what was expected of him even on the darkest night. Although sung all over the world, chanteys were used most frequently on the fast-moving big passage makers, square-rigged vessels that traveled long distances. But with the advent of the donkey, or steam engine, chanteys no longer served a purpose and became relics of a bygone age.

Fo'c'sle songs, sung for entertainment during off hours, often set stories of incidents at sea to melodies popular on dry land. Disasters, strange events, and the sailing ship itself were frequent subjects. Each marine occupation had its own songs—for instance, "The Horton's In" for fishermen, "Greenland Whale Fishery" for whalers, and "The Liverpool Packet" for the flyers on square-riggers.

Legends and tales dealing with life on the

Boats decorated for the annual blessing of the fleet, New Bedford, Mass., 1981

sea abounded. Many told of disasters, specters, miraculous rescues, fast passages, great skippers, or exceptional catches. Others tried to explain why certain ships were unlucky, what caused phosphorescence in the water, or where seals, mermaids, and mermen came from.

All seamen shared certain superstitions, customs, and beliefs. Among well-known hazards were sailing on Friday and allowing women, ministers, corpses, or crippled people aboard ship. Stowaways and murderers were also considered bad luck, as was Saint Elmo's Fire, the electrical glow that could appear at the tip of the ship's mast in stormy weather. Good luck, by contrast, came to those born with the caul, who believed they couldn't drown, or those who underwent certain initiation rituals. Fishermen who drank a cup of gurry from the barrel full of codfish livers every morning were sure to have good health. Certain words and actions were taboo. Others were considered indispensable. The first sailor to spot a whale was expected to drive a gold coin into the mast. The cod fishermen who caught the first fish had to throw it back into the water over his shoulder, or else bad luck would ensue.

Humor was also an important part of maritime folklore. Sailors often made jokes at the expense of their skipper, deriding him for being unable to find his position, for getting caught in a compromising situation, or for committing any number of dim-witted acts. Ignorant passengers and novice sailors were also fair game. One tale from the 19th and early 20th centuries ridicules the young helmsman who steers toward the brightly colored lights of a drugstore, believing they are navigation signals. Then, of course, there is

the unsuspecting passenger who is sent aloft to gather eggs from the crow's nest or down below to polish the "golden rivet under the bilge water."

More serious were the practical jokes and horseplay visited upon any number of living beings. To cure seasickness the inexperienced mate would be instructed to swallow a chunk of pork on a string, which an old salt would haul back out a few minutes later. Sailors sometimes set a comrade afire to see what he would do. Another grisly source of fun was cutting off a shark's left pectoral fin and then releasing the creature back into the water to swim widdershins until it died, or getting two gulls to swallow hook-bearing fish attached to each other by a stout piece of line. Such stunts may have been cruel, but the sailor's life was, too. Less painful pranks would have interested no one.

Seafaring had its own language, too, overlaid with the specialized vocabulary of the particular trade. Many are the sea creatures whose names are unknown to landlubbers—the skip-jack (a bluefish), cunner (an ugly little fish with spots), blue Jimmey (a small blue fish), and skillagalee (a swordfish). Sometimes objects were named for individuals—the Charlie Noble, for example, was a smokestack—but for the most part terms were those that could be easily pronounced and readily distinguished from other words above the ocean racket. "Port" and "starboard," for example, are not easily confused.

Nor is marine lore confined to the sea. It follows sailors ashore, touching everything from the conditions under which the child who may someday go to sea is born to when the "butt sprung and rotten" old salt will die. The dying sailor with a few more hours left

will "most probably hang on through the turn of the tide and go out on the ebb." It determines the kinds of material with which a ship is built, its design, where construction is started and under what conditions, who works on it, who comes near it, and the conditions prevailing at its launch. Are the omens good? Are the wind and tide right? Does it run down the ways cleanly? If these factors are not propitious, the ship will be unlucky and no decent crew will board it, although sometimes it can be cleansed of its faults through magical means.

Today, seafaring as a way of life has all but vanished from the New England scene. Fish stocks are nearly depleted, whaling days are done, sealing is forbidden, and freight is moved by other means. One sees the odd tanker hauling road salt or scrap metal, an occasional tow of barges. Only lobster boats and a few diehard fishers are on the water every day. But more vessels than ever are afloat in New England waters. It is said that if all the boats registered in Long Island Sound were to appear at the same time, they could not all fit in that waterway. Their yachtsman and yachtswoman owners, who venture forth only on pleasant summer days, may imagine that they are reliving a romantic experience, or they may be demonstrating their success. Very few are left who "goes foreign don't'cha know."

Roger D. Abrahams, Kenneth S. Goldstein, and Wayland D. Hand, eds., *By Land and by Sea: Studies in the Folklore of Work and Leisure Honoring Horace P. Beck on His 65th Birthday* (1985); Fletcher S. Bassett, *Legends and Superstitions of the Sea and of Sailors in All Lands and at All Times* (1885); Horace Beck, *Folklore and the Sea* (1996 [1973]); Joanna Carver Colcord, *Sea Language Comes Ashore* (1977 [1945]); Charles Nordhoff, *Sailor Life on Man of War and Merchant Vessel, Comprising "Man-of-War Life" and "The Merchant Vessel"* (1884).

Horace P. Beck

Music and Dance Traditional music making in New England (with the exception of Native American music history, which forms a related but separate stream) began, like other aspects of the region's expressive culture, as an offshoot of British practice before gradually taking on an American identity. African, French, Irish, and other peoples contributed to the mainstream British American music culture and created ethnic music cultures of their own, while popular, mass-mediated music, meant to transcend ethnic boundaries, profoundly affected music making in New England as elsewhere. Today, most New Englanders' daily involvement in music making embraces musical traditions from many regions and cultures, with varying degrees of integration among them.

Colonial New Englanders took pleasure in

singing songs. Psalm singing took place in the home as well as in houses of worship. The *Bay Psalm Book* (1640) was the first book published in New England. In 1644 the Westminster Assembly of Divines recommended the practice of "lining-out" for psalm singing in Britain and the colonies, a procedure operating in New England since the earliest British settlements whereby a song leader gave out, or chanted, the lines of the psalm one at a time and the congregation repeated them. The tunes were sung more or less in unison, not in harmony, and they were learned orally, by imitation rather than by note reading. For this reason they have come to be known as folk hymns, even though their texts were fixed and transmitted by the medium of print. Nonetheless, the tunes were printed in some collections, and it is possible to trace some old favorites, such as the hymn of thanks titled "Old Hundred."

Eventually various reformers introduced music literacy and part singing into church music, displacing the lined-out psalmody in favor of a more learned, print-based music culture, and by the early Federal era the old way of singing was largely obsolete in the region. For the singing of ballads and songs we have less direct evidence during the colonial period; however, written reminiscences of people like Boston-born Benjamin Franklin indicate that most people knew, and sang, the same popular songs and ballads—"Chevy Chase" is one example—that their British counterparts held dear.

In 1823 a small songbook titled *The Green-Mountain Songster*, "by an Old Revolutionary Soldier," was published in Sandgate, Vt. This was the first collection of traditional folk songs from a singer's repertoire to be printed in the United States, and it consisted of 49 compositions: British ballads; a few American ballads, such as "Brave Wolfe"; and a local ballad, "Joel Baker," about a New Hampshire lad who committed suicide. The anonymous author also included some humorous songs and love songs and seemed particularly fond of songs that took a political stand.

Not only did singing continue as a popular pastime during the Federal era, but gradually a body of American song entered tradition. Perhaps the best-documented 19th-century New England singing tradition is that of the North Woods lumber camps, where men spent four winter months harvesting timber. Songs served as evening entertainment, and many told of lost loves, shipwrecks, and other disasters. Local songs and ballads were composed by people working in the camps or sailing the ocean, some of whom got their songs printed and sold. Sea chanteys, work songs built on patterns of call and response, were designed to coordinate group tasks on sailing ships. African Americans worked on the ships, and their influence may be heard in these songs, whether in the call-and-response patterns or in the short phrases. Most sea chanteys were British until the 19th century, when American versions grew more numerous.

During the 20th century folk-song collectors such as Phillips Barry and Helen Hartness Flanders sought and found more of the Child ballads—canonical English and Scottish popular ballads gathered by Harvard scholar Francis James Child during the 19th century—in New England than had been found in the Appalachian South, while Fannie Hardy Eckstorm and Eloise Linscott published collections including children's songs, sea chanteys, and lumber-camp songs. Edward D. Ives's later studies of song makers Larry Gorman, Lawrence Doyle, and Joe Scott shifted the scholarly focus from the collection of anonymous texts to an exploration of creativity within folk tradition.

Folk songs were sung well into the 20th century in lumber camps, on coastal schooners, in women's domestic and work circles, and at rural general stores and Grange halls; but with the rising popularity of recorded music, particularly after World War II, British-American singing in New England gradually entered a revival phase. Now New England's traditional music is heard at folklife festivals, sometimes in schools or homes, and frequently at living-history museums, where it serves as a means of exhibiting or connecting with an earlier heritage. Related in spirit if not in subject matter to the woodsmen song makers, many contemporary New England singer-songwriters take sustenance from traditional music while penning lyrics that acknowledge the ironies of modern relationships. They tend to accompany themselves on acoustic guitars, perform in coffeehouses, and seek alternatives to the commercialized music industry.

Many colonial New Englanders also enjoyed dancing, as long as it was graceful and proper; amorous dancing was regarded as sinful. Longways country dancing, known today as contra dancing, was a common evening's entertainment. In addition to the country dancing, usually done to the music of a violin, flageolet, or fife, fancy ballroom dancing was popular among the wealthy in New England cities, where dancing masters taught fashionable European steps. The instrumental music for these dances was like that used in the British Isles. John Playford's *The English Dancing Master*, first published in 1651 and reissued more than 20 times through 1727, is the earliest inventory of dance tunes. A few late-18th-century colonial New England dance-tune manuscripts survive, while the earliest surviving published dance and tune book was John Griffiths's *Collection of the Newest and Most Fashionable Country Dances and Cotillions*, which appeared in Providence in 1788.

Most of the tunes fall into two or three parts, each part consisting of eight or 16 beats. This structure facilitated the dance, for each dance figure occupied eight beats. Among the tunes in the Griffiths collection is "Fisher's Hornpipe," a melody that spread throughout North America and is still in use. Others from the 18th-century books that are still played include the well-known "Soldier's Joy" and "Haste to the Wedding," but the overwhelming majority of these notated tunes from the 18th century fell out of fashion during the 19th. Playing the fiddle or fife was both a gentleman's amateur occupation and something that the lowest classes, notably African Americans, took up as a profession. The dance tunes existed in notation and also in oral tradition, but it does not appear that composing melodies then was a particularly widespread occupation; rather, tunes were chosen from among a common stock.

Early in the 19th century the cotillion, an American variant of the French quadrille, gradually replaced the longways contra dance; at midcentury fashionable European couple dances such as the waltz, polka, schottische, and galop (which later developed into the two-step) gained favor in the cities. A solo, or fancy-dance-step, tradition also existed; sailors' hornpipes, played to a particular rhythm, are an example; and solo dancing ("Negro jigs") was a staple of the minstrel show, perhaps the most popular entertainment in the North. Minstrel music, however, was developed by white composers increasingly on African American models and sounded different from the music for the gala balls.

By the 19th century's end couple dances had replaced quadrilles ("square dances") in urban areas, while quadrilles and contra dances—the latter especially in northern New England—held on in rural regions. Whereas the violin had dominated musical ensembles in the North early in the century, small bands including wind and brass as well as stringed instruments became the norm after the Civil War, when public halls grew larger, gatherings increasingly took place outdoors, and the need for louder music was apparent. It seemed there was no public occasion during which the town or community band failed to provide a mix of marches and patriotic airs; arrangements of popular parlor songs, such as those of Stephen Foster; and dance tunes. Bandmasters arranged the music, and many musicians read it in manuscript or printed form. At the same time, more informal dances (kitchen junkets) took place inside large country houses, where

Shaker dance, ca. 1835

a fiddler and piano player (or pump organist) could be found holding forth.

Nineteenth-century traditional dance music was very much affected by the influx of Irish immigrants. Casual references to New England dancing in the writings of the period usually mention that the fiddler was Irish (or in many instances Negro). The mid-19th-century dance-tune collections published by Elias Howe of Boston included Irish jigs and reels, Scottish dance melodies, and minstrel-show songs, along with more elaborately structured pieces for fashionable ballroom dancing that invited instrumental flourishes worthy of classical virtuosos. By the time of the two monumental collections put out by Howe—*Howe's 1,000 Jigs and Reels* (1867) and Sidney Ryan's *Mammoth Collection* (1883)—the Irish influence was strongly felt, and the Playford-type tunes had largely disappeared.

French Canadians came to work in the 19th-century New England woods and factories, and eventually they constituted the largest group of nonnative English speakers in the region. They sang their chansons and played their dance music in "little Canadas" that sprang up in pockets throughout New England, and while their French-language songs did not enter the mainstream, their dance music cross-fertilized the already amalgamated British and Irish ("Yankee") dance tunes to the point where today a traditional French song such as "Saint Anne's Reel" is as much a part of a New England fiddler's repertoire as is "Soldier's Joy."

In the 20th century the New England quadrille bands gradually changed into small dance bands, playing for dances in town halls everywhere. The most popular instrumentation included a piano, violin, and trumpet, to which could be added a guitar, four-string banjo, clarinet, small drum set, or string bass. Popular couple dances such as the two-step, waltz, and fox-trot predominated, but no evening was complete without an old-fashioned square dance or such contra dances as the Portland Fancy or Lady of the Lake. Another strong influence on New England's dance music came from the Canadian Maritime Provinces, where Scottish fiddling traditions mingled with the burgeoning country-music industry, and fiddlers such as Don Messer exerted enormous influence. Since World War II it has been possible to speak of a Yankee repertory that includes French, Scottish, Irish, and English traditional dance tunes.

Dance fiddling, old-time fiddle contests, square dancing, and contra dancing were the subject of several 20th-century revivals, the first occurring in the 1910s in large part thanks to the efforts of Elizabeth Burchenal, author of *American Country Dances* (1916). Later revivals, including one in the 1920s sponsored by the automobile manufacturer Henry Ford, kept the older tunes going in a few rural pockets in Maine, New Hampshire, and Vermont, as well as around Boston, until contra dancing was embraced in the 1970s by the back-to-the-land movement. Then a new generation of musicians began to learn the Yankee dance tunes, and many contra dance bands sprang up throughout New England. The fiddle and piano were the mainstays of these bands, but traditional folk instruments such as the guitar, mandolin, tin whistle, accordion, flute, fife,

and even the five-string banjo were also included in various additional combinations. The influence of the folk music revival also made itself felt in the expansion of the Yankee tune repertoire to include southern Appalachian, Canadian, and especially Irish traditional dance music. The contra dance revival in New England has continued apace, spreading to communities in many other parts of the United States.

The ethnic music traditions of other populations likewise influence musical culture in New England. Today, Polish polkas, for example, are popular in Massachusetts and New Hampshire; Portuguese and Cape Verdean music in Rhode Island and southeastern Massachusetts; Cape Breton music in Waltham and Watertown, Mass.; Finnish dance music in Massachusetts and Maine; Jewish klezmer music in Boston; Greek music throughout southern urban New England; and so forth. The immigrants from Southeast Asia during and after the wars in Indochina during the 1960s and 1970s brought a variety of ethnic music to New England, and one can attend, for example, Cambodian New Year's celebrations in Providence and in Lowell, Mass. Beginning in the late 1960s a "roots" movement in American culture gave ethnicity a positive connotation, with the result that music, one of the most tenacious of ethnic markers, was revived and strengthened throughout the region. The Stockholm–New Sweden–Westmanland area of Aroostook County, Maine, settled in the late 19th century, provides a case in point. Though first- and second-generation Swedes there kept traditional dances and dance music alive, interest subsequently waned until the 1980s, when a new consciousness of Swedish identity in the area called forth a revival of the old music.

Phillips Barry, ed., *The Maine Woods Songster* (1939); Phillips Barry, Fannie Hardy Eckstorm, and Mary Winslow Smyth, *British Ballads from Maine: The Development of Popular Songs with Texts and Airs* (1929); Wilberforce Eames, ed., *The Bay Psalm Book: Being a Facsimile Reprint of the First Edition, Printed by Stephen Daye at Cambridge in New England in 1640* (1903); Helen Hartness Flanders, Elizabeth Flanders Ballard, George Brown, and Phillips Barry, eds., *The New Green Mountain Songster: Traditional Folk Songs of Vermont* (1939); Edward D. Ives, *Joe Scott, the Woodsman-Songmaker* (1978); Eloise Hubbard Linscott, ed., *Folk Songs of Old New England* (1993 [1939]); *Ryan's Mammoth Collection: 1,050 Reels and Jigs, Hornpipes, Clogs, Walk-Arounds, Essences, Strathspeys, Highland Flings, and Contradances, with Figures, and How to Play Them; Bowing and Fingering Marked; Together with 40 Introductory Studies for the Violin* (1995 [1883]); Beth Tolman and Ralph Page, *The Country Dance Book: The Old-Fashioned Square Dance, Its History, Lore, Variations, and Its Callers* (1937).

Jeff Titon

Narrative Narrative most often takes the form of a story and features a beginning, a middle, and an end. Narrators inherently know, or else learn, that stories must be told in a meaningful order. New Englanders love to tell stories. The region is home to a rich heritage of traditional and personal storytelling.

Ageless and multicultural, narratives have survived throughout the millennia because they often express an important truth about life. Not only are narratives found in all cultures, they play a central role in maintaining community life and giving meaning to individual lives. Oral tales, the most universal of all narrative forms, have served a vital role in the lives of those who tell and listen to them.

Traditional narratives pass on enduring values and life lessons. All narrative genres—sacred stories, myths, legends, folktales, fairy tales (*märchen*), personal-experience narratives, and life stories—bring people more into accord with themselves, with others, with the mystery of life, and with the universe around them. Narratives can connect both the teller and the listener to the psychological, social, mystical, and cosmological realms. They illustrate that one person's experience or situation in life, though seemingly unique, is most likely common to others as well.

New England narratives contain the entire range of motifs identified and classified by Stith Thompson in the *Motif-Index of Folk Literature* (1932–36). Used to identify similarities across narratives, motifs are the smallest narrative elements that persist across generations. There are literally thousands of possible motifs, and they are usually of three main types: characters, background elements, and incidents. Examples of just a few motifs common to New England narratives include sea serpents, which were encountered at various places along the coast; magicians, who could make water burn, rocks move, or trees dance; mountain spirits, who were called upon for assistance; and ghost ships, New England's most famous apparition.

The first storytellers of New England were the Wabanaki, or people of the Dawnland (consisting of the Passamaquoddy, Penobscot, Micmac, Maliseet, and Abenaki tribes), the Massachusett, Wampanoag, Natick, Narragansett, Pequot, Pawtucket, Mashpee, and other native peoples of the region. Their traditional narratives tell how creation, as well as storytelling, came into being; they impart the values, virtues, beliefs, sacred knowledge, and practices that sustain the people. All events of importance were held in the collective memory of community elders and passed on through storytelling. The ability to tell a story was and still is one of the most admired skills in Indian communities. Storytelling was an occasion for quiet intimacy among the members of the group, a time for teaching what mattered most to them.

Many myths in the native tradition recount the origin of the world or tell of sacred beings, animal or human. When the subject, or hero, is purely human rather than divine, the narrative becomes a legend. Myths are connected to religious beliefs, while legends tend to be more historically based. The central character in the sacred stories of the Eastern Woodland Indian people is the giant Glooscap, who created the features of the landscape, tamed the winds, secured water and food for his people, and brought forth the people themselves from the ash tree. In this story Glooscap took his bow and arrows and shot at the trunks of ash trees, from whose bark emerged dancing men and women with light-brown skin and black hair. Glooscap also fought a water monster and turned it into a small bullfrog. He is known even to behave like a trickster, especially when asked to perform frivolous deeds.

Traditional native folktales also include stories of ghosts, treasures, witchcraft, shamans, and little people, among others. The Natick, Mashpee, and Wampanoag told stories of native folk healers who practiced herbal cures, often using secret ingredients from roots and plants to expel spirits from the bodies of patients. Another story tells of the Indian spirit Cheepi, who appeared to natives in the Boston area around the period of European contact to warn them against departing from the ancestral ways, to uphold custom, and to safeguard traditional values.

In 1996, for the first time ever, five young Native American storytellers from New England toured the region presenting traditional tales—creation stories, fables, and legends—handed down over generations, as well as personal narratives of Indian experience today. Called "First Things First," the touring production celebrated the cultural heritage of native New Englanders.

Settlers from Europe brought many traditional narratives with them, along with a wealth of tall tales. Colonial tales often recounted the fantastic and wondrous exploits of folk heroes, and competitive story swapping fast became a New England pastime. Yankee yarns developed from the tradition of European and English rogue tales but acquired their own special twist. Narrators in coastal towns told of heroic family members, local characters, and maritime incidents, conveying beliefs shared by deep-sea sailors in other parts of the world.

Figuring prominently in early New England stories was the resourceful Yankee, whose craftiness was mixed with a dash of the country bumpkin. Folk humor found its most popular outlet in the tall tale and the exaggerated personal experiences of the storyteller, often shared in the comfortable surroundings of village square or kitchen. The Maine form of that tradition, with its down east accent and dry, understated wit, lives on in the many *Bert and I* recordings of Robert Bryan and Marshall Dodge.

Personal narratives dealing with the themes and issues of contemporary life are recounted everyday in every corner of New England. They relate everything from true experience to oral history to family lore to occupational incidents to autobiography. A story swap is born every time one personal story leads to another.

New England is well known throughout the United States for its personal-narrative raconteurs. Once primarily the province of community elders, storytelling today is open to all. In 1998 Maine's public television network aired a four-part documentary titled *Our Stories* that featured in-depth, highly personal profiles of members of the Passamaquoddy community, a lobstering family on Little Cranberry Island, a western Maine farming family, and a Franco-American potato-farming family in northern Maine's Saint John River valley. The series featured people of all ages telling stories of struggle, of prejudice and discrimination, of alcoholism, of hope, and of survival. Throughout New England such narratives, each one part of a collective truth, still serve to unite individuals, families, and generations.

One type of personal narrative, that of New England immigrants and refugees, has been growing in significance. New England cities, and indeed villages, today struggle to move beyond the melting-pot metaphor of assimilation and toward a flower-garden metaphor of difference in which people of various colors, backgrounds, and histories can flourish side by side. The archive of the Center for the Study of Lives at the University of Southern Maine may be an indication of this trend; within its collection of nearly 500 life stories, 40 ethnic groups are represented.

The immigrant epic is a contemporary narrative form that relates the immigrant experience from life in the homeland to arrival in and adaptation to the new country. The increasingly diverse communities of New England have now become a nurturing ground for the refugee epic as well, a rich and powerful form of the personal-experience narrative. A noteworthy repository of refugee epics is the Fortunoff Video Archive for Holocaust Testimonies at Yale University.

Many current initiatives attest not only to the power of stories but also to the strength of New England's renewed interest in storytelling. The six-state region boasts more than 50 professional storytellers and hundreds of others who tell their own, their families', or their communities' stories in relaxed, impromptu settings. Countless numbers of raconteurs informally maintain and pass on the living heritage of folk storytelling in New England from front porches, kitchen tables, or wherever else there are listening ears.

Numerous individuals and community organizations in New England are currently engaged in regular activities that will keep the region's distinctive genre of narrative alive for a long time to come. In Maine alone, there is the Maine Folklife Center in Orono, which has been recording stories for more than 30 years; the Center for the Study of Lives at the University of Southern Maine, which has a growing, diverse archive of life stories; and the Acadian Archives of the University of Maine at Fort Kent. Connecticut is home to the Center for Oral History at the University of Connecticut in Storrs; Mystic Seaport in Mystic, which preserves the oral histories of whalemen; and the Ethnic Heritage Center Archives at Southern Connecticut State University. Massachusetts hosts the LANES (League for the Advancement of New England Storytelling) Festival at Simmons College in Boston; and New Hampshire, the annual gathering of Keepers of the Lore in Milford. And the Vermont Folklife Center has long coordinated storytelling efforts in that state, drawing from the Abenaki, Cuban, Franco-American, Italian, Lebanese, and Vietnamese communities.

At the beginning of the 21st century, the New England experience as told in its storytellers' narratives reflects a rich cultural, occupational, communal, and personal diversity. At the heart of each personal narrative still is the region's enduring ethic of self-determination and self-reliance, coupled with a strong sense of place and community.

Robert Atkinson, *The Gift of Stories: Practical and Spiritual Applications of Autobiography, Life Stories, and Personal Mythmaking* (1995); Linda Degh, "Folk Narrative," in *Folklore and Folklife*, ed. Richard Dorson (1972); Richard Dorson, *American Folklore* (1959); Richard Erdoes and Alfonso Ortiz, *American Indian Myths and Legends* (1984); Edward Ives, ed., *Symposium on the Life Story, Folklife Annual* (1986); Maine Indian Program of the New England Regional Office of the American Friends Service Committee, *The Wabanakis of Maine and the Maritimes: A Resource Book about Penobscot, Passamaquoddy, Maliseet, Micmac, and Abenaki Indians* (1989); William S. Simmons, *Spirit of the New England Tribes* (1986); Stith Thompson, *The Folktale* (1977 [1946]).

Robert Atkinson

National Heritage Fellows

To be named a National Heritage Fellow is to receive the highest public honor the United States reserves for traditional folk artists. This award means that the quality, effect, and traditional nature of the honoree's artistic achievements qualify him or her for recognition as a living national treasure. Established by folklorist Beth Lomax Hawes under the aegis of the National Endowment for the Arts (NEA), the fellowship program gave out its first awards in 1982. By 2001, 10 New Englanders had been named National Heritage Fellows. Paradoxically, recipients are not necessarily famous: known mainly within their regional or ethnic groups, they embody particular, locally meaningful traditions. Each one—of approximately 12 Fellows nationwide every year—receives a $10,000 stipend and is honored at a special ceremony in Washington, D.C.

New England's National Heritage Fellows reflect the region's dynamism and its storied traditions. Individual New England folk masters have been honored in the familiar arts of fiddling, quilting, and basketry, as well as the less familiar arts of Hmong weaving and embroidery, Greek lyra music, and South Indian flute playing.

"Make it right, or make it over"; so says 1987 Fellow Newton Washburn, a fourth-generation split ash basket maker from Bethlehem, N.H., citing his mother's rule. These words of solid, traditional craft wisdom in an aesthetic form bring to mind the baskets themselves. Washburn's ancestors, the Sweetsers (from Vermont), have been known for sturdy baskets pleasing to the eye since at least 1850.

"Mother started me out with a flat bottom," Washburn recalls. "Then we went to round baskets. Each one you had to do 'til it was right. The first one you did was right because if it wasn't you took it apart and started over again. There was never nothing said about how many you made. . . . It was quality, not quantity."

Washburn brought his family's tradition through a difficult phase. During the 1930s the demand for baskets dwindled because cheap, galvanized containers became available. It was impractical for the Sweetser family to continue making the baskets, and the tradition lapsed. It wasn't until Washburn returned to it later in life, laboring to remember and reconstruct the repertoire, that the art was revived.

National Heritage Fellow Mary Mitchell Gabriel, of Princeton, Maine, learned from her grandmother how to make baskets of brown ash splints at age seven. Gabriel was self-motivated: "I pestered her to teach me." Gabriel was born into the Passamaquoddy tradition of using sweetgrass combined with split ash to make baskets, and birch bark to make canoes, paddles, and snowshoes. In her early years she gathered sweetgrass from the coastal salt marshes of Maine and pounded brown ash logs to make splints.

The same manufacturing of cheap, practical products that curtailed the Sweetser basket tradition in New Hampshire and Vermont—and many other folk crafts throughout the country in the early 20th century—reached Native American communities in Maine as well. Thanks in large part to Mary Gabriel and others like her, native basketry in Maine survived a discouraging century, gradually adapting and emerging today as a revival supported not only by native peoples and artists but by state agencies, art exhibitors, and culture advocates.

Mary Gabriel knows her tradition so well that she can innovate within it without violating its unspoken aesthetic parameters. Thus she invents harmonious elements such as the braided frog handle. Yet, like so many folk artists, she judges her own work mainly by its technical proficiency and its ability to remain "stout and sturdy" and carry its beauty for years: "If I am to be remembered for my baskets, I want them to live forever."

Gabriel's sentiment is echoed by the Shakers, who say, "Do all your work as though you had a thousand years to live and as if you will die tomorrow." Sister Mildred Barker, New England's first National Heritage Fellow in 1983, was the embodiment of Shaker values. Raised in the Shaker community at Alfred, Maine, she devoted herself from the age of seven to traditional Shaker music, fulfilling the community's imperative "Hands to work and hearts to God." In 1981, when Sister Barker was 83 years old and the principal leader of the Shaker Society in Maine, the folklorist Daniel Patterson wrote: "Her love of learning songs has not abated. One Christmas I sent up a tape of performances of long-forgotten songs I had found in early Shaker manuscripts. On my visit the next summer I found that she had learned all of them, and excited the other members of the Society to learn them too. The songs were now part of the repertory spontaneously sung in worship."

Sister Barker's musical memory and enthusiasm were matched by her sweet voice, musical skill, and enthusiasm. A fellow Shaker once commented, "Sister Mildred always said the vim and vigor was in music and that's what attracted her to Shakerism."

The English Shakers arrived in New England as immigrants, and they were by no means the last to bring remarkable folk artistic traditions to the region. Yang Fang Nhu, a 1988 Fellow, came to Providence from a mountain village in northern Laos, by way of France, in 1984. Sewing and weaving were fundamental women's skills in her traditional Hmong society, but Fang Nhu was exceptional and became not only a master weaver but also a builder of looms.

Displaced by the Vietnam War, Yang Fang Nhu was unable to weave for many years. After 1984, with the help of the Rhode Island State Council on the Arts and the NEA, she built a traditional loom and returned to weaving, dying, and batiking her own cloth. At the time of her award, she was teaching her skills to members of the first American-born Hmong generation.

Ilias Kementzides, a Pontic Greek lyra player who was named a National Heritage Fellow in 1989, also journeyed across physical and cultural distances before settling in New England. Kementzides was born in a Greek community in the Caucasus region of the Soviet Union. He was 11 years old in 1940 when his family moved to a location near Thessaloníki, Greece.

The music of Kementzides's lyra—a bottle-shaped violin with three strings—played an important role in nurturing a stable sense of identity within the community, no matter where its members found themselves: "In Russia, every weekend the whole neighborhood would gather in the courtyard. . . . If someone heard an instrument starting up, everyone would come running. It was joyous. That's how it was in Greece too. Not a blade of grass could grow in our courtyard, there was so much dancing."

In 1974 Kementzides immigrated to Norwalk, Conn., home to another Pontic Greek community, and soon he was performing at Pontic weddings and other celebrations throughout the Northeast and in Chicago. "There was a place for the lyra here," he said. "Not only that, I was able to give a gift, in a sense, to pass on an ancient tradition."

Another Connecticut Fellow, playing an equally fundamental and ancient instrument, is T. Viswanathan, a South Indian *kuzhal* flute master. The subtlety of this South Indian (Karnatic) bamboo instrument depends on the touch of the fingers and the movement of the head. It has seven or eight openings, and its pitch varies with the length of the flute. As with the Greek lyra, musicianship lies in the performer's mastery of a complex tradition rather than a complex technology.

Viswanathan was named a National Heritage Fellow in 1992, after he had toured India, Europe, and North America for more than 40 years. For 25 of those years, in the United States, he played for his own Indo-American community, helping to sustain its identity, and for welcome outsiders, communicating the South Indian soul to the general public.

Tradition need not be threatened to be folk, but it should be community-based, informally communicated, and subject to dynamic varia-

tion. Thus National Heritage Fellowships acknowledge American master artists whether they are "the last practitioners of dying traditions" (which they are often thought to be but rarely are) or influential artists within thriving communities.

Two New England fiddlers, 1984 Fellow Joseph Cormier and 1983 awardee Simon St. Pierre, are good examples of the latter. Fiddling occasions have changed since their youth, when they played for dances. Joe Cormier of Waltham, Mass. (but originally from the Acadian fishing village of Cheticamp, Nova Scotia), still considered himself a "dance fiddler." In the 1980s he was playing for weekly maritime-style quadrilles at the French American Victory Club in Waltham, a local tradition since the 1930s in the Boston area.

St. Pierre, originally from Quebec but living in Aroostook County, Maine, since the 1950s, also played dance tunes: the reel, the two-step, and rare French Canadian waltzes. His audience was lumberjacks and his setting the bunkhouses of logging camps.

If there are many fine fiddlers practicing local and regional styles throughout New England, there may be even more excellent quilters. To be named a National Heritage Fellow for quilting, as Amber Densmore of Chelsea, Vt., was in 1988, is to join a select group. Densmore was chosen at age 87, 82 years after her mother taught her to mend. She had gone on to make bedspreads, lace doilies, and hooked rugs, as well as patchwork quilts.

Densmore's needlework is expressive of beauty, anchored in utility, and serves memory. Her "Farm and Home Memory" quilt of 172 embroidered blocks depicts elements of farm life such as "sugaring-off" and bringing in the hay. Her art was also an act of generosity: when folklorists sought to document her life's production, they were told, "I've given it all away! You'll just have to go and see my grandchildren."

Peter Kyvelos of Belmont, Mass., joined the list of New England's National Heritage Fellows in 2001. Kyvelos makes traditional musical instruments by hand. His specialty is the oud, a cousin to the lute that is native to Southwest Asia and North Africa. Kyvelos bought his first oud after falling in love with the instrument's unfamiliar sound when he was 16 years old. Forty-odd years later, when he became a Fellow, he was building new ones, repairing broken ones, and playing them in concert. Using natural woods along with high-tech plastics in his handcrafted pieces, Kyvelos both continues and extends an ancient tradition.

The NEA selects National Heritage Fellows from public nominations. Nominations

can be made by any U.S. citizen and must include an essay or cover letter describing the artist's career and life, the traditional character of his or her art, its community basis, and other related aspects, such as artistic quality and significance. Nominations should be accompanied by documentation of the artist's performance (audio- or videotape recordings) or material (slides or photos) art. Letters of support, often from scholars knowledgeable about the particular tradition, are usually solicited by the nominator. New Fellows are named annually.

The Art of Traditional Fiddle [audio CD] (Rounder Records, 2001); Jane Beck, ed., *Always in Season: Folk Art and Traditional Culture in Vermont* (1982); Ken Burns, *The Shakers: Hands to Work, Hearts to God* [videocassette] (1983; VHS release, 1996); Marjorie Hunt, "Masters of Traditional Arts," *National Geographic*, January 1991; Daniel W. Patterson, *The Shaker Spiritual* (2000 [1979]); Chuck Rosenak and Jan Rosenak, *Museum of American Folk Art Encyclopedia of 20th-Century Folk Art and Artists* (1990); Steve Siporin, *American Folk Masters: The National Heritage Fellows* (1992).

Steve Siporin

Native American Music and Dance

The native peoples of New England are in the Algonquian linguistic group, including the nations of the Wabanaki Confederacy: Abenaki, Penobscot, Passamaquoddy, Maliseet, and Micmac. Other major surviving groups are the Narragansett, Wampanoag, Nipmuck, Pequot, and Mohegan. Tribal identities are problematic, because Europeans who first encountered these peoples found a well-developed political structure, but did not use consistent names for the groups they met and later wrote into treaties, censuses, and other legal documents. Before widespread acculturation, native peoples of this region practiced similar lifeways, including song and dance styles that have continued to the present. Northeastern Native Americans were among the earliest in contact with Europeans, who by the 16th century were regularly fishing and trading along the coast. From their accounts the earliest descriptions of indigenous musical styles can be drawn.

Among northeastern peoples, songs and dances are an important part of political protocols. Many of these ceremonies have survived five centuries of European occupation, and have been important in reestablishing tribal sovereignty today. There are trading ceremonies, including welcome songs and line formation dances. The Wampum Ceremonial complex shared among the Wabanaki, Mohawk, and their Algonquian neighbors involved a Welcoming Dance, Greeting Dance between leaders, various songs in council such as the Peace Pipe Ceremony used today, women's shawl dances, and a song or dance whereby a newly installed leader greets the people. Marriages involve special songs and formation dances in squadrons signifying the blending of the two families.

Northeastern Indians have played a prominent role in the comparative study of world music. The first notation of a song in North America was made by Marc Lescarbot (part of the Pierre du Gua de Monts expedition) around 1607. The first field recordings in the world were made by J. W. Fewkes in 1890 of Passamaquoddys Noel Josephs and Peter Selmore singing in Calais, Maine. Transcriptions and recordings were made in the Northeast throughout the 20th century; audio and video recording have proven more useful to native communities.

In the Northeast region, musical genre is identified with the function of a song. Although function governs such aspects as rhythm, pace, and text, there are some prominent general characteristics of northeastern native musical style. The tune is the most important organizing principle rather than an abstract concept of scale or key. When analyzed, songs from the Northeast use a variety of scale types; some are pentatonic and others have seven or eight different pitches in one octave (for example, both the minor and major third). Pitches in the surviving and recorded songs conform to the scale degrees of mainstream European American culture. In antiphonal sections, the responders must match the pitch of the leader even if he changes it from verse to verse (a feature also found in powwow song performance).

Traditional singing styles of northeastern peoples feature a relaxed chest voice, used by both men and women; this is in marked contrast to Plains styles imported with powwow singing. Traditional accompaniments are handheld shakers, various drums, and drumming with logs, bark rolls, or shakers on the ground. The pattern is often duple, but the relation between the beat and the rhythm of the singing ranges from simply synchronized to complicated; singing may be "swung" over the beat.

Individual variations are a crucial element of singing style. While many songs follow archetypes, in performance they are often extemporized to a degree with new text composed for each occasion, tag endings, and exclamations. Extemporization is a crucial aspect of a singer's skill. Most songs have repeated sections or strophic verses. The function a song is used for influences style, and the same tune when sung for different purposes may have a different rhythm.

Of the major genres, social dance songs are often antiphonal, with a leader answered by a chorus; they are also often sectional, with each section repeated. Song lyrics often mix lexical texts and vocables, and the lyrics signal dance motions. Personal and charm song genres include hunting songs, canoeing songs, and love songs. Other important genres are game songs and lullabies.

There are also common features in traditional northeastern dancing styles. The "stomp dance" is the most common step: each foot is tapped once or twice on the ground before the dancer steps out on it. Men's dancing styles feature deliberate motions, and pantomime dance types such as hunting dances are common. Women's dancing styles tend toward graceful motions—for example, in shawl dances, such as the Passamaquoddy Tuhtuwas. There are many mixed-sex dances, including formation dances in squadrons. Line dances, round dances, and serpentine dances are all documented from the earliest contact period and are still performed today.

Instruments used in the Northeast are principally shakers and drums. Traditional drum types include water drums, log drums with or without heads, and single- or double-headed hand drums. Traditional shakers are of two types and have been made of a variety of materials: strings of animal hoofs and claws, used by shamans; and turtle shells, gourds, hollowed wood, and cow horns filled with stones, seeds, or gun shot. The Abenaki recognize two styles of songs, one accompanied by drums and the other accompanied by shakers.

Traditional music in the Northeast was affected by Christian missionary activity beginning in the 17th century. Both Protestant and Catholic catechetical material and hymn texts were produced in various northeastern languages by Europeans and Native Americans: John Eliot's Bible in Massachusetts, Eugene Vetromile's *Ahiamihewintuhangan* (*The Prayer Song*) in Abenaki and Maliseet dialects, Micmac hieroglyphic prayerbooks, and Thomas Commuck's Narragansett hymns. In the 19th and 20th centuries, funeral rites used mostly Christian songs.

Among the best-documented musical styles in the Northeast are those of the Passamaquoddy and Penobscot. Many groups, such as the Wampanoags, have preserved traditions within their own communities. Federal recognition claims are driving much documentation at present. The Mashantucket Pequot Nation has played a major role in musical renewal in the Northeast through its yearly competitive powwow, its museum, and other ongoing cultural activities.

Bruce Bourque, *Twelve Thousand Years: American Indians in Maine* (2001); Jesse Walter Fewkes, "A Contribution to Passamaquoddy Folk-Lore," *Journal of American Folk-lore* 3, no. 11 (1890); *The History of New France by Marc Lescarbot, with an English Translation, Notes, and Appendices by W. L. Grant* (1907–14); Lewis Mitchell, Robert M. Leavitt, and David A. Francis, *Wapapi Akonutomakonol / The Wampum Records: Wabanaki Traditional Laws* (1990); Frank G. Speck, *Penobscot Man: The Life History of a Forest Tribe in Maine* (1997 [1940]); Bruce G. Trigger, ed. *Northeast*, vol. 15 of *Handbook of North American Indians*, gen. ed. William C. Sturtevant (1978).

Ann Morrison Spinney

Portuguese American Folklife

Portuguese American folklife assumes one of the most colorful and expressive forms of ethnic pride and identity in southeastern New England. Folklore, music, and art customs are embedded in a ritual calendar of popular saints' festivals held at Catholic churches in the heart of most Portuguese communities.

Portuguese immigration originated from the rural sectors of the Azores, Madeira, Cape Verde, and the Continent. Regional pride, called *bairrismo*, prevented Portuguese immigrants to America from sharing a uniform national identity; this bias generated intense rivalries and social tensions between mainlanders and islanders, and between those from different islands. Bairrismo persists in Portuguese American communities where immigrants from the same islands or the Continent cluster and settle.

Portuguese immigrant communities of New England are distinguished by the multigeographical origins of their residents. Initial migrations occurred during the 18th and 19th centuries when Yankee merchants and whalers traded with the Portuguese Atlantic islands. Many Portuguese sailors who joined the crews on these vessels eventually settled in the New England port cities of Boston, New Bedford, and Nantucket, Mass., and Newport, R.I., obtaining jobs in the maritime trades and later sending for their families. The first period of mass immigration occurred between 1880 and 1921. This wave corresponded to the emergence of the textile industry and innovations in shipping, notably packet steamers. Agents for New England merchants actively recruited rural Azoreans and Madeirans to work in the mills. Passage of the Emergency Restriction Law of 1921 and the National Origin Act of 1924 curtailed immigration with restrictive quotas until the 1960s, but a second wave of Portuguese mass migration followed the modification of quotas by the Immigration and Nationality Act of 1965. The construction of international airports in the Azores and Madeira also led to a revitalization of Portuguese settlements in New England.

The new influx of Portuguese immigrants brought more diversity and conflict to existing Portuguese American communities. In addi-

Procession of Portuguese Americans enters the Church of Espirito Santo on the patronal feast day, Fall River, Mass., 1976

tion to regional identity, there were significant differences between the "modern" immigrant culture and the memories of "the old country" maintained by Americanized second- and third-generation descendants. In the mill towns where job opportunities had been scarce since the Depression, Luso-American descendants expressed their contempt for newcomers by calling them "greenhorns." Many children of recent immigrants nevertheless have sustained their linguistic and cultural ties to the homeland.

At Catholic churches throughout Portugal, the islands, and the immigrant communities, parishioners conduct public rituals devoted to the images of saints, the Blessed Virgin, Jesus Christ, and the Holy Ghost. These figures are viewed as intermediaries to God. Devotees pray to their favorite patron for divine intervention (as in the Blessing of the Fleet in Stonington, Conn., or Gloucester, Mass.). In return, the Portuguese pledge sacred vows, called *promessas,* to sponsor or celebrate a specific feast. These observances combine medieval Roman Catholic liturgy with ancient pagan agricultural festivities.

Portuguese feasts provide a convenient framework for exploring the relationships linking family, economics, politics, folklore, and religion. A committee of adult men and their families transform mundane village and neighborhood life into sacred experience by coordinating ritual performances. The Por-

tuguese mark ritual space with ephemeral folk art. They festoon the streets leading to their churches with arches of greens, colored lights, banners, flags, and flowers. The altar and images of the saints are also adorned and surrounded by flowers, candles, and incense. Many feasts begin with novenas, a week of prayer and recitation of the rosary, and culminate with a solemn High Mass and procession of the saints on the feast day. A carpet of flowers traditionally marks the procession route. The processional retinues are virtual profiles of the social organization of the immigrant community. At the conclusion of religious ceremonies, Portuguese gather at the *arraial* on the church grounds, where they indulge in eating, drinking, and gambling while listening to brass bands, Portuguese folk songs (fado) and folk music, or singing duels.

Portuguese American communities throughout New England also observe *festas,* extraordinary events featuring elaborate decorations, music, singing, dancing, gambling, ceremonial eating, and ritual drinking. These secular activities are punctuated with religious rituals in the church and a devotional service and procession on the feast day. The Festas do Divino Espirito Santo are the most prevalent events celebrated by Azoreans in the spring. During the seven Sundays following Easter, the silver crown and scepter of the Holy Ghost pass from one household shrine to another. The sponsors provide a ceremonial meal of *massa*

sovada (sweet bread) and *sopas* (soup) to the needy in memory of Queen Isabela, the originator of the festa. These Azorean celebrations are followed by the Festa do Senhor Santo Cristo, the patron of S T o Miguel, in May, at Ponta Delgada and several Portuguese churches in New England.

The largest celebration of the Festa do Espirito Santo is currently held in Fall River, Mass., in August. The Madeiran community of New Bedford, however, claims to celebrate "the largest Portuguese feast in the world." Their annual observance of the Feast of the Blessed Sacrament is held on the first weekend of August. These festivals, with the exception of the Holy Ghost Feast in Fall River, have been conducted for nearly a century in New England.

The ceremonial meals and ritual foods shared at festas have preserved the culinary traditions of rural gardeners. Before a feast, traditional Portuguese conduct *matancas* (ritual killings), where they kill and prepare fresh chickens, rabbits, pigs, goats, or cows for ceremonial meals made with fresh herbs and vegetables from the neighborhood gardens. Grapes, picked from arbors covering the garden patches, are pressed in local wine cellars called *adegas. Carne assada* (roast beef), *carne guisada* (stewed beef), *cacoila* (marinated pork), *favas* (broad beans), *linguica* and *chourico* (pork sausage), and *carne de espeto* (Madeiran shish kebob) are standard offerings at festas, with ample cups of wine, beer, or *aguardiente* (moonshine).

Folkloric groups, brass bands, *ranchinhos,* and fado are four of the most popular forms of musical entertainment at festas. Nearly a dozen folkloric groups perform traditional Portuguese songs and dances in native regional costumes on the New England feast circuit. Three of the most popular groups representing the spectrum of regional styles are the Rancho Folclorico da Clube Portugues de Hartford, the Madeiran Folkloric Group of the S.S. Santissimo Sacramenteno Club in New Bedford, and the Lusitanos, an Azorean troupe from Fall River. Members of the Lusitanos also perform an innovative fusion of traditional and modern Azorean and Portuguese music under the name Gerasons. The Madeirans are famous for their national dance, the *bailhino.* Azoreans, on the other hand, prefer the *chamarrita, sapateia,* and *pezinho.*

Brass bands are an integral part of any Portuguese feast, at which they lead processions and perform concerts on stage afterwards. The bands originally formed during the 19th and early 20th centuries and have been revitalized by recent mass migration. Brass bands now include young boys and girls as well as adult men. Some of the most notable marching bands include the Portuguese American Band, Our Lady of the Angels Band, and the Senhor da Pedra Club Band from New Bedford; the Banda do Santo Antonio, the Acoreano Band Club, and Our Lady of the Light Band from Fall River; and the Holy Rosary Band from Providence.

Folk musicians frequently bring guitars, mandolins, and accordions to the feast grounds and engage in improvisational sessions with relatives and friends. These groups are called *ranchos* or *ranchinhos*, depending on their size. The rhythm accompaniment from the crowd might include tambourines, castanets, iron triangles, drums, and clapping. These casual sessions may erupt into singing duels known as *cantigas ao desafio*; the object of the duel is to outplay and mock your adversary publicly in verse.

Portuguese fado music, which emerged from the Moorish quarters of Lisbon, is reserved for the formal dinner crowd at festas and local Portuguese restaurants. The leading area fado singers are continental Portuguese: Ana and Jose Vinagre from New Bedford, Fernando Alberto from Fall River, and Natercia de Conceicao from Providence. They are usually accompanied on *guitarra* and *viola* by Azorean musicians who have mastered this continental music form.

Three folkloric beliefs and customs are highly visible at Portuguese feasts: the *mal olhado* (the evil eye), *mal de inveja* (jealousy), and *quebranto* (weakness). These influences are often attributed to those who stare too intensely at people attending the feast. These folk "superstitions" are countered by a combination of pagan talismans and Catholic prayer. At Portuguese feasts, it is not uncommon to find infants, who are thought to be most susceptible to these malevolent influences, adorned with gold bracelets bearing a *figa* (the fist), a crescent moon, a pentacle, and *o corno*, the twisted goat horn. Protective mothers and grandmothers stop at churches to light votive candles and submit final prayers to their favorite patron saint before leaving for home.

All Portuguese festas are ritual performances that depend on the fulfillment of social and religious obligations. They heighten Portuguese awareness of shared sentiments, values, and regional ethnic identity and simultaneously sustain their folk art, music, and culinary traditions. The continuity of Portuguese feasting and folklife depends on the inclusion and socialization of children in adult activities through the preparation and celebration of the festivals. Subsequent modifications and transformations result from the degree that Portuguese descendants accept, reinter-

pret, and act on the customs and meanings imparted to them by their immigrant parents or grandparents. Portuguese American feasts and folklife, therefore, are not simply an extension of traditional Portuguese culture, but rather dynamic ritual dramas continuously recreated by successive generations responding to their unique and changing circumstances in New England.

Stephen L. Cabral, *Tradition and Transformation: Portuguese Feasting in New Bedford* (1989); Cecilia Cardoza Emilio, *Azorean Folk Customs* (1990); Manuel J. Esperanca, *Madeira: The Majestic and Mysterious Island* (1992); Rodney Gallop, *Portugal: A Book of Folkways* (1961); Donna Huse and James Sears, "Urban Cottage Gardens," in *The Portuguese Spinner: An American Story*, ed. Marsha McCabe and Joseph Thomas (1998); Leo Pap, *The Portuguese-Americans* (1981).

Stephen L. Cabral

Powwows The modern powwow can be traced to the Algonquian word *pawwaw*, referring to a formal or informal council for dialogue and ceremony. Traditionally, gatherings for community celebration and ritual were held around changes of season. Native American leaders with healing abilities were also called pawwaws in southern New England. The singing and dancing that often accompanied native healing practices have become part of our contemporary understanding of the term. In 1646, in an effort to suppress Indian religions and encourage native peoples to adopt European ways, the Massachusetts General Court made it illegal to hold a pawwaw

and to "worship false gods" or the devil. Even today one finds *powwow* associated with witchcraft in dictionary definitions of the term.

With the passage of the American Indian Religious Freedom Act in 1978, the public became more accepting of and interested in Native American ways. Contemporary New England powwows are secular events predominantly focused on intertribal exchange. Many are open to the public and incorporate educational programs for tourists. Drug- and alcohol-free, modern-day powwows feature craftsmen and women, honoring ceremonies, singing, and dancing; sometimes traditional musicians, such as flutists, give special performances or tribal storytellers give presentations. Powwows are typically weekend-long events, although larger gatherings can last as long as a week.

Music and dancing are central. While the Native American music of New England was traditionally sung only with the accompaniment of rattles or hand drums, contemporary powwows have adopted the styles of western and southern Indian groups. Large drums, averaging the circumference of a marching band's bass drum, are played by four to a dozen singers. Most powwows feature two or three drum groups. Larger events in recent years, often hosted by colleges or tribal reservations, hold drumming competitions, which attract many more drum groups.

Dancing competitions are popular, too. During the warmer months dances can be held outdoors in fields or arbors; winter ushers

Getting acquainted at the Planting Moon Powwow, Topsfield, Mass., 1992

them indoors, to gymnasiums or recreation centers. Men, women, and children all take part. A lot of time and effort are invested in each dancer's regalia, which is fashioned in accordance with the style of dance to be performed. Many styles have been adapted from early traditions, but modern styles are always developing. They include men's and women's fancydancing, jingle dress, and the grass dance.

On average, a committee needs nine months to a year to organize a powwow. Most powwows employ a master of ceremonies to coordinate the flow of activities, and an arena director to oversee grounds maintenance and advise attendees regarding protocol.

Powwows have been an important part of the revitalization of American Indian identity in New England over the past 100 years. They continue to provide both a public presence of native ways for European Americans and a means of cultural exchange and renewal for New England's Indian peoples.

Charlotte Heth, ed., *Native American Dance: Ceremonies and Social Traditions* (1992); Ben Marra, *Powwow* (1996); Josephine Paterek, *Encyclopedia of American Indian Costume* (1994); Chris Roberts, *Powwow Country: People of the Circle* (1998).

Susie Husted

Proverbs

Proverbs—or concise statements of apparent truths that have currency among people who share a certain geographic, ethnic, or even national identity—reflect at least in part jointly held attitudes, mores, and experiences. In the case of New England, early settlers established a lifestyle based on Puritan ethics, commonly held religious beliefs, high moral principles, and a set of characteristics that came to be widely viewed as Yankee values: independence, ingenuity, thriftiness, ruggedness, tenacity, simplicity, pride, and a particularly dry sense of humor. The mindset or worldview of New Englanders is to a certain degree reflected in the unique proverbial wisdom of this northeastern region of the United States.

Of course, New Englanders also use such nationally and internationally known proverbs as "Big fish eat little fish," "In wine there is truth," or "One hand washes the other." And the original settlers of New England brought an entire stock of English proverbs with them. Expressions such as "The early bird catches the worm," "A stitch in time saves nine," and "The proof of the pudding is in the eating" are used to this day in the region and throughout the country. Generations of immigrants also brought Gaelic, Italian, Portuguese, and other foreign-language proverbs to New England, where some are still in use among native speakers or as loan translations into English.

It is thus difficult to ascertain which proverbs might in fact be indigenous to New England. Sayings such as "If you don't like the weather in New England, just wait a minute and it will change" and "Snow on Mount Mansfield and in six weeks the valley will be white" are obviously attached to the region. And we know that Ralph Waldo Emerson coined "Hitch your wagon to a star" in 1870. But the origins of other proverbs used in the area, such as "Money is flat and meant to be piled up" and "Out of old fields comes new corn," are much less clear. Trying to locate certain proverbs in a particular New England state can be even more complicated. Maxims such as "Sap runs best after a sharp frost" and "The world is your cow, but you have to do the milking" have been identified as originating in Vermont on account of their rural nature, but they could also have been coined in New Hampshire. Even the origin of the well-known proverb "Good fences make good neighbors," used by Robert Frost in his 1914 poem "Mending Wall," is not certain. An earlier variant, "A good fence helps to keep peace between neighbors," appeared in 1640 in England, and the similar text "Good fences preserve good neighborhoods" dates from 1815. But today only Frost's version is current in New England and the United States. Summarizing both the landscape of stone walls and the reserved nature of some New Englanders, it can fairly be considered a true New England proverb.

Although proverbs are always best observed and studied in oral communication, New England's rich tradition of proverbial lore has been published in widely circulated farmer's almanacs, whose purpose is to provide education, moral uplift, and entertainment. Benjamin Franklin recorded and reformulated many proverbs into classic and enduring form in his *Poor Richard's Almanack* and even created an essay, "The Way to Wealth," consisting almost entirely of proverbs spoken by "Father Abraham" in the 25th anniversary issue of the *Almanack* in 1757. The works of such New England writers as Edward Taylor, Cotton Mather, Ralph Waldo Emerson, Nathaniel Hawthorne, Henry Wadsworth Longfellow, John Greenleaf Whittier, Oliver Wendell Holmes, Harriet Beecher Stowe, Henry David Thoreau, James Russell Lowell, Herman Melville, Emily Dickinson, Louisa May Alcott, Rowland Evans Robinson, Mark Twain, and Dorothy Canfield Fisher contain many regional proverbs in context. Emerson in particular, the New England preacher, rhetorician, essayist, Transcendentalist, philosopher, pragmatist, and humanist, was deeply interested in and intrigued by proverbs. He collected specimens himself and inter-

spersed them freely in his letters, journals, sermons, lectures, and essays.

What follows is a sampler of proverbs that comment on various aspects of New England life. They represent traditional wisdom about life's concerns and tribulations, and they continue to be used as fitting observations on human relationships, be they personal, social, or materialistic: "Use it up, wear it out, make it do, or do without"; "If it ain't broke, don't fix it"; "Boston is a state of mind"; "Independence is better than riches"; "If you want to get to the top of the hill, you must go up it"; "An empty purse puts wrinkles in the face"; "You can't tell whether an egg is good by looking at its shell"; "If you wish to see Old England, you must go to New England"; "Handsome apples are sometimes sour"; "When the well is dry, we know the worth of water"; "There are many witty men whose brains can't fill their bellies"; "Talking will never build a stone wall or pay taxes"; "Talk less and say more"; "A warm-back husband and a cold-foot wife should easily lead a compatible life"; "Matrimony is not a word but a sentence"; "An apple pie without cheese is like a kiss without a squeeze"; "The lazy dog leans to the wall to bark"; "There are lazy minds as well as lazy bodies"; "What is worth doing is worth doing well"; "A crooked road won't get you far"; "Don't throw away the bucket until you know if the new one holds water"; "Mud thrown is ground lost"; "Don't swallow the cow and worry with the tail"; "Other people's eggs have two yolks"; "Make money honestly if you can, but make money"; "Dirty hands make clean money"; "Many a fair flower springs out of a dunghill"; "Dunghills rise and castles fall"; "Two small lobsters make a big one"; "It is hard for an empty sail to stand upright"; "Only Yankees and fools predict the weather"; and "In New England we have nine months of winter and three months of damned poor sledding." To a degree these proverbs reflect the mind and character of New Englanders, and as such they represent a treasure trove of Yankee folk wisdom.

Wolfgang Mieder, *American Proverbs: A Study of Texts and Contexts* (1989); Mieder, *Yankee Wisdom: New England Proverbs* (1989); Wolfgang Mieder, Stewart A. Kingsbury, and Kelsie B. Harder, eds., *A Dictionary of American Proverbs* (1992); Bartlett Jere Whiting, *Early American Proverbs and Proverbial Phrases* (1977).

Wolfgang Mieder

Public Folklore

Public folklore, the public dimension of the academic field, arrived on the scene in the late 1970s and grew in strength during the 1980s and 1990s, when it became firmly established. Through the development of state- and community-level folk arts programs and educational programs, public folklore underscores cultural expressive traditions passed down through generations within a family or a community, traditions that frequently symbolize cultural identity. Public folklorists typically work in arts and culture agencies such as arts councils, museums, historical societies, and humanities councils, or in private consulting organizations. Today, all six New England states have public folklore programs.

A cultural strategy was initiated during the New Deal, resulting in the Works Project Administration folklore programs that were carried out during the 1930s. Folklorists began "to contemplate the relationship between government and culture," thus laying the underpinnings for public folklore. Three major influences shaped public folklore as we know it today: the Smithsonian Institution's Folklife Festival, with its coherent aesthetic and political vision of diversity; the nation's 1976 Bicentennial, which spearheaded a resurgence of interest in family heritage and roots, and with it the establishment—through a congressional legislative act—of the American Folklife Center at the Library of Congress; and Bess Lomax Hawes becoming director, in 1976, of the Folk Arts program at the National Endowment for the Arts (NEA). With the NEA's matching grant policy, Hawes saw a way to integrate the traditional arts into state arts councils.

The Bicentennial ushered in a new emphasis on cultural conservation at the national level that touched local communities and resonated throughout the country. In 1978 Vermont became the first New England state to initiate a folk arts program at the arts council with an NEA grant. Through an intensive survey of folk arts in Vermont and a statewide exhibition, Vermonters discovered a strong history of traditional arts and numerous fine traditional artists at work in the state. Although the Vermont program did not become a part of the state government as Hawes had hoped, it developed into a private, nonprofit organization, which was much more risky because of the lack of steady funding. In 1984 the Vermont Folklife Center became a reality under the protective wing of the arts council; it later found a home in Middlebury, where it undertook its first fledgling fund-raising efforts, and today is a stable organization.

In neighboring New Hampshire, public folklore efforts endured a number of false starts, but a state program eventually blossomed. As early as 1980 a folk arts coordinator was hired, but after three years of NEA support, the position was dropped because of the lack of state funding. In 1993 it was reinstated, again through the NEA, and by 1997 it had finally become a permanent position at the New Hampshire State Council on the Arts through the state budgeting process. This position was predicated on the interest of the Smithsonian's Folklife Festival in featuring New Hampshire on the Mall in Washington, D.C., and New Hampshire's determination to have this happen. Thus the groundwork was laid in the years leading up to 1997, but funding ran out a second time before a permanent position was approved. In 1998 a new traditional arts coordinator was hired to fill the position, and Lynn Martin Graton was plunged into the maelstrom of festival politics and the job of producing the festival on the Mall, then restaging it in New Hampshire in the summer of 2000. The festival brought credibility and visibility to the arts council and through extensive fieldwork provided a traditional arts directory database. Today, the program is well known, well established, and in demand.

As in New Hampshire, the Maine Arts Commission applied to the NEA to fund a folk arts coordinator in the mid-1980s and maintained the position for three years, but the commission was then unwilling to continue funding it. Finally, in 1989, Kathleen Mundell was hired by the Maine Arts Commission with state money to head a traditional arts program. Over the next 12 years, Mundell built a model program. She worked extensively with the Wabanakis, helping them to establish the Maine Indian Basketmakers Alliance in 1993. She established a Traditional Arts Apprenticeship Program and also helped a number of communities survey their cultural resources, which in turn led to community programs. In 2001 the Maine Arts Commission began to move away from the traditional arts, placing greater emphasis on community arts. Mundell's original job was redefined with minimal emphasis on the traditional arts; she resigned the position, and her departure was a setback for traditional arts programming at the state level. More recently, Community Arts Associate Keith Ludden began stewardship of public folklore programs at the Maine Arts Commission.

The Maine Folklife Center grew out of an academic program in the anthropology department at the University of Maine at Orono. It is best known for its archives, which were compiled by Edward Ives and his students. The center has also begun to mount traveling exhibits and to present programs, particularly on traditional music, on Maine Public Radio. The Maine Folklife Center hopes to continue the trend, but unfortunately it does not have the influence of the arts commission.

In 1979 the American Folklife Center began a fieldwork project in Rhode Island. One result was the partial funding of a folklife consultant by the Rhode Island Historical Preservation and Heritage Commission. Program money was generated through grants, which continue today. The NEA initially funded a folk arts coordinator for the Rhode Island State Arts Council in 1982; while such funding was usually limited to three years, Rhode Island received support for five years. Finally, in 1986 the legislature voted on a full-time, salaried, union position for identifying, documenting, and presenting traditional artists. Over the years, Winnie Lambrecht, who has held this position since the beginning, has built an apprenticeship program and a traditional arts component to the council's educational programming. Folklorist Michael E. Bell has worked with the Rhode Island Preservation and Heritage Commission since 1980. The traditional arts remain a well-integrated part of the council's overall programs.

Connecticut has taken a different road entirely. The Institute for Community Research, an organization concerned with community health and social issues, wanted to establish a program for exploring community artistic expression. The director first established the Cultural Heritage Arts Program in 1991 through an NEA grant. In 1994, the institute assumed its funding. Over the years, the program has focused on locating and documenting traditional artists and their communities, and on public programming through exhibitions, publications, CDs, and radio shows.

Like New Hampshire, Massachusetts has experienced ups and downs in its efforts to establish a state traditional arts program. A strong program was initiated at the Massachusetts Cultural Council through an NEA grant in 1984. During the late 1980s, the Folklife and Ethnic Arts program flourished under Dillon Bustin, and Massachusetts was to be featured at the Smithsonian's Folklife Festival in 1988. During the same year, Lowell, Mass., was chosen as the site for the National Folk Festival, and the American Folklife Center conducted a yearlong documentation project in that city. With 1988 came the restaging of the Smithsonian Folklife Festival and a host of public programming. In 1989, the New England Folklife Center was established as a program of the Lowell Historic Preservation Commission, under the auspices of the U.S. Department of the Interior. It was federally funded for four years with the anticipation that it would partner with other governmental and private institutions. Eventually the New England Folklife Center joined with Middlesex Community College; after five years, however, Middlesex withdrew its funding and the New England Folklife Center disappeared—a lost opportunity. The Lowell Folk Festival, on the other hand, was a major success, drawing audiences from Cambridge Mass., to Portland, Maine. In 1990 the city of Lowell took over the festival, which continues today as a city initiative and a major New England event, perhaps the largest cultural event in the region.

In 1990 the New England Foundation for the Arts (NEFA) hired a traditional arts coordinator, initially through an NEA grant, to reach the region's many different ethnic communities. The traditional arts were featured in apprenticeships, touring, and technical assistance and an innovative project designed to help new traditional performing artists find mainstream venues. NEFA also played an important role in fostering communication among New England folk arts coordinators from different states. The traditional arts program was unfortunately lost with a change in directorship.

Sustainability has always been a major concern for public cultural programs; without state support, few programs have been viable. Likewise, unless local projects were initiated with a sustained funding source, they could not be maintained. Today, the climate is positive. In 1998, for instance, the Massachusetts Cultural Council received a grant from the NEA that called for the reestablishment of a permanent folklorist position on its staff, the renewal of a focused fieldwork effort, and the integration of folk and traditional arts into grant programs throughout the agency. By 2000, the program was well entrenched and activity had increased statewide.

Public folklore has infused the field with a new vitality, but progress has not always been smooth. Bess Hawes, through her position as director of the Folk and Traditional Arts Program at the NEA, was a major influence in fostering state programs. Even with that support, fledgling programs sometimes proved too weak to survive on their own. State monies seem the most reliable funding stream. Despite the various failures, several strong programs and an infrastructure of public folklorists remain throughout the region. Public folklore will continue to be a visible part of New England culture.

Robert Baron, "Multi-Paradigm Discipline, Inter-Disciplinary Field, Peering Through and Around the Interstices," *Western Folklore* 52 (1993); Robert Baron and Nicholas R. Spitzer, eds., *Public Folklore* (1992); Jane C. Beck, "Taking Stock," *Presidential Address for the American Folklore Society* (1996); Burt Feintuch, *The Conservation of Culture: Folklorists and the Public Sector* (1987); Elizabeth Peterson for the NEA, *The Changing Faces of Tradition: A Report on the Folk and Traditional Arts in the United States* (1996).

Jane C. Beck

Quilts Since colonial times New England women have been responsible for household textile production. Early family inventories and wills document their quilts, three-layer bedcovers generally consisting of a patchwork or appliquéd top; a soft, insulating material in the center called *batting;* and a plain backing, all sewn together with as many as 12 to 14 tiny stitches per inch in sometimes elaborate patterns. Quilting bees, at which needleworkers gather to complete a quilt's construction collectively, have provided social interaction as well as practical assistance.

The appreciation of quilts has endured into modern times. Throughout American history girls have prepared for adulthood by sewing quilts for their dolls, adolescents have made quilts for their hope chests, mature women have made quilts for their families and friends, and older women have produced them for younger generations. In the late 1980s and 1990s New Englanders joined people from all states and of all nationalities in contributing to the enormous AIDS Memorial Quilt, constructed and displayed to commemorate lives lost to AIDS throughout the United States and the world.

The styles, construction, and uses of quilts have evolved over time, especially since the mid-19th-century manufacture of blankets rendered handmade bedding a luxury rather than a necessity and the sewing machine speeded construction in the average household. Many quilters forsook remnants and patches of material in favor of fine wool or cotton fabrics and produced extraordinary showpieces. Friendship or album quilts, to which inked, stamped, or embroidered inscriptions were applied, became a way of remembering departed friends or celebrating special events. Groups of reform-minded quilters auctioned or raffled off their creations to raise money for church-related or charitable endeavors, antislavery and temperance activity, and soldiers' aid during the Civil War. Crazy quilts, which depart from the traditional three-layer structural scheme, combining silks and satins in asymmetrical patterns, enjoyed a vogue in the late 19th century.

New England industries facilitated the making of quilts. The Boott Mill of Lowell, Mass., produced cotton prints that were purchased by quilters. Coats and Clark, Inc., manufactured thread in Stamford, Conn. And the Fairfield Processing Corporation in Danbury, Conn., manufactures Poly-fil for quilt batting today.

Quilts can be viewed today throughout New England. Permanent collections can be found at the Connecticut Historical Society and Wadsworth Atheneum in Hartford; the Litchfield (Conn.) Historical Society; the Shelburne (Vt.) Museum; in Deerfield and Sturbridge, Mass.; and at the Peabody Essex Museum in Salem, Mass. Annual agricultural fairs, such as the Eastern States Exposition in Springfield, Mass., display both antique and modern quilts.

Since the 1970s quilts have enjoyed a renaissance. Great numbers of local quilting clubs have formed, with members meeting regularly to exchange information, hear lectures or take classes from guest quilters, and create quilts to raise money for causes ranging from AIDS babies to women's shelters to public television. In 1976 several local groups united to form the New England Quilters Guild, whose museum in Lowell, Mass., features a library, quilt collection, and rotating exhibits. By 1997 1,000 people had joined 60 chapters of the organization.

Lynne Z. Bassett and Jack Larkin, *Northern Comfort: New England's Early Quilts, 1780–1850* (1998); Lilian Baker Carlisle, *Pieced Work and Appliqué Quilts at Shelburne Museum* (1957); Richard L. Cleveland and Donna Bister, *Plain and Fancy: Vermont's People and Their Quilts as a Reflection of America* (1991); Laurel Horton and Bryding Adams, eds., *Quiltmaking in America: Beyond the Myths* (1994).

Karen J. Blair

Scrimshaw The origin of the term *scrimshaw* remains unknown, but its use in America to identify decorative and functional objects made from whalebone, whale ivory, or walrus ivory dates to the 1820s when the whaling industry rose to prominence in New England. Thousands of surviving examples of scrimshaw produced between that time and the decline of the whaling industry after the Civil War serve as reminders of the importance of whaling to the New England economy, the popularity of scrimshaw as a vernacular art form, and the artistry of numerous—largely forgotten—scrimshanders who created it.

Whale hunting worldwide by coastal New Englanders was prompted by a market for the oil that whale blubber yielded. Whale oil was promoted by some for medicinal purposes, but its primary value was as a fuel for lamps and a lubricant for machinery. The discovery of this relatively clean-burning oil may have prompted improvements in artificial domestic lighting, and its lubricating properties were critical to the development of new mechanized manufacturing processes in the Northeast.

After the oil was rendered from the whale's blubber, many seamen saved various parts of the skeleton as raw material for scrimshaw. The teeth and bone of the sperm whale along with baleen, a material resembling plastic used by the right whale to filter ocean water for food, were crafted by scrimshanders into an impressive array of articles intended for shipboard and domestic purposes. Carpenters', riggers', coopers', and sailmakers' tools, along

Scrimshaw on walrus tusks

with navigational instruments, were among the most common items made for shipboard use. Popular household items intended as gifts for loved ones or to be sold ashore included jagging wheels used to crimp and pierce pie dough, which often featured handles sculpted in human and animal forms; bodkins for piercing holes in fabric and leather; knitting needles; clothespins; boxes; and intimate tokens of affection, such as corset busks bearing engraved designs. Small scrimshawed objects were likely crafted by many working seamen, while more ambitious items, such as swifts (yarn winders) and birdcages, were likely made onshore by retired whalers or those between voyages.

In addition to making useful wares, scrimshanders also ornamented sperm whales' teeth with images and inscriptions, and these may be the most widely known examples of the art. The engraving of whales' teeth possibly derived from the custom of engraving images and sentiments on powder horns during the 18th and early 19th centuries, for the techniques are similar. Using a pointed tool, the scrimshander first incised a design on the surface of the tooth. He then applied ink to the tooth and wiped off the excess to highlight the engraving, whose lines retained the ink. Teeth bearing portraits of famous individuals or loved ones; depictions of whale hunts, ships, or battles; written sentiments; erotic images; and geometrical designs are most common.

Sometimes scrimshanders transferred popular illustrations to a tooth by applying the picture to the surface of the tooth, scratching a series of dots to outline the image, and then connecting the dots to complete the transfer.

During the 20th century scrimshaw persisted in decorative carvings affixed to the top of Nantucket lightship baskets made by Jose Formosa Reyes, who came to Nantucket from the Philippines. Reproductions of famous scrimshaw items are made in various composite materials, but little work in ivory is done in New England, given the protection of whales and other ivory-producing animals. Superb collections of the folk art are housed in the Peabody Essex Museum and the New Bedford Whaling Museum, both in Massachusetts.

Richard C. Malley, *Graven by the Fishermen Themselves: Scrimshaw in the Mystic Seaport Museum* (1983); Michael McManus, *A Treasury of American Scrimshaw: A Collection of the Useful and Decorative* (1997).

Richard Miller

Smithing The tools and traditions of blacksmithing came to New England in the 17th century with the first European immigrants. Blacksmiths provided essential services to the new colonial settlements, fabricating metal goods that were an integral part of domestic and work life. Before the Industrial Revolution the smithy produced basic building supplies—hinges, latches, screws, and nails—as well as such essential tools as the ax, froe, and saw. Blacksmiths forged weather vanes—the first one in New England was a cockerel, reportedly made from two old copper kettles in 1721 by Boston craftsman Deacon Shem Drowne for a Hanover Street church—iron implements for cooking and illumination, iron parts for horse-drawn conveyances, and iron tools for a variety of occupations. Lock- and gunsmiths specialized in precision-made parts, and wheelwrights used blacksmithing skills to band wooden wheels with iron tires. Related metalworking trades included working with copper, silver, and tin.

In the second half of the 19th century local craft shops like the one described in Henry Wadsworth Longfellow's 1841 poem "The Village Blacksmith" declined because of a shift to factory production. During this period machine-made goods replaced metal objects forged by hand, but blacksmith shops survived by specializing in building wagons, sleighs, and carriages and by shoeing horses and oxen. Blacksmiths also functioned as local fix-it men and acted as vernacular engineers in devising solutions to practical problems; a Vermont blacksmith, Thomas Davenport, is credited with developing the prototype of the first electric motor.

With the rapid adoption of the automobile in the early 20th century, the blacksmith's role in a horsepower-based transportation system quickly became obsolete. But blacksmiths also had the right tools and experience to respond to the emerging technology of the automobile, and as older New Englanders observe, "Blacksmith shops became garages." In rural areas horses continued to be used on farms well into the 1940s. The blacksmiths who served farm communities fabricated tools, shod horses, built sap sleds, and kept farm equipment up and running. But even in the countryside as the tractor gained ascendancy, blacksmithing became an anachronism.

In the 1960s blacksmithing received an unexpected burst of life when young people rediscovered it as they searched for meaningful work. Some sought out older smiths, often of their grandparents' generation, from whom they learned the trade as informal apprentices. Over the decades leading up to the turn of the 21st century blacksmithing not only persisted but flourished. Today, the time-honored tools, techniques, skills, and knowledge of the village blacksmith are being put to a wide variety of uses. Some contemporary smiths work exclusively as farriers, but the livelihoods of most depend on decorative ironwork—from chandeliers to towel racks—for urban and suburban consumers.

Despite the changes brought by the 20th century, blacksmiths explain that the line of continuity, the "tradition" of blacksmithing, lives not in the objects made but in the processes by which they were made. Contemporary blacksmiths, like their predecessors, have mastered a system of knowledge that enables them to manipulate metal in the creation of new forms. Thus hand-forged objects are linked over the span of centuries: the S-curve of a 21st-century table leg and that of a 19th-century wagon brace are one and the same.

Alex Bealer, *The Art of Blacksmithing* (1995); Mabel E. Reaveley, *Weathervane Secrets* (1984); H. R. Bradley Smith, *Blacksmiths' and Farriers' Tools at the Shelburne Museum: A History of Their Development from Forge to Factory* (1981); Eliot Wigginton, ed., *Foxfire 5: Ironmaking, Blacksmithing, Flintlock Rifles, Bear Hunting, and Other Affairs of Plain Living* (1979).

Gregory L. Sharrow

Smuggling Geography is destiny. Bounded by the indented, island-encrusted Atlantic coast to the east, the Hudson River and Lake Champlain waterways to the west, and the rough, often deeply wooded boundary with Canada to the north, New England's borders are virtually impossible to protect against the illegal trafficking of goods or people. Couple this with the independent nature of the quick-witted, taciturn, Yankee trickster-hero figure, and smuggling becomes an inevitable outcome. Indeed, one of the first acts of the American Revolution was the sinking of HMS *Gaspee* in Bristol, R.I., after it had chased local smugglers. Rhode Island had an early reputation as a center to fence stolen and smuggled goods.

Much of New England well into the 20th century was a rural backwater with a fluctuating low-cash economy, where smuggling and its entrepreneurial handmaidens—piracy, profiteering, and poaching—diversified one's options for survival. Thus, the imposition of federal restrictions on trade actually served as a boon to the shadow economy, giving rise to a romantic image of the popular smuggler. Thomas Jefferson's Embargo Act (1807–10), which prohibited trade with Great Britain and its Canadian territories, was a case in point.

Before the embargo there was a hefty legal exodus from New England's northern tier to the Province of Lower Canada (Quebec) of grain, pork, cheese, butter, lumber, and the potash used in making glass and especially the soap vital to the large British wool industry. At its height, a load of potash was worth 10 times a comparable load of wheat, in those days a considerable sum. Tons and tons of potash from New England's trees went to Britain via Canada. Return loads brought a multiplicity of manufactured goods from Britain. (Mount Mansfield's Smuggler's Notch derived its name from its use as a smuggling route.) The embargo stimulated local manufacture of many of these same items; the smuggling that swiftly followed was popularly tolerated and supported. When in 1808 the Lake Champlain patrol vessel *The Fly* captured the notorious single-masted cutter *The Blacksnake*, Vermonters were enraged. Newspaper accounts of the incident condemned the embargo as an infringement of individual rights and liberties. Pete Sutherland's award-winning 1991 folk song "The Black Snake and the Fly" recounts the story and popular sentiment:

So raise your glass to smugglers,
for they've helped small towns survive,
And now the lake's alive with "snakes"—
the potash business thrives.

The Prohibition era (1920–33) ushered in another period of general disregard for the law. Passed as the 18th Amendment to the U.S. Constitution (New Hampshire was the last state to ratify), the law prohibited the possession and trade of liquor. Despite the concerted efforts of temperance organizations nationwide, the law was overwhelmingly unpopular. Smuggling began at once. Bootlegging, so called because of the long practice of smuggling flat whiskey bottles in boots, burgeoned throughout New England as did both the production and carrying of liquor. Certain hidden stills that began their careers during this era continue to operate today in the region's countryside. The Italian granite-working families of Barre, Vt., accustomed to turning boxcar loads of grapes into wine and grappa, continued to receive their freight shipments, avowedly for making grape juice. Apprehending rural perpetrators was more a game of hide-and-seek than the staged raids performed in cities. The romantic figure of the rural bootlegger had its dark counterpart in the serious criminal developments in cities nationwide; Boston and Providence were New England's ties to organized crime.

During Prohibition, schooners would load cargoes of alcohol onto speedboats disguised as fishing boats to run the liquor ashore where fast trucks would haul it to New York and other destinations. Legends developed about the trickery used to hide cargoes in unusual places. New England folklore often views the acquisition of sudden wealth as ill-gotten gains. The homes of wealthy sea captains from the China trade are seen as the result of running opium on clipper ships to the Far East. A persistent legend from the Prohibition era holds that money from bootlegging would lead to personal harm in the long run, and the misfortunes of the Kennedy family are still seen as a testimony to this fact, based on Joseph Kennedy's alleged involvement in smuggling.

People, too, have been contraband. Vermont, first among states to ban slavery, was a committed participant in the Underground Railroad during the decades before the Civil War, passing runaway slaves from station to station until they reached safety in Canada. During the late 20th century the region continued its sanctuary tradition, taking in and passing on to Canada illegal political refugees, many from Central America. A dark side existed to this work as well, with profiteering from the import of Asians, primarily to urban centers. The smuggling of arms, tobacco, and drugs did not have the popular support of earlier periods. Nevertheless, during hard times in the fisheries during the 1970s and 1980s, the smuggling of marijuana and cocaine along New England's coast increased. Given the combination of opportunism and a border impossible to seal, smuggling is probably an inextricable part of the region's culture.

Scott Corbett, *The Sea Fox: The Adventures of Cape Cod's Most Colorful Rumrunner* (1956); H. Nicholas Muller III, "Smuggling into Canada: How the Champlain Valley Defied Jefferson's Embargo," *Vermont History* 38 (Winter 1970); Wilber Henry Siebert, "The Underground Railroad in Massachusetts," *American Antiquarian Society Proceedings*, new series, 45 (1935); Pete Sutherland, "The Black Snake and the Fly," *Vermont Life*, 46, no. 1 (Autumn 1991).

Eleanor Kokar Ott

Social Protest New Englanders have long voiced their dissatisfaction with existing social conditions through various forms of traditional expression. Native Americans are known to have responded to European encroachment by way of time-tested oratorical practices. Narragansett chief Miantonomo, for example, was aiming to instill intertribal unity in a speech he made to fellow Indians after the near decimation of the Pequot by both English and Native American forces in the 1630s. Miantonomo complained that "the English have gotten our land," observing, "So are we all Indians as the English are, and say brother to one another; so must we be one as they are, for we shall be all gone shortly." Latter-day attempts at pan-Indian unity in New England and throughout North America have generated intertribal powwows, among whose symbols of solidarity and protest is the prominently placed portrait of imprisoned American Indian rights activist Leonard Peltier. Ironically, when in 1773 a group of colonial rebels protesting British taxes staged their legendary tea party in Boston Harbor, they dressed as Native Americans with painted faces and inspired tavern songs with such lyrics as "Rally, Mohawks, and bring out your axes,/and tell King George we'll pay no taxes."

Independence from the Crown did not, however, free factory workers from exploitation. In the early 1800s young women recruited from farms to work in textile mills sang songs such as "Lowell Factory Girl," protesting conditions and wages in the mills and expressing a longing to return to "my native dell." In a 1912 strike in Lawrence, Mass., immigrant workers expressed their anger on colorful placards in different languages, inspiring the song "Bread and Roses," which became something of a labor anthem. It may also have inspired the name of the Bread and Puppet Theater, a collective founded by the German-born sculptor Peter Schumann and based in northern Vermont since 1970. Bread and Puppet has joined protest marches and has staged performances with political themes throughout New England and the world, using masked, costumed performers, musicians, and larger-than-life-size puppets and combining such elements as agitprop theater, folk drama, and the pageantry of mummers' parades.

The parade also served as a form of veiled protest for African Americans, whose exclusion from "civil society" in colonial and antebellum New England prompted black coronation festivals during which slaves held parades

Women's liberation march, Boston, 1970

and mock elections following the supposedly general election day of white New Englanders. New England women found creative ways to protest slavery as well. In 1836, for example, Massachusetts abolitionists put the traditional skill of quilting to work on a cradle quilt inscribed with a protest message that was offered for sale at the Ladies Anti-Slavery Fair. Quilts also served the temperance and suffrage movements.

Women who supported Dorr's Rebellion against the Rhode Island government's failure to liberalize an outdated constitution in the 1840s used other domestic skills, organizing clambakes as festive suffrage fund-raisers. Well over a century later, during the late 1970s and 1980s, traditional regional seafood was used to symbolize opposition to a nuclear energy plant in Seabrook, N.H., organized by the Clamshell Alliance. That group's unofficial anthem was the reworked folk song "Acres of Clams," with new lyrics transforming it into a song of antinuclear protest.

Pat Ferrero, Elaine Hedges, and Julie Silber, *Hearts and Hands: The Influence of Women and Quilts on American Society* (1987); David M. Rosen, *Protest Songs in America* (1972); Peter Shaw, *American Patriots and the Rituals of Revolution* (1981); Melvin Wade, "'Shining in Borrowed Plumage': Affirmation of Community in the Black Coronation Festivals of New England (c. 1750–c. 1850)," *Western Folklore* 40 (1981).

David Shuldiner

Soirées

For a traditional *tourtière*, you will need 2 lbs. of lean ground pork; 1 lb. of ground beef (optional); three large cooked potatoes, mashed; one medium onion; ½ teaspoon cinnamon or nutmeg; salt and pepper to taste; and 2 cups of water. Place the meat in the water and simmer for 45 minutes. Add chopped onion and seasonings and simmer for 15 more minutes. Remove from heat, discarding any excess liquid. Mix in the mashed potatoes. Place filling in a double crust and bake at 375 degrees for 30 to 40 minutes.

When Franco-Americans gather for a party in the evening, it is called a soirée. In the 1800s and early 1900s, when Franco-American families were larger than they are today, 30 to 100 family members of every generation might attend. Some families had soirées almost weekly; others held them once or twice a year.

Soirées are most common, now as in the past, around New Year's Day, when Franco-Americans living in New England often travel to Quebec to celebrate the holiday. Some must rent halls to accommodate many generations. Other New Year's festivities still occur at home.

A typical soirée begins with a meal. Traditionally, that meal is provided by the host, but soirées these days are often potluck. Among the common foods served at soirées are *tour-tière* (pork pie), *cretons* (a pork spread served on toast or crackers), pea soup (made with whole yellow peas and a ham bone), turkey, ham, meat loaf, and farm-fresh or canned vegetables. For dessert or a snack one might have maple syrup pie, sweet custard pie, maple rice pudding, *tire* (maple taffy), potato candy (potato, powdered sugar, and peanut butter), or *pouding au chômeur* (poor man's pudding, cake that floats on a base of syrup made with brown sugar, water, butter, and vanilla).

The beverages consumed at a soirée are often homemade and can be very potent. *Caribou*—one measure of alcohol, two measures of water, and three measures of wine—is one of the strongest. There are also delicious wines made from celery, rice and raisins, or wild cherries. It is usually after such beverages start flowing that storytelling begins. Stories can take the form of one-person skits or one-act plays with several participants. Sometimes they become more elaborate and include singing and costumes. Often the stories recount a bit of family history or poke fun at a community or family member.

Once the meal has been eaten and everyone is socializing, someone will begin to sing a song. A *chanson à répondre,* or response song, needs no formal introduction. Anyone may start it off. He or she begins with the chorus or first line, waits for everyone to repeat it, then goes on to the next verse. Respondents usually sing the first line of each verse and the chorus. Many soirée-goers are singers, dancers, or storytellers, and all are expected to perform at each soirée. It is common, for instance, for vocalists to sing the same songs soirée after soirée. Such repetition assures that the songs will be passed on from one generation to another.

While singers are performing, seated listeners often keep time with their feet. Percussion is an important part of a soirée. There may or may not be any instrumental music, but there are always clapping hands or tapping feet, and sometimes spoons providing a beat. The rhythmic foot tapping, done with both feet, sounds like a galloping horse. The right foot taps the toe and heel alternately, while the left foot taps once between beats. A person first taps the right toe, then the left, then the right heel, and then repeats the pattern: toe-toe-heel, toe-toe-heel. The spoons player follows along, holding two spoons back to back in one hand while hitting them against his or her thigh and the other hand. These forms of percussion help keep everyone singing together in large family gatherings when it sometimes can be hard for people on two sides of a room to stay synchronized. Soirée participants often clap their hands during the chorus or repetition segments of a song or while instrumental music is being played on a fiddle, accordion, or harmonica.

The Irish have lilting, the Swiss have yodeling, and Franco-Americans have what is called *turlutte*. Turlutte is a series of rhythmic sounds made with the mouth, although they are not words. Turlutte is sometimes found within a song or may be used as a substitute for instrumental music. There are as many forms of turlutte as there are people who sing it.

Besides vocal and instrumental music, soirées often include a form of dancing called quadrille. Like square dancing, the quadrille usually involves four couples organized in square formation. Large soirées may use a caller; family gatherings can do without, as almost everyone knows the dances by heart. Another traditional dance is called the *gigue,* French step dancing. The primary difference between American clogging and the gigue is that clogging involves the use of the heel, whereas the gigue uses mostly the ball of the foot. Franco-Americans today are more apt to learn the gigue from a dance master than a family member. But there once was a time when young people learned from their elders steps that had been in the family for generations.

Gerard J. Brault, *The French-Canadian Heritage in New England* (1986); C. Stewart Doty, *The First Franco-Americans: New England Life Histories from the Federal Writers' Project, 1938–1939* (1985); Robyn Holman, ed., *Franco-American Music Traditions* (1996); New Hampshire Writers' Program, *Festal Days, Songs, and Games of the Franco-Americans of New Hampshire* (1940s).

Martha Pellerin Drury

Thanksgiving In nearly all agricultural communities some form of harvest home is celebrated to mark the end of seasonal tasks and offer thanks for the crops. Depending on when a particular crop is brought in and the climate of a given region, thanksgiving festivities may occur as early as the British Lammas (loaf mass) on the first day of August or as late as our own holiday in the latter part of November. Such celebrations can include a wide range of activities, from the games and frolics of a cornhusking to processions, bonfires, and symbolic dances. Participants may enjoy a simple meal and a day off from work, or they may indulge in a three- or four-day orgy of eating and drinking.

As Americans we learn that our first Thanksgiving was observed by early Pilgrims who had migrated to Massachusetts and wished to thank God that the new land had proved so bountiful. The picture we receive features settlers, their families, and local Indians feasting on wild turkey, venison, and an array of fruits and vegetables, *pompion* (pumpkin) foremost among them. Legend has it that

Winslow Homer, Thanksgiving Day—Ways and Means *(1858)*

Americans have celebrated accordingly from that day on.

The truth is somewhat different. The Pilgrims did observe a harvest home in 1621, but the affair did not then become an annual one. In fact, two types of thanksgiving had been known to Europeans from antiquity: the season-ending harvest-home feast and the more spontaneous celebration day proclaimed in response to a military victory or other favorable event. Thus in July 1623 the colonists feasted to give thanks for the end of a long drought. During colonial times the two sorts of thanksgiving were generally independent of each other, movable, and certainly not national. But in New England a tradition was haltingly beginning to form. Historical records from the Connecticut River valley indicate, for instance, the proclamation of a "solemne day of Thanksgiving to be kept throwout this Colony" in late November dating back to 1665. It was in response to the need for specifically American holidays during the early years of the new nation that something more like the modern Thanksgiving began to evolve based on both ancient and colonial models.

But a national holiday was slow in coming. Regionalism was strong, and local governors and national leaders proclaimed various dates for giving thanks for a host of reasons. In 1789 George Washington and Congress chose Thursday, November 26, as the day for a nationwide observance. New England, and later

eight southern states, maintained the day. But regional quibbling accentuated by the Civil War made it difficult for an enduring consensus to be reached. Finally, in 1863, after many years of lobbying by the influential *Godey's Ladies' Book* editor Sarah Josepha Hale, Abraham Lincoln set aside the last Thursday of November as a day to offer thanks for "fruitful fields and healthful skies," without reference to matters regional or military. In time, most Americans accepted the date. The day after Thanksgiving, now called Black Friday, became the start of the Christmas shopping season; in 1939 Franklin Delano Roosevelt moved the holiday to the fourth Thursday in November to guarantee the merchants a longer shopping period.

Several aspects of the modern celebration can be traced back to New England historical roots. The holiday occurs, for example, on a Thursday, when midweek church meetings took place in the colonies of Plymouth and Massachusetts Bay. A strong link between New England and Thanksgiving has also been forged in the popular imagination by such artworks as "A Boy's Thanksgiving Day," the traditional song based on Lydia Maria Child's poem and sung by generations of American schoolchildren, and the well-known 1867 etching of G. H. Durrie's *Home to Thanksgiving* produced by Currier and Ives.

Thanksgiving today features a copious meal centering on turkey and pumpkin, the foods supposedly feasted upon in 1621, to which we add all manner of vegetables and other edibles, many of them introduced by immigrants. Americans often attend church services on Thanksgiving, although televised football games probably draw a larger audience; the Macy's Thanksgiving Day Parade in New York City attracts thousands. Thanksgiving is a major family occasion, with travel in America reaching its height right before and during that extended weekend. It is not universally beloved, however, in a highly mobile culture whose single-parent and two-earner households often make it difficult for families to live up to the ideal depicted in Norman Rockwell's 1943 painting of three smiling generations gathered around a mammoth roast turkey lovingly placed on the table by grandma. Native Americans, too, without whom there would probably have been no thanksgiving feast in 1621, sometimes view the celebration as a painful reminder of the atrocities that followed. Others, however, like their mainstream American counterparts, take advantage of the day to give thanks or to pray that all the world's peoples may live in abundance and harmony.

Diana Karter Applebaum, *Thanksgiving: An American Holiday, an American History* (1984); Hennig Cohen and Tristram Potter Coffin, eds., *Folklore of the American Holidays*, 2d ed. (1991); W. De Loss Love, *The Fast and Thanksgiving Days of New England* (1895).

Tristram Potter Coffin and Joan E. Howard

Vampires Vampire lore developed in New England as a regional variant of diverse ancient worldwide traditions whose common element is the belief that a corpse, perhaps undead, perhaps animated by an evil spirit, is responsible for a deadly epidemic. The vampire typically finds victims among its immediate family. Folk tradition defines two major responses to a vampire threat: inter the corpse in such a way as to prevent it from returning to the realm of the living—by decapitating the body, burying it face down, staking it to the earth, or breaking its limbs—or else destroy the evildoer by exhuming and burning the cadaver or certain of its parts. In New England consumption (most likely pulmonary tuberculosis) was the plague that vampires were believed to spread, and exhumation was the favored response. In fact, the vampire was a scapegoat.

Evidence of vampirism in New England during the 18th and 19th centuries includes eyewitness accounts, memorates (personal narratives of supernatural experiences incorporating traditional beliefs), family folklore, local legends, old newspaper articles, published local histories, town records, journal entries, unpublished correspondence, genealogies, and even an archaeological excavation of one family cemetery. Almost all of the recorded examples of vampire exhumation in North America occurred in New England: Manchester, Vt. (1793); Dummerston, Vt. (ca. 1794 or 1798); Cumberland, R.I. (1796); Exeter, R.I. (1799); Plymouth, Mass. (ca. 1807); Loudon, N.H. (ca. 1810); Barnstead, N.H. (1810); South Woodstock, Vt. (ca. 1817); Foster, R.I. (1827); Woodstock Green, Vt. (1830); Jewett City, Conn. (1854); Griswold, Conn. (mid-1800s); Peace Dale, R.I. (1874); West Stafford, Conn. (before 1888); West Greenwich, R.I. (1889); and Exeter, R.I. (1892). The other three occurred in Chicago, Ill. (1875); Ontario, Canada (before 1893); and Seneca Lake, N.Y. (before 1898). These exhumations probably represent only a small percentage of those carried out to halt the spread of tuberculosis in North America.

The case of Mercy Brown is typical. Mercy's father, George T. Brown, was a respected farmer in rural Exeter. In 1883 his wife died of consumption; seven months later so did his daughter, Mary Olive. Within a few years Brown's only son, Edwin, began to show signs of the disease. Alarmed, Brown took Edwin to the doctor, knowing all too well that a diagnosis of consumption was practically a death sentence. In the meantime 19-year-old Mercy had contracted the galloping variety of the illness; she died quickly and was buried in the family plot on Chestnut Hill in January 1892. By mid-March Brown was at his wits' end and under pressure from relatives and neighbors to take action. In an attempt to save his remaining child and protect the community at large, Brown finally consented to an exhumation of his family. Under the direction of the medical examiner from the nearby village of Wickford, Dr. Harold Metcalf, the three bodies were uncovered. The mother and oldest daughter were nothing but skeletons, but Mercy, buried only two months earlier, appeared to have liquid blood in her heart. Despite Dr. Metcalf's assurances that the condition of Mercy's corpse was unremarkable, attendants at the scene burned her heart to ashes on a nearby rock. Edwin was said to have drunk the ashes in water shortly thereafter. He must have been too ill with the disease by that time, however, for he died two months later. Family lore would have it that since Edwin was the last in the community to die in that outbreak, the exhumation "took care of the problem."

Variants of this folk remedy include burning organs other than the heart (among them lungs and liver) and incinerating the entire corpse (while those afflicted inhale the smoke). The body exhumed in early-19th-century Plymouth was simply turned face down and reburied. No evidence suggests that the participants in any of these episodes knew of or referred to these beliefs and practices as vampirism, even though the term almost invariably was used by commentators from outside the community.

The recent archaeological excavation of an abandoned family burial ground in Griswold, Conn., used in the 1700s and early 1800s, provides physical documentation for the vampire tradition. Of the 29 whole or partial skeletons unearthed, that of "J.B." is particularly interesting. The complete skeleton of this 50- to 55-year-old man, buried in a stone-lined grave, was the best preserved in the cemetery. On the coffin lid an arrangement of tacks spelled out "JB-55," presumably the initials and age at death of this individual. When the grave was opened, J.B.'s skull and thighbones were found in a skull-and-crossbones pattern on top of his ribs and vertebrae, which had also been rearranged. An examination of J.B.'s remains revealed indications of chronic respiratory disease. The archaeologist, forensic anthropologist, and folklorist who reviewed the evidence came to the following collective conclusion: J.B., a 55-year-old adult male, died of pulmonary tuberculosis or a similar infection interpreted as tuberculosis. Several years after his interment one or more of his family members contracted the disease (including, possibly, his 45-year-old wife and 13-year-old child). As a last resort, to spare the lives of the family and keep consumption from spreading into the community, J.B.'s body was exhumed so that his heart could be burned. When the body was unearthed, however, J.B. was found to be in an advanced stage of decomposition. Perhaps his ribs and vertebrae were disarranged in the desperate search for the remains of his heart. With that organ nowhere to be found, exhumers crossed J.B.'s femurs over his chest and placed his skull between them, a practice with precedents in northern Europe, including Great Britain.

To understand why this folk medical practice was a reasonable response to a fatal disease, one must set aside current medical thinking and view events through the eyes of participants. Before the 20th century New Englanders were unaware that tuberculosis was caused by a microscopic organism, even though they knew that it was contagious and almost always killed its victims. At a time when about one in every four deaths was attributable to consumption, a New England farmer likely would have seen neighbors, close friends, and kin die without hope of cure. The head of a consumptive family no doubt felt enormous pressure to stop the plague before it decimated his family and engulfed the community. His options were few: accept the medical establishment's death sentence, or heed the advice of a local belief specialist and hope the folk remedy would work. Better to do something than nothing at all.

By the 20th century vampires had disappeared from their habitat in the New England countryside. Ironically, those who had argued in the late 19th century that civilization was on the verge of eradicating the last vestiges of those "primitive survivals from a barbaric past" were in a sense at least partially correct: an empirically tested bacterium had banished this traditional scapegoat. As the vampire tradition became a historical oddity rather than "a horrible superstition" actually practiced by folks living down the road, Hollywood was beginning to teach people how to enjoy it. Even though the writer H. P. Lovecraft alludes to Mercy Brown in his short story "The Shunned House," current tales of vampires in New England are sustained primarily through formulaic newspaper and television stories that transform dead victims of pulmonary tuberculosis into fanged fiends haunting the countryside. With few models to draw on, the mass media cast these victims into the mold of the cinematic Dracula, an image supported by neither folklore nor history.

John McNab Currier, "Contributions to New England Folklore," *Journal of American Folklore* 4 (1891); Nancy Kinder, "The 'Vampires' of Rhode Island," in *Mysterious New England*, ed. Austin N. Stevens (1971); Rockwell Stephens, "The Vampire's Heart," in *Mischief in the Mountains: Strange Tales of Vermont and Vermonters*, ed. Walter R. Hard, Jr., and Janet C. Greene (1970); George R. Stetson, "The Animistic Vampire in New England," *American Anthropologist*, o.s., 9 (1896).

Michael E. Bell

Weather Lore New England's fickle weather plays an important role in the lives of many people. For the most part the region's weather lore evolved from that of Europe and then spread from New England to the rest of the nation. New England's lengthy coastline and its several mountain ranges make for sometimes legendary weather phenomena that, like the folklore associated with them, are specific to the region.

Weather lore comes in two forms: long-range forecasts, which are reasonably accurate, anticipate conditions over the course of a month or a season, while short-range predictions deal with everything from the imminent blizzard to conditions one to three days hence. The latter have often proved superior to the meteorological prognostications of the weather bureau, especially in narrow geographic areas. New England's *Old Farmer's Almanac*, which since 1792 has based predictions on a "secret weather forecasting formula," has done much to call attention to New England's weather lore. The publication claims an 80 percent accuracy rate.

Good weather predictions, whatever their nature, are based on multiple signs. The accuracy of a forecast is often in proportion to the number of indicators used. Folkloric predictions of long-range weather depend on natural cycles and signs: for instance, geese flying south; the size of muskrat houses in the fall; or prevailing weather conditions on special dates, such as Saint Swithin's Day (July 15), when "just so far as the sun shines in, just so far will the snow blow in." Forecasts sometimes involve divination: How much fat is on the hog? In what condition is the keel bone of a fowl? The direction and strength of the wind "when the sun crosses the line [equinox]" are traditionally viewed as foretelling the general force and direction of the wind for the season.

Most weather lore is local. Bad weather is likely, for example, when Long Island appears to be riding high above the water from the Connecticut shore; when Block Island, R.I., is visible from Newport in the same state; when the rote of the sea can be heard in Padenarum, Mass. Gales may be anticipated when the sea is roily or when there is a large ocean swell. Northern lights mean that the weather will turn cold, and snow fleas signal the imminent arrival of spring.

Certain signs are more local still. Suds in Cohasset Harbor, Mass., predict a gale whose intensity can be measured by their height. "If the anvil comes up over Dan Dragon's [farm] you'll get a thunderstorm," people say in Ripton, Vt. "If the Squeakerguzzle [a cleft in a tidal rock] gurgles, it will storm on Matinicus" is folk wisdom on an island in Maine.

The condition of the moon and the sun

Weather-vane maker Alfred Blais at work on a novelty weather vane in Lewiston, Maine, 1974

when those bodies rise and set is extremely important. "When the sun sets clear as a bell,/ It will be cold sure as hell," old-timers in New Englanders intone. Clouds, too, can serve as portents. Most Yankee fishermen and farmers know that "mackerel skies and mares tails make tall ships carry low sails." The amount of summer fog, always a concern of mariners, along the Maine coast is thought to be ruled by the water temperature at Mount Desert Rock on Decoration (or Memorial) Day.

The weather prophet, as individuals skilled in the art are called, uses two primary tools: the weather vane and the barometer. A falling glass and an easterly wind bring dirty, or stormy, weather, while a west wind and a rising glass bring fair skies. Various seemingly unrelated natural signs can indicate barometric change and reveal wind direction. None is too minuscule to overlook: the number and pattern of extra lines in a spider's web, pain in a wound, how long it takes a kettle to boil, rising smoke, a sputtering fire, feeding sheep, hatching flies, chickens feeding in the rain, cows lying down to sleep, the behavior of cats, dew, seabirds ashore, the way plants respond to the sun, the brightness of stars—even dreams are triggered by wind direction and barometric pressure. The skill resides in being attuned to, and knowing how to interpret, these nuances.

Lee Albert, *Weather Wisdom: Being an Illustrated Practical Volume Wherein Is Contained Unique Compilation and Analysis of the Facts and Folklore of Natural Weather Prediction* (1976); Ken Fitzgerald, *Weathervanes and Whirligigs* (1967).

Horace P. Beck

Women's Folklife Much of New England's traditional culture has been formed and transmitted, preserved and interpreted—indeed, sometimes transformed and subverted—by women. When Europeans first came to New England, women's home-manufacturing skills made survival possible. Young girls learned these skills early on. Women made stocking yarn; bed and table linens; coarse woolen work clothes for men and boys; various linen and woolen garments for infants and young children; linen shirts, shifts, petticoats, aprons, and summer pantaloons. They knitted stockings, garters, gloves, and caps. They washed clothes, made soap, and fashioned hats and bonnets from braided straw, palm leaf, and cloth. They made cheese, slaughtered pigs, and preserved meat. They made apple cider as well as small beer, ready to drink in just 24 hours. They dipped or molded candles until kerosene became widely available in about 1869.

When Mary Rowlandson was captured by the Nipmuck, Narragansett, and Wampanoag in February 1676 at her Lancaster, Mass., home, she grabbed her knitting needles—then put them to use almost daily during her captivity. Women also took their knitting along as they waited for babies to be born. In the mid-1800s young women knitted while they visited with friends, often showing off their finest, most elaborate work.

Industrialization and male professionalism changed the face of women's traditional practices. As factory production of textiles in Britain and New England increased in the early 1800s, weavers in more prosperous families, freed from marketplace demands, experimented with complex weaving patterns. Although garments of all kinds became available in stores, women continued to knit, especially occupational clothing. Minnie Doughty of Chebeague Island, Maine, for example, knitted "wet mittens" in the early 1900s that fishermen wore while hauling traps. When first made, wet mittens are one-third larger than a person's hand; then they are shrunk in boiling water, so their stitches become tighter than what anyone could knit.

Traditional medical practices also shifted. Midwives, such as Maine's Martha Ballard, had used herbal remedies, perhaps laced with wine or rum. They called in friends of a laboring mother-to-be, for most early American women literally gave birth in the arms or on the laps of their neighbors. By the last decade of the 1700s, young male physicians began delivering babies, though without displacing midwives altogether.

Women's traditional stories, songs, and artifacts often aim to chronicle women's lives, negotiate for women's rights, or celebrate women's accomplishments. Women who immigrated to Lowell, Mass., around the turn of the 19th century to work in textile mills there created folk art from their personal experience. "My quilt," one young mill worker wrote in her diary, "is a bound volume of hieroglyphs, each of which is a key to some painful or pleasant memory."

Singers such as Mabel Worcester, of Hanover, Maine, honor—and exemplify—women's endurance. In 1965 at age 86 Mabel was still performing "Margery Grey," a 25-stanza song about a woman who, lost in the woods in the 1760s, survived a seven-month, 320-mile journey from Vermont north to Canada and south to Charlestown, N.H., on the other side of the Connecticut River.

Mrs. George Tatro of Springfield, Vt., sang one of her mother's favorite songs, "John Grumlie," to her grandchildren. When the song's Farmer Grumlie complains to his wife of doing more work in a day than she does in three, she promptly challenges him to a contest. Grumlie gets his comeuppance when she beats him hands down. Bertha McKeown's favorite story about her legendary father, Maine hunter and poacher George Magoon, brings to life the day McKeown hid five partridges in the butter she was churning to keep wardens from finding Magoon's illegal cache. Afterward, even her father stormed about looking for the lost birds: apparently, no man could imagine that he would find anything dubious inside a woman's butter churn.

When there is work to be done in families and communities, women and men have often divided up the tasks. In the basket-making Sweetser family of Vermont, men cut down the brown ash trees and prepared the wooden strips, but men and women both made the baskets, in distinctive personal styles. In Aroostook County, Maine, Donald and Mary Lafford Sanipass of the Micmac nation, like other basket makers among the Maliseet, Passamaquoddy, and Penobscot, often divide their work along gender lines: Don collects and prepares the ash, Mary does the weaving, and they both hoop and handle their work baskets. With the emergence of the resort industry during the last quarter of the 19th century, native women began making miniature baskets and "fancy" ones such as the "porcupine curlicue."

Women also transform tradition as they create spaces for themselves in primarily male domains. Although men tended the fire for generations at the Allen's Neck Clambake in Massachusetts, women have now claimed the right to work in this center of dramatic action. Women have also established major roles for themselves in religious centers, often becoming advocates for their communities. In 1980 Marta de Jesus of Hartford founded the Centro de Espiritismo in her Puerto Rican American neighborhood. As a spiritist healer in the circum-Caribbean tradition, Marta communicates with the spirits of people who died young or failed to reach their full spiritual potential during their lifetimes and who sometimes cause illness and misfortune among the living.

Women have long used their traditional arts to work for peace and social justice. "May the use of our needles prick the conscience of the slave holder," read the quilt of one New England abolitionist. Although some feminists of the 1800s argued that sewing was a symbol of women's oppression, temperance and suffrage leaders displayed handmade banners and quilts as emblems of their struggle. New England women quilted panels opposing the nuclear arms race for the Ribbon Project of the 1980s and banners for the Gulf War Peace March of 1990. In 1985 Marty Tracy and her husband set up Peace Fleece, a yarn company in Kezar Falls, Maine, in hopes of helping to diffuse the threat of nuclear war by increasing mutual understanding through trade. They sell products made by people all over the world, such as yarn that blends Russian wool with American or Palestinian with Israeli, as well as hand-painted knitting needles and wooden buttons made by Moscow-area artisans.

Women have long been passionate about documenting and preserving their New England heritage. As folk-song collector Eloise Hubbard Linscott wrote during her 1940 letter campaign to get the Archive of Folk Music to loan her a portable recording machine: "Mr. [John] Lomax has done so much for his part of this country [the Southwest]; is there some one who can give a little time to MY part? It is as different in its characteristics and problems as other sections better advertised." Linscott's fervor was matched by other song collectors, such as Fannie Hardy Eckstorm, Helen Hartness Flanders, Joanna Colcord, Mary Winslow Smyth, and Margaret MacArthur.

Gender issues were always with them. Linscott funded her research with money left over from her household budget: "Lots of things I've done haven't been very ladylike, [but] . . . housework irritates me so," Linscott commented in 1976. When Eckstorm and Smyth published their *Minstrelsy of Maine: Folksongs and Ballads of the Woods and the Coast* in 1927, they wrote, with more than a little irony: "The editors of this volume fully realized that collecting these songs was a man's job. . . . Had a man competent to perform the task expressed an intention of preserving these songs, we should not have undertaken the work. But no man appeared. . . . So we volunteered."

Rug hooking in the New Hampshire exhibit, Smithsonian Folklife Festival, 1999

The women performers whom these collectors met were themselves documenters of traditions. Carrie Grover of Gorham, Maine, sang and fiddled from her repertoire of more than 400 songs. Susie Carr Young of Orland, Maine, performed and wrote down more than

a hundred Anglo and Irish traditional tunes. Women listeners also documented songs, approaching relatives, neighbors, and strangers in their quest to help collectors. Mrs. Guy R. Hathaway of Mattawamkeag, Maine, questioned three local loggers until she had a version of "The Jam on Gerry's Rock" to send to Eckstorm and Smyth. And 96-year-old Jane Chase of Jeffersonville, Vt., lay awake at night, remembering "The Half Hitch" a line or two at a time so she could send it to Helen Flanders. Some listeners had begun collecting songs in scrapbooks long before any stranger came collecting. Phianna Hopkins of West Wardsboro, Vt., filled an 18-page notebook with verses of old songs sung by her grandfather, Hezekiah Coates, born in 1790, and her aunt. In Lewiston, Maine, many Franco-American women are still filling scrapbooks with songs.

New England women also highlight and interrogate cultural practices by including women's folklife in their fiction and nonfiction writings. From Catharine Sedgwick in the 1820s to Harriet Beecher Stowe, Louisa May Alcott, Elizabeth Stuart Phelps, Sarah Orne Jewett, Amy Lawrence Lowell, Louise Dickinson Rich, Ruth Moore, and Elizabeth Coatsworth in the late 19th and early 20th centuries, women have offered their own images of the region through their representations of women's lives and concerns. Ann

Petry, Grace Metalious, Kate Barnes, Carolyn Chute, and Cathie Pelletier, among many others, have carried on that tradition.

Today, women professionals document, teach, and preserve folklife in institutional settings. All of New England's state folklorists are women; the first, Jane Beck of Vermont, took up her post in 1978. Professors Rayna Green and Karen Baldwin offered the first women's folklore course in the United States during the spring of 1975 at the University of Massachusetts in Amherst.

Jane C. Beck, ed., *Vermont Recollections: Sifting Memories through the Interview Process,* special issue of *Northeast Folklore* 30 (1995); Kristin Langellier, "Contemporary Quiltmaking in Maine: Re-fashioning Femininity," *Uncoverings* 11 (1990); Bunny McBride, *Our Lives in Our Hands: Micmac Indian Basketmakers* (1990); Jane C. Nylander, *Our Own Snug Fireside: Images of the New England Home, 1760–1860* (1993); Merrill Singer and Roberto Garcia, "Becoming a Puerto Rican Espiritista: Life History of a Female Healer," in *Women as Healers: Cross-Cultural Perspectives* (1989); Laurel Thatcher Ulrich, *The Age of Homespun* (2002); Ulrich, *Good Wives: Image and Reality in the Lives of Women in Northern New England, 1650–1750* (1980); Ulrich, *A Midwife's Tale: The Life of Martha Ballard, Based on Her Diary, 1785–1812* (1990); Margaret R. Yocom, "'Awful Real': Dolls and Development in Rangeley, Maine," in *Feminist Messages: Coding in Women's Folk Culture,* ed. Joan Newlon Radner (1993).

Margaret R. Yocom

Gender

Barbara A. White, Section Editor

INTRODUCTION

In 1638, when Anne Hutchinson was excommunicated by her Boston church and driven from the Massachusetts Bay Colony, the minister Hugh Peter made the cause of her expulsion unmistakably clear: "You have stept out of your place, *you have rather bine a Husband than a Wife and a preacher than a Hearer; and a Magistrate than a Subject.*" In so doing, he expressed the Puritan conception of gender, of what it meant to be male or female. New England's early European settlers saw a vast gulf between men and women (note the minister's binary oppositions—husband/wife, preacher/hearer—as though no one could be both) and a natural hierarchy: men should be dominant and women submissive; men were husbands, preachers, magistrates, and women were wives, hearers, subjects. Of course, the early settlers did not use the word *gender,* as we do today, to express the meanings that a culture assigns to a person's sex. To them the few anatomical differences between the sexes were essential. Although some societies might minimize these differences, the Puritans chose to maximize them. Anatomy was destiny and gender the prime determinant of a person's life, more important than age, class, or race.

Male dominance was enshrined in the English common-law tradition the settlers brought with them. The law of domestic relations was "Baron and Feme." As Linda Kerber notes, "The very wording implies a political relationship: lord and woman, not husband and wife. One party had status as well as gender; the other had only gender. As 'Baron,' husband stood to wife as king did to baron." The marriage relationship was based on "coverture," the idea that once a woman wed, her identity was enveloped by her husband's. Husband and wife were legally one person, and because he "covered" her, she could not independently own property or exercise political rights. By the same token, the husband, as the responsible party, could be sued or punished for his wife's bad behavior. An unmarried woman, or "feme sole," could own property, though she had no political rights; in practice, her autonomy was limited because she was expected to live in a household under the authority of a male relative. Puritan New England did not look kindly on the single state: both "old maids" and bachelors were pressured to marry.

Ironically, only widows could approach the status of independent womanhood. A widow was guaranteed a third of her husband's real estate, could inherit his business, and had the right that other women did not to take an apprentice. Scholars have found that New England widows were more likely than those in other regions "to push and redefine gender boundaries." Many were left desperately poor, however, and struggled just to support themselves, for coverture had far-reaching economic as well as legal implications for both women and men. If a wife's property and earnings belonged to her husband and he was the one responsible for providing for the family, the husband played the central economic role; the wife had only to use appropriately what he produced. Even if a spinster or a wife wanted to act as provider, or a widow needed to, few opportunities were open to her beyond the bounds of the household. A wife, who could not legally negotiate a contract, and a "feme sole," unable to read or write, could hardly expect to earn an independent living.

In fact, Native American women exercised more economic power than did female colonists. Although the New England Indians and the English both divided labor along gender lines, the two cultures differed on the kinds of work assigned to each group. Native American women took the primary responsibility for agriculture, carried heavy loads, and engaged in trade. Because the English considered these men's jobs, they tended to see Indian men as lazy and women as oppressed and degraded. But the women gained "a large degree of authority within the clan" from their economic centrality. They occasionally became religious leaders (*shamans*) or even tribal heads (*sachems*). In King Philip's War (1675–76), the last of the New England Indians' attempts to hold their land, there were at least three female chieftains. Weetamoo, who was once married to the brother of Metacom ("King Philip"), commanded more than 300 Pocasset male warriors. She and her last husband, the Narragansett leader Quinnapin, captured Mary Rowlandson, who later described them in *The Soveraignty and Goodness of GOD . . . a Narrative of the Captivity and Restauration of Mrs. Mary Rowlandson* (1682). Rowlandson, a minister's wife, was astonished at the dominance of Weetamoo and the male Indians' avoidance of sexual assault. *The Soveraignty and Goodness of God* became the most popular secular narrative of the 17th and 18th centuries.

Not many white women could read it, however, because education was another area in which women were greatly disadvantaged. Puritan New England has always been celebrated for the value it placed on literacy and the heroic efforts it made to found schools in the "wilderness." What a remarkable feat to have established Harvard College as early as 1636! But higher education was strictly for men. When he was governor of the Massachusetts Bay Colony, John Winthrop wrote in his *Journal* of the insanity that afflicted the wife of the governor of neighboring Connecticut. Like Anne Hutchinson, she had stepped out of her place, devoting herself "wholly to reading and writing, and had written many books." According to Winthrop, "if she attended her household affairs, and not such things as are proper for men, whose minds are stronger, etc., she had kept her wits." Although this judgment seems ludicrous today and we might attribute the woman's insanity to the weight of Winthrop's "etc.," the statement made some sense during the 17th century. If a woman was to marry, as the great majority did, and be "covered" by her husband, what would be the purpose of educating her? She need not know how to write, for example, if she was prohibited from signing a contract. It might be nice if she could read the Bible, that great Puritan justification for education, but if she couldn't, her husband, as the religious leader within the family, could instruct her himself. This negative attitude regarding the education of women resulted in a gap between male and female literacy rates. Kenneth Lockridge estimates that half of the men but only a third of the women in the first generation of New England settlers could sign their names. Interestingly, this gap only widened during the 17th and 18th centuries; by the time of the Revolution, 80 percent or more of the men, but only 40 to 45 percent of the women, were literate.

The widening of the literacy gap can be traced in part to the declining influence of religion during the 1600s and 1700s. In some ways the Puritan religious establishment legislated the separation of the sexes and the subordination of women; as Laurel Thatcher Ulrich notes, it "perpetuated the Anglican custom of 'seating' the congregation in ranked order, according to sex, wealth, and age. Gender was the first distinction among God's children. The gospel of damnation and grace intoned from the pulpit was the same for all Christians, but men and women heard it from different sides of the room." Women might be morally weaker than men and in greater danger of being possessed by devils (therefore most of the accused witches in New England were female), but the gospel's being "the same for all Christians" still had subversive potential. Women possessed individual souls to be saved, souls that were equal before God to those of men. Ulrich went on to discuss the growing imbalance in church membership in the 1700s; in Hampton Falls, N.H., in 1712, for instance, 70 percent of the church members were female. While they still sat separately and could not preach or bear titles, membership had to be earned, and women who succeeded gained a public status apart from their husbands.

Thus there were conditions that mitigated women's subordination in the church, as there were in other institutions. Wives' lack of legal identity, for example, was softened somewhat by the existence of equity courts in which judges were not bound by coverture and husbands could be sued. Massachusetts forbade wife beating, and a woman could obtain a divorce in New England more easily than in any other region (the Puritans saw marriage as a civil rather than a religious contract). Although women were less likely to be literate than men, the female literacy rate was higher in New England than it was in other regions. Even in the economic realm, where men held sway completely, women's work had some value. On farms men and women often worked side by side at complementary tasks that allowed the household to survive as an interdependent unit. According to *The Office and Duty of an Husband* (1529) by Juan Luis Vives, an author popular in both England and the colonies, complementarity applied everywhere, even inside the home as "both husbands and wives . . . have certain things in the house that only pertain to the authority of the husbands . . . [and] there are other things in which the husband giveth over his right unto the woman."

By the time of the Revolution distinctions between the sexes had been heavily elaborated, and men and women were widely seen to be separated by inborn characteristics. They were opposites: men excelled in reason, for example, and women in intuition (or a man represented the head and a woman the heart, as the concept was often expressed). In a century that exalted reason, this made women lesser beings. As Linda Kerber states, "Female qualities were commonly made the measure of what a good republican ought to avoid." Any kind of "effeminacy" was decried in men. It is thus not surprising that when the founding fathers proclaimed "all men are created equal," they meant all male humans. But the ideology of the Declaration of Independence was to spread much further than the authors of the document intended. In 1776 Abigail Adams wrote to her husband, John: "I desire you would Remember the Ladies, and be more generous and favourable to them than your ancestors. Do not put such unlimited power into the hands of Husbands. Remember all Men would be tyrants if they could." Perhaps she was joking when she added that the ladies "are determined to foment a Rebellion, and will not hold ourselves bound by any Laws in which we have no voice, or Representation," but she had made an important connection, applying the ideology of the Revolution to the status of women. Other writers began to do so in a more formal way, among them, Judith Sargent Murray of Gloucester, Mass. In her "Essay on the Equality of the Sexes" (1790), Murray argued that although men's and women's minds are by nature equal, men have been elevated by a superior education denied to women. This same argument was emphasized by England's notorious Mary Wollstonecraft, whose *Vindication of the Rights of Woman* (1792) was widely read in New England and was applied to African American women in the 1820s by Boston's Maria Stewart.

Between 1790 and the mid-1830s major changes occurred in women's education. The issue was hotly debated, and girls began to attend public schools for longer intervals—not just during growing season when the places were vacated by boys. Seminaries for women were founded, some of which offered instruction that went as far as the early college level. In the 1820s Catharine Beecher employed her sister Harriet (later to become Harriet Beecher Stowe) as a teacher in her famous seminary in Hartford; one of their pupils would become the celebrated feminist journalist Fanny Fern. The Wheaton Female Seminary opened its doors in 1835, and some years later Lucy Larcom, the poet who as a girl had worked in the textile mills of Lowell, Mass., was hired to teach there. In 1837 Mary Lyon opened the first real equivalent of a four-year college, the Mount Holyoke Female Seminary. As women built their educational networks, the female literacy rate, half that of men at the time of the Revolution, had climbed to parity by 1850.

Linda Kerber has named the rationale that allowed these changes to happen "Republican Motherhood." The new republic was thought to be fragile and dependent on a virtuous, educated citizenry. If the Republican Mother was to properly raise the next generation of citizens, especially sons, then she, too, had to be educated. Kerber explains that on the one hand, "Republican Motherhood was a progressive ideology. Women were redefined as more than 'helpmates' to their husbands. . . . It allocated an assertive role to women. . . . The ideology of Republican Motherhood seemed to accomplish what the Enlightenment had not by identifying the intersection of the woman's private domain and the public order." Still, the Republican Mother was granted education not to enhance her own condition but to prepare her to perform a service for men, and her access to the public order remained very limited.

Other changes were taking place during the first part of the 19th century that would push women more firmly back into the private domain. The industrial development of New England, beginning with the textile industry, led to the separation of work from home and the rigid differentiation of these "spheres" by gender. In the be-

Mount Holyoke Female Seminary, 1851

ginning the mills seemed a boon to young farm women, who tasted the joys of greater independence and a paycheck of their own; but as wages fell and working conditions worsened, these women gradually left the mills and were replaced by men and immigrant women. On New England farms, as Nancy F. Cott explains in *The Bonds of Womanhood,* "The expansion of nonagricultural occupations drew men and grown children away from the household, abbreviating their presence in the family and their roles in child rearing. Mothers and young children were left in the household together just when educational and religious dicta both newly emphasized the malleability of young minds." As goods were bought with men's wages and household production declined, women devoted more time to child care: "More than ever before in New England history, the care of children appeared to be mothers' sole work and the work of mothers alone."

Of course, these transformed conditions did not apply to all women. Lower-class women always had other duties besides child care; most black women were either slaves in the South or domestic laborers in the North. The rationale that has been called the "cult of domesticity" or the "ideology of separate spheres" was applied to middle-class men and women. The men were to enter the cold, rational, competitive world of work, which was increasingly seen as aggressive and immoral, whereas women had to stay at home; they were to elaborate their domestic space, care for the children, keep the family morals, and provide a comfortable retreat for the working men. For men this system brought considerable gain, staving off competition from women in the workplace and the world of public affairs, for example. At the same time, however, men lost influence over their children and their position as guardians of morality; they also had to adjust to a new, strictly metered workday very different from the old seasonal or task-oriented work patterns. For women separate spheres meant some losses, allowing them only limited use of their new educations, and some gains—they had always been unwelcome in the public realm, but in taking charge of the children and their morals, women had new domestic responsibilities that had formerly belonged to their husbands. Gradually they would be viewed as more moral and "spiritual" than men, and eventually they would use this perception to venture out of their assigned sphere. In the early part of the 19th century they had only to be "true women," as Barbara Welter defines it, and cultivate the virtues of piety, purity, submissiveness, and domesticity.

The cult of domesticity was originally a New England phenomenon, though it gradually spread to the rest of the country. Cott notes in *The Bonds of Womanhood* that "New Englanders proselytized so vigorously on behalf of their religious and secular values, through the dissemination of printed literature, and migrants, that they consciously contributed to the making of a nation (the northern part of it, at least) in their image." The tremendous growth in printing and publishing that coincided with the cult of domesticity helped propagate the trend. An increasing amount of advice literature was available in the form of sermon collections and manuals of conduct and etiquette. This literature had traditionally promulgated gender roles and continued to do so, benefiting now from a broader circulation.

One person who was instrumental in spreading cult values, and whose career illustrates many of the contradictions of Republican Motherhood and the cult of domesticity, is Sarah Josepha Hale of New Hampshire. Hale grew up in a rural area and was unable to take advantage of the late-18th-century rise of dame schools in urban centers. She was educated at home. Like Judith Sargent Murray, she studied alongside her brother as he prepared for and completed college. Hale married but was widowed at the age of 35. With five children to support, she wrote a successful novel and became editor of *Ladies' Magazine* in Boston. Eventually the Philadelphia publisher Louis Godey bought out this magazine and united it with his own *Lady's Book* under Hale's editorship. She edited *Godey's Lady's Book* for 40 years, raising its circulation from 10,000 in 1837 to 150,000 by 1860, an amazing figure for the time. Hale did not generally approve of women taking as public a role as her own and claimed that she would never have left her fireside had she not been obligated to earn money to educate her children (a variation of the Republican Motherhood rationale that female writers would use well into the 20th century). Hale opposed woman suffrage and other rights for women because she felt that women were by nature morally superior to men and might be contaminated if they entered the public sphere. She championed women's education in the pages of *Godey's*, however, advertising the new female academies and helping her friend Matthew Vassar found his college for women. Women, she thought, had to be well educated to bring up their children properly. It is no wonder that some of Hale's biographers have labeled her a "militant feminist" and others a "true conservative."

If women were morally superior and had taken over men's former role as moral guardians of society, it was inevitable that they would need to move out of the domestic sphere on occasion to combat bad influences threatening the home. And so it occurred, first in the form of charitable work with poor women and children, then in "female moral reform," or aid to prostitutes. Women began to join social-reform movements, such as those favoring temperance and abolition. Susan B. Anthony worked in the temperance movement during the 1840s, while Elizabeth Cady married an antislavery lecturer, Henry Stanton. The occasion for both women to start thinking about gender and their own rights as women was being denied the right to speak at international conferences: Stanton (and her mentor, Lucretia Mott) at the World Anti-Slavery Convention in 1840 and Anthony at the World Temperance Convention of 1853. The beginning of the organized women's rights movement is generally thought to be the gathering that Stanton and Mott called in 1848 in Seneca Falls, N.Y.

New England was very influential in the origin of the women's movement, however. Lucretia Mott had been born and brought up on Nantucket Island, whereas Stanton had spent the years from 1840 to 1847 living in Boston and imbibing the atmosphere of reform. She says in her autobiography that she met "many of the noble men and women among reformers, whom I had long worshiped at a distance" and "attended all the lectures, churches, theaters, concerts, and temperance, peace, and prison-reform conventions within my reach. I had never lived in such an enthusiastically literary and reform latitude before, and my mental powers were kept at the highest tension." The third woman who could be credited with founding the women's movement, Lucy Stone, lived in Massachusetts. She graduated from Oberlin College in 1847 and started lecturing in New England on abolition and women's rights that same year. According to Susan B. Anthony, Matilda Joslyn Gage, and Elizabeth Cady Stanton's *History of Woman Suffrage* (1881–87), Stone was "the first who really stirred the nation's heart on the subject of women's wrongs."

For a time Lucy Stone was friendly with Stanton and Anthony. They held annual conventions during the 1850s and formed the Woman's National Loyal League during the Civil War. The only point of contention was Anthony's resentment of Stone's marriage, though Stone thereby brought to the movement a husband (Henry Blackwell) and daughter (Alice Stone Blackwell) who would dedicate their lives to the cause. The split in the women's movement occurred after the war when the male Republicans, including former abolitionists and supporters of women's rights, abandoned woman suffrage to back suffrage for black men. All the feminist leaders protested the 14th Amendment, which inserted the word "male" into the Constitution for the first time. The feminists were told it was "the Negro's hour," though Stanton pointed out the effacement of black women—it was really the "Negro man's hour." Although Lucy Stone felt betrayed by the male abolitionists and said a nail went through her breast when they excluded women, she could not finally break with her old friends, such as Wendell Phillips and William Lloyd Garrison, in the New England–based abolitionist movement. Stanton and Anthony, on the other hand, chose to put gender first and in 1869 called a meeting of their followers to form the National Woman Suffrage Association (NWSA). A year later Stone, Julia Ward Howe, and other Boston-based feminists excluded from the NWSA formed a second organization, the American Woman Suffrage Association (AWSA).

This split in the movement, which would last for 20 years, was thus very much a regional one. Stanton and Anthony's supporters came primarily from small towns in New York and the Midwest, whereas Stone's organization was based in Boston. Partly because of the presence of old-time abolitionists, the AWSA included men in its leadership, while the NWSA did not. The AWSA also attracted a number of black women, including the writer Frances E. W. Harper; Caroline Remond Putnam, who helped found the Massachusetts Woman Suffrage Association; and Josephine St. Pierre Ruffin, a Bostonian who praised the AWSA leaders. According to Rosalyn Terborg-Penn, "more African American women . . . affiliated with the AWSA rather than the NWSA." During the years of the split, the NWSA tended to grab the headlines, but the AWSA was quietly successful in local organizing for state suffrage battles. Stone also established a women's rights newspaper in 1870, the *Woman's Journal*, which became the main paper of the movement.

When Stone's daughter Alice Stone Blackwell came of age in the late 1870s, she faced a different world from the one her mother had on leaving Oberlin. New vocations were open to her. In their Civil War work, fellow New Englanders Clara Barton and Dorothea Dix had led the way for women to become nurses. Thousands of women went South during and after the war to teach the freedmen and women; the black scholar W. E. B. Du Bois later paid them tribute, saying, "This was the gift of New England to the freed Negro: not alms, but a friend; not cash, but character." Stone Blackwell was able to graduate from Boston University, as more colleges and universities opened their doors to women. Several elite women's colleges opened their doors, including Wellesley (1870), Smith (1871), and Radcliffe (1879), and the professions gradually opened to women.

By 1890 the suffrage associations were filled with younger women who had no memory of the reasons for the existence of rival organizations and saw the practical advantages of union. Political realities forced Stanton, Anthony, and Stone, despite their personal disagreements, to agree and unite the two organizations as the National American Woman Suffrage Association (NAWSA). On the face of it, the agreement was an equitable one: Stanton would be president, Stone head of the executive committee, and Anthony vice president; Stone would continue to edit the *Journal*. In reality, however, Susan B. Anthony was the one who had the power base from which to direct the movement. Stanton soon found herself chastised by NAWSA for her antireligious *Woman's Bible* (1895–98), and Stone felt increasingly out of touch until her death in 1893. She believed that her role in founding the movement had been forgotten, and indeed Stanton and Anthony compiled the later volumes of the *History of Woman Suffrage* with little attention to Stone or the AWSA or New England. When she came to write a biography of her mother, Alice Stone Blackwell would be reduced to arguing that Seneca Falls was just a small local meeting and the first *national* women's rights meeting occurred in 1850 in Worcester, Mass., with Stone in attendance.

With the advantage of hindsight, it can be said that the demise of the AWSA and its union with the NWSA to form the NAWSA in 1890 marked the end of strong New England participation and influence in the first phase of the women's movement. The first suffrage successes took place in the West (Wyoming, 1869; Colorado, 1893; Utah, 1896), and the West and Midwest produced the massive Woman's Christian Temperance Union (WCTU), which the midwesterner Frances Willard led to a prosuffrage stand. New York City and Washington, D.C., were the sites of huge demonstrations and parades during the 1910s, when many women turned to direct action. Tennessee, where a dramatic struggle took place in 1920, was the last state to ratify the 19th Amendment. Ironically, New England's contributions at the turn of the century were mainly negative. The Massachusetts Association Opposed to Further Extension of the Suffrage to Women, the first antisuffrage organization, which had been founded in 1882, grew stronger and managed to defeat a state referendum on woman suffrage in 1895 and again in 1915. The only important positive New England influences that lasted into the 20th century were the *Woman's Journal,* edited by Alice Stone Blackwell until 1917, and Charlotte Perkins Gilman of Rhode Island, grandniece of Catharine Beecher and Harriet Beecher Stowe, who became the premier feminist theorist at the turn of the century. Gilman's emphasis on the service to the world that economically independent women could perform had clearly been influenced by her famous New England antecedents.

If New England's influence on the suffrage movement was waning, the region, or at least its capital, Boston, was breaking new ground in the area of tolerance for different sexual orientations. Catharine Beecher and Harriet Beecher Stowe, one a spinster, one a married woman, occupied the two primary cultural niches that were open to 19th-century women; but Charlotte Perkins Gilman was bisexual, and Alice Stone Blackwell was involved for many years with her cousin Kitty Barry in a so-called Boston marriage. The term *Boston marriage* was coined to describe women who lived together for a sustained period of time and had their primary relationship with each other, whether or not the relationship included sex. During most of the century women had been allowed a great deal of latitude in their relations with each other. It was considered normal for female friendships to be "long-lived, intimate, and loving," in the words of Carroll Smith-Rosenberg; women might sleep in the same bed, write each other passionate letters, and even accompany a close friend on her wedding trip. But by the latter part of the century, sexologists and psychiatrists had begun to label such behavior deviant. Nancy Sahli states, "As long as women loved each other as they did for much of the nineteenth century without threatening the system itself, their relationships either were simply ignored by men or were regarded as an acceptable part of the female sphere." But when women began to graduate from college in large numbers, live together without depending on men, and demand their political rights, they became a threat to the established order. By the 1920s, same-sex friendships, to say nothing of Boston marriages, were actively discouraged.

Gay men also had their historical moment of openness, as homosexuals began to group together in large cities. Boston's gay subculture has been called "Boston Bohemia." Douglass Shand-Tucci argues that Boston was the center of aestheticism (the "art for art's sake" movement) in the United States and that *aesthete* was "almost a euphemism for homosexual." He symbolically dates the flourishing of Boston Bohemia from 1882, when the notorious British homosexual Oscar Wilde visited the city, to 1909, when Sigmund Freud came to speak: "What Wilde had started Freud ended." The Freudian view of homosexuality as a kind of arrested development fit very well with changing standards of masculinity in the late 19th century. Everyone who has written about men's roles at the time has emphasized a new definition of manliness. Whether it be called the "manliness movement," "passionate manhood," or "masculinism," the new standard of masculinity had less to do with male character and its assertion in the public sphere than with the male body and physical strength and courage. Physical culture, especially body building, became a fad, along with the martial arts and rough competitive sports. Men's "animal instincts" and tendencies toward violence, once thought to be in need of control, now appeared in a positive light.

Both Michael Kimmel and E. Anthony Rotundo view the new masculinism as a reaction to the women's movement and the doctrine of separation of spheres. Most notably, men put increased emphasis on fathering and developed institutions such as the Boy Scouts that were designed to remove boys from the feminizing influence of "women's sphere." Rotundo states, "The fear of womanly men became a significant cultural issue in the late nineteenth century, one discussed by men in a new gendered language of manly scorn." Men were increasingly sorted out into strong masculine types and weak feminine types, and the latter were associated, no matter how unrealistically, with homosexuality. According to Rotundo, there was "a need to create a category of person who could represent men's unacceptable feminine impulses." The image of the effeminate homosexual filled this need and "provided a negative referent for the new masculinity, with its heavy emphasis on the physical marks of manliness." A sharp line between heterosexuality and homosexuality was thus drawn for both genders; homosexuality and even romantic friendship were driven underground.

The changes that have affected gender in the United States since 1920 have seldom been seen as regionally distinctive. During the 20th century, as Patricia Nelson Limerick notes, a tendency developed to view each region as an "interchangeable part of a homogenized nation-state." To some extent developments in New England paralleled what occurred in other regions—such as married women shuttling back and forth between the home and the workforce as the perceived needs of society changed. During the 1920s women in New England as elsewhere were supposed to be learning how to balance career and marriage, but the Great Depression sent them home to prevent them from taking "men's jobs." With World War II married women were urged to replace men even in industry, but when the soldiers returned, an enormous propaganda campaign sent Rosie the Riveter back to full-time housewifery. According to Lois Scharf, it was the Depression decade that brought the "erosion of feminist rhetoric and thought," as women's organizations were forced to make more and more defensive and conservative justifications of women working. "Married women's right to employment was based, it was said, on their overriding concerns for their families and not on earlier hopes of enhancing women's status," Scharf writes. With economic recovery and World War II this question became moot, but feminism was a more lasting casualty as "a positive ideology encouraging personal and occupational progress and equality had vanished."

Other historians view the debilitating conflicts between women's organizations themselves as contributing to the demise of feminism. After 1920 the National Woman's Party (NWP), which had used aggressive tactics in working for suffrage, turned its attention to trying to pass an Equal Rights Amendment (ERA); but NAWSA, now the League of Women Voters (LWV), opposed the amendment, fearing that protective legislation for women and children in the workforce would be invalidated. During the 1920s and 1930s the two groups fought each other to a standstill. The conflict is often described as wholly class based, with the NWP being made up of upper- and middle-class women and the LWV of working-class women, but in fact numerous working-class women supported the ERA and numerous LWV members were upper-class reformers. The issues were complex. To use a New England example of the 1920s, members of the Massachusetts LWV took pride in the progressivism of their state, which was the first to enact a minimum-wage law for women. When the law set women's wages at 37 cents an hour, however, Harvard scrubwomen were replaced by men earning 34 cents an hour, and the NWP had reason to complain that minimum-wage laws deprived working-class women of jobs.

The opposition between the NWP and the LWV was thus reflected by events in New England, as were its attendant issues and trends. A few New England women held prominent national positions in these organizations, such as Maud Wood Park, the first president of the LWV. Yet the most distinctive fact about New England in gender-based movements of the first half of the 20th century is its relative unimportance. Of the 17 women included in *The Nation*'s 1926 survey of feminists, nearly half were born in New England. But only one, the journalist Inez Haynes Irwin, spent a significant portion of her life in the region; the others gravitated to Philadelphia or New York, complaining of the isolation and loneliness of their backwater birthplaces. The child psychologist Phyllis Blanchard opens her 1927 memoir "The Long Journey," reprinted by Elaine Showalter, with the comment that "farm life in New England is—or was, before the day of the automobile—lonely and isolated . . . at best." In her study of feminist women active during the 1930s, Susan Ware includes 28 who formed a network within the New Deal. Of these, two were native New Englanders: Frances Perkins, Franklin Roosevelt's secretary of labor and the first female cabinet member, and Molly Dewson, an economist and prominent Democrat. Yet both women left New England after college, and Ware lists their "home state" as New York.

New England was more visible in its antifeminism. Massachusetts and Connecticut, for instance, were the only two states in the nation not to participate in the Sheppard-Towner Act of 1921, which provided matching federal funds for maternity and pediatric clinics. (Sheppard-Towner was one of the first federally funded health-care programs and had been guided through Congress by a coalition of women's groups; it expired in 1929, by which time women had lost the political power to push a renewal through Congress.) Massachusetts and Connecticut repeatedly failed to pass women's jury service bills, and sometimes the New England states even legislated away previous rights. While Connecticut passed a law forcing married women to adopt their husbands' legal residence, Maine legislation required a woman to take her husband's name in registering to vote. In the 1930s Massachusetts became the center for opposition to married women working. The Massachusetts Women's Political Club, an ultraconservative group, lobbied for various measures against working wives in order to preserve conventional gender roles. In 1937 they persuaded the state assembly to pass a bill barring wives from the civil service, but the measure did not make it through the senate. The same scenario occurred in Connecticut, where the LWV and other women's groups persuaded the senate not to adopt a similar measure. Although these bills ultimately failed, traditionalists kept on trying to pass discriminatory legislation, and de facto exclusion of married women in private industry and public employment was widespread in the two states.

One might expect this conservative drift to have been countered by New England's elite women's colleges—after all, they had educated several New England women leaders: Maud Wood Park graduated from Radcliffe, where Inez Haynes Irwin also studied; Frances Perkins graduated from Mount Holyoke and Molly Dewson from Wellesley. Smith College in the 1920s funded the highly innovative Institute for the Coordination of Women's Interests, headed by the feminist Ethel Puffer Howes. The institute was designed to study and promote means by which women could combine a career with marriage and motherhood. It established a pioneering day-care facility, a cooked-food service for women, and a pilot program to train women for part-time and freelance work at home. But after six years Smith closed the institute; as Nancy Cott explains in *The Grounding of Modern Feminism,* "Founded when the elite women's colleges were adjusting to the fact that most of their graduates would become not scholars but wives and mothers, the institute was a casualty of the dissension aroused in that transition." Howes had also been interested in "how to incorporate women's perspectives into every college course"; if she had been able to implement her ideas, speculates the historian of education Barbara Solomon, women's studies might have developed much earlier than it did.

The loss of Smith's institute turned out to be only a symptom of the decline in women's status in the women's colleges as the 1930s progressed. In 1937 the Mount Holyoke board of trustees appointed a man to succeed retiring president Mary E. Wooley, and members of both the NWP and the LWV protested to no avail. At all the colleges the number of male faculty and administrators increased as the number of women decreased. When Adlai Stevenson gave the commencement address at Smith in 1955, he could confidently assume the graduates' "vocation of marriage and motherhood." Students who attended Smith during the 1950s, such as the New England poet Sylvia Plath and the feminist-to-be Gloria Steinem, found little support for their ambitions. There were, of course, exceptional women such as Margaret Chase Smith of Maine, who in 1948 became the first woman to have been elected to both houses of Congress. But she gained her position by succeeding her husband when he died. The first woman to hold a state governorship in her own right, Ella Grasso of Connecticut, did not do so until 1975, after the resurgence of the women's movement.

The so-called second wave of the women's movement came to life in the late 1960s on the campuses and in the cities of New England, as it did throughout the country.

Nancy Platt, Minister at St. Matthew's Episcopal Church, Hallowell, Maine, 1991

The two most important women's groups in New England were the Boston-based Bread and Roses and Cell 16. Bread and Roses, founded in the summer of 1969, was a socialist-feminist group that came out of the New Left. The Bread and Roses women opposed male supremacy but also believed that the women's movement should continue to work against the Vietnam War. Cell 16 was a smaller, more exclusive vanguard group started by Roxanne Dunbar in the summer of 1968. According to Alice Echols, it was "among the first radical feminist groups in the country." Cell 16 was influential beyond its numbers, as it published one of the earliest feminist journals, *No More Fun and Games: A Journal of Female Liberation.* The journal spread Cell 16's program of independence from men, including celibacy, all-female communes, and karate, and established the reputation of Dunbar's organization as "the most militant of all women's liberation groups." Dunbar moved away, however, weakening the group, and by 1973, both Bread and Roses and Cell 16 were defunct. The next New England organization to exert a nationwide influence was the Combahee River Collective, a gathering of African American women led by Bostonian sisters Barbara and Beverly Smith. In 1977 the collective issued "A Black Feminist Statement," which became well known for asserting that gender oppression cannot be analyzed separately, apart from race and class, because women of color experience interlocking systems of oppression.

During the 1970s the initial "women's liberation" groups of the second wave gave way to associations organized along occupational or topical lines or promoting specific types of change. Boston was again a pioneer, much as it had been during the first wave a century and a half earlier. In 1973 a new kind of labor organization was founded in Boston. The National Association of Working Women, Nine to Five, concentrated on organizing clerical, or "pink-collar," workers, who had generally been ignored by the male-dominated "blue-collar" unions. The organization drew up an "office workers' bill of rights" demanding equal pay and promotion opportunities for women, maternity benefits, and the right to refuse employers' requests to make coffee or do personal errands. According to the labor historian Philip Foner, Nine to Five focused on organizing women working in Boston's large publishing and insurance industries; it won a key victory in 1977 when it unionized the 160-worker Allyn and Bacon Company, a publishing house.

Bostonians also took a leadership role in areas in which the city had always been strong, health and religion. A group of women who would eventually call themselves the Boston Women's Health Book Collective began meeting to explore women's health issues. They jointly wrote a manual to help women make informed decisions about their health care. After selling 200,000 copies of a nonprofit newsprint edition, the collective revised and expanded the work that would become the bible of the women's health movement, *Our Bodies, Ourselves* (1973). This book, which has grown more massive with each new edition, is arguably the best known and most significant book to come out of the women's movement. It has inspired women's health organizations and publications in all regions of the United States and the world; at the time of its 25th anniversary edition in 1998, the book had been "adapted and adopted by women in many different countries and cultures" and translated into 14 languages.

In the area of religion and spirituality, Mary Daly, a professor of theology at Boston College and an early member of the National Organization for Women (NOW), was highly influential. Her first book, *The Church and the Second Sex* (1968), argued for the reform of Catholicism from within. But by the time of *Beyond God the Father* (1973), Daly had become more radical and advocated moving "beyond the father" to build a female counterculture, a space where female spirituality and feminist values would prevail. In subsequent books Daly has used her interest in etymology to create a veritable new language for women. Meanwhile, on the other side of the Charles River in Cambridge, the Harvard Divinity School was feeling the effects of the women's movement and inaugurating (in 1976) its influential program Women's Studies in Religion. In the early 1980s an associate professor at Harvard, Carol Gilligan, became internationally known for her research on women's moral decisions; in her book *In a Different Voice* (1982) Gilligan concludes that women are not less moral than men but less abstract and rule-bound in decision making, basing their morality on the importance of human relatedness.

Apart from the work of Gilligan, New England was not particularly prominent in the gender movements of the 1980s and 1990s. The rise of the gay and lesbian rights movements has been most visible in New York and California (except, perhaps, for the tiny city of Provincetown, Mass., on Cape Cod); it was in Greenwich Village in 1969 that a police riot at the Stonewall Inn, a gay bar, inaugurated the gay liberation movement. New England has also experienced, simultaneously with the rest of the country, the growth of women's studies in academia and of new community institutions, such as feminist health centers, support services for victims of rape and sexual assault, and shelters for battered women and children. Men have also organized on the basis of gender. Some are "pro-feminist," to use Michael Kimmel's designation; that is, they support feminists and the feminist position on most questions. In New England the New England Men's Emerging Network (NEMEN) has sponsored regional conferences for men working on feminist-defined issues. Profeminist men tend to be centered in academia, a fact that associates them with one of the most popular 20th-century images of New England manhood, the WASP prep-school type portrayed in the works of John Irving, John Cheever, and other writers.

Other men strive to emulate the traditional strong seaman type. They are masculinist, in a throwback to the late 19th century when men strove to become "real men" and resist any "feminizing" influences. According to Anthony Rotundo, the ideal of the "spiritual warrior," as expressed by Robert Bly, leader of the movement, signifies a "turning away from women" to pursue a "ritual quest for manhood in an all-male setting." This masculinist movement is much larger and more popular among men than its profeminist counterpart. Like the work of Carol Gilligan and her colleagues, it places heavy emphasis on the differences between men and women, which are often presented as inborn or essential. As New England enters a new century, both women and men have transformed the Puritan churches, but they still sit on opposite sides.

Susan D. Becker, *The Origins of the Equal Rights Amendment: American Feminism between the Wars* (1981); Boston Women's Health Book Collective, *Our Bodies, Ourselves for the New Century: A Book by and for Women* (1998); Russell Bourne, *The Red King's Rebellion: Racial Politics in New England, 1675–1678* (1990); Nancy F. Cott, *The Bonds of Womanhood: "Woman's Sphere" in New England, 1780–1835*, 2d ed. (1997); Cott, *The Grounding of Modern Feminism* (1987); John Putnam Demos, *Entertaining Satan: Witchcraft and the Culture of Early New England* (1982); W. E. B. Du Bois, *The Souls of Black Folk: Essays and Sketches* (1903); Alice Echols, *Daring to Be Bad: Radical Feminism in America, 1967–1975* (1989); Larry D. Eldridge, ed., *Women and Freedom in Early America* (1997); Sara M. Evans, *Born for Liberty: A History of Women in America* (1989); Philip S. Foner, *Women and the American Labor Movement* (1979–80); James Kendall Hosmer, ed., *Winthrop's Journal: "History of New England," 1630–1649* (1908); Linda K. Kerber, *Women of the Republic: Intellect and Ideology in Revolutionary America* (1980); Michael S. Kimmel and Thomas E. Mosmiller, eds., *Against the Tide: Pro-Feminist Men in the United States, 1776–1990: A Documentary History* (1992); Lyle Koehler, *A Search for Power: The "Weaker Sex" in 17th-Century New England* (1980); Patricia Nelson Limerick, "Region and Reason," in *All over the Map: Rethinking American Regions,* ed. Edward L. Ayers and Peter S. Onuf (1996); Kenneth Lockridge, *Literacy in Colonial New England: An Enquiry into the Social Context of Literacy in the Early Modern West* (1974); Lonna M. Malmsheimer, "Daughters of Zion: New England Roots of American Feminism," *New England Quarterly* 50 (1977); J. A. Mangan and James Walvin, eds., *Manliness and Morality: Middle-Class Masculinity in Britain and America, 1800–1940* (1987); Judith Sargent Murray, *Forming a New Era in Female History: Three Essays* (1999); Carole Nichols, *Votes and More for Women: Suffrage and after in Connecticut* (1983); E. Anthony Rotundo, *American Manhood: Transformations in Masculinity from the Revolution to the Modern Era* (1993); Leila J. Rupp and Verta Taylor, *Survival in the Doldrums: The American Women's Rights Movement, 1945 to the 1960s* (1987); Nancy Sahli, "Smashing: Women's Relationships before the Fall," *Chrysalis* 8 (1979); Lois Scharf, *To Work and to Wed: Female Employment, Feminism, and the Great Depression* (1980); Douglass Shand-Tucci, *Boston Bohemia, 1881–1900,* vol. 1 of *Ralph Adams Cram: Life and Architecture* (1995); Elaine Showalter, ed., *These Modern Women: Autobiographical Essays from the Twenties* (1978); Carroll Smith-Rosenberg, "The Female World of Love and Ritual: Relations between Women in 19th-Century America," *Signs* 1 (1975); Barbara Miller Solomon, *In the Company of Educated Women: A History of Women and Higher Education in America* (1985); Elizabeth Cady Stanton, *Eighty Years and More: Reminiscences, 1815–1897* (1971 [1898]); Elizabeth Cady Stanton, Susan B. Anthony, and Matilda Joslyn Gage, eds., *History of Woman Suffrage* (1881–87); Adlai Stevenson, "A Purpose for Modern Women," *Woman's Home Companion* (September 1955); Louise L. Stevenson, "Women Antisuffragists in the 1915 Massachusetts Campaign," *New England Quarterly*

(March 1979); Sharon Hartman Strom, "Leadership and Tactics in the American Woman Suffrage Movement: A New Perspective from Massachusetts," *Journal of American History* 62 (1975); Rosalyn Terborg-Penn, *African American Women in the Struggle for the Vote, 1850–1920* (1998); Laurel Thatcher Ulrich, *Good Wives: Image and Reality in the Lives of Women in Northern New England, 1650–1750* (1982); Susan Ware, *Beyond Suffrage: Women in the New Deal* (1981); Barbara Welter, "The Cult of True Womanhood, 1820–1866," *American Quarterly* 18 (1966); Marjorie Spruill Wheeler, ed., *One Woman, One Vote: Rediscovering the Woman Suffrage Movement* (1995); Barbara A. White, "Sarah Josepha Hale," in *American Women Writers: A Critical Reference Guide from Colonial Times to the Present,* ed. Lina Mainiero (1979–94); Nancy Woloch, *Women and the American Experience,* 3d ed. (2000).

Barbara A. White

Alcott, William Andrus (1798–1859)

Educator, physician, and writer. Born on a farm in Wolcott, Conn., William Alcott taught school until concern for his own and his students' health inspired him to study medicine. A second cousin and close friend of the Transcendentalist Bronson Alcott, whose daughter was Louisa May Alcott, William was the nation's most published and reprinted advice author before the Civil War. In more than 100 books and pamphlets, he developed notions of gender, morality, and health that typified and disseminated the New England Protestant vision of a perfect society achieved through individual self-restraint. He died in Auburndale, Mass., after spending his life in New England.

As a physician in western Connecticut, Alcott rejected the era's drug-heavy therapies in favor of lifestyle prescriptions: outdoor exercise, frequent bathing, vegetarianism, and cold water as one's only beverage. Punctuating his medical career were further stints of teaching, during which Alcott promoted inductive learning rather than rote memorization and introduced practical improvements to the learning environment, including blackboards, ventilated school buildings, and comfortable seats. Finding the pen to be a more effective tool of reform than either his medical practice or classroom teaching, however, he soon embarked on a variety of writing projects.

Although Alcott wrote tracts and edited journals on many subjects for children and educators, he became most famous for his advice literature. Here he perfected his conception of the temperate life appropriate to men and women. *The Young Man's Guide* (1833), reprinted 20 times, and *The Young Husband* (1838) steered young men toward the righteous, responsible persona that was Alcott's masculine exemplar. Alcott advocated early rising, frugality, industrious habits, and a respectful marriage. Swearing, using tobacco and alcohol, running up debts, and going to the theater were unacceptable, as were displays of anger, overbearing behavior, and dishonesty in business. He gravely repeated the medical belief of his day that masturbation caused an overall decline in physical and mental health.

In his frank *The Physiology of Marriage* (1856) Alcott admitted that sexual desire struck both men and women. Even in marriage, though, according to him, exuberant passion was physically and morally harmful to both spouses, and sexual activity of any kind would indirectly damage an unborn or breast-feeding child. When a woman was not pregnant or lactating, married couples should have sexual relations no more than once a month.

Whereas men received guidance on business dealings and money management, women were told that their work as mothers could profoundly, but always invisibly, change the world. In *The Young Woman's Guide to Excellence* (1840) and *The Young Wife* (1837) Alcott urged women, like men, to practice frugality, cleanliness, efficiency, and healthy habits. Unlike men, women had a duty to pass these values on to their families. Alcott repeatedly counseled against anger and faultfinding. Conceding that a husband could try a wife's patience and acknowledging that men, too, had to sacrifice self-interest to make a happy marriage, Alcott still maintained that women should be more submissive than men. Women should also feel a strong attraction for life in the home, preferring private pursuits to public ones. Nevertheless, a woman should develop her mind and be ready to support herself if necessary. Alcott prized a gentle and self-sacrificing woman, but he appreciated neither the clinging vine nor the then-fashionable sickly waif.

Alcott's writings helped to crystallize the Victorian ethic of sexual self-control, high moral expectations, and gender difference according to which people judged themselves and others. He believed that most Americans would follow his advice only partially at best, and he was right. Nonetheless, he urged constant effort. During his lifetime and for several decades after his death, Americans strove to live up to William Alcott's deeply gendered and thoroughly New England ideals of proper behavior.

Joan Burbick, *Healing the Republic: The Language of Health and the Culture of Nationalism in 19th-Century America* (1994); Harvey Green, *Fit for America: Health, Fitness, Sport, and American Society* (1986); Louis Salomon, "The Least-Remembered Alcott," *New England Quarterly* 34 (1961); James C. Whorton, *Crusaders for Fitness: The History of American Health Reformers* (1982).

Rebecca R. Noel

American Woman Suffrage Association

The American Woman Suffrage Association (AWSA) was one of two suffrage groups to emerge in 1869 from a split in the women's rights movement. In its representative organizational structure and in its state-by-state work for suffrage, it differed from the National Woman Suffrage Association (NWSA), which concentrated early efforts on a suffrage amendment to the federal Constitution.

The formation of two rival suffrage organizations grew out of the failure of Reconstruction reform politicians to include women in the push for increased civil rights for freed slaves. Instead of backing universal suffrage, Congress passed amendments intended to guarantee the suffrage rights of male former slaves. Bitterly disappointed, Elizabeth Cady Stanton and Susan B. Anthony responded by accepting the support of a racist demagogue, George Francis Train. Stanton and Anthony's women's rights newspaper, the *Revolution*, published editorials urging women to oppose ratification of the 15th Amendment, guaranteeing the vote to freedmen, and to campaign instead for educated suffrage. In a moving speech at the 1869 convention of the American Equal Rights Association, Lucy Stone, one of the three principal leaders of the movement, argued, "We are lost if we turn away from the middle principle and argue for one class. . . . I thank God for the Fifteenth Amendment." At the convention the overwhelming majority of suffragists voted in favor of a resolution endorsing ratification of the 15th Amendment.

After Stanton and Anthony formed the NWSA, whose first resolution called for defeat of the 15th Amendment, New England Woman Suffrage Association leaders decided that a second national organization "at once more comprehensive and more widely representative" was "urgently called for." Its leaders worried that the NWSA's anti–15th Amendment campaign gave the impression that the women's movement was "opposed to the Negro," to the political harm of both causes. A circular letter inviting delegates from throughout the United States to a November 1869 organizational convention in Cleveland, Ohio, met with widespread enthusiasm, and the AWSA was formed.

From association headquarters in Boston, AWSA leaders Lucy Stone, Julia Ward Howe, and Margaret Campbell directed a national organizing campaign. Paid AWSA lecture agents canvassed towns, cities, and rural enclaves, forming suffrage clubs, distributing tracts, and directing petition drives. The association became a single-issue lobby with roots in every political district. "Organize! Organize!" Stone exhorted week after week in the *Woman's Journal*, the newspaper that served various women's and human rights causes from 1870 until 1931.

After the 1875 Supreme Court decision in *Minor v. Happersett*, which reserved the power to enfranchise to the states, the AWSA increased its efforts to secure state and municipal suffrage for women. The model suffrage club charter urged members to circulate tracts and newspapers, hold public meetings, and work to elect friends of woman suffrage to legislatures while laboring to defeat suffrage opponents. Each AWSA district had its own political action group, which actively lobbied and petitioned with the help of the Boston office.

By the 1880s differences between the two rival suffrage organizations had diminished, and in 1890 the two groups joined to form the

National American Woman Suffrage Association (NAWSA). One unfortunate legacy of the schism is the lack of historical attention to the work done by the Boston-based AWSA.

Andrea Moore Kerr, *Lucy Stone: Speaking Out for Equality* (1992); Lois Bannister Merk, *Massachusetts and the Woman-Suffrage Movement* (1961).

Andrea Moore Kerr

Beecher Sisters

In the span of their years and the breadth of their interests, the four daughters of influential Presbyterian minister Lyman Beecher—Catharine Esther (1800–1878), Mary Foote (1805–1900), Harriet Elizabeth (1811–96), and their half sister Isabella Homes (1822–1907)—epitomized the complex public and private commitments that characterized the lives of educated women in 19th-century New England. Although none of the sisters ultimately accepted their father's strict Calvinism, three of them—Catharine, Harriet, and Isabella—were inspired by his example to become important figures in national reform movements.

A pioneer in women's education, Catharine Esther Beecher founded the Hartford (Connecticut) Female Seminary (1823), the Western Female Institute in Cincinnati, Ohio (1833), and the Milwaukee (Wisconsin) Female Seminary (1850). In addition, she was a prominent author and lecturer on subjects ranging from family life to moral philosophy to women's health. Catharine, who never married, both embodied and expanded the growing range of choices available to single educated women in the 19th century. Despite her own life choices, however, Beecher insisted that women were naturally mothers and homemakers, a theme developed in many of her most important published works, including *A Treatise on Domestic Economy* (1841) and *The American Woman's Home* (1869). She opposed the participation of women in abolition and the growing women's rights movement.

Harriet Elizabeth Beecher, later Harriet Beecher Stowe, taught for a time in her older sister's first two schools, but in 1836 she married the college professor Calvin Stowe. Prompted in part by the financial burden of a growing family, Harriet combined the work of running a household and raising eight children, one of whom died in infancy, with a distinguished career as an author. The first piece of writing to be published under her own name, "A New England Sketch," appeared in *Western Monthly* magazine in 1834. In 1843 she published her first full-length work, *The Mayflower; or, Sketches of Scenes and Characters among the Descendants of the Pilgrims.* Her most famous novel, *Uncle Tom's Cabin; or, Life among the Lowly,* published serially in the *National Era* in 1851 and under separate cover in

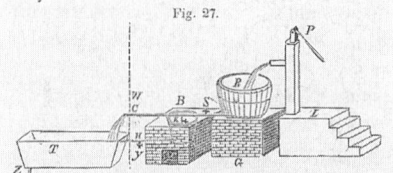

Fig. 27, represents the accommodations for securing water with the least labor. It is designed for a well or cistern under ground. The reservoir, R, may be a half hogshead, or something larger, which may be filled once a day, from the pump, by a man, or boy.

Fig. 27.

P, Pump. L, Steps to use when pumping. R, Reservoir. G, Brickwork to raise the Reservoir. B, A large Boiler. F, Furnace, beneath the Boiler. C, Conductor of cold water. H, Conductor of hot water. K, Cock for letting cold water into the Boiler. S, Pipe to conduct cold water to a cock over the kitchen sink. T, Bathing-tub, which receives cold water from the Conductor C, and hot water from the Conductor H. W, Partition separating the Bathing-room from the Wash-room. Y, Cock to draw off hot water. Z, Plug to let off the water from the Bathing-tub into a drain.

"Securing water with the least labor," a page from Catharine Beecher's Treatise on Domestic Economy *(1841)*

1852, was written in protest of the Compromise of 1850, whose accompanying Fugitive Slave Law required officers in nonslave states to assist in the capture of fugitive slaves. The book helped galvanize growing antislavery sentiment among white northerners. Harriet's plots, characters, and themes were always deeply positioned in New England, a characteristic that often led critics to dismiss her work as mere regionalism. Most of her writings, both fiction and nonfiction, expounded the broadly redemptive values of a sentimentalized domesticity. Her last novel, *Poganuc People,* was published in 1878.

Isabella Homes Beecher, later Isabella Beecher Hooker, was an active woman suffragist who based women's claim to equal legal rights on a belief in the innate superiority of women as mothers. In 1841 Isabella married John Hooker, a lawyer. She subsequently gave birth to four children, one of whom died in infancy. Throughout her married life Isabella maintained a public career as a suffrage speaker and an author. She was active in the founding of the Connecticut Woman Suffrage Association in 1869. Her publications included *Womanhood: Its Sanctities and Fidelities* (1873); *The Constitutional Rights of the Women of the United States,* delivered as a speech before the International Council of Women in 1888 and published in 1890; and *An Argument on United States Citizenship* (1902). In 1873 Isabella broke from her close-knit family to join growing criticism of her brother, the minister Henry Ward Beecher, for his alleged adultery with a member of his Brooklyn congregation, an act of independence that permanently alienated her from her siblings. In her later years Isabella became interested in spiritualism.

Of the sisters, only Mary Foote Beecher, later Mary Beecher Perkins, chose a relatively quiet, nonpublic life. Although as a young

woman Mary offered music and drawing lessons for a time in New London, Conn., and taught briefly at Catharine Beecher's Hartford Female Seminary, in 1828 she married Thomas Clap Perkins and withdrew from paid labor. Mary remained interested in reform causes and opposed the Fugitive Slave Law, but for the most part she eschewed active participation in reform societies. Like most women in prosperous 19th-century New England families, Mary focused her attention on housework, managing domestic servants, and raising her four children and, for much of the period 1835–41, her half sister Isabella. Yet the Beecher legacy of female activism persisted in Mary's line: her granddaughter was the noted author and activist Charlotte Perkins Gilman.

Jeanne Boydston, Mary Kelley, and Anne Margolis, *The Limits of Sisterhood: The Beecher Sisters on Women's Rights and Woman's Sphere* (1988); Joan D. Hedrick, *Harriet Beecher Stowe: A Life* (1994); Milton Rugoff, *The Beechers: An American Family in the 19th Century* (1981); Kathryn Kish Sklar, *Catharine Beecher: A Study in American Domesticity* (1973); Barbara A. White, *The Beecher Sisters* (2003).

Jeanne Boydston

Blackwell, Henry

(1825–1909) Suffrage leader and abolitionist. Of all the male reformers involved in the woman suffrage movement, Henry Browne Blackwell was the most consequential. For more than 40 years, from 1866 until his death in 1909, the struggle for national woman suffrage was the focus of his activism. A resident of Dorchester, Mass., for most of his adult life, Blackwell was born in 1825 in Bristol, England. His family emigrated to the United States in 1832. His father, Samuel, a British antislavery reformer, immersed himself in the American abolitionist movement. Although the family lived in Long Island, N.Y., and Cincinnati, Ohio, Blackwell grew up surrounded by New England abolitionists, which inspired him to embrace antislavery reform. His father's death forced Blackwell to pursue a business career while a young teenager. A frustrated entrepreneur all his life, Blackwell frequently invested in businesses and real estate, though his ventures were seldom profitable.

Like a number of male abolitionists, he was attracted to the women's rights movement, delivering his first women's rights address in 1853 at the Fourth National Woman's Rights Convention in Cleveland. Two years later, when he wed the prominent Massachusetts abolitionist and women's rights reformer Lucy Stone, Blackwell formally promised to support her women's rights work. In 1866 he and Stone embarked on their suffrage careers when they helped found the American Equal Rights Association, an organization dedicated to securing universal suffrage. In the spring of 1867 the couple stumped through Kansas to rally support for a woman suffrage referendum. As a loyal Republican during the late 1860s Blackwell insisted that he and Stone postpone agitating for woman suffrage until the ratification of the 14th and 15th Amendments guaranteed African American rights. Yet during this time he and Stone formed the New England Woman Suffrage Association (1868), the American Woman Suffrage Association (1869), the Massachusetts Woman Suffrage Association (1870), and their newspaper, the *Woman's Journal* (1870). He participated in uniting the woman suffrage movement through the formation of the National American Woman Suffrage Association in 1890, becoming one of the organization's most active campaign leaders.

Although Blackwell was often eclipsed by Stone's brilliant oratory and prominence in the movement, he was an aggressive campaigner and a shrewd strategist. In his all-out pursuit of woman suffrage, he proposed a controversial strategy to break the South's unified antisuffrage bloc, arguing that the enfranchisement of southern white women would allow the South to retain white political supremacy. Like the vast majority of suffragists and social reformers of the late 19th century—but unlike his celebrated wife—Blackwell became a proponent of "educated suffrage," believing that the ballot should be withheld from illiterate immigrants and African Americans until they received a rudimentary education.

Blackwell's greatest contribution was his unique, intuitive understanding of the politicians and businessmen who were the most steadfast opponents of woman suffrage. Backroom politicking was his forte, and, unlike Stone, he thrived on the adventure and physical hardships of state suffrage campaigns, leading efforts in Vermont, Nebraska, South Dakota, Colorado, Rhode Island, and Washington state. Blackwell remained an active suffragist until his death. In his final years he also protested the persecution of Russian Jews and Armenians, American imperialism, and the deportation of political refugees.

Andrea Moore Kerr, *Lucy Stone: Speaking Out for Equality* (1992); Michael S. Kimmel and Thomas E. Mosmiller, eds., *Against the Tide: Pro-Feminist Men in the United States, 1776–1990: A Documentary History* (1992); Suzanne M. Marilley, *Woman Suffrage and the Origins of Liberal Feminism in the United States, 1820–1920* (1996); Leslie Wheeler, ed., *Loving Warriors: Selected Letters of Lucy Stone and Henry B. Blackwell, 1853 to 1893* (1981).

Judith E. Harper

Boston Gay and Lesbian History

Insofar as sexuality is held today to be a central aspect of human life and a crucial ingredient of individual identity, Michel Foucault was surely right to say that the subject was *discovered* in the 19th century. Since then, inevitably, it has been ceaselessly explored. This encyclopedia entry, a necessity from the point of view of the early 21st century, would hardly have been conceived of even a generation ago, though the subject encompasses Boston's history back to the earliest days of the 17th century.

What the 19th century dubbed "homosexuality" is of course discernible throughout all historical eras in Boston as elsewhere, despite 17th-century antisodomy laws that made the "unclean practice" punishable by death. At Harvard, for example, the anguished soul-searching of the Puritan minister and tutor Michael Wigglesworth on the subject of same-sex desire in his (miraculously) surviving journal from 1653 to 1657 is well known. Similarly, the Boston artist Washington Allston, a student in the late 1700s, seems to some scholars to have demonstrated a life pattern suggestive of homosexuality. Also of considerable interest are the sometimes intensely homoerotic musings of Ralph Waldo Emerson and Henry David Thoreau during the 1830s and 1840s, respectively, an era during which the acceptance of homosexuality, at least in the Ivy League, has been well established by the work of the Yale historian Peter Gay. A decade later the poetic effusions of the Harvard undergraduate Henry Adams document as well the effect of the notoriety of Lord Byron's sexuality on one level of New England life during the 1850s. The distinctly more serious work of Herman Melville has also attracted scholars' attention, as have the romantic friendships between the actor Charlotte Cushman and the sculptor Emma Stebbins, for example, and another midcentury Boston sculptor, Anne Whitney, and the painter Abby Adeline Manning.

Those relationships point directly to the role of New England's hub in the historical development of an emerging gay and lesbian subculture in the West in the later years of the 19th century, particularly in England and America. No small part of that history involved the female same-sex unions such as Whitney and Manning's that, though certainly not unique to any one place, came to be called Boston marriages, thus identifying the city with the most prominent same-sex relationship of the era. They existed, moreover, at the highest levels, with notable examples being the couples formed by the wealthy Boston poet and social reformer Annie Adams Fields and the Maine author Sarah Orne Jewett, who lived and traveled together from 1882 until Jewett's death in 1909, and that of Katharine Loring and Alice James, sister of Henry James—considered by many to have been homosexual—whose novel *The Bostonians* (1886), the masterpiece of his middle years, describes such a Boston marriage.

The Boston men's clubs, several of which had a distinctly bohemian repute (chiefly the Tavern, St. Botolph, and the Papyrus), nurtured a number of similarly devoted male couples—the playwright T. R. Sullivan and Theodore Dwight, director of the Boston Public Library, for example. Here, too, a novel of the period, though much less of a work than *The Bostonians*, celebrates such a relationship: Frederic Loring's *Two College Friends* (1871), the story of two Harvard men who fall in love as undergraduates and then enlist in the Union Army together in the Civil War and are conspicuous for their courage and effectiveness. It is a tale of "comradely" or "athletic" love very much in the spirit of Walt Whitman, who in the 1860s became the prophet of the modern concept of gay identity (though it was not his term, *adhesiveness*, that stuck but that of a Swiss physician: *homosexuality*). Indeed, it was on Boston Common in 1860 that Whitman and Emerson engaged in a dialogue about *Leaves of Grass* from which Whitman emerged surer than ever that to censor or shorten the work in any way was to admit there was something wrong with it. Published in Boston that year in what Whitman felt was its first complete form, the book in many places celebrated his concept of love between men.

That concept (the inspiration, of course, of *Two College Friends*), referring as it does to the archetype of the warrior (and by extension the athlete), contrasts strikingly with the other gay archetype of the aesthete (and by extension the artist), embodied by Oscar Wilde, who lectured in Boston in 1882. Both archetypes are evident in the several bohemian circles of Boston identifiable in the late 19th century. First, there was the group that formed around the noted patron of the arts Isabella Stewart Gardner, which included at varying times not only Henry James and the renowned Edwardian portrait painter John Singer Sargent but the architects Harold Peto and Ralph Adams Cram, the Boston Pops conductor T. Adamowski, the painter Dennis Bunker, the composer Charles Loeffler, and the art museum administrator Matthew Prichard. Prichard was a friend of Lord Alfred Douglas and Edward Perry Warren, a wealthy Boston gay man of the time who gave the Museum of Fine Arts one of America's great collections of classical sculpture—several pieces of which celebrate men engaged in same-sex erotic pursuits. Two of Gardner's nephews were also gay, William Amory Gardner, one of the three founders of the Groton School, and Joseph Peabody Gardner, who died in 1886, four years after graduating from Harvard. Amory Gardner commissioned the architect Henry Vaughan, another gay man, to design the Groton School's Chapel of Saint John (1899–1901) in memory of his brother. That so famous a landmark was the product of one gay man memorializing another with a building designed by a third aptly illustrates the nature and character of the contribution of the newly emerging gay subculture to New England's intellectual and cultural history.

The "bachelor don," whether homosexual or not, was in fact a distinct turn-of-the-century social type, especially at Harvard, where another circle, often overlapping with Gardner's, centered on the philosopher George Santayana. That group combined aspects of both the Whitmanian and the Wildean archetypes. Two novels that depicted bohemian Harvard in the 1880s and 1890s, Charles Flandrau's *Harvard Episodes* (1897) and Shirley Johnson's *The Cult of the Purple Rose* (1902), are quite a bit more Wildean, certainly, than *Two College Friends*. A third bohemian circle, again somewhat overlapping with both Gardner's and Harvard's, existed on Boston's North Shore in Gloucester, where what has been called something of a New England Bloomsbury gathered around the scientist and inventor John Hays Hammond, Jr., and his partner, the actor Leslie Buswell, and Congressman A. Piatt Andrew, Jr. (later a founder of the American Field Service on the Western Front during World War I), and his partner, the interior designer Henry Sleeper, whose brilliant and labyrinthine house Beauport, of major importance in the history of the American decorative arts, is so clear an example of what is nowadays often called "queer space." One wonders, however, if the house that the architect Philip Johnson built for himself on Ash Street in Cambridge while studying architecture at Harvard—herald of his later Glass House—is not another, though it is so very different in its crisp, lucid openness.

Women also figured in this North Shore group, and indeed the Boston marriage remained a vital institution into the 20th century. Two Wellesley College professors who forged such relationships, for example, were Vida Scudder, the Anglican Marxist thinker who may have been the first woman to study at Oxford University, and Katherine Lee Bates, author of *America the Beautiful*. Others were the poet Amy Lowell, who lived with the actress Ada Dwyer Russell from 1912 until Lowell's death in 1925, and the novelist Alice Brown and poet Louise Imogen Guiney. The last two were luminaries of another Boston bohemian circle, this one centered in 1880 and 1890 on Pinckney Street and led by Guiney, the architect Ralph Adams Cram, and Fred Holland Day, the pioneering pictorialist photographer whose publishing house, Copeland and Day, brought Oscar Wilde's work to America. Other notables from this group included the Harvard poets Richard Hovey and Bliss Carman (coauthors of *Songs of Vagabondia*), the architects Henry Vaughan and Bertram Goodhue (during the years he was Cram's colleague), the book designer D. B. Updike, and the composer Frederick Field Bullard. Although documentation of these various circles has just begun, it is no wonder that Xavier Mayne declared in his book *The Intersexes* (1908) that only New York was ahead of Boston as one of America's "homosexual capitals."

Whitman and Emerson's dialogue on Boston Common provides an important early indication of the extent and depth of Boston's role in the emergence of a gay subculture. As the gay literary historian Byrne R. S. Fone has written, the British gay thinkers of the era J. A. Symonds and Edward Carpenter regarded Whitman's poetry as virtually "an announcement of a program in which homosexual love was to be an instrument for spiritual growth, social change and political reform." The writings of James M. Pierce, the distinguished mathematician and the second dean of Harvard's Faculty of Arts and Sciences (1895–97), were also influential. Given that Pierce wrote, anonymously but boldly (as recorded by Havelock Ellis), that "passion is not characterized or differentiated by the nature of its object, but by its own nature," Fone is correct to place him among the first in the modern era to propose "a theory of sexual orientation rather than sexual preference"—of homosexuality, in other words, not as a deviation from heterosexuality but as a part of "a larger spectrum of desire."

Post–World War I figures associated in some way with gay culture and Boston include the composers Aaron Copland and Leonard Bernstein; the poets May Sarton, Elizabeth Bishop, and John Wheelwright; the journalist Joseph Alsop; the architects Eleanor Raymond, Philip Johnson, and Paul Rudolph; the sportswoman Eleanor Sears; the painter Margaret Sargent; the novelist John Cheever; the scholars A. Kingsley Porter and F. O. Matthiessen; and the founder of the New York City Ballet, Lincoln Kirstein.

The latter decades of the 20th century were a time of change for gay and lesbian Boston. In 1973 one of the nation's first and most influential gay periodicals, the weekly *Gay Community News,* was founded; it is now published quarterly. In 1974 Boston's Elaine Noble became the first openly gay person elected to the Massachusetts legislature. Since then gay men and lesbians have grown more numerous at all levels of government. In 1989, after a 17-year legislative battle, Massachusetts became the second state to pass a law, signed by the Democratic Governor Michael Dukakis, prohibiting discrimination based on sexual orientation. While fundamentalist and conservative forces reminiscent of the city's Puritan founders have protested every political and legislative advance for homosexuals, there can be little doubt that Boston will continue to

Gay liberation march, Boston, 1972

play a leading role in American gay and lesbian history.

Byrne R. S. Fone, *Masculine Landscapes: Walt Whitman and the Homoerotic Text* (1992); The History Project, *Improper Bostonians: Lesbian and Gay History from the Puritans to Playland* (1998); Douglass Shand-Tucci, *The Art of Scandal: The Life and Times of Isabella Stewart Gardner* (1997); Shand-Tucci, *Ralph Adams Cram: Life and Architecture*, vol. 1, *Boston Bohemia, 1881–1900* (1995).

Douglass Shand-Tucci

Boston Marriage

Boston Marriage The term *Boston marriage*, designating a pattern of single women's relationships and living arrangements, originated in late-19th-century New England. That same region had already provided the cultural and historical context for *spinster,* itself a word that recognized the emerging presence of single women in the antebellum U.S. society and workforce. A Boston marriage involved two single, unrelated, and self-supporting women who shared an intense, enduring, and possibly sexual relationship that often included cohabitation. Usually educated and professional women, the two may have chosen to live together because they were emotionally attached to one another or because lower pay for women undermined their individual ability to support an urban middle-class lifestyle.

The emergence of Boston marriages in the latter 19th century was linked to two important aspects of this period in U.S. women's history: the increased numbers of single educated women who had joined the workforce, especially in the professions; and the Victorian trend that segregated independent, unmarried women within society, assigning separate spheres to men and women. The separate woman's sphere nurtured prolonged relationships between unrelated women, allowing them to bond within the domestic circle, sex-segregated educational institutions, women's professions (most of which barred married women), and all-female organizations dedicated to civic, social, and political reform.

One of the most famous Boston marriages was that of Annie Adams Fields, the widow of the publisher James T. Fields, and the author Sarah Orne Jewett, who became famous in the late 19th century for her portrayals of strong, independent New England spinsters. Gradually the term *Boston marriage* came to be used beyond New England, but Henry James emphasized its origin in his satirical novel *The Bostonians* (1886), which attacked both feminism and female couples, associating the two phenomena.

Lillian Faderman, *Surpassing the Love of Men: Romantic Friendship and Love between Women from the Renaissance to the Present* (1981); Micaela di Leonardo, "Warrior Virgins and Boston Marriages: Spinsterhood in History and Culture," *Feminist Issues* 5, no. 2 (1985); Esther D. Rothblum and Kathleen A. Brehony, *Boston Marriages: Romantic but Asexual Relationships among Contemporary Lesbians* (1993).

Angela M. Howard

Boston Women's Health Book Collective

Boston Women's Health Book Collective The Boston Women's Health Book Collective is a nonprofit education and advocacy organization devoted to issues of consequence to women's health. Inspired by the second wave of feminism during the late 1960s and early 1970s, the collective is most famous for its publication *Our Bodies, Ourselves,* first issued in 1973. Since that time, the collective has undergone many changes, but the goals and focus of the group remain unchanged.

Founders of the collective, including Nancy Miriam Haley, Wendy Sanford, Norma Swenson, Jane Pincus, Judy Norsigian, and Paula Doress-Wortes, were first inspired to organize after a 1969 Boston conference on women and their bodies. Using concerns raised at that forum to guide them, this small group met to share stories, compare experiences, and write a series of papers that would constitute *Women and Their Bodies,* the first version of their book. Initially aiming to "do something about those doctors who were condescending, paternalistic, judgmental and non-informative," according to the introduction to the 1984 version of the work, the group compiled women's health data from textbooks, medical journals, physicians, and nurses. In the fall of 1969 this information was offered to the public as part of a free course titled "Women and Their Bodies," which allowed collective founders to share their health resources with others.

As public interest in the course materials grew, the group approached the New England Free Press, a nonprofit alternative publisher, about printing them. In December 1970 that press issued a first, 138-page newsprint edition of *Women and Their Bodies.* Demand for the publication was so strong that it strained the resources of the Free Press and forced collective members to seek a larger publisher. The collective signed on with Simon and Schuster in 1971, and the first, 276-page edition of *Our Bodies, Ourselves* appeared two years later. By 1998 the newly revised and updated *Our Bodies, Ourselves for the New Century: A Book by and for Women* was 780 pages long, with the collective maintaining an average annual budget of well over half a million dollars. The collective has for some years included African American and Hispanic women both on its pages and among its authors. Consequently, the health concerns of minority women are better reflected in more recent editions of the book.

As collective members state in the introduction to the 1998 *Our Bodies, Ourselves,* their focus has not wavered since the text was first published in 1973: "As the millennium approaches, our original goals for this book remain as important as ever: to fit as much information about women's health between the covers of this book as we can, providing women with tools to enable all of us to take charge of our health and lives; to support women and men who work for progressive change; and to work to create a just society in which good health is not a luxury or a privilege but a human right."

The primary objective of the Boston Women's Health Book Collective remains providing women of all ages, backgrounds, races, ethnicities, and sexual orientations with vital information about their health and with the tools they need to evaluate the institutions and people that furnish medical care, including hospitals, clinics, doctors, health maintenance organizations, medical schools, nursing schools, and public health departments. Fertility control, childbearing, sexuality, and older age are constant themes of their book, which also addresses topics as varied as nutrition, exercise, on-line women's health resources, AIDS, eating disorders, domestic violence, and organizing for change.

Joyce Antler and Sari Knopp Biklen, eds., *Changing Education: Women as Radicals and Conservators* (1990); Boston Women's Health Book Collective, *Our Bodies, Ourselves for the New Century: A Book by and for Women,* rev. ed. (1998); Sara Rimer, "They Talked and Talked, and Then Wrote a Classic," *New York Times,* June 22, 1997.

Marion J. Coffey

Bundling

Bundling Bundling was a controversial 18th-century New England courting ritual, brought over from the British Isles, that allowed unmarried couples to sleep in the same bed wrapped up in individual covers and separated by a board. New England families used bundling, or "staying with," as the practice was sometimes called, to negotiate the boundaries between parental control and autonomy for young people, who were thus able to express their sexual desires. Bundlers were expected to remain clothed, though an undetermined number circumvented the expectation.

While many bundling couples planned to marry, the practice was not the equivalent of an engagement. A few wooers even stayed with more than one person at a time. Bundling was not a private event—as few things were in colonial New England. Hopeful suitors took careful note of others seen leaving their love interest's home early in the morning.

Eighteenth-century standards of acceptable behavior were more lenient than those of either Puritan or Victorian America. By the mid-1700s New England courts were rarely if ever charging individuals with fornication. But there was no shortage of proof that young people were often engaging in premarital sex. It is estimated that 30 to 40 percent of brides were pregnant on their wedding day in the decade preceding the American Revolution. In most cases no shame was attached to premarital pregnancy as long as marriage occurred before the child was born. Despite the era's greater leniency, parental and societal pressure usually ensured that it did.

There were some practical reasons for parents to let young sweethearts stay overnight together. Parents knew that they would never be able to control the feelings, desires, and actions of their children. Young people could act on their sexual desires by secretly meeting a lover on their way to or from work or a neighbor's house. If pregnancy resulted from such an encounter, paternity was harder to establish when a suitor was unwilling to own up to his actions. If he was known to have stayed with a young woman who got pregnant, however, it would be more difficult for him to deny responsibility. By allowing young people to explore some of their physical desires in the safety of their homes, parents were affording them added protection in the case of a premarital pregnancy. Daughters in particular needed that protection, as unmarried mothers faced severely restricted opportunities in 18th-century society.

Not everyone approved of bundling, however. Many New England ministers, including Jonathan Edwards, railed against the practice as encouraging lewdness and disorder among the young. Churches offered alternative opportunities and settings for socializing, but more often than not these options supplemented rather than eliminated the practice of bundling.

The custom of bundling reveals 18th-century tensions between parents and children over the right to choose one's marriage partner and control one's sexuality. For many families it was the common ground on which the rules of courtship, marriage, and independence were set.

Jane Nylander, *Our Own Snug Fireside: Images of the New England Home, 1760–1860* (1993); Milton Rugoff, *Prudery and Passion* (1971); Laurel Thatcher Ulrich, *Good Wives: A Study in Role Definition in Northern New England, 1650–1750* (1980); Laurel Thatcher Ulrich and Lois K. Stabler, "'Girling of It' in 18th-Century New Hampshire," in *Families and Children*, ed. Peter Benes and Jane Montague Benes (1987).

Beth A. Kaputa

Clothing Clothing has been called a language, though it is an imprecise one with multiple, ever shifting meanings. Personal attire can identify its wearer geographically and historically. It can also signify inclusion in or exclusion from certain groups, often indicating social and economic status or positioning its wearer in a hierarchy of power and subservience. Clothing frequently sends messages about personal status and religious, ethnic, or other group identities. Overlaying all other identities, however, is that of the sex of the wearer. Gender, to a great extent, makes clothing. When garments are created, chosen, or observed by others, the first distinction made, usually unspoken, pertains to gender. Clearly, clothing is an important means of communicating a person's sense of self and of his or her role in society. It is also one of the most potent and easily recognizable symbols of a particular culture. For many Americans New England culture can be summed up by its clothing symbols, from the soberly dressed Puritans of the 17th century to the ruggedly attired L.L. Bean "preppies" of the 20th.

By the 1800s images of Puritans not only represented a unique New England experience but had become a symbol of American values in general. The stern, industrious, anti-aristocratic Puritans, depicted in somber dress relieved only by touches of white at sleeve and collar, embodied the democratic principles of the entire nation. Today, while certain details have changed, the stereotypical New Englander has much the same image. Shirts made of chamois, a soft, durable cotton; canvas duck-hunting coats; and rubber-bottomed hunting shoes demonstrate their wearer's adherence to utilitarian virtues.

Puritans never wore the costumes in which countless murals, public statues, and Thanksgiving decorations have attired them. These depictions are usually based on 19th-century interpretations of the past. The severe garments, stripped of any adornment, are exaggerations based on the Puritan dislike of excess. Although Puritan writings speak of making garments in "sadd colours," rich, warm tones of russet, green, scarlet, and purple were often used for clothing in addition to dull gray, brown, and black. Puritans dressed simply if one judges by the fashionable excesses of their day, but overall the cut of their attire was not unlike that of their contemporaries. Women wore long, gathered skirts with a separate bodice. Men wore long hose resembling modern-day tights, knee-length breeches, and doublets, which were close-fitting garments that covered the body from the neck to just below the waist. Women sometimes wore doublets, too, but not without criticism. Like most people of the 17th century, Puritans believed that certain items of dress were proper only for one sex. One English Puritan remarked disapprovingly about women who chose to wear doublets, "Though this be a kind of attire proper only to a man, yet they blush not to wear it."

Nevertheless, certain kinds of garments served both sexes. Women and men alike wore sturdy cloaks of similar cut and undergarments that were exposed to view in the form of white linen collars and sleeves. Edging this linen with lace or embroidery was common, though Puritan ministers and magistrates lectured against such extravagance. In Connecticut and Massachusetts during the 1630s, laws were passed that prohibited immoderate display of costly finery, but people largely ignored them. Contemporary portraits, for example, often depict subjects adorned in elaborate lace collars and sleeves. In most respects, then, 17th-century New Englanders looked very much like their British or southerly colonial counterparts.

The harsh climate of New England did affect styles, however, dictating heavier clothing made of stouter fabric than may have been worn in England. A scarcity of material also affected the Puritans' choices. Homespun linens and wools, available from native sources, filled many clothing needs. Taking their cues from Native American modes of dress, settlers made men's doublets out of native deerskin.

Native American women and men in fact used deerskin for many of their garments. Edward Winslow, a Puritan settler in New Plymouth, described the deerskin cloaks, long hose, and aprons of leather worn by Samoset, an Indian visitor to the settlement, and five Massasoit men. Winslow later observed that the dress of Native American women, who wore deerskin breeches, stockings, and shoes, was similar to that of their male counterparts. He also noted that Indian women, unlike men, always wore strings tied about their legs.

By the time the Puritans arrived in Massachusetts in the 1620s, coastal Native Americans had long been exposed to European ways of dress by sailors who had fished cod off the shores of North America since the late 15th century. These contacts may have influenced the Indian style of leggings described by early European settlers. Native Americans often traded beaver skins for articles of clothing. By the 1640s Roger Williams of Providence, R.I., noted that Indians had added English wool cloaks to their wardrobes. European settlers were less likely than Indian natives to adopt alien ways of dressing, but cultural contact did lead to new attire for both groups.

Over time certain kinds of distinctions become more, and sometimes less, important than others. Until the 18th century in New England, as in the rest of the colonies and western Europe, clothing predominantly high-lighted distinctions between social ranks. Women's and men's garments differed in cut and form but basically complemented each other. Farmworkers of both sexes wore earth-toned or undyed cloth garments. Lavish bro-cades and satins primarily connoted class po-sition, not gender. Lace, which in the 20th century came to connote femininity, signified instead aristocratic affluence and was worn by both women and men of high rank. But dur-ing the 18th century gender distinctions be-came paramount. This was the era of what costume historians have labeled "the great masculine renunciation" of fashion. Middle- and upper-class men in New England and the rest of the United States, like their counter-parts in western Europe, gave up their finery, adopting increasingly modest and sober dress. Now not only did the cut of male garments differ from women's; so, too, did the fabrics and colors, with dark wools replacing bright satins.

Women continued to wear the elaborate fashions that most men now eschewed. By the early 19th century clothing had come to differ-entiate the sexes markedly, underscoring com-monly held cultural assumptions concerning the nature of women and men. Men clothed themselves in "practical" suits and adopted a fashion for facial hair—mustaches, beards, and side whiskers—that was thought to em-phasize manliness. In sharp contrast, notwith-standing the New England cold, women at-tired themselves in delicate, pale muslin dresses, which were thought to coincide with the current notion of womanliness. As the 19th century progressed, these gender distinc-tions in clothing would become more pro-nounced in accordance with the then perva-sive notion of separate spheres for each sex. Men began wearing a recognizable precursor of today's business suit, a form of clothing that, despite subtle variations through the years, has shown remarkable endurance and consistency. Women's clothing, by contrast, underwent ever more rapid transformation. The wide, fancifully trimmed sleeves of the 1830s gave way to narrow, plain ones by the early 1840s. By midcentury the tubular silhou-ette characteristic of dresses at the turn of the century was replaced by tight bodices and wide skirts that emphasized and exaggerated the curves of the female body. Skirts became so voluminous that a cagelike hoop was re-quired to support their enormous expanse of fabric. Despite the impracticality of this style, hoopskirts were the first truly democratic fashion. Because its steel components were relatively cheap, all but the poorest women were able to afford some sort of hoop.

By the 19th century most regional clothing distinctions had given way to an "American" style. The suits donned by New England men might be cut from heavier cloth, but in shape they were essentially the same as those worn by their southern and western counterparts. Women in every state followed fashions in such magazines as *Godey's Lady's Book,* edited by New Englander Sarah Josepha Hale, which circulated styles throughout the country. New England also played a role in setting national trends at the century's end when the Shaker knit sweaters developed for athletes at Dart-mouth, Harvard, and other Ivy League schools helped create a 20th-century masculine ideal.

Although clothing became increasingly ho-mogeneous in the United States of the 20th century, dress ways and their meanings con-tinued to evolve. For example, when women appropriated trousers, once the symbol of masculinity in western culture, they changed both what trousers signified and what it meant to be a woman. In the 21st century clothing conventions remain an integral part of our so-cial structure, as new or more subtle distinc-tions replace the old. Puritan goodwives of the 1690s may seem the antithesis of 1890s Gibson Girls, but both images express versions of the feminine ideal of their day. The "bourgeois lumberjacks" of present-day Boston may look a lot like 19th-century Maine woodsmen, but their lifestyles have little in common. Cloth-ing remains a fluid language, always changing as it constructs and reflects culture.

Michael Batterberry and Ariane Batterberry, *Fash-ion: The Mirror of History* (1982); Fred Davis, *Fashion, Culture, and Identity* (1992); Anne Hollander, *Sex and Suits: The Evolution of Modern Dress* (1994); Claudia Brush Kidwell and Valerie Steele, eds., *Men and Women: Dressing the Part* (1989); James Laver, *A Con-cise History of Costume and Fashion* (1969); Alison Lurie, *The Language of Clothes* (1981); Diana de Marly, *Dress in North America* (1990); Philippe Per-rot, *Fashioning the Bourgeoisie: A History of Clothing in the 19th Century* (1994).

Lisa Purcell

Combahee River Collective

The Combahee River Collective was a fitting des-ignation for the group of African American feminists who came together in Boston during the early 1970s. Named after the fearless guer-rilla action planned and led by Harriet Tub-man in 1863 in the Port Royal region of South Carolina, the collective was distinguished by a unique blend of intellectual and grassroots activism. In many ways the group followed in the tradition of Tubman's historic raid, which, in addition to liberating 750 enslaved Africans, was the first American military ac-tion planned and led by a woman.

The Combahee River Collective was founded in Boston in 1974 and flourished through the late 1980s. Its groundbreaking es-say, *The Combahee River Collective Statement* (1986), not only eloquently expressed the po-litical and intellectual ideologies of its mem-bers but demonstrated a progressive philoso-phy of anti-oppression that went far beyond other statements, scholarly or otherwise, that were produced during the period.

These courageous feminists held that black feminism was the logical political movement to combat what the *Statement* calls the "mani-fold and simultaneous oppressions that all women of color face." The group advocated the inherent value of African American wom-anhood and the necessity to struggle against all forms of oppression. Composed of African American feminists and lesbians, the collec-tive renounced fractionalization based on gen-der and collaborated with other progressives of color, both male and female. The group's ideology was particularly innovative in its cri-tique of biological essentialism, according to which biology is destiny, and in its limited re-course to politics based on identity, which has often been found to conflict with a progressive agenda for social change. At the same time, however, the collective built a theoretical framework, and created a language, that in-corporated the importance of culture and community. It also asserted that all major sys-tems of oppression were inextricably linked: true feminists must struggle to destroy not only patriarchy but also the capitalist, imperi-alist structures bound up with racism, poverty, and homophobia. This level of analytic inge-nuity placed the collective ahead of its time.

The collective's ideology led to grassroots organizing and activism, while individual members continued to grapple with issues such as abortion, domestic violence, rape, and health care. The group also led educational workshops aimed at combating oppression in high schools, colleges, and universities across the country and held retreats for African American women writers and activists. Its ability to blend theory and activism has rarely been matched. While the collective may never, like Tubman, have waged a military bat-tle, it certainly embodied an equally spirited commitment to human liberation.

Combahee River Collective, *The Combahee River Collective Statement: Black Feminist Organizing in the Seventies and Eighties* (1986); Barbara Smith, ed., *Home Girls: A Black Feminist Anthology* (1983).

Kali N. Gross

Courtship and Marriage

Recent re-search has revised previous stereotypes of Pu-ritan and Victorian behavior in courtship and marriage, proposing that Puritan as well as later Victorian marriages were often based on love and saw sexual expression as an integral, although potentially dangerous, part of marriage. But the courtship and marriage practices of those eras still differed considerably from those of today. Industrialization and personal mobility have dramatically changed the circumstances by which individuals find suitable marriage partners. Bundling, for example, the 18th-century New England courtship custom that allowed fully clothed, unmarried couples to sleep in the same bed, has been replaced by computerized wooing that takes place in Internet chat rooms and dating services that let clients proclaim themselves on videotape to be available for possible "long-term relationships."

During the early colonial period, Protestantism, which wielded enormous political and cultural authority, favored the establishment of families, and unmarried women and men were both rare. Unmarried women at the age of 25 were considered spinsters, and unmarried men could not choose their own residence but were housed within the homes of families. Well beyond the late 18th century, women generally remained in the home of their parents until their wedding day. By contrast, in the United States by 1990 only one single woman in eight still lived with her parents, according to marriage license applications.

Unlike other regions in colonial America, such as the Chesapeake Bay area, New England had no imbalance between the sexes because it was a destination to which entire families, not just individuals, generally immigrated. There was thus no shortage of white marriage partners. African Americans were fairly few in number during New England's early colonial period, and in some states, such as Massachusetts, marriage between African Americans or Native Americans and whites was illegal until the mid-19th century. Their relatively small numbers and disadvantaged legal status made for a shortage of marriage partners for African American New Englanders.

Courtship in colonial New England, which could last as long as 10 years, was strictly supervised, with women enjoying less freedom than men. Sexual intercourse outside of marriage was a very serious offense against the mores of the community and the church, but it was not entirely unheard of for a bride in New England to be pregnant on her wedding day. In 17th-century Massachusetts, married couples whose first child was born less than seven months after the wedding day were suspected of premarital fornication and were sometimes prosecuted and fined.

The laws of Puritan New England gave parents substantial power over the disposition of their children in marriage. Gradually over the 18th and 19th centuries, parental control

declined as the growth of business and commerce diminished the dependence of young men on family land, but parental wishes remained a factor in marriage choices. Parents exercised their authority over unmarried children in a number of ways, controlling matters such as land, capital, and the timing of their disposition that could importantly affect their sons' marriage plans. Marriage negotiations between families frequently involved the father of a suitor giving a house and land to the newly married couple. Marriage records from the 17th century in New England indicate that many new husbands were well past their 21st birthday, suggesting parental unwillingness to part with land, capital, and their sons' labor contributions to the household of origin.

For sons and daughters alike birth order was also a determining issue in marriage. The oldest son was often in an economically favored position, and his disproportionate share of family wealth often permitted him to marry a woman with a handsome dowry from a relatively prosperous family. In early colonial times the wealthier the family, the younger the bride. In the New England region, as well as throughout the United States generally, women have traditionally married younger than men. In early-17th-century New England the average age of first marriage for women was 22 years and 26 for men, a figure that rose during the 18th century. Sisters were expected to marry in birth order, lest the community believe an older, unmarried daughter was in some way impaired or deficient.

The only legal form of marriage was a civil contract involving property rights that was executed by a magistrate. In colonial times weddings were not performed in churches. For nearly 200 years every New England state except New Hampshire required that public announcements of a couple's intention to marry, called banns, be published three times before a marriage could take place. In the absence of such banns a union was not considered respectable. Marriage was a contract rather than a sacrament and thus could be dissolved, but divorces were not easy to obtain. If one spouse died, remarriage was prompt, sometimes occurring in a matter of weeks. Serial monogamy, or marriage to one spouse at a time but several spouses over the course of one's lifetime, was practiced during colonial times and remains fairly common today.

Over the first few decades of the 19th century, attitudes toward marriage and gender roles began to shift. American Victorian culture (roughly 1830 to 1890) dictated that marriage should be based on personal happiness, mutual affection, and respect between spouses. Women were viewed as spiritually and morally superior to men. Wives were to nurture

and maintain their families and make the home a sanctuary for their husbands. This "cult of domesticity" is well documented in the diaries, memoirs, and letters of New England's white middle- and upper-class women of English Protestant heritage.

Once married, women found motherhood almost inevitable. During colonial times women were usually either pregnant or lactating until menopause, but during the Victorian era they managed to have smaller families. Wealthy Victorian women married later than less prosperous young women, in a reversal of the earlier pattern. More and more, women made their own decisions about marriage choices and were not merely "married off" by their parents.

For men marriage meant enhanced status as the head of a household. For women, by contrast, marriage meant leaving one's family of origin and taking on responsibility for the physical, emotional, and moral needs of others. Even though marriage was not always seen as a gain for women, the decision not to marry was still a serious one for women as well as men. Few saw being single as an enviable condition. A study of Massachusetts in 1830 reported that less than 13 percent of that state's women failed to marry before the age of 50.

In the early 1880s New England was being transformed into an industrial society. Technological change profoundly affected the socioeconomic system of the 19th century as well as courtship and marriage. Unmarried young women went to live and work in the textile mills of Lowell and Waltham, Mass., and men entered wage labor, ending their financial dependence on their parents. In addition, waves of European immigrants began to arrive in New England, especially from 1865 through 1917. Regional industrialization created class distinctions that combined with social, ethnic, religious, and political diversity to transform many cultural practices.

The post-Victorian era, sometimes described as having lasted from 1890 to 1960, further modified courtship and marriage patterns, as education levels increased and men and women entered the labor force in unprecedented numbers. Assumptions about courtship and marriage changed, as did the rules and rituals that governed these relations, in response to economic changes and global events, especially world wars. As women entered the workforce and sometimes lived outside the home, silver trays for suitors' calling cards disappeared from New Englanders' front halls, courtship moved from private homes to public places, and the era of dating began. As early as the 1930s the automobile began contributing significantly to that trend. Attitudes toward premarital sexual activities became more moderate, but a double standard still prevailed that gave men more latitude to explore sexuality free from cultural judgment.

In the 20th century, marriages became based on personal, social, and cultural companionship. In 1951 the United States had the second-lowest age at first marriage of any record-keeping country in the history of the 20th century, 22.6 years for men and 20.4 years for women. By 1959, 47 percent of all brides were marrying before their 19th birthday.

In the last four decades of the 20th century patterns of courtship and marriage changed dramatically both regionally and nationally. In 1994 the number of marriages per 1,000 people in New England states was generally lower than the national rate of 9.1 percent, with the exception of Vermont, at 10.1 percent. Connecticut had the lowest marriage figure in the region at 6.7 percent. Not only has the marriage rate been falling, but by the 21st century the average age at first marriage for both men and women had risen above 26 years. In the past, marriage was considered a prerequisite for having children. Today, though some stigma still attaches to single mothers, New England newspapers publish birth announcements of single mothers. Consistent with national trends, the region's birthrate from 1990 to 2002 dropped from 16.7 to 13.9 per 1,000; approximately 33 percent of all births were to unmarried women. Cohabitation before marriage in the United States is now the norm rather than the exception. With the national divorce rate running as high as 50 percent, cohabitation appears to be an important stage in or alternative to the contemporary courtship and marriage.

Same-sex partnering has also met with growing acceptance in some parts of New England. In the early 21st century, Maine was the only state that had not passed some sort of civil rights bill for same-sex unions, and in 2003 the Massachusetts Supreme Judicial Court ruled that same-sex marriage was legal in the commonwealth.

Nancy Bonvillain, *Women and Men: Cultural Constructs of Gender* (1995); Nancy F. Cott, *The Bonds of Womanhood: "Woman's Sphere" in New England, 1780–1835,* 2d ed. (1997); Nancy F. Cott and Elizabeth H. Pleck, eds., *A Heritage of Her Own: Toward a New Social History of American Women* (1979); Carl N. Degler, *At Odds: Women and the Family in America from the Revolution to the Present* (1980); Joseph M. Hawes and Elizabeth I. Nybakken, eds., *American Families: A Research Guide and Historical Handbook* (1991); Ellen K. Rothman, *Hands and Hearts: A History of Courtship in America* (1984); Steven Seidman, *Romantic Longings: Love in America, 1830–1980* (1991); U.S. Department of the Treasury, Bureau of Statistics, *Statistical Abstract of the United States* (1990).

Nancy Johnson Black

Daly, Mary (1928–) Radical feminist writer, theologian, and philosopher. Mary Daly is a

Mary Daly, 1989

self-named radical feminist "Nag-Gnostic philosopher" who emerges, and radically departs, from a tradition of New England intellectuals known for their iconoclasm, astute social commentary, and dissent. Born in Schenectady, N.Y., Daly attended working-class Catholic schools. While a student, she dreamed of being a philosopher, but because she was female she was denied access to philosophy programs. Daly studied philosophy via English and theology, earning a bachelor's degree in English (College of Saint Rose, 1950), a master's in English (Catholic University of America, 1952), and doctorates in religion (Saint Mary's College, 1954), theology (University of Fribourg, Switzerland, 1963), and philosophy (University of Fribourg, 1965). As a professor of feminist ethics at Boston College, Daly has influenced feminist critiques of theology, philosophy, and rhetoric. As a popular feminist writer and lecturer in the United States and Europe, Daly has influenced women from all walks of life.

Although Daly credits Thomas Aquinas with teaching her to think philosophically, she also credits his sexism with teaching her to think for herself. In 1966 Daly began teaching at Boston College where, amid legendary battles over tenure and promotion, she has offered the first women's studies courses in theology, taught courses for the Women's Institute of the Boston Theological Institute (a consortium of theological schools), and written progressively more radical critiques of patriarchal myths and language.

In *The Church and the Second Sex* (1968) Daly calls for sexual equality within the Catholic Church. In *Beyond God the Father: Toward a Philosophy of Women's Liberation* (1973) she redefines God as a space of "human becoming," and in *Gyn/Ecology: The Metaethics of Radical Feminism* (1978) she articulates an ethics that allows women to refuse patriarchal

history and "re-fuse" their own interconnected histories. In *Pure Lust: Elemental Feminist Philosophy* (1984), Daly provides women with strategies for challenging patriarchal passions and reconnecting with each other and the earth. *Websters' First New Intergalactic Wickedary of the English Language* (1987) is a "metapatriarchal" dictionary Daly wrote with Jane Caputi that records Daly's language theory and lexicon. And *Outercourse: The Be-Dazzling Voyage* (1992) is Daly's autobiography, a record of her own radical feminist journey.

Daly's radical feminism continues a New England tradition of individualism. She defines radical feminism as a self's journey from foreground (patriarchal consciousness) to background (radical feminist consciousness). This journey is effected via "Spinning," or feminist language play. In *Gyn/Ecology* Daly offers a model of this process: "Women's minds have been mutilated and muted to such a state that 'Free Spirit' has been branded into them as a brand name for girdles and bras rather than as the name of our verb-ing, being Selves." Daly uses the phrase "commuting to Boston" as her metaphor for reentering the patriarchal foreground. Although accused (often unfairly) of essentialism, idealism, lesbian separatism, and even unintentional racism, Daly will be remembered for extending the boundaries of radical feminism and for spurring a famous debate about methodology in which she championed commonalties among women while the African American feminist poet Audre Lorde upheld differences.

Vivian Harrower, *Feminist Critiques of a Male Savior* (1985); Audre Lorde, "An Open Letter to Mary Daly," in *Sister Outsider,* ed. Audre Lorde (1984); Krista Ratcliffe, *Anglo-American Feminist Challenges to the Rhetorical Traditions* (1996); Dale Youngs, "What's So Good about the Goddess?" *Christianity Today* 37 (1993).

Krista Ratcliffe

Domesticity Domestic ideology, especially as it came to be understood in the early-to mid-19th-century United States, emphasized the exalted position of women as wives and mothers. Centered in the home, the domestic woman attended to her family's material comfort and emotional well-being. Exercising influence on her male relatives and affectionately training her children in the paths of morality, she maintained social virtue. This concept of a woman's role emerged from and was a function of New England's history, economy, and culture. After the Industrial Revolution moved production from individual family farms to urban manufacturing centers, the barter system gave way to an economy whose primary medium of exchange was cash. Thus men abandoned farming, moved to cities and suburbs, and began to work for pay in the newly burgeoning capitalist industries. Women, once integral to a self-sustaining domestic economy, now became primarily responsible for spending the family's capital and maintaining the home as a refuge to which tired wage earners could return after a hard day's work. Children, who once had assumed adult responsibilities within a family economy, now enjoyed an extended childhood during which their mothers' job was to mold their character with loving discipline. Ultimately, then, men moved into a public sphere whose values were capitalist and competitive, while women occupied a private sphere whose values were selflessly Christian.

A descriptive model derived from a regional phenomenon, domestic ideology has often been extended by implication to describe the experience of all mid-19th-century women. Yet even a cursory examination suggests its limits. Many of the first laborers to move into cities and earn wages in the new capitalist system were the daughters of New England farmers, who sought work in the textile mills of the Northeast. The domestic ideal that emerged as a result of the new division of labor does not adequately account for them or for the lives of other single women. Moreover, domestic ideology overlooks its own inherent conflicts, requiring as it did that women have servants to help run the home at the same time that it urged them to revel in their household duties. It assumes a cultural order dominated by heterosexuality and Protestant upper-class values. In its sometimes uncritical and universal application, such an ideology does not describe the lives of people of color, laborers, or immigrants.

Domesticity was promulgated by New England writers, who articulated its details in fiction, prescriptive literature, nonfiction, and journalism. These writers identified New England as the primary seat of domestic virtues. Both Catharine Beecher and Harriet Beecher Stowe, for example, lauded the merits of New England housekeeping—Beecher's *A Treatise on Domestic Economy* (1841) sought to extend regional practices to the new western settlements, while Stowe's novels and journalism, particularly her *House and Home Papers* (1865), located happiness within homes that mirrored New England's architecture, customs, work patterns, and values. Many of the texts most closely identified with domestic ideology were published in the Northeast: Sarah Josepha Hale's *Ladies' Magazine* (1828–37), one of the first periodicals for women, was published in Boston; *Godey's Lady's Book,* which Hale edited from 1837 until 1877, was published in Philadelphia but vaunted New England history, heroes, heroines, and regional virtues.

New England's part in the formulation of domestic ideology has been understood in three ways. During the 1940s and 1950s literary historians labeled the mid-19th century, the period of domesticity's greatest influence, "the Feminine Fifties," following the title of Fred Lewis Pattee's dismissive literary history. Focusing on the literary productions of New England writers, they endorsed Nathaniel Hawthorne's condemnation of the "damned mob of scribbling women" who had competed with him and his contemporaries in the rapidly expanding field of magazine fiction. Subsequent literary historians, who understood Hawthorne to be objecting to the inferior quality of domestic writing by women, elevated less popular fictions by Hawthorne and his contemporary Herman Melville, positing that although the mass of 19th-century readers could not appreciate these writers' iconoclasm, ambiguity, and density, these authors had nevertheless captured the qualities that were most typically American. At the same time literary histories devalued the works of many of the women writers of the period—the so-called domestic sentimentalists—because they lacked these qualities.

During the late 1960s and 1970s the feminist literary theorists and historians who engaged in rescuing "forgotten" works written by women in the previous century used domestic literature to forge a wide-ranging historical and sociological description of women's culture. Paradoxically, they shared the assumption of earlier scholars that 19th-century women were confined to a world separate and different from that of men. For example, on the basis of her extensive reading of fiction, gift books, and periodical writings published in New England between 1820 and 1860, Barbara Welter identified the four "cardinal virtues" thought to constitute an all-pervasive domestic ideology, or what she called "the cult of True Womanhood" (the term "cult" is Wel-ter's; the phrase "True Womanhood" is common to the period). These virtues were "piety, purity, submissiveness and domesticity."

A pious Christian woman believed that her subordination to man was a matter of divine fiat. A pure woman was chaste before marriage and faithful to her husband; her purity would serve as a corrective to mens' naturally licentious nature. A submissive woman obeyed her parents, husband, and social superiors. A domestic woman confined herself to her home and to such public duties as were consistent with her womanly nature, notably charity work and church-related activities. Her access to political power was understood to derive from her influence on her husband and sons. Welter's description has exhibited remarkable staying power and is still cited as accurately characterizing both 19th-century domestic texts written by New England writers and the patterns of 19th-century social structure across the United States.

Other scholars saw in the concept of separate spheres an opportunity for feminine community and political activism. Carroll Smith-Rosenberg's pathbreaking essay "The Female World of Love and Ritual" (1975), for example, affirmed the psychological power of same-sex relationships. In *The Bonds of Womanhood* (1977) Nancy F. Cott saw feminine identification as a necessary precondition of feminist political involvement, while in *Sensational Designs* (1985) Jane Tompkins reread domestic fiction by New England writers as the basis of a woman-centered politics of reform.

Most recently domestic ideology has been reexamined with an eye toward precisely defining its pervasiveness. Emphasizing its New England origins and ideals and considering the diversity of 19th-century women, scholars such as Linda Kerber have concluded that the idea of separate spheres was primarily "employed by people in the past to characterize power relations . . . and by historians in our own time . . . [to] impose narrative and analytical order on the anarchy of inherited evidence." In "Separate Spheres, Female Worlds, Woman's Place" (1988), Kerber locates the American understanding of separate spheres in Alexis de Tocqueville's description of American society—an account based solely on that French author's brief visit to the United States. She argues that the model was imprecise even in Tocqueville's day but that its imaginative force served to differentiate American women from their purportedly more liberated European counterparts.

Subsequent work on domesticity has followed Kerber's lead, undertaking a broad-ranging critique. Hazel Carby's *Reconstructing Womanhood: The Emergence of the Afro-American Woman Novelist* (1987) demonstrates the race-based assumptions of domestic ideology, while Christine Stansell's *City of Women: Sex and Class in New York, 1789–1860* (1986) demonstrates its limited application to urban working women. Both studies, although not focused specifically on New England, suggest a more complex understanding of the region's society and culture. Laura McCall's "'The Reign of Brute Force Is Now Over'" quantifies the supposed adherence of *Godey's Lady's Book* to Welter's four "cardinal virtues." McCall concludes that "*not one*" of the female characters in *Godey's* fiction "possesses all four features that purportedly made up the 'true woman' of antebellum America." Nicole Tonkovich's *Domesticity with a Difference* (1997) reexamines works written by four New England writers, attending particularly to the class and regional identities of women supposedly addressed by domestic ideology. Considering the contradictions between the texts they wrote and the practices those writers and others of their class engaged in, the book exposes the contradictions undermining any textual description of domesticity.

Thus, although domestic ideology has not been dismissed out of hand as a 19th-century phenomenon, scholars have begun to question and outline its limits. Attending to its New England origins and biases, they have argued that its first articulations derived from ideals that were white, upper-class, Protestant, and urban, while its power to describe or to control the lives of slaves, immigrants, women of color, or working women is severely limited. Moreover, recent work has shown that the very texts thought to be most representatively "domestic" may also pursue complex agendas, promoting the ideologies thought to characterize upper-class domesticity while arguing for more radical political agendas that illustrate women's abilities as independent thinkers and actors. Finally, the most recent scholarship demonstrates that women who wrote, whether they favored the limited behaviors described by domestic ideology or penned subversive texts, were necessarily involved in public negotiations, were aware of this public dimension to their lives, and saw the limits of the domestic ideology that supposedly described and circumscribed the lives of 19th-century women.

Nancy F. Cott, *The Bonds of Womanhood: "Woman's Sphere" in New England, 1780–1835*, 2d ed. (1997); Mary Kelley, *Private Woman, Public Stage: Literary Domesticity in 19th-Century America* (1984); Linda K. Kerber, "Separate Spheres, Female Worlds, Woman's Place: The Rhetoric of Women's History," *Journal of American History* 75 (1988); Laura McCall, "'The Reign of Brute Force Is Now Over': A Content Analysis of *Godey's Lady's Book*, 1830–1860," *Journal of the Early Republic* 9 (1989); Carroll Smith-Rosenberg, "The Female World of Love and Ritual: Relations between Women in 19th-Century America," *Signs* 1 (1975); Jane Tompkins, *Sensational Designs: The Cultural Work of American Fiction, 1790–1860* (1985); Nicole Tonkovich, *Domesticity with a Difference: The Nonfiction of Catharine Beecher, Sarah J. Hale, Fanny Fern, and Margaret Fuller* (1997); Barbara Welter, "The Cult of True Womanhood," *American Quarterly* 18 (1966).

Nicole Tonkovich

Early Feminism and Feminists Some of the earliest expressions of feminist thought in North America came from New England during and immediately after the American Revolution. In the 1830s abolitionism led, particularly in New England, to the growth of feminism and the development of a strong feminist-abolitionist cadre. In 1845 Margaret Fuller published her visionary work on ideal gender relations, *Woman in the Nineteenth Century,* and from 1848 to the Civil War a series of women's rights conventions focused feminist activism, with one of the most important taking place in Worcester, Mass. After the war fierce controversy over the 15th Amendment, which enfranchised black men, split the movement into the Massachusetts-based American Woman Suffrage Association (AWSA) and the New York–centered National Woman Suffrage Association (NWSA). Reunification of the two groups in 1890 and a new generation of leaders, many of them from New England, generated the energy and creativity that led to ratification of the 19th Amendment, granting women the right to vote, in 1920.

The Protestant emphasis on reading scripture created an unusually large number of literate women in New England. Early in the revolutionary period Abigail Adams shrewdly counseled her husband John Adams to "remember the ladies" when formulating laws for a newborn country. Ostensibly, this was a reminder of the tyranny of men over their wives that was sanctioned by common law; but Abigail's threat to revolt if she was not granted the right to consent to the new government bespoke a larger vision of woman's role. After the Revolution Judith Sargent Murray published a number of full-length works advocating that women be educated for economic independence. Her writings of the late 18th century provided a grounding for the expansion of thought that would occur during the 19th century.

A disproportionate number of first-generation feminists were daughters of New England. Most were descendants of Puritans, a good number of them Unitarians or sometimes Transcendentalists. Many were Quakers. Indeed, without New England's unusually fertile environment for social activism, the growth of feminism would have been significantly slower. With the Second Great Awakening encouraging both perfectionism and reform, another campaign for equal rights had a tremendous influence on the development of the early women's movement: abolitionism. William Lloyd Garrison's Boston antislavery paper, the *Liberator,* advocated putting an immediate end to slavery. In 1837 South Carolina natives Sarah and Angelina Grimké were attracting mixed audiences to their antislavery parlor talks in New England. The Massachusetts clergy's opposition to those talks led Sarah Grimké to develop a compelling biblical defense of women's equality and to become a champion of women's rights. Subsequently, women such as Massachusetts natives Abigail Kelley Foster and Lucy Stone began to speak for the antislavery movement.

Like radical abolitionism, Transcendentalism was also native to New England. It was this philosophy of self-reliance and freedom from institutional beliefs that provided the source for Margaret Fuller's *Woman in the Nineteenth Century,* which was the fullest exposition of feminist philosophy to date in the United States and had a major influence on early feminist thought. In favor of complete emancipation, Fuller argued for educational opportunity, access to occupations, and political rights for women.

Fuller influenced Lucretia Mott and Elizabeth Cady Stanton, who organized and led the first women's rights convention in Seneca Falls, N.Y., in 1848. That gathering was prompted primarily by the misogyny of the 1840 World Anti-Slavery Convention in London, which had barred the two feminist leaders from participating; but some of the seeds for a women's rights conference had been planted in Boston, where Stanton spent the years 1844 to 1847 early in her married life. Mott, who was born in Nantucket, Mass., also had strong links to New England. The Seneca Falls gathering inspired a series of conventions, one of the most important of which was held at Worcester, Mass., in 1850. The Worcester meeting was celebrated as the first national convention, while the New York assembly, though precedent-setting, was considered a local affair. No organizations for women's rights were founded, but delegates continued to convene until the Civil War.

Until the 14th and 15th Amendments to the Constitution were passed, the women's rights movement was united in its philosophy, goals, and strategies. Women advocated for married women's property acts, education, employment, and suffrage, as well as for complete equality with men. Harriot Hunt's protests against taxation without representation and Stone's refusal to take her husband's name when she married were two of the many ways in which New England women publicized the principles of feminism.

After the Civil War the 14th and 15th Amendments, guaranteeing the rights of male former slaves, split the New York and New England wings of the feminist movement. The American Equal Rights Association, to which most of the feminists belonged, supported these amendments, though they entered the word "male" into the Constitution for the first time and though the 15th Amendment enfranchising African American men did not grant the vote to women. That omission led Stanton and Susan B. Anthony to form the NWSA in 1869. In response to the founding of the NWSA, members of the New England Suffrage Association, including Stone, Foster, and Julia Ward Howe, formed the AWSA, which sought to avoid the conflict between suffrage for women and suffrage for freedmen by taking a state-by-state approach. Stone believed that the 15th Amendment could be a stepping-stone to woman suffrage.

The two organizations would be at odds with one another for the next 21 years. Hallmarks of the AWSA were its federal organization, its devotion to working state by state for woman suffrage, its exclusive focus on suffrage, and its inclusion of men in both leadership and membership. Its *Woman's Journal* was published in Boston for half a century. Suffrage gains, primarily in the West, were slow but incremental. The NWSA, by contrast, was noted for its espousal of a federal amendment for woman suffrage, the wide range of radical causes that constituted its agenda, and a distrust of men.

The deep split between the two groups was finally bridged in 1890, when Alice Stone Blackwell, daughter of Lucy Stone and Henry Blackwell, finally negotiated a truce with Anthony. The two organizations then merged into the National American Woman Suffrage Association (NAWSA). At first NAWSA placed more emphasis on campaigns for state suffrage than the federal amendment and focused on the vote to the exclusion of other issues, leading many to believe that AWSA principles dominated the new organization. The 1890s were marked by a number of successes, with Wyoming, Colorado, Utah, and Idaho entering the union as woman-suffrage states. An 1895 defeat in Massachusetts proved to be a turning point in the New England movement, however. In that year a mock referendum on woman suffrage was held in conjunction with municipal elections. Both men and women cast ballots, but the vote against woman suffrage was overwhelming. Strong antisuffrage groups forced movement leaders to completely rethink their strategies. Maud

Wood Park and Inez Haynes Gillmore, young members of the Massachusetts Woman Suffrage Association, devised one new approach to the issue when they founded the College Equal Suffrage League in an effort to appeal to college women and alumnae.

With the deaths of Stone in 1893, Stanton in 1902, and Anthony in 1906, NAWSA needed new leadership and fresh tactics to give it life. New England provided many of the new leaders. Anna Howard Shaw, for example, an immigrant of Scottish descent who had been raised in Lawrence, Mass., and earned degrees in theology and medicine from Boston University, became a protégé of Anthony's and served as president of the NAWSA from 1904 to 1915. New tactics, developed in England by the Pankhursts, also crossed the ocean from the British Isles. In 1909 the Massachusetts Suffrage Association and the Boston Equal Suffrage Association for Good Government sponsored tours of New England by speakers who held spontaneous open-air meetings at popular town gathering places in an effort to bring the woman-suffrage issue to the people. Activist organizations also began questioning politicians about their position on woman suffrage and working to defeat those who opposed it. Rhode Island and Maine granted presidential suffrage to women in 1917 and 1919, respectively.

When Carrie Chapman Catt succeeded Shaw as president of the NAWSA in 1915, she put into effect a "winning plan" with the help of Park, one of her chief deputies. Once the suffrage amendment had passed Congress—much to the credit of Park, who was in charge of the congressional committee—Catt rallied her troops to fight for ratification. She considered most New England states to be doubtful ratifiers. Massachusetts, however, distinguished itself by becoming the eighth state to ratify. All the New England states eventually ratified the amendment, although the struggle was intense in nearly every state.

When the history of woman suffrage was compiled by Stanton, Anthony, and Matilda Joslyn Gage, it naturally favored the New York–based movement and shortchanged New England. Recently, however, interest in the AWSA has undergone a resurgence. In any case, no one can deny that New England origins were crucial to the rise and rapid growth of early feminism or that, through schism and reunification, New England contributed mightily to feminist strategy and success.

Ellen Carol DuBois, *Feminism and Suffrage: The Emergence of an Independent Women's Movement in America, 1848–1869* (1978); Eleanor Flexner, *Century of Struggle: The Woman's Rights Movement in the United States* (1975 [1959]); Blanche Glassman Hersh, *The Slavery of Sex: Feminist-Abolitionists in America* (1978); Suzanne M. Marilley, *Woman Suffrage and the Origins of Liberal Feminism in the United States, 1820–1920* (1996); Marjorie Spruill Wheeler, ed., *One Woman, One Vote: Rediscovering the Woman Suffrage Movement* (1995); Jean Fagan Yellin, *Women and Sisters: The Antislavery Feminists in American Culture* (1989).

Bonnie L. Ford

Ecofeminism Connecting the women's movement with the ecological movement, ecofeminism links the worldwide oppression of women to the global oppression of nature, arguing that both have been devalued by patriarchy. Although their political agendas, goals, and theoretical orientations vary widely, ecofeminists are wary of the ways in which the feminization of nature and the perception of women's close connection to the earth have been used to rationalize the domination of women and nature.

The word *ecofeminism* was first coined in 1974 by the French feminist Françoise d'Eaubonne in *Le Féminisme ou la mort;* the concept was further developed by Ynestra King at the Institute for Social Ecology in Plainfield, Vt., during the mid-1970s. Rachel Carson's earlier works—*The Sea around Us* (1951), *The Edge of the Sea* (1955), and *Silent Spring* (1962)—had already demonstrated the connection between planetary well-being and political action, issuing an eloquent plea on behalf of a damaged earth.

Boston, with its long history of liberationist movements (temperance, abolitionist, suffrage), has provided the setting for a particularly rich culture of ecofeminist thought and activity. The Massachusetts Audubon Society was formed in 1896 in part as a response to Victorian society's cruelty toward birds. The New Hampshire writer Celia Thaxter's "Woman's Heartlessness," published in the first issue of *Audubon* magazine (1887), had scolded women for decorating their hats with bird feathers.

One of the first scholarly works to link women and environmental issues was the Boston College professor Mary Daly's *Gyn/Ecology* (1978). Carolyn Merchant's *Ecological Revolutions* (1989) brings an ecofeminist sensibility to bear on the capitalist and environmental transformations that occurred in New England between 1600 and 1850, examining patterns of exploitation and dominance and their links to economics, nature, culture, and gender.

Some ecofeminists argue for the importance of animal rights to a movement that condemns exploitation of any kind. Marti Kheel critiques hunting as a sport, while Carol Adams, in *The Sexual Politics of Meat* (1990), and New Hampshire ecofeminist Josephine Donovan, in *Animals and Women* (1995), a volume coedited with Adams, link animal rights, feminist theory, and vegetarianism.

Yet another faction of ecofeminists embraces spiritualism, revitalized goddess worship, and rituals borrowed from indigenous religions. They experience a holistic kinship with all of the earth and advocate transformed consciousness and heightened spiritual awareness as necessary adjuncts to social and political change. Spiritual ecofeminists emphasize an ethics of caring and interconnectedness.

Ecofeminism has been criticized for its seeming separation of ecological issues from feminism in general, although it goes beyond the social justice concerns of mainstream feminism. The ideology's lack of historical analysis tends to universalize women's experience, thereby ignoring racial and class differences as well as First World feminists' participation in the oppression of nature and other people. Critics of the spiritual dimension of ecofeminism maintain that the appropriation of indigenous religions by whites constitutes cultural imperialism and that taking symbols and rituals out of context offends native peoples.

Although New England writers such as Henry David Thoreau, Celia Thaxter, Sarah Orne Jewett, and Robert Frost wrote of the transcendence of nature, ecofeminist literary criticism is attuned to the interconnections, whether celebratory or confining, between women and their environment as portrayed in works of literature.

Irene Diamond and Gloria Feman Orenstein, eds., *Reweaving the World: The Emergence of Ecofeminism* (1990); Greta Gaard, ed., *Ecofeminism: Women, Animals, Nature* (1993); Ynestra King, "Engendering a Peaceful Planet: Ecology, Economy, and Ecofeminism in Contemporary Context," *Women Studies Quarterly* 23 (1995); Carolyn Merchant, *Earthcare: Women and the Environment* (1996).

Debra J. Rosenthal

Fern, Fanny (1811–72) Newspaper columnist and novelist. Sara Payson (Willis) Eldredge Farrington Parton, who used the pseudonym "Fanny Fern" throughout her professional life, was born in Portland, Maine. By the time she died in New York City, she had published two novels, six collections of journalistic essays, and three volumes of stories for children. Both her father, Nathaniel Willis, and her brother, N. P. Willis, were prominent in New England publishing circles. From the mid-1850s through the 1860s, she was the highest-paid newspaper columnist in the United States. Although she was never a political activist, many of her columns advocated women's rights.

Shortly after Fern's birth, her family moved to Boston, where her father established a religious newspaper, the *Puritan Recorder,* and a magazine for children, the *Youth's Companion.* She attended Catharine Beecher's Female Seminary in Hartford from 1828 to 1831 and in 1837 married Charles Harrington Eldredge, with whom she had three daughters. After Eldredge's death in 1846, Fern struggled to support herself and her children by working as a seamstress. She was married, briefly, to the Boston merchant Samuel P. Farrington; the couple divorced in 1853.

Noted for her skill as an essayist while a student at the Hartford Female Seminary, Fern's career as a writer began with newspaper columns in Boston papers in 1851. In the absence of strict copyright restrictions, her sometimes sentimental but increasingly witty columns on motherhood, religion, women's fashions, and a wide range of other topics were reprinted in other newspapers in the Northeast. Her popularity grew with the publication of two collections of her columns—*Fern Leaves from Fanny's Port-Folio* (1853) and *Fern Leaves, Second Series* (1854)—and her novel *Ruth Hall* (1854), which depicts a young widow determined to work to keep her family together. This highly autobiographical novel was immediately controversial because of its satiric portraits of Fern's father and brother, both of whom refused to support her career aspirations. Nonetheless, Fern's spirited writing caught the attention of Nathaniel Hawthorne, who exempted her from the "damned mob of scribbling women" about whom he complained in the 1850s. Her talent was also recognized by Robert Bonner, who hired her as a weekly columnist for the *New York Ledger* in 1855 at 100 dollars per week—a position she held until her death. In 1856 Fern married the biographer James Parton and the same year published her second novel, *Rose Clark.*

Fanny Fern espoused in her columns a number of the causes that women's rights organizations advocated in the middle of the 19th century. Using humor and satire, she supported temperance, female suffrage, women's economic independence, and the betterment of women's health. She also defended the right of women to speak in public and to remain single if they chose. Not all of her causes were related specifically to women; she was a staunch supporter of the Union during the Civil War, deplored the conditions in urban prisons, and advocated clothing reform, dietary reform, and regular exercise. So complete had her identity as a writer become by the end of her life that "Fanny Fern" is the only name on her tombstone. Fern's work was rediscovered in the 1980s as part of a reassessment of 19th-century women writers, and hers is now regarded as a significant feminist voice.

Nancy A. Walker, *Fanny Fern* (1993); Joyce W. Warren, *Fanny Fern: An Independent Woman* (1992); Ann D. Wood, "The 'Scribbling Women' and Fanny Fern: Why Women Wrote," *American Quarterly* 23 (1971).

Nancy A. Walker

Fraternal and Sororal Organizations During the final third of the 19th century, New England had hundreds of diverse oath-bound voluntary organizations for both men and women, although those for men are perhaps better known. Among the most notable were the Freemasons, the Odd Fellows, the Knights of Columbus, the Knights of Pythias, the Benevolent and Protective Order of Elks, the Improved Order of Red Men, the Order of the Eastern Star, and the Patrons of Husbandry, better known as the Grange. While the fraternal movement in New England can be traced to the establishment of the first Masonic lodge in Boston in the 1730s, its period of greatest popularity and influence occurred between 1865 and 1930. During its heyday, as much as 40 percent of the male population may have been members of fraternal organizations.

The practice of graduated ritual initiation of new members and a tendency toward ceremony and elaborate titles characterize fraternal and sororal organizations. The Knights of Pythias, for example, ceremonially induct members into three separate levels of membership and refer to the presiding officer of a local group as the Chancellor Commander. Similarly, the Knights of Columbus confer four degrees of membership and refer to the presiding officer as the Grand Knight.

Through the enactment of quasi-religious ritual initiations, these groups tutor individuals in systems of thought and bestow symbolic identities and fictive familial relationships upon their members. On joining such an organization, an individual is metaphorically transformed. Having experienced the initiation ceremony, the new member is privy to the group's defining knowledge and attains a newly augmented status. Before joining, the new member is simply an individual; but upon initiation, he or she becomes a "brother" or a "sister," a Knight or a High Priestess, an Elk or a Moose, a Noble of the Mystic Shrine, or even a Veiled Prophet of the Enchanted Realm.

The modern fraternal and sororal model, which ties individuals together by providing them with shared cultural experiences and metaphoric vocabularies, originally was developed by Freemasons in Britain during the 17th and 18th centuries to teach morality and ethics within a nonsectarian context. Over the past two-and-a-half centuries, numerous organizations administering a range of ideologies

Newly installed officers of the Grand Lodge of Masons, Boston, ca. 1970

have embraced this ritual structure. The Sons of Temperance, for example, ritually promoted sobriety while the Knights of Labor used ceremony to cultivate worker solidarity. Members of the Loyal Men of American Liberty, a small group founded in Boston in 1890, used the fraternal model to foster patriotism.

Fraternal and sororal organizations tend to group individuals along lines of ethnicity, class, and gender. Some groups develop ties among individuals of similar background as part of their mission. The Ancient Order of Hibernians, for example, self-consciously serves to bind together Catholic men of Irish descent. Similarly, the bylaws of the Daughters of the American Revolution restrict its membership to female descendants of men who served in the American Revolutionary War, while the Patrons of Husbandry draw membership from agricultural communities.

In many cases, the demographic identity of an organization has been determined by day-to-day practice, rather than by formal policy. Common fraternal and sororal custom requires new enlistees to be recommended by a member of the group and approved by the local membership as a whole. These prerequisites produce a proclivity toward homogenous local memberships. Economic barriers to entry, such as annual dues and initiation fees, also work to ensure socioeconomic similarities within groups. This does not mean that only wealthy individuals belong to fraternal and sororal organizations, but rather that a range of associations exist to meet the financial

means of different segments of New England society. Masonic lodges, for example, historically have charged slightly higher annual dues than have the Odd Fellows.

Endemic racism in 19th-century New England led to the creation of parallel black and white fraternal structures. Individuals of African descent with claims to fraternal status were denied entry into most groups. In response, organizations of African Americans were established closely resembling those of Anglo-American communities. The Grand United Order of Odd Fellows, a fraternity of African Americans, for example, was founded in 1843 by Peter Ogden, a black sailor who had been initiated into Odd Fellowship in Liverpool. The most prominent of the black fraternal organizations, the Prince Hall Freemasons, has roots in Massachusetts stretching back into the 18th century and carries the name of a prominent Bostonian, African American minister Prince Hall. The black and white societies largely practice identical rituals and have similar regalia but maintain distinct memberships and institutional loyalties. Although African American voluntary organizations historically have been viewed as a means toward assimilation and middle-class respectability, recent scholarship has indicated that during the 19th century they also served as resources for the development of a black consciousness.

Membership in many of New England's oath-bound voluntary organizations was long restricted to men. Many fraternities, such as

the Freemasons, the Knights of Columbus, and the Odd Fellows, admit only males to this day; a recent court decision now mandates that women be admitted to the Elks. Other groups, such as the Colonial Dames, allow only women to participate. Recently historians and sociologists have argued that single-sex fraternal and sororal organizations help shape gender identities. In the process of teaching concepts of morality, ethics, and correct modes of behavior, it has been posited that all-male groups convey definitions of masculinity to their members. By enacting rituals featuring knights, laborers, and biblical patriarchs, fraternal men have the opportunity to immerse themselves in idealized, traditionally masculine roles. Similarly, the many women's groups established for the female relatives of male fraternalists, such as the Pythian Sisterhood founded in Concord, N.H., in 1883, or the Order of the Golden Circle, a 20th-century institution composed primarily of women of African descent, have been perceived as resources for indoctrinating women in proper behavior within the "women's sphere."

Although ceremonial forms and ritual practices define fraternal and sororal organizations, these activities represent only one facet of their institutional life. Social and recreational events have always been prominent features of fraternal and sororal culture. During the 19th century, groups regularly sponsored banquets, dances, picnics, and evenings of amateur theatricals. In the 20th century, bowling leagues and golf tournaments were added to the older forms of entertainment. Regional and national conventions possibly are the most characteristic, and publicly visible, fraternal and sororal social activity. During the boom years of fraternalism, meetings assumed spectacular proportions. The 1895 Triennial Conclave of the Masonic Knights Templar, for example, held in Boston over five days in August, featured a parade of 26,000 uniformed participants.

New England's fraternal and sororal organizations have a strong tradition of benevolence. Throughout the 18th century and during the antebellum period, charity was practiced informally within local groups. Financial support was extended to destitute members, their widowed spouses, and orphans, as local group finances allowed. After the Civil War, fraternal benevolence became systematized in two primary modes: some groups established institutions, often called "homes," to care for the needy. For example, in the years between 1887 and 1927 the Odd Fellows established homes in Auburn, Maine; Concord, N.H.; Ludlow, Vt.; Worcester, Mass.; East Providence, R.I.; and Groton, Conn. Other groups, such as the Knights of

Columbus and the Ancient Order of United Workmen, established insurance or mutual benefit plans that made payments when members became ill or died.

Although fraternal and sororal benevolence was concentrated within the ranks of the members and their immediate families during the 19th century, in the 20th century the focus broadened to include the general public. The Order of the White Shrine of Jerusalem, a Masonic group of Christian women active in Maine, for example, was proud to assert in its publication *200th Anniversary of Masonry in Maine and of Portland Lodge No. 1* (1962) that "help was given to rehabilitate any needy person found worthy, regardless of race, creed, color, age, or affiliation." The Shriners' Burn Institute in Boston and the Shriners' Orthopaedic Unit in Springfield, Mass., both supported by the Ancient Arabic Order of Nobles of the Mystic Shrine, are among the most notable examples of fraternal public benevolence in New England.

During the 20th century, many organizations with fraternal and sororal origins deemphasized ceremonial practices. While the Freemasons and Odd Fellows have continued to perform ritual into the 21st century, other groups, following the lead of service clubs such as the Rotary and the Jaycees, have discontinued formal initiations. The Benevolent and Protective Order of Elks, for example, greatly simplified its ritual between 1895 and 1911 and now practices it only occasionally. Similarly, in an attempt to propagate a more contemporary image, during the 1980s the Loyal Order of Moose changed its corporate name to Moose International and replaced its ceremonial headgear and robes with color-coded blazers and neckties.

Fraternal and sororal organizations have existed in New England since the 18th century and will persist for the foreseeable future. This organizational model has proved an effective vehicle for binding individuals for group action, whether to achieve social change or to support the status quo. Through ritual initiation, these organizations provide their members with ways for helping them understand the human condition and the individual's place within society. These ceremonially forged conceptual structures are manifested in the initiates' public and private behavior and thus influence civic discourse. Although often overlooked by historians, these omnipresent groups have played an important role in shaping the behavior, belief systems, and personal identities of significant portions of New England's population.

Mrs. S. Joe Brown, *The History of the Order of the Eastern Star among Colored People* (1997); Steven C. Bullock, *Revolutionary Brotherhood: Freemasonry and the Transformation of the American Social Order, 1730–1840* (1996); Mark C. Carnes, *Secret Ritual and Manhood in Victorian America* (1989); Mary Ann Clawson, *Constructing Brotherhood: Class, Gender, and Fraternalism* (1989); Christopher J. Kauffman, *Faith and Fraternalism: The History of the Knights of Columbus* (1992); William D. Moore, "The Masonic Lodge Room, 1870–1930: A Sacred Space of Masculine Spiritual Hierarchy," in *Gender, Class, and Shelter*, ed. Elizabeth Collins Cromley and Carter L. Hudgins, *Perspectives in Vernacular Architecture* 5 (1995); Albert C. Stevens, *The Cyclopedia of Fraternities* (1907).

William D. Moore

Gay and Lesbian History When late-20th-century homosexuals first searched for historic homosexual or gay role models, they inevitably adopted historical figures into a modern perception that hadn't existed during previous times: although homosexuality has been around for millennia, the word *homosexual* was coined in the 19th century, and the modern concept of a gay group identity emerged during the 20th. To find past New Englanders who could be identified as having had same-sex interests, such as the 17th century's William Plaine of Guilford, Conn.; Michael Wigglesworth of Cambridge and Malden, Mass.; Elizabeth Johnson of Essex County, Mass.; Sarah Norman and Mary Hammon of Plymouth Colony; John Alexander and Thomas Roberts, also of Plymouth Colony; and possibly some of Thomas Morton's followers at Merrymount in Wollaston, Mass., it was necessary to examine surviving diaries or publications and criminal trial records. New England's colonial legal culture, shaped by the Puritan outlook, made expressing or acting on same-sex interest hazardous in the extreme. A series of colonial antisodomy laws—enacted in 1636 in Plymouth Colony, in 1641 in Massachusetts Bay, in 1642 in Connecticut, in 1647 in Rhode Island, in 1656 in New Haven Colony, and in 1680 in New Hampshire—confirmed England's law of 1533. Like their English prototype, most of these laws explicitly defined sodomy as a capital offense, though only few New Englanders, among them William Plaine, were executed for it. Whipping and public confessions were the regional norm.

During the 18th century the influence of Puritan clergy on the government gradually diminished as royal charters replaced business charters after 1689, while the debacle of the Salem witch trials in 1691–92 further eroded it. In the 18th century the church punished same-sex activity through chastening public confessions or excommunication, rather than by civil procedure.

The Puritans had made instrumental use of the stigma then associated with same-sex relations to defame unrelated activity. This was probably the case for many of the claims made against Thomas Morton and his maypole revelers at Merrymount in 1637 and against the followers of Anne Hutchinson in 1638. Similarly, clergy at the turn of the 18th century unsuccessfully claimed false connections to defame the introduction of wigs for men. Late-18th-century newspapers used comparable associational innuendo to defame the fringed silk cravat of the exaggerated "macaroni style" in men's dress.

The meaning of mutual expressions of passionate love among men or women is obscured by an Enlightenment culture that separated the supposed rationalism of men from the supposed emotionalism of women and encouraged same-sex friendships in gender-separated spheres. The later Romantic movement provided men with acceptable models for literary expressions of mutual love. For the historian, these developments muddy the waters when trying to distinguish between the "brotherly" love called *philia* by the Greeks and sexual, erotic love. Were historic figures to be transported to an early-21st-century New England culture that identifies distinct sexualities, some would probably emerge as merely best friends while others would almost certainly fit the modern concept of gay couples.

By the late 19th century, lifelong same-sex relationships were available to women independently wealthy enough to live outside of a male-headed household. This impromptu institution, called a Boston marriage, may often have been sexual, though economic and other factors could be involved as well. A number of educated women entered into such relationships, including the author Sarah Orne Jewett and Annie Adams Fields; the sculptor Anne Whitney and the painter Abby Adeline Manning; and the poet Amy Lowell and the actress Ada Dwyer Russell. Newly emerging women's colleges provided congenial environments for other 19th-century female couples, including the poet and Wellesley professor Katherine Lee Bates and Katharine Coman. Still others chose expatriatism, where their intimacy might be dismissed as foreign eccentricity. In the 1850s one such circle of lesbian Yankees living abroad included the sculptors Harriet Hosmer, Emma Stebbins, and Edmonia Lewis and the actor Charlotte Cushman in Rome.

By the end of the 19th century the bohemian or artistic movement provided a social context for people with same-sex attractions, especially men. Artists, architects, designers, performers, and literary figures could form congenial circles while still presenting themselves to the heterosexual world in whatever degree of traditional, overt, or ambiguous style they chose. Many members of the large

A gay couple is married in a state-sanctioned wedding at the Arlington Street Unitarian Universalist Church, Boston, 2004

Boston bohemian circle overlapped with a Gloucester, Mass., contingent headed by the designer Henry Davis Sleeper and his neighbor and apparent partner, the Harvard professor and congressman A. Piatt Andrew, Jr. Many in this circle came together under the patronage of the socialite art collector Isabella Stewart Gardner.

Extended communities of gay identity began to emerge in New England in the late 19th and early 20th centuries in cities, where "French flats" (purpose-built apartments), residential hotels, and clubs provided prosperous single men and women with respectable dwelling alternatives to the family mansion. Laboring women and men could choose to live in Young Men's and Women's Christian Association housing or take single rooms in boardinghouses to escape living in tenements with families or sharing rooms with other boarders. Unregulated by the usual authorities, this generation of unattached men and women could act on sexual and emotional inclinations for which they might not previously have found the privacy. In New England, the large internal migration that took place during World War I and (especially) World War II resulted in growing populations of gay people in the cities.

Throughout this period old laws remained on the books and new layers of control were added. Late-19th-century vice squads and social reformers alike responded to the increased numbers of men and women who had escaped the watchful family eye by trying to track illicit sex. Preoccupation with prostitution caused neighbors, self-appointed moral-reform societies, and police to team up to scorn, report, and prosecute opposite-sex "visitors" while naively overlooking same-sex visitors. That changed as the first decades of the 20th century progressed, with new scientific and social definitions of homosexuality.

In the 1890s the German physician Richard von Krafft-Ebing had concluded that homosexuality was a mental abnormality, a view accepted by Sigmund Freud, who advocated psychoanalytic treatment. The latter suggestion fit comfortably with Americans' discomfort with the newly defined identity. This was particularly true among New England's many variants of reform Protestantism and the region's burgeoning Roman Catholic population, dominated by traditionally conservative Irish Catholics. Vice squads and reform societies expanded their efforts to control or even put an end to homosexual activity. In New England, as elsewhere, this included increased censorship and banning of books, plays, and films; indeed, "banned in Boston" became something of a cultural parody of the New England outlook.

Increased authoritarian repression built pressure for opposition, but the first advocates of equal civil rights for homosexuals were confronted with the realization that the act of advocacy itself might be classified and treated as illegal. Short-lived organizations that formed during the 1920s and again just after World War II were followed by longer-lasting groups in the 1950s. Two California organizations, the Mattachine Society, founded in 1950, and the Daughters of Bilitis, founded in 1955, advocated social, legal, and individual reappraisals of homosexuality. A nationwide umbrella group, the North American Conference of Homophile Organizations (NACHO), was founded in 1966. Foster Gunnison, then of Hartford, was the first chairman of the credentials committee that evaluated the admittance petitions of the proliferating local and regional organizations.

After the June 1969 riots at the Stonewall Inn bar in New York City, which were followed by weeks of police crackdowns on gay bars, a Gay Liberation Front was organized in New York, and a year later the riot was commemorated by the first public marches for gay civil rights in New York, Boston, and other large cities around the country. By the mid-1970s marches were an annual event in major cities nationwide and through the 1980s and 1990s were organized in most New England state capitals. The presence of gay groups in other parades, however, was resisted, most notably in the 1990s in South Boston's Saint Patrick's Day parade, where the organizers secured a court order to ban gay participation.

But social attitudes were changing. In 1969 (the year of the Stonewall riots), a panel of the National Institute of Mental Health recommended repealing all laws concerning private sex between consenting adults, and in 1973 the board of the American Psychiatric Association (APA) removed homosexuality from its list of recognized mental illnesses. Liberal Protestants, following the church's model of taking a stand against race-based bigotry, had begun to question the legitimacy of homophobia even before the APA did, widening the gulf between liberal mainstream Protestantism and conservative evangelical Protestantism. New England, with its long tradition of ethnic and working-class Democrats and as home to many universities, briefly emerged as a newly liberal region of the country. New Englanders elected an openly gay congressman, Barney Frank of Massachusetts, in 1981, and gay candidates ran for statewide offices. In the late 1990s, New Hampshire's general court had the largest number of gay legislators in the nation.

All this coincided with the reemergence of diverse voices after the apparent but temporary unity of the eras after World War II and the Cold War. The successful grassroots methods of the Civil Rights movement provided a model for civil rights advocacy, and through the 1980s and 1990s petitions and bills to legislatures brought about modest gay civil rights bills in each of the New England states except Maine. These narrowly defined bills generally provided gay men and women with equal access to public accommodation in housing and employment. The bills were made palatable to voters by explicit exemption of religious organizations from compliance, distinguishing these bills from earlier civil rights bills on which they were modeled. Petitioning to revoke these bills is an annual ritual in many state legislatures.

During the 1990s the scope of public discussion about gay issues widened, including the questions of whether to allow gays in the military and same-sex marriage. Although Congress passed the Defense of Marriage Act (1996), which allowed states to define marriage solely as a union between a man and a woman, Vermont passed a civil union bill in 2000 that made available to same-sex couples most of the privileges enjoyed by heterosexual couples in matters of health, hospital visitation, property, bequests, tax filing, and (for public servants) employment. In autumn 2003—not long after a U.S. Supreme Court decision overturned a Texas sodomy statute—the Massachusetts Supreme Judicial Court found that the state constitution could not be interpreted to exclude same-sex couples from marriage. The Massachusetts decision immediately gave rise to a proposed amendment to

Homosexual Rights Laws in New England, 2004

	Connecticut	Maine	Massachusetts	New Hamphire	Rhode Island	Vermont
State antidiscrimination law	Yes	No	Yes	Yes	Yes	Yes
Year passed	1991	1997	1989	1997	1995	1992
Year repealed		1998				
Towns with antidiscrimination law	3	7	6	0	3	1
State employee domestic partner benefits available	Yes	No	Yes	No	No	Yes
Town employee domestic partner benefits available	1	1	6	0	0	2
Defense of Marriage Bill adopted	No	Yes	Pending	No	No	Yes
Year adopted		1997				Text in Civil Union Bill, 2000
Marriage or civil unions recognized	No	No[a]	Yes 2003	No	No	Yes 2000
Law prohibiting sex between consenting adults	No	No	Yes	No	No	No
Year repealed	1971	1976		1975	1978	1977
Sexual orientation included in state hate crimes law	Yes	Yes	Yes	Yes	Yes	Yes

[a]In 2004 the Maine legislature passed a law establishing a domestic partnership registry available to same-sex couples as well as heterosexual couples and granting the registrants various legal rights.

the U.S. Constitution that would prohibit same-sex marriage, based in part on the fear that couples who had married legally in Massachusetts could sue for recognition of their marriage if they moved to other states and thus perhaps overturn state statutory prohibitions based on the Defense of Marriage Act. The Massachusetts decision became a kind of litmus test as the public split more or less evenly over the reelection of George W. Bush, who supported the constitutional amendment. Legislatures in states adjacent to Massachusetts entered into vigorous debate about gay marriage; most of them passed state Defense of Marriage acts if they were not already in place.

The Massachusetts finding took effect in May 2004, but implementation was complicated by rediscovery of a dormant 1913 law on interracial marriage. In the 1840s Massachusetts was the first state to allow interracial marriage, but the 1913 law prohibited such marriages for nonresidents if the couple's home state did not recognize the union. In May 2004, as gay couples began marrying, public debate grew up throughout New England over the word *marriage,* though without reference to the Puritan notion that marriage was a secular, rather than a sacred, institution. The Massachusetts legislature passed a constitutional amendment that would annul same-sex marriages while converting them to and allowing same-sex civil unions. This amendment would require passage in two

consecutive legislatures and then ratification by the voters before it could take effect. Currently, opponents of same-sex unions under either name are seeking to dominate the state legislature in the 2004 elections in hope that the amendment—or an even narrower amendment forbidding and annulling same-sex marriages and prohibiting civil unions—can receive its second passage.

Maine remains the sole New England state with no equal civil rights law. In the spring of 2004, however, in the midst of the highly publicized amendment debates, the Maine legislature passed without fanfare a bill for the protection of families and children that creates a domestic partnership registry available to both heterosexual and same-sex couples. Registration grants partners primary medical power of attorney for each other in cases of incapacitation, including decision making on the termination of life-support systems and rights of disposal of the remains of the deceased. The bill also allows the estate of a person in a domestic partnership who died intestate to be probated in the same way it would the estate of a married person. The law is seen, in part, as a way to protect survivors and children of unmarried couples from loss of material support, such as the home and financial assets. It is unofficially anticipated that the bill will work in opposition to a common practice in which courts void the wills of gay people at the request of relatives, removing assets from surviving partners and children of gay couples. As

the battles heat up over these emotionally charged issues, gay culture continues to grow in visibility and acceptance in New England.

Allan Berube, *Coming Out under Fire: The History of Gay Men and Women in World War Two* (1990); Martin Duberman, *Stonewall* (1994); Will Fellows, *Preservation Comrades: Gay Men as Keepers of Culture* (forthcoming); Charles Kaiser, *The Gay Metropolis, 1940–1996* (1997); The History Project, *Improper Bostonians: Lesbian and Gay History from the Puritans to Playland* (1998).

Mark J. Sammons

Gender Segregation Throughout history women and men have had unequal access to particular environments or have performed different roles within them. New England experiences have been significant in four areas where gender has mattered: educational institutions, workplaces, social clubs, and social service organizations.

Education has long been differentiated by sex. In the 18th century New England girls, if they received an education at all, were taught at different times of day and for shorter periods than boys; in the 19th century they were frequently seated on opposite sides of the room from boys or in different rooms altogether. Until well into the 19th century colleges and universities were formally the domain of men, although female domestics might be present. Separate women's colleges eventually provided an alternative to male-only schools or to what was initially a small number of coeducational institutions. New England's women's colleges included four of the "Seven Sisters": Mount Holyoke, the first women's college in the United States, opened in 1837; Smith and Wellesley in 1875; and Radcliffe, in 1879. Although, with their small enrollments, these elite private colleges never educated a large number of women, they had continuing cultural importance.

For much of New England's colonial history agricultural and domestic production occurred at home, which left little opportunity for segregation by sex. With industrialization women began working in mills, continuing to do so in large numbers throughout the 19th and into the 20th century. Lowell, Mass., for example, attracted a large population of single women, who lived in boardinghouses and worked in factories. There were still significant numbers of men at Lowell's mills, however. In 1844 the only sex-segregated factory in the Lowell complex employed exclusively men.

Despite the importance of the mills, much production still occurred in the home. The 19th-century cult of domesticity, according to which middle-class women's work consisted of nurturing and moral uplift, was fostered in New England. Although many women also did their own housekeeping—by the 1880s only 20 to 25 percent of U.S. urban and suburban homes had household help—paid domestic service was an important source of employment for a large number of women. In general women and children were the primary daytime residents of suburban homes until after World War II.

Today, women and men share the same workplaces more often than they did in the past, although some occupations, such as trucking and clerical work, are still highly segregated by sex. Nationally, women are prominent among the owners of small businesses, and New England boasts some interesting examples of this phenomenon. Northampton, Mass., for instance, is known throughout the country for its high concentration of women- and lesbian-owned businesses in the center of town.

Clubs and social service groups have also created domains specific for both women and men. In the late 19th century, men's fraternal organizations boomed, and women became a dominant force in the settlement-house movement, which aimed to improve the welfare of disadvantaged urban residents. Women's clubs had a wide-ranging influence on civic and educational matters at the turn of the 20th century, with African American New Englanders creating separate groups such as the Woman's Era Club, which met on Boston's Beacon Hill. Voluntary and professional social services in the form of women's shelters and women's health clinics continue sex-segregated spaces in the 21st century.

Gail Dubrow, "Claiming Public Space for Women's History in Boston: A Proposal for Preservation, Public Art, and Public Historical Interpretation," *Frontiers* 13 (1992); Dolores Hayden, *The Grand Domestic Revolution: A History of Feminist Designs for American Homes, Neighborhoods, and Cities* (1981); Daphne Spain, *Gendered Spaces* (1992); Gwendolyn Wright, *Building the Dream: A Social History of Housing in America* (1981).

Ann Forsyth

Gilman, Charlotte Perkins (1860–1935)

Social critic and writer. Charlotte Anne Perkins—one of the leading feminist reformers of her day—was born in Hartford to Mary Westcott Perkins and Frederick Beecher Perkins. Proud of her New England roots and family heritage, Charlotte described the sons and daughters of her great-grandfather Lyman Beecher as "world-servers" and drew strength and courage from the example of her great-aunts Catharine Beecher, Harriet Beecher Stowe, and Isabella Beecher Hooker.

Perkins attended the Rhode Island School of Design in 1878, married the artist Charles Walter Stetson in 1884, and gave birth to Katharine Beecher Stetson in 1885. In 1887 she was diagnosed as a hysteric and subjected to a lengthy rest cure during which she was admonished "never to touch pen, brush, or pencil again." After several weeks, her condition growing steadily worse, Perkins rejected the orders of her doctor and went back to writing. Divorced from Stetson in 1894, Perkins married her cousin George Houghton Gilman in 1900.

Gilman wrote more than 2,700 poems, novels, plays, short stories, essays, and booklength treatises, as well as an autobiography. Many of these works touched on the topic of gender inequality or what she called the "sexuo-economic oppression of women." "The Yellow Wallpaper" (1892), one of Gilman's best-known works, is the semi-autobiographical account of a young woman's descent into madness caused by the social and economic constraints imposed on women in marriage. Today the story is a staple in women's studies and literature courses and the subject of intense scholarly attention. Ironically, Gilman's forbears Catharine Beecher and Harriet Beecher Stowe had made important contributions to the cult of domesticity that their grandniece in the Victorian era came to view as a form of slavery.

Gilman referred to herself as a sociologist, was a reform Darwinist, and believed that social progress should be accelerated. *Women and Economics: A Study of the Economic Relation between Men and Women as a Factor in Social Evolution* (1898), written in Belmont, N.H., called for the end of sexual oppression and the full economic independence of women. The book, which challenged the leading "scientific" assumption of the day that the condition of women was a natural one, made her an international celebrity. It was translated into seven languages and used as a textbook at Vassar College.

Many of Gilman's later works originally appeared in serial form in the *Forerunner*, a journal that she edited and wrote herself from 1909 to 1916. In other major nonfiction works, such as *The Home* (1903), *The Man-Made World* (1911), and *His Religion and Hers* (1923), Gilman elaborated on her criticism of androcentric culture and gender inequality. *Herland* (1915), a fictional account of three young men who discover a thriving, humane, peaceful, and cooperative all-woman society, provided a vision of what women could achieve if given freedom from gender bias and stratification.

Houghton Gilman died in 1934 while the couple were living in Connecticut. Charlotte, having learned she had breast cancer, moved to Pasadena, Calif., to be near her daughter and grandchildren that same year. At age 76, Gilman took her own life. Her fame had been eclipsed by the time of her death, and none of her books remained in print. Today, however, a number of her prodigious writings have been reprinted and many of her achievements reclaimed. In 1993 Gilman was voted one of the 10 most influential women of the 20th century; the following year she was inducted into the National Women's Hall of Fame in Seneca Falls, N.Y.

Polly Wynn Allen, *Building Domestic Liberty: Charlotte Perkins Gilman's Architectural Feminism* (1988); Charlotte Perkins Gilman, *The Living of Charlotte Perkins Gilman: An Autobiography* (1991 [1935]); Mary A. Hill, *Charlotte Perkins Gilman: The Making of a Radical Feminist, 1860–1896* (1980); Ann J. Lane, *To Herland and Beyond* (1997).

Mary M. Moynihan

Girlhood

The subject of girlhood in New England immediately raises questions about the relationship between ideals and reality and the connection between literary description and actual experience. The Puritans who first settled New England had specific ideas about the roles of children and women in a covenanted community and communicated those ideas through religious writings, laws, and literature. In the 19th century, educators such as Catharine Beecher wrote long treatises on the nature of the female vocation and the necessity to educate girls for their role as keepers of the domestic flame. In the 20th century some of the most influential research and writing on the nature of girls and their lives came from New England universities and research centers. Trying to determine whether the lives of New England girls actually reflected the literature written for and about them is the work of social historians.

For historians New England girlhood during the colonial period means uncovering the stories not only of Puritan girls but also of the indentured servants and African American girls who sometimes populated their households and of Native American girls whose lives were changed by those who named their region New England. During the 19th and 20th centuries, as historians note, the mix of girls in New England underwent changes. Girls from Ireland and later eastern and southern Europe arrived, French Canadian girls came down from Quebec, and many girls left New England with their families to settle the western frontier. By the middle of the 20th century, New England's major cities were racially and ethnically diverse. While it is impossible to give a full picture of New England girlhood in a brief sketch, the attempt must include both historical and literary sources; recognition of class, ethnic, regional, and racial distinctions; attention to changes over time; and the realization that some aspects of New England girlhood are probably peculiar to the region, while others are more characteristic of the nation as a whole.

New England's colonial period began in the early 17th century with settlements established by Pilgrims and Puritans, dissident English religious groups. For the girls in these families the ideal was a life centered on religious duty and myriad household tasks. By the age of six most girls were participating in the household economy, gardening, spinning, cooking, and tending younger siblings. While most common schools, the public primary schools of the era, were not open to girls during the 17th century, a Massachusetts law passed in 1642 required that parents teach their children to read so that they could be familiar with the Bible. Some parents did teach their daughters to read, but female literacy rates were not high and remained lower than those of males throughout the colonial period. By the 1730s private schooling was available to girls with the requisite means, and some evidence suggests that more affluent families saw education as a means of upward mobility for their daughters as well as their sons. But while the sons of prominent families often marked their teenage years by entering Harvard or Yale, the daughters were most likely to signal their maturity by experiencing religious conversion. The next milestone in a Puritan girl's life was almost always marriage, on average at the age of 23.

Between early childhood and marriage girls did not always live with their immediate families; many were sent out to help relatives or to work as servants in other households. In poorer families girls as young as four were expected to start taking care of still younger siblings. In the crude pioneer environment of colonial New England, girls were not always well protected or lucky. And, like boys, they often died in household accidents or from diphtheria, measles, whooping cough, and intestinal worms. Girls could also be victims of child abuse. One father, according to court records, was fined for excessively beating his 11-year-old daughter. Orphaned girls were frequently placed in the homes of strangers and, lacking dowries, often faced uncertain futures. As the historian Carol Karlsen points out, most of the accusers during the Salem witch trials were young girls who had lost parents to Indian attacks on the Maine frontier and were living tense, unhappy lives as domestics in Salem households. By claiming "possession," they were able to act out their fear and anger without risking banishment from the community. Another indication that not all girls' lives fit completely into the Puritan mold is the fact that premarital intercourse, though formally forbidden, was widespread and usually tolerated if marriage occurred before the birth of the first child.

The Revolutionary War, along with the beginnings of the Industrial Revolution in New England, eventually led to increased education for girls, a gradual decrease in the amount of domestic labor expected of the very young, and the possibility of factory employment for many young girls. According to Nancy F. Cott, the years between 1780 and 1835 brought changes to the lives of New England women while still keeping intact the ideal of women's essentially domestic and subordinate role in society. The ideology of Republican motherhood that developed after the Revolution emphasized women's role in raising children to be worthy citizens. As a result, educational opportunities for women grew more numerous, and more women were employed as schoolteachers.

Although economic and social changes during the early 19th century meant that New England girls might spend more time in schoolrooms, those changes also thrust many into factories and domestic service. In fact, from the beginning of large-scale textile manufacture in New England in the early 1800s through the Civil War period, most mill operatives were girls and women between the ages of 15 and 30, and many girls were no older than 10 when they entered the workforce. The number of New England girls employed in factories or as "hired girls" outside the home

increased still further during the 1840s with the arrival of desperately poor Irish immigrants.

At the same time that New England girls were receiving more schooling and participating in the Industrial Revolution as textile workers, New England writers, educators, and ministers were developing a middle-class culture of girlhood. Lydia Maria Child founded *Juvenile Miscellany* in 1826, the nation's first magazine for children, replete with games, whimsy, and moral and social instruction. Other women wrote stories for girls steeped in domestic values and virtues. In 1868 Louisa May Alcott produced *Little Women*, a novel whose characters and plots seemed more realistic than the era's didactic, sentimental children's literature and that decisively shaped images of New England girlhood from then on. It was so popular that Alcott's publisher elicited a second volume of the work from her in 1869. Drawing on her own girlhood experiences but softening some of the harsher realities, Alcott painted a picture of a girlhood characterized by economic hardship, spiritual vitality, intellectual idealism, and domestic harmony. Her heroines, Meg, Jo, Beth, and Amy March, represented the range of temperaments and possibilities available to white middle-class girls in 19th-century New England. The book may have romanticized Alcott's own life and that of her sisters, but it seems to have inspired many girls in New England and elsewhere to strive to find a balance between the expression of individual personalities and conformance to socially acceptable roles. Lucy Larcom's *A New England Girlhood* traced that author's journey from a rural New England family through the mills to a career as a writer, suggesting possibilities of economic and intellectual independence for New England girls.

While native-born Protestant New England women such as Louisa May Alcott, Lydia Maria Child, and Catharine Beecher were describing and creating ideals for New England girls to follow, girls with very different backgrounds were arriving in New England. The first immigrant girls to appear in large numbers were Irish; in the famine years they arrived with their families and later came alone as teenagers seeking work. These girls enjoyed certain advantages that later immigrant girls did not share. As early as the 1860s and 1870s, many were attending high schools run by nuns; in fact, Irish girls were more likely to be educated than their brothers. During the late 19th and early 20th centuries, they were becoming nurses and teachers. For a variety of reasons Irish girls usually married late and were more likely than their counterparts from other ethnic groups to lead independent lives, at least for a while. Immigrant girls from southern and eastern Europe, meanwhile, usually sacrificed education to family economic needs. French Canadian girls came with their families to work in the textile mills throughout New England and rarely received much schooling; Italian girls usually worked in factories or did piecework in the home, but in neither case was school part of their daily routine.

During the early 20th century a Polish Jewish immigrant girl, Mary Antin, continued the New England tradition of providing ideals and models for girls. In 1912 she published *The Promised Land*, an account of her journey to America and her experiences as an adolescent in Boston. The book details Antin's steady educational progress and her identification with such American icons as George Washington, Horatio Alger's rags-to-riches heroes, and Louisa May Alcott. It also depicts the family divisions that immigration can cause. Since Antin's book was regularly assigned in civics classes, its sensitive descriptions of the immigrant experience resonated throughout America.

The 20th century brought changes in the lives of all American women, and it can be argued that those changes were not as regionally distinctive as they had been in earlier, more provincial periods of American history. Ethnicity continued to affect the experience of girlhood, but in the 20th century race took on a new importance in New England. With the black migration from the South that began before World War I and continued into the 1960s, New England's cities became more racially mixed and divided. Harriet Wilson had chronicled the hardships of African American girlhood in her 1859 novel *Our Nig*; Dorothy West's 1948 work *The Living Is Easy* looked back at the 1910s and 1920s to chronicle girls coming of age in a mixed African American community of old New England families and newcomers from the South. Anthony Lukas's *Common Ground: A Turbulent Decade in the Lives of Three American Families* examines the turmoil created by court-mandated busing by depicting the effects of forced integration on one white and one black schoolgirl in 1970s South Boston.

New England girlhood today may exist more as a memory or an ideal than as a distinct reality. Clearly, girls still grow up in New England, but they may be more affected by the economic and social realities and the nationwide ideals and images of late-20th- and early-21st-century America than by regional factors. Even stories that focus on New England girls, such as the three teenagers in the movie *Mystic Pizza*, are as likely to come from Hollywood as Boston. In fact, the 1994 film

version of *Little Women* was directed by an Australian. One may note, however, that the educational achievements of today's American girls have their roots in such New England–based developments as the Puritans' determination to teach their daughters to read the Bible, Catharine Beecher's decision to open a female academy and lay down rules for educating girls, and the efforts of largely anonymous Catholic nuns who founded high schools and colleges for girls throughout the region. Certainly, the literary depiction of girlhood had strong roots in New England, beginning with the letter writing and journal keeping of literate Puritans, continuing with the writings of Louisa May Alcott and other 19th-century women, and moving into the 20th century with immigrant autobiographies and journals. Beyond that, many New England girls in their own lives contributed to an evolving concept of American girlhood that stressed educational achievement, independence, and the expansion of women's roles beyond the home.

Nancy F. Cott, *The Bonds of Womanhood: "Woman's Sphere" in New England, 1780–1835*, 2d ed. (1997); Roger Daniels, *Coming to America: A History of Immigration and Ethnicity in American Life* (1990); Hasia R. Diner, *Erin's Daughters in America: Irish Immigrant Women in the 19th Century* (1983); Carol F. Karlsen, *The Devil in the Shape of a Woman: Witchcraft in Colonial New England* (1987); J. Anthony Lukas, *Common Ground: A Turbulent Decade in the Lives of Three American Families* (1985); Martha Saxton, *Louisa May: A Modern Biography of Louisa May Alcott* (1977); Werner Sollors, ed., *"The Promised Land" by Mary Antin* (1997); Laurel Thatcher Ulrich, *Good Wives: Image and Reality in the Lives of Women in Northern New England, 1650–1750* (1982).

Barbara A. McGowan

Hale, Sarah Josepha (Buell) (1788–1879) Writer and editor.

Born in Newport, N.H., Sarah Josepha Buell was an avid student from an early age. Educated primarily by her self-taught mother and brother Horatio, who attended Dartmouth College, young Sarah acquired the equivalent of a college preparatory education.

In 1813 she married David Hale, a lawyer, and continued her independent studies. Widowed by age 35 with five small children, she turned to writing and editing as a means of supporting her family. A first book of poems, *The Genius of Oblivion and Other Original Poems*, was published in 1823 with the help of her husband's Masonic colleagues and met with moderate success. Shortly thereafter Hale published her first novel, which led to editorial opportunities in Boston and Philadelphia.

As she moved to those antebellum cultural and publishing centers, Hale brought her New Hampshire Yankee heritage along with her.

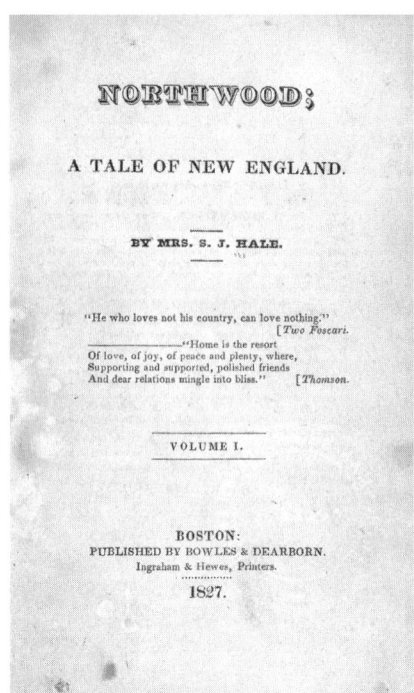

Title page of Sarah Josepha Hale's Northwood *(1827)*

Among the first American novels by women, Hale's *Northwood: A Tale of New England* (1827) exalted the traditions of rural New England. One of those traditions, the yearly celebration of Thanksgiving, later became a national holiday because of Hale's persistent petitioning of U.S. presidents and governors between 1844 and 1863.

Her literary career reflected the cultural influence exerted by the women writers who dominated women's popular literature in the United States before and after the Civil War. As both a writer and an editor, she used her unique position to persuade readers of the importance of "granting to females the advantages of a systematic and thorough education." Hale used her prominence as a social and literary critic to recognize the past and present accomplishments of women. As an editor, first of the *Ladies' Magazine* in Boston (1828–37) and later of the merged *Godey's Lady's Book* and *American Ladies Magazine* in Boston and Philadelphia (1837–77), Hale was a conservative advocate of the national trend toward increased education and employment opportunities for women, a trend for which New England set the standard.

On the basis of Calvinist principles, Hale interpreted woman's proper place for white middle-class women whose lives were transformed by antebellum industrialization and urbanization. Her religious convictions and political conservatism permeated Hale's fiction, poetry, and nonfiction, which instructed several generations of women in their domestic duties. In Boston, Hale was active in the women's civic and social reform organizations that were responsible for completing the Bunker Hill Monument and for founding the Seamen's Aid Society to help the wives, widows, and children of lost or disabled sailors. Her American patriotism was affected by a regional pride in New England as the "cradle of the nation."

During her 40 years as the editor of the major 19th-century women's magazine of Victorian America, Hale became a nationally influential supporter and purveyor of the antebellum concepts defining womanhood for the mainstream middle class; she publicized and made respectable reform movements that promoted women's educational institutions such as Vassar College and women's entry into the professions of teaching, medicine, and other fields suitable for single and married "ladies" seeking to support themselves and their families. Twentieth-century historians would not classify Hale, who opposed the women's rights movement, as a feminist; however, none contest the significance of her contribution to increasing women's access to education and paid employment outside the home.

Ruth E. Finley, *The Lady of Godey's: Sarah Josepha Hale* (1931); Sherbrooke Rogers, *Sarah Josepha Hale: A New England Pioneer, 1788–1879* (1985); Nicole Tonkovich, *Domesticity with a Difference: The Nonfiction of Catharine Beecher, Sarah J. Hale, Fanny Fern, and Margaret Fuller* (1997); Helen Rosen Woodward, *The Lady Persuaders* (1960).

Angela M. Howard

Homophobia In 1972 George Weinberg defined *homophobia* as "the dread of being in close quarters with homosexuals—and in the case of homosexuals themselves, self-loathing." Twenty years later Warren J. Blumenfeld, a Boston gay activist, edited *Homophobia: How We All Pay the Price* (1992), an extensive analysis of how homophobia affects both its agents and its targets. Drawing on the work of Cooper Thompson, founder of the Campaign to End Homophobia (then based in Cambridge, Mass.), Blumenfeld identified four levels of homophobia: *personal* (an individual belief that homosexuals are sick, sinful, or disgusting), *interpersonal* (verbal and physical harassment, discrimination in housing and employment), *institutional* (systematic discrimination by governmental, educational, professional, or religious organizations, sometimes called *heterosexism*), and *cultural* (social norms and assumptions that make homosexuals invisible or deviant). Closely related to homophobia is *internalized homophobia*, the hatred of their own sexuality that some gay, lesbian, bisexual, or transgendered people feel

Spontaneous shrine in Victory Garden section of the Fens, Boston, 1980

when they accept society's evaluation of them as unworthy.

Homophobia is closely related to attitudes about gender, the expression of masculinity or femininity through social behavior. Rigid ideas about what types of dress, speech, behavior, or occupational and social preferences are masculine or feminine reinforce all forms of homophobia, since society labels men and women who defy them abnormal. The devaluing of women and of the values traditionally associated with femininity (nurturing, gentleness, concern for relationship rather than competition) means that men who possess these so-called womanly qualities are often labeled gay regardless of their actual sexual or romantic orientation; the same goes for women who display the supposed manly attributes of strength and independence.

Since the current concept of homosexuality did not exist until the late 19th century, when the word was coined, early New England laws were aimed at "sodomitical practices," which included bestiality along with same-sex relationships. In 1629 the Reverend Francis Higginson reported the discovery of five "sodomiticall boys" on a voyage to New England; they were eventually sent back to England, where the punishment for sodomy for anyone older than 14 was hanging. In 1646 William Plaine of New Haven Colony became the first New Englander executed for sodomy. Sexual relations between women were equally strongly

condemned by religious and civil authorities, but a 1636 proposal by John Cotton to place sex between women on a par with sex between men as a capital offense failed to win approval in the Massachusetts Bay Colony. New Haven Colony's sodomy statute was the most extreme of the early New England laws, making lesbianism, heterosexual anal intercourse, and masturbation crimes punishable by death.

In recent years institutionalized homophobia has been less prevalent in New England than in many other regions of the country. As of June 1999 five of the six New England states had laws on the books prohibiting discrimination based on sexual orientation in housing and in public and private employment, and Maine was the only New England state with a law explicitly prohibiting same-sex marriage. In 2000 Vermont was the first state to pass a civil union bill, and in November 2003 the Massachusetts Supreme Judicial Court ruled that the state constitution permits same-sex marriage, revitalizing legislative battles over this issue throughout New England and the rest of the country.

Cultural and personal attitudes change more slowly, however. New England has long been the site of two value systems that tend to conflict: the Puritan heritage of social and religious conformity and discomfort with sexuality, and the politically and religiously liberal, antislavery, pro–civil rights legacy associated with many of the nation's founders. Attitudes toward homosexuals reflect these two traditions. Boston's gay pride parade, for example, is one of the largest in the country and usually features participation by local and state officials, some of them openly lesbian or gay. Nonetheless, when lesbian and gay Irish Americans sought to march as a group in that same city's Saint Patrick's Day parade, they were harassed by sidewalk hecklers and eventually barred from taking part by an edict that the U.S. Supreme Court upheld. New England's most notorious antigay crime occurred in Bangor, Maine, in 1984, when three teenagers pushed 23-year-old Charlie Howard off a bridge into the Kenduskeag Stream, where he suffered an asthma attack and drowned. Anger over his death sparked the founding of the organization now known as the Maine Lesbian and Gay Political Alliance.

New England is home to Gay and Lesbian Advocates and Defenders (GLAD), one of the nation's few legal organizations devoted exclusively to supporting the legal rights of lesbian, gay, bisexual, and transgender people and people living with HIV and AIDS. GLAD responds to calls from people in all six New England states with questions regarding discrimination, harassment, violence, and censorship. Over the course of the 1990s, parents in Amherst, Mass., sought to prohibit an elementary school display of "Love Makes a Family," an exhibition of photographs featuring families that included lesbians and gay men; a dentist in Bangor, Maine, refused to treat any man, woman, or child with HIV; and the school board in Merrimack, N.H., passed a policy prohibiting any neutral discussion of gay and lesbian issues in schools. Although all these cases ended in upholding the legal rights of homosexuals, they indicate that homophobia has far from disappeared in New England.

Nan D. Hunter, Sherryl E. Michaelson, and Thomas B. Stoddard, *The Rights of Lesbians and Gay Men: The Basic ACLU Guide to a Gay Person's Rights* (1992); Suzanne Pharr, *Homophobia: A Weapon of Sexism* (1988); George H. Weinberg, *Society and the Healthy Homosexual* (1972).

Rita M. Kissen

Howe, Julia Ward (1819–1910) Social reformer and writer.

Julia Ward Howe was born in New York City to the Wall Street banker Samuel Ward, Jr., and his wife, Julia Rush (Cutler) Ward. Privileged with an education, Julia began her writing career with essays on Goethe, Schiller, and Lamartine in the *New York Review* and *Theological Review* before 1840; later publications included various memoirs and a biography of women's rights advocate Margaret Fuller. In 1843 she married Samuel Gridley Howe, the progressive Boston educator who founded the Perkins School for the Blind. The socially conscious Julia Ward Howe established herself within the Boston environment of philosophers, poets, and liberal theologians, including such prominent reformers as Theodore Parker, Charles Sumner, and James Freeman Clarke. During the 1840s Howe also wrote—but did not publish—an extraordinary novel titled *The Hermaphrodite*, in which she explores social and sexual strictures for both men and women.

Although best known as the author of the "Battle Hymn of the Republic," Julia Ward Howe won public recognition by enacting reform in areas ranging from women's rights to world peace. Her public reform activities began with abolition; Howe coedited the antislavery newspaper *Commonwealth* with her husband and opened Green Peace, their Boston residence, as a center of antislavery activity. No movement or cause involving women, from suffrage to pure milk for babies, was launched or promoted without her. Howe's feminism was premised on a concern for women's total relationship to their culture.

After her children's marriages and with the death of her husband in 1876, Howe devoted the majority of her time and energy to public service, especially woman suffrage and the women's club movement. The New England Women's Club, one of the earliest such institutions, was formed in 1868 to provide educational and organizational opportunities to its members, with Howe serving as its first vice president and later as president. Howe also joined in establishing, and in 1881 became president of, the Association for the Advancement of Women. A founder of the General Federation of Women's Clubs and president of that organization from 1893 until 1898, Howe was also the first president of the Massachusetts Federation of Women's Clubs.

Active in the woman suffrage movement, especially in establishing both local and national organizations such as the Massachusetts Woman Suffrage Association, of which she twice served as president, Howe also helped found and twice presided over the New England Woman Suffrage Association. Giving speeches at conventions and legislative hearings, Howe became a leading voice in the American Woman Suffrage Association. For 20 years she edited and contributed to the weekly *Woman's Journal* (1870), official organ of the National American Woman Suffrage Association. *Sex and Education,* a defense of coeducation edited and with an introduction by Howe, appeared in 1874.

Howe's *Appeal to Womanhood throughout the World,* a pamphlet issued in September 1870, called for a general congress of women to promote peace and was translated into five languages. In December 1870 Howe delivered the opening address for the New York planning meeting for a World's Congress of Women in Behalf of International Peace; in 1871 she became president of the American branch of the Woman's International Peace Association. A consummate reformer, Julia Ward Howe was the first woman elected, in 1908, to the American Academy of Arts and Letters. She died in Newport, R.I.

Deborah Pickman Clifford, *Mine Eyes Have Seen the Glory: A Biography of Julia Ward Howe* (1979); Mary H. Grant, *Private Woman, Public Person: An Account of the Life of Julia Ward Howe from 1819–1868* (1994); Julia Ward Howe, *The Hermaphrodite,* ed. Gary Williams (2004); Howe, *Reminiscences, 1819–1899* (1969 [1899]); Wendy Hamand Venet, *Neither Ballots nor Bullets: Women Abolitionists and the Civil War* (1991).

Diane Apostolos-Cappadona

Livermore, Mary Ashton Rice (1820–1905) Reformer, suffragist, and teacher.

Mary Ashton Rice was born in Boston, the daughter of Timothy Rice, a Calvinist minister who educated his children in strict Calvinism. From age 10, Mary read the Bible from beginning to end at least once a year. She attended various private schools and Boston's coeducational Hancock Grammar School until she was 14 years old. At the Baptist Female Seminary of Charlestown, Mass., she became a paid "assistant pupil," teaching younger students by the end of her first year.

After graduation she taught for four years in a southern Virginia plantation school, returning to Boston a convinced abolitionist. Hired in 1842 to run a private academy in Duxbury, Mass., Rice created a self-governing classroom without punishments or rewards. It was at Duxbury in the early 1840s that she first became involved in temperance work, helping to organize children into what was called a Cold Water Army and writing stories for the group's paper.

In 1845 Mary Rice married the Reverend Daniel Parker Livermore, a Universalist whose antislavery and protemperance sermons appealed to her. While at their first pastorate in Fall River, Mass., Livermore won a temperance story competition. After spending more than 10 years at various churches in New England, the couple moved to Chicago, where Livermore helped her husband promote their views in his Christian newsletter the *New Covenant.*

She was in Boston on April 15, 1861, when Lincoln called for volunteers at the beginning of the Civil War. In her narrative *My Story of the War,* Livermore wrote, "I had never dreamed that New England, slow to wrath, could be fired with so warlike a spirit." The only hopeful sign appeared to her to be the "regeneration of its [the nation's] women." Her local aid society in Chicago merged with the northwestern branch of the newly formed Sanitary Commission, which was providing supplies to soldiers and operating battlefield hospitals. Livermore traveled extensively during the war, tending soldiers, visiting hospitals, raising money, and lecturing. Her work with the women of the Sanitary Commission convinced her that woman suffrage would provide the votes necessary for social reform.

In 1869, just four years after the war ended, Livermore was elected president of the Illinois Woman Suffrage Association, and she started and edited a suffrage paper, the *Agitator*, which merged with the *Woman's Journal* in Boston. In 1870, when the Livermores moved to Melrose, Mass., she began her 25-year career on the lecture circuit, advocating the education of women, temperance, and suffrage. She was president of the Massachusetts Woman's Christian Temperance Union and the Massachusetts Woman Suffrage Association, working also with the Women's Educational and Industrial Union and the National Conference of Charities and Corrections. Her best-known lecture—"What Shall We Do with Our Daughters?"—promoted the education and training of women. Livermore died in Melrose, Mass., on May 23, 1905.

Mary Ashton Rice Livermore, *My Story of the War* (1972 [1887]); Livermore, *The Story of My Life* (1899); Livermore, *What Shall We Do with Our Daughters? Superfluous Women, and Other Lectures* (1883).

Tina Hummel

Murray, Judith Sargent (1751–1820)

Poet, essayist, and playwright. Judith Sargent Murray was a major contributor to the conversation about gender issues that dominated elite public discourse during the late 18th century. She is most famous for her essays on women's equality, including "On the Equality of the Sexes" (1790) and the four-part "Observations on Female Abilities" (1798). Blaming women's weaknesses on nurture, not nature, she insisted that with proper education women could surmount any obstacle.

Judith Sargent was born in Gloucester, Mass., to Winthrop and Judith (Saunders) Sargent and lived nearly all of her life in coastal New England. Although New England was America's most literate region, women had only limited access to formal education, and Sargent's parents provided her with unusual educational opportunities for the time: she and her oldest brother were tutored together by the Reverend John Rogers, minister of Gloucester's Fourth Parish Church. Nonetheless, while Winthrop, Jr., went on to Harvard College, Judith's formal education ended.

At age 18 Sargent married Captain John Stevens. After his death in 1786 she lived alone, doing her best to fend off her husband's many creditors. In 1788 she married the Reverend John Murray, who had come to Gloucester in 1774 as an itinerant preacher. Reverend Murray converted the Sargent family and others to the new doctrine of Universalism and became the founding pastor of the town's Universalist church, the first in America. The Murrays remained in Gloucester until 1793 when they moved to Boston with their only child, Julia Maria, to found a church there.

In Boston, Judith Sargent Murray's writing accelerated. She already had a number of essays and poems in print, and she now became a regular contributor to the *Massachusetts Magazine* under the pen name Constantia. Her most important and influential writings are the essays of the fictional Mr. Vigillius, a "gleaner" of wisdom from many sources. The essays were later gathered into a three-volume collection, *The Gleaner: A Miscellaneous Production*, in 1798. Using fictional characters as vehicles for the discussion of a wide range of subjects—from odes to beauty to a defense of Federalism—Murray stressed the importance of female education and asserted her belief that a woman could comment on any topic, that women's intellectual ability knew no bounds. She expounded on native talent and innate goodness while repeatedly bemoaning the fate of good people who suffered economic losses through no fault of their own. Suffused with regionally specific images—farms, small villages, sailors, and merchants—Murray's works reflect her knowledge of a life in which fortunes were tied to the uncontrollable rhythms of the sea. Her two plays—a comedy titled *The Medium; or, Happy Tea-Party* (1795), published in *The Gleaner* as *Virtue Triumphant* in 1798, and a drama titled *The Traveller Returned* (1796)—were the first plays by an American woman to be performed onstage.

John Murray died in 1815, and Judith Sargent Murray spent the next three years editing his letters and sermons and completing his autobiography. She then traveled to Natchez, Miss., with her daughter Julia Maria, who had married the planter Adam Bingaman. Murray lived with her brother, Winthrop Sargent, Jr., first governor of the Mississippi territory, and died at his plantation. Her 20 recently discovered letter books, now in the Mississippi Department of Archives and History, reveal Murray to have been an even more extraordinary and radical thinker than her published works indicate. Her home in Gloucester is now open to the public as the Sargent House Museum.

Sharon M. Harris, ed., *Selected Writings of Judith Sargent Murray* (1995); Amelia Howe Kritzer, "Playing with Republican Motherhood: Self-Representation in Plays by Susanna Haswell Rowson and Judith Sargent Murray," *Early American Literature* 31 (1996); Sheila L. Skemp, *Judith Sargent Murray: A Brief Biography with Documents* (1998).

Sheila L. Skemp

New England Women's Club

The New England Women's Club was one of the earliest and most influential women's organizations in America's club movement. It was founded in Boston in 1868 by Caroline Severance to provide social interaction and intellectual stimulation for its members and civic reform for the community. Club activities challenged social norms dictating that women's interests should be confined to the domestic arena. Immediately the group attracted a distinguished slate of 118 women (and 17 men) who sought to mold the public sphere outside the home. The most prominent reformer in the club, the abolitionist Julia Ward Howe, presided over the organization from 1871 until her death in 1910. The club grew to include other reform-minded members such as the novelist Louisa May Alcott, the physicians Marie Zakrzewska and Harriot Hunt, the kindergarten founder Elizabeth Peabody, the suffragist Lucy Stone, the temperance advocate Mary Livermore, the Transcendentalist Ednah Dow Cheney, the philosopher Ralph Waldo Emerson, and the writer Henry James. James satirized the clubwomen in his novel *The Bostonians* (1886).

Not surprisingly, the members used their collective knowledge, experience, ingenuity, courage, and connections to champion a wide range of reforms, many of them designed to expand women's roles in society. They funded scholarships for women at Boston University and pressured Harvard University to support Radcliffe College for women. They sponsored a dress-reform store to offer an alternative to fashionable but tyrannical corsets, and they pressured the Boston Public School Board to yield positions to women. Members suffered criticism for these activities outside their households. According to the group's publication *History of the New England Women's Club from 1868 to 1893* (1894), which can now be consulted at the Schlesinger Library in Cambridge, the *Boston Transcript* complained that because of the club "Homes will be ruined, children neglected, woman is straying from her sphere." Such attacks did not deter members from addressing pressing social questions, including health, immigration, labor, education, poverty, housing, war, and women's rights. This they have never ceased to do, although club influence in shaping law, public policy, and Boston's institutions waned after the mid-1920s.

For all their success in improving their region, members met other goals as well. Social interaction enjoyed an important place in club programming. Picnics, teas, receptions to honor visitors, and birthday parties for distinguished women, living or dead, provided an opportunity for relaxation and dialogue. Self-improvement was fostered as well in the form of speeches made by members or noted guest lecturers on art, literature, science, and contemporary issues. Formal classes facilitated the study of foreign languages, social problems, and poetry.

The New England Women's Club also played a major role in hosting regional and national conventions of women's organizations. Its format and goals, widely admired, inspired emulators throughout the country.

Karen J. Blair, *The Clubwoman as Feminist: True Womanhood Redefined, 1868–1914* (1980); Deborah Pickman Clifford, *Mine Eyes Have Seen the Glory: A Biography of Julia Ward Howe* (1979).

Karen J. Blair

Noyes, John Humphrey (1811–86)

Social reformer. A social reformer who tried to restructure Victorian gender relations, John Humphrey Noyes was born in Brattleboro, Vt., amid the social and religious changes that accompanied the growth of capitalism in 19th-century New England. He was raised in Putney, Vt., by an agnostic father and a deeply religious mother who was watchful of her children's spirituality.

Like most middle-class male social reformers of the mid-19th century, Noyes was well educated. He graduated from Dartmouth College in 1830 and, after undergoing a religious conversion in 1831 during a wave of revivals, enrolled at Andover Theological Seminary in Massachusetts. In 1832 he left Andover for Yale, where the theologian Nathaniel Taylor was modifying traditional Calvinism by emphasizing the human capacity to overcome sin.

Carrying Taylor's belief in human perfectibility much further, Noyes decided in 1834 that the Second Coming of Christ had occurred in A.D. 70, that the divine social state was being achieved on earth, and that complete salvation from sin was attainable in this life. After traveling through New England and New York in search of converts, he returned to Putney in 1837, where he sought to spread his radical perfectionist doctrines by establishing first a Bible school, then a Society of Inquiry, and, finally, in 1841, a community devoted to realizing his vision of the kingdom of heaven on earth.

Noyes rejected contemporary gender relations and what he considered the socially disruptive influences of individualism. Like other New England utopian communities created during the first half of the 19th century, such as the Roxbury, Mass., Brook Farm and Fruitlands in Harvard, Mass., Noyes's Putney community sought to reorganize gender and family relations in a communal context. Convinced that divine law required universal love, he insisted that his followers replace the personal attachments of monogamous marriage with loyalty to a wider "family." In 1846 he introduced the practice of "complex marriage," in which marital ties, sexual relations, and child care were expanded beyond the individual couple to the community level. In sharp contrast to the celibacy practiced by another group of religious dissenters, the Shakers, whose New England roots went back to the late 18th century, Noyes institutionalized in community life the practice of "amative" (nonreproductive) intercourse, characterized by a form of birth control called "male continence" (withdrawal without ejaculation), as an expression of spiritual love. After publishing his doctrines in 1847 as *The Berean*, he fled to New York state to escape charges of adultery. There he continued the social experiment begun in New England by establishing the long-lived Oneida community in 1848.

Noyes's progressive views reflected a wider rethinking of gender in Victorian New England. But because his paramount concern was establishing communal loyalty and his personal leadership rather than reorganizing gender-based authority structures, his restructuring of gender relations was limited. On one hand, he promoted sexual liberation and women's rights by freeing his female followers from the fear of unwanted pregnancies and the strains of child care, offering them greater sexual parity with men than they could find in the larger society. On the other, he declared that men were superior to women, included only men among his top advisers, required that sexual relationships be initiated by men, limited educational opportunities for community women, and adhered to traditional notions of "women's work." He died at Niagara Falls, Ontario.

Lawrence Foster, "Free Love and Feminism: John Humphrey Noyes and the Oneida Community," *Journal of the Early Republic* 1 (summer 1981); Marlyn Klee-Hartzell, "Family Love, True Womanliness, Motherhood, and the Socialization of Girls in the Oneida Community, 1848–1880," in *Women in Spiritual and Communitarian Societies in the United States*, ed. Wendy E. Chmielewski, Louis J. Kern, and Marlyn Klee-Hartzell (1993); Ernest R. Sandeen, "John Humphrey Noyes as the New Adam," *Church History* 40 (March 1971); Robert Thomas, *The Man Who Would Be Perfect: John Humphrey Noyes and the Utopian Impulse* (1977).

Bret E. Carroll

Park, Maud Wood (1871–1955)

Suffragist, lobbyist, and lecturer. Born in Boston, Maud Wood graduated from Saint Agnes School in Albany, N.Y., and Radcliffe College. While still an English major at Radcliffe, she married Charles Edward Park, who died of pneumonia in 1904. Four years later she married Robert Hunter, a theater manager. She concealed both of her marriages from all except her closest friends, though she took Park's name.

Park devoted her life to women's rights in honor of the first generation of women who opened higher education to women. In 1900 she attended the last meeting of the National American Woman Suffrage Association (NAWSA) to be held under the leadership of Susan B. Anthony. Shortly after the NAWSA meeting she cofounded the College Equal Suffrage League in Boston with Inez Haynes Gillmore (later Irwin) to recruit her generation of college women into the suffrage movement and help them recognize the accomplishments of early women's rights activists. To further that effort, she also worked with the Massachusetts Woman Suffrage Association and the Boston Equal Suffrage Association for Good Government, and lectured at colleges and NAWSA meetings. In 1906 the annual NAWSA meeting voted to create a National College Women's Equal Suffrage League. Park had been traveling in Europe for two years when Gillmore wrote her in 1910 to tell her of the news and advise her to return home to continue their work.

In 1917 Park became vice chair of the NAWSA congressional committee in Washington, D.C. Along with her colleagues, Park pioneered the "front door lobby," which

Maud Wood Park, 1951

helped persuade members of Congress to vote for the 19th Amendment, granting women the right to vote, through an open, straightforward, and well-organized approach to lobbying. Her best-known work, *Front Door Lobby* (published posthumously in 1960), details her suffrage campaign in Washington. After the amendment became law in 1920, Park became the first president of the newly formed National League of Women Voters (later League of Women Voters of the United States), a post she held until 1924. She lobbied for social welfare legislation and independent citizenship for women and set up the Women's Joint Congressional Committee, which coordinated women's lobbying efforts.

As president of the National League of Women Voters, Park worked toward the "unification of laws relating to the civil status of women, child welfare, food supply, social hygiene, and protection of women in industry." Although suffrage had been gained, Park continued to lecture on the importance of getting women to the polls, comparing nonvoters to army deserters. She also helped organize the first parent-teacher association in Boston and advocated a role for women in the police force.

Later in life Park became a playwright at her home in Cape Elizabeth, Maine, where she wrote under both her own name and the pseudonym C. J. Maywood. She died in Melrose, Mass.

Sara Hunter Graham, *Woman Suffrage and the New Democracy* (1996); Suzanne M. Marilley, *Woman Suffrage and the Origins of Liberal Feminism in the United States, 1820–1920* (1996).

Tina Hummel

Rowlandson, Mary (ca. 1637–1711) Writer.

Mary White Rowlandson wrote the first and most popular account in English of captivity by New England Indians. In 1682 four editions appeared of *The Soveraignty and Goodness of GOD, Together with the Faithfulness of His Promises Displayed; Being a Narrative of the Captivity and Restauration of Mrs. Mary Rowlandson.* The narrative remained a best-seller into the 19th century.

Mary White was born to Joan and John White in Somerset, England, around 1637. With her parents and siblings, she emigrated to New England, settling first in Salem and finally in Lancaster, Mass. She married the Reverend Joseph Rowlandson and the couple had three children.

The event that changed her life occurred during King Philip's War (1675–76), the most serious conflict of the century between the European settlers and the indigenous people of the region. The colonists' encroachment onto land occupied by the Algonquian Indians led the Narragansett, Nipmuck, and Wam-panoag of southern New England to rebel. Their leader was Metacom, a Wampanoag chief called "King Philip" by the English. In February 1676 the Rowlandsons' frontier town of Lancaster was attacked. Joseph had gone to Boston, but Mary and the children were wounded and captured. She witnessed her brother-in-law and nephew being murdered and later described in her narrative the sight of her friends and relatives "lying in their blood . . . like a company of sheep torn by Wolves."

Her captors took Rowlandson through some 20 "removes," as she calls their travels, to central Massachusetts and up to New Hampshire in the three months of her imprisonment. Her "babe" Sarah (age six) died within a fortnight of the attack and had to be left "buried . . . in the Wilderness." Rowlandson was separated from her other children, Mary (age 10) and Joseph (age 14), although she was occasionally allowed to see them. Rowlandson proved to be a resourceful captive, using her sewing skills to make clothing, for which she was paid in food; she also acted as servant to Weetamoo, sister-in-law of Metacom. While Rowlandson continued to view the Indians as "Barbarous Creatures," she noted that "not one of them ever offered me the least abuse of unchastity." Her captors did not harm her and shared the little they had.

Rowlandson was ransomed in May 1676 and several weeks later got her children back. Her husband accepted a call from Wethersfield, Conn., where the family moved. Before his death in 1678 Mary wrote her narrative. Its publication was supported by leading ministers, including Increase Mather, because of the spiritual lessons she drew from her experience. Her main consolation and support during captivity was the Bible that one of the Indians gave her on the journey. She read it continuously and trusted "in the presence of God . . . Gods Power is as great now, and as sufficient to save, as when he preserved Daniel in the Lions Den."

After a year of widowhood Rowlandson married Captain Samuel Talcott; she lived in Wethersfield until her death. Although she lived quietly, she said she never again slept soundly.

Mitchell Robert Breitwieser, *American Puritanism and the Defense of Mourning: Religion, Grief, and Ethnology in Mary Rowlandson's Captivity Narrative* (1990); Tara Fitzpatrick, "The Figure of Captivity: The Cultural Work of the Puritan Captivity Narrative," *American Literary History* 3 (1991); David L. Greene, "New Light on Mary Rowlandson," *Early American Literature* 20 (1985).

Barbara A. White

Second-Wave Feminism What is often called the second wave of feminism

emerged in New England during the late 1960s, as it did throughout the country, among two different groups of women. The activists who identified with women's liberation were closely allied with the peace and Civil Rights movements of the sixties and were most comfortable organizing outside established institutions. They developed a radical critique of the position of women in the private world of personal relationships as well as the public world of education, work, and politics and articulated a vision of a radically transformed world. Other activists, often called equal rights feminists, who sought to be included within mainstream institutions and worked to effect change through litigation and legislation, identified with the National Organization for Women (NOW). The two strands of feminism moved closer together during the early 1980s, as NOW incorporated many of the ideas of women's liberation and the political climate in the country made confrontational strategies and radical visions difficult to sustain.

Although NOW was formed in 1966, local NOW chapters did not appear in New England until the early 1970s, after interest in feminism had been rekindled by the activity and writing of women's liberation activists. Women's liberation groups sprang up in towns and cities throughout the region in 1968 and 1969. Cell 16, a Boston-based group founded in 1968, published an influential radical feminist journal, *No More Fun and Games,* that urged women's liberation activists to learn karate and practice celibacy as ways of reducing their vulnerability and to devote their energy to creating a feminist revolution. The Boston women's liberation organization Bread and Roses, named for a slogan made famous in the 1912 strike of textile workers in Lawrence, Mass., was formed in 1969 and became one of the most successful citywide socialist feminist groups in the country. Composed of about 30 small groups, Bread and Roses ran orientation sessions for new recruits, coordinated political projects, and sponsored demonstrations.

Women's liberation activists worked on a wide variety of issues. They founded women's centers, educated one another about women's health, worked to legalize abortion, supported the struggles of welfare recipients for decent allowances, pressured institutions to provide child care, and organized against the discriminatory practices of restaurants, newspapers, colleges, and workplaces. In November 1969 a demonstration in New Haven, Conn., in support of seven jailed women who were members of the militant African American organization the Black Panthers drew national attention, as thousands of women marched, chanting "Free our sisters, free ourselves." In

Cambridge, Mass., in 1971 women's liberation activists conducted a referendum in which residents voted two to one that the Cambridge city government should provide free 24-hour child care.

In 1970 the Boston Women's Health Book Collective, which was holding workshops that combined medical information with frank discussions about women's experiences, decided to broaden their audience by publishing a book about women's health. *Women and Their Bodies,* selling for 25 cents, reproduced the atmosphere of women's health workshops by integrating current scientific information with women's reflections.

Two events in 1970 stimulated the proliferation of women's liberation activities in the New England region: a conference in Boston sponsored by Cell 16 and the demonstrations, fairs, and celebrations held on August 26, the 50th anniversary of the ratification of the woman suffrage amendment. Called by NOW, the August 26 activities marked the growing visibility of women's liberation and increased interaction between women's liberation activists and members of NOW, who began organizing local chapters that year. Twelve thousand people joined the Boston demonstration, and new groups were formed in the demonstration's wake. At the event in New Haven, the newly formed New Haven Women's Liberation Rock Band made their debut. Composed of eight women, the band was one of the two women's liberation musical groups that sought to use the energy of rock music to communicate the ideas and spirit of feminism. The band played for audiences throughout the country and, in collaboration with the Chicago Women's Liberation Rock Band, recorded an album, *Mountain Moving Day,* that was produced by Rounder Records in Boston in 1972.

During the early 1970s African American women began to organize their own feminist organizations and to generate theory that spoke to their particular experience as African American women. One of the most influential and widely reprinted statements about black feminist politics was published in 1974 by the Combahee River Collective, a Boston group that began as a chapter of the short-lived National Black Feminist Organization and later became an independent group.

The campaign to ratify the Equal Rights Amendment stimulated the formation of several NOW chapters in the New England states, all of which had at least one chapter by the mid-1970s. Every New England state ratified the Equal Rights Amendment, with New Hampshire, the second state to ratify, taking the lead. Several New England states adopted their own statewide equal rights amendments.

New England played an important role in the dissemination of feminist ideas through pamphlets, journals, and newspapers. The New England Free Press, a Boston printing and publishing group, issued many of the early pamphlets articulating the ideas of women's liberation. The *Second Wave,* a Cambridge-based magazine covering both Boston-area and national events, was published sporadically from 1971 to 1983. *Sinister Wisdom,* a lesbian feminist literary journal, was published in Massachusetts, Maine, and Vermont throughout the 1980s before moving to California in 1987. *Sojourner,* a monthly feminist newspaper founded in 1975, and the *Women's Review of Books,* established in 1983, remain influential periodicals for feminist activists and intellectuals.

Feminism spawned a number of interrelated movements addressing particular aspects of women's subordination. Since self-determination is a core concept of feminism, a woman's right to control her body has been a central facet of second-wave feminism. In the early 1970s this took the form of campaigns against state anti-abortion statutes. In Rhode Island and Connecticut groups of women plaintiffs filed suits contesting their state's abortion laws in an effort to stimulate public discussion about abortion. Those lawsuits, *Doe v. Israel* and *Abele v. Markle,* were decided in the plaintiffs' favor in lower courts and were on their way to the Supreme Court when the finding in *Roe v. Wade* in 1973 rendered all state anti-abortion statutes unconstitutional.

From the early days of the second wave of feminism, the need to improve the disadvantaged position of women in the workplace has been an essential part of the feminist program. Workplace discrimination was attacked through litigation and legislation, but the wage gap between men and women persisted, largely because of the concentration of women in low-wage jobs such as office work. As the growing feminist movement challenged the assumption that women's jobs were secondary to their roles as wives and mothers and questioned the tradition of the "office wife," clerical workers began organizing both to improve their economic status and to demand respect on the job. A newsletter begun in Boston by a small group of clerical workers in 1972 laid the groundwork for a citywide organization, Nine to Five, founded in 1973. Nine to Five quickly grew into a national organization that served as a clearinghouse for the complaints of office workers, conducted several studies, and published guides for office workers about office survival and sexual harassment. In 1981 Nine to Five moved to Cleveland, Ohio, where it helped to create District 925, a nationwide union for office workers affiliated with the Service Employees International Union.

Violence against women emerged as an issue within the feminist movement in the early 1970s. One of the earliest organizations in the country to focus on domestic violence was Spruce Run, a battered-women's project in Bangor, Maine, which was launched in 1972 and is still in operation. By the mid-1970s all the New England states had established organizations and services to address the needs of the survivors of male violence.

While activism for women's liberation declined during the mid-1970s in New England, reflecting a national trend, groups of women seeking to translate feminist goals into legislative action became more active. Women's lobbies, chapters of the National Political Caucus, and branches of NOW worked in all six New England states to strengthen antiviolence legislation, institute comparable-worth laws for state workers, improve regulation and state funding for child care, protect women's reproductive rights, secure funding for rape crisis centers and battered women's shelters, and promote legislation against workplace and educational discrimination.

In the 1980s women's organizations mobilized to counter the antifeminist backlash that threatened many of the gains of the previous decades, to defeat referenda and legislation limiting the rights of lesbian and gay people, and to protect women's health centers from anti-abortion violence. In 1988 3,000 people, "standing up for choice," formed a line from Boston to Brookline in response to Operation Rescue's efforts to blockade abortion clinics. A major victory for reproductive rights was achieved in 1990, when Connecticut enacted a statute codifying the provisions of *Roe v. Wade.*

In the 1990s and into the 21st century, feminist organizations continue to mobilize to protect women's access to abortion and health care, contest funding cuts in programs that support poor women and children, work with local police departments to combat violence against women, push for laws against sexual harassment, and strengthen antidiscrimination legislation and enforcement. A renewed interest in feminism among young women has stimulated the growth of women's studies programs in the region, and feminist organizations have begun seeking to address the concerns of young women, who sometimes describe themselves as a "third wave" of feminism.

Rosalyn Baxandall and Linda Gordon, eds., *Dear Sisters: Dispatches from the Women's Liberation Movement* (2000); Susan Brownmiller, *In Our Time: Mem-*

oir of a Revolution (1999); Flora Davis, *Moving the Mountain: The Women's Movement in America since 1960* (1991); Ruth Rosen, *The World Split Open: How the Modern Women's Movement Changed America* (2000).

Amy Kesselman

Sexualities Contemporary views of sexuality are dominated by the notion that there are two authentic forms of sexual expression, heterosexuality and homosexuality. This conception of sexuality is rooted in the fundamental assumption that there are two genders corresponding to two biological sexes; that is, if all people are clearly either female or male, then all romantic and sexual attractions or relationships must be either between people of the same gender and sex or between people of different genders and sexes, and hence clearly either homosexual or heterosexual.

However, bisexuality is increasingly recognized as a common behavioral pattern and an authentic sexual orientation. Sexuality can also be culturally specific. For instance, many Americans of Latin descent see the position one assumes when engaging in the sex act as the primary determinant of homosexuality; a man who takes the active role in male-male sex is not considered homosexual. Furthermore, people of all sexual orientations differ in terms of the types of romantic or sexual relationships they wish to enter into, the amount of sexual activity they like, the particular sexual practices they prefer, and the importance and meaning of sexuality in their lives. Classifying someone as lesbian, gay, bisexual, or heterosexual reveals little about the complexity of that person's sexuality. Recognizing the wide variety of sexual cultures and practices, scholars now refer to *sexualities* instead of *sexual orientations*.

Social scientists' critiques of simplistic notions of sexual orientation and gender reflect a questioning that began outside academia. The early gay liberation and second-wave lesbian feminist movements of the late 1960s and early 1970s, in New England as well as throughout the country, hoped to break down distinctions between gays and straights and between men and women. Today, challenges to traditional notions of gender and sexuality are coming from the bisexual, transgender, and sex-radicalism movements.

Although the West Coast is usually thought of as the hotbed of revolutionary sexual politics and practices, New England has generated its fair share of them. Early feminists and lesbian feminists found encouragement in the intellectual atmospheres of college campuses, a disproportionate number of which are located in New England, including

four of the so-called Seven Sisters. Today's bisexual and transgender movements are also well represented in New England. The Bisexual Resource Center, an epicenter of bisexual political activity, is located in Cambridge, Mass., and the International Foundation for Gender Education, which publishes a journal for cross-dressers and transgenderists called *Transgender Tapestry*, is located in Waltham, Mass.

Despite scientific and cultural challenges to rigid definitions of homosexuality and heterosexuality, the distinction is still incorporated into the moral, legal, and political institutions of New England society. Children are generally raised with the assumption that they will be heterosexual. Those who practice other forms of sexuality must reject such heterosexual identity and socialization and embrace their own sexuality, sometimes by "coming out," or revealing their sexuality, to friends, family, or the larger society. Negative social attitudes toward alternative sexualities often make coming out difficult. It can be especially complex for racial or ethnic minorities. Those who already suffer one form of discrimination may be reluctant to take on an additional minority identity and cannot assume that lost family support, especially important in the face of societal racism, will be replaced by support from a predominantly white lesbian and gay community.

Negative attitudes toward sexual diversity are changing, however, especially in New England. Nationwide, the most dramatic evidence of change is the increasing media coverage of lesbian, gay, and bisexual concerns, including public discussion of the U.S. military policy on homosexuality that began in the 1990s. In almost all New England states legislation has been passed protecting gays, lesbians, and bisexuals against various forms of discrimination.

Richard J. Hoffman argues that our cultural attachment to simplistic and distinct gender categories and our preference for heterosexuality stem from monotheistic religious traditions such as that of the Protestantism so central to the colonization of New England. Things are changing, however. Increasing numbers of faith communities, including the Unitarian Universalist Association, headquartered in Boston; some Quaker and United Church of Christ congregations; and Reform Jewish synagogues, now welcome lesbian and gay members without condemnation and offer to bless same-sex partnerships. But many New Englanders belong to religions that have officially denounced homosexual practice, along with other sexual behaviors that have traditionally been frowned upon, such as premari-

tal sex and the use of birth control; 50 percent belong to the Catholic Church, and nearly 10 percent are Baptist or Methodist.

The most reliable survey of sexual activities in the United States, the National Health and Social Life Survey, begun in 1992, found that a smaller percentage of people have what it called "traditional" sexual attitudes in New England than in any other region of the United States. Their survey also found that "sexual libertarian" views, which involve acceptance of a broad range of sexual activities, among them sexual expression between people of the same gender, are more prevalent in New England than anywhere else in the country.

John Boswell, "Concepts, Experience, and Sexuality," in *Forms of Desire: Sexual Orientation and the Social Constructionist Controversy*, ed. Edward Stein (1990); Michel Foucault, *The History of Sexuality*, trans. Robert Hurley (1978); Richard J. Hoffman, "Vices, Gods, and Virtues: Cosmology as Mediating Factor in Attitudes toward Male Homosexuality," *Journal of Homosexuality* 9, nos. 2 and 3 (1984); Edward O. Laumann, John H. Gagnon, Robert T. Michael, and Stuart Michaels, *The Social Organization of Sexuality: Sexual Practices in the United States* (1994); David J. McKirnan, Joseph P. Stokes, Lynda Doll, and Rebecca G. Burzette, "Bisexually Active Men: Social Characteristics and Sexual Behavior," *Journal of Sex Research* 32, no. 1 (1995); Jay P. Paul, "Bisexuality: Reassessing Our Paradigms of Sexuality," *Journal of Homosexuality* 11, nos. 1 and 2 (1985).

Paula C. Rodriguez Rust and Andrew Lane

Spinsters Originally attached to one whose occupation was spinning, the word *spinster* was by 1617 the common-law term for an unmarried woman. In the 18th century it came to designate a woman who remained unmarried beyond the usual age and, like its synonym *old maid*, to carry a negative connotation. By the 1820s the word evoked the presumed characteristics of such an individual.

The percentage of spinsters—either not yet or never married—in colonial New England was always low. Numbers began to rise, however, in the last decades of the 18th century and continued to increase through the 19th; they were particularly high in areas where unmarried women found work in newly mechanized textile mills. The percentage of unwed native-born white women in Massachusetts, for example, was virtually double that of the U.S. population generally: 16.9 compared with 7.7 percent in 1850. Immigrant Irish and free black populations also had high rates of singleness, the former owing to working conditions that separated women from men as live-in domestics and the latter to the sex ratio of men to women. The high rate of singleness among native-born white women began to decline early in the 20th century.

Increased singleness among women during the antebellum period was due in part to changes in the mate-selection process, as parents granted more authority to their daughters to make such a choice. Additionally, romantic ideation in fiction, advice books, and female behavior manuals influenced young women's view of the eligibility of potential marriage partners. Middle-class women sought a male "beau ideal," whose rarity delayed or discouraged some from marrying. Nineteenth-century New Englanders such as Sophia Smith, whose fortune established Smith College in Northampton, Mass.; Maria Mitchell, America's first female professional astronomer; and the poet and hymnist Lucy Larcom voiced a rationale for remaining unwed that included social factors (the need to care for family members, the constraints of marriage), financial requirements (the importance of their wages to the family economy), and concerns linked to gender expectations (the desire to pursue a vocation or avoid motherhood, the restrictiveness of housework).

As a growing number of women chose not to marry, the stigma attached to spinsterhood was undercut by an ideology of "single blessedness," which valued the decision not to wed when its motive was Christian benevolence or familial devotion—or a reasonable facsimile thereof. In the New England novels of Louisa May Alcott, Harriet Beecher Stowe, and Sarah Orne Jewett, for example, the sister of charity and the maiden aunt served as positive alternatives to "wife" and contrasted with more negative portraits of similar figures in the work of Nathaniel Hawthorne or Henry James.

The use of *spinster* declined when *new woman*, a positive term coined by Sarah Grand in the 1893 British novel *The Heavenly Twins*, caught on in the early 20th century. Nonetheless, even as social and economic opportunities expanded for unmarried women, reliance on sexual and psychiatric explanations for singleness in American culture made it difficult for the unwed or later-wed woman to see herself in a positive light.

After 1950 the term *single woman* took precedence. Second-wave feminists recast her as a heroine whose rejection of marriage signified her sexual liberation, economic and social independence, and political critique of patriarchy. In 1978 the Boston College theologian Mary Daly reclaimed the spinster as a joyful, creative, and radical being in *Gyn/Ecology*: "She who has chosen her Self, who defines her Self, by choice, neither in relation to children nor to men, who is Self-identified, is a spinster." For Daly the spinster's rejection of centuries-old patriarchal dogma and language, the effects of which had undermined female spirituality and creativity, would emancipate

women. By the late 20th century, as permanent or periodic singleness emerged as an alternative to marriage or long-term coupling in America, the use of *Ms.* instead of *Miss* or *Mrs.* deemphasized women's marital status as a social marker. Nevertheless, divergent representations of the unmarried female—heroine or failure, independent or neurotic, assertive or autocratic—continue to clamor for cultural precedence.

Lee Chambers-Schiller, *Liberty, a Better Husband: Single Women in America: The Generations of 1780–1840* (1984); Laura L. Doan, ed., *Old Maids to Radical Spinsters: Unmarried Women in the 20th-Century Novel* (1991); Sally L. Kitch, *Chaste Liberation: Celibacy and Female Cultural Status* (1989); Susan Koppelman, ed., *Old Maids: Short Stories by 19th Century U.S. Women Writers* (1984).

Lee Chambers-Schiller

Stewart, Maria W. (Miller) (1803–79)

Lecturer, writer, and teacher. Maria W. (Miller) Stewart, a lecturer and writer, was a pioneer black abolitionist and a defiant champion of women's rights. A forerunner of the champions of black activism, she is recognized as the first American-born female public lecturer on political themes to leave extant copies of her texts.

Born Maria Miller in Hartford, Stewart was orphaned at the age of five and, until she was 15, was bound out as a servant in a clergyman's family. There she acquired the rudiments of a formal education and a strong religious faith. She moved to Boston and in 1826 married James W. Stewart, a successful black businessman some years her senior, adopting his middle initial as well as his surname.

Widowed after barely three years of marriage, Stewart experienced a religious conversion and believed that God had called her to become a "warrior" for the "cause of oppressed Africa." Pronouncing herself to be a "strong advocate for the cause of God and for the cause of freedom," she began to write and lecture against slavery in the South and the oppression of blacks in the North. She urged blacks to demand their human rights and argued that African Americans needed to establish strong, self-sufficient educational and economic institutions within their own communities. She called on black women to fully participate in religion, education, politics, and business and urged them to defy prevailing notions of female subservience by developing their highest intellectual capacities.

Stewart's ideas, and particularly her public lectures, were highly controversial in the Boston black community. Lamenting that she had been unable to make herself useful to her own people, she left Boston for New York City in 1833. She supported herself as a teacher

there and later in Baltimore, where she also contributed to the African Methodist Episcopal Church's publication *The Christian Register*. At the start of the Civil War, Stewart established a school for black children in Washington, D.C., and later wrote a brief memoir of that era called "Sufferings during the War."

The abolitionist editor and printer William Lloyd Garrison published Stewart's 12-page political manifesto *Religion and Pure Principles of Morality, the Sure Foundation on Which We Must Build* in 1831 and a collection of her meditations on religion, *Productions of Mrs. Maria W. Stewart*, in 1835. Stewart delivered four public lectures in Boston—at Franklin Hall (1832) to the Afric-American Female Intelligence Society (1832), at the African Masonic Hall (1833), and a farewell address at the African Meeting House on Beacon Hill (1833). Stewart acknowledged that the greatest influences on her were the Bible; the writings of David Walker, author of *Appeal . . . to the Coloured Citizens of the World* (1829); and the Englishman John Adams, author of *Sketches of the History, Genius, Disposition . . . of the Fair Sex, in All Parts of the World.* (1790). Many of Stewart's speeches and essays were published in Garrison's *Liberator*. A new edition of her works, *Meditations from the Pen of Maria W. Stewart*, including letters and testimonials from friends and various dignitaries, appeared in 1879, just months before her death.

Marilyn Richardson, ed., *Maria W. Stewart, America's First Black Woman Political Writer: Essays and Speeches* (1987); Lora Romero, *Home Fronts: Domesticity and Its Critics in the Antebellum United States* (1997); Rodger Streitmatter, *Raising Her Voice: African-American Women Journalists Who Changed History* (1994).

Marilyn Richardson

Stone, Lucy (1818–93)

Feminist, orator, and journalist. Born on a small farm in West Brookfield, Mass., Lucy Stone rose from humble rural origins to power and fame first as an abolitionist and orator and later as an organizational leader and journalist. In 1870 she founded the *Woman's Journal*, a chronicle of women's political and professional accomplishments. Stone was known as the "morning star" of the woman suffrage movement, having delivered her first public address on behalf of women's rights in Gardner, Mass., in 1847, almost a full year before the women's rights meeting in Seneca Falls, N.Y.

Stone entered Oberlin College in the autumn of 1843. After graduation in 1847 she divided her time as a speaker between women's rights and abolition. Her oratorical skills brought her instant fame and notoriety, and her name was soon being advertised alongside those of orators Wendell Phillips and Theodore Parker, two of the greatest 19th-century public speakers. By 1854 Stone's verbal prowess had P. T. Barnum seeking to represent her, an offer she declined.

Stone was also a consummate political organizer. Beginning in the 1840s she set up education committees and later political clubs in cities, towns, and rural hamlets, using proceeds from her lectures to print and distribute women's rights propaganda. Stone was instrumental in organizing the first National Woman's Rights Convention, held in Worcester, Mass., in 1850, an event that drew worldwide attention. She went on to stage national conventions every year until the outbreak of the Civil War. Stone was also a skilled lobbyist, addressing legislatures throughout the United States and Canada on behalf of greater legal and political rights for women. In 1855 she used the occasion of her marriage to Henry Blackwell, brother of the pioneering physicians Elizabeth and Emily Blackwell, to launch a public protest against women's legal disabilities in marriage. She refused to be known as Mrs. Blackwell, keeping her birth name throughout her life. Women who kept their own names after marriage became known as "Lucy Stoners."

In the years immediately following the Civil War, when Reconstruction amendments failed to enfranchise women, concentrating instead on freedmen, some woman suffrage leaders tried to defeat the ratification of the black suffrage amendment. Stone led the majority of suffragists in resisting these tactics. A schism developed in 1869; Stone led the American Woman Suffrage Association, the larger and more politically organized suffrage group, until 1889. In 1870 she began publishing the *Woman's Journal,* a woman suffrage weekly. For the next 60 years it chronicled women's progress week by week, providing an invaluable record.

Stone's fame has been partially eclipsed as a result of the division of suffragists. In their *History of Woman Suffrage* (1881) Elizabeth Cady Stanton, Susan B. Anthony, and Matilda Joslyn Gage, leaders of the other wing of suffragists, marginalized Stone's pioneering contributions. Stone continued to lobby, petition, and lecture on behalf of woman suffrage until her death, in Dorchester, Mass.

Alice Stone Blackwell, *Lucy Stone: Pioneer of Woman's Rights* (1930); Andrea Moore Kerr, *Lucy Stone: Speaking Out for Equality* (1992); Carol Lasser and Marlene Deahl Merrill, eds., *Friends and Sisters: Letters between Lucy Stone and Antoinette Brown Blackwell, 1846–93* (1987); Leslie Wheeler, ed., *Loving Warriors: Selected Letters of Lucy Stone and Henry B. Blackwell, 1853 to 1893,* (1981).

Andrea Moore Kerr

Transsexuality Transsexuality is both a medical syndrome and a cultural phenomenon. Although throughout history some people have lived as members of the other sex or wanted to become members of the other sex, transsexualism as we know it today emerged in the mid-20th century as a result of advances in medical technology and the development of terms that distinguish the psychological experience of sex from biological sex. Transsexuals seek physical sex change (hormonal treatment, genital and other forms of plastic surgery) because they believe that their psychological sex (gender) differs from their anatomical sex.

Many transsexuals endure financial hardship and social stigma in order to obtain sex reassignment. Numerous university research programs studying transsexualism and related "gender disorders" shut down in the late 1970s and 1980s after conflicting reports about the psychological advisability of sex-reassignment treatments. Medical and operative options for transsexuals remain available through private clinics and physicians, although these are few in number and of varied reputation.

During the 1980s and 1990s some transsexuals began to agitate for a political understanding of their experience. Organizations such as GenderPac and Transsexual Menace placed gender nonconformity and transgender rights on the national political agenda, linking transsexuals with homosexuals and bisexuals as politically repressed sexual minorities.

New England has been an important center for transsexual support and transgender activism since the late 1970s. The International Foundation for Gender Education, founded in 1978 and located in Waltham, Mass., addresses issues pertinent to cross-dressers, transsexuals, and other transgender people: its stated values include "individual uniqueness and dignity; personal wholeness; respect for human diversity; freedom from society's arbitrarily assigned gender definitions; and respect, acceptance, enforcement, and protection of gender-related Human and Civil Rights for all." The organization publishes *Transgender Tapestry,* a magazine that features informational articles as well as personal advertisements.

Since 1974 Provincetown, Mass., has been the site of the Fantasia Fair. Occurring each October, the fair is a weeklong party and conference for cross-dressers and others who wish to experiment with gender or live as a member of the other sex. Many transsexuals also participate in gay and lesbian pride events (now often described as lesbian, gay, bisexual, and transgender pride events), such as the parades that occur to commemorate the Stonewall Riot each June in most major New England cities and many of its larger towns.

The Tiffany Club, founded in 1978 and also located in Waltham, provides outreach and support for members and helps people with "issues of gender confusion, cross-dressing, and transsexualism." A chapter of Gender Education and Advocacy called It's Time, Massachusetts is a public advocacy organization whose goal is "legal protections for people with gender-variant expressions in the Commonwealth of Massachusetts."

Kate Bornstein, *Gender Outlaw: On Men, Women, and the Rest of Us* (1994); Vern L. Bullough and Bonnie Bullough, *Cross Dressing, Sex, and Gender* (1993); Holly Devor, *FTM: Female-to-Male Transsexuals in Society* (1997); Bernice L. Hausman, *Changing Sex: Transsexualism, Technology, and the Idea of Gender* (1995).

Bernice L. Hausman

Women's Clubs New England women have been in the forefront of the women's club movement for 200 years. They have participated in church-based ladies' aid societies, informal quilting bees, pro- and antisuffrage associations, patriotic societies, garden clubs, sororities, alumnae associations, the women's auxiliaries of fraternal and Masonic orders; in organizations devoted to abolition, temperance, charity, and benevolence; in trade unions, working girls' clubs, civic reform societies, arts and crafts guilds, music-making alliances, literary and amateur theater groups, and professional associations. As early as 1801 the Female Charitable Society for Benevolence formed in Salem, Mass., to aid the needy, and in 1848 the Ladies' Physiological Institute in Boston provided women with a course in female physiology. In Lowell, Mass., in the 1820s early female factory workers formed study groups. Slavery and alcohol consumption inspired antebellum women to unite for reform, and New England women distinguished themselves in leadership for abolition and temperance.

The New England Women's Club and Julia Ward Howe placed Boston in the forefront of the post–Civil War movement for literary and civic-reform societies, which flourished during the late 19th and early 20th centuries. Clubs quickly formed both in the local area and all over the region for the enjoyment and education of women members and the improvement of the community. For example, Josephine St. Pierre Ruffin organized the Woman's Era Club for African American women with the goal of establishing kindergartens in Boston. The Concord Woman's Club in New Hampshire and Montpelier Woman's Club in Vermont devoted considerable effort to supporting public libraries. The

The Women's Van, a health-care program by the Junior League of Boston, 1983

Rhode Island Woman's Club in Providence pressed Brown University to open Pembroke College for Women. In settlement houses and ethnic neighborhoods women's clubs were organized for immigrant women.

In undertaking municipal reforms, members transformed their communities and defied the popular belief that women were suited only for household concerns. In clubs women developed organizational skills used to bring about an extensive list of civic improvements in towns and cities, including public parks and playgrounds, vocational training in the schools, drinking fountains, shelters and clinics, scholarships for youth, protective legislation for women and children, public art and memorial statuary, and tree planting on Arbor Day. Evidence of clubwomen's efforts, in countless forms, is found throughout New England, whether it be cottages for composers, writers, and artists that music clubs funded at the Mac-Dowell Colony in Peterborough, N.H.; the outdoor amphitheater established by drama-loving club members in Camden, Maine; or the DAR State Forest in the western Massachusetts town of Goshen preserved by the Daughters of the American Revolution.

Special-interest groups of every stripe attracted women at the turn of the century, and many of these united into larger networks as a means of maximizing the influence that members might have on social issues. Boston was home to the Association of Collegiate Alumnae (now the American Association of University Women), founded by Marion Talbot in 1881; the American Woman Suffrage Association, led by Lucy Stone and Julia Ward Howe from 1869 to 1890; the Women's Educational and Industrial Union, founded in 1877 and still in operation; the New England Woman's Press Association; and the Massachusetts Association Opposed to the Further Extension of the Suffrage to Women, founded in 1895. In 1895 Josephine Ruffin organized the National Federation of Afro-American Women, a group that later merged with the Colored Women's League of Washington to form, first, the National Association of Colored Women and then the National Association of Colored Women's Clubs. Maine women pioneered in consolidating that state's literary and civic reform clubs into the Maine Federation of Women's Clubs in 1892; soon following were Massachusetts (1894), New Hampshire and Rhode Island (1895), Vermont (1896), and Connecticut (1897).

Strong branches of national organizations have abounded throughout New England and have represented a wide array of political opinion, ranging from the pacifist Women's International League for Peace and Freedom, generally ostracized for its stance during World War I, to the Daughters of the American Revolution, who engaged in incendiary red-baiting during the 1920s. Most have taken a moderate path in pressing for the socially significant changes of their era.

Women's clubs, in addition to initiating and maintaining civic improvements in extraordinary number, have provided a wealth of opportunities for their members. During their heyday in the late 19th century, clubs were one of the only venues in which women could master such skills as public speaking, establishing and running committees, fund-raising, managing organizational finances, publicizing programs, and legislative lobbying. In clubs women enjoyed the company of like-minded neighbors and affected local public policies. Often called "universities for middle-aged women," clubs also served an educational function, soliciting members to research and report on subjects of interest to the group and inviting notable guests to lecture or give classes on contemporary issues and literary and historical topics.

Many clubs tended to attract privileged white Protestant middle-class women whose husbands enjoyed local prominence as professionals, elected officials, and businessmen. These were the women who felt free to join associations in middle age after their children had enrolled in school. They were also the ones who could afford to pay club dues and devote energy to club projects. By inviting their neighbors to fill vacancies on the membership roster, they usually ensured the homogeneity of their groups and generally excluded minority women. However, considerable numbers of other women—immigrants, African Americans, laborers, Jews, and Catholics—formed clubs of their own, addressing social issues of significance to them.

Since the 1920s women have enjoyed increasing opportunities throughout society, in education, politics, the professions, and business. With more choices before them, fewer have elected to devote their time to club activity. Nonetheless, many early women's clubs continue to exist, if not to flourish, with their membership devoted to the educational, social, and civic goals pursued by women's clubs in the past.

Karen J. Blair, *The Clubwoman as Feminist: True Womanhood Redefined, 1868–1914* (1980); Sarah Deutsch, "Learning to Talk More Like a Man: Boston Women's Class-Bridging Organizations, 1870–1940," *American Historical Review* 97, no. 2 (1992); Massachusetts State Federation of Women's Clubs, *Progress and Achievement: A History of the Massachusetts State Federation of Women's Clubs, 1893–1962*, 2d ed. (1962); New Hampshire Federation of Women's Clubs, *A History of the New Hampshire Federation of Women's Clubs, 1895–1940* (1941); Marion Talbot and Lois Kimball Mathews Rosenberry, *The History of the American Association of University Women, 1881–1931* (1931).

Karen J. Blair

Women's Publishing Women have been part of the world of printing, publishing, and letters since early colonial times. Not until the 1890s, however, did a woman make a serious effort to establish a press that was deliberately and self-consciously feminist in philosophy and content, while gay and lesbian presses did not appear before the 1970s.

Today's clear distinction between printer, publisher, and bookseller did not exist during the colonial era. All aspects of getting a written work to press and to an audience were usually under the control of an individual owner with the full right to decide what and how to publish and distribute. Even well-populated areas were likely to contain no more than one or two printers. Thus being a printer meant holding a powerful and influential position in a society where there were far fewer means of disseminating information than we now enjoy.

King James II of England well understood the power of the press. He instructed the governor of New York not to allow any unauthorized presses into the colonies. One was brought to Boston in 1638, however, by the Reverend Jose Glover and his family. Glover died en route to America, however, leaving his wife proprietor of the Cambridge (later Harvard) Press for two years, after which it was taken over by her new husband.

Ann Franklin of Newport, R.I., was the first working woman printer in New England. Ann's apprenticeship came with her role as the wife of James Franklin, brother of the much-renowned Benjamin. In addition to running the home and raising five children, Ann worked in the print shop alongside her husband. When she was widowed in 1735, she thus had a means of providing for her family. Over the years she began to assert herself as owner of the business and to sign her work, "Printed by Ann Franklin."

Other prominent early women printers were Sarah Goddard, who published the *Providence Gazette* in 1767; Hannah Bunce Watson, who helped found the *Hartford Courant* in the 1770s, a newspaper continuously published since that time; Margaret Green Draper, who continued publication of the *Boston News-letter* after her husband's death during the American Revolution; and Mary Wilkinson Crouch, who published the *Salem (Mass.) Gazette* in 1781.

The New Hampshire–born Sarah Josepha Hale came to wield enormous national influence during her long career (1837–77) not as printer but as editor of *Godey's Lady's Book*. In *Godey's,* and in her 1827 novel *Northwood,* Hale encouraged women to obtain an education, though she failed to challenge her society's basic assumption that a woman's place was in the home. Margaret Fuller, who helped found the Transcendentalist journal *The Dial* in 1840 and served as its editor until 1842, based her feminist theories and her work as a journalist on the belief that women must have and use the power of the press to change society. It was not until the late 19th century, however, that women gained full control over publications.

An outstanding contribution to feminist publishing in New England was the *Woman's Era,* a monthly newspaper established in 1890 by Josephine St. Pierre Ruffin in Boston. *Woman's Era,* addressed to an audience of middle-class African American women, was decidedly feminist in nature and intended to promote the advancement of African American women in particular. The newspaper gained national prominence when it became the official publication of the National Federation of Afro-American Women, which launched the important black women's club movement in American history. The paper survived under the editorship of Ruffin until 1897.

The distinctive story of feminist publishing in New England is of more recent date. One of the important features of any activist movement is the need to disseminate information, and the feminist movement of the 1960s and 1970s was no exception. New England's longest standing and most successful feminist press is Alice James Books, founded in Cambridge, Mass., in 1973 by a cooperative made up of five women and two men who had all been in a poetry workshop together. It is named for William and Henry James's sister Alice, whose posthumously published diary made her a feminist icon. The cooperative

provided women with access to publishing and enlisted their assistance as readers or editors for the press as part of their publication contract. In 1994 Alice James Press decided to affiliate itself with the University of Maine at Farmington. The mission statement of the organization also changed at that time: while maintaining its New England emphasis, Alice James would henceforth publish poetry by both women and men. The press took this controversial step to widen its scope and thereby ensure its continued survival. The members of the cooperative continue to share an aesthetic and philosophical commitment to feminism. In 1998 the press celebrated its 25th anniversary; it is one of the longest operating private presses in America.

Also in 1973 the Boston Women's Health Book Collective published the first edition of its groundbreaking compendium on women's wellness, *Our Bodies, Ourselves.* The 1998 edition of *Our Bodies, Ourselves for the New Century* marked two-and-a-half decades of providing vital health information to women in New England and throughout the world.

In 1975 a lesbian-feminist press was established in Lebanon, N.H. Initially called New Victoria Printers, one year later New Victoria Publishers was formally organized. It was accorded nonprofit status as an educational and cultural corporation to publish books by and about women in 1977. The house, now located in Norwich, Vt., takes its name from the Victoria Press, an all-women print shop in England founded in 1860 by the women's rights activist Emily Faithful.

A gay and lesbian press now called Alyson Publications was launched in Boston by Sasha Alyson in 1977; when it was sold in 1995, it moved to Los Angeles. Elysium Press of North Pomfret, Vt., was founded in 1980 and publishes mostly neglected or overlooked gay literature of the 20th century. Madwoman, a publisher in Northboro, Mass., of lesbian mysteries and fiction, started in 1991 and publishes only works written by lesbians. Hysteria Publications of Bridgeport, Conn., opened in 1993 with a quarterly magazine called *Hysteria* devoted to women's humor. It put out its first book, *Getting in Touch with Your Inner Bitch* by Elizabeth Hilts, the following year. Hysteria describes itself as a publisher of relevant humor for irreverent women, though it is not exclusively a feminist publisher. Circlet Press in Boston focuses on erotic science fiction and fantasy, preferably with gay or lesbian emphasis.

Paris Press, founded in 1995 in Ashfield, Mass., like Alice James and New Victoria, is a nonprofit organization. Jan Freeman established the press to publish neglected or undervalued writers when she discovered that the

Spring Fashions, *from* Godey's Lady's Book *(1854)*

works of the poet Muriel Rukeyser were out of print. The press publishes in all genres and is particularly interested in contemporary feminist works of high literary merit.

Some presses founded since the 1970s have been forced to close shop. These include Astarte Shell Press of Portland, Maine, which grew out of the Feminist Spiritual Community in 1989. This press finally folded in December 1997 after publishing 15 books. They attribute their demise to a decline in feminist bookselling and the rise of large corporate bookstores, which bought large numbers of their books and then returned them for a refund when they did not sell. Astarte went out in a blaze of glory, however, when its last book won the Best Small Press Award in 1997.

Small presses are unusually labor intensive and require a high degree of commitment from their employees to flourish in a competitive market. That and their sensitivity to economic reversals make many of them short-lived.

Many periodicals are produced for feminist and gay or lesbian audiences. They include the *Women's Review of Books,* founded in 1983 as a project of the Wellesley College Center for Research on Women, and *Teen Voices,* which was launched in 1990 to give 12- to 19-year-old girls and young women a magazine with a more feminist perspective than that of most others addressed to the teenage market. Publications with a smaller readership range from *Valley Women's Voice* at the University of Massachusetts, Amherst, founded in 1979, to *Erotic Earthbody,* begun in 1993 in Camden, Maine. Among the many gay and lesbian periodicals currently being published in New England are the Boston-based *Fag Rag* (1970), *Gay Community News* (1973), *Bay Windows* (1983), and *Harvard Gay and Lesbian Review* (1994).

Susan Albertine, ed., *A Living of Words: American Women in Print Culture* (1995); Marie Harris, "Alicejamesbooks: A Cooperation of Poets," *Poets and Writers* 24 (1996); Leona M. Hudak, *Early American Women Printers and Publishers, 1639–1820* (1978); John Tebbel, *Between Covers: The Rise and Transformation of Book Publishing in America* (1987).

Robin Lent

Geography
and Environment

Victor A. Konrad and Theodore L. Steinberg, Section Editors

John E. Carroll, Consulting Editor, Environment

Throughout the United States and abroad, one of the most popular images of the American landscape derives its natural setting, spatial arrangement, and cultural features from New England. The small town clustered around a village green on which stand a white-steepled church and clapboard buildings, surrounded by wooded hills and gently rolling farmland, instantly evokes not only "New England" but "America."

Long before the United States reached to the Pacific Ocean, the country was being identified as an amalgam of discrete "regions": the settled East and the frontier West, the "Yankee" North and the "Confederate" South. As the United States evolved, much of this regional character changed, but New England seemed stuck in a regional identity that had been mostly fixed in the 17th century. Once the six New England states had been established, only minor adjustments to the borders with British North America in the largely uninhabited northern area changed the political boundaries of the region. Yet the definition of New England as a region did not depend merely on this aggregation of six states with common features of settlement, geography, economy, and outlook. Those who came to settle New England fashioned a concept of region defined by its oppositions between arable land and wildland, lowland and upland, coast and inland. This concept expanded the realm of possibility in resource use and settlement, and it allowed for a basic American imperative toward expansion. New England is a region that continues to remake its geography and is a model for regional evolution in other parts of the United States.

PATTERN FOR AMERICA

The geography of New England is filled with examples of transported European practices in the division and use of land. The early colonial arrangement of settled territory within a managed wilderness was reminiscent of the comfortable juxtaposition of cultural and natural areas found in Europe. Today settlements still extend along the region's accessible coast and up river valleys of the Connecticut, Androscoggin, Kennebec, Merrimack, and Penobscot Rivers, avoiding land that is poorly drained and otherwise unsuitable for agriculture. Most towns and villages are established in the valleys—only rarely on ridges or heights of land. The arrangement of New England states, however, reveals a pattern for a national design in state boundaries that cut across rather than conform to natural area boundaries.

European traditions often led to American innovations. The European method of land division by "metes and bounds" forms the irregular survey pattern found in areas settled before the 19th century. After this time, rectangular survey systems were introduced to measure and divide the unoccupied land remaining in the northern and western parts of the region. Early on, public commons were important, but as the emerging United States embraced individual property ownership, New Englanders were in the vanguard of claimants expressing personal rights to land and resources. At the same time, they translated the mutual good of the commons into an ethic of land conservation that would extend across the United States.

On the land and along the coastal waterways, modes of travel and transportation derived from European traditions of wheel and sail. But New Englanders then extended sail transportation to its farthest reach. European innovations of steam and rail were incorporated rapidly and then transferred westward, where their full potential was realized in America's vast open spaces. Waterways also provided energy in the form of waterpower that was harnessed through capturing the force of tidal surges, but most often this power was claimed at the fall line where upland-born streams and rivers descended rapidly down slopes to alluvial valleys and coastal plains. Again, the concept and practice originated in Europe, but New England, with its substantially greater waterpower potential, refined this form of energy production. Waterpower, too, was adapted for hydroelectric production in the region and directed westward.

Although this European inheritance can make America's cultural landscape appear merely derivative, New England was crucial to the emergence of an "American" geography in two primary ways: in the creation of distinctive places and as a cultural hearth. Places that have a distinctly American form or function were first defined in New England—for instance, the mercantile city, with a commercial waterfront at its core and rings of financial, retail, accommodation, administration, and residential space surrounding it. Eighteenth-century Boston is the model, but most New England coastal towns and cities fit this mold. Similarly, New England's early towns and villages established the features characteristic of the American town: a "downtown" area, with central services extending from commerce to worship space to residential neighborhoods. The manufacturing town was developed in this region, as were basic forms of American rural settlement ranging from coastal farm villages to river valley towns and agricultural hamlets. America's resort communities, mining towns, lumber camps, fishing villages, transportation centers, sporting locations, and marketplaces can be traced to initial forms in New England. The definition of *place* in America—as a form of settlement or as a place with a specific function—is rooted in the expression of place, which originated in New England.

New England's cultural geography and its traits have been carried by migrants from the region, adopted by others, and communicated by media ranging from handwritten letters to the Internet. In this way, New England functions as a cultural hearth, or territorial cradle, that helps define and shape American culture generally. Wilbur Zelinsky's essay "New England as Cultural Hearth" in this section explains how this hearth is apparent through inventions, settlement forms, and architectural traditions, but more significantly in the mix of ideas, ideals, and perceptions expressed in everything from speech patterns to spiritual values.

ICE-ALTERED APPALACHIA

Unlike other northern areas of the country, which were only partially buried by ice, New England was covered entirely by the last continental glaciation. In New England, therefore, evidence of glaciation is found in all aspects of the region's physical geography, from its rearranged surface geology to the unique habitats created for humans and animals.

Glaciation created or affected the features that characterize the landscape of New England and shape its geography, from its distinctive islands and inlets to its many smaller bodies of water and ponds to its mountain ridges and polished slopes. Although the ice is gone, the characteristic visual marks of its presence continue to define the region's geography. Landmarks and landscapes acknowledge this powerful glacial legacy. Mount Monadnock's rounded summit, Mount Katahdin's ice-gouged flanks, the scoured valleys of the White Mountains, and the smoothed contours of the heights in Acadia National Park are all defined by the effect of the ice. In Acadia, Jordan Pond is formed behind a moraine—a deposit of gravel and soil at the edge of glacial advance—and ice-borne boulders, or erratics, stand out in the contemporary landscape as features of curiosity in the lore of the park. Cape Cod is a moraine, and Martha's Vineyard and Nantucket Island are composed of glacial deposits. Thousands of modest bodies of water such as the well-known Walden Pond are found in the region's glacial outwash plains, resulting in a distinctive landscape of reflective serenity. Their spirit extends to the mythical and has helped to create powerful images such as those in the film *On Golden Pond.* The landscape of ice-altered Appalachian ridges, glacial deposits, and captured water that formed the physiographic inheritance of New England offered meager resources for traditional agriculture but challenged New Englanders to forge innovative livelihoods from the land and the penetrating sea.

Regional development through resource extraction, land clearance, settlement, and even urbanization has not managed to change the persistent physiographic characteristics of New England much. North-south belts remain distinct: the Green Mountains, the Connecticut River valley, the White Mountains, the eastern hilly belt, and the coastal district. Relief is enhanced from south to north with peaks higher than 4,000 feet in the Green Mountains and one exceeding 6,000 feet in the White Mountains. The coastal plain in southern New England is narrow in Connecticut and enlarged in the Narragansett and Boston Basins of Rhode Island and Massachusetts. North and east of the Boston Basin, the coastal plain is drowned in the Gulf of Maine to produce thousands of islands and peninsulas, abrupt relief alternating with coastal marshlands, and the estuaries of numerous smaller streams. Contained by the curve of eastern New England, Nova Scotia, and New Brunswick and the shallows of Georges Bank, the Gulf of Maine and adjacent Bay of Fundy act

Connecticut River valley, 1956

as an immense aquatic engine with energy unleashed in massive tides and rapid currents to sustain a highly developed food chain of sea life. This offshore component of New England continues to contribute to the region's geographical definition, which includes mountain, valley, and sea.

LANDSCAPE TRANSITIONS

To achieve its stability of regional definition and character, New England has endured more than four centuries of transition. Landscape transitions may be measured on related scales of forestation and agricultural land use, where forest has given way to farms and in time reclaimed abandoned farmland. Transitions may also be traced through changing concepts of settlements, from rural village to industrial town and back again to the celebration of smaller places such as Woodstock, Vt., and Litchfield, Conn.

Transitions may be experienced most readily on the land as an observer moves across the lines that differentiate the geography of the region. Despite the fact that maritime areas have been an integral part of the region since European settlement, most New Englanders today tend to look landward. The landscape transitions from urban to suburban that they encounter in their daily routines are similar to the changes from central city to bedroom community found in any American city.

Beyond the city, one encounters the first landscape transition characteristic of New England: wildland, generally reforested or abandoned from agricultural use, is found adjacent to even the largest cities, providing a sharp contrast to the urban fabric. Although this wildland is most visible from the highways that have been designed to speed up travel between larger centers, it is the local roads, winding their way through strands of towns and villages, that move to the next transition line and lead the observer through agricultural enclaves and gentrified rural landscapes.

At points where these roads climb out of river valleys or off the coastal plain, they encounter slopes and uplands reclaimed by forest and poorly drained swales in between the uplands. In Connecticut, Massachusetts, and Rhode Island, these residual lands form enclaves between broad corridors of movement and settlement that extend north and west from the coast. In the northern states, "up-country" New England predominates, with landscapes of enveloping forest punctuated here and there by mill towns.

In the northwestern corner of the region, roads leave the forest, drop into the Lake Champlain valley, and lead to Burlington, Vt. At the northeastern tip of Maine, the forest gives way to potato fields in the Aroostook and Saint John River valleys and accommodates a cluster of Yankee farming communities near a string of Acadian French street villages. These northern agricultural enclaves remain more viable than most of the surviving farmland in southern New England, where only the Connecticut River valley retains a significant commitment to agricultural production, ranging from specialized shade tobacco and fruit growing to generalized mixed farming. Although vigorous farmland preservation policies are in effect throughout New England, the average farm acreage declined by approximately 80 percent during the 20th century.

Forests, by contrast, cover most of the region, and more than 30 million acres, or approximately 75 percent of the region, is classified as commercial forest. Almost all this forest is regenerated, following numerous cuttings, and the main product now is wood pulp rather than timber. The forest landscape is more pervasive today than at any time during the 20th century, but it is mostly a landscape of smaller deciduous trees rather than the original coniferous species.

These forests cloak substantial evidence of transitions in land use, such as the miles of abandoned stone walls and unused roads found under their canopy. Remnants of buildings, usually cellar holes and foundations, also survive beside an early industrial infrastructure of dams, millworks, canals, kilns, and railroad grades. But also in the forest landscape of today are recreational facilities and camps for every conceivable wilderness pursuit. They circle accessible lakes and ponds to herald a new, prevailing pattern in the geography of New England: throughout the region, recreational landscapes are coming to predominate.

The use of the land for recreation, with an associated emphasis on historic preservation, conservation, and transportation improvements, has made New England a major destination for activities ranging from canoeing to exploring historic districts in towns. This transition has contributed substantially to regional stability and prosperity, for unlike many other economic activities, recreation and tourism prevail in every state as major contributors to New England's economy. In recent years, more recreational facilities have become "four-season destinations," combining golf courses, ski slopes, hiking trails, and water sports. Recreational land use has merged with retailing in popular destinations from Freeport, Maine, to Brattleboro, Vt., to Newport, R.I. Places throughout New England are stacking and integrating recreational opportunities in order to attract visitors from inside and outside the region. Nowhere is this more evident than along coastal Route 1, where attractions are displayed in a veritable market lane for the passing motorist. In sharp contrast, the Appalachian Trail follows the height of land and moves through wilderness southwest from Mount Katahdin in Maine to the New York boundary and on down to Georgia.

Some analysts see New England as a "bypassed" region, claiming that its relative economic position sagged as people, companies, and capital moved west and south. For instance, the decline that occurred as the textile industry relocated to southern states persuaded observers, particularly those outside the region, that New England could not adjust. Yet the region has been adapting to the loss of its initial advantages of geography and history throughout the 20th century and into the 21st. The industrial sector, for example, has abandoned most basic manufacturing and retained only profitable industries that depend on highly skilled labor, much of it in high-tech industries. Some basic processing of natural resources remains viable throughout northern New England. This transition in function is most apparent in southern New England, for much of its industry has disappeared and the economic landscape is concentrated with service and information and management functions. In the fields of insurance services and education, for example, New England is a national leader, particularly in Boston and specialized centers such as Hartford (although back-office operations, for example, an MBNA bank-processing center, have moved out of Boston and Hartford to places such as Belfast, Maine). The industrial landscape remains visible—some sites preserved, such as Lowell National Historical Park; some recycled, as in the case of Digital Equipment Corporation's old mill headquarters—but most is in decay. The relic industrial landscape in most New England towns and cities extends from the former workplaces to rows of one-story mill housing and three-decker tenements.

Some might say that New England has withstood the inevitable change and rejuvenation that come with transition because the region's forms have been created from rock and brick and stubborn "Yankee" intentions. These markers of successive industrial accomplishment—the creation of larger and more complex mills, for example, or the persistence of accumulated and connected farm buildings—attest to the durability of New England's past but also draw a rich, detailed map of the region in space and time. These touchstones of the past mark the points of significance, establishing and sustaining the formative American region. Furthermore, they record the milestones of economic and social achievement and the values inherent in creating a national dream of power and wealth.

GEOGRAPHICAL VALUE

New England is a storehouse of geographical features, patterns, landmarks, and processes, and the region portrays these geographical elements in landscapes that are easy to read, with rewarding insights for observers. Herein lies the geographical value of New England. A great deal may be learned about human and cultural geography by examining the characteristics of New England's patterns of religious affiliation, arrangement of ethnic groups, concentrations of language, expressions of political viewpoints, and distribution of the general population. Each of these dimensions reveals the cumulative diversity of historical ties and the dynamic reality of interaction on the continuum from work pressure in the metropolis to the sublimity of life in the hinterlands.

The six-state region contains a population of 13.9 million (2000 census)—the smallest census division in the United States with the slowest growth rate. New England is a region in the mature stage of demographic development, with low, stable levels of fertility and mortality, a small net loss in population because of limited internal U.S. migration, and few international immigrants in recent years (see table). Massachusetts, Connecticut, and Rhode Island are among the most densely populated states in the country, but Maine, New Hampshire, and Vermont have population densities well below the region's average of 211 people per square mile. In these northern states, the population is also increasingly elderly. The relatively small minority population of New England is concentrated in urban areas, accounting for less than 2 percent of the population in rural areas.

Recent immigrants from Asia, Africa, and the West Indies; African Americans; and large ethnic groups of Portuguese and Polish ancestry are found almost exclusively in urban areas. Irish, Jewish, and Italian groups have a longer history in the more heavily populated states. People of Irish ancestry are found throughout New England's cities and towns, and along with those who claim English, Scottish, German, French, and Swedish ancestry they form the ethnic tapestry that accounts for most of the population throughout the region. Although ethnic group settlements may be found in places ranging from New Sweden, Maine, to the Irish neighborhoods of South Boston, most New Englanders who claim western European ancestry have allowed their ethnic identities to fade. The French, and particularly the French Canadians, are the exception. Canadians from Quebec and Acadians, largely from Atlantic Canada, often merged in large, exclusive communities of French Canadians in mill towns throughout the region, including Waterville, Augusta, Lewiston, and Biddeford, Maine; Woonsocket, R.I.; Lowell, Fall River, and New Bedford, Mass.; Nashua and Manchester, N.H.; New Haven and Bridgeport, Conn.; and Winooski, Vt. Traditional rural French settlement areas are found in

Demographics of New England

	Connecticut		Maine		Massachusetts		New Hampshire		Rhode Island		Vermont		New England	
	Number	%	Number	%	Number	%	Number	%	Number	%	Number	%	Number	%
Population	3,405,565	100	1,274,923	100	6,349,097	100	1,235,786	100	1,048,319	100	608,827	100	13,922,517	100
Males	1,649,319	48	620,309	49	3,058,816	48	607,687	49	503,635	48	298,337	49	6,738,103	48
Females	1,756,246	52	654,614	51	3,290,281	52	628,099	51	544,684	52	310,490	51	7,184,414	52
0 to 19 years old	925,702	27	335,485	26	1,675,113	26	344,165	28	282,616	27	166,257	27	3,729,338	27
20 to 34 years old	639,211	19	227,273	18	1,331,067	21	228,827	19	212,139	20	112,419	14	2,750,936	20
35 to 54 years old	1,061,856	31	405,576	32	1,936,348	31	405,165	33	312,173	30	195,721	32	4,316,839	31
55 to 84 years old	714,523	21	283,273	22	1,289,877	20	242,398	19	220,494	21	124,434	25	2,874,999	21
Over 85	64,273	2	23,316	2	116,692	2	18,231	2	20,897	2	9,996	2	253,405	2
Race/ethnicity														
White	2,780,355	82	1,236,014	97	5,367,286	85	1,186,581	96	891,191	85	589,208	97	12,050,905	87
Black or African American	309,843	9	6,760	0.5	343,454	5	9,035	0.7	46,908	5	3,063	0.5	719,063	5
American Indian and Alaska native	9,639	0.3	7,098	0.6	15,015	0.2	2,964	0.2	5,121	0.5	2,420	0.4	42,257	0.3
Asian	82,313	2	9,111	0.7	238,124	4	15,931	1	23,664	2	5,217	0.9	374,340	3
Hispanic (any race)	320,323	9	9,360	0.7	428,729	7	20,489	2	90,820	9	5,504	0.9	875,225	6
School enrollment (population 3 years and older enrolled in school	910,869	100	321,041	100	1,726,111	100	332,888	100	290,605	100	164,156	100	3,745,670	100
Nursery school and kindergarten	115,886	13	33,040	10	209,409	12	36,767	11	30,650	11	17,256	11	443,008	12
Elementary school	401,109	44	146,178	46	703,094	41	151,310	46	118,468	41	70,680	43	1,590,839	42
High school	189,662	21	74,607	23	340,205	20	69,979	21	54,478	20	35,902	22	767,833	20
College or graduate school	204,212	22	67,216	21	473,403	27	74,832	23	84,009	29	40,318	25	943,990	25
Educational attainment (age 25 and older)	2,295,617	100	869,893	100	4,273,275	100	823,987	100	694,573	100	404,223	100	9,361,568	100
High school graduate or higher	1,927,961	84	742,605	85	3,622,182	85	720,233	87	541,487	78	349,317	86	7,903,7859	84
Bachelor's degree or higher	720,994	31	198,960	23	1,418,295	33	236,104	29	177,817	26	119,025	29	2,871,195	31
Marital status (population age 15 and older)	2,969,250	100	1,028,823	100	5,091,369	100	978,641	100	841,503	100	488,281	100	11,397,867	100
Never married	732,266	27	245,864	24	1,581,452	31	243,840	25	249,556	30	130,410	27	3,183,388	29
Now married	1,483,688	55	579,456	56	2,631,643	52	560,995	57	433,554	50	269,304	55	5,959,640	54
Separated	42,556	2	12,555	1	100,839	2	13,320	1	16,022	2	6,161	1	191,453	2
Widowed	188,033	7	73,012	7	354,485	7	57,763	6	63,120	8	30,836	6	767,249	7
Divorced	249,707	9	117,936	12	422,950	8	102,723	11	79,251	9	51,570	11	1,024,137	9
Veterans (population age 18 and older)	310,068	12	154,590	16	558,933	12	139,038	15	102,494	13	62,809	14	1,327,932	12
People with a disability (population age 5 and older)	546,813	18	237,910	20	1,084,746	19	193,893	17	195,806	20	97,167	17	2,356,335	19
Nativity														
Native to United States	3,035,598	89	1,238,232	97	5,576,114	88	1,181,632	96	929,042	89	585,582	96	12,546,200	90

(continued)

Demographics of New England (continued)

	Connecticut		Maine		Massachusetts		New Hampshire		Rhode Island		Vermont		New England	
	Number	%	Number	%	Number	%	Number	%	Number	%	Number	%	Number	%
Born in state of residence	1,940,576	57	857,515	67	4,196,702	66	534,558	43	643,912	61	330,528	54	8,503,791	61
Foreign born	369,967	11	36,691	3	772,983	12	54,154	4	119,277	11	23,245	4	1,376,317	10
Region of birth of foreign born (excluding born at sea)	369,961	100	36,689	100	772,972	100	54,154	100	119,277	100	23,245	100	1,376,298	100
Europe	141,141	38	11,000	30	248,614	32	18,248	34	39,221	33	8,971	39	467,195	34
Asia	70,156	19	6,949	19	201,598	26	13,481	25	19,578	16	4,455	19	316,217	23
Africa	9,748	3	1,067	3	47,770	6	1,864	3	12,066	10	511	2	73,026	5
Oceania	1,388	0.4	239	0.7	2,517	0.3	350	0.6	397	0.3	173	0.7	5,064	0.4
Latin America	128,267	35	2,197	6	231,759	30	7,759	14	43,892	37	1,210	5	415,084	30
Northern America	19,261	5	15,237	42	40,714	5	12,452	23	4,123	4	7,925	34	99,712	7
Language spoken at home (population 5 years and older)	3,184,514	100	1,204,164	100	5,954,249	100	1,160,340	100	985,184	100	574,842	100	13,063,293	100
English only	2,600,601	82	1,110,198	92	4,838,679	81	1,064,252	92	788,560	80	540,767	84	10,943,057	84
Language other than English	583,913	18	93,966	8	1,115,570	19	96,088	8	196,624	20	34,075	6	2,120,236	16
Spanish	268,044	8	9,611	0.8	370,011	6	18,647	2	79,443	8	5,791	1	751,547	6
Other Indo-European language	251,335	8	76,079	6	529,784	9	64,067	6	91,449	9	24,334	4	1,037,048	8
Asian and Pacific Island language	47,993	2	5,737	.5	171,253	3	9,891	1	19,926	2	3,015	.5	257,815	2
Occupation (Employed, age 16 and older)	1,664,440	100	525,690	100	3,161,087	100	650,871	100	500,731	100	317,134	100	6,918,274	100
Management, professional, and related	651,385	39	196,862	32	1,298,704	41	232,927	36	169,994	34	115,136	36	2,665,008	39
Service occupations	237,406	14	95,601	15	444,298	14	84,618	13	78,539	16	46,384	15	986,846	14
Sales and office	440,288	27	161,480	26	818,844	26	173,282	27	135,754	27	77,608	25	1,807,256	26
Farming, fishing, and forestry	3,446	0.2	10,338	2	6,642	0.2	2,902	0.4	1,715	0.3	4,160	1	29,203	0.4
Construction and maintenance	132,878	8	64,064	10	235,876	8	60,988	9	38,437	8	29,562	9	561,805	8
Production, transportation, and material moving	199,037	12	95,666	15	356,723	11	96,154	15	76,292	15	44,284	14	868,156	13
Income (dollars)														
Median household income	53,935		37,240		50,502		49,467		42,090		40,856		45,682	
Per capita income	28,766		19,533		25,952		23,844		21,688		20,625		23,401	
Median male income for full-time, year-round workers	45,787		32,372		43,048		39,689		37,587		32,457		38,490	
Median female income for full-time, year-round workers	33,318		24,251		32,059		27,488		27,583		25,322		28,299	
Poverty status														
Families	49,983	6	26,611	8	105,619	7	13,498	4	23,608	9	9,925	6	229,694	6
Families with female householder	29,897	20	13,327	28	61,880	22	7,237	18	14,611	29	5,107	24	132,059	22
Individuals	259,514	8	135,501	11	573,421	9	78,530	7	120,548	12	55,506	9	1,223,020	9

Source: U.S. Census (2000)

northern Vermont, where they spilled over from Quebec during the 19th century, and in northern Maine, where the Acadian community that formed during the 18th century was divided by the international boundary in 1842.

French Canadians also have shown the greatest resistance to linguistic assimilation, for French is still spoken in the region more than any other language except English and Spanish. Newcomer linguistic groups include more than a dozen from Asia, with Chinese, Indic, and Arabic heading the list. Languages spoken by immigrants early in the 20th century—Italian, Polish, Yiddish, German, Swedish, Russian, and others—have either been lost or are spoken by substantially smaller numbers of people. Portuguese is one of the few languages that has grown in the number of speakers because of the sustained infusion of new immigrants. Except for French, all these languages are spoken mainly in urban areas of the region.

New England is primarily Anglophone throughout. Its distinct English dialect had its roots in southwestern England but evolved a unique nasal twang and vocabulary. Regionally specific terms such as *brook* and *pond,* as well as numerous references to the Native American geography, and the clustering of settlement names (for example, Conway, North Conway, and Conway Station) characterize the map of New England place-names.

The map of religion in New England is less distinctive, as its patterns reflect those of the United States in general. In urban areas, religious affiliation is linked to ethnic distribution, particularly of groups arrived recently from Asia and Europe. Mosques and inner-city church buildings recycled by other Eastern religions speak to the religious diversity of the immigrant communities. Catholicism remains unusually strong in the cities and mill towns with active Irish, Italian, Portuguese, Hispanic, and French parishes. New Englanders of French Canadian descent retain the faith more strongly than their Quebec cousins. Also apparent in the geography of religion in New England is a growing acceptance of evangelical Protestant ministries in the northern tier of states. Churches and congregations are large, often with associated Christian schools and media ministries similar to those found in the southern United States.

The political map of New England similarly traces lines of religious and ethnic distribution. Parts of Maine, Vermont, and particularly New Hampshire are acknowledged for conservative political viewpoints expressed in Republican and often independent voting patterns. Liberal Republicanism has a strong New England base. Swings to the right are accompanied by equally strong swings to the left or center and shade the political map as Democrat territory more often than not. Massachusetts, in particular, is generally characterized by liberal leanings from local to national politics. Overall, New England's highly educated and politically astute population participates actively in politics at all levels. The region introduced the town meeting to the nation and continues to provide "bellwether" readings on national political affairs from all its states, but particularly from the incisive opinions of Maine, New Hampshire, and Vermont residents.

Throughout New England, as in other parts of the country, cultural values often come from and are nurtured by the community. If ethnic group identification is strong within a community, ethnicity may guide the development of cultural values. Similarly, religion, language, political orientation, and demographic characteristics such as age may help fashion outlook and identity. In New England, particularly for longtime residents, geography also contributes to the process of shaping and integrating concepts of identity. Many residents of northern New England, for instance, align an explicit sense of identity with state allegiance, often summed up in state mottoes such as New Hampshire's "Live Free or Die" and Maine's "The Way Life Should Be."

Geography has profoundly influenced the development of regional affiliation and cultural identity in New England. New Englanders align themselves and establish their cultural positions within the geographical continuum from urban core, with Boston's centrality, to upland periphery. The Yankee identity is constructed in part by knowing one's location on this continuum and is further detailed relative to the places, landmarks, and landscapes that New England's residents experience. Expressions such as "round the pond," "upside the lighthouse," and "next door" still hold substantial meaning.

Perhaps the most compelling motive revealed in the geography of New England is its residents' sustained commitment to access, yet conserve, the wilderness. These words written by Henry David Thoreau in September 1853 on the occasion of his trip to Chesuncook in Maine capture the sentiments that would lead him and other New Englanders to spread this emerging conservation ethic across the United States: "Why should not we, who have renounced the King's authority, have our national preserves, where no villages need be destroyed, in which the bear and panther, and some even of the hunter race, may still exist, and not be 'civilized off the face of the earth,'—our forests, not to hold the King's game merely, but to hold and preserve the King himself, the Lord of Creation,—not for idle sport of food, but for inspiration and our own true recreation? Or shall we, like villains, grub them all up, poaching on our own national domains?"

New England's future as a viable region depends on the continued enshrinement of this fundamental value of enlightened conservation. It guides the persistence of a regional geography that is mature in its patterns and sustainable in its structure and design.

James P. Allen and Eugene J. Turner, *We the People: An Atlas of America's Ethnic Diversity* (1988); Emerson W. Baker, Edwin A. Churchill, Richard S. D'Abate, Kristine L. Jones, Victor A. Konrad, and Harald E. L. Prins, eds., *American Beginnings: Exploration, Culture and Cartography in the Land of Norumbega* (1994); Dona Brown, *Inventing New England: Regional Tourism in the 19th Century* (1995); Michael Conzen and George K. Lewis, *Boston: A Geographical Portrait* (1976); William Cronon, *Changes in the Land: Indians, Colonists, and the Ecology of New England* (1992); Bruce C. Daniels, *The Connecticut Town: Growth and Development* (1979); Ron Fisher, *The Appalachian Trail* (1972); Stewart H. Holbrook, *The Yankee Exodus: An Account of Migration from New England* (1950); Stephen J. Hornsby, Victor Konrad, and James Herlan, eds., *The Northeastern Borderlands: Four Centuries of Interaction* (1989); Lloyd C. Ireland, *Wildlands and Woodlots: The Story of New England's Forests* (1982); Donald S. Janelle, ed., *Geographical Snapshots of North America* (1992); Hans Kurath, *Handbook of the Linguistic Geography of New England* (1973); Richard Lingeman, *Small Town America: A Narrative History, 1620–the Present* (1980); Dean R. Louder and Eric Waddell, eds., *French America: Mobility, Identity, and Minority Experience across the Continent* (1993); Joseph McCarty, *New England* (1967); Lois K. Mathews, *The Expansion of New England: The Spread of New England Settle-*

ment and Institutions to the Mississippi River, 1620–1865 (1962); Douglas R. McManis, *Colonial New England: A Historical Geography* (1975); Donald W. Meinig, *Atlantic America, 1492–1800,* vol. 1 of Meinig, *The Shaping of America: A Geographical Perspective on 500 Years of History* (1986); David R. Meyer, *From Farm to Factory: Urban Change in Central Connecticut* (1976); J. H. Paterson, "New England," in *North America* (1989); Neal R. Peirce, *The New England States* (1976); William F. Robinson, *Abandoned New England* (1978); Howard S. Russell, *A Long Deep Furrow: Three Centuries of Farming in New England* (1976); Dean R. Snow, *The Archeology of New England* (1980); John R. Stilgoe, *Borderland: Origins of the American Suburb, 1820–1939* (1988); Stilgoe, *Common Landscape of America, 1580 to 1845* (1982); Henry D. Thoreau, *The Maine Woods* (1972 [1864]); James E. Vance, Jr., *Capturing the Horizon: The Historical Geography of Transportation since the Transportation Revolution of the 16th Century* (1986); Joseph S. Wood, *The New England Village* (1997); Wilbur Zelinsky, *The Cultural Geography of the United States* (1992).

Victor A. Konrad

INTRODUCTION, ENVIRONMENT

"Wherever [man] plants his foot," wrote the Vermont statesman and conservationist George Perkins Marsh, "the harmonies of nature are turned to discords." In his book *Man and Nature; or, Physical Geography as Modified by Human Action* (1864), at that time the most thorough treatise on land management ever written, Marsh wrote both of humankind's abuse of nature and of its moral obligation to find a more stable way of conversing with the natural world. "The equation of animal and vegetable life," he cautioned, "is too complicated a problem for human intelligence to solve, and we can never know how wide a circle of disturbance we produce in the harmonies of nature when we throw the smallest pebble in the ocean of organic life." Marsh advised his readers to deal discreetly and humbly with nature or perhaps risk losing species whose potential benefit to human beings might not yet be understood.

Marsh, a native of Woodstock, Vt., based his prescription for establishing harmony between humankind and nature on his own firsthand experience as a farmer and observer of the New England landscape. During his lifetime, New England's agricultural mode of production gave way to industrialization, a process that left deep, lasting marks on the region's landscape and waterscape. By the mid-19th century, economic development had forged its way across the region, leaving in its wake vast expanses of cutover land, widespread pollution, and the early stages of urban sprawl. It is no surprise that both Marsh and kindred spirit Henry David Thoreau, two of the nation's earliest and greatest environmental thinkers, developed their ideas within a region being racked by the demands of a burgeoning economic order. New England has long been the scene of both profound environmental change and conservationist thinking.

A popular New England saying has it that "if you don't like the weather, wait a minute, and it will change." There was and continues to be a great deal of truth in this observation. Often determined by a clash of cold, dry air bearing down from the north with warm, moist air flowing up from the south, New England's weather patterns can change in the blink of an eye, a fact that has cost the life of many an Atlantic fisher. Generally speaking, most of the region has a temperate climate, fairly evenly divided into four discrete seasons. Each year the skies can also be counted on to yield an average of 40 to 45 inches of precipitation, an abundance of moisture that, in this respect at least, makes the region more suitable for farming than the arid sections of the American West.

Inland New England is dominated by mountains, all of them part of the Appalachian system. Most famous are the White Mountains, which begin in western

Maine and continue on a northeast-southwest diagonal into northern New Hampshire. The White Mountains are home to the Presidential Range and Mount Washington, the highest point in the northeastern United States, at 6,288 feet. The mountains take their name from their grayish-white granite peaks and sides. The Green Mountains, so dubbed for the lush foliage that dominates them, extend from the Connecticut River, which separates Vermont from neighboring New Hampshire, to the border of New York state. Overall, the Green Mountains have been subject to heavy erosion over the years and thus rise to less lofty heights than the White Mountains. Their tallest peak, Mount Mansfield, is only about 4,400 feet high.

Among New England's other major resources is a coastline whose 6,000 miles of inlets, peninsulas, and bays stretch from the eastern tip of Maine to Stamford, Conn., on Long Island Sound. Along this expanse are the countless harbors that have allowed New Englanders to harvest—at times too aggressively—the rich bounty of the sea. Offshore fishing spots such as the Grand Banks and Georges Bank, until the mid-20th century, were among the most productive fisheries within striking distance of U.S. shores.

New England's major rivers—the Connecticut, Merrimack, Housatonic, and Kennebec, all of which flow in a southerly direction through the region—have been valuable resources, too. Until the 19th century migrating species of fish pushed their way upstream, providing New Englanders, and before them Native Americans, with an ample source of food. Meanwhile, Native Americans and Yankee farmers reaped plentiful crops in some of the river valley lowlands, such as those of the Connecticut River. These lowlands have been abundantly productive, agriculturally speaking— far more so than the stonier uplands, which are suited only for growing trees.

When Europeans first settled New England in the 17th century, the area consisted of three basic vegetative regions. Most of Maine, northern and central New Hampshire, Vermont, and the extreme western part of Massachusetts were dominated by a spruce and hardwood forest. White pine and hemlock covered southern Maine, southern New Hampshire, three-fourths of Massachusetts, and the northern reaches of Connecticut and Rhode Island. Along the coastal region of Massachusetts, southern Connecticut, and Rhode Island lay a forest made up chiefly of oak and chestnut trees. In short, New England's original forest was both rich and diverse, a fact that impressed more than a few European explorers and settlers.

On the whole, the Native Americans who inhabited the region before European colonization survived by practicing agriculture, hunting game, and gathering nuts and berries. There were regional differences, however. Those Indians north of the Kennebec River in Maine were exclusively hunters and gatherers. In the spring these northern Indians would migrate to river and coastal areas to avail themselves of smelt, alewives, sturgeon, and salmon. Men of these villages set up weirs made of brush across the region's rivers to snag their prey. They also took to the water in canoes to spear fish from New England's many lakes. During the summer months women collected clams and other shellfish as well as raspberries, strawberries, blueberries, wild plums, and cherries. In the fall the villages moved inland again, breaking into smaller groups to hunt moose, deer, bear, beaver, and caribou. Typically, men hunted and killed the game, and women slaughtered and prepared the meat.

The Indians of southern New England practiced a more diverse form of subsistence. In addition to hunting and gathering, they also planted crops. Because their food base was far more varied, it is not surprising to find that population densities in the south tended to be significantly higher than they were in the north.

Villagers broke into bands during the fall and winter, and adult males, like their northern counterparts, tracked game through the snow. But instead of simply fishing and gathering wild foods in the summer and fall, the Indians of southern New England practiced a form of shifting agriculture. Under this system of farming, fields were planted and tilled for eight to 12 years and then were abandoned and allowed to return to forest. Although the Indians may not have been aware of the ecological benefits of this farming method, their decision to migrate after several years of land use gave the soil a chance to recover its nutrients. The main crops—corn, beans, and squash—were often mixed together in the field. This helped lessen the likelihood that they would fall prey to insects, another way in which native agriculture proved itself sustainable. The crops were often planted—between March and June—by women, who had a more important role in the system of subsistence than Indian women in the north. Thus New England's early European settlers found numerous cleared and cultivated fields along the region's river valleys. Indeed, the colonists were evidently so impressed with the areas Native Americans had cleared that they chose precisely these spots for their own towns.

Fire proved an important tool for the southern Indians as they carved out a living on the land. It was used to clear areas for planting and to drive game so that they could be hunted more efficiently. Whether by chance or by design, burning the land had at least one positive ecological effect: it recycled nutrients into the ground and increased the soil's fertility. The burned-over landscape also helped the Indians improve their hunting prospects by creating a congenial habitat that attracted deer, beaver, turkey, and other species. Thus when the Europeans arrived, they found not a completely untouched expanse of forest but a landscape punctuated by huge areas that had large trees and no shrubs and were filled with grass, much like a park.

When European ships arrived on the shores of New England, they brought with them the makings of what the historian Carolyn Merchant has called a full-scale "ecological revolution." The most devastating change was caused by the diseases Europeans brought ashore, which would eventually kill four-fifths of New England's native population. Before the Europeans came, Indians had never been exposed to smallpox, plague, yellow fever, or other illnesses common in Europe, so they had no immunity to them. Mortality rates of 80 percent or more were not unheard of among New England natives. In 1633 a smallpox epidemic in southern New England killed 95 percent of the residents of some villages. The population of Native Americans decreased from roughly 70,000 in 1600 to only 15,000 in 1675.

Apart from new diseases, the colonists also brought with them an array of plants and animals that were previously unknown in New England. Horses, sheep, goats, cows, and pigs came over in large numbers and were set free to forage in pasture-lands. The increase in livestock led in turn to a rise in predators such as bears, foxes, and wolves, which made short work of the domesticated animals. To lower the number of predators, towns offered bounties. Lynn, Mass., for example, paid a per-head price for most of the 428 foxes killed in the town between 1698 and 1722.

The domesticated animals were just one element in an entirely new agricultural regime—at least for New England—that involved the cultivation of grains such as rye, wheat, barley, and oats, none of which had been planted in the region before the colonists arrived. The Europeans also brought with them carrots, turnips, cabbage, lettuce, and cucumbers, among other vegetables unfamiliar to the Native Americans. The new and abundant crops—much like the imported livestock—swelled the ranks of other predator populations. Gray squirrels, raccoons, blackbirds, and crows feasted on the colonists' croplands.

A few unwanted plants—dandelions, stinging nettles, sow thistles, wormwood, and other weeds—were unintentionally brought to New England among the new-comers' luggage. Pests such as the black rat and the cockroach stowed away aboard the colonists' ships. By 1740 the rat population had spread as far inland as Pomfret, Conn. Together, these new arrivals helped to further change the makeup of New England's ecology.

But next to the devastating effect of disease, it was the colonists' cultural baggage that made the biggest imprint on the way the New England landscape looked and functioned. Two institutions in particular were central here, both of which had a long, enduring history in western Europe: the market and private property.

While it is true that Native Americans were no strangers to trade, it is also true that for them trade was entirely local, revolving mainly around exchanges between neighboring villages. The Europeans, however, succeeded in forging a much broader regional and international economy. The fur trade, for example, involved the creation of trading links between Britain, where beaver hats were popular during the 17th century among the commercial elite, and Indian hunters in northern New England, who traded the pelts for corn and other material goods. Within the new trade context, beavers, which had once been used simply to satisfy native subsistence needs, had a price attached to them. The ecological consequences of this change were dramatic. Now pressures that transcended local needs and boundaries compelled Indians in New England to kill more game than ever before. By 1800 the region's population of beaver, fox, mink, and other fur-bearing creatures, transformed into market commodities, had been annihilated.

Apart from having no conception of price, the Indians also did not think of land itself as something one could own to the exclusion of others. In other words, the concept of private property was foreign to their way of relating to the environment. The Indians claimed only the limited right to use land for hunting, gathering, and farming. Thus different villages could use the same hunting grounds without any of them asserting an exclusive property right. Indians claimed the resources of the land—game, nuts, berries, fish—but did not possess or own the land.

The colonists saw things differently. To them land was something with discrete boundaries that could be fenced and owned and, ultimately, exchanged. Over the course of the 17th and 18th centuries, the colonists drew more and more of New England's landscape into the legal domain of private property, carefully recording the boundaries of various property interests in deed books located in county courthouses. As the historian William Cronon has observed, "More than anything else, it was the treatment of land and property as commodities traded at market that distinguished English conceptions of ownership from Indian ones."

Perhaps nowhere in New England did the Europeans' capitalist culture have a more apparent effect than on the region's forests. European travelers and explorers were initially struck by the incredible expanse of forest that existed in the region when they came despite the Indian custom of thinning the woodlands by fire. John Winthrop, the governor of Massachusetts Bay Colony, commented on the dense knot of trees and brush found along the coast to the north and south of Boston. Thick woods lay near at hand throughout the area. Yet as early as 1637 the timber supply in the immediate vicinity of Boston had been logged out, and lumber had to be shipped in by boat from Cape Ann. It was primarily the colonists' use of wood for fuel that had put such a huge dent in the available supply.

During the 1630s commercial lumbering operations began on the rivers north of the Merrimack in Maine and New Hampshire. Britain was in the middle of a major timber shortage at this time, and many saw New England's vast forest reserves as a ready source for ships' masts, planks, clapboards, and other construction materials. Seventeenth-century material culture depended heavily on wood, and demand for the resource was great. New England's trees, much like the region's fur-bearing animals, were thus transformed into commodities to be exchanged on a trans-Atlantic market. Sailing ships generally needed enough wood for 23 masts, cross-yards, and a bowsprit. A large vessel might need a mast some 120 feet in length, a dimension that no longer could be found in the forests of Russia or Germany. Seventeenth-century New England, by contrast, had plenty of tall trees for the taking.

Export figures for the period from 1768 through 1772 make New England's major role in commercial lumbering in the Atlantic economy amply clear. During those five years 233 million feet of boards and planks were exported from ports up and down the East Coast. Significantly, one-third of the colonies' timber exports came from the hinterlands along the Piscataqua River, along the border between New Hampshire and Maine.

Relentless pressure on the forest resources of New England led inevitably to their destruction. Thoreau noted as early as the first half of the 19th century that only second-growth forest existed around his home at Walden Pond. As he quipped, the original forest was being cut down so quickly that "we shall all be obliged to let our beards grow at least, if only to hide the nakedness of the land and make a sylvan appearance." When Charles Dickens visited the area in 1842, he remarked on the miles of cutover land that he saw as he traveled north from Boston by train. By 1880 only 27 percent of Connecticut and 34 percent of Rhode Island were still forested. Moreover, the ecological effects of this exploitation were becoming increasingly clear. Deforestation tended to make the land warmer in summer and colder in winter. It led to increased flooding and caused some streams simply to dry up. It also increased erosion in some places. In short, the pillaging of New England's woods had by the 19th century led to a thoroughgoing change in the region's ecology.

In the midst of the wholesale destruction of the region's forestlands, another stunning change—with far-reaching consequences for the New England environment—was taking place. Beginning early in the 1800s merchant capitalists in Boston began to turn their attention to manufacturing, investing in textile mills that relied on waterpower for energy. The Industrial Revolution was set to begin.

The city of Lowell, Mass., on the banks of the Merrimack River played a key role in New England's early industrial history, serving as a model for textile cities on waterways throughout the region. Lowell was founded and developed by the Boston Associates, a small group of prominent, wealthy New England entrepreneurs who invested in textile factories there in the 1820s. Like land, furs, and lumber, water was transformed into a commodity and sold to companies that manufactured cotton cloth. To change water into a commodity involved controlling it to a degree never before attained in New England. The Boston Associates built an elaborate water-control infrastructure at Lowell consisting of a complex network of dams and power canals. Eventually the system pioneered at Lowell was exported to textile cities throughout New England. Up and down the Merrimack River at places such as Lawrence, Mass., and Nashua and Manchester, N.H., and on other rivers, such as the Androscoggin, Saco, Cocheco, Chicopee, Taunton, and Connecticut, textile mills sprouted like mushrooms.

The industrial control of water had profound environmental and social consequences. For example, dams and millponds created for supplying waterpower to factories tended to flood land upstream, especially valuable meadowland from which farmers had customarily harvested hay. Conflict thus erupted between farmers with hay to cut and downstream mill owners concerned with maintaining an adequate supply of waterpower for their mills.

Dams across the region's rivers also helped block the passage of migrating species of fish, spoiling New England's river fisheries, which had served even as late as the early 19th century as an important source of food for the region's farmers. In 1820, before the creation of the factory towns along the Merrimack, one observer estimated that some 2,500 barrels of salmon, shad, and alewife were caught each year at East Chelmsford, Mass., the rural town that would eventually become the city of Lowell. However, the building of dams on the Merrimack, especially the Great Stone Dam in Lawrence, completed in 1848—more than 30 feet wide and 900 feet across—finished off the river fisheries. The dams not only blocked the passage of fish, they affected the river's stream flow, which may have reduced the spawning runs. Fish are likely to migrate upstream when stimulated by rising water. The retention of the water to conserve waterpower may have hindered their upstream migration.

The factories and their dams not only blocked the passage of fish, they also contributed to the pollution of the region. Organic pollution made up most of the waste emitted by printing and dying works found in textile factories across New England. But a substantial amount of more toxic, inorganic waste also entered the region's streams, including sulfuric and muriatic acids and arsenate of soda. Worse water polluters than the textile mills were the paper factories that dotted streams throughout New England. Paper mills released wastewater heavily laden with caustic alkali as well as lime chloride and sulfuric acid.

The toxic effects of industrial development were rivaled only by the harmful pollution generated by the accompanying urbanization of the region. In the Merrimack River valley in 1880 the population of Lowell had swelled to nearly 60,000; Lawrence had close to 40,000 people; Manchester, more than 32,000. To meet the water needs of all these people, cities were forced after the Civil War to develop public water supplies. In 1873, for example, the Lowell Waterworks was completed. Three years later Lawrence finished work on a similar system. By the 1880s the creation of public water systems throughout New England had increased household water use. With the rise in consumption came an increase in the amount of wastewater generated. Privies and cesspools were no longer adequate for the growing quantities of waste they were called on to handle. In response, cities constructed sewer systems that shifted the burden of pollution, as historian Joel Tarr has observed, from the land to the region's rivers. Cities downstream of major urban areas were now especially at risk from contaminated water supplies, courtesy of their upstream neighbors.

By the 1880s the waters of New England were more thoroughly controlled than ever before. The ever-mounting problems of water pollution and flooding were slowly making New Englanders see that the region's ecology linked them to people who were sometimes many miles away. This growing sense of ecological interdependence may have laid the foundation for the conservation movement, which showed signs of emerging as early as the late 19th century.

The earliest attempts to help conserve and restore New England's natural resources—devastated by some 250 years of economic development—date from the 1860s. By 1867 all the New England states except Rhode Island had formed fish commissions to help supervise the restoration of migrating species of fish to the region's waters. The commissions took various conservation measures, including moratoriums on fishing for salmon and shad in certain rivers. They also engaged in artificial propagation programs to help rejuvenate the resource and required the construction of fishways to enable fish to ascend over dams along the region's rivers. Yet by the 1890s it was clear that efforts to restore the region's former fish ecology had failed, largely because of continued attempts to dam rivers—now to generate hydroelectric power—without properly designed systems to allow fish to pass upstream.

Attempts to conserve the region's forest resources date from the turn of the century. In 1893 New Hampshire established a permanent forestry commission. The Massachusetts Forestry Association was formed in 1898; the Vermont Forestry Commission was set up in 1905. These organizations tried to discourage the setting of fires and encourage the planting of trees. They also purchased tracts of forestland to help preserve them. In addition, a great deal of attention was paid at this time in New England to educating people on the virtues of wise forest use. In 1897 B. E. Fernow offered the country's first forestry course at the Massachusetts Agricultural

Delivering a toilet system to the Appalachian Mountain Club's Greenleaf Hut, Mount Lafayette, N.H., 1970s

College. Yale established a forestry school three years later; Harvard opened one in 1906. Forest conservation in New England reached something of a high point in 1911, when Congress purchased the land to establish the White Mountain National Forest.

By the 1920s New England's forest area was 13 percent greater than it had been 60 years earlier, although this was probably more a function of the abandonment of farms and their reversion to forest than of conservation measures. (In Rhode Island, for example, the number of farms dropped sharply, from 5,292 according to the 1910 census to 4,083 10 years later.) Still, the trend toward increasing reforestation continued over the course of the 20th century, as more and more farms were given up. By the 1970s, approximately 85 percent of Maine and New Hampshire and 66 percent of Massachusetts, Rhode Island, Connecticut, and Vermont were classified by the U.S. Forest Service as woodland.

But returning tree cover alone did not mean all was well with the region's forests. In the 1950s some tree species, such as the red spruce and sugar maple, began to die off in the mountainous areas of Vermont and New Hampshire. The problem seemed to worsen with increasing elevation. Scientists eventually determined that acid rain was to blame for the massive forest declines. A dramatic rise in the use of fossil fuel, especially during the period after World War II, produced extremely high emissions of sulfur. In the American Midwest, the nation's industrial heartland, factories and increasing numbers of automobiles spewed pollutants into the atmosphere, where prevailing westerly winds eventually carried them to the eastern part of the country. New England's forests thus paid the price as the nation shifted to a new energy regime that depended more and more on the use of coal and oil.

The marring of the region's forests took on added importance after World War II, as New England residents increasingly came to see nature as something that, apart from aiding production, they could enjoy in their leisure time. Clean air and water, as well as a generally more healthy environment, were at the heart of a new drive, fueled by rising living standards, to make nature conform to the needs of postwar suburbanization and increased leisure for the middle class. A shift was occurring from conservation, founded on the rational and efficient use of water and forest resources, to environmentalism, a concern with nature as an amenity that could be enjoyed. New England eventually emerged as a leading center of this new environmental consciousness. In 1977 the League of Conservation Voters placed New England at the top of its regional list for the votes cast by its congressional delegation on environmental measures (the Gulf states were at the bottom). Not all New England states pledged unqualified support for the environment, however. New Hampshire, for example, tended to lag behind the other states in this regard.

Nonetheless, New England was clearly a bastion of environmentalism. During the 1960s the region pioneered the use of conservation commissions: citizen bodies appointed to find ways of identifying and raising money to protect undeveloped land from falling victim to real estate developers. During the same decade the Massachusetts Audubon Society, the most vibrant chapter in the country, built network-of-nature facilities for educating the public and raising environmental consciousness throughout the region.

It is probably no coincidence that one of the leading environmental thinkers of the 20th century, Rachel Carson, made New England her spiritual home. Born in Springdale, Penn., in 1907, Carson journeyed to Massachusetts in the 1930s to work as a marine biologist for the U.S. Bureau of Fisheries (later the Fish and Wildlife Service). During the summer of 1953 she built a cottage on Southport Island off the coast of Maine, where she summered for the rest of her life. Carson's groundbreaking work *Silent Spring*, published in 1962, changed the face of environmentalism. In that book Carson condemns the irresponsibility of modern industrial society in its dealings with nature. That society, as she saw it, was so in love with itself and its technological prowess that it had forsaken humbleness in the face of natural forces. The untoward effects of an arrogant industrial culture and its chemicals were deeply apparent in Carson's chosen home. *Silent Spring* describes, for instance, once beautiful routes that a roadside weed-spraying program had transformed into "a sere expanse of brown." Like Marsh and Thoreau before her, Carson saw a New England landscape in the process of profound ecological destruction. Like them, she issued an eloquent plea for a more gentle, reverential approach in our dealings with nature.

But this time what developed was one of the most influential strains of activism in all of U.S. history: the environmental movement. Tapping into the radical political climate of the 1960s, with its sit-ins and demonstrations against racial discrimination and the Vietnam War, *Silent Spring* helped bring about a sea change in environmental attitudes all over the country. The result was a massive legislative outpouring on the federal level, with Congress passing bills to deal with clean air and water, toxic waste, pesticides, endangered species, solid refuse, safe drinking water, coastal management, and more in the years following 1970. This unprecedented legislative initiative was joined by a corresponding upsurge in the membership rolls of environmental organizations. The Audubon Society, for example, which was particularly strong in New England, grew from 120,000 to 400,000 members during the 1970s, an increase of more than 300 percent.

Nuclear power soon emerged as a major focus of concern for the burgeoning environmental movement. In 1974 Sam Lovejoy, who lived in a rural commune in Massachusetts, used a crowbar to topple a 450-foot utility tower in Montague, Mass., where a nuclear power plant was being built. With plans moving forward for two reactors in the town of Seabrook on New Hampshire's meager 18 miles of seacoast, activists mobilized to form the Clamshell Alliance in 1976. That same year nearly 200 antinuclear protesters occupied the grounds of the proposed Seabrook plant. In 1977 more than 2,000 activists carried out a similar protest, entering the site and digging latrines to show that they planned to be there for the long haul. These events galvanized the antinuclear movement and helped inspire other grassroots groups, such as the Abalone Alliance in California, to engage in similar direct-action tactics. Although protesters did not prevent Seabrook from completing one of its two planned reactors, their long and costly resistance to the facility contributed to the reason why no new nuclear power plant has been ordered in the United States since 1978.

New England is also home to approximately 12 percent of the nation's Superfund sites, locations at which pollution of the water or soil is so severe that it may threaten the health of nearby residents. Many of these sites are the current or former locations of military or industrial facilities. At the largest Superfund site in the region, on upper Cape Cod, toxins from the Massachusetts Military Reservation are contaminating groundwater at a rate of 3 million gallons a day. Cancer rates in towns neighboring the post are 24 percent higher than the state average. In the 1980s Woburn, Mass., was home to New England's worst Superfund site—the fifth most polluted in the country—a 225-acre Industri-Plex site where animal hides had been processed into glue, chemicals, and insecticides. By April 2000 environmental cleanup had reached the point at which ground could be broken for a regional transportation center.

The environmental movement combined with federal legislation has unquestionably bolstered the ecology of contemporary New England. The Clean Air Act of 1990, for example, providing for a 50 percent reduction in sulfur dioxide emissions, has reduced acid rain. But some of the most important changes in the region's landscape have resulted less from organized activism or legislation than from major shifts in land use. The clearing of forest for farming and fuel has decreased dramatically as the region has become less dependent on agriculture. The woods have returned, and so have the animals that once occupied the region—deer, beaver, and bear, among others. Moose have grown so numerous in some northern areas that collisions between the animals and automobiles occur several times a year. The return of wildlife has caused some New England states to institute driver education programs intended to help residents safely navigate their roads in this new ecological setting.

Near the turn of the 21st century the state of Maine was the site of a unique environmental occasion. On July 1, 1999, the 972-foot-long Edwards Dam across the Kennebec River in Augusta, built in 1837, became the first such structure in U.S. history to be dismantled against the wishes of its private owner. Early in 2001 salmon redds, or nests, were being spotted in shallow-water areas 17 miles upriver from the former location of the dam. The path to their spawning grounds having been largely blocked for 162 years, Atlantic salmon and several other species of migratory fish were on the verge of making a comeback. Populations of osprey and bald eagles are also on the rebound along Maine's down east coast and elsewhere in New England, thanks to a 1972 federal ban on the insecticide DDT.

Like most regions in America, New England still suffers the ills of an automobile-centered culture—subsidized by government tax policy and postwar loan programs—that has devastated cities, clogged roadways, and covered untold miles of open space with asphalt. But ecological change is complex. Despite suburban sprawl, New Englanders today probably have more contact with creatures of the forest than Henry David Thoreau, who lived through the years of heaviest deforestation, ever did—a point worth remembering on the next drive into town.

Jan Albers, *Hands on the Land: A History of the Vermont Landscape* (2000); Charles F. Carroll, *The Timber Economy of Puritan New England* (1973); William Cronon, *Changes in the Land: Indians, Colonists, and the Ecology of New England* (1983); Alfred W. Crosby, Jr., *The Columbian Exchange: Biological and Cultural Consequences of 1492* (1972); Brian Donohue, *Reclaiming the Commons: Community Farms and Forests in a New England Town* (1999); David R. Foster, *Thoreau's Country: Journey through a Transformed Landscape* (1999); David R. Foster and John F. O'Keefe, *New England Forests through Time* (2000); Robert Gottlieb, *Forcing the Spring: The Transformation of the American Environmental Movement* (1993); Samuel P. Hays, *Beauty, Health, and Permanence: Environmental Politics in the United States, 1955–1985* (1987); Richard W. Judd, *Common Lands, Common People: The Origins of Conservation in Northern New England* (1997); Carolyn Merchant, *Ecological Revolutions: Nature, Gender, and Science in New England* (1989); Diana Muir, *Reflections in Bullough's Pond: Economy and Ecosystem in New England* (2000); Howard S. Russell, *A Long, Deep Furrow: Three Centuries of Farming in New England* (1976); Kent C. Ryden, *Landscape with Figures: Nature and Culture in New England* (2001); Kirkpatrick Sale, *The Green Revolution: The American Environmental Movement, 1962–1992* (1993); Theodore Steinberg, *Nature Incorporated: Industrialization and the Waters of New England* (1991); Joel A. Tarr, *The Search for the Ultimate Sink: Urban Pollution in Historical Perspective* (1996); Tom Wessels, *Reading the Forested Landscape: A Natural History of New England* (1997); Michael Williams, *Americans and Their Forests: A Historical Geography* (1989); Donald Worster, *Nature's Economy: A History of Ecological Ideas* (1977).

Theodore L. Steinberg

Acid Rain Acid rain (or, more accurately, acid precipitation, as much of it arrives in snow and fog) is any form of precipitation that measures less than 5.6 on the pH scale. Precipitation in its pure form is naturally slightly acidic (pH 5.0–5.6). About 10 percent of the acidity in acid rain is from natural sources, with 90 percent caused by humans. Human generation of sulfuric and nitric acids can significantly increase the normal acid level. Sulfuric acid, deriving from sulfur dioxide gas, constitutes two-thirds of the acidic composition of acid rain. This acid originates from a small number of large sources, most significantly from coal-fired and oil-fired electric power plants burning high-sulfur coal or oil without stack gas controls and from large metal smelters, with a much less significant amount deriving from other industrial sources. Nitric acid, deriving from nitrous oxide gas, constitutes about one-third of the acidic composition of acid rain. This acid originates from a large number of small sources, most significantly from motor vehicles and aircraft and from all industrial processes involving internal combustion.

The New England environment lies downwind of significant sulfur dioxide and nitrous oxide sources arriving from the west and south and itself generates a considerable amount of nitrous oxide on its own, in direct proportion to its population distribution and density. New England's ecosystems of forests, lakes, ponds, and thin soils atop granite bedrock are also highly vulnerable to damage, being naturally acidic and containing little capacity to chemically buffer arriving acid. The biological acidification is, therefore, rapid in New England, and serious environmental, economic, and political issues have resulted.

Beginning with the New Hampshire presidential primary of 1980 and continuing through the late 1980s, the New England states were involved in political disputes with acid-originating states to the south and west, and particularly with Ohio and other upwind midwestern industrial states. The New England states also formed a strong alliance with Canada and its provinces on this matter, given Canada's similar geographical situation of being downwind of much acid pollution and its equal if not even greater vulnerability to damage. Both New England (particularly northern New England) and Canada actively voiced complaints to the acid-originating regions until the latter 1980s. At that time, although the issue did not disappear, scientifically speaking, it did fade politically, given the significant change in political climate in both Canada and the United States. Canada's desire for a bilateral free trade agreement with the United States and the increasing severity of the economic recession in New England toward the end of the decade defused the issue, which eventually became subsumed in broader social concerns over climate change and holes in the ozone layer.

An established trend in spruce and fir decline along the pollution gradient from New York to Maine is believed to be due to nitrogen saturation, acidification, or the long-term effects of the 1960s drought. A strong circumstantial case can be made for the interactive and synergistic effects of different pollutants in contributing to this decline. There is no evidence that this effect differs on different sides of the mountains. Recent reviews in changes in stream quality in Europe and the United States, including New England, show declining sulfate concentrations in response to reductions in sulfur dioxide emissions. Several streams in Europe show increasing pH (that is, reduced acidity), as well. In the United States, sulfate declines in streams have not generally been accompanied by increasing pH. The Hubbard Brook research site in the White Mountains of New Hampshire continues to provide the best long-term data on these matters and contains the oldest series of acidity records in the northeastern United States.

New England continues to suffer from incoming acidity and acid damage, with threats to its tourist and inland sport fishing economies. Continued acidification may well represent a long-term cumulative threat to the New England forest and forest soils, and perhaps also to surface water resources, given the ability of acidity to release toxic aluminum from granite bedrock into the water column and thus into drinking water.

John E. Carroll, *Acid Rain: An Issue in Canadian-American Relations* (1982); Carroll, *Environmental Diplomacy: An Examination and Prospective of Canada-U.S. Transboundary Environmental Relations* (1983); Carroll, *International Environmental Diplomacy* (1990); Gregory S. Wetstone and Armin Rosencranz, *Acid Rain in Europe and North America: National Responses to an International Problem* (1983).

John E. Carroll

Appalachian Mountain Club

The Appalachian Mountain Club (AMC) was founded in Boston in 1876 by a group of university professors, including Edward Pickering and Charles Fay, who wished to foster interest in outdoor activities including mapping, trail building, scientific studies, conservation, and exploration in the mountainous regions of northern New England. Once a regional group, the AMC is now the oldest nonprofit conservation and recreation organization in the United States. The group promotes the protection, enjoyment, and wise use of the mountains, rivers, and trails of the Northeast and has more than 85,000 members in 12 regional chapters from Maine to Virginia. The AMC maintains more than 1,400 miles of trails (including 350 miles of the Appalachian Trail) and more than 30 shelters in the Northeast, largely through the help of volunteers.

Throughout its history, the AMC has worked hard to protect the highland regions of the Northeast. The group is dedicated to the belief that the mountains and rivers have intrinsic worth and can also provide recreational opportunity, spiritual renewal, and ecological and economic health for the region. By encouraging its members to enjoy and appreciate nature the organization promotes concern for the conservation of fragile natural resources. The AMC works to influence legislation that enforces conservation and supports environmentally sensitive policies and regulations. In 1911, for instance, AMC members were successful in fighting for the passage of the Weeks Act, which led to the creation of the White Mountain National Forest, the first national forest east of the Mississippi. During the 1920s, AMC members helped establish the Appalachian Trail, which extends from Maine to Georgia.

In 1888, the AMC built its first mountain hut, Madison Hut, initiating the only alpine hut system in the northeastern United States. Today, the AMC operates eight huts in the Presidential Range of New Hampshire, each a day's hike apart, providing shelter, bunks, blankets, and hearty meals for hikers. The use of these huts also minimizes the effect that hikers and campers have on the sensitive natural areas in the region's woodlands. In 2003 the AMC opened a full-service lodge, the Highland Center, in Crawford Notch.

The AMC is active in backcountry and environmental education, mountain ecology and river research, and conservation policy and advocacy. The group is currently working to ensure the protection of the 26 million acres that make up the Northern Forest of Maine, New Hampshire, Vermont, and New York, the last remaining undeveloped wildland in the Northeast. The AMC offers hundreds of workshops in subjects ranging from mountain safety to leadership skill building. The AMC research department is involved with scientific research in several areas, including air-quality monitoring, endangered alpine species preservation, and forest ecology.

The AMC is well known for its outstanding publications, including its popular maps and guidebooks. AMC publications range from the "bible" of the White Mountains, the *AMC White Mountain Guide*, currently in its 27th edition, to books on nature trails and hikes throughout New England, as well as books on canoeing, kayaking, backcountry skiing, and children's books. Since 1876 the AMC has published *Appalachia*, the country's oldest journal of mountaineering and conservation. The AMC's library in Boston houses one of the country's most extensive collections of mountain-related books, maps, and images, including old postcards, slides, personal journals, summit registers, and other artifacts of the organization's long history and the history of mountaineering in New England.

Appalachian Mountain Club, *Appalachia*, 75th Anniversary Issue 17 (May 1851); Appalachian Mountain Club, *The AMC: A Working Society* (1973); William Reifsnyder, *High Huts of the White Mountains: A History of the Appalachian Mountain Club's High Hostels* (1993); Laura and Guy Waterman, *Forest and Crag: A History of Hiking, Trail Blazing, and Adventure in the Northeast Mountains* (1989).

Louise Levy

Appalachian Trail

The idea for the creation of the Appalachian Trail—a mountain footpath along the crest of the Appalachian Mountains—was born in New England, largely in response to the industrial growth of the Northeast and the increasing mechanization of turn-of-the-20th-century society. Conceived in 1921 by native New Englander Benton MacKaye, a regional planner, forester, and early conservationist, the trail had its roots in the hiking or "tramping" movement in New England that had emerged to improve the quality of America's increasing leisure time. The first mountaineering organizations in the country—clubs such as the Appalachian Mountain Club of Boston and the Green Mountain Club of Vermont—contained urban, intellectual members who sought recreational opportunities in the nearby Appalachians. As an adjunct to the groups' social activities, trail building became a primary activity for these organizations. The 270-mile Long Trail, cutting through Vermont from the Massachusetts state line to the Canadian border, was built by the Green Mountain Club under the leadership of James P. Taylor and served as the inspiration for the Appalachian Trail, which would eventually stretch from Maine to Georgia.

MacKaye originally planned the Appalachian Trail as a greenway community, with both camps and residential areas for hikers. He envisioned workers using their spare time to build the trail and its camps—that this "work" would organically become "play" and that this wilderness refuge would then replenish the spirits of its visitors. Despite the utopian intellectual climate of the day, only the hiking trail component of MacKaye's sweeping vision gained popularity. A relatively small group of people across 14 states wanted to create a "wilderness" hiking trail of an ambitious length of more than 2,000 miles. In 1925 the Appalachian Trail Conference (ATC) was established in Washington, D.C., and under the stewardship of chairman Myron H. Avery oversaw the completion of the trail just 12 years later.

In general, the idea for the Appalachian Trail spawned the organizations that built it. This was not the case, however, in New England, for these entities existed well before 1921. Completion of the project through most of the New England states was made significantly easier because some of the existing trail systems, such as Vermont's Long Trail, were incorporated into the larger Appalachian Trail as it progressed. The New England stretch of the trail, through Maine, New Hampshire, Vermont, Massachusetts, and Connecticut, is steep and craggy and tends to follow the fall line up the mountainsides, direct and unyielding.

MacKaye's philosophy of "work becoming play" has been realized in the building, maintenance, and management of the trail, for club volunteers today still carry out most of these activities along the 2,158-mile-long trail. The clubs' management activities are coordinated by the nonprofit ATC, with its national headquarters now in Harpers Ferry, W.V., and regional offices in New Hampshire, Pennsylvania, Virginia, and North Carolina. The ATC ultimately reports all activities to the National Park Service, which maintains administrative responsibility for the Appalachian Trail. In addition, the conference has 31 affiliated organizations, among them the Appalachian Mountain Club, which holds maintenance responsibilities for specific portions of the trail.

In 1968, with the passage of the National Trails System Act, the Appalachian Trail became a federally protected national scenic trail. It continues to be traversed primarily by weekend or short-term hikers, although a number of "through-hikers" start from the south in the early spring and complete the entire trail in about six months. In keeping with tradition, New Englanders continue to use the names of the original trail systems, such as the Hunt Trail in central Maine and the many sections of the trail in the White Mountains of New Hampshire that still bear the names that originated in the late 19th century.

Jane Curtis, Will Curtis, and Frank Lieberman, *Green Mountain Adventure: Vermont's Long Trail* (1985); Ron Fisher, *Mountain Adventure: Exploring the Appalachian Trail* (1988); Benton MacKaye, *The New Exploration: A Philosophy of Regional Planning.* (1962 [1928]); Laura Waterman and Guy Waterman, *Forest and Crag: A History of Hiking, Trail Blazing, and Adventure in the Northeast Mountains* (1989).

Valerie Shrader

Arnold Arboretum

The Arnold Arboretum of Harvard University—established in 1872 as a research institute and living museum by the trustees of wealthy New Bedford merchant James Arnold—is the oldest public arboretum in the United States. It is part of Frederick Law Olmsted's Emerald Necklace, the series of parklands that run through Boston, and is a functioning part of the Boston Parks and Recreation Department. Designed by Olmsted, America's first landscape architect, and the institution's first director Charles Sprague Sargent, the Arnold Arboretum is dedicated to the study and appreciation of woody plants and is well known for careful documentation of its collections. In its bequest, its founders specified that the arboretum should contain "all the trees [and] shrubs . . . either indigenous or exotic, which can be raised in the open air."

As a world leader in botanical research, the institution hosts international programs for studying floras of the North Temperate Zone. A library and an herbarium that houses tens of thousands of pressed, dried plant samples complement the living collections. Throughout its history, the arboretum has served as a leader in plant exploration and collection domestically and abroad. Distinguished for its introduction of numerous woody ornamental plants to North America, the institution continues to participate in plant exploration expeditions, including recent trips to Taiwan and Tibet.

Located on 265 acres in Jamaica Plain, Mass., the living collections include more than 15,000 documented specimens of temperate trees, shrubs, and vines. The living collections are remarkable for the individual specimens' sizes and maturities; many date back to the late 19th century. Collections of special note include the lilac collection, the Eleanor Cabot Bradley Collection of Rosaceous Plants, the Larz Anderson Bonsai Collection, and the Chinese Path, which features many outstanding Asiatic trees and shrubs. The Larz Anderson Bonsai Collection includes bonsai trees from the 18th century, and the arboretum's famous lilac collection has more than 500 lilac plants, including 190 cultivars (a race or variety of plant created or selected intentionally and maintained through cultivation) and 23 species and their botanical varieties; the public can enjoy them all when the arboretum hosts its annual Lilac Sunday in the spring.

Educational outreach has been an important function of the arboretum since 1891 when Sargent initiated a program of horticultural instruction. Today, the arboretum offers educational programs to adults and children, teacher training seminars, public tours, and an intern program. The arboretum's Field Studies Experiences program engages elementary students in basic botany topics. More recently, the arboretum has developed innovative programs designed to help improve the teaching of science in the schools themselves. One such project is Seasonal Investigations, a yearlong, Internet-supported study of school yard trees.

In addition to its strong emphasis on science and education and its range of public programs for diverse audiences, the arboretum is an unusual public resource that provides an environment offering respite and reflection for an urban population at no charge, from dawn to dusk 365 days a year.

Ellen S. Bennett

Aroostook County, Maine

Aroostook County, the largest county east of the Mississippi River, is couched in the arc of the Saint John River, which makes up most of Maine's northern border. The sparsely populated western half is drained by the Saint John, Allagash, and Aroostook Rivers and is heavily forested with spruce, balsam, and northern hardwoods. The fertile eastern section hosts a vigorous agricultural economy. Aroostook County is distinctive for its unique ethnic mix of Acadian, Irish, French Canadian, Scandinavian, and Yankee populations; its strong ties to Canada; and its unpopulated forests that attract both loggers and recreationists.

Before the arrival of Europeans, the area was inhabited primarily by Micmac Indians. French-speaking Acadians, Aroostook's first European settlers, moved up the Saint John River through the province of New Brunswick, Canada, during the 1780s, after the arrival of British loyalists on the lower river. Founding a series of communities known as the Madawaska Territory on the current border of Maine and Canada, the Acadians remained isolated from ports on the Saint Lawrence River and from settlements in Maine. Later migrants from Ireland, Quebec, Sweden, and Maine contributed to the county's diverse ethnic composition. Houlton, the first Yankee village, was established between 1805 and 1810 largely by settlers from New Salem, Mass.

The focal event of the county's early history was the "bloodless Aroostook War," which climaxed a boundary dispute between the United States and Great Britain that had troubled the Northeast since the American Revolution. Diplomacy reached a crisis in 1839 and was resolved under the 1842 Webster-Ashburton Treaty, which gave Maine the fertile Aroostook River valley, most of the heavily timbered upper Saint John, and the right of free navigation through New Brunswick on the lower Saint John, an important consideration for the landlocked county. Aroostook lumber also gained duty-free status in both British and U.S. ports, a concession that helped forge a unique international timber trade along the Saint John River.

The first roads were cut from central Maine into the Aroostook in the early 1830s, and the county was incorporated in 1839. In the mid-1840s, state lands in the western county were sold to lumber operators in quarter, half, or whole townships. Farmers in eastern Aroostook County worked off-season in the lumber camps and sold produce, hay, and grains to lumber operators. During the 1870s the establishment of railroads running across the border from New Brunswick stimulated potato and potato starch production. In December 1893 the Bangor and Aroostook Railroad reached Houlton, connecting the county to coastal Maine ports. Subsequently, Aroostook potatoes gained national importance, constituting one-eighth of the U.S. crop by the late 1920s. During these years pulpwood replaced lumber as the region's primary forest product.

The Great Depression devastated Aroostook County's heavily mortgaged potato farms. In addition, farmers faced long-term declines in potato consumption and increasing competition from potato-growing states in the West. After World War II, pulpwood producers also encountered problems in the form of labor recruitment, declining softwood stocks, and budworm infestations of spruce.

During the late 1960s rising public use of Maine's North Woods spurred creation of the state Land-Use Regulation Commission, which helped preserve the wild character of western Aroostook County. A lingering controversy over the state's so-called public lots—lands set aside in each township during the state's formative years to be sold by the towns for schools and other public expenses—was resolved by consolidation of several tracts under state recreational management. In 1966 the state legislature created the Allagash Wilderness Waterway to protect the wild quality of Aroostook County's most famous river.

Potatoes, forest products, and recreation continue as the foundations of northern Maine's economy. Consequently, the major themes in the history of the county—cooperation and conflict across the border, close ties to the natural landscape, and a search for economic diversity—are no less evident today than they were a century ago.

Beatrice Craig, "Early French Migrations to Northern Maine, 1785–1850," *Maine Historical Society Quarterly* 25 (1986); Helen Hamlin, *Pine, Potatoes, and People: The Story of Aroostook* (1948); Richard W. Judd, *Aroostook: A Century of Logging in Northern Maine* (1989); Charles Morrow Wilson, *Aroostook: Our Last Frontier* (1937).

Richard W. Judd

Audubon Societies

The Audubon Societies, named after John James Audubon, the famed 19th-century ornithologist and artist, were founded in Boston in 1896. In protest against the excessive killing of long-legged wading birds, terns, and songbirds for use in the flourishing millinery trade of the day, two prominent Boston Brahmins, Harriet Lawrence Hemenway and Minna B. Hall, formed a society that would eventually become one of the largest and most effective nonprofit bird-conservation organizations in North America.

Working as pioneer environmental activists at the turn of the century, Hemenway and Hall quietly rallied the financial backing and moral support of 900 other women and then persuaded the Boston scientific establishment to join their cause. The focus of their effort was to bring about protective bird legislation that would halt the slaughter of birds for use of their feathers. Using their social prominence and collective financial resources, the women were eventually able to persuade ornithologists such as Edward Howe Forbush, Charles S. Minot, and William Brewster of the importance of their campaign. In 1896 the Massachusetts Audubon Society was formed to carry on the efforts initiated by Hemenway and Hall.

By 1897 similar groups had been formed in Colorado, the District of Columbia, Maine, New York, and Pennsylvania. In 1905, through the increased urgings of the "Mothers of Conservation," the National Association of Audubon Societies for the Protection of Wild Birds and Animals was formed; in 1940 it became known as the National Audubon Society.

The crusade against the feather trade gained momentum in 1898 when Senator George Hoar of Massachusetts introduced a bill that would prohibit not only the sale and shipment of bird plumes within the United States but also their import or export. Hoar's bill did not pass, but a bill introduced in 1900 by Congressman John Lacey of Iowa was successful. To this day, the Lacey Act prohibits the interstate shipment of animals killed in violation of state laws.

From these early beginnings, the Audubon movement grew in two distinct organizational directions. The National Audubon Society, headquartered in New York City, developed a network of membership-supported chapters throughout the United States. Audubon Societies in states such as Massachusetts, New

Hampshire, and Rhode Island, however, chose to remain independent and to this day lack any affiliation with the national organization.

Originally concerned exclusively with bird protection, the Audubon program currently focuses on much broader conservation issues. Member groups now take an active role in environmental advocacy issues, maintain sanctuaries and nature centers nationwide, sponsor educational outreach opportunities, and publish journals and various scientific materials. One of the National Audubon Society's most visible programs is the annual Christmas Bird Census, an ongoing survey of winter bird populations that has been conducted since 1900.

Land protection is an especially important function of the Audubon movement. The Massachusetts Audubon Society, for example, protects more than 28,000 acres in that state; several other states also have extensive acreage under Audubon stewardship. This continuing legacy of bird protection and conservation makes the Audubon movement one of the oldest and most important environmental initiatives in the United States.

Frank Graham, *The Audubon Ark: A History of the National Audubon Society* (1990); Christopher Leahy, John Hanson Mitchell, and Thomas Conuel, *The Nature of Massachusetts* (1996).

Wayne R. Petersen

Baxter State Park Baxter State Park, a wilderness preserve of 201,018 acres, surrounds 5,271-foot Mount Katahdin, Maine's highest mountain and the northern terminus of the Appalachian Trail. The park is located 20 miles northwest of Millinocket in east central Maine and contains an outstanding diversity of wildlife, plants, and landforms. Katahdin, meaning "main mountain," was important to Abenaki legend as home to the malevolent spirit Pamola and had been climbed only a few times when Henry David Thoreau compiled his vivid account of a partial ascent in 1846. A distinctive feature of Katahdin is its glacial basin, along the edge of which the Knife Edge Trail proceeds to Baxter Peak, the highest of Katahdin's several summits. The mountain's mystique was enhanced by a rich folklore of logging and river driving on the Penobscot River's West Branch. Theodore Winthrop's *Life in the Open Air* (1876) and Frederic E. Church's paintings added to the mountain's reputation. Construction of the Bangor and Aroostook Railroad at the turn of the century facilitated access to the mountain, and the railroad promoted wilderness recreation through its annual guide, *In the Maine Woods*.

In 1905 the Maine Federation of Women's Clubs proposed a federal forest reserve around Katahdin, linking their campaign to a similar proposal for the White Mountains. Percival P. Baxter, the scion of a family of wealthy philanthropists, had first become interested in preserving Katahdin in 1903 during a fishing trip to the region. He was elected to the state legislature in 1905 and introduced the first of many unsuccessful bills calling for a state reserve in 1919. When Governor Frederick H. Parkhurst died in office in 1921, Baxter, as president of the Senate, succeeded him. Baxter continued to promote the park concept until he left office in 1925.

In 1930 Baxter purchased 6,000 acres of timberland, including Katahdin, from Great Northern Paper Company and deeded it to the state. It was designated Baxter State Park in 1931. Baxter continued purchasing land around the peak, deeding the parcels to the state as soon as each title was clear. Since timberlands were held in common and undivided interests by a number of owners, including multiple heirs of the original landowners, negotiations were complex. Baxter completed the last purchase of 7,764 acres in the summer of 1962, finally realizing his dream of a vast wilderness park at age 87. Baxter's practice of deeding over individual parcels as he acquired them created a variety of management problems. The land was to be "forever . . . left in the natural wild state," but over the three decades during which the deeds of trust were drafted, Baxter altered specific regulations to accommodate local pressures, various landowners' conditions, and his own changing attitudes toward park use. Vacillations regarding forest management, roads, firearms, snowmobiling, hunting and trapping, aircraft, and predator elimination fueled incessant controversy.

The Appalachian Mountain Club served the park by sponsoring annual excursions and marking and maintaining trails. During the 1930s the Civilian Conservation Corps maintained roads and built parking areas, shelters, fireplaces, and latrines. The National Park Service periodically considered federal purchases in the region, a threat that left landowners more favorably inclined toward Baxter and forced the people of Maine to face the challenge of managing the park. In the late 1930s state funds were allocated to hire a ranger, and the park was put under joint supervision of the state forest commissioner, the commissioner of inland fisheries and game, and the attorney general. With meager state appropriations, administration languished, but when Baxter died in 1969 his bequest for a Maintenance and Improvement Fund became available. A small but dedicated staff met the challenge of preservation and public use.

In the years following Baxter's death the park authority tried to balance his original vision against the demands of different public groups. As the environmental movement took shape during the 1970s, the authority became embroiled in controversy over modern ecological philosophies. Issues such as the use of snowmobiles, all-terrain vehicles, motorcycles, or trailers and campers in the park; spruce budworm control; salvage logging in a 510-acre blowdown that occurred in 1975; and timber cutting in the park's Scientific Forest Management Area led to a fascinating if sometimes acrimonious dialogue over the meaning of wilderness in an eastern context. In recent years, serious concern over acid rain damage to the forest and lakes has been added to this list.

John W. Hakola, *Legacy of a Lifetime: The Story of Baxter State Park* (1981); Henry David Thoreau, *The Maine Woods* (1909).

Richard W. Judd

Berkshires The Berkshire area of western Massachusetts includes Berkshire County and the Berkshire Hills. It is delineated on three sides by state borders—Vermont to the north, New York to the west, and Connecticut to the south; the eastern border is topographical, but no less distinct. Heading west from the north-south meanderings of the Connecticut River, the fertile lowlands of tobacco fields in the Pioneer Valley are quickly left behind, and the land rises abruptly into the rocky foothills of the Appalachians. This so-called Berkshire Barrier slowed western colonial expansion into the region for 100 years. Berkshire retains a remoteness today, if not in travel time to nearby cities, then in the insular tendency among the venerable "Berkshirite."

Independent minds, personal expression, and individualism are well-entrenched ingredients in the culture of Berkshire. For instance, it comes as no surprise that the Berkshire Convention of 1774 voted to boycott British-made goods, among the first such decrees in the colonies. Likewise, most Berkshire towns still use the time-honored "town meeting" form of government where local citizens convene to debate and vote on town business. Any voting citizen may address the meeting, and people certainly do so, often at length, despite obviously holding a minority opinion. Although the total population of Berkshire has never exceeded 150,000, and some of its towns reached their peak populations long before 1900, the effect of a succession of singular personalities, plus distinct and evolving places, has been particularly formative to Berkshire culture.

Nineteenth-century Berkshire saw the proliferation of industry—tanning, glass, iron, paper, and textiles—in the towns dotting the hills and waterways. In 1801, Zenas Crane started a paper mill and contracted with the U.S. government to supply the special paper required for currency stock. Such was his success that both the family ownership and the contract continue to this day.

In the mid-19th century, drawn by the pastoral landscape, Berkshire became the home of Nathaniel Hawthorne, who wrote *The House of Seven Gables* there, and Herman Melville as he worked on *Moby-Dick*. Melville purportedly was inspired as he gazed from his window by a silhouette of a whale formed by the slopes of nearby Mount Greylock, the highest peak in the Berkshire Hills. Other literary greats soon followed, establishing a literary legacy in the area.

Among Hawthorne's and Melville's friends was Samuel G. Ward, a wealthy man who became a summer resident of Berkshire starting in 1846. The area's favorable summer climate and ease of access by rail from Boston, New York, and Hartford, led to the "cottage era"— another key to Berkshire culture. Bridging the gap between social prominence and literary importance was Edith Wharton, author of the *Age of Innocence* and the first woman to win the Pulitzer Prize. Wharton became a Berkshire "cottager" in 1901. The Carnegies, the Vanderbilts, and others also built and played in the area. The days of the "Inland Newport" are now long past, but the resort status of Berkshire continues.

By the 1930s, the next great period of Berkshire was beginning to flower, bringing leisure pursuits and entertainment of the highest order to the emerging middle class. The snowy winters and gentle hills of the Berkshire Hills were ideal for the new sport of skiing. Facilities were pioneered on Berkshire slopes, and the area became busy with skiers taking advantage of the landscape in a new way.

Under the direction and vision of Serge Koussevitzky, the Boston Symphony Orchestra established a great musical institution on the land once occupied by Samuel Ward's summer estate. The Berkshire Music Festival in Tanglewood, Mass., has become a world-class attraction where audiences enjoy excellent music in an outdoor setting. Tanglewood has become synonymous with musical greats such as Aaron Copland, Leonard Bernstein, Seiji Ozawa, and John Williams.

Through these changes, Berkshire culture has been adept at adaptation and preservation. Some of the early cottages were razed, and some have remained private residences; but others have found new life as schools or health centers. Edith Wharton's home, The Mount, was saved from the wrecking ball by director and actress Tina Packer. In the 1970s she founded a professional theater group, Shake-

speare & Company, which performed theater outdoors on the grounds of The Mount for more than 20 years before moving down the street to another former cottage, allowing the property to be transformed yet again into a Wharton museum. In the 1990s, the Guggenheim Museum, searching for a site for its oversized collection of contemporary art, transformed some long-disused and massively scaled 19th-century Berkshire textile mills into stunning display space. The result is a postmodern mix of old and new: high-tech film and computer companies flourish alongside art galleries, all housed within the rambling manufacturing space of a now vanished era.

Modern mentalities may encourage short memories and emphasize rapid change, but Berkshire culture runs counter to both. The Berkshire area, just 49 miles north to south and ranging from only 12 to 24 miles in breadth, remains distinct. Owing to its unique landscape, small population, and the history of visionary individuals, Berkshire remains a resilient, vibrant, and unique cultural realm.

Sam Bittman and Steven A Satullo, eds., *Berkshire: Seasons of Celebration* (1982); Carole Owens, *The Berkshire Cottages: A Vanishing Era* (1984); Roderick Peattie, ed., *The Berkshires* (1948); Richard Wilkie, *Historical Atlas of Massachusetts* (1991).

George Roberson

Bird's-Eye Views Bird's-eye views are aerial landscape perspective drawings of settlements, generally cities, towns, and villages, published by itinerant graphic artists largely during the 19th century. They show the general spatial structure of these urban places by depicting streets, buildings, landmarks, and land uses seen obliquely from an imaginary vantage point high above and just beyond the town. Most of the surviving prints of New England localities, nearly 800 in number and covering just over 500 different places, are monochrome lithographs prepared from pencil-and-ink drafts, though many contain a color wash for accent and a few are polychrome. While they range in size from book illustrations to large, framed wall panoramas, their usual size approximates 19 by 25 inches. They were produced for local sale by advance subscription, with artists soliciting sales directly or through a paid agent. The artist made a view by rendering the town's general layout in perspective on a master drawing and then filling it with simplified representations of the buildings previously sketched from the street, a process whose duration ranged from a few days to a few weeks, depending on the size and complexity of the town and the artist's skill.

The genre enjoyed national appeal from 1835 to 1915 because lithography brought landscape art in this form, priced between $1.50 and $3.00, within reach of the broad middle class. As parlor decorations and public advertisements, bird's-eye views portrayed the unique urban character that a community had achieved at the time of printing. In addition, marginal vignettes and numerically indexed features in the main view highlighted many businesses, institutions, and prominent residences that swelled personal and local pride.

Bird's-eye views had their roots in the low-angle perspective drawings of large towns created during the 18th century, such as the London-engraved prospects of Boston produced

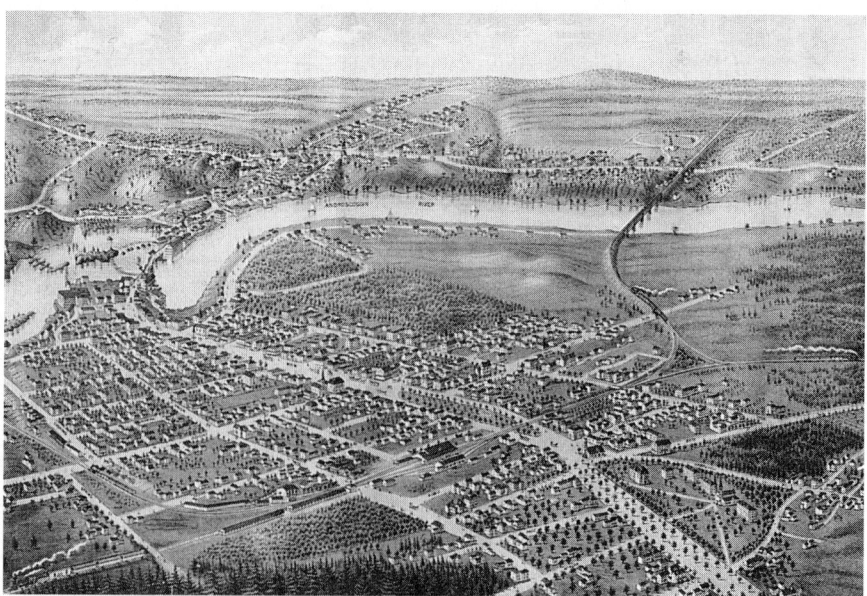

Bird's-eye view of Brunswick and Topsham, Maine, 1877

by William Burgis beginning in 1723. But by the 1830s higher-angled views, popularized first in the Midwest by English, American, and German artists, affected New England tastes. Production in New England, which represented one-sixth of the national total, surged during the urban prosperity of the period 1845–60 and even more so during the high industrial period of 1875–99. The region's peak year was 1878, when 57 separate views were published.

New England's bird's-eye views were drawn primarily by prolific artists specializing in this form of art who were active on a national scale and traveling wherever opportunity knocked. The most productive by far was Oakley H. Bailey, who sketched 248 separate places in New England, but other major figures included George E. Norris, Lucien R. Burleigh, James C. Hazen, and Albert Poole. Collectively, these men accounted for 481 views, or 60 percent of the region's total. Also active were a few New England practitioners, such as John B. Bachelder, Henry P. Moore, and Fitz Hugh Lane, the only artist with a broader reputation, based on his marine paintings. The genius of these views lay in their intricate graphic portrayal of cities and towns for an appreciative mass audience in the era before photography.

Christine B. Podmaniczky, *Through a Bird's Eye: 19th Century Views of Maine* (1981); John Reps, *Views and Viewmakers of Urban America, 1825–1925* (1984); David Ruell, "The Bird's Eye Views of New Hampshire, 1875–1899," *Historical New Hampshire* 38 (1983); James R. Warren and Donald A. Wise, "Two Bird's-Eye-View Artists: The Bailey Brothers," *Bulletin of the Special Libraries Association Geography and Map Division* 124 (1981).

Michael P. Conzen

Blights and Pests Perhaps the most discussed pest in New England is the black fly, a tiny native that gives a painful bite. However, of all the pests and blights that have afflicted the New England landscape, the most devastating have been caused by those that are not native. These imported diseases have ravaged indigenous plants that never developed natural defenses or resistance to the introduced pests.

Chestnut blight, caused by a fungus (*Cryphonectria parasitica*), is among the most destructive forest diseases ever known. At the turn of the 20th century, it was estimated that every fourth tree in the Appalachian forest was a chestnut. The nuts produced by this tree were an important source of food for wildlife, livestock, and humans. Its wood resisted rotting and thus became the choice for fence posts, shingles, railroad ties, telegraph and telephone poles, and coffins. Chestnut bark,

University of New Hampshire Professor John F. Burger with black flies, 1998

rich in tannic acids, was an important resource for the tanning industry.

The chestnut blight fungus was accidentally introduced into the United States on Asian chestnut trees brought to New York City early in the new century. The first diseased American chestnuts were discovered in the Bronx Zoological Park in 1904. The fungus quickly spread. By 1917 most of the trees in Connecticut, western Massachusetts, and western Rhode Island were dead or dying, and by 1945 the disease had killed several billion trees (the equivalent of 9 million acres) from the Canadian border to Georgia. Small chestnut trees can still be found throughout New England, however.

The fungus causes a girdling canker that occurs only on aboveground parts of trees; thus new shoots readily develop from the roots. The poet Robert Frost wrote of this phenomenon:

Will the blight end the chestnut?
The farmers rather guess not.
It keeps smoldering at the roots,
And sending up new shoots,
Till another parasite,
Shall come to end the blight.

Frost's poem was prophetic. A canker-healing strain of the fungus was discovered in Europe in the 1950s. Scientists today are still trying to develop a practical way to establish that strain in the United States, and breeding programs hold promise for the development of a blight-resistant American Chestnut.

American elms were once the most important landscape tree in New England. They lined the main thoroughfares of many cities and towns, hence the abundance of Elm Streets and Elm Avenues. Visit any of these thoroughfares today, however, and you will find them devoid of their namesake. Dutch elm disease, also caused by a fungus (*Ophiostoma ulmi*), was introduced into the United States in 1930 or 1931 on elm saw logs from France. It was identified in Connecticut in 1933 and Massachusetts in 1941, and by 1952 it was killing elms from New England to Kentucky. The heavy use of DDT in an attempt to control the beetle carrying the fungus overland was one of the factors that prompted Rachel Carson to write *Silent Spring* (1962). Many trees that survived the initial contagion succumbed to a more aggressive strain of the fungus that began killing trees during the 1970s. The millions of lost trees have drastically altered New England's urban landscape, and the cost of removing them has run into millions of dollars. There is hope for the return of the American elm, however, thanks to breeding efforts that have succeeded in developing several disease-resistant cultivars—that is, plants that are selected intentionally and maintained through cultivation.

A naturalist's attempt to start a silkworm industry in the United States resulted in the release of one of the most destructive insect pests ever introduced into North American forests, the gypsy moth (*Lymantria dispar*). The insects escaped from a laboratory in Medford, Mass., in 1869. By 1890 they were so prevalent and had wreaked so much destruction in Massachusetts that the state legislature appropriated $25,000 for a pest-control program that included burning infested trees and shrubs and applying creosote to egg masses. Control efforts appeared to be working so well that the program was abandoned in 1900. This was a fatal mistake, however, for within five years the pest had spread to Rhode Island, Connecticut, and southern New Hampshire. In 1990 upwards of 700,000 acres of New England forests were defoliated by the moth's voracious larvae.

Gypsy moth caterpillars feed on the foliage of more than 500 species of trees and shrubs. Oaks are among their favorite foods, but the hungry larvae will attack and defoliate almost any tree or shrub during a serious outbreak. Trees weakened by repeated defoliation usually die. And forests are not the only targets. Defoliation and tree loss also occur in urban areas, where the caterpillars become a major nuisance, crawling over homes, outdoor furniture, and gardens and leaving droppings in their wake. Luckily, in the years around the turn of the 21st century, a naturally occurring fungus began to reduce gypsy-moth population explosions and their damage. It is hoped that in the future these naturally occurring controls and integrated pest management will keep this devastating pest in check.

Other plant diseases caused by fungi have also left their mark on the culture and history of New England. One writer has suggested a link between the witchcraft hysteria in Salem, Mass., in 1692 and ergot, a grain fungus that can produce hallucinations and convulsions like those suffered by the victims of the accused witches. Late blight (*Phytophthora infestans*), the disease that caused the Irish potato famine and the death of millions in Ireland during the 1840s, also precipitated the emigration of more than a million Irish to North America, many of whom settled in New England, particularly near Boston.

Although blights and pests often go unnoticed during our daily lives, they will no doubt continue to affect the people and landscape of New England aesthetically, economically, and culturally.

Linda. R. Caporael, "Ergotism: The Satan Loosed in Salem?" *Science* 192 (1976); George W. Hudler, *Magical Mushrooms, Mischievous Molds* (1998); Warren T. Johnson and Howard H. Lyon, *Insects That Feed on Trees and Shrubs,* 2d ed. (1988); Wayne A. Sinclair, Howard H. Lyon, and Warren T. Johnson, *Diseases of Trees and Shrubs* (1987).

Cheryl A. Smith

Blizzards, Hurricanes, and Floods

New England has been host to a number of extreme weather events. Hurricanes, blizzards, floods, tornadoes, and other more occasional or even exotic phenomena have claimed lives, wreaked havoc on natural and human structures, and left a deep impression on those who have witnessed them, thereby passing from the meteorological record into the general history of the region.

Responses to these often tragic events have contributed in a modest but distinct way to the evolution of a regional culture. Chroniclers from Cotton Mather to Sebastian Junger (*The Perfect Storm,* 1997) have preserved the details of particular episodes of elemental fury. Creative artists from John Greenleaf Whittier to Winslow Homer to Ang Lee (director of the 1997 film *The Ice Storm*) have fashioned images and metaphors from the details. What is more, the memory of such events has become embedded in the folkways of the region. Whether told through Native American legends or articles in *Yankee* magazine or simple word-of-mouth, stories of great storms, of snow in August, or of killing heat on the Fourth of July find their way to newcomers and to the young as part of the heritage of a shared place.

The table conveys something of the range and variety of New England's experience with calamitous weather, although it should be noted that it relies upon facts rather than the descriptive richness of scholarly, artistic, and folk traditions. As a means of keeping what may seem a grim litany in perspective, it may be well to consider that the region has actually been less vulnerable to calamity of this sort than some other areas of the world, where thousands of lives and entire communities are all too frequently lost to a single sweep of wind or wave. It may also help to hold in mind the words of Sidney Perley, who prefaced his pioneering history of New England storms with the reassurance that, across the region, the "annual average number of pleasant days [has been shown to be] one hundred and ninety-seven, three-fifths of them being very pleasant."

Robert P. Emlen, "The Great Gale of 1815," *Rhode Island History* 48 (1990); Donald Hall, "New England's Calamitous Weather (and Why We Love It)" *Yankee* (September 1988); David Ludlum, *The Country Journal New England Weather Book* (1976); Sidney Perley, *Historic Storms of New England* (1891).

Gerald T. Burns

New England's Disastrous Weather

Familiar Name	Date	Description	Area(s) of Maximum Effect	Casualties	Damage and Description
Legendary Flood	Prehistory	Native American legend of flood covering all but Mount Washington; dubious authenticity, but possibly traceable to Paleo-Indian experience of preglacial lake(s) in the Northeast	General	Entire human population of the region, with the exception of two survivors	Presumably extensive
Great Storm of 1635	August 25, 1635	Likely a hurricane; probable landfall Rhode Island; violent winds and rain; storm tide estimated at 14 ft.	Narragansett and Massachusetts Bays	At least 27 dead, including at least eight Narrangansett Indians	Shipping losses; thousands of trees torn up by the roots; ripening crop of Indian corn largely destroyed; structural damage to houses
Great Snow of 1717	February 27–March 7, 1717	Four successive snowfalls, two major; up to 5-ft. depth, 14-ft. drifts	Eastern coastal and adjacent inland areas	Unknown	Estimated 95% of deer population perished; extensive loss of livestock and fruit trees; church services, postal delivery, and public meetings suspended for weeks in many areas
The Dark Day	May 19, 1780	Four to six hours of obscured daylight, equivalent to "Darkness of a common Starlight Night," caused by forest-	Southern half of the region	None reported (although many initially expected by those for whom darkness portended	Much public, commercial, and domestic activity halted for the duration of the phenomenom

(continued)

New England's Disastrous Weather (*continued*)

Familiar Name	Date	Description	Area(s) of Maximum Effect	Casualties	Damage and Description
Great September Gale	September 23, 1815	clearing fires in northern Northeast and New York Hurricane; landfall Saybrook Conn.; worst effects from winds and tides east of storm track	Southern coastline, especially Narragansett Bay and Providence	the biblical Day of Doom) Total unknown but likely substantial, both at sea and on land; 12 killed at Point Judith, R.I.	In Providence, 35 vessels and 500 buildings wrecked; damage estimated at $1.5 million (one-quarter of all taxable property); massive environmental damage to shorelines, inland forests, and freshwater supplies
Year without Summer	June–September, 1816	Pronounced cooling of atmosphere over the Northeast caused by volcanic ash from eruption of Mount Tambora in Southeast Asia; killing frosts and snow during every summer month	General across region, with greatest severity in Vermont, where drought compounded the effects	None reported directly attributable to the phenomenon	Widespread crop failure and loss of livestock; acute food shortages in some areas; marked acceleration of farm out-migration from the Northeast to the Midwest
Great New Hampshire Whirlwind	September 9, 1821	Tornado; from descriptions, likely F5 (highest) on Fujita Intensity Scale; track 30+ miles long, 1/2 mile wide	West central New Hampshire, especially Sunapee, New London, and Warner	At least seven killed, 20 or more injured	Damage recorded to 27 farms, some virtually obliterated; destruction of forest trees and orchards; loss estimated at $10,000 in New London
October Gale	October 3, 1841	Probable hurricane; track out to sea, east of Cape Cod	Eastern coast from Portland to Nantucket, especially offshore fishing grounds	At least 128 lost at sea, 57 from Cape Cod village of Truro	More than 100 vessels wrecked; $50,000 damage to fishing fleet and stores at Pigeon Cove, Mass.; shore installations on Nantucket battered
Wallingford Tornado	August 9, 1878	Short-lived but powerful tornado; 2-mile track cut through residential area	Wallingford, Conn. (north of New Haven)	34 killed (all but one, Irish immigrants); 100 injured	30 homes, a school, and a church serving the immigrant colony destroyed; $200,000 damage
Blizzard of '88	March 12–14, 1888	Massive nor'easter; became stalled over Block Island; snow depths up to 50 in. (Middletown, Conn.), gale force winds, near-zero temperatures	Connecticut, western Massachusetts, southern New Hampshire and Vermont	400 deaths from storm on eastern seaboard (separate figures for the Northeast not available)	Extensive damage to shipping, railroads, telegraph facilities; food and fuel shortages; normal transportation and communications blocked for up to a week; $20 million total damage (eastern seaboard)
Portland Storm	November 27, 1898	Nor'easter; up to 27 in. snow inland; 70 mph winds over Cape Cod and islands, higher at sea	Eastern and southeastern coasts, especially offshore fishing grounds and shipping lanes	191 killed when S.S. *Portland* sank off Cape Cod; total lost at sea estimated at 400	Heavy shipping losses; gale damage in coastal areas; morbid imagination of public stirred by sensational accounts of storm and sinkings
Fourth of July Heat Wave	July 1–12, 1911	12 consecutive days of temperatures higher than 90° and 100°; July 4 high of 106° (Nashua, N.H., and Lawrence, Mass.)	General across region, with effect most pronounced in major cities ("heat-island" effect)	Estimated 1,100 heat-related fatalities in Massachusetts alone	Pace of urban life slowed; July 4 celebrations subdued; Boston Common transformed into "vast dormitory" by thousands

(*continued*)

New England's Disastrous Weather (*continued*)

Familiar Name	Date	Description	Area(s) of Maximum Effect	Casualties	Damage and Description
					fleeing stifling tenements for cooler sleeping space
Vermont Flood	November 3–4, 1927	Widespread flash flooding of rivers and streams brought on by rainfall amounts exceeding 9 in. in 24 hours	Vermont	84 killed	Widespread destruction and damage to buildings, roads and highways, bridges, railroad lines; $28 million total
All–New England Flood	March 9– 21, 1936	Massive, sustained spring flooding; combination of early snowmelt and heavy rains; record crests reached in numerous locations	Major river basins, e.g., Kennebec, Merrimack, Connecticut	Small loss of life	Very extensive structural damage, especially to mills and factories lining waterways; downtown Hartford inundated; property damage estimated at $100 million
New England Hurricane (also Great Hurricane of '38)	September 21, 1938	Probable Category 3 (extensive damage potential) hurricane; arrival unpredicted; landfall Milford, Conn.; maximum winds 121 mph, 17-ft. storm tide, torrential rains	Southern coast, especially Rhode Island (devastated by tide); approximately 150-mile corridor to Burlington, Vt.	At least 600 dead (in the Northeast), 1,750 injured	4,500 homes; 15,000 other buildings, 6,000 vessels destroyed or damaged; estimated 275 million trees downed in central Northeast; 63,000 people in emergency shelters; total damage (includes Long Island) $306 million (in 1998 dollars, $1.78 billion)
Worcester County Tornado	June 9, 1953	Probable F5 event; track 46 miles long, up to 1 mile wide; "explosive"-type destruction observed	Worcester County, Mass., especially Holden, Worcester and Shrewsbury	94 killed, 400 seriously injured	Extensive destruction in residential areas, including suburban housing development; Assumption College (Worcester) heavily damaged; total damage $53 million
Hurricane Diane	August 17– 19, 1955	Storm track south of Long Island; up to 20 in. rain in some inland areas, triggering catastrophic flooding	Inland southern areas, especially Torrington and Waterbury, Conn., Woonsocket, R.I.	82 dead	Inundations of populated areas; severe structural and infrastructural damage; disruption of services; $800 million damage ($1.1 billion in 1998 dollars)
Pre-Christmas Ice Storm	December 16–17, 1973	Nor'easter producing freezing rain; ice sheaths on trees and power lines more than 1 in. thick	Connecticut, especially central sections	At least five deaths	Worst power outages to date in Northeast history; 250,000 temporarily forced from homes; tree damage greater in Connecticut than during 1938 hurricane
Blizzard of '78	February 6, 1978	Nor'easter with aspects of a "snow hurricane"; snow depths of 27 in. in Boston, up to 4 ft. in northern Rhode Island; wind gusts to 79 mph in Boston, 110 mph at sea; significant storm tides	Southern and eastern coastal areas; Boston and Providence areas especially hit hard	99 deaths	Extensive beach erosion and shore damage (including destruction of famous landmarks); transportation paralyzed for days; 53 arrested for looting in the Boston area; $500 million damage

(*continued*)

New England's Disastrous Weather (*continued*)

Familiar Name	Date	Description	Area(s) of Maximum Effect	Casualties	Damage and Description
Hurricane Bob	August 19, 1991	Hurricane; Rhode Island landfall, then cutting across southeastern Massachusetts	Southern New England, especially Rhode Island and southeastern Massachusetts	18 deaths	One of the top 10 costliest hurricanes; $900 million in property damage; 2.1 million businesses and homes lost power for more than 24 hours
January Ice Storm	January 5–9, 1998	Slow-moving weather systems producing extensive icing; sheaths 1–3 in., up to 9 in. on tower structures	Northern Northeast, especially Maine	Six dead; upwards of 400 treated for CO_2 poisoning	840,000 Maine residents (70%) without power up to three weeks; widespread damage to trees, power and communications facilities; estimated $330 million damage

Boston Harbor Boston Harbor consists of 45 square miles of shallow waters enclosed by the Nantasket peninsula to the south and Winthrop peninsula and Deer Island to the north. The harbor achieved notoriety during the 1980s as one of the nation's worst pollution problems, but before that it had been many things. From the first European settlement of the Massachusetts Bay Colony in 1630 until the 19th century, Boston's well-protected harbor made the town a focal point for American trade. Boston boats harvested flounder, lobster, shellfish, and herring from the harbor and cod from nearby Stellwagon Bank and shipped their catches to ports throughout the world. Despite serious pollution and a high incidence of pollution-related cancers in harbor fish, Boston is still an important fishing port, with significant commercial harvests of lobster, clams, and flounder. Only specially licensed commercial gatherers, restricted to 40 percent of the existing local beds, may dig for clams.

Forty-five islands dot the harbor, housing a city shelter, sewage treatment plants, swimming beaches, a state park, an environmental education center, a condominium development, and a variety of navigational aides. Some are legacies of efforts to cure the sick and reform the poor and criminal by isolating them from urban life. Others reflect a long history of using Boston Harbor for garbage and waste disposal. Archeologists have found historic or prehistoric artifacts in every test pit excavated on the harbor islands.

Boston Harbor's deteriorating water quality first attracted attention in the 1870s when public health officials concluded that odors from a failing sewer system threatened to spread epidemics throughout the city. To remove wastewater from the waterfront, the city created a network of intercepting sewers that sent Boston's sewage out to sea with every outgoing tide, an approach so revolutionary that it won many awards. By 1889, however, Bostonians had realized that this system did not go far enough. That year, the Massachusetts legislature incorporated Boston's sewage system into a regional network of sewers servicing towns throughout the Mystic, Charles, and Neponset River drainages. Extending the sewer network inland protected river quality but significantly increased the pollution loads of water flowing into the harbor.

Regional sewers dramatically improved water quality in Boston-area rivers but seemed only to concentrate wastes in the harbor. In 1939, the sixth report on pollution since 1900 declared the harbor "revolting to the aesthetic sensibilities." In 1952 and 1968 regional sewer officials built two of the three plants recommended in 1939; however, neither of these improved water quality as expected.

By the 1980s, population growth had grossly overextended sewage facilities. Raw sewage from 43 percent of Massachusetts's population and untreated wastes from more than 5,000 industrial plants flowed directly into the harbor from 108 overflow pipes, many still located along Boston's waterfront. In 1982 the South Shore community of Quincy sued the Metropolitan District Commission in an effort to halt further pollution. Finding in Quincy's favor, the courts forced the state to create the Massachusetts Water Resources Authority, which initiated the Boston Harbor cleanup. In a subsequent suit the courts also determined that Massachusetts was in violation of the 1972 Clean Water Act and required the state to develop a plan for new primary and secondary sewage treatment facilities. Beginning in 1995, partially treated wastes were diverted from the harbor into a huge pipe emptying into Massachusetts Bay, and by 1996 water quality had improved enough to permit swimming at harbor beaches. Since 1999 sewage overflows have been processed at a secondary treatment facility on Deer Island that uses microorganisms to digest organic matter. These new sewage treatment facilities have provided the first real improvement in harbor waste disposal since the 19th century.

The cleanup has cost more than $3 billion in addition to the $2.5 billion spent since 1967, a huge investment in environmental quality that represents an important acknowledgment of the harbor's significance to the region. Nonetheless, these efforts will not undo damage caused in the past. Landfill has drastically reduced vital salt marsh acreage, and dams and river pollution have eliminated fish spawning in harbor tributaries.

Massachusetts Bay Programs, *Massachusetts Bays 1991 Comprehensive Conservation and Management Plan: An Evolving Plan for Action* (1991); Massachusetts Water Resources Authority, *The Boston Harbor Project's Effluent Outfall: Overview of the Issues and Introduction to Phase I of the Monitoring Plan* (1992); Seth Rolbein, "Dangerous Waters: Boston's Floating Crap Game," *Boston Magazine* (May 1987).

Sarah S. Elkind

Canals and Turnpikes The period of canal and turnpike construction in New England began in the 1790s and had largely ended by the 1820s, although most water- and roadways built during this era were still in use many years later. Leading New England merchants of the late 1700s envisioned a network of improved highways that would enable teams to transport increased loads at higher speeds, on wheels in summer and on runners in winter. They also proposed to channel New England's water into canals that would allow heavy cargoes of goods and animals to be carried through the countryside to market on boats resembling the freight gondolas and passenger packets used along the seacoast.

Such projects were beyond the power of the limited government of the period, so private corporations, empowered to charge tolls, became the means through which canals and improved highways were financed and built. Canal corporations levied tolls at locks; turnpike corporations placed gates or pikes at stated intervals; bridge corporations erected tollhouses at the portals of their spans. Legislatures granted powers of eminent domain to these corporations, allowing the companies to design extensive projects without fear of being thwarted by individual landowners.

New England's most ambitious canal was the Middlesex, completed in 1803 under the supervision of Loammi Baldwin, Sr. This 27-mile route, from Charlestown to the Merrimack River at Pawtucket Falls (later the site of Lowell), Mass., pioneered large-scale canal building in the United States. North of Pawtucket Falls, the natural bed of the Merrimack River was made navigable by completion of Blodgett's Canal at Derryfield (later Manchester), N.H., in 1807, followed by other locks around upstream waterfalls and rapids. In 1815 boats began regular runs between Concord, N.H., and Boston via the Middlesex Canal. Improved transportation on the Connecticut River began when the first inland navigation canal to be chartered in the United States was built around Bellows Falls on the upper Connecticut River between 1791 and 1802. Corporations built locks around rapids on the Connecticut River at South Hadley (opened in 1795), Turner's Falls (1800), and other falls as far south as Windsor Locks, Conn. The Blackstone Canal, connecting Providence, R.I., and Worcester, Mass., opened in 1828.

The turnpike era began in New England when toll roads were established between New London and Norwich, Conn., in 1792 and between Glocester, R.I., and the Connecticut state line in 1794. By 1830, when turnpike profits began to decline and some corporations abandoned their roads to town control, more than 380 turnpikes had been chartered in New England.

The technology of the time was barely adequate to complete such works. Both canal and turnpike construction depended largely on human and animal muscle, aided by simple tools such as plows, shovels, crowbars, wheelbarrows, and dump carts. Completion of such projects required improvements in surveying instruments and techniques; blasting, stone splitting, and stone masonry; and bridge design.

Canal and turnpike projectors remained sanguine even as earlier corporations began to experience financial losses. Schemes to connect Lake Champlain with the sea at Portsmouth by canal, or Boston with Providence, were still being advanced in the 1820s. New turnpike corporations sought charters in the 1830s, even as other planners were beginning to promote railroads.

Although the Cape Cod Canal (1914) remains important as a shipping route, older canals are seen mostly as marshy traces, abandoned locks, or short, restored remnants. Those with adequate water supplies were sometimes converted to power canals for mills or hydroelectric plants. Many former turnpikes remain in use as town or state highways, often transformed into major arteries of travel. Others, by contrast, have been abandoned and exist only as trails.

Canal and turnpike corporations were the first public utilities of New England. They were authorized by law and accountable to the governments that chartered them. These corporations pooled the investments of shareholders into large reserves of capital and completed projects that had great economic and social significance in their era. The experience gained by these corporations in finance, management, civil engineering, and land surveying established models for the planning and construction of the railroads, which supplanted turnpike and canal alike. Turnpikes and canals bound distant regions through common financial and cultural interests, breaking down the insularity that had characterized much of New England from the time of early settlement.

Hayden L. V. Anderson, *Canals and Inland Waterways of Maine* (1982); Charles Rufus Harte, *Connecticut's Canals* (1938); Christopher Roberts, *The Middlesex Canal, 1793–1860* (1938); Frederic J. Wood, *The Turnpikes of New England,* (1997 [1919]).

James L. Garvin

Cape Cod National Seashore

Occupying a substantial area, mainly on the Atlantic side of the Cape Cod peninsula, from below Chatham, Mass., in the south to Provincetown, Mass., and its environs in the northwest, the Cape Cod National Seashore conserves land that was touched by Captain Myles Standish and the *Mayflower* Pilgrims in November 1620, was visited by Henry David Thoreau in the mid-19th century, and is beloved of generations of American artists and vacationers.

The comment made by Thoreau in his 1865 work *Cape Cod* is still apt: "I did not see why I might not make a book on Cape Cod, as well as my neighbor on 'Human Culture.' It is but another name for the same thing, and hardly a sandier phase of it." The interaction of nature and culture is very much in evidence on the Cape Cod National Seashore, created by an act of Congress and signed into law by President John F. Kennedy on August 7, 1961.

Conservationists first broached the idea of protecting this area in the 1950s. The eventual act passed by Congress focused on both conservation and recreation. In the beginning the National Seashore covered primarily the less populated Lower Cape, particularly the extensive sand dune and beach areas of Wellfleet, Truro, and Provincetown. Marked by the exhilarating combination of sea, sand, light, and air for which Cape Cod has long been reputed, the seashore is also rare in the national park system for its proximity to large population centers in the Northeast. Under the general jurisdiction of the Department of the Interior, it now covers nearly 45,000 acres.

In its planning stages the proposed seashore was unpopular with many Cape towns and residents, who, embracing a materialist version of American individualism, feared the loss of private property. It has won overall acceptance, however, illustrating, in the words of Charles Foster, that "a national park can enjoy an effective and even symbiotic relationship with adjacent communities. . . . The stable land base represented by the Seashore has encouraged private investment and reinvestment both outside its boundaries and for those remaining within but subject to protective zoning." The Cape Cod National Seashore was the first major national park for which acquisition funds were authorized by Congress. That enabled certain state lands—notably, the "Province Lands" of rolling dunes and grasses near Provincetown—to be incorporated into the conservation area and set a pattern for future instances of federal, state, and local cooperation. Indeed, Cape Cod was the model for a series of national seashores, from Point Reyes, California, to Padre Island, Texas, and Fire Island outside New York City.

Concluding his book, Thoreau judged Cape Cod far superior to "a ten-pin alley, or a circular railway, or an ocean of mint-julep. . . . A man may stand there and put all America behind him." Creation of the Cape Cod National Seashore has gone a long way toward preserving what Thoreau so highly valued. But the Cape is not immune today from hazards posed by both natural forces and visitors who expect to recreate in as well as conserve

Cape Cod National Seashore, Nauset Light Beach, Eastham, Mass., 1988

the Cape's fragile ecology. Increasing numbers of tourists—nearly 5 million in 1998—threaten to overrun unspoiled horizons as surely as the sea erodes the peninsula's beaches and dunes. Soon it may no longer be possible for a person to stand, like Thoreau, on Cape Cod and "put all America behind him." All America may soon be standing there, too.

Charles H. W. Foster, *The Cape Cod National Seashore: A Landmark Alliance* (1985); Henry David Thoreau, *Cape Cod,* ed. Joseph J. Moldenhauer (1988).

George K. Romoser

Carson, Rachel (1907–64) Writer, biologist, and environmentalist. Rachel Louise Carson was born in Springdale, Penn., educated at Pennsylvania College for Women (now Chatham College), and received a master's degree in zoology from the Johns Hopkins University in 1932. Although she made her home in Silver Spring, Md., Maine was her spiritual home. Its coast and marine life were her research laboratory, and she drew upon its beauty in her popular natural histories of the sea. Carson's love of nature ultimately compelled her to challenge the accepted idea of the value of technological progress and to speak out against the wide-spread misuse of pesticides, which she believed endangered the future well-being of the living world.

Carson first saw the ocean in 1929 when she went to New England to work at the Marine Biological Laboratory in Woods Hole, Mass. For 15 years Carson was employed as an aquatic biologist and editor at the U.S. Bureau of Fisheries (later the Fish and Wildlife Service) in Washington, D.C. She published her first book on marine life, *Under the Sea-Wind: A Naturalist's Picture of Ocean Life,* in 1941. A decade later her best-selling book *The Sea Around Us* (1951) won the National Book Award and established her as a leading authority on the earth's oceans. The book's success enabled Carson to buy land on Southport Island off Boothbay Harbor, Maine, where she built a summer cottage. In 1952 she resigned from her post at the Bureau of Fisheries to devote her time to writing. Her research in the tide pools and rocky shores of the Maine coast provided much of the material for *The Edge of the Sea* (1955), an ecological approach to life along the shore.

Carson's lifelong interest in conservation and preservation was heightened by her summers in Maine. In 1956 she tried to save a tract of forest on Southport Island. Although this effort failed, Carson helped establish the Maine chapter of the Nature Conservancy. In July 1958 she published an influential article, "Our Ever-Changing Shore," in *Holiday* magazine, in which she drew attention to the rapid loss of pristine seashore areas in the United States, such as the ones she had written about, and argued for their preservation.

Carson began *Silent Spring* (1962), her most influential book, in 1958. Her decision to write a book attacking the pesticide policies of government and industry sprang in part from her fear that all she held precious in nature would be destroyed by the overuse of chemical biocides. Her achievement in *Silent Spring* was to make the complex science of ecology understandable to the general public and to awaken people to their individual responsibilities. The contemporary environmental movement can be dated from the controversy that surrounded Carson's book and its eventual validation.

Carson's posthumously published book *The Sense of Wonder* (1965) conveys her deeply held belief that appreciation for the beauty and wonder of the earth could halt the course of humankind's senseless destruction of the natural world. She died of cancer and heart disease at her home in Maryland at the age of 56.

Martha Freeman, ed., *Always, Rachel: The Letters of Rachel Carson and Dorothy Freeman, 1952–1964* (1995); Linda Lear, *Rachel Carson: Witness for Nature* (1997); Linda Lear, ed., *Lost Woods: The Discovered Writing of Rachel Carson* (1998); Mary A. McCay, *Rachel Carson* (1993).

Linda Lear

Catamounts The catamount (*Felis concolor*), or eastern mountain lion or cougar, has long been a powerful symbol of the New England wilderness. A large, graceful cat that can live in various habitats, the catamount ranges in size from 70 to 200 pounds in adulthood; the male may measure up to 9 feet long nose to tail, and 24 to 30 inches tall at the shoulder. Even before Europeans arrived in New England, indigenous peoples such as the Abenaki wove tales about the big cat into their legendry. Colonial French and Anglo settlers feared the beast and hunted it persistently. Catamounts, with their eerie howls and stealthy ways, haunted the woods that early homesteaders hoped to turn into productive farms. Tales circulated about the cats stalking people on paths and leaping high barrier fences to steal and kill lambs and calves. Towns organized communal hunts, and each state placed substantial bounties on catamounts. Even on exhibit—for instance, when an entrepreneur brought one to Boston in 1741—the feline was fearsome.

But for all their fear of the lions, some New Englanders also appreciated and identified with their wild ways. Vermonters, in particular, adopted the cat as a symbol of their own independence. In the 1760s and 1770s, the Green Mountain Boys gathered at Stephen Fay's tavern in Bennington, which had a stuffed catamount on a platform in front. The cat was allegedly posed snarling toward the despised Yorkers to the west. Later Vermonters named the establishment the Catamount Tavern. During the Revolutionary War, Ethan Allen, according to some accounts, compared himself to a catamount and let loose a howl for his British captors. In the 1920s Bennington constructed a catamount statue on the site of the old tavern, Vermont issued a sesquicentennial coin with the cat on one side, and the University of Vermont adopted the feline as its mascot.

The actual catamount fared less well during these times. Relentless pressure from hunters and human encroachment cut down numbers severely; the cats were exterminated because of their attacks on domestic animals, especially as sheep raising became popular in the region. By the end of the Civil War, catamount hunts throughout most of New England became rare and noteworthy. In Vermont, for example, hunts in Weathersfield in 1867, West Wardsboro in 1875, and in Barnard in 1881 attracted much attention. Northern New England states—first New Hampshire in 1853, then Vermont in 1881 with the Barnard hunt, and next Maine in 1906—all declared the cat extirpated. That has remained the "official" view of state fish and wildlife departments, despite mounting numbers of sighting claims. In 1934 a group of Boy Scouts and their minister Scoutmaster touched off a region-wide debate with their assertions of spotting a catamount near Chester, Vt.

Increasingly over the next six decades stories of sightings have poured in from Vermont and Maine, and occasionally from New Hampshire and western Massachusetts. State officials and some zoologists have scoffed, maintaining that the observers were drunk or deluded or that the cats they saw were dogs, fishers, escaped pets or circus animals, or strays from Canada. Believers, including Middlebury College biologist Harold Hitchcock, retorted that the catamount had reestablished its former range because the percentage of forested acreage and number of deer had increased in the region. Fish and wildlife departments have loosened their stance lately; Vermont now keeps records of sighting reports. In September 1994 analysis of some scat found near Craftsbury, Vt., confirmed the presence of a catamount, but the department still suspects it was a stray. In the meantime several schools retain the catamount, panther, or wildcat as a mascot. Controversy over a

catamount sighting plays a key role in Vermont writer Chris Bohjalian's novel *Water Witches* (1995). The Catamount Brewery flourishes, and the stuffed catamount, the one that Alexander Crowell shot in 1881 in Barnard, remains the most popular exhibit at the Vermont Historical Society in Montpelier.

Thomas L. Altherr, "'Will's Panther Club': Rev. William J. Ballou, the Irrepressible and Uncompromising Order of Pantherites, and the Chester, Vermont, Catamount-Sighting Controversy, 1934–1936," *Vermont History* (1998); Altherr, "The Catamount in Vermont Folklore and Culture, 1760–1900," in Jay W. Tischendorf and Steven J. Ropski, eds., *Proceedings of the Eastern Cougar Conference, 1994* (1996); Robert Busch, *The Cougar Almanac* (1996); John Lazenby, "The Cat Is Back," *Vermont Life* 49 (1994).

Thomas L. Altherr

Civilian Conservation Corps Established in 1933 as part of a package of New Deal programs, the Civilian Conservation Corps (CCC) tried to solve two Depression-era crises simultaneously. Young, unemployed men stirred popular fears of groups of shiftless, amoral youth wandering the country, committing crimes in the absence of work. At the same time, the nation's forested and wild land was disappearing and losing its productivity at an alarming rate, a fact not lost on the burgeoning ranks of American conservationists who sought to turn the tide of human exploitation. The CCC sought to put this large population of at-risk youth to work restoring the health and productivity of America's forests and natural areas. Few New Deal programs enjoyed such near-universal popularity, and the CCC would set the stage for future government-sponsored youth programs such

as the Peace Corps and the Student Conservation Association.

Perhaps nowhere in America was the environmental damage resulting from human exploitation worse than in the New England states. Soil erosion and forest fires had taken their toll on the region many times during the previous century, and the CCC helped in such varied efforts as flood damage control, reforestation programs, and road building.

In 1933, New England had 90 CCC camps, with more than 18,000 enrollees. Many of the young men, aged 18 to 25, who signed up for the New England CCC were from impoverished northeastern urban areas such as Boston, Providence, and New York. Maine, New Hampshire, and Vermont had too few local enrollees to meet state needs, so the CCC imported workers from more populated areas. Some New England CCC detachments were composed of southern blacks, while others successfully integrated blacks into predominately white outfits.

In addition to the CCC's conservation success, the program also left New England well prepared for the postwar tourist boom. CCC units cleared ski trails, erected cabins, and set up picnic areas all over New England. Many of the region's state parks and trail systems owe their existence to the corps. Construction materials for most CCC building projects, including cabins, picnic shelters, and ranger stations, came from whatever was locally available, giving the structures a distinctly regional flavor. One such cabin has been preserved on the grounds of the Deerfield Fair in Deerfield, N.H., for use in historical exhibitions on the former CCC camp at this site, and as a piece of Deerfield Fair history.

Members of the Civilian Conservation Corps at a forestry camp in Danbury, N.H., 1934

The corps was not universally admired, despite its popularity. Efforts to make the CCC a permanent institution were opposed by various New England politicians and ultimately unsuccessful. Other controversies connected with proposed CCC expansion included the debate over Camp William James, established in 1941 in Sharon, Vt. Designed to be an experiment in mixing privileged youth with CCC enrollees in an effort to break down class barriers, the project was supported by such influential women as First Lady Eleanor Roosevelt and Vermont writers Dorothy Canfield Fisher and Dorothy Thompson. The camp drew the ire of many politicians, however, some of whom drew parallels between the fledgling experiment and Nazi youth camps. The project was eventually abandoned. Cost-cutting in the face of World War II brought the popular, although weakened, program to an end in 1942.

David D. Draves, *Builder of Men: Life in CCC Camps of New Hampshire* (1992); Jack Preiss, *Camp William James* (1978); John A. Salmond, *The Civilian Conservation Corps, 1933–1942: A New Deal Case Study* (1967); Frederick W. Stetson, "The Civilian Conservation Corps in Vermont," *Vermont History* 46 (1978).
Ryan McMillen

Climate

As Mark Twain noted in his "Speech on the Weather," "One of the brightest gems in the New England weather is the dazzling uncertainty of it. There is only one thing certain about it: you are certain there is going to be plenty of it—a perfect grand review; but you never can tell which end of the procession is going to move first." The region is known for the intensity and variety of its climatic conditions. Temporally significant climate changes have occurred over millennia, but weather in New England can also fluctuate from hour to hour. Spatially, the region has a strong climatic gradient from north to south, which is modified by dramatic climate changes with elevation. Also, proximity to the ocean strongly influences temperature and patterns of precipitation.

New England's modern climate is generally classified as Humid Continental, that is, characterized by warm summers, very cold winters, and a lack of strong seasonal variation in the distribution of precipitation. The region is classified as humid because its annual precipitation is greater than its potential evapotranspiration, which is the climatic demand for water through evaporation and/or transpiration given the temperature and length of daylight. Thus the region has an excess of moisture annually that recharges soil and groundwater or is converted into stream flow.

New England's location between the warm, moist equatorial climate to the south and the frigid climate of the Arctic to the north results in its climatic variability. Here in the mid-latitudes, air masses from opposing climates clash, producing several types of harsh, turbulent weather conditions that may take the form of tropical storms and hurricanes, tornadoes, drought, heat waves, frigid temperatures, nor'easters, blizzards, high winds, heavy rainfall, and flooding.

The climatology of New England is also significantly influenced by proximity to the ocean. The region's southern shore, including Connecticut, Rhode Island, and southern Cape Cod, is modified by the Gulf Stream, which is a warm water current flowing from south to north along the eastern coast of the United States. In contrast, the region's eastern shore, including coastal Maine, New Hampshire, and eastern Massachusetts, is influenced by the cold water Labrador current that flows southward from eastern Canada toward New England. These two currents, which meet near the southeastern tip of Cape Cod, play a major role in the specific climate patterns across the region.

Average annual temperatures range from near 50° F along the south shore of Rhode Island and Connecticut, to about 40° F in northern Maine but change little at locations of similar latitude and elevation. Decreases in temperature toward the north occur because lower solar angles at higher latitudes attenuate solar energy. Temperature averages decrease with elevation, however, as the result of lower atmospheric pressure; for example, the annual average temperature at the summit of Mount Washington (at an elevation of 6,288 feet, the highest point in the White Mountains) is 26.5° F, which is lower than temperatures found in extreme northern Maine.

Seasonal changes in temperature are largely controlled by the number of daylight hours and by solar intensity. Temperatures are warmer during the summer because the days are longer and the sun's rays are more direct than at any other time of the year. In Concord, N.H., daylight ranges from 15 hours and 24 minutes on the summer solstice (June 21–22) to 8 hours and 59 minutes on the winter solstice (December 22–23). On the summer solstice the sun reaches its highest point in the sky, peaking near 70 degrees above the horizon at solar noon (at 90 degrees the sun would be directly overhead), resulting in high-intensity radiation at the surface. In contrast, on the winter solstice when there are fewer hours of daylight, the sun rises only to near 23 degrees above the horizon. The change in day length throughout the year is greater to the north of Concord and less to the south.

Annual temperature ranges (the difference between the warmest and coldest average monthly temperature) are near 50° F in New England. Coastal sites tend to have smaller ranges than inland locations. Burlington, Vt., and Portland, Maine, for example, have similar annual averages (44.6° F and 45.8° F, respectively). Portland, however, is warmer in the winter and cooler in the summer than Burlington, resulting from the modifying maritime influence of offshore water, which experiences relatively small temperature fluctuations in both daily and seasonal cycles. Afternoon sea breezes during the spring and summer are an important component of this reduction in range; transported inland from the cool ocean surface, this cool ocean air tempers high afternoon temperatures in the coastal zone.

Northern New England is also noted for having the highest day-to-day variability in winter minimum temperatures. Northern Vermont is particularly subject to temperature extremes because of its distance from the coast. As a result, it is common for warm, moist, tropical air to invade the region from the south, only to be replaced rapidly by brutally cold and dry air from the polar regions of northern Canada or even Siberia. Polar air transported on northwesterly airstreams into the region remains frigid because it undergoes only slight modification as it moves over the cold and dry continental surface of Canada. The warmest temperature recorded in New England was 107° F measured at both Chester and New Bedford, Mass., on August 2, 1975, and the coldest was −50°F, measured at Bloomfield, Vt., on December 30, 1933.

Annual precipitation patterns across New England are very complex because of the effect of elevation. Elevation seems to enhance precipitation by forcing air currents to rise and cool, thereby producing condensation, clouds, and precipitation. Most of New England averages between 35 and 45 inches of precipitation annually; values are generally higher near the coastline and lower toward the north and west. Several areas, however, have significantly higher precipitation because of the effect of mountains. The summit of Mount Washington has the highest average annual precipitation in the region: 98.96 inches.

Central and southwestern New England experience the lowest month-to-month variations in average precipitation, as records for Hartford, Conn., show. In northern and northwestern New England, precipitation values are greater in the summer because of enhanced convective storms (that is, storms that are intensified by the transfer of heat, usually upward, by massive motion in the atmosphere). In the winter, the persistent flow of cold, dry air from Canada inhibits precipitation. This cold Canadian air is associated with high pressure, clear skies, and a general reduction in the capacity of the local atmosphere to carry moisture. The net result is lower precipitation during the winter than during the summer.

The eastern coastal zone of New England (Portland, Maine, for example) receives more precipitation in winter than summer and experiences peak precipitation in November. From late fall through early spring, powerful cyclones tracking near or across New England produce precipitation. During fall, relatively warm sea surface temperatures cause an increase in the evaporation of ocean water. This in turn increases the amount of atmospheric moisture carried by these cyclones, thereby increasing the possibility of heavy rainfall. The storm of late October 1996 is an example of this climatic process: it produced between 12 and 19 inches of rain along the eastern New England coast from Newburyport, Mass., to Portland, Maine. In contrast, summer precipitation is reduced in this coastal region because of the atmospheric stability induced by cold offshore water from the Labrador current and the resultant afternoon sea breeze. Consequently, the cooler afternoon temperatures suppress afternoon convective storm activity. This is the only area in the eastern United States where winter precipitation exceeds summer precipitation. Tropical storms and hurricanes, however, can occasionally produce intense summer and fall rainstorms anywhere within New England; Hurricane Diane, for example, generated more than 19 inches of rain in parts of Connecticut and Massachusetts in August of 1955.

Elevation and proximity to the coast also affect snowfall patterns. Approximately 30 inches fall annually along the southern shore of Connecticut, Rhode Island, and Massachusetts, whereas in northern Vermont, New Hampshire, and Maine annual snowfalls can range up to approximately 110 inches. Coastal locations generally have lower annual snowfalls than inland sites at the same latitude because of their relatively warmer winter temperatures. This is particularly true along the southern coast of New England, but periodically the cold water associated with the Labrador current is sufficiently warm in winter to convert snowfall to rain in the northern coastal zone

Snowfall totals also tend to increase with elevation because of the uplift of air over mountains and the overall cooler temperatures at higher altitudes. This is noticeable in both the White and Green Mountains. Mount Washington, for example, averages 254 inches of snow per year; during the winter of 1968–69, the total was an impressive 566 inches. There also seems to be some "lake effect" enhancement of snowfall from Lake Ontario, located on the northern border of New York state and perhaps from Lake Champlain in northwestern Vermont. Lake effect snowfalls are produced when warm surface water evaporates, creating moisture that is rapidly converted to snow just downwind from the source. Most of the largest snowstorms in New England, however, are produced by coastal nor'easters.

Over the past 2 million years New England experienced periods of glaciation, interrupted by interglacial epochs. Although the causes of these shifting patterns are much debated, they were probably associated with changing orbital relationships between the earth and the sun, as postulated by the Serbian astrophysicist Milutin Milankovitch. The paleoclimatology of New England is significant because the relentless advance and retreat of ice across the area shaped the modern landscape through erosion and deposition and created dramatically different climate regimes that have persisted for thousands of years.

David Ludlum, *The Country Journal New England Weather Book* (1976); Glenn T. Trewartha, *The Earth's Problem Climates* (1981); Mark Twain, "Speech on the Weather," *The Family Mark Twain* (1935).

Barry D. Keim

Connecticut River Valley

Draining more than 11,000 square miles, the Connecticut River originates 1,880 feet above sea level at a series of small lakes on the U.S.-Canadian border and flows 400 miles south until finally spilling into Long Island Sound at Saybrook, Conn. The northern section of the river, which serves as the border between Vermont and New Hampshire, courses over a hard-rock base through a narrow valley with high hills on either side; tributary valleys lead into the main river basin. Once in Massachusetts, the valley widens into gently sloping hills and meadows. Below Hadley Falls, at Holyoke Dam in southwestern Massachusetts, the land flattens into a broad expanse that encompassed a glacial lake at the end of the last ice age. Below Middletown, Conn., the valley again narrows, slicing through hard rock on its last leg to the sea.

The abundant flora and fauna of the valley sustained a significant population of Native Americans—Western Abenaki to the north and Agawams to the south—and also made the area attractive to Europeans. Adriaen Block and his Dutch traders sailed up the lower Connecticut River in search of furs in 1614. Beginning in 1615, the first of many European epidemic diseases decimated the Native American population. The remaining Indians exchanged furs for manufactured goods with the increasing numbers of European settlers moving into the valley. By the middle of the 17th century English Puritans had settled communities in Hartford, Middletown, Windsor, and Wethersfield, Conn., and Springfield and Westfield, Mass.

Early settlers combined farming with fur trading, but excessive trapping soon obliterated the fur-bearing animals and drove native people to sell land in return for trade goods. During the 18th century farmers cut trees, constructed dams to provide power for milling lumber and grinding grain, mowed and drained meadows for pastureland, and turned the Connecticut River valley north of Middletown, Conn., to Vermont and New Hampshire into farmland. As the only area of New England to produce an agricultural surplus during these years, the valley's products (wheat, fish, wool, pork, and beef) found their way to distant markets, particularly in the West Indies.

The valley's agriculture became increasingly commercial during the early 19th century, and rural manufacturing developed. The success of the mills in Lowell, Mass., and the westward expansion of railroads resulted in heavy industrial investment in the valley by midcentury. Textile mills in Chicopee, Mass., and textile, paper, rubber, and machine shops in Holyoke utilized the river's waterpower. Brass, iron, and armament works were built in Springfield, Mass., and in Windsor and Hartford, Conn. In 1785 Enoch Hale erected the first bridge across the Connecticut River, connecting Walpole, N.H., with Bellows Falls, Vt. By 1796 bridges crossed the river at Springfield, Mass.; Windsor, Vt.; and Hanover, N.H.

The valley's economy changed significantly during the late 19th and 20th centuries. Toward the end of the 19th century, grain and beef production diminished as truck farming emerged to meet the needs of growing urban areas. At the same time, dairy farming became significant to the economy of the northern valley, becoming Vermont's leading industry by 1900. Vermont's farms supplied first butter and later fresh milk to urban markets to the south and east. But the valley's manufacturing base began to decline during the 1920s. Northern Connecticut increasingly relied on the insurance business, as industrial jobs became scarce.

Although industry brought jobs to the region, it also brought pollution and urban crowding. Factories dumped industrial wastes into the Connecticut River and its tributaries, and crowded tenements emptied sewage directly into whatever ditch, creek, or stream was convenient. By 1900 the pristine river—which once teemed with fish and supported a significant shad fishery—was so badly polluted and dammed that few fish could survive, and the river developed the reputation of being a "most beautiful sewer."

After years of excessive pollution, the Connecticut River has begun to experience a mild recovery. The Clean Water Act of 1972 helped to transform the river from a Class C river (no fishing or swimming) to a Class B river (both allowed). Although it is now a viable recreation site, the river still faces threats of pollution from residential sewage as surrounding communities spring up before adequate sewage treatment is available. Flooding, a problem for valley residents for 200 years, culminated in the devastation of 1927 (including the famous Vermont Flood of 1927), and the federal government built a series of flood-control dams during the 1930s and 1940s.

By contributing to the remodeling of old mills and the development of new homesteads, academic institutions and high-tech companies have helped revitalize the valley in recent years. A haven for artists and writers in the 19th century, the valley is again attracting intellectuals, craftspeople, and artists who appreciate the semirural setting and cultural offerings of the area's universities and colleges.

Despite its scenic tranquillity and intellectual excitement, the valley is still haunted by the collapse of its older industrial base. Cities such as Holyoke, Hartford, and Chicopee suffer from high levels of unemployment, declining tax revenues, and shrinking services.

Jan Albers, *Hands on the Land: A History of the Vermont Landscape* (2000); Christopher Clark, *The Roots of Rural Capitalism: Western Massachusetts 1780–1860* (1990); Timothy Dwight, *Travels in New England and New York* (1821–22); Walter Hard, *The Connecticut* (1947); Jerold Wikoff, *The Upper Valley: An Illustrated Tour along the Connecticut River before the 20th Century* (1985); Michael Tougias, *River Days: Exploring the Connecticut River from Source to Sea* (2001).

John T. Cumbler

Earthquakes New England and adjacent regions have experienced numerous significant earthquakes. While most have been minor, some were strongly felt and a few were violent enough to damage property. The first European settlers in the region were frightened by a strong earthquake in 1638 although no damage was reported. In 1727 an earthquake strongly shook Newburyport, Mass., and was felt throughout all of New England. In 1755 a larger earthquake centered off Cape Ann, Mass., and with an estimated magnitude of 6.25 on the Richter scale damaged buildings along the coast from Scituate, Mass., to Portland, Maine, and was felt from Nova Scotia to Maryland. In 1904 a strong earthquake centered near Eastport, Maine, caused minor damage near its epicenter, and in 1940 a pair of moderately strong shocks that were centered in the Ossipee Mountains of New Hampshire damaged chimneys throughout the epicentral region. Strong earthquakes in southeastern Canada—in 1663, 1732, 1870, 1925, and 1988 in Quebec and 1982 in New Brunswick—were felt in New England.

New England is riddled with faults from past geologic activity, and as in other seismically active parts of the earth, earthquakes of small magnitude are much more frequent than those of larger magnitude. Each year about half a dozen earthquakes are felt somewhere in New England, most of Richter magnitude 3.5 or less. These minor shocks cause no damage. Earthquakes above magnitude 5.0, capable of at least minor damage, occur, on average, once every 55 to 60 years in New England. Earthquakes above magnitude 6.0, the estimated size of the 1755 shock, probably occur only once every 500 or so years. No earthquake above magnitude 7.0 has been recorded in the region; such a large shock would probably be a once-in-5,000-year occurrence.

While some states are more active than others, all New England states have experienced earthquakes. Maine experiences approximately half of New England's earthquakes annually, with most activity in the central, western, and coastal parts of the state. Earthquakes have occurred in all parts of New Hampshire; most happen between the lakes region and the Massachusetts border. Most quakes felt in Vermont have occurred along the eastern border or in the northwestern corner of the state. Most earthquakes in Massachusetts happen in the northeastern and southeastern parts of the state, with some epicenters in central Massachusetts. Earthquake activity has been felt along coastal Rhode Island and Connecticut and in central Connecticut. Current earthquake data are insufficient to verify which faults in the region are seismically active.

In New England, as in all of the eastern two-thirds of North America, earthquakes are caused by plate tectonic forces. North America is spreading at the center of the Atlantic Ocean away from Europe and Africa and is pushing against the Pacific Ocean plate on the west. This squeeze gradually builds up pressure in the North American plate, and earthquakes happen when pressure is released that has accumulated over geologic time.

Although New England is typically associated with natural disasters such as nor'easters, floods, blizzards, and hurricanes, earthquakes continue to fascinate regional geologists and the public alike. Native American references to earthquakes survive in some New England place-names, such as Moodus ("place of noises") in Connecticut and Nashoba ("hill that shakes") in Massachusetts. The events in 1727 and 1755 provoked religious revivals and momentary panic as fervent colonists believed the quakes to be an expression of God's anger, perhaps auguring the end of the world. Today, structures in New England are designed to withstand earthquake shaking, many children learn about earthquake safety in school, and felt earthquakes get widespread media coverage.

John E. Ebel and Alan L. Kafka, "Earthquake Activity in the Northeastern United States," in *Neotectonics of North America* (1991); Massachusetts Emergency Management Agency, *Earthquakes in New England* (1986); Carl W. Stover and Jerry L. Coffman, *Seismicity of the United States, 1568–1989*, rev. ed. (1993).

John E. Ebel

Endangered Species Although New England hosts myriad natural habitats, few species are native to the region. Human activity, including overharvesting, alteration of habitats, and pollution, has placed some of the native and often naturally rare species perilously close to extinction. These same activities have also caused local extinction of more common species such as the sea-beach amaranth, the eastern cougar, and the gray wolf. The federal Endangered Species Act of 1973 and state endangered species laws were enacted to stop this trend. As of December 1998, 33 species of plants and animals in New England were listed as threatened or endangered and receive varying levels of protection. Equally as important as protection, however, is official recognition of the rarity of a species and the need for its conservation. This recognition prompts widespread efforts toward the recovery of federally listed and many state-listed endangered and threatened species.

Some of the first species listed as endangered in New England include the peregrine falcon, bald eagle, small whorled pogonia, and two endemic plants: the Furbish lousewort and the Robbins' cinquefoil. The Furbish lousewort occurs only along the banks of the Saint John River in northern Maine and has been affected by dams, bank stabilization, and commercial development of its habitat. Unfortunately, little of its remaining habitat is permanently protected. On the other hand, Robbins' cinquefoil, an alpine plant found in three sites in the White Mountains of New Hampshire, occurs entirely on U.S. Forest Service lands. Populations of this plant have recovered from previous overcollecting by botanists and trampling by hikers. Soon it will be delisted, its recovery the result of measures taken by the U.S. Forest Service, the Appalachian Mountain Club, the New England Wildflower Society, and the U.S. Fish and Wildlife Service.

The small whorled pogonia, a small, green orchid, was known to exist in only 17 locations when it was first listed as endangered in 1982. Government agencies, conservation groups, academia, and interested landowners worked hard to recover this species. In 1994 the small whorled pogonia was downlisted to threatened with the discovery of more than 85 additional sites and protection of more than 60 percent of its populations.

The status of two other species has also dramatically improved since listing. The bald eagle, almost eliminated from New England, now nests in Connecticut, Massachusetts, New Hampshire, and Maine. By 1995 the bald eagle had sufficiently recovered throughout its range for it to be reclassified to threatened. The peregrine falcon, another bird that had disappeared from the East because of pesticide poisoning, was taken off the endangered species list in 1999 and now nests on mountain cliffs and ledges of high-rise buildings in all of the New England states.

Several species found on beaches—the threatened northeastern beach tiger beetle (Massachusetts), the threatened piping plover (Maine, New Hampshire, Massachusetts, Connecticut, and Rhode Island), and the endangered roseate tern (Maine, New Hampshire, Massachusetts, and Connecticut)—declined because of commercial and residential development of their habitats and an increase in recreational activities, coupled with increased nesting competition with other seabirds. These species are also found outside of New England, and rangewide efforts are slowly bringing them back. The piping plover population in New England has increased far more than anywhere else in its range, primarily because of strong state protection and a cadre of dedicated biologists and volunteers.

Recently, partnerships among the U.S. Fish and Wildlife Service; other federal, state, and local agencies; conservation organizations; schools; private entities; and citizens' groups have been forged to work toward the conservation of endangered species. The New England Plant Conservation Program, for example, is a coalition of 68 different organizations dedicated to the conservation of regionally rare plants. The survival of New England's only Karner blue butterfly population in Concord, N.H., rests in the hands of a coalition formed by developers, local government, the Nature Conservancy, and the U.S. Fish and Wildlife Service, all working toward restoring its population and protecting its habitat. The slow, steady recovery of many of New England's endangered species suggests the efficacy of these and other innovative approaches to conservation.

Garrett E. Crow, *New England's Rare, Threatened, and Endangered Plants* (1982); David W. Lowe, John R. Matthews, Charles J. Moseley, eds., *The Official World Wildlife Fund Guide to Endangered Species of North America* (1990).

Susanna L. von Oettingen

Environmental Disease

In light of current medical knowledge, any historic disease process must be understood as environmental—whether transmitted by germs, induced by toxins, or encouraged by diet, whether epidemic or endemic. During the four centuries of New England's documented history, the diseases of the region have varied with the historic transformations of its societies and ecologies, usually in a fashion parallel to those of other American regions. From the 1500s well into the 1800s, New England inhabitants seldom considered the modern notion of environmental disease—that of agents or conditions in an organism's physical environment causing a specific pathology. They did, however, conceive of their ailments in terms of interaction between the body and its surroundings.

Pre-Columbian Native Americans in New England suffered from diseases that medical science would later identify as environmentally caused—ranging from infectious maladies such as pneumonia and roundworm to nutritional diseases such as pellagra. Nonetheless, they, like other Native American groups whose exposure to biological exchanges from intercontinental trade remained limited, stayed remarkably free of the deadly infectious ailments that plagued Europe and Africa. And, like Indians in other sections of North America, they viewed environmental influences on these ailments in terms of animistic universes specific to each culture.

In New England, as in other parts of the Americas, the first great documented epidemics of environmental disease occurred in the 16th and 17th centuries, as Native Americans were exposed to and intermixed with Europeans. New germs from Europe and Africa—notably smallpox but also plague, cholera, influenza, and perhaps tuberculosis and yellow fever—attacked the unprepared immune systems of Native Americans, leaving communities devastated. Although New England's Indians probably battled epidemics during the initial century of European contact, the first documented epidemic struck the Massachusetts, Abenakis, Pawtuckets, and other groups beginning in 1617. When the Pilgrims arrived in Plymouth in 1620, they found a field of bones where a village had once stood. What may have been smallpox, yellow fever, or bubonic plague decimated as much as 90 percent of some Indian groups. The Pilgrims took these events as divine sanction for their new settlement. Epidemics throughout the colonial period weakened Native American resistance to European settlement.

From the 16th into the 19th century, European settlers in New England, though less vulnerable to the ailments that ravaged the Indians, continued to suffer from these as well as other environmental diseases. As epidemics of yellow fever and cholera swept through New England's cities during this era, inhabitants recognized that many of these diseases were caused or worsened by environmental agents, from malevolent atmospheres to fellow human beings. Taking action against epidemic outbreaks, ports and other towns whose traffic in people (and germs) made them especially susceptible set up quarantines. In the case of smallpox, the Puritans anticipated New England's later eminence in medical innovation by becoming the first, in 1721, to introduce a crude form of inoculation to North America. Yet New Englanders made little or no distinction between physical agents and divine influence in the occurrence of disease; hence, prayer and devotion seemed equal, or even superior, to more worldly measures. Indeed, behind some of colonial New England's most famous religious episodes—for example, the Salem witchcraft trials or the Great Awakening—lay an ever-present anxiety about how suddenly and capriciously disease could strike, and sometimes kill.

During the past century and a half, New Englanders have contributed significantly to the understanding and control of environmental diseases. By the late 18th and early 19th centuries, medical and nonmedical practitioners, as well as many laypeople, had come to understand most human ailments in terms of a dynamic equilibrium between body and environment. They tended to interpret any perceived imbalance of bodily substances (which they called "humours") or of temperature in terms of asymmetries between internal and external conditions. Efforts to alleviate these imbalances centered around diet and ventilation, to control what the body took in, and purgatives or laxatives, among other therapies, to regulate evacuation. Although early 19th-century doctors in Philadelphia enjoyed a more privileged status, elite New England physicians, especially those associated with medical schools at Harvard, Yale, and other centers of medical learning, played important roles in appropriating the more anatomically discrete and localized notions of disease. Based on autopsies and pathological studies, this new approach, which was then being developed on the Continent, especially in

France, focused on the body and its internal workings—what the physiologist Claude Bernard would call the *milieu intérieur*. In addition, during the first half of the 19th century in New England this method helped to reinforce and diversify environmental hypotheses about disease, as patients and doctors increasingly began to question the number and variety of localized environmental influences that might be deleterious or therapeutic to one's health.

Pulmonary tuberculosis, or phthisis, the most common cause of death at the time, is a case in point. Thought to be largely hereditary in origin, its alleviation or cure involved environmental manipulation. Male sufferers went to sea or to the arid West; females, confronted by the limits to their environmental options, raised their children to become, upon a mother's early death, orphans in others' homes. The built environment of New England also came to be implicated in disease. Early textile enterprises at Lowell and elsewhere were suspected as breeding grounds for new as well as old varieties of factory-related environmental disease. In the cities, the increased construction of hospitals, mental asylums, and sewage systems during this era also reflected an attempt to reduce disease through deliberate environmental change. Instead of remaining at home, the sick entered institutions whose grounds, interiors, facilities, and staff aimed, at least in theory, to correct the internal imbalances responsible for their sufferings.

Toward the latter half of the 19th century, New England's elite doctors and other health professionals emerged as national leaders in the new styles of medical and public health science that aspired to a less regionally specific and more universalized approach to environmental influences on disease. Long-established centers for medical education such as Harvard and Yale became some of the earliest to integrate new experimental sciences such as physiology and bacteriology into medical teachings. Along with changes in the knowledge base came changes in governmental practice. Local and state governments in New England, along with New York City, were among the first in America to integrate bacteriological techniques and insights into state interventions to prevent disease, thereby forging the modern model for public health initiatives. William Sedgwick, a bacteriologist at the Massachusetts Institute of Technology who collaborated with sanitary engineers at the Massachusetts State Board of Health; and Charles Chapin, who undertook an antibacterial campaign as health commissioner of Providence, R.I., were among the first to combat infectious diseases through the use of water filtration, antitoxins, and vaccinations.

Partly because of the growing use of these methods, but more because of improvements in nutrition and general living conditions, infectious diseases became less of a threat after the turn of the century. New England's medical and public health schools and its strong tradition of health-related state interventions established the region as a leader in the field of environmental influences on health, both at home and around the world. In 1918 Harvard became the first American university to have an academic department devoted to industrial hygiene—which became a crucial foundation for the later field of environmental health—partly as a result of pioneering compensation laws instituted by the state of Massachusetts within its industrial workplaces. After World War II, New England doctors and public health officials furthered their efforts to understand the environmental origins of chronic degenerative diseases such as cancer and heart disease, which dominated mortality statistics nationwide. Massachusetts was the second state in the country to inaugurate a cancer-control program, and the small Massachusetts town of Framingham became the site for a pathbreaking study of environmental and other risk factors predictive of heart disease. Exemplifying a new perspective and an experimentalist style of epidemiology, the Framingham investigation also helped link the nation's leading killer disease to environmental influences such as fat and salt in the diet.

Even as this post–World War II epidemiology was helping to pinpoint environmental causes of the two leading killer diseases of that era, increasingly sophisticated statistical capabilities helped stimulate new interest in the regional, and even local, nature of disease as well as of medical perceptions and practices. Again, New England's medical elite led the way, among them Alvan Feinstein, at the Yale–New Haven Hospital, who concentrated on elucidating specifically clinical (as opposed to laboratory or experimental) claims to knowledge; and John Wennberg, at Dartmouth's Mary Hitchcock Hospital, who demonstrated wide variances in medical procedures across the region. New Haven doctors, for instance, were far less likely to consider a disease hospitalizable than were their counterparts in Boston. Undoubtedly, this growing awareness of regional differences and the limits of medical universalism reinforced the post-1960 upsurge of skepticism toward medical authority. So did revelations about medical abuses of human experimentation, much of it spearheaded by New England clinicians such as Henry Beecher at Harvard's Massachusetts General Hospital. New England doctors thereby paved the way toward greater lay involvement in environmental health.

Nonmedical New Englanders also pioneered in this area. Rachel Carson drew heavily upon her New England ties in depicting pesticidal threats to humans as well as animals in her book *Silent Spring*. Olga Huckins, whose letter to Carson inspired the book, lived in Duxbury, Mass., and Morton Kisking, Carson's chief medical adviser, in Westport, Conn. During the 1970s, New England students and citizens organized the New Hampshire–based Clamshell Alliance, whose protests against the Seabrook nuclear power plant in southern New Hampshire moved the antinuclear movement to the forefront on the East Coast. The town of Woburn, Mass., also gave rise to a trailblazing and well-publicized branch of the environmental justice movement in the 1980s. When a number of local children developed leukemia, residents of the town joined with experts from the Harvard School of Public Health to document the association between contaminated well water and the local cancer rate, pursuing their grievances in court.

These upsurges of activism over environmental toxins in New England (and elsewhere in the United States) differed in important ways from those of the mid-19th century. Occurring at a time when medicine and public health had gained increasing authority in dealing with disease, these concerns often became enmeshed in the statistical, laboratory, and medical methods used to define and detect disease. They also focused more on the effect of industry and other human activities on the environment and were more apt to result in governmental interventions, especially on the federal level. Risk-factor conceptions of disease elaborated within public health and medicine after World War II may have represented an expert effort to address these anxieties. Historians have only begun to explore how these popular concerns about environmental threats to the human body draw upon a long tradition that extends to our forebears of the 19th century and earlier.

James Cassedy, *Charles V. Chapin and the Public Health Movement* (1962); Alfred Crosby, *The Columbian Exchange: Biological and Cultural Consequences of 1492* (1972); Jonathan Harr, *A Civil Action* (1995); W. B. Kannel, "The Framingham Experience," in *Coronary Heart Disease Epidemiology* (1992); Barbara Rosenkrantz, *Public Health and the State: Changing Views in Massachusetts, 1842–1936* (1972); Sheila Rothman, *Living in the Shadow of Death: Tuberculosis and the Social Experience of Illness in American History* (1995); Theodore Steinberg, *Nature Incorporated: Industrialization and the Waters of New*

England (1991); John Harley Warner, *The Therapeutic Perspective: Medical Practice, Knowledge, Identity in America; 1820–1885* (1986).

Christopher Sellers

Environmentalism

Environmentalism is the popular social and political movement to preserve, improve, and restore the presence and function of the natural environment and the resources people use. Early roots of environmentalism are found in the organized opposition to deforestation and industrial blight during the last decades of the 19th century that helped give rise to the progressive political movement. For example, efforts to pass the Weeks Act in 1911 resulted in an organization dedicated to protecting New Hampshire's White Mountain forests. This action also spawned conservation in both its utilitarian and scientific/rationalistic forms and in its preservationist/romanticist form. The term *environmentalism* came into modern usage during the mid-1960s in New England and throughout North America and continues to be used. Thus, it was a utilitarian form of conservation thought, a human reaction to the extraordinary waste, inefficiency, corruption, and greed associated with early large-scale industrialization during the era after the Civil War. Environmentalism was intended to be rational, efficient, and scientific; it yielded modern natural resource management and environmental management in all their forms.

Growing from the thought of Ralph Waldo Emerson, Henry David Thoreau, and other Transcendentalists, as well as the pathbreaking scientific and philosophical work of George Perkins Marsh in *Man and Nature* (1864), New England environmentalism has had a national impact that has fueled the public's reaction against resource depletion and destruction. Environmentalism had, and continues to have, a moderating effect on the pace and intensity of such resource depletion and ecological destruction. With this spiritual and religious history, it has been a reaction of the heart as much as of the mind.

Today's environmentalism draws first from early- to mid-20th-century thoughts and actions of John Muir, John Burroughs, Bob Marshall, William O. Douglas, Mary Austin, Aldo Leopold, Rachel Carson, Carl Sauer, William H. Whyte, and Henry Caudill. Rachel Carson is sometimes credited with bringing the word "environmentalist" into common parlance in 1962 with her book *Silent Spring;* the terms "conservationist" and "preservationist" represent pre-1962 usage. Modern environmentalism, however, was also boosted during the 1960s when questioning of and dissatisfaction with the post–World War II status quo—that of racial segregation, the nu-

clear arms race, and political witch-hunting—led to the Civil Rights, peace, and disarmament movements. Because these movements shaped many values, conservation of forests and soil, preservation of wilderness, and protection of endangered species of animal and plant life for the first time merged with a serious desire to curb and ultimately eliminate water and air pollution and natural resource waste worldwide. In particular, Barry Commoner's book *The Closing Circle* (1971) demonstrated that there was no place to hide from the consequences of pollution. To Commoner, environmentalists needed to go beyond simple awareness of problems to discover and eliminate pollution's life-threatening causes, even if that meant significantly redirecting society's economic and social goals or its applications of new technology.

Commoner's analysis was anticipated by Ian McHarg's book *Design With Nature* (1969). Both of these books helped give rise to environmentalists who had both a local and global view and who ultimately divided into "shallow" (or "reform") ecologists, who believe that the environment can be saved through rules, regulations, research, and money; and "deep" ecologists, who believe that modern social and political systems need to be completely replaced. Reformers tend to have faith in scientific, technological, economic, and political remedies, whereas deep ecologists believe that only a change in values and operating paradigms will bring solutions. Despite these differences, all environmentalists transform their concerns and beliefs into action and can precisely describe how environmentalism has changed their lives and perceptions of the world around them.

As mentioned, New Englanders contributed to early environmentalism in North America by giving birth to transcendental thought, which, among other things, extolled the beauty of and divinity in nature. New England has also been home to the town forests movement, town conservation commissions, land trusts, and some of the oldest private environmental organizations in the United States (for example, the Appalachian Mountain Club; Massachusetts, New Hampshire, and Rhode Island Audubon Societies; and the Society for the Protection of New Hampshire Forests). New England colleges and universities also created numerous and early environmental studies and conservation degree programs, with Dartmouth, the University of Vermont, Williams, the University of New Hampshire, Middlebury, and Yale among the earliest in the nation. The New England congressional delegation and federal regional agencies have on average been more environmentally involved and sensitive than counter-

parts elsewhere. Finally, private support of environmentalism (both large donor and grassroots) has been uncommonly strong in New England.

In New England, as in the nation, environmentalism is concerned with the quality of air and water, the prevention and control of pollution, and the restoration of watersheds, topsoil, forests, wetlands, and shorelines. Environmentalism is allied with sustainable agriculture, recycling, energy conservation, and renewable energy systems; with wilderness designation and preservation; with species and habitat protection; with conservation of the marine and estuarine environment; and with the legal, political, scientific, economic, and ethical questions pertaining to these topics. Many environmentalists can be found in federal government agencies in New England, including the regional offices of the Environmental Protection Agency, the National Park Service, the U.S. Fish and Wildlife Service, the Army Corps of Engineers, the Natural Resource Conservation Service (formerly Soil Conservation Service), the White Mountain and Green Mountain National Forest offices of the U.S. Forest Service, and their counterparts in state government. Professional and voluntary groups in New England include chapters of the Sierra Club, Wilderness Society, Clean Water Action, and The Greens. Other environmental groups include independent state-based organizations such as the state Audubon Societies, various natural resources councils, the Society for the Protection of New Hampshire Forests, Save the Bay (Rhode Island), and active regional organizations such as the League of Conservation Voters, the Appalachian Mountain Club, numerous public land trusts, the Clamshell Alliance, and organic farmers' organizations. Finally, local and grassroots organizations are numerous and perhaps play a bigger role in New England than in most other regions. Town conservation commissions, which originated in New England, are also active participants.

Major regional environmental threats have galvanized New England environmentalism in recent decades: nuclear power (notably Seabrook in New Hampshire and Millstone in Connecticut); pollution of Long Island Sound; coastal oil refineries and deep-water ports (notably the Onassis proposal for a port in New Hampshire's Great Bay estuary); Connecticut River dams and water quality; highway construction and widening (for example, the Maine Turnpike and an east-west highway across New Hampshire); logging (particularly clear-cutting) on private timberlands in Maine and in national forests of New Hampshire and Vermont; overfishing; Boston Harbor sewage pollution; hazardous air quality along the seacoast and in many inland areas; acid rain, especially in the mountains and in lakes; ski resort effects on water supply and quality, energy, and forests; coastal erosion; freshwater and coastal wetlands destruction; groundwater depletion and contamination (especially on Cape Cod and other coastal locations); waste incineration and toxic waste dumping; and the uncertain future of the region's northern forests. All of these issues and more sustain New England environmentalism.

Central to the idea of environmentalism is the debate over limits to growth, a debate with which all environmentalists are intimately allied. All scientific evidence suggests that there are tangible physical limits to growth. However, cultural belief dictates, in practice, that there are no limits to growth and that the belief in such limits is heretical to the doctrine of growthism (that is, an unfettered belief in unlimited growth) that we all know. Principal research on limits to growth has been done at New England institutions (MIT, Dartmouth, University of New Hampshire) under the auspices of Jay Forrester and Dennis and Donella Meadows. Given the pressure to conform to the worship of growth, a very shallow environmentalism might adhere to the idea of no limits, but most environmentalists by definition would more likely accept the notion that infinite growth in a finite environment is an absurdity, thus contributing another definition to the term "environmentalist."

In sum, contemporary environmentalism, in New England as elsewhere, ranges from reform or shallow environmentalism, which assumes that the system is flawed and can be fixed (via money, regulation, habitat acquisition, etc.), and a deeper form of environmentalism based on ecological principles which argues that the value system itself and ingrained assumptions upon which it is based are at fault and can be checked only through the embrace of a wholly new set of assumptions or values. The latter rejects the notion of unlimited economic growth and accepts the four ecological principles: that everything is connected to every other thing, that all waste must go somewhere, that there is a price to pay for every environmental abuse, and that the study of nature is the best guide for people seeking to protect it. Environmental statutes, regulatory authority, and virtually all institutions, public and private, adhere to the former—the essentially status quo paradigm. But a growing number of grassroots citizens' organizations and environmental education programs are adhering to or are at least seriously considering the more fundamental and radical change, the true paradigm shift, that is associated with the latter, with serious consideration of ecological principles. More New

Englanders are reaching the conclusion that a change in fundamental values, rather than the simple expenditure of funds, passage of statutes and regulations, or creation of institutions, will be necessary if environmental challenges, both within the region and around the globe, are to be successfully addressed.

John E. Carroll, *Environmental Diplomacy* (1983); John E. Carroll, ed., *International Environmental Diplomacy* (1988); John E. Carroll, Paul Brockelman, and Mary Westfall, eds., *The Greening of Faith: God, the Environment and the Good Life* (1997); John E. Carroll and Keith Warner, eds., *Ecology and Religion: Scientists Speak* (1998); William Cronon, *Changes in the Land: Indians, Colonists and the Ecology of New England* (1983); Samuel P. Hays, *Beauty, Health and Permanence: Environmental Politics in the United States, 1955–1985* (1987); *International Environmental Affairs: A Journal for Research and Policy* (quarterly since 1988); Richard W. Judd and Christopher S. Beach, *Natural States: The Environmental Imagination in Maine, Oregon and the Nation* (2003); Robert Paehlke, ed., *Conservation and Environmentalism: An Encyclopedia* (1995).

John E. Carroll

Ethnic Geography Ethnicity or ethnic identity refers to the sense of a shared heritage based on national origin or origins outside the United States that is transmitted through such things as family history, customs, and language. Because geography focuses on the similarities and differences among places (either localities or larger regions), ethnic geography describes and explains the variations in the ethnic composition of places and how these relate to other characteristics of those places. Two general statements can be made: First, variations in the strength of ethnic populations from place to place are significant and result in differences in culture from one part of New England to another. Second, the real patterns of ethnic populations have been remarkably stable during the 20th century and reflect the general locations of settlement by specific immigrant groups a century or more ago.

Despite the strong association in many people's minds of New England with its English colonial societies, the ethnic composition of the region has been almost completely reshaped since 1830 as a result of net migration: immigration from many different countries plus a large out-migration of descendants of early colonists. In the 2000 U.S. census only 13 percent of New Englanders reported that their primary or secondary ancestry was English. If primary and secondary ancestries are again taken into consideration, an Irish origin was most common and was reported by 2.7 million New Englanders. Next in ranking were approximately equal numbers of residents claiming French (including French

Canadian), Italian, or English ancestry, each totaling about 1.8 million in the region. More than 700,000 New Englanders had German, Polish, or African American ethnicity. People of Portuguese or Scottish ancestry numbered about 400,000, also the estimated size of New England's Jewish population according to the American Jewish Year Book of 2001. In recent decades a range of Asian peoples and others from various islands in the West Indies have settled in New England, thus augmenting its ethnic diversity. This essay will restrict itself, however, to the most important aspects of the ethnic geography of the region's largest groups.

Ethnic geography looks at the patterns of net migration of various ethnic populations. For the most part these patterns are closely connected to the locations of relative economic opportunity that different groups have perceived. As people of various origins entered and settled in New England, they concentrated in some areas and bypassed others. Ethnic concentrations occurred because migrants, in a process called chain migration, typically chose destinations where friends and relatives had told them they could find good opportunities. In this way migrants sometimes linked localities in a country of origin with others in New England. For example, most of the French who settled in Augusta and Waterville, Maine, grew up in Beauce County, Quebec, while those who came to Brunswick typically originated in L'Islet County.

Ethnic geography is interrelated with the culture, politics, and economy of different parts of New England. Where any ethnic group settled in large numbers, it left a heritage of religious and national identity and culture. Patterns of ethnic-group strength help explain variations in political attitudes, party affiliation, and voting behavior. Different ethnic groups also came to New England bringing particular skills and other resources from their countries of origin. Their occupations were thus frequently related to their ethnic origins. Other job-related variations can be seen to result from the location and timing of employment and entrepreneurial opportunities in New England.

The distinctiveness of the New England region derives partly from the cultural characteristics of colonial New Englanders and the continued cultural and economic influence wielded by their descendants, an ethnic group often called Yankees. Late-19th- and 20th-century in-migrations of people from England, Canada's Maritime Provinces, and other parts of the United States supplemented the numbers of Yankees and obliterated most distinctions between colonial-stock New Englanders and later arrivals of British extraction.

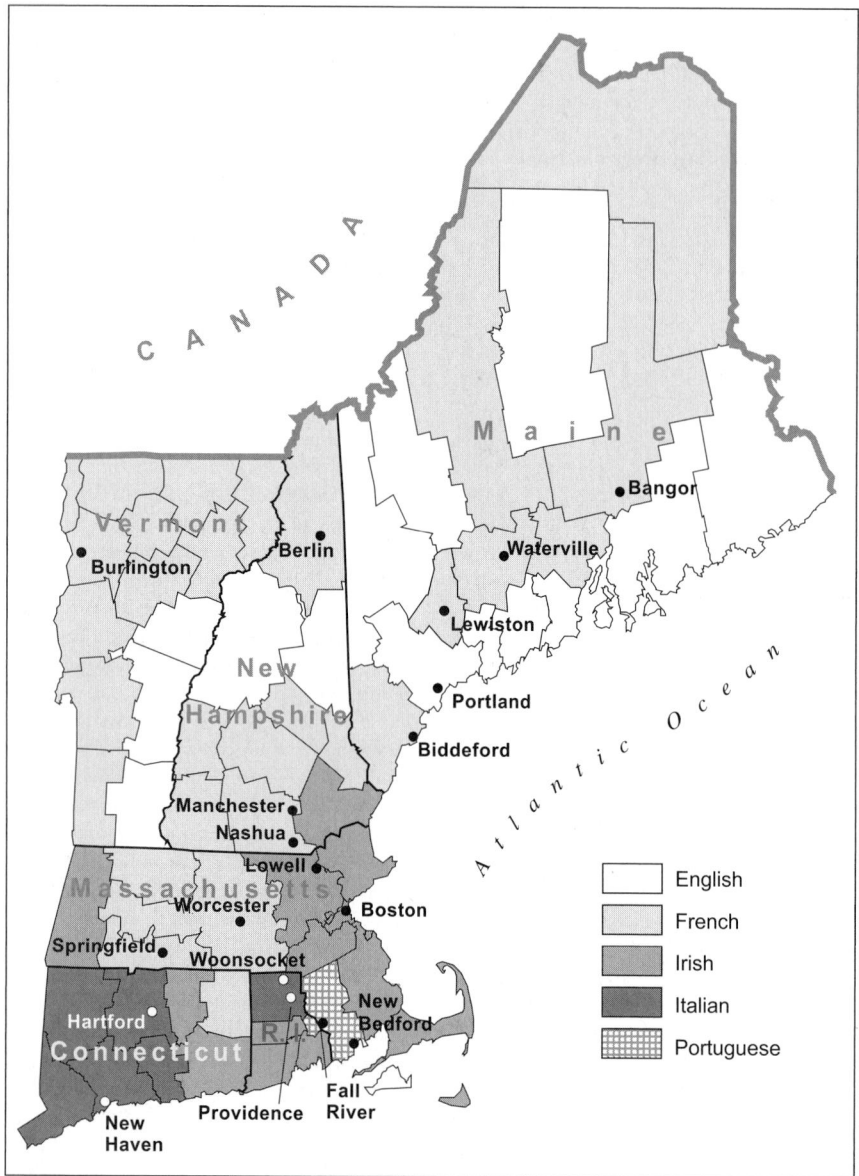

Leading ancestry: New England counties, 2000
Note: *French and French Canadian ancestries are combined*
Source: *U.S. Census (2000) data on total ancestries reported*

While New Englanders were still colonial subjects of the king, they defeated by one means or another the Native Americans who had previously controlled most of Massachusetts, Connecticut, and Rhode Island. After the Revolution, their descendants forced most native peoples in New Hampshire, Maine, and Vermont to give up their lands. By 1830 English-speaking whites, the majority of whom were descendants of the same old English colonial stock, had cleared farm plots and developed trading towns throughout New England. Thus a dominant culture spread over most of the region, leaving only scattered settlements of Indians on tiny parcels of land,

many of which were later administered as reservations by the different states.

Beginning about 1830, however, there was a major exodus from rural New England. Many Yankees sought either the newly opened superior farmland south of the Great Lakes or employment in the cities. Within southern New England especially, the expansion of cities and manufacturing remolded the economic geography, with the result that since that time most immigrants and others looking for work have chosen urban destinations. Thus the fact that English ancestry is still predominant only in more rural areas, mainly in northern New England, derives from the relative lack of em-

ployment and business opportunities in those areas (see map).

In the 1830s men and women from Ireland began to arrive, eager to take whatever jobs might be available. Sailing ships dropped off their cargo of Irish at many coastal ports, particularly Boston, whose population swelled with thousands of destitute immigrants, especially after Ireland was struck by famines during the 1840s. By the 1850s the Irish presence sparked strong anti-Catholic sentiment and nativist reactions on the part of many people of English ancestry. Thus began an era of social separation between Catholic and Protestant in New England. The special strength of Irish ancestry in the Boston area, which continues today, makes the name Celtics very appropriate for Boston's National Basketball Association team.

The Irish dispersed from the ports into all New England cities, searching for opportunities. They also settled in small numbers in many interior towns. Some had taken the cheaper and shorter passage to Canadian ports and worked their way south, a few walking most of the way to Massachusetts. Many Irish arrived just at the time their labor was needed for railroad construction, and gangs of Irish laborers fanned out along major routes. Some settled down in towns along the way, either assimilating into the local Yankee society or establishing a tiny Irish Catholic community. In towns with textile mills Irish women slowly replaced the Yankee farm girls who had been the original textile workers, and in many New England cities well-to-do Yankee families had Irish maids. Scotch-Irish, or Protestants from Northern Ireland, generally settled west and south of New England, so that being Irish in New England has generally meant being Catholic.

French speakers who migrated into New England were 30 times more likely to have lived previously in Canada than in France. Settlements along the Saint Lawrence River in Quebec and coastal areas of the Maritime Provinces were the major sources of French migrants to New England. In New England "Canadiens" from the Saint Lawrence area merged with the lesser numbers of "Acadiens."

New England has two rural areas of French settlement, visible on a map of ethnic identities but home to relatively few people. The older one lies along Maine's northern border in what was once disputed land claimed by both Maine and British North America. The French settlement along the Saint John River was actually split lengthwise by the final international boundary, established in 1842, so that the northernmost part of Maine remains distinctive in having been very strongly French since the late 18th century. The second area of rural French habitation is northern Vermont, where French settlement spilled over from Quebec during the 19th century. Manual work on farms and in towns and later business opportunities, especially in dairy farming, attracted settlers, and proximity to Canada and to French-language television has resulted in a greater maintenance of the French language in these areas than in the urban settlements to the south.

Most Canadian immigrants settled in New England's industrial specialty towns and cities. With the expansion of manufacturing after the Civil War and the success of many Irish in moving up the occupational ladder, the French found a wide range of jobs. However, they were especially likely to work in the widely scattered shoe factories and cotton mills. Thus the French settlement pattern showed special concentrations in the large mill cities of Waterville, Augusta, Lewiston, and Biddeford, Maine; Nashua and Manchester, N.H.; Woonsocket, R.I.; and Lowell, Fall River, and New Bedford, Mass. Around the turn of the century, the new pulp and paper industry offered better jobs, attracting French families and others to such new places as Berlin, in the northernmost county of New Hampshire.

Regional concentrations of other European groups in 2000 are also similar to those of 1900. Portuguese settlement in the New Bedford area began in the 1820s with the hiring of Azorean young men to work in the whaling industry, which was based in New Bedford. The migration flow continued to focus somewhat on the New Bedford and Fall River areas, where many Portuguese farmed or worked in textile mills. During the late 19th century many families connected with the fishing industry settled in or near Boston, and during the 20th century others sought work in the industrial cities of Connecticut. In the 1890s Italians settled mainly in major coastal cities such as Boston, New Haven, Conn., and Providence, where large numbers of men became construction laborers, replacing many Irish, who were then moving into better jobs. The 2000 predominance of Italian ancestry in southwestern Connecticut can be viewed partly as an outflow from New York City.

Immigrants from Germany and Sweden during the late 19th century often came with some industrial skills and moved to manufacturing cities. The largest German settlements were in Boston; New Haven; Bridgeport, Conn.; Lawrence, Mass.; and Providence. For Swedish immigrants the leading destination in all New England was Worcester, Mass., the result of two different chain migrations of

skilled machinists and engineers. Boston, Providence, and Brockton, Mass., had the next largest Swedish populations. The ancestry map does not show these groups, but their population centers and those of other ethnic groups in 1980 can be seen in *We the People: An Atlas of America's Ethnic Diversity.*

Although some skilled workers were recruited for certain jobs in New England's industry, most migrants from Europe, the Middle East, the American South, and Puerto Rico who arrived during the 20th century lacked experience in manufacturing. Industrial workers from older immigrant groups often moved into supervisory or white-collar positions when a new immigrant group arrived. Within two or three generations most descendants of immigrants assimilated in many ways to the dominant culture, a process sometimes called Anglo-conformity. Residentially, new groups with little money or skills typically moved into the older, cheaper housing near city centers as earlier immigrants dispersed to the suburbs.

Especially since World War II, ethnic concentrations have become blurred and weakened by suburbanization and migration, with the result that groups are more geographically mixed. In several counties the two or three leading ethnic or ancestry groups have almost equivalent numbers. Since the late 1960s, professionals and other highly educated immigrants, frequently from Asia, have settled in the larger metropolitan areas of New England. They have often opened businesses or worked in advanced technical fields for private

companies or universities but have had no need to form ethnic concentrations.

Although cultural and geographical assimilation have been substantial, regional ethnic patterns reflecting 19th-century migrations are still evident when the numerically largest ancestries are mapped by counties (see map). Moreover, most New Englanders have found that assimilation has in no way obliterated the memory or meaning of their ethnic identity.

James P. Allen and Eugene J. Turner, *We the People: An Atlas of America's Ethnic Diversity* (1988); Stephan A. Thernstrom, Ann Orlov, and Oscar Handlin, *Harvard Encyclopedia of American Ethnic Groups* (1980).

James P. Allen

Floods River and coastal flooding is a natural phenomenon that has been occurring in New England throughout geologic time. In hilly New England, river floodplains have traditionally offered the most fertile agricultural land and the most attractive sites for settlement and transportation routes. The earliest flood documented occurred in 1639, in Hartford, Conn., when the Connecticut River overflowed its banks. Since then, significant floods have happened in the region on the average of about one every four to five years.

Coastal flooding in the form of tidal surges is caused by high onshore winds and intense low pressures associated with extratropical or tropical storms and hurricanes. In the spring, snowmelt causes relatively modest high flows in most New England rivers; rivers whose flows are not regulated by dams overflow their

Flooding in Weymouth, Mass., 1968

Major Riverine Flooding in New England between 1900 and 1990

State	November 1927	March 1936	September 1938	March 1953	August 1955	October 1955	October 1959	May 1961	March 1968	June 1973	January 1979	April 1979	June 1982	April 1987
Connecticut		X	X		X	X							X	
Maine		X		X				X				X		X
Massachusetts		X	X		X				X					X
New Hampshire	X	X	X				X							X
Rhode Island		X			X				X			X	X	
Vermont	X	X	X								X			
Deaths	84	11	600	0	82	17	0	0	0	3	0	0	11	0
Damage[a]	29	100	387	<1	800	36	<1	1	44	64	6	<1	250	100

[a]In millions of then-current dollars
Source: U.S. Geological Survey, *Water-Supply Paper 2375*

banks every two to three years. A number of conditions can bring about major river floods: prolonged intense rain from slow-moving coastal extratropical cyclones (the famed nor'easters) in fall, winter, and spring (as in October 1955 and October 1996); heavy rain from tropical storms and hurricanes in late summer and fall (November 1927, September 1938, August 1955); or heavy rain plus rapid snowmelt due to warm, moist air in spring (March 1936, April 1987). Intense summer thunderstorms also cause significant river floods over smaller areas. Soil frost and significant antecedent rain reduce the absorption capability of the soil and increase the stream of water produced by a given volume of rain; the formation and breakup of ice jams often increase flood depths and flood damage locally. The widespread clearing of land for agricultural purposes that occurred before 1850 and the poor management of logging—particularly in the White Mountains before 1900—exacerbated the flood potential of affected lands. Twentieth-century urbanization has had the same effect on a more local level.

Statistics on the four or five most significant river floods in each of the six New England states, including the number of deaths and the damage caused, are shown in the table. The two largest and most devastating floods occurred within a period of two-and-a-half years, between March 1936 and September 1938. The deluge of March 1936 brought the most severe riverine flooding in the region since glacial times (14,000 years ago). That year the winter was cold and the ground was frozen under a deep snowpack. A pronounced temperature rise began about March 9, and the first of two heavy rains spread over the region on March 11 and 12, raising river levels and causing the breakup of thick river ice. The second rain began on March 17, and the accompanying warm, moist air caused simultaneous rapid snowmelt that produced wide-spread record stream flows and river levels, the latter made worse by ice jams. Bridges, roads, railroads, and riparian structures were badly damaged, but warnings via telegraph, telephone, and radio kept the loss of life low.

The hurricane of September 21, 1938, caused more deaths, disruption, and destruction than any other natural catastrophe in New England's history. Taking an unexpected inland course and traveling at unprecedented speed, the storm traveled from Long Island Sound up the Connecticut River valley and then northwest across Vermont to Canada in about five hours. Most of the deaths and damage were caused by high winds and tidal surges along the southern coast and by the lack of forewarning. In the Connecticut and Merrimack River basins the accompanying rains (of up to 9 inches) produced record flood levels in some areas and many that were second only to those of 1936. Flooding associated with storm-enhanced tidal surges led to the construction of large barriers on the Charles River in Boston and at the head of Narragansett Bay in Providence.

Local floods have also had significant effects. The flood of March 1, 1896, for example, so damaged the commercial waterfront area of Dover, N.H., that subsequent development shifted to areas above tidewater. It was, however, the extensive destruction wreaked by the larger-area floods of 1927, 1936, and 1938 that led to calls for federal flood-control measures. In 1935 the U.S. Army Corps of Engineers began construction of the first of 36 flood-control dams (the last was completed in 1967), thereby regulating the flow of water from more than 4,000 square miles of the region's land. These impoundments flood, or have the potential to flood, a total of 100 square miles. In most cases construction of these dams involved some relocation of roads and other utilities; for example, the Franklin Falls Dam on the Pemigewasset River required the reloca-

tion of the village center of Hill, N.H. Although many of the dams built by the corps are in upstream states (New Hampshire and Vermont), they were constructed largely for protection of development in downstream states (Massachusetts and Connecticut). To provide compensation for the property taxes lost, the legislatures of the states involved have entered into the Merrimack River and Connecticut River Flood Control Compacts.

Between 1934 and the present, the corps also built 70 local-protection projects (levees, channel modification, and the like) along some 140 miles of river. In Warwick, R.I., protection involved moving or eliminating 61 homes. Along the Charles River in Massachusetts, citizen activists persuaded the corps that the most cost-effective and environmentally sound approach to flood-damage reduction was the preservation of more than 8,000 acres of wetlands for storage of floodwaters. To date, corps-engineered dams and local projects in New England have cost nearly $3 billion (in 1997 dollars). In addition, the U.S. Soil Conservation Service (now the Natural Resource Conservation Service) has constructed a number of flood-control dams as small watersheds. During the late 1960s, the corps proposed that an additional seven flood-control dams be constructed and that local protection of major cities within the Connecticut River basin be enhanced. Citizen concern over the economic justification for and environmental effects of these projects induced the New England River Basins Commission to conduct a comprehensive study of alternative approaches to flood-damage reduction in the basin. The results indicated that the proposed dams and levees were not justified and that flood damages are best reduced via improved flood warning, provision of flood insurance for existing structures, and restriction of future floodplain development. Such development is now regulated by state statutes in Connecticut, Maine, and Massachusetts and by local zoning in most flood-prone communities in all six states.

David Ludlum, *The Country Journal New England Weather Book* (1976); U.S. Army Corps of Engineers New England Division, *Water Resources Development* (NEDEP-360-1-31 through 37) (1995); U.S. Geological Survey, *Water-Supply Paper 2375* (1991).

S. Lawrence Dingman

Forests and Forestry

The forests of New England today look remarkably like those seen by the Native Americans and colonists centuries ago despite enormous changes in the ways they have been used by humans and altered by natural forces. Covering more than 80 percent of the region, New England's forests are a complex mixture of species and forest types unsurpassed in ecological diversity anywhere except in the tropical rain forests. This richness is reflected in the myriad ways New England forests are used—for example, in the manufacture of paper, as building material and fuel, and for recreation—and in their essential ecological role in sustaining wildlife habitats, protecting watersheds, and giving New England its distinctive scenic heritage.

The New England forest is a product of its turbulent past—a history written on the landscape. Several million years ago powerful geologic forces initially shaped the valley and mountain landscapes that have come to characterize the region; glaciers some 14,000 years ago reshaped them; and subsequent and ongoing mountain erosion has continued the process. The resulting differences in soil, climate, and elevation across New England created a wide variety of forests, from the scrub oaks and pitch pine along the coast to the spruce, fir, and hardwoods of the north. In each of the region's distinctly different types of forests one finds thousands of associated tree, shrub, and plant species that support an abundance of wild creatures that depend on the forest for their habitats.

The activities and practices of early native inhabitants—limited essentially to hunting, fishing, agriculture, and the use of fire—had little effect on the forests. The first colonists, however, quickly altered the face of the region. They soon realized that forest products were a source of valuable exports, such as ship masts, timbers, barrels, and potash, to ready markets abroad. In the post-Revolution years, the earlier pattern of settlement along the coast and the major rivers rapidly expanded inland as agriculture changed from subsistence farming to commercial enterprises, and the advent of industry based on waterpower stimulated new settlements on inland rivers. Vast areas of forest were cleared for farming, settlements, fuel, and wood products, and by the mid-19th century 3 out of 4 acres were being farmed in much of New England (the exceptions being northern Maine and the higher mountains). In some areas, such as Vermont, 90 percent of the forests were cleared for farming and sheep grazing. This extensive cutting threatened a severe fuelwood shortage in southern New England; this shortage was forestalled only by the shipping of coal south from the tidewater rivers of Maine and the decline of the region's agriculture brought on by industrialization and the opening of the West.

Cheap transportation on the Erie and Champlain Canals, and later by railroad, meant that farmers on the deep, rich, and stone-free soils in western New York and the Ohio River valley could compete with Yankees who farmed thin, poor, and stony soils. As a result, thousands of acres of cleared land were abandoned to the forest, reversing the trend of deforestation in the region by the time of the Civil War. Forests reclaimed these old fields so rapidly that new forest industries were possible by the early 1900s, at about the same time that the old-growth pine and spruce forests of Maine were cleared. The need for wooden containers in a region heavily active in manufacturing and rail shipment created a market for these second-growth forests well into the 20th century, until human and natural change intervened once again. Market loss during the Great Depression and the devastating hurricane of 1938 caused a severe decline in the wood-consuming industries of southern and central New England, and rural land once again reverted to woodlands.

Judging from historical records and pollen deposits gathered from bogs, Native Americans and colonists in New England saw just about the same tree species one sees today. Although chestnut blight and Dutch elm disease have decimated those species, most other species live in about the same places (or ecological niches) that they have occupied for several millennia.

The oaks and hickories of the central hardwood region extend northward from the Appalachians and dominate southern New England; spruce, birch, beech, and maple are found in the north. In between, these species mingle to form rich transitional hardwood forests, generously interspersed with hemlock and white pine. Although the colonists surely found more large trees than one finds today, the difference is surprisingly less than many might imagine. New England has been swept by tropical hurricanes at least once every century; as a result, few large trees endure for more than a few centuries, although remnant trees up to 400 years old do exist. Likewise, although human activities have continually caused changes in the forests, the richness and diversity of the ancient forest remain, if not in terms of age and scale.

The uses of these forests have been as varied as the trees that grow there and the changing needs of the people who depend on them. For the early Yankee, the forests were an integral part of daily life, providing firewood, furniture, cooperage, building materials, innumerable tools, tableware, clocks, and even food in the form of sugar and nuts. Later these forests provided the raw materials for vigorous industries that produced matches, shoe heels, toys, boxes, barrels, sports equipment, furniture, lumber, railroad ties, fence rails, solvents, paper, charcoal, and chemicals for tanning leather. During the time the region was powered primarily by water and wood, these forested watersheds were the basic source of energy. Today, this forest supplies lumber and wood fiber for papermaking and serves as a source of enjoyment for millions of people.

Recreation has long influenced forest usage in this region, beginning in the late 19th century with the Old Home Week movement, which encouraged individuals to visit rural areas. The resulting invasion of urban people, whose aesthetic values and romantic view of the countryside differed from those of rural residents, changed the landscape dramatically. Among the most important contributions was the introduction of forestry management to the region, through passage of the historic Weeks Act of 1911, which led to the establishment of the Green Mountain National Forest in Vermont and the White Mountain National Forest in New Hampshire. These new national forests brought protection to major watersheds of northern New England from

Fighting a forest fire, Manomet, Mass., 1969

the exploitative logging that had swept the region during the late 19th and early 20th centuries. Floods, fires, and decimation of wildlife and fish habitats threatened both local industries and the growing tourist economy. The Clarke-McNary Act of 1924 further encouraged forestland management by assisting states in the establishment of forestry agencies; this measure led to the development of state and local park and forest systems, stimulating both scientific forest management and recreational use of public lands. Citizen conservation organizations, such as the Society for the Protection of New Hampshire Forests and local Audubon Societies and garden clubs, supported continual expansion of public park, forest, and wildlife refuge systems; these organizations were early models for the thousands of conservation, environmental, and land-trust organizations that exist today. The development of private recreational areas for skiing, camping, and second homes further changed the nature of forestlands, making nonconsumptive uses increasingly competitive with traditional lumbering.

Although public agencies play a major role in managing and protecting the New England forest today, ownership remains largely private: 75 percent of forestland is owned by more than half a million small landowners, the remainder consisting of large corporate holdings mostly in northern areas. The average small landowner holds fewer than 50 acres and does not use his or her holding primarily for wood production. Efforts by state foresters to improve the condition of these smaller, private forests and to increase their output of wood products have not been overly successful. Consequently, the region's forests produce less than half of their potential in quality wood fiber. Some conservationists see this as a positive trend, noting that forests are more important for recreation, wildlife habitat, and watershed protection than for the production of wood. These conflicting views have prompted increasing debates in New England about the future of the forests, leading to referendums and proposed legislation. Several major regional study projects are under way to plan for the future by carefully weighing alternatives in light of past experience and changing public values. The most important contribution of these forests to the nation could well be the demonstration of effective forest policies for small, private woodlands and corporate holdings as well as public lands that are economically, ecologically, and culturally sustainable.

Mollie Beattie, Charles Thompson, and Lynn Levine, *Working with Your Woodland* (1993); Sheila Connor, *New England Natives: A Celebration of People and Trees* (1994); William Cronon, *Changes in the Land: Indians, Colonists, and the Ecology of New England* (1983); David F. Foster and John F. O'Keefe, *New England Forests through Time* (2000); Christopher Klyza and Stephen Trombulak, *The Future of the Northern Forest* (1995); Tom Wessels, *Reading the Forested Landscape: A Natural History of New England* (1997).

Carl Reidel

Furbish, Kate (Catherine) (1834–1931)

Botanist and artist. Kate Furbish was born in Exeter, N.H., and then moved with her family to Brunswick, Maine, where her father became a successful hardware store owner. A botanist and artist, Furbish produced *Flora of Maine*, a collection of paintings of the state's flowering plants, which she presented as a gift to Bowdoin College in 1908. Two plants, both her discoveries, bear her name: *Pedicularis furbishiae* (Furbish lousewort), so rare that construction of a dam was scuttled to protect it, and *Aster cordifolius var. furbishiae* (heart-leaved aster). Near the end of her life, Furbish presented 4,000 mounted plant specimens to the Harvard (Gray) Herbarium in Cambridge, Mass., where they were added to the New England Botanical Club collection.

A veteran of solitary fieldwork, Furbish asserted that nature was her teacher. However, she stayed informed of developments in her field and corresponded with New England's preeminent botanists, Asa Gray, Merritt Lyndon Fernald, and George Edward Davenport. Eschewing any artistic motivation, Furbish studied painting in Boston and Paris for the primary purpose of rendering plants accurately rather than decoratively.

The increasingly esteemed science of botany was an accepted, if limited, endeavor for women at the time Furbish emerged as an accomplished, prolific, and dedicated amateur botanist. Although women were barred from membership in the New England Botanical Club until 1964, Furbish's female contemporaries were active in botany. Among the more well known are the writers Emily Dickinson, who created an herbarium, and Celia Thaxter, who rendered botanical paintings on ceramic ware.

Furbish's arduous travels and physical bravura when collecting specimens, county by county, gave counterpoint to quiet hours of classifying and recording. She lectured and published and was a founding member of Maine's Josselyn Botanical Society, for which she served as president in 1911 and 1912. She also held the professional position of botanist at Poland Spring House, one of the state's therapeutic resorts.

Furbish's lifework, *Flora of Maine*, which she worked on from 1870 to 1908, comprises 1,326 watercolors and sketches whose veracity of structure and color documents the keen powers of observation she focused on each individual plant in its habitat. Furbish's *Flora* serves the serious student as an object of beauty as well as utility.

Kate Furbish died in Brunswick, Maine, at the age of 97.

Ada Graham and Frank Graham, Jr., *Kate Furbish and the Flora of Maine* (1995).

Nancy Wetzel

Geographers

Much of the early geographical knowledge of educated New Englanders was derived from the writings of Ptolemy, Sebastian Münster, Philipp Cluver, and Nathanael Carpenter. In the mid-1600s, this was augmented by the work of Bernhardus Varenius. New England whalers arguably became proto-Antarctic geographers early in the 19th century. Farmers and families who farmed came close to the physical environment in each of its moods: they learned much of soils, slope, weather, and climate. Once geography entered the academy, its learning was various; there seemed to be no core, no margins, to "geography." A vast body of learning lacked structure. Numerous proto-geographers wrestled with the problem. Then came William Morris Davis.

Davis (1850–1934) was appointed instructor in geology at Harvard in 1878. Physical geography had been adopted as an admissions subject and a college-level course in 1870. The Department of Geology harbored a group of men sympathetic to the geographers' cause; N. S. Shaler, who functioned as mentor to Davis, was the most notable of these.

At Harvard, Davis developed his ideas concerning physiography as the end product of the geologic schema and provided the idea of the "cycle of erosion"—an intellectual device that facilitated comprehension of how the landscape came to be, and that became the essential concept around which American geography developed. The cycle—sometimes referred to as the geographical cycle—elaborated the work of running water, which, over time, transforms the topography of the earth's surface. Davis distinguished resultant landscapes, such as open valleys in humid New England and steep-sided valleys (such as the Grand Canyon) in semi-arid environments.

Davis lectured, published, worked with schoolteachers, arranged field trips, and developed a student-disciple record without comparison in the history of American geography. He enlarged the notion of the geographic beyond the cycle of erosion by studying human response to physical environments, a genre then known as human geography. Although he did not dwell on this sort of geography very long, he inspired some of his students to undertake this work. Many of his students were a significant part of the first generation of professional geographers in the United States, becoming department heads, founding and editing journals, and developing their mentor's thought. Fifteen of Davis's 48 students became founding members of the Association of American Geographers (1904). Davis was responsible for the foundation of the latter (which recently celebrated its centennial), held visiting professorships in Paris and Berlin, and led the Liverpool-Rome Geographical Pilgrimage (1911) and the U.S. Transcontinental Excursion (1912). He resigned from his Harvard post in 1912, produced another 200 publications, and lectured across the country (most often in the far West).

Ellsworth Huntington (1876–1947), one of Davis's students, had studied ontography. He joined Yale University in 1907 and remained there throughout his career, seeking to understand how, and to what degree, the physical environment determined the life of humans. This work was tied to studies of climate change and the relative merits of different climates. Most of this work was accomplished from about 1900 to the early 1920s and included *The Pulse of Asia* (1907), *Palestine and Its Transformation* (1911), *Civilization and Climate* (1915), and *World Power and Evolution* (1919).

Huntington's concern with the quality of people emerged at the end of World War I. His design for geography was to study root causes for the varied degrees of success that came to different civilizations. Climate had been his first investigation, and now people themselves became a second investigation. He began to feel that democracy was threatened by higher birthrates among Mediterranean and Alpine populations compared with the Nordic stock. He studied eugenics and genetics and then wrote *The Character of Races* (1924), *The Builders of America* (with Leon Whitney, 1927), and *Season of Birth: Its Relation to Human Abilities* (1938), among other books and many articles.

The third of Huntington's determinants of civilization was "culture," which he regarded as the field of recorded history. This completed his triadic causation study of civilization. In 1945 he summed his life's work in *Mainsprings of Civilization*, which presented his view of geography. He started with the effect of the physical environment on humankind and then moved among the disciplines, chasing a problem—for him, the determinants of civilization.

Isaiah Bowman (1878–1950) was another of Davis's students who worked at Yale University, where he remained for 10 years (1905–15). As was typical of much of American geography at the time, Bowman sought specific instances of "influence" exerted by the physical environment on human society. Regionally, he turned his attention to South America, where he made three extended field trips (1907, 1911, and 1913). He published considerably on that part of the world. As the years passed, the main thrust of geography seemed to settle on the study of regions of the world, while emphasis on the study of influences declined markedly beginning in the 1920s.

In 1915, Bowman was appointed director of the American Geographical Society, a post that he held for 20 years. Then he moved to Johns Hopkins University, where he served as president until 1948. He never ceased being a geographer, although his thrust after 1915 was toward practical application of the discipline. At the American Geographical Society, he developed three major team undertakings: the millionth map of Hispanic America, study of the polar lands to the north, and pioneer fringe areas of the world. Each of these studies proved to be of much practical value, and each project left behind it a trail of first-rate published work on the subject.

Special mention must be made of Bowman's work with The Inquiry—an organization of intellectuals established to prepare the American delegation for negotiation at the Paris Peace Conference (1918–19). He was a major figure on this occasion, and on his return to the United States he wrote *The New World* (1921), a book widely read and adopted for history and geography classes on a number of college campuses. During World War II, he once again played a notable role in advising President Roosevelt and his officers at Dumbarton Oaks, the Stettinius Mission to London, the U.N. Conference at San Francisco, and elsewhere. Nowhere does Bowman try to define geography precisely, but he makes his point of view explicit in *Geography in Relation to the Social Sciences* (1934).

Wallace W. Atwood (1872–1949) graduated from the University of Chicago and came under the influence of Rollin D. Salisbury, who helped instill in him a keen and lifelong interest in the Rocky Mountains. In 1913 Atwood left Chicago and went to Harvard University, where he followed the recently retired Davis and was given the title professor of physiography. Atwood worked with teachers of physical geography (as we might now term physiography) and wrote numerous school geographies. At this he was very successful, both in presenting himself clearly and in writing of people living in distant lands. Such titles included *Home Life in Faraway Lands* (1928), *Nations beyond the Seas* (1930), and *Nations Overseas* (1946). He realized that an intense physical geography would not succeed in the school system; later, however, he wrote *The Physiographic Provinces of North America* (1940), which was successful at the college level. In 1920 Atwood left Harvard to assume the presidency of Clark University in Worcester, Mass.

There, he established the graduate school of geography, which opened in 1921, with Atwood as its director. His staff included a number of accomplished geographers. While he was director, some 70 doctorate degrees and nearly 200 master's degrees were awarded. Many of these students would take positions of significance in the profession. Substantively, Atwood placed a human geography on a physical base. This worked well and he helped to advance geography in the schools. Furthermore, he passed on his interest in ecology and conservation to his students.

Each of these four geographers served as president of the Association of American Geographers and received numerous honors, as well as helped set the stage for the continuance of geography as an important discipline and area of research.

John E. Harmon and Timothy J. Rickard, eds., *Geography in New England* (1988); William A. Koelsch, "Wallace Atwood's 'Great Geographical Institute,'" *Annals of the Association of American Geographers* 70 (1980); Geoffrey J. Martin, *Ellsworth Huntington: His Life and Thought* (1973); Martin, "The Emergence and Development of Geographic Thought in New England," *Economic Geography* (extra issue, 1998).

Geoffrey J. Martin

Geology Many think the discipline of geology to be the study of rocks. But this definition is too restrictive because the word *geology* translates as the science *(logos)* of the whole earth *(geo)*, not merely its *petra*, which is short for its rock. Geologists try to understand how all of earth's materials—rock, air, water, and life—interact as components within a single global system. Furthermore, geology is much more than a technical field allied with mining, oil exploration, mineral collecting, geological hazards, and paleontology. It is also the explanation of physical geography, a field that concerns itself principally with the descriptive mapping of landscapes. If geography is the house in which regional culture makes its home, then geology is its basement, plumbing, and wiring.

In the United States today, geology is most often associated with the parched and mountainous landscapes of the American West where the rocks are plainly visible and where the dynamic forces responsible for these rugged landscapes are self-evident. But geology is just as important in New England, though the rocks are less visible in this vegetated, well-watered region.

Although broken into countless towns, New England is unified as a region by its geology. Its bedrock is mostly the exposed crustal root of an ancient mountain system that developed between 300 and 500 million years ago and was continuous with mountains in Britain. The crest of the former mountain range bisects New England in a sweeping curve that begins at the Connecticut shore, extends north-northeast to the White Mountains of New Hampshire, and then northeast to the highlands of Maine beyond Mount Katahdin. The Hudson-Champlain lowland defines the western edge of this ancestral range. The sandy archipelago from Long Island to Nantucket marks its southern limit as the moraine-studded edge of the coastal plain. The Dutch and French were limited to the western and northern margins of this crustal block, respectively. Conversely, the British colonies of this region were unified, in part, by the unified geology.

New England is the daughter country of old England. The success of settlement was due in part to the similarity between old and new worlds, places on opposite Atlantic shores where the climate, soils, streams, coasts, and stones were similar. The preconditioning of early British immigrants to America was due to the common geological history between the two places. Previously united as part of the same mountain range on the supercontinent Pangaea, England and New England were rifted apart and then drifted apart as the Atlantic widened between them.

Early New England settlements were almost exclusively along the coast and tidewater rivers because of safe harbors, a rich fishery, and rich estuarine soils. The typical harbor lies behind a resistant, glacier-scoured, wave-beaten headland flanked by a sandy beach on one side and a broad tidal inlet on the other, providing both access to and protection from the stormy Atlantic. The fishery was rich because it lay above the famous offshore banks (Georges Bank in particular) that were formed by the submergence of the glaciated portions of the continental shelf, the boulder-studded details of which provided habitat for fish, especially cod. Meanwhile, the coastal estuaries and marshes near shore that were nurseries for the marine food web were created by stream responses to a rise in sea level.

Early colonists also explored inland, hoping to find great mineral wealth, but were quickly disappointed. Except for some fairly restricted deposits of iron and copper ore, and localized mines of garnet, graphite, and mica, the region is generally without concentrated mineral wealth. The same was true for its energy resources. Hence, the New England industrial economy became and remained principally dependent on hydropower manufacture, rather than on mineral or fuel extraction. The one exception to this trend was the deep underground mines in Cheshire, Conn., which produced most of the national supply of the mineral barite, used principally as a thickener for the white paint on so many early American clapboard houses. The ubiquity of building stone facilitated hydropower development by providing erosion-proof materials for mill-dams, canals, and foundations.

New England's three largest metropolitan areas—Boston, Providence, and the corridor between New Haven, Conn., and Northampton, Mass.—developed in geological basins where the rocks were softer and more deeply eroded than adjacent terrains. The same is true for the basin from Newark, N.J., to New York City, which lies at the southwestern corner of the region. Areas of soft rock and low topography connected with the broadest bays and largest rivers, giving room for the economic and demographic expansion of urban New England. Other weak spots in the earth's crust helped align the grid of early canals, railroads, and auto turnpikes.

The economic power that drew farmers inland from rivers and coasts was the suitability of the terrain for an agricultural economy dependent on livestock grazing, and to a lesser extent tillage fields and orchards. The success of this effort was largely due to the underlying layer of glacial hardpan, technically called *lodgment till.* This compacted, silty, stony layer prevented the downward percolation of rain and snowmelt, creating year-round moist soils and abundant springs. New England's legendary rolling hills are glacially streamlined accumulations of this substance, which also contain glacially scattered stones. Hence, the iconic image of rural New England—stone walls on gracefully curved hillsides—is a result of glacial action that simultaneously smoothed the surface and dropped a load of stones. The small size of New England fields and their exaggerated stoniness derive from glacial action as well.

The tradition of town rule is related to the spatial detail, or texture, of the landscape. In New England, the bedrock grain runs generally from the south-southwest to the north-northeast. Belts of strong and weak rock create ridges and valleys along this trend, respectively. In contrast, the glacial grain runs from north-northwest to south-southeast and is responsible for deepening the valleys and streamlining the hills in that direction. The intersection of these two grains yielded an inland landscape partitioned into thousands of small topographic "cells," each surrounded by fairly narrow valleys. With locally dramatic relief between upland and lowland, and with streams running anything but straight, travel was rendered difficult, especially east to west. This reduced the scale of human communities, which eventually coalesced into hundreds of towns.

Although later eclipsed during the era of Manifest Destiny, New England was a place of exciting developments in geology and natural history, particularly during the early 19th century. The discovery of natural curiosities—fossilized footprints, plant fragments, and fish and dinosaur bones in the Connecticut River valley—by Reverend Edward Hitchcock of Amherst College helped lay the groundwork for evolutionary theory. The discovery of unusual minerals and lava flows by Benjamin Silliman of Yale University helped create the discipline of geology as the marriage of natural history and crystal chemistry. The prominent moraines, erratic boulders, and "boulder-clay" of Cape Cod and the islands allowed Louis Agassiz of Harvard University to extend his glacial theory from Europe to North America. In fact, the rise of New England culture coincided with the emergence of geology as a discipline, a time when the region's leading intellectuals—Timothy Dwight, Noah Webster, Ralph Waldo Emerson—were giving the natural landscape as much attention as they had previously given to the ecclesiastical landscape.

Geology, the meat and bones of science, gave natural history the depth of time and the universality of process that would help transition European Calvinism into American Transcendentalism. The story of Pliny Moody, a farmer from Hadley, Mass., is a case in point. In 1802 he discovered enormous three-toed footprints in the Jurassic red sandstone of the Connecticut River valley. At the time, they were interpreted as the tracks of Noah's raven. Two decades later, these same tracks, together with what we now know to be dinosaur bones, were being properly interpreted as vertebrate fossils. The connection between geology and visual art was important as well, particularly in the case of the Hudson River School and the American impressionist movement, most of which developed along or near the New England coast. Rock headland, sandy shore, meadow and marsh, bouldery streams, conifer forest glades: all are beautiful, and all are geological phenomena characteristic to the region. All have become fused with its identity. The soul of New England perches on a rock.

In an era before widespread use of fossil fuels, the hydropower resources of the region assured the industrial success of New England. The flow of meltwater at the base of the glacier diverted preexisting streams to positions where they were forced to flow over hard-rock ridges, producing narrow reaches with small waterfalls that were easily exploited as sites for millponds and mills. In places where the bedrock was less resistant, however, glacial action broadened and deepened preglacial stream courses, later filling them with deposits of sand and gravel that became important aquifers. The combination of easy-to-exploit narrows and the steady flow from aquifers yielded nearly ideal conditions for mills at the scale of small villages. The same was true for New England's larger rivers—especially the Merrimack and the Connecticut—which had the added advantage of negligible down-valley gradient between developed mill sites.

The growth of the interstate highway system and the straightening and shortening of earlier road networks have, ironically, made geology more visible than at any time in the past. Thousands of road cuts, each an artificial canyon, provide views of the stony viscera that lie beneath the earth's surface. The typical views are either of massive granites or marbles or of tightly banded gneisses and slates, many of which are cut through by veins and shattered into jagged blocks. These rocks were formed deep within the roots of the former New England mountain ranges, where they were transformed by metamorphism. The fractures speak of the cooling and decompression experienced by the earth's crust as it rose upward during eons of erosion. The survival of such ledges against the onslaught of one ice age after another is testament to the strength of this land. Conversely, the artificial exposure of these rocks is testament to the power of petroleum and the ingenuity of material scientists and mechanical engineers. These canyons proclaim the notion that human beings have, during the past half century, become the most important geological agent operating in the region.

William Cronon, *Changes in the Land: Indians, Colonists, and the Ecology of New England* (1983); Christopher J. Lenney, *Sightseeing: Clues to the Landscape History of New England* (2003); Stephen Marshak, *Earth: Portrait of a Planet* (2001); Robert M. Thorson, *Stone by Stone: The Magnificent History in New England's Stone Walls* (2002).

Robert M. Thorson

Georges Bank   Georges Bank is an off-shore bank east of Cape Cod approximately 150 nautical miles long by approximately 90 nautical miles wide. Its shallow depths range from about 650 feet to as little as 13 feet and separate the Gulf of Maine to the north from the open waters of the North Atlantic to the south. The bank is bounded to the west by the Great South Channel and to the east by the Northeast Channel. Jurisdictionally, the United States owns the seabed southwest of

the Hague Line (the popular name for the international boundary that divides U.S. and Canadian waters on Georges Bank), and Canada owns the northeast portion. During glacial periods, the bank was above sea level, and mammoths and humans roamed its sandy shores; tusks and bones still occasionally surface in fisher trawls. Today, the shallow waters can pose a threat to shipping during great storms, when wave action can expose rocks and ledges.

In historical times, the fish and shellfish fisheries over the bank (including cod, haddock, flounders, and scallops, among other species) sustained colonial New England. Stories of cod so large and so numerous that they practically "jumped into the boat" reached England and attracted colonists to the growing colonies. Generations of fishers along the New England coast learned the habits and habitats of the fish. Finally, during the 1970s, the development of new and more efficient fishing methods and gear and the invasion of large foreign fishing vessels into U.S. coastal waters sent the fisheries, already heavily exploited, into rapid decline.

During the 1980s, environmental groups and legal action narrowly averted placement of oil-drilling rigs on the bank after exploratory drilling was completed. The moratorium, due to expire in 1999, was extended to 2012 by executive order. These pressures led to new research efforts to understand the dynamics of this very productive and disturbed ecosystem. Oceanographic research has revealed that the primary reasons for the bank's productivity include a clockwise eddy that retains organisms over the bank during spring and summer and strong tidal currents that mix the water and nutrients, keeping organisms suspended in the well-lighted surface waters and fostering photosynthesis. This combination of retention and suspension ensures high concentrations of the planktonic plants (phytoplankton) at the base of the food chain. These in turn support tiny planktonic animals (zooplankton), which are eaten by the young commercial fish species. The young fish thrive on this rich and predictable food source, surviving to mate and produce another generation of commercially valuable fish.

Despite the enormous biological productivity of Georges Bank, heavy fishing pressure and disturbed deep-water habitats—and perhaps natural climatic variability—reduced stocks of spawning fish and eventually gave rise to a food chain dominated by skates and sharks. Stringent fisheries management practices (including time-area closures, gear restrictions, and targeted fisheries) have been put in place to try to restore commercial fish stocks to their historically productive and

healthy state. New ecosystem management strategies using sustainable practices and unprecedented cooperation between fishers, managers, and scientists are being forged so that once again Georges Bank can support commercial and recreational fishing while preserving traditional ways of life in New England. The sharp reduction in fishing on Georges Bank and in other areas, nevertheless, has devastated down east Maine communities, as well as commercial fishers from New Bedford to Portland.

Richard H. Backus and Donald W. Bourne, eds., *Georges Bank* (1987); J. Boreman, B. S. Nakashima, J. A. Wilson, and R. L. Kendall, eds., *Northwest Atlantic Groundfish: Perspectives on a Fishery Collapse* (1997).

Ann C. Bucklin and Peter H. Wiebe

Glaciation   Globally, the beginning of the current Ice Age is marked by the first advance of continental glaciers southward into the mid-latitudes about 2.5 million years ago. By that time the Appalachian Mountains in New England had been reduced by weathering and erosion to a landscape of low relief close to sea level with scattered peaks up to 5,000 feet in elevation. Sparse evidence indicates that up to the onset of cooling and glaciation during the Late Cenozoic Era, the climate of the Northeast resembled that of the present-day state of Georgia.

The most recent ice sheet, the Laurentide, expanded across New England and reached its maximum extent about 21,000 years ago. This position is marked by terminal moraine segments making up Long Island, N.Y., and Martha's Vineyard and Nantucket, Mass., and by concentrations of coarse gravels on the continental shelf to the east. Subsequently, the climate began warming about 18,000 years ago, and the region was free of glaciers by 10,000 years ago.

· Glaciers altered the landscape of New England through erosion and deposition. Bedrock erosion by the last glacier, flowing toward the southeast, was locally severe. This can be seen in the widespread abrasion and quarrying, for example, that asymmetrically shaped hills which are now characterized by abraded, striated up-ice slopes facing the northwest and ragged, ripped apart down-ice slopes facing southeast. However, it is estimated that on the average only about 4 feet of bedrock was eroded from the area, much of which was deposited as unsorted basal till unevenly blanketing the landscape. Although erosion was minimal because of the high resistance of New England's crystalline bedrock, the glacier was responsible for removing most of the softer preglacial soils and for streamlining the landscape in the direction of ice flow. Meltwater deposits of sand and gravel are focused in the valleys, and like the basal till, the rock fragments tend to be coarse because of their resistance to attrition. This coarseness is broadly reflected by the rocky soils and in the vast network of stone walls composed of large rocks taken from the fields. The final retreat of the ice margin was accompanied by a short marine transgression of the coastal zone north of the terminal moraine. This can be seen in the emerged shorelines and a discontinuous blanket of fossiliferous ocean bottom glacial-marine mud present in coastal areas.

Generally, glacial sediment blocked the preglacial drainage system of the region. The great numbers of lakes and the many waterfalls of today resulted from the disruption and reestablishment of a youthful regional drainage system. In human terms glaciation provided the basis for farming that developed throughout colonial New England. The rocky soils, however, eventually proved to be inferior, resulting in a significant migration of farmers westward to more fertile lands after the Civil War.

Contemporaneously, the demand for textiles, wood products, and paper rapidly increased, and the waterfalls provided both hydropower and hydroelectricity for mills. The relatively poor rocky soils and rolling landscape, although not ideal for farming, provided an adequate basis for widespread forestry, producing both lumber and cellulose for papermaking, while the emerged glacial-marine mud supported a local brick and tile industry. And finally, the rolling landscapes, extensive forestlands, and numerous lakes and rivers of the interior, along with the beauty of the coastal zone, have provided for the long-term recreational industry.

Bjørn G. Andersen and Harold W. Borns, Jr., *The Ice Age World* (1997); B. D. Stone and Harold W. Borns, Jr., "Pleistocene Glacial and Interglacial Stratigraphy of New England, and Adjacent Georges Bank and Gulf of Maine," in *Quaternary Glaciations in the Northern Hemisphere*, ed. V. Sibrava, D. Q. Bowen, G. M. Richmond (1986).

Harold W. Borns, Jr.

Global Warming

Not all New Englanders would agree with Henry David Thoreau's portrayal of winter in his 1854 journal: "Is not January alone pure winter? December belongs to the fall; it is a wintry November: February belongs to the spring; it is a snowy March." That may change, however, as so-called greenhouse gases amass in the atmosphere and produce global warming. Acting like a blanket, these gases (carbon dioxide [CO_2], methane, nitrous oxide, and chlorofluorocarbons [CFCs]) trap heat as it radiates outward from the earth's surface. In the past

century, mining, agricultural expansion, industrial growth, the burning of fossil fuels, and the increased generation of wastes have dramatically increased greenhouse gas concentrations.

Changes in climate have been a consistent feature of the earth's history. Eighteen thousand years ago, at the peak of the last glaciation, New England was buried under thousands of feet of ice. Global temperatures were then about 7° to 9° F cooler than at present. In recent decades climatologists have used global climate models to project future changes brought about by the human-related activities that generate greenhouse gases. Current models generally support the theory that over the next century a mean global warming of about 2° to 7° F will occur, affecting winters more than summers. New England's mean annual temperature may rise from 45° F to between 47° and 52° F, which is higher than most annual means of the past century. Because warmer air is able to carry more water, precipitation is expected to increase by about 5 to 15 percent, mostly during the winter months.

Per capita greenhouse gas emissions in New England are lower than the average for the United States owing to the region's limited industrial base, its small geographical size (which means shorter transportation routes), and its relatively low dependence on fossil fuels for the generation of electricity. They are, nonetheless, much higher than the global average. The main source of greenhouse gas in New England is the fossil fuel used for transportation and heating, which generates CO_2 when burned; landfills, a distant second, produce methane, some of which is now recovered for use as fuel. New trees produced by reforestation probably absorb (into plant biomass and organic soil matter) about one-tenth the CO_2 emitted by fossil fuels. CFC emissions are declining in New England and elsewhere because of replacement by other compounds.

The changing composition of the atmosphere is a global issue; no matter where CO_2 originates, for example, it eventually becomes part of the earth's atmosphere and thereby influences climate worldwide. The Framework Convention on Climate Change, adopted at the 1992 United Nations Convention on Environment and Development, proposed that developed nations return CO_2 emissions to 1990 levels by the year 2000 (unfortunately, this did not happen). The long-range goal is to stabilize atmospheric concentrations of greenhouse gases at levels that do not adversely influence climate. Current mitigation plans include international trading of CO_2 emissions and reductions. (Under an emissions trading scheme, a company can exceed the

amount of emissions it is allowed by buying emissions rights from other companies that do not exceed their allocation.)

The potential effect of global warming is hard to quantify because of the uncertainty of the changes predicted, the adaptability of human society, and unforeseen changes that may lie ahead. Sea level is expected to rise between 1 and 3 feet during the next century, as glaciers melt and seawater undergoes thermal expansion. These events could lead to above-normal coastal erosion and vulnerability to major storms. The winter ski season, a major component of the tourism industry in northern New England, may become shorter or more intermittent, despite the possibility of more snow. Agriculture may benefit from a longer and warmer growing season, but timber harvests could be adversely affected by shifts in the range of species in the northern forests. Distributions of wild plant, animal, and insect species are also expected to change. Indeed, climatic changes may affect those features of the New England landscape that have traditionally composed its popular image.

J. T. Houghton, L. G. Meira Filho, B. A. Callendar, N. Harris, A. Kattenberg, K. Maskell, *Climate Change, 1995: The Science of Climate Change* (1996); University of Maine Water Resources Program, *A Regional Response to Global Climate Change: New England and Eastern Canada* (1993); U.S. Environmental Protection Agency, *Inventory of U.S. Greenhouse Gas Emissions and Sinks, 1990–1994* (1995).

Steve Frolking

Great Auk

The great auk, a large, flightless seabird that once migrated up and down the Atlantic coast of North America, became extinct on June 3, 1844, when three Icelandic fishermen, commissioned to obtain a specimen for a private collection, killed the last nesting pair and crushed their only egg. Since its extinction, the great auk has served as a vivid reminder of the power of humankind to alter the course of nature, as well as a powerful tool to educate people about the possible fate of threatened and endangered species.

In prehistoric times, the great auk (*Pinguinus impennis*) wintered as far south as Florida on the west Atlantic coast and the Canary Islands on the east. Paintings of the bird have been found in ancient caves in France and Spain, testifying to its importance to prehistoric peoples both as a harbinger of changing seasons and as an important and abundant resource. By the time of the European settlement of North America, the great auk's territory had shrunk to its historic migration routes along the East Coast.

The great auk was extremely easy to catch while on land, where it came mainly to lay eggs. In the water, however, the great auk

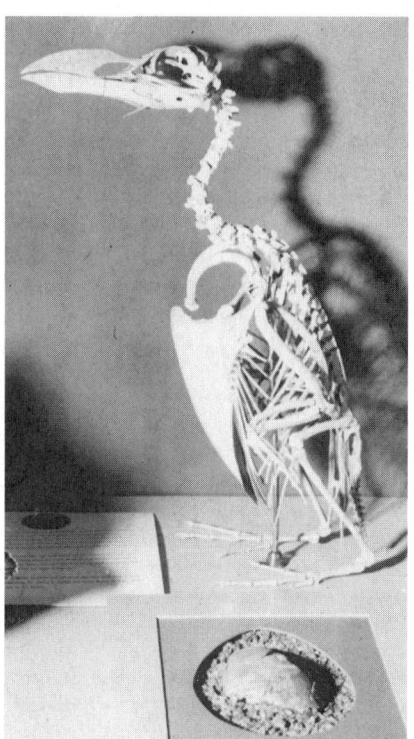

Skeleton and egg of a great auk

could swim powerfully, an ability vital to making the long journey every year from its nesting grounds on the islands and coast of Newfoundland to the warmer waters of the Carolinas. Hunters prized the great auk for its tasty meat and thick layer of fat, which was used for fuel. In addition, the bones of the great auk served as excellent fishhooks, its feathers were gathered for pillows, and its eggs were considered a delicacy.

Its scarcity finally drove the auk into extinction. When European and American collectors realized that the bird's numbers were declining precipitously, they sought valuable specimens to stuff and display as a sign of prestige, rather than trying to save those birds that were left. The birds and their eggs fetched fantastic sums once it was clear that they were extinct; two stuffed specimens went for $4,615 (more than $63,000 in 2003 dollars) at a 1934 London auction.

The ghost of the great auk now haunts the Atlantic seacoast. The conservation and environmental movements of the late 20th century use the fate of the auk as a cautionary tale of what can happen when a valuable resource is overexploited for short-term financial gain. Allan W. Eckert's fictionalization of the life of a single auk, *The Great Auk* (1963), quickly became an environmental and animal-rights classic. Inspired by this account, Richard Wheeler, a kayaker and conservationist from

Cape Cod, traced the migration route of the great auk for a 1993 public television documentary in an effort to draw attention to the lessons of the great auk's extinction for modern-day fishers. To Wheeler and other environmentalists, present-day drops in Atlantic fishing stock from overfishing resemble the last days of the great auk. In both cases, people and governments once thought the resource so abundant that no amount of hunting could deplete it beyond the point of viability. Today, the great auk's ghost serves as a vivid reminder of human hubris in the face of exploitable nature and as a warning to contemporary fishers of the possible disappearance not only of their catch, but of their livelihood as well.

W. R. P. Bourne, "The Story of the Great Auk, *Pinguinus impennis*," *Archives of Natural History* 20 (1993); Allan W. Eckert, *The Great Auk* (1963); "Haunted Cry of a Long Gone Bird" [videocassette], *NOVA* (1994); Robert Silverberg, *The Auk, the Dodo, and the Oryx: Vanished and Vanishing Creatures* (1967).
Ryan McMillen

Green Mountains The Green Mountains, part of the Appalachian Mountain range, run the entire 160-mile length of Vermont and are the physical and spiritual backbone of the state. The very name *Vermont* derives from the old French *vert* (green) and *monts* (mountains). The main range and three subranges have five peaks over 4,000 feet, including Vermont's tallest (Mount Mansfield at 4,393 feet), and many over 3,000 feet. The Green Mountain Club's 270-mile Long Trail traverses the high ridges; the Appalachian Trail follows the high ridges of the southern half of the state. Countless streams and small rivers course down the mountain slopes, and three major rivers—the Missisquoi, Lamoille, and Winooski—cut them from the east to the west.

Most of the Green Mountains date to between 445 and 345 million years ago, even though they contain billion-year-old worn remnants of former higher ranges, some of the most ancient rock in North America. Continental-plate collisions transformed the previous peaks and ocean sediments into today's mountains, which are predominantly made up of metamorphic rock (schist and gneiss).

Glaciers have periodically waxed and waned in North America. At its maximum 20,000 years ago, the latest (Wisconsin) glaciation buried all of Vermont under a mile or more of ice. As the climate warmed, the glaciers receded northward, departing the region some 13,000 years ago and leaving behind smoothed peaks, broad U-shaped valleys, bedrock showing deep gouges from dragged-over boulders, rock-strewn soil, river terraces of sand and gravel, and thousands of water

bodies and wetlands. Forests slowly reclaimed the lands.

Today, 75 percent of the Green Mountains are covered with hardwood forests from the lowlands to an elevation of about 2,500 to 2,800 feet. Predominant climax species (those that are current and stable) are sugar maple, red maple, American beech, yellow birch, and eastern hemlock. Quaking aspen, paper birch, and gray birch are common pioneer species entering disturbed locations, such as abandoned fields and burned areas. In southern Vermont, oaks and hickories are significant components. The forests harbor myriad spring wildflowers and diverse wildlife, including white-tailed deer, moose, black bear, fisher, beaver, bobcat, and scores of woodland birds.

Between 2,800 and 3,000 feet, northern hardwoods yield to montane boreal (subarctic) forests of balsam fir, red spruce, and understory mosses, lichens, and a few wildflowers. Near timberline (3,800–4,000 feet) the trees, mostly firs, become more stunted and tangled, snow is deeper, temperatures are colder, and food is scarcer. There are few birds and mammals.

The treeless summits of Mount Mansfield (250 acres) and Camel's Hump (10 acres) support vestiges of post–Ice Age landscape, alpine tundra that has much in common with that of the arctic: a frost-free season only a few weeks in length; sparse, peaty soils; and dwarfed plants clumped to reduce exposure to wind and abrading ice. Very few animals frequent this region, as conditions are too harsh and food too meager.

After the last glaciation, seminomadic hunter-gatherers entered the region, pursuing species such as caribou, elk, and even mammoth. Later Native American groups hunted the mountains for deer, moose, and smaller game. Still later, more settled native groups focused on agriculture, hunting game and gathering nuts in the mountain forests to supplement their diet.

During the late 1600s and early 1700s, increasing numbers of European immigrants converted mountainside forests into pastures and croplands. Settlers cut the huge white pines for ship masts. By the mid-1800s, Vermont was mostly deforested, even high into the mountains. Many woodland-dependent wildlife species disappeared, including mountain lions, wolves, moose, deer, beavers, passenger pigeons, and wild turkeys.

But the Industrial Revolution, Civil War, and lure of rich Midwest agricultural lands caused many mountain farmers to abandon their lands over the next half century. Fledgling forests, especially white pine, reclaimed the fallow lands. By 1900 the pines had grown to a size desirable to the emerging logging industry. When the overtopping pines were removed, young hardwoods underneath matured into forerunners of today's forests, and much of the wildlife returned.

Much of the area is in some way protected. The Green Mountain National Forest, established in the southern half of the state in 1932, covers approximately 366,721 acres and is a federal forest reserve; state forests and parks account for an additional 130,000 acres, and private organizations conserve another 25,000 acres. In addition, almost 300,000 acres of private forestland are conserved through the state's "current use" tax program, all land above 2,500 feet has special protection (Vermont's land-use law, Act 250), and clear-cutting generally is restricted.

The mountains have been mined (and some still are) for deposits of granite, marble, asbestos, talc, copper, and other earth resources. They now support a strong timber industry, the leading industry in the state, and attract sightseers, tourists, and those seeking recreation such as skiing, hunting, hiking, and fishing.

Jan Albers, *Hands on the Land: A History of the Vermont Landscape* (2000); Charles W. Johnson, *The Nature of Vermont: Introduction and Guide to a New England Environment*, 2d ed. (1998); Peter J. Marchand, *North Woods: An Inside Look at the Nature of Forests in the Northeast* (1987); Harold A. Meeks, *Vermont's Land and Resources* (1986); Bradford B. Van Diver, *Roadside Geology of Vermont and New Hampshire* (1987).

Charles W. Johnson

Hay, John (1915–) Writer, naturalist, educator, and activist. Acclaimed as New England's contemporary heir to Henry David Thoreau, John Hay has written 15 books focusing on natural history and human relations to the natural world. From his home in Brewster, Mass., and a small farm in Waldoboro, Maine, Hay writes with remarkable beauty of the interconnections among animal populations, plant communities, and human culture.

John Hay was born in Ipswich, Mass., to Clarence Hay, an archeologist at the American Museum of Natural History, and Alice (Appleton) Hay. His grandfather, the American diplomat, statesman, and author John Milton Hay (1838–1905), built a family summer home on Lake Sunapee in Newbury, N.H. It was there, and at the Appleton family home in Ipswich, that the young John Hay learned to love nature. Educated at Saint Paul's School in Concord, N.H., Hay graduated from Harvard College in 1938. He then worked as Washington correspondent for the Charlestown, South Carolina, *News and Courier* before entering the army during World War II.

After the war, Hay returned to the United States and became a literary apprentice to the Cape Cod poet Conrad Aiken. Hay's eloquent writings retain a poetic quality as they concentrate on examining relationships among species, cultures, and places in which natural rhythms and cycles play a central role. *The Run* (1959), for example, explores the annual journey of spawning herring, while *The Bird of Light* (1991) contemplates the global language of migrating terns. *The Great Beach* (1963), a collection of essays on tidal rhythms and seasonal affinities, won Hay the John Burroughs Medal in 1964. One of his more recent works, *A Beginner's Faith in Things Unseen* (1995), concentrates on the North American continent and the "magical and ceremonious past" of the land and its people.

Throughout his work, Hay cites the disproportionate influence of a single century of rapid economic and industrial expansion on the world around him and laments the way morally unrestrained technology threatens complex ecosystems that have taken hundreds of centuries to evolve. Hay's books abound with images of formerly distinct places that have been homogenized by mass communications and high-speed transportation. For evidence of this, Hay notes diminished populations of birds, fish, and mammals, as well as the slow disappearance of traditional cultures with significant ties to the land, from the Lakota Sioux to the Cape Cod Yankee. He leaves his readers to ponder the relationship between ecological and cultural impoverishment.

As heir to his family's literary and scientific legacy, Hay is a dedicated conservationist and educator. Founder of the Cape Cod Museum of Natural History, he served as first president of its board of trustees from 1958 to 1980. From 1972 to 1987, Hay was an adjunct professor of environmental studies at Dartmouth College, and for nearly 40 years he has worked actively with conservation organizations to protect habitats for native wildlife and to develop conservation education programs in Maine, Massachusetts, New Hampshire, and Costa Rica.

In 1960, the Hay family deeded 675 acres of forest on Lake Sunapee—the Hay Forest Reservation—to the Society for the Protection of New Hampshire Forests. In 1972, Alice (Appleton) Hay bequeathed an adjacent 162 acres to the U.S. Fish and Wildlife Service as the John Hay National Wildlife Refuge in honor of John Milton Hay. The refuge is an education center with exhibitions and programs exploring historical, environmental, and horticultural themes.

Contemporary Authors: A Bio-Bibliographical Guide to Current Authors (new rev. series), s.v. "John Hay"; North Cairn, "The Light that Guides Him: Writer John Hay Reflects on Mysteries of the Earth," *Cape Cod Times*, March 6, 1998.

David Anderson

Hurricanes and Tropical Storms In an average year, approximately 100 tropical disturbances form over the North Atlantic Ocean Basin. Any one of these could develop into a tropical storm or hurricane and could strike somewhere in New England. Fortunately, an annual average of only six develop into hurricanes, with minimum wind speeds of 74 mph. Furthermore, only a small fraction of these events strike New England. When they do, however, the effect can be dramatic because of high population densities along coastal New England.

Origins of the most powerful tropical cyclones can typically be traced to tropical waves developing off the West African coast between June and November. These systems often intensify as they organize and progress westward in the easterly trade winds across the warm tropical Atlantic, with slight drifting toward the north. Eventually, the storms drift sufficiently north that they exit the westward-moving tropical trade wind belt and enter the zone of the westerlies, which flows from west to east, where they begin to turn northward and then eastward. This causes the storms to follow a parabolic curve around the North Atlantic subtropical high. Most of these tropical cyclones either strike the southeastern United States or curve before landfall and drift northeastward into colder Atlantic waters where they dissipate.

New England–bound hurricanes generally trace their origins to the region near the Cape Verde Islands or in the southwestern part of the North Atlantic Basin near Bermuda. They are unique in that they exhibit very little curvature when passed from the trade winds to the westerlies and generally take a northerly path toward the New England coast. Along this trajectory, tropical storm systems are able to maintain much of their intensity from the energy provided by the warm Gulf Stream current that produces warm sea surface temperatures from Florida to the shores of Connecticut, Rhode Island, and the south shore of Cape Cod. For this reason, the southern New England coastline is most vulnerable to hurricanes, with Cape Cod having the highest occurrence rate, averaging one hurricane every 14 years, while most of Rhode Island and Connecticut (including Long Island) average one every 17 years. Given New England's coastal configuration, direct landfall of hurricanes has extremely low probabilities along the eastern Massachusetts and New Hampshire coastline northward from the Cape, although these areas are affected by hurricanes making initial

Boats deposited in streets and front yards by the Hurricane of 1938, Onset, Mass.

landfall elsewhere in the region. The occurrence rates increase along the central and northern Maine coast, however, averaging approximately one in 20 years.

Between 1900 and 1995, 11 tropical cyclones crossed the New England shoreline at hurricane strength, while another eight systems struck New England at tropical storm strength (with wind speeds between 38 and 73 mph). Surprisingly, four of these hurricanes are among the 50 most powerful to strike the United States in the 20th century. These include Hurricanes Gloria (1985), Edna (1954), and unnamed hurricanes in 1938 and 1944. The deadliest hurricane to strike this region was the Hurricane of 1938, which crossed Long Island to hit Connecticut and then entered Massachusetts and Vermont, killing at least 600 people and producing $306 million (unadjusted) of damage. The effect from this hurricane was felt across the region and even leveled stands of trees as far inland as the White Mountains in New Hampshire. In the aftermath of the Hurricane of 1938, major flood-control projects were undertaken, including a barrier along the Connecticut River to protect downtown Hartford, a tidal floodgate to protect downtown Providence (it saved the city when closed for the first time during the blizzard of 1978), dams along the upper Connecticut River, and numerous projects in New Hampshire and Vermont. The costliest storm to strike New England, however, was Hurricane Bob, which, in 1991, made landfall in Rhode Island and then cut across southeastern

Massachusetts, causing $1.5 billion worth of damage (adjusted for inflation).

David L. Ludlum, *Early American Hurricanes: 1492–1870* (1963); Joe McCarthy, *Hurricane!* (1969); Charles J. Neumann, Brian R. Jarvinen, Colin J. McAdie, and Joe D. Elms, *Tropical Cyclones of the North Atlantic Ocean, 1871–1992* (1993); Anthony J. Vega, and Mark S. Binkley, "Tropical Cyclone Landfall in the United States 1960–1989," *National Weather Digest* 19 (1994).
Barry D. Keim

Industrial Landscape Off the interstates, along narrow highways through the backwoods, New England's industrial landscape is like that of no other region in the United States. In river valleys throughout the area, isolated mill towns feature standard brick or granite factories two to five stories tall and the single-story cottages or two- and three-decker tenements that were built to house workers in the mills.

Although virtually all the extant mill structures and housing were erected after 1850, many sites date from earlier industrial efforts. Here and there one can still find the groundwork of gristmills hidden along streambeds or factory attachments to larger structures left over from the period before 1850. But this early layer of construction is obscured for the most part by the major textile and manufacturing centers built during the second half of the century. Fortunately, however, the 1793 cotton mill and 1810 machine shop at Slater Mill in Pawtucket, R.I., as well as the 1830s gristmill at Sturbridge Village, Mass., have been preserved and are open to the public.

Most of New England's post-1850 industrial infrastructure can be found in Massachusetts, Connecticut, and Rhode Island, but scattered industrial concentrations reach up the Merrimack River valley into New Hampshire and along the Maine coast to the Kennebec River and north into its valley. In the rest of Vermont, New Hampshire, and Maine, despite exceptions in Springfield and St. Johnsbury, Vt., for example, factories are more sporadic.

Textile manufacturing set New England's industrial development in motion. Starting around 1790, merchants and mechanics began to manufacture cotton yarn for New England markets, and they soon expanded their sales to the rest of the East Coast. The Brown family of Providence, leading merchant wholesalers, financed the early mills, sometimes in cooperation with Samuel Slater, a textile mechanic. Others copied their approach, and by 1820 cotton mills had scattered through the Blackstone River valley of Rhode Island (Cumberland, Slatersville) and into eastern Connecticut (Hopeville, Moosup, Danielson), eastern Massachusetts (Lancaster, Uxbridge, Taunton), and southern New Hampshire (New Ipswich). These mills and numerous others sold their yarn in markets outside New England. Because the yarn had high value relative to its weight, transportation costs remained trivial. Owners could therefore build factories in their hometowns as long as they had access to water power, and New England abounded in suitable sites. Merchant wholesalers such as the Brown family handled distribution. With the industry's shift to larger-scale production, primarily after 1820, when mills started weaving cotton cloth, large textile cities proliferated in places such as Chicopee, Lowell, Fall River, and New Bedford, Mass.; Nashua and Manchester, N.H.; and Saco and Augusta, Maine.

During the early 19th century shoe manufacturing began in many eastern Massachusetts villages. Small shops sold their shoes both to the South and to other East Coast markets through wholesalers. Like cotton yarn, shoes had high value relative to their weight, so transportation costs to the wholesale hub of Boston posed no problem. Small towns relying on shoemaking therefore came to litter the landscape. Some of them, such as Lynn and Brockton, Mass., later grew into large centers of shoe manufacturing.

Similarly, manufacturers in Connecticut during the first several decades of the 19th century started producing a wide range of consumer goods for markets along the East Coast. Tinware, clocks, silverware, pins, needles, hardware, and other products became the foundation of many factory villages. Meriden, New Britain, Bristol, and Waterbury, Conn.,

Springfield, Mass., 1881

are among those that developed into industrial cities after 1850.

Many of these industrial centers reached their zenith during the 1890s. After World War I a number of old industries, trapped in outmoded mill technology and multistory factory buildings, either grew slowly or declined. Both textile and shoe manufacturing plummeted in the mid-20th century, as increased automation and overseas competition caused plant closures in New England, leaving multitudes of vacant mills. From 1900 until the 1960s surviving firms in other industries gradually added new capacity in one-story plants adjacent to old, abandoned mill buildings or expanded along major highways. New England lacked the industries that required the construction of plants on an enormous scale: the iron and steel industry, starting in the 1880s, and automobile manufacturing, beginning about 1920. Most of those factories scattered across the Midwest from western Pennsylvania to Chicago. Connecticut's two exceptions to the New England pattern were both rooted in military defense: the airplane-engine works of Pratt and Whitney in East Hartford, now a division of United Technologies, and Electric Boat in Groton, now a division of General Dynamics. The cessation of the Cold War forced retrenchment at both firms.

Since 1950 changes to New England's industrial landscape resemble those that have occurred elsewhere in the nation. Low-slung factories in industrial parks and on isolated sites house computer, software, and biotechnology firms in areas such as eastern Massachusetts and central Connecticut. Highly visible factories, almost indistinguishable from offices, line Route 128 and Interstate 495, the expressways that encircle Boston. But many firms in Massachusetts and Connecticut nestle in wooded, parklike settings and are often invisible from the highways. The place-names

hark back to old New England villages, but the places have now become exurbs of Boston, Hartford, and New York City.

Some cities, such as Meriden and New Britain, Conn., destroyed their industrial architectural heritage in the 1950s and early 1960s during an orgy of urban renewal. In most cities and towns of southern New England, however, factories built between 1850 and 1920 still stand, providing mute testimony to the prominent place they held in American industrialization. Vast acres of multistory brick and granite mill buildings fill medium-sized cities such as Manchester and Nashua, N.H.; Lowell, Lawrence, Worcester, Holyoke, Fall River, and New Bedford, Mass.; Providence and Pawtucket, R.I.; and Bridgeport, New Haven, and Waterbury, Conn. Many of these buildings are partially occupied by warehouses and small firms, as are some in mill villages, but scores of others stand empty. Owners are afraid to sell because they are liable for environmental cleanup, and buyers are reluctant to take ownership of sites that might have severe undetected pollution for which they may in the end become responsible. This impasse condemns many relics of New England's industrial landscape to a living death.

Widespread enthusiasm to preserve the industrial past undergirded the creation of the Lowell National Historical Park, which memorializes the most famous example of large-scale textile industrialization, whose beginnings date back to the 1820s. Such projects can be difficult to fund, however, and attention has turned to the recycling of former mill buildings. Advocates point to such successes as Digital Equipment Corporation, a former computer firm whose corporate headquarters along with certain production facilities were located in old mills in the suburbs of Boston, and Cheney Mills, a large, formerly derelict silk-manufacturing complex in Manchester,

Conn., whose many buildings were transformed into housing for moderate-income residents. Such renovations are extremely costly, however, and often must be privately or publicly subsidized. Because federal funds can be tapped for such purposes, old mills are frequently turned into housing for the elderly.

Life goes on as well in the areas surrounding erstwhile factories, whether in large cities or former mill villages. Some neighborhoods of old, elegant Victorian homes formerly occupied by mill owners, managers, and local business elites attract middle- and upper-income professionals eager to restore the houses to their former glory. These groups make up a tiny percentage of the population in old industrial cities and villages, however. It is much more common to find original one-story mill housing or two- and three-decker tenements providing inexpensive homes for people with low or moderate incomes, just as they did more than a century ago. Residents these days tend to be African American, Hispanic, and Asian.

The industrial landscape built between 1850 and 1920 retains a prominent physical presence in New England although many suburban and exurban residents avoid contact with it. For the casual traveler passing through the region's cities and towns, it remains to be discovered.

Michael P. Conzen, ed., *The Making of the American Landscape* (1990); Robert B. Gordon and Patrick M. Malone, *The Texture of Industry: An Archaeological View of the Industrialization of North America* (1994); David R. Meyer, "Emergence of the American Manufacturing Belt: An Interpretation," *Journal of Historical Geography* 9 (1983); Meyer, *From Farm to Factory to Urban Pastoralism: Urban Change in Central Connecticut* (1976).

David R. Meyer

Industries Among its many claims to distinction, New England was the first U.S. region to confront the problems of industrial pollution. Long before the advent of modern industry during the 19th century, New Englanders already had considerable experience in dealing with the tradeoffs between economic expansion and environmental degradation. To the early colonists New England's natural resource base seemed inexhaustible. Not surprisingly, many of the first documented environmental problems relate to deforestation and the use of sawmills. As technological advancements created new opportunities for industry, they placed new burdens on the environment. In the 20th century industrial pollution has affected larger and larger areas, become more difficult to detect and treat, assumed a larger array of different forms, and become more toxic to plant and animal life.

Despite these changes, New England communities have remained steadfast in their determination to balance economic prosperity and environmental protection.

From the colonial period through the end of the 19th century, deforestation and mill dams were blamed for more environmental problems than perhaps any other preindustrial or industrial activities. Deforestation occurred for a variety of reasons. During the colonial period the region's vast timber resources supported a thriving mercantile economy. New England became the major supplier of timber to Britain, which was already mostly deforested, and the West Indies, whose climate could not sustain key timber species. Forests also were cleared to provide fuel for industrial, agricultural, and domestic purposes. The pig-iron industry relied heavily on timber resources, and a typical New England household could consume up to 40 cords of firewood annually. The accelerated rate of deforestation caused regional timber scarcities by the end of the 18th century, forcing communities to switch to coal for fuel and heating. Unquestionably, the environment suffered. Deforestation caused streams to dry up, soil temperatures to fluctuate more widely, and soils to erode severely. Incident radiation on deforested areas increased the rate of snowmelt and the frequency and severity of flooding. Despite fair warnings of deleterious consequences by naturalists such as Samuel Williams, Peter Kalm, and George Perkins Marsh, New England communities were slow to react to deforestation. Colonists viewed the clearing of land, as William Cronon has noted, not as deforestation but as "the progress of cultivation."

Like deforestation in the forestry sector of the colonial economy, mill dams were the primary environmental issue in the manufacturing sector. Despite the elementary state of waterpower technology in the preindustrial era, the number of sawmills, gristmills, and full mills grew rapidly, especially on the smaller tributaries of major rivers. By 1665, 20 sawmills were operating along New Hampshire's Piscataqua River. As the state of water technology advanced, mills and mill dams began to appear everywhere in the Merrimack River valley, especially along the Concord and Merrimack Rivers. Flooding caused by the mill dams became a major problem. During the 17th and 18th centuries, regulations were passed to protect meadowlands from flooding (the mill acts of 1713 and 1796, for example), but they were largely ineffective, often shielding mill-dam owners from litigation rather than enforcing flood controls. Flooding therefore continued unabated in many areas, and community animosity toward mill owners

eventually led to direct, sometimes violent confrontation.

Dams also posed an environmental hazard because they blocked fish from migrating to their spawning grounds. Toward the end of the 18th century salmon were extinct in many stretches of New England rivers. Again, communities were driven into conflict with mill owners. In heated debates mill owners argued that fishing represented a lesser economic activity than manufacturing. This was the controversy in 1790 when a bill was considered in the Massachusetts legislature to secure free passage of fish up the Charles River. Like other bills that would follow, it required the mill owner to construct a "fishway," a steplike structure that would allow the fish to pass over the dam. Mill owners objected to this requirement, primarily because it reduced the available waterpower, but also because of the high construction costs and uncertainty about the structure's effectiveness. Many fishways simply did not work. In 1845, for example, the Essex Company began building the Lawrence Dam, which would be the era's largest dam on the Merrimack River. The original 1845 Act of Incorporation required the Essex Company to construct a fishway, but the company delayed, hoping to sidestep the requirement. In 1847 county officials forced Essex to comply with the original plan and build the fishway, which proved to be largely ineffective.

Since the mid-19th century New England communities have regularly sought legal recourse against industries for environmental damages, but direct-action tactics have often proved more effective. In 1849 Henry David Thoreau was one of the first to suggest this

form of environmental activism. Thoreau was angry over the newly constructed Billerica Dam on the Concord River because it compromised the shad's ability to migrate upstream. Motivated by the shad's "just cause," he contemplated using a crowbar to dismantle the dam. Thoreau's version of environmental monkey wrenching matured as time went on, with many protesters patterning their own environmental advocacy after his. By the latter half of the 20th century, direct-action tactics had become a common response to industry-related problems. During the mid-1970s, for example, a series of direct-action protests in Massachusetts and New Hampshire drew national attention to the potential environmental risks posed by nuclear power generation. In the spirit of Thoreau, Sam Lovejoy used a crowbar in 1974 to knock down a Northeast Utilities weather tower in northwestern Massachusetts, built to test the area for a planned dual-reactor nuclear facility. In 1976 18 members of the Clamshell Alliance occupied another proposed twin-reactor site at Seabrook, N.H., in an act of civil disobedience; the following year more than 2,000 environmental activists followed suit, 1,400 of whom were arrested.

While these tactics were effective in the short run, regional environmental groups had more long-term success, especially when local communities could be rallied in support. During the mid-1980s the Boston-based National Toxics Campaign (NTC) organized Superdrive for Superfund, a community-based effort aimed at influencing a key piece of environmental legislation—the Superfund Amendments and Reauthorization Act (SARA). The

Harvesting wood, Perry, Maine, 1987

effort paid off, and the final passage of SARA in 1986 contained right-to-know provisions, technical-assistance grants, and emergency-planning requirements—all direct results of NTC's community-based efforts. The NTC was also successful in influencing other environmental policies, being one of the first community-oriented environmental groups to advocate reducing the use of toxic substances rather than trying to treat them after use (end-of-the-pipe treatments). Much of this thinking was incorporated into what the federal Environmental Protection Agency (EPA) now calls "pollution prevention."

Since the mid-1980s federal and regional government agencies have been increasingly effective in dealing with environmental problems in New England. The water pollution caused by dioxin discharges from paper mills provides a good example. Dioxin is a compound produced by the bleaching process, and it is suspected of causing cancer, reproductive anomalies, birth defects, and immune-system damage. Paper mills and the pollution they cause are an integral part of New England's history. Beginning in 1850 paper mills started sprouting up in Fitchburg, Clinton, and Leominster, Mass. Early on, they were suspected of polluting river water, and in 1876 the Massachusetts State Board of Health found the Nashua River basin to be, in Theodore Steinberg's words, "extensively polluted by the wash of nine paper mills." As recently as 1985, high dioxin levels were discovered in fish in Maine's Penobscot, Kennebec, Androscoggin, Presumpscot, and Saint Croix Rivers, pollution attributed to the effluent of seven "bleach kraft" paper mills, which make kraft paper fibers and bleach them. This discovery led to a concerted effort to deal with the dioxin problem once and for all. The Natural Resources Council of Maine was particularly effective in raising awareness of the problem, pushing for state regulations to completely eliminate dioxin from discharges. The effort paid off. In 1999 the S. D. Warren paper mill in Westbrook, Maine, received the first permit in the country mandating the complete absence of dioxin in wastewater discharge.

Despite obvious progress, the environmental challenges that New England communities face today are very different from their historical counterparts, and in many ways more complex. As foretold in Rachel Carson's *Silent Spring* (1962), industrial pollution has become less visible and more toxic. It has also become more difficult to detect and treat. Some organic chemicals, such as TCE (trichloroethene) and PCBs (polychlorinated biphenyls), can stubbornly remain in the environment for decades, poisoning food and water supplies and making rivers and lakes unfit for human use. Moreover, the financial cost of dealing with chemical pollution can be enormous. In 1999 General Electric agreed to pay $250 million to clean up the Housatonic River in Massachusetts and Connecticut, its sediments having been contaminated with PCBs from a plant in Pittsfield, Mass. In Falmouth, Mass., the U.S. military has already spent more than $200 million cleaning up jet-fuel contamination from the former Otis Air Base. Up to 100 billion gallons of groundwater could be tainted, and some local cranberry bogs have been almost completely destroyed. Perchlorate pollution left over from years of grenade and rocket training on what has become the Massachusetts Military Reservation is now believed to have seeped into Cape Cod's primary aquifer, creating yet another, quite possibly more serious environmental problem.

Another headline-making case involved W. R. Grace, a chemical company whose toxic waste found its way into the Woburn, Mass., water supply. Contaminated with TCE and PERC (perchloroethylene), the groundwater is thought to be linked to an increased incidence of childhood leukemia between 1969 and 1978. In 1990, having settled $8 million with affected families, Grace agreed to spend $69 million to clean up contaminated public wells. The legal actions leading up to the settlement were documented in Jonathan Harr's *A Civil Action* (1996), which was later turned into a movie.

Today, at the beginning of the 21st century, the EPA struggles to balance the cost of environmental protection with the goal of economic prosperity. As a result, the agency turns increasingly to market-based instruments as a means of obtaining regulatory compliance. The use of "tradable permits," a system originally tested with power plants in the West, is gaining acceptance in the East. With tradable permits, power plants receive so-called pollution credits, which can be traded or sold to dirtier plants that have difficulty meeting compliance requirements. Another emerging trend is voluntary compliance. Companies that participate in the EPA's National Environmental Performance Track Program, for instance, enjoy relaxed regulatory oversight and are encouraged to limit air, soil, and water pollution voluntarily. The EPA has found that program participants tend to display a higher rate of compliance with environmental regulations than their nonparticipating counterparts. Efforts to educate and collaborate with industry in reducing pollution have also been successful. In the Chemical Industry Audit Project, companies in Connecticut, Rhode Island, and Massachusetts worked with the EPA to implement more effective management practices for hazardous chemicals, and the result was greater compliance.

The long-term effectiveness of these programs remains to be seen, however. Many New Englanders find the shift to incentives and voluntary measures to be troublesome. The task of proving that such measures lead to greater compliance will be left to government agencies. Nonetheless, history has shown that local communities can effectively organize, protest, and bring about change when necessary. For New Englanders, the burden of environmental stewardship is not simply a government responsibility, it is a duty bestowed on every citizen. Having dealt with industrial production and its attendant environmental challenges longer than any other region in the country, New Englanders are uniquely aware of the benefits, and potential harms, of industry.

William Cronon, *Changes in the Land: Indians, Colonists, and the Ecology of New England* (1983); John T. Cumbler, *Reasonable Use: The People, the Environment, and the State, New England, 1790–1930* (2001); Environmental Protection Agency, *The State of the New England Environment* (annual, 1995–); Lois Marie Gibbs, *Dying from Dioxin: A Citizen's Guide to Rebuilding Our Health and Reclaiming Democracy* (1995); Robert Gottlieb, *Forcing the Spring: The Transformation of the American Environmental Movement* (1993); Roderick Frazier Nash, *The Rights of Nature: A History of Environmental Ethics* (1989); John Perlin, *A Forest Journey: The Role of Wood in the Development of Civilization* (1989); Theodore Steinberg, *Nature Incorporated: Industrialization and the Waters of New England* (1991).

James Henson

Islands Islands, resulting from the effects of the last ice age, are a significant feature of the New England landscape. Retreating glaciers and a rising sea level created the rocky islands of the Maine coast; in southern New England, glacial moraines created the major islands of Nantucket and Martha's Vineyard. Clusters of islands—those in Boston Harbor, Narragansett Bay, Casco Bay, and the Isles of Shoals—have distinctive stories related to the economic and defense histories of their mainland cities. Most early New England island communities depended on fishing and farming. During the 19th century, industrial activities such as quarrying, whaling, and fish processing developed. The 20th century saw a decline in population on many islands, but on others major resorts, tourism, and second homes have transformed the population and the economy.

Maine's Mount Desert Island has an area of 108 square miles and 18 summits, including Cadillac Mountain. Bar Harbor, a popular tourist destination, is located on Mount Desert Island, as is Acadia National Park, the first national park of the eastern United States, established in 1919. Farther south, the Isles of Shoals, divided between Maine and New Hampshire, are composed of nine islands and rocky ledges. Some of these islands are wildlife refuges, and several are owned by the Star Island Corporation. Maine's Appledore, the largest of the Isles of Shoals, is the site of poet Celia Thaxter's cottage and garden as well as a fresh water spring. The long, narrow Smuttynose Island is where Blackbeard is believed to have honeymooned; this island was also the site of the 1873 murder of two women popularized in Anita Shreve's best-selling 1997 novel *The Weight of Water.* Star Island in New Hampshire is the only one of the Isles of Shoals that is served by ferry service and accessible to tourists, and White Island is the site of one of only two lighthouses in New Hampshire. Other Maine islands include Damariscove, Maine's first permanent colonial settlement, and Crotch Island, which is the site of a wildlife sanctuary and one of the region's last island stone quarries.

Boston Harbor is home to some 30 islands, 17 of which were recently designated a national park. Six of the Boston Harbor Islands are accessible by ferry; all are located within 4 to 10 miles of Boston. Most of these islands exist in a semiwilderness condition, each some combination of rocky shore, salt marsh, and vegetation. Many of the Boston Harbor Islands are populated by various species of wildlife.

In southern New England, Martha's Vineyard, located 7 miles off the coast of Cape Cod, was formed by glacial action 10,000 years ago and is Massachusetts's largest island. Triangular in shape, the island is 9 miles wide and 23 miles long and has a total area of 100 square miles, with 124.6 miles of tidal shoreline. Its neighboring island, Nantucket, is located 30 miles south of Cape Cod and 15 miles from Martha's Vineyard across the Muskaget Channel. Nearly 15 miles long and roughly 3 to 6 miles wide, Nantucket was also formed by glacial movement and is characterized by its wide, sandy beaches and moderate climate. Rhode Island's Block Island is located 9 miles south of the mainland and is about 7 miles long and 3.5 miles wide. Once settled by the Narragansett Indians, the island is now primarily a tourist destination. Tourists access the island by ferry and enjoy visiting its Monhegan Bluffs—185-foot-high chalk cliffs.

Because early New England colonists feared attack from the natives and from roving Spanish vessels, islands were favorable locations for early settlement. The sea served as a moat against the former, and it was easier to scurry away from an island than to beat out of a bay with a Spaniard sitting in its mouth. The first English settlement in the region was on the island of Cuttyhunk, which Bartholomew Gosnold fortified in 1602. The last in the chain of the Elizabeth Islands stretching westward from the elbow of Cape Cod, Cuttyhunk is located 14 miles off the coast of New Bedford, Mass. A mere 2 miles long by a mile wide, only one-third of the island is settled by its 26 year-round residents; the rest is inhabited by native flora and fauna.

The idea of protection was a fatuous one, for island settlers were subject to attack by both natives and pirates. Massacres occurred on Block Island, the Isles of Shoals, Richmond, Jewel, Aroostook, and Vinalhaven, as well as others. From time to time these islands were sacked by pirates and plundered by the British during the American Revolution and the War of 1812. Islands were nonetheless popular settlements because they lay close to fishing grounds, facilitating a major New England industry. Moreover, in the absence of adequate roads or ground transportation, nearly all travel and commerce was by sea; thus, island folk lived, literally, "by the side of the road."

Most of the region's larger islands were populated early, and the smaller ones were used to raise livestock, dry fish, or cut timber. The outer islands developed complete communities with schools, churches, stores, shipyards, and so on. Although islands were sometimes densely populated, the islanders were usually descendants of the original settlers and family names were sparse: Dodges and Littlefields on Block Island; Beals on Beals Island, Maine; and Stanley, Hadlock, and Spurling on Cranberry Isles, Maine.

Because of the nature of island life, each island tended to develop a subculture of its own, and its residents held singular views of neighboring islanders or strangers. There were, for example, distinct boat designs for various islands—the Block Island Cowhorn, the No-Man's Land Boat, and the Isles of Shoals boat. There was the Old Jakey Turnip from Eagle Island, Maine, and the Block Island potato. Each island, too, had its own lore, heroes, superstitions, beliefs, and customs. Each laid claim to its own fishing grounds, which were guarded to the death if necessary, and often developed relations with neighbor islands. It was customary for boys from one island to marry girls from another island and vice versa, which served to secure territory.

The mainlander's view of an island was often different from that of the islander. Block Islanders and the people of Long Island, Maine, for instance, gained the distinction of being shipwreckers and nefarious characters—characteristics still held to be true. A "Cranberry Island clam digger" was the most contemptuous evaluation of character in Maine. Until well into the 20th century islanders were amphibians who were more at home afloat than ashore. Young Nantucket boys were told, "Yanders [Yonder] lie the green pastures whence cometh your bread." They all went to sea, some in the fishery, some whaling, and some foreign trades and some in coasting vessels. Many, like Charlie Barr, who skippered the schooner *Atlantic,* became famous as professional yacht captains, while many more were lost at sea.

With the coming of electricity, railroads, highways, and automobiles, islanders have found themselves in an odious backwater, and many have moved to the mainland to be near supplies, entertainment, hospitals, and employment. The subsistence life of a fisher-farmer no longer appeals. Island children prefer their own car to a dory or a lobster boat, and the long periods of isolation brought on by the stress of harsh weather are no longer acceptable.

The plight of the traditional islander is made more difficult by the coming of outlanders for whom island life and owning an islet have become fashionable. Newcomers want to rearrange a lifestyle that has evolved over centuries to suit their own view after a few months on an island. For instance, they would prefer to allow no drying of nets ashore, permit only regulated farming, institute harbor and wharf restrictions, and so on, all of which have invariably led to stress for native islanders.

In an effort to preserve island life and ecosystems, the Island Institute of Rockland, Maine, conducts educational and community service programs and produces related publications, including the *Island Journal.* The singularity of island life, however, is rapidly becoming a memory. Islands once heavily populated are now deserted, and others remain home to only a few families. Cattle and sheep no longer graze the islets. More and more islands are being bought up for summer camps, while many more have been claimed by conservation groups hoping to return them to original conditions. The way of life on those islands that accommodate both native islanders and newcomers is slowly changing to suit off-island ideals.

John D. Bardwell, *The Isles of Shoals: A Visual History* (1989); Philip W. Conkling, *Islands in Time: A Natural and Human History of the Islands of Maine* (1981); John Stilgoe, *Alongshore* (1994); Hazel Young, *Islands of New England* (1954).

David H. Watters

Isles of Shoals The Isles of Shoals, located approximately 6 miles off the coast of Rye, N.H., consist of nine islands and numerous rocks and ledges. The islands now known as Duck, Appledore, Smuttynose, Malaga, and Cedar are in Maine; while Star, Lunging, White, and Seavey's islands lie in New Hampshire waters. Known for their rich fishing grounds during the 17th century, by the 19th century the Isles of Shoals had lost their commercial value and were home to a popular summer colony and resorts. During the 1970s, oil interests threatened to turn the islands into an offshore terminal for super tankers. Through the efforts of numerous groups of concerned citizens, voters at local town meetings, and the New Hampshire legislature, these plans were thwarted, and the islands, most of which are privately owned, have been allowed to retain their natural beauty.

Captain John Smith first mapped the rocky islands in 1614. The huge cod teeming in the surrounding waters attracted European fleets, and the archipelago became an important commercial port. By the mid-17th century its 600 inhabitants included many wealthy entrepreneurs. The town of Gosport, on Star Island, was founded in 1715 and became the center of population for the islands. Fishing remained an important industry until the American Revolution, when the islands were evacuated. Some residents returned after the war, but by the early 19th century most depended on charity and the help of missionaries for survival.

In 1839 Thomas Laighton purchased several of the islands and became keeper of the lighthouse on White Island. Recognizing the natural beauty of the Shoals, Laighton and his partner, Levi Thaxter, constructed a large hotel on Appledore Island in 1847. Thaxter married Laighton's daughter Celia in 1851. The couple lived in the Boston area during the winter, and Celia, lonely for her childhood home, began to write poetry. Her work received critical acclaim, and she became one of America's best-known female poets. Her presence turned her family's hotel on Appledore Island into a popular gathering place for New England's leading writers, painters, musicians, and academics. Guests included authors Nathaniel Hawthorne, Henry Wadsworth Longfellow, Sarah Orne Jewett, and John Greenleaf Whittier; publisher James Fields; and artists William Morris Hunt, Ross Turner, and Childe Hassam.

When developers purchased most of Star Island to build the Oceanic Hotel in 1873, the few fishing families still living on the island moved to the mainland. With Celia Thaxter's death in 1894 and competition from mainland resorts, the popularity of the Shoals declined. Another era began in 1897 when the first Star Island summer religious conference was organized. In 1916 members of the Unitarian and Congregational denominations formed the Star Island Corporation to purchase the island. Now a permanent conference center, Star Island has daily summer ferry service and welcomes casual day trippers to explore its rocky shores.

From 1928 until 1940, the University of New Hampshire operated a summer marine zoology program on Appledore Island. In 1973 UNH joined with Cornell University to establish the Shoals Marine Laboratory, now one of the largest undergraduate marine science field stations in North America. The laboratory also sponsors occasional programs for the general public.

Duck Island, maintained as a wildlife refuge by the Star Island Corporation, is home to a winter colony of harbor seals. The islands support large colonies of double-crested cormorants, herring gulls, and great black-back gulls, as well as smaller nesting populations of glossy ibis, black-crowned night heron, snowy egrets, and various seabirds. During the spring migration, as many as 120 bird species have been identified.

John D. Bardwell, *The Isles of Shoals, A Visual History* (1989); Peter E. Randall, *Out on the Shoals: Twenty Years of Photography on the Isles of Shoals* (1995); Lyman V. Rutledge, *The Isles of Shoals in Lore and Legend* (1965); Celia Thaxter, *Among the Isles of Shoals* (1873).

Peter E. Randall

Lake Winnipesaukee Surrounded by New Hampshire's White Mountains to the north and draining into the Atlantic coastal plain to the south, picturesque Lake Winnipesaukee is one of the largest and best-known lakes in New England. The lake was formed some 14,500 years ago as the last continental glacier melted northward, leaving a deeply scoured, largely granite basin that was gradually filled by the more than 60 streams that presently supply its water. Ancient shorelines seen on adjacent hills indicate that the lake was once considerably larger, although its present area of about 72 square miles is more than twice that of the more than 1,000 other lakes and ponds in New Hampshire combined. The 28-mile-long lake has a basin dissected by numerous bays and 274 islands, with a combined shoreline length of 240 miles.

Long before Europeans arrived in North America, Native Americans were enjoying the abundance of fish and wildlife on the shores of the "beautiful water in a high place" or, more poetically, "smile of the Great Spirit," two of numerous translations of the word *Winnipesaukee* from the language of the Abenaki Indians. Fearing attacks from other Indians and a colonial raiding party, the Winnipesaukees left their lakeside village of Aquedoctan, then the largest settlement in the Northeast, and fled to Canada in 1696, never to return.

The second period of human activity on Lake Winnipesaukee began about a half century later with a wave of settlers moving into what is now the town of Wolfeboro. Lake Winnipesaukee became a hub of activity after the Revolutionary War. A thin horizon of fossilized sawdust buried about 2 feet deep in the lake sediments reveals the widespread decimation of lakeside forests that occurred at this time. During the 1850s and after, water rights to the lake were controlled by various compa-

Early burial ground and Oceanic Hotel on Star Island, Isles of Shoals, N.H., 1987

nies, and when purchased by Boston Associates, an organization that controlled Massachusetts mills along the Merrimack River, the manipulation of water flow through the dam drastically affected lake levels and surrounding property.

For the next 100 years, traveling to Lake Winnipesaukee to cruise its waters on one of its many steamboats or to stay in a luxury hotel became the pinnacle of tourist goals. During its 67 years of service, the 178-foot steamboat *Mt. Washington* is said to have transported nearly half a million people across the waters of Lake Winnipesaukee. In 1887, for a four-dollar round-trip train ticket, one could leave Boston at 8:30 in the morning and arrive by noon at the Weirs Hotel. An additional dollar allowed for a "stopover of pleasure at places of interest along the route." Today, the lake remains an important tourist attraction, and although the automobile has replaced the train and myriad smaller recreational watercraft ply the lake's waters, one can still take a sunset ride aboard the *Mt. Washington II*.

Lake Winnipesaukee is known regionally for its wildlife and sport fishing, featuring numerous angling derbies in the summer and ice fishing in the winter. Large flocks of ducks and geese stop at the lake during spring and fall migrations. Canada geese, four duck species, and the common loon—a threatened species in New Hampshire—have nesting populations on the lake. Native fish species in Lake Winnipesaukee include rainbow smelt, cusk, and lake trout. Many introduced fish species such as landlocked salmon, largemouth bass, and rainbow trout have become popular sport fishes.

The water quality in Lake Winnipesaukee is remarkably good, considering its intensive recreational activity. Water clarity is generally between 25 to 30 feet, and although water milfoil occurs in the lake, it is limited to a few shallow areas such as Alton Bay. The lake's overall resilience is in large part due to its depth of 180 feet and its great volume of water, estimated at 625 billion gallons. Also, its watershed has recovered from the period of intensive logging and is now 88 percent forested. The greatest threat to the water quality in Lake Winnipesaukee is the rapid development of the shoreline and nearby watershed, releasing excessive nutrients such as phosphorus into the lake. Typical of the lakes in northern New England, acid rain has caused significant losses in the lake's naturally weak buffering system over the past 40 years, but as yet there are no obvious signs of damage to aquatic communities in the lake. To protect the lake's water quality, large-scale projects have improved disposal of municipal wastes,

and since 1980, changes in water quality are being tracked by the New Hampshire Lake Lay Monitoring Program, the first volunteer monitoring program in New England.

Paul H. Blaisdell, *Three Centuries on Winnipesaukee* (1975); Ronald W. Gallup, *Lake Winnipesaukee: The Smile of the Great Spirit* (1969); W. S. Hawkes, *Winnipesaukee and about There: Descriptive of the Lake Region of Central New Hampshire* (1887); Lakes Region Planning Commission, *Lake Winnipesaukee and Its Watershed* (1997).

James F. Haney

Land Division The manner in which land is divided and distributed has an enduring effect on the landscape. The pattern created by the early lots, and by the roads laid out to access them, is still evident in much of New England.

One of the more durable conventions of settlement geography in the United States derives from the fact that New England, like the rest of the Atlantic seaboard, is an area of irregular land survey, often referred to as "metes and bounds." But the New England practice of granting land in the form of townships to proprietors who then distributed parcels to individuals produced a pattern of land division more regular than in colonies where grants were made to individuals who were free to choose and define their plots. In New England, towns customarily laid out their lands in an orderly fashion before distribution. The need to define and measure tracts gave rise to rectilinear land survey, producing a landscape composed of straight lines.

Some of New England's early settlements were organized around villages, clusters of dwellings situated on uplands adjacent to marshes and accessible by water. The inhabitants of these villages were allotted land for dwelling houses, for tillage, and for cutting hay, and they also had rights in common fields, pastures, woodlands, and marshes. In consequence, each landholder had a number of noncontiguous parcels dispersed over the area of the settlement. House lots, upland for tillage, and meadow and marshlands were generally apportioned in long, narrow strips—that is, in rows referred to as *ranges*—that were uniform in length but often varied in width. Waterside lots were customarily laid out as long rectangles running back into the land. After the accessible waterside lots had been granted, ranges of lots were laid out in interior locations. The resulting pattern has customarily been described as irregular land survey, but it was an irregularity composed of rectilinear parcels that were often distributed in ranges. It was not a maze of irregular, randomly shaped lots.

Independent farms, which had been pre-

sent even at the beginning of settlement, became increasingly common as the 17th century advanced. From 1650 on, new divisions of land in early settlements were more and more commonly laid out in ranges. By 1700 large unitary farms were the norm in New England, and newly granted land was apportioned accordingly. Eighteenth-century townships were generally laid in ranges of large lots.

In general, townships laid out all at once by nonresident proprietors were characterized by the greatest degree of uniformity; they were typically a single division of uniform lots. Towns laid out by resident proprietors as settlement progressed usually had several divisions of land with a separate set of ranges for each division. Because land division was meant to apportion all the land within a town, the pattern of ranges and lots was often derived from the boundaries of the town. This practice produced a variety of lot shapes, most often rectangles or parallelograms. But in a few cases the rhomboid outline of the land granted to the town produced diamond-shaped lots, surely one of the more unusual patterns in American land survey.

Range is overwhelmingly the dominant form of land division in northern New England, where more than 70 percent of the territory was laid out according to that pattern. But range survey is also common in southern New England, where it is dominant inland from the earliest settled coastal towns.

Lots extending inland from the water are the other general feature of land division in New England. These were generally rectilinear parcels of 50 to 100 acres and can be found everywhere along the coast, estuaries, and larger rivers and lakes of the region. On the coast and along the large rivers, lots of this kind afforded easy access and often contained the best land. In the hills and mountains of the interior, where the most important variation in land quality is that between floodplain and upland, river lots were a means of parceling out the flat, fertile intervales as arable or meadowland. Here small intervale lots were often coupled with larger tracts of upland laid out in ranges. It should be noted that the New England practice of laying lots inland from the water is not related to the *rangs* of the Saint Lawrence River valley. Rangs were a product of the French seigneurial system, and lots were characteristically very long and narrow. English lots were much wider and larger and were not part of large estates.

The greatest departure from orderly land division, indiscriminate location, occurred where settlers were allowed to select and define their own lots. This practice, often called "choice pitching," was a feature of the end of the colonial period, not its beginning. Although the earliest cases were in eastern Massachusetts during the second half of the 17th century, most pitched lots were laid out in the 1720s and 1730s. In northern New England the earliest pitched lots were laid in 1736, and the practice was most common after 1760. The right to choice pitch lots was often a concession made to attract new settlers or to reward those who came early. It was also primarily a feature of towns in which land divisions were made by resident proprietors as settlement progressed. And it may be that pitching was a part of the general loosening of communal bonds and restrictions and the increasing individualism that characterized the end of the colonial era. This tendency to discard the restraint of orderly land division late in the colonial period is a curious countercurrent to the generally perceived progression from irregular to orderly land survey as the settlement of New England progressed.

Two other colonial powers settled and laid out land on the fringes of New England: the French and the Dutch. Despite French grants of *seigneuries* on the shores of Lake Champlain, there is no evidence that rang, or longlot, survey survived in Vermont. Apparently the seigneuries had not developed to the point where the small number of long lots that had been laid out could survive the English conquest in the 1760s. There is one area, however, where permanent French settlement was antecedent to English, or, more accurately, American, control. That was the Madawaska settlement in the upper Saint John River valley of Maine and New Brunswick. Here Acadian settlers arrived in approximately 1785, laid out rangs, and farmed for 60 years before the international boundary was finally established in 1842. Rangs line the Saint John River, and in some places second, third, and fourth rangs reach inland as far as 5 miles.

The Dutch domain was the valley of the Hudson River, and that country's slowly expanding settlements rarely extended into New England. A few settlers from manors near Albany moved eastward, however, establishing Dutch farms in areas that were later confirmed as parts of Massachusetts or southwestern Vermont.

The lines that were laid when the land was first distributed are still evident in much of New England. Despite its natural variety and despite the impression of irregularity that those who view it generally receive, there is an underlying linearity in the countryside. Lot lines are the most widespread feature of the New England landscape. They are also remarkably durable. Once land was granted and taken up, property lines were rarely discarded. This true even though property has changed hands many times and individual holdings

have increased or decreased in size. Changes have generally been accomplished by aggregating or subdividing original lots and laying out new boundaries parallel to the old. In this way the basic land divisions created in the early days of settlement remain in the landscape today. Where the land was laid out in ranges, initial survey usually provided "range roads" to give access to the lots. Range roads are a pervasive feature of the New England countryside; oftentimes in rough country one finds them running in straight lines directly up and over steep hills.

Lots are features on maps, but they are also evident in the landscape, even in areas that have remained forested or, more commonly, have reverted to woodland with the decline of agriculture. Lot lines are most clearly evident in field patterns deriving from land survey. Where farming has ceased, contrasts in wild vegetation often reflect differing uses of the land or differing dates of field abandonment in adjacent lots. Even in dense mature woodlands, lot patterns remain inscribed on the land by the thousands of miles of stone walls that march endlessly over the hilly countryside.

A comparison of two New Hampshire towns, Hampton and Strafford, illustrates the effect of differing kinds of land survey. Hampton, settled in 1638 and laid out as an agricultural village, typifies coastal New England. Systematic rectilinear land survey is unusual along the coast, although small groups of rectilinear lots were laid in ranges. Roads were developed to focus on town centers. The most conspicuous straight line in this gently rolling countryside is the Boston and Maine Railroad's right-of-way, built through Hampton in 1840.

Thirty miles to the northwest, Strafford, which was laid out in 1730, provides a striking contrast to the 17th-century settlements of the seacoast. Despite a rough, hilly landscape, the impress of range survey is manifest. Rectangular fields and range roads dominate the settlement pattern even into the Blue Hills. As these examples show, initial land survey is more important than landforms in determining the pattern of the landscape in New England. The lines laid by surveyors at the beginning of settlement have endured.

Ralph H. Brown, *Historical Geography of the United States* (1948); Jere R. Daniell, *Colonial New Hampshire: A History* (1981); Anthony N. B. Garvan, *Architecture and Town Planning in Colonial Connecticut* (1951); Richard C. Harris, *The Seigneurial System in Early Canada* (1966); Terry G. Jordan and Lester Rowntree, *The Human Mosaic: A Thematic Introduction to Cultural Geography*, 5th ed. (1990); Douglas R. McManis, *Colonial New England: A Historical Geography* (1975); Edward T. Price, *Dividing the Land:*

Early American Beginnings of Our Private Property Mosaic (1995); Howard S. Russell, *A Long, Deep Furrow: Three Centuries of Farming in New England*, 2d ed. (1982).

William H. Wallace

Language Patterns The history and geography of language in New England fall neatly into three phases: the prolonged, preliterate aboriginal period; a 210-year interval, 1620 to approximately 1830, during which the English language almost totally dominated the scene; and, finally, the years since the 1830s, when substantial influxes of immigrants from non-Anglophone lands have added much linguistic variety without effectively challenging American English.

We know woefully little about the languages spoken by the original inhabitants of New England when European explorers, sojourners, and settlers first encountered them in the 16th and 17th centuries. Except for a few Protestant missionaries who learned some of the native tongues expressly for the purposes of preaching and producing printed versions of the Bible and other religious materials in those languages, little systematic effort was made to collect vocabularies or investigate phonology, syntax, and grammar. What is quite certain is that throughout the region all the languages—including Abenaki, Massachusett, Mohegan-Pequot, and Narragansett—belonged to the Algonquian linguistic family; less certain is the contention that they were all mutually intelligible. Depopulation, acculturation, and social disintegration likely led to the virtual extinction of these languages by the 19th century. The 2000 census reports 42,257 Native Americans in the region, and 2,854 speak Native American languages at home, an increase from the 2,288 so reporting in 1990.

Today, the most important and durable legacy of the aboriginal speech is to be found in New England's place-names. In many hundreds of instances the names borne by streams, ponds, hills, islands, and other physical and settlement features are obviously of American Indian origin, even though their spelling and pronunciation may be badly garbled and their original meanings obscure. And, of course, Connecticut and Massachusetts have our earlier Americans to thank for their names.

From the onset of serious European interest in the region, the English language has prevailed wherever the newcomers settled. Indeed, aside from a few speakers of Welsh and possibly Scottish Gaelic, the initial, crucial influx was entirely Anglophone. A great many distinct dialects of English were (and still are) spoken in Great Britain; but it is safe to assume, despite the lack of adequate scholarly investigation, that the distinctive New England dialect that developed during the colonial period originated in the various forms of speech prevalent in the southeastern portions of the island from which the great bulk of the colonists emigrated. The only other languages used by white residents would have been the Latin, Greek, and Hebrew read and occasionally written by some of the learned elite.

Even as early as the 18th century, visitors to the region became aware of a recognizable New England brand of American English, with its familiar nasal twang among other attributes too technical to be described here, and this distinctiveness has certainly persisted to the present day. In the 1920s, as American linguists grew in numbers and professional expertise, a group of them became deeply involved in studying the geographic variations in spoken language within the country and launched the still ongoing Linguistic Atlas of the United States project. Not too surprisingly, and in a manner consistent with the region's reputation for cultural innovation and enterprise, New England was the initial focus of attention. After extensive field interviews with predominantly older rural subjects, a massive atlas and accompanying handbook materialized setting forth in much detail local variations in and regionalization of vocabulary and pronunciation. The work done in New England, in combination with surveys conducted elsewhere in the eastern United States, firmly documented the existence and basic geographic dimensions of New England speech. Lacking, however, was specific analysis of such important and universal variables as age, gender, ethnicity, education, social class, occupation, and position along the rural-metropolitan spectrum.

A more recent research project, the *Dictionary of American Regional English* (*DARE*), offers the possibility not only of updating the status of New England speech but also of remedying many of the deficiencies in our knowledge noted above. Initiated in 1965, the *DARE* project has made an essential contribution to our understanding of the American vernacular in the form of a computerized database containing the responses to a remarkable, far-ranging questionnaire administered to a representative sample of the population over five years. As of this writing, four alphabetic volumes, including many maps and covering items A through Sk, have appeared. In Craig Carver's *American Regional Dialects*, which exploits *DARE*'s massive collection of data on vocabulary, we find confirmation of the subregions of New England speech established in the earlier survey—most significantly the division between eastern and western sections of the region—and of the seminal role of New England in shaping the linguistic character of an "upper north" region that embraces all of New York and the upper Midwest along with portions of Pennsylvania and New Jersey.

Further evidence of the singularity of the New England vocabulary—certain generic terms used in place-names and a special pattern for naming sets of neighboring settlements, for example—is inscribed on maps. Such regionally specific terms as *brook* and *pond*, along with names for lesser geographical features, abound in the region and in places settled by New England migrants but are rare or nonexistent elsewhere in the land. Similarly, when we encounter a cluster of satellite villages and hamlets spun off from a nearby place and bearing its name plus a distinguishing North, West, Center, Station, or the like, we can bet on their New England identity.

If New England received only a trickle of immigrants during the late colonial period and early years of national independence, the situation changed decidedly from the 1830s onward. The Irish accounted for most of the trans-Atlantic newcomers during the middle third of the 19th century, and their particular version of English has undoubtedly affected speech patterns in specific localities, though in ways not yet studied. Arriving shortly after the Irish wave were considerable numbers of Germans, then Scandinavians, and eventually substantial streams of natives of the lands of central, eastern, and southern Europe and the Russian empire, along with some Middle Easterners and a scattering of Asians. The result, obviously, was the creation of much complexity in the linguistic scene, at least temporarily, and perhaps some as yet undetermined effect upon the speech patterns of the host Anglophone community.

If all immigrants did not succeed in becoming fluent in English, their U.S.-born offspring certainly did, and few members of the third generation could speak or understand more than some scattered words and phrases in their ancestral tongues. Such linguistic assimilation has failed to operate fully in one significant case—that of Franco-Americans. If virtually all the migrants from Quebec and other Francophone areas who settled in the cities and mill towns ultimately came to be absorbed into the English-speaking community, such was not the outcome in northern Maine's Aroostook River valley or northernmost Vermont and New Hampshire, areas in close proximity to the Quebec homeland, where the French language has taken deep root and bilingualism prevails to this day.

By 1920, toward the close of the era of America's greatest intake of immigrants, New England had attained its polyglot peak. The numbers in the table provided refer to "foreign white stock," that is, foreign-born whites plus people with one or both foreign-born white parents. We have no information from the census as to the extent of bi- or multilingualism, but it must have been considerable. The diversity of languages is impressive, as is the sheer number of people speaking French, Italian, Polish, Yiddish, German, and other languages. The great majority of the linguistically unassimilated lived in urban centers, while comparatively few found their way into the villages and countryside.

Since Congress enacted legislation in 1965 that relaxed restrictions on source areas and, indirectly, volume of immigration, and with the advent of refugees from Southeast Asia and elsewhere, the ethnic, and thus linguistic, composition of New England has undergone a great deal of change, as has happened elsewhere in the nation (see table). It is rather startling to discover that Spanish (751,547) has overtaken French (264,631) as New England's second most important language, presumably as the result of people entering from other parts of the United States as well as from

Language Spoken by "Foreign White Stock" in New England, 1920

Language	Number	Language	Number
English and Celtic	1,981,954	Greek	44,710
French	651,788	Finnish	31,051
Italian	494,924	Slovak	25,834
Polish	275,342	Magyar	23,418
Yiddish and Hebrew	211,232	Syrian and Arabic	20,846
German	185,564	Armenian	18,603
Swedish	142,307	Danish	16,703
Portuguese	124,252	Norwegian	15,274
Lithuanian and Lettish	75,185	Czech	8,306
Russian	67,745		

Source: U.S. Bureau of the Census, *Fourteenth Census of the United States*, vol. 2: *Population* 1920 (1922)

Language Spoken at Home in New England by Persons Aged Five and Older, 2000

Language	Number	Language	Number
English only	10,943,057	Russian	45,768
Spanish	751,547	Vietnamese	41,176
French	264,631	Mon-Khmer	30,562
Portuguese	231,119	Korean	20,050
Italian	129,784	Japanese	16,291
Chinese	96,385	Tagalog	13,937
Polish	72,923	Scandinavian	11,014
Indic	49,075	Hungarian	6,385
German	48,586	Yiddish	4,828
Greek	44,619	Native North American	2,854
Arabic	28,058		

Source: U.S. Census (2000)

Latin America and the Caribbean. Many of these Hispanic newcomers live in Connecticut River and Merrimack River valley cities in a pattern resembling developments in New York's Hudson River valley. Other speakers of alien tongues may be clustered in specific localities, as, for example, the Portuguese in New Bedford, Mass., and Providence or Yiddish speakers in larger metropolises. New England has largely avoided the public rancor over designating English as an official language that has so embittered interethnic dealings in other parts of the country, but New Hampshire did enact such legislation in 1996, which, ironically, had to be translated into French to comply with another state statute. The unspoken, and valid, assumption elsewhere in the region is that American English will prevail among the progeny of the latest newcomers, as it has in the past. In any event, according to the 2000 census, only 6.4 percent of New England's population speak English "less than very well," suggesting a very small percentage speaks English "not at all."

Much remains to be learned about linguistic phenomena in New England, past and present. When we consider the identity of New England's linguistic regions, several trends will dominate future discussion. We may, for example, find regional speech patterns converging with national ones given the effect of mass communications. Internal, as well as international, migration may also affect language in the region. The influence of black English in such cities as Boston and Hartford could well become more pronounced. And the extension of the New York City commuting area into Connecticut may alter speech ways in that corner of New England. Even though it is probable that more is known about the language of New England than of any other

region of the United States, the research agenda remains long and challenging.

Craig M. Carver, *American Regional Dialects: A Word Geography* (1987); Frederick G. Cassidy, ed., *Dictionary of American Regional English*, 4 vols. to date (1985–); Ives Goddard, "Eastern Algonquin Languages," in *Northeast*, ed. Bruce G. Trigger, vol. 15 of *Handbook of North American Indians*, gen. ed. William C. Sturtevant (1978); Hans Kurath, *Handbook of the Linguistic Geography of New England* (1973); Kurath, *Linguistic Atlas of New England* (1939–43); Hans Kurath and Raven I. McDavid, Jr., *The Pronunciation of English in the Atlantic States* (1961); Wilbur Zelinsky, "Some Problems in the Distribution of Generic Terms in the Place-Names of the Northeastern United States," *Geographical Review* 45 (1955); U.S. Bureau of the Census, *Census 2000.*

Wilbur Zelinsky

Long Island Sound Long Island Sound is a body of seawater formed more than 8,000 years ago by the retreat of glacial ice and a resultant rise in sea level. Three sides are bordered by land: to the north are Connecticut and Rhode Island (west of Narragansett Bay); to the south, Long Island, N.Y.; and to the west, Westchester County, N.Y., and New York City. On the western end, its waters become part of the Throgs Neck and New York Bay–East River system, which opens into the Atlantic Ocean. To the east is the Atlantic Ocean; there, the Sound is geographically defined by Orient Point; Long Island; and Plum, Gull, and Fishers Islands, all part of New York State.

The important port cities of New Haven, Bridgeport, and Stamford, Conn., border Long Island Sound; their proximity to metropolitan New York has tended to separate them from New England life and affairs. Historically part of New England, these cities are now more culturally related to New York.

The Sound covers 1,180 square miles, is 90 miles long, and varies in width from 3 to 20 miles. It is more than 100 feet deep, except at the eastern opening to the sea, where the depth reaches a maximum of 330 feet. Tides range from less than 3 feet in the east to more than 6 feet in the west. Freshwater from the Housatonic and Thames Rivers of Connecticut make up more than one-third of the Sound; the largest source is the Connecticut River. Unlike a typical estuary, the Sound has no major source of freshwater at its head.

Daniel Webster dubbed Long Island Sound the "American Mediterranean." Contemporary writers sometimes refer to it as the "urban sea." Adriaen Block, the Dutch captain for whom Block Island is named, was probably the first European to navigate its waters in the early 17th century, sailing west to east. In the 18th century, sailing ships developed commercial trade on the waterway; by the 19th and early 20th centuries, with the advent of steam, shipping had developed into heavy passenger and freight transport. Historically, menhaden, oysters, and whaling dominated commercial fishing.

Present-day activities on the Sound center on recreational activities such as sport sailing, although barge and ferry traffic continues to be important. In addition to industrially developed areas, Long Island Sound has its share of luxury mansions and estates along the Gold Coast of northern Long Island as well as in many less concentrated sites along the Westchester and Connecticut shorelines. The Sound is also part of the Atlantic Intracoastal Waterway extending along the East Coast of the United States from New England to Florida.

The shallowness of the Sound has encouraged flora and fauna, a rich food source for fish, and has resulted in local commercial fishing enterprises, which are now discouraged because of serious pollution. Fishing for weakfish, bluefish, crabs, oysters, clams, and lobsters, long a tradition, continues on a limited commercial and recreational basis only along the Connecticut shore.

One of the most important functions of the Sound is waste disposal for the more than 8 million people living in the immediate region as well as for the many towns along its tributaries. Sources of pollution include the major Connecticut rivers, all of which drain important industrial areas in addition to carrying sediment and agricultural runoff; the heavily polluted East River and New York Bay, which contain large volumes of industrial and urban waste; and shipborne elements on the Sound itself, including barges and tugs.

The waters of Long Island Sound have been degraded by oil spills and leakage from vessels, thermal pollution, dredging and dumping, destruction of coastal wetlands, the discharge of raw sewage, and emissions and discharges from nuclear power plants. Pollution from these as well as riverine sources had become so severe that during the early 1970s the federal government established an intergovernmental commission to study the future of the Sound. Further work, prompted by alarm over deteriorating water quality, led to the Long Island Sound Regional Study, begun during the 1970s. In 1985 Congress provided the U.S. Environmental Protection Agency with funds to research, monitor, and assess water quality in the Sound. In 1988, under Section 320 of the U.S. Clean Water Act Amendments of 1987, Long Island Sound was designated an "Estuary of National Significance." These programs have revealed three serious problems regarding water quality in the Sound: low levels of dissolved oxygen (hypoxia), contamination by toxic substances, and the degradation of habitat and the health of humans and all other living things. More recently, pathogenic contamination and floatable debris have also been identified as serious environmental issues. These ecological problems in Long Island Sound are of such magnitude that they dwarf other concerns pertinent to this body of water.

Lee Koppelman, *The Urban Sea: Long Island Sound* (1976); U.S. Environmental Protection Agency, *Comprehensive Conservation and Management Plan: Draft—The Long Island Sound Study* (1993); Marilyn E. Weigold, *The American Mediterranean: An Environmental, Economic and Social History of Long Island Sound* (1974).

John E. Carroll

Long Trail Vermont's Long Trail extends 270 miles from the Massachusetts border to Canada. The trail follows the spine of the Green Mountains, crossing the tops of all of the major peaks in Vermont. A primitive "footpath in the wilderness," the trail crosses both public and private land and is open to all. Lodges and shelters, available on a first-come, first-served basis, line the trail at intervals of 7 to 10 miles. There is no charge for using most of the Long Trail's shelters, with the exception of a few heavily used sites where caretakers are stationed and a modest fee is charged. The trail crosses a variety of terrain, including lowland swamp, northern hardwood forest, boreal forest, and Vermont's only areas of Arctic tundra vegetation, located on the peaks of Mount Mansfield, Camel's Hump, and Mount Abraham. The first 100 miles of the trail also form part of the Vermont section of the 2,158-mile-long Appalachian Trail, which runs from Georgia to Maine.

The Long Trail was conceived of by James P. Taylor, a private-school teacher. Frustrated by a paucity of hiking trails and believing it would do Vermonters good to recreate in the mountains and escape what he termed their "valley-mindedness," Taylor proposed the Long Trail. In 1910 he and 22 others founded the Green Mountain Club with the intended purpose of making the mountains "play a larger part in the life of the people." By 1930 the trail had been completed, largely through the efforts of club volunteers. In 1971 Vermont's legislature declared that the Green Mountain Club, a nonprofit, membership-based organization, was the "founder, sponsor, defender, and protector" of the Long Trail and charged it with the responsibility of preserving the trail and promoting its use. Club members and other volunteers maintain much of the footpath plus an additional 175 miles of side trails. The club also issues a detailed guidebook to the trail and its facilities.

The first long-distance hiking trail in the nation, the Long Trail has faced several challenges in its history, including an attempt during the 1930s to build a scenic highway parallel to it. The Green Mountain Club was instrumental in defeating this project. Beginning in the 1980s fears that private development would close parts of the trail to hikers caused the club to embark on an ambitious plan to acquire land or easements where the trail crossed private holdings. With the aid of both public and private funds, the club has been extremely successful in securing protection for most of the trail in perpetuity.

Jane Curtis and Frank Lieberman, *Green Mountain Adventure: Vermont's Long Trail, an Illustrated History* (1985); Green Mountain Club, *Guide Book of the Long Trail* (1996); Laura Waterman and Guy Waterman, *Forest and Crag: A History of Hiking, Trail Blazing, and Adventure in the Northeast Mountains* (1989).

Hal Goldman

Maine Forest Fires, 1947 Most forest fires in New England come during two weeks in the spring when only a thin scum of leaves beneath the trees is dry enough to burn. Usually such blazes can be stopped with relative ease. Catastrophic forest fires have been few. Nearly all have broken out in broad areas of sandy soil laid down by glacial meltwater streams or in woodlands rooted in organic matter accumulated for decades on previously barren ledges. Maine was the site of bad fires in July 1762 and in October 1825, 1827, 1837, and 1903. Not many structures were lost in those blazes, however. Although houses burned to the ground all too commonly in earlier times, the fires usually started within their walls.

But in October 1947 hundreds of Maine townspeople had to flee for their lives before conflagrations that came roaring out of forests. The preceding summer had been nearly rainless, something rare in New England. Leaf litter on forest floors was deep and dry as dust. Even as the summer's drought had grown worse, small fires, including those smoldering in town dumps, had been casually allowed to burn. By October 20 of some 50 fires were burning in Maine, and they began to spread rapidly. October 21 and 22 were terrible days when winds reached speeds as high as 65 mph. Flames shot hot and fast above the tree crowns in the forest, as winds shifted violently from northwest to southwest and back again.

The sandy lands of southwestern Maine and bedrock ledges of Mount Desert Island bore the brunt of the damage. Sixteen people died in southern Maine, and major parts of several towns and villages were leveled. Nothing was left of the homes that were in the path of the fire except chimneys and foundation stones.

In major parts of Brownfield, Waterboro, Saco, Biddeford, and Kennebunkport almost all structures burned. On Mount Desert Island a fire that bared the rocky knob of Cadillac Mountain destroyed many buildings and mansions around Bar Harbor, as well as the famous Jackson Laboratory; the town center was spared only by a shift in the wind. About 400 people were evacuated by boat from Bar Harbor. Brownfield lost 250 homes; Lyman, 192 year-round houses and 100 summer camps; Kennebunkport, more than 100 cottages. The village of Newfield was destroyed; Alfred lost hundreds of acres of forest and farmland; 700 people were evacuated from Waterboro. In all of Maine, 2,500 people became homeless; 1,182 homes, 280 barns, and 1,193 other buildings were razed. In late-20th-century dollars, the damage reached nearly $2.5 billion.

Maine towns were not accustomed to forest fires in the fall and were not prepared for massive, fast-burning conflagrations. In population centers local fire departments were responsible for controlling fires. Not only were they ill prepared for the blaze, but no framework existed for cooperation, coordination, or sharing of equipment between towns.

Structural changes took place in the wake of the disaster. The Maine Forest Service, which previously dealt with fires in areas with no town government, was put in charge of training and statewide coordination of forest-fire control. The Northeastern Interstate Forest Fire Protection Compact was established to respond to very large fires in the northeastern United States, New Brunswick, and Quebec. These reforms, in addition to modernized equipment, faster means of telecommunication, and advanced fire-fighting techniques, will presumably prevent the recurrence of a disaster like the far-reaching and unexpected fire of 1947.

Joyce Butler, *Wildfire Loose: The Week Maine Burned* (1979); Charles B. Fobes, "Historic Forest Fires in Maine," *Economic Geography* 24 (1948); A. G. Hall, "Four Flaming Days," *American Forests* 53 (1947).

David M. Smith

Maps New England is a cartographic creation. The region was not a predefined stage for English colonization; rather, it was constructed during the colonial period as a territory and was imbued with spatial meaning through maps. After the American Revolution the conceptual primacy of the region was eclipsed by the new republic's primary spatial idea of the sovereign state. The region has nonetheless persisted as a secondary spatial structure within popular geographic theory and practices. Overall, New England has had the most sustained cartographic presence of all of North America's extragovernmental territorial entities. This presence is well recorded in the substantial cartographic collections found in the libraries of several of the region's universities, including Harvard, Yale, Brown, and (most recently) Southern Maine, as well as at several state historical societies and the American Antiquarian Society in Worcester, Mass.

European images and spatial concepts of the eastern seaboard of North America remained unstable and malleable well into the 17th century, allowing advocates of colonization to establish several new geographic entities. Those covering the central seaboard included Norumbega (falsely construed as an authentic, indigenous name), New France, New Netherlands, and New England. The last was literally created by John Smith after his 1614 voyage to the "north part of Virginia." Smith christened the coastline in his *Description of New England* (1616), and he gave it a concrete geographic identity with a map. Dependent like all European explorers on indigenous guides, Smith recorded in his text numerous Abenaki place-names. But he replaced all these on his map with English and Scottish names assigned by the future Charles I. The resultant image established a powerful, unequivocal, and royally approved bond between a particular geographic area, English settlement, and the name New England. This bond was cemented through a series of published tracts whose texts celebrated English colonization of a territory defined in their maps: William Wood's *South Part of New-England* in his *New Englands Prospect* (1634); John Seller's *A Mapp of New England*, with his *Description of New-England* (1675); and John Foster's *Map of New-England* in William Hub-

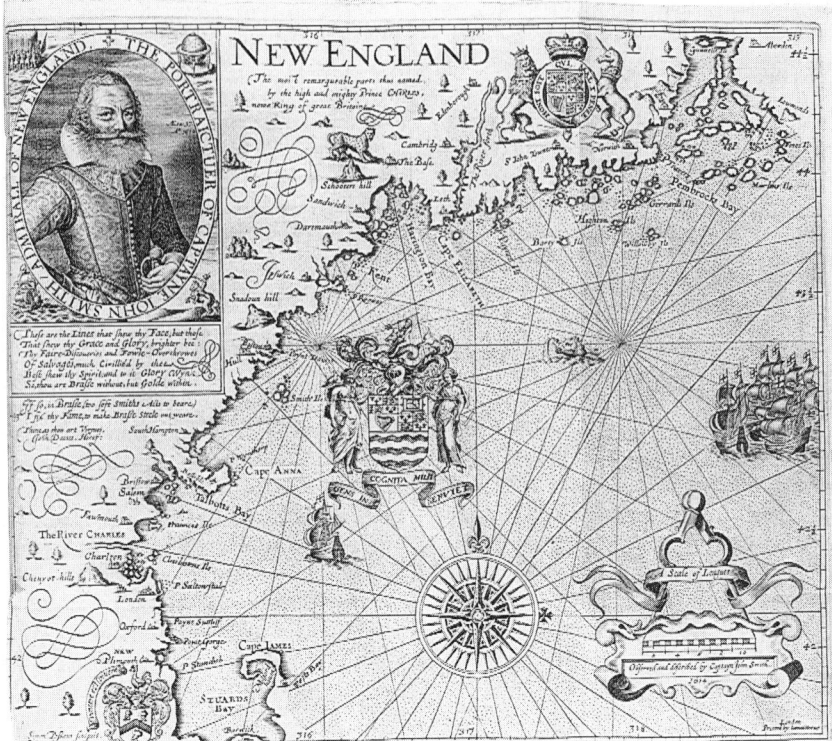

Captain John Smith's map of New England, 1616

bard's *Narrative of the Troubles with the Indians* (1677). The concept of New England was thus political as well as cultural: these tracts constituted the English response to the imperial claims, and to the associated geographic configurations, advanced by the Dutch and the French.

Smith's exclusion of native peoples from his cartographic vision was an idealization of colonial settlement that was not sustained during the actual settlement process. The initial spatial definition of towns and other grants in so-called Indian deeds was both verbal and highly schematic, owing as much to the landscape practices of the indigenous peoples from whom the land was appropriated as it did to practices imported from England. Again, the few general maps made by the colonists depended heavily on indigenous sources for their representation of areas beyond English settlement; as a result the printed maps of New England all embodied complex economic, cultural, and political exchanges between colonists and natives.

The geographic concept of New England developed in concert with English settlement. This is evident in both the distinct cartographic modes of detailed land surveys and general regional mapping. First, the archival and legal task of defining landownership, integral to the expanding commercial land market, produced an array of detailed surveys of

towns and individual properties. Second, the expansion of settlement away from eastern Massachusetts led to the progressive expansion of the territorial framing of New England. In this respect New England was an unstable entity. After the English annexation of the New Netherlands (New York) in 1664, several maps, like the anonymous one inserted into Cotton Mather's *Magnalia Christi Americana* (1702), yoked together New England and New York. Alternatively, the establishment of English colonies in the Canadian Maritime Provinces, together with anti-French claims, led some mapmakers in the early 1700s to extend New England eastward so as to encompass Nova Scotia.

New England was firmly fixed as a region only after 1750. In an effort to implement the Enlightenment's epistemological ideologies, William Douglass rejected existing techniques of regional mapping, together with their reliance on indigenous sources, and compiled surveyed "plans" of towns into a single large map of the region that was posthumously published as *This Plan of the British Dominions of New England* (1753?). Douglass pursued an overtly political agenda. He sought to subvert the political importance of the individual colonies, with their royally appointed governments and charters, by denying them any spatial significance. Instead, Douglass gave preference to the local assemblies whose legitimacy rested in the towns, which he construed to be coherent agricultural, religious, and politically autonomous communities. Douglass presented New England as the realm of a distinct form of self-government that excluded New York, Nova Scotia, and indeed the rest of Europe's American colonies. His image of New England was subsequently popularized in a form that undid his political agenda. Published by Thomas Jefferys in London during the anti-French, pro-imperial fervor of late 1755, John Green's *A Map of the Most Inhabited Part of New England* included much of New York along the Hudson River and symbolically relocated New England within the larger realm of the Atlantic economy; the map nonetheless highlighted the town as New England's characteristic territorial component. Between them Douglass and Green created the mythic, rational township that would be reified in surveys of the public domain after 1787 and that would until the early 20th century give all but the smallest regional maps of New England and its states a look quite distinct from maps of the other areas of colonial settlement.

Maps of individual colonies were made despite New England's predominance as a geographic concept, but they were all strictly administrative in function, and few were printed. With the American Revolution, however, New England was eclipsed as a spatial category by the new republic's creation of two politically charged spatial concepts: the sovereign state and the United States. Soon after independence geographic entrepreneurs began to publish large, detailed maps of each state in the region, such as William Blodget's maps of Vermont (1789) and Connecticut (1791). Moses Greenleaf's 1815 map and description of Maine were instrumental in reconceptualizing the district as a legitimate state. Several early state maps were sponsored by state governments seeking to establish an official image of their territories. As one of the wealthiest states in the union, Massachusetts played a particularly important role in this process. Its first statewide survey was undertaken in the 1790s, the results being published by Osgood Carleton; a second survey was undertaken in 1830–44 and was revised in 1855–60. (All these maps point to the highly regional nature of map production in New England: excluded from the national book-distribution network created by New York publishers and in place by 1840, New England publishers have produced maps for strictly local consumption; the first map publisher to break into national distribution was DeLorme Mapping Company, of Yarmouth, Maine, which has successfully applied the innovative format of its atlas of that state to the rest of the country.)

Large wall maps of each state continued to be made until the Civil War. Their replacement by compact state atlases after 1865 signaled both changes in the ethnography of reading maps and the diminished sovereignty of the state, with the constitutional realignment of federal and state government. It was exactly at this time that federal mapping agencies became involved in state mapping projects. Most notably, when Massachusetts undertook a complete resurvey of its territory (1884–90) in response to the landscape changes and economic needs of continued industrialization, it did so in conjunction with the U.S. Geological Survey (USGS). The result was a highly detailed topographic survey of the state structured according to the USGS's plan for a nationwide survey. The other New England states all soon contracted with the USGS to map their territories, excluding those parts of Maine and New Hampshire whose low population did not warrant detailed mapping. Considered together, these surveys integrated the states into the federal union in a spatial hierarchy that left no scope in official geographic theories for midlevel concepts such as New England.

Even so, New England has persisted as a spatial concept for organizing public geographic theory. Starting with the first general atlas published in North America—Mathew Carey's *American Atlas* (1795)—general atlases have represented states as distinct entities, each on its own page. Large atlases, since about 1840, have ordered their state maps alphabetically, with no regard to geographic contiguity or region, as does the present-day *Rand McNally Road Atlas*. But for smaller or cheaper atlases the strictures of economics and format have required the use of larger spatial conglomerates, and New England is almost always one of them. The region has been most tenacious at the furthest remove from formal geographic discussion, specifically in popular geographic works intended for mass consumption. The 19th-century geography texts used in schools, for example, generally included a section on New England while devoting separate sections to New York, Pennsylvania, and so on; indeed, the region as a whole was the subject of special supplements to geography textbooks after 1890. Again, early road books issued by the American Automobile Association and other automobile societies addressed all of New England rather than its individual states, while a steady number of regional road atlases have appeared since 1918. Despite the predominant representations of politically defined states, New England remains a culturally potent cartographic concept.

Popular maps have perpetuated New England's existence as a meaningful, if precarious, spatial category. Lacking political significance as a geographic entity, New England has maintained its regional cohesion on the strength of its persistent cartographic image and the cultural associations that are rooted in that cartographic conception.

David Grayson Allen, *"Vacuum Domicilium"*: The Social and Cultural Landscape of Seventeenth-Century New England," in *Introduction: Migration and Settlement*, vol. 1 of *New England Begins: The 17th Century*, ed. Jonathan L. Fairbanks and Robert F. Trent (1982); Emerson W. Baker, Richard D'Abate, Edwin Churchill, and Harold E. Prins, eds., *American Beginnings: Exploration, Culture, and Cartography in the Land of Norumbega* (1994); Peter Benes, *New England Prospect: A Loan Exhibition of Maps at the Currier Gallery of Art, Manchester, New Hampshire* (1981); Peter Benes and Jane Montague Benes, eds., *New England Prospect: Maps, Place Names, and the Historical Landscape* (1982); Susan L. Danforth, "The First Official Maps of Maine and Massachusetts," *Imago Mundi* 35 (1983); Matthew H. Edney, "Politics, Science, and Government Mapping Policy in the United States, 1800–1925," *American Cartographer* 13 (1986); Barbara McCorkle, *New England in Early Printed Maps, 1513 to 1800: An Illustrated Carto-Bibliography* (2001); Margaret Wickens Pearce, "Native Mapping in Southern New England Deeds," in *Cartographic Encounters: Perspectives on Native American Mapmaking and Map Use*, ed. G. Malcolm Lewis (1998).

Matthew H. Edney

Marsh, George Perkins

Marsh, George Perkins (1801–82) Diplomat, legislator, and environmentalist. George Perkins Marsh, born into a prominent family in Woodstock, Vt., was the author of *Man and Nature; Or Physical Geography as Modified by Human Action* (1864), the earliest significant work examining the history of the relationship between human culture and the natural environment. A voracious reader by the age of five, Marsh received his early education from his father and older brother, studying classical languages, geography, morality, and natural science. At Dartmouth College, from which he graduated in 1820, he pursued a conventional course of further study in languages, science, and moral philosophy.

After teaching for a year at Norwich Academy in Vermont, Marsh studied law and was admitted to the bar in 1825. He practiced in Burlington for 10 years before his election to the Vermont legislature in 1835, and to the United States House of Representatives as a Whig in an 1843 special election. While in Congress, Marsh was instrumental in passing the legislation establishing the Smithsonian Institution.

In 1849 President Zachary Taylor appointed Marsh minister to Turkey. While serving in this post, Marsh traveled extensively, studying in particular the disastrous erosion that almost inevitably followed deforestation of steep slopes. In 1853 his tenure in Turkey was ended by Democratic president Franklin Pierce, and he returned to Vermont, where he accepted the post of state fish commissioner. His work there led to a *Report on the Artificial Propagation of Fish* (1857), in which he explored the effects of deforestation on fish habitat. Marsh returned to the Mediterranean in 1861 when President Lincoln appointed him the first U.S. minister to Italy.

As a child in Vermont, and as an adult in southern Europe and western Asia, Marsh witnessed the indiscriminate clearing of mountain forests. While the original forests were still largely intact, the runoff of rain and melting snow was gradual, but once the mountains were deforested, the runoff occurred rapidly, leading to cycles of flood and drought. Depicting nature as a complex and interconnected system, Marsh anticipated the modern science of ecology.

In *Man and Nature*, Marsh argued that continued abuse of nature would lead to a degraded environment, agricultural collapse, and even human extinction. An expanded second edition appeared in 1874 as *The Earth as Modified by Human Action: A New Edition of Man and Nature*. A third edition, incorporating a further expansion of text and notes, appeared posthumously in 1882. Marsh died in 1882 while visiting a forestry school at Vallombrosa in the Italian Apennines.

The logical conclusion of *Man and Nature* was that reform and conservation were essential to the future of human civilization. In the United States, Marsh's book inspired early efforts to protect natural resources and was a factor in the 1885 establishment of New York's Adirondack Forest Preserve. In New England, Marsh's call for conservation encouraged the creation of the White Mountain National Forest in 1918 (which grew out of the passage of the Weeks Act in 1911) and the Green Mountain National Forest, established in 1932.

Jane and Will Curtis, *The World of George Perkins Marsh, America's First Conservationist and Environmentalist* (1982); David Lowenthal, *George Perkins Marsh: Versatile Vermonter* (1958); Caroline Crane Marsh, *Life and Letters of George Perkins Marsh* (1888).

Philip G. Terrie

Merrimack River Valley The Merrimack River is the fourth largest in New England, draining an area of 5,014 square miles (75 percent in New Hampshire, 25 percent in Massachusetts) that extends from Franconia Notch, N.H., to Newburyport, Mass. The name Merrimack, derived from an Abenaki Indian phrase meaning "swift water place," is applied to the main-stem river of this drainage basin below the junction of the Pemigewasset

and Winnipesaukee Rivers. Other principal tributaries are the Contoocook, Nashua, and Concord Rivers.

The region was first inhabited about 9000 B.C. by Paleo-Indians. By 6500 B.C. a hunter-gatherer culture had been established, centering on the Pawtucket and Amoskeag falls as important sources for fish and as the focus of social life. At the time of European contact (ca. A.D. 1600), the Merrimack River valley was occupied by tribes of the Pennacook Confederation.

The English land grants of the 1620s were based on the misconception that the Merrimack flowed from west to east for its entire length (rather than from north to south above Lowell, Mass.), which led to confusion in sorting out land-ownership in New Hampshire. In 1642 the Massachusetts General Court commissioned a survey that discovered one of the sources, Lake Winnipesaukee.

The first European settlement occurred at the mouth of the river (at present-day Newburyport, Mass.) in 1635; by 1750 other communities had been built on the sites of Indian villages. The river's abundant fish—especially salmon, shad, sturgeon, and alewives—provided food for settlers and Native Americans alike.

Because sandbars at the mouth and falls not far upstream made navigation impossible, the valley remained of secondary economic importance until the 1780s. The 27-mile Middlesex Canal, the first great feat of canal engineering in North America, was constructed between 1794 and 1803 to divert the valley's growing trade in granite, timber, and agricultural products from Newburyport to Boston. With the completion of canals around the falls at Amoskeag, Hooksett, and Bow—which took place between 1807 and 1815—the river was navigable to Concord. However, river transport was soon replaced by railroads, which reached Concord by 1842; commercial navigation came to an end in 1851. Henry David Thoreau's *A Week on the Concord and Merrimack Rivers* (1839) evokes the pastoral preindustrial riverscape and a sense of the vitality of its inhabitants at that time.

Attempts to harness the Merrimack's waterpower for textile manufacture began around 1800, and by 1850 extraordinary industrial and concomitant cultural revolutions were under way. In 1823 the Pawtucket Canal at Lowell was built to power a mill, and by 1836 the city had developed a unique communitarian culture built around textile manufacture. The construction of mills in Lawrence, Mass., during the 1840s also promoted its growth into a major city. Derryfield, N.H., was a town of a few hundred people until 1810, when its name was changed to Manchester in anticipation of its emulation of the English

manufacturing city. In addition to its textile industry, Manchester became known for the manufacture of locomotives, fire engines, and rifles. The Merrimack was said to be the busiest river in the world. The hydropower developed at its falls is responsible for the distinctive cultural development of New Hampshire and northeastern Massachusetts and contributed to the cultural differences between New Hampshire and the more agrarian Vermont.

By 1950 the availability of other sources of power and of cheaper labor in the South had diminished the importance of the mills. The old mill cities, which have changed over to new industries, and their suburbs remain the economic and population centers of the basin, but highways now link them to Boston and the northeastern megalopolis. Industrial activities have taken their toll, however. By the 1950s the Merrimack and some of its tributaries were among the most polluted rivers in the country. Other consequences of industrial development and population growth have been the diversion of water supplies both within and outside the drainage basin and the construction of some 350 dams that alter the natural stream-flow patterns and affect habitats (especially for migrating fish). Today, 17 of these dams generate about 270 million kilowatt-hours annually, enough to supply energy for about 45,000 households.

Major problems in water quality were addressed largely through federal programs of the 1970s and 1980s; however, this progress, along with population and economic growth, has exacerbated conflicting demands on the Merrimack for waste transport and treatment, hydropower, industrial and domestic water supply, development of riparian land (with consequent increases in flood damages), recreation, and fish and wildlife habitat (including major efforts to reintroduce salmon). Competition among these demands creates the need for an integrated river-basin approach to water-resource management. However, the institutional infrastructure for such an approach that was developed under federal leadership during the mid-1970s is no longer in place, and needed management programs are today left to the advocacy of private organizations such as the Merrimack River Watershed Council, with some assistance from state and federal agencies.

George Waldo Browne, *The River of Broken Waters: The Merrimack* (1918); Raymond P. Holden, *Rivers of America: The Merrimack* (1958); J. W. Meader, *The Merrimack River: Its Source and Its Tributaries* (1869); Gary Samson, *Merrimack Valley, New Hampshire: A Visual History* (1989).

S. Lawrence Dingman

Merritt Parkway Of all the highways in the United States, only one relatively modest

37.5–mile stretch of road, Connecticut's Merritt Parkway, has been listed on the National Register of Historic Places. The parkway (named for many-termed Fairfield County congressman Schuyler Merritt) was conceived in the early 1920s as an alternative to the traffic-choked Boston Post Road (U.S. Route 1). The proposal survived a decade of political wrangling in Hartford and Fairfield County before construction began in the depths of the Great Depression, part of the Works Progress Administration's public works program. The first half of the road opened with great ceremony on June 30, 1938; the remaining portions were opened as completed, until the final link, the Housatonic River Bridge in Stratford, Conn., was inaugurated on September 2, 1940.

Called the Gateway to New England, the parkway was created to handle the explosive growth of automobiles: the number in the United States mushroomed from just four in 1895 to 32 million by 1940, not counting a concomitant rise of trucks and buses. By the late 1920s, some 25,000 vehicles per day were counted on the Post Road in Greenwich, Conn. The road could comfortably handle only half that number.

Numerous problems beset the parkway's early planning and construction. Some wanted a no-nonsense, efficient, railroadlike commuter highway; others insisted that the new road should be an asset to the county's rolling hills and woodlands. The wealthy landowners, fearing an invasion of New Yorkers, opposed any road that threatened their bucolic way of life; those from outlying parts of the county and state opposed the project, reasoning that the traffic problem was not theirs to fix.

Once the legislature appropriated money for land acquisition and initial construction in 1931, the real problems began to surface, including a notorious land scandal that rocked Fairfield County and the entire state. John MacDonald, the Connecticut highway commissioner, cloaked in secrecy the proposed route of the new road and the actual land-acquisition process for the 300-foot-wide right-of-way, bypassing the state land-acquisition agency and its procedures in favor of a special independent procurer. G. Leroy Kemp, a real estate broker and former Republican assemblyman, was appointed to the position and augmented his own modest salary with a kickback scheme. Kemp offered greatly sweetened deals, which reached 10 times the assessed property value, through carefully chosen realtors to select landowners—some ranking Republicans—and they then split the realtor's commission among themselves. Rumors of these sweetheart deals began circulating; in January 1938, after titillating reports of "irregularities" appeared in local papers, Democratic governor Wilbur Cross convened a grand jury, and despite Republican efforts at damage control, Kemp was tried and sentenced to three to seven years. Cross requested MacDonald's resignation.

If land acquisition got off to a rocky start, the actual construction was a spectacular success. An exceptionally talented group of young designers worked with a crew of some 2,000 workers hired from the welfare rolls. Chief project engineer Warren Creamer deserves much of the credit for the finished roadway, but hardly less notable for their contributions are architect George Dunkelberger and landscape architect Weld Thayer Chase. The winding, hill-climbing route was largely dictated by the topography, but these two men contributed the constructed features that enhance the Merritt Parkway, fitting it into the natural beauty of the area.

Many first-time travelers on the parkway are struck by the 68 original bridges, each one unique. All were designed by Dunkelberger, a rather eclectic architect with a taste for the Art Deco style of the time. Technically, the bridges are not particularly innovative, but Dunkelberger brought imagination and wit to disguising the rigid steel-frame structures using wrought iron, precast concrete panels, and a number of other often ingenious means. Chase, working in the tradition of Frederick Law Olmsted and the English landscape park, brought unusual sensitivity to repairing the construction scars by planting native trees, shrubs, and wildflowers along the entire route, including the median strip, to give the road a more natural appearance.

The end product is more than a highway through beautiful, scenic countryside. It is a design in which civil engineering, architecture, and landscaping are integrated into a remarkable work of art. It is no less significant as an example of regional planning that successfully united local, state, and federal resources along with the enthusiasm for a better solution to a vexing problem that local residents demanded. That similar effects were not achieved 20 years later in building the interstate highway system is regrettable; certainly, the Merritt Parkway provided the model. As Schuyler Merritt said of his namesake, "A beautiful parkway is not wholly or primarily a means for quick transit, but it should be constructed so as to add beauty to the landscape."

Bruce Radde, *The Merritt Parkway* (1993).

Bruce Radde

Mount Desert Island On Frenchman Bay in southeastern Maine, Mount Desert Island is the primary site of Acadia National Park (1919), the first national park to be established east of the Mississippi. A unique blend of freshwater lakes, mountains, valleys, and majestic coastlines, the island was discovered by Samuel de Champlain in 1604. Champlain described the scoured, glaciated landscape, nearly cut in half by Somes Sound, as "high and cleft in seven or eight mountains, all in line . . . bare of trees, nothing but rock." He named the landmass l'Isle des Monts-déserts (the Isle of Bare Mountains). At present-day Otter Creek he encountered the Penobscot and Passamaquoddy Native Americans on their annual migration to the coast to dig, shuck, and smoke clams and oysters for Maine's long inland winters. Evidence of such activity is found in the remnants of 14 middens, or shell heaps, that experienced eyes can detect on and around contemporary Mount Desert Island.

For 200 years the French and British vied for this part of the Province of Massachusetts Bay. In 1688 the governor of French Canada gave the island to La Mothe de Cadillac, who later founded Detroit. In 1713 Louis XIV ceded Acadia, a region stretching from the Saint Lawrence River to the Atlantic Ocean, to the English. With the end of the French and Indian War, New Englanders, most of

Merritt Parkway, White Oak Shade Road overpass, New Canaan, Conn.

English origin, began the systematic settlement of the easternmost border of what in 1820 became Maine.

In the early 1760s Governor Bernard of the Province of Massachusetts Bay became the sole proprietor of Mount Desert Island. Bernard had set the stage for permanent colonization by inducing loyal men of the Boston area to locate there. One such was Abraham Somes of Gloucester, who founded Somesville, the island's oldest permanent settlement, at the head of Somes Sound in 1761.

With its many harbors, the unspoiled setting of the island became a base for local fishers and shipbuilding. It remained remote and inaccessible until it was "rediscovered" in 1844 by Thomas Cole and his Hudson River School of painters, among them Albert Bierstadt, Thomas Birch, Frederic Church, Charles Dix, and William Hart. Their paintings helped attract to this idyllic spot visitors from major eastern cities. In the beginning farms took on boarders, and then farms were purchased by guests; by 1882 18 large hotels (one with 600 rooms) were the core of a burgeoning summer colony.

As large mansions were built between 1880 and 1920, wealthy rusticators converged upon Bar Harbor, which rivaled Newport as a mecca for the affluent. Famous owners included the Vanderbilts, Pulitzers, Searses, Proctors, Astors, and Rockefellers, who referred to their "modest" summer homes as cottages. Joining the group were academicians and clergy, who formed the nucleus of the movement that preserved a large part of the island from private interests. Harvard University was well represented by naturalists, who during the late 19th century were the first to examine the geologic origins of Mount Desert Island.

In October 1947 the Great Fire, one of many raging forest fires in New England during that particularly dry fall, consumed much of peripheral Bar Harbor, including most of the mansions along Millionaires' Row. The island's principal city is now home to the College of the Atlantic (1972) and is the terminus for ferry service to and from Yarmouth, Nova Scotia.

The attractions of Mount Desert remain the same but the visitors have changed. Mount Desert's rugged natural beauty makes it a perfect venue for sightseeing, hiking, and climbing. Motels, campgrounds, shops, and restaurants cater to some 3 million yearly visitors. Acadia National Park, occupying more than 30,000 acres on the island, is the area's main tourist destination. Among its prominent attractions are a nature center, featuring wildflowers and plants indigenous to the area, and the Abbe Museum, displaying Native American artifacts. From the summit of Aca-

dia's Cadillac Mountain (at 1,530 feet, the highest spot on the Atlantic coast north of Brazil), one has a sweeping view of Mount Desert, its surrounding islands, and the mainland. Isle au Haut and the Schoodic Peninsula, which house the other segments of Acadia National Park, lie respectively to the south and north. The park also boasts coastal scenic overlooks of shoreline granitic cliffs anchored to the sea, plus 45 miles of carriage roads, built to accommodate horse-drawn vehicles and open only to nonmotorized traffic. Gone now are tycoon families in the elegant conveyances of bygone days. Since the Great Fire masses of American and Canadian tourists have made their way to Mount Desert Island on less rustic roadways in the ubiquitous family automobile, entree to worlds far beyond the confines of their familiar neighborhoods.

George B. Dorr, *Acadia National Park: Its Growth and Development* (1948); Judith S. Goldstein, *Tragedies and Triumphs: Charles W. Eliot, George B. Dorr and John D. Rockefeller, Jr. and the Founding of Acadia National Park* (1992); G. W. Helfrich and Gladys O'Neil, *Lost Bar Harbor: Photographs from the Collection of the Bar Harbor Historical Society* (1982); Samuel Eliot Morison, *The Story of Mount Desert Island, Maine* (1972); Robert Rothe, *Acadia* (1979).

Maynard Weston Dow

Mount Washington Mount Washington (elevation 6,288 feet) is the crown jewel of New Hampshire's White Mountains and the highest point in the Appalachian Mountains north of the Great Smokies. Presiding over the 52-acre Mount Washington State Park, it joins the eight other loftiest White Mountains to form the Presidential Range. Touted as home to the world's worst weather, this legendary peak is a popular destination for scientists, tourists, and outdoor enthusiasts.

The mountain once lay at the bottom of a large inland sea. About 390 million years ago heat and pressure from accumulated sediment raised the underlying rocks and turned them into mountains. Erosion and glacial ice subsequently scoured the range, giving the primarily quartzite and mica-schist peaks their current form.

The retreating ice cap of the last great ice age (12,000 to 15,000 years ago) carved out huge chunks of rock from the sides of Mount Washington. Great Gulf to the north, Tuckerman and Huntington Ravines on the east, and Ammonoosuc Ravine on the west are distinguishing features of the mountain. Three main rivers drain Mount Washington's slopes, the Saco, Androscoggin, and Ammonoosuc, with many lesser streams collecting snowmelt and rainwater from the mountain's sides.

Native peoples of the Abenaki nation called the peak *Agiocochook*, "home of the Great

Spirit." Early European explorers may have first set eyes on it in 1524. Samuel de Champlain wrote of seeing the snow-covered mountain from Casco Bay in 1604. Darby Field of Exeter, N.H., was the first European to climb Mount Washington, led by Pennacook Indian guides in 1642. In 1784 a group of scientists and intellectuals conducting the first official exploration of the peak renamed it Mount Washington in honor of the Revolutionary general who five years later would become the first U.S. president.

White exploration and settlement of the area followed the end of the French and Indian War (1763). The accidental discovery of a passage through Crawford Notch (to the west) in 1771 opened the way for freight transport, travelers, and settled villages. By the mid-19th century the scenery and wildness of the White Mountains were attracting artists and writers such as Thomas Cole and Nathaniel Hawthorne, who helped popularize the region as a summer resort. Crawford Notch, Pinkham Notch (to the east), and surrounding towns such as North Conway and Bethlehem developed into fashionable tourist centers with grand hotels and regular train service from eastern cities. The Mount Washington Hotel at Bretton Woods is the last of these great resort hotels still in operation.

The first trail on Mount Washington was cut in 1819 by Abel and Ethan Allen Crawford, local tavern owners, who led groups on horseback to a simple shelter on the summit. Parts of the old Crawford Path are still in use and form a segment of the 2,158-mile Appalachian Trail, which traverses the Presidential Ridge and Mount Washington on its way from Springer Mountain, Ga., to Maine's Mount Katahdin.

The Appalachian Mountain Club developed a system of huts in the White Mountains, beginning on Mount Madison at the northern end of the Presidentials in 1888. They built the Lakes of the Clouds hut, about a mile below Mount Washington's summit, after two of their most experienced members died in a severe ice storm in June 1900. The club also operates a visitor center in Pinkham Notch that provides lodging, education services, and an operations base for mountain search and rescue.

Mount Washington lies within a day's drive of 70 million people; tens of thousands seek recreation on its slopes every year, with hikers traversing its extensive trail network in all seasons. Skiers flock to Tuckerman Ravine for world-famous spring skiing. The first manmade tourist attraction in the United States, an 8-mile-long road built originally for carriages (1861), makes it possible for visitors to reach the summit by car, van, or motorcycle during the warmer months. They can also ride the historic cog railway (1869), the world's first rack-and-pinion railroad, whose locomotives are still powered by coal-fired steam. Foot, automobile, and bicycle races up the mountain take place every year.

Washington's summit lies in the path of three major storm systems. Clouds or fog are present at least 300 days a year. The average year-round temperature is 27 degrees; the yearly snowfall, 21 feet. On April 12, 1934, the highest wind gust ever recorded, 231 miles per hour, occurred on Mount Washington's summit. Fierce storms can develop within minutes in all seasons, and it is not uncommon for people caught in them to die. A sign at the summit lists those who have perished on the mountain, usually the victims of intense cold, wind, and snow. Since the first death in 1849 more than 120 people have died, bearing witness to the harsh conditions and enduring popularity of the peak. Eight people were also lost in a tragic cog railway accident on September 6, 1967.

Much of Mount Washington is above the tree line, and wildlife is scarce on its open plateaus and rock fields. Vegetation is limited to hardy, low-growing plants such as diapensia, Lapland rosebay, and alpine azalea, which produce a carpet of blossoms in early summer. One species, *Potentilla robbinsiana*, grows nowhere else in the world. Many plants native to Mount Washington are more typical of northern Labrador than of New England.

Those who visit the mountaintop encounter a sprawl of transmission towers, weather-monitoring equipment, buildings, parking lots, and boardwalks. The stone Tip Top House (1853), the oldest building still standing on the summit and one of the oldest mountaintop hostelries in existence, became a state-run museum in 1998. The concrete Sherman Adams Building (1979), operated by the New Hampshire Division of Parks and Recreation, houses the Mount Washington Observatory and a museum, snack bar, gift shop, and post office. The observatory, a private research and educational facility, has compiled weather data on the summit continuously since 1932.

Mount Washington and the nearly 780,000 acres of land that surround it make up the White Mountain National Forest. We in the 21st century must find a way to meet the challenge of balancing habitat protection and wilderness values with commercial logging and escalating recreational use.

Frank Allen Burt, *The Story of Mount Washington* (1960); Gene Daniell and Jon Burroughs, eds., *AMC White Mountain Guide: Hiking Trails in the White Mountain National Forest*, 26th ed. (1998); Maggie Stier and Ron McAdow, *Into the Mountains: Stories of New England's Most Celebrated Peaks* (1995).

Maggie Stier

Narragansett Bay Narragansett Bay is a 28-mile inlet that extends northward from Rhode Island Sound and divides the state of Rhode Island into two unequal parts. The width of the bay varies from 3 to 12 miles, and two navigable rivers, the Providence and the Seekonk, flow into it from the north. Many islands dot the bay, including Rhode, Prudence, and Conanicut Islands. Providence, the state capital, is located at the northern end of the bay, while the popular resort city of Newport is located at the south end. Since the colonial era Narragansett Bay has been one of the most significant focal points for population growth, commercial expansion, and industrial development in the northeastern United States.

The bay's evolution has mirrored that of much of New England. Originally, the land around the bay and many of its islands were settled by the Narragansett Indians, for whom it is named. Their displacement began peacefully with the sale of lands to religious refugees from the Puritan colony of Massachusetts. Roger Williams, Anne Hutchinson, and others founded independent settlements along its shores. With its good soil and relatively mild climate, the southwestern mainland of the bay evolved during the colonial era into a slave-holding plantation society, controlled by the elite Narragansett Planters. The bay region also became a hub of shipbuilding and vigorous commercial activity that spread its influence into many parts of the world, including Africa, the Caribbean, and, eventually, the Far East. One of the mainstays of the Narragansett system was the lucrative slave trade for which Rhode Island became infamous.

During the mid-19th century, commerce declined in the area and funds were increasingly directed into manufacturing. The rivers and streams that flowed into Narragansett Bay, particularly the Blackstone and the Pawtuxet, provided the waterpower necessary to drive the region's booming textile mills during America's Industrial Revolution. The eventual decline of textiles from the 1920s through the 1950s led to the enhancement of another New England industry—tourism. As early as the 1890s Narragansett Bay had already grown into a major resort center; Newport became a haven for the business elite of America who built palatial "cottages" overlooking the bay. In time, however, all classes enjoyed the recreational attractions of Narragansett Bay through amusement parks, fishing piers, boat rides, and waterfront hotels. This phase of the bay's history expanded dramatically after World War II.

The by-products of this evolution were not all positive, for at each stage the bay region paid a price. The displacement of the aboriginal population turned violent and extermina-

tory. The booming trading system contained the stigma of New England's largest slave market. Nineteenth-century industrialization led to the pollution of the bay and its river system and the destruction of its fish stocks. Opposition to proposals for oil drilling and the development of a nuclear reactor on Narragansett Bay, however, led to a drive to control environmental spoilage and to "Save the Bay."

When the U.S. Navy closed and abandoned many of its fortifications and munitions depots on Narragansett Bay's islands in the early 1970s, nearly 2,000 acres of land was deeded to the state for the Bay Islands Park System. Today, state, federal, and private organizations continue to work to reestablish the health of the bay's estuarine habitats, to reduce toxic contaminants, and to restore nutrient balances. Salt marshes and wildlife areas are increasingly being protected in an effort to maintain the bay's ecological equilibrium. Despite historical industrial pollution, the effects of global climate change, and the stresses of human activity, the return of marine mammals and some migratory fish to the bay attests to gradual improvement.

Peter J. Coleman, *The Transformation of Rhode Island, 1790–1860* (1963); Daniel P. Jones, *The Economic and Social Transformation of Rural Rhode Island, 1780–1850* (1992); William G. McLoughlin, *Rhode Island: A Bicentennial History* (1978); *The Smithsonian Guide to Historic America: Southern New England* (1989).

Eric Jarvis

Native Americans and the Environment Fifteen thousand years ago New England lay concealed beneath the last continental ice sheet of the Pleistocene. As temperatures and sea levels rose over the next 5,000 years, ice retreated northward for the final time, and the region's coastline began to resemble what one sees today. Mosaiclike communities of vegetation formed and succeeded one another both in southern New England, where tundra gave way to a mix of conifers and finally to oak-dominant deciduous forests, and in the north, where tundra was eventually replaced by mixed-conifer and hardwood forests.

Indians arrived in New England some 11,000 to 12,000 years ago. For millennia their economies were based exclusively on hunting, fishing, and gathering. Shellfish were especially important for people who lived along the coast, and massive quantities of this resource, together with fish, waterfowl, and other foods, allowed permanent settlement in southern New England's coastal and estuarial regions. Sometime before A.D. 1000, New England Indians slowly and unevenly adopted domesticated crops such as maize, beans, sunflowers, and squash, adding farming to their repertory of subsistence techniques.

The relation between native people and the environment before New England's colonization is unfortunately obscured by five centuries of transformation traceable to people of European descent. European explorers and colonists did, however, extensively record their impressions of the environment and of numerous local kin-based Indian communities, some that were politically autonomous and others that paid tribute to authoritative hereditary leaders in other societies. But Europeans also created new epidemiological, economic, and political conditions, immediately placing these small sovereign nations at risk and over time effacing most aboriginal cultural variation in the region. Many Native Americans died from disease. Some communities disappeared entirely; others consolidated in new alignments, their changing identities resulting as much from turmoil as from continuity. The best-known names of these native groups are Maliseet, Passamaquoddy, Penobscot, Eastern and Western Abenaki, Nipmuck, Wampanoag, Narragansett, Mohegan, and Pequot.

One of the most poignant themes of European descriptions of the region's environment is a sense of awe. Rarely, observers said, had they seen such natural bounty: trees so towering; berry bushes so laden; oyster and mussel beds so vast; lobsters, sturgeon, bass, cod, and whales so plentiful; and wolves, deer, and bears so abundant. Some who witnessed animals teeming or passenger pigeons, migratory waterfowl, and other birds darkening the sky were predisposed to find a menacing wilderness, but many more invoked imagery of Eden. Some of these were propagandists, their promotional hyperbole intended to encourage other settlers to join them. Not all were exaggerating, however, for Europeans did indeed encounter an unprecedented wealth of plant and animal life.

But New England was not beyond the human pale when Europeans arrived. Far from untouched or virgin, it bore the indelible imprint of aboriginal people who had manipulated and transformed it. One of the most important means of alteration was fire, which New England Indians used principally to enable them to hunt deer and bears more easily. According to *New Englands Prospect* (1634) by William Wood, Indians in early-17th-century Massachusetts burned hunting areas each November when grasses and leaves were like tinder, eliminating undergrowth that would otherwise choke woods and make hunting difficult. In wet marshy places and in fields left unburned because the native inhabitants had died in epidemics, Wood found thickets. Other Europeans also remarked that Indians held burns once or twice each year. They described open grassy ground between regularly spaced trees in hardwood forests and were reminded of managed parks in England. There is no doubt that fire eliminated vegetation obstructing the hunt, or that it encouraged the growth of meadows bordering open forest, edge habitats that were ideal for browsing deer and other animals.

New England Indians transformed their environment through domesticated crops, even though much of the northern and interior mountainous parts of the region were unsuited for intensive maize cultivation. About 1,000 years ago Indians living in coastal Connecticut, Massachusetts, and southern Maine and in the lower Connecticut River valley began to cultivate food by turning forests into fields; after six centuries they were growing corn, beans, and squash in fields prepared with hills and ridges. When Europeans arrived, some Indians may have intensified agricultural practices in order to be able to trade corn for the newcomers' metal tools. Corn yields were evidently between 25 and 60 bushels per acre; stored in baskets and other containers in underground pits, the crop was consumed between harvests. Changes to habitat from farming were greatest in fields where crops were grown several years in succession and then fallowed; Indians then slashed forests to create new fields, the trees and brush they burned providing ash for the next growing cycle. During the 17th century some Indians living along the coast used fish to fertilize fields nearing exhaustion, thereby extending productivity.

Although some New England Indians did farm, domesticated crops rarely composed more of their diet than all other resources combined before Europeans arrived, and even then Indians throughout New England continued to hunt, fish, and gather. Diets were probably always sensitive to changing environmental and ecological conditions; for example, 1,500 to 2,000 years ago Indians living at Narragansett Bay shifted their diet from oysters, whose beds were apparently obliterated by silt flowing into the bay, to soft-shelled clams.

New England Indians no doubt possessed extensive knowledge of the natural world. They collectively defined as edible an extraordinary variety of terrestrial, riverine, and marine resources, including seals, white-tailed deer, moose, beavers, rabbits, turkeys, passenger pigeons, migratory waterfowl, and various crustacea, shellfish, and fish, as well as nuts, seeds, and berries. Many resources varied seasonally and geographically, and Indians developed diverse strategies to exploit them. During the 17th century people often moved according to season from coastal sites near crops and maritime food supplies to inland sites near deer and other terrestrial and riverine resources. Some native people may have remained in relatively permanent villages, obtaining most of their needs from the sea, the shore, the woods, and the fields. Hunting parties also went on extended forays in search of game.

The pressures aboriginal New England peoples placed on animal and plant species and land, though largely unknown, should not be underestimated. The large expanse of cleared land along the coast that in 1524 so greatly impressed Giovanni da Verrazano began to take form at Narragansett Bay a millennium ago, as open fields displaced forests. Here is evidence of human-induced biotic change, a result perhaps of a combination of factors, including deliberately set fires, trees cut for fuel, and the fallowing cycle.

Demands on land and resources were surely a function of demography, at least in part. The link between population and pressure on resources, though complicated everywhere by ecological, cultural, and historical factors, seems intuitive and direct: the greater the size and density of a population, the greater its potential demand on fuel, water, animals, plants, and other basic resources of the region. In the centuries immediately preceding the arrival of Europeans, the aboriginal population in southern and coastal New England probably increased because of the rich shellfish and other resources; on the eve of European discovery some 125,000 people may have lived in the region in densities ranging from a low of 31 people per 100 square miles in the north to a high of 689 people per 100 square miles in the coastal south, where, not coincidentally, we find the most evidence of habitat alteration.

Epidemics set off by microbes transported by Europeans shattered this population, killing some 67 to 95 percent of native people in one century. Arriving in Massachusetts, 17th-century colonists encountered empty villages surrounded by graves and cleared fields lying unharvested or fallow; some thanked God for relieving them of the burden of turning forest into arable fields. That some also described this region as Eden may not now be so surprising. In 1650 the population density of England, from which many settlers came, was 11,650 people per 100 square miles, or up to 375 times that of aboriginal New England—at a time when the first wave of epidemics in the colonies had not yet occurred. Moreover, Europeans were arriving from a continent whose environment they had transformed by draining marshes, destroying forests for fuel and arable land, mining coal that darkened the sky with soot as it burned, and eliminating predators that threatened the few species reserved for sport. In contrast, the minuscule aboriginal populations in New England placed relatively modest demands on the environment, and after disease reduced the population, the survivors had even less effect on the land.

By 1720, 100 years after the *Mayflower* arrived in Plymouth, 150,000 people of European descent had overwhelmed the decimated native New England population. Their numbers greatly reduced, Indians developed new relations with European neighbors who possessed an almost unquenchable thirst for arable and grazing land, beaver pelts, timber, and other commodities. In the 17th century, through almost every conceivable means of transaction, Indian land fast became European-owned land. Meeting the immigrants' demand for meat and furs meant a reduction in the abundance of deer, turkeys, and beavers. Indians, unrestrained by their social relation with animals and as interested in guns and other manufactured European goods as Europeans were in furs and food, helped hunt beaver and other animals to local extinction. In part as a result of faunal declines, 18th-century native people established family hunting territories in northern parts of New England as a conservation measure. During the 19th century the Maliseet added waste of game to other personal actions considered responsible for poor luck in hunting. Throughout the region, New England Indians came to participate in the economy as laborers, domestics, producers of crafts, and small-scale rural trappers and garden farmers.

David J. Bernstein, *Prehistoric Subsistence on the Southern New England Coast: The Record from Narragansett Bay* (1993); Kathleen J. Bragdon, *Native People of Southern New England, 1500–1650* (1996); William Cronon, *Changes in the Land: Indians, Colonists, and the Ecology of New England* (1983); Shepard Krech III, *The Ecological Indian: Myth and History* (1999); Howard S. Russell, *Indian New England before the Mayflower* (1980); Dean R. Snow, *The Archaeology of New England* (1980); Frank Gouldsmith Speck, *Penobscot Man: The Life History of a Forest Tribe in Maine* (1970); Bruce G. Trigger, ed., *Northeast*, vol. 15 of *Handbook of North American Indians*, gen. ed. William C. Sturtevant (1978).

Shepard Krech III

Native Americans and the Landscape

Much of New England was tundra when the first Paleo-Indian hunters arrived some 12,000 years ago. Their descendants and later waves of Indians adapted to a changing landscape, albeit one evolving geologically at such a slow pace that long-term changes would have been obscured by more dramatic seasonal ones. The landscape was also being modified by its human inhabitants. As young forests matured across the region, early inhabitants of North America are believed to have carried out controlled burns in order to clear vegetation and maintain meadows that would attract deer and elk. In addition, streams were modified to facilitate the harvesting of fish runs. As native populations grew more familiar with the resources of the region, they settled into routines that brought them back to the same sites year after year in a cycle that permanently altered the landscape.

By 6000 B.C., Native Americans were conveying food plants beyond their natural habitats into portions of the eastern woodlands, an area stretching from the Mississippi River eastward to the Atlantic Ocean. Squash and wild onions, for example, have been identified at archaeological sites where they would not have naturally occurred. The interaction of humans with plants and animals during this remote time was not considered a form of agriculture, but it did set the stage for later agricultural developments.

What archaeologists refer to as the Archaic era lasted from the end of the Paleo-Indian period, around 8000 B.C., until about 700 B.C. A well-known culture popularly attributed to the Red Paint people flourished in northern New England from around 3200 to 2100 B.C. This late Archaic cultural development has been related to similar ones in the Canadian Maritime Provinces and in the interior west of New England. The culture is best known for its cemeteries, in which finely made ground- and chipped-stone tools were typically deposited with the dead on beds of red ocher. Excavations at coastal sites such as the Turner Farm on Penobscot Bay in Maine have shown that these people were also adapted to maritime hunting. Ground-stone adzes and gouges, some of which have been recovered, were presumably used to build large dugout canoes. Bayonetlike slate blades mimicking the rostra (swords) of swordfish allow us to glimpse part of a maritime culture that disappeared when changes in the ocean currents and climate rendered its adaptation obsolete.

The New England Indians encountered by the earliest European travelers spoke one or another of several Eastern Algonquian languages. Early Algonquian peoples spread out of southeastern Canada and into the Great Lakes region, New England, and the Maritimes sometime after 1000 B.C. They may have been better adapted than others to emerging environmental conditions and possibly carried technology—namely, the bow and arrow—that enabled them to displace earlier inhabitants. The names of lakes and streams in New England often derive from Eastern Algonquian words. Hills and mountains have Algonquian names less frequently. Modern place-names can often be traced back to Native American terms, although the words for towns and counties are more likely to be European imports. Both Massachusetts and Connecticut owe their names to Native Americans.

Perhaps as recently as A.D. 900, a wedge of Iroquoian speakers intruded into the lower Great Lakes region and isolated the Eastern Algonquian from the rest of the Algonquian family of languages to the west. The Eastern Algonquian then spread southward along the eastern seaboard as far as North Carolina, a territorial expansion that may have been fueled by their acquisition of domesticated plants.

By the early 17th century the Eastern Algonquian of New England had diversified into seven broad groupings. Then epidemics spread by the European population began to devastate them. Most 17th-century descriptions of the Eastern Algonquian reveal groups already much reduced in size and adapting rapidly to the changing conditions brought on by European colonization. The Massachusett peoples, including the Narragansett, Wampanoag, and other local groups in eastern Massachusetts and Rhode Island, were ravaged by a hepatitislike illness shortly before the arrival of the founders of Plymouth colony in 1620. The disease spread to, but not beyond, the Mohegan-Pequot nation of eastern Connecticut. In the 1630s smallpox reduced these populations again, along with the native peoples of western Connecticut and Massachusetts. There, a confusion of personal names, place-names, and local ethnic names such as "Quiripi" and "Pocumtuck" in sparse written records make it hard for us to understand the ethnic divisions of the time.

What can be determined is that southern New England was inhabited by horticulturists who lived in large villages or bark wigwams for at least part of the year. Family groups dispersed seasonally to special-purpose camps in order to harvest fish runs, waterfowl, or other short-lived resources. They lived in little farmsteads in the summer where they tended fields of maize, beans, and squash, the trio of plant domesticates that dominated native horticulture in the region. Giovanni da Verrazano visited southern New England in 1524 and later described thriving communities living at a regional density that probably approached 500 people per 100 square miles. A century later epidemics would inflict convulsive change on their descendants.

The growing season is longer than 150 days only in the southern Connecticut River valley, along coastal Connecticut and Rhode Island, through eastern Massachusetts, and northeastward along a narrow strip of the New Hampshire and Maine coasts. Native horticulture was not effective north of this line, which is to say, throughout Vermont and in most of New Hampshire and Maine. Consequently, the adaptation of New England native peoples to this part of the region focused mainly on hunting and fishing. That economy supported only an eighth to a quarter of the population density that southern New England sustained.

Most of the Indians of northern New England belonged to a far-flung group usually referred to as Abenaki. The Western Abenaki lived mainly in the interior of New Hampshire and Vermont. The Eastern Abenaki lived primarily in Maine. Other Eastern Algonquian peoples, the Maliseet and closely related Passamaquoddy, lived primarily in what is now New Brunswick but extended their territory into portions of eastern and northern Maine. All of them were strongly oriented to the main rivers of the region, and they tended to concentrate in villages located near seasonal fishing stations in the spring and fall. Horticulture was not a dependable option in most of Abenaki country, and it was only rarely attempted. Families dispersed to interior hunting camps in the winter and to coastal locations in the summer.

To get from place to place natives in southern New England traveled mostly over well-established paths that were probably created many centuries ago. These later served European immigrants, and many paths were eventually widened and made into paved roads that are still used today. Overland travel was less common in northern New England, where it was impeded by dense forests. Paths in the north were mainly portages between lakes and streams, with birchbark canoes providing the principal means of travel. In that part of the region where the American white birch is common, the Abenaki mastered the manufacture of lightweight birchbark canoes. When European contact stimulated the fur trade, hunting and trapping territories crystallized around traditional winter camps and the Abenaki became major North American suppliers.

A combination of the European demand for land and disease-induced depopulation forced the native peoples of southern New England into early dependency. King Philip's War (1675–76) ended their independence from the colonies of Massachusetts, Connecticut, and Rhode Island. Many surviving natives were forced into small, marginalized communities, while others were absorbed into the growing colonial populations. A few communities survive: Wampanoag, Narragansett, Pequot, Mohegan, Nipmuck, Paugusset, and Scaticook. Some are undergoing ethnic revitalization that has attracted both popular and scholarly attention.

The Abenaki of northern New England kept their independence much longer than their southerly counterparts. Their lands were not much sought after by colonial farmers, and their location between competing English and French powers enabled them to survive in part by playing the Europeans off each other. The Western Abenaki tended to gravitate toward the French, and many moved to refugee communities near the Saint Lawrence River during the colonial wars of the 18th century. These communities were mainly at Saint Francis and Becancour, both on the south bank of the Saint Lawrence in Quebec. Small surviving communities of Western Abenaki have reasserted themselves in Vermont and New Hampshire in recent years.

Some Western Abenaki shifted eastward in Maine with the result that Eastern Abenaki communities along the Penobscot River came to be dominated by Western Abenaki speech and custom. Contacts continued with the Passamaquoddy and Maliseet, with whom the Eastern Abenaki had long maintained close relations that persist today. The Penobscot were gradually divested of their landholdings in Maine during the late 18th and early 19th centuries. Legal action brought in the 1970s on behalf of the Penobscot and their Passamaquoddy and Maliseet neighbors in that state eventually led to partial compensation for these losses, however. Communities of all three survive in Maine locations.

Bruce J. Bourque, *Diversity and Complexity in Prehistoric Maritime Societies: A Gulf of Maine Perspective* (1995); Dean R. Snow, *The Archaeology of New England* (1980); Bruce G. Trigger, ed., *Northeast*, vol. 15 of *Handbook of North American Indians*, gen. ed. William C. Sturtevant (1978).

Dean R. Snow

Nearing, Helen and Scott (1904–95, 1883–1983) Homesteaders and social critics.

Helen (Knothe) Nearing and Scott Nearing embodied and promoted a philosophy that constituted the most significant expression of the benefits of simple living and homesteading to emerge in 20th-century America. Together they wrote nearly 50 books, including their most influential work, *Living the Good Life: Being a Plain Practical Account of a Twenty-Year Project on a Self-Subsistent Homestead in Vermont, Together with Remarks on How to Live Sanely and Simply in a Troubled World* (1954). When it was reissued in 1970, *Living the Good Life: How to Live Sanely and Simply in a Troubled World* was embraced by the youth of the counterculture and sold more than 200,000 copies. Like Henry David Thoreau, the Nearings are examples of people whose conscientious practical living illuminates a powerful cultural critique.

Scott Nearing was born in Morris Run, Penn., and received a bachelor's degree and doctorate from the University of Pennsylvania. He taught economics at the University of Pennsylvania's Wharton School and became involved in progressive social causes in Philadelphia. Because of his outspoken views on social reform, he was fired from his position as

Helen and Scott Nearing, 1970

an assistant professor in 1915 in one of the first major cases involving academic freedom of the 20th century. From 1915 to 1917, Nearing taught at the University of Toledo in Ohio, but in April 1917 he was fired from that position as well, this time for his opposition to American involvement in World War I. He joined the Socialist Party and in March 1918 was indicted under the Espionage Act for writing an anti-war pamphlet. Continuing his involvement in left-wing politics, he drifted away from the Socialists and joined the Communist Party in 1927 but was expelled for his independent radicalism in 1930. With his first wife, Nellie Seeds (who died in 1946), Nearing had two sons: John (born 1912) and Robert (adopted 1914). He became estranged from his wife during the 1920s, and in 1928 met Helen Knothe. Nearing and Knothe lived together for many years before marrying in 1947.

Helen Knothe was born in New York City to a family active in business and civic circles. Her parents were Theosophists, gardeners, vegetarians, and intellectuals, and her childhood home in Ridgewood, N.J., was a center for political and social interchange. Helen pursued classical violin studies in Europe and also traveled in India and Australia before meeting Scott Nearing.

Beginning in 1932, when they left New York City during the depth of the Depression, the Nearings lived a life of self-sufficiency. Their spartan existence united New England simplicity and determined self-reliance and combined hand labor with intellectual work aimed at personal and social transformation. The trademarks of what they called "the good life" were stone buildings, organic gardens, native cash crops (maple sugar in Vermont, blueberries in Maine), and the absence of domestic animals and power tools. The Nearings continued their homesteading in Maine, moving to Forest Farm on Cape Rosier in 1952. After Scott's death, Helen carried on their tradition of gardening, writing, teaching, speaking, and greeting the scores of visitors who made pilgrimages to the Nearings' farm. Their books *Living the Good Life* and *Continuing the Good Life: Half a Century of Homesteading* (1979) and Helen Nearing's *Loving and Leaving the Good Life* (1992) offer both the Nearings' philosophy of life and practical examples of simple living. Their Maine home, now The Good Life Center, is open to the public and administered by the Trust for Public Land, a national conservation organization. It is a living center dedicated to perpetuating self-sufficiency, simplicity, peace, ecological and economic sustainability, and social justice for the future.

John Hoskyns-Abrahall, *Living the Good Life* [video recording] (Bullfrog Films, Oley, Pa., 1977); Ellen LaConte, *On Light Alone: A Guru Meditation on the Good Death of Helen Nearing* (1996); John A. Saltmarsh, *Scott Nearing: An Intellectual Biography* (1991); Stephen J. Whitfield, *Scott Nearing: Apostle of American Radicalism* (1974).

John A. Saltmarsh

New England and Canada Before considering the interrelations between New England and Canada, it is worth remembering that the political units and boundaries that Europeans imposed on the Northeast had little meaning for the native peoples. At the time of European contact, Algonquian-speaking Micmacs, Maliseet, Passamaquoddy, Penobscot, and Abenaki occupied extensive territories in the Northeast. Their seasonal rounds of hunting and fishing took them from the shores of the Gulf of Maine and Atlantic Ocean into the interior throughout much of what is now Maine and the Canadian Maritime Provinces. Even today the Canadian-U.S. border is not seen as a boundary between native peoples, and links are close between bands in northern New England and eastern Canada.

Almost from the beginning of European settlement, some sort of border has existed between New England and Canada. Nevertheless, the boundary that was established in 1783, dividing the continent into two, has been in Graeme Wynn's words "remarkably porous." People, goods, and ideas have flowed back and forth, influencing both New England and the neighboring Canadian provinces. Certainly the influence of New England over Maritime Canada has been pervasive. Columbia University historian John Bartlett Brebner considered French Acadia (present-day eastern Maine, Nova Scotia, New Brunswick, and Prince Edward Island) to have been "New England's outpost" in the 17th and early 18th centuries; geographer D. W. Meinig has argued that a "Greater New England" had emerged by 1750, stretching from the core of southern New England eastward through Nova Scotia to Saint John's on the Avalon Peninsula in Newfoundland. During the Acadian period Boston served as a major market for Acadian agricultural produce, and Yankee traders operated in the Bay of Fundy. After the British expulsion of the Acadians from Nova Scotia in 1755, farmers and tradesmen from crowded agricultural townships in New England were encouraged to settle the vacant farmlands around the Bay of Fundy, while fishermen from eastern Massachusetts settled on the rocky South Shore of Nova Scotia. What had once been French Catholic settlements became English-speaking Yankee Congregational and Baptist areas. The Yankee influx was reinforced after the American War of Independence, when Tories or loyalists (the Canadian term), many of them from New England, moved to the safety of British territory. Some settled in Quebec, carving out the eastern townships along the Vermont border, but many moved to the Maritimes, settling in Nova Scotia and in the new loyalist colonies of New Brunswick and Cape Breton. A notable feature of this migration was the sizable community of freed and escaped slaves that formed at Africville, just outside Halifax, Nova Scotia, many of whose descendants remain in the region. During the early 19th century New Englanders continued to spill over the Quebec and New Brunswick borders, looking for agricultural land or jobs in the woods and sawmills.

At least until the massive immigrations of settlers from the British Isles after the end of the Napoleonic Wars in 1815, the Maritime Provinces bore many of the hallmarks of the New England cultural landscape. In Nova Scotia much of the settled area in the western part of the province was divided into townships of approximately 12 miles square (100,000 acres), following the pattern found in northern Maine. In the agricultural townships of the Annapolis River valley land was allocated in rectangular lots of various sizes, but on the South Shore fishermen divided up "beach rooms," lots used for setting up a fishing stage and drying flakes, and neglected the rocky interior. Timber-framed Cape Cod houses of one and a half stories and with a central chimney were built in both fishing and agricultural areas of the province, becoming the prototype for the Maritime small house of the 19th century. After the loyalist influx larger, two-story houses in the Georgian style were constructed. Meetinghouses, such as those in Barrington on the South Shore and at Horton in the Cornwallis Valley, and Anglican churches, particularly those in the Annapolis River valley, closely followed New England designs. Gravestones also reflected New England styles, with the death's head and angel motifs common on late-18th-century stones. Across the Bay of Fundy in New Brunswick, the loyalist imprint was considerable. In Saint Andrews and Saint John two-story Adam- or Federal-style houses, in brick or wood, were common, while the architecture of the magnificent Greenock Presbyterian Church in Saint Andrews owed much to New England prototypes. The influence of New England was also felt on the orientation of buildings along main streets. Influenced by the early-19th-century Greek Revival in the United States, many stores in the Maritimes were built with their gable ends turned toward the street, faint echoes of Greek temple facades.

Toward the end of the 19th century, New

England's influence over the cultural landscape of the Maritimes reasserted itself, although not to the same degree as a century earlier. The development of a tourist "pleasure periphery" in coastal and upland New England spilled over into the Maritimes. Indeed, it was the New England poet Henry Wadsworth Longfellow who helped shape the tourists' image of Nova Scotia when he published in 1847 his hugely successful poem *Evangeline* about the Acadian deportation. Even though Longfellow never visited Nova Scotia, his poem single-handedly created "Evangeline Country" in the Annapolis River valley, an area still marketed under that name today. Large hotels, such as The Pines in Digby, Nova Scotia, and Algonquin in Saint Andrews, were built to cater to the American tourist influx, while camps in the woods housed American sportsmen. The summer homes built mainly for Americans at Campobello and Saint Andrews, New Brunswick; Baddeck on Cape Breton Island; and Dalvay, Prince Edward Island, owed much in their architecture to the Queen Anne–style and shingle-style cottages common along the Maine coast. Elsewhere in the region it is difficult to isolate specifically New England influences amid the pervasiveness of American architectural styles, but it could be argued that the main administrative buildings of Dalhousie University and King's College in Halifax, Nova Scotia, designed by Massachusetts Institute of Technology–trained architect A. R. Cobb, owed much to the Colonial Revival sweeping New England in the early 20th century.

Although Maritimers came in droves to New England during the late 19th and early 20th centuries, their influence on the New England cultural landscape was relatively slight. A common language and similar culture made them largely invisible in the melting pot of immigrant Boston. The influence of French-speaking Canadians on New England, however, was much more marked. From the early 19th century, French Canadians from Quebec had worked seasonally in northern New England, bringing in the harvest on farms in Vermont and New Hampshire and working in the woods in Maine. French Canadians and Acadians in the Upper Saint John River valley also spilled over the border, taking up agricultural land and creating the distinctive cultural landscape of the Madawaska area. Here long lots running back from the river, large Roman Catholic churches, and twin barns were common features. Yet these seasonal and permanent incursions into northern New England were soon dwarfed by the massive migrations of French Canadians to mill towns in the south. As the

textile industry in New England boomed, there was an increasing demand for cheap labor, and much of it was supplied by French Canadians. By 1900 French Canadians could be found working in textile towns from New Bedford, Mass., to Old Town, Maine, with especially large concentrations in Fall River, Holyoke, and Lowell, Mass.; Manchester, N.H.; and Biddeford-Saco and Lewiston-Auburn, Maine. The proportion of French Canadians in Woonsocket, R.I., was so great that the city came to be called the "Quebec of New England." In these immigrant "Petit Canadas," the French language and Roman Catholicism took hold. Large Catholic churches with their parochial schools and seminaries began to be built, frequently under the influence of architectural styles prevalent in Quebec. In Lewiston, Maine, the juxtaposition of the enormous Continental Mill and Saint Mary's Catholic Church, hard by the three-decker tenements of the town's Petit Canada, is one of the most symbolic cultural landscapes in New England. Combined with the substantial Irish and Italian immigrations at about the same time, the French Canadian influx helped recast the religious geography of the region. From being overwhelmingly Protestant, New England had become predominantly Catholic. The stereotype of a New England inhabited by Puritan Yankees could hardly be further from the truth.

Today, the spread of an urbanized American culture, little of it recognizably from New England, is helping to undermine the distinctiveness of the cultural landscapes of Quebec and the Maritimes. The same automobile-based landscape of fast-food restaurants, gas stations, suburbs, and shopping malls can be found on both sides of the border. The attempt to create a joint Canadian-U.S. international park encompassing historic sites relating to the Acadians on either side of the border only highlights the need to set off and preserve historic landscapes before they are overwhelmed by a homogenized North American culture. The spread of gas stations belonging to the New Brunswick–based oil giant Irving into Maine reflects the new economic realities of cross-border trade under the North American Free Trade Agreement and the cultural convergence in the Northeast. Although Canadian, the stations proudly fly Old Glory.

John Bartlett Brebner, *New England's Outpost: Acadia before the Conquest of Canada* (1927); Naomi Griffiths, "Longfellow's *Evangeline*: The Birth and Acceptance of a Legend," *Acadiensis* 11 (1982); Stephen J. Hornsby, Victor A. Konrad, and James J. Herlan, eds., *The Northeastern Borderlands: Four Centuries of Interaction* (1989); Victor A. Konrad, "Against the Tide: French Canadian Barn Building Tradition in the St. John Valley of Maine," *American Review of*

Canadian Studies 12 (1982); Lewiston Historical Commission, *Historic Lewiston: Franco-American Origins* (1974); Dean R. Louder and Eric Waddell, eds., *French America: Mobility, Identity, and Minority Experience across the Continent* (1993); D. W. Meinig, *Atlantic America, 1492–1800*, vol. 1 of *The Shaping of America: A Geographical Perspective on 500 Years of History* (1988); Graeme Wynn, "A Province Too Much Dependent on New England: Northeastern America, 1755–1775" and "A Region of Scattered Settlements and Bounded Possibilities: Northeastern America, 1775–1800," *Canadian Geographer* 31 (1987).
Stephen Hornsby

New England as Cultural Hearth A

cultural hearth can be defined as the territorial cradle or matrix within which the essential elements of a cultural system evolve and crystallize to achieve a distinctive identity—and then spread outward to shape the character of an extended area. Under this definition, New England is the finest example of a cultural hearth in the Western Hemisphere. Furthermore, despite its off-side location, relatively small size, and (at least in recent times) unimpressive fraction of the nation's total population, the region has in many ways profoundly affected the remainder of the United States, both in the past and in the present day.

The significance of New England as a cultural hearth is apparent at two levels: the tangible—consisting of social and historical artifacts—and, perhaps more important, the intangible—consisting of ideas, ideals, and perceptions that set the United States apart from the rest of the world. Beginning with the immediately verifiable, it is clear that the cultural and demographic core of New England came into existence during the century and a half between the founding of the Plymouth Colony in 1620 and the eve of the American Revolution. The early, enduring heart of the region was colonized almost entirely by individuals from the southern and eastern sections of Great Britain, who also established themselves in parallel fashion within the southern and eastern portions of the region—in the more accessible and productive tracts of Massachusetts, Connecticut, and Rhode Island (and segments of Long Island). The newcomers may initially have maintained the particularities of their English roots, but gradually such localisms faded away under the influence of the dominant religious and social ethos, and by interaction with a new habitat. Thus a common, identifiable New England culture was born.

The major components of a cultural system can be propagated outward from a cultural hearth into a receptive territory in three basic ways: group migration, contagious diffusion (that is, the direct observation and then adoption of a cultural innovation by a succession of near neighbors), and long-distance communication. All three have operated in the case of New England.

With the passage of time, a burgeoning population streaming out from southeastern New England occupied the remainder of the three oldest colonies and then moved northward to claim New Hampshire, Vermont, and the more exploitable portions of Maine. By the closing decades of the 18th century, driven by the meagerness of the region's physical resources and a remarkably high rate of natural increase, many New Englanders had ventured past the bounds of New England proper. In northern New Jersey, northeastern Pennsylvania, and much of upstate New York, native New Englanders eventually accounted for many of the area's early European occupants. The turmoil of the American Revolution set off an exodus in other directions, as loyalists escaped to Nova Scotia, New Brunswick, and the eastern townships of Quebec, among other places, where they were to make a lasting imprint upon the sociocultural personality of their new homes.

After the Revolutionary War New Englanders and migrants from the other two major colonial American cultural hearths, the Midland and the Chesapeake Bay area, began moving inland from the original 13 states. Their migration routes tended to run latitudinally, so that New Englanders are particularly prevalent in northern Ohio and the upper Midwest, even though intermixture with people from other cultural hearths (and eventually immigrants from Ireland, Germany, Scandinavia, and other European lands) became stronger and more complex the greater the distance from the Atlantic seaboard. Nonetheless, traces of New England culture can be discerned as far afield as the Pacific Northwest and other places frequented by the active 19th-century merchant seamen and whalers sailing from ports in the home region. Evidence of this migration can be read in the landscape—in the layouts of certain settlements in New York, Ohio, and Michigan that mimic the design of the much-celebrated New England village—as well as in the many place-names borrowed from New England.

In keeping with its leadership role in the American Industrial Revolution, New England, along with the Middle Atlantic states, pioneered in the development of mass-production factories and their associated mill towns, providing models to be copied elsewhere. The region was also once at the forefront of mechanical invention and industrial technology, conspicuously so in textiles, shipbuilding, and lumbering, while parallel advances occurred in banking, insurance, and finance. Thanks in part to such early momen-

tum, it has managed to keep abreast of competitors in certain types of high-tech research, development, and manufacturing to the present day.

Linguists have detected and carefully mapped the audible patterns of New England speech (specifically vocabulary and pronunciation) throughout much of the northeastern quadrant of the nation and even past the Mississippi River. In the case of religion, however, the influence on other regions has been much less striking than has been true for settlement landscape or language. Although Yankee missionaries have been as energetic as any among Native Americans and heathen foreigners, the Congregational faith that once dominated New England has not fared nearly as well outside the region as have the Methodists, Baptists, Presbyterians, and Roman Catholics. It is noteworthy that Unitarianism, essentially a 19th-century New England derivative of Congregationalism, has diffused throughout the land but primarily as a faith appealing to elite segments of the population. However, even with New England's relatively small contribution to the map of American religion, the picture changes when we consider its indirect effect as a progenitor of the so-called burned-over district of central New York, an area of significant religious revival that grew out of New England's First and Second Great Awakenings in the early to mid and late 1700s. In addition to the various denominations that originated or gained momentum in the region during the early 19th century, New England also spawned a surprising number of reform movements with religious overtones, temperance and abolitionism among them.

New England's contributions to the more sophisticated modes of culture, mainly the circulation of printed words and images, have been significant. This is especially true in the case of education. Literacy flourished early in colonial New England, and the region soon outdistanced all others in terms of the number and quality of colleges and preparatory academies. Indeed, the prestigious schools of New England, most of them privately supported, continue to attract a considerable influx of students from other parts of the world. Moreover, in earlier times a disproportionate share of college presidents and primary and secondary school teachers serving outside the region were born, reared, and trained in New England.

Even more potent a method for instilling New England's ideals and values throughout the land has been the region's initial domination of the school-textbook market. Within the broader field of publishing, 19th-century New England was preeminent in the number, quality, and effect of its books and periodicals.

New England publishers furnished the means whereby a galaxy of poets, novelists, and authors of nonfiction won the hearts and minds of a national public. The printed page also reinforced the region's strong role in science, medicine, philosophy, theology, politics, the arts, history, and other fields of scholarship. New England writers and publishers were successful in establishing the region as the nation's moral standard-bearer during the formative years of the republic.

As Alexis de Tocqueville wrote tellingly in the 1830s, "The two or three main ideas which constitute the basis of the social theory of the United States were first combined in the northern British colonies, more generally denominated the states of New England. The principles of New England spread at first to the neighboring states; they then passed successively to the more distant ones; and at length they imbued the whole Confederation." Tocqueville noted that the civilization of New England was "like a beacon lit upon a hill, which, after it has diffused its warmth around, tinges the distant horizon with its glow."

If New England had far transcended the spatial and ideological bounds of the standard cultural hearth by the early 19th century, its image and influence spread even farther along a somewhat different path thereafter. The crucial iconic ingredient in this latter-day development has been the romanticized New England village. In the words of author Donald W. Meinig, "An idealized image of the New England village became so powerfully impressed upon such a broad readership as to become a national symbol, a model setting for the American community."

Further enshrining the somewhat imaginary old-time New England as the quintessence of the American dream has been the popularity of such journals as *Yankee,* Thornton Wilder's emotionally riveting play *Our Town,* Norman Rockwell's scores of poignant and persuasive New England–based illustrations, various film and television productions, and a thriving tourist industry that focuses on the hallowed sites of the American Revolution, homes of eminent authors, and such clever re-creations of an endearing colonial past as Plimoth Plantation. What remains certain about New England as a cultural hearth is that despite its weakened economic and political clout, New England still casts its spell nationwide and may continue far into the future to be an indispensable component of each American's self-image and sense of rootedness.

Stewart H. Holbrook, *The Yankee Exodus: An Account of Migration from New England* (1950); John B. Leighly, "Town Names of Colonial New England in the West," *Annals of the Association of American Geographers* 68 (1978); George Wilson Pierson, "The Obstinate Concept of New England: A Study Denudation," *New England Quarterly* (March 1955); Lois Kimball Mathews Rosenberry, *The Expansion of New England: The Spread of New England Settlement and Institutions to the Mississippi River, 1820–1865* (1909); Thomas J. Schlereth, "The New England Presence on the Midwestern Landscape," *The Old Northwest* (1983); Alexis de Tocqueville, *Democracy in America* (1945 [1838]); Christina Tree, *How New England Happened: A Guide to New England through Its History* (1976); Wilbur Zelinsky, *The Cultural Geography of the United States*, rev. ed. (1992).

Wilbur Zelinsky

New York and New England

New York may now exert a powerful influence on New Englanders, but in earlier centuries New England culture determined the course of settlement and culture in large areas of that state. Seeking new vistas, opportunities, and—most of all—land, New Englanders migrated to many areas of New York, bringing with them an established though evolving material and social culture. Once aboriginal populations were driven out, and in the absence of other European settlers, New England migrants were able, particularly after the American Revolution, to establish their own patterns of community and economy on what was in many ways a clean slate. Wilbur Zelinsky has called this endeavor the "first effective settlement" of the area.

By 1800 settlers had gained a strong foothold in the southern and eastern portions of New England, a region that in many ways lived up to its name as an extension of old England. Integrating English crops, animals, and building types with American realities such as maize, native peoples, and a vast scale of space and resources, New Englanders created a culture very different from the one that evolved in the Tidewater region of eastern Virginia to the south, for example, or in Nouvelle France to the north. A number of factors made New England what it was, including small, dispersed family homesteads; a political organization of space based on townships; an egalitarian and close-knit community life; and, in later years, widespread development of urbanism, mercantilism, and industrialism. Strong population growth served to further the spread of these characteristics.

There were limiting forces, however. Foremost among them were New England's small size and the region's often difficult agricultural conditions. Colonial-era conflicts with French and Native American foes also hindered the expansion of New England's frontiers. Land hunger could finally be sated after 1763, when these conflicts came to an end, allowing New Englanders to move north, northeast, and northwest into Maine, New Hampshire, Vermont, and western Massachusetts.

The movement of New Englanders into New York actually began before the start of the American Revolution. It was, however, a very uneven and selective flow. Much of the lower Hudson River valley south of Albany, including the western half of Long Island and the New York City area, was already inhabited by a mainly Dutch-Flemish population, and a great deal of its land was encumbered in large estates and holdings. New Englanders from Connecticut and Massachusetts seeking land and opportunities moved across Long Island to what is today Suffolk County, migrated to the uninhabited hills and valleys of the Taconic region close to New York–New England borders, or leapfrogged westward into the frontier areas of the Mohawk River and Schoharie Creek valleys.

Settlers were halted in their westward migration by the "Iroquois Wall," however, and by the particularly dangerous and bloody conflicts that occurred in New York during the Revolution. Like earlier frontiers in New England, the New York settlement frontier collapsed backward toward older settled areas. But during the 1770s and 1780s New York, in its abbreviated form, was a major military theater for American forces. Thousands of New England soldiers served in the Champlain River valley, the Mohawk-capital district, the Hudson-Catskill area, and the west. Many fought in the Sullivan-Clinton campaign against the Iroquois in 1779. These soldiers were directly exposed to the potentials and opportunities offered by New York lands and resources, and they took their knowledge home. With the end of hostilities, many discharged soldiers came back. This process was facilitated further by the expulsion or out-migration of most Iroquois.

After the region's native inhabitants, along with British military control, were removed, state government and other institutions set about securing the region. A complex array of land grants, speculators, and military tracts emerged. Speculators rapidly began selling lands that the Iroquois had cleared and made productive. New York simply did not have the population during the 1780s and 1790s to settle its upstate regions quickly, and New England's available land was beginning to run out. New Englanders thus simply "went west." And they continued to do so well into the 1830s, transforming the semiwilderness area beyond the Hudson River valley corridor into a prosperous, heavily settled, and culturally complex landscape.

The diffusion of New Englanders into New York was not a single, monolithic, or homogenized phenomenon. Rather, people came from different areas and settled in specific subregions of New York, often separated from one another by long distances and environmental features. Into the military district of the Champlain River valley, eastern Adirondacks, and the northern tier along the Quebec–New York border came large numbers of Vermonters and a scattering of New Hampshire residents. Indeed, so many Vermonters settled this largely empty area that it was often called New Vermont. Maine, with its own uninhabited frontier to fill, was least represented in New York, with New Hampshire doing only slightly better. Those New Hampshire citizens who did make their way into New York were often migrants once removed, having first settled in Vermont before moving on again to New York.

After 1783 migrants from Connecticut and Massachusetts flooded into specific parts of upstate New York. After filling the last empty pockets near the New York–New England borders, these newcomers moved through the valleys of the Catskills, the Susquehanna River, and particularly the Mohawk River toward the newly opened lands of the Chenango Twenty Townships, the Finger Lakes, and the Rochester and Buffalo areas. Subtle differences existed between the two groups, with those from Connecticut tending more often to settle together and their Massachusetts counterparts spreading out in various directions. Rhode Islanders were a minor subset of migrants, generally heading for the same target areas as their neighbors from Massachusetts. Gradually, these New Englanders mingled with people from New Jersey and Pennsylvania in the case of central New York and with Canadians in the case of northern New York, thereby approaching a cultural plurality and complexity usually associated with later eras of settlement and regional development in New York. It is striking to note, however, that for 50 or 60 years after the Revolution, the most important source area for upstate New York settlers was New England. Much of New York north and west of the Hudson had essentially become an extension of New England.

But what cultural baggage did these New Englanders bring with them to New York, and what did they re-create as they settled there? Probably the primary icons of a New England–style cultural landscape were the newcomers' individual farmsteads focusing on crop-oriented agriculture and set among a quickly developing array of hamlets and villages. Spotted with village greens and centrally located Congregationalist, Baptist, or Presbyterian churches, these communities were often planned and built according to familiar patterns and endowed with familiar political and social institutions. What evolved socially, politically, and spatially stood in sharp contrast to what developed in the lands south of Maryland. Commercial ventures soon gained the upper hand, however, transforming what once had been subsistence communities.

Along with settlers, New England social zealotry and fire for religious reform also traveled westward into New York. By the 1780s, as the flow of New Englanders spilled into that state, the Great Revival had already begun in New England. Migrants brought with them to New York their New England conscience, their Calvinism, and their willingness to take part in social movements such as abolitionism, feminism, and the personal perfectionism practiced by members of New York's Oneida Community. The areas of upstate New York that were settled by New Englanders became hotbeds of religious and social movements, generating new faiths such as Mormonism and Millerism.

By the dawn of the 19th century New York north and west of the Hudson River valley was intellectually, culturally, and materially an evolving extension of New England society. That early influence set the stage for many subsequent developments in the region and continues to make itself felt in upstate survey patterns, transportation systems, and land uses. It can also still be seen in the architectural styles of homes, barns, churches, businesses, and public buildings extant from this era, styles often copied today. It is present in speech patterns, social mores, and belief systems. Although often forgotten and mixed with other traditions and changes, New England's cultural influence was firmly in place by 1800 and remains evident even today.

Whitney R. Cross, *The Burned-Over District: The Social and Intellectual History of Enthusiastic Religion in Western New York, 1800–1850* (1950); James W. Darlington, "Peopling the Post-Revolutionary New York Frontier," *New York History* 74 (1993); Donald W. Meinig, "The Colonial Period, 1609–1775," in *Geography of New York State*, ed. John Thompson (1977); Robert D. Mitchell and Paul A. Groves, eds., *North America: The Historical Geography of a Changing Continent* (1987); Richard H. Schein, "Urban Origin and Form in Central New York," *Geographical Review* 81 (1991); Lewis D. Stilwell, *Migration from Vermont* (1948); William Wyckoff, *The Developer's Frontier: The Making of the Western New York Landscape* (1988); Wilbur Zelinsky, *The Cultural Geography of the United States*, rev. ed. (1992).

Thomas A. Rumney

Nor'easters A nor'easter is a type of cyclone—called an *extratropical cyclone*—that has counterclockwise winds that converge on an area of deep low pressure at the surface of the earth. These storms occur primarily between October and April, peaking in February, though they are occasionally observed be-

Route 128, Dedham, Mass., following the blizzard of 1978

tween June and August. The most powerful nor'easters tend to happen near the beginning and end of the season.

This seasonal pattern is associated with the changing positions and shapes of the eastward-flowing polar jet stream. In winter, when the jet stream is in its southernmost location, it meanders more crookedly than in summer to the north and south. Nor'easters are particularly likely to develop when cold polar air moves across the southeastern United States at a time when warm air and warm Gulf Stream water prevail at similar latitudes along the East Coast. When this occurs, the jet stream often flows northeastward along the eastern seaboard. The dynamics of this atmospheric configuration create strong fronts and zones of intense instability in the coastal zone. Nor'easters are known to form in particular off the coast of Hatteras, N.C., but they may also originate in the Gulf of Mexico or off the coast of Florida.

Once formed, nor'easters generally move northeastward from the point of origin. Their name comes, however, from the cold northeasterly wind flow (blowing from northeast to southwest) in the northern and western portions of the storm system, which is frequently located over land. The southern and eastern sectors are typically warm and laden with moisture. The instability generated by these colliding air masses can provide some of New

England's most severe weather conditions, including heavy snowfalls, high winds, and coastal flooding and erosion. Slow-moving or stalled nor'easters tend to inflict the most damage because the atmospheric conditions associated with them remain in a given area for an extended period of time.

Perhaps the longest lingering nor'easter in recent memory occurred February 22–28, 1969, when a storm developed in the Gulf of Mexico, moved northeastward, intensified along the East Coast, and then passed New England very slowly. More than 30 inches of snow fell over extensive portions of eastern Massachusetts, New Hampshire, and Maine. The deepest snowfalls were recorded at Mount Washington (98 inches) and Pinkham Notch, N.H. (77 inches), and Long Falls Dam, Maine (56 inches); even Boston got 26 inches of the white stuff.

Other notorious nor'easters have made their mark in the annals of New England weather. The blizzard of March 11–14, 1888, produced between 40 and 50 inches of snow in some New England locations. The blizzard of 1978 dumped more than 3 feet of snow across Rhode Island, Connecticut, and Massachusetts between February 5 and 7, leaving 99 people dead in its wake. Another major storm hit in March 1993, affecting all of New England as well as points beyond and paralyzing major urban centers.

High winds along the New England coastline, occasionally in excess of hurricane strength (that is, sustained winds above 75 mph), are also commonly associated with nor'easters. In early February 1961, for example, wind gusts of 96 and 83 mph were recorded at Blue Hill Observatory in Milton, Mass., and Block Island, R.I., respectively. In the coastal zone strong winds typically produce 5- to 30-foot waves whose destructive force is often exacerbated by high tides or storm surges induced by the nor'easter. Enhanced wave activity has accounted for extensive beach erosion and flood damage to homes all along the New England coastline and may ultimately lead to the total demise of Nantucket Island sometime during the new millennium.

Judd Caplovich, *The Great Storm of '88*, ed. Wayne W. Westbrook (1987); Robert E. Davis and Robert Dolan, "Nor'easters: These Cyclonic Storms Batter the East Coast from October through April, Yet Their Destructive Potential Remains among the Most Difficult to Predict," *American Scientist* 81 (1993); Paul J. Kocin and Louis W. Uccellini, *Snowstorms along the Northeastern Coast of the United States, 1955 to 1985* (1990); National Oceanic and Atmospheric Administration, *Northeast Blizzard of '78, February 5–7, 1978: A Report to the Administrator* (1978).

Barry D. Keim

Northeast Kingdom, Vermont

Vermont's three northeastern counties (Caledonia, Essex, and Orleans), which surround St. Johnsbury and extend north to the border with Canada and east to the border with New Hampshire, are often referred to as the Northeast Kingdom. This is a densely forested area with many lakes and open valleys. Numerous secondary roads extend across the ridges to connect small villages that service the woods industries and agricultural economy. In the fall, the area attracts visitors who view the brilliant foliage of the diverse species of deciduous trees. The Northeast Kingdom Fall Foliage Festival—an archetypal New England celebration with harvest suppers, flea markets, bazaars, and auctions over the period of a week—is centered in the villages of Barnet, Cabot, Groton, Marshfield, Peacham, Plainfield, Walden, and St. Johnsbury.

Settlements of distinction in the region include Danville, the home of the American Society of Dowsers, and Brownington, with its historic district surrounding Brownington Academy, a private school founded by an African American, Alexander Twilight, in 1836. While some villages are nestled in the valleys, a significant number of settlements are perched on hills where they provide panoramic vistas along valleys and across ridges. Peacham provides an outstanding view of this landscape, but the perspectives from other villages, including Barnet Center and Brownington, are striking as well.

St. Johnsbury is the small city at the center of the Northeast Kingdom. It is the birthplace of the platform scale, which was invented by Thaddeus Fairbanks and distributed worldwide. After the 1830s, the city prospered as the Fairbanks manufacturing company grew and the Fairbanks family became patrons of education and the arts. The Athenaeum still serves as public library and art museum, with an excellent collection of Hudson River School and native Vermont painters. Founded by Franklin Fairbanks in 1889 and opened in 1891, the Fairbanks Museum and Planetarium contains numerous eclectic collections, including 4,500 mounted birds and mammals and an extensive collection of antique dolls. The Douglas B. Kitchel Center for the Study of the Northeast Kingdom is also part of the Fairbanks Museum. The center is housed in an ornate Romanesque Revival building designed by Vermont architect Lambert Packard.

St. Johnsbury retains much of the manufacturing and service functions of the past while adding contemporary businesses that benefit from its location at the junction of the cross-regional Route 2 and Interstate 91. Manufacturing and processing facilities of the maple syrup and sugar industries are located in St. Johnsbury and throughout the area. Maple trees dominate the Northeast Kingdom and symbolize two economies that form a mainstay for the area: the sugaring industry in the spring, and foliage tourism in the fall.

The Northeast Kingdom's remoteness and its residents' fierce individualism and commitment to tradition have made the region symbolic of the entire state, even as it attracts outsiders. Many of the 50,000 people in the area trace their ancestry to earlier generations of Scots and French Canadian immigrants who came to work in the region's forests. Many Kingdom families have hunted for generations at hunting camps on land leased from paper companies that own hundreds of thousands of acres. Several writers have found a home there, including David Mamet and Howard Frank Mosher. Mosher's novel *Where the Rivers Flow North* (1978) was filmed in the area; another of his Kingdom novels, *A Stranger in the Kingdom* (1989), tells the story of a 1940s racial incident. The Northeast Kingdom is also home to the renowned Bread and Puppet Theater, which draws thousands of visitors to an annual festival. In recent years, as forces of change enter the region, the area has seen debates over the consolidation of small schools, economic development, and state intervention at a religious commune.

Richard Brown and Reeve Lindbergh, *The View from the Kingdom: A New England Album* (1987); Virginia Campbell Downs, *Voices from the Kingdom* (1997); Scott E. Hastings, Jr., *The Last Yankees: Folkways in Eastern Vermont and the Border Country* (1990); Peter S. Jennison, *Roadside History of Vermont* (1989).

Victor A. Konrad

Northwestern Connecticut

Northwestern Connecticut is basically wooded and bucolic and includes the 26 towns of Litchfield County, the state's largest county. This area of ebb contrasts with the densely populated mainstream cities along Connecticut's coast and the Connecticut River valley to the east. The Litchfield hills include Connecticut's highest elevations and are more rugged than the state's eastern highlands. Connecticut's coldest temperature, −37 degrees Fahrenheit, was recorded in the county at Norfolk in 1943.

The Housatonic River is the major river in northwestern Connecticut. Its upper-valley towns remain scenic and largely undeveloped. The spectacular autumn colors here draw visitors from parts near and far. The southern tier of the Litchfield Hills include numerous glacial bogs, lakes, streams, and meadows that bring to mind the foothills of the Alps.

Iron plantations were established in the extreme northwestern corner of the county in the 1740s, but by the end of the 19th century, they and other industries in the upper Housatonic—including those producing hats, knives, carriages, and textiles—were declining. Today, empty factories and other industrial detritus are a common part of the middle and lower part of the Housatonic River valley landscape and in the Naugatuck River valley to the east between Waterbury and Naugatuck.

Even while industrial decline was occurring, the area was seen as an island of retreat. The newly rich built cottages and villas modeled after those in Europe. Artists, writers, musicians, and foreign royalty were attracted to the Litchfield Hills, an appeal that continues to this day. The middle rich also came, buying ruined farms and giving them new life.

The town of Litchfield, situated in the center of the region, is often seen by visitors as a surviving example of a late colonial New England town. In fact, its orderly, manicured green and streets, stately museums, and congregational church spire are the products of the romantic era of the late 19th century largely inspired and saved by transplanted summer people. This process was common throughout New England during the Colonial Revival.

Litchfield is rich in history. America's first law school was established there in 1784, and many well-known Americans—including vice presidents, members of Congress, Supreme Court justices, and governors—went through its doors before it closed in 1833. Historic homes abound, such as that in which Harriet

Beecher Stowe was born and one in which Oliver Wolcott, Sr., lived. It is possible to get lost in the 4,000-acre White Memorial Conservation Center in Litchfield, the largest wildlife and nature center in Connecticut.

About 10 miles northwest of Litchfield center is Cornwall, where approximately one-third of the property owners are part-time residents. Cornwall has no single center but is composed of three villages—each with its own post office—and several smaller hamlets with names like Yelping Hill, Cornwall Hollow, and Calhoun Corner. One of the three covered bridges still left in Connecticut is in West Cornwall. Designed by Ithiel Town, it has been in use since 1864. Another in the northwest area, Bulls Bridge, in Kent crosses the Housatonic and serves traffic between Bulls Bridge and the New York state line.

Just outside of Cornwall is the Cathedral Pines Preserve. These old-growth white pine and hemlock trees point 150 feet into the air and remind one of the redwoods of northern California. Unfortunately, the area was devastated by tornadoes in 1989, and some of the damage can still be seen.

The Appalachian Trail enters Connecticut in Salisbury and winds for 56 miles along the Housatonic River to the New York state border at Kent.

The southern towns in Litchfield County are more urban and densely populated than those to the north. All but one of the towns along the county's southern border experienced population gains from 1990 to 2000. On the other hand, six towns in the northern group experienced population declines during the same period. One of these, Norfolk, showed a 19 percent decrease, the largest decline of any of Connecticut's 169 towns. The decline in the northern group was largely due to year-round residents selling to buyers planning to use the property seasonally. The growth in the southern-tier towns is owing to their proximity to Interstate 84, the growth of related technology firms, and the ease of commuting to firms outside the county. All but one of the Connecticut towns without cell phone towers in 2003 were in Litchfield County, a further indication of how the northwest corner contrasts with other parts of the state.

Michael Bell, *The Fare of Connecticut* (1985); Thomas R. Lewis and John Harmon, *Connecticut: A Geography* (1986).

Thomas R. Lewis

Peterson, Roger Tory (1908–96) Artist, writer, and photographer. Beginning with *A Field Guide to the Birds* (1934), Roger Tory Peterson did more to popularize birds and bird watching than any ornithologist past or present. Using a system today known as the Peter-

Roger Tory Peterson revising an illustration of gulls, 1994

son System, this book introduced the use of diagnostic arrows to point out individually unique markings on birds shown in illustrations. Subsequently, this technique has been applied to many groups of organisms, from plants to insects and mammals to fish. Peterson established the Houghton Mifflin Company's Peterson Field Guide Series.

Born to parents of Swedish extraction in Jamestown, N.Y., Peterson demonstrated a passion and talent for drawing birds at an early age. At 17, he took a temporary job painting intricate Chinese designs on lacquered furniture for the Union Furniture Company, but by 1927 he was in New York City attending the Art Students League. He studied there for two years before joining the National Academy of Design from 1929 to 1931.

In New York Peterson made the acquaintance of several individuals who profoundly influenced his burgeoning career as an artist and ornithologist. One of these, the eminent ornithologist Ludlow Griscom, a figure legendary for his ability to identify birds in the field, was especially helpful. Among those to take early notice of the developing young bird painter was Clarence E. Allen, founder of Maine's Camp Chewonki and director of the Rivers School in Brookline, Mass. Allen provided Peterson with crucial education and field experience by making him a nature counselor for five summers at Camp Chewonki. Peterson's enthusiasm was so infectious that in 1931 Allen invited him to teach natural history and painting at the Rivers School. It was during his tenure at the Rivers School that Peterson, with support from Griscom and others,

completed the illustrations and text for his first book.

While teaching in Massachusetts, Peterson met Francis H. Allen, then editor of Houghton Mifflin and the individual who would guide his success as an artist and author. Convincing Houghton Mifflin that his system for identifying birds in the field would work, without first shooting them, launched his career. It is no accident that Peterson's books found a publisher in Boston. New Englanders, who had founded Audubon Societies to protest the killing of birds for feathers to decorate hats, provided a ready audience for Peterson's field guides. In three weeks, the initial print run of 2,000 copies of *A Field Guide to the Birds* was sold out. Today, the guide is in its third edition with more than 4 million copies sold.

In addition to writing six titles in the Peterson Field Guide Series, Peterson wrote or cowrote 10 other books, including *Birds Over America* (1948) and *The Birds* (1963), and served as a contributing author and illustrator to countless others. His work was recognized with numerous awards, including the World Wildlife Fund Gold Medal (1972) and the Medal of Freedom (1980), and the establishment in his honor of the Roger Tory Peterson Institute in Jamestown, N.Y. He died in Old Lyme, Conn.

John C. Devlin and Grace Naismith, *The World of Roger Tory Peterson* (1977).

Wayne R. Petersen

Plants New England's contemporary natural landscape would have comforted early

European settlers with thoughts of home: lawns carpeted with Kentucky bluegrass and dotted with dandelions and roadsides bedecked with ox-eye daisies, Queen Anne's lace, and chicory. But early settlers encountered a landscape that was wild and unfamiliar to them. Over time, many plant species that settlers needed but were not available locally were transplanted from Europe. Consequently, many plants identified with the region today are nonnative, sometimes invasive, and in many cases endanger native species and habitats.

Early settlers looked to New England's native plants for food, flavorings, clothing, dyes, medicines, and beauty aids. Many were familiar; some plant species grew on both sides of the Atlantic and others were represented by a different species in the Americas but the differences were often negligible. Jam, for example, could be made as easily from European red raspberry as from American. Native plants also provided colonists with valuable goods for export. Sassafras root bark was a highly popular cure-all in Europe, and its export was economically significant to the early colonies. At the beginning of the 18th century the colonies began exporting native ginseng species to China. Although this wild ginseng was different from the Chinese species, the Chinese found it acceptable.

Most of the plants grown for hay in New England today, from grasses (including Kentucky bluegrass) to clover, were brought over from Europe. Stowaway seeds that made the trip in hay bales, seed bags, and even ship's ballasts included many of the flowers that now commonly color roadsides and vacant lots: dandelions, buttercups, mullein, daisies, Queen Anne's lace, common Saint-John's-wort, yarrow, and chicory. These plants are relatively harmless, but other plant species from Europe and Asia are destructive to their surroundings. Bittersweet, several species of Asian honeysuckle, and English ivy—all beautiful vines—have spread from gardens and overrun the surrounding countryside. Of the New England states, Connecticut has been particularly hard-hit by invasive vines.

New England's wetlands in particular have been invaded by purple loosestrife, a tall plant topped in summer by a spike of deep purple or magenta flowers, and the common reed, or *Phragmites,* an even taller plant, topped by a large, feathery tassel. Each of these species pushes out the cattails and other native plants that are vital to wetland wildlife. Other invasive plant species that are damaging New England's natural environments include mustard garlic, Eurasian milfoil, leafy spurge, and multiflora rose.

As damaging as these invasive plants are, the region's threatened, rare, and endangered plants are jeopardized more by loss of habitat than by other plant species. For example, among New England's state-listed threatened or endangered plants are the lady's slipper, particularly the ram's-head lady's slipper, the showy lady's slipper, and the moccasin flower or pink lady's slipper. These large and strikingly beautiful pink or pink and white orchids are found in deep, moist woods and were never common. Similarly, at least one species of aster is threatened in each New England state. Many of these asters are at the edge of their range or require a particular habitat that is rare in that state; the species of aster that is threatened in one state is sometimes common elsewhere in New England. And goldenseal, used as an herbal remedy, is receiving state attention in both Vermont and Connecticut. The sandplain gerardia is perhaps New England's most endangered plant and is one of the few plants native to the region that appears on the federal list of endangered plants. Other federally listed endangered or threatened plants in New England include the small whorled pogonia, Jesup's milk-vetch, the northeastern or barbed-bristle bulrush, chaffseed, the Furbish lousewort, and the prairie white-fringed orchid.

Vermont and Maine have selected commercially important plants for their official state trees and flowers, reflecting a modern appreciation for the plant world. Vermont's red clover is important forage for farm animals and its sugar maple makes it the nation's leading producer of maple sugar. Maine's state flower is the white pine cone and tassel, and its state tree is the white pine. The other states' choices emphasize beauty and symbolism. Connecticut's choice of the mountain laurel is particularly apt. Each June the flowers of this small tree turn the woodlands of Connecticut and Massachusetts into a floral wonderland. The Charter Oak, Connecticut's state tree, refers to the ancient white oak tree in which was hidden Charles II's royal charter granting land rights to Connecticut residents.

The New England aster deserves special mention. This hardy plant blooms from late summer until the first snows, brightening the fall landscape with its intense purple blossoms. It tolerates a variety of growing conditions from roadside to forest clearing and is found throughout the region. Most cultivated asters grown in gardens are hybrids derived from the New England aster and the New York aster, also common. Although this tree is often overlooked, it is difficult to imagine the New England countryside in autumn without the deep purple accent of the New England aster.

In spring, New England's woods produce the season's first flowers. The trout lily or adder's tongue with its spotted leaves, the pale yellow clintonia, and the red and painted trilliums, sometimes known in New England as "benjamins," bloom under the early spring sun before the forest leaves shade them. In later spring, wild lupine displays its blue spikes, and the striking yellow mark on the lower lip of the elegant blue flag belies its native, wild origins. Lilacs also abound in New England. Although not a native plant, the lilac is closely associated with the New England farmhouse doorway, and New Hampshire chose the purple lilac as its state flower. Harvard University's Arnold Arboretum hosts an annual lilac festival in May, showcasing more than 200 varieties of the fragrant flower.

Plants such as the beach pea, sea rocket, seaside goldenrod, beach grass, and dusty miller (though a nonnative) provide color and texture at the beach, while sea-lavender washes its color over the nearby sea marshes in late summer. Many rare plants, some native to the northern tundra areas, are found on New England's highest peaks and granite summits, but the tiny white blooms of mountain sandwort are among the most conspicuous and widespread summit flowers. New England's blackberries, or, more specifically, black raspberries, not only provide humans with a natural treat but are an important late summer food for birds preparing for migration and black bears for hibernation. Purple or white asters and goldenrod provide points of color in the green landscape during the late summer. A short growing season means that New England is not as lush as other parts of the world or as rich in plant species; adapted to their environment, however, its native plants have developed ways to survive the harsh winters.

New Englanders may no longer rely on wild, native plants or introduced species for food or medicine, but the region's plants have significant commercial and cultural value, particularly in their effect on the region's foodways, as they did during early settlement. A new age of herbalists and food collectors has taken to the region's woods and fields in search of edible mushrooms such as morels, chanterelles, and chicken-of-the-woods; foods such as leeks and wild ginger; and medicines, especially ginseng and goldenseal. Maine's potatoes and wild blueberries, northern New England's apples, Vermont's maple syrup, Massachusetts's cranberries, and pears and tobacco leaf, to name but a few, play an important role in the economic market. Boston baked beans, traditional squash and pumpkin dishes, the New England boiled dinner with a slew of homegrown vegetables, and many fruit and berry pies—strawberry rhubarb, mince, apple—are some of the plant-based foods commonly identified with the region. And for their aesthetic value alone—the pale clintonias and bold red trilliums of spring and the vibrant colors of the maple leaves in autumn—New England's plants continue to be culturally significant.

Timothy Coffey, *The History and Folklore of North American Wildflowers* (1993); New England Wildflower Society, *Flora Conservanda: New England* (1997); Nancy G. Slack and Allison W. Bell, *Appalachian Mountain Club Field Guide to the New England Alpine Summits* (1995); Donald W. and Lillian Q. Stokes, *A Guide to Enjoying Wildflowers* (1985); Alice F. Tryon and Robbin C. Moran, *The Ferns and Allied Plants of New England* (1997); Jeff Wallner and Mario J. DiGregorio, *New England's Mountain Flowers: A High Country Heritage* (1997).

Madeline Bodin

Population New England has progressed through most of the stages of demographic transition and can be characterized as a mature and stable region with low fertility, relatively long life expectancy for most of its residents, and only minor fluctuations in the rate of population growth. It is a bimodal region in demographic terms: the three southern states, Massachusetts, Connecticut, and Rhode Island, are more densely populated and more urban and suburban in nature, whereas the three northern states, Maine, New Hampshire, and Vermont, are more rural, distinguished by small towns and villages, and much less densely populated than the southern tier. This duality is frequently and clearly reflected in New England's demographic patterns.

The six-state region contained in 2000 a total population of 13.9 million people and is the smallest of nine U.S. census divisions. From 1990 to 1995, New England's population growth rate of 0.5 percent was the slowest of any census area; the growth rate for the decade 1990 to 2000 was 5.6 percent, still the lowest of the divisions.

The history of demographic change in New England has been mixed. The total population of the region increased from about 1 million in 1790 to nearly 14 million by 2000. The most rapid rate of growth occurred during the two decades beginning in 1790 and 1840, although in absolute numbers the greatest increase (1.3 million) was recorded between 1960 and 1970. Massachusetts and Connecticut have historically had the majority of New England's population, and their share of the total has increased significantly during the 20th century. In 2000 these two states were home to 70 percent of New England's residents.

New England had the highest urban population in that census division until 1910 but came in fifth on that measure in 1990. The urban population increased from 66 percent of the total to 74 percent, which represents only a slight increase relative to that of other divisions during the same period. Urban population in the West South Central division, for example, increased from 22 to 75 percent of the total; in the Mountain division it went from 36 to 80 percent. However, by 2000, urban population had increased to 81 percent.

The rural population of New England changed very little during the 20th century, having decreased only 6 percent since 1900. Today New England's three northern states are primarily rural; according to the 2000 census, rural dwellers made up 62 percent of the population in Vermont, 60 percent in Maine, and 41 percent in New Hampshire, compared with 12 percent in Connecticut, 19 percent in Massachusetts, and 10 percent in Rhode Island.

Contemporary demographic trends are affected by prevailing rates of fertility and mortality as well as by population growth and mobility. In 1990 fertility in New England was the lowest in the United States, with 14.3 births per 1,000 persons; the national average is 15.9 per 1,000 persons. The total fertility rate (TFR), the average number of children a woman will bear in her lifetime at prevailing rates, for New England is the lowest in the United States at 1.8, while the U.S. average is 2.08. The highest TFR in New England is found in Connecticut, at 1.85, and the lowest in Massachusetts, at 1.77. Fertility both in New England and in the United States as a whole increased by approximately 0.3 between 1980 and 1990. This picture has changed little according to the 2000 census. The U.S. average has increased to 2.13, but the New England average remains 1.8.

As expected in a mature demographic context, the overall death rate in New England in 2000 was 9.1 per 1,000 persons, a figure that is higher than the national average of 8.7 per thousand. The region's infant-mortality rate, a measure of the number of children who die before their first birthday, is the lowest in the country. The infant-mortality rate in 2001 was 5.5 per thousand live births for the region, compared with a U.S. average of 6.8. Among the New England states, the lowest infant-mortality rate is that of New Hampshire at 3.8, while Rhode Island has the highest rate, at 6.8. These rates are a marked improvement over 1991, when data showed pockets of inordinately high infant mortality in cities in Rhode Island and Connecticut. The infant-mortality rate for the black metropolitan population of Rhode Island in 1991 was 19.8, and in Connecticut it was 14.8. Another measure of mortality is life expectancy at birth, which averaged 76.9 years for the region in 2000, compared with a national life expectancy of 77 years.

New England's population growth rate from 1980 to 1990 was 7 percent, which made the region fifth among the 9 census divisions. Between 1990 and 1995, however, New England had only a 0.8 percent growth, the lowest divisional growth rate in the country and one that was considerably lower than the national average of 5.6 percent. Within the region, the north-south divide is reflected in the positive rates of growth for Vermont (3.9 percent) and New Hampshire (3.5 percent), which contrast with negative growth rates in Rhode Island (−1.4 percent) and Connecticut (−0.4 percent). Intermediate rates are found in Massachusetts (0.9 percent) and Maine (1.1 percent).

It is important to note that during the early 1990s, for the first time in the history of New England, the three states of the southern tier experienced an absolute decline in population. Between 1990 and 1992 the population of Massachusetts went from slightly more than 6 million to slightly less than that number. That of Connecticut declined by 0.4 percent between 1990 and 1995, and that of Rhode Island went down by 1.4 percent. This trend was reversed in the late 1990s, and population for the region increased by 5.6 percent from 1990 to 2000. Between 2000 and 2003, the population of Connecticut increased 2.3 percent; that of Massachusetts, 1.3 percent; and that of Rhode Island, 2.7 percent. These states still lag the regional and national average.

The region's projected rate of growth from 1990 to 2010, at 4.1 percent, is the lowest in the United States. The growth projection for the entire country, by contrast, is 20.8 percent, with the largest increase, 40 percent, expected to occur in the Mountain division. Within New England, the highest growth rates are projected for the northern tier (New Hampshire, 15.4 percent; Vermont, 10.7 percent; and Maine 6.6 percent, compared with a 2.7 percent average in the three southern states).

Between 1990 and 1994, New England experienced a net loss of 365,000 people as a result of internal migration; more people have left the region than have moved into it from other areas. The large majority of these departures were from Massachusetts, which experienced a net loss of 184,000, and Connecticut, with a net loss of 126,000. The majority of out-migrants from New England between 1985 and 1990 moved to the South Atlantic region (41 percent), most of whom (23 percent) went to Florida. The second and third major recipient areas were the abutting Middle Atlantic region (23 percent) and the Pacific region (14 percent). Approximately 410,000 residents moved within the six-state region. The most popular intraregional destinations were New Hampshire (115,000) and Massachusetts

(109,000). This trend continued at a slower rate from 1995 to 2000, as economic conditions improved. The net out-migration rate for these years was 6.4 per 1,000 residents, accounting for 82,285 people. The concentration was largest in Connecticut, with a −20.5 rate, and Massachusetts, with a −9.4 rate.

Another perspective on population movement can be seen in the proportion of each state's residents born in the state. The average for the United States in 2000 was 61.8 percent. Two New England states have rates that are higher than the national average (Massachusetts at 66 percent and Maine at 67 percent). Rhode Island is at 61 percent. But the rates for Vermont (54 percent), Connecticut (57 percent), and New Hampshire (43 percent) are lower than the national average. The New Hampshire figure reflects the large number of in-migrants that came to that state during the 1980s and 1990s. From 1990 to 2000, 536,828 legal international migrants entered the region, two-thirds of whom went to Massachusetts, with somewhat less than one-third settling in Connecticut. Few international migrants move to the northern tier.

Population density in 2000 in New England again reflects the region's dual nature. Overall, there are 228 people per square mile, but the figures for the southern-tier states are many times higher than those for the North. In fact, with the exception of New Jersey, the states of Rhode Island, Massachusetts, and Connecticut have the highest population densities in the United States (with 1,003, 810, and 702 people per square mile, respectively). New England's metropolitan areas, those with more than 50,000 people, lie primarily in the southern three states.

Minority populations in 2000 in New England remain small compared with those of other regions. All minorities taken together make up only 13.4 percent of the region's population, with the largest proportions being found in Connecticut (18.4 percent), Massachusetts (15.5 percent), and Rhode Island (15 percent). The minority population in all three northern-tier states amounts to less than 4 percent.

New England's population is relatively old; the median age of 37.1 years is the second highest of all the census regions; the U.S. median age is 35.3. Whereas the portion of the U.S. population older than 65 is 12.4 percent, the corresponding figure in New England is 13.6 percent. New Hampshire, where only 12.0 percent of residents are older than 65, has the region's smallest elderly population, and Rhode Island has the largest (14.5 percent).

The 2001 marriage rate in New England is low at 8.4 per 1,000 people. The divorce rate is also the lowest in the country, at 3.8 per thousand. The Commonwealth of Massachusetts has the lowest divorce rate of any state in the union, at 2.4 per thousand. According to 1996 data, New England's abortion rate is near the national average at 22.9 for every 1,000 women aged 15 to 44. The three southern, more urban states have significantly higher abortion rates than the northern tier (in Maine, for example, the rate is 9.7 per thousand, compared with 29.3 in Massachusetts). Teenage motherhood in 2000 in New England, at 8.1 percent of all births, is low compared to the national average of 11.8 percent. The percentage of children born to unwed mothers is also relatively low in New England, at 28.1 percent of the total births, compared with a national average of 33.2 percent.

New England's population in 2001 is the most highly educated in the country, with 28.2 percent holding a bachelor's or more advanced degree. The U.S. average is 22.6 percent. New England also has significantly fewer people living in poverty than does the United States as a whole. In 2003, 12.5 percent of the nation's population lived below the poverty line, compared with a New England regional average of 8.3 percent. The figures for New Hampshire and Connecticut were particularly low, at 5.1 and 8.1 percent, respectively. In terms of 2003 median income per household, New England ranks first among the 9 census divisions. Among the 50 states, Connecticut, Massachusetts, and New Hampshire rank in the top five, all at just over $55,000. Maine, by contrast, ranks 41st, at $37,619. The national average is $43,527.

The total active labor force in New England in 2000 numbered just over 6.9 million persons, 868,000 in manufacturing and 5.1 million in nonmanufacturing industries (service, trade, and so on). The remainder fell into other categories. Seventy percent of New England's total manufacturing employment was in Massachusetts and Connecticut. Of those outside the manufacturing sector, 39 percent worked in management, professional, and related jobs, 26 percent worked in sales and office, and 14 percent worked in service jobs. Despite the rural nature of the population, the proportion of New England's labor force employed in agriculture, forestry, and fishing was 0.4 percent in 2000. In Maine these laborers made up 1.2 percent of the total workforce, with Vermont not far behind, at 1 percent. Massachusetts and Connecticut (0.2 percent), New Hampshire (0.4 percent), and Rhode Island (0.3 percent) employed substantially fewer in these areas. The regional decline from 0.9 percent in 1990 is due in part to substantial decreases in the fisheries. The unemployment rate for the region in 2002 hovered at about 4.6 percent (the U.S. average in 2002 was 5.8 per-

cent). Rates were lowest in Vermont and Connecticut (4.3 percent) and highest in Rhode Island (5.1 percent).

While most similar to the mid-Atlantic region, and perhaps most different from the rapidly changing Mountain region, New England is unique on a variety of demographic measures. It is important to note, however, that its demographic characteristics and processes vary widely from one part of the region to another. New England can clearly be divided into two distinct subregions: a very urban, densely populated South and a rural yet nonagricultural North characterized by a plethora of small cities and villages. By narrowing the focus even further, one finds unique pockets or areas that vary significantly from regional and state patterns. The southern rim of New Hampshire, for example, is much more urban than the rest of the state and is intrinsically tied to the Boston metropolitan area in terms of economic and demographic processes. Western Massachusetts is decidedly more rural than the rest of that state and has more in common with New England's northern tier. Finally, there exist urban distressed areas where large minority populations show significant levels of poverty and associated demographic characteristics such as high infant mortality and high fertility. Only by considering the region's wide variety of population characteristics can we arrive at an accurate demographic picture of New England.

Kimberly Crews and Kelvin Pollard, *The United States Population Data Sheet of the Population Reference Bureau* (1998); Carol J. De Vita, *The United States at Mid-Decade, Population Bulletin 50, no. 4* (1996); U.S. Bureau of the Census, *County and City Data Book, 1994* [CD-ROM] (1995); Census Bureau, *Historical Statistics of the United States: Colonial Times to 1970* (1975); Census Bureau, *Statistical Abstract of the United States* (1995, 2000); U.S. Census (2000).

George J. Demko and Priscilla S. Dana

Quabbin Reservoir Quabbin Reservoir, located in central Massachusetts, is the largest reservoir in the Greater Boston metropolitan area water system, with a maximum capacity of 412 billion gallons. Drawing on 186 square miles of watershed, the Quabbin covers 25,000 acres, is 18 miles long, and has 118 miles of shoreline and 60 islands. Between 1919 and 1939, taxpayers spent $50.3 million to build Winsor Dam on the Swift River and create the Quabbin system. Land acquisition alone took 10 years—from 1926 to 1936—and accounted for nearly a quarter of the initial cost. Construction displaced 2,500 people from 650 homes, required relocating 7,613 bodies from 34 cemeteries, and completely flooded the towns of Enfield, Dana, Greenwich, and Prescott. The Massachusetts legislature officially dissolved these four towns on April 27, 1938.

Currently managed by the Massachusetts Water Resources Authority and the Metropolitan District Commission, the Quabbin network delivers water to 46 communities and nearly half of the population of Massachusetts. Demands for Quabbin water are expected to continue to increase as contamination has forced more and more towns to abandon their wells and reservoirs. Current management policies emphasize the preservation of water quality and wildlife habitat, as the area surrounding the reservoir provides vital habitat to species ranging from bald eagles and wild turkeys to bear, fox, and an occasional cougar. Visitors enjoy hiking, birding, and fishing in limited areas of the Quabbin watershed.

The history of the Quabbin begins with Boston's earliest efforts to improve water supplies for the city. In 1848, Boston completed the Cochituate Reservoir and built an 11-mile aqueduct connecting the reservoir to the city; running water promised to attract new businesses to Boston and control epidemic disease. Within a few years, however, the city's water use ballooned beyond all projections. In 1872, the city annexed Charlestown's Mystic River network and tapped the nearby Sudbury River. But soon, however, industrial and domestic pollution of these rivers sent Boston leaders looking for other sources of water. In the 1880s, after Boston lost a heated battle for rights to the Shawsheen River, public health leaders, engineers, and political reformers advocated the construction of a regional waterworks. In 1895, voters in 13 cities and towns approved the creation of the Metropolitan Water District. With the construction of the Wachusett Reservoir in 1906, the district began implementing its plan to supply clean water to Boston from outlying areas. The Wachusett site, located on the Nashua River near the towns of Boylston, Clinton, and West Boylston, was well suited to projected reservoir development farther west, and Wachusett engineer Frederic P. Stearns actually anticipated and planned the Quabbin Reservoir system. The Wachusett and Quabbin Reservoirs are connected to one another via the Quabbin Aqueduct.

The Quabbin, like its antecedents, was designed to redistribute the state's water resources from west to east. When community residents learned that the state planned to take their land and move their cemeteries, they became outraged at what they saw as an objectionable extension of Boston's political and material power far beyond its municipal boundaries. Resentment grew as these towns tried to absorb thousands of workers brought into the area to build the waterworks. The political implications of the Quabbin and Wachusett projects were much like those created by similar water-rights controversies in other parts of the United States. Water disputes usually have been settled in favor of urban and industrial areas, resolutions reflecting the close association between political and economic power in the struggle for control of natural resources.

Thomas Conuel, *Quabbin: The Accidental Wilderness* (1981); John R. Greene, *The Creation of Quabbin Reservoir: The Death of the Swift River Valley* (1981); Donald W. Howe, *Quabbin: The Lost Valley* (1951); Fern Nesson, *Great Waters: A History of Boston's Water Supply* (1983).

Sarah S. Elkind

Regional Planning The popular image of New England is that of an eclectic but essentially coherent part of the American landscape. Maine's rocky coast, Vermont's village greens, gritty mill towns, Beacon Hill, and all the rest merge into a unified whole when the idea of New England enters the imagination. Each piece of the regional mosaic is, of course, a distinct entity reflecting its own cultural, economic, and geographic forces. From a planning standpoint few regions in America harbor such diverse and contrasting circumstances. Three of the country's four most densely populated states occupy the southern quarter of New England, while the region's northern tier contains 25,000 square miles of upland terrain whose population density is less than that of Utah. Overlaid on the mosaic are the transcendent realms—the coast, the forests, the river basins, the metropolitan corridors.

Planning in New England has traditionally mirrored the diversity of the place, spawning a myriad of seminal concepts that have produced a remarkable legacy. Lowell, Mass., was America's first planned industrial city, built in 1822 as a private investment opportunity that organized living and working functions around the harnessing of waterfalls. After Lowell the face of New England became that of industrial urbanization, as integrated mill complexes sprang up in every location where water could be captured to work looms and spindles. Boston's Back Bay, arguably one of America's masterpieces of urban design, is the consequence of a planned campaign to fill a fetid tidal backwater and create needed real estate for the expanding 19th-century city. Frederick Law Olmsted, hired by the country's first city park commission in Boston, turned an assignment to remedy a festering drainage problem into the "Emerald Necklace," the continuous system of parks and open spaces stretching from Boston Common to Franklin Park. Progressive planning in 19th-century Boston went on to create the country's first railway, first subway, and first metropolitan water and sewer systems.

During the early 20th century an unlikely alliance of conservationists and Merrimack River valley mill owners led a quest to end the rapacious timbering, chronic fires, and erosion in the White Mountain headwaters of the Merrimack that jammed the millraces with silt and debris, threatening the viability of New England's industrial heartland. The resulting Weeks Act of 1911 called for the federal government to protect the waterways by acquiring the headwater backcountry, a step that culminated in the creation of the White Mountain and Green Mountain National Forests. During the 1920s and 1930s Percival Baxter single-handedly acquired and deeded 200,000 acres of forest to the people of Maine, protecting what is now Baxter State Park from the predations of overlogging.

Regional planning in New England during the closing decades of the 20th century was grounded primarily in the environmental and social activism for which the region has long been noted. Planning continues to reflect the complex layering of many provinces—political, economic, social, and geographic—of which New England consists. At the base are the six sovereign states with their widely diverging political philosophies, coupled with the fiercely coveted local home-rule prerogatives of their 1,600 constituent communities. Only the states can enact laws enabling land to be zoned, regulated, and preserved; promulgate tax laws; or produce much of the infrastructure that directs development. The localities are left to implement zoning, a situation that too often results in urban sprawl and exclusionary land-use patterns.

The New England states have been bellwethers in establishing regional planning districts and statewide and environmental planning policies. Vermont and Maine pioneered rigorous statewide land-development regulation. Vermont became a national trailblazer in 1970 with the passage of Act 250, which mandated the formulation of state land-capability, development, and land-use plans, together with stringent permitting procedures for large-scale developments anywhere in the state. The law grew out of citizen concerns over rampant development that took place in the state's southern ski country during the 1960s. Maine's watershed year for state land-use planning and regulation was 1971, when two pieces of legislation were enacted: one requiring localities to adopt subdivisions and zoning controls for all lands adjacent to coastal and navigable inland waterways and one applying environmental and development regulations to the largest contiguous geographic area in New England, the 11-million-acre unorganized North Woods.

Among planning initiatives that traverse state boundaries, two federally sponsored agencies were mandated during the 1960s to engage in regional and resource planning for New England. The New England Regional Commission (NERCOM) was established in 1967 as one of eight regional bodies nationwide to address issues of social and economic distress. Administered jointly by the six governors and a federal cochair, NERCOM had a spotty history. Cited in an investigative report in the *Boston Globe* in 1972 as a heavily politicized pork-barrel operation, the agency underwent modest reforms leading to more substantive research and technical assistance. Its 1981 document *The New England Regional Plan: An Economic Development Strategy* was the most comprehensive and up-to-date analysis of the region's needs and prospects to be produced in a number of years. Within months of the report's publication, NERCOM's federal funding was terminated.

The New England River Basins Commission (NERBC) was also formed in 1967, under provisions of federal legislation calling for regional river basin planning. Reputed nationally to be an effective natural resource–planning entity, NERBC developed an exceptionally lucid picture of the relationship of land use, transportation, energy, and environment to water use, quality, and supply. Its studies attended to those matters, of tremendous importance in a water-dominated setting like New England, at a scope previously unmatched. Alas, NERBC was eliminated as well in 1981.

The New England Governors' Conference absorbed the functions of NERCOM and NERBC in somewhat abbreviated forms after federal funding for both agencies was eliminated. That conference, founded in 1937 as a forum for cooperation among New England's state governments, focuses on issues of prevailing interest among the six states. In recent years these issues have included acid rain, fisheries and coastal development, energy, transportation, forestry, and environmental matters. The Governors' Conference is the only regional entity whose research and policy agendas are tied to the interests of duly elected state administrations and can be translated into state policies. It remains, however, an issues forum, subject to the disparate interests of ever-changing state administrations.

The New England Council is the business community's regional umbrella, founded in 1925 to address economic problems stemming from the exodus of the New England textile industry. Today, the council's concerns revolve around regional competitiveness and the effect of public policy on regional economic development, tracking legislation in Washington, and lobbying the region's business viewpoint. With its emphasis on economic growth, it is occasionally at odds with New England's environmental interests.

The New England Board of Higher Education (NEBHE) exists under an interstate compact chartered by Congress, with the mission to promote the welfare and development of higher education in the region. In addition to supporting interstate enrollments and developing research data, NEBHE is a tireless exponent of higher education as an instrument of regional economic development. The board's agenda has enormous currency, given the role that higher education and knowledge-intensive business play in the economy and the quality of life in New England.

With the new millennium, regional planning in New England continues to rest on a three-legged stool. One leg includes the individual states and their respective powers to legislate statewide and subregional planning (notable examples being Vermont's Act 250 and the Cape Cod Commission, created in 1990 to formulate a land-use policy for that unique Massachusetts region). The second consists of the formal organizations constituted to think about particular sectors of regional interest (the New England Governors' Conference, NEBHE, and so on). The third leg is made up of the collaborative efforts that led to the historic formation of the White Mountain National Forest and the Cape Cod National Seashore. Citizen coalitions reacting to threats to the essential character of their regions demonstrate a quintessentially New England approach to regional planning—diverse and often parochial cultures rallying to a common sense of place. Grassroots initiatives can be as formal as the Northern Forests Land Study, a comprehensive assessment of the northern woodland areas of Maine, New Hampshire, Vermont, and New York carried out by the U.S. Forest Service between 1988 and 1990, or as informal as the 1,000 Friends of Massachusetts, a planning-advocacy group. One environmental advocacy organization, the Conservation Law Foundation, leverages federal and state laws to forge sweeping legal agreements that protect the region's fisheries, coastlines, wilderness areas, and urban air quality. Ad hoc alliances of disparate interests have been effective in warding off an onslaught of proposals for ports and refineries that would industrialize Maine's pristine eastern coast and, through litigation, in reclaiming Boston Harbor from its status as one of America's most polluted harbors.

The impact of government, environmental, and citizen planning interests can be seen in changes affecting three parts of New England's transportation infrastructure: inter-state highways, mass transit, and high-speed rail. Major interstate highway projects have been redirected in response to objections raised by environmental and community-advocacy groups. Their diligence during the early 1970s persuaded the governor of Massachusetts to abandon well-advanced plans for an inner-belt freeway around downtown Boston and Cambridge fed by three radial interstates that would have obliterated thousands of homes and businesses. That action set the stage for the first significant transfer of federal interstate highway funds to urban mass transit construction. It resulted in four major rail extensions of the metropolitan Boston transit system and the revitalization of several urban districts flanking station stops.

As a result of deft maneuvering by most of the New England congressional delegation, downtown Boston at the end of the 20th century and the beginning of the 21st was the site of America's largest public works project, the replacement of the 50-year-old elevated central artery that would have been the linchpin of the ill-fated inner-belt project. The aptly nicknamed "Big Dig" installed a new, underground artery and a tunnel under Boston Harbor connecting Interstate 90 to Logan International Airport. The project was intended both to reclaim the downtown fabric of Boston and to upgrade two critical New England highway links. Despite numerous setbacks, it is scheduled for completion in 2005.

The quest for high-speed rail service between Boston and New York has been pursued by planners and advocacy groups since the early 1960s. The Regional Plan Association (RPA), a citizen-based organization chartered to promote interstate planning for the New York metropolitan region, has consistently promoted high-speed rail service to relieve highway and airport congestion in the northeast urban corridor. Numerous plans and studies by the RPA during the 1960s were instrumental in drawing the federal government into the discussion. The New England Regional Commission began high-speed-rail studies for the region's governors in 1969, advocating the development of a new 90-mile link between Providence, R.I., and New Haven, Conn., that would bypass the circuitous rail route along the Connecticut shore. That ambitious plan fell victim to economics and political resistance, but the concept of high-speed-rail travel endured. During the early 1990s Congress authorized a $2.4 billion upgrading of Amtrak rail passenger service in the northeast corridor between Boston and Washington, reducing travel time between Boston and New York by 90 minutes with electrification, advanced trains, and roadbed improvements.

Entering the new millennium, New England does not lack formal bodies at state and regional levels that perform useful planning, research, and monitoring functions; nor is the region short of grassroots constituencies poised to debate, litigate, and forge consensus around a given planning issue. The collective instincts to conserve and preserve will continue to sustain the area reasonably well. The challenge is to evolve new institutions and civic forums that can frame overarching visions of what the region must be in the 21st century. New England is uniquely positioned to demonstrate to all regions how an array of distinct but fragile resources—old urban places, countrysides, coasts, upland wilds, and a knowledge-based economy—can be brought together in their diversity as a unified, livable, vital environment.

Charles H. W. Foster, *The Cape Cod National Seashore: A Landmark Alliance* (1985); Rudolph W. Hardy, "The Ideal Form of Regional Cooperation," in *Prospects for New England: Highlights of Proceedings and Supplementary Papers from a Conference at the Woodrow Wilson International Center for Scholars, October 7, 1974,* ed. Neal R. Peirce and Jeffrey I. Mayer (1975); Lloyd C. Irland, *Wildlands and Woodlots: The Story of New England's Forests* (1982); Lawrence W. Kennedy, *Planning the City upon a Hill* (1992); Ian Menzies, "Regionalism: The Next Step," *New England Journal of Public Policy* 2, no. 1 (1986); Neal R. Peirce, *The New England States* (1976).

Perry Chapman

Religious Regions

Say "New England" and "religion" in the same sentence, and most Americans will conjure black-clad Puritans or simple white spires of the Congregational variety. While such pictures merely oversimplify the colonial religious landscape, they utterly distort religion in contemporary New England. If we must add to our image of colonial religion a few hanging Quakers and many adult baptisms, we must also replace today's picture-book Congregational houses of worship with the stained glass and crucifixes of the Catholic Church.

During the colonial era, Massachusetts and Connecticut were the bastions of Congregationalism. Even these two colonies, however, were challenged early on by other flavors of Protestantism. The first Anglican church in New England, for example, was established in Boston in 1689 under the unpopular leadership of Governor Edmund Andros. If Anglicanism did not flourish in Massachusetts, it carved out a spot in Connecticut's religious landscape, with 1724 heralding the establishment of an Anglican church in Stratford, Conn., to be followed by another the next year and a third in 1732; by 1736, 700 Anglican families lived in Connecticut. Meanwhile, Rhode Island, adopted home of Puritan dissenters

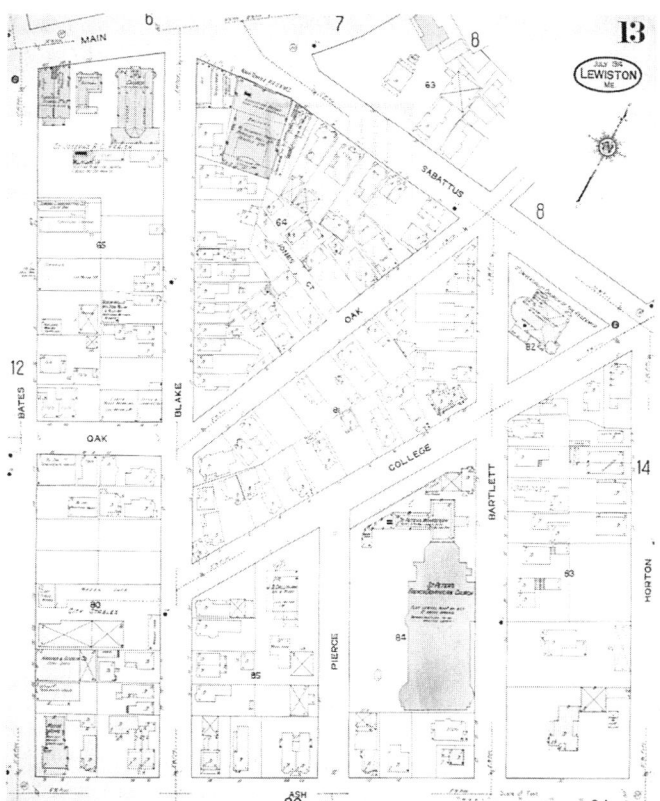

13

Town plan showing church denominations, Lewiston, Maine, 1914

Roger Williams, Samuel Gorton, and Anne Hutchinson, was busy earning a reputation as a miasma of sectarianism. In 1702 Cotton Mather described Rhode Island as a hotbed of "*Antinomians, Familists, Anabaptists, Antisabbatarians, Arminians, Socinians, Quakers, Ranters,* everything in the world but *Roman Catholics,* and *Real Christians.*"

Although Rhode Island earned a singular reputation as a center of religious dissent, Massachusetts Bay authorities sent Christians who did not toe the orthodox Puritan line to other far-flung destinations. Devotees of Anne Hutchinson landed in New Hampshire as well as Rhode Island, and Presbyterians were sent to Essex County. But Puritans shaped the religious landscape—and future—of New England not simply by expelling outsiders but by dispersing missionaries to bring "everything in the world but . . . *Real Christians*" to orthodoxy. Dispatched by leaders of the Massachusetts Bay Colony, missionaries traveled to the coast of Maine to combat French Catholic settlements there.

The 18th-century Great Awakening contributed more than any other single factor to the religious diversity of New England. What historian Steven Marini has termed "radical evangelicals" became prominent in southeastern New England and the Connecticut River valley. The New Lights congregated in the Connecticut River valley and central New En-

gland. Between 1745 and 1770 almost 100 congregations (roughly a quarter of all New England's parishes) separated from the established church. These new congregations were particularly prominent in eastern Connecticut and southeastern Massachusetts, which were developing agrarian areas, and the townships in central Massachusetts and New Hampshire. Rhode Island continued to be a haven for dissenters: Jews were a significant if small presence in colonial Rhode Island, with Sephardic Jews establishing Touro Synagogue, America's first Jewish house of worship, in 1763. Baptists, naturally, were more visible in Rhode Island than anywhere else in New England; in 1767 the Warren, R.I., Baptists Association was formed, providing a stable institutional structure for the faith.

Baptists would grow only stronger over time: in 1850 Maine, New Hampshire, and Rhode Island would boast more Baptist congregations than churches of any other denomination. Rhode Island alone had 106 Baptist congregations; the Baptists' nearest denominational competitor was the Congregationalists, with a mere 21 churches. A century earlier, neither Maine nor New Hampshire claimed a single Baptist church. Vermont, Massachusetts, and Connecticut, however, remained strongholds of Congregationalism, the latter two states weighing in with more than twice as many Congregational as Baptist churches.

The most striking change since the colonial era, however, was the presence of Methodists; by 1850 no state in New England would be home to fewer than 100 Methodist churches. Other newly prominent religious bodies included the Unitarians: by 1850 eastern Massachusetts boasted more than 10 Unitarian churches in almost every county. (This is no surprise: the Unitarian church was born of a schism in the Congregational churches. In 1810 there were 361 Congregational churches in Massachusetts, and in the next few years 96 of these became Unitarian.)

Into the 20th century, Massachusetts would remain a center for innovative religious experimentation. The Christian Scientists, for example, were established in Boston in 1879, and their headquarters remain there today. Jews of Ashkenazic extraction constituted another new group in the pastiche of New England religion, making up 10 percent of Boston's population by 1920. Arabic-speaking Christians who fled from the Turks in Syria and Lebanon made their way in the early years of the 20th century to Rhode Island. The Lutherans, who had no churches in New England in 1850, had established at least one congregation in most of the counties of New Hampshire, Massachusetts, Rhode Island, and Connecticut by 1950.

Without question, however, the most important change in New England's religious landscape has been the influx of Catholics, which began in the 19th century with large Irish and French Canadian populations immigrating to New England. Today, there are more than 1,900 Catholic churches in New England; 43 percent of New England's total population is affiliated with the Roman Catholic Church, and 72 percent of all people who are affiliated with some church or synagogue in New England identify as Catholics. Pockets of Catholicism dot New England, and especially urban New England, where ethnic neighborhoods, be they the Irish Catholic sections of Boston or Italian Catholic enclaves in Connecticut, have an influence that goes beyond the narrowly religious. If other religious groups are represented in New England's landscape primarily through houses of worship, no less important for Catholics are the parochial schools (and, especially in Massachusetts, institutions of higher education) that have long been American Catholicism's strongest defense against assimilation.

No religious group in the region rivals Catholic hegemony; Jews come in a distant second, claiming 3.3 percent of the total population (434,721 people). The United Church of Christ (UCC)—Congregationalists—is third, with 2.8 percent of the total population, and Episcopalians come in fourth, with 2.1 percent of the population.

These figures are approximated throughout the region. In Connecticut 41.8 percent of the total population is Catholic, 49.2 percent in Massachusetts, 63.1 percent in Rhode Island, 25.6 percent in Vermont, 26.8 percent in New Hampshire, and 21.5 percent in Maine. In Connecticut the UCC claims the second largest following (4.1 percent of the total population). In Maine United Methodists are Catholicism's closest contenders, with 2.9 percent of the total population. In Massachusetts Jews make up 4.7 percent of the total population; UCC is the largest Protestant group, with 437 churches and 2.3 percent of the total population. In New Hampshire UCC claims 3.3 percent of the entire population, whereas in Vermont the United Methodists claim just 0.1 percent more New Englanders than the Congregationalists, with 4.4 percent of the total population identifying as Methodist and 4.3 percent as Congregationalist. In Rhode Island Episcopalians run a distant second to Catholics, garnering 3.2 percent of the total population, with 2.2 percent of Rhode Islanders remaining loyal to the American Baptists.

Other denominations are not without a presence in New England: The Church of Jesus Christ of Latter-day Saints (Mormons) is strongest in Maine and Vermont, where it claims 0.5 percent of the total population of each state. The largest New England following of the Evangelical Lutheran Church in America is found in Connecticut, with 1.1 percent of the total population. Other denominations, such as the Presbyterians and the Quakers, have even smaller memberships in New England. Of course, variations abound on the local level: The African Methodist Episcopal (AME) Zion church has a relatively strong following in New Haven County, Conn., where 1 percent of the total population claims that affiliation, and in New London County, Conn., where 1.2 percent of the population worships at AME Zion. The Southern Baptists Convention claims 0.7 percent of the population of Windham County, Conn. In Franklin County, Maine, 0.9 percent of the total population identifies with the Church of the Nazarene, as do 1.9 percent of the residents of Sagadahoc County and 2.1 percent of Somerset County in the same state.

To put New England Protestantism in perspective, it is worth remembering that the UCC's position as the largest Protestant group in New England means little: in recent years rumors have been flying that owing to low membership and empty coffers, UCC seeks to merge with its liturgical cousin, the Episcopal Church. It would be a great historical irony if the spiritual heir of the Puritans were forced to embrace the descendant of the Church of England as its only means of survival in the very region the Puritans settled almost four centuries ago.

The New Englander W. E. B. Du Bois wrote that religious denominations are the great differentiating factor for black Americans. The same can be said for New England and New Englanders. Although generally imagined to be a monolith, New England is in fact a patchwork of many regions, and religion has arguably been the largest force in shaping what distinguishes them. Cities, for example, continue to be home to a disproportionate number of Catholics and Jews (including some homegrown groups such as the Bostoner Hasidim), with suburbs comprising a mix of Catholics and Protestants. Rural areas, by contrast, are primarily Protestant, with the exception of places historically settled by Catholics. Maine, for instance, has claimed a sizable French Catholic population, although the rural Catholic parishes now often serve more Spanish speakers than Francophones. In inner-city areas such as Boston's Roxbury, black churches are not simply religious institutions but cultural centers of communities. So, too, are inner cities seen as the ripest targets for evangelization by groups ranging from evangelical Protestants, who have converted to Eastern Orthodoxy and now hope to find followers among urban youth, to the Episcopal Church, not historically noted for its proselytizing zeal.

Martin B. Bradley, Norman M. Green, Jr., Dale E. Jones Mac Lynn, and Lou McNeil, *Churches and Church Membership in the United States, 1990: An Enumeration by Region, State, and County Based on Data Reported for 133 Church Groupings* (1992); Edwin S. Gaustad, *Historical Atlas of Religion in America*, rev. ed. (1976); Philip F. Gura, *A Glimpse of Sion's Glory: Puritan Radicalism in New England, 1620–1660* (1984); Stephen A. Marini, *Radical Sects of Revolutionary New England* (1982).

Lauren Frances Winner

Rivers and Waterways New England was an economically prosperous place largely because of the abundant resources provided by local rivers and waterways. For centuries, the people of the region depended on rivers as sources of drinking water, food, power generation, transport, and irrigation. Without the myriad of waterways, it is doubtful that many local populations, industries, or urban centers would have flourished. Unfortunately, the biologic health of many rivers declined with each new societal demand. It is clear that rivers evolved dramatically from the period immediately after glaciers retreated from New England to the present day. It is also clear that rivers have suffered to a large degree at the hands of humans.

To fully understand the societal impact on

Principal Rivers of New England

River (State)	Point of Origin	Point of Termination	Length (miles)
Allagash (Maine)	Piscataquis and Aroostook Counties, Maine	Saint John River	92.5
Ammonoosuc (N.H.)	Coos and Grafton Counties, N.H.	Connecticut River, SW N.H.	100
Androscoggin (Maine)	Umbagog Lake, N.H.	Kennebec River, Maine	157
Aroostock (Maine)	Piscataquis County, Maine	Saint John River, New Brunswick	140
Charles (Mass.)	Eastern Massachusetts	Boston Bay, Mass.	47
Chicopee (Mass.)	Hampden County, Mass.	Connecticut River, Chicopee, Mass.	17
Concord (Mass.)	Junction of Sudbury and Assabet Rivers	Lowell, Mass.	29
Connecticut (Conn.)	New Hampshire, near Canadian border	Old Saybrook, Old Lyme, Conn.	407
Deerfield (Mass.)	Windham County, Mass.	Connecticut River, Franklin County, Mass.	100
Farmington (Conn.)	Otis, Mass.	Connecticut River, Windsor, Conn.	13
Hoosic (Mass.)	Berkshire County, Mass.	Hudson River, Troy, N.Y.	70
Housatonic (Conn.)	Berkshire County, Mass.	Long Island Sound, Stratford, Conn.	148
Kennebec (Maine)	Moosehead Lake, Maine	Atlantic Ocean, Bath, Maine	150
Lamoille (Vt.)	Franklin County, Vt.	Lake Champlain, Chittenden County, Vt.	75
Machias (Maine)	Hancock County, Maine	Machias Bay, Washington County, Maine	70
Merrimack (Mass.)	Franklin, N.H.	Newburyport, Mass.	110
Millers (Mass.)	Southern New Hampshire	Connecticut River, Franklin County, Mass.	60
Missisquoi (Vt.)	Orleans County, Vt.	Lake Champlain, Franklin County, Vt.	90
Nashua (N.H.)	Wachusett Reservoir, Mass.	Nashua, N.H.	80
Otter Creek (Vt.)	Bennington County, Vt.	Lake Champlain, Addison County, Vt.	100
Passumpsic (Vt.)	Caledonia County, Vt.	Connecticut River, St. Johnsbury, Vt.	43
Pawcatuck River (R.I.)	Western Rhode Island	Narragansett Bay, R.I.	23
Pemigewasset (N.H.)	Grafton County, N.H.	Franklin, N.H.	70
Penobscot (Maine)	Central Maine	Atlantic Ocean, Penobscot Bay, Maine	101
Piscataqua/Salmon Falls (N.H./Maine)	Portsmouth, N.H.	Coastal Maine	12
Piscataquis (Maine)	Dover-Foxcroft, Maine	Builford, Maine	43
Quinebuag (Conn.)	Hampden County, Mass.	Joins Shetucket, Norwich, Conn.	100
Quinnipiac (Conn.)	Hartford County, Conn.	New Haven Harbor, Conn.	38
Saco (Maine)	West of Mount Washington, N.H.	Saco, Maine	104
Seekonk/Blackstone (R.I.)	Northeastern Rhode Island	Pawtucket, R.I., to Narragansett Bay, R.I.	5
Shepaug (Conn.)	Litchfield County, Conn.	Housatonic River, Southbury, Conn.	35
Shetucket (Conn.)	Willimatic, Conn.	Joins Quinebaug to form Thames	20
Saint Croix (Maine)	Chiputneticook Lakes, New Brunswick	Passamaquoddy Bay, Maine	129
Saint John (Maine)	Somerset County, Maine	Bay of Fundy, New Brunswick	418
Taunton (Mass.)	Plymouth County, Mass.	Mount Hope Bay, Fall River, Mass.	44
Thames (Conn.)	Norwich, Conn.	Long Island Sound, New London, Conn.	15
West River (Vt.)	Windham County, Vt.	Connecticut River, Brattleboro, Vt.	50
Westfield (Mass.)	Berkshire County, Mass.	Connecticut River, Springfield, Mass.	80
White River (Vt.)	Addison County, Vt.	Connecticut River, White River Junction, Vt.	50
Winooski (Vt.)	Northeastern Vermont	Lake Champlain, Chittenden County, Vt.	100

rivers in New England during the past half millennium, it is first necessary to paint a clear picture of the status of rivers before humans began to manipulate the streamside environment. Seventeen thousand years ago, a mere blip in geologic time, glaciers covered all of New England and rivers flowed unseen beneath the ice. Climate change brought glacial melting and a northerly retreat of the front end of the glacial ice. Rivers that emanated from the ends of the glaciers soon swelled and turned milky gray from their voluminous load of glacially ground rock. Sediment from the rivers deposited in wide, flat layers that form many current and former floodplain areas. Warmer climates also brought a return of widespread vegetation cover in New England that culminated in extensive forested channel banks. Meanwhile, flow to the rivers gradually dwindled as precipitation began to replace glacial melting as the primary source of river flow. Water clarity improved, and biological communities evolved into complex, interdependent systems.

Human effects on rivers began with the first landscape modifications for agriculture by Native Americans. By the time European settlers arrived, the rivers had already adjusted to these influences to an unknown degree. The more intensive farming practices colonists used, with greater degrees of deforestation and tillage, changed the volume of both sediment and water delivered to local channels. In the mid-19th century Henry David Thoreau provided an early perspective on changes in New England rivers with his well-known journal detailing a trip along the Concord and Merrimack Rivers. The most productive farming occurred on the wide floodplain areas immediately adjacent to the rivers and required removal of the existing forest areas. This change in streamside forests influenced waterways for more than a century because the input of fallen timber to rivers, which is critical in the formation of aquatic habitat, was reduced. As early as the 1800s, people raised concerns that fish populations were dwindling because of this deforestation and agriculture, and similar concerns still exist today.

Perhaps the most critical period for New England rivers dates from 1677, when the first dam in the United States was completed in Connecticut, to the 1980s, when construction of new dams in the nation began to taper off. The growth of New England industry, especially textile production, relied on water power, with many negative consequences for the steeper waterways in the region. Dams were constructed for mechanical waterpower, electrical generation, transportation, and public water supplies. Currently, the number of dams per unit area is higher in New England than in any other region in the United States; and Worcester County, Mass., has a larger number of dams than any other U.S. county. Dams blocked migration for Atlantic salmon, American shad, alewife, blueback herring, and other fish and trapped upstream sediments that were often contaminated with industrial waste. In fact, the overall effect of these dams on the flow of water in New England channels probably exceeds any possible effect related to the continued problem of global warming.

Waterpowered industry was largely responsible for the urbanization of many locations in New England. In other situations, marshlands along rivers were filled to accommodate urban growth. Higher population densities created sewage disposal problems and increased demands for clean sources of water supply. Rivers served as the original sewage disposal mechanism, with predictable consequences for downstream municipalities that relied on the same rivers for their water supply. Biologic communities often adjusted to more pollution-tolerant species as water quality decreased. Local efforts and the Clean Water Act of 1972 helped to reduce the dumping of raw sewage and industrial waste, but more diffuse sources of pollution from road surfaces, agricultural fields, and suburban lawns have proved much more difficult to regulate and reduce. The gradual process of development with the associated increased abundance of pavement also progressively increased flood flows because rain flows through storm water drains to rivers instead of into the forested soils of precolonial New England. As a result of the increased quantity of paved areas, the size of annual floods has more than doubled in some areas of New England, with a greater chance for economic loss.

In response to many of the abuses to New England rivers, conservation and restoration efforts have developed at various times. Early concerns over the loss of fish resulted in the construction of fish passages on some New England dams and more recent efforts at dam removal. Meanwhile, trout anglers began small local projects designed to benefit trout populations as early as the late 1880s. Restoration programs were vastly expanded by the Civilian Conservation Corps during the 1930s and state fisheries agencies since the 1950s. Currently, environmental concerns over rivers continue in areas that include the impacts of diverse sources of pollution, reduction of flow by dams during seasonal droughts, migration barriers to fish, and changes in flood flows due to urbanization. The future environmental health of New England waterways is still uncertain, but clearly human activities in the past few centuries scarred rivers in ways that may take another glacial period to fully erase.

R. E. Bilby and G. E. Likens, "Importance of Organic Debris Dams in the Structure and Function of Stream Ecosystems," *Ecology* 61 (1980); J. T. Cumbler, *Reasonable Use* (2001); W. L. Graf, "Dam Nation: A Geographic Census of American Dams and Their Large-Scale Hydrologic Impacts," *Water Resources Research* 35 (1999); D. M. Thompson and G. N. Stull, "The Development and Historical Use of Habitat Structures in Channel Restoration in the United States: The Grand Experiment in Fisheries Management," *Géographie Physique et Quaternaire* 56 (2002); H. D. Thoreau, *A Week on the Concord and Merrimack Rivers* (1849).

Douglas M. Thompson

Route 1 Route 1 is the oldest and easternmost federal highway in the United States. It was established by Congress in 1921 and officially named in 1925. Major parts of the roadway had existed for at least two centuries as the Colonial Post Road, interconnecting the most advantageous bridge points over tidal rivers adjacent to the coast from northeastern New York through New Haven, Conn.; Providence; Boston; and Portsmouth, N.H. By 1774 what became Route 1 extended to Portland, Maine, and by 1804 as far as Eastport in that same state. The highway currently stretches all the way to Fort Kent, in Maine's Aroostook County.

From 1500 on, the resources of the sea had attracted Europeans seeking cod and other products to the land and waters of what is now known as the Gulf of Maine. Overland transport became more secure in 1763, with the conclusion of the French and Indian War. Colonial settlers on the interface of tidewater and solid ground relied increasingly on a dual, ship- and roadway-based system of transport.

Coastal counties abutting Route 1 afford a convenient measure of New England's population concentration along this key regional highway. If we exclude landlocked Vermont for the moment, in 1830 Route 1 counties were home to 50 percent of New England's population. That figure had risen to 60 percent by 1890 and 68 percent in 1930, just five years after the highway received its official designation. Today, despite interstate highways' attracting growth throughout New England, the concentration of population along Route 1 is still 63 percent. Bringing Vermont back into the picture does not seem to affect the percentage figures much: in 1930, for example, the region-wide population density of Route 1 counties, at 65 percent, was only three points lower than the five-state figure, according to the U.S. census.

From the start Boston has been the urban hub of New England's Route 1. But every settlement on Route 1, from the tiniest village to the most major population center, was initially a port. Movement, both seaward and landward, radiated from each one. In several cases the penetration far inland of New England's tidal waterways—the Penobscot River to Bangor and the Kennebec River to Augusta in Maine, the Rhode Island Sound to Providence, the Connecticut River past Hartford and well into Massachusetts past Springfield—aided such movement. Any road map clearly shows the manner in which radial lines of inland transport are interconnected by the earliest coastal alignment, which served as the backbone of New England's entire territorial organization.

During the 20th century Route 1 became home to almost every imaginable commercial venture that tourists and locals alike could reach by car. Fast-food restaurants and miniature golf courses, fruit stands and outlet malls, lobster shacks and Internet service providers sprouted up side-by-side along a roadway that can sometimes seem in summer less a thoroughfare than a two- to four-lane parking lot. But through it all Route 1 has retained its vitality. From the earliest wooden ships to the jet aircraft departing from Bangor, Portland, and Boston International Airports, Route 1 has continued to hold a central place in the New England transportation system.

Philip W. Conkling, ed., *From Cape Cod to the Bay of Fundy: An Environmental Atlas of the Gulf of Maine* (1995); Charles O. Paulin, *Atlas of the Historical Geography of the United States* (1932).

Allen K. Philbrick

Route 128 Route 128, "America's Technology Highway," is a highway stretching in a 65-mile arc around the cities of Boston and Cambridge that has come to symbolize the proliferation of high technology–based companies throughout eastern Massachusetts. The region is home to nearly 3,000 firms that provide products and services in such diverse

Route 128 and Route 1, Dedham, Mass., 1972

areas as computers, software, telecommunications, artificial intelligence, advanced materials, biotechnology, electronics, photonics, and medicine.

At its southern end, Route 128 begins at an intersection with Interstate 95, 2 miles due south of the southernmost tip of the city of Boston. It remains coincident with Interstate 95 all the way to historic Salem, where 95 then veers north to New Hampshire. Route 128 continues on to Gloucester at the tip of Cape Ann, the far end of what is known as Boston's North Shore. Due west of the city, Route 128 intersects Route 90, the Massachusetts Turnpike, and as it swings through the northwest it cuts through Lexington, not far from the birthplace of the American Revolution. For much of its length, the route is bordered by rolling hills covered by trees that often partly mask the presence of high-tech facilities ranging from Polaroid in Waltham to the sprawling Lincoln Laboratory complex, a research facility operated by the Massachusetts Institute of Technology for the U.S. Air Force, in Bedford.

When the first 27-mile segment was completed in 1951, the road was the beginning of the first limited-access circumferential highway in the nation. Route 128 replaced an older and much smaller road of the same name that meandered from town to town just outside of Boston, usually going right through the town centers. Although it is not clear that the new highway alleviated traffic congestion in the city as intended, it did provide easy access to

largely underdeveloped land located conveniently near the metropolitan area.

At the same time, entrepreneurs with commercial ideas based on technologies developed primarily at MIT and Harvard as part of the World War II research effort were looking for affordable space to start up and expand their companies. By 1957, 17,000 people were employed by 99 companies located along Route 128, and parts of the road were widened in 1958 to accommodate the unexpected traffic flow. Companies such as CBS Hytron, Sylvania, EG&G, High Voltage Engineering, M/A-Com, Millipore, and Thermo Electron sprang up alongside Route 128 during this period.

The continuing start-up of companies along the highway and throughout the region and extending into southern New Hampshire came to be known as "the Route 128 phenomenon." The road itself, also known as the Yankee Division Highway, was marked with signs dubbing it "America's Technology Highway." The easier access to the land around Boston fueled so much development and so much growth in traffic that another ring road, Route 495, was constructed approximately 12 miles farther out during the 1970s. A number of high-tech companies have located along that highway as well. The widespread commercial success of the minicomputer in the 1960s and 1970s, developed initially by locally based Digital Equipment Corporation and subsequently by such area firms as Data General, Wang Laboratories, and Prime Computer, drew international attention to the start-up activity in

the region. The economic effect of the high-tech sector on the economy, led by minicomputers and software, came to be known as "the Massachusetts Miracle."

In a broader context, the construction of Route 128 accelerated a process of technology-based company creation that began in 1886 with the founding of Arthur D. Little, the world's first high-tech consulting firm, in Cambridge. Over the course of the decades before World War II, such diverse companies as Bell Telephone, General Radio (GenRad), Polaroid, and Raytheon also started up in the area. Many of the companies established in the region rely on the fundamental technological expertise developed at area universities, affiliated hospitals, and government research laboratories. The process is further fueled by the venture capital community, which was founded in 1946 with the establishment in Boston of American Research and Development, the world's first high-tech venture capital firm.

The combination of these resources has created a unique infrastructure that sustains the process of new company creation. This, in turn, not only draws entrepreneurs from other areas to start their companies in the region, but also encourages existing firms to acquire promising start-ups and to locate research and development facilities in the area to capitalize on emerging technologies with commercial promise.

Over time, the name "Route 128" has come to signify the entrepreneurial high-tech industry throughout eastern Massachusetts as much as it does the highway itself. It has been estimated that 60 percent of Massachusetts's economy is found in the Route 128 region, loosely defined as the area inside the ring of Route 495. Along with Silicon Valley south of San Francisco, Route 128 is one of the most active spawning grounds of new technology companies in the world.

Susan Rosegrant and David R. Lampe, *Route 128: Lessons from Boston's High-Tech Community* (1992); AnnaLee Saxenian, *Regional Advantage: Culture and Competition in Silicon Valley and Route 128* (1994).

David R. Lampe

Saint John River Valley The main stem of the river that names the Saint John River valley begins with the confluence of two branches, the Southwest and Baker, about 7 miles east of the Quebec border in Maine's northern woods. From there, the Saint John River flows sharply to the northeast and then finds a more gradual west-to-east route for approximately 75 miles before it courses southeasterly and empties into the Bay of Fundy at Saint John, New Brunswick.

Rising from the banks of this nearly 450-

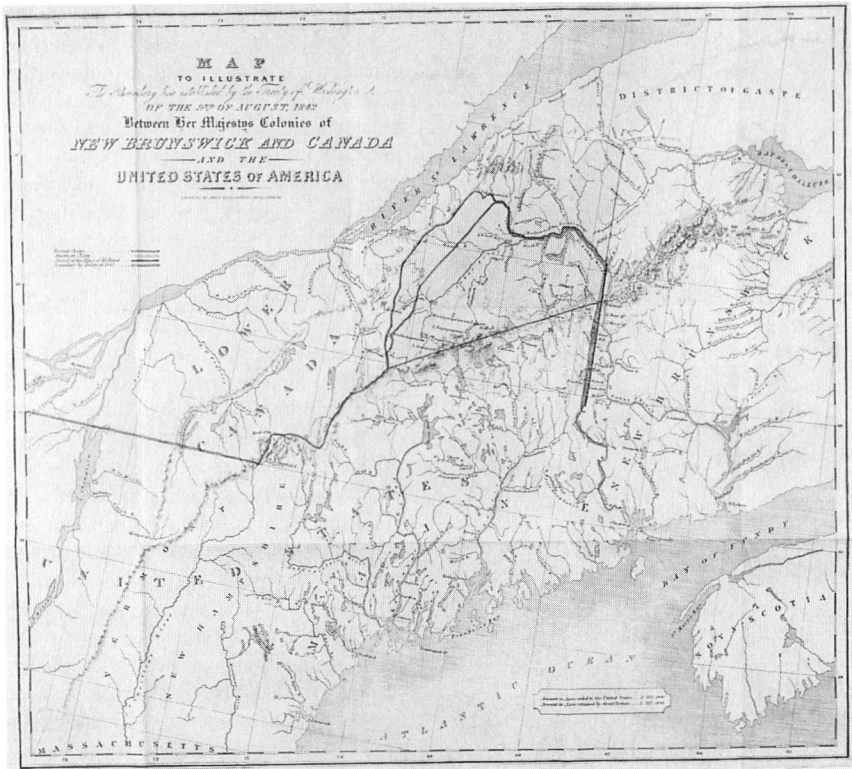

Saint John River valley and the Treaty of Washington boundary line, 1843

mile-long international river, the Saint John River valley possesses dramatic topography. In Maine, however, the valley is also an area defined by culture. The "valley," as it is popularly known, generally refers to the settlements and surrounding land (with a total population of approximately 27,000) along the Saint John River's south shores, from the spruce-fir forests of Allagash to Hamlin's farmland expanses. The area's culture is even more defined by the Acadians, French-speaking people who immigrated to what is now known as Nova Scotia from France in the 16th century and later migrated to the Saint John River valley. In fact, in the communities east of Saint Francis, the term *Acadian* is synonymous with the Saint John River valley.

Many valley residents, with names such as Cyr, Hebert, Violette, and Daigle, trace their ancestry to the first Acadian settlers who migrated to the area more than 200 years ago. But the valley's Acadian culture transcends the limits of direct genealogical links. Others throughout the 18th and 19th centuries joined the Acadian settlers, coming in large numbers from Quebec (with French-Canadian roots distinct from the Acadians) and in smaller numbers from New Brunswick and elsewhere in Maine. These groups mixed and intermarried with the Acadian population over two centuries. Nonetheless, the valley sustained a predominantly Acadian cultural identity that

has grown even stronger in recent decades, with preservation efforts, such as the Acadian Village in Van Buren, Maine, spurred by local historical societies, family reunions, and festivals. The people of the Saint John River valley share many characteristics, most significantly an association with and use of the French language, a commitment to religion (specifically Catholicism), a strong sense of family and home, a sense of place rooted in the valley and its natural resources, and an importance placed on history. One notable exception to the predominance of an Acadian cultural identity is the area surrounding Allagash, the valley's most westerly town, which was established by early American loyalist, English, and Scots-Irish settlers.

The Saint John River valley's culture has also been shaped by its identity as a borderland, dividing Maine and New Brunswick. The international border was created in 1842 by the Webster-Ashburton Treaty following decades of diplomatic and, at times, armed conflict. Control of the region's vast and valuable forests lay at the heart of the conflict. The current border, the Saint John River from Saint Francis to Hamlin, was reached in compromise but enforced a political separation of a culturally unified area. The border's placement had very different economic, social, and political implications depending on what side of the river people found themselves. On the

Canadian side, the area was central, serving as an important east-west commerce and communication route between the Maritime Provinces and Lower Canada. On the Maine side, however, the area became isolated, as it was more than 200 miles north of Bangor, through virtually uncharted wilderness. While railroads traveled along the valley's New Brunswick shores by 1870, it was not until 1899, and the beginnings of a commercial potato industry, that they stretched north through Maine to Van Buren.

With the Saint John River valley's remoteness, outside influences were slow in diluting the valley's culture. As a result, the culture's richness and distinctions, many surrounding the Acadian identity found there, flourished relatively undisturbed and continue to be celebrated, nourished, and preserved today.

Thomas Albert, *The History of Madawaska* (1985); Guy F. Dubay, *Chez-Nous: The St. John Valley* (1983); Victor A. Konrad, "Against the Tide: French Canadian Barn Building Traditions in the St. John Valley of Maine," *The American Review of Canadian Studies* 12, no. 2 (1982).

Sheila McDonald

Salmon and Shad The Atlantic salmon (*Salmo salar*) belongs to the family Salmonidae, a large family of fish made up of salmon, trout, char, whitefishes, and graylings. The Atlantic salmon is an anadromous fish; that is, it reproduces in freshwater after long periods in the ocean, migrating between the two. In North America, Atlantic salmon are found from Greenland and Labrador to Maine, originally occurring as far south as Delaware. Landlocked populations of Atlantic salmon can also be found in New England; these fish were first introduced to New Hampshire lakes in 1866 and remain in freshwater their entire lives.

The anadromous salmon spend between two to four years, depending on water temperature, in freshwater streams after hatching from fertilized eggs. The fish grow slowly during this period and weigh no more than a few ounces. Toward the end of the freshwater phase, the young salmon begin to undergo many biological changes that enable them to live in seawater. Salmon generally migrate in April and May to the ocean where they spend between one and three years feeding extensively. They then return to freshwater streams in the spring and early summer and generally spawn in October and November, laying their eggs in shallow nests of the stream where the current is fast and the bottom is composed of coarse gravel.

Atlantic salmon are an important biological and economic resource and are considered to be among the most valued game and food fishes in the world. Salmon were also an important staple food of some northeastern Native Americans who taught European settlers how to fish for them. Once relatively plentiful in the Northeast, the species is now restricted to a few New England rivers including the Connecticut River, which originates in the Connecticut lakes near the Canadian border and forms the boundary between New Hampshire and Vermont, and then flows through central Massachusetts and central Connecticut. The Penobscot River was once the richest salmon river in Maine.

The dramatic decrease in the great salmon runs is due to many factors, including overfishing, logging, damming, and pollution of rivers. With the construction of a large dam across the Merrimack River in Concord, N.H., in 1895 and the failure of fish ladders at dams in Lowell and Lawrence, Mass., during the 1890s, a once-thriving fishery on this river was destroyed. In the late 1800s an average of 150,000 pounds of salmon were landed yearly in the rivers of Maine. By this time, very few salmon were caught elsewhere in New England. Since 1950 the total commercial catch for salmon has never exceeded 1,000 pounds. Recreational sports fishing probably takes another few hundred pounds of salmon annually.

Approximately $2 billion to $3 billion have been spent in efforts to reestablish Atlantic salmon in New England during the past 30 years by improving the habitat, expanding biological research, and installing fish passageways at dams. In addition to these enhancement efforts by state, federal, and international agencies, commercial Atlantic salmon rearing has grown in recent years and the annual stocking of hatchery-reared fish continues. These efforts have yet to result in a substantial comeback of the sea-run Atlantic salmon to New England.

The American shad (*Alosa sapidissima*) is an anadromous member of the family Clupeidae (herrings) which includes the blueback herring and alewife. Shad are native to the Atlantic coast from southern Labrador to northern Florida but were introduced into the Sacramento River in the 1870s and have since spread along the Pacific coast from Kamchatka to Todos Santos Bay, Mexico.

American shad, like the salmon, spends the majority of its life in the ocean and then migrates into freshwater tributaries and rivers to spawn. In New England, spawning runs of shad enter rivers between late April and late June, depending on spring weather conditions and geographic location. Spawning usually occurs in deep areas of a river where currents are moderate to strong. Juveniles spend their first summer in the river and migrate to the ocean as the temperature drops in the fall.

Shad remain at sea until they mature at four or five years and attain an average length of 16 to 20 inches. Shad at sea feed on planktonic organisms. During spawning migrations, adults eat little.

American shad have historically been exploited for their flesh and roe (*sapidissima* means "most delicious"); Atlantic coast landings exceeded 22,000 tons in 1896, but overfishing, damming, and pollution of rivers led to dramatic population declines. Commercial landings had a recent peak of 3,000 tons in 1970 but have since declined to less than 1,000 tons. Despite the population decline, shad remain a popular sport fish wherever they are available.

Between 1848 and 1952 state and federal hatcheries were operated to produce shad in most of the Atlantic seacoast states to help support local populations. Currently, a federally implemented management plan for American shad and river herring seeks to facilitate cooperative management and restoration strategies among states. Restoration efforts have involved habitat improvement, fish passageways at dams, and stocking programs. Despite a brief period of improved returns, the number of American shad continues to decline.

Gary J. Anderson and Ann E. Brimer, *Salar: The Story of the Atlantic Salmon* (1976); Anthony Netboy, *The Atlantic Salmon: A Vanishing Species?* (1968); The Shad Foundation, *The Shad Journal* (published quarterly); Lawrence Stolte, *The Forgotten Salmon of the Merrimack* (1981).

Stacia A. Sower and Caleb Slater

Salt Marshes Salt marshes are a distinctive geographical feature of the New England landscape. They appear in tidal locations where their most well-known feature is a graded series of salt-tolerant plants that provide a habitat for many animals and fish. These locations are also a source of food and economic profit to people who cultivate and manage them. In recent times salt marshes have proved to be a significant study area for ecologists, botanists, historians, and anthropologists.

Humans have used the grasses and peat of the marsh since Roman times, especially in Britain and the Low Countries. There, salt marsh areas were diked to control the level and salinity of the tidal saltwater. This process created large areas of rich, arable land, as well as fields producing both fresh and salt hays.

When North American settlement became substantial, farmers from the Low Countries and Essex County in England brought the techniques of diking and harvesting of salt hay to the Bay of Fundy, the coast of New England, and south to the Carolinas.

Techniques of using and managing salt marshes have changed relatively little during the past 300 years, except that more energy is applied to some portions of the work. Many of the basic tools used in this work have a history of three centuries of use, and it is only in very recent years that these tools have fallen into disuse. Salt marshes are still managed in parts of Massachusetts and still bring in cash income. Obsolete words describing the grass and the processes of diking are still occasionally heard along the coast of northern New England. But for the most part, the aesthetic aspect of salt marshes for art and literature and the use of the knowledge of the past by ecologists have supplanted most traditional agricultural uses.

Salt marsh hay, which traditionally was used on farms to feed and bed animals and for banking houses against the winter, has been the primary product of the marsh. The earliest settlers both in Plymouth and in Massachusetts Bay were attracted to salt marshes because they intended to raise cattle. By 1630 salt marsh hay was annually harvested in large amounts along the north coast of Massachusetts. Whenever settlement moved to new areas, the salt marsh land was prized, and proprietary records of the first land companies and their settlers indicate the careful lotting of salt marshes so that each new family would have access to the hay. Little evidence of common land usage is found in the salt marsh.

Essex County in Massachusetts and York County in Maine were significant sources of salt marsh hay in New England. Later, Washington County in Maine also became active in salt marsh economy. Early court records provide a number of accounts of hay being stolen from the marsh. On several occasions the sheriff's posse had to be called out to catch the miscreants.

Salt marsh hay was a significant cash crop as well, auctioned regularly in markets centered in Portsmouth and Boston but also throughout New England. Cattle feed, bedding, packing for fragile goods (such as Sandwich glass), and nursery bedding stock provided a constant market for the hay. Salt marsh hay was also often fed as a supplemental food to stabled animals during winter, especially animals associated with the ubiquitous small breweries that were the norm.

The salt marsh was usually harvested in September after the regular hay harvest. The hay was cut with heavy scythes manufactured for this purpose. Workers using poles transferred the hay to central locations where 10- to 15-foot oval cylindrical haystacks were erected on staddles (sometimes staddels) so that the sea at high tide did not harm the hay. The word *staddle* is closely related to the word for tree trunk in Anglo-Saxon, indicating that the first such uses were probably stumps from cut-down trees.

When animals were used in the harvesting, they were fitted with bog or marsh shoes, usually constructed from a flat piece of elm with an animal shoe attached to the wood. These shoes differed from animal to animal, as oxen have cloven hooves, for instance, and demand a different shoe. The bog shoes were strapped to the animal hooves, allowing the wet marsh to bear their weight.

Later in the year, the hay was moved from the staddles and transferred usually to river or seacoast, normally by horses and oxen. The hay was then taken to the sale site by wide, flat-bottomed scows called gundalows. Such scows, powered by sails, were a prominent sight along the coast. In the most lucrative days of salt marsh hay, as much as 20,000 tons at a time were taken to market, at one time by gundalows lashed together and propelled by schooners at each corner.

In order to enhance the business, people often diked the salt marshes to control the salinity of the hay. Dikes were built from peat blocks dug from the immediate area that were laid like bricks in a wall, wider at the bottom, tapering on the seaward side from perhaps 4 feet to 2.5 feet wide. Usually, construction crews consisted of three men, one digging, one passing, and one laying the peat blocks. It was traditional practice to change positions every 20 minutes.

These dikes were penetrated every 30 or 40 feet by a wooden box constructed usually of elm, cedar, or hemlock in which swung a gate, called a flapper valve. This swinging valve allowed water to escape under pressure, controlling the interior salinity, while closing against the rising tide, to limit the amount of water taken in. These valves operated through a combination of water flowage and the difference in specific gravity of saltwater and freshwater. Once in place these tools did their work twice each day and repair work was seldom necessary. Some of these flapper valves, built into bridge structures, are as much as 30 feet in diameter and are constructed of steel.

Once a dike was built, it needed repair only after hard winters or ice damage. Dikes on the Maine coast constructed as early as 1815 may still be seen. When large areas of land were to be diked, diking companies were frequently franchised by the state, and at times of high usage, such diking companies abounded. There was, for instance, a boom period in diking companies from 1810 to 1830 and again from 1860 to 1880.

Although some diking efforts were conducted by the elite as a way of land "improvement," most dikes were designed to provide a cash crop and a valuable resource for local farmers and others who had a financial interest in the dikes and their adjacent produce. In the Bay of Fundy area, dikes were important enough so that they affected family life (large families to ensure labor requirements) and marital patterns (local-area marriages to ensure cooperation in dike maintenance). In New England this does not appear to be the case.

Diking and controlling salt marsh hay was a significant activity before the Revolutionary War in Cohasset and Marshfield and along the north shore of Massachusetts. In Maine towns such as York, Wells, Scarborough, and Machias were centers of diking enterprises. Even in a country with seemingly unlimited land and new prospects, local farmers used centuries-old knowledge to make a living.

David C. Smith, Victor Konrad, Becky Koulouris, Edward Hawes, and Harold W. Borns, Jr., "Salt Marshes as a Factor in the Agriculture of Northeastern North America," *Agricultural History* 63, no. 2 (1989); John and Mildred Teal, *Life and Death of the Salt Marsh*, (1969); Betsey Woodman, *Salt Haying, Farming and Fishing in Salisbury, Massachusetts: The Life of Sherb Eaton (1900–1982)*, (1983).

David C. Smith

Seabrook Station In 1971 several New England electric utilities, led by the Public Service Company of New Hampshire (PSNH), announced that a nuclear generating station with two 1,110-megawatt reactors would be built at Seabrook, N.H. The partners expected construction to cost less than $1 billion and operation to begin before the end of the decade. But costs increased to more than $6 billion before a single reactor started operating commercially in 1990.

In the interim, public perception of nuclear power, initially hospitable, shifted dramatically. A general respect for political, corporate, and scientific authority collapsed in the wake of failures associated with Vietnam, Watergate, and the accident at the Three Mile Island nuclear power plant near Harrisburg, Pa. Research detailing the risks of radiation and the inability of government to provide assuredly safe disposal of radioactive waste contradicted promoters' assertions that nuclear electricity was the best way to meet the nation's energy needs. Furthermore, the complexity, scale, and location of the plant seemed to threaten established fishing and tourist businesses and to undermine traditions of local political control.

The shifting popular mood was as much a part of the Seabrook environment as were the surrounding waters, marshes, and beaches. Opponents of the plant included the town of Seabrook, several other New Hampshire communities, and the Commonwealth of Massachusetts. Environmental protection was the focus of initial regulatory hearings, out of which a more explicit opposition to nuclear power developed; after Three Mile Island, and especially after the 1986 explosion and partial meltdown of a Soviet reactor in Chernobyl, emergency planning became the central concern.

To obtain state approval of the Seabrook site, PSNH scrapped its original cooling scheme and substituted tunnels that would transport ocean water without disturbing intervening wetlands. Federal proceedings eventually modified the new design to reduce potential damage to marine life. Environmental groups used the courts and the Environmental Protection Agency in their attempts first to prevent construction and then halt it. That effort ultimately failed, but the delay did result in an improved plant design. Plant opponents concluded that the protracted environmental deliberations, lasting from 1975 until 1978, revealed incompetent corporate managers whose forecasts of cost, schedule, and product demand were invariably inaccurate and regulators who were determined to approve the sponsors' plans.

Convinced that further legal opposition was futile, area residents Guy Chichester, Robert Cushing, and Catherine Wolff and other anti-Seabrook activists formed the Clamshell Alliance, which proposed to seize the site and halt construction of the reactor. In April 1977, on the order of New Hampshire Governor Meldrim Thompson, state police arrested 1,400 trespassing demonstrators. A second occupation, planned for June 1978, evolved into an orderly rally in the face of the state's unyielding stance and divisions within the alliance itself. The participatory decision-making process of the Clamshell Alliance failed to find a way to halt construction or to realize the group's broader vision of a decentralized society. But the alliance did shift the focus of public debate from environmental protection to the risks posed by nuclear technology to society and public health.

Those dangers seemed more real after the 1979 accident at Three Mile Island. Subsequent federal requirements for emergency planning revived legal efforts to keep Seabrook from operating. Governor John Sununu, a vigorous champion of the project, submitted New Hampshire's evacuation plans over the objections of officials from Hampton and other nearby communities, who maintained that the plans were impractical, especially during the summer when bathers thronged the beaches adjacent to the plant. Governor Michael Dukakis of Massachusetts eventually agreed and declined to submit an emergency plan for affected Commonwealth communities. That decision, which delayed

Seabrook nuclear generating station and Hampton Beach in New Hampshire, 1989

operation for months, precipitated more permissive federal rules.

During the long struggle to license Seabrook Station, fuel costs, interest rates, and the project's budget rose substantially, while demand for electricity declined. Several sponsoring utilities, sometimes at the urging of state regulatory agencies, withdrew their support. In 1988 PSNH declared bankruptcy. Although corporate reorganization allowed commercial operation to begin at Seabrook two years later, the long, expensive battle discouraged future expansion of the nuclear industry in New Hampshire and elsewhere in the United States.

Henry F. Bedford, *Seabrook Station: Citizen Politics and Nuclear Power* (1990); Barbara Epstein, *Political Protest and Cultural Revolution: Nonviolent Direct Action in the 1970s and 1980s* (1991); Samuel P. Hays, *Beauty, Health, and Permanence: Environmental Politics in the United States, 1955–1985,* (1987); Donald W. Stever, Jr., *Seabrook and the Nuclear Regulatory Commission: The Licensing of a Nuclear Power Plant* (1980).

Henry F. Bedford

Society for the Protection of New Hampshire Forests

One of the first citizen conservation organizations in the United States, the Society for the Protection of New Hampshire Forests (SPNHF) was founded in 1901 by residents of Massachusetts and New Hampshire to "preserve the forests, protect the scenery . . . and cooperate in other measures of public improvement." This purpose was refined in 1904 to read, "The Society for the Protection of New Hampshire Forests

seeks to perpetuate the forests by their wise use and their complete reservation in places of special scenic beauty."

The founders' original goal was to create a federal reserve in the White Mountains, where 50 years of logging and forest fires had denuded the forest and befouled the headwaters of the state's rivers. Leading a coalition of women's clubs, hotel owners, industrialists, journalists, and other conservation groups (most notably the Appalachian Mountain Club), the SPNHF lobbied Congress for 10 years, culminating in 1911 with the passage of the Weeks Act, which authorized the federal government to buy land from private owners, thus enabling creation of the entire eastern National Forest system.

Through the middle decades of the 20th century, the SPNHF led numerous land preservation campaigns, placing into public ownership such landmarks as Mount Monadnock, Franconia Notch, Mount Kearsarge, and Mount Sunapee. At the same time, the organization held true to its utilitarian side as expressed in the "wise use" clause of the 1904 mission statement. The organization taught forestry to landowners, lobbied for reduced taxes on growing timber, led public campaigns to eradicate forest pests, and represented forest landowners. In 1950 the SPNHF brought the Tree Farm program (to recognize and encourage reforestation on private land) to New Hampshire.

During the 1960s and 1970s the SPNHF became involved in myriad conservation problems, including land use, energy, litter,

and water and air pollution. In the 1980s, as more specialized groups emerged to tackle those issues, the SPNHF rededicated itself to its 1904 mission of protecting land and caring for forests. Of particular note was the Trust for New Hampshire Lands/Land Conservation Investment Program. Initiated by the SPNHF, this private/public partnership invested $47 million between 1987 and 1993 to conserve 100,000 acres of land for recreation, wildlife, scenery, agriculture, and forestry.

As of 2000, 10,000 members and donors supported the SPNHF's four program areas—land protection, education, advocacy, and forestry. The organization is directed by a volunteer Board of Trustees and operated by a full-time professional staff of 40. The annual budget is approximately $3 million. The SPNHF, headquartered in Concord, N.H., owns approximately 36,500 acres in more than 137 reservations and holds interests in an additional 88,000 acres.

Paul E. Bruns, *A New Hampshire Everlasting and Unfallen* (1969); Society for the Protection of New Hampshire Forests, *Forest Notes* (quarterly journal).

Richard Ober

Towns and Villages

New England has a settlement landscape of marked regional individuality and burdensome symbolic value. This landscape is a precious asset linking 350 years of historical development of place and region. It is also composed of veneers—literally, settlement built upon settlement, and figuratively, symbol built upon symbol.

New England settlers experimented with various models of town and village settlement, and by the 1660s a relatively standardized form had developed. A town or village was created when freehold farmers on dispersed farmsteads formed a political corporation and ecclesiastical parish. Consequent communal ties and a high degree of localized economic interdependence characterized this type of community and allowed it to function successfully despite the distances between farmsteads. Commerce, churchgoing, and social interaction focused on the town or village center, which was not itself a village in the contemporary sense of the term, consisting of a meetinghouse and, occasionally, community structures such as a town house. Towns and villages thus provided the geographic as well as social frames for this landscape of dispersed settlement.

Town in New England referred specifically to geographic spaces and to the communities that held charters to inhabit those spaces. New England town communities established exclusive church congregations, organized town meetings at which political expression was exercised, and served as vehicles for distributing land to a population made up largely of families intent on farming. The latter function was economically critical, as no family could support itself well without access to land.

Like New England towns, New England's colonial villages were also chartered communities inhabiting specific locations. And as villages have always been hierarchically secondary to towns, so were they, too, in New England. The point is important. Colonial villages were secondary parishes or districts of towns, though in time they might become towns in their own right. Salem, Mass., offers an apt illustration. Within the town of Salem developed early on Salem town and the village of Salem. Salem town was the port and marketplace that became the core of the present city of Salem. In the village of Salem farmers settled on dispersed homesteads of enclosed or contiguous farmland, petitioned for their own parish and church, and eventually were chartered as the town of Danvers.

Regional variations in settlement form did exist but reflected functional differences, as in certain areas of England. Farmers concentrated linearly along valuable intervale land in wide alluvial valleys, such as that of the Connecticut River. New Englanders engaged in coastal trading and fishing formed settlement nucleations within towns in which other inhabitants also farmed. But most towns and villages throughout the colonial period consisted mainly of dispersed agricultural settlement, again as in parts of England. Thus colonial New England towns and villages were not so much a deviant form of settlement as they were an early American manifestation of English antecedents. The interlarding of community-sanctioned individual farmsteads and homesteads within a community's bounded space manifested itself in 19th-century agricultural settlement expansion and continues today to shape Americans' relation with the land.

If New England towns and villages of the colonial period were preurban spaces, the New England villages we recognize today were protourban places. With a quickening of commerce during the 1790s and after, increasing numbers of full-time nonfarmers congregated at points of high accessibility to engage in trade. Across New England these high-traffic areas were colonial town and village centers, often created on hilltops where townspeople had placed their meetinghouse and burying ground and to which they had built their town and village roads. This 19th-century gathering of commercial activities and residences around meetinghouse lots in town and village centers, in addition to interconnected town and village roads, created a protourban system of nucleated center villages, market towns, and small cities.

The form of center villages varied according to site conditions and road networks that had been laid down for other reasons in an earlier time. Rebuilt roads and new turnpikes intersected where colonial town and village centers were evolving into center villages, reinforcing the locational advantages of centrality and solidifying the form. Nineteenth-century disestablishment separated meetinghouse and burying ground from the remainder of the meetinghouse lot to form the secular village common. Stately homes dressed main thoroughfares framing village commons and leading from the center village. Center villages underwent continued construction, and after a period of relative economic stability during the 1830s and 1840s, residents in some towns undertook village beautification.

During the 19th century some center villages remained small, but many, such as Pittsfield, Mass., and Bristol, Conn., became cities; others grew more and more industrialized, often relocating downhill to mill sites or turnpike crossings. Some, like Roxbury, Mass., by Boston, were eventually enveloped by expanding urban centers, while others, like Litchfield, Conn., inspired the design of suburbs. New England villages continue to stimulate suburban development. One need only read the real estate pages of any local newspaper to find repeated reference to the New England town and village landscape in subdivision names, landscaping, and domestic architecture.

Suburban inspiration derives from an invented tradition. Nineteenth-century Romantic elites who built center villages also fashioned a corresponding myth of Puritan antecedence, democratic society, and patriotic fervor, which became tradition in the powerfully nostalgic search for national and local identity that occurred during the centennial years of the 1870s. The tradition is the consequence of quite deliberate attempts to create a mythical landscape at both the local level—by families and communities—and the national level—by the influential, self-conscious promoters of a new literary, aesthetic, and historical ideology. The tradition was specifically expressed in an architectural vision that selected individual houses and places of New England as representative of the whole. Scholars seeking the origins of American democracy in the New England town meeting and the roots of American-vernacular building traditions further elaborated on this past and linked New England to a larger Anglo-Saxon tradition. Center villages with town commons surrounded by substantial dwelling houses became the historical landmarks and monumental constructions that served as contrived symbols of an imaginative colonial past.

As a consequence the postcard-perfect town and village landscape we observe in New England today—in Woodstock, Vt., for instance—with its white-painted, black-shuttered, classic dwellings, churches, and stores abutting a tree-shaded village green, has come ironically to reflect continuity with more than change from the past. For the first century and a half of New England settlement, the Europeanized landscape of towns and villages was filled with single-family farms linked to town and village centers, but few were nucleated settlements akin to contemporary villages. The center villages that epitomize this landscape today arose during the 19th century to mark New England's rural ascendancy. That they remain today suggests the passing not of New England's colonial past but of its industrial past.

Bruce C. Daniels, *The Connecticut Town: Growth and Development, 1635–1790* (1979); Richard Lingeman, *Small Town America: A Narrative History, 1620–the Present* (1980); Kenneth Lockridge, *A New England Town: The First Hundred Years: Dedham, Massachusetts, 1636–1736* (1985); Sumner Chilton Powell, *Puritan Village: The Formation of a New England Town* (1963); Page Smith, *As a City upon a Hill: The Town in American History* (1966); John Stilgoe, *Common Landscapes of America, 1580–1845* (1982); Stilgoe, *Borderland: Origins of the American Suburb, 1820–1939* (1988); Joseph S. Wood, *The New England Village* (1997).

Joseph S. Wood

Transportation From earliest colonial settlements through the present day, evolving methods and means of transport and transportation have influenced the development of regional culture and identity. Competition among settlements for markets and among transport agents for economic survival is a persistent feature of transport history.

Trade among coastal settlements and river ports defined New England commerce during the 17th and 18th centuries. Tidewater access was critical for linkage with Europe and with the colonies; post roads and native trails provided paths for communication, but a shift to a broad diffusion of land transport began in the 1790s with the construction of turnpikes and canals.

Turnpikes, noted for their straightness, serviced stage lines from Boston and other centers. Charters specified tolls, and turnpike legislation introduced precedents of tax exemption for transport agents, eminent domain, and public rights-of-way. However, public roads and railroad competition forced the abandonment of most turnpikes by the mid-19th century.

The canal era was important to the extension of port hinterlands. Through a series of canals in the early 1800s, Hartford and New Haven vied with each other and with Boston for access to the Connecticut River valley. The Middlesex Canal linked Boston with the upper Merrimack by 1803, providing raw materials for early cotton-mill expansion at Lowell, Mass. Along the Blackstone River, a canal completed in 1828 helped industrial development in Providence but intruded on Boston's trade area.

In Maine, a canal to Lake Sebago was part of Portland's unfulfilled dream for water access to the Saint Lawrence. Boston-based plans for canals between the Merrimack and the Connecticut and from Boston to the Hudson River did not proceed. Instead, it was New York, aided by the Erie (1825) and Champlain (1827) Canals, that gained access to western continental expansion and to the western lowlands of Vermont. Early railroads paralleled New England's canals, ending their transport role by the 1840s.

The rise of Boston as a rail terminus occurred in 1835, when separate railroads were completed to Lowell, Providence, and Worcester, Mass. Boston's legacy as a "hub" was fixed by stage and rail lines converging on the port, making it a major terminus for freight and passengers. The Western Railroad reached the Hudson in 1841. But the city of Troy, N.Y., blocked a rail bridge to Albany, N.Y., until 1866, assuring New York's superior access to the Erie Canal. The Western was intended to divert traffic from the Connecticut River valley and from the West (via the Erie Canal) to Boston. But competition ensued with fast New York–based packet ships that sailed down the Hudson to coastal southern New England.

Maine tried a rail policy independent of Boston and New York. The line to Montreal in 1853 that made Portland a terminus for Canada's grain trade used the British broad gauge. Plans for extensions to the Connecticut River and to New London, Conn. (from Bangor, Maine, to Nova Scotia for carriage by Atlantic ferry and rail) did not succeed. By 1870, Maine railroads adopted the American standard gauge, thereby committing their commercial orientation to Boston.

Towns and regions linked by rail gained commercial advantages, a factor that encouraged their purchase of stocks in rail lines and their grants of land and donations to secure local terminals. Duplication of routes by competing firms and overoptimism about traffic led to poor investment outcomes. However, a notable success of rail expansion was its contribution to tourism. Excursion trains, evident in the 1850s, became popular after the Civil War, with narrow gauge lines being extended to mountain, lake, and coastal resorts.

After the Civil War, New England's trade moved increasingly through New York and Albany. Albany's gateway status followed construction of a rail tunnel through Hoosac Mountain in western Massachusetts in 1875. This improved Boston's access to the Hudson-Champlain lowlands but was met with New York legal restrictions on rail competition.

By the late 19th century, continental rail expansion allowed farmers in other states to market produce in New England more cheaply than could local farmers, ushering in the abandonment of farmland and related freight. Regional railroads and narrow gauge lines suffered from automobile competition by the 1920s, when rail mileage peaked in most parts of New England. An extended period of railway abandonment and consolidation followed, augmented by bankruptcies, mergers, and acquisitions.

Success of the automobile relates to the flexibility of individualized transport and to the improvement of roads. Bicycle enthusiasts encouraged better roads and the issuance of bonds to finance construction, but motorization of road vehicles accelerated these practices. During the 1890s New England states introduced aid for roads. Highway commissions were organized before World War I, federal aid for highways followed, and gasoline taxes appeared in the 1920s.

"Superhighways" in the 1930s (such as the Worcester-Boston Turnpike) failed to control access from, and commercial use of, adjoining properties, leading to extreme congestion. Clearing the way for limited-access roads, an amendment to Rhode Island's constitution in 1937 set the legal basis for restricting access to highways by abutting landowners.

Connecticut used state funds to build the Merritt Parkway, started in 1934, but charged tolls for further highway development. An early limited-access highway, the Merritt was beautifully landscaped, zoned to prohibit commercial land uses, and restricted to non-commercial vehicles. Turnpikes built shortly after World War II did allow commercial traffic and were integrated later into the interstate highway system. The Highway Act of 1956 initiated construction of a 45,000-mile interstate network, with 1,800 miles in New England.

Automobiles and highways led to major landscape changes. Population spread far beyond city boundaries, and average commuting distances increased. Circumferential roads (for example, Route 128 around Boston) and limited-access beltways (for example, Interstate 495) became magnets for the expansion of manufacturing and service firms, many moving from central cities. They attracted employees from an extended region, with

most commuting by automobile. Widespread use of automobiles led to a broad diffusion of home, work, and play locations. Weekend and seasonal traffic escalated to areas of high natural and cultural amenities.

Complementing the automobile, scheduled ferry service to outlying islands, more than 400 licensed air landing strips, and dozens of heliports and seaplane bases give popular access to all corners of New England. In addition, the expansion of private logging roads lures the traffic of camper vans and tenters, hikers, and hunters into northern forest regions.

Interstate highways have changed practices for distributing goods, with interchanges becoming focal points for commerce and freight transshipment. Warehouses moved to the urban periphery to avoid congestion in central cities. Former rail freight yards are now intermodal terminals that allow fast truck-rail transfer of trailers and containers. Shipment by boxcar has declined in response to the greater use of intermodal containers.

The shift to multimodal transport systems is a significant outcome of deregulation. Federal deregulation during the 1980s made it easier for railroads to solicit traffic, to form alliances with truckers and intermodal shippers, and to run trains on tracks owned by other companies. In trucking, deregulation resulted in new carriers during the late 1970s, but the share of business has concentrated in a few major firms.

Most New England exporters use the Port of New York, but shipping is still important to Boston and Portland (mostly tankers feeding the oil pipeline to Montreal). Boston port traffic includes direct calls to Europe, South America, and the Middle East as well as feeder and barge services via New York to other parts of the world. New York's port terminals are also linked to intermodal transport systems for efficient container transfer to and from inland centers.

During the 1980s air cargo express couriers entered competition with motor carriers, offering competitive rates and fast delivery. Regional passenger airlines formed to take advantage of the routing and pricing flexibilities of deregulated markets. By the 1990s, subsidiaries to major airlines were the primary carriers from outlying centers. However, because of easy highway access, many travelers bypass local airports and either drive or take buses to Kennedy, LaGuardia, and Logan airports, the three hub terminals serving New England. Boston's Logan International Airport serves more than two dozen scheduled airlines. A quarter of its domestic traffic is to New York, creating one of the nation's busiest air corridors.

The Boston–New York corridor is also a

primary market for Amtrak, the federally subsidized rail passenger corporation, created in 1970 and operational in 1971. Its Metroliner from Boston to New York faces competition from price-aggressive air carriers. Planners hope that now this line has been electrified for high-speed trains that cut the trip from four to three hours, traffic from roads will be diverted and possibly offset the need for a second Boston airport.

After four centuries of transport expansion, access to New England's prized countryside poses threats of overcrowding and ecological destruction. Increasing numbers of people and automobiles combine with earlier retirements from the workforce and flexible work arrangements (including telecommuting) to put further pressure on amenity environments. New technologies and desires for global competitiveness propel decision makers toward just-in-time production systems, automated transport infrastructure, larger freight carriers, and faster vehicles. Transportation and communication unquestionably bond New Englanders beyond local identities, but continued exploitation of these space-adjusting technologies may also intrude on the region's cultural and environmental integrity.

Edward Chase Kirkland, *Men, Cities and Transportation: A Study in New England History, 1820–1900* (1948); Balthasar Henry Meyer and Caroline E. MacGill, *History of Transportation in the United States Before 1860* (1917); James E. Vance, Jr., *Capturing the Horizon: The Historical Geography of Transportation since the Transportation Revolution of the 16th Century* (1986).

Donald G. Janelle

Trustees of Reservations

Founded in 1891, the Trustees of Reservations is a member-supported, nonprofit conservation organization dedicated to the preservation of properties of exceptional scenic, historic, and ecological value in Massachusetts for public use and enjoyment. The Trustees of Reservations also works to save privately held open land across the state.

On March 5, 1890, the periodical *Garden and Forest* carried a letter titled "The Waverly Oaks"; its author was Charles Eliot, a young landscape architect then practicing in Boston, who proposed the establishment of what would become the Trustees of Reservations, the first private organization of its kind in the world devoted solely to the preservation of open space for public purposes.

In earlier decades, conservationists had focused on how to prevent pillage of the natural wonders of the American West. But at the end of the 19th century, efforts turned to ways to mitigate the continuing destruction of human resources, particularly in the densely settled urban East. Boston had become one of the nation's largest manufacturing centers, its population swelled by tens of thousands of people who had come from farms and villages as well as from foreign countries. Living conditions in the city were, for the most part, deplorable. Eliot, an associate of the celebrated planner Frederick Law Olmsted, believed, as Olmsted did, that parks, with their fresh air, scenic beauty, and quiet repose, offered an antidote for the ills of urban life. It was with this in mind that he wrote his letter.

Although Eliot ultimately envisioned the city with a series of "country parks" of 50 acres or more in size, he urged that action begin immediately to preserve "special bits of scenery" still remaining "within ten miles of the State House which possess uncommon beauty and more than usual refreshing power." As examples he mentioned a steep moraine in Waverly, "set with a group of mighty oaks" as well as a site in Sherborn where the Charles River narrows and flows dramatically between high ledges crowned with hemlock.

To protect these places, Eliot urged the creation of a unique, not-for-profit organization. It was to be "an incorporated association" composed of citizen representatives "of all the Boston towns . . . empowered by the State to hold small and well distributed parcels of land free of taxes, just as the Public Library holds books and the Art Museum pictures for the use and enjoyment of the public."

On May 21, 1891, the legislature voted to establish the Trustees of Reservations (originally called the Trustees of Public Reservations) "for the purpose of acquiring, holding, maintaining and opening to the public . . . beautiful and historic places . . . within the Commonwealth [of Massachusetts]." A year later, the Trustees of Reservations successfully urged the legislature to establish a Metropolitan Park Commission (now the Metropolitan District Commission). As the first regional park agency in the United States, it gave Eliot what he wanted within a decade: an outstanding collection of public beaches and open space reservations, many of them, such as Blue Hills and Middlesex Fells, large enough to qualify as "country parks."

The Trustees of Reservations celebrated yet another first as its charter became the model for England's great National Trust, founded in 1895. Today, there are national trusts and land trusts throughout the world. In North America, citizen interest in the protection of open space has resulted in more than 1,000 land trusts in 45 states from New England to California. All owe their beginnings to the Trustees of Reservations.

More than a century after its birth, the organization is still hard at work in Massachusetts. It preserves more than 38,000 acres of extraordinary open space from Berkshire County to Cape Cod, from Cape Ann to the islands of Martha's Vineyard and Nantucket. Included are 94 properties totaling some 23,612 acres. These properties range from beaches, wetlands, woodlands, river corridors, and rolling pastures to historic houses and formal gardens. All are open to the public for a variety of activities and are visited by more than 1 million people annually. Another 14,885 acres are protected by 224 conservation restrictions, and another 96 properties totaling 14,730 acres are protected with its assistance. The Trustees of Reservations relies for support on membership dues, charitable contributions, admission fees, grants, and endowment income. With headquarters in Beverly and regional offices in Stockbridge, Leominster, Canton, Ipswich, and Vineyard Haven, the Trustees in 2003 had a household membership of more than 37,500.

Gordon Abbott, *Saving Special Places: A Centennial History of The Trustees of Reservations* (1993); Charles W. Eliot, *Charles Eliot, Landscape Architect* (1902); Albert Fein, *Frederick Law Olmsted and the American Environmental Tradition* (1972); Libby Ola Hopkins and Richard Cheek, *Land of the Commonwealth: A Portrait of the Conserved Landscapes of Massachusetts* (2000).

Michael Triff

"Up-Country" New England

Although many New Englanders would recognize a backcountry or up-country part of their region, defining "up-country" New England is somewhat difficult because this part of New England has typically been viewed through its relation to the more densely settled and urbanized coastal plain of southern New England. Whether celebrated as rustic and primeval or criticized as unsettled and backward, *up-country* takes its meaning from longstanding oppositions in New England, as in American culture more generally, between nature and society, wilderness and the city, savagery and civilization.

The large tracts of undivided forestland that distinguish the up-country from the rest of New England are largely a product of its settlement history. Whereas European colonists quickly displaced native peoples from the lower Connecticut River valley and the coastal plain around Boston, most of what is now Maine, New Hampshire, and Vermont remained under the control of the Abenakis and their Native American allies, who violently resisted the encroachments of colonial settlers. By the late 18th century, when the Abenakis had been displaced and northern New England was opened for settlement, prospective settlers from Connecticut and Massachusetts were already beginning to move westward onto the more fertile lands of the Midwest. As a result, large portions of northern New England, especially the thin-soiled uplands between the major river valleys, were never settled at all or were sold off in large lots to speculators who made their profits from logging rather than from developing the land. By the middle of the 19th century, many second- and third-generation settlers, especially in the uplands, were also moving westward, such that in 1860 there were nearly as many Vermont-born people living elsewhere than in the Green Mountain State itself. Those who stayed behind in up-country New England were disproportionately older and more white Anglo-Saxon Protestant than in the region at large; the majority of Catholic immigrants from Ireland and Quebec bypassed the area for the cities and mill towns of southern New England.

At the turn of the 20th century, with the advent of wood-pulping technology, the rapidly growing paper industry was drawn to the sparsely inhabited forests of the up-country. The International Paper Company, one of the first multinational corporations, led the way in buying out landowners and consolidating the control of the large paper companies over the waters and forests of the up-country. In a region with little public land, these large industrial owners still own more than 8.5 million acres of forestland in Maine, New Hampshire, and Vermont. Large paper mills were established in Berlin, N.H., Millinocket and Rumford, Maine, and other places where previously there had been little industry. This growth of paper production in up-country towns also marked the decline of tidewater towns such as Bangor, Maine, that had depended on spring floods to deliver logs from upriver forests to provide jobs in the local sawmills. The novelist Holman Day remembered the bitter struggle between the locals and out-of-state interests to control the forests, but the Great Northern Paper Company, like its competitors, won workers' loyalty with a tradition of corporate paternalism. Unionization brought higher wages to male mill workers, while their wives and daughters were trapped in single-industry towns with little opportunity for steady employment. Despite a century of economic change and the more recent development of tourism in the up-country, the local economies remain heavily dependent on pulp and paper.

Outside the mill towns, life was harder still, especially on the back roads and hardscrabble farms of this mostly rural region. Restructuring and specialization opened New England agriculture to competition from western markets for beef, fruit, and dairy products. Farmers throughout New England, but particularly in the hill country, found it difficult to compete in these new national markets. Although Americans continue to venerate the idea of the family farm, in reality, farms depend on a patchwork of government-assistance payments, subsistence production, market sales, and off-farm wage labor to survive. While up-country New Englanders remain proud of their independent thinking and determination in the face of an often harsh environment, they also suffer from having some of the most chronically poor counties in the nation, whether measured in terms of per capita income, unemployment rates, or infant mortality statistics.

Conditions of hardship have provided fertile soil for the new realism of contemporary writers such as E. Annie Proulx and Caroline Chute, who, in Faulknerian style, depict the quiet suffering of New England's forgotten rural poor. Their gritty portrayal of rural life runs counter to a considerable tradition of nostalgia and romanticism about the up-country. Transcendentalists such as Henry David Thoreau and the artists of the Hudson River School led the mid-19th century "rediscovery" of the primitive New England up-country. They sought spiritual redemption in the wild mountain peaks of Katahdin and the White Mountains. Turn-of-the-century outdoor enthusiasts looked more to the forests than to the mountains for a taste of the primitive. They came north in droves to visit a wilderness near at hand, where they might get away from it all and re-create the primitive pioneer virtues of the frontier settler, lost to a growing generation of white-collar managers trapped by desk jobs. Today, 70 million Americans live within a day's drive of these northern forests. For them, it still provides the nearest accessible wilderness experience, and they put an enormous recreational pressure on the up-country. Their interest in conserving the forest and in using government regulation to protect its recreational values has put them in conflict with local people and the powerful forest industry that for generations have looked to the forest for fiber, profits, and jobs. Debates over conservation, tourism, and forestry remain bitter and deeply divisive, in part because they play on long-standing tensions between up- and down-state interests, in-staters, and those from away.

The up-country's remaining pastoral landscape of fields and rolling hills has also been incorporated into a growing tourist trade that both connects and divides up-country folk and their neighbors in southern New England. Abandoned farms have become vacation homes for urbanites who wish to spend the summer in the nourishing countryside, but like the outdoors enthusiasts who looked to the woods as wilderness, they celebrate the up-country in romantic terms as an uncontaminated remnant of the way America used to be. The primitive conditions of the up-country are a boon to tourists who come to experience the simple life. To a large extent the "Americana" of the antiques industry represents the regional material culture of up-country New England. In part, this reflects the fact that New England was a hearth area for migration to the upper Midwest, but it also reflects the success of elite historic preservationists, such as the Boston-based Society for the Preservation of New England Antiquities (now Historic New England), in defining American identity in terms of the simple and sturdy New England "Yankee." Visitors to Maine are still welcomed by a sign on Interstate 95 announcing, "Maine. The Way Life Should Be."

This recent migration into the up-country by exurbanites from southern New England and across the country has made distinctions between natives and those from away harder to uphold. As interstate highways have brought more of the up-country into commuting distance from Boston and the high-tech industries, small rural towns are being transformed into suburban bedroom communities. This migration reverses more than a century of population decline in the up-country. Newcomers are attracted by a variety of factors: a traditional rural lifestyle, a slower pace, schools untroubled by urban and racial strife, wide-open spaces, lower housing prices, and so forth. Ironically, these exurbanites have brought with them many of ills that they sought to escape, specifically traffic, noise, and suburban sprawl. They also bring some different values to the up-country. Residential development has seen the posting of subdivided farm and woodland once open to the public for hunting and fishing. Zoning regulations and property tax rates have also pitted farmers and others dependent on traditional, extractive land uses against newcomers with different expectations about the landscape and the level of local services. Now, as in the past, these struggles turn on the shifting and contested identity of the up-country itself. Is it a pastoral retreat from the urban blight of the south? Is it a traditional, working landscape, producing commodities for a world market? Or does it represent something else entirely? The answers to these and other questions about its nature and history will determine the future of up-country New England.

Hal S. Barron, *Those Who Stayed Behind: Rural Society in 19th-Century New England* (1984); Dona Brown, *Inventing New England: Regional Tourism in the 19th Century* (1995); William Cronon, *Changes in the Land: Indians, Colonists, and the Ecology of New En-*

gland (1983); David Dobbs and Richard Ober, *The Northern Forest* (1995); Stephen C. Harper, Laura L. Falk, and Edward W. Rankin, *The Northern Forest Lands Study of New England and New York: A Report to the Congress of the United States on the Recent Changes in Landownership and Land Use in the Northern Forest of Maine, New Hampshire, New York, and Vermont* (1990); A. E. Luloff and Mark Nord, "The Forgotten of Northern New England," in *Forgotten Places: Uneven Development in Rural America,* ed. Thomas A. Lyson and William W. Falk (1993); Harold F. Wilson, *The Hill Country of New England: Its Social and Economic History* (1936).

David Demeritt

Vermont's Act 250

Vermont's beautiful and rugged landscape has played a crucial role in how Vermonters have defined themselves from the earliest period of settlement. Because of this, debates about how that landscape should be used and who should make those decisions have been among the most contentious in the state's history. Periodically, issues such as whether or not to build a skyline drive along the crest of the Green Mountains ("the Green Mountain Parkway") have forced Vermonters to come to terms with the complexities and contradictions inherent in managing the state's landscape.

Statewide land-use planning first came under serious consideration in the early 1960s during the administration of Democratic Governor Philip H. Hoff. By the late 1960s, Vermonters realized that their existing laws provided almost no way to regulate several massive residential projects proposed by developers. Responding to what was considered to be a crisis, Republican Governor Deane Davis sponsored legislation to address issues raised by large-scale development. Davis understood that Vermonters valued decision making at the local level, but his planners emphasized that large developments could have an effect at the regional and state levels. A highly respected jurist and businessman, Davis worked hard to balance these concerns and was able to win bipartisan support for his proposed legislation. The result was the passage of a statewide land-use control law universally referred to as Act 250, which became effective on April 4, 1970.

The original act included three major components. First, a "capability and development plan" was to be drawn up to identify and inventory Vermont's resources and land-use needs. Second, this capability and development plan was to be used to design a statewide "land use development plan" that would identify appropriate types of development for all areas in the state. Finally, Act 250 established a statewide permitting system to keep development or subdivision of land in conformance with the capability and development plan and

with the statewide land-use plan, as well as other criteria. The legislature passed a capability and development plan in 1973 but refused to adopt the extremely controversial land-use plan. In 1983 the legislature repealed the portion of the act requiring a land-use plan. As a result, Act 250 has become a case-by-case permitting system rather than a comprehensive land-use control law.

In order to obtain a permit under Act 250, a project must first be reviewed by one of nine regional district environmental commissions. Composed of local citizens appointed to two-year terms by the governor, these commissions reflect Governor Davis's original desire to keep decision making on land-use questions at the local level to the fullest extent possible. Commissions may grant permits, deny them, or grant them with various conditions. Environmental commission decisions may be appealed to a statewide environmental board made up of nine members appointed by the governor with the advice and consent of the state senate. The board's decisions may be appealed to the Vermont Supreme Court.

Act 250's permitting requirements apply only to certain types of development or subdivision: generally, construction for commercial or industrial purposes involving more than 10 acres of land; construction for commercial or industrial purposes on more than 1 acre of land in any municipality that has not adopted permanent zoning and subdivision laws; construction of housing projects of more than 10 units; construction for commercial or industrial purposes involving more than 10 acres that is to be used for municipal or state purposes; and commercial, industrial, or residential development above 2,500 feet. An Act 250 permit is also required for the subdivision of a tract or tracts of land for resale into 10 or more lots. The act exempts projects that involve construction for farming, logging, or forestry below an elevation of 2,500 feet. In reviewing an application for an Act 250 permit, the district environmental commission evaluates the project's expected contributions to water and air pollution and soil erosion and effect on water resources, transportation networks, schools, municipal or governmental services, scenic or natural beauty, and wildlife, among other concerns.

Act 250 has been controversial almost from its inception. Applications for large retail and housing developments outside Vermont's cities and ski-area expansion typically stir public debate on the law's efficacy. Act 250's detractors argue that it imposes delays and raises the cost of development, making Vermont less effective than neighboring states in attracting businesses, and that the review process usurps local control and gives outside

parties too much power. Proponents assert that without Act 250, Vermont's rural beauty and quality of life would be quickly eroded and believe that the costs of the act to developers and the public are outweighed by the negative effect overdevelopment would have on the state's tourist industry.

Cindy Corlett Argentine, *Vermont Act 250 Handbook: A Guide to State and Regional Landuse Regulation* (1993); John McClaughry, "The Land Use Planning Act: An Idea We Can Do Without," *Environmental Affairs* 3 (1974); Thomas R. McKeon, "State Regulation of Subdivisions: Defining the Boundary between State and Local Land Use Jurisdiction in Vermont, Maine, and Florida," *Boston College Environmental Affairs Law Review* 19 (1991); *Vermont's Act 250: A 25 Year Retrospective* [video recording] (Colchester, Vt., ETV, 1995).

Hal Goldman

Village Commons and Greens

The New England village or town common evolved from the colonial meetinghouse lot, the centrally located land reserved or designated for the ecclesiastical society. Here settlers located their meetinghouse, burying ground, and nooning sheds, used for warming or eating during breaks in services or for community gatherings. A tavern sometimes served as the sole public building on the site and the seat of government. Thus the meetinghouse lot was the social and political as well as the geographic center of the community. It was not, however, part of the colonial common land for cultivation or pasturage.

Commons as we know them today emerged only in the 19th century with the rise of center villages and disestablishment, which severed the official ties between church and town. Center villages formed during the early years of the American republic as protourban places focusing on agricultural trade and commerce. Disestablishment produced secular town commons from the portion of meetinghouse lots not retained by the congregation. Center village residents removed the remains of previllage nooning sheds, stables, and other relics of the colonial town center. They seeded commons—literally turning them into greens—built walls about burying grounds, and discarded rubble. True center village improvement and purposeful creation of village greens awaited the second half of the century, however. Meanwhile, center village dwellers also erected stately and stylish homes that dressed the main thoroughfares leading to and from the center village and thereby framed the new village common.

Congregations, of course, retained the remainder of the former meetinghouse lots and on these sites often removed boxlike colonial houses of worship, replacing them with classically proportioned churches. In the latter half of the 19th century businesses in many towns migrated downward from hilltop center villages, forming areas of concentrated industrial activity. In the most extreme cases—Cummington, Mass., is an example—this downhill slide left only the old burying ground and a small, open remnant of the former village common at an intersection of roads.

The U.S. Centennial in 1876 initiated a new phase of improvement for those villages and commons that had survived. Commemorative "centennial" trees and monuments honored New England's contribution to the Revolution and the Civil War, enhancing the national symbolism as well as the beauty of these historical spaces. Elms were especially popular because of their distinctive branching pattern and rapid growth. Victorian gazebos, bandstands, fountains, and sculptured flower beds, along with fences to keep traffic off plantings, enabled townspeople and villagers to use commons—or greens, as they were known in northern New England—for such community activities as carnivals, auctions, fairs, games, and patriotic celebrations.

As the U.S. population moved westward, so, too, did the village green or common. Wherever congregations of New Englanders established settlements during the 19th century—in upstate New York, the Western Reserve, or further west along the migration path often called the "Yankee runway"—like their forbears, they configured open public space in central places.

David D. Brodeur, "Evolution of the New England Town Common, 1630–1966," *Professional Geographer* 19 (1967); John D. Cushing, "Town Commons in New England, 1640–1840," *Old Time New England* 51 (1961); John B. Meyer, "The Village Green Ensemble in Northern Vermont," *Vermont Geographer* 2 (1975); Joseph S. Wood, *The New England Village* (1997).

Joseph S. Wood

Walden Pond and Woods

Walden Pond in Concord, Mass., was created during the Pleistocene epoch as glaciers retreated from present-day New England. The pond covers approximately 61 acres and reaches a maximum depth of 100 feet. Walden Woods, which extends from Concord to Lincoln, Mass., is a forest of about 2,680 acres made up mostly of second-growth white pines and mixed hardwoods. In 1845 Henry David Thoreau moved to a cabin next to Walden Pond in an attempt to practice the Transcendentalist philosophy introduced to him by his friend and mentor Ralph Waldo Emerson, whose landmark essay espousing that philosophy, "Nature," appeared in 1836. Thoreau's two-year experiment yielded *Walden; or, Life in the Woods,* published in 1854. Today, Walden

Thoreau's Cove, Walden Pond, and Walden Woods, Concord, Mass., ca. 1908

Pond attracts visitors inspired by Thoreau's life and writings; in tribute to him, many leave stones at the cabin site.

Historically, Native Americans hunted in Walden Woods, and during the 18th century freed slaves and white misfits built hamlets there. For years, the forest was viewed as wild and forbidding, and townsfolk dreaded traveling on Walden Road, the shadowy horse path linking Concord and Lincoln. Beginning in the 1820s, however, Emerson, Nathaniel Hawthorne, Bronson Alcott, the young Thoreau, and others among Concord's cultural elite often sauntered through Walden Woods, and sometimes to Walden Pond, for solitude, communion with nature, and inspiration for philosophical inquiry and literary endeavors.

During the time Thoreau lived at Walden Pond, construction of a section of the Boston-Fitchburg Railroad began. Workers cut a broad swath through the forest for the track and harvested additional trees for railroad ties, shanties, and firewood. Walden Woods would be further reduced over the next several decades by logging and wildfires.

In 1866 the railroad company expanded its project by building a park and picnic grounds, which became a popular destination for Bostonians during summer months. Although that facility burned down in 1902, swimmers and picnickers—sometimes as many as 2,000 a day—continued making trips to the pond; to accommodate them, a bathhouse and sandy beach were constructed in

1917. To prevent further commercialization and to commemorate Thoreau, by then internationally known for *Walden,* a coalition of local families, literary aficionados, and sympathetic state representatives proposed legislation that in 1922 officially designated 80 acres beside Walden Pond as a state reservation.

The growing use of automobiles over the next decade led to a huge increase in tourism in the area; by the mid-1930s, crowds numbering 25,000 were not uncommon on summer Sundays. Yet recreational overuse was only one form of environmental abuse that was to threaten the area during the 20th century. In 1938, for example, the town of Concord established a landfill near the pond. During the late 1950s the government of Middlesex County, Mass., which had been assigned the task of managing the state reservation at Walden Pond, began altering the shoreline to improve the swimming beach. Conservation groups and literary societies, however, soon brought legal action to halt the work. A 1960 ruling ordered the county to restore the reservation to its original condition. With that task still uncompleted in 1974, responsibility for the reservation was transferred to the Massachusetts Department of Environmental Management, which corrected some of the problems caused by previous mismanagement, including the heavy volume of daily visitors to Walden Pond.

Meanwhile, much of Walden Woods remained unprotected, a situation made glaringly apparent in the mid-1980s by the announcement that two developments, an office complex and a condominium suite, would be built in the area. In the process of alerting the American public to the problem through the media, conservationists and preservationists attracted the attention of musician Don Henley. In 1990 Henley founded a nonprofit organization, the Walden Woods Project, which by 1996 had raised $14 million, enabling the organization to purchase 96 acres of the historic forest and effectively block the two developments. The project also financially underwrote the costly Thoreau Institute, a research center in Lincoln. Critics were vocal in their insistence that those funds should have been spent securing additional parcels of Walden Woods for preservation, a move that would have better reflected the philosophical and ethical position of that institute's namesake.

Joseph L. Andrew, Jr., "The Struggle for Walden," *The Humanist* 57 (1997); Thomas Blanding, "Giving Walden to the World, 1921–22: Four Contemporary Reports," *Concord Saunterer* 17 (1984); Blanding, "Historic Walden Woods," *Concord Saunterer* 20 (1988); Steve Knopper, "The Battle for Walden Woods," *Rolling Stone* 732 (April 18, 1996).

Ted Olson

Waste Management Waste management refers to the collection and disposal of unwanted materials or by-products of human activity. Although wastes may be generated in urban or rural settings and may be in the form of liquids, solids, or gases, most collection and disposal has been designed to handle residential and commercial refuse (solids), as well as sewage and industrial runoff (liquids) in and around cities.

In colonial New England, individuals were responsible for disposing of their own wastes. As in Europe, garbage (such as kitchen and food scraps), dirt, and sewage were dumped in streets and common areas. The earliest sanitary ordinance came in 1634 when Boston officials prohibited garbage disposal near the Town Dock. As Boston's population increased, officials created the most comprehensive waste management measures in the American colonies. In 1652 they forbade animal entrails in streets and banned privies within 20 feet of homes or highways unless constructed with an underlying vault 6 feet deep. A year later, the town restricted the location and disposal practices of slaughterhouses, tanneries, and other so-called nuisance industries that generated foul odors and wastes.

Despite Boston's lead in sanitary affairs, its streets remained dirty and benefited more from heavy rains and roaming swine that fed off garbage than from any human cleaning effort. To augment individual responsibility, in 1662 Boston officials began hiring "scavengers" to remove dead animals and other offensive matter from roadways. In 1666 all forms of refuse from the streets were banned and citizens were directed to cast garbage off the drawbridge at Mill Creek. The latter requirement reflected a popular notion that marshes and other wetlands represented unproductive real estate desirable only for development with solid wastes. Rural New Englanders, too, used swamps, rivers, and ponds as waste disposal sites.

Urban sanitation improved in the 18th century with paved roads and better drainage; once again, Boston led the way by constructing cobblestone streets and wastewater gutters. Although it was customary for citizens to clean roadways in front of their homes, dirt often combined with litter to bury paved thoroughfares. Therefore, in 1725 Boston officials forced residents to perform their civic cleaning duty or face heavy fines. By 1750 Boston had the finest sewage system in the American colonies, thanks to property owners who constructed, at their own expense, roughly 500 sections of sewers and drains. Despite progress on land, though, sewers and drains commonly emptied into the nearest waterway and helped establish an historic pattern of harbor pollution.

The next major step in waste management occurred in 1799, after an outbreak of yellow fever, with the formation of the Boston Board of Health. Motivated by the belief that decomposing wastes caused contagious disease—popularly known as the filth or miasmic theory in the 19th century—the board ordered clean, popular dump sites such as Frog Pond at Boston Common and the Town Dock. Other Massachusetts communities followed suit and formed their own local health boards—Salem in 1799, Marblehead in 1802, Plymouth in 1810, Lynn in 1821, and Cambridge in 1828.

In 1850 Boston bookseller and statistician Lemuel Shattuck issued a landmark report to the Massachusetts legislature on the connection between poor waste management and disease. Although the state moved slowly on his 50 recommendations for sanitary improvement, the fear of epidemics did motivate many local communities to remove foul nuisances. During the late 1850s and 1860s, Boston's swampy Back Bay, which had deteriorated into an unsightly and pungent dump, was filled with solid wastes and leveled for real estate development. Rag pickers, who traveled city streets in search of salvageable materials, assisted gravel contractors and deposited rubbish (dry and nonputrescent waste products composed of wood, glass, metal, and paper) into the Back Bay.

In 1869 Shattuck's most visionary recommendation became a reality with the formation of the Massachusetts State Board of Health (MSBH), America's first comprehensive state health agency. Beginning in the 1870s, New Englanders also pioneered the science of sanitary engineering. The country's first sewage farm, which spread sewage on level land for absorption and purification by soil, was instituted near Augusta, Maine, in 1872. Between 1876 and 1885, Boston expanded its sewage system with 25 miles of new drains and several large holding tanks on Moon Island that discharged stored effluent with the tides.

Throughout the 1870s and 1880s, the MSBH investigated the connection between inadequate sewage treatment and poor water purity. The board became a major force behind an 1878 Massachusetts law prohibiting the discharge of pollutants within 20 miles of a public water supply. Unfortunately, political and economic interests altered the act to exempt numerous businesses and municipalities that already discharged wastes into waterways.

Significant advancements in sewage treatment also came about through the work of Ellen Swallow Richards, a Massachusetts Institute of Technology instructor who helped create the nation's first sanitary engineering curriculum, and the establishment in 1886 of the MSBH's Lawrence Experimental Station at Lowell. The Lawrence Station emerged during a period of intense concern over sewage and industrial pollution along the Merrimack River and the effects of such contamination on cities downstream, especially since epidemics from waterborne diseases such as typhoid and cholera could devastate entire communities. The Lawrence Station became one of the nation's leading research centers in water purification as it pioneered the process of intermittent filtration whereby sewage is laid on a bed of fine materials and then passed through filters and exposed to aerobic bacteria. At the local level, many New England communities such as Danbury and Meriden, Conn.; Marlboro and Brockton, Mass.; and Pawtucket and Woonsocket, R.I., adopted this method as their primary means of sewage treatment.

The 1880s and 1890s brought improvements in street cleaning, refuse collection, and waste disposal, all of which had advanced little since the colonial era. Smoother pavements, horse-drawn sweeping machines, and watering carts augmented hand sweeping, although urban population growth and the increased use of streets resulted in ephemeral cleanliness. Many municipalities hired private contractors to clean roadways, collect refuse, or dispose of waste, a practice that continues today.

Recycling of wastes became so profitable that many large New England cities required the collection of rubbish, household ashes from stoves and furnaces, and garbage in separate receptacles. Rag pickers or private contractors generally sorted through rubbish and then sold it to junk or scrap-metal dealers to be reprocessed into new commercial products. Municipalities and private developers used ashes in the construction of roads and buildings or as landfill. Farmers purchased the bulk of garbage as feed for swine, but in larger cities such as Boston, Providence, and Bridgeport, Conn., a process known as "reduction" boiled garbage down into industrial greases and fertilizer. A few seaside communities, most notably Newport, Boston, and Lynn, even dumped garbage and other refuse into the sea. Ocean dumping, however, failed to generate income and resulted in so much beach and harbor pollution that the U.S. Supreme Court banned the practice for household wastes in the 1930s.

Garbage reduction also ceased by the 1930s because of a flat recycling market and the trend in many cities to construct refuse incinerators. Most communities, though, continued to rely on hog farms or old-fashioned dumps well after World War II. The city of Worcester, Mass., operated its own profitable hog farm, and despite concerns over diseases such as trichinosis, such piggeries remained uniquely popular in New England. In fact, a 1965 survey of Rhode Island disposal methods revealed that 38 percent of all municipalities relied in part on swine feeding while just 13 percent used incineration. Remarkably, 92 percent of cities and towns depended on outdated and hazardous open-faced dumps that were nothing more than pits that harbored rats, flies, and continuous fires.

Federal clean air and solid waste acts in the 1970s and 1980s forced municipalities throughout New England to replace open dumps with sanitary landfills in which refuse is buried between alternate layers of dirt and gravel. Landfills, however, represent a major source of pollution because harmful materials can percolate into nearby water supplies. To prevent further contamination, stringent state and federal regulations resulted in the closure of many local landfills, beginning in the late 1980s, in favor of regional sanitary landfills, incinerators, or recycling facilities.

Regardless of whether waste disposal facilities are local or regional, New Englanders have historically used these sites as social gathering points. In many rural and suburban communities, refuse collection is often a function of individual initiative rather than a municipal or contractual service, with residents required to drive their household garbage, recyclable items, and yard wastes to disposal sites. As such, town dumps, lately known as waste transfer stations, often with "swap shops," have served as valuable meeting places for residents of rural communities to meet, exchange information, and often swap second-hand items. In fact, perhaps no practice better symbolizes the so-called Yankee tradition of thrift and frugality than "dump picking" or "dumpster diving," whereby one person's discarded trash is sorted through by another for items to be recycled, resold, or used at home.

Increased government regulation and infrastructure investment also resulted in substantial progress in sewage treatment and water quality. For example, in 1970, 69 percent of all municipal sewage systems in Vermont discharged raw wastes into waterways; currently all of these communities provide some form of treatment. In addition, the 1972 federal Marine Protection, Research, and Sanctuaries Act severely limited the use of coastal waters as disposal sites for toxic and radioactive wastes.

The 1988 presidential campaign brought the centuries-old pollution of Boston Harbor to the forefront of national debate. For years the Metropolitan District Commission and its successor, the Massachusetts Water Resources Authority (MWRA), dumped raw sewage sludge into the harbor despite legislation to the contrary. As part of a federal mandate to clean up the harbor, in 1991 the MWRA began to divert sludge to the Fore River treatment plant in Quincy, to be dried and sold as fertilizer. In July 1994, the MWRA opened the first phase of the new Deer Island treatment plant designed to process more than 1 billion gallons of sewage each day. By the end of 2000, the cleanup of the harbor was nearly 99 percent complete, with a price tag of almost $4 billion, making it one of the largest public works projects in New England history and the second most expensive behind the Central Artery/Ted Williams Tunnel Project, or the so-called "Big Dig."

New England achieved fame in the 1980s and 1990s for being on the forefront of recycling and incineration. In 1986 Rhode Island became the first state in the nation to mandate recycling, and by 1995 New England's 34 incinerators (located in every state except Rhode Island and Vermont) gave the region a 41 percent incineration rate—far above the national average of 10 percent. In 2000 the Central Landfill in Johnston, R.I., New England's largest sanitary landfill, accepted roughly 3,500 tons of municipal and commercial waste per day and exceeded 22 stories in height, inadvertently becoming one of the state's most unique tourist attractions. By 2003, only 39 percent of municipal solid wastes in New England were sent to landfills, the lowest regional rate in the country.

Scott Allen, Davis Butler, and Richard Sanchez, "Where It All Goes," *Boston Globe,* December 13, 1993; Ellis J. Armstrong, ed., *History of Public Works in the United States, 1776–1976* (1976); Carl Bridenbaugh, *Cities in the Wilderness: The First Century of Urban Life in America 1625–1742* (1960); John T. Cumbler, "Whatever Happened to Industrial Waste? Reform, Compromise, and Science in 19th-Century Southern New England," *Journal of Social History* 29 (1995); Heather Hepler, "Dredging up the Past: Cleaning Historical Boston Harbor," *American City & Country* (June 1994); Martin Melosi, *Garbage in the Cities: Refuse, Reform, and the Environment, 1880–1980* (1981); Melosi, *The Sanitary City: Urban Infrastructure in America from Colonial Times to the Present* (2000); Lemuel Shattuck, *Report of the Sanitary Commission of Massachusetts 1850* (1948 [1850]).

Steven H. Corey

Water Pollution The English began to use the word *pollution* to describe human contamination of the natural environment during the 1850s and 1860s. Massachusetts's public health officials were among the first Americans to adopt the usage. In the 1870s, Massachusetts became the first state to conduct official studies of river pollution; these studies inspired similar investigations around the nation. More than a century later New Englanders continue the fight against pollution despite their often complex, ambivalent relationship with the contaminants and irritants of modern life.

The region has historically struggled with the burden of polluted rivers, harbors, and coastlines. To New England's industrial pioneers, a river was a resource to be exploited for profit, whether as a source of power or a repository for manufacturing wastes. Water pollution grew as industry grew. By the mid-19th century, the region's fast-growing mills and factories were depositing tons of dye, acid, pickling liquor, sludge, and sawdust into nearby waters.

The explosive growth of urban populations also led to serious pollution problems. At first, city residents disposed of domestic wastes on land, in cesspools and privies. But after public health officials linked the disposal of wastes in increasingly crowded neighborhoods to outbreaks of cholera, cities began to build sewer systems. By the 1870s, dozens of New England cities were dumping their untreated waste into rivers and coastal waters.

New England's sport fishers sporadically complained about water pollution in the years after the Civil War, but the first powerful movement to control the problem was led by the patrician reformers of the Massachusetts

In 2003 Connecticut's Housatonic River, near Kent, presented an idyllic picture of pastoral New England, but anglers were warned not to eat the fish caught in its waters because of the heavy pollution

Board of Public Health. Inspired by British precedent, the board undertook the nation's first studies of river pollution in the mid-1870s. Although the state's rivers were not nearly as polluted as the principal rivers of England, the board pressed for antipollution legislation, and Massachusetts passed the nation's first water pollution law in 1878.

Unfortunately, the law had little effect. Because of perceived financial risks to the textile industry, the three major manufacturing rivers in the state—the Merrimack, the Connecticut, and the Concord—were exempted. The law also made no provision for enforcement. Moreover, a group of leading industrialists campaigned to wrest control of the health board away from the doctors who sought to purify the state's water, thereby negating what little control the state had over pollution. The doctors were reluctant to attack their social peers in high office, and they recognized the industry's importance to the state's economy—but the struggle was nevertheless hard-fought. According to historian John Cumbler, neither side was able to win a decisive victory; control of the board therefore seesawed back and forth throughout the 1880s.

For decades, doctors had assumed that filth and foul odors alone could cause disease, but by the late 1880s the germ theory of disease was gaining acceptance, and the board of health began to consider ways to kill germs in polluted water. In 1888 Massachusetts established the nation's first experimental water-treatment laboratory. The outbreak of typhoid epidemics in Lowell and Lawrence gave re-

searchers a chance to test the germ theory in practice. The water supplies for both cities came from river taps a few miles downstream from sewer outlets, so investigators concluded that residents were thus exposed to typhoid germs. They urged both cities to use new treatment methods to sanitize their water. The advice proved sound: in both cities, the death rate from typhoid fell dramatically. The board of health shifted its focus from reducing water pollution to improving water-treatment techniques. The triumph of this new paradigm reduced the tension between public health officials and industrialists.

Throughout New England, the response to pollution was similar. Public officials acted to ensure the quality of drinking water either by treating river supplies or by building pipelines to remote reservoirs. But no state acted vigorously to stop pollution. As a result, the pollution load on the region's waters increased decade by decade. By the 1950s, many of New England's rivers were all but dead; they were unsafe for swimming, and the fish had disappeared. Nashua residents sometimes bet on the daily color of the river: depending on the dyes dumped by paper factories, the water might be red, orange, blue, green, white, or black. The Connecticut River became known as "the most beautifully landscaped sewer in the country." In 1970 the Federal Water Quality Administration put two New England rivers—the Merrimack and the Androscoggin—on a list of the 10 most polluted rivers in the nation.

Municipalities were as culpable as industry. Between 1900 and 1939, the Massachusetts

legislature investigated pollution in Boston Harbor six times, repeatedly finding that conditions were "revolting to the aesthetic sensibilities and violate all public health requirements." The 1939 report recommended the construction of sewage treatment plants on three harbor islands, but the municipal water authority delayed to avoid the expense. The first treatment plant finally was built in 1952, and the second in 1968. Even after the passage of the federal Clean Water Act in 1972, local authorities stalled. In 1985, after years of interagency wrangling, a federal judge finally set a long-term schedule for a multibillion-dollar project to end pollution of the harbor. Although the Massachusetts Water Resources Authority missed its December 31, 1999, deadline, the cleanup, which included the establishment of a state-of-the-art waste treatment facility on Deer Island, has vastly improved harbor conditions. Similar plans have been executed to clean up Long Island Sound, Narragansett Bay, and Lake Champlain.

The region has had more success in cleaning polluted rivers. Indeed, environmentalists and journalists often cite three New England rivers as examples of what might be done to overcome decades of environmental damage. Today, the Merrimack is clean enough to drink, people can swim in the Nashua, and the Connecticut is attractive enough to be the source of a real estate boom. The Environmental Protection Agency has set an Earth Day 2005 deadline for its initiative to clean up the historic Charles River. But the path to reform has taken many twists and turns.

In Maine, for example, the first campaign to pass antipollution legislation began in 1941, but the state did not take strong action against polluters until the 1960s. At first, the call for cleaner rivers came from a group of business leaders eager to diversify the economic base of the state. If the state acted to control pollution, the group argued, the tourist and service sectors of the economy might grow rapidly. But the business leadership of the state responded with ambivalence or hostility because the economic argument could cut both ways—though cleaner rivers might attract new business, the costs of pollution control might devastate major industries already struggling to make do. Accordingly, the first efforts at reform came to nothing. By the mid-1950s, however, a significant number of individuals and civic groups had begun to protest pollution on aesthetic and environmental grounds, and their efforts led the legislature to adopt water-quality standards for the state's industrial rivers in the early 1960s. To overcome the objections of the paper industry, however, the state did not require manufacturers to meet the new standards until the 1970s.

The most successful efforts to clean up polluted rivers have required the involvement of local citizens, not just the passage of legislation. The campaign to revive the Nashua River ultimately brought together conservationists, business executives, union leaders, engineers, and government officials in both Massachusetts and New Hampshire. The goal was not simply to improve the quality of the water, but also to establish greenways and wildlife sanctuaries along the banks; the far-sightedness of the effort has won national acclaim. The cleanup even inspired a children's book: Lynne Cherry's *A River Ran Wild: An Environmental History* (1992).

To be sure, the Nashua River still has scars from a century of injuries—the bottom sediments remain contaminated with pollutants, for example—but the transformation of the past 30 years testifies to a number of historic changes in attitudes. Although not all of one mind, New Englanders are much less willing now to tolerate pollution of the region's waters and are more likely to value the beauty of their rivers as a community resource.

John J. Berger, "Mother Nashua," in *Restoring the Earth: How Americans Are Working to Renew Our Damaged Environment,* ed. John J. Berger (1979); Richard Conniff, "The Transformation of a River—From 'Sewer' to Suburbs in 20 Years," *Smithsonian* 21 (1990); John Cumbler, "Whatever Happened to Industrial Waste?: Reform, Compromise, and Science in 19th Century Southern New England," *Journal of Social History* 29 (1995); Eric Jay Dolin, "Boston Harbor's Murky Political Waters," *Environment* 34 (1992); Richard W. Judd, "The Coming of the Clean Waters Acts in Maine, 1941–1961," *Environmental History Review* 14 (1990); Barbara Gutmann Rosenkrantz, *Public Health and the State: Changing Views in Massachusetts, 1842–1936* (1972); Theodore Steinberg, *Nature Incorporated: Industrialization and the Waters of New England* (1991).

Adam W. Rome

Watersheds A watershed (also called a *drainage basin, river basin,* or *catchment*) is the region that contributes the water that passes through a given cross section of a stream. The boundary of a watershed is called a *divide,* and the area of a watershed is called the *drainage area* of the stream at (or above) the cross section. A watershed is a natural landscape unit because its geology, topography, and vegetation determine the amount, timing, and quality of water flowing to the stream network. In 1899 the New England geographer William Morris Davis, writing in *Geographical Journal,* noted that "ordinarily treated, the river is like the veins of a leaf; broadly viewed it is like the entire leaf," in other words, the watershed.

The sizes of the principal drainage basins of New England, defined as an area that exceeds 100 square miles and discharges to the sea, are given in the table. Many of New England's major watersheds cross state boundaries and, like most watersheds, constitute natural landscape units unto themselves, a fact that was largely ignored when political boundaries in the region were being delineated. The only state boundary that follows a divide is a short portion of the border between New Hampshire and Quebec; few town boundaries even approximate divides. Although this arbitrary designation of political units had little consequence in the early history of the region, it has

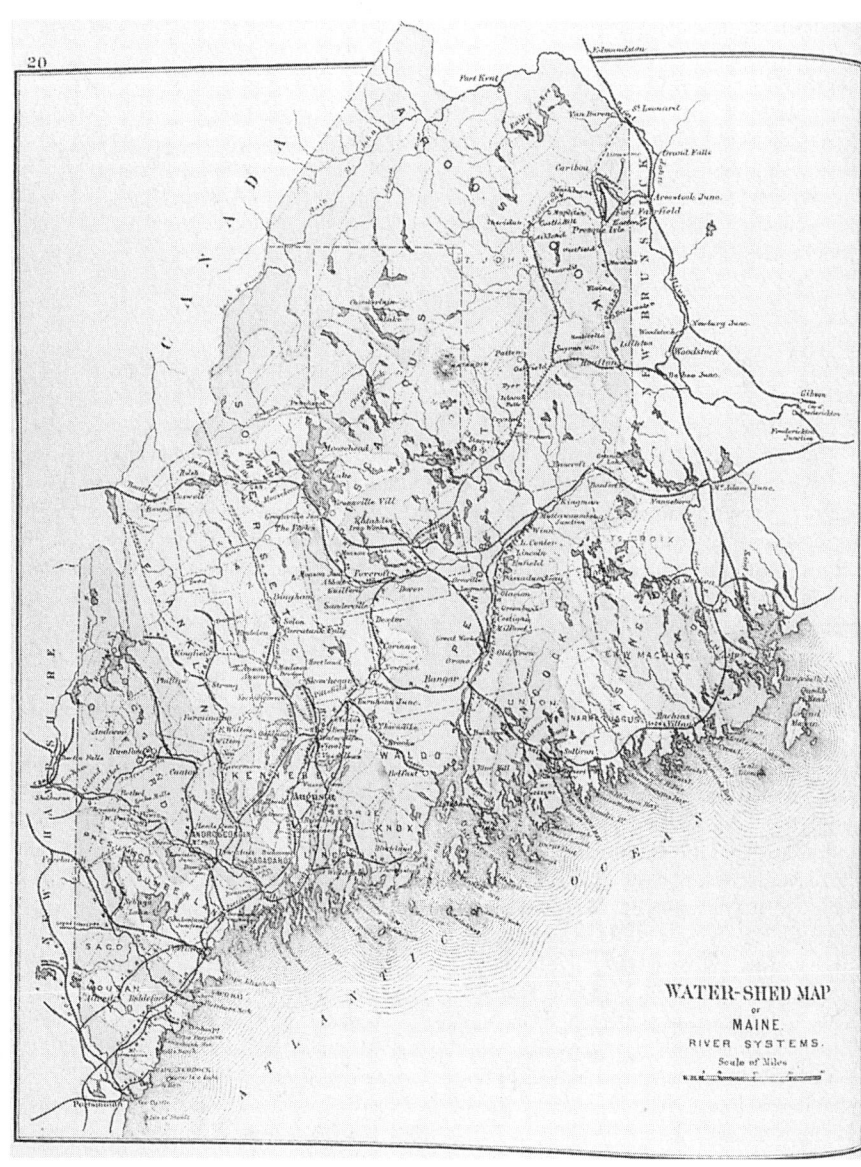

"Water-Shed Map of Maine River Systems," Stuart's Atlas of the State of Maine *(1901)*

Areas of Principal New England Watersheds (in Square Miles)

Watershed	Connecticut	Maine	Massachusetts	New Hampshire	Rhode Island	Vermont	Outside Region	Total
Lake Champlain						4,640	3,594	8,234
Saint François						255		
Saint John		7,360					14,000	21,360
Saint Croix		1,010					625	1,635
Machias		692						692
Narraguagus		227						227
Union		545						545
Penobscot		8,570						8,570
Sheepscot		192						192
Kennebec		5,910						5,910
Androscoggin		2,730		720				3,450
Presumpscot		920						920
Saco		827		870				1,697
Piscataqua		246		776				1,022
Merrimack			1,200	3,800				5,010
Ipswich			140					140
Charles			311					311
Neponset			117					117
Taunton			562					562
Blackstone			382		158			540
Pawtuxet	230							230
Pawcatuck	57				246			303
Thames	1,162		251		61			1,474
Connecticut	1,436		2,726	3,046		3,928	114	11,250
Quinnipiac	166							166
Housatonic	1,232		500				218	1,950
Hudson	36		190			450	12,690	13,366

Note: Watersheds are listed from north to south, by location of mouth of river

Source: U.S. Army Corps of Engineers, New England Division, *Water Resources Development* (NEDEP-360-1-31 through 37) (1995)

created significant land-use and water-resource management problems as the population has grown. In particular, differing land-use regulations by adjacent towns can hamper effective watershed management, especially control of pollution that originates outside a defined area.

Although the boundaries of states and towns, which have legal authority to regulate water resources and land use, do not follow watershed boundaries, all water-resource and land-use planning agencies recognize that effective management of water requires a joint perspective. Courts in Connecticut, Rhode Island, Massachusetts, and Maine have generally ruled that diversions of water outside of a watershed are violations of the common-law principle of "reasonable use" of water by riparian landowners; in New Hampshire and Vermont, however, law permits such diversion if the use is otherwise reasonable. State legislatures have often authorized specific diversions, usually in response to public demand for more water. Recently, Connecticut and Massachusetts passed laws that regulate such diversions, and Massachusetts has designated 27 river basins for water-resource planning.

From time to time, public and private institutions have been organized to focus on water- and land-management issues specifically related to watersheds. In 1953, the Vermont, New Hampshire, Massachusetts, and Connecticut legislatures entered into the Connecticut River Flood Control Compact, which cleared the way for the construction of flood-control dams by providing a mechanism whereby the lower-basin states, where most of the benefits of flood-damage reduction are concentrated, could compensate Vermont and New Hampshire towns for property taxes forgone on the land behind the dams. The Merrimack River Valley Flood Control Commission, involving New Hampshire and Massachusetts, was formed for the same purpose in 1957.

A major step toward including consideration of watersheds in water-resource and related land-resource management issues was undertaken in the region in 1967, when all six states agreed to establish the New England River Basins Commission under the provisions of the federal Water Resources Act of 1965. The commission was made up of representatives from each state and from the major federal water-resource agencies, including the Army Corps of Engineers, the Soil Conservation Service, and the Fish and Wildlife Service. Among the commission's major projects was a comprehensive review of flood problems in the Connecticut River basin, prompted by citizens' concern about the environmental and economic costs of a proposal to construct seven dams in the upper part of the watershed to reduce flood damage in the areas of Springfield, Mass., and Hartford. The study concluded that nonstructural approaches such as floodplain zoning, flood warning, and flood insurance were the most cost-effective measures to reduce damage, and the dams were not built. The commission also examined other contemporary problems, such as those involving regional water supplies (particularly finding alternative solutions to impending shortages in eastern Massachusetts) and water conservation, and prepared a comprehensive overview of water- and land-use issues for many of the region's major basins. President Ronald Reagan's administration opposed the regional watershed perspectives, however, and Congress terminated the commission in 1981.

In many parts of the region private organizations have been formed to promote environmental activities centering on watersheds. The Charles River (Massachusetts) Watershed Council successfully lobbied the Corps of Engineers to preserve the flood-storage capacity of riparian wetlands through the purchase of land rather than through the construction of flood-control structures. The Nashua River (Massachusetts and New Hampshire) Watershed Council has promoted water-quality improvement. The Merrimack River Watershed Council, along with the private New England Interstate Water Pollution Control Commission, has worked closely with state and federal agencies on water quality, habitat, recreation, and water-use issues.

Watersheds are natural systems and as such can be carefully monitored. Two New England research programs have achieved world renown for their contributions to the understanding of hydrologic processes and ecosystem functions. The Hubbard Brook Experimental Forest (HBEF), in West Thornton, N.H., was established in 1955 by the U.S. Forest Service to study the effects of forest practices on stream flows. During the early 1960s, pioneering ecologists and earth scientists from Dartmouth, Yale, Cornell, and the U.S. Forest Service expanded the scope of research at HBEF by establishing the Hubbard Brook Ecosystem Study. Researchers at HBEF have maintained the longest continuous record of precipitation chemistry in North America and were the first to document the phenomenon of acid rain. Studies based on HBEF research have helped establish the interdisciplinary science of biogeochemistry and have guided forest-management practices in the Northeast. The Hubbard forest is now designated as a U.S. Long-Term Ecological Research site and as a Biosphere Reserve under the Man and the Biosphere Program of the United Nations.

The Sleepers River Research Watershed (SRRW), in Danville, Vt., was established in 1957 by the U.S. Agricultural Research Service. Beginning in 1966, SRRW was the site of a cooperative study by the U.S. Agricultural Research Service and the U.S. National Weather Service that significantly improved the understanding of snowmelt and the flooding it may cause. Another study, also begun in the 1960s, by researchers from Johns Hopkins and Cornell universities, has led to major advances in understanding how rain and snowmelt travel to streams in humid regions. Such studies are continuing under the auspices of the U.S. Geological Survey, the U.S. Army Cold Regions Research and Engineering Laboratory, and the University of Vermont.

William Morris Davis, "The Geographical Cycle," *Geographical Journal* 14 (1899); Gene E. Likens and F. Herbert Bormann, *Biogeochemistry of a Forested Ecosystem*, 2d ed. (1995); Theodore Steinberg, *Nature Incorporated: Industrialization and the Waters of New England* (1991); U.S. Army Corps of Engineers New England Division, *Water Resources Development* (NEDEP-360-1-31 through -37) (1995); U.S. Geological Survey, *Water-Supply Paper 2300* (1986).

S. Lawrence Dingman

Water Supply New England is one of the most water-rich regions of the United States, and the availability of freshwater has been central to its environment, culture, and economic development. Despite this relative abundance, significant conflicts over the resource have occurred almost since the beginning of European settlement and are intensifying as populations grow and industrial development continues.

The source of all water is precipitation delivered by the global hydrologic cycle. New England has an annual average precipitation of 45 inches, most of which soaks into the ground; of this, 20 inches per year is extracted by the region's extensive forests and returned to the atmosphere through evapotranspiration. Almost all of the remaining 25 inches eventually enters the river network; a small fraction flows directly to the sea as groundwater.

The water available for human use varies according to space, based on differences in geology and climate, and time, depending on weather and water storage, withdrawal, and diversion by humans. Degradation of quality, usually caused by human activities, also affects water availability. In New England, significant groundwater sources (known as *aquifers*) are found principally in sand and gravel deposits in the larger river valleys; well yields of 100 to more than 500 gallons per minute are commonly achieved from such aquifers. In a few places, large groundwater supplies can be obtained from zones of intense fracturing in otherwise dense, impervious bedrock. Because the locations of the best aquifers are also usually the most attractive areas for development, groundwater supplies are often threatened by contamination from hazardous wastes, septic systems, leaking underground storage tanks, and road salt.

Although average annual stream flow is very high by world standards, the seasonal variability of flows imposes major restrictions on water supplies. Typically, average monthly stream flows during the low-flow season (August or September) are one-tenth to one-twentieth of those during the high-flow season (March or April). Reliable surface-water supplies therefore require the construction of reservoirs; the region has more than 200 dams that store more than 30 million gallons of water, and the flows of most of the larger rivers are regulated.

In the past 100 years, New England has experienced nine severe droughts: those of 1880–85, 1905–20, 1929–36, 1939–45, 1947–51, 1955–59, 1960–69, 1979–83, and 1984–88. The drought of the 1960s was the most widespread and severe. Local water shortages requiring restrictions on nonessential water use are common summer occurrences. Humans may use water that flows naturally through the stream network (known as *in-stream use*) for hydropower generation, transport, fish and wildlife habitat, recreation, navigation, and the treatment of wastewater; or they may extract water from groundwater or surface-water sources (*withdrawal use*) for domestic or industrial supplies, manufacturing, agriculture, and the cooling of fossil-fuel and nuclear power plants. A portion of the water withdrawn evaporates, is transpired by crops, or is incorporated in manufactured products (*consumptive use*); the remainder is discharged back to the hydrologic system (*return flow*).

The first extensive use of rivers for transport involved getting logs to sawmills. Initially, felled trees were piled on frozen rivers and carried downstream by the high flows of spring breakup. During the early 1800s in Maine, small dams were built to regulate flows so that the season for log runs could be extended. During the mid-1800s, as the demand for timber grew, larger dams were built on the Kennebec, Androscoggin, and other rivers, thus ending the runs of migrating salmon. A violent conflict over water, known as the Telos War, erupted in Maine during the 1840s, when loggers from the Penobscot area diverted flow from a portion of the Saint John River basin into the Penobscot River basin; in response, loggers from the Saint John basin tried, unsuccessfully, to destroy the diversion dam. River drives of pulp logs continued well into the 20th century in northern New Hampshire and Maine but ended in the 1960s because of the effect of the practice on water quality. Water-borne transportation played a significant role in the region's commerce beginning about 1800, and canals were constructed on many of the larger rivers. However, the growth of railroads made the canal systems obsolete by about 1850.

European settlers quickly exploited the waterpower of smaller streams by building mills, most of which were located at natural falls or rapids and required the construction of low dams for water diversion and storage. During the 17th and 18th centuries, the mill was the center of village social life. An 1816 map of New Hampshire shows nearly every stream lined with small sawmills, gristmills, woolen mills, and a few larger cotton mills. By the mid-1800s, Connecticut had 203 mill towns. The supply of water to these mills was so important that most New England states passed laws (known as the Mill Acts) giving mill owners the right to flood the lands of upstream landowners without penalty.

In the last half of the 19th century, water powered the Industrial Revolution in New England. More than half the energy that industry used in 1900 was mechanical waterpower. In 1891 a hydroelectric power plant was built at Farmington, Conn., and became a research center for the industry. Currently, 178 billion gallons per day of stream flow are used to generate 8.6 billion kilowatt-hours of electricity within New England.

Beginning in the 1970s, conflicts between the regulation of stream flow for hydroelectric power and the maintenance of in-stream flows for fish and wildlife habitat and recreation have emerged as a central water-resource issue in the region. The federal government has the right to require minimum stream flows downstream of hydroelectric dams, and the six states have varying degrees of legal authority to assure adequate flows to protect habitats and water quality.

The first community water supplies were shallow wells or springs at central locations, though these were subject to contamination from human waste. Epidemics from waterborne diseases, along with the need for fire control, provided the incentive for the creation of larger systems capable of providing purer water. The first so-called fountain society, which sold clean water distributed through wooden pipes, was chartered in Providence in 1772. By 1796 Boston's water supply was dispersed through some 40 miles of wooden pipe from its source several miles to the south. Other municipal supplies were established in Nashua, N.H., in 1852; Burlington, Vt., in 1867; Providence in 1871; and Manchester, N.H., in 1874. Today, about 75 percent of domestic and commercial water use is publicly supplied, mostly from surface-water sources.

The development of Boston's public water supply has significantly affected the politics and economics of both the city and the state of Massachusetts and suggests the direction of future water-supply policies for the region. Early on, Boston adopted the policy of assuring a pure water supply by using distant upland sources, and by 1848 the city was being supplied via an 11-mile-long aqueduct from a reservoir west of Boston. Within 25 years the city's growth required new supplies, and reservoirs further west of the city were added to the system. By 1890 those supplies had also become inadequate, and although effective water-treatment methods were becoming available, people still did not want to drink anything but pristine, untreated water. The

only acceptable potential new sources were even farther away: Lake Winnipesaukee, in central New Hampshire, and the Merrimack and Nashua Rivers, which flow through Massachusetts and New Hampshire. In 1895 the latter choice was selected, in part because it opened the possibility of future expansion farther west, which, according to an 1893 report by the Massachusetts State Board of Health, would "forever settle the water policy of the [Metropolitan] District." Construction of the Wachusett Reservoir, 40 miles away, required the flooding of parts of four towns. Still, Boston continued to grow. In 1927 the legislature voted to construct the Quabbin Reservoir, impounding the Swift River, 85 miles west of Boston; completed in 1939, it required the obliteration of four rural towns. This reservoir, which holds some 400 billion gallons and forms a lake 18 miles long and 4 miles wide, is said to be the largest water-supply reservoir in the world. But the population served by the Boston system continued to expand, and by 1970 usage exceeded the safe yield. Once again, studies identified potential new sources, including the Merrimack River, groundwater, and the Connecticut River, which runs through the western section of Massachusetts. The most economical solution appeared to be the latter, involving use of the pumped-storage hydroelectric plant in Northfield, Mass., and an aqueduct from atop Northfield Mountain to the Quabbin.

Environmentally concerned citizens in western Massachusetts had seen enough of Boston's water imperialism, however, and pointed out the danger of the degradation of Quabbin's water quality and the inefficient use of water by Bostonians. Ultimately, the conservationists prevailed, and the Massachusetts Water Resources Authority, with the guidance of an official citizen advisory committee, implemented conservation measures that have at least temporarily prevented the need for new supplies.

Despite the relative abundance of water in New England, the limits of the resource are increasingly apparent. Options for development of future surface-water sources are limited owing to the difficulty of obtaining and protecting the large watershed and reservoir areas required and the costs of mandated treatment. Possibilities for groundwater development are restricted by the limited extent of productive aquifers and by the growing threats of contamination from septic systems and hazardous wastes. The availability of future water supplies is a particular concern in southwestern Connecticut, southeastern and central Massachusetts, Cape Cod and the islands, southeastern New Hampshire, and

northern and central Rhode Island. In-stream-flow resources are increasingly at issue as demands for withdrawal for industry (including snowmaking at ski areas) and regulation for power generation conflict with concerns about conserving the region's distinctive habitats and recreational opportunities. Conservation, higher water prices, and the use of treated wastewaters will play increasing roles in assuring water supplies for future generations.

Donald W. Howe, *Quabbin: The Lost Valley* (1951); Fern L. Nesson, *Great Waters: A History of Boston's Water Supply* (1983); U.S. Geological Survey, *Circular 1081* (1993), *1200* (1998); U.S. Geological Survey, *Water-Supply Papers 2300* (1986), *2350* (1990), *2375* (1991).

S. Lawrence Dingman

Waterways Waterways, passages on water that people use as routes of transit, traverse New England and connect the region with the rest of the world. These passages—on rivers and canals; lakes, brooks, and creeks; and along coasts and across oceans—have provided a means of transportation and communication for as long as humans have inhabited the region.

Waterways were a characteristic of the landscape that framed the economic development of New England. A highly mobile indigenous population used many of the routes while traveling from dispersed interior winter hunting camps to seaside summer gathering and planting sites. With the settling of Europeans during the 17th and 18th centuries, waterways became the first and best routes inland as well as paths to encounters with Native Americans. William Pynchon built his fur-trading post in 1636 at Springfield, Mass., on the banks of the Connecticut River, a waterway extending from northern New Hampshire southward the full length of New England and emptying into Long Island Sound. To the northwest Lake Champlain, a route of both threat and promise, invasion and trade, became the focus of European-American contention for a century.

New England's economy, dependent on the commodification of its natural resources for success, relied on waterways for transport. Timber, bulky to move and as important to trade as it was to building and heating, could be transported best on rivers. According to Henry David Thoreau's *The Maine Woods* (1864), by 1837, on the Penobscot River alone, logs for 200 million board feet of lumber were floating to mills for cutting and shipping. Fishing, however, was the leading commercial enterprise for New Englanders. Ranging for a thousand miles toward the northeast, hundreds of small schooners plied the waters from

Georges Bank off Massachusetts to the inshore fishing grounds of the Gulf of Saint Lawrence. Larger schooners fished the Grand Banks to the southeast of Newfoundland. Salted cod was marketed to Catholic Europe and to the slave economies of the Caribbean.

New England's staples—fur, fish, and lumber—were processed at locations that bordered on waterways. New England established its industrial base through the cycle of sawing timber into lumber that was used to build ships and then using ships to catch fish or transport staples to market. Artisans constructed wooden vessels in the estuaries along the coast, first on Massachusetts Bay and later on the Gulf of Maine as supplies of timber were depleted.

In the 18th and 19th centuries, waterpower drove the mills and factories that clustered on the banks at fall lines on the Blackstone, Merrimack, and Connecticut Rivers as well as myriad lesser streams. Fabricated metal instruments—tools and weapons—were needed by Americans moving west. Cotton from the South was woven into textiles, and leather from Latin America was cobbled into shoes. The falling water that powered the factories also restricted passage, indicating a place to settle on the boundary between the agrarian and the maritime, the rural and the urban. Canals, though often commercial failures, circumvented the falls and linked the interior and the coast, connecting all New Englanders. Bordering a waterway meant access to the rest of the world. Waterborne traffic brought trade and capital for local investment, immigrants seeking a new life, and information on the arts, politics, and technology. Until the advent of the railroad in the 1840s and commercial telegraphy in the 1850s, inaccessibility to waterways meant economic backwardness and cultural isolation.

Only in the 20th century did the role of waterways in the development of New England decline. Manufacturing fled south for cheaper labor, bitter longshore struggles deflected the flow of shipping, and overexploitation brought the fishing industry to a near standstill. Waterways remain central to the region, however, having been repositioned as major icons of heritage, tourism, and recreation. No longer a means of survival in economically sparse surroundings, waterways have now come to symbolize a culturally quaint environment. Places such as Connecticut's Mystic Seaport; the Maine Maritime Museum in Bath; the textile mills of Lowell, Mass.; and Slater Mill in Pawtucket, R.I., all waterside centers of industry during the 19th century, are now sites of preservation and learning that may provide visitors a respite from today's

defining economic activities, provoking thoughts of how waterways contributed to the economic activities of the past.

William Cronon, *Changes in the Land: Indians, Colonists, and the Ecology of New England* (1983); Ronald E. Shaw, *Canals for a Nation: The Canal Era in the United States, 1790–1860* (1990); Theodore Steinberg, *Nature Incorporated: Industrialization and the Waters of New England* (1991); Daniel Vickers, *Farmers and Fishermen: Two Centuries of Work in Essex County, Massachusetts, 1630–1850* (1994).

Bradford Hunter

White Mountains

A century ago, steam-driven trains rumbled through northern New England's secluded mountain valleys, carrying logs to the region's mills or rivers. Today, evidence of this activity can barely be seen in the dense underbrush and rejuvenated forests of the scenic White Mountain region. Indeed, a hiker on the trail into the lush Zealand Valley or along the banks of the East Branch of the Pemigewasset River explores the White Mountains with the aid of flat railroad beds that once were heavy with engines heading into timber country, or hikes along ancient logging roads now turned into footpaths.

The White Mountain region of north and central New Hampshire is composed of some 1,700 square miles. It includes the Presidential Range of 86 peaks over 2,000 feet, centered on Mount Washington (which, at 6,288 feet, is the highest peak in the Northeast), and the Franconia Range. Forty-eight of the White Mountains are higher than 4,000 feet. The spectacular Franconia Notch separates the two ranges, and Crawford Notch is a similarly

dramatic pass through the Presidential Range. Granite is the primary geological feature of the mountains, which were shaped by glaciation. The environment consists of many forest zones, which are well irrigated because of the region's proximity to the coast and its maritime weather patterns. The area features boreal spruce-fir and deciduous forests, with zones changing according to elevation. At high elevations, many peaks have krummholz, or the kind of stunted forest that is characteristic of such elevations, and Mount Washington and other peaks in the Presidential Range have extensive alpine meadows with many species of alpine flora. The weather on the peaks is known for its extremes, particularly Mount Washington, which boasts the "world's worst weather"; the weather station atop Mount Washington recorded a wind of 231 miles per hour on April 12, 1934.

The White Mountain region was well known to Native Americans who guided the first European explorer, Darby Field, to Mount Washington in 1642. The Europeans could see the mountains from the sea, but apart from occasional accounts by explorers and captives who traversed them with Native Americans during colonial wars, the region was largely unmapped and unknown until the late 18th century. By the 1820s, increasing trade with Canada through Crawford Notch, increasing demand for timber, and scientific curiosity had opened the region. A landslide in 1826 that killed the Willey family in Crawford Notch brought national attention to the region, and romantic writers and painters, including Nathaniel Hawthorne and Thomas Cole, visited the site. Ethan Allen Crawford,

Pemigewasset Wilderness, White Mountains, N.H., 1980

who ran an inn in the Notch and guided parties up Mount Washington, hosted the first of what would become a flood of tourists. Guidebooks by Thomas Starr King and others attracted visitors to famous sites, including the Flume and the Old Man of the Mountain, and grand resort hotels accommodated them. Artists of the White Mountain School popularized scenic views of the "Switzerland of America." Development of the tourism industry during the antebellum era was made possible by railroads built to exploit forest resources. This dual use of the White Mountains continues to characterize the area today.

From the summit of 4,680-foot Mount Carrigain, once dubbed the "Watchtower of the Wilderness," one may scan the surrounding country and see not only 45 of the White Mountain region's 48 highest peaks, but also the valleys and hillsides that for many years were littered with the slash and debris of the forest worker. Few ventured into many of these regions 60 or 70 years ago, undoubtedly influenced by graphic descriptions of the destruction wrought by the logger's ax and also subsequent forest fires. But the White Mountains have attracted visitors and vacationers for 150 years and more, and did so even during the years that mountain valleys and slopes were being devastated by lumber barons such as James Everill Henry and George Van Dyke. Indeed, it was their effect on the mountains that spurred New Englanders, both in northern New Hampshire and in other states, to seek permanent federal protection of the land that is now part of our National Forest system.

The Weeks Act of 1911, named for Massachusetts Congressman John Weeks, a New Hampshire native, established the first national forest preserve in the East. Modeled in part after the Adirondacks state preserve, the act was fostered by the Society for the Protection of New Hampshire Forests. The society had responded to deforestation that threatened the famed Old Man of the Mountain, urging schoolchildren to donate pennies to purchase land for preservation. The society and other organizations, such as the Appalachian Mountain Club and the New Hampshire Audubon Society, have formed partnerships with state and national government officials to add lands to the national forest and to state forests when sales of vast tracts of timber company land have threatened the region. New Hampshire has taken a distinctive approach by preserving a working forest while setting aside some lands for wilderness designation and opening others to recreational use.

White Mountain National Forest, covering some 800,000 acres, including 112,000 acres of congressionally designated wilderness area, stretches across the middle part of New Hampshire and extends a short distance eastward into Maine. It is home today to abundant wildlife (including moose, deer, black bear, and the endangered peregrine falcon), a mixed variety of hardwood and softwood trees, and even rare alpine plants. Humans also have a place in the area, with cross-country and downhill ski areas and hiking trails—more than 1,000 of them—throughout the mountains. The modern-day lumber worker has a place in the region, too, although not as such a dominant force as a century ago, as tourism has replaced the wood products industry as the lifeblood of the White Mountains.

For the approximately 6 million people who visit the White Mountains every year—be it to breathe the fresh mountain air; ride the old cog railway, more than 100 years old, to the summit of Mount Washington; marvel at the annual show of fall colors; or climb to the top of Mount Carrigain—the region's past is mostly hidden among the abundant white birches, sugar maples, and coniferous trees at both the higher and lower elevations. In these maturing woodlands, rusting crosscut saws, railroad spikes, and abandoned cast iron camp stoves rest where they were set down three and four generations ago, an aging symbol of what once was. The legacy of logging's threat to the White Mountains is an awareness of the complex ecosystem of the region. In recent years, local residents, politicians, scholars, and leaders of environmental and recreational organizations have debated the best ways to conserve this environment, attentive to the important interconnection of human communities and the White Mountain environment.

Appalachian Mountain Club, *AMC White Mountain Guide: A Guide to Trails in the Mountains of New Hampshire and Adjacent Parts of Maine* (1992); C. Francis Belcher, *Logging Railroads of the White Mountains* (1980); David Dobbs and Richard Ober, *The Northern Forest* (1995); Laura Waterman and Guy Waterman, *Forest and Crag: A History of Hiking, Trail Blazing, and Adventure in the Northeast Mountains* (1989).

Mike Dickerman

Wildlife New England has a diverse wildlife fauna, with approximately 340 regularly occurring inland species and many other coastal ones. New England's geography, topography, physiography, and land-use history all influence the region's fauna. For example, northern species, including mink frog, northern bog lemming, and moose, reach their southern distribution limits in New England; others meet their northern limits here, including five-lined skink, timber rattlesnake, and least shrew. Their distributions reflect New England's latitudinal and elevational gradients, which together provide an extremely wide array of habitats, ranging from northern boreal forests to temperate coastal forests, and from alpine tundra on the highest peaks to tidal marshes.

Recorded observations of New England's wildlife date from the earliest European settlement. William Wood (1634) provided the first comprehensive record of New England's natural resources at the beginning of European settlement and focused on edible, useful, or pest species, especially those that might depredate livestock. Birds are similarly addressed, but amphibians and reptiles, except for rattlesnakes, are scarcely noted. In all, Wood includes more than 50 recognizable species—20 mammals and more than 30 birds. Some species are curiously missing, including woodchucks, bats, and rodents such as white-footed mice, which surely would have infested stored grain or barns. Similarly, it is difficult to imagine such an observer not noticing robins, house wrens, or blue jays, but these species may not have adapted to human habitation or were uncommon in earliest settlement times. Wood's omissions, of course, do not mean that these species were not present; writers of the period typically noted only those species that were dangerous, useful, or peculiar.

It wasn't until Alexander Wilson and John James Audubon in the 19th century that substantial increases in the knowledge of New England's fauna occurred. Not until the late 19th and early 20th centuries was New England's birdlife adequately described by the economic ornithologists, notably Edward Howe Forbush. The first complete account of New England's mammals was compiled in 1977, and of amphibians and reptiles in 1983. For a region so long settled, the natural histories and current distributions of its fauna are only recently fairly well known, and the distributions of most amphibians are still rather poorly known.

Now mostly forested, the New England landscape has undergone dramatic changes over the past 350 years. Before European settlement, substantial parts of southern New England were quite open because of native prairies, Native American agricultural clearing, and periodic hurricanes. Throughout the region, abundant beaver meadows and periodic natural fire on dry sites imparted a shifting mosaic of open habitats to the forested landscape. The heath hen, an extinct subspecies of the greater prairie chicken, occupied scattered grasslands, native prairies, and blueberry barrens from Virginia north to Massachusetts and possibly to southernmost Maine and on the larger offshore islands.

With settlement, forests were cleared for agriculture, slowly until the 1750s and then more rapidly until, between 1800 and 1860, 75 percent of the arable land in southern and central New England was in pasture and farm crops. A century later, New England was again mostly forested—the result of an era of land abandonment that began soon after the opening of the Erie Canal in 1825 and the growth of New England industrial cities.

Most of the faunal changes in the past 350 years were due to the vast scale and intensity of habitat change that swept New England during settlement and subsequent land abandonment and reforestation. Extirpations of large predators, fur bearers, and game are well documented as the landscape was settled. White-tailed deer were reduced to very low levels soon after settlement; by 1646 hunting of deer was prohibited in Rhode Island, and in 1694 harvest seasons were set in Massachusetts and in 1698 in Connecticut. Wolves were gone from New England by about 1850. The last reported mountain lion was killed in Maine in 1891. Beaver were gone from southern New England soon after settlement; 8,992 beaver pelts were shipped from the Connecticut River drainage between 1652 and 1657. Land abandonment in the mid-1800s produced abundant habitat for early-successional species such as vesper sparrows and young forest species such as ruffed grouse.

Most game species, however, reached extremely low population levels in New England around the turn of the 20th century, following the so-called era of exploitation, from 1850 to 1900. The second half of the 19th century was a period of intense market hunting of deer in Maine and of waterfowl, passenger pigeons, shorebirds, and game birds, as well as plume hunting of herons elsewhere. Laws to protect wildlife were largely established in the 20th century; recovery from persecution has been rapid and dramatic. Nowhere else in the world was so large an area cleared and rapidly abandoned as in New England, yet there were relatively few extinctions, and virtually all extirpated wildlife species later recolonized the region.

Reintroductions of extirpated native species have occurred over time. White-tailed deer were released as early as the late 19th century in Vermont and elsewhere, having been rare or absent for a century or more. Beaver were successfully reintroduced in Lenox, Mass., in 1932, having been eradicated in the early 1800s. After 1932 beaver also naturally reoccupied their former Massachusetts range from New York. Wild turkeys were reestablished from transplanted wild birds from New York in the 1970s and now are widespread throughout and beyond their former range. Peregrine falcons,

Highway sign in the White Mountains, N.H., 2002

gone from most of eastern North America by 1960 because of eggshell thinning caused by the accumulation of DDT and other persistent pesticides, were successfully reestablished during the 1970s and 1980s.

Current general trends in New England wildlife populations, notably the increases in forest species and the declines of open-habitat species, underscore both the dynamic nature of the landscape and the long-term effects of past human activities.

Grassland and shrubland species, especially birds, are the most rapidly declining species in New England. Examples include bobolink, meadowlark, vesper sparrow, upland sandpiper, and eastern towhee. Resident forest birds have increased in abundance; the pileated woodpecker, which requires large trees for nest and roost cavities, has steadily increased in abundance over the past 50 years.

House finches spread rapidly throughout New England in the 1970s to early 1980s from caged birds released in New York City in the 1940s. Along the Atlantic Coast, many formerly southern birds, including the great egret, blue heron, oystercatcher, and willet, have spread northward into New England. Inland, red-bellied woodpeckers have become common in much of southern New England. Winter bird feeding has probably allowed southern species such as the cardinal and tufted titmouse to colonize New England by reducing mortality during severe winter weather.

Some mammals have shown dramatic changes in abundance and distribution. Population increases are more obvious than decreases, and perhaps no changes are more apparent than those of moose and black bear. In the past 30 years moose have extended their range from northern Maine to Massachusetts and now occur in Connecticut, as they did at the time of European settlement. In the past

20 years, black bear have been increasing throughout their range and are now commonly seen in suburbs. Coyotes now occupy all of New England, after first arriving in northern Maine in the 1930s and Vermont in the 1940s. Fishers have expanded their range southward into Connecticut.

The New England cottontail has become much reduced in distribution with the decline of old field and brushy habitats and now has a quite spotty distribution in much of the region. Over the 350 years of European settlement and early exploitation of wildlife, only three species, all birds, have become extinct: the Labrador duck, great auk, and passenger pigeon. The heath hen was a subspecies and is also extinct. Among mammals, only the sea mink and eastern elk, both subspecies, are extinct. Changes in reptile and amphibian populations are less well known. Some species are greatly reduced in range. Rattlesnakes, for example, were once found in Maine; and five-lined skinks, now found in southwestern Connecticut and the West Haven area of Vermont, were formerly found in Barre and New Bedford, Mass.

Changes in the landscape have exerted lasting effects on more species than did direct exploitation. A century and a half after the peak of land clearing, the effects of forest regrowth are still occurring, as revealed by declining open-country species and increasing forest species. All species populations are in constant flux, now responding for the most part to human activities and uses of the land. Those activities that fundamentally alter land cover have far-reaching and long-term effects on wildlife.

As subsistence agriculture gave way to modern society, people's relationships to the land and wildlife changed. Consumption and persecution of wildlife have greatly diminished; modern society largely values wildlife for its aesthetic, ecologic, and scientific attributes. These values are not found in the early literature as utilitarian values prevailed in our early history: deer were used for meat and leather, beavers were valuable for their fur, and wolves were considered vermin. Some conflicts between people and wildlife remain; deer, beaver, and bear populations are increasing in suburban areas, for instance. But the main threats to many species today are habitat availability and benign neglect. Many early-successional species are quietly disappearing from New England as forests grow in extent and age. Acceptance of such changes as "natural" will reduce populations of early-successional rabbits and grouse as surely as snares or guns.

Robert A. Askins, *Restoring North America's Birds: Lessons from Landscape Ecology* (2000); Richard M. DeGraaf and Deborah D. Rudis, *Amphibians and Reptiles of New England: Habitats and Natural History* (1983); Richard M. DeGraaf and Mariko Yamasaki, *New England Wildlife: Habitat, Natural History, and Distribution* (2001); Edward H. Forbush, *Birds of Massachusetts and Other New England States* (1925, 1927, 1929); David R. Foster et al., "Wildlife Dynamics in the Changing New England Landscape," *Journal of Biogeography* 29, (2002); Alfred J. Godin, *Wild Mammals of New* England (1977); William Wood, *New England's Prospect*, ed. Alden T. Vaughan (1977 [1634]).

Richard M. DeGraaf

Woods Camps In the forests of northern New England, the traditional woods camp served as a months-on-end home for the labor force that cut and moved wood to lumber mills during the late 19th and early 20th centuries. These camps were located in the deep woods of northern New England near the lakes and rivers—including the Androscoggin, Kennebec, and Penobscot—on which timber or pulpwood was floated to the mills. These three major tributaries carried an average of 540 million board feet of lumber cut annually between 1890 and 1900. Another 322 million board feet came from 11 other waterways, including the Piscataqua and the Saco in the west and the upper Saint John and Aroostook in the east. The Connecticut River's last drive in 1915 approached 65 million board feet. The largest harvests occurred near those large rivers that eventually flowed to the lumber mill centers in Berlin, N.H., and Westbrook, Skowhegan, Augusta, Millinocket, Old Town, and Bangor, Maine.

Although independent timber owners such as J. E. Henry in New Hampshire and John Ross of Bangor, Maine, invested heavily in the early lumber industry, large corporations such as Saint Regis and Great Northern began the systematic purchase of northern New England forests early in the 20th century. These companies depended on skilled woods camp bosses like the legendary Albert "Jigger" Johnson (1879–1935) and W. R. Brown (1875–1955). Camp bosses were responsible not only for getting the harvest to the mill, but for the management of a large crew of men, a physical facility that could house and feed that crew, a stable of hard-working horses, and a blacksmith shop that maintained essential equipment and tools.

Oral history, historic archaeology, and contemporary descriptions of life in the lumber woods provide detailed descriptions of the traditional lumber woods camp. One building, perhaps 30 by 60 feet, depending on the size of the operation, housed the woodsmen's sleeping quarters on one end and the cook room on the other, with food storage at the center of the building. One woods operation in Washington County, Maine, in the 1940s, housed 75 men in a camp 95 feet long by 32 feet wide with 18 windows. A woods operation of this size also included a hovel for the horses, a teamster's shack, and an office for the managers, clerks, and bosses. A woods operation was always located near a steady supply of timber or, in later years, pulpwood for paper production.

The older, larger, extensive network of sorting operations on the Penobscot River known as the Argyle Boom was another style of woods camp. Logs from deep in the Maine woods were driven more than 100 miles to a series of sorting booms that sent the logs to the sawmill that owned them. The heyday of this operation spanned some 80 years until the 1930s when the era of lumbering on the Penobscot River ended.

The boom house was similar to the traditional woods camp but accommodated approximately 250 men; it was approximately 25 feet wide, 30 feet deep, and two-and-a-half stories high. The cooks, the wood scalers, and the bosses slept on the second floor. The dining room took up the entire first floor, and the kitchen occupied a 15-by-35-foot ell. Large kitchen woodstoves and brick ovens handled baking and the cooking of such staples as baked beans. A storehouse and icehouse were located nearby. The bunkhouses, which were separate buildings, were located about 100 feet away and measured approximately 75 feet long, 30 feet wide, and two-and-a-half stories high. Twelve-by-12-foot rooms ran the length of the building with a central corridor. Men slept four to a room in double bunks on the first two floors, but the attic was often one long room full of bunks. Woodsman Ernest Kennedy of Argyle, Maine, remembers the attic as the "ram-pasture"—the place where transients, drunks, and troublemakers would find rest.

As the 20th century pressed on, the forest economy changed. Throughout northern New England, as settlement continued, more subsistence farming and smaller scale forestry operations developed, and traditional woods camps disappeared. Family operations often included work in the woods and on the farm to produce raw materials or homemade paper and wood products. The woods camp evolved during the 20th century from the legendary deep woods shelter to the rural New England home.

Stephen Ballew, Joan Brooks, Dona Brotz, and Edward D. Ives, "Suthin': An Oral History of Grover Morrison's Woods Operation at Little Musquash Lake, 1945–1947," *Northeast Folklore* 18 (1977); William Robinson Brown, *Our Forest Heritage: A History of Forestry and Recreation in New Hampshire* (1958); Edward D. Ives, "Argyle Boom," *Northeast Folklore* 17 (1976); Robert E. Pike, "Log Drive on the Connecticut," *Atlantic Monthly* (July 1963).

Michael P. Chaney

Woods Hole Oceanographic Institution Founded in 1930, the Woods Hole Oceanographic Institution (WHOI) is part of a continuing scientific tradition in Woods Hole, Mass. Spencer Fullerton Baird, the first U.S. Commissioner of Fish and Fisheries, began studies of fish and invertebrates in the area in 1871, and his work led to the construction of the first U.S. marine station at Woods Hole in 1885. Three years later the first building of the Marine Biological Laboratory—a center for the study of marine animals—was erected. The work at these two institutions had already established Woods Hole as a center for scientific research when WHOI was founded.

The institute was formed as a private, non-profit corporation after the National Academy of Sciences Committee on Oceanography recommended establishing a well-equipped oceanographic institution on the Atlantic coast. The Woods Hole site had many advantages: a long history of scientific goodwill and cooperation in the community, a small but deep water harbor providing ready access to the deep sea and to the contrasting conditions north and south of Cape Cod, and proximity to numerous universities.

Henry B. Bigelow, professor of zoology at Harvard University, became the first director of WHOI, and Frank R. Lillie, who also served as president of the Marine Biological Laboratory, became chairman of the board. A $2.5 million grant from the Rockefeller Foundation provided endowment, 10 years of operating funds, and moneys to support construction of the first building, a 142-foot research sailing vessel, and a 40-foot collecting vessel.

During its first decade, WHOI drew professors and graduate students from various universities, primarily for summer research.

Woods Hole Oceanographic Institution researchers retrieve equipment during a survey of Nantucket Harbor, Mass., 1992

World War II brought the first great expansion of the institution's facilities and programs. The U.S. Navy, realizing that many of its operations depended on the environment, initiated related research programs, many of them at WHOI. The institution's 60-member summer staff expanded to a year-round complement of more than 300, and the annual operating budget skyrocketed from $107,000 in 1940 to more than $1 million in 1944.

After the war, the navy's continuing interest in the marine environment supported WHOI research in areas such as the physics of the North Atlantic (including the movement of the Gulf Stream), delineation of the structure of the earth beneath the oceans, and studies of marine meteorology. The establishment of the National Science Foundation in 1950 created a new source of research funding, and from the late 1950s through the 1980s WHOI continued to grow.

At the beginning of the 21st century, WHOI comprises five science departments and four research centers and operates one small and three large research vessels as well as the deep submersible *Alvin* and several remotely operated and autonomous vehicles. With a support staff of nearly 500 and a scientific and technical research staff of about 300, WHOI collaborates with colleagues from universities across the United States and throughout the world. A joint graduate program with the Massachusetts Institute of Technology was established in 1968 and in 2003 awarded 28 graduate degrees.

Woods Hole village continues to attract scientific endeavors as well as marine-based businesses. In addition to a modern National Marine Fishery Service laboratory and a branch of the U.S. Geological Survey, the village is home to several private institutions, including the Marine Biological Laboratory, the environmentally oriented Woods Hole Research Center, and the Sea Education Association, an organization offering a semester-long multidisciplinary undergraduate program that combines navigation, oceanography, and sailing.

Victoria A. Kaharl, *Water Baby: The Story of "Alvin"* (1990); Susan Schlee, *On Almost any Wind: The Saga of the Oceanographic Research Vessel "Atlantis"* (1978).

Robert B. Gagosian

History

Charles E. Clark, Section Editor

INTRODUCTION

Every culture is a product of its past, but in New England the past is especially tangible. Almost everywhere in the region, the physical landscape evokes other times. Abandoned barns and covered bridges, stone walls snaking through woodlands that were once fields and pastures, coastal hamlets, carefully pruned village greens, moss-covered gravestones, proudly preserved urban mansions, and rows of recycled red-brick mill buildings all speak eloquently, often sadly, of a New England that used to be. So do the other, more deliberately contrived artifacts of place: lineal societies like the Mayflower Descendants and the Piscataqua Pioneers, Boston's Freedom Trail, local and state historical societies and museums, a plethora of bound genealogies, and the historic preservation movement.

The regional historical consciousness, moreover, has not escaped the purview—indeed, the participation—of the professional scholar. From the immense compilation of biographies and providential interpretations of events that constituted Cotton Mather's *Magnalia Christi Americana* in 1702, to a cluster of scientific New England community studies of the 1970s, to various "new narrative" histories of people and events in the 1990s, the place of New England on the agenda of American historians has remained high.

New Englanders as a whole, therefore, whatever their occupation or descent or place of residence within the six states, are surrounded by reminders of their region's past and may tend in large part to identify the region with that past. History, in other words, not only shapes New England's identity but in many minds actually constitutes that identity.

THE BEGINNING

Both the name and the idea of New England originated with Captain John Smith in 1614. The name, with quite a different meaning attached, was maintained energetically and self-consciously by his Puritan successors. As a label for a geographic region, the name has stuck. Its meanings—for *New England* has always been much more than a geographic description—continue to evolve.

When Smith and the later Puritan immigrants and their English contemporaries used the name New England, the context was imperial. Their exploration and settlement of the region were carried out under the color of claims established earlier by the English Crown in its competition with other European powers for pieces of the New World. Such competition omitted from consideration the occupancy of the native inhabitants, consisting entirely in the region that became New England of subgroups of the woodland Algonquian (or Algonkian or Algonquin) linguistic family.

Estimates of the number of native people who lived in the region at the time of European settlement have varied widely. Some recent scholarship has put the figure as high as 144,000, perhaps 90,000 of whom lived in what are now Massachusetts, Rhode Island, and Connecticut. That, however, was before the disastrous epidemic of 1616–18 that arrived with the English ships and carried off between 70 and 90 percent of the native inhabitants. Thus it appeared to the English settlers that the land was relatively empty, a fact that some of them attributed to divine providence.

It oversimplifies the matter to say that the story of Native American and European relations can be reduced to a tale of destruction and dispossession. Thanks in part to William Bradford's history of the Plymouth Colony and its copiers, almost every American, including most schoolchildren, can cite a few documented instances of early peaceful contacts and even cooperation between the original Americans and the European immigrants. Beyond that, recent scholarship has begun to make inroads on the long-standing assumption that when Indian lands were transferred to European hands, it was done in every case without a shared understanding of the meaning of ownership. Interracial resentments and misunderstandings, in full flower by 1675 in the regionwide native uprising known as King Philip's War (1675–76), were exacerbated by international conflict in the decades that followed. By 1763 the native presence in New England had been reduced to an almost invisible and entirely powerless collection of tiny communities on the margins of the dominant society. The rest had either died or continued a century-old pattern of migration to Canada.

For white New England, the 17th-century encounter between peoples produced lasting cultural consequences. Such native crops as Indian corn (maize), pumpkins, squash, and tomatoes, as well as the technique of making syrup and sugar from the sap of the maple tree, have become staples of New England agriculture. Stalking game, trapping fur animals, certain fishing techniques, and the tactics of wilderness warfare were all adopted from native instruction or example, as were the canoe, the hatchet, moccasins, and snowshoes. The region's language has been enriched by terms such as those of some of the crops and tools just noted and especially by adaptations of Algonquian place names.

The English claim to the region, along with much of the rest of eastern North America, rested on the voyages in 1497 and 1498 of the Bristol-based mariner John Cabot. They preceded by a quarter of a century the first recorded description of the coastline by Giovanni da Verrazano, who sailed in 1524 under the sponsorship of France. Verrazano's brief contacts with Native Americans along the way suggest that Europeans may have been there before. Probably not long after Verrazano's voyage, fishermen from the West County of England began undocumented seasonal visits to the rich fishing grounds of the western North Atlantic, coming ashore at places from Newfoundland to Cape Ann to dry and pack their catches and repair equipment.

In 1607 the newly organized Plymouth Company, a corporation of English stockholders, sent out George Popham to lead what might have been the first permanent English settlement in America. The tiny Sagadahoc colony on the coast of Maine did not last. It was left to the rival London Company to sponsor the first permanent English colony in America at Jamestown, Va.

The western Atlantic fishery, however, continued to flourish, resulting at least as early as 1610 in the establishment of a few year-round fishing and trading stations. The first such settlement south of Newfoundland may have been at Monhegan Island, which served as the base for John Smith's map-making expedition of 1614 that gave New England its name.

Smith's imperial vision of New England, articulated in several promotional tracts beginning with *A Description of New-England* (1616), was of colonies that would strengthen England economically and militarily as well as tighten the national moral fiber. His proposed communities would combine a communal fishery with part-time farming on individual landholdings. Such a fishermen's yeoman republic would not only produce a profitable export trade but at the same time accommodate some of England's surplus population, employ the idle gentry, provide a "nursery of seamen" well prepared for England's naval battles, and afford a vigorous way of life in healthful surroundings.

For lack of financial backing, Smith never realized his vision. A few little English colonies in the early 17th century such as the ones at Pemaquid and Richmond Island, Maine, were roughly similar to the model that Smith had proposed, with the addition in some cases of an important Indian fur-trading component. There is no evidence, however, that settlements such as these were prompted by anything like the moral and patriotic vision of a John Smith rather than the simple commercial motives of their sponsors.

PILGRIMS AND PURITANS

Behind the largest and most important movement to settle New England, on the other hand, was an energizing motive not greatly different from Smith's. But at the heart of Puritanism there was also the powerful ingredient of religion.

The founders of the Plymouth Colony, settled in 1620 by about 100 passengers on the *Mayflower*, were of a wing of the Puritan movement so radical as to profess their complete separation from the Church of England. To avoid persecution, a Separatist congregation had fled England for Holland, where in Leyden the concerned elders eventually felt the once-tight bonds of a persecuted religious community beginning to loosen. Thus some in the congregation decided to move again, negotiating with the London Company for a tract near the Hudson River.

Thirty-five Leyden church members, joined by about 40 more Separatists and a few others, sailed from Plymouth in the *Mayflower* on September 16, 1620. They arrived by accident on November 11 at the tip of Cape Cod. Despite being more than 200 miles northeast of their planned destination, a scouting party from the ship settled on the site that became Plymouth for the colony. Before going ashore in December, 41 of the ship's passengers signed the famous Mayflower Compact, by which they acknowledged their continuing allegiance to King James and agreed to form "A Civil Body Politic" for self-government, to which all would submit. To historians of many subsequent generations, this first actual "social contract" has been seen as a significant precedent in the formation of the American political ethos.

Thus began the settlement of southern New England by those to whom their historian and long-term governor William Bradford referred in one passage of his history as pilgrims, a name that has become an indelible part of the American historical-mythological vocabulary since an orator's invocation of the "Pilgrim Fathers" during a Plymouth Forefathers' Day celebration in 1799.

In 1630 Plymouth Colony became overshadowed at once by the far larger neighbor into which it was finally absorbed, the Massachusetts Bay Colony. Unlike the Plymouth band, the Massachusetts Bay Company, composed of solid Puritan businessmen and gentry, managed to get its own charter directly from the Crown. It emerged out of an earlier New England Company, which had sent a settlement to

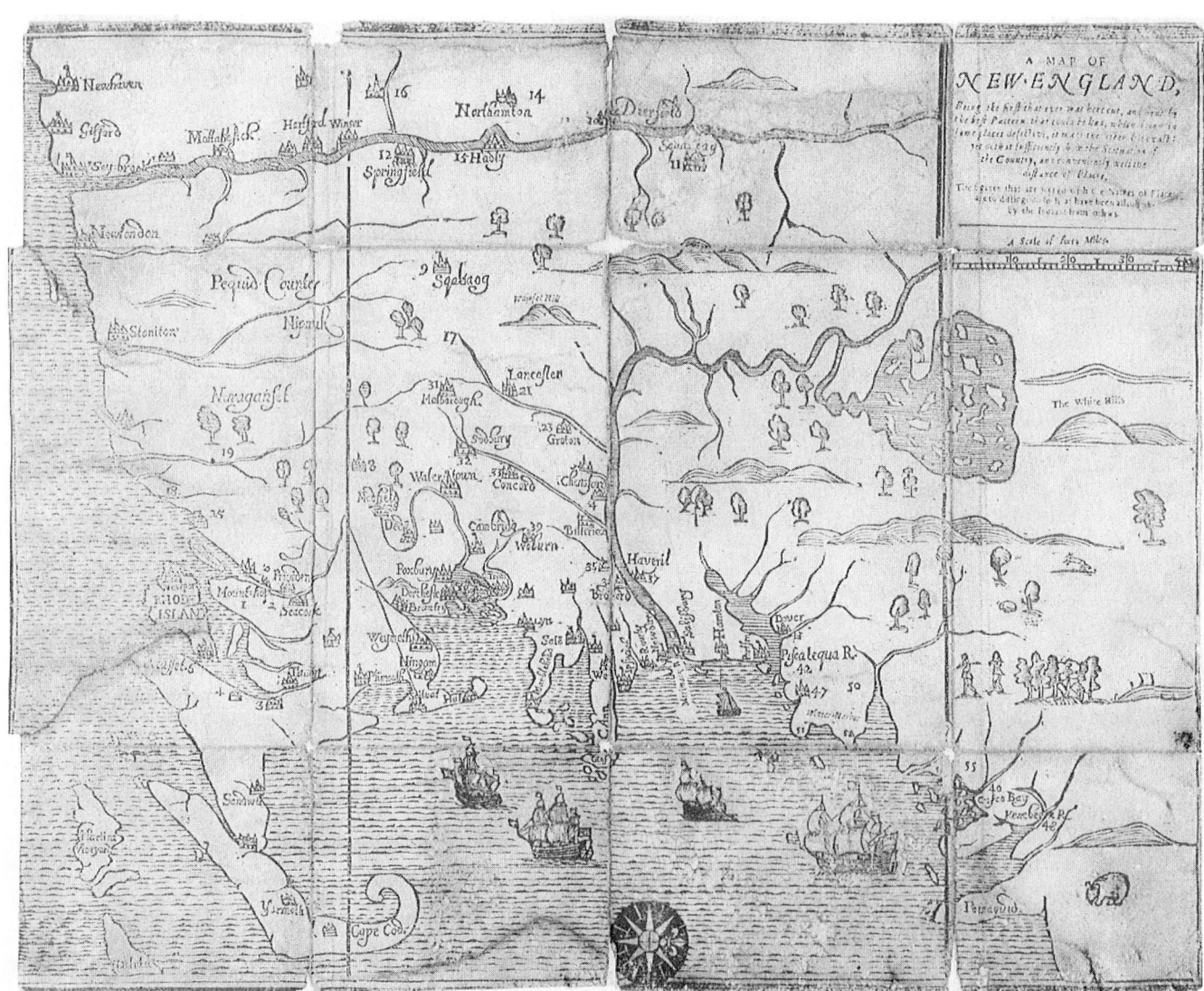

John Foster's "Map of New England, Being the first that was ever here cut, and done by the best Pattern that could be had, which being in some places defective, it made the other less exact: yet doth it sufficiently shew the Scituation of the Country, and conveniently well the distance of Places. The figures that are joyned with the Names of Place are to distinguish such as have been assaulted by the Indians from others," from William Hubbard, A Narrative of the Trouble with the Indians in New England *(1677)*

Salem in 1628 to prepare the way for a migration. In its renamed and newly chartered form, achieved in 1629, the company elected John Winthrop, a landed gentleman from East Anglia, as governor and agreed that members who did not wish to emigrate to America would sell out to those who did. Thus when a fleet of 11 ships sailed with a thousand passengers in the spring of 1630, the entire Massachusetts Bay Company, charter and all, sailed with it. Under Winthrop's leadership, the charter's provisions for managing the affairs of a business corporation were transformed into the government of a commonwealth. Over the next dozen years, some 20,000 persons sailed from old to New England.

Both the timing of the "great migration," of which Winthrop's fleet was the vanguard, and the decision to move the company charter itself to New England were responses to what from the Puritan point of view was the deteriorating state of affairs in England. Whatever hope there might have been for reforming the English church along the lines favored by mainstream Puritans, or even achieving toleration for reformed practices in selected parishes, was dashed by the rigidity of Charles I, who succeeded to the throne in 1625, and his chief adviser, William Laud, who eventually became archbishop of Canterbury.

Winthrop's vision for New England, one that governed the aspirations and practices of the region's dominant population for several generations, was that it should serve as an example for the rest of the world by establishing a truly reformed Christian society based on biblical example and precept. In "A Modell of Christian Charity," the sermon he addressed to his fellow passengers in the mid-Atlantic, Winthrop declared that the colony's success or failure would be a test of divine favor. In the decades that followed, some of the most eminent Puritan divines of all time would elaborate on Winthrop's vision by portraying their experiment as the latest chapter in Christian history and New England as the means by which God was forwarding the work of reformation and human redemption.

Through the 17th century, the Massachusetts Bay Colony became by far the most dominant force in the region. The General Court prescribed by the company charter became the colony's legislative body, which, under the tutelage of the ministers, enacted a capital code based on Leviticus, demanded strict Sabbatarian observance, required towns to educate their children, and in 1636 chartered Harvard College to provide the churches with an educated ministry.

The Massachusetts Bay Colony's main economic base was agriculture. Scores of rural towns soon covered much of eastern Massachusetts. In these largely farming communities, each self-governing and each with its own established church and town-supported minister, the majority of Massachusetts families lived, worshiped, made their livings, and conducted their public affairs. Meanwhile, a lively mercantile economy based on fishing, trade, and shipbuilding began to flourish in Boston and smaller ports, spawning a prosperous merchant class that by the end of the 17th century rivaled the clergy as the leading influence in the colony.

The expansion of Puritan Massachusetts was not confined within its own borders. Roger Williams and Anne Hutchinson were the most prominent of the dissenters from Massachusetts orthodoxy who were exiled in the 1630s to Rhode Island, where

Williams embarked upon the daring experiment to found a colony that provided not only for a broader participatory democracy than that in Massachusetts but also for freedom of conscience "in matters of religious concernments." Thomas Hooker, minister of Newetowne (later Cambridge), led his flock in 1636 to Hartford, which became the nucleus of the new colony of Connecticut. The separate colony of New Haven was founded two years later by a newly arrived Puritan group from London under John Davenport. New Haven Colony finally joined with Connecticut in 1665.

Meanwhile, Massachusetts began to extend its influence, and finally its authority, over the scattered settlements that lay within John Mason's proprietary grant of New Hampshire and Sir Ferdinando Gorges's virtually ungoverned province of Maine. By 1643 the four towns of New Hampshire were included within the Massachusetts county of Norfolk. Between 1650 and 1658, commissioners secured agreement in every tenuous Maine settlement between the Piscataqua River and Casco Bay to acknowledge the jurisdiction of Massachusetts. Thus northern New England was drawn within the powerful orbit of Puritan Massachusetts. In the case of New Hampshire, political separation came in 1680 with the establishment of a royal province of that name, but the cultural influence of Massachusetts, abetted by continued northward migration from that time to this, endured. Maine continued to be a part of Massachusetts until it achieved statehood in 1820.

As for Plymouth, because of cultural and religious affinities between the elder but much weaker sister and Massachusetts Bay, friendly and mutually influential relations were carried on between the two from the beginning. Plymouth's dependence upon Massachusetts was formalized in 1691 when the Bay Colony, having lost its first charter in 1684 and suffered through a brief period of royalist rule under the Dominion of New England, was incorporated together with the old Plymouth Colony and Maine into a new Province of Massachusetts Bay.

THE MAKING OF YANKEE NEW ENGLAND

The new Massachusetts charter of 1691 marked the beginning of a new era for New England. The region now contained four political entities: the royal province of Massachusetts Bay, including the former Plymouth Colony and what would eventually be called the district of Maine; the much smaller royal province of New Hampshire, whose boundary with Massachusetts was still in dispute and would not be settled until 1740; the charter colony of Rhode Island; and the charter colony of Connecticut, including the former New Haven Colony.

Although the region retained its distinctive religious orientation, the chief tendencies of the day were toward secularization, tolerance, and, in the coastal capitals, a degree of cosmopolitanism. The merchants were quickly rising to political dominance and would soon be displaying their wealth and tastes in elegant houses, furnishings, clothing, and hospitality. The colonial establishment of William and Mary and their successors brought a host of new royal appointees to British America to administer the mercantile laws, the post office, and the military and naval presence that increasingly became a factor in colonial life as the chief powers of Europe entered a period of sustained conflict. The new Massachusetts charter provided for religious toleration for all Protestants, a toleration that worked itself out slowly and painfully during the next few decades.

Many of the clergy saw the shift toward a more secular and a more tolerant society as a decline from holier and sturdier times, either evidence or cause of divine disfavor. Death and destruction on the northeastern frontier during King William's War (1689–97), the first in a protracted series of international and intercolonial conflicts, seemed to confirm the notion that God was indeed angry with his once-chosen people of New England. The most lastingly notorious manifestation of the insecurity and confusion of these difficult times was the outbreak in 1692 in the Massachusetts town of Salem of a local hysteria that ended with the hanging of 14 women and five men for witchcraft. Another man, Giles Corey, was pressed to death for refusing to answer the charge.

Painful though the transition had been, the new century that New England now entered was one of expansion and prosperity. Whenever a break in hostilities with the French and their Indian allies made it possible, new generations of New Englanders moved into western Massachusetts, eastern Connecticut, New Hampshire, and Maine. Some of the northward migrants from Connecticut settled on the west side of the Connecticut River in territory that eventually would become Vermont. Migration within the region by the descendants of earlier settlers was augmented by the arrival of modest numbers of immigrants from northern Ireland, the so-called Scotch-Irish, who established important communities in New Hampshire. Less well publicized new arrivals in this period included Irish and German immigrants to Maine and Jewish arrivals in Rhode Island, where that colony's distinctive religious freedom had welcomed the first Jewish immigrants at least as early as the 1670s. Every New England colony also imported small but far from negligible numbers of African slaves, who worked on farms, on ships, in urban crafts, and as household servants for rich merchants.

By far the most numerous of New England's inhabitants in the 18th century, however, were of English Puritan stock, most of them farmers and their families. Although the piety and the severe Calvinist theology of their grandparents had become more lax and perhaps more humane for most of them, these were still a religious people. By and large they still heard weekly sermons, read their Bibles, held family devotions, and in many cases, as far as we can judge from surviving documents, continued the introspective spirituality of their ancestors. New Englanders as a group, however, were an intensely practical as well as a spiritual people. In the 18th century, it was this practical side of the regional character—enforced by the hard necessities of rural life, encouraged by the secularizing tendencies of the day, and nurtured by the opportunities for making good—that took the ascendancy. Combining the moral athleticism and inclinations toward both spiritual and secular self-reliance of his Puritan forebears with a shrewdness in economic affairs, an elevation of the virtues of frugality and hard work, a town-based civic consciousness, an economy of speech, and a dry wit, the Yankee emerged as a recognizable regional type.

Meanwhile, the hegemony of Congregationalism and the church-town system became strained both by divisions within and by challenges from Anglicans, Baptists, Quakers, and others from without. In the middle of the 18th century, the intercolonial revival movement known as the Great Awakening divided many New England communities into New Light and Old Light factions, resulting in some cases in a separation within the church and in others in the strengthening or the emergence of a rival denomination. Religious turmoil brought into question the nature of the New England town itself. The presence of dissenters from the local establishment, even in some cases of entire dissenting congregations, meant that about 1750 many towns started to shed their nature as sponsors of supposed religious uniformity. There began, therefore, a slow movement toward the decline of the town minister, congregation, and meetinghouse as the prime symbols of the community's identity. The burden now shifted gradually to entirely secular expressions—the town meeting, the militia company, the schools, and eventually a civic building to be used for public purposes after the meetinghouse had been turned over to one or another of competing religious societies. It was with this emerging secularized civic identity, a consciousness that was beginning to define the community mainly in political rather than religious terms, that Yankee towns throughout the region faced the crisis that became the American Revolution.

REVOLUTION AND THE NEW REPUBLIC

By 1763 the most highly politicized community in British America was Boston. The Boston Caucus was the most sophisticated and successful of the factions that had contested for power in the Massachusetts General Assembly for the past 40 years. Over the same period, a newspaper and pamphlet press had developed a forum for debating controversial public issues, often in light of the theories of the Whig opposition party in England. Royal governors were constantly scrutinized by assemblymen and the writers of political tracts for the slightest evidence of the improper exercise of authority. Urban craftsmen, apprentices, sailors, and laborers formed a critical mass that was available to respond to some popular leader's call for a demonstration or protest.

Thus it was Boston that first responded to the American Revenue Act, or Sugar Act, of 1764 by initiating nonimportation agreements, and it was Boston that was the center of tumultuous resistance to the Stamp Act the following year. Over the next decade, the most dramatic episodes of opposition to British policy and its consequences were likely to be located in Boston or its immediate vicinity—the so-called massacre of 1770, the Boston Tea Party of 1773, Britain's punitive response in the form of the various Intolerable Acts aimed directly at Boston and Massachusetts, the military occupation of the town, the British garrison's fatal attempt to seize stores at Lexington and Concord in April 1775, the siege of Boston by colonial troops, and the Battle of Bunker Hill that June. Other early acts of resistance that raised the tensions leading to independence included the burning of the British revenue ship *Gaspee* in Narragansett Bay in 1772 as well as inflammatory episodes in New Hampshire in 1774 and Maine in 1775. New England representatives, most notably John Adams and

John Hancock of Massachusetts, were prominent in the Second Continental Congress, which declared independence and supervised most of the war.

Military actions in the region after 1775 were for the most part peripheral to the main campaigns of the war. New England troops, however, were conspicuous in every theater, and the region produced a disproportionate number of leading commanders, perhaps none more praised than Nathanael Greene of Rhode Island and certainly none more condemned than Benedict Arnold of Connecticut, who performed signal services for the American cause before his conversion to the British side. As vital to the outcome of the war as the contributions of any general, however, was Connecticut's logistical support of the Continental Army, inspired and coordinated by its wartime governor, Jonathan Trumbull. Loyalist sympathies, quite strong in the Middle Colonies and the lower South, were notably weak in New England despite the prominence of two native-born royal governors who were forced into exile, Thomas Hutchinson of Massachusetts and John Wentworth of New Hampshire.

Although all New Englanders recognized that in the War for Independence they were engaged in common cause with nine other colonies to the southward, the tone of their resistance had a distinct regional coloring. The clergy, New England's "black regiment," preached revolutionary doctrine from the pulpit. The historian Edmund S. Morgan has identified in the nonimportation agreements and subsequent patriotic sacrifices willingly undertaken a strain of asceticism and eagerness to struggle in adversity that he has called the "Puritan ethic" in the American Revolution. The best known of many versions of "Yankee Doodle," which satirically describes the wondering visit of a thoroughly provincial New England farm boy to Washington's army besieging Boston, was adopted by American troops everywhere as a rallying tune. Lest there could be any doubt about the precise nature of the regional ethos in its fight against tyranny, the Boston composer William Billings ended the first stanza of his militant patriotic hymn "Chester" with the ringing phrase, "New England's God forever reigns."

As the British American colonies became transformed into independent states, and as the states joined into nationhood, they were plunged into one of the most creative political eras in the history of the Western world. Everyone involved in the debate over the polity to come agreed that the new United States should be a republic—or at least a confederation of republics. Within that broad consensus, however, there were differences based on economic interest, geography, orientation toward Europe, and political philosophy. No better index to the polarities within the republican consensus of the era can be found than in the respective positions of Thomas Jefferson of Virginia and John Adams of Massachusetts.

Although it cannot be claimed that Adams spoke for every Yankee, his political insights as disclosed in *Thoughts on Government* (1776), *Defence of the Constitutions of the United States* (1787), and letters to Jefferson and to his remarkable wife, Abigail, give the fullest expression to a regionally based republicanism descended not only from classical sources but also from New England Puritanism. His ideas about government were based on a skepticism about human nature, a devotion to the ideal of equal rights balanced by a realistic acceptance of inevitable differences in human condition and consequent abilities to govern, an orientation toward the English rather than the French political culture, and a conviction that a balanced constitution was the people's best safeguard against their own folly and self-interest and the only sure guarantor of individual and civic virtue. Adams's attitude of cautious pragmatism toward self-government may be taken, along with an insistence *upon* self-government, as an underlying political assumption in many parts of New England, especially north of Boston, to this day.

In the winter of 1786–87, the debtors' uprising in western Massachusetts known as Shays's Rebellion became one of the chief immediate stimuli of the movement to strengthen the national government. One especially important New England delegate to the Constitutional Convention in Philadelphia the next autumn turned out to be Roger Sherman of Connecticut, whose proposal for different methods of representation in the two houses of Congress became the basis for the key compromise that produced a draft of the federal Constitution. Among the 13 states, only Rhode Island refrained from sending delegates to the convention; it was also the second slowest state to ratify. In Connecticut, a convention voted quickly for ratification in January 1788, making that state the fifth to ratify. A month later, the Federalist delegates to the Massachusetts convention overcame strong Antifederalist opposition with a proposal to accompany the convention's approval with recommendations for amendments. New Hampshire Federalists followed the same strategy in June 1788, giving that state the honor of becoming the ninth and decisive state to ratify. Rhode Island reluctantly joined the union in May 1789, six months before North Carolina finally made it unanimous. In 1791, the new Republic of Vermont, having cast off allegiance to both New York and New Hampshire during the revolutionary years, became the 14th state.

The next two decades were times of economic expansion and population growth. The postwar revival of New England's ocean commerce, having suffered a temporary setback, now came back with yet greater vigor. New England ships began sailing around the Horn to the Pacific Northwest to take on furs, which were then traded for goods in China. In the interior, farmers who had once operated not far above the subsistence level now began producing surpluses that made their way to Boston and New York markets along a rapidly developing system of turnpikes and canals. Pioneering families moved in sizable numbers into previously unsettled areas. In Maine violent confrontations sometimes occurred between the new settlers and representatives of the large companies of proprietors that claimed ownership of the land.

This brief era of prosperity, in which New England's economic dynamism was matched by its political eminence during the presidency of John Adams, came to a shocking halt in 1807. Britain and France were at war, and both belligerent powers had been disrupting American shipping. The American response, recommended by the Jefferson administration, was the Embargo Act, which in effect put an end to all legitimate foreign trade and devastated New England ports. Revival had scarcely begun when shipping interests were dealt the crowning blow by the War of 1812. The war intensified New England–based Federalist opposition to Republican national policy, manifested finally in the Hartford Convention of 1814–15. The convention adopted several resolutions proposing constitutional and policy changes but did not, contrary to popular belief at the time, seriously consider the notion of New England's seceding from the union. The war also served to reinvigorate a latent movement for statehood in Maine, where resentment against Massachusetts ran high for its failure to provide adequate defense against British raids on the coast.

The end of the war, which came while the Hartford Convention was still sitting, brought some discredit upon New England Federalism and initiated the so-called Era of Good Feelings, during which New England joined with the rest of the nation in warm support of President James Monroe, the last member of the once-feared Virginia Dynasty. The economic structure of the region, however, had changed forever. Agricultural and rural interests surpassed the devastated seaports in importance in several of the states, but the more dramatic and ultimately decisive economic shift came with new developments in waterpowered manufacturing.

Beginning with Samuel Slater's cotton-spinning mill in Rhode Island in 1790 and Eli Whitney's revolutionary introduction of interchangeable parts for his firearms factory in Hartford in 1798, New England quickly became the nation's workshop. While the embargo and the War of 1812 badly damaged the region's shipping interests, they also created a demand for domestic manufactured goods. The timing could not have been better for entrepreneurs like Boston's Francis Cabot Lowell, who went to Waltham in 1814 to build the world's first integrated textile mill—one, that is, that combined all the processes in producing fabric under one roof and one ownership. By 1820, the year that Maine finally rounded out the region's present complement of states by its separation from Massachusetts, New England was a manufacturing region.

There was a dark side to the achievement of Maine statehood. Maine's admission to the union was made part of a package called the Missouri Compromise as a way to maintain the balance in the U.S. Senate between slave and free states. Thus unexpectedly was New England thrust into complicity in raising the specter of a great national division over slavery.

YANKEE EMINENCE AND YANKEE DECLINE

The antebellum decades brought a strange mixture of developments bearing upon New England's standing in the nation and upon the position of the descendants of the Puritans within the region itself. New England not only took its place as the nation's workshop; it also built upon a long tradition of scholarship and literature to reaffirm its unquestioned role in American culture as the nation's schoolmaster. Of the nine American colleges founded before the Revolution, four were in New England, and now others were swiftly being added—no fewer than three in the new, thinly populated state of Vermont alone. The academy movement flourished, as did significant reforms in the public schools under the stimulus of Horace Mann, secretary of the Massachusetts State Board of Education, and his Connecticut counterpart, Henry Barnard. In 1833 the town of Peterborough, N.H., established a free public library, today the oldest of thousands of such institutions nationwide in continuous use. Of the eight state historical societies founded between 1791 and 1832, five were in New England, not counting the American Antiquarian Society in Worcester, Mass., begun in 1812.

All these developments, in keeping with the democratic tendencies of the day, were aimed at broadening access to learning. By now literacy in the region was practically universal in all classes and among both sexes, as was attendance during at least some span of childhood at a public primary school. Although collegiate education was still largely confined to males, young women attended academies and the new normal schools for the training of teachers, a New England invention. The founding of Mount Holyoke Female Seminary in 1837 set the stage for the dramatic advances in higher education for women, mostly from privileged families, that would soon follow. Many young women of humbler circumstances, usually from farms in which the products of domestic manufacturing were being replaced by factory-made fabrics and clothing, found work in the burgeoning textile mills of the antebellum era. Such employment, most famously in Lowell, Mass., entailed close social supervision and the encouragement of cultural and literary development, which were intended to offer some of the same intellectual and moral advantages that others got in academies and colleges.

While egalitarian ideals influenced much of the thought of New England's leading intellectuals, they themselves were mainly of a fairly narrow, Harvard-based elite. Mostly they were writers—the "schoolroom poets" who established the American genteel tradition in poetry, the writers of Romantic fiction (whose assured place in the canon of American letters remains unassailed except by postmodern scholars who challenge any canon at all), and the small community of Transcendentalist essayists, poets, educators, social experimenters, and reformers who by their influence and close identification with their place made their ideas and their works virtually synonymous with a redefined New England.

This lively intellectual strain in New England life combined with the region's persistent moralism, certain currents of evangelicalism, and the emerging sectionalism in national politics to produce a hothouse of reform enthusiasm. The central cause was the abolition of slavery. New England names associated with abolitionism are legion, but none more decisively than those of William Lloyd Garrison and Harriet Beecher Stowe. Garrison, best remembered for his role in founding the American Anti-Slavery Society and for his 34-year editorship of the militant Boston-based *Liberator,* also provided the first forum for the passionate speeches of Frederick Douglass, the influential former slave who later founded the abolitionist newspaper *North Star* in Rochester, N.Y. Stowe's antislavery novel *Uncle Tom's Cabin* (1852) was so profoundly affecting that Abraham Lincoln was once heard to remark that it brought on the Civil War. Abolitionism, however, was only the brightest star in a whole galaxy of reform movements ranging from temperance to women's rights, almost all of which either originated in New England or are otherwise closely associated with Yankees.

Between 1820 and 1860, therefore, New England not only maintained but strengthened its leadership in the economic and cultural life of the nation. At the same time, the eminent persons who were reshaping the economy and culture within the region were practically all of the same Yankee stock that had predominated there ever since their English Puritan ancestors had displaced the native inhabitants two centuries earlier. But there were signs of change.

Farming, the staple occupation of most inland Yankees, had always been a chancy business in New England. Except in a few areas such as the lower Connecticut River valley, soil and climate were more favorable for cultivating the region's famed strenuous virtues than surplus crops. For a short while in the 1820s and 1830s, the farmers of northern New England found an alternative to tilling reluctant soil in clearing huge areas of forestland and raising sheep whose wool fed the new textile mills. Even that, however, proved but a brief moment of prosperity. Flatter and more fertile lands to the west had been attracting farmers from New England's hill country for some time. With the opening of rail connections between western farmlands and eastern markets, the "moving out" began in earnest. Sheep pastures became forests once again, now laced through with crumbling stone walls.

The Yankee occupation of the upper Midwest, a pattern eventually to be repeated in the Pacific Northwest, was instrumental in the westward spread of the regional culture. The emigrants were soon joined by Congregational and Presbyterian missionaries. New England–inspired colleges such as Grinnell in Iowa and Oberlin in Ohio (which turned coed in 1833, a first in the nation) became, among other things, centers of abolitionist fervor. This expansion of New England, however, came at the expense of New England itself. The region's proportion of the national population declined steadily from 17 percent in 1820 to less than 12 percent in 1850.

The growth that New England did experience was due in part to the arrival of new peoples. The largest contingent by far was from Ireland. The stream of Irish immigration began in the 1820s, arousing xenophobic passions to the extent that an anti-Catholic mob burned the Ursuline Convent in Charlestown, Mass., in 1834. For a decade beginning with the great Irish famine of 1846, a thousand poor Irish farming people arrived in Boston every month. By 1860, more than a third of Boston's population was Irish. Although Winthrop's former Puritan "city upon a hill" was and still is the great center of New England's Irish American population, the immigrants spread out all over the region in search of work. For males, construction jobs on roads, canals, and railroads were typical; females tended to take up domestic service in the homes of some of the most prosperous Yankees.

The region's small quota of blacks, who had always relied on such menial jobs, was undercut in the process. The great new source of employment for immigrants, however, was New England's textile industry, which employed men and women alike, and their children as well. The famed "Lowell system," with its paternalistic supervision of dormitory-housed "mill girls," soon fell victim to the opportunities for hiring cheap immigrant labor.

The Irish were not the only new arrivals in the antebellum years. To mill towns from Maine to Rhode Island came migrants from rural Quebec, responding to industrial recruiters and taking advantage of rail connections between Canada and

New England. Their particular linguistic and geographic circumstances discouraged the kind of rapid integration into New England society at which the Irish eventually excelled. What the Irish and the French Canadians did have in common—and what distinguished both from old stock New Englanders—was Roman Catholicism. By the end of the century, with the beginnings of the massive new immigration from southern and central Europe, the Catholic Church would be the largest single religious denomination in every New England state except Maine and Vermont and one of the most powerful political and social institutions in the region.

All these changes, begun in the decades before the Civil War, signaled the decline of New England's leadership in the nation and of the original stock of New Englanders within the region, even as both achieved the apex of their influence. New England sent two presidents to the White House, John Quincy Adams of Massachusetts and Franklin Pierce of New Hampshire, each of whom served one term. Adams, the dignified son of the second president, a proven diplomat, and an advocate of national expansion and government-sponsored internal improvements, was defeated in 1828 by a coalition that emerged as the Democratic Party and elected Andrew Jackson.

By the time of Pierce's election in 1852, the hottest national issue of the day had become the debate over slavery. Pierce opposed abolitionism and while in office tried too hard for sectional reconciliation for the tastes of even his fellow northern Democrats, who nominated James Buchanan in 1856 instead. Like Adams, who inspired an opposition that became one of the two great modern political parties, Pierce was instrumental in consolidating an opposition that became the other such party. In 1860 the new Republican Party that emerged from the conflicts of the Pierce-Buchanan era elected Abraham Lincoln, the event that provoked the southern states to secession.

While the political influence of New England on the national stage declined, the region was conspicuous in its contributions to the Union cause during the Civil War. Enthusiasm for the fight was not unanimous; among other things, New England cotton manufacturers and their employees understood their symbiotic relationship with the slaveholding cotton planters of the lower South. New England, however, was the historic center of abolitionist fervor; the regional sentiment, especially in rural areas, was overwhelmingly both abolitionist and Unionist. The war's enormous casualties were part of the price. In Maine and New Hampshire, the census figures of 1870 actually reported a drop in the population from 1860, the year the war began.

After the war and the abandonment of Reconstruction in 1877, the nation's attention shifted from racial justice and the repairing of political wounds to the profoundly transforming processes of industrialization and urbanization. It now seemed to many thoughtful New Englanders that their region was less relevant to national tendencies than ever before. New England did participate in these national developments, becoming ever more industrial and urban, but the spur for change was elsewhere. The New England–based textile industry, which in any case would begin to move south within a few decades, was dwarfed by the empires of steel, oil, meat packing, flour milling, national railroads, and national finance that were forged by the new entrepreneurs of the age—none of whom was associated with New England except as a summer visitor who used the region's mountains or seashore as a vacation retreat.

Located at the edge rather than in the heart of the nation's great new continental transportation system, New England could no longer remain central to any national concern except in its traditional strong suit, the related areas of education, scholarship, science, and literature. Not even Progressivism, the one great reform movement of the age, had New England origins. Among the eastern states, only New Hampshire, whose government had been transformed for a time into a serf of the Boston and Maine Railroad, translated indignation over the preposterous political excesses of the Gilded Age into a vigorous, broad-gauged program of reform. Even there, however much the Progressive reaction was prompted from within, the inspiration came from elsewhere.

Within the region, the population became ever more diverse. The new immigration brought waves of arrivals from central, eastern, and southern Europe. Like the earlier immigrants, the new arrivals to New England settled where the jobs were, which in most cases meant the ever-growing industrial cities, especially in the southern tier. For many of the Irish, whose large core of children and grandchildren of earlier immigrants was now being augmented by newer arrivals, the rise out of humble circumstances had been facilitated by participation in local and state politics and by the appointments to police, fire, and public works departments that such participation entailed. By the end of the century, Irish politicians were holding electoral office themselves and were well along in the process of dominating public life in Boston and several other urban centers of the region. In their usage, the term *Yankee,* applied to employers and political opponents, had become merely another ethnic slur.

Immigrants arriving in Boston, ca. 1920

As the 19th century approached its end, no Yankee summed up the sense of decline better than the historian Henry Adams, the last eminent member of what had once been the definitive New England family. His education up to now, he believed—the education of a 19th-century New England gentleman with intellectual roots in the 18th century—had done nothing to prepare him for the new 20th century, which was now upon him.

THE 20TH CENTURY

For individual New Englanders, the first half of the 20th century was exactly what it was for the rest of the country: a time of rapid change in daily life, resulting in most cases from the industrial and technological developments that had begun in the Gilded Age. Those who remained on the farms of northern New England were affected more slowly than most, but the rural electrification program of the New Deal eventually dragged even the most recalcitrant of traditional Yankees into the 20th century.

In the more heavily populated parts of New England, the change was even more profound. On the eve of World War I, the proportion of foreign-born inhabitants in the three southern New England states reached about 65 percent, the highest in the nation. Practically all the central, east, and south European nations from which millions of emigrants fled to North America between 1870 and 1920 sent at least some representatives to southern New England. Meanwhile, more arrivals from French Canada joined their compatriots in industrial towns in Maine, New Hampshire, and Vermont as well as in southern New England, while smaller numbers of selected nationality groups spread into northern New England from their original ports of arrival.

One result of this transformation of the New England population was a period of ethnic politics that lasted at least until some years after World War II. In Massachusetts especially, where by the turn of the century the Irish influence had become the determining influence in the Democratic Party, the Yankee minority became even more conscious of its own ethnicity and embraced the Republican Party with renewed zeal. One such Republican, Vermont-born Calvin Coolidge, was elected vice president in 1920 after two terms as governor of Massachusetts. On the death of Warren G. Harding in 1923, he succeeded to the presidency, where he combined frugal policies with a taciturn style and a reputation for personal honesty that for a time endeared this almost archetypal Yankee to the mainly prosperous and conservative America of the 1920s. On the state and municipal levels, electoral politics in southern New England, with some local variations depending upon the prevalence of the newer ethnic groups other than Irish, became reduced largely to a contest for policy and patronage between Yankee Republicans and Irish Democrats.

One softening influence on this stark division was the combination of Depression-era programs and wartime leadership of Franklin D. Roosevelt, who attracted sufficient support in southern New England and New Hampshire to lead many Republicans to at least a temporary abandonment of their traditional party—not, however, in Maine and Vermont, the only two states in the union to cast their electoral votes for Alf Landon in 1936. A much more decisive influence was the election and brief presidency of John F. Kennedy, a Massachusetts Irish Catholic, but a stylish and apparently thoroughly assimilated one. Questions of ethnicity and religion have seldom figured seriously in ticket-building and campaign rhetoric since 1960, although in some cities and on some occasions matters of race have replaced them.

Another result of the transformation of the population was the post–World War I Red Scare and its associated manifestations of xenophobia, of which New England contributed several. Among these were the forcible defeat of the Boston police strike in 1919 (by Governor Coolidge), the New England version of the roundup of supposedly radical aliens ordered by Attorney General Mitchell Palmer in January 1920, and the passionately debated conviction in 1921 and execution in 1927 of the Italian anarchists Nicola Sacco and Bartolomeo Vanzetti for armed robbery and murder.

A different side of the Yankee political tradition emerged during the Cold War version of the Red Scare when, in 1950, Margaret Chase Smith of Maine, the first woman elected to the U.S. Senate, spearheaded a Declaration of Conscience against the terrorizing tactics of her fellow Republican senator Joseph R. McCarthy. Of the seven GOP senators who signed a courageous statement condemning McCarthy's unprincipled harnessing of the fear of subversion for political advantage, three represented the northern New England states.

During and after World War II, another transformation in the urban population of New England occurred with a significant northward migration of African Americans from the rural South. Boston's black population tripled between 1940 and 1960, resulting in a challenge to the preexisting black community, including its peaceful and usually friendly relations, despite its second-class status, with the city's whites. Other New England cities whose white residents, like Boston's, counted their enlightened race relations a mark of superiority over the rest of America were similarly affected. The bubble of complacency burst with the crisis over court-ordered busing as a solution to de facto school segregation in Boston. Racial animosities ran high on both sides as this issue, with its accompanying demonstrations and violence, dominated the 1970s and transformed the political culture of Boston as profoundly as the emergence of the Irish as a political force a century before.

Throughout most of the first 30 years of the 20th century, New England experienced a booming economy. Textile and shoe manufacturing led the way in northern and eastern New England, supplemented by papermaking and dairy farming in the northern tier and by the production of machines, tools, and other technological goods throughout the region. Connecticut, the historic center of the nation's firearms industry, achieved dramatic new levels of productivity as a result of World War I and during and after the war added parts for the automotive, aviation, and electrical power industries to its manufacturing capacity. By the eve of World War II, Connecticut had become a center of aircraft production and submarine building as well.

In some parts of New England, the Great Depression began early. By 1920 there were already signs that the textile industry on which much of the region depended would not stay in New England forever. Fourteen of Connecticut's 47 cotton mills, for example, moved south between 1919 and 1929. These losses were less noticeable there, however, where other industries were humming along, than in places like Lowell, where many mills either relocated or shut down during the 1920s, and Manchester, N.H., the home of the largest textile manufacturing complex in the world. A crippling strike in Manchester in 1922 set the stage for a series of subsequent disasters, culminating in the final shutdown in 1935. A nearly dead textile industry was revived temporarily during World War II. The war also created demands for everything that New England's variegated industrial plant could produce. Vacant factory space was pressed into round-the-clock use, idle machinery was refurbished and reactivated, and a fully employed civilian workforce went to work at everything from spinning cotton thread to building ships and military aircraft. As in other parts of the country, in New England the recruitment of women to formerly male-dominated manufacturing jobs as well as into the military worked the beginning of a profound social change that had yet to run its course at the end of the century.

After the war, textiles finally left New England for good, except for a few specialty mills, and the shoemaking industry declined drastically. The region was saved from a prolonged postwar depression, however, by the demands of the Cold War. The region's new industrial base became electronics and high technology, fed by the great scientific and technological research centers in New England's eminent universities. In these same postwar years, the region became much more adept at developing and promoting its potential as a mecca for tourism, continuing a trend that had begun during the Gilded Age and taken a more democratic turn with the coming of paid vacations and the family automobile. Now the tourist and recreation industry became a four-season affair, responsible for large contributions to the economies of all six states.

The selling of New England to visitors who came to fish, hunt, swim, sail, hike, ski, see autumn foliage, shop for antiques, patronize bookshops, hear an outdoor symphony, photograph covered bridges, and study family genealogies entails an effort, once more, to define the region. The effort is shared even by those who have nothing to sell, especially those whose ancestral roots in New England are deep or who by adoption have found in stone walls or in pounding surf or in the village green and meetinghouse the sense of permanent place that they had found lacking in the mobile and transient America of the late 20th century. Usually these efforts concentrate on the regional past and its artifacts, a quest to recapture and understand a simpler and quieter time that is associated especially with rural New England. An idea of New England that stresses such a past has powerful appeal for visitors and residents alike. For the most thoughtful New Englanders, however, even those who acknowledge their own captivation by such an image, it is an image that lacks completeness because it rests on the pretense that history can be made static, a proposition that Henry Adams in his sad wisdom knew a century ago could not stand.

Penobscot Princess Watawaso (left) and her sister preparing brown ash for weaving, 1947

THE FUTURE

At the opening of the 21st century, New England faces special new regional challenges, themselves the product of recent changes. The end of the Cold War, upon which much of the region's economy depended for two generations, brought the closing of military bases and an abrupt decline in defense production. Yet another important change in the population has occurred with the immigration of significant numbers of Southeast Asians, whose sacrificial work ethic and way of life are reminiscent of the Puritan-Yankee ethos that brought success to the region's once-dominant population.

Changes in costs and in revenue sources—and in public attitudes—have presented states and localities with difficult questions of public finance. The competing demands of industry, recreation, and environmental conservation continue to pose unresolved questions about the proper use, or nonuse, of the region's natural resources. The debate over such questions as well as the region's continued confrontation with issues of ethnic relations has been enriched and complicated by the reemergence into the public consciousness of the very dispossessed peoples who were thrust onto the geographic and economic margins of society, and thus into near invisibility, by the European conquest of this part of America three centuries ago.

Beginning in the 1970s, a series of successful land claims initiated an era of new prosperity and cultural assertiveness on the part of several Native American tribal communities from Maine to Connecticut. The moral, economic, political, and even environmental and cultural implications of this dramatic, largely unexpected development have yet to be fully understood and confronted by any of the sides in the resulting transformed relations among peoples.

The ideas of New England that were formed by John Smith, the Puritans, and the reformers and Transcendentalists all looked to the future. At the beginning of the 21st century, the most vital regional activity of all is being carried on by men and women in a wide range of fields who are trying to imagine a sane and fruitful future that will be grounded wisely in New England's complicated past.

Henry Adams, *The Education of Henry Adams* (1973 [1904]); James Axtell, *The Invasion Within: The Contest of Cultures in Colonial North America* (1985); William Billings, *The New-England Psalm-Singer; or, American Chorister* (1770 [rep. in *The Complete Works of William Billings*, vol. 1, ed. Karl Kroeger (1981)]); Paul Boyer and Stephen Nissenbaum, *Salem Possessed: The Social Origins of Witchcraft* (1974); Francis J. Bremer, *The Puritan Experiment: New England Society from Bradford to Edwards*, rev. ed. (1995); Dona Brown, *Inventing New England: Regional Tourism in the 19th Century* (1995); Richard D. Brown, *Massachusetts: A Bicentennial History* (1978); Richard L. Bushman, *From Puritan to Yankee: Character and the Social Order in Connecticut, 1690–1765* (1967); Charles E. Clark, *The Eastern Frontier: The Settlement of Northern New England, 1610–1763* (1970); Clark, *Maine: A Bicentennial History* (1977); David Hackett Fischer, *Paul Revere's Ride* (1994); Doris Kearns Goodwin, *The Fitzgeralds and the Kennedys* (1987); Robert A. Gross, *The Minutemen and Their World* (1976); Oscar Handlin, *Boston's Immigrants, 1790–1865: A Study in Acculturation* (1991 [1941]); Tamara K. Hareven and Randolph Langenbach, *Amoskeag: Life and Work in an American Factory-City* (1978); Francis Jennings, *The Invasion of America: Indians, Colonialism, and the Cant of Conquest* (1976); John F. Kasson, *Civilizing the Machine: Technology and Republican Values in America, 1776–1900* (1976); Bert James Loewenberg, *American History in American Thought: Christopher Columbus to Henry Adams* (1972); J. Anthony Lukas, *Common Ground: A Turbulent Decade in the Lives of Three American Families* (1985); David McCullough, *John Adams* (2001); William G. McLoughlin, *Rhode Island: A Bicentennial History* (1978); Edmund S. Morgan, "The Puritan Ethic and the American Revolution," *William and Mary Quarterly*, 3d ser., 25 (1967); Elizabeth Forbes Morison and Elting E. Morison, *New Hampshire: A Bicentennial History* (1976); Charles T. Morrissey, *Vermont: A Bicentennial History* (1981); Thomas H. O'Connor, *The Hub: Boston Past and Present* (2001); William D. Piersen, *Black Yankees: The Development of an Afro-American Subculture in 18th-Century New England* (1988); David M. Roth, *Connecticut: A Bicentennial History* (1979); Howard S. Russell, *A Long, Deep Furrow: Three Centuries of Farming in New England* (1976); Robert Sobel, *Coolidge: An American Enigma* (1998); Alan Taylor, *Liberty Men and Great Proprietors: The Revolutionary Settlement on the Maine Frontier, 1768–1820* (1990); Laurel Thatcher Ulrich, *Good Wives: Image and Reality in the Lives of Women in Northern New England, 1685–1750* (1982); Walter Muir Whitehill and Laurence W. Kennedy, *Boston: A Topographical History* (2000).

Charles E. Clark

Precolonial Settlement At the time of the first English settlement, New England was home to peoples whose ancestors had arrived there some 12,000 years earlier. Generally known as Indians by the English, these native groups referred to themselves by a variety of names, among them Micmac, Penobscot, Abenaki, Pawtucket, Massachusett, Pokanoket, Narragansett, Pequot, Nipmuck, Quiripi, and Mohegan. All spoke Eastern Algonquian languages. Archaeologists suggest that settlement of this region began soon after the withdrawal of the last glacial ice. In the Paleo-Indian period small, mobile bands of settlers hunted abundant large game, leaving such artifacts as leaf-shaped, fluted projectile points throughout New England. Native hunters appear to have lived in camps near deposits of chert, jasper, and other lithic materials used in tool manufacture.

Either these or later hunters established themselves permanently in New England, initiating an archaeological period known as the Archaic (ca. 7000–200 B.C.). During this time native people adapted their tools and diets to what was available locally. Coastal inhabitants of New England in particular depended heavily on fish, shellfish, and marine mammals and developed a highly sophisticated technology to exploit these resources. Peoples of the interior hunted deer, moose, bear, and other fur-bearing animals. Because these groups were more populous and more sedentary than their predecessors, their archaeological remains are more numerous. Vestiges of their culture indicate that they lived in circular dwellings with central hearths, wore tailored clothing, and, in the more northern regions, practiced elaborate burial rituals that included the use of powdered red and yellow ocher.

The most recent archaeological period in southern New England, the Woodland (ca. A.D. 500–1500), was characterized by a series of innovations and adaptations. In the early centuries of this period, native peoples of the region were heavily influenced by the important ritual and religious developments of the Ohioan peoples to the west and south; members of the Adena culture, in particular, probably traded with New England natives for shell and may have had diplomatic or tributary ties with them as well.

At about the same time people living in southern New England adopted a new language, Proto-Eastern Algonquian. That language soon spilt into daughter languages, which eventually developed into the languages known as Micmac, Passamaquoddy, Abenaki, Loup, Massachusett, Narragansett, Pequot-Mohegan, and Quiripi-Unquachog. As the Woodland period progressed, people

in the northern regions of New England moved seasonally between the coast and interior locations, exploiting game and fish, wild plants, and other resources. Groups in the south, ancestors of the modern-day Massachusett, Pokanoket (Wampanoag), Narragansett, Pequot, Nipmuck, and Mohegan, were more sedentary but developed two distinct adaptations. Those on the coast became increasingly dependent on local shellfish and other marine resources as well as on native plants like hickory and acorns. Coastal people were able to live in semipermanent communities in the rich estuarine environments common to these areas. Those living near the fertile bottomlands of the Connecticut River valley became accomplished farmers, establishing large, permanent villages and living in clustered dwellings that resembled the longhouses of the Iroquois. Like the Iroquois, they came to depend on maize, beans, and squash as their principal crops.

Both inland and coastal peoples used ceramics, which through time became increasingly well adapted for cooking grains and other plants. Like their ancestors, they traded with the great Ohioan urban centers to the west, traveling along established inland waterways. By the end of the Woodland period, even coastal peoples had adopted maize, and the population of southern New England had grown to almost 120,000 people. The more sparsely settled northern territories had a population of close to 20,000.

Europeans began exploring the New England coast in the early 16th century, although natives of the region may have had earlier, sporadic contact with Basques or even Norse from Greenland. Giovanni da Verrazano first sailed the coast of New England in 1524, but explorations did not begin in earnest there until Bartholomew Gosnold's voyage of 1602. Visits by Martin Pring in 1603, Samuel de Champlain in 1604 and 1606, and George Weymouth in 1605 followed. Henry Hudson also explored the southern New England coast in 1609, as did Adriaen Block in 1612 and 1614. The early explorers bartered beads, metals, and cloth for fur and corn; the European items, beyond their practical uses, are believed to have had religious significance for the native people.

The first European descriptions of the native peoples of New England were full of praise for the dress, physical strength, and beauty of the natives, the technology of their culture, and the richness of their natural resources. It was these very riches, however, that Europeans, particularly English settlers, were eager to exploit. Inevitably, their pursuit of economic and political hegemony at the ex-

pense of the indigenous inhabitants of New England brought natives and newcomers into conflict.

Early English settlers in Plymouth, Boston, and the newly established colony of Rhode Island found that the natives were organized into communities led by hereditary rulers known as sachems (from the Massachusett word *sontimoog*). These men (and, less often, women) allocated resources, conducted diplomacy, made decisions concerning war, and administered justice within the community. Some of them, known as *ketasontimoog*, or great sachems, controlled larger territories and maintained tributary relations with subordinate sachemships. To the north, native peoples were organized in patrilineally related bands led by charismatic individuals who were active in trade and warfare. Inland farming people may have been organized in a more egalitarian, lineage-based fashion.

All native groups shared a deeply rooted spirituality based on the concept of *manitou*, an animating force manifested in nature, animals, and remarkable acts by human beings. Manitou were believed to take human or animal forms—frequently a snake, a bird, or other water or sky dwellers. Native people sought contact with manitou through prayer, fasting, trances, and dreams. Religious leaders, known in southern New England as powwows, had especially strong relationships with manitou and called on their many powers in their healing and divination.

The material culture of the Native Americans was extremely well adapted to their diet and environment, with a strongly marked division of labor. Men were responsible for the manufacture of stone tools, traps, and fishing equipment. Women made pottery, wove the mats that covered the interior and exterior of their homes (called in southern New England *wetuwamash*, one of the sources for the English word *wigwam*), and prepared all foods. Women were also the farmers in southern New England.

Social customs in various parts of New England varied. Among the Micmac, for instance, a man who wished to marry was required to live with his intended's family for one to three years before the union could take place. In southern New England brides' families received a gift, known as a bride-price, when a marriage was contracted. In some areas women went to live in their husbands' communities; in others, above all those in which farming was important, men sometimes moved in with their wives. Parents and other family members taught children the skills appropriate to their sex.

Although there was social inequality in

some coastal communities (especially those in the south), native people were noted for their generosity to friends and strangers alike. Warfare, although frequent, was waged on a small scale and focused on the acquisition of captives, who were often adopted into the captors' communities, and on revenge. Trading was active in the region, and travel was common even over great distances. Many people spoke more than one language and maintained ties with remote communities.

The remarkable balance of native life was unalterably disrupted by the coming of English explorers and settlers. In 1617–19, before the establishment of colonies, a terrible epidemic of European import swept through the Massachusetts Bay area, wiping out up to 90 percent of the native population. In 1633 another epidemic raged, causing similar losses along the Connecticut River.

Survivors found their lands increasingly encroached upon by English settlers, their game and fish disappearing, and their freedom restricted. Although some moved north and west in an effort to preserve their culture, many more remained. With time some of those living among the new settlers became Christian, and many adopted their English neighbors' ways of life.

Kathleen J. Bragdon, *The Native People of Southern New England, 1500–1650* (1996); Paul J. Lindholdt, ed., *John Josselyn, Colonial Traveler: A Critical Edition of "Two Voyages to New-England"* [1674], by John Josselyn (1988); Dean R. Snow, *The Archaeology of New England* (1980); Bruce G. Trigger, ed., *Northeast*, vol. 15 of *Handbook of North American Indians*, gen. ed. William C. Sturtevant (1978); Roger Williams, *A Key into the Language of America*, critical introduction by John J. Teunissen and Evelyn J. Hinz (1973 [1643]); William Wood, *New England's Prospect*, ed. Alden T. Vaughan (1977 [1634]).

Kathleen J. Bragdon

European Settlement and Development, 1620–1775
Permanent colonial settlement began in 1620 with Plymouth, the first of the religious colonies in New England. The lessons learned by Plymouth's colonists during their early hardships later contributed to the Massachusetts Bay Colony's success; established in 1630, it quickly overshadowed Plymouth in sheer numbers. Because of the vast numbers of immigrants who moved to New England between 1630 and 1643 the period is known as the Great Migration. After 1643 migration declined significantly, and by midcentury most English immigration to New England was complete. This wave of migration was a critical factor in the survival and growth of 17th-century New England colonies; the approximately 20,000 English who arrived during the Great Migration brought goods and money, causing town populations to soar.

The Sarah Swan stone, 1767, Bristol, R.I.

Most English migrants to New England were Puritans who came primarily for religious reasons. Although they typically made the trip in family groups, some were unmarried young adults who came as indentured servants. Ratios of men to women in these 17th-century New England communities were unequal, though more balanced than in other regions of colonial North America. The healthful climate and more favorable sex ratios in New England enabled the populations to increase more by reproduction than immigration. New England's colonial population reached 23,000 by around 1660, 90,000 by around 1700, and more than 500,000 by the American Revolution.

While the English population of New England grew, however, the Native American population decreased dramatically, as native communities were hit by wave after wave of epidemic disease against which they had little immunity. Moreover, the numbers of enslaved Africans in New England increased throughout the colonial period with perhaps 1,000 by 1690, 4,000 by 1720, and 15,000 on the eve of the Revolution.

Settled along rivers and coastlines, colonial New England was blessed with waterways that offered ease of transportation and access to trade and communication networks. Agriculture, fishing, fur trade, and timber extraction each played important roles in New England's development and provided the impetus for much colonial expansion during the 17th century. Colonial settlement expanded rapidly in the 1630s and 1640s; English settlements in New Hampshire, Connecticut, and Providence Plantations (later Rhode Island) all took root between 1634 and 1638. Gradually, settlement also spread south to Long Island and north to what would become Maine.

New England began to develop an export trade in the 1640s that would continue throughout the colonial period, exporting livestock, fish, timber and timber products, and New England–built ships. Faced with a short growing season, rocky soil, and plant diseases, most New England farmers were less involved with export agriculture than farmers in other regions of colonial North America, particularly

during the 18th century. Inheritance practices—which rejected primogeniture and entail in order to divide holdings among all children—along with large family sizes, low mortality, and the land's marginal fertility pushed many to migrate north and west in search of land.

Though it now seems clear that the framework of New England colonization was established by the mid-17th century, a sense of insecurity long persisted among colonists, many of whom made plans in the 1640s and 1650s to abandon New England and migrate to the West Indies. This insecurity led to the formation of the United Colonies of New England, an intercolonial defensive alliance against Indian, Dutch, and French threats that lasted until the 1670s. The United Colonies was primarily a military coalition; there was otherwise little political contact among the New England colonies until the political crisis of the 1760s.

Most political interaction flowed between individual colonies and England; while some colonies existed under a charter that allowed them to choose their own governors and councilors, others were royal colonies with officials appointed by London. Similar hierarchical but participatory political institutions developed at the local level throughout the region. All colonial New England towns, for instance, held town meetings. Town authority and each colony's political autonomy were threatened briefly during the Dominion of New England (1686–89), which consolidated New England, New York, and New Jersey under the administration of Sir Edmund Andros. The Dominion was short-lived and unpopular with most colonists.

New England's settlement and development were intertwined with wars in the colonial era; colonial settlements, for example, expanded into Connecticut rapidly after the Pequot War (1636–37). As the first major Anglo-Algonquian war in New England, the Pequot War was a watershed event because the English victors set a tone of ruthlessness and distrust that haunted Indian-English relations throughout the colonial period. King Philip's War (1675–76), or Metacom's War, carried this bitter legacy further. King Philip's War eventually spread through most of New England, and most of the Algonquian people of southern New England joined in an attempt to force colonists to return to England. The war was devastating on all sides. More than 500 English noncombatants were killed. More than 50 of approximately 90 English towns were attacked and at least a dozen were destroyed. The ensuing destruction and fear, exacerbated during the Anglo-French conflicts that followed, caused the New England frontier to contract until the eve of the Revolution, with New Englanders reluctant to expand further into native territories.

For Native Americans, King Philip's War was disastrous. An estimated 3,000 were killed, and English victors sold many Native American captives into slavery in the West Indies. In 1676 political independence for Native Americans in colonial New England came to an end, and many fled to French Canada or to New York, while those who stayed did so as a despised minority. Native Americans who remained in New England managed, against overwhelming odds, to preserve important aspects of their culture.

Proximity to New France meant that New England bore the brunt of the Anglo-French imperial rivalry. New Englanders participated in a series of wars with France from 1689 until 1763 that contributed to further economic and social problems. By the 18th century, Massachusetts (with Maine), New Hampshire, and Rhode Island were forced to import grains from the middle and southern colonies. Throughout the 18th century, Boston faced increasing competition from other ports, costly wars with France, and growing poverty. Fewer New England colonists could afford to buy enough land to support a family; to address this problem some colonies offered land for military service. Wars in the 1740s had a high social as well as economic cost, particularly in Boston, where one of every three adult women was widowed and almost one-fourth of taxpayers were unable to pay taxes. These conditions worsened in the 1760s and 1770s.

Meanwhile the spread of slavery in New England prompted some discussion. Although New Englanders generally shared the same attitudes toward Africans as colonial Europeans elsewhere, New England farmers, because they lacked a staple export crop, did not need large numbers of enslaved laborers. Thus, most enslaved blacks worked in urban households or on the docks of seaports, and significant free black communities sprang up in the cities. Although New England had a smaller slave population than other regions, the slave trade reached higher levels in maritime New England, where Rhode Island and Boston merchants developed the infamous triangle trade of New England fish, beef, barrel staves, and rum for West Indian molasses and African slaves. Merchants in Newport, R.I., became the leading carriers of slaves on mainland North America, relying on Boston merchants as intermediaries until the 1750s, when they began trading through alternate networks.

Religion served as both a cohesive and a divisive force in colonial New England communities. New England's earliest religious immigrants sought to create harmonious church-based communities, but with varying degrees of success and with considerable social and religious coercion. Early Puritan leaders in Massachusetts used harsh penalties to enforce religious conformity; Anne Hutchinson was banished from the colony for questioning authority, and Roger Williams was exiled for his Anabaptist beliefs. Rhode Island became a haven for those with Quaker or other religious beliefs not tolerated elsewhere in New England. Beginning in the 1730s, the Great Awakening became a source of social and religious conflict, as communities, churches, and households split between New Light believers of the new, more emotive evangelical expression of Protestant Christianity that swept New England and Old Light adherents to an older, less expressive, and more hierarchical version of Puritanism.

Philip J. Greven, Jr., *Four Generations: Population, Land, and Family in Colonial Andover, Massachusetts* (1970); David D. Hall, *Worlds of Wonder, Days of Judgment: Popular Religious Belief in Early New England* (1989); Daniel R. Mandell, *Behind the Frontier: Indians in 18th-Century Eastern Massachusetts* (1996); Mary Beth Norton, *Founding Mothers and Fathers: Gendered Power and the Forming of American Society* (1996); William D. Piersen, *Black Yankees: The Development of an Afro-American Subculture in 18th-Century New England* (1988); Neal Salisbury, *Manitou and Providence: Indians, Europeans, and the Making of New England, 1500–1643* (1982); Laurel Thatcher Ulrich, *Good Wives: Image and Reality in the Lives of Women in Northern New England 1650–1750* (1982); Daniel Vickers, *Farmers and Fishermen: Two Centuries of Work in Essex County, Massachusetts, 1630–1850* (1994).

Cynthia J. Van Zandt

American Revolution and Early National Period, 1775–1820

No region of the United States is more closely associated with the American Revolution than New England. Decades before the outbreak of the Revolution, the colonial wars (especially the French and Indian War of 1754–63) both strengthened and weakened the American colonists' ties to England. Offended by British arrogance and rising taxes, inspired by Enlightenment ideas and radical whiggery, New Englanders forged the crucible of the Revolution. The region was the site of the Stamp Act Riots (1765), the Boston Massacre (1770), the burning of the customs schooner *Gaspee* (1772), the Boston Tea Party (1773), and the closure of Boston Harbor by the Coercive Acts (1775). The opening of formal hostilities at Lexington and Concord, Mass., on April 19, 1775, and the fighting prowess displayed by patriots at Boston's Bunker Hill in June of the same year attest to the central role of New England in the Revolution.

When Ralph Waldo Emerson's grandfather William visited the Cambridge military encampment that housed soldiers from across New England in 1775, the differing forms of shelter caught his attention. Allen French cites a letter of July 17, 1775, from William to his wife: "Every tent is a portraiture of ye temper and taste of ye person that came in it," noting tents made of boards, stone, turf, birch, brush, and sailcloth.

As William Emerson discovered, Americans lived and waged war differently. Just as diverse types of shelter made up the Cambridge encampment, diverse cultures contributed to the pattern of the war. In contrast

Artist's rendering of the Battle of Bunker Hill, 1881

to the one-dimensional conflict portrayed in most accounts, the Revolution was fought by disparate peoples bound more closely to community than to a young nation.

This cultural patchwork at times inhibited the patriot cause. Vermont communities, for example, were divided by differing cultural values. Some patriots believed in deference to authority, whereas others, like the Green Mountain Boys and the New Lights, a group of religious revivalists inspired by the English divine George Whitefield and New England's Jonathan Edwards, adopted more egalitarian values. Patriarchalism limited women's active involvement in the fighting and forced many military recruiters to secure parental permission before sons could enlist.

Regional weather played an important role in the fighting. A series of cold winters leading up to the Revolution resulted in limited stocks of food when British forces required them. Maine's severe weather wreaked havoc with Colonel Benedict Arnold's wilderness march to and retreat from Quebec. Big campaigns were planned for milder seasons. Inspired by the Roman general Cincinnatus and agrarian virtue, farmers often left their ranks to return home for the harvest.

If some elements of New England culture impeded mobilization, others facilitated it. Like their Puritan and colonial forebears, many New Englanders went to war believing in providentialism and persuaded that God was on their side. A tradition of covenants and town meetings gave New Englanders more motivation and independence of thought than their opponents possessed. Patriots living on the coast were well prepared for sea duty, whether on privateers, in their state's naval forces, or in the Continental Navy.

Although the geographic center of fighting shifted after the spring of 1776, New England's early involvement was crucial. Upon hearing of the battle at Lexington, 20 men from Gageborough, Vt., elected a captain and marched to Cambridge to join the patriot army forming under George Washington. Richard Buel, Jr., points out in *Dear Liberty: Connecticut's Mobilization for the Revolutionary War* (1980) that between May and November 1776, 18,915 men from that state entered the Continental Army, the militia, and the patriot navy. Within a week of Lexington, 46 of Connecticut's 72 towns sent 3,716 recruits to Boston. Brunswick, Maine, dispatched one-third of its able-bodied men that same year.

Like Boston, northern New England played a critical role in the fighting. In May 1775 Ethan Allen, Benedict Arnold, and Allen's rambunctious Green Mountain Boys captured the dilapidated and weakly garrisoned Fort Ticonderoga, located where Lake Champlain joins Lake George, from the British. In June 1775 New York and Connecticut irregulars led by General Richard Montgomery left Ticonderoga to take Montreal and other British forts. A second patriot invading force of 1,050, under Benedict Arnold, left Cambridge with orders to advance up the Kennebec River in Maine and the Saint Lawrence to assault Quebec. The poorly coordinated pincer maneuver had failed by late 1775; New England musketeers endured serious hardships, and the patriots lost 5,000 men to battle, disease, and desertion, along with vast stores of equipment and supplies.

Reinforced in Canada by 1776, the redcoats foresaw recapturing Ticonderoga and launching a three-pronged squeeze on Albany, N.Y. New Englanders helped thwart British plans to seal off New England and crush the Revolution, however. Benedict Arnold successfully attacked a British fleet on Lake Champlain in October 1776, and Vermont's Fort Independence helped keep England's forces at bay until the summer of 1777. Built in 1776 to reinforce Fort Ticonderoga, Fort Independence held 12,000 to 13,000 troops along with women and children, making it a sort of military city and the colonies' fourth largest population center. The resumption of the British offensive against New England and Albany sent shock waves through the United States. New Englanders were dispatched to buttress the patriots in New York, and revolutionaries evacuated Ticonderoga on July 5, as General John Burgoyne led 9,400 redcoats, Hessian mercenaries, Indians, and camp followers south toward Albany.

In mid-August 1777 General John Stark and his force of 2,600 New Hampshire militiamen and allies dealt Burgoyne a serious blow when they destroyed a Hessian foraging party and relief force at the Battle of Bennington. The defeat cost Burgoyne a tenth of his expeditionary force and helped set the stage for the huge patriot victory at Saratoga in October 1777, the turning point of the war.

Bennington and Saratoga also made a strong impression on New England's native peoples, who tried to remain neutral or play the British off against the patriots. The Abenaki had guided Arnold's army through the Maine woods, but British coercion induced them to join Burgoyne's force. Burgoyne's disastrous campaign made the Abenaki less willing to assist the British, however.

Burgoyne's defeat also solidified the patriotism of Massachusetts's Stockbridge Indians, who had fought at Bennington and volunteered as minutemen even before the war began. Although the Mashpee of Cape Cod, the Penobscot of Maine, and the Pequot and Mohegan of Connecticut also fought alongside the patriots, the number of Native Americans who allied themselves with the revolutionaries fell far short of the estimated 13,000 who fought with the British.

Blacks also had mixed feelings about the Revolution. They saw little reason to assist the country that had enslaved them and had little to lose in helping the British, who were not dependent on black slave labor. Furthermore, colonial enlistment laws of the time frequently barred blacks from military service. A proclamation by the royal governor of Virginia in 1775 was to change the colonies' stance on such exclusionary policies; in it, according to Benjamin Quarles's *The Negro in the American Revolution* (1961), the British promised freedom to all "indentured servants, Negroes, or others . . . that are able and willing to bear arms . . . [to reduce] the Colony to a proper sense of duty to His Majesty's crown and dignity." Although tens of thousands of blacks joined the British forces, many chose to side with the patriots. Crispus Attucks died at the Boston Massacre, Prince Estabrook was wounded at Lexington, and Peter Salem fought at Bunker Hill. Reluctance on the part of some Continental officers to enlist blacks disappeared as vacancies in the American ranks grew. Desperate for recruits in 1778, Rhode Island created a regiment of 138 black soldiers, who fought ably. Accustomed to going to sea as mariners, blacks also made important contributions to patriot navies.

New England's participation in the war came at a heavy price, however. To take one example, of the 831 men and boys from Marblehead, Mass., serving with the patriots in 1780, 121 went missing in action and 166 became prisoners of war. The war widowed 378 of Marblehead's 1,069 women and orphaned 672 of its 2,242 children. Laurel Thatcher Ulrich notes that Marblehead women found it especially hard to discharge their duties because the war had followed fast on the heels of a series of local disasters. A shortage of firewood led some women to dismantle a portion of Marblehead's fishing wharves, the economic lifeblood of that seafaring community.

Like Marblehead, other New England towns had to fend for themselves while meeting the demands of mobilization. James Leamon contends that isolated settlements and limited economic and military resources made Maine's experience somewhat like that of the frontier, or "conflicted," societies of the lower South. In October 1775 a British fleet bombarded Falmouth, Maine, destroying 130 homes, an Anglican church, the new courthouse, and the fire station. Many helpless residents were forced to flee when their homes were looted and pillaged by neighboring militia.

Rhode Islanders may have endured even greater hardships. Effectively regulating the molasses trade, the Sugar Act of 1764 crippled Rhode Island's economy. The situation worsened in 1776, when the British captured Newport and imposed martial law, ultimately destroying this and other coastal Rhode Island communities. Elaine Crane writes in *A Dependent People: Newport, Rhode Island, in the Revolutionary Era* (1985) that the French author, reformer, and future revolutionary Jean Pierre Brissot de Warville, visiting Newport after the war, found "a reign of solitude . . . only interrupted by groups of idle men standing with folded arms at the corners of the streets, houses falling to ruin, miserable shops . . . grass growing in the public squares . . . rags stuffed in the windows."

Although the conflict undeniably disrupted New England's established trade and economic patterns, James Henretta has found evidence that the production of household and artisanal goods, undertaken to meet individual and military needs, rose substantially in many parts of the region during the Revolution. Women like the daughters of Martha Ballard of Hallowell, Maine, became involved in weaving. Known for their resilience in the face of hardship, wives in Marblehead bore the responsibility of securing food and fuel while their husbands were at sea. During the 1780s peddlers and traders appeared in growing numbers in the Connecticut River valley. Wartime exigencies and opportunities made thousands of farmers more calculating and allowed merchants to invest in privateering, government bonds, and new productive enterprises such as banks, textile factories, ships, gristmills, and sawmills. The chartering of the Massachusetts Bank in 1784, an exclusive franchise granted to the Charles River Bridge Company in 1785 by the General Court of Massachusetts, and the victories of entrepreneurial ironmasters and cotton mill owners over farmers testify to New England's accelerated economic development and commercial culture.

If the Revolution hastened the transition to capitalism and made the government more responsive to the interests of America's moneyed ranks, it also promoted popular sovereignty in America and the world. Concerned about England's new imperialism in the 1760s, ordinary New Englanders became increasingly involved in politics. The Declaration of Independence—with contributions by Roger Sherman of Connecticut and John Adams of Massachusetts and influenced by other declarations of independence issued in New England between April and early July 1776—brought immediate political changes to New England. On January 15, 1777, Vermont declared itself an independent republic. Forced to create a new government based upon the people as the constituent power, the state adopted a constitution on July 8, 1777. A wave of constitutional writing and constitutional conventions ensued.

The Massachusetts Constitution of 1780 sprang from the Revolution and served as a model for other key instruments of American democracy. The words "We the people ordain and establish," making governmental power emanate from the people, first appeared in the Massachusetts document and were subsequently used in the preamble to the U.S. Constitution in 1787 and the new Pennsylvania Constitution of 1790. The drafters of the U.S. Constitution also turned to the Massachusetts text in devising provisions for a system of checks and balances and a strong executive branch. The Massachusetts Constitution also served as a source of the U.S. Bill of Rights. Suffrage in the popular referendum to affirm the Massachusetts convention's work was extended to all free adult males.

Other important democratic changes occurred in the immediate aftermath of the war. Following the example set by Vermont's constitution, which forbade involuntary servitude, Massachusetts abolished slavery with revolutionary swiftness. By 1804 Connecticut, Rhode Island, and the other northern states had taken steps toward abolition. New Hampshire did not explicitly outlaw slavery, but the institution gradually disappeared after the Revolution. In the legislatures of New England, the less well-to-do were gaining seats, newly settled areas were winning representation, and voters were selecting many more representatives. By 1784 the number of Massachusetts legislators who were wealthy had dropped from the 1765 figure of 50 percent to only 21.5 percent. New Hampshire's legislature experienced even more radical changes. Whereas merchants, lawyers, and large landowners dominated the New Hampshire Assembly in 1765, 20 years later ordinary farmers with moderate properties controlled a majority of the seats.

From the Revolutionary War, American culture inherited some remarkably persistent attributes. The Civil War historian Grady McWhiney argues in *Attack and Die: Civil War Tactics and the Southern Heritage* (1984) that when the North and the South went to war in 1861, the South's Celtic heritage culturally conditioned the Confederate states to fight aggressively. Southerners fought like Cavaliers, and northerners like Puritans. Like George Washington, leaders of both sides opposed guerrilla warfare, although southern states possessed many of the conditions important for successful partisan warfare. Similarly, Washington's influence helped ensure that civilians would always hold the reins of military power and that military coups d'état would not threaten America.

Whether struggling for independence a second time in 1812 or battling enemies in Europe and Asia in the 20th century, the United States waged war in a distinctive manner. Enamored of the Cincinnatus model, America placed a premium on the militia and volunteerism, eschewing a large professional army until World War II. Ill-prepared for war at sites as diverse as Lexington, Fort Sumter, Havana Harbor, Pearl Harbor, and Kuwait, Americans eventually rallied to achieve complete military victory. This pattern was not to be repeated in the post–World War II era, however, when Americans became enmeshed in Korea and Vietnam. In both these cases America was doomed by its crusading spirit, its aversion to nonconventional warfare, and a hubris born of total victory in every war since the country's inception. Ironically, the United States confronted many of the same obstacles in Vietnam that the British faced in trying to suppress the American Revolution.

Colin Calloway, *The American Revolution in Indian Country* (1995); Allen French, *The First Year of the American Revolution* (1934); Robert Gross, *The Minutemen and Their World* (1976); James Henretta, *The Origins of American Capitalism* (1991); James Leamon, *Revolution Downeast: The War for Independence in Maine* (1993); Robert Shalhope, *Bennington and the Green Mountain Boys* (1996); Florence Simister, *The Fire's Center: Rhode Island in the Revolutionary Era* (1934); Laurel Thatcher Ulrich, "Daughters of Liberty: Religious Women in Revolutionary New England," in *Women in the Age of the American Revolution*, ed. Ronald Hoffman (1989).

William A. Baller

Antebellum New England, 1820–60

From 1820 to 1860, New England was the economic, political, legal, and cultural nerve center of the United States. The flowering of antebellum New England followed the War of 1812 and the Hartford Convention (1814–15), which had brought about the crippling of the region's economy and the nadir of its national reputation and political influence. This Yankee renaissance began symbolically with the Missouri Compromise of 1820, which created the sixth and final New England state—Maine.

During this era, the New England textile industry revolutionized manufacturing and set the trend for other budding industries and for the evolving wage-based economy: it improved textile machinery and waterpower generators, transformed the organization of production, and introduced the concept of time-discipline into the developing factory system. The mills of Lowell, Mass., Manchester, N.H., and Biddeford, Maine, to name just

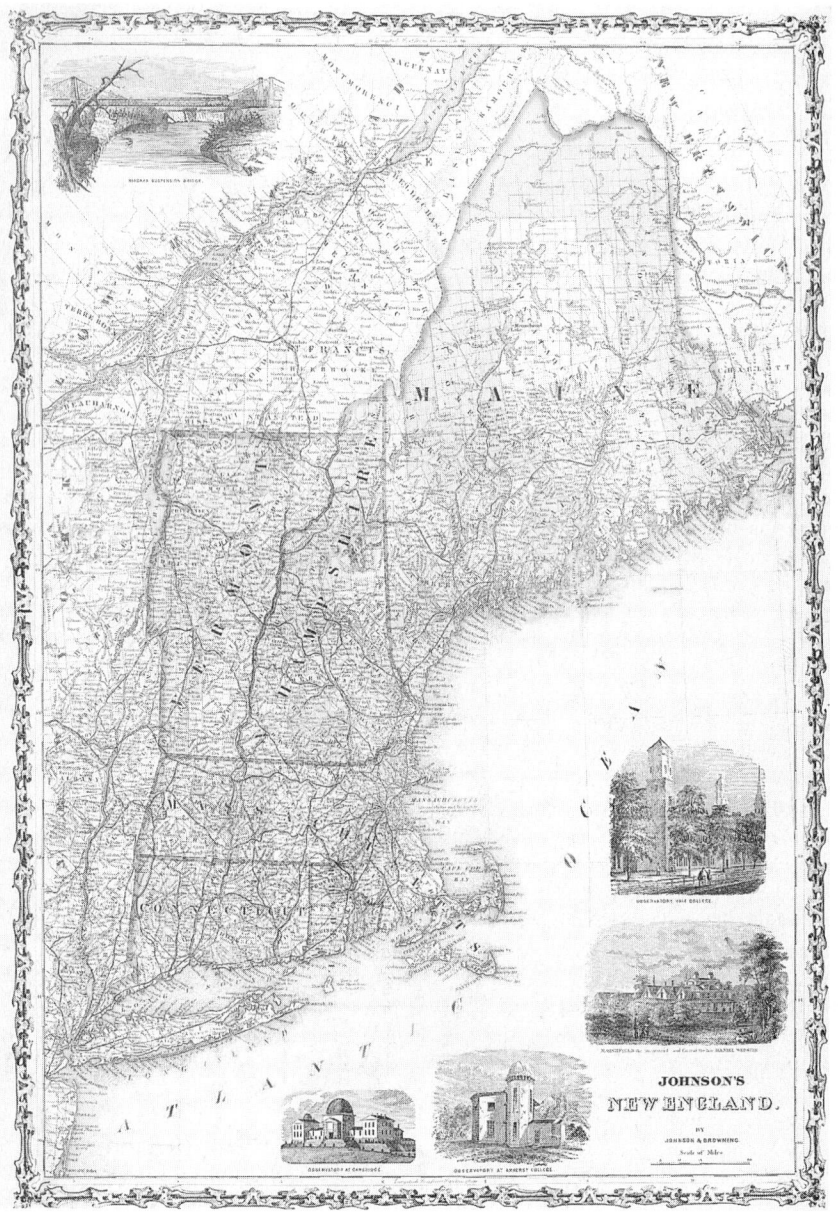

New England in 1860

a few of the larger enterprises, employed tens of thousands of farmers' daughters, who lived in a paternal-corporate dormitory setting that, ironically, contributed to both their collective sense of sisterhood and their economic independence.

This transference of labor from farm to mill was feasible because sheep pastures in northern New England took over family farmland and decreased the need for daughters' labor at home; for example, in 1840, there were 1.7 million sheep in Vermont alone, almost six animals for each Vermonter. Industrialization also occurred in rural areas such as Oxford and Dudley, Mass., where a tense power struggle developed between community and corporation. Other factories, such as the Amoskeag

Mills of Manchester, were magnets for French Canadian and Irish immigrants; this influx of immigrant workers marked the beginning of an increasingly heterogeneous New England population—a harbinger of the ethnic politics that came to fruition in later decades.

Industrialization was just one element of the market economy that was tightening its grip on antebellum America. Technological developments in transportation, infrastructure, and communications; urbanization and immigration; new legal precedents regarding the sanctity of contracts and the autonomy of corporations; and a more sophisticated financial system were all particularly felt in New England. One result of this rapid economic and social transformation was that middle-

and upper-class New Englanders felt as though they were losing control of their world; they especially feared an increasing dearth of order and self-discipline among the lower classes. Such misgivings sparked myriad reform movements that focused on individual improvement, thereby attempting to counteract the perceived negative effects of economic change and social discord.

Benevolent and moral reform societies multiplied throughout New England; temperance, reform of asylums and penitentiaries, improvements in medical care and education, and women's suffrage were all prominent causes. These humanitarian endeavors were informed by the fervent evangelical desire of the Second Great Awakening (which peaked during the 1820s and 1830s) to rescue the human spirit from depravity and bring the world closer to perfection—all in preparation for the Second Coming. Pious women reformers, in particular, functioned as America's conscience, female moral suasion crusading against masculine sins like gambling and sexual vice.

This activist sense of obligation and stewardship saw no greater expression than in the antislavery movement. Abolitionists judged slavery a dangerous blight upon the republic, a hypocritical betrayal of the ideals expressed in the Declaration of Independence, and a sin that condemned slave owners and deprived African Americans of their moral free agency. Yankee abolitionist leaders such as William Lloyd Garrison, Harriet Beecher Stowe, and Wendell Phillips brought the evils of slavery to the forefront of public consciousness. Stowe's phenomenally popular novel *Uncle Tom's Cabin* (1852) brought vile images of slavery directly into northern parlors and convinced an increasing torrent of northerners that the South's "peculiar institution" was immoral.

New England's politicians provided critical leadership throughout the antebellum era. Daniel Webster—scion of New Hampshire, Whig, congressman (1813–17, 1823–27), legal scholar, U.S. senator from Massachusetts (1827–41, 1845–50), orator, U.S. secretary of state (1841–43, 1850–52)—was one of the Great Triumvirate (consisting of Webster, Henry Clay of Kentucky, and John C. Calhoun of South Carolina), which dominated national politics for nearly 30 years. In 1830, goaded by a southern senator's claim to states' rights that could justify nullification or secession, Webster resoundingly defended the constitutional union as the creation of the people and thus not subordinate to the states' whims. This conflict foreshadowed the winter of secession (1860–61), and Webster's defense of 1830 was reiterated and lifted to new heights by President Abraham Lincoln at Gettysburg in 1863.

As sectionalism intensified during the 1850s, most New Englanders adhered to free-labor ideology, which extolled equal opportunity for social mobility, progress, and economic independence and abhorred the slave labor society propagated by the South. Small-town Yankees were unflinching supporters of radical-abolitionist Whig-Republicans, such as Henry Wilson of Massachusetts (U.S. senator, 1855–73), Israel Washburn of Maine (U.S. representative, 1851–61), John P. Hale of New Hampshire (U.S. representative, 1843–45, U.S. senator, 1847–53, 1855–65), and Francis Gillette of Connecticut (U.S. senator, 1854–55), who collectively exerted enormous influence in Congress on behalf of Yankee ideology. Charles Sumner of Massachusetts (U.S. senator, 1851–74) led the region's political struggles for abolition and against the supposed efforts of the South's so-called slave power to corrupt the national government and extend slavery to the Pacific, thereby transforming the republic into a "slaveocracy."

Outside the political arena, U.S. Supreme Court Associate Justice Joseph Story ensured that Yankee legal culture would become America's legal culture. Through his writings, his decisions from the bench, and his teaching, Story modernized American jurisprudence and rescued it from the centrifugal forces inherent to a rapidly expanding, fragmented legal system in its formative stage. From his chair at Harvard Law School (1829–45), Story trained a generation of lawyers, amassed the finest academic legal library in the nation, established Harvard as the country's preeminent law school, and published a magisterial series of commentaries on virtually all the major branches of American law. He nationalized New England's version of law by making American jurisprudence more scientific and instrumentalist—that is, practical and flexible, with an eye toward the real-life consequences of its decisions—which accommodated the development of the country's market economy. Story also attempted to fend off the South's aggressive constitutional theories. In his *Commentaries on the Constitution* (1833), he refuted the South's contract theory of the Constitution and the idea of state sovereignty underpinning it. His pedagogical methods and legal vision shaped the teaching and practice of American law for the remainder of the 19th century.

While Justice Story doctored the country's legal infirmities, the New England Transcendental movement of the 1830s and 1840s ministered to the American soul; it breathed new life into the nation's culture and helped change the direction of religion, literature, and social thought in the United States. Centered in Boston and Concord, Mass., the movement

had neither formal doctrine nor membership. Indeed, it borrowed from an eclectic variety of European schools of philosophy, particularly the German transcendentalists and their chief architect, Immanuel Kant. The most important American Transcendentalists included Henry David Thoreau, William Ellery Channing, Bronson Alcott, Margaret Fuller, Theodore Parker, and Ralph Waldo Emerson, the central figure of the movement. American Transcendentalists emphasized the innate value and autonomy of the individual; in part, theirs was a spiritual extension of the political ideology of the Revolution. They generally believed in an intuitive idealism, personal freedom, the idea of an organic universe permeated by an immanent God, the divinity of humankind, and the importance of individual moral insight, as opposed to the rule of many.

Although Transcendentalists believed that reform must originate from within the individual, most joined social-reform organizations that worked in such causes as temperance, pacifism, abolition of slavery, and universal suffrage. Some also became interested in communitarian experimentation, the most famous example of which is George Ripley's Brook Farm, established in 1841 in West Roxbury, a suburb of Boston. Artists from every field banded together, sharing their work and ideas, in order to stimulate intellectual and aesthetic fermentation. Their small-scale utopian experiment, however, was neither financially stable nor entirely harmonious, and the endeavor collapsed in 1847. A similar, more short-lived affair was founded in 1843 by Bronson Alcott at Fruitlands in Harvard, Mass.

Even at its zenith, Transcendentalism never quite achieved the status of a grassroots movement. Nonetheless, its influence was far-reaching and has reverberated through the years, enriched and reexpressed through the lives of such luminaries as Walt Whitman, Emily Dickinson, Nathaniel Hawthorne, John Dewey, Mary Baker Eddy, Mohandas K. Gandhi, and Martin Luther King, Jr.

During the antebellum era, New England rose from the ashes and humiliation of the 1810s to achieve national leadership, leaving an unmatched record of achievement and influence for a region in American history. New England's identity has never been more vibrant and confident than during the antebellum period, its social and moral endeavors never so profound, its cultural contributions never so unique, its legal and political guidance never more crucial.

Thomas Dublin, *Women at Work: The Transformation of Work and Community in Lowell, Massachusetts, 1826–1860* (1979); Eric Foner, *Free Soil, Free Labor, Free Men: The Ideology of the Republican Party before the Civil War* (1970); R. Kent Newmyer, "Harvard Law School, New England Legal Culture, and the Antebellum Origins of American Jurisprudence," *Journal of American History* 74, no. 3 (December 1987); Charles G. Sellers, *The Market Revolution: Jacksonian America, 1815–1846* (1991); Ronald G. Walters, *American Reformers, 1815–1860* (1978); Walters, *The Anti-Slavery Appeal: American Abolitionism after 1830* (1976).

David A. Cecere

Industrialization and Urbanization, 1865–1914

In her autobiography, *Loom and Spindle* (1898), Harriet H. Robinson, a first-generation Lowell, Mass., "mill girl," identified profound changes that had transformed urban industrial life in New England since the Civil War. The factories, in her opinion, were "not so agreeable nor so healthful to work in as they used to be." She commented that the "children of the land of Dante, of Thomas Moore [*sic*], of Racine, and of Goethe" now replaced the "children of New England ancestry" and that neither "the church of their parents" nor the strict moral paternalism of the mill owners guided the lives of these new workers as they had Robinson's native-born contemporaries. Although employees worked fewer hours, manufacturers now required them "to do a far greater amount of work in a given time" than had been true in Robinson's day. Their souls, she lamented, "seemed starved." Robinson believed that New England manufacturers needed to "mix a little conscience with their capital" to ensure that factory operatives would receive "better homes than they find themselves in [in] too many of our factory towns and cities, and a better social atmosphere, that they may be lifted out of their mental squalor into a higher state of thought and feeling." Only then, grieved Robinson, could New England's "lost Eden" be restored.

In the decades between the Civil War and World War I the emergence of large-scale industry, along with rapid urban growth and increased immigration, remade New England and the nation. Many individuals shared Robinson's sense of loss, particularly among such social elites as the Boston Brahmins. Before the Civil War the textile magnate Abbott Lawrence could proudly boast of his $50,000 contribution to Harvard University. After the war individual gifts of $3.5 million to Johns Hopkins University, $24 million to Stanford University, and $34 million to the University of Chicago made Lawrence's gift pale by comparison. Observing the rise in the staggering fortunes of the millionaire entrepreneurs Cornelius Vanderbilt, John D. Rockefeller, Jay Gould, and Andrew Carnegie elsewhere in the United States, the Harvard professor Barrett Wendell bemoaned that New Englanders were "vanishing into provincial obscurity." "It is time that we perished," confided the historian Brooks Adams to his brother Henry. "The world is tired of us."

New England nonetheless remained the most densely populated urbanized industrial region in the country. The percentage of New England's population that was foreign born or had foreign-born parents was higher than in any other part of the country. Regional cities grew dramatically, pushing outward and recasting themselves internally. Between 1870 and 1900 many cities enlarged their boundaries by thousands of acres. Boston, for instance, originally occupied a peninsula of 783 acres but by the late 19th century had spread over almost 24,000 acres. New households and businesses strained existing services and created an urgent need for water, gas, street lighting, transportation, and sewer systems, for additional streets, schools, and government buildings, and for more police officers, firefighters, and teachers.

The newcomers came from eastern and southern Europe, French-speaking Canada, the Cape Verde Islands, and the West Indies. By World War I growing numbers of African American migrants from the rural South were joining them. The large influx of Jews and Catholics was one of the most consequential new features of urban immigration. New immigrants tended to live initially in older, inner districts of the region's cities, frequently creating crowded ethnic enclaves. In many of New England's urban areas, particularly Boston, Worcester, Mass., and Providence, a new, distinctive form of working-class vernacular architecture emerged, the three-decker. Consisting of three long, narrow apartment units stacked on top of each other, these three-story buildings became commonplace in New England industrial centers by the end of the period. Also clustered within the urban landscape were whole networks of voluntary

ethnic institutions, including clubs, churches, and mutual benefit societies, that provided sick and death benefits to their members. Crowded and cut off from their native-born counterparts, immigrants brought vastly dissimilar cultures, languages, and customs to the region. As they became preponderant, the old order disappeared.

Divergent patterns of production characterized New England industry. Throughout the region single-industry mill towns maintained their notable place. Lowell, for example, continued to be a center for the manufacture of staple cloth, but newer textile centers came to dwarf the City of Spindles. Lawrence, Mass., developed by Boston investors before the Civil War, specialized in the production of woolens and by the 1880s housed three of the largest textile mills in the country. Unlike Lowell, where firms maintained separate identities, the textile factories of Lawrence consolidated in 1899 to form the American Woolen Company with more than 12,000 workers. In Manchester, N.H., another initiative funded by Boston investors became the nation's largest textile factory. Consisting of 30 major buildings and employing 17,000 people, the Amoskeag Manufacturing Company dominated both the economic and social life of the city.

A third great textile center emerged after the Civil War in Fall River, Mass., which boasted scores of cotton mills by the late 1870s. Fall River's waterpower resources proved inadequate as the city's mills proliferated; local manufacturers responded by pioneering the extensive use of steam power. Fall River mill owners also developed new, highly automated ring-spinning machinery. Such technological innovation, however, spurred a series of strikes by highly skilled groups such as the English mule spinners—operators of special machines used in spinning fine and delicate yarns—who resisted what they felt was a dilution of their

craft. In the shadows of these industrial giants, smaller textile cities also emerged, such as Woonsocket, R.I., which specialized in woolen and worsted production.

Following the Civil War many New England cities diversified their industry. By the early 20th century Bridgeport, Conn., had become famous for the manufacture of specialized metal products, particularly machine tools, rifles, and ammunition casings, and it claimed one-fifth of the world's corset market. North of Bridgeport a band of towns—Bristol, Waterbury, and Meriden, Conn.—became national leaders in brass, clock, and silver manufacturing.

Providence also emerged from the Civil War as an important manufacturing center. It distinguished itself in many areas: machine tools from the Brown and Sharpe Company, files from the Nicholson File Company, steam engines from the Corliss Steam Engine Company, and flat and hollow silverware from the Gorham Manufacturing Company were respected around the world. Powering all of the equipment in Machinery Hall and rising almost 30 feet above the display floor, the Corliss Company's giant 1,500-horsepower twin-cylinder steam engine was the most celebrated exhibit at the 1876 International Centennial Exhibition in Philadelphia. Providence was also a leader in woolen manufacture and furnished a quarter of the nation's total jewelry production by 1900.

After the Civil War, Worcester also joined the list of prominent northeastern industrial cities. Product diversity marked Worcester's manufacturing, but more than 40 percent of the city's workforce produced machinery, tools, and metal wire. Many claimed that Washburn Wire Company had helped win the West, since by 1890 wire-fenced pastureland had virtually replaced the open range. By the early 20th century Worcester, Providence, and Bridgeport were all engaged in the small-batch production of specialty goods. They now resembled the diverse industrial centers of New York City and Philadelphia more than the single-industry textile towns that had traditionally characterized New England manufacturing.

Notable changes in the organization of production occurred in Lynn, Mass., another great industrial center of New England with only one predominant industry, shoe manufacturing. Early firms relied heavily on outworkers who did piecework at home. Not until the late 19th century did Lynn shoe manufacturers begin to centralize production in factory complexes and replace outworkers with factory operatives. With the consolidation of the workforce under one roof, ever greater numbers of married and single women

Lowell, Mass., 1881

were brought into the factories to labor alongside men. But centralization and mechanization did not turn all shoe workers into mere machine tenders. Many still directly handled the tools and materials of their trade, and artisanal sensibilities survived. Skilled laborers made an effort to form labor unions, among them the Knights of Saint Crispin, and in Lynn and other Massachusetts cities such as Boston and New Bedford labor coalitions contended for political power. Between 1885 and 1889 coalitions in Lynn secured significant political victories.

Group solidarity affected daily life in many urban workplaces. Immigrants often segregated themselves into individual departments, perpetuating their separation by recruiting fellow ethnics into similar jobs. The American Federation of Labor was not interested in organizing unskilled employees, many of whom were blacks or new immigrants. As a result these workers responded to the appeals of more militant labor organizations like the Industrial Workers of the World, sometimes crossing ethnic lines to work together in a collective struggle. The Lawrence Bread and Roses strike of 1912, in which workers fought for higher wages and better working conditions in the mills, is an excellent example of such interethnic cooperation. In other circumstances ethnic loyalties precluded worker solidarity, and corporate use of Asian and black workers as strikebreakers confirmed many unions' racist and exclusionary practices.

In New England and elsewhere urbanization created political chaos, as contending groups vied to determine public priorities. Political machines, based in wards in which one ethnic group usually composed a majority, dispersed jobs through vast patronage systems that rewarded ethnic loyalty and rejected outsiders. Throughout the 19th and early 20th centuries workers endured overcrowding, ill health, poverty, and substandard housing. Tensions between workers and employers increasingly exploded in strikes, confrontations between native-born and immigrant workers, and increased criminal activity in tenement neighborhoods. Many believed there was a crisis in public order.

Downtown business interests and professional leaders organized to intervene in the political process. Chambers of commerce, boards of trade, good government associations, and municipal reformers strategized to restore urban rule to the so-called better elements. At a time when immigrant representatives of working-class wards were enjoying a prominent voice on many city councils, new municipal charters circumscribed the authority of the councils and shifted authority from

elected officials to expert commissions and executive appointees. These officials were either appointed or elected at large by a citywide constituency, as reformers worked to circumvent the ethnic majorities that dominated individual wards and to ensure that downtown and professional interests would prevail. Furthermore, new groups of nonelected urban professionals—civil engineers, landscape architects, public health officials, and school administrators—generated permanent urban bureaucracies.

New England elites adopted other responses to this tumult. Some tried to halt change by forming the Immigration Restriction League. Some left urban areas and moved to surrounding suburbs. Others moved into or created fashionable sections within cities, for example, Boston's Back Bay, Providence's East Side, Manchester's North End, and Bridgeport's Seaside Park. Wealthy residents reclaimed downtown areas by creating an impressive array of new structures, including, in Springfield, Mass., H. H. Richardson's Hampden County Courthouse, Richard Upjohn's Memorial Church, and George Hathorne's City Library. Elites also commissioned the construction of urban parks such as Boston's Emerald Necklace, Providence's Roger Williams Park, Bridgeport's Seaside Park, and Hartford's Colt Park to uplift the urban masses by introducing pastoral elements to city life. Still others, particularly new professionals like Robert Woods of Boston's South End Settlement, joined their counterparts throughout the nation in efforts to Americanize the foreign born and eliminate overcrowding, poverty, dangerous working conditions, and ill health through planning, zoning, and progressive reform.

Ironically, just as New England was maturing as an urban industrial region, it was also taking the lead in deindustrialization, as textile factories beat a path to the South as early as the 1870s. New England persisted in pointing the way to the future but abandoned forever Robinson's "lost Eden."

Alan Dawley, *Class and Community: The Industrial Revolution in Lynn* (1976); Walter Licht, *Industrializing America: The 19th Century* (1995); Thomas H. O'Connor, *Bibles, Brahmins, and Bosses: A Short History of Boston*, 3d ed. (1991).

Robert L. Macieski

World Wars and Depression, 1914–45

New Englanders who came of age between 1914 and 1945 confronted world war, economic depression, and numerous social and cultural upheavals. Though occasionally local in origin, the challenges they faced were often part and parcel of national trends and calamities. The rise of the automobile and the

Ku Klux Klan, chronic joblessness and the New Deal, their sons fighting and sometimes dying on distant battlefields—New Englanders knew each of these and more and lived through so much history as to defy a concise retrospective assessment of their times.

In August 1914, Great Britain, France, and Russia went to war against Germany and Austria-Hungary, and the New England reaction was decidedly mixed. Many inhabitants felt an affinity toward England and the Allies, although this sentiment was hardly universal given the anti-British tradition of Boston's Irish community. The initial tendency was to respect President Woodrow Wilson's proclamation of America's neutrality in the conflict. In the presidential election of 1916, however, New Englanders supported the losing candidacy of Charles Evans Hughes, a Republican who criticized the Democratic president for failing to uphold America's rights on the high seas in the face of Germany's submarine campaign. And when the United States finally declared war on the Central Powers in April 1917, New Englanders enthusiastically rushed to mobilize their region for war—the results of which were immediate and dramatic. The local textile industry enjoyed a temporary revival as venerable operations like the Amoskeag Mills in Manchester, N.H., increased production to meet the national demand for uniforms and blankets. The Springfield Armory in Massachusetts manufactured thousands of firearms for the U.S. military, and the state of Connecticut, with its shipyards and heavy industry, led the nation in wartime production per person.

In addition to economic boom, however, the war brought a sustained assault on the region's cherished sense of isolation from outside forces and disasters. The mostly Maine men of the 72d Artillery, Coast Artillery Corps, after spending a quiet year guarding the entrance to Portland Harbor, were sent to join thousands of their fellow Yankees already serving in the American Expeditionary Force in France. The people of Onset, Mass., on Cape Cod, witnessed the shelling of their local Coast Guard station by a German submarine. Bostonians found themselves part of an international medical catastrophe late in the war: Spanish influenza, which eventually killed millions worldwide, first appeared in the American Midwest during the spring of 1918 and was brought to the Northeast by the thousands of soldiers and sailors who passed through Boston on their way to Europe. By late August the illness had raged through the crowded barracks on Commonwealth Pier and sent hundreds of men to the Chelsea Naval Hospital. In early September, sailors from the nearby navy yard marched through the streets of Boston as part of a "Win the War for Freedom" parade, thereby spreading the flu into the local population. By the end of the month Boston was a city on the edge of panic, with shuttered stores, churchless Sundays, and more than 1,000 people dead.

Fortunately, the Spanish influenza epidemic vanished with the end of World War I. Shortly thereafter Boston experienced another tragedy, this time local in origin. On January 15, 1919, in the immigrant neighborhoods of the city's North End, a huge cast-iron tank owned by the Purity Distilling Company burst open and sent a wave of raw black molasses pouring down Commercial Street. The Great Boston Molasses Flood killed 21 people, injured 150, and left the nearby harbor brown for months.

As in the rest of the country, in New England the intense patriotism cultivated during World War I often degenerated into a suspicion of anyone or anything not deemed 100 percent American. In addition to condemning all things German, public opinion viewed with alarm any organization, be it political party or labor union, that featured a significant foreign-born contingent. This apprehension continued to flourish after the war, augmented by widespread belief that Communism, then triumphant in Russia, was being imported into the nation through immigration. Exacerbating the concerns of Americans fearful of socialist agitation was the prevalent labor unrest in the immediate postwar years. Massachusetts governor Calvin Coolidge found himself the center of much national acclaim when he authorized the use of the state police to break Boston's police strike of September 1919. A fear of foreign influence also explains the local appearance of the Ku Klux Klan, especially in northern New England, where the organization's anti-Catholicism won adherents among those unsettled by the influx of French Canadians into the region during the previous decades. By the mid-1920s the Klan claimed 50,000 supporters in Maine alone, a membership roll that was perhaps exaggerated but nevertheless large enough to make mischief in local politics throughout the decade.

Perhaps the best-known example of nativism in New England, however, is the Sacco and Vanzetti case. Two Italian immigrants, Nicola Sacco and Bartolomeo Vanzetti, were convicted in 1921 for robbing a shoe company in South Braintree, Mass., and murdering two men. The defendants' guilt or innocence seemed a side issue during the trial, as much testimony centered on the pair's foreign birth and anarchist political beliefs. For many, Sacco and Vanzetti symbolized American xenophobia at its most extreme, and, when the two men were executed in August 1927, tens of

thousands of mourners wearing red armbands marched in the funeral procession through the streets of Boston.

Yet the popular imagination often remembers the 1920s as a decade of optimism and prosperity presided over by the Vermont native and longtime Massachusetts resident Calvin Coolidge. Assuming the presidency following Warren G. Harding's death in 1923, Coolidge was elected in his own right in 1924 and remained in office until March 1929. Many New Englanders, living in an age of unbridled growth and change, found comfort in a president who epitomized the frugal, honest, and taciturn Yankee, an image Coolidge himself did little to dispute. And to a certain extent, New England benefited from the prosperity associated with its native-son president. A seemingly robust economy plus the increased availability of the automobile, for example, brought thousands of middle-class tourists to Cape Cod beaches and the coast of Maine. Nevertheless, many of the region's farm families lived out the decade in dismal poverty, and high unemployment plagued New England's mill towns as the textile industry began relocating jobs to the South.

The stock market crash of 1929 was an economic earthquake felt instantly along Boston's State Street financial district. By the following March unemployed workers were staging demonstrations on Boston Common to draw attention to their plight. For many New Englanders, the Great Depression did not descend immediately but crept over the landscape like a leisurely blight. During the political campaigns of 1930, Maine newspapers reported that the most debated local issue was not the economy but Prohibition. Lillian M. N. Stevens, the future president of the National Women's Christian Temperance Union, was leading a fierce but ultimately losing effort to prevent the repeal of the state's ban on intoxicating beverages.

Also garnering headlines that year was the legal ordeal of the Massachusetts native Mary Ware Dennett, a longtime women's rights advocate and an early organizer, in 1915, of the National Birth Control League. Convicted on obscenity charges in 1929 for sending sex education materials through the mails, Dennett's case was publicized nationally by the American Civil Liberties Union, and she was eventually exonerated.

Still, by the time Franklin D. Roosevelt became president in 1933, New Englanders were consumed by economic worries as their region became increasingly marked by farm failures, a declining fishing industry, massive unemployment, and towns staggering under the burden of relief to the poor. The New Deal programs that subsequently arrived in the Northeast

brought a measure of relief, and no small challenge to long-held notions of Yankee self-sufficiency. Local politicians like Boston's mayor James M. Curley, for example, welcomed federally funded public works projects but resisted strenuously calls for direct financial relief for those impoverished by hard times. In addition, many New England entrepreneurs strongly resented the regulations governing wages, working conditions, and management-labor relations that often accompanied federal intervention in the local economy. In the 1936 presidential race, in which the Democratic president was smashingly reelected, two New England states provided the only tallies for the Republican challenger, leading national political observers to alter an earlier statement on the down-easter's talents as an election day prognosticator to "As Maine goes, so goes Vermont."

The New Deal brought much to New England, however, with the National Recovery Act of 1933, for example, funding 700 jobs to build three bridges across the Cape Cod Canal. The Civilian Conservation Corps (CCC) put hundreds of young New Englanders to work building roads, planting trees, and completing sections of the Appalachian Trail. One CCC project in particular involved clearing trees felled by the Great Hurricane of 1938, a storm that caused millions of dollars in damage and killed 600 people.

New England finally shook off the effects of the Great Depression in the early 1940s as America was drawn into World War II. Maine's Bath Iron Works employed 30,000 men and women in building hundreds of ships for the Allied war effort. The Springfield Armory contracted with the U.S. military to produce the reliable M1 rifle, and the firm Pratt and Whitney contributed thousands of aircraft engines to Connecticut's overall reemergence as an "Arsenal of Democracy." New England was also the home of several companies involved in developing the new technologies of modern warfare. The Raytheon Manufacturing Company of Cambridge, Mass., led the nation in the production of radar tubes and perfected for the navy an effective shipboard radar system. Unemployment vanished in this wartime economy as New England offered jobs to the local workforce and to the thousands who relocated to the region during the war years.

As coastal defense was heightened, the residents of Cape Cod experienced the installation of gun emplacements at both entrances of the canal and the presence of sentries patrolling their once tranquil beaches under the glare of spotlights. The Newport (R.I.) Navy Base, long the home of the Naval War Col-

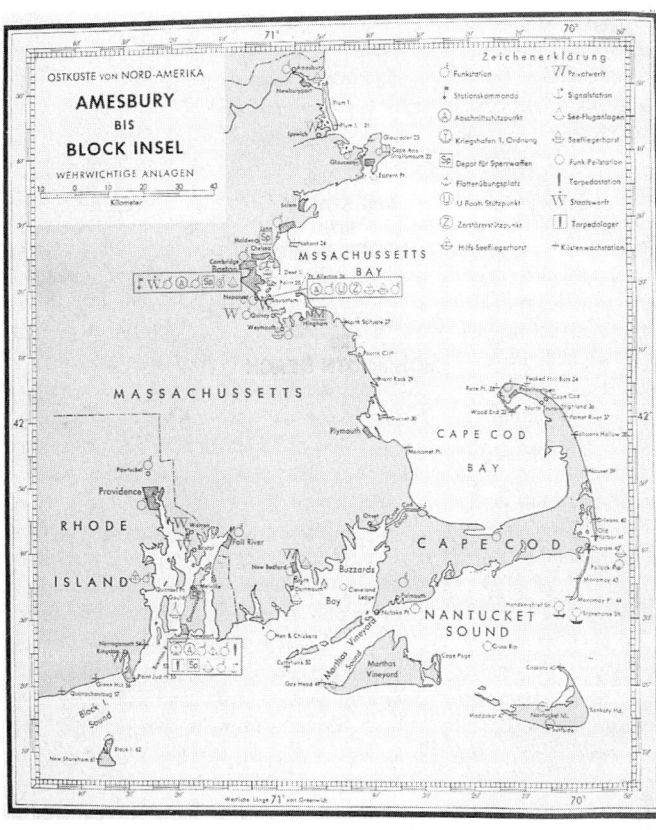

German war map of southern New England, 1943

erated from the Great Depression. Many feared a return to hard times should federal government spending and direct involvement in the economy come to an end. In Connecticut, where the state's commitment to heavy industry had produced one of the more reliable components of the "Arsenal of Democracy," the rapid postwar cancellation of military contracts proved a calamity to workers and management alike. Pratt and Whitney Aircraft, a company that employed nearly 40,000 wartime employees in several Connecticut and Massachusetts communities, lost $400 million in orders within days of the war's end. The lifting of wartime price controls coupled with the demands of postwar consumers created both high inflation and shortages of goods. Faced with a long list of exuberant potential customers, a Portland, Maine, automobile dealer raffled off the right to purchase the only new car available on his lot. And with the end of wartime wage controls, labor unions used work stoppages to combat the massive layoffs and inflation-eroded wages faced by their members. A division of Pratt and Whitney in East Hartford, Conn., endured a strike by workers over higher wages that lasted more than six months.

In response to labor unrest in his state, Massachusetts governor Robert F. Bradford established a nine-person committee, representing the interests of both management and labor, to investigate ways to stabilize the labor situation in the Bay State. The results, which were submitted to the governor in March 1947, called on the state legislature to pass laws that placed local government in a better position to mediate labor disputes. Clearly this effort, along with similar actions in other New England states, did little to prevent the further decline of such regional industrial stalwarts as shipbuilding, shoe manufacturing, and the textile industry. The closing of textile mills had a particularly devastating effect on communities in Rhode Island, Massachusetts, New Hampshire, and Maine. Nashua, N.H., for example, lost nearly 4,000 jobs when the Nashua Manufacturing Company closed its doors at the end of 1948. Ultimately, the decision on the part of many postwar textile mill owners to seek lower labor costs and high tax benefits in the South, coupled with increased foreign competition after 1960, reduced industry employment, which as late as 1950 had numbered 300,000 New Englanders, to 75,000 workers by the 1970s.

But several firms carried on, often with new fabrics and a determination not to abandon struggling New England communities. The Hathaway Company shirt factory, which survived for 165 years in Waterville, Maine, finally closed its doors in 1998 after the owners suc-

lege, became an essential part of the Allied struggle for control of the North Atlantic. As the nation mobilized for total war, thousands of New Englanders became part of an American military that fought all over the world. In Massachusetts, Mildred H. McAffee, president of Wellesley College, joined the more than half a million residents of the Bay State who served when she accepted a commission in the U.S. Naval Reserve and assumed the directorship of the WAVES (Women Accepted for Volunteer Emergency Service). The state of Vermont, which declared war on Nazi Germany two months before the rest of the nation, sent 49,942 of its citizens into the military; 1,233 did not return. More than 80,000 Mainers enlisted; 1,634 died for their country. The memory of these sacrifices was yet another tempering influence on a generation of New Englanders who, with the coming of peace in 1945, faced the task of leading their region into a new era.

Gerald J. Brault, *The French-Canadian Heritage in New England* (1986); Francis X. Busch, *Prisoners at the Bar: An Account of the Trials of the William Haywood Case, the Sacco-Vanzetti Case, the Loeb-Leopold Case, the Bruno Hauptmann Case* (1998); Richard Collier, *The Plague of the Spanish Lady: The Influenza Pandemic of 1918–1919* (1996); Richard W. Judd, Edwin A. Churchill, Joel W. Eastman, eds., *Maine: The Pine Tree State from Prehistory to the Present* (1995); David M. Kennedy, *Freedom from Fear: The American People in Depression and War, 1929–1945* (1999); Duane Lockard, *New England State Politics* (1959); Charles H. Trout, *Boston, the Great Depression, and the New Deal* (1977).

Paul D. Nygard

Reorientation and Revival, 1945 to the Present While serving overseas during World War II, a Bowdoin College alumnus wrote home to urge the president of his alma mater not to "let anybody change" the ways and nature of a beloved Maine institution known in youth. In replying to this cry from the heart, President Kenneth C. M. Sills put into words the dichotomy of thought typical of New Englanders throughout the second half of the 20th century and the beginnings of the 21st: a desire to retain and celebrate those characteristics believed to distinguish their corner of the United States from the rest of the country coupled with a recognition of their region's obligations to national trends and demands. Although sympathetic to his correspondent's search for continuity in dearly held beliefs and traditions, Sills suggested that it was "wishful thinking to believe that we shall return to the situation that existed before the war. We must gird ourselves for new tasks, new problems, new responsibilities."

A major task confronting New Englanders as peace returned in 1945 involved the reorientation of a regional economy only recently lib-

cumbed to market pressures and moved operations overseas. Malden Mills in Lawrence, Mass., run by the Feuerstein family since 1906, escaped bankruptcy in the early 1980s and prospered through the development of Polartec, a popular synthetic fabric. The company survived a devastating fire in 1995, but the debt incurred during rebuilding finally forced the company into bankruptcy, from which it emerged under ownership of a creditors' group in 2003. Former mill towns eventually found new industries but the effects of this industrial dislocation lingered on in such Massachusetts towns as Lawrence, Lowell, and New Bedford well into the 1970s. (Lowell native Jack Kerouac once described his hometown's Saint John de Baptiste Church as the "ponderous Chartres Cathedral of the slums.")

In some regions of New England, Cold War spending by the United States military provided a degree of economic salvation in decades after World War II. A decision by the U.S. Navy to station a portion of the Atlantic Fleet in Newport, R.I., helped make the Defense Department the largest civilian employer in the state until 1973. Other avenues for the postwar regional economic development often emerged from the computer technology and other scientific industries that grew up during 1940–45. In 1946 State Street financiers in Boston provided the funding for Tracerlab, a pioneer in radiation-detection instrumentation that set the standard for subsequent high-tech endeavors by tapping into the talent pool graduating from the Massachusetts Institute of Technology, Harvard, and the region's other major universities. In 1951 the Sperry Rand Corporation, working out of an old barn in Stamford, Conn., produced the world's first working computer designed specifically for business. The commitment of southern New England to high-tech industries expanded dramatically during the postwar decades, with the web of companies along Route 128 near Boston constituting nation's initial Silicon Valley.

During the 1980s, the technology produced and sold by such companies as Digital Equipment and Data General provided the impetus behind the Massachusetts Miracle, an economic boom that not only signaled the turnaround of a sagging regional economy but also helped propel Massachusetts governor Michael Dukakis to the Democratic presidential nomination in 1988. Though misjudgments concerning the future of the personal computer plus the national recession of 1990–91 ended the Miracle, New England's high-tech sector had reasserted itself by 2000 in the fields of computer software and biotechnology. Jenzabar, for example, located in Cambridge, had established itself by the turn of the

21st century as the largest provider of Internet software for American higher education. More remarkable still than this success was the story of Jenzabar's founder, president, and chief operating officer, Ling Chai—a student dissident from China who survived the massacre at Tiananmen Square, then escaped to America, and found a home in New England.

A catalogue of the problems faced by New England during the second half of the 20th century would find similar issues throughout the United States. The troubles that plagued Providence, for example,—"white flight," failing infrastructure, diminished tax base—shared much with the rest of urban America, though the revitalization of the city in the 1990s as a center for tourism and the arts owed much to the controversial reign of Providence's mayor Vincent "Buddy" Cianci, a New England original,. Regional turmoil over race and civil rights also reflected national issues and events. During the late 1960s Hartford and New Haven as well as other urban areas in Connecticut experienced several "long, hot summers" of racial tensions. In Boston a 1974 federal court ruling that advocated busing as a means of achieving racial integration in the public school system sparked years of contentious protest. The ensuing racial conflict, powerfully illustrated by photojournalist Stanley Forman's 1976 image of an antibusing protester wielding an American flag as a lance during a scuffle outside Boston City Hall, seemed to render any claim to New England exceptionalism less than compelling.

Indeed, one problem particular to Yankeedom in recent decades could best be described as a frequent inability to adapt a traditional regional identity to the reality of a changing and diverse human society. This identity, in addition to much-noted attributes as shrewdness in commerce and directness in speech, also suggested a commitment to hard work and achievement, clear notions concerning social justice, a devotion to public service over private interest, and a welcoming attitude to new ways of doing things—all imbued with an affection for a unique physical landscape. Not surprisingly, the history of the region since 1945 frequently documents the struggle of women, immigrants, African Americans, and the members of the gay community to claim their right to the regional identity through increased visibility in the realms of public service and social change. John F. Kennedy served Massachusetts in the U.S. House of Representatives (1947–53) and Senate (1953–61) and, in 1961, became the first Irish American Catholic elected president of the United States. Margaret Chase Smith represented Maine in the U.S. Senate from 1948 to 1972 and distinguished herself from her political

colleagues not only because she was the first woman elected to that body but in publicly denouncing the excesses of Senator Joseph McCarthy in her 1950 "Declaration of Conscience." Edmund S. Muskie, the son of Polish immigrants from the paper-mill town of Rumford, Maine, was the surprise winner of the 1954 election for governor of Maine. Muskie won reelection in 1956 and later served his state as a U.S. Senator and the nation as secretary of state. In 1966 and 1972, the people of Massachusetts elected Edward W. Brooke to U.S. Senate—the first African American in history to be chosen for that office by popular vote. In the 1974 elections, Connecticut voters chose Italian American Ella T. Grasso as the state's first female governor while approving at the same time an amendment to the state constitution outlawing discrimination based on sex. And, at the beginning of the 21st century, the region placed itself at the forefront of the national debate concerning gay rights. In 2000 Vermont became the first state to allow same-sex couples the rights and benefits of marriage through a legally recognized civil union. Less than four years later the Massachusetts Supreme Court ruled that no "constitutionally adequate reason" existed to deny same-sex couples the rights held by traditional couples and ordered a rewriting of the state's marriage laws to accommodate the new legal landscape. As the 2004 presidential campaign unfolded (with Massachusetts senator John Kerry as the Democratic nominee), New England, the cradle of revolution and abolition, once again found itself at the center of a national controversy.

Though "Yankee" originally described the people of Protestant Anglo-Saxon ancestry who dominated the region for the 200 years after the Pilgrims landed, the term has since been used by all New Englanders, whatever their race, ethnicity, or sex, to lay claim to a distinctive cultural belief system. Though at times individualistic, such a mindset tends to be fiercely protective of those things New England calls its own. Tourism, for example, remains forever a part of the regional landscape, but efforts to preserve fragile regional landscapes have manifested themselves many times since 1945. In 1961 President Kennedy, who loved the beauty of the coastline of southeastern Massachusetts, signed legislation creating the Cape Cod National Seashore. And though development seems an unavoidable aspect of economic expansion, the Vermont legislature in 1970 passed Act 250 to protect the state's resources and character from rapid, unplanned growth. In 1990 the residents of Cape Cod, concerned that a dramatic expansion in population during the 1980s had overburdened their region's natural resources, created the Cape Cod Commission to develop strategies to control the proliferation of new businesses and new housing.

Major league sport franchises can be found all over America, but New England's baseball fans insisted that the Boston Red Sox labored under "the Curse of the Bambino," a reference to the team's sale of Babe Ruth to the hated New York Yankees in 1919; in 2004 an ecstatic "Red Sox Nation" celebrated its first World Series win since 1918. And though Walden Pond in Concord, Mass., offers little in terms of aesthetic distinctiveness, the Thoreau Country Conservation Alliance and the Walden Woods Project have fought tenaciously to preserve from suburban sprawl this living link to the region's most celebrated philosopher and writer, Henry David Thoreau. Perhaps, ultimately, being "Yankee" means living in a state of grace with the very idea of New England.

James A. Aloisi, Jr., *The Big Dig* (2004); Dona Brown, *Inventing New England: Regional Tourism in the 19th Century* (1995); Herbert Ross Brown, *Sills of Bowdoin: The Life of Kenneth Charles Morton Sills, 1879–1954* (1964); Judith Freeman Clark and Robert J. Allison, *Massachusetts, from Colony to Commonwealth: An Illustrated History* (2002); Robert Dallek, *An Unfinished Life: John F. Kennedy, 1917–1963* (2003); Ron Formisano, *The Great Lobster War* (1997); Herbert F. Janick, Jr., *Connecticut: 1914 to the Present* (1975); Richard W. Judd, Edwin A. Churchill, and Joel W. Eastman, eds., *Maine: The Pine Tree State from Prehistory to the Present* (1995); Frank F. Lee, *Negro and White in Connecticut Town* (1961); W. Barksdale Maynard, *Walden Pond: A History* (2004); William Moran, *The Belles of New England: The Women of the Textile Mills and the Families Whose Wealth They Wove* (2002); Neal R. Peirce, *The New England States: People, Politics, and Power in the Six New England States* (1976); Douglas W. Rae, *City: Urbanism and Its End* (2003); Mike Stanton, *The Prince of Providence: The True Story of Buddy Cianci, America's Most Notorious Mayor, Some Wiseguys, and the Feds* (2003).

Paul D. Nygard

Abolitionism

New England played a prominent role in the campaign against slavery even though the numbers of abolitionists were sparse. Many abolitionists joined the movement after embracing the Second Great Awakening (ca. 1795–1835), a widespread religious revival. Others espoused abolitionism after abandoning ineffectual and halfhearted efforts to liberate slaves and "uplift" free blacks. William Lloyd Garrison, the most prominent New England abolitionist, exhibited evangelical zeal as well as scorn for the American Colonization Society (1817), which he and others viewed as a cynical ploy to maintain slavery and rid America of free blacks.

A former colonizationist, Garrison wasted little time in attacking slavery in an uncompromising and forceful manner, most prominently in his newspaper *The Liberator*. With the premier issue on January 1, 1831, Garrison fired the first salvo against slavery and colonization, launching a crusade that would last until the end of the Civil War, 34 years later. That same year Garrison and other abolitionists founded the New England Anti-Slavery Society, which was followed two years later by the creation of the American Anti-Slavery Society. By the mid-1830s, all six New England states boasted a variety of antislavery societies at the state, county, and town levels.

New England abolitionists exhibited a great deal of courage when promoting their cause. As abolitionists exhorted churches, governments, and individuals to join the crusade, anti-abolitionists—especially strong in New England—responded with increased hostility. For them, abolitionists alienated southern slaveholders and, as a result, threatened sectional peace and perhaps the union itself. Anti-abolitionists tried to silence them with congressional gag rules in Washington, D.C., and physical intimidation locally. Angry Bostonians paraded Garrison through the streets at the end of a rope, while townspeople of Canterbury, Conn., pressured Prudence Crandall to abandon her boarding school for black girls. Noyes Academy in Canaan, N.H., met a similar fate, while the poet John Greenleaf Whittier and the English abolitionist George Thompson bolted out of Concord, N.H., in the wake of a howling mob. Most abolitionist speakers, men and women alike, faced a variety of intimidating behavior, but to the chagrin of anti-abolitionists these attacks merely strengthened the abolitionists' resolve.

As the physical threat to New England abolitionists grew, the movement split along ideological lines. Led by Garrison, many New England abolitionists extended the platform of antislavery to include women's rights and nonresistance (or pacifism). In addition, they stepped up their criticism of the clergy for abandoning the fight against the sin of slavery. Conservative abolitionists bristled at these "extraneous issues," and by 1840 antislavery organizations throughout New England had split into rival camps.

To compound the schism within abolitionist ranks, Garrison and his followers, as pacifists, insisted that slavery could not, nor should not, be voted out of existence because such actions ultimately relied on force. The duty to abolish slavery rested with individual slaveholders, not with Congress; only through "moral suasion" could abolitionists push the issue. Not all New England abolitionists agreed, however. The Liberty Party, an abolitionist third party, fielded candidates for a variety of offices, including president, as early as 1840. Many of these political abolitionists rejected Garrison's approach and enthusiastically championed political action. Led by John Parker Hale of New Hampshire, these and other abolitionists drifted into the Free-Soil Party by 1848 and eventually were absorbed by the Republican Party in the mid-1850s, even though the Republicans made no claim of endorsing immediate emancipation.

Scholars have argued that too much emphasis has been placed on the split within the ranks of abolition. True, individual members held a variety of views regarding the nature and direction of the movement. But abolitionists of all persuasions, despite their differences, fervently confronted the "peculiar institution" at considerable personal risk. Always a minority within New England and the nation, the abolitionists succeeded in combating slavery through a vigorous press and dedicated organizers. Differences of opinion among various factions seldom muffled the abolitionist critique of American slave society, and disagreements did not dampen their vision of a biracial society based on freedom and equality.

Laurence Lader, *The Bold Brahmins: New England's War against Slavery, 1831–1863* (1973); Henry Mayer, *All on Fire: William Lloyd Garrison and the Abolition of Slavery* (1998); Joanne Pope Melish, *Disowning Slavery: Gradual Emancipation and "Race" in New England, 1780–1860* (1998); Benjamin Quarles, *Black Abolitionists* (1991).

Stephen L. Cox

Adams, Abigail

(1744–1818) Patriot and First Lady of the United States. Abigail (Smith) Adams was the wife of one American president (John Adams, 1797–1801) and the mother of another (John Quincy Adams, 1825–29). Her independent reputation largely derives, however, from the letters she wrote for more than half a century. Adams's letters compare with those of the great correspondents of her age, which explains why they have been in print since 1840.

Abigail Smith was born in Weymouth, Mass., to the Reverend William and Elizabeth Smith. Her youth—indeed, most of her adult life—was spent in the countryside around Boston. As was typical for most women of the time, she was educated at home. She married John Adams in 1764 after a lengthy courtship during which the two exchanged delightfully witty and amorous letters.

During the next decade, while Abigail Adams cared for their four children, John Adams became increasingly active in revolutionary politics. For the last 25 years of the 18th century, John Adams was engaged in political affairs that often took him to distant places.

Abigail Adams remained at home in Braintree (later named Quincy) during the Revolutionary War, supporting her family, maintaining their farm, and writing the torrent of letters that are still the best surviving record of a New England woman's wartime experiences. In a letter written on March 31, 1776, while her husband was involved in drafting the Declaration of Independence, Abigail Adams admonished him to "Remember the Ladies" in the new "Code of Laws which I suppose it will be necessary for you to make." This signature statement has resonated as a beacon for American advocates of women's rights for more than two centuries.

In 1784 Abigail Adams traveled to Europe to join her husband, who was then a member of the U.S. delegation to the peace negotiations in Paris. After a 10-month sojourn in Paris, the Adamses moved to London to preside over the first U.S. mission to the Court of St. James's. Soon after returning to America in 1788, John Adams was elected vice president. During his tenure in that office (1789–97), Abigail lived for several years in the temporary national capitals of Philadelphia and New York. When John was elected president in 1797, Abigail again returned to Philadelphia and for one season to the new capital city of Washington. "This House is built for ages to come," she wrote of the presidential mansion that was still under construction.

As First Lady, she presided over public events, hosted visitors, and attended receptions. Most important, she served as confidante and counselor to her husband during his beleaguered one term in office. She was not, as some have suggested, an architect of his politics, for John Adams had strong opinions and programs. She was, however, when the president felt his cabinet members had betrayed him, the one person whom he trusted as an intelligent, informed, and partisan supporter.

All the while, Abigail Adams wrote letters to family and friends that not only captured the events, the spirit, and the consciousness of her time, but also revealed her own character. She was intelligent, witty, religious, practical, tolerant, and wise—qualities she often referred to as New England traits. She was a keen observer of the political scene and a commentator on social life and customs. Her correspondents included famous public figures, including Mercy Otis Warren and Thomas Jefferson, as well as New England neighbors, among them Harriet Storer and Royall Tyler.

The final decades of her life were spent in her beloved Quincy, where she took care of her household and family, gardened, attended worship, observed political developments, engaged in social activities, and recorded all in an endless stream of letters.

Charles Francis Adams, ed., *Letters of Mrs. Adams, the Wife of John Adams* (1977 [1840]); L. H. Butterfield, Wendell D. Garrett, and Marjorie E. Sprague, eds., *The Adams Papers: Adams Family Correspondence*, 4 vols. (1963–73); Edith B. Gelles, *Portia: The World of Abigail Adams* (1992); Phyllis Lee Levin, *Abigail Adams* (1987).

Edith B. Gelles

Adams, John (1735–1826) President of the United States. Born in Braintree (now Quincy), Mass., John Adams, the nation's second president and first vice president, was a noted political thinker. In these roles, Adams worked on behalf of forming and strengthening national institutions. He would become the controversial leader of the Federalist Party, a political party that would eventually lose its status, first becoming a regional party with strength only in New England and then disappearing altogether from the political landscape.

Attending Harvard College at the age of 15, Adams went on to study and practice law. His father's influence was substantial, and in later years Adams would write that his father's devotion to public service influenced his manner of thinking. Adams married Abigail Smith in 1764, and, although separated geographically for much of their early marriage, their lifelong partnership is documented in their amorous, often humorous correspondence to each other.

Adams's many published writings in defense of colonial rights, the first one prompted in 1765 by the Stamp Act, influenced the rise of revolutionary opinion in New England and raised him to a conspicuous place in the resistance to British authority.

Adams was elected to the First Continental Congress in 1774, and when it reconvened as the Second Continental Congress the following year, he assumed a leading role in the movement for independence. He was a member of the committee to draft the Declaration of Independence, although the actual writing was done by Thomas Jefferson, and he was the most strenuous defender of Jefferson's handiwork in the ensuing debate in Congress. During the War for Independence, Adams represented the new United States in diplomatic posts in France and the Netherlands. In 1783, with Benjamin Franklin and John Jay, he negotiated and signed the Treaty of Paris, which ended the war. He was the first U.S. minister to Britain from 1785 until 1788 and succeeded in negotiating a commercial treaty with the former mother country.

Adams was committed throughout his life to a version of republicanism that emphasized the necessity of civic virtue to the preservation of free societies. In the absence of individual public spirit and a willingness to sacrifice personal gain for the public good, he and many of his revolutionary colleagues feared, republican government would eventually fail. Adams was less optimistic than some about human nature, however, and therefore urged a form of government that by a balanced constitution would place checks upon both individual ambition and a potential tyranny of the majority. In his later years, Adams expressed regret that American society had become more concerned with commerce than with republican civic virtue. He laid out his political theory in numerous letters, essays, and books, including *Thoughts on Government* (1776) and *A Defence of the Constitutions of Government of the United States* (1786–87), and as the principal author of the Massachusetts Constitution of 1780.

Adams's presidency, from 1797 to 1801, witnessed the moving of the capital from Philadelphia to Washington, D.C., a naval conflict with France, enactment of the Sedition Act of 1798, and the collapse of the Federalist Party. Under the Sedition Act, individuals could be prosecuted for "any false, scandalous and malicious writing . . . against the government of the United States, or either house of Congress . . . or the President . . . with intent to defame . . . or to bring them into contempt, or disrepute." Federalist Party leaders claimed that the legislation was essential in view of the heightened tensions with France.

Before the congressional elections of 1798, Adams, in an effort to secure a peaceful settlement of the dispute with France, sent a delegation to Paris to protect U.S. trading interests. The French foreign minister refused to receive the American diplomats; as a prerequisite to meeting with the diplomats, French agents known only as X, Y, and Z demanded a payment of $250,000 and a loan of $10 million. The XYZ affair became an issue during the 1798 campaign and resulted in the defeat of pro-French Jeffersonian candidates for Congress. The French question remained very important during the election of 1800, some Federalists supporting war with France as a way to win the national election. In actuality, the Federalist campaign of 1800 was hampered by internal party tensions between the supporters of Alexander Hamilton and those loyal to Adams. Following the election of Thomas Jefferson in 1800, the Federalist Party faded as a national party and increasingly was confined to New England. Eventually, even this New England base would be lost, and the Federalist Party would disappear as a force in American politics.

Adams returned to Massachusetts following his defeat for reelection. He remained interested in politics, however, as evidenced by his correspondence with Jefferson and his participation in the Massachusetts Constitutional Convention of 1820, called to consider revisions in the constitution of 1780. During the debates of the 1820 convention, Adams adopted a conservative position on the question of suffrage, arguing that ownership of property should remain a prerequisite for the franchise. In this matter, Adams was supported by Joseph Story, a U.S. Supreme Court justice, and Daniel Webster, a future U.S. senator. He also, however, introduced and unsuccessfully urged passage of an amendment guaranteeing complete religious freedom in Massachusetts. He died in Quincy on the 50th anniversary of the nation's independence, July 4, 1826. By dramatic coincidence, Thomas Jefferson died the same day.

David McCullough, *John Adams* (2001); Peter Shaw, *The Character of John Adams* (1976); Stephen Skowronek, *The Politics Presidents Make: Leadership from John Adams to Bill Clinton* (1997); Page Smith, *John Adams* (1962); Gordon S. Wood, *The Radicalism of the American Revolution* (1992).

Michael E. Meagher

Adams, John Quincy (1767–1848)

President of the United States. John Quincy Adams, diplomat, senator, secretary of state, sixth president of the United States, and Massachusetts congressman, was a dominant political figure in early national and antebellum America. Born in Braintree (now Quincy), Mass., the eldest son of John and Abigail Adams, John Quincy Adams received much of his early education in Europe, where he accompanied his father on diplomatic missions. He returned to America, entered Harvard College, and after graduation in 1787 studied law. Unhappy as a lawyer, he became a diplomat in the Netherlands and Germany, returning to Boston in 1801 to enter politics. In 1803 Adams was elected to the U.S. Senate, and as a marginal Federalist like his father he alienated many in his party with his independent-minded voting. When he supported President Jefferson's infamous embargo of 1807, the Federalists in the Senate removed him from the party's ranks in the body, and then, under pressure from the Federalist-dominated Massachusetts legislature, he resigned his Senate seat before his term expired. President James Madison appointed John Quincy Adams minister to Russia in 1809, and in 1814 he served as one of the peace commissioners who negotiated the treaty ending the War of 1812. After serving two years as minister to Britain in 1815–17, he was named secretary of state by President James Monroe.

Adams's tenure as secretary of state was active and controversial. He aggressively supported General Andrew Jackson's campaign against Florida's Seminole Indians (an ironic twist considering his bitter relations with Jackson after the election of 1824), negotiated

John Quincy Adams, daguerreotype by Matthew Brady, 1847

a treaty for Florida's cession to the United States, and was the originator of the Monroe Doctrine. In 1824 Adams, Jackson, Secretary of the Treasury William H. Crawford, and House Speaker Henry Clay all vied for the presidency. Adams received 84 electoral votes, all from New England districts, and this put him 15 electoral votes behind Jackson. When no candidate received a majority, the election was thrown into the House of Representatives. There, Henry Clay, a bitter rival of Jackson, gave his support to Adams, and the New England candidate was elected president. When Adams made Clay his secretary of state, many claimed a "corrupt bargain" had been struck, a charge that would hang over both men for the rest of their lives.

Adams's four years as president were frustrating. His aggressive program for federal improvements frightened those who saw enhanced federal powers as a threat to liberty and, in the South, to slavery. Skeptical of party politics, he refused to remove political opponents from office. This, combined with the congressional elections of 1826, which elevated anti-Adams forces into the majority, left the administration vulnerable to attack from all directions. In 1828 Adams was easily defeated for a second term by Andrew Jackson and returned to Massachusetts.

In 1830 he was elected to Congress, where for 18 years he gained great fame as a prominent critic of the Democratic Party. Much of this prominence came from his nearly 10-year battle to overturn the so-called gag rule, a par-

liamentary restriction passed in 1836 forbidding the presentation of antislavery petitions in the House. Adams considered the rule a gross violation of the Constitution and waged a spirited and successful campaign for its removal. Adams further contributed to the abolitionist movement by successfully arguing the *Amistad* case in front of the U.S. Supreme Court in 1841; his eloquent defense of a group of African slaves who had taken over the Spanish slave ship *Amistad* resulted in their being freed and subsequently returned to Africa. Considered cold and distant by some, an inspiration to abolitionists like Charles Sumner, Old Man Eloquent, as he was called, collapsed in the House chamber and died two days later, on February 23, 1848.

Mary W. M. Hargreaves, *The Presidency of John Quincy Adams* (1985); Daniel Walker Howe, *The Political Culture of the American Whigs* (1979); William Earl Weeks, *John Quincy Adams and American Global Empire* (1992).

Michael J. Connolly

Adams, Samuel (1722–1803)

Revolutionary, writer, state politician. The basic facts of Samuel Adams's life have never been in dispute, yet the interpretations of Adams have diverged widely. To some he was the quintessential American revolutionary, a man whose inability to embrace postrevolutionary America attests to the purity and rigor of his commitments. To others he was an inflexible, domineering rabble-rouser. To assess Adams is, in many ways, to assess America's revolutionary past.

Samuel Adams was born in Boston to a prominent merchant and brewer, Samuel Adams, Sr., and his wife, Mary. These Adamses belonged to an established Massachusetts family that traced its ancestry back to one of the original Massachusetts Bay Puritans, Henry Adams.

Adams graduated from Harvard College in 1740. He became a member and clerk of the Massachusetts Assembly in 1766. One of five Massachusetts men to sign the Declaration of Independence, Adams served in the Continental Congress until 1781. In the 1790s Adams served Massachusetts as president of the state senate, lieutenant governor, and governor.

Samuel Adams has always been best known for his active role in the decade leading to American independence. During these years Adams adeptly articulated dissent and organized dissenters through the Committee of Correspondence, Society of the Bill of Rights, and Continental Congress. He corresponded with other revolutionary figures like John Dickinson, Richard Henry Lee, and Elbridge Gerry. Adams rarely delivered orations; public letters, committee work, and informal persuasion in eateries like the Green Dragon Tavern made up most of his revolutionary activity.

In the mythologized version of his life, Adams was the archrevolutionary who admonished the Boston mob never to compromise with Englishmen and to destroy anything in its path. Yet he was a deliberate man who came to his revolutionary perspective gradually and reluctantly. Like most revolutionaries for American independence, Adams admired the British system of government and agitated for reform. Only after hostilities broke out in 1775 did he become an ardent revolutionary. In addition, Adams considered forcible resistance and destruction of property to be dangerous last resorts of a revolutionary movement; he opposed Shays's Rebellion and the Whiskey Rebellion, popular uprisings in 1786 and 1794, respectively.

An austere and principled man, Samuel Adams flourished in the crisis of revolution. Yet postrevolutionary America quickly shifted from a republic of virtue to an aggregate of individualistic strivers. Even before his death in 1803, Adams was seen as a relic of a variety of vanished ages. He symbolized the classical republicanism of the Boston Federalists, the rigid moral probity of the Puritans, and the virtuous self-effacement of Roman republicans like Cicero. Even in Adams's own day, Americans had difficulty reconciling a revolutionary beginning with a settled and productive United States. The radicalism of the American Revolution was and is usually obscured, and a revolutionary like Adams is either misremembered or maligned. Indeed, most Americans today know Adams only as the namesake of a popular beer brewed in Boston. Yet Samuel Adams exemplified a now-vanished American identity essential to the creation of an independent American state.

Samuel Adams, *The Writings of Samuel Adams*, ed. Harry Alonzo Cushing (1907); John K. Alexander, *Samuel Adams: America's Revolutionary Politician* (2002); Pauline Maier, *The Old Revolutionaries: Political Lives in the Age of Samuel Adams* (1980); John C. Miller, *Sam Adams: Pioneer in Propaganda* (1936); Gordon S. Wood, *The Radicalism of the American Revolution* (1991).

Robert Battistini

Adams Family When John Adams, a lawyer practicing in Boston, and Abigail Smith, a parson's daughter from nearby Weymouth, married in 1764, they founded a lineage whose members have served New England and America with unrivaled distinction across six generations. Annually, thousands of persons visit the Adams National Historic Park in Quincy, Mass., to see the birthplaces, residences, and burial vaults of a still-flourishing family whose forebears came to America in the 1630s. Among the site's 11 historic buildings is the Adams Stone Library: housing 14,000 volumes, it reflects the importance that succeeding generations of Adamses have attached to the written word.

The family's achievements, beginning when John Adams advocated colonial rights, have ranged from statesmanship and diplomacy to conservation and literature. After serving as one of the authors of the Declaration of Independence, John Adams helped draft the treaty that ended the American Revolution. He served as the first U.S. minister to Great Britain and then became the new nation's first vice president, a post in which he served for eight years. Narrowly defeating Thomas Jefferson, Adams was elected president in 1797. In 1801, having lost his second presidential contest against Jefferson, he retired to his farm in Quincy, where for 25 years he continued a lifelong practice of writing political essays and commentary.

Over the course of her husband's career Abigail Adams became one of America's most gifted letter writers and advocates for improving the status of women. She also was mother to the second generation of Adamses, whose most famous member was John Quincy Adams. He served as U.S. minister to Holland, Prussia, Russia, and Great Britain and as secretary of state for eight years. After one term as president (1825–29), he became a leader in Congress and a vocal foe of slavery until his death in 1848. In 1841, when the U.S. government appealed the Hartford federal court's decision to free the *Amistad* captives, Adams argued before the Supreme Court on behalf of the African rebels.

Both John Quincy Adams and his wife, Louisa Catherine, preferred a literary life to politics. Louisa wrote but never published drama, poetry, brilliant letters, and a memoir. John Quincy's diary of 70 years is the most famous journal ever kept by an American, and his voluminous scientific and literary treatises were widely admired. He was Harvard's first Boylston Professor of Oratory.

John Quincy passed along his passion for planting trees in New England to his son Charles Francis Adams, whose memorable career in politics and literature began with essays against slavery. Charles Francis served in Congress and in posts abroad, including that of U.S. minister to England during the Civil War. He was also successful in intellectual life, becoming America's first modern historical editor.

The sons of Charles Francis were less active in politics, preferring literary endeavors. The most memorable results were Henry Adams's historical treatises and *The Education of Henry Adams* (1907). Henry's brother Brooks Adams wrote pathbreaking books in economics and history. Charles Francis Adams II had a more diversified record, serving with distinction as a cavalry officer in the Civil War. Afterward he wrote about economics, became president of the Union Pacific Railroad, pioneered in conserving natural resources and strengthening public education, and closed his labors as a historian and public speaker. A fourth brother, John Quincy Adams II, was a popular political and business figure in New England.

The Adamses have been the subject of continuous scholarly and popular interest. In 1975 public television aired *The Adams Chronicles*, a 13-hour documentary drama on the family. Anthony Hopkins brought John Quincy Adams to life in the film *Amistad* (1997), directed by Steven Spielberg. The historian David McCullough won a Pulitzer Prize for his best-selling biography *John Adams* (2001).

Twentieth-century members of the family, male and female, have included a professor at Harvard, a poet, a medical scientist, several officeholders, business leaders, and, of course, historians. It is no wonder President John F. Kennedy described the Adams family's record as daunting.

James Truslow Adams, *The Adams Family* (1930); Paul C. Nagel, *The Adams Women: Abigail and Louisa Adams, Their Sisters and Daughters* (1987); Nagel, *Descent from Glory: Four Generations of the John Adams Family* (1983); Jack Shepherd, *The Adams Chronicles: Four Generations of Greatness* (1975).

Paul C. Nagel

Allen, Ethan (1738–89) **and Ira** (1751–1814) Vermont soldiers and statesmen. Ethan Allen led the charge to establish Vermont as an independent state. Ira Allen drafted Vermont's constitution, which remains in force today. Both were born in Connecticut, Ethan in Litchfield and Ira in Cornwall. Their parents, Joseph and Mary Baker Allen, also had three other sons. Joseph was a poor farmer whose ancestor Samuel Allen had emigrated from England to America in 1632.

In 1762 Ethan married Mary Bronson, with whom he had five children. After Mary died in 1783, he wed Frances Buchanan and fathered three more offspring with her. Ira and his wife, Jerusha Enos, had three children, only one of whom lived to maturity. In their late youth both brothers were engaged in land surveying and developing.

In 1763 the Allens left Connecticut for Vermont and settled in Bennington. New York and New Hampshire were hotly disputing the Vermont territory at the time, with New York's governor extracting heavy fees, if not confiscating land, from farmers there. The Allens supported New Hampshire but ultimately lost a court battle in favor of its claim. In order to avoid dispossession of family land and certain ejection, in 1770 Ethan Allen formed a citizens' militia called the Green Mountain Boys, which included all the Allen brothers as well as other settlers, to fight for the right to stay on the land. Although they advocated forming a new colony, the American Revolution interrupted their efforts. The Green Mountain Boys fought as patriots and were best known for capturing Fort Ticonderoga from the British in a bloodless battle on May 10, 1775. From that captured fort came the cannon used by General George Washington to expel the British from Boston.

Ethan and Ira continued to push Congress to recognize Vermont's statehood. After the colony declared its independence on January 17, 1777, Ira drew up the state constitution, wrote the preamble, and acted as the state's first treasurer. When the Continental Congress did not recognize Vermont as a state in 1778, Ethan and Ira attempted to form an alliance with Great Britain that would annex Vermont to Canada. It is unclear whether the brothers really wanted to become part of Britain or simply used the threat of such an alliance to force Congress to formally accept Vermont's statehood. Either way, the British gave up their claim to Vermont in the Treaty of Paris (1763), which put an end to the French and Indian War.

Both Ethan and Ira Allen published political pamphlets and books. Ira wrote *The Natural and Political History of the State of Vermont* (1798), a valuable account of how Vermont gained its statehood. Ethan is known for his *Vindication of the Opposition of the Inhabitants of Vermont to the Government of New York* (1779) and for his deistic work *Reason the Only Oracle of Man* (1784), which outlines the principles of natural religion.

While Ira died in relative obscurity in Philadelphia in 1814, Ethan died a hero in Burlington in 1789, two years before Vermont finally became a state. In 1885 Vermont commissioned a monument at Montpelier to the Green Mountain leaders' legacy, and in 1893 another was unveiled in Burlington. The Allens' fight for Vermont statehood highlights the democratic nature of northern frontier life. The brothers were not bred to be political leaders but rather rose from the ranks of the common people. As a result, they helped create one of the most democratic of U.S. state constitutions, second only to that of Pennsylvania.

Michael A. Bellesiles, *Revolutionary Outlaws: Ethan Allen and the Struggle for Independence on the Early American Frontier* (1993); Charles A. Jellison, *Ethan Allen, Frontier Rebel* (1969); Robert E. Shalhope,

Bennington and the Green Mountain Boys: The Emergence of Liberal Democracy in Vermont, 1760–1850 (1996).

Leslee K. Gilbert

Arnold, Benedict (1741–1801) Continental Army general, traitor.

More than two centuries after his death, Benedict Arnold remains one of the American Revolution's most controversial figures. By the war's third year Arnold was a hero. His tactical brilliance, energetic leadership, and courage propelled him to the rank of major general in the Continental Army and won him the admiration of George Washington. Other, less estimable aspects of Arnold's character included an overblown sense of personal honor, which forced him to respond to any perceived affront. Arnold's far more tragic betrayal of the Revolution resulted in his name becoming forever synonymous with treason.

Arnold was born in Norwich, Conn., a descendant of William Arnold, one of the original proprietors of Rhode Island, and a great-grandson of William's son Benedict, a governor of that colony. The younger Benedict Arnold's father (also named Benedict) achieved means and respectability as a merchant, but by the mid-1750s the Arnold family's economic decline forced young Benedict into an apprenticeship with his mother's cousins, Daniel and Joshua Lathrop. With their help Arnold started his own business in New Haven, Conn., in 1761. By the outbreak of the Revolution, Arnold had established himself as a successful merchant, shipmaster, and occasional smuggler.

As the Revolution began, Arnold's martial abilities quickly emerged. Eager for action, he took part in the attack on Fort Ticonderoga on Lake Champlain. In September 1775 Arnold, now a colonel, led a 1,000-man contingent on a grueling march through the Maine wilderness to invade Canada. Outside Quebec, Arnold's men joined Richard Montgomery's army and on December 31 assaulted the city. Despite the failure of the attack and a wound to his left leg, Arnold gained recognition for his attempt; his reputation soared and Congress promoted him to brigadier general. Arnold's rise continued through 1776. In response to an enemy thrust down Lake Champlain, he constructed a naval fleet and fought the British at Valcour Island in October. Arnold lost the battle, but his small navy helped forestall further British operations that year. In 1777 Arnold played a crucial role in the American victory at the Battle of Saratoga, where he was again wounded.

Despite his battlefield achievements, Arnold feuded with his superiors. In July 1777 Arnold resigned briefly after a quarrel with

Congress concerning the seniority of five junior brigadier generals who were promoted ahead of him. At Saratoga, Arnold angrily confronted his commander, Horatio Gates, for failing to mention him in official reports of the battle. Gates relieved Arnold of command. Later, as military commander of Philadelphia, Arnold faced court martial in part for using government wagons to haul personal property. Smarting from these and other perceived insults and unable to maintain the affluent lifestyle of his new wife, the young Margaret "Peggy" Shippen, whose father was Judge Edward Shippen, a prominent Tory, Arnold began corresponding with the British. By late September 1780, as commander in the Hudson Highlands, Arnold conspired to hand over the crucial fortifications at West Point, N.Y. Arnold's plot unraveled when militiamen captured his contact, Major John André, with the plans to West Point and a pass signed by Arnold. André was tried and hanged, but Arnold escaped to New York City, where he continued to fight as a British brigadier general, conducting raids against his former comrades in Virginia and Connecticut. After the war he lived in Canada and later England, where he died in 1801.

George Athan Billias, ed., *George Washington's Generals and Opponents: Their Exploits and Leadership* (1994); James Kirby Martin, *Benedict Arnold, Revolutionary Hero: An American Warrior Reconsidered* (1997); Willard Sterne Randall, *Benedict Arnold: Patriot and Traitor* (1990).

Thomas A. Rider

Balch, Emily Greene (1867–1961) Feminist peace activist and sociologist.

Emily Greene Balch, the daughter of Ellen Maria Noyes and Francis Vergnies Balch, descended from 17th- and 18th-century English immigrants to New England and grew up as part of the socially and intellectually privileged elite during the post–Civil War era. She was born, reared, and died in the Boston area, spending most of her life in Jamaica Plain and Wellesley. Balch was the 1946 Nobel Peace Prize Laureate, the second U.S. woman to achieve this recognition. She engaged in reform work for all of her adult life, but her ardent peace activism, most notably for the Women's International League for Peace and Freedom (WILPF), brought her international renown during World War I and the interwar period.

Like many of the white, middle-class women of the Progressive Era who opened new opportunities for women as activists and professionals, Balch attended college and chose a reform-oriented career. After graduating from Bryn Mawr College in 1889, Balch pursued graduate study at universities in Paris and Berlin, where she focused her studies upon poverty. She helped to found the Denison House settlement in Boston in 1892, but given her scholarly inclination, she decided to accept a job teaching economics in 1896 at Wellesley College, where she remained for more than 20 years. Her contract was terminated by the college's trustees in 1918, after she requested a leave of absence to campaign in opposition to World War I. This left her without a job or a pension.

Balch felt a lifelong duty to promote improved human relations, first as a socialist and then, with the advent of the Great War, as a pacifist. Her ideas and dedication to reform were shaped initially by her New England family and Unitarian upbringing, which stressed the importance of conscience and a call to service. Her sense of mission was subsequently influenced by her association with Jane Addams and other reform-minded women, while her association with the Quakers, who opposed war as a basic tenet of their faith, probably strengthened her devotion to pacifism. At first, like Addams, she was interested in the poor and working classes, composed mostly of the many immigrants who experienced poverty and unjust, inhumane economic and social conditions as they settled in U.S. cities. Aside from her teaching and civic service, Balch wrote her most significant work, *Our Slavic Fellow Citizens* (1910), which is considered a pioneering study of immigration. This survey, intended to counter prevailing nativist views, included her firsthand observations of immigrant communities in the United States as well as of east European cultures and conditions.

World War I caused Balch to redirect her efforts toward peace. She, her close colleague Jane Addams, and many progressive women viewed the war as a terrible catastrophe, which made clear the need for women's equal participation in international affairs if there ever was to be a peaceful world. With the founding of the WILPF in 1919, Balch directed its newly established headquarters in Geneva, where she represented the group at the League of Nations. Thus began her second career as a peace activist, and for the next 30 years she held leadership positions in the WILPF and participated in the wider peace movement. She contributed vitally to rethinking the concepts of peace, freedom, social justice, and internationalism. Peace work for Balch entailed not only applying nonviolent means of conflict resolution, but working toward a just social order in which basic human needs were met and human rights respected. During the 1940s, she made numerous innovative proposals, among them a recommendation for the internationalization of polar regions, waterways, and strategic bases. When she won the Nobel

Peace Prize, she articulated her transnational vision of a world of freely cooperating peoples, who, freed from war and the threat of it, would create a "planetary civilization" which went far "beyond nationalism." Her approach to peace is probably best summed up in her 1922 definition of the WILPF: "Lovers of our lands, we are citizens of the world, conscious partakers in the sacrament of all human life, or more truly of all sentient life."

Harriet Hyman Alonso, "Nobel Peace Laureates, Jane Addams and Emily Greene Balch: Two Women of WILPF," *Journal of Women's History* 7 (1995); Anne Marie Pois, "Foreshadowings: Jane Addams, Emily Greene Balch, and the Ecofeminism/Pacifist Feminism of the 1980s," *Peace and Change: A Journal of Peace Research* 20 (1995); Mercedes Randall, *Improper Bostonian: Emily Greene Balch, Nobel Peace Laureate, 1946* (1964); Linda K. Schott, *Reconstructing Women's Thoughts: The Women's International League for Peace and Freedom before World War II* (1997).

Anne Marie Pois

Blaine, James G. (1830–93) Journalist, politician, U.S. secretary of state. Born in West Brownsville, Penn., James Gillespie Blaine graduated from Washington College (now Washington and Jefferson) in Washington, Penn., in 1847. He then taught school for six years while studying law. After marrying Harriet Stanwood, Blaine moved with her to Maine in 1853. The influence and financial assistance of Stanwood's family enabled Blaine to become part owner of Augusta's *Kennebec Journal* in 1854. He turned the newspaper into a strong voice for the emerging Republican Party.

In 1856 Blaine became a delegate to the first Republican National Convention and rapidly turned his attention from journalism to politics. He served as chairman of Maine's Republican committee from 1859 to 1881 and was elected to the Maine House of Representatives in 1858, becoming its speaker in 1860. Blaine left in 1863 after being elected to the U.S. House of Representatives, where he served until 1876. He was Speaker of the House from 1869 to 1875 and a U.S. senator from 1876 to 1881.

A charismatic leader and brilliant orator, Blaine supported black suffrage during Reconstruction and established a reputation as a Unionist. He opposed general amnesty for Confederates but disagreed with the most repressive aspects of the Radicals' Reconstruction plan, becoming leader of the party faction known as the Half-Breeds. When President Grant retired, many Republicans favored Blaine, dubbed the Plumed Knight, for the presidency.

While Speaker of the House, however, Blaine had been involved in transactions that would frustrate his presidential ambitions. Af-

ter helping the Little Rock and Fort Smith Railroad win a land grant from Congress in 1869, Blaine asked to sell the railroad's bonds for a generous commission. When the arrangement came to light, Blaine was charged with corruption. He insisted he had not been bribed but had, rather, sought a reward after the fact. The charges nevertheless thwarted his bids for the presidential nomination in 1876 and 1880 and may have cost him the election in 1884.

In 1880 James A. Garfield, Blaine's friend and congressional ally, became president. Garfield appointed Blaine secretary of state, and Blaine worked hard to strengthen commercial and cultural ties with Latin America. When Garfield was assassinated in 1881, Blaine resigned and retreated to private life. His political influence remained strong, however, and he was chosen as the Republican candidate for president in 1884. Although Blaine began the campaign as the frontrunner, the old allegations of corruption came back to haunt him, and his candidacy was soon in trouble. To compound his problems, outraged Catholic voters turned against him when a Blaine supporter called Democrats the party of "Rum, Romanism, and Rebellion."

After his defeat by Grover Cleveland, Blaine turned his energies to building Stanwood, a family home in Bar Harbor, Maine, and to finishing his two-volume memoir, *Twenty Years of Congress: From Lincoln to Garfield* (1884–86). Still the titular head of the Republican Party, Blaine promoted Benjamin Harrison of Indiana for the presidential nomination in 1888. Harrison rewarded Blaine for his support by appointing him secretary of state (1889–92). As secretary Blaine enthusiastically advanced Pan-Americanism and organized the First International Conference of American States, held in 1889–90. The conference established the Bureau of American Republics, parent organization of the Organization of American States. After losing the presidential nomination in 1892, Blaine retired from politics. He died in Washington, D.C. Blaine's Augusta home is now the official residence of the governor of Maine.

H. Wayne Morgan, *From Hayes to McKinley: National Party Politics, 1877–1896* (1969); Edward Stanwood, *James Gillespie Blaine* (1908); Alice Felt Tyler, *The Foreign Policy of James G. Blaine* (1965).

Richard S. Offenberg

Bradford, William (1590–1657) Founder, many-time governor, and historian of Plymouth Plantation. No record exists of the birth of William Bradford, but we know he was baptized on March 19, 1590, in Austerfield, England, a small Yorkshire farming community. When his parents, William and

Alice (Hanson), died in Bradford's early childhood, he became a regular participant by the age of 12 in meetings of Puritan dissenters, who advocated separation from the national church. In 1606 Bradford became a full member of a separatist congregation in nearby Scrooby. Fearing persecution, he emigrated in 1608 with other members of his congregation to Holland, where they eventually settled in Leyden and took up labor primarily as artisans. Dutch life afforded the congregation a sanctuary in which to forge unity and religious purpose. Yet economic hardships exacted a high toll on the English group, and in 1620 Bradford and other leaders of the community began to seek financing and a charter for a settlement in the New World.

After weathering a treacherous Atlantic passage, Bradford, together with 40 fellow separatists and 61 "strangers," harbored at Cape Cod on November 11, 1620, on board the *Mayflower.* On that day, Bradford was among the 41 signers of the Mayflower Compact, a covenant in which the signers declared their allegiance to God, king, and the "Civil Body Politic" that would be their governing authority in their new land. During the ensuing months the settlers suffered famine and disease; half of them did not live through the winter. Bradford's wife fell to her death in the harbor, either by accident or suicide. With assistance from the local Wampanoag Indians, the colonists managed to eke out a meager existence that got them through the difficult winter. Despite the adversity the settlers faced in their first years in the colony, Plymouth Plantation would become the first viable settlement north of Virginia.

Bradford was first elected governor of Plymouth Plantation in 1621 and served in that office for nearly every consecutive term until 1656. During his tenure, the colony grew from a beleaguered assembly of a few dozen settlers to a prosperous colony engaged in the international trade of furs and fish. In 1630 Bradford began writing a history of the settlement, a work known today by the title *Of Plymouth Plantation.* Using a "plain style" characteristic both of his prose and the religion to which he ascribed, Bradford placed the establishment of Plymouth Plantation within the context of the Protestant Reformation, recounting the persecution of the Scrooby congregation in England, its reestablishment in Holland, and its migration to the New World. Bradford attributes the success of the colony to the "Lord which upheld them," yet his narrative is also replete with the worldly business of the plantation, describing in detail its debts and creditors, its financial misfortunes, and its many varied attempts to achieve prosperity.

Bradford ceased work on his memoir about 1650 and died in 1657, shortly after leaving the office of governor. The latter portions of his narrative are marked by passages lamenting the death of his dear friend William Brewster and decrying outbreaks of "wickedness" among the colonists. What began for Bradford as an attempt to establish a truly Christian outpost in a new land had dissolved as strangers settled in increasing numbers among the original Pilgrims, who were themselves often at odds with one another. Bradford's history stands out as a masterwork of early American literature that would influence students of New England culture for centuries to come.

Douglas Anderson, *William Bradford's Books: "Of Plimmoth Plantation" and the Printed Word* (2003); George D. Langdon, Jr., *Pilgrim Colony: A History of New Plymouth: 1620–1691* (1966); Ruth A. McIntyre, *Debts Hopeful and Desperate: Financing the Plymouth Colony* (1963); Bradford Smith, *Bradford of Plymouth* (1951); Perry D. Westbrook, *William Bradford* (1978).

Nancy F. Sweet

Bretton Woods Conference From July 1 through July 22, 1944, representatives of 44 nations gathered at the Mount Washington Hotel in the White Mountain resort town of Bretton Woods, N.H., for the United Nations Monetary and Financial Conference. The Bretton Woods agreements on economic recovery, currency stability, and world economic growth laid the groundwork for international economic relations in the post–World War II era. The conference also launched both the International Monetary Fund (IMF) and the International Bank for Reconstruction and Development, more commonly known as the World Bank.

The United States and Great Britain had been working together since 1941 on many of the proposals codified at Bretton Woods. It was the United States, however, under the leadership of Franklin D. Roosevelt and with the assistance of Treasury Secretary Henry Morgenthau, Jr., and Morgenthau's chief aide, Harry Dexter White, that dominated the agenda and the conclusions of the conference. Bretton Woods was part of the emerging United Nations organization and an expression of American postwar leadership. Among other things, the conference established the American dollar as the central world currency. The Soviet Union signed the Bretton Woods accords but did not join the IMF or World Bank.

Despite differences between the famed British economist John Maynard Keynes and White, his American counterpart, both the United States and Great Britain agreed that economic growth and a degree of government management of monetary, developmental, and trade policies were necessary ingredients of a postwar financial order intended to promote lasting peace and prevent future world depressions. In his opening address as chairman of the conference, Morgenthau proclaimed that "prosperity has no fixed limits," summoning world leaders to a global economy of growth that remains the prevailing philosophy to this day.

The World Bank has sparked controversy on the political left on account of the detrimental environmental and social impact its loans have often had on poor developing countries. But both it and the IMF, reflecting the preoccupations and postwar plans of the United States and Great Britain, have stood the test of time.

In recent years so-called free-market doc-

Bretton Woods Conference room, Mount Washington Hotel, New Hampshire, 1994

trines have called into question the Keynesian (and Rooseveltian) notion that government should play a role in steering economic life, while critics of globalized economics argue that postwar economic institutions and policies have increased corporate power and the privileges of wealth at the expense of the poor and democratic practices. Nevertheless, the postwar economic consensus symbolized by Bretton Woods still dominates many international policies.

A. L. K. Acheson, J. F. Chant, M. F. J. Prachowny, eds., *Bretton Woods Revisited: Evaluations of the International Monetary Fund and the International Bank for Reconstruction and Development* (1972); Henry Hazlitt, *From Bretton Woods to World Inflation: A Study of the Causes and Consequences* (1984); Raymond F. Mikesell, *The Bretton Woods Debates: A Memoir* (1994); Miklos Szabo-Pelsoczi, ed., *Fifty Years after Bretton Woods: The New Challenge of East-West Partnership for Economic Progress* (1996).

George K. Romoser

Brown, John (1800–1859). Abolitionist. John Brown was a radical abolitionist and an important antislavery martyr. Born in Torrington, Conn., Brown was the son of a tanner and the grandson of a soldier killed in the Revolutionary War. In October 1859, attempting to liberate slaves and end American slavery, Brown led 21 recruits (16 white men and five black men) in an attack on the Federal Armory at Harper's Ferry, in what is now West Virginia. Thirty-six hours after the attack began, federal troops led by Robert E. Lee stormed the engine house, ending the raid. After a widely publicized trial, Brown was hanged on December 2, 1859.

Brown's early life was marked by frustration and failure. In 1842, after several decades of unsuccessful business ventures, a federal court declared him bankrupt. Although devastating to his large family, bankruptcy freed Brown of his creditors and enabled him to devote himself to his true passion, abolitionism.

Unlike that of mainstream abolitionists, Brown's activism often involved close relationships with northern blacks. After the Compromise of 1850 and the passage of the Fugitive Slave Law, Brown organized the black community of Springfield, Mass., into the League of Gileadites, a group intended to guard against slave catchers. Brown assisted the wealthy congressman Gerrit Smith in the parceling out of land in upstate New York to free blacks. Brown maintained close friendships with the black abolitionists Frederick Douglass and James McCune Smith.

In 1854 the Kansas-Nebraska Act rendered Kansas a battlefield. Brown's sons were already there, and Brown decided to join the fight. After the city of Lawrence was burned by proslavery forces in May 1856, Brown and his men retaliated, dragging five men from their homes and executing them with swords. Brown denied involvement in what became known as the Pottawatomie murders. In June 1857, Brown secured his reputation as a military hero by winning the Battle of Blackjack while vastly outnumbered.

In 1858 Brown's Kansas celebrity helped him raise money for his ambitious plan to attack the South and end slavery. The specifics of Brown's plan are still the subject of debate, particularly whether he intended to initiate a large-scale exodus of freed slaves to the North or whether he intended a chain reaction of slaves liberating and arming other slaves that would ultimately force the South to acknowledge the end of slavery. Gerrit Smith and Franklin Sanborn formed a secret committee of six to fund Brown's actions. In January 1858, Brown raided a Missouri farm and transported 11 slaves over 1,000 miles to Canada. At a conference in Ontario, Brown drafted a "provisional constitution" for the reborn United States that he hoped would emerge after his raid.

The six weeks between the raid and execution were the most significant of Brown's life. Brown's pretrial interview, sentencing speech, and prison letters, communicated via telegraph lines, captured the nation's attention as have few events in American history before or since. Whereas many northerners were critical of Brown's military means, many felt sympathy for Brown himself. From his prison cell, Brown orchestrated the national conversation about the raid, demanding that it be one about the religious foundations of his actions, his interpretation of God's will. He denied charges that he was motivated by revenge for the death of his son in response to an abolisitionist raid in Kansas or that he was insane. He insisted that he aimed to free the slaves but not to foment a violent insurrection, a distinction few of his detractors were willing to accept in the wake of Nat Turner's slave rebellion. The distinction was significant to Brown, who believed that any violence on the part of the slaves would be in defense of their innate freedom.

The question of means, whether slavery should be opposed by force or by nonviolence, had divided the abolitionist movement for decades. Brown's religious rhetoric, informed by his devoted reading of Jonathan Edwards and aggressively interpreted by supporters such as Lydia Maria Child, James Redpath, Henry Thoreau, and Wendell Phillips, enabled Brown to inhabit simultaneously the position of Old Testament avenger and New Testament martyr. Brown's execution galvanized a divided North and laid the foundation for the violence of the Civil War.

Louis A. DeCaro, *"Fire from the Midst of You": A Religious Life of John Brown* (2002); Robert M. DeWitt, *The Life, Trial and Execution of Captain John Brown, Known as Old Brown of Ossawatomie, With a Full Account of the Attempted Insurrection at Harper's Ferry* (1859); Stephen B. Oates, *To Purge This Land with Blood: A Biography of John Brown* (1970); James Redpath, *A Public Life of Captain John Brown* (1859); Redpath, ed., *Echoes of Harper's Ferry* (1860); Franklin B. Sanborn, *Life and Letters of John Brown* (1885); John Stauffer, *The Black Hearts of Men: Radical Abolitionists and the Transformation of Race* (2002).

Joshua Goren

Brown Family The Brown family of Rhode Island descends from Chad Browne, an English immigrant who settled in Providence in 1638. Established early as landowners, farmers, mariners, and community leaders, the Browns of Providence Plantations rose to regional prominence in the 1730s when the fourth generation of Browns founded the mercantile house of Obadiah Brown and Company.

Obadiah Brown (1712–62) brought his nephews Nicholas (1729–91), Joseph (1733–85), John (1736–1803), and Moses (1738–1836) into the business he had founded with his late brother, their father James Brown (1698–1739). By the close of the colonial period Nicholas Brown and Company, as it was renamed in 1762, encompassed both shipping and manufacturing interests. Through their counting house on the Providence River they imported goods in their own ships from England, France, Holland, Spain, and their colonies in the Americas and exported articles manufactured at their own rum distillery, spermaceti candle manufactory, rope works, and iron foundry. In their home waters of Narragansett Bay they were adept at evading British revenue agents, and during the Revolutionary War they continued to prosper when the Continental Congress licensed them to operate their ships as privateers. At the conclusion of hostilities they initiated the Rhode Island trade with China.

The family firm's few ventures into the African slave trade proved unprofitable and ceased after 1765, though John Brown avidly espoused the slave trade and continued to pursue it on his own, even after it was outlawed in Rhode Island. Moses Brown, a Quaker and a founder in 1789 of the Providence Society for Promoting the Abolition of Slavery, sought his brother's prosecution for slave trading. In 1790 Moses Brown brought Samuel Slater to Rhode Island to build a cotton-spinning mill, thus introducing the Industrial Revolution to America. In 1791 the family founded one of the nation's first banks, the Providence Bank, whose successor institution survives to this day.

The initiative and vision of these fifth-generation members of the Brown family have been reflected ever since in the cultural landscape of Providence. The Browns were founders and substantial supporters of the Library Company of Providence, now the Providence Athenaeum. They were instrumental in funding, designing, and constructing the most important buildings of colonial-era Providence—the Market House (1773), the First Baptist Meeting House (1775), and the College Edifice (1770) of the College of Rhode Island, which was renamed Brown University in 1804. Their mansions on College Hill are among the most notable examples of 18th-century domestic architecture in America.

The male heirs of Joseph, John, and Moses Brown died without issue, and the Brown family line descended with Nicholas Brown, Jr. (1769–1841). In partnership with his brother-in-law Thomas Poynton Ives (1769–1835), he turned the family's business interests to cotton manufacturing and real estate investment. The financial rewards of this strategy were substantial and allowed succeeding generations of the Brown family to delegate the daily management of the family business while they pursued philanthropic and leisure interests. Throughout his life John Carter Brown (1797–1874), the second son of Nicholas Brown, Jr., maintained the family's legacy of support to Brown University, donating and endowing campus buildings.

With the deaths in May 1900 of both John Nicholas Brown (b. 1861) and his brother Harold Brown (b. 1863), the family's fortunes passed again to a single male heir, three-month-old John Nicholas Brown II (1900–1979), labeled by the popular press "the World's Richest Baby." John Nicholas II eventually undertook graduate studies in art history at Harvard before returning to Providence to head the family business. He was a founder of the Medieval Academy of America and served as assistant secretary of the navy for air under President Harry Truman. In 1930 he married Anne Seddon Kinsolving (1906–85), who donated her private library—the preeminent collection of military costume history—to Brown University following her husband's death in 1979. Their three children, Nicholas Brown (b. 1932), a career naval officer before becoming executive director of the National Aquarium in Baltimore; J. Carter Brown III (1934–2002), director of the National Gallery of Art from 1969 to 1992; and Angela Bayard Brown Fischer (b. 1937), partner in the family firm Brown and Fischer, were the last of their line to be raised in Providence. Their ancestral home, the Nightingale-Brown House (1791), is now owned by Brown University and is occupied by the John Nicholas Brown Center for the Study of American Civilization.

Among the descendants of Chad Browne are some 650 families with surnames other than Brown, many of whom continue to live in Rhode Island.

James B. Hedges, *The Browns of Providence Plantations: The Colonial Years* (1952); Hedges, *The Browns of Providence Plantations: The 19th Century* (1968); Martha Mitchell, *Encyclopedia Brunoniana* (1993); Calvin Tomkins, "For the Nation: Profile of J. Carter Brown," *New Yorker* 66, no. 29 (September 3, 1990).

Robert P. Emlen

Chamberlain, Joshua Lawrence

(1828–1914) Civil War general, educator, politician. Joshua Lawrence Chamberlain was born in Brewer, Maine. In 1848 he entered Bowdoin College, where he met his future wife, Fannie Adams. He took courses with Calvin Stowe, the young professor whose wife, Harriet Beecher Stowe, Chamberlain heard read early drafts of *Uncle Tom's Cabin*. In 1856 Chamberlain accepted a teaching position at Bowdoin. In August 1862, he left, ostensibly to take a sabbatical, and volunteered to become lieutenant colonel of the 20th Maine Volunteer Infantry Regiment.

During the Civil War, Chamberlain performed meritoriously in several engagements. He is best known for his actions on the second day of the Battle of Gettysburg (July 1–3, 1863), when he led the flagging 20th Maine in a bayonet charge against onrushing Confederates at Little Round Top. Following Gettysburg, he was made a brigade commander in the 5th Corps. Throughout the war, Chamberlain took part in more than 24 battles and suffered six wounds, including a severe one to his hip at Petersburg, Va., in June 1864, for which Gen. Ulysses S. Grant gave him a rare field promotion to brigadier general. He left the war a major general, having served meritoriously in the final stages of the conflict outside of Richmond, particularly in the Appomattox Campaign of March–April 1865. On April 12, 1865, he was given the honor of accepting the formal surrender of Confederate weapons and colors; in a gesture of "honor answering honor," he ordered his men to salute his Confederate adversaries.

After the war Chamberlain parlayed his military success into the governorship of Maine (1866–70), which he served as a moderate Republican, and the presidency of Bowdoin College (1870–83), where he became frustrated with the failure of his efforts to institute an engineering curriculum and military drill. In January 1880, as commander of the Maine state militia, he helped resolve the "twelve days" crisis over the state gubernatorial election by publicly daring disgruntled political foes to shoot him down. In his later years Chamberlain tried his hand at several business ventures, none of which proved very lucrative. In 1905 he became surveyor of the Port of Portland.

Wartime memories consumed Chamberlain's later years. He spoke frequently before veterans' groups and worked tirelessly to promote the memory of his old comrades. His reminiscences, most notably *The Passing of the Armies* (1915), reflected on the meaning of the cataclysm of 1861–65. For Chamberlain, battle was a test of character in which "the highest qualities of manhood are called forth—courage, self-command, sacrifice of self for the sake of something held higher." A strong sense of Victorian masculinity and Christian civilization dictated his conservative politics and permitted a relatively easy reconciliation with former Confederates. Unlike those of his generation whose faith in humanity was destroyed by the war, Chamberlain came to see it as a source of personal and national greatness. In 1893 he was awarded a Congressional Medal of Honor for valor at Gettysburg. In 1914, at the age of 85, Chamberlain died as the result of a wound he suffered at Petersburg, the last direct casualty of the Civil War.

John J. Pullen, *Joshua Chamberlain: A Hero's Life and Legacy* (1999); Diane Monroe Smith, *Fanny and Joshua: The Enigmatic Lives of Frances Caroline Adams and Joshua Lawrence Chamberlain* (1999); Alice Rains Trulock, *In the Hands of Providence: Joshua L. Chamberlain and the American Civil War* (1992).

Patrick Rael

Civil War

At the close of the Civil War (1861–65) almost every town in New England erected some sort of monument on the village common or in the local cemetery to commemorate the deeds of those who served in the nation's most terrible war. Most were simple memorials, much like the bronze statue of a soldier at parade rest that still stands in Antrim, N.H. The inscription at the base of that monument reflects the patriotism of the day: "In memory of the men of Antrim who on land and sea fought for liberty, union and equal rights for all mankind and gave their lives that future generations might enjoy the benefits thereof." There is no attempt to mask an underlying pride, for New Englanders of the late 19th century felt that they had awakened the conscience of the nation by leading the fight against slavery and had saved the country from disunion at the same time. Joshua Lawrence Chamberlain, Maine's most prominent Civil War hero, wrote of Confederate soldiers surrendering at Appomattox Courthouse in Virginia, "Whoever had misled these men, we had not. We had led them back, home."

Citizens in other regions of the country not only failed to share this view of New England's moral supremacy but complained about the region's economic power. "Shall we sink down as serfs to the heartless, speculative Yankees," wrote the editor of the *Columbus (Ohio) Crisis*, "swindled by his tariffs, robbed by his taxes, skinned by his railroad monopolies?" Indeed, southerners felt that prime responsibility for what they called the War of Northern Aggression lay at the feet of a puritanical, money-hungry, radical Yankee majority intent on trampling the rights of the South's simple yet sturdy agrarian minority. A "conglomeration of greasy mechanics, filthy operatives, small-fisted farmers, and moonstruck theorists," according to the editor of the *Muscogee (Ga.) Herald* in 1856, New Englanders seemed to be at the center of every sectional conflict of the 1840s and 1850s. William Lloyd Garrison, Elijah P. Lovejoy, John Quincy Adams, the Massachusetts Emigrant Aid Company, Benjamin Curtis—the Supreme Court justice who wrote the most powerful dissent in the Dred Scott Case—Charles Sumner and, finally, John Brown (born in Torrington, Conn.) are just a few examples of this phenomenon. New England fishing fleets monopolized the southern fisheries, New England businesspeople depressed the price of cotton, New England bankers raised the price of credit, New England merchants charged exorbitant rates to move southern products, and New England legislators pushed higher tariffs through Congress.

The truth, or at least historical accuracy, is somewhere in the middle. It is fair to say, however, that in the 1850s and 1860s New England's economic, political, and social influence far exceeded its 10 percent of the U.S. population. Economically, the area was the workshop of the country. According to the census of 1860, there were 19,514 industrial establishments in the region, 1,500 more than in all 11 states of the Confederacy. New England was a giant in textile manufacture (a true indicator of industrial power at the time), boasting 4 million spindles and dwarfing the number found in any other region of the country. Massachusetts alone produced more goods, at a higher value, than the entire South. In addition, much of the important machine-tool industry was located in the Northeast. Given that the North had the finest educational system in the country (more than 95 percent of adults could read and write), it should come as no surprise that over half of the important patents granted between 1790 and 1860 were held by New Englanders. That kind of "Yankee ingenuity" and industrial might served the North well during the war. Early in the conflict, for example, Connecticut firms and factories alone turned out 1,000 rifles a month—and soon doubled that figure. In 1864 the Springfield Armory in Massachusetts produced 300,000 rifles.

Socially, New England experienced a true golden age before the war. Boston, whose population exceeded that of Charleston, S.C.; Richmond, Va.; Montgomery and Mobile, Ala.; and Memphis, Tenn., combined, was the most cosmopolitan city in the county. It had more institutions of higher learning than did Alabama, Mississippi, Arkansas, and Texas put together. Providence and Hartford also provided citizens with excellent educational opportunities. In addition, Dartmouth College (N.H.) and Bowdoin College (Maine) both had national reputations (in 1852, Harriet Beecher Stowe, a Connecticut native, published *Uncle Tom's Cabin* while her husband was a professor at Bowdoin).

Economic and social power, of course, went hand in hand with political influence. As a hotbed of political activism, the birthplace of the Free-Soil Party, and a stronghold of the new Republican Party, New England controlled a disproportionate share of the federal government just before and during the Civil War. Of 22 Senate committees in the U.S. Congress, 16 were chaired by men born in New England. Galusha Grow, father of the Homestead Act and Speaker of the House of Representatives, was born in Ashford, Conn. Hannibal Hamlin of Maine, after serving as president of the Senate, became vice president of the United States. Gideon Welles of Connecticut became secretary of the navy, and Lincoln's second secretary of the treasury, William Pitt Fessenden, who was born in New Hampshire, represented Maine in the Senate. Thaddeus Stevens, chairman of the Ways and Means Committee, was a native of Danville, Vt.

Further proof of New England's political sway is evidenced by the nomination and election of Abraham Lincoln to the presidency in 1860. The eight states whose popular votes gave Lincoln his greatest majorities in that crucial election were, respectively, Vermont, Minnesota, Massachusetts, Maine, Rhode Island, Connecticut, Michigan, and New Hampshire. Remarkably, Lincoln and the Republican Party swept all 67 counties in New England that year. Never again would the region command such political clout.

Following the first shots at Fort Sumter, near Charleston, in 1861, which signaled the start of the war, New Englanders demonstrated their devotion to the Union cause. Approximately 370,000 men from the region served in the federal forces, more than 100,000 of whom were missing, wounded, or killed before the conflict came to an end. Half the men of military age in New Hampshire, for example, joined one of that state's 19 regiments or served in the navy. Connecticut suffered a casualty rate of more than 35 percent. Men from Maine and Massachusetts made up over half the regiments that New England sent to war. A few of these deserve mention. The 22d Massachusetts, 14th Vermont, 17th Maine, and 20th Maine regiments were crack units that performed heroically at Gettysburg and in other battles. The 54th Massachusetts Colored Regiment, trained by Colonel Robert Gould Shaw, proved the gallantry of black soldiers in its assault on Battery Wagner at Morris Island, S.C., in July 1863. The Fifth New Hampshire suffered more casualties (295, including 19 officers) than any other northern infantry regiment, while the First Maine Heavy Artillery had the most killed or fatally wounded (210) in any one engagement of the war, the June 1864 battle at Petersburg, Va.

Several prominent Civil War leaders and personalities hailed from New England. Generals Nathaniel P. Banks, Edwin Sumner, and Joseph Hooker were from Massachusetts. General Ambrose Burnside, the unfortunate commander of the Army of the Potomac at the Battle of Fredericksburg and owner of the most famous whiskers in the country, was a Rhode Islander. General Joseph Mansfield, killed at Antietam, was born in New Haven, Conn., as was Admiral Andrew Foote. Generals Oliver Otis Howard and Joshua Lawrence Chamberlain, both Medal of Honor winners, were natives of Maine. General Benjamin Butler, the "beast of New Orleans," was born in Deerfield, N.H., and became a resident of Massachusetts. Dorothea Dix (Maine), Isabella Fogg (Maine), Mary Jane Safford (Vt.), Mary Livermore (Mass.) and Clara Barton (Mass.) were key figures in the nursing corps and the U.S. Sanitary Commission. Even the music of the war was composed by New Englanders. George Frederick Root, born in Sheffield, Mass., wrote 28 wartime songs, including "The Battle Cry of Freedom" and "Tramp! Tramp! Tramp! or, The Prisoner's Hope." The most popular poem of the war, "Battle Hymn of the Republic" by Julia Ward Howe of Massachusetts, was set to the tune "John Brown's Body."

Except for a brief "invasion" at Saint Albans, Vt., a foiled bank robbery at Calais, Maine, and naval actions off the coast, no armed battles took place on New England soil during the Civil War. Nonetheless, the conflict had a profound impact on several segments of the New England economy. The coastal shipping trade, which depended heavily on raw materials from the South, was shattered. In addition, the textile industry withered (especially in Maine and New Hampshire), as did wooden shipbuilding. Even New England's population, which had steadily increased for several decades at a rate of about 20 percent, showed a lag, its growth slowing to 11.2 percent. The census of 1870 reported only two states that lost population during the 1860s, neither one of them Confederate; they were Maine and New Hampshire.

At no other time in these states' histories did population decline. Only Rhode Island came anywhere near the 22.6 percent increase experienced by the country as a whole.

Oliver Wendell Holmes, Jr., a veteran of the 20th Massachusetts Infantry and a Supreme Court justice, wrote after the war, "We have shared the incommunicable experience of war. We have felt, we still feel, the passion of life to its top.... In our youths, our hearts were touched with fire." The Civil War offered New Englanders the opportunity to complete the revolution started by their ancestors in 1775. Slavery was abolished, and the federal union restored. The price for this incommunicable experience, as restless New Englanders left for opportunities south and west, was a gradual decline in the economic and political influence of the region.

Bruce Catton, *The Army of Potomac Trilogy: A Stillness at Appomattox, Glory Road, Mr. Lincoln's Army* (1951–53); Eric Foner, *Free Soil, Free Labor, Free Men: The Ideology of the Republican Party before the Civil War* (1970); Shelby Foote, *The Civil War: A Narrative,* 3 vols. (1958–75); Herman Hattaway and Archer Jones, *How the North Won* (1983); Allan Nevins, *Ordeal of the Union,* 8 vols. (1957–71); David M. Potter, *The Impending Crisis, 1848–1861* (1976); John J. Pullen, *The Twentieth Maine* (1957); Geoffrey C. Ward, with Ric Burns and Ken Burns, *The Civil War: An Illustrated History* (1991).

Jerry R. Desmond

Colonial Revival The renewal of interest in the material culture, landscape, and architecture of the colonial period during the late 19th century was a widespread movement that gained momentum following the nation's centennial celebrations in 1876. Spurred by industrialization, urbanization, and immigration, architects, writers, and painters as well as members of the upper classes retreated to rural areas for rejuvenation, allying themselves with what was perceived to be a more pure and less harried past.

Several regions in New England provided restful havens and bucolic imagery for colonial revivalists. These included Deerfield, Salem, and Concord, Mass.; Litchfield, Conn.; and the Piscataqua region of New Hampshire and Maine. In these retreats men and women created paintings, photographs, buildings, gardens, and landscapes based on a conception of colonial simplicity and harmony. These activities forged a new version of New England's past.

Often the New England villages to which urban visitors withdrew were found to be somewhat disappointing. They lacked modern amenities such as electricity and water and were less attractive than the new urban suburbs. Visitors thus established village improvement societies, whose goal was to beau-

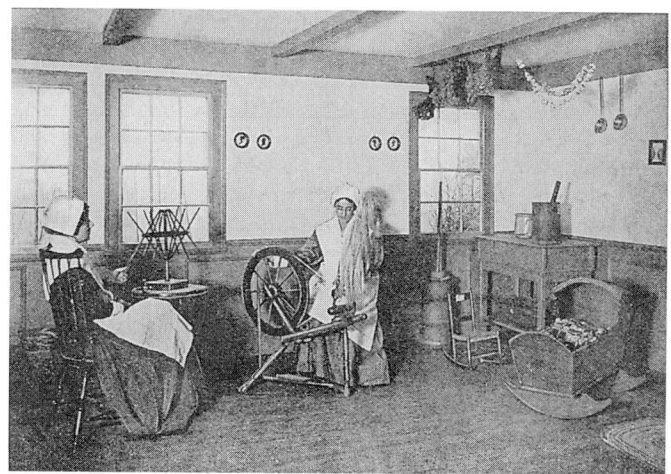

"Domestic Industry," from Della R. Prescott, A Day in a Colonial Home *(1929)*

tify, restore, and preserve. The New England village, complete with white clapboard houses, town common, elm trees, and steepled Congregational church, is the signature production of Colonial Revival improvement societies.

One of the best-known New England towns to be transformed by such a society during this period was Litchfield, the birthplace of Ethan Allen and Harriet Beecher Stowe. A frontier town, Litchfield reached its peak during the 1820s, when the population had grown to 4,600 and its residents had built several handsome houses. This early-19th-century period supplied the imagery for the so-called restoration of the town during the Colonial Revival. Improvement society activities included the planting of elm trees, installing of plaques to identify historic houses, and exhibiting of historical artifacts. Restorers painted their houses white, added black exterior shutters and dormers, and enlarged chimney stacks. By the turn of the century Litchfield had become a "white city upon a hill."

The Colonial Revival is most often associated with architecture, and the forms it took varied greatly. The design of new houses, ranging from suburban homes to the summer "cottages" of wealthy vacationers, which might have 40 rooms, often incorporated supposedly colonial details such as elaborate Palladian windows, widow's walks, and exposed beams. Architects also remodeled and restored older homes, adapting them for modern use with such amenities as screened porches while at the same time preserving interior woodwork and other details. If a house was seen to be lacking certain desirable features, the architects or builders often simply added them.

Perhaps one of the most famous Colonial Revival architectural firms was McKim, Mead and White. In the summer of 1881 Charles McKim and William Mead made a tour of

New England, stopping at Salem, Marblehead, and Newburyport, Mass., and Portsmouth, N.H. At each stop they studied the surviving Georgian buildings. The four-square, rational design was reminiscent of Europe's finest Palladian architecture, lending an air of restrained dignity to the urban landscape of these New England towns. McKim and Mead used the drawings made during their tour as models for new Colonial Revival buildings ornamented with arched and pedimented windows, columns, hipped roofs with dormers, roofline balustrades, and ornate interior carving.

The interior of houses also was a locus for many Colonial Revival activities. During the late 19th century the home was seen as a retreat from the modern world, and if it was decorated with relics, so much the better. The ideal New England home was nestled in the countryside, protected from the influx of modern amenities, and representative of the rugged individuals who had built it. In *Oldtown Folks* (1869) Harriet Beecher Stowe peopled the New England home with frugal, hardworking folk. These qualities—frugality, stern morality, and rugged individualism—highly valued during the Colonial Revival period, are what rural New Englanders are known for still.

The Colonial Revival's most widely celebrated interior space was the New England kitchen. It appeared in private homes, in novels, and at fairs. First publicized at the Philadelphia International Centennial Exhibition in 1876, the New England kitchen featured a wide chimney mantel adorned with candlesticks, an old-fashioned spinning wheel, a small flax wheel, a cradle, a long wooden bench called a settle, and herbs hanging from exposed beams. Boston baked beans and brown bread were prominent items on the menu. New England kitchen exhibits gave women a public yet domestic role at fairs and provided a baseline from which to measure modern progress.

In addition to local color writers like Connecticut's Stowe and Maine's Sarah Orne Jewett, painters made the New England home an important artistic motif. The Boston School impressionist Edmund Tarbell created several historically oriented canvases, including *My Family* (1914). The living room depicted in *My Family* is a late-19th-century early American New England interior. Colonial woodwork and diamond-paned casement windows as well as antique furnishings are part of the scene. Seated in the living room is the artist's family, mother sewing serenely with her children gathered round.

Antiques symbolized the high quality of colonial home life. In the period after the Centennial collectors began to search for relics that were associated with famous men and events. They also collected articles that would remind them of the daily habits of their forefathers. These practical tools of daily life in colonial times, including candlesticks, spinning wheels, and warming pans, were enshrined in parlors as important ancestral relics. Old china was perhaps the most widely collected antique, as evidenced, for example, by the formation in Worcester, Mass., of the China Hunters Club in the 1870s.

While many antiques found their way into the Colonial Revival home, a large number entered the collections of historic houses and museums. In Deerfield, Mass., the Pocumtuck Valley Memorial Association opened Memorial Hall in 1880. There a spinning wheel, household utensils, and domestic artifacts were displayed in a colonial parlor, kitchen, and bedroom. At the Essex Institute in Salem, Mass., George Francis Dow created a series of period rooms in 1907. These rooms consisted of a 1750s kitchen and a parlor and bedroom furnished in the style of 1800. The rooms were created with old woodwork and were livened up with such personal effects as gloves, eyeglasses resting on a book, and a newspaper to give the viewer the impression he or she had just stepped into the past. Such rooms provided visitors with important images of how New Englanders lived during the colonial period.

Many of New England's historic house museums were also founded during the height of the Colonial Revival. In Portsmouth five historic houses were opened between 1908 and 1932. These agencies of "instruction and inspiration" were often established by upper-class women interested in educating the working class. When the National Society of the Colonial Dames of America in the State of New Hampshire opened Portsmouth's second historic house museum, known as the Moffatt-Ladd house, in 1913, the house was described as "magnificent. About it cluster historic memories, making of it a fitting home for a society whose object is to inspire patriotism in a new generation by recalling the virtues of the old." During the restoration of the house gas chandeliers were removed, the woodwork was painted white, the floors were stripped, and the parlor was painted yellow and blue, "a beautiful combination . . . much used in Colonial days."

The Colonial Revival peaked in the 1930s, reviving somewhat, primarily in its architectural guise, in the 1950s and 1980s. It lives on in the smart-stepping fife and drum corps that often appear in New England's Independence Day parades and as an adjunct to other patriotic rituals. The revival has played an important role in creating a New England identity. Architects, writers, painters, and collectors created a vision of New England that included a white steepled landscape, serene Georgian houses, kitchens filled with the utensils needed for a self-sustaining lifestyle, and a hardworking New England folk guided by a strict moral compass.

Alan Axelrod, ed., *The Colonial Revival in America* (1985); John Durel, "'Historic' Portsmouth: The Role of the Past in the Formation of a Community's Identity," *Historical New Hampshire* 41 (1986); Sarah L. Giffen and Kevin D. Murphy, eds., *A Noble and Dignified Stream: The Piscataqua Region in the Colonial Revival, 1860–1930* (1992); William Rhoads, *The Colonial Revival* (1977); Elizabeth Stillinger, *The Antiquers: The Lives and Careers, the Deals, the Finds, the Collections of the Men and Women Who Were Responsible for the Changing Taste in American Antiques, 1850–1930* (1980).

Sarah Rooker

Colonial Wars and Captivities

In the century and a half between the landing of the Pilgrims and the American Revolution, New England suffered through seven wars. The first occurred just a few years after the arrival of John Winthrop's great fleet in 1630. The Pequot War (1636–37) involved control of the land along the Connecticut River and the European belief that any Native American violence, no matter how trivial or justified, must be nipped in the bud to discourage further attacks. The Pequot were slaughtered or sold into slavery. Relations between settlers and Indians remained calm until the outbreak of King Philip's War (1675–76), which proved to be the bloodiest of all the colonial conflicts. Again the initial controversy concerned land, as the Wampanoag and their chief, Metacom (King Philip), found themselves caught between two colonies wishing to expand: hemmed in by Connecticut and Massachusetts, Rhode Island and Plymouth had no choice but to push into the Wampanoag land that lay between them. What began as a localized skirmish, however, soon escalated into a clash involving all the major tribes in New England.

A war begun in the fall of 1688 against the Eastern Abenaki Indians soon expanded into the first of the international conflicts that collectively became known as the French and Indian wars. The Glorious Revolution in England brought the Dutch stadtholder William and his English wife, Mary, to the throne in 1688, enabling William to add England to his war against Louis XIV. This in turn pitted the English colonies against their northerly neighbor, New France. Because the population of the French colony was so low, the inhabitants relied on Native American allies to bolster their defense. The first of these French and Indian wars, King William's War (1689–97), the American phase of the War of the League of Augsburg in Europe, was followed closely by a second, Queen Anne's War (1702–13), part of the War of the Spanish Succession. The 31-year interlude of international peace that followed 1713 was marred by a local conflict between Massachusetts and the Eastern Abenaki known as Dummer's War (1722–27) after the lieutenant governor of the province.

In the next quarter century both the English and the French attempted to improve their defenses. The government of Massachusetts built several forts along their frontier line, and the French constructed the fortified city of Louisbourg on Cape Breton Island, Nova Scotia. In 1745, at the start of King George's War (1744–48), or the War of the Austrian Succession, a force of 3,500 New England provincial soldiers, aided by a squadron from the Royal Navy, laid siege to and captured the great prize of Louisbourg, which the English government returned to France at the peace.

In 1754 a new war broke out between the English and the French in western Pennsylvania, expanding quickly into a widespread European and North American conflict. Alternately known as the French and Indian War, the Seven Years' War (the name of the concurrent European conflict), and the Great War for Empire, it is probably best referred to simply as the Last French War insofar as its manifestations in New England are concerned.

Indeed, it was the last French war because the British, by committing large numbers of regular troops and the Royal Navy, captured New France and refused to relinquish it at the peace table. Although most of the conflict occurred outside New England, French and Indian raiding parties did strike at New England communities. In addition, New England contributed a significant number of soldiers to the Battle of Lake George (1755), the capture of Fort Beauséjour in Nova Scotia (1755), and the siege of Fort William Henry on Lake George (1757).

Throughout the earlier of these wars the French, enlisting Eastern Abenaki alone or French-led Indian parties, attacked communities along the New England frontier. During these attacks many English settlers were captured and marched back to New France or to native villages; some historians place the number of captives as high as 1,500. A few of those held prisoner published their stories, and such narratives became a popular form of entertainment in a world that frowned on frivolous fiction. By means of these narratives two captives in particular became famous in New England history: Mary Rowlandson, captured in an attack on Lancaster, Mass., during King Philip's War, and the Reverend John Williams, captured at Deerfield, Mass., at the beginning of Queen Anne's War. Hannah Dustin, who was taken in a raid on Haverhill, Mass., near the end of King William's War, did not publish a narrative, but Cotton Mather's account of her capture and escape was well known.

These hostilities affected all New Englanders, both European and Native American. The cost of soldiers and supplies, the redemption of captives, and the support of widows drove up taxes. New England's Indian populations paid a devastating price for the disruption in settlement patterns caused by the wars, as they were forced to accept a frontier line whose inhabitants had concerns and agendas very different from those of the older, more protected communities. Although the wars temporarily brought New England closer to the mother country, they also fostered a military ethos and confidence that would carry New England into the War for Independence.

Fred Anderson, *A People's Army: Massachusetts Soldiers and Society in the Seven Years' War* (1984); Douglas Edward Leach, *Arms for Empire: A Military History of the American Colonies in North America, 1607–1763* (1973); Patrick M. Malone, *The Skulking Way of War: Technology and Tactics among the New England Indians* (1991); Francis Parkman, *France and England in North America*, 2 vols. (1983 [1892]).
Steven C. Eames

Connecticut Connecticut became the fifth state in the union on January 9, 1788. Its capital is Hartford, its land area is 5,018 square miles, and its population at the 2000 census was 3,405,565. When European explorers made their way up the pristine Connecticut River to investigate a dense and unknown land, they found beauty that a harsh Ice Age had left behind: majestic hills, lakes, and fertile soil upon which new settlers could attempt to eke out a living. The first Europeans to arrive were the Dutch. In 1614 Adriaen Block

Soldiers and Sailors Memorial Arch (1886), Hartford, a Civil War monument

guided a small ship up the Connecticut River to a point just north of present-day Hartford. A man with an eye for profit, Block immediately recognized opportunities for trade with the local Indians. It would have been hard not to take notice of the natives living in the area; at the time there resided within the state's present-day boundaries the densest concentration of Native Americans in the region, some 6,000 to 7,000 from approximately 16 tribal groups. Block traded a variety of goods for beaver pelts, and thus began the Dutch interest in the new territory.

By the 1630s other Dutch had made their way up the river the Mohegans called Quinnehtukqut, or "long tidal river." The only river that runs the full length of New England, the Connecticut, as settlers later translated it, was so named because of its tidal effects from Long Island Sound. The river rises and falls with the changing tides as far north as Enfield, some 60 miles from the river's mouth on the Sound. In 1633 the rising water brought Jacob Van Curler, who purchased a small tract of land from the Pequot Indians. He quickly erected a fort, the House of Hope, located at the confluence of the Connecticut and Park Rivers. The Dutch also established Kievits Hoeck, a post on the mouth of the river where Old Saybrook is now located.

In 1632 an Englishman named Edward Winslow ventured from his home in the Plymouth Colony to explore the lush Connecticut River valley. Winslow's glowing account of the area prompted the colony to send a settle-

ment party the next year. Leading the expedition was William Holmes, who traveled up the river with parts for a house that had been crafted in Plymouth. He landed north of the Dutch fort, purchased land from the local Indians, assembled the house, and in doing so founded Windsor, the first English settlement in Connecticut. Migration to the new area, however, really began in the summer of 1635 when citizens from Massachusetts began settling around the Windsor house.

Other colonists soon followed Holmes's lead. In the fall of 1634 John Oldham, an explorer from Dorchester, Mass., founded Wethersfield, and in 1636 the Reverend Thomas Hooker settled Hartford with approximately 100 followers. The new settlements were not without their difficulties. The two most pressing problems were the Dutch and the natives; neither appreciated English encroachment. The new inhabitants were simply too numerous for a handful of Dutch traders, who were soon forced to abandon their outposts. War between the English and the Pequots raged throughout the mid-1630s. Colonists ensured their safety only after defeating the Pequot in 1637, opening the way for even more English settlements. New Haven was founded in 1638 under the guidance of John Davenport, and from that town flowered a host of other hamlets, including Guilford, Milford, Branford, and Stamford.

As the various Connecticut towns grew, a number of prominent leaders judged it prudent to tie the settlements together for their mutual prosperity. As one of the preeminent proponents of the movement, Thomas Hooker insisted that a doctrine of fundamental law was needed that would grant authority to the government but that would exist only with "the free consent of the people." In 1639 leaders from the towns of Windsor, Wethersfield, and Hartford joined and created the Fundamental Orders. The document included a preamble and 11 orders so that "there should be an Orderly and decent Government established according to God and Order and dispose of the affayres of the people." Among the various provisions were guidelines for the election of a governor, magistrates, and representatives from the three towns. The historical significance of the Fundamental Orders was marked, representing the first time in history that a group of people came together to form a social compact that created a new and independent commonwealth with specific governmental officers, structures, and rules. Many scholars consider the Fundamental Orders to be the first written constitution; the Connecticut General Assembly concurred by adopting the name Constitution State in 1959.

In the years following the creation of the

Fundamental Orders, Connecticut and the rest of New England continued steady growth and organization. In 1642 commissioners from Massachusetts Bay, Plymouth, Connecticut, and New Haven convened in Boston to draw up articles for "the United Colonies of New England" to secure a "perpetual league of friendship and amity, for offence and defence." In 1650 Connecticut added to the Fundamental Orders by passing a Magna Charta that listed the rights of the people. Notwithstanding these strides toward governmental organization, Connecticut lacked legality in the eyes of the British Crown, and the colony's longevity was in question.

In 1660 Charles II acceded to the throne, and Connecticut's leaders believed their best chance for safeguarding the colony was to petition the king for a royal charter. Connecticut's governor, John Winthrop, Jr., the oldest son of the famous Massachusetts leader, was chosen as the emissary to plead the colony's case in England. He left for London in July 1661 and by May 1662, he had succeeded in his mission. The royal charter designated the corporate body as the "Governour and Company of the English Colony of Conecticut [*sic*] in New England in America" and granted not only legitimacy but also a high degree of self-government. The charter also set the colony's boundaries: Narragansett Bay to the east, the Massachusetts border to the north, Long Island Sound to the south, and all the way to the South Sea, or Pacific Ocean, on the west. (Connecticut later yielded its western land claims to the Congress of the Confederation in 1786.)

The royal charter also helped to consolidate the colony. After struggling to maintain its autonomy, and after a number of its own towns had already joined the Connecticut Colony, the colony of New Haven submitted to Connecticut's rule in December 1664. The increase in population during these years reveals the steady, prosperous growth of Connecticut. In 1636 Connecticut had 800 residents. By 1640 settlers had increased to some 2,000, and in 1675 the number reached 12,000. As it had in the past, increased English immigration produced tension with the native peoples. Native American anger over white encroachment caused uprisings throughout New England in the late 1660s, and in 1675 minor scares exploded into outright warfare. Under the leadership of Metacom, known to colonists as King Philip, the Wampanoags waged what became known as King Philip's War to retake the lands stolen by white settlers. Although the war began in the Massachusetts and Plymouth colonies, it quickly spread to other colonies and native peoples, and the inhabitants of Connecticut were faced once again with protecting their new homes. As in the

first war, they were successful, and with the conclusion of hostilities in the spring of 1676 came the end of Indian power in the region. The census of 1774 revealed the extent to which English settlement ultimately overwhelmed the native population. Whereas in 1630 there were some 6,000 to 7,000 Indians and only about 300 colonists, by 1774 there were a mere 1,363 natives left, all of whom lived on reservations. White settlers had reached 197,842.

As Connecticut grew, so did the rest of the American colonies. Yet with prosperity and sovereignty came conflict with England. When war ultimately broke out in 1775 Connecticut proved to be a model of efficiency in supplying militia. The Continental Congress subsequently turned to Captain Joseph Trumbull of Connecticut to serve as commissary general of the army to ensure proper provisions for the American troops. Indeed, it was Trumbull to whom General George Washington turned when the army endured a fateful winter at Valley Forge. As a result of both Trumbull's and the state's success, Connecticut was dubbed the Provision State.

If Connecticut revealed its patriotism during the Revolution, the state showed only obstinacy during the War of 1812, in which America renewed its conflict with England. A bastion of Federalism (the political party dominated by such men as Alexander Hamilton and John Adams), the Connecticut congressional delegation voted unanimously against war and thwarted the federal government's efforts to wage the war by withholding supplies, refusing to procure funds, and not allowing the state's troops to fight in Canada. The height of Connecticut recalcitrance, however, came with the infamous Hartford Convention of 1814–15, when delegates came to Hartford from a number of New England states to condemn President James Madison's war policies. New England, and especially Hartford, was the object of much ridicule when the war ended abruptly. The convention was touted as the ultimate example of disloyalty.

In the wake of the war Connecticut continued growing, and new times ultimately called for a new constitution. The state was in fact well overdue; even after the Revolution it had continued to operate under its royal charter of 1662. Thus in 1818 leaders gathered and drafted a new state constitution. They were unable to decide on a capital city and finally determined to keep the colonial plan of having two capitals, one in Hartford and the other in New Haven. Some 50 years later, in 1873, Hartford was chosen as the state's sole capital when it offered $500,000 for a new capitol building.

By 1818 residents were deeply involved in a variety of mercantile ventures. The cotton in-

dustry boomed in the 67 mills spread throughout the state. Other businesses included tanneries, glassworks, and paper mills, as well as pottery, small arms, button, rubber, and hat factories. For a time, even silk was a product of Connecticut. Though it was difficult to farm the rocky terrain—as the myriad stone walls throughout the region attest—agriculture was also a staple of the state. Competition from western lands caused further problems for farmers, but they managed by specializing their crops. As a result, Connecticut produced perishables like tomatoes, onions, lettuce, apples, and milk. Another crop was fine tobacco, a product at which the state continues to excel.

These many ventures made for a diverse economy, yet one of the state's earliest trades was associated with life at sea. The first Connecticut-made ship, the *Tryall*, was launched from Wethersfield in 1644, and the navy's first warship, the *Oliver Cromwell*, was built in Essex at the beginning of the Revolution. From this auspicious beginning the state's sailors and shipbuilders continued to be among the nation's best. During the height of American whaling in the mid-1850s, New London ranked third among U.S. ports.

Shipping, another growing industry, was always risky as boats were prey to storms, pirates, and belligerent nations. In the 1790s a group of enterprising men pooled their interests so that many rather than one shipowner would assume losses. Thus was born the American insurance industry. In later years the idea was applied to fire protection for homes and life coverage for individuals. Today Hartford is known as the insurance capital of the world.

The novelty of insurance is one of many ingenious ideas brought to fruition by Connecticut's residents. Inventing new methods and products has always been a mainstay of the state's people. In fact, from the establishment of the U.S. patent office in 1790 to the 1930s, Connecticut regularly led all states in the number of patents granted relative to population. In one period alone, from 1820 to 1845, more than 20 patents of major importance were granted to such men as Samuel Colt, the inventor of the repeating pistol, and Charles Goodyear, the creator of the process to vulcanize (cure) rubber. Famous Connecticut patents also included Eli Whitney's cotton gin and Christian Sharps's breech-loading rifle. Other inventors were perhaps more obscure, but no less important: Ebenezer Jenks created steel fishhooks in 1813, and in 1858 Ezra J. Warner received the first U.S. patent for a can opener. Today the quest for new products and ideas remains a focal point in the state, with some 100 independent and 400 corporate laboratories.

In addition to its leadership in Yankee ingenuity, Connecticut can claim a number of other firsts. In 1647 Alse Young of Windsor was the first person to be hanged for witchcraft in New England. In 1764 publication of the *Hartford Courant* began, and today it is the oldest American newspaper in continuous existence. Tapping Reeve of Litchfield began the nation's first law school in 1784, and in 1780 Benedict Arnold of Norwich became America's first traitor. The outbreak of the Civil War precipitated the launching of the first ironclad ship in Mystic, and in 1939 Igor Sikorsky constructed the first helicopter at his plant in Stratford.

Connecticut has also been a leader in education. In 1795 the state was the first to take the proceeds from western land sales and fund public schools. Earlier in the century Puritan leaders established one of the nation's earliest colleges when in 1701 a charter was granted and a school established in Saybrook. Fifteen years later it was moved to New Haven and ultimately named after one of its benefactors, Elihu Yale. In 1861 Yale University became the first to confer an American doctoral degree. During the early part of the 19th century other religious sects were prompted to form institutions of higher learning. In 1823 an Episcopalian college was founded as Washington College in downtown Hartford. It became Trinity College in 1845, and in 1872 was moved from its original site when the trustees sold the property to the city so that a new state capitol could be built. Methodists continued the educational movement by establishing Wesleyan College in 1831.

The early 20th century brought increased ethnic diversity to the state. Indeed, by 1910 foreign-born residents accounted for some 30 percent of Connecticut's 1,114,756 people. Immigrants came from Italy, Russia, the Austro-Hungarian Empire, and Poland. Later decades brought individuals from Puerto Rico and Asia. Notwithstanding this diversity, the 2000 census report revealed that the state's residents were largely Caucasian—some 81 percent. Other ethnic groups consisted of 9.4 percent Hispanic, 9.1 percent African American, 2.4 percent Asian, and .2 percent Native American.

Connecticut's industry remains diverse. In 2000 there were some 4,200 farms; mining contributes significantly to the state's economy; and various corporations make their homes in Connecticut's 21 cities. Seafaring is still a large part of the state's life: one of the navy's largest submarine facilities is located in Groton. Despite its successful development, much of the state's pristine beauty witnessed by the first settlers remains. The "long tidal river" endures as a source of serenity, and many of the state's forests are largely intact.

Ellsworth S. Grant, *The Miracle of Connecticut* (1992); Thomas R. Lewis, *Near the Long Tidal River: Readings in the Historical Geography of Central Connecticut* (1981); Forrest Morgan, ed., *Connecticut as a Colony and as a State* (1904); Norris Galpin Osborn, ed., *History of Connecticut*, vols. 1, 4, 5 (1925); Robert J. Taylor, *Colonial Connecticut: A History* (1979); Albert E. Van Dusen, *Connecticut* (1961).

Matthew Warshauer

Coolidge, (John) Calvin (1872–1933)

President of the United States. Calvin Coolidge, the 30th president of the United States (1923–29), was born in Plymouth, Vt., on July 4, 1872, the first child of John and Victoria Coolidge. His father, the owner of a general store, was also a farmer and local politician. Although prosperous by rural Vermont standards, the Coolidges lived an austere life. The Coolidge homestead had no running water, electricity, plumbing, central heating, or telephone. When Vice President Coolidge succeeded to the presidency upon the death of Warren G. Harding in 1923, the oath of office was administered by his father, a local notary, in the family parlor by the light of a kerosene lamp.

Young Coolidge, always painfully shy, graduated from Amherst College in 1895 with a reputation for wit and a commitment to public service. Settling in Northampton, Mass., he married Grace Goodhue and entered law and politics. Although rooted in conservative Vermont values, Coolidge was a practical politician rather than a rigid ideologue, and in his roles as legislator, senate president, and governor of Massachusetts between 1906 and 1920

he supported many progressive reforms, including the direct election of senators, regulation of child labor, workmen's compensation, legalization of picketing, women's suffrage, a state income tax, and pensions for state workers. Writing to a friend in 1915, he asserted, "I think I have a reputation of being conservative, which I am, because I do not make so loud a noise as some others. I think I have been in sympathy with practically all legislation to improve living conditions." In his first speech as governor, Coolidge advised the legislature, "Let there be a purpose in all your legislation to recognize the right of man to be well-born, well-nurtured, well-educated, well-employed, and well-paid."

Coolidge's often progressive record as governor has been overshadowed by the Boston police strike of 1919. Although Coolidge supported the grievances of the police, his assertion that "there is no right to strike against the public safety by anybody, anytime, anywhere" captured the public imagination and secured him the Republican vice presidential nomination in 1920. President Harding's unexpected death in August 1923 put Coolidge in the White House.

In his first address to Congress, Coolidge endorsed lower taxes and lower government expenses, rejecting any "suggestion that the Government should, or could, assume for the people the inevitable burdens of existence." But, declaring "our National Government is not doing as much as it legitimately can do to promote the welfare of the people," Coolidge

President Calvin Coolidge back at the Vermont farm, 1924

also called for antilynching legislation, a commission to mediate labor disputes, hospital care for veterans, oil slick laws to protect coastal waters, a minimum wage for women, a constitutional amendment to permit federal regulation of child labor, and the establishment of a cabinet department of education and welfare. "We want idealism," he told Congress, "we want that vision which lifts men and nations above themselves."

Coolidge became extremely popular, even though his style and temperament were the antithesis of the Roaring Twenties. Despite his personal reserve, "Silent Cal" averaged eight press conferences each month, was the first president to use radio effectively, and gave more speeches than any previous president. An idealist with a strong belief in human progress, he exhorted the American people to value public service, civic involvement, education, and character, and to reject materialism and prejudice. Coolidge never said, and did not believe, that the business of America is business. He was convinced that the federal government should first encourage citizens to solve their problems at the local and state levels.

Coolidge was elected to a full term in 1924. But the death of his 16-year-old son, Calvin, Jr., from blood poisoning shattered the president, who had never gotten over the loss of his mother and younger sister during his adolescence. "When he went," the grieving father wrote, "the power and the glory of the Presidency went with him." Nevertheless, Coolidge continued to seek economical and effective government. Tax cuts exempted 98 percent of the people from federal income taxes; the wealthiest Americans paid 93 percent of income taxes when Coolidge left office. The national debt was reduced by $2 billion. Coolidge vetoed the McNary-Haugen farm bill, which he believed would encourage overproduction, higher prices, and a federal bureaucracy. Although concerned about speculation in stocks, he rejected federal intervention in the stock market. But he did support regulation of the new radio and aviation industries. Coolidge enforced Prohibition without enthusiasm, observing that "bad laws" tend to undermine respect for good laws.

In foreign affairs, Coolidge supported membership in the World Court, improved relations with Mexico, and vetoed a cutoff of Japanese immigration to the United States. In 1928, 15 nations signed the Kellogg-Briand Pact, sponsored by the United States and France and supported by Coolidge, renouncing war as a means of settling international disputes. World War II exposed the naïveté of the treaty.

Dispirited after his son's death, the president chose not to seek reelection in 1928. The Coolidges returned to their two-family house in Northampton. Coolidge completed his autobiography, wrote a newspaper column, and served as president of the American Antiquarian Society until his death, at the age of 60.

Hendrik Booraem, *The Provincial: Calvin Coolidge and His World, 1885–1895* (1994); Robert E. Gilbert, "The Trauma of Death: Calvin Coolidge," *The Mortal Presidency: Illness and Anguish in the White House* (1992); Donald R. McCoy, *Calvin Coolidge: The Quiet President* (1967); Sheldon M. Stern, "The Struggle to Teach the Whole Story: Calvin Coolidge in American History Education," *New England Journal of History* 53 (1996).

Sheldon M. Stern

Dorr Rebellion In Rhode Island, industrialization and its corollary, urbanization, combined by the 1840s to produce a crisis in constitutional government known as the Dorr Rebellion. Rhode Island's royal charter, still in effect at the time, gave disproportionate influence to rural towns—which by then were in decline—conferred almost unlimited power on the General Assembly, and contained no procedure for amending the charter. To preserve their power and influence, state legislators, regardless of party, insisted on upholding an antiquated real estate requirement for voting and officeholding, even though all other states had abandoned it. As Rhode Island became more urbanized, this statutory freehold qualification became increasingly restrictive. By 1840, on the eve of the rebellion, about 60 percent of free adult males in the state were disenfranchised by it.

Because earlier moderate efforts at change (beginning as early as 1817) had been virtually ignored by the General Assembly, reformers decided in 1841 to bypass the legislature and hold a People's Convention to be equitably apportioned and chosen by an enlarged electorate. Thomas Wilson Dorr, a lawyer from Providence and the scion of a distinguished family, assumed leadership of the movement in late 1841 and drafted much of the progressive People's Constitution, which was ratified in a popular referendum in December 1841 by the overwhelming mandate of 13,944 to 52. In April 1842 Dorr was elected governor under this document.

The reformers, or Dorrites, were resisted by a so-called Law and Order coalition of Whigs and rural Democrats, who returned the incumbent governor, Samuel Ward King, to office in a separate election and then used force and intimidation to prohibit the implementation of the People's Constitution. When Dorr responded in kind by unsuccessfully attempting to seize the state arsenal in Providence on May 18, 1842, most of his followers deserted, and Dorr fled into exile. When he returned in late June to reconvene his People's Legislature in the Glocester village of Chepachet, a Law and Order army of 2,500 marched to Glocester, sending the People's governor into exile a second time.

The agitation against the charter that had produced the Dorr Rebellion influenced the victors to consent to a popularly written constitution, which was overwhelmingly ratified in November 1842 by a vote of 7,024 to 51 and became effective in May 1843. Although the margin of victory was huge, voter turnout was meager in a state with more than 23,000 adult male citizens. That the opposition, in mute protest, refrained from voting explains in part the apathetic reception of the constitution and the lopsided vote. This document retained the old real estate requirement for naturalized citizens, a restriction aimed openly at Irish Catholics. It allowed each town only one senator regardless of its population, giving rural towns a stranglehold on the state senate, a situation that remained in effect until the tumultuous state-governmental reorganization in 1935 known as the Bloodless Revolution. Cumbersome procedures made the amending of the constitution difficult, and the legislative branch retained much of its power.

Dorr returned in October 1843 to surrender to local authorities. He was arrested immediately and jailed until February 1844, then prosecuted for treason against the state. Following a short trial, a jury composed entirely of his political opponents found him guilty and sentenced him to hard labor in solitary confinement for life. This harsh treatment produced a national outcry and became an issue in the presidential campaign of 1844. Dorr had served one year of his sentence when Governor Charles Jackson authorized his release in June 1845.

A Democratic General Assembly restored Dorr's civil and political rights in 1851 and in 1854 reversed the treason conviction. But these gestures did little to cheer the vanquished reformer, whose spirit and health had been broken by his defeat and incarceration. Disillusioned, Dorr died in December 1854 in the midst of a local Know-Nothing campaign directed against immigrant Irish attempts, which he supported, to secure the vote.

Patrick T. Conley, *Democracy in Decline: Rhode Island's Constitutional Development, 1776–1841* (1977); George M. Dennison, *The Dorr War: Republicanism on Trial, 1831–1861* (1976); Russell J. DeSimone and Daniel C. Schofield, comps., with an introduction by Patrick T. Conley, *The Broadsides of the Dorr Rebellion* (1992); Marvin E. Gettleman, *The Dorr Rebellion: A Study in American Radicalism, 1833–1849* (1973).

Patrick T. Conley

Earle, Alice Morse (1851–1911) Author, antiquarian, social historian. Alice Morse Earle was born in Worcester, Mass., the daughter of Edwin and Abigail (Clary) Morse. She was educated at Worcester High School and at Dr. Gannett's boarding school in Boston. In 1874 she married Henry Earle of Brooklyn, N.Y., with whom she had four children. Earle lived much of her life in Brooklyn, passing summers at her father's home in Worcester. After her husband's death she traveled extensively in Europe with her sister, with whom she was shipwrecked in 1909 when their steamer, the *Republic,* was rammed and cut in half by the *Florida.* Morse fell out of the lifeboat and narrowly escaped drowning; the incident weakened her health considerably, and she died at Hempstead, Long Island, N.Y., in 1911.

Earle's professional life was spent preparing and publishing books about the colonial history of America. Her first article, about her ancestors' church in Chester, Vt., based on family materials, was published in the *Youth's Companion* in 1890. An expanded version on the New England meetinghouse was printed in the *Atlantic Monthly* (1891); her book *The Sabbath in Puritan New England* was published by Scribners the same year. This was the first in a long series of publications, including *China Collecting in America* (1892); *Customs and Fashions in Old New England* (1893); *Costume of Colonial Times* (1894); *Margaret Winthrop* (1895); *Colonial Dames and Good Wives* (1895); *In Old Narragansett* (1896); *Colonial Days in Old New York* (1896); *Curious Punishments of Bygone Days* (1896); *Home Life in Colonial Days* (1898); *Child Life in Colonial Days* (1899); *Stagecoach and Tavern Days* (1900); *Old-Time Gardens* (1901); *Sun Dials and Roses of Yesterday* (1902); and *Two Centuries of Costume in America, 1620–1820* (1903), a two-volume work that she considered one of her most significant. Earle also assisted in the compilation of *Early Prose and Verse* (1893) and *Diary of Anna Green Winslow, a Boston School Girl of 1771* (1894) and contributed to *Historic New York* (1897) and *Chap-Book Essays* (1897). She became a noted lecturer whose articles frequently appeared in such magazines as *Atlantic Monthly, New England Magazine,* and *Chap-Book.* She also contributed book reviews to *Dial.*

Earle focused her research on one phase of American history until she had mastered all the available material, including correspondence, court records, diaries, and laws. Moreover, she focused on the lives, manners, and customs of early Americans, a departure from professional historians' practices of the day. She was a popular consultant on American antiques, and during the Colonial Revival her works helped shape an image of New England domestic life that was re-created in the house museums of Wallace Nutting, the Society for the Preservation of New England Antiquities

(now Historic New England), and local historical societies. Later scholars in the fields of folklore, material culture, and women's history found in her work an essential resource for reshaping their fields. The renewed interest in America's colonial past developed alongside patriotic hereditary societies, such as the Daughters of the American Revolution, of which Earle was a member.

Esther C. Averill, "Alice Morse Earle," *Old-Time New England* (January 1947); John A. Garraty and Mark C. Carnes, eds., *American National Biography,* s.v. "Earle, Alice Morse" (1998); Edward T. James, ed., *Notable American Women, 1607–1950: A Biographical Dictionary,* s.v. "Earle, Alice Morse" (1971).

Martin J. Manning

Emancipation Emancipation was achieved gradually in New England, through custom as much as through law. By 1800, roughly 160 years after the introduction of slavery in the region, the institution had been phased out through various emancipation laws. New England became involved in the slave trade in 1638, the most active ports being Boston and Newport, R.I. The majority of New Englanders, however, were not slaveholders: for example, only about one-eighth of the households in Massachusetts owned slaves by the mid-18th century. Furthermore, slaves in New England generally worked much more directly with their masters than did southern slaves and served at all levels of the economy—as house servants, factory workers, farm laborers, blacksmiths, carpenters, and shipbuilders. Although some large farms in Connecticut and Rhode Island had 40 slaves or more, the average number of slaves in New England was two per slaveholding household.

Both Connecticut and Rhode Island ended slavery through gradual emancipation laws. Although it is unclear when the first slaves arrived in Connecticut, laws appearing in the 1660s and 1670s indicate the existence of slavery in the state at that time. The Act of 1784 provided that all slaves born after March 1, 1784, could be held as servants only until the age of 26. A 1792 law prevented circumvention of emancipation by prohibiting residents from selling their slaves out of state. Slavery was abolished outright in Connecticut in 1848. In 1652 Rhode Island attempted to moderate slavery by limiting a slave's service to 10 years, though this law was mostly ignored. In 1779 the state prohibited the sale of slaves outside its borders and in 1784 passed a gradual emancipation law similar to that of Connecticut.

Slavery was not widespread in either Vermont or New Hampshire. Vermont's first constitution (1777) prohibited slavery; nonetheless, legislation passed in 1786, which prohibited the sale of slaves outside its territory, indicates that slavery did exist there to some

Susan Sedgwick's portrait of Elizabeth Freeman (1842), the first slave in the United States to be legally set free from her masters as the result of a suit brought by Sedgwick's husband, the Stockbridge attorney Theodore Sedgwick

extent. It is clear, however, that from its inception Vermont discouraged the practice of slavery within its borders. Although slavery was never formally abolished in New Hampshire, it gradually disappeared. Yet, as late as 1840 the federal census lists one slave in New Hampshire, five in Rhode Island, and 17 in Connecticut.

Despite indications that slaves were held in Massachusetts as early as 1624, most scholars agree that the first definitive evidence of slaves in the Bay State appears in 1638. Beginning in the 1760s, many slaves successfully sued masters for their freedom on grounds ranging from unfulfilled promises of manumission to the absence of specific laws that legalized the institution; an example of these "freedom cases" is *Brom and Bett v. Ashley* (1781), also known as the Elizabeth Freeman case. A series of 18th-century legal suits known as the Quock Walker cases culminated in the Massachusetts Supreme Court decision *Commonwealth v. Jennison* (1783), in which Chief Justice William Cushing declared that slavery was incompatible with the free-and-equal clause in the state constitution. For a variety of complex reasons, this case did not end slavery in Massachusetts, but it did signal that the legal system would not protect slavery in the state. Because Maine remained a territory of Massachusetts until it entered the union as a free state in 1820 (as part of the Missouri Compromise), slavery, strictly speaking, was never legal in this New England state.

In the 1770s, assertions of natural rights associated with the American Revolution helped prompt groups of slaves in New Hampshire and Massachusetts to petition their legislatures to outlaw slavery. These petitions were unsuccessful, but many slaves in New England became free after serving in the Revolutionary War.

Overall, New England was more a center of the slave trade than of slave labor. By the end of the 18th century, slavery had largely ceased to exist in the region. The rhetoric of freedom that surrounded the American Revolution, along with growing moral objections to slavery on the part of abolitionists, the unsuitability of the institution to the regional economy, and increasing opposition by the white working class to competition from slave labor combined to increasingly delimit the existence of the institution until it faded from the New England landscape.

Lorenzo Johnston Greene, *The Negro in Colonial New England* (1968 [1942]); William D. Piersen, *Black Yankees: The Development of an Afro-American Subculture in 18th-Century New England* (1988); Robert B. Shaw, *A Legal History of Slavery in the United States* (1991); Robert M. Spector, "The Quock Walker Cases (1781–83): Slavery, Its Abolition and Negro Citizenship in Early Massachusetts," *Journal of Negro History* 53 (1968).

Christine Brooks Macdonald

Federal Constitution At the time of the Constitutional Convention of 1787 the four New England states (Connecticut, Massachusetts, New Hampshire, and Rhode Island) made up about 24 percent of the population of the 13 more or less United States. Although all four had in common commercial economies and antislavery sentiments, these shared viewpoints were not enough to cause them to join forces at the convention. Rather, New England's contributions to the U.S. Constitution must be viewed as a function of individual delegations and indeed individual delegates; the impact of New England, whose seven delegates constituted 12.7 percent of the 55 who attended, therefore amounted to a good deal less than the sum of its parts.

Only two of New Hampshire's four delegates showed up at the convention. They did not arrive until it was half over and then contributed little to the discussions. Rhode Island's legislature, dominated by holders of state bonds and other antinationalists, chose not to participate. Vermont and Maine were not represented because they did not become states until after the convention, in 1791 and 1820, respectively.

Because the Massachusetts delegation represented the third most heavily populated of the 13 states, one would expect it to have played a significant role at the convention. But Francis Dana did not attend, and those who did—the nationalists Rufus King and Na-

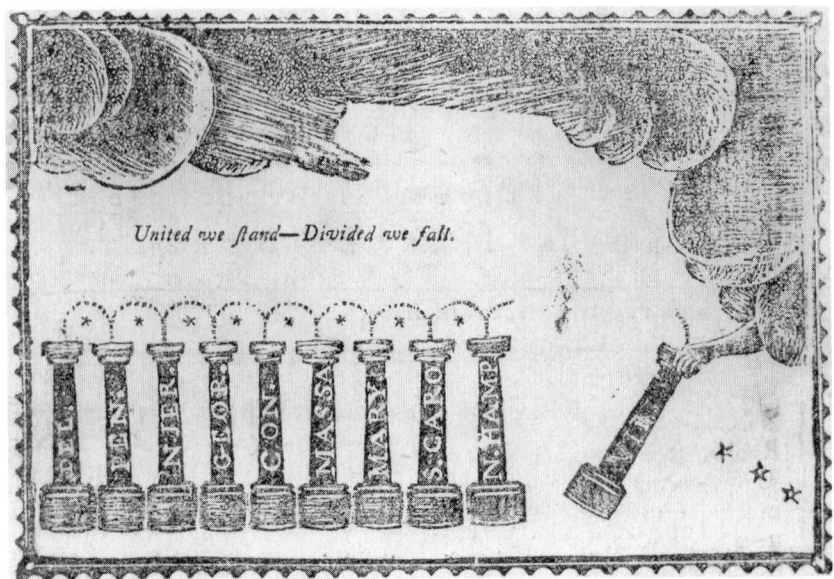

Advocacy for ratification of constitution, New Hampshire Gazette, *June 26, 1788*

thaniel Gorham and the headstrong Elbridge Gerry, all wealthy merchants from the coastal east, along with the westerner Caleb Strong—often split the vote, with Gerry and Strong siding together against King and Gorham, thereby neutralizing Massachusetts's influence. The New Hampshire delegates, John Langdon and Nicholas Gilman, followed the Massachusetts nationalists on most issues. The Connecticut delegation, consisting of the tightly knit team of Roger Sherman, William Samuel Johnson, and Oliver Ellsworth, carved out its own path, frequently as a compromising balance between nationalist and antinationalist delegations, heavily and lightly populated states, and northern and southern states.

The U.S. Constitution as sent to the states for ratification reflected the strong nationalist consensus among the 55 delegates. Convention participants differed, however, on how much to centralize the government and restrict state powers, issues on which New Englanders themselves did not agree. Nevertheless, Gerry, who finally refused to support the document, and Sherman were major forces in moderating the high nationalism of the Madisonians, a group that included King.

New England's sectional interests focused principally on protecting foreign commerce, as conducted at the time and as a subject for future international treaties. The New England delegates agreed that Congress should have authority to regulate interstate and foreign commerce. Efforts by southerners to block such powers resulted in a requirement that treaties (of all kinds) with foreign nations be ratified by a two-thirds vote of the Senate rather than by a simple majority.

Connecticut split with Massachusetts, however, on export duties. Most nations relied on the income from such taxes, and Massachusetts assumed that both import and export levies would fall under the authority of Congress. But Connecticut derived much of its revenue from trade with the West Indies, which would have been severely inhibited by export duties. Sherman and his colleagues struck a bargain with delegates from the Carolinas and Georgia to forbid export taxes entirely. In exchange the Connecticut delegates agreed to help the southerners get a fugitive-slave clause written into the Constitution and ward off attempts to prohibit the importation of additional slaves. King, one of the convention's three most vocal opponents of slavery, fought this bargain, though in vain.

The Connecticut delegates were instrumental in resolving the central political issue of the convention—that of striking a balance between large and small states and between the state and central governments. It took this moderating position not as a New England state but as a middle-sized state that was fundamentally in favor of states' rights. The famous Connecticut Compromise undermined James Madison's basic principle of proportional representation in both houses of Congress. The Connecticut delegates had to strive for a government that could control the commercial might of neighboring Massachusetts and New York yet make it impossible for the new central government to run roughshod over the states. The Connecticut delegates successfully sought to balance a House in which the large, populous states would dominate with a Senate in which every state would have an equal vote to protect its special interests and local self-government. This compromise not only provided both of these controls and protections but probably saved the convention from dissolution at its most critical moment.

Divisions within the Massachusetts delegation, Connecticut's trek along its own path, New Hampshire's tardy arrival and lack of innovative participation, and Rhode Island's absence meant that New England presented no strong, unified point of view at the convention. The region's influence was manifest, however, in the work of the Connecticut delegation and of individuals such as Gerry and King.

George Athan Billias, *Elbridge Gerry, Founding Father and Republican Statesman* (1976); Christopher Collier and James Lincoln Collier, *Decision in Philadelphia: The Constitutional Convention of 1787* (1986); Charles R. King, ed., *The Life and Correspondence of Rufus King; Comprising His Letters, Private and Official, His Public Documents, and His Speeches*, 6 vols. (1971 [1894–1900]); Elizabeth P. McCaughey, *From Loyalist to Founding Father: The Political Odyssey of William Samuel Johnson* (1980).

Christopher Collier

Forbes, Esther (1891–1967) Novelist and historian. Born in Westborough, Mass., Esther Forbes was the daughter of William Trowbridge Forbes, a judge, and Harriette Merrifield, a local historian. Forbes grew up in Worcester, graduated in 1912 from Bradford Academy in Haverhill, Mass., and then took writing courses at the University of Wisconsin (1916–18). From December 1919 until mid-1926, Forbes worked on the editorial staff of Houghton Mifflin in Boston, an experience that helped her develop her writing craft. Forbes left the publishing company to marry Albert Hoskins, a lawyer, in January 1926; they lived in New York until their divorce in 1933, when Forbes returned to the family home in Worcester.

Forbes's first important success was a short story, "Break-neck Hill," which won an O. Henry Award in 1920. *O Genteel Lady!* (1926), her first novel, explored a young woman's struggle to reconcile her literary aspirations with her sexual passions and the social conventions of 19th-century Boston; it garnered critical acclaim and sold well.

Forbes added to her professional reputation with what many consider her finest work of fiction, *A Mirror for Witches* (1928), the story of a tormented girl in 17th-century Salem, Mass., written from the point of view of an apologist for the Salem witchcraft trials. *Miss Marvel* (1935) traced the life of an unmarried woman who retreats into a world of fantasy and imaginary lovers and was followed by the less successful *Paradise* (1937) and *The General's Lady* (1938).

Esther Forbes, 1948

Forbes's next novel was to be about a man who remained neutral during the American Revolution, but the onset of World War II caused her instead to explore the nature of freedom and warfare. The result was the nonfictional *Paul Revere and the World He Lived In* (1942). Her mother collaborated on the extensively researched book, which won a Pulitzer Prize for history in 1943. Forbes also used a Revolutionary War setting for *Johnny Tremain* (1943), the story of a silversmith's apprentice that won the Newberry Medal in 1944 and has become a classic of American children's literature and a popular motion picture.

Forbes's later books were also well received. *America's Paul Revere* (1946) was revised for children from her earlier biography. *The Running of the Tide* (1948) traced the decline of a Salem family in early-19th-century America; it won the Metro-Goldwyn-Mayer Novel Award (1948). *Rainbow on the Road* (1954) described the making of American folklore through the experiences of an itinerant limner. In 1960 Forbes became the first female member of the American Antiquarian Society. At the time of her death in Worcester she was at work on a history of witchcraft in New England.

Esther Forbes earned the respect of historians and reviewers, who praised her lively recreation of the past, her meticulous treatment of historical detail, and her skillful delineation of character. She preferred life in Worcester with her family to the literary circles of large cities but was nevertheless a serious artist whose best work added new dimensions to the historical novel.

Jack Bales, *Esther Forbes: A Bio-bibliography of the Author of "Johnny Tremain"* (1998); Margaret Erskine, *Esther Forbes* (1976); David D. Hall, "Esther Forbes," in *Notable American Women: The Modern Period*, ed. Barbara Sicherman and Carol Hurd Green (1980); Edward J. Jennerich, "Esther Forbes," in *Dictionary of Literary Biography*, vol. 22 (1983).

Martin J. Manning

Franklin, Benjamin (1706–90) Printer, inventor, statesman. A native of Boston, Benjamin Franklin was the 10th and youngest son of Josiah and Abiah Franklin. Although usually associated with his adopted city, Philadelphia, Franklin was in many ways shaped by his New England upbringing. One of his greatest creations, Poor Richard of *"Poor Richard's" New Farmer's Almanac*, edited by Franklin from 1732 until 1757, gave national voice to New England proverbial expressions by means of an English form, the almanac, that was already well established in the repertoire of the region's printers. The famous section of Franklin's *Autobiography* (1771–88) detailing his daily ritual of self-examination has forever linked him to the utilitarian and materialistic tendencies inherent in the popular conception of the so-called Puritan ethic.

After only two years of elementary education Franklin was apprenticed to his brother James, printer and publisher of the weekly *New-England Courant*. Franklin attributed his lifelong love of learning, debate, and satire as well as his rationalism to his experiences as an apprentice. Growing up in a culture that was becoming less Puritan and more Yankee, Franklin wrote a series of humorous essays at the age of 16 under the pen name Silence Dogood satirizing the austere Puritanism of local celebrities like the Boston minister Cotton Mather. Nonetheless, Franklin would later list Mather's *Bonifacius; or, Essays to Do Good* (1710) as a central influence on his decision to undertake a life of public service.

In 1723 Franklin ran away from home and eventually established a successful printing business in Philadelphia. He became devoted to the city's civic life and to social improvement and helped found the Library Company of Philadelphia (1731), the American Philosophical Society (1743), the Philadelphia Academy (1751, now the University of Pennsylvania), and the Pennsylvania Hospital (1752). A keen observer and inventive genius, he conducted the famous kite experiment proving that lightning was electricity, a discovery that earned him election to the Royal Society of London in 1756.

Franklin was an early champion of intercolonial cooperation and a leader of the patriot cause during the American Revolution. He served as London agent for Pennsylvania (1764–75) and was soon asked to represent the interests of Georgia (1768), New Jersey (1769), and Massachusetts (1770) as well. In 1773

Nineteenth-century commemoration on the building occupying the site of Benjamin Franklin's birthplace, Boston

Franklin exposed letters written by Thomas Hutchinson, the royal governor of Massachusetts, to various British officials that, when published, brought about the governor's downfall. With British–American tensions mounting, Franklin returned home in 1775 and became a delegate to the Second Continental Congress; the following year Congress dispatched him to Paris to attempt to negotiate an alliance with France. Regarded by many as a steadying influence, Franklin is unique in having signed all four critical documents establishing the new nation: the Declaration of Independence (1776), the Treaty of Alliance and the Treaty of Amity and Commerce with France (1778), the Treaty of Paris (1783), and the Constitution of the United States (1787). He retired from public service in 1787 and died in Philadelphia. His best-known writings include *The Way to Wealth* (1758) and his *Autobiography*, both of which have been translated into many foreign languages.

Although Franklin left Boston while still a youth, New Englanders were among the first to celebrate his accomplishments. In 1778 Franklin, Mass., was named for him; in 1790 Boston developers created Franklin Street and erected a memorial urn for him there; and the first full-figure bronze statue of Franklin was unveiled in front of Boston's Old City Hall in 1856. In his will Franklin left £100 to the town of Boston, the interest on which was to fund yearly Franklin Medals encouraging scholarship, and £1,000 that in accordance with Franklin's detailed instructions would eventually be used to establish the Franklin Institute, a technical college, in 1908. The Boston Athenaeum, Boston Public Library, and Mas-

sachusetts Historical Society all have rich materials related to Franklin; Yale University has been home to the Franklin Papers project since 1954.

Nian-Sheng Huang, *Benjamin Franklin in American Thought and Culture, 1790–1938* (1994); Ellen R. Cohn, ed., *The Papers of Benjamin Franklin*, 37 vols. to date (1959–); Walter Isaacson, *Benjamin Franklin: An American Life* (2003); Claude Anne Lopez, *Mon Cher Papa: Franklin and the Ladies of Paris* (1966); Edmund S. Morgan, *Benjamin Franklin* (2002); Gordon S. Wood, *The Americanization of Benjamin Franklin* (2004).

Nian-Sheng Huang

Genealogy New Englanders have long been interested in their ancestry. Beginning in the early colonial period settlers regularly had births, marriages, and deaths recorded in town records. Families sometimes composed more extensive accounts in manuscript form, which might even be printed. In the early 19th century underlying interest in New England genealogy was captured in John Farmer's *Genealogical Register of the First Settlers of New England* (1829), the first major attempt to trace the region's earliest settlers.

In 1845 the New England Historic Genealogical Society (NEHGS) was founded in Boston, the first such organization in the Western world. Intended as the principal resource for the study of families of New England ancestry, NEHGS laid the foundation for genealogical scholarship not only in New England but throughout the nation. Its journal, the *New England Historical and Genealogical Register*, created the standard format used for scholarly genealogy today. The society

rapidly began to acquire books and manuscripts on local and family history and to publish towns' vital records. Along with such institutions as the Massachusetts Historical Society and the New Hampshire Historical Society, NEHGS encouraged a generation of antiquarian scholarship on New England families and towns.

In 1898 the society opened its membership to women and was soon attracting members from around the country. By the early 20th century NEHGS had become the foremost center of genealogical studies in the nation. Interest in genealogy continued to grow throughout the first half of the century, generated by NEHGS and organizations like the New York Genealogical and Biographical Society, established in 1869.

By the turn of the century genealogical scholarship was being increasingly viewed as distinct from other scholarly disciplines. Whereas such fields as history and sociology came to be dominated by men and women trained in university graduate programs, genealogy remained a subject largely for amateurs. This image was enhanced by lineage societies like the Mayflower Society and the Daughters of the American Revolution, both established in the 1890s. Henceforth the stereotypical genealogist became the amateur searching for prominent ancestors.

Genealogy's reputation was further damaged, at least in the minds of professional scholars, by its uneven publishing record. Most of the research in the field was published privately by individual genealogists. These vanity publications, over which there was little or no editorial control (the exceptions being those prepared by well-known professional genealogists such as Donald Lines Jacobus and Mary Lovering Holman), often contained errors and in a few cases even presented bogus accounts of ancestors. By 1960 New England genealogy had fallen from its late-19th-century glory days.

Since the 1970s interest in the subject has undergone a great resurgence, prompted in part by the nation's Bicentennial celebrations and by the publication in 1976 and subsequent televised broadcast of Alex Haley's *Roots: The Saga of an American Family*. Along with renewed interest has come a new image. Active genealogists and genealogical societies can now be found in nearly every U.S. county. Since 1894 the Church of Jesus Christ of Latter-day Saints has been collecting records for genealogical research from around the world, and the expansion and availability of this collection (now largely on microfilm) has been a major factor in broadening the appeal of genealogical research to Americans of all ethnic backgrounds. Because of the many scholarly genealogical journals now being published, the major conferences held nationally and regionally, and the formation of accrediting bodies such as the Board for Certification of Genealogists, scholarship in the field has steadily improved.

Genealogical research in New England has been even further accelerated by the personal computer; desktop publishing, for example, has made the private printing of family histories easier than ever before. Specialized software programs facilitate the creation and formatting of complex genealogies. New databases available online and especially on CD-ROM have dramatically enhanced the accessibility of genealogical information that was previously difficult or impossible to find.

Robert Charles Anderson, *The Great Migration Begins: Immigrants to New England, 1620–1633*, 3 vols. (1995); Ralph J. Crandall, *Shaking Your Family Tree: A Basic Guide to Tracing Your Family's Genealogy* (1986); Crandall, ed., *Genealogical Research in New England* (1984); James Savage, *A Genealogical Dictionary of the First Settlers of New England*, 4 vols. (1998 [1860–62]).

Ralph J. Crandall

Hancock, John (1737–93) Merchant, philanthropist, president of the Continental Congress, signer of the Declaration of Independence, first governor of Massachusetts. John Hancock was born in Braintree, Mass., in 1737, the son and grandson of influential Congregational ministers. After his father's death in 1744, young Hancock was adopted by his uncle Thomas, a former bookbinder's apprentice who amassed a fortune in trade and real estate. John took residence with Thomas and his wife, Lydia, in their Beacon Hill mansion in Boston.

Hancock received a gentleman's education, studying classics at the Boston Latin School and later matriculating at Harvard College. After graduating in 1754, he entered the family business, ultimately assuming control of the House of Hancock upon his uncle's death. He traded in whale oil, potash, and naval stores, and earned considerable income from shipping, banking, and real property. Though he inherited a small number of slaves, Hancock did not regularly, if ever, traffic in them.

As Thomas's successor, Hancock enjoyed tremendous prestige in Boston. In 1765 the townspeople voted him selectman; the following year they elected him representative in the General Court. From these posts, Hancock opposed the Stamp Act; he also joined forces with the Sons of Liberty, presumably financing much of their activity. The Townshend Act turmoil of the late 1760s drew Hancock further into resistance politics when customs officials seized his sloop *Liberty* on smuggling charges.

After the retirement of his nemesis, Governor Francis Bernard, and in the wake of the Boston Massacre (1770), Hancock began to withdraw from radical politics. He accepted a royal appointment as colonel of cadets, the Massachusetts honor guard, and nearly agreed to serve on Governor Thomas Hutchinson's council but was dissuaded by Whig leaders eager to reconcile Hancock and the Adams-Otis faction. In 1773 Hancock played a prominent role in disseminating several politically embarrassing letters written by Hutchinson. That December, Hancock supported the destruction of East India tea, known as the Boston Tea Party. Decades later, Tea Party member George Robert Twelves Hewes remembered, improbably, that Hancock helped dump the tea overboard.

In 1775, Hancock joined the Adams cousins and other Massachusetts delegates in the Continental Congress. Having narrowly avoided British troops at Lexington, Mass., and soon to be heralded along with Samuel Adams as the only rebels exempted from General Gage's amnesty proclamation, Hancock arrived in Congress at the height of his popularity and was promptly elected president. Though the first signer of the Declaration of Independence, Hancock fell out of favor with his Massachusetts colleagues, who resented his ostentatious governance.

Upon returning to Boston in 1778, Hancock quickly shored up broad political support. Under the new Massachusetts Constitution, he was elected the state's first governor, a position he held almost continuously until his death. Only briefly, in 1785–87, did Hancock retire, citing poor health, and in so doing he happened to avoid the crisis of Shays's Rebellion. Hancock initially resisted the proposed U.S. Constitution, which threatened to diminish state power and lacked a bill of rights, but he was persuaded to support it by Massachusetts Federalists.

Hancock died in his home on October 8, 1793. He was survived only by his wife, Dorothy Quincy, their two children having both died at an early age.

William T. Baxter, *The House of Hancock: Business in Boston, 1724–1775* (1965); William M. Fowler, *The Baron of Beacon Hill: A Biography of John Hancock* (1980).

Benjamin H. Irvin

Hartford Convention During the final days of the War of 1812 a group of disgruntled Federalists gathered in Hartford to voice their opposition to that conflict. In many ways events conspired to turn this council of Federalists, known as the Hartford Convention, into a political fiasco. Because of poor communications in the early republic most Americans learned simultaneously of General Andrew Jackson's rousing victory at New Orleans, the signing of the Treaty of Ghent to end the war, and the ill-fated assembly of war-weary Federalists at Hartford. Relieved that the inglorious war was over and sparked by patriotism over Jackson's triumph, most Americans outside New England viewed the Hartford Convention as an act of treason. Many historians have concurred with this view.

Before the war broke out, New England shipping had been devastated by President Jefferson's 1807 embargo on trade with warring European nations. Federalist dismay over the conduct of the war climaxed in fall 1814, when Massachusetts and Connecticut declared the withdrawal of their state militias from federal jurisdiction. Eager to air their grievances, several Massachusetts radicals had called for a meeting as early as 1813. The huge Federalist victories in the 1814 elections, however, finally forced moderates to assent to a convention. By the time the delegates met, many New Englanders were ready to quit the war if not the union.

Twenty-six delegates met in Hartford from December 15 to January 5 to discuss New England's disaffection with "Mr. Madison's War." Of New England's five states at the time only three, Massachusetts, Connecticut, and Rhode Island, officially sent representatives. The convention also seated unofficial delegates from Vermont and New Hampshire. Harrison Gray Otis, the Boston lawyer who along with George Cabot led the convention, opened the meeting with a set of moderate proposals that became the group's final declaration. The convention ultimately adopted a seven-part resolution that defended sectional rights in matters of defense, repeated New England's grievances with President Madison's conduct of the war, in particular the federal government's failure to protect New England, and proposed a series of actions to rebuild faith in the union.

Given the compromising tone of the published declaration, moderates clearly dominated the debates. Although the day-to-day discussions were never revealed—delegates were pledged to strict secrecy—it seems that the participants never seriously considered secession. The very restraint of the final document suggests that the Hartford Convention must be understood as a successful attempt to reign in extremists in order to forge a Federalist consensus based on New England demands for a quick end to an unpopular war. In this sense the convention achieved its aims. At least within New England, Federalists continued to dominate state politics for another decade.

Taking a broader perspective, historians

have correctly called the Hartford Convention a political blunder of the first order. Jackson's victory at New Orleans greatly overshadowed both the British burning of Washington and Madison's inept handling of the war. In the ensuing upsurge of patriotism, most Americans' suspicion of the Hartford Convention grew; after the war the convention became synonymous with secession. Outside of New England, Federalism proved a dead letter in its wake.

Henry Adams, *History of the United States of America during the Administrations of Jefferson and Madison,* abridged ed., ed. Ernest Samuels (1967); Henry Adams, ed., *Documents Relating to New England Federalism, 1800–1815* (1905); James M. Banner, Jr., *To the Hartford Convention: The Federalists and the Origins of Party Politics in Massachusetts, 1789–1815* (1970); David Hackett Fischer, *The Revolution of American Conservatism: The Federalist Party in the Era of Jeffersonian Democracy* (1965).

Peter S. Field

Historical Societies

In 1855 the Reverend George E. Ellis, a Congregational minister in Boston, an avid amateur historian, and a future president of the Massachusetts Historical Society, wrote to an official of the New-York Historical Society, "The truth is Massachusetts has always been remarkable for the number of its chroniclers, annalists and historical contributors. It is the only state in the union which possesses elaborate histories contemporaneous in their authorship with all the epochs and incidents through which it has passed in two centuries and nearly a half."

Despite his obvious boosterism, Ellis was right to call Massachusetts a leader in the production of historians, the publication of historical writings, and the preservation of historical materials. It is therefore not surprising that Massachusetts was home to this country's first historical society. The Massachusetts Historical Society was founded in Boston in 1791, seven years after the end of the American Revolution.

Inspired by and patterned after the Society of Antiquaries of London, the oldest historical organization in the world (founded in 1572), the Massachusetts institution began its existence as a nationally oriented program. Its professed mission was "to collect, preserve and communicate, materials for a complete history of this country." In time it would limit its geographic range to Massachusetts and New England.

What occasioned the founding of the Boston society? To a considerable extent, it was the zeitgeist of the 18th century. The Enlightenment produced a new spirit of philosophical inquiry resulting in the formation of a rash of academies and learned societies in western Europe, the American colonies, and,

later, the United States. Benjamin Franklin's Junto, or Leather Apron Club (1727), the American Philosophical Society (1743), and the American Academy of Arts and Sciences (1780) were but three American manifestations of this intellectual reawakening. The founding of the Massachusetts Historical Society was a further expression of this movement.

Puritanism also played a role. Massachusetts was the home of American Puritanism, and Boston was its intellectual nerve center. The Puritans were driven by a sense of history. They viewed their migration to New England in the 17th century, the "errand into the wilderness," as part of God's master plan for humankind. John Winthrop's sermon of 1630, composed aboard ship en route to the New World, underscored the special status of the "city upon a hill" that the Puritans believed themselves called upon to build. Their view of themselves as main actors in one of the most momentous episodes of world history was the essence of the Puritan notion of exceptionalism.

Governor Winthrop told the story of the colony's development in his own extensive journals. Generations of Puritans schooled their children on the importance of history and of their clan's unique historical mission. Both parents and ministers participated in this intensive educational effort. The result was a heightened historical consciousness among the Puritans. The eight founders of the Massachusetts Historical Society, especially the principal catalyst, the Reverend Jeremy Belknap, derived from this tradition.

Another essential factor in the founding of the Boston society was the powerful surge of nationalism that swept through the United States following the Revolution and the creation of new state and federal governing bodies. The residents of Massachusetts, including the founders of the Massachusetts Historical Society, firmly believed that the American victory over Great Britain and the subsequent establishment of the new nation were two of the most significant events in world history. They shared Thomas Paine's view, expressed in *Common Sense* (1776), that "the Cause of America was the cause of mankind," that there never was a "Cause of greater worth. It is not the affair of a City, a County, a Province, or a Kingdom, but of a Continent—of at least one eighth part of the habitable Globe."

Furthermore, many historical materials were being rapidly—and alarmingly—lost, to neglect, fires, natural disasters, and the "ravages of unprincipled or mercenary men." Before and during the American Revolution, Massachusetts alone sustained severe losses of historical treasures. A fire in 1747 leveled the

Town House, or courthouse, in Boston, destroying a huge body of vital legal records. Another conflagration in 1764 destroyed the Harvard College Library, which had housed the largest collection of books in New England and the American colonies. This was a devastating blow to American scholarship; it also affected the learned gentry of Boston and Cambridge who utilized this repository. In 1765, during the Stamp Act crisis, a mob of unruly patriots sacked the beautiful Georgian home of Lieutenant Governor Thomas Hutchinson in Boston and dispersed a large body of valuable historical sources painstakingly collected by that learned royal official for his projected history of the Massachusetts Bay Colony. The British army scattered many records of the Court of Common Pleas in the streets of Boston as they prepared to evacuate the city in 1776. During this same period British soldiers dispersed a "greater part" of the Reverend Thomas Prince's "noble collection of manuscripts," which Prince had stored in the steeple of his hallowed Old South Church. Belknap called it a "sacrifice to British barbarity." One of the most capable Puritan historians of the 18th century and a discriminating acquisitor of Americana, Prince had spent his life amassing this incomparable collection.

Belknap was among the first Americans to recognize the need for U.S. repositories in which documents and other vital historical materials could be safely housed and preserved for researchers of his generation and the future. An accomplished historian and cultural nationalist of the first rank, Belknap made it his life's mission to establish such a facility, realizing that goal in 1791.

Belknap's organization served as the model for the five other New England state historical societies and the American Antiquarian Society of Worcester, Mass., all of which were founded in the first half of the 19th century: the American Antiquarian Society in 1812; the societies of Maine and Rhode Island in 1822; New Hampshire's society in 1823; Connecticut's in 1825 (although this organization remained moribund until 1839, when it was revived); and Vermont's in 1838.

Following the Massachusetts example, these societies concentrated on collecting historical materials and publishing historical works. In their collection and membership policies, the Massachusetts society and American Antiquarian Society had a national orientation, while the other institutions focused on their respective states. There were other subtle differences among the seven New England organizations, but all were fundamentally alike in purpose, composition, and programs.

A profile of the founders of the historical societies established in New England reveals a remarkable consistency. Initially, all were men. They were relatively young, mostly in their thirties and forties. Almost all had formal educations and were prominent in their respective communities. They ranked at the top of the social and economic order: lawyers, clergymen, educators, businessmen, doctors. Almost all were of Anglo-American stock and could trace their ancestry to the early colonial period. Many were descended from the first generation of Pilgrims and Puritans. Many had family members who had served in the American army during the American Revolution. All had an acute sense of history and place; many were collectors of historical materials and writers of history.

Ralph Waldo Emerson's well-known aphorism "An institution is the lengthened shadow of one man," although now considered gender-biased, applied to the early New England historical societies. With a few exceptions, one or two men played salient roles, either in founding these institutions, breathing life into them, sustaining them when they appeared to be on the verge of dissolution, or pushing them to new heights of development. Jeremy Belknap, for example, fit Emerson's description to a tee. He was the life force of the Massachusetts society in its formative years, earning the sobriquet "Father of American historical societies." A man of prophetic vision, Belknap proposed a national system of state historical societies in the United States even before organizing the Massachusetts society.

There were other leaders with vision, unusual energy, and a profound love of history. Isaiah Thomas, the founder of the American Antiquarian Society, and Christopher Columbus Baldwin, its librarian in later years, were the lifeblood of that institution in its formative stages. The Reverend Ichabod Nichols was the key figure in the early years of the Maine Historical Society. Henry Barnard and the Reverend Thomas Robbins can be credited with reviving and spurring the development of the Connecticut Historical Society after it had sunk into the doldrums of inactivity.

With the passage of time, a host of small local historical institutions, limited in geographic scope, were founded in New England, all deriving inspiration from the state societies. Currently, hundreds of such organizations dot the rugged landscapes of Yankeedom. A few, such as the Essex Institute of Salem, Mass. (merged with the Peabody Museum in 1992), and the Colonial Society of Massachusetts, sponsor substantive programs and have a strong professional bent. The bulk, however, have a more amateur character. They boast a handful of members, possess few phys-

ical assets, and confine their programs to meetings, lectures, and an occasional publication. The values that sustain and energize these organizations nonetheless are closely linked to those that led to the 18th-century founding of the Massachusetts Historical Society.

Reflecting an upsurge of interest among recent immigrants to New England in their group's growth and development, many ethnic historical societies have been founded, for example, the Rhode Island Black Heritage Society; the Jewish Historical Society of Greater New Haven, Conn.; and the French Canadian Genealogical Society, located in Tolland, Conn. Taken together, these local and ethnic societies have immeasurably broadened and enriched the history of New England.

Julian P. Boyd, "State and Local Societies in the United States," *American Historical Review* (1934); Leslie W. Dunlap, *American Historical Societies, 1790–1860* (1944); John F. Jameson, "History of Historical Societies," *Seventy-fifth Anniversary Report of the Georgia State Historical Society* (1914); Louis Leonard Tucker, *The Massachusetts Historical Society: A Bicentennial History, 1791–1991* (1995); Walter Muir Whitehill, *Independent Historical Societies: An Enquiry into Their Research and Publication Functions and Their Financial Future* (1962).

Louis Leonard Tucker

Historiography The writing of history about New England began as early as English settlement itself. In the eyes of the Puritan leadership, "New England" was a divinely guided episode in the history of redemption. For its proper understanding and for the discernment of the divine instructions contained in the smiles and frowns of Providence, God's work needed to be faithfully recorded. Thus William Bradford's *Of Plymouth Plantation* (1630) and John Winthrop's journal set the standard for providential history. Though neither governor's history saw print for two centuries after its author's death, both manuscripts provided grist for several Puritan authors. With some exceptions, such as the historically based promotional literature of Capt. John Smith and the satirical portrayal of the Plymouth Pilgrims by Thomas Morton, the main theme of most historical writing about New England in the 17th century was providentialism. It came to a climax in Cotton Mather's *Magnalia Christi Americana* (1702), a collection of biographies and historical sketches designed to return Mather's readers to the pious designs and heroic qualities of their grandfathers.

During the 18th century, New England's historians developed a newly scientific use of documentary sources and an attempt at something like historical objectivity. Under the influence of the European Enlightenment and

of an emerging English ideal of urbane, learned, and moderate "polite" literature, some Americans entered an anglicized and largely secularized tradition of history writing. There are signs of this tendency in New England as early as midcentury, most notably in a two-volume history of the British American colonies by the Scottish-born Boston physician William Douglass and the Reverend Thomas Prince's annalistic *History of New-England* (1736), though the latter was hardly secularized. The best New England contributions to enlightened history writing were undoubtedly the loyalist governor Thomas Hutchinson's *History of the Colony and Province of Massachusetts-Bay* (1767) and the Reverend Jeremy Belknap's *History of New-Hampshire* (1792), both of which, except for Hutchinson's first volume, came out soon after the American Revolution. While the political and religious preferences of both authors are clear, these histories nevertheless disclose a systematic and even scientific use of evidence along with an obvious immersion (despite Hutchinson's loyalty to Britain) in the powerful English Whig tradition with its stress on civil liberty, civic virtue, and the limitation of political power. The American Revolution naturally stimulated a number of efforts in the following decades to write about it and understand it in retrospect. Particularly notable among such efforts by New Englanders, both because of her gender and because it is a vivid example of strong Whiggish history, was Mercy Otis Warren's three-volume *History of the Rise, Progress, and Termination of the American Revolution* (1805).

Belknap's and Warren's histories, along with those of several other American writers, including James Sullivan's *History of the District of Maine* (1794), were attempts to explore and express an American national identity. But it was left to the Massachusetts-born George Bancroft, the first professionally trained American historian, to construct a full-blown idealistic view of the American experience. In his ten-volume *History of the United States* (1834–74), Bancroft paid scrupulous regard to the facts and to scholarly methods. Nevertheless, its earliest volumes appearing at the height of the Romantic movement and of the Jacksonian enthusiasm, this monumental work celebrated the origins and glorious destiny of an Anglo-Saxon America, returning even to a kind of providentialism. Bancroft later toned down both the Romantic vision and florid prose while his Boston Brahmin contemporary Francis Parkman was working on the last volumes of his great *France and England in North America* (1851–92). Meanwhile, the Unitarian minister John G. Palfrey, another Bancroft contemporary, produced a five-volume chronological history of New England.

New Englanders dominated the formation of a university-based organized historical profession in America in the late 19th century. Although American historians of that era tended to write on national rather than regional themes, American history more often than not was being told from a New England perspective. "The history of the United States has been written by Boston," complained the southern historian Ulrich B. Phillips in 1903, "and largely written wrong." In the 1880s and 1890s, for example, the New Englanders Herbert Baxter Adams, Edward Channing, and John Fiske had all asserted in one way or another the so-called germ theory of American history, attributing the most characteristic American political institutions, including their region's town meeting, to "Teutonic" origins. A muted variation on the theme can be discerned even among the so-called imperial historians a bit later. In his four-volume *Colonial Period of American History* (1934–38), the Yale historian Charles M. Andrews stressed the British context of the American colonies and the institutions by which they were founded and regulated from London. His slightly older contemporary, Maine-born Herbert Levi Osgood, also of the imperial school, laboriously produced a joyless history of political institutions and war in colonial America in seven comprehensive volumes.

The emergence around 1900 of what was called the new history, directing attention to nontraditional areas of study, and of the contemporaneous and partly overlapping school of progressive history, was not by and large a New England movement—with the important exception of William B. Weeden's *Economic and Social History of New England, 1620–1789*, published early in the new history movement in 1890. In part under the influence of Frederick Jackson Turner's frontier hypothesis of 1893 (both new and progressive), the interests of the historical profession as well as of the popular imagination were drawn westward.

One of the giant progressive historians, the westerner Vernon L. Parrington, opened the first volume of his huge *Main Currents in American Thought* (1927–30) with a protracted negative portrayal of the Puritan founders of New England. Thus he was able to construct an exceptionally low starting point in his saga of the three-century progress of American culture to enlightenment, liberalism, and democracy—pausing in mid-18th century long enough to declare the brilliant New England theologian Jonathan Edwards an "anachronism." Parrington's contemptuous dismissal of New England's founders as bigots and tyrants brought to a climax a brief tradition of Puritan

denigration best exemplified previously by James Truslow Adams, who in *The Founding of New England* (1921), the first in a three-volume history of the region, had described the 17th century as "New England's glacial age."

The rehabilitation of the Puritans was not long in coming. Perry Miller, who like Parrington was officially a professor of literature rather than history, began a lifelong project of understanding the mind of New England Puritanism with the publication in 1933 of *Orthodoxy in Massachusetts, 1630–1650*. Developing his analysis much further in *The New England Mind* (1939, 1953), Miller set in motion a remarkable scholarly industry in Puritan studies that at the end of the 20th century had not run its course. His successors, even those who have disagreed with his findings or attacked his methods, have all had to acknowledge Miller as their point of departure.

Historical writing in America between the wars began to show the immense variety in subject and approach that presaged still greater diversity in the decades after World War II. That variety very much included New England writers and topics. As early as 1921, to take one example, the renowned Harvard historian Samuel Eliot Morison launched one side of his long career with *The Maritime History of Massachusetts*. In addition to continuing with maritime and naval themes for the rest of his long life, in the 1930s he produced several volumes on the history of Harvard and with titles such as *Builders of the Bay Colony* (1930) and *The Puritan Pronaos* (1936) helped reinforce Perry Miller's rehabilitation of the Puritans. The nonacademic historian Esther Forbes, who favored New England themes, wrote best-selling and prize-winning biographies and histories, most notably *Paul Revere and the World He Lived In* (1942). The literary and cultural historians Van Wyck Brooks and F. O. Matthiessen attracted large reading audiences with critical and historical works centering on New England topics, including especially the Transcendentalist writers of the 19th century. Some social historians focused on urban life, while Oscar Handlin led the way in immigration history with his pathbreaking *Boston's Immigrants* in 1941.

In most cases the various and often conflicting historiographical currents of the 1950s and 1960s—consensus history, radical history, and the reinterpretation of slavery and race—did not involve specifically New England topics except as parts of larger themes. Late in that period, however, a movement toward a new, more rigid scientism in history came to be directed to an extraordinary degree on an old, old subject: the colonial New England town. In 1970 alone, a number of New England "community studies" burst upon the

scene, all based on social science methods including computer-based techniques of quantitative analysis. The early New England past has also figured conspicuously in the women's history movement that flourished in the 1980s and 1990s, especially in the work of Laurel Thatcher Ulrich. The contemporaneous interest in a vastly revised Native American history has often focused on early New England, as has the innovative field of environmental history, especially under the influence of William Cronon's *Changes in the Land* (1983).

At the beginning of the 21st century, the practice of history in America is perhaps more diverse and fragmented that at any previous time. Special interests, political positions, ethnic attachments, cultural and intellectual enthusiasms, and favorite "sister disciplines" all have roles in a discipline engaged in a seemingly futile quest for some new paradigm. In such a milieu it is striking that in John Demos's *The Unredeemed Captive* and David Hackett Fischer's *Paul Revere's Ride*, both appearing in 1994, two prominent New England–based historians writing on New England subjects have returned to narrative—the skillful telling of dramatic stories—the oldest and most fundamental historical form of all.

Oscar Handlin et al., *Harvard Guide to American History* (1954, 1969); Richard Hofstadter, *The Progressive Historians: Turner, Beard, Parrington* (1968, 1970); E. Brooks Holifield, *Era of Persuasion: American Thought and Culture, 1521–1680* (1989); Bert James Loewenberg, *American History in American Thought: Christopher Columbus to Henry Adams* (1972); Peter Novick, *The Noble Dream: The "Objectivity Question" and the American Historical Profession* (1988).

Charles E. Clark

Kennedy, John Fitzgerald (1917–63)

Politician, writer, president of the United States. In 1960, at the age of 43, John Fitzgerald Kennedy became the 35th president; he was the youngest man elected U.S. president, the first president born in the 20th century, and the first Roman Catholic to occupy the Oval Office. He personified youthful strength and leadership for millions worldwide. Kennedy's memorable inaugural address, amid heightened cold war tensions, enjoined fellow Americans to "ask not what your country can do for you—ask what you can do for your country."

Kennedy was born in Brookline, Mass., the second of Joseph and Rose (Fitzgerald) Kennedy's nine children. He grew up in an atmosphere of wealth and privilege. Sickly through adolescence and often hospitalized, "Jack" Kennedy developed a love of reading, an ironic sense of humor, and extraordinary personal charm. At boarding school he was a discipline problem and an average student before entering Harvard College in 1936. Once there he gradually became interested in writing and history. His senior thesis on Britain's failure to respond to Nazi aggression was published with support from his father, the U.S. ambassador to Great Britain from 1937 to 1940, as *Why England Slept* in 1940.

Kennedy joined the navy in September 1941 and became commander of a patrol boat in the South Pacific. He received the Navy and Marine Corps Medal for leadership and bravery after his craft was sunk by a Japanese destroyer. When the war ended, Kennedy worked briefly as a correspondent for the International News Service. Although often in pain from wartime injuries and Addison's disease, a debilitating failure of the adrenal cortex, he ran for Congress from Massachusetts's 11th District in 1946 and easily won. During his three terms in Congress Kennedy took a special interest in veterans' issues and foreign affairs. In 1952 he ousted the incumbent Republican Henry Cabot Lodge, Jr., to win a seat in the Senate.

The following year Senator Kennedy married the socialite Jacqueline Lee Bouvier and in 1954 underwent risky spinal surgery. While convalescing, with assistance from his wife and staff, he wrote *Profiles in Courage* (1956), which won the Pulitzer Prize for biography in 1957. Narrowly missing the Democratic vice presidential nomination in 1956, the senator decided to run for president in 1960. Kennedy entered several primaries to prove he could win voter support in spite of his youth and Catholicism. His solid victory in Protestant West Virginia launched Kennedy toward a first-ballot nomination at the 1960 Democratic national convention.

Trailing in the polls, Kennedy challenged his Republican opponent, Vice President Richard Nixon, to an unprecedented series of television debates, which most viewers felt that Kennedy won. The religious issue would not disappear, however, despite Kennedy's assurances that he was committed to the separation of church and state. It may be that his efforts to secure the release of the jailed civil rights leader Martin Luther King, Jr., which mobilized black voters, gave Kennedy the winning margin in an extremely close election.

Although President Kennedy failed to persuade Congress to enact federal aid to education and medical insurance for senior citizens, his New Frontier initiatives, especially the Peace Corps and space program, seized the public imagination. Hoping to maintain southern congressional support, the president moved cautiously on the issues of racial segregation and discrimination. In 1963, after police attacked peaceful demonstrators in Birmingham, Ala., and Governor George Wallace attempted to block integration of the state's university, public support for laws to guarantee civil rights grew stronger. Kennedy declared racial justice a moral issue and sent legislation to Congress to outlaw racial, religious, and gender discrimination in public places.

Kennedy's commitment to winning the cold war was shaken by the failure of the Bay of Pigs invasion, a plan by the Eisenhower administration to topple the regime of Cuba's leader Fidel Castro, which Kennedy implemented in April 1961. After a tense summit meeting between Kennedy and the Soviet premier Nikita Khrushchev, the Communists constructed the Berlin Wall in August 1961. In October 1962 the USSR began secretly sending offensive nuclear weapons to Cuba; Kennedy responded with a U.S. naval blockade to interdict the shipments. The ensuing crisis brought the two nations to the brink of war. Conflict was averted when Khrushchev agreed to withdraw the missiles from Cuba in return for Kennedy's public pledge not to invade the island nation and his private agreement to remove American missiles from Turkey. U.S.–Soviet relations improved in 1963, when the United States, Great Britain, and the Soviet Union ratified the Limited Test Ban Treaty, outlawing nuclear tests in the atmosphere, under water, and in outer space. A communications hotline between Washington and Moscow was created to prevent misunderstandings, and the president authorized the sale of surplus wheat to the USSR. He was also responsible, however, for augmenting the U.S. arsenal of nuclear weapons and for sending 16,000 military advisers to assist South Vietnam in its war against communist North Vietnam.

On November 22, 1963, Kennedy was touring Texas, where he hoped to heal a rift in the Democratic Party that posed a threat to his reelection. While riding through Dallas in an open limousine with his wife and the Texas governor John Connolly, Kennedy was shot by a sniper and killed. The nation mourned its fallen president, whose televised funeral transfixed the entire world. Decades after his death the debate over Kennedy's personal and political legacy continues to divide historians and fascinate the American people.

James N. Giglio, *The Presidency of John F. Kennedy* (1991); Nigel Hamilton, *JFK: Reckless Youth* (1992); Herbert S. Parmet, *Jack: The Struggles of John F. Kennedy* (1980); Geoffrey Perret, *Jack: A Life Like No Other* (2001); Richard Reeves, *President Kennedy: Profile of Power* (1993).

Sheldon M. Stern

Luce, Clare Boothe (1903–87) Journalist, playwright, and politician.

Ann Clare Boothe Luce, known for her wit, humor, and ability to create memorable and acerbic phrases, was prominent in the theater, publishing, and politics throughout her life. She was born in New York City to a former show dancer and a traveling musician. Her father, William F. Boothe, deserted the family, and in 1919 her mother, Ann Clare (Snyder) Boothe, married Albert E. Austin, a surgeon who later served as a Connecticut congressman. Luce graduated from Miss Mason's School in Tarrytown, N.Y., that same year and studied theater briefly in New York City. She was introduced to the women's movement by Mrs. O. H. P. Belmont, a suffragist leader. In 1923 she married George Tuttle Brokaw. They divorced in 1929, and Luce's settlement made her financially independent. The couple had one daughter, Ann.

In 1930 Luce became an editorial assistant at *Vogue* magazine. Later that same year she joined the staff at *Vanity Fair,* quickly becoming an associate editor, and was promoted to managing editor in 1933. Although known for her satirical essays, Luce began to write for the theater after resigning her editorship in 1934. Her first Broadway play, *Abide with Me,* staged in 1935, was not well received, but *The Women* (1936), a comedy satirizing New York's idle rich, was a great success and was later made into a movie. Other plays by Luce include *Kiss the Boys Goodbye* (1938), *Child of the Morning* (1951), and *Slam the Door Softly* (1972).

In 1933 Clare Boothe met Henry R. Luce, president of Time, Inc., and later editor in chief of *Time, Life,* and *Fortune* magazines; they married in 1935 and moved to Connecticut. Covering the war under contract to *Life,* she visited Europe in 1940, publishing her experiences in *Europe in the Spring* (1940). In 1941 she witnessed the devastation caused by the Japanese invasion of China; in 1942, while on assignment in Africa, India, China, and Burma, Luce interviewed Generalissimo and Madame Chiang Kai-shek and the future Indian prime minister Jawaharlal Nehru.

Clare Boothe Luce entered politics in 1940. Attacking President Franklin Roosevelt for failing to prepare the United States for the threat of war, she supported Wendell Willkie and criticized the "ramsquaddling, do-gooding New Deal bureaucrats" in Washington. Two years later she was elected to Connecticut's Fourth District seat in the U.S. House of Representatives. She supported Thomas E. Dewey's bid for the presidency in 1944, telling voters that a Republican victory would sweep away the "dictatorial bumbledom" of the Democrats. A member of the Military Affairs Committee during her two terms in Congress (1943–47), she showed more interest in world affairs than in her western Connecticut constituency. She had already advocated early entry into World War II and as a member of Congress demanded a strong challenge to the Soviet Union after the war. On the domestic side she sponsored a bill to ensure equal pay for equal work, asked for increased immigration quotas for East Indian and Chinese refugees, and served as a member of the Joint Commission on Atomic Energy.

After taking a brief respite from politics to write about her conversion to Roman Catholicism, Luce returned to public life. In 1952 she campaigned for Dwight D. Eisenhower, who as president appointed her ambassador to Italy. She thus became only the second woman in U.S. history to hold an ambassadorship and the first to serve as ambassador to a major power. A member of the President's Foreign Intelligence Advisory Board in the 1970s and 1980s, she received the Presidential Medal of Freedom from Ronald Reagan in 1983. Clare Boothe Luce died in Washington, D.C., at the age of 84.

Ralph G. Martin, *Henry and Clare: An Intimate Portrait of the Luces* (1991); Sylvia Jukes Morris, *Rage for Fame: The Ascent of Clare Boothe Luce* (1997); Stephen Shadegg, *Clare Boothe Luce: A Biography* (1970).

Alfred B. Rollins, Jr.

Maine Maine became the 23d U.S. state in 1820. It covers 33,265 square miles and is both the largest and the most sparsely populated state in New England, with 1,274,923 inhabitants according to the 2000 census. Portland served as Maine's capital until 1831, when the more centrally located Augusta gained that distinction.

Maine's first human inhabitants, the Paleo-Indians, arrived in the area in the wake of the glaciers some 12,000 years ago. They were replaced between 8000 and 6500 B.C. by the Archaic culture. Adapting to richer land and sea resources, the Late Archaic (so-called Red Paint) people, known for their ocher-lined burial sites, developed distinctive woodworking tools and polished-stone projectile points. Around 1800 B.C. this culture was replaced by members of the Susquehanna tradition, forebears of the modern Abenaki.

The first clearly documented European visit to the Maine coast occurred in 1524, when Giovanni da Verrazano claimed the land for France. In 1604 Pierre du Gua, Sieur de Monts, and Samuel de Champlain established a French colony on the Saint Croix River. Devastated by scurvy, the colonists resettled across the Bay of Fundy in 1605. English explorations in 1602–5 paved the way for the short-lived Popham Colony, at the mouth of the Kennebec River, in 1607. This settlement, too, was abandoned within a year. Hopes for

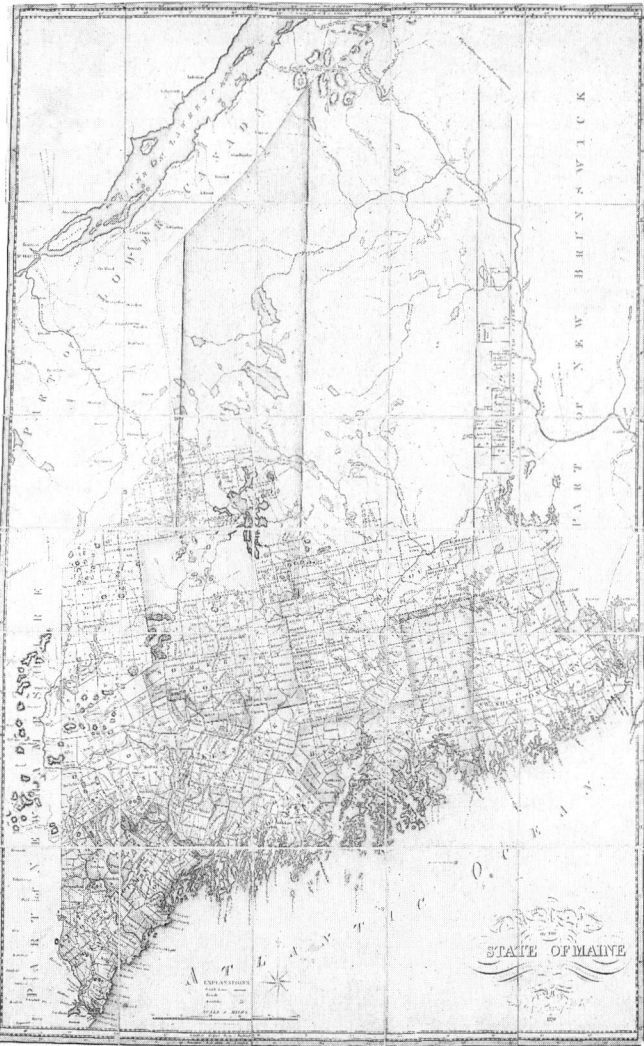

Moses Greenleaf's 1820 "Map of the State of Maine from the Latest and Best Authorities" helped establish the boundaries of the state of Maine

colonization were rekindled by the explorer John Smith, who mapped the coast in 1614. Fishing stations and fur-trading posts, established in the 1620s, were the first English settlements. These outposts gradually diversified, fostering an export economy based on fish, furs, lumber, cooperage, grain, ship timbers, and cattle.

In 1635 the English proprietor Ferdinando Gorges dissolved the Council for New England and took for himself the Province of New Somerset, stretching from the Piscataqua to the Kennebec. Gorges's land grants led to the establishment of several towns on the southern coast, and in 1639 Thomas Gorges, Ferdinando's nephew, instituted a system of government for the colony. In 1652–53 the Massachusetts Bay Colony absorbed southern Maine, extending its jurisdiction to the Kennebec by the 1670s. In Penobscot Bay, French colonists built Fort Pentagoet to secure the western boundary of Acadia. The fort was destroyed by Dutch marauders in 1676, but the

fur trader Jean Vincent d'Abbadie, baron de Saint-Castin, continued to exert French influence in Penobscot Bay.

For the Abenaki the mid-1600s brought increasingly hard times. Epidemics, beginning in 1616, killed at least 75 percent of Maine's Native American inhabitants. Frustration with English encroachments, trading abuses, and free-roaming English livestock led to a series of clashes following the opening of King Philip's War in 1675. Abenaki forces drove the English from all but a few settlements in Maine before peace was restored in 1678. Similar tensions led to King William's War (1689–97), Queen Anne's War (1702–13), Dummer's War (1722–27), King George's War (1744–48), and the French and Indian War (1754–63), during which many Abenaki fled to Jesuit missions near the Saint Lawrence River. Others left for more remote interior village sites or dispersed into family bands.

The American Revolution brought only limited engagements in Maine. In June 1775 radicals in the small down east port of Machias captured three British warships, an incident ranked as the first naval engagement of the war. On October 18, 1775, British vessels bombed and destroyed the coastal town of Falmouth. In 1779 a British expedition invaded eastern Maine, hoping to secure a place of refuge for dispossessed loyalists. A Massachusetts armada sent to expel the small British force at Castine encountered a British relief fleet and was scuttled in the Penobscot River, an engagement recognized as the worst naval defeat of the American Revolution. The Treaty of Paris of 1783 renounced British claims to Maine but left the state's northeastern boundary vague.

Thoughts turned to separation from Massachusetts shortly after the Revolution, but social and political divisions in Maine slowed the process. Prosperous seacoast merchants favored a new state guided by their own conservative principles and economic interests, while backwoods farmers, plagued by inequitable taxes, debts, and conflicts with absentee landlords, saw independent statehood very differently. Maine's emerging Democratic leadership, spearheaded by William King of Bath, rallied the interior towns, and the movement quickened after Massachusetts failed to defend its eastern territories against British invasion during the War of 1812. In 1819 separationists prevailed, and Maine joined the union in 1820 as part of the Missouri Compromise.

Once statehood had been obtained, Maine politics was racked by factionalism related to the temperance movement and abolitionism. In 1851 Portland mayor Neal Dow pushed through the state legislature a prohibition statute called the Maine Law, which became a national model. In 1856 antislavery Whigs and Democrats abandoned their respective parties, joined Dow's prohibitionists and the nativist Know-Nothing advocates, and boosted the state Republican Party to victory. Republicans ruled Maine almost without interruption for the next century.

In the years after statehood, farming occupied most Maine people. Farmers responded to rising western competition by growing mixed crops or by specializing in hay, potatoes, dairy products, apples, and blueberries. Nonfarm work—lumbering for men and domestic industries for women—tided families over long winters. By the 1920s Maine was producing about one-eighth of the total U.S. potato crop.

Maine's wealth also stemmed from an extractive economy based on granite, lime, slate, and ice. Abundant white pine and rivers suitable for log drives placed the state among the nation's top lumber producers. As lumbering operations spread into the northeastern part of Maine, disagreements over the still undefined border with New Brunswick sparked the so-called Aroostook War, a deployment of militia and federal troops on both sides of the Saint John River in 1839. The skillful diplomacy of General Winfield Scott and Lieutenant Governor John Harvey of New Brunswick averted hostilities, and the boundary was settled by the Webster-Ashburton Treaty in 1842.

Proximity to the prime fishing grounds of the Grand and Georges Banks, excellent harbors, and a long seafaring tradition placed Maine among the nation's top fish producers. Shipbuilders, too, benefited from protected building sites, nearby supplies of mixed timbers, and a favorable location for the West Indies and cotton trades. Maine pioneered the great square-rigged down-easters, fast-sailing commercial ships built primarily for the Pacific grain trade.

Maine entered the Industrial Revolution in a variety of ways, ranging from home-based and small-shop operations to some of the largest textile factories in New England. Maine's first large cotton textile mill was built in 1826 at Saco. The industry spread rapidly as investors took advantage of the state's many waterpower sites. Lewiston became the state's leading textile center. Labor consisted initially of young farm women, but those workers were replaced in the 1870s by French Canadian immigrants.

Approximately 73,000 Mainers served in the Union Army and navy during the Civil War, the highest figure per capita of any northern state. Maine's contribution to the war is exemplified by Joshua Lawrence Chamberlain of the 20th Maine Regiment, best remembered for withstanding a fierce Confederate attack at the Battle of Gettysburg and for being chosen by Ulysses S. Grant to receive the formal surrender of Lee's army at Appomattox. Hamden's Dorothea Dix, famous as an advocate for reform in prisons and insane asylums, served as superintendent of women nurses during the war.

Maine made important contributions to national politics during and after the war, its most prominent statesmen being Hannibal Hamlin, vice president in Lincoln's first administration, and Senator William Pitt Fessenden, Lincoln's secretary of the treasury and chair of the Joint Committee on Reconstruction. In addition, the charismatic James G. Blaine served twice as secretary of state. Portland's Thomas Brackett Reed, Speaker of the House during the 1890s, became one of the most powerful political figures in America.

The second half of the century brought changes in Maine's economy. Deep-sea fishing gave way to near-shore fishing for lobsters, herring (sold as sardines), and clams. After 1880 lumbering was supplemented by paper production, a capital-intensive industry that fundamentally altered Maine landownership patterns. Tourism, encouraged by Maine's scenic coastal vistas, cooling breezes, abundant fish and game, and relative lack of development, supported a mix of small-scale guiding, camp operation, and boarding, along with some of the largest hotel and resort developments in the nation, including the sumptuous Bar Harbor cottages built in the 1880s.

The Great Depression created opportunities for Maine's lackluster Democratic Party. In 1932 the Lewiston Democrat Louis J. Brann won the race for governor. Still, Maine was one of only two states to vote Republican in the 1936 presidential election (Vermont was the other). Despite the nationwide upsurge of unionism during the late 1930s, Maine workers suffered brutal defeats in the textile and shoe industries. World War II revived Maine's economy: Bath Iron Works, Maine's leading shipbuilder, launched over 250 ships, while Maine's wooden-boat builders produced torpedo boats, minesweepers, and patrol craft for the war effort.

During the early postwar years Maine lagged behind the rest of the nation economically, following declines in strategic industries like fishing, lumbering, and textile production. Advocating state programs to reinvigorate Maine business, the Democrat Edmund S. Muskie won a startling upset victory in the gubernatorial election of 1954. In 1958 Muskie joined the Republican Margaret Chase Smith in the U.S. Senate. Smith, first elected to the Senate in 1948, gained fame for her "declaration of conscience" speech of June 1, 1950, condemning the tactics of her fellow Republican Joseph McCarthy and national anticommunist hysteria. Muskie distinguished himself in the 1970s as a champion of federal environmental legislation.

The 1970s brought economic expansion and a building boom for second homes, condominiums, marinas, ski areas, and other resort facilities. Portland revitalized its waterfront, dubbing it the Old Port and bringing new life to the city's hard-hit downtown. During the 1970s Maine assumed a leading role among states in environmental protection, implementing water pollution regulations based on a classification system developed in the 1950s. A proposal to dam the largely pristine Saint John River was widely debated and then abandoned, as were plans for oil refineries along the coast. On July 1, 1999, an American environmental first occurred when crews began dismantling a dam across the Kennebec River in Augusta against the wishes of its private owner, opening the way to spawning grounds for several species of migratory fish that had been blocked for 162 years.

Franco-Americans, Maine's most significant minority population, demonstrated new ethnic awareness, establishing cultural centers at the University of Southern Maine's Lewiston-Auburn College and at the University of Maine in Fort Kent. Maine's other large minority, the Penobscot and Passamaquoddy Indians, launched a land-claims suit in 1964 and in 1980 were awarded $81.5 million in federal compensation with which to purchase land and create trust funds. As resource-based and heavy industries were eclipsed by light industry in the 1980s, Maine's economy responded more directly to the ups and downs of the national economy. In 2003 the Dirigo Health Reform Act was passed as part of a state initiative to provide universal health coverage.

Ronald F. Banks, *Maine Becomes a State* (1970); Alaric Faulkner and Gretchen F. Faulkner, *The French at Pentagoet, 1635–1674: An Archaeological Portrait of the Acadian Frontier* (1987); Richard W. Judd, *Aroostook: A Century of Logging in Northern Maine, 1831–1931* (1989); Richard W. Judd, Edwin A. Churchill, and Joel W. Eastman, eds., *Maine: The Pine Tree State from Prehistory to the Present* (1995); James S. Leamon, *Revolution Downeast: The War for American Independence in Maine* (1993); Kenneth M. Morrison, *The Embattled Northeast: The Elusive Ideal of Alliance in Abenaki-Euramerican Relations* (1984); Alan Taylor, *Liberty Men and Great Proprietors: The Revolutionary Settlement on the Maine Frontier, 1760–1820* (1990); Laurel Thatcher Ulrich, *A Midwife's Tale: The Life of Martha Ballard, Based on Her Diary, 1785–1812* (1990).

Richard W. Judd

Massachusetts Archaeological evidence suggests that humans have inhabited present-day Massachusetts for more than 10,000 years. Gradually the original population increased in number and became highly organized and mobile societies developing tools, textiles, leather, basketry, canoes, complex religious beliefs, and advanced techniques related to agriculture, hunting, and fishing. By the time of European arrival around 1500, tens of thousands of Native Americans lived in Massachusetts from Cape Cod to the western mountains. The largest tribes were the Massachusett (meaning "great mountain," probably a reference to the highest point of the Blue Hills, where they resided), Mahican, Narragansett, Nauset, Nipmuck, Pennacook, Pocumtuck, and Wampanoag, all of whom spoke dialects of Algonquian.

Europeans introduced diseases to which natives had no immunity, resulting in a rapid decline in native populations. The first recorded epidemic began in coastal areas in 1616, wiping out as much as 90 percent of the native

Massachusetts State Seal

population. By the time the Pilgrims arrived in 1620, many settlements had been abandoned including the site at which Plymouth Plantation was founded. Disease, warfare, hunger, and oppression continued to cause declines in Native American communities throughout the 17th and 18th centuries. Many tribes including the Massachusett had ceased to exist as organized groups by the 1800s.

Early European exploration may have begun with the Norseman Leif Ericsson, who is rumored to have sailed the New England coast in the year 1000, though no concrete evidence exists. In 1498 the Englishman John Cabot undertook exploration of the area, which served as the basis of England's original claims to North American lands. Fishermen from France and Spain probably made periodic stops beginning in the 1500s, either fishing local waters or in transit to the abundant Grand Banks. Bartholomew Gosnold landed in Massachusetts in 1602. He explored the bay and named Cape Cod in honor of the prized fish teaming in its waters. Three years later Samuel de Champlain began preparing detailed maps of the New England coast, which would help attract more explorers and colonists to the area.

The colonial era began with the arrival of the Pilgrims. Religious reformists who were unhappy with the Church of England, the Pilgrims, led by William Bradford, sought to establish a society in the New World in which they could practice their beliefs without persecution. In September 102 men, women, and children sailed from Plymouth, England, in crowded conditions aboard the *Mayflower*. The voyage was financed by a group of London merchants who had obtained rights from the Virginia Company. In exchange the settlers were to supply furs, timber, and other goods.

On November 9, the colonists arrived at Cape Cod, 200 miles north of their intended destination. Having landed outside the jurisdiction of the Virginia Company, the Pilgrims drafted a document that became known the Mayflower Compact, which established guidelines for self-governance. The Pilgrims arrived too late in the season to plant crops and about half died before contact was established with the Wampanoag the following spring. With the help of the Indians conditions at Plymouth Colony gradually improved, but it remained a small settlement and was soon overshadowed in importance.

Massachusetts Bay Colony was founded in 1630 by Puritan reformers. Led by John Winthrop, the Puritan colony was much better organized than Plymouth. Massachusetts Bay grew rapidly, with some 12,000 colonists arriving in the 1630s. The colony possessed its own charter and was financed by the Puritan community, which freed it from the control of London merchants. As the result, Massachusetts Bay colonists devoted much energy to developing a model community, which they felt would serve as an example for reform elsewhere.

But owing to both the growth of the colony and factionalization, Puritans soon began settling adjacent lands. In search of economic opportunity, Reverend Thomas Hooker and a group of his followers founded Connecticut in 1636. Conflicts soon arose with the local Pequot Indians over land ownership and trade. The Pequot War of 1637 resulted in the decimation of the Pequot at the hands of the settlers and their Narrangasett and Mohegan allies.

Dissent among the settlers of Massachusetts Bay had become increasingly common by the late 1630s and resulted in two more offshoots. Critical of many of the political and religious policies of the Puritan government, particularly their usurping of Indian lands, the minister Roger Williams fled Massachusetts. Joined by many of his followers, he founded Rhode Island in 1636. Viewing the Puritan government of Massachusetts Bay as too lenient, Reverend John Davenport left Boston and together with his followers founded New Haven Colony in 1638.

Massachusetts resisted an attempt to establish greater control by the English government beginning in the 1660s, foreshadowing the American Revolution. After colonial resistance to increased regulation from abroad, the colony's charter was revoked in 1684. Seven years later it became a royal province controlled by a governor appointed by the Crown.

In addition to its importance as a focal point of political activity, Massachusetts was a population and economic center as well. The colony's population doubled approximately every 20 years and by 1700 had surpassed 80,000, giving it the largest population of any English colony in North America. Maritime trade, particularly with Caribbean ports, increased as rapidly as the population, and Boston became known as the market town of the West Indies and one of the most important ports in the Americas.

The economic productivity of Massachusetts and the other colonies, combined with Britain's preoccupation with wars in Europe, meant that new political and economic restrictions imposed by London were seldom enforced. But Britain's national debt, partly incurred in the defense of the colonies, precipitated a stricter policy of colonial control and the passage of new taxes. The Sugar Act (1764) severely limited the foreign trade upon which the Massachusetts economy depended. The Stamp Act of the following year further burdened and angered an increasingly defiant population.

Many of the most important triggers of the American Revolution occurred in Massachusetts. In March 1770 British soldiers stationed in Boston fired upon a group of disorderly protesters. The "Boston Massacre" as the event was described throughout the colonies, fanned the flames of revolution. The Tea Act (1773) prompted Samuel Adams to organize a group of Bostonians disguised as Indians to dump the newly arrived tea on three British cargo ships into Boston Harbor. In response, Britain closed Boston's port and implemented what became known in the colonies as the "Intolerable Acts," designed to punish Massachusetts. When the Constitutional Congress convened, shortly thereafter, members demanded a boycott of British products.

The first shots of the Revolution were fired on April 19, 1775, by Massachusetts farmers who had been warned by Paul Revere that British troops were coming to seize weapons caches at Lexington and Concord. Patriots laid siege to the British garrison in Boston and won a decisive victory at the Battle of Bunker Hill, leading British forces to evacuate Boston the following March. Following early victories, the British were expelled from the colony for the remainder of the war.

The war years were nonetheless hard for Massachusetts, which initially functioned under an Executive Council, considered inadequate by many of the population. In June 1780 a new constitution, crafted primarily by John Adams, was ratified; it is the world's oldest written constitution still in effect. In the 1780s many Massachusetts farmers struggled with debt and taxes; one, Daniel Shays, led a group of farmers to the capital in protest, and fighting erupted. "Shays's Rebellion" ended the following year when the farmers surrendered.

Massachusetts prospered in the early national period as the result of maritime trade with Europe and China. However the U.S. Embargo Act of 1807, which prevented U.S. ships from trading in foreign ports in retaliation for foreign interference with U.S. shipping, hurt the state's maritime economy. During the War of 1812, which most Massachusetts residents opposed, the shipping economy ceased completely. The embargo and war forced the United States to manufacture many of the goods that could no longer be imported. Thanks to abundant waterpower, availability of quality labor, and access to seaports, the new industries increasingly located in New England, Massachusetts in particular. The first modern factory in the United States was a textile mill constructed in Waltham in 1814.

The 1820s were a period of continued change. Maine separated from Massachusetts in 1820, providing a "free-state" counterbalance to Missouri, which had just been admitted as a "slave-state." Agriculture in Massachusetts and New England began a steady decline with the opening of the Erie Canal in 1825 and the subsequent arrival of cheaper farm products from the West. Massachusetts farmers moved to cities in increasing numbers, seeking factory work, or sought opportunities elsewhere in the western United States.

Abolitionism appeared early in Massachusetts, and during the Civil War, the state furnished more than 125,000 troops to the Union war effort. But its industrial capacity was arguably its most important contribution. In the late 1800s, Massachusetts produced half the shoes and one-third of the woolen goods in the United States and was also an important center in the production of machinery, cotton textiles, and other goods.

As the economy grew, so did the rate of immigration. Beginning in the early 19th century, immigrants seeking economic opportunities transformed the once predominantly English demography of Massachusetts. Finnish, Scots, Irish, and Turkish immigrants were the predominant groups before the turn of the 20th century; French, German, Italian, and Polish immigrants arrived in significant numbers later. By 1930 approximately two-thirds of Massachusetts's population consisted of first- or second-generation Americans.

Massachusetts was an important center of social activism in the 20th century. Many leaders of the suffrage movement, including Susan B. Anthony, came from the state, and the mill towns were the sites of some of the earliest organized labor movements. Massachusetts was among the first states to enact laws preventing the exploitation of women and children and to protect the health and safety of laborers. Early

in the Great Depression, it was one of the first states to establish a relief program for displaced workers. Massachusetts was also a model for education, boasting public schools in every locale, widespread public libraries and museums, and numerous colleges and universities.

The past century of the state's history has been economically varied. The first decades were characterized by frequent strikes and labor unrest. The Great Depression and the devastating hurricane of 1938 caused additional hardships. The onset of World War II galvanized production in Massachusetts shipyards and industries, enabling the state to achieve early recovery from the national economic crisis. Continued demand in the state's military-industrial complex, combined with increasingly diversified and high-tech industries, kept the economy energized. The national economic downturn of the late 1980s proved only a temporary setback as the Massachusetts economy experienced growth through the turn of the millennium.

Richard D. Brown and Jack Tager, *Massachusetts: A Concise History* (2000); Christopher Clark, *The Roots of Rural Capitalism: Western Massachusetts, 1780–1860* (1992); James Deetz and Patricia S. Deetz, *The Times of Their Lives: Life, Love, and Death in Plymouth Colony* (2000); R. A. Douglas-Lithgow, *Native American Place Names of Massachusetts* (2000); Larry B. Pletcher, *It Happened in Massachusetts* (1999); Scholarly Press, *Encyclopedia of Massachusetts Indians* (1999); Walther M. Whitehill and Lawrence W. Kennedy, *Boston: A Topographical History* (2000)

Barry D. Mowell

Mather Family The Mather dynasty of New England Puritan ministers began with Richard Mather (1596–1669), who was born to yeoman parents in Lowton, Lancashire, England. He matriculated at Brasenose College, Oxford, in 1618 and was ordained in the Church of England. Forced out of his post in Toxteth as a Puritan refusing to conform to Anglican practices, he emigrated to New England in 1635. He became preacher of the Dorchester, Mass., church, where he was known more for his efficient parish administration than for his preaching style. Along with John Eliot and Thomas Mayhew, Mather produced the *Bay Psalm Book* in 1640. He wrote most of *A Platform of Church Discipline Gathered Out of the Word of God* (1649), known as the *Cambridge Platform*, which established the autonomy of individual congregations as the basic tenet of Congregationalism.

Richard Mather had four sons who became ministers, the most famous of whom was Increase (1639–1723), minister of Boston's North, or Second, Church from 1661 to 1723 and president of Harvard College from 1685 to 1701. After graduating from Harvard in 1656, Increase Mather took a master's degree at Trinity College, Dublin, preached at several churches in England, and briefly held a post on the island of Guernsey. He returned to Boston in 1661, was ordained by the Second Church, and married Maria Cotton, daughter of the Reverend John Cotton, in 1662.

When the Massachusetts Bay Colony's original charter was revoked in 1684 and replaced by the government of the Dominion of New England in 1686, Increase Mather emerged as one of the most strident defenders of the Old Charter. Badgered and arrested by the Dominion governor Sir Edmund Andros, he traveled to England in 1688 to plead the colony's case before James II. Although he failed in his attempt to have the Old Charter reinstated, Increase Mather was able to secure the appointment of an American, Sir William Phips, as governor of the colony. Few of his fellow colonials appreciated Mather's efforts, however, and when he returned to Boston in May 1692, he was widely criticized. Mather returned to the Harvard presidency but was forced out in 1701, probably as a result of his theological controversy with the liberal ministers of Boston's Brattle Street Church, founded in 1699.

The author of some 100 printed works, Increase Mather held firmly to the "New England Way" of earlier Puritanism and was known for his jeremiads—powerful attacks on evil and backsliding—of which *Ichabod; or, A Discourse Shewing What Cause There Is to Fear That the Glory of the Lord Is Departing from New-England* (1702) is one of his finest. He had a deep interest in science and its reconciliation to revelation in scripture, which he expressed in *Kometographia; or, A Discourse Concerning Comets* (1683) and *An Essay for the Recording of Illustrious Providences* (1684). As a historian he wrote *A Brief History of the Warr with the Indians in New-England* (1676) and *A Relation of the Troubles Which Have Hapned in New-England by Reason of the Indians There* (1677).

Cotton Mather (1663–1728), son of Increase and grandson of Richard Mather and the Reverend John Cotton (1585–1652), is perhaps the most famous of all the Mathers. Graduated from Harvard College in 1678, he was ordained as his father's assistant at Boston's Second Church in 1685. During Increase Mather's trip to England (1688–92) Cotton moved into his father's position of prominence, not only preaching effectively but exerting considerable political influence as well. He was a leader of the uprising that resulted in the overthrow of Governor Andros in 1689 and became involved in both criticizing and explaining the prosecutions for witchcraft that began in Salem Village (now Danvers) early in 1692.

Both Increase and Cotton Mather believed in the reality of witchcraft, but Cotton came to interpret the Salem outbreak as evidence of a broad conspiracy by the devil to destroy New England, while his father did not. Early in 1692 Cotton Mather led Boston's ministers in condemning the use of spectral evidence—testimony that the accused had visited the victim as a specter, or spirit—in the trials while still supporting the prosecutions. In September, Increase, who had viewed events with increasing alarm since returning from England, wrote *Cases of Conscience Concerning Evil Spirits Personating Men* (1693), asking Governor Phips to call a halt to the trials. Twelve ministers signed this document, but Cotton Mather withheld his signature because his own *Wonders of the Invisible World* (1693), a justification of some of the verdicts in the Salem trials, was about to appear in print. By the time *Wonders* was published, the public had become disillusioned with the proceedings, and Cotton Mather's account was largely discredited. In his *Magnalia Christi Americana; or, The Ecclesiastical History of New-England* (1702) he joined the general denunciation of the Salem trials, admitting that innocent people had been executed.

Cotton Mather was extraordinarily prolific: he published more than 450 works and left many more manuscripts, including his voluminous *Diary* (1911). Although he wrote many sermons, some of his most famous works are on secular topics. *Bonifacius; or, Essays to Do Good* (1710), which promoted the concept of public service, strongly influenced the young Benjamin Franklin. Cotton Mather shared his father's intense interest in science and, like him, struggled to reconcile it with his religious beliefs. Cotton Mather became a Fellow of the Royal Society of London and earned notoriety for promoting inoculation to prevent the spread of smallpox. *The Angel of Bethesda* (1722) is his chronicle of the use of inoculation during the Boston epidemic of 1722.

Cotton Mather was succeeded in his ministry by his son Samuel Mather (1706–85). Cotton's nephew Mather Byles (1707–88), whom he raised almost as a son, was a noted poet and wit before becoming pastor of Boston's Hollis Street Church until he was dismissed in 1776 as a loyalist. His great-nephew Mather Byles Jr. (1735–1814), originally a Congregationalist minister in New London, Conn., was ordained in the Anglican Church in 1768 and served as rector of Christ Church, Boston (1771–76), during the stormy days leading up to the Revolution, before going into exile as a loyalist. From the beginnings of the Massachusetts Bay Colony through the Revolution the Mathers were passionate, committed leaders who made a

marked contribution to the development of New England culture.

Sacvan Bercovitch, *The Puritan Origins of the American Self* (1975); Mason I. Lowance, Jr., *Increase Mather* (1974); Robert Middlekauff, *The Mathers: Three Generations of Puritan Intellectuals, 1596–1728* (1971); Kenneth Silverman, *The Life and Times of Cotton Mather* (1984).

Mason I. Lowance, Jr.

Miller, Perry (1905–63) Historian. One of the most enduringly influential scholars and teachers of early American literature, history, and culture, Perry Miller devoted his career to an intellectual mission that he hoped would explain "the innermost propulsion of the United States." His first books were monumental histories of the intellectual and theological work of the 17th-century settlers of the Massachusetts Bay Colony known as the Puritans. With his two-volume *The New England Mind* (1939, 1953), Miller kindled intense and lasting academic interest in the life and writings of the Puritans, who had previously been known mainly for their religious intolerance and their curiously rigid version of Protestant Christianity. Miller's work is important in that it implicitly asserted the primacy of New England to the nation's life, after decades of historical studies had followed the lead of Frederick Jackson Turner in defining the frontier as the exceptional feature of American experience.

Miller was born in Chicago and earned his bachelor's and doctoral degrees at the University of Chicago. He served on the faculty of Harvard College from 1931 until his death in 1963, with only a brief interruption for military service in the Office of Strategic Services during World War II. At Harvard he was the Powell M. Cabot Professor of American Literature. After producing his magisterial histories of Puritanism, Miller next turned his attention to the later phases of American intellectual and theological development, always emphasizing what he termed the "life of the mind in America." *Jonathan Edwards* (1949), a landmark intellectual biography of the 18th-century Calvinist clergyman and philosopher, was followed by critical anthologies of Puritanism and edited volumes on American Transcendentalism, the 19th-century philosophical movement led by such figures as Ralph Waldo Emerson, Margaret Fuller, Henry David Thoreau, William Ellery Channing, and Amos Bronson Alcott. In many of his books and essays Miller employed a characteristic method of showing the continuities and affinities between the earlier Puritan thinkers of the 17th century and the better-known writers of what has come to be known as the American Renaissance in literature during the 19th century, among them Emerson, Thoreau, Herman Melville, Nathaniel Hawthorne, and Walt Whitman. Miller's influence continues today through his students, a generation of Harvard-trained historians who teach and publish studies of New England intellectual history.

Although some recent historians have disputed Miller's claims about the intellectual links between the different generations of American thought and others reject his view of a homogeneous New England Puritan theology, his work as a whole nevertheless continues to be a compelling scholarly model for the interdisciplinary study of American religion, literature, and intellectual history. An enormous body of scholarship on American Puritanism has appeared and continues to grow, much of it still responding to the principles and premises of Miller's seminal work suggesting that the 17th-century ideas and writings of the Puritans in America were the intellectual seed from which a distinctively American literature eventually would grow. Miller received many honors during his lifetime, and a posthumously published study, the first volume of Miller's never-completed *Life of the Mind in America* (1965), won the Pulitzer Prize in 1966. Miller died in Cambridge, Mass., at the age of 58.

Ann Douglas, "The Mind of Perry Miller," *New Republic*, February 3, 1982; David Levin, "Perry Miller at Harvard: The Grandeur of a Literature Professor," *Southern Review* 19 (1983); Kenneth Lynn, "Perry Miller: In Memoriam," *American Scholar* 52 (1983); Stanford J. Searl, Jr., "Perry Miller as Artist: Piety and Imagination in *The New England Mind: The 17th Century*," *Early American Literature* 12 (1977–78).

James Emmett Ryan

New Deal During the summer of 1933 a flamboyant Blue Eagle flag, symbol of the National Recovery Administration (NRA), could be seen flying in parades throughout New England, hailing a hoped-for new economic age. The stock market crash of 1929 had ushered in a catastrophe that cut the U.S. gross national product in half and sent unemployment rocketing from 1.5 to 12.8 million. New England's textile and shoe businesses were swamped by low-wage competition at home and abroad. Its shipbuilding industry was dying, and its rugged small farms were being driven out of the market by mechanized western competition. The policy crafted by Franklin D. Roosevelt to combat the Great Depression was known as the New Deal.

The New Deal was an experimental, haphazard program. Between 1933 and 1936 the focus nationwide was on relief and recovery. Thereafter it shifted to economic and social reform. Much New Deal legislation challenged the powers reserved to the states. In New England, as elsewhere, state policies had to be rethought and new state-federal relations built. Roosevelt was initially committed to economy in government and a balanced budget, but chaos in the financial system and the exhaustion of state relief resources forced him to change course.

During the first few months of the new Roosevelt administration, a period that has come to be called the Hundred Days, the president and Congress stabilized the banking system and created the Civilian Conservation Corps, the Federal Emergency Relief Administration, and the Agricultural Adjustment Administration to support farm markets and prices. Legislation was passed to regulate securities exchanges, support home mortgages, insure bank deposits, set up a national employment system, create thousands of public works jobs, and provide new credits for farmers. The NRA, created to stabilize industry by implementing codes of fair competition, was at the center of Roosevelt's program. By midsummer the NRA Blue Eagle had become a ubiquitous symbol of recovery.

Meanwhile Roosevelt had created the National Labor Relations Board. Steps had also been taken to control the money supply and insulate America from the world economy. In 1934 Congress passed appropriations for recovery, farm mortgages, and new housing and authorized reciprocal trade agreements to lower tariffs.

Democratic victories in the congressional elections of 1934 led to the creation of the Works Progress Administration; soil conservation, rural resettlement, and electrification programs; public utilities regulation; and passage of the Wagner Act, also known as the National Labor Relations Act, as well as Social Security. But in May 1935 the Supreme Court declared the NRA unconstitutional. It outlawed the agricultural support program in January 1936. The Court's narrow view of clauses governing interstate commerce and general welfare and of the appropriate range of presidential power seemed to permanently stall Roosevelt's plans. But in the 1936 elections only Maine and Vermont went Republican. Roosevelt had strong majorities in both the Senate (76–16) and the House (331–89).

When two Supreme Court justices modified their views, Roosevelt's program, and the authority of the judiciary, were saved. The Court approved minimum wages for women, the Wagner Act, Social Security, a new agriculture act, and the Tennessee Valley Authority, which provided federal flood control and electrical power to a seven-state region in the South.

Roosevelt was expected to run poorly in New England in 1936, in part because only Massachusetts and Rhode Island had supported him in 1932. The region had not profited as much from the New Deal as the West and South. With the exception of Connecticut, its percentage of national personal income had slipped badly. Maine was 32d nationally in per capita federal spending, Vermont being the only state in the region to fare better. This was partly the result of endless factional fights within the local Democratic parties. In Massachusetts, Roosevelt supporters were split by a vicious rivalry between James Curley, the mayor of Boston, state party leaders, and the congressional delegation. New Deal programs had exacerbated class and regional divisions: working-class, urban, and large farming regions were antagonistic to business and small-town interests. Roosevelt was booed by Harvard students, but he had heavy support from ethnic minorities. Maine and Vermont notwithstanding, he won 54 percent of the New England vote in 1936. His principal strength lay in the cities, where he was identified with traditional Democratic bosses like Thomas J. Spellacy in Hartford. He carried New Haven, Conn., by 15,000-plus votes, while the margin in the whole state of New Hampshire was only slightly more than 4,000.

Washington could do little about New England's economic decline. Unions grew stronger under New Deal laws, and labor conflict increased. Both owners and labor wanted higher tariffs. They opposed Roosevelt's trade agreements and fought against the processing taxes that were paying for the agriculture program. Price supports and crop controls belatedly helped only northern Maine potato farmers and tobacco growers in the Connecticut River valley.

All six New England states were rescued from enormous relief bills, however, and thousands of men and women found employment at federal agencies. New public construction in the region ranged from a 300-bed City Hospital, subway lines, slum clearance, and a handsome south-side beach for Boston to new district schools in places like Grand Isle, Vt., and Whitefield, N.H. Federal funds paid for channeling of the Cape Cod Canal. Town halls, bridges, swimming pools, and parks were constructed all over New England. College students found part-time work through the National Youth Administration. State tourist guides were published, and artists were paid to create post office murals, play in local orchestras, and act in city theaters.

Designed to put people to work quickly, the relief programs were not uniformly popular. Many viewed leaf raking as less than bona fide employment and criticized sewer lines dug through frozen ground that collapsed with the arrival of spring. Federal attacks on local control were resented by town governments. Yet only Massachusetts successfully defended its relief distribution system—and paid a heavy price in lost revenue. Rivalry among agencies caused painful delays. But in 1935 federal money paid 55 percent of the relief bill for Massachusetts, where 16 percent of the population was on welfare. In rural Vermont, where only 8 percent of the population was on relief, Washington paid more than 60 percent of the bill.

The Civilian Conservation Corps, which sent $25 a month directly home for each of its recruits, was the most popular New Deal program. It left a handsome legacy of national parks and forest conservation throughout the New England states. But dreams of harnessing the enormous tides on the Maine coast fell apart over conflicting technical estimates and political mismanagement. Flood control became the most divisive issue for New Deal supporters in New England. In 1935 the president derailed a proposal for a Connecticut Valley Authority like the TVA. He insisted on an interstate compact among the four states involved, which Vermont sabotaged. The 1936 flood, which left 77,000 people homeless, and the 1938 hurricane demanded action. Roosevelt thus restored control of waterpower to the national government. Federal money built a system of dikes that saved cities along the Merrimack and Connecticut Rivers from future disaster. But Democratic congressmen suffered in 1938 from having opposed the state-controlled approach and supported public utilities regulation. Prominent Roosevelt supporters in both houses of Congress were defeated, and Republicans regained control of governorships and legislatures in every New England state.

Despite a momentary recovery in 1937, the Depression did not go away, and many lost faith in the New Deal. Although it had given many Americans new hope, maintained political stability, and saved millions from the most extreme hunger and poverty, it had not brought the crisis to an end. World War II did. In 1940 Boston still had 36,000 unemployed. That year Roosevelt bid desperately for New England votes by promising not to send American boys into a foreign war, a promise he would not be able to keep. He carried the three industrial states but lost Maine, Vermont, and New Hampshire. Employment returned to 1929 levels only at the peak of military spending in 1943–44. In the long term, the New Deal programs and spirit built the foundation of the welfare state and opened the door to massive increases in federal and executive authority over the economy. Roosevelt's political coalition lived on long after his death

in 1945 and set the framework for a half century of economic and social policy.

Lyle W. Dorsett, *Franklin D. Roosevelt and the City Bosses* (1977); Harold Gorvine, "The New Deal in Massachusetts," in *The New Deal*, vol. 2, *The State and Local Levels*, ed. John Braeman, Robert H. Bremner, and David Brody (1975); Richard W. Judd, *The New Deal in Vermont: Its Impact and Aftermath* (1979); Richard W. Judd, Edwin A. Churchill, and Joel W. Eastman, eds., *Maine: The Pine Tree State from Prehistory to the Present* (1995); William E. Leuchtenburg, *The F.D.R. Years: On Roosevelt and His Legacy* (1995); Leuchtenburg, *Flood Control Politics: The Connecticut River Valley Problem, 1927–1950* (1953); Harvard Sitkoff, ed., *Fifty Years Later: The New Deal Evaluated* (1985); Charles H. Trout, *Boston: The Great Depression and the New Deal* (1977).

Alfred B. Rollins, Jr.

New Hampshire New Hampshire achieved statehood on June 21, 1788. In 2001 its population was estimated at 1,259,181. Its land area is 8,968 square miles, and its capital is Concord. To most of the world, New Hampshire mainly adds up to two things, bold scenery and eccentric politics. Yet throughout most of the state's history the very physical features that now attract visitors and generate revenue served as an obstacle rather than an asset. As for New Hampshire's stubborn attachment to certain defining political features, including a tax code that in most places would be considered antiquated, it has been only in fairly recent decades that any movement toward change in these sensitive areas has been paralyzed by the rhetoric of standpattism. Such rigidity, moreover, was challenged as the state faced the new millennium.

New Hampshire's history also discloses other realities that confound conventional assumptions. For example, although one persistent image of the state may involve an agrarian way of life centered on family farms and sleepy villages, New Hampshire became predominantly urban and industrial as early as 1850. Though New Hampshire, along with its northern New England neighbors Vermont and Maine, is often portrayed as a last stronghold of the Yankee, the state's population in fact has been composed of a broad ethnic mix for more than a century. And although the cheek-to-jowl positions of New Hampshire and Vermont give rise to the notion of the "twin states," the two have little in common demographically, economically, or politically except in the immediate vicinity of their shared Connecticut River valley.

New Hampshire is one of the four New England states (and the only one in the northern tier) that were among the original 13. Its settlement by Englishmen began in 1623, only three years after the Plymouth Colony. The predominant Native American people at the time

were the Pennacooks, centered in the Merrimack River valley, with whom the first English fishermen and traders enjoyed friendly relations. The Pennacooks remained neutral during the New England–wide King Philip's War in 1675, but they did abandon their traditional village sites in south-central New Hampshire and move northward. Between 1689 and 1713, during King William's and Queen Anne's Wars, the settlements of New Hampshire and Maine bore the brunt of frontier raids by French-led Native Americans.

New Hampshire took its name from the English county that was the home of its first proprietor, Captain John Mason, but it did not become a distinct political entity until 1680, when the English Crown created a jurisdiction to try competing land claims. During most of its first 60 years as a royal province, New Hampshire shared governors with the much larger and more prosperous Massachusetts. In 1741, however, a long-standing boundary dispute with Massachusetts was settled to the great advantage of New Hampshire, and the province acquired a royal governor of its own. During the quarter century–long administration of Benning Wentworth and the much briefer term of his nephew John Wentworth, the Portsmouth merchant elite gained nearly absolute political power within the province and important influence in Britain.

Despite the early popularity of the young John Wentworth, his administration ended as the revolutionary crisis neared its climax. After a crowd of New Hampshire men raided and looted Fort William and Mary in Portsmouth Harbor on two successive nights in December 1774, he became politically helpless and soon fled the province.

In the period of political creativity that followed the American Revolution, New Hampshire's role turned out to be a crucial one. When the federal Constitution was proposed late in 1787, most New Hampshire people had little enthusiasm for the strengthening of a distant government—but the superior political abilities of the seaboard-based proponents eventually carried the day. A New Hampshire convention meeting in Concord in June 1788 voted for ratification, thus providing the ninth and final vote necessary to put the new Constitution into effect.

Economic recovery after the Revolution was slow, but a resumption of maritime commerce in the 1790s brought about a brief new era of prosperity. When that era was ended by the Embargo of 1807 and the War of 1812, the effects of which were exacerbated in New Hampshire by a disastrous fire that destroyed much of the Portsmouth waterfront in 1813, the focus of the state's economy, along with its center of political gravity, shifted inland. Ex-

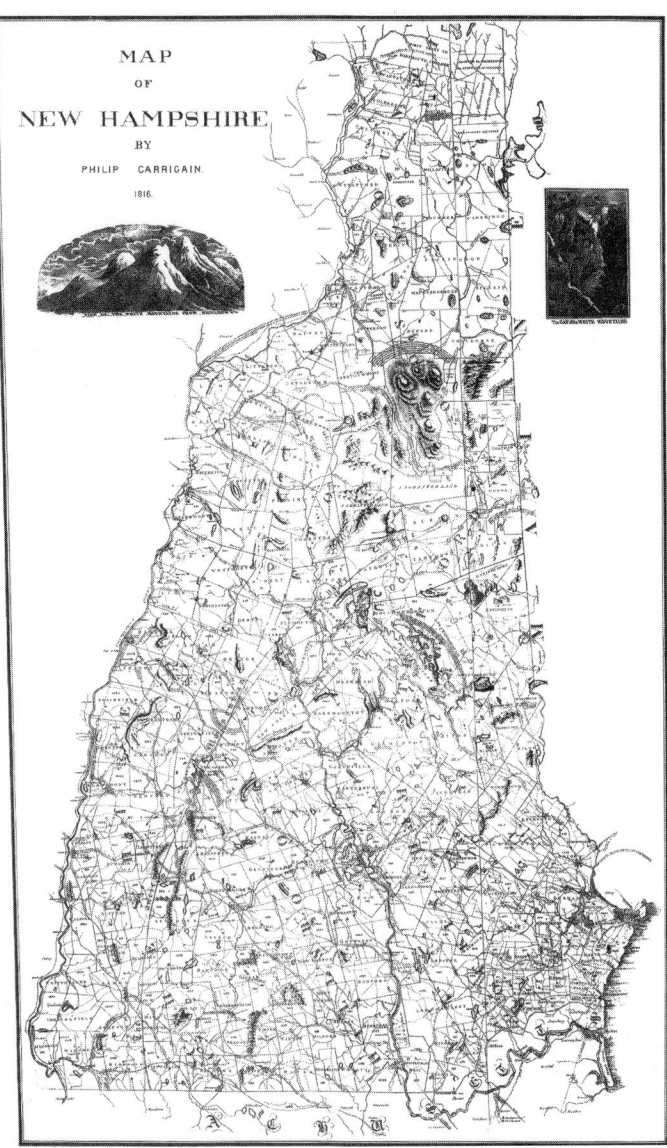

Philip Carrigain, a former New Hampshire secretary of state and state surveyor and the first to call New Hampshire the Granite State, was commissioned to create this map of New Hampshire in 1816

local operators began the systematic exploitation of mineral resources, including iron, mica, quartz, and the raw materials for a glassworks. By 1820 mills were being absorbed and expanded by financiers from out of state who recruited their labor force wherever it could be found. The most dramatic growth occurred at the Amoskeag Falls on the Merrimack River, where a small cotton spinning mill founded in 1809 eventually grew into the world's largest textile plant, located in New Hampshire's largest city, Manchester. Farmers, meanwhile, transformed thousands of acres of woodland into cleared sheep pastures. This definitive alteration of the New Hampshire landscape, occurring mainly between 1810 and 1840, began a slow process of reversal when sheep raising (along with part of New Hampshire's rural population) moved westward beginning shortly before the Civil War.

With the growth of the textile industry, supplemented by shoe manufacturing and various industries based on forest products, including paper, the state's population became altered significantly by immigration. French Canadian and Irish workers began arriving before the Civil War, and by 1900, New Hampshire was home to contingents of most of the major European immigrant groups of the Gilded Age.

By about the same time, the state's industrial plant, having outgrown local sources of capital, was becoming owned and controlled largely from the outside, especially from Massachusetts. Most conspicuously, the Boston and Maine Railroad had acquired sufficient control over New Hampshire's political and judicial processes that for several decades it was able to have its way in matters of regulation and taxation. It was mainly that situation, effectively satirized by the Cornish author Winston Churchill and attacked vigorously by reform elements in the Republican Party, that nudged New Hampshire, almost alone among the eastern states, into its own version of the national Progressive movement. Eventually the reformers managed the introduction of direct primary elections, in the first of which, in 1910, the reform leader Robert Bass won the Republican gubernatorial nomination and the election. That accelerated a series of reforms aimed at democratizing and cleansing the government and curbing the power of industry. Progressive Republicans also led a New Hampshire–based forest conservation movement resulting among other things in the creation in 1911 of the White Mountain National Forest, the first in the nation.

In 1924 John G. Winant, heir to the still-vigorous progressive wing of the party, became governor. He was not reelected in 1926 but served again for two terms in the early 1930s,

cept for a brief return to Federalist ascendancy in response to the unpopular embargo and war, political dominance passed for most of the first half of the 19th century to the Jeffersonian Republicans and their successors the Democrats, whose main strength was in the agricultural interior. In 1808 the state capital moved from Exeter to Concord, some 40 miles from the coast.

The climax of Democratic supremacy, followed by its swift demise, came during the era of Franklin Pierce, who fought vainly within his state to preserve party unity against the rise of antislavery activism. Pierce was the Democratic nominee for president in 1852, opposed by the Whig candidate Winfield Scott and also by his fellow New Hampshireman John Parker Hale, his former rival within the party who now split from the Democrats to accept the Free-Soil presidential nomination. Pierce won the three-way race, becoming New

Hampshire's only U.S. president, but his policy of southern reconciliation was popular neither in his home state nor in the rest of the North, and he failed to be renominated in 1856. The various antislavery factions that formed the modern Republican Party in 1854, some historians argue, took their first crucial steps in Exeter, N.H. Whether Exeter or Ripon, Wis., its rival for that honor, was the actual birthplace of the GOP, there is little doubt that the enthusiastic response to Abraham Lincoln during his visit to New Hampshire in February 1860 gave an early push to the bandwagon that handed Lincoln the nomination that year.

The industrial development of New Hampshire began not long after the state capital moved from the seacoast to Concord. Entrepreneurs in some of the southern New Hampshire villages introduced water-driven machinery for the manufacture of textiles. Other

during which time he broke with his party's policies to embrace much of the New Deal program and instituted state-level recovery measures of his own. During World War II, he was ambassador to Great Britain.

New Hampshire's textile industry, the backbone of the economy, began to falter even before the Great Depression, and other traditional industries followed suit. The great Amoskeag mill complex finally shut down in 1935. After a temporary recovery during World War II, textiles for the most part moved out of New Hampshire for good, and shoe making, another industrial staple, was waning.

Postwar development programs by state and local governments and by quasi-public development corporations were dramatically successful in filling the breach by attracting new industries, largely electronic and other high-tech products served by interstate highways rather than by the dying railroad. In the 1970s, Aristotle Onassis's proposed oil refinery on Durham Point and the construction of a nuclear power plant in Seabrook led to political protest and, in the case of Seabrook, civil disobedience. At the same time, again through deliberate promotion by the state, tourism became a four-season industry while the state's natural amenities from seacoast to lakes to mountains became a kind of mantra for the luring of business and industry as well.

The new economy attracted newcomers to the state by the thousands. Some came not to take the well-paying jobs that were being created in New Hampshire, but to settle in communities north of the Massachusetts border that were becoming extensions of Boston's commuting suburbs. With the closure of Pease Air Force Base in 1991, prime real estate became available for development. But in the north, the sale of paper company lands and the precarious condition of the mills in Berlin threatened the preservation of forestland and the economies based on it. Political change came to the state with the election of its first woman governor, Jeanne Shaheen, in 1996. The first-in-the-nation presidential primary continued to play an important role, both in the nomination process and in attracting attention and money to New Hampshire, though in the wake of the 2004 campaign season there was pressure within both major national parties for a reassessment.

Part of the attraction of New Hampshire for new businesses and residents was the absence of a state-level broad-based tax. Largely through the admonitions of the *Manchester Union Leader*, the conservative newspaper owned from 1946 to 1981 by the flamboyant William Loeb, attempts to introduce a state income tax were invariably shouted down and their proponents usually defeated at the polls.

Meanwhile, the relative paucity of state funding of public schools was burdening local communities dependent almost entirely on property taxes. In 1997 the state's supreme court declared the existing system of school financing unconstitutional, thus forcing a reconsideration of a long-held tenet of taxation and even of New Hampshire's fundamental tradition of localism. The legislature, in an effort to spread the educational tax burden more evenly, responded in 1999 with a statewide property tax. When added to the local tax, the new tax simply exacerbated the burden on wealthier communities, which mounted legal protests. Other voices challenged judicial authority on the matter as Democrat John Lynch, who pledged to oppose new state taxes, prepared to enter the governor's office in 2005.

Political and economic rivalries based on geography, such as those occasioned by the moving of the capital, have been a consistent New Hampshire phenomenon. Topography discourages travel from east to west, while the valleys of the major south-flowing rivers provide well-bounded natural settings for cultural regions linked less with other regions in New Hampshire than with small pieces of Vermont and Maine or to the parts of Massachusetts to which the Connecticut and Merrimack Rivers lead. The most isolated of all New Hampshire regions remains the area north of the White Mountains, accessible from the south only along the Connecticut River or through the three narrow notches, the New Hampshire term for mountain passes. This small state, therefore, is divided by nature into distinct socioeconomic units, each with its own history of settlement and development, its own political interests, and to some extent even its own political makeup. This profound regionalism has combined with the even stronger pattern of localism to hamper political consensus. In recent decades, regional isolation has been overcome to some extent by electronics and asphalt, but geographic divisions and their consequences remain.

Jeremy Belknap, *The History of New-Hampshire*, 3 vols. (1972 [1792]); Charles E. Clark, *The Eastern Frontier: The Settlement of Northern New England, 1610–1763* (1970); Donald B. Cole, *Jacksonian Democracy in New Hampshire* (1970); Jere R. Daniell, *Colonial New Hampshire: A History* (1981); Daniell, *Experiment in Republicanism: New Hampshire Politics and the American Revolution, 1741–1794* (1970); Tamara K. Haraven, *Amoskeag: Life and Work in an American Factory-City* (1978); Evan Hill, *The Primary State: An Historical Guide to New Hampshire* (1976); Lynn Warren Turner, *The Ninth State: New Hampshire's Formative Years* (1983).

Charles E. Clark

Pierce, Franklin (1804–69) President of the United States. Franklin Pierce, the 14th president, was the son of a Revolutionary War soldier and community leader, General Benjamin Pierce, and Anna Kendrick Pierce. Benjamin, an influential figure in Hillsborough County, N.H., was a supporter of Thomas Jefferson and a determined opponent of the Federalists. Although Hillsborough was an isolated area, this did not deter Benjamin Pierce from sending his son to two academies and then to Bowdoin College, where young Franklin formed a friendship with the author Nathaniel Hawthorne.

An attorney and obscure politician from New Hampshire, Pierce assumed the presidency during an era of political change. The acquisition of Texas, California, and other western territories from Mexico changed the balance of power between North and South. By 1850, tensions between the two regions over the extension of slavery were addressed by Congress in a series of bills known as the Compromise of 1850. The compromise admitted California as a free state, organized the areas of Utah and New Mexico without federal restrictions on slavery, fixed the Texas boundary, and authorized a new Fugitive Slave Act.

Southern political leaders gained influence in the Democratic Party during the presidential administration of James K. Polk (1845–49). This, in turn, created frustration in the North. Martin Van Buren, reflecting this sentiment, ran for president in 1848 as a Free-Soil candidate against the Democrat Lewis Cass and the Whig nominee, Zachary Taylor. The Free-Soil movement opposed the extension of slavery in the West, claiming that slavery threatened the agricultural development of these regions. The Free-Soil controversy weakened the Democratic Party and contributed to the Whig victory of 1848.

Accordingly, in 1852 the Democrats nominated Franklin Pierce for president. Party leaders anticipated that Pierce would run a national campaign based on his New England background and his prosouthern attitudes. As party leaders had anticipated, Pierce was a successful candidate in all regions of the nation. He carried 26 of the 30 states, amassing a total of 254 out of 296 possible electoral votes. In addition, the Democrats won large majorities in the House of Representatives and the Senate.

Pierce had been seen as a dark horse. Although he had served in the House and the Senate, his primary accomplishment was as an attorney. In 1848, however, he had opposed Free-Soilers, feeling that they threatened the unity of the Democratic Party. As president, he was determined to follow the provisions of the Compromise of 1850, including enforcement of the increasingly controversial Fugitive Slave Act. In 1854 Pierce ordered federal

President Franklin Pierce, ca. 1853

troops to Boston to assist in the return of a fugitive slave, Anthony Burns, to the South. This action provoked harsh reaction in Boston and was widely resented. The Pierce administration contained many cabinet secretaries with southern sympathies, including the future Confederate president, Jefferson Davis, who served as secretary of war. The administration's policies were designed to satisfy southern objectives.

In 1853 Pierce's representative to Mexico, James Gadsden, signed an agreement acquiring southern Arizona and southern New Mexico for the United States. The Gadsden Purchase was viewed favorably by the South, for southern elites envisioned a transcontinental railroad from New Orleans to California. For this reason, the Gadsden Purchase faced substantial opposition in the northern states. Even more controversial was Pierce's desire to acquire Cuba, an action widely favored in the South. The desire to purchase Cuba would persist, and in 1859 the administration of President James A. Buchanan tried to gain congressional approval for such a policy.

Buchanan secured the Democratic nomination in 1856, as the party refused to renominate Pierce. Even so, the presidency of Franklin Pierce saw far-reaching changes, including heightened tensions between North and South and the disintegration of the Whig party. The newly formed Republican Party became active in the 1856 campaign, nominat-

ing John Charles Frémont for the presidency. Four years later, the party would gain the presidency with the election of Abraham Lincoln.

Pierce returned to New Hampshire and watched as the nation was plunged into civil war. He was critical of Lincoln and believed the war could have been avoided. His opposition to the war caused New Hampshire to largely ignore Pierce's contributions until the early 20th century. He died in Concord, N.H.

John and Alice Durant, *The Presidents of the United States: A History of the Presidents of the United States* (1976); Sidney M. Milkis and Michael Nelson, *The American Presidency: Origins and Development, 1776–1990*, 2d ed. (1994); Roy Franklin Nichols, *Franklin Pierce: Young Hickory of the Granite Hills*, 2d ed. (1988 [1958]); Stephen Skowronek, *The Politics Presidents Make: Leadership from John Adams to Bill Clinton* (1997).

Michael E. Meagher

Pilgrims The Pilgrims were English Protestant refugees who established Plymouth Colony in 1620. As puritan Separatists, they thought the existing Church of England was beyond reform and chose to leave the established church and form new congregations of devout believers. The English Crown and religious authorities saw this move as a challenge to legitimate authority and religious truth and, in response, instituted a series of persecutions to stop the spread of such beliefs. Unwilling to compromise their faith, the Pilgrims fled persecution by emigrating to the more tolerant Dutch Republic, where they lived for over a decade. Eventually, they felt

dissatisfied with the difficult economic conditions there, and many feared that their children were losing their English heritage and becoming too much like the Dutch. Some of the community decided to emigrate to North America, where they could preserve both their English character and religious freedom. Their chief spiritual leader, the Reverend John Robinson, remained in the Dutch Republic, however, with those who chose not to emigrate again. In preparation for the journey, the Pilgrims returned to England and obtained a patent from the Virginia Company, which provided them with the necessary permission to settle on England's new territories abroad. Of the two ships that left Plymouth, England, only the *Mayflower* made the entire trip, landing at Cape Cod in November 1620.

Whether by accident or design, the Pilgrims landed outside the bounds of their Virginia Company patent. Because the patent no longer applied, the free men in the group agreed to a new pact by which community members would abide. This was the Mayflower Compact, a document revered by later generations of New Englanders as a forerunner of American democratic government. The Pilgrims settled on land left vacant by a devastating epidemic, which had killed entire Native American communities shortly before the *Mayflower*'s arrival. The Pilgrims regarded the vacant land as a sign of God's favor, and many subsequent generations of European American New Englanders embraced the Pilgrims' interpretation that God had favored the success of the colony. Plymouth's early years were difficult nonetheless. Many died during the

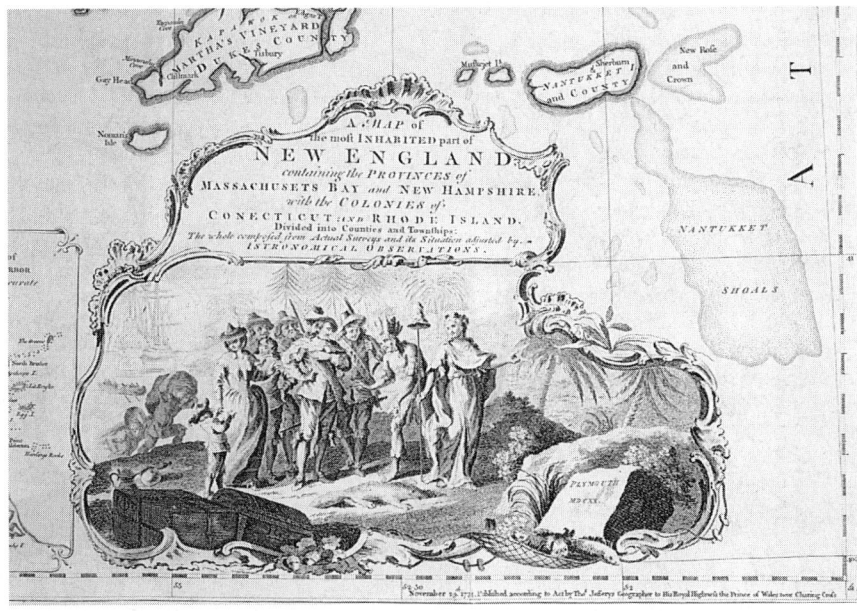

Cartouche from a 1755 map of "the inhabited parts of New England" depicting the arrival of the Pilgrims at Plymouth Rock

Atlantic crossing, and almost half of the colonists died in the first year's harsh winter, when food supplies were meager. The colonists survived their first few years largely through the aid of the neighboring Algonquians. As a result of Plymouth's tenuous early years, such colonists as the longtime governor William Bradford and Miles Standish, the colony's military leader, became best known to later generations. This was partly the influence of Bradford's eloquent history of Plymouth's first years, which details the colonists' tribulations and the measures they undertook to survive in the face of adversity. During Plymouth's second and third decades, the larger puritan colonies of Massachusetts Bay and Connecticut overshadowed it, and the Massachusetts Bay Colony eventually absorbed Plymouth in 1691. The Pilgrims' influence on New England culture, however, stems less from their role in the early colonial era than from their importance to later generations as a symbol of a New England identity.

The Pilgrims attained renewed importance in the early 19th century, as New Englanders sought increasingly to establish their regional identity and history as the cornerstone for a national identity. The New Englanders Daniel Webster and Henry Wadsworth Longfellow played a crucial role in this campaign to establish a national history on a firm New England foundation. Webster helped to bring the name *Pilgrim* into widespread use for the first time. The tremendous popularity of Webster's Plymouth Bicentennial Oration of 1820 and of Henry Wadsworth Longfellow's narrative poem *The Courtship of Miles Standish* (1858) firmly established the Pilgrims as icons of American history and culture. Through the 19th and early 20th centuries, the Pilgrims served as exemplars of the American ideal. In the wake of growing immigration, nativist and anti-Catholic groups embraced the Pilgrims as progenitors of their vision of America. Many groups claimed Protestant Christianity as the country's founding religion, and the Pilgrims became Pilgrim Fathers of the nation. For others, the Pilgrims symbolized a uniquely American commitment to freedom of conscience. In 1863 President Lincoln declared Thanksgiving Day a national holiday, and this annual commemoration of the Pilgrims institutionalized New England's place in the nation's cultural memory.

William Bradford, *Of Plymouth Plantation, 1620–1647*, ed. Samuel Eliot Morison (1952); John Demos, *A Little Commonwealth: Family Life in Plymouth Colony* (1970); John Seelye, *Memory's Nation: The Place of Plymouth Rock* (1998); Eugene Aubrey Stratton, *Plymouth Colony, Its History and People, 1620–1691* (1986).

Cynthia J. Van Zandt

Popular History New Englanders are surrounded by popular interpretations of history. Revolutionary War reenactments, Currier and Ives prints, and colonial-style housing developments are just a few of the ways New England's history has been interpreted by and assimilated into U.S. popular culture. But while early schoolbooks such as *The Tales of Peter Parley about America* (rev. ed. 1860) ascribed American character to its Puritan heritage, and state historical societies had flourished within limited circles since early in the 19th century, the past was not a popular subject outside academia until the late 19th century, when industrialization and immigration radically changed both New England's landscape and its population, making many nostalgic for an older order. Since that time popular history has resulted in such diverse endeavors as newly energized historical societies, house museums, artworks, pageants, monuments, movies, and novels. The prevalence of its representations of the past helps define New England as a region.

Popular history in New England has long been tied to old homes and historic architecture. In 1847 residents of Deerfield, Mass., banded together to save the Ensign John Sheldon House (1699), popularly known as a symbol of the Deerfield Massacre of 1704. While unsuccessful, this first attempt at historic preservation in America helped establish a pattern of preserving homes associated with great men or women, romantic tales, and important historical events. Often run by women's groups such as the Daughters of the American Revolution, historic house museums became the setting for teas, costume balls, and old-time cooking demonstrations. Such romantic images of colonial life were also popularized around the turn of the 20th century by such writers as Sarah Orne Jewett, Alice Morse Earle, and Thomas Bailey Aldrich as well as by the photography of Mary and Frances Allen, Wallace Nutting, Emma Lewis Coleman, and, more recently, Samuel Chamberlain.

While it was New England's upper classes that first promoted history, the pursuit became more popularized during the 1930s, with the creation of government-sponsored projects such as the American Guide series of the Works Progress Administration (WPA) and the Historic American Building Survey. By the 1950s and 1960s, automobile travel fueled the heritage tourism industry, as middle-class families visited historic sites like Strawbery Banke in Portsmouth, N.H., and Old Sturbridge Village in Massachusetts. By creating an ideal image of New England life, these museum villages helped assure Cold War America of its cultural superiority.

In addition to spawning elaborate Bicentennial productions such as PBS's $5.2 million series *The Adams Chronicles*, the 1970s also opened history to previously excluded groups. Lowell, Mass., began preserving its industrial heritage and celebrating the contributions of Irish, French Canadian, and East European immigrants. Boston saw the restoration of the

Puritan Sabbath reenactment, 1977

African Meeting House, America's oldest extant black church. At the same time, young professionals angered by the demolition of historic structures by federal urban renewal programs moved to the city and restored Victorian homes. Urban redevelopment projects like Boston's Faneuil Hall capitalized on this new interest in historic urban architecture, and old areas of the city were marketed as tourist attractions.

Today, popular interest in the past has received a new boost from the multicultural movement, which encourages individuals to celebrate their personal heritage. With its emphasis on ethnic and racial diversity, however, the history promoted by multiculturalism is very different from turn-of-the-20th-century interpretations that honored New England's colonial past and Anglo-Saxon traditions.

Dona Brown, *Inventing New England: Regional Tourism in the 19th Century* (1995); Sarah L. Giffen and Kevin D. Murphy, eds., *A Noble and Dignified Stream: The Piscataqua Region in the Colonial Revival, 1860–1930* (1992); David Glassberg, *American Historical Pageantry: The Uses of Tradition in the Early Twentieth Century* (1990); Michael Kammen, *Mystic Chords of Memory: The Transformation of Tradition in American Culture* (1991).

Briann G. Greenfield

Praying Indians During the 17th century, the label "Praying Indians" identified members of the Massachusett, Wampanoag, and Nipmuck tribes in the Massachusetts Bay Colony who had adopted Puritan ways. From 1650 to 1675, they established 14 "praying towns" in eastern and central Massachusetts. Their significance is a point of academic controversy, however, as scholars disagree over the extent to which native peoples willingly or truly embraced Puritan religion, politics, and labor practices. Although few New Englanders today would recognize the term, the tragic history of these people is part of the bedrock of regional consciousness. Their relationship with the Puritan population of Massachusetts concretized the forms through which New Englanders would deal with outsiders and, in particular, with racial minorities.

Beginning with a "grievous plague" that took place between 1616 and 1619, waves of European-borne epidemics such as smallpox, measles, and dysentery decimated Algonquian villages along the coast and estuaries of Massachusetts Bay. Villages like Patuxet (resettled as Plymouth by Separatist emigrants) lost as much as 90 percent of their populations. Furthermore, the plague disrupted essential patterns of living and undermined core values and institutions, fundamentally unraveling the indigenous culture of the affected native peoples.

The struggle of severely anomic survivors to find meaning in their plight dovetailed with the emergence of a long-promised Puritan mission during a critical smallpox year, 1646–47. Evangelists like John Eliot of Roxbury promised a restoration of order based on Puritan religious practices. Gradually, the traumatized Algonquian people began to graft Puritan religious and civic practices onto their traditions. The praying towns they established emerged as both refuges from land-hungry colonists and centers of eclectic acculturation.

The potential for acculturation evaporated with the outbreak of King Philip's War (also known as Metacom's War) in June 1675. As disgruntled Wampanoag and Nipmuck warriors along the frontier—including some of Eliot's converts—took arms against colonial domination, Puritan hysteria erupted against a more accessible scapegoat, the loyal Praying Indians. Local militias captured many and forced them into internment camps on the bleak islands of Boston Harbor, where wretched conditions created "want and sickness" among the exiles. By February 1675, however, Puritan military leaders refused to lead the colony's army without Christian Indian scouts. The subsequent Praying Indian participation through the spring of 1676 contributed significantly to shift the tide of war to favor the colony's army.

For the Praying Indians, however, acculturation remained an uncompleted journey. Metacom's uprising replicated the conditions that ensued from the earlier epidemics. In the aftermath, the General Court reduced the number of Praying Towns to just three; covetous English neighbors absorbed the remainder. Recurrent pestilence, particularly smallpox, continued to compromise the survival of the remaining towns. At the end of the French and Indian War, in 1763, only 37 members of the Massachusett tribe could be counted in town records. Finally, in 1855, the town of Natick reported only one living descendant.

The history of the Praying Indians is largely forgotten. In the 19th century, it lingered only in such oblique references as Hawthorne's *Mosses from an Old Manse* (1864). Even so, the events surrounding the Praying Indians established a precedent in New England's racial consciousness. The region's people continued to follow the example laid down in the aftermath of King Philip's War, subordinating New England's own laws and institutional missions to the imperatives of economic development and material gain and exiling Native Americans to the bleak recesses of marginality.

Francis Jennings, *The Invasion of America: Indians, Colonialism, and the Cant of Conquest* (1975); Dane Morrison, *A Praying People: Massachusett Accultura-*

tion and the Failure of the Puritan Mission, 1600–1690 (1995); James P. Ronda, "'We Are Well As We Are': An Indian Critique of 17th-Century Christian Missions," *William and Mary Quarterly* 34 (1977); Neal Salisbury, *Manitou and Providence: Indians, Europeans, and the Making of New England, 1500–1643* (1982).

Dane Morrison

Reed, Thomas B. (1839–1902) Politician, Speaker of the House of Representatives. The future parliamentarian and congressional leader Thomas Brackett Reed was born in Portland, Maine, educated in public schools, and graduated from Bowdoin College in 1860. Upon completing his studies, Reed taught school and studied law. In 1861 he traveled to California and in 1863 gained admission to the California bar. He never felt at home in California, however, and soon returned to Portland.

Although Reed did not succumb to the great waves of patriotism that lured many of his college classmates away from school and into the Civil War, he did join the navy in April 1864, serving as acting assistant paymaster of the gunboat *Sybil* on the Mississippi River. In November 1865 Reed returned to Portland to practice law. He served as a state representative and senator and was Maine's attorney general from 1870 to 1873. He married the widow Susan (Merrill) Jones in 1870. Between 1873 and 1876 Reed served the city of Portland as its solicitor.

In 1876 Reed entered the national political arena. Elected to represent Maine's first congressional district, he quickly secured a reputation as a keen student of parliamentary tactics. He became a member of the House Rules Committee in 1882 and during his tenure helped to make that committee one of the most powerful in the House. Reed became Republican minority leader in 1885 and was elected Speaker of the House for the first time in December 1889. He is best remembered for the parliamentary reforms he introduced during the 51st Congress, known as the Reed Rules. Designed to eliminate obstructionism, the rules required that all members present on the House floor vote on a measure unless they were financially interested in it; that a quorum be determined by the number of members actually present whether voting or not; and that the speaker be allowed to ignore motions meant to delay action on a particular motion.

Reed was a dark horse for the Republican presidential nomination in 1892, but his candidacy never materialized. He tried again in 1896 but lost to William McKinley. He nonetheless supported McKinley and was instrumental in shepherding the president's domestic measures through Congress.

Reed's economic views were in tune with

those of the conservative leadership in the Republican Party. He cared little for reform and felt that the federal government should not interfere with private business. Reed believed that laissez-faire and rugged individualism were sound and sensible doctrines. He failed to realize that there could be a satisfactory balance in the relations between the federal government and private business.

Although Reed rarely discussed foreign policy, his views on the subject were well known. He ardently opposed expansion and believed the United States should avoid foreign entanglements. Therefore, he opposed both the Spanish-American War and the addition of new territories, both of which his party supported. Disillusioned with the Republican leadership, Reed retired from politics in 1899 to practice law in New York. In private life Reed continued to criticize the government's imperialistic designs and was particularly outspoken in his opposition to the administration's Philippine policy. Reed died in Washington, D.C., on December 8, 1902.

Reed's greatest accomplishment was to revive the House of Representatives as an effective legislative body. He reestablished the concept of majority rule without destroying minority rights and transformed the House into a constructive deliberative body in which action prevailed over obstructionism.

Samuel W. McCall, *The Life of Thomas Brackett Reed* (1914); William A. Robinson, *Thomas B. Reed, Parliamentarian* (1930); Barbara W. Tuchman, *The Proud Tower: A Portrait of the World before the War, 1890–1914* (1966).

Richard S. Offenberg

Revere, Paul (1734–1818) Patriot, craftsman. Paul Revere, patriot, goldsmith, and early American industrialist, is best known for a one-and-a-half-hour ride he made on April 18–19, 1775, the night before the first battles of the American Revolution. Yet Revere had made much longer rides in the years leading up to the Revolutionary War, traveling as far as New York and Philadelphia to carry important news and documents for various patriot groups and committees. Revere would probably have remained a relatively minor Revolutionary War figure had not Henry Wadsworth Longfellow (1807–82) published his celebrated poem "Paul Revere's Ride" in 1861. Reprinted in Longfellow's *Tales of a Wayside Inn* in 1863 and many times since, this poem, combined with Americans' increasing interest in their colonial past, eventually transformed Revere from a figure of local importance into a national folk hero.

Paul Revere was born in the North End section of Boston, then the largest city in the British colonies of North America. Revere's father, also named Paul Revere (originally Apollos Rivoire), was a descendant of Huguenots from the Bordeaux region of southwestern France. In 1715 Apollos's family sent him to the colonies, where he apprenticed with a Boston goldsmith (as silversmiths were known at the time). Paul Revere's mother, Deborah Hichborn, was the descendant of several well-to-do New England families, some of whose ancestors had been among the earliest English settlers. Revere attended school near his home and then apprenticed with his father. When the elder Revere died in 1754, Paul, then 19, was too young by custom to take over the family goldsmith shop. He took over the family business in his own name in 1756, following service as an artillery officer during the French and Indian War.

In the 1760s and 1770s Revere operated one of the largest goldsmith's shops in Boston, where he crafted a variety of gold and silver items for wealthy customers and persons of more modest means. In addition, Revere produced numerous commercial engravings such as trade cards, bookplates, and illustrations for magazines, and even served as a dentist for a time (although he never made a set of teeth for George Washington, as is sometimes suggested; such a task was beyond his ability). In 1757 he married his first wife, Sarah Orne, with whom he had eight children, six of whom survived. Following Sarah's death, Revere married Rachel Walker, with whom he also had eight children, five of whom survived. Many of Revere's sons became involved in his various business activities, and several of his daughters married neighbors, business associates, or apprentices. In 1768 Paul Revere sat for a portrait by John Singleton Copley; the painting, depicting Revere in craftsman's clothes, is among the best-known American works of portraiture.

Revere first became involved in radical political activity in the 1760s. In the beginning he confined most of his efforts to engraving political cartoons, including his famous "Boston Massacre" print (1770). This print dramatized a violent confrontation in downtown Boston in which British soldiers fired into an unruly crowd, killing and wounding several persons. In the early 1770s, Revere became active in several radical political groups, including the North Caucus, which met most often at the Green Dragon Tavern on Union Street. According to tradition, much of the planning for the incident known as the Boston Tea Party took place at these meetings in November and December 1773.

Paul Revere undertook his first messenger ride on the day after the Boston Tea Party, carrying news of the event to New York and Philadelphia. In December 1774, Revere rode 60 miles to Portsmouth, N.H., to warn the local militia that the British planned to reinforce Fort William and Mary. In the winter of 1774 and spring of 1775, Revere and several of his neighbors formed their own spy ring to observe the actions of British authorities in Boston. In the spring of 1775 it became clear that something was about to happen. On the evening of April 18, 1775, a messenger contacted Revere and told him to go to the house of Dr. Joseph Warren, one of the last patriot leaders still in Boston at the time and also a personal friend of Revere's. Dr. Warren dispatched Revere to Lexington, Mass., with a message warning Samuel Adams and John Hancock that British troops were marching to arrest them. Warren also informed Revere that he had already sent another messenger, William Dawes, to Lexington by another route. Two friends rowed Revere across the river, where he borrowed a horse from a local family. After evading capture by a British patrol just outside of Charlestown, Revere alarmed the countryside all the way to Lexington, where he arrived about one o'clock in the morning.

Following the outbreak of hostilities, Paul Revere served the Massachusetts government in several capacities, printing currency and supervising the procuring of cannon and gunpowder. In the spring of 1776, Revere received a commission as an officer in the Massachusetts artillery. For the next three years, he served as commander of Castle Island, a fort in Boston harbor, and took part in several local expeditions.

In the early 1780s Revere attempted to operate a hardware store business, with indifferent success. In the late 1780s he established a foundry in Boston's North End, where he cast cannons and bells and manufactured ship fittings for the many local shipyards. In 1800, at age 65, Revere embarked on perhaps his riskiest business venture. He purchased an old gunpowder mill in the town of Canton, south of Boston, which he converted into a mill for rolling sheet copper. Although at one point the new business almost drove him into bankruptcy, the copper mill soon made Revere quite wealthy. Revere copper was used to plate the hulls of ships (including the USS *Constitution* in 1803) and to cover the roofs of buildings. Robert Fulton of New York City used heavy Revere copper plates for the boilers of many of his steamboats. In 1811 Paul Revere retired from his copper mill and foundry businesses, turning them over to his son Joseph and two of his grandsons. Paul Revere died at the age of 83, and was buried next to his second wife, Rachel, in Boston's Granary Burying Ground.

David Hackett Fischer, *Paul Revere's Ride* (1994); Esther Forbes, *Paul Revere and the World He Lived In*

(1942); Patrick M. Leehey et al., *Paul Revere—Artisan, Businessman, and Patriot: The Man behind the Myth* (1988); Jayne E. Triber, *A True Republican: The Life of Paul Revere* (1998).

Patrick M. Leehey

Rhode Island

One of the 13 original colonies, Rhode Island became the 13th state on May 29, 1790. It is the smallest state in the union, with a total area of 1,214 square miles. Nonetheless, it is remarkably diverse. Although it is the country's second most densely populated state (after New Jersey), nearly two-thirds of its acreage consists of agricultural, forest, and undeveloped land. Its population is heterogeneous, consisting of approximately 20 major ethnocultural groups. In 2000, Rhode Island had 1,048,319 inhabitants, making it the 43d most populous of the 50 states. Well over 60 percent of that number declared their affiliation with the Catholic Church, making Rhode Island, proportionately, the most Catholic state in the union. The state capital is Providence, New England's second-largest city.

The shores and islands of Narragansett Bay were a haven for Rhode Island's earliest European settlers. In 1636 the Englishman Roger Williams, with the acquiescence and assistance of the Wampanoag and Narragansett Indians, established Providence as a refuge for people persecuted elsewhere because of their religious beliefs. Seekers and other dissenters followed Williams to the Narragansett Bay region, among them William Coddington and Anne and William Hutchinson, who founded Portsmouth in 1638 on the island of Aquidneck. Coddington moved to the southern end of Aquidneck in 1639 to establish Newport, and in 1642 Samuel Gorton, another Portsmouth dissident, settled Warwick, originally Shawomet, on the mainland south of Providence. Under the aegis of a 1644 parliamentary patent a colony soon developed, pioneering the principles of religious liberty and the complete separation of church and state. Quakers (1657) and Jews (1658) were among Newport's early settlers. The royal charter obtained for the colony by Dr. John Clarke in 1663 reaffirmed these principles. This liberal document also made Rhode Island a self-governing colony. Throughout the colonial and revolutionary eras, individualism, self-reliance, democratic localism, and resistance to external control were characteristic Rhode Island traits.

Like all of England's North American colonies, Rhode Island was primarily agricultural. In the mid-18th century the sizable plantations of South County, utilizing black slave labor, reached the peak of their prosperity. Here and in the undulating fields surrounding island towns, colonial farmers raised livestock, especially sheep and the renowned carriage horses named Narragansett pacers, and cultivated such commodities as apples, onions, flax, and dairy products. The virgin forests yielded lumber for boards, planks, timber, and barrels, and the sea offered whales and an abundance of fish for use as food and fertilizer. Most of these items soon became valuable exports in Rhode Island's fast-expanding trade network.

By the end of the colonial era Rhode Island was engaged in brisk commerce with the entire Atlantic community, including England, the Portuguese islands, Africa, South America, the West Indies, and other British mainland colonies. Commercial activities flourished in Newport, Providence, and Bristol and in lesser ports such as Pawtuxet, Wickford, East Greenwich, Warren, and Westerly. A lucrative if nefarious aspect of this commerce was the slave trade, an enterprise in which Rhode Island merchants outdid those of any other mainland colony. Their traffic formed one leg of a triangular route that brought molasses from the West Indies to Rhode Island, whose distilleries turned it into rum. This liquor was bartered along the African coast for slaves, who were carried in crowded, pest-ridden vessels to the West Indies, to the southern colonies, or back to Rhode Island for domestic service in the mansions of wealthy merchants or on South County plantations.

When Britain imposed administrative controls that threatened the colony's prosperity and autonomy in the 1760s, Rhode Island took the first halting steps toward revolution and independence. Having exercised more local self-government than any other British colony since the royal charter of 1663, Rhode Island became an early leader in the revolutionary movement and then a reluctant participant in the new federal union. Rogues Island, as James Madison and other founding fathers called it, was the last of the 13 original colonies to surrender its self-determination by ratifying the federal Constitution.

The year 1790 was marked by an event that served as the catalyst for the state's economic transition: the installation and operation of a cotton-spinning frame similar to those used in England in a mill at Pawtucket Falls on the Blackstone River. It was the first time cotton yarn was spun by waterpower in America. The chief participants in this promising venture

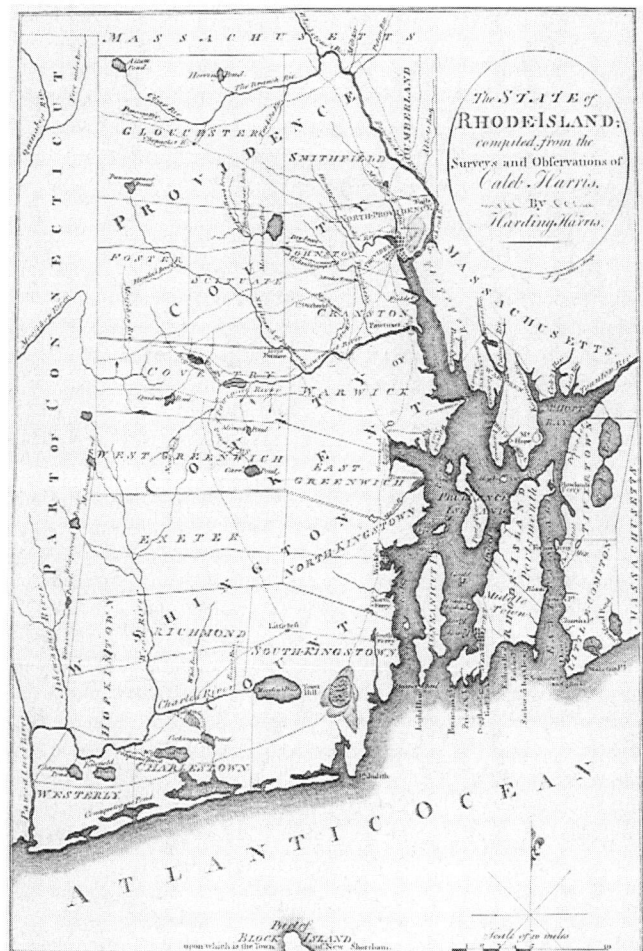

Map of Rhode Island from Mathew Carey's American Atlas *(1795), the first general atlas published in North America*

were the Providence merchants Moses Brown, Smith Brown, and William Almy; Samuel Slater, a young English immigrant with technical knowledge and managerial experience acquired in his native land; and local craftsmen such as the carpenter Sylvanus Brown and metalworker Oziel Wilkinson.

The Rhode Island cotton industry developed slowly, Providence businessmen supplying most of its funds, managers, and expertise. Commercial capital began shifting into cotton manufacturing in 1804, before the Embargo Act closed U.S. ports to export shipping and even before the state's maritime operations, now including trade with China, reached their peak. By the late 1820s the processing of cotton had displaced commerce as the backbone of Rhode Island's economy; river valleys in the northeastern quadrant of the state hummed with industrial activity.

In this era woolen production also flourished, especially in South County, and the need for textile machinery gave rise to a base-metals industry centered in Providence. Another early and important area of industrial endeavor was the manufacture of precious metals, especially gold and silver jewelry. For a century these four industries—cottons, woolens, base metals, and precious metals—steadily expanded, dominating the state's economic life. Meanwhile, agriculture declined, a large number of farms reverted to forest, and many rural towns experienced a substantial out-migration.

The principal trends in 19th-century Rhode Island were toward industrialization, immigration, and urbanization. By the 1840s these forces combined to produce a constitutional crisis known as the Dorr Rebellion. The state's royal charter, then still in effect, gave disproportionate representation to the declining rural towns, conferred almost unlimited power on the legislature, and contained no procedure for its own amendment. Lawmakers, regardless of party, insisted on retaining the old real estate requirement for voting and office holding, even though all other states had abandoned it. As Rhode Island grew more urban, this freehold qualification became more restrictive. By 1840 about 60 percent of free adult males were disfranchised.

Because earlier moderate efforts at change had been virtually ignored by the General Assembly, the reformers of 1840–43 decided to bypass that body and hold a People's Convention, equitably apportioned and chosen by an enlarged electorate. Thomas Wilson Dorr, a patrician attorney, assumed the leadership of the movement in late 1841. A coalition of Whigs and rural Democrats used force to block the implementation of Dorr's basic law, called the People's Constitution, but they were pressured into making limited changes in the form of a written constitution that became effective in May 1843. That document was designed to disfranchise Irish Catholics, then migrating to the state in increasing numbers, by retaining the real estate requirement for the foreign-born.

By the 1850s Dorr's movement had resulted in a realignment of political parties. Native-born Whigs, rural Democrats, and urban workingmen who opposed both slavery and the Irish flirted with Know-Nothingism and then coalesced within the newly formed Republican Party, led by the archnativist Henry Bowen Anthony, editor of the *Providence Journal*. A minority of long-established Yankees and those Irish who had acquired real estate or were American-born adhered to Dorr's wing of the Democratic Party.

The last half of the century was an era of Republican dominance. When the native-born Irish grew numerous enough to challenge that party's ascendancy, the Republicans (led from 1884 by Senator Nelson Aldrich and Charles R. "Boss" Brayton) did away with the real estate requirement in order to recruit and enfranchise certain sociocultural foes of the Irish: immigrants from French and British Canada, England, and Sweden. By the end of the century the political battle lines between WASP Republican and Irish Catholic Democrat were sharply drawn, newer immigrants tipping the balance of power temporarily in favor of the Republican Party. In few (if any) other states were ethnoreligious factors so politically influential.

Fashionable Gilded Age Newport, summer retreat of America's upper class, contrasted sharply with the turbulent urban-industrial milieu and with the quiet farms of South County and Rhode Island's western hills. Astors, Vanderbilts, Belmonts, Whitneys, and their peers built spectacular "cottages" on Newport's Bellevue Avenue and Ocean Drive, held lavish balls and other galas, and popularized such sports as tennis, golf, polo, and sailing. Satellite summer colonies in Jamestown, Narragansett Pier, and Westerly's Watch Hill, though less elegant than Newport, enhanced coastal Rhode Island's image as one of America's premier vacation resorts for the well-to-do.

In the late 19th century Rhode Island's four big industries continued to boom. Cotton textiles evidenced a trend toward consolidation—bigger mills, more employees, and more spindles. This enterprise dominated the economy of the Blackstone and Pawtuxet Valleys, and the Providence-based cotton textile empire formed by Benjamin B. and Robert Knight was allegedly the largest in the world. In 1900, this industry boasted 90 establish-ments and an average yearly workforce of 24,192.

Woolen production experienced a wartime expansion in the 1860s and continued to flourish at century's end. With entrepreneurs like Charles Fletcher leading the way, Providence ranked first among the cities of the nation by 1900 in the production of woolen and worsted goods, and Rhode Island, with 54 establishments employing 16,738, ranked third nationwide in this area of manufacture.

In the base-metals trade the state was also prominent. Brown and Sharpe (based in Providence until its relocation in 1964 to North Kingstown) was the largest producer of machine tools in the nation; its managers, Joseph Brown and Lucian Sharpe, earned renown for producing the micrometer and the vernier caliper.

Rhode Island also boasted the country's largest steam-engine factory, founded and run by George Corliss of Providence. The crowning achievement of this noted inventor and his firm was the construction of the gigantic steam engine used to power the machinery displayed at the mammoth Philadelphia International Centennial Exhibition of 1876.

Other giants of the base-metals industry included the file company of William T. Nicholson, the world's largest producer of metal files and rasps, and William G. Angell's American Screw Company, whose three large Providence plants turned out more wood and machine screws during this era than any other company in the world. By 1900, Rhode Island had 144 machine shops and foundries employing 8,799 workers.

The precious-metals industry also enjoyed exceptional growth. The Gorham Manufacturing Company in Providence was the country's largest producer of silverware, and its statues, memorials, and architectural bronze work were famous nationwide. Among the best known of Gorham's creations is *The Independent Man*, the statue that has stood atop Rhode Island's capitol dome since 1899. While Gorham was the giant, many smaller jewelry and silverware firms also flourished—enough of them to make Providence and its environs the world's leading costume-jewelry manufacturing center. By 1900, this industry claimed 249 establishments employing 8,767 people throughout the state.

During the Gilded Age the big-four industries were joined by a fifth major area of manufacturing: rubber goods, especially footwear. Woonsocket, Providence, Bristol, and Warren contained this industry's principal plants, while the entrepreneurs Joseph Banigan, Joseph Davol, Samuel P. Colt, and Governor Augustus O. Bourn provided the fledgling industry with either inventive genius or managerial expertise.

Early in the 20th century Rhode Island again underwent important demographic and economic changes. Before World War I south and east European immigrants poured in from Italy, Portugal (including the Azores and Cape Verde), Greece, Armenia, Syria, Poland, Lithuania, the Ukraine, and Russia (mainly Jews). In the postwar decade the state's burgeoning population suffered through a precipitous decline in the dominant textile industry.

Politics were also eventful. Led by Providence business interests and rural politicians from South County and Connecticut-border farming towns, a conservative Republican Party blocked the local implementation of most Progressive Era reforms. During the 1920s and 1930s, however, came a major transition from Republican to Democratic control.

Economic unrest stemming from such factors as the decline of textiles, the Great Depression, and the rise of local organized labor coupled with the development of cultural antagonisms between so-called natives and recent immigrants weakened the initial allegiance of Franco-Americans, Italian Americans, and Jewish Americans to the Republican Party. The vigorous efforts of the Irish-led Democratic Party, key constitutional reforms, the 1928 candidacy of Al Smith, the first Catholic to run for president, and the social programs of the New Deal also helped bring the newer immigrant groups within the Democratic fold by the mid-1930s.

Democratic leaders such as Theodore Francis Green, Thomas P. McCoy, and Robert Emmet Quinn staged a governmental reorganization known as the Bloodless Revolution of 1935. After their excesses drew a brief electoral rebuke, the Democrats consolidated their power during the 1940s under Governor J. Howard McGrath and Providence mayor Dennis J. Roberts. From that time until the mid-1980s, Democrats captured most state and congressional elections (with the notable exception of the victories of the Republican John H. Chafee) and maintained a lopsided edge in both houses of the General Assembly, especially after the reapportionment occasioned by the one man–one vote decisions of the U.S. Supreme Court in the 1960s.

World War II made Rhode Island a hothouse of defense-related industrial growth. Between 1945 and 1973 the navy was the state's largest civilian employer, and the arrival in Newport of the cruiser-destroyer force of the U.S. Atlantic Fleet in 1952 produced a major influx of naval personnel. But the military bubble burst in 1973 with the Nixon administration's decision to relocate the force to southern ports. It was by far the most severe economic jolt to the state since the stock market crash of 1929. The support facilities at

Quonset were soon closed, and Davisville was cut back drastically, with a resulting loss of 16,000 civilian jobs. During 1973 and 1974 more than 20,000 navy personnel left the state. Middletown suffered a 41 percent decline in population. The Department of Defense did, however, upgrade Newport as an education and training center, with the Naval War College as its nucleus. It also turned the Naval Undersea Warfare Center into the world's premier science and technology laboratory for undersea warfare; in 2000, the facility employed nearly 3,000 Rhode Islanders.

Ethnic diversity, long a hallmark of Rhode Island life, has been augmented since the late 1960s by new waves of immigrants. While Azorean Portuguese, Irish, Russian Jews, and blacks from the West Indies and Africa (especially Liberia and Nigeria) have joined older ethnic communities, the most significant modern migration to Rhode Island has come from Latin America and Southeast Asia. The Hispanic population hails from Puerto Rico and a score of Latin American nations, most notably Colombia and the Dominican Republic. Members of the Asian community come mainly from Vietnam, Cambodia, and Laos (including Laotian hill people known as Hmong) and, in smaller numbers, from China, Korea, Japan, India, and the Philippines. Ethnic and racial clashes have been minimal, and ghettolike neighborhoods are nonexistent in Rhode Island's cities.

Despite the corruption and turbulence that have marred its political life and the trauma caused by the economic transformation from manufacturing to service-oriented businesses, Rhode Island possesses a kind of vitality that bodes well for its future. Among the service-oriented enterprises, higher education is paramount. The state maintains three public colleges. The University of Rhode Island, established in 1892 as the Rhode Island State College of Agriculture and Mechanic Arts, has a main campus in the village of Kingston, a major extension division in Providence, and satellite programs elsewhere in the state. One of its most notable academic resources is its Graduate School of Oceanography. Rhode Island College, founded in 1854 as a normal school, is located in Providence; and the Community College of Rhode Island, established as Rhode Island Junior College in 1964, has campuses in Warwick, Lincoln, and Providence.

Major colleges not run by the state are Brown University (1764), an Ivy League institution of international renown, with a wide range of excellent programs, including a medical school; Providence College (1917), a liberal arts school with undergraduate and graduate divisions, founded by the Dominican fathers,

which has educated more of the state's professional class than any other college; Rhode Island School of Design (1877), highly acclaimed for excellence in the fine arts, architecture, and design; the U.S. Naval War College (1884), which is the center of a large naval-education complex in Newport; Roger Williams University (1919), noted for its school of architecture and the home of the state's only law school; and Bryant College (1863), a top-rated business school.

Other colleges and their special areas include Johnson and Wales College (1914), business and culinary arts; and Salve Regina University in Newport (1947), a Catholic liberal arts college. The American Mathematical Society, a major scholarly institution, is based in Providence.

By way of vigorous programs of historic preservation and environmental protection, economic diversification, and intergroup cooperation, present-day Rhode Islanders seek to preserve the best of their heritage while striving to improve the quality of life for generations yet to come.

Charles Carroll, *Rhode Island: Three Centuries of Democracy,* 4 vols. (1932); Peter J. Coleman, *The Transformation of Rhode Island, 1790–1860* (1963); Patrick T. Conley, *An Album of Rhode Island History, 1636–1986* (1986); Conley, *Democracy in Decline: Rhode Island's Constitutional Development, 1776–1841* (1977); Edward Field, ed., *State of Rhode Island and Providence Plantations at the End of the Century,* 3 vols. (1902); Sydney V. James, *Colonial Rhode Island* (1975); William G. McLoughlin, *Rhode Island: A History* (1978); Marion I. Wright and Robert J. Sullivan, *The Rhode Island Atlas* (1982).

Patrick T. Conley

Sacco and Vanzetti On May 5, 1920, in the wake of the nationwide anticommunist and anti-immigrant frenzy known as the Red Scare, authorities arrested the Italian immigrants Nicola Sacco and Bartolomeo Vanzetti for two murders committed during an armed robbery in South Braintree, Mass., on April 15, 1920. Scholars and journalists still argue over whether the two were guilty. Sacco, a shoemaker, and Vanzetti, a fish peddler, were known as draft dodgers and political radicals with an interest in anarchism. Their trial, which took place in Dedham, Mass., between May 31 and July 14, 1921, was dominated by bigotry and antiradical hysteria. In spite of conflicting eyewitness accounts and a lack of hard evidence that Sacco and Vanzetti were even at the scene of the crime, the two were convicted and sentenced to death. Transcripts indicate that at his sentencing trial Vanzetti proclaimed his innocence, firmly declaring, "I have struggled all my life . . . to eliminate crime from the earth." The case became a political cause célèbre.

Bartolomeo Vanzetti (left) and Nicola Sacco on their way to trial, Boston, 1921

Defense attorneys appealed the verdict, insisting that witnesses had wrongly identified the two, but their efforts failed. While incarcerated in the Charles Street Jail, Sacco and Vanzetti studied and wrote about their case; their eloquent pleas helped arouse worldwide sympathy. The reporter Philip G. Strong quoted Vanzetti's words in the *New York World* on May 13, 1927: "Never in our full life, could we hope to do such work for tolerance, for justice, for man's understanding of man as now we do by an accident. . . . The taking of our lives—lives of a good shoemaker and a poor fish peddler . . . That last moment belongs to us—that agony is our triumph."

The liberal Harvard professor and future Supreme Court justice Felix Frankfurter insisted that anti-immigrant and antiradical sentiments had governed the case and that the two defendants had been denied their constitutional right to a fair trial. Intellectuals at home and abroad, including Albert Einstein and the Czech president Thomas Masaryk, protested the verdict. On November 18, 1925, the convicted murderer Celestino Madeiros confessed that he had committed the crime with members of a Rhode Island gang, but Judge Webster Thayer still refused to grant Sacco and Vanzetti a new trial. Governor Alvan Fuller appointed a special commission to review the case and advise him on whether to grant clemency. A. Lawrence Lowell, president of Harvard, Samuel Stratton, president of MIT, and the former probate judge Robert Grant concluded that the trial had been fair and the sentence appropriate.

This decision triggered violent demonstrations in major cities throughout the United States and Europe. In Boston, police arrested 150 picketers, and in New York City and Philadelphia protestors set off bombs. Local opinion, however, still ran against Sacco and Vanzetti. Many Bostonians resented outside criticism, and the violent protests only deepened their conviction that Sacco and Vanzetti were alien agitators and enemies of the Roman Catholic religion. Sacco and Vanzetti were executed on August 23, 1927.

Journalists and scholars still argue over new evidence, some claiming that Sacco was guilty and Vanzetti innocent. In an official proclamation in 1977 Massachusetts governor Michael Dukakis formally acknowledged that the state had treated Sacco and Vanzetti unfairly. The names Sacco and Vanzetti nonetheless have become a metaphor for the recurring struggle between civil liberty and antiradical rage. The trial continues to remind Americans how fragile constitutional rights can be in times of extreme national hysteria.

G. Louis Joughin and Edmund M. Morgan, *The Legacy of Sacco and Vanzetti* (1948); Francis Russell, *Sacco and Vanzetti: The Case Resolved* (1986); Robert P. Weeks, ed., *Commonwealth vs. Sacco and Vanzetti* (1958); William Young and David E. Kaiser, *Postmortem: New Evidence in the Case of Sacco and Vanzetti* (1985).

Alfred B. Rollins, Jr.

Salem Witchcraft Cases The last major outbreak of witchcraft accusations and prosecutions in the English-speaking world began in the winter of 1691–92 when two girls in Salem Village (now Danvers), Mass., a community of 500 people, began to suffer fits. By the time the episode came to an end, 19 people had been hanged and one had succumbed after two days of torture. Sometimes involving convulsive behaviors, the afflictions of nine-year-old Elizabeth Parris and 11-year-old Abigail Williams also consisted of violent tantrums and long periods of unresponsiveness. Both girls lived in the house of the Reverend Samuel Parris, whose parish was located in the northwest portion of Salem Town, the seat of Essex County, about 17 miles northeast of Boston. As the girls' condition worsened, adults prayed and fasted in an unsuccessful attempt to cure them. A village doctor, unable to determine a natural cause for their distress, suggested that the children were bewitched. When adults asked the girls to identify their tormentors, they named three Salem Village women: Sarah Osborne, Sarah Good, and Tituba, the Reverend Parris's Carib slave.

At the end of February 1692 the Salem magistrates John Hathorne and Jonathan Corwin arrested the women, subjecting each one to a verbal examination. Tituba confessed under questioning that the devil had asked her to make a covenant with him and that she had seen four familiar names in the devil's book. Unable to remember all four, she testified that the signatures of Osborne and Good were among them. Osborne corroborated some elements of Tituba's story by suggesting that Good was a witch, but Good denied the allegations. On March 1, 1692, the magistrates committed all three women to a Boston jail, then turned their attention to a new problem: tracking down the two witches who remained at large. The Salem witchhunt had begun.

During the next few months the witchhunt expanded dramatically. By the end of March the girls began accusing people from outside Salem Village; by May the magistrates had investigated more than 50 people from throughout the eastern part of the Massachusetts Bay Colony. While the number of accused kept growing larger, so too did the number of victims. By the middle of the summer at least eight girls and women had been afflicted. Practicing witchcraft was a capital crime according to the laws of England and the Massachusetts Bay Colony, and as such was more

T. H. Matteson, The Trial of George Jacobs, August 5, 1692 *(1855), depicting one of the Salem witchcraft trials*

than a local concern: it would be addressed at the highest levels of colonial justice.

Ongoing investigations attracted the attention of colony leaders, some of whom went to Salem to witness the afflictions and inquiries firsthand. The unprecedented number of cases and confessions persuaded many persons in authority that they had uncovered a devil's plot to destroy the Massachusetts Bay Colony. God, it seemed, had been communicating his displeasure with the colony through omens since the 1670s. Such portents included wars, famines, smallpox epidemics, droughts, fires, the 1684 revocation of the colony charter, and the tyranny of a royally appointed governor, Sir Edmund Andros. When the findings of the witchcraft magistrates were added to this list, many leaders came to believe that the devil had established a vast network of servants in the Massachusetts Bay Colony who must be unearthed and defeated if the colony was to survive. Thus in the continuing examinations magistrates sought evidence of demonic pacts among the accused, while at the same time they encouraged confessed witches and afflicted persons to identify other individuals who might be in league with the devil.

By May 1692 eastern Massachusetts prisons were crowded with accused witches, but colony magistrates were unable and unwilling to begin trying the accused without a charter from England—Sarah Osborne in fact died in jail while awaiting trial. Although the original charter of 1629 was replaced in 1691, the new charter and the colony's new governor, Sir William Phips, did not arrive in Massachusetts Bay Colony until May 14 the following year.

Before the end of May, with scores of people in prison, Phips and his council created a temporary court to hear the witchcraft cases. This Special Court of Oyer and Terminer, consisting of seven associate justices led by Lieutenant Governor William Stoughton, convened five times during the summer of 1692. In its initial session, which began on June 2, the court tried, convicted, and condemned its first victim, Bridget Bishop, a Salem Village innkeeper. Bishop, who had often appeared before local magistrates for entertaining guests at late hours and disturbing the peace, was hanged on June 10, 1692. By the end of its fifth session the court had condemned more than 20 people to death, including Sarah Good, Rebecca Nurse, the Reverend George Burroughs, Mary Easty, John Proctor, and Martha Carrier. In all, 14 women and five men were hanged, and one man, Giles Corey, whose wife, Martha, was executed on September 22, was pressed to death for failing to complete his not-guilty plea.

Serious evidentiary questions plagued the entire trial process, and in September the court finally faced them. One such question had to do with "spectral evidence." Witches were thought to afflict their victims through spirits or specters visible to the bewitched. Because many pious people were accused, some

colonists came to believe that the devil could assume the form of any person, even an innocent one, and afflict someone. This revelation meant that the devil may have tricked the afflicted into accusing an innocent individual of practicing witchcraft. Such treachery could result in the execution of a virtuous person. The Court of Oyer and Terminer also called into question the wisdom of relying on confessed witches to implicate those who would not confess. Many executions had been based on this type of evidence. But in September, with confessors beginning to recant their confessions, the court finally realized the error of its ways.

By the end of October 1692, amid these and other difficulties, the governor and council had dissolved the special court. In 1693 the recently created Superior Court heard the unresolved cases that remained. After addressing the questions raised about spectral evidence and the confessors' testimonies, the new court reviewed its predecessor's indictments and declared half of them, including that of Tituba, invalid. Of the remaining cases, the court found only three people guilty, and the governor suspended their executions.

By the end of the Salem witchcraft trials in 1693, legal action had been taken against more than 140 people, and many more had been unofficially accused of practicing witchcraft. Within 10 years some participants disavowed or apologized for their participation in the affair. Samuel Sewall, for example, a judge who served on both courts, issued a public apology. One of the afflicted girls, Ann Putnam, also made a public statement acknowledging that she had been deceived by the devil and that some of those executed were probably not witches. Ultimately, the Massachusetts Bay Colony government attempted to make restitution to the families of witch-hunt victims by reversing the attainder against many executed witches. Some attempts were also made to compensate the accused or their families for losses suffered during their ordeals.

Although the witchcraft trials had concluded by 1694, they have never ceased to be a source of fascination. Authors and artists have been among those most inspired. Nathaniel Hawthorne, for example, a 19th-century descendant of Judge John Hathorne, referred often to the trials in his writing. According to myth, it was to distance himself from his infamous ancestor that the younger Hawthorne added the *w* to his name. In the 20th century numerous plays, movies, novels, and visual artworks featured Salem witchcraft, including Shirley Barker's *Peace, My Daughters* (1949) and Arthur Miller's *The Crucible* (1954). Modern-day Salem hosts dozens of witchcraft-related attractions.

As early as the 1890s, some 200 years after the witchcraft trials, Salem was earning a reputation as the Witch City. The Essex Institute offered an exhibition on the trials in 1892, and Salem manufacturers soon began using witch imagery on everything from skin cream to board games. In Salem today the high school mascot is a witch, witches on broomsticks adorn police cars, and interest in the trials is the cornerstone of the city's active tourist industry. Monuments to witchcraft trial victims exist in both Salem and Danvers, although Danvers has not embraced its witch-related history the way Salem has.

The most significant historical work on the Salem witchcraft trials was accomplished in the last four decades of the 20th century, when a vast array of books were published. In *Salem Possessed* (1974), for example, Paul Boyer and Stephen Nissenbaum explore the social context in which the witch-hunt accusations were made. Chadwick Hansen's *Witchcraft at Salem* (1969) examines the psychological side of the girls' afflictions, arguing that witchcraft was indeed practiced in colonial Massachusetts. Carol Karlsen looks at the Massachusetts history of witch prosecution in *The Devil in the Shape of a Woman* (1987) and uncovers a society grappling with economic, social, and religious tension. Finally, John Demos's *Entertaining Satan* (1982) seeks to understand the place that witchcraft occupied in 17th-century life and in colonial New England society. The Salem witchcraft trials remain one of the most frequently explored events in American colonial history.

Paul Boyer and Stephen Nissenbaum, eds., *The Salem Witchcraft Papers: Verbatim Transcripts of the Legal Documents of the Salem Witchcraft Outbreak of 1692* (1977); Richard Weisman, *Witchcraft, Magic, and Religion in 17th-Century Massachusetts* (1984).

Thomas E. Conroy

Shays's Rebellion

Shays's Rebellion, an armed uprising that occurred in Massachusetts in 1786–87, was a turning point in the era of the Confederation. The rebellion—or regulation, as it was called—was sparked by concerns over the payment of debts both private and public, the legal status of paper money, and the organization of the state courts. The outcome of this uprising and others of its kind spurred the formation and adoption of the Constitution of the United States in 1787–88.

Though such grievances were common throughout the Confederation, only in Massachusetts did this unrest grow to full-scale rebellion. In the winter of 1780–81, the legislature, which had long been controlled by the older, more affluent eastern towns, voted to repay the state's war debt through taxes imposed on land and the population, payable only in

Marker at site of 1787 Shays's Rebellion battle, Springfield, Mass.

hard currency. In response, protesters in the western counties first met in convention to draw up legislative petitions, and in 1782 the Hampshire County convention sent regulators to forcefully close the county courts, which had been in the hands of the entrenched elite for many years. This protest, named Ely's Rebellion after one of its leaders, Samuel Ely, was the immediate model for Shays's Rebellion.

In July 1786 new taxes were voted in by the state legislature to help pay the debt of the Confederation government. Daniel Shays, a farmer and former Continental officer from the hilltown of Pelham, was the reluctant leader of the regulation that broke out in August. Working with the county conventions, he attempted to keep the courts closed while negotiating with the state government for both legislative action and debtor pardons for his followers. The critical moment in this struggle came in January 1787, when, after attempting to seize the federal armory in Springfield, most of Shays's men were captured at Petersham. Shays himself escaped to Vermont, and though there were scattered disturbances until the following April, the rebellion was suppressed by a powerful army sent from Boston and led by the American general Benjamin Lincoln.

The rebellion's aftermath had as much significance as its origins. Incensed by the violation of civil rights in the suppression of the regulators, voters elected a new government that met many of the original demands of the conventions. The rebellion set the stage for the debate over the federal Constitution the

following year. Conservatives, who had been lukewarm to a new constitution, now embraced it passionately, while the regulators and their sympathizers stood uniformly opposed. This opposition explains why Massachusetts just barely ratified the Constitution in January 1788. Ironically the new federal government's broad powers, specifically in assuming state war debts, quieted grievances in Massachusetts. But if Shays's Rebellion rapidly faded from political memory, it remains both a textbook example of the breakdown of constitutional politics and a romantic symbol of social resistance to unregulated capital accumulation.

John L. Brooke, "'To the Quiet of the People': Revolutionary Settlements and Civil Unrest in Western Massachusetts, 1774–1789," *William and Mary Quarterly* 3d ser., 46 (1989); Richard Brown, "Shays's Rebellion and the Ratification of the Federal Constitution in Massachusetts," in Richard Beeman, Stephen Botein, and Edward C. Carter II, eds., *Beyond Confederation: Origins of the Constitution and American National Identity* (1987); Robert A. Gross, ed., *In Debt to Shays: The Bicentennial of an Agrarian Rebellion* (1993); David P. Szatmary, *Shays' Rebellion: The Making of an Agrarian Insurrection* (1980).

John L. Brooke

Sherman, Roger

(1721–1793) Statesman, drafter of the Declaration of Independence, U.S. congressman, U.S. senator. Roger Sherman was a merchant and statesman who figured prominently in the establishment of a federal government in the new United States. Born to poor farmers in Newton, Mass., Sherman later moved to Connecticut to pursue a career as a surveyor. His timely occupation brought considerable dividends, and Sherman, buoyed also by income from investment in his brother's general store, was soon the largest landowner in Litchfield County. In 1749 he married Elizabeth Hartwell with whom he had four children who survived infancy. That same year he began a career in public office that would continue until his death. Early offices as selectman, deputy, and justice of the peace in Litchfield County whetted his appetite for greater things, and in 1760, following Elizabeth's death, Sherman relocated to New Haven, the busy port city and co-capital of Connecticut.

Having been admitted to the bar in 1754, Sherman was soon appointed a New Haven County justice, an extraordinary honor for such a new arrival. He also remarried, fathering eight children with Rebecca Prescott, a woman 20 years his junior. From his position within the Connecticut judiciary, Sherman assumed an ever more active role in politics. During the Stamp Act controversy of 1765, Sherman helped draft the colony's instructions to its delegates to the Stamp Act Congress. A moderate radical, Sherman held views that were closely in step with public opinion, and in 1766 he was elected to Connecticut's upper house to replace a previous conservative legislator. Eight years later, Sherman was sent to the Continental Congress to represent the colony and, viewed by his fellow delegates as a sensible and clear-headed patriot, was selected to serve on the five-man committee that drafted the Declaration of Independence.

While retaining his political offices in Connecticut, Sherman continued to strut on the national stage. He helped to draft the Articles of Confederation and, in 1787, represented his state at the Constitutional Convention in Philadelphia. Now one of the most experienced statesmen in the country, Sherman made 185 speeches to the assembly and brokered countless backroom compromises to enable the constitutional negotiations to advance. His agenda, it seems, was to so strengthen the central government that it could operate successfully while preserving states' rights.

This agenda was parlayed into several strategic caveats in the Constitution that tipped the balance from a national government toward a federal system. Most notably, he engineered the famous Connecticut Compromise to secure equal representation among the states in the upper house. By blocking James Madison's effort to create proportionality in the Senate, Sherman struck a lasting blow for states' rights.

Always a respected figure in his home state, Sherman won election to the U.S. House of Representatives in the first Congress and then later to the U.S. Senate. From there he unsuccessfully resisted the creation of the Bill of Rights, fearing the unnecessary growth of federal power. He died of typhoid in 1793, after 45 years of public life. Honored by colleagues of all stripes at his death, Sherman is best remembered for having signed more of this nation's founding documents than any other person: the Declaration and Resolves of 1774, the Declaration of Independence, the Articles of Confederation, and the U.S. Constitution.

Roger Sherman Boardman, *Roger Sherman, Signer and Statesman* (1938); Julian P. Boyd, "Roger Sherman: Portrait of a Cordwainer Statesman," *New England Quarterly* 5, no. 2 (1932); Christopher Collier, *Roger Sherman's Connecticut: Yankee Politics and the American Revolution* (1971); Charles A. Goodrich, *Lives of the Signers to the Declaration of Independence* (1829); John G. Rommel, *Connecticut's Yankee Patriot: Roger Sherman* (1979).

Richard J. Bell

Smith, Captain John (1580–1631)

Colonial governor, explorer, cartographer. Captain John Smith was born in Willoughby, Lincolnshire, England, to a yeoman family. He received a good basic education through the patronage of the local lord of the manor and was apprenticed to a merchant in King's Lynn. Bored and longing to travel, Smith, still in his teens, went to France, where he fought in the religious wars. Later captured by Turks while fighting in Austria-Hungary, he escaped and traveled through much of Europe and in North Africa before returning to England. In addition to his well-known role in founding Virginia, Smith was involved in promoting English colonization of America broadly.

In 1607 Smith, recruited as an expert at surviving in alien cultures, joined the Virginia Company of London's first expedition to establish the colony of Jamestown. When the other councilors died or fell prey to the disease and despair that overcame the colony in its first year, Smith took charge, restored the colonists' health, and rebuilt the settlement's infrastructure. Smith also worked hard to establish relations with the Indians. After what was probably an adoption ceremony in which Smith thought Pocahontas had saved his life, Smith and the Native American leader Powhatan developed a mutual wariness and respect for one another. Nonetheless, Jamestown's leaders never trusted Smith, and when he was injured in 1609 by a powder explosion, his rivals used the incident as an excuse to ease him out of the colony.

Disappointed in Virginia, Smith became a promoter of colonization in the North. The Virginia Company of Plymouth's colony at Sagadahoc in Maine, founded in 1607, failed in one of the coldest winters of the century. From that time forward Norumbega, as the region was called, was considered undesirable. In 1614 two London merchants commissioned Smith to survey the eastern coast of North America and assess its economic potential. Smith mapped the northeastern portion of what is now the United States and renamed it New England, in part to distinguish the region from Virginia, whose climate and resources he represented as alien to English culture, and in part to designate it as a place in which settlers might live as they had in their homeland. In *A Description of New-England* (1616) Smith argued that fishing and farming, occupations suitable for England's solid middling people, would be the chief enterprises of the region and portrayed it as "the Paradise of these parts." His book has been credited with inspiring the founding of the first successful New England colonies.

We know Smith largely through his own books. He was the first participant-eyewitness to write a coherent history of the English colonies, and on the basis of his own observations he published the first accurate English maps of Virginia and New England. Smith was also the first to argue vehemently that the old gold-and-glory model of colonization was foolish; he recognized that only solid commodities created by the labor of immigrants would build true societies.

Philip L. Barbour, ed., *The Complete Works of Captain John Smith (1580–1631)*, 3 vols. (1986); Barbour, *The Three Worlds of Captain John Smith* (1964); Karen Ordahl Kupperman, ed., *Captain John Smith: A Select Edition of His Writings* (1988); J. A. Leo Lemay, *The American Dream of Captain John Smith* (1991).

Karen Ordahl Kupperman

Captain John Smith, from his map of New England (1616)

Sumner, Charles (1811–74)

Orator, politician, U.S. senator. Born in Boston to a prominent family, Charles Sumner graduated from Harvard College (1830) and Harvard Law School (1833). He traveled widely in Europe and met many leading political figures there before entering public life. Before his election to the U.S. Senate in 1851 he practiced law and argued several significant cases before the Massachusetts Supreme Court. He became one of the nation's most radical opponents of slavery and most consistent proponents of full constitutional rights for African Americans South and North.

Sumner was first exposed to the abolitionists William Lloyd Garrison and Wendell Phillips as a Harvard undergraduate. His own involvement in antislavery activities began in the 1840s, when he led New Englanders in opposing the Mexican War (1846–48). Believing that the war was being fought to gain additional slave territories, Sumner eloquently argued before the Massachusetts Supreme Court that military enlistments for the war were illegal. His antiwar statements brought him to the attention of the state's political leaders. Also a proponent of prison and educational reforms and world peace, he ran for Congress on the Free-Soil ticket in 1848. The following year he argued before the Massachusetts Supreme Court that the state's black children were entitled to attend school with whites, and in 1850 he vehemently attacked the Fugitive Slave Act, which compelled all citizens under threat of imprisonment to assist in the capture and return of runaway slaves.

Sumner was instrumental in moving the slavery debate into the political mainstream. His biting oratory, his unswerving commitment to the cause, and most of all his willingness to attack the privileged world of his forebears made him the ideal candidate for a movement that desperately sought status, legitimacy, and a spokesman of stature. With the help of Henry Wilson, the self-made Natick Cobbler, and other political insiders, Sumner was elected to the U.S. Senate by a coalition of conscience consisting of Whigs, antislavery Democrats, and Free-Soilers. Once in Washington he delivered a series of blistering tirades against slavery. The most explosive of these was a three-day-long speech, "The Crime against Kansas," delivered in May 1856, in which Sumner attacked the Kansas-Nebraska Act of 1854. Sumner described the act, which allowed slavery in Kansas and asked settlers to decide whether the territory would join the union as a slave or free state, as "the rape of virgin territory, compelling it to the baneful embrace of slavery." He also called the authors of the act, Senators Andrew P. Butler and Stephen A. Douglas, swindlers. Two days later Preston S. Brooks, a congressman from South Carolina and Butler's nephew, stormed into the Senate chamber and mercilessly beat Sumner with a cane.

Severely injured, Sumner was unable to return to the Senate for three years in spite of his almost unanimous reelection in 1857. His vacant seat became a potent visual symbol of intensifying sectional hostility. "The Crime against Kansas" and "The Crime against Sumner" became rallying cries of the newly formed Republican Party, which exploited the event to help galvanize northern public opinion against slavery and the slave power.

With Lincoln's election in 1860 Sumner became chairman of the Senate Committee on Foreign Relations (1861–71) and was instrumental in keeping England from joining the Civil War on the southern side. Sumner urged Lincoln to repeal all fugitive slave laws, abolish slavery in the District of Columbia, and create a Freedman's Bureau to assist emancipated slaves. Sumner thought Lincoln was well intentioned though slow to initiate reform, but he attacked outright Andrew Johnson's plan for moderate Reconstruction. Sumner helped form the radical wing of the Republican Party and called for a Reconstruction plan that would completely reorganize southern society by redistributing the land of former slaveholders, granting full political rights to all native-born white and black males, and opening public schools to all races. Sumner's devotion to principles placed him at odds with Presidents Johnson (whose impeachment proceedings he supported) and Grant (who removed Sumner as chairman of the Foreign Relations Committee after he had helped defeat Grant's proposed annexation of Santo Domingo) and with his own party, which in the 1870s was becoming the champion of business interests. Still plagued by his caning injuries and disaffected by his party, Sumner died of a heart attack in Washington, D.C.

David Herbert Donald, *Charles Sumner and the Coming of the Civil War* (1981 [1960]); Eric Foner, *Free Soil, Free Labor, Free Men: The Ideology of the Republican Party before the Civil War* (1995); Charles Sumner, *Charles Sumner: His Complete Works*, introduction by George Frisbie Hoar, 20 vols. (1969).

Richard Kazarian

Town Histories The writing of town histories began in the early 19th century as a means of preserving the past at a time of deep transition in the social history of New England. Although in centennial sermons ministers had sometimes briefly recounted the history of a town or a congregation, the earliest town history to be printed as a book was John Farmer's *An Historical Memoir of Billerica* (1816). In 1791 a group of Bostonians founded the Massachusetts Historical Society, an institution whose mission included publishing articles on local history as well as preserving original documents and reprinting them in its ongoing collections. But it was not until the

1830s, when many towns witnessed the passing of the revolutionary generation and celebrated the bicentennials of their settlement, that the genre of the town history took off. Fourteen such books dealing with Massachusetts towns were published in that decade, another 17 in the 1840s, and many more in the years thereafter.

These undertakings occurred within a wider context of antiquarian and genealogical activity. The Essex Historical Society, the first historical society devoted to a county, was founded in 1821, followed by the New England Historic Genealogical Society in 1845; other state and local societies were established throughout the region in subsequent decades. Beginning with the records of Connecticut in 1850, local historians, institutions, and even town and city governments launched efforts to print colonial records and to edit and publish important diaries, letters, and early writings, such as Massachusetts governor John Winthrop's settlement journals, first issued as *History of New England* in 1825.

As a genre the town history drew on three narrative traditions, the oldest being that of the annal, which dates back to antiquity. The influence of this tradition is readily apparent in such works as Joseph Felt's *Annals of Salem* (1827) and more broadly in the efforts of early antiquarians to record the dates of public events and arrange them in sequence. A second tradition, having many English precedents from the 18th century, was that of the topographical description or account of the natural history, architecture, relics, and curiosities of a locality. Thus did 19th-century town histories often begin with a chapter on topography and move on to discuss buildings that had survived from earlier times. A third tradition was that of the ecclesiastical or church history, exemplified in Cotton Mather's massive *Magnalia Christi Americana* (1702). Invariably, town histories detailed the founding of churches and provided biographies of former, for the most part Puritan or Congregational, ministers.

After 1840 another common feature of these histories was the inclusion of genealogical information on the founding families of a town and their descendants. These books almost always incorporated documents—records of town and church meetings, land transactions, and vital statistics; personal letters; diaries—whose originals are now lost. They remain an indispensable source of knowledge. Native Americans make an appearance in some early town histories but usually only in the context of the colonial wars. The Revolution and its heroes always held an important place in the story.

The publication of town histories was most

certainly connected to the commemoration of anniversaries, but much deeper social forces were also at work in these years, transforming the nature and significance of the town. New Englanders had been migrating west ever since the end of the Revolution. As the decline of the New England rural economy and the pace of migration accelerated, once strong intergenerational family ties began to weaken. In some towns the connections between past and present were ruptured by the arrival of textile mills and the advent of the railroad. In response to the demand for workers that these technological changes created, immigrants from Europe soon flooded the region. Political and religious conflict, especially the schism between orthodox Congregationalism and newly emergent Unitarianism, made cultural homogeneity a thing of the past.

A sense of loss and a palpable effort to stanch the flood of change through the power of memory pervade 19th-century town histories. David N. Camp's *History of New Britain* (Conn.) (1889) proposes, for example, "to preserve the memory of local events, traditions, and enterprise, and of notable persons, to glean from old records, from perishable manuscripts, crumbling monuments, and the memory of the aged, material which would soon be lost." These words could have been written by any of the authors of 19th-century town histories, all of whom felt that the present was becoming unhinged from the past—and all of whom wondered, amid the hustle and bustle of American society, who would pause to read their books. We ourselves should read them with careful attention. Although they celebrate the moral and political character of the region, they are far from being hymns to progress or expressions of ancestor worship.

As a new, "scientific" way of writing history emerged from research universities, the earlier genre became vulnerable to satire. Americans began to mock their Victorian ancestors. John P. Marquand's novel *The Late George Apley* (1937), notable in this respect, includes a scene in which the eponymous Apley reads a dry, pointless paper on the history of a single plot of land to the assembled members of an upper-crust Boston literary society. Within this context town history was interesting only for what it disclosed about the development of institutions, especially town settlement and town government. Dormant between World War I and the 1950s, the genre underwent a spectacular revival after 1960.

Emerging in tandem with the renewal of social history and a resurgence of interest in the colonial period was a new field, historical demography. Inspired by the work of French social historians, scholars studying early America put the genealogical information in the old histories to new uses in analyzing family structures and their psychological and social dimensions. The information about family structure assembled by Philip J. Greven, Jr., in *Four Generations: Population, Land, and Family in Colonial Andover, Massachusetts* (1970) undercut long-standing arguments about differences between early America and early modern Europe. Continuity, not disruption or change, marked the social experience of the New England colonists, an argument strongly advanced in Kenneth A. Lockridge's *A New England Town: The First Hundred Years, Dedham, Massachusetts, 1636–1736* (1970), which employed the anthropological concept of peasant culture. David Grayson Allen's explicitly comparative *In English Ways: The Movement of Societies and the Transferral of English Local Law and Custom to Massachusetts Bay in the 17th Century* (1981) also made the argument for continuity.

In the hands of these scholars local history was not an end in itself or a genre arising from a social crisis within small-scale communities but an experimental means of asking larger questions about the organization of the entire society. The method led to a question none of these studies could resolve: Which, if any, of the patterns uncovered in a particular case study were typical of the whole? The new social history diverged from 19th-century antiquarianism in seeking larger social patterns as well as in its concern for social conflict rooted in economic difference. In *Salem Possessed: The Social Origins of Witchcraft* (1974) Paul Boyer and Stephen Nissenbaum linked the Salem witch-hunt of 1692 to a factionalism based on economics; in this work and in local studies of towns during the Great Awakening of the 1730s and 1740s, the thesis emerged that economic opportunity began to diminish by the end of the 17th century. This argument was extended in a study of Boston and other 18th-century urban communities, Gary B. Nash's *The Urban Crucible: Social Change, Political Consciousness, and the Origins of the American Revolution* (1979). Wishing to approach history "from the bottom up," Nash focused on the discontents of ordinary people and the ways in which they gradually challenged an ethos of deference.

Other social historians turned their attention to the mill towns and industrial cities that emerged in the 19th century, exploring the shape of the new economic order and its consequences. *Boston's Immigrants, 1790–1865: A Study in Acculturation* (1941) by Oscar Handlin was a pioneering volume of this kind. Thomas Dublin's study of "mill girls," *Women at Work: The Transformation of Work and Community in Lowell, Massachusetts, 1826–1860* (1979), shifted the focus to women.

The town histories written after 1960 by professional historians and those of their 19th-century predecessors differed not only in their research strategies and organizing themes but also in their politics. The role of the genre in the earlier period was paradoxically both liberal and conservative: conservative in imagining continuity and homogeneity, liberal in commemorating the political and moral activism typical of Yankee culture. Town histories written after 1960, by contrast, were not written for a popular audience, and few invoke a sense of place or region. While the new social history was democratic and inclusionary in its sympathies, the narrative techniques of the academic case study limited the reach of its message.

David D. Hall and Alan Taylor, "Reassessing the Local History of New England," in *New England: A Bibliography of Its History*, ed. Roger Parks (1989).

David Hall

Trumbull Family

The Trumbulls were a distinguished family from colonial, revolutionary, and early national Connecticut descended from John Trumble, who migrated to Roxbury, Mass., in 1639. Jonathan Trumbull (1710–85) of Lebanon graduated from Harvard in 1727 with designs on a ministerial career. The death of his older brother, however, prompted him to enter into the family mercantile enterprise. First elected to the General Assembly in 1733, he used his political connections to secure lucrative military contracts during the colonial wars. While the return of peace in the 1760s and overextended credit led him to the brink of financial bankruptcy, his political fortunes flourished. He was elected governor in 1769. An early supporter of the patriot cause, Trumbull played a major role throughout the war in provisioning American troops. In 1784 he declined another term as governor, in part because of failing health. General George Washington gave him his famous nickname, Brother Jonathan, which was popularized as a name for plain-speaking rural Yankees in Royall Tyler's play, *The Contrast*. Among Jonathan Trumbull's children were Joseph (1737–78), a member of the Connecticut Committee of Correspondence and commissary-general of the American army; Jonathan; and John.

Jonathan Trumbull (1740–1809) graduated from Harvard in 1759 and entered the family mercantile enterprise. During the Revolution Congress appointed him the first comptroller of the Treasury, and in 1781 he became secretary to General Washington. He sat in the first three Congresses, being elected Speaker in 1791. After brief service in the U.S. Senate, he was elected deputy governor in 1796. An ardent Federalist, he succeeded to the governorship a year later upon the death of Oliver Wolcott and was reelected annually until his own death.

John Trumbull the artist (1756–1843) graduated from Harvard in 1773 and after brief military service decided upon an artistic career despite his father's admonition that "Connecticut is not Athens." Studying in London in the 1780s under Benjamin West, he began work on a series of grand historical paintings of the American Revolution that would be his claim to fame. These included *The Death of General Warren at the Battle of Bunker's Hill* (1786) and *The Declaration of Independence, July 4, 1776* (1787). His inability to support himself as an artist in America prompted a return to Europe in 1794 for a decade of work on the Jay Treaty Commission and artistic endeavors. In 1817 Congress commissioned him to execute the four life-sized Revolutionary War scene paintings that still decorate the walls of the capitol rotunda in Washington. From 1817 to 1836, he also served as president of the American Academy of the Fine Arts.

Other prominent members of the Trumbull family included Benjamin Trumbull (1735–1820) and John Trumbull (1750–1831), both first cousins to the elder governor Trumbull. Benjamin served as Congregational minister in North Haven from 1760 to 1820 and was the author of *A Complete History of Connecticut . . . to the Year 1764* (2 vols., 1818). John Trumbull gained notoriety for his literary talents, before abandoning belles lettres for a legal career. One of the so-called Connecticut Wits, he is most famous for *The Progress of Dullness* (1772–73), a satire on academic life, and *McFingal* (1775–82), a humorous narrative of the ill fortunes of a Boston loyalist.

The Trumbull family influenced the politics of the revolutionary and early national periods as well as the popular imagery of that period in art and literature. Thus they blended the politics and cultural expression of Federalism, which defined in part the image of Connecticut and the region.

Helen A. Cooper, *John Trumbull: The Hand and Spirit of the Painter* (1982); Victor E. Gimmestad, *John Trumbull* [poet] (1974); John W. Ifkovic, *Connecticut's Nationalist Revolutionary: Jonathan Trumbull, Junior* (1977); Glenn Weaver, *Jonathan Trumbull, Connecticut's Merchant Magistrate* (1956).

Robert J. Imholt

Utopian Communities

The desire to create a more perfect society has motivated countless New Englanders to found communities that stem from a utopian vision. Such idealized settlements have attempted to combine a novel social arrangement with the traditional elements of community, family, and religion. Differing in size, philosophy, longevity, and inspirational source, New England's utopian communities have provided an alternative to what are perceived to be the shortcomings of established society.

Early utopian groups challenged mainstream religious structures and practices. Best known among them from the revolutionary period are the Shakers, who originated in England and were led to America in 1774 by Ann Lee, the founder; this celibate sect developed a society based on communitywide bonds rather than individual ties. By the late 18th century Shaker leaders had established communities in New York, Connecticut, Massachusetts, New Hampshire, and Maine, one of which (at Sabbathday Lake in New Gloucester, Maine) remains active.

In the 1840s a rapidly increasing number of utopian experiments grappled with social and economic reform, attempting to create alternatives to the rising capitalist, individualistic, materialistic society. Transcendentalist philosophy inspired Brook Farm (West Roxbury, Mass., 1841–47). A joint-stock venture under the leadership of the social reformer George Ripley, Brook Farm attracted the attention of numerous literary and religious leaders, including Bronson Alcott, Charles Dana, Ralph Waldo Emerson, Margaret Fuller, Nathaniel Hawthorne, Theodore Parker, and Orestes Augustus Brownson. From 1843 until 1845 Brook Farm was a center of the Fourierist movement, based on a utopian theory developed by the French social reformer Charles Fourier.

At Fruitlands near Harvard, Mass., in 1842, Bronson Alcott, Charles Lane, and Henry Wright sought a self-sufficient, agricultural lifestyle. Because of personality conflicts, however, their experiment failed after only eight months. Adin Ballou's Hopedale Community (near Milford, Mass., 1841–56) offered a life of "practical Christianity." John Humphrey Noyes developed the Putney (Vt.) Society in 1841, a semicommunal group that preceded Noyes's New York–based Oneida Community, which during the 1860s and 1870s maintained a branch in Wallingford, Conn.

Several utopian communities were founded in New England in the late 19th century and early 20th. Although little known, these enclaves document the continued attempt to work cooperatively in an individualistic society. Examples in Massachusetts include Adonai-Shomo (1861), Northampton (1842–46), the Esoteric Fraternity (1870s), New Clairvaux (1897), and several collective farms. In Maine the Industrial Brotherhood (Thomaston, ca. 1900) envisioned cooperative stores, colonies, and cities. Frank Sandford organized the Church of the Living God and built a community known as Shiloh (Durham, Maine,

1893). Sandford's vision of sailing to Jerusalem with his followers came to an end when he failed to provide adequate supplies for the transatlantic voyage and several passengers died during the journey.

In the 20th century the search for utopia faded from public view but did not disappear. The movement regained visibility in the 1960s with the establishment of communes like Sunrise Hill (Greenfield, Mass., 1966). Inspired by the same issues as their 19th-century predecessors, these communes endeavored to reform class, gender, racial, and work relations while dealing with the same problems that had plagued earlier experiments, including financial difficulties, personality clashes, and hostility from the surrounding community.

Despite challenges the quest for utopia continues to be a vital facet of New England life. In the 1980s and 1990s numerous communities were established, many of them religiously based, such as the Messianic Communities in Hyannis, Mass., and Rutland, Vt., and Island Pond, Vt. A long-standing theme in New England life, the desire to create utopia remains strong.

Robert S. Fogarty, *Dictionary of American Communal and Utopian History* (1980); Rosabeth Moss Kanter, *Commitment and Community: Communes and Utopias in Sociological Perspective* (1972); Timothy Miller, *American Communes, 1860–1960: A Bibliography* (1990); Donald E. Pitzer, ed., *America's Communal Utopias* (1997).

Elizabeth A. De Wolfe

Vermont

The 14th state to join the union, in 1791, Vermont covers 9,614 square miles and had 608,827 residents in 2000. Montpelier, with a population of 8,035, is the smallest capital city in the United States.

Vermont's history and culture are closely tied to its geology and topography. Created by glacial action, the state's rocky terrain is dominated by the Green Mountains—or *verts monts*, the French term from which Vermont got its name—and interrupted by long, narrow valleys dotted with lakes. The mountains, running north to south through the center of the state, controlled settlement patterns, funneling people up the Connecticut River valley to the east and into the Vermont Valley to the west.

The first human inhabitants, Paleo-Indians, appeared some 12,000 years ago in the heavily forested area of what is today northern New England and lower Canada. Banding together, these peoples formed the Abenaki nation. By the early 17th century the Western Abenaki, engaged in farming as well as traditional hunter-gatherer activities, had established as many as 20 villages on accessible waterways in the northwestern regions of Vermont.

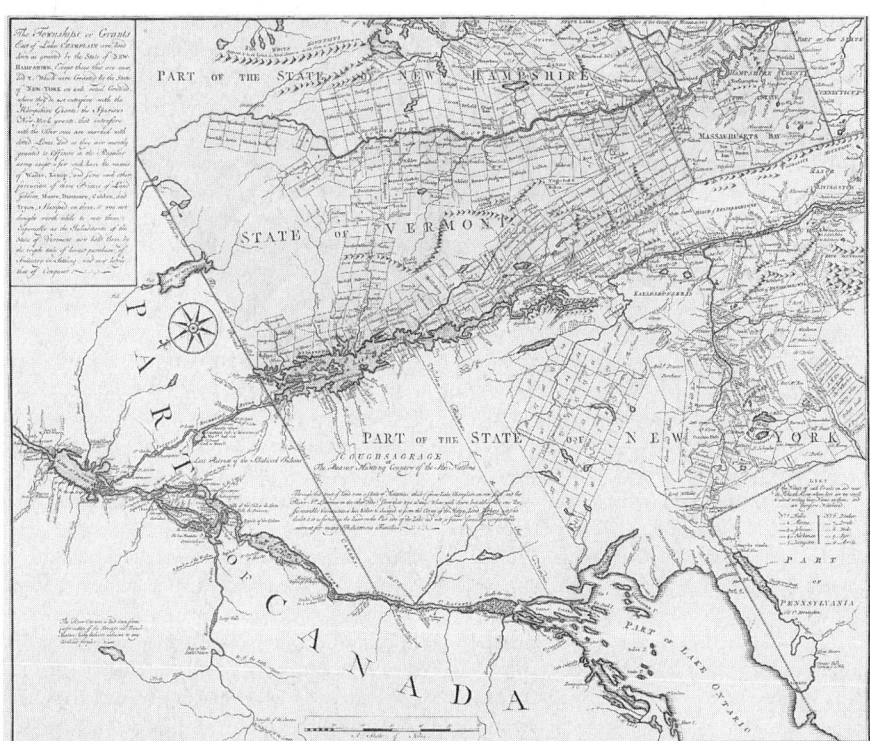

In this 1780 map of Vermont, drawn in Amsterdam, Vermont was identified as a state and the map was oriented with north in the lower left (southeast)

The 4,000-year-old Abenaki way of life was disrupted by the coming of the French. Initial contact probably occurred in the 1640s, when French trading sites were established along the eastern shore of Lake Champlain. In 1664–65 colonists from France built and occupied the first permanent European settlement in Vermont, Fort Saint Anne, on Isle La Motte. While the French were making inroads in Vermont's northern reaches, their English counterparts were slowly moving northward from Massachusetts. In 1724 the British established their first settlement in Vermont at Fort Dummer on the west bank of the Connecticut River. Twenty-five years after that fort's founding, Benning Wentworth, royal governor of the New Hampshire colony, began selling land grants in the future Vermont, most of which were purchased by speculators from Connecticut and Massachusetts.

Settlement of the territory was delayed by the French and Indian War (1754–63). Once the French had retreated into Canada in late 1759, newcomers gradually began to arrive from lower New England. The Treaty of Paris granted the area to the British in 1763. A land-ownership dispute soon broke out between New Hampshire and New York, whose charter claimed all land west of the Connecticut River. King George III upheld New York's claim in 1764, and that colony imposed burdensome fees on territorial residents.

Prominent in both legal negotiations and armed skirmishes over the land were the grants' largest resident speculators, the Allen family. As general agent for the New Hampshire titleholders, Ethan Allen organized a defense that resulted in a loss for the grantees. That decision prompted him to form the Green Mountain Boys, a citizens' militia. Led by Allen and other large landholders, these militiamen protected recalcitrant grantees from eviction and discouraged "Yorkers" from becoming settlers. Growing tension between Great Britain and its colonies eventually diverted the Green Mountain Boys from the land war to revolutionary activities, however. When a petition for statehood was rejected by the newly established government after independence was declared in 1776, grantees declared their own independence on January 15, 1777, and inaugurated the Republic of Vermont.

The new republic adopted a constitution that differed from all others of the period by prohibiting slavery and granting universal manhood suffrage. For 14 years the republic acted as a sovereign power—coining money, maintaining a militia, and naturalizing citizens. Vermont also conducted a separate foreign policy, entering into negotiations with the British in the 1780s for readmission to the empire but always avoiding annexation. On March 4, 1791, after striking a deal with New York for title to the long-disputed lands, Vermont finally gained its statehood.

During the next two decades Vermont's population increased by 150 percent, jumping from 85,000 in 1791 to 218,000 in 1810. A flurry of road building (1795–1810) and the construction of a canal near Bellows Falls in 1802 further expedited settlement. Lumbering and potash production for the processing of soap and lye provided consistent employment for all. The development of gristmills, sawmills, tanneries, and quarrying operations added to the manufacturing capacity of the state.

A brisk trade with Canada also augmented Vermont's growing prosperity. To avoid involvement in the Napoleonic Wars, Thomas Jefferson issued a series of embargo acts (1807–10) prohibiting trade with either France or Britain. In the beginning these measures served only to drive the thriving Canada-Vermont trade underground, but when the United States was finally drawn into the War of 1812, Vermont's economy collapsed. By 1820, between the declining fertility of farmland and bad weather, Vermont's farming boom, too, had come to an end.

The opening of the canals in the 1820s, especially the Champlain and Erie Canals, resulted in the loss of grain markets to the West and encouraged emigration from Vermont to western farmlands. During this period more people left the state than were born in it. Population figures remained stable, however, thanks to an influx of newcomers, many of them non-Yankee or foreign-born. To fill the economic void left by declining farm production and markets, Vermonters sought other means of invigorating the economy. During this time Vermont's stonecutting, iron-casting, and furniture-making industries developed.

Sheep became Vermont's staple crop and its major industry. In 1811 William Jarvis, U.S. consul to Portugal, surreptitiously exported 3,000 merino sheep to the United States, 300 of which went to his farm in Vermont. Noted for the high quality of their wool, merinos flourished in rocky Vermont. In the 1830s and 1840s Vermont was a major supplier and processor of wool, which brought prosperity to those involved in its production. At the height of the merino craze in the 1840s, sheep outnumbered humans six to one. In the 1850s the lure of western lands better suited to large-scale ranching and the abolition of protective tariffs on wool threatened the profitability of the sheep industry; by 1870 it was moribund.

Between 1820 and 1850 economic uncertainty and the state's changing social complexion created an unstable environment in Vermont. Opposition to Masonry proved strong in the state, which cast its seven electoral votes for the anti-Masonic presidential candidate in 1832 and elected an anti-Masonic governor (1831–35). Anti-immigrant sentiment rumbled, as foreigners and non-Yankees moved into the state to work in the developing extractive industries (marble, granite, and slate), in lumbering, and on the railroads. The large influx of French Canadian refugees fleeing in the wake of the unsuccessful patriot uprising in Quebec (1837–38) also exacerbated nativist feelings.

Vermont did not escape the religious revivalism of the period, producing its share of evangelists and sects, among them Joseph Smith, founder of Mormonism, and John Humphrey Noyes, leader of the Perfectionists. To facilitate another type of social reform, Vermonters established their first temperance society in 1828. By 1852 the public outcry against drink had led to a statewide prohibition of alcohol sales that was not repealed until 1902.

In the 1830s canal fever gave way to passion for the railroad. Vermonters decided that a rail network was key to the state's economic revival. The state's first railroad was not completed until 1848, however. It was a mixed blessing. While transporting perishable farm goods, cut stone, and lumber to distant markets, the railroad also made it easier for opportunity seekers to leave the state. Between 1850 and 1900 two of every five Vermonters did just that. As goods and people flowed out of the state, immigrants flowed in. A new potential source of income, tourists—bound for mineral springs and spas—also arrived by train.

Another railroad, of the underground variety, changed Vermont's way of life. Antislavery sentiment dominated Vermont's social concerns. Having banned the practice in its constitution, Vermont actively campaigned against slavery. The Vermont Anti-Slavery Society was launched in 1834. In 1843, as if anticipating the Fugitive Slave Act of 1850, the legislature made it illegal to recapture escaped slaves in Vermont. In 1857 it defied federal laws again, declaring that any slave entering the state was free. In 1860 Vermonters cast 75.8 percent of their votes for Lincoln; less than 20 percent went to the Vermont-born Steven A. Douglas.

In its enthusiasm for the Union cause, Vermont appropriated $1 million to support the war effort. Of a population of 315,000, some 35,000 Vermonters enlisted. The equipping of troops with rifles, gunpowder, and woolen cloth gave a big boost to the economy, establishing the basis for postwar textile and machine-tool industries. But high casualties—5,000 dead and an equal number disabled—and many veterans' unwillingness to return home provoked widespread concern for

Vermont's agricultural future and rural way of life. The Vermont Board of Agriculture was formed in 1870 to help the state shift from farming to dairying.

By the 1890s Vermont had assumed a leadership role in the production of butter and cheese in New England. Thirty years later dairying was the mainstay of Vermont's agricultural economy, a reality reinforced by the fact that some 83,000 more cows than people resided in the state. The introduction in the 1950s of the bulk tank car to transport milk allowed larger dairying concerns to expand their markets further. As late as 1980 more than 80 percent of Vermont's population was engaged in dairying or dairy-related activities.

Near the turn of the 20th century, while Vermonters searched for viable ways to earn a living, the landscape of the Green Mountain State underwent a major change. Primarily owing to the logging boom of the 1870s and 1880s, land that in 1790 had been 75 percent forested was 75 percent cleared. Isolated voices that had long been calling for the protection and conservation of a vanishing Vermont landscape were finally heard. The Board of Agriculture joined the railroads in promoting tourism, which was seen as an environmentally sound and economically profitable source of income. Vermont established the Bureau of Publicity in 1911 to assist in promotional efforts.

The development of the tourist trade was profoundly affected by the automobile, which opened the entire state to visitation and created new industries designed to serve a mobile clientele. Tourist cabins, roadside stands, and gas stations sprouted along major roadways. Summer camps and resorts developed even in Vermont's remotest areas.

The Vermont Commission on Country Life, created in 1928, published *Rural Vermont: A Program for the Future*, which recommended land-use planning and conservation. Polluted lakes and rivers should be cleaned, abandoned farmlands reforested, and scenic highways built. Not everyone relished the idea of Vermont becoming a four-season tourist attraction, however. After three years of discussion (1933–36) a statewide referendum defeated the idea of a Green Mountain Parkway. The state nonetheless established a service in 1941 to encourage the production of Vermont-made arts and crafts and in 1946 created *Vermont Life*, a magazine promoting the notion that "Vermont Is a Way of Life" nationwide.

With the help of the Civilian Conservation Corps (1933–42), Vermont constructed many assets of its outdoor recreation program: campgrounds and hiking trails, along with ski trails, lodges, and lifts. The interstate highway system (1957–82) further facilitated tourism

and the ski industry but also put an end to the state's self-imposed isolation. Between 1960 and 1990 Vermont's population increased by nearly 45 percent. Vermont became a magnet state, exceeding both California and Florida in attracting new immigrants.

Concerned by this influx of newcomers and tourists, the legislature passed a series of statutes that placed Vermont in the vanguard of the national struggle to control growth and preserve the environment. In 1968 Vermont passed the Billboard Law, which regulated outdoor advertising. Two years later Vermont's Land Use and Development Act (known as Act 250) established a statewide process for dealing with environmental and land-use problems. The Beverage Container Deposit Law was enacted in 1972. And in 1988 Vermont passed Act 200 to encourage consistent local, regional, and state agency planning. Known as the Growth Management Law, it provided incentives for local and regional planning to protect communities, farmland, wildlife, and overall quality of life.

Late in the 20th century two landmark bills were crafted in response to rulings handed down by the Vermont Supreme Court. In 1997 came the passage of Act 60, which restructured the state's funding of public schools in an effort to reduce economic inequities between rich and poor communities. In 2000 the legislature passed a law, the first of its kind in the United States, creating marriagelike civil unions for gay and lesbian couples.

There continues to be tension between the protection of Vermont's environment and the promotion of economic development. And controversy over civil unions is not likely to dissipate anytime soon. Even the merits of a supposedly nonpolluting industry such as tourism have come under scrutiny. In 1993 and again in 2004 the National Trust for Historic Preservation designated Vermont an endangered historic treasure. What both the trust and many Vermonters fear is the loss of the small-town or rural lifestyle preserved in Vermont's 237 towns, 49 villages, nine cities, three townships, three gores, two unorganized towns, and one grant, which today are home to slightly more than half a million people.

Jan Albers, *Hands on the Land: A History of the Vermont Landscape* (2000); Lynn A. Bonfield and Mary C. Morrison, *Roxana's Children: The Biography of a 19th-Century Vermont Family* (1995); Howard Coffin, *Full Duty: Vermonters in the Civil War* (1993); Nancy L. Gallagher, *Breeding Better Vermonters: The Eugenics Project in the Green Mountain State* (1999); J. Kevin Graffagnino, Samuel B. Hand, and Gene Sessions, eds., *Vermont Voices, 1609 through the 1900s: A Documentary History of the Green Mountain State* (1999); William A. Haviland and Marjory W. Power, *The Original Vermonters: Native Inhabitants, Past and Present* (1994); Robert E. Shalhope, *Bennington and the*

Green Mountain Boys: The Emergence of Liberal Democracy in Vermont, 1760–1850 (1996); Robert Sobel, *Coolidge: An American Enigma* (1998).

Gainor B. Davis

War of 1812 On June 18, 1812, following years of uneasy relations between the two nations, the United States declared war on Great Britain. The issues dividing the countries included the Royal Navy's impressment of American sailors and violation of neutral rights during the Napoleonic Wars, British agents' incitement of the western Indians against American settlers, and American expansionism in Canada and Florida.

The war proved extremely unpopular in New England, one of the last bastions of Federalist strength. At the heart of the opposition was the reliance of New England's maritime industry on trade with the British Empire. In the short run the war greatly harmed the New England economy. This dissension led the New England states to cooperate less fully than they might have with the administration in Washington. New England governors were slow in organizing state militias, and smuggling between Canada and the United States along the New England border was prevalent.

Much of the military action took place at sea, and although New Englanders may not have been enthusiastic about the war, they did celebrate notable American naval victories. In August 1812 the frigate *Constitution* sailed from Boston and made naval history in the months that followed, capturing HMS *Guerrière* on August 19, *Java* on November 29, and HMS *Levant* and HMS *Cyane* on February 20, 1815. These victories made the *Constitution* a national icon. Another Boston frigate did not fare so well, however. On June 1, 1813, the *Chesapeake* was taken by HMS *Shannon* off the coast of Marblehead, Mass.

One of the most decisive battles of the war took place on Lake Champlain, located between Vermont and New York. On September 11, 1814, an American squadron under the command of Commodore Thomas Macdonough defeated a British squadron. This important victory prevented the British from taking control of Lake Champlain, which would have allowed them to launch a campaign down the Hudson River valley. British forces also harassed the New England coast. In September 1814 they landed near Castine, Maine, and advanced a short distance inland. The Royal Navy was also active in Long Island Sound and in the waters off the Massachusetts island of Nantucket.

New England's unhappiness with the war culminated in the Hartford Convention. Delegates from all the New England states met between December 15, 1814, and January 5, 1815, at Hartford to express their grievances and propose a series of resolutions supporting states' rights. Their proposals arrived in Washington when the war had just ended and the news of Andrew Jackson's victory at New Orleans was being celebrated. The seemingly disloyal behavior manifested at Hartford, coupled with New England's reluctance to support the war, hurt the region's image in the eyes of the rest of America.

The war helped New England economically, however, by hastening development of its textile industry. Unable to invest in maritime enterprises during the war, New Englanders placed considerable capital in mills. This phenomenon has sometimes been referred to as the movement "from wharf to waterfall."

The war came to an inconclusive end in 1815. Great Britain and the United States agreed to begin peace negotiations in January 1814, but the talks were delayed until July. Both nations entered the talks with unrealistic demands. The United States wanted an end to all objectionable British maritime practices and demanded cessions of Canadian territory. Britain sought a neutral Native American buffer state in the American Northwest and wanted to revise both the American-Canadian boundary and the 1783 Treaty of Paris, which had established U.S. independence. In a treaty signed at Ghent, Belgium, on December 24, 1814, they finally agreed to return to the antebellum status quo. The treaty was ratified by Britain four days later and by the U.S. Senate on February 16, 1815. Between these dates a final battle was fought on January 8, when a British army landed at the mouth of the Mississippi River and was defeated near New Orleans by forces under the command of Andrew Jackson.

Although the Treaty of Ghent failed to secure U.S. maritime rights, these rights were not seriously threatened during the century of peace that followed in Europe (from 1815 until World War I), and Britain never again pursued its disputes with the United States to the point of risking another war. The United States did not conquer Canada, but Native American opposition to American expansion in the Northwest and Southwest was broken. Both the United States and Canada emerged from the war with an increased sense of national purpose and awareness.

James M. Banner, Jr., *To the Hartford Convention: The Federalist Party and the Origins of Party Politics in Massachusetts, 1789–1815* (1970); William S. Dudley, ed., *The Naval War of 1812: A Documentary History*, 2 vols. (1985–92); John C. Fredriksen, comp., *Free Trade and Sailors' Rights: A Bibliography of the War of 1812* (1985); Donald R. Hickey, *The War of 1812: A Forgotten Conflict* (1989).

William M. Fowler, Jr.

Warren, Mercy Otis (1728–1814) Historian, playwright, political satirist. Mercy Otis Warren came of age at the center of the revolutionary maelstrom. Born in Barnstable, Mass., Warren received an unusual education for a girl. She was privately tutored along with her oldest brother, James Otis, in Greek and Roman history as well as English literature. James was a dominant force in her life. Even after leaving home for Harvard College he continued to guide his sister's reading and encourage her intellectual interests. Warren's life was typical in other respects, however. In 1754 she married a substantial gentleman from nearby Plymouth, moved into his household, and bore five sons over the next 12 years.

James Otis emerged as an early patriot leader, but by the late 1760s he had become mentally unstable and was unable to continue his leadership role in the resistance movement. Warren carried on her brother's work in her own way. With the encouragement of her husband and family friends such as John Adams, Warren began to employ her literary skills for the patriot cause. Writing anonymously, she published political satires like *The Adulateur* (1773), *The Defeat* (1773), and *The Group* (1775), which appeared in the form of plays. Newspapers printed her poems, most of which were largely political. In 1776, inspired by the British historian Catharine Macaulay, Warren began to write a history of the American Revolution. This project would preoccupy her off and on for the next quarter century.

After the war ended, Warren became increasingly alienated from national politics. In writings signed "A Columbian Patriot," she opposed the ratification of the U.S. Constitution, arguing that the proposed system would undermine republican government and threaten revolutionary ideals. Even after the Constitution went into effect, Warren found it hard to reconcile herself to the new order. Yet the postwar era also brought her a measure of fame. In 1790 Warren issued a volume containing her collected poems and plays. Celebrated as a literary hero, she basked in the praise of famous men.

In 1805 Warren published her three-volume *History of the Rise, Progress and Termination of the American Revolution: Interspersed with Biographical, Political and Moral Observations*. Warren had little to say about the status or condition of women in her book. Rather, her *History* melded a magisterial narrative of political events with a strong moral statement about the Revolution's meaning and significance. She urged Americans to reaffirm the basic principles of the Revolution—simplicity, frugality, and republican virtue—and to avoid the temptations of prosperity, European decadence, and aristocratic pretension. She also criticized what she saw as the monarchical tendencies of the Federalist presidents George Washington and John Adams.

For many decades Warren's *History* was overshadowed by other works that were neither as comprehensive nor as distinctive. Partly because she was a woman and partly because she was a Jeffersonian publishing in the bastion of Federalism, her tome met with public indifference and private criticism. John Adams accused her of misrepresentation, inaccuracy, and personal betrayal. Only the mediation of Abigail Adams enabled the two old friends to settle their differences.

Warren died in Plymouth, never having traveled outside Massachusetts. Her writings, however, reveal that she understood a world far beyond her personal experience. Subsequent generations have honored her as one of America's first prominent writers and cited her as a precedent for later "scribbling women." Thus Warren's life and works have produced a diverse and multifaceted legacy.

Katharine Susan Anthony, *First Lady of the Revolution: The Life of Mercy Otis Warren* (1958); Lester H. Cohen, "Explaining the Revolution: Ideology and Ethics in Mercy Otis Warren's Historical Theory," *William and Mary Quarterly* 37 (1980); Jeffrey H. Richards, *Mercy Otis Warren* (1995); Rosemarie Zagarri, *A Woman's Dilemma: Mercy Otis Warren and the American Revolution* (1995).

Rosemarie Zagarri

Webster, Daniel (1782–1852)

Lawyer, orator, U.S. representative and senator, secretary of state. One of New England's most illustrious statesmen, Daniel Webster was descended from English ancestors who came to America in 1635. He was born in Salisbury (now Franklin), N.H., the son of the Revolutionary War veteran Ebenezer Webster and his second wife, Abigail. Daniel Webster graduated from Dartmouth College in 1801 and in 1807 moved to Portsmouth, N.H., where he practiced law. He became one of the nation's most prominent constitutional lawyers, arguing a number of landmark cases before the U.S. Supreme Court. As a congressman, senator, and U.S. secretary of state he was a strong voice for unionism and compromise in the emerging sectional controversies of the early 19th century. Known for his dark features and sharply chiseled countenance, Webster was a consummate speaker, who through his historical orations became the nation's spokesperson and best-known popular historian.

Webster achieved prominence in New Hampshire by opposing the War of 1812 and was elected to Congress as a Federalist. He was reelected in 1814 but moved to Boston in 1816 and returned to private law practice. Now concerned with the broad interests of the mer-

Daniel Webster, engraving by S. A. Schoff, ca. 1831

chants and manufacturers of Massachusetts, he began to speak from a national rather than a local point of view. Representing his alma mater before the Supreme Court in *Dartmouth College v. Woodward,* he successfully argued that the state of New Hampshire had violated a contract when it altered the charter of Dartmouth College to make it a state university. The Court's decision to uphold the original contract was later used to protect corporations against the states. In the cases of *McCulloch v. Maryland* (1819) and *Gibbons v. Ogden* (1824), Webster convinced the Supreme Court to reduce the taxing power of the states and increase the power of the national government over interstate commerce.

Meanwhile Webster's fame as an orator was spreading. In 1820 he stood alongside Plymouth Rock to celebrate the landing of the Pilgrims. Five years later at the dedication of the Bunker Hill monument he recreated the battle for a rapt audience of 20,000. In 1826 he delivered a eulogy for John Adams and Thomas Jefferson in Boston. With his powerful voice and dark glowing eyes he was so awe-inspiring that many called him godlike.

Webster made his greatest contribution to American nationalism after he was elected to the U.S. Senate. During a debate on land policy in 1830 Senator Robert Y. Hayne of South Carolina presented a doctrine contending that individual states had the right to nullify federal laws. In replying to Hayne, Webster repudiated the doctrine and defended the union. He is best remembered for the ringing peroration of his second reply, "Liberty *and* Union, now and forever, one and inseparable," which generations of northern schoolchildren committed to memory.

The remainder of Webster's career was less satisfying. A leader of the Whig party, he ran unsuccessfully for president in 1836. As secretary of state he succeeded in settling the northeastern boundary dispute with Great Britain in 1842 but resigned soon afterward because of policy disputes with President John Tyler. Critics accused Webster of making policy decisions driven more by his desire to become president than by sound principles of governance. Although opposed to slavery, he angered antislavery northerners by supporting the Fugitive Slave Law and other provisions of the Compromise of 1850 in order to preserve the union. John Greenleaf Whittier was so disgusted that he wrote a poem entitled "Ichabod" in which he called Webster "so fallen! so lost!" Two years later Webster died at his home in Marshfield, Mass.

But Webster was not forgotten. Because Webster was so firmly identified with unionism, his fame increased during the Civil War and endured into the 20th century. In the voting for the first inductee to the Hall of Fame for Great Americans in 1901 he tied with Abraham Lincoln, placing second only to George Washington. And in 1957 the members of the Senate ranked him second to his colleague Henry Clay of Kentucky as the leading American senator.

Irving H. Bartlett, *Daniel Webster* (1978); Maurice G. Baxter, *One and Inseparable: Daniel Webster and the Union* (1984); Robert V. Remini, *Daniel Webster: The Man and His Time* (1997); Daniel Webster, *The Papers of Daniel Webster,* ed. Charles M. Wiltse and Harold D. Moser, 14 vols. (1974–89).

Donald B. Cole

Williams, Roger (ca. 1603–83)

Clergyman, religious controversialist, founder of Rhode Island and Providence Plantations. In the 300-plus years since his death Roger Williams has achieved nearly mythical status as a champion of "troubled consciences" and an advocate for Native American rights. Born into a London merchant family, Williams earned a bachelor's degree from Cambridge University in 1627 and was ordained as a minister in the Church of England. In 1629 he became chaplain of Sir William Masham's household, where he met John Cotton and John Winthrop, Puritan leaders who sought to reform the state church from within. Concerned about the direction of the established church under William Laud, archbishop of Canterbury, Williams emigrated to New England, reaching Boston in February 1631.

Williams's Separatist beliefs led him to accept church positions in Salem and Plymouth, Mass., between 1631 and 1635. While at Salem, Williams attacked Puritan authorities for their unwillingness to fully reject Anglican "popish rituals," their illegal occupation of Indian lands, and their decision to allow magistrates to exercise power over religious matters. His criticisms precipitated a major political crisis that pitted the Salem church against colony leaders and provoked the Massachusetts general court to banish him in October 1635.

Williams escaped to the southern frontier, purchased land from the Narragansett Indians, and founded the town of Providence in 1636. A master of Indian dialects, Williams frequently negotiated peaceful ends to intertribal disputes and averted potentially disastrous native attacks on colonial settlements. His studies of Narragansett language and culture resulted in his first book, *A Key into the Language of America* (1643). A catalog of native words and phrases and a sympathetic description of tribal customs, the *Key* reflects Williams's high regard for the "remarkably free and courteous" Indians he encountered as well as his desire to impart to them "the Knowledge of Christ."

Williams's work on behalf of Providence and the surrounding towns was similarly extensive. In 1643 he traveled to England to secure the parliamentary patent that incorporated the Narragansett Bay communities into the single colony of Rhode Island. Between 1644 and 1647, and from 1654 to 1657, Williams served as the colony's president. He helped to write Rhode Island's first legal code and led the fight against territorial incursions from neighboring colonies. After 1657 he retired from the colony's service, though he continued to participate in political life. He died in Providence in 1683.

Williams's enduring legacy springs from his tireless advocacy of religious liberty. Influenced by English Baptists and Separatists, Williams believed that civil order could be maintained even when individuals differed in "religious concernments" and welcomed exiles from Bay Colony churches to Rhode Island, including Anne Hutchinson and her followers. In 1644 Williams defended the establishment of a haven for "persons distressed of conscience" against the attacks of the Boston cleric John Cotton and argued for the complete separation of civil and spiritual spheres. His half of the debate, published as *The Bloudy Tenent of Persecution* (1644), was expanded in *The Bloudy Tenent yet more Bloudy* (1652), in which Williams ridiculed the concept of coerced uniformity and indicted American Puritans for quashing the discussion of religious principles. Williams built a colony in which the free exchange of religious ideas was possible and thus played a crucial role in legitimizing ecclesiastical diversity in New England.

Edwin S. Gaustad, *Liberty of Conscience: Roger Williams in America* (1991); Glenn W. LaFantasie, ed., *The Correspondence of Roger Williams* (1988); Perry Miller, *Roger Williams: His Contribution to the American Tradition* (1953); Edmund S. Morgan, *Roger Williams: The Church and the State* (1967).

Raymond D. Irwin

Winthrop, John (1588–1649) Political leader.

John Winthrop, the son of Anne Browne and Adam Winthrop, was a leader of the Great Migration to New England in the 1630s and a leading figure in shaping the region's political culture. His father was a barrister and small landowner and the youngest son of the elder Adam Winthrop, master of the clothworkers, who in 1544 purchased Groton Manor, a former monastic property in the county of Suffolk. Like his father, Winthrop matriculated at Cambridge University, studying at Trinity College from 1603 until 1605. In 1610 he purchased Groton Manor from his uncle John, who had resettled in Ireland. In 1613 Winthrop was admitted to Gray's Inn to study law and was then appointed commission of the peace for Suffolk. He served as a justice from 1617 until the mid-1620s, when he was omitted from the commission, only to be reappointed in 1626. He also served on the Sewer Commission (responsible for public works) and in 1627 was appointed an attorney at the Court of Wards and Liveries.

Winthrop was raised a Puritan at a time when the movement was rising in Suffolk, but in the 1610s the religious tide changed. Puritans were marginalized and in response began to develop a more intense piety that led to further alienation. Winthrop's position made it increasingly difficult for him to reconcile his faith with his public life, so he joined the Massachusetts Bay Company along with others considering migration. Following the Cambridge Agreement of leading stockholders to migrate and take the company charter with them, Winthrop was elected company governor in 1629. In April 1630 he sailed for the colonies on the *Arbella*. His lay sermon given to fellow adventurers, "A Modell of Christian Charity," set forth his vision of New England as a communal society covenanted with God to be an example of right order to England and the world—"a city upon a hill."

Winthrop was reelected governor each year until 1634 and served again from 1637 to 1640, 1642 to 1644, and from 1646 until his death on March 26, 1649. His experience in county administration in England provided a model for the workings of the Massachusetts government as he took the lead in transforming a corporate charter into a frame of civil government. He defended the right of magistrates to exercise discretionary leniency as opposed to the more rigid views of such leaders as Thomas Dudley, but also spoke forcefully against liberty that stretched to license. He took a strong stand against the views of Roger Williams but maintained a personal friendship with him even after Williams was banished from the colony and resettled in Rhode Island. Winthrop was the leading lay opponent of Anne Hutchinson and justified the Bay Colony's treatment of her in his *A Short Story of the rise, reign, and ruine of the Antinomians, Familists and Libertines* (1644). He was hopeful about the outcome of England's Puritan Revolution of the 1640s but did not live to see the rise of Oliver Cromwell to power in the 1650s.

Winthrop kept a private spiritual diary while in England, his *Experiencia*. On leaving England he began a more secular journal, which was first published in 1790 and has been issued in a definitive edition as *The Journal of John Winthrop, 1630–1649* (1996). Even in manuscript form, this work was the most important source for those who have written the history of the first decades of Massachusetts.

Richard S. Dunn and Laetitia Yeandle, eds., *The Journal of John Winthrop, 1630–1649* (1996); Massachusetts Historical Society, *Winthrop Papers*, multivolume series in progress (1929); Edmund S. Morgan, *The Puritan Dilemma: The Story of John Winthrop*, 2d ed. (1999); Lee Schweninger, *John Winthrop* (1990).

Francis J. Bremer

Woman Suffrage

Although New England has been the center of various reform movements, the region did not lead the way in the fight for woman suffrage. Nevertheless, women activists made their presence felt there. Marilla Young Ricker of New Hampshire, who represented her state at national suffrage conventions and became a practicing lawyer in Washington, D.C., insisted that her payment of taxes made her eligible to vote; she successfully cast a ballot in 1871, although in subsequent years her attempts to vote were denied. Another prominent New Englander, the author Louisa May Alcott, argued for women's rights in her fiction and was the first woman to register when Massachusetts gave women school, tax, and bond suffrage in 1879.

The emergence of the woman suffrage movement was closely linked to the abolitionist movement. Members of female antislavery societies compared the position of white women in society to that of slaves. After the Civil War many shifted their activist energies to the cause of woman suffrage, continuing to challenge rules of decorum by organizing public meetings, speaking in public, and lobbying Congress. They viewed suffrage, or the right to vote in local and national elections, as a mark of full participation in a democratic society and as a means to further other reforms, including increased legal rights for married women, control over wages and property, and joint guardianship of children. Although the first women's rights convention, held in Seneca Falls, N.Y., in 1848, determined that women should agitate for suffrage in addition to other reforms, women did not gain the vote nationwide until the ratification of the 19th Amendment to the Constitution in 1920. Throughout this 70-year period, however, New England failed to exert the leadership it had shown in the abolitionist movement. Thirty of the 48 states had some form of woman suffrage before the amendment was ratified, but by 1920 only two New England states had granted women the limited right of presidential suffrage: Rhode Island in 1917 and Maine in 1919.

The debate over the 15th Amendment to the Constitution, designed to give black men the franchise, split the suffrage movement into two camps. On one side were the supporters of Elizabeth Cady Stanton and Susan B. Anthony, who decided not to support this amendment because it excluded women. On the other side were Lucy Stone, her husband, Henry Blackwell, and Thomas Wentworth Higginson, who formed the New England Woman Suffrage Association (NEWSA) in 1868, the first major political society to make woman suffrage its goal and whose first president was Julia Ward Howe. NEWSA believed it could gain woman suffrage with the help of the reform-minded Republican Party, but Republicans were focused primarily on the Reconstruction agenda of gaining the franchise for black men. NEWSA thus agreed to subordinate woman suffrage to black suffrage. Stanton and Anthony responded by forming the National Woman Suffrage Association, with the goal of establishing woman suffrage through a federal constitutional amendment. In 1869 the New England association became a national organization, the American Woman Suffrage Association, whose strategy was to attain the vote for women state by state. The National and the American Woman Suffrage Associations remained separate organizations with separate strategies until 1890, when Alice Stone Blackwell, the daughter of Lucy Stone and Henry Blackwell, facilitated their merger into the National American Woman Suffrage Association.

In the 20th century the National American Woman Suffrage Association worked to increase the number of states in which women could vote and eventually led a successful effort for passage of the federal woman suffrage amendment in both houses of Congress in 1919. After a series of close votes, the states ratified the amendment in 1920.

Ellen Carol DuBois, *Feminism and Suffrage: The Emergence of an Independent Women's Movement in America, 1848–1869* (1978); Eleanor Flexnor, *Century of Struggle: The Woman's Rights Movement in the United States,* rev. ed. (1975); Anne Firor Scott and Andrew M. Scott, *One Half the People: The Fight for Woman Suffrage* (1982 [1975]); Elizabeth Cady Stanton, Susan B. Anthony, Matilda Joslyn Gage, eds., *History of Woman Suffrage,* 6 vols. (1970 [1881–1922]).

Christine Brooks Macdonald

Images and Ideas

David H. Watters, Section Editor

INTRODUCTION

There were images and ideas about New England before there was a New England. Captain John Smith named the region in 1616 in the hopes that it might attract a different sort of settler from the gentlemen and servants who had struggled in Virginia. He created one of the first myths of New England as a land in which sound yeomen, craftsmen, fishermen, and their families would settle free of England's social problems. Another myth inscribed on the land came from Puritan pens describing New England as the New Israel, to be settled by a vanguard that would create, in John Winthrop's terms, a model of Christian charity, a city upon a hill, for the eyes of the world to see. In mapping such images over the land of New England and the complex Native American societies there, these Europeans set a pattern of inventing New England that has characterized its culture for nearly four centuries. Americans know many of these images: Pilgrim founders, revolutionary patriots, rebels and reformers, ingenious tinkers and industrialists, Boston Brahmins, and quaint Yankees mixed with summer folk.

Americans may be less aware of New England's long history as a multiethnic and multiracial society. New England boasted one of the first global societies in the 17th century in which Native Americans, Europeans, and Africans met, and by the Civil War it was America's first industrialized and most urbanized region. Images of New England communicate and mask ideas about the meaning of the region. Immigrants were haunted by nostalgia for lands left behind and by an idealized memory of an earlier England they hoped to reproduce. Biblically inspired images of New England as a new Eden or New Israel contained within them a narrative of declension and failure, in which an avenging God punishes a backsliding people whose corruption has seeped from consciousness. As Nathaniel Hawthorne noted in *The Scarlet Letter* (1850), a burying ground and a prison marked Boston's earliest landscape. The massacre of the Pequots in 1637 and the defeat of King Philip (Metacom) in 1676 still haunt the land. Indeed, the historically powerful images and ideas of Yankee New England are deeply rooted in challenges to that very Yankee dominance.

The environment is also central to the development of New England images and ideas. Glacial moraine and broad river valleys in the south merge with a rocky coast and mountain-crusted north. Climatic extremes are legendary. Extraordinary natural resources from the sea and the timberlands and the availability of waterpower shaped lifeways. The ecological diversity of the region foreshadowed social and economic diversity as well as an independent, entrepreneurial spirit. New England's work ethic is rooted in such environmental realities as much as it is a result of the Protestant concept of vocation and the get-ahead spirit of immigrant entrepreneurs.

New Englanders are made, not born, and images and ideas communicate a rich historical consciousness of the competing claims of communities to represent an authentic regional identity. As cultural historians have argued, region is an invention or construction that has a social function, as do the categories of race, ethnicity, gender, and class. At least as early as the revolutionary era, New Englanders asserted pride of place for the origins of American values. Robert Frost claimed that New England "was the first little nation that bade fair to be an English speaking nation on this continent." Such statements homogenize differences within the region and silence competing voices. Even in Frost's work we see historical forces shifting the focus in New England literature to where the "true" New England can be found: along its rocky coast and in its maritime heritage; in its towns, those cradles of democracy; in its up-country Yankee areas; and in its urban centers. Each generation challenges definitions of the true New England and inexorably creates new ones.

Given the region's early obsession with literacy and its later embrace of the newest technologies of communication, competing stories and images about New England's past and present identities find ready markets. New images may subvert the received pieties, but they also may lead to a rediscovery of forgotten stories of New England's earlier diversity. For example, in its special 60th-anniversary issue for September 1995, *Yankee* magazine featured the 60 people who "made" New England. A reader had to search for non-Yankee faces. The editor, Judson Hale, described the process of finding 60 living New Englanders whom visitors would "be likely to talk about back home, people who somehow help define the New England communities in which they live." It was the 1990s, so more specific consideration was given to "things like gender, ethnic backgrounds, age, geographic representation, and occupation." But when the final cut was made, all criteria were put aside for a consensus that developed around the vanilla ice cream of the Yankee, with a sprinkling of others—an Italian gardener, black women basketball players, Lebanese clothiers, cooks, quarriers, and the African American writer Dorothy West. One Native American, Squanto, appears in a group held responsible for what is bad about the region.

It is easy to make fun of such lists, but *Yankee*'s attempt to broaden the definition of *Yankee* and its frequent coverage of new New Englanders are instructive. In many ways, the list reflects what visitors might see in tourist literature and in Colonial Revival images of New England, but the exercise also reveals the inner workings of regionalism as a way of understanding American life. Regional stereotypes often mask the complexities of New England life, but they can also reveal the process whereby regional identity has been formed. The challenge in studying images and ideas of New England is to reconstruct concepts of the region to include the diversity of its people and places, past and present.

The materials in this section suggest the strength of regionalism in American life even as they display its artifice. New England is a text and a cultural map that have to be read, interpreted, and represented to diverse publics. The challenge to residents and scholars alike is to master the archive of symbols to tell old and new stories that shape the identity of audience and teller. This process has sometimes been obscured by claims that New England is more than just a region. Nancy Shoemaker, in "Regions as Categories of Analysis," notes that the Northeast has been an unmarked category, the default for America as a whole, against which other regions are defined as such. The literary critics Jane Tompkins and Lawrence Buell have noted much the same tendency in the creation of a canon of American literature in the 19th and early 20th centuries that collected New England writers as a core of national tradition. Joseph Conforti provides an authoritative history of the inner workings of these inventions of New England from the Puritan era to the mid-20th century.

Regionalism is not just a New England story. In a pluralistic, democratic society on a vast and diverse land, people feel the need to create a sense of place. The popularity of the idea of regions and sections to explain American political culture has waxed and waned, from debates over the Constitution to the speeches of Daniel Webster, the writings of Alexis de Tocqueville, and the theses of Frederick Jackson Turner. The concept of region has proved unstable, and the definitions of regional culture are subject to debate. For each revival of the idea of region over the past century, whether in the scholarly work of Van Wyck Brooks, of Perry Miller, or of David Hackett Fischer, there has been a countercurrent of criticism and reconstruction. Dona Brown, James Lindgren, Stephen Nissenbaum, and Joseph Conforti challenge Yankee homogeneity by unpacking the inventions of New England in response to ethnic diversity.

It is significant that many historical studies of New England peter out after World War I, as if the constituents of regional images and ideas are finally diluted by urbanization and a national media. The real New England in some contemporary accounts resides in ever smaller Yankee rural enclaves, a few urban neighborhoods, and select institutions. Scholars today point to the rise of tourism and the power of the national media to show how New England identity has been put to the service of a consumer economy. This debate itself matches the lived experience of New Englanders today, who are highly conscious of the region's preserved history, its distinctive lifeways, and its environments, but who are also cognizant of the national and international forces that have shaped the lives of their families and communities. To use the terms of the anthropologist Mary Louise Pratt, New England has long been a contact zone, and the history of those contacts constitutes a regional identity evidenced in the people, places, and things identified as New England. The challenge here is to present the historical development of New England images and ideas without embalming them in local history or neglecting the deep diversity of competing images, past and present. Given the *Encyclopedia*'s organization, by which many images and ideas have been parceled out to other sections, what appear here are a core of items and a suggestive miscellany. A reader can move from these entries to those in other sections, pulling on one thread without unraveling the whole.

The idea and then the fact of New England in the 17th century were the creation of global forces of nationalism, exploration, and imperialism. The sea made it possible for New England to become one of the first societies composed of Native Americans, Europeans, and Africans. New England's regional consciousness was formed in the colonial era with the establishment of political, economic, and cultural ties as directed by and in resistance to dictates from London. Puritan religion and English folkways blended to create what Perry Miller called "the New England mind." New England was defined by who was excluded as much as by who was included. The Dutch were pushed out of Connecticut, and Native Americans were enslaved, subjugated, and pushed to the margins after the so-called civil war of 1676–77. Until 1763, the French were a constant threat to the north. The professed Puritan ideal of a covenanted community had fractured by the end of the 17th century over religious, national, and racial exclusion. Intense self-scrutiny, moral idealism, and the tension between individualism and corporate responsibility outlived the Puritans. A fierce independence and an intolerance of outsiders complete the mixed legacy of the colonial era.

As ethnic and religious exclusion faded in the 19th century and were overwhelmed by the arrival of the Irish in the 1840s, an increasingly self-conscious Yankee and Brahmin culture contributed to the Colonial Revival movement's image of a persistently Yankee New England. The presence of Yankee culture shaped the experience of arriving immigrant groups. The stories of ethnic groups with histories just as long, who arrived in greater numbers in other hubs of immigration, such as New York, Chicago, and Philadelphia, may obscure the fact that the New England experience of these groups shaped their consciousness. The sequence and numbers in New England make a difference, as does the character of the Catholic Church hierarchy, with the dominance of the Irish in Massachusetts, French Canadians in New Hampshire and Vermont, and Italians in Rhode Island and Connecticut, to cite only a few examples. In more recent decades, groups as diverse as Haitians, Cambodians, Puerto Ricans, Dominicans, Somalis, and Ukrainians have established significant New England enclaves, but they also have distinctive trajectories of experience depending on the circumstances and location of these enclaves.

The struggle over New England identity has been marked for centuries by the presence of New York City and Canada. The growth of New York City as a cultural and economic capital in the 19th century eclipsed the influence of Boston. New York City was and is a center of gravity for ethnic groups who make a home in New England. New Yorkers, however, as creators and consumers of New England, are invested in the sustenance of regional identity. Canada has played a critical role in setting New England's boundaries. New England's colonial military campaigns against French Canada, and its forays during the American Revolution and the War of 1812, set political and cultural boundaries. The influx of people from Canada to New England, however, whether French Canadians from Quebec or Nova Scotians and Cape Bretoners working or settling in the "Boston States," and a constant flow back and forth, have forged shared regional communities and interests. Today, New England's state governors and the premiers of Canada's eastern provinces meet to shape regional policies.

In this section are entries on distinctive regional places by which people locate New England and themselves as New Englanders. These are also locations that visitors wish to experience, so the look of the place is often preserved to meet these needs. Guidebooks lead people to regional destinations by scenic routes and explain the history and culture that make place meaningful. The Geography and Environment and the Tourism sections of the encyclopedia offer a fuller roster of such sites, but in this section are places that resonate as icons, such as Plymouth Rock, the Old Man of the Mountain, and Peyton Place. Most significant in the creation of place are images of the states themselves, and of the de facto capital of the region, if not hub of the universe: Boston. The states are a product of many historical and political forces that persist remarkably in creating local identities, and they also function in relation to one another to shape regional identity.

The colonies of Massachusetts, Connecticut, Rhode Island, and New Hampshire emerged as original states, and after a brief period as a republic, Vermont joined the union in 1791. Maine was transformed from a district of Massachusetts into a state in 1820 as part of the Missouri Compromise that foretold the region's eventual role in the Civil War. New Englanders contemplated leaving the union in 1815 in response to disastrous embargo policies and the effects of war with Great Britain. The 1815 Hartford Convention also symbolized New England's recognition that the center of gravity in America was shifting west and south.

Massachusetts claims many firsts, with a Puritan past and a preservationist impulse lingering in a history of dynamic demographic change, political ferment, and educational and technical expertise. Rhode Island is small, radical, and ingrown, a clambake of Catholics and Protestants, Italians, Portuguese, Yankees, Franco-Americans, and Native Americans. Connecticut distinguishes its colonial history from that of its neighbors, and Hartford declared its independence from Boston as a cultural and industrial leader in the 19th century. The overwhelming pull of New York City, however, has for a century contested the identification of the state with New England. The northern tier states also have deeply held traditions and stories of origins. Maine's statehood in 1820, Vermont's brief existence as an independent republic after the American Revolution, and New Hampshire's libertarian, if not contrarian, spirit, especially in relation to Massachusetts, have created a region within a region. Each generation has provided a voice of northern New England, from Robert Frost and Dorothy Canfield Fisher to Carolyn Chute, Stephen King, and Howard Frank Mosher. Such diversity coexisting with recognition of strong common bonds among the states further strengthens images and ideas of New England. Boston, of course, is a special place, dominating in size, complexity, and influence, so its story is told separately here and in many other sections.

The development of Boston and state identities is most notable in the region's literature. The Boston area has always been the hub of New England literature, for here were the first presses and the first college, an educated elite, the ministry, and the availability of books imported from England. Over the centuries, Boston has sustained a literary culture with nationally prominent publishers and magazines and a concentration of educational institutions, which are now supporting writers in residence as well as other arts, patrons, and readers. Harvard's dominance is evident not only in the roster of American authors among its graduates but also in the presence of scholars. From Henry Wadsworth Longfellow in the 19th century to F. O. Matthiessen, Lawrence Buell, and Helen Vendler in the 20th and 21st, Harvard scholars have proposed powerful interpretive models of the region's writing.

Other centers of literature thrive. In Hartford, the Connecticut Wits of the early republic gained renown, followed after the Civil War by a cluster that included Mark Twain, Harriet Beecher Stowe, Charles Dudley Warner, and Rose Terry Cooke. Connecticut is still known for towering figures with deep local roots, and for authors who left New York City to make their home in the state, among them Wallace Stevens, Eugene O'Neill, Ann Petry, and Arthur Miller. Connecticut has been the focus of the so-called suburban realists along the route of the New Haven Railroad, such as John Cheever and Ann Beattie.

In Massachusetts, the Concord Transcendentalists were gathered around Ralph Waldo Emerson and Bronson Alcott, providing a fertile ground for such figures as Henry David Thoreau and Louisa May Alcott. In the Berkshires, New York writers from Herman Melville to Edith Wharton encountered New England's darker elements, even while celebrating a rural retreat from the city.

From the time of Roger Williams, Rhode Island has fostered a distinctive literary tradition in opposition to Boston's idealized images of New England. Rhode Islanders give voice to the conflicts of immigration and ethnicity. H. P. Lovecraft was a pioneer in writing Gothicized science fiction and horror to capture Providence life, and today Geoffrey Wolff is an example of writers who find fertile material in the conflicts between white Anglo-Saxon Protestant Brahmins and Italian Americans in the blood sport of politics. Brown University is home to some of America's preeminent writers.

Maine, Vermont, and New Hampshire are often mythologized as a last bastion of Yankee culture, an image that belies the prominence of Franco-Americans and reinvigorated Native American nations. Nevertheless, this image has attracted such writers as Robert Frost and the so-called local color writers, including Sarah Orne Jewett, Mary Wilkins Freeman, and Edwin Arlington Robinson. Throughout the 20th century, writers found retreat in the region from what Maxine Kumin called the po-biz (poetry business) of New York and from the academy. Indeed, art colonies have provided a literal retreat for many writers, among them Thornton Wilder and John Updike, who crafted their defining New England visions in part at the MacDowell Colony in Peterborough, N.H. Donald Hall, Howard Frank Mosher, Carolyn Chute, Galway Kinnell, and Stephen King, to name a few, have mined the region's image for materials and moods, often inverting traditional images through wit, irony, and Gothicism. Grace Metalious's *Peyton Place* shattered forever the *Our Town* image of the region, and Stephen King's works imagine a vampire in every person "from away" who opens an antique shop.

Although literary images and ideas have shaped regional identity, many Americans know the region best through the images of visual artists, tourist guidebooks and brochures, and advertising. The Art, Tourism, and Media sections of the *Encyclopedia* trace the historical development of such images, but it is important to note here how the region developed what might be called a brand name through the conjunction of images, advertising, and tourism. By the 19th century, the image of the Yankee peddler had become popular in genre painting and newspaper advertisements, communicating negative views of sharp Yankee traders and positive views of the region's commercial spirit. Similarly, the image of the Yankee schoolmaster, lampooned in John Quidor's paintings and Washington Irving's "The Legend of Sleepy Hollow" in the early 19th century, set a New England brand name on education. New England "schoolmarms" could market their credentials across the country, and by late in the century, the image of New England educational institutions, from preparatory schools to universities, appeared in popular prints and schoolbooks.

New England products, from clocks, textile machinery, and textiles to candy, salt cod, and Shaker herbs, were advertised for their quality based on their New England origins. In the 20th century, with the rise of modern marketing techniques in manufacturing and tourism, New England brand names were identified with the iconic places and events of the region. One can buy any number of products with a Plymouth Rock logo or name, and the state of Vermont carefully guards the use of its name on products. People expect purity and authenticity in products produced in New England, and handcrafted items fetch a premium. Images of sailing vessels, a rocky coast, villages, and rural vistas sell New England in many media.

If literary and popular images have been significant means of presenting New England places, its political culture, from images of the Boston Tea Party to the Kennedys and the New Hampshire presidential primary, indicate the region's influence on national life. The region's influence in national politics has waned since the Kennedy administration, but powerful leaders in Congress, such as Senators Judd Gregg (R-N.H.) and Joseph Lieberman (D-Conn.), offset the growth of political power in the South and West. Moreover, the New Hampshire presidential primary has brought national focus to the state's voters, who boosted the campaigns of Eugene McCarthy, Jimmy Carter, and Ronald Reagan. Connecticut elected Ella Grasso as the region's first woman governor, starting a trend of women in state and federal office that has included the governors Madeline Kunin (Vermont), Jeanne Shaheen (New Hampshire), and Jane Swift (Massachusetts) and the U.S. senators Olympia Snowe and Susan Collins (both Maine), among others.

A sense of place is also created in the region through things, whether possessed for personal use or aesthetic appreciation, preserved and displayed for the public, or mediated for display as regional signifiers. Many New England objects have governmental or institutional status, as we read in the entries "Old Man of the Mountain" and "Plymouth Rock." Antiques, wooden toys, decoys, dolls, samplers, lighthouse souvenirs, Shaker boxes, lobster traps, and gravestone rubbings are coin of the realm for those who display a New England taste. Food is another entrée to the region's culture. The doughnut, dunked, has replaced pie for breakfast. (A New Hampshire menu in the 1970s listed a bagel as a "Jewish donut.") Toll House cookies are baked, and cabinets, Moxie, and tonic slake the thirst. Cuisine has become national and international, but the region still shows its preference for foods originating in Native American and colonial English foodways, as entries in the Folklife section reveal. New England gave Fannie Farmer to the nation, and Julia Child brought France to America by means of a Boston public television station.

Images of New England are inseparable from the ideas they represent, and ideas themselves have a special status in the construction of regional identity. New En-

The first soft drink mass-marketed in the United States, Moxie was invented by Dr. Augustin Thompson of Union, Maine, and bottled in Lowell, Mass. Like some other soft drinks, Moxie was originally touted as a medicine, or "nerve food"; today it can be found mainly in northern New England, although the word has entered the language as a synonym for "pep" or "spunk."

gland is a place in which ideas are seen to matter a great deal; they have a status and a history. Ideas exhibited a peculiar force in the founding of New England, and in their name social revolutions, such as the Great Awakenings and the abolition movement, discipline and liberate individual identities. One can speak of the New England conscience, and intellectual historians trace the New England heritage of the Protestant ethic. Philosophers discuss New England's Puritanism, Transcendentalism, and pragmatism.

Ideas, of course, are embodied in people and their artifacts. New England images and ideas are the constructs of people and social institutions, but surely the images and ideas exist in a complex ideology that shapes individual identities and stereotypes. Behaviors are historically located with historical figures to create myths, and these figures then inspire imitation. Stereotypes of the Yankee give us black Yankees, frugal Yankees, Yankee peddlers, Yankee hermits, Yankee radicals, and Yankee dreamers. Many of the embodiments of these identities and stereotypes are found in the Politics, History, Gender, and Ethnic and Racial Identity sections, but in this section a few figures hold pride of place for the power they have had in shaping the regional image. Ideas know no borders, but New England would not be New England without the particular mix of historical philosophies that are commonly seen as constituent of regional thinking. As Herman Melville wrote of the force behind Hawthorne's work, "the shadow of Puritan gloom" falls across the region at certain seasons and times of life (for Boston Red Sox fans, by midsummer). Introspection and the examination of conscience are still seen as regional characteristics, long after the doctrinal Calvinism of the Puritans has faded.

New England has a long history of religious ferment and invention. Puritans, Unitarians, Universalists, Shakers, Christian Scientists, Free Will Baptists, and Mormons found fertile soil in New England. Argument over the depravity and perfectibility of human nature heated many a winter night in a region where people commonly believe it is possible to have an original relationship with the universe. As the philosopher George Santayana noted in his essay "The Genteel Tradition in American Philosophy," it is the conjunction of Puritanism, Transcendentalism, and pragmatism that gives New England and America a distinctive life of the mind. Innumerable intellectual institutions still foster ideas in New England, and town meetings still serve as an occasional forum for momentous issues, such as the Vietnam War or nuclear weapons policy.

Perhaps the strongest regional idea in New England is that literacy is an essential gateway to identity, citizenship, and salvation. The breadth of New England literature is the most visible effect of high levels of literacy. As early as the 1640s, Puritan legislation joined social custom to support literacy; in the 19th century, Horace Mann's common-school movement was followed by John Dewey's educational philosophy in stamping educational reform with the New England hallmark. Two hundred years ago, literacy was strengthened by the revolutionary idea of free public libraries, and indeed New England's public libraries are still vital cultural centers. High rates of literacy ensured a supply of writers and readers to propagate the New England story.

New England's literacy also afforded a context in which groups denied power—including Native Americans, African Americans, and women—could make their stories known. In the 1770s, Phillis Wheatley wrote her way to freedom, setting a pattern for African American writers to follow, from education to publication to protest. The long roster includes David Walker, Frederick Douglass, Maria Stewart, W. E. B. Du Bois, and Pauline Hopkins. The example of Malcolm X reveals how the region's traditions could be used to transform its image. In 1948 the inmate Malcolm Little began copying a dictionary in the library of the Norfolk Prison Colony in Massachusetts to improve his vocabulary and reading skills. Little, later Malcolm X, also read the pamphlets of the abolitionist Anti-Slavery Society of New England, the works of W. E. B. Du Bois, the Harvard Classics, and one novel, *Uncle Tom's Cabin*. He wrote that a "new world opened to me, of being able to read and *understand*," and he decided to "devote the rest of [his] life to telling the white man about himself—or die." The state's penal tools are turned against the masters to tell the truth, an impulse an earlier imprisoned writer, Henry David Thoreau, would have understood.

These African American writers imbibed New England culture and values even as they revealed the injustices that had denied them full citizenship and free voices. Similarly, the voices of the Native American authors Samson Occom and William Apess ring through the centuries, attacking the myth of the disappearing Indian. In defense of their rights, they were joined by women writers like Lydia Maria Child. Indeed, New England women writers were at the forefront of New England's reform movements. Despite limitations, New England women could get an education from the time of early dame schools and female academies through the founding of Mount Holyoke, Smith, and other women's colleges. As the examples of Harriet Beecher Stowe and Sara Josepha Hale demonstrate, women writers transformed American culture and gave New England some of its most distinctive voices.

Educational reform movements led by Horace Mann, John Dewey, and Theodore Sizer became national in scope. Influential presidents of premier research institutions such as Harvard and Yale have shaped higher education nationally, and the region has been strongly associated with higher education for women from the time of Mary Lyons and Catherine Beecher before the Civil War. Vannevar Bush of the Massachusetts Institute of Technology created partnerships between federal research, especially in the area of defense technologies, and university and private research entities that shaped the growth of technology in New England and the nation. Despite the assertions of its founders, New England has no special claim on the national conscience, but it continues to produce more than its share of individuals who challenge the status quo, presenting the potent mix of individualism and community responsibility familiar from such figures as John Winthrop, Thoreau, and Margaret Chase Smith. In New England the personal is political, as the founders of the Boston Women's Health Cooperative would agree, but the local is also political, when it comes to voicing individual and community rights against outside intrusion.

New England images and ideas often come together for public display in communal celebrations. Some are rooted in specific historical events associated with the region, such as Patriot's Day and Thanksgiving, but others are the artful inventions of groups, governments, and institutions, such as Old Home Day and the awarding of *Boston Post* Canes. These celebrations are but some of the public expressions of New England's highly developed historical consciousness. Historic preservation is deeply embedded in the region, and it creates the archive from which images and ideas of New England are drawn. The depth of historical record, the number of local historical sites and societies, the support of governments and educational institutions, and the many individuals doing history work make the images and ideas of New England's past a palpable reality for its residents today. Cotton Mather claimed in his *Magnalia Christi Americana* (1702), an epic history of New England, "Whether New England may live any where else or no, it must live in our History!" History has been a cottage industry of New England since the days of William Bradford. New England writers have been profoundly political in their vision, from the Puritan jeremiads to the revolutionary tracts, abolitionist lectures, and moralistic chronicles of desegregation and the economic and environmental crises of the 1970s.

A preservation ethic was submerged in the Puritan impulse to restore a lost community of saints, and surely nostalgia was packed away in the sea chests of immigrants. Plain speech, biblical quotation, and nostalgia joined to create one of New England's first literary forms, a sermon called the jeremiad. Named for the Old Testament prophet, this sermon castigated backsliding and called for the restoration of old ways before God's wrath destroyed modern innovations.

Preservation is the lesson learned in any region's school of loss, but it became a New England political philosophy during the early national and antebellum eras. American freedoms and community values were located by such writers as John Adams and Timothy Dwight in the New England town. The townscape of a central green flanked by a white church, civic buildings, shops, and domestic dwellings became a New England brand for export to other regions and for use as a national icon. As the scholars John Seelye, Joseph Wood, and Michael Kammen have shown, this cultural landscape became a repository of American memory, home to a consecrated host of Pilgrim ancestors and Revolutionary War patriots. Historians, authors, artists, and civic leaders in the antebellum period joined to preserve New England's past, to support social development meant to partake of a New England spirit, and to prepare New England for future, and perhaps decisive, struggles with other regions over the soul of America. Their efforts created a preservation movement with profound effects on the images and ideas of New England.

Early evidence of a preservation ethic includes the founding of village improvement societies and historical societies. Sons of New England clubs formed, and in

Church (ca. 1790) and burying ground in South Shaftsbury, Vt.

Portsmouth, N.H., a "return of the sons" event was held on July 4, 1853. Before the Civil War, Lydia Maria Child, Nathaniel Hawthorne, and Harriet Beecher Stowe wrote early examples of what would become the local color movement. Bicentennial histories, orations, and celebrations of the founding of New England began in 1620. Daniel Webster's great orations at Plymouth and Bunker Hill set the tone for political and cultural battles over the meaning of American freedom that would culminate in the Civil War. After the war, historic preservation gained enormous cultural force in what has come to be known as the Colonial Revival movement. Catalyzed by the display of a New England hearth and spinning implements worked by costumed women at the International Centennial Exhibition of 1876, the desire for a usable and seemingly stable past took the form of colonial architecture and artifacts. The Colonial Revival was also a creative reconstruction of the past based on contemporary political and social situations. New Hampshire's Old Home Week, for example, was established in 1899 in an attempt to counter a crisis of farm abandonment and general rural economic and educational decline.

During the 20th century, New Englanders made historic preservation a major regional cultural force. Some, like William Sumner Appleton and Wallace Nutting, focused on the preservation of historic buildings and artifacts as part of a cultural program to strengthen the authority of New England's Anglo-American roots in the face of ethnic immigration. Others, such as Alice Morse Earle, sought to recover and preserve domestic ways, joining with local color writers who emphasized domestic life. With the rise of modernism around the time of World War I, many preservation activities were relegated to the margins of an increasingly national and international culture, and it was not until the regionalism movement of the 1930s that New England recovered from an image of being a cultural backwater.

Many modernists, particularly visual artists, sought in rural New England, especially along the Maine coast and in the hill country of New Hampshire and Vermont, an authentic spirit of folk culture. With the political challenges of communism and fascism compounding the loss of faith in American democracy attendant on the Depression, New England's traditions of town meeting and religious freedom gained renewed cultural appeal. The founding of *Yankee* magazine (1935), the popularity of Norman Rockwell's *Four Freedoms* series (1943), and the success of Thornton Wilder's *Our Town* (1938) are but a few of the cultural markers of a revival of New England's rural town values. Outdoor museums, such as Old Sturbridge Village and Plimoth Plantation, were vehicles for the display of collections, for new scholarship, and for tourism.

A primary voice of the New England idea was Robert Frost, but a host of other authors, such as Dorothy Canfield Fisher and Esther Forbes, contributed as well. Critics and scholars argued for the roots of many American traditions, whether defining a "New England mind," in Perry Miller's magisterial studies, or aesthetic principles in Van Wyck Brooks's books, or the new demographic methods in studies of towns and family life by Philip Greven. Several of New England's most cogent analysts after World War II, among them Malcolm Cowley and E. B. White, were transplanted from New York City, but they established an intellectual counterpoint to New York in their rural New England residences.

By the 1960s, historic preservation had developed an important field of academic study, primarily on New England's colonial past, but it also flourished in the public sphere with the movement to celebrate Americans' racial and ethnic roots. A revitalized high-tech and biotechnological economy and an expanding system of higher education went hand in hand with efforts to preserve and reuse New England's architectural heritage. Now the factory, mill town, and urban areas became the focus of a preserved New England image, especially after the devastations of urban renewal projects in Hartford and Boston's West End. The planned bicentennial celebrations of 1976 gave New England a head start, with a massive celebration in Concord, Mass., on April 19, 1975, attended by President Gerald Ford, thousands of militia reenactors, People's Bicentennial Commission protesters gathered at the North Bridge, and hundreds of thousands of spectators. In 1976 the Fourth of July concert on the Charles River Esplanade by Arthur Fieldler and the Boston Pops was America's national celebration. Many of the ethnic divisions of New England's past seemed melted together in a new New England, whose prosperity would be based on technology (especially fueled by defense spending), an expanding service industry, education, and tourism.

The image of New England, however, was offset by disturbing images emerging from Boston in the context of school desegregation. In the mid-1970s, America witnessed riots over busing, attacks on schoolchildren, and depressing reports about abysmal conditions in the cradle of American public education. A positive result of Boston's busing crisis was the emergence of a new generation of African American political leaders, not just in Massachusetts but across New England. Such scholars as Robert Hayden, James Oliver Horton, Lois E. Horton, and Valerie Cunningham put black history on the New England map, and the success of Steven Spielberg's film *Amistad* (1997) led to an *Amistad* black history trail, the building of a replica for educational cruises, and a new appreciation of the complexities of New England's abolitionist past. The film *Glory* (1989) restored to public view the contributions of free people of color in the Massachusetts 54th Regiment to the Union cause in the Civil War. These examples indicate the need to reconstruct received images and ideas of New England, both to correct and deepen regional memory and to respond to new challenges to regional identity.

By the 1970s, many of New England's cities suffered from urban blight and environmental issues—from the wreck of the oil tanker *Argo Merchant* (1976) to the identification of toxic industrial sites—while the decline and sale of northern forestlands belied the poster image of the New England town. Vermont passed landmark environmental legislation to preserve farmland, and other states responded with conservation trusts and easements. New England set about reinventing itself once again in the 1990s; this time the images and ideas presented a quality of life based not only in the Yankee rural and vacation landscapes and family-oriented suburbs near restored towns and cities. Quality of life centers increasingly on a diverse, multicultural place with the amenities cities can provide, all on a foundation of regional historical awareness. Popular television shows like *Cheers* and *Providence* as well as a spate of movies filmed in Boston neighborhoods did much to erase the negative images of the 1970s.

The replica of the Amistad *(2000) in New London, Conn., 2004*

The transformation of an old industrial city, Lowell, Mass., is emblematic of the change. Lowell was revitalized economically by the growth of Wang Industries and the location nearby of major offices for Digital Equipment Corporation and Raytheon. Through the efforts of Congressman and then Senator Paul Tsongas and a host of local officials, Lowell became the home of America's first urban national park, highlighting the city's industrial past. Waves of new immigrants, most notably one of America's largest populations of Cambodians, added vitality to the city. The 49th National Folk Festival was in Lowell in 1987–89.

Folk arts are a special window on the process of ethnic identity formation in New England. As Jane Beck writes, folk artists "create work that is rooted in another artistic tradition. In that respect it is not necessarily reflective of New England, but it is indicative of new artistic traditions flowing into the area and entering into a dynamic relationship with it. . . . Because these narratives of folk art are so intensely personal, rooted in an individual sense of place and identity and shaped by expressive traditions of older generations, they can be viewed as embodying an essence of New England." In 1948, for example, José Reyes, a basket maker from the Philippines, adapted Nantucket scrimshaw and lightship basket forms to create a New England icon. The evangelist and lawyer John Greco endeavored to shape Holy Land USA on a hillside in Connecticut, appropriating for his faith the vision of John Winthrop. It is in hands such as these that images and ideas of New England are preserved, revitalized, and transformed.

In northern New England, environmental issues challenge the continuity of communities whose way of life gave rise to potent New England images. The decline of fisheries on the Gulf of Maine, the sale of timberlands, the loss of dairy farms, and the closure of paper mills erode the economic base of traditional employment. Since the 19th century, New England's nature writers—George Perkins Marsh, for example—have understood that a working landscape of interwoven human and natural histories, rather than the wilderness, defines the region's natural resources. In the early 21st century, writers, scientists, and government officials struggle to accommodate deeply held beliefs about how New England's landscape should look and how its natural resources should be used to new realities of environmental degradation and the global economy. In response, new images and ideas of the northern region have developed, combining an appreciation of scenic beauty, deep scientific knowledge, lyrical writing, and, on occasion, political advocacy. This approach characterizes the works of Rachel Carson, John Hay, Henry Beston, Helen and Scott Nearing, John Elder, and Maxine Kumin, to name only a few who speak, or write, for the land.

In each case, a way of life and a cherished image of New England invested with ideas about its meaning are threatened. Without an economic base, people cannot live the lives they value, the lives that tourists travel to see. As Charles E. Clark notes in his history of Maine, ironic, self-deprecating humor has a long tradition as a defense against sophisticated urbanites. It also masks the anger of country people who may have more education and mother wit than the wealthy rusticator, tourist, or summer resident. As tourism has intensified the demand for "authentic" New England places and experiences, Yankee humor deflects and subverts the tourist gaze.

The humor of Marshall Dodge in the *Bert and I* series became popular when down east Maine was being opened by new highways. One Maine bumper sticker states, "If It's Tourist Season, Why Can't We Shoot Them?" This ironic self-consciousness, however, is not limited to down east humorists. It also characterized the performance art of Spaulding Gray's recollections of suburban life in Barrington, R.I. Development pressures—whether for urban renewal and gentrification, suburbanization, or second-home construction—are chronicled with dark humor in the works of Geoffrey Wolff, Carolyn Chute, and Ernest Hebert.

A profound transformation of the New England image at the end of the 20th century was the result of the reemergence of native peoples. Successful land-claim settlements in the 1970s for the Penobscot and Passamaquoddy tribal nations in Maine were followed by the recognition and land claim settlement by congressional legislation of the Mashantucket Pequot tribal nation in Connecticut. Formerly "disappeared" native communities began to reshape the region's history and its contemporary identity. The Pequot's Foxwoods Casino has given the tribe an economic base. The casino also has helped Connecticut's economy at a time of economic depression following cutbacks at the submarine-manufacturing facilities in Groton. The spectacular Mashantucket Pequot Museum and Research Center presents Pequot history and supports research for native and nonnative scholars. Such modern developments have revitalized both scholarship and public understanding about the significance of Native Americans to the images and ideas of New England throughout its history.

In the 21st century, the best image of New England's cultural presence is still that of an old house that has served many inhabitants, with an attic full of the bricolage of history and memory. Such places are recycled—Paul Revere's house began as the home of an immigrant French Huguenot family, became the home of a patriot, was next a tenement in an Italian neighborhood, then, under Mayor Curley, was one of many symbols of Irish American political power, and is now a restored museum site dwarfed by skyscrapers. New England's old house, caught between restoration and destruction, is at once a symbol of decline and renewal. Images of loss sell in the New England tourist market, and nostalgia haunts New Englanders, who sense that other regions own the future.

Nevertheless, rather than basking in Indian-summer images of quaint decline, New Englanders follow the lead of Robert Frost in returning to a core Puritan value, a belief in the power of old words, like an old house, to contain new meanings: New Englanders persist in "a stubborn clinging to meaning; to purify words until they meant again what they should mean. Puritanism had that meaning entirely: a purifying of words and a renewal of words and a renewal of meaning." If New England images and ideas continue to have meanings, they will do so by incorporating the words and experiences of the Puerto Ricans of Hartford, the Cambodians of Lowell, and the Dominicans of Boston. Regional consciousness is now a congeries of nostalgia and innovation in which the newest voices will engage the tradition in conversation and rewrite the region's history.

The Puritan legacy may have marked New England with intolerance, but it also fostered a healthy libertarianism in which good fences make good neighbors who keep their own counsel and speak their minds. Given its complex geography, distinctive state cultures, contested history, and centuries of diversity, the old house of New England culture is still recognizable in form, even if we can't be sure who will open the door.

Gerard J. Brault, *The French-Canadian Heritage in New England* (1986); Van Wyck Brooks, *The Flowering of New England, 1815–1865* (1936); Brooks, *New England: Indian Summer, 1865–1915* (1940); Dona Brown, *Inventing New England: Regional Tourism in the 19th Century* (1995); Lawrence Buell, *New England Literary Culture from Revolution through Renaissance* (1986); Charles E. Clark, *Maine: A History* (1990); Joseph A. Conforti, *Imagining New England: Explorations of Regional Identity from the Pilgrims to the Mid-20th Century* (2001); Malcolm Cowley, *New England Writers and Writing* (1996); Andrew Delbanco, ed., *Writing New England: An Anthology from the Puritans to the Present* (2001); Jonathan L. Fairbanks and Robert F. Trent, eds., *New England Begins: The 17th Century*, 3 vols. (1982); David Hackett Fischer, *Albion's Seed: Four British Folkways in America* (1989); William J. Gilmore, *Reading Becomes a Necessity of Life: Material and Cultural Life in Rural New England, 1780–1835* (1989); Lisa Weber Greenberg, ed., "Stories to Tell: The Narrative Impulse in Contemporary New England Folk Art." Exhibition brochure, DeCordova Museum and Sculpture Park, Lincoln, Mass. (1988); Philip J. Greven, *The Protestant Temperament: Patterns of Child-Rearing, Religious Experience, and the Self in Early America* (1977); James Oliver Horton and Lois E. Horton, *Black Bostonians: Family Life and Community Struggle in the Antebellum North*, rev. ed. (1999); Michael Kammen, *Mystic Chords of Memory: The Transformation of Tradition in American Culture* (1991); James M. Lindgren, *Preserving Historic New England: Preservation, Progressivism, and the Remaking of Memory* (1995); Cotton Mather, *Magnalia Christi Americana; or, The Ecclesiastical History of New-England, from Its First Planting in the Year 1620 unto the Year of Our Lord 1698, in Seven Books*, 2 vols. (1967 [1702]); Perry Miller, *The New England Mind: From Colony to Province* (1983 [1953]); Miller, *The New England Mind: The 17th Century* (1983 [1954]); Stephen Nissenbaum, "New England as Region and Nation," in *All over the Map: Rethinking American Regions*, ed. Edward L. Ayers, Patricia Nelson Limerick, Peter S. Onuf, and Stephen Nissenbaum (1996); William D. Piersen, *Black Yankees: The Development of an Afro-American Subculture in 18th-Century New England* (1988); Mary Louise Pratt, *Imperial Eyes: Travel Writing and Transculturation* (1992); Kent C. Ryden, *Landscape with Figures: Nature and Culture in New England* (2001); George Santayana, "The Genteel Tradition in American Philosophy," in *The Genteel Tradition: Nine Essays* (1967); John Seelye, *Memory's Nation: The Place of Plymouth Rock* (1998); Nancy Shoemaker, "Regions as Categories of Analysis," *Perspectives: American Historical Association Newsletter* 34 (1996); William S. Simmons, *Spirit of the New England Tribes: History and Folklore, 1620–1984* (1986); Alexis de Tocqueville, *Democracy in America* (2000 [1835]); Jane Tompkins, *Sensational Designs: The Cultural Work of American Fiction, 1790–1860* (1985); William H. Truettner and Roger B. Stein, eds., *Picturing Old New England: Image and Memory* (1999); Frederick Jackson Turner, *The Significance of Sections in American History* (1932); Laurel Thatcher Ulrich, *The Age of Homespun: Objects and Stories in the Creation of an American Myth* (2001); Daniel Webster, *The Writings and Speeches of Daniel Webster* (1903); Malcolm X and Alex Haley, *The Autobiography of Malcolm X* (1992 [1965]).

David H. Watters

Alger, Horatio, Jr. (1832–99) Writer of juvenile fiction. Horatio Alger, Jr., wrote more than 100 juvenile novels featuring a poor boy who overcomes all obstacles to become a successful businessman, novels that sold tens of millions of copies and infused the name Horatio Alger with a cultural meaning it retains today.

Alger was born in Chelsea, Mass., and moved to nearby Marlborough in 1844, where he enrolled at the Gates Academy. The strong classical education he got there supplied the knowledge of Latin, Greek, and mathematics that enabled Alger to pass the entrance examination for Harvard College in 1847. Marlborough also exposed Alger to the early impact of industrialization in New England, for although it was still largely a farming community, shoe factories had begun to employ a significant number of the town's citizens.

By the time Alger began his studies at Harvard, he had already developed ambitions of becoming a writer. During his teenage years he had written poetry, and while an undergraduate he supplemented his income by publishing stories and essays in local newspapers and magazines. Upon graduation in 1852 he enrolled at the Harvard Divinity School, but, distracted by his freelance activities and lacking funds, he soon dropped out. After working for a time as a journalist and schoolteacher, Alger reentered Harvard Divinity, graduating finally in 1860.

He had no pulpit of his own until 1864, when he secured a position in Brewster, Mass., and settled into what he undoubtedly thought would be a long career as a minister. In 1866, however, he was forced to resign from the ministry after being accused of "unnatural familiarity" with at least two teenage boys. Alger never specifically acknowledged or denied the charges, but he later expressed feelings of guilt over what he termed his "imprudent" actions while in Brewster.

Defrocked and humiliated, Alger arrived in New York City and sought to make his living as a writer. He became fascinated by the lives of homeless boys who roamed the city selling newspapers and shining shoes; their struggles and triumphs provided Alger with material for his first great success, *Ragged Dick,* published in serialized form in 1867.

Ragged Dick established the formula that Alger would endlessly repeat, with minor permutations, over the course of the next three decades. "Ragged Dick," a young orphaned boy of generally good character acquires over the course of the novel the values he needs to succeed in an urbanized, industrialized society: hard work, perseverance, and the ability to delay personal gratification. These characteristics, though necessary for success, do not

guarantee it; at critical (and convenient) points in the story, an older, successful man comes forward to provide financial aid or a job. The novel closes with the hero achieving his goal—respectability—in the form of a new suit of clothes, a job (clerical in *Ragged Dick*), and a new name (Ragged Dick becomes Richard Hunter).

The enduring significance of Alger's writings does not derive from their literary merit. Rather, Alger's work is more properly situated in the long tradition of the literature of moral instruction for children, a direct descendant of the New England Puritan schoolteachers' nursery rhymes and grammars. Alger's achievement lay in showing how the older ethic valued by preindustrial New Englanders—hard work, perseverance, prudence, self-denial—also could lead to success in the new capitalistic, industrializing, and urbanizing America.

Alger spent his writing career in New York City but frequently returned to New England, often staying with his sister and her family in Natick, Mass. In 1896, his health failing, Alger moved permanently to Natick.

Gary Scharnhorst, *Horatio Alger, Jr.* (1980); Gary Scharnhorst with Jack Bales, *The Lost Life of Horatio Alger, Jr.* (1985); Michael Zuckerman, "The Nursery Tales of Horatio Alger," *American Quarterly* 24 (1972).
Christopher Berkeley

André the Seal André was a harbor seal who swam 200 miles each year from his winter home in a southern New England aquarium to Rockport, Maine, to rejoin his adoptive human family. André's life was celebrated in the children's book *A Seal Called Andre* (1975), and a 1994 movie, *André* (though the Paramount film actually starred a California sea lion and was filmed in Vancouver, British Columbia). Named Rockport's honorary harbormaster, André was once ranked by the *Portland Press Herald* as "second only to Andrew Wyeth as the state's most acclaimed summer resident."

The Rockport tree surgeon and professional scuba diver Harry Goodridge found the two-day-old seal pup apparently abandoned or orphaned on a rock ledge on a summer day in 1961. He named his new pet after André Cowan, a trainer at Marineland in Florida. At first, André lived in the house and yard with Goodridge, his wife, and their five children, and would ride in the back seat of the family car to the harbor for twice-daily swims. Eventually, audiences gathered by the hundreds at the harbor to watch André shoot baskets, roll over, clap his flippers, assume striking poses, and balance toys on his nose.

Rockport residents often found the seal sleeping on top of their fishing gear or in their skiffs. In the water, André would swim alongside rowboats, rolling over to invite fishermen

André the Seal and admirers at the New England Aquarium, Boston, 1979

to rub his belly. He would embrace scuba divers with his flippers or put his nose up to their facemasks. Most residents and tourists were so delighted with his antics that the Rockport Chamber of Commerce once named him Outstanding Citizen of the Year. But a few were dismayed. One day the seal appropriated the town constable's dingy; when the constable's son tried to move the seal, André nipped the boy's hat from his head and flung it overboard. (André later retrieved the hat, at Goodridge's request.) A similar fate befell a shiny brass button on the new coat of one of the Goodridge children, Toni: André nipped it off and tossed it in the water, to the child's distress. The next day, however, Goodridge found his seal waiting for him at the waterfront, the button in his mouth. André dropped it at his trainer's feet.

When André was 12 years old, measuring 5 feet long and weighing 250 pounds, Goodridge decided to board the seal at an aquarium for the winter. Thereafter, André spent most of his winters at either the New England Aquarium in Boston or the Mystic Marinelife Aquarium in Mystic, Conn. But each spring, aquarium staff would release the seal to the wild, and he would swim the 200 miles north to Penobscot Bay. When he was first released, he made the trip from Boston in less than four days.

André lived to old age for a seal. He was blind from cataracts when he made his final swim from Massachusetts in 1985. He died in the summer of 1986 at age 25 after losing a mating season fight with another seal; he was found on a deserted stretch of shore in Rockport. André was buried in Goodridge's backyard after a short ceremony, and his obituary was carried in dozens of newspapers. Harry Goodridge died in 1990.

Harry Goodridge and Lew Dietz, *A Seal Called André* (1975).

Sy Montgomery

Antiques and Decorative Arts

The accumulation, study, and display of antiques played a key role in the creation of a collective memory in New England. To this day, real or imagined ancestral relics serve as talismans of shared experience that not only prescribe identity within the region, but also contribute to the image of New England as a historic cultural and geographic landscape seemingly immune to change. Whether on view in public institutions or presented at home, antique furniture, silver, ceramics, pewter, glass, and other domestic accessories are sought-after commodities and tangible history lessons that have dramatically shaped popular understanding of the past.

Although a handful of diarists made occasional reference to hoary old chairs or chests in the course of the 18th century, the passing of the revolutionary generation in the 19th century sparked widespread introspection and interest in objects associated with historical figures and events. Historical societies, often founded as libraries for genealogical purposes, began to collect three-dimensional objects in the early republic. The Essex Institute (now part of the Peabody Essex Museum) in Salem, Mass., organized in 1821, included a joined chair from 17th-century Ipswich in its collections. The Pilgrim Society of Plymouth, Mass., acquired a turned chair purportedly owned by founding colonial governor John Carver sometime between the organization's inception in 1820 and 1828. As the society's Pilgrim Hall evolved into a cabinet of historical curiosities, other famous seating forms were donated in the 1830s, including another turned chair ascribed to the ownership of 17th-century elder William Brewster. The public display of these and other mnemonics of the colonial past in New England popularized the preservation of historic objects. Embedded in local myths, such pieces owed their existence to historical connections rather than to aesthetic preference and were soon incorporated in the literary culture of the region.

Publishing played a key role in nurturing a popular antebellum interest in antiques. Poetry and other forms of fiction provided a delivery system for local myth to become national history. Historical settings furnished with antiques became recognizable motifs familiar to readers throughout the United States. New England writers of national reputation such as Henry Wadsworth Longfellow and John Greenleaf Whittier animated colonial material culture by placing grandfather's clock at the head of the stairs or grandmother's spinning wheel in the parlor. Visual artists such as Eastman Johnson and Edward Lamson Henry and sculptors such as John Rogers concretized this imagery and made antiques increasingly accessible to the middle class.

Public displays fueled popular interest in antiques. The Philadelphia Centennial Exposition of 1876, often identified as a national coming of age, included two important installations that received widespread attention. The Connecticut Cottage, a state pavilion, and the New England Kitchen contained antiques that would become icons, including a desk reportedly owned by John Alden and a 17th-century cradle descended ostensibly from Peregrine White, the first child born in Plymouth Colony. Depicted in both *Frank Leslie's Illustrated* and *Harper's Weekly,* the domestic tableaux at the Centennial brought New England antiques to the nation.

The antiquarian movement achieved Rotarian respectability in the decades after the Civil War. Such authorities as the critic and journalist Clarence Cook began to advocate decorating with antiques. Writing in *The House Beautiful* in 1881, Cook explained that "everybody can't have a grandfather, nor things that came over on the *Mayflower*." The answer, for Cook and countless others, was to purchase this missing ancestry while touring New England. Antique shops began to dot the region as local communities adopted a tourist economy. Books like Annie Trumbull Slosson's *The China Hunters Club* (1878) and Mary Brine's *Grandma's Attic Treasures* (1882) narrate the growing mania for collecting "blue and white" china and period furniture.

The China Hunters organized as a club in the industrial city of Worcester, Mass., in the mid-1870s. Dedicated to the collection and study of period ceramics and porcelain, they produced several volumes aimed at a popular audience as well as important museum installations. By the 1890s, the home of good taste required an antique plate or two on the mantle as an act of domestic filial piety in the Victorian interior.

Antiques dealers, responding to the demands of the market, began to congregate in specific communities and neighborhoods. In Boston, Charles Street at the foot of Beacon Hill evolved into an antiques row. Hartford became a center of the antiques trade by the turn of the century. Pickers brought antique goods to restoration specialists and dealers in the city who, in turn, serviced a growing cadre of collectors. Irving Whitall Lyon, a physician for an insurance company, inaugurated the modern era of connoisseurship of American antiques when he published the lavishly illustrated *Colonial Furniture of New England* in 1891. Lyon promoted a scientific study of New England styles and types and pioneered the use of probate inventories in an attempt to revise the often-romantic family histories given to pieces as they descend through the generations. By the turn of the century, Hartford was home to a number of scholar-collectors, including George Dudley Seymour and Henry Wood Erving, the man responsible for coining the name Hadley chest for the distinctive early carved case furniture of the Connecticut River valley.

Hartford served as the site in 1910 of the first annual meeting of the Walpole Society, an exclusive club dedicated to collecting. Drawing its small membership from the elite collectors of Connecticut, Massachusetts, and New York, the Walpole Society played an important organizing role in the creation of major private collections that eventually formed the decorative arts galleries of large urban museums such as those of the American Wing at the Metropolitan Museum of Art in New York and the Museum of Fine Arts in Boston. To serve such discriminating collectors, Hartford supported a population of cabinetmakers specializing in the restoration trade. Often East European in origin and trained in their native lands, these little-known craftsmen defined an aesthetic that presented 18th-century furniture with glowing refinished surfaces.

The Roaring Twenties, stereotypically depicted as a jazz age of frantic modernity, proved to be the renaissance for interest in antiques. Heretofore gathered primarily for their historical associations, antiques began to be sorted according to aesthetics, value, and quality. Wallace Nutting, the erstwhile Congregational minister turned decorative arts authority, published landmark texts including *Furniture of the Pilgrim Century* (1921) and the three-volume *Furniture Treasury* (1928–33). Baedekers for the field of collecting, Nutting's books provided a popular ready reference and further organized the antiques market. In 1922 the magazine *Antiques* began serialization and provided a regular forum for the exchange of information as well as a platform for dealers, many of whom sought a national clientele. Overlooked styles such as the neoclassical furniture of the Federal era gained in popularity as latter-day Pilgrims sought a more refined aesthetic for the modern era.

The rise of suburbia in the decades after World War II established decorating with antiques as appropriate for the middle-class home. As the American dream took the form of a Colonial Revival house in a development approximating the landscape of a historic New England town, countless families lent an air of authenticity to their homes with a china cupboard filled with transfer-printed ceramics purchased on vacations to Maine or cut glass gathered in antique shops on Cape Cod. Regional auction houses and large-scale outdoor flea markets such as Brimfield in central Massachusetts provided an infrastructure for the trade. Droves of Americans, schooled in the "Good, Better, Best" paradigm promoted by the 1950s writings of Albert Sack—whose father had been a dealer in Boston—set out for New England looking for both a bargain and a sense of identity in the ever-changing 20th and 21st centuries.

Irving Whitall Lyon, *The Colonial Furniture of New England* (1891); Elizabeth Stillinger, *The Antiquers* (1980); William H. Truettner and Roger B. Stein, eds., *Picturing Old New England: Image and Memory* (1999).

Thomas Andrew Denenberg

Arts and Crafts Movement

The Arts and Crafts movement, an international initiative for social and aesthetic reform, found a welcome home in New England beginning around 1900. Spearheaded by the Society of Arts and Crafts, Boston, local craft societies and village industries peppered the region from pastoral villages to gritty urban neighborhoods. This revival of hand craftsmanship in textiles, wood, and metals profoundly influenced the curriculum of educational institutions, from schools to settlement houses. These programs, varied and geographically diverse, shared an ideology that promoted the return to traditional craft techniques as an antidote to the vicissitudes of 20th-century life. Placing a unique emphasis on local styles and forms, the craft revival in New England served to reinforce regional identity in an increasingly modern, increasingly heterogeneous world.

As a search for meaning in preindustrial patterns of art and labor, the handicraft revival was by no means a new phenomenon nor was it unique to New England. The mid-19th-century efforts of John Ruskin and William Morris in Great Britain launched a revolution in social thought and practice that quickly gained currency in America. Ruskin, a professor of fine arts at Oxford and the author of such landmark volumes as *The Seven Lamps of Architecture* (1849) and *The Stones of Venice* (1853), focused attention on the banality of industrial labor while defining, for generations of Victorians, the aesthetic and spiritual im-

portance of premodern art and architecture. Morris, a designer, poet, and activist, emphasized the secular over the spiritual and became a prominent socialist voice in the last decade of the 19th century.

The English foundations of the Arts and Crafts movement were, therefore, firmly embedded in the political discourse of the day. "The Nature of the Gothic," an essay from Ruskin's *Stones of Venice,* became an international manifesto for the movement. Ostensibly architectural history, the essay was in fact contemporary cultural criticism with a profound socialist bent. "When fingers measure degrees like cog wheels," declared Ruskin (sounding much like his contemporary Karl Marx), workers become "unhumanized." The answer for Ruskin, Morris, and their followers was a return to hand craftsmanship.

The Arts and Crafts movement found an American champion in the Harvard professor Charles Eliot Norton, the first professor of fine arts at an American university. Not only did Norton model his lectures on Ruskin's teachings, but he also sought to inspire an appreciation of Italian culture among his students by emphasizing the moral and spiritual values of earlier periods of art and architecture. Ruskin's approval of Norton's efforts was made clear when Norton was named to be Ruskin's literary executor after his death in 1900.

Because he was an author and activist, Norton's sphere of influence extended well beyond the classroom. In 1897 he cofounded the Society of Arts and Crafts, Boston (SACB), with a group of like-minded Brahmins and was chosen to serve as the organization's first president. Echoing Ruskin, the society sought, in the words of its mission statement, "to bring Designers and Workmen into mutually helpful relations, and to encourage Workmen to execute designs of their own." A hint of the tensions within the Boston group, and in the Arts and Crafts movement in general, is evident as the incorporation document proceeds to recommend "an appreciation of the dignity and value of good design." From its very genesis, the question arose: Should the society work to better the lot of the working classes, or just to improve their aesthetic judgment?

Although the SACB oscillated between aesthetic and social concerns, the group never wavered in its mission as an educational institution or in its commitment to its artisan-members. Organized as an idealized medieval guild, SACB members were grouped as Masters, Craftsmen, and Associates. The understanding implicit in this trinity was that skilled woodworkers, silversmiths, jewelers, and bookbinders would educate journeymen and apprentices to design and produce objects

of lasting value. Associates, originally called Patrons, supported the organization. The SACB marketed its members' work through the Handicraft Shop, sponsored important exhibitions, organized lectures, provided a lending library, and published a nationally known journal called *Handicraft.*

Although the SACB provided an organizational structure to the movement in New England, grassroots craft enterprises gave the region its unique style and ideology. With rare exception, New England craft organizations employed vernacular styles that reinforced regional identity. Boston's Paul Revere Pottery was one such effort that successfully married local myth with the reform impulse of the Progressive Era to create the blend of aesthetics and social purpose that Ruskin and Morris had called for decades earlier. Founded in 1908 by Edith Guerrier and Edith Brown, the Paul Revere Pottery evolved out of a literary club called the Saturday Evening Girls. Based in Boston's North End, an immigrant neighborhood, the Saturday Evening Girls provided respectable leisure activity for the teenage daughters of Italian and Slavic immigrants. The group turned to art pottery in 1908 and opened a shop around the corner from the Paul Revere House "in the shadow of the Old North Church." By taking the name of the famous colonial craftsman, the Paul Revere Pottery not only tapped into the rich vein of history and myth exploited a generation earlier by Henry Wadsworth Longfellow and his contemporaries, but also declared its members to be good immigrants in the same way as Revere, a first generation Franco-American, was. The ceramic goods produced by the pottery were marketed in the SACB showrooms, included in its exhibitions, and sold by department stores.

The blend of historical myth and craft exemplified by the Paul Revere Pottery was repeated throughout the region. In Salem, Mass., the House of the Seven Gables was restored in 1908–10 to house a social settlement. Designed to facilitate assimilation of immigrants into the community, the building was renovated to recall Nathaniel Hawthorne's famous romance, while the educational program of the institution followed the Arts and Crafts precepts of the progressive Sloyd system of manual training. Developed by Otto Salomon, a German educational theorist, the Sloyd curriculum sought to teach life skills though a progression of manual exercises such as woodworking and leatherwork. The House of the Seven Gables Settlement Association thus employed the most up-to-date of pedagogies, while relying on historical symbols of local meaning to add value to the arts and crafts.

The most complete example of the transmission of Arts and Crafts ideology into practice came not in a city but in the pastoral village of Deerfield, Mass. A frontier outpost in colonial times, Deerfield enjoyed a healthy agricultural economy until the mid-19th century. Passed over by the railroad in 1846 in favor of neighboring mill towns such as Greenfield, old Deerfield was left to wither on the economic vine. New England tourism dramatically increased after the Civil War, however, and the same rail line that deprived Deerfield of economic nourishment at mid-century guaranteed its success as a summer colony in the 1890s, making the town's undeveloped Main Street a short buggy, then streetcar, ride from the railhead.

Arts and Crafts ideology came to town with the summer folk, and Deerfield was soon host to no fewer than four craft organizations; the Society of Blue and White, the Pocumtuck Basket Makers, the Deerfield Basket Makers, and the Deerfield Society of Arts and Crafts (later renamed the Deerfield Industries). All found inspiration in the town's unique colonial history. The Society of Blue and White initially copied historic textiles housed in Deerfield's Memorial Hall, while the Pocumtuck Basket Makers traded on Deerfield's reputation as a colonial outpost—and its long history of violent conflict with Native Americans—by producing an "Indian" product. Ambitious members of the local Society of Arts and Crafts reproduced and reinterpreted major pieces of local furniture, such as a 17th-century oak Hadley chest on display in Memorial Hall.

The Arts and Crafts movement spread north in the 1920s. In New Hampshire, for example, a committee of the local historical society founded the Sandwich Home Industries in 1926. Organized to produce hooked rugs, woven textiles, baskets, and wrought iron, the Home Industries sought to afford local residents a means of making a living while reviving traditional craft practices. Other New Hampshire communities, such as Wolfeboro, followed this example. By 1931 the governor, John Winant, institutionalized the movement when he appointed a Commission of the Arts and Crafts, an administrative organization that soon changed its name to the League of New Hampshire Arts and Crafts. Increasingly important during the economic hard times of the Great Depression, the league listed 886 members in 1932. One year later, the group boasted 1,452 members committed to the craft revival, with nine shops throughout the Granite State.

New Hampshire was by no means unique. Rug-making endeavors dotted the Maine landscape from Sabatos rugs in Center Lovell to the Cranberry Isles rug industry near Northeast Harbor. The Maine Seacoast Missionary Society encouraged rug hooking in the 1920s as an income-producing activity for the residents of the remote maritime region. In 1939, Maine followed New Hampshire and organized statewide support for craft initiatives under the Department of Education. Vermont followed suit in 1941 and established a state commission as well. The Arts and Crafts movement was therefore fully institutionalized in New England by the eve of World War II.

The Arts and Crafts movement played an important role in defining New England as a traditional, productive region in the early decades of the 20th century. Manual training was combined with regional history to offer a tangible means of education for New England's rising immigrant population and rural poor. Settlement houses and village industries provided economic uplift in both urban and rural settings—support that gained importance during the Great Depression as basket making and rug hooking helped support the region. Taken in sum, the handicraft revival reinforced the perception of New England as a region with a long tradition of craft production, a reputation that belied the fact that the area was indeed the earliest and most industrial region of the country.

Eileen Boris, *Art and Labor: Ruskin, Morris, and the Craftsman Ideal in America* (1986); Bert Denker, ed., *The Substance of Style: Perspectives on the American Arts and Crafts Movement* (1996); Suzanne L. Flynt, Susan McGowan, and Amelia F. Miller, *Gathered and Preserved* (1991); Wendy Kaplan, ed., *"The Art That Is Life": The Arts and Crafts Movement in America, 1875–1920* (1987); T. J. Jackson Lears, *No Place of Grace: Antimodernism and the Transformation of American Culture, 1880–1920* (1981); Marilee Boyd Meyer, ed., *Inspiring Reform: Boston's Arts and Crafts Movement* (1997).

Thomas Andrew Denenberg

"Banned in Boston" "Banned in Boston" is a derisory phrase alluding to the legendary powerful and pervasive force of local censorship in the notoriously puritanical city during the 1920s. The phrase came into common use in the context of early-20th-century reactions to New England's rigid Puritanism, manifest in such diverse expressions as H. L. Mencken's vitriolic essays "The American: His Morals" (1913), "The New American Puritanism" (1914), and "Puritanism as a Literary Force" (1917); Victor Seastrom's film *The Scarlet Letter* (1926); and the first volume of Vernon L. Parrington's *Main Currents in American Thought: The Colonial Mind, 1620–1800* (1927). Twenties America caricatured New England Calvinists as sternly inflexible, self-righteous inquisitors who were motivated— in Mencken's acerbic words—by "the haunting fear that someone, somewhere, may be happy."

This popular characterization was not totally divorced from historical fact. As early as 1628, Governor William Bradford had dispersed Thomas Morton's out-settlement at Merrymount (now Quincy, Mass.), exiling Morton because of his promiscuous and lascivious lifestyle. Puritans considered drama frivolous and immoral, and Boston did not welcome theatrical productions during its first 150 years; stage plays were banned by the General Court from 1750 to 1797. Indeed, that early thespian ban gave rise to a companion catch phrase (also prominent in the 1920s)—"Boston version"— that referred to a play from which offensive words or stage business had been cut in order to satisfy local censorship authorities.

Late-19th-century attitudes provide more immediate historical background for Boston's censorious reputation. As a result of the federal Comstock anti-obscenity law (the Postal Act of 1873), the New England Watch and Ward Society, modeled on the New York Society for the Suppression of Vice (1873), was organized in 1876. This nongovernmental body took as its mission protecting the moral purity of the citizens of Boston by banning materials—books, plays, magazines, and pictures—it considered impure or indecent and that threatened to subvert traditional family values. Its members and supporters composed a social register of the Brahmin elite, and among its officers were presidents of Yale and Harvard as well as such noted Protestant clergy as the Massachusetts Episcopal bishop William Lawrence.

The Watch and Ward Society assumed a more efficient censorship role in 1907 when the Reverend Jason Franklin Chase became its secretary. Under Chase, the Watch and Ward Society developed a system of self-censorship (on the society's recommendation) by the Boston Booksellers' Committee. By the mid-1920s, however, control of censorship in Boston had shifted to municipal authorities, who relied on the police and courts to enforce their decrees. The chief municipal drama censor was John M. Casey, head of the Licensing Division of Mayor James M. Curley's office from 1920 to 1926.

The Boston ban was most effective in the 1920s; between 1918 and 1926, an estimated 75 books were banned; more than 100 were proscribed in the years 1928–29. Ironically, the Old Howard (Athenaeum), which introduced burlesque in the 1890s, was largely unhindered by municipal restriction until the 1930s. By that time, the (Edward W.) Weeks bill had liberalized the Massachusetts obscenity law, dramatically reducing the overzealous banning of literary materials and rendering the slogan that had rallied the anticensorship forces, "banned in Boston," a faded memorial of a bygone era.

Cleveland Amory, *The Proper Bostonians* (1947); Carl Bode, ed., *The Editor, the Bluenose, and the Prostitute: H. L. Mencken's History of the "Hatrack" Censorship Case* (1988); Paul S. Boyer, *Purity in Print: The Vice-Society Movement and Book Censorship in America* (1968); William Noble, *Bookbanning in America: Who Bans Books?—And Why?* (1990).

Louis J. Kern

Barnum, P. T. (Phineas Taylor) (1810–91) Entertainer, impresario.

One of the most recognizable 19th-century New Englanders, P. T. Barnum played a central role in the development of mass entertainment and the modern variety of fame. His career took shape against what he perceived to be the elitism of dominant New England culture. Barnum was born in Bethel, Conn. After a tumultuous stint as editor of the populist Jacksonian newspaper the *Herald of Freedom* (1831–34) in conservative Danbury, Conn., he moved to New York. His first act of showmanship was a tour of the North Atlantic states in 1835–36 with Joice Heth, an elderly African American woman purported to be the 161-year-old former nurse of the baby George Washington. When Heth died, Barnum arranged to have an autopsy performed in public (for which, of course, he charged admission); the postmortem revealed that her story was a hoax. Barnum's handling of this affair reflected his media savvy and his callous attitude toward African Americans (as well as that of his audiences), and it foreshadowed his future exhibits of freaks, curiosities, and wonders.

Statue of Barnum at P. T. Barnum Museum, Bridgeport, Conn.

From 1841 until 1868 Barnum owned the American Museum in New York, which housed an animal menagerie, a lecture room, dramatic stages, artwork, antiquities, exotic artifacts, and displays of human and natural oddities. Many exhibits, such as the Feejee Mermaid, were "humbugs" that tested his audience's abilities to distinguish the genuine from the inauthentic. Furthering his growing national fame, Barnum toured Europe with General Tom Thumb (actually Charles S. Stratton, a diminutive child from Connecticut) in 1844; "the little General" famously delighted Queen Victoria and King Leopold of Belgium at Buckingham Palace with his jokes, dances, impersonations, and a duel with the queen's poodle. Barnum's next great tour was with Jenny Lind, "the Swedish Nightingale," whose rapturous soprano and charming public manner (combined with Barnum's massive publicity campaign) won her an unprecedented American audience in 1850–51. Henceforth, Barnum's productions were cast as respectable entertainment, suitable for the famously prudish middle-class Victorian family.

As Barnum became a more established figure, he grew increasingly involved in politics. He joined the Republican Party in 1860 and supported enfranchisement for blacks after the war. He became Fairfield's representative to the Connecticut legislature in 1865, lost campaigns for the U.S. Congress and Senate in 1867 and 1876, and in 1875 was elected to a one-year term as mayor of Bridgeport, where he owned an elaborate mansion on a 17-acre estate. During his mayoral tenure he focused (with minimal results) on cleaning up the town's saloons and brothels.

Between episodes of his intermittent political career came lavish spectacles: the Traveling World's Fair (1873–74) and the Great Roman Hippodrome (1874–76), noted for its "Congress of Nations," in which actors portraying monarchs of "all civilized nations" were shown in native dress riding in caravans. In 1876 he began "the Greatest Show on Earth," which was merged with rival showman James A. Bailey's circus in 1881 and bought by the Ringling family in 1906.

Barnum's autobiographies, which he revised and updated throughout his life, were among the most widely read books of the 19th century and have become classics of the genre. Additionally, Barnum has been the subject of numerous biographies, scholarly studies, a feature-length film, and a Broadway musical. The Barnum Museum in Bridgeport presents Barnum's life, career, and influence on 19th-century American culture. His legacy is part of our everyday language, kept alive in part by the circus and animal crackers that continue to bear his name.

Bluford Adams, *E Pluribus Barnum: The Great Showman and the Making of U.S. Popular Culture* (1997); P. T. Barnum, *The Life of P. T. Barnum, Written by Himself* (2000 [1855]); Barnum, *Struggles and Triumphs; or, Forty Years' Recollections of P.T. Barnum* (1987 [1869]); Benjamin Reiss, *The Showman and the Slave: Race, Death, and Memory in Barnum's America* (2001).

Benjamin Reiss

Boston Post Cane

The *Boston Post* Cane was the advertising brainchild of Edwin A. Grozier, publisher of the *Boston Post*. In a letter to 700 towns in Maine, Massachusetts, New Hampshire, and Rhode Island dated August 2, 1909, and in a newspaper article of August 18, 1909, Grozier announced his plan to give a fine cane to the oldest citizen of the town. Canes were not distributed to all towns; 258 went to Massachusetts, and perhaps another 200 went to towns in New Hampshire, Rhode Island, and Maine, where the *Post* was circulated. Only two canes were presented in Vermont, but none in Connecticut.

The cane was to be given to the oldest citizen, a male voter. Upon that person's decease, the cane was to go to the next oldest male voter. After the passage of the 19th Amendment giving women the vote, and following complaints by women, Edwin Grozier's son Richard opened the honor to women in the 1930s. To gain further publicity for the paper, Grozier published photos of recipients and accounts of ceremonies marking presentations of canes, starting with Solomon Talbot, 95 years of age, of Sharon, Mass. A notice accompanying a subsequent photo display elaborated Grozier's motives for honoring the elderly, noting that the canes "are intended as a tribute to honored and useful lives, to thrift, temperance, and right living, and above all, to the superb vigor of New England manhood." This language countered developing popular imagery of a decrepit New England countryside of declining villages and native stock and complemented attempts by advocates of the Colonial Revival and Old Home Week movements to rehabilitate New England traditions.

The canes themselves were made by J. F. Fradley and Company of New York City from "Gaboon ebony from the Congo, Africa." The head is 14-karat gold with ornamental swags on the sides and is engraved on top:

Presented
By the *Boston Post*
to the OLDEST CITIZEN
of

———————

(To be transmitted).

The town was to engrave its name in the blank and return a form to the *Post* with information on the recipient, including interesting incidents, Grand Army of the Republic membership, and his reasons for longevity. This was not Grozier's first attempt to increase circulation by recognizing the elderly. As Barbara Staples reports, he previously had awarded a rocking chair and a Morris chair to the oldest couple in New England. He also boosted circulation in 1894 with a special edition written and edited entirely by women. Grozier had a storied newspaper career, beginning in 1881 with the *Boston Globe,* followed by stints at the *Boston Herald* and as editor-in-chief for the evening and Sunday editions of the *New York World.* He bought the *Boston Post* in 1891 and rapidly built its circulation.

The cane, however, is the lasting legacy, having outlived the *Boston Post,* which closed in 1956. The canes are still actively distributed in the region. Barbara Staples, in *The Bay State's Boston Post Canes,* surveyed Massachusetts towns and determined that 161 canes survive. This book presents the stories of the first recipients in Massachusetts towns. Some communities still award the cane to the oldest citizen; other canes have been retired and donated to local historical societies; other towns present a replica or a certificate; in others, the family of the last recipient has kept the cane. In some towns, the presentation of the cane has a deep significance, as when Sister Ethel Hudson, the last of the Canterbury (N.H.) Shakers, received the cane at age 96 in 1992. In some towns, however, the cane is considered a "kiss of death," viewed with bemusement and superstition.

"The *Boston Post* Gold Head Canes: Presented to the Oldest Citizens of 700 New England Towns through the Selectmen," *Boston Post* (August 18, 1909); Tim Clark, "Keepers of the Cane," *Yankee* (1983): 191; Barbara Staples, *The Bay State's Boston Post Canes: The History of a New England Tradition* (1997).

David H. Watters

Brother Jonathan Originating in the Revolutionary War, "Brother Jonathan," later usually "Jonathan," was a name given to the figure of the rustic New England Yankee who became the representative American throughout much of the 19th century. By the Civil War he had been replaced by the figure of Uncle Sam.

Brother Jonathan first appeared in the writings of loyalists and British soldiers to identify and satirize New Englanders who fought for the American cause. Subsequent characterizations in the 18th century appeared in British and American songs, including versions of "Yankee Doodle"; on stage, most notably in Royall Tyler's *The Contrast* (1787); and in mock pastorals by Federalist writers in the 1790s. With the War of 1812, however, Americans made the figure their own as the youthful, democratic counterpart to, and often the an-

tagonist of, the English archetypal character, John Bull. "Jonathan may be described as the finishing model of the Anglo-Saxon, of which John Bull is the rough cast," declared *Putnam's Magazine* in 1853.

Although Jonathan was predominantly a humorous literary figure who appeared in songs, poems, stories, and letters and on stage over the years, some of his peculiarities, as they were called, had roots in folklore. Giving "a Yankee answer," for example, meant evading a question, often by asking another one. Yet at the same time, Jonathan was known for being intrusively inquisitive and compulsively garrulous. His most enduring peculiarity, perhaps, was his bent for ingenious peddling and shrewd trades. In *A Trip to New England* (1699), Edward Ward wrote that although the Saints of New England "wear in their faces the Innocence of Doves, you will find them in their dealings . . . as Subtile as Serpents." In the 19th century, this legendary skill was called Yankee "cuteness" (for "acuteness") and celebrated what was considered on both sides of the ocean as a national trait that affirmed the material promise of America. Travel books recounted purportedly true stories of wood nutmegs, pit-coal indigo, and sandbags painted to sell as hams, but such stories also appeared widely in print and on stage, suggesting an active exchange between literary sources and oral tradition.

Brother Jonathan also had an important visual history in the evolution of the figure of Uncle Sam, who replaced the Yankee as the national type. Illustrations of the Yankee, for example, often portrayed him dressed in striped trousers, top hat, and waistcoat or swallowtail coat, features that became ultimately identified with Uncle Sam. Uncle Sam originated in the War of 1812, but he appeared only occasionally, and as the representative of the government, not its people. With the coming of the Civil War, as Brother Jonathan's New England origins were increasingly identified with the Northern cause, Uncle Sam emerged as the national icon for Americans. For many years, however, the British preferred Brother Jonathan in that role.

Alton Ketchum, *Uncle Sam: The Man and the Legend* (1959); Winifred Morgan, *An American Icon: Brother Jonathan and American Identity* (1988).

Cameron C. Nickels

Candy New England's tradition of candy making is long and distinguished, and today the oldest candy manufacturers and shops in the nation still operate in the region. The candy-making tradition was first built on maple sugar, "the great New England contentment," in the words of the food writer Fred

Halliday: "It sits so sweetly and lightly on the tongue that it never cloys the palate. It is delicate, and it has a body, in its pure early spring rendering, that is almost ethereal." The earliest reference to New England sugaring goes back to 1609: "The Indians get juice from the trees and from it distil a sweet and agreeable liquid." By the 1760s, British periodicals were carrying accounts of New England maple sugaring.

Candy making in early New England was a social occasion, often reserved for holidays when neighbors would gather for taffy pulls and to make caramels, molasses taffy, maple-syrup candy, pralines, and maple nut fudge. At maple-sugaring time, "sugar-on-snow" and other maple candies made spring a favorite time of the year for children. Local foods—cranberries, walnuts, apples, and blueberries—were used in candy making, and New England's extensive shipping trade provided the rest of the ingredients that became staples of the region's candy-making traditions—rum, raisins, vanilla, cinnamon, and molasses.

The commercial manufacture of candy began in 1765, when Dr. James Baker of Dorchester, Mass., financed the first chocolate mill in America and founded the company still known as Baker's Chocolate. Ye Olde Pepper Companie, established in 1806, is the oldest candy store in the country, still operating on Derby Street in Salem, Mass., just a few doors from the House of the Seven Gables. The shop's signature candy, the Salem Gibraltar, a soft lemon- or peppermint-flavored bite-sized piece with a sugar base, was carried by the city's fleet to the far corners of the world.

New England's queen of candy, Fannie Farmer, was born in Boston and became, despite suffering from childhood paralysis, the nation's leading cooking authority at the turn of the 20th century. Farmer wrote the nation's leading recipe book, *The Boston Cooking-School Cook Book* (1896), which has now sold more than 3 million copies worldwide. The candy maker Frank O'Connor, owner of Laura Secord Candy Shops, Canada's largest retail company, opened the first Fannie Farmer Candy Shop in Rochester, N.Y., in 1919, four years after Farmer's death. In the 1920s, O'Connor expanded through the upper Midwest and the Dakotas; Fannie Farmer Candies continue to be sold today, primarily in New England.

In the 1880s, the Charles N. Miller Company made its candy in the Paul Revere House and christened a chewy peanut-butter and chocolate bar with the name Dearo, taken from a political group in Boston's North End whom Mayor John "Honey Fitz" Fitzgerald had taken to calling his "dear ol' North

Enders." Perley G. Gerrish, of Cambridge, Mass., made the first peanut bar, Squirrel Brand, in 1905. Seavey's Sweets brought out the Needham, a chocolate-covered coconut square named after a Massachusetts preacher of the 1870s. Old Nick, a nut roll from the Schutter Candy Company, was popular in New England in the 1920s. Washburn Candy Corporation, of Brockton, Mass., is the oldest family-owned candy manufacturer in the United States, and it holds the distinction of being the country's only large-scale maker of Christmas ribbon candy.

The Peter Paul Candy Manufacturing Company was established in 1919 in New Haven, Conn., having grown from a home-made-chocolate shop founded by Peter Paul Halajian and five Armenian associates who sold their freshly made candy door to door. In 1922 the company moved to nearby Naugatuck. In 1978 Peter Paul merged with Cadbury, and in 1988, Hershey Foods Corp purchased the corporation. PEZ candy, manufactured in Orange, Conn., is sold in more than 60 countries around the world, and its collectible dispensers have become a staple of American pop culture. The candy was originally made in Vienna, however, and its name derives from the German word for peppermint.

The New England Confectionary Company (NECCO), established in Boston in 1847, is the nation's oldest continuously operating candy company and is renowned for its famous NECCO wafers. In 1866 the company introduced their "conversation candies," initiating a tradition that continues today with 8 billion Valentine hearts produced each year. Originally cut into various shapes, including postcards, baseballs, and horseshoes, the Valentines included such messages as "Please send a lock of your hair by return mail." Still-popular pithier messages were soon introduced—"Be Mine," "Kiss Me," "Sweet Talk," and the like—supplemented in recent years by such sentiments as "Fax Me." Charlestown's landmark Schrafft's building was once home to the William F. Schrafft and Sons candy company, possibly the first American makers of jellybeans; Schrafft, a shrewd marketer, ran an advertisement in 1861 urging people to send jellybeans to soldiers fighting in the Civil War.

Ray Broekel, "Land of the Candy Bar," in *American Heritage* (October–November 1986); Fred Halliday, *The New England Food Explorer* (1993); Georgia Orcutt and Sandra Taylor, eds., *Desserts: The Flavor of New England* (1982); Sara B. B. Stamm, *Favorite New England Recipes* (1991).

Louis Mazzari

Celebrations of New England's Past

The poet Oliver Wendell Holmes had his native New England in mind when, commenting in 1880 on the vogue of celebrating sundry historical dates, he observed, "One might think the patron saint of America was Saint Anniversary." By the late 19th century, the celebration of regional and local anniversaries had become part of the historical consciousness and retrospective tradition that had long characterized New England.

The region's historical consciousness and celebratory tradition have their origins in Puritan practices. During the middle and late 17th century, as the members of the first generation of Puritans gradually died, ministers and political leaders increasingly celebrated the seemingly heroic founding of the region. New England's founders were commemorated as magistrates and ministers whose courage, piety, and virtue singled them out as God's new "chosen people." The settlement of New England came to be viewed as the consequence of a "Great Migration," a movement of devout pioneers in the 1630s that resembled the Christian spiritual quests of biblical times.

This heroic historical narrative of the founding of the region was intended not only to celebrate the past but also to offer inspiration to the present. Second- and third-generation New Englanders were criticized for falling away from the piety and virtue of the founders and were urged to rededicate themselves to the lofty standards of their ancestors. Such celebratory and didactic invocations of the past were not tied to specific dates. Rather, the heroic achievements of New England's founding generation were commemorated in sermons on various occasions—election day and fast days, for example—and in such written histories as Cotton Mather's *Magnalia Christi Americana* (1702).

It was not until the 18th century that a specific historical date emerged for the celebration of an important aspect of New England's past. In Plymouth, Mass., Forefathers' Day, December 22, became an official anniversary for commemorating the landing of the Pilgrims in 1620. During the American Revolution, the celebration of Forefathers' Day acquired political significance. It served the patriot cause by reminding Americans that the religious persecution of the Pilgrims established a historical precedent for English assaults on political liberty in the 1760s and 1770s. Americans were urged to emulate the courage, virtue, and love of liberty of their Pilgrim forefathers.

In the decades after the Revolution, migrating New Englanders carried the celebration of Forefathers' Day beyond the region's boundaries. The bicentennial of the founding of Plymouth in 1820 added to the Pilgrim mystique. Plymouth staged a major celebration, and Daniel Webster, perhaps New England's greatest orator, delivered a lengthy address that located in Plymouth the origins of New England institutions and Yankee ideals. He also named the Plymouth Colony the seedbed of the American republic, and the source of Americans' love of political and religious liberty. The bicentennial of Plymouth's founding encouraged New England Societies, which were formed by migrating Yankees in southern and midwestern cities, to popularize both the commemoration of Forefathers' Day and the Pilgrim myth that Webster so eloquently explained. Forefathers' Day, however, was gradually eclipsed by the celebration of Thanksgiving, which had been observed by colonial New Englanders on different dates and which became a national holiday in 1863.

In the first half of the 19th century came a variety of other historical anniversaries that occasioned celebrations and the dedication of commemorative markers. Centennials and bicentennials of towns and churches were widely celebrated across the region. In 1835, for instance, Concord, Mass., organized an elaborate commemoration of the town's bicentennial. Concord's citizens listened to Ralph Waldo Emerson deliver a major address that praised the town's Puritan roots and contributions to the American Revolution. On the Fourth of July two years later, Emerson participated in a local commemoration that dedicated an obelisk to the town's patriots. For this occasion Emerson composed his "Concord Hymn," which contained the famous description of the "embattled farmers" who "fired the shot heard 'round the world." The power and enduring influence of this depiction suggest how 19th-century commemorations profoundly shaped popular understanding of New England's past. One astute 19th-century observer of these pre–Civil War historical commemorations commented that public understanding of the New England past was not formed primarily by "our formal and elaborate histories" but by "our Plymouth Rock and Fourth of July orations, our town and church centennials, and our New England festivals, now observed in the chief cities of the land."

The patriotic historical narratives that emerged from these celebrations uniformly linked the settlement of New England and the American Revolution into an epic account that shaped popular understanding of regional identity and explained the origins of the antebellum Protestant republic. But these commemorations also produced exclusionary interpretations of New England's past. William Apess, a Connecticut descendant of Pequot Indians and an itinerant Methodist minister, appropriated the patriotic rhetoric of 19th-century historical commemorations for a countercelebration. In a kind of protest of self-congratulatory New England historical observances, Apess publicly celebrated the 160th anniversary of the death of King Philip (Metacom). In his "Eulogy on King Philip" (1836), which he delivered twice and also published, Apess commemorated the Wampanoag chief who attempted to forge a Pan-Indian alliance against the depredations of land-hungry New Englanders. Apess held up this "son of the forest" as the George Washington of his people, "a martyr to his cause, though unsuccessful, yet as glorious as the American Revolution." Apess challenged the high-flown commemoration rhetoric of popular speakers like Daniel Webster and retold the story of the settlement of New England from a Native American perspective.

Such minority historical views, however, were increasingly overwhelmed not only by the swell of antebellum patriotic celebrations but also by the progress of "Saint Anniversary" in New England after the Civil War. The arrival of revolutionary anniversaries sparked a new round of historical commemorations, some intended to heal the wounds of the Civil War. In 1875, for example, former Confederate soldiers from South Carolina not only joined the parade marking the centennial of the Battle of Bunker Hill, but planted a palmetto tree next to a northern pine in ritualistic affirmation of sectional friendship within the union.

In 1876 the nation's centennial celebration helped launch the Colonial Revival, a commemorative, nostalgic, even reactionary movement that extolled the virtues and accomplishments of the colonial past. Particularly in New England, a changing landscape of mills, cities, and non-Protestant immigrants provoked concerns for the passing of "old New England." Many descendants of the region's colonial settlers were disquieted by the demise of the rural, seemingly stable, and culturally homogeneous world of their ancestors. In the late 19th and early 20th centuries, local, regional, and national historical anniversaries provided occasions for celebrating New England's Anglo-Protestant foundation. Colonial Revival historical commemorations were also designed to promote the Americanization of growing numbers of immigrants.

Colonial Revivalists were particularly proud of the religious origins of New England and the spiritual and political aspirations of its Anglo-Protestant founders. While Plymouth and the Pilgrim forefathers continued to gain stature in the regional historical imagination, the Puritans also were commemorated for the virile character, rock-ribbed sense of duty, and spiritual ideals they embodied. Such values were memorialized in impressive bronze statues to the Puritan founders of New England.

As part of the 250th anniversary of the establishment of the Massachusetts Bay Colony, for instance, the sculptor Richard Greenough completed an imposing statue of John Winthrop in downtown Boston in 1880. Seven years later Augustus Saint-Gaudens's magnificent bronze *The Puritan* was dedicated in front of the public library in Springfield, Mass. Even in those parts of the region where Puritanism had been less influential, Colonial Revivalists found other ways to celebrate the New England values and traditions that seemed increasingly threatened by heavy immigration and its attendant changes. Rhode Island officials, for example, erected a statue entitled *Independent Man* on their new statehouse in 1899, a secularized symbol of many of the same New England virtues commemorated in Puritan statuary.

By the turn of the 20th century historical pageants had become a central part of local, state, and regional celebrations in Colonial Revival New England. These pageants were usually theatrical reenactments of important historical events. Pageants were typically staged on the Fourth of July, during country fairs, or as part of Old Home Week—the summer celebration that began in the 1890s and encouraged migrating New Englanders to acknowledge and return, at least temporarily, to their roots. Handbooks such as *Celebrating the Fourth of July by Means of Pageantry* (1912) spurred commemoration organizers across the region. In Vermont, pageants often focused on the Green Mountain Boys and the spirit and commitment to liberty that brought the state into existence during the American Revolution. Some pageants involved multiple reenactments depicting a broad sweep of local history. Portsmouth, N.H., organized a 12-episode historical pageant in 1923 that celebrated the community's experience back to 1789. A similar 12-episode pageant in Bath, Maine, in 1928 reviewed the city's history up to the arrival of statehood in 1820.

The New England heritage that was celebrated in Colonial Revival pageants and in earlier historical commemorations was overwhelmingly if not exclusively white. Only occasionally did African Americans receive the kind of prominence accorded them in the historical pageant of Newburyport, Mass., in 1913: African Americans marched with floats celebrating the local abolitionist hero William Lloyd Garrison and portraying the hardships of slavery, the Emancipation Proclamation, and the progress achieved since slavery had been outlawed.

The arrival of tercentennial anniversaries in the 20th century initiated yet another cycle of pageantry, oratory, and memorializing. New statues, bronze plaques, and granite monuments appeared on the New England landscape. Saint Anniversary in the 20th century extended the patterns that earlier commemorations of New England's past had firmly established. First, the colonial period remained the privileged historical era of New England celebrations. Second, New England's Anglo-Protestant heritage was understandably commemorated but usually in exclusionary ways. Third, localism continued to characterize celebrations of the New England past. As historical pageants suggested and as the bicentennial commemorations of 1976 confirmed, regional and even national experience and identity frequently acquired meaning by being grounded in the celebration of local history.

John E. Bodnar, *Remaking America: Public Memory, Commemoration, and Patriotism in the Twentieth Century* (1992); Dona Brown, *Inventing New England: Regional Tourism in the 19th Century* (1995); Lawrence Buell, *New England Literary Culture from Revolution through Renaissance* (1986); David Glassberg, *American Historical Pageantry* (1990).

Joseph A. Conforti

Child, Julia (1912–2004)

Cookbook author and television chef. No culinary celebrity wrought a greater influence upon the American palate than Julia (McWilliams) Child. She delighted both professional and amateur cooks with her series of television cooking shows, best-selling cookbooks, and numerous articles and columns on the pleasures of the table.

Born in Pasadena, Calif., Child graduated from Smith College in 1934. She worked in advertising until 1942, when she procured a position with the Office of Strategic Services in China. In China she met Paul Child, also a government employee, and they were married in 1946.

In 1948 the Childs were transferred to Paris. Julia Child began studying under the famed chef Max Bugnard at the Cordon Bleu and was soon immersed in a circle of expatriate Francophiles and local cuisiniers. Among these were Simone Beck and Louisette Bertholle, who, along with Child, opened a cooking school, L'Ecole des Trois Gourmandes, in 1951 for Americans. Child, Beck, and Bertholle are best known as the authors of *Mastering the Art of French Cooking*, volume 1 (1961). This comprehensive tome and its sequel, volume 2 (1970), introduced the American public to French foods and cooking techniques and earned rave reviews.

To increase sales, Child publicized the book through personal appearances and demonstrations. She first appeared on television in 1961 on NBC's *Today* show. The following year WGBH, Boston's public-television station, asked Child, who was now a resident of Cam-

Julia Child begins a cooking demonstration, 1978

bridge, Mass., to give a half-hour television demonstration of her cooking techniques. The show proved popular, and WGBH commissioned Child to do a full-length series in the hope that she would be able to tap into Americans' growing interest in French cuisine, a trend generated in part by First Lady Jacqueline Kennedy's decision to hire a French chef for the White House. *The French Chef*, which aired in 1963, was not the first show of its kind, but it proved more marketable than earlier shows. Its success derived largely from the novelty of fancy European cooking enlivened by Child's unpretentious style. Her folksy, sometimes goofy sense of humor demystified the elegant, complicated dishes she prepared. While she sought to elevate audiences' tastes by championing seasonal foods and butter over margarine, she put amateur cooks at ease by admitting her own (sometimes visible) culinary mistakes and sneaking in the occasional bouillon cube when fresh stock was not available. By 1964 the black-and-white series was airing in more than 50 cities. In 1965 Child received the George Foster Peabody Award for distinguished achievement in educational television, and in 1966 she won the first Emmy awarded to a personality on an educational program.

Child cemented her status as a celebrity chef in the 1960s and 1970s. She continued to write for the *Boston Globe, McCall's,* and *Parade. The French Chef Cookbook* appeared in 1968, and her new color-television series,

French Chef, aired between 1970 and 1974. *Julia Child and Company* and its sequel, *Julia Child and More Company,* both geared to increasingly sophisticated tastes, appeared in 1978 and 1979. In 1980 Child ventured into commercial television, taping a series of segments for ABC's *Good Morning America.* Until this time Child's reputation had been built on her down-home, no-nonsense approach to food, but in response to a growing number of affluent viewers Child pitched her next series, *Dinner at Julia's,* to a tonier crowd. Filmed at a Santa Barbara, Calif., seaside estate, the series, with its accompanying videocassettes and cookbook, featured a chic Child hobnobbing with celebrities and bantering with famous guest chefs. The show drew criticism for abandoning her homespun image and catering to culinary glitterati but still developed a sizable audience. *Dinner at Julia's* also spawned *The Way to Cook* videocassettes in 1985, which helped to publicize her newest book, *The Way to Cook* (1989). *Cooking with Master Chefs* (1993) further diverged from earlier shows by showcasing celebrity chefs exclusively; Child rarely cooked on this show, choosing instead to trade tips and questions with her guests. The series resulted in two books, *Cooking with Master Chefs* (1993) and *In Julia's Kitchen with Master Chefs* (1995). In 1996 she launched a similar series called *Baking with Julia,* which focused on master bakers and pastry chefs and generated an eponymous cookbook (cowritten with Dorie Greenspan). Child also published

two books in 1998: *Julia's Delicious Little Dinners* and *Julia's Menus for Special Occasions* (cowritten with E. S. Yntema). Child retired to California in 2001. She donated the contents of her kitchen to the Smithsonian Institution and her collection of cookbooks and papers to the Schlesinger Library of the Radcliffe Institute in Cambridge. To celebrate her 90th birthday, 20 restaurants across the country gave dinners in her honor to raise funds to allow the International Association of Culinary Professionals, in which Child was active, to conduct research in France.

Julia Child revolutionized the way Americans eat. She introduced new foods and techniques and changed the way we talk, think, and learn about food through her pioneering work as a popular cookbook writer and television chef. Child will be remembered as much for her love of haute cuisine as for her inimitable accent, which harks back to a New England blueblood tradition and connotes a warm, down-home lifestyle. Most crucial, by making French cuisine accessible to amateur cooks and highlighting the joys of commensalism and fresh food, Julia Child brought lasting pleasure and diversity to the American table.

Noel Riley Fitch, *Appetite for Life: The Biography of Julia Child* (1997); Joan Reardon, *M. F. K. Fisher, Julia Child, and Alice Waters: Celebrating the Pleasures of the Table* (1994).

Jennifer L. Jang

Connecticut Connecticut, the third smallest state in the union with its 5,009 square miles, presents a pleasant face to the world. Its natural environment has more charm than drama. Water is everywhere: the state has 253 miles of coastline, nearly 20,000 lakes and ponds, and more than 12,000 miles of rivers and streams. Gentle hills dot every view, even in the Connecticut River valley, the central lowland that bisects the state. A rich blend of hardwoods color the fall with brilliant foliage, and softwoods make most of Connecticut a fit subject for a winter holiday card. Though its bays, lakes, mountains, beaches, gorges, and forests may not be spectacular, their abundance gives Connecticut a look that is typically New England throughout.

The social and residential environment is similarly homogeneous. More than 80 percent of Connecticut's 3.4 million residents (2000 census) live in urban communities, making this one of the most densely populated states in the country despite its lack of a real metropolis. Hartford, New Haven, and Bridgeport are small compared with New York, Chicago, and Los Angeles, and they're not much larger than many of Connecticut's 18 other cities and 169 towns. Hartford, New Haven, and Bridgeport have impressive skylines, many cultural institutions, and areas of deep poverty; suburbs of the three range from wealthy, prestigious bedroom communities to industrial manufacturing centers. Much of Fairfield County functions as a suburb of New York City, and eastern Connecticut is more rural than the rest of the state.

The dominance of New York City sometimes creates competing cultural affiliations that give the state a split identity. Should Nutmeggers (as residents are called) root for the Red Sox or the Yankees, for example? The dramatic growth of minority populations also challenges traditional assumptions about the Connecticut Yankee. Yet as the 21st century opens, most Nutmeggers live in medium-sized towns or small cities, drive cars to work, and aspire to middle-class status. Connecticut consistently has the highest per capita income of any state and one of the lowest poverty rates. If any state could serve as a model for New England town life and 21st-century affluence, it would be Connecticut.

In one form or another Connecticut has nearly always been a positive role model for New England and the nation. Founded in the 1630s as part of the Puritan migration to America, Connecticut was overshadowed throughout its colonial history by its parent colony, Massachusetts. Three clusters of Puritan settlements—one on the Connecticut River, consisting of the towns of Hartford, Windsor, and Wethersfield; one at the mouths of the Connecticut and Thames Rivers, consisting of Saybrook, New London, and Norwich; and one along the western shore of Long Island Sound, consisting of New Haven, Branford, Milford, Greenwich, Guilford, Stratford, and Fairfield—were brought together in 1662 to form a single colony under a charter issued by the Restoration government in England. New Haven and the towns around it, which had been an independent colony since 1638, briefly resisted amalgamation under the Charter of 1662 but by 1664 had acquiesced to what appeared to be inevitable.

Relief of the Charter Oak, State Capitol Building, Hartford

In 1687, to stem a growing tide of colonial independence, the royal official Sir Edmund Andros tried to seize the charter, but Captain Joseph Wadsworth safely hid it in a large white oak on the Wyllys estate in Hartford. A symbol of resistance to tyranny, the tree came to be called the Charter Oak. When it was blown down in a windstorm on August 21, 1856, its wood attained the status accorded to pieces of the true cross and was fashioned into innumerable souvenirs and pieces of furniture. In 1947 Connecticut adopted the white oak as its state tree.

Defining moments in the assertion of an English identity in colonial Connecticut were the British conquest of the Dutch colony on Manhattan, which negated that country's claims to the region, and the massacre of Pequot Indians in 1636. Over the 114 years between the union of 1662 and the issuance of the Declaration of Independence, Connecticut grew to include 75 towns. Hartford and New Haven served as co-capitals; New London was the most important port; and Middletown, Fairfield, and Norwich were major trading centers. But colonial Connecticut was primarily a land of Puritan villages with appended outlying farms. The Congregational spirit of Puritanism infused the colony with a sense of localism and autonomy that became embedded in the town meeting and the church meetinghouse.

Colonial and early national Connecticut had four nicknames: the Constitution State, the Land of Steady Habits, the Provisions State, and the Nutmeg State. Each one represents a feature of Connecticut's early years; collectively, they create an accurate composite. The name Constitution State comes from the adoption in 1639 of a written compact, the Fundamental Orders of Connecticut, that prescribed the structure of government for the three river towns. Whether the Fundamental Orders was indeed a constitution is a much-debated but moot point. By issuing that document, Connecticut's founders manifested a degree of political independence unequaled by any other colony, with the possible exception of Rhode Island. Only these two neighbors in southern New England preserved their royal charters throughout their colonial histories and governed themselves without any direct interference from British authorities.

The sentiments expressed in the nickname Land of Steady Habits suggest how well Connecticut's independent governing arrangements worked. Colonization produced turbulence everywhere Englishmen tried to transplant fragments of their own fractious culture. Connecticut had its share of quarrels—Congregationalists and Presbyterians debated the form of orthodoxy in the founding

generation, Anglicans and Baptists fought bitterly to wrest toleration from the established church in the mid-18th century, eastern and western Connecticut divided over the Great Awakening in the late colonial period—but Connecticut's squabbling, vexatious as it may have been, paled in comparison to that of every other colony. Nutmeggers recoiled in horror at the vicious strife characteristic of Rhode Island, "the land where people think otherwise." Connecticut enjoyed the most tranquil, stable history of any English American colony.

The Provisions State nickname attests to another successful aspect of early Connecticut: its remarkably productive agricultural economy. Connecticut exported a diversified array of grains, processed meat and dairy products, and fish to the West Indies in exchange for molasses and cash credits with English merchants. During the Revolution, Connecticut diverted the supplies that normally would have been shipped to the Caribbean to the patriot armies. The state provided soldiers, money, militia units, and ships to the Revolution; it endured military attacks and coastal shelling; but its most important contribution to the war effort came from its ability to feed the soldiers of the Continental Army.

The sobriquet Nutmeg State was first used by the generation after the Revolution: it reflected evolutionary changes occurring in Connecticut's social and economic sense of self that are often summed up by the phrase "from Puritan to Yankee." The unflattering nickname arose when unscrupulous traveling tinsmiths from Connecticut allegedly sold wooden nutmegs throughout the southern states. The original Yankee peddlers were indeed usually from Connecticut, and they did become known for enterprise and sharp trading, traits that define the Yankee character. Undoubtedly apocryphal, the nutmeg swindle nevertheless bespoke underlying sentiments that contained a new truth for 19th-century Connecticut. In the years after the War of 1812 it was a center of hustling, bustling commercial activity that sent ships around the world, as well as one of the main centers of the milling activity that began the Industrial Revolution in the United States. Such distinguished industrial pioneers as Samuel Colt and Eli Whitney were among the residents of Connecticut who created hundreds of mills to mass-produce goods and employ thousands. By the Civil War period, manufacturing led all sectors of the Connecticut economy.

Connecticut's politics during the early national period continued the well-established tradition of stability. The state furnished several distinguished revolutionary leaders, including Jonathan Trumbull, the only person to serve as governor of a state throughout the entire war; Samuel Huntington, a president of the Second Continental Congress; Roger Sherman, author of the Connecticut Compromise, which broke the logjam between large and small states in the Constitutional Convention; and General Israel Putnam, a major general in the Continental Army and the commander of American troops at the Battle of Bunker Hill.

Connecticut was one of the few states not to write a constitution during the revolutionary era, continuing to govern itself under the Charter of 1662. The state voted staunchly Federalist and was one of only two states not to vote for Thomas Jefferson when he ran for reelection in 1804. The Federalist Party weakened its hold on the electorate by flirting with secession from the union at the Hartford Convention of 1814–15 and died in Connecticut after opposing unsuccessfully the adoption of a new state constitution in 1818. Democrats and Whigs enjoyed an approximate parity in Connecticut during the debates of the second-political-party system, but in 1858 the newly formed Republican Party captured control of the state government.

Social changes reflected economic and political currents: racial, ethnic, and class divisions became manifest and enduring. Connecticut began emancipating its slaves in 1784 and played a leading role in the movement to abolish slavery elsewhere in the nation. But it also disenfranchised freed blacks and tolerated systematic racial discrimination. Connecticut furnished one of the ugliest symbols of oppression in American history when it prosecuted Prudence Crandall for opening a school to educate black girls in the 1850s.

Massive Irish immigration in the 1840s fragmented Connecticut's white ethnic homogeneity and gave rise to virulent bigotry against Roman Catholics. German immigration in the 1850s and an influx of southern and eastern Europeans and of French Canadians in the late 19th century began the transformation of Connecticut into the multicultural state it is today. At the high point of immigration, in 1910, more than one-fourth of Connecticut's residents were born outside the United States. In the 1920s a large number of southern blacks migrated north to Connecticut to work in its prosperous industries. In the post–World War II era more southern blacks moved to the state, joined by Hispanics and northern New Englanders attracted by jobs in the high-paying defense industries. As the 21st century begins, what was once a primarily Puritan English Connecticut has a majority of Roman Catholics among its religiously affiliated citizens, large Irish, Italian, and Polish ethnic communities, and a population that is 9.1 percent black and 9.4 percent Hispanic and contains a small but rapidly increasing percentage of Asians.

Among the icons, persons, and accomplishments that stand out in Connecticut's development are a few that exemplify its culture. The most distinctive type of building in the state is the white Congregational church, with its tall pillars, clapboard exterior, green shutters, and clock-tower steeple. More than 200 of these simple, elegant churches were constructed between 1820 and 1860. They are often selected as cover pictures for books and brochures about the state. The Travelers tower in Hartford, a symbol of the city's preeminence in the insurance industry, is the state's best-known building. Many consumer items that were once or still are household names, such as the Colt .45, the Fuller Brush, and the Thermos bottle, were Connecticut products. More recently, Pratt and Whitney aircraft engines, Electric Boat atomic submarines, and Sikorsky helicopters all illustrate Connecticut's extraordinary role in the Cold War defense industry.

Connecticut has not distinguished itself in supplying political leaders to the United States. No citizen of the state has been elected president, although the older George Bush was raised in Greenwich and George W. Bush was born in New Haven. Among Connecticut's famous citizens are Benedict Arnold and Nathan Hale, two men who defined alternative images of character during the Revolution. Connecticut's figures of national importance have tended to be from the world of letters and education. The Connecticut Wits, a group of satirists, poets, and essayists, the most famous of whom were John Trumbull, Timothy Dwight, and Joel Barlow, are often referred to as the first school of American literature. Noah Webster's name has become nearly synonymous with American dictionaries. Catharine Beecher and Harriet Beecher Stowe, two of the 19th century's most influential authors and social reformers, formed the nucleus of a vibrant literary circle in Hartford at midcentury. Mark Twain also lived in Hartford for a portion of his adult life and worked as a reporter for the *Hartford Courant*. More recently, Wallace Stevens, Arthur Miller, William Styron, Barbara Tuchman, and Robert Penn Warren lived and wrote in Connecticut.

Intellectual accomplishments are a fitting symbol for a state that hosts Yale University, one of the world's great institutions of higher learning; the American School for the Deaf, the first such school in the world; Trinity College, the first American Episcopal college; Wesleyan University, the first American Methodist college; and an enviable system of other private colleges, public institutions, and vocational schools. From its Puritan founding to the present, Connecticut has maintained a strong commitment to education and has been a net importer of students and exporter of graduates. It has the highest percentage of private high school graduates in the nation. In addition to a network of some 190 parochial schools maintained by the Catholic Church, Connecticut has such distinguished prep schools as Cheshire Academy, Hopkins School, Choate Rosemary Hall, Miss Porter's School, Kent School, the Hotchkiss School, Suffield Academy, the Taft School, and the Loomis Chaffee School.

Politically, Connecticut has been one of the more liberal states in the country since the New Deal. The Depression-era Democratic governor Wilbur Cross, a former dean of the Yale Graduate School, reoriented the state's political alignment and made the Democrats the majority party. Connecticut's multicultural and multiracial society, its industrial manufacturing base, and its strong educational traditions made the state a perfect fit for the New Deal coalition. After the Cross years, in response to the Democrats' success at the ballot box, Connecticut Republicans generally subscribed to the moderate wing of their party. In 1974 Connecticut elected the reformer and social advocate Ella Grasso, a Democrat, to the governorship; she was the first woman governor in the country whose husband had not preceded her in the position.

In the early 21st century, the state is grappling with the impact of the decline in defense-industry spending occasioned by the end of the Cold War and experiencing many of the problems associated with racial tensions, crime, poverty, underemployment and unemployment, and urban decay that seem endemic to the nation. The remarkable re-emergence of the Mashantucket Pequot in the 1970s, and the construction of that tribe's Foxwoods Casino and Resort, has transformed the economy of southeastern Connecticut, however. Revenues from the Pequot casino, along with those of the Mohegan Sun complex nearby, have substantially boosted state finances. The casinos and the Mashantucket Pequot Museum and Research Center are recreating the image of the Native American presence in the state. Connecticut remains one of the most prosperous and progressive states in the country and one of the most desirable places to live.

Ellsworth S. Grant, *The Miracle of Connecticut* (1992); William Hosley and Gerald W. R. Ward, *The Great River: Art and Society of the Connecticut Valley, 1635–1820* (1985); David M. Roth, *Connecticut: A Bicentennial History* (1979); Albert E. Van Dusen, *Connecticut* (1961).

Bruce Colin Daniels

Conservatism While conservatism is often unified across national borders by common themes, prejudices, and inclinations, much of its energy and enduring appeal emanates from its regional history, traditions, and peculiarities. Equally as important as regional variation is its evolution through time, from a "regional ideology" and preference for particular religious, social, and political institutions to a culturally conservative "regional attitude" that critiques modern values from a regional perspective. Conservatism may be defined as a set of mutually dependent principles, arguments, and images stressing human imperfection and natural inequality, the necessity of community institutions to channel irrational human passions, and the importance of judging the effect of institutions and policies on their ultimate consequences and not their original intentions. Understood in this way, as a conscious philosophy bounded by time, one can identify strands of a New England conservatism from the first settlements in the region.

In many ways, the Puritans were the region's first conservatives, devoutly localist in outlook and dedicated to consultative yet authoritative institutions like the Congregational Church and the town meeting. Called by one historian "decentralized Calvinists," Puritan Congregationalists came together in tight communities, accepted and denied individuals' entrance into their spiritual compact by group vote, elected ministers to be their spiritual and social, but not political, leaders, and were intensely involved in the governing of church affairs. The church was a careful balance between communal needs and individual participation, as the faithful melded the commands of the Bible, their transplanted British traditions, and the needs of a frontier society with their recognition of the Holy Spirit's ability to affect individual lives. "In America," writes William Cullen Dennis, "the opposing, though not contradictory values of consolidation and separation, of community good and individual rights, would exist in a restless, tenuous balance over the centuries as the Puritan influence spread across the land. Because this balance would so exist, ordered liberty would remain possible in America."

New England town meetings also grew out of the "congregational tradition." Assembled as political bodies in their various towns, they elevated prominent townsmen to political leadership. Paramount to political decision making, however, was the character and quality of the leaders. Democracy was openly rejected, and educated, socially prominent, respected public men were elected to town positions to govern for the people. Such an arrangement made towns into miniature republics. As David Hackett Fischer writes, "The New England way was government by consent, but the people consented to men rather than to measures. It was representative government, but the concept of representation was *in personam*." The "best men" or "the elect" directed the institutions of New England society, not an unruly, potentially passionate and irrational populace. The "Congregational way" or "consultative tradition" endures.

The charge of utopianism is too often aimed at Puritan New Englanders. Congregationalists were not perfectionists bent on creating a utopian, otherworldly "city upon a hill." Instead, as Christopher Lasch once noted, they were a gathering of local communities, aware of their moral shortcomings as imperfect humans, subjecting themselves to the rigorous ethical standards of the Old Testament. Their often severe refusal to recognize other religious faiths or to tolerate deviance from their way of life (although this has been exaggerated in historical accounts) spoke more to their deep understanding that men needed institutions to govern their passions and preserve the civil society than to a penchant for creating the perfect society on earth.

While not direct intellectual descendants, the 18th century New England Federalists grew out of the same conservative tradition: conviction of unalterable human inequality, skepticism of social mobility, and belief in the necessity of institutional control of passions. New England Federalism jelled as a political and social force during the disorderly 1780s, when dissatisfaction arose with a new independent America barely governed by the loose and ineffective Articles of Confederation. More particularly, civil disturbances like Shays's Rebellion in 1786 united conservative New Englanders into a cohesive body and ignited, according to Forrest McDonald, a resurrection of "pristine Puritanism whose central concern was the imposition of authority of the righteous over the lawless and the sinful." Centered on such prominent regional leaders as John Adams, Fisher Ames, William Plumer, Theodore Sedgewick, and Timothy Pickering, New England Federalism dominated national politics during the 1790s.

At first dedicated to an older style of "deferential politics," New England Federalists successfully adapted Jeffersonian politics and organized themselves into the party of ordered liberty against what they considered a disgraceful clique of French-inspired Jacobins and "mobocrat" radicals. As steadfast statists, Federalists aggressively defended state intervention in social and economic matters. They boosted the creation of a national bank, boomed high tariffs and government support for business, and backed the building of a national infrastructure of roads, turnpikes, and canals. National government became the Puritan New England town writ large—highly institutionalized yet allowing for individual participation. Although the Federalist Party declined nationally after John Adams's defeat by Thomas Jefferson in 1800, they remained in power in New England (particularly in Massachusetts) for another 20 years. With the rise of Andrew Jackson, the Federalists had disappeared and a new conservative force was being born in New England circles: Whiggery.

Originating as a group of anti-Jacksonians in the late 1820s, New England Whigs were a diverse group. While many liberal Whigs stressed the reformable nature of human life and molded religious and philosophical systems to fit their vision of social organization, conservative Whigs built on the concerns of their Puritan and Federalist intellectual forefathers. Incorporating communal needs with individual desires, New England Whig leaders like Daniel Webster, Edward Everett, and Rufus Choate posited a paternal, organic American society in which citizens had moral and communal duties rather than equality and rights apart from society. Inspired by the writings of the Scottish commonsense philosophers, the English conservative Edmund Burke, and the theology of the Harvard Unitarians, Whiggery dominated New England society and politics throughout the antebellum era (particularly in Boston) and vigorously upheld the necessity of firm institutions—like the government, law, church, banks—to guide irrational Jacksonian passions.

While upholding a deferential social order, New England Whiggery simultaneously argued for aggressive economic and technological development. Some historians and commentators have seen this combination as a lack of principle or the presence of radical and innovative tendencies at the heart of Whiggery. Whigs, however, saw no contradiction between social conservatism and economic development. These "progressive conservatives" sponsored technological advances like railroad development and steam power and used them to bulwark an organic conservative social order of deferential politics and a hierarchical social life. As Everett declared of himself and his fellow Whigs, they sought "the rule of a bold and safe progress from the records of a wise and glorious experience."

As economic expansion, industrialization, and social upheaval complicated American life after 1865, many New Englanders began to search for cultural meaning and stability in the region's past. The invention of Old Home Week in northern New England during the 1890s not only brought much-needed economic relief to a depressed region by importing tourists, it also acted as a culturally conservative reminder of an idealized old New England. People began to vacation at quiet, slower, nostalgic locations like Nantucket, the White Mountains, coastal Maine, and rural Vermont to rediscover local institutions and traditions they (or their ancestors) had left behind. In addition, Colonial Revival architecture and furniture gained immense regional popularity. "The aesthetic language of symmetry, order, and harmony translated for many colonial enthusiasts into a social language," relates the cultural historian Dona Brown. Writers in national journals and magazines at the end of the 19th century celebrated New England community as an antidote to modern ills, as "New England's countryside was imagined as a kind of underground cultural aquifer that fed the nation's springs of political courage, personal independence, and old-fashioned virtue."

Conservative New England intellectuals also gained national prominence after the Civil War. Henry Adams both flourished and cringed under the weight of his ancestry—it was as much a source of inspiration as it was daunting. In his two classics, *The Education of Henry Adams* (1918) and *Mont Saint Michel and Chartres* (1912), Adams rejected his ancestral Whiggery and pessimistically regarded a world of greed, technology, and Darwinian science as beyond hope. Corporate capitalism and the avaricious pursuit of scientific truth doomed America to a socialistic future without beauty or God. Adams bemoaned the decline of American leadership. "The progress of evolution from President Washington to President Grant, was alone evidence enough to upset Darwin," Adams sneered. Yearning for a past more deferential, ordered, and beautiful, he began to admire and study Roman Catholicism as the last institution of cultural meaning in the world.

While Adams was cranky and aloof, Robert Frost was witty and widely revered. His poems were simple dedications to country life in rural New England and were often politically charged. He liked to call himself a Grover Cleveland Democrat and criticized Franklin Roosevelt's New Deal in many of his poems, especially his controversial collection *A Further Range* (1936). In "A Roadside Stand," he berated New Deal social engineering:

> While greedy good-doers, beneficent
> beasts of prey,
> Swarm over their lives enforcing benefits
> That are calculated to soothe them out of
> their wits.

In another poem, "Departmental," he satirized federal bureaucrats by comparing them to dutiful ants disposing of a carcass. Content with being a cultural critic, Frost declined a more open political role, begging off once with the excuse that "it is not the business of the poet to cry for reform."

Harvard and Yale Universities produced several major conservative thinkers. Irving Babbitt, a Harvard professor of classics and French literature from 1894 to 1933, bitterly condemned the direction of American society and letters in the Progressive Era. His ideas, presented in *Literature and the American College* (1908), *Rousseau and Romanticism* (1919), and *Democracy and Leadership* (1924), helped found a conservative countercultural movement in the 1920s called the New Humanism. The Harvard graduate and fellow New Humanist Paul Elmer More retreated to the Vermont woods when not teaching in Pennsylvania. Here he produced the influential "Shelburne Essays," which commented on Greek history, the unity of pagan and Christian philosophy, and the American founding. Babbitt, More, and the New Humanists were "cultural traditionalists, defensive of classical principles in art, deeply skeptical about human nature, and neo-Burkean in their political and social views," according to the political historian Patrick Allitt. The movement had limited popularity and influence during its members' own lifetimes—H. L. Mencken ruthlessly mocked them, and Sinclair Lewis's famous novel *Babbitt* (1920) was titled for the Harvard professor—but gained a considerable following within the American intellectual right after World War II.

In 1951 a recent Yale graduate named William F. Buckley published *God and Man at Yale,* a determined and articulate attack on left-wing ideas within the prestigious New England university. Buckley soon founded the irreverent conservative monthly *National Review,* which introduced its readers to a mix of anticommunist politics, procapitalist economics, and trenchant criticism of American society, manners, and culture. Buckley's fellow Yale graduate Jeffrey Hart also wrote for the *National Review* and taught English at Dartmouth College in New Hampshire. Hart defined conservatism as an intellectual process: "Under pressure from liberal abstractions—and the pressure has increased daily—conservative ideas have more and more exhibited themselves, emerging from habits of behavior, from actual experience, and from historical pieties, to become available *as ideas.*" Buckley and Hart, along with other Yale graduates such as John Chamberlain, L. Brent Bozell, and M. Stanton Evans, helped shape the postwar conservative movement that led to both the Goldwater nomination in 1964 and the Reagan victory of 1980.

None of this is to deny the New England presence in conservative politics after the Civil War. After all, the 1936 Republican presidential candidate Alfred M. Landon carried only two states against the wildly popular Franklin D. Roosevelt: Maine and Vermont. The region supplied the Republican Party with some of its more prominent conservative leaders from 1865 to 1930: James G. Blaine, Thomas B. Reed, Eugene Hale, Henry Cabot Lodge, Nelson Aldrich, and Calvin Coolidge, to name just a few. In fact, Reed, Hale, Lodge, and Coolidge became symbols in their own lifetimes of an enduring New England conservatism: Reed and Hale, the tight-lipped Mainers, both resolutely opposed to the moralism and jingoism of the pretentious Theodore Roosevelt; Lodge, the embodiment of the coldly realistic, irascible, aristocratic politician who defeated the overly idealistic Woodrow Wilson; Coolidge, the popular and quintessential Vermont Yankee of thrifty government, quiet self-reliance, and biting, sarcastic wit. New England conservatives have also dominated post–World War II American politics, particularly New Hampshire governors Meldrim Thompson and John Sununu, New Hampshire senator Judd Gregg, and Vermont senator George Aiken, all three wielding influence greater than the electoral power of their respective states.

By the 1980s and 1990s, the region's conservatives had gained a reputation for economic conservatism combined with social liberalism. This trend is best seen in Massachusetts governor William Weld, who rescued state finances from disaster in the early 1990s, and New Hampshire senator Warren Rudman, who teamed up with Texas senator Phil Gramm in 1985 to pass congressionally mandated reductions in the federal budget deficit (later weakened by the Supreme Court). For these men, conservatism was fiscal restraint, low taxes, and balanced budgets, not a broader fight for traditional institutions and mores.

But New England is often still regarded as a culturally conservative region, its stereotypical white Congregational church set neatly in front of an orderly, well-trimmed town common often used as a regional image. People move into or tour the region to rediscover a slower, more conservative "small town life" and escape the noisy movement of the cosmopolitan world. *Yankee* magazine, *This Old House,* and leaf-peeping are nostalgic signals that New England remains to many a traditional and authentic corner of America. Apparently the Puritan urge for the ordered life has not perished.

Patrick Allitt, *Catholic Intellectuals and Conservative Politics in America: 1950–1985* (1993); Dona Brown, *Inventing New England: Regional Tourism in the 19th*

Century (1995); William Cullen Dennis, "Puritanism as the Basis for American Conservatism," *Modern Age* (Fall 1974); Edward Everett, *Stability and Progress: Remarks Made on the Fourth of July, 1853, in Faneuil Hall* (1853); David Hackett Fischer, *The Revolution of American Conservatism: The Federalist Party in the Era of Jeffersonian Democracy* (1965); Robert Frost, *Collected Poems of Robert Frost* (1942); Jeffrey Hart, *The American Dissent: A Decade of Modern Conservatism* (1966); Daniel Walker Howe, *The Political Culture of the American Whigs* (1979); Forrest McDonald, *Novus Ordo Seclorum: The Intellectual Origins of the Constitution* (1985); Jerry Z. Muller, *Conservatism: An Anthology of Social and Political Thought from David Hume to the Present* (1997); Peter J. Stanlis, "Robert Frost: Social and Political Conservative," *Chronicles* (August 1992).

Michael J. Connolly

Cookies Some of the nation's most popular cookies originated in New England. The term first appeared in print in 1796 as *cookey*, and the earliest cookies in New England were probably butter or shortbread cookies that closely resembled English teacakes. Maple sugar from the northern-tier states and molasses (imported from the West Indies to supply New England rum distilleries) gave regional flavors to many popular cookies, such as hermits, gingerbread, and spice cookies. A perennial favorite, the chocolate chip cookie, also known as the Toll House cookie, was invented by accident in Whitman, Mass. Ruth Wakefield and her husband, Kenneth, bought a house there in 1930, where they established the Toll House Inn (so named because it had once been a place where horses were changed on the route from Boston to New Bedford). Ruth added some chopped chocolate to the butter cookies that she regularly baked to serve to her inn's guests, but rather than melting during the baking process and blending throughout the cookie as she had expected, the pieces remained whole. The cookie's popularity spread, and the Nestlé Company began to produce morsels for the cookies, printing the original recipe on the package.

Another national favorite (the third most popular cookie in the United States) is the Fig Newton. According to legend, Fig Newtons were first produced in 1891, when the Philadelphia inventor James Henry Mitchell brought his double-funneled dough-sheeting machine to the Kennedy Biscuit Works in Cambridge, Mass. His invention allowed dough to be wrapped around a filling, in this case, fig jam. James Hazen, manager of the bakery at the Kennedy Biscuit Works, named the cookies Newtons, after the neighboring town of Newton, Mass. Subsequent Kennedy Biscuit Works cookie inventions were named after towns and communities around Boston, including the Needham, a coconut cookie wrapped in chocolate. Another incarnation of this cookie is the Maine Potato Needham, a candylike concoction with mashed potatoes, coconut, and confectioner's sugar, dipped in chocolate. The National Biscuit Company (now Nabisco) bought the Kennedy Biscuit Works in 1898, renaming its famous cookie the Fig Newton; in 1991, Nabisco celebrated the cookie's hundredth birthday in Newton, Mass.

Cookie baking and trading contribute to social culture and tradition making; they are, for instance, at the center of an annual event in Wellesley, Mass.: the Christmas cookie exchange. Each year since 1971, two women from Wellesley, Mass., Mary Bevilacqua and Laurel Gabel, have hosted a gathering of friends in which guests bring their specialty cookie and trade samples and recipes. The Wellesley cookie exchange attracted the notice of *Yankee* magazine, and so great was the demand for recipes that the *Wellesley Cookie Exchange Cookbook* was published in 1986. The cookie exchange continues in Wellesley and elsewhere; the once all-female event now includes some male bakers.

Cookies have not been without controversy in New England. In a project meant to help them understand how legislation is enacted, a group of Somerset, Mass., schoolchildren proposed that the chocolate chip cookie be named the official state cookie. Few expected the firestorm that developed; indeed, some Bay State residents (including the governor) protested the choice, preferring the beloved Fig Newton. In the end, a compromise was struck: while the chocolate chip cookie did become the commonwealth's official cookie on July 9, 1997 (Massachusetts Bill S-1716), the Fig Newton was unofficially named the state's fruit cookie.

The diverse population of New England naturally contributes to the wide variety of authentic ethnic cookies that arrived over the course of several centuries with various immigrant groups and over time have gained popularity throughout the region and the nation. Examples include the Italian biscotti, the Jewish mandelbrot, and the Portuguese morgados and suspiros.

Susan Mahnke, *The Wellesley Cookie Exchange Cookbook* (1986).

Rachelle Friedman

Covered Bridges The covered bridge, an image evocative of the New England countryside, is a wooden truss bridge with a roof, siding, and, occasionally, decorative portal trim added. The purpose of the cover is solely to protect the trusses from deterioration owing to excessive moisture from rain and snow. The overwhelming majority of all bridges built in New England from the late 18th through the early 20th centuries were wooden trusses, and almost all wooden bridges that have survived are covered. As recently as 1927 there were approximately 1,500 wooden truss bridges in use in New England. In 1998, 191 remained, 101 of which are in Vermont. If well maintained, covered bridges have remarkable longevity; the average age of the surviving bridges in New England is 130 years.

Wooden trusses were known to the Romans, and in the 16th, 17th, and 18th centuries were used for bridging rivers in Italy, Switzerland, and Germany. Great timber resources quickly made North America the leader in wooden bridge development and New England its point of origin. The "geometry work bridge," built in Norwich, Conn., in 1764, is thought to be America's first wooden truss bridge. The period of rapid expansion and settlement following the Revolutionary War led to a high point for wooden truss designers, patented designs, and the construction of unprecedented clear spans. Timothy Palmer of Newburyport, Mass., began building large trussed arches in the 1790s with an uncovered 244-foot clear span near Portsmouth, N.H. Palmer also built the bridge over the Schuylkill River in Philadelphia, believed to be the first long covered bridge in America.

Theodore Burr, born in Connecticut, patented the Burr Arch in 1804 and spanned large rivers like the Hudson and Susquehanna. Ithiel Town of New Haven, Conn., patented the Town Lattice Truss in 1820, which was subsequently constructed by the hundreds throughout the United States and Canada. Other notable patented trusses include the Howe, Long, Pratt, and Paddleford, all originating in New England.

In the 19th century, thousands of short-span bridges were built in the traditional, unpatented, king- and queenpost truss forms, and many of these were uncovered, with the intent of avoiding the expense and additional dead load of a roof system and boarding. Larger structures spanning wider rivers or carrying railways involved great capital expenditure, and these were increasingly covered as a means of protecting the investment. In winter, however, covered bridges would have to be "snowed" by carting in snow to permit sleighs and sleds to slide across them. The Cornish-Windsor Bridge, which carries traffic across the Connecticut River between Vermont and New Hampshire, is the world's longest two-span wooden bridge, each span measuring 208 feet in the clear. The second longest single span is the 228-foot North Blenheim Bridge in New York State, built in 1855 by Nicholas Powers of Brandon, Vt. As late as 1908, long after the introduction of steel and concrete designs,

The Cornish-Windsor covered bridge (1866) spanning the Connecticut River, between Cornish, N.H., and Windsor, Vt., 1984

New England railroads were still constructing wooden spans such as the 103-foot-span double-lattice covered truss at Wolcott, Vt. Because of their complexity and expense, most wooden bridges longer than 40 feet were built by specialists in heavy timber framing and were often constructed off the river and rolled into position across temporary falsework.

Covered bridges are a tourist attraction in New England, and their importance as examples of historic engineering guarantees a commitment to preserve those that remain, most of which now see only moderate or light vehicular use. Once destroyed by the thousands to make way for modern road systems, they are today threatened by fire, flooding, and lack of maintenance. The disappointing performance of concrete highway bridges has led to some interest in new wooden bridges, which are relatively unaffected by road salt. New covered wooden highway bridges have been constructed in Maine, Vermont, and New Hampshire in the past decade, and others are presently being designed for Massachusetts.

Richard Sanders Allen, *Covered Bridges of the Northeast* (1957); American Society of Civil Engineers, *American Wooden Bridges* (1976); Herbert Wheaton Congdon, *The Covered Bridge* (1973); Milton S. Graton, *The Last of the Covered Bridge Builders* (1990 [1978]); Joseph C. Nelson, *Spanning Time: Vermont's Covered Bridges* (1997); Lee H. Nelson, *The Colossus of 1812: An American Engineering Superlative* (1990).

Jan Leo Lewandoski

Diners Diners, movable restaurants featuring simple, homey meals, originated in Providence in 1872, when Walter Scott began to sell hot food from a horse-drawn wagon to hungry newspaper workers. Scott operated his cart business until 1917 and ushered in one of New England's most popular types of eateries and one of its most distinctive manufacturing industries. Eventually, horse-drawn carts became enclosed "lunch-wagon" restaurants on wheels that could seat almost 30 people. Many of these wagons were manufactured in Worcester, Mass., by the Worcester Lunch Car Company, which operated from 1906 to 1961. By 1940 more than 6,500 diners operated

throughout the United States, but their numbers declined dramatically during the 1960s and 1970s. Late in the 1970s a movement to restore old diner cars as working restaurants began in New England, and diners once again became a respected and familiar part of the local culinary landscape.

Immediately after Scott started his food-wagon business, his idea spread throughout Providence and southern New England, and New Englanders vied to create ever-more-elaborate lunch carts. Charles H. Palmer of Worcester entered the diner business in 1889 and was to become one of the most important figures in New England diner history. Beginning in 1891, Palmer patented several lunch-wagon designs that were to become the industry standard. His long, narrow diners featured wheels that allowed the restaurants to be moved easily, and offered both sit-down and take-out service. With Palmer's help, diners by the turn of the century had become a signature feature of New England.

Although diner cars were manufactured in several factories around the United States, Worcester retained its central importance to the industry. Worcester Lunch Cars, among the most popular diners in the country throughout the 20th century, were built primarily by French Canadian immigrant craftsmen and factory workers. As the diner became an icon of American culture between the 1920s and the 1950s, it retained its New England identification.

Though challenged by fast-food restaurants during the late 1960s, many New England diners continued to operate even as the

Miss Bellows Falls Diner, in Bellows Falls, Vt., was made by the Worcester Lunch Car Company

eateries grew less popular nationwide. It is no surprise, then, that the renewed historical and culinary interest in diners that began in the late 1970s was centered in New England. Restored diner cars offering both authentic and updated versions of diner fare began to reopen all over the region, many of them serving such traditional regional dishes as steamers, johnny-cakes, and coffee milk. Notable New England diners include the Moran Square Diner (a Worcester Lunch Car diner) in Fitchburg, Mass., Jigger's Diner in East Greenwich, R.I., and the Central Diner in Worcester, Mass.

In 1985 the Modern Diner, a Sterling Streamliner that first opened in Pawtucket, R.I., in 1940, became the first diner included on the National Register of Historic Places, opening the way for 14 more diners to be declared historic sites. Today, diners are appreciated as unique forms of American architecture and as culinary and cultural institutions with New England roots.

Richard J. S. Gutman, *American Diner: Then and Now* (1993); Gutman, "The Diner," *American Heritage* 44 (1993); John F. Mariani, "The Return of the Great American Diner," *Esquire* 123 (1995).

Sarah J. Purcell

Doughnuts Long a staple of New England breakfasts, doughnuts are also the stuff of New England verse:

> Cut in diamonds, twists or rings,
> Drop with care the doughy things
> Into the fat that swiftly swells
> Evenly the spongy cells.
> Watch with care the time for turning,
> Fry them brown, just short of burning.
> Roll in sugar, serve when cool,
> This is the never failing rule.

Legend has it that the doughnut was invented in the mid-19th century by a Maine sea captain, Hanson Gregory, who, needing both hands to right his ship's course, stuck his piece of fried bread onto a spoke of his ship's wheel. The more prosaic version is that Gregory cut out the middles of his mother's fried-dough cakes because they were not cooked through. Either way, doughnuts have been fodder for New England folklore ever since. Among the folktales of Maine is the legend of the famous Coffin family, who invented doughnuts that turned themselves over in the cooking fat and jumped out of the pan when they were done.

In the era before franchise restaurants, spiced doughnuts were a breakfast mainstay in northern and eastern New England, while muffins held sway in the south. Eventually doughnuts made their way throughout the region and the nation. Traditionally served with cold cider, milk, or coffee, the fried confec-

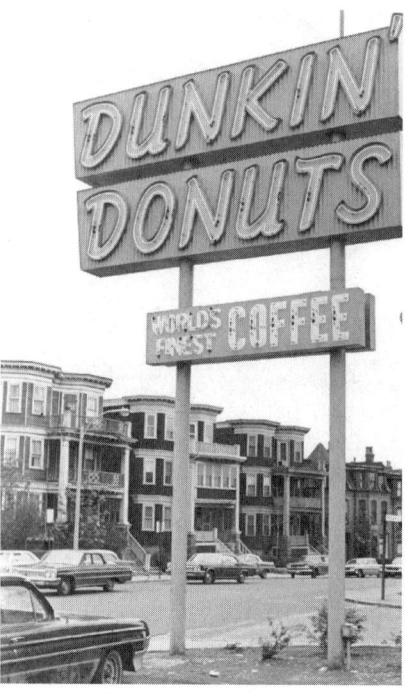

Dunkin' Donuts shop in Dorchester, Mass., 1967

tions come in any number of shapes and flavors, as rings, rounds, or twists, plain, sugared, spiced, glazed, or filled with jelly. The Philbrook family, for instance, innkeepers since the mid-1800s near Shelburne, N.H., perfected the White Mountain doughnut, a small, featherlight variety. The secret to good doughnuts, they contend, is using sour milk or buttermilk in the batter, seasoning it with a little bacon fat, taking care not to add too much flour, and cooking the doughnuts in lard. Frederick Wiseman's four-hour film *Belfast, Maine* (2000) features a lengthy segment on doughnut making in that small midcoast city.

One gets a sense of the doughnut's place in New England folk culture from the reminiscences of Gertrude E. Olsen, of Mansfield, Mass. "My mother was always known as 'Auntie' or 'The Doughnut Lady' to the people of our community," she told the food writer Sara Stamm. "Each Saturday, she replenished our doughnut crock, and each Saturday the paperboy, the mailman, the milkman, and the grocer lingered to chat a bit and enjoy some hot doughnuts straight from the kettle on the old wood-burning range. We children could hardly wait for the first doughnut holes, which she would fry on the pretext of testing the fat, but really to see our delight in savoring their goodness to the accompaniment of ice-cold milk."

In 1946 William Rosenberg founded Industrial Luncheon Services, a company that delivered meals and coffee-break snacks to factory workers on the outskirts of Boston. The

success of that enterprise led Rosenberg to open his first coffee and doughnut shop, the Open Kettle, in Quincy, Mass. In 1950 Rosenberg changed its name to Dunkin' Donuts. The shop was first franchised in 1955, and the chain went public in 1968. The company raised its profile considerably in 1978, when it aired its first network television commercials. A British conglomerate, Allied Domecq, bought Dunkin' Donuts in 1990. Dunkin' Donuts, with corporate headquarters located in Randolph, Mass., is now the largest chain of coffee shops in the world, operating 5,000 franchises in 40 countries. In one year Dunkin' Donuts serves enough freshly brewed coffee for every person in Rhode Island to have 577 cups.

Doughnut legends are still being created, and Massachusetts is the scene of an ongoing battle over the popular sweet. In 1998 the eight-year-old schoolgirl Emma Krane of Somerville launched a campaign to name Boston Cream the state's official doughnut. Legislators from the Berkshires, trying to level the commonwealth's tilt toward the metropolis, stalled the effort, however—despite a nationwide poll conducted by Dunkin' Donuts, which conclusively determined that America's favorite doughnut is what that chain terms the Boston Kreme.

Brooke Dojny, *The New England Cookbook: 350 Recipes from Town and Country, Land and Sea, Hearth and Home* (1999); Federal Writers' Project of the Works Progress Administration, *Maine: A Guide "Down East"* (1937); Fred Halliday, *Halliday's New England Food Explorer: Tours for Food Lovers* (1993); Sara B. B. Stamm, *Favorite New England Recipes,* 2d ed. (1991).

Louis Mazzari

Down East "Up to Boston," they say, and "down to Maine." Some swear that *down east* is a seafaring phrase dating back to the 1700s. With prevailing winds blowing from the west, when you sail from Boston to Bar Harbor, you're sailing to the east and downwind. Londoners, too, used to travel down to Edinburgh. Bostonians may go down to Gloucester, but one thing is clear: down-easters are Mainers—from Kittery to Fort Kent, from Calais to Coburn Gore. Such, at least, is the reigning philosophy at *Down East* magazine.

Down east Yankees are busy, thrifty, and averse to squandering anything, whether time, energy, or words. They employ a language that is direct and concise but also rich and vividly graphic. Generally nasal, slurred, and hesitant, down east speech used to encompass a great variety of patterns. *Maine: A Guide "Down East"* (1937), issued by the Works Progress Administration, found "as many Maine dialects as there are States in the Union." Today, the most familiar traits of native speech include *ayuh* (meaning "yes"), the removal of *r* from most words that contain it ("nawtheastuh" for *northeaster*), and the insertion of *r* into words that do not ("Auguster" for *Augusta*, Maine's capital city).

Traditional down-easters heartily lack the hail-fellow-well-met exuberance one might encounter elsewhere in the United States. Louise Dickinson Rich in *State O'Maine* (1964) disputes their reputation as dour, however. "This is frequently a false impression," says Rich, "rising from Down-easters' disinclination to expose their feelings. Ever since they first came to the Maine coast, they have necessarily been on guard against unexpected attacks from a variety of quarters, including Indians, the weather, the wrath of God, and smooth-talking, out-of-state salesmen." Down east Yankees fear that a casual smile could lead to a commitment they have no desire or intention to make.

Maine, of course, is famous for its weather. Down-easters say they have two seasons, winter and the Fourth of July. The state's brutal weather, like the harsh lessons of the sea, has left its mark on Mainers, shaping their character and unadorned outlook on life. "Sometimes epic fogs move in from the Bay of Fundy in a mile-high wall to shroud the land for days on end," writes Rich. "Visitors find these fogs depressing, but to Down-easters they are restful, beautiful and right."

The popular perception of down-easters owes a great deal to the works of several 19th-century writers who were either born in Maine or moved to the state: *Way Down East; or, Portraitures of Yankee Life* (1854), by the Portland journalist Seba Smith, who founded the state's first newspaper in 1829; *The Pearl of Orr's Island: A Story of the Coast of Maine* (1862), by Harriet Beecher Stowe; and *The Country of the Pointed Firs* (1896), by Sarah Orne Jewett. The paintings of N. C. Wyeth and William and Marguerite Zorach, among others, disseminated artistic images of down east nationwide.

The region's humor might come closest to defining the down east turn of mind. Dry as a bone and radically understated, it often uses tourists and know-it-alls as foils whose hubris is turned to absurdity. Maine humor harks back to Seba Smith, who invented the humorous rural Maine character Major Jack Downing, and Artemus Ward, who in the 1860s became the country's first deadpan comic lecturer and pointed American literature toward its humorists. In recent years Tim Sample, Kendall Morse, Joe Perham, and Robert Skoglund, among others, have brought down east humor to a national audience.

Since the early 1940s, John Gould, a resident of Friendship, Maine, has written a down east column for the *Christian Science Monitor*. A collection of the essays was published in 1994 as *Dispatches from Maine, 1942–1992*. Gould related the story of Farmer Wadell, for example, who one day decided to paint his silo with huge red, white, and blue stripes, like a giant barber pole, on the tallest hill for miles around. None of the town folks thought to comment on it to him. But a traveling salesman from Worcester stopped one day to ask why he had painted the structure that way. "To preserve the wood," Wadell responded. "Time and again," Gould wrote, "there has been evidence that our neighbors are willing to indulge each other in whimsy."

To the 20th-century Maine writer Gerald Warner Brace, there is a philosophical aspect to the down east cast of mind that has attracted people for centuries now. Brace saw the down-easter as a person living close to the elements, one whose livelihood required a working knowledge of nature: "The people on the old coast of Maine were not romantic philosophers or poets—they were not at all bookish or self-conscious—but they did seem to provide the evidence on which philosophy could build. They illustrated what could be done when the right people and the right place and climate and conditions all collaborated in a harmonious and at best beautiful way of life."

For many years bright blue road signs at border crossings proclaimed, "Maine, the way life should be," to all who left or entered the state. While many down-easters might agree, they would likely see no need to waste words on something so obvious.

Gerald Warner Brace, *Between Wind and Water* (1966); Jonathan Daniels, *A Southerner Discovers New England* (1940); Neal R. Peirce, *The New England States: People, Politics, and Power in the Six New England States* (1976); Neil Rolde, *Maine: A Narrative History* (1990).

Louis Mazzari

Drinan, Robert F. (1920–) Jesuit priest, U.S. congressman, law professor. Born in Boston to James and Ann Mary Drinan, Robert F. Drinan earned his B.A. from Boston College in 1942 and became a Jesuit seminarian at Weston College. After earning his M.A. at Boston College in 1947, he took an LL.B. in 1949 and an LL.M. at Georgetown University Law Center before being ordained to the priesthood in 1953. The following year he earned a doctorate in sacred theology at Rome's Gregorian University and took a fellowship in theology at Florence in 1954–55. Having been admitted to the bar in Washington, D.C., and in Massachusetts as well as having earned the right to practice before the Supreme Court, he became associate dean and professor at Boston College Law School in

Father Robert F. Drinan celebrates his election to Congress, 1970

1955 and was made dean a year later, a position he held until 1970. During his deanship, Drinan brought the school from merely local significance to being one of the top 20 in the country and was instrumental in developing the proposal that made Boston College the site of one of the four Social Welfare Regional Research Institutes in the country.

Through his books, which analyze religion and public policy, defend the public expression of dissent, and criticize national policy in Vietnam; his activity in the American Bar Association's family law section; his vice presidency of the Massachusetts Bar Association; his editorship of the *Family Law Quarterly;* and his chairmanship (1962–70) of the Massachusetts advisory committee to the U.S. Commission on Human Rights, Drinan attracted attention as a thoughtful, forceful proponent of liberal positions. In 1970 he challenged Philip J. Philbin, the hawkish Democratic congressman from Massachusetts, for the Fourth District seat. After a highly sophisticated campaign, Drinan became the first Roman Catholic priest elected to the U.S. Congress. During five terms, he served as the only civil libertarian on the House Internal Security Committee, was active in the Environmental Study Conference and the Steering Committee of Members of Congress for Peace through Law, and chaired the Subcommittee on Criminal Justice of the House Judiciary Committee. He filed the original impeachment complaints against Richard Nixon and, as a member of the House Judiciary Committee, voted for Nixon's impeachment. Because of his support of abortion rights he was barred by the Vatican from seeking reelection in 1980 and left Congress in 1981.

Since 1981 Father Drinan has been professor of law at the Georgetown Law Center. Continually publishing books and articles on legal ethics, human rights, civil liberties, and public policy, he has participated in human rights activities in Central and South America, Vietnam, and the Philippines, and has served as an election observer in Panama and Armenia. He chaired the American Bar Association's Standing Committee on World Order under Law and the International Committee for the Release of Anatoly Shcharansky; helped found the Lawyers' Alliance for Nuclear Arms Control; and advised the U.S. Holocaust Memorial Commission.

Congressional Directory, 96th Congress (1979); Robert F. Drinan, *Democracy, Dissent and Disorder* (1969); Drinan, *The Fractured Dream: America's Divisive Moral Choice* (1991); Drinan, *God and Caesar on the Potomac: A Pilgrimage of Conscience* (1985); Drinan, *The Mobilization of Shame* (2001); Drinan, *Can God and Caesar Coexist?* (2004).

Joseph M. McCarthy

Eden The myth of New England as a biblical Eden dominated language and discourse from the earliest settlements until the Civil War, when all aspirations for a utopian land of abundant natural resources "flowing with milk and honey" and a harmonious community of enlightened citizens were shattered on the battlefields of Gettysburg and Atlanta.

Early Puritan histories chronicled events that paralleled episodes in the Old Testament; the migration from Egypt through the wilderness into Canaan, for example, was recapitulated in the Puritan migration from England across the Atlantic to the "New English Israel," as Thomas Morton titled his history in 1637. Similarly, William Bradford's *Of Plimoth Plantation* (1630) compares the Pilgrims to ancient Israelites, and John Winthrop's "Modell of Christian Charity" (1630) prophesies the coming of the New Jerusalem to New England, that "city upon a hill," a vision of the future paradise that is also established in John Cotton's "God's Promise to His Plantations" (1630).

These early histories and sermons are the most visible examples of New England's appropriation of biblical mythology; poems, letters, diaries, biographies, and autobiographies also reflected the essential New England vision of itself as a reiteration of the experience of Israel found in the Old Testament. This biblical identification permitted strong theocratic control of the expanding New England community; it also enabled writers and theologians to establish their accounts in the richly metaphorical and prophetic language of Scripture, the language of Canaan, as it was called. This scriptural vocabulary allowed a loose conflation of the concept of the Garden of Eden with the Land of Canaan, that mythic paradise toward which the Israelites were constantly struggling. In New England, this paradise would be realized on earth through a process of progressive historical improvement toward a millennium, which would be attended by the Second Coming of Christ in spirit.

Eden, then, represented a return to innocence, the incarnation of the second Adam, a leaving behind of the values, governments, traditions, monarchies, and aristocracy of the Old World and the assumption of new values by a community transformed by its experience of migration and the promise of the New World. The new Adam, the American, would occupy a special place in history, and the New English Israel would be a blessing to the New World, just as Old Israel had brought the Messiah to the Old World. Eden and Canaan grew closer together in the New England self-conception, and these representations abound in writings from the earliest settlements to

the work of Henry David Thoreau and Walt Whitman in the 19th century.

At the end of the 17th century, Cotton Mather composed his *Magnalia Christi Americana* (1702), which contains some 60 biographies of the "saints" who had settled New England. In this work, Mather regularly compared such leaders as Winthrop and Bradford to Old Testament figures: Bradford and Winthrop are both Moses, and the title of his life of Winthrop is "Nehemias Americanus." These parallels were so powerful in the literature of New England that long after the American Revolution was fought and the Constitution had replaced the Bible as the font of governing principles, the rhetorical strategies and language of literature continued to reflect the essential New England impulse to represent both its history and that of the nation as a forward movement toward Eden and Canaan.

These images abounded from 1750 to 1865; two prominent examples are most representative. In 1771 Philip Freneau read a poem at the commencement exercises of Princeton College called "The Rising Glory of America." There he prophesied that the promise of America was both biblical and progressive:

> Paradise anew
> Shall flourish, by no second Adam lost,
> No dangerous tree with deadly fruit shall
>   grow,
> No tempting serpent to allure the soul
> From native innocence. . . . The lion and
>   the lamb
> In mutual friendship linked, shall browse
>   the shrub,
> and Timorous deer with softened tigers strat
> O'er mead, or lofty hill, or grassy plain.

These pastoral images from Isaiah 53 and Psalms 23 suggest an American purity that will bring Eden (and Canaan) to the New World. Another poet, Joel Barlow, would add technological innovation to the Edenic myth in *The Vision of Columbus* (1788) and *The Columbiad* (1806).

The American Eden was thus momentarily realized, even as slavery had undermined the ideal represented by this myth. In the turbulent antebellum years (1820–60) there was a transformation of Eden, and the Civil War years turned Eden, Canaan, and Paradise into a political empire that required extensive bloodshed to survive. The language of Canaan continued to inspire writers, but Eden as a mystic force was lost. Recalling this lost image became a trope for later writers like Robert Frost in "Nothing Gold Can Stay," Sarah Orne Jewett in *The Country of the Pointed Firs,* Edith Wharton in *Summer,* and Donald Hall in such poems as "Maple Syrup" and "The Black-Faced Sheep." The remembered vision of the New England Eden resonated among 20th-century New Englanders who contemplated the region's seeming fall from grace and authority in the national economy and political life.

Mason I. Lowance, Jr., *The Language of Canaan: Metaphor and Symbol in New England from the Puritans to the Transcendentalists* (1980); Leo Marx, *The Machine in the Garden* (1964); A. W. Plumstead, *The Wall and the Garden* (1968); John Seelye, *Prophetic Waters* (1977).

Mason I. Lowance, Jr.

Farmer, Fannie Merritt (1857–1915)

Cookbook author. Fannie Farmer learned to cook as a mother's helper when she was in her twenties. At 39 she wrote *The Boston Cooking-School Cook Book* (1896), and her name became a household word.

Farmer was born in Boston and lived in the area most of her life. The oldest of four sisters, she grew up in Medford, Mass. At 16 she had an illness (probably polio) that paralyzed her left leg; she regained her ability to walk but always had a limp. Farmer lived with her parents until she was 28, when she went to work as a household helper for a family friend. She had never cooked but discovered an aptitude for the craft and entered the two-year course at the Boston Cooking School, a training program for professional cooks and schoolteachers. She stayed on to teach and in 1894 became the school's director.

The publisher of *The Boston Cooking-School Cook Book* so doubted the success of "a cookery book" that he required Farmer to contribute to its publication costs. To his surprise, it was an instant best-seller. It did not include witty remarks, helpful hints, or a conversational tone; its purpose was to give clear, exact, foolproof instructions that would produce consistent results. Other cooks' recipes called for a piece of butter the size of a walnut or a heaping dessert spoon of sugar, but Farmer allowed no room for error. She became famous as "the mother of level measurements." "A teaspoon is a teaspoon, leveled flat," she said. That was that. She helped to bring the tools of science into American kitchens and hoped to convey to her readers "a knowledge of the principles of diet." The recipes ranged from lengthy instructions for making soup stock with beef bones to advice for making dainty salads and tea-party sandwiches. The book explained how to build and maintain the wood-and-coal fire that fueled the stove, recommended a basic inventory of cooking tools, and advised on food shopping. Farmer thus joined a tradition of practical New England cookbook authors dating back to Lydia Maria Child and her *American Frugal Housewife* (1833).

In 1902 Farmer resigned from the Boston Cooking School to open Miss Farmer's School of Cookery, where weekly lectures and demonstrations were the means of training housewives and not-yet-married young ladies. A student scribbled in her notebook, "Miss F. says if a cook can make a good cream cake, baking-powder biscuit & creamed codfish she can cook anything." Red-haired and blue-eyed, wearing pince-nez, Fannie Farmer had an enthusiasm that made her a popular speaker at women's clubs. Today she would surely have a television cooking program; in her own time, she traveled the lecture circuit, speaking to packed houses. With her sister, she wrote a column for *Woman's Home Companion.*

Having been an invalid herself, Farmer took great interest in cooking and nutrition for the sick. In 1904 she published *Food and Cookery for the Sick and Convalescent,* a book she considered more important than her more famous work. Twenty-one editions of *The Boston Cooking-School Cook Book* were published before her death in 1915; since renamed *The Fannie Farmer Cookbook,* it is still being published, kept current with other editors' revisions, and is a standard guide for new cooks. Most recently, Marion Cunningham revised the book and released its 100th-anniversary edition in 1996. The name Fannie Farmer has become synonymous with New England cooking. Farmer died in Boston and is buried in Mount Auburn Cemetery in Cambridge, Mass.

Edward T. James and Janet Wilson James, eds., *Notable American Women, 1607–1950: A Biographical Dictionary* (1971); Mary Drake McFeely, *Can She Bake a Cherry Pie? American Women and the Kitchen in the 20th Century* (2000); Laura Shapiro, *Perfection Salad: Women and Cooking at the Turn of the Century.* (1986).

Mary Drake McFeely

Frugality

The high estimation that New Englanders have long accorded frugality comes from multiple sources. Foremost it was a religious value inscribed in the souls of colonial Puritans, Quakers, and evangelicals. These rigorous Protestants esteemed diligence, industry, and frugality as crucial aspects of the holy life; the disciplines of working assiduously, avoiding idleness, and living modestly with the fruits of this labor were signs of sanctification. Prosperity was a dangerous source of temptation, a common stimulant for neglecting devotion and for absorption in the distractions of the world. Luxuries, especially fashions in dress, were the bugbear of this austere Protestant piety; Puritans, Quakers, Baptists, and their varied heirs in New England (Methodists, Adventists, right on down to 21st-century Pentecostals) have drawn and redrawn the line against an endless number of supposed superfluities: from fancy ruffs to trifling jewelry. Modest adornment of the body has long been a hallmark of frugal Christian living in these New England Protestant traditions.

The politics of republican virtue matched Puritan and evangelical asceticism as a wellspring of New England frugality. Republican political theorists, whether Thomas Paine or Benjamin Franklin, shared the same emphasis on simplicity, diligence, and frugality with their more spiritually ardent counterparts (Paine had grown up in a Quaker family and easily transferred that religious vision into revolutionary politics). The two ethics—one from civic republicanism, the other from fervent Protestantism—flowed together in New England, so that by the early 19th century they were all but indistinguishable. One New England religious reformer, Elias Smith, gave them coterminous vocabularies; his *Herald of Gospel Liberty,* published in Portsmouth, N.H., from 1808 to 1818, threaded republican and evangelical didacticism into a characteristically homegrown synthesis. Avoiding corrupting luxuries and cultivating frugal disciplines became both a political and a religious obligation of the virtuous citizen.

Transcendentalists such as Ralph Waldo Emerson and Henry David Thoreau added a romantic, antimodern dimension to understandings of frugality. Seeing the advance of the market revolution as disordering social relations and agrarian life, they looked to the simplicity of nature to provide a check on the rampant money-getting and self-indulgence of the expanding economy. Puritan frugality was reinvented in a new idiom—one of woodsy retreat, flinty self-reliance, and village sturdiness. Avarice and incessant trade were thought to deaden the spirit, while thrift was the handmaiden of poetic inspiration and renewed tranquility. These romantic mutations of Protestant austerity led both to individualistic quests after simplicity through solitude and to such communitarian endeavors as Brook Farm and Fruitlands, in which frugality was made part of corporate routine. Living frugally in a community of common purpose often fired the utopian imagination of New England Transcendentalists.

Few ideals have proven more resilient in New England culture than those of simplicity, industry, and frugality. Though often seen as imperiled, they have proven to be enduring values, despite (or perhaps because of) the omnipresence of Yankee prosperity, competing gospels of wealth, and the spreading paradise of consumer pleasures. Indeed, frugality itself has become a commodified export of New England culture, available for all in the rugged plaids and sensible thriftiness of L. L. Bean's outdoor wear.

David E. Shi, *The Simple Life: Plain Living and High Thinking in American Culture* (1985); Max Weber, *The Protestant Ethic and the Spirit of Capitalism* (1958).

Leigh E. Schmidt

Gothic New England

The Gothic vision of New England in history, literature, and folklore combines nostalgia for a medieval or colonial golden age with the stronger belief that the past, however longed for, is the source of horror and evil. Abandoned burial grounds, crumbling gabled mansions, and Puritan persecutions have shaped the popular image of New England as horror capital, with Stephen King of Maine as its recent chronicler.

King continues the tradition of collecting and transforming supernatural tales begun by Cotton Mather and John Greenleaf Whittier. Nineteenth-century writers who drew on such legends include Nathaniel Hawthorne, Harriet Beecher Stowe, Charlotte Perkins Gilman, and Mary Wilkins Freeman. In the 20th century, the Rhode Island writer H. P. Lovecraft peopled the landscape with monsters and the reanimated dead.

Origins of the current Gothic revival lie in the 17th century. Most early New Englanders shared a fear of necromancy and the malevolent powers of the dead. In addition, belief in a devil who delighted in tempting good Puritans led to witch-hunts and executions in Connecticut, Massachusetts, and New Hampshire, and to the Salem witch trials of 1692. Some colonists continued to dread Europe's legendary monsters: the merfolk, ocean serpents and lake dwellers, vampires, and werewolves. Such fears have not entirely disappeared, though they are expressed today as fear of alien abduction or satanic ritual abuse.

Less malevolent medieval traditions also persisted in New England: the belief in fairies, Maypoles, and the search for and acceptance of signs, wonders, and "wonderful Providences." Intellectuals pursued the "real Gothic" connections seen in Longfellow's poem "The Skeleton in Armor," which recounts the Viking discovery of Newport. In the 1840s, Gothic Revival mansions like Roseland Cottage in Woodstock, Conn., echoed the spires and pointed arches of medieval cathedrals. Today, such Romanticism is manifested by Neo-Pagans, the Society for Creative Anachronism, fantasy writers, and paraarchaeologists who seek out Celtic Culdee settlements and find Ogham writing in glacial scratches on fieldstones.

New Englanders endowed the native peoples, the fields and the forests, and later the factories, towns, and cities with shapes of fear. The forests were frightful places for the first settlers; no less frightful were the original inhabitants, the Indians who seemed like forest demons.

The Indians' attempts to win back their lands in the Pequot Wars and King Philip's War were seen by Puritans as campaigns by the devil against the Kingdom of God.

The darker aspects of Gothic medievalism are exemplified in New England's obsession with the dead, from Puritan gravestones to ancestor worship. The Mathers recorded poltergeist activity, while later folklorists chronicled ghosts in farmhouses and factories. Nineteenth-century spiritualism raised the dead in a more hopeful guise, where mediums could report that the "undiscovered country" looked like home. Not all New Englanders shared the spiritualists' sunny view of the afterlife; in the 19th century, some believed that tuberculosis might be caused by the depredations of the uneasy dead. Archaeological evidence from Griswold, Conn., has confirmed that bodies were exhumed and mutilated to prevent the occupants from returning as vampires.

Regional decline captured by New England's writers and philosophers reflects the Gothic vision of decay and fall. Quakers, Indian wars, demonic possession, and contentions among the "elect" reminded the Mathers of their failure to create in Massachusetts John Winthrop's "city upon a hill." In the 19th century, the fall was seen as an economic one, evident in the mass westward migration from New England farms. Such writers as Hawthorne and Henry Adams chronicled the perceived loss by their generation of the Puritan founders' and revolutionary patriots' strength of purpose.

Popular magazines of the 1890s portrayed rural New England as a backwater whose population had become inbred and sinister, and Edith Wharton's *Ethan Frome* (1911) became an American classic by linking Gothic themes to regional psychological characteristics of guilt and sexual repression. By the 1930s, urban industries that had attracted women from farms and immigrants from Europe were beginning to leave. The textile mills were among the earliest, followed by manufacturers of shoes, machine tools, hats, jewelry, and other products. Industrial cities like Fall River, Mass., and Pawtucket, R.I., and regions like northeastern Connecticut and the Merrimack River valley seemed left behind by history. The abandoned factory joined the abandoned farm as proof of New England's continued decline.

Though economic conditions have since improved, this Gothic picture of New England persists in the fiction of Shirley Jackson, Howard Frank Mosher, Carolyn Chute, and Stephen King, authors whose images have created a mass media market for New England Gothicism in film and television. The Gothic legacy still draws intrigued tourists to "America's Stonehenge" in Salem, N.H., and to the Witch Museum and Halloween celebrations in Salem, Mass.

Joseph A. Citro, *Passing Strange: True Tales of New England Hauntings and Horrors* (1996); Gary Hoppenstand and Ray B. Browne, eds., *The Gothic World of Stephen King: Landscape of Nightmares* (1987); Faye Ringel, *New England's Gothic Literature: History and Folklore of the Supernatural from the 17th through the 20th Centuries* (1995); John Greenleaf Whittier, *The Supernaturalism of New England* (1847).

Faye Ringel

Gravestones, Burying Grounds, and Cemeteries

When Thornton Wilder set a scene of *Our Town* in a New Hampshire burying ground, he evoked both the physical landscape of death and the popular image of New Englanders under the burden of the past. The earliest settlers of Massachusetts, Connecticut, and Rhode Island punctuated town commons with burying grounds, in contrast to the Anglican and Catholic traditions of sanctified churchyards or interment inside the church. In remote areas of New England and throughout New Hampshire and Rhode Island, family burying plots, frequently more than 100 in a town, are often the only reminders of earlier settlement. With the establishment of the first Jewish cemetery in Newport, R.I., in 1759; some African American burying grounds; the nation's first nondenominational "rural" or garden cemetery, Mount Auburn in Cambridge, Mass., in 1831; and Catholic cemeteries in urban areas, the landscape of death created before the Civil War represented New England's complex, evolving religious and social history. In the 19th century, creation of rural cemeteries like Mount Auburn fit the mood of the nature-loving Transcendentalists, while evoking a landscape ideal of class and culture based on Protestant founding traditions, during a time of mass Catholic immigration, especially from Canada and Ireland. These historic landscapes persist. For example, Providence's Swan Point Cemetery (1847) offers commemo-

The Cuffe Gibbs stone, Newport, R.I., 1768, signed by the African American carver Pompe Stevens

ration for the dead and quiet recreation for the living in a setting that blends memory and modern life.

The progressive styles of grave markers—from death's head to soul image to urn and willow in the colonial period; and from neoclassicism, the Egyptian Revival, and Victorian Gothicism to the mass-produced modernism of the 20th and 21st centuries—have been interpreted as indexes to the changing religious sensibilities and tastes of the region. In comparison to other regions, New England styles are often more conservative and understated.

Individual gravesites and graveyards function today in the tourist industry and popular literature for New Englanders and other Americans to confirm stereotypes about the New England psyche. Pilgrimages to various sites also may serve to solidify individual identification with place. Literary pilgrims visit Authors Ridge in Sleepy Hollow Cemetery (1855) in Concord, Mass., to see the graves of the Alcotts, Thoreau, Emerson, and Hawthorne. The cenotaphs in the Seaman's Bethel, New Bedford, Mass., still serve to remind New Englanders, as they did Melville in *Moby-Dick*, of those lost at sea. Many New Englanders can recite favorite epitaphs, grave or humorous, from colonial times as well as more contemporary examples, such as Robert Frost's epitaph in Bennington, Vt., which reads, "I had a lover's quarrel with the world."

Many traditions of colonial and revolutionary New England draw visitors to Salem, Boston, and Plymouth, Mass., Newport, and Hartford. The monuments for early African Americans, such as Crispus Attucks, Amos Fortune, and John Jack, and those cut by Pompe Stevens for Newport's colonial slave and free black population, are often the only physical survivals of the community. Graveyards also persist as part of the popular and folk culture of the region in the literature of Stephen King and Robert Frost, the plaster replicas of stones for sale in gift shops, and the homemade Halloween graveyards that sprout on suburban lawns each October.

Blanche Linden-Ward, *Silent City on a Hill: Landscapes of Memory and Boston's Mount Auburn Cemetery* (1989); Allan I. Ludwig, *Graven Images: New England Stonecarving and Its Symbols, 1650–1815* (1999); Dickran and Ann Tashjian, *Memorials for Children of Change: The Art of Early New England Stonecarving* (1974); David H. Watters, *"With Bodilie Eyes": Eschatological Themes in Puritan Literature and Gravestone Art* (1981).

David H. Watters

Green, Hetty (1834–1916) Financier. Hetty Green, known as "the witch of Wall Street," was born Hetty Robinson in 1834 in New Bedford, Mass. Her mother, Abby Howland, inherited a fortune from her father, Isaac Howland, Jr., who made his fortune in the whaling and merchant-shipping business. Raised a Quaker, Hetty Robinson was educated first at the Friends School on Cape Cod and later at James Lowell's School in Boston, run for the daughters of wealthy New England aristocrats.

When her father, Edward Mott Robinson, moved his business concerns from New Bedford to New York City, Hetty went along to help manage his financial affairs. Edward Robinson died in 1865, leaving his entire $6 million fortune to Hetty. Shortly thereafter, Hetty Robinson's unmarried aunt, Sylvia Ann Howland, died. Although her aunt's will allotted her a substantial stipend, Robinson laid claim to her aunt's entire fortune by producing a second will allegedly drawn up at her aunt's deathbed. Written entirely in Robinson's own handwriting but signed in two places by her aunt, the second will did not convince other Howland family members, who declared that the signatures were forged. Robinson filed suit to secure her aunt's entire fortune, estimated at more than $2 million. At the height of the controversial case Robinson married her financial adviser, Edward Henry Green of Bellows Falls, Vt., with whom she fled to London during the trial. The Howland will case dragged on for five years; in 1870 the court dismissed her claim on the grounds that there was insufficient evidence of a contract between Robinson and her aunt.

Upon returning to America in 1875, Hetty Green once again took up obsessive management of her fortune, becoming a major operator on Wall Street, where she was feared for her ruthless financial dealings. She had extensive holdings in railroad stocks and government bonds and maintained considerable liquid assets that she used for lending. She owned more than 8,000 parcels of real estate throughout the country. Despite being a multimillionaire, she appeared in public in shabby clothes, carried odd bits of food around with her, haggled with shopkeepers over petty purchases, sought medical treatment at charity clinics, and lived in run-down boardinghouses. When her husband went bankrupt in 1885, she initially refused to underwrite his losses; they separated shortly afterward. She continued to live with her son and daughter in inexpensive lodgings in New York and New Jersey, avoiding any display of wealth and shunning most of society.

Her eccentricities made her the topic of numerous gossip columns across the country, and her miserly behavior literally cost her only son his leg, which became infected following a sledding accident; Green refused to hire a physician and instead made the rounds of every free medical clinic in Manhattan and Brooklyn. Turned away, she attempted to treat the leg with home remedies. When she finally called on a doctor, it was too late; gangrene had set in and the leg had to be amputated.

Her husband died in 1902, and in 1908 Green drew up her own will. She died in 1916, the richest woman in America, alone in a small apartment in Hoboken, N.J., at the age of 81 and was buried at the family cemetery in Bellows Falls, Vt. She bequeathed her approximately $100 million estate to her son and daughter.

William Kendall Clarke, *The Robber Baroness* (1979); William Emery, *The Howland Heirs* (1919); Arthur Lewis, *The Day They Shook the Plum Tree* (1963); Boyden Sparkes, *The Witch of Wall Street: Hetty Green* (1936).

J. North Conway

Hermits Hermits distinguish themselves from other vagrants and homeless people in New England by establishing long-term identification with one place and permitting the development of a history, a mythology, and perhaps even celebrity status, often attracting tourist interest. Known for their self-reliance and eccentricity, hermits typically hunger for union with either God or nature. Simultaneously spiritual and intensely practical, the traditional hermit's temperament parallels what Austin Warren considers "the two strains in the New England character: the Yankee trader and the Yankee saint"; The New Englander has a mind that "is shrewd in its lower ranges, speculative in its upper." Consequently, the New England hermit both perpetuates an age-old tradition and provides a distillation of regional character. Relatively unmodified by social influence, he or she is a more independent, ingenious, and spiritually committed version of the archetypal New Englander.

Solitary preoccupation with sacred reality, be it transcendent or immanent, is historically characteristic of New England hermits. Sarah Bishop, a recluse of early-19th-century Ridgefield, Conn., was noted for her piety; her trances were interpreted as communication with the spirit world. Charles Lambert, the 19th-century hermit of Mosquito Pond, N.H., lived in solitude for more than 70 years, meditating on nature. Henry David Thoreau famously preached simplification and conservation, while Henry Beston, alone in a Cape Cod beach house in the 1920s, wrote of our deep need for "elemental" things. More recently, Bill Britt, the hermit of Chestnut Hill in Newton, Mass., from 1969 to 1988, planted trees and communed with the natural world from a woodland near a shopping mall.

This spiritual hunger frequently coexists with an intense practicality. In his journals,

Thoreau related exactly how he built his hut and planted his beans. Lambert kept a vegetable garden, sold herbs, trapped, chopped wood, and herded 1,200 sheep. The 19th-century "giant hermit" of Isle au Haut, Maine, maintained a comfortable refuge that rivaled Robinson Crusoe's, a hideaway he ingeniously destroyed at death with a fire started with a magnifying glass. In December 1998, Thomas Johnson, the "subterranean hermit" of Nantucket, drew considerable attention with his underground bunker, a hidden woodland lair complete with paneling, books, stove, bed, portable generator, and television. His story, once a front-page feature of the *Boston Globe* complete with instructions on how to build your own hideaway, appeals to New England sensibilities—it chronicles both a spiritual quest and an ingenious experiment in construction.

The New England character is not purely spiritual. Austin Warren perceives it as also "ungracious": the native is more liable to resemble "a crank than a libertine." For all their interest in spiritual matters, long-term recluses often retreated because of personal maladaptation: Bishop mourned the death of her fiancée; Lambert failed in wooing his beloved; the giant hermit fled upon discovering his wife's unfaithfulness; Britt took to the woods after a divorce. Their estrangement from society might have a libertarian bent, such as Britt's rejection of governmental assistance; be harmlessly bizarre, as in Daniel Pratt's insistence that he was actually the elected president of the United States; or be darkly obsessive, as in the case of Jules Bourglay, a 19th-century Frenchman who roamed the hills of Connecticut in a leather suit meant to recall a failed leather investment. Britt's greatest fear was that, if evicted from his woods, he would become "just another street person."

Hermitic traits of spirituality, self-reliance, and a crankiness born of either principle or mental disquiet (or both) persist. Britt, who wrote poetry and constructed his own shelters, also resisted both eviction and governmental assistance, insisting, in effect, on the right to "live free or die." (He froze to death in his wigwam in 1988.) Johnson, who constructed a warren in the middle of woods he called his "place of schooling and of worship," also smuggled drugs and fled an Italian prison. His claim that he had "gone into the earth, almost like a seed, to regerminate," could apply to most New England hermits—reticent, sometimes lost in darkness, they likewise have the ingenuity necessary to preserve a precarious liberty. They are New Englanders writ large: fascinating enactments of Americans' deeper character.

Judith Evans, "Bill Britt," *Boston Globe* (June 13, 1987); Brian MacQuarrie, "The Underground Man," *Boston Globe* (December 3, 4, 6, 1998); Edward Rowe Snow, *Fantastic Folklore and Fact: New England Tales of Land and Sea* (1968); Austin Warren, *New England Saints* (1956).

Christopher A. Fahy

Holy Land USA

Built by the attorney and evangelist John Baptist Greco, Holy Land USA illustrated the life of Jesus Christ, represented biblical scenes and miracles, and simulated the cities of Bethlehem and Jerusalem on 18 acres of rocky land in Waterbury, Conn. An expression of Greco's faith as a Roman Catholic, Holy Land functioned not only as a religious sanctuary but also as a tourist attraction and venue of environmental folk art from 1958 until 1984. It still stands atop Pine Hill, marked by an illuminated 32-foot stainless-steel cross, visible to travelers heading into or out of New England on Interstate 84. This site is one of Connecticut's few examples of environmental folk art, and at the height of its popularity it attracted more than 40,000 visitors a year.

John Greco envisioned an accessible space to share with others of similar religious background; through his creation, with its traditional content and intention of bringing pleasure to others, he created folk art. In 1946 Greco purchased land on Pine Hill and slowly began collecting previously used materials such as cast-off lumber, tires, old church pews, plastic sheeting, garbage cans, and copper tubing to construct the site. These materials assumed new meaning when arranged into scenes that reflected the Judeo-Christian tradition. In 1958 Holy Land opened to the public, complete with 200 buildings making up miniature replicas of Jerusalem and Bethlehem, biblical ornaments, statues, scenes, and didactic signs. Greco wanted visitors to worship there and share his enthusiasm for their faith. Holy Land was unique because it represented a traditional catechism through an unconventional composition.

Although Greco intended to build an accessible place of worship, his creation also attracted secular tourists. The American Automobile Association listed Holy Land USA in its tour books, and thousands of visitors arrived each year. Some visitors appreciated the space as environmental folk art, a work that surrounded and interacted with its audience as they walked through the art.

Conflict over its religious and artistic function grew as Holy Land fell into disrepair and closed to the general public in 1984. In 1972 Greco relinquished the perpetual care of Holy Land to an order of Catholic nuns, the Religious Teachers of Saint Lucy Filippini, even though he visited the site almost daily until it closed. After 26 years the site was too costly to maintain and lacked funds for renovation. In the late 1980s, after Greco's death, folk art restoration groups and the religious order maintaining the site argued over who should care for and preserve Greco's creation. The religious order still retains control of the site, but no restoration is planned. Although the site has not been open to the public since 1984, the steel cross remains illuminated atop Pine Hill to remind New Englanders of what was once Holy Land USA.

Sando Bologna, *The Italians of Waterbury: Experience of Immigrants and Their Families* (1993); Heather Heston, "Land's Sisters to Move," *Waterbury Republican-American* (July 6, 1997); Mark Muro, "Jerusalem, Connecticut," *Boston Globe* (October 14, 1986); Tena Tyler, "Group Looks for Ways to Restore Holy Land," *Waterbury Republican-American* (November 14, 1993).

Sheila A. Brennan

Home

The archetypal image of the New England home recalls the region's colonial past and is evocative of the simple, tranquil ways of rural life. This image, though based in part on historical reality, was constructed in the mid-19th century to fulfill nostalgic ideals in a time of rapid industrialization and demographic change. This, by implication and practice, resulted in an image that was rural, not urban, Anglo-Protestant, not ethnic or racial. This ideal satisfied the American urbanite's need for refuge, sanctuary, and safe haven from the hustle and bustle of the marketplace and the Industrial Revolution. Influenced by traditions of Calvinism and Puritanism, the iconic New England home resonated with the spirit of Thanksgiving all year long. Home, according to Robert Frost, in his "The Death of the Hired Man," is the place where, "when you have to go there, they have to take you in."

An influx of immigrants in the 1820s and 1830s brought new languages and cultures and a new heterogeneity to the established social hierarchy in Puritan New England, promoting the stereotyping of a traditional New Englander and likewise the image of calm domesticity. In 1826, forces of nature conspired to promote a tiny rural house as the symbol of the hardworking New Englander's confrontation with the unsympathetic environment: located in New Hampshire's Crawford Notch, the Willey House was left unscathed although its farming family was killed seeking safety from a landslide. The house remained standing until 1890, its sparse interior and few simple, functional possessions intact and undisturbed, just as the family had abruptly left them. For 70 years visitors toured the Willey House, a monument to the family's hard work, frugality, and helplessness in the face of nature. Its image was widely circulated as a testament to New Englanders' independence and determination; the story was celebrated in fiction while the house was reproduced in lithographs and stereopticon images.

But the New England home was usually pictured in a more cheerful context. Within, the New England home reflected the Yankee qualities of self-reliance, resourcefulness, and cleverness. Debates among regions over the best model of American familial, social, and political values began in the 1790s in such works as Timothy Dwight's poem "Greenfield Hill" (1794); by the 1820s, the components of the ideal New England home in a village setting were in place. According to early popular advice books of the 1820s, the New England home was the moral center of the nation, a sheltered, secluded refuge run by the mother, who was responsible for raising the new republic's citizens. In the very early days of the republic, when gentility was prized, the New England home was often pictured with a three-generation family seated before the hearth, all reading or doing handiwork. After the 1840s, however, adults were more often pictured actively producing foodstuffs and household goods while children read and studied or helped their parents.

Three New England women helped to popularize the New England home as a national icon. Lydia Maria Child wrote *The American Frugal Housewife* (1833), which taught women across the country reliable methods of housekeeping, food preparation, and caring for the family. Catharine Beecher and Harriet Beecher Stowe wrote *The American Woman's Home* (1869), which provided moral guidance and admonishments for spiritual training that reflected traditional New England values. Another Beecher family member, Henry Ward Beecher, contributed *Norwood; or, Village Life in New England* (1868), sealing the connection between the New England home and an idealized version of New England womanhood that had developed in advice books, literature, and art by the Civil War.

As the art historian Sarah Burns has demonstrated, artists and printers popularized the image of the New England home after the Civil War, when casualties, nostalgia, and anxieties about urbanization and immigration were assuaged by reassuring images of rural homes. George Henry Durrie's images of Connecticut and Eastman Johnson's poetic Nantucket interiors adorned urban parlors. E. B. and E. C. Kellogg of Hartford printed

thousands of copies of New England home scenes, often in a seasonal setting. Later, the popular hand-colored lithographs of Nathaniel Currier and James Ives brought images of picturesque rural New England scenes into parlors all across the country. In many other popular renditions, notably in *Ballou's Pictorial*, the New England home was pictured as remote from cities and towns, abounding with character and detail: a large room, at once perhaps a kitchen and sitting room, with a yawning fireplace, the large family's adults gathered before its blazing pile of cordwood and merry children meeting in the chimney corner. Practical objects might include a row of flatirons and candlesticks on the mantelpiece, strings of dried apples festooning the ceiling, a cat, and a gun rack. Often the image was captioned, "From such firesides great and noble men have gone forth in the world." The most important functional objects of the New England colonial home became recognizable to a host of readers of advice books, periodicals, and newspapers as these images circulated throughout the enlarging republic. The spinning wheel, the kitchen fireplace, the tall case clock, the cradle, and the butter churn became domestic icons, celebrated in poetry and art.

The earliest homes built by colonists were adapted to the skills of a primarily rural society. Simple in design, small and adaptable, the traditional rectangular two-story configuration was easily recognized by its three- or five-bay exterior, with one or a pair of windows on either side of a central door. A central core of fireplaces provided heating, and the hearth was the center, both literally and figuratively, of the home. Often its exterior was pictured as a comfortable village dwelling with overarching trees, a tidy dooryard, bountiful fields, and a large barn, and the house itself was either a two-story mansion or a quaint saltbox; both had multiple rooms clustered about a central chimney. In reality, the typical 18th- and 19th-century New England home was much smaller.

Literary representations of the New England home, including Henry Wadsworth Longfellow's *The Courtship of Miles Standish* (1858), Harriet Beecher Stowe's *Oldtown Folks* (1869), John Greenleaf Whittier's *Snow-Bound* (1866), and Louisa May Alcott's *Little Women* (1868–69), portrayed New Englanders as frugal, hardworking, guided by stern moral principles, and at the same time warm and focused on home and family. Elizabeth Stuart Phelps's *The Gates Ajar* (1868) consoled Civil War widows by describing heaven as a New England village in which loved ones would be reunited in their homes. Sarah Orne Jewett's *Country of the Pointed Firs* (1896) portrayed

home as a place with "chairs in all their places"—a place where there was internal order in an ever-changing, rapidly industrializing region and nation. The New England home continues to be celebrated during the Thanksgiving and Christmas seasons with Lydia Maria Child's nostalgic *The New-England Boy's Song about Thanksgiving Day*, commonly known by its lyric, "Over the river and through the woods, to grandfather's house we go."

In the last half of the 19th century, artists and photographers began documenting the pastoral New England landscape and the idealized activities of home, ignoring the surrounding hubbub of the city and the noisy confusion of the factory. They produced tranquil images that reflected unchanging ideals. These images ignored the existence of modern technology in favor of an imagined everyday life governed by the weather and the rhythms of agriculture. Featuring Deerfield, Mass., and York, Maine, Emma Coleman and the sisters Frances S. Allen and Mary E. Allen produced narrative photographs that, capturing a mood of old-fashioned simplicity, documented household processes like flax processing and candle dipping that seemed endangered. More detailed prose descriptions of the New England home abounded in the photographs of Wallace Nutting and the books of Alice Morse Earle, which met the public demand for information about ways of life in the days of New England forebears. Earle's work brought together masses of obscure and diverse information and reinforced the icons of the spinning wheel, the hearth, and the rocking chair. Efforts to preserve this material culture and the houses that contained it inspired William Sumner Appleton, Wallace Nutting, and others to restore houses to reflect the nostalgic values of the Colonial Revival movement in the early 20th century. The house museum became a standard of tourist and educational activities, thus assuring the survival of an iconic version of the New England home into the 21st century.

The New England home chronicles unique patterns of material culture. Architectural contributions include the extended farmhouse of northern New England documented by Thomas Hubka in his *Big House, Little House, Back House, Barn* (1984), and the three-decker, an architectural form unique to New England. Although the canonized forms are the saltbox, the garrison colonial, and the Cape Cod, the extended farmhouse perhaps best exemplifies regional identity: simple, refined, and adaptable to change. The three-decker, common in Worcester, Mass., reflects New England's patterns of immigration and ethnic population, and its porches reveal a public culture connected to the urban community and neighborhood.

Given the power of the images and ideas of the New England home, critical appraisal, parody, and deconstruction of its official cultural status are also characteristic of the region. Nathaniel Hawthorne's *House of the Seven Gables* (1851) suggests the history of expropriation of lands and the pursuit of wealth that is the corrupt foundation of New England homes. Harriet Wilson, in *Our Nig* (1859), and Sarah Josepha Hale, in *Northwood* (1827), explored the corruption that slavery could bring to the regional, and the national, home. Louisa May Alcott's *Little Women* even evokes themes of violence and despair. After the Civil War, local-color writers revealed repressed and, on occasion, corrupt lives, especially those of women trapped on the farm as economic vitality drained away. This counter-image of the New England home in part inspired the Old Home Week movement, beginning in the 1890s.

The persistent image of the idyllic home remained strong enough for each new generation of writers to shock readers with revelations of the dark side. The national audience consumed a darker idea of the New England home in Robert Frost's *North of Boston* (1914) and Edith Wharton's *Ethan Frome* (1911). Hidden secrets clutter shelves, cupboards, and attics, along with chipped china and spinning wheels. The secrets may be sexual, as in Grace Metalious's *Peyton Place* (1956), Carolyn Chute's *The Beans of Egypt, Maine* (1985), and John Irving's *The Cider House Rules* (1985), or they may be economic and political, as in the works of Russell Banks and Ernest Hebert. John Cheever's *The Wapshot Chronicle* (1957) is a satirical and nostalgic look at the peculiar shaping power of the traditional images of the home on contemporary New England families. Stephen King has made the Gothic version of the New England home his stock in trade, brilliantly extending images and ideas of New England to include contemporary anxieties.

In recent years, critics, museum curators, authors, and artists have reexamined the images and ideas of the New England home in light of the ethnic and racial diversity of the region, past and present. New England house museums now present Jewish, African American, Native American, and Franco-American settings, to name just a few examples. Nevertheless, the New England home and its values still resonate in many images with the colonial, rural past.

Each year millions of magazines advertise items and images that reflect the New England quaintness of hearth, rocker, and kitchen. Tourists can visit historic homes and even stay overnight in them. The image of the New England home, while originally developed as a salve to rapid industrial and population change, has nevertheless absorbed that change throughout time. A region that once rejected its ethnic population has expanded its accepted icons to include the Kennedy rocker and the three-decker, and today its multitudes of mass-produced, oil-heated homes still boast the now unnecessary but nonetheless time-honored fireplace, its hearth always available for the re-creation of the New England Thanksgiving.

Alan Axelrod, ed., *The Colonial Revival in America* (1985); Clifford Edward Clark, Jr., *The American Family Home, 1800–1960* (1986); Sarah Burns, *Pastoral Inventions: Rural Life in 19th-Century American Art and Culture* (1989); Alice Morse Earle, *Home Life in Colonial Days* (1993 [1898]); Sarah L. Giffen and Kevin D. Murphy, eds., *"A Noble and Dignified Stream": The Piscataqua Region in the Colonial Revival, 1860–1930* (1992); Thomas C. Hubka, *Big House, Little House, Back House, Barn: The Connected Farm Buildings of New England* (1984); Jane C. Nylander, *Our Own Snug Fireside: Images of the New England Home, 1760–1860* (1993).

Cynthia Watkins Richardson

MacArthur Fellows of New England (Table, opposite)

Maine Maine has long been saddled with—and has promoted—its image as a place apart. Depending on your point of view, the state is isolated or secluded, narrow-minded or free-thinking, stubborn or independent, a stern vacationland. No matter what your perspective, however, Maine holds a unique place in the national mind.

All of Maine's corners have been roughly tugged and pulled at by a number of forces. Glaciers clawed its tall mountains into thousands of coves and bays. The most populous and warlike of the Native American nations of New England made their home in Maine. The French and the English fought for decades over Maine's timber and fish, and then the Revolution ruined its economy. Massachusetts ruled Maine as a colony and in the War of 1812 abandoned it to British warships. While the state's coastline and rivers have been a source of wealth, its hardscrabble farms have yielded equal harvests of potatoes and poverty. Maine's wild countenance and fearful weather have been seen over the centuries as shaping Mainers' moral fiber and unadorned outlook on life.

Almost as big as the other five New England states put together, Maine is a gigantic wilderness with bounteous tracts of thick forest, more than 2,000 lakes, and a smattering of small to medium-sized communities. Its inland waters alone cover an area twice the size of Rhode Island. But Maine is also the end of the line, the only state among the lower 48 to border only one other state. Neal Peirce has called it a "continental cul-de-sac." Vast and impenetrable, Maine offered early visitors indomitable nature. In the 1500s European ships, many of them French, charted the coast without leaving a settlement. In 1607 the British sponsored a colony at the mouth of the Kennebec River—as they did the same year in Jamestown, Va.—but Popham, Maine, proved less hospitable than its southerly counterpart and was quickly abandoned. Still, permanent English settlements affiliated with Plymouth Colony were established along the Maine coast in the 1620s. Unlike the Massachusetts colonists, whose communities took root and grew, Maine settlers were constantly at war with the French and the Indians; by the 1690s, only four poor settlements remained. Maine's long coast rendered it vulnerable to attack, and during the Revolutionary War Maine suffered more than any other state in New England. Its image as a land of hard-bitten survivors dates back at least to that time.

Maine agitated for statehood in the years following the War of 1812, when Massachusetts left it undefended from British attack and occupation. By 1820 Massachusetts had decided that there was little to gain from the large, remote, unruly region and willingly let the province go. At that time Maine had 300,000 people. The expansion of the logging and shipbuilding industries had tripled its population since the Revolution. Maine's population continued to expand rapidly through the middle of the 19th century.

Boat building had become a major industry early on because of Maine's extraordinary seacoast and vast forests, a seemingly inexhaustible source of masts and timber. By the 1840s, Maine was the nation's preeminent shipbuilder, a fact that helped shape its paradoxical character. This land of primitive forests and isolated logging camps was also home to ships' crews and captains' families who had traveled the world. Maine was more cosmopolitan in the 1830s, 1840s, and 1850s than it would be in the corresponding decades of the 20th century. In his book *The Maine Woods* (1864), Henry David Thoreau wrote that Bangor in the 1840s was "already overflowing with the luxuries and refinement of Europe, and sending its vessels to Spain, to England, and to the West Indies for its groceries—and yet only a few axemen have gone 'up river,' into the howling wilderness which feeds it." That sense of an unbridgeable cultural distance between coastal and inland Maine has never been erased; it is one of the primary components of Maine's contradictory character.

MacArthur Fellows of New England

	Name	Profession	Affiliation or Residence
1981	Joseph Brodsky	Poet and Andrew W. Mellon Professor of Literature	Mount Holyoke College South Hadley, Mass
	John Cairns	Retired from Department of Cancer Biology	Harvard School of Public Health Boston
	Robert Coles	Research psychiatrist	Harvard University Cambridge, Mass.
	Howard Gardner	Codirector, Harvard Project Zero Professor of education Professor of neurology	Harvard University Cambridge, Mass. Boston University School of Medicine Boston
	Henry Louis Gates, Jr.	W. E. B. Du Bois Professor of Humanities and chair of Afro-American studies	Harvard University Cambridge, Mass.
	Stephen Jay Gould	Professor of zoology	Harvard University Cambridge, Mass.
	Ian Graham	Assistant curator of Mayan hieroglyphics	Peabody Museum Harvard University Cambridge, Mass.
	John P. Holdren	Professor of environmental policy Director, Program in Science, Technology, and Public Affairs	John F. Kennedy School of Government Harvard University Cambridge, Mass.
	John Imbrie	Henry L. Doherty Professor Emeritus of Oceanography	Brown University Providence
	Robert W. Kates	Retired as professor of geography Director emeritus, World Hunger Program	Brown University Providence Resides: Ellsworth, Maine
	Elma Lewis	Artistic director	Elma Lewis School of Fine Arts Roxbury, Mass.
	Roy P. Mottahedeh	Professor of Islamic history	Harvard University Cambridge, Mass.
	Richard Mulligan	Professor of molecular biology Professor of genetics	Massachusetts Institute of Technology Whitehead Institute Cambridge, Mass. Harvard University Medical School Cambridge, Mass.
	David Pingree	Professor of the history of mathematics and of the classics	Brown University Providence
	Derek Walcott	Poet and playwright	Boston University Boston
	Robert Penn Warren	Writer	Fairfield, Conn.
1982	Persi Diaconis	Professor of mathematics	Harvard University Cambridge, Mass.
	Robert Parris Moses	Educator	The Algebra Project Cambridge, Mass.
	Frederick Wiseman	Documentary filmmaker	Zipporah Films Cambridge, Mass.

(continued)

MacArthur Fellows of New England (*continued*)

Year	Name	Profession	Affiliation or Residence
1983	Randall Caroline and Watson Forsberg	Founder and director, respectively	Institute for Defense and Disarmament Studies Cambridge, Mass.
	William C. Clark	Environmental scientist Director, Center for Science and International Affairs	John F. Kennedy School of Government Harvard University Cambridge, Mass.
	Brad Leithauser	Lecturer Lawyer, poet, and writer	Mount Holyoke College South Hadley, Mass.
	Irene J. Winter	Professor of fine arts	Harvard University Cambridge, Mass.
1984	Shelly C. Bernstein	Professor of pediatrics Associate in medicine (hematology/oncology) Clinical associate	Harvard University Medical School Dana-Farber Cancer Institute Boston
	J. Bryan Hehir	Parker Gilbert Montgomery Professor of the Practice of Religion and Public Life President	John F. Kennedy School of Government Harvard University Cambridge, Mass. Catholic Charities of the Archdiocese of Boston Boston
	Sara Lawrence-Lightfoot	Professor of education	Graduate School of Education Harvard University Cambridge, Mass.
	Heather Nan Lechtman	Professor of archaeology and ancient technology and materials science and engineering	Massachusetts Institute of Technology Cambridge, Mass.
	Matthew Meselson	Professor of the natural sciences	Harvard University Cambridge, Mass.
	David R. Nelson	Professor of physics	Harvard University Cambridge, Mass.
	Roger S. Payne	Research scientist President	Whale Conservation Institute Lincoln, Mass.
	Michael J. Piore	Mitsui Professor of Contemporary Technology Professor of economics	Massachusetts Institute of Technology Cambridge, Mass.
	Judith N. Shklar	John Cowles Professor of Government	Harvard University Cambridge, Mass.
	Charles Simic	Professor of English Poet	University of New Hampshire Durham, N.H.
	David Stuart	Linguist and epigrapher	Peabody Museum Harvard University Cambridge, Mass.
	Frank Sulloway	Visiting scholar, Department of Brain and Cognitive Sciences	Massachusetts Institute of Technology Cambridge, Mass.
	Alar Toomre	Professor of mathematics	Massachusetts Institute of Technology Cambridge, Mass.
1985	Harold Bloom	Sterling Professor of the Humanitites Berg Professor of English	Yale University New Haven, Conn. New York University New York, N.Y.
	Valery Chalidze	Publisher, writer, physicist, and human rights activist	Fair Haven, Vt.

(*continued*)

MacArthur Fellows of New England (*continued*)

Name	Profession	Affiliation or Residence
Robert M. Hayes	Human rights attorney	Moon, Moss, McGill, and Bachelder Portland, Maine
Shing-Tung Yau	Professor of mathematics	Harvard University Cambridge, Mass.
1986 Richard M. A. Benson	Professor of photography	Yale University School of Art New Haven, Conn,
Benedict H. Gross	Professor of mathematics	Harvard University Cambridge, Mass.
David C. Page	Molecular geneticist Whitehead Fellow	Whitehead Institute Cambridge, Mass.
Jay Wright	Poet and playwright	Bradford, Vt.
1987 Huynh Sanh Thông	Director, Vietnamese studies	Yale University New Haven, Conn.
Eric Steven Lander	Director	Whitehead Institute Center for Biomedical Research
	Professor of biology	Massachusetts Institute of Technology Cambridge, Mass.
David Mumford	Professor of mathematics	Brown University Providence
Muriel Sutherland Snowden	Community affairs and education and cofounder	Freedom House Dorchester, Mass.
William Julius Wilson	Malcolm Wiener Professor of Social Policy	Malcolm Wiener Center for Social Policy Harvard University Cambridge, Mass.
Richard Walter Wrangham	Professor of biological anthropology	Peabody Museum Harvard University Cambridge, Mass.
1988 Ran Blake	Jazz pianist and composer Professor, Third stream studies department	New England Conservatory of Music Boston
Andre Dubus	Writer	Haverhill, Mass.
Naomi Pierce	Hessel Professor of Biology	Harvard University Cambridge, Mass.
Max Roach	Professor of music and dance	University of Massachusetts Amherst, Mass.
Jonathan Dermot Spence	Sterling Professor of History	Yale University New Haven, Conn.
1989 Leo William Buss	Curator of invertebrates Professor of biology, geology, and geophysics	Peabody Museum Yale University New Haven, Conn.
Jay Cantor	Professor of English Writer	Tufts University Medford, Mass.
John Harbison	Composer, conductor, and professor of music	Massachusetts Institute of Technology Cambridge, Mass.
Aaron Lansky	Founder and president, National Yiddish Book Center	Amherst College Amherst, Mass.
Errol Morris	Documentary filmmaker	Cambridge, Mass.

(*continued*)

MacArthur Fellows of New England (*continued*)

Name	Profession	Affiliation or Residence
George Russell	Professor Composer and conductor	New England Conservatory of Music Boston
Pam Solo	Executive director	Institute for Civil Society Newton, Mass.
Claire Van Vliet	Graphic artist	West Burke, Vt.
1990 Martha Clarke	Director and choreographer	Sherman, Conn.
Margaret Joan Geller	Professor of anatomy	Harvard-Smithsonian Center for Astrophysics Cambridge, Mass.
John Hollander	Sterling Professor of English Poet	Yale University New Haven, Conn.
David Kazhdan	Professor of mathematics	Harvard University Cambridge, Mass.
Nancy Kopell	Professor of mathematics	Boston University Boston
Marc Shell	Professor, Department of English and American Literature and Language	Harvard University Cambridge, Mass.
Richard Stallman	Software developer and president	Free Software Foundation Cambridge, Mass.
1991 Mari Jo Buhle	Professor of American civilization and history	Brown University Providence
Harlan Lane	Distinguished University Professor	Northeastern University Boston
Gunther Schuller	Artistic director Composer and conductor	Sandpoint Idaho Music Festival Sandpoint, Idaho Newton Centre, Mass.
Joel Schwartz	Environmental epidemiologist	Harvard School of Public Health Boston
1992 Stanley Cavell	Walter M. Cabot Professor of Aesthetics and the General Theory of Value Writer	Harvard University Cambridge, Mass.
Evelyn Fox Keller	Professor, Program in Science, Technology, and Society	Massachusetts Institute of Technology Cambridge, Mass.
Laurel Thatcher Ulrich	Professor of early American women's studies	Harvard University Cambridge, Mass.
Günter P. Wagner	Professor of biology	Yale University New Haven, Conn.
1993 Paul E. Farmer	Physician Anthropologist and community health activist	Harvard University Medical School Boston
Thomas M. Scanlon, Jr.	Professor of philosophy	Harvard University Cambridge, Mass.
Leonard W. J. van der Kuijp	Professor of Tibetan and Himalayan studies, Department of Indian and Sanskrit Studies	Harvard University Cambridge, Mass.
John Edgar Wideman	Professor of English Writer	University of Massachusetts Amherst, Mass.

(*continued*)

MacArthur Fellows of New England (*continued*)

	Name	Profession	Affiliation or Residence
	Heather Williams	Associate professor of biology Neuroethologist	Williams College Williamstown, Mass.
1994	Anthony Braxton	Professor of African American music Composer	Wesleyan University Middletown, Conn.
	Donella H. Meadows	Lecturer, Department of Environmental Studies	Dartmouth College Hanover, N.H.
	Jack Wisdom	Professor, Department of Earth, Atmospheric, and Planetary Sciences	Massachusetts Institute of Technology Cambridge, Mass.
1995	Jed Z. Buchwald	Professor of the history of science Director, Dibner Institute	Massachusetts Institute of Techonology Cambridge, Mass.
1996	Dorothy Stoneman	Founder and president	YouthBuild U.S.A. Boston
1997	Peter Galison	Mallinckrodt Professor of the History of Science Professor of physics	Harvard University Cambridge, Mass.
	Michael Kremer	Associate professor of economics	Massachusetts Institute of Technology Cambridge, Mass.
	Kara E. Walker	Artist	Providence
1998	Tim Berners-Lee	Director	World Wide Web Consortium (WC3) Cambridge, Mass.
	Bernadette Brooten	Professor of Christian studies	Brandeis University Waltham, Mass.
	Nancy Folbre	Professor of economics	University of Massachusetts Amherst, Mass.
	Karl Sims	Computer scientist	Cambridge, Mass.
1999	John Bonifaz	Lawyer, executive director	National Voting Rights Institute Boston
	Shawn Carlson	Physicist and educator, founder and executive director	Society for Amateur Scientists East Greenwich, R.I.
	Jacqueline Jones	Professor, Department of History	Brandeis University Waltham, Mass.
	Juan Maldacena	Professor, Department of Physics	Harvard University Cambridge, Mass.
2000	Daniel Schrag	Professor of geochemistry	Harvard University Cambridge, Mass.
	Gina Turrigiano	Assistant professor, Department of Biology and the Center for Complex Systems	Brandeis University Waltham, Mass.
2001	Lene Hau	Optical physicist, Gordon McKay Professor of Applied Physics	Harvard University Cambridge, Mass.
2002	Ann Blair	Intellectual historian and professor of history	Harvard University Cambridge, Mass.
	Karen Hesse	Novelist	Brattleboro, Vt.
	Sendhil Mullainathan	Economist and associate professor of economics	Massachusetts Institute of Technology Cambridge, Mass.
	Daniela Rus	Roboticist and associate professor of computer science and cognitive neuroscience	Dartmouth College Hanover, N.H.

(*continued*)

MacArthur Fellows of New England (*continued*)

	Name	Profession	Affiliation or Residence
2003	James J. Collins	University professor, professor of biomedical engineering	Boston University Boston
	Erik Demaine	Assistant professor of computer science	Massachusetts Institute of Technology Cambridge, Mass.
	Osvaldo Golijov	Associate professor of music	College of the Holy Cross Worcester, Mass.
	Nawal Nour	Founder and director, African Women's Health Practice	Brigham and Women's Hospital Boston
	Anders Winroth	Associate professor of medieval history	Yale University New Haven, Conn.
	Xiaowei Zhuang	Assistant professor of chemistry and chemical biology	Harvard University Cambridge, Mass.

Source: "Complete List of MacArthur Fellows, 1981–2003." The John D. and Catherine T. MacArthur Foundation. www.macfound.org/programs/fel/fel_overview.htm MacArthur Fellows (1981–2003)

Other contradictions are woven throughout the state's history. In Maine's early years, a frontier atmosphere prevailed. "Rum was the common beverage," confides *Maine: A Guide "Down East"* (1937), published by the Federal Writers' Project of the Works Progress Administration, "and spirits were consumed on all occasions." By the mid-19th century, though, Maine had adopted prohibition laws that would not be repealed until 1934. And as prohibitionists were gaining ground in the state in the 1840s, Maine was also taking a strong stand against slavery. In the 1850s a virulent anti-Catholicism came to the fore, linked to prejudice toward the Irish, and by the 1920s the state had acquired a sizable Ku Klux Klan contingent, devoted to American nativism.

When shipbuilding shifted from wood to metals, Maine began a long decline; in every decade since 1850, its economy has fallen below the national growth rate. Farming began to fade soon after the Civil War, and the textile mills and shoe factories built on Maine rivers could absorb only some of the able-bodied young men and women no longer needed on the farms. French Canadian labor was cheaper, in any case, and this group eventually came to make up 20 percent of the state's population. "The essential fact," writes Peirce, "was that once the United States became an industrialized and rail-borne (and later highway-borne) nation, Maine would be at the end of the line—and fail to grow apace. For decades, its prime export was its young people."

Timber was still the state's predominant industry. But after shipbuilding failed and the economy declined, the new Maine Central Railroad began spreading tourism. Following the Civil War, tourists were visiting Rangeley Lakes, Moosehead, and Rockland and the summer resort at Bar Harbor on Mount Desert Island. Americans came to view Maine as a place to hunt and fish, relax, and, at a time of great change, commune with nature. They went to Maine to rediscover a fast-receding simpler life, solid and hard-won.

For most of its history Maine has been quintessentially Republican: rock-ribbed, conservationist, favoring the practices of free labor. Its reputation was for decades only slightly less Republican than that of Vermont, these being the only two states to vote for Alf Landon in Franklin Delano Roosevelt's 1936 landslide. During the latter half of the 19th century, Maine's reputation in the national political and cultural arenas was bolstered by three Republican statesmen of great stature—Hannibal Hamlin, Lincoln's first vice president, and two immensely powerful Speakers of the U.S. House, James G. Blaine and Thomas B. Reed, who served during the 1870s and 1880s–90s, respectively. No Maine Republican has had a comparable impact on the national scene since that time.

The next national figure, Edmund Muskie, served as governor of Maine, U.S. senator, and U.S. secretary of state but may be best known for losing the Democratic presidential nomination in 1972. The son of a Polish-born tailor, Muskie indicates the partial shift in Maine's population from Yankee Republican to ethnic Democrat. According to the political analyst Michael Barone, quoted by Peirce, Muskie's "serene and plain manner, coupled with his clearly honest idealism, persuaded many Yankee Republicans that not all Democrats were big-city hacks, and that some like Muskie were decent men who could be trusted with government."

A number of notable persons either born in or drawn to Maine have contributed to the state's image as a place where independent, often contrary ideas take root. Maine has fostered the crusading progressivism of Scott and Helen Nearing, who came to homestead on Penobscot Bay in 1952, bringing their radical politics and commitment to social justice with them. The couple's book *Living the Good Life: How to Live Sanely and Simply in a Troubled World* (1970) attracted counterculture readers all over the United States. Margaret Chase Smith, a congressional leader in both the House and the Senate, came to national attention in 1950 when she became the first Republican senator to denounce the tactics used by Joseph McCarthy in his anticommunist smear campaign. Rachel Carson's *Silent Spring*, published in 1962, is viewed by many as the book that launched the U.S. environmental movement. Carson spent much of her adult life near West Southport, finally building a cottage on the Sheepscot River. The naturalist Peter Matthiessen wrote in a *Time* magazine article (1999) that "she had a mischievous streak, a tart tongue and confidence in her own literary worth. . . . Secure in the approval of her peers, she remained remarkably serene in the face of her accusers." Through such personalities Maine has stood, in the national consciousness, for firm ideals and a strain of moralism, sometimes stubborn or idiosyncratic but always deep-seated and strongly held.

"This is the forest primeval," Henry Wadsworth Longfellow intoned, describing the spectacular desolation of Maine's age-old woodlands in the poem *Evangeline* (1847). "Loud from its rocky caverns the deep-voiced neighboring ocean/Speaks, and in accents disconsolate answers the wail of the forest." Maine remains the most undeveloped state east of the Mississippi. Some 90 percent of Maine's surface is covered by woods, and even today, half or more is designated as wildlands, outside the jurisdiction of any municipal government. These "unorganized territories" are mostly owned by huge paper companies, semisovereignties within the state. The Maine woods are home to some magnificent mountains, almost 100 of them rising more than 3,000 feet above sea level and nine of these towering to heights over 4,000 feet. The most famous is Mount Katahdin, at 5,269 feet the highest point in Maine, set in a seemingly limitless wilderness. Katahdin's isolated summit affords views unobstructed by other peaks; when the sky is clear, you can see more land and water from the peak than from any other point of land in America.

Traveling through the forests of Maine in 1846, Thoreau noted, "Very few, even among backwoodsmen and hunters, have ever climbed [Katahdin], and it will be a long time before the tide of fashionable travel sets that way. . . . Some hours only of travel in this direction will carry the curious to the verge of a primitive forest, more interesting, perhaps, on all accounts, than they would reach by going a thousand miles westward."

The Maine coast, by contrast, has attracted fashionable travelers, artists, writers, and summer vacationers of every stripe since the 19th century. From Kittery to New Brunswick, Canada, is less than 250 miles. But the rugged coastline wends its way in and out for more than 3,500 miles, giving Maine half the shoreline of the whole East Coast. That fact may partially explain why a relatively unimportant industry, lobster fishing, is the primary image of Maine in the eyes of the rest of the nation. All the products of Maine's lobster and fish industries combined fall far short of the economic importance of paper, tourism, textiles, and agriculture, but the lobsterman incarnates the Maine of rugged individualism in a setting of stern beauty, representing a distinctive way of life.

Following World War II more and more people began to see in Maine an unvarnished beauty that called into question modern America's urban civilization. Many moved to the state, seeking a more direct communication with primitive nature and a sense of rootedness perceived to be lacking in contemporary urban and suburban life. Maine's towns and rural areas, unlike its cities, thus have benefited from the state's once lethargic economy. Maine's isolation, while impoverishing many of its natives, has attracted the relatively affluent to Maine's repose. These transplants have adopted and transformed Maine's traditional strain of environmental conservatism, and protests often accompany proposals for development. Maine's image in the nation's mind is still informed by the belief, as Thoreau wrote in 1846, that "there still waves the virgin forest of the New World."

Gerald Warner Brace, *Between Wind and Water* (1966); Samuel Adams Drake, *Nooks and Corners of the New England Coast* (1969 [1875]); John Gould, *Dispatches from Maine, 1942–1992* (1994); W. Storrs Lee, ed., *Maine: A Literary Chronicle* (1968); Neal R. Peirce, *The New England States: People, Politics, and Power in the Six New England States* (1976); Kenneth Roberts, *Trending into Maine* (1938); Neil Rolde, *Maine: A Narrative History* (1990); Caskie Stinnett, *One Man's Island: Reflections on Maine Life from Slightly Offshore* (1984).

Louis Mazzari

Maine Coon Cat The Maine Coon cat is popular well beyond New England and enjoys international distinction. Usually a large, hardy feline, the Maine Coon appears solid and rectangular and sports a semilong, smooth, shaggy coat with shorter hair on the head and shoulders. The ears are distinctively tufted and the tail is plumed. Excluding Siamese patterns, chocolate, and lilac, almost every color or color combination is acceptable. Variations of the tabby pattern dominate, but the solid color class includes pure white, black, blue, red, and cream. In the particolored class are such patterns as tortoise shell, calico, and blue cream; other color classes include chinchilla, shell cameo, and black smoke. The paws are large and tufted, with five toes in front and four in back. Breeders tend to shun six-toed cats. Maine Coon owners describe their pets as intelligent, amiable, affectionate, serene, and independent.

A significant factor in the fascination with Maine Coon cats is the mystery surrounding their origin. Many theories abound. Because the tabby markings of early Maine Coons resembled those of raccoons, legend held that the Coon was a cross between a house cat and a raccoon; this theory has been dismissed as physically impossible. Another discounted theory held that the Maine Coon was a cross between a house cat and a bobcat or lynx. Also unlikely is the speculation that the Coon cat descends from Norwegian Forest cats, or Skogkatts, that Vikings brought to North America on their ships. Perhaps more plausible is the story that Captain Samuel Clough of

Maine Coon cat

Wiscasset, Maine, planned to bring French queen Marie Antoinette to a safe haven in America. Although the alleged plan failed, Captain Clough did sail with many of the queen's household furnishings and six of her long-haired cats. Let loose in the Maine countryside, the cats mated with resident tabby cats and thus propagated offspring that would logically resemble the Maine Coon. One variation of this story suggests that Marie Antoinette sent six Angora cats to America during the Revolutionary War as a gift to the Marquis de Lafayette; another variation is that the queen sent Norwegian Forest cats to the United Sates. An eponymous theory suggests that a Captain Coon from England brought his favorite Persians and Angoras when he sailed to New England; thus the offspring were called Coon cats. Probably most plausible is Marilis Hornidge's speculation that "the Maine Coon is the result of nature working on a wide genetic pool on the North American continent."

Although the Maine Coon cat was very popular in the 1800s and in the second half of the century won awards in many competitive cat shows, Persians and Siamese cats became preferred breeds late in the 19th century, nearly consigning Maine Coons to oblivion. Renewed interest in the breed, however, led to the founding of the Maine Coon Cat Club in 1953 and the Maine Coon Breeders and Fanciers Association in 1968. Today the Maine Coon is recognized and respected as an outstanding show cat and a beautiful, faithful pet.

Sharyn P. Bass, *This Is the Maine Coon Cat* (1983); The Cat Fanciers' Association, *Cat Encyclopedia* (1995); Marilis Hornidge, *The Yankee Cat: The Maine Coon* (1991); Desmond Morris, *Cat World: A Feline Encyclopedia* (1996).

Sally C. Hoople

Massachusetts "I shall enter on no encomium upon Massachusetts; she needs none. There she is. Behold her, and judge for yourselves. There is her history; the world knows it by heart. "The past, at least, is secure. There is Boston, and Concord, and Lexington, and Bunker Hill; and there they will remain forever." The soaring rhetoric of Senator Daniel Webster of Massachusetts in 1830, in his celebrated "Reply to Hayne" speech on the floor of the U.S. Senate, while admittedly an expression of provincial excess, spoke volumes for the historical stature of the Bay State in the early 19th century. At the start of the 21st century, of the 50 American states, none has received the historical attention that Massachusetts has. As a result, the history of early America became, to some writers and to many readers, the history of Massachusetts writ large. Indeed, the images of Massachusetts and the ideas associated with its people and history resonate in many ways, forming a state identity for its citizens and an image of that identity for all Americans.

The dominant images of Massachusetts are rooted in a series of historical periods and connected intimately to key ideas articulated at those times and by subsequent scholars. The images have not been created solely by intellectual or political leaders; they have also been the result of populist movements, ethnic groups, and folk culture. As new images arise and old ones fall in and out of favor, Massachusetts has become a collage with motifs located in the colonial era, the American Revolution, education, the Industrial Revolution and the era of reform, the arrival and rise to dominance of the Irish, historic preservation movements, and the transformation of the economy and the population at the end of the 20th century. Boston has always had a disproportionate place, owing to its dual roles as state capital and de facto capital of New England itself.

The reason for the primacy of Massachusetts in the national historical narrative well into the 19th century was that, for many generations, beginning in the colonial period and extending into Webster's time, Massachusetts produced more historians than any other state, and these men—and they were primarily men—wrote the historical books read by students and the general American public. This group became known as the Massachusetts school of historians, and their influence continued well beyond Webster's era. It has often been said that other states had interesting, rich histories but Massachusetts had the historians. Some modern historians from other regions have resented the dominance of Massachusetts chroniclers and challenged their narrative of events and interpretations. As Arthur M. Schlesinger, Jr., has written, "Scholars to the south and west have often rather irritably found a Yankee bias in the writing of American history, what it would be

politically correct these days . . . to call New Englandcentrism." The southern historian Ulrich B. Phillips spoke directly to the point: "The history of the United States has been written by Boston and largely written wrong."

The historians of Massachusetts were responsible for implanting a multitude of indelible images of early Bay State historical events in the American psyche. These images were first produced by words and then reinforced by a vast number of artworks, both contemporaneous and of later times. First and foremost is the image of the Pilgrims. There is the arrival of the *Mayflower* at the "stern and rockbound" coast of Massachusetts in 1620, and the landing of the Pilgrims at Plymouth on December 26 near a rock that was destined to become one of the most famous physical symbols in American history. The dour Pilgrim Fathers, attired in their severe dark clothes and stovepipe hats, attend Sabbath services, a Bible in one hand, a musket in the other. The first Thanksgiving at Plymouth Plantation is commonly depicted with the Pilgrims sharing their harvest with the then-friendly Wampanoag Indians. A dark, Puritan counterimage is presented in images of the witches of Salem being led to their deaths on Gallows Hill.

The visual images of the American revolutionary era are even more profoundly embedded in the American mind. They include the Boston Massacre of 1770 in which five patriots, including the first to fall, Crispus Attucks, of African American and Natick Indian heritage, were killed by a contingent of British troops. This scene was immortalized by Paul Revere in an engraving that ranks as one of the most effective propaganda works of American history. Henry Wadsworth Longfellow created an icon of the lamp swinging from the belfry of Boston's storied Old North Church on the evening of April 18, 1775, signaling Paul Revere and the other night riders that the British troops had begun their ill-fated march to Lexington and Concord. Histories, fiction, poetry, art, and scholarly writings celebrate the nearly 70-man contingent of poorly equipped minutemen, under the command of Captain Jonas Parker, huddled on the Lexington Green on the dawn of April 19, 1775, awaiting the arrival of General Thomas Gage's well-trained force of 700, part of the most vaunted military power in the world at that time.

The subsequent skirmish on the green, fraught with confusion, was the first spilling of American blood in the American Revolution: eight minutemen died and 10 were wounded. The two-minute clash at the North Bridge in Concord and the firing of the "shot heard 'round the world" proved for Massachusetts

historians that once again, in the battle for men's minds, the pen is mightier than the sword. Massachusetts claims as its own General George Washington, America's Cincinnatus, when he arrived in Boston to take command of the American army and to begin the campaign to drive the British from that strategic city. The bloody Battle of Bunker Hill (actually Breed's Hill), in which Colonel William Prescott ordered his undisciplined, undermanned, ragtag army not to fire on the superior British troops until they saw the "whites of their eyes," has echoed through American military history. These and many other scenes have projected the view that Massachusetts and the American Revolution are synonymous terms. "Where the Revolution began," "Birthplace of Democracy," and "Cradle of Liberty" bellow the modern boosters of Boston as they seek to lure American and foreign tourists to the Bay State.

The early Massachusetts historians placed their focus upon the history of the white people of their colony and state and consciously disregarded one group of human beings: the native population. Only in recent times have scholars examined the Native Americans of Massachusetts in depth. There were Indians in present-day Massachusetts thousands of years before the arrival of European explorers and settlers, but little is known about the culture or civilization of these people. Much has become known about the Indians who inhabited Massachusetts when the first French and English explorers arrived. These natives engaged in agricultural pursuits, producing corn, pumpkins, squashes, and beans, and practiced a system of crop rotation to revitalize the soil. Archaeologists have uncovered a large body of evidence on their cooking utensils, eating habits, household possessions, clothes, and artistic endeavors. Historians have underscored their agricultural and dietary contributions to the first settlers.

The Indians encountered by the Pilgrims at Plymouth and by the Puritans at Massachusetts Bay belonged to the Algonquian linguistic stock. During the early colonial period, seven Algonquian groups resided in Massachusetts: the Massachusett, Wampanoag, Nauset, Pennacook, Nipmuck, Pocumtuc, and Mohegan. The Pilgrims settled on land occupied by the Wampanoag. With assistance provided by two members of this group, Samoset and Squanto, the Pilgrims enjoyed peaceful relations with the Wampanoag during the first half century of their settlement. Samoset played a key role in a treaty effected between the Pilgrims and the Wampanoag in 1621; Chief Massasoit was the leader of the Indians. Squanto, who had lived in England for several years and acquired a knowledge of English,

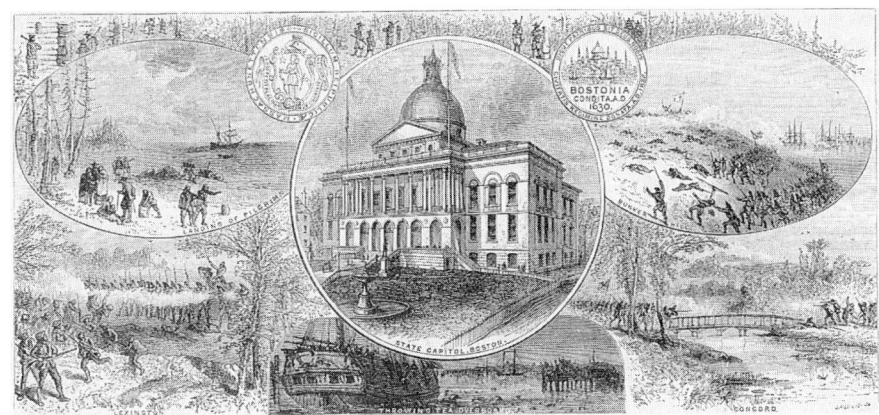

Images of Massachusetts from Harper's School Geography *(1881)*

served as an interpreter for the two groups and helped resolve differences when they arose.

The era of peaceful coexistence ended when Massasoit's son, Metacom (King Philip), assumed leadership of the Wampanoag in 1662, following the death of his brother. An implacable foe of the English settlers, Metacom was convinced that the steady growth of the colonists' settlements in southern New England would lead to the extermination of the Indians. In 1675 hostilities began between various tribes allied with Metacom and the three settlements making up the New England Confederation (Massachusetts Bay Colony, Plymouth Colony, and Connecticut). Rhode Island was soon drawn into the conflict. Thus began King Philip's War, a vicious struggle that persisted for almost three years and resulted in numerous atrocities by both sides, the destruction of many white and Indian settlements, and heavy casualties. The Native American presence in Massachusetts persisted in several communities, and the images of Native Americans in Massachusetts have been contested as communities have reemerged through cultural and political activities. Most notable are the "Day of Mourning" parades and protests on Thanksgiving Day in Plymouth.

Unlike the colonial era and American Revolution, educational developments in Massachusetts have no striking images associated with them, yet in this field the Bay State has ranked as the leading center in the nation since its first years. Public education in the United States began in Puritan Massachusetts. The Puritans placed a transcendent value on education and learning. In 1642 the General Court required the selectmen of each town to assume the responsibility of training or apprenticing all boys whose parents were financially unable to provide this help. Five years later, the General Court went further, passing legislation requiring each township of 50 families to maintain a primary school and each township of 100 families to establish a grammar school. This may have been the first time in history that a government had decreed that all boys must receive an education at public expense. In time, this policy would be extended to girls.

The Puritans can also be credited with founding the first school of higher education in America, Harvard College, established in 1636 for the twin purposes of training young men for the Congregational ministry and giving these prospective clerics, and all other students, a broad liberal education so that they could cope with the vagaries of the secular world.

The greatest spurt in public education in the history of the United States occurred in the early 19th century when Horace Mann became secretary of the Massachusetts Board of Education. Mann was an educational reformer of the first rank. His revolutionary improvements in public education elevated Massachusetts to a position of leadership in the nation. He established schools for the blind, the deaf, and "wayward" boys; upgraded the public high schools in the state; and founded the nation's first colleges for the training of teachers. Mann's policies and programs profoundly influenced educational systems in many other states and countries. He was largely responsible for making Massachusetts world-renowned as a pioneer of public education in secondary schools.

The dominant images and ideas of Massachusetts in the 19th century are those of a rapidly modernizing society, a state that assumed industrial and intellectual leadership in many fields. Although the Industrial Revolution in New England started in Rhode Island and advanced quickly there and in Connecticut, its most identifiable symbol is the planned industrial city for textile manufactures, Lowell, Mass. The Boston Associates, dubbed the "lords of the loom" by John Greenleaf Whittier for supporting the cotton plantations of the "lords of the lash," were identified with the brick mill towns and cities across the commonwealth. Like the fisheries of the 18th and 19th centuries, symbolized by the "sacred Cod" hanging in the statehouse, an industry not unique to Massachusetts became a symbol of the state.

A spirit of reform and freethinking, rooted in Puritan and revolutionary times, took on a distinctly individualistic tone. Massachusetts led the way in the abolitionist movement, through the presence of such great leaders as William Lloyd Garrison and Frederick Douglass. Movements for temperance, hospital reform, public health, improved treatment of the insane, and so on, were part of the special ferment centered in Concord, Boston, and Cambridge. Important intellectual movements—Transcendentalism, identified with Ralph Waldo Emerson, Henry David Thoreau, Bronson Alcott, and Margaret Fuller, and pragmatism, identified with William James—contributed to the image of Massachusetts as a place of ideas. Women transformed their lives, claiming a heritage that stretched back into earlier times in such figures as Anne Hutchinson, Abigail Adams, and Judith Sargeant Murray.

Women gathered in conventions to discuss rights in Massachusetts, setting the stage for the Seneca Falls, N.Y., convention of 1848. Margaret Fuller, editor of the Transcendentalist journal *The Dial*, wrote a foundational theoretical text on women's identity and rights, *Woman in the 19th Century* (1845). In education, the Peabody sisters of Salem worked with Bronson Alcott and Horace Mann on school reform, and such leaders as Mary Lyon founded women's colleges. Mary Baker Eddy established the Church of Christ, Scientist. The image of the Massachusetts woman as independent thinker, suffragist, reformer, "schoolmarm," and artist became a stereotype that authors such as Nathaniel Hawthorne, Henry James, and Charlotte Perkins Gilman could examine in their works throughout the 19th century. Women historians, among them Alice Morse Earle and Esther Forbes, penned popular works, especially during the Colonial Revival movement. The identification of Massachusetts with leadership in women's history continues through the annual Berkshire Women's History Conference and the presence of major research institutions at Harvard (Radcliffe) and at Brown University, and at numerous women's studies programs. Indeed, Laurel Thatcher Ulrich, in her *Age of Homespun* (2001), proposes an alternate set of women-centered images to define the development of New England.

Like every state in the union, Massachusetts was a land of immigrants; the native population was decimated by disease and warfare and largely dispersed after King Philip's War.

From 1620 to the middle of the 19th century, the social composition of the state was heavily English, reflecting its close ties with Great Britain. There was a smattering of other ethnic groups but the Anglo-Americans were the dominant force.

This dominance began to decline in the 1840s with the entry of a heavy flow of Catholic-Irish immigrants. These people had left Ireland because of severe economic problems, principally caused by the Great Famine of the 1840s, one of the worst agricultural disasters in the history of western Europe. The alternative to remaining and dying was emigration to America. More than 1.5 million Catholic-Irish boarded rickety "coffin ships" and crossed the Atlantic in search of the heavily publicized American dream. Boston became the main destination of these destitute people, many of whom were afflicted with serious diseases. In 1847, Black '47, as it was called, the worst year of the famine, more the 25,000 Catholic-Irish refugees arrived in Boston. Thousands of others disembarked in Canadian ports, and many of these soon resettled either in Boston or in such neighboring communities as the mill towns of Lowell and Lawrence, where there were possibilities for employment. By 1850, 43 percent of the foreign-born population of Boston was Catholic-Irish, as was much of eastern Massachusetts.

The Catholic-Irish profoundly altered the character and social, economic, religious, and political history of Boston and the commonwealth. Within half a century, Yankee dominance came to end, and a new social and political order was established.

Boston felt the greatest impact from this massive immigration. Impoverished, uneducated, disease-ridden, and lacking the skills and capital to assimilate into Boston's highly developed economic structure, the immigrants lived in abject poverty. Mostly of peasant stock, the men were relegated to menial day labor, and the women eked out a meager existence as domestic servants for affluent Yankee families. In Boston's economic and social structure, the Catholic-Irish ranked even below blacks.

Life was "poor, nasty, brutish, and short" for these new immigrants. The American dream did not materialize. Living in poor housing without adequate sanitary conditions, many contracted tuberculosis and intestinal diseases. Their death rate was excessively high: after reaching Boston, the immigrants lived an average of only 14 years. Poverty gave rise to alcoholism, prostitution, illegitimate children, and mental disorders. The social disintegration of the Catholic-Irish, plus a bias against them, led Boston businessmen to scorn them as employees. "No Irish need apply" signs were prominently displayed in the windows of Boston business establishments and factories, and newspaper employment ads frequently began "N.I.N.A." There was no need to spell out the words.

The political success the Catholic-Irish achieved in Boston and Massachusetts politics in the next half century was slow but inexorable. History was on the immigrants' side. The initial breakthrough came in 1857, when John C. Tucker became the first Catholic-Irishman to win a seat in the Massachusetts House of Representatives. Other firsts soon followed. In 1869 Patrick Collins became the first Catholic-Irishman to enter the state senate. In 1884 Hugh O'Brien became the first Irish-born Catholic mayor of Boston. In 1889 the Irish attained a majority in the 75-member city council. In 1905 John "Honey Fitz" Fitzgerald became the first Boston-born Catholic-Irish mayor of Boston. From that point on, the Catholic-Irish became the dominant force in city and state politics. James M. Curley, John W. McCormack, Thomas P. "Tip" O'Neil, John F. Kennedy and his brothers and nephews, Raymond L. Flynn, John Joseph Moakley, William M. Bulger: the list of 20th-century Catholic-Irish political leaders is long and impressive.

In modern times, the Catholic-Irish have been fully assimilated into all aspects of Boston and Massachusetts life. The leading scholar on the Boston Irish, Thomas H. O'Connor, has written, "They are no longer immigrants and exiles of the Famine era. The Boston Irish have become people of education, culture, and refinement. To a great extent, in their prolonged struggle for survival and achievement, they did turn Boston into an Irish city."

In the 20th and early 21st centuries, images and ideas of Massachusetts are a mixture of the old and the new. The Colonial Revival movement found a home in Massachusetts through leading scholars and preservationists, including William Sumner Appleton, who established the Society for the Preservation of New England Antiquities (now Historic New England) in 1910. The preservation movement and the developing tourism industry went hand in hand to create an enduring image of Massachusetts as a place of Yankee values, centered on Salem and Plymouth, along Boston's Freedom Trail, in Deerfield, and on Nantucket. The creation of Old Sturbridge Village solidified the role of Massachusetts as the conservator of the region's "official" past. The Massachusetts economy went through a cycle of transformations, with a new emphasis on high-tech industries, especially in computing. The presidential candidacies of Michael Dukakis in 1988 and John Kerry in 2004 presented the nation with familiar Massachusetts images of liberal politics and an educational elite.

The most significant challenge to the received images of Massachusetts has come with dramatic demographic change, especially in the period following World War II and continuing today. The "new immigration" presents a new set of images and ideas of Massachusetts, including the Cambodians of Lowell and the Dominicans of Boston, among others. Ethnic immigration to Massachusetts has been fueled by a search for employment, education, and quality of life. In some sense, these new groups follow familiar paths, since Lowell, for example, has long been a city of immigrants, but surely newer residents of Massachusetts will sort through the received images and ideas of the state and ultimately contribute their own.

Charles Francis Adams, *Massachusetts: Its Historians and Its History* (1893); Charles E. Banks, *The Planters of the Commonwealth: A Study of the Emigrants and Emigration in Colonial Times* (1930); Alden Bradford, *History of Massachusetts for 200 Years: From the Year 1620 to 1820* (1835); Federal Writers' Project, *Massachusetts, a Guide to Its Places and People* (1937); Oscar Handlin, *Boston's Immigrants, 1790–1865: A Study in Acculturation* (1959); Samuel E. Morison, *Builders of the Bay Colony* (1930); John Seelye, *Memory's Nation: The Place of Plymouth Rock* (1998); Walter M. Whitehill, *Boston, a Topographical History* (1968).

Louis Leonard Tucker

McAuliffe, Christa (1948–86) Teacher.

Known to millions of Americans as the "teacher in space," Sharon Christa (Corrigan) McAuliffe became a national figure when, after an extensive search that included the review of 11,000 applications and videotaped interviews, she was chosen to be the first private citizen to fly a space-shuttle mission. When the shuttle *Challenger* exploded 73 seconds after takeoff on January 28, 1986, McAuliffe was killed along with the other six members of the crew.

A civics, history, and English teacher, the Boston-born McAuliffe received a bachelor's degree from Framingham (Mass.) State College (1970) and a master's degree from Bowie (Md.) State College (1978). McAuliffe began her career in Maryland while her husband, Steven, was pursuing a law degree. In 1978 the couple returned to New England, settling in Concord, N.H., where they had two children and McAuliffe taught at local junior high and high schools. At Concord High, she taught classes in economics, law, and American history, as well as a course she had developed on the American woman.

After she was chosen for the shuttle program, which she called "the ultimate field trip," McAuliffe gave many interviews in

Christa McAuliffe boards a test flight plane at Kennedy Space Center, 1986

which she accomplished what school boards and NASA officials had tried for decades to achieve: she captured the imagination of students, teachers, parents, and others who, like her, had witnessed the birth of the space age and dreamed that space travel would one day be accessible to everyone. She also used her newfound access to the media to discuss the value of education, working to alter the public's perception of her profession. Her personal motto, "I touch the future, I teach," became an inspiration to fellow teachers and a signal to young people that teaching was a rewarding career. At a time when public interest in the space program was flagging, McAuliffe's sense of wonder generated renewed enthusiasm for space exploration.

In testimony to McAuliffe's dual role as a teacher and *Challenger* crew member, many institutions and awards carry her name. Most notable in New Hampshire is Concord's Christa McAuliffe Planetarium (est. 1988), visible from McAuliffe's gravesite across the Merrimack River. Framingham State College is home to the Christa Corrigan McAuliffe Center for Education and Teaching Excellence and to one of the many *Challenger* Centers for Space Education established by Steven McAuliffe and the families of the other *Challenger* crew members as living memorials. The *Challenger* Centers give school-age children firsthand experience in planning and carrying out a space mission.

Each year 50 federally funded Christa McAuliffe Fellowships, along with various other fellowships and scholarships and the

Christa McAuliffe Sabbatical for New Hampshire teachers, are awarded in memory of the first teacher in space. Today schools across the country carry her name.

Grace George Corrigan, *A Journal for Christa: Christa McAuliffe, Teacher in Space* (1993); Robert T. Hohler, *I Touch the Future: The Story of Christa McAuliffe* (1986).
Grace George Corrigan

Memory The perceptions, values, and meanings New Englanders attach to their region are created through memories and historical associations. Forms of cultural heritage—rites, beliefs, skills, or traditions that may take a material or an intangible form—have been used to establish and affirm a Yankee identity and forge a regional sense of place. In New England, the past lives in memories, often as narratives centered on activities in particular places. The various ways that cultural memory has been created, institutionalized, disseminated, and understood in New England include—among other manifestations—place-names, family reunions, town histories, monuments, commemorations, and historical reconstructions.

The evolution of place-names in New England reflects complex interactions between English settlers and Native Americans. It is difficult to reconstruct the Algonquian place-names for the landscape encountered by 17th-century English colonists. Only in naming major landmarks did the English imitate the sounds of the language. On his 1616 map of New England, for example, the explorer John Smith retained use of the authentic native term *Massachuset* as a name for the Boston basin as well as the Charles River and the Blue Hills. Otherwise, the colonists applied common English landscape terms of the post-medieval period to secondary features of the region's glaciated topography. By eradicating Native American place-names and renaming New England places in a way that recalled localities in their homeland, the English settlers clearly documented their political possession of the land.

Although New England did not fully emerge as a self-conscious region until the mid-19th century, some New Englanders did write local histories during the colonial period. Before 1800, chroniclers of local history worked within one of three literary models: topographical description, "annals," and providential history. Topographical descriptions were written by and for educated gentlemen. Following well-established formal conventions (specifically lists), this mode of narration focused on everything from natural history to church history. The writings were dominated by more of an interest in the present than the

past. Like cartography and toponymy, topographical descriptions largely excluded Native Americans from the New England landscape.

Annals, a second narrative tradition, portrayed the past as a sequence of events arranged chronologically. Change for writers of annals was orderly, precise, and linear. Their broad sweep of events suggests that New Englanders perceived a fundamental continuity between past and present. Providential historians, including such self-acknowledged cultural spokesmen as John Winthrop and Cotton Mather, thought of history as manifesting God's interventions to redeem the fallen. Through a distinctive rhetoric, the increasingly sophisticated 17th-century narratives they wrote used the past to shape the history, meaning, and purpose of the Puritan community and the idea of New England. Successively rewriting the past, providential historians sought to advance the myth that proclaimed New England chosen. These texts generated and regenerated a collective memory by revising the meaning of past events and accommodating more recent, often disturbing, events. In *Magnalia Christi Americana* (1702), for example, Cotton Mather lamented the moral decline of New England. The late 17th century was an uncertain time during which society was distressed by the Salem witch trials, battles with the Indians and French, and a government in transition. By preserving the piety and patriotism of the fathers, Mather argued, New England could restore its status as a city upon a hill.

While cultural authorities in Boston wrote local histories during the colonial period, English settlers on New England's frontier created meaning and identity by commemorating the past in different ways. Major events in Deerfield, Mass., were the source of stories lodged in collective memory and memorialized in landmarks and artifacts. The massacre and abduction of the town's residents by Indians in 1704 achieved an immediate place in the consciousness of New Englanders with the publication of an autobiographical account by the Deerfield pastor, John Williams. More than a personal memoir animated by a private search for self or even a simple family history, Williams's narrative persisted as a prototype when Americans, pressing westward, confronted Native Americans. Between 1715 and 1720, a brick and stone monument was erected in memory of the town's devastating Battle of Bloody Brook (1675). The symbolic commemoration of these events embodied a new memory, both individual and communal, concerned with justifying the presence and expansion of English colonists throughout the New England landscape.

Even before the famous Indian attack on

Deerfield, English colonists eagerly followed Samuel Sewall's order to the readers of his 1677 almanac to preserve the memory of King Philip's War (1675–76), a conflict with Algonquians that was probably the most significant event in the history of colonial New England. In addition to etching the war on the land, English colonists also marked the end of the war with gruesome memorabilia. They displayed the decapitated head of King Philip (Metacom) throughout the colonies and made pilgrimages to view the body parts of other Indian enemies. Although King Philip's War inevitably receded in importance for the colonists, no peace treaty officially ending the hostilities was ever signed, and visible reminders of the war, in fact, affirmed the fragility of the colonists' victory.

The Charter Oak, an inherently impermanent site in Hartford, preserves the memory of early political battles in New England. When Sir Edmund Andros, appointed governor of all New England colonies in 1686, sought to force Connecticut officials to relinquish the colony's royal charter on October 31, 1687, legend claims that they secreted the parchment in the hollow of a tree thereafter known as the Charter Oak. A portion of the original charter survives, and a tablet marks the spot where the tree formerly stood. During the 20th century, entrepreneurs made the wood of the Charter Oak into chairs, gavels, and various other mementos now in museums and private collections, and also appropriated the name Charter Oak for all manner of merchandising efforts from soft drinks and cigars to a horse-racing track.

Likewise, the tradition of Roger Williams's well has enshrined the authority of Rhode Island origins. A place at North Main Street in Providence memorializes the landing of Roger Williams and his followers in June 1636 at what was a spring. According to a Proprietors' Grant of 1721, "Liberty is reserved for the inhabitants to fetch water at this spring forever." In 1869, however, the spring was walled up and a pump placed nearby. A building was erected over the site but was torn down when the land was donated as a public park. During the early 20th century, the Rhode Island historical architect Norman M. Isham designed the present terrace, well-curb, and steps.

As the Industrial Revolution gained momentum 50 years after America had become a nation, the center of power shifted away from New England. Some towns were beginning to experience economic decline as young people moved south and west as well as to large cities. Nostalgia was both the response and indeed the antidote to these economic and demographic changes, among both those who left and those who stayed behind. By documenting and reaffirming their origins New Englanders reassured themselves of their rightful place. They sought to use history to redefine their regional identity. With the emergence of modern capitalism and the concomitant sense of profound cultural change, New Englanders perceived a distance and discontinuity between past and present. A heightened self-consciousness and introspection accompanied a new historicism during the middle and late 19th century.

Literary and artistic elites constructed the image of the New England village, a community of Puritan yeoman farmers on the colonial green, which became the icon of New England's exceptionalism in America. New Englanders incorporated this image as fact into their reminiscences of the preindustrial past. In the physical evidence of a town's past, history becomes palpable. Infused with this historical consciousness, Litchfield, Conn., exemplifies the transformation of the landscape according to this idealized conception of the colonial past. Quaint villages are littered with monuments to local heroes, war memorials to the town dead, and cemeteries, places inhabited by former residents. Similarly, the storied annual town meeting is a living tradition. This image of the New England village is emblematic of the region's public memory of its ritualized past. These collective memories reveal what New Englanders want to believe about themselves. In particular, many New Englanders continue to perceive their region as a moral beacon and a political model for the nation.

From 1870 to 1930 disturbing levels of urbanization, immigration, and industrialization spawned a colonial revival in New England. Americans, and especially New Englanders, sought asylum from the cultural turbulence by turning to their historical past. At the forefront of the new, middle-class interest in ancestral traditions were antiquarians who produced factual local histories. In addition, New Englanders established local historical societies where they could research family genealogies, restore family homesteads with historical associations, and collect and display memorabilia. Architectural and guidebook writers described, through sketches and photographs, the early mansions of New England's old maritime centers, such as Newport, R.I., Salem and Newburyport, Mass., Portsmouth, N.H., and Portland, Maine. Along the decaying waterfront in Portsmouth, for example, summer gentry preserved and opened many historic houses to the public. These artifacts and family trees were the material remains of the region's colonial past and the essence of its collective memory.

During the Colonial Revival, American culture became increasingly commercialized. New Englanders actively produced and marketed an image of their region as a place with a special history that dated back to the nation's origins. They advertised and sold New England as a tourist attraction. Returning sons and daughters as well as tourists could partake of the local heritage by reenacting the past in historical pageants, attending homecoming celebrations, and visiting historic sites.

While New England's cultural elite attempted to use history to escape the advancing effects of modernity, French Canadians similarly tried to maintain their traditions as they migrated to mill towns and industrial centers of northern New England in great numbers. The nationalist motto *Je me souviens* (I remember) memorializes their history. Rather than seeking assimilation into American culture, they remained in enclaves where they celebrated their cultural patrimony. Many French Canadians were concerned about *survivance,* the protection of the group's religion, language, and customs from American influences. On Saint-Jean-Baptiste Day, a traditional French Canadian religious and patriotic holiday that falls on June 24, Franco-Americans returned to their roots. The celebration usually consisted of a mass followed by a parade, picnic, and speeches. In Lewiston, Maine, for example, the occupants of one decorated float, members of the parish choir, sang traditional French airs as the procession wound through Little Canada.

The ethnic memory that French Canadians, one of New England's largest minority groups, sought to perpetuate foreshadowed the forceful, identity-based cultural politics of the late 20th century, celebrated today in the Lowell (Mass.) Folk Festival. These commemorations of heritage have served as expressions of collective memories that, as they have proliferated, have become increasingly more personalized, more local, more family oriented, and more democratic.

Stephen Carl Arch, *Authorizing the Past: The Rhetoric of History in 17th-Century New England* (1994); Emerson W. Baker, Richard D'Abate, Edwin Churchill, and Harald E. Prins, eds., *American Beginnings: Exploration, Culture, and Cartography in the Land of Norumbega* (1994); Gerard J. Brault, *The French-Canadian Heritage in New England* (1986); Federal Writers' Project, *Connecticut; A Guide to Its Roads, Lore, and People* (1938); Michael G. Kammen, *Mystic Chords of Memory: The Transformation of Tradition in American Culture* (1991); William H. Truettner and Roger B. Stein, eds., *Picturing Old New England: Image and Memory* (1999); W. Lloyd Warner, *The Living and the Dead: A Study of the Symbolic Life of Americans* (1959); Joseph S. Wood, *The New England Village* (1997).

Paige W. Roberts

New-England Primer Few pieces of material culture have contributed more to the New England worldview than the aptly named *New-England Primer,* an illustrated children's alphabet to which sermons, moral sketches, and other aids to right living were joined. From the 1680s to 1830, between 6 million and 8 million copies of *The New-England Primer* were printed and sold.

The origins of *The New-England Primer* have been difficult to establish. The New York Public Library houses the earliest surviving (though incomplete) copy, printed in 1727. In October 1683 the London publisher John Gaine went on record as having issued *The New-England Primer; or, Milk for Babes.* This work may have been compiled by the Englishman Benjamin Harris, who had published a children's reader, the *Protestant Tutor,* in 1679. The object of the *Protestant Tutor* was to teach young readers to "spel [*sic*] and read English" and to recognize "the errors and deceits of the papists." "A Catechism against Popery" and verses on the Protestant martyr John Rogers appear both in the *Protestant Tutor* and in most editions of *The New-England Primer.* Harris moved to Boston from London in 1686, and in 1690 placed an advertisement for a second edition of *The New-England Primer* in a Boston newspaper. No 17th-century edition of *The New-England Primer* has been found, however, and it is unknown whether the 1727 edition is a later version of Harris's text or whether it was patched together from existing alphabets, catechisms, and picture books. In any event, it is likely that at least portions of the 1727 *New-England Primer* were in wide circulation among the children of British colonists in New England before the end of the 17th century.

To grasp the enormous power of *The New-England Primer* it is necessary to recall that early generations of colonists taught children their ABC's so that they could eventually read the Bible, and that apart from sermons and aids to biblical literacy, adult reading matter was generally in short supply. This meant that the narrative resources of the colonists for making sense of their experiences were relatively limited, widely shared, and theologically fraught. *The New-England Primer* tied religious instruction to the alphabet ("In *A*dam's fall, / We sinned all") and from there to spelling and reading, so that children would absorb the anxious lessons of Puritan theology along with the basic information they required to participate in the social world. Children learned to read by learning to discern the presence and designs of God, represented to them, in part, as the constant threat of death and the concomitant requirement of spiritual vigilance. The child's prayer "Now I Lay Me Down to Sleep," which children on reflection must have found rather frightening ("If I should die before I wake . . ."), was first printed in *The New-England Primer.*

The New-England Primer's introduction of vivid language and graphic images to its readers was eventually its likely undoing. Pious textbooks occasionally did what one might now regard as the secret—because forbidden—work of fiction in the Calvinist republic. In the case of *The New-England Primer,* for example, generations of readers thrilled to the illustrations of the burning of John Rogers in front of his wife and 10 small children (whom children were invited patiently to count) at the hands of the Catholic Queen Mary ("Bloody Mary") Tudor. For these readers, Rogers was both a martyr for the Protestant cause and a pulp fiction hero. The pulp fiction quality of the *Primer* is evident not only in the fact that it was cheaply produced, massively circulated, and often read literally to pieces, but also in the rather lurid quality of its teachings. Even before they had mastered the alphabet, the *Primer*'s small readers had encountered attacking *D*ogs in pursuit of a thief, learned forthrightly of David's adultery with Bathsheba (U for *U*riah, her husband), and had their innocence reflected back to them through curtains of Gothic doom ("*T*ime cuts down all, / Both great and small"; "*Y*outh forward slips, / Death soonest nips").

Between 1800 and 1830 *The New-England Primer*'s circulation reached its height, but its audience's tastes had already been primed for more fantastic, increasingly secular fare, and by the 1850s editions of the *Primer* were being sought for their antiquarian interest. The *Primer* was often either viewed with nostalgia by adults or held up as a negative example of Puritan child-rearing practices seemingly based on fear and guilt.

Paul Leicester Ford, ed., *The New England Primer* (1962 [1897]); Charles F. Heartman, *The New-England Primer Issued Prior to 1830* (1934); Elisa New, "'Both Great and Small': Adult Proportion and Divine Scale in Edward Taylor's 'Preface' and *The New England Primer,*" *Early American Literature* 28 (1993); David H. Watters, "'I Spake as a Child': Authority, Metaphor, and *The New England Primer,*" *Early American Literature* 20 (1985–86).

Tracy Fessenden

New Hampshire

New Hampshire lies at the geographical center of New England. In many ways its history, institutions, and culture resemble those of its regional neighbors. The state's Native American inhabitants, in the precontact era, spoke Algonquian dialects, lived in bands, and were alternately nomadic and sedentary. The Europeans, who gradually began replacing native peoples in the early 1600s, were for the most part Protestant Christians from the British Isles primarily interested in establishing agricultural communities united by church, family, and the common commitment to individual land ownership. Many of New Hampshire's English pioneers migrated from southern New England colonies and brought with them such regional institutions as the town meeting and public taxation for ministerial salaries. During the 1770s citizens of the colony not only followed the lead of Massachusetts in rebelling against the mother country but even used the constitution of the Bay Colony as a model for their own.

Postrevolutionary developments also paralleled regional developments. New Hampshire participated fully in the 19th-century Industrial Revolution, utilizing New England's abundant water power, the entrepreneurial skills of the state's inhabitants, and the expansion of both national and international markets. New Hampshire organized a flexible pattern of public authority based on democratic principles and an educational system financed by both private and public sources. Non-English immigrants provided needed labor for industrial growth; their children helped fill the schools. Many of New Hampshire's rural towns, like those in surrounding states, lost population to the West and to America's fast-growing cities. City folks, in turn, vacationed with increasing frequency at the seashore and in the mountains, as they did

G–M from The New-England Primer Improved for the More Easy Attaining the True Reading of English *(1777)*

in Rhode Island, Connecticut, Massachusetts, Vermont, and Maine. In general, agriculture declined steadily after the 1840s, industry and recreation grew as economic activities, and New Hampshire shared the general fate of the region it centered well into the 20th century.

Similar observations could be made about recent history. New England as a whole made a successful transition from an industrial to a postindustrial economy; so did New Hampshire. The region featured clean manufacturing, educational and service-oriented occupations, easy access to recreational activity, technological experimentation, and speedy transportation. New Hampshire could take pride in its developments in all these areas. In short, the Granite State—a popular label for New Hampshire—has always been very much part of New England.

New Hampshire also has distinctive qualities. Like all states, it contains its own set of formal cultural institutions as well as clusters of less formal organizations reflecting its peculiar demographic mix. The MacDowell Colony in Peterborough is a mecca for musicians, artists, and writers. Manchester's Currier Art Gallery, the Hood Museum at Dartmouth College in Hanover, and the New Hampshire Historical Society in Concord all have valuable art collections on permanent display and a changing array of temporary exhibits. The historical society, in addition, features a large exhibit tracing the history of New Hampshire. The state's 11 four-year colleges, 16 private prep schools, and numerous public schools all sponsor artistic and theatrical projects. Many vacation centers have summer theaters. The former home of the 19th-century sculptor Augustus Saint-Gaudens in Cornish serves both as a National Historic Site and the venue for concerts and exhibitions. Nashua and Manchester have independently incorporated arts and science centers. Dozens of small towns have organized historical societies, many of which manage their own small museum.

Race and ethnicity shape cultural institutions in all societies. Few Native Americans in what is now New Hampshire survived the European invasion, and neither colony nor state has developed a large African American, Asian, or Hispanic population. The seacoast city of Portsmouth has nonetheless been home to a small African American community since colonial times, and the Merrimack River valley cities of Nashua and Manchester had large increases in Hispanic and Asian populations over the last decade of the 20th century. Still, racially based organizations have been relatively few and limited in size.

Ethnic institutions, by contrast, have thrived. Scots and the Scotch Irish began ar-

riving in large numbers as early as the 1720s, spread westward from their initial settlement in Londonderry, and carried the traditions of Presbyterianism with them. In the late 19th and early 20th centuries clusters of Irish, Greeks, Finns, Italians, Poles, and Jews settled in New Hampshire. Each group founded organizations to help preserve its ethnic traditions.

The two dominant ethnic groups were English and French Canadian. The former pioneered initial European settlement, reproduced at a rapid rate, gathered in Congregational, Unitarian, Baptist, and Episcopal churches, owned most of the large farms and industries in the state, and in general served as the model for the emerging image of the New England Yankee. French-speaking Canadians flooded into New Hampshire in the late 19th century. Many worked in the numerous textile mills along the Merrimack, Salmon Falls, and Connecticut Rivers and their tributaries. Others settled in the north country, where lumbering and the pulp and paper industry offered jobs. Franco-Americans brought with them their own cultural institutions, soon dominated an increasingly powerful Roman Catholic Church, and were influential in the creation of a Catholic-run private educational system. In communities such as Berlin, West Manchester, Allenstown, and Pembroke, French was spoken as much as English.

In recent years ethnicity has become less important in New Hampshire. The broad process of Americanization has weakened divisions among the state's various ethnic groups. As late as the mid-20th century, however, if one were asked to describe the typical Granite State resident, Franco-Yankee would not have been a bad response.

New Hampshire contains a richly varied landscape, elements of which resemble the dominant features in all the other regional states. The coastal plain (part of a larger entity including southern Maine, eastern Massachusetts, and most of Connecticut and Rhode Island) is stony, fertile, and laced with rivers, several of which join to form the Piscataqua estuary. The Connecticut River valley shares geologic and soil conditions with eastern Vermont. New Hampshire, like Maine, contains numerous large lakes, including Winnipesaukee, Sunapee, and Ossipee. The White Mountains, dominate the north-central section. North of the Whites lie hundreds of square miles of wilderness.

Varied landscape has shaped much of New Hampshire's cultural life, including, for example, its literature. The most famous literary shaper of New Hampshire's image is Robert Frost, whose early books of poetry portrayed the land and the lives of his neighbors at his

farm in Derry. Thomas Bailey Aldrich wrote about the Piscataqua's maritime world in *An Old Town by the Sea* (1893); LeGrand Cannon, in *Look to the Mountain* (1942), wrote about community building in the shadows of Mount Chocorua; Ernest Hebert, in a series of novels, described the gentrification of an area once dominated by farming. John Irving's New Hampshire novels gain much of their richness from the author's familiarity with the state's varied landscape. The same observation could be made of Maxine Kumin's poetry and Donald Hall's essays and poems.

Among the components of the varied landscape, one, the White Mountains, has dominated the manner in which outsiders have come to think of New Hampshire and its inhabitants. In the second quarter of the 19th century painters began flocking to the Whites and either set up shop in one of the growing number of grand hotels or became part of the well-established art colonies in Conway and Franconia. These artists—John Kensett, Thomas Cole, Jasper Cropsey, Benjamin Champney, Albert Bierstadt, and many others—exhibited and sold their works throughout United States, thus reinforcing the popular perception that New Hampshire's most exceptional feature was its mountainous landscape.

One trait New Hampshire seems to lack is a cultural stereotype. Everyone knows what Vermont farmers, Maine lobstermen and lumberjacks, and Boston Brahmins are supposed to look and act like. There are, however, no stereotypical New Hampshire people. The best that national pundits can come up with is "craggy individualists." The individualist part of that phrase applies as well to folks from Vermont and Maine, but the "craggy" part is uniquely New Hampshire. New Hampshire's most widely recognized visual icon was the geologic formation known as the Old Man of the Mountain, a revealing fusion of landscape and persona whose once natural crags were held together until 2003 by cables and pulleys in the Granite State's Franconia Notch.

Several individuals, craggy or otherwise, have been identified with the state in the national mind for their actions and ideas. The prominent 19th-century lawyer and Whig leader Daniel Webster was one, even after he had represented Massachusetts for years in the U.S. Senate. The writer and editor Sarah Josepha Hale, whose campaigning led to the establishment of Thanksgiving as a national holiday in 1863, was another, along with Mary Baker Eddy, who founded the Church of Christ, Scientist in the 19th century, and Christa McAuliffe, who would have been the first teacher in space had her life not been tragically cut short in the 1986 explosion of the space shuttle *Challenger*. David H. Souter, nominated to the Supreme Court by President George H. W. Bush, was expected to take a moderate to conservative stance on such issues as abortion; instead, he has had one of the most independent records on the Rehnquist court. William Loeb linked the state to a flinty brand of conservative Republican politics with his prominent daily newspaper, the *Manchester Union Leader*.

New Hampshire is New England's (and probably the nation's) most decentralized state. The decentralization has deep historical roots. New Hampshire's 100-plus incorporated towns functioned during the American Revolution with little interference from a rudimentary state government. Popular suspicion of centralized authority first produced, then preserved, a state constitution emphasizing the power of the state's current 234 towns and cities. For a complex set of reasons New Hampshire never adopted either a general sales or a general income tax, even though all the other states in New England have had one or both of these sources of revenue. Meager resources have meant meager expenditures: for example, legislators earn only a token salary of $100 a year for their services. Meanwhile, a powerful ethic of public-private cooperation in funding such institutions as orphanages, hospitals, and schools arose. By the 1960s, New Hampshire had developed a system in which the relation between state and local authority and assumptions about public financing set it apart from states elsewhere in New England. And New Hampshire's craggy individualists thrived on the distinctiveness. The legislature approved "Live Free or Die" as the automobile license plate logo, a clear expression of commitment to as little central authority as could be managed.

In recent years New Hampshire's pattern of decentralized governance has gained national visibility. A first-in-the-nation presidential primary (itself a source of pride) has attracted hundreds of out-of-state reporters, who frequently describe for their readers this strange land of town meetings, unpaid legislators, no broad-based sales or income tax, and happy but unpredictable voters. Most observers label the mix conservative and package the Granite State not with its regional and more liberal neighbors but with the likes of Montana and Alaska. Reportage in the last few years, however, has begun to shift. The *New York Times* ran a column by David E. Rosenbaum on February 18, 1996, headlined "Now New Hampshire Finds Itself in Vanguard," which argued that in a nation and world increasingly disillusioned by central governmental authority,

New Hampshire had become a model for the future.

Jeremy Belknap, *History of New Hampshire*, vol. 3: *A Geographical Description of the State* (1973 [1792]); Charles Brereton, ed., *New Hampshire Notables: Presenting Biographical Sketches of Men and Women Who Have Helped Shape the Character of the Granite State* (1986); Paul Eric Bruns, *New Hampshire Everlasting and Unfallen: An Illustrated History* (1969); Edwin A. Charlton, comp., *New Hampshire as It Is* (1997 [1885]); Federal Writers' Project, *New Hampshire: A Guide to the Granite State* (1938); Wallace Nutting, *New Hampshire Beautiful* (1923); Peter E. Randall, *New Hampshire, a Living Landscape: Panoramic Photographs* (1996); F. B. Sanborn, *New Hampshire: An Epitome of Popular Government* (1973 [1904]).

Jere Daniell

Nobel Laureates of New England (Table, next page)

Norton, Charles Eliot (1827–1908)

Writer, editor, critic. The influential Harvard University professor Charles Eliot Norton was born in Cambridge, Mass., the only son of Andrews Norton, a professor at Harvard Divinity School, and his wife, Catharine Eliot. After graduating from Harvard in 1846, Norton worked in a Boston importing firm and traveled, in 1849, as supercargo on a clipper ship to India. He then toured Egypt and Europe, acquiring such influential friends as George William Curtis and Robert Browning. Returning to Boston in 1851, Norton operated his own East Indies import firm until 1855, when he committed himself to a life of letters. Having assisted Francis Parkman in preparing *The Oregon Trail* for publication in 1846, Norton then edited his father's papers and poems. He escorted his mother and two sisters to Rome and England in 1855, forming close friendships with John Ruskin, William Makepeace Thackeray, and the Pre-Raphaelites in London. From these travels came a translation of *The New Life of Dante Alighieri* (1859) and *Notes on Travel and Study on Italy* (1860).

Back in Cambridge, Norton was coaxed from his lamplit study on Shady Hill by his close friend the poet James Russell Lowell to contribute to the *Atlantic Monthly* in 1857. An opponent of slavery, Norton led the Loyal Publication Society for three years, publishing material in support of President Lincoln and the Civil War. Norton married Susan Ridley Sedgwick in 1862, and they had three sons and three daughters before her death in 1872. In 1864–68, coeditors Norton and Lowell revived the senescent *North American Review*, a quarterly published by conservative Boston Brahmins of their own class. Like Emerson, Longfellow, Lowell, and Oliver Wendell Holmes, Norton was an aristocrat who could not ap-

preciate literature or art that had not been created in an atmosphere of refined leisure. Populist and progressive critics of the new economic and social order—writers like Henry George, Edward Bellamy, Hamlin Garland, and William Dean Howells—were alien to him. Despite his love of Italy, his lifelong anti-Catholicism limited his political life and aesthetic judgments.

One mark of Norton's status as a literary lion was that E. L. Godkin asked his help in founding the journal *The Nation* in 1865. When Charles Dickens came to Boston in 1867, Norton hosted a memorable dinner for the author at his estate. Like many antebellum Bostonians, however, Norton feared that foreign travel would corrupt his American virtue and hoped to return home undamaged by European Catholicism, lax morals, and indifference to reform and progress. But Europe drew him often, and Ruskin taught him to admire Gothic art and to despise the High Renaissance. Norton became the first professor of art history in the United States in 1873 and was a popular teacher who interpreted European culture to generations of Harvard students from 1873 to 1897. His 1878 lecture series inspired Isabella Stewart Gardner to create her art museum on Boston's Fenway.

As captain of the cultural community in Boston, Norton taught his students and friends his belief in the moral power of art and the social value of good taste. He passed these ideas on to the new Museum of Fine Arts, the Society for the Preservation of New England Antiquities (now Historic New England), the Society of Arts and Crafts in Boston, and eminent leaders in the American Arts and Crafts movement (1890–1930) and the Colonial Revival movement, leaders like Theodore Roosevelt, Bernard Berenson, and Wallace Nutting. Norton was a talented reactionary and the charming center of a wide circle of influential friends on both sides of the Atlantic.

Norton edited important works and correspondence by William Blake, Anne Bradstreet, Thomas Carlyle, George William Curtis, John Donne, and Ralph Waldo Emerson and wrote a prose translation of Dante's *Divine Comedy* (1891–92). He also recognized the early work of Henry James, Walt Whitman, and Rudyard Kipling. His most significant books include *Historical Studies of Church Building in the Middle Ages* (1880) and *History of Ancient Art* (1891). A freethinker in religion and a Mugwump Republican in politics, Norton was at times too controversial for staid Boston, but he received honorary degrees from Cambridge, Oxford, Yale, Columbia, and Harvard. He served as vice president of the New England Anti-Imperialist League

Nobel Laureates of New England

	Year Awarded	Name	Awarded For	Affiliation or Residence
Chemistry	1914	Theodore W. Richards	The determination of many atomic weights	Harvard University Cambridge, Mass.
	1965	Robert W. Woodward	Contributions to the art of organic synthesis	Harvard University Cambridge, Mass.
	1968	Lars Onsager	Work in the science of thermodynamics	Yale University New Haven, Conn.
	1976	William Nunn Lipscomb, Jr.	Work on the stereochemistry of enzyme-catalyzed reactions and organic molecules	Harvard University Cambridge, Mass.
	1980	Walter Gilbert	Jointly with Paul Berg and Frederick Sanger for biochemical studies of nucleic acids	Biological Laboratories Cambridge, Mass.
	1986	Dudley R. Herschbach	Jointly with Yuan Tseh Lee and John C. Polanyi for research on chemical reaction dynamics	Harvard University Cambridge, Mass.
	1989	Sidney Altman	Jointly with Thomas R. Cech for the discovery that ribonucleic acid (RNA) can act as an enzyme to facilitate chemical reactions	Yale University New Haven, Conn.
	1990	Elias James Corey	The synthesis of chemical compounds based on natural substances	Harvard University Cambridge, Mass.
	2001	Wolfgang Ketterle	Jointly with Eric A. Cornell and Carl E. Wieman for the achievement of Bose-Einstein condensation in dilute gases of alkali atoms and for early fundamental studies of the properties of the condensates	Massachusetts Institute of Technology Cambridge, Mass.
Economic Sciences	1970	Paul A. Samuelson	Developments in static and dynamic economic theory and contributions to raising the level of analysis in economic science	Massachusetts Institute of Technology Cambridge, Mass.
	1971	Simon Kuznets	The development of the gross national product as a measure of economic output	Harvard University Cambridge, Mass.
	1972	Kenneth J. Arrow	Jointly with John R. Hicks for contributions to general economic equilibrium theory and welfare theory	Harvard University Cambridge, Mass.
	1973	Wassily Leontief	The development of the input-output method of economic analysis	Harvard University Cambridge, Mass.
	1975	Tjalling C. Koopmans	Jointly with Leonid V. Kantorovich for contributions to the theory of optimum allocation of resources	Yale University New Haven, Conn.
	1981	James Tobin	Analysis of financial markets and their behaviors	Yale University New Haven, Conn.
	1985	Franco Modigliani	Theories of savings and of financial markets	Massachusetts Institute of Technology Cambridge, Mass.
	1987	Robert M. Solow	Contributions to the theory of economic growth	Massachusetts Institute of Technology Cambridge, Mass.

(continued)

Nobel Laureates of New England (*continued*)

	Year Awarded	Name	Awarded For	Affiliation or Residence
	1997	Robert C. Merton	Jointly with Myron S. Scholes for a new method to determine the value of derivatives	Harvard University Cambridge, Mass.
Literature	1936	Eugene O'Neill	"The power, honesty and deep-felt emotions of his dramatic works, which embody an original concept of tragedy"	New London, Conn.
	1992	Derek Walcott	"A poetic oeuvre of great luminosity, sustained by a historical vision, the outcome of a multicultural commitment"	Boston University Boston
Medicine and Physiology	1934	George Richards Minot William Parry Murphy	Jointly with George Hoyt Whipple for discoveries concerning liver therapy for anemias	Harvard University Cambridge, Mass.
	1953	Fritz Albert Lipmann	Discovering coenzyme A and its importance for intermediary metabolism	Harvard University Cambridge, Mass. Massachusetts General Hospital Boston
	1954	John Franklin Enders	Jointly with Frederick Chapman Robbins for the discovery of the ability of poliomyelitis viruses to grow in cultures of various types of tissues	Harvard Medical School Boston
		Thomas Huckle Weller		Children's Medical Center Boston
	1961	Georg von Bekesy	Discoveries concerning the physical mechanisms of stimulation within the cochlea	Harvard University Cambridge, Mass.
	1962	James Dewey Watson	Jointly with Francis Harry Compton Crick and Maurice Hugh Frederick Wilkins for the discovery of the molecular structure of nucleic acids and its significance for the transfer of information in living material	Harvard University Cambridge, Mass.
	1964	Konrad Bloch	Jointly with Feodor Lynen for discoveries concerning the mechanism and regulation of cholesterol and fatty acid metabolism	Harvard University Cambridge, Mass.
	1967	George Wald	Jointly with Ragnar Granit and Halden Keffer Hartline for discoveries concerning the primary physiological and chemical visual processes in the eye	Harvard University Cambridge, Mass.
	1969	Salvador E. Luria	Jointly with Max Delbruck and Alfred D. Hershey for discoveries in the replication mechanism and the genetic structure of viruses	Massachusetts Institute of Technology Cambridge, Mass.
	1974	George Emil Palade	Jointly with Albert Claude and Christian René de Duve for discoveries concerning the structural and functional organization of the cell	Yale University New Haven, Conn.
	1975	David Baltimore	Jointly with Howard Martin Temin and Renato Dulbecco for discoveries concerning the interaction between tumor viruses and the genetic material of the cell	Massachusetts Institute of Technology Cambridge, Mass.

(*continued*)

Nobel Laureates of New England (*continued*)

Year Awarded	Name	Awarded For	Affiliation or Residence
1979	Allan M. Cormack	Jointly with Geoffrey N. Hounsfield for the development of computer-assisted topography	Tufts University Medford, Mass.
1980	Baruj Benacerraf	Jointly with Jean Dausset for discoveries concerning genetically determined structures on the cell surface that regulate immunological reactions	Harvard University Cambridge, Mass.
	George D. Snell		Jackson Laboratory Bar Harbor, Maine
1981	David H. Hubel	Jointly with Roger W. Sperry and Tosten Wiesel for discoveries concerning information processing in the visual system.	Harvard University Cambridge, Mass.
2002	H. Robert Horvitz	Jointly with Sydney Brenner and John E. Sulston for discoveries concerning genetic regulation of organ development and programmed cell death	Massachusetts Institute of Technology Cambridge, Mass.
Peace 1946	Emily G. Balch	Work with the Women's International League for Peace and Freedom	Boston
1973	Henry A. Kissinger	Negotiation of the Vietnam cease-fire agreement	Harvard University Cambridge, Mass.
1986	Elie Wiesel	Dedication to peace, atonement, and human dignity	Boston University Boston
1997	Jody Williams	Jointly with the International Campaign to Ban Landmines for work in the banning and clearing of antipersonnel mines	Putney, Vt.
Physics 1946	Percy W. Bridgman	Discoveries in high-pressure physics	Harvard University Cambridge, Mass.
1952	Edward M. Purcell	Jointly with Felix Bloch for methods of measuring magnetic fields of atomic nuclei	Harvard University Cambridge, Mass.
1964	Charles H. Townes	Jointly with Nikolai G. Basov and Aleksandr M. Prokhorov for research on laser and maser beams	Massachusetts Institute of Technology Cambridge, Mass.
1965	Julian S. Schwinger	Jointly with Richard P. Feynman and Sin-Itiro Tomonaga for work on defining basic theories of quantum electrodynamics	Harvard University Cambridge, Mass.
1972	Leon N. Cooper	Jointly with John Bardeen and John R. Schrieffer for the development of the theory of superconductivity	Brown University Providence
1976	Samuel Chao Chung Ting	Jointly with Burton Richter for the discovery of the subatomic J particle	Massachusetts Institute of Technology Cambridge, Mass.
1977	John H. Van Vleck	Jointly with Philip W. Anderson and Sir Nevill F. Mott for contributions to understanding the behavior of electrons in magnetic, noncrystalline solids and for discovering the use of economical materials, such as amorphous silicon, in the development of computers	Harvard University Cambridge, Mass.

(*continued*)

Year Awarded	Name	Awarded For	Affiliation or Residence
1979	Sheldon L. Glashow Steven Weinberg	Jointly with Abdus Salam for contributions to the theory of unified weak and electromagnetic interaction between elementary particles	Harvard University Cambridge, Mass.
1981	Nicolaas Bloembergen	Jointly with Arthur L. Shawlow and Kai M. Siegbahn for discoveries in electron spectroscopy for chemical analysis and for work in the field of laser spectroscopy	Harvard University Cambridge, Mass.
1989	Norman F. Ramsey	Jointly with Hans G. Dehmelt and Wolfgang Paul for the development of methods to isolate atoms and subatomic particles for study and for the development of the atomic clock.	Harvard University Cambridge, Mass.
1990	Jerome I. Friedman Henry W. Kendall	Jointly with Richard E. Taylor for the discovery of atomic quarks	Massachusetts Institute of Technology Cambridge, Mass.
1994	Clifford G. Shull	Jointly with Bertram N. Brockhouse for the development of neutron-scattering techniques	Massachusetts Institute of Technology Cambridge, Mass.

Source: Nobel e-museum, the official Web site of the Nobel Foundation: http://www.nobel.se; The Nobel Prize Internet Archive: http://www.nobelprizes.com/nobel/nobel.html; "Nobel Laureates in the Sciences: A Guide to Reference Sources," Louisiana State University Libraries: http://www.lib.lsu.edu/sci/chem/guides/srs118

(1898–1904) and of the reorganized Anti-Imperialist League (1904–8).

At the time of his death at his Cambridge birthplace, Shady Hill, on October 21, 1908, Norton had exerted a profound influence on American literature, art, and architecture. As an apostle of Old World culture, he was a dominant figure in the waning Boston-Cambridge-Concord intellectual circles. The Charles Eliot Norton Papers are held at Harvard University's Houghton Library and at the University of Virginia Archives.

Martin B. Duberman, *James Russell Lowell* (1966); Sara Norton and M. A. DeWolfe Howe, eds., *Letters of Charles Eliot Norton* (1913); Kermit Vanderbilt, *Charles Eliot Norton: Apostle of Culture in a Democracy* (1959).

Peter C. Holloran

Nutting, Wallace (1861–1941) Minister, photographer, antiquarian. Wallace Nutting, a Harvard-educated Congregational minister turned photographer, antiquarian, and entrepreneur, served as a tireless promoter of historic New England in the first half of the 20th century. As the foremost popular authority on early American life, Nutting employed the growing culture of consumption to sell an idealized view of New England's past to the nation in a variety of interrelated media. From hand-colored photographs to books and reproduction colonial furniture, Nutting provided images, texts, and objects that reinforced middle-class desires for a soothing, golden age past in an era of uncertainty and change.

Nutting presented himself as a Yankee archetype—intelligent, taciturn, and always correct. Born in the sleepy village of Rockbottom, Mass., he grew to maturity in Industry, Maine, before attending Exeter, Harvard, and the Hartford and Union Theological Seminaries. After a decade of service to the Congregational Church in cities throughout the United States, Nutting returned east to Providence.

The minister, suffering from neurasthenia, retired from the pulpit in 1904 and looked to his hobby of photography for relaxation. An avid shutterbug since the late 1890s, Nutting began to copyright his photographs and sell them to magazines and print shops at the turn of the century. Seeking the fresh air of the New England countryside, Nutting and his wife, Mariet Griswold Nutting, moved to an old farm in Southbury, Conn., in 1906. After a period of living as genteel farmers, they established a photography studio in their barn and perfected a method of hand-tinting platinum prints that employed young women from the surrounding countryside as colorists. Nutting traveled incessantly throughout the region to capture views and issued progressively larger catalogs of his photographs in 1906, 1912, and 1915. By 1915 approximately 20 percent of his line was composed of "colonials," or images of young women in traditional dress posed in historic interiors.

Nutting's photographs sold hand over fist and spawned other historically themed enterprises under his banner. Concerned that his colonials lacked authenticity, Nutting purchased and restored five historic houses in three New England states and opened the Wallace Nutting Chain of Colonial Picture

The Wallace Nutting Collection of Early American Furniture, Morgan Building, ca. 1928

Houses to serve as settings for his images as well as museums. Nutting acquired over a thousand period objects to furnish these houses and soon moved to maximize his investment by organizing a reproduction furniture business based upon these Early American prototypes. Consumers could buy Nutting's photographs, visit his museums, and purchase his furniture. In 1925 Nutting sold his furniture collection to J. P. Morgan, Jr., who gave it to the Wadsworth Atheneum in Hartford, thus endowing the minister's reputation with institutional gravitas.

Nutting turned to publishing in the 1920s with great reward. He wrote landmark volumes on American decorative arts, including *Furniture of the Pilgrim Century* (1921) and *The Furniture Treasury* (1928–33), as well as a series of highly popular travelogues that recycled his images of idyllic streams, timeless villages, and genteel ancestors. Individual volumes, such as *Vermont Beautiful* (1922), *Connecticut Beautiful* (1923), *Massachusetts Beautiful* (1923), *New Hampshire Beautiful* (1923), and *Maine Beautiful* (1924), extolled the region's historic landscape and collectively contributed to the creation of New England as an organizing myth for modern America.

Joyce P. Berendsen, "Wallace Nutting, an American Tastemaker: The Pictures and Beyond," *Winterthur Portfolio* 18, nos. 2–3 (1983); Thomas Andrew Denenberg, *Wallace Nutting and the Invention of Old America* (2003); William L. Dulaney, "Wallace Nutting: Collector and Entrepreneur," *Winterthur Portfolio* 13

(1979); Beverly Seaton, "Beautiful Thoughts: The Wallace Nutting Platinum Prints," *History of Photography* 6, no. 3 (July 1982); Marianne Berger Woods, "Viewing Colonial America through the Lens of Wallace Nutting," *American Art* 8 (1994).

Thomas Andrew Denenberg

Old Farmer's Almanac When the first edition of the *Farmer's Almanack,* as it was then titled, appeared in Boston bookstores and in peddlers' wagons around New England during October 1792, George Washington was still the president of the United States. "Fitted to the town of Boston," it proclaimed, "but will serve for any of the adjoining states."

Its founder was Robert Bailey Thomas (1766–1846), a bookseller and schoolteacher who loved astronomy. He lived on a farm that, owing to boundary changes, was at one time or another located in no fewer than four Massachusetts towns: Shrewsbury, Lancaster, Sterling, and West Boylston. The foundations of the Thomas homestead now lie beneath the waters of the Wachusett Reservoir, while Thomas himself lies in the Sterling cemetery next to his wife, Hannah Berman Thomas (1774–1855).

Although *The Old Farmer's Almanac,* as it was called starting in 1848, is today the oldest continuously published periodical in North America, it had hundreds of competitors during the first half century of its existence. The majority of these early American almanacs, known collectively as "farmer's almanacs," not

only were published in New England (Benjamin Franklin's *Poor Richard's Almanack,* published in Philadelphia from 1733 to 1756, was the most famous exception), but also seemed to both advocate and celebrate those New England attributes that have come to be associated with the region's culture: thrift, independence (particularly financial), a certain contrariness, hard work, respect for education, a "no frills" approach to life, and the ability to make do contentedly with very little. Again and again, particularly in the famous "Farmer's Calendar" section each year, Thomas or one of his contributors gently, subtly—sometimes humorously—preached these New England values to a rapidly growing readership.

His first edition was 48 pages long; it sold for sixpence (about nine cents) per copy or 40 shillings a gross; and its initial circulation of 3,000 copies tripled in just one year. The editorial fare then, as now, included astronomical information for each day of the year, planting tables, history, recipes, country advice, odd facts, and, from the start, weather forecasts. "Cold and frosty . . . looks like snow" was the very first prediction—for January 1–9, 1793.

Why Thomas's almanac thrived while so many other similar New England almanacs fell by the wayside is not clear. The demise of the competition was perhaps accelerated when a rumor spread around New England in 1815 that the *Farmer's Almanack* would predict snow for July and August 1816. And, indeed, because of a printer's error, the word *snow* apparently did appear throughout those summer

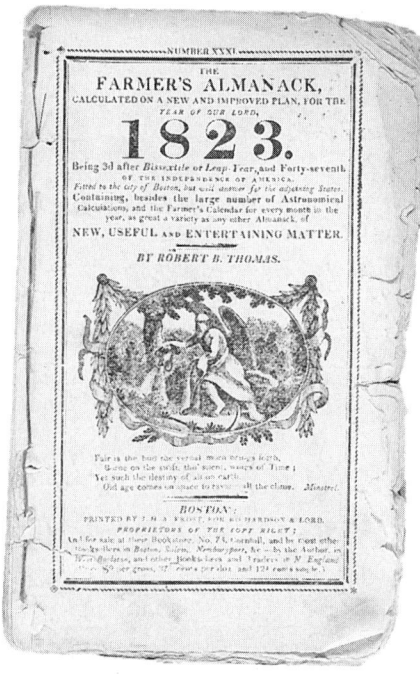

The Farmer's Almanack *(1823)*

forecasts. After discovering the error, Thomas reportedly destroyed the "snow" copies and had the entire 1816 edition reprinted. Nonetheless, the rumor persisted. Then, owing to dust circling the globe from a volcanic eruption in what is now Indonesia, the summer of 1816 turned out to be one of the coldest in recorded history—it snowed several times. Thomas became a forecasting genius.

Even after this stroke of good fortune, however, Thomas rarely mentioned his weather forecasts when addressing readers on the "To Patrons" page of each edition. His goals were more conservative and modest. "We strive to be useful," he said simply in 1829, "but with a pleasant degree of humor." From his extant notes and letters, however, we know that his weather forecasting "secret" lay in the observation of certain solar cycles, including those of sunspots, that seemed to closely correlate with weather patterns and cycles on earth.

After Thomas's death in 1846, a succession of nine editors, all natives of Massachusetts, guided the almanac through the Civil War years, into the 20th century, and up through the 1930s. The almanac's modern era began in 1939, when Robb Sagendorph, who had founded *Yankee* magazine four years earlier, purchased *The Old Farmer's Almanac* for his company, Yankee Publishing Incorporated, then—and now—located in Dublin, N.H. During the 1950s and 1960s, Sagendorph broadened the weather forecasts as well as newsstand distribution from strictly New England and the Northeast to all the United States and Canada.

Today, the *Almanac* has some 13 million readers annually, of whom approximately 18 percent reside in the Northeast, 25 percent in the Midwest, 42 percent in the South, and 15 percent in the West. A recent survey revealed that a whopping 76.5 percent own gardens versus only 9 percent who are farmers. (Then again, only 4 percent of the U.S. population farms for a living.) In 2000, roughly 4.3 million *Old Farmer's Almanac* readers owned computers and could visit the almanac's Web site, which is updated daily.

Contemporary readers remain responsive to the *Almanac's* old-fashioned advertisements; they are typical of late-19th-century advertisements in New England publications, including almanacs. In addition to the more standard fare of gardening and household products, these have, in recent years, featured glass eyes, false teeth, chickens that lay colored eggs, and some sort of pick-me-up known as Rooster Pills.

To survive in modern times, however, *The Old Farmer's Almanac* must be entirely brand-new each year. In fact, if Thomas were to rise from his grave to peruse the 256 pages (usu-ally) of the 21st-century editions, he would recognize as his own only the title page and the 24 calendar pages. These present, along with a hodgepodge of traditional data relevant to the year, the astronomical structure of each of the forthcoming 12 months. In doing so, incidentally, they make *The Old Farmer's Almanac* a true almanac, loosely defined in the ancient Arabic language as "a calendar of the heavens." But they serve another purpose, too. Through their traditional format and old astronomical symbols, they serve to remind readers of the fact that, with the advent of the 21st century, *The Old Farmer's Almanac* can be said to have participated in no fewer than four centuries of American history—that is, four centuries of American history as observed from the distinct perspective of an enduring New England spirit that has truly nurtured this beloved publication from George Washington's time to the present day.

Marion Barber Stowell, *Early American Almanacs: The Colonial Weekday Bible* (1976).

Judson D. Hale

Old Home Day Old Home Day is a day set aside each summer by many New England communities for the celebration of hometown history, culture, and family. It is rooted in hometown reunions sponsored by New Hampshire communities from as early as the 1850s. Since 1899, Old Home Day has been both a progenitor of regional culture and an event that has fixed specific images of rural New England in the American mind.

The current tradition of Old Home Day began in 1899, at a time when rural New England was suffering from severe depopulation, farm abandonment, and other signs of economic transition. Recognizing the need to repopulate and to inject capital into the countryside, New Hampshire governor Frank West Rollins proposed that the state set aside a week, called Old Home Week, during which every New Hampshire community would invite natives who had moved west or to cities to visit the "old home town." At the state level, Rollins proposed two days of parades, musical programs, speeches, and other events in Concord. Following the celebrations in the state capital, individual communities—with the aid of the state Board of Agriculture—would sponsor family and school reunions, picnics, and other entertainment to celebrate the return of their native sons and daughters. On one day chosen as the local Old Home Day the bulk of a community's ceremonies would be held. Rollins believed that this plan would stimulate visitors' interest in rural communities, promote rural tourism, and bring in money for community needs.

Initially, Rollins's proposal proved to be successful as more than 70 towns participated in Old Home Week. Other New England states copied it, most notably Maine, Vermont, and Massachusetts, each one choosing a different week in the summer so as not to overlap with other Old Home Weeks. In nearly all instances, Old Home Week observances equated the concept of New England with those of family, patriotism, history and tradition, nature, and agriculture. The movement shared with the Colonial Revival a concern that New England's white Anglo-Saxon Protestant heritage might be overwhelmed by immigrants of Catholic, south European, and African heritage. Moreover, Governor Rollins's call for people to return to their native communities suggests the tension that results in a rural society when its youth have moved away. These concepts were repeated in Old Home Week invitations, literature, speeches, and especially in song and poetry, most notably in Robert Frost's "The Generations of Men" (1914), Edith Wharton's *Summer* (1917), and Donald Hall's *Old Home Day* (1996). In fact, nearly all celebrations included the reading of poetry and the singing of songs written specifically for the occasion by local residents.

Within 30 years Old Home Week's popularity had subsided, in part because many communities could not afford to hold the celebration every year, but also because the week no longer was deemed necessary for attracting tourists. Nevertheless, the tradition of Old Home Day has continued in many parts of New England, especially in New Hampshire, where some communities still hold Old Home Weekends in August. In recent years, some communities, such as Newmarket, N.H., have generated new traditions to build community across ethnic lines. Parades, community suppers, sporting events, musical performances, craft demonstrations, and family reunions blend the old and the new. The tradition continues to promote the idea of New England as a historical, tradition-laden region that values community.

Dona Brown, *Inventing New England: Regional Tourism in the 19th Century* (1995); Thomas Curren, *Old Home Day in New Hampshire, 1899–1998: Celebrating the Living Heritage of New Hampshire's Communities* (1998); New Hampshire Old Home Week Association, *Let's All Sing* (1947); "Old Home Week: New Hampshire's Great Midsummer Festival," *New Hampshire: The Granite State Monthly* 61 (June 1929).

Scott Roper

Old Man of the Mountain Before he tumbled down the mountainside on or about May 3, 2003, the Old Man of the Mountain embodied a unique combination of natural phenomenon, humanmade artifact, and cultural icon. Overlooking Franconia Notch in

New Hampshire's White Mountain National Forest, the Old Man was composed of five granite ledges on the northeast side of Cannon Mountain and measured 40 feet 5 inches in height. He could be seen in profile about 1,200 feet above the floor of the Notch only from a specific vantage along the northern shore of Profile Lake.

The first recorded sighting of the Old Man occurred in 1805 by members of a road crew working in Franconia Notch. The actual first sighting by a European remains disputed, although the purported discoverers, Luke Brooks and Francis Whitcomb of Franconia, were noted as remarking upon the profile's likeness to the current president, Thomas Jefferson.

The profile was not immediately popular. With the exception of a few admirers (among them the New Hampshire abolitionist Nathaniel Peabody Rogers, who some believe coined the profile's name, Old Man of the Mountain), it was deemed largely unremarkable by travel writers of the early 19th century. By midcentury, the Old Man began to be considered both a tourist destination and a symbol of New Hampshire itself. William Oakes's *Scenery of the White Mountains* (1848) identifies the "Profile Rock" as "perhaps the greatest object of popular curiosity and admiration in the vicinity of the White Mountains." The most renowned addition to Old Man literature was Nathaniel Hawthorne's publication of "The Great Stone Face" in 1850.

In the 1850s local residents noticed that the large stone that constitutes the Old Man's forehead was slipping forward and was in danger of eventually falling into the Notch below. It was not until 1915, however, that Edward H. Geddes, a quarry superintendent in Quincy, Mass., closely inspected the slipping stone and contrived a way to affix it more permanently to the main rock face. Over eight days in the fall of 1916, Geddes installed three giant turnbuckles to prevent, only temporarily as it turned out, further slippage.

The Old Man's celebrity continued to grow as the profile was adopted as New Hampshire's state emblem in 1945 to accompany the state's motto, "Live Free or Die," and has since appeared on public documents, buildings, and highway signs throughout the state. Thirty years after its initial facelift, officials decided the Old Man was in dire need of additional reinforcement, and in 1957 the state allocated $25,000 for repairs. In the face of growing concern about the Old Man's preservation, substantial work and money went into supporting the Old Man on his perch. But the improvements turned out to be temporary.

The profile became a widely appropriated symbol, the meaning of which shifted with the times. When the land around the profile

was for sale in 1923, and thus vulnerable to potential exploitation, the Society for the Protection of New Hampshire Forests used the image in its campaign to buy 6,000 acres in Franconia Notch in order to protect the site as an environmental treasure. President Eisenhower invoked the Old Man as a symbol of democracy during the Cold War. The image is known to millions of tourists through state publications and from the tokens used on New Hampshire's toll roads.

Even after the Old Man's demise, which evoked shock and mourning in New Hampshire and across New England, the profile remains as much a symbol of natural wonder as of human ingenuity and regional ideology. Its place in New Hampshire culture was perhaps best expressed by Daniel Webster, who, during a visit to the White Mountains in 1831, reportedly offered the following accolade: "Men hang out their signs indicative of their respective trades. Shoemakers hang out a gigantic shoe, jewelers, a monster watch, even the dentist hangs out a gold tooth; but up in the Franconia Mountains, God Almighty has hung out a sign to show that in New England, He makes men."

Dona Brown, *Inventing New England: Regional Tourism in the 19th Century* (1995); Frances Ann Johnson Hancock, *Saving the Great Stone Face: The Chronicle of the Old Man of the Mountain* (1984); John T. B. Mudge, ed., *The Old Man's Reader: History and Legends of Franconia Notch* (1995).

Pavel Cenkl

Patriot's Day Patriot's Day, an official Massachusetts state holiday since 1894, marks the anniversary of the April 19, 1775, Revolutionary War battles of Lexington and Concord. From 1776 to the present day, April 19 has been observed as a day of prayer and fasting accompanied by civic celebration throughout Massachusetts. Now celebrated officially on the Monday closest to April 19, Patriot's Day celebrations include battle reenactments, public ceremonies and picnics, and the running of the annual Boston Marathon. A commemoration of the Revolutionary War's New England origins, Patriot's Day celebrates regional pride and national patriotism.

On April 19, 1775, British forces led by Lieutenant Colonel Francis Smith attacked militia forces mustered in Lexington, battled a larger militia group in Concord, and were chased under fire back to their Boston headquarters. Forty-nine American minutemen were killed in the fighting, but the British suffered heavier casualties and a blow to their reputation by losing one of the first battles of the Revolutionary War.

New Englanders first marked the battle anniversary in Lexington on April 19, 1776. The

"Paul Revere" meets Mayor James M. Curley, Boston, Patriot's Day, 1932

local Congregational minister Jonas Clarke delivered the first of many sermons on what became an annual day of fasting to commemorate the battle. The largest celebration of April 19 before the official 1894 Patriot's Day designation came in 1825, when Lexington and Concord vied with one another to produce elaborate public celebrations.

By the late 19th century, the celebrations of April 19 had become increasingly secularized, even as they retained their patriotic overtones. In its official 1894 proclamation, the Massachusetts legislature dubbed April 19 "a day rich with historical and significant events which are precious in the eyes of patriots." The first celebration of the official state holiday included parades, civic ceremonies, orations, battle reenactments, picnics, fireworks, church services, foot races, and a re-creation of Paul Revere's ride to warn the citizens of Massachusetts of the British troop movements, all of which were to remain features of Patriot's Day celebrations 100 years later.

During the mid- to late 20th century, Patriot's Day continued as a holiday celebrating the local, state, and regional pride of Massachusetts residents and as a day of festivity and fun. Modern Patriot's Day celebrations include well-attended battle reenactments in all towns that contributed minutemen to the fight, from Waltham and Acton to Lexington and Concord. The Boston Marathon, a major stop on the international marathon circuit, enhances the publicity and celebratory spirit of the day.

Patriot's Day has also become a day to celebrate the heroes of subsequent wars and, in the 1990s, a sacred day for right-wing militia groups. In 1975 the Bicentennial celebration featured an appearance by President Gerald Ford, who was met at the Old North Bridge by antiwar protesters and advocates of a People's Bicentennial. Still, for more than 200 years and in remarkably consistent fashion, the celebration of Patriot's Day has enhanced the feeling among many Massachusetts residents that they deserve a special place in the history of the Revolutionary War and in the annals of patriotism.

Todd Balf, "It's the Best Day of the Year," *Yankee* 57 (1993); Edward Tabor Linenthal, *Sacred Ground: Americans and Their Battlefields* (1993); Robert Sullivan, "Early on an April Morning," *Yankee* 60 (1996); George J. Varney, *The Story of Patriot's Day* (1895).

Sarah J. Purcell

Peyton Place Through a series of popular novels, films, and television programs, the fictional small town of Peyton Place, N.H., has become synonymous with scandals, secrets, and frank sexuality hidden beneath a picturesque New England exterior. The phenomenon began in 1956 when Grace Metalious's first novel, *Peyton Place*, became an immediate best-seller and was quickly followed by a successful motion picture in 1957. The novel sold 60,000 copies in its first 10 days; over the years it has sold 12 million copies. Although Metalious wrote a less-acclaimed sequel, *Return to Peyton Place* (1959), which was adapted for the screen in 1961, her opus received its biggest boost when the first primetime television soap opera, *Peyton Place*, premiered on September 15, 1964, and continued for 514 episodes, until June 2, 1969.

Born on September 8, 1924, to French Canadian parents in Manchester, N.H., Grace de Repentigny graduated from Central High School, married George Metalious in 1943, gave birth to three children, divorced in 1958, and died from cirrhosis of the liver on February 24, 1964. But having dreamed since childhood of becoming a writer, she used her experience of living in several New Hampshire towns (including Durham, Belmont, and Gilmanton) to create a literary sensation.

As described by Metalious, the landscape of Peyton Place is marked by tall church spires, tree-shaded streets, white Cape Cod houses, red-brick textile mills along the Connecticut River, and old-growth forests. But this idyllic image belies the melodramatic misfortunes of many of the town's 3,675 inhabitants. Selena Cross kills her drunken stepfather when he tries to assault her and is acquitted when the town's physician reveals that several years earlier he illegally aborted a pregnancy resulting from her being raped by her stepfather. The indiscretions of Rodney Harrington, the licentious son of the town's mill owner, are reg-

ularly repaired by his father's money, until he fatally collides with a truck while ogling a bare-breasted woman in the car seat next to him. Constance MacKenzie operates a successful apparel shop but lives in fear that her own dark secret—the illegitimate birth of her sensitive but adventurous daughter, Allison—will eventually become grist for the Peyton Place gossip mill. The novel revealed another dirty New England secret: the fierce class and ethnic divisions that undermine the image of a model New England community symbolized by the democratic town meeting and the placidity of picturesque town commons.

Although the plot was sanitized for the 1957 film version (Selena's abortion became a miscarriage, and Rodney died in World War II combat), much of the New England flavor was retained, thanks in part to the fact that the movie was shot on location in Camden, Maine, and that many locals appeared as extras. The television series was sanitized even further by eliminating the Cross family entirely, keeping Rodney alive to love again, and constructing a generic New England village on a Hollywood studio lot.

The Peyton Place phenomenon left an important legacy. Published after Alfred Kinsey's *Sexual Behavior in the Human Female* (1953) but before Betty Friedan's *Feminine Mystique* (1963), *Peyton Place* boldly expressed an incipient feminist vision of greater independence (including sexual liberation) for women. Also enduring is the notion that small towns—like Peyton Place in the 1950s and 1960s (or Twin Peaks in the 1990s)—are complex microcosms of American society.

Otto Friedrich, "Farewell to *Peyton Place*," *Esquire* (December 1981); Kenneth MacKinnon, *Hollywood's Small Towns: An Introduction to the American Small-Town Movie* (1984); George Metalious and June O'Shea, *The Girl from Peyton Place: A Biography of Grace Metalious* (1965); Emily Toth, *Inside Peyton Place: The Life of Grace Metalious* (1981).

James I. Deutsch

Philanthropists and Philanthropy

John Winthrop, founder of the Massachusetts Bay Colony, hoped to create a New World utopia centered on religion and bonded by a spirit of charity. Many other colonial New Englanders echoed Winthrop's vision of a special leadership role for the region. While New Englanders prospered through trade and manufacturing and abandoned visions of communities of saints living simply and self-sufficiently as village farmers, many retained Puritanism's emphasis on the need for cooperatively run communities to act as exemplars for the larger society.

As a result, philanthropic traditions in America have deep roots in New England.

Philanthropy in colonial New England included efforts by wealthy individuals to create worthy memorials to themselves or family members. In 1638, for instance, John Harvard gave his collection of 400 books to a new college in the Massachusetts Bay Colony, stipulating that in turn the school be named after him. Throughout the colonial period other prosperous New Englanders similarly endowed libraries, reading societies, and schools, all of which benefited their communities while bearing their names. While these philanthropic activities displayed traditional distributive charity, others were original. In the 17th and 18th centuries New England clergymen, in alliance with their wealthy parishioners, created definitions of public spiritedness that demanded not only that individual rich people obey biblical injunctions to good works, but that communities themselves organize philanthropically. Cotton Mather's *Bonifacius; or, Essays to Do Good* (1710) emphasized humanitarianism, compassion, and charity and influenced Benjamin Franklin in his public service and political writings.

By the beginning of the 18th century, charity societies, particularly those to aid and educate the poor, thrived throughout New England, supplementing publicly funded municipal almshouses with private, church-led charity. Unique to colonial New England was the degree to which philanthropic giving was a cooperative and highly organized activity. The rich shipbuilders who worshiped at Boston's Old South Church, for instance, cooperated annually to supply the city's indigent with firewood in winter. Members of other prominent Boston congregations raised funds by declaring monthly fasts, donating the amount their households would have otherwise spent for food. Charity in New England extended beyond distribution of food and firewood to education. As early as 1728, all of Boston's churches agreed to an "evangelical treasury" plan that pooled funds to create a system of free schools for the education of poor children.

New England's 19th-century industrial prosperity meant that many more families could contribute to education. Dominated by names like Phillips, Otis, Shattuck, Lyman, Eliot, and Quincy, New England's first families established a host of schools and colleges. Moreover, by the early 1850s, such families were significant patrons of hospitals, orchestras, and museums as well as parks and gardens meant for public enjoyment.

If colonial New England philanthropy established an important model of cooperative charity work by private societies, its 19th-century successor created another: the philanthropic foundation. No 19th-century philanthropist had more lasting influence than George Peabody. Born in 1795 in South Danvers, Mass., Peabody's life exemplified the opportunities the Industrial Revolution offered the ambitious. Unlike most philanthropists, Peabody belonged to the working class; he was the son of a drapery worker. It was, however, a world he soon abandoned, as, from scratch, he built a transatlantic transportation and commercial banking empire and founded, in partnership with a young Boston merchant named Junius Morgan, the House of Morgan.

By the end of the Civil War, Peabody's investments in banks, railroads, steamship lines, and the first telegraph cable system across the Atlantic had created a huge fortune. Although he spent most of his adult life in Europe, supervising his business enterprises from London, Peabody was deeply troubled by the devastation the war had caused throughout the South. His concern caused him to sponsor a new kind of philanthropic institution: the charitable foundation, an institution structured on a corporate model with a board of trustees, an annual report, hired staff, and a government-issued charter. Established in 1867 with what was contemporaneously judged to be an enormous, $2 million endowment, the Peabody Education Fund sought to improve the education of poor southerners, both white and black. In alliance with other prominent New Englanders, most importantly the Rhode Island textile manufacturer John Slater, Peabody vigorously extended to another part of the nation the unique New England philanthropic emphasis on education as a crucial tool for social improvement.

After 1890, when the Peabody and Slater funds merged, the New England philanthropic mission to the American South focused on education of African Americans. In 1907 another wealthy northerner, Anna Jeanes, established a third major foundation, the Jeanes Fund, which funded teacher training among rural black southerners. These three foundations left a significant legacy. At a time of overwhelming race prejudice, they sought to better the lives of America's black population. Worth noting, however, is the fact that they each did so without challenging ideas about black inferiority. Whites generally ran the segregated schools established for black education. Students learned practical vocational skills. Courses for boys emphasized better ways to grow crops, along with industrial skills like carpentry and shoe repair. Girls learned to cook and clean.

In creating the most important 19th-century foundation, Peabody thus established an even more important tradition—one that was followed by most 20th-century foundations. The philanthropy he and his fellow New Englanders championed sought improvement of conditions for those deemed less fortunate, but rarely endorsed real revolutions in the social or economic status quo.

Between 1900 and 1910 the axis of philanthropic influence shifted, as New York, not Boston, became home to many of the nation's most significant philanthropic families. At the beginning of the 21st century the greatest number of foundations in the United States still located their central offices in New York. In 1999 *Fortune* magazine's annual list of the nation's top 10 corporate and individual givers failed to mention a single person or company based in New England. But that fact demands the frame of another: philanthropists and philanthropy by the late 20th century had changed. Regional patterns of influence had far less importance than did the reality that gifts from individual Americans and philanthropic bequests from estates, rather than corporations, provided the vast majority of all contributions to charitable causes.

In interesting ways, however, philanthropy based in New England continued to exercise significant influence nationally in the 20th century. Although the region's institutional and family philanthropies were no longer the country's best known, New England philanthropy nevertheless innovated in two crucial areas: creating alliances between nonprofits and governments and offering new financial models for charity.

Before the 1950s most philanthropies and nonprofit agencies received little or no public funding. For instance, the revenues for the Judge Baker Guidance Center of Boston, arguably the country's top child-psychology clinic, came principally from its investment income. By the end of the century, the center's most important source of funding was state and federal tax dollars. A pattern first seen strongly in New England spread across the nation in the last three decades of the 20th century, as state and federal agencies signed contracts with nonprofits for delivery of services. The Baker Center provided counseling for abused teenagers under an agreement with the Massachusetts Department of Public Welfare. Thousands of other philanthropies and nonprofits followed suit. Private agencies and philanthropic institutions actually ran a host of government programs ranging from drug and alcohol treatment to runaway shelters to adult day care for Alzheimer's patients. At the beginning of the 21st century the lines defining public, private, and nonprofit sectors have become difficult to distinguish. A pattern that started in Massachusetts typified delivery of tax-payer-provided social services countrywide. Many states depended almost exclusively on nonprofits for this.

If New England philanthropies and nonprofits promoted this closer alliance with government, they also pioneered in creating new and highly influential financial vehicles for charity. Throughout most of American history charity had meant outright donations, either in cash or in kind. But by the end of the 20th century loans competed with grants as vehicles for philanthropic giving. Led by Fidelity Investments of Boston, whose Fidelity Funds managed some $240 billion in assets, and by the New Hampshire Charitable Fund, a number of New England philanthropies organized their endowments as revolving loan funds.

The New Hampshire Fund, dedicated to environmental and architectural preservation in the state, created six permanent loan funds. In addition to the more than $10 million available from these sources, the foundation extended its resources by borrowing funds for re-lending. In the 1980s, for instance, Amoskeag Industries loaned the fund $60,000 for an energy conservation program in Manchester, while other companies loaned capital to preserve historic theaters throughout the state. Repaid loans returned to revolving capital. The idea of substituting revolving loan funds for onetime grants was financially sophisticated. A director of the New Hampshire Fund correctly asserted that it increased philanthropy's potential "fire power" and allowed charitable and nonprofit institutions to engage in issues on a much larger scale than by simply writing a check.

It is fitting that the region that lauded philanthropic giving in the 17th century continues to reshape the ways it is accomplished nearly 400 years later. Despite deficits in charitable giving, the region has a higher concentration of nonprofit and grantmaking organizations than any other in the country. New Englanders are more likely to work for nonprofit organizations than are Americans in other regions; in 2002, 11.8 percent of Maine workers had nonprofit jobs, versus 7.2 percent nationally. New England is home to many academic research centers dedicated to the nonprofit sector, including Yale University's Program on Non-Profit Organizations, Boston College's Social Welfare Research Institute, Harvard University's Hauser Center on Nonprofit Organizations, and Tufts University's Lincoln Filene Center for Citizenship and Public Affairs. At the start of the 21st century, many organizations and institutions are devoted to tracking and increasing patterns of philanthropic giving in New England.

Dwight Burlingame and Dennis Young, eds., *Corporate Philanthropy at the Crossroads* (1996); Deborah Gardner, "Practical Philanthropy: The Phelps-Stokes Fund and Housing," *Prospects* 15 (1990); David

Hammack, ed., *Making the Nonprofit Sector in the United States: A Reader* (1998); Christine Heyrman, "The Fashion among More Superior People: Charity and Social Change in Provincial New England, 1700–1740," *American Quarterly* 34 (1982); Melinda Marble, *Social Investment and Community Foundations* (1988); Bruce McCully, "Governor Francis Nicholson, Patron par Excellence of Religion and Learning in Colonial America," *William and Mary Quarterly* 39 (1982); Waldemar Nielsen, *Inside American Philanthropy: The Drama of Donorship* (1996); Elizabeth Schaff, "George Peabody: His Life and Legacy," *Maryland Historical Magazine* 90 (1995).

Judith Sealander

Plymouth Rock

The subject of scores of poems, plays, orations, and paintings, Plymouth Rock, in Plymouth, Mass., has become one of the most prominent secular icons in America. Inseparably linked with the Pilgrims and what is often erroneously hailed as the first landing of British citizens in the colonies, it has become the metaphorical cornerstone upon which the nation has been built and will continue to build. As Daniel Webster observed in 1820, on the bicentennial of the Pilgrims' landing, "Two thousand miles westward from the rock where their fathers landed, may now be found the sons of the Pilgrims, cultivating . . . the patrimonial blessings of wise institutions, of liberty, and religion." In years to come, he continued, "the voice of acclamation and gratitude, commencing on the Rock of Plymouth, shall be transmitted through millions of the sons of the Pilgrims, till it loses itself in the murmur of the Pacific."

Plymouth Rock has become the symbol of America's great faith and greater hope as well as a brand name for a wide range of products that producers hope will be associated with the nation's founding and stability (for example, the Plymouth Rock Assurance [Insurance] Corporation). In the 1830s, Alexis de Tocqueville, a French visitor to the United States, would observe, "This rock has become an object of veneration in the United States. . . . [It has] become famous; it is treasured by a great nation; a fragment [of the rock] is prized as a relic." But the rock has also had its detractors—some in jest, others in earnest. Mark Twain described the Pilgrims as "a simple and ignorant race . . . [who] never had seen any good rocks before, [thereby explaining their] hopping ashore in frantic delight and clapping an iron fence around" it. In commenting on the tendency of those whose ancestors had "come over on the *Mayflower*" to lord it over others, Dorothy Parker suggested that it would have been better if Plymouth Rock had landed on the Pilgrims rather than the other way around. Indian rights activists, lamenting their fate at the hands of those who arrived on the *Mayflower*, have often protested

Plymouth Rock in its 1930 shrine

the annual Pilgrim's Progress reenactment of the Pilgrim landing at Plymouth Rock. Thanksgiving is their Day of Mourning.

Plymouth Rock is neither mentioned by the chroniclers of Plymouth's first century, nor made note of in any other way, until the second decade of the 18th century, whereupon the location of the rock was marked on a town map. It was not recognized for its historic importance until the 1770s. In the early years of that decade, an elderly town resident, Ephraim Spooner, stepped forward to tell the story of Thomas Faunce, who, as a young man, had known many of the Pilgrim Fathers. When in 1741 Thomas Faunce, then 95, heard of plans to build a new wharf in Plymouth, Spooner recalled, Faunce had identified the 10-ton granite boulder located at the end of Plymouth Bay as marking the spot where the Pilgrims had landed on December 26, 1620.

In 1774, in the spirit of the imminent American Revolution, residents relocated the rock to a site next to the liberty pole erected in front of the Town Hall. When the rock was raised, however, it split in two, and the lower part was left in the original spot. On July 4, 1834, the Pilgrim Society moved the upper part to the front of the recently constructed Pilgrim Hall and, finally, in 1880 it was reunited with its other half at its original site. Plymouth Rock became the victim of zealous tourists who chiseled pieces of the landmark for souvenirs, so the society erected a fence and a Victorian canopy to protect it. The original canopy was replaced upon the tercentenary of the Pilgrim landing by another canopy, designed along

neo-Grecian lines by McKim, Mead and White.

Robert D. Arner, "Plymouth Rock Revisited: The Landing of the Pilgrim Fathers," *Journal of American Culture* 6 (1983); Rose T. Briggs, *Plymouth Rock: History and Significance* (1968); Francis Russell, "The Pilgrims and the Rock," *American Heritage* 13 (1962); John Seelye, *Memory's Nation: The Place of Plymouth Rock* (1998).

Bryan F. Le Beau

Postage Stamps

Since the first U.S. postage stamp was issued in 1847, New England's principal figures, institutions, icons, and significant events have been a major source of images for American stamps. The Boston native Benjamin Franklin, for example, has been an enduring image on American postage, and other images, such as Daniel Chester French's *Minute Man* statue, have been issued and reissued as symbols of New England history. Numerous literary and political figures and inventors from the region, including such notable African Americans as Jan Matzeliger, Ernest Everett Just, and W. E. B. Du Bois, have appeared in the U.S. Postal Service's Famous American, American Presidential, Literary American, and Black Heritage series. New England sites and buildings—for example, the Boston State House and the Old Windmill in Portsmouth, R.I.—have been included in the American Architecture and Historic Windmills series. (See the table on the next page for a selected list.)

Scott E. Green

Pragmatism

The pragmatic spirit may be located as far back as Socrates and Aristotle; it informs Immanuel Kant's *Critique of Pure Reason* (1781) and infuses the essays of Ralph Waldo Emerson, celebrant of personal change and growth. As a distinct philosophical movement, pragmatism evolved in Cambridge, Mass., in the 1870s, largely from the work of Charles Sanders Peirce and William James. It was later taken up, revised, and expanded by such philosophers as Giovanni Papini in Italy, F. C. S. Schiller in England, and John Dewey, George Herbert Mead, Horace Kallen, and Sidney Hook in America. Contemporary pragmatists include Richard Rorty, Hilary Putnam, Richard Poirier, Cornel West, and Stanley Cavell. Historians of philosophy locate the work of Peirce, James, and Dewey as significant points in the development of pragmatism from a theory of meaning to a theory of truth to a theory of inquiry.

Derived from the Greek *pragma*, meaning "deed" or "action," pragmatism, as its originators saw it, was a method, a technique, or a disposition rather than a system of propositions. Pragmatism holds that the truth of an idea is

Postage Stamps Featuring New England Figures, Events, and Images

Subject	Issue Date(s)	Series	Subject	Issue Date(s)	Series
Benjamin Franklin	1847	—		1981	(prestamped postal card)
	1851–57	—			
	1860	(prestamped envelope)	John Quincy Adams	1938–43	American Presidential
	1861	(official carrier stamp)	Calvin Coolidge	1938–43	American Presidential
	1861–66	—	Franklin Pierce	1938–43	American Presidential
	1865	(newspaper stamp)	Louisa May Alcott	1940	Famous American
	1870	(prestamped envelope)	Alexander Graham Bell	1940	Famous American
	1870–71	—	Charles W. Eliot	1940	Famous American
	1873	(franking stamp)	Ralph Waldo Emerson	1940	Famous American
	1873–79	(official prestamped envelope)	Daniel C. French	1940	Famous American
			Mark Hopkins	1940	Famous American
	1874–76	(prestamped envelope)	Elias Howe	1940	Famous American
	1875	—	James Russell Lowell	1940	Famous American
	1875	(official carrier stamp)	Edward A. MacDowell	1940	Famous American
	1879	(franking stamp)	Horace Mann	1940	Famous American
	1881–82	—	Augustus Saint-Gaudens	1940	Famous American
	1887–99	(stamped letter sheet)	Gilbert C. Stuart	1940	Famous American
	1902–3	—	James A. Whistler	1940	Famous American
	1903	National Postal Museum Issue	Eli Whitney	1940	Famous American
	1908–15	—	John Greenleaf Whittier	1940	Famous American
	1918–20	—	Vermont Statehood	1941	—
	1918–21	(savings stamp)	USS *Constitution*	1947	—
	1922–26	—		1985	(prestamped envelope)
	1938–43	American Presidential	Battle of Fort Ticonderoga	1955	—
	1947	(prestamped airmail envelope)	Old Man of the Mountain	1955	—
			Virginia of Sagadahock	1957	—
	1954–66	Liberty	Paul Revere	1958	Liberty
	1956	—		1971	(message and reply card)
	1958	(prestamped postal card)	Bunker Hill Monument	1958	Liberty
	1976	—	Noah Webster	1958	—
	1997	Pacific 97	Horace Greeley	1961	—
Daniel Webster	1870	(prestamped envelope)	Dr. James Naismith	1961	—
	1870–71	—	Winslow Homer	1962	Fine Art
	1873	(franking stamp)	Brian McMahon	1962	—
	1873–79	(official prestamped envelope)	Robert H. Goddard	1964	(airmail stamp)
			John F. Kennedy	1964	—
	1879	(franking stamp)		1965	(prestamped airmail envelope)
	1882–88	—			
	1894	—		1965–68	Prominent American
	1902–3	—		1967	(prestamped airmail envelope)
Commodore Oliver H. Perry	1870	(prestamped envelope)			
	1873	(franking stamp)	John S. Copley	1965	Fine Art
	1879	(franking stamp)	Oliver Wendell Holmes	1965–68	Prominent American
	1890	—	Eugene O'Neill	1965–68	Prominent American
John Adams	1898	(prestamped postal card)	Francis Parkman	1965–68	—
				1975–81	—
	1938–43	American Presidential	Henry David Thoreau	1967	—
Nathan Hale	1922–26	—	Battle of Bunker Hill	1968[2]	—
	1977	(prestamped postal card)		1975[3]	—
			Bennington Flag	1968	Historic Flag
	1977	(message and reply card)	Bunker Hill Flag	1968	Historic Flag
			Rhode Island 1775 Flag	1968	Historic Flag
Great Heag, Acadia National Park	1934	National Park	John Trumbull	1968[2]	Fine Art
			Washington's Cruisers	1968	Historic Flag
	1935	(stamp souvenir sheet)	Herman Melville	1970	(prestamped envelope)
Nathanael Greene	1936–37[1]	Army Commemorative		1984	Literary American

(continued)

Postage Stamps Featuring New England Figures, Events, and Images (*continued*)

Subject	Issue Date(s)	Series	Subject	Issue Date(s)	Series
Emily Dickinson	1971	American Poets	Igor Sikorsky	1988	(airmail stamp)
Whaling Ship *Charles W. Morgan*	1971	Historic Preservation	Isaac Royal House, Medford, Mass.	1990	(prestamped postal card)
Gloucester, Mass.	1972	(prestamped postal card)	West Quoddy Head (Maine) Lighthouse	1990	American Lighthouse
Samuel Adams	1973	(prestamped postal card)	Jan E. Matzeliger	1991	Black Heritage
	1973	(message and reply card)	University of Vermont	1991	(prestamped postal card)
Charles Thomson	1975	(prestamped postal card)	Vermont Statehood	1991	—
Robert Frost	1976	American Poets	W. E. B. Du Bois	1992	Black Heritage
State Flag Set	1976	—		1998	Celebrate the Century, 1900s
Nathan Hale	1977	(prestamped postal card)	Wadsworth Atheneum	1992	(prestamped postal card)
John Hancock	1978	(prestamped postal card)	Bowdoin College	1993	(prestamped postal card)
	1978	(message and reply card)	James Thurber	1994	Literary Arts
			Alice Hamilton	1995	Great American
			Ernest E. Just	1996	Black Heritage
USCG *Eagle*	1978	(prestamped postal card)	Thornton Wilder	1997	Literary Arts
			Martha Chase Doll	1997	Classic American Dolls
Boston State House	1979	American Architecture	The Freake Limner	1998	Four Centuries of American Art
Robert F. Kennedy	1979	—			
Windmill, Eastham, Mass.	1980	Historic Windmills	John Foster	1998	Four Centuries of American Art
Old Windmill, Portsmouth, R.I.	1980	Historic Windmills	Winslow Homer	1998	Four Centuries of American Art
State Birds and Flowers	1982	—			
Gropius House, Lincoln, Mass.	1982	American Architecture	Northeastern University	1998	(prestamped postal card)
Touro Synagogue	1982	—	Brandeis University	1998	(prestamped postal card)
Nathaniel Hawthorne	1983	Literary American			
Boston Bull Terrier	1984	American Dog	Redwood Library and Athenaeum	1999	(prestamped postal card)
Herman Melville	1984	Literary American	Justin S. Morrill	1999	—
Norman Rockwell	1984	—	Block Island Lighthouse	1999	(prestamped postal card)
	2001	American Illustrators			
Abigail Adams	1985	—	Frederick Law Olmsted	1999	—
Broadbill Decoy by Ben Holmes, Stratford, Conn.	1985	Duck Decoy	Middlebury College	2000	(prestamped postal card)
Marblehead Lighthouse	1985	American Lighthouse	Fenway Park	2001	Baseball's Legendary Playing Fields
Morgan Horse	1985	American Horse	Rockwell Kent	2001	American Illustrators
New England Neptune	1985	Seashell Booklet	Maxfield Parrish	2001	American Illustrators
Red Head Decoy by Keyes Chadwick, Martha's Vineyard, Mass.	1985	Duck Decoy	N. C. Wyeth	2001	American Illustrators
			Norman Rockwell	2001	American Illustrators
Stanley Steamer	1985	Transportation	Acadia National Park	2001	—
Atlantic Cod	1986	Fish Booklet	Each New England State	2002	Greetings from America
John Harvard	1986	Great American			
Settling of Connecticut	1986	(prestamped postal card)	Minor White, Albert Sands Southworth, and Josiah Johnson Hawes (last two on one stamp)	2002	Masters of American Photography
Settling of Rhode Island	1986	(prestamped postal card)			
Julia Ward Howe	1987	Great American			
Mary Lyon	1987	Great American	Walter Camp	2002	Early Football

[1]The 1936–37 Army Commemorative stamp used Trumbull's portrait of Nathanael Greene
[2]The 1968 Fine Art series stamp issued in Trumbull's honor featured a detail from his *Battle of Bunker Hill*
[3]The 1975 stamp of the Battle of Bunker Hill used a detail from Trumbull's painting
Source: Scott E. Green, *Specialized Catalogue of United States Stamps* (1997); U. S. Postal Service Web site.

inextricably connected to the consequences of that idea; that the personality and context of a thinker are inextricably connected to what is thought; and that transcendent abstractions do not suffice in describing reality.

Pragmatism resulted from discussions undertaken by a group of young men living in the Boston area in the third quarter of the 19th century. Calling themselves the Metaphysical Club, the members included, in addition to Peirce and James, three lawyers—Oliver Wendell Holmes, Jr., Nicholas St. John Green, and Joseph Bangs Warner—and the historian John Fiske. All were or had been associated with Harvard, either through the college itself, its law or medical school, or the Lawrence Scientific School.

The Metaphysical Club built upon the tradition of Emerson's Transcendental Club, begun in 1836, in which such provocative thinkers as Bronson Alcott, George Ripley, Orestes Brownson, and assorted writers and students came together to discuss philosophical, theological, ethical, and literary issues. Topics included "What is the essence of Religion as distinct from morality?" and "Does the species advance beyond the individual?" By the 1860s, intellectual clubs proliferated in the Boston area: members of the Saturday Club, the Town and Country Club, the Atlantic Club, and the Radical Club held energetic, often heated conversations in Back Bay parlors and hotel dining rooms.

The Metaphysical Club, despite its stately name, was notable for its informality and youth. Although none of its members was trained as a philosopher—Peirce was a mathematician and James's degree was in medicine—all were interested in prevailing philosophical debates, especially about the impact of Darwin's theory of natural selection on metaphysics. This theory asserted that nature, rather than behaving according to immutable laws, was spontaneous and random; that individuals and the environment acted upon each other reciprocally; and that the choices made by individuals caused a difference in the universe as a whole. The Darwinian universe, therefore, was characterized by change and novelty.

Skeptical and intellectually audacious, the members of the Metaphysical Club shared a sense of rebellion against German idealism and British rationalism—both discussed widely at the time—and any other philosophy that proposed a system of universal abstractions and held that nature and human nature have fixed characteristics. Georg Hegel and Herbert Spencer, both of whom attempted to respond to Darwinian theory while positing a stable and orderly universe, seemed to the Metaphysical Club entirely unsatisfactory.

Besides questioning the relation between science and philosophy, the members of the Metaphysical Club were concerned with the practical consequences of holding one philosophy rather than another. They were aware of the growing social and economic problems throughout the country, especially in the industrial centers of New England—labor unrest, for example, characterized by recurring strikes and disputes—as well as the increasingly heterogeneous population resulting from large waves of immigration. Pragmatism appeared to be a method that could serve to guide moral and ethical decisions, foster consensus, and lead to social stability.

Although all of the members of the Metaphysical Club considered these to be social issues, Peirce focused his attention on ways that a community of individuals formulates a consensus about reality and communicates that consensus through language. Impatient with metaphysical abstractions that he called "meaningless gibberish," Peirce sought a way to clarify the signs by which we convey meaning to one another. A technique that fostered clarity necessarily would help to distinguish significant and resolvable intellectual problems from meaningless problems that result from the use of vague, abstract language.

In two articles published in the *Popular Science Monthly* in 1877–78, "The Fixation of Belief" and "How to Make Our Ideas Clear," Peirce, while never using the term *pragmatism,* put forth one of its most important principles: the truth of ideas can be known only by considering the consequences of those ideas in concrete experience. For Peirce, the consequences of an idea meant its empirical reality rather than its practical effects in altering or having an impact upon reality.

William James, eagerly attentive to Peirce's propositions, took up and revised the notion of consequences when he formulated his own version of pragmatism. For James, the consequences of an idea meant the practical effects of holding that idea, the consequences for the individual in terms of a feeling of well-being or satisfaction, or the consequences for the community in terms of cohesiveness and stability. A great popularizer of philosophy through his lively writings and well-attended lectures, James promoted his own version of pragmatism for his own generation and those that followed.

James first used the term *pragmatism* rather late in his career in a lecture he delivered at the Philosophical Union in Berkeley, Calif., in 1898. In "Philosophical Conceptions and Practical Results," James made two important points. First, he said that philosophical affinity was influenced by an individual's temperament: a person's needs and interests inspired

attention to one philosophical issue over another and to one theory rather than another. That personal impetus gave philosophy an immediate connection to an individual's everyday life. Second, one's philosophy determined how one made ethical decisions and affirmed a sense of authority to take action—or not—in the face of moral dilemmas. Beliefs must make a difference and have perceptible consequences or they are not worth arguing over. James's focus on the individual caused some contemporaries to suggest that his pragmatism might be better called humanism.

Although James called for "civic courage" in the face of concrete social problems, pragmatism, as he saw it, also could help one consider the most compelling unresolved philosophical problem: God's existence as one or as many. James suggested that individuals consider their personal stake in the answer to that question: What difference would it make if God were one Absolute? How would one's daily life, behavior, and sense of well-being change? As he considered this issue in his published works, notably *Pragmatism* (1907) and *The Meaning of Truth* (1909), James proposed a distinction between tough-minded and tender-minded thinkers, the tough-minded being empiricist and pluralistic, but pessimistic and fatalistic; and the tender-minded being rationalistic and idealistic, yet optimistic and "free-willist." James posited pragmatism as a method of justifying religious belief no matter which perspective one took.

James's student John Dewey, a native of Burlington, Vt., revised both Peirce's and James's definitions of pragmatism. For Dewey, pragmatism was significant as a theory not so much of meaning or of determining truth, as of inquiry. Concerned with ways that individuals learn to become productive participatory citizens, Dewey applied pragmatism to education, translating the pragmatic spirit into an educational pedagogy that he called instrumentalism. He believed that learning occurs most successfully in environments in which students engage in activities inspired by their own curiosity and growing interests. Generative and active learning, he believed, would transform children into active, civic-minded adults who could solve problems creatively and face the challenges of an increasingly pluralistic democracy. At the University of Chicago and at Columbia University, Dewey established primary schools that focused on teaching through activity.

Pragmatism has proven to be both controversial and resilient; since its 19th-century beginnings, philosophers have debated the definition of the term. Arthur O. Lovejoy, a philosopher who had been James's student at Harvard, came up with 13 definitions of pragmatism from the work of James alone. Within social and political discourse, pragmatism often has been misunderstood to mean mere expediency or justification for relativism and subjectivism. Yet because of its potential to serve as a guide for public life, to allow for multiple and diverse perspectives, and to affirm each individual's significance to the community, its attraction has continued, especially among the liberal political community. As a method of inquiry, it has influenced literary, feminist, and cultural theory. Such New England writers as Robert Frost and Wallace Stevens reflect Jamesian pragmatism in their questioning of the authority of language to represent reality and their interest in the subjectivity of experience and perception; indeed, some scholars believe that the pragmatist spirit informs literary and artistic modernism.

John Dewey, *Philosophy and Civilization* (1931); John Patrick Diggins, *The Promise of Pragmatism* (1994); Russell B. Goodman, ed., *Pragmatism: A Contemporary Reader* (1995); Charles Hartshorne and Paul Weiss, eds., *Collected Papers of Charles Sanders Peirce* (1965); Louis Menand, *The Metaphysical Club: A Story of Ideas in America* (2001); Richard Rorty, *Consequences of Pragmatism* (1982); Philip Weiner, *Evolution and the Founders of Pragmatism* (1949).

Linda Simon

Preppies *Preppy,* a term referring originally to a preparatory, or prep, school student, later became a label for a certain style of bearing, clothing, and class consciousness. Although not exclusively associated with New England, the region's preparatory schools and hence preppy style loom large in the images and ideas associated with the preppy. By a strange and perhaps appropriate twist of fate, the word *preppy,* according to the *Oxford English Dictionary* (*OED*), originally meant "silly or immature." But this meaning derives from the fact that *preppy* described preparatory school students and their youthful behavior. The current meaning evolved in the early 1980s, with the publication and phenomenal success of Lisa Birnbaum's guide to life among the Izod- and khaki-clad sailing crowd, *The Official Preppy Handbook* (1980).

Private preparatory schools in New England, both boarding and so-called country day schools, were founded after the English model to prepare male children for entrance to elite colleges and universities. Venerable male institutions like Phillips Exeter (Exeter, N.H.), Phillips Andover (Andover, Mass.), Deerfield (Mass.), Groton (Mass.), Saint Mark's (Southborough, Mass.), and Saint Paul's (Concord, N.H.) were joined by distinguished female academies such as Miss Porter's (Farmington, Conn.). The association of these schools with "preppiness" is primarily a phenomenon of the 20th century, in a combination of media images in books and movies and the marketing of that image by manufacturers of clothing and accessories. By the time Birnbaum's book appeared, preppiness was reduced to a cultural style of attitudes and consumer preferences. The ideal preppy is depicted as the scion of an old New England White Anglo-Saxon Protestant family with privileges matched by a sense of entitlement, a young man or woman whose prep school education affords access to inner circles of business, law, education, and government. Perhaps as a defensive reaction against such evidence of class privilege in a democracy, the preppy is also seen as someone silly or immature, as the *OED* has it, someone whose clothes are square and whose background might not have prepared him or her for the realities of life outside preppy environs.

As is the case with many other elements of New England's identity, the preppy image was presented to national audiences at a time when the schools themselves were undergoing changes, as coeducation and the ethnic and economic diversification of student bodies and faculty gained steam in the 1960s and 1970s. J. D. Salinger's *Catcher in the Rye* (1951) and John Knowles's *A Separate Peace* (1959) were best-sellers, but the prep school world they depicted would not survive the 1950s. By the 1970s, such writers as John McPhee, John Irving, and Geoffrey Wolff combined nostalgia with absurdist or satirical touches. Nevertheless, as Irving has shown in his autobiographical writings and, more recently, as Lorene Cary has described in *Black Ice* (1991)—about her years as one of the first black women at Saint Paul's School—preppies see the true character of the institutions that profoundly shape the character of some of America's future leaders. Films featuring preppy characters and settings, most notably *Love Story* (1970) and *The World According to Garp* (1982), based on the 1978 Irving novel, reinforced the literary images for a national audience.

Birnbaum's book spotlighted the preppy set, inspiring would-be preppies around the country. Teenagers learned which clothes to wear, which hobbies and sports were preppy enough to pursue (tennis and skiing, yes; track and basketball, no), and where most of their summering country-club chums could be found (at the Vineyard [Martha's Vineyard] and 'tucket [Nantucket]). What Birnbaum's guide failed to convey, however, was the elusive nature of preppiness. Being preppy was, in its heyday, not so concerned with the overt display of wealth. Preppiness was, rather, perfectly represented by old money trappings: rumpled linen and khaki, blond hair windblown from a day of sailing, and expensive but weathered loafers worn without socks.

As preppy style spread across the country, its original spirit was watered down, becoming barely recognizable behind newly purchased tennis shirts and boat shoes. Once characterized by a lifestyle of privilege, preppiness had become a mere fashion trend. Suddenly, midwesterners were snapping up Izod shirts and squeaking new Docksiders—shoes that they not only wore *with* socks but that would probably never touch the deck of a boat. Once preppiness strayed too far from its New England roots, it stopped making much sense; belts with whales stitched on them, boat shoes, "duck" boots, sailboats, yacht clubs, and rope bracelets had little meaning when the nearest seashore was a thousand miles away.

At the start of the 21st century, the most obvious signifiers of preppidom, boat shoes, raised collars, and pink and green Bermuda bags, are long gone. Instead, the word itself has evolved into a catchall term describing conformist teenagers who sacrifice their individuality to popular style. Fittingly, *The Official Preppy Handbook* has been out of print for years. Despite the obvious erosion of the class, racial, gender, and regional boundaries of preppiness, New England prep schools continue to prepare leaders. Influential families like the Bushes are associated with these schools, and new family dynasties will inevitably emerge from New England's prestigious preparatory schools.

Donna A. Danielewski

Pulitzer Prize Winners of New England (Table, next page)

Rhode Island The most enduring images and ideas of Rhode Island radiate from the state's geographic features and the circumstances of its founding as a haven for nonconformists and freethinkers. Having almost 250 miles of coastline bordering the Atlantic Ocean, Rhode Island has long been known as the Ocean State. Among its prominent features are Narragansett Bay, a fabled finger of water dividing Rhode Island's tiny land mass into eastern and western sections, the Sakonnet River, offshore islands such as Aquidneck, Conanicut, and Block, abundant seafood, picturesque lighthouses, sailboats, and other sights and sounds of the shore.

When Roger Williams was banished from the Massachusetts Bay Colony for his avowal of "soul liberty," the right to maintain religious beliefs free from government coercion, he secured title for land at the head of Narragansett Bay from the resident Native Americans and founded the town of Providence in 1636. After

Pulitzer Prize Winners of New England (Selected)

Category	Year	Prize Winner(s)
Journalism		
Beat Reporting	1995	David Shribman of *Boston Globe*
Breaking News Reporting	1999	Staff of *Hartford Courant*
	2002	Staff of *Lawrence (Mass.) Eagle-Tribune*
Commentary	1980	Ellen H. Goodman of *Boston Globe*
	1997	Eileen McNamara of *Boston Globe*
Criticism	1980	William A. Henry III of *Boston Globe*
	1994	Lloyd Schwartz of *Boston Phoenix*
	1996	Robert Campbell of *Boston Globe*
	2001	Gail Caldwell of *Boston Globe*
Editorial Cartooning	1962	Edmund S. Valtman of *Hartford Times*
	1973	Paul Szep of *Boston Globe*
	1974	Paul Szep of *Boston Globe*
	2002	Clay Bennett of *Christian Science Monitor*
Editorial Writing	1924	No author named of *Boston Herald*
	1927	F. Lauriston Bullard of *Boston Herald*
	1945	George W. Potter of *Providence Journal–Bulletin*
	1948	John H. Crider of *Boston Herald*
	1954	Don Murray of *Boston Herald*
	2001	David Moats of *Rutland (Vt.) Herald*
Explanatory Journalism	1992	Robert S. Capers and Eric Lipton of *Hartford Courant*
Feature Photography	1976	Staff Photographers of *Boston Herald American*
	1985	Stan Grossfeld of *Boston Globe*
General News Reporting	1988	Staff of *Lawrence (Mass.) Eagle-Tribune*
International Reporting	1950	Edmund Stevens of *Christian Science Monitor*
	1967	R. John Hughes of *Christian Science Monitor*
	1996	David Rohde of *Christian Science Monitor*
Investigative Reporting	1994	Staff of *Providence Journal–Bulletin*
Local Investigative Specialized Reporting	1972	Timothy Leland, Gerard M. O'Neill, Stephen A. Kurkjian, and Ann Desantis of *Boston Globe*
	1978	Anthony R. Dolan of *Stamford (Conn.) Advocate*
	1980	Stephen A. Kurkjian, Alexander B. Hawes, Jr., Nils Bruzelius, Joan Vennochi, and Robert M. Porterfield of *Boston Globe Spotlight Team*
	1984	Kenneth Cooper, Joan Fitz Gerald, Jonathan Kaufman, Norman Lockman, Gary McMillan, Kirk Scharfenberg, and David Wessel of *Boston Globe*
Local Reporting, Edition Time	1953	Editorial Staff of *Providence Journal and Evening Bulletin*
National Reporting	1968	Howard James of *Christian Science Monitor*
	1968	Robert Cahn of *Christian Science Monitor*
	1986	*Boston Globe*
Photography	1948	Frank Cushing of *Boston Traveler*
	1957	Harry A. Trask of *Boston Traveler*
Public Service	1921	*Boston Post*
	1940	*Waterbury (Conn.) Republican and American*
	1966	*Waterbury (Conn.) Republican and American*
	1975	*Boston Globe*
	2002	*Boston Globe*
Spot News Photography	1976	Stanley Forman of *Boston Herald American*
	1977	Stanley Forman of *Boston Herald American*
	1984	Stan Grossfeld of *Boston Globe*
Letters, Drama, and Music		
Biography or Autobiography	1917	*Julia Ward Howe*, Laura E. Richards and Maude Howe Elliott, assisted by Florence Howe Hall

(continued)

Pulitzer Prize Winners of New England (Selected) (*continued*)

Category	Year	Prize Winner(s)
	1918	*Benjamin Franklin, Self-Revealed,* William Cabell Bruce
	1919	*The Education of Henry Adams,* Henry Adams
	1925	*Barrett Wendell and His Letters,* M. A. Dewolfe Howe
	1931	*Henry James,* Charles W. Eliot
	1934	*John Hay,* Tyler Dennett
	1936	*The Thought and Character of William James,* Ralph Barton Perry
	1938	*Pedlar's Progress,* Odell Shepard
	1939	*Benjamin Franklin,* Carl Van Doren
	1941	*Jonathan Edwards,* Ola Elizabeth Winslow
	1945	*George Bancroft: Brahmin Rebel,* Russell Blaine Nye
	1950	*John Quincy Adams and the Foundations of American Foreign Policy,* Samuel Flagg Bemis
	1957	*Profiles in Courage,* John F. Kennedy
	1961	*Charles Sumner and the Coming of the Civil War,* David Donald
	1963	*Henry James,* Leon Edel
	1965	*Henry Adams,* 3 vols., Ernest Samuels
	1966	*A Thousand Days,* Arthur M. Schlesinger, Jr.
	1971	*Robert Frost: The Years of Triumph, 1915–1938,* Lawrance Thompson
	1974	*O'Neill, Son and Artist,* Louis Sheaffer
	1976	*Edith Wharton: A Biography,* R. W. B. Lewis
	1985	*The Life and Times of Cotton Mather,* Kenneth Silverman
	1995	*Harriet Beecher Stowe: A Life,* Joan D. Hedrick
	1997	*Angela's Ashes: A Memoir,* Frank McCourt
	2002	*John Adams,* David McCullough
Drama	1920	*Beyond the Horizon,* Eugene O'Neill
	1922	*Anna Christie,* Eugene O'Neill
	1928	*Strange Interlude,* Eugene O'Neill
	1938	*Our Town,* Thornton Wilder
	1957	*Long Day's Journey into Night,* Eugene O'Neill
	1959	*J.B.,* Archibald MacLeish
Fiction	1921	*The Age of Innocence,* Edith Wharton
	1938	*The Late George Apley,* John Phillips Marquand
	1979	*The Stories of John Cheever,* John Cheever
	1982	*Rabbit Is Rich,* John Updike
	1989	*Breathing Lessons,* Anne Tyler
	1991	*Rabbit at Rest,* John Updike
	2002	*Empire Falls,* Richard Russo
	2003	*Middlesex,* Jeffrey Eugenides
History	1922	*The Founding of New England,* James Truslow Adams
	1937	*The Flowering of New England, 1815–1865,* Van Wyck Brooks
	1939	*A History of American Magazines,* Frank Luther Mott
	1941	*The Atlantic Migration, 1607–1860,* Marcus Lee Hansen
	1943	*Paul Revere and the World He Lived In,* Esther Forbes
	1944	*The Growth of American Thought,* Merle Curti
	1946	*The Age of Jackson,* Arthur M. Schlesinger, Jr.
	1956	*The Age of Reform,* Richard Hofstadter
	1964	*Puritan Village: The Formation of a New England Town,* Sumner Chilton Powell
	1966	*The Life of the Mind in America,* Perry Miller
	1968	*The Ideological Origins of the American Revolution,* Bernard Bailyn
	1973	*People of Paradox: An Inquiry Concerning the Origins of American Civilization,* Michael Kammen
	1980	*Been in the Storm So Long,* Leon F. Litwack
	1981	*American Education: The National Experience, 1783–1876,* Lawrence A. Cremin
	1991	*A Midwife's Tale,* Laurel Thatcher Ulrich

(*continued*)

Pulitzer Prize Winners of New England (Selected) (continued)

Category	Year	Prize Winner(s)
	1993	*The Radicalism of the American Revolution*, Gordon S. Wood
	2001	*Founding Brothers: The Revolutionary Generation*, Joseph J. Ellis
	2002	*The Metaphysical Club: A Story of Ideas in America*, Louis Menand
Nonfiction	1962	*The Making of the President, 1960*, Theodore H. White
	1966	*Wandering through Winter*, Edwin Way Teale
	1973	*Children of Crisis*, vols. 2 and 3, Robert Coles
	1979	*On Human Nature*, Edward O. Wilson
	1982	*The Soul of a New Machine*, Tracy Kidder
	1986	*Common Ground: A Turbulent Decade in the Lives of Three American Families*, J. Anthony Lukas
	1991	*The Ants*, Bert Holldobler and Edward O. Wilson
	2003	*A Problem from Hell: America and the Age of Genocide*, Samantha Power
Poetry	1922	*Collected Poems*, Edwin Arlington Robinson
	1923	*The Ballad of the Harp-Weaver; A Few Figs from Thistles; Eight Sonnets in American Poetry, 1922. A Miscellany*, Edna St. Vincent Millay
	1924	*New Hampshire: A Poem with Notes and Grace Notes*, Robert Frost
	1925	*The Man Who Died Twice*, Edwin Arlington Robinson
	1926	*What's o'Clock*, Amy Lowell
	1928	*Tristram*, Edwin Arlington Robinson
	1931	*Collected Poems*, Robert Frost
	1933	*Conquistador*, Archibald MacLeish
	1936	*Strange Holiness*, Robert P. Tristram Coffin
	1937	*A Further Range*, Robert Frost
	1943	*A Witness Tree*, Robert Frost
	1947	*Lord Weary's Castle*, Robert Lowell
	1953	*Collected Poems, 1917–1952*, Archibald MacLeish
	1955	*Collected Poems*, Wallace Stevens
	1957	*Things of This World*, Richard Wilbur
	1966	*Selected Poems*, Richard Eberhart
	1967	*Live or Die*, Anne Sexton
	1973	*Up Country*, Maxine Kumin
	1974	*The Dolphin*, Robert Lowell
	1982	*The Collected Poems*, Sylvia Plath
	1983	*Selected Poems*, Galway Kinnell
	1984	*American Primitive*, Mary Oliver
	1989	*New and Collected Poems*, Richard Wilbur
	1990	*The World Doesn't End*, Charles Simic
	1993	*The Wild Iris*, Louise Gluck
Music	1943	*Secular Cantata No. 2, A Free Song*, William Schuman, performed by the Boston Symphony Orchestra and published by G. Schirmer, New York
	1944	*Symphony No. 4, Opus 34*, Howard Hanson, performed by the Boston Symphony Orchestra on December 3, 1943
	1947	*Symphony No. 3*, Charles Ives, first performed by Lou Harrison and Chamber Orchestra in New York, April 1946
	1948	*Symphony No. 3*, Walter Piston, first performed by the Boston Symphony Orchestra in January 1948
	1961	*Symphony No. 7*, Walter Piston, first performed by the Philadelphia Orchestra on February 10, 1961, and commissioned by the Philadelphia Orchestra Association
	1962	*The Crucible*, Robert Ward, an opera in three acts. Libretto by Bernard Stambler, based on the play by Arthur Miller. First performed at New York City Center, on October 26, 1961, by the New York City Opera Company
	1963	*Piano Concerto No. 1*, Samuel Barber, premiered with the Boston Symphony at Philharmonic Hall on September 24, 1962
	1970	*Time's Encomium*, Charles Wuorinen, premiered in its entirety at the Berkshire Music Festival on August 16, 1969

(continued)

Pulitzer Prize Winners of New England (Selected) (continued)

Category	Year	Prize Winner(s)
	1971	*Synchronisms No. 6 for Piano and Electric Sound (1970)*, Mario Davidovsky, premiered on August 19, 1970, at the Berkshire Music Festival
	1982	*Concerto for Orchestra*, Roger Sessions, first performed by the Boston Symphony Orchestra on October 23, 1981, Seiji Ozawa, conductor
	1987	*The Flight into Egypt*, John Harbison, premiered by the Cantata Singers and Ensemble on November 21, 1986, at the New England Conservatory in Boston
	1989	*Whispers Out of Time*, Roger Reynolds, premiered on December 11, 1988, at Buckley Recital Hall, Amherst College, Mass.
	1996	*Lilacs, for Voice and Orchestra*, George Walker, premiered on February 1, 1996, by the Boston Symphony Orchestra; commissioned by that orchestra
	1997	*Blood on the Fields*, Wynton Marsalis, premiered on January 28, 1997, at Woolsey Hall, Yale University, New Haven, Conn.
	2000	*Life Is a Dream, Opera in Three Acts: Act II, Concert Version*, Lewis Spratlan, premiered on January 28, 2000, by Dinosaur Annex in Amherst, Mass. Libretto by James Maraniss
	2001	*Symphony No. 2 for String Orchestra*, John Corigliano, premiered by the Boston Symphony Orchestra on November 30, 2000, at Symphony Hall, Boston

Source: The Pulitzer Prizes, www.pulitzer.org

only four months, Williams left the American Baptist Church, which he helped start in 1639, and became a Seeker, a searcher for the good in any faith practice. Williams irked many with his views, but he worked assiduously to establish a legitimate government for the colony that provided order without impinging on religious beliefs; Rhode Island was one of

The Independent Man *atop the Rhode Island State House dome, Providence*

the only colonies to welcome Jews. His success as colony agent in obtaining from the British government the Charter of 1663, which contained such protections, had lasting consequences.

The traits for which Williams was known, dissidence and distinctiveness, persisted in Rhode Island. Coming soon after Williams, Anne Hutchinson and her antinomian followers brought their controversial belief in the Inner Light, direct communication between God and individuals, to the town of Portsmouth on the northern portion of Aquidneck Island. They so disturbed the community that a group broke off and founded Newport on the fine harbor at the southern end of that island. Samuel Gorton, another religious Seeker, founded Shawomet, today's Warwick, west of Narragansett Bay in 1642. An influx of Quakers, border disputes with neighbors, and erratic royal governance kept these early settlements in social and political turmoil.

Nothing, however, surpassed the turmoil that stemmed from conflict with Native Americans, whose cultural and economic values clashed with those of the colonists. The brutal Great Swamp Fight of December 19, 1675, fought on land now within Rhode Island, gave the colonists an advantage over local tribes and prompted retaliation. The prominent sachems, or chiefs, Metacom (King Philip) of the Wampanoag and Canonicus of the Narragansett, abandoned their previous policies of accommodation and attacked settlements, burning much of Providence in

March 1676. King Philip's War ended in August 1676 with Metacom's death near Mount Hope in Bristol. Remembered often in story, symbol, and place-names, Native American peoples have only recently regained genuine stature in Rhode Island, with the reassertion of tribal rights through court actions and federal recognition.

Rhode Islanders became famous, or notorious, for their assertion of rights and independence during the revolutionary period. In 1764 Stephen Hopkins, a multiple-term governor, wrote *The Rights of Colonies Examined*, a tract that justified a break from England. The burning of the grounded revenue ship *Gaspee* in 1772 vented local anger toward imperial tax policies and heightened emotions throughout the colonies. Rhode Islanders declared their independence from England on May 4, 1776, two months before the Declaration of Independence. Many from Rhode Island fought on land and sea during the Revolutionary War. None, perhaps, gained greater fame than Nathanael Greene, whose generalship loosened British control over the Carolinas. Newport suffered greatly from British occupation between 1776 and 1779, losing a profitable trade built on molasses, rum, and slaves carried between the Caribbean, Rhode Island, and Africa to aggressive competitors in Providence and Bristol such as the Brown and DeWolf families. Largely content to act as a shipping entrepôt and scornful of outside interference, Rhode Islanders resisted pressure to ratify the federal Constitution until 1790. A narrow vote in convention approved the new national government.

Rhode Island's political course has lent credence to its early denunciation as Rogue's Island. The Charter of 1663, retained as the fundamental law until 1842, limited suffrage to male landholders and their firstborn sons. As immigrants arrived in large numbers during the early decades of the 19th century and propertyless artisans and mill hands crowded cities and towns, only a small percentage of adults exercised political control. Thomas W. Dorr, scion of an old Rhode Island family, led a revolt of the disenfranchised in 1841 and 1842, known as the Dorr Rebellion, that failed to overthrow the established government but provoked implementation of a less restrictive constitution. Dorr was arrested for treason and imprisoned; it was not until national adoption of the "one man, one vote" principle in the 1960s that Rhode Island eliminated voting restrictions based on property, sex, nativity, and race.

Henry Bowen Anthony, editor of the *Providence Journal* and a Republican senator in the late 1800s, harbored a nativist streak that relegated Rhode Island's growing foreign population to the political margin. Blacks, largely invisible to the white majority, suffered equal indignities and occasional violence. Nelson W. Aldrich, a senator whose influence earned him the nickname "General Manager of the United States," and Charles R. "Boss" Brayton, head of Rhode Island's Republican political machine, were kingpins following Anthony's death in 1884, receiving national attention from muckraking journalists for buying and selling votes, patronage manipulation, legislative intrigues, and brazen indifference to reformers. More recently, Vincent A. "Buddy" Cianci astonished observers by rising to prominence as mayor of Providence, falling from grace amid allegations of corruption and crude behavior, and then returning to office to preside over a stunning cultural and commercial renaissance of the state's capital city. In 2002 Cianci's fortunes turned again, when the mayor was convicted of racketeering conspiracy.

Political and social tensions and trends have been interconnected with economic developments. Samuel Slater, an English millwright, established the first commercially successful textile factory along the Blackstone River in Pawtucket in 1789 with Moses Brown's capital. The availability of waterpower across Rhode Island, as well as investment capital seeking ventures less susceptible to the vagaries of foreign policy than the China trade and overseas shipping, instigated mill construction and a turning away from mercantile and agricultural pursuits. Women and children from surrounding farms worked in these mills until they were increasingly displaced by Irish and French Canadian immigrants less willing to demand better pay and treatment.

Most of these immigrants were Catholic. Subsequent immigration from Italy, Portugal, and Poland increased Catholic numbers, and for many years Rhode Island has been the only U.S. state with a majority Catholic population. Providence, Pawtucket, Woonsocket, Central Falls, and West Warwick grew into major centers of cotton, wool, and specialty textile manufacture; the related industries of machine and tool making evolved on a parallel course, with George H. Corliss standing out as an inventor and entrepreneur. Jewelry and related products—beginning with Jabez Gorham's successful silversmith shop in the late 18th century—also contributed to Rhode Island's becoming the most industrialized and densely populated state in the nation by the start of the 20th century.

Relations between management and labor, always uneasy because of a split between Yankee leaders and ethnic workers, worsened with the advent of southern competition, more militant unionization, and the Great Depression. This cleavage was perhaps best exemplified by the contentious trial in 1844 of three Irish workers for the murder of the prominent mill owner Amasa Sprague and the hanging of one of them, John Gordon, which spurred so great an outcry of justice wronged that the state legislature subsequently outlawed capital punishment. General strikes in 1922 and 1934 sparked violent clashes and began the unraveling of the textile industry in Rhode Island.

Military installations offset some lost employment, but the abandonment of Newport as a major naval base in the 1970s and the elimination or scaling back of other facilities caused new economic distress. The creative reuse of old industrial structures, the reclamation of river corridors and shoreline, the aggressive promotion of tourism, and entrepreneurial efforts to exploit new technologies display anew the spirit, work ethic, and inevitable friction that have characterized Rhode Island's economy. Some economic development has emanated from educational initiatives and programs at Brown University and the Rhode Island School of Design in Providence, two renowned institutions of higher learning.

No depiction of Rhode Island's political, social, or economic travails has ever removed the sea from view. Repasts of quahogs, the large hard-shell clams with a peculiarly strong flavor, and lobster, traditionally steamed with potatoes and corn at clambakes, have delighted many. (Another culinary treat, johnnycake, made from precisely ground white flint corn, has been the subject of books, poems, and songs.) The glorious coast and temperate weather attracted summer visitors as early as the late 18th century, but it was the magnificent excess of the late 19th and early 20th centuries that stamped Newport and, to a lesser extent, Narragansett as playgrounds of the rich. Numerous pretentious mansions, known as cottages, survive in Newport and are a focal point for tourists. Their opulence contrasts with the restrained elegance of architectural gems surviving from Newport's colonial heyday—among them the Redwood Library, Holy Trinity Church, and Touro Synagogue—and unwittingly frames the story of class divisions in this harbor city when set against the miraculously preserved neighborhoods of modest artisan and worker homes from both the revolutionary period and later Irish immigration. Others besides the elite enjoy Rhode Island's coastal resources. Public beaches and fishing areas abound and dot the map with melodious, evocative names like Misquamicut, Quonochontaug, Moonstone, and Matunuck.

An 11-foot-high bronze statue known as the *Independent Man* has sat atop the capitol dome in Providence since 1899, and the state flag and seal feature an anchor that bears the word *Hope*, devices adopted in the 17th century. Independence, stability, and hope have been more than symbols for Rhode Island; these ideals have guided its people through their highs and lows, as well as their times of magnanimity and ignobility, and certainly will play a significant role in the future.

Paul Buhle, Scott Molloy, and Gail Sansbury, eds., *A History of Rhode Island Working People* (1983); Federal Writers' Project of the Works Progress Administration for the State of Rhode Island, *Rhode Island: A Guide to the Smallest State* (1937); Rowland Gibson Hazard, comp., *The Jonny-Cake Papers of "Shepherd Tom" Together with Reminiscences of Narragansett Schools of Former Days by Thomas Robinson Hazard* (1968 [1915]); Sydney V. James, *Colonial Rhode Island: A History* (1975); Gary Kulik and Julia C. Bonham, *Rhode Island: An Inventory of Historic Engineering and Industrial Sites* (1978); Glenn W. LaFantasie, ed., *The Correspondence of Roger Williams* (1988); William G. McLoughlin, *Rhode Island: A History* (1986); Marion I. Wright and Robert J. Sullivan, *The Rhode Island Atlas* (1982).

William M. Ferraro

Samplers Making a sampler—a piece of cloth embroidered in cross-stitch with numerals, letters of the alphabet, and often a pictorial scene rendered in more elaborate stitches—was an essential part of a young lady's education in New England throughout the 17th, 18th, and first half of the 19th centuries.

One of the few acceptable forms of artistic expression permitted women, samplers were worked by those whose family possessed the financial means to secure tutelage. Most of the girls were the daughters of merchant-class families. Their average age was 11, with instruction often beginning at about five but rarely continuing beyond 15.

Seventeenth-century samplers were stylistically English in manner. Narrow bands of about 18 to 20 inches in length by 12 inches in width, the form could easily be rolled for storage and referred to later as a guide for duplicating stitches and decorative patterns for bands and borders. Surviving examples of New England samplers of this period are rare; they include those worked by Loara Standish of the Plymouth Colony, about 1640–50, and by Mary Hollingworth of Salem, Mass., around 1664.

By the early 18th century, the stitching of samplers embellished with flowers, fruit, decorative banding, and pictorial scenes was frequently included in a young woman's course of study. Public buildings often served as the sampler's central decorative focus, while the use of a moral verse extolling virtue or the need to prepare to meet the Lord was common. Allusions to death in an age of high childhood mortality rates were pervasive. Among the more common verses found on cross-stitch samplers was the popular

[Child's name] is my name
England is my nation
Portsmouth is my dwelling place
And Christ is my salvation.

Between 1750 and 1775 a uniquely New England freedom of form began to characterize samplers. American sampler makers never again looked to England for direction in creating these unique needleworks. The finished product, which by this time had assumed either a squarer or a broader, shorter oblong shape, served as a lasting emblem of the maker's abilities. In the days preceding the advent of the sewing machine and mass-produced consumer goods, most women made regular use of the needle in their roles as wives and mothers. Household linens and clothing needed constant attention.

After the American Revolution, the number of seminaries for female education increased greatly. The benefits of educating females was widely embraced, and sermons, treatises, and discourses on female education together with regular newspaper items reached a groundswell in the final decade of the 18th century in every major New England center. Alexander Pope's quotation "'Tis education forms the common mind / Just as the twig is bent, the tree's inclined" commonly appeared on embroidery samplers and in advertisements for schools.

The number of schools offering instruction for young women, both public and private, burgeoned during the first quarter of the 19th century. Many of these schools included instruction in the "useful and ornamental arts." These included needlework, painting, and drawing. Male instructors engaged the services of a preceptress to provide instruction in needlework. The preceptress prepared the linen ground for the child by marking the selected pattern and then tutored her in the proper use of the needle to achieve the desired effect. Like institutions catering to the education of males, some young women's schools earned reputations recognized beyond their state's borders, including Susanna Rowson's Academy in Boston; Mrs. Saunders and Miss Beach's Academy in Dorchester, Mass.; Mary Balch's School in Providence; the Reverend Timothy Alden's Academy in Portsmouth, N.H.; and the Misses Martin's School in Portland, Maine.

As the 19th century progressed, the vogue for making samplers faded, giving way to new forms of schoolgirl art, some of which were geared to a faster, simpler method of achieving similar needlework effects. Berlin work and its punch card "Home Sweet Home" technology offered instant gratification. After 1840 ornamental needlework as a primary subject in the education of girls ceased to occupy a place of prominence. Samplers were seldom produced after this time, and women's education began to emphasize the academic over the ornamental.

Although the tradition of making samplers can be traced over time to all American states, New England produced the vast majority, and, consequently, most surviving examples can be found here in local museums and town historical societies. Samplers and needlework pictures, rarely exhibited today by major art institutions, are nonetheless among the most visible and engaging objects composing the legacy of schools that existed in early New England and of the young needlewomen who populated them.

Ethel Stanwood Bolton and Eva Johnston Coe, *American Samplers* (1921); Glee F. Krueger, *New England Samplers to 1840* (1978); John F. LaBranche and Rita F. Conant, *In Female Worth and Elegance: Samplers and Needlework Students and Teachers in Portsmouth, New Hampshire, 1741–1840* (1996); Betty Ring, *Girlhood Embroidery: American Samplers and Pictorial Needlework, 1650–1850* (1993).

Rita F. Conant and John F. LaBranche

Seafood

In the old City Hall in Boston, an imposing wooden carving of a codfish hangs high in the public gallery of the historic House of Representatives. Nearly 5 feet in length and referred to as the Massachusetts Sacred Cod, the carving was presented to the legislature in 1784 by the Boston merchant Jonathan Rowe to remind the members of the importance of seafood, a commodity that brought economic prosperity to Massachusetts and the other New England colonies—as well as to Rowe himself, after whom a major commercial pier in Boston is named. The economic, political, and social roles seafood has played in the development of New England as a region are vital.

From the time of the earliest colonial settlements (and even earlier), seafood was a major source of food for New Englanders. Finfish and shellfish were not only readily available, they were also highly popular elements in the diets of all classes of society. An early example of how widespread the consumption of seafood was in New England can be found in 1652, when the Puritan legislators decreed that codfish, haddock, hake, and pollack could not be taken during the winter months because these were their time for spawning.

Recipe collections and cookbooks from colonial and early American times show that seafood was enjoyed year-round in a variety of dishes. Fish cakes, such as salt-cod cakes, were extremely popular, as were fish stews and chowders. Recipes for fried fish, fish hash, scalloped fish casseroles, and pickled, roasted, or boiled fish were common. Oysters, cod, haddock, mackerel, lobster, halibut, bluefish, and shad were also popular in 19th-century New England.

Chowder, which today might be considered the quintessential New England dish, did not originate in New England. Food historians tell us that references to chowder are centuries old; the word itself is of French origin, deriving from *chaudière*, the cauldron in which the fish stew was cooked. Although today New England chowder is almost always identified as clam chowder, until the mid-19th century New England chowders were made with fish; clams were added only occasionally. Old New England recipes for chowders call for fresh fish, salt pork, onions, water, and either potatoes or (more commonly) hard biscuits to thicken the chowder. Chowder recipes did *not* call for milk or cream; milk was not used in chowder until the mid-19th century, and its use was not widespread until the early 20th century. The popular chowders of today, made with hard-shell clams (quahogs), potatoes, and lots of milk or cream—and no salt pork!—are a far cry from their antecedents. But whether made with fish or clams, clear or milk broth, "genuine" New England chowder never has tomatoes.

Through the early 20th century, seafood was more standard in the New England diet than it is today. And narratives, cookbooks, and restaurant menus reveal that a much greater variety of seafood was eaten earlier than is the case now. Approximately three dozen species of finfish and shellfish were enjoyed by New Englanders during the 18th and 19th centuries, compared to the scant dozen that are popular today. Some of the most popular choices today—swordfish, scallops, mussels, and tuna, for example—were not favored in earlier times. Seafood is now one of the more expensive "meat" choices, but in colonial times and through the early part of the 20th century, the price of most seafood made it accessible to even the poorest.

Before commercial refrigeration, fish had to be sold as soon as they were unloaded from the boat. The fish could be either fresh or preserved—until the middle of the 19th century, this usually meant salted and dried, the primary method of preserving fish. Acres of land in coastal New England were devoted to drying salted fish on flakes, long wooden racks set up off the ground, with good exposure to sunlight. Old photographs of New England ports show fish flakes stretching back endlessly from the piers and fish houses. But in the 1920s Clarence Birdseye introduced his quick-freezing process, and that advance, along with commercial-scale filleting, helped make "fresh" ocean fish available across the nation.

Seafood harvested in the waters off New England is considered a delicacy around the world. Maine lobster is famous in places as far away as Norway and Japan, and the state is the country's leading supplier of fresh lobster, producing more than 62 million pounds in 2002. Oyster farming in Long Island Sound off the coast of Connecticut, which has been done commercially for more than 150 years, remains a strong business today. Rhode Island is the nation's largest supplier of squid, selling more than 18 million pounds in 2002. During the 1980s, New Bedford, Mass., was the country's most profitable fishing port. This was due not only to the size of the fleet and the catches but also to the quantities of scallops and yellowtail flounder in the total landings, both of which command high prices. Fishing still plays a strong role in Massachusetts; it is responsible for nearly a third of the state's economy. According to the National Oceanic and Atmospheric Administration (NOAA) Division of Fisheries, in 2002 New England produced about 29,000 tons of seafood. The opportunity to eat fresh seafood is regularly cited by tourists as one of the top reasons for visiting New England.

More than a third of America's supply of seafood comes from waters off New England, even though this area makes up only 7.3 percent of the total U.S. coastline. There are more than 2,000 species of finfish in these coastal waters, but of this number only about 500 are harvested for human food. Out of that 500, fewer than 20 are popular with American consumers today, although recent nutritional advice to increase seafood consumption for better health—seafood is low in calories and high in Omega-3 fatty acids, potassium, calcium, phosphorous, and zinc—has brought about an increased demand for seafood. To help meet that demand, New Englanders are being reintroduced to underutilized species such as hake, skate, and squid and may soon find that their choices in the fish market are as varied as those of their ancestors.

Kim Bartlett, *The Finest Kind* (1977); Russell Bourne, *The View from Front Street* (1989); Jeremy Collie, *The Changing Face of New England Fisheries* (1994); James B. Connolly, *The Book of Gloucester Fishermen* (1927); William Finn, *The Dragger* (1970); Andrew German, *What's the Catch?* (1994); Mark Kurlansky, *Cod* (1997); Raymond McFarland, *The Masts of Gloucester* (1937); Martha W. Murphy, *A New England Fish Tale* (1997); Sandra L. Oliver, *Saltwater Foodways: New Englanders and Their Food, at Sea and Ashore, in the 19th Century* (1995).

Martha W. Murphy

Seasons New England's four distinct seasons have helped define the region for natives and visitors alike. The same is true for the region's writers, many of whom have looked to the climate for subject matter and inspiration. From the depths of a Maine winter to the glories of autumn in Vermont, seasonal change has enabled writers to tie their works closely to the rhythms of the year. From the earliest days of colonization through the present, awareness of the seasons has been a hallmark of New England creative life. The seasons provide powerful images of New England identity, often representing the psychology or character of the region's people, but the experience of the seasons in New England has also generated powerful ideas over the centuries about human nature and American life that transcend the region.

The artistic and literary use of New England's seasons generally takes one of two principal forms. One form uses the cycle of seasons to metaphorically explain the patterns of birth, death, and renewal that operate at all levels of the landscape. With its predictable repetition, the flow of the seasons enables writers and artists to organize their materials in meaningful ways for their audience. Moreover, close attention to the unfolding cycle of life focuses the literary and artistic eye on specific features of the land. The second form concentrates on the experience and meaning of one season as it stands for the essential image and idea of New England. In both configurations, one can see a conflict of regional philosophies about human nature and the environment. In the Puritan view, nature and its cycles were evidence of the presence of sin and death: redemption is possible, and nature's cycles are a metaphor for that, but salvation transcends the seasons. The Transcendentalist view connected the human spirit to nature's seasons, affirming the significance of the seasons to the formation of character in those closest to nature. Surely these images are mixed in New Englanders' individual dispositions as well as in philosophies based in pragmatism and the modern ecological sciences, from William James to Rachel Carson.

Anne Bradstreet is an example of an early New England writer consciously organizing

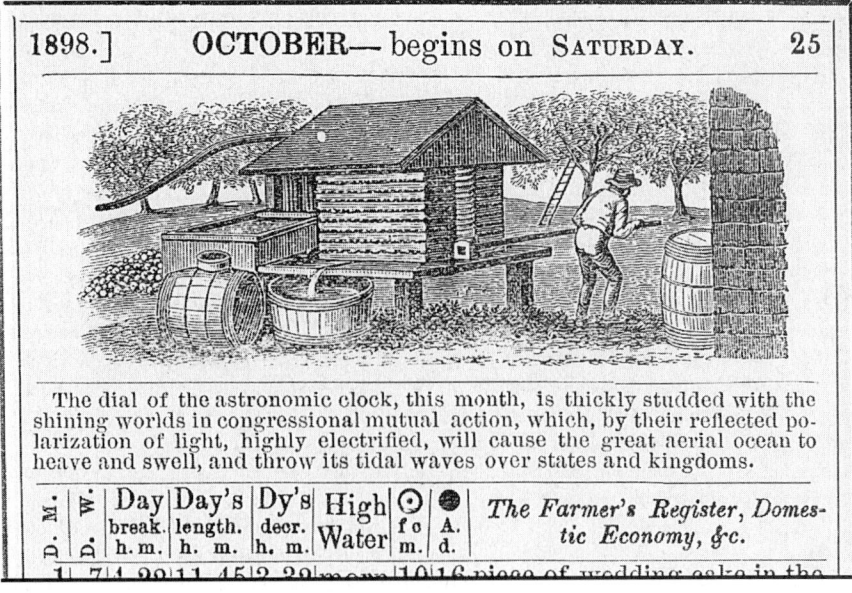

"October," Leavitt's Farmer's Almanac (Improved) *(1898)*

her work around the calendar. Although its details are not specifically drawn from New England, her early poem "The Four Seasons of the Year" connects a typical 17th-century agricultural economy to the segments of the year. She marks each season by the fruits of its harvest. Bradstreet's year unfolds in an orderly manner as she devotes one section of nearly equal length to each of the four seasons. An almanac conceived as poetry, each section notes the monthly position of the sun and the temperature one can expect as the year progresses. Throughout the poem she organizes the physical materials of her landscape—its colors, sounds, and textures—by indicating the time and sequence of the emerging fauna. Thoreau follows a similar plan in *Walden* (1854), although he traces a less rigidly structured pattern of seasons than Bradstreet does. Thoreau frees himself to devote far more time to his summer meditations than to those at other times of the year. He expands or compresses discussions of fall, winter, and spring depending on the overall need of the narrative. Still, Thoreau maps his exploration of the simple life against the seasonal cycle of time.

In *The Twelve Seasons of the Year* (1949), the nature writer Joseph Wood Krutch used the yearly cycle in ways that combined the order of Bradstreet and the flexibility of Thoreau. He offers comparable chapters for each month while paying particular attention to the disparities between the calendar and his own sense of the changing seasons on his Connecticut farm. Rather than marking the start of spring by the equinox, Krutch hails the new season only when the peepers begin to sing. Since the songs can first be heard any time between the middle of March and the beginning of April, Krutch cannot predict the precise arrival of spring. He knows it will come, but must pay close attention to the natural world to know when that time is.

In the second, more common, method of presenting New England's seasons authors meditate on specific seasons rather than the cycle. Because of its legendary severity, New England's winter has received more such attention than its counterparts. Early European colonists were struck by the depth of the region's cold. While exploring the coast of Maine in 1604, for example, Samuel de Champlain complained, "There are six months of winter in this country." Although some writers such as William Bradford believed that the climate grew warmer as the 17th century progressed, the early accounts of New England winter proved hard to dispute. They helped solidify the popular image of a cold and harsh climate.

Whether harsh or not, New England winters have often been presented as a season that tests one's endurance. Emily Dickinson found the winter months particularly difficult. She likened frost to a "blond Assassin" that "beheads" all in its path. Encouraged by "an Approving God," Dickinson's winter checks the exuberance displayed in her poems of summer and spring. Elsewhere she wrote that the sharp "Slant of light" common to winter afternoons "oppresses, like the Heft / Of Cathedral Tunes." Robert Frost's several winter poems also remark on the season's capacity to isolate. By forcing us to draw deeply on our own resources, Frost's winter encloses us in what Emerson called the "tumultuous privacy of storm." In "Stopping by Woods on a Snowy Evening," for example, the speaker, drawn equally by the eerie beauty of the storm and the sense that he should be moving on, resignedly reminds himself that he has "miles to go" before he can sleep. In "An Old Man's Winter Night," Frost presents a winter chill that "looked darkly in" at an old man who forgets why he has gone to the window to gaze out. Frost offers a terrifying vision, one in which we can imagine a landscape filled with old men shut in by New England's wintry gales. In Edith Wharton's *Ethan Frome* (1911) and Ernest Hebert's *The Dogs of March* (1995) such winter brooding climaxes in violence.

Others, however, have seen aesthetic and intellectual power in New England winters. William Cullen Bryant, for example, claimed that winter "boasts / Splendors beyond what gorgeous Summer knows." In his 1842 essay "A Winter Walk," Thoreau discovered that "primeval nature is still working and making tracks in the snow." If we know where and how to look, Thoreau claimed, the winter rewards us with a "sturdy innocence, a Puritan toughness." John Greenleaf Whittier's *Snow-Bound* (1866) is the classic presentation of the domestic intimacies and cultural renewal a blizzard's isolation can foster. The poet and essayist James Russell Lowell also believed that winter's austerity revealed beauties that other seasons concealed. While many people associate winter with old age or death, Lowell called the season a "wide-awake boy" for the wondrous possibilities present in the otherwise quiet landscape.

While winters have been represented in various ways, nearly everyone agrees on the beauty of New England's autumns. Thoreau's late essay "Autumnal Tints" offers both a naturalist's and a poet's view of the season's charms. Thoreau describes autumn as an unfolding work of art that progresses from one type of flora to another. The earliest to turn are the grasses, which by late August reveal the first signs of summer's end. By late September the red maples "have been conspicuously changing for a week," followed in turn by the several varieties of elm. As the leaves begin to fall, the ground becomes part of the celebration of color. "A queen," Thoreau remarks, "might be proud to walk where these gallant trees have spread their bright cloaks in the mud."

The minister and novelist Henry Ward Beecher viewed autumn as a beautiful release from other yearly concerns. From the hills above the Housatonic River valley, Beecher imagined the sun looking down "upon the labors of its fiery hands with complacency." Free to simply marvel at the surroundings, Beecher describes an endless autumn in which the work of the year has been done and the days can be spent in a guilt-free idyll.

The portion of fall that most confounds the sense of the orderly progress of time is Indian summer, the period of unseasonable warmth following the first killer frosts. "These are the days when Birds come back," Dickinson wrote, a time "when skies resume" the "old sophistries of June." The 20th-century poet Philip Booth likened Indian summer in Vermont to "days lost / somewhere in August"; it is the "other summer / summer twice come." The sensual delights of Indian summer, however, betray sexual unease in the Puritan tradition, in the provocative opening of Grace Metalious's *Peyton Place* (1956): "Indian Summer is like a woman. Ripe, hotly passionate, but fickle, she comes and goes as she pleases so that one is never sure whether she will come at all, nor for how long she will stay."

Summer and spring have received slightly less attention, no doubt because they seem less obviously dramatic than New England's winter and fall. While Thoreau ended the cyclical *Walden* with spring, he did so less in celebration of the sounds and textures than for the sense of renewal that it brings. "In a pleasant spring morning all men's sins are forgiven," he wrote at the end of the book. Of the major New England writers, Dickinson offers perhaps the most consistent celebration of the region's milder seasons. In "A Little Madness in the Spring" she praises "This Whole Experiment of Green," associating the "tremendous scene" with the majesty of God. Elsewhere, she writes that the sheer exaltation of the returning migratory bird fills the air with "shouts for joy to Nobody / But his seraphic self." New Englanders do associate the joys of spring with two particular difficulties that combine hope and despair: mud season and baseball's opening day. Mud season ranges in date from late February to early April and is so named because of the depth of mud on unpaved roads caused when the upper layers of the earth thaw while the deep frost of winter lingers below. Firm roads at dawn are quagmires by noon. As Mark Twain said, "In the spring I have counted one hundred and thirty-six different kinds of weather inside of four-and-twenty hours."

Robert Frost's "Two Tramps in Mud Time" locates the uncertainty of spring as a defining feature of northern New England, where one still chops firewood in March and April. This characteristic of spring and mud season suggests that no joy in New England is unalloyed, no hope unshadowed by the prospect of failure and black flies, all of which somehow build character. New England's nature writers have made spring their season, since particular features of the landscape, including spring pools, migrating birds, and fish runs, define the region. For example, David Carroll's "wet-sneaker trilogy" chronicles the fate of turtles and salamanders in the fragile spring environment. Rachel Carson's *Silent Spring* (1962) evokes environmental catastrophe to question assumptions about the continuity of the seasons.

New England's summer lacks the metaphoric richness that has made the other seasons such popular literary subjects. Moderately warm and nearly always pleasant, the season offers a three-month respite from the intensity of its counterparts. Other than Dickinson, who wrote upward of 200 poems for which summer serves as a major theme, few New England writers have turned to the physical nature of the season for subject matter. In William Dean Howells's novel *The Rise of Silas Lapham* (1880), summer was a time when the wealthy left Boston. Even Thoreau's *Walden,* in which summer occupies most of the narrative, the most intense descriptions of the landscape occur in the sections devoted to winter. There are notable exceptions, such as Edith Wharton's *Summer* (1917), a steamy, erotic interlude, as well as Donald Hall's *String Too Short to Be Saved* (1979), *Seasons at Eagle Pond* (1987), and his baseball poems. Each season apparently has its literary function: winter tests our endurance, fall captivates our eyes, and spring allows us to begin again, but New England's summer seems beyond the power of art. Its serenity works well in such paintings as the Gloucester seascapes of Fitz Hugh Lane, but the region's writers—Dickinson excepted—have found the other seasons more imaginatively rich.

The Hartford-based poet Wallace Stevens, however, turned summer's apparent lack of drama into verse. In "Credences of Summer" the speaker says of summer, "Let's see the very thing and nothing else. / Let's see it with the hottest fire of sight." Demanding a seasonal vision that finds meaning in the specific, Stevens wished to "Trace the gold sun about the whitened sky / Without evasion by a single metaphor." By turning to "the essential barrenness" of summer—by emphasizing the very lack of metaphor—Stevens found rich-

ness in this New England season. His lines prove what the Puritan poet Anne Bradstreet wrote in the middle of the 17th century: "Every season has its charms."

Artists no less than writers have defined the image of New England's seasons. From the first paintings by Thomas Cole of autumn foliage in New Hampshire's Crawford Notch, fall's beauties were favored by Hudson River and White Mountain School artists who followed him. Frederick Edwin Church and Edward Shapleigh painted luxuriant fall scenes, communicating to 19th-century viewers the mingling of Christian and romantic spiritual values to be found in the landscape. As New England's social and economic fortunes declined in the late 19th century, the fall palate darkened in the works of George Inness and Winslow Homer. Winter genre scenes of New England were the stock in trade of such genre painters as John Durrie, whose scenes became Currier and Ives prints in the 1800s and are still reprinted. Images of fortitude amid frost and country occupations and pleasures like ice cutting, maple sugaring, skating, and sleighing seemed to assure city dwellers in industrial America that traditional life persisted in New England. Such images are perpetuated in films and television. Certain holidays, such as Thanksgiving and Christmas, and certain psychological conditions or character types dominate New England films, from *White Christmas* (1954) to *Affliction* (1997). New England's dramatic seasonal changes, with seasons that embody a distinctive set of cultural values, drive the plots and characters of many of Stephen King's books and movies.

Popular images of and ideas about New England's moody seasons might best be represented by Mark Twain's famously ironic remarks: "If you don't like the weather in New England, just wait a few minutes," and "I reverently believe that the Maker who made us all makes everything in New England but the weather."

Tim Armstrong, "'A Good Word for Winter': The Poetics of a Season," *New England Quarterly* (1987); Lawrence Buell, *The Environmental Imagination: Thoreau, Nature Writing and the Formation of American Culture* (1995); William Cronon, *Changes in the Land: Indians, Colonists, and the Ecology of New England* (1983); L. Edwin Folsom, "'The Souls That Snow': Winter in the Poetry of Emily Dickinson," *American Literature* (1975); Ernest Sanden, "Delight Delayed by Retrospect: Emily Dickinson's Summer Poems," *New England Quarterly* (1967); Adam W. Sweeting, *Beneath the Second Sun: A Cultural History of Indian Summer* (2003); Mark Twain, "New England Weather," in *Mark Twain's Speeches* (1910).

Adam W. Sweeting

Secular Shrines and Other Sacred Places

Sacred places are associated with the perceived, physical presence of some form of supernatural force or transcendent power; according to the historian of religion Mircea Eliade, they are sites where a "hierophany," or "irruption of the sacred," occurs. Shrines have a more specific function; they are places used for various forms of devotion, like the commemoration of holy persons or special events, and are usually found in conjunction with relics, monuments, or the tombs of glorified individuals. They often elicit feelings of esteem, veneration, and attachment in the individual who visits them.

The sacred has appeared in myriad ways in the region that is now New England. Most of the sacred spaces of Native Americans who occupied the region before contact—the Narragansett, Pequot, and Wampanoag—have been destroyed by European American settlement. The tourist industry and local historical societies have shaped the landscapes of the sacred in a manner that fuses religious veneration with both national memory and consumer ideology. Shrines and sacred places in New England take many forms: places in the natural environment, monuments and landmarks, and religious buildings.

Although there are numerous places in New England that have acquired particular symbolic power in the American imagination, before European Americans "tamed" the wilderness much of the natural world had, and still has, sacred significance for local Native Americans. Intimacy among the social, natural, and supernatural worlds, expressed in myths of origin, seasonal celebrations, and food rituals, characterized native cultures. Unlike the cosmology of the Christian settlers, the natural realm was not separate from the human and the divine; special powers circulated throughout the cosmos and linked humans with the natural world. Potentially, all places could be considered sacred. Along streams and rivers, up and down the eastern coastal region, in mountains, forests, and pastures, native peoples perceived special powers throughout their environment and tried to live in harmony with them. Some sacred natural and built environments still remain; the Narragansett have preserved their early meetinghouse and gather annually to commemorate the site in what is now Southport, Conn., of the Great Swamp Fight (1675), and Gay Head Wampanoags revere the clay cliffs of Martha's Vineyard, Mass.

Most European Americans do not assume that the sacred permeates all nature; there are, however, places on the landscape that have acquired a sacred significance in New England culture. Walden Pond in Massachusetts is one prominent example of how a specific natural site has become a revered place. Even though

Henry David Thoreau lived in a one-room cabin as an experiment in solitude and self-sufficiency in the 1840s, by the 1990s Walden Pond had become a tremendously popular tourist destination for travelers, many of whom felt a peculiar attachment to this famous body of water in the New England countryside. Plans for development around the pond in the 1980s were thwarted by a range of local and national organizations; representatives from these groups understood the area as a hallowed place with a unique, culturally powerful significance in American history in general and New England history in particular.

The White Mountains in New Hampshire and southern Maine define another natural region in New England that has long drawn people from all over the country. This national forest has been one of the most visited in the United States, and from the beginning visitors have expressed their sense of wonder in religious terms. As one 1856 guidebook states, the White Mountains were "consecrated to freedom"; a more recent guidebook includes the following, attributed to Daniel Webster, referring to the (now toppled) Old Man of the Mountain: "In the mountains of New Hampshire, God Almighty has hung out a sign to show that there He makes men." Hikers, skiers, backpackers, and other outdoor enthusiasts have appreciated the natural scenery and found adventure, rejuvenation, and mystery in the highest mountains in the northeast, several of which are named after local Native American leaders, such as Mount Passaconaway and Mount Kancamagus.

Natural locations offer one kind of sacrality; humanmade monuments throughout New England possess a similar religious meaning that makes them stand out from their environment. These sites have more to do with human milestones in New England and American history than natural locations do, but they evoke similar feelings of wonder, reverence, and respect. Sites associated with New England's founders, for instance, are frequently marked by monuments, such as Plymouth Rock in Massachusetts. The sacred adheres to these sites because they bring to mind the mysteries of death, the continuity of national identity, and the mythology of American origins; they also provide a ritual space for the perpetuation of a shared sense of history and American community.

Historic graveyards abound in New England. And while there are numerous burial grounds containing the famous dead in New England history, such as Mount Auburn Cemetery in Cambridge, Mass., and Sleepy Hollow Cemetery in Concord, Mass., where pilgrims leave offerings at the graves of Thoreau, Hawthorne, and Emerson on Authors Ridge, smaller, more anonymous graveyards can be found throughout the region. Visitors traveling the highways and byways of New England often stop to take pictures or examine gravemarkers in old burial grounds. The seemingly ancient iconography, which includes hourglasses, winged cherubs, and skulls and crossbones, combined with the stark textual reminders of mortality that frequently begin "Here lyes the body of . . . ," are simultaneously prosaic and exotic, contributing to the attraction many have to these locations. New England graveyards are imbued with the sacred because they evoke a distant society's familiarity with death and suggest generational continuities between the past and the present.

Museums can also be imbued with the sacred, especially when they are linked to both national history and present vitality. There are a variety of well-known, distinguished museums throughout New England that remind visitors of the region's illustrious place in American culture. Some, like the Submarine Force Museum located on the Thames River in Groton, Conn., celebrate military might and technological ingenuity—an increasingly potent mixture in the production of sacred places. The only submarine museum operated by the U.S. Navy, it contains documents, photographs, and exhibits that offer testimony to American control of the seas. The USS *Nautilus*, the world's first nuclear-powered ship, was built in Groton in 1954 and is adjacent to the museum. Now decommissioned, it is open to visitors who can stand in awe of America's military strength and expertise in harnessing nuclear power.

New England is also intimately linked to the birth of the nation, and landmarks commemorating the Revolutionary War are especially potent for visitors and tourists who travel through the area. While these landmarks can be found in a number of places, the towns of Lexington and Concord in Massachusetts are integral to the myth of origins in American public memory. The town green in Lexington and the North Bridge in Concord played a central role in the first battles between the minutemen and the British; they have subsequently became objects of patriotic veneration. The association between the New England minutemen, republican ideology, and national destiny in the local texts and monuments is especially critical to the sacralization of these and other landmarks of the American Revolution.

In a more conventionally religious sense, some of the most sacred places in New England are religious structures used specifically for various forms of devotion. These buildings may not have historic or national value, although many are tourist attractions for these very reasons; rather, the variety of religious structures offer sanctuaries where rituals and ceremonies that link humans with a divine, transcendent realm can be performed. In the increasingly multicultural environment of New England, and especially in larger cities where religious diversity has become a social reality, mosques, temples, gurdwaras, and synagogues share the local terrain with the more numerous Christian churches.

Various religious structures have their own characteristics and distinctive architectural styles. Some date from before the Revolution, while others have been dedicated within the past decade; some have a special significance for the religious community alone, others have particular value for reasons beyond communal usage by the local congregation. The oldest extant Jewish synagogue in the United States is the Touro Synagogue in Newport, R.I. This house of worship, built in 1763, has served the local Jewish population from the colonial era to the present. Although its plain exterior conveys little of the elegance found inside, it is an impressive building. The colonial design gives it a stately appearance, and the symbolism found within links worshipers to the Judaic tradition. The twelve Ionic columns that support the gallery where women worship represent the Tribes of Israel, and the Holy Ark directs congregants eastward toward Jerusalem. The Mother Church of Christian Science draws many visitors to Boston. The African Meeting House on Beacon Hill in Boston has become a shrine to the struggle for freedom. Monuments, plaques, and piles of stones left by pilgrims mark spots associated with the founders of religious movements, including the Mormon founder Joseph Smith, the Christian Science founder Mary Baker Eddy, and Shaker founders Mother Ann Lee and Father William Lee.

There are numerous historic Christian churches in New England, with many of the most famous concentrated in downtown Boston. Believers, patriots, and tourists visit these sacred sites both because of their association with the nation's history and because they continue to be used for religious purposes. Christ Church, also known as the Old North Church, is situated in Boston's North End and is a site on the Freedom Trail; it was built in 1723 and is the city's oldest standing church. An architectural treasure, the Old North Church is also celebrated in American history: the lanterns warning Paul Revere about the British military movement were hung in its steeple.

New England hosts a wide assortment of religious traditions from all over the world. While many immigrant religious communities worship in houses, community centers, or office parks—transforming secular space into sacred space—some have tried to build religious structures that carry on stylistic traditions from their home countries. One example of this can be found in Ashland, Mass. The Sri Lakshmi Temple was the first Hindu temple in New England constructed according to a typical Hindu model. Consecrated in 1990, the temple is home to four shrines that contain images of four Hindu deities. Indian immigrants from all over New England visit and worship at this sacred site, where lectures, pujas, and communal celebrations take place throughout the year.

As a result of both historical forces and contemporary demographic change, New England culture has provided a context for the appearance of numerous hierophonies. Shrines and sacred places do not appear according to one common cosmic vision and religious sensibility; instead, multiple religious communities have found, and tried to maintain, the presence of the sacred in a variety of settings in the New England region.

Catherine Albanese, *Nature Religion in America: From the Algonkian Indians to the New Age* (1990); Dona Brown, *Inventing New England: Regional Tourism in the 19th Century* (1995); David Chidester and Edward T. Linenthal, *American Sacred Space* (1995); Diana Eck, ed., *World Religions in Boston* (1996); Mircea Eliade, *The Sacred and the Profane: The Nature of Religion* (1987); John A. Grim and Donald P. St. John, "The Northeast Woodlands," in *Native American Religions: North America*, ed. Lawrence E. Sullivan (1987); Edward Tabor Linenthal, *Sacred Ground: Americans and Their Battlefields* (1991).

Gary Laderman

Souvenirs A souvenir is a concrete reminder of the intangible. When one purchases a souvenir, the goal ostensibly is to possess something that will evoke memories of a place and of the buyer's experiences there or to demonstrate to a loved one that he or she was thought of in that place. A souvenir is also representative of the place where it was obtained, in its use or design or by the words and images on it. The "Made in China" sticker on the bottom of the Maine moose coffee mug seems to contradict the authenticity of the item.

Some souvenir buyers are collectors who create and order a world of antique spoons and china or snow globes and shot glasses. But even when buying a single item, a buyer is choosing from a selection of cultural markers that influence his or her reading of a place to create an imagined world in which that place holds a specific meaning. The New England constructed by most of its souvenirs occupies a mental space that tourists and natives alike literally buy into, perhaps to reassure themselves of a place where life is imagined to be

Souvenirs of Maine for sale in Kittery, 2002

slower and values more traditional, and where history—embodied by Revolutionary War soldiers, accused witches, and escaped slaves—still walks. In the act of purchasing the souvenir, the buyer engages in an interpretation of a place. Throughout the past 150 years, souvenirs have been tied tightly to identity, class, commercialization, and the complex role New England has played in American culture.

Before tourism began, souvenirs as we know them didn't exist. Dona Brown points out that when wealthy 18th-century travelers came to New England, they stopped in Hartford or Boston as part of their tour of major American cities. Wealthy and well connected, tourists engaged in social activities with other notable citizens, attending church, visiting institutions, and making excursions to the mills of Lowell or the shipyards of Salem, Mass. New England was known for its thriving industrialism and modern cities, rather than for its lakes, mountains, or shore.

In the first half of the 19th century, demand for a concrete representation of New England grew as wealthy urban elites from Boston and New York came for the summer season. Nahant, Mass., and Newport, R.I., were established as seaside destinations by the 1830s, but the White Mountains were by far the nation's favorite tourist destination, second only to Niagara Falls. Travel to the mountains was seen as a pilgrimage to encounter the sublime, and souvenirs were relics of that experience. Paintings were, for their owners, a claim to the scenery or at least identified them as possessing higher sensibilities.

Besides paintings, the only souvenirs to depart in the trunks and pockets of these early White Mountains visitors were ephemera—paper goods from hotels or railroads, such as menus and brochures. By the mid-1850s, guidebooks were produced for various New England destinations as an interest in history grew along with national consciousness. These early pictorial guides canonized local legends, some part fact and some part myth, and established the content and format that continue to define area guides to the present. Tourists could also purchase cartes de visites, small photos and prototypes for the later postcard, but they were not the de facto travel correspondence and souvenir they are today.

Some natural or homemade items served as souvenirs. In the O'Connor souvenir collection displayed at the Flume Gorge and Gilman Visitors' Center in Franconia Notch, N.H., are a 19th-century walking stick carved by Hermit Jack and locally made spruce gum. Locals and travelers chipped pieces off of Plymouth Rock, as Alexis de Tocqueville observed in 1835. In Connecticut, visitors pocketed acorns and leaves from the Charter Oak, which, after it fell in 1856, was turned into numerous objects that were sold as souvenirs. But these local and unique examples are the exceptions, not the rule. Most New England souvenirs were mass-produced, often manufactured abroad, and followed national trends.

The souvenir industry exploded with three successive popular culture trends after the Civil War: stereoscopic views, souvenir china, and spoons. Until this time, collecting was an idiosyncratic hobby of a few individuals. But with the ability to mass-produce inexpensive consumer items and the increasing democratization of travel with railroads, the collecting impulse turned into a cultural fervor.

The first mania was the collecting of stereoscopic views, long cards with two images that create a three-dimensional illusion. Stereoscopic views became hugely popular in 1865 and continued to be a source of home entertainment for 40 years. Many of their photographers were located in the White Mountains, including perhaps the most famous among them, the Kilburn brothers of Littleton, N.H. But interest in White Mountains paintings and the particular appreciation for landscape began to fade.

The International Centennial Exhibition of 1876 and the Colonial Revival triggered a new enthusiasm for commercially produced souvenir items of all types, particularly souvenir china. These ceramic plates, pitchers, and other items were made in English, German, and eventually Japanese factories. Drugstores in virtually every town, large and small, sold ceramic wares bearing a local image, usually from a stereoscopic view or photograph and ranging from a banal shot of a downtown rotary to Charlestown's Bunker Hill Monument and Newport's Old Stone Mill. Unlike earlier historical china, which was used on the table, these souvenir pieces were for show and were often placed on the railing running beneath the dining room ceiling or along the wainscoting. The mass production of images on ceramics coincided with a change in the perception of New England: from a place of modern cities and awe-inspiring mountains it became one of nostalgic quaintness.

A jewelry store in Salem, Mass., Daniel Low and Company, launched America's souvenir spoon craze with the Salem Witch spoons in 1891. Through spoons, iconographic depictions of the region's history and topography gained currency. Very often these spoons showed historic homes and birthplaces of such writers as Longfellow and events like Roger Williams's purchase of Providence from the Narragansett. Even while local silver manufacturers such as Gorham Manufacturing Company of Providence, Towle Manufacturing Company of Newburyport, Mass., and the William B. Durgin Company of Concord, N.H., were producing souvenir spoons in great numbers, New England's formerly thriving cities were in recession. Interest spread from the mountains to the older fishing towns along the coast, from a view of New England as a place of industrial progress and progressive ideas to a place of old homes and simple ways.

Although even 18th-century travelers collected Native American "curiosities" to put in their cabinets, increased travel in the late 19th century greatly increased the production and consumption of these items. Abenaki and Micmac Indians traveled seasonally from Canada to resorts in New Hampshire and Maine to sell baskets, miniature canoes, beadwork, and embroidery—all specifically created for tourist consumption. What Ruth B. Phillips terms "souvenir art" created by Native Americans was a complex synthesis of popular culture and traditional art, both influenced by and influencing the other.

After World War I, the souvenir market expanded with a staggering variety of designs and materials. Native American art was replaced by manufactured versions using similar symbols. The postcard replaced the stereoscopic view. Souvenir china and spoons continued to be bought and sold along with an avalanche of playing cards, pennants, figurines, coasters, salt and pepper shakers, and dolls. Most souvenir collectors bemoan the decline they see in the quality and taste of souvenirs since Victorian times. The change in the value and quality of these items reflects the budgets of the middle- and working-class "day-trippers" who were able to visit tourist areas in automobiles.

The variety of souvenirs could also be seen as reflecting the more individualized pattern that tourism was taking. Whereas 19th-century tourists all arrived at the same destination following the train schedules, motorized tourists, who were free to take any route and stop anywhere they liked, created different patterns. Instead of flocking to grand resorts, 20th-century tourists of various classes went camping, stopped at sleep-away cabins and motels along the highway, and rented summer homes. They might sightsee, hike mountain trails, swim at the beach, visit a museum or theme park, or do little else but shop for souvenirs. Souvenirs increasingly sentimentalized the region as a place old and simple, removed from the modern marketplace. These cultural trends sometimes pleasingly intersected in such oddities as miniature Pilgrims enduring the eternal Plymouth winter within a snow globe.

Another explanation for the more whimsical nature of souvenirs is their heavy consumption by children. Susan McConnel suggests that children's particular interest in souvenirs is owing to their desire to obtain markers of their own histories. Some shop owners have observed that adults may buy an inexpensive souvenir because it reminds them of their childhood, thereby establishing another function of the tourist souvenir as a remembrance of one's childhood or an idealized version of it.

Until recently, the version of New England celebrated by New England souvenirs reflected the Anglo-Saxon experience. But since the Civil Rights movement, a conscious attempt has been made to debunk the myth of white, middle-class New England. Historical interpretations at Strawbery Banke in Portsmouth, N.H., and Plimoth Plantation in Massachusetts have widened to include the original Native American communities as well as Jewish, African American, and immigrant experiences. African American freedom trails commemorate New England's participation in the Underground Railroad. The image of New Haven's *Amistad,* a ship reconstructed in 2000 after the vessel was made famous in Steven Spielberg's movie depicting the historic slave rebellion and its aftermath in 1839–40, adorns fleece vests and mouse pads.

The owner of the Afro-American Museum of History store in Boston claims that she doesn't carry souvenirs in her shop, just high-end jewelry, T-shirts, and gifts. To her, the word *souvenir* has become synonymous with inauthentic or cheaply made items. But as a growing corporate culture results in the "malling" of historic downtowns, a sense of nostalgia is rising for midcentury America's unabashed celebration of the road and its tacky souvenirs. Such books as *Roadside America* and *Road Trip USA* resist the McDonald's and Disney versions of the tourist experience. In this perspective, the snow globe would be seen as an authentic souvenir, much more so than the polo shirt or baseball cap with an embroidered theme park logo.

The most popular souvenirs in New England today are probably postcards and T-shirts. Some favorite T-shirts carry the names of local microbreweries, such as Gritty McDuffs in Portland, Maine, or the Nutfield Brewing Company in Derry, N.H. Souvenir ceramics and spoons still sell as well as bumper stickers proclaiming "I Brake for Moose" and "This Car Climbed Mount Washington." In Rhode Island, the pineapple—a symbol of hospitality—and the Old Stone Mill appear frequently on key chains and patches. The very name Newport retains its suggestion of affluence and summer idylls and can sell a sun visor or coffee mug. In Connecticut, magnets and shot glasses bear images of the Charter Oak and the state's many lighthouses in Old Saybrook and New London. The romantic name Mystic Seaport goes home on sweatshirts and towels.

In Maine, the association with Native American commerce persists with Quoddy Moccasins. Balsam fir incense and stuffed pillows sell well, as do images of blueberries on pottery and linen. Outdoor sportsmen might buy or receive clothing adorned with a moose or fish, and an L. L. Bean emblem on a shirt suggests Maine just as much as the state's name does.

In Massachusetts, the Black Dog of Martha's Vineyard is ubiquitous, appearing on golf balls, windsocks, clothing, and travel mugs, as do Pilgrims, cranberries, and the name Cape Cod. Boston Red Sox, Celtics, and New England Patriots hats and shirts go home with sports fans. Beer mugs with emblems from the television show *Cheers* are still popular, years after the series ended. The Vermont cow is an international ambassador on the Ben and Jerry's logo designed by Woody Jackson. Maple sugar products are always on display or have whole stores devoted to them. Covered bridges are still major sellers on calendars, posters, and prints throughout the region.

In New Hampshire, one of the earliest symbols of New England, the Old Man of the Mountain, went from being a sign of God's hand to being a nationally recognized symbol of New England's firm abolitionist stance to being a quick roadside curiosity worth about a half hour's time on the way to more scenic destinations. Although it fell down in 2003 the profile of the "Great Stone Face" still appears on New Hampshire highway signs and license plates, but souvenir vendors have remarked that the image isn't as popular as the moose, lobster, or even the lowly seagull. Vendors do report an increased demand for items bearing the state motto, which shares space with the profile on New Hampshire's license plates: "Live Free or Die." Whether the tourist's feeling about these words is one of sarcasm or reverence, this new demand is an indication of what the country wants to see when it sees New England.

Dona Brown, *Inventing New England: Regional Tourism in the 19th Century* (1995); Richard Hamilton, "The Hotel Marketing Phenomenon: Souvenirs, Mementos, Advertising and Promotional Materials," *Historical New Hampshire* 42 (Spring 1995); Jamie Jenson, *Road Trip USA: New England* (2001); Thomas Starr King, *The White Hills; Their Legends, Landscape and Poetry* (1868); Ken Kirtby, *The New Roadside America* (1992); Werner Muensterberger, *Collecting: An Unruly Passion* (1995); Ruth B. Phillips, *Trading Identities: The Souvenir in Native North American Art from the Northeast, 1700–1900* (1998); Susan Stewart, *On Longing* (1984).

Laura Cuozzo

Stewart, Martha (1941–) Media personality and entrepreneur. Martha Stewart was born in Jersey City, N.J., to Edward and Martha Kostyra, second-generation Polish Catholics. She was reared in the small northern New Jersey town of Nutley, where she learned many of the domestic skills that would make her a household name. While studying art history at Barnard College in New York City (financed through scholarships and modeling jobs), she married a Yale law student, Andrew Stewart, with whom she had a daughter, Alexis. The "diva of domesticity," as fans have dubbed the multimedia personality, had a brief but successful career as a stockbroker in Manhattan. Like many young urban professionals in the late 1960s, she and her husband purchased and remodeled a weekend retreat in the Berkshire Mountains.

Stewart transformed her personal interest in architectural remodeling, organic gardening, chicken raising, tag sale shopping, and catering into business ventures that would ultimately lead her to write *Martha Stewart's New Old House,* a pictorial personal essay and how-to restoration manual, and several cookbooks. In 1973 she moved with her family to Westport, Conn., where she restored a Federal-style 1805 farmhouse, Turkey Hill. Stewart began a catering business in 1976 that became a billion-dollar venture within 10 years. She ran the business out of her basement kitchen, eventually opening a specialty shop in Westport.

In 1982 Stewart published her first book, the beautifully illustrated and extremely successful *Entertaining* (with Elizabeth Hawes), which would fuel her success as a media celebrity. Its high price, large size, and elaborate photography—from Stewart toiling in garden and kitchen to wedding cakes layered with fresh flowers and greenery—make *Entertaining* a coffee table book rather than a utilitarian guide to homemaking. Although Stewart has published more than 20 subsequent hardcover and paperback cooking and craft texts, *Entertaining* remains a paean to the work ethic and the aesthetic presentation of distinctly fresh cuisine through casually elegant entertaining. Although much of her subsequent work suggests a more urban and minimalist cuisine and aesthetic, *Entertaining* marks Stewart's appropriation and mass marketing of New England living as traditional American living. The groaning board visuals for "Our Farmhouse Thanksgiving for Eight" or "A Christmas Open House for Fifty" supply many subchapters in *Entertaining* that celebrate nostalgia for New England hearth and historical home. This romanticized image of New England has become more complex with the proposed sale of Turkey Hill—due, Stewart wrote, to the diminished quality of life in a town now more often lauded for its suburban proximity to New York than for its friendly charm—and with the purchase of Edsel Ford's summer estate on Mount Desert Island, Maine.

Having constructed herself as *the* resource for domestic instruction, Stewart has inspired millions in the United States and Canada with expert home-keeping advice on everything from gardening, cooking, and collecting to household repair and craft projects through Martha Stewart Living Omnimedia, a publicly traded company since 1999. Her glossy magazine *Living* has garnered top honors for magazine design, and her daily one-hour television show, *Martha Stewart Living,* received two Emmys. She has expanded these media ventures to include an interactive World Wide Web site, syndicated *Ask Martha* newspaper columns and radio spots, and a Martha Stewart Everyday line of paints and products for garden, kitchen, and bed and bath at K Mart.

At the height of her success, Stewart became embroiled in a securities fraud investigation. She was indicted in 2003, went to trial, and was convicted in 2004 of lying to government investigators about her sale of certain stock. She resigned as chair and CEO of Martha Stewart Living Omnimedia and began serving her five-month prison sentence in 2004.

While her fans are effusive in their admiration, her critics are less generous. Stewart has most often been taken to task for promoting overly fussy, time-consuming projects that invoke class- and race-bound privileges better left to the 19th century. But even her most practical, if excessive, busyness in the home has inspired a cottage industry of parodic publications and performances, to which she has often contributed in self-parodic performances on television talk shows.

Tom Connor, Jim Downey, and J. Barry O'Rourke, *Martha Stuart's Better Than You at Entertaining* (1996); Martha Stewart, "Fed Up in the Burbs, Martha Stewart Leaving," *New York Times Magazine,* April 9, 2000; Stewart, *Martha Stewart's New Old House: Renovating with Style* (1993).

Lynda Goldstein and Virginia A. Smith

Toys and Games Diversions and amusements in colonial New England were often born from labor. Children might turn arduous chores such as carrying wood or water into a race or contest; other games and toys were inventions of children's imaginations, and some, like tag, hide-and-seek, and hopscotch, are still played today. Toys were often made from found materials such as cornhusks, rags, and dried fruit. Children made many of their own toys spontaneously, creating chains with flowers or cradles and pillows with milkweed pods and seeds. Girls played cat's cradle, a yarn game allowing for a wide variety of figures, while boys played with popguns made from the twigs of elderberry bushes, whistles made from chestnuts, and toy weapons such as clubs, slingshots, and bows and arrows.

Early New England games such as tennis, cricket, and blindman's buff probably involved the entire family. Despite the threat of stiff fines, adults played card games at taverns, the social centers of the day, and cockfighting and animal baiting were also popular. Colonial sporting matches called "rough and tumbles" included maiming and eye gouging, while gentler pastimes included singing and playing music. Early board games were played on flat surfaces with pieces moved according to a roll of the dice or the turn of a card, and before the middle of the 19th century many provided religious and social instruction. After the Civil War, board games offered lessons in business success. All ages played "goose," an Italian pastime similar to Parcheesi.

The earliest New England dolls were cornhusk dolls, painted and costumed, the remnants of harvest festivals. Diaries reveal that children later played with wooden or rag dolls. Penny woodens, stiff and clumsy dolls carved from pine or maple, were popular even after the manufacture of more attractive dolls. Colonists also made dolls from dried apples, an art derived from the Iroquois. During the

Federal period, shops offered wigs for dolls as well as naked dolls so that children might dress them, usually in a manner resembling their owners. Some families had Sunday dolls that appeared once a week dressed in their best. As recreation gradually became acceptable on Sundays, children held tea parties for their dolls. Dollhouses made from birch bark and model kitchens initiated girls into the arts of housewifery. Children also played with toys having no evident social purpose: wooden tops, kites, hoops, balls, and jackstraws.

Few 17th- and 18th-century toys survive. Before 1850 New England toys were usually one-of-a-kind pieces, made by hand or in workshops. Small, carved figures of animals and humans were popular. Rarely signed, they ranged from a few inches in size to several feet. With a piece of wood and a jackknife, craftsmen could whittle individual pieces or groups for toy zoos or farmyard arrangements. Often containing more than 100 pieces, the Noah's Ark was a toy to be enjoyed only on the Sabbath. Toward the end of the 19th century, the Willimantic Thread Company in Connecticut offered Noah's Arks in paper cutouts. In the 1820s, Connecticut tinsmiths made simple tinplate toys such as bubble pipes and whistles. A decade later, William Tower, along with Joseph Jacobs and Crocker Wilder, organized the Tower Guild in South Hingham, Mass., a cooperative of craftsmen who made small toys and doll furniture.

Push and pull toys made of carved and painted woods were simple to make and use. Children pulled or pushed horses and other animals, and later planes and boats, set on wheels. The New England rocking horse, the most popular of carved toys, had broad plank rockers and a carved head; often it was difficult to distinguish from the European model. Later examples were fully carved, mounted on long, curved rockers. Mason and Converse Toy Company in Winchendon, Mass., at one time the world's largest wood toy factory, created horses on spring-drive frames that produced a bouncing motion. The bicycle was inspired by the velocipede, a horse-shaped seat mounted on a tricycle-like device. Horse designs later served for kiddie-cars, wagons, and ships.

Colonial children played with wooden toys animated by hand. Jumping jacks moved when the strings attached to their extremities were pulled. Stick-mounted figures had many forms: animals climbing a tree or ladder, chickens and birds pecking the ground in search of food. After 1850 toys were made with techniques developed during the Industrial Revolution and modeled after items in the real world. The Industrial Revolution saw the widespread manufacture of toys, and the production techniques of the 19th and 20th centuries allowed for tremendous output.

The Joel Ellis doll was the first wooden doll to be made commercially. In the largest manufacturing plant in Springfield, Vt., Ellis made doll carriages, wagons, hoops, sleds, small toys, and dolls. He patented 13 inventions, including a child's cab and the mortise-and-tenon joint for his wooden doll. This joint allowed the doll to pose in a variety of ways. Made in small, medium, and large sizes, the dolls were made in equal numbers of blondes and brunettes, the smaller sizes being the most popular. As financial depression struck and confidence in the doll market fell, Ellis manufactured the dolls for only one year, 1873.

Several New England firms made dollhouses, usually modeled after contemporary architectural rural styles. R. Bliss of Pawtucket, R.I., used lithographed paper to decorate wooden houses and mass-produce them for a larger audience. A major dollhouse producer, the firm created large, colorful houses in more than 40 styles and in sizes ranging from nine inches to 28 inches. Bliss also produced a variety of buildings, including barns, churches, skyscrapers, and stores, as well as board games. Morton and Converse printed dollhouse designs directly on wood, while Cass, a wooden toy manufacturer in Athol, Mass., produced simple dollhouses. Converse also made hobbyhorses and Noah's Arks and indeed produced so many toys in Winchendon that the town became known as Toy Town, USA.

Construction toys have many parts and are seldom found in complete sets today. W. S. Reed Toy Company, founded in 1875 in Leominster, Mass., was one of the first companies to manufacture construction toys. Some toys incorporated elements of education: blocks, for instance, in cubes or cylinder shapes, had the alphabet printed on them. Tower blocks came with the materials to build a 5-foot tower and a pulley system for an elevator, while kits provided the materials to make log-cabin playhouses. The Buddy L Corporation, founded in 1910 in Salem, Mass., made a pressed-steel pickup truck, eventually expanding into cranes, steamrollers, and other construction toys over the years.

Real-life prototypes gave rise to cast-iron toys, trains, and wheeled vehicles. Manufactured chiefly in New England, where waterpower and steam were used to operate lathes, presses, and other tools, these toys became as much a part of American life as machines were. New England boys played with cap pistols, the earliest cast-iron toys. Reflecting the importance of engines to American industry, toy engines began to appear. Weeden Manufacturing in New Bedford, Mass., one of the earliest makers of steam toys, created both horizontal and vertical engines, live-steam fire engines and complete steam plants. Most steam engines had brass boilers, but Russell Frisbie, a J. E. Stevens employee in Cromwell, Conn., patented a cast-iron steam engine in 1871.

As New England, particularly the Connecticut River valley, was the center of the clockmaking industry, many mechanical toys had clock mechanisms with springs operating levers and rods. In Connecticut, George W. Brown of Forestville and Edward Ives of Ives, Blakeslee and Company, in Bridgeport made toy vehicles and trains with surplus clockwork motors from New England clock factories. Using leftovers from the New Haven Clock Company, Ives became a leading manufacturer, creating tinplate dancers, ships, and animals. Ives's spring-motivated toys included jack-in-the-box and squeak toys. Nathan S. Warner, an Ives employee, patented a clockwork rowboat and swing for the firm. Albert H. Dean, another Ives employee, patented a toy woman churning butter, and Arthur Hotchkiss of Cheshire patented a walking-device mechanism; he sold the rights to Ives, who made eight other walking toys based on the patent. Jerome B. Secor, a sewing machine manufacturer in Bridgeport who made toys on the side, created many mechanical toys, including a clockwork piano player who, when wound, rocked back and forth to the music. A. C. Gilbert Company in New Haven, founded in 1908, manufactured boxed magic sets and in 1913 introduced the instantly successful Erector Set.

Connecticut also had a long history of horse-drawn toys, including tinplate circus toys. These toy wagons contained lions, tigers, and zebras and their trainers. Firefighting vehicles, modeled after those used by early companies, came in matching sets, complete with pump and hose carriage. Galloping horses pulled drays, carriages, buggies, and soldiers. In the 20th century these favorite toys gave way to toy cars, warships, and planes. New England companies such as Keystone Manufacturing in Boston and the Pressed Metal Company of Pawtucket, R.I., made different types of automobiles, replacing the horse-drawn carriage. Keystone, for example, manufactured Packard-style fire trucks, mail vans, dump trucks, and steamrollers. They were usually made from cast iron because this process allowed for greater accuracy in depiction than sheet metal did.

Toy trains reflected America's romance with this mode of transport, and several New

England firms, including Ives, Weeden, and R. Bliss, made locomotives and passenger cars from tin and later, to reduce handiwork, iron. Complete with smokestacks and headlamps, they were often accurate representations of full-size engines and their component parts. Makers sometimes capitalized on current events to market a train; R. Bliss, for example, named the Lincoln Park train after the site of the 1893 Columbian Exposition in Chicago.

Perhaps to teach children to save, craftsmen began making toy banks as soon as hard currency was introduced in America. Designed either in tin or the more intricate cast iron, banks depicted buildings, people, and animals. Mechanical banks had levers or switches that activated springs to set the bank in motion once a coin was deposited. For example, J. E. Stevens of Cromwell, Conn., manufactured an acrobat bank in which the pressing of a lever caused an acrobat's feet to swing forward, striking a clown's stomach and allowing a coin to drop in a slot. The design for this bank and for others was patented by Edward L. Morris of Boston, who then assigned it to the Stevens firm. Stevens produced 21 models of banks ranging in price from $2.50 to $3.00.

In 1860 Milton Bradley, a lithographer in Springfield, Mass., invented the Checkered Game of Life and sold it. Milton Bradley's zoetrope and the kaleidoscope, patented by Charles G. Bush in Providence in 1874, were popular. In 1880 Bradley turned to making jigsaw puzzles. Today, Milton Bradley is the top maker of toys and games in the world. Bradley died in 1911, but his business was so successful that in 1962 the firm opened a multimillion-dollar plant in East Longmeadow, Mass. Today they produce such games as Chutes and Ladders, Candyland, and Twister. In 1984 Hasbro acquired Milton Bradley and its subsidiary Playskool, the manufacturer of toys for infants and grade-school children. Based in Pawtucket, Hasbro designs and manufactures children's and family's leisure-time toys, including action figures, vehicles, and play sets. Hasbro games range from the traditional to the hi-tech; the company continues to produce puzzles and card games, but it also produces electronic learning aids, handheld electronic games, and interactive software. In 1989 Hasbro purchased the assets of Coleco industries, which allowed Scrabble and Parcheesi to join the Milton Bradley line. Hasbro also has joined with Tonka, Kenner Toys, and Parker Brothers Games. Parker Brothers, which manufactured games in Salem until 1991, is the maker of Monopoly (developed in 1934), a game based on buying and renting property; probably the most famous of all board games, it is now produced in several languages and sold around the world.

Marshall B. Davidson, ed., *The American Heritage History of Colonial Antiques* (1967); Priscilla Sawyer Lord and Daniel J. Foley, *The Folk Arts and Crafts of New England* (1965); Eleanor St. George, *The Dolls of Yesterday* (1948); Elizabeth Stillinger, *The Antiques Guide to Decorative Arts in America, 1600–1875* (1972); Robert W. Swedberg and Harriett Swedberg, *American Clocks and Clockmakers* (1989); Blair Whitton, *Toys* (1984).

Suzanna Nyberg

Transcendentalism Transcendentalism arose in the 1830s in New England as a religious and literary and philosophical movement. It received its name in derision. Critics claimed that in their enthusiasm for German philosophical idealism, Transcendentalists walked with their heads in the clouds. The specific beliefs of American Transcendentalists varied. They kept no membership rolls and required no doctrinal allegiance. Members did share, however, certain fundamental ideas, orient their lives around common rituals, and meet for conversation in the so-called Transcendental Club. Moreover, club members understood their movement to be, first and foremost, spiritual.

Prominent members of the Transcendental Club included Ralph Waldo Emerson, Frederic Henry Hedge, Bronson Alcott, George Ripley, James Freeman Clarke, Convers Francis, and Orestes Brownson. Other who appeared at meetings or were associated with the movement included Henry David Thoreau, Margaret Fuller, William Henry Channing, William Ellery Channing, Elizabeth Palmer Peabody, Jones Very, and William Henry Furness. Fuller served as editor of the *Dial*, the principal journal of American Transcendentalism.

American Transcendentalists were in many ways children of the past. First, they were children of the Puritans, who had early exhibited a mystical strain and an ability to find God in nature. The Puritans were sensitive to the God who was immanent as well as transcendent in the self or in nature. They gave to their Transcendentalist heirs a religious culture in which nature and the interior life were respected in the light of divinity, and they encouraged a seriousness and intensity of purpose in the pursuit of spiritual things. And, finally, Puritan philosophical thinking had favored the Platonic tradition with its idealism and its system of analogy between material world and spiritual realm.

Second, the Transcendentalists were children of the Unitarians, who had emerged from the liberal wing of Puritanism. Unitarians embraced the Enlightenment philosophy of John Locke. Lockean philosophy had rejected the traditional theory that one gains knowledge through innate ideas. It argued instead for the mind as a tabula rasa, a clean slate on which knowledge was recorded through the impression of the senses and then subjected to reflection to give rise to ideas. This sensationalist philosophy became central to the Unitarians' theological quest for certainty, for a ratio-

Main house at Brook Farm, West Roxbury, Mass., site of a Transcendentalist communitarian experiment, 1932

nal argument for the faith of a liberal 19th-century person.

Unitarians not only turned from the trinity to the unity of God but also created a theological milieu free of dogma, making space for an intellectual and spiritual freedom that the Transcendentalists would harvest anew. Moreover, freedom from dogma was related to the further Unitarian emphasis on individual responsibility. A person, Unitarians thought, was intrinsically capable of acting responsibly and thus was innately good.

Finally, Unitarians refined their moral theology through their appropriation of Scottish commonsense philosophy. As expounded by Thomas Reid, Dugald Stewart, and Thomas Brown, Scottish common sense adhered to much of Locke's empiricism but argued for the self-evidence of fundamental rational principles (common sense) as grounds for acquiring knowledge of the objective world. It argued, too, for a moral sense, a basic intuitive understanding by means of which people distinguished between good and evil.

Transcendentalists, many of whom were Unitarians in background, came to regard Lockean sensationalism, as mediated through the rationalism of Unitarian preaching, as the enemy to be destroyed in the service of the spirit. As seen in Ralph Waldo Emerson's "Divinity School Address" (1838), Transcendentalists continually railed against the barrenness and coldness that they found in the doctrinal message of the Unitarian Church. Rejecting Lockean sensationalism for an intuitional philosophy, Transcendentalists argued that the truth of the Gospels was confirmed by the moral character of Christ there revealed and intuitively grasped.

The Transcendentalists found other sources for their thought and spirituality in Europe, especially in Romanticism. They embraced the philosophy of Immanuel Kant, which challenged the epistemological doctrine of Locke. For Kant, knowledge was mediated through a series of mental categories that shaped the raw data of experience. Thus, knowledge was partly ideal (the product of the mind) and partly empirical (the product of the senses).

The Transcendentalists turned as well to three other German thinkers: Friedrich Jacobi, who argued for the direct and immediate knowledge of intuition; Johann Fichte, who exalted the human mind as the ultimate reality, going beyond Kantian idealism by denying the existence of an objective, external world; and Friedrich Schleiermacher, the theologian of Pietism who identified religion with feeling.

German influences reached the Transcendentalists in various ways. The New Englanders Edward Everett, George Ticknor, and George Bancroft all studied in Germany, while Charles T. C. Follen taught German at Harvard. Among the founding members of the Transcendental Club, Frederic Henry Hedge spent four years studying in Germany, but the Transcendentalists got much of their German secondhand, through the work of Samuel Taylor Coleridge and, to a lesser extent, that of Thomas Carlyle and William Wordsworth.

James Marsh introduced Coleridge to an American audience in 1829, when he published Coleridge's *Aids to Reflection*. In a preliminary essay and notes, Marsh stressed Coleridge's distinction between Reason and Understanding based on a simplification and transformation of Kant. For Coleridge, Reason was the high faculty of intuition and could have direct, positive knowledge of spiritual things, while Understanding was the lesser faculty that dealt with the material world. The American Transcendentalists made this distinction basic to their religious understanding.

French eclecticism, especially in the work of Victor Cousin, found a congenial audience among some Transcendentalists as well. Cousin combined Scottish common sense with German idealism and other sources, arguing that each possessed truths that could be understood intuitively.

The Neoplatonic and metaphysical tradition of Europe was discovered by many American Transcendentalists, creating new spiritual heroes like Emanuel Swedenborg and Jakob Böhme. The Transcendentalists read Plato with the aid of the introductions and translations of Thomas Taylor, a British scholar who gave his readings a Neoplatonic and mystical cast. They also discovered Sampson Reed, a young Swedenborgian whose speaking and writing introduced the Transcendentalist leaders to the Swedish mystic.

The Orient acted not as a first teacher but as a corroborator of what the Transcendentalists already knew. The excitement of discovering insights and experiences similar to their own among strange and distant peoples was strong, and both Emerson and Thoreau have left literary records of their encounters with the East. From India the Bhagavad Gita, certain texts of the Vedas, and the *Laws of Manu*, and from China even the sayings of Confucius whetted Transcendentalist appetites for the East. Read in inaccurate translations and mingled eclectically with other sources, Eastern works proved malleable to Transcendentalist reconstruction.

Finally, American Transcendentalists were children of their contemporary America. The new nation was living through an era of material and mental ferment, the Industrial Revolution, rapid urbanization, a dramatic increase in immigration, and significant strides toward a new age of popular democracy. Some Americans immersed themselves in reform movements for causes like temperance, antislavery, peace, and women's rights. Others turned to revivals and new religious movements, while a few experimented with more radical ways of living, among nontraditional communitarian groups.

American Transcendentalists feared the materialism of the era and the absence of more lasting values. Nevertheless, they shared the excitement of their times and held to a vision in which flux was at the heart of things, a vision reflected in the language of motion they preferred when speaking of religious truth.

Thus, although they inherited much from the past, American Transcendentalists moved beyond their inheritance to offer ideas of their own. They developed a distinctive spirituality, a lived expression of their religious vision. They grounded their thought in the ancient worldview of correspondence, seeing the relation of human life to what lay beyond it as that of microcosm to macrocosm, but they also derived practical religious consequences from this theory of correspondence.

First, respect and reverence for nature and spirit became cardinal moral requirements. Second, correspondence suggested that the way to learn the truth about human life was to look at the universe, taking note of what it was and what rhythms it kept. Third, human life acquired greater reality when grounded on the larger pattern of the cosmos. And, fourth, since correspondence taught that the microcosm was simply a small-scale replica of the macrocosm, there could be no radical break between sacred and profane. All of human life was religious.

Transcendentalist religion did not require formal worship. Some Transcendentalists found it more appropriate to contemplate nature, catching there a glimpse of the spirit that animated all things. That meant living in tune with the divinity within oneself and being open to intuitive knowledge and aware that intuition corresponded to reality outside the self. Their living in harmony with cosmic law cultivated the ground for mysticism. Primarily, however, it allowed American Transcendentalists to be empowered by their divinity and thereby to live expansively, learning to control and order their lives and environments.

Catherine L. Albanese, *Corresponding Motion: Transcendental Religion and the New America* (1977); Paul F. Boller, Jr., *American Transcendentalism, 1830–1860: An Intellectual Inquiry* (1974); Arthur E. Christy, *The Orient in American Transcendentalism: A Study of Emerson, Thoreau, and Alcott* (1932); Philip F. Gura,

The Wisdom of Words: Language, Theology, and Literature in the New England Renaissance (1981); William R. Hutchinson, *The Transcendentalist Ministers: Church Reform in the New England Renaissance* (1959); Nathaniel Kaplan and Thomas Katsaros, *The Origin of American Transcendentalism in Philosophy and Mysticism* (1975); Arthus Versluis, *American Transcendentalism and Asian Religions* (1993).

Bryan F. Le Beau

Tudor, Tasha

Tudor, Tasha (1915–) Author and illustrator. Tasha Tudor, born in 1915 in Boston, portrays historic New England in her children's books and illustrations. The daughter of the yacht designer William Starling Burgess and the portrait painter Rosamond Tudor, she was originally named Starling Burgess. Her eccentric parents and their eclectic friends encouraged her to explore her picturesque Marblehead, Mass., environment when she was a child. Her parents divorced when she was nine years old, and while her mother pursued artistic ambitions in New York City's Greenwich Village, Tudor lived with an unconventional family in Redding, Conn. There she participated in the family's theatricals, sketched New England wildflowers, and savored the rural lifestyle. Inspired by Hugh Thompson's illustrations in *The Vicar of Wakefield*, she decided to become an illustrator and studied briefly at the Museum of Fine Arts School in Boston.

Tudor met her future husband, Thomas Leighton McCready, Jr., in 1936, and in 1938 she wrote *Pumpkin Moonshine*, a story about an escaped jack-o'-lantern, for his niece Sylvie Ann. Tudor convinced Oxford University Press to publish the book, and thus began her prolific career as an illustrator. She used royalties earned from illustrating an edition of *Mother Goose* to buy a 1789 farmhouse on 450 acres near Webster, N.H., where she reared her four children. Wishing to live in the style of 1830s and 1840s New England settlers, Tudor insisted on being self-sufficient, raising her own flax and weaving cloth on her loom. Her gardens, often illustrated in her books, are famous for her cultivation of old-fashioned varieties.

According to her daughter Bethany, Tudor's "impressions of rural New England life are the inspiration for her artwork." Tudor brought New England flora and fauna into her farmhouse kitchen to observe and draw authentically. She also sketched nearby villages; Harrisville, N.H., for instance, was the model for Corgiville, the setting of several of Tudor's books. In *Becky's Birthday* (1960), her characters visit a typical New England country store and churn ice cream. Tudor's *First Delights: A Book about the Five Senses* (1966) presents common New England images such as maple syrup and cornstalks. Holidays are among Tudor's themes: *Snow before Christmas* (1941), for example, reveals Tudor's holiday customs of roasting apples, making candles, and baking plum pudding.

Tudor's books promote the New England values of thrift and industriousness and depict well-behaved, polite children who express reverence for adults. She has also illustrated editions of such children's classics as Frances Hodgson Burnett's *The Secret Garden* (1962). While some critics feel that Tudor's work is too quaint, dated, and idealized, most have been receptive. Twice the runner-up for the prestigious Caldecott Medal, Tudor received the Catholic Library Association's Regina Medal in 1971 for her contribution to children's literature.

After divorcing her husband, Tudor relocated to Marlboro, Vt., where her son built a home for her on a remote farm. She owns Corgi Cottage Industries, which sells reprints of her works, handmade toys, the videos *Take Joy! The Magical World of Tasha Tudor* and *Take Peace! A Corgi Cottage Christmas*. A television special about the artist aired on ABC's *Primetime Live* for Thanksgiving, 1997. Tudor released her 91st book, *The Great Corgiville Kidnapping*, for Christmas, 1997.

Tudor's celebration of preindustrial values links her to the Colonial Revival movement as well as to 1930s socialists, such as Helen and Scott Nearing, who sought the simple life in Vermont. By blending images of childhood with images of traditional New England ways, she is one of a number of authors, including Louisa May Alcott, Robert McCloskey, and E. B. White, who have created an image of New England as an embodiment of a national childhood.

Bethany Tudor, *Drawn from New England: Tasha Tudor, a Portrait in Words and Pictures* (1979); Tasha Tudor, *Tasha Tudor's Sampler* (1977); Tasha Tudor and Richard Brown, *The Private World of Tasha Tudor* (1992).

Elizabeth D. Schafer

Vermont

Vermont Vermont occupies a unique place in the national consciousness. Beloved even by people who have never set foot in it, Vermont has the power to evoke what the historian Charles Morrissey, borrowing Abraham Lincoln's phrase, has called "the mystic chords of memories." Its quaint villages, rolling farmland, and picturesque landscape are potent, contemporary reminders of the nation's agrarian past and of a spirit that many Americans fear has been lost. Within the state, however, where there is less sentimentality and more practicality, most Vermonters would probably agree with the historian Ralph N. Hill that Vermont is "contrary country."

Known as the Green Mountain State for the two dominating and parallel ridges of mountains that run down its spine from the Canadian border in the north to the Massachusetts border in the south, Vermont has also been profoundly influenced by the waters that delineate its borders. The Connecticut River, running the length of the state's eastern border, and Lake Champlain, running much of the length of the western border, are responsible for fertile lowlands that continue to make farming possible in a place where mountains are a metaphor for what someone has called "hard living in a hard place." So cleanly divided are the two flanks, the eastern side oriented to Boston and southern New England, and the western side to New York, that the Vermont government operated from the mid-19th century to the mid-20th century under the unwritten Mountain Rule, which decreed that governors must come from alternate sides of the state in order to fairly represent the population.

The state has north-south divisions, too, however, each with its own character. Ever since the first ski tow in the country began operating in Woodstock in 1934, the southern part of the state has been developing as a playground for southern New England's urban masses. The northern part takes its relation to Canada so casually that the international border runs through the middle of towns and even through the middle of a store and an opera house. The three northeasternmost counties, named collectively the Northeast Kingdom by the former governor George Aiken in 1949, remain a beautiful, sparsely settled land of moose, timber, and hardscrabble communities.

For many years Vermont has ranked as the most rural of the 50 states, and Vermonters have turned this to their commercial advantage by advertising an idealized, pastoral landscape on everything from chocolates to ice cream containers to calendars. The truth, however, is that even in this most rural state a significant number of Vermonters can go for weeks without seeing a cow. This is particularly true in and around Burlington, on Lake Champlain, where almost a quarter of the state's population is clustered in old communities struggling to retain their historic identities against the rising tide of development and growth.

Most citizens of Vermont live in towns, which may or may not look like one of the familiar picture-postcard communities that have been successfully promoted around the country for decades. Photographs of white-steepled churches, bandstands on the green, and patchwork farmland tucked under the chins of majestic mountains accurately portray some of Vermont's much-heralded physical charms, but they misrepresent the complexi-

Taking a break during driveway pickup repair, Searsburg, Vt., 1994

ties of contemporary rural life in a state where native Vermonters are increasingly hard to find. Some much-photographed towns— such as Woodstock, which has been polished to a high sheen with Rockefeller money— have become too expensive for average Vermonters to live in. Other towns, those beyond the photographer's lens, are still engaged in fierce, stubborn struggles more than a century old to live up to their founders' hopes.

This stubbornness and independence have long been a part of Vermont's mystique. Vermonters began cultivating their image as independent thinkers even before statehood, when with the help of the state's one mythic hero, the bombastic Ethan Allen, they finally wrested control of the territory in 1777 from New Hampshire and New York and organized as an independent republic. Their constitution included provisions, unique in America at that time, prohibiting slavery and granting universal suffrage to every white man. Although Vermont gained statehood in 1791, the path of its freewheeling thinking was set. In 1941, for example, the Vermont legislature declared war on Germany even before Pearl Harbor determined the nation's course, and in 1936 Vermonters voted to reject the Green Mountain Parkway, a plan as ambitious as Virginia's Skyline Drive, which would have laid a federal highway the length of Vermont and brought tourists and their dollars in by the millions. By doing so, they expressed their abiding love for their land and their willingness to fight a century of rural depression on their own terms. They also attracted attention to themselves in

ways that added color to the image of Vermonters that President Calvin Coolidge had personified.

Vermonters continue to distinguish themselves as freethinkers in national and state politics. A Republican stronghold from the middle of the 19th century until the Democrat Phil Hoff won election as governor in 1962, Vermont has taken a lead role in restoring the definition of *conservative* to its original meaning—namely, one who protects and preserves—in the national debate. Ironically, the vigor with which Vermonters have practiced their conservatism over the years has made Vermont one of the most politically liberal states in the union. As early as 1864 George Perkins Marsh of Woodstock launched the environmental movement by arguing in *Man and Nature* for a more scientific and sympathetic approach to the environment. Senator Ralph Flanders, alone in the U.S. Senate, challenged Senator Joseph McCarthy as he spiraled out of control in 1954. In 1997 Jody Williams of Putney won the Nobel Peace Prize for her international work to ban land mines. Vermont's natural and built landscapes are conserved from ill-conceived development by Acts 250 and 252, passed in 1970, and by some of the earliest and most aggressive land-use legislation in the country. In Washington, D.C., its national interests are represented by liberal senators and by a socialist representative, the only one in the country.

Vermont's image today is built upon a history that unfolded at the periphery of the nation's explosive growth in the 19th century.

From the middle of the century onward, Vermont grew at approximately one-quarter of the rate of the nation as a whole. So bleak were these years for many Vermont hill towns that historians have called the period the "winter of Vermont." The effect of poverty and Vermont farmers' desperate but not hopeless effort to find a place in the national economy changed the state's landscape relatively little while much of the rest of the nation was being transformed by expansion and development.

Shrewd Vermonters had found a way by the late 19th century to make stagnation look bucolic to the growing number of urban vacationers coming up from New York and southern New England, but it was not until after World War II, when Americans began to question the benefits of progress, that Vermont's lack of change was suddenly noticed by tourists zipping along its new highway system and by people all over the country who saw in Norman Rockwell's paintings Vermont as an island of stability in a seething ocean of social upheaval. People began to see the wisdom in a remark made by Sinclair Lewis, a Vermont resident in the 1930s, that a town of 4,000 was not necessarily twice as good as a town of 2,000.

Vermonters moved quickly to cultivate and preserve what the state had to offer. *Vermont Life,* the state's hugely successful promotional magazine, was launched in 1946. The Shelburne Museum, founded in 1947 by Electra Havemeyer Webb to showcase the American spirit, truly stopped time with its vast Americana collections, but hordes of new urban and suburban dwellers in southern New England and New York did not need a museum. To them, the whole of Vermont was a nostalgic reminder of a romanticized past that never was.

For 150 years most Vermonters bent their backs to soil and stone in all kinds of weather, and they survived only by tending to their work with a ferocious faith in the future. If they were not already independent, hardy, frugal, practical, and tolerant by virtue of their Calvinist heritage, then adversity and the challenging environment made them so. During the coldest time of the Vermont "winter," they exported their most precious resource, their sons and daughters, men and women like Stephen Douglas, John Deere, Joseph Smith, Dorothea Dix, Horace Greeley, and John Dewey. These and tens of thousands of others left Vermont between 1840 and 1950 in search of opportunities unavailable at home, but in their exodus they unwittingly carried with them across the country the model of a character that became the enduring image of a Vermonter.

At the opening of the 21st century, Vermonters worship that image with a reverence comparable only to their love of the land and with hardly a backward glance at the human cost. Although every image is always vulnerable to changing realities, Vermont's image persists in part because the state attracts thousands of immigrants annually, many of whom come not to change the way of life but to share it. Recently, however, that way of life appeared threatened; in 2004 the National Trust for Historic Preservation declared the entire state "endangered," claiming that its "special magic" could disappear under the onslaught of "big box" retailers whose stores "often overwhelm their surroundings and [whose] impersonal corporate identity too often trumps community character." For Vermonters, who take what John Calvin would regard as unseemly pride in their state's image, the coming years could be decisive.

Jan Albers: *Hands on the Land: A History of the Vermont Landscape* (2000); Charles Edward Crane, *Let Me Show You Vermont* (1937); Federal Writers' Project, *Vermont: A Guide to the Green Mountain State* (1937); Dorothy Canfield Fisher, *Vermont Tradition: The Biography of an Outlook on Life* (1953); Nancy Price Graff, ed., *Celebrating Vermont: Myths and Realities* (1991); Ralph N. Hill, Murray Hoyt, Walter R. Hard, Jr., *Vermont: A Special World* (1969); Charles T. Morrissey, *Vermont: A History* (1981); Maria Newman, "Endangered: Quaint Towns. Green Hills. Vermont!" *New York Times*, May 24, 2004; Neal R. Peirce, *The New England States* (1976); Susan Bartlett Weber, ed., *The Vermont Experience* (1987).

Nancy Price Graff

Vermont Life For many non–New Englanders, the images in *Vermont Life* have come to represent their notions of the quintessential New England. Since publication of its first issue in the autumn of 1946, *Vermont Life* has reflected the beauty of Vermont's natural landscape as well as the quaint and quirky aspects of the state's people and culture. The magazine strikes a balance between nostalgia and a more honest examination of change and occasional decline in the state. With its stunning photography and crisp writing, *Vermont Life* has come to rank with other superb state magazines such as *Arizona Highways* and Maine's *Down East*.

Vermont Life relies primarily on visual imagery to tell the state's stories. Each issue typically contains six or seven photo essays, one of which is a panoramic look at the current season: foliage-season photographs of Peacham, spring shots of the Jenne Farm in Reading, or winter scenes of the ski areas, for example. In addition to the usual photo essays, *Vermont Life* has also chronicled 60 years of change in the state, examining disturbing trends in agriculture (especially dairying), wildlife, hunting,

and tourism. Paradoxically, the magazine presents Vermont as at once a sort of magical kingdom impervious to outside influences and a place caught in the flow of modernization.

Some critics of *Vermont Life* have accused the glossy magazine of ignoring the very real poverty-stricken rural areas in favor of the touristy towns; of concentrating on the picturesque to the exclusion of the typical. Others chide the editors for making Vermonters seem a bit extraheroic, downplaying their foibles and shortcomings, turning taciturnity into a virtue, and forgetting some of the uglier, xenophobic episodes of Vermont's past.

Earle Newton launched the magazine in 1946; in 1950 Walter R. Hard, Jr., became editor and guided the publication for the next two decades. In 1972 Brian Vachon, an editor at the *Saturday Review* in New York, took over. Charles Morrissey succeeded Vachon as editor in 1981, and in 1983 Nancy Price Graff became editor. Her tenure, too, was short, but since 1985, Tom Slayton has added a measure of continuity. *Vermont Life* celebrated its 50th anniversary in 1996.

During its first 20 years, *Vermont Life* ran a small operating deficit that necessitated funding from the Vermont legislature; today the magazine is still published by the state. In 1960 *Vermont Life* ventured into the calendar trade, packaging 12 or so vibrant scenes of Vermont for each year. Later the magazine published occasional books, such as the best-selling *Vermont: A Special World* in 1969, but by the late 1980s such extra marketing was not enough to avoid deficits. In 1991, despite protest from purists, the magazine solicited advertising to increase its profitability. Although the ads can be distracting, *Vermont Life* still holds to its original goal of promoting the Green Mountain State.

Walter Hard, Jr., *Green Mountain Treasury: A Vermont Life Sampler* (1961); William C. Lipke, "From Pastoralism to Progressivism: Myth and Reality in 20th-Century Vermont," in *Celebrating Vermont: Myths and Realities,* ed. Nancy Price Graff (1991); *Seasons of Change: 50 Years with Vermont Life, 1946–1996,* special supplement to *Vermont Life* (1996); Susan Bartlett Weber, ed., *The Vermont Experience* (1987).

Thomas L. Altherr

WPA Guides The WPA Guides, also known as the American Guide Series, are a series of travel guides that were written in the late 1930s and early 1940s by members of the Federal Writers' Project (FWP), a New Deal Works Progress Administration (WPA) program designed to provide work for unemployed writers and research workers. Aimed at automobile tourists, the WPA Guides were

written for the 48 states and Alaska as well as Washington, D.C., and Puerto Rico (there was no guide for Hawaii). In addition to the state books, individual guides were produced for some interstate highway routes, cities, and towns, such as U.S. Route 1, Boston, and Milford, Conn.

The state guidebooks are divided into three sections. The first section reviews the state's natural setting, culture, and people in essays on such subjects as history, industry, geography, art, architecture, folklore, and religion. The second section describes the state's major cities and towns, while the third and largest section is devoted to tour itineraries complete with route maps, mileage, and detailed descriptions of what visitors would encounter. Photographs are also an integral part of the books. The New England series abounds with picturesque scenes of rustic farms, ivy-covered colleges, and colonial architecture.

Although the guide series was national in scope, the New England volumes offer a detailed portrait of the region, its people, and its history. Readers of the New England guides will discover barn dances in Connecticut, curious rock formations in Vermont, clam tapping in Maine, high-society parties in Rhode Island, textile factories in Massachusetts, and bean-hole dinners in New Hampshire. Even though the guides celebrated what was special about each town and city, editors at the FWP's Washington headquarters discouraged hyperbole and restricted the use of words like *interesting, quaint,* and *famous.* Instead, editors urged writers to transcend the dry historical accounts of most tour books and capture contemporary America. The New Hampshire guidebook, for example, addressed strikes and labor laws, and the Rhode Island volume tackled economic decline. As a result, the guides foster contradictory images of New England as historic yet faced with modern challenges.

The New England guides, the first to be completed as a regional unit, were published between 1937 and 1938. Sales were steady, considering the hard economic times of the period. By 1940 the Vermont guide had sold more than 10,000 copies, and it went into a second edition. All have been revised and reprinted as recently as 1989. Although the books were often praised by critics, the states were not always happy with their portrayal. Governor Charles F. Hurley of Massachusetts protested references to the Sacco-Vanzetti case—a controversial murder trial of the 1920s that cast doubt on the workings of the Massachusetts judicial system—so vehemently that he eventually forced the editors to make minor changes. Charges of communist sympathies also followed FWP staff throughout the federal agency's existence and contributed to the 1939 budget cuts, which left the agency dependent on state sponsorship. The agency was completely disbanded in 1943, when the wartime economy's low unemployment rates made such programs unnecessary.

While political pressures plagued the FWP, the agency's biggest problem was its inexperienced staff. Of the 6,500 people employed at the FWP's height, few were professional writers. Most were simply educated individuals in need of employment. Despite editors' efforts to check facts, eliminate omissions, animate dull prose, and create clarity from a confusing mass of individual copy, the lack of experienced writers for some books gave the series an uneven quality. The Massachusetts project did, however, benefit from the talents of the writers Conrad Aiken, Josef Berger, Merle Colby, and George Willison.

Archie Hobson, ed., *Remembering America: A Sampler of the WPA American Guide Series* (1985); Jerre Mangione, *The Dream and the Deal: The Federal Writers' Project, 1935–1943* (1972); Monty Noam Penkower, *The Federal Writers' Project: A Study in Government Patronage of the Arts* (1977).

Briann G. Greenfield

Yankee Magazine

"For the Yankee this is perhaps the age of bewilderment," wrote the founder Robb Sagendorph in his first edition of *Yankee* magazine in September 1935. Sagendorph and his wife, Beatrix, an artist, had recently moved from Boston to their Italian-style stucco home in Dublin, N.H., overlooking Mount Monadnock. The Yankee "sees individuality, initiative, natural ingenuity," Sagendorph continued, "about to be 'swallered inter' a sea of chain stores, national releases, and nation-wide hookups. It is in return for a mass economy and the homogenization of our regional cultures that the Yankee is being asked these days to sell his Yankee soul, his birthright."

Although his own magazine experience was confined to being editor of the *Harvard Lampoon* during his undergraduate days, Sagendorph obviously knew exactly what he was doing—and why. "Thus, *Yankee* Magazine is born today," he concluded. "Its destiny is the expression and perhaps, indirectly, the preservation of our New England culture."

Since the first issue with its total circulation of 612 subscribers, *Yankee: The Magazine of New England Living* has grown to be the third largest regional magazine in the country (after *Southern Living* and *Sunset*), with some 500,000 monthly subscribers. More than half of these readers live outside the six New England states, but survey after survey shows clearly that they don't want to read about anything in *Yankee* that isn't "New England."

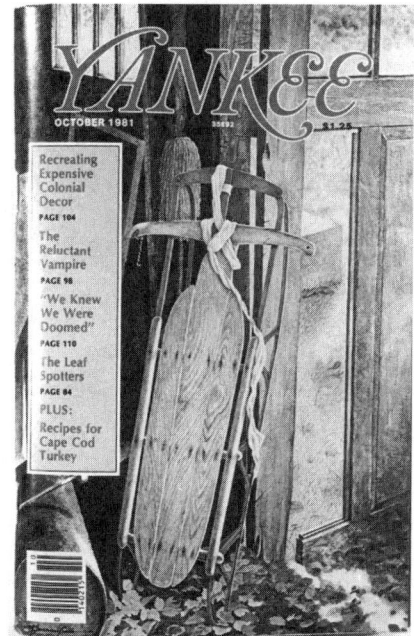

Yankee *magazine (October 1981)*

Despite its phenomenal growth over the years, *Yankee* is still headquartered in the tiny village of Dublin (with an additional office in Boston) and is still wholly owned by Sagendorph family descendants, the Trowbridge, Kaupi, and Hale families. Most important, its mission remains exactly as articulated by Sagendorph back in 1935.

Each issue of *Yankee* attempts to address, either directly or indirectly, the definition, expression, and preservation of New England culture. The editors of *Yankee* magazine strive to reflect the distinct role that each of the region's six states plays within that culture. A *Yankee* feature article about former Massachusetts governor Michael Dukakis, for example, might examine how the Puritan work ethic and conscience may have had an effect on this son of a Greek immigrant during his formative years. A piece about a small New Hampshire seacoast town successfully defeating a popular governor's plan for an oil refinery within its borders can reveal a little of New Hampshire's fierce aversion to any kind of higher (human) authority. A description of the annual New Hampshire road-kill auction surely says something about the state's frugality. From various angles, *Yankee* attempts to touch on the personalities of each of the New England states—from Vermont's common sense to Rhode Island's tolerance, from Connecticut's Yankee ingenuity to Maine's often-quoted unique brand of coastal humor.

Interwoven with and often a part of these themes are photographs, poetry, and fiction and extensive service material covering New

England travel, food, homes, and gardens. So while the "homogenization" of America, as described by Sagendorph in 1935, may be continuing today, *Yankee* continues its dedication to expressing and preserving the unique culture of New England.

Judson Hale, *The Education of a Yankee: An American Memoir* (1987); Hale, *Inside New England* (1982); Yankee, *A Little Book of Yankee Humor* (1977); Yankee, *Mad and Magnificent Yankees* (1973).

Judson D. Hale

Yankees

Who exactly is a Yankee? To New Englanders, a Yankee is someone of "original" New England heritage. To the foreign-born American, the term refers to a native of the United States. To a European or Asian, a Yankee is an American; to a southern American (below the Mason-Dixon Line), a Yankee is a northerner; to a northerner, a Yankee is a New Englander; to a New Englander, a Yankee is a Vermonter; to a Vermonter, a Yankee is a person who eats apple pie for breakfast; to a Vermonter who eats apple pie for breakfast, a Yankee is someone who eats it with a knife. As this popular definition indicates, the term is nebulous, its definition changing over time and responding to shifting images and ideas about the character of the region. The origin of the term itself is steeped in controversy.

Before the American Revolution, the word was probably the first effort of the Massachusetts Indians to imitate the sound of the national name of the English, which they pronounced "Yengees." The Indians would say that "they know the Yengees [the New Englanders], and can distinguish them by their dress and personal appearance, and that they were considered to be less cruel than the Virginians, or Long Knives. The English proper they called Saggenash." This may be a mythological derivation, as was the invention of a Yankos Indian tribe that reportedly gave their name to the brave English who had defeated them in battle. One theory holds that the Dutch name *Janke* (Johnny) may be a source, while some point to the Flemish and German term *Jan Kees,* referring to a country bumpkin. One of the first documented uses of the term to refer to New Englanders is found in a letter by General James Wolfe written in 1758. The term was later adopted by the Dutch on the Hudson River, who applied it contemptuously to all people of New England.

During the American Revolution, the term was used by the British soldiers. In 1775, at the skirmishes at Concord and Lexington, British troops were roughly handled by the "Yankees"; the term was a reproach when applied by the regulars. During the Civil War the word acquired wide currency as a nickname or

Maine Yankees in a general store, North Jay, 1976

contemptuous epithet among the Confederates for Union soldiers. The Confederates, in turn, were dubbed Johnnies or Rebs by the Union soldiers.

The term is also used to designate a particular profession, especially in New England, such as Yankee preacher, Yankee schoolmaster, and the still-popular Yankee peddler, which now appears as the name of furniture and craft shops that claim to sell original products from New England, even if the store is located in a Deep South shopping mall.

Perhaps the best-known use of the word is in the popular American song of the colonial era, "Yankee Doodle." The well-known words were composed in the 1750s and were used by the British to make fun of the provincial colonial troops, but it became very popular with Americans as well. The first complete rotation of the verses in America appeared in the *New York Journal* on October 12, 1768. The British continued to use the song in derision of American troops during the Revolution, but after the victory at Concord (1775), Yankees sang it to the retreating enemy to the disgust of the British general, Thomas Gage, who allegedly exclaimed, "I hope I shall never hear that tune again." After this event, "Yankee Doodle" became an American patriotic air, and American schoolchildren continued to sing the song in celebration of their national heritage. During the Civil War the song, a

negative and unbearable tune to the southern ear, represented humiliation and defeat to the occupied South and was hissed and forbidden in many theaters.

Finally, *Yankee* is used in nicknames, although this usage is relatively obscure today. Early in the 18th century Jonathan Hastings, a Cambridge, Mass., farmer, used the word to designate excellence; this usage led, according to one theory, to the popularity of the term as a nickname for New Englanders, such as Yankee Hastings or Yankee Jonathan. The term *Yankee Jonathan* is interchangeable with *Brother Jonathan*, a nickname popularized in part by the first stage Yankee, Brother Jonathan, in Royall Tyler's play *The Contrast* (1787).

A famous archetypal variation is *Boston Brahmin*, a colloquial expression for New Englanders whose ancestors allegedly arrived on the *Mayflower* in 1620. *Brahmin*, a term borrowed from the Hindus to identify the intellectual elite, was applied to the New England man of letters in the 19th century but soon became a rather derogatory term used by less affluent Bostonians to distinguish the rich upper class ("old cave dwellers") who inhabited Boston from the earliest days of colonial settlement. This class was best personified in the old ditty "Here's to dear old Boston, the home of the bean and the cod, where Cabots speak only to Lodges, and Lodges speak only to God." Typical examples of Brahmins include

the poet and dean of Harvard Medical School Oliver Wendell Holmes, Sr.; the U.S. congressman and state senator Leverett Saltonstall; and the U.S. senator and Harvard professor Henry Cabot Lodge. Theodore Roosevelt's first wife, Alice Hathaway Lee, the daughter of George Cabot Lee, was a Brahmin, as was the United Nations ambassador and socialite Marietta Peabody Tree. The actress Katharine Hepburn has always represented the quintessential Brahmin Yankee in the performing arts; her characters, and especially her diction, rarely deviated from the New England flavor of her Hartford, Conn., education and upbringing.

Another stereotypical image of the Boston Brahmin recalls the skinflint image associated with Yankee Jonathan and the Yankee peddler—the Brahmin who handles millions of dollars all day and then goes to the coffee shop in his office building and orders a cheese sandwich. This Yankee image includes such non-Brahmins as the financier Hetty Green of Vermont. Think also of the Vermonter Calvin Coolidge, governor of Massachusetts and U.S. president, whose thrifty manners and nearly pathological silence in public represented to many Americans another type of Yankee. Being a member of the New England aristocracy did not necessarily guarantee entrance into the Yankee category, for Yankee implied Protestant Anglo-Saxonism as a bulwark against Catholic immigration. Thus John F. Kennedy's grandfather and father may not have been Yankees in the public mind, but Kennedy's own image as a Yankee Brahmin developed during his career, perhaps cemented by the appearance of Robert Frost at his inauguration in 1961. For the record, John F. Kennedy was not considered a part of the Boston Brahmin class, but the Adamses—father John and son John Quincy—definitely were.

During most of the 19th century, regional differences attracted Americans. The subtle differences of the Yankee, the backwoodsman, the New England bluestocking, the New York Dutchman, and the southern aristocrat were all sources of humor and literary image. According to Walter Blair, the Yankee was traditionally portrayed as self-effacing and laconic. When such characters traveled, the humor became obvious: Yankee figures like Joe Strickland (created by George W. Arnold); Enoch Timbertoes; Major Jack Downing (the first great comic Yankee and the model for Uncle Sam, from the pen of Seba Smith, whose character represented the United States in cartoons for years); and Sam Slick (Thomas Chandler Haliburton's Nova Scotia peddler) journeyed into various New England towns and cities as mystified observers and reported home about the wondrous and peculiar ways of city residents.

Similar situations occurred when the Yankee, portrayed as shrewd and cunning on his own turf, left New England. Yankees were sympathetic yokels when described by other New Englanders but were fodder for the frontier humorist. Nathaniel Hawthorne (*The House of the Seven Gables, The Scarlet Letter*), Henry Wadsworth Longfellow ("The Midnight Ride of Paul Revere," *Evangeline, Hiawatha*), and John Greenleaf Whittier (*Among the Hills, Snow-Bound: A Winter Idyll*) were famous New England writers who emphasized the stern, Puritan, thrifty Yankee character in their writing. Mark Twain's *A Connecticut Yankee in King Arthur's Court* (1889) was a more humorous portrayal but with darker undertones about the implications of Yankee technology and social engineering. The Yankee humorists Oliver Wendell Holmes ("The Deacon's Masterpiece; or, The Wonderful 'One-Hoss Shay'") and James Russell Lowell ("the tongue of the people in the mouth of the scholar") wrote patrician humor for a high-powered, well-educated New England audience. Ralph Waldo Emerson wrote an essay, "The Comic," which highlighted such Yankee characteristics as aloofness, high moral insight, and a certain degree of superiority toward the rest of the world.

Harriet Beecher Stowe wrote regional novels such as *House and Home Papers* (1864), *The Mayflower* (1843), *The Minister's Wooing* (1859), *Oldtown Folks* (1869), *The Pearl of Orr's Island* (1861–62), *Pink and White Tyranny* (1871), *Poganuc People* (1878), and *Sam Lawson's Oldtown Fireside Stories* (1871), but her most famous book, *Uncle Tom's Cabin* (1852), written from the perspective of someone who had never witnessed southern life in the dying days before the Civil War, did much to heighten southern negative feelings toward the Yankees up north. Likewise, such people as Davy Crockett made fun of his preconceptions of New England in his *Account of Colonel Crockett's Tour to the North and Down East* (1835): he found New Englanders "a selfish, cunning set of fellows, that was fed on fox ears and thistle tops; that cut their wisdom-teeth as soon as

they were born; that made money by their wits, and held onto it by nature; that called cheatery mother-wit."

The Yankee as a humorist creation appeared in various sketches, songs, plays, anecdotes, magazines, films, and dramatic works. The image of the homespun, cracker-barrel New England type soon became a richly colored comic portrait. In 1825 George W. Arnold created his comic character Joe Strickland and placed him in a series of letters that appeared in the New York *National Advocate* and *Enquirer,* while several magazines that described the Yankee character sprang up with *Yankee* in their title: *Yankee Miscellany* in Boston, *Yankee Blade* in Portland, and *Yankee Notions* and *Yankee Doodle* in New York. For nearly 60 years, *Yankee* magazine, published by Yankee Publishing in Dublin, N.H., has been the authority on life and travel in New England, preserving regional culture while propagating the image that persists today.

Such films as *The Scarlet Letter* (1926) with Lillian Gish depicted the stern convictions and hypocrisy of 17th-century New England; Arthur Miller's *The Crucible* (1953), the classic drama of the McCarthy period, used the 17th-century Salem witch trials to present the author's condemnation of the period. Happier depictions include *The Magnificent Yankee,* the play (1946) and film (1950) based on the life of Oliver Wendell Holmes, and the classic *Little Women,* Louisa May Alcott's autobiographical 1868 novel of family life in Concord, Mass., which has been adapted to film several times since 1936. The first version starred Katharine Hepburn in one of her most representative character interpretations. One of the best and most entertaining portrayals of the political and social tensions between Boston Brahmins and the increasingly powerful Boston Irish is Edwin O'Connor's *The Last Hurrah* (1956), the fictionalized life of a big city mayor now generally accepted to be James Michael Curley, the legendary mayor of Boston; the 1958 motion picture version featured Basil Rathbone.

O'Connor's novel suggests the continuing mutability of the term's meaning today. On one hand, Yankee character was held up as a

bulwark against the transformation of the New England population and characteristics by immigrants. Proponents of the Colonial Revival movement, with its accompanying lineage societies, historical societies, and museums, saw New England values as embodied in colonial families and their English descendants. It became popular to celebrate and lament the northward-retreating true Yankees. On the other hand, some treated the inevitable decline of the Yankee, especially the Brahmin, in the face of modern life with humor, as in Dorothy Canfield Fisher's *Seasoned Timber* (1939), John Marquand's *The Late George Apley: A Novel in the Form of a Memoir* (1937), and John Cheever's *The Wapshot Chronicle* (1957). In more recent years, the image of the Yankee has come to include immigrant groups who seem to resurrect valued characteristics of the Yankee, such as ingenuity, entrepreneurial skills, self-improvement, and education. Thus Yankee rituals such as Patriot's Day, Old Home Day celebrations, and Thanksgiving take on an ethnic flavor.

According to Royal Ford, many New Englanders still exhibit the qualities that have so long defined their region, but Yankees may not be what one expects them to be. Today, many of the region's best fishermen are of Portuguese and Cape Verdean descent, while the New England work ethic is personified by French Canadian, African American, Irish, Italian, and other immigrants. But you would still know a Yankee anywhere by the characteristics of frugality, resourcefulness, industriousness, self-reliance, tenaciousness, and neighborliness that all share.

Walter Blair and Hamlin Hill, *America's Humor: From Poor Richard to Doonesbury* (1978); Catherine Fennelly, ed., *New England Character and Characters as Seen by Contemporaries* (1965); Royal Ford, "Who's a Yankee?" *Boston Globe* (November 1, 1998); Henry Harrison, *The Origin of Yankee* (1917); Mitford M. Mathews, ed., *Dictionary of Americanisms on Historical Principles* (1966); Edwin V. Mitchell, *Yankee Folk* (1948); Stephan Thernstrom, ed., *Harvard Encyclopedia of American Ethnic Groups* (1980); Clarence M. Webster, *Town Meeting Country* (1970 [1945])

Martin J. Manning

Industry, Technology, and Labor

Gary Kulik, Section Editor

INTRODUCTION

COLONIAL BACKGROUND

Colonial New England lacked a single staple crop comparable to wheat in the Mid-Atlantic region and tobacco in the South. Although New Englanders worked assiduously throughout the colonial period to develop single-crop economies, circumstances forced them instead to develop a complex, mixed economy roughly balanced between agriculture and manufactures, tied together by an active, intricate pattern of trade. In the early-17th-century Connecticut River valley, merchants initiated an aggressive fur trade, but as supplies dwindled leadership passed to New York, and the trade had become moribund by the 1650s. The region's great stands of white pine were ideal for an active mast trade, but the long Atlantic passage worked against a broader timber trade. John Winthrop, the first governor of the Massachusetts Bay Colony, and others sought to establish iron-making in eastern Massachusetts, but the absence of skilled workers and capital doomed the enterprise.

The closest New England came to a staple was the cod fishery, the region's first substantial sustained economic enterprise. In the short term, cod fishing assisted the region in its balance of payments with England, spurred shipbuilding, and increased trade with the Wine Islands and the West Indies. In the longer term, it served as a nursery for sailors and merchants, and promoted significant technological change as smaller ships gave way in the early 18th century to larger, two-masted ketches and schooners able to sail farther and stay out longer.

The whaling business, although smaller than the cod fishery, actually had a broader impact on the region. With Nantucket as its center, the business grew sharply over the course of the 18th century and like the cod fishery promoted trade, shipbuilding, and technological change. Because whales were hunted not as food but for their oil, bone, and ambergris, the whale fishery was also key to secondary manufactures, such as candles, stays, and perfume. Between 1730 and the 1770s the region's whaling fleet almost tripled in size, supporting 12 colonial candleworks as well as other businesses.

New England agriculture was characterized by small-scale mixed farming, with some exceptions. During the 17th century the Narragansett region of southern Rhode Island developed a slave-based plantation dairy economy. But in general farmers grew corn and rye, tended small flocks of sheep and herds of cattle, and practiced a mix of subsistence and market agriculture.

The easy availability of land and the relative scarcity of labor led to extensive rather than intensive cultivation, which worked against efforts to increase yields, through either better management or new technologies, and also led to practices that seemed careless and wasteful to British observers used to less abundant resources. Through most of this period, New England farmers girdled trees, allowing them to die slowly, rather than clear-cutting their lands, used extensive amounts of wood for fuel and fencing, and rarely practiced field rotation.

Although New England farmers do not seem to have made any significant technological advances in this period, the region's agriculture did foster critical technical skills in the milling industry. Sawmills, gristmills, and fulling mills dotted the landscape, and virtually every small town had at least one mill to grind grain, saw wood, or finish woolen cloth. The region's geography, with a fall line close to the coast and many small streams, ponds, and tidal ponds, provided innumerable sites suitable for mills and dams. As New Englanders developed the mechanical skills necessary for building dams, waterwheels, and gearing, they created a fund of technical knowledge that would prove important to the region's development.

In the towns and cities a broad range of craft skills developed. New England had fewer ironworks than the middle colonies, but significant clusters developed south and west of Boston and in the Salisbury area of northwest Connecticut. These works led to important secondary manufactures, including bell foundries and edged-tool works in Massachusetts and a wide array of metal-forming crafts throughout western Connecticut. Once established, the metal trades of both areas remained significant well into the 20th century. Other small-scale colonial crafts laid the groundwork for major 19th-century industries. Shoemaking, for instance, was prominently associated with Lynn, Mass., by the mid-18th century. Connecticut clockmakers began their work even earlier.

New England's port cities also spurred manufacture. A maritime economy needed ships, and shipbuilding became the single largest manufacturing enterprise of the era. A host of shipyards sprang up: between 1769 and 1771 alone, 60 percent of all the tonnage produced in the colonies came from New England. With the shipyards came ropewalks, sailmakers, and iron founders. The wealth that shipping helped create paid for skilled housewrights, furniture makers, coach makers, silversmiths, and portrait painters. It was no accident that the great centers of high-style furniture making were Newport, R.I., Portsmouth, N.H., and Boston and Salem, Mass.

It was the merchants who tied the whole economy together. They provided the means for the Atlantic trade in fish, whale parts, manufactured goods, lumber, and agricultural products. Perhaps as important, they were at the center of an intricate intraregional and intracolonial transportation trade, the outlines of which are still only dimly perceived. In 1770 New England's commodity exports were worth only £0.85 per capita, well below the mid-Atlantic and the South, yet earnings from shipping services brought the figure up to £1.56, on par with the middle colonies. And the personal tastes of these merchants, both in the big ports and the smaller provincial cities, could be satisfied only by increasingly sophisticated consumer goods. The absence of a single agricultural staple, then, pushed New England into a complex, multifaceted economy that served the region well in the next century.

At the beginning of the American Revolution, New England was, by several measures, the poorest of the three seaboard regions. Yet its 19th-century economic growth was not hindered by that. In part, this suggests that industrial advance did not rigidly depend on large amounts of capital. More than that, New England benefited from high levels of literacy, mechanical aptitude, and the skills produced by a complex, interdependent economy. By the beginning of the 19th century, New England boasted an impressive, savvy corps of merchants and sea captains, a growing number of industrious, creative artisans, farmers, and mariners, and the rough beginnings of a population poor enough to welcome the coming of industrial labor.

INDUSTRIAL NEW ENGLAND

A substantial part of New England's industrial history can be told through the textile industry. Beginning at Pawtucket Falls, R.I., in 1790, with the well-known works of Samuel Slater, cotton and woolen mills spread west and north into the river valleys of Connecticut, Massachusetts, New Hampshire, Maine, and Vermont. Mill villages clustered near dams, with mills rising several stories above the water flanked by rows of worker houses, came to characterize New England. Although other regions had their mill towns, few areas were as densely settled—Ashton, R.I., Putnam, Conn., Blackstone, Mass., Winooski, Vt., Harrisville, N.H., and a host of others formed linked series of towns running down New England's lesser river valleys.

By the 1820s the mill towns had become mill cities. Within a generation, the footprint was clear. Long stretches of red brick spread out along the region's major rivers: the Merrimack, the Chicopee, and the Connecticut. Manchester, N.H., and Lowell and Lawrence, Mass., were the largest and best-known of the new mill cities. With the increased use of steam power by midcentury, Fall River, Mass., joined the ranks of major cotton cities, and many other New England cities, no longer hindered by the lack of waterpower, added a mill or two.

These villages and cities created an economy with a national, even an international, dimension. Capital flowed from the major regional mercantile and banking centers of Boston, Providence, Hartford, and New York. Cotton came from the plantation South and wool from the Midwest; machinery from a growing number of specialized works in Taunton, Whitinsville, and Worcester, Mass., and, when necessary, from England. The workers came initially from the farms and port cities of New England, but by midcentury they were emigrating from the rural districts of Ireland, Quebec, Italy, and Poland, as well as the farms and factories of England, Scotland, and Belgium. Cotton and woolen goods, and the silks and synthetics of a later period, flowed south and west in great volume.

At their peak in the early 20th century, the factory enclaves of city and town were marked by bustle, vitality, and occasional strife. Ralph Fasanella, a self-taught painter of Brueghelesque vision, captured the essence of this in his paintings of the Lawrence textile mill strike of the early 20th century.

During their century-long dominance, the mills gave rise to a host of specialty industries. In the cities, leather-belt companies, reed makers for power looms, card-clothing companies, and bobbin-and-spindle and shuttle makers arose. The mills

Mico Kaufman's Homage to Women *(1984) in Lowell, Mass., celebrates women's role in Lowell's industrial society*

created the need for specialized engineering skills, waterwheel and later turbine specialists, mill-construction specialists, and waterpower experts, even specialty insurance companies.

More than this, the mills nurtured the mechanical skills that helped give rise to new industries. For more than a century, New England was the center of the textile machinery industry. The metalworking skills and practical inventiveness of the latter easily transferred to machine-tool companies like the nationally prominent Brown and Sharpe or to steam-engine works like Corliss. The first textile machine works, at Lowell and Taunton, even built some of the region's first locomotives.

The New England economy depended, of course, on more than just textiles. A nationally important arms industry emerged in the Connecticut River valley, centered in Springfield, Mass., with the establishment of the Springfield Armory in 1798. The armory played a major role in the development of the American system of manufacture. Private arms makers also flourished. The Colt works in Hartford pioneered the development of the American revolver. Smith and Wesson, located first in Norwich, Conn., and then in Springfield, was the first to develop a revolver with a contained metallic cartridge. The New Haven Arms Company in Connecticut, later the Winchester Repeating Arms Company, achieved fame with the Winchester lever-action repeating rifle, advertised as "the gun that won the West."

New England also emerged as the center of the American clock and watch industry. Beginning in the colonial era, Connecticut's clockmakers became world leaders in this manufacture. Specializing in mass-produced and inexpensive clocks, the firms were technological pacesetters and dominated the U.S. market in the years af-

Quarrying for granite in Vermont, 1984

ter the Civil War. The Waltham Watch Company, which emerged at midcentury, mass-produced affordable, accurate watches, increasing production tenfold by 1877.

A significant metalworking industry developed at several places in southern New England. A critical segment stretched along the north shore of Long Island Sound, in Bridgeport and Waterbury, Conn. Waterbury, closely linked to the clock industry, became the brass capital of the United States, producing buttons, lamps, and a host of stamped or rolled brass products. South of Boston, several important companies emerged, including the Ames Company, a leading ax and shovel maker. By the 1870s Ames was producing three of every five shovels sold in the world. New Britain, Conn., became the home of Stanley Tools, while Worcester, Mass., emerged as a diversified metalworking city. Providence became a center for jewelry and, along with Boston, developed a high-end consumer silver and silverplate industry.

Other cities and regions became closely associated with particular industries. The paper industry flourished in the Berkshires. By midcentury, Holyoke, Mass., became a major paper town and so too did several towns in Maine. Danbury, Conn., was the national center of hat production. Along the margins of the region, active and lesser-known extractive industries prospered. Timber and pulpwood drove the economy of northern Maine. Charcoal iron production would survive in Salisbury, Conn., well into the 20th century. Large marble and granite quarries developed in Vermont. Rutland's Vermont Marble Company had become the largest marble works in the world by 1903. Westerly, R.I., had a cluster of granite quarries, while Portland, Conn., was home to the largest quarry district in the world. Stretching over 175 acres and employing 1,500 workers, the brown freestone quarry supplied building materials to the nation's major East Coast cities.

New England developed a well-earned reputation for inventiveness. In a cynical age, it is too easy to dismiss such terms as "Yankee ingenuity" as self-advertising. New England did in fact have its share of prominent inventors, including Eli Whitney, Samuel Colt, and Charles Goodyear, men whose names continue to be recognized. Far more important, however, was the depth and pervasiveness of Yankee ingenuity. In the early 19th century, Connecticut and Massachusetts led the nation in patents per capita. Both states had rates of invention twice the national average. Countless lesser-known New Englanders increased the efficiency of textile machines, steam engines, machine tools, shoe production, ax and edged-tool making, bridge building, and clock- and watchmaking. The roots of such mechanical inventiveness probably lie in New England's high rates of literacy and numeracy, which are closely linked to the visual learning made possible by its myriad waterpowered mills.

The region's economic growth and extraordinary inventiveness were not without their costs. The rise of the mills and the emergence of wealthy mill owners aroused suspicion and some hostility. Cotton-mill owners in southern New England asserted use rights to water that contravened traditional rights and overrode those of farmers, fishermen, and small mill owners. The rise of cotton-mill villages, and the control mill owners exercised over them, called into question republican principles. From the 1820s on, the labor question continually recurred. Long hours, low wages, dangerous working conditions, and child labor fueled the debate. Strikes became commonplace; trade-union organizing increased. In the early- to mid-20th century, New England's industrial labor movement reached its peak, just as its industrial economy began to decline.

DECLINE

The industrial economy of New England began to show significant symptoms of decline by the 1920s. As economic opportunities emerged in the South and West, fueled in part by population growth, New England's share of the national economy inevitably shrank. Boston declined in importance as an exporter of both goods and capital. The cotton textile industry, which produced 68 percent of all U.S. cotton goods in 1860, produced only 36 percent by 1927. The region's wealth increased only five times between 1880 and 1927, compared to a national increase of seven times.

But New England's decline was more than relative. The textile and shoe industries experienced absolute decline. Between 1919 and 1929, Massachusetts alone lost 154,000 manufacturing jobs, 94,000 of those in shoes and textiles. These losses were felt acutely in one-industry cities like New Bedford, Fall River, Lawrence, and Lowell, where textile workers made up 62–82 percent of all workers, and in Haverhill and Brockton, where shoe workers totaled more than 80 percent of all workers.

As New England's industrial economy entered its slow, prolonged decline, the Great Depression of the 1930s exacerbated tendencies already in place. The loss of jobs continued. Seventy-nine shoe firms left Massachusetts in the 1930s, while Boston, which had a relatively diversified economy, lost one-quarter of its industrial jobs in the same period. World War II brought only temporary relief to industries that had been dominant in the 19th century. By the 1950s, the last vestiges of the old factory economy were visible only in underused and slowly decaying mills.

What caused the decline of New England's industrial economy? The essential outlines are clear. The core of the region's economy rested on industries for which labor costs were relatively high and capital entry costs relatively low. The rise of the southern textile industry in a region with historically low labor costs dramatically increased competition. Increased competition in turn led to overcapacity, lowering prices and putting further pressure on already slim profit margins.

Over the course of the 20th century, business leaders came to decry New England's labor militancy, relatively high costs, and (by the 1950s) inflexible work rules. Some of their complaints were valid. From the 1920s on, a growing number of companies abandoned New England in search of more tractable workers and lower costs.

Over the same period, a parallel critique developed regarding New England's business leaders, who were depicted as too conservative and averse to risk, unwilling to innovate and wedded to past practice. Leaders in the shoe industry, for example, never saw the potential in children's shoes. Some criticisms were far harsher. The senior management of Waltham Watch was publicly derided as incompetent or even criminal. In addition, the quality of business leadership declined across the board. Many of the rich had sent their sons to schools like Harvard, where they had been educated away from business.

RECOVERY

World War II had few long-term consequences for New England's old industrial economy, but it did spur the growth of a science-based defense industry. Emerging from the region's metalworking and engineering traditions, three geographical areas rose to prominence. Around Boston, General Electric and Raytheon, drawing on the expertise of the Massachusetts Institute of Technology, built aircraft engines and radar, respectively. In the Connecticut River valley, Pratt and Whitney emerged as a major aircraft engine producer. Along Long Island Sound, General Dynamics and United Aircraft (later United Technologies) played important roles. After the war, these companies maintained their prominence. Raytheon became an important missile manufacturer, and General Dynamic's Electric Boat Division at Groton, Conn., built the first nuclear submarine.

Innovations in defense technologies had important effects in the postwar growth of New England's technology and computer companies. Employment in direct defense and aerospace industries remained high until the early 1960s, when it began to decline. From 1969 on, the fastest-growing sector of the economy was high technology, centered on the Route 128 corridor surrounding Boston. By 1986 the three most valuable companies in Massachusetts were Digital Equipment, Raytheon, and Wang Laboratories.

Regional differences continued to matter. The high-technology economy of the Boston area spread both west and north, helping to create pockets of prosperity along Route 495 and stretching into southern New Hampshire and southern coastal Maine. New York City's expanding economy kept most of southwestern Connecticut prosperous, although the old industrial cities of Bridgeport and Waterbury continued to struggle. The Connecticut River valley towns of Hartford and Springfield, the former a national center for the insurance business for most of the 20th century, could not keep pace and suffered declines. Rhode Island's economy also lagged, but harbor-front renewal in Providence and Newport were hopeful signs. Tourism, recreation, and the growth of second homes marked the economy of wide stretches of northern New England, where high levels of prosperity coexisted with pockets of stark rural poverty. The vast reaches of northern Maine showed the least change, as pulp, paper, and potatoes remained at the center of the north woods' economy.

In the years after World War II, New England's economy took on the general outlines of the national economy. Manufacturing gave way to service industries. In Massachusetts, for example, several banks, the Stop and Shop grocery chain, the Zayre retail chain, and General Cinema movie theaters were all ranked in the top 25 most valuable companies. The region's labor movement peaked, and trade union membership declined . In many ways, the region was losing its economic distinctiveness.

Silversmith Edwin Leinonen making a spoon, 1969

In two areas, however, New England remained strongly linked to its past. The post–World War II emergence of science-based industry, with its close ties to the universities, reflected a depth of expertise similar to the great fund of practical knowledge once so prevalent among Yankee artisans. The region also led the nation in the imaginative reuse of its industrial buildings. In hundreds of New England towns 19th-century mills and factories have been converted into attractive, functional apartments, homes for the elderly, retail shops, college classrooms, and even small-scale manufactories devoted to the preindustrial crafts. Often obscuring, and at times romanticizing, their 19th-century purpose, these reclaimed buildings remain mute witnesses to a way of life long gone and monuments to the depth of New England's industrial history.

C. W. Barron, *What Ails New England? The Remedy* (1927); Mary H. Blewett, *Men, Women, and Work: Class, Gender, and Protest in the New England Shoe Industry, 1780–1910* (1988); Carl Bridenbaugh, *The Colonial Craftsmen* (1950); Edward Byers, *The Nation of Nantucket: Society and Politics in an Early American Commercial Center, 1660–1820* (1987); Carolyn C. Cooper, *Shaping Invention: Thomas Blanchard's Machinery and Patent Management in 19th-Century America* (1991); Thomas Dublin, *Women at Work: The Transformation of Work and Community in Lowell, Massachusetts, 1826–1860* (1979); George S. Gibb, *The Saco-Lowell Shops: Textile Machinery Building in New England, 1813–1949* (1950); Robert B. Gordon and Patrick M. Malone, *The Texture of Industry: An Archaeological View of the Industrialization of North America* (1994); Laurence F. Gross, *The Course of Industrial Decline: The Boott Cotton Mills of Lowell, Massachusetts, 1835–1955* (1993); Tamara K. Hareven and Randolph Langenbach, *Amoskeag: Life and Work in an American Factory City* (1978); Seymour E. Harris, *The Economics of New England: Case Study of an Older Area* (1957); Bennett Harrison, *Rationalization, Restructuring, and Industrial Reorganization in Older Regions: The Economic Transformation of New England Since World War II* (1982); Donald R. Hoke, *Ingenious Yankees: The Rise of the American System of Manufactures in the Private Sector* (1990); David A. Hounshall, *From the American System to Mass Production, 1800–1932* (1984); David Jeremy, *Transatlantic Industrial Revolution: The Diffusion of Textile Technologies Between Britain and the United States, 1790–1830s* (1981); Alice Hanson Jones, *Wealth of a Nation to Be: The American Colonies on the Eve of the Revolution* (1980); Edward Kirkland, *Men, Cities, and Transportation: A Study in New England History, 1820–1900* (1948); Gary Kulik, Roger Parks, and Theodore Z. Penn, eds., *The New England Mill Village, 1790–1860* (1982); Gary Kulik and Julia C. Bonham, *Rhode Island: An Inventory of Historic Engineering and Industrial Sites* (1978); David S. Landes, *Revolution in Time: Clocks and the Making of the Modern World* (1983); John J. McCusker and Russell R. Menard, *The Economy of British America, 1607–1789* (1985); Judith McGaw, *Most Wonderful Machine: Mechanization and Social Change in Berkshire Paper Making, 1801–1885* (1985); Marc Scott Miller, *The Irony of Victory: World War II and Lowell, Massachusetts* (1988); Jonathan Prude, *The Coming of Industrial Order: Town and Factory Life in Rural Massachusetts, 1810–1860* (1983); Matthew Roth, *Connecticut: An Inventory of Historic Industrial and Engineering Sites* (1981); Daniel Vickers, *Farmers and Fishermen: Two Centuries of Work in Essex County, Massachusetts, 1630–1850* (1994); Vickers, "The Northern Colonies: Economy and Society, 1660–1775," in *The Colonial Era*, vol. 1 of *The Cambridge Economic History of the United States*, ed. Stanley L. Engerman and Robert E. Gallman (1996); Caroline F. Ware, *The Early New England Cotton Manufacture: A Study in Industrial Beginnings* (1931); Richard W. Wilkie and Jack Tager, eds., *Historical Atlas of Massachusetts* (1991).

Gary Kulik

Industrial Revolution, 1790–1860

Industrial Revolution is a convenient term used to describe a series of interrelated transformations—most notably the rise of the city, the replacement of handicrafts with machines, the emergence of the working class, and the birth of the factory—that occurred during the late 18th century. Although there is much truth to these generalizations, they fall short of describing the unique path New England followed in its initial period of industrialization. Although the region would eventually acquire its share of smokestacks and polluted cities, industry coexisted with and complemented more traditional, agrarian ways of life to a degree not seen elsewhere in the United States.

In 1790 New England was not, by most conventional indicators, a region poised on the threshold of a capitalist revolution. Many people in rural areas worked on small-scale, family-owned and operated farms, producing much of what they needed. However, a vibrant market economy led to the creation of town centers with blacksmiths and other crafts- and tradespeople. The countryside was dotted with grist mills, lumber mills, and small manufactures, such as furniture makers, wagon makers, and tanners. On the coast, New England's cities and towns featured shipyards and small-scale manufacturers supporting the maritime trade and provisioning trades. The large urban industrial centers that would later dominate the landscape—Lowell and Lynn, Mass., most prominently—either did not exist or had yet to outgrow their origins as sleepy villages.

Nonetheless, subtle changes in the regional economy had already paved the way for industry's arrival. Throughout the 18th century, a burgeoning population had prompted the subdivision of farms, creating a class of landless laborers and making farming less profitable for those who remained on the land. Increasingly, households throughout the region looked for ways to supplement their incomes. At the same time, declining commercial prospects encouraged many wealthy families in New England to consider investing money in new, industrial ventures.

These conditions—a growing supply of surplus labor and the availability of investment capital—figured in the success of Samuel Slater's pioneering cotton textile factories. Beginning in 1790, Slater, a British mechanic, formed a partnership with the merchant Moses Brown to build a waterpowered textile mill in Pawtucket, R.I. Completed three years later, the mill used carding machines and spinning frames built by Slater to process the raw cotton into yarn. It was the first of dozens of such factories, many of which would farm out the finished yarn to be spun into cloth in households throughout the region.

Such mills brought industry to New England without the usual drama of the "industrial revolution." Slater's use of quiet waterpower, his continued reliance on outwork, his hiring of entire families rather than individual workers, and his creation of quaint "mill villages" (complete with workers' cottages, churches, stores, and artisan shops) eased the acceptance of the machine and the new social order it represented. It was an attempt—and a largely successful one—to reconcile the rural heritage of New England with an emergent industrial order. Wary of the squalor and pollution of Britain's new industrial cities, New England entrepreneurs cloaked their industrial revolution in the trappings of an agrarian past.

The most ambitious and successful attempt to achieve such a balance came with the founding of the Boston Manufacturing Company in 1814 by the merchants Francis Cabot Lowell and Nathan Appleton. Making use of a corporate charter, Lowell and Appleton pooled the savings of friends and relatives to underwrite the construction of a waterpowered mill in Waltham, Mass. Unlike Slater's mills, their factory integrated and mechanized all steps of textile production under one roof: carding, spinning, and weaving. In an additional departure from Slater's practices, the Boston Manufacturing Company tapped a different pool of surplus labor: young, unmarried women who supplemented their families'

income with wages earned in the mills. These "mill girls" usually worked for a short while before moving on and getting married, an arrangement intended to avoid the creation of a landless working class. To further minimize the "evils" of the factory system, Lowell and his partners housed the women in company-owned and operated boardinghouses.

The experiment proved a success, and Lowell and his partners raised additional capital to build a series of factories on the Merrimack River in the 1820s and 1830s. Thus, the eponymous city of Lowell was born, bearing little resemblance to most cities of the age, being neat, well planned, and the home of a relatively stable social order of young, unmarried women. Though that order would eventually disintegrate with growing competition and the influx of low-paid Irish immigrants in the 1840s, the city of Lowell stood out at the time as an alternative urban industrial vision.

Shoe manufacturing cities like Lynn developed in a different fashion, one that more accurately foreshadowed the future of industry in the region. Beginning in the late 18th century, entrepreneurs—mostly merchants and shoemakers—began providing raw materials to farm families eager to earn a little extra cash by working at home sewing shoes. Over the next few decades, entrepreneurs gradually abandoned the outwork system, and began hiring men and women to work within central shops. The entrepreneurs subsequently replaced these workshops with manufactories that centralized all the different steps of shoe

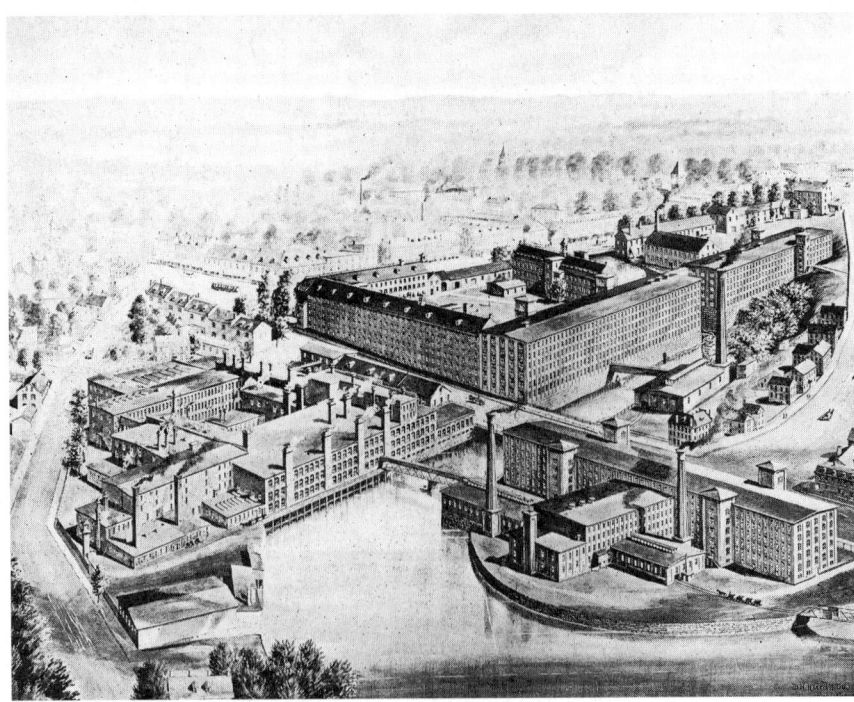

Cocheco Mills, Dover, N.H., ca. 1900

manufacturing under one roof. Finally, in the 1850s, factory owners introduced labor-saving machinery that automated much of the shoe-production process. Such a pattern of gradual industrialization and urbanization was paralleled in smaller shoe-manufacturing centers throughout Massachusetts, New Hampshire, and Maine.

Other industries, such as papermaking, followed different paths to maturity. Berkshire County, Mass., emerged as the center of the papermaking industry in the antebellum era. Factories in the region pursued a path of almost total mechanization. In the 1820s and 1830s, entrepreneurs introduced cylinder papermaking machines, followed in the 1840s by the famous Fourdrinier papermaking machine—a contraption that Herman Melville described as "a miracle of inscrutable intricacy." Despite their technological sophistication, however, such enterprises remained small, locally owned, and reliant on waterpower—relatively unobtrusive clusters of industry compared to places like Lynn.

A more famous monument to New England's industrialization is the Springfield Armory in Massachusetts, home of the "American System" of interchangeable parts. The new system arose with the development of precision machines that produced identical copies of the many parts that made up a typical gun. These technological advances complemented and fostered a growing division of labor; in Springfield, for example, the number of separate operations involved in making a gun went from 36 in 1815 to 100 in 1825 to more than 400 in 1855, each employing a separate class of worker.

Over the course of the antebellum era, the system of interchangeable parts was adopted by many industries centered in New England, including such famous establishments as Samuel Colt's Patent Fire-Arms Manufacturing Company in Hartford and many of Connecticut's clock and watch factories. Clock manufacturers like Eli Terry and Seth Thomas used interchangeable parts in order to mass-produce cheap wooden and metal clocks, thus obviating the need for skilled craftsmen and paving the way for the growing specialization and division of labor.

In general, workers in industries throughout New England resisted such transformations, resenting the loss in wages, the obsolescence of craft traditions, and the growing drudgery of industrial labor. In the Slater mills, for example, workers resorted to absenteeism, theft of raw materials, and arson to protest unfair working conditions. Even in more paternalistic workplaces like Lowell, the mill girls resisted management's attempts to improve productivity and went on strike. Though these

actions rarely succeeded, they proved a harbinger of things to come. Throughout the industries for which New England became most famous—textiles and shoes, especially—the 1840s and 1850s were dominated by a rise in labor activism spurred by worsening labor conditions and an influx of low-paid, unskilled Irish workers, many of whom replaced the earlier generation of workers. In the closing decades of the antebellum era, laboring people formed increasingly radical workers' parties and unions that fought for better pay, a 10-hour workday, free public schools, abolition of imprisonment for debt, protection of wages by lien laws, and control over local banks. On the eve of the Civil War, massive strikes broke out in Lowell (1857) and Lynn (1860), developments that foreshadowed the increasingly tense labor relations of the coming decades.

New England looked very different on the eve of the Civil War from the way it had some 70 years earlier. An influx of unskilled, predominantly Irish immigrants had swelled the ranks of the working class; sprawling industrial cities had replaced the pastoral factory towns of earlier decades; and the region had become an industrial powerhouse. By 1860 Massachusetts and Rhode Island had the most workers per factory of any states in the union as well as the largest capital investment per factory. New England as a whole produced 60 percent of all boots and shoes in the country and employed 105,000 workers in a textile industry that produced some 940 million yards of cloth a year—three times as much as the rest of the nation combined. By 1860 there was no disputing that despite several decades in which the ambitions of industrialists and the rural heritage of New England had coexisted a profound change had come across the region: the Industrial Revolution had arrived.

Alan Dawley, *Class and Community: The Industrial Revolution in Lynn* (1976); Thomas Dublin, *Women at Work: The Transformation of Work and Community in Lowell, Massachusetts, 1826–1860* (1979); Brooke Hindle and Steven Lubar, *Engines of Change: The American Industrial Revolution, 1790–1860* (1986); Walter Licht, *Industrializing America: The 19th Century* (1995); Judith A. McGaw, *Most Wonderful Machine: Mechanization and Social Change in Berkshire Paper Making, 1801–1885* (1987); Jonathan Prude, *The Coming of Industrial Order: Town and Factory Life in Rural Massachusetts, 1810–1860* (1983).

Stephen Mihm

Industrial New England, 1861–1918

By 1861 New England's economy depended heavily on textile manufacturing, fed by America's cotton crop from the South. When the supply was cut off by the Civil War, New England's textile mills shifted production to wool uniforms and blankets or began manufacturing rifles and other war materials to maintain

prosperity. Industry reorganized generally into either large-scale mechanized textile, paper, or shoe mills powered by technological advances or small-scale manufactories supported by skilled labor using sophisticated techniques to produce specialized products such as machine tools or jewelry. From 1861 to 1918 New England matured industrially, even as cost advantages shifted to other regions of the country.

The changes in New England's textile industry influenced the broader industrial development of the region and also reflected industrial growth throughout the United States. Despite its dearth of diverse natural resources, New England had an industrial head start on the rest of the country, and was gifted with an abundance of waterpower and a versatile, efficient, and competitive population that made it a leader in technological innovation. This combination of adaptability and innovation would cast the region in a continuing role of economic leadership.

A tremendous increase in immigration between 1861 and 1918 also helped service the region's extraordinary industrial growth. Factories soon became filled with men and women from southern and eastern Europe and the Middle East. In 1850 Connecticut's foreign-born population accounted for 10 percent of the state's population of 38,518. In 1870 native-born Americans accounted for 75 percent of the state's population, but by 1918 that figure had declined to only 35 percent. In northern New England the steady influx of immigrants came mainly from French-speaking Quebec or New Brunswick, Canada. Waves of Irish and French Canadians immigrated to Rhode Island, but after 1890 a great influx of Italian immigrants shifted the balance again. By 1910 only 30 percent of Rhode Island's population was of Yankee stock; one-third had been born abroad and 36 percent had at least one foreign-born parent.

The region's population shifted again when many workers from northern New England migrated to find work in the mills of Lowell and Lawrence and in the shoe towns of Essex County, Mass. In Haverhill they were joined by many Italians, Armenians, and East European Jews. Some 75 percent of the stitchers in the Haverhill Shoe Strike of 1894–95 were native born, most of Anglo-Saxon heritage, although some were the children and grandchildren of Irish and Canadian immigrants. In Vermont, French Canadians settled in Burlington to work in the mills, and Italians filled the quarries in Barre, where Emma Goldman spoke to the anarchists in 1911 and the town elected a socialist mayor in 1912. But despite efforts to recruit more immigrant workers, aside from a few Swedish and Finnish farmers

Vermont did not experience the same effects of immigration as other areas of the region.

The drastic population shifts in industrial areas caused relations between ethnic groups to become increasingly strained, often resulting in labor agitation. The great strike of 1877, partially a result of the depression of 1872, brought renewed union activity to the region, as did the depression years of 1893 and 1894. During the Haverhill Shoe Strike, 3,000 workers walked away from their machines and filled the streets in protest. Perhaps most dramatic and symbolic of the strained relations between labor and management, the so-called Bread and Roses strike against the American Woolen Company of Lawrence, Mass., in 1912 achieved worldwide notoriety.

Textile production—focused largely in New England—was second only to the nation's iron and steel industry, and Massachusetts was the preeminent center of wool and cotton manufacturing in the nation. The Amoskeag Manufacturing Company, with its mills in Manchester, N.H., and its offices in Boston, was the world's largest cotton manufacturing firm. The American Woolen Corporation, also with offices in Boston and some 35 mills throughout the region, was the world's largest wool manufacturing company. Lowell, Lawrence, Fall River, and New Bedford, Mass.; Providence, R.I.; Willimantic, Conn.; and Lewiston, Maine, were also great textile centers.

In 1905, of the 23 million cotton spindles in operation that year, New England had 14 million—8 million of them in Massachusetts. In 1860 New England was home to 81,000 cotton mill workers. In 1905, 155,981 of the 310,458 cotton mill operatives in the United States were located in New England. In 1860, 25,583 wool mill workers lived in New England; in 1905, of the 179,967 wool operatives nationally, the region had 98,263. The silk industry in New England had approximately 70 establishments employing some 12,000 workers.

The manufacture of leather products, primarily shoes, was the second-ranked industry in New England, and the first in Massachusetts, which was the leading shoe and leather center of the world. The leather industry was also firmly established in Maine and New Hampshire. By 1900, an estimated 1,000 establishments in more than 100 New England communities contributed to shoe production. Brockton, Lynn, and Haverhill, Mass., dominated the shoe industry, and women dominated the labor force in these towns. Haverhill was also the wood heel capital of the world. In 1908 Haverhill became the first city east of the Mississippi River to adopt the commission form of government. The other shoe cities of the region included Marlboro, Rockland,

A New England manufacturing town, 1881

Whitman, and Newburyport, Mass.; Auburn and Gardiner, Maine; and Manchester, Nashua, and Dover, N.H.

Unlike textile firms, the United Shoe Machinery Corporation of Beverly, Mass., held a monopoly on shoe machinery production and leased its machines on a per-shoe cost. The resultant low capitalization required to make shoes permitted the growth of mobile small-scale operations specializing in piecework by contract. By 1911 New England was turning out between 5 million and 6 million cases of shoes per year.

Papermaking was also a major New England industry. An increasingly literate population meant an increased demand for paper for newspapers, magazines, and books. Maine continued to increase its pulp production, but other areas of the nation, meanwhile, became more competitive. Nevertheless, by 1900 Massachusetts and Maine were second and third nationally in paper production. Holyoke, Mass., was the leading paper center in the world, with an international reputation for producing fine and book papers. Dalton, Mass., was also famous for its production of fine paper, including the paper used for U.S. government banknotes. Paper production was greatly affected, however, when New England began experiencing decreased water supply, labor strikes, and tariff changes.

Attleboro, Mass., and Providence were the centers of jewelry production in New England, and second in the nation. By 1894 the jewelry industry was the economic base of this area. A small operation that offered relatively easy entry for the intrepid entrepreneur, the jewelry business could be housed in a small

space, and each business seemingly gave birth to another as individual jewelers used new techniques, became more creative in design, and experimented with different metals. New immigrants arriving after 1900, especially skilled German jewelry workers, dramatically changed the industry. But jewelry, like women's shoes, was often a casualty of fluctuating styles.

The manufacture of machinery and machine tools in New England was equally important to all the states, including Vermont, where the Springfield Valley area was known as "precision valley." Ninety percent of the textile machinery used in the United States was made or invented in New England. Lowell, Whitinsville, Hopedale, Worcester, and Hyde Park, Mass., dominated the industry.

The 1900 census reported that the American wool trade consumed 483 million pounds of wool, with New England using 263 million pounds. Of the $380,934,030 total value, New England's share was $218,108,733, or 59 percent. Similarly, New England cotton textiles were valued at $224,072,562, or 51 percent of the $442,451,218 total.

Despite these statistics, however, industrial New England was constantly in flux, largely because of shifting population patterns. Although the region experienced a steady increase in the labor force from 1870, wage differentials in comparison with other regions—in part owing to the region's prosperity, unionization, and relatively slow overall population growth—led to the continual outmigration of industries to other regions. By the end of World War I, New England's industries faced growing economic pressures that the prosperity of the war years only masked temporarily.

Mary H. Blewett, *The Last Generation: Work and Life in the Textile Mills of Lowell, Massachusetts, 1910–1960* (1990); Robert W. Eisenmenger, *The Dynamics of Growth in New England's Economy, 1870–1964* (1967); George French, ed., *New England: What It Is and What Is It to Be* (1911); Laurence F. Gross, *The Growth of Industrial Decline: The Boott Cotton Mills of Lawrence, Massachusetts, 1910–1960* (1990); Seymour E. Harris, *The Economics of New England: Case Study of an Older Area* (1952); William F. Hartford, *Where Is Our Responsibility? Unions and Economic Change in the New England Textile Industry, 1870–1960* (1996); Patricia Trainor O'Malley and Paul H. Tedesco, *A New England City: Haverhill, Massachusetts* (1987); Paul H. Tedesco, *The Hub of the Jewelry World: Attleboro, Massachusetts, 1894–1975* (1979).

Paul H. Tedesco

Industrial Decline, 1919–45

Economic decline and pessimism have often seemed the natural state in New England. In 1836 William Ellery Channing remarked of Boston, "We are a city too much given to croaking. I have been told that we were on the brink of ruin ever since I knew the place." Seymour Harris, in 1952, echoed him: "The miracle of New England is not how badly she has performed, but, in the face of barren natural resources and unfavorable location relative to raw materials and markets, how remarkably she has moved ahead." The region has constantly encountered serious problems of adjustment.

Although New England's industries benefited greatly from the U.S. involvement in World War I, they suffered proportionately from the immediate stoppage of defense contracts and the demobilization of the military when the armistice was declared. The region soon experienced labor strikes, unemployment, and general economic depression. Any competitive advantage that New England industries might have had before 1919 also slipped with the western geographic shift of industrial and consumer markets, the introduction of new power sources, and the general transition to a metals-based economy. Between 1919 and 1947 the market shift from nondurable goods like textiles, shoes, and paper to durable goods like airplanes and machinery resulted in an increase of some 97,000 workers in durables and the release of 30,000 workers to nonmanufacturing occupations. This expansion of employment in the durable-goods industries offset the reduction of employment in nondurable-goods industries. Diverse industrial development in New England also meant that many of its cities concentrated on the production of a single commodity, while smaller communities became one-industry and even one-firm towns.

Although large-scale industries such as textiles and leather are often credited with the region's growth, the economic history of New England is largely a history of small business. Small enterprise has always played an important role in the region's economy and has influenced New England's remarkable growth in the technology industry. The small-business sector functioned as a laboratory for new technologies and processes and a competitive testing ground for new ideas. In the 1930s, academic research institutions, particularly the Massachusetts Institute of Technology, developed an impressive array of guidance and navigation systems, metallurgy, optics, and electronics. Nevertheless, as World War II approached, the New England economy was still in decline and its major industries steadily migrated to other regions.

President Franklin Roosevelt's New Deal did not stop this general industrial decline. The advent of World War II, however, and the impact of increased government outlays stanched the nation's economic bleeding. The Springfield Armory, for example, which had 1,000 workers in 1936, grew to 14,000 by 1943. The war also reinforced labor unions as a powerful American institution despite constant labor-management struggles. Even more dramatic was the movement of women back into the labor force to fill the shortages caused by the draft and enlistments. With the war's end in 1945, industry in New England once again began to decline.

Haverhill, Mass., provides a good example. In 1890 Haverhill produced 7.3 percent of the total value of shoes manufactured in the United States, ranking it among the top five shoe centers; in 1923 it produced only 3.6 percent. On January 1, 1920, 122 firms were doing business in Haverhill; by December 31, 1928, only 102 remained, and during these years, many firms went out of business or moved to nonunion communities. From 1849 to 1933 New England's total shoe distribution declined from 51.3 percent to 35 percent, while the Midwest's distribution rose from 7.6 percent to 36.3 percent. After 1919 the growing importance of style as a factor in the production of women's shoes emphasized the nearness-to-market argument, the migratory nature of the shoe industry, and increased foreign competition. Companies such as T. and A. Bata of Czechoslovakia began using American technology to produce cheaper shoes with cheaper labor.

In general, this same period was marked by constant agitation over wages, hours, and job security. Management, unable to reduce production costs by finding cheaper materials or lowering transportation costs, fought the workers constantly about wages and union

organizing. Brockton and Haverhill, Mass., became centers of union discontent and socialism in the shoe industry. Among shoe workers, union membership reached a national high in 1920, then began a general decline. The nature of the industry, with its small shops and piece-rate system, is partially responsible for the development of an independent shoe union movement and experimentation in socialist government. The citizens of Haverhill elected the first socialist mayor in the United States and saw the Socialist Labor Party take control of city government for a time. Municipal socialism also took hold and was taken up by other industrial communities in the region.

The postwar slump affected New England's industry powerfully between 1921 and 1941. Textile mills continued to move south. New England's production of cotton goods, which was 75 percent of the nation's output in 1880, was down to 20 percent by 1939. New England began specializing in finer grades of product as unemployment and union strife increased. The woolen industry maintained a dominant position by its easy access to foreign supplies of wool, the position of Boston as the central wool market of the United States, and the region's nearness to consuming centers. Paper manufacturing, New England's most important industry based on regional natural resources, produced pulp in New Hampshire and Maine while the Connecticut River valley in Massachusetts, especially Holyoke, concentrated on high-grade paper.

The shoe industry was localized in a few centers: Brockton, Boston, Haverhill, Lynn, and Salem, Mass.; Nashua and Manchester, N.H.; and Auburn, Maine. Despite the effects of the two World Wars, production and employment in the boot and shoe industry continued to decline. The rubber industry produced mainly footwear and tires and tubes. Plants in Massachusetts, Connecticut, and Rhode Island produced more than 50 percent of the nation's rubber. Electrical equipment machinery led the metal-producing industries; Massachusetts produced 60 percent of the region's income in this area, followed by Connecticut, Rhode Island, and New Hampshire. New England's gain in machinery was greater than in the nation at large during the 1930s and was not affected by outside competition. New England's rubber-production plants were large units within national corporations.

The area of greatest expansion during the years 1941 to 1945 was in transportation equipment and electrical machinery, mainly in the Connecticut airplane industry and the Massachusetts textile industry. The region produced more than 50 percent of the national output of textile machinery, but in 1945 this industry was in decline also. Machine tools were produced in Connecticut, Massachusetts, and Rhode Island. Mechanics' tools were produced in Vermont, Connecticut, and Massachusetts. And although the general expansion of manufacturing in New England from 1939 to 1945 coincided with an increase in the number of industrial workers, this expansion was well below the national average. The war years continued to impede New England's economic growth because the War Department made a special effort to assign war plants evenly throughout the country. It was apparent that other regions had begun to gain a clear advantage over New England, which had established lines of production.

During World War II, the federal government awarded a substantial number of military contracts to small research and development firms throughout New England. To develop new weaponry, these companies had to design new production techniques and become familiar with new technologies. This impetus, coupled with the region's industrial history, its specialized labor force, and a plethora of research institutions, formed the basis for the computer revolution that swept the region, the nation, and the world after 1945.

John Donald Black, *The Rural Economy of New England: A Regional Study* (1950); Robert W. Eisenmenger, *The Dynamics of Growth in New England's Economy, 1870–1964* (1967); Laurence F. Gross, *The Course of Industrial Decline: The Boott Cotton Mills of Lowell, Massachusetts, 1835–1955* (1993); Seymour Harris, *The Economics of New England: Case Study of An Older Area* (1952); Tom Juravich, William F. Hartford, and James R. Green, *Commonwealth of Toil: Chapters in the History of Massachusetts Workers and Their Unions* (1996); *The Economic State of New England: Report of the Committee of New England of the National Planning Association* (1954); Paul H. Tedesco, "An Experiment in Labor Peace: Haverhill, 1890–1930," *Historical Journal of Massachusetts* 15 (1987); Tedesco, *Economic Change and the Community: Canton, Massachusetts, 1797–1965* (1970).

Paul H. Tedesco

Postindustrial New England, 1945 to the Present

As New England's economy of textiles and shoes declined, other industrial strengths surfaced. Precision metalworking industries, a skilled labor force, and major research universities linked to industry slowed the region's economic decline. During World War II, the military gave the Massachusetts Institute of Technology and Harvard a disproportionate share of its research and development funding to develop fire control and guidance systems, radar and information technologies. This included federal funding to start MIT's Lincoln Laboratory in 1950 and to fund MIT's Draper Laboratory and Harvard's Computational Laboratories. These research centers and other regional institutions remained vital to the Department of Defense (DOD) in conducting the Cold War.

Through these war experiences, many researchers affiliated directly or indirectly with MIT (and to a lesser extent Harvard and other universities in the region) developed ongoing relations with the federal government's major research agencies (such as the DOD and National Institutes of Health), with industrial firms working in high technology, and with venture capitalists who were looking to profit from emerging industries. These networks encouraged entrepreneurial action, and DOD contracts in aerospace, shipbuilding, and electronics revived New England's industrial economy. Entrepreneurs used this know-how to initiate the minicomputer industry. When these entrepreneurs failed to keep pace with the personal computer march, others made use of the region's resources to generate new industries in advanced health care, biotechnology, software, and communications.

New England's postindustrial economy no longer relies on connections to particular industries or production processes. Instead it has effectively become knowledge- and innovation-based, an economy in which individuals draw on the region's past to reconfigure its future. The challenge is how to retain this enviable position with increased competition from elsewhere in the nation (most notably California's Silicon Valley) and the world. While the region's knowledge and innovation infrastructure remains in place, increased competition and internal weaknesses could negatively affect the economy over the next decades.

Throughout the 1980s and 1990s and into the 21st century, while population growth lagged behind the national average, the region's per capita income and productivity grew at rates significantly above the national average. New England also had relatively high high-technology employment, research and development funding, venture capital investment, and numbers of university graduates during this period.

The major trends in the New England economy over the past decades include slow overall growth in population and employment relative to the nation; decline in regional manufacturing employment while it increased in the nation; growth in other employment at approximately the same rate as the nation's except for the deep recession during the late 1980s and early 1990s; relatively strong income and productivity economies in Massachusetts, Connecticut, and New Hampshire and less vibrant economies in Maine, Rhode Island, and Vermont; and a shift of employment, (a) away from manufacturing to services and the financial, insurance, and real estate industries, (b) within manufacturing from nondurable to durable goods, and (c) within durable goods to high-technology products.

Most notably, gross state product (GSP) and per capita income have increased faster in New England than in the nation, both for the long term (last two decades of the 20th century) and during the growth period after the 1988–92 recession to the end of the century. All six New England states rank in the top third among U.S. states in GSP per capita change and change in median income for four-person families from 1980 to 1999. Leading the region and the nation are New Hampshire, Massachusetts, and Connecticut, ranked first, second, and third, respectively, in change in GSP per capita and ranked among the top six in the nation in per capita income in 2000. Coupled with its relatively high-income averages, New England has relatively low poverty. All six New England states rank in the bottom third of all states in this measure.

Fundamental to its high income and low poverty is the region's employment concentration in relatively high value-added activities. The region retains above-average employment in instrumentation, transportation equipment (other than motor vehicles), electronics, and industrial machinery. The services sector has been the fastest growing in the New England economy. Well over 40 percent of the region's jobs are now in services, higher than the national average. New England has twice the concentration of employment as the nation in education services. Other significant industries within the services sector in which New England has a higher employment concentration than the nation include health services, management and engineering services, legal services, and business services.

Also strong in the postindustrial regional economy are finance, insurance, and real estate. These industries employ about 10 percent of New England workers and have risen from below to above the national average since 1980. This is particularly impressive given the sharp decline in employment in depository institutions and real estate in the region during the deep recession of the late 1980s and early 1990s. The strength of these industries is largely a product of the rapid growth in securities and mutual funds and related industries, which rose more than 50 percent since 1992.

One of the fastest-growing segments of the New England economy is high-technology industry. In the absence of a standard U.S. Census classification, several definitions of high-technology industries have emerged. One of the more comprehensive definitions is that of the American Electronics Association (AEA), which includes services as well as manufacturing industries. Using the AEA classification, the region's employment concentration in high-technology industries was approximately 50 percent above the national average at the turn of the 21st century. Moreover, in the AEA's ranking of individual states by percentage of total private-sector employment in high-technology industries, three of the New England states rank in the top seven: Massachusetts (second, with 8.8 percent), New Hampshire (third, with 8.6 percent), and Vermont (seventh, with 6.4 percent). The most significant components of New England's high-tech industries include software, computer equipment, electronics, communications equipment, and services.

In fact, much of the explanation for the region's high per capita income and low poverty is that high-technology and knowledge- and innovation-based industries have thrived in New England for decades. Firms in the region share access to a multifaceted high-technology infrastructure, including funding from the DOD and other federal agencies, venture capitalists, and New England's colleges and universities, which have helped to fuel the region's strong research and development base and supply entrepreneurial talent.

The region experienced a decline in its share of federal research and development funds during the late 1980s as support in defense-related fields declined. In 1985 New England accounted for approximately 10 percent of total federal research and development dollars. This percentage fell to 6.6 by 1990 but increased back to 9 percent in 1996. In terms of total research and development, which includes corporate expenditures, the region continues to be strong. In 1999 four New England states—Massachusetts, Rhode Island, New Hampshire, and Connecticut—ranked among the top third in the nation in research and development funding per capita. Massachusetts ranked third among the 50 states, with funding more than 2.5 times the national average. Yet over the last five years of the 1990s the increase in research and development spending in the same four states was below the national average. The region's ability to maintain a strong position in research and development will be critical in the postindustrial economy.

Another aspect of the region's high-tech economy is venture capital. A high percentage of the nation's venture capital dollars have flowed into New England for many years. The region broke the $2 billion mark for venture capital monies for the first time in 1998, a year in which venture capitalists put approximately 50 percent more funds into the region than in

1995. This is more than twice the rate of increase nationally during that period. In 2001 Massachusetts (ranked first), New Hampshire (fourth) and Connecticut (ninth) were in the top tier of the states in venture capital invested as a percentage of GSP.

The third critical component of the high-technology infrastructure—higher education—feeds the high-technology economy with research and labor supply. The region has almost 300 institutions of higher education; in 1998 New England colleges awarded 46,700 graduate degrees, 79,900 bachelor's degrees, and 26,700 associate's degrees. The key to New England's economic advantage is not the numbers of degrees awarded but rather the relative concentration and nature of degrees granted. New England awards a higher percentage of the nation's total degrees than its share of the U.S. total population at all levels beyond the associate degree. In 1998 New England awarded 35 percent more bachelor's degrees per capita than the U.S. average, 75 percent more master's degrees, 62 percent more doctorates, and 40 percent more professional degrees. And though not all members of New England graduate programs end up staying in the region, many do. With the exception of Maine, New England states all rank in the top third in the nation in percentage of adults with a graduate degree.

Slow population and labor-force growth put a lid on the regional economy at the end of the period of strong growth during the late 1990s (with a regional unemployment rate of 3 percent in 1999, more than a full percentage point below the national unemployment rate). Foreign immigrants have been an important alternative source of skilled labor. One-third of foreign immigrants to Massachusetts between 1990 and 1996 were employed in highly skilled occupations by 1996, compared to 25 percent nationally.

The postindustrial New England economy faces some key challenges. The region's strong position in the research and development infrastructure is in question. Contract awards from the DOD have declined, and while a high proportion of New Englanders work in knowledge-based and high-technology industries, growth in these industries lags behind the national average. During the 1993–2000 economic boom period nationally, high technology in the region grew at half the national rate.

During the 2000–2001 national recession, high-technology industry employment in New England declined 2.6 percent compared to the national average of 2.3 percent, though the early 2000s recession was much milder than that of the late 1980s and early 1990s. During the earlier recession the region experi-

enced a much more pronounced decline in high-technology employment than the nation, 17 percent compared to 2 percent. The main factor in the sharp technology downturn in the late 1980s was the region's high concentration in minicomputer manufacturing. The stronger relative performance in the early 2000s downturn suggests that the region at the end of the 20th century was benefiting from a more diversified and well-balanced high-technology sector.

In sum, retaining a high share of federal and corporate research and development funding and activity, excellence in higher education, and a skilled, educated workforce pose both the biggest challenges and the biggest opportunities to New England at the beginning of the 21st century.

American Association for the Advancement of Science, *National Science Foundation Patterns of R and D Resources* (1997); American Electronics Association (AEA) *Cyberstates 2002: A State-by-State Overview of the High Technology Industry* (2002); Massachusetts Institute for a New Economy, *The Road Ahead: Emerging Threats to Workers, Families and the Massachusetts Economy* (1998); Progressive Policy Institute, *The 2002 State New Economy Index* (2002); Edward B. Roberts, *Entrepreneurs in High Technology: Lessons from MIT and Beyond* (1991); Susan Rosengrant and David R. Lampe, *Route 128: Lessons from Boston's High-Tech Community* (1992); Peter Temin, ed., *Engines of Enterprise: An Economic History of New England* (2000).

Ross Gittell and Allen Kaufman

Ames Tools In the 19th century Americans recognized the name Ames as a leader in politics, the railroad industry, and particularly the production of high-quality shovels. From their beginnings as blacksmiths and yeoman farmers, the Ameses rose to become one of New England's most prominent and influential 19th-century families.

Captain John Ames (1738–1805) made some of this country's first metal shovels in his blacksmith shop in West Bridgewater, Mass. In 1803 his son Oliver (1779–1863) established a shovel-making manufactory in nearby North Easton, Mass. Although best known as a manufacturer of shovels and spades, the company and its local affiliates at one time made a variety of hand tools, including hoes and knives. Company and Ames family members were also part or full owners of numerous industrial enterprises; in New England their workers produced locomotive and steamboat components, cannons, plows, and paper.

The ironworking tradition of the Ames family had begun in England. In 1635 brothers William and John Ames brought their trade to Braintree, Mass., where William worked at one of North America's earliest colonial ironworks. For generations their descendants were connected with industrial enterprises throughout New England: south of Boston (West Bridgewater, Easton, Braintree, Canton, and Sharon, Mass.), Springfield, Mass., and northwest Connecticut. The Ameses were active in local, state, and national politics and in the construction and management of American railroads, and were prominent investors in big business. Most notable politically was Oakes Ames (1804–73), who served in the U.S. Congress for ten years and was instrumental in the building of the Union Pacific Railroad. His good reputation was tarnished, however, in the 1873 Credit Mobilier scandal. His son Oliver (1831–95) was governor of Massachusetts from 1886 to 1889.

The Ames company manufactured a wide variety of shovels recognized for their quality. The company was well poised to meet the growing demand for shovels from agriculture, western expansion, canal, turnpike, and railroad construction, gold mining, and the military. In 1833 the company produced 78,000 shovels with 65 employees, and by 1865 Ames was manufacturing 786,000 shovels a year and employed 250 persons. In the 1870s they manufactured three-fifths of the world's shovels. At the 1893 World's Columbian Exposition, Ames shovels won first prize. The company underwent major mergers and acquisitions in both 1901 (becoming Ames Shovel and Tool Company) and 1931 (becoming Ames, Baldwin, and Wyoming Company). It left New England in the 1950s when its Easton facility shut down; Ames Lawn and Garden Tool Company, located in Parkersburg, W. Va., has no current family affiliation. In 2000 Ames Lawn and Garden Tools merged with True-Temper Hardware of Pennsylvania to form Ames–True-Temper, a division of U.S. Industries and the world's largest manufacturer of nonpowered lawn and garden tools.

The Ames company left an enduring mark on the New England landscape, particularly in the village of North Easton. Many of the shovel-shop buildings survive (most ca. 1850), as does much worker housing. Private Ames estates and exceptional examples of public architecture, including five Ames-funded buildings designed by H. H. Richardson, can be seen as well. The Ames office building still stands in Boston. The Stonehill Industrial History Center at Stonehill College in Easton contains extensive primary materials on the Ames family and company (including 800 shovels) in its Arnold B. Tofias Industrial Archives and Ames Family Collection. The family's legacy extends beyond the physical to the region's historic landscape; financial, business, and political success along with social prominence and deep Yankee roots ensured that Ameses were present at innumerable important events and movements in American history.

Winthrop Ames, *The Ames Family of Easton, Massachusetts* (1938); W. L. Chaffin, *History of Easton, Massachusetts* (1975 [1886]); Edmund C. Hands, *Easton's Neighborhoods* (1995).

Gregory J. Galer

Amoskeag Manufacturing Company

The Amoskeag Manufacturing Company and the city of Manchester, N.H., which the company planned and began developing in 1837, were products of the new industrial order launched in New England by a closely knit group of entrepreneurs known as the Boston Associates. At its peak in the early 20th century, the Amoskeag was the world's largest textile plant, employing up to 17,000 workers. It used approximately 30 major mills with a total of 8 million square feet of floor space. The Amoskeag housed 74 separate cloth-making departments, three dye houses, 24 mechanical and electrical departments, three major steam-power plants, and a hydroelectric power station. The company was almost completely self-sufficient in its operations, design, and construction. For a time it manufactured locomotives and rifles in addition to textile machinery.

In the 1830s the Boston Associates purchased the waterpower of the entire Merrimack River and assembled a 15,000-acre plot across the Amoskeag Falls as a site for the planned city, which would be named after Manchester, England, the world's largest textile city. Manchester's urban plan reflected the social program of its developers. As in Lowell, Mass., and elsewhere the company established a community of young rural women who worked in the mills and lived together in boardinghouses. This community was governed by a social system of corporate paternalism—a philosophy of benevolent control—that treated workers as the corporation's "children" and permeated all aspects of life: the organization of work, the strict management of boardinghouses, the founding of charities, and the endowment of churches. In the mid-19th century, when the majority of the labor force consisted of young unmarried women, the company also regulated employee behavior after work hours: boardinghouse doors were locked at 10 o'clock in the evening, church attendance was compulsory, and alcohol consumption was prohibited.

For most planned New England industrial communities the "utopian" period of company control ended shortly before the Civil War. Irish immigrant families willing to work for lower wages replaced the "mill girls," and speculative housing gradually replaced corporation boardinghouses. But while management became fragmented among many small factory units in Lowell, it remained consolidated in Manchester. During the 1880s and 1890s, the Amoskeag began to annex mills that had originally been constructed as separate corporations founded by the Boston Associates and managed by overlapping directorships. Thus, by 1905 the Amoskeag Company had become the only large textile corporation in the city. To encourage the development of business and private housing in Manchester, the company auctioned land to private buyers for stores and residences, and endowed churches and various social clubs with land. Until the 1930s no new industry could be established in Manchester without the Amoskeag's permission, as the company controlled nearly all available industrial land and supplied more

The former Amoskeag Mills are still a landmark of Manchester, N.H.

than two-thirds of Manchester's employment opportunities.

The Amoskeag Company's control of Manchester's economic life gave it great influence over the city's political life as well. Amoskeag overseers and other officials served on the board of aldermen, and management retained close ties with the police force, which proved useful during strikes. But absentee management and remote control also had an impact on the spirit of both the mill and the city, and led eventually to the company's demise. Many of the Amoskeag's board of directors were prominent Boston financiers, few of whom had more than small investments in Amoskeag securities. The treasurer—who was almost solely in charge of the management of the Amoskeag—ran the mills from his Boston office. In Manchester, the agent, a local, salaried official, had charge of executing—and to some extent planning—most aspects of production as well as handling all matters concerning personnel and labor relations, but he answered to the Boston office. Nonetheless, the longevity and loyalty of its agents helped account for the Amoskeag's success and phenomenal sense of continuity. Three generations of the Straw family served the Amoskeag as agents between 1856 and 1924.

Beginning in the 1870s French Canadian immigrants, driven from rural Quebec by land scarcity, depleted farms, and poverty, began to enter the labor force of the Amoskeag mills. By 1900 the steady recruitment of French Canadians into the Amoskeag had significantly altered Manchester's population. By 1910 French Canadians made up 35 percent of the Amoskeag's labor force and 38 percent of the city's population. Yet despite the prominence of French Canadians in the mills' labor force, the ranks of overseer and second hand were still filled by native-born Americans, English, Scottish, and second-generation Irish, with an occasional sprinkling of Germans and Swedes.

At the beginning of the 20th century, Polish immigrants began coming to Manchester, first from other New England communities and later directly from Poland. By 1920 the city's Polish population had grown to 2,000, and Poles made up approximately 10 percent of the Amoskeag's labor force. Greeks constituted another 10 percent. By 1910 company foremen and overseers had become accustomed to speaking or understanding some French, but most other immigrant groups had to depend on translators and were more firmly locked into the lowest skilled and unskilled positions. Tensions between immigrant groups frequently led to name calling and occasionally to fighting.

To combat these difficulties, the Amoskeag launched a corporate welfare and efficiency program in 1910. These paternalistic measures were devised to attract additional laborers to the city, socialize them to industrial work, instill loyalty to the company, curb labor unrest, and prevent unionization. The efficiency program, inaugurated simultaneously with the welfare program at the peak of the corporation's expansion, introduced an employment office that centralized the hiring process of all workers and kept systematic personnel records. The employment office checked on employees' backgrounds and activities, thus helping screen out unwanted elements, especially blacklisted workers and "agitators." The welfare program, vivid in the memories of most workers, touched their lives in numerous ways. It included the Textile Club, which published the *Amoskeag Bulletin;* a textile school and a cooking school; and a dental service, as well as a limited superannuation plan. The Amoskeag Company also established a family playground and sponsored a visiting-nurse service. As an incentive to greater work stability, the company introduced a home-ownership plan, offering house lots for sale to workers who had been with the company for five years or longer, along with a reasonable mortgage plan.

One of the Amoskeag's most important contributions to its workers was undoubtedly the provision of corporation tenements, in which workers, usually those with large families, rented apartments. The "corporations," as the workers called them, were three-to-five-story brick houses strung along the streets leading down from the center of the city to the millyard. These substantial structures were originally built as boardinghouses for the first "mill girls." Some were subsequently remodeled into flats for large families while the rest continued to serve as boardinghouses for single workers. The rent, which amounted to about a dollar a room per month, was always substantially lower than the market rate for the rest of the city. The buildings were carefully kept up by the Amoskeag's maintenance crews. But by 1910 only about 15 to 20 percent of the Amoskeag's labor force lived in these buildings; most workers rented city housing, and a significant number owned their own homes.

Except for minor unrest in the 1880s, the corporation's paternalistic programs and the overall Amoskeag "spirit" effectively discouraged unionization until World War I. The United Textile Workers of America (UTW) made its first inroads into Manchester in 1917, a time when labor shortages coincided with high demand for production, both due to the war effort. Union membership, although small, was drawn from strategic positions in the mill. In 1919 the UTW organized the first strike at the Amoskeag since an 1885 strike led by the Knights of Labor. Because the mills were working primarily on war orders, the secretary of war dispatched an arbitrator, who granted the workers their demand for a 15 percent pay increase instead of the 12 percent the Amoskeag had offered. The strike was settled within five days, but in the process the union added 5,000 new members to its rosters. The union's foothold in the corporation, however, remained limited.

Although the Amoskeag made the greatest profits in its history during World War I, in the industrial demobilization that followed the company, along with most other New England textile corporations, began to experience a gradual decline. By the 1920s, a period of surface prosperity in the United States, Amoskeag workers were already rehearsing for the Great Depression. The announcement in February 1922 that the company was increasing work hours while cutting wages 20 percent succeeded in galvanizing a large majority of workers. (Similar wage cuts were being made in most of the New England textile cities at the same time and were also precipitating strikes.) The resulting bitter, nine-month strike was the first long-term general strike in the Amoskeag's history and marked the turning point for the company and its workers. The workers were ultimately forced to return to work under terms imposed by the company.

On September 4, 1934, the workers joined a national general textile strike, which was called off after three weeks without significant results. From that point on the arena of labor protest shifted from organized strikes to sit-down strikes in various departments. These continued until September 1935, when the Amoskeag shut down operations with the proclaimed intention of reopening. In December, the corporation applied for reorganization in state bankruptcy court, but in July 1936 the court ordered liquidation of the company's assets. The Amoskeag's shutdown in the midst of the Depression destroyed the economic base of Manchester, by then a city of 75,000, dealing it a devastating blow.

George Waldo Browne, *The Amoskeag Manufacturing Co. of Manchester, New Hampshire: A History* (1915); James P. Hanlan, *The Working Population of Manchester, New Hampshire, 1840–1886* (1981); Tamara K. Hareven, *Family Time and Industrial Time: The Relationship between the Family and Work in a New England Industrial Community* (1982); Tamara K. Hareven and Randolph Langenbach, *Amoskeag: Life and Work in an American Factory-City* (1978); Arthur M. Kenison, *Dumaine's Amoskeag: Let the Record Speak* (1997).

Tamara K. Hareven

Axes and Edged Tools

Immigrants arriving in New England brought scythes, axes, and saws to supply themselves with food, fuel, and shelter, but these soon wore down, or proved unsuitable for use on the frontier. Since the immigrants could not easily import replacements, artisans like Joseph Jenks, who by 1646 was making scythes at his Saugus, Mass., smithy, began filling local needs. Artifacts reveal that successive generations of blacksmiths well into the first decade of the republic used traditional methods to turn out edged tools of indifferent quality. Although the failure of a badly made tool was an inconvenience for a town dweller, it was a matter of life or death on the frontier. Most American men and women in the 19th century depended on the performance of their tools, which they handled every day.

Growing demand among an expanding, westward-moving population for uniformly reliable edged tools that would fit American conditions and tastes created opportunities for Yankee mechanics. As they developed new techniques for making edged tools, they created a paradigm for New England manufacturing culture. In the 1790s they began to use waterpower to reduce the arduous physical labor of hammering out an iron scythe or ax blade and welding the steel edge on it. Simeon North, later famous as a leader in the development of interchangeable-parts manufacture, began his industrial career near his family farm in Berlin, Conn., with the purchase of a sawmill on Spruce Brook that he converted to a scythe shop in 1795.

After applying mechanical power to their work, edged-tool makers next concentrated production into shops, where a manager could closely control the quality of the product. Thus, after John and Joseph Farwell began making scythes with trip-hammers in Fitchburg, Mass., in 1796, two of their apprentices, Alpheus Kimball and John Thurston Farwell, set up their own works, producing 9,600 scythes a year by 1820. John T. Farwell later joined with former apprentice Abel Simonds to start a third scythe works in Fitchburg. The three shops had a production capacity of 84,300 scythes per year.

Yankee edged-tool makers thrived by emphasizing the quality as well as the efficient production of their products. The Collins brothers of Connecticut began factory production of axes in 1826. Samuel Collins recognized his American customers' demand for quality and superior design when he observed that Yankee woodcutters were scientific choppers who appreciated good axes, would pay more for them, and would use them with care. Unlike their English competitors, who stuck with traditional designs, New England edged-tool makers responded to their customers' needs and preferences by making tools in a wide range of styles and patterns. The Collins brothers expanded their business worldwide both by building a reputation for the quality of their products and by making axes, machetes, and other tools in the patterns that customers in different parts of the world preferred.

Edged-tool makers had to confront a major health concern as they concentrated production into large shops. Artisans finished edged tools on large, water-cooled grindstones. The rapidly revolving stones would sometimes burst, often killing the grinder, who sat astride the stone. Artisans who remained on the job for extended periods contracted silicosis from inhaling the wet stone and steel particles. The need to retain workers led Yankee mechanics to devise safer production methods. Beginning in 1832 at the Collins works, Elisha K. Root designed forging and shaving machinery that so closely shaped an ax that little additional grinding was required. Like Root many New England mechanicians who got their start making edged tools later contributed new manufacturing techniques in other industries. After scythe maker Simeon North began making pistols for the government in 1799, he initiated mechanization of armory work. In 1864 Abel Simonds's sons converted their father's scythe shop into the Simonds Manufacturing Company in Fitchburg, Mass., later famous for making saws. In Millbury, Conn., Elijah and Asa Waters set up a scythe works that in 1808 became the nucleus of the armory in which Thomas Blanchard made his first irregular-turning lathe. By offering a salary of $5,000 a year, the highest yet paid in a New England industry, Samuel Colt lured Elisha Root away from the Collins works in 1849 to develop new production methods for his Hartford armory; these were copied in England and Europe a decade later.

New England's edged-tool makers reached their peak in the late 19th century. Benjamin Jenkins and James Boyd had started scythe production in Winsted, Conn., in 1792. Others followed, and by 1881 the largest of the town's three works made 120,000 scythes a year. New farming and woodcutting methods, however, soon jeopardized the industry. When edged-tool makers failed to bring out new products, woodsmen adopted the two-man saw in place of the ax as their primary felling tool. Improved sawmills eliminated the need to shape timber with adzes. Farmers who bought mowing machines no longer needed scythes. Additionally, inexpensive steam engines and, later, central-station electric power diminished the competitive advantage of New England's abundant waterpower. Other regions had lower transportation and labor costs. The Simonds works in Fitchburg prospered with sawmaking. But as the 20th century advanced, such famous ax makers as Douglas in Massachusetts and, in 1967, Collins in Connecticut, closed, sometimes selling their names to others. Collins machetes are now made in Mexico. And if a customer needs a scythe blade, a New England hardware store must import it from Austria.

Robert B. Gordon and Patrick M. Malone, *Texture of Industry: An Archeological View of the Industrialization of North America* (1994); Donald R. Hoke, *Ingenious Yankees: The Rise of the American System of Manufactures in the Private Sector* (1990); Paul B. Kabakian, *American Woodworking Tools* (1978); Henry J. Kauffman, *American Axes* (1972).

Robert B. Gordon

Banking and Financial Services

New England's banking and financial services industries have been an important and abiding element in the region's survival of the challenges imposed by the demanding physical environment. Poor soil, short growing seasons, and bitter winters provided strong incentives for the accumulation of surpluses as protective buffers against the vicissitudes of nature. The virtues of thrift and prudence guided not only the earliest 17th-century Puritan settlers but also later immigrant groups in their flight from poverty. These beliefs, combined with the Yankee spirit of innovation, led to the establishment of savings and lending institutions to reduce risk and maximize returns in financial contracting.

The regional takeoff in banking occurred immediately after the end of the Revolution with the creation in 1784 of the Bank of Massachusetts (forerunner of the Bank of Boston). This marked the beginning of widespread banking formation throughout the region; 21 banks were chartered by 1814 in Massachusetts alone. The prerevolutionary economy had been beset by limited sources of currency and credit. Although both Massachusetts and Connecticut had issued their own state currencies during the early 1700s, this practice was prohibited by the Crown with the extension of the imperial system. Attempts to develop land and commodity banks were also short-lived. The credit system had depended heavily on large merchant-trading business, which, in turn, looked to London to discount bills of exchange and credit instruments. During the Revolution, finance had been in disarray largely because of the wartime exigencies faced by the Continental Congress. But after independence, the new federal government sought stability through the formation of the

First and the Second Banks of the United States.

Banking organizations in the early republic advanced New England's economy, reducing financial risk and lowering transaction costs by providing four basic services. First, they accepted deposits and transferred funds. Second, they extended short-term credit by discounting notes primarily for self-liquidating commercial transactions such as the financing of seasonal inventories. Third, they issued notes that effectively served as paper currency during a period when the federal government's currency involvement remained limited to the minting of coins. And finally, they exchanged notes issued by other banks as well as foreign currencies.

Investment banking began to flourish in the 1820s in response to the need to finance the region's first railroads. New Englanders became early proponents of railroad development after the decline of their ports when the Erie Canal was completed in 1825. Success in floating railroad bonds and, to a lesser extent, preferred and common stock by Boston firms such as Kidder Peabody and Company, John M. Forbes and Company, and Lee, Higginson, and Company, prepared regional investment bankers to play leading roles in the later financing of western roads. Rail finance also helped these companies resolve long-term financing questions for clients in other rising industries, such as shoe and textile manufacture, power generation, and telephone communication. Although New England investment banking maintained close correspondent relations with institutions in both New York and London, the demand for liquid markets for local securities became so great that a stock exchange was formed in Boston in 1834. And investment banking expertise enhanced regional income by enabling local investors to capitalize on the economic expansion of other U.S. regions and foreign lands.

Trust companies were another specialized financial market intermediary that emerged during the 19th century. Both the Massachusetts Hospital Trust and the Rhode Island Hospital Trust, formed during the first two decades of the century, were early prototypes that began accepting deposits as an adjunct to their life insurance and annuity businesses. Not until the 1870s, however, did the modern trust company begin to make its appearance in New England. Trusts were attractive because they were generally required to maintain lower reserve assets than commercial banks. Besides providing safety deposit boxes and personal trust services for the wealthy, the trusts were allowed to make real estate loans and could extend more credit to individual borrowers. With the expansion of regional industry, these firms offered corporate trust services such as disbursing interest and dividend payments and transferring and registering securities.

Changes in the size and financing of banks in the second half of the 19th century created new needs for information and professional knowledge for New England banks. One aspect of this was the drive by leading organizations to maximize profits and reduce risk by creating branch networks through the acquisition of local banks. Although many states allowed branch development for trust companies and state-chartered commercial banks in their home cities, nationally chartered banks were generally prohibited from these practices until the passage of the McFadden Act in 1927. Branch building helped to increase deposits, which had overtaken equity as the main source of investment capital. The traditional mode of lending based on informal assessments of character and financial capacity gave way to a system that was more dependent on professional knowledge and was constrained by the requirements of state regulation. Knowledge of accounting and finance acquired through training in new professional schools of business like Harvard's Graduate School of Business Administration and Dartmouth's Amos Tuck School of Business became vital to aspiring bankers who were called upon to evaluate financial data submitted by prospective borrowers lacking ties to a bank's executive leadership.

Speculation in stocks and bonds also led to greater interdependence between country and city banks in New England, creating, at times, great strains on the financial system. During summer months country banks often transferred their surplus balances to correspondents in money centers like New York or Boston for investment in call loans to brokers. When they recalled these transfers to finance the harvests each fall, credit shortages developed. Such seasonal tightness, however, could lead to panic if the financial system also experienced a major shock, such as a contemporaneous collapse of a major business. The frequency and dislocations caused by such panics eventually encouraged the formation in 1913 of the Federal Reserve (Fed) to maintain, among other duties, liquidity in the financial system during periods of stress. Operating through a regional structure, banking policy with respect to New England became the focus of the Federal Reserve Bank of Boston.

During the 1920s strong public interest in preferred and common stock investment further modified the structure of New England banking and finance. The boom induced two major developments. First, some commercial banks became involved in investment banking by underwriting the flotation of bonds and stocks. The First National Bank of Boston, for example, formed for this purpose in 1918 what eventually became known as First National Corporation–Old Colony Trust (now Credit Suisse–First Boston Corporation). Second, it encouraged the growth of investment trusts, a form first perfected in England during the 1860s and a precursor of the modern mutual fund. These entities sold shares to investors, who benefited from the investment trust's financial expertise in creating diversified portfolios of securities. Some were subsidiary activities of local investment banking houses such as Kidder Participations, an arm of the Kidder, Peabody Banking concern, or local commercial banks like Shawmut National Investment Trust (1928) and Shawmut Associates (1929), both formed by the Shawmut National Bank. Other investment trusts were organized by specialized management companies such as Massachusetts Financial Services (now MFS, Inc.), organized in 1924, or the State Street Investment Management Company. These latter pioneers established a firm foundation for the subsequent strong rise of mutual and money market funds in the region after World War II.

The Great Crash of 1929, however, reversed the diversification movement in favor of a more tightly regulated banking system that was less susceptible to major dislocations. Investor ardor for stocks understandably cooled with the 90 percent decline registered in the Dow Jones Industrial Average between 1929 and 1933. In reaction the Glass-Steagall Act of 1933 mandated the complete separation of commercial from investment banking. This would lower default risk and, thus, reduce the likelihood that banks would need to draw on the resources of the newly organized Federal Deposit Insurance Corporation. The safety net was further strengthened through the Banking Act of 1935, which, among other powers, allowed the Federal Reserve to specify the level of reserves for chartered banks and the maximum interest rates payable on deposits. This, along with its ability to influence short-term rates through its open market operations, gave the Fed substantial leverage in dealing with the problem of an overheating economy. As rates rose, banks experienced reductions in deposits as customers shifted their funds, often offshore, to secure higher rates than those allowed the central bank. Leading banks like the Bank of Boston and BayBanks responded to the growing internationalization of finance by opening foreign branches and increasing their offshore lending activities.

A concern emergent in the 1950s, however, that the regulatory safety nets were actually contributing to a decline in international competitiveness by keeping financing costs too high induced substantial innovation which affected the basic character of New England finance. Leading corporations discovered that it was cheaper to raise short-term capital through direct sales of their commercial paper to investors. They could also avoid restrictive U.S. banking regulations by borrowing in the Eurodollar market that developed during the 1960s. The Stock Exchange Commission's shelf registration rules also facilitated the flotation of secondary offerings of stocks and bonds. Such changes affected the institutional distribution of financial assets. Banking share of the nation's asset pool fell from 52 percent in 1950 to 38 percent in 1970. Mutual, money market, and pension funds, on the other hand, increased their collective hold from 5 percent in 1950 to 29 percent by 1990. New England, with its strong capacities in professional finance, was able to capitalize on this major shift. It was during the long period of post–World War II prosperity that the names of such investment management companies as Fidelity, Putnam, and Scudder joined the trailblazing enterprises of the 1920s as pillars of the new consumer financial capitalism. Their achievement was the ability to structure specialized securities portfolios that satisfied a broad spectrum of investor risk preferences.

The quest for more efficient finance, especially among midsized corporations that had traditionally been financed by banks, encouraged the formation of innovative business organizations. Two such developments that influenced New England banking were the rise of conglomerates in the 1960s and the rise of leveraged-buy-out partnerships (LBOs) in the 1980s. Conglomerates were entities that consolidated a group of enterprises in diverse businesses. One successful New England example was the Textron Corporation of Providence, which merged subsidiaries in the manufacture of textiles, helicopters, and military electronics.

The way the region's commercial banks responded to the changing circumstances in finance after 1945 was also conditioned by new state and federal legislation that revived the trend of forming larger and more diversified banking institutions. Besides enhancing the regulatory powers of the Federal Reserve, the passage of the Bank Holding Company Act of 1956 and the Bank Merger Act of 1960 made possible the formation of two types of growth-enhancing holding company structures. The drive to establish larger and more diversified institutions was responsive to the perception that U.S. banking was too fragmented compared to other advanced economies. In branch banking states (which had spread throughout New England by 1961), single bank holding companies allowed the consolidation of merged banking entities and also the diversification into allied service lines. In addition, new state legislation in the 1980s made possible interstate branch banking. Initially, most of the New England states allowed out-of-state banks into their territories under banking reciprocity agreements. But two states, Maine and Rhode Island, took the lead in allowing nationwide banking. The alternative, multistate bank holding companies, was more popular in the Midwest and South as a means for overcoming state unitary banking restrictions.

These and other federal regulatory changes led to the greater concentration, diversification, and safety of New England banking. By 1987 the top 10 banks in each of the six New England states accounted for upward of 85 percent of commercial bank deposits. Fleet Financial Corporation of Providence, seventh largest in 1987, later pursued an aggressive merger policy that eventually transformed it into one of the nation's superregional banks, operating major subsidiaries in New England and the Middle Atlantic states. Moreover, in 1984 the deposits of the top six banks centered either in Boston (4), Hartford (2), or Providence (1) ranged from $2.1 billion to $7 billion. Besides growth through branching, the bank holding company structure allowed leading banks to expand the range of their business activities to include leasing, factoring, insurance and stock brokerage, mortgage banking, trust services, credit cards and consumer finance, real estate management, economic and investment advisory services, loan processing, and data processing services. The Garn–St. Germaine Depository Institutions Act of 1982 liberalized the range of services that thrift institutions could offer beyond mortgage finance and reduced significantly reserve requirements to foster industry expansion. Later, the Financial Reform, Recovery and Enforcement Act of 1989 reacted to the higher risks of default because of more aggressive lending and declining institutional solvency endemic in contemporary banking by raising reserve requirements to 8 percent of risk-adjusted assets, as had been recommended earlier by the Bank for International Settlements. One major culmination of these changes in the banking environment was the formation of Fleet Boston Corporation through the merger of the highly diversified Fleet Financial Group of Providence and BankBoston (formerly the Bank of Boston) in 1999. The new entity, which had $180 billion in assets and a market capitalization of $40 billion, ranked eighth in size among U.S. banks and accounted for about a third of the New England banking market.

Banking in New England has been subject to the same merger pressures that have characterized American banking for the past 30 years. In March 2004 Bank of America, based in Charlotte, N.C., bought FleetBoston, thus creating the nation's largest bank.

George J. Benston, *The Separation of Commercial and Investment Banking: The Glass-Steagall Act Revisited and Reconsidered* (1990); Helen M. Burns, *The American Banking Community and New Deal Banking Reforms, 1933–1935* (1974); Norman S. B. Gras, *The Massachusetts First National Bank of Boston, 1784–1934* (1976); William F. Hixson, *Triumph of the Bankers: Money and Banking in the 18th and 19th Centuries* (1993); Benjamin J. Klebaner, *American Commercial Banking: A History* (1990); Alpheus Thomas Mason, *The Brandeis Way: A Case Study in the Workings of Democracy* (1938); Elmus Wicker, *The Banking Panics of the Great Depression* (1996).

Paul J. Miranti, Jr.

Batterson, James Goodwin (1823–1901) Industrialist.

James Goodwin Batterson, industrialist and pioneer of accident and life insurance, was born in Wintonbury (now Bloomfield), Conn., to Simeon S. and Melissa Roberts Batterson. His father, who operated two stone-cutting businesses in New Preston and later in Litchfield, Conn., provided him with a classical education in the local public schools and academy, but could not afford to send his son to college. His early training, however, left young Batterson with a lifelong enthusiasm for classical antiquities and literature. In later life he would produce a number of English paraphrases of Greek and Latin classics as a relief from the cares of business.

After three years as an apprentice printer in Ithaca, N.Y., and a brief period reading law under O. S. Seymour at Litchfield, Batterson associated himself with his father in the latter's stone-cutting and monument business. In 1845 he moved to Hartford, where he established himself as a dealer in marble and granite, and as a manufacturer of monuments and statuary. Among his early patrons was the rising Hartford industrialist Samuel Colt, with whom he was associated in founding the Hartford Arts Union. Interested in all aspects of his trade, Batterson had done fieldwork under James G. Percival in the first geological survey of Connecticut (1842), and would tour the archaeological sites of the Nile Valley in 1858–59 with the British engineer Isembard Kingdom Brunel.

During the 1860s Batterson expanded his operations to include contract work for homes, business premises, and public buildings, and in 1875 he incorporated his enterprise as the New England Granite Works. Among his most successful ventures in the post–Civil War era were the Connecticut State Capitol (1878), the granite stonework of the Library of Congress (1897), and the New York State Capitol in Albany (1867–1904), whose granite columns Batterson produced by means of a mechanical lathe he invented. Batterson's outstanding monuments include the Connecticut Battle Monument at Antietam, Md., and the Soldiers' National Monument at Gettysburg, Pa.

In 1863, influenced by the English practice of issuing accident insurance to railroad travelers, Batterson organized the first accident insurance firm in the United States. Chartered by the state of Connecticut as the Travelers Insurance Company, the firm issued its first policy to a Hartford associate of Batterson's at a premium of two cents. Initially ridiculed for his venture, Batterson succeeded in developing Travelers into one of America's leading life and casualty insurers.

A "sound money" fiscal conservative, Batterson published a tract entitled *Gold and Silver as Currency* (1896), which was adopted by Republicans in that year's presidential campaign to counter William Jennings Bryan's free-silver plank in the Democratic platform. In the year of his death, however, Batterson joined progressives in Connecticut advocating a state constitutional convention to redress the imbalance in legislative representation whereby approximately 10 percent of the population could control a majority in the General Assembly.

An ardent student of literature as well as political and economic issues, Batterson produced a considerable body of original poetry as well as translations of the classics and tracts on insurance and fiscal issues.

James G. Batterson, *The Beginnings* (1901); William F. Henney, *James G. Batterson* (1901); William N. Hosley, *Colt: The Making of an American Legend* (1996).

Gary E. Wait

Ben and Jerry's   How did two Jewish baby boomers from Long Island found a multimillion-dollar business that captured some of the popular sense of New England? Mostly by accident. In 1977 Ben Cohen and Jerry Greenfield decided to start a bagel store, but they couldn't afford the equipment. Their second choice was an ice cream shop in Saratoga Springs, N.Y.; someone beat them to it, however, and they headed for the college town of Burlington, Vt.

Initially, their association with Vermont was not deep. When they opened their shop in an old gas station in May 1978, they used the slogan "Vermont's Finest All Natural Ice Cream," but that was mostly a joke—they knew that

they made the only all-natural ice cream in the state. They preferred the slogan "Lick It," which they put on bumper stickers and T-shirts. But when members of Burlington's lesbian community were offended by radio disc jockey Don Imus's plug of the ice cream, the slogan returned to "Vermont's Finest."

As Ben and Jerry's became dramatically more successful—helped by the booming demand for high-butterfat, super-premium ice cream, the opening of franchise shops (in 1981), the move into national distribution in the mid-1980s, and a talent for attracting favorable media coverage—it began to take on its distinctive "hip capitalist" style. Some of its fame derived from the innovative, often counterculturally suggestive flavor names: Cherry Garcia, Rainforest Crunch, and Chunky Monkey. As bearded (in Ben's case) and long-haired members of the sixties generation, the two entrepreneurs viewed big business skeptically. Their first response to their growing success—fueled by Jerry's decision to follow his girlfriend to graduate school in Arizona—was a suggestion that they sell the business after it grew beyond the small community-oriented store they had started. Instead, Ben decided to try to reconcile the business with his counter-culture values. Ultimately, those values became embodied in the corporate mission statement, which, in addition to its commitment to making money ("profitable growth"), also calls for "initiating innovative ways to improve the quality of life of a broad community." In practical terms, this means that Ben and Jerry's gives away 7.5 percent of its pre-tax earnings through three philanthropic ve-

hicles—the Ben and Jerry's Foundation, Employee Community Action Teams, and corporate grants—and supports such causes as the Children's Defense Fund and opposition to the Seabrook nuclear power plant and the first Gulf War. Until 1994, when Robert Holland was hired as the first CEO from outside the company, no executive could make more than seven times the salary of the lowest-paid employee.

The company's social mission has not undercut—and has probably underwritten—its quest for profits by projecting the image of a fun and deserving product that is worth buying at a premium price. By the end of 1998, the original $12,000 investment had grown into a huge corporation with sales exceeding $209 million, profits of $6 million, more than 150 franchise shops in the United States and abroad, and a large Vermont manufacturing plant—the state's most popular tourist attraction. Although the company was acquired by Unilever in 2000, Ben and Jerry have become more firmly ensconced in the state's public image than Calvin Coolidge or the Green Mountain Boys.

Fred Lager, *Ben and Jerry's: The Inside Scoop* (1994); Hanna Rosin, "The Evil Empire: The Scoop on Ben and Jerry's Crunchy Capitalism," *New Republic* (September 11, 1995); Ed Barna, "Ben and Jerry's Copes with a Changing Marketplace," *Vermont Business Magazine* (May 1995); Paul C. Judge, "Is It Rainforest Crunch Time?" *Business Week* (July 15, 1996).

Roy Rosenzweig

Boston Associates   The Boston Associates were a group of Boston-based industrialists who played a seminal role in America's Industrial Revolution. From careers in merchant trade, they turned to manufacturing, particularly the New England textile industry, and profoundly influenced the development of the Merrimack River valley from 1821 through midcentury. They were renowned not only for the success of their enterprises but also for innovative practices in labor relations, industrial technology, business organization, and finance. They also achieved prominence in politics and philanthropy. Including names such as Lowell, Lawrence, Cabot, Appleton, and Jackson, their families became the backbone of the elite "Boston Brahmins."

Named later by historians, the Boston Associates were not a formally constituted group. They had, however, one undisputed founder: Francis Cabot Lowell (1775–1817). To escape the risks and demands of mercantile trade, Lowell undertook an enterprise that was revolutionary in several respects. Lowell's Boston Manufacturing Company, located in Waltham, Mass. (1813), was an "integrated" cotton textile mill, performing all the processes of converting raw cotton into finished cloth by waterpowered machinery. To allay fears of recreating England's degraded factory workforce, Lowell recruited young women from the declining farms of New England for temporary factory employment. He provided supervised boardinghouses for these "mill girls," with regulations concerning their behavior. Lowell raised a massive amount of capital by inviting other investors into a joint-stock corporation, still a novel form for American manufacturing. Finally, he mass-produced coarse goods for a broadening market.

After Lowell's death, the remaining investors expanded operations at a new site on the Merrimack River. Later named Lowell, Mass., this development repeated the labor, technological, and business approach of Waltham, but on a larger scale. These practices became known as the "Waltham-Lowell system," in contrast to the "Rhode Island system" of smaller mills employing family labor.

Various combinations of the growing group of Boston Associates undertook new textile developments throughout New England in the 1830s and 1840s. But when overcapacity and business fluctuations threatened profits, Francis Cabot Lowell's paternalism eroded. The mill girls departed, replaced by waves of immigrants. The Boston Associates, meanwhile, reaped dividends and profited from land development and stock trading. They also diversified their investments into railroads, banking, and insurance.

Politically, the Boston Associates dominated the Massachusetts Whig Party, assuring their access to charters of incorporation and land and water development rights. Daniel Webster took up their cause on national issues such as a protective tariff. Abbott Lawrence, a leading figure among the Associates, nearly became vice president of the United States, and later served as ambassador to Great Britain. The compromise position of the Boston Associates in the sectional debate over slavery proved untenable, however, and their political influence declined with that of the Whigs.

Philanthropy to such institutions as Harvard University and Massachusetts General Hospital augmented their social position. Later generations achieved prominence in education, the arts, science, medicine, and law, often holding leadership positions in the same institutions. Although their accomplishments would later be overshadowed by those of the barons of the Gilded Age, the Boston Associates had set America on the course to large-scale industrialization.

Robert F. Dalzell, Jr., *Enterprising Elite: The Boston Associates and the World They Made* (1987); Steve Dunwell, *The Run of the Mill: A Pictorial Narrative of the Expansion, Dominion, Decline and Enduring Impact of the New England Textile Industry* (1978); Ferris Greenslet, *The Lowells and Their Seven Worlds* (1946); Frances W. Gregory, *Nathan Appleton: Merchant and Entrepreneur, 1779–1861* (1975).

James Beauchesne

Boston Police Strike Sparked by the suspension of 19 union leaders, the September 1919 Boston police strike cost 1,117 officers their jobs and catapulted Massachusetts governor Calvin Coolidge to national prominence. Part of a nationwide struggle over postwar labor relations, the walkout fueled antilabor jeremiads and badly damaged public employee unionism.

During World War I, labor unrest had spread to police and other public employees. Municipal officials across the country vehemently opposed police unionization. In September 1918 National Guard troops had replaced striking Nashua, N.H., officers. The postwar Red Scare, sensational headlines, and massive firings distinguished the Boston strike from these disputes.

Complaints about wages and working conditions spurred organizing among Boston police. Officers worked under a 1913 pay scale and put up with long hours, insect-infested sleeping quarters at station houses, and favoritism. Off-duty police needed permission to leave the city.

Former mayor Edwin Upton Curtis became Boston's police commissioner in December 1918, as the officers' Boston Social Club stepped up pressure for a raise. Although willing to improve conditions, Curtis bristled at challenges to his authority. In June 1919 the American Federation of Labor (AFL) voted to enroll police unions. Ignoring Curtis's warnings, Boston officers joined more than 60 police unions requesting AFL affiliation, which Curtis prohibited on August 11. When the police accepted an AFL charter and elected union officers, Curtis launched disciplinary hearings and began recruiting volunteer strikebreakers.

Hoping to avoid a showdown, Mayor Andrew Peters appointed a commission headed

Calvin Coolidge, governor of Massachusetts, reviews troops during the Boston police strike, September 1919

by investment banker James J. Storrow. Police responded favorably to Storrow's proposal for an independent local union, fact-finding for disputes over working conditions, and no penalties for past AFL membership. Spurning the compromise, Curtis suspended 19 union leaders. On September 9, 1,117 of Boston's 1,500 police officers went on strike.

The first night of the strike Curtis did not call out his volunteers. Some looting and other disturbances occurred—although less than reported by the press. On September 10, Mayor Peters mobilized Boston National Guard units. During the next two days, eight residents died in strike-related incidents—seven shot by National Guardsmen—and 70 people were injured. With the Guard in control of the streets, Coolidge asserted his command over the troops and dispatched additional units. Reclaiming his authority from Peters, whom he and Coolidge feared might seek a compromise, Curtis immediately fired the 19 suspended leaders and barred other strikers from returning to work. Before the walkout, the Boston Central Labor Union, the local coordinating council for AFL unions, had pledged to support the police. Its failure to vote on a sympathy strike doomed the officers' hopes of regaining their jobs.

Amid sensational press accounts of police "Bolshevism," Coolidge built a reputation as a defender of law and order. Proclaiming that there was "no right to strike against the public safety by anybody, anywhere, anytime," he rode the strike to reelection in 1919, the vice presidency of the United Sates in 1920, and eventually the White House. After the strike, Boston recruited a new force. It was not until 1968 that the unaffiliated Boston Police Patrolmen's Association won a union contract.

Robert Murray, *Red Scare: A Study in National Hysteria, 1919–1920* (1955); Francis Russell, *A City in Terror: 1919, the Boston Police Strike* (1975); Joseph Slater, "Public Workers: Labor and the Boston Police Strike of 1919," *Labor History* 38 (1997).

Dexter Arnold

Brass America's brass industry was born in Waterbury, Conn., and Connecticut's Naugatuck River valley. Each New England state responded in its own way to the decline of agriculture through the 19th century; Maine turned to shipbuilding, Vermont to dairy farming, and Connecticut to the brass industry. In the 19th century, in spite of the lack of readily available raw materials, metalworkers from Waterbury supplied the nation with a variety of brass articles, from oil lamps to cutlery. As much as any other New England enterprise, Connecticut's brass industry offers a fine example of Yankee ingenuity.

Brass is used as a generic name for any copper alloy. It is harder than copper but costs more than iron or steel, and it cannot be tempered the way steel can. Brass can be subjected to cold or heat, however, and it is malleable, exhibits great resistance, and takes on a fine surface finish. It has many uses, therefore, and is widely chosen as a medium for small wares or where its color or durability makes it attractive.

Connecticut's brass industry was made possible in the mid-18th century by Yankee peddlers, famous throughout the country for selling tinware household articles and cutlery to rural families from Montreal to Charleston, S.C., and west to the Mississippi. By 1800 most of the nation's tableware came from Connecticut, and peddlers had developed fully organized operations to market brass household items from buttons to oil lamps. These peddlers plied their trade with a business acumen that spread the Yankee reputation for shrewdness across the country.

Early in the 19th century, makers of pewter buttons began to manufacture buttons from sheet brass. They obtained copper by melting old stills, kettles, and ship sheathing, and added zinc. Brass buttons were at first sold from house to house; then tinware peddlers added them to their stock in trade. By 1811, the Porter and Grilley families, pioneering Waterbury metalworkers, had retired, and their company was bought out by Frederick Leavenworth, David Hayden, and James Mitchell Lamson Scovill; this partnership was later reorganized as the Scovill Manufacturing Company.

In 1837 the brass clock was developed, and it revolutionized both the clock and the brass industries. Cheaper than any other clock available, the brass clock was an instant success and greatly expanded the market for brass at a time when mills had been built with the capacity to supply the new demand. Soon afterward, the invention of photography required copper plated with silver, opening another major market for Connecticut's brass mills. In 1855 the development of petroleum expanded the market for brass lanterns. For each new use, the industry adapted and expanded rapidly to fit the new market conditions.

The larger markets and their increasing profits drew competition, and during the mid-19th century several new plants were established. The first operations were organized around production of buttons, kettles, and other specific household items, but new companies were formed in the 1840s and 1850s to manufacture brass on a large scale. As late as 1900, four-fifths of the nation's brass was produced in Connecticut, while few brass plants in the United States had been organized without workmen and managers drawn from Connecticut.

In the late 19th century the industry's titan was Charles F. Brooker. By the close of 1901, Brooker had bought and merged company after company, organizing the American Brass Company, second-largest to Scovill, and preparing the way for the Anaconda Copper Mining Company to purchase the Connecticut brass mills. In 1922 Anaconda became the first corporation to mine, manufacture, and sell copper and brass materials to the consumer. Through the 20th century, aluminum, steel, and plastic severely diminished the use of household brass, but producers have adapted production to industrial uses.

Why did the brass industry flourish in a region where no raw materials were available? Its pioneers were metalworkers from Waterbury (often referred to as "Brass City"). Their access to the Naugatuck River as a power source and their proximity to the New York market also influenced the industry's success. The adaptability of brass lent itself to development by men who were inventive, commercially minded, and mechanically oriented, making Connecticut's brass industry quintessentially Yankee.

Cecilia Bucki, *Metal, Minds, and Machines: Waterbury at Work, 1820–1920* (1980); Watson Davis, *Story of Copper* (1924); William Gilbert Lathrop, *The Development of the Brass Industry in Connecticut* (1936); Isaac F. Marcosson and Cooper Heritage, *The Story of Revere Copper and Brass, Inc.* (1955).

Louis Mazzari

Breweries and Distilleries In his *History of the American People* (1902), Woodrow Wilson wrote of New England, "Out of cheap molasses of the French Islands, she made the rum which was the chief source of her wealth—the rum with which she bought slaves for Maryland and the Carolinas, and paid her balances to the English merchants."

In the 1720s rum imported from the West Indies began to displace cider as New England's most popular alcoholic beverage. Before long, rum was being manufactured in New England, with far-reaching social and economic consequences. In the late 1730s eight distilleries in Boston and Newport, R.I., were conducting a thriving business in molasses and rum. Boston's Long Wharf, wrote William Taussig in *Rum, Romance, and Rebellion* (1928), "was alive with molasses coming in and rum going out."

Rum was the currency of New England's slave trade. By 1750, at the height of the slave-trading era, 63 Massachusetts distilleries were turning West Indies molasses into rum. The rum in turn was traded in Africa for slaves to be sold in the West Indies, where the cycle started all over again. The so-called triangle trade became the backbone of New England commerce.

New England's colonists began distilling spirits as far back as 1650, fermenting apple whiskey, rum, cider, and brandy. By the Revolution, distilled spirits had been widely accepted in the American colonies. But between 1790 and 1830 the nature of distilling in New England and America changed. Whiskey, produced from grain, gradually replaced rum as the country's preeminent distilled beverage. Irish and Scottish immigrants, who had been distilling grain for decades, began moving westward and distilling spirits from a mash of rye and corn grown in the mid-Atlantic states and Kentucky. With the abolition of the slave trade in 1808, grain became more readily available than imported molasses. Whiskey thus became cheaper and easier to produce than rum. The westward movement of settlers encouraged the growth of whiskey and bourbon—made from locally produced rye, corn, and other grains—and contributed to the decline of New England's distilleries.

Hiram Walker provides an example of the industry's migration from the region. Walker was from East Douglas, Mass., where he worked in a dry-goods store in the 1830s. In 1838 he moved west to Detroit, where he began selling whiskey through a grocery business. By 1858 he had established a flour-milling and distilling operation across Lake Michigan in Ontario. His successful Walker's Club Whisky was later renamed Canadian Club.

New Englanders have been brewing beer since soon after the *Mayflower* landed, most often in small batches made at home. This was the first alcohol in New England; the Indians in eastern North America had none. Commercial brewing began early in the region's colonial history, but beer was also imported from England. By the Revolutionary War, though, people were drinking more rum, whiskey, and other distilled spirits than beer. The corn and rye used in distilling were easier to grow in New England than the malt and hops needed for brewing. And because beer is a perishable food product, before the advent of pasteurization towns had to brew their own beers. As beer drinking became more popular in the growing cities, the demand for brewer's hops expanded, helped along by the development of a new transportation system. In Vermont, farmers had been searching for alternatives to crops that had been migrating west, and between 1850 and 1865 Vermont experienced a boom in hops, producing the second-largest annual crop in the nation after New York. By the end of the 19th century, German immigrants had entered the industry and were working to consolidate smaller breweries. National companies grew at the expense of New England's local breweries, a trend that contin-

ued until Prohibition virtually destroyed the alcoholic-beverage industry in 1920.

Boston had a few breweries before the Revolution, but the city became primarily a distribution center for other beers throughout much of the 1800s. A number of German lager breweries were established there, though. In 1890, for example, 21 breweries were operating in Boston, although none would be classified as a national brewer. One of the largest, Haffenreffer and Company, was founded in the 1880s. New England Breweries, another conglomerate, formed in 1890, was dissolved at Prohibition but continued to operate three plants after Repeal in 1933. All were closed by 1973.

Larger-than-life Frank Jones of Portsmouth, N.H., entered the brewing business in 1856 and founded the Frank Jones Brewing Company three years later. He remained chairman of that firm, brewing ale and porter, until his death in 1902. In 1895 Frank Jones was the nation's 10th-largest brewery. After Repeal, the company was known as the Eldredge Brewing Company and later as the Frank Jones Brewing Company. It closed in 1950. In 1988 Don Jones, a member of the family, began distributing Frank Jones Portsmouth Ale, derived from an old Jones recipe and brewed at the Catamount Brewery in White River Junction, Vt.

In 1956 Carling Black Label built a state-of-the-art brewery in Natick, Mass., but in the 1970s the company succumbed to Anheuser-Busch, Schlitz, Pabst, and, later, Miller, Stroh, and Coors. Established in 1890 in Cranston, R.I., the Narragansett Brewing Company survived Prohibition to regain its title as New England's largest-selling beer. In 1963, for instance, two-thirds of the beer sold in the region was Narragansett. The primary sponsor of Red Sox baseball, 'Gansett became a household name throughout the region. Among the sounds of New England daily life in the 1950s and 1960s was the company's advertising catchphrase, "Hi, neighbor, have a 'Gansett!" In 1964 Narragansett purchased the Haffenreffer name. The Falstaff Brewing Corporation of Saint Louis, Mo., bought Narragansett the following year, however, and marketed both the Narragansett and Haffenreffer brands. While Budweiser and Michelob constructed new facilities in New Hampshire, by 1970 Narragansett's old brewery, and its focus on tried-and-true brewing methods, had left the company at a commercial disadvantage. After its market share in New England dropped to 17 percent, the 91-year-old operation closed in 1981.

Prompted by the success of imported beers, by the impressive track record of boutique wineries, and by the legalization of home

Samuel Adams Boston lager

brewing in 1977, small brewers began to appear throughout the country, beginning in California and the Pacific Northwest, but catching on quickly in New England, where brewpubs and microbreweries have opened throughout the region. Starting in the mid-1980s, the Boston Beer Company's Samuel Adams beers and ales, brewed both within and outside New England, came to regional and national prominence. Today the company is a leading example of craft brewing.

Will Anderson, *Beer, New England: An Affectionate Look at Our Six States' Past and Present Brews and Breweries* (1988); Stanley Baron, *Brewed in America: A History of Beer and Ale in the United States* (1962); Kate Cone, *What's Brewing in New England: A Guide to Brewpubs and Microbreweries* (1997); Thomas Rumney, "The Hops Boom in 19th-Century Vermont," *Vermont History* 56 (1988).

Louis Mazzari

Brown and Sharpe In 1833 David Brown, a Yankee peddler from Warren, R.I., established a clockmaking and clock-repair business with his son Joseph, first in Pawtucket, later in Providence. It would become one of Rhode Island's longest-standing and best-known companies, exemplifying the character of traditional New England industry. Now owned by the Swedish firm Hexagon, Brown and Sharpe produces some of the world's most accurate measurement devices.

In the 1830s David Brown sold clocks, watches, and silverware in villages throughout New England before going into business with his son. Many of the clocks in New England's public buildings and churches were manufactured by the Browns before the Civil War. Among those still working are the clock in the Methodist Church of Warren, installed in 1849, and the clock built in 1853 for the Newport Colony House, Rhode Island's State House until 1901. By the 1850s, the company had begun precision machine-shop operations, specializing in extremely accurate workmanship. Young Brown developed the pocket caliper, the first practical tool for exact measurement that was cheap enough to allow the ordinary machinist to adopt techniques of fine work.

Lucian Sharpe began as a shop apprentice in 1848 and became a full partner in 1853, adding business acumen to the firm, which was renamed J. R. Brown and Sharpe. Brown continued to develop precision measurement devices, standardizing production of the tools that fueled the mechanization of 19th-century America and making Brown and Sharpe an industry leader.

In the 1850s the company developed the first single-thread sewing machine and thus led the way toward new methods that improved the quality and efficiency of manufacturing tools. The firm expanded tremendously beginning in 1858, producing both household sewing machines and intricate machines designed for specific purposes. The production of machine tools provided the company's next growth spurt, soon augmented by the machinery and firearms required for the Civil War. Brown and Sharpe's milling and grinding machines were exhibited at the Philadelphia Centennial Exposition in 1876 as examples of the high standards of American manufacture.

The company reached its peak around World War II, when it employed nearly 11,000 people. In the 1970s and 1980s Brown and Sharpe began producing such equipment as three-dimensional scanning probes and shop-floor measuring robots. In 1981 the company experienced a long, bitter strike. It recovered in the 1990s to develop Microsoft Windows–based measuring software.

The turn of the 21st century found Brown and Sharpe in reduced financial circumstances, however. In 2001, having changed its name to BNS Company, the former industrial icon, along with the name Brown and Sharpe, was sold to the Stockholm-based investment firm Hexagon A.B. for $170 million. BNS, relocated in Warwick, R.I., continues to operate its metrology-software subsidiary under the name Xygent.

Duane Clinker, *Standing Together: Union Busting at Brown and Sharpe, a Photo Essay with Strike Documents* (1982); Henry Dexter Sharpe, *Joseph R. Brown, Mechanic, and the Beginnings of Brown and Sharpe* (1949).

Louis Mazzari

Bush, Vannevar (1890–1974) Electrical engineer. Vannevar Bush was born in Everett, Mass., in 1890. Descended from an early New England family of merchants and ministers, he became one of the most important academic engineers and scientists in the United States during the 1930s and 1940s, remaining influential until his death in 1974. His policies, especially when he led the National Defense Research Committee during World War II, helped establish the value of academic science and research to national goals and bolstered the high-tech industry of New England. Bush also helped to change the relation between the federal government and American universities. His vision of permanent government support for research projects selected by leading university scientists, rather than politicians, was only faintly realized with the establishment of the National Science Foundation, but Bush's ideas, expressed in *Science, the Endless Frontier* (1945), continued to be influential.

Bush was more than a policymaker. He was a technological entrepreneur, an educator, an inventor and, in the eyes of some, one of the first computer scientists. He joined MIT's electrical engineering department in 1919, where he wrote a pathbreaking engineering text and guided MIT into the field of automated computing. Bush laid the groundwork for New England's influence in the electronic computer industry and much more: his famous article, "As We May Think" (1945), published in the *Atlantic Monthly,* has been saluted as the intellectual foundation of hypertext and other aspects of advanced personal computing.

As a result of Bush's encouragement and his ability to gain funding from leading foundations and industrial corporations, MIT built the most powerful analog computing devices of the 1930s, the Differential and Rockefeller Analyzers. Bush and his students also hoped to merge electronics and microfilm to revolutionize information storage and retrieval. His library machine, the Rapid Selector, was soon molded into a series of prototype devices for the super-secret codebreaking agencies of the army and the navy.

Bush became a central figure among the nation's scientific and policy elites. In 1939 he assumed the leadership of the Carnegie Institution in Washington, D.C., whose reputation helped him persuade Franklin Roosevelt to create a scientist-led agency to develop advanced military technologies. Bush's direction of the civilian National Defense Research Committee led America's elite universities to become entwined with the atomic bomb, and, more deeply, radar.

Bush's influence declined after the war. Although he remained at the Carnegie Institu-

tion and was called upon to help reshape the military and the patent system, he did not maintain the power or the visibility of the war years. He retired in 1955 and used his energies to turn long-held ideas into inventions and to warn of the dangers of political and military directed science.

Colin Burke, *Information and Secrecy: Vannevar Bush, Ultra and the Other Memex* (1994); Vannevar Bush, *Science Is Not Enough* (1967); James M. Nyce and Paul Kahn, eds., *From Memex to Hypertext: Vannevar Bush and the Mind's Machine* (1991); G. Pascal Zachary, *Endless Frontier: Vannevar Bush, Engineer of the American Century* (1997).

Colin Burke

Business Ethics and Traditions Business practices in New England can be traced to their Puritan origins in the 17th century and, even more directly, to the China trade in the 19th century. By the turn of the 20th century, however, as Boston, New England's commercial and financial capital, yielded leadership to New York, business ethics in New England lost distinctiveness, becoming absorbed instead into the national pattern. While differences persist between and among regions and industries, the nationalizing of the economy during the 20th century emphasizes similarities rather than differences.

New England business practices were puritanical not only in the 17th and 18th centuries but even after the Revolutionary War and the War of 1812. The first governor of Massachusetts Bay Colony, John Winthrop, asserted that Christian business ethics, such as charging no interest on loans and giving to the poor, should distinguish New England society, and Benjamin Franklin's proverbial expression "Honesty is the best policy" epitomizes the blending of Puritan values with Yankee shrewdness. New England's active maritime trade further influenced the region's business practices. Boston and Salem, for example, dominated the China trade; with long voyages and slow communication, China traders had to trust agents, correspondents, and partners, and selected them from friends and kin. Character was an absolutely essential ingredient for successful stewardship.

During the mid-19th century, former China traders transferred their capital back to New England. John P. Cushing, resident in Canton for a quarter century, returned to Massachusetts and invested his capital in railroads and other enterprises with Bryant, Sturgis and Company, a Boston merchant firm that pioneered in money management. Similarly, Boston's John Murray Forbes, a China trader, mobilized capital from the China trade community to build the Chicago, Burlington and Quincy Railroad.

The Boston capital market strengthened other existing impulses for superior business ethics. Imputations of improper business behavior might result in the disenchantment of potential investors. So in 1875 Forbes ousted high-level insiders from the Chicago, Burlington and Quincy for breaching conflict-of-interest rules. Admittedly, Forbes knew that the rules were imprecise and adherence less than perfect, but he recognized that Burlington investors had to be assured that everything would be open and aboveboard.

During the 20th century the moral ties that bound the business community together attenuated; even the elite classes became less homogeneous. Also, New York established its primacy, inevitably affecting Boston standards. Still, distinctions between insiders and outsiders persisted. Business standards became internalized so that sanctions, or even the mere threat of sanctions, had the desired effect. As prudent bankers in New England adhered to standards different from wildcat bankers in the West, so New England merchants did not act or think like oil wildcatters. New England financial institutions therefore experienced greater longevity than those elsewhere despite the similarity of regulatory laws. Internalization, the quality of enforcement, and the continuity of fortunes combined to make the difference.

Cleveland Amory, *The Proper Bostonians* (1947); E. Digby Baltzell, *Puritan Boston and Quaker Philadelphia* (1979); Saul Engelbourg, *Power and Morality: American Business Ethics, 1840–1914* (1980); Paul Goodman, "Ethics and Enterprise: The Values of the Boston Elite, 1800–1860," *American Quarterly* 18 (1966).

Saul Engelbourg

Clocks and Watches

In the early years of the 19th century, New England mechanics and entrepreneurs reinvented the way clocks and watches were made. In this formative phase of the American Industrial Revolution, clockmaking changed from a handicraft to a factory process in which unskilled workers operated specialized machines to produce large quantities of uniform and interchangeable parts. As a result, for the first time since the invention of the mechanical clock around 1300, nearly everyone could afford a timepiece.

Emulating armory practices used by the government, Eli Terry of Plymouth, Conn., helped recast manufacturing in the private sector by applying waterpowered machinery in clock production, making clocks the first complex consumer products to undergo this transformation. After completing a first contract in 1809 for 4,000 mass-produced tallcase clocks with wooden movements, Terry designed a smaller clock for a shelf or mantel

in 1815. Many competitors, most of them in Connecticut, emerged to make wooden-movement clocks, which sold for as little as $7.50 apiece. After working for Terry, Seth Thomas established his own business. Eager consumers purchased his clocks in such numbers that by the late 1830s the market was saturated. The Seth Thomas Clock Company, in Thomaston, Conn., grew to be one of the country's largest clock manufacturers in the second half of the 19th century.

Watchmaking had been at the height of advanced technology since the mid-17th century, with centers in England, France, and Switzerland. But despite high consumer demand for imported watches, fewer than 1,000 were made in America before 1849. In that year, Aaron Dennison and Edward Howard began to redesign the pocket watch and invent gauges and machinery to manufacture it. Their enterprise would result in the American Waltham Watch Company of Waltham, Mass., which perfected its product line and manufacturing processes in the 1850s, making about 30 watches a week and selling them for $50 or less.

Improvements in making steel springs and rolling sheet brass led to other types of smaller, even less expensive clocks, and by midcentury affordable New England clocks enjoyed a worldwide market. Seven Connecticut-born clock companies, each making hundreds of thousands of clocks per year, dominated the U.S. market after 1860: Seth Thomas Clock Company, New Haven Clock Company, E. N. Welch Manufacturing Company, Ansonia Clock Company, E. Ingraham Company, William L. Gilbert Clock Company, and Waterbury Clock Company.

By 1930 hundreds of millions of watches had been produced in the United States, and the average price had steadily declined. Waltham and its competitor the Elgin Watch Company, of Elgin, Illinois, led the American watch industry into the 20th century, with technical innovations and the production of jeweled mechanical watches. Previously, unjeweled watches made in Connecticut by the Waterbury Watch Company had brought the price of a watch down to about $3.50 by the early 1880s.

Despite advances in the 19th century, the American clock and watch industry did not fare as well as the 20th century progressed. Watchmaking production peaked in 1910, when the market became saturated and a slow slide began toward the Great Depression. Contributing to the decline was competition from the Swiss, who had captured more than half of the world's watch market in the 19th century. In line with American watchmakers, the Swiss took up mass-production tech-

niques, first for pocket watches and then for wristwatches. Between 1929, when Ansonia Clock Company was sold to the Amtorg Trading Corporation in the Soviet Union, and 1983, when Seth Thomas Clock Company moved to Georgia, the major clock manufacturers left New England, merged into other enterprises, or failed altogether. Today, the sole surviving timepiece giant in the region is Timex Corporation, a direct descendant of Waterbury Clock Company, which maintains its headquarters in Middlebury, Conn.

Chris H. Bailey, *Two Hundred Years of American Clocks and Watches* (1975); Michael C. Harrold, *American Watchmaking: A Technical History of the American Watch Industry, 1850–1930* (1981); Donald Hoke, *Ingenious Yankees: The Rise of the American System of Manufactures in the Private Sector* (1990); Philip Zea and Robert C. Cheney, *Clock Making in New England, 1725–1825* (1992).

Carlene E. Stephens

Colt, Samuel, and Colt Firearms

Beginning in 1855 Colt revolvers were manufactured in the brownstone armory that Samuel Colt built near the Connecticut River in Hartford. At the time it was the largest private armory in the world, crowned with the blue onion-shaped dome that has been a Hartford landmark ever since. The inventor, entrepreneur, and promoter Samuel Colt was born in Hartford in 1814. As a youngster, his passion for firearms and explosive devices made him an indifferent student, much to the chagrin of his father, Christopher, who, in desperation, apprenticed him as a sailor on the brig *Corvo* sailing from Boston to Calcutta and back. While aboard, the 16-year-old youth conceived of the revolver by watching the action of the ship's wheel and carved a wooden model of a six-shooter. His father financed the making of two prototypes. Both failed.

Undeterred but penniless, Colt decided to earn money to carry on his experiments by becoming a performer. Billed as "the celebrated Dr. Coult of New York, London, and Calcutta," he toured Canada and the East Coast for three years giving demonstrations of "laughing gas." He engaged a competent mechanic, John Pearson, to make improved models of his revolver and, borrowing $1,000 from his father, sailed to Europe to apply for patents. Still only 21 years old, he received patents in London and France in December 1835, and U.S. Patent No. 138 the following February. On the strength of these he obtained $200,000 in capital from New York and New Jersey investors.

His first attempt at manufacturing took place in Paterson, N.J., in a leased section of a silk mill. But his company failed in 1842, even

Colt Firearms factory, Hartford

though 100 of his revolvers had met with success against the Seminole Indians in Florida and in the hands of Texas Rangers against the Comanches. Five years later, seeking good firearms for use in the Mexican War, the army gave him an order for 1,000 revolvers. Still lacking money and production facilities, Colt turned to Eli Whitney, Jr., in Whitneyville, Conn., where the Colt-Whitney-Walker model was manufactured.

Colt returned to Hartford, rented quarters, and produced the Colt Dragoon Model. In 1852 he purchased 250 acres of flood-prone land in the South Meadows and began planning the construction not only of a great armory but also a self-sufficient community called Coltsville. Ignoring the skepticism and hostility of the city leaders, he built a dike along his property for flood protection, laid out streets, erected houses for his employees, and even built a hall for their entertainment.

Always on the lookout for more business, Colt saw an opportunity to furnish guns for both sides in the Crimean War. The first American to manufacture abroad, in 1853 he opened a factory in London to make the Model 1849 Pocket and the Model 1851 Navy. The plant was mismanaged and closed in 1857.

The operating genius of the Colt Armory was Elisha K. Root, the most brilliant machinist of his era in New England. Adapting the system of interchangeable parts pioneered by Eli Whitney and the Springfield Armory, Root developed equipment and processes that made it possible to mass-produce firearms on machines except for the finishing and final as-

sembly. By 1857 Colt Armory turned out 250 guns a day. It also became a training center for a succession of gifted mechanics like Pratt and Whitney, who went on to apply Root's methods in companies of their own.

Colt himself functioned as president and salesman extraordinary by aggressive marketing and close relations with military officials, legislators, and foreign heads of state. Thousands of his revolvers were shipped to California during the Gold Rush. He traveled abroad, wrangling introductions to government officials and making them gifts of beautifully engraved weapons.

In less than a decade Colt had become America's first tycoon, a millionaire, rather bibulous, cigar-smoking bachelor who had everything but a wife and home. These he acquired with his usual dispatch and pomp. He chose as his bride Elizabeth Jarvis, the daughter of a Middletown minister. The extravagance of their wedding on June 5, 1856, shocked Hartford's staid society, as did his building of the palatial Armsmear on the western end of his domain.

As North and South raced toward cataclysm, Colt was busy making enormous profits by filling the demands of both sides right up to the firing on Fort Sumter. A Democrat, he opposed the election of Abraham Lincoln for fear the union would be destroyed—and a lucrative market thereby lost. In his view slavery was not a moral wrong but an inefficient economic system. Anticipating the onset of conflict, he shrewdly prepared the armory for a five-year struggle and the arming of a million men by erecting a second factory.

By then his immense business responsibilities had begun to wear down his seemingly inexhaustible energies. Bothered by frequent attacks of inflammatory rheumatism, he drove himself as if he knew his days were numbered. He died in January 1862 at the age of 47, leaving his widow and son Caldwell an enormous estate for that time.

A catastrophe almost put an end to Colt Armory two years after his death when 1,500 men were working two 10-hour shifts to keep General Grant's troops supplied with muskets and revolvers. Fire destroyed the original factory and most of the machines. Colt's widow, Elizabeth, ordered a new armory built. At the height of the Civil War annual production had reached 100,000 revolvers and nearly 50,000 muskets. During peacetime, however, the military's demand for munitions declined sharply. The company tried to keep its workforce busy making machine tools, steam engines, sewing machines, printing presses, and both the Gatling and Browning machine guns. The six-shot Colt .45, or "Peacemaker," appeared in 1872, becoming a legend among cowboys

and frontiersmen. It was said that while Lincoln made all men free, Colts made all men equal.

In 1901 Elizabeth Colt sold Colt's to Boston and New York financiers. The company earned huge profits until the end of World War I, paying its investors annual dividends averaging 22 percent. During the war the Colt Armory achieved the best records in its history. Before America's entry, because of demand from Canada and Great Britain, the company's order backlog extended to three years, employment rose to nearly 4,000, and its stock quintupled in value. By the end of the war it had delivered 425,500 automatic pistols, 151,700 revolvers, 13,000 Maxim-Vickers machine guns, and 10,000 new Browning machine guns, while handling the subcontracting of nearly 100,000 more. Employment peaked at 10,000. The three men most responsible for this spectacular achievement were company president William C. Skinner; Fred Moore, head of production; and the inventor John Browning. Browning's .45-caliber pistol was the army's standard sidearm. In addition to his .30-caliber machine gun, Browning invented a lightweight automatic rifle. His son Lieutenant Val A. Browning was the first to fire both weapons in France.

Peacetime called for a different strategy. Anticipating a severe drop in military sales, Skinner and his successor, Samuel Stone, set in motion a diversification program similar to the one used following the Civil War. They obtained contracts for adding machines and commercial dishwashers to be marketed under names other than Colt. Stone acquired a company engaged in molding hard plastics, which he renamed Coltrock, and another company that made electrical products.

Colt's weathered the Great Depression better than other Hartford manufacturers, reducing the work week, cutting salaries, keeping more men on the payroll than needed, and eating up surplus. On the day Pearl Harbor was attacked, December 7, 1941, the company was still the largest private armory in the United States and the only one turning out machine guns. As it had in two previous conflicts, Colt's stretched itself to the limit, winning the army-navy "E" for outstanding production in 1942. But a few months later it was evident that Colt's was in the incipient stage of its eventual downfall. It began losing money every month. The root of the trouble was partially its fatigued and strife-torn labor force, but more important was the obsolescence of both management and manufacturing techniques.

In September 1955 the directors voted to merge Colt's with an upstart conglomerate called Penn-Texas, which had acquired Pratt and Whitney Machine Tool the same year. Under the new ownership the most significant achievement was the introduction of the M-16 automatic rifle, which became the standard army and air force weapon. Following this Colt's suffered one blow after another: mismanagement, heavy deficits, obsolete products, loss of markets and contracts, defense cutbacks, a four-year strike, another buyout, and bankruptcy. Yet it recovered from all these reversals and now operates, not in the old downtown armory, but in a modern plant in West Hartford. The 1994 move marked an end to 147 years of gunmaking in Hartford, during which not only Colt's but also Sharps, Pope Manufacturing, and Pratt and Whitney Machine Tool had led the state to an unprecedented era of power and prosperity. The armory is being renovated for small businesses, artists' studios, and possibly a museum of industrial technology.

Henry Barnard, *Armsmear: The Home, the Arms, and the Armory of Samuel Colt* (1866); William B. Edwards, *The Story of Colt's Revolver* (1953); Ellsworth S. Grant, *The Colt Armory* (1995); Charles T. Haven and Frank A. Belden, *A History of the Colt Revolver* (1940); William Hosley, *Colt—The Making of an American Legend* (1996); Phyllis Kihn, "Colt in Hartford," *Connecticut Historical Society Bulletin* (1959); Jack Rohan, *Yankee Arms Maker: The Incredible Story of Samuel Colt,* (1948); R. L. Wilson, *The Colt Heritage* (1979).

Ellsworth S. Grant

Columbia Records

Columbia Records has the longest continuous history of any brand name in the sound recording industry. The American Graphophone Company was first organized in 1887 to manufacture and market the "graphophone," an improvement on Thomas Edison's tinfoil phonograph developed by a group of inventors assembled by Alexander Graham Bell. In 1888 the company leased a factory in Bridgeport, Conn., which was to remain its company's manufacturing headquarters for decades. Meanwhile, the Columbia Phonograph Company was established in 1889 as a local agency licensed to market both graphophones and the new Edison wax cylinder phonographs in the District of Columbia, Maryland, and Delaware. Another agency, the New England Phonograph Company of Boston, enjoyed similar rights in Massachusetts, Connecticut, Rhode Island, New Hampshire, Vermont, and Maine. Both agencies marketed prerecorded entertainment cylinders in the early 1890s, Columbia focusing on the U.S. Marine Band and local Washington whistler John Yorke AtLee while the New England company specialized in Baldwin's Cadet Band of Boston and comic Irish routines by Russell Hunting of the Boston Theater.

In the mid-1890s the Columbia Phonograph Company and American Graphophone Company merged to form a single enterprise. Columbia also relocated the center of its recording program to New York City in 1897, giving it access to a wider range of prestigious talent. By pursuing exclusive contracts with the leading recording artists of the day and relentlessly suing competitors (including the New England Phonograph Company) for patent infringement, the Columbia group had emerged by the late 1890s as a leading force in the cylinder phonograph field, rivaled only by Edison's own National Phonograph Company. Competition from the alternative disc format developed by Emile Berliner and the Victor Talking Machine Company next induced the Columbia group to collaborate with a succession of disc record manufacturers, finally purchasing the Globe Record Company outright in 1902 and relocating it from Milburn, N.J., to Bridgeport. Six years later, Columbia set a new trend by marketing an inexpensive "double disc" with a recording on both sides rather than just one.

Columbia flourished alongside Edison and Victor as one of the "big three" whose control of key patents allowed them to monopolize the American recording industry of the early 20th century. Eventually, however, the postwar recession of the early 1920s, the loss of exclusive patent protection, and the advent of radio took their toll on the company's fortunes. Forced into receivership in 1923, Columbia changed owners several times over the next 15 years as a brief recovery was wiped out by the onset of the Depression. In 1938 the label was purchased by the Columbia Broadcasting System (CBS), which succeeded in reestablishing it as an industry leader. Over the next half century, Columbia/CBS Records pioneered important new media formats, developing the long-playing record (LP) in 1948 and collaborating with the Sony Corporation of Japan to introduce the compact disc in the early 1980s. In 1988, CBS sold its recording division to Sony, which today continues to use the Columbia Records name.

Tim Brooks, "Columbia Records in the 1890s: Founding the Record Industry," *ARSC Journal* 10 (1978): 4–31; Brooks, "High Drama in the Record Industry: Columbia Records, 1901–1934," *ARSC Journal* 33 (2002): 21–76; Timothy C. Fabrizio, "District of Columbia: The Graphophone in Washington, D.C.," *ARSC Journal* 27 (1996): 1–10; Allan Sutton and Kurt Nauck, *American Record Labels and Companies: An Encyclopedia (1891–1943)* (2000).

Patrick Feaster

Computer Industry

New England has played a vital role in the creation and development of the computer industry worldwide. The demands of World War II, along with the

initiative and drive of computer developers, made the 1940s and early 1950s a revolutionary time in the evolution of computer technology. The first computing projects during this period were designed to meet military goals and received federal support. They were carried out for the most part by university-affiliated researchers at Harvard, the Massachusetts Institute of Technology, and the University of Pennsylvania. These early ventures generated technical knowledge and laid the foundation for the unique relation between government, universities, and industry that still exists today.

The first digital computer, the Mark I, a programmable, electromechanical calculator, was designed and built by the Harvard professor Howard Aiken, who worked directly with IBM engineers in the basement of the university's physics research laboratory. In 1944 the Mark I was installed at Harvard and continued to function until 1959, when it was finally retired. IBM then licensed the machine's technology, with the result that core memory became commonplace in first- and second-generation computers.

In the late 1940s Richard Bloch, who worked with Aiken, brought the Mark I know-how to Raytheon Manufacturing Company in Lexington, Mass. As manager of Raytheon's computer department, Bloch, under contract to the U.S. Navy, designed Raytheon's first electromechanical calculator for missile operation, the RADAC. In the early 1950s, after successfully completing this project, Raytheon developed its first commercial computer, the Datamatic 1000, for the First National Bank of Boston. First National then placed an order for 15 Datamatics, at a cost of $1 million apiece. To fulfill this order, Raytheon sold more than 50 percent of its computer department to Honeywell, located in Needham, Mass., which later purchased the rest of the department.

During the mid-1940s engineers and scientists at MIT's federally funded Lincoln Laboratory began work on Project Whirlwind. Designed by Jay Forrester and Ken Olsen and funded by the U.S. Navy, the Whirlwind computer was originally intended to be part of a general-purpose flight simulator that would be used to train bomber crews. Instead, it evolved into the first real-time, general-purpose computer and became operational at MIT in 1951.

From Project Whirlwind developed the idea for SAGE (Semi-Automatic Ground Environment), an air-defense system linking hundreds of radar stations in the United States and Canada in the first large-scale computer communications network. SAGE made important contributions to computer graphics, computer time-sharing, digital communications, and ferrite-core memories. Although Lincoln Laboratory was given primary responsibility for SAGE, companies such as IBM, Rand, Burroughs, Western Electric, RCA, and AT&T also participated. In this way SAGE technologies worked their way into commercial products and helped establish industry leaders.

Long a leader in electronics, Lincoln Laboratory applies science and technology to critical problems of national security. One measure of the laboratory's contribution to the nation's economy is its success in transferring technology to spin-offs like Arcon Company (located in Waltham, Mass.), Computer Corporation of America (Framingham, Mass.), Digital Equipment Corporation (founded in Maynard, Mass.; acquired by Compaq in 1998), Mitre Corporation (Bedford, Mass.), and Sycamore Networks (Chelmsford, Mass.), to name a few.

Lincoln Laboratory was also influential in establishing a precedent for organizational management. On the SAGE project, for example, researchers had a great deal of freedom to devise their own solutions to the problems they encountered. This management style represented a departure from traditional American bureaucracy and was adopted by the laboratory's engineers and scientists who later started their own companies, as well as by many of the technology companies located in the suburban Boston area.

The 1960s ushered in third-generation computers that substituted microelectronic or integrated circuits for transistors, minicomputers, and the first time-sharing computer. In 1957 two engineers from the lab at MIT, Ken Olsen and Harlan Anderson, founded Digital Equipment Corporation in a converted woolen mill in Maynard with the goal of creating and producing an alternative to IBM's mainframe. In 1965 Digital introduced the PDP-8, the world's first commercially successful minicomputer, which sold for one-fifth the price of a small IBM 360 mainframe. The speed, small size, and attractive price enabled the PDP-8 to be used in manufacturing plants, small businesses, and scientific laboratories. In 1970 the PDP-11 became the most widely used minicomputer.

As the minicomputer market grew, a group of engineers from Digital Equipment, led by Ed deCastro, founded Data General in Westborough, Mass., in 1968. Data General introduced the Nova, the first 16-bit minicomputer with four accumulators. The Nova line helped expand the market for low-priced computers—computers costing less than $100,000. This was a period when minicomputers were expected to make mainframes obsolete. Other companies, such as Prime Computer (Natick, Mass.) and Wang Laboratories (Lowell, Mass.), introduced their own minicomputers.

Some software firsts occurred at this time. In 1963 the Dartmouth College mathematicians Thomas Kurtz and John Kemeny created BASIC, an easy-to-learn programming language, to meet their students' needs. Since they did not copyright or patent their creation, BASIC later became the standard for early personal computers. That same year Ivan Sutherland, while at Lincoln Laboratory, published a program called Sketchpad, an interactive, real-time computer system that contributed to the beginning of the computer graphics field. In 1967 MIT's Seymour Papert designed a computer language for children called Logo.

The 1970s were a period of change: semiconductor memories replaced magnetic cores, computer time-sharing was further developed, minicomputers continued to sell, and the VAX was introduced. In 1963 MIT had been awarded federal funding for Project MAC (Multi-Access Computer), whose goal was to design a time-sharing system that would allow users to share a single, larger computer as a mainframe instead of using several smaller machines. MIT was chosen because it offered courses on such topics as artificial intelligence, computer-aided design, computer languages and devices, and human-machine systems. Project MAC led to many advances in these areas, including the groundwork for word processors and interactive programming, the idea for spreadsheets, the development of the first real networking of the personal computer, the first version of Internet protocols for the personal computer, and the creation of the UNIX operating system. By the mid-1970s, almost every mainframe computer had incorporated time-sharing technology. Previously computing was available only to large businesses, academic institutions, and the government. Now, as more users could simultaneously perform tasks on a single machine, the cost of computing dramatically decreased, while usage increased. Project MAC played a large role in changing the public's philosophy regarding the use of computers.

In the late 1970s, as a follow-up to the popular PDP-11 minicomputer, Digital Equipment Corporation introduced a family of VAX machines that provided hundreds of times the capacity of most minicomputers. The VAXes represented an important departure from IBM's mainframe-host-to-dumb-terminal computing model. They ranged from desktop personal computers to mainframes, all using the same operating system. Their software compatibility caused them to achieve success during the 1980s. For the first time executives and engineers worldwide could work on the same project, creating a vast computer network. The distributed computing concepts developed by Digital paved the way for the Internet.

The fast-growing Digital Equipment Corporation retained the atmosphere of a small company in which only a few engineers were responsible for product development. As Digital became one of IBM's major competitors, it continued to project a spartan image. Many customers, scientists, and engineers found that image extremely appealing. Digital represented everything that was liberating about computers, from its work areas to its casual dress. IBM, by contrast, continued to project a formal image and to enforce a traditional dress code.

Another successful company at this time was Wang Laboratories, founded by An Wang in 1951. Many of the office technologies and devices that have today become commonplace, such as word-processing programs and other office software, first emerged from Wang Laboratories. Wang aimed its products at the office workers who did the actual typing and filing. This approach led to practical rather than cutting-edge technology, which later became a disadvantage.

In the 1980s personal computers were beginning to be recognized as the machines of the future. IBM, Apple Computer, Digital Equipment, and Wang Laboratories were among the companies offering personal computers to businesses and the public. By the end of the decade, advances in microchip technology caused a shift from proprietary systems, such as those of Wang and Digital, to open systems that could accommodate many vendors.

Beginning in the 1980s a new class of computers using microprocessors and costing less than VAXes but more than personal computers became available. Whereas the VAX brought the power of a scientific machine into the engineering division of a company, these new machines brought such power to the individual workstation. These systems used the UNIX operating system and could be networked for the sharing of data and peripherals. Apollo Computer, founded in Chelmsford by Prime Computer's creator, Bill Poduska, unveiled the first workstation, which offered more power than some minicomputers at a fraction of the price. By the mid-1980s, Apollo was encountering competition; in 1989 it was acquired by Hewlett-Packard, which had entered the market with a workstation of its own design.

In 1979 the first electronic spreadsheet, VisiCalc, developed by Harvard Business School and MIT graduates to run on the Apple computer, had become an instant success. Shortly afterward Mitch Kapor developed the Lotus 1-2-3 spreadsheet for the IBM personal computer; it quickly became a new industry standard. In 1982 Kapor and Jonathan Sachs cofounded Lotus Development Corporation in Cambridge, Mass.

By the late 1980s companies were downsizing, merging, reinventing themselves, or closing. Those that were unable to adapt to the new technologies and marketplace simply went under. Companies like Digital, Data General, Prime, and Wang Laboratories, despite their previous dominance, were unable to build on the foundations they had established. Mainframe computing held its ground, but the era of minicomputers had ended.

The demise of the minicomputer market contributed to the closing of Prime Computer in 1992 and the merging of its subsidiary, Computervision Corporation, with Parametric Technology. With this merger Parametric, founded in 1985 in Needham, became the world's sixth-largest independent supplier of software tools for automating the mechanical development of a product from its conceptual design through production.

Data General's decline actually began in the early 1980s. In 1999 EMC Corporation acquired Data General and integrated its line of information-storage systems into the EMC product line. EMC was founded in 1979 in Newton, Mass., as a supplier of add-on memory boards to the minicomputer market. By 1989 the company had moved to Hopkinton, Mass., and revised its strategy to address the world's growing reliance on electronic data; soon it became a world leader in information-storage systems.

In 1988 Digital Equipment Corporation had been the second-largest computer company in the world, with IBM in first place. Although Digital's technology was the best of its day, it did not win the needed market share for its computers. In 1990 the company posted its first quarterly loss and layoffs followed. The company ceased to exist in 1998, when Compaq Computer Corporation of Houston purchased Digital Equipment for $9.6 billion.

Wang Laboratories began to reorient itself to address the changing market but suffered heavy operating losses. In 1992 Wang declared Chapter 11 bankruptcy but reorganized, reinvented itself, and recovered 12 months later. Through acquisitions and partnering, Wang became a global information-technology leader known as Wang Global. In 1999 Wang Global was acquired by Getronics of Amsterdam, a leading provider of vendor-independent computer solutions and services to professional users of technology.

Although Lotus Development Corpora-tion still exists, the company was acquired in 1995 by IBM. In this new context Lotus Development Corporation is known as Lotus Software from IBM.

Other companies have continued to grow with the changing technology or have reinvented themselves. Analog Devices of Norwood, Mass., established in 1965, continues to be a leading manufacturer of precision high-performance integrated circuits for analog and digital signal-processing applications, changing and expanding as the technology and market dictate. Banyan Systems, founded in 1983 in Westborough, initially made its name with its VINES network operating system software. Banyan grew until the early 1990s but by 1997 had lost market share for its trademark product, found itself in serious financial jeopardy, and could not compete with industry giants Microsoft and Novell. In September 1999 Banyan discontinued operations and focused its efforts on building a service business. In May 2000 Banyan changed its name to ePresence and became a leading technology-service company that provides directory-based solutions for Fortune 1,000–class enterprises.

The development of the computer industry in New England has been and is greatly influenced by the area's major research universities. The federal government, especially the Department of Defense and the National Science Foundation, continues to provide important financial support for computing research and development. The technology advances and the companies that have been established in New England have had an impact on the region, the country, and the world. As new technologies emerge, so, too, will new and reinvented companies.

Paul E. Ceruzzi, *A History of Modern Computing* (1998); Committee on Innovations in Computing and Communications, *Funding a Revolution: Government Support for Computing Research* (1999); James W. Cortada, *The Computer in the United States: From Laboratory to Market, 1930–1960* (1993); Tracy Kidder, *The Soul of a New Machine* (1981); Raúl Rojas and Ulf Hashagen, eds., *The First Computers: History and Architectures* (2000); Annalee Saxnian, *Regional Advantage: Culture and Competition in Silicon Valley and Route 128* (1994).

Eleanor Hollis Tedesco

Corliss Steam Engines The Corliss Steam Engine Company was incorporated in 1856 in Providence. For the next 32 years George H. Corliss manufactured high-grade steam engines in a factory that grew to cover more than 9 acres and employed upward of 1,000 workers. By 1870 it was the largest industrial complex in New England and the most important center of steam engine production in the country. Engine building was a vital business to both the region and the na-tion during the 19th century as American industry grew to rely more and more heavily on steam rather than waterpower to drive its machines. Unfettered by conditions imposed by nature or weather, steam-driven factories could run continuously and be located in virtually any area. Corliss mill engines were some of the best built, and its unique valve gear, patented in 1849, made them the most economical to run.

George Henry Corliss (1817–88) was born in Easton, N.Y. He was educated in village schools and later attended Castleton (Vt.) Academy. Although he was not trained as an engineer, he showed a great aptitude for mechanics. Corliss opened a general store in 1838, and when customers complained about the quality of the stitching in the boots he sold, he set about building a machine to improve them. While in the process of promoting his stitching machine in 1844, he traveled to Providence. There he was subsequently hired by the machinery-building firm of Fairbanks, Bancroft and Company, where he was employed as a draftsman and, eventually, a designer of steam engines. The company in turn became Bancroft, Nightingale and Company, and in 1847 the name was changed to Corliss, Nightingale and Company, reflecting Corliss's significant role in the firm. During the next several years a new Corliss-engineered factory was constructed in which steam engines were built to his designs and based on his patented improvements. The resulting product revolutionized the construction of steam engines. Corliss was so confident of his engine's economy that he offered buyers a novel method of payment: purchasers were given the option of paying a set price outright or making payments based on the savings in fuel over a given time. Wise buyers chose the former.

Although Corliss engines were popular throughout industry in general, their smooth running and responsive characteristics were especially useful in textile mills. Their ability to maintain a constant speed meant fewer broken threads, less down time, and a more uniform product. The speed of Corliss engines was not controlled by a simple throttle valve situated in the incoming steam line, as was common practice. Semirotary or oscillating valves were used instead of the traditional slide valve, and their operation was linked to closing devices and the engine's flyball governor. Corliss achieved an engine more sensitive to changing power needs that used steam more completely, thereby saving fuel and money.

George Corliss was granted approximately 70 U.S. patents, including several for machine tools and boilers, but the majority were for improvements in steam engines. As his most basic early patents expired in the 1870s and no further extensions were possible, countless other engine builders, recognizing the significance of his work, incorporated Corliss-type valve gears in their own designs. Thus, the Corliss name came to be associated with a specific type of steam engine, which remained popular long after the death of the inventor in 1888.

J. Leander Bishop, *A History of American Manufactures from 1608 to 1860* (1966); Eugene S. Ferguson, "Power and Influence: The Corliss Steam Engine in the Centennial Era," *Annals of the New York Academy of Sciences* (1984); "George H. Corliss," *Scientific American* (June 2, 1888); H. F. Mueller, "The 'One Hundredth Anniversary' of George Henry Corliss," *Power* (May 14, 1918).

William E. Worthington, Jr.

Defense Industry The defense industry has played a crucial role in New England's modern economic and social evolution. Founded in the engineering tradition of the 19th century's gun and ammunition industry, its impact became especially important during World War II and the following decades of the Cold War, when military spending increased dramatically. These war and near-war conditions caused a reorientation of New England's aging industrial base. They also linked the region's economy to world diplomatic relations, such that any change in these relations would have a serious impact. For instance, cutbacks following the end of the Vietnam War led to a contraction in military production and a regional depression. Likewise, the thaw in the Cold War led to a decrease in defense spending that hurt New England's economy. On the other hand, the military buildup of the Reagan era translated into a bonanza for New England's military-industrial complex during the 1980s. This dependence on the defense industry has left the region vulnerable to a boom-bust cycle in which its economic health became linked to external events and policies.

New England's vital textile and shoe industries of the 19th and early 20th centuries were in sharp decline before World War II, when idle and boarded-up mills and rising unemployment seemed to symbolize the region's future. The growth of the defense industry helped to change this situation. The engineering and aircraft firms that had survived the Great Depression in the 1930s were the beneficiaries of a steep increase in military spending brought on by the war; this increase continued into the 1950s and 1960s, and New England's economy was revitalized within the emerging nexus of Pentagon budgets and high-technology research. The production of radar, aerospace technology, nuclear submar-

ines, and missiles—and the federal money pouring into the region—resulted in another "industrial revolution" for New England.

The rise of the defense industry since World War II has particularly affected Massachusetts and Connecticut. In Massachusetts, the boom was felt along Route 128, which encircles metropolitan Boston. In Connecticut, industry is clustered along the shores of Long Island Sound at Stamford, Norwalk, and especially Groton. The two states share a third cluster along the Connecticut River valley, including cities such as Springfield, Mass., and Hartford and New Haven, Conn. A somewhat less significant area of defense production lies just to the north of Boston in southern New Hampshire.

The Boston cluster has been historically linked to the presence and activities of the Massachusetts Institute of Technology in Cambridge. As early as World War II, MIT actively pursued military research contracts and began to spin off production companies based on that research. The reputation of MIT was, and is, a crucial factor in locating and keeping defense firms in the greater Boston area, providing a magnet for high-tech growth and the recruitment of first-rate scientists and engineers from around the nation.

Several cities within the 65-mile arc of Route 128 are heavily involved in military production, including Lynn, where General Electric developed aircraft engines, and Waltham, a Raytheon center for radar and missile production including the Patriot missile used in the 1991 Gulf War. The city of Lowell has had a particularly uneven connection to the defense industry; a classic textile city in serious decline before World War II, Lowell received the first significant break in its economic plight during the war. The federal government established munitions and other military factories in Lowell, and by so doing challenged the dominance of the mill owners and presented their employees, both male and female, with new opportunities. Workers began leaving the dying textile mills for the higher wages of the defense industry. But although the new firms brought a degree of prosperity to the city, most did not stay beyond the end of the war, merely postponing the erosion of Lowell's prewar textile base. The Cold War, however, encouraged the continued presence of some firms, like Raytheon; finally, during the Reagan boom of the 1980s, Lowell received the military-industrial base promised since the war.

In the Connecticut River valley, Pratt and Whitney in East Hartford became one of the major defense contractors in New England, building airplane engines during the Depression. World War II was an important turning

point for Pratt and Whitney, as government orders vastly expanded its production. The company began developing jet engines during the early Cold War years and, in the 1980s, grew enormously, employing more than 30,000 people as a division of United Technologies Corporation.

Connecticut's Long Island Sound region has had a long relation with the U.S. Navy, particularly as a result of General Dynamics' Electric Boat Division at Groton. Electric Boat inherited Groton's role in the development of submarines for the navy that had begun during the 1890s. The Groton shipyard also prospered during World War II and in the 1950s produced the first nuclear-powered submarine—the USS *Nautilus*. Following the 1970s defense lull, Electric Boat built ballistic-missile nuclear submarines as well as attack submarines, both of which contributed to a great expansion at Groton yards and at the company's facilities in Quonset Point, R.I. The economic importance of military procurement became obvious in the late 1970s when a dispute between General Dynamics and the navy that threatened to close the Groton site was mediated by the governor of Connecticut and the state's senior senator; such high-level political intervention demonstrated the crucial financial stake that Connecticut had in maintaining its defense contracts. Similar situations throughout New England, at the Portsmouth Naval Shipyard in New Hampshire and the Bath Iron Works in Maine, for example, were likewise symptomatic of the region's economic dependence on the defense industry.

Since World War II, New England's economy has depended on Pentagon largess. Throughout the 1980s Massachusetts and Connecticut were among the top 10 states in obtaining prime military contracts. Both states have had substantially higher per capita shares of federal defense dollars than any other area of the nation; this has translated into higher per capita income levels and dramatically lower unemployment rates. Among the other states, only southern New Hampshire has shared in this kind of defense patronage.

By the beginning of the 1990s New England, with only 5 percent of the nation's population, had received 12 percent of the Pentagon's military budget. All the region's largest employers were connected to this spending. The dissolution of the Soviet Union and the subsequent end of the Cold War, however, led to a decrease in the need for military hardware. The federal defense spending that was once responsible for a new industrial revolution in New England gave way to drastic cutbacks in military procurements and a diminution in defense production.

Joel Garreau, *The Nine Nations of North America* (1981); Jacob Goodwin, *Brotherhood of Arms: General Dynamics and the Business of Defending America* (1985); Ann Markusen, Peter Hau, Scott Campbell, and Sabina Deitrick, *The Rise of the Gunbelt: The Military Remapping of Industrial America* (1991); Marc Scott Miller, *The Irony of Victory: World War II and Lowell, Massachusetts* (1988); Henry Wiencek, *The Smithsonian Guide to Historic America: Southern New England* (1989).

Eric Jarvis

Department Stores The birth of the department store in New England paralleled the rise of business and urbanism in the late 19th century. Retailing establishments, which survived the arrival of the shopping mall but now face the formidable competition of online shopping, are monuments to the phenomenal growth of the American city at the turn of the 20th century. During the 1850s and 1860s, the burgeoning economy in urban centers resulted in increased factory production of a wider range of goods and an expanded buying public. Transportation advancements increased the mobility of this middle-class clientele, bringing consumers from far afield to thriving commercial centers. While bazaars and street arcades had previously made a variety of goods available in one area, the notion of consolidating various "departments" under one administrative body was introduced in Paris, most notably in the Bon Marché, established by Aristide Boucicault. While A. T. Stewart in New York is regarded as the first entrepreneur to bring the idea of the department store to the United States, in 1862, his modern store on lower Broadway was quickly followed by similar enterprises, including Macy's, also in New York, Wanamaker's of Philadelphia, and Marshall Field's in Chicago.

In New England, several large dry-goods businesses also became department stores in the 1870s and 1880s, notably those of Edward Filene (William Filene's Sons) and Eben Jordan, in partnership with Benjamin L. Marsh (Jordan, Marsh and Company) in Boston; Gershon Fox (G. Fox and Company) in Hartford; and John Shepard (Shepard's) and the Samuels Brothers (Outlet Company) in Providence. While textile mills in northern New England provided the raw materials for the dry goods and clothing that were the main product line, the addition of varied mass-produced, low-priced items such as household goods and home furnishings transformed the dry-goods shop into the department store. Using the retailing practices established at the Bon Marché, these modern emporiums were distinguished from specialty shops by the fact that they sold a wide variety of goods at a low markup and fixed price because they were permitted merchandise returns, and by the prin-

Jordan Marsh department store building, Boston, 1975

ciple of free entrance, meaning customers could enter the premises without pressure to buy.

Department stores typically were family owned and operated, often founded by immigrants like William Filene, a tailor, and Gershon Fox, a peddler, both from Germany. Most New England retailers were self-taught, learning the department store business even as they defined it. These entrepreneurs were masters of promotion, making use of merchandising schemes, advertising, and special events to forge a strong identity for their business ventures as more family than company, casting themselves in the role of beneficent patriarch. This personalizing strategy provided a sense of identity for the employees who powered the engines of commerce and inspired loyalty in the middle-class clientele. Advertisements for G. Fox and Company often recounted that when account records were destroyed in a catastrophic fire in 1917, customers came to the store's temporary office voluntarily to pay their bills: "They paid from memory and from their hearts." The department stores became prominent local institutions and tourist landmarks, often actively involved in the political and cultural life of the New England cities they served. Eben Jordan, Jr., who succeeded his father as president of Jordan Marsh, financed the building of the Boston Opera House and also built Jordan Hall, a new auditorium for the New England Conservatory of Music.

The department store in New England was linked with the rise and fall of the fortunes of the city, architecturally as well as economically. As individual dry-goods shops were expanded, they grew beyond their ground-floor locations to fully occupy existing buildings, taking over adjacent structures and eventually entire blocks. By the turn of the century, neighbors Filene's and Jordan Marsh physically dominated Boston's Downtown Crossing shopping district, which had formed around the intersection of Washington, Summer, and Winter Streets. Shepard's and its major competitor, the Outlet, both subsumed entire city blocks in downtown Providence, acquiring and converting existing structures in order to present a massive unified front to entice customers. The gradual but consistent growth resulted initially in collections of haphazard structures that had to use signs and display windows to distinguish themselves.

But in the early 20th century, new purpose-built structures took advantage of the latest stylistic trends and technological innovations in American commercial architecture. The need for open floor space for selling, large windows to display merchandise, and mechanisms to facilitate the transportation of people and goods resulted in the use of building innovations such as cast iron or steel construction and sheet glass production, and new conveying and communication systems such as elevators, escalators, telephones, and pneumatic tubes. Filene's hired the nationally known architect Daniel Burnham to design its new building, which still stands at Washington and Summer Streets. Opened in September 1912, the eight-story structure had an additional two levels below ground with an underground connection to the subway system. The classical Renaissance stone-and-brick facade, decorated with roses for the grand opening, bestowed the respectability of a public institution on what was at heart a machine for selling.

These sites for the exchange of goods in the modern New England city also became places for the consumption of culture. Shopping was transformed into a leisure activity, beginning on the street, where display windows presented the ideal life of the aspiring middle class and, as at Filene's, uniformed doormen assisted customers to the entrance. Inside, the department stores provided libraries, art galleries, and auditoriums, sacrificing valuable selling floor in order to act as local museum, school, and theater. Centinel Hill Hall, G. Fox's 11th-floor auditorium, complete with stage and theatrical lighting, sat 500 for concerts and lectures. After World War I, Filene's held popular tea dances, complete with orchestra, in the afternoons in its auditorium. Filene's opened a Paris office in 1910 and established itself as the purveyor of taste in women's fashion, publishing a clothing magazine and holding fashion shows and grooming lectures. With the aim of offering "relaxation and recreation" to its customers, the Jordan Marsh store provided a well-stocked library and reading room, a game room for gentlemen, and a comfortable lounge for ladies to listen to music.

The department stores even took on the promotion of good health for customers and staff; Jordan Marsh offered a physician, a dentist, a chiropodist, and a dental hygienist always on duty, while G. Fox and Company's 10th-floor hospital had a staff of six registered nurses and a medical secretary. For the middle class, particularly women, the department store promised to fulfill all needs, material and spiritual, providing a public forum for interaction and a safe haven in the modern city.

The influential role the department store played in the development of downtown business districts in major cities and small town Main Streets expanded in the early 20th century. Filene's opened its first branch store in 1923 in Wellesley, Mass., pioneering expansion into the suburbs. But these small stores in town centers, an outgrowth of resort shops and traveling shows at hotels in places like York Harbor, Maine, and Falmouth and Northampton, Mass., were eventually superseded by the large regional shopping centers that sprang up after World War II. Transportation continued to impel the development of retailing as the rise of the automobile and demise of public transportation systems made suburban centers with ample parking a necessity.

Although Jordan Marsh displayed an optimistic confidence in downtown retailing when it decided to build a new store on Washington Street in 1947, it was the only large store in the eastern United States to undertake such a major reconstruction in several decades. Attempts to consolidate resulted in local alliances; Filene's bought B. Peck Company of Lewiston, Maine, in 1947 and eventually merged with G. Fox's, but most family-owned stores were sold to large out-of-town corporations that stressed bottom lines rather than historical significance. Providence's once-vital retail shopping district also fell victim to suburban developments; Shepard's went bankrupt and closed in January 1974, and the Outlet was first sold to United Department Stores of Trenton, N.J., in 1980, then closed in October 1982. The May Company decided to close G. Fox's—once the nation's sixth-largest department store—in September 1992, leaving Hartford's downtown without a large department store. The Jordan Marsh chain of stores merged with Macy's in 1994 and now operates under the Macy's name.

Whereas Boston, with its downtown workforce and tourist traffic, continues to support arch rivals Filene's and Macy's, their long-term viability is questionable. The department store continues to be challenged by its own offspring, which have taken retailing innovations to new extremes: low-price discounters offering bargains, high-end specialty shops promising personal service, and electronic superstores assuring a more global reach than suburban branches. But these retailing establishments have yet to challenge the department store's critical role as a center of communal life in New England towns and cities and as a defining monument of modernity in the United States.

Meredith L. Clausen, "The Department Store: Development of the Type," *Journal of Architectural Education* 39 (Fall 1985); Richard H. Edwards, Jr., *Tales of the Observer* (1950); John Ferry, *A History of the Department Store* (1960); Michael B. Miller, *The Bon Marché: Bourgeois Culture and the Department Store, 1869–1920* (1981); Hrant Pasdermadjian, *The Department Store, Its Origins, Evolution and Economics* (1954); Douglas W. Rae, *City: Urbanism and Its End* (2003); William McKenzie Woodward and Edward F. Sanderson, *Providence: A Citywide Survey of Historic Resources* (1986).

Louisa Iarocci

Domestic Work Most obviously, "domestic work" refers to housework: tasks like cooking, cleaning, and mothering, usually performed by women as an extension of their role as wives. Beyond this definition, domestic work also covers the jobs performed in the home to sustain the family economy. They include household production of food and clothing as well as taking in "outwork," such as stitching shoes in the 1840s or word-processing in the 1990s. Domestic work is also an occupation, generally of poor or minority women, who are employed by wealthier women eager to escape the drudgery of housework or who need time to participate in the market economy. Most fundamental, domestic work is a social, political, and cultural concept, with deep roots in New England's history that continues to define contemporary lives.

The domestic routine of Beatrice Plummer, a 17th-century New England woman, began early in the morning with milking and continued throughout the day with cooking, baking, cleaning, pickling, butter churning, cheese making, spinning, laundering, and childcare. Although Plummer and her husband, Francis, worked together in close proximity to maintain their self-subsisting home, Beatrice was primarily responsible for the household chores, while her husband's domain extended beyond the homelot to the orchard, the cornfields, and the fishing stages. This gendered division of labor reflected the respective social value placed on women's and men's work in colonial New England. A husband's labor was a manifestation of an economic, social, and legal status that subsumed his wife's and ensured the continued invisibility of her domestic work.

More than 300 years later, women continue to be responsible for the majority of domestic work. Statistics show that 67 percent of mothers in New England have full-time jobs, perform two-thirds of household tasks, and undertake most of the daily childcare. On average, in dual-income households women work a full month longer per year than their husbands. Specific tasks may have changed since colonial times, but women still perform a litany of intensive, repetitive, physically debilitating work in the home. Research that crosses racial and class boundaries shows that—among many other responsibilities—women cook dinner, vacuum, do the laundry, scrub the toilet, make doctors' appointments for their children, and check in with the babysitter. Moreover, although household tasks are shared more often than previously, domestic work is normalized as an extension of a woman's role in contemporary New England, just as it was in the 17th century.

The social devaluation of domestic work also belies its fundamental importance as a means of sustaining family life and supplementing the wider economy. In mid-19th-century Providence, for example, developing industries relied on the ingenuity of working-class women to bolster the below-subsistence wages paid by factory and mill owners. Women added to their husbands' meager incomes by making candles, hauling wood, carrying water, sewing clothes, collecting rags, taking in boarders, and scavenging or stealing necessary items. It is estimated that this kind of domestic work provided as much as half of the household income in New England's working-class communities.

In 1993, 13 percent of single mothers receiving Aid to Families with Dependent Children in New England worked to make up the shortfall between welfare payments and necessary expenditures. Some of these women cultivated connections with family and friends or utilized resources at church and community agencies. They also found ways to combine their household responsibilities with off-the-book employment, often taking on paid domestic work like housecleaning, childcare, catering, and home sewing. Some women worked in the "underground" economy: selling stolen goods or working as occasional prostitutes. As in the 19th century, financial necessity and the conception that domestic work is naturally a female responsibility lead women to take extraordinary measures to provide for their families.

Women of all classes have to balance time spent on household tasks with attention given to activities outside the home. Consequently, acquiring the necessary organizational skills for managing domestic work has been a consistent concern of New England women. In the 19th century, Catharine Beecher paid meticulous attention to this process. In *A Treatise on Domestic Economy* (1858), she outlined various household tasks in great detail and suggested how her readers might instruct their domestic employees to perform them correctly. Beecher believed that domestic work was a manifestation of women's superior virtue and a reflection of their capacity to influence the moral character of their families and wider society. Nevertheless, this "cult of domesticity" was predicated on the unfeminine nature of physical labor. Middle-class women, therefore, had to delegate household tasks to working-class women in order to pursue the ideal of "true womanhood."

Domestic service has always been integral to domestic work in New England. In the 17th century, colonial families often hired young women or brought in cousins to help with spinning or laundry. "Hired girls" were treated as equals by their employers and usually ate at the same dinner table. African American women were also employed to do domestic work, but they were designated "servants" rather than with the more equitable term "help" that referred to native-born white women. In the 1840s, immigrant women from western and northern Europe were usually hired for domestic work in New England

homes. Correspondence among wealthy women of this era expresses prejudicial dissatisfaction with these new employees, particularly Irish immigrants. Typical was a complaint made by Caroline Barrett White of Brookline, Mass.: "My cook left today and the one I had engaged to take her place failed to keep her engagement. Irish fidelity!" From the perspective of a domestic servant, housework was a double responsibility performed at her place of employment and in her own home. The difficulties inherent in maintaining this double shift of domestic work are made obvious in the experience of Chloe Spear, an African American employed by a Boston family in the late 18th century. Every day Spear came home from work and began the household chores for her family and for the boardinghouse she ran with her husband. She also took in outside washing that dried while she slept for a couple of hours before preparing breakfast and returning to her paid job.

In contemporary New England, 38 percent of women in households employ some kind of domestic help, usually daycare. There are almost 6,000 daycare centers in the region and more than 20,000 licensed daycare providers. There are also countless cleaning services and temporary agencies that provide help with household chores. Domestic work continues to be a racially segregated occupation. Most employers are white and most employees are members of minorities; in particular, the number of Hispanic employees has increased dramatically. Employers are eager to hire minority women because they will work for less money. An employment agent in Newton, Mass., explained this exploitative motivation in simple terms: "I just had one woman come in who requested a Cambodian or Vietnamese. Why? Because she can get them cheap!"

In the absence of domestic employees, some women are able to combine housework with paid employment. The psychological consequences of managing domestic and paid work in 21st-century New England are also clear. A contemporary mother, secretary, and University of Massachusetts student noted, "I enjoy my family, I don't want to feel like it is a job, but when I come home from the office and have to make dinner and take care of the baby, it feels like just another thing I have to do." The mixed feelings expressed by this woman resonate through New England history to Harriet Beecher Stowe, who, despite myriad public accomplishments, remained anxious about domestic work: "I wish I had the same strength and ability for household matters as my grandmother.... My mother was less than her mother, and I am less than my mother."

Catharine Beecher, *A Treatise on Domestic Economy for the Use of Young Ladies at Home and at School* (1858); Mary H. Blewett, *We Will Rise Together in Our Might: Working Women's Voices from 19th-Century New England* (1991); Jeanne Boydston, *Home and Work: Housework, Wages and the Ideology of Labor in the Early Republic* (1991); Nancy F. Cott, *The Bonds of Womanhood: "Woman's Sphere" in New England, 1780–1835* (1977); Faye E. Dudden, *Serving Women: Household Service in 19th-Century America* (1983); Arlie Hoschild and Ann Machung, *The Second Shift* (1989); Judith Rollins, *Between Women: Domestics and Their Employers* (1985); Laurel Thatcher Ulrich, *Good Wives: Image and Reality in the Lives of Women in Northern New England, 1650–1750* (1982).

Jacqueline Ellis

Electric Power and Electrification

The development of electric power in New England paralleled the larger evolution of the electric industry throughout the United States but also differed from it in several key ways. First, New England electrified relatively early, thanks to its (commercially desirable) dense population and endowment of industrial entrepreneurs, scientists, institutions of higher learning, and leading electric equipment producers. Second, from the electric industry's founding to the present, the region has been burdened with some of the nation's highest power rates because of its lack of fossil fuels (coal, oil, and natural gas), its great distance from major sources of those fuels, and its limited number of hydropower sites. In addition, despite its costly electric power, New England quickly became electric-energy intensive in its commercial, residential, and industrial sectors. The region's electric utilities also forged an unusual number of "power pools" in the late 1960s and early 1970s in an effort to increase efficiency and meet demand peaks. Finally, the New England states embraced nuclear power more aggressively than any other part of the country following World War II and later became a hotbed of antinuclear protest.

Reflecting larger patterns, electric light and power came to New England in the late 1870s and 1880s. First came small boiler-dynamo units ("isolated plants") that produced direct current (D.C.) for the arc lighting of a street, open space, or individual building; the Brush Electric Company, for example, installed Boston's first commercial application (1878) and street lights (Scollay Square, 1881). By the end of the decade, small central-station companies also were producing direct current or alternating current (A.C.) for arc lights, incandescent lights, and low horsepower motors. Competition among firms and rival technologies was fierce. In 1886 the Westinghouse interests opened the nation's first commercial A.C. system in Great Barrington, Mass., while Edison's backers established the nation's

Power station and industrial landscape, Bellows Falls, Vt., 2002

second central-station incandescent lighting company in a major city (following New York's Pearl Street Station) in Boston. By the turn of the 20th century, Edison systems (after adopting A.C.) were dominant in Boston—then the best-lighted city in the world—and elsewhere in the region.

Hydropower came to New England through the efforts of Malcolm Chace and Henry Harriman, whose companies built dams along the Deerfield and Connecticut Rivers beginning in 1907 and transmitted the power down to industrialized central Massachusetts. The enterprise grew into the New England Electric System, which—though it later operated fossil fuel and nuclear plants—remained the region's largest supplier of hydropower. In 1930, 30 percent of New England's electricity came from its rivers, the remainder from coal.

The dominant utilities expanded territorially in the early 1900s, and by the 1930s had settled into a stable pattern of privately owned regional giants, interspersed with a few small (sometimes municipal) utilities. Having grown by adding territory and new customers, the power companies now focused on increasing per-customer consumption of power. The large utilities—particularly Boston Edison, which emerged as a national leader in the promotion of electricity—built large marketing and public relations organizations that employed aggressive campaigns—often coordinated by the New England Section of the powerful National Electric Light Association—to encourage the use of industrial motors, store lighting and electric signs, appli-

ances and electric cooking, and electric automobiles and delivery wagons.

Consumption of electricity dipped briefly during the Great Depression, then began an uninterrupted climb as one of the region's most robust industries in World War II and the postwar period. As high-technology firms (many spawned by the Massachusetts Institute of Technology) were built along Massachusetts's Route 128 in the 1950s and 1960s, some became large consumers of power. By 1961, 500 of the region's electronics firms (total revenues: $1.25 billion) dotted Route 128, including the giant defense contractor Raytheon, the largest employer and power user in Greater Boston. The new high-tech sector helped decouple economic growth from electric energy consumption but did not compensate fully for losses from the region's declining industrial base.

As demand for electricity burgeoned, the region's utilities increasingly turned to formalized and centrally controlled power-sharing arrangements. Power sharing dated back to the industry's founding and received a boost in New England during World War I, when mobilization put heavy demands on the region's electrical capacity. But it was not until the late 1960s and early 1970s that the electric utilities formed comprehensive and sophisticated "power pools." On the technical side, the pools involved the interconnection of high-voltage transmission lines and the shifting of load among separate utility companies through a central command post by means of new computer technology. Operationally, the pools enabled member utilities to improve their oper-

ating efficiencies to better meet pockets of high demand within the system, and to safeguard against a recurrence of cascading outages, as in the Great Northeastern Blackout of 1965. The Eastern Massachusetts and Vermont Energy Control (EMVEC) was formed in 1967, followed by Rhode Island–Eastern Massachusetts–Vermont Energy Control (REMVEC) in 1969, New England Power Exchange (NEPEX) in 1970, and New England Power Pool (NEPOOL), which included 42 utilities, in 1972.

The region's electric utilities converted rapidly from Appalachian coal to lower-cost imported oil after the Johnson administration lifted the residual oil import quota in 1965. Even so, electric energy costs in New England remained much higher than the national average. It is not surprising, therefore, that the region's utilities, especially in Massachusetts, pursued nuclear power more aggressively than other regions or states in the nation. Lacking indigenous fossil fuels but rich in engineering know-how, New England's industrial interests eagerly embraced the atom as a possible way to lower energy costs and attract new industry. Even before the Atomic Energy Commission opened its doors in 1946, the New England Council (a group of educators and business leaders) formed an "atomic energy committee" that included MIT president Karl Compton. In 1954 the New England Governors Council also established an atomic energy committee (made up of scientists, attorneys, and industrial and utility leaders). The committee's July 1955 report strongly advocated atomic power development "at the earliest opportunity," and included a widely adopted model act for state regulation and promotion.

By that time, the region's leading utilities had taken action. In late 1954, 11 New England electric utilities (which together supplied 90 percent of the region's power) formed the Yankee Atomic Electric Company, which soon announced plans to build a light-water power plant in the western Massachusetts town of Rowe. Public reaction was overwhelmingly positive, as was the response from Washington. Atomic Energy Commission chair Lewis Strauss, who would become famous for his 1954 public declaration that atomic power might become "too cheap to meter," told a gathering of 400 New England industrialists that when it came to nuclear power, their region possessed a "great historic and geographic industrial advantage," and assured them that the new kind of energy was no more dangerous than other kinds of industry. Yankee Rowe went on line in July 1961.

The 1970s were the most troubled times in the industry's history. The growth of nuclear power in New England began to draw fire in the late 1960s from environmentalists, scientific activists, and ordinary residents living near atomic plants. The New England Coalition on Nuclear Pollution (1971) began working through the courts with some success; in a 1974 referendum, a third of Vermont and Massachusetts voters called for the dismantling of nuclear plants in their state. In April 1977, some 2,000 antinuclear activists, organized by the Clamshell Alliance, descended on the Public Service Company's nuclear plant at Seabrook, N.H.; the largest protest of its kind, it helped ignite a nationwide antinuclear movement. Seabrook Station did not go on line until 1989.

By that time, nuclear power interests were retreating in the face of massive cost overruns, and the industry itself was suffering severely—even in the public relations realm—because of spiraling costs associated with the 1973–74 oil crisis. Demand for electricity in New England, after growing at an annual average rate of 7.6 percent between 1960 and 1972, fell to 1.6 percent after the oil embargo. Meanwhile, the regulatory terrain began to shift, first with passage of the Public Utility Regulatory Policy Act of 1978—which opened the field to competition from solar power, cogeneration, and other nonutility sources—and then with further policy steps toward wholesale deregulation.

In response to these challenges, the region's utilities launched conservation and load-management programs designed to encourage customers to use less energy and shift consumption to off-peak hours. This provided some public relations relief, but more important, it allowed the utilities to avoid new construction, which had become prohibitively expensive and politically perilous. The utilities also formed new strategic alliances. New England Electric System sold its generating capacity in 1998 and is now a British-owned transmission and distribution company. The electric power and gas facilities in 80 eastern Massachusetts cities and towns were combined into Nstar, a diversified energy services company, in late 1999. Although the region's total electric generating capacity has grown rapidly in recent years, the once-staid utility companies must adjust to the eclipse of a stable economic and political paradigm, and growing concern over the massive failures of the region's power grid in 1998 and 2003.

Brian Balogh, *Chain Reaction: Expert Debate and Public Participation in American Commercial Nuclear Power, 1945–1975* (1991); Stephen Doheny-Farina, *The Grid and the Village: Losing Electricity, Finding Community, Surviving Disaster* (2001); John T. Landry and Jeffrey L. Cruikshank, *From the Waters: The Origins and Growth of the New England Electric System* (1996); Henry Lee, "Energy: The Challenge," in *New England Prospects,* ed. Carl E. Reidel (1982); Harold C. Passer, *The Electrical Manufacturers, 1875–1900* (1953); Richard Rudolph and Scott Ridley, *Power Struggle: The Hundred-Year War over Electricity* (1986); David B. Sicilia, *Selling Power* (2003).

David B. Sicilia

Fidelity Investments   In the last quarter of the 20th century Fidelity Investments, a financial-services firm headquartered in Boston, emerged as the nation's (and the world's) largest sponsor of open-end mutual funds. The company's Magellan Fund, under the guidance of financial guru Peter Lynch from 1977 to 1990, produced spectacular returns for investors, and its stellar performance encouraged executives to introduce more than 200 additional mutual funds in the 1980s and 1990s to meet the surging public demand.

Launched in 1930, near the onset of the Great Depression, the original firm began modestly with a single mutual fund, appropriately titled Fidelity Fund. At this time, open-end mutual funds—which had no limitations on the issuance of shares and allowed investors to redeem them directly from the issuer—were a novelty in financial circles. Only Massachusetts Investors Trust, introduced in the 1920s, has a longer history as a sponsor of open-end funds. The managers of Fidelity Fund invested their customers' savings in a diverse group of marketable securities, thereby relieving individual investors of all responsibility for selecting specific stocks and prudently timing purchases and sales.

In 1943 a former lawyer, Edward C. Johnson, took over the management of Fidelity Fund, assuming ownership three years later. He and his team of securities analysts were successful managers, and in 1947 they added a second fund, Puritan, that invested in a mix of stocks and bonds. Two additional stock funds were introduced in the late 1950s. In 1963 the company created an innovative fund with an international focus, but tax considerations led to a shift in emphasis. Retitled the Magellan Fund, the revised goal was to seek out stocks with outstanding growth potential—for example, corporations like IBM. Peter Lynch assumed the position of fund manager for Magellan in 1977, and his performance was so outstanding that Fidelity, and indeed the entire mutual fund industry, received a tremendous boost from the favorable publicity.

Edward "Ned" Johnson III succeeded his father as president of Fidelity Investments in 1972. Under his leadership the firm introduced a money market fund with check-writing privileges, and soon thereafter it initiated a new direct-marketing strategy for all its funds that bypassed brokerage firms and lowered sales fees for customers. Many of the mutual funds managed by Fidelity became "no-load" funds: investors paid no sales commissions.

Fidelity Management and Research Company remains a private corporation owned by the Johnson family and a few hundred employees. The Fidelity Foundation, an independent philanthropic organization, was established in 1965 and has donated—usually anonymously—more than $40 million to community development, arts and cultural organizations, and medical research. By the late 1990s Fidelity earned management fees on more than 230 mutual funds with assets totaling over $600 billion, or approximately 3 percent of the entire capitalization of the U.S. equity market and just over 1 percent of world equity markets. Fidelity serves more than 3 million households around the globe. Many American families with 401 and 403 retirement plans have their savings invested in the mutual funds managed by this Boston-based enterprise.

Diana Henriques, *Fidelity's World: The Secret Life and Public Power of the Mutual Fund Giant* (1995).

Edwin J. Perkins

Firearms   Although countless individual gunsmiths worked throughout the New England states during the 1700s, it was not until the last decade of that century that the region emerged as the center for arms production in the United States. This change was brought about by four factors. While three of these—reliable sources of waterpower, excellent port facilities, and a highly talented labor pool—existed elsewhere, though not in as high concentrations, the fourth was almost unique to New England. This was the early realization that machine tools could be used to manufacture arms in quantities far beyond the capabilities of any single gunmaker.

The first arms maker to successfully employ machinery on a large scale was Eli Whitney, now better known as the inventor of the cotton gin. Whitney is widely credited for introducing the concept of interchangeable parts to the American arms industry. Producing parts of consistent dimension and construction was especially vital in the case of military arms, where field repairs were common. If, for example, the parts of a broken musket lock could not be replaced on the spot with similar pieces, the musket became useless for the rest of the battle. Standardization was essential to the maintenance of arms in the new republic's military forces.

While Whitney was able to achieve a remarkably high degree of standardization through the use of specialized machinery at his factory in New Haven, Conn., from 1798 onward, true interchangeability generally remained a matter of luck. In particular, the internal mechanisms of gun locks had to be hand finished to ensure that they functioned properly. Nevertheless, Whitney set the stage not only for his contemporaries but for those who followed.

In Berlin, Conn., Simeon North employed machinery to produce flintlock pistols for the U.S. government between 1813 and 1829. Nathan Starr used the same methods to produce government-issue firearms and swords in Middletown, Conn. Successful production of consistently dimensioned small parts finally came about when the firearms industry employed skilled machinists from another New England industry, clockmaking. Though their role in the firearms industry is often overlooked today, New England's clockmakers provided the technical expertise needed to design machines that could cut precisely formed parts from iron bar stock. This, combined with a dramatic change in the construction of gun locks (the old flint system had been replaced by the much simpler percussion cap), resulted in what only can be termed a revolution in gun design. Multishot arms, which previously had been somewhat cumbersome affairs, now were practical. In addition, the guns' more sophisticated lock work could be manufactured without difficulty.

In the 19th century, realizing that the future of the arms industry did not lie in the production of military arms but rather in the civilian market, a number of makers concentrated their efforts on manufacturing personal sidearms. Perhaps the most famous of these was the percussion pepperbox. Constructed using a revolving group of barrels machined from a single piece of steel, these pistols provided their owners with five or six shots instead of the one or two previously available in flintlock pistols. The first practical designs for pepperboxes were patented by two Massachusetts residents, Benjamin Darling of Bellingham in 1836 and Ethan Allen of Worcester the following year.

Concurrently, a former Connecticut native named Samuel Colt patented the first design for a pistol that was to become the quintessential American firearm: the revolver. The revolver consisted of a short cylinder drilled with holes to hold loose powder and balls, a frame containing the lock mechanism, and a separate barrel mounted in front of the cylinder. Despite being compact and easily disassembled for cleaning, Colt's first efforts suffered from an overly complicated cylinder-turning system. It was not until 1847 that he perfected a simple pawl-and-hand mechanism to rotate the cylinder as the pistol was cocked. (The first revolvers of this kind were made for Colt by Eli Whitney, Jr.) Their suc-

cess caused Colt, a flamboyant entrepreneur, to open his own factory in Hartford the following year.

Colt's venture exemplified the American system of manufacture. Workers performed specialized tasks and often spent their entire careers manufacturing one specific part. Barrels, frames, and cylinders were made in dedicated departments, lock parts in another, finishing in a third, and assembly a fourth. This compartmentalization ensured the production of consistently dimensioned components, as well as a final product that was, for all intents and purposes, identical to the one next to it. More important, Colt's reliance upon machine-made parts allowed a level of production Eli Whitney could never have dreamed possible. Yet even with the degree of industrialization Colt achieved, certain parts still had to be hand finished. To function properly, the cylinder of a revolver needs to turn a precise distance each time the pistol is cocked so that the chambers holding the powder and ball are in exact alignment with the barrel. A difference of as small as 1/1,000 of an inch in any of the parts involved in turning the cylinder could effect this alignment. Consequently, one of the primary responsibilities of the assemblers employed at the Colt factory was to make sure these parts were properly tuned so that each revolver functioned perfectly. Despite the inventor's efforts to improve the precision of the machinery at his works, the goal of eliminating hand labor remained elusive.

Simpler arms, such as single-shot rifles and muskets could, however, be made almost completely with machines. This was demonstrated conclusively by the firm of Robbins and Lawrence in Windsor, Vt. Though now remembered for its pepperboxes and rifles, Robbins and Lawrence was better known in the 19th century for machine tools. Indeed, at the 1851 Exhibition of the Works of Industry of all Nations held in London, Robbins and Lawrence were awarded a medal for their machinery, rather than their firearms.

Just as the introduction of the percussion cap had changed the New England arms industry in the 1830s, the development of the self-contained metallic cartridge in the late 1850s was to have a profound effect. This cartridge combined the ignition priming, powder, and bullet in one unit. In 1857 the Springfield, Mass., partnership of Smith and Wesson was the first firm to market a revolver chambered for metallic cartridges. These small-caliber pistols proved an immediate success and the patent covering their construction gave Smith and Wesson a virtual monopoly on their manufacture until 1872.

The metallic cartridge also made other types of firearms possible. In New Haven,

Oliver F. Winchester began manufacturing repeating rifles in 1862. By the early 1870s, his company dominated this segment of the industry both in the United States and abroad, and the company's advertisement of the Winchester repeating rifle as "the gun that won the West" was more appropriate than many advertising slogans. Winchester also displayed a business acumen which typified successful arms makers of the post-1860 era. Instead of relying on the American market, Winchester directed his energies abroad after 1865. He also actively purchased firms that could affect his sales (including the firm established by Eli Whitney). By following these policies the Winchester Repeating Arms Company became the world's largest manufacturer of firearms by 1900.

Smaller companies also found industrialization to be the key to arms manufacture. The Darling Brothers of Bellingham, Mass., and Woonsocket, R.I., made revolving pepperboxes using machine tools. William W. Wetmore of Windsor, Vt., used templates to manufacture the components of his target rifles.

While the Connecticut River valley was the site of New England's major arms manufacturers, the industry was not restricted to that region. Norwich, Conn., was the focal point for manufacturing the inexpensive cartridge pistols now known as "Saturday Night Specials." Allen and Thurber made tens of thousands of pepperboxes in Worcester, Mass. Christian Spencer made repeating cartridge rifles in Boston, and the Providence Tool Company made a variety of rifles in Rhode Island.

Today, New England remains a center of arms production. Colt pistols are still made in Hartford both by the original firm's namesake successor and a new firm called the U.S. Fire Arms Company. Smith and Wesson maintains its factory in Springfield, Mass. Winchester rifles are still made in New Haven though by U.S. Repeating Arms Company. And other companies emerged during the 20th century that still operate in the 21st, chief among them Sturm, Ruger and Company of Southport, Conn., and Newport, N.H.

Felicia Johnson Deyrup, *Arms Makers of the Connecticut Valley: A Regional Study of the Economic Development of the Small Arms Industry, 1798–1870* (1948); Claude E. Fuller, *The Whitney Firearms* (1946); James E. Hicks, *Nathan Starr Arms Maker 1776–1845* (1940); William Hosley, *Colt: The Making of a Legend* (1996); Herbert G. Houze, *Firearms and Edged Weapons at the 1851 London International Exhibition* (forthcoming); Roy G. Jinks, *The History of Smith and Wesson* (1977); Roy M. Marcot, *Spencer Repeating Firearms* (1990); Harold R. Mouillesseaux, *Ethan Allen, Gunmaker: His Partners, Patents and Firearms* (1973); Stuart M. Mowbray, *The Darling Pepperbox: The Story of Samuel Colt's Forgotten Competitors in Bellingham,*

Mass., and Woonsocket, R.I. (2004); S. N. D. North, and Ralph H. North, *Simeon North, First Official Pistol Maker of the United States* (1913); Robert L. Wilson, *Ruger and His Guns: A History of the Man, the Company and Their Firearms* (1996); Robert L. Wilson and Robert Q. Sutherland, *The Book of Colt Firearms* (1971); *The Winchester Repeating Arms Company: Its History from 1865 to 1981* (2004 [1994]).

Herbert G. Houze

Food Franchises

Indigenous New England cuisine extends beyond the bean and the cod to include ice cream, doughnuts, and submarine sandwiches. In fact, some of the country's most popular food franchise operations had their start in New England.

A pioneer in the concept of franchising (a form of licensing in which the franchiser agrees to provide a franchisee with a name, logo, operational standards, advertising, and products, for a percentage of the profits) was Howard Deering Johnson of Quincy, Mass. In 1925 Johnson hit upon the idea of offering home-made ice cream, with a higher than usual butterfat content, in an unprecedented variety of 28 flavors. Recognizing the importance of the automobile in American culture, he promoted the revolutionary idea of franchising restaurants to feed the traveling public. Older New Englanders still reminisce about Howard Johnson's fried clam strips, invented in Ipswich, Mass., and the company's signature clam chowder, perfected by Jacques Pepin, Howard Johnson's corporate chef. Although the familiar orange-roofed restaurants had disappeared by 1990, Howard Johnson's ice cream and prepackaged frozen foods, including the company's famous macaroni and cheese, are still available in retail markets.

During the summer of 1935 the brothers Prestley and Curtis Blake opened an ice cream shop in Springfield, Mass., that they called Friendly Ice Cream. To keep customers coming back during the cool months they added hamburgers to the menu. By the time the Hershey Foods Company purchased the company in 1979, the franchise had 600 shops. In 1988 a group of investors purchased the company from Hershey and added an "s" to the name; Friendly's retains its image as a family restaurant chain a notch above other fast food outlets and the place to go for premium ice cream.

Another ice-cream maker to enter the franchise field was Ben and Jerry's Homemade, founded in 1978 in Burlington, Vt., by childhood friends Ben Cohen and Jerry Greenfield. As part of its countercultural image, Ben and Jerry's uses creative names to distinguish the ice cream flavors: Cherry Garcia is named after the Grateful Dead's Jerry Garcia, and

Phish Food, which contains a school of fudge fish in every pint, celebrates the band, which had its start in Vermont. Ben and Jerry's scoop-shop chain is now a subsidiary of Unilever, a global consumer goods company and the world's leading ice cream producer.

Arthur Cores and Steven Kolow hatched Boston Market in 1985 as Boston Chicken in Newton, Mass. Their concept was to offer consumers high-quality, home-style food as take-out. This alternative to existing fast food outlets offered consumers the ability to put a fully prepared family dinner on the table without cooking. The Boston Market concept was an immediate success and expanded to more than 1,100 franchised restaurants before it declared bankruptcy in 1998. The McDonald's Corporation purchased the company in 2000.

Call them grinders, submarines, subs, or torpedoes, but don't call them hoagies in New England. One of the first persons to franchise the submarine sandwich was Fred DeLuca of Bridgeport, Conn., founder of Subway. In 1965, at age 17, he borrowed $1,000 from Dr. Peter Buck, a family friend, to open Pete's Super Submarines. The name was soon shortened to Subway, and the first franchise opened in 1974. Today there are over 20,000 outlets in more than 75 countries, making it the largest submarine sandwich chain in the world. Subway still maintains its corporate headquarters in Milford, Conn.

The D'Angelos Sandwich shop franchise had its start in 1967 as Ma Riva's Sub Shop in Dedham, Mass. The name was first changed to Angelo, and then a "D"—for "delicious"—was added. In 1997 Papa Gino's, which had its beginning as a single-slice East Boston pizzeria, acquired D'Angelo's 200 sandwich shops.

Operating out of Dorchester, Mass., Bill Rosenberg opened a mobile lunch operation in 1946 selling sandwiches, doughnuts, and coffee at factory gates. In 1950 he opened a doughnut shop called Open Kettle in Quincy, Mass. Deciding the name wasn't catchy enough, he renamed the shop Dunkin' Donuts. Years later, Bill Rosenberg reminisced, "I figured that if Howard Johnson's could offer 28 varieties of ice cream, we could do the same thing with doughnuts. In fact, we expanded that number to 52 different doughnuts—one for every week of the year." Rosenberg licensed his first franchise in Worcester, Mass., in 1955 and went on to found the International Franchising Association in 1959 to promote the industry. Today Dunkin' Donuts is the world's largest coffee and baked goods chain. In 1982 Fred the Baker ("Time to make the doughnuts") was one of the most recognized personalities in advertising history. In 1990 Dunkin' Donuts was purchased by Allied

Domecq, of Great Britain, the world's second-largest spirits company.

Carrie Shook and Robert L. Shook, *Franchising: The Business Strategy That Changed the World* (1993); Tina Grant, ed., *International Directory of Company Histories* (2003); Andrew F. Smith, ed., *Oxford Encyclopedia of Food and Drink in America* (2004).

Joseph M. Carlin

Founding Families

An important aspect of New England's economic growth was the formation and development of industrial elites connected by family, marriage, or friendship. The two major sources of venture capital upon which the region's industrial growth was based were family wealth and mercantile profits derived from these elite groups, the best known of which was the Boston Associates. These elite relationships continue to have an impact on the economic, political, social, and cultural life of New England.

Examples of important elite industrial families in the region's development abound. Paul Revere, a craftsman and hero of the American Revolution, was also a ship chandler, a bell manufacturer, and the owner of the first copper-rolling mill in the United States, the Revere Copper Company, built in 1801 in Canton, Mass. Revere's first large job was the 6,000 feet of copper sheathing to cover the newly completed dome of the Bulfinch State House in Boston in 1803. The business was incorporated in 1825 with an intimate group of stockholders including Revere's son Joseph, his nephew Frederick W. Lincoln, James Davis, a brass founder long associated with the Revere family, James Davis, Jr., and Henry Winsor, James Davis, Jr.'s, brother-in-law. These two families controlled the company until it was sold at auction in 1909.

The Ames family of Easton, Mass., manufactured the "four-star" shovel made famous in the building of the Union Pacific Railroad. The family was active in politics and was a dominant force in the local community. Another family in the same area, the Drapers of Canton and Hopedale, Mass., were prominent textile and machinery manufacturers. Hopedale became a model communitarian community in 1841 under the leadership of the Reverend Adin Ballou, remaining under Draper family control until after World War II, when the townspeople voted for political freedom, while still receiving Draper philanthropy.

In the Blackstone River valley in Rhode Island, William Sprague II, a prosperous farmer whose family began cotton spinning, dominated the Cranston area and made it into the center of calico cloth manufacturing. The family controlled banking, railroads, and marketing through commission houses nationally. The Spragues were involved in local and national politics, working to maintain the protective tariff and to encourage the industrial development of the state. Their real competition was from Brown and Ives, the firm of two prominent old mercantile Rhode Island families whose influence is still felt.

William Sprague IV was governor of Rhode Island as the Civil War opened; Rhode Island's militia under Sprague's command was the first to respond to President Lincoln's call to arms. After the First Battle of Bull Run, Sprague turned down Lincoln's offer of a brigadier's commission. Sprague was reelected governor and then elected to the U.S. Senate in 1863. He courted and married Kate Chase, the daughter of Secretary of the Treasury Salmon P. Chase, who used the Sprague family wealth and influence in a failed attempt to gain the Republican presidential nomination in 1868; Sprague was reelected that same year, and Kate Chase Sprague initiated divorce proceedings. After leading financier Jay Cooke's bank collapsed, leading to the credit crunch that became the panic of 1873, the Sprague empire went into receivership, then folded in 1882, and disappeared. William Sprague IV, the last of the Civil War governors, died in 1915 while escaping the German invasion of Paris.

The Dennison Manufacturing Company of Framingham, Mass., is another example of an elite industrial family's evolution. In 1844 Andrew Dennison, a shoemaker in Brunswick, Maine, unable to compete with mass production, began working with his sons Aaron and Eliphalet, who were manufacturing paper jewelry boxes. Aaron was also a successful watchmaker who later helped establish the Waltham Watch Company. By 1855 the Brunswick location was hurting the Dennison operation, so Andrew sold the business to Eliphalet, who moved it to Boston, added merchandise tags to the product line, patented his own tag design, and quickly expanded the business nationally. In 1878 the company was reorganized as a corporation. The company prospered, weathered the Depression, and expanded its paper product line successfully to meet World War II needs. It became a diversified corporation, converting paper into useful products to satisfy market needs while cooperating with RCA to produce a copier that utilized newer and advanced paper products. Like Ames and Draper, Dennison became a dominant force in the Framingham area.

In 1815 Major Joseph Fairbanks, his wife, and his two sons left Brimfield, Mass., and moved to St. Johnsbury, Vt., to join their third son. Here, with sons Erastus and Thaddeus, he laid the foundation of the E. and T. Fair-

banks Company, which came to dominate the platform scales business. They were joined in 1850 by the 17-year-old Charles Hosmer Morse (a distant relative of the famous inventor Samuel F. B. Morse), who transformed the company into a diversified manufacturing firm. It survived the depression of 1873 in part because it received an order from the U.S. Postal Service for 3,000 postal scales to weigh newspapers. Winner of numerous national and international awards, Fairbanks, Morse and Company products included railroad scales, turbines, pumps, locomotives, generators, electric motors, and diesel engines. St. Johnsbury's growth was closely aligned with that of the company, which gave generously to the community, establishing a private school, an athenaeum, a museum, and a YMCA building. The family's impact on the city was not unmixed, however, and following World War II, the community voted for political independence while the firm remained family owned. Eventually the company was taken over by an outside organization, but the family's influence remained.

Captain Nathaniel Stevens, the founder of the Stevens textile empire, established a small country store in 1810 in North Andover, Mass. He married Harriet Hale, whose father, Moses Hale, had established a carding and fulling mill in East Chelmsford (now Lowell), Mass. In 1813, with two business partners, Stevens established a factory, hiring James Scholfield as overseer; Scholfield belonged to the same family that had built the country's first power-driven carding machine in Newburyport, Mass.

In 1832 Stevens bought out his partners, and the Stevens Company became an exclusively family-run operation. He also began investing in other areas, such as steam engines and railroads. In 1850 he expanded into neighboring Haverhill and named his third son, Moses T., a partner. A second son, Horace, was admitted to partnership in 1860 and the firm's name changed to Nathaniel Stevens and Sons.

The firm was very successful during the Civil War, but Captain Stevens died in 1865, leaving his sons Moses T., George, and Horace in control. They expanded the firm and consolidated all commission activity in Faulkner, Kimball and Company under Henry Page, an old family friend. The deaths of George and Horace left Moses T. sole proprietor during the 1870s, but he was joined by his sons, Nathaniel and Samuel D., as partners in 1885, and the firm's name changed to M. T. Stevens and Sons. A Democrat, Moses T. had a keen interest in politics, and was elected to Congress in 1891. As a freshman representative, he was an active member of the Ways and

Means Committee, where he introduced a bill for placing raw wool on the free list.

In 1899 J. P. Stevens and Company, a new commission house, was organized under family control. In 1901 that house and M. T. Stevens and Sons were incorporated together to respond to the reorganization of the American Woolen Company. When Moses T. died in 1907 at age 82, he had served in both state and national legislatures, had been a bank director and an insurance trustee, and was involved in various charitable activities, including a home for the elderly, a town hall, library, and high school, and the Unitarian North Church in North Andover.

The firm continued under the leadership of Nathaniel II and expanded into new areas like rayon. When Nathaniel II died in 1946, production and selling merged into J. P. Stevens and Company, still under family management although no longer under the family's financial control. Under the chairmanship of Robert T. Stevens, the company was the oldest diversified textile company in the world and a leading advocate for tariff protection. Although no longer strictly a family firm, J. P. Stevens, now international in scope, is a striking example of the perseverance of New England's industrial strength. The Stevens family continues to contribute to the North Andover community.

The family was the basic unit in New England society and an important factor in the industrial development of the region. The importance of family, marriage, and friendship to business growth in the six states is clear and continues to have an impact on the region. The industrial revolution began in New England for three reasons: the region had more skilled workers in traditional industries from which the new technologies developed; investment capital was available from overseas trade; and entrepreneurs who had made money in commerce understood the risks involved in putting capital and mechanical skills to work. These entrepreneurs became the region's industrial elite, developing networks that were essential to the region's growth. In the 20th century, during the region's second industrial revolution in high technology, these linkages helped diffuse innovations among older firms and revitalize New England's technological base.

Victor S. Clark, *History of Manufactures in the United States*, 3 vols. (1929); Robert F. Dalzell, Jr., *Enterprising Elite: The Boston Associates and the World They Made* (1987); Lloyd C. Ferguson, *From Family Firm to Corporate Giant: J. P. Stevens and Company, 1813–1963* (1970); John S. Hekman and John S. Strong, "The Evolution of New England Industry," *New England Economic Review* (March–April 1981); Francis X.

Ryan, *Crisis in a One-Industry Town: St. Johnsbury, Vermont, and Fairbanks, Morse and Company, 1815–1965* (1974); Paul H. Tedesco, *Economic Change and the Community: Canton, Massachusetts, 1797–1965* (1970).
Paul H. Tedesco

Gaming Gaming in one form or another is legal in every New England state. Gaming options run the gamut from state-sponsored lotteries to Native American casinos and include slot machines, video lottery terminals (VLTs), keno machines, bingo, pari-mutuel horse and dog tracks, jai alai, and simulcast wagering.

Official lotteries were conducted in New England as far back as the 1700s before the founding of the country and flourished in the New England states intermittently until they were abolished about 1890. Then, in 1964, New Hampshire created a state sweepstakes patterned after the famed Irish Sweepstakes. When New York introduced a successful lottery several years later, New Hampshire changed its sweepstakes to a lottery. The remaining New England states eventually joined in, finding lottery proceeds a good way to fund state needs from education to assisting local communities with funds to purchase such things as fire trucks and other emergency vehicles. State-run lotteries exist in all six states, and several states have joined forces to offer combined lottery games.

Pari-mutuel wagering has been present in New England since the early 1930s and is controlled in each state by the State Racing Commission. Some of the most famous racetracks for flat (thoroughbred) racing existed in the region; a few still survive, including Narragansett Park in Pawtucket, R.I.; Rockingham Park in Salem, N.H.; Suffolk Downs in East Boston, Mass.; and Lincoln Park in Lincoln, R.I. Although thoroughbred racing was the main attraction, these tracks would often offer standard-bred harness racing during other meets. Other harness tracks are located in Vermont, Maine, Rhode Island, and Massachusetts. Green Mountain Park operated in Pownal, Vt., from 1963 to 1992, first as a venue for flat racing, and then switching to harness racing and, in 1977, greyhound racing. Maine hosts 10 county fair meets and has two harness tracks. Other New England states also offer county fair meets of harness racing—for example, the Topsfield (Mass.) Fair, America's oldest fair.

Dog racing remains popular in the New England states despite a movement to outlaw the activity as cruel to animals. Connecticut has two dog tracks, Rhode Island one, Massachusetts two, and New Hampshire three. The dogs share the track with horses at Lincoln Park and at Hinsdale Park in New Hampshire. Gaming at Lincoln Park is not confined to betting on races, however; 2,400 VLTs help keep track patrons—and revenues—from draining away to the nearby Indian casinos operating in Connecticut.

The success of Foxwoods Casino, in Mashantucket, near Ledyard, and Mohegan Sun, in Uncasville, near Montvale, Conn., has inspired other Native American tribes residing in New England to seek federal recognition in order to build casinos. (Although casino gambling is illegal in all six New England states, Indian reservations are sovereign territory and exempt from state gaming laws.) Major casino operators including Harrah's, MGM, and Caesar's, Carnival have offered to assist the tribes gain federal recognition in exchange for the rights to operate the casinos for a percentage of the profit.

No New England state has been left untouched by the success of Connecticut's two Indian casinos, whose history is as much a story of Native Americans in the late 20th century as it is of the casino gambling industry. In 1987 there were only two half-sisters living on the Mashantucket Pequot Reservation near the banks of the Mystic River in southeastern Connecticut when a monumental piece of legislation was being considered by the U.S. Congress to address issues of Indian gaming prompted by two lawsuits (*Seminole Tribe v. Butterworth* [1980] and *California v. Cabazan Band* [1987]). The Indian Gaming and Regulatory Act (IGRA) of 1988 allowed Native American tribes to "compact" gaming with the state in which their reservations were located. The act also specified that if certain games were permitted within the state, even at charity events, these were also allowable on reservations. That same year the Pequots—who include anyone who is at least one-sixth Pequot—obtained a $4 million loan from the Arab American Bank to build a bingo hall, which brought in $13 million the first year and earned a $2.6 million profit. Initially these funds were used to help rebuild the infrastructure on the reservation. By 1992 the profits had enabled the tribe to build a full gaming casino, Foxwoods. The distribution of the new gaming income has made the 350 members of the Pequot tribe among the richest residents of New England. The Pequots secured a loan for $142 million from Genting International, a rubber producer in Malaysia and owner of the world's largest casino, and in 1997 Foxwoods opened a 17-story, $400 million hotel tower. The casino, now the largest in the United States, employs more than 12,000 workers and attracts gaming patrons throughout the Northeast.

The other federally recognized tribes in New England have yet to enter this gaming arena, although tribes in southeastern Massachusetts have campaigned for a casino in Fall River or New Bedford while tribes in Maine have attempted to push through legislation to allow a casino in Sanford, and more tribes in Connecticut are seeking federal recognition. The Narragansett tribe in Rhode Island may soon own a competing casino in nearby West Warwick.

The Indian Gaming and Regulatory Act was passed to help the tribes reduce their dependence on the federal government. Instead, sovereignty has become the central issue for tribal members as they seek exception from state and federal laws. IGRA maintains that tribes must solely own their casinos although they may contract management to outsiders. The act also allows tribes to establish their own gaming commissions, but they must report to the National Indian Gaming Commission. Because tribal sovereignty allows the casinos to operate tax free, gaming has provided these Native Americans with vast wealth, which they are using to challenge these laws.

When the act was passed, many tribal members saw gaming as the "return of the white buffalo"—a way to preserve Indian lands, customs, and traditions. State governments, however, viewed Indian casinos as undeclared revenue on which no taxes could be collected. Anxious for a share of the pot and suspicious of illegal activity, the states began to seek gaming compacts with the tribes. The IGRA had established three classes of gaming: wagering on traditional tribal games whose prizes have minimal value (Class I); bingo, lotto, pull tabs and other "non-banked" games (Class II); and "banked" games and slot machines (Class III). In Connecticut, where slot machines were illegal, the state found a way to benefit from casino revenues by allowing the Pequot and Mohegan tribes the exclusive right to operate slots for 25 percent of the annual slot revenues. The Pequots, who had previously run only bingo games, quickly agreed to this provision and signed a compact with the state that allowed Class III gaming and slots. The success of these games enabled the tribe to secure the Genting International loan, fueling Foxwoods's expansion.

The Mohegan Tribes gained federal recognition in 1994 and, after years of negotiation, acquired a site in trust of a closed atomic parts plant near Montvale as their reservation. After signing a compact with Connecticut, the 1,100-member tribe contracted with Sun International of South Africa to reconstruct the plant into the world's third largest casino. The first Indian casino to fund itself entirely through a Wall Street offering, Mohegan Sun opened in 1997, drawing 75,000 patrons on opening day. The immense success of both casinos has provided an economic boon to the state of Connecticut through increased employment and tourism. In 2000 joint casino revenue was $2.3 billion with $288 million going to the state as slot tax.

For a period in the 1970s and 1980s, New Englanders flocked to jai alai frontons to bet on this fast, agile sport, an ancient ball game. Although jai alai was played in a fronton at the Newport Grand in Rhode Island until 2003, the game also ended in the other New England frontons. Milford Jai Alai closed its doors in 2001, and the Bridgeport Jai Alai converted to greyhound racing in 1995. Both now rely on revenues from simulcast jai alai and racing. The Newport Grand has similarly expanded its gambling options and now offers simulcast horse, dog, and jai alai wagering as well as 1,000 VLTs.

In the 21st century, gaming has proliferated in New England. The passage of gaming legislation in one state prompts legislation in neighboring states. Slots or VLTs have been authorized by referendum in Maine, edging out the proposed Indian casino. New Hampshire has entertained legislation for VLTs at its horse and dog tracks, and the owners of the defunct Green Mountain Racetrack in Pownal are investigating ways to reopen the track and introduce slot machines. Keno machines have been authorized in Massachusetts and joins bingo in many locations. The other New England states also allow bingo at many licensed locations. The reason is not far to seek; revenues from legalized gaming are staggering. The Indian casinos are expected to bring in over $1.6 billion and the lotteries $2.65 billion in 2004.

Bureau of Indian Affairs, Department of the Interior, *Mohegans to Receive Land in Trust for Connecticut Reservation* (1997); Arthur W. Wright and Associates, Connecticut, *Statistics and Economic Impact of Indian Gaming* (1997); "Massachusetts Could Lose $1 Billion to Neighbors," *Boston Herald*, July 2004; "From Lotteryville to Powerball: Secretary of State Announces Archives Exhibit on 300 Years of Lotteries in R.I.," press release, Rhode Island Department of State, September 12, 2003; Abraham McLaughlin, "Even in Puritan New England, Casino Profits Call," *Christian Science Monitor*, September 6, 2002; "Maine Signs Slot Bill," *Bangor (Maine) Daily News*, April 14, 2004; Judith Nies, "Casualty of Gaming," *Conservation Matters* (Fall 1998).

Emery H. Trowbridge

Gillette   One of the great marketing success stories of the 20th century, the Gillette Company of Boston was founded by the salesman, utopian theorist, and inventor King Camp Gillette and William Emery Nickerson, an MIT graduate, as the American Safety Razor Company in 1901. With the help of Nickerson, Gillette devised a disposable safety razor and began production at a South Boston factory in 1903 under the name of the Gillette Safety Razor Company. In the company's early years, Gillette came up with a number of successful promotions, including giving away razors to increase the sale of blades and distributing razors and blades to the American armed forces during World War I. Gillette also took early advantage of the world market, opening a branch office in London in 1905. By the 1920s Gillette could boast that his razors could be found in towns above the Arctic Circle and "in the heart of the Sahara."

Gillette was a utopian visionary. His *The Human Drift* (1894) argued for a corporate utopia, managed by a "United Company," in which the majority of the population would be clustered in 40,000 circular skyscrapers occupying the space between Rochester and Buffalo, N.Y. This "Metropolis" would banish the need for prices, money, and competition, he claimed, while providing everyone with both equality and a measure of aesthetic choice. The company Gillette founded, however, thrived on competition and price. Gillette himself aggressively defended his patent rights while buying out competitors.

With his picture on every packet of blades, Gillette became a corporate celebrity. He lost his personal fortune in the 1929 stock market crash, and corporate infighting reduced his authority in the company. Gillette spent his last years in a failed effort to extract oil from shale, and died in 1932.

The company moved on, continuing to expand its market share and reaching its peak in 1962, when it commanded roughly 70 percent of the U.S. razor blade market. When the stainless steel blade developed by Wilkinson Sword began to threaten Gillette's market, the company responded by buying much of Wilkinson's blade business. Gillette also began to diversify during the late 1950s to early 1970s, acquiring Braun AG, the Toni Company, Paper-Mate, and Buxton Leather goods, among others, with mixed results. In the 1970s Gillette brought out a series of successful products—the Trac II razor, the Atra razor, the Good News! disposable razor, and the Daisy razor for women—while establishing a stronger position in skin and hair care products.

The years since 1980 have been marked by continuing acquisitions—Oral B toothbrushes (1984), Waterman Pen (1987), Parker Pen Holdings (1993), and Duracell International batteries (1998)—and continuing innovation, developing the Sensor family of shaving systems in 1990 and the Mach3, its most successful new product ever, in 1998. Successfully beating back a hostile takeover attempt by Revlon in 1986, Gillette remains the world leader in blades and razors and has begun to buy blade companies in Russia and the Czech Republic. The company still has a factory in South Boston.

Russell B. Adams, *King C. Gillette* (1978); Gordon McKibben, *Cutting Edge: Gillette's Journey to Global Leadership* (1998); Rita Ricardo-Campbell, *Resisting Hostile Takeovers: The Case of Gillette* (1997); Don Roy and Michael D. Hartline, "The Gillette Company," in O. C. Ferrell, Michael D. Hartline, and George H. Lucas, *Marketing Strategy*, 2d ed. (2002).

Gary Kulik

Granite and Marble Quarrying   New England's marble and granite industries are today a small, specialized part of the region's economy, but they were important components of rural development and industrialization in the 1800s and early 1900s. Their key role is evident in significant alterations in the natural landscape; thousands of abandoned quarries reflect the hundreds of small and large stone operations that, in turn, changed the built environment of the United States. Courthouses, banks, streets, monuments, and gravestones in nearly every city and town were made of New England granite or marble. A relic of the preindustrial period, the folkloric image of the solitary Yankee stonecutter, like the stone itself, reminds New Englanders of their character and their past. New Hampshire's nickname, "the Granite State," was coined by the marquis de Lafayette in 1825 when he visited the quarries of Concord, N.H., which had received the stone contract for Boston's Quincy Market. By the Great Depression, however, most quarrying operations had ceased, and stone production today is carried out principally by a few large firms.

Granite (and gabbro, gneiss, and basalt) is found in every New England state, and major quarrying operations were developed along the coast of Maine; Cape Ann and Quincy, Mass.; Westerly, R.I.; Waterford, Conn.; and Barre, Vt. Marble (and some limestone), restricted to the far-western portion of the region, was quarried early in Connecticut and Massachusetts, but operations became principally located in a few sections of Vermont, especially the Rutland area. While some quarries were worked intermittently before 1800, their purpose was mostly local consumption. Substantial production awaited, and was an impetus for, the extension of transportation systems to rural areas in the form of canals and railroads. Quarries near Boston, or with access to water, such as at Cape Ann, Mass., or near the Champlain Valley in Vermont, developed early.

Early technologies for quarrying and shaping stone involved a repertoire of hand tools, explosives, and water- or oxen-powered ma-

Illustration of a column of granite being shaped on a turning lathe, Wallace W. Atwood, New Geography *(1922)*

chinery. The practice of splitting granite with shims and wedges was apparently introduced by German stoneworkers around 1800 and rapidly became the standard method. Solomon Willard is credited with developing the industry in Massachusetts, and he brought a number of innovations to bear in supplying stone for the Bunker Hill Monument. The project also demonstrated the use of granite for decorative purposes. Marble, softer and easier to work than granite, was cut to size by waterpowered toothless saws, fed sand and water for abrasion. Used more for decorative and ornamental purposes, marble became the favorite stone for monuments, especially gravestones, its classical look rapidly replacing slate and other stone in the early 1800s.

In 1800 Redfield Proctor combined two companies in the Rutland area to form the Vermont Marble Company, which entered into pooling arrangements to control most marble production in the state. By purchasing other companies and importing Italian marble, Vermont Marble grew to be the largest marble company in the world by 1903. Gravestones were a major component of the industry until innovations in granite polishing made that stone the preferred choice. Granite also came to be used extensively as paving stone for city streets, a significant part of production. New Englanders also quarried the brown freestone of the Connecticut River valley. The Portland, Conn., quarries were the largest in the world in 1876, producing brownstone for buildings in Boston, New York, and Philadelphia, and, most notably, for the Washington Monument.

Mechanization increased rapidly after 1865, with the introduction of pneumatic drills and channeling machines, improved abrasive tech-

niques, stone crushers, cable railways, wire saws, and a host of other technologies. Current methods, less labor-intensive, include jet channeling and thermal finishing.

Successive waves of immigrant workers changed the makeup of quarry communities. Stonecutting is a highly skilled occupation, and companies brought trained cutters from Scotland, Italy, and other countries throughout the 1800s. In addition, thousands of laborers were needed, and Irish, Swedish, Finnish, and French Canadian workers were hired. Ethnic and religious conflicts were not uncommon. Conflict between management and labor over contracts and work weeks led to the formation of the Granite Cutters Union, the Quarry Workers Union, and the Paving Cutters Union. Major lockouts or strikes occurred in 1892, 1899, and 1922. Although both marble and granite workers suffered from occupational injury, the granite sheds where stone was worked were the most dangerous places because the rock dust from pneumatic tools caused silicosis. Regulation came slowly, with dust-removal equipment common only after the 1920s.

In the 20th century several forces combined to bring about a decline in stone industries. Changing architectural styles and technologies made steel and concrete cheaper and more appealing, while concrete and asphalt replaced granite paving on streets. Many companies went out of business, while others consolidated. In 1930, 10 Vermont granite companies formed Rock of Ages, a firm that continues today and promotes both the industry and the historical images that come to mind when one thinks of stone. High technology has replaced most of the earlier workforce, and while dimension stone is still quar-

ried, current demand is usually for the less romantic crushed stone.

Arthur W. Brayley, *History of the Granite Industry of New England* (1913); Barbara H. Erkkila, *Hammers on Stone: A History of Cape Ann Granite* (1980); Roger L. Grindle, *Tombstones and Paving Blocks: The History of the Maine Granite Industry* (1977); Middlebury Historical Society, *The Marble Border of Western New England* (1885).

Jeff Wanser

Hats Zadoc Benedict is credited with being the first to move hatmaking from a New England home craft to a manufacturing enterprise when in 1780 he established a shop in Danbury, Conn., devoted solely to hat production. Benedict employed three men to create 18 hats a week. Other hatmakers soon followed, and eventually Danbury produced 25 percent of the nation's finished hats and 75 percent of hat bodies for finishing elsewhere, earning it the nickname "Hat City."

As early as 1808 there were as many as 50 businesses in Danbury's hat trade; by the mid-1830s dozens of mills were devoted to the industry. Hat manufacture also dominated neighboring Bethel, Conn., and not far to the south hats were made in Norwalk, where the durable derby, with its rounded shape, was introduced in 1850. Connecticut became so closely associated with hat manufacture that in 1949 the state legislature established a Hat Day, marked by gubernatorial proclamations. The tradition lasted almost 30 years.

To make hats, hatters first cleaned and trimmed animal skins, then treated them chemically to prepare them for felting: the creation of the hat fabric by use of moisture, heat, and pressure. Felt, unlike cotton or wool, was neither spun nor woven. The product was made through wetting, steaming, shaping on molds, and sewing.

The hat business was volatile, and a firm's success depended on both technological innovation and the vagaries of fashion. Mallory and Company of Danbury began as a cottage operation in the 1820s and survived to become a major 20th-century producer because of its willingness to respond to changes in style and technique. The company was the first to introduce sewing machines into hat manufacture in 1861. When bonnets fell out of vogue in the 1850s in favor of formed hats, no machinery was available to make the new product. Determined not to let opportunity pass by, Mallory temporarily hired older hatters skilled in hand methods while developing a mechanized production that again made traditional hand workers obsolete.

The industry developed a skilled labor force overseen by paternalistic employers. Children followed their parents into the shops from generation to generation. Hatters plied their trade in a steamy atmosphere, where they smelled of wet fur and inhaled chemical fumes, most injuriously mercury, which damaged the nervous system and caused "hatters' shakes."

Organized labor was long active in Danbury. A bitter strike at D. E. Loewe and Company in 1902 became a landmark in American labor history when the U.S. Supreme Court ruled that a labor boycott created a restraint of trade, which in turn violated the Sherman Anti-Trust Act, originally designed to combat corporate monopolies.

As clothing became less formal after World War II, the industry fell victim to a fashion trend that rendered it obsolete when first men and later women elected not to wear hats. Although some mark the industry's demise from January 1961, when President Kennedy broke tradition and was inaugurated bareheaded, hat manufacture was already in rapid decline and New England's dominance in the industry had ended.

William E. Devlin, *We Crown Them All: An Illustrated History of Danbury* (1984); Donald B. Robinson, *Spotlight on a Union: The Story of the United Hatters, Cap and Millinery Workers International Union* (1948); Matthew Roth, *Connecticut: An Inventory of Historic Engineering and Industrial Sites* (1981).

David K. Leff

Howard Johnson's Howard Deering Johnson, of Quincy, Mass., was 27 years old when in 1925 he assumed his late father's business debts and took over a failing patent-medicine store with a soda fountain and a newsstand. In an old-fashioned freezer in the basement Johnson developed a recipe for ice cream that ensured his success. Soon he was selling his ice cream on beaches south of Boston, and by the end of the 1920s he had added hotdogs, hamburgers, and sandwiches to his menu. In 1929 Johnson opened a second restaurant, with a wider menu, in downtown Quincy, with plans to expand further.

Johnson foresaw a successful market among America's increasing highway travelers. In the 1930s he gambled that—despite the Depression—better highways would mean more motorists, who would be looking for economical food that would meet a reliable standard of quality. To finance this chain, Johnson conceived of franchising. He agreed to lend the Howard Johnson's name to a Cape Cod restaurant in return for a fee and an agreement to buy food and supplies from him. By 1935 Johnson had franchised 25 roadside ice cream and sandwich stands in Massachusetts. In the next five years, Howard Johnson's logo—Simple Simon and Pieman—appeared on weathervanes on more than 100 full-service restau-

rants, and the chain had spread down the East Coast to Florida.

Johnson opened the first toll-road restaurant in the United States in 1940 on the Pennsylvania Turnpike and for years ran the most turnpike restaurants in the country. World War II cut off supplies, and gas rationing reduced the number of travelers, but Johnson sold food to military installations, defense plants, and schools. More Howard Johnson's restaurants opened in the prosperity of the postwar years. Facing a labor shortage of skilled chefs, Howard Johnson's was a pioneer in the development of the fast food industry, shipping standardized and pre-portioned food from company-operated central plants to restaurants for final preparation, ensuring consistent quality throughout the chain.

While serving standardized food, Howard Johnson's used the color and variety of the 1950s to create a distinctive image. Celebrating choice and consistency, each Howard Johnson's restaurant served 28 flavors of ice cream. Each sported an orange-porcelain tiled roof crowned with ornamented cupolas, white walls, and turquoise shutters and trim. The company had 400 restaurants by 1954, when it franchised its first motor lodge in Savannah, Ga. A well-known brand-name motel with a reliable restaurant next door became a successful combination.

The chain soon developed an innovative approach to the motor lodge. Howard Johnson's was the first to fully package motels, tying exterior and interior motifs into a total design concept launched in the late 1950s; the rooms were at once distinctive and easily duplicated, leading to prefabricated construction, which revolutionized the motel-chain industry.

Howard B. Johnson took over from his father in 1959, and the company went public in 1961. Well into the 1960s, the orange roofs were ubiquitous. In 1965, Howard Johnson's did more business than McDonald's, Burger King, and Kentucky Fried Chicken combined. The company developed its Red Coach Grill restaurants, and in 1969 the Ground Round chain was created. By the late 1970s, Howard Johnson's operated more than 1,000 restaurants and 500 motor lodges, as well as a number of vending and turnpike operations. Despite its growth, however, competition from fast food chains had cut deeply into the company's business.

In 1980 a British tobacco and food conglomerate, the Imperial Group, bought Howard Johnson's for $630 million, squeezed it for profits, and then sold it to the Marriott Corporation in 1985. Marriott sold the hotels and lodges to Prime Motor Inns, and attempted to convert the restaurant locations from Howard Johnson's to its own concept. In response,

Howard Johnson's franchisees negotiated a settlement to allow them to incorporate as Franchise Associates, in South Weymouth, Mass., and continue to use the name and original ice cream recipes. In 1990 a company now known as the Cendant Corporation, which operates more than 500 motor lodges across the country, acquired the corporate hotel chain. Howard Johnson's prepackaged frozen foods and ice cream are still available in grocery store chains.

John A. Jakle, Keith A. Sculle, and Jefferson S. Rogers, *The Motel in America* (1996); John Mariani, *America Eats Out* (1991).

Louis Mazzari

Ice "In the winter of '46–7 there came a hundred men of Hyperborean extraction swoop down on to our pond one morning, with many carloads of ungainly-looking farming tools— sleds, plows, drill-barrows, turf-knives, spades, saws, rakes, and each man was armed with a double-pointed pike-staff, such as is not described in the New-England Farmer or the Cultivator," noted Henry David Thoreau in *Walden* (1854).

During the 19th century, harvesters carved ice from dozens of lakes and rivers throughout New England, and from even smaller bodies of water with rail access, such as the pond from which Thoreau observed the scale and efficiency of the industry. "To speak literally, a hundred Irishmen, with Yankee overseers, came from Cambridge every day to get out the ice. They divided it into cakes by methods too well known to require description, and these, being sledded to the shore, were rapidly hauled off on to an ice platform, and raised by grappling irons and block and tackle, worked by horses, on to a stack, as surely as so many barrels of flour, and there placed evenly side by side, and row upon row, as if they formed the solid base of an obelisk designed to pierce the clouds."

The natural ice industry—the business of harvesting, transporting, storing, and selling the frozen lakes and rivers of the North—was a 19th-century American phenomenon. Before 1800 New England farmers had used axes and crosscut handsaws to cut ice for their meat, milk, and cheese. In January or February rural New Englanders would set aside time to harvest the ice from a local lake or pond, just as they would raise a barn, joining their horse teams for the task.

Intent on filling the icehouse of his family's hotel on Fresh Pond in Cambridge, Mass., Nathaniel Jarvis Wyeth developed tools and cutting methods that allowed him to contract with Frederick Tudor for large quantities of ice accessible to rail transport. Establishing trade throughout the South and later Europe and India, Tudor became known as the Ice

Ice harvesting on the Kennebec River, 1881

King. The son of a prominent Boston family, at age 13 Tudor chose business over attending Harvard with his brothers. In 1805 Tudor began to ship ice south from a pond in nearby Lynn, Mass. Early on, he realized the importance of well-designed and well-constructed icehouses, gambling that ice could be stored in a warm climate. By 1834, with rights to cutting throughout New England and New York, Tudor owned a network of ships, icehouses, and distribution agencies in such cities as Charleston, S.C., Mobile, Ala., and New Orleans. He also developed a prosperous foreign trade with several cities in the West Indies, South America, and eventually Europe.

By 1830 iceboxes had become commonplace throughout the United States, allowing Americans to add more milk, meat, and vegetables to their diet, and by the 1840s giant six-story icehouses loomed over the Kennebec and Penobscot Rivers. Complex networks of rail and ship had been established to keep ice cool on its voyage from Wolfeboro, N.H., to New Orleans or Calcutta.

For years Maine produced more ice than any other state. Its lakes and rivers were clean and unpolluted, and its severe winters were ideal for freezing dense, clear ice. And the Kennebec, Sheepscot, and Penobscot Rivers, which yielded most of Maine's ice, were nonetheless always accessible to Atlantic shipping. In 1890, at the industry's peak, 26 icehouses had been built along the Penobscot. Fifty-three lined the Kennebec. Throughout the state 25,000 men cut 3 million tons of ice. Harvests from the Kennebec River and from nearby lakes were promoted as "colder, clearer, and better tasting" than ice from any other

source. Kennebec Ice wagons were common throughout New England, and icemen sold the product at a premium price.

In Massachusetts ice came chiefly from lakes and ponds. Large firms harvested ice in Worcester and Fitchburg, but the trade was concentrated in Boston, which bought and exported most of the state's production. Boston's supply, for both home consumption and export, came primarily from nearby Fresh Pond in Cambridge, Spy Pond in Arlington, and Walden Pond in Concord. By 1856, 100 wagons and 50 horses were part of the network that sold ice throughout the city and its outlying towns. Ice was sold to families, hotels and restaurants, stores, saloons, and factories. Once regarded as a luxury, it had become a necessity. By the 1860s, metropolitan Boston was buying 100,000 tons a year.

New Hampshire's ice industry was more modest than its counterparts in other states, but harvesting was the economic mainstay in a number of towns, including Milton, Sanbornville, Wolfeboro, and Wakefield. In the 1850s the railroads, looking for new business, built sidings at the edge of a number of New Hampshire lakes, so their ice could be loaded directly onto railcars. The Tudor Company cut much of New Hampshire's ice and transported it to Boston, where it was shipped south or abroad.

All through Victorian New England the iceman's familiar horse and brightly painted wagon were part of the town and city scene. Making a delivery, tracking through a kitchen, the iceman used large tongs and carried the blocks over his shoulder, on which he wore a leather sheepskin. All along town and city

streets, houses displayed a square white card out front that told the iceman how much ice was needed—25, 50, 75, or 100 pounds.

New England's ice industry reached its peak in the 1880s. By the turn of the 20th century old icehouses were becoming dilapidated. Manufactured ice came to replace natural ice; Jacob Perkins of Newburyport, Mass., built the first refrigerator in 1834. But it wasn't until World War I that mechanical refrigeration became widely available to homes and businesses. Once it did, refrigerators moved into kitchens across the country. By the early 1920s, the New England ice industry was only a memory.

Joseph C. Jones Jr., *America's Icemen: An Illustrative History of the United States Natural Ice Industry, 1665–1925* (1984); Neal R. Peirce, *The New England States: People, Politics, and Power in the Six New England States* (1976).

Louis Mazzari

Industrial Preservation and Reuse

Serious efforts to preserve significant features of New England's industrial heritage began with the restoration of the Old Slater Mill in Pawtucket, R.I., in 1924 and are most apparent today at Lowell National Historical Park in Massachusetts. Preservation in a museum or park setting is only feasible, however, for a few historic landmarks. But industrial structures have lasting value in a variety of roles. Examples of successful adaptations include former factories providing housing for the elderly, seaside warehouses offering fine dining, railroad stations converted to offices, and a trolley bridge landscaped as a promenade for pedestrians. The architectural quality, rugged construction, dramatic interior spaces, and historical associations of many industrial buildings argue strongly for "adaptive use." There is also growing recognition that recycling still useful structures conserves valuable materials, saves energy, and keeps collective memories vibrant. Starting in the 1960s, New England architects like Simeon Bruner, Lee Cott, and Tim Anderson earned national reputations by giving new life to decayed working places.

New England has a large share of empty or underutilized industrial buildings. These are concentrated in urban centers but may also be found at mill villages and rural waterpower sites. This region prospered with the rapid industrial expansion that began in the 1790s but suffered declines in its principal manufacturing sectors after World War I. Even before the collapse of large industries became common, individual firms often failed, and technological changes made some existing buildings no longer suitable for a particular process. Entrepreneurs have always practiced industrial reuse, converting abandoned structures for some other type of manufacturing or transportation function. Modern production of both basic and high-tech goods is still carried on in many older buildings. Established companies sometimes take over entire mills, while startup businesses usually rent only a single floor or room.

The Historic Preservation Act (1966) recognized the importance of America's historic built environment and gave an emotional boost to rehabilitation efforts in New England. More important, however, were various federal policies, state-run preservation programs, and local initiatives providing economic incentives for adaptive-use projects. With the passage of the Tax Reform Act (1976), which allowed rapid depreciation of historic properties, developers and investors began looking for older buildings to convert. Programs that subsidized the development of elderly or low-income housing provided additional incentives and reduced financial risks. Another law in 1981 offered direct tax credits for certified rehabilitation of historic buildings. Federal tax policy continues to encourage reuse but no longer allows passive investors to share in the tax benefits through syndication. As a result, it has become more difficult to find financing for projects. The best hope on the horizon may be new state and local "brownfields" laws that reduce developers' liability for and promote realistic solutions to the environmental problems at numerous industrial sites. Selective, sensitive reuse of features from New England's industrial heritage offers many economic and cultural benefits, but it requires public support. Examples of such work can be found throughout New England. Factory buildings have been converted to apartments in Central Falls, R.I., and Willimantic, Conn.; to a shopping mall in Winoski, Vt.; and to an art museum in North Adams, Mass.

James Marston Fitch, *Historic Preservation: Curatorial Management of the Built World* (1990); Robert B. Gordon and Patrick M. Malone, *The Texture of Industry: An Archaeological View of the Industrialization of North America* (1995); Walter C. Kidney, *Working Places: The Adaptive Use of Industrial Buildings* (1976); Jennifer Trainer, ed., *MASS MoCA: From Mill to Museum* (2000).

Patrick M. Malone

Industrial Utopian Communities

During the middle decades of the 19th century, a handful of small manufactories established model environments for managers, workers, and their families. Their example influenced other businesses at the turn of the 20th century and captured the attention of both American and foreign visitors who wrote about labor issues and the living conditions of industrial workers.

Hopedale and Ludlow, Mass.; Peace Dale, R.I.; South Manchester, Conn.; and Fairbanks Village at St. Johnsbury, Vt., although probably not unique, were nonetheless among the earliest and best of these industrial utopian communities or model company towns. Each was established by a resident family of industrialists who exhibited an abiding interest in the environmental surroundings of their mills. Four were associated with textiles or textile machinery and the fifth with machine scales. Each family held the controlling interest in the community, thus owning the land and constructing the housing. Eventually, new additions were planned and landscaped with practical as well as aesthetic considerations in mind. Streams and reservoirs needed for operating steam engines and turbines were protected and made an amenity for the community. In some cases, the water's edge was landscaped and trees planted to buffer the houses from the mills. Parks were provided and workers were encouraged to enjoy them.

Comparatively small, these communities rarely exceeded a population of more than 2,000–3,000, and because the industry maintained the controlling interest, consistency in the appearance of buildings and grounds tended to set them apart. Unlike rural villages, large factories—occasionally built of stone though more often of brick—dominated the landscape and overshadowed churches and public buildings. The din of the factory and the presence of skilled and unskilled workers walking to work in small groups from boardinghouses and cottages created a very different street setting from neighboring mixed-economy and farming villages.

The architecture was simple and utilitarian, although well designed and carefully maintained. Local architects were employed to design the mills, the homes of management and labor, and schools, libraries, and community centers. The largest homes belonged to the mill owners and were usually set apart from those of the workers. Modest cottages, often apportioned into two-family or duplex dwellings and usually identical in appearance, were rented to the mill workers at affordable rates. Regardless of whether the mill owners had set out to build model dwellings, they were encouraged by state and, eventually, federal labor officials to enter drawings, photos, and other descriptions of their cottages at world trade fair exhibits, such as those in Paris in 1878, 1889, and 1900. The American entries competed well and sometimes received medals.

Hopedale began as a social communitarian experiment in 1842; it was acquired in 1856 by the Draper family, who expanded the industrial operation and reestablished the settlement on a capitalist footing. Although the

Drapers had sympathy for Fourierist principles of organization, they dismissed such egalitarian measures as profit sharing. The Hazards, who founded Peace Dale and established their enterprise in 1848, were Quakers, a sect that had a history of founding enlightened industrial concerns in England, Northern Ireland, and America. On the other hand, the Cheneys who established South Manchester in 1838, the Fairbanks who established their village near St. Johnsbury in the 1830s, and the Ludlow Associates—Charles T. Hubbard, C. N. Wallace, and John E. Stevens—who founded Ludlow in 1868 appear to have been driven not by social or religious theories of the period but rather by economic opportunity helped in large measure by Yankee ingenuity.

A feature of the communities that operated at several levels of social involvement was paternalism. In an effort to achieve a utopian vision in which business prospered and workers went contentedly about their tasks, management exercised considerable control over the lives of their employees. Since many workers were immigrants, management believed it had a responsibility to instruct and acculturate them to American ways. Not all workers welcomed this meddling, especially in their private affairs. But others welcomed an education for their children, libraries with free lending privileges, and evening entertainment at the town hall or community building. The company would also encourage participation in village improvement, awarding prizes in competitions for gardening, yard maintenance, and the like. But such communities were exceptions in an industrial era in which management rarely paid sufficient attention to the condition of labor. The idealism that marked their founding waned in the late 19th and early 20th centuries as economic pressures overtook utopian vision.

John S. Garner, *The Model Company Town: Urban Design through Private Enterprise in 19th-Century New England* (1984); William Alfred Hinds, *American Communities and Co-operative Colonies* (1908); Edwin L. Shuey, *Factory People and Their Employers: How Their Relations Are Made Pleasant and Profitable* (1900).

John S. Garner

Insurance

How Hartford became the "insurance capital" of New England and, some claim, of the United States, is a tale of risk-taking Yankee merchants, river captains, and entrepreneurs. In the 18th century, small ships built on the Connecticut River carried horses, cattle, hay, lumber, and farm products from the busy port of Hartford to the West Indies and returned laden with salt, sugar, molasses, and rum. Upon learning that marine risks

The Travelers building, Hartford

were underwritten by Lloyds of London, Ezekiel Williams, Jr., began insuring vessels and cargoes by persuading wealthy citizens in the city to share the risks. The investors met regularly at John Morgan's coffeehouse near the wharves. If a voyage was successful, they shared the profits; if not, they lost their investment.

Commercial marine and fire insurance were the next logical steps, but these were giant moves indeed for a city of only 6,000 persons. In 1794 Colonel Jeremiah Wadsworth, Hartford's wealthiest citizen, and three others organized the Hartford and New Haven Insurance Company, pledging their personal fortunes to pay all claims. This informal arrangement led in 1810 to the formation of Hartford Fire, the city's first insurance corporation. Nine years later Aetna Fire was chartered.

In December 1835 Hartford made insurance history when a disastrous fire broke out in New York City, destroying nearly 700 buildings. The president of Hartford Fire, Eliphalet Terry, went to New York and found that most other insurance firms had collapsed under the burden of enormous claims. To the despairing homeowners and merchants Terry made the dramatic announcement that "the Hartford" stood ready to pay all claims in full. Confidence was restored and Hartford's reputation for integrity solidified.

The success of Terry's trip led to the creation of new insurance companies. Connecticut Mutual Life (now merged with Massachusetts Mutual of Springfield) was founded

in 1846—the first company to sell life insurance. In 1851 one its founders, Barzillai Hudson, started a competitive firm. His intention of selling policies only to teetotalers was a marketing failure, and the American Temperance Life Insurance Company did not prosper until its name was changed to Phoenix Mutual. Three other firms that would become giants in the insurance industry appeared during the next few years: Aetna Life (1853), Travelers (1864), and Connecticut General (1865). All were stock rather than mutual companies.

Ambition and personality conflicts among the pioneers fueled expansion. When Eliphalet Bulkeley, the first president of Connecticut Mutual, was not reappointed to the presidency, he quit in a rage and formed Aetna Life. Failing to receive a promotion, Henry Kellogg, a Connecticut Mutual bookkeeper, also resigned and incorporated the Phoenix Insurance Company to sell fire policies.

The widespread use of steam power to run factories and steamboats and the alarming frequency of explosions inspired the formation of Hartford Steam Boiler Inspection and Insurance Company in 1866. By the turn of the century it was the undisputed leader in its specialized field.

The great Chicago fire of 1871 again tested the soundness and reliability of Hartford companies. More than 17,000 buildings were reduced to ashes and 250 people killed before the whirlwind blaze could be controlled. Though Hartford Fire, Phoenix Fire, and Aetna Fire suffered heavy losses, they were saved by bank loans and the sale of additional stock. Not so fortunate were their out-of-state competitors, 200 of which could pay off only half their obligations, and 68 of which never recovered. Another even greater challenge to the solvency of Hartford fire insurance companies came in 1906 as the result of the San Francisco earthquake and fire; Hartford companies again met the challenge.

The chief executives and major investors of Hartford's leading insurers made up a small but elite group who knew one another, served as directors on one or more of the boards, and were actively involved in local and state politics and in supporting charitable institutions. In the middle of the 20th century they were referred to as "the bishops" because of their dominant roles in setting local policies. Among them was the independent-minded E. Clayton Gengras, a former automobile mechanic and car dealer who rose to be head and principal stockholder of Security-Connecticut Insurance Group and was regarded as Hartford's leading philanthropist.

Four men in particular stand out for their exemplary leadership spanning more than a century. James Goodwin Batterson, the

founder in 1864 of Travelers, the first casualty company, learned about railroad accident insurance on a trip to England. The erudite Batterson was a poet, a Greek scholar, an architect, and a builder, as well as an entrepreneur. As president of Travelers until his death in 1901, he acted during its fledgling years as his own underwriter, actuary, claims adjuster, auditor, and advertising department. Travelers sold the country's first accident insurance policy in 1864, and the following year began to sell life insurance. Its first policyholders included such distinguished persons as John Wanamaker, P. T. Barnum, Josh Billings, William Lloyd Garrison, Harriet Beecher Stowe, and General George A. Custer. The name Travelers quickly became known throughout North America. Some 70 rivals sprang into existence but most folded. Batterson persuaded the rest to unite under his leadership, making his company the sole survivor in 1866.

Morgan Gardner Bulkeley was the most colorful, dominant, and politically active insurance president in Hartford's history. Some suspected that he had three aims: one to rule a prospering multiple-line company, another to head the Republican Party in Connecticut, and the third to engage in a variety of athletic, antiquarian, civic, and philanthropic pursuits. With his handsome face and handlebar mustache, he was the very model of the Victorian tycoon, formidable yet affable, with a conviction that might makes right. During his 43-year tenure as its president (1879–1922) Aetna Life and Casualty forged ahead at a phenomenal rate—from 29 to 2,000 employees and from $6 million to $80 million in annual income.

As successful as he was in managing a growth enterprise, Bulkeley loved politics even more. For nearly 40 years he was in and out of public office, successively serving as Hartford mayor for four terms, governor for two terms, and U.S. senator for one term. Throughout his life he had a genius for doing big things expeditiously in response to urgent needs. An ardent baseball fan, he became the first president of the National Baseball League in 1876. He was also responsible for building a new bridge across the Connecticut River, the largest stone structure of its kind at the time, which is now named for him. Because of a legislative impasse over the election of his successor as governor, he was obliged to remain in office for another term and had to borrow $300,000 from Aetna to run the state.

Bulkeley's successor was his nephew Morgan Brainard. Though lacking his uncle's charisma—he never lost the image of the "aw shucks" country lad—Brainard shared Bulkeley's down-to-earth approach to running the nation's seventh-largest insurance group. His common sense and calmness under fire carried the company through the Great Depression with minimum loss. Salaries were reduced 10 percent and dividends stopped, but no employees were laid off. Of equal significance for the welfare of Hartford was Brainard's bold decision in 1931 to build a new home office, the largest Colonial style building ever constructed. During World War II, when Aetna's employment totaled 30,000, the company was the major provider of protection for the Manhattan Project. By 1955 Aetna had $15 billion of insurance in force, 12 times greater than in 1922.

For 71 years Frazar B. Wilde was closely identified with Connecticut General. Joining the company as a mail clerk at age 19, he rose to the presidency 22 years later. Personal service, he once said, was the difference between Connecticut General and other life insurance firms. His policy concerning claims was: "We don't adjust claims, we pay them." Always a fresh, independent thinker, he believed that insurance was a risk-taking business, and as early as 1926 Connecticut General had started to insure airline passengers and pilots. During the Depression, when competitors were cutting back, he took the opposite tack, hiring and training sales managers. As CEO he initiated coverage for atomic-energy workers, individual pension plans, and estate planning. In the 1960s he teamed with the developer James Rouse to develop the new city of Columbia, Md.

Realizing that Connecticut General had outgrown its downtown home, he purchased 280 acres of farm and wooded land in Bloomfield, Conn., where he built a modern structure of aluminum, granite, and white marble, with glass walls, interior courts, and movable paneling—all of which combined to provide a superb environment and smooth work flow. Following its dedication in 1957, the "office of the future" was praised as "one of the most carefully planned buildings of the age."

Wilde's influence extended far beyond the company. A self-educated economist, he became a nationally respected expert on monetary and fiscal policy, serving as adviser to governors and presidents. His economic philosophy was disarmingly simple: "good old-fashioned common sense to not spend beyond one's means." Modest yet outspoken, thoughtful and wry, he once told an interviewer, "I've always been a freak Yankee, full of ideas, an absolute maverick. The other thing I had was an above average capacity to pick good lieutenants." Under his leadership Connecticut General became the third-largest stockholder-owned insurer in the country.

Hartford insurance companies have pioneered coverage for accidents, automobiles, aviation, rain, renewal term life, pension plans, and health care. Their experience with the Manhattan Project enabled them to underwrite innovative policies for the development of atomic power for peacetime use and the exploration of outer space. As good corporate citizens they have contributed generously to the communities in which they thrive. Travelers financed Hartford's first urban renewal project, Constitution Plaza, in 1960; Aetna built the Hartford Civic Center in 1974; and Phoenix Mutual initiated a billion-dollar complex called Adriaen's Landing for the commercial and recreational revitalization of the city's old waterfront, planned to open in 2005.

In the late 20th century insurers were forced to try mergers, consolidation, and radical shifts in market strategy to compete in the rapidly changing global economy. The real estate collapse in the 1980s decimated the portfolios of companies like Travelers. Connecticut General merged with the Insurance Company of North America to become Cigna; Connecticut Mutual merged with Massachusetts Mutual; Aetna Life sold its property and casualty business to Travelers for $4 billion; Travelers itself merged with Citicorp; and Lincoln National, a newcomer to Hartford, took over both Aetna's and Cigna's life insurance businesses.

With the introduction of Medicare in 1966, the industry was asked to handle medical payments to hospitals and help administer benefits. The emergence of private health-care plans has transformed Aetna into the largest health-care provider in the country. In 1996 it bought U.S. Healthcare for $8.9 billion; in 1998 it acquired the health-care subsidiaries of New York Life and Prudential HealthCare.

In 2004 Hartford's top three insurance companies—Aetna, the Hartford, and Travelers—had combined sales of $49.6 billion.

William Cain, *A Matter of Life and Death* (1970); Connecticut General, *One Hundred Years in Perspective* (1965); Hawthorne Daniel, *The Hartford of Hartford* (1960); Henry R. Gale and William G. Jordan, *One Hundred Years of Fire Insurance, 1819–1919* (1919); Ellsworth S. Grant and Marion H. Grant, *The City of Hartford, 1784–1984* (1986); H. Richard Hooker, *Aetna Life Insurance Company* (1956); W. Glenn Weaver and J. Bard McNulty, *An Evolving Concern* (1991); P. Henry Woodward, *Insurance in Connecticut* (1897).

Ellsworth S. Grant

Iron Abundant wood in North America and increasingly costly fuel in England made iron smelting an attractive economic opportunity for immigrants to the colonies. After 17th-century failures at Falling Creek, Va., and Saugus, Mass., English investors backed colonists in Maryland to start making iron for export in the 1720s. New Englanders followed several decades later, and by 1775 had forges and furnaces making iron for their own needs and overseas customers. They had improved their metallurgical technique so that they could use several of their blast furnaces to cast cannon for the Continental Army.

By the first decade of the early republic, New Englanders had mastered the skills they needed to make castings for machinery and to forge wrought iron to close, uniform dimensions. With their furnaces, forges, and rolling mills they supplied the iron products needed by pioneering manufacturers like Eli Whitney. In subsequent decades New England ironmasters never matched the large-scale production achieved by their colleagues in the Middle Atlantic states. Instead they made a niche for themselves as suppliers of high-quality iron, meeting the stringent requirements of the nation's new manufacturing industries. Thus they supplied the Harpers Ferry Armory in Virginia with gun iron needed for musket barrels and forged large anchors for the navy, shafts for steamboat engines, and, later, axles for locomotives and railway cars.

Initially, New England ironmakers had smelted bog ore dug from shallow ponds and wetlands. Bog ore often formed rapidly enough that a forge or furnace proprietor could reharvest the same area within a decade or so, and could match production to a continuous ore supply. Bog ore tended to be rich in phosphorus and produced a pig iron that was particularly suitable for casting hollow ware. But works using it remained dispersed because the ore sources were small. By 1735 adventurers in western Massachusetts and Connecticut had discovered extensive deposits of rich ore in the area later known as the Salisbury district. The industry concentrated around these ores achieved national prominence in the 19th century, first as suppliers of the highest grades of bar iron, and later as makers of railway-car wheels.

Because of their easy access to nearby woodlands, American ironmasters did not face the same need to convert to mineral fuel that their European counterparts did. Charcoal making was, however, labor intensive, and ironmasters could afford it only if they could sell their charcoal-smelted iron at superior prices. By the mid-19th century, ironmakers in Pennsylvania had learned to match the quality of New England bar iron with metal they made more cheaply with mineral coal fuel. The forge branch of the New England industry was the first to close. The established but declining market for railroad-car wheels kept some New England blast furnaces going until 1923, when their proprietors abandoned furnaces in North Canaan, Conn., and Richmond, Mass.

Land clearance for agriculture meant that initially wood for making charcoal was abundant. Ironmasters in the Salisbury district, in Vermont, and in Maine drew on the nearby forested mountains for their fuel. But as they consumed the local woodland, they had to either import fuel or establish a system of continuous wood production adequate to their needs. They did both. Ironmasters in western Connecticut and Massachusetts used specially built railway cars to bring in charcoal from Vermont, and in addition they acquired large parcels of woodland that they managed on the coppice system. With some 20,000 acres in wood production, a furnace manager could have a continuous fuel supply by cutting 1,000 acres a year. Although environmentalism was not a concern at the time, the ironworks were sequestering as much carbon from the atmosphere as they were releasing in their coaling and smelting. Those that used bog ore ran a truly sustainable industry.

As ironmasters abandoned their furnaces early in the 20th century, wealthy individuals looking for rural retreats bought up huge tracts of forest at low prices. Their heirs subsequently made some of these into nature reserves, while others were acquired for state parks and forests. Thus ironmaking, which helped launch New England manufacturing, created wealth that allowed later generations to take an interest in the environment and assemble the large areas of woodland that later became state parks and forests.

Today, the Saugus (Mass.) Iron Works National Historic Site, a popular tourist attraction, includes a reconstructed blast furnace, a forge, a rolling mill, and a restored 17th-century house. The museum interprets early industrial engineering and the importance of iron manufacturing to America's industrial prosperity.

Robert B. Gordon, *American Iron, 1607–1900* (1996); Edward N. Hartley, *Ironworks on the Saugus* (1957); James A. Mulholland, *A History of Metals in Colonial America* (1981).

Robert B. Gordon

Labor Movements During the region's first 200 years of settlement, New England citizens looked to the sea and land for traditional ways of making a living. By the beginning of the 19th century, the region began an economic transformation that no longer necessitated the use of compass or plow. The revolutionary experiments of Samuel Slater and Moses Brown in Pawtucket, R.I., created a foundation for the factory system in North America during the 1790s. The ingenuity of Slater's mill and the fledgling industrial orbit

in the Blackstone Valley of Rhode Island and Massachusetts convinced many an investor to turn inland along the myriad tributaries that flowed into the Atlantic Ocean. Freshwater streams and waterfalls—not saltwater and sea winds—would churn the next economic gale in New England and change the workplace forever.

The incremental transition from maritime and agricultural ways of life to manufacturing was as insurrectionary as the American Revolution itself—and longer lasting. As textile mills mushroomed across the region, a controversial workforce assembled at the new three- and four-story structures that challenged the area's churches for physical elevation and spiritual dominance. Young children and teenaged girls recruited from local farms joined a smaller number of skilled males in the factories. Industrial discipline and mechanical time could be hard on a citizenry that was used to personal independence and seasonal rhythms, and owners wisely paid wages in hard currency, a rare commodity in an agrarian region still practicing commercial bartering.

With a sense of destiny, new masters of the changing rural landscape built dams to harness waterpower and interfered in the spawning of fish, an important source of free food to local families. Mill owners flooded public grazing land without permission and woke New England towns every morning with the inexorable ringing of factory bells. Community resentment over such intrusions combined explosively with employee grievances about child labor, harsh discipline, and other working conditions. Young women working at Slater's Mill went on strike in 1824 to the activist cheers of local inhabitants. Antebellum female textile operatives frequently led similar protests elsewhere in the region. A few years after the "turnout," as the 1824 strike was called, Pawtucket citizens raised enough money to place a clock in the steeple of the Congregational Church to compete with the suspected misregulation of time by the company's bells. Time became public.

Until about 1850 most mill workers in New England were native born and of English ancestry. They had a sense of political rights and perhaps a vague knowledge of the ancient European guild system, the solidarity of which was evident in the traditions of local craftsworkers. When the vagaries of financial conditions or the venality of local owners upset the balance of power between employer and employee, these pioneer factory hands banded together in primitive and short-lived labor organizations.

By the 1830s the emerging textile industry, and the social and cultural changes it engendered, had created a counterinsurgency

among the workers. The New England Association of Farmers, Mechanics, and other Workingmen established branches throughout the region's mill towns. This inclusive group agitated for the 10-hour workday, the right to vote, and political reform. Seth Luther, an early labor protagonist, printed a searing pamphlet for the New England working class that intelligently portrayed the new way of life as a sophisticated form of wage slavery. The Panic of 1837 undid much of this early organizing while the Potato Famine in Ireland a decade later unleashed a wave of immigrants who undercut fledgling class unity among American mill workers by accepting lower wages. Newcomers, whatever their cultural differences, usually leapfrogged ahead of the region's small, segregated African American community because of the relative whiteness of their skin.

Successive migrations of similarly desperate refugees—French Canadians, Jews, Italians, Portuguese, and Cape Verdeans—found a slice of economic salvation and a loaf of discrimination in New England. These "adopted citizens," as they were sometimes called, often tolerated conditions that native-born Americans found unacceptable. Ethnic groups banded into neighborhoods and communities where language, faith, and culture outlasted several generations of Americanization and created nativist tension with earlier inhabitants. Few immigrants possessed a trade to enter the craft world of iron molders, railroad brotherhoods, or construction unions. However, common labor, factory work, and domestic service—especially for the thousands of women, who constituted the highest percentage of females in the nation's industrial workforce—expanded during and after the Civil War in New England. Immigrants with European industrial experience fared better than their agrarian-trained counterparts.

The factory system followed waterpower to its source in the hinterlands of New England, where an exceptional firm like the Amoskeag Mills or the American Woolen Company could dominate host cities like Manchester, N.H., or Lawrence, Mass., sometimes for more than a century. Smaller companies and concentrated industries could achieve similar influence over a town or area by baptizing the region occupationally: the Danbury, Conn., hatters; the Barre, Vt., granite workers; the Lynn, Mass., shoemakers; or the Naugatuck Valley, Conn., brass workers. Paternalism and its 20th-century offspring, welfare capitalism, throve in New England's industrial valleys from the onset of the Industrial Revolution until the New Deal cleansing.

By the early 1880s the first modern labor movement had coalesced into an unusual amalgamation of skilled and unskilled workers that cut across race, ethnicity, religion, and gender. The Knights of Labor harnessed the anxiety and class-consciousness created by the disintegration of traditional workplace relationships, the permanence of company towns, and political corruption. The "Order" organized employees on the shop floor and in ethnic, urban communities. They formed Gilded Age collaboratives, libraries, and even a day-care center in at least one city. They embraced arbitration and boycotts and implemented an internal court system to settle disputes among members and local assemblies. The Order also drew significant numbers of women and people of color to its ranks with an early espousal of equal pay for equal work.

The Knights attacked traditional New England power structures by championing sympathetic working-class candidates for public office. In Boston, for example, they endorsed the labor writer George McNeil for mayor; in Rutland, Vt., quarry workers became the backbone of an insurgent political organization; and in Rochester, N.H., mill workers formed a phalanx of proletarian voters. In Connecticut the Knights signed up rubber workers and elected 37 state representatives. Shoe workers signed on in Maine. Under pressure from the Order even stodgy Rhode Island liberalized voting qualifications for workers. Although progressive candidates and political bodies in this era and later periods occasionally instituted legal change and protective labor laws, the judicial system remained a conservative, antiworker bulwark until the coming of the Great Depression, the New Deal, and the Congress of Industrial Organization (CIO).

A vicious employer counteroffensive eventually toppled the Knights in the 1880s. As the Order faltered, the American Federation of Labor (AFL) solidified a base of strength in the white, male, English-speaking skilled trades. British, German, and Scandinavian journeymen created an organizational structure of state federations and city labor councils that endures today. The new "business unionism" proved popular among the skilled trades, which now had a partial monopoly on good jobs the same way corporate giants controlled some industries. The AFL eschewed class struggle, but it militantly demanded a share of the fruits of industrial society, participating in some of the country's most memorable socioeconomic battles during the Progressive Era.

Trolley wars especially punctuated the New England urbanscape as members of the AFL's Streetcarmen's Union mobilized angry citizens during the period 1890–1910. Transit walkouts frequently ignited popular protest against public utilities that symbolized the era's political malignancy. Boycotts and riots shook Providence and Pawtucket, R.I.; Boston and Worcester, Mass.; Bridgeport, Hartford, and New Haven, Conn.; Portland, Maine; and Berlin, N.H. Union organizers in other sectors often followed the tarnished trolley tracks to success in these prolabor strongholds.

Although descendants of the old-stock ethnic groups had climbed the economic ladder by the end of the 19th century, the new immigrants from southern and eastern Europe and the Middle East encountered prejudice at work and in unions. Some turned to the militant and inclusive Industrial Workers of the World (IWW), also known as the "Wobblies." Ephemeral victories like the monumental Bread and Roses strike against the American Woolen Company of Lawrence, Mass., in 1912 contributed more to Wobbly legend and a literary legacy than it did to any permanent organizing thrust. Three of the nation's most urbanized, industrialized states—Connecticut, Massachusetts, and Rhode Island—served as a magnet for job seekers near and far who transformed Yankee society into a Catholic majority. Maine, New Hampshire, and Vermont, on the other hand, maintained their rural character and reacted less hospitably to workers' struggles and immigrant problems.

Wartime working conditions in unskilled industries during World War I triggered innumerable strikes. In Connecticut, 76 of the state's 422 walkouts in 1915 and 1916 were from Bridgeport industries. Authorities throughout the region suppressed radical outbursts, especially in the munitions industry, while stepping up Americanization campaigns to wean immigrants from their home ties. The 1920s Red Scare put the lid back on militant unionism, although for a time the IWW bogeyman made the AFL, with its skilled trades, acceptable. In the region's hub, the unusual—and unsuccessful—Boston police strike of 1919 ironically served as a general exercise for the repression of labor. At the other end of the spectrum the legendary labor anarchists Sacco and Vanzetti were electrocuted in 1927 by the Commonwealth of Massachusetts on charges of robbery and murder that many believed were false. Elsewhere during that schizophrenic decade railroad shop workers went on strike throughout New England in 1922. A constellation of textile walkouts permeated the 1920s capped by a New Bedford, Mass., job action in 1928.

The Great Depression of the 1930s ended the ambiguity in the lives of New England workers. With little to lose, the CIO emerged from the economic wreck to offer hope to all

Marchers during the Lawrence strikes, 1912

toilers regardless of skill, color, or sex. Following the tradition of the Knights and the Wobblies, the CIO and its offshoots seemingly organized everyone, including Cape Verdean cranberry pickers on Cape Cod and Irish weavers in Olneyville, a section of Providence. In Woonsocket, R.I., where workers literally fought each other hand-to-hand for the right to work, the Independent Textile Union signed up an incredible 80 percent of the predominant and previously uninterested French Canadian population.

World War II brought a new respectability to industrial workers, now soldiers of production, in a drive to outproduce fascism. Depression-era labor battles like the 1934 general textile strike, when state militias suppressed walkouts in almost every New England state, set the stage for a postwar national social contract in which the region's profits were finally shared with its hourly producers. Political power matured, as union drives became a blue-collar civil rights movement. Rhode Island, for example, elected the bricklayer and union leader John E. Fogarty to Congress, where for 14 terms he joined other New Deal legislators who maintained their working-class sympathies and votes. Unions helped partially topple the last bastions of Yankee political power, though not the wealth that nurtured that influence. The well-to-do divided themselves culturally between old money and new entrepreneurial fortunes.

During the 1950s, the house of labor was joined together into the AFL-CIO. The minimum wage reached a dollar an hour, six-figure salaries were taxed at a rate of more than 90 percent, and the service sector surreptitiously crept past manufacturing as the number one employer in New England. The New England labor movement grew substantially despite a string of runaway shops—which departed seeking cheaper labor in the South—that had signaled the beginning of deindustrialization. Tens of thousands of federal employees, municipal workers, firefighters, police officers, health-care employees, and other white-collar professionals joined unions, camouflaging, at least temporarily, the decline of membership in basic manufacturing. Schoolteachers, often the first members of immigrant families to graduate from college, used the organizational tactics of their parents and grandparents in a new work setting to make traditional gains. Like their counterparts in the mills more than a century earlier, women spearheaded the charge through high-profile strikes and ended some of the sexist practices that denied them seniority and security.

By the time global competition became a buzzword in the last third of the 20th century,

neither labor nor management was prepared for the economic bruising of New England. Strike after strike unleashed an old-style labor fury in the remaining union strongholds that still employed machinists, textile operatives, and steelworkers. In some conflicts workers initiated corporate campaigns that economically pressured companies outside the traditional confines of the picket line. Some efforts merely attempted to impede runaway shops and maintain the status quo through concessionary bargaining. Despite substantial defeats at Morse Tool in New Bedford, Mass.; Brown and Sharpe in North Kingstown, R.I.; and International Paper in Jay, Maine, the union movement survived. But the family-owned manufactories had passed to multinational conglomerates.

New England, the quintessential labor region, lost its manufacturing identity as the computer replaced the micrometer. Old private-sector adversaries, employers and unions, found themselves not locked in deadly embrace but leaning against one another for support like exhausted fighters. Government workers were pitted against overburdened taxpayers as an eroding property base and corporate tax breaks set neighboring states against one another in a downward spiral. The New Deal Democratic Party, stamped for decades with the union label, had splintered into independent, free-agent campaigns fending for individual success. By the 1980s the Democrats took labor for granted as the union density rate plummeted in the region. "Looking out for number one" replaced the spirit of the timeless labor anthem "An injury to one is an injury to all."

As old jobs disappeared, traditional ethnic neighborhoods splintered, and retired workers headed for the Southwest. A wave of newcomers arrived from the Americas, Southeast Asia, and remnants of the Soviet Union. This latest influx provided the usual challenge to a crisis-ridden labor movement: how to incorporate people of color, women, and changing cultural mores into a hidebound labor organization. At the dawn of the 21st century, unions returned to their roots in search of a rainbow coalition.

In recent years support personnel at prestigious institutions like Boston, Yale, and Harvard Universities have scored impressive representation victories while most of the region's hospital workers, skilled and unskilled, carry a union card. In 1988 construction workers in Massachusetts beat back a statewide political referendum that would have substantially reduced their wages on government jobs. Workers in New England are making the transition to the high-tech jobs that seem to follow

highways into rural areas while unions work furiously to organize the grandchildren from labor's golden years.

Donald Bell and Herbert Gutman, eds., *The New England Working Class and the New Labor History* (1987); Jeremy Brecher, Jerry Lombardi, and Jan Stackhouse, eds., *Brass Valley: The Story of Working People's Lives in an American Industrial Region* (1982); Leon Fink, *Workingmen's Democracy: The Knights of Labor and American Politics* (1983); Gary Gerstle, *Working-Class Americanism: The Politics of Labor in a Textile City, 1914–1960* (1989); Tom Juravich, William F. Hartford, and James R. Green, *Commonwealth of Toil* (1996); Scott Molloy, *Trolley Wars: Streetcar Workers on the Line* (1996).

Scott Molloy

Lawrence Strikes For workers in the 19th and 20th centuries, "going on strike" represented labor's most potent weapon against corporate exploitation and abuse. By withdrawing their labor from the mill, the factory, or the shop, wage-earning men and women sought to demonstrate its importance to those who profited from it. Because Lawrence, Mass., became one of the nation's largest textile manufacturing centers, workers there helped hone this weapon, eventually crafting it into a dramatic and effective tool against wage reductions, arbitrary increases in work loads, and the dehumanizing effects of efficiency experts. Beginning with the Pacific Mills strike in 1882, when more than 5,000 operatives walked out, Lawrence's workers staged significant strikes in 1894, 1902, 1912, 1919, 1922, 1931, and 1937. Extraordinary both for their tactics and in the quantity and diversity of the participants, the strikes in Lawrence, especially its most famous strike, in 1912, have accorded the city a special place in the nation's history as a center of working-class activism, female militancy, and ethnic solidarity.

Before 1912 strikes in textile manufacturing typically involved a specific group of operatives from a particular mill rather than all mill operatives regardless of skill or the location of their employment. Nonemployees seldom participated. In 1912, however, workers in Lawrence captured the attention of the nation and the world when 25,000 textile operatives, most of them women and children, joined with neighbors and kin to shut down the city's "monster" mills, virtually crippling the textile industry throughout the region. Popularly remembered as the Bread and Roses strike, the confrontation struck at the heart of one of America's largest, most ruthless trusts, the American Woolen Company, which by 1910 had accumulated hundreds of woolen and cotton textile mills throughout New England. When Massachusetts passed a law in 1912 reducing the maximum work week for women and children from 56 hours to 54, the company sought to make up for the loss in production by reducing wages throughout the region. In response, factory women in Lawrence threw down their aprons and marched out of the mill, shouting, "Strike! Strike!" By January 13, more than 25,000 men, women, and children speaking dozens of languages had gone out, igniting one of the country's most inspiring and dramatic strikes. "What we saw in Lawrence," recalled reformer Mary Heaton Vorse, "affected us so strongly that this moment in time in Lawrence changed life for us."

The most famous leaders of the strike—"Big Bill" Haywood, Carlo Tresca, and Elizabeth Gurley Flynn—came from the Industrial Workers of the World, or Wobblies, but it was the many local leaders like Annie Welzenbach, Josephine Lis, Sarah Axelrod, Angelo Rocco, and James Brox who emerged from the city's immigrant neighborhoods and provided the grassroots organizing necessary to unite so diverse a community. The arrests of union organizers and the efforts of police to prevent parents from sending children to live with families in other cities turned public opinion against the owners. The settlement in March gave more than 150,000 workers a one-cent hourly raise.

The strike of 1912 put Lawrence's textile operatives at the center of New England's organizing efforts, providing both a model for collective action and a seasoned corps of activists in the decades that followed. When the Wobblies left the region, local leaders of 1912 continued to organize the industry, turning up in New Hampshire, Rhode Island, New York, and again in Lawrence during the strikes of 1919, 1922, and 1931. Their legacy is perhaps best remembered in the slogan from the 1912 strike: "Give Us Bread but Give Us Roses Too."

Ardis Cameron, "Bread and Roses Revisited: Women's Culture and Working-Class Activism in the Lawrence Strike of 1912," in *Women, Work and Protest: A Century of Women's Labor Activism*, ed. Ruth Milkman (1985); Cameron, *Radicals of the Worst Sort: Laboring Women in Lawrence, Massachusetts, 1860–1912* (1993); William Cahn, *Lawrence, 1912: The Bread and Roses Strike* (1980); David J. Goldberg, *A Tale of Three Cities: Labor Organization and Protest in Paterson, Passaic, and Lawrence, 1916–1921* (1989).

Ardis Cameron

L. L. Bean   Founded in 1912, L. L. Bean was named for its founder, Leon Leonwood Bean, a native son of Greenwood, Maine. Bean grew up an avid outdoorsman, enjoying camping, hunting, and fly fishing. After one particularly cold, miserable hunting trip, Bean was inspired to create the Maine Hunting Shoe—a boot with waterproof rubber bottoms and leather uppers. Starting up a business from the basement of his brother's dry-goods store in Freeport, Maine, Bean acquired a list of Maine hunting-license holders and mailed 1,000 fliers advertising his one product, offering a guarantee of "perfect satisfaction." He received 100 orders for the boots. When 90 pairs were returned because the bottoms separated from the uppers, Bean refunded his customers' money, honoring his guarantee. Undaunted, he perfected the boots and mailed more fliers.

In 1917 L. L. Bean's retail store opened in Freeport. Over time, Bean's single-page flier increased to become a full-fledged catalog, advertising not only the Maine Hunting Shoe but other outdoors equipment, clothing, and advice from the owner himself. Bean felt that by offering excellent quality and service in a timely fashion and by eliminating the guesswork in product choice, customers would keep coming back. This policy led him, in 1951, to open his store 24 hours a day, 365 days a year.

Bean's target market became the out-of-

Leon A. Gorman, president of L. L. Bean and grandson of its founder, holding a Maine Hunting Shoe, 1975

state sportsman who needed the proper equipment and clothing to hunt or fish correctly and fashionably. Bean himself, and by default his company, appealed to these sportsmen because both embodied the aura of Maine. He marketed an image of Maine as a sportsmen's paradise, and of himself as the holder and distributor of its secrets. He wanted his customers to know that the work had already been done for them—the flies chosen, the clothing tested, the advice received. By using targeted lists and customer referrals, Bean essentially created the direct-mail catalog business. L. L. Bean's products became so well known and respected that they could be found in presidents' wardrobes, in MacMillan's Arctic expedition of 1923, and on American soldiers during World War II. When Bean died in 1967 at the age of 94, leadership of the business passed to his grandson, Leon A. Gorman.

By the end of the 20th century, L. L. Bean catalogs and products had been sent all over the world, and the company had become not only a corporate giant with a down-home New England image but a major tourist attraction in Freeport, where its flagship store received more than 3.5 million visitors a year. Today L. L. Bean sells more than 16,000 home and outdoor products through its catalogs (whose covers often feature New England scenes commissioned from noted artists), its 16 U.S. factory outlet stores—seven in New England—and its 9 stores in Japan. Bean's presence has attracted other outlet businesses to Freeport, making the town itself a major tourist destination.

Leon Leonwood Bean, *My Story: The Autobiography of a Down-East Merchant* (1960); Leon A. Gorman, *L.L. Bean, Inc.: Outdoor Specialties by Mail From Maine* (1981); M. R. Montgomery, *In Search of L.L. Bean* (1984).

Judith Livingston Loto

Matzeliger, Jan E. (1852–89) Inventor. Jan Matzeliger was born on a plantation in Dutch Guiana (now Surinam) in 1852. His mother, Alitta, was a native of Surinam and his father was a Dutch engineer. At age 10, Matzeliger went to live with his father in the capital city of Paramaribo, where he trained as a mechanical engineer, becoming a wizard with machines. Matzeliger left home at 19, working as a merchant sailor for several years and then as an apprentice cobbler in Philadelphia before he settled in 1877 in Lynn, Mass., which had a thriving shoe manufacturing industry. He eventually found work in P. J. Harney's shoe factory.

A deeply religious man, Matzeliger tried to attend a white Catholic church but was turned away because of his race. He then tried to join an Episcopal and afterward a Unitarian church, but his reception was equally cold. In an abolitionist city where Frederick Douglass had once lived and lectured, intolerance was seemingly prevalent. Matzeliger did find a religious home at the North Congregational Church, but he never forgot his early experience of racial intolerance.

Shoe lasting was the only process in shoe manufacturing that was not mechanized at that time. Matzeliger often watched the hand lasters painstakingly attach the soft leather uppers to the inner sole of the shoe. Although major shoe manufactories had spent large sums attempting to develop lasting machines, they had failed. Matzeliger realized that the only way to invent a machine to last shoes was to duplicate the movements of the lasters' hands. Working endless hours in his attic room or by candlelight in his makeshift cellar laboratory, Matzeliger built his first lasting machine models with cigar boxes, elastics, and other discarded materials. His invention was so astounding that when he applied to the U.S. Patent Office, officials were skeptical; the drawings were so complicated that a patent official was dispatched to Lynn to see the machine operate.

Matzeliger received a patent for his invention on March 20, 1883, and his Hand Method Lasting Machine was purchased by the United Shoe Machinery Corporation. He also received patents for several other shoe-manufacturing machines, including an improvement on his original lasting machine model. Ironically, Matzeliger's invention displaced white craftsmen and so weakened the Lynn Lasters' Union that workers called it the "Niggerhead" machine.

Matzeliger was diagnosed with tuberculosis and died in 1889 at age 37. He willed most of his new fortune and stock holdings to the North Church, stipulating that the money be used "toward the support and comfort of those Christian poor of said Lynn, irrespective of religious denomination, except that it shall not knowingly be given or expended for any member of the Roman Catholic, Unitarian, and Episcopal Churches." Matzeliger's lasting machine ensured New England dominance of the shoe industry for decades to come, and his contribution to industrial history, and to African American history, was great.

Sidney Kaplan, "Jan Earnst Matzeliger and the Making of the Shoe," *Journal of Negro History* 40, no. 1 (January 1955); Robert Alexander Smith, "Jan Matzeliger and the Lasting Machine," in *No Race of Imitators: Lynn and Her People, an Anthology,* ed. Elizabeth Hope Cushing (1992); *A Lasting Impression— Jan Matzeliger and the Shoe Lasting Machine* (video, 1993).

Robert Alexander Smith

Military Bases The presence of military bases has profoundly affected New England culture. But today most of the region's major military bases are either closed or face an uncertain future. Perhaps the most famous New England military base, past or present, is Bunker Hill, a hastily prepared wood and earthen fort on the Charlestown heights overlooking Boston. From this position, militia held off three determined attacks by the British regular army. The Battle of Bunker Hill on June 17, 1775, was technically a colonial defeat, but it rallied the new Continental Army that had formed three days earlier. Although residential housing and urban development cover the original battlefield, a granite obelisk standing 221 feet tall now marks the site of the fort.

Founded on June 12, 1800, the Portsmouth Naval Shipyard is one of the oldest permanent military bases in the nation, perhaps the oldest in New England. The shipyard is located on Seavey Island in Kittery, Maine, but it was named for the city of Portsmouth, N.H., where the nearest post office was located. The shipyard motto, "Sails to Atoms," highlights the base's original purpose of building wooden warships and its transition to building and later overhauling nuclear-powered submarines. The Portsmouth Naval Shipyard has always had a tremendous economic impact on the region. In December 1943, the shipyard reached peak employment with 20,466 employees; today, the shipyard employs only a few thousand people.

Many of New England's small forts are products of the War of 1812, fought largely in the Northeast, and the preceding years of tension and threat that led to war. Typical of the region's forts is Fort Preble in South Portland,

Maine, which overlooks Portland Harbor and Casco Bay. Constructed in 1808 from earth and stone the star-shaped Fort Preble is a classic example of early 1800s military construction. Because Portland Harbor was considered a strategic area, Fort Preble was continually upgraded as technology changed. Today the Fort Preble site is part of the Southern Maine Technical College campus.

Fort Preble was also the site of military action during the Civil War. In 1863 a small naval force under the command of Confederate Lieutenant Charles W. Read raided Portland Harbor and commandeered the revenue cutter *Caleb Cushing.* As the action developed, the *Cushing* was hunted by the steamship *Chesapeake* and several other ships. A small naval skirmish occurred, and the Confederates set the *Cushing* on fire before surrendering. The prisoners were imprisoned at Fort Preble for several months and then transferred to other facilities.

Newport, R.I., was also the site of major naval operations from the time of the Civil War. Its greatest importance, however, was during World War II, when the navy established an operating base there, with peak employment of 162,000. After the war, the Newport Naval Yard continued operation until 1974. During World War II, Casco Bay in Maine became a major naval station, hosting the flagship of the North Atlantic Fleet. Liberty ships were constructed in South Portland, and Long Island was a major fueling base. Aside from gun emplacements and bunkers on Peaks Island and former military buildings on Chebeague and other islands, little remains of this major base.

In the late 1800s, tensions with Spain began to rise, and Congress moved to strengthen coastal defenses following an 1886 recommen-

A sign in Limestone, Maine, advertises Maine potatoes and the Loring military base

dation by the secretary of war. After the Spanish American War, however, politicians were eager to spend money in their districts by building fortifications to defend their city harbors. As a result, a series of coastal defense forts were built around the Portsmouth Naval Shipyard, including Fort Foster in Kittery, Maine, and Forts Stark and Constitution in New Castle, N.H. Unlike previous fortifications, which were constructed of stone and earth, these new forts were built of concrete reinforced with granite. In some places the concrete was 45 feet thick. These fortifications, often camouflaged to look like hills from the sea, mounted 3-, 6-, 8-, and 12-inch naval guns and had a series of observation towers that ranged from Salisbury, Mass., to Wells, Maine.

Fort Preble was also rebuilt as a coast artillery post, and in 1891 construction began on Fort Williams, which was later upgraded to meet new requirements. Like their New Hampshire counterparts, these formidable Maine forts were made of reinforced concrete. None of these forts was ever used in battle; nonetheless, the army made gradual improvements to prepare for World War I, including the addition of two 16-inch naval guns in Rye, N.H., increasing the range of harbor defenses.

Improvements continued through World War II with the addition of anti-aircraft guns and other enhancements, but the mission remained the same. Yet despite their continual improvement, these forts were all obsolete before the end of World War II. The arrival of long-range aircraft and aircraft carriers meant that hostile forces no longer had to approach U.S. shores by ship. Consequently, these forts were gradually declared surplus. Fort Preble was deactivated in 1950, Fort Dearborn was purchased by the state of New Hampshire in 1961, and Fort Williams was deactivated in 1962. Today the ruins of these forts can be visited in state parks that bear their names.

In order to support the mass mobilization of soldiers for World War I, the army established Fort Devens in Ayer, Mass., in 1917. Fort Devens eventually became home to the U.S. Army Military Intelligence School and the 10th Special Forces Group, and was also a key facility for training Army Reserve and National Guard soldiers. The U.S. Congress selected Fort Devens for deactivation in 1989; today, Fort Devens is the town of Devens, Mass. The Devens area is being developed primarily as a commercial resource, but part remains as the Devens Reserve Forces Training Area, which will continue to carry out the original Fort Devens mission of training soldiers and units.

During World War I, the military began to experiment heavily with aviation. As a result, the army and navy both established airfields, which eventually gave way to concrete airstrips capable of landing the large bombers that fought in World War II. Because the New England states were a logical refueling stop for aircraft en route to Europe, several airfields were located to the region. After World War II many of these airfields became surplus property and were given back to the states and towns. In many cases, these airfields still serve as regional, municipal, and international airports. The Manchester Airport, located at Grenier Industrial Park (formerly Grenier Field), N.H., is one such example. Its military mission is gone but the facility still serves the community. Some other examples include the Sanford Regional Airport, Maine; Pease International Tradeport, Newington, N.H.; and Bangor International Airport, Maine.

The Pease International Tradeport is a prime example of the military legacy in New England. The air force built Pease in the 1950s to deter the Soviets during the Cold War, choosing Newington because of its strategic location on the flight path to Europe. In 1989 the Base Realignment and Closure Commission of Congress decided to close Pease. What killed it was a combination of the winding down of the Cold War and changing technology that reduced the strategic significance of its location. In short, the base became obsolete. What remains today is the Pease International Tradeport, which houses a growing collection of corporations and businesses. The Tradeport is also the home of Pease Air National Guard Base, which continues the military mission.

The Cold War defense buildup included the establishment of a Strategic Air Command at Westover Air Force Base in Chicopee, Mass. By the early 1980s SAC capabilities had been consolidated elsewhere, but Westover remains a large Air Reserve Base. Similarly, Loring Air Force Base in Limestone, Maine, was established in 1952 to support B-52 bombers and refueling tankers. The base closed in 1994, contributing to economic hardship in northern Maine.

The Boston Navy Yard, located in nearby Charlestown, was established in 1799. Through World War II it was a major facility for shipbuilding and submarine construction. It closed in 1974, and some of its facilities were dedicated for use as a National Park site for the USS *Constitution*. The Massachusetts Military Reserve, Camp Edwards, covers some 22,000 acres on Cape Cod, and it has been used extensively for military training since 1911. The reserve was also the site of Otis Air Force Base. Since the late 1970s, environmental concerns over groundwater pollution have led to protests and cleanups.

The history of military bases in New England started with revolution and continues with evolution. Today, there are only a few active military bases remaining in New England, and many doubt they have a future. What remains, though, are more than memories. Many of the old forts have become state parks and recreation areas. Children play at Fort Foster and wonder what the concrete structures were once used for. Other bases, like Fort Devens and Pease Air Force Base, have become centers of economic development. And some, like Sanford Regional Airport, continue to serve their communities with few reminders of their military past. In short, the military bases have evolved from part of New England's superstructure to part of its infrastructure—a fitting contribution by any measure.

Marcus Cunliffe, *Soldiers and Civilians: The Martial Spirit in America, 1775–1865* (1968); Marvin A. Kreidberg and Merton G. Henry, *History of Military Mobilization in the United States Army, 1775–1945* (1975); Emanuel Raymond Lewis, *Seacoast Fortifications of the United States: An Introductory History* (1979); Maurice Matloff, ed., *American Military History* (1996); Donna L. McKinnon and Joel W. Eastman, *A Guide to Fort Preble, 1808–1950* (1991); John B. Wilson, *Armies, Corps, Divisions, and Separate Brigades* (1999); Jack P. Wysong, *The World, Portsmouth and the 22nd Coast Artillery: The War Years, 1938–1948* (1997).

Ralph J. Huber

Mill Girls

The term *mill girls* most often referred to the female factory workers of Lowell, Mass., during the 1840s. The factories in Lowell were designed by the Boston Associates, a group of wealthy businessmen, as centers of both industrial productivity and intellectual and spiritual growth in the predominately unmarried female workers. Most mill girls lived in factory-owned, single-sex boardinghouses where they shared meals and a sense of community. In the second half of the 19th century, these workers were known as factory girls, a name also used for women in factories in England and Scotland.

Many of the young women who came to Lowell were from Yankee farming families of northern New England states like New Hampshire and Vermont. Their reasons for seeking employment were varied: some needed extra income to send to financially struggling families; some wanted to build a dowry; some hoped to pay the tuition of a brother in college at Harvard, Bates, or elsewhere; still others had no other means of support. Although some historians have maintained that most of these daughters of freemen saw their employment in the mills as a temporary stage in their lives, recent studies have shown that a significant number of the mill girls continued to labor in the Lowell factories for the greater part of their adult lives.

Among the most notable mill girls were

Mill operatives, Dover, N.H., ca. 1900

Lucy Larcom, Harriet Hanson Robinson, Harriet Farley, and Sarah Bagley, contemporaries who were at one time or another associated with the literary magazine the *Lowell Offering*. Larcom, who spent approximately 12 years in the Lawrence Company Mills, began writing poetry for the *Offering*. Later a friend and business associate of John Greenleaf Whittier's, Larcom was a member of the New England literati, an editor for Ticknor and Fields publishing house, and a popular poet. In 1884 Houghton Mifflin published the *Household Edition of Larcom's Poetical Works*. Harriet Hanson Robinson, also a contributor to the *Offering*, chronicled the life of the mill girls' community in her book *Loom and Spindle* (1898). Both Harriet Farley and Sarah Bagley distinguished themselves in the position of editor: Farley of the *Lowell Offering*, and Bagley of the labor-union newspaper *The Voice of Industry*. The relationship between Farley and Bagley was often contentious because their views differed on such issues as the social role of women, the working conditions in the mills, and whether women writers should enter the political sphere. Later in life Sarah Bagley became superintendent of the Lowell telegraph office and is believed to have been the nation's first female telegrapher.

Labor activism began among mill girls of Dover, N.H., and Lowell in the early 19th century. About 400 workers staged a walkout in Dover in 1828 to protest "obnoxious regula-

tions"; the first walkout in Lowell was in 1834. Throughout the 1830s and 1840s, mill girls agitated against pay cuts, rent increases for company housing, longer work hours, production speedups, and regulations restricting women's freedoms inside and outside factories. Poems and speeches evoked the rhetoric of the American Revolution, claiming that Yankee women would not be treated as slaves. Some 2,000 workers struck in 1836, forming the Factory Girls' Association. Labor activism among native-born women peaked in the 1840s.

Most agitation failed, however, when owners advertised for new operators and turned out leaders, or when weak markets undercut the workers' bargaining position. Owners also responded by hiring immigrants—Irish in the 1840s and 1850s, and French Canadians and other immigrant groups after the Civil War. Nevertheless, a tradition of female labor agitation had been established that would rise again with the famous Bread and Roses strike against the American Woolen Company of Lawrence in 1912.

Mary Blewett, *We Will Rise in Our Might: Working-women's Voices from 19th-Century New England* (1991); Thomas Dublin, *Women at Work: The Transformation of Work and Community in Lowell, Massachusetts, 1826–1860* (1979); Dublin, *Transforming Women's Work: New England Lives in the Industrial Revolution* (1994); Shirley Marchalonis, *The Worlds of Lucy Larcom, 1824–1893* (1989).

Susan Alves

Museums of Industry, Technology, and Labor (Table, opposite)

Plastics Plastics are synthetic materials molded, cast, or extruded into various shapes. Production of celluloid plastic in Massachusetts began about 1890, 21 years after its discovery. The most successful celluloid firm was Viscoloid, founded in 1901 when Bernard Doyle, who supplied horn to combmakers in Leominster, realized that celluloid was an excellent substitute for increasingly scarce horn and ivory. Made from nitrated cellulose and camphor, the celluloid was molded and pressed in blocks, cut into sheets similar to horn or tortoiseshell, and then processed by traditional combmaking techniques. By 1925, when Du Pont purchased Viscoloid, several Leominster firms fabricated objects from celluloid sheet. One successful company was Foster Grant, headed by Samuel Foster, Jr., and his son Joseph, who commercialized injection molding of finished objects from cellulose acetate in 1934.

Injection molding transformed the plastics industry during the 1940s. No longer "the comb city," Leominster became "the plastic city," a center of molders, fabricators, and companies like Standard Tool, which made molds and presses. Opposing integration of supply by petrochemical companies, in 1954 Foster Grant opened a plant at Baton Rouge, La., to produce styrene monomer, the source of polystyrene, for the firm's trademark sunglasses. After American Hoechst purchased Foster Grant in 1974, gradually phasing out local production, Leominster remained home to molding companies like Union Products, known for its polyethylene pink flamingos.

Other New England cities entered plastics manufacture after Bakelite phenolic resin was commercialized in 1909. Waterbury, Conn., known for brass manufacturing, attracted molders of phenolic because it could be substituted for brass in some applications. Plastic molding also developed in areas with a concentration of machinists to provide molds, presses, and other equipment, such as Bridgeport and Hartford, Conn., and the mill towns of Rhode Island and southeastern Massachusetts. Reed-Prentice of Worcester, Mass., became a leading U.S. manufacturer of molding presses. Makalot, a Boston resin supplier, sold phenolic compounds to several local molding firms, such as Northern Industrial Chemical. General Electric, which molded plugs, switch plates, and bases of radio tubes in Pittsfield, Mass., also became a large national "custom molder," providing other manufacturers with molded parts to order. After World War II,

Museums of Industry, Technology, and Labor

	Museum	Location	Theme/Highlights
Clocks	American Clock and Watch Museum	Bristol, Conn.	Inexpensive wooden clocks, social impact of mass production and marketing
Guns and Machine Tools	Springfield Armory National Historic Site	Springfield, Mass.	1850 arsenal building, major small arms collection, development of interchangeable parts
	American Precision Museum	Windsor, Vt.	Large machine tool collection housed in 1846 Robbins and Lawrence armory
	Eli Whitney Museum	Hamden, Conn.	History of manufacturing and effects of technology on society, firearms collection
Ironmaking	Saugus Ironworks National Historic Site	Saugus, Mass.	17th-century house and reconstructed blast furnace, forge, and slitting mill
	Katahdin Iron Works State Historic Site	Brownville Junction, Maine	Restored 19th-century blast furnace and charcoal kiln
	Sloane-Stanley Museum and Kent Furnace	Kent, Conn.	Early American tools, ruins of 1826 iron furnace
Mining/Stoneworking	Vermont Marble Museum	Proctor, Vt.	History of quarrying and marble product manufacture, working factory
	Western Gateway Heritage State Park	North Adams, Mass.	Building of Hoosac Tunnel for railway
Papermaking	Crane Museum	Dalton, Mass.	History of papermaking, models of historic processes
	Holyoke Heritage State Park	Holyoke, Mass.	Paper manufacturing history, planned industrial city, water power technology
Plastics	National Plastics Center and Museum	Leominster, Mass.	History and technology of plastics manufacturing
Shoemaking	Lynn Heritage State Park	Lynn, Mass.	Shoemaking, early jet engines
Steam engines	New England Wireless and Steam Museum	East Greenwich, R.I.	Large collection of steam engines, early radios
Textiles	Lowell National Historical Park	Lowell, Mass.	First planned U.S. industrial city, restored factory and boardinghouse, canal tours
	American Textile History Museum	Lowell, Mass.	Large collection of textiles and machinery, re-created mill, warehouse, and factory spaces
	Lowell Heritage State Park	Lowell, Mass.	Waterpower
	Slater Mill Historic Site	Pawtucket, R.I.	First waterpowered textile mill in America, early machine shop, Rhode Island factory system
	Windham Textile and History Museum	Willimantic, Conn.	Material culture of workers and owners of Willimantic Linen Company
	Museum of Work and Culture	Woonsocket, R.I.	French Canadian immigration, textile work, labor organizing and unionization
	Lawrence Heritage State Park	Lawrence, Mass.	Textile factories and work, 1912 Bread and Roses labor strike
	Blackstone River and Canal Heritage State Park	Uxbridge, Mass.	Impact of early mill development on countryside, intact section of canal and towpath
	Fall River Heritage State Park	Fall River, Mass.	Cotton textile manufacture
	Old Belknap Mill	Laconia, N.H.	Water turbines, textile machinery, knitting

(continued)

Museums of Industry, Technology, and Labor (*continued*)

	Museum	Location	Theme/Highlights
Woodworking and Lumbering	Gardner Heritage State Park	Gardner, Mass.	Furniture making and silversmithing
	Patten Lumbermen's Museum	Patten, Maine	Work and technology of logging, logging camp and blacksmith shop
	Old Schwamb Mill	Arlington, Mass.	19th-century millwork and woodworking machinery, operating firm making picture frames
	Frye's Measure Mill	Wilton, N.H.	1858 waterpowered mill with associated machines for box making, operating company
Diverse Industries	Charles River Museum of Industry	Waltham, Mass.	Textiles, watches, automobiles, machine tool, first fully integrated textile mill in United States
	Maine State Museum	Augusta, Maine	Permanent exhibition on textile, lumbering, and fishing industries
	Worcester Historical Museum	Worcester, Mass.	Permanent exhibition on diverse industries, including steel and wire, diverse social experience

General Electric's research complex at 1 Plastics Avenue, Pittsfield, developed Lexan polycarbonate and other advanced engineering plastics.

New England's most famous postwar plastic product was Tupperware, developed by Earl Tupper of Berlin, N.H., while he was experimenting with injection molding of polyethylene for Du Pont in the late 1940s. Popular attention focused on Tupperware home parties administered from Orlando, Fla., but the patented food containers were manufactured in Massachusetts and Rhode Island for several decades. At the opposite end of the spectrum was the Monsanto House of the Future, a fiberglass-reinforced polyester shell engineered by Albert Dietz at MIT's Plastics Research Laboratory in Cambridge, Mass. Intended as a mass-production prototype, the futuristic Monsanto House was installed at Disneyland in 1957 and visited by 20 million people. New England's plastics industry suffered during the 1980s and 1990s as manufacturing moved outside the United States. The region's historical importance was recognized in 1992 when the industry-funded National Plastics Center and Museum opened at Leominster.

Alison J. Clarke, *Tupperware: The Promise of Plastic in 1950s America* (1999); J. Harry DuBois, *Plastics History U.S.A.* (1972); Robert Friedel, *Pioneer Plastic: The Making and Selling of Celluloid* (1983); Jeffrey L. Meikle, *American Plastic: A Cultural History* (1995).

Jeffrey L. Meikle

Pratt and Whitney A unit of United Technologies, Pratt and Whitney is one of Connecticut's most famous manufacturers and a significant contributor to the state's economy. Headquartered in East Hartford, the company, whose motto is "Dependable Engines," produces and services space-propulsion systems and jet engines for the military, commercial, and general-aviation markets. Plants are located in North Haven, Middletown, and Cheshire, Conn.; North Berwick, Maine; Columbus, Ga.; West Palm Beach, Fla.; San Antonio, Tex.; San Jose, Calif.; and Montreal, Halifax, and Toronto, Canada.

In 1925 Frederick Rentschler, a former president of Wright Aeronautical and an aviation pioneer, traveled to Hartford to seek funding for the production of a revolutionary new airplane engine. Rentschler chose Connecticut because it was home to many small tool companies and a skilled labor force, crucial elements of his business plan.

Rentschler bought both the name and the physical plant of Pratt and Whitney, a machine-tool and gun manufacturer founded in 1860 by Francis Pratt and Amos Whitney, cousin of the famous Connecticut inventor and entrepreneur Eli Whitney. Rentschler quickly assembled a team of aviation visionaries, and in only six months Pratt and Whitney unveiled the Wasp, a revolutionary 425-horsepower engine weighing less than 650 pounds.

The radial air-cooled Wasp, which made a buzzing noise in flight, was a radical departure from the heavier, more cumbersome engines of its day. It powered record-setting flights by Amelia Earhart, Charles Lindbergh, and Jimmy Doolittle. In 1926 the Wasp's performance prompted the U.S. Navy to order 200 of the impressive engines, thus cementing the company's reputation as an innovator in the nascent aviation industry.

In 1929 a merger between Pratt and Whitney, Boeing Air Transport, Chance Vought Aircraft Corporation, and Hamilton Aircraft (later Hamilton Standard) resulted in the creation of United Aircraft and Transport Company (UATC). UATC's aim was to produce under one corporate roof all the parts needed to build planes and a new airline, United, to fly them. Antitrust legislation in 1934 forced the breakup of UATC into three separate companies, with United Aircraft retaining Pratt and Whitney, Chance Vought, Sikorsky (brought on board after the initial merger), and Hamilton Standard.

Following quickly on the heels of the Wasp's remarkable success, the company produced the Hornet, the Wasp Junior, and the Twin Wasp, which was used in many World War II–era military planes. Pratt and Whitney and its sister companies contributed more than 363,600 engines to the war effort. Over 600 million horsepower, fully half the total U.S. aerial horsepower during World War II, was produced by Pratt and Whitney engines.

Having put all its resources into developing

Working on a jet engine at Pratt and Whitney, 1980s

piston engines, which by war's end were becoming obsolete, the company scrambled to regain ground after the war by focusing on emerging jet-engine technology. In 1948 Pratt and Whitney shipped its first jet engine, the J-42 Turbo-Wasp, which was used in the navy's F9F-2 Panther aircraft. In 1952 the company was once again an industry leader, winning the highly coveted Collier Trophy for its turbojet designs. In 1958 its JT-3 engine was used in the first transatlantic flight of the Boeing 707. In the 1960s and 1970s the company continued producing experimental engines, including the JT8-D, for commercial aircraft, and the F-100 military engine.

During the late 1960s, however, the company experienced costly setbacks with its engine designs for the Boeing 747, prompting in part a corporate restructuring in 1975. Pratt and Whitney continued as a unit of the new corporation, United Technologies. In the 1980s the company introduced more fuel-efficient commercial turbofan engines. In addition, its turbopumps are used on the NASA space shuttles.

In the early 1990s Pratt and Whitney engines were selected to power the U.S. military's F-22 and Joint Strike Fighter combat aircraft. Pratt and Whitney continues developing new technology for commercial aviation as well. Its Connecticut workforce is shrinking, however: the number of machinists fell from 13,600 in 1991 to 5,100 in 2001. The company operates maintenance and overhaul shops in Singapore, Taiwan, and Ireland, and

joint manufacturing ventures in Chengdu and Xian, China, and Perm, Russia.

Gary Hoover, *Hoover's Handbook of American Business, 2000* (1999); Jacob A. Vander Meulen, *The Politics of Aircraft: Building an American Military Industry* (1991); Frederick B. Rentschler, *An Account of the Pratt and Whitney Aircraft Company, 1925–1950* (1950); United Aircraft Corporation, *The Pratt and Whitney Aircraft Story* (1950).

Lisa Stepanski

Pulp and Paper Pulp and paper manufacture is an important part of New England's heritage and continues to be crucial to the survival of many towns and cities, particularly in Maine and northern New Hampshire. The industry began late in the 17th century when there was local demand for paper for writing and printing. Some of the earliest mills were located in Massachusetts, which had developed into a major paper-production center by the middle of the 19th century. Early mills were built on waterways that provided power and a good supply of clean water. The small, labor-intensive mills were also located near population centers in order to be close to paper markets and rag supplies that provided fiber for making paper. Small paper mills, like their early textile counterparts, often drew on a local female workforce that labored in poor conditions, as noted in Herman Melville's biting satire "The Paradise of Bachelors and the Tartarus of Maids" (1855).

With mechanization, the paper industry quickly expanded. The Fourdrinier paper ma-

chine was invented in France in 1799 by Louis Robert, improved and patented in England by Henry and Sealy Fourdrinier, and introduced to New England in 1829. Later, severe shortages of rag supplies caused by the Civil War led to widespread experimentation with vegetable fibers. By 1880 new processes using wood to produce paper pulp had cut the price of paper in half; this caused a boom in pulp and paper production in northern New England, especially Maine. The industry expanded into the vast northern forests, using spruce and fir for pulp and, later, increasing amounts of hardwoods.

From the Civil War to the end of the 19th century, large mills were constructed on the great river systems like the Androscoggin and the Kennebec. The rivers supplied process water and power, and the pulpwood was transported to mills in huge drives. Industrialists created major plants in the Maine wilderness to manufacture pulp and paper. European immigrants supplied labor for these developments and remained to work in the mills with Canadians and native New Englanders. Meanwhile, the mills grew as electricity replaced waterpower, and paper companies bought large areas of forest land in northern New England and eastern Canada to satisfy the increased demand for fiber and ensure future wood supply. The required heavy capitalization and falling paper prices caused by overproduction at the end of the 19th century ushered in a period of merger. Independent mills were merged into giant corporations such as International Paper Company and Great Northern Paper Company, and the industry began to mature into its present structure.

By World War I, the industry in the North showed signs of decline as expansion and relocation to the southern and western United States began, largely in response to cheaper labor and wood. The supply of woods labor, always short, grew worse during World War II. In New England this shortage was alleviated by permitting more French Canadians to cross the border and using German prisoners of war. Woods labor shortages after World War II and the end of river drives led to increased mechanization in harvesting.

The extent of the industry relocation has been compared to the better-known migration of the cotton textile industry that occurred at about the same time. During this period, the pulp and paper industry in New England began to specialize in high-quality paper products in which it enjoyed a competitive advantage. The Crane Company in Dalton, Mass., for instance, has supplied the U.S. Treasury since 1879 with paper made of a special blend of 75 percent cotton and 25 percent

The Champion International Paper Company mill, Bucksport, Maine, 1993

linen for all paper money. Papermaking in southern New England relied on purchased pulp. Some mills turned to paper conversion, producing products from purchased paper. New England production and employment in pulp and paper continued to grow, particularly after World War II, but not as rapidly as in the South and West. New England towns that remained closely associated with the pulp and paper industry included Rumford, Maine, where one of the country's largest paper mills was located, and Berlin, N.H., where the Northern Forest Heritage Park was established in 1994 in an effort to preserve and present the history of the industry.

Since the 1960s, corporations located in the South and West and later overseas acquired established companies in New England; the pulp and paper industry in New England is now largely owned by multinational corporations. These corporations expanded and modernized old mills, added new capacity, and installed technology to meet stricter air- and water-pollution standards. Before this period of acquisition and investment, the industry had done little to control pollution. The pulp and paper industry now produces high-quality products, pays high wages, and manages large forest landholdings.

Thomas M. Beckley, "Pluralism by Default: Community Power in a Paper Mill Town," *Forest Science* 42 (1996); Lloyd C. Irland, *Wildlands and Woodlots: The Story of New England's Forests* (1982); Nancy Kane Ohanian, *The American Pulp and Paper Industry, 1900–1940: Mill Survival, Firm Structure, and Industry Relocation* (1993); David C. Smith, *History of Papermaking in the United States (1691–1969)* (1970).

Paul E. Sendak

Railroads The railroad has been a touchstone of New England culture since the first regional lines were built during the early 19th century. New England was among the first to create an interurban system of rail routes that reached beyond the city centers to the rural districts. Likewise, it was among the earliest to suffer decline of the system with the rise of the highway culture in the 20th century.

The development of the railroad enterprise can be attributed to true Yankee innovation. The first American railroad charter was granted in 1826 when the Granite Railway carried materials from the quarries of Quincy, Mass., to the Neponset River for the construction of the Bunker Hill Monument in Charlestown. An industrial tramway of English design, the Granite Railway served as a model for future railroad projects undertaken by Boston investors. A trio of railway routes opened from Boston in 1835—the Boston and Worcester, the Boston and Providence, and the Boston and Lowell—all modeled on the success of the steam-driven Liverpool and Manchester in England (1830). These first three "rail-roads" revolutionized travel from Boston, providing hourly service to nearby cities. The routes featured the stone-arched Canton viaduct over the Neponset River, engineered by William McNeill in 1834 and still in use by Amtrak trains today.

In Maine individual lines were set from coastal cities, such as the Bangor and Old Town in 1832 and the Machiasport and Whitneyville in 1836. Within five years the first Massachusetts railroads had expanded to a regional scale—the Boston and Maine to Portsmouth, the Boston and Albany to Troy, and the Providence and Stonington (Conn.) to Long Island Sound—linking New England with New York and the Erie Canal and westward. A second pulse of railroad construction was chartered from New Haven, Conn., up the Connecticut River to Hartford and Springfield, Mass., as local branch lines linked cities such as New Bedford, Mass., Concord, N.H., and Fitchburg, Mass., to the expanding regional system. The railroads also provided access to the winter ice ponds around Boston, most notably in Concord, where Henry David Thoreau watched the Fitchburg cars steam past Walden Pond. By 1850 the New England railroad network had become the most complex in the nation, extending from Waterville, Maine, to New York, and from Cape Cod to Burlington, Vt., with key interchanges at Worcester and Springfield that helped these cities emerge as innovative industrial centers.

The railroad served as the hallmark of New England technology, and major locomotive manufactories opened in Taunton, Mass.,

Portland, Maine, and Manchester, N.H., producing elaborately crafted engines decorated in colorful Victorian styles. In the cities grandly towered depots marked the railroad gateways to distant points, with monumental Gothic examples in Salem, Mass., and Boston, Italianate brick complexes in Providence and New Haven, a handsome Greek Revival station in Worcester, and an Egyptian-style facility in New Bedford. The largest railroad project of the era was the Hoosac Tunnel, along the Mohawk Trail in the Berkshire Hills, connecting Fitchburg and Boston with Troy, N.Y. Conceived in 1854, the "Great Bore" required the efforts of Welsh miners working in the deep shaft under Hoosac Mountain for more than 20 years.

Before the Civil War, the railroads had extended to the mountain resorts of New Hampshire and Maine via the Atlantic and Saint Lawrence from Portland. Scenic routes were cut through Crawford Notch to the White Mountains, and grand hotels were built to house summer tourists in elegant style. To reach the mountain summits, ingenious rack railways were constructed on timber trestles, most notably the Mount Washington Cog Railroad (1869), which is still in operation today. On the islands off Cape Cod, narrow-gauge lines, with quaint toy engines and tiny cars, were built along the sandy shores to transport passengers from the ferry terminals on Martha's Vineyard and Nantucket, Mass. These narrow-gauge lines were also built on the down-east coast of Maine with lines from Wiscassett and Gardiner as well as Sebago and Rangley Lakes, for carrying both tourists and lumber. More practical logging lines were run into the White Mountains with the help of French Canadian labor, creating a web of temporary tracks that changed with each cutting season.

In Boston the railroad provided the means for extending suburban commuter service to the estate farms of the North and South Shores. Daily trains carried passengers from North and South Shore stations to the rustic depots in the neighboring suburbs of Newton, Wellesley, Hingham, Cohasset, Beverly, and Ipswich. These depots were designed in the latest styles, most notably the Romanesque stations of the Boston and Albany line, created by H. H. Richardson, the architect of Boston's Trinity Church. In Connecticut the exodus from New York City also served a commuter population along the coastal route to Stamford and Bridgeport. With the completion of the Connecticut River Bridge in 1872, the shoreline route to Boston was formed as the New York, New Haven, and Hartford Railroad. Still other routes to New York were offered by the boat train of the Fall River Line, beginning in 1847, and the Air Line of the New York and New England Railroad through Willimantic, Conn., in 1884. With electrification of the line along the coast from New York to New Haven in 1908, passengers awaited seating in parlor cars en route to Boston.

In northern Vermont the waiting connections to Burlington proved endemic, prompting a popular verse by Edward Phelps: "I hope in hell, / Their souls may dwell, / Who first invented Essex Junction!" The advent of the automobile after World War I slowly eroded the necessity of New England railroads. While the major lines, such as the Boston and Maine and the New Haven, survived well into the postwar prosperity of the 1950s, the construction of high-speed highways gradually reduced passenger travel to the immediate lines from Boston and New York. Most smaller cities were without scheduled service by 1970. Freight lines were maintained on the major routes, such as the Canadian-owned Central Vermont from Montreal to New London, Conn., and the Grand Trunk across northern Maine between the Maritime Provinces and Quebec.

A few local lines managed to reinvent familiar names, like the Providence and Worcester, which served the Blackstone Valley textile towns. Gradually, however, even these secondary lines succumbed to highway traffic, reducing them to tourist lines for fall foliage or summer amusement. Today commuter service from central Boston still runs to the suburbs of Middlesex and Essex counties, many with restored Victorian stations as landmarks of local pride. Full electrification of the New Haven line to Boston for the high-speed Acela service was inaugurated in 2000 to compete with air travel to New York, and the Downeaster service between Boston and Portland began in 2001. While the white table-clothed meals have been reduced to fast food, New England's railroad culture has maintained itself as the dense urbanization of the region continues to offer advantages for intercity travel.

Donald H. Bray, *They Said It Couldn't Be Done: The Mount Washington Cog Railway and Its History* (1984); Carl R. Byron, *A Pinprick of Light: The Troy and Greenfield Railroad and Its Hoosac Tunnel* (1978); Robert H. Farson, *Cape Cod Railroads: Including Martha's Vineyard and Nantucket* (1990); Alvin F. Harlow, *Steelways of New England* (1946); Ronald Dale Karr, *Rail Lines of Southern New England* (1995); Donald D. Keyes, ed., *The White Mountains* (1980); Carol L. V. Meeks, *The Railroad Station: An Architectural History* (1995, [1956]).

Arthur Krim

Raytheon Founded in Cambridge, Mass., in 1922 as the American Appliance Company, the firm took the name Raytheon ("light from the gods") in 1925. A science-based company that first flourished in the age of hot and cold wars, Raytheon's history is suggestive of the ways in which New England businesses adapted to the opportunities of the mid-20th century. Its founders were Lawrence K. Marshall, his college roommate Vannevar Bush (who became a nationally prominent scientist), and Charles G. Smith, all educated in New England. Smith developed the radio tube, turning radios from battery-operated to electrical instruments. That tube, or gaseous rectifier, would be the company's principal product through the 1930s. Capital and managerial skill came from the sons of old New England families, especially William Gammell, Jr., a Providence textile-mill owner. One of Raytheon's most valuable employees was Percy Spencer, a machinist from Maine who had little formal schooling but a pronounced ability to solve engineering problems.

Raytheon's breakthrough came with World War II. Spencer devised a superior way of mass-producing magnetron tubes, the essential component of radar systems. By the end of the war, Raytheon was producing 80 percent of all magnetrons. The company also developed improved shipboard radar, eventually outfitting all U.S. PT boats. From 1940 to 1945, production increased 40 times, employment 16 times.

After the war, the company's reliance on military contracts continued. Under the leadership of Charles Francis Adams, a former investment banker and Adams family descendant, Raytheon maintained its radar production while developing new missile guidance systems. In 1950 the Lark became the first guided missile to destroy an airplane in flight. Raytheon's success led to contracts to develop the navy's Sparrow and the army's Hawk. By 1958 sales and staff had reached all-time highs of $375 million and more than 40,000 employees, while government contracts amounted to 85 percent of its business.

From the 1960s to the present, Raytheon's history has been marked by efforts to expand its commercial businesses. By 1969, under the direction of Thomas L. Phillips, the company had increased its commercial activity to 55 percent of sales. A key acquisition in 1965 was Amana Refrigeration, a purchase that finally allowed Raytheon to take full advantage of its 1947 invention of the first microwave oven, the Radarrange. Two years later, the first countertop 110-volt microwave ovens went on sale under the Amana name for under $500. Raytheon also established itself in commercial marine electronics, publishing, power-plant construction, household appliances, and oil and gas exploratory services.

Raytheon, however, remains best known for its missiles. The Patriot, first produced in 1976 and initially designed as a ground-to-air anti-aircraft missile, was pressed into service during the 1991 Gulf War to shoot down Iraqi Scud missiles. The initial glowing reports of the Patriot's success were later called into question by a number of sources and now appear to have been greatly exaggerated. Whatever the merits of this criticism, Raytheon later sold substantial numbers of Patriots while continuing to make improvements, and Patriot batteries remain in place.

In the aftermath of the Cold War, under the business pressures of the 1990s, Raytheon sought to divest itself of certain noncore businesses such as publishing. In response to a sharp decline in defense procurement and the shakeout of the defense industry, it successfully sought mergers in 1997 with the defense systems of Texas Instruments and Hughes Electronics. It continues to produce commercial marine electronics and provide engineering and construction services. Raytheon has also moved into such commercial sectors as air traffic control systems, microelectronics and satellite technology, and the manufacture of business aircraft.

Stephan Budiansky, "Playing Patriot Games," *U.S. News and World Report*, November 22, 1993; Raytheon, "Raytheon Historical Backgrounder" (1998); Otto J. Scott, *The Creative Ordeal: The Story of Raytheon* (1974); Jennifer Weeks, "Patriot Games: What Did We See on Desert Storm TV," *Columbia Journalism Review* (July–Aug. 1992).

Gary Kulik

Sawmills and Lumbering During the first half of the 17th century, Englishmen with little experience living in a wooded environment settled a tree-covered land that had been modified by Native American woodcrafters for more than 12 millennia. Within 200 years, few Native Americans remained, but many of the progeny of European settlers had become lumbermen and woodcraftsmen, and much of the biota had become strikingly different. By harvesting the trees for fuel, construction timber, and a long list of domestic, agricultural, and industrial items, the transatlantic settlers had transformed millions of forested acres into farms, pastures, and manufacturing enclaves.

Previous successes in plant and animal domestication in Europe gave the Puritan settlers an unquestioning assurance that God had assigned them a near-juridical role over all orders of life. Preoccupation with predestination drove many merchants into assiduous efforts to prove worthiness for divine election by successfully fulfilling growing demands for timber in both domestic and overseas markets. Timber dealers conceptualized trees and other naturally occurring items as commodities with

Sawing white pine in Epping, N.H., 1992

of New England sawmills today are affected by global forces, such as changes in the pulp market and the profitability of exporting sawlogs to Europe and Japan. Some have found a niche serving specialty markets for hardwoods used by furniture makers.

Charles F. Carroll, *The Timber Economy of Puritan New England* (1973); Brooke Hindle, ed., *America's Wooden Age: Aspects of Its Early Technology* (1975); Lloyd C. Irland, *Wildlands and Woodlots: The Story of New England's Forests* (1982); David C. Smith, *A History of Lumbering in Maine, 1861–1960* (1972).

Charles F. Carroll

Shoes The manufacture of shoes has played an integral part in the economic development of New England. Shoe manufacturing began in shops and workhouses as early as 1750; one of the first shoe factories opened in Brockton, Mass., in 1760. Between 1760 and 1850 Massachusetts became the leading manufacturer of shoes in the nation and Boston the shoe and leather center of the world. All New England states, with the exception of Vermont, developed viable shoe manufacturing centers. The chief footwear producing communities were Brockton, Lynn, Haverhill, and Marlboro, Mass.; Manchester and Nashua, N.H.; and Gardiner, Maine. Brockton became the leading manufacturer of men's shoes; Haverhill, often referred to as the Queen Slipper City, became the world's greatest slipper and low-cut footwear producer; Lynn was the Commonwealth's second shoe city and led the world in women's footwear. Brockton and Haverhill were centers of the Socialist Labor Party movement in the shoe industry; the latter became the first city in the nation to have a socialist mayor and the first city east of the Mississippi River to have a commission form of government.

Shoes were part of the agricultural base of New England from the beginning of settlement. Although cobblers were prevalent in many areas, including itinerants who visited homes to make or complete homemade shoes, farmers with large families often made shoes for their own uses. As the region became more urbanized and mercantile capitalism more prevalent, the demand for these handcrafted shoes increased and became a major part of the 19th-century household economy. More and more farmers-turned-craftsmen organized the shoe trade in individual "10-footers"—small wood-frame workshops—alongside their farmhouses. Increasing demand was among the factors that led to the great Lynn shoe strike of 1860, the first truly national labor crisis, which reflected the industrialization and mechanization of the shoe industry as well as the increasing use of female labor.

During the Civil War, increased demand

an abstract value, and the result was a philosophy, carried on through generations, that ensured a continuous process of forest destruction, land transformation, and the emergence of an almost totally cultural landscape in southern New England.

Whereas the Native Americans had brought about limited ecological changes by using stone implements, the new forest dwellers created a built landscape using efficient iron and steel cutting tools. Even the first single-bladed, vertical, reciprocating saws, integrated with water-driven mechanical systems, could rip through soft white pine 20 times more efficiently than pit or trundle saws. Over time, New England's premier industrial machine, the sawmill, underwent a series of improvements that allowed greater speed with less wobble. Millwrights eventually added a series of parallel blades to form gang mills, and by the early 19th century they also were developing more effective circular blades, some with replaceable teeth. These machines, together with a host of newly invented woodworking tools, tore through diminishing supplies of soft- and hardwoods. By the mid-19th century, well over half the trees in southern New England, including much of the white

pine, white oak, white cedar, and chestnut, had been cut and shaped into buildings, fences, and factories, or had sailed away to foreign ports as ships, masts, barrels, boxes, shingles, and boards. Millions of cords had also been felled and burned directly as domestic and industrial fuel, or converted to charcoal for blast furnaces and forges.

The inhabitants of southern New England would have one last fling with the lumber industry in the late 19th century when they used waterpowered turbines or steam engines to drive saws through logs cut from the extensive tracts of white pine that had seeded on abandoned farmland. In the meantime, much of the commercial lumber industry had shifted to the north. For a time Maine was the nation's largest commercial timber producer and Bangor the world's leading timber-shipping port. Although leadership in commercial lumbering shifted to the western states, the heavy demands for construction timber, the growth of the plywood, particle board, and pulp-based paper manufacturing industries—and the emergence of scientific forest management—ensured that the less heavily populated regions of northern New England would continue to participate in the lumber industry. Operators

Stitching vamps at Stride Rite Shoe Company, Lexington, Mass., ca. 1985

for footwear led to competition, mechanization, and expanded factory organization. Subsequently, the industry became even more specialized as workers such as cutters, stitchers, and lasters were defined by the task they performed and the cost of labor became closely associated with the piece-rate system. As a consequence of this specialization, the New England boot and shoe industry took a leading position in the production of the machinery necessary to make modern footwear. Almost 100 different machines were developed, including the McKay sole-sewing machine, the Matzeliger lasting machine, the Goodyear welting machine, and a host of special machines for rolling soles, cutting outsoles and heels, trimming, and polishing. Industry machinery had matured by 1895, and although the powerful lasters' union resisted, keeping lasting a hand operation into the 1880s, mechanization shortened and simplified production. One worker with a machine that could sew to the welt was able to accomplish the work of 54 workers with an awl.

Shoemaking, unlike textiles, did not require large capitalization. The machinery required to make shoes faster, cheaper, and better was owned by the United Shoe Machinery Corporation, which held a monopoly on the machines and preferred to lease them on a per-shoe cost basis rather than sell them outright. This action removed the biggest expense for an enterprising shoemaker and created a huge USM complex in Beverly, Mass., with some 5,000 workers. The development of the railroad supported the expansion of the New England shoe industry, as well as the tanning and

machine tool industries, by making it economical to continue production in a resource-lacking region.

In the late 19th century, more and more immigrants (French Canadians, Irish, Italians, and Greeks, in particular) flooded New England to take up jobs in the shoe trade. The industry became marked by extreme union labor friction, eventually leading to the closure or relocation of many New England firms. By the 1920s it was apparent that shoemaking was driven by a capricious buying public whose whims designers tried to anticipate twice a year. The Great Depression exacerbated an already difficult situation. More than ever, industry priority became low-cost manufacture and the interplay of materials, labor, transportation, and competition.

Consequently, competition from western shoemaking centers, such as Saint Louis, Mo., and foreign competitors, especially the Bata Corporation of Canada, began causing difficulties that continued to plague the New England shoe industry through the 1930s, with only slight relief during World War II. The industry began a major shift to cheaper materials and a more central location in the national transportation net. Eventually, overseas sites such as Brazil and Korea, with lower labor costs and cheaper and more proficient machines, became the new production leaders.

Despite this loss of leadership in the industry, specialty New England firms remain active and viable through increased efficiency, inventiveness, and progressive competition. Signature New England firms like Bass, Dexter, Rockport, and Timberland are known

worldwide. Reebok, the athletic shoe manufacturer, is based in Massachusetts. But it is L. L. Bean of Freeport, Maine, and its Maine Hunting Shoe, a rubber bottom sewn to a leather upper, that since its invention in 1911 has not only captured market share but solidified New England's reputation as a leader in rugged, durable shoe manufacture.

Henry F. Bedford, *Socialism and the Workers in Massachusetts, 1886–1912* (1966); Mary H. Blewett, *Men, Women, and Work: Class, Gender, and Protest in the New England Shoe Industry, 1780–1910* (1988); Essex Institute, *Life and Times in Shoe City: The Shoe Workers of Lynn* (1979).

Paul H. Tedesco

Sikorsky Aircraft Corporation The Sikorsky Aircraft Corporation of southern New England, a subsidiary of United Technologies Corporation, is the oldest continuous manufacturer of helicopters in the world. Based in Stratford, Conn., this pioneering company built ocean-spanning flying boats in the 1930s before abandoning fixed-wing manufacture. During World War II it initiated the world's first mass production of helicopters and today remains a world leader in the design and manufacture of helicopters for commercial, industrial, and military uses.

Sikorsky Aircraft was founded by Igor I. Sikorsky, an aviation pioneer whose stature in the industry rivals that of the Wright brothers. Born in Kiev, Ukraine, in 1889, Sikorsky built and flew the world's first multi-engine airplane in 1913, then manufactured biplane bombers for Imperial Russia during World War I. After fleeing the Russian Revolution of 1917, he immigrated to the United States and resumed airplane manufacture on Long Island, N.Y., in the 1920s. Within a decade, his company had risen to prominence, building four-engine "flying clipper ships" for Pan American Airways.

In 1929 Sikorsky Aircraft moved to Stratford, Conn., where the Housatonic River flows into Long Island Sound. In July of that year, the company joined the United Aircraft and Transport Corporation (UATC), a newly formed aviation holding company based in Hartford. Engine maker Pratt and Whitney (also based in Hartford) and Boeing Aircraft of Seattle were the key components of UATC, which also included airplane manufacturers Northrop, Stearman, Chance Vought; the Hamilton Standard Propeller Company; and an airline then known as Boeing Air Transport.

In 1934 New Deal legislation reshaped U.S. aeronautics by forcing the breakup of the nation's "aviation trusts." Passed to promote competition, the Air Mail Act of 1934 forced UATC to split into three separate compo-

A Sikorsky Skycrane delivers a sailboat to a marina for repairs, Marion, Mass., 1985

nents: Boeing in Seattle and its Stearman subsidiary in Wichita; United Air Lines in Chicago; and the United Aircraft Corporation in Connecticut. Sikorsky Aircraft has remained a part of the New England conglomerate, which in May 1975 became the United Technologies Corporation.

Having first performed rotary-wing experiments in 1909, Igor Sikorsky resumed his quest for practical vertical flight in 1938 amid decreasing demand for flying boats. In September 1939 he hovered his single-seat VS-300 prototype, a test bed that flew with a variety of rotor configurations before emerging as America's first successful helicopter in December 1941. Based on this success, Sikorsky Aircraft manufactured the two-seat R-4—history's first production helicopter—which had limited use during World War II. Subsequent Sikorsky rotorcraft were widely employed in the Korean and Vietnam conflicts.

Although known for large turbine-powered helicopters, such as the U.S. Marine Corps CH-53E Super Stallion, Sikorsky Aircraft also builds the midsize army UH-60 Black Hawk utility helicopter and its naval cousin, the SH-60 Seahawk. Current commercial product offerings include the S-76 corporate helicopter and the S-92 Helibus.

Since the 1990s, Sikorsky, with facilities in Connecticut, Florida, and Alabama, has increasingly focused on integrating advanced electronic systems and capabilities into its helicopters, often in partnership with other

manufacturers. The army's cancellation in 2004 of the RAH-66 Comanche armed reconnaissance helicopter was a blow to the company, but it continues to be a leading helicopter manufacturer, and in 2004 began exploring the Asian market.

Dorothy Cochrane, Von Hardesty, and Russell Lee, *The Aviation Careers of Igor Sikorsky* (1989); Frank J. Delear, *Igor Sikorsky: His Three Careers in Aviation* (1969); Jay P. Spenser, *Whirlybirds: A History of the U.S. Helicopter Pioneers* (1998).

Jay P. Spenser

Silver Brilliantly lustrous, extremely malleable and ductile, the element silver has the highest thermal and electrical conductivity of any substance. Throughout history, ownership of silver table and ornamental wares has been an important indication of social status, communicating the possessor's wealth and position. Silversmiths and goldsmiths (the titles were used interchangeably in New England until the late 18th century) were respected and trusted craftsmen in their communities. The first silversmiths in the American colonies were John Hull and Robert Sanderson, Sr., who formed their Boston partnership in 1652 when Hull was appointed master of the Massachusetts mint.

In its natural state, silver is usually found as silver ore, and in minerals such as argentite, polybasite, and prousite, all mined in the western United States during the 19th century. Earlier, silversmiths in the New England states relied on old, worn, or damaged articles of silver and miscellaneous silver coins to provide the raw material for their craft. The silver alloy typically consisted of approximately 90 percent silver, 10 percent copper (for strength) and trace amounts of lead and gold, although significant fluctuations were possible, depending on what was thrown into the melting pot. This alloy was known as "coin silver" and was slightly below the British "sterling" standard of 92.5 percent silver, adopted in the year 1300.

Molten silver alloy was poured into molds for ingots or, better yet, shallow molds capable of producing a rough sheet of silver. Silversmiths then hammered the metal into thin sheets, scribed a circular area on this sheet, and cut out the piece to be worked. Various sizes of hammers were used to raise the silver dish over a variety of wooden forms, called stakes, held in a vise. The silver became brittle as it was hammered repeatedly; to compensate for this, the metal was frequently annealed by heating it until it turned cherry red and then immersing it in cold water. When the body of the silver article was formed and planished (smoothed), cast handles, feet, and so forth were soldered to the piece to produce the finished article. Common domestic objects were

tankards, cups, porringers, pitchers, bowls, jewelry, and spoons, while ecclesiastical forms included chalices, flagons, and dishes.

Among the most prominent silversmiths in the colonial and federal eras were Pygan Adams (1712–76) of New London, and Robert Fairchild (1703–94) of Stratford, Conn.; Daniel Russell, Sr. (ca. 1698–1750), and Daniel Russell, Jr. (1726–78) of Newport, and Saunders Pitman (1732–1804) of Providence, R.I.; Benjamin Burt (1729–1805), Paul Revere, Sr. (1702–54), and Paul Revere, Jr. (1734–1818), of Boston; Samuel Drowne (1749–1815) of Portsmouth, N.H.; Roswell H. Bailey (1804–86) of Woodstock, Vt.; and Zebulon Smith (1786–1865) of Bangor, Maine. British silver was the strongest influence in style for the silversmiths of New England, in part because so many of them were trained in England or apprenticed to British emigrant craftsmen. Boston was dominant in its influence during the colonial period, and the quality of its finest silver rivaled that of London-made goods.

Innovation and experimentation marked the development of silver manufacture in the 18th and 19th centuries. Rolling mills were used to produce the necessary sheet silver for craftsmen, and this, in turn, directed the shape and style of the finished product. Presses were invented in 1801, and the Newburyport, Mass., firm of Theophilus Bradbury and Son was using a roller press by 1815. O. J. Seymour of Hartford and Newell Harding and Company, Boston, employed steam-powered rolling mills to prepare their silver stock. The presses also permitted a wide range of ornamental designs to be molded into the sheet silver, creating an explosion of Gothic, Egyptian, Rococo Revival, and neoclassical patterns in the 19th-century wares.

Perhaps the most important technological development was the perfection of silver plating by means of electrolysis. A base metal form could be coated with a thin layer of silver using an electrical current and a solution containing dissolved silver. New England was the center of this new industry. In November 1842 the *Hartford Times* announced that Summer Smith was using galvanism for silver plating and gilding. Soon the Gorham Manufacturing Company of Providence, Reed and Barton of Taunton, Mass., Meriden Britannia Company of Connecticut and others were competing with established silversmith shops for the market in fine tablewares. By the 1859 census of manufactures, 128 electroplating firms employing more than 2,500 workers were in business, and the production of silver plate had surpassed that of solid silver wares.

Science and technology have diverted much of the silver used in America from its traditional role as tableware and jewelry. The total use of silver for wrought utensils and jewelry has decreased to 6.5 percent, while its use in photographic film and electrical circuitry has risen to 51.7 percent and 16.7 percent, respectively. Among the few early New England silver companies to continue operating to the present are Gorham, Reed and Barton, and Towle Silversmiths of Newburyport, Mass., which traces its history as far back as 1690.

Patricia E. Kane, *Colonial Massachusetts Silversmiths and Jewelers* (1998); Charles S. Parsons, *New Hampshire Silver* (1983); Charles L. Venable, *Silver in America, 1840–1940: A Century of Splendor* (1995); Barbara McLean Ward and Gerald W. R. Ward, *Silver in American Life* (1979).

Bert R. Denker

Slater, Samuel (1768–1835) Industrialist.

President Andrew Jackson once addressed Samuel Slater as "the father of American manufactures." He had good reason. When the 21-year-old Slater landed in New York City in 1789 fresh from an apprenticeship in the cotton textile mills of his hometown in Belper, England, Americans manufactured little yarn or cloth outside the home. British laws against the export of textile machinery and factory plans had stymied American manufactures, but Slater had sufficient knowledge to produce machines based on the spinning and carding machines designed in England by Richard Arkwright. In December 1790, after 11 months' work with Rhode Island artisans at the Almy and Brown mill in Pawtucket, Slater completed construction of the first commercially successful, American-built, waterpowered spinning machinery. By so doing, Samuel Slater established the 19th-century American cotton textile industry's earliest form and focus.

Under Slater's direction, the small Pawtucket spinning mill soon became a viable manufacturing operation. With the support of his partners, William Almy and Smith Brown, Slater introduced English mill management methods to go with his just-completed Arkwright machinery. The Pawtucket mill employed a factory workforce consisting of children aged eight to 14 along with their parents, resulting in a family system of labor. Slater established a dawn-to-dusk workday, standardized yarn production necessary to supply Almy and Brown weavers and customers, and personally supervised the mill's year-round operations. His approach, eventually called the Slater system, gradually spread throughout southern and central New England, providing a foundation for the larger mill complexes developed in Waltham, Mass., and along the Merrimack River by Boston Associates.

Slater remained a successful industrial

The Slater Mill, Pawtucket, R.I., 1949

leader until his death in 1835 in Webster, Mass. His cotton and woolen mills were important models of diversity and flexibility. He manufactured yarn and cloth, relied on both water and steam power, and employed hand-loom weavers and the power loom to finish his cloth. At various times Slater owned or actively supervised mills in Rehoboth, Oxford, and Dudley, Mass.; Smithfield and Providence, R.I.; Jewett City, Conn.; and Pawtucket. He also was involved in other Massachusetts mills at Ludlow, Fitchburg, and Sutton; in a Rhode Island mill at Central Falls; and in New Hampshire's Amoskeag mills. Nevertheless, Slater was not immune to financial difficulties; fluctuations in mill property values in 1829 nearly caused his financial collapse and did ruin many of his fellow mill owners.

Concerns about the mill society's moral direction caused Slater to adopt an aggressive, paternalistic approach. He introduced a Sunday School for Pawtucket child workers, supported a number of different religious organizations, promoted various educational institutions, and organized several banks to encourage individual savings. All, he felt, strengthened the moral fiber of his mill people.

Opportunistic Americans followed Slater's example and capitalized on his pioneering efforts. After the War of 1812 this group included builders of larger, fully integrated mills that appeared in locations such as Waltham and Lowell, Mass. Gradually, Americans turned from spinning wheels and hand looms

to dependence on yarn and cloth manufactured by Almy, Brown, and Slater and their competitors. Not surprisingly, the cotton textile industry quickly emerged as America's premier manufacturing industry and placed its permanent stamp on 19th-century New England, its people, landscape, and future. The Slater Mill Historic Site, created in 1951, in Pawtucket is today a museum and tourist attraction.

E. H. Cameron, *Samuel Slater: Father of American Manufacturers* (1960); James L. Conrad, Jr., "'Drive That Branch': Samuel Slater, the Power Loom, and the Writing of America's Textile History," *Technology and Culture* 36 (1995); Barbara Tucker, *Samuel Slater and the Origins of the American Textile Industry, 1790–1860* (1984); George S. White, *Memoir of Samuel Slater: Father of American Manufacturers* (1967 [1836]).

James L. Conrad, Jr.

Springfield Armory In 1794 President

George Washington established two national armories to make small arms for the U.S. Army—one at Springfield, Mass., and the other in Harpers Ferry, in what was then Virginia. Located at the site of a Revolutionary War supply depot, Springfield Armory was among the oldest continuously operated factories in the United States, producing standard-issue shoulder arms from 1795 to 1963. The armory was most significant for its role in designing and producing the army's principal shoulder arms, and for its antebellum development of a large factory system with closely controlled production of uniform precision metal and wood products. The Harpers Ferry

Armory rarely attained Springfield's production levels or mechanical and organizational improvements. After the Virginia site was destroyed early in the Civil War, Springfield Armory remained the only national armory until early in the 20th century.

Springfield Armory made five major types of weapons: single-shot, smoothbore flintlock muskets (1795–1842); single-shot weapons with locks adapted for percussion ammunition, manufactured as smoothbore (1842–55) and rifled (1857–65) muskets; single-shot breechloading rifles with a so-called trapdoor mechanism (1865–93); two kinds of bolt-action magazine, or repeating, rifles including the Krag (1894–1902) and the famous Model 1903 (1903–31); and two kinds of rifles with breech mechanisms operated by combustion gas from fired cartridges: the semi-automatic M1 or Garand (1937–57) and the selective-fire full automatic M14 (1959–63). Armory inventor John C. Garand's eight-shot M1 was the world's most powerful military rifle during World War II. Springfield Armory had manufactured approximately 843,000 Springfield '03 rifles by World War I, and approximately 4.5 million M1 semi-automatic rifles during its entire production history.

Undeveloped manufacturing standards, variations among federal and private suppliers, and lack of well-defined government authority limited army shoulder arms quality and output before 1815. When the Army Ordnance Department gained control of all arms procurement after severe problems during the War of 1812, it insisted on weapons with dimensionally interchangeable parts. To meet this demand, Springfield Armory managers introduced new production and management methods. By 1849 the Armory was making essentially uniform weapons based on the grad-

ual introduction of more mechanized manufacturing, a practical gauging system, and tight management controls on the output of workers usually paid per acceptable piece. Armory inventiveness was greater in management than in manufacturing methods; the latter were marked by sophisticated adaptations rather than innovations. Despite mechanization, skills needed to meet demanding Armory standards gave workers considerable control over shop procedures well into the 20th century.

The Armory's large-scale operations and its role as a central information exchange among private arms makers dependent on public contracts made "Armory practice" an antebellum standard from which many American industries drew important but selective lessons. As private small arms and other precision industries grew after 1850, Springfield Armory's commercial influence began to wane. The Armory's relative indifference to manufacturing costs and insistence on full interchangeability inhibited private use of Springfield methods and made Armory managers extremely cautious about introducing new weapons designs. Following a remarkable record of Civil War output, including a twentyfold increase in production with a sevenfold increase in workers, Armory production and design generally lagged behind commercial practice. Procrustean manufacturing standards contributed to rifle supply problems during the Spanish American and First World Wars. Renewed adaptation of commercial technology in the 1930s helped Springfield reach astonishing M1 output figures during World War II.

The wartime importance of commercial arms manufacture decreased after 1945, however, and Springfield Armory was less successful in a research, design, and pilot production

capacity supporting private industry. Amid cost-cutting and bureaucratic battles within the army, the Armory was closed in 1968. Today the Armory Museum preserves and presents the history of mass production and weaponry in America.

Felicia Johnson Deyrup, "Arms Makers of the Connecticut Valley: A Regional Study of the Economic Development of the Small Arms Industry, 1798–1870," *Smith College Studies in History* 33 (1948); Edward C. Ezell, *The Great Rifle Controversy: Search for the Ultimate Infantry Weapon from World War II Through Vietnam and Beyond* (1984); Michael S. Raber, "Conservative Innovators, Military Small Arms, and Industrial History at Springfield Armory, 1794–1918," *IA: The Journal of the Society for Industrial Archeology* 14 (1988); Robert M. Reilly, *United States Military Small Arms, 1816–1865* (1970).

Michael S. Raber

Stanley Works In 1843 Frederick Trenck Stanley (1802–83) established a small shop in his hometown of New Britain, Conn., to manufacture bolts using machinery. A steam engine, probably the first in use in Connecticut, powered his small metalworking shop. In 1852 he established a joint stock company under the name Stanley Works with a capital of $30,000 and expanded production to include hinges. The design and finish of Stanley Works hardware attracted a larger market. By 1866 the company had begun producing bolts and butt hinges, and it began exporting its products in 1870. By 1876, when Stanley Works was honored at the Philadelphia Centennial, the company occupied a four-story brick factory, had a capital of $300,000 and was producing well-designed ornamental hardware. Looking aggressively at a world market, Stanley established a separate export sales office in New York and factories in Canada (1914), Germany (1926), and England (1937).

Stanley was able to establish its special niche in the hand-tool market because of a 1920 merger with its neighbor, the Stanley Rule and Level Company, founded in 1857 by Henry Stanley, a cousin of Frederick's. Stanley Rule and Level had earned an excellent reputation for the manufacture of boxwood and ivory rules, levels, Try squares, T-bevels and mallets. In 1869, Stanley Rule and Level acquired the patent to the Bailey iron plane, the first easily adjustable planing tool and now highly prized by collectors.

During the 1930s, the Stanley Works began to develop portable electric tools and photoelectric door openers; it continued to expand its products in the second half of the century to include pneumatic nailing and fastening tools, industrial hand tools, and a full range of tools for consumers. Now the leading toolmaker in the United States, the company owns a number of trademarks, including Bos-

Springfield Armory, 1965

titch, Husky, Monarch, and Mac Tools. In 1966 Stanley Works became a public company, and shortly after developed the slogan "Stanley helps to do things right."

The Stanley Works aroused controversy in 2002 after its shareholders, encouraged by management, voted to change its place of incorporation from Connecticut to Bermuda, hoping to save $30 million a year in taxes on its international earnings. Under severe public pressure, including legal action by the state's attorney general alleging irregularities in the voting process, the company backed down. Stanley's business was not noticeably affected by the controversy: the company announced record first-quarter sales and profits in 2004.

Gary Kulik

Textile Machinery The production of textile machinery in New England was a regional specialty closely intertwined with trends in two allied fields: textile mills sought improved equipment for converting various fibers, especially cotton, into yarn or cloth, and metalworking processes were improved for forming and assembling the assorted components of capital goods equipment.

The chronology of firms and figures in the textile machinery industry parallels New England's industrial ascent and decline. The origins of the trade can be traced back to 1790 when the Wilkinson clan of Pawtucket, R.I., and other local artisans built the initial water-powered yarn-spinning machines associated with English immigrant Samuel Slater. This episode contained several of the threads that would later form the pattern associated with the textile machinery industry, including the balance between imported innovations and domestic contributions as well as the personalized process of technology transfer between nations and generations.

The imprint of the textile machinery industry on New England's landscape took the form of dispersal followed by concentration. Though many new mills were equipped by machinists working onsite through the War of 1812, the remainder of the antebellum era featured a process of consolidation as a number of large independent shops achieved prominence. The locations of the principal firms included both urban and village settings in Pawtucket and Providence; Lowell, Fall River, Taunton, and Whitinsville, Mass., and Saco, Maine, for cotton machinery; and Worcester and North Andover, Mass., for woolen machinery.

During the early stages of their existence, these textile machinery manufacturers differed considerably in their access to capital, managerial ethos, manufacturing methods, relations with customers, and scope of product line. These antebellum factories tended to take one of two architectural forms: on one hand was the integrated foundry and machine shop complex, which combined a variety of industrial buildings that housed the thermal processes and metalworking operations necessary for fabricating textile machinery. On the other were the less extensive facilities for more specialized makers of smaller key components such as spinning rings, drawing rolls, and shuttles.

Perhaps the most distinctive aspect of textile machinery manufacturing was its method of internal production management, known in various guises as inside contracting or the job system. The inside contractor was the platypus of Victorian industry: part skilled worker, part project manager, part entrepreneur. In their specialized areas contractors exercised an unusual degree of authority. Beginning in the late 19th century, managerial reformers sought to redefine the relationship between the shop floor and the front office by whittling down the prestige and prerogatives of contractors. Even with the advent of more centralized controls, however, 20th-century textile machine shops still retained an identifiable occupational subculture.

When the initial wave of disinvestment in textiles hit New England in the 1920s, many machinery makers were swamped as well. But some historic firms managed to continue on into the era of high technology. The Draper works at Hopedale, Mass., where the automatic loom was invented, and the 150-year-old firm of Davis and Furber at North Andover, Mass., did not shutter their works until 1980 and 1982, respectively. Idle plants looming over placid millponds now provide opportunities for further reflection. At its height in the 19th century, however, the region's textile machinery industry exerted a wide influence. It was not only a center of innovation for the textile industry but the incubator of metal-working skills that helped shape the manufacture of locomotives, steam engines, machine tools, and weapons.

George O. Draper, "Textile Machinery," in *Lamb's Textile Industries of the United States*, ed. E. Everton Foster (1916); George S. Gibb, *The Saco-Lowell Shops: Textile Machinery Building in New England, 1813–1949* (1950); Thomas E. Leary, "Industrial Ecology and the Labor Process: The Redefinition of Craft in New England Textile Machinery Shops, 1820–1860," in *Life and Labor: Dimensions of American Working-Class History*, ed. Charles Stephenson and Robert Asher (1986); Thomas R. Navin, *The Whitin Machine Works Since 1831: A Textile Machinery Company in an Industrial Village* (1950).

Thomas E. Leary

Textiles From earliest settlement, New England colonists saw textile production as one of the keys to survival and success. They made sure that their towns included people with the skills to produce the materials they needed. They produced miles of rope to rig the ships in which they traded. They processed linen, wool, and cotton into acres of cloth for sails, clothing, bedding, and myriad other uses. Around the mid-17th century, fulling mills harnessed waterpower to produce a warmer, more durable felted woven cloth. Late in the 18th century carding mills prepared wool for spinning on domestic spinning wheels. These operations did not necessarily alter social or economic relations, but they did make cloth production less arduous. Most people continued to farm and produce goods for sale or trade, seeking a "competence"— that is, a sufficient income for a life of reasonable comfort.

The Industrial Revolution radically changed the bases of both production and fundamental social relations. In the late 18th century Great Britain began producing yarn and cloth in factories through a succession of powered processes. Efforts to mimic this success occupied mechanics and investors in New England during the closing decades of the century. Finally, in a Pawtucket, R.I., factory, the industrialist Samuel Slater combined his knowledge of the English process with the skill of local machinists and artisans and the financial backing of local investors to produce cotton yarn successfully by power. "Successful" now meant profitable.

With agriculture in decline, laborers arrived to toil for the low hourly wages Slater offered, making yarn sold for the profit of investors, and Slater's production system based on the mill village spread throughout the region. A cash economy began to emerge. Factory workers no longer organized production, determined products, or owned what they made. No sooner had the system emerged than workers and owners or managers came into conflict over time, wages, and other elements of factory practice, and eventually they devised new social relations to accommodate the demands of the new form of production.

A second model of factory production emerged when Boston merchants sought new investments after Britain's reassertion of control over the maritime trades following the War of 1812. Francis Cabot Lowell and his cohorts, known as the Boston Associates, formed the Boston Manufacturing Company and built a factory in Waltham, Mass., which added power weaving to Slater's yarnmaking. This integrated factory processed raw cotton into finished cloth. The Boston Associates developed their joint-stock company to facilitate the huge investment needed for large-scale production and to protect investors. They lob-

Sewing at a garment factory, Fall River, Mass., ca. 1980

bied successfully for government protection through tariffs, incorporation law, and subsidized transportation networks. Their successful system was repeated in large textile-producing cities across New England: Lowell, Lawrence, Holyoke, and Chicopee, Mass.; Manchester and Nashua, N.H.; and Lewiston and Saco-Biddeford, Maine, to name a few. The financial networks they created facilitated the movement of their profits into various industries across the country.

Each of these single-industry cities involved heavy capital investment to harness waterpower and build giant factories capable of producing the vast quantities of cloth needed to return a profit on such an investment. The Boston Associate's company built boardinghouses for single female workers and machine shops to make the equipment. They devised increasingly complex machinery to lessen the importance, cost, and independence of individual workers. This technology aimed to minimize skill but not effort, cheapening rather than saving labor. Over time, workers' assignments grew, as did machine speeds, decried by the workers as the "stretch-out" and the "speed-up."

Absentee owners (residing primarily in Boston) delegated authority for the operation of these factories and demanded steady returns despite a lack of reinvestment to maintain and improve operations. Here accommodation was not achieved, and the workforce of Yankee women gradually rejected the owners' terms and left the mills. The large number of Irish immigrants, forced to leave their famine-stricken homeland, provided replacement labor. The new workers, however, also rejected the working conditions and within a generation or so left the mills. This pattern repeated itself steadily as nonindustrial peoples around the globe, their home lives disrupted by the encroaching market economy, fled to the "land of opportunity" and jobs they too would reject as soon as they were able. French Canadians, Italians, Greeks, and Poles were just a few of the groups following the pattern more recently adopted by Hispanics and Southeast Asians. Neighborhoods, and in some cases whole cities such as French-speaking Lewiston, Maine, and Woonsocket, R.I., reflected the languages and customs of these groups.

Both models of production and labor-management relations continued as steam-powered cities like Fall River and New Bedford, Mass., came to outproduce Lowell, and eventually all New England states were dotted by textile mills, large and small. The industry's impact remains widely visible in the factories and housing of the former mill cities and towns of each state. Gradually most of the small mills became producers of woolens or specialty goods. The larger mills generally produced bulk cottons, woolen carpeting, and occasionally silk. In nearly every case, each factory operated with formal independence, although common ownership led to cooperation among the biggest producers. The trusts that consolidated other major U.S. industries had little success in the highly cyclical and easily entered textile industry, with the notable, temporary exception of the 50-odd factories organized into American Woolen Company in the early 20th century.

The industry boomed with the domestic and foreign demand of World War I but declined afterward. Just as the region had pioneered industrial development, it now initiated the movement toward runaway industry, always seeking the cheapest available environment. Lack of reinvestment allowed plants and machinery to deteriorate; this style of operation led to accidents and irregular employment, which resulted in taxes for workers' compensation and unemployment insurance. Federal law slowed the immigration that had brought the new workers who would be temporarily forced to accept the unsavory conditions. Investment once funneled into the New England mills gradually shifted to the South, which lacked the degree of industrial experience and thus the taxes and the worn-out plants and equipment. The South offered instead new "immigrants" from its failing agricultural sector who were desperate enough to accept low "family" wages in the new company towns of the American textile industry. Northern textile machine builders and investors gradually invested in and took over the textile factories founded as part of the "New South" movement; in the teens and twenties they supplanted much of the production in New England. The New England textile industry, however, did not disappear. World War II provided another boom period for mills that had hung on. During and after the war, Royal Little bought factory after factory at fire-sale prices and used them first for textile production and then as pieces of the puzzle from which the giant Textron conglomerate would emerge.

One of the textile companies that did not leave for the South was Malden Mills, the Massachusetts manufactory that became a symbol of industrial integrity when owner Aaron Feuerstein vowed to rebuild it and to continue paying the company's 3,200 workers after it burned down on December 11, 1995. At the time of the fire, Malden Mills manufactured fabrics for apparel and upholstery but was best known for its Polartec fabric, made from recycled plastic products. Feuerstein kept his promise until forced into bankruptcy in 2003; now owned by a creditors' group, Malden Mills operates one of the most highly advanced mills in the world.

Most of the large producers of bulk textiles closed their doors in New England, as did many of the village-based factories. Although most of the region's remaining textile manufactures produce synthetic material, the traditional textile industry still has a presence. Woolen mills still produce fashion goods and new materials such as fabric for office divider partitions. A cluster of factories produces millions of labels for garment makers. Fabric for recreational outerwear, material for high-tech sails and bulletproof vests, automobile and domestic upholstery, braid for everything from military uniforms to shoelaces, and fabric for industrial filters, blankets, and innumerable other uses still flow from New England mills.

As production has declined, interest has grown in the history of textiles, evident in such institutions as the American Textile History Museum in Lowell and the Francis Cabot Lowell Mill site in Waltham. The textile industry's mark is found not only in the architecture of many cities and towns but also in the region's ethnically diverse populations, even though the textile industry now employs tens of thousands rather than the hundreds of thousands of workers of earlier days.

Mary H. Blewett, ed., *The Last Generation: Work and Life in the Textile Mills of Lowell, Massachusetts, 1910–1960* (1990); Robert F. Dalzell, Jr., *Enterprising Elite: The Boston Associates and the World They Made* (1993); Robert Dublin, *Women at Work: The Transformation of Work and Community in Lowell, Massachusetts, 1826–1860* (1993); Laurence F. Gross, *The Course of Industrial Decline: The Boott Cotton Mills of Lowell, Massachusetts, 1835–1955* (1993); Hannah Josephson,

The Golden Threads; New England's Mill Girls and Magnates (1949); Jonathan Prude, *The Coming of Industrial Order: Town and Factory Life in Rural Massachusetts, 1810–1860* (1983).

Laurence F. Gross

Town, Ithiel (1784–1844)

Engineer, architect, and entrepreneur. Born in Thompson, Conn., Ithiel Town invented the lattice-truss bridge, one of the earliest internationally known industrialized bridge systems. Sent to live in Boston with an uncle when his father died in 1792, Town worked as a carpenter and schoolteacher before studying under the Boston architect Asher Benjamin. Town became one of the most prominent Greek Revival architects in the United States during the early 19th century. Most important, however, is his significance in the development of building construction systems, an importance comparable to that accorded to Henry Ford in the history of manufacturing.

Town's lattice-truss bridge, patented in the United States in 1820, consisted of rectangular frameworks of multiple, diagonally intersecting boards. These frameworks, which resembled lattices, allowed relatively short members, pinned at the intersections with wooden pegs, to form a structure that crossed long spans. This widely built type of covered bridge represented a crucial step in the development of industrial structures and methods of construction. The assembly on land of uniform parts into a framework that could be launched over an opening enabled the rapid construction of thousands of bridges. Reports of Town's bridge appeared in numerous European engineering publications. It became the prototype for the frame structure today known as a truss and inspired theorists to devise standard methods of structural analysis. The lattice design was subsequently translated into iron and steel. Thousands of lattice-truss bridges of wood and metal were built on the expanding networks of roads and railways in the United States and Europe during the 19th century.

Between 1812 and 1815 Town designed the Georgian-style Center Congregational Church and the Gothic-style Trinity Church, both on the New Haven Green in Connecticut. With Isaac Damon of Northampton, Mass., he built many wooden bridges, including a toll bridge across the Connecticut River in Springfield, Mass. His other important designs included the Connecticut State Capitol (1827–31) in New Haven, and the Wadsworth Atheneum in Hartford. Although it was never completed, New Haven's Eagle Bank (1824) was designed by Town in the Greek Revival style; many of his subsequent designs demonstrated this influence, including the Hillhouse Estate

(1828), Skinner Villa (1830), and the Whitney Estate, all in New Haven. In his own villa, Town amassed an enormous private art and architecture library, which he made available to the public and to young architects. His neighbors and friends included Samuel F. B. Morse, with whom he traveled throughout Europe. One of Town's first lattice-truss bridges was built on Eli Whitney's New Haven property. From 1829 through 1835 Town worked in partnership with architect Alexander J. Davis and was based largely in New York, although he retained his ties to New Haven.

Town sought and employed ideas developed throughout the world and contributed substantially to the technology and culture of industrializing nations. Moreover, his lattice-truss bridge helped to shape the idea of what it meant to be a New Englander: practical, efficient, and innovative. Town's work, influenced by an international exchange of ideas, had an impact far beyond the borders of region.

Gregory K. Dreicer "Influence and Intercultural Exchange: The Case of Engineering Schools and Civil Engineering Works in the 19th Century," *History and Technology* 12 (1995); Robert Fletcher, and J. P. Snow. "A History of the Development of Wooden Bridges," *Transactions of the American Society of Civil Engineers* 99 (1934); R. W. Liscombe, "A 'New Era in My Life': Ithiel Town Abroad," *Journal of Society of Architectural Historians* 50 (1991); Roger Hale Newton, *Town and Davis, Architects* (1942).

Gregory K. Dreicer

Waltham and Pawtucket Strikes

In 1815 the first fully mechanized textile mill began production in Waltham, Mass., less than 10 miles west of Boston on the Charles River. By May 1821 the same mill was the scene of the first factory workers' strike in New England. Perhaps in response to the lingering effects of the depression of 1819, the mill owners cut the wages of unmarried men and all women without advance notice. When payday came, the women left work, halting production for two days. Although few details are known about this walkout, its pattern was repeated frequently in the mills of antebellum New England. These strikes were all directed at the textile industry; they focused on a large mill near an urban market; they revolved around female operatives; and they were called to protest a reduction in wages.

Three years later, in May 1824, female weavers in Pawtucket, R.I.—where Samuel Slater first used power-driven machinery to spin thread in 1790—led a strike against lower piece rate wages and longer working hours owing to shorter meal breaks. The weavers, who were severely affected by the 20 percent reduction in piece rates, held a meeting and

agreed not to tend their looms until the old wage standards were restored.

One evening shortly after the strike began, a crowd of workers and sympathetic townsfolk marched through the streets of Pawtucket shouting at the mill owners' houses—stark symbols of wealth and power—and breaking windows in one factory. The following day, concerned that future demonstrations might be even more destructive, mill owners closed their gates and shut down operations until a settlement could be reached. The strike dragged on into a second week with reports of continued unrest and even a case of suspected arson at Edward Walcott's mill. No one was apprehended for setting that fire, and the factory sustained only minor damage.

In the wake of this turbulence, the strike was settled in the early days of June with a compromise between mill owners and workers. Although not all changes in wages and hours were reversed, the owners discovered that they could not unilaterally alter the conditions of employment for a population of determined workers backed by the community. Although strikes in the 1820s, especially by women, were considered bold and even shocking according to prevailing standards of public conduct, owners felt compelled to issue a statement defending their financial decisions after the strikes were settled. The Pawtucket workers—especially the women weavers—learned that solidarity within their ranks and support from the surrounding community were crucial to protect the interests of labor in its growing conflict with the demands of industrial capitalism. This pattern would be repeated among future generations of workers in the mills of New England.

Gary Kulik, "Pawtucket Village and the Strike of 1824: The Origins of Class Conflict in Rhode Island," *Radical History Review* 17 (1978); David Zonderman, *Aspirations and Anxieties: New England Workers and the Mechanized Factory System, 1815–1850* (1992).

David A. Zonderman

Waterpower

Waterpower played a formative role in the physical and economic development of New England from the colonial period, when watermills provided essential products for home consumption and export, through the region's growth as an international center of industry in the 19th century. Once the only alternative to animal or wind power, waterpower declined in importance with the rise of steam power, but in the form of hydroelectricity it remains a valuable regional resource.

New England geography is highly favorable for waterpower. The region's rivers and streams, fed by ample precipitation and descending rapidly over frequent falls, drain the hilly terrain. Most of these watercourses are small, but they are widely distributed and easily harnessed, which made them valuable in the early stages of industrial growth. The tide also provided waterpower for coastal tide mills.

Colonists transplanted European waterpower technology with the first settlements. Although more primitive forms existed, most watermills had a dam to concentrate the water's fall and form a reservoir; raceways to carry the water to and from the waterwheel; and the wheel itself, which was turned by water striking its paddles or filling its buckets. The early forms of the wheel were wooden; by the 1850s iron turbines had proven more efficient. The turning wheel transferred the water's energy to the process machinery through a system of gears, shafts, belts, and pulleys. The local watermill was an important part of the technological knowledge that underlay Yankee ingenuity.

Exploitation of waterpower intensified after Samuel Slater introduced the English factory system to New England in the 1790s. Investors in new industries, especially textiles, colonized the region's watersheds, building hundreds of new mills and associated villages, often in remote locations. Although most industrial villages were small, the power potential of the largest rivers inspired capitalists to undertake unified industrial developments on a scale unmatched elsewhere in the world. The commercial development of large waterpowers created several new industrial cities, beginning with the establishment of Lowell, Mass., in 1822. The proliferation of dams and factories seriously affected the natural environment, disrupting fish migrations, flooding land, and polluting waters. Successful protests against these effects dwindled as industry grew in economic importance.

Water was the principal source of industrial power through the 1860s, aided by many valuable contributions to hydraulic engineering from New England mechanics. Thereafter, industry relied increasingly on the steam engine, with its lower infrastructure costs, greater mobility, and higher capacity for expansion. Steam power was also more reliable; even with improved reservoir systems, waterpower was vulnerable to drought and flood. By 1880 even Lowell obtained more power from steam than water. With the growth of steam power and large-scale urban manufacturing, small rural watermills were gradually abandoned.

In the 1890s waterpower assumed an important role in the new electric power industry, as long-distance electrical transmission systems finally overcame waterpower's geographical constraints. New Englanders used their extensive waterpower experience to develop interconnected systems of central power stations that used hydrogeneration to balance expensive steam generation. New England's major rivers continue to generate hydroelectricity today, while earlier forms of waterpower technology are represented in museum settings.

Robert B. Gordon and Patrick M. Malone, *The Texture of Industry: An Archaeological View of the Industrialization of North America* (1994); Louis C. Hunter, *A History of Industrial Power in the United States, 1780–1930*, vol. 1: *Waterpower in the Century of the Steam Engine* (1979); Hunter, *A History of Industrial Power in the United States, 1780–1930*, vol. 3: *The Transmission of Power* (1991); Theodore Steinberg, *Nature Incorporated; Industrialization and the Waters of New England* (1991).

Richard Greenwood

Whitney, Eli (1765–1825) Inventor. Born

in Westboro, Mass., on December 8, 1765, raised on his family's farm (where he showed more interest in mechanical than agricultural activities), educated at Yale College, and recognized as the inventor of the cotton gin and an espouser of the concept of interchangeable parts, Eli Whitney has come to personify Yankee ingenuity in the minds of many Americans. Although he lived briefly in Georgia, where he devised his cotton gin, Whitney spent almost his entire adult life in New Haven, Conn.; there he won renown for the firearms he produced.

Whitney's mechanical aptitude nearly cost him his college education. Although his father was financially able to pay his tuition, Whitney decided he would rather remain a businessman, manufacturing nails and hatpins in his father's shop, than continue his studies. When he finally entered Yale, he had to underwrite the cost of much of his education, in part by repairing machinery and equipment around the campus. After his graduation in 1792, he decided to become an attorney and moved south to accept a position as a tutor, hoping to simultaneously read law. In Georgia he learned of the need for a machine to remove the seed from upland, or "greenseed," cotton. By the spring of 1793 Whitney had devised such an apparatus. He then returned to New Haven to perfect his invention and begin manufacturing it.

Although he obtained a patent for his cotton gin on March 14, 1794, his invention failed to make Whitney a wealthy man. Because of the simplicity of his machine, southern planters could easily copy it and thus avoid buying his product. By 1798 he realized that protecting his patent rights in court was impossible, and he began to look for another way to make a living.

Facing the possibility of war with France in 1798, the U.S. government needed more muskets than its armories at Harper's Ferry, Va., and Springfield, Mass., could make. Whitney persuaded the government that he could produce 10,000 stands of arms within two years; he would, he told federal officials, introduce to his manufacturing process the concept of interchangeable parts—a concept Thomas Jefferson had heard discussed in France more than a decade before. Whitney eventually took 10 years to deliver the 10,000 muskets. Never during his lifetime was he able to manufacture muskets using interchangeable parts or to devise machines that would cut metal to the tolerances required for them. Still he continued to win contracts from both federal and state governments. By the time of his death in 1825, he had become one of New Haven's leading citizens.

Edwin Battison, "Eli Whitney and the Milling Machine," *Smithsonian Journal of History* 1 (1966); Carolyn C. Cooper, "Eli Whitney's Armory: Myth, Machines, and Material Evidence," *Journal of the New Haven Colony Historical Society* 31 (1984); Constance McLaughlin Green, *Eli Whitney and the Birth of American Technology* (1956); Robert S. Woodbury, "The Legend of Eli Whitney and Interchangeable Parts," *Technology and Culture* 1 (1960).

Thomas J. Farnham

Yankee Ingenuity The heyday of Yankee

ingenuity was in the 19th century, when New Englanders led the nation in industrial innovation. French economist Michel Chevalier noted while visiting in 1834 that there was hardly a Connecticut artisan who could not claim credit for the invention of a novel tool or machine. Early 19th-century New Englanders already had the reputation for inventiveness and enterprise they would enjoy for the next 100 years.

Indeed, between 1790 and 1841 Connecticut residents took out more patents per capita—44 for each 10,000 persons—than those of any other state. Massachusetts followed with 40; industrialized Pennsylvania had 20, and the national average was only 17. The typical New England patentee came from a family of farmers or mechanics and had attended high school; a quarter had completed college. Southern New England's leadership continued through the century: the commissioner of patents noted that through 1891 Connecticut residents still led the country in patents per person. The availability of natural resources, economic factors expressed in capital and markets, and cultural influences encompassing attitudes toward work and novelty all contributed to New Englanders' inventiveness.

The New England that produced so many ingenious Yankees in the early decades of the 19th century also had productive farms on the coastal plain and in the large river valleys. These farms exported food to New York and

Boston, and grew the grain for production of distilled spirits, the region's leading manufactured product. Unlike their counterparts in other regions, however, New England upland farmers, while raising sheep and producing butter and cheese for export, often engaged in manufacturing enterprises, such as ironmaking. The relatively short growing season, long winter nights, and availability of adequate interior lighting gave these farmers time for tinkering. Curiously, however, few of their innovations were farm machinery.

New England had only one natural resource unmatched by other regions: its abundant, reliable water supplies. At its numerous small waterfalls, innovators with modest capital developed mechanical power for tasks that others might have to do by hand. Young people who grew up surrounded by mill mechanisms could appreciate the release from manual labor that machinery could bring. Observing millwork function was a practical introduction to the principles of mechanics.

Yankee ingenuity extended beyond invention to include prowess in both manufacturing and sales. Innovators such as Eli Terry (the clockmaker), the Collins brothers (producers of edged tools), and Samuel Colt (inventor of the revolver) devised ways of producing their wares cheaply enough that ordinary Americans could easily afford them. Rapid population growth outside New England offered potential markets if an inventor could interest people in buying new products. The barter and credit economy New Englanders developed to deal with the scarcity of money in the 18th century had honed their trading instincts. Some entrepreneurial innovators traveled widely to bring their products to new markets; others hired agents. Unlike many of their European competitors, the New Englanders promptly redesigned their products to meet customer preferences reported back to them by their sales staff.

An innovator who built up a growing market had to hire other artisans to help make the products. Before the influx of immigrants late in the century, New England manufacturers found they had to pay relatively high wages to attract youths who would otherwise seek greater opportunities in the West. Hence, Yankee innovators found economic opportunity in creating devices and techniques that reduced the labor needed to produce goods. Stark necessity sometimes inspired inventions that improved the conditions under which artisans worked. Yankee artisans discovered that grinding metal parts to shape was both unpleasant and unhealthy work; to keep their grinding shops staffed, managers at the Springfield Armory and the Collins ax works devised machinery to eliminate much of this hazardous work.

The primary industries New Englanders had established in the 18th century provided essential services that entrepreneurs needed. Thus, when Waterbury, Conn., makers of brass buttons first wanted to have metal rolled, they took it to a mill up the road in Litchfield that had been making nail rod since the first days of the republic. The network of turnpike roads New Englanders had started building at this time made it possible for manufacturers to get such specialized services at acceptable cost.

Favorable physical and market factors would not have supported Yankee innovation without a regional culture that provided incentives and made invention and manufacturing socially acceptable. The largely rural population of New England retained customs and prac-tices established in colonial times. Migration and immigration to manufacturing cities began to alter these established cultural patterns only late in the 19th century. For many decades New Englanders could be conservative in politics and religion and at the same time progressive in their attitudes toward the material world. New Englanders valued education, achieving literacy rates well ahead of those in other regions. They traveled and read widely, conversed and exchanged information freely. New Englanders admired determination and drive, and held both intelligence and craftsmanship in high regard. An innovator could gain respect through success, and neighbors in an otherwise conservative community would admire new devices and techniques. Artisans remained free of the restrictions that factory managers and labor unions later enforced with rigid job descriptions.

Although some, like Charles Goodyear, succeeded with physical and chemical processes through persistent trial and error, Yankee innovators usually did best with mechanical devices, which lent themselves to tinkering. In the 20th century, innovative New Englanders carried their mechanical skills to new industries throughout the United States.

Carolyn C. Cooper, *Shaping Invention: Thomas Blanchard's Machinery and Patent Management in 19th-Century America* (1991); Robert B. Gordon and Patrick M. Malone, *Texture of Industry: An Archeological View of the Industrialization of America* (1994); Donald R. Hoke, *Ingenious Yankees: The Rise of the American System of Manufactures in the Private Sector* (1990); David A. Hounshell, *From the American System to Mass Production, 1800–1932* (1984); Otto Mayer and Robert C. Post, eds., *Yankee Enterprise: The Rise of the American System of Manufacturing* (1981).

Robert B. Gordon

Law

Alfred L. Brophy, Section Editor
Katherine Hermes, Alexandra Maravel, and James Walsh, Consulting Editors

INTRODUCTION

Legal thought has been a principal export and a central part of New England's intellectual culture since European settlers first arrived. John Winthrop's 1630 sermon aboard the *Arabella*, "A Modell of Christian Charity," one of the earliest statements of New England principles, centered on moral laws. For generations, the Bible provided a basic text to guide New Englanders; the need for obedience to law and what this means has been a central theme throughout New England's history. Conflicts over both religious freedom and the role of religion in civic life, from the expulsion of Roger Williams to the abolition of slavery to gay marriage, have resonated beyond New England's borders.

RELIGIOUS INSPIRATION AND LOCAL PRACTICE IN COLONIAL NEW ENGLAND

From the founding of the Plymouth Colony in 1620, law has been a central feature of New England colonial life. There were strict laws governing behavior, regulating trade with Native Americans, and controlling such issues as inheritance and trade with other colonists. Court officials enforced laws about church attendance, dress, and the sale of weapons to Native Americans; restricted work on the Sabbath; and regulated the treatment of servants and the sale of alcohol. The *Lawes and Libertyes* of Massachusetts, compiled in 1648, illustrates the colonists' concern with order. Based on the Old Testament as well as on English customary and statute law, the *Lawes* ordered, among other provisions, that Anabaptists (those who rejected the Puritan sacrament of infant baptism) be banished because they were "the Incendiaries of Commonwealths and the infectors of persons in main matters of religion and the troublers of Churches in most places where they have been." The *Lawes* permitted slavery and made capital crimes of adultery as well as blasphemy, rebellion by a son against his father, and witchcraft. Murder was also a capital crime.

Yet capital punishment was extremely rare in colonial New England, much rarer than in England at the time. It was only occasionally imposed on adulterers, and, based on the very limited evidence, women adulterers seem to have been sentenced to death more frequently than men. The debate in New England over capital punishment, particularly in the case of adultery, illustrates the divisions within the community over the extent to which the Old Testament standards of the *Lawes* were accepted. While we often think of New England as a godly community, in which the Bible provided a "rule to walk by," many departed from biblical injunctions. Nonetheless, the colonists believed, as the foreword to the *Lawes* stated, that laws were necessary for good government. "A Commonwealth without laws," to borrow a metaphor from the time, "is like a Ship without rigging and steeradge." And it was the magistrates who had to be good navigators of the ship of state, for they were seen as guides to the community.

So although the death penalty was rarely imposed, prosecutions for adultery and fornication (for which the punishment might be an order of marriage or a whipping) were common, probably in large part because these crimes threatened Puritan social control. Women were subject to a double standard in adultery cases, for adultery was defined as a crime involving a married woman. Hence, a married man who had an affair with an unmarried woman was guilty only of fornication, while a married woman who had an affair with an unmarried man was guilty of adultery. Men and women tended to face different punishments as well. Typically, men guilty of fornication were required to pay child support, while women were whipped.

Civil authorities tried cases involving religious beliefs. Two early prominent cases were the trials before the Massachusetts General Court of Roger Williams (1635) and Anne Hutchinson (1637). Williams had advocated such heresies as expanded communion, while Hutchinson had criticized the colonists' narrow, legalistic focus on morality. Denounced as an antinomian (one who acts according to divine inspiration rather than law), Hutchinson, like Williams, threatened the Puritan theological consensus; her religious crime led to her banishment, and she settled in Rhode Island. She was killed by Native Americans in 1643 in what some saw as divine vengeance. The trials of Williams and Hutchinson, as well as similar cases involving Quakers, tended to bring the idea of the rule of law into ill repute. As the foreword to the *Lawes and Libertyes* reminded colonists, it was not enough to have laws, "except they be also just." At least in their application, many of the 17th-century laws were not.

Perhaps the most notorious linking of religion and the law was the Salem witchcraft trials of 1692. Although recent research reveals that witchcraft trials took place throughout the 17th century in Connecticut and Massachusetts, none are as famous as the Salem trials. The trials—colored by fear of foreigners (like the slave Tituba) and Native Americans, as well as by disdain for poor and weak members of the community who were accused of witchcraft—represented a remarkable breakdown of justice, even as the community turned to the legal process to uphold the social order. The trials are synonymous in American history with unjust prosecutions. Convictions based on "spectral" evidence (testimony by accusers that defendants appeared in a dream or vision) led to capital punishment. Nineteen people were hanged and one pressed to death during the course of the crisis, which began in February and lasted to September. Yet even as fear gripped the community, some tried to halt the proceedings. The respected minister Increase Mather published a pamphlet urging that it "were better that ten suspected witches should escape than one innocent person should be condemned." In the fall of 1692 the community realized it had been too zealous and began a period of atonement. Samuel Sewall, one of the judges at the trials, apologized in 1697, as did some of the accusers. It is unclear how strongly Sewall's infamous role in the trial might have affected his beliefs in human rights, but there may be a connection between his acknowledgment of wrongdoing in 1697 and his publication in 1700 of an antislavery tract, *The Selling of Joseph.*

It was in deciding less well-known, but very important everyday cases that the courts established their authority and brought order to New England. The thousands of criminal and civil cases decided during the colonial period established the importance of the rule of law. The work of those early courts can be seen in the manuscript notes of cases kept by justices of the peace. William Pynchon's notebooks offer a particularly clear look at the legal system in the late 17th century. Pynchon served as a justice in western Massachusetts along the Connecticut River, where he dealt with land transactions and disputes over debts. From Pynchon's notebooks, we can see that the courts served as a way of airing disputes and teaching participants about community values. Many people attended the court meetings, and they were able to see who was being punished for criminal offenses and how civil disputes (such as defamation, mistreatment of servants, breach of contract, failure to pay mortgages, questions about paternity, and claims among heirs to an estate) were handled.

The volume of litigation reached extraordinary levels in the colonial era, with sometimes half or more of the adult male members of the community serving as jurors, witnesses in lawsuits, or parties to lawsuits each year. Disputes between neighbors were usually settled informally, although courts handled disputes between neighbors and between colonists from neighboring towns. The judges were always white men, but the other participants in the court system were surprisingly diverse. Women participated frequently as litigants and as witnesses. In some cases involving paternity of children, women served as jurors. Native Americans and African Americans appeared sometimes as litigants (even against whites) or witnesses and at other times as defendants. For instance, in the 1710s, a court in Edgartown, Mass., adjudicated a dispute between two Native Americans who both claimed the right to lease grazing rights to colonial settlers on Chappaquiddick Island. It is sometimes difficult to interpret such high rates of participation. In part they reflect widespread conflicts within the community. But they also reflect a well-functioning court system, which funneled potentially dangerous disputes into a forum where they could be resolved without violence. The high rate of participation in the administration of justice, including jury service, correlates to the growth of the idea of participatory democracy, whose most visible New England symbol was the town meeting.

Sometimes disputes within families became legal cases. Parents in New England frequently held on to their estates until they died, which meant that children frequently did not receive their inheritance until they were well into middle age. The practice led to conflicts over inheritance, which appeared in courts in many ways, including criminal trials. Thomas Cornell of Rhode Island, for example, may have murdered his mother, Rebecca, in 1673 to obtain his inheritance. Over the course of Thomas Cornell's murder trial the court heard a variety of evidence, including testimony from one of Cornell's neighbors that Cornell's specter had appeared in a dream and testimony that Cornell had quarreled with his mother. Cornell was convicted and executed.

The courts were also notorious for their informality in the 17th century. Few colonists had much formal training in law, and magistrates and litigants relied on manuals created for justices of the peace that told how courts should operate and on books of forms for real estate transactions, wills, and contracts. Until around 1820 the availability of law books in New England was limited. Even well-stocked libraries had at best a few dozen volumes; almost all volumes were printed in England. Few people had access to much more than William Blackstone's *Commentaries on the Laws of England* (1765–69). People learned law by seeing it in operation, with local knowledge supplemented by law books. Law was thus particularly susceptible to modification in New England. Rather than a code of laws, legal actors relied on principles that seemed to them correct. This pragmatism is illustrated by the remark of an 18th-century New Hampshire judge that the jury should "do justice between the parties, not by any quirks of the law out of Coke or Blackstone—books that I never read and never will—but by common sense as between man and man."

The courts also worked within an imperial context, for they were established pursuant to royal charters. Colonists could even appeal to the Privy Council, a privilege that reminded them of their connections (even if remote) to Great Britain. The courts were places where colonists were tutored in rules, the power of their superiors and the crown, and their community's values. The colonists sometimes challenged their place in the empire, such as when they deposed the royal governor Edmund Andros, who in 1686 had been installed over an entity called the Dominion of New England (combining New England, New York, and New Jersey), which was intended to consolidate the crown's power in America. Andros was overthrown in 1689, and Massachusetts received a new royal charter in 1691.

At certain times, social norms proved to be as important as law in regulating behavior. In 1639, for example, the merchant Robert Keayne was fined by a Massachusetts court and subsequently censured in a sermon by John Cotton for charging too much for certain commodities. Keayne's 1653 will sought to explain his actions.

REVOLUTION AND CONSTITUTION

As Americans headed into the Revolution, conflicts over law—who were the legitimate lawmakers and what were the rights of the colonists—arose again. Many of the ideological origins of the Revolution lie in New England arguments about rights to representation and freedom from imperial domination. These arguments increased and took on stronger force over the course of the 18th century. In 1761, for instance, the Boston lawyer James Otis argued that "writs of assistance"—in essence, general search warrants that permitted British customs officials to search merchants' warehouses and even private homes without probable cause—violated the colonists' natural rights. Otis lost the case, but his ideas took hold. In 1768 Otis and Samuel Adams issued a letter against the newly passed Townshend Acts, which imposed new taxes on the colonists. Tensions continued to mount until in March 1770 a minor dispute between a merchant and a British sentry escalated into what was later called the Boston Massacre, leaving five Americans dead and four British soldiers on trial for murder. John Adams, soon to be famous as a defender of revolution, here defended the soldiers and won their acquittal. Still, tensions simmered. Bostonians began to take action on their own to protest what they believed were unfair laws, including the act that quartered 4,000 British troops in Boston. Calling themselves the Sons of Liberty, the group, which may have had thousands of members, staged a number of protests, including the famous Boston Tea Party of December 1773, led by Samuel Adams. Less than two years later the Revolution began.

One might construct an argument about the intellectual descent of legal thought from John Adams to Henry David Thoreau that parallels the historian Perry Miller's thesis in "From Edwards to Emerson" that the changes in New England theology descend from Jonathan Edwards to Ralph Waldo Emerson. For there was much in common between Adams's legal thought—and that of other New England lawyers of the revolutionary generation—concerning the rights of the colonists and the ideas of the abolitionist generation, characterized by Henry David Thoreau, about the need to obey only just laws. Those conflicts between law and justice, between internal moral compass and the dictates of government, reappear periodically throughout American history.

The Revolution led to several substantial changes in New England law. Most important, slavery was abolished following the decision of Chief Justice William Cushing of the Massachusetts Supreme Judicial Court in the Quock Walker cases (1783). The cases arose when Quock Walker, a slave, ran away from his owner, Nathaniel Jennison; when Jennison found Walker he beat him. Claiming that he had been promised his freedom when he reached the age of 25, Walker sued and won. Later,

The Boston Massacre as depicted by engraver Paul Revere (1770)

Jennison was also charged with assault and battery; for purposes of the prosecution, it was important to know whether Walker was a slave at the time he was beaten or whether he was free. Cushing charged the jury that "perpetual servitude can no longer be tolerated in our government." Revolutionary ideology had touched slaves as well as free people—slaves had even petitioned the Massachusetts governor for relief.

After the Revolution there were also reforms in inheritance law. Rhode Island revised its intestacy law to provide for equal distribution of property among children, rather than awarding the oldest male child a disproportionate share. Such changes corresponded to changes in how the revolutionary generation viewed established wealth. Where English society celebrated long-established wealth and the right of inheritance, the revolutionary generation, on the whole, did not. The Americans' Enlightenment vision of society was at odds with the inheritance of privilege. As with so many other themes that recur throughout American history and law, the new sentiments toward inheritance were captured by Nathaniel Hawthorne. His short story "My Kinsman, Major Molineaux" concerns the revolutionary generation's desire to depose its previous rulers. Another change ushered in by the Revolution was the increase in enfranchisement, as states eliminated discriminatory voting requirements. In 1784 New Hampshire eliminated the property requirement; Massachusetts adopted a similar reform. In 1820 Massachusetts simplified its voting requirements to allow males over 21 who paid any taxes to vote.

One of the most significant changes for New England was the postrevolutionary alteration in the relation of religion and government. That change is best seen in the First Amendment of the Constitution prohibiting Congress from making any law respecting religion. Massachusetts maintained Congregationalism as the state religion until 1833; Connecticut did not disestablish its church until 1818; and New Hampshire did not do so until 1819. Conflict over religious freedom—in which freedom was not always the winner—cropped up throughout the antebellum period. In 1848, for example, New Hampshire citizens petitioned the legislature to restrict the rights of Shakers, but Franklin Pierce successfully defended the Shakers. In 1834 an anti-Catholic mob burned the Ursuline Convent in Charlestown (now Somerville), Mass.; Catholics unsuccessfully sought compensation for the destruction.

New England also contributed important leaders to the judiciary, the Congress, and the bar of the new nation. Early U.S. Supreme Court justices from New England include William Cushing, Oliver Ellsworth, and Joseph Story. Other important leaders of the early bar were Jonathan Trumbull and Daniel Webster.

Even New England fictional literature explored key questions of law and jurisprudence. Royall Tyler, a justice on the Vermont Supreme Court from 1801 to 1813 and professor of law at the University of Vermont from 1811 to 1814, examined the moral choices made by King Solomon in his play *The Judgement of Solomon*. Nathaniel Hawthorne published *The Scarlet Letter* (1850), a densely complex novel that presented a female adulterer as a flawed heroine, rather than a criminal. Hawthorne condemned the community's rigid laws and attitudes more than the fallen Hester Prynne, who struggles to atone for her sin.

Periodical literature, like the *North American Review,* published in Boston, frequently commented on changes in legal thought. The *Review* focused on the disputes between Whigs and Democrats, such as the radical New York Democrat William Sampson's critique of the law as unfair or arguments over changes in Supreme Court doctrine. Similarly, the Massachusetts lawyer and later U.S. senator Robert Rantoul's "Oration at Scituate," delivered on July 4, 1836, urged codification as a way of reducing the uncertainty and irrationality of the common law. Although moderate in stance, the *Review* frequently focused attention on radicals who were seeking to reform the law.

Even as New England was changing the law of inheritance, slavery, and religion, there were changes at the national level. The U.S. Constitution established national courts, which were favorable to established property interests. The Judiciary Act of 1789 allowed the U.S. Supreme Court to hear appeals from state supreme courts, thus establishing federal judicial supremacy. The Constitution also established a powerful federal government, which was capable of enforcing laws against agrarian interests. The Constitution was inspired in part by Shays's Rebellion in western Massachusetts in late 1786 and early 1787. Daniel Shays, a farmer, had petitioned with other farmers for relief from taxes, as well as from the burden of paper currency and judicial reform, which would have treated debtors more favorably. Denied legal redress, the farmers began an armed insurrection, preventing courts from meeting in Northampton, Worcester, Concord, and elsewhere. By February 1787, however, Massachusetts troops had dispersed the rebels and most had been offered general amnesty. Two rebels were executed for their role in the rebellion.

Later, under Chief Justice John Marshall of Virginia, the Supreme Court, in *Dartmouth College v. Woodward* (1819) and a series of similar cases, protected Dartmouth College's corporate charter—and by extension other contracts—from interference by the state. And in late 1814 and early 1815, angered by the loss of trade caused by the maritime embargo imposed during the War of 1812, Federalists met in what became known as the Hartford Convention to consider a series of proposals to address their concerns over war and the power of southern states, although the delegates rejected resolutions supporting secession. The movement died with the end of the war, but it illustrates the rich constitutional theorizing that took place in New England during the early years of the United States.

EDUCATION, LEGAL CHANGE, AND SLAVERY

In the colonial and early national periods, many judges had limited knowledge of the law and indeed expressed hostility to formal law, but this attitude changed in the early 19th century. The first law school in New England was established in Litchfield, Conn., by Tapping Reeve. The Litchfield Law School operated from 1784 to 1833 and educated nearly 1,000 students, including John C. Calhoun, Aaron Burr, and more than 100 future members of Congress. Reeve lectured and held moot courts; he later published some of his lectures in *The Law of Baron and Femme* (1816), an early legal text. Harvard began its law school in 1817 and had as its first professor the Supreme Court justice Joseph Story. At the time, legal thought was becoming better developed. Increasingly sophisticated doctrines were published in admiralty law, commercial and real estate law, and constitutional law. A major development of the early 19th century was the publication of reports of court cases. Those "reporters" made available well-reasoned judicial decisions on a variety of subjects, and each year more precedents became available that lawyers and judges could—and had to—cite. Around 1820 printed reports of cases became so numerous that it became necessary to publish reference works that catalogued and analyzed them.

Beginning in the early 19th century, Boston became a publishing center of legal texts. The most important early U.S. catalog of case law is Nathan Dane's multivolume *General Abridgment and Digest of American Law* (1823–29), which made the entire case law accessible. Treatises also digested the (often conflicting) precedents. Much like Francis Lieber's *Encyclopaedia Americana* (1829–33), another New England publishing project of the antebellum era, Joseph Story's treatises on such topics as constitutional law and contracts made it possible for people far removed from libraries to have access to the most sophisticated legal ideas. The leading legal periodical of the 1820s through the 1840s was the *American Jurist,* published in Boston. It represents the attempts to bring the law into line with modern commercial principles and to direct legislation toward the promotion of economic growth and middle-class values of morality and industry. If William Blackstone's *Commentaries* represented the "mysterious science of the law" (in the historian Daniel Boorstin's phrase), American law in the early 19th century could be said to represent the "understandable science of the law." For American judges sought to make the law understandable.

Karl Llewellyn, one of the leading scholars of law in the 20th century, called the antebellum period the "golden age of American law." It was a time when judges and lawyers vowed not to be bound by outmoded rules. They tested precedents against reason and experience and adopted new ways of thinking. If this sounds like Ralph Waldo Emerson's proposal for the best way for students to proceed, it is because Emerson's 1837 Phi Beta Kappa oration at Harvard, "The American Scholar," captured what Americans were doing in all areas of thought. No longer would they be bound by outmoded ideas or ancient precedents. For, as Joseph Story said in his Phi Beta Kappa oration at Harvard (1826), "The civil and the common law have yielded to the pressure of the times, and have adopted much, which philosophy and experience have recommended, although it stood upon no text of the Pandects, and claimed no support from the feudal policy. Commercial law, at least so far as England and America are concerned, is the creation of the eighteenth century." The Transcendental emphasis on reason over precedent was so influential in law that we might speak of this period as the "Transcendentalization" of American law.

Yet Phi Beta Kappa orators frequently mocked Transcendental ideas. Timothy Walker, who brought New England legal ideas to Cincinnati, where he opened a law school (the forerunner of the University of Cincinnati), captured in an 1850 Phi Beta Kappa lecture at Harvard the Transcendentalists' contempt of precedent: "We will no longer walk in the ancient paths. . . . We must reform them altogether. To this end, we pronounce antiquity a humbug, precedent a sham, prescription a lie, and reverence folly. We have been priest-ridden, and king-ridden, and judge-ridden, and school-ridden, and wealth-ridden, long enough." Walker went on to argue against legal reforms in such areas as women's rights and criminal punishment. One important mid-19th-century reform was the restriction of "coverture," the right of a husband to control his wife's property. Through married women's property acts legislatures throughout the country protected wives' property from attachment by their husbands' creditors. Walker thought that the changes in law were too great and too rapid.

Thus, while Emerson and the New England jurists shared a common desire to remake precedent to serve their present values, they disagreed on what those values were and how great the changes should be. Many jurists seem to have been engaged in a mission to make American law receptive to commercial interests, a goal at odds with much of Transcendental thought. Thus, we hear judges remaking the rules regarding contracts and torts to promote economic growth. In contracts, no longer could someone plead that he or she had received an unfair bargain as a way of avoiding performance on a contract. Where in the 18th century judges appeared (and the emphasis here is *appeared*—subsequent research may show that there was no golden era of fairness in New England law) to offer some mitigation of harsh rules, in the commercial 19th century jurists made few such calculations. Similarly, in employment law, judges limited the rights of employees to recover for workplace injuries. The fellow-servant rule, for instance, established in the 1837 case of *Farwell v. Boston Railroad*, prohibited a railroad employee injured by the negligent acts of another employee from recovering against his employer. Another popular doctrine used to limit recovery was contributory negligence. However, on the side of the employees, the Massachusetts Supreme Judicial Court upheld the legality of trade unions in 1840 in *Commonwealth v. Hunt*. During this period, distinguished jurists such as Story and Justice Lemuel Shaw of the Massachusetts Supreme Judicial Court set precedents that were followed by the rest of the nation. Other important antebellum jurists from New England include U.S. Supreme Court justices Levi Woodbury, Benjamin R. Curtis, and Nathan Clifford.

The Supreme Court altered somewhat the protection given by Massachusetts to property rights in 1837 in the *Charles River Bridge* case. The Supreme Court, under the leadership of newly appointed Chief Justice Roger Taney of Maryland, a Democrat, allowed a new bridge over the Charles River to compete with another, existing bridge. Many feared that the decision, over a dissent by Justice Story, would allow legislatures to infringe on vested property rights. Meanwhile, many Democrats hailed the decision as promoting "improvement" and reducing the price of crossing the river.

As judges were remaking precedent to comport with their new, probusiness values, disputes arose over what values they should respect. One of Harriet Beecher Stowe's first published stories, "Love versus Law," dealt with the conflict between warm sentiments of the heart and cold legal calculations. The story concerns a property dispute between Deacon Enos Dudley, the Jones family, and their neighbor Uncle Jaw. Dudley had purchased a prime piece of property from Jones, but Jones died before delivering the deed. Jones's daughters then inherited his property. Meanwhile, Uncle Jaw was upset because Jones's property had a dam, which periodically flooded his property. Because of his anger about the flooding—as well as his jealousy of the Joneses wealth—Uncle Jaw refuses to allow his son to marry Jones's daughter. Deacon Enos settles the dispute by giving up his claim to the Jones land. The lesson, which Uncle Jaw has difficulty understanding, is that love is more important than property.

Those conflicts appeared in much more dramatic form in Stowe's 1852 novel *Uncle Tom's Cabin*. For there Stowe took on the Fugitive Slave Act of 1850, which gave slaveowners extraordinary powers in recovering runaway slaves. The act became a major site for the conflict between respect for law versus individual conscience, one of the hallmarks of New England legal thought. Through hundreds of sermons, pamphlets, and public addresses, New Englanders explored the conflict between the duty to uphold a federal statute and individual feelings of humanity. The act had important support from Senator Daniel Webster of Massachusetts, and the controversy surrounding it involved much of New England in discussion of jurisprudence. Even many, like Webster, who opposed slavery saw value in the union. Justice Lemuel Shaw ordered the return of the fugitive slave Thomas Sims in April 1851, arousing the anger of abolitionists, who were incensed by his implication of Massachusetts in the return of human beings to slavery. In 1854, as President Franklin Pierce's administration was taking strenuous action to enforce the act, the fugitive Anthony Burns was arrested by the U.S marshal in Boston and, amid violent protests by abolitionists, was returned to the South. We get a hint of the conflicts Shaw felt in Herman Melville's novella *Billy Budd*, which ostensibly concerns the trial of a seaman for homicide. Though Captain Vere, who presides at the hastily held trial, believes it unjust to sentence Budd to death, he nevertheless complies with the Articles of War (the law) and orders Budd's execution, an action that haunts him the rest of his life. *Billy Budd* speaks to the conflict between justice and law. Perhaps it is really about the Fugitive Slave Act and the conflicts that judges faced who enforced that law; it is noteworthy that Shaw was Melville's father-in-law.

The act led many to take up their pens, including Ralph Waldo Emerson and Henry David Thoreau. Though neither had legal training, both engaged in questioning the jurisprudence that called for such inhumane actions. In so doing they took part in an important critique of legal thought: questioning whether one should follow the law or one's conscience. Stowe's solution was to touch the heart, to move people to do what was right, regardless of the law. Indeed, much of *Uncle Tom's Cabin* is a critique of law. Stowe notes early in the novel that "over and above" the institution of slavery "there broods a portentous shadow—the shadow of law." Stowe's words may be the source of a famous phrase by Justice Oliver Wendell Holmes, Jr.: law is "not a brooding omnipresence in the sky, but the articulate voice of some sovereign or quasi-sovereign that can be identified." In New England legal discourse was general; not only could Harriet Beecher Stowe criticize the law but Oliver Wendell Holmes listened to her. Four years after *Uncle Tom's Cabin* appeared, Stowe published *Dred: A Tale of the Great Dismal Swamp*, which engaged specifically with the conflict between duty to law and duty to humanity. In *Dred,* Stowe portrayed a judge who was privately against slavery but felt compelled to issue a proslavery decision. The judge, based in some ways on Justice Thomas Ruffin of North Carolina, followed the law rather than his own internal moral compass. *Dred* was Stowe's explanation of why judges and legislators would not act on humane sentiments.

Another important slave case, arising from the admiralty court in Connecticut, concerned the *Amistad* mutiny, in which slaves on the Spanish ship *Amistad* seized control of the ship. They were captured and tried in Hartford; the case ended up in 1841 in front of the U.S. Supreme Court, where the defendants were represented by former president John Quincy Adams. His argument centered on the claim that the slaves were not slaves under Spanish law and hence had the right to use violence to secure their freedom. Adams prevailed, but the Supreme Court's opinion did not implicate the legality of slavery, only the status of the people on the ship. Perhaps the single most important slave case was *Dred Scott v. Sandford,* decided by the Supreme Court in 1857. Over a dissent by Justice Benjamin R. Curtis of Massachusetts, the court struck down the Missouri Compromise and held that slavery was legal throughout the territories. The lines between New England antislavery and southern proslavery legal thought were drawn, and the issue could be settled only by war.

HOLMES, HARVARD, AND THE PROGRESSIVES

After the Civil War, New England continued to dominate the legal culture of the United States. Much of the agenda for Reconstruction was driven by ideas associated with New England, including those of Senator Charles Sumner of Massachusetts. For the abolitionists based in New England and places settled by New Englanders set the nation on the path toward abolition, then remade American law with the 13th, 14th, and 15th Amendments, which outlawed slavery, guaranteed equal rights regardless of race, and provided for voting rights regardless of race.

The postwar period of legal thought was dominated by Oliver Wendell Holmes, Jr., and the Harvard Law School. Holmes was a member of Boston's Metaphysical Club, which studied pragmatism. His famous book *The Common Law* (1881), based on the Lowell Lectures given in Boston, sought to explain legal development as a phenomenon that responded to history and to the positive commands of the state, rather than to natural law. Holmes later delivered an important lecture at Boston University, "The Path of the Law," which further explored the centrality of human experience to legal development. Although the origins of this thinking appeared in antebellum opinions, Holmes, who served on the Massachusetts Supreme Judicial Court from 1882 until 1902 and then on the U.S. Supreme Court until 1932, made American law modern: something that could be self-consciously shaped and that responded to the commands of the legislature. For example, Holmes opposed minimum wage and maximum hour legislation as an interference with property rights.

While Holmes was working as a jurist in Massachusetts, Harvard Law School was remaking legal education. In 1871 Christopher Columbus Langdell introduced the "case law method," which taught students law through study of judicial cases.

Langdell's method, which survives at law schools more or less intact to this day, made it possible for law schools to educate large numbers of students relatively inexpensively. Other notable Harvard professors of the time included John Chipman Gray and James Barr Ames. Gray became so outraged at an opinion of the Massachusetts Supreme Judicial Court that permitted a wealthy but spendthrift heir to receive money from a trust but avoid creditors that he wrote a treatise, *Restraints on the Alienation of Property* (1883) opposing the case. Professor Gray's ideas were rejected by many states, but his treatise *Rule against Perpetuities* (1886) has dominated the field for more than a century. Later Roscoe Pound served as professor and dean of Harvard Law School (1916–36) and popularized "sociological jurisprudence," which focused on the connections between law and social conditions.

While Cambridge's elite were engaging in such high-level theorizing about law, Boston was facing much more mundane crises. Immigration from Ireland beginning in the 1840s and from southern Europe beginning in the 1880s had led to class and ethnic conflicts, as concern rose over poverty and crime. Sometimes those tensions appeared in labor union conflicts, such as the Boston Police Strike of 1919; at other times they manifested themselves in criminal trials, such as the 1927 trial of Nicola Sacco and Bartolomeo Vanzetti, two Italian immigrants, whose arrest, conviction, and execution for murder and armed robbery was believed to be politically motivated. During the Progressive Era, New England was a place of strict moral regulation, and the region became known for its frequent use of government power to regulate the health and safety of its citizens. Prohibition and the popular "science" of eugenics notwithstanding, such regulation could be positive: the Progressive Era was also a time of reforms in child labor and of minimum wage and maximum hour legislation. The Boston attorney Louis Brandeis fought for unions' and women's rights. His brief in favor of the state in *Muller v. Oregon,* decided in 1908 by the Supreme Court, was based on an exploration of the effect of long working hours on women's health. Today briefs that explore the sociological implications of a law are still known as "Brandeis briefs." In 1916 President Woodrow Wilson nominated Brandeis to the U.S. Supreme Court. Following contentious Senate hearings, which focused on his "fitness" (which many took to be a code word for his religion and progressive stances), Brandeis was confirmed as the first Jew on the court. Paradoxically, given the racism of many of the leaders of the Progressive Era, the fight for equal rights for blacks also became more vocal; one leader was the Boston corporate attorney Moorefield Story, the first president of the National Association for the Advancement of Colored People.

NEW DEAL, CIVIL RIGHTS, AND BEYOND

The New Dealers brought the legal realists—those who like Brandeis focused on the connections of law to society—to power in Washington. The legal realists, successors to both Justice Holmes's pragmatism and Roscoe Pound's sociological jurisprudence, were well represented on the faculty of the Yale Law School, which was by the 1930s one of the most progressive law schools in the country. These thinkers' concerns with humanity and the effects of law on society led them to seek government intervention in the economy and public welfare across a broad spectrum. What the legal faculty had in common was a concern about the social effects of law and the effects on law of social forces, as well as a skepticism regarding the role of rules in law and a focus on "nonlegal" explanations of "legal" phenomena. William O. Douglas left the Yale Law School faculty to serve at the Securities and Exchange Commission and then as a justice on the Supreme Court (1939–75). Other important realists on the Yale faculty were Jerome Frank, author of *Law and the Modern Mind* (1935), who later served as a judge on the U.S. Court of Appeals, and Thurman Arnold, author of *The Symbols of Government* (1935) and *The Folklore of Capitalism* (1937), who later headed the Justice Department's Antitrust Division and served as a judge on the Court of Appeals. Felix Frankfurter of the Harvard Law School faculty, another progressive, replaced Louis Brandeis on the Supreme Court in 1939.

The post–World War II period, with the optimism born of the Allies' victory, soon changed to a time of fear over the alleged presence of communists in the government. During the Army-McCarthy hearings in 1954, held to investigate a series of charges by Senator Joseph McCarthy of Wisconsin against the U.S. Army, the Boston attorney Joseph Welch confronted McCarthy over his accusation that Welch's young assistant Fred Fischer was a communist sympathizer. The hearings, which placed a New England corporate lawyer against a midwestern senator, led to McCarthy's downfall.

In the 1960s, as the sexual revolution and the Civil Rights movement gripped the nation, New Englanders contributed in important ways to both. In the early 1960s, the director of Connecticut's Planned Parenthood and a Yale Medical School professor challenged an 1879 state statute prohibiting the use or distribution of contraceptives. Justice William O. Douglas's opinion for the court in *Griswold v. Connecticut* (1965) struck down the statute on the grounds that it interfered with a married couple's privacy rights. The opinion is credited, along with Douglas's 1945 opinion in *Skinner v. Oklahoma,* which struck down an act permitting the sterilization of repeat offenders, with starting the line of reasoning that led to the Supreme Court's 1973 decision in *Roe v. Wade,* which guaranteed the right of a pregnant woman to an abortion. The Justice Department under President John F. Kennedy from Massachusetts took major steps toward integrating public schools in Little Rock, Ark., and public universities in Alabama and Mississippi. Later, President Richard Nixon's Justice Department pushed for the integration of public schools in Boston, which led to busing and violence in 1974. New England, then, both led and mirrored the nation.

New England's influence in the legal culture of the nation continues. One of the most respected U.S. Supreme Court justices, David H. Souter, is from New Hampshire. Souter has served on the court since 1990, when he was nominated by President George W. Bush on the recommendation of Bush's chief of staff, John Sununu of New Hampshire. Souter, who has been a leading moderate on the court, served as a judge on the New Hampshire Supreme Court and then briefly as a judge on the U.S. Court of Appeals before his appointment.

Close connections between law schools and the bench can still be found in New

England. Supreme Court Justice Stephen G. Breyer is a former Harvard Law School professor; another Harvard Law School professor, Charles Fried, served on the Massachusetts Supreme Judicial Court; Guido Calabresi, formerly dean of Yale Law School, now serves on the U.S. Court of Appeals; and Ellen Ash Peters, who recently retired as chief justice of the Connecticut Supreme Court, served as a professor at Yale. Many legal academics in New England, particularly at Harvard and Yale Law Schools, are leading legal theorists, including Akhil Reed Amar, Bruce Ackerman, and Carol Rose of Yale and Lawrence Tribe, Martha Minow, Randall Kennedy, and Mary Ann Glendon of Harvard. A core characteristic of much of their work is the belief that law ought to serve humane values—a belief hardly unique to New England law but one that has received special reverence in the region, especially in the recent work of faculty like Yale's William Eskridge and Stephen Carter and Harvard's Charles Ogletree and Morton Horwitz. That belief is central to the Critical Legal Studies movement of the 1970s and 1980s and its successor the Critical Race movement of the 1990s and today. Critical Legal Studies also emphasized the political nature of legal decisions and the indeterminacy of legal rules.

Perhaps the best recent evidence of the search for humanity in law is the 2003 *Goodridge* decision of the Massachusetts Supreme Judicial Court, which ruled that it was unconstitutional to deny marriage to same-sex partners. The decision surprised many but reaffirmed the role of state courts in defining constitutional rights, even as members of the Massachusetts legislature scrambled to overturn the decision through legislative action or constitutional amendment. As courts around the country explore *Goodridge*'s implications for their states and as legislatures respond, we are reminded that New England courts are continuing to shape doctrine as they have throughout the nation's history.

Jerold S. Auerbach, *Unequal Justice Lawyers and Social Change in Modern America* (1977); Bernard Bailyn, *The Ideological Origins of the American Revolution* (1967); Mary Sarah Bilder, *The Transatlantic Constitution: Colonial Legal Culture and the Empire* (2004); Paul Boyer and Stephen Nissenbaum, *Salem Possessed: The Social Origins of Witchcraft* (1974); Alfred L. Brophy, "Reason and Sentiment: The Moral Worlds and Modes of Reasoning of Antebellum Jurists," *Boston University Law Review* 79 (1999); Elaine Forman Crane, *Killed Strangely: The Death of Rebecca Cornell* (2002); Cornelia Hughes Dayton, *Women before the Bar: Gender, Law, and Society in Connecticut, 1639–1789* (1995); Robert Ferguson, *Law and Letters in American Life* (1987); William W. Fisher III, Morton J. Horwitz, and Thomas Reed, eds., *American Legal Realism* (1993); Julius Goebel, "King's Law and Local Custom in 17th-Century New England," *Columbia Law Review* 31 (1931); David D. Hall, *Witch-Hunting in 17th-Century New England: A Documentary History, 1638–1692* (1991); Oscar Handlin and Mary Flug Handlin, *Commonwealth: A Study of the Role of Government in the American Economy—Massachusetts, 1774–1861* (1962); George Haskins, *Law and Authority in Puritan Massachusetts* (1962); Peter Hoffer, *Law and People in Colonial America* (1992); Morton J. Horwitz, *The Transformation of American Law, 1780–1860* (1977); Horwitz, *The Transformation of American Law, 1870–1960* (1992); Laura Kalman, *Legal Realism at Yale, 1927–1960* (1986); Peter Karsten, *Heart versus Head: Judge-Made Law in 19th-Century America* (1997); David T. Konig, *Law and Society in Puritan Massachusetts: Essex County, 1629–1692* (1979); Anthony T. Kronman, ed., *History of the Yale Law School: The Tercentennial Lectures* (2004); Roger Lane, *Policing the City: Boston, 1822–1885* (1967); Leonard W. Levy, *Law of the Commonwealth and Chief Justice Shaw* (1987); Bruce Mann, *Neighbors and Strangers: Law and Community in Early Connecticut* (1987); Perry Miller, *The Life of the Mind in America: From Revolution through Civil War* (1966); William E. Nelson, *The Americanization of the Common Law: The Impact of Legal Change on Massachusetts Society, 1760–1830* (1975); Nelson, *Dispute and Conflict Resolution in Plymouth County, Massachusetts, 1725–1825* (1981); Mary Beth Norton, *Founding Mothers and Fathers: Gendered Power and the*

Forming of American Society (1996); Ann Marie Plane, "Legitimacies, Indian Identities, and the Law: The Politics of Sex and the Creation of History in Colonial New England," *Law and Social Inquiry* 23 (1998); L. A. Powe, *The Warren Court and American Politics* (2000); Howard H. Schweber, *The Creation of American Common Law, 1850–1880: Technology, Politics, and the Construction of Citizenship* (2004); Christopher L. Tomlins and Bruce H. Mann, eds., *The Many Legalities of Early America* (2001); Gordon S. Wood, *The Creation of the American Republic* (1969).

Alfred L. Brophy

Abortion There is perhaps no greater moral, ethical, philosophical, or religious controversy in the United States today than that over abortion. The legal approach to abortion in this country from its inception to about the mid-1800s had its roots in New England via the benchmark Massachusetts case *Commonwealth v. Bangs* (1812).

Abortion, the termination of a pregnancy that results in the death of an embryo or fetus, was not a criminal offense in English common law unless the fetus had moved in the womb, or "quickened," which was usually during the fourth or fifth month of pregnancy. In 1803 England abandoned this traditional approach and criminalized abortion at any stage of gestation with the passage of Lord Ellenborough's Act. The United States, however, retained the quickening doctrine. In *Commonwealth v. Bangs,* the Massachusetts Supreme Judicial Court dismissed charges against a doctor who had performed an abortion because the indictment failed to allege "that the women was quick with child at the time." *Commonwealth v. Bangs* remained the decisive precedent on the issue of abortion in the United States throughout the first half of the 19th century and, in some states, well into the late 1800s. In 1822, for example, Connecticut became the first state to enact abortion legislation; the state made it a crime for a person to try to induce an abortion in a woman "quick with child." This legislation in effect preserved the quickening doctrine.

Two Massachusetts cases in the mid-1840s spurred anti-abortion legislation. The first was the 1845 decision by Chief Justice Lemuel Shaw in *Commonwealth v. Parker* that a female abortionist, Luceba Parker, could not be punished because there was no evidence that the babies had quickened. Shaw condemned Parker's practices but held that she had not committed a crime. The second case involved the death of Maria Aldrich of Smithfield, R.I. After Aldrich became pregnant, her lover, Fenner Ballou, brought her to Boston, where he paid a physician $100 to perform an abortion. Aldrich contracted an infection and died. In a subsequent prosecution for homicide, both Ballou and the physician were acquitted. The two highly publicized cases led Massachusetts to make it a crime to procure an abortion; the sentence was enhanced if the woman died as a result. The law was apparently aimed in part at protecting women from men who might seduce them and then coerce them into having an abortion. An important part of the purpose was to protect the mother's safety.

In the middle of the 19th century, attitudes toward abortion at any stage of pregnancy became more hostile. This was spurred primarily by the sharp increase in the incidence of abortion in the mid- to late 1800s among white, married, Protestant, native-born, middle- and upper-class women and by pressure from the so-called "regular" physicians' movement, which opposed abortion. While states nearly uniformly criminalized abortion in the period from 1870 through the early 1960s, abortions continued. In contrast to the current call among prochoice advocates for abortions to be "safe, rare, and legal," in that period they were sometimes unsafe, rather common, and illegal. Recent research also demonstrates that many viewed them as both available and acceptable if performed at home. During the Depression, abortions increased; at the same time they drew increased scrutiny. That scrutiny led to efforts from both physicians and the emerging feminist movement to reform abortion law and make abortions safer and legal.

In the post–World War II era, feminists urged expanded access to contraception and choice as issues related to personal autonomy. The U.S. Supreme Court's 1965 decision in *Griswold v. Connecticut* recognized the right of a married couple to have access to contraception. It arose from the prosecution and conviction of the executive director of Connecticut's Planned Parenthood and the head of the Obstetrics and Gynecology Department at Yale Medical School who were prosecuted for violating a Connecticut statute that prohibited counseling and medical treatment for contraceptive purposes. The court overturned both the convictions and the statute.

Less than a decade later, the U.S. Supreme Court's landmark decision in *Roe v. Wade* (1973) struck down a Texas statute criminalizing abortions. Justice Harry Blackmun, writing for the majority, agreed that a state has a "compelling interest" in protecting the health and safety of its citizens but argued that a pregnant woman also had a constitutionally protected right of privacy. Citing *Griswold v. Connecticut,* Blackmun referred to the "penumbra" cast by the Bill of Rights that created a zone of privacy closed to state intrusion. Blackmun also conceded that a state has a legitimate interest in protecting "potential life" but noted that there was no agreement on when life began and no precedent for extending constitutional protections to a fetus. The court ruled that a state could not interfere with a woman's right to have an abortion during the first trimester of pregnancy; could regulate abortion, without prohibiting it, during the next trimester; and could prohibit abortion during the last trimester, unless the procedure was necessary to save the life of the mother.

The Supreme Court's decision had parallels with the concept of quickening. While many celebrated this decision, others, especially those in the Roman Catholic Church, opposed the new doctrine. The terms *prolife* and *prochoice* came to define these two differing ideologies. The latest battle emerging in the debate concerns a form of late-term abortion called partial-birth abortion by its critics. From 1995 to 2000, the U.S. Congress repeatedly passed a bill that would ban such abortions, but President Bill Clinton vetoed the bill every time. In 2003 Congress passed another bill banning the procedure; President George W. Bush signed the bill into law.

Cornelia Hughes Dayton, "Talking the Trade," in *Colonial America: Essays in Politics and Social Development,* ed. Stanley N. Katz, John M. Murrin, and Douglas Greenberg, 5th ed. (2001); James C. Mohr, *Abortion in America: The Origins and Evolution of National Policy, 1800–1900* (1978); Leslie J. Reagan, *When Abortion Was a Crime: Women, Medicine, and Law in the United States, 1867–1973* (1997); David T. Smith, ed., *Abortion and the Law* (1967); Laurence Tribe, *Abortion: The Clash of Absolutes* (1990); Glanville Williams, *The Sanctity of Life and the Criminal Law* (1957).

Adoption The origin of adoption laws in the United States can be traced to the landmark 1851 statute An Act to Provide for the Adoption of Children, more commonly known as the Massachusetts Adoption Act. Before this statute, legal adoption was not widely practiced in the United States. Instead, Americans followed informal adoption practices that gave poor or orphaned children to better-off families, usually in return for their labor. Like indentured servitude or the apprentice system, informal adoption was primarily an economic arrangement designed to supply the adopting family with additional labor and to provide the adopted children with a home where they would learn valuable skills. At the same time, there was the gradual emergence of private informal adoptions and laws governing name changes, which slowly paved the way for legal adoption. The most famous early example was in 1693, when the governor of Massachusetts, Sir William Phips, adopted his nephew, who was named in Sir William's will as his son.

Given the relative lack of laws governing adoption in early America, the treatment of adopted children varied widely. Although loving families were created through indenture, cases of abuse, neglect, and even death were also frequently reported. Because children were seen primarily in economic terms as a source of labor, they were often exploited.

In time, however, a constellation of cultural factors combined to create the right environment for new laws governing adoption. Care for homeless children shifted to almshouses and orphanages (with poor results) as America changed in the mid-19th century into an industrial society. At the same time, a declining birthrate and the cult of romanticized motherhood increased the demand for adoption. Along with these changes came a shift in the culture's perception of children. In place of the Calvinist belief that all humans, including children, were sinners, there developed a view of infants as innocents needing protection. Adoption laws were enacted against this backdrop, with the primary emphasis shifting from the property rights of the adult to the "best interests of the child."

The Massachusetts Adoption Act required courts to oversee adoptions and to ensure that the welfare of the child was the primary outcome of custody arrangements. The law also provided for the screening of adoptive parents and sought to ensure that adoptive parents were able to offer adequate care for the child. In adoption cases, the courts began to act on behalf of children, making sure that their interests governed the outcomes of the cases. In addition, the law required the written consent of the child's biological parents or nearest living relative for the adoption to take place, thus legally eliminating any claims the biological parents might make in the future.

E. Wayne Carp calls the Massachusetts Adoption Act a "watershed in the history of the Anglo-American family and society," reasoning that it changed the way the American family could be defined. A family was no longer defined only by blood kinship but as the individuals responsible for the well-being of the child. The 1851 Massachusetts Adoption Act became a model and spurred 25 other states to adopt similar statutes in the 25 years that followed. Perhaps the most important effect of this law is that it created modern-day adoption's guiding principle—that the best interests of the child should govern all custody arrangements.

LeRoy Ashby, *Endangered Children: Dependency, Neglect and Abuse in American History* (1997); E. Wayne Carp, *Family Matters: Secrecy and Disclosure in the History of Adoption,* (1998); Carmel Shalev, *Birth Power: The Case for Surrogacy* (1989).

Lisa Sisco

Animal Rights As early as the 17th century, New Englanders were concerned about protecting animals from abuse. The Massachusetts Bay "Body of Liberties" (1641) included a provision that made it criminal to "exercise any tyranny or cruelty toward any brute creatures which are usually kept for man's use." Bearbaiting, a form of entertainment in which dogs were set on a restrained bear, was criticized, and efforts were also made to ease the suffering of draft animals. The work of the 17th-century English humanitar-

ian and vegetarian Thomas Tryon also influenced New England readers. Later, the Shakers were known for their protection and gentle treatment of animals based on the belief of their founder, Ann Lee, that cruelty to animals fueled brute passions in humans. In the 19th century, the beginnings of a true animal rights movement developed with the founding of the New England Anti-Vivisection Society (NEAVS) in 1895; its first president, Philip Peabody, published a significant attack on the practice in that year. The society was formed in opposition to an animal experimentation lab at Harvard established by Henry Bowditch. The Massachusetts Society for the Protection of Cruelty to Animals (MSPCA) also opposed the practice.

In recent years, New England has experienced growing grassroots activism and organizational support for advancing the rights and furthering the protection of animals. An increasingly popular device that activists use is the citizen initiative process. An important example of this was the passage of a citizen-sponsored ballot in 1996 that prohibited the use of specific kinds of traps and the use of dogs in bear hunting. Sponsored by the MSPCA, the Massachusetts Audubon Society, and the Humane Society of the United States, this measure also enabled the governor to choose any citizen to serve on the state's wildlife regulatory board, a departure from the prior practice of only seating members who had sporting licenses. Other New England states have challenged the traditional dominance of wildlife management by hunting, trapping, and fishing interests. In 1997, Connecticut passed a law that required training for wildlife control operators and the humane euthanizing of "nuisance animals," such as skunks, squirrels, or stray dogs and cats.

New England animal rights activists also have continued the early work of NEAVS, protesting what they perceive to be the abuse of animals in medical research laboratories and trying to establish a citizen voice in the regulation of animal experimentation. In the late 1980s, the Cambridge Committee for Responsible Research managed to pass a local ordinance that created the only municipal-level commissioner of laboratory animals in the country. This ordinance called for National Institutes of Health guidelines to be applied to all public and private laboratories in Cambridge, Mass., and extended these guidelines to cover mice, rats, and birds. It also enabled the commissioner to appoint the public member of animal care and use committees, when formerly the research institutions themselves made these appointments.

New England activists have supported ef-

forts of protectionist groups to improve animals' lives by trying to reclassify animal cruelty as a felony, rather than a misdemeanor. The 1990s saw Connecticut, Rhode Island, New Hampshire, and Massachusetts pass stiffer laws in this regard. In turn, the presence of organizations such as NEAVS has complemented grassroots animal rights activism.

Of course, grassroots efforts on behalf of animal rights and protection in New England have not always fully succeeded. In the 1990s, activists in Cambridge failed to achieve a ban on the use of primates in research, and Citizens to End Animal Suffering and Exploitation could not prevent a state-sanctioned culling of deer at the Quabbin Reservoir in Massachusetts. Rhode Island banned calf roping and "bloodless" bullfights, but it has been the only New England state to do so. Activists in several New England states have sought to ban greyhound racing but have succeeded only in Maine and Vermont, where there were no racing interests to challenge. Nevertheless, during the 1990s there were many important advances in animal rights and protection in New England, and there is reason to be optimistic about the future.

Andrew Linze and Paul Barry Clarke, eds., *Animal Rights: A Historical Anthology* (2004); Philip G. Peabody, *The Experiences of Two American Anti-Vivisectionists in Various Countries* (1895); Tom Regan, *The Case for Animal Rights* (1983); Peter Singer, *Animal Liberation* (1975); Cass R. Sunstein and Martha C. Nussbaum, eds., *Animal Rights: Current Debates and New Directions* (2004); Stephen M. Wise, *Rattling the Cage: Toward Legal Rights for Animals* (2000).

Arnold Arluke

Associated Industries of Massachusetts v. Snow Environmental issues gained prominence in the late 20th century as the states and the national government moved to address newly recognized problems, but laws created in response to such issues were often challenged. In Massachusetts, asbestos was recognized as a health problem as early as 1975, when the legislature created an Asbestos Commission in the Department of Health to assess the hazard of exposure to the substance in schools and public buildings. Eventually, the state's Department of Labor and Industries assumed the duties of the Asbestos Commission, and in 1987 the department announced detailed regulations related to training requirements for asbestos handlers that were challenged in court, giving rise to the case of *Associated Industries of Massachusetts v. Snow*.

The state discovered that 12 percent of its school buildings contained friable asbestos and created a statute designed to regulate asbestos abatement throughout the state. The Associated Industries of Massachusetts (AIM), an employers' association dedicated to improving the economic climate of Massachusetts, tried to invalidate this statute and the regulations promoted under its authority when it brought suit in September 1988. The original case was called *Associated Industries of Massachusetts v. James F. Snow;* Snow was at the time commissioner of the Department of Labor and Industries.

In its decision of July 12, 1989, the U.S. District Court determined that certain Massachusetts regulations were expressly preempted, and an appeal was taken. AIM contended that state regulations were excessive and should be superseded by federal Occupational Safety and Health Administration (OSHA) regulations. AIM also claimed that mandatory training could tie up as many as 120,000 workers in two-day training classes, thereby imposing on them a heavy financial burden. The challenge was supported by Associated Builders and Contractors, which represented about 750 construction-related businesses.

The appeal, cited as *Associated Industries of Massachusetts v. Snow,* was heard in January 1990 and decided in March. In the appeal ruling, which supported the right of a Massachusetts state agency to enforce its own asbestos abatement, the U.S. Court of Appeals for the First Circuit determined that state regulations that have the dual effect of protecting both state workers and citizens are not preempted by federal OSHA provisions. The ruling specifically affirmed state provisions for the mandatory training and licensing of workers involved in asbestos removal, for monitoring areas undergoing such work, and for strengthening worker and public protection against contamination from asbestos and lead paint. The case had broader national implications as states tried to fend off preemption for their laws by federal law in regulatory matters involving public safety.

Associated Industries v. Snow is just one of the growing number of case laws that will determine the shape of environmental regulation in the foreseeable future.

Steve Marantz, "U.S. Court Backs State on Asbestos Removal," *Boston Globe,* March 17, 1990; Maggie Mulvihill, "First Circuit Gives Nod to State Asbestos Regs," *National Law Journal* (April 2, 1990).
Martin J. Manning

Beach Access Access to shores and beaches in New England, as elsewhere, is controversial and finds various resolutions depending on local customs and politics. During early settlement, some New England colonies departed from English common law, recognizing private property rights below the high tide line, establishing rights of access and use

Sign restricting access to a private beach in Milford, Conn., 2004

for large ponds or boatable waters, and developing what became known as the public trust doctrine. In modern times, however, New England states have been relatively conservative, typically refusing to extend traditional public trust rights of access and use in any generalized way to accommodate increasing demands for beach-related recreation. Rights of beach access remain fragmented and contested in New England.

In earlier times, access to the shore was essential for navigation and waterborne commerce. Fishing likewise required access to the shore, as did the gathering of shellfish and the hunting of waterfowl. A right to "pass and repass"—that is, to walk along the shore—was also traditionally recognized. Other uses requiring shore access that were once important in New England included skating, cutting ice, gathering seaweed, cutting sedge, and driving cattle. In the 20th century, recreational beach users such as sunbathers, boaters, swimmers, and surfers have tried to claim the status of customary users entitled to beach access, although not always with success.

The European American tradition dealt with conflicts over access to shores and beaches with a morass of formal and informal customs, local solutions, and generalized laws. English custom traces its roots back to Roman laws that provided for general public access to the water for navigation, commerce, and fishing and held that the ocean could belong to no one. The Magna Charta reflected these principles, which were further developed in medieval common law customs relating to common areas. By the 17th century in England it was widely recognized that land under the ocean up to the high tide line belonged to the king and that this land was burdened with an *ius publicum,* a public right of access for navigation, fishing, and fowling. This principle eventually became the modern public trust doctrine.

The American colonies adapted English

law and custom regarding shore access to local conditions. The Massachusetts Bay Colony permitted private ownership of lands below the high water mark by as much as 100 rods (1,650 feet). This change from common law property rules was intended to spur the construction of wharves and thus to promote commerce. Even though Massachusetts provided for the traditional public rights of access for navigation, fishing, and fowling, it set itself apart from the other New England colonies in that there was no longer an intertidal zone along the beach to which the state had legal title and the public had uncontested rights of use.

In another adaptation to local conditions, Massachusetts deviated from traditional English legal doctrine by granting public rights of access to "great ponds"—that is, ponds more than 10 acres in surface area—even though the ponds were privately owned. Maine and New Hampshire also recognized common rights of access and use for large ponds, and Vermont developed similar rights for "boatable waters."

Maine tended to follow Massachusetts in its beach access laws, but other New England states approached beach access in different ways. Rhode Island's 1663 colonial charter provided for ocean access for fishing and commerce, and its 1843 constitution guaranteed access to the ocean. New Hampshire and Connecticut courts early recognized both intertidal public ownership and the public access aspects of the public trust doctrine.

Throughout the coastal United States, conflicts over shore use and access intensified during the 1960s and 1970s because of increased population, changing vacation habits, the availability of automobiles, the improved interstate highway system, and increasing permanent suburban or retirement populations in shore towns. This increasing conflict prompted a number of interesting developments. Federal guarantees of beach access were proposed in Congress, but went nowhere. In Massachusetts, and eventually in New Hampshire and Maine, legislatures considered amending state law to provide a greater right of public access to beaches for recreational purposes. In each of these states, an opinion of the state supreme court held that legislative readjustment of public and private property rights in order to increase public access to beaches would result in the taking of private property, and thus would require compensation by the state. The legislatures backed off. Traditional rights of public access, such as the right to pass and repass, continued but were strictly limited instead of being expanded to accommodate the new demand for recreational beach use.

The old laws and customs of access still had some effect. In many urban areas—including Boston and Providence—development had occurred on filled land, that is, land deposited by the tide and thus subject to the *ius publicum* of access. The Massachusetts Supreme Judicial Court decided in 1979 that where any portion of a real estate parcel consisted of filled land, the public still held a right of access. Consequently, developers had an obligation to consult with the state so as to provide appropriate water access to satisfy the public right. Similarly in Vermont, land along the shore of Lake Champlain, ceded to a railroad in the 19th century to encourage the building of wharves, could not simply be converted by the railroad to condominiums in the 1980s. The shore land remained burdened with a public trust requirement that it be used for public purposes, to be determined by the legislature. In Rhode Island, certain filled lands are likewise subject to a right of public access.

Many conflicts about beach access are extremely local in nature, involving questions of whether particular easements or shore rights are created in deeds or covenants or have developed as the result of customary practice over a period of years. They are typically resolved on specific facts, not broad principles.

Municipalities also became players in disputes over beach access. Many municipalities own beaches, and their access policies have varied. In Connecticut, for example, some town beaches were generally open to all in the 1970s. Other towns reserved their beaches for residents, and yet other shore towns made deals with one or two inland towns to allow their residents in as well. Somewhat more subtle means of keeping beaches for limited populations included reserving the only convenient parking for local residents or charging high beach access fees or parking fees to nonresidents.

The creation of more and better federal and state beaches was another response to the de-

mand for better access to beaches for recreation. From the 1970s on, federal and state funding to aid local projects often came with strings attached, requiring public access to beaches. This led some towns—Greenwich, Conn., in particular—to refuse all federal funding so as to retain control of their beaches. Greenwich's exclusive "residents-only" policy was overturned in 2001. The Connecticut Supreme Court, however, rejected using the public trust doctrine to impose a general obligation of public access to beaches above the high tide line. Instead, it decided the case on a narrower ground, holding that the particular beach at issue was within a public park that was a public forum, so that any member of the public must be allowed access under federal and state constitutional principles of free speech and assembly. Greenwich subsequently sought to impose exorbitant beach fees on nonresidents but under pressure reduced the fees to a reasonable level.

An overlooked development in modern contests over beach access is the civil rights–style challenge mounted in Connecticut during the 1970s. Rather than arguing that the public generally had a right to use the shore as a public resource, the Revitalization Corps of Hartford, led by Ned Coll, compared the exclusion of nonresidents from town beaches in Connecticut, Rhode Island, and Massachusetts to suburban exclusionary zoning. The corps sometimes relied on disruptive, attention-getting tactics, such as bringing busloads of inner-city children to targeted beaches, leafleting at railroad stations, and picketing political representatives. After a few years this movement lost steam. But it may have had a point, as recreational beach access often is stratified along race and class lines. It can be expected that beach access will remain a source of legal litigation well into the 21st century.

Jack A. Archer, *The Public Trust Doctrine and the Management of America's Coast* (1994); Coastal States Organization, *Putting the Public Trust Doctrine to Work*, 2d ed. (1997); Marc R. Poirier, "Environmental Justice and the Beach Access Movements of the 1970s in Connecticut and New Jersey: Stories of Property and Civil Rights," *Connecticut Law Review* 28 (1996); "Public Access and the New England Shoreline," *Maine Law Review* 42 (1990).

Marc R. Poirier

Blue Laws Strict regulation of personal and public behavior, especially on the Sabbath, was a foundation of the Puritan mission to create a godly society. Daily life in an English village could be violent and dissolute, and the Sabbath was no exception. The Anglican Sabbath was not a day given up largely to prayer; indeed, the Crown encouraged recre-

ation and sports for the masses as innocuous diversions from more serious and potentially revolutionary activities. Such behavior, accompanied by heavy consumption of alcohol, left many villagers injured, pregnant, or so drunk that they could not work and had to take "Saint Monday" as a day of rest. To the Puritans, such behavior not only defiled the sanctity of the "Lord's Day" but also challenged their mission to reform society along godly lines.

Once in New England, the Puritans were able to pursue their program of social regulation through rules dubbed blue laws. Received historical tradition has it that this term derives from the blue paper covers on the general code of laws published by the New Haven Colony in 1656. The popular meaning of the term, however, applies more narrowly to Sabbatarian prohibitions. "'Tis Gods Time," wrote Cotton Mather of the Sabbath, "and will not admit any Pastime." Attendance at Sunday church services became mandatory, while travel, work, and recreation were banned from sunset Saturday to sunset Sunday. Throughout the 17th century penalties and enforcement mechanisms were adopted to combat widespread evasion and lax enforcement. Nonattendance at church was usually not punished unless absences were prolonged, nor were prohibited activities penalized unless they were open and notorious.

The notoriety of the blue laws as an excessive and characteristically "puritanical" repression of all enjoyment stems largely from a myth created by a disgruntled Tory, the Anglican minister and missionary Samuel Peters. Driven from his home in Connecticut by the threat of a tarring and feathering in 1775, he took revenge by writing a satirical history of that colony in 1781; in it he included a mock list of offenses, such as a mother's kissing her child on the Sabbath, that were said to be punishable by the "Blue Laws of Connecticut."

Many blue laws continue as limits on Sunday business to this day, though they are largely shorn of their religious impulse. Challenges to them during the first half of the 20th century gained popular support by attacking the ban on Sunday baseball games; but later in the century pressures from commercial and consumer interests led to the ending of most laws that required stores to be closed on Sundays, either through legislative repeal or judicial decisions based on grounds of due process or equal protection, not religious freedom. Today's surviving laws thus hark back more to those of colonial Rhode Island, where the separation of church and state made Sunday a secular day of rest, with no compulsory church attendance or bans on travel or personal labor.

William Addison Blakely, *American State Papers Bearing on Sunday Legislation* (1911); David Laband and Deborah Heinbuch, *Blue Laws: The History, Economics, and Politics of Sunday Closing Laws* (1987); Samuel Middlebrook, "Samuel Peters: A Yankee Munchausen," *New England Quarterly* 20 (1947); Edwin Powers, *Crime and Punishment in Early Massachusetts, 1620–1692: A Documentary History* (1966).

David Thomas Konig

Borden, Lizzie

Borden, Lizzie (1866–1927) Murder suspect. Lizzie Borden, who was born, reared, and died in Fall River, Mass., belonged to one of the city's old, established families. Her father, Andrew, was a rich but parsimonious businessman, the very model of a thrifty Yankee. Lizzie, a Sunday-school teacher and member of the Woman's Christian Temperance Union, also sat on the board of Fall River Hospital. The turning point in her quiet, respectable, upper-class life came on August 4, 1892.

On that Thursday morning Lizzie's 65-year-old stepmother, Abby, was hacked to death in her second-floor bedroom, and an hour or so later her 70-year-old father suffered the same fate in the downstairs sitting room (though receiving fewer blows). Lizzie, who was unmarried, and Bridget Sullivan, the Irish-born family maid, were the only other people known to have been in the house at 92 Second Street. After an inquest, the police arrested Borden for the homicides.

The prosecution's case was not a particularly strong one. Although the rooms where the slayings took place were splattered with blood, authorities found no blood on Borden or her clothes. But Borden had hired George D. Robinson, a skilled, experienced, and politically connected lawyer, to defend her. After a 12-day trial, the all-male jury took an hour to reach a verdict of not guilty, apparently concluding, as Robinson had suggested in his closing arguments, that it was "morally and physically impossible for this young woman defendant" to commit such a crime. "To foully murder her stepmother and then go straight away and slay her own father," Robinson continued, "is a wreck of human morals: it is a contradiction of her physical capacity and certainty."

The acquittal should have settled the matter, but the case has refused to die—perhaps because Borden had apparently tried to purchase poison the day before the murders and was believed to have burned a dress in a stove a few days later. In the more than 100 years since that August day, numerous books, articles, and plays have been written about the crime. The case has also inspired a ballet (Agnes de Mille's *Fall River Legend*), an opera (Jack Beeson's *Lizzie Borden*), a 1975 made-for-TV movie, a musical (Christopher McGovern's *Lizzie Borden*), and a journal (the *Lizzie Borden Quarterly*). Indeed, the house where the Bordens were murdered has become a bed-and-breakfast establishment. Many New England children have jumped rope to the rhyme

Lizzie Borden took an ax
And gave her mother forty whacks.
When she saw what she had done,
She gave her father forty-one!

Borden's likeness has even appeared on a T-shirt.

What explains this fascination with a century-old crime? The fact that it has never been solved—and probably never will be—certainly accounts for much of the continuing interest in these gruesome murders. Theories about the case abound. Some have suggested that Lizzie Borden's sister, Emma, or the maid Bridget or a phantom stranger did the bloody deed. Most students of the slayings agree that Lizzie was the culprit, but why she committed the murders has generated much speculation. Perhaps the most popular theory is that Lizzie, fearful that her father intended to leave his fortune to Abby, was motivated by greed. Some have argued that Lizzie killed her stepmother and father after having been discovered in bed with Bridget. Others contend that she committed the murders in a raging epileptic fit. A more recent conjecture has her murdering her father after years of being sexually molested. No solid documentary evidence is available to support any of these theories. But with or without evidence, Lizzie Borden and the Fall River homicides will continue to attract investigators.

Mary Cantwell, "Lizzie Borden Took an Ax," *New York Times Magazine*, July 26, 1992; Marcia R. Carlisle, "What Made Lizzie Kill," *American Heritage* 43 (1992); David Kent, *Forty Whacks: New Evidence in the Life and Legend of Lizzie Borden* (1992); Jules R. Ryckenbusch, ed., *Proceedings, Lizzie Borden Conference: Bristol Community College, Fall River, Massachusetts, August 3–5, 1992* (1992).

Richard P. Harmond

Boston Massacre Trials

Boston Massacre Trials On the night of March 5, 1770, soldiers of the British 29th Regiment fired into a threatening crowd of Boston civilians, killing five. The Boston Massacre, as the incident was quickly dubbed, showed the growing anger of the colonists over laws and taxes imposed upon them by a distant government in which they had no representation. But the trials of Captain Thomas Preston and eight British soldiers had a significance beyond the punishment of the perpetrators. Among the longest in colonial America and the most important in the nation's history, the trials demonstrated to both the colonists and the British government the commitment of Massachusetts to the rule of law, not mob justice. In fact, two future signers of the Declaration of Independence who argued the cases took opposite sides, one appearing for the prosecution and one for the defense. As Governor Thomas Hutchinson insisted to angry Bostonians on the night of the massacre, "The law shall have its course."

There were other important aspects to the trials. The idea of "reasonable doubt" was established as a legal criterion in one of the earliest recorded instances of the phrase's use. The dying testimony of a massacre victim, normally not admissible, was admitted as evidence. And, in one of its final appearances, the medieval concept of "benefit of clergy" allowed two convicted soldiers to escape hanging.

The trials—*Rex v. Preston* and *Rex v. Wemms*—took place before the Massachusetts Superior Court of Judicature. (The commanding British officer during the massacre, Captain Preston, was tried separately from his men.) Because of the tension between Boston's loyalists, who wanted the soldiers to be acquitted, and patriots, who wished them to be executed, the trials were delayed for seven months in the hope that the situation would calm down.

Captain Preston's trial began on October 24. Counsel for the prosecution were Solicitor General Samuel Quincy, a loyalist, and Robert Treat Paine, a patriot and future signer of the Declaration of Independence. Their task was to prove that the captain had issued the command to fire and was thus responsible for the deaths of the civilians. Defending him were Robert Auchmuty, Jr., the loyalist judge of the Vice-Admiralty Court; Josiah Quincy, Jr., a talented young attorney and ardent patriot (and Samuel Quincy's younger brother); and John Adams, the future president and signer of the Declaration, who was Boston's foremost attorney and a recognized leader of the patriot cause. The case was tried before four justices—two political moderates, a scholarly patriot sympathizer, and an outspoken loyalist. The defense counsel concentrated on proving that Captain Preston did not give the command to fire, citing the confusion of the dark and crowded street. The prosecution failed to prove that he issued the command. After five days of trial, the jury—stacked in Preston's favor—found the captain not guilty.

The soldiers' trial began on November 27. The jury, which did not contain a single Boston resident, had the task of deciding which of the soldiers had fired, and whether they had fired with malice or in self-defense. The prosecution built its case on the soldiers' hatred of the townspeople, while the defense stressed the hostility of the crowd. The dying testimony of one of the victims, Patrick Carr, related how intensely the mob had threatened the soldiers. After eight days, six of the soldiers were acquitted. Two soldiers were found guilty of the lesser charge of manslaughter: Private Matthew Kilroy for killing Samuel Gray and Private Hugh Montgomery for killing Crispus Attucks. Kilroy and Montgomery "prayed benefit of clergy," which allowed those who were convicted of manslaughter to be branded with an *M* on the thumb and released. John Adams later described his work in these trials as "one of the best pieces of service I ever rendered my country."

The Legal Papers of John Adams, vol. 3, ed. L. Kinvin Wroth and Hiller Zobel (1965); Hiller Zobel, *The Boston Massacre* (1970).

Stephen C. O'Neill

Boston Strangler Albert DeSalvo, born in Chelsea, Mass., in 1931, is generally believed to have been the serial rapist and murderer responsible for the deaths of 13 women between June 1962 and January 1964. The first victim was Anna Slesers, aged 55, who was found strangled in her apartment with a bathrobe sash tied in a bow around her neck. She had been raped and her body left in a pornographic pose. Subsequent victims were Helen Blake, aged 65; Nina Nichols, 68; Ida Irga, 75; Jane Sullivan, 67; Sophie Clark, 25; Patricia Bissette, 23; Beverly Samans, 23; Evelyn Corbin, 57; Joann Graff, 23; and Mary Sullivan, 19. They were strangled, stabbed with a knife, and penetrated with objects such as broom handles. The killer, who became known as the Boston Strangler, left their bodies in grotesque poses, on one occasion with a note reading "Happy New Year." The lurid and pornographic nature of these crimes was seen as existing in particularly ironic counterpoint to the puritanical image of Boston.

DeSalvo had previously been charged with assault and battery, lewd conduct, and attempted breaking and entering. In November of 1964 he was brought in for questioning in a series of Green Man rapes (so called because of the color of the perpetrator's work clothes) in Massachusetts, Rhode Island, New Hampshire, and Connecticut. He confessed and was placed under observation in Bridgewater State Hospital, where he was befriended by the convicted murderer George Nassar. After a series of conversations with Nassar, DeSalvo confessed to the Strangler slayings and added two victims to the list. One was Mary Mullen, 85, whose death had been attributed to heart failure; the other was Mary Brown, 69, who was beaten and stabbed to death in her home. DeSalvo never stood trial for the Strangler

Albert DeSalvo, the "Boston Strangler," being escorted to a cell at Walpole State Prison, 1967

crimes, but in a deal negotiated by his lawyer, F. Lee Bailey, he drew a term of life imprisonment for the Green Man rapes. In 1973 he was stabbed to death by a fellow inmate at Walpole Prison. Some critics doubt that DeSalvo was the Strangler, suggesting that Nassar was the killer and coached DeSalvo for the role. Others refuse to believe that one man was responsible for all the murders and argue that some were the work of a copycat killer or killers. In 2001, DeSalvo's brother and the sister of one of the victims moved to reopen the case through new tests of evidence and an examination of Mary Sullivan's exhumed body. The examination showed no DNA link to DeSalvo.

During the two-year siege, chilling reports appeared in the press, rumors flew, and many Boston-area women lived in a state of terror. A medical-psychiatric team of experts was formed to construct a profile of the killer. In its majority opinion, the murders were the works of at least two men, one responsible for the older women, and another for the younger. The team put forth the theory that the killer had been brutalized by a dominant and seductive mother, whom he symbolically attacked through his victims in a manner "both sadistic and loving." A novelization of the case, *No Way to Treat a Lady,* by William Goldman (subsequently filmed), featured a killer based on these projections. Feminist critics including Susan Brownmiller have scorned the inherent sexism of these constructions and pointed to the fact that DeSalvo's father was extremely abusive and regularly beat his son and wife.

Like Jack the Ripper, the Boston Strangler has become a mythic celebrity/monster, functioning as an icon of sexist terror. Brownmiller analyzes the performance of the Rolling Stones's classic 1970 song "The Midnight Rambler" as a re-creation of the rape-murder of Beverly Samans, with the rock star playing the role of the hero/strangler. The lyrics are taken almost directly from the reported confessions of DeSalvo. Blithe references to the Boston Strangler continue in the national popular culture. A specialty cocktail called the Boston Strangler is listed on the menu at Boston's, a restaurant in Florida. An MTV host once announced that he was going to deliver some news from Boston, "home of baked beans, BU, and at least one renowned serial strangler."

Harold K. Banks, *The Strangler: The Story of Terror in Boston* (1967); Susan Brownmiller, *Against Our Will: Men, Women, and Rape* (1975); Jane Caputi, *The Age of Sex Crime* (1987); Gerold Frank, *The Boston Strangler* (1967).

Jane Caputi

Brandeis, Louis D. (1856–1941) Jurist. Louis Dembitz Brandeis was appointed associate justice of the Supreme Court of the United States in 1916 by President Woodrow Wilson. He was the first Jew to serve on the court. Brandeis became known for defending liberal causes, often in dissent, and for writing detailed opinions that focused as much on facts as on principles of law, reflecting his conviction that law should be studied and practiced with a recognition of its effects on society. At the time of his appointment, he had

Louis D. Brandeis, ca. 1916

already earned a national reputation as a brilliant advocate and progressive reformer.

The son of a prominent family in Louisville, Ky., Brandeis settled in Boston after graduating from Harvard Law School (1877). He clerked for Massachusetts chief justice Horace Gray, established a successful law practice, and became friends with a wide circle of prominent people, including Oliver Wendell Holmes, Jr., with whom he later served on the Supreme Court.

His commitment to public interest law led Brandeis to intervene in labor-management disputes. In 1902, for example, he was asked to mediate a strike at a New England shoe factory that resulted from announced wage cuts. He conducted a careful investigation that revealed that work—though generally well paid—was seasonal, leaving workers without any income for 10 to 15 weeks during the year. With the cooperation of both management and labor, Brandeis developed a schedule to space the work evenly and eliminate regular layoffs.

In the case of *Muller v. Oregon* (1908), Brandeis submitted a famous brief, the "Brandeis Brief," based on sociology and statistics to defend a state law limiting the hours a woman could work. His brief established the standard for legal argument in the 20th century.

After the election of Woodrow Wilson, Brandeis became an important presidential adviser. He supported the Federal Reserve System and government regulation of trusts, including the Clayton Antitrust Act and the

Federal Trade Commission. He used the expression "the curse of bigness" to describe the problem of institutions that become too large to manage properly. His opposition to big business and defense of workers' rights nearly derailed his appointment to the Supreme Court. He was confirmed after four months of hearings.

As a justice, Brandeis's commitment to democracy generally found expression in a philosophy of judicial restraint. Believing, however, that the right to speak and publish freely was essential to the survival of democracy, Brandeis took an activist role in a series of First Amendment cases decided in the decade after World War I. In 1928 he wrote a powerful dissent in *Olmstead v. United States,* insisting that the police be held to the highest standards in carrying out their responsibilities, especially with regard to the Fourth Amendment and an individual's right to privacy; he recognized the right of an individual "to be let alone."

Influenced by Jacob De Haas, editor of the *Jewish Advocate,* the leading Jewish newspaper in Boston, Brandeis became an outspoken supporter of Zionism and, in 1914, the leader of the American Zionist movement. He was inspired by the dream of a Jewish homeland, democratically governed, and his commitment to this goal intensified as persecution of Jews in eastern Europe increased. After he retired from the Supreme Court in 1939, he devoted the rest of his life to the Zionist movement.

His insistence that all members of the community be given fair treatment and equal opportunities under the law earned him the name "The People's Attorney." Throughout his life, Brandeis gave generously of his time, his talents, and his fortune to achieve these objectives. Shortly after his death, the trustees of Middlesex University in Waltham, Mass., in recognition of Brandeis's interest in furthering the foundation of a Jewish homeland, renamed their institution in his honor.

Samuel J. Konefsky, *The Legacy of Holmes and Brandeis: A Study in the Influence of Ideas* (1956); Alpheus T. Mason, *Brandeis: A Free Man's Life* (1946); Philippa Strum, *Louis D. Brandeis: Justice for the People* (1984); Melvin I. Urofsky and David W. Levy, eds., *Letters of Louis D. Brandeis* (1971–78).

Christine L. Compston

Case Law Method The case law method is a model of legal education devised and implemented by Christopher C. Langdell, dean of Harvard Law School, in the last quarter of the 19th century. Often referred to as the "casebook" method, Langdell's case law approach to legal education takes the record of selected appellate court cases, studies the facts and extracts the legal principles of the cases,

and, by analogy, applies the established principles to existing legal problems in order to understand why the established rules of law apply or do not apply.

Until Langdell's innovation, legal education in the United States was a product of apprenticeship or clerking with an established lawyer for an indeterminate time. The lawyer's apprentice performed rudimentary legal tasks, such as drafting routine documents. In return, the lawyer tutored the apprentice in practical legal skills and assigned readings in a small number of established legal treatises, such as William Blackstone's *Commentaries,* and in relevant state statutes. When lawyer and apprentice felt the time was right, the apprentice went before state bar authorities and answered a few questions or took an exam. If successful, the apprentice was admitted to practice.

This type of education was inconsistent and produced attorneys with widely varying levels of knowledge and skill. Moreover, much of the substantive base of the law was limited to arid, dated legal treatises. By 1870 the organized bar in the United State was advocating the establishment of law schools closely affiliated with colleges and universities. The curriculum of these early university law schools, however, such as those at the University of Maryland and Harvard, remained bound by the concept of legal education as simple mastery of a body of legal principles.

Langdell added more analytical content to legal education. He wanted students to have access to specific recorded cases that could illustrate principles in specific areas of law, such as contracts, Langdell's specialty. Assigning students to find such cases on their own was too time-consuming, so Langdell himself combed volumes of recorded cases and selected those cases that illustrated basic principles of contract law. The result was the first "casebook" in American legal education: *A Selection of Cases on the Law of Contracts* (1871).

Langdell's deductive use of case law remains relatively simple. Students find similarities between a casebook example and the case facts at hand. Then, the legal rule or principle of the casebook example is explained. Finally, the established rule of law is applied to the present set of facts to decide the case.

Practitioners of the case law approach view law as a science consisting of certain legal principles. For the case law advocate, a successful legal education must involve students mastering these principles and developing analytical skill so they can apply appropriate legal principles to a changing set of human events.

Critics of Langdell's method reject the concept of law as an antiseptic analysis of cases to extract binding legal principles. Oliver Wendell Holmes, Jr., an early critic of Langdell, viewed law as a product of the social setting in which it operated. To Holmes, law could not be properly understood apart from social and political factors. "The life of law has not been logic," sniffed Holmes; "it has been experience." The case law method and its corresponding Socratic method (so-called) has also been criticized by feminists and scholars of critical legal studies.

Nevertheless, the effect of Langdell's case law method on American legal education is profound. Substantive courses offered in virtually every American law school follow a modified casebook format that includes "materials" to accompany the cases. The method was introduced to the popular media in the Harvard Law School classroom of Professor Kingsfield (John Houseman) in the movie *The Paper Chase* (1973), based on the novel by John Jay Osborn, Jr. Langdell's emphasis on the rule of case law is likely to remain the norm in American legal education and legal practice through the 21st century.

Laura Kalman, *Legal Realism at Yale* (1986); Frederick G. Kempin, Jr., *Historical Introduction to Anglo-American Law* (1990); William LaPiana, *Logic and Experience: The Origin of the Modern American Legal Education* (1994); Brian L. Porto, *The Craft of Legal Reasoning* (1998).

Paul D. Marsella

Charles River Bridge v. Warren Bridge

The history of the *Charles River Bridge* case is very much the history of Jacksonian democracy. The issue was simple: Did private interests outweigh the needs of the people? Did certain individuals or corporations have a right to special privileges above and beyond the rights of others and of the public at large? Andrew Jackson had answered the question plainly when he vetoed the bill to recharter the Bank of the United States on the grounds that it was a monopoly and that "every monopoly and all exclusive privileges are granted at the expense of the public, which ought to receive a fair equivalent." With such definitive views it was not surprising that Jackson's secretary of the treasury, Roger B. Taney, the man who helped deliver the death blow to the bank by removing its federal deposits, was the same man who rendered the famous 1837 Supreme Court decision that ended the seemingly exclusive charter possessed by the Charles River Bridge Company in Boston, Mass. Indeed, it was even more fitting that Taney had been placed on the high court as its chief justice by Jackson.

The case stemmed from the Massachusetts legislature's approval in 1828 of a second bridge over the Charles River to speed the growing traffic between Boston and Charlestown. The plan to build the second bridge was opposed from the start by the owners of the Charles River Bridge. They insisted that the legislative charter granted to them in 1785 was exclusive and that the construction of a competing bridge violated the contract made by the state and subsequently violated the contract clause of the U.S. Constitution.

There was no question that the new bridge, named after the hero of Bunker Hill, Joseph Warren, would be a source of competition for the Charles River Bridge. When completed, the new structure would be only 260 feet away from the old bridge on the Charlestown end and 916 feet away at the Boston end. Moreover, the roads leading to the Boston end of the bridges would come within 26 feet of one another. Also at issue was the question of tolls. Once the cost of construction plus 5 percent had been recovered, or after six years, the Warren Bridge would be free of tolls.

Before the Warren Bridge began operation on Christmas Day, 1828, the proprietors of the Charles River Bridge filed suit. More than a year later, on January 12, 1830, the Massachusetts Supreme Judicial Court rendered a split decision in the case: two justices upheld the constitutionality of the new charter, and two opposed it. The road was paved for the case to travel to the U.S. Supreme Court with Chief Justice John Marshall presiding. At the bar of the high court stood the incomparable Daniel Webster for the Charles River Bridge. John Quincy Adams led the team representing the Warren Bridge. Each side gave electrifying arguments concerning the sanctity of contracts versus the importance of public progress, but the court could not render a decision because the justices were evenly divided. For the next six years, the case sat in a kind of legal limbo, while justices died, most notably, John Marshall.

The case was retried at the beginning of 1837, this time with Roger Taney as chief justice. On February 12, 1837, he spoke for the majority of the tribunal, which was split four to three. "While the rights of private property are sacredly guarded," explained Taney, "we must not forget that the community also have rights, and that the happiness and well-being of every citizen depends on their faithful preservation." The original charter granted to the Charles River Bridge proprietors said nothing about exclusivity, explained the chief justice, and "any ambiguity in the terms of the contract must operate against the adventurers, and in favor of the public." Finally, Taney insisted that if implied monopolies were sanctioned by law, every "old turnpike" company would contest the building of new transportation improvements such as canals and railroads.

Taney's ruling against the Charles River Bridge was a landmark decision representing the Supreme Court's shift from the views of the Marshall court. In *Dartmouth College v. Woodward* in 1819, Marshall had declared that the charter granted to Dartmouth College was in fact a contract and was thus protected by the contract clause of the Constitution. Marshall probably would have defended the charter granted to the Charles River Bridge. Taney's ruling in the case transformed the court's view of private versus public rights. The sanctity of contracts would still be upheld, but not at the expense of the people's rights. The tenets of Jacksonian democracy had found expression through the Taney court.

Henry F. Graff, "The Charles River Bridge Case," in *Quarrels That Have Shaped the Constitution*, ed. John A. Garraty (1962); Stanley Kutler, *Privilege and Creative Destruction: The Charles River Bridge Case* (1971); Wallace Mendelson, ed., *The Constitution and the Supreme Court* (1965); R. Kent Newmyer, *The Supreme Court under Marshall and Taney* (1968).

Matthew Warshauer

Christian Science and the Law

Christian Science, a religion founded in New England by New Hampshire native Mary Baker Eddy, is commonly identified by the reliance of its adherents on spiritual healing. In the *Church Manual* (1906), Eddy states that she founded the Church of Christ, Scientist, in 1879 to "reinstate primitive Christianity and its lost element of healing." Its teachings, as distinguished from faith healing, assert that spiritual healing can be understood and practiced "scientifically."

Christian Science case law has followed the principles and guidelines developed by courts to adjudicate a broad range of church-related cases. Decisions involving Christian Science practice have taken into account both the individual's right to free exercise of religion and a state's authority to act in the interest of citizens. Yet judges have also been aware of First Amendment constraints that preclude special treatment, viewed by some as violating the Establishment Clause, and prohibit government entanglement in religious matters.

The founding of the church coincided with the growing influence of the medical profession. State legislatures during the late 19th century passed laws to restrict medical practice to licensed physicians, and in a number of states Christian Science practitioners were charged with violating these laws. An 1898 decision by the Supreme Court of Rhode Island, *State v. Mylod*, concluded that reliance on prayer could not be construed as medical practice. The New York Court of Appeals, the most prestigious state court at the time, grounded a similar ruling in the free-exercise provision in the New York Constitution in *People v. Cole* (1916).

Cases involving the right of parents to rely on Christian Science treatment for their children have compelled judges to define more precisely the role of the state in family life. The decisions reached in Christian Science cases shed light on society's increasingly complex discussions regarding the right of individuals to choose differing modes of health care.

While taking into account the rights of parents, judges also recognize parental responsibilities and weigh these in their deliberations. In *Commonwealth v. Moyse* (1924) the court placed a teenage boy from Massachusetts under medical observation in response to a complaint brought against the parents. The child's significant improvement under Christian Science care led to dismissal of the complaint and a 40-year period of legislative and judicial accommodation of Christian Science healing practice. This accommodation was called into question, first, in the 1967 *Sheridan* case—in which jurors found a Christian Science mother guilty of manslaughter after her daughter died from pneumonia—and, more significantly, in *Commonwealth v. Twitchell* (1993). In the latter case, the judge overseeing the trial refused to inform the jurors of a 1971 statute designed to permit parents to rely on "spiritual means alone" in caring for their children. As a result, the parents were found guilty of manslaughter. Their appeal raised questions of due process, and the Supreme Judicial Court of Massachusetts, recognizing the good-faith efforts of the parents to abide by state law, overturned the convictions. The justices determined that, in the future, parents in similar circumstances have the duty to seek medical services.

Two suits brought against the Christian Science board of directors in 1919 raised questions of church governance, challenging the authority of the board to remove officers. In both cases the Supreme Judicial Court of Massachusetts relied on what would later be termed the doctrine of "neutral principles," according to which courts may decide nondoctrinal matters related to trust and property law without violating the First Amendment. Christian Science case law has also been influenced by Supreme Court decisions on other cases of religious freedom, such as the 1972 Amish case *Wisconsin v. Yoder,* which relied on the Free Exercise Clause of the Constitution to protect the right of parents to home-school their children.

Christian Science Publishing Society, *Christian Science: A Contemporary Sourcebook* (1990); Thomas C. Johnsen, "Christian Scientists and the Medical Profession: A Historical Perspective," *Medical Heritage* 2 (1986); Robert Peel, *Health and Medicine in the Christian Science Tradition: Principle, Practice, and Challenge* (1988); Jean Kinney Williams, *The Christian Scientists* (1997).

Christine L. Compston

Civil Disobedience

Civil Disobedience   Civil disobedience is a nonviolent method of protest that individuals or groups use who are seeking to effect social or political change. Protesters knowingly refuse to obey a law that they believe to be unconstitutional or morally wrong in its substance, terms, or effects.

Although many have practiced civil disobedience before and since, the term was popularized in the 19th century by the actions and writings of Henry David Thoreau, who in July 1846 opted to pass a night in the jail in Concord, Mass., rather than pay a poll tax to a government that tolerated slavery and waged an unprovoked war with Mexico. In January 1848 Thoreau gave a lecture titled "The Relation of the Individual to the State" at the Concord Lyceum in which he explained his refusal to comply. The text was published after Thoreau's death as "Civil Disobedience," although Thoreau never used that term. In that work, Thoreau asked the principal question and articulated the moral imperative behind acts of civil disobedience: "Unjust laws exist: shall we be content to obey them, or shall we endeavor to amend them, and obey them until we have succeeded, or shall we transgress them at once?" Thoreau's own actions served as an answer to this question, as did his now famous words, "Under a government which imprisons any unjustly, the true place for a just man is also a prison."

Thoreau's experience represents only a single example of civil disobedience, and certainly not the earliest known in New England. Only three years earlier, his Concord neighbor and fellow abolitionist Amos Bronson Alcott (father of the author Louisa May Alcott) refused to pay his poll tax, thus inspiring Thoreau to take action himself. Although Thoreau did not invent civil disobedience, his articulate defense of his actions has made his the more memorable, and eventually inspirational, transgression.

Thoreau's words lived on to inspire Mohandas Gandhi, who encountered "Civil Disobedience" as a lawyer in South Africa, where he defended Indians who had violated discriminatory laws. Gandhi was deeply impressed by Thoreau and became a lifelong exemplar of civil disobedience, further refining this means of peaceful protest to include passive resistance to unjust authority. Through Gandhi, Thoreau's ideas became an effective instrument of political action. Later in the 20th century, Rosa Parks and Martin Luther King, Jr., successfully adopted and adapted the concept of passive resistance for the U.S. Civil Rights movement. In his landmark "Letter from Birmingham Jail" (1963), the imprisoned King echoed the dissident from Concord who, a century before him, had passed a single night in jail: "There are *just* laws and there are *unjust* laws. I would be the first to advocate obeying just laws. One has not only a legal but a moral

Defendants leave federal court in Boston after the sentencing of Dr. Benjamin Spock (second from right), one of five Vietnam War protesters charged with conspiracy, 1968

responsibility to obey just laws. Conversely, one has a moral responsibility to disobey unjust laws."

In New England's recent past, civil disobedience has often been linked to national issues: the Vietnam War, for example, in the highly publicized conspiracy trial in 1968 of Benjamin Spock, William Sloane Coffin, Jr., Mitchell Goodman, Marcus Raskin, and Michael Ferber for aiding and abetting draft resistance; the Civil Rights movement, with protests in the 1970s against court-ordered busing as a means of racially integrating Boston's public schools; U.S. involvement in El Salvador and Guatemala in the 1980s, with the Sanctuary movement protecting refugees from those countries; and, most notably, nuclear power, with the construction of nuclear reactors for a power station in Seabrook, N.H., drawing protesters en masse. During the 1970s and 1980s anti-Seabrook activists organized by the Clamshell Alliance were arrested in large numbers for trespass, and they offered defenses including the right to revolution enshrined in the New Hampshire Constitution. Civil disobedience has a long history in New England, and will probably have a healthy future.

Abe Fortas, *Concerning Dissent and Civil Disobedience* (1968); Martin Luther King, Jr., "Letter from Birmingham Jail," in *The American Reader: Words That Moved a Nation,* ed. Diane Ravitch, rev. 2d ed. (2000); Henry David Thoreau, *The Variorum Civil Disobedience,* annotated by Walter Harding (1967); Elliot M. Zashin, *Civil Disobedience and Democracy* (1972).

Donna A. Danielewski

Cocoanut Grove Fire

Just after 10 o'clock on the evening of November 28, 1942, fire broke out in the Melody Lounge, a basement bar in Boston's fashionable Cocoanut Grove nightclub. Flames raced upstairs to the former speakeasy's show floor and cocktail lounge. In minutes, 490 patrons and employees were dead or dying; scores more were injured. No definitive cause was established. Faulty wiring installed by unlicensed electricians was one possibility, or a busboy may have inadvertently ignited a decorative palm tree.

The fire's lethality was less mysterious. A thousand Saturday night revelers packed a building licensed for half that number. Wall and ceiling decorations burned so quickly that firefighters found some victims still sitting on bar stools, killed before they had the chance to flee. Some survivors who escaped without apparent injury succumbed minutes or hours later; investigators determined that they had inhaled deadly fumes released when the imitation leather throughout the Grove was exposed to heat. The lights also failed, adding to

Aftermath of the fire at the Cocoanut Grove nightclub, Boston, 1942

the panic. Finally, many exits were concealed, locked, or poorly designed; 200 people died trying to escape through a jammed revolving door, while 100 more were bunched behind a door that opened only inward. Boston's war mobilization may have reduced the death toll; in preparation for enemy attacks on Boston and military casualties, city and volunteer agencies made personnel, supplies, and other resources available to aid the injured. Survivors of the fire may have been the first civilians treated with the new antibiotic, penicillin. The injured also received experimental burn treatments being tested at Massachusetts General Hospital and Boston City Hospital. These techniques, used to treat injured soldiers and sailors during the war, worked well.

Lax inspection was another contributing factor to the fire. Although the Grove had passed a safety inspection shortly before the fire, the owner, Barnett Welansky, often boasted about his city hall connections. Several officials were indicted, but none was convicted. Welansky was eventually convicted of manslaughter, however, and an architect involved in renovating the club was convicted of conspiracy, and in an influential decision, the Massachusetts Supreme Judicial Court upheld Welansky's manslaughter conviction. Although Welansky was away on the night of the fire, the court found him responsible for recklessly disregarding the safety of patrons. On

the basis of this decision, landlords in many states have been prosecuted after their poor maintenance caused the deaths of tenants.

The Cocoanut Grove fire still lives in Boston's memory. Boston papers continue to publish obituaries of survivors and rescuers, and the cause of the tragedy is still investigated and debated. But the effect of the fire extended well beyond Boston, as the nation recognized how easily the tragedy could have been avoided. The Boston-based National Fire Prevention Association suggested that sprinklers, lighted exits, and outward-opening, unlocked exit doors would have prevented many deaths. The disaster in Boston led to fire code reform across the country.

Paul Benzaquin, *Fire in Boston's Cocoanut Grove* (1967); Edward Keyes, *Cocoanut Grove* (1984); *Management of the Cocoanut Grove Burns at the Massachusetts General Hospital* (1943) (rpt. *Annals of Surgery* 117, no. 6 [1943]); National Fire Protection Association, *The Cocoanut Grove Nightclub Fire, Boston, November 28, 1942* (1943).

Gabriel J. Chin

Colonial Law

Law stood at the center of the Puritan reformation of church and society. Cotton Mather summed up almost a century's efforts when he reiterated what had guided his grandparents' generation and continued to shape his own. "The *Reformation of the Law,* and more *Law* for the *Reformation of the*

World," he wrote in 1710, "is what is mightily called for." Building a Bible Commonwealth demanded the most minute attention to regulation; failure to eradicate sin not only threatened individuals' souls but imperiled the "city upon a hill" that was to lead a vast reformation of humanity. Puritan theology placed enormous responsibility on the individual to seek his or her own salvation, but it also taught that all saints "preparing" for salvation must accept the guidance and assistance of others. Clear and well-known laws would provide the support for this endeavor.

Theology, however, did not lead the founders of New England to create a theocracy (rule by clergy) nor to ground their laws entirely—or even largely—in the Bible. They retained a powerful attachment to local English customs and the common law, as well as an abiding hostility to prerogative courts and public officials who had persecuted them. In addition, the social and economic crisis of 16th- and 17th-century England had left them with painful memories of a world in collapse. Together, Puritan faith and secular goals gave form to a comprehensive program of laws and legal institutions. The laws of the several New England colonies differed in details, but a shared English and Puritan background shaped them all and produced a general pattern of lawmaking; social order under law and religious purity according to the Bible were inseparable aspects of this common purpose.

The "godly" society that represented the primary goal of Puritan laws thus required godly institutions as a foundation: family, congregation, and town all received the careful attention of lawmakers seeking to reinforce them as pillars of communal authority. Marriage became a secular matter that emphasized the compatibility of mates capable of living together in harmony and not ungodly strife. Under the authority of magistrates, laws made the process of getting married more difficult but also allowed bad marriages to be ended more easily through divorce. Parental authority over children was strengthened by laws providing harsh penalties for disobedience, but the inheritance of property was made more equal among heirs so as to enable sons to start families of their own. Churches of likeminded saints were to be "gathered" under rules set by law, and heterodoxy was suppressed. Ecclesiastical authority benefited from statutes criminalizing heresy, blasphemy, and disrespect of ministers. Church and state were separate but mutually reinforcing institutions. Statutes regulated town affairs to assure orderly governance by elected officials and worked to promote adherence to law by guaranteeing the free participation of all heads of households. Even judicial officers were

elected in the 17th century before the royalization of Massachusetts Bay and New Hampshire.

Memories of their English experience combined with fears of desolation and disorder in a wilderness environment to produce many new laws. Sabbath and sumptuary laws were designed to promote regular habits, proper dress, and sober appearance and to impose order through a hierarchy of class, gender, and piety. Recalling the scourge of wandering English vagabonds and facing a severe labor shortage, colonial leaders in New England passed strict laws against idleness and made it lawful to compel labor (with compensation) at harvest time. Precise rules regulated the consumption of alcohol and tobacco; others banned hunting for mere recreation as a waste of ammunition and food.

In creating such a program of reinforced collective authority, New England legislators also provided for communal enforcement of the law: not only were grand jurors enjoined to present offenders but neighbors were directed to report violations and to provide neighborly watchfulness for sin and crime. Punishment exposed offenders to the shame of public humiliation in pillory or stocks, while branding (for example, *B* for Burglarie) enabled the community to recognize malefactors and watch them closely for any repetition of an offense.

Colonial New England laws also provided control over property rights as a means of promoting communal values against what Thomas Hobbes described as the war of all against all in England. The scarcity of essential foodstuffs and other products threatened to vastly worsen the price gouging and inflation of the competitive society that the colonists had experienced before emigration. Economic regulations therefore fixed many wages and prices and dictated trade policy. At the same time, other colonial laws affecting property can be said to have stabilized their communities by assuring personal rights and a stake in society. Insecurity of land tenure was a nightmare memory of the English past, when enclosure and rising rents had destroyed communal village life and set tens of thousands adrift and homeless. Colonial lawmakers thus acted to secure property rights by abolishing feudal obligations and by making land grants in freehold, with the requirement that conveyances be recorded. Early Massachusetts laws even required that all homes be built within a half mile of the meetinghouse and that sales of land to outsiders be approved by the town. Social and economic growth, however, overwhelmed these efforts in the 18th century; older restraints were repealed as property lost its communal purpose and be-

came more a guarantee of individual status and security. As poverty and population increased, laws were passed expelling the "strolling poor."

Much of the legacy of colonial laws continued beyond the 17th century into the next century and the national period. Just as the behavior of private individuals was to be constrained by law and the authority of family, congregation, or town, so, too, were public officials made subject to the rule of law. Distrust of human authority—a distrust drawn from a belief in original sin, and from the persecution of Puritans in the Court of Star Chamber and before the High Commission—lay at the root of many colonial statutes. Insistence on common law principles and procedures guaranteed colonists' lives and property and produced an unremitting opposition to prerogative courts and procedures. The New England colonies were unique in their hostility to the chancellor's equity courts, whose "law" they regarded as arbitrary—measured more by the length of the chancellor's foot than by any consistent principle, observed one of its harsher critics. Refusing to create equity courts, and insisting on the common law as their guide, the New England colonies continued to reject such courts and their jurisprudence well into the 19th century.

Their concern for known and consistent laws led colonial New Englanders to spell out—literally—the extent of legal authority. One major lack in common law jurisprudence was its unwritten nature, and by 1636 Massachusetts Bay began to set down in writing many of its rules of governance and civil and criminal laws. Governor John Winthrop of Massachusetts Bay feared the rigidity that such a compilation might produce, and he urged the colonists to allow laws to develop "*pro re nata*, upon occasion." The General Court (the colonial assembly) nonetheless ordered publication of the "Body of Liberties" (1641), which was succeeded by the *Lawes and Libertyes*, published in 1648. Connecticut had compiled its political laws in 1639 with its "Fundamental Orders" and in 1650 repeated the Massachusetts pattern with a more comprehensive code. The publication of the Massachusetts code also began a tradition of making printed laws available. Lacking their own printing presses, Plymouth (in 1672 and 1685), Connecticut (in 1673), and New Hampshire (in 1699) contracted to have their laws published in the Bay Colony. Throughout the colonial period, presses provided colonists with printed copies of orders, proclamations, and resolutions.

Written laws thus were at the foundation of the New England colonies, which jealously protected their legacy of English law. From the receipt of their first charters, which guaranteed rights consistent with those enjoyed in England, the colonists repeatedly cited their entitlement to the rights of English subjects. By restricting public authority clearly within the bounds of expressly provided procedures, colonial legislators established basic standards of due process and certain libertarian protections. Although these limits drew upon religious and political impulses, they presaged the later and more purely secular notion that John Adams described as a government of laws and not men. Evidence in court was to be given in person but recorded, and absent witnesses were required to have their testimony submitted as sworn before an official. At the same time, courts were not permitted to inquire into opinions held privately, or to compel self-incrimination. The right to a jury was made a hallmark of trial procedure. Litigants enjoyed the right of appeal in civil matters, and by the 18th century appellate cases flooded the Superior Court of Judicature, the highest tribunal in the colony.

David Grayson Allen, *In English Ways: The Movement of Societies and the Transferral of English Law and Custom to Massachusetts Bay in the 17th Century* (1981); Stephen Botein, *Early American Law and Society* (1983); Daniel R. Coquillette, ed., *Law in Colonial Massachusetts, 1630–1800* (1984); Cornelia Hughes Dayton, *Women before the Bar: Gender, Law, and Society in Connecticut, 1639–1789* (1995); George L. Haskins, *Law and Authority in Early Massachusetts: A Study in Tradition and Design* (1960); David Thomas Konig, *Law and Society in Puritan Massachusetts: Essex County, 1629–1692* (1979); Bruce H. Mann, *Neighbors and Strangers: Law and Community in Early Connecticut* (1987); Edgar J. McManus, *Law and Liberty in Early New England: Criminal Justice and Due Process, 1620–1692* (1993).

David Thomas Konig

Connecticut's Black Law

On May 24, 1833, Connecticut's General Assembly in Hartford passed an act that made it illegal for a private school to enroll an African American child from outside the state. Those violating the law were liable for a $100 fine, which would be doubled for each subsequent offense. The law was passed because there was one, and only one, person committing the offense.

The so-called Black Law was a direct response to the attempts of Quaker-educated Prudence Crandall to establish a private academy in 1833 for "young ladies and little misses of color" in the eastern Connecticut town of Canterbury. Local officials objected to the school because, they said, it would bring about a large black migration, increased crime, pauperism, and the decline of property values. Local groups mounted a white terrorist campaign against Crandall and her students that

included rock throwing, attempted arson, death threats, and numerous acts of vandalism. Under pressure from the town's political leaders, the state legislature passed the Black Law. Crandall was arrested, served a night in jail before posting bond, and was then acquitted in two different jury trials. On appeal, a local superior court reversed the acquittals, but the state's supreme court then threw out the convictions. The General Assembly soon repealed the law but only after Crandall had been driven from the state by constant harassment.

The case drew national attention to the issue of black citizenship in antebellum America some 20 years before the Supreme Court's *Dred Scott* decision denied citizenship to blacks. The Black Law tacitly recognized a second class of citizenship for blacks in the state and violated Article IV, Section 2, of the U.S. Constitution, which entitles the citizens from each state to the rights enjoyed by those of another. In 1838, amid growing antislavery sentiment in New England, the Connecticut General Assembly repealed the infamous law. It was not until the passage of the 14th Amendment in 1867 that the citizenship of African Americans was recognized, however.

The arguments in favor of full black citizenship put forth by the prominent Connecticut attorney William Ellsworth (son of the former U.S. chief justice Oliver Ellsworth) in Crandall's defense were used again by Thurgood Marshall in *Brown v. Board of Education* (1954), which outlawed segregated schools in the United States.

In 1886, at the urging of journalists and noted figures such as Mark Twain, the Connecticut legislature awarded the 83-year-old Crandall a pension of $400 a year. Today, the original building of the Canterbury Female Boarding School is the Prudence Crandall House, a National Historic Landmark and museum. On October 1, 1995, in honor of her efforts toward racially integrated education in Canterbury, lawmakers named Crandall Connecticut's state heroine.

Philip S. Foner and Josephine F. Pacheco, *Three Who Dared: Prudence Crandall, Margaret Douglass, Myrtilla Miner, Champions of Antebellum Black Education* (1984); Edmund Fuller, *Prudence Crandall: An Incident of Racism in 19th-Century Connecticut* (1971); Joanne Pope Melish, *Disowning Slavery: Gradual Emancipation and "Race" in New England, 1780–1860* (1998); Susan Strane, *A Whole-Souled Woman: Prudence Crandall and the Education of Black Women* (1990).

Ronald Lettieri and Richard Mandel

Courts of Appeals for the First and Second Circuits

The U.S. Courts of Appeals for the First and Second Circuits are the

lower federal appellate courts with jurisdiction over the New England states. As such, they hear appeals in federal cases, usually cases litigated in the federal district courts of those states. Maine, Massachusetts, New Hampshire, and Rhode Island (along with Puerto Rico) make up the jurisdictions in the First Circuit; Connecticut and Vermont (along with New York) are in the Second Circuit. Because the U.S. Supreme Court offers only a tiny proportion of litigants the opportunity to appeal decisions of the courts of appeals, those decisions are final for most appellate litigants.

Until late in the 19th century, federal circuit courts (the predecessors of today's courts of appeals) were relatively weak institutions. The circuit courts heard appeals from federal district courts and also had original (or trial) jurisdiction over most federal criminal cases and certain federal civil cases with more than $500 in controversy. There were, however, no judges specifically assigned to the circuit courts; for most of the century the circuit courts were presided over by one judge from a federal district court and one justice of the U.S. Supreme Court "riding circuit." Moreover, the circuit courts (along with the district courts) were narrowly limited in their jurisdiction. In particular, they did not have jurisdiction over civil cases raising questions of federal law. Consequently, the most important 19th-century federal cases from New England (including the Dartmouth College case and the Charles River Bridge case) came to the U.S. Supreme Court from state courts rather than from the lower federal courts of the First and Second Circuits.

In the 20th and 21st centuries the lower federal courts have come to play a more central role in New England and in U.S. law more generally. The Evarts Act of 1891 created the U.S. Courts of Appeals as we know them today and set in motion their rise as the final forum for dispute resolution for most federal court litigants. In both the First and Second Circuits, appellate caseloads have risen sharply during the 20th and 21st centuries as a result of the development of a wider sphere for federal law. The growth of the federal appellate dockets has been especially strong since the 1960s. In the Court of Appeals for the First Circuit, approximately 100 appeals per year were filed between 1925 and 1960. By 2001, more than 1,700 appeals were being filed each year, about 1,000 of which came out of New England jurisdictions. In the Second Circuit, 674 appeals were filed in 1961, but by the mid-1980s in excess of 2,000 appeals were being filed each year. (In the Second Circuit growth has been driven largely by cases from New York.)

In U.S. law, lower federal courts function as

the carriers of national norms into the states. This role has often placed lower federal courts at the center of controversy over issues such as racial segregation in the South and natural resource allocation in the West. In New England, however, the federal courts have been less controversial as the importer of national norms. In fact, whereas federal courts usually bring outside values to bear on local contexts, federal courts in the First and Second Circuits have frequently reversed the trajectory of influence. Nonetheless, they have also stepped into controversy by requiring busing to achieve racial integration in Boston schools and made debatable rulings in cases involving beach access and legislative redistricting.

Both the First and Second Circuits have long been the home of some of the nation's most respected judges. Historically, a strong majority of the First Circuit's judges have been trained at Harvard, and a considerable number of Second Circuit judges have been trained at Yale. Moreover, each circuit has had among its judges a number of former law teachers and deans at those institutions. As a result, both the First and Second Circuits have often been recognized not just as conduits for federal law, but also as innovators in its development.

George Dargo, *A History of the United States Court of Appeals for the First Circuit, Vol. 1, 1891–1960* (1993); Jeffrey B. Morris, *Federal Justice in the Second Circuit: A History of the United States Courts in New York, Connecticut and Vermont, 1787–1987* (1987); Edward A. Purcell, *Litigation and Inequality: Federal Diversity Jurisdiction in Industrial America, 1870–1958* (1992).

John Fabian Witt

Criminal Justice and Crime

The European colonists who settled New England in the early 17th century established communities maintained through vigilant enforcement of social norms. Because several of the colonies were founded by individuals who were fleeing religious and political persecution, the tension between personal liberty and the government's mandate to protect the public interest has long fueled debate over criminal justice policy. Today, New England has attained a reputation for tolerance while still possessing what some have called a puritanical streak.

Two famed instances of injustice and intolerance defy the prevailing mores in the region and perhaps provide the proverbial exceptions that prove the rule. In the 17th century, many colonial communities were organized around particular religious beliefs and practices. The witch trials of 1692 in Salem, Mass., demonstrated the repercussions of overzealous efforts to maintain a rigid sense of community

March protesting the conviction of Sacco and Vanzetti, 1925

standards. The prosecution of witches also came at a time when the courts were closed because of an interruption in the government. The first court to open heard only cases of witchcraft. Nineteen people, most of them women, were convicted of engaging in witchcraft and most were hanged; one died in prison. Another suspect was pressed to death. Modern explanations of the hysteria in Salem point to political and religious anxieties and animosity among opposing community factions.

In the 20th century, intolerance may be the best explanation for the persecution of Nicola Sacco and Bartolomeo Vanzetti, Italian immigrants who embraced anarchistic political views. Accused of the 1920 murders of a paymaster and a guard in South Braintree, Mass., and convicted at a critically flawed jury trial in 1921, the two were sentenced to death. The case took place amid the post–World War I era of antiradical hysteria and divisive U.S. immigration policy. Many saw the case as a conflict between the traditional, Anglocentric New England and a changing society experiencing an influx of immigrants from southern and eastern Europe, rather than a matter focused simply on the facts at hand. The international outcry over the case led the governor of Massachusetts to appoint an advisory committee to investigate. The committee concluded that the two convicted men did not deserve clemency, a decision seen by many as more intent on preserving the status quo than

on pursuing justice. Sacco and Vanzetti were executed in August 1927.

Today, crime rates in New England are lower than the national averages, largely because of three factors. First, the median age of the population in New England is slightly older than the national average (crime rates are highest among men in their late teens and early twenties). Second, the region's population is more stable than the nation's as a whole (crime tends to be more common in relatively transient communities). Third, New England's economy has generally been more robust than the national economy over the past several decades. Scattered throughout the region, however, are several communities that have suffered postindustrial decline, as major employers have abandoned aging factories and mills, leaving many people out of work. These communities typically have higher crime rates relative to other communities in the region.

All six New England states reported incarceration rates below the 2003 national average of 429 prisoners per 100,000 population; the overall regional rate is 304 prisoners per 100,000 population. Connecticut has the highest rate in the region, with 403 prisoners per 100,000, while Maine has the lowest rate in the nation, with 148 prisoners per 100,000. With a relatively well-educated professional workforce in the corrections field, alternatives to incarceration are frequently introduced in New England. These have included the use of so-called boot camps for youthful offenders and mediation programs for certain violent offenders.

Probation, the most common alternative to incarceration, was pioneered in Boston in 1841. John Augustus, a shoemaker, offered to help a man in trouble with the law for drunkenness by promising to supervise the man's behavior and guarantee his subsequent reappearance in court. The experiment proved successful, and between 1841 and 1859, Augustus and a group of volunteers under his guidance were estimated to have helped nearly 2,000 men and women. Today, far more offenders are on probation than incarcerated in New England.

The low incarceration figures are also explained in part by the low rate of violent crime in the region, relative to the rest of the country. New Hampshire, Maine, and Vermont have, respectively, the 46th-, 48th-, and 49th-lowest violent crime rates in the country. The most urbanized New England state, Massachusetts, ranked 31st in the nation in 2001, with 479.5 violent crimes reported per 100,000 population. The nation's 49th-ranked state, Vermont, had 105 crimes per 100,000 population, nearly one-eighth the rate of the highest-ranked state, Florida.

Between 1930 and 1976, a total of 52 executions were carried out in New England, mostly in Massachusetts and Connecticut, the region's most urbanized states. Despite a significant increase in the rate of capital punishment nationally after the U.S. Supreme Court allowed reinstatement of the death penalty in 1976, no executions have taken place in New England since then. Only Connecticut and New Hampshire currently have enforceable death penalty statutes. Both states restrict the application of the death penalty to cases involving aggravated murder and provide for execution by lethal injection. The general lack of acceptance of execution as a means of punishment in the region may be explained in part by the powerful presence of the Roman Catholic Church, which proscribes the death penalty, as does the much smaller yet long-established Unitarian Universalist Association.

Another explanation for the comparatively moderate punishments meted to criminals in the region may be the relatively apolitical nature of its courts. Although many states provide for popular election of judges, trial and appellate judges in all of the New England states are appointed, either by nominating committees or by the states' governors. Some critics of judicial appointments point to a distrust of the voting public among the political elite. Those who support the appointment process argue that "down ballot" races such as those for judicial posts receive little public scrutiny and thus many voters are uninformed and apathetic about these races.

Trials and appeals for federal crimes such as bank robbery and drug trafficking are heard in a U.S. district court, the federal trial court of general jurisdiction. Each of the region's states has at least one U.S. district court. Appeals of cases tried in Maine, New Hampshire, Massachusetts, and Rhode Island are heard by the U.S. Court of Appeals for the First Circuit, headquartered in Boston. Federal cases tried in Vermont and Connecticut are appealed to the Second Circuit.

Some of the more spectacular court cases tried in the region have involved organized crime groups, which have long fascinated the public, frustrated authorities, and provided in-demand illicit services in New England. Gaspare Messina founded the Mafia's New England family in Boston in 1916. The organization involved itself in traditional Mafia activities such as gambling and loan-sharking; and bootlegging operations during Prohibition were particularly widespread owing to the region's location on the Atlantic Coast and its shared border with Canada.

The New England Mafia moved its headquarters to Providence during the 1950s, under the leadership of Raymond L. S. Patriarca. Besides controlling illegal gambling in New England, Patriarca had financial interests in several Las Vegas casinos. Patriarca ran the organization from 1954 until his death (of natural causes) in 1985. Raymond J. "Junior" Patriarca succeeded his father after a brief power struggle. However, Junior was imprisoned after a 1992 federal conviction for racketeering. The prosecutor's case was boosted by the introduction of a tape secretly recorded at a Mafia induction in which Junior participated in Medford, Mass., in 1989. This, coupled with the 1986 conviction of underboss Gennaro "Jerry" Angiulo, whose office in Boston's North End had also been bugged by the FBI, substantially weakened the organization. Francis "Cadillac Frank" Salemme was thought to have been the boss of the New England Mafia at the time of his arrest in 1996. Testimony related to the accusations against Salemme and several others brought public scrutiny to the relationship between the FBI and a number of informants who themselves were major organized crime figures. Louis "Baby Shacks" Manocchio of Providence is believed to be the current head of the New England Mafia.

Recent developments in organized crime in the region include the growth of the Latin Kings, a burgeoning gang active primarily in the southern, more urban parts of New England. The Latin Kings have been heavily involved in drug trafficking in the region. Law enforcement officials also express concern about Asian tongs, or associations, some of which have been involved in a variety of criminal activities, including drug trafficking and gambling. Currently neither of these factions seems to have captured the public's interest as the declining Mafia did.

Discussion of crime in New England must distinguish between circumstances in the three urbanized states in the southern part of the region, Connecticut, Massachusetts, and Rhode Island, and circumstances in the predominantly rural northern states of New Hampshire, Vermont, and Maine. Although the urbanized states have more significant problems, social and historical conditions in general have led to a regional crime rate below the national average, allowing New England's criminal justice system to focus on preventing crime rather than merely reacting to its occurrence.

Paul Boyer and Stephen Nissenbaum, *Salem Possessed: The Social Origins of Witchcraft* (1974); Kai T. Erikson, *Wayward Puritans: A Study in the Sociology of Deviance* (1966); G. Louis Loughlin and Edmund M. Morgan, *The Legacy of Sacco and Vanzetti* (1948); Edgar J. McManus, *Law and Liberty in Early New England: Criminal Justice and Due Process, 1620–1692* (1993).

Peyton Paxson

Criminal Law The criminal laws of early New England closely reflected the political hegemony of puritanism over most of the region. The Pilgrim and Puritan founders came to New England not just to colonize but to create model Christian communities living in perfect harmony with the laws of God. Since the best source of divine law was the Bible, many of the first criminal statutes were based on biblical models. The laws enacted by Massachusetts, New Plymouth, Connecticut, and the New Haven Colony put far greater emphasis on moral behavior and good Christian living than on the protection of property. Drunkenness, fornication, lewdness, cursing, Sabbath-breaking, and even smoking received more attention than the various forms of larceny. The reliance on Scripture for moral guidance is most apparent in laws providing for the death penalty, a punishment that Puritans hesitated to impose without express scriptural authority. While their capital crimes included many Old Testament offenses such as adultery, blasphemy, and idolatry, they omitted numerous crimes punishable by death in England for which scriptural precedents could not be found. Eleven of the 12 capital offenses listed in the Massachusetts "Body of Liberties" of 1641 carried scriptural citations, and the capital laws adopted by Connecticut the following year did the same. The law code enacted by ultra-Puritan New Haven Colony in 1656 specifically made Scripture binding in all capital cases.

But Scripture was by no means the only

source of law in Puritan New England. The Puritans revered the legal and constitutional traditions of England's common law, and their lawmakers sought to combine what was morally essential in Scripture with the traditional rights of English people in the 17th century. One of the key provisions of the Massachusetts "Body of Liberties" and the more comprehensive *Lawes and Libertyes* of 1648 was the principle enshrined in the Magna Carta that no one should be deprived of life, liberty, or property without due process of law. Both codes put more explicit limits on governmental power than the vague guarantees of the English common law did. The list of guarantees is familiar and impressive: no unreasonable search or seizure, no double jeopardy, no compulsory self-incrimination, and no cruel or barbarous punishments. The right to bail, grand jury indictment, and trial by jury; the presumption of innocence; and the right to confront accusers in open court were all protected. Indeed, most of the rights taken for granted by Americans today took root and flourished in the legal culture of early New England.

Massachusetts took the lead in regional legal development. Although New Plymouth adopted a rudimentary body of laws in 1636, five years before the first Massachusetts code, by midcentury undisputed leadership had passed to Massachusetts. Maine and New Hampshire fell into line as territories claimed and governed by Massachusetts. Even after New Hampshire became a separate jurisdiction in 1679, most of the Massachusetts laws previously in force were reenacted. Massachusetts law entered Connecticut and New Haven Colony with the first settlers, many of whom had lived in the Bay Colony and had no desire to abandon familiar forms of law and government. The capital laws that Connecticut adopted in 1642 were taken almost completely from the capital list enacted by Massachusetts the year before. When a more comprehensive code was adopted in 1650, whole passages were copied almost verbatim from the Massachusetts code of 1648. Although New Haven Colony relied primarily on Scripture in dealing with criminal offenses, the civil provisions of the code adopted in 1650 were based on the Massachusetts model.

Only Rhode Island remained completely outside the orbit of Massachusetts law. Many Rhode Islanders were religious refugees from the Bay Colony with bitter memories of Puritan law and justice. Their commitment to religious freedom and their need, because they had no charter, to demonstrate loyalty to the Crown caused them to follow English legal practices as closely as possible. Maintaining good relations with England was furthermore important because both Massachusetts and

New Plymouth had territorial claims that might have obliterated Rhode Island as an independent jurisdiction. Therefore, the first list of criminal laws adopted in 1647 was based almost entirely on English common law and statutory models. Although certain crimes were listed under New Testament captions, their substantive provisions were English, not scriptural. The Bible citations that punctuated the Puritan codes were notably lacking. Nor did Rhode Island enact the death penalty for scriptural offenses that were not capital crimes in England. Sodomy, bestiality, and witchcraft made the capital list not because they were scriptural offenses but because they were punishable by death under English law. Rhode Island never strayed very far from English legal models. A statute enacted in 1673 required a copy of the English laws in force to be available at all legislative and judicial sessions.

The treatment of offenders in the 17th century was not complicated by modern notions of societal responsibility for individual wrongdoing. The prevailing view was that criminals were innately wicked, and neither Puritans nor non-Puritans had any qualms about punishing them severely. The penalties inflicted in New England ranged from fines and admonitions for minor offenses to corporal punishments and death for more serious crimes. Whipping was the most common form of corporal punishment because it could be calibrated according to the seriousness of the offense. The most serious noncapital crimes might be punished by branding and ear cropping. Although no colony prescribed an official method of execution, the common law method of death by hanging was virtually automatic in capital cases. One punishment almost never ordered was long-term incarceration. Colonial jails were primarily holding facilities for prisoners awaiting trial or punishment. The preference for corporal punishments was at least partly driven by economics, as colonial society did not have the resources needed to support a prison population. But such punishments probably would have been favored in any case because they closed the books on the offense completely. To prolong punishment by incarcerating the offender long after the offense had been forgotten hardly had the deterrent effect of a public whipping or hanging.

Puritan criminal law remained a powerful force in New England well into the 18th century. Even after the Puritan political hegemony ended, the courts continued to function as defenders of public morality. The court records of Massachusetts show that most of the changes that transformed Puritan law into the criminal law of today occurred after 1760, when the law's function shifted from the de-

fense of morality to the defense of property. Although fairly common in the 17th century, crimes of theft usually involved only petty pilferage that was not serious enough to cause economic problems. Nor did such thefts usually involve violence. When violence occurred at all, it usually resulted from personal disputes that the tight social networks of the time prevented from getting out of hand. All this changed with the accumulation of wealth and the breakdown of moral constraints as populations dispersed beyond the old centers of social control. Crimes against property and antisocial behavior generally increased sharply during the late 18th century, necessitating changes in the criminal codes. New offenses such as bribery, embezzlement, and various forms of larceny were added to the criminal lists, and penalties were increased for crimes of violence. By 1866 crimes against people accounted for 38 sections of the statute law of Massachusetts, while crimes against property accounted for another 91 sections. Although numerous morals offenses remained on the books, offenders were seldom prosecuted. The resources of the justice system had by now been almost fully mobilized to deal with the more pressing problem of secular crime.

The theory that criminals were innately wicked also began to change in the late 18th and early 19th centuries. The generation after the Revolution looked more to social and economic factors to explain criminal behavior. Criminal law came to be viewed as more than an instrument of deterrence and vindictive justice; it could also be used to rehabilitate and restore the offender to society. Corporal punishments were replaced by confinement in penitentiaries, where offenders could be reclaimed as useful citizens through hard labor and moral reflection. The new approach led to a drastic reduction in the list of capital crimes. In 1684, 27 offenses called for the death penalty in Massachusetts; by 1866 only first-degree murder was punishable by death.

The emphasis on rehabilitation led to provisions for probation and parole. In 1878 Massachusetts became the first state to enact a probation statute. This formalized what had been a long-standing practice of assigning minor offenders to people who would supervise them in the community instead of sending them to prison. Provisions for parole were also enacted under which prisoners could earn early release for good behavior. The remission of jail time had originally been a function of the governor's pardoning power. Between 1828 and 1866, 12.5 percent of all inmates released from prison in Massachusetts got out on pardons. Regularizing parole relieved overcrowding and made room in prisons for recently convicted offenders.

The influence of Massachusetts on legal developments in the rest of New England diminished considerably during the 19th century. Maine became a state in 1820, and the rest of the region looked increasingly to local needs when enacting criminal statutes. By the end of the century, repeated legislative tinkering and revisions had produced distinctively local bodies of criminal law. Connecticut, New Hampshire, Maine, and Vermont have by now removed most of the old morals offenses from their criminal laws, while the Massachusetts statutes still devote considerable space to such offenses. Adultery remained a felony in Massachusetts long after the rest of New England reduced it to a misdemeanor or removed it from the criminal list completely. Only Rhode Island and Massachusetts continue to list blasphemy and profanity as punishable offenses. Maine, Vermont, and Rhode Island have abolished capital punishment, while Connecticut, New Hampshire, and Massachusetts have retained it, the last by a state constitutional amendment specifically authorizing the death penalty.

Perhaps the most important development in 20th-century criminal law was the imposition of national due process standards by the U.S. Supreme Court. Expansive interpretations of the 14th Amendment and the federal Bill of Rights have drastically reduced the sovereign discretion of the states in the administration of criminal justice. The right of jury trial, rules of evidence, police practices, and even what may be criminalized must now conform to national constitutional standards. The court struck down a Connecticut statute outlawing contraceptives in *Griswold v. Connecticut* (1965), and in *Memoirs v. Massachusetts* (1966) it reversed a Massachusetts ruling that the 18th-century novel *Fanny Hill* was obscene and therefore subject to state suppression. Notwithstanding the homogenizing influence of national constitutional constraints, New England criminal law has managed to retain some of its original Puritan flavor. The regulation of morality is still visible in the classification of certain acts as "lewd" or "lascivious." Although no longer capital crimes, sodomy and other forms of unconventional sex remained punishable offenses in Massachusetts until 2003. The Puritan hegemony that ended three centuries ago still resonates occasionally in the criminal laws of New England.

Bradley Chapin, *Criminal Justice in Colonial America, 1606–1660* (1983); Lawrence M. Friedman, *A History of American Law* (1973); Kermit L. Hall, *The Magic Mirror* (1989); George L. Haskins, *Law and Authority in Early Massachusetts* (1960); Adam Hirsch, "From Pillory to Penitentiary: The Rise of Criminal Incarceration in Early Massachusetts," *Michigan Law Review* 80 (1982); Edgar J. McManus, *Law and Liberty in Early New England: Criminal Justice and Due Process, 1620–1692* (1993); William E. Nelson, "Emerging Notions of Modern Criminal Law in the Revolutionary Era: An Historical Perspective," *New York University Law Review* 42 (1967); Edwin Powers, *Crime and Punishment in Early Massachusetts, 1620–1692* (1966).

Edgar J. McManus

Dartmouth College v. Woodward One of the most important cases in American jurisprudence, the Supreme Court's 1819 decision in *Trustees of Dartmouth College v. William H. Woodward, Esq.* had profound and far-reaching effects, both educationally and commercially, on the young republic and New England in particular. What began as a quarrel between the president of a small, remote New Hampshire college, which had as its original mission the education of Native Americans, and the college's board of trustees blossomed into a Supreme Court precedent subsequently used to uphold the rights of private corporations and entities in the face of legislative action.

In 1815, John Wheelock, son and presidential successor of Eleazar Wheelock, the college's founder, began a political campaign to pack the college's board of trustees with legislative appointments more sympathetic to his often whimsical and nepotistic interests. The increasingly intransigent board of trustees, eager to see Dartmouth develop into an important intellectual institution and not merely a

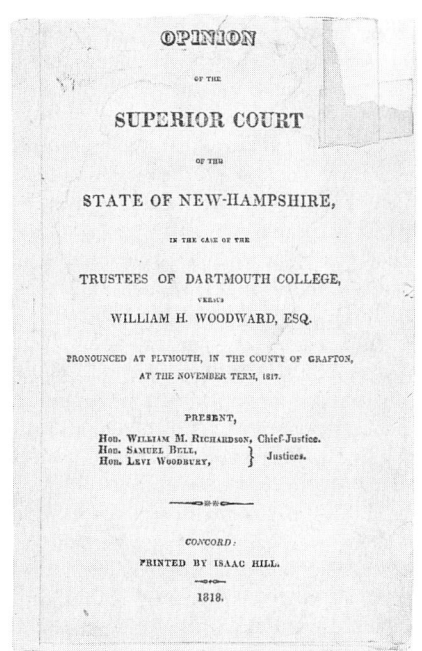

Title page of the Dartmouth College v. Woodward *case report, 1818*

family enterprise, removed Wheelock from his position. Wheelock enlisted the help of the New Hampshire legislature, which passed a bill in 1816 to establish Dartmouth University as a state-controlled, state-supported, and secular institution, with Wheelock as president.

The trustees resisted, refusing to recognize the validity of the act, and sued William H. Woodward, formerly secretary of the college, who had defected to the new university, carrying with him all of Dartmouth's records and official seal. After the state judiciary ruled in favor of the new university, the case moved to the Supreme Court in 1818, with Dartmouth graduate Daniel Webster arguing on behalf of Dartmouth. Webster's words from his closing address became a talisman for Dartmouth students and alumni: "It is, Sir, as I have said, a small college. And yet there are those who love it!" Chief Justice John Marshall overturned the lower court's decision, stating that the Dartmouth College charter was a contract and, as such, could not be infringed upon by the state government without violating the U.S. Constitution.

The implications of Marshall's opinion were not immediately recognized. In later years, the precedent set by the case would become known as the Dartmouth College doctrine and would be used to argue on behalf of the sovereignty of private institutions of all sorts, including schools, charities, and, perhaps most importantly for American history, business corporations.

Private schools in New England felt the effect of the ruling most immediately, as many of them, including Harvard and Yale, had previously weathered damaging attacks by state legislatures seeking expanded control owing to various religious and political disagreements. These attacks mellowed considerably after the ruling, especially after the court cemented the Dartmouth College doctrine by deciding for Bowdoin College in a similar case, *Allen v. McKean*, in 1831.

The *Dartmouth College* ruling not only allowed New England to preserve its small-town collegiate flavor but also helped set a powerful cultural precedent for the region's pride in academic freedom. In addition, the decision gave New England industrial and mercantile interests greater autonomy and latitude in their business affairs by protecting them from the threat of power-hungry and opportunistic state legislatures.

Leon Burr Richardson, *History of Dartmouth College* (1932); John M. Shirley, *The Dartmouth College Causes and the Supreme Court of the United States* (1971); Francis N. Stites, *Private Interest and Public Gain: The Dartmouth College Case, 1819* (1972).

Ryan McMillen

Dawes, Henry Laurens (1816–1903)

U.S. representative and senator. Henry Laurens Dawes, chief author of the Dawes Severalty Act of 1887, designed to end Indian reservation life, was born in Cummington, Mass. Despite a haphazard education at home and in the district schools, he passed Yale's entrance exam—and walked 100 miles in three days to enroll there. Upon graduating in 1839, Dawes taught school and studied law; in 1842 he passed the bar examination and opened a law office in North Adams, Mass.

Active in Whig politics in Berkshire County, the young lawyer gained prominence as a temperance orator and editorialist for the *Weekly Transcript.* He served several terms in the Massachusetts House and Senate, where he was an early advocate of state funding for the Hoosac Tunnel, which in 1874 opened the railroad from Boston to the West. After serving four years as district attorney for western Massachusetts (1853–57), he was nominated by the Republican Party as its candidate for Congress and was elected to the House of Representatives in 1856.

In his 18 years in the House (1857–75), Dawes carved out a reputation as a cool and deliberate legislator. During the Civil War he served with distinction on the War Contracts Committee. He visited encampments, comforted the wounded in hospitals, and so zealously exposed corruption that Abraham Lincoln once protested to Senator Henry Wilson that Dawes "has done more to break down the Administration than any other man in the country." Years later, Dawes wrote the introduction to James L. Bowen's book *Massachusetts in the War, 1861–1865* (1889).

During Reconstruction, Dawes seemed as ill at ease with the radical wing of the Republican Party as he was with the corruption of the Grant administration. His work as chairman of the Elections Commission and with other committees earned him the name "Father of the House." He helped shape legislation that created the "Weather Bulletin," which collected and compared weather reports from around the country; a fish commission; Yellowstone National Park; and Arlington National Cemetery. In 1869 Dawes's career in the House came to a climax when he served one term as chairman of the House Committee on Appropriations.

Dawes was elevated to the U.S. Senate upon the death of Charles Sumner in 1874. There, he earned his somewhat dubious fame as chairman of the Committee on Indian Affairs. He was influenced by eastern reformers such as Lyman Abbott and Helen Hunt Jackson, who mourned the injustice of the treatment of American Indians and called for immediate action to prevent their extermination.

The General Allotment Law of 1887, also known as the Dawes Severalty Act in honor of its principal congressional sponsor, was designed to ultimately replace the communal ideal of the reservation system with a way of life dominated by individualistic values and private property. The law created a 25-year trust during which Indian land could not be sold, but as soon as the restriction was removed, the rush to buy Indian land began.

The Dawes Act represents a failure of good intentions all too common in the history of New England reform: motivated by sincere concern for Indian welfare, the law proved ineffective against the greed of western land grabbers and led to the loss of much valuable Indian land. Ninety million acres of Indian-owned land passed into white ownership as a result of the act.

Henry Dawes served three terms in the Senate (1875–93) and retired to his home in Pittsfield, Mass. "My foe is inactivity, idleness," he once noted in his diary. He was a workhorse, not a show horse, a pure product of 19th-century New England. Dawes died in Pittsfield on February 5, 1903.

Steven J. Arconti, "To Secure the Party: Henry L. Dawes and the Politics of Reconstruction," *Historical Journal of Western Massachusetts* 5 (1977); Kent Carter, "Federal Indian Policy: The Dawes Commission, 1887–1898," *Prologue* 22 (1990); Fred H. Nicklason, "The Shaping of Values in 19th Century Massachusetts: The Case of Henry L. Dawes," *Historical Journal of Massachusetts* 11 (1983); Francis Paul Prucha, *American Indian Policy in Crisis: Christian Reformers and the Indian, 1865–1900* (1976).

Richard S. Taskin

Doe, Charles (1830–96)

Jurist. Charles Doe was born in Derry, N.H., the youngest child of Joseph Doe and Mary Bodwell (Ricker) Doe. He attended Harvard College but transferred to Dartmouth College, where he graduated in 1849. He then joined the law office of Daniel M. Christie in Dover, N.H., and subsequently attended Harvard Law School but did not complete a degree. He became solicitor for Strafford County, where his family name brought him many cases. Doe was admitted to the bar in 1854.

As an active Democrat, Charles Doe became assistant clerk to the New Hampshire state legislature (1853–54). In 1856 he was removed from his position as county solicitor, but three years later he joined the Republican Party after his growing dissatisfaction with the Democratic Party's attitude toward the secession crisis. In 1859 he was appointed an associate justice of the Supreme Judicial Court of New Hampshire, where he developed a reputation as a judge who wanted to reform the existing legal system, an idea that was not popular with members of the legal profession.

Doe declined to modify his views on legal reform and, eventually, earned the grudging respect, if not the assent, of his peers and impressed the public with his absolute sincerity of purpose, his efficiency, and his competence, all traits demonstrated from the outset of Doe's judicial career. He never overcame the animosity of his political opponents, however. In 1874, the Democrats won back control of the legislature; they reorganized the state courts, abolishing the supreme judicial court and replacing it with a superior court to which Doe was pointedly not appointed. He did not resume his law practice but retired to his home in Rollinsford, where he declined a nomination for Congress. In 1876, the Republican Party regained power, created the Supreme Court of New Hampshire, and appointed Doe its chief justice. During his tenure, he worked primarily on appellate matters and drafted opinions renowned for their originality.

Doe delighted in research, frequently investigating legal principles to their foundation; his influence was especially felt in the field of procedure. He believed that common law rights existed independently of any particular writ, that a mistake in procedure was a mere formality and not substantive, and that the court had power to make any necessary amendments independently of the legislature. On this principle, historically untrue, he brought about procedural reforms that were effective, though radical, by means of court decisions and without recourse to legislation.

Doe died suddenly in Rollinsford on March 9, 1896.

John Philip Reid, *Chief Justice: The Judicial World of Charles Doe* (1967); Reid, "The Touch of History: The Historical Method of a Common Law Judge," *American Journal of Legal History* 8, no. 2 (1964); Jeremiah Smith, *Memoir of Hon. Charles Doe* (1897).

Martin J. Manning

Frankfurter, Felix (1882–1965)

Jurist and legal scholar. Born in Vienna, Austria, Felix Frankfurter immigrated to the United States when he was 12 years old. His family settled in New York City, where he attended public schools and the City College of New York. Frankfurter, who graduated from Harvard Law School first in his class, spent one year in private practice before realizing that his interests lay in public policy and government service. He assisted Henry L. Stimson, U.S. attorney in New York, and then became solicitor for the Bureau of Insular Affairs when Stimson became secretary of war. In 1914 he was invited to join the faculty at Harvard Law School. Although not a native New Englander, Frankfurter's career and legal thought were shaped by his mentors, Louis Brandeis and Oliver Wendell Holmes, Jr., and he be-

Felix Frankfurter, 1948

came deeply involved in New England legal affairs through his years at Harvard Law School and his criticism of the Sacco and Vanzetti trial.

Frankfurter had a distinguished career at Harvard, where he taught constitutional and administrative law, examining a few cases in great detail. His students learned to consider not only legal doctrine but also relevant social and economic factors. He produced numerous books and articles, many in collaboration with former students or faculty colleagues. A landmark study, *Criminal Justice in Cleveland*, written with Roscoe Pound (1922); *The Business of the Supreme Court*, with James Landis (1928); and *The Labor Injunction*, with Nathan Green (1930) demonstrate the breadth and depth of his scholarly interests. With Henry Hart and Henry Weschler he formed the "legal process" school of jurisprudence, which bemoaned the loss of judicial restraint during the New Deal era.

Politically, Frankfurter was a Progressive. He was a founder of *The New Republic* magazine, a charter member of the American Civil Liberties Union, legal adviser to the National Association for the Advancement of Colored People, and counsel for the National Consumers' League. Disturbed by the procedures used in the Sacco and Vanzetti trial, he lobbied intensely but unsuccessfully to secure a new trial for the two immigrants.

During the 1930s, Frankfurter helped to shape policy, draft legislation, and identify bright, young lawyers to administer new federal agencies. He turned down Franklin Roosevelt's offer to appoint him solicitor general, realizing that he might carry more influence as a private adviser. When the president proposed to "pack" the Supreme Court by raising the number of justices from nine to 13, Frank-

furter refused public comment; Roosevelt was his hero, but Justice Louis Brandeis—an outspoken opponent of the plan—was a close friend. Indeed, Brandeis had once referred to Frankfurter as "half brother, half son."

In 1939 Roosevelt appointed Frankfurter to the Supreme Court, a position he held until his retirement in 1962. He may have breached the wall that is supposed to separate the executive and judicial branches of the federal government by continuing to advise Roosevelt on matters of public policy, but as a justice, Frankfurter usually deferred to state legislatures. For example, in 1943 he refused to hear a challenge to Connecticut's ban on contraceptives even though he considered the law ridiculous. With the exception of cases involving the Establishment Clause, involving religion, he found few reasons to overrule state legislation that threatened individual rights. A notable exception was *Sweezy v. New Hampshire* (1957), in which Frankfurter upheld a claim of academic freedom, finding that the state's attorney general had exceeded his authority in questioning a university professor with unpopular ideas. Despite a strong commitment to procedures used to investigate federal criminals, Frankfurter generally refused to apply the Fourth Amendment to the states. He did not view the Constitution in absolute terms but relied on "standards of civilized behavior" and "reasonableness" when judging.

Joseph Lash, ed., *From the Diaries of Felix Frankfurter* (1975); Bruce Allen Murphy, *The Brandeis/Frankfurter Connection* (1982); Michael E. Parrish, *Felix Frankfurter and His Times: The Reform Years* (1982); Melvin I. Urofsky, *Felix Frankfurter: Judicial Restraint and Individual Liberties* (1991).

Christine L. Compston

Fugitive Slave Laws Although the problem of how to treat those fleeing from slavery arose in colonial times, it became a much more complicated legal problem when some of the states after 1776 abolished slavery, and some did not. In those states that did, fugitive slave laws became ineffective. When Quock Walker, an African American, left his supposed master in 1781 to take a job elsewhere, he was physically seized in an attempt to return him to slavery. The "master" was then convicted of assault because Walker was declared by the court to be a free man under the state constitution of 1780. By the time the U.S. Constitution was ratified, all of the New England states had made provisions to abolish slavery. The problem then arose as to whether African Americans fleeing from the slave states would find legal refuge in New England.

Under the Articles of Confederation states

were not obligated to return fugitive slaves. The U.S. Constitution, however, declared that fugitive slaves be "delivered up on claim of the party to whom such service or labor may be due." Before the 1830s there were few cases involving runaway slaves in New England, but by the end of that decade the region had become the home of many abolitionists, as well as a haven for southern fugitives, including the soon-to-be-famous Frederick Douglass.

In Massachusetts, Chief Justice Lemuel Shaw in *Commonwealth v. Aves* (1836) held that slaves voluntarily brought into the state were free but that fugitives should be returned because of the constitutional clause. In response to that decision, the Massachusetts legislature passed a personal liberty law allowing those seized as runaway slaves to go to the courts for an order that would release them. That same year, two Maine sailors helped a slave escape from Georgia. The slave's master followed the ship to Maine, seized his slave, and returned home. However, successive Maine governors refused to extradite the sailors to Georgia, where they had been indicted for theft. The "Maine-Georgia Controversy" continued as a war of words, pamphlets, and resolutions until it fizzled out in 1842.

In 1842 Justice Joseph Story, who held the "New England seat" on the Supreme Court, delivered a stunningly proslavery opinion in *Prigg v. Pennsylvania*, for which he was denounced by an abolitionist newspaper as "the Slave-Catcher-In-Chief for the New England States." The decision struck down all state laws interfering with the return of fugitive slaves, including the personal liberty law passed by Massachusetts. A year later, Chief Justice Shaw of Massachusetts refused to issue an order to release George Latimer, who had been seized as a fugitive slave. When the case was appealed to the U.S. circuit court, one of the judges was Joseph Story. Not surprisingly, the circuit court ordered Latimer returned to the man who claimed to own him. Fortunately for Latimer, the threat of mob violence persuaded his supposed owner to sell him at a nominal price to a purchaser who had already agreed to give Latimer his legal freedom. Shortly after this incident the Massachusetts legislature passed the 1843 "Latimer law," which prohibited holding a fugitive slave in any state facility and prohibited any state official from participating in the return of a fugitive slave. All other New England states passed similar laws.

In 1850 Congress adopted a new fugitive slave law, with the crucial support of Senator Daniel Webster from Massachusetts, providing new and more arbitrary rendition procedures and harsher penalties for those who helped fugitive slaves. Under this law, accused fugitives could not testify on their own behalf and were not allowed a jury trial. Furthermore, federal commissioners were appointed in every county in the country to enforce the law, and these commissioners were paid $5 if they decided that the alleged fugitive before them was not a slave, but were paid $10 if they found in favor of the claimant. The standards of evidence under this law were also extremely lax.

The 1850 law led to new personal liberty laws in all of the New England states, and to riots and rescues in Boston. In 1851 a mob rescued the fugitive slave Shadrach from inside a courtroom. Although a number of the alleged rescuers were charged and tried, no one was convicted. Later that year federal authorities succeeded in removing Thomas Sims from Boston and taking him back to Georgia, but only after Boston lawyers led a spirited resistance.

The most famous fugitive slave case of the last antebellum decade was the rendition of Anthony Burns. Boston police arrested Burns in 1854, hoping to remove him quickly and quietly to Virginia. Richard Henry Dana, Jr., however, found out about the hearing before U.S. Commissioner Edward G. Loring and imposed himself on the court, demanding a recess in order for Burns to decide whether he wanted counsel. This led to a weeklong hearing into his status, finally leading to a determination that Burns was indeed the slave of the claimant, Charles Suttle of Virginia. During the week a mob, in part led by the Rev. Thomas Wentworth Higginson, almost set Burns free. In the melee, a federal deputy was killed. The hearing into the status of Burns took place in a heavily guarded courthouse ringed with soldiers and members of the militia. Nearly 1,000 armed men guarded Burns during his walk from the courthouse to the wharf, where he was placed on a revenue cutter and sent to Virginia.

In the aftermath of the Burns affair, the Massachusetts legislature removed Commissioner Loring from his position as a probate judge. Loring left his native Boston to spend the rest of his life in Washington, D.C. Burns was the last fugitive slave taken from Boston and became a symbol in the North of the oppressive nature of the fugitive slave law. After 1854 the fugitive slave law was, in fact, a dead letter in New England.

Stanley Campbell, *The Slave Catchers* (1968); Paul Finkelman, "Legal Ethics and Fugitive Slaves: The Anthony Burns Case, Judge Loring, and Abolitionist Attorneys," *Cardozo Law Review* 17 (1996); Finkelman, *Slavery in the Courtroom* (1985); James O. Horton and Lois Horton, *Black Bostonians: Family Life and Community Struggle in the Antebellum North* (1979).

Paul Finkelman

Gray, John Chipman (1839–1915) Lawyer and law professor. Born to an elite Boston family, John Chipman Gray was educated at the Boston Latin School, Harvard College, and Harvard Law School. His half-brother, Horace Gray, served on the U.S. Supreme Court from 1881 until 1902. William James, the famous psychologist and pragmatic philosopher, and Oliver Wendell Holmes, the nation's leading jurist and judge, were lifelong friends.

After graduating from law school, Gray joined the Union Army. When the Civil War ended, Gray founded the still prominent law firm of Ropes and Gray. In 1866, Gray and John Ropes also founded the *American Law Review*, which became a leading journal of legal news and analysis. Gray joined the Harvard Law School faculty in 1869, serving there for 44 years, all the while maintaining his active practice with Ropes and Gray.

At Harvard, Gray taught the three-year sequence of property courses. As the occasion arose, he also taught agency, conflict of law, constitutional law, evidence, and jurisprudence. As a popular professor and eminent practitioner, Gray held leadership positions in university alumni organizations and in Boston legal, civic, and cultural institutions.

Gray is most known for his work in the law governing the transmission of wealth through generations. He wrote two treatises on the subject: *Restraints on the Alienation of Property* (1883) and *The Rule against Perpetuities* (1886). Both books were immediately accepted as definitive statements of the law in both England and America. Although now more than a century old, Gray's treatises are still regarded as the leading scholarly treatment of their subjects.

Part of the explanation for the popularity of Gray's treatises is that they are paradigmatic expressions of "classical orthodoxy," the jurisprudential style that dominated American and English legal thought during the late 19th and early 20th centuries. Gray's treatises depict restraint and perpetuities law as founded on a few fundamental principles and conceptions that were elaborated with remorseless deductive logic into a myriad of binding rules. In restraint and perpetuities cases, there was "a definite recognized rule. If a decision agrees with it, it is right; if it does not agree with it, it is wrong." Analysis of restraints and perpetuities problems, Gray said, was like "do[ing] . . . sums correctly."

Gray, however, was not entirely a classical jurist. Late in life, he published a book on legal philosophy, *The Nature and Sources of Law* (1909), that in many ways anticipates legal realism, the jurisprudence that supplanted classical orthodoxy in the 1930s.

In *Nature and Sources*, Gray says that law is not some brooding and transcendent omnipresence. Law is simply "the opinion of judges on matters of ethics and public policy." In determining what the law is, judges consider a variety of sources, such as statutes, precedent, custom, expert opinion, morality, and public policy. But ultimately law consists of the rules that judges choose to enforce.

Scholars have long been puzzled by the apparent conflict between the legal philosophy underlying Gray's doctrinal treatises and the philosophy expressed in his jurisprudential writing. It is not possible to reconcile them by saying that his views changed over time. Gray had been teaching the views he published in *Nature and Sources* in his Harvard jurisprudence courses all during the time he worked on his doctrinal treatises.

Gray believed that the reconciliation lay in the fact that law ultimately reflects the judges' moral convictions about what the law should be. Restraint and perpetuities law were two areas of law in which Anglo-American judges had come to agree about basic governing principles. Restraint and perpetuities law, therefore, assumed the geometric form of mature bodies of law. But unlike many classical legal scholars, Gray did not believe this had to be so. There could be, and were, bodies of law that legal scholars could not truthfully depict according to the tenets of classical legal thought. Those areas were not yet based on a judicial consensus about a consistent set of fundamental principles and their deductive elaboration.

Moreover, because Gray believed that law would always be subject to shifts in the judiciary's moral beliefs, it was possible for law that had assumed a perfectly classical form to lose it. Living during the era of classical orthodoxy's dominance, but friends with the philosophers and jurists who first essayed the more pragmatic and positivist future, Gray wrote about areas of law that had assumed a mature form but also knew that those doctrines may not "be in entire harmony with the Social Code of the next century."

Stephen A. Siegel, "John Chipman Gray and the Moral Basis of Classical Legal Thought," *Iowa Law Review* 86 (2001).

Stephen A. Siegel

Griswold v. Connecticut The case of *Griswold v. Connecticut* (1965), which articulated for the first time that the Constitution guarantees Americans a right of privacy, grew out of an 1879 Connecticut statute that prohibited the sale or use of contraceptives and the provision of medical advice about avoiding conception. Doctors could not prescribe birth control pills or contraceptive devices even for married women whose lives and health were endangered by pregnancy. For years the Planned Parenthood League of Connecticut (PPLC) had tried and failed to get the Connecticut legislature to repeal the law. Many opponents of repeal were Roman Catholic legislators who supported the official position of the church that artificial means of birth control were immoral.

Consequently, the PPLC decided to pursue the matter in the state's courts, but in 1940 the Connecticut Supreme Court in *State v. Nelson* upheld the law. There was now no other recourse but the federal courts. The problem, however, was that Connecticut did not enforce the law, so there was nobody aggrieved enough by fine or imprisonment to have standing in a federal court. Opponents of the law therefore sought a declaratory ruling from the U.S. Supreme Court that the law was unconstitutional. In two cases, *Tileson v. Ullman* (1943) and *Poe v. Ullman* (1961), the justices refused to hear challenges to the law. Justice Felix Frankfurter, for example, said he would not allow himself to become involved "in debates concerning harmless, empty shadows."

At that point Estelle Griswold, the executive director of PPLC, and Dr. Lee Buxton, a practicing physician who was also head of the Department of Obstetrics and Gynecology at Yale Medical School, opened a birth control clinic in New Haven. Buxton treated the patients, and Griswold gave them birth control literature. Within days both Griswold and Buxton were arrested. They were found guilty at trial, and the Connecticut Supreme Court upheld both convictions. When the case reached the U.S. Supreme Court, the justices voted seven to two to overturn the convictions and invalidate the Connecticut statute. The majority could not agree on their reasons for voting as they did, however, and only five of the justices could find a right of privacy in the Constitution. The lead decision, written by Justice William O. Douglas, focused on the "penumbra" or "zone" of privacy created by the First, Fourth, and Fifth Amendments and, most surprisingly because it is so open-ended, also the Ninth Amendment. Although Justice Arthur Goldberg preferred to base the right of privacy on the Ninth Amendment, the argument by Justice Douglas that the Bill of Rights casts a penumbra in which unspecified rights exist has become more persuasive.

Critics of *Griswold v. Connecticut* charged that it was an egregious example of judicial activism that created a right where none had existed. But the case has withstood the proverbial test of time. Almost all commentators would now agree that the Constitution guarantees a right of privacy. Moreover, the court has affirmed such a right in other major decisions concerning marriage and contraception, such as *Loving v. Virginia* (1967), which invalidated laws that prohibited interracial marriages; *Eisenstadt v. Baird* (1972), which protected unmarried people from discrimination; and the celebrated *Roe v. Wade* (1973), which restricted the ability of states to prohibit abortions. Thus the right defined in *Griswold v. Connecticut* limits the power of state legislatures to pass laws intruding on the rights of Americans to decide whom to marry and whether or not to have children.

David J. Garrow, *Liberty and Sexuality: The Right of Privacy and the Making of "Roe v. Wade"* (1994); Darien A. McWhirter and Jon D. Bible, *Privacy as a Constitutional Right: Sex, Drugs, and the Right to Life* (1992); David M. O'Brien, *Privacy, Law, and Public Policy* (1979); Richard C. Turkington, George B. Trubow, and Anita L. Allen, *Privacy: Cases and Materials* (1992).

Roger D. Hardaway

Hartford Circus Fire

The Hartford circus fire of July 6, 1944, was the most devastating incident to occur in Connecticut since the state's ports were shelled during the Revolutionary War. The Ringling Brothers and Barnum and Bailey Circus was one of the few diversions available to war-weary mothers and children during that hot summer. One month after D-day, and two days after the Fourth of July, the circus made its annual trip to Hartford. At 2:20 P.M., just after the wild animals had been led out of the big top, a fire broke out on a portion of the canvas tent. Within moments it became an inferno in which 169 people died and more than 550 were seriously injured. This disaster would significantly alter the state of Connecticut and its legal system.

Many people were hurt in the panic that the fire touched off. Exits blocked by chutes used to take animals out of the tent were a major cause of injury and death. Sloppily set up chairs and fire extinguishers, owing to a wartime worker shortage, also contributed to the calamity. Another serious fault was the way in which the tent was waterproofed. The Ringlings, unable to obtain fire-retardant chemicals reserved for military use, had treated the big top with 1,800 pounds of liquid paraffin mixed with 6,000 gallons of gasoline. Once lit, the tent burned like a giant candle.

Raymond Baldwin, Connecticut's governor at the time of the fire, compared the human suffering brought on by this tragedy to a bomb attack on the cities of Europe. Despite extraordinary publicity, relatives did not come forward to identify one child who had died of smoke inhalation. The unknown girl was buried in the city cemetery as tag number 1565. Not until 1991 did the Hartford firefighter Rick Davey, after many years of investigating, identify the child as Eleanor Cook. Little Miss 1565, as Eleanor had been called for many years, became the circus fire's grim symbol, and her photograph, widely circulated by the authorities, became known throughout the world.

The legal reforms brought about by the fire included changes in the regulatory codes pertaining to outdoor performances, an increase in the number of inspections required for shows taking place under tents, and an augmented presence of police officers, firefighters, and equipment at a show location. New laws mandated large liability-insurance policies for canvas-covered entertainment. In Connecticut today circuses must carry at least $6 million in insurance, a statutory requirement that is often prohibitive for smaller companies. Corporate law was also improved and modernized. Six circus executives were convicted of involuntary manslaughter in connection with the fire, which led companies to set higher standards of corporate administration.

One of the most significant outcomes of the Hartford fire was the development of an alternate dispute-resolution process for resolving the civil suits brought against the circus. Facing liability of $15 million and a never-ending stream of attachments, the circus was about to collapse, leaving fire victims with no hope of recovery. Three enterprising Hartford attorneys, Julius Schatz, Arthur Weinstein, and Edward Rogin, were able to persuade the scholarly judge John Hamilton King to order the circus into state receivership. Simultaneously, the Hartford bar and Dan Gordon Judge, a New York attorney representing the circus, met in a courtroom of the superior court and developed an arbitration plan to substitute for standard trial processing of the victims' claims. Instead, the plan called for a panel of three judges (one chosen by the victims, one chosen by the circus, and one chosen by Connecticut's chief justice) to hear claims and set the amount of compensation for each victim or family. Arbitration awards were paid from circus earnings over a six-year period and distributed under the direction of the receiver, Edward Rogin.

This settlement was the first of its kind for a mass tort. It led to the development of the federal Chapter 11 bankruptcy law we know today. It was also used as a model for settling claims associated with the sinking of the Italian luxury liner *Andrea Doria,* which went down after colliding with another ship in the waters off Nantucket in July 1956, and in the efforts of U.S. District Court judge Robert C. Zampano of New Haven, Conn., to resolve complex securities-related litigation during the 1980s and 1990s.

Henry S. Cohn and David Bollier, *The Great Hartford Circus Fire: Creative Settlement of Mass Disasters* (1991); Don Massey and Rick Davey, *A Matter of De-*

gree: *The Hartford Circus Fire and the Mystery of Little Miss 1565* (2001); Stewart O'Nan, *The Circus Fire: A True Story* (2000).

Henry S. Cohn

Holmes, Oliver Wendell, Jr. (1841–1935)

Jurist and legal scholar. Oliver Wendell Holmes, Jr., known for his vast legal knowledge and directness of expression, spent nearly five decades of his life on the judicial bench, serving first on the Supreme Judicial Court of Massachusetts (1882–1902; chief justice from 1899) and then on the Supreme Court of the United States (1902–32).

Holmes not only was a native of Boston but was closely connected to a half dozen of the city's oldest families. His grandfather Charles Jackson served on the state's highest court, and his father, a physician and poet, wrote *The Autocrat of the Breakfast Table*. The younger Holmes graduated from Harvard College in 1861 and then served for three years as an officer in the 20th Massachusetts Regiment. The Civil War shaped his outlook. He was wounded three times—at Ball's Bluff, Antietam, and Fredericksburg—and lost many of his closest friends. Years later, in his 1895 Memorial Day speech, he would speak of "a soldier's faith" and lessons learned from war, but the real legacy was a profound skepticism that influenced his private and public life.

After graduating from Harvard Law School in 1866, he entered private practice. His inclinations, however, lay in scholarly pursuits, and he soon distinguished himself as editor of the *American Law Review* (1870–73), editor of the 12th edition of *Kent's Commentaries on American Law* (1870–73), and author of *The Common Law* (1881). He taught law briefly at Harvard.

Oliver Wendell Holmes, Jr., ca. 1910

His circle of friends included Henry Adams, whose own investigation of European American law guided Holmes's research for *The Common Law*, as well as fellow members of the Metaphysical Club, an informal group of talented and original thinkers that included William James and Charles Sanders Peirce.

His scholarly works organized, categorized, and analyzed private law as it was practiced in England and the United States. The extraordinary knowledge of case law and understanding of legal concepts that he acquired through research enabled him, as a judge, to grasp quickly the issues in a case and to identify relevant precedents. As a result, his opinions—nearly 2,000 in all—are characterized by directness in terms of both substance and language.

Holmes's reputation, at least among the general population, rests largely on pithy phrases—often insensitive or superficial—that nevertheless capture the attention. In one of his most controversial decisions, *Buck v. Bell* (1927), Holmes upheld a statute that allowed for the involuntary sterilization of those labeled "mental defectives," declaring that "three generations of imbeciles are enough." His conservatism was evident but less strident in *Adkins v. Children's Hospital* (1923). "It will take more than the Nineteenth Amendment," he wrote, "to convince me that there are no differences between men and women." He explained the need to limit free speech by arguing that there is no right to cry "Fire!" in a crowded theater, and he defended the right to express unorthodox opinions because the marketplace of ideas would eliminate those that were useless. He also coined the phrase "clear and present danger" to define when the government could act to restrict personal freedoms.

His philosophy of judging found expression in deference to legislative decisions unless state-made policies were plainly unconstitutional. His understanding of democracy placed responsibility for making law with elected officials, except insofar as freedom of expression was concerned, and assigned judges the task of deciding whether legislative policy was a legitimate exercise of the state's police power and was consistent with precedent. His dissent in *Lochner v. New York* (1905) illustrates this reluctance to override state law; that in *Gitlow v. New York* (1925), his qualified support for civil liberties.

Albert Alschuler, *Law without Values: The Life, Work, and Legacy of Justice Holmes* (2000); Liva Baker, *The Justice from Beacon Hill: The Life and Times of Oliver Wendell Holmes* (1991); Sheldon M. Novick, *Honorable Justice: The Life of Oliver Wendell Holmes* (1989); G. Edward White, *Justice Oliver Wendell Holmes: Law and the Inner Self* (1993).

Christine L. Compston

Labor Law

Labor law defines the rights and duties of employer and employee. It is usually divided by jurists into two subcategories. *Labor law*, as the phrase has come to be used by 20th-century lawyers and judges, generally comprises the collective spheres of employment: unions, management, and the collective bargaining process. *Employment law*, on the other hand, usually denotes the rules governing the individual employment contract between employer and employee. Both categories, however, leave out much of the "labor" that goes on in any society, especially the housework, child rearing, and other work traditionally designated as women's labor. Labor law is thus more aptly described as being the law of paid labor. As such, labor law has helped to shape economic production in New England and to allocate its rewards. Historically, the principles and rules laid down by New England courts have formed the basis of much of U.S. labor law.

In the 17th and 18th centuries, New England took its labor law from the English common law. The relationship of master and servant was one of legally binding authority. As Sir William Blackstone noted in his famous 1765 commentary on the common law, the relationship of employer and employee was the relation of "master and servant," which, along with the relations of husband and wife and parent and child, constituted the "three great relations in private life." The employment relationship was thus a relationship of formalized inequality. Masters exercised over their servants a legally constituted disciplinary authority similar to that which they exercised over wives and children, including the power to discipline servants by corporal punishment. Masters could also obtain specific enforcement of a labor contract; thus, an employee who quit could be forced at pain of imprisonment to return to work.

In early- and mid-19th-century New England, courts were central players in the construction of a new conceptual model in the law of labor relations. Under labor law's new dispensation, the employment relation was reconceptualized as being governed by the free competition of employer and employee. In theory, the new law of employment placed employer and employee in positions of formal legal equality. In practice, however, the new labor law had an intricate mix of formal equality, on one hand, and persistent traces of formal and informal inequality, on the other.

Two Massachusetts cases capture the ambiguous transformation of New England labor law and of U.S. labor law more generally. The 1842 *Commonwealth v. Hunt* decision announced the legality of combinations among workers to raise wages. Early trade unions had faced the threat of criminal prosecution for conspiracy. Thus, in *Hunt* members of the Boston Journeymen Bootmakers' Society were convicted for conspiracy "to form an unlawful club" and "unjustly to extort great sums of money by means thereof." Chief Justice Lemuel Shaw of the Supreme Judicial Court of Massachusetts, however, reversed the conviction and ruled that workers, like commercial competitors more generally, could wield their economic power in free competition with the employers of labor. Almost 30 years later, however, the Massachusetts Supreme Judicial Court still viewed employers as having property rights with regard to their employees. In *Carew v. Rutherford* (1870), the court ruled that an employer could recover damages from employees for inducing other employees to strike, even when the striking employees had been at-will employees, able to quit at any time. Employees, then, were ostensibly free to combine and to bargain with employers; yet persistent ideas about employers' entitlement to the labor of their employees undermined that market freedom and reintroduced older patterns of legal inequality into the labor relation.

As the 19th century progressed, the idea that employers had a legally protected entitlement to workers' labor manifested itself in injunctions prohibiting or severely curtailing strike activity. Some New England courts—despite the ruling in *Hunt*—continued to uphold criminal indictments against workers for labor organizing. But more often it was the labor injunction that reinforced a hierarchy of entitlements and obligations in the workplace by restricting labor activism. In Massachusetts alone courts issued 260 injunctions in labor disputes between 1898 and 1916. The Massachusetts Supreme Judicial Court—the most important court in New England—led the way by upholding labor injunctions even in the absence of evidence of physical force or threats by the striking workers.

With regard to individual employment contracts, 19th-century courts continued to play an important role in setting the terms of employment. In theory, the rules of the free market labor relationship were set privately by the parties to the employment contract. But courts were continually required to fill the gaps in contracts and to supply terms for which private parties had made no express or implied agreement. In the process, courts created default rules that governed the relationship of employer and employee. Most notoriously, courts held that employees could not recover damages from employers for workplace injuries arising out of the ordinary risks of employment. Courts also ruled that employees were not entitled to back pay when they quit before the end of the term of an em-

ployment contract, and that employer work rules were binding terms of the employment contract even when the rules had been modified during the course of employment. These default rules, in turn, appear to have shaped the agreements of the parties by creating legally sanctioned templates for employment contracts. Few employment contracts, for example, shifted the risk of workplace injuries back to employers. Thus, even as the new 19th-century law of employment purported merely to enforce the prior agreements of private parties, it also gave shape and substance to those agreements, sanctioning certain contract terms at the expense of others, and participated in the construction of the 19th-century employment relation.

In the 20th century, New England's role as a leading region in the field of labor law waned. To be sure, some of the most important early federal labor law cases arose in New England. In the famous 1908 Danbury Hatters case, for example, the U.S. Supreme Court elicited the fury of organized labor by holding that individual members of the United Hatters of North America were jointly and severally liable for damages arising out of a union boycott of D. E. Loewe and Company of Danbury, Conn. And lawyers such as Louis Brandeis, Felix Frankfurter, Archibald Cox, and Derek Bok helped to shape national labor law reform from their positions in New England. Labor law, however, has increasingly become the domain of federal law and thus national rather than regional norms.

At the beginning of the 21st century, the cutting edge of labor law in New England (as elsewhere in the United States) has shifted from the arena of unions, management, and collective bargaining to new developments in the sphere of the individual employment relation. Most dramatically, federal law since 1964 has established an antidiscrimination principle prohibiting discrimination in employment on the basis of race, color, religion, sex, national origin, and, in more recent years, age and disability. Federal law has also exerted new controls over other areas of employment. Employee benefits are governed by federal law under the exceedingly complex rules set out in the Employee Retirement Income Security Act of 1974. Workplace safety regulations have been governed by federal law since 1970 by the Occupational Safety and Health Act.

As the labor market of New England has been integrated into a national and increasingly international economy, it has become difficult for individual states and regions to exert the kind of control over the labor relationship that New England courts and legislatures exercised during the 19th century. Moreover, the future of labor law may be increasingly dif-

ficult to predict. The employment relation has always been touched by numerous and varied areas of the law not squarely defined as labor law per se. Social insurance laws, for example, create a social safety net that can improve labor's bargaining position; so, too, the law of plant closings and mergers and acquisitions shapes employers' capacity to shift production away from a unionized labor force. As changing labor markets in the 21st century prompt employers and employees to develop new and untraditional work arrangements, legal rules not specifically applying to the labor relation will probably become still more important. The underlying issues of equality and power, however, will remain unchanged.

Daniel Ernst, *Lawyers against Labor: From Individual Rights to Corporate Liberalism* (1995); William E. Forbath, *Law and the Shaping of the American Labor Movement* (1991); Karen Orren, *Belated Feudalism: Labor, the Law, and Liberal Development in the United States* (1991); Robert J. Steinfeld, *The Invention of Free Labor: The Employment Relation in English and American Law and Culture, 1350–1870* (1991); Christopher L. Tomlins, *Law, Labor, and Ideology in the Early American Republic* (1993); Christopher L. Tomlins and Andrew J. King, eds., *Labor Law in America: Historical and Critical Essays* (1992); Paul Weiler, *Governing the Workplace: The Future of Labor and Employment Law* (1990); Weiler, "Promises to Keep: Securing Workers' Rights to Self-Organization under the NLRA," *Harvard Law Review* 96 (1983).

John Fabian Witt

Langdell, Christopher Columbus

(1826–1906) Lawyer, professor of law, and law school dean. Christopher Columbus Langdell was born in New Boston, N.H. His early years were filled with misfortune, including the failure of the family farm and the death of his mother and two brothers. Nonetheless, with hard-earned savings, Langdell graduated from Phillips Exeter Academy and attended Harvard College for 15 months before he was forced to withdraw for lack of funds. After working as a laborer and reading in a law office, he entered Harvard Law School in 1851, received his degree, and remained for postgraduate study until 1854.

Early in 1855, Langdell began legal practice on Wall Street in New York City, where he remained for 15 years. A shrewd and effective attorney, he appears to have been among the midcentury pioneers recognizing that the highly technical written brief would supplant oral arguments in litigating increasingly complex cases arising in commercial centers. But he became alienated from legal practice by the widespread complicity of leading lawyers and judges in the corruption of New York City courts by Tammany Hall in the 1860s and left New York.

In 1870 Langdell was appointed professor

(and dean soon thereafter) of Harvard Law School. At that time, the main features of law education at Harvard, as well as at virtually all university law schools in the country, did not differ from those he had experienced in the early 1850s. There were no academic requirements for admission beyond English literacy; the length of the course was, in theory, 18 months but could easily be shortened to a year or less through personal testimony of outside reading or clerking in a lawyer's office. The curriculum consisted of a cycle of elementary courses, which students entered and exited at any point; there were no course prerequisites. There were also no examinations or other academic requirements, even mere attendance, in order to complete a course or receive the degree. Teaching was done by lecturing, and the faculty taught part-time while maintaining a full schedule of legal or judicial work, although Harvard was an exception to this widespread norm in having three professors who devoted most of their time to teaching. Finally, the library was regarded as a repository of textbooks that students borrowed and rarely returned.

In his second semester, Langdell began reforming this system by introducing case law method teaching and publishing the first casebook for teaching law: *A Selection of Cases on the Law of Contracts* (1871). This inductive method—through which a process of Socratic questioning led students to formulate and then refine generalizations abstracted from reading the original case reports—was initially resisted and ridiculed by most students, faculty, and alumni. However, a small group of leading students were won over by the intellectual challenge presented by Langdell's case law method, and their example induced other students to follow. Chief among those early leaders was James Barr Ames, who became Langdell's protégé, colleague, and ultimately successor as dean of Harvard Law School. During the 1870s, Langdell worked prodigiously and published several casebooks.

Meanwhile, with the help of President Charles Eliot, Langdell led the faculty to institute a number of other changes. Between 1870 and 1878 the law school introduced requirements that all successful applicants for admission either hold a bachelor's degree or pass a demanding examination, that all students pass written examinations in their subjects in order to receive their degree, that the courses be organized in a graded sequence with prerequisites for advanced courses, and that the course of study be extended to three years for a degree. In addition, Langdell guided a full-time librarian in transforming the library from a textbook repository into a scholarly resource. Finally, Langdell and Eliot

created the professorial career track in U.S. law schools by hiring in 1873 the first law professor in the United States who had studied law but never practiced: James Barr Ames.

While he was undertaking these reforms Langdell published *A Summary of Equity Pleading* (1877) and *A Summary of the Law of Contracts* (1880). Together with his casebooks, these treatises, particularly the latter, have been regarded as his most significant contribution to legal scholarship. But at the age of 57, Langdell underwent a marked change. His eyesight began to deteriorate, and he published nothing between 1883 and 1888 until he started issuing articles in the *Harvard Law Review* on the topic of equity jurisdiction. In 1892 he again stopped publishing, having become nearly blind. In 1895 he retired as dean of the law school, and in 1897 he began issuing another group of articles on a variety of topics, which continued to appear until his death.

By that time the reforms that Langdell introduced to Harvard Law School were regarded as exemplary, and they would be adopted by virtually every university law school in the United States over the next two decades. Furthermore, his innovations became the norm to which medical schools and other professional schools in the 20th century aspired, making Langdell arguably the most influential figure in the history of legal education in the United States.

W. Burlette Carter, "Reconstructing Langdell," *Georgia Law Review* 32 (1997); Grant Gilmore, *Ages of American Law* (1977); Gilmore, *The Death of Contract* (1974); Thomas C. Grey, "Langdell's Orthodoxy," *University of Pittsburgh Law Review* 45 (1983); Patrick J. Kelley, "A Critical Analysis of Holmes' Theory of Contract," *Notre Dame Law Review* 75 (2000); Bruce A. Kimball, ". . . The Inception of Case Method Teaching in the Classrooms of the Early C. C. Langdell, 1870–1883," *Law and History Review* 17 (1999); Bruce A. Kimball and R. Blake Brown, "'The Highest Legal Ability in the Nation': Langdell on Wall Street, 1855–1870," *Law and Social Inquiry* 29 (2004); William P. LaPiana, *Logic and Experience: The Origin of Modern American Legal Education* (1994); Kevin M. Teeven, *A History of the Anglo-American Common Law of Contract* (1990).

Bruce A. Kimball

Law Enforcement New England is home to some of the oldest law-enforcement agencies in the United States. As society's needs evolve, the region's demographics change, and crime in general becomes increasingly complex, New England's law enforcement efforts have had to keep pace. Accordingly, the region's law enforcement agencies have undertaken continual innovation and reorganization since the colonial period. The science of criminology, too, was fostered in New England at Harvard University by W. E. B. Du Bois.

Suffolk County, Mass., has had a sheriff since 1692. The sheriff and deputies had powers of arrest at that time but were not otherwise involved in fighting crime. A night watch, charged with maintaining public order and guarding against frequent fires, was created in Boston by state statute in 1801; patrols lasted from around 10 P.M. until dawn. Boston was one of the first cities in the United States to establish a police force distinct from the night watch. The first formal police officer powers, allowing day patrols, were defined by the Massachusetts legislature in 1838, and during the 1850s, the distinction of duties between night watchmen and police diminished. The Boston Police Department, established in 1854, was the first paid professional public safety department in the nation.

Most police responsibilities at the time centered on the quelling of small demonstrations, regulating liquor, and protecting public health. For example, during a cholera epidemic in 1834, Boston police visited every house to check for illness, and police stations served as temporary hospital facilities. Police emptied more than 3,000 privies during this period.

During the early part of the 20th century, the working conditions of Boston police officers were so poor—with low salaries, filthy stations, work weeks longer than 70 hours, a requirement that officers pay for their uniforms, and unabashed political favoritism among supervisors and officers—that most officers joined the American Federation of Labor (AFL). When the city refused to recognize the union in 1919, more than 1,100 officers—three-quarters of the force—went on strike. Rioting and looting ensued, several lives were lost, and property damage totaled more than $1 million. President Woodrow Wilson publicly condemned the striking officers, and Massachusetts Governor Calvin Coolidge had all of the strikers fired. The public's antipathy toward the strikers brought a revocation by the AFL of its police charters and effectively stalled the national police labor movement for 20 years. The strike did improve the working conditions at the Boston Police Department, however; annual salaries were increased by $300, officers were no longer required to pay for their uniforms, and a pension system was implemented.

Today, although fewer than 40 percent of the nation's local police departments are unionized, all six New England states allow local and state police officers to engage in collective bargaining. Most states specifically prohibit strikes by public employees, although informational picketing is permitted. Epidemics of the so-called blue flu, in which large numbers of officers call in sick, presumably to

Graduation ceremony at the Vermont Police Academy, Pittsford, Vt., includes Vermont's first black officer, 1993

promote bargaining demands, are not unknown to the region. Another alternative to striking includes the tactic used in 1969 in New Bedford, Mass., where members of the local police association successfully pressured the city administration to raise their salaries by boycotting New Bedford businesses.

New England has more than 34,000 sworn state and local full-time officers today and more than 1,100 full-time civilian police personnel. Sheriffs' departments tend to play a much smaller role in New England, relative to much of the rest of the country, with a little over 3,000 sworn officers in the region, a number comparable to the number of sheriffs' deputies in New Jersey alone. County sheriffs' departments in rural areas of the region maintain an active, somewhat autonomous role in law enforcement. However, Massachusetts's sheriffs have seen their duties limited to maintaining correctional facilities, and with the abolishment of county government in 1998, they have become state employees. Connecticut abolished its sheriff system in a referendum in 2001.

New England's six state police departments were typically created for two reasons. In the early period, state police departments were organized to enforce laws that local officers would not or could not enforce for political reasons; the Connecticut State Police, one of the nation's oldest state police forces, was created in 1903 in response to this concern. More recent efforts to organize law enforcement activities at the state level tended to focus on assembling the increasingly sophisticated resources needed to combat crime, as in the case of the Vermont State Police. Repeated attempts to assemble a state police force in Vermont during the 1930s and early 1940s had been delayed because of opposition by the politically powerful county sheriffs of the state. After public outcry following an unsolved murder in Bennington, the Vermont legislature shifted its position, and the state police department was created in 1947.

State police departments are primarily charged with enforcement of traffic laws on state highways. Yet state officers also typically possess broad law enforcement authority as a means of providing assistance to small rural communities when necessary. Commonly, state police agencies also have responsibility for arson investigation because of the need for technical expertise and interagency cooperation. In addition, state police departments maintain increasingly complex computer information systems, providing data to other agencies as needed on criminal activity and current and former criminals.

Some of the most significant changes in the role of law enforcement agencies occurred during Prohibition. The 1920s saw the emergence of organized crime, as the legal supply of liquor ceased while public demand remained unabated. The tremendous spirit of lawlessness that arose during Prohibition particularly affected New England, with its large population connected through familial and commercial ties to foreign countries that were still producing alcoholic beverages, and with its many miles of international border and coastline. State and local law enforcement agencies added radio communications, hired more officers, and accelerated the mechanization of their departments in order to battle racketeers. The traditional police role of providing service to the public diminished as the emphasis shifted to crime fighting. The presence of federal law enforcement increased significantly, in an effort to counter smuggling activity in the region.

Some 2,000 agents with arrest and firearms authority today provide the federal law enforcement presence in New England. These include FBI agents, border patrol and customs officers, agents of the Bureau of Alcohol, Tobacco, and Firearms, and the U.S. marshals. More than half of the region's federal agents are based in Massachusetts.

Civil unrest during the 1960s brought a new federal response to crime. The Law Enforcement Assistance Administration (LEAA), created by Congress in 1965, and the Omnibus Crime Control and Safe Streets Act of 1968 provided large amounts of federal funds to state and local agencies. The LEAA was the first significant federal program designed to help state and local police departments, and it allowed those departments to add equipment, personnel, and programming that was otherwise unaffordable. A series of federal initiatives followed; many local law enforcement officials resented the political reality that with desired federal funding comes undesired federal control. The "new federalism" of the Republican Party in 1994 that proposed to give back state control has not materialized.

Partly because of prodding by federal authorities, diversity has been a stated goal among the region's law enforcement agencies over the past several decades. Female officers joined the Connecticut State Police during the World War II era; the Vermont State Police added its first female troopers in 1977. Many departments maintain affirmative action hiring programs, although political patronage, which tends to favor European American candidates, remains a common way of gaining employment in law enforcement. Today, women and members of minority groups still compose less than 10 percent of the region's law enforcement forces.

As is true in the United States in general, the region increasingly has emphasized the professionalism of law enforcement personnel. Over the past several decades, state laws have required longer and broader training of officers in areas such as computer literacy, family relations, stress management, and multicultural awareness. Statewide training councils have been created to oversee the many training requirements mandated by state and federal legislation over the past 30 years. Some agencies, such as the Massachusetts Criminal Justice Training Council, have deemphasized the traditional quasi-military model of training, promoting instead human services and community policing.

The New Hampshire State Police is the only state law enforcement agency in the region that requires its officers to have some college education as a minimum requirement for employment. Most New England police forces still require entry-level officers to possess no more than a high school diploma, although many departments provide financial incentives, such as tuition reimbursement and salary increases, to officers who pursue a college education.

Law enforcement in New England will undoubtedly undergo continued change, and at an accelerated pace. As the technological capabilities of both criminals and law enforcement personnel develop, the need for increasingly educated officers and other staff intensifies. In an era of community policing, traditional models of law enforcement are giving way to new methods of preparing officers for the field, methods that will help them face 21st-century challenges.

John H. Burpo, *The Police Labor Movement* (1971); Shaun L. Gabbidon, "W. E. B. DuBois, Pioneering American Criminologist," *Journal of Black Studies* 31, no. 5 (2001); Roger Lane, *Policing the City: Boston, 1822–1885* (1967); Wilbur Miller, *Cops and Bobbies: Police Authority in New York and London, 1830–1870* (1977).

Peyton Paxson

Lawes and Libertyes of Massachusetts

The Book of the General Lawes and Libertyes concerning the Inhabitants of Massachusetts (1648) was one of the first law codes to be published in the English colonies. Like Puritans in England, those in Massachusetts wanted to curb the arbitrary powers of various officials, prerogative judges in England, and magistrates in New England. The *Lawes and Libertyes* was the culmination of that endeavor.

Governor John Winthrop and several magistrates led the opposition to codification. They not only objected to the curbing of their powers but also wanted some incorporation of Mosaic law into the new system. Furthermore, they argued that discretionary justice was necessary to ensure that crimes and punishments fit the circumstances of a new society. The opponents of codification also feared that the adoption of a code of laws might violate the colonial charter granted by England. Nonetheless, the *Lawes and Libertyes* was adopted in 1648 both to curb magisterial discretion and to guide these societal arbiters, who, unlike their English counterparts, preferred a legal system free of those schooled in

the law, so their judgments would be less legalistic.

Unlike modern codes of law, which are arranged by subject matter, the *Lawes and Libertyes* is an alphabetical text, a handbook for ready reference to be used by magistrate and colonist alike. It covers a wide range of subjects, identifying capital crimes (including murder, blasphemy, and rape), regulating trades and businesses (such as baking, agriculture, and innkeeping), and defining the relationships among church, colonist, and state. On the last subject, it is possible to note early indications of a separation of church and state, as the civil authority is charged with granting marriage and divorce but is prohibited from prescribing church doctrine.

Although the *Lawes and Libertyes* was intended for wide distribution—the General Court ordered 600 copies—that intention was not realized. Many copies of the text were destroyed by the General Court itself, which may have been leery of retaliation by English authorities. In fact, printed copies of the *Lawes and Libertyes* were feared lost for 250 years, until one surfaced in England at the turn of the 20th century. Nonetheless, a comparison of subject matter and wording reveals that the *Lawes and Libertyes* served as the model for codifications later adopted by the colonies of Connecticut and New Haven and strongly influenced similar efforts in New York and Pennsylvania.

Mark D. Cahn, "Punishment, Discretion, and the Codification of Prescribed Penalties in Colonial Massachusetts," *American Journal of Legal History* 33 (1989); Carol F. Lee, "Discretionary Justice in Early Massachusetts," *Essex Institute Historical Collections* (1976); Ronald G. Walters, "New England Society and *The Laws and Liberties of Massachusetts, 1648*," *Essex Institute Historical Collections* (1970); Thorp L. Wolford, "The Laws and Liberties of 1648," in *Essays in the History of Early American Law*, ed. David H. Flaherty (1969).

Ronald Lettieri and Richard Mandel

Litchfield Law School

Founded by Tapping Reeve (1744–1823) in the early 1780s, the Litchfield Law School in Connecticut was the first place where students could, in a classroom setting, learn the legal profession. Until Reeve opened the school, prospective lawyers trained by clerking with a practicing lawyer. Reeve himself had learned the trade by working under the supervision of Jesse Root of Hartford.

Within a year of setting up his law practice in 1773 in the town of Litchfield, Reeve began supervising Aaron Burr, his brother-in-law, in his legal studies. Over the next few years, Reeve accepted more and more young men into his law office. By 1784 the transition from

supervising clerks to teaching students was complete: in that year Reeve opened, next to his home, a small, one-room schoolhouse for his lectures.

During the early years of the Litchfield Law School's existence, Reeve was the sole instructor, and enrollment averaged 15 students a year. In 1798 Reeve invited James Gould, a local lawyer who had attended the school, to become his partner. By sharing teaching responsibilities, Reeve was able to accept more students and to serve as a part-time judge for the Connecticut Superior Court. Enrollment peaked in the early 1810s at 55 students.

Reeve and Gould lectured throughout the year, recessing for four weeks each spring and fall. New students, applying for admission by producing a letter of introduction, joined the school when it was convenient for them. The instructors lectured in a cyclical fashion, working their way through a list of topics and then returning to the beginning. Students attended lectures until they had heard all of the subjects. The length of the cycle varied depending on the year, but for most students, it lasted from one to one-and-a-half years.

The law school was an important source of income for both instructors, and beyond the initial costs of constructing the law school buildings (Gould built his own classroom next to his home when he started teaching), the two lawyers had few expenses. For the students, attending the Litchfield Law School could be costly. Not only did the students pay tuition, but out-of-town students also contracted with local families for room and board. Travel expenses placed an additional burden on the students. While travel costs were fairly moderate for the New England students, such as the future educator Horace Mann and the future Supreme Court justice Levi Woodbury, they could be substantial for those making the lengthy trip from the South or West. South Carolinians such as John C. Calhoun and Augustus Baldwin Longstreet spent as much as three weeks and $50 on their transportation to the school. Many other students were willing to undertake the expense: approximately 1,000 students, hailing from 24 states, attended the school before it closed in 1833.

Unlike university-based schools, the Litchfield Law School had no life beyond the participation of its original instructors. Upon Gould's retirement, a decade after Reeve's death, the school closed. By that time, prospective lawyers had many choices for their training. Some clerked with practicing lawyers. Others attended the proprietary schools that had opened in competition with the Litchfield Law School. A growing number of students chose to attend the new university law schools. During the tenure of the Litchfield Law School and after, many law students combined the practical experience of clerking with classroom instruction.

The Litchfield Law School launched the careers of many well-known Americans, including vice presidents, members of Congress, and Supreme Court justices. Many more graduates held state and local political office, while others became leaders of the nation's emerging corporate, mercantile, industrial, and financial establishments. Thomas Kimberly Brace, for example, used his knowledge of the law to help him found an insurance company. More than 20 alumni of the school, including the Cincinnati Law School founder Edward King, started or were early professors in new law schools.

Lynne Templeton Brickley, "The Litchfield Law School," unpublished lecture, Litchfield Historical Society (1998); Samuel H. Fisher, *Litchfield Law School, 1774–1833: Biographical Catalog of Students* (1946), John H. Langbein, "Blackstone, Litchfield, and Yale: The Founding of the Yale Law School," in *History of the Yale Law School: The Tercentennial Lectures*, ed. Anthony T. Kronman (2004).

Rebecca Martin

Maine Law and Prohibition

On June 2, 1851, the Maine legislature passed "An Act for the Suppression of Drinking Houses and Tippling Shops" prohibiting the sale of alcoholic beverages. It was the first statewide prohibition law that allowed successful prosecution and created significant criminal penalties, and the term *Maine Law* came to designate prohibition laws passed throughout the northern and western states during the 1850s. The Maine Law ranked with the Fugitive Slave Law of 1850 as one of the most controversial political issues of that decade, creating conflicts that played an important role in the destruction of the era's two-party system and the rise of the Republican Party.

Neal Dow, the Portland temperance crusader who wrote the Maine Law, specifically designed it to solve problems that had weakened previous prohibitory legislation. Maine had passed a law in 1846 that, while banning the sale of spirits and wine in small quantities, did not apply to wholesalers and established only minimal fines. Dow's bill not only prohibited the sale and manufacture of liquor but liberally allowed for search and seizure, mandating jail time and heavy fines for repeat offenders. When criticized for increasing governmental power and curtailing civil liberties, Dow denigrated individual rights that conflicted with the general welfare.

The American Temperance Union (ATU) saw the Maine Law as a way to revitalize the stagnant temperance movement. Relying on tens of thousands of tracts and the proselytiz-

Guarding illegal stills seized in 1920, Trowbridge, Vt.

ing of such figures as Dow, the ATU popularized the Maine Law throughout the North and West. Within five years 13 states and territories and two Canadian provinces had passed versions of the Maine Law. Massachusetts was the first to copy the bill in late 1851, while Vermont, Rhode Island, and the Minnesota Territory followed suit in 1852. Michigan passed a Maine Law in 1853 and Connecticut in 1854. Over the course of 1855 New Hampshire, Indiana, Delaware, Iowa, New York, and the Nebraska Territory all instituted versions. Indeed, every northern and western state enacted some form of prohibition law or constitutional amendment during the 1850s. In other states only gubernatorial vetoes and a failure to respond to referendums blocked the passage of similar bills.

Several forces quickly mobilized to protest the new legislation. For the first time distillers and brewers organized to form trade and lobbying organizations. Working-class groups, especially immigrant Irish, engaged in numerous violent demonstrations. The liberal search-and-seizure provisions of most prohibition laws exposed them to many successful constitutional challenges. Recognizing the potential divisiveness of the issue in an already explosive political climate, political parties refused to take any official stand on the issue.

Ultimately, it was the prohibitionists' own extreme measures that brought about a reversal of public opinion. In Maine, for example, the fanatical Dow used his position as mayor of Portland to engage in almost continual searches. In 1855, however, he became a victim

of his own system when a lawful city purchase of medicinal liquors in Dow's name inadvertently broke the crusading mayor's law. When Dow blocked indictment against himself, an angry mob arose at Portland City Hall. The boisterous crowd refused to disperse until the militia, on Dow's direct order, fired into its midst, killing one man and wounding seven others. The peace and social harmony the Maine Law had promised proved elusive, and the laws throughout the nation were quickly either repealed or amended into impotence. By the end of the Civil War, even these emasculated laws existed only in Maine, Vermont, and New Hampshire. Indeed, the failure of state efforts to enforce a prohibitory law that was significantly at odds with public opinion served as a cautionary tale for the next generation of prohibitionists, who returned to moral persuasion. It was a lesson that the generation after them learned at considerable cost.

Jack S. Blocker, Jr., *American Temperance Movements: Cycles of Reform* (1989); Frank L. Bryne, *Prophet of Prohibition: Neal Dow and His Crusade* (1961); Ernest H. Cherrington, *The Evolution of Prohibition in the United States of America: A Chronological History* (1920); Ian R. Tyrell, *Sobering Up: From Temperance to Prohibition in Antebellum America, 1800–1860* (1979).

Mark C. Smith

Native Americans and the Law

In 1681 the Gay Head Wampanoag of Martha's Vineyard expressed in writing the importance of two legal concepts that have characterized the relationship of law and New England's native peoples throughout the years. Wrote the sachem, or leader, Mittark, who would die two years later: "I am Mittark, sachem of Gay Head and Nashaquitsa as far as Wanemessit. Know this all people. I Mittark and my chief men and my children and my people, these are our lands. Forever we own them, and our posterity forever shall own them. I Mittark and we the chief men, and with our children and all our people, have agreed that no one [shall] sell land. . . . But if anyone does not keep this agreement, he shall fall [and] have nothing more of this land at Gay Head and Nashaquitsa at all forever." Mittark and his people defined their identity as strong and forever lasting, and they tied that identity to their lands. These twofold social, economic, and legal considerations have grounded the societies of New England's Indians from time immemorial.

The Algonquian-speaking native peoples of New England had a variety of traditional legal systems. In the south the hereditary quasi-autocrat known as the sachem, such as Mittark, was the acknowledged leader. Sagamores, lower-level sachems, ruled on the village level. Without wielding the arbitrary and totalitarian power of a contemporaneous European king, the sachem was responsible for administering justice. He or she (there were a few female sachems and sagamores) served in a judicial capacity and in some instances was called on to make certain decisions and punishments. A strain of direct democracy prevented sachems and sagamores from ruling capriciously, for these leaders were bound not only by traditional law (what some call "custom") but also by the opinions of an advisory council. Indeed, consensus was often needed in important matters, be they domestic or international.

This force of democracy was even stronger in northern New England among such peoples as the Abenaki, Passamaquoddy, and Penobscot. Although the title of sachem was still hereditary, its legal status was sometimes reduced to that of an adviser or even a figurehead north of what became the state of Massachusetts. This fluid nature of native leadership and decision making would prove problematic for European settlers accustomed to more rigid and linear forms.

Many non-Indians, from the general public to scholars to jurists, have misunderstood these basic elements of Native American existence, particularly with reference to New England's Indians. "There was no law" is a rather crude interpretation of traditional Indian legal cultures that gives short shrift to the complexity and legitimacy of Indian legal systems as compared with their European-derived counterparts. There were, to be sure, many dissimilarities between the two systems; nonetheless,

there were also many areas of overlap. With the advent of colonization, however, native peoples were subjected to the strictures of a newly imported legal framework.

Other aspects of traditional legal systems were altogether beyond the Europeans' willing comprehension or acceptance. Because Indian land-law practices in southern New England were concerned with usufruct rather than the rights conveyed by deeds, fences, and continuous occupancy, native law came into conflict with the English-based system that settlers brought with them to colonial New England. Contentious legal issues included property rights, fiscal liability, and criminal and civil law. In the latter two areas especially, Puritan cultural biases often prevented the colonists from acknowledging the legitimacy of Indian frameworks.

Two turning points are worthy of note. The first involved the Pilgrims and a Nipmuck boy named Penowanyanquis who was running an errand on behalf of the Narragansett. In the summer of 1638 a group of escaped Plymouth Colony servants led by Arthur Peach, "a lusty and desperate young man," stole wampum beads and three woolen coats from Penowanyanquis and murdered him in the forest. Before the boy died, Indians in Massachusetts Bay Colony were able to capture Peach and his friends. After some discussion among sachems and representatives of Massachusetts Bay, Peach and the others were sent to Plymouth Colony to be tried for murder. The trial raised a crucial question: Could an English person be tried by Indians? Peach and two others were found guilty and sentenced to death, but it was by a colonial court, not by an Indian tribunal. After the Peach decision Plymouth began to pass laws that took more and more civil and criminal jurisdiction away from Indians, for whom English authorities developed a separate legal system.

King Philip's War (1675–76) was the second turning point in the evolution of legal relations between New England's Indians and the European settlers. The war brought great devastation, and the colonists used the law to punish Indian captives. Many were sold into slavery. The legal system, which had been evolving into a separate yet jurisprudential means of regulating Indian-white relationships, now became a tool of revenge and self-protection for the colonists. Evenhanded justice no longer had any force of law. The colonists refused to be subjected to native criminal jurisdiction regardless of the circumstances, insisting that all crimes be arbitrated in their own forums. In the civil arena the Puritans initiated antimiscegenation laws that refused to acknowledge the legality of marriages between whites and Indians. In this un-

yielding atmosphere, misunderstanding led predictably to conflict, and conflict culminated in the conquest of native New England, the dissolution of indigenous legal systems, and the imposition of foreign ones under European American hegemony.

In light of how far removed the English Crown was from the conflicts in New England, the natives were left to the rules established by the colonial courts until the Crown began to exercise jurisdiction over Indian affairs in the late 17th century. Mainly because of the importance of the Iroquois in the rivalry between France and England, the British government treated some Indians as allies as well as subjects. The British claim to almost all of North America east of the Mississippi River was originally by right of Christian occupation, but this claim was now buttressed by land cessions made by the Six Nations.

In effect, the federal government under the U.S. Constitution inherited the Crown's exclusive authority to regulate Indian affairs. Its first attempt to do so was the 1790 Act to Regulate Trade and Intercourse with the Indian Tribes. Among other things, the 1790 statute forbade states and individuals from signing treaties with Indian nations without first obtaining federal sanction. It simultaneously solidified tribal sovereignty and marked an early federal encroachment on it. Many Indian issues were placed under federal authority because of their international status, but the law also limited native legal prerogatives by regulating Indian commerce and criminal jurisdiction.

Discontent simmered among New England's native peoples, culminating in the Mashpee Revolt of 1833. The Mashpee Wampanoag of Massachusetts regained some of their lost sovereignty and legal control the following year, but the gain would prove only temporary. Indigenous legal rights in the region, as in the rest of the nation, would continue to decline.

The assimilation policy in force during the last quarter of the 19th century and the first three decades of the 20th was especially detrimental to native sovereignty. The Major Crimes Act of 1885 impinged on Indian legal systems by selectively removing seven crimes, including murder, from their exclusive jurisdiction, even when only Indians were involved. The list of seven crimes originally chosen has expanded prodigiously since 1885. Another benchmark case during this era gave Congress the power to revoke the terms of treaties unilaterally. The government was now making official what had been the de facto reality for New England native peoples for more than two centuries: they were at the legal mercy of the European settlers.

The introduction of the Indian New Deal during Franklin Roosevelt's administration turned this tide somewhat, but native nations in New England remained for the most part politically and legally impotent. Not until the late 1960s did the situation begin to change. The Mashpee of western Cape Cod decided to seek the return of 11,000 acres of land on the basis of the Indian Trade and Intercourse Act of 1790. Their land had been ceded without federal sanction in a treaty made with the state of Massachusetts. The Mashpee seemed to have a solid legal case, except for the crucial fact that they were not a federally recognized tribe. A jury found them ineligible on those grounds in 1978, but New England had not seen the last of such matters.

The Passamaquoddy, the Penobscot, and the Houlton Band of Maliseet claimed approximately two-thirds of the state of Maine, pronouncing invalid three land-cession treaties signed with the states of Massachusetts (1794 and 1796) and Maine (1818), the last of which featured bogus signatures. They had fought on the side of the United States in the Revolutionary War as the Wabanaki Confederacy, which proved instrumental in holding Maine for the patriots, but they had been forgotten at the Treaty of Paris when the boundary was drawn severing the Maliseet and placing some Micmacs on the Canadian side. Over the course of the 20th century Maine had taken lands away from the Passamaquoddy without permission and only grudgingly granted Indians the right to vote in state elections in 1967, the last state in the nation to do so. Thus Maine's Indians sought to rectify many wrongs.

In *Joint Tribal Council of the Passamaquoddy Tribe v. Morton* (1975) the federal appellate court accepted the argument that the Indian Trade and Intercourse Act of 1790 voided the treaties. Out-of-court negotiations that involved President Jimmy Carter's administration constructed the Maine Indian Claims Settlement Act, which Congress passed in 1980. The law gave Maine's Indians $81.5 million in restitution and the opportunity to purchase up to 300,000 acres of land.

To pursue their claims, the Passamaquoddy had to prove that they constituted a tribe of Indians as defined by the court. They met the criteria, but the need for more formal guidelines precipitated an administrative ruling by the U.S. Department of the Interior. Within five years, more than 70 tribes throughout the United States had applied for federal recognition. Several New England tribes sought vindication of their land rights. Those attaining tribal status included the Wampanoag of Gay Head in Massachusetts; the Micmac in Maine; the Schaghticoke, the Mohegan, and

the Mashantucket Pequot in Connecticut; and the Narragansett of Rhode Island. The Narragansett gained federal recognition and $3.5 million to purchase 900 acres through the Rhode Island Indian Claims Settlement Act of 1978, and the Mashantucket Pequot Indian Claims Settlement Act of 1983 allowed that tribe to consolidate its landholdings. Thus New England's Indians have embraced U.S. legal institutions to legitimize their identities, long tenaciously held, as well as to regain their lost lands.

Increasing access to money and power continued with the passage of the Indian Gaming Regulatory Act of 1988. This act cleared the way for reservations to offer gambling to the public despite state prohibitions. The most successful endeavor in New England so far has been by the Mashantucket Pequot, who run the highly profitable Foxwoods Resort Casino in southeastern Connecticut. By 1997, approximately 45,000 people were using the facility every day, and slot machine revenues alone were projected at $140 million for the year. By 2004 the casino was the largest in the United States, employing more than 12,000 workers. There have been inconsistencies, however, as the ongoing case of the Narragansett of Rhode Island shows. Their attempts to build a casino have thus far been thwarted, with the failure of a proposal for a state referendum in 2004.

The Native American Graves Protection and Repatriation Act (NAGPRA) of 1990 offered a degree of belated respect to traditional Indians by protecting ancient cultural artifacts and the skeletal remains of Native American ancestors. The result has been a sometimes heated struggle with the museum and archaeological communities over the return of items long in their possession and the termination of certain research activities. Given the significant number of very old museums in New England and the important roles those institutions have played in the accumulation of Indian artifacts, grave goods, and skeletal remains, this legislation has had a profound effect on the region. Harvard University's Peabody Museum anticipated the 1990 law when, shortly before the passage of NAGPRA, it returned to the Omaha of Nebraska the Omaha sacred pole, the Omaha white buffalo robe, and numerous other sacred artifacts that had been taken from the tribe nearly 100 years ago by the anthropologist Alice Fletcher. Many other institutions have since followed suit.

State authorities have traditionally compounded their ignorance of Indian law by taking a proprietary view of "their" Indians, often disregarding federal preeminence in Indian affairs. For instance, in 1996 a Canadian Mo-

hawk, Bernadine Norton, was repeatedly told by the University of Massachusetts at Lowell that she needed a green card in order to receive financial aid—a flagrant violation of the 1794 Jay Treaty, which explicitly excludes members of the Canadian Iroquois Confederacy from such regulations. The case is sadly typical of the failure of state bureaucracies to properly understand and negotiate native legal issues.

In another example, this one involving the Saint Francis–Sokoki Band of Abenaki, the New England Indian Task Force requested in September 1988 that the state of Vermont and the U.S. government try to work with Abenaki leadership to resolve issues regarding fishing rights. The attempt did not succeed, and the ensuing litigation culminated in a Vermont district court judge ruling in August 1989 that Vermont Abenaki retained their original fishing rights and had not ceded them to the state. The Supreme Court of Vermont overturned that decision in 1992, and the U.S. Supreme Court refused to hear an Abenaki appeal the following year.

Like Vermont, Rhode Island has pressed disputes with Native Americans. In 1996 the city of Providence persuaded a Rhode Island superior court judge to issue an order allowing it to reclaim an ancient Hawaiian wooden carving a scant three weeks after a NAGPRA review board unanimously decided that the object should be returned to native Hawaiians. Only after two years of legal wrangling, court-ordered mediation, and a $125,000 donation to the city's museum of natural history did Providence agree to return the object to Hawaii. While this conflict ended in a successful resolution, many such cases do not, with the United States serving as the final arbiter. A 1996 ruling by the U.S. Court of Appeals for the Second Circuit in New York declared, for example, that the Mashantucket Pequot Reservation is not exempt from federal workplace safety regulations. While one may make an ostensibly moral argument about why the Pequot should be forced to comply, it would be specious to ignore the double standard at work and the sovereign implications it has "for the niche the federal government has carved out for the Indian tribes," to quote the judge in the case.

The federal government may have reduced native sovereignty to a "niche," but that state of affairs is not necessarily permanent. Recent legal gains noted above, though countered by setbacks, have ushered in a dynamic new legal era for the Indian peoples of New England as they seek to maintain and retain their time-honored native identity and their homelands.

Jeff Benedict, *Without Reservation* (2000); Kathleen J. Bragdon, *Native People of Southern New England, 1500–1650* (1996); Paul Brodeur, *Restitution: The*

Land Claims of the Mashpee, Passamaquoddy, and Penobscot Indians of New England (1985); Colin G. Calloway, ed., *After King Philip's War: Presence and Persistence in Indian New England* (1997); Jack Campisi, *The Mashpee Indians: Tribe on Trial* (1991); Patrick Frazier, *The Mohicans of Stockbridge* (1992); Francis Jennings, *The Invasion of America: Indians, Colonialism, and the Cant of Conquest* (1976); Howard S. Russell, *Indian New England before the Mayflower* (1980); Leslie Francis Stokes Upton, *Micmacs and Colonists: Indian-White Relations in the Maritimes, 1713–1867* (1979).

John R. Wunder and Akim D. Reinhardt

New England Seat The existence of a "New England seat" on the U.S. Supreme Court ensured the representation of New Englanders and offered an opportunity to bring to the process of judicial decision making a unique sensibility, forged somewhat by the culture of the northeastern states. New Englanders Joseph Story and Oliver Wendell Holmes, Jr., rank as two of the best-known and most important Supreme Court justices in American history. As Senator George Hoar of Massachusetts, wrote, "We have contributed from New England some very tough oak timbers to the bench."

President George Washington was the first to consider geographical representation vital to the court's legitimacy and competence in resolving disputes. Geographic diversity was crucial during the early years when anti-Federalist hostility to the fledgling federal court system remained strong. Moreover, the federal court system was less developed then and necessitated that Supreme Court justices adjudicate cases in states with which they were most familiar, usually the ones from which they were appointed. They did this by "riding circuit." Today we have a three-tiered system of federal courts: district (trial), intermediate appellate, and Supreme, with individual judges selected specifically for each judicial position. Supreme Court justices of the past performed both trial and appellate functions. This arrangement saved salaries, strengthened national identity, and exposed justices to the reality of people's legal problems. An additional benefit of limiting the number of federal judges was that wrangling between nationalists and states' rights proponents over the growth of the national government was diminished. Thus, the system of federal organization that classifies regions of the country into judicial circuits was an arrangement that enabled New Englanders to have guaranteed Supreme Court appointments.

With the Judiciary Act of 1789, Congress divided the country into three judicial circuits: the Eastern, Middle, and Southern. The business for each circuit (including major federal crimes, trials of large cases involving citizens of different states, and appeals from district courts) was handled by one federal district judge and two Supreme Court justices. Part of New England—New Hampshire, Connecticut, and Massachusetts—was put in the Eastern Circuit with New York. Maine was not incorporated into a circuit; it was left as a district by itself. The Maine district court had the same power as a circuit court. Because Rhode Island and Vermont had not entered the union when the circuits were created (Rhode Island joined in 1790, Vermont in 1791), they could not be placed in the Eastern Circuit. As the country expanded, new districts and circuits were added and states realigned. With the Judiciary Act of 1802, Congress placed Connecticut, Vermont, and New York in the Second Circuit; Massachusetts, Rhode Island, and New Hampshire went into the First Circuit. When Maine became a state in 1820, it was placed into the First Circuit. In 1915 Puerto Rico, a territory, was also added to the First Circuit.

Although the shape of the First Circuit never encompassed all of New England, the First Circuit's structure constrained presidents when choosing occupants for the seat. Beginning with Washington's selection of William Cushing of Massachusetts in 1789, the third seat on the court was designated the New England seat, and after Cushing's death in 1810, only jurists drawn from the states in the First Circuit were eligible. Reserving the sixth seat for southerners was another guarantee of regional representation on the court. Even westerners had a seat on the court for a time. So powerful was the regional tradition that Oliver Wendell Holmes, Jr., after years on the Massachusetts Supreme Judicial Court, despaired of being nominated to the national Court because President William McKinley had promised to appoint a Boston lawyer, Alfred Hemenway, to replace retiring Associate Justice Horace Gray. But McKinley was assassinated and the new president, Theodore Roosevelt, appointed Holmes.

Massachusetts was overrepresented on the New England seat, by Associate Justices William Cushing (1790–1810), Joseph Story (1812–45), Benjamin Curtis (1851–57), Horace Gray (1882–1902), and Oliver Wendell Holmes, Jr. (1902–32). New Hampshire produced Levi Woodbury (1845–51), and Maine was represented by Nathan Clifford (1858–81).

Cushing had served as the vice chair of the Massachusetts ratification convention for the U.S. Constitution as well as on the Massachusetts Supreme Court. His knowledge of the document, his judicial experience, and his New England roots recommended him to President Washington. His years on the court were uneventful. The court had little business and low prestige and rarely commanded attention; the chief justiceship was considered a particularly unimportant post, and Cushing refused Washington's offer of it, claiming ill health. He joined in the 1803 opinion in *Marbury v. Madison*, written by Chief Justice John Marshall, establishing the power of the judiciary to void legislation on the grounds that it violated the U.S. Constitution.

President James Madison's choice for the New England seat, Joseph Story, was confirmed in 1811. The youngest person ever appointed to the court, he served for 33 years. A renowned legal scholar, Story published nine treatises on the law, each of which became an authoritative guide for lawyers and judges. In particular, they provided uniformity in commercial and admiralty law. Story sought to reconcile the opposing forces of governmental power and vested property rights in a manner suited to an industrializing economy, as shown in *Dartmouth College v. Woodward* (1819), which protected Dartmouth's corporate charter from the state. He reworked ancient common law principles to suit the conditions of the energetic American economy.

Levi Woodbury, appointed by President James Polk in 1845, served five years. Little remembered for jurisprudence, he is notable for his political experience before appointment. Woodbury served as New Hampshire's governor, as U.S. senator, and as secretary of both the navy and the treasury.

Benjamin Curtis was appointed by President Millard Fillmore in 1851. He crafted "The Cooley Rule" in *Cooley v. Board of Wardens* (1852), which resolved conflicts between federal and state power to regulate commerce. Curtis left the court after six years, his resignation prompted by the infamous 1857 *Dred Scott* case, in which the court held that Congress lacked power to prohibit slavery in the territories. Curtis dissented, affirming congressional power over territories and citing evidence that blacks in some of the original 13 states were citizens at the time of ratification and that they were therefore citizens of the United States, contrary to the court's opinion.

Nathan Clifford, succeeding Curtis, is one of the more obscure occupants of the third seat. Clifford served as speaker of the Maine legislature as well as attorney general of both Maine and the United States. Nominated by President James Buchanan in 1857, he took his seat in early 1858, serving the court for 23 years.

President Chester A. Arthur chose Horace Gray to fill Clifford's vacancy in 1881. Gray had served as chief justice of the Massachusetts Supreme Judicial Court. A report prepared under his supervision recommended that Congress establish autonomous circuit courts of appeal, with circuit court judges chosen specifically for each circuit. Appeals from the district courts would go to the new courts of appeals. The 1891 Evarts Act enacted these reforms and the system established continues today.

The last occupant of the seat, Oliver Wendell Holmes, Jr., was the legendary "Yankee from Olympus." Having served on the Massachusetts Supreme Judicial Court for 20 years, the last three as chief justice, Holmes was appointed by President Theodore Roosevelt in 1902 and retired in 1932. Skeptical of ultimate truths, Holmes exercised judicial review sparingly. Recognizing his status as a nonelected judge, he would allow citizens, through their elected officials, to legislate for the accomplishment of desirable social ends, even if he disagreed with their choices. For Holmes the role of law was to enhance people's lives, not to serve as an intellectual exercise for judges. His philosophy took policymaking out of the hands of the conservative, probusiness courts and into progressive legislatures and administrative agencies. Economic abuses spawned by an unrestrained free market could thus be eliminated democratically. Holmes presented some of his most important ideas in dissents, as in *Hammer v. Dagenhart*, a 1918 case in which the majority refused to allow the federal government to discourage child labor. Holmes is also known for his jurisprudence concerning the First Amendment of the U.S. Constitution. Rather than simply accepting the view of the majority as he did on economic issues, Holmes used judicial review to enhance freedom of expression for individuals. In his dissent in *Abrams v. United States* (1919), Holmes advocated a marketplace of ideas, unconstrained by one person's ideas of truth, in which competing ideas vied for acceptance. Only if the spoken ideas presented a "clear and present danger" to society was government justified in outlawing it.

Three factors during the late 19th century diminished the importance of geographic representation on the court: congressional elimination of circuit riding in 1891; the rising demand for ethnic, religious, or racial representation, rather than geographic; and the dilution of state identity among the American people. The New England seat vanished in 1932, with President Herbert Hoover's controversial decision to fill Holmes's seat with the New Yorker Benjamin Cardozo on the grounds that only someone of the highest jurisprudential stature, regardless of regional origin, could succeed Holmes.

The appointment of David Souter of New Hampshire in 1990 brought a New Englander back to the court. Souter served New Hampshire as assistant attorney general under Warren Rudman (1971), as attorney general (1976–78), and on the New Hampshire Superior (1978–83) and Supreme Courts (1983–90). Given his reputation as a jurist with an independent streak and his close connections with Rudman and New Hampshire governor John Sununu, he was a logical choice for appointment to the U.S. Court of Appeals by President George H. W. Bush; on the other hand, Bush's choice of Souter five months later to fill the seat vacated by the retirement of Justice William J. Brennan was something of a surprise. Called at the time a "stealth justice," Souter presented his moderate stance on abortion in his first major decision, *Planned Parenthood of Southeastern Pennsylvania v. Casey* (1992). The formation of a moderate bloc composed of Souter, Sandra Day O'Connor, and Anthony Kennedy has sometimes provoked the ire of conservatives. But Souter's decisions are noted for their respect for precedent and history. His New England character is evidenced by a quick wit and habit of storytelling, as well as by a simple lifestyle, whether it be packing a daily lunch for work at the court or hiking the White Mountains when home in Weare. His decisions, balancing the rights of individuals with those of the states and corporations, may also reflect deep New England traditions.

In 1994 President Bill Clinton's nomination of Stephen G. Breyer added another New England resident to the court. Although Breyer was born and reared in California and attended Stanford University, he spent much of his career in Massachusetts as a professor at Harvard Law School and a judge on the U.S. Court of Appeals. In keeping with the tradition of thoughtfulness and humanity often associated with justices from New England, Breyer is respected for the craftsmanship of his opinions as well as for his attention to human interests beyond the questions the court confronts.

Henry Abraham, *Justices and Presidents* (1992); John A. Fliter, "Keeping the Faith: Justice David Souter and the First Amendment Religion Clauses," *Journal of Church and State* 40 (Spring 1998); Linda Greenhouse, "Changed Path for Court? New Balance Is Held by Three Cautious Justices," *New York Times*, June 26, 1992; Scott P. Johnson and Christopher E. Smith, "David Souter's First Term on the Supreme Court: The Impact of a New Justice," *Judicature* 75 (February–March 1992); David M. O'Brien, *Storm Center: The Supreme Court in American Politics* (1993); William Rehnquist, *The Supreme Court: How It Was, How It Is* (1987); Bernard Schwartz, *A History of the Supreme Court* (1993); G. Edward White, *The American Judicial Tradition: Profiles of Leading American Judges* (1976).

Susan J. Siggelakis

Penitentiaries Although the colonies sometimes held accused or convicted criminals for short periods in houses of correction, New England's earliest prisons emerged in the aftermath of the Revolution. By the 1830s, the crude facilities constructed in the first decades of the century gave way to penitentiaries. New England's penitentiaries were modeled after the famous example at Auburn, N.Y.—which featured individual cells and silence among prisoners—but they came to exert a particular influence on 19th-century prison reform, owing in large part to the zealous advocacy of the Rev. Louis Dwight, leader of the Prison Discipline Society of Boston.

New England's first prisons were adaptations of military or other facilities. In 1773, Connecticut used an abandoned copper mine as its own Newgate prison (the notorious English prison that held the prisoners of the continental government) for loyalists during the Revolution. In 1785, Massachusetts locked its convicts in the Castle Island fortress in Boston Harbor. Connecticut held to its crude form of underground incarceration until 1827, but in 1805, Massachusetts moved its prisoners from Castle Island to Charlestown, where it had constructed the region's first state prison built specifically for the purpose. Vermont followed in 1809 with a prison at Windsor, and New Hampshire opened its Concord state prison in 1812. All of these early institutions drew upon emerging theories of crime that sought to rehabilitate criminals by putting them to work.

It was not until the 1820s and 1830s, however, that penitentiaries under the Auburn system wholeheartedly embraced this notion. Prisoners at these institutions were sentenced to "hard labor," which they were to perform under a rigid rule of silence. They spent their nights in solitary confinement to preclude nocturnal conspiracies that might undo their daytime rehabilitation. In 1823, three years after Maine separated from Massachusetts and acquired statehood under the Missouri Compromise, it built an Auburn-style prison at Thomaston. The rest of New England soon followed suit: Connecticut with a new prison at Wethersfield (1827), then Massachusetts (1829), Vermont (1831), and New Hampshire (1832).

By the time of the Civil War, New England's penitentiaries were run down, overcrowded, and strangers to the ideals of their founders. A new generation of reformers called for more specialized institutions, which would classify prisoners according to their potential for rehabilitation and confine them, not for fixed terms, but for indeterminate sentences that ended only when reformation was successful. These efforts on behalf of the reformatory prefigured the penology of the Progressive Era, which placed its faith in the use of scientific methods to rehabilitate criminals.

Inmates play basketball at the Nashua Street prison in Boston, 1980s

Massachusetts established the Women's Reformatory Prison at Framingham in 1877 and the Concord Reformatory for young men in 1884. In the early 20th century, these institutions, along with the Norfolk (Mass.) Prison Colony (begun in 1927), were nationally recognized examples of the Progressive approach to individualized rehabilitation. By the end of the century, however, they too had fallen far short of their founders' ideals. New England turned away from its history of rehabilitation and reform, following a national trend that greatly expanded the use of long-term incarceration meant only to be punitive and custodial.

Artistic portrayals have contributed to popular images of the region's penitentiaries. Maine's Thomaston prison was featured in Stephen King's novella *Rita Hayworth and Shawshank Redemption,* the basis for the 1994 film *The Shawshank Redemption.* Frederick Wiseman's controversial documentary about the Massachusetts State Prison for the Criminally Insane, *Titicut Follies* (1967), was banned by the Massachusetts Supreme Judicial Court until 1992 but ultimately contributed to the reform of that institution.

Estelle B. Freedman, *Their Sisters' Keepers: Women's Prison Reform in America, 1830–1930* (1981); Adam Jay Hirsch, *The Rise of the Penitentiary: Prisons and Punishment in Early America* (1992); David J. Rothman, *Conscience and Convenience: The Asylum and Its Alternatives in Progressive America* (1984); Rothman, *The Discovery of the Asylum: Social Order and Disorder in the New Republic* (1971).

Larry Goldsmith

Property and Commercial Law
The law that governs interests in property and commercial matters is both vast and fundamental to the American economic system. Property law governs ownership—the legal rights to possess, use, benefit from, exclude others from, and dispose of things both tangible and intangible. It is generally subdivided into two broad categories: the law governing real property, or land, and the law concerning personal property, both tangible (like an automobile) and intangible (such as the intellectual property rights to a book). Commercial law, in the most general sense, is that body of law governing all aspects of commerce in property. Historically, commercial law has encompassed the law of contracts, sales, commercial paper and banking, bulk sales and fraudulent conveyances, documents of title, investment securities, secured transactions, bankruptcy, admiralty, and agency and business organizations. Both property law and commercial law have existed for millennia. The American law of real property developed within the English system of feudalism; and American law governing commercial practices grew out of the *lex mercatoria,* or the Law Merchant, also inherited from England, which, in its time, provided a uniform and efficient legal system for roving merchants who transacted business internationally in the medieval world.

The basic law of property inherited from England continued in the New England colonies, as in the other colonies, and much of that legal tradition remains intact today. Interests in real property are classified into "estates" and generally may vary with respect to the time the interest may be realized (such as on the death of the current possessor), limitations on the transfer of ownership (such as restrictions on sale), the extent of permissible use of the property (such as restrictions of property to single-family residential use), and the duration of the interest involved. Interests in real property may be held singly or jointly with other people and may be divided between people who have the right to control the property and those who have the right to benefit from it. Property may be acquired privately, with public grants, or by adverse possession. Personal property includes both tangible and intangible things other than land, including chattels, contract rights, accounts receivable, and infinite other possibilities; therefore, interests in personal property may be quite complicated.

Although property law in New England continues to be characterized by concepts and rules that emerged from the English feudal system, it has of course evolved to adapt to contemporary circumstances and the changing needs of society. Thus, ancient doctrines governing classifications of interests in land continue in effect, yet new adaptations have emerged to accommodate recent innovations in ownership such as condominiums, timeshares, and cooperatives. And while the fundamental principles of interests in personal property have survived the centuries, the law has been forced to adapt those principles to developing interests in intellectual property, including property interests associated with computer software and the Internet.

One of the more significant developments in U.S. property law in which New England played a substantial role was the emergence of strong constitutional protections of private property ownership from governmental interference. During the revolutionary period and through the early 19th century, New England strongly influenced the development of fundamental constitutional protections of private property. For instance, in their state constitutions Vermont and Massachusetts pioneered protections against government takings of private property, commonly referred to today as eminent domain. During the revolutionary era, attitudes toward governmental interference with private ownership strengthened. In 1777, owing to an emerging distrust of government and a growing sense of individual freedom, Vermont became the first state whose constitution required that just compensation be paid to an owner deprived of property by the government. Massachusetts followed suit in 1780. National agreement with this broad ideological shift concerning the relationship between government and private property became manifest with the ratification of the U.S. Constitution, which itself contained a "takings clause." The clause provided that the federal government could take land from citizens only when it did so for a public purpose and if it paid just compensation. In the late 20th and early 21st centuries the U.S. Supreme Court has been slowly extending the Constitution's protections of private property, such as limiting the government's power to regulate property. In the spring of 2005, the U.S. Supreme Court will hear a case arising from the decision of the city of New London, Conn., to condemn the property of a working-class community and resell it to developers for a shopping mall and upscale housing. The case turns on the Constitution's requirement that property can be taken only for "public use." The question is thus whether it is a legitimate "public use" for state and local communities to replace communities of modest means with wealthier private communities. Part of the answer may turn on the increased tax revenues that the new community will generate.

While the law of property remains relatively stable, the need for the law to continually reinvent itself is far more apparent in commercial law. Indeed, the Law Merchant, the ancestor of modern commercial law, represented the customary practices of merchants, and to this day trade custom and usage inform the commercial law, ensuring that the law keeps pace with changing business practices. The development of commercial law, however, is somewhat constrained by a competing interest that is not prominent in the law of property: the need for the law to be roughly uniform to facilitate commerce in an ever-expanding economy. As a region of significant commercial importance, New England commercial law conforms to the broad uniformity that exists nationally.

Historically, perhaps the most important development in the homogenization of commercial law has been the adoption in 49 states of the Uniform Commercial Code (UCC), which uniformly codifies the law of sales and leases, bank deposits and collections, fund transfers, negotiable instruments, bulk sales, investment securities, documents of title, letters of credit, and secured transactions. Several areas of commercial law not covered by the UCC are also made uniform under federal jurisdiction. These areas include admiralty law under the constitutional grant of admiralty jurisdiction to the federal judiciary, and bankruptcy under the federal bankruptcy code. Thus, the only bodies of commercial law that can differ substantially from state to state are the law of contracts and the law governing agency and business associations. Still, the necessity for commercial law to reflect contemporary business practice means that trade custom and usage continue to inform the law, resulting in revisions to the UCC.

Because the UCC continues to respond to changes in commercial practice, important innovations in commercial law by states often affect revisions in the UCC. States are free to adopt all or parts of the UCC and may modify sections adopted within their own statutory framework; these nonuniform adaptations may later serve as the basis for revisions to the UCC. For example, Massachusetts has long been recognized nationally as the predominant state of organization for mutual fund companies. The reason that so many mutual fund companies organize in Massachusetts is to take advantage of a form of business organization that is unique to that state, the business trust. As a consequence of being home to more than 50 percent of mutual fund companies, Massachusetts has incidentally developed significant expertise in the law governing investment fund securities. Consequently, Massachusetts's enactment of nonuniform amendments to its UCC provisions pertinent to mutual funds were later adopted in subsequent revisions of the UCC by its drafters.

Massachusetts has also been influential in an area of commercial law not governed by the UCC—the law of business organizations, which generally governs the formation, functioning, and dissolution of business enterprises, including, for instance, corporations, partnerships, limited liability entities, and joint ventures. The law of business organizations, like the commercial law generally, must respond to the changing needs of business practice, and Massachusetts has contributed significantly to the development of business law. For instance, during the latter half of the 20th century an increasing number of small business enterprises chose to organize as corporations rather than use the more traditional structure of a partnership to reduce their exposure of personal liability for business obligations. The corporate form of organization, originally intended for large business conglomerates encompassing thousands of shareholders, presented numerous problems when applied to these new entities with small numbers of shareholders, called closely held corporations. Of principal concern was the relatively harsh manner in which minority shareholders (shareholders who do not control a majority of the corporation's stock) could be treated by the majority shareholders under traditional corporate law. Recognizing that closely held corporations are, in substance, often no more than partnerships organized as corporations, in the case of *Donahue v. Rodd Electrotype* (1975), Massachusetts pioneered the rule that shareholders in closely held corporations must treat each other in a manner similar to that of partners in a partnership.

Gregory Alexander, *Commodity and Propriety: Competing Visions of Property in American Legal Thought, 1776–1970* (1997); Roger A. Cunningham, William B. Stoebuck, and Dale A. Whitman, *The Law of Property*, 2d ed. (1993); Harry G. Henn and John R. Alexander, *Laws of Corporations and Other Business Enterprises* (1983); Seldon A. Jones, Laura M. Mauret, and James M. Story, "The Massachusetts Business Trust and Registered Investment Companies," *Delaware Journal of Corporate Law* 14 (1988); Marylynn Salmon, *Women and the Law of Property in Early America* (1986); Alphonse M. Squillante and John R. Fonseca, *The Law of Modern Commercial Practices* (1980); David A. Thomas, ed., *Thompson on Real Property*, 2d ed. (1998); William M. Treanor, "The Original Understanding of the Takings Clause and the Political Process," *Columbia Law Review* 95 (1995).

Michael D. Blanchard

Railroad Regulation During the 19th century the railroads emerged as the first large-scale industrial corporations and assumed increasing importance as a means of facilitating transcontinental expansion and the Industrial Revolution. The combination of concentrated wealth and public importance that characterized the railroads would ultimately precipitate the first federal administrative agency in U.S. history, the Interstate Commerce Commission. But long before the federal government began attempts at regulation, New England states pioneered managing the growth and consolidation of their railroads, both by passing laws and by creating the first state railroad commissions in the country.

From their inception New England's railroads tended toward consolidation. The consolidation trend was not unique to New England, however, but characteristic of the railroad industry. Railroad owners and investors recognized early that longer and more numerous lines led to greater economies of scale, reducing operating costs and thus enhancing profits. The drive toward consolidation also represented the railroads' efforts to diminish competition from other lines. In New England, as in the rest of the country, the presence of competing railroads spawned price wars aimed at attaining greater market shares. The price wars themselves were often catalysts for consolidation, cutting into profits or even resulting in losses. When competing lines merged, they could cease battling for market share and charge prices for freight and fare alike that permitted them to operate with wider profit margins.

The trend toward consolidation and the overwhelming economic importance of the railroads at both the national and regional levels thus provided the impetus for government regulation. But while the incentives to regulate were uniform, responses to them varied by region. The patchwork of state regulation that developed in New England during the 19th century included general legislation, oversight by state judiciaries, and, perhaps most notably, state railroad commissions. In 1839 Rhode Island became the first state in the nation to form a commission, followed in time by the other New England states. These commissions possessed little actual power over the railroads, however; their authority tended to be limited to making recommendations with respect to rates, safety, and the development of new lines.

Beyond administrative authority, it was the philosophical approach to regulation, articulated most notably by Charles Francis Adams of the Massachusetts commission, that distinguished New England railroad regulation. Unlike the grangers and the populists of the Midwest, who attacked the railroads' monopoly power and sought to regulate rates and increase competition between lines, New England railroad regulators adopted what in their view was a more enlightened approach, which recognized the harm that could result from raw competition and the benefits that could result from consolidation. The New England philosophy of regulation emanated from the view that the railroads were quasi-public entities that by nature functioned best as natural monopolies. The region was therefore more permissive of consolidation, particularly where the emerging line promised benefits to New England's economy. Thus the New England regulators' approach focused on improving the railroads rather than reining them in.

As the railroads consolidated further and inevitably transcended regional boundaries, it became apparent to the New England commissions that if regulation were to be effective, it had to be imposed on a national level. Contrary opinions voiced by legislators and the public in general quickly became irrelevant when the U.S. Supreme Court issued a number of decisions in the 1880s severely limiting the power of states to regulate the railroads. With the establishment of the Interstate Commerce Commission in 1887, the state regulation of railroads became secondary in importance.

George Pierce Baker, *Formation of the New England Railroad Systems: A Study of Railroad Combination in the 19th Century* (1968); James W. Ely, Jr., *Railroads and American Law* (2002); Edward Chase Kirkland, *Men, Cities, and Transportation: A Study in New England History, 1820–1900* (1948); Gabriel Kolko, *Railroads and Regulation, 1877–1916* (1965).

Michael D. Blanchard

Religious Freedom Religious freedom as we understand it today hardly existed in New England during the colonial era. Although church membership was not compulsory, church attendance was, and in Massachusetts and Connecticut, the Congregational clergy were tax-supported. While church and state were seen as separate entities, they were linked in God's higher plan for humanity; thus those who were responsible for civil governance of the colonies (being firmly Puritan themselves) saw no conflict of interest in intervening in religious affairs.

Many of the early Puritan migrants to New England engaged in a range of religious experimentation that tested the limits of Puritan beliefs and practices. In 1637–38, Anne Hutchinson, a charismatic student of the teachings of John Cotton, argued that individual salvation depended on the inward spirit of God and suggested that those ministers lacked true divinity who did not possess that spirit themselves. She presented a uniquely feminine voice in a public sphere that had been defined as properly the regard of men and thus roused the scrutiny of civil authorities who perceived her arguments as a direct challenge to the authority of the ministers. This early period of religious experimentation resulted in growing contention over the rules of the church and the privileges accorded to its members. Some Puritan innovators and radicals were quietly suppressed, while others were brought to trial on charges of sedition and heresy for ideas and activities that conflicted with existing standards of Puritan religious practice or authority. These trials typically resulted, as they did for both Anne Hutchinson and Roger Williams, in a sentence of banishment from the Puritan colonies.

Under pressure from their English cohorts to institute discipline within the church, New England's civil leaders called a synod of ministers in 1646 that ultimately adopted a platform for church governance. Under the Cambridge Platform of 1648, religious authority was placed firmly in the hands of the ministers, and laypeople were admonished to exercise restraint until given leave to speak by a minister. Thereafter, when confronted with the active presence of evangelical Anabaptists (beginning in 1651) and Quakers (beginning in 1656), Massachusetts Bay led the way in coordinating the Puritan response to "heretical threats." Quakers became especially conspicuous because they sometimes disrupted Congregational Sunday services. The punishment for Quaker and Anabaptist evangelicals included imprisonment, fines, mutilation (such as cutting off the ears or branding the tongue), public flogging, and, in Massachusetts, in the case of those who resisted all other warnings to desist, public hanging. These acts were humorously defended by Nathaniel Ward, who joked that "All Familists, Antinomians, Anabaptists, and other Enthusiasts" did have religious freedom—the freedom to "keep away from us." Official policy toward toleration did not change significantly during the next four decades; laws requiring conformity in worship and a uniform system of belief remained in effect, although enforcement declined precipitously. Some dissenting groups were thus able to quietly increase their numbers, but others were stymied. Anglicans, for example, made no headway in New England before 1686, when the first Anglican liturgy was read in Boston, and that was only after Charles II revoked the colony's original charter in 1684.

Only Rhode Island—where Roger Williams sought to put into effect his belief that each individual should have the liberty to follow the dictates of his or her own conscience, and where no church received support from the civil government—established what might be deemed a tolerant stance toward religious dissenters. From its humble founding in the late 1630s by antinomians and Anabaptists rejected and despised by the Puritans of Massachusetts Bay, Rhode Island became a haven for those of "distressed conscience." This devotion to "soul liberty," as Williams called it, attracted a variety of sects not welcome elsewhere in New England, including not only Protestant groups but also Jews, who established a community at Newport in 1677 and later built New England's first synagogue there in 1763.

The Revolution of 1689 in England had only a limited effect in New England. The Massachusetts charter of 1691 now linked voting rights to the ownership of property rather than to membership in the Congregational Church, but the Congregational clergy were still paid from tax collections. Nor was this condition changed by the American Revolution in Massachusetts, Connecticut, Vermont, or New Hampshire.

The process of eliminating state support and limiting the status and privileges of the church began earliest in frontier portions of New England, particularly Vermont, which officially separated church and state in 1807. Connecticut and New Hampshire completed the process in 1818 and 1819, respectively. But it was not until 1833 that Massachusetts finally amended its constitution to eliminate state support for the Congregational Church and thus remove the subordinate footing of other religious groups. The civil disabilities imposed on Jews and Catholics, however, continued in some states and were not eradicated in New England until 1875, when New Hampshire amended its constitution to remove the prohibition against voting and office holding by non-Protestants. The free exercise of religion is always a controversial matter, but the right is recognized in the Constitution, and no American today is forced by law to support a church.

Mary Louise Greene, *The Development of Religious Liberty in Connecticut* (1905); Timothy D. Hall, *Separating Church and State: Roger Williams and Religious Liberty* (1998); Jane Kamensky, *Governing the Tongue: The Politics of Speech in Early New England* (1997); William G. McLoughlin, *New England Dissent, 1630–1833: The Baptists and the Separation of Church and State* (1971).

Holly Snyder

Ricker, Marilla (Marks Young) (1840–1920)

Lawyer and voting rights activist. Born in New Durham, N.H., Marilla Ricker was one of the country's first female lawyers. She gained the right for women to practice law in New Hampshire and in 1910, at the age of 70, tried to run for governor of that state.

In becoming a suffragist and freethinker, Ricker followed the example of her parents, Jonathan and Hannah Stevens Young, who were educated farmers. She married John Ricker, an older man (56 to her 23) and inherited a substantial fortune when he died five years later. In her writings Ricker often remarked on the value of financial independence for women.

In 1869 Ricker attended the first convention of the National Woman Suffrage Association in Washington, D.C., and "hurried home to New Hampshire," she said, to try voting. Although she was refused, Ricker would continue to present herself at the Dover polls year after year, arguing her right as a citizen and taxpayer to vote.

After reading law in a private office in Washington, Ricker was admitted to the bar in 1882, having submitted what the chairman of the entrance committee called "an unusually creditable examination." Nine years later she was certified to argue before the U.S. Supreme Court. Ricker pleaded several important test cases: her challenge of the Sunday closing law failed, but she had more success in prison reform, gaining rights for indigent convicts, including prostitutes.

During the presidency of William McKinley (1897–1901), Ricker also became the first woman to seek a major diplomatic post in the U.S. foreign service when she tried unsuccessfully to be named minister to Colombia. Ricker's platform as gubernatorial candidate in 1910—woman suffrage and taxation of churches—enshrined her two main interests, but state officials ruled that if women could not vote, they could not appear on the ballot. Ricker spent her last decade lecturing and writing. Her essays on free thought were collected in *The Four Gospels* (1911), *I Don't Know, Do You?* (1916), and *I Am Not Afraid, Are You?* (1917).

Bennie L. DeWhitt, "A Wider Sphere of Usefulness: Marilla Ricker's Quest for a Diplomatic Post," *Prologue* 5 (1973); Karen Berger Morello, *The Invisible Bar: The Woman Lawyer in America, 1638 to Present* (1986); Barbara A. White, "Marilla M. Ricker," in *American Women Writers: A Critical Reference Guide from Colonial Times to the Present*, ed. Lina Mainiero (1979–94).

Barbara A. White

Roberts v. City of Boston

At issue in the landmark 1849 case *Roberts v. City of Boston* was the constitutionality of racial segregation in the Boston public schools. The Boston school committee had maintained separate schools for African American pupils since the early 19th century. In 1848 black parents launched a new effort to eliminate segregated schools. In this connection, five-year-old Sarah Roberts sought permission to attend the public school nearest her home instead of a more distant "colored" school. When this request was denied, Benjamin F. Roberts filed suit against the city in his daughter's name, seeking damages under a state statute for illegally excluding the child from a public school. Charles Sumner, a noted abolitionist and later U.S. senator, represented Roberts. Sumner argued that segregated schools violated the Massachusetts Declaration of Rights, which provided that "all men are born free and equal." He contended that the school committee had no power to segregate students by race and that separate schools carried a stigma of inferiority.

Speaking for a unanimous Supreme Judicial Court, Chief Justice Lemuel Shaw sustained the authority of the school committee to impose segregation. He asserted that Sarah was not unlawfully denied instruction because there was a public school she could attend. Shaw emphasized that the newly refurbished school facilities for blacks were equal to those available for whites. He ruled that the committee possessed discretionary power to classify students by race and that the wisdom of this policy was a matter for the committee to determine. Conceding that blacks were entitled to equal rights, Shaw nonetheless insisted that the maintenance of separate schools did not violate the state constitution. The chief justice concluded that any feelings of racial prejudice, should they exist, were not created by law and probably could not be changed by legal means. Accordingly, the action by Roberts was dismissed.

Despite the outcome in this case, the power of local school boards in Massachusetts to separate students on the basis of race did not last long. In 1855 the state legislature prohibited public schools from making distinctions among pupils on account of race, effectively superseding the *Roberts* decision.

On the national stage, however, Shaw's opinion in *Roberts* had an enduring effect. Shaw's commanding reputation lent considerable prestige to the view that racial segregation was constitutional. Both state and federal courts repeatedly cited the decision during the late 19th century as authority for upholding segregated schools. The U.S. Supreme Court heavily relied on the *Roberts* case in *Plessy v. Ferguson* (1896), in which the court ruled that racial segregation did not violate the 14th Amendment. Hence, the *Roberts* opinion provided the legal rationale for racial segregation. Not until *Brown v. Board of Education* (1954) was the separate but equal doctrine implicit in *Roberts* pronounced unconstitutional under the Equal Protection Clause of the 14th Amendment.

Elijah Adlow, *The Genius of Lemuel Shaw, Expounder of the Common Law* (1962); Leonard W. Levy, *The Law of the Commonwealth and Chief Justice Shaw* (1970 [1957]); Leonard W. Levy and Douglas L. Jones, eds., *Jim Crow in Boston: The Origin of the Separate but Equal Doctrine* (1974); George R. Metcalf, *From Little Rock to Boston: The History of School Desegregation* (1983).

James W. Ely, Jr.

Robinson (Sawtelle), Lelia (Josephine) (1850–1891)

Lawyer and writer. Born in Boston to Daniel and Mary Robinson, Lelia Robinson was known as "the lawyer" at her elementary school after defending a classmate accused of lying. However, journalism was Robinson's first calling, and she worked for a number of Boston newspapers. At age 17, Robinson married Rupert Chute, but their marriage was brief; Robinson divorced her husband on the grounds of adultery. Because divorce carried a great stigma at the time, Robinson fought in court for the right to keep her maiden name, which the court granted in 1877. This exposure to the law may have prompted Robinson to venture into the legal profession, and in 1878 she enrolled at Boston University School of Law. In 1881, Robinson graduated cum laude, the first woman graduate of the law school.

After graduating from law school, Robinson became the first woman to seek admission to the bar in Massachusetts. In 1881, the Supreme Judicial Court of Massachusetts denied her admission because the law did not explicitly state that women could practice. Robinson worked to secure the unanimous passage of new legislation that would allow women to practice law, and in 1882 she became the first woman admitted to the bar in Massachusetts.

Robinson opened a law office in Boston but had very little business. Hoping that the progressive West would prove more amenable to a woman practitioner, in 1884 Robinson opened a law practice in Seattle, Wash. Robinson found success in Seattle, a city that offered her the opportunity to be the first woman lawyer to argue before a mixed jury of men and women. Robinson immediately realized the importance of women serving on juries, which instilled a deep and lifelong interest in suffrage and the rights of women. Despite this success, Robinson moved back to Boston in 1885 to attend to family obligations.

In Boston, Robinson began to write popular works on legal topics. In 1886, she wrote the critically acclaimed *Law Made Easy: A Book for the People*. Making law accessible to women was also a personal crusade for Robinson. She wrote a series of columns for the *Woman's Journal* and *The Chautauquan* on "points of law a woman should understand" and also published her second book, the widely read *The Law of Husband and Wife* (1889).

Promoting the cause of women and of women in the legal profession became themes in Robinson's career. Robinson hired women to work in her law office and joined women's professional organizations, including the Equity Club, a correspondence club of women lawyers from across the country. The advancement of women in the profession was celebrated by Robinson's 1890 article in the *Green Bag*, "Women Lawyers in the United States," which was the first written attempt to survey the accomplishments of women lawyers across the country. Robinson struggled to collect data on the 208 women lawyers listed in the 1890 U.S. census; she was able to gather information depicting the achievements, both professional and personal, of 120 women lawyers, including herself.

In 1890, Robinson married the businessman Eli Sawtelle. Sawtelle encouraged Robinson's professional aspirations; during their honeymoon, Robinson was admitted to the U.S. Supreme Court bar, becoming the sixth woman authorized to practice law before the court.

Robinson's flourishing career was tragically cut short. She suffered from sleeplessness and died from an overdose of sleeping medication on August 10, 1891. She was 41.

As a lasting tribute, Robinson's words are inscribed in the entrance of the U.S. District Courthouse in Boston: "The best administration of justice may be most safely secured by allowing the representation of all classes of the people in courts of justice."

Virginia G. Drachman, "'My "Partner" in Law and Life': Marriage in the Lives of Women Lawyers in Late 19th- and Early 20th-Century America," *Law and Social Inquiry* 14 (1989); Mary A. Greene, "Mrs. Lelia Robinson Sawtelle: The First Woman Lawyer of Massachusetts," *The Chautauquan* 14 (December 1891); Douglas Lamar Jones, "Lelia J. Robinson's

Case and the Entry of Women into the Legal Profession in Massachusetts," in *The History of the Law in Massachusetts: The Supreme Judicial Court, 1692–1992*, ed. Russell K. Osgood (1992).

Erika V. Wayne

Schools of Law New England is home to 16 law schools, with each of the region's states represented. Nine are in Massachusetts, three are in Connecticut, and the four other New England states have one each. These schools range from the oldest and largest in the country to some of the newest and smallest. The older, larger law schools have adopted a generalized approach to curriculum offerings, while several of the smaller schools have attained prominence by emphasizing legal specialization. Typically for a region dominated by private higher education institutions, all but two of New England's law schools—those of the University of Connecticut and the University of Maine—are private.

The nation's first law school was founded in Litchfield, Conn., in 1784, by Tapping Reeve. The nation's oldest continuously operating school of law, Harvard Law School, was founded in 1817. Today, with approximately 1,650 full-time students pursuing the Juris Doctor (J.D.) and 200 others seeking specialized degrees, Harvard Law is also among the nation's largest. Harvard Law's students and the school's faculty members are served by the largest academic law library in the world, with nearly 2 million volumes. Many outsiders' perceptions of Harvard Law School are based on John Jay Osborn, Jr.'s 1971 novel, *The Paper*

Chase, and the 1973 film and subsequent television series of the same name, together with best-selling author Scott Turow's memoirs of his first year at Harvard Law, *One L* (1977); the school has developed the reputation of being not merely rigorous, but intellectually brutal. Few graduates have made an effort to dispel this notion.

Yale Law School, while as prestigious and venerable as its Ivy League rival, is much smaller, with an enrollment of approximately 600. Students enjoy a student-to-faculty ratio of less than 10 to 1. The Yale experience has long been recognized as lacking much of the harsh competition attributed to Harvard, although Yale admits an even smaller percentage of applicants than does Harvard (8 percent of Yale applicants are admitted, versus Harvard's 12 percent). Yale admitted its first African American student in 1880; one-third of its student body today is composed of minority-group members. Clarence Thomas, the second African American to serve on the U.S. Supreme Court, is a graduate of Yale Law School. President Bill Clinton and his wife, Hillary, met while both were students there.

The University of Maine Law School, located in Portland, is one of the smallest in the country, with approximately 250 students. The Vermont Law School is a private institution founded in the 1970s. The school's Environmental Law Center has earned a national reputation, and students can obtain both a J.D. and a master's degree in environmental law. In keeping with its theme of environmentalism, in 1998 the school opened Oakes Hall, a class-

The original school building of Litchfield Law School (1784– 1833), the first law school in the country, which was operated by Tapping Reeve and James Gould

room building with the latest in energy- and resource-conserving technologies as well as electronic and distance-learning facilities.

The Franklin Pierce Law Center, located in Concord, N.H., was founded in the 1970s and has chosen to remain one of the nation's smallest independent law schools. Its program in intellectual property has earned national recognition, and it has the largest full-time intellectual property faculty in the country. Originally founded as a unit of Franklin Pierce College, the Law Center soon became an independent institution.

Boston College Law School was established in 1929. Although Boston College maintains its original affiliation with the Jesuit order of Roman Catholic priests, the school attracts a national student body from a variety of religious traditions. The Massachusetts legislature has long had the reputation of being dominated by Boston College Law grads. John Kerry, the 2004 Democratic presidential candidate, is a graduate of the school.

The law school at Boston University was established in 1872 and draws students from across the country. The school maintains a national orientation, with more than half of its graduates leaving New England. The Northeastern University School of Law, also in Boston, offers its students a unique cooperative program. After the first year of course work, students alternate every three months between the classroom and full-time externships that approximately 800 employers in 40 states and countries offer. Another unusual feature is that professors give students narrative evaluations of their efforts rather than grades. The school was founded in 1898 as a component of the Young Men's Christian Association (YMCA) and has the reputation of being liberal in its viewpoint. For instance, it requires a public interest component in all students' programs; it also has the Tobacco Products Liability Project and clinical programs in poverty law and prisoners' rights.

The New England School of Law was established in 1908 as the all-female Portia Law School. The school had more than 200 students by 1922, and all of the women who passed the December 1921 bar exam in Massachusetts were Portia graduates. The Boston school became coeducational in 1938; today, nearly half of its students are male. The name was changed to the New England School of Law in 1969. Like its neighbor Suffolk University, New England offers extensive evening programs for working students, as well as a full-time day division. Students may also apply for special part-time status, designed for those with sole or primary child-care responsibilities.

The history of Suffolk University and its law school is unlike that of most institutions; that is, the law school came first (1906) and the institution's other programs followed. Suffolk is one of the largest law schools in the country and has traditionally emphasized its evening program. Located near the Massachusetts State House in Boston, the school points to its accessibility to positions in the Massachusetts government and also maintains a tradition of extensive clinical programs.

The Western New England University School of Law began in 1918 as a satellite program of Northeastern College (now Northeastern University) with courses offered to students in the evening at the Springfield Central YMCA. The law and undergraduate programs became independent from Northeastern in 1951. The law school remained exclusively an evening program until 1973.

The Massachusetts School of Law is located in Andover, north of Boston. The school was established in 1988 and licensed by the state in 1990, allowing its graduates to sit for the Massachusetts bar exam. The school is unusual in that it does not require prospective students to take the Law School Admission Test (LSAT), one of the factors that led to the school's failure to win provisional accreditation from the ABA in 1992. The school responded with a $90 million lawsuit against the ABA, claiming that the accreditation criteria established monopolistic practices among accredited programs. The lawsuit brought scrutiny to the ABA's rigid standards and calls for reform from several deans of accredited schools, as well as a suit by the Justice Department. Although the ABA did modify its accreditation standards in response, the Massachusetts School of Law ultimately failed to convince the courts of the merits of its complaint. Massachusetts School of Law graduates, though unable to apply for bar membership in every state because of the school's lack of ABA accreditation, are eligible to sit for the bar exam in Massachusetts, Connecticut, and Vermont.

The other unaccredited law school in Massachusetts has taken a much more traditional approach. The Southern New England School of Law, established during the 1980s in North Dartmouth, Mass., has embraced ABA standards and expects to gain accreditation soon. The school aggressively recruits top students by offering substantial scholarships for candidates with high LSAT scores.

Roger Williams University's Ralph R. Papitto Law School, the only law school in Rhode Island, has significant curriculum offerings in maritime law and houses the Marine Affairs Institute. Students may also pursue a joint J.D.–master of marine science degree program in conjunction with the University of Rhode Island. Founded in 1993, the law school gained accreditation in the shortest time possible under ABA guidelines.

The University of Connecticut Law School, founded in 1921, is located in Hartford. Its emphasis on small class size has created a student-to-teacher ratio of 12 to 1. The school is one of the least expensive in the region and offers preferential tuition to non-Connecticut residents of all New England states except Maine, which supports the region's only other public law school.

The private Quinnipiac University School of Law, located in Hamden, Conn., arose from the law school at the University of Bridgeport. Bridgeport found itself in severe financial straits during the early 1990s, and in 1991 the law school faculty voted to leave Bridgeport. The move met with resistance from Bridgeport's administration, which tried to fire the law dean, who refused to leave.

Four of the current nine U.S. Supreme Court justices (Stephen Breyer, Anthony Kennedy, Antonin Scalia, and David Souter) were graduated from Harvard Law School, and one (Thomas) from Yale. Justice Ruth Bader Ginsburg attended Harvard Law School for two years before transferring to Columbia. The last two U.S. presidents who were lawyers—Gerald Ford and Clinton—both attended Yale. Although the two Ivy League institutions in the region have drawn the most national attention, all 16 New England law schools have played a role in educating many successful lawyers, judges, and political leaders.

Laura Kalman, *Legal Realism at Yale, 1927–1960* (1986); William P. LaPiana, *Logic and Experience: The Origin of Modern American Legal Education* (1994); Robert Bocking Stevens, *Law School: Legal Education in America from the 1850s to the 1980s* (1983); Charles Warren, *History of the Harvard Law School and of Early Legal Conditions in America* (1908).

Peyton Paxson

Shaw, Lemuel (1781–1861) Jurist. Born in West Barnstable, Mass., on Cape Cod, Lemuel Shaw was raised in a rural parsonage. His father, a Congregational minister, was Shaw's only teacher until the boy reached the age of 14. Shaw ultimately graduated from Harvard College in 1800. He studied law for three years in Boston and New Hampshire under the tutelage of a leading attorney and was admitted to the New Hampshire bar in 1804. Shortly thereafter Shaw returned to Boston and began the practice of law. He was named a justice of the peace in 1810 and was elected as a Federalist to the lower house of the Massachusetts legislature. He was a member of the Massachusetts constitutional convention of 1820 and served two terms in the state senate during the early 1820s. Then Shaw devoted his energy to the practice of law, focusing on commercial law and gaining a prominent place at the bar. Governor Levi Lincoln appointed Shaw chief justice of the Supreme Judicial Court of Massachusetts in 1830, and he dominated that bench until his resignation in 1860.

Widely regarded as one of the most significant jurists of the antebellum era, Shaw played a pivotal role in shaping the principles of English common law to the needs of a society undergoing economic transformation. Since New England was at the forefront of economic change, Shaw was frequently called upon to adapt the law to new conditions. He did much to formulate early railroad law, for example, defining the status of railroads as common carriers, examining the exercise of eminent domain, and upholding state regulatory authority. In the famous case of *Farwell v. Boston and Worcester Railroad* (1842), Shaw adopted the fellow-servant rule, under which an employee injured by the negligence of a coworker could not recover damages from the employer. The injured worker would have to sue the coworker who actually caused the accident. Shaw's opinion led to wide acceptance of the fellow-servant doctrine in American law.

Although instinctively conservative, Shaw sometimes embraced a reformist approach to legal issues. This was demonstrated by his important opinion in *Commonwealth v. Hunt* (1842), which rejected the common law rule that combinations of employees constituted a criminal conspiracy. This decision in effect recognized the right of employees to organize unions. Yet in other areas of law Shaw's conservative side came to the fore. In *Commonwealth v. Kneeland* (1838) he sustained a conviction for blasphemy, rejecting a defense of religious liberty. Likewise, Shaw upheld the practice of racial segregation in the Boston public schools in *Roberts v. City of Boston* (1849). The *Roberts* ruling became an important precedent for the constitutionality of separate schools. In 1851, Shaw refused to issue a writ of habeas corpus to release a fugitive slave held under a federal warrant. He regarded the fugitive-slave provision of the Constitution as an essential element in the formation of the union.

In sum, Shaw profoundly affected the development of American law. He made his mark as an expositor of common law principles. Shaw generally deferred to legislative authority and rarely used judicial review to invalidate statutes because he believed that states should generally be allowed the vigorous exercise of their police powers.

Elijah Adlow, *The Genius of Lemuel Shaw, Expounder of the Common Law* (1962); Joseph Henry Beale, Jr., "Lemuel Shaw," in *Great American Lawyers*, ed. William Draper Lewis (1907–9); Leonard W. Levy, *The Law of the Commonwealth and Chief Justice Shaw* (1970 [1957]); G. Edward White, *The American Judicial Tradition: Profiles of Leading American Judges* (1976).

James W. Ely, Jr.

Story, Joseph (1779–1845) Jurist. An acclaimed legal scholar who ranks among the great Supreme Court justices in U.S. history, Joseph Story was born in Marblehead, Mass., the son of locally prominent parents. He graduated from Harvard College in 1798. After reading law in the office of a local congressman and completing an apprenticeship, Story was admitted to the bar in 1801 and opened his practice in Salem. He soon earned a wide and favorable reputation. In 1805 he was elected to the first of three terms in the Massachusetts House of Representatives, serving until 1808. The following year he secured election as a Jeffersonian Republican to the 10th Congress to fill the vacancy occasioned by the death of his political ally Jacob Crowninshield, holding this seat from May 23, 1808, to March 3, 1809. During his brief congressional service, he managed to infuriate President Thomas Jefferson and acquire some political enemies by his opposition to the administration's foreign trade embargo. Disheartened by political subterfuge and squabbling in Washington, Story declined to seek renomination in 1808, but three years later he returned to the Massachusetts legislature, where he emerged as speaker for a brief period in 1811.

The death of Associate Justice William Cushing in 1810 created an opening on the U.S. Supreme Court. President James Madison considered several possibilities, but late in 1811 he nominated Story, who easily won Senate confirmation. At 32 years of age, Story, a banker, legal writer, poet, and opponent of slavery, achieved the distinction of being the youngest person ever appointed to the U.S. Supreme Court. He served on the nation's highest judicial bench from 1812 until his death.

Story's 33 years on the Supreme Court were a crucial epoch in the constitutional life of the new republic. His constitutional vision coincided with Chief Justice John Marshall's nationalism. The two colleagues became friends and allies, affirming the doctrine of judicial review and the implied powers of Congress (*McCulloch v. Maryland*, 1819). Story defended the existence of broad federal power by claiming that a strong national government was essential for the growth of commerce and industry, a matter of concern to New England. Altogether Story wrote 286 Supreme Court opinions, of which 269 were majority decisions. In the process of expounding on the origin and nature of the federal union, he wrote many groundbreaking opinions and enlarged federal court jurisdiction. He upheld the property rights of private corporations (*Terrett v. Taylor*, 1815). His landmark ruling in *Martin v. Hunters' Lessee* (1816) established the power of the Supreme Court to review and reverse the opinions of state courts in matters relating to the Constitution, thereby upholding the appellate jurisdiction of the Supreme Court while guaranteeing that federal law would be uniformly interpreted in the United States. In this important case, Story not only embraced an expansive view on the authority and role of the Supreme Court as the harmonizer of decisions emanating from lower courts but also persuasively argued his nationalist doctrine that the powers of the national government in the revered Constitution were derived from the people and not from the states. He unmistakably sanctioned the concept that the people did not intend to make the national government dependent on the states.

During his years on the Supreme Court, Story remained active in various endeavors. He was a delegate in 1820 to his state's constitutional convention. In 1829 he accepted a teaching appointment as the first Dane Professor of Law at the Harvard Law School and relocated to Cambridge, Mass. Two years later he refused the chief justiceship of the Massachusetts Supreme Judicial Court. Meanwhile, Story was publishing voluminous works. His great three-volume treatise *Commentaries on the Constitution* (1833) attained notable success and widely influenced the shaping of American legal education and jurisprudence.

When Marshall died in 1835, Story seemed the logical heir to succeed him as chief justice. This failed to happen, however, because of the personal and political hostility between Story and President Andrew Jackson, whom Story contended was unqualified for the presidency. Jackson's states' rights agenda countered Story's nationalism, and Roger B. Taney was appointed chief justice in 1836.

Story was a passionately faithful and principled guardian of the Constitution and one of the commanding figures in American judicial history. A wise justice who understood the connection between practical realities and cherished principles, Story did nothing less than ensure that the Constitution evolved and endured. He died in Cambridge, Mass., leaving a legacy for his successors.

Gerald T. Dunne, *Justice Joseph Story and the Rise of the Supreme Court* (1970); James McClellan, *Joseph Story and the American Constitution: A Study in Political and Legal Thought* (1990); R. Kent Newmyer, *Supreme Court Justice Joseph Story: Statesman of the Old Republic* (1985); Alan Watson, *Joseph Story and the Comity of Errors: A Case Study in Conflict of Laws* (1992).

Leonard Schlup

Sumptuary Laws European societies had a long tradition of regulating dress and appearance through sumptuary laws. These rules usually served one or more of several purposes—religious, economic, or social—but New England's laws were unusual in serving all three. Decreeing what one could or could not wear not only advanced Puritan religious goals, but also conserved scarce goods in a wilderness environment and preserved hierarchical distinctions between rich and poor and male and female in a society far removed from the force of traditional authority. Unlike many other Puritan social regulations that generally repeated or strengthened conventional laws operating in England in the 17th century, the first New England sumptuary laws revived a tradition dying in England, where most clothing regulations had been repealed in 1604.

The earliest regulations in the 1630s in Massachusetts Bay restricted "superfluous and unnecessary clothing" but also enjoined citizens to identify men who wore certain "new fashions, or long hair . . . to be uncomely, or prejudicial to the common good." Together, these restrictions reflected the Puritans' opposition to worldly pride as well as to the waste of resources involved in such extravagance. Soon they introduced a more obviously sexual concern in their ban on uncovered arms.

Though Massachusetts Bay repealed its sumptuary laws in 1644, it renewed and expanded them in 1651, when it noted, "Intollerable excess and bravery hath crept in upon us, and especially amongst people of mean condition." The preservation of class hierarchy thus led the colony to limit what one wore according to one's status. By a statute of that year, people with annual incomes of less than £200 were forbidden to wear lace or buttons of gold or silver, hoods or scarves of lace, and other expensive or scarce materials. The law provided significant exceptions, however. Anyone below the £200 threshold wearing those items might pay for the privilege by paying a tax proportionate to that income. Aware that status involved more than money, the General Court exempted from the law those who held public office (and their families), active military personnel, those who possessed education or employment "above the ordinary degree," and those "whose estate have been considerable, though now decayed."

Sumptuary laws never received widespread or even consistent support in New England. The colonies of Rhode Island, Plymouth, and New Haven did not enact any such laws; enforcement was generally lax in Massachusetts Bay, although women of the lower class were prosecuted more than others. Only periods of alarm about social disintegration provoked stricter enforcement and greater attention, as in 1651 or 1662 (when concerns over "the Rising Generation" targeted youths' apparel). With the onset of King Philip's War in 1675, prosecutions increased as Massachusetts added restrictions on wigs and "Naked Breasts and Arms." In 1676 Connecticut abandoned its vague 1641 sumptuary laws and adopted the Massachusetts code, and in 1679 a New Haven county court heard the only case ever presented in the colony. By the end of the century all such laws had fallen into disuse, and in 1720 an observer labeled them all "obsolete."

David H. Flaherty, *Privacy in Colonial New England* (1967); Alan Hunt, *Governance of the Consuming Passions: A History of Sumptuary Law* (1996); Edgar J. McManus, *Law and Liberty in Early New England: Criminal Justice and Due Process, 1620–1692* (1993); Carole Shammas, *The Pre-Industrial Consumer in England and America* (1990).

David Thomas Konig

Vermont Statehood On March 4, 1791, Vermont became the 14th state. Before admission, Vermont had existed as a "territory" disputed by New York and New Hampshire and as a self-proclaimed sovereign republic.

The geographic region known before the Revolutionary War as the New Hampshire Grants was claimed by New York and New Hampshire, leading to legal battles and intermittent armed conflict. In 1764, the British Privy Council awarded the disputed territory to New York, but townships west of the Green Mountains and along the Connecticut River valley rejected that decision. In May 1775, Vermonters actively engaged in the American Revolution with the capture of Fort Ticonderoga and sought to trade their pro-American stance for recognition as an independent state. Because the Continental Congress was unwilling to alienate New York, the impasse over Vermont statehood simmered until 1791. Unwilling to continue to exist in the legal limbo of a disputed territory, representatives of 28 towns in Vermont met in July 1777 and declared Vermont an independent sovereign state. Over the next six years, Vermont never wavered from its pro-American military support but was the scene of a series of forced annexations of pro–New York towns and the arbitrary arrests of all remaining New York officials by the paramilitary force under the leadership of Ethan and Ira Allen, known as "the Green Mountain Boys." These extralegal actions led to a full-scale border war between Vermont and New York in 1781–82 over possession of the "Yorker towns" in southeastern Vermont. With the end of the Revolutionary War in 1783, the 80,000 inhabitants of Vermont awaited entrance as the newest member of the United States.

For the next eight years, Vermont existed as an independent republic, conducting its own diplomatic, judicial, political, and economic affairs while the American Confederacy debated its constitutional status. Vermont's first governor, Thomas Chittenden, contended that Vermont's independent statehood was firmly established in 1777 when the people of the region exercised their sacred right as a constituent power and declared their political independence from the oppressive government of New York. As such, pro-independence Vermonters depicted themselves as a constitutional microcosm of the newly independent American states in their actions against England. Vermont became the 14th state in 1791 only after adjudication by an ad hoc congressional commission and payment of $30,000 to New York as settlement for all pending land claims. Later that year, a convention of Vermont towns meeting in Bennington ratified the U.S. Constitution in a close election that finally admitted Vermont as a state.

Michael Belleseiles, *Revolutionary Outlaws: Ethan Allen and the Struggle for Independence on the Early American Frontier* (1993); Charles Jellison, *Ethan Allen: Frontier Rebel* (1969); Peter Onuf, "State Making in Revolutionary America: Independent Vermont as a Case Study," *Journal of American History* 67, no. 4 (1981); Robert Shalhope, *Bennington and the Green Mountain Boys* (1996).

Ronald Lettieri and Richard Mandel

Literature

Paul Lauter and Sandra A. Zagarell, Section Editors

David H. Watters, Consulting Editor

INTRODUCTION

In *Oldtown Folks* (1869), Harriet Beecher Stowe identified the revolutionary era as "the seed-bed of New England," epitomizing New England's essence in the fictional revolutionary village of Oldtown, a Congregationalist, predominantly Anglo-Saxon, harmonious community. Here, as in her other New England narratives, Stowe engages in an activity in which many New England writers took part: defining New England. Conjuring up one or another version of New England has been a preoccupation of New England writers for close to 400 years. From Puritans such as John Winthrop and Cotton Mather through 20th-century and contemporary poets like Robert Frost, Robert Lowell, and Maxine Kumin, many of New England's writers have explicitly or implicitly characterized the region in which they lived.

Defining New England was not always as celebratory an action as it was for Stowe. Mather and other Puritans decried New England's faults, and many later writers—Henry David Thoreau, Elizabeth Stoddard, and Mark Twain among them—satirized the region's self-righteousness, materialism, and provincialism. Sometimes defining New England took on a reformist character. The racially diverse and nonpatriarchal model New England community of Lydia Sigourney's *Sketch of Connecticut, Forty Years Since* (1824) put pressure on the homogeneous model that predominated in the early 19th century. Much Romantic and Transcendentalist literature, grounded most strongly in the perceptions and experiences of the individual, reached beyond the region and was a part of national and international cultural and political movements. Still, New Englanders have generally identified themselves as such, and much, though by no means all, of the region's writing displays a consciousness (sometimes positive, sometimes uneasy) of being written in New England. Much of it, moreover, has contributed to images of New England that are prominent beyond the region as well as within it. As we consider New England's vast and diverse literature, defining New England will be a bass note, sounded with others—the exploration of personal experience, the promotion of national as well as regional reform, the expression of aesthetic creeds and commitments—in various strains of harmony and dissonance.

The concept of "New England" was formulated via a set of defining images even before the colonists had reached the shores of their new home. In a lay sermon preached aboard the *Arabella* in 1630, John Winthrop, governor-to-be of the Massachusetts Bay Colony, articulated the ideal of New England as a homogeneous community, fused by common convictions, that resonated for centuries. "We must be knit together in this work as one man," Winthrop proclaimed, "always have before our eyes . . . our community in the work, our community as members of the same body." This image was intended to mold Winthrop's quarreling fellow passengers into a collective body, but it also anticipated the cultural work of many later representations of New England as a cohesive community. At least as resonant has been the promise that New England would be "as a city upon a hill" before the eyes of the world, blessed if it remained unified, but punished "if we shall deal falsely with our God."

Explicitly or implicitly, the image of New England as a uniform community, united in common religio-providential purpose, fused emotionally and spiritually and forming a single organism, influenced the public utterances and devotional and doctrinal writing produced in New England throughout the 17th century and for a significant period thereafter. Combining argument, exhortation, and promise in rich, often biblical and emotional language, much of this discourse served to consolidate and reconsolidate the colonies in the face of internal conflict and increasing dissent, severe physical and material hardships, frequent warfare with Native Americans, and much-resented strictures imposed by the British, as well as inevitable diffusion as people moved away from the original settlements. In sermons and other forms of public address, many of them widely circulated in written form, Puritan leaders from John Cotton to Cotton Mather stated and restated New England's status as a divinely covenanted community. Often they used the Puritan-developed jeremiad form, which emphasized the collective identity of "God's people," calling members to task for their lapses, sometimes pointing to God's punishments of them, but also casting "the New England way" as sustaining and divinely sanctified and predicting that if the colonists reformed, they would find God's kingdom on earth. Indeed, by the end of the century—especially in the writing of Cotton Mather—predictions of the fulfillment of the colony's covenant with God had become a sort of Christian myth, with New England's eventual glorification as a combined New Eden and New Jerusalem.

As the foundation of the orthodox Puritan culture, the Word (the Bible) and the word (the wide array of religiously based writings) were almost as instrumental in forging the settlers into a "cohesive" community when the city on the hill was *not* an explicit subject as when it was. Written material encouraged the colonists' identification with Puritan New England but also affected them individually by way of their constant Bible reading in circumstances ranging from the private (individual study) through the domestic (household readings) to the public setting of the church. Beyond the Bible, orthodoxy informed all major genres of the culture: tracts; biographies of early Puritan leaders (Increase Mather's life of his father, Richard; Cotton Mather's *Magnalia Christi Americana*); histories of New England; psalms, of which early Massachusetts Bay religious leaders produced their own translation, the *Bay Psalm Book* (1640); sermons and the texts that shaped daily routines, the catechism; and the *New-England Primer* (ca. 1683), which taught many a New England child to read.

Yet Bible reading, while fostering cohesion, allowed for difference in the form of individual interpretation of God's word. And despite tight government control over what was published and circulated in New England, some dissonant voices surfaced in print. In his *New English Canaan* (published in England in 1637), the Anglican Thomas Morton, founder of the short-lived colony of Ma-re Mount, challenged the orthodox community, condemning the Puritans as narrow-minded fanatics and encouraging non-Puritan settlement. Even within Puritan New England colonists criticized New England life in letters and in some locally available pamphlets and treatises. Late in the century the image of the covenanted community was tarnished seriously by the Salem witch trials and their aftermath. Although the only authorized account, Cotton Mather's *Wonders of the Invisible World* (1693), fully justified the proceedings, criticisms soon began to circulate, perhaps most damagingly the recantation of Samuel Sewall, special commissioner to the trials, in a public bill in 1697.

Furthermore, the emphasis of Protestant theology on personal salvation and the need for each person to experience for himself or herself God's "free grace" led to a profound commitment to forms of individualism. This is illustrated in the section of William Bradford's *Of Plymouth Plantation* (for 1623) describing how within three years of its establishment the *Mayflower* community abandoned collective holding of farmland and turned instead to private plots such that "they should set corn every man for his own particular, and in that regard trust to themselves." The ethos of individualism that marks America—perhaps more than anything else—was thus early set into place in the material circumstances of 17th-century New England farming. And it has remained, sometimes in exaggerated ways, a central feature of New England culture, as some of the characters painted by Robert Frost and Amy Lowell illustrate 300 years later.

In the 17th century, individualism was manifest in a variety of cultural forms. Diaries, for example, could be quite idiosyncratic. Sewall's, which was reproduced and circulated in several manuscripts, vividly describes the dynamics of a complicated family life and details a failed courtship after the death of his first wife. Although the diary of the poet and minister Michael Wigglesworth expresses exemplary Puritan attitudes, it also uses a cryptographic shorthand to voice tormented homoerotic desire. In the era's most famous captivity narrative, *The Sovereignty and Goodness of GOD . . . a Narrative of the Captivity and Restauration of Mrs. Mary Rowlandson* (1682), Rowlandson properly mobilizes her conviction of sin and punishment to awaken readers to a greater sense of religious commitment, but the intensity with which she recounts her harrowing experience aligns her gripping narrative with the entertaining prose of novels popular in the next century. And while poetry often expressed doctrinaire thinking—Wigglesworth's apocalyptic *The Day of Doom* (1662) was phenomenally popular—it, too, accommodated a variety of private subjects and attitudes. Ballads often explored the privations of life in New England in robust and irreverent ways. The cultivated poetry of Edward Taylor and Anne Bradstreet was often highly personal. Taylor's poems can be intensely subjective, even mystical, with community and religious orthodoxy merely peripheral subjects. Indeed, Taylor's "Preparatory Meditations" can be viewed as his efforts to discipline, in poetic form, personal urges and anxieties in order to prepare himself for his duties of ministering to a congregation. The domestic and familial focus of much of Bradstreet's work can sideline attention to New England life as a whole. A number of her poems, moreover, express marked ambivalence about doctrinal religious sentiment, and some exhibit a decidedly cosmopolitan temperament and a yearning to live in England, not New England.

Were the vital oral tradition of the original native inhabitants of New England available today, the texture and variety of 17th-century New England native culture would be more apparent. Elements of these original cultures have been preserved in some native tales, legends, and songs although serious Anglo-American attempts to record them did not take off until the 19th century, by which time many New England Native American communities had been nearly destroyed. Although Puritan writing routinely demonized Native Americans, it does contain information about contemporary native cultures. Roger Williams's *A Key into the Language of America* (1643), William Wood's *New Englands Prospect* (1634), and several of the missionary John Eliot's studies of Indian languages provide some sense of native life during the early period of contact. Rowlandson's *Soveraignty and Goodness of GOD* is informative for a slightly later time. Morton's *New English Canaan* gives a generally positive picture, comparing native habits of moving with the seasons to those of English gentlemen. Since the English were generally less interested in native life than, say, the French or Spanish, however, the ethnographic "record" about native cultures in New England not only reflects vehement bigotry, it is also lamentably thin. Native American writers such as Samson Occom in the 18th century and William Apess in the 19th century wrote to challenge Anglo-American depictions and histories of New England's Native Americans.

By the turn of the 18th century, defining New England through the written word became less of a preoccupation as New England's culture and religion began to diversify because of increased immigration and growing cosmopolitanism. Although Congregationalism, as Puritanism had become, would produce a potent strain of writing throughout the century, by the early 1700s belles lettres—polite literature associated with genteel society—and other forms of more secular writing flourished alongside religious writing. Furthermore, several Protestant denominations not dedicated to preserving the image of the covenanted community took hold, notably Methodism. With the advent of the religious revival known as the Great Awakening of the 1730s, even Congregational ministers' writings and sermons concentrated most intensely on cultivating individuals' awareness of their precarious spiritual state and prompting their experience of conversion. The most famous sermon of the era, Jonathan Edwards's "Sinners in the Hands of an Angry God" (1741), was designed to terrify Edwards's audiences and readers into recognizing their sinfulness—though a more joyous, even ecstatic expression of religious sentiment was more characteristic of Edwards's work. But as British rule became increasingly onerous, Congregationalist sermons tended to reflect more generally on the nature of New England by becoming more political. Gad Hitchcock's Massachusetts Election Sermon of 1774, for example, expressed local resentment of British abuse of authority. A number of sermons printed and circulated beyond New England also contributed to the swelling of colonywide anti-British sentiment and a sense of common identity among American colonists. Dissenting ministers' writings about, and eventual organization on behalf of, resistance to the spread of the British episcopacy similarly cultivated a more general sense of Americanness beyond the region.

Belletristic writing (often, but not always, secular) was not, as a rule, expressly political; moreover, as a dimension of New England cosmopolitanism, it was oriented to New England's Anglo-American gentility, not New England uniqueness. In Boston, as in several other American port cities, cosmopolitan social circles cemented by literary culture and institutionalized in gendered forms—such as men's club and tavern groups and women's tea tables and salons—began to flourish in the early 18th century. Spurred by the popularity of belles lettres in post-Restoration England, by the spread of literacy and relative prosperity in the American colonies, and by Enlightenment associations between literary culture and sociability, this culture was self-consciously urbane and genteel. It placed a high premium on classical and British literature, which circulated in both print and manuscript forms, and devoted much of the refined conversation on which it prided itself to this literature. Yet American belletristic circles reflected their local environments sharply even without characterizing them as local. Mather Byles, the self-appointed laureate of Massachusetts and a Christian belles letterist (to use David Shields's phrase), worked hard to cultivate a literary reputation in London but did so partly through poems commemorating events in Massachusetts. And Byles's work became part of a decidedly local literary scene when a fairly broad readership came to relish the witty satires that Bostonian Joseph Green produced in response to the perceived pretentiousness in Byles's verses. In a less public medium, Sarah Kemble Knight's urbane *Journals of Madam Knight* (1825) affirms a strongly New England center of gravity. Written during a five-month business trip that Bostonite Knight took through Connecticut and New York in 1704–5, this literary masterwork was designed to appeal both to Knight's family and, recent scholars suggest, to women of her tea table. Knight's wit and style reflect her identification with transatlantic metropolitan culture, yet she expresses a very Boston-centered sense of identity, comparing customs, dress, and living standards in various parts of Connecticut unfavorably with "our" Boston life, while savoring New York's superiority to Boston in fashion, architecture, and sociability.

The career of the first published African American woman writer, Phillis Wheatley, calls attention to New England's continued involvement in transatlantic networks even as, on the eve of the Revolution, many of its leaders proclaimed the region politically and economically autonomous. Wheatley was brought to Boston as a slave. Her poetry's appeal in New England was enhanced by its English readership: the countess of Huntington, an important figure in evangelicalism, was instrumental in the initial publication in England of the Methodist Wheatley's *Poems on Various Subjects* (1773). Religious sentiment and Wheatley's accomplished writing style contributed to her popularity overseas, but her New England identification was also clear, whether in her encouragement to Harvard students to become more pious or in her drawing of cautionary parallels between the enslavement of Africans and the abuse by the British of their authority over New England. Her writing also suggests the existence before the Revolution of a community of New Englanders of color that dissented from the tradition of a New England sense of superiority. In 1774 she wrote a much-reprinted open letter to her friend, the Mohegan Reverend Samson Occom, that condemns the hypocrisy of white Americans who call for their own "liberty" while supporting the enslavement of African Americans.

After the Revolution, the American nation became a central focus of writing in New England, as it was throughout the nation-to-be. The most coherent revolutionary-era body of New England writing with a national scope was produced by the Connecticut Wits, a Hartford-based group of conservative Republicans—John Trumbull, Joel Barlow, David Humphreys, and Timothy Dwight among them—whose neoclassical verse advocated Federalist politics. Several elite Boston women also participated prominently in this "literary" creation of the new nation. Mercy Otis Warren, who would later compose an anti-Federalist history of the American Revolution, wrote several plays in the 1770s supporting the patriots' cause, excerpts of which were circulated in the much-read magazine *The Massachusetts Spy*. Later, despite women's exclusion from citizenship, Warren and Sarah Wentworth Morton took part, via their writing, in national conversations about the character of the new republic, and their Boston colleague, the feminist poet and essayist Judith Sargent Murray, insisted, audaciously, on some equality for women, proclaiming, "The soul unfetter'd/Is to no sex confin'd" ("On the Equality of the Sexes," 1790).

Some early federal writing also shows beginning signs of defining New England as a distinct section within the new nation, though not yet a bona fide region. A number of the Connecticut Wits used belles lettres as a political medium to advocate one kind of new England: republican, stratified, antidemocratic. The jointly written *Anarchiad* (1791–1805) and several other Wit poems condemned Shays's Rebellion, an uprising of farmers against postrevolutionary taxes and debt collection that served the interest of the wealthy. Dwight's *Greenfield Hill* (1794) idealized Greenfield, Conn., as a conservative utopia: a stable, religious, agrarian village that distilled specifically New England virtues. Stock New England characters also began to make appearances. In his play *The Contrast* (1790), Vermonter Royall Tyler created what would become an enduring New England type, Brother Jonathan, an awkward but honest country bumpkin. The glimmering of New England regionalism was also fostered by the early federal increase in the number of newspapers and magazines, which encouraged the production of writing with some local orientation. Some of the poetry published by Warren and Murray in Boston-based magazines refers to local places, events, and people. As a regular feature of the rural newspapers that appeared in great numbers (many only to fold quickly), poetry also provided local writers with a public medium. Their verse often mentioned such local matters as births, deaths, and the condition of neighbors who had fallen ill.

Novels also contributed to this early regionalism. Popular, if not yet fully respectable, novels placed a premium on "fact," thereby encouraging a New England feel in some of the many early national novels published in New England. A Worcester, Mass., setting flavors Sukey Vickery's *Emily Hamilton* (1803), a critique of sexual mores governing women's lives. Both William Hill Brown's *The Power of Sympathy* (1787) and Hannah Foster's phenomenally popular *The Coquette* (1797) refer to a Connecticut woman, Elizabeth Whitman, who died in childbirth after having been seduced and abandoned. Foster's novel is plotted around Whitman's story, and the (New England) originals of several of her male characters were readily identifiable by those who knew or knew of them.

The trend of representing New England as a distinct region increased during the second decade of the 19th century. Given the uneasiness within the area about its weakened national status after the War of 1812 and tensions among New Englanders over what their defining characteristics were, considerable literary energy was focused on representing New England's culture and history. From the 1820s through the 1840s, poetry and prose as well as historical, religious, and didactic writing took up these subjects; and two prominent, popular forms of prose fiction, the village sketch and historical fiction, were in effect dedicated to the work of defining New England.

Village sketches memorialized old-fashioned village life and reflected a fairly conservative, Puritan-descended Congregationalism. They generally appealed to long-time New Englanders' emotional and ideological attachment to a tradition-based image of the region during a time when New England was undergoing visible alteration through industrialism and further religious and ethnic diversification. Descendants of the Puritan "city upon a hill," the villages of the more conservative sketches are typified by Timothy Dwight's description in *Travels in New England and New York* (written, 1796–1815; published, 1821–22) of the region as a realm of look-alike villages "composed of neat houses, surrounding neat schoolhouses and churches, adorned with gardens, meadows, and orchards, and exhibiting the universally easy circumstances of the inhabitants." The equation of New England with traditional village life also played to the loyalties of the increasing number of New Englanders emigrating to the newly opened West, to which conservative Congregationalists such as Dwight and Lyman Beecher wanted to extend New England's influence. Beecher's *A Plea for the West* (1835) demands that New Englanders win the soul of the West to preserve America as a Protestant nation (*A Plea* is haunted by the perceived threat of Catholic expansion); this objective also informs the village sketches of Beecher's daughter Harriet Beecher (Stowe), the consummate antebellum creator of village sketches.

Mobilizing nostalgia, Stowe's "The Old Meeting House" (1840) invokes an imaginary revolutionary-era "Yankee village" to encourage readers within the region and outside it to identify with a New England resembling that of Dwight's *Travels*. All the residents of the exemplary New England village of this sketch have Yankee-sounding names—Israel Scran, Zedekiah Morse—and their social life centers on Sunday worship in the lovingly described meetinghouse. But the village sketch also accommodated less orthodox definitions of the region. Eliza Lee, in *Sketches of a New England Village, in the Last Century* (1838), emphasizes the diversity of the residents of her village and portrays the minister's daughters, not the minister, as the mainstays of village life. Lydia Sigourney's *Sketch of Connecticut* celebrates a New England town composed of a racially and religiously diverse population and beneficially presided over by a genteel widow.

The New England represented in historical fiction was perhaps more conspicuously ideological, for New England history provided writers with a medium for advancing their positions on religious doctrine and democracy in contemporary New England via their versions of the past. (A prominent controversy at the turn of the 19th century pitted Hannah Adams's *Summary History of New England* [1799], which was critical of Puritan narrowness and applauded the greater liberalism of contemporary New England, against conservative Jedidiah Morse and Elijah Parish's *Compendious History of New England* [1804], which endorsed Puritan orthodoxy of the past as well as orthodox Calvinism in the present.) Historians of New England of various persuasions often cast the Puritan quest for religious freedom and self-determination as the wellspring of revolutionary-era resistance to English tyranny. This view of the region's origin and character formed a defining framework for New England historical fiction. Some narratives, including Harriet Vaughn Cheney's *A Peep at the Pilgrims* (1824), celebrated fairly doctrinaire concepts of New England; others directed sharp criticism at New England's history, illuminating together the intolerance of Puritan New England and present-day New Englanders' penchant toward smugness.

Whether critical or celebratory, the focus of these fictions attested to New England's importance, past and present. By contrast, writers from outside New England, such as Washington Irving and James Fenimore Cooper, created characters attesting to a certain bemused hostility to New England's cultural and commercial expansionism. One thinks, for example, of figures of fun such as Ichabod Crane, the gangling Connecticut schoolmaster done in by Brom Bones in "The Legend of Sleepy Hollow" (1819), and of the equally extended figure of David Gamut, who in *The Last of the Mohicans* (1826), teaches the "youth of the Connecticut levy" the true New England version, and only the New England version, of the psalms. Likewise, much of the short fiction that Nathaniel Hawthorne published during the 1830s and 1840s expresses skepticism about New England's Puritan traditions. Going beyond merely questioning New England traditions, other writers used historical fiction to promote liberal reform, local and national. Lydia Maria Child's *Hobomok, a Tale of Early Times* (1824) scrutinizes Puritan practices with parallels in the 1820s, including restrictions on white women's lives and racism toward Native Americans. Catharine Maria Sedgwick's *Hope Leslie* (1827) challenges New England chauvinism by characterizing Puritan forefathers like John Winthrop as misogynistic and racist and placing white women and Native Americans at the center of this narrative "of early times in Massachusetts" (the novel's subtitle). Associating 17th-century New Englanders' treatment of Native Americans with the nation's contemporary practice of Indian removal, both novels also suggest that New England is culpable in the current treatment of Native Americans, even if the nation's leaders hail from elsewhere.

A few antislavery writers put especially strong pressure on New Englanders' traditional sense of superiority. Mobilizing a staple of New England culture, religious discourse, the Methodist activist David Walker's implacable *Appeal* (1829) in effect repudiates New England exceptionalism, for Walker indicts all whites, northern as well as southern, as members of a slaveholding, Christianity-betraying race and seeks to spur resistance to slavery by African Americans throughout the United States. Maria W. Stewart's spiritual-abolitionist autobiography, *Productions of Mrs. Maria W. Stewart* (1835), urges her New England audience to oppose slavery actively. Child's *Appeal in Favor of That Class of Americans Called Africans* (1833) details racist laws and practices in the state of Massachusetts. New Englanders responded with far more outrage than self-correction, and in Boston, the Athenauem, an elite literary club, withdrew permission for Child to use its library.

In much of the earlier 19th century, and increasingly by midcentury, then, New England was caught up in pressing national questions and international intellectual and political currents. Writers were less directly involved in defining New England than they were in drawing on New England traditions as they engaged with these trends in a "New England" kind of way—or "New Englandly," as Emily Dickinson would put it. Nevertheless, slavery and its abolition were on New England's agenda, and a series of events and publications kept it there. In 1831 William Lloyd Garrison had established *The Liberator* in a Boston print shop, asserting, correctly, that he would be heard. From that office, a stream of pamphlets, speeches, manifestos, and poems demanding immediate, unconditional abolition of slavery would flow forth over the next 30 years. They were inspirations to those increasingly determined to end the South's "peculiar institution" and were incitements to those, especially in New England, whose businesses depended on southern cotton.

Periodic organizing campaigns—such as those to establish a national antislavery society; to defend the Africans from the schooner *Amistad;* to resist the Fugitive Slave Law (1850) and so free men like Anthony Burns taken by slave catchers—kept the issue before New England's citizens. Many of the region's most persuasive writers and speakers, including Wendell Phillips, Thomas Wentworth Higginson, and John Greenleaf Whittier, devoted themselves to the antislavery cause, often in deed as well as word. To be sure, there was intense resistance to Garrisonian abolitionism. Garrison was himself led down the streets of Boston with a rope around his neck by a mob of men of property and substance; meetings of the Boston Female Anti-Slavery Society were disrupted by similarly respectable gentlemen. Indeed, Harriet Wilson's *Our Nig* (1859) chronicles the vicious racism of a typical New England family. But this passionate conflict over slavery and race helped force intellectuals and writers to engage vigorously with these and other issues of their moment.

The most important of such issues for New England was probably the advent of industrial capitalism. New England was a central site for the development of wide-scale changes in work, production, distribution, and wealth that would reshape the country as a whole. The responses of New England writers, drawing on their heritage and on international currents of reform, helped establish America's distinctively individualistic ways of coping with the revolutionary changes brought about by capital. A factory system was also emerging elsewhere in the United States—as, for example, in Wheeling, then Virginia, as chronicled in Rebecca Harding Davis's story "Life in the Iron Mills" (1861), and in New York and Pennsylvania—but the primary development of the factory system occurred in New England towns. Yet New Yorker Herman Melville's brilliant depiction in "The Paradise of Bachelors and the Tartarus of Maids" of a paper factory tucked away in the Berkshire mountains captures the exploitation by many postbellum New England factories of young female laborers—and the ineffectual hand-wringing of some observers made uncomfortable by the new industrialism.

The economies of more centrally located towns—for instance, Lowell and Lawrence, Mass.—were supported by large-scale mills from which flowed cotton textiles and similar products that would transform the production of clothing and other home commodities across the country. Out of these mills came increasing wealth, especially for the comfortable classes of merchants and manufacturers in New England and elsewhere. In them would form, especially during the 1830s and 1840s and despite the misgivings of some of the owners, a "permanent factory population" of workers, many of them Irish immigrants—men, women, and children—who possessed nothing but the labor of their hands and who were subject to the most brutal exploitation, especially during little-comprehended and recurrent times of economic collapse. This new system of industrial capitalism would produce in the United States, as it had in Europe, increasingly sharp divisions of class that appalled and frightened men of relatively comfortable circumstances such as Ralph Waldo Emerson and Thoreau; it threatened the very character of American democracy. "The spirit of the American freeman," Emerson would write in "The American Scholar" (1837) at the depth of a financial panic, "is already suspected to be timid, imitative, tame. Public and private avarice make the air we breathe thick and fat. The scholar is decent, indolent, complaisant. See already the tragic consequence. The mind of this country, taught to aim at low objects, eats upon itself. There is no work for any but the decorous and the complaisant. Young men . . . are hindered from action by the disgust which the principles on which business is managed inspire."

"What is the remedy?" Emerson would ask. Characteristically, perhaps, as the inheritors of the earlier New England tradition of presuming to define values and directions for the nation, he and the others in the Transcendentalist circle in and around Concord, Mass.—Thoreau, Margaret Fuller, Bronson Alcott, Theodore Parker, and William Henry Channing among them—would see themselves obligated to offer remedies for the current social malaise. At the same time, however, they would maintain a certain distance from daily struggles for, as Thoreau put it, "I came into this world, not chiefly to make this a good place to live in, but to live in it, be it good or bad" ("Civil Disobedience," 1849). Nonetheless, few of New England's midcentury writers could, or indeed wished to, avoid the issues of slavery, class conflict, and also women's rights. Even Hawthorne, conservative on most directly political issues, engages new questions of science and technology and their social effects in *The House of the Seven Gables* (1851) and in many stories, such as "The Birth-mark" and "Rappaccini's Daughter," and issues of reform in *The Blithedale Romance* (1852). Orestes Brownson portrays the rise of class conflict in essays like "The Laboring

Classes" (1840), though his solutions were rather more utopian than those of his contemporaries Karl Marx and Friedrich Engels.

New England writers of the Transcendental Club and those, somewhat more of the establishment, at Cambridge, Mass., effectively saw themselves as a kind of secular clergy, chosen like their Massachusetts Bay Colony predecessors to lead, if not a revolution, certainly a way of transforming or at least transcending the corruption of everyday life. But their common wisdom was that the remedies for the social issues presented by slavery, industrial capitalism, and gender inequality were rooted in individual transformation rather than collective action. Social experiments like Brook Farm and Fruitlands offered opportunities for communal living that might model ways of life not infected by the diseases of the time. But Emerson and Thoreau would not participate in them. The former emphasized, as the title of his most famous essay says, "Self-Reliance": "To believe your own thought, to believe that what is true for you in your private heart is true for all men—that is genius. Speak your latent conviction, and it shall be the universal sense; for the inmost in due time becomes the outmost, and our first thought is rendered back to us by the trumpets of the Last Judgment." This is not the language of social reform, though it is a powerful inspiration for the individual writer. As Walt Whitman said of such passages, "I was simmering, simmering, simmering; Emerson brought me to a boil."

Nor would Thoreau join his friends Alcott at Fruitlands and Margaret Fuller and others at Brook Farm. How, then, might one counter the outrage of slavery or the Mexican war? In "Civil Disobedience," Thoreau answers: "If the injustice has a spring, or a pulley, or a rope, or a crank, exclusively for itself, then perhaps you may consider whether the remedy will not be worse than the evil; but if it is of such a nature that it requires you to be the agent of injustice to another, then, I say, break the law. Let your life be a counter friction to stop the machine. What I have to do is to see, at any rate, that I do not lend myself to the wrong which I condemn." And what of the increasing pull of material goods, wealth, and comfort, or the poverty, alienation, and "quiet desperation" that are their necessary counterparts? "Simplify, simplify, simplify," Thoreau argues in *Walden* (1854), as much his example of and model for change as "The Communist Manifesto" (1848) was for Marx and Engels.

In seeking to reform their times, like many of their contemporaries in America and abroad, the men and women of New England's intelligentsia drew upon models perhaps familiar to them from an earlier New England. James Russell Lowell's *Biglow Papers* (1846–48) uses Yankee dialect verse to speak out against slavery, the Mexican war, and land-grabbing in Texas and California:

Ez fer war, I call it murder,—
There you hev it plain an' flat;
I don't want to go no furder
Than my Testyment fer that.

Both Henry Wadsworth Longfellow (for example, in *Poems on Slavery*, 1842) and Whittier (for example, in *Voices of Freedom*, 1846) turn their considerable poetic skills

Monument to Henry Wadsworth Longfellow, Portland, Maine

to argue the abolitionist cause, in ways perhaps reminiscent of Wigglesworth. In *Uncle Tom's Cabin* (1852) Harriet Beecher Stowe writes an extended Christian parable wherein New Englanders, Simon Legree and Miss Ophelia, play critical roles. And her later novel *The Minister's Wooing* (1859) consciously addresses the question of whether the values of Puritan New England can be sustained without its terrorizing theology. Bronson Alcott sought to set people on the road to redeeming society by transforming the education they provided their children, as in his *Conversations with Children on the Gospels* (1836–37). Margaret Fuller, recognizing that most women had been denied the opportunity of a full, much less a liberating, education, held her "conversations" in Elizabeth Peabody's bookshop as one means of compensating for such deprivations and wrote "Woman in the Nineteenth Century" (1844) to open alternatives to gender stereotyping and prejudice. These were, in their different ways, agitational and educational ventures, in a certain sense mid-19th-century equivalents of what collections of psalms and sermons, captivity narratives, and the *New-England Primer* had been for the settler community of two centuries before.

This flourishing of literary work, especially in New England and New York, to which F. O. Matthiessen has given the name American Renaissance, raises a question: Why these things in this way at this time? There is no definitive answer, of course, even for the somewhat more restricted case presented by New England. We have suggested one set of influences by placing this account of the "Flowering of New England," as Van Wyck Brooks called it, in the context of the fierce social and political issues being contested across the United States in the quarter century or so before the Civil War. Social change, which disrupts old norms and assumptions, can often be the parent of a newly flourishing culture, stimulating literary and artistic production even by those who might personally prefer an older way of life. Yet standing aside from concern with political and social ills, Emily Dickinson adapted traditions of resistance and reform to create an individualistic poetic self hearkening back to Puritan self-examination. Despite characterizing herself as a writer who embodies the region's culture by "seeing New Englandly," she published virtually none of her poetry during her lifetime.

On the whole, though, the flowering of New England owed much to the technological changes that enabled it. The rotary press, for example, allowed the mass production and wide circulation of novels like *Uncle Tom's Cabin,* long poems like *Hiawatha* (1855), and popular periodicals; and these developments allowed at least some people, including some women, to make their living as writers, a much harder task earlier in the 19th century. Similarly, the rapid spread of rail transportation enabled Emerson and New England poets such as Lowell, Oliver Wendell Holmes, Sr., and Longfellow to bring their works—and their values—to audiences across the United States.

These developments should be set against the international trends to which the name Romanticism has generally been given. Most of the New England intelligentsia about whom we have been writing were familiar not only with the work of English Romantics such as Wordsworth and Byron but with those of German writers such as Goethe and Schiller. The word *transcendentalism* was in fact derived from Immanuel Kant's *Critique of Pure Reason,* and a number of these New Englanders had, like Longfellow, studied in Germany. The writings of Emerson, Thoreau, and Fuller in particular reveal the influence of Hindu and other Asian texts. Moreover, as the revolutionary political movements of the late 1840s reached a crescendo in Europe, American writers became increasingly familiar with their rise and fall. Fuller, for example, reported in long, passionate letters to the *New York Herald* on the cause of Italian independence and its suppression by French forces. And while most New Englanders were probably not familiar with the writings of Marx and Engels, they did come to know of the aspirations for change of European socialist movements. We cannot know to what extent these international currents shaped New England culture of the antebellum period, nor even the extent to which the uprisings of 1848 in Europe inspired American resistance to the Fugitive Slave Act of 1850. But it is fair to say that the American Renaissance should be seen less as an artifact of individual writers and more as an outgrowth of material and intellectual forces at play in New England and elsewhere in the years leading up to the Civil War.

The war and its aftermath brought about large-scale changes everywhere in the United States. These differed from region to region; indeed, one major characteristic of postbellum American culture was the tension between a trend toward the production of a national culture and a contrary tendency to emphasize and thereby sustain regional differences. Nowhere, perhaps, were these trends stronger than in New England. The editors of New England–based magazines such as the *Atlantic Monthly* and the *North American Review*—men who included James Russell Lowell, William Dean Howells, Charles Eliot Norton, Henry Brooks Adams, and Henry Cabot

Lodge—spoke from their Boston and Cambridge breakfast tables and easy chairs to a national, indeed an international, audience. They, with critics and novelists like Henry James and Thomas Bailey Aldrich, sought to erect a definition of literature as a professional and generally masculine enterprise, for which a very few predecessors such as Hawthorne offered models.

Many of these Boston Brahmins would be dismissed as provincial by the likes of Mark Twain and later George Santayana, but in their time they linked the cultural work they produced and encouraged to national politics. Lowell served as minister to both Spain and England, where he was greeted by an English newspaper as "His Excellency the Ambassador of American Literature to the Court of Shakespeare." Norton was one of the founders of *The Nation* magazine as well as a longtime professor at Harvard and a key advocate of modernizing university curricula. Lodge, a powerful senator from Massachusetts who played a central role in the U.S. rejection of the League of Nations, wrote biographies of Alexander Hamilton, Daniel Webster, and George Washington. Adams, in addition to his important historical work, wrote a scathing fictional indictment of Washington corruption, *Democracy* (1880), as well as the autobiographical *The Education of Henry Adams* (1907), a book that was key to establishing the modern notion that art might offer a way to stabilize, or at least cope with, a disintegrating world: "One controlled no more force in 1900 than in 1850, although the amount of force controlled by society had enormously increased. . . . In such labyrinths, the staff is a force almost more necessary than the legs; the pen becomes a sort of blind-man's dog, to keep him from falling into gutters. The pen works for itself, and acts like a hand, modeling the plastic material over and over again to the form that suits it best. The form is never arbitrary, but is a sort of growth like crystallization, as any artist knows well." Although these men and others of their circle disagreed on some issues, they were a powerful cultural force that projected traditional New England values, especially to the "better kind" of people and those who imitated them across the country.

In his day, Howells was perhaps the most influential in strictly literary terms. With the *Atlantic Monthly* and *Harper's Magazine* he promoted the careers of many of the important writers of the time, among them Abraham Cahan, Charles W. Chesnutt, Stephen Crane, Paul Laurence Dunbar, Mary E. Wilkins Freeman, Hamlin Garland, Charlotte Perkins Gilman, and Frank Norris. His many novels— once taken to exemplify realism in fiction but later dismissed as (in Norris's words) "the drama of a broken teacup"—may also be seen as his way of translating into narrative the New England obsession with questions of ethics. In his career, Howells was among the first truly national writers, projecting a pattern of life and work that would come to characterize 20th-century intellectuals. Born in Ohio, he became an active supporter of Abraham Lincoln (writing a campaign biography) and lived overseas as consul in Venice. He then established himself in Boston, where he replaced the publisher James T. Fields as editor of the *Atlantic Monthly*. After 15 years in that post, he moved to New York, where he continued his work promoting reform both in literature and in the political world. Ultimately, he served for 13 years as the first president of the American Academy of Arts and Letters.

Howells's slightly younger colleague in fiction, Henry James, can be seen to embody this cosmopolitan tendency even more strongly. Little in James's fiction registers even the scenery of his native New York, much less the particularities of its culture, although he satirizes aspects of the New England reform mentality nastily in his novel *The Bostonians* (1886). James and Howells may be taken to represent one major tendency of American culture, including that of New England, as it turned toward the 20th century: its absorption into larger national and international trends, the breaking away from any definitively local or regional character.

To be sure, other New England writers dedicated themselves during the period after the Civil War to characterizing their own region with renewed energy. They were participating in a regionalist movement that was at once local and national: a nationwide commemoration of the region's vernacular cultures and long-standing social arrangements that were apparently about to be extinguished by the accelerating forces of modernization, including industrial and agricultural capitalism; national networks of finance, transportation, and communication; increased immigration and urbanization; the dramatic sharpening of class differences; and the spread of consumerism and its commodity culture. Postbellum New England did suffer from serious economic decline: the hard conditions of small farming rendered the region largely uncompetitive in the developing national market; its small ports were unable to handle larger ships or compete with more convenient railheads; its manufactories became increasingly marginal to the expansion of basic industries such as steel. The region's male population, too, had dropped, a casualty of the war, of westward migration, and of the decline of opportunities now seen as taking place elsewhere. Regionalists wrote against this tide. Far from simply capturing a disappearing New England culture on paper, the work of writers such as Sarah Orne Jewett, Thomas Bailey Aldrich, and Alice Brown also made a pitch for a definition of New England that hearkened back to the conservative antebellum village sketches: as the habitat of a "traditional" way of life descended, more or less intact, from the region's colonial origins and still surviving in rural village communities peopled by English-descended Protestant New Englanders. Asserting national heritage, traditionalist regionalism affirmed New England's role as the nation's proper leader even as it was being displaced by the political, economic, and cultural ascendancy of New York and Chicago.

This (re-)invention of New England tradition had many dimensions, with regionalist literature completing the Colonial Revival movement in architecture and design, the historical preservation movement, "heritage" tourism, and other related cultural movements. In conjunction with New England's long history, the continuity of much of its population, and the visible presence of the past, especially in rural areas, traditionalism appeared long-lived and organic. But however traditional it seemed, the postbellum invention of New England was paradoxically and inextricably enmeshed within contemporary capitalism, and regionalist literature conspicuously so. It was a profitable commodity underwritten by the publishing industry, which had consolidated as a major business after the war. Regionalist literature was promoted in New England by influential editors such as Howells, Horace Scudder, and Aldrich, all at some point affiliated with Boston's premier publishing house,

Houghton Mifflin, and with the prestigious *Atlantic Monthly* magazine; and it was purchased primarily by a large, urban-based readership who yearned for images of "untouched" rural life. Fiction such as Aldrich's *An Old Town by the Sea* (1893), Brown's *Meadow-Grass: Tales of New-England Life* (1895) and *Tiverton Tales* (1899), and Jewett's *Country of the Pointed Firs* (1896)—all published by or by arrangement with Houghton Mifflin—characterized New England country life as uncontaminated by change or outside influences and as preserving much of the English-derived culture and community of the early settlers. Jewett's elegant *Country,* the height of New England regionalism, celebrates the coastal Maine community of Dunnet Landing as a complete, English-descended "world" held together by "a golden chain of love and friendship" that links together everyone who belongs in the community by birthright. (*Country*'s edginess about the intrusion of "foreigners" into the New England for which Dunnet stands is evident both in the much-emphasized Englishness of this "world" and by an undercurrent of anxiety about "others.")

Even in the most traditionalist regional literature, though, a more modern consciousness is apparent. From Jewett's first book, *Deephaven* (1877), through her last collection of short fiction, *The Queen's Twin* (1899), her writing both asserts that rural life is the storehouse of New England's heritage and reflects the presence of railroads and modern commerce (in the obvious form of tourism but also more subtly in such details as trade between the country and the city). Some of it refers quite positively to the ethnic diversification of the rural population. Some regionalist writing actively disputed the idea that rural New England was purely traditional. Much of the fiction by the extremely popular Mary E. Wilkins Freeman centers on the interplay between long-standing and modern ways in country villages, often accentuating the pros and cons of each. Even Freeman's famous "A New England Nun" (1887), which centers on a character who is utterly remote from any aspect of modern cosmopolitan life, appeared in the pages of *Harper's Bazar* [*sic*] alongside expressions of that life—patterns for the latest fashions in lace and dresses and ads for cosmetics. Other regionalist fiction was openly critical of restrictions characteristic of the kind of rural New England that the traditionalists commemorated. Short fiction by Rose Terry Cooke—"Mrs. Flint's Married Experience" (1880) and "How Celia Changed Her Mind" (1891)—levels a harrowing critique of the grim consequences for women of traditional village ideas about gender and marriage. The groundbreaking dissection of the modern, urban phenomenon of divorce in Howells's *A Modern Instance* (1882) is inseparable from the novel's hard-hitting portrait of the hidebound nature of New England provincial life, including its old-fashioned, durable marriages. At the same time, the "country" humor of the popular Rowland Robinson showed a rural New England that was more rough-edged and crusty than the genteel version promoted by highbrow inventors of tradition such as Aldrich.

Thus the processes of defining New England in late-19th-century regionalist literature were complex and to some extent contradictory. They had the effect of helping make the region available for tourism by "charging the landscape with meaning," but they also projected New England onto the national cultural stage *as* a distinctive region, marked by distinctive local characters who spoke and thought in distinctive local ways. In many respects, as we have pointed out, such localism projected positive images of New England as a major repository of underlying national values. But the region and its inhabitants could also emerge as more quaint, even grotesque, than powerful. Given the creative energy of Massachusetts during the 1840s and 1850s that helped shaped the first truly national literature, how does it come about that by 1923 archetypical New Englanders are—to quote another New Englander and adopted New Yorker, e. e. cummings—"the Cambridge ladies who live in furnished souls," believing "in Christ and Longfellow, both dead," the last sterile Puritans, importing poetry, religion, consumables, and visitors?

While idyllic versions of the New England village persist in works like those of Dorothy Canfield Fisher, certainly by 1909, with Mary E. Wilkins Freeman's "Old Woman Magoun," the New England village of her childhood has become the hamlet of Barry's Ford, situated above hills that "lie in moveless curves like a petrified ocean"; at its center is a "miserable little grocery, wherein whiskey and hands of tobacco were the most salient features of the stock in trade." Or, a few years later, it emerges as North Dormer: "There it lay, a weather-beaten sunburnt village of the hills, abandoned of men, left apart by railway, trolley, telegraph, and all the forces that link life to life in modern communities. It had no shops, no theatres, no lectures, no 'business block'; only a church that was opened every other Sunday if the state of the roads permitted, and a library for which no new books had been bought for twenty years, and where the old ones mouldered undisturbed on the damp shelves" (*Summer*, 1917). To be sure, these are the words of yet another New Yorker, Edith Wharton, recasting the staples of the village sketch into emblems of physical and cultural decline.

This transformation of New England images from a radiating center of republican values to a queer backwater populated by reticent if not altogether inarticulate folk can be taken to mark fundamental power shifts—not just in the location of cultural and political power but in the very nature of power in the United States. For during the 19th century, the country moved from a set of regional economies and related institutions and values to a national economy dominated by images of consumption and the cultural production of desire, especially among a growing middle class. In this context, certain places came to be associated with the dynamic modern on one hand and the declining—but still charming—conventional on the other. In the 1890s, mass-circulation magazines such as *Munsey's, Cosmopolitan,* and *Ladies' Home Journal* were gaining a certain kind of cultural authority, especially among that middle class, over traditional journals such as the Boston-based *Atlantic Monthly*. Through these mass-circulation magazines, New York City began to take precedence, as Richard Ohmann writes: "They drew the reader's knowing (or envious, or naive, or wondering) gaze to its theaters and concert halls, its performers and millionaires, its police and politicians. . . . These magazines assumed and helped promote an interest in New York as a cultural magnetic field, influential throughout American society." By contrast, in Ohmann's words, "*McClure's* and the *Journal*, especially, constructed Boston and rural New England as significant because they offered glimpses of a residual culture seen as 'our' heritage."

Robert Frost (at podium), with President John F. Kennedy, 1961

Many in New England, especially in Boston, were hardly willing to give up cultural predominance and devised a variety of institutional means, from university centers to writers' colonies and from museums to symphonies, for sustaining their authority. But increasingly, the image of New England was not that of the urban, glamorous world: its cities were older, gritty with the residue of almost a century of manufacturing, and its heritage was that of the village in a more and more rapidly urbanizing America. Envisioning New England thus, one discovers folk such as Edwin Arlington Robinson's Old Eben Flood:

> . . . The weary throat gave out,
> The last word wavered; and the song being done,
> He raised again the jug regretfully
> And shook his head, and was again alone.
> There was not much that was ahead of him,
> And there was nothing in the town below—
> Where strangers would have shut the many doors
> That many friends had opened long ago. ["Mr. Flood's Party"]

Mr. Flood is but one of the many comical, pathetic, yet touching New England characters of the time. In significant ways during the 20th century, the region comes to be a site in literature for nostalgia, comedy, pathos, queerness, and—what quickly grows from it—the psychic depravity and local grotesques featured in the work of Eugene O'Neill or some of the region's more recent writers, including Stephen King and Carolyn Chute. Such regional images, once created, take on a life of their own and persist long beyond the time in which material realities have altered. Indeed, so strong do such images become that they are no longer forced, as it were, upon a region's artists but become the substance of their own production.

The strong national and regional trends we have been describing have to some extent blocked a full view of the rich diversity of New England writing from the 19th century onward. Other writers, representing New England along more diverse lines than its regionalists or its Brahmins, openly or tacitly rebuked the cultural and racial narrowness of New England traditions. The socialist and feminist Florence Converse's *Diana Victrix* (1897) pointed New England forward in new directions: its two "new woman" protagonists are involved in a Boston marriage, and their relationship and their professionalism figure the future of the region and the nation, as the critic Kate McCullough shows. Pauline E. Hopkins's novel *Contending Forces: A Romance Illustrative of Negro Life North and South* (1900) represented the heterogeneity of class and culture of Boston's African American community, a group of New Englanders rarely acknowledged by regionalism. Hopkins pointedly refers to some of her African American characters as "Yankee." Written at a time of escalating southern brutality against African Americans, *Contending Forces* resembles writing by earlier black New Englanders such as David Walker, insisting that white New Englanders, as citizens of the nation, had an obligation to intervene in the disenfranchisement, lynching, and general brutalizing of blacks in the South. Dorothy West's later book *The Living Is Easy* (1948) portrays the marginalization even of well-to-do African Americans in supposedly cosmopolitan turn-of-the-century Boston.

New England writers such as West and Ann Petry in *The Street* (1946) and in short stories like "The Witness" (1971) focus questions of race and racism not in a distant South but in northern cities and towns. In many respects, therefore, they offer continuingly relevant patterns for the late-20th- and early-21st-century New England writing that emerges from the decaying mill towns and the new ethnic inhabitants who have increasingly populated them.

Indeed, difference—particularly of class and ethnicity—even more than commonality marks much New England writing of the past half century. The confessional poetry of Robert Lowell, Sylvia Plath, Anne Sexton, and others can be seen in relation to John Gilgun's *Music I Never Dreamed Of* (1989), a semi-autobiographical novel about growing up working-class, Catholic, and gay in South Boston, or to Susan Eisenberg's poetry about breaking gender barriers to work as an electrician. The literature emerging from New England's many academic centers—as, for example, the poetry of Harvard graduates Wallace Stevens, T. S. Eliot, and cummings or of the many writers who work in the creative writing programs of many New England colleges and universities—might be contrasted with the fiction of a Chute or of French Canadian–descended Jack Kerouac. But little is distinctive to New England in these contrasts, or in much of the work itself. Nor is its audience regional. As American culture has itself become more homogeneous, sharp regional differences like the ones that once marked New England literature have diminished and are preserved most self-consciously by historical societies, regional centers, educational institutions, and the publications of organizations such as the Mark Twain and Harriet

Beecher Stowe houses in Hartford. Lowell's resonant historical poetry, as in *For the Union Dead* (1964), represents an exception rather than the rule in how New England lives today in the books of its citizens. All the same, because "tradition" can be a valuable commodity in consumer and tourist economies and because the idea and the lingering realities of regions *do* continue to fire imaginations, literary writing will surely continue to reflect on New England—and to reinvent it.

William L. Andrews, *To Tell a Free Story: The First Century of Afro-American Autobiography, 1769–1865* (1986); Sacvan Bercovitch, *The American Jeremiad* (1979); Richard H. Brodhead, *Cultures of Letters: Scenes of Reading and Writing in 19th-Century America* (1993); Van Wyck Brooks, *The Flowering of New England, 1815–1865* (1979 [1936]); Dona Brown, *A Tourist's New England: Travel Fiction, 1820–1920* (1999); Lawrence Buell, *The Environmental Imagination: Thoreau, Nature Writing, and the Formation of American Culture* (1995); Buell, *New England Literary Culture: From Revolution through Renaissance* (1986); Michelle Burnham, *Captivity and Sentiment: Cultural Exchange in American Literature, 1682–1861* (1997); Hazel Carby, *Reconstructing Womanhood: The Emergence of the Afro-American Woman Novelist* (1987); Joseph A. Conforti, *Imagining New England: Explorations of Regional Identity from the Pilgrims to the Mid-20th Century* (2001); Patricia Crain, *The Story of A: The Alphabetization of America from* The New England Primer *to* The Scarlet Letter (2000); Cathy N. Davidson, *Revolution and the Word: The Rise of the Novel in America* (1986); Andrew Delbanco, ed., *Writing New England: An Anthology from the Puritans to the Present* (2001); Josephine Donovan, *New England Local Color Literature: A Woman's Tradition* (1983); Ann Douglas, *The Feminization of American Culture* (1977); Philip Gould, *Covenant and Republic: Historical Romance and the Politics of Puritanism* (1996); David D. Hall, *Worlds of Wonder, Days of Judgment: Popular Religious Belief in Early New England* (1989); Mary Kelly, *Private Woman, Public Stage: Literary Domesticity in 19th-Century America* (1984); Jill Lepore, *The Name of War: King Philip's War and the Origins of American Identity* (1998); Kenneth A Lockridge, *Literacy in Colonial New England: An Inquiry into the Social Context of Literacy in the Early Modern Era* (1974); Mason I. Lowance, Jr., *The Language of Canaan: Metaphor and Symbol in New England from the Puritans to the Transcendentalists* (1980); Wendy Martin, *An American Triptych: Anne Bradstreet, Emily Dickinson, Adrienne Rich* (1984); F. O. Matthiessen, *American Renaissance: Art and Expression in the Age of Emerson and Whitman* (1941); Louis Menand, *The Metaphysical Club: A Story of Ideas in America* (2001); Perry Miller, *The New England Mind: The 17th Century* (1968 [1939]); Miller, ed., *The American Transcendentalists: Their Prose and Poetry* (1981 [1957]); William H. Robinson, *Black New England Letters* (1977); Ivy Schweitzer, *The Work of Self-Representation: Lyric Poetry in Colonial New England* (1991); John Seelye, *Memory's Nation: The Place of Plymouth Rock* (1998); Jane P. Tompkins, *Sensational Designs: The Cultural Work of American Fiction, 1790–1860* (1985); Robert von Hallberg, *American Poetry and Culture, 1945–1980* (1985); Perry D. Westbrook, *The New England Town in Fact and Fiction* (1982).

Paul Lauter and Sandra A. Zagarell

Adams, Henry (1838–1918) Writer and historian. One of the most important American historians of the 19th century, an autobiographer, a novelist, and a political journalist, Henry Brooks Adams was born in Boston to Charles Francis Adams and Abigail Brooks Adams. His heritage placed him firmly among the New England elite; his maternal grandfather was allegedly the richest man in Boston, while his paternal grandfather and great-grandfather were John Quincy Adams and John Adams, the sixth and second presidents of the United States, respectively. His father continued the family's involvement in national politics as a member of the House of Representatives and as minister to England during the Civil War. Although he called his own lack of participation in government a "failure," Henry was not interested in running for office; instead, he transferred the Adams's concern with the nation to scholarship and writing.

After graduating from Harvard, Adams worked as secretary to his father in Washington and London (1861–68), where he wrote articles on British politics, economics, and Darwinian theory. On his return to the United States he began a career as a journalist in Washington, but in 1870 he accepted an appointment at Harvard as assistant professor of medieval and American history and editor of the influential journal *The North American Review*. In 1872 he married Marian Hooper, also of an old Massachusetts family. In 1877 he resigned his position and moved to Washington to be near his research sources and at the center of American politics; Washington was his home base for the rest of his life. The next dozen years were a period of extraordinary productivity. Adams wrote biographies of Albert Gallatin (1879) and John Randolph (1882); two novels of contemporary political and cultural life, *Democracy* (1880) and *Esther* (1884); and his major work of history, *History of the United States of America during the Administrations of Thomas Jefferson and James Madison* (nine vols., 1889–91). The focus and stability of this period of his life were shattered by Marian's suicide in 1885, and Adams embarked on what he called his "posthumous" existence, a peripatetic life with travels to Japan, Cuba, the American West, Hawaii, Tahiti, Australia, Ceylon, Europe, and Russia.

He is now best known for two later works: *Mont-Saint-Michel and Chartres* (1904) and *The Education of Henry Adams* (1907). They represent his "dynamic theory of history," which rejected 19th-century progressive models for such scientific models as thermodynamics; he argued that history moved along lines of mechanical "force" and that the role of the historian was to chart these lines and to suggest possibilities for action within them. In addition to charting a movement from medieval "unity" to 20th-century "multiplicity," these hybrid texts, which fuse passionate historical study with ironically detached autobiography, invoke women as a unifying focus for symbolic thought, as in the medieval cult of the virgin. The *Education* is a powerful study of modern fragmentation; it also illuminates a New England mind worried about elite decline in the face of class and ethnic multiplicity. Adams knew a wide range of political, literary, scientific, and artistic figures; among his closest associates were John Hay, Clarence King, and John La Farge. He died in his home in Washington.

J. C. Levenson, Ernest Samuels, Charles Vandersee, and Viola Hopkins Winner, eds., *The Letters of Henry Adams*, 6 vols. (1982–88); John Carlos Rowe, *Henry Adams and Henry James: The Emergence of a Modern Consciousness* (1976); John Carlos Rowe, ed., *New Essays on The Education of Henry Adams* (1996); Ernest Samuels, *The Young Henry Adams* (1948); Samuels, *Henry Adams: The Middle Years* (1958); Samuels, *Henry Adams: The Major Phase* (1964).

Brigitte Bailey

African American Literature African American literature has long been distinguished by its ability to maintain a racially conscientious approach while simultaneously satisfying the demands of a white reading public. Among the writers who emerged from New England a variety of genres, agendas, and traditions are evident; some of this writing is more literary than others, some more explicitly political. For many years, the absence of slavery in the North provided for a greatly reduced, but also highly selective, black presence in New England. Thus, while there may not have been as many African American writers in New England as in the South for many years, those who did live and write in New England proved important and influential, the product of a free society.

The earliest African American literature in New England was poetry that successfully used the European forms that white readers valued. New England's first known poem written by an African American was Lucy Terry's "Bar's Fight," composed in 1746 and maintained by oral tradition to commemorate a Native American ambush on two white families in Deerfield, Mass. Kidnapped as an infant, Terry was a slave herself; she became a skilled orator later in life, arguing passionately against racial discrimination. The poem, however, empathizes with the white families under attack, an identification that implicitly argues that oppression is not bound by race. The poet and essayist Jupiter Hammon was the first published African American; his essay *An Evening Thought, Salvation, by Christ, with Penitential Cries* and his first poem, "Salvation Comes by Christ Alone," both appeared in 1760. The precocious and brilliant poet Phillis Wheatley also embodied the conflicting characteristics of her place, race, and time. Although a slave, Wheatley was educated by her owner's wife and was unusually well-read; when she began writing poetry at age 12, she quickly mastered neoclassical conventions and focused on religion, nature, and patriotism, rather than condemning slavery. However, Wheatley used her African origins as the basis of her understanding of freedom, a common topic in her poetry. Still, her status largely defined her work's reception; Wheatley's first collection, *Poems on Various Subjects, Religious and Moral* (published in London in 1773), required the authorizing "Attestation" of 18 distinguished white gentlemen before appearing in print. In general, poets may have been restrained from undertaking racial themes by the requirements of form; many important autobiographical narratives, diaries, and plays of the next several decades are far more assertive in portraying racial experience.

For many antebellum African American writers, politics, life, and literature were inextricably interconnected. Boston's African Lodge No. 459, the African American Masonic order that was organized and led by Prince Hall and made official in 1787, helped shape the cultural and intellectual climate for northern blacks, as it agitated, lobbied, and petitioned for increased educational opportunities. Against such a background, abolitionist fervor took hold. Religious passions that developed during the Second Great Awakening revived New England's long-standing commitment to reform, and black writers took full advantage of the opportunities thus created. When the American Anti-Slavery Society was founded in 1833, its moral commitment to abolition and, perhaps more importantly, its financial strength created valuable publishing venues for black writers. African American radicals such as Maria Stewart, whose controversial *Religion and the Pure Principles of Morality* (1831) called for active resistance, and David Walker, whose *Appeal* (1829) was outlawed as seditious in the South, rose to prominence through the publishing opportunities created by William Lloyd Garrison, John Brown, and other white abolitionists. Historian William C. Nell, who came from a strongly abolitionist Boston family and was inspired by Garrison's moral commitment to the cause, exerted a multifaceted and wide-ranging influence on the region's African American culture. Nell wrote several pamphlets in the 1850s documenting black Americans' contributions to the military. His access to many prominent New Englanders shaped literary history as well; it was Nell who introduced Harriet Jacobs to editor Lydia Maria Child, and Nell who helped Jacobs find a Boston publisher for her *Incidents in the Life of a Slave Girl* (1861).

While southern writers produced many slave narratives, northern presses published them and northern activists promoted them. Still, New England's African Americans did document their experiences: Nancy Prince's 1850 autobiographical narrative, for instance, offers insights into the abuses and oppressions that defined her life as a free black in Newburyport, Mass., thereby illustrating the limits of freedom in the antebellum North. Charlotte Forten Grimké's diaries (1854–92) demonstrate intellectual integrity and political commitment, reflecting the values of her excellent New England education. A similar political activism informs William Wells Brown's *The Escape; or, A Leap for Freedom* (1858), the first African American play to be published. Although never produced, the play was often read aloud at antislavery meetings in Boston and Chelsea, Mass. Brown was an escaped slave himself whose free life was defined by abolitionist activities and whose antislavery propaganda included plays, fiction, history, and autobiography.

Many slave narratives—Brown's included—were influenced by the estimable *Narrative of the Life of Frederick Douglass* (1845), a wildly popular and effective chronicle that not only underscores the slave's desire for freedom, but also emphasizes the value of literacy in acquiring full selfhood. The different demands on male and female writers are most evident in comparing southern slave narratives and northern novels of the pre–Civil War years, a comparison that also highlights the blurring of boundaries between genres. New Hampshire native Harriet Wilson's *Our Nig* (1859), the first novel published by an African American woman, shares numerous characteristics with Jacobs's *Incidents in the Life of a Slave Girl;* indeed, *Incidents* was long believed to be a fictional account. Both works invoked the redemptive power of Christian virtue to illustrate the potential for their protagonists' salvation; both used pseudonyms to protect actual people; both opened with testimonials from prominent (usually abolitionist) personages; and both conveyed the complicated process of establishing authenticity in terms of racial identity and authorship for a largely white audience. Wilson's *Our Nig* and Jacobs's *Incidents* maintain a strong, arguably gendered connection to Harriet Beecher Stowe's *Uncle Tom's Cabin* (1852), a novel that, while not written by an African American, certainly strongly influenced African American history:

Stowe's best-selling sentimental serial galvanized Christians (including many women) nationwide on behalf of abolition. Two late-19th-century novels by Emma Dunham Kelley follow in this didactic Christian tradition, yet their lack of political or social protest separates them from Stowe. The importance of religion also appeared in Amelia Johnson's late-19th-century Sunday school fiction, which emphasizes the social value of an evangelical ministry.

Literary production that wasn't beholden to attestation or advertisement from prominent whites was often supported by African American magazines and newspapers, which played a central role in providing both a forum and support for African American writers. Here, too, many writers wrote in a variety of genres and styles. The confluence of literature and politics is best exemplified in Archibald Grimké (brother-in-law of Charlotte Forten Grimké), the biracial nephew of prominent white abolitionists who was born a slave and in 1874 was graduated from Harvard Law School. As editor of the Republican Boston *Hub,* as a racially conscientious social activist, and as author of major biographies of abolitionists such as Charles Sumner and William Lloyd Garrison, Grimké helped shape the region's discussion of emancipation, segregation, and racial discrimination. Similarly influential but less prominent (perhaps because as a woman, much of her effect was under- or unacknowledged) was Pauline Hopkins, whose contributions to African American literature, culture, and political empowerment were profound. Hopkins's serialized novellas appeared in the *Colored American Magazine,* a widely distributed Boston-based journal, and her fiction—notably, *Contending Forces: A Romance Illustrative of Negro Life North and South* (1900)—combined social protest with a sentimental melodramatic narrative. In addition to this fiction, and to numerous editorials and biographical profiles of black Americans, Hopkins elaborated her vision of African America's potential through a series of articles on "The Dark Races of the Twentieth Century" that appeared in *The Voice of the Negro* in 1905.

Propagandistic literature designed to emphasize the intelligence, moral virtue, and social value of black America embraced the Victorian values shared by white America while emphasizing the distinctive characteristics of black experience. Massachusetts native W. E. B. Du Bois, the first African American to earn a Harvard doctorate and the nation's single most influential African American thinker, exerted a powerful literary and political influence at the turn of the century. Although Du Bois published poetry and fiction, his greatest contribution is *The Souls of*

Black Folk (1903), a vibrant collection of essays that presciently declared, "The problem of the Twentieth Century is the problem of the color-line" and that proposed the resonant metaphor of "the Veil" to convey a sense of the double-consciousness that separates "American" from "Negro."

Du Bois's influence extended to writers of the post–World War I renaissance in Harlem, where he established *The Crisis,* the literary journal of the National Association for the Advancement of Colored People (NAACP) and a formidable arena for black literature. A number of Boston natives are associated with this literary movement. William Stanley Braithwaite challenged the connection between art and politics that characterizes much turn-of-the-century black literary expression. His *Anthology of Magazine Verse* actively promoted black writers while maintaining his antipolemicist view that the best poetic expression marries truth and beauty. Helene Johnson's poetry grew out of the Harlem Renaissance, and Angelina Weld Grimké (daughter of Archibald) also made valuable contributions, writing poetry, essays, and short fiction in addition to her work with the NAACP's drama committee. Grimké's play *Rachel* (produced in 1916 and published in 1920), a sentimental protest against racism, was the first play written by an African American to be performed for a white audience by an African American cast.

Small magazines and literary journals became important sources for black literary expression in Harlem, and Boston's Dorothy West—Helene Johnson's cousin—helped publish *Challenge* and *New Challenge,* two ambitious if short-lived literary journals. West was best known for her fiction, however, and her work is distinguished by its piercing irony. Her autobiographical novel *The Living Is Easy* (1948), for instance, demonstrates the complex interconnections between class and race conflict within Boston's black middle class. Connecticut native Ann Petry, best known for her highly acclaimed urban novel *The Street* (1946), also engages the racial, social, and gender dynamics of her small New England community in her writing, particularly *The Narrows* (1953). Petry's work continues to be noteworthy, as does West's. Indeed, the 1995 publication of West's novel *The Wedding* attracted considerable attention, not only for its literary value but also for the fact that she completed the work—which she had begun composing in the 1930s—at the strong encouragement of her Martha's Vineyard neighbor Jacqueline Kennedy Onassis, to whom she dedicated the book, noting "Though there was never such a mismatched pair in appearance, we were perfect partners."

New England homes and New England educations have nurtured a number of contemporary African American writers, and their work demonstrates the variety of genres, approaches, and treatments that characterize postmodern literature. The range of their concerns is evident, for instance, in the contrast between the work of novelist Trey Ellis, with his attention to educated, middle-class blacks; poet Melvin Dixon, whose work grapples with racial ancestry; and poet Jewelle Gomez, who writes about women's lives and sexuality. Lorene Cary's memoir *Black Ice* (1991) eloquently documents the struggles she faced in trying to reconcile herself to issues of race, class, and gender in an elite and aristocratic New England school. A number of prominent black writers adopted New England homes after achieving some literary success, and they chose New England in part because of the academic appointments offered them: poets Sam Cornish and Michael Harper, playwright Ed Bullins, Nobel laureate Derek Walcott, essayists and fiction writers Jamaica Kincaid and Michael Thelwell are a few examples. But other significant African Americans, such as science fiction writer Samuel R. Delany and mystery writer Barbara Neely, have also relocated to New England without the draw of academic affiliation.

New England has indeed become a center for the study of African American literature and culture, and many New England–based African Americanist scholars have developed innovative critical analyses to promote the understanding, interpretation, and dissemination of black literature. The University of Massachusetts at Amherst, for example, houses the original papers of Du Bois. Harvard and Yale in particular have played central roles: Yale's James Weldon Johnson collection was founded by Carl Van Vechten in 1941 and contains numerous important manuscripts, correspondences, and rare books. The Yale School of Drama has nurtured many black playwrights, and in 1986 the Yale Repertory Theatre was the first to produce August Wilson's Pulitzer Prize–winning drama *Fences.* Harvard's W. E. B. Du Bois Institute for Afro-American Research was founded in 1975 and, under the direction of the influential scholar and essayist Henry Louis Gates, Jr., is dedicated to the study of African and African American history, culture, and society.

Thus New England–born and –educated writers and New England institutions have not only shaped African American cultural expression, but also—and perhaps more significantly—have directed the critical analysis and popular understanding of African American experience today. In New England, black literary expression was shaped by the particu-

larities of the region's political, cultural, and intellectual tradition: the 18th century's concentration of abolitionist agitators, the 19th century's socially progressive reformers, and the 20th century's Ivy League universities have had a direct and lasting effect on all forms of African American writing.

Houston A. Baker, Jr., and Patricia Redmond, eds., *Afro-American Literary Study in the 1990s* (1989); Hazel Carby, *Reconstructing Womanhood: The Emergence of the Afro-American Woman Novelist* (1987); Frederick Detweiler, *Negro Press in the United States* (1968); John Ernest, *Resistance and Reformation in 19th Century African-American Literature* (1995); Henry Louis Gates, Jr., *Figures in Black: Words, Signs, and the 'Racial' Self* (1987); Blyden Jackson, *A History of Afro-American Literature* (1989); Saunders J. Redding, *To Make a Poet Black* (1939); William H. Robinson, *Black New England Letters* (1977).

Kathleen Pfeiffer

Alcott, Louisa May (1832–88) Writer.

Louisa May Alcott's status as an icon of American and New England childhood was established shortly after the appearance of *Little Women* (1868–69), a novel drawn largely from the youthful experiences of Alcott and her three sisters. As many critics have noted, *Little Women* stands as Alcott's masterpiece not just because it has remained continuously in print and been read by successive generations of readers, but also because it has been intensely beloved by so many of these readers. Alcott's more recent status as a feminist icon taught in college courses stems from the rediscovery and republication in the mid-1970s of very different writing: the adult thrillers featuring subversive female protagonists that Alcott wrote under a pseudonym. This rediscovery has led in turn to a more nuanced appreciation of her children's fiction, particularly *Little Women* and its sequels, *Little Men* and *Jo's Boys,* as well as to increased critical attention to and new editions of her serious works for adults.

Alcott was born in Germantown, Penn.,

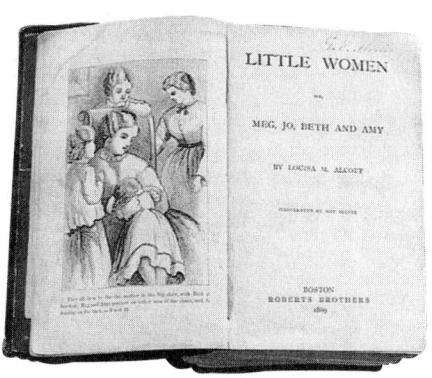

Title page of the first edition of the complete Little Women *(1869)*

but her parents, the Transcendentalist and educator Amos Bronson Alcott and Abigail "Abba" May Alcott, a descendant of prominent Bostonians, moved their family to Massachusetts by the time Alcott was two. Most of her life was spent either in Boston or Concord, with one important interlude in 1843: an experiment in communal living at Fruitlands, in Harvard, Mass. Here, she was tutored by her father's associate, Charles Lane, whom she disliked, correctly intuiting that his communitarian ideas and influence over her father threatened to break up her family. Henry David Thoreau's tutoring was more to her liking, as were the ideas of other leading minds such as Ralph Waldo Emerson, Margaret Fuller, Lydia Maria Child, Nathaniel Hawthorne, and Alcott's abolitionist uncle, Samuel Joseph May. Emerson's library was almost as important to Alcott as his personal influence, particularly his loan of volumes of Goethe, a favorite writer along with Charlotte Brontë and Charles Dickens. Alcott read widely—the Greek classics, the Bible, Shakespeare, Dante, John Bunyan's *Pilgrim's Progress* (her father's favorite), works by Carlyle, Charlotte Yonge, the British and German Romantics—and her writing is peppered with allusions to these texts.

By the time of Alcott's success with *Little Women,* she was halfway through her life as a published author but just on the cusp of earning enough money through writing to make it her primary occupation. Earlier, various other employments (as governess, domestic servant, teacher, seamstress, Civil War nurse, and paid companion) had limited her time and energy for writing but nevertheless provided subjects and prompted Alcott to experiment with a variety of genres for both children and adults. Moreover, Alcott's location near Boston meant that a number of outlets for publication were near at hand. Her children's verse and stories appeared in *Our Young Folks, The Youth's Companion,* and *Merry's Museum,* the latter of which she edited for a short time; and George W. Briggs published *Flower Fables* (1855), a book of fairy tales dedicated to Ellen Emerson. The poetry, short stories, and nonfiction/reportage she wrote for adults were published in such respectable Boston-based venues as *Olive Branch, The Commonwealth,* and most prestigious of all, the *Atlantic Monthly.* James Redpath brought out *Hospital Sketches* (1863), Alcott's reworked abolitionist letters from *The Commonwealth* about her Civil War nursing experiences, and A. K. Loring published *Moods* (1864), a novel inspired by Emerson, Thoreau, and Alcott's own moody nature. Given their overt sexuality, manipulative protagonists, and lurid themes (revenge, murder, insanity, mind control, drug use, the will to power), Alcott sent her less respectable writing, her "sensation fiction" or thrillers, to illustrated weeklies such as Boston's *The Flag of Our Union* and *Saturday Evening Gazette,* as well as to *Frank Leslie's Illustrated Newspaper,* based in New York. Alcott enjoyed writing the sensation fiction and it paid well, but this use of her talents conflicted with her desire to be successful as a serious author for adults.

So too did spending her time on a request from Thomas Niles (of Roberts Brothers publishers) for a girls' book. Alcott overcame her reluctance with the thought that she would be addressing an underserved audience in need of "lively" reading, though she worried that the first chapters were "dull." She revised her opinion upon reading the manuscript of *Little Women* in proof, finding it "not a bit sensational" but true to the lives of the four Alcott sisters (Anna, Louisa, Elizabeth, and May), the models for the book's Meg, Jo, Beth, and Amy March. Despite her disdain for sequels, *Little Women's* instant popularity upon publication in October 1868 inspired Alcott to complete *Little Women* Part 2, by January 1, 1869.

Reasons for the book's success are not hard to find. Alcott's account of the March girls and their rich next-door neighbor, Theodore "Laurie" Laurence, was lively, especially compared with the day's standard for children's literature: didactic lessons thinly disguised as fiction, with one-dimensional "model" children and equally stereotypical bad boys and girls. *Little Women* Part 1 follows the sisters over the course of a year during which their father is away serving as a chaplain in the Civil War, and their mother (Marmee) is preoccupied with her volunteer efforts on the home front. The girls have plenty of opportunity to misbehave or get into tricky situations. Alcott doesn't completely disregard the notion that fiction for young people should be uplifting, but her references in Part 1 to Bunyan's *Pilgrim's Progress* secularize and transform Bunyan's allegory. In place of the soul's pilgrimage to heaven, *Little Women* shifts the focus to the benefits of self-improvement. The sisters move closer to realizing their individual ambitions through curbing their respective flaws; they don't so much become better young women as they become successful young women. Having legitimated female ambition in Part 1, Alcott explores its conflict (and less extensively, its compatibility) with the role of wife and mother in Part 2. Meg and Amy each marry, then Jo weds, but famously *not* to Laurie, and not until she is heartsick and lonely after the death of her beloved Beth.

After the publication of *Little Women,* Alcott wrote another significant novel for adults, *Work: A Story of Experience* (1872), and satirized the utopian experiment at Fruitlands in "Transcendental Wild Oats" (1873), but the bulk of her work was for youth. *Little Men* (1871) and *Jo's Boys* (1886) continued and brought to a close the saga of the March family; in addition, she published five other children's novels and numerous collections of short stories. While all were popular in their time, *Little Women* is the book that set a new standard for American children's literature and that prompted the greatest degree of adulation and the most adaptations.

Scenes from *Little Women* were staged as plays within several years of the book's publication, and live productions (some musical) continue into the 21st century. Among the most notable are the 1912 Broadway play, *Little Women* (produced by William A. Brady, script by Marion De Forest), and the 1998 opera, *Little Women,* by Mark Adamo. *Little Women* on film has almost as extensive a history: at least two silent movies of *Little Women* before 1920, three Hollywood feature films (in 1933, 1949, and 1994), and two made-for-television productions (one by the BBC in 1970 and a 1978 NBC/Universal Studios version). Of these film versions, the three Hollywood movies stand out for their popularity with contemporary audiences. Each recasts Alcott's novel in terms that speak to the cultural concerns of the day. George Cukor's 1933 film (with Katharine Hepburn as Jo) reassures Depression-era audiences that families can survive hard times, while Mervyn LeRoy's postwar 1949 film focuses on the girls' romances and starting new families. Gillian Armstrong's 1994 version highlights Alcott's feminism and her interest in progressive reforms.

Like Cukor's film and a 1918 silent movie version, Armstrong's *Little Women* features shots of Orchard House in Concord, Mass., the Alcott family residence most closely associated with the novel. Orchard House, along with Concord's Sleepy Hollow Cemetery (Alcott's burial site after her death in Roxbury, Mass.), has become a place of pilgrimage for *Little Women* fans. Alcott's admirers leave mementos and notes at her grave and tour the house for glimpses of the desk at which Alcott wrote and the sketches her sister May drew on the walls. Visitors to Orchard House come to find traces of Alcott, but also to find themselves, so closely has Alcott's portrait of middle-class New England girlhood become the model for American girlhood.

Janice M. Alberghene and Beverly Lyon Clark, eds., *Little Women and the Feminist Imagination: Criticism, Controversy, Personal Essays* (1999); Gregory Eiselein and Anne K. Phillips, eds., *The Louisa May Alcott Encyclopedia* (2001); Joel Myerson and Daniel Shealy, eds., *The Journals of Louisa May Alcott* (1989); Madeleine B. Stern, *Louisa May Alcott: A Biography,* rev. ed. (1999).

Janice M. Alberghene

Bellamy, Edward (1850–98) Writer and social reformer. Born in Chicopee Falls, Mass., to the Baptist minister Rufus Bellamy and his wife, Maria (Putnam), Edward Bellamy is best known for his futuristic novel *Looking Backward* (1888). After the fashion of Rip Van Winkle, the novel's protagonist, Julian West, falls asleep for 113 years and then wakes in the year 2000 to a Boston he hardly recognizes. Blending progressive utopianism and romance, the novel demonstrates Bellamy's remarkable prescience about the changes that permanently altered New England between the mid-19th and late-20th centuries. Bellamy's unorthodox views on woman suffrage, labor relations, and the Industrial Revolution's imprint on the social, political, and economic fabric of American society place him in a long line of prominent New England thinkers that includes Jonathan Edwards, Ralph Waldo Emerson, and Henry David Thoreau.

Bellamy's mother, a stern Calvinist, impressed on Edward and his three brothers the importance of Christian duty and instructive reading. The Bellamy household's proximity to the factories of Chicopee Falls allowed the young Edward to observe firsthand the many benefits accruing to mill owners at the expense of overworked, underpaid laborers. This experience, combined with a religious conversion at the age of 14 and extensive spiritual training, shaped Bellamy's reformist views.

After failing the West Point entrance exam because of frail health, Bellamy spent 1867 at Union College in Schenectady, N.Y., where he was exposed to socialist thinking and the works of François-Marie-Charles Fourier. In 1868 he traveled to Germany as companion to his cousin William Packer. On his return he studied law, passing the Massachusetts bar in 1871. That same year he contributed an article, "Woman Suffrage," to Theodore Tilton's publication *Golden Age,* thus launching his literary career. During 1872 he worked briefly in New York City as a journalist, returning to assume an editorial position with the *Springfield Union.* Over the next decade Bellamy contributed editorials, book reviews, and short stories to such publications as the *New York Evening Post, Scribner's, Appleton's Journal,* and *Lippincott's.* In 1882 Bellamy married Emma Sanderson. The couple had two children, Paul (born 1884) and Marion (born 1886).

With his brother Charles, Bellamy founded the *Springfield Daily News,* where he was an editor from 1880 to 1884. He left that publication to devote himself to writing and social reform. Bellamy wrote six novels—*Six to One: A Nantucket Idyl* (1878), *The Duke of Stockbridge* (serialized in 1879, republished as a book in 1900), *Dr. Heidenhoff's Process* (1880), *Miss Ludington's Sister* (1884), and *Looking Backward* and its sequel *Equality* (1897)—as well as 23 short stories. Bellamy's fiction was lauded in print by William Dean Howells.

Bellamy's most celebrated work, the bestselling *Looking Backward*, envisioned a harmonious, egalitarian America and inspired a worldwide movement known as "Bellamyism" (nationalism) that promoted utopian socialism. The new society that Bellamy describes in *Looking Backward* is remarkably free of conflict caused by economic or social inequities. Harmony reigns and social ills such as strikes, poverty, and class warfare have been eliminated. Even more striking to modern readers is the way in which the novel foresees such technological innovations as debit card transactions, shopping malls, and the electronic media. A sequel, *Equality*, was published in 1897. Increasingly committed to a radical leftist agenda that embraced feminism, environmentalism, and labor and animal rights, Bellamy founded the socialist weekly *New Nation* in 1891. His progressive ideas remained popular until World War I and influenced writer-reformers such as Charlotte Perkins Gilman, Upton Sinclair, and Eugene Debs. For health reasons, Bellamy and his family moved to Denver in 1898. He died of tuberculosis in May of that year and is buried in Chicopee Falls.

Sylvia E. Bowman, *Edward Bellamy* (1986); Nancy Snell Griffith, *Edward Bellamy: A Bibliography* (1986); Daphne Patai, ed., *Looking Backward, 1988–1888: Essays on Edward Bellamy* (1988).

Lisa Stepanski

Bishop, Elizabeth (1911–79) Poet.

One of the most original voices in this century's American poetry, Elizabeth Bishop was born of Canadian American parents in Worcester, Mass. Her father died when she was still an infant, and her mother was committed to a mental institution when she was five years old. Bishop never saw her again. Kept from school by various illnesses, she was educated at home and raised by her maternal grandparents in Nova Scotia and an aunt in Boston. Her official education began at the age of 16 when she enrolled at Walnut Hill School in Natick, Mass. Three years later she entered Vassar, from which she graduated in 1934. During this period she wrote her first poems and met the poet Marianne Moore, who remained her lifelong friend and mentor. After college, Bishop lived in New York for several years, making long trips to England, France, Spain, Italy, and North Africa, settling finally in Key West in 1939. Her first book of poems, *North and South*, was published in 1946. Bishop worked as consultant in poetry at the Library of Congress from 1949 to 1950 and then moved to Brazil in 1951, where she lived until the death of her companion, Lota de Macedo Soares, in 1967. Her last years were spent teaching at Harvard and living in Boston.

Her other books of poetry include *Poems: North and South—A Cold Spring* (1955), which earned a Pulitzer Prize; *Questions of Travel* (1965); *The Complete Poems* (1969), which won the National Book Award; and her final volume of poems, *Geography III* (1976). In addition to the poetry, Bishop wrote stories, articles, and reviews and translated both Brazilian poetry and prose.

Bishop once told a reviewer that the poetry she admires most has a naturalness of tone; she herself possessed a talent for writing such poetry. Her much anthologized poem "The Fish" begins:

I caught a tremendous fish
and held him beside the boat
half out of water, with my hook
fast in a corner of his mouth.
He didn't fight.
He hadn't fought at all.
He hung a grunting weight,
battered and venerable
and homely.

Bishop's sharp eye for detail, verbal precision, and formal control give her poetry a lightness of touch that disguises the gravity of the subject matter. Bishop took the world as she found it: full of contradictions. She never complained or moralized in her work. "Auden's later poetry is sometimes spoiled for me," she said, "by his didacticism. I don't like modern religiosity in general; it always seems to lead to a tone of moral superiority."

As a poet, Bishop had too much respect for fact and sense to give herself over completely to the imagination, while at the same time, she had too much imagination to resist its temptations. Her poetry, Octavio Paz wrote, "satisfies a double thirst: thirst for reality and thirst for marvels." In its understatement and in smallness of scale, her poetry belongs with that of Emily Dickinson and Robert Frost. "Something needn't be large to be good," she said, and her poems prove that to be the case.

Several of Bishop's best-known poems are set in New England, and her writing represents a continuing conversation with earlier New England writers, such as Emerson, Thoreau, and Frost, as well as her contemporaries, most notably Robert Lowell, who dedicated his famous poem "Skunk Hour" to Bishop.

Elizabeth Bishop, *The Complete Poems: 1927–1979* (1983); Robert Giroux, ed., *One Art: Letters/Elizabeth Bishop* (1994); Brett C. Millier, *Elizabeth Bishop: Life and the Memory of It* (1993); Lloyd Schwartz and Sybil P. Estess, eds., *Elizabeth Bishop and Her Art* (1983).

Charles Simic

Bradstreet, Anne (ca. 1612–72)

Writer of poems and prose meditations. The first writer in British North America to publish a book of poems, Anne (Dudley) Bradstreet was born in Northampton, England, to Thomas Dudley and Dorothy Yorke. When she was seven years old, her father became steward to the earl of Lincoln, a situation that gave her access to tutors and a large library, and encouraged her to acquire a solid classical and nonconformist religious education. She married Simon Bradstreet in 1628 and emigrated to the Massachusetts Bay Colony with her husband and parents in 1630. In this new environment, Bradstreet wrote poetry and prose meditations, raised eight children, and managed a busy household with a husband whose career included agriculture, commerce, and public service.

Because of her family connections, Bradstreet was involved in many significant political events of her day. Her father alternated with John Winthrop in the positions of governor and deputy governor for nearly 20 years and quarreled acrimoniously with Winthrop over the future direction of the colony. Bradstreet's husband held a variety of administrative positions in the colony and after her death served for several years as governor.

In this politically charged atmosphere, Bradstreet produced a substantial body of work, spanning some 40 years. Her first collection of poems was carried to London by her brother-in-law, John Woodbridge, apparently without her knowledge, and published as *The Tenth Muse Lately Sprung Up in America* (1650). The volume includes most of her poems on public subjects such as politics and history: quaternions, or four-part series, on nature and the seasons, human nature, and the stages of life; and dialogues that showcase her classical education and reveal the influence of the poets Francis Quarles, Guillaume DuBartas, Sir Philip Sidney, and Edmund Spenser. The collection was well received and earned a regional reputation for its author. An American edition, *Several Poems Compiled with Great Variety of Wit and Learning* (1678), was augmented with some of her more private poetry, including poems that explored themes of family life, parental and marital love, grief, nature, and religious faith and doubt.

From the relatively early "Dialogue between Old England and New" to the later "Contemplations," Bradstreet struggled as both a spiritual and worldly pilgrim. Many of her writings deal with her journey toward redeeming faith. As she wrote in "To My Dear Children," "Many times hath Satan troubled me concerning the verity of the Scriptures, many times by atheism how I could know whether there was a God." But other writings deal with her struggle as a woman who felt the sting of community sanctions against her for being a writer: "I am obnoxious to each carping tongue / Who says my hand a needle better fits."

Bradstreet's identities as woman, Puritan, and metaphoric pilgrim facing a strenuous and beautiful frontier shaped how she saw her home and how she wrote about it. Her poems and prose meditations open a window on the early Anglo–New England community—its daily life, its family and gender structures, its intellectual and literary paradigms, its religious and political conflicts. Bradstreet's complex vision has engaged generations of readers, and her poetry and prose appear in numerous anthologies of American literature. Her collected works have been republished frequently—two editions in the 17th century, one in the 18th century, two in the 19th century, and three in the 20th century—and she has been celebrated in the work of the 20th-century American poets John Berryman and Adrienne Rich.

Pattie Cowell and Ann Stanford, eds., *Critical Essays on Anne Bradstreet* (1983); Joseph R. McElrath, Jr., and Allan P. Robb, eds., *The Complete Works of Anne Bradstreet* (1981); Rosamond Rosenmeier, *Anne Bradstreet Revisited* (1991); Elizabeth Wade White, *Anne Bradstreet: "The 10th Muse"* (1971).

Pattie Cowell

Bread Loaf Writers' Conference

Each August since 1926 the Bread Loaf Writers' Conference has offered aspiring writers an opportunity to enjoy the counsel, criticism, and advice of notable writers. This annual summer gathering is held at the Bread Loaf campus of Middlebury College, located in the Green Mountain National Forest in Ripton, Vt. The land was originally owned by Vermont native Joseph Battell who, during his lifetime, acquired nearly 30,000 acres of New England countryside. In 1866 Battell established the Bread Loaf Inn, a Victorian farmhouse with a number of guest cottages for summer visitors; upon his death in 1915 he willed the inn and surrounding lands to nearby Middlebury College.

In 1920 the college opened the Bread Loaf School of English, a six-week summer program for graduate students of English and American literature, with additional courses in composition. Several writers who taught there—Willa Cather, Katherine Lee Bates, and Louis Untermeyer among them—envisioned the Bread Loaf campus as a place where emerging poets, novelists, and others could immerse themselves both in the study of writing and in a community of fellow writers. The president of Middlebury College, Paul Dwight Moody, knowing that the campus was deserted during the late summer, eventually offered his support and in 1925 asked New Yorker John C. Farrar, an editor and instructor at the Bread Loaf School, to organize a two-week conference on creative writing for the following August.

Conferees who attended one of the first three Bread Loaf Writers' Conferences (and paid $100 for the privilege) found that John Farrar had gathered faculty and speakers who offered an interesting blend of theory and practice. Lectures by writers including Sinclair Lewis and Stephen Vincent Benét competed with talks by publishers and literary editors on the practicalities of earning a living as a writer. After Farrar resigned to cofound the publishing company Farrar and Rinehart in 1928, Robert M. Gay became director, followed by poet and Harvard professor Theodore Morrison, who served as director from 1932 to 1955. Despite economic depression and world war, Morrison's tenure as director was marked by growth and notoriety; its success inspired the creation of similar conferences throughout the United States. Theodore and Kathleen Morrison's close relationship with Robert Frost brought the famous poet to every conference session from 1938 to 1962. The editor and poet John Ciardi succeeded Morrison and served as director from 1956 to 1972, an era distinguished both by a steady increase in participants and by challenges to an entrenched hierarchy that had isolated conferees—even those attending on fellowships or scholarships—from the senior faculty. The poet and teacher Robert Pack, director from 1973 to 1994, and his successor Michael Collier have introduced further changes, building on the successes of their predecessors.

The celebrity that the Bread Loaf Writers' Conference enjoys is perhaps inspired by the reputations of those who have graced and continue to grace its faculty. More impressive still, however, is the catalog of writers—including Carson McCullers, Eudora Welty, Theodore Roethke, Anne Sexton, John Irving, Toni Morrison, Tim O'Brien, Rita Dove, and others—who, in their formative years, benefited from their immersion in this community of writers.

David Haward Bain and Mary Smyth Duffy, *Whose Woods These Are: A History of the Bread Loaf Writers' Conference, 1926–1992* (1993); Theodore Morrison, *Bread Loaf Writers' Conference: The First 30 Years: 1926–1955* (1976).

Paul D. Nygard

Brooks, Van Wyck (1886–1963) Writer and critic.

Born in Plainfield, N.J., Van Wyck Brooks adopted New England as both his home and the subject of many of his writings. Brooks, a nationally known literary critic, editor, and biographer, graduated from Harvard in 1907 and spent much of his adult life in Connecticut. In 1937 he received the Pulitzer Prize in history for *The Flowering of New England, 1815–1964* (1936), the first of his five-volume history of American literature, *Makers and Finders: A History of the Writer in America, 1800–1915* (1936–52). Sounding a theme that would dominate Brooks's later writing, *The Flowering of New England* idealizes the American past as a foundation for its future literature while establishing Ralph Waldo Emerson and the Transcendentalist school as a model for American writers. The sequel, *New England: Indian Summer, 1865–1915* (1940), solidified a cultural image of New England as a nostalgic repository of national character in a time of immigration and industrialization. For Brooks, who was more interested in literature's social significance than its artistic quality, the New England literary tradition represented a "usable past," a past that could enrich contemporary American literature and society.

Brooks's search for a usable past began when he was a boy. The son of the stockbroker Charles Edward and Sallie Bailey (Ames) Brooks, Van Wyck grew up surrounded by business concerns. At the age of 12, Brooks traveled to Germany, France, Italy, and England and was overwhelmed by the richness of European art. Brooks's European experience came to convince him that the arts require a supportive culture, and he began to seek such a culture in America.

Disappointed by the literary communities at Harvard and in New York, Brooks's early career is marked by his dissatisfaction with American culture. At age 23, he wrote his first book, *The Wine of the Puritans* (1908), while working as a journalist in England. The book, which is loosely based on Brooks's own experiences, attacks the Puritan mindset for its lack of artistic appreciation. By the 1920s Brooks had become a prominent member of a group of radical socialist writers who sought a new American art based on a new social order. Brooks joined other critics of his generation, such as H. L. Mencken, in attacking New England Puritanism as the source of the puritanical aspects of Victorian culture, especially as reflected in literature. He believed American writers often failed to bridge the artistic and the materialistic impulses in American life, a split resulting from Puritanism's separation of spirituality and worldliness.

From 1926 to 1931 Brooks's career was interrupted by a period of mental illness, which he called his "season in hell." Brooks emerged from the experience a changed man; his characteristic cynicism was transformed into respect for America's artistic past and hope for its future. During this period Brooks wrote not only *Makers and Finders* but also *The Writer in America* (1953) and *From a Writer's Notebook* (1958), in which he reflects on a personal philosophy of life and literature. While this new Brooks met popular acclaim, critics derided his work as nostalgic and sentimental. Brooks died in his Bridgewater, Conn., home in 1963.

Van Wyck Brooks, *An Autobiography* (1965); James Hoopes, *Van Wyck Brooks: In Search of American Culture* (1977); Raymond Nelson, *Van Wyck Brooks: A Writer's Life* (1981).

Briann G. Greenfield

Captivity Narratives

The earliest published account of a European's capture by Native Americans dates from 1542. But the captivity narrative came into its own as a genre in New England partly because there captivity was a historical reality. Hundreds of New England settlers were taken captive, many—especially children, young women, indentured servants, and blacks—sometimes choosing never to return from an Indian culture that offered them a different, perhaps more fulfilling, social identity. Native Americans took captives back to New England for ransom, in exchange for money or goods with other tribes or the French and later the British in Canada, to replace lost family members, and in some cases for revenge in "mourning" raids instigated by family members of Indians lost in combat.

Returned captives often wrote or dictated narratives of their experiences. Mary Rowlandson's *The Sovereignty and Goodness of GOD . . . a Narrative of the Captivity and Restauration of Mrs. Mary Rowlandson* (1682) was the first published, with 15 editions by 1800. Early examples such as Rowlandson's, or Cotton Mather's strategic use of captivity narratives in his sermons and in *Decennium Luctuosum* (1698), or John Williams's *Redeemed Captive Returning to Zion* (1707), are as much documents of religious conversion and faith as they are accounts of native-white culture clash. Indian capture was made to fit a Chris-

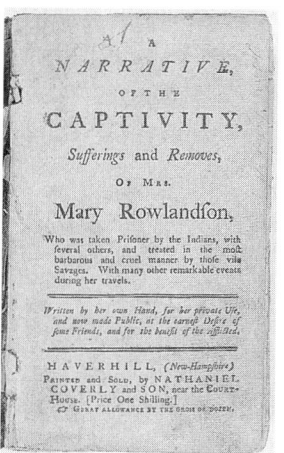

Title page of the 1796 edition of Mary Rowlandson's Narrative *(1682), with the title that was adopted in the late 18th century*

tian typological project. Just as Israelites wandered in the desert before recovering the Holy Land, so the captives' estrangement from and ultimate return to "Zion" proved that although God tested the Puritans in New England, he would ultimately redeem and deliver them. Some narratives offered alternative views of captive experience with their tales of self-reliance, adventure, and respect for Indian ways. In two examples, Hannah Dustin, for example, kills and scalps her captors and is rewarded financially, and Quaker Elizabeth Hanson develops a respect for Indian women. In another narrative, John Gyles spends enough years with an Indian group in Maine to become deeply knowledgeable of Native American social life and survival skills, and he lives the rest of his life on the border between the races.

The genre also revealed the limits and fragility of the European presence and cultural identity in New England. The voluntary attrition of many underprivileged New Englanders, women, and children was disconcerting to settlers who understood "savagery" as incompatible with "civilization." Stories recounting a captive's sojourn into otherness and return to New England celebrated the spiritual and emotional commitment of those who rejected native life to return and claim New England as their own. Therefore, the "unredeemed captives" who could not or would not return haunted New Englanders. The most famous case was that of Eunice Williams, daughter of the Reverend John Williams of Deerfield, Mass. Taken captive as a child in the Deerfield massacre of 1704, she was adopted by a Mohawk family and had several children with her Mohawk husband.

As the threat of capture in New England

receded through the 18th century—as Indians were decimated by disease and warfare, relocated to some settlements in Canada, and lost French and British allies as colonial wars and the American Revolution ended—the religious framework of the narratives fell away, to be replaced by sentimental concerns. This turn from religious fervor to emotional passion was a means for women writers of both factual and fictional captivity narratives to examine new, potentially liberating, emotions. At the same time, the genre facilitated Indian-hating by recounting acute suffering—often of women—at native hands. Many of the narratives from the time of the French and Indian War and the Revolutionary War present tales of incredible experiences on the New Hampshire and Vermont frontiers. The most famous is the story of Susannah Johnson, taken captive in 1754 at Fort Number 4, in Charlestown, N.H. She gives birth to a child on the hard trip to Canada, her husband is killed, and she endures four years of captivity in French Canada. Nevertheless, by the 1820s, the genre had changed so much that Catharine Sedgwick in *Hope Leslie* (1827) and Lydia Maria Child in *Hobomok* (1824) could use the conventions of captivity narratives in sentimental fictions sympathetic to native concerns.

The first narrative by an American slave is a black New Englander's tale of Indian captivity, *A Narrative of the Uncommon Sufferings and Surprizing Deliverance of Briton Hammon, A Negro Man* (1760). Although Hammon was a New England slave, by the time slavery was abolished in New England the conventions governing captivity narratives had shifted to define slave narratives. The moral—that only savages hold other people captive—remained the same. New England, or more broadly, the North, remained "Zion," the place to which the captive wished to escape. Harriet Wilson's *Our Nig* (1859) contested this easy recasting of New England as the Promised Land, reminding readers that black servants remained oppressed and captive even in New England. But Harriet Beecher Stowe in *Uncle Tom's Cabin* (1852) referenced the captivity narrative genre in a more conventional way. "I wonder, if the Indians should come and take you a prisoner . . . if you'd think it your duty to abide in the condition in which you were called. I rather think you'd think the first stray horse you could find an indication of Providence." In this transformation of the captivity narrative, the Indians became slaveholding southerners, the captives runaway slaves, and the white, civilized North remained the Holy Land it had been for Mary Rowlandson almost 200 years earlier.

In the 20th century, captivity narrative fiction became primarily a genre for young readers, in works such as Mary P. Wells Smith's *The Boy Captive of Old Deerfield* (1904) and Conrad Richter's *The Light in the Forest* (1953). It has recently been revived for adults by Ernest Hebert in *The Old American* (2000), a novel based on a Keene, N.H., captivity story. The novel envisions American, and hence New England, identity as a blending of European and native cultures.

Michelle Burnham, *Captivity and Sentiment: Cultural Exchange in American Literature, 1682–1861* (1997); Christopher Castiglia, *Bound and Determined: Captivity, Culture-Crossing, and White Womanhood from Mary Rowlandson to Patty Hearst* (1996); John Demos, *The Unredeemed Captive: A Family Story from Early America* (1995); Gary L. Ebersole, *Captured by Texts: Puritan to Postmodern Images of Indian Captivity* (1995); John Sekora, "Red, White, and Black: Indian Captivities, Colonial Printers, and the Early American African-American Narrative," in *A Mixed Race: Ethnicity in Early America,* ed. Frank Shuffleton (1993).

Bethany Schneider

Cheever, John (1912–82)

Writer. A writer of short fiction and novels, John Cheever was hailed by the *New York Times* book critic John Leonard as "a Chekhov of the exurbs" for his chronicles of New England suburban life. Cheever has been viewed as the archetypal New England writer, a 20th-century exemplar of a belief in purity and a sensitivity to evil that has been characteristic of New England writers since Nathaniel Hawthorne.

Cheever was born and grew up in Quincy, Mass., in what he considered to be the marginal branch of an old Boston family, during what he termed "the Athenian twilight" of New England culture. His storytelling gift was shown when, at age eight, he improvised tales to entertain his classmates; by age 10, he began to write his stories down. His dismissal from Thayer Academy in Braintree, Mass., provided the subject for his story "Expelled," which was published in *The New Republic* in 1930 when he was only 18. Cheever married Mary Winternitz in 1941 and they raised three children. He lived in the New York suburb of Ossining until his death in 1982.

Cheever published a near record number of short stories in *The New Yorker,* many of which satirized white postwar suburban conventions and mores. His stories have been collected in *The Way Some People Live* (1943), *The Enormous Radio and Other Stories* (1953), *The Housebreaker of Shady Hill and Other Stories* (1958), *Some People, Places and Things That Will Not Appear in My Next Novel* (1961), *The Brigadier and the Golf Widow* (1964), and *The World of Apples* (1973). *The Stories of John Cheever* (1978; winner of the National Book Award and a Pulitzer Prize) assembles many of the best-

John Cheever, 1974

known and most highly praised of his stories, including "The Country Husband," "The Enormous Radio," and "The Swimmer."

Cheever's novels, even when they are not set in New England, reflect morals and mores indicative of his regional literary heritage. *The Wapshot Chronicle* (1957), an episodic comic novel about the male line of a wealthy Massachusetts family in which Cheever explored New England's past and present, received a National Book Award in 1958. Its sequel, *The Wapshot Scandal* (1964), continues the tale of the family's decline. *Bullet Park* (1969), a nightmare of drug addiction and breakdown in suburban New York, is a caustic, pessimistic dissection of American upper-class life. *Falconer* (1977), set in a New York prison (Cheever taught writing classes at Sing Sing prison in the late 1970s) is about an ex-professor incarcerated for fratricide and frankly expresses the homoerotic and homosexual desires underlying much of Cheever's writing. Cheever's last published work, the novella *Oh What a Paradise It Seems* (1982), is about environmental pollution in a northeastern suburb and an aging man's redemption through homosexual love.

Cheever's letters and journals, edited respectively by his son Benjamin, an editor for *Reader's Digest,* and his daughter, the writer Susan Cheever, were published posthumously in the late 1980s. Susan Cheever quotes exten-

sively from her father's journals and letters in her biographical memoir of her father, *Home before Dark* (1984), to reveal his homosexuality and his ordeals with alcoholism. This information has deepened scholars' understanding of his homosexual themes, especially in his last novels.

In a 1982 *New Yorker* review, fellow writer John Updike wrote that Cheever "speaks in the cranky, granular, impulsive, confessional style of our native wise men and exhorters since Emerson." New England traditions and influences are evident in Cheever's cultural conservatism about heterosexual marriage, the nuclear family, and personal display; his capacity for darkness; and his ambition to use his writing to ameliorate the harsh Puritanism of some of his forebears.

R. G. Collins, ed., *Critical Essays on John Cheever* (1982); John Hersey, "John Cheever, Boy and Man," *The New York Times Book Review,* March 26, 1978; John Leonard, "Cheever Country," *The New York Times Book Review,* March 7, 1982; John Updike, "On Such a Beautiful Green Little Planet," *The New Yorker,* April 5, 1982.

Ronna C. Johnson

Child, Lydia Maria (1802–80)

Writer and abolitionist. Lydia Maria Francis (Child) was born in Medford, Mass., and her career as an abolitionist and writer spanned more than 50 years and propelled the development of writing as both a commercial and activist enterprise. The daughter of a prosperous baker, she received little formal education in her youth. After the death of her mother, 12-year-old Lydia lived with a sister in Norridgewock, Maine, where she shared the household duties, enjoyed the wilderness setting, and maintained a correspondence with her older brother Convers. Lydia would later share a home in Boston with Convers, who provided intellectual guidance and introductions into the homes of that city's upper class.

The 1824 publication of *Hobomok*, a work of historical fiction set in Puritan New England, brought immediate public recognition to Child. Featuring miscegenation as a topic, *Hobomok* presented a sympathetic portrayal of Native Americans. After the success of *Hobomok*, she wrote several additional works of historical fiction, including *The Rebels; or, Boston before the Revolution* (1825). Child also established herself as a writer for children, publishing *Evenings in New England* (1824), a collection of moralistic short stories, and editing from 1826 to 1834 the *Juvenile Miscellany*, the first successful children's periodical in the United States. She returned to an examination of Native American life in *The First Settlers of New England* (1829). In this work, she addressed the Puritans' inhuman treatment of Native Americans, a thinly disguised critique of Andrew Jackson's Indian removal policy.

By the age of 26, Child had established herself as an acclaimed author and clever entrepreneur. She was one of the first women to be admitted to Boston's elite literary club, the Athenaeum. She married David Child in 1828, and the couple lived in and around Boston until debts he incurred forced them to move to western Massachusetts. Child's work received critical acclaim but varied financial rewards. Part of her success was due to her business acumen and skill at crafting books for selected audiences. Recognizing the growing commercial market for printed material and responding to the confusion created by rapid social change, in *The American Frugal Housewife* (1829), Child wrote for new wives bewildered by changing roles, although she herself disdained domestic duties.

An ardent abolitionist, Child wrote an elegant, scholarly overview of the history of slavery in the world and argued for an immediate end to American slaveholding in *An Appeal in Favor of That Class of Americans Called Africans* (1833). This book increased support for abolition but also cost Child her popularity. Her book sales plummeted, and when proslavery subscribers canceled their subscriptions to the *Juvenile Miscellany*, Child was forced to resign as editor. Her outspoken stance also angered the Boston Athenaeum, which re-

scinded her membership. When the Childs' sugar-beet farm, established to provide an alternative to slave-produced sugar, failed, Lydia Maria Child moved to New York to edit the *National Anti-Slavery Standard* in 1841. Editorial disputes, however, led her to resign in 1843. Despite public disapproval, she remained faithful to the cause, writing many works of fiction and nonfiction with abolition themes. In *The History of the Condition of Women in Various Ages and Nations* (1835), the last two volumes of the five-volume *Ladies Family Library*, Child pioneered the use of minority biographies as role models for her readers. In 1861 Child edited Harriet A. Jacobs's *Incidents in the Life of a Slave Girl*, an autobiographical account of the horrors of slavery.

Child continued to write and publish throughout her life. Continuing to market her books to specific audiences, in *Looking toward Sunset* (1865), she collected poems and stories for an elderly audience. She and her husband, reunited after several lengthy separations, spent their later years in a small cottage in Medford, just west of Boston. They had no children. Over her lengthy career, Child, through her numerous works of fiction, nonfiction, and poetry, espoused religious tolerance and civil rights for African Americans, Native Americans, and women. Lydia Maria Child died in 1880.

Deborah Pickman Clifford, *Crusader for Freedom: A Life of Lydia Maria Child* (1992); Carolyn L. Karcher, *The First Woman in the Republic: A Cultural Biography of Lydia Maria Child* (1994); Bruce Mills, *Cultural Reformations: Lydia Maria Child and the Literature of Reform* (1994).

Elizabeth A. De Wolfe

Children's Literature to 1900

New England stood at the forefront of nearly every major development in the history of American children's literature from the colonial era until the mid-1870s. During this period most of America's important children's authors lived in New England, and most American novels and stories written for children were set in the region. After the mid-1870s, New England's continued role in children's literature, although important, was no longer dominant.

When the Puritans moved to New England in the mid-1600s, they brought with them two beliefs that fostered the development of children's literature. First, they believed that everyone who belonged to their theocracy needed to know how to read—so that they could read the Bible. They also believed that children and adults differed in an important way. Drawing on the teachings of the Swiss theologian John Calvin, many Puritans embraced the concept of "infant depravity," that

is, the idea that because the Bible says "we are all born in sin," young children must be the most sinful of all. These beliefs led the Puritans to create and widely distribute reading material that was intended specifically for children to teach them about the Bible and to impress upon them the seriousness of their innate sinfulness.

The earliest example of this type of reading material was John Cotton's famous catechism titled *Milk for Babes, Drawn out of the Breasts of both Testaments*, which was first published in New England in 1656. This pamphlet-length work consisted of a series of questions and answers dealing with theological issues. Another notable example of Puritan literature for children was Cotton Mather's *A Token for Children of New England*, which originally appeared in 1700.

The Puritans' first important book-length work intended for children was *The New-England Primer*, the first American edition of which was printed in Boston between 1686 and 1690. Over its long history, *The New-England Primer* underwent many revisions. Most versions, however, included a syllabary, or table of syllables; the Lord's Prayer; *Milk for Babes* or some other catechism; and a series of short rhymes, one for each letter of the alphabet, such as "In Adam's Fall / We sinned all," for the letter *A*.

Although the Puritans wrote very little fiction for children, one notable exception was *The Prodigal Daughter*. First published anonymously in Boston in the late 1730s, this rhymed story features a disobedient girl who becomes angry when her parents try to correct her misbehavior. While she is sulking in her room, Satan visits her, and together they devise a plan to poison her parents. When this plan fails, the girl falls into a deathlike trance, during which she visits both hell and heaven. She finally revives after renouncing her evil ways. This story was so popular that it went through 29 American editions, the last of which came out in 1820.

Beginning in the late 1700s, the influence of the Puritans on New England culture gradually diminished. As more New Englanders began to identify with the new nationalism that was then taking root, the nature of New England children's literature began to change. Noah Webster, for example, promoted American culture in his famous primer *The American Spelling Book* (1783). This change can also be seen in the new children's magazines that came out of New England during the early 19th century. The two most prominent examples were Lydia Maria Child's *The Juvenile Miscellany*, which began publication in 1826, and Nathaniel Willis's *The Youth's Companion*, which began in 1827. Both of these magazines tried to instill a sense of patriotism in their readers.

Religious themes continued to figure prominently in much of the children's literature New Englanders wrote during the early decades of the 19th century, but the concept of infant depravity appeared less and less in these children's books. John S. C. Abbott's *The Child at Home,* first published in Boston in 1833, is a good example of a book that was at the cusp of this change. The author, a Congregational minister who grew up in Maine and served as the pastor of a church in central Massachusetts, portrayed children as being innocent but easily corrupted. His book is filled with cautionary tales of innocent children who are "ruined entirely" by associating with "bad boys."

John S. C. Abbott's older brother, Jacob Abbott, shared his brother's desire to provide children with moral and religious instruction, but he felt that his brother placed too much emphasis on telling children how *not* to behave. Jacob Abbott believed that children's writers should take a more positive approach to teaching morality and proper behavior. Thus, when a publisher asked him to write a book for young children, he welcomed the opportunity to apply his theory. This book, titled *The Little Scholar Learning to Talk* (1835, later republished as *Rollo Learning to Talk*), introduced a young boy named Rollo and his family. Other Rollo books soon followed, including *Rollo Learning to Read* (1835), *Rollo at Play* (1836), *Rollo at Work* (1837), and *Rollo at School* (1839). The setting for all of these books is a New England farm, and farming activities figure in the books' rambling stories. Abbott's goal, however, was not to tell riveting stories but to cultivate the "amiable and gentle qualities of the heart" by providing his young readers with "character and conduct to be imitated." Abbott's Rollo books attracted a vast readership, making Abbott the best-selling children's author in America before the Civil War.

With the rise of the Romantic movement during the mid-19th century, the notion of childhood innocence gained more supporters among New England's writers for children. In some cases, these writers were influenced by Jean-Jacques Rousseau's rather sentimental view of childhood, as presented in his classic work *Emile.* The image of the innocent child figures in many children's books written by New Englanders during the antebellum period, including Lydia Howard Sigourney's *The Girl's Reading-Book* (1838), Catharine Maria Sedgwick's *Love Token for Children* (1839), Lydia Maria Child's *Flowers for Children* (1844), and Rebecca Sophia Clarke's *Little Prudy* (1864). In many cases, the child char-

acters in these books seem almost saintly by contemporary standards.

In addition to promulgating the notion of childhood innocence, followers of the Romantic movement often promoted the cultivation of children's imaginations. This idea led a number of New England romantics to write fantasy books for children, a trend that reached its height during the 1850s. Nathaniel Hawthorne led the way with the publication of *A Wonder Book* in 1851 and *Tanglewood Tales* in 1853. Both books consist of retellings of Greek myths that are introduced by a frame story set in New England. In 1853, Richard Henry Stoddard, a protégé of Hawthorne's, published a collection of original fairy tales under the title of *Adventures in Fairy-Land.* A few years later, Louisa May Alcott published a book of fairy tales titled *Flower Fables* (1855). Christopher Pearse Cranch soon followed with two extended works of fantasy: *The Last of the Huggermuggers* (1856) and its sequel, *Kobboltozo* (1857). Although not a native of New England, Cranch was educated at Harvard and spent much of his adult life in Maine and Massachusetts. As the decade came to a close, Jane G. Austin brought out *Fairy Dreams* (1859), a collection of six original fairy tales.

The fantasy stories that New Englanders wrote for children sold reasonably well at the time of their original publication, but they were soon eclipsed by realistic children's books written in the area during the late 1860s and 1870s. This development began in 1868–69 with the publication of Louisa May Alcott's *Little Women.* This largely autobiographical tale about the domestic activities of four sisters growing up in a small New England town became one of the best-selling children's books of the 19th century. In addition to attracting a wide readership, *Little Women* drew praise from literary critics who argued that Alcott's March sisters were among the first fully developed and truly believable characters from American children's literature.

The success of *Little Women* spawned a subgenre of realistic domestic stories intended primarily for girls. Alcott's other contributions to this subgenre include *An Old-Fashioned Girl* (1870), *Little Men* (1871), *Eight Cousins* (1875), *Rose in Bloom* (1876), *Under the Lilacs* (1878), *Jack and Jill* (1880), and *Jo's Boys* (1886). A number of other New England children's authors also wrote domestic stories similar to *Little Women.* Four noteworthy examples are Sarah Chauncy Woolsey's *What Katy Did* (1873), Lucretia Peabody Hale's *The Peterkin Papers* (1880), Margaret Sidney's *Five Little Peppers and How They Grew* (1881), and Sarah Orne Jewett's *Betty Leicester, a Story for Girls* (1890).

At the same time that Alcott was writing *Little Women* in her family home in Concord, Mass., Thomas Bailey Aldrich was at work in the neighboring state of New Hampshire, writing an autobiographical novel about his boyhood in Portsmouth, New Hampshire. Titled *The Story of a Bad Boy,* Aldrich's book came out in 1869 and quickly achieved bestseller status. Like *Little Women,* Aldrich's book won praise for its realistic characters and vivid depiction of New England life. Aldrich's central character struck readers as a real boy, full of mischief and energy. Also like *Little Women, The Story of a Bad Boy* inspired other children's authors to write similar books. Many literary historians credit Aldrich for launching the subgenre of the boys' adventure story, but his achievement in this area was eventually overshadowed by Mark Twain's classic *The Adventures of Tom Sawyer* (1876).

Although Twain wrote *Tom Sawyer* during his Connecticut years, the book cannot be claimed as an example of New England children's literature because its midwestern setting is such an integral part of the story. In fact it can be argued that the publication of *Tom Sawyer* marked the end of New England's dominance in the field of children's literature.

New England authors continued to write children's books during the final quarter of the 19th century, but few of these books became classics. Nevertheless, the many important children's books written in New England before 1900 earn the region its place as a fountainhead of classic American children's literature.

Gillian Avery, *Behold the Child: American Children and Their Books 1621–1922* (1994); Jerry Griswold, *Audacious Kids: Coming of Age in America's Classic Children's Books* (1992); Rosalie V. Halsey, *Forgotten Books of the American Nursery: A History of the Development of the American Story Book* (1911); Virginia Haviland and Margaret N. Coughlan, eds., *Yankee Doodle's Literary Sampler of Prose, Poetry, and Pictures* (1974); Alice M. Jordan, *From Rollo to Tom Sawyer and Other Papers* (1948); Monica Kiefer, *American Children through Their Books* (1948); Anne Scott MacLeod, *A Moral Tale: Children's Fiction and American Culture 1820–1860* (1975); Mark I. West, ed., *Before Oz: Juvenile Fantasy Stories from 19th-Century America* (1989).

Mark I. West

Children's Literature, 1900 to the Present Children's literature had strong origins in New England but gradually became more geographically diverse in terms of both authors and subject matter. By 1900, New England children's literature had ceased to be American children's literature, but continued to be a dominant force in the genre. This is demonstrated by the large number of New England children's authors and illustrators awarded either the Newbery Medal for best children's book of the year or the Caldecott Medal for most distinguished picture book of the year. Furthermore, through the founding in Boston in 1924 of the *Horn Book*, the oldest and most influential children's literature journal in the country, New England writers and illustrators continued to be at the forefront of children's literature.

Two major themes that unify many examples of New England children's literature are the celebration of rural landscapes and the investigation of historical events or figures. Kate Douglas Wiggin's *Rebecca of Sunnybrook Farm* (1903) and Eleanor H. Porter's *Pollyanna* (1913) feature the adventures of independent orphans. Wiggin's spirited protagonist disrupts the calm world of her spinster aunts in Riverboro, Maine, while enchanting the older, wealthy Adam Ladd. Porter's optimistic protagonist, whose favorite word is "glad," brings the power of positive thinking and change to Beldingsville, Vt. Dorothy Canfield Fisher's *Understood Betsy* (1917) reverses this formula when a sheltered and insecure girl arrives at her relatives' farm in Putney, Vt., where she gains self-reliance.

Doll stories that reconstruct childhood from earlier historical periods include Rachel Field's *Hitty, Her First Hundred Years* (1929), in which a Maine doll recounts her adventures while resting in an antique shop, and Carolyn Sherwin Bailey's *Miss Hickory* (1946), which features a stubborn doll recording her life in rural New Hampshire.

Elwyn Brooks (E. B.) White wrote three animal fantasies that are all partly set in New England. White wrote *Charlotte's Web* (1952) on his farm in Blue Hill, Maine, and considered his novel a "hymn to the barn." His lyrical prose reflects careful attention to detail; he consulted reference books to make Charlotte a spider native to the barns of northern New England. Like a New Englander, Charlotte is laconic, but the few words she weaves into her web save Wilbur the pig in this extraordinary story of friendship. A more realistic rendering of a similar situation is Robert Newton Peck's *A Day No Pigs Would Die* (1972), in which a young boy in a Vermont Shaker family in the 1920s has a pet pig; despite winning a ribbon at the Rutland Fair, however, the animal must be slaughtered. White's *Stuart Little* (1945) begins in New York City, but the protagonist follows his quest to the idealized New England village of Ames Crossing, which is described as "the loveliest of all towns" and reflects White's appreciation for rural New England. White's *The Trumpet of the Swan* (1970) is set in Boston, where the mute swan Louis learns to play the trumpet for passengers on the swan boats.

Robert McCloskey's charming picture

book *Make Way for Ducklings* (1941), with recognizable bird's-eye views of Boston, is closely associated with the Boston Public Gardens where the Mallard family rears its young. McCloskey's humorous illustrations of the ducklings are now immortalized as bronze statues there. McCloskey moved with his family to an island on the Maine coast, where he created a series of stunningly beautiful picture books, including *Blueberries for Sal* (1948), *One Morning in Maine* (1952), and *Time of Wonder* (1957), that celebrate the beauty of that rugged landscape.

New England folklore appears in McCloskey's *Burt Dow, Deep-Water Man* (1963), the tall tale of a fisherman swallowed by a whale who escapes by his painting skills. Stephen Vincent Benét's frequently anthologized short story "The Devil and Daniel Webster" (1939) remains a popular tall tale that celebrates a New Englander's ability to argue a hard bargain. Chris Van Allsburg's picture book *The Stranger* (1986) is a mysterious story of the arrival of a stranger who can stop the seasons on a small New England farm.

Barbara Cooney's picture books evoke a deep appreciation for the New England seacoast. The autobiographical *Miss Rumphius* (1982) features an independent protagonist who travels the world and returns to her house overlooking the sea in Damariscotta, Maine; she then decides to plant five bushels of lupine seeds around the state to make the world more beautiful. Cooney's *Island Boy* (1988) is based on the historical account of Matthais Tibbetts, who grew up with his family on a remote Maine island. Her illustrations for Donald Hall's *Ox-Cart Man* (1979) provide an appropriate folk art counterpart to Hall's narrative of life on a New Hampshire farm in 1832. Hall has written several picture books, including *Old Home Day* (1996), which traces the development of Blackwater Pond, N.H., from the Ice Age to the present, and *The Milkman's Boy* (1997), which is based on his family's dairy business during the early 1900s.

While Robert Frost did not write specifically for children, his poetry is widely used in schools and a selection appears in Hall's *The Oxford Book of Children's Verse in America* (1985). Other significant children's poets include Laura E. Richards, who is considered to be one of the best writers of American nonsense. *Tirra Lirra: Rhymes Old and New* (1932) is the best of her collections. Boston's David McCord published 10 volumes of children's verse, beginning with *Far and Few: Rhymes of the Never Was and Always Is* (1952), and is best known for his clever wordplay.

Humorous verse is also at the heart of Dr. Seuss's first picture book, *And to Think I Saw it on Mulberry Street* (1937). Theodor Seuss

Geisel started using his famous pseudonym for his cartoons while a student at Dartmouth. A college friend in publishing helped him get his first children's book published after 27 other publishers had rejected it. Children's author Oliver Butterworth, also a Dartmouth graduate, wrote *The Enormous Egg* (1956), which recounts the misadventures that occur when an egg on a chicken farm in Freedom, N.H., hatches a baby triceratops.

The author-illustrator Robert Lawson provides cockeyed versions of American history in *Ben and Me* (1939), in which the career of Benjamin Franklin is recounted by the inventor's trusty confidant, the aptly named mouse Amos, and in *Mr. Revere and I* (1953), in which the famous midnight ride is narrated by Revere's horse. Lawson also wrote and illustrated *Rabbit Hill* (1944) and its sequel, *The Tough Winter* (1954), which are animal fables that explore the vicinity around Lawson's home in Westport, Conn., from the animals' points of view.

The most famous children's novel dealing with the American Revolution is Esther Forbes's *Johnny Tremain* (1943), which tells the story of a young crippled silversmith's apprentice who becomes a messenger for key political figures. Forbes's novel is carefully researched; she had previously won the Pulitzer Prize for history for her book *Paul Revere and the World He Lived In* (1942). Forbes's novel reflects the patriotic atmosphere of the World War II period in which it was written, but James Lincoln Collier and Christopher Collier's *My Brother Sam Is Dead* (1974), about a Connecticut family's experiences during Shays's Rebellion, takes a more critical view of patriotism, reflecting the moral ambiguity of the Vietnam War era.

Jean Fritz is one of the writers most responsible for revising the manner in which history is written for children. Using accurate and sometimes unflattering details, Fritz has artfully introduced new historicism to biographies for children in her series of "question biographies" such as *And Then What Happened, Paul Revere?* (1973) and *Will You Sign Here, John Hancock?* (1976). Fritz's accurate use of historical documents has helped put an end to idealized and distorted American history for children.

The growing importance of women's history is reflected in works such as Joan W. Blos's *A Gathering of Days: A New England Girl's Journal, 1830–32* (1979), which is the story of a young girl on a farm in Meredith, N.H. Elizabeth George Speare's *The Witch of Blackbird Pond* (1958) is the tale of a lively girl raised in Barbados who cannot adjust to the Puritanism of the Connecticut Colony in 1687 and is accused of being a witch. Patricia

Clapp's *I'm Deborah Sampson: A Soldier in the War of the Revolution* (1977) is based on the account of a woman who disguised herself as a man in order to fight in the Revolutionary War. Cornelia Meigs's *Invincible Louisa* (1933) remains a popular biography of Louisa May Alcott, the author of *Little Women* (1868–69). Katherine Paterson's *Lyddie* (1991) is an unflinching examination of the harsh labor conditions of female mill workers in Lowell, Mass., during the 1840s. A useful companion to *Lyddie* is David Macaulay's *Mill* (1983), which details the construction and technology necessary for running a cotton-spinning mill in New England in 1810.

While famous New Englanders are featured in children's books, so are less familiar individuals. Jacqueline Briggs Martin's *Snowflake Bentley* (1998), illustrated by Mary Azarian, is a picture book celebrating Wilson Bentley, of Jericho, Vt., who photographed snowflakes for 50 years. Elizabeth Yates's *Amos Fortune, Free Man* (1950) records the struggles of an African prince who was captured in 1725 and brought as a slave to America where he earned his freedom and became a tanner in Jaffrey, N.H. Virginia Hamilton's *Anthony Burns: The Defeat and Triumph of a Fugitive Slave* (1988) deals with the 1854 court case of the African American put on trial in Boston under the Fugitive Slave Act of 1850. Elizabeth George Speare's *Calico Captive* (1957) is based on the journal of Susanna Johnson, published in 1807, which records her capture by Native Americans in 1754 and her journey from New Hampshire to Montreal, Canada, during the French and Indian War. While visiting the public library of Milo, Maine, Speare read in a local history of the town the account of 14-year-old Theophilus Sargent, who survived the summer of 1802 in the local woods with the help of members of the Penobscot tribe. Speare developed this into the survival story *The Sign of the Beaver* (1983). Jean Lee Latham's *Carry On, Mr. Bowditch* (1955) is the remarkable history of the self-educated seaman who made major contributions to navigation.

In addition to historical fiction, many family stories occur in more recent times. Eleanor Estes's three-book series featuring the Moffat family of Cranbury, Conn., during World War I began with *The Moffats* (1941). She also wrote *Ginger Pye* (1951), which features a family's search for a lost dog. Lois Lowry's Anastasia series began with *Anastasia Krupnik* (1979) and features the adventures of two precocious children living in Cambridge, Mass. Helen Dore Boylston's *Sue Barton, Student Nurse* (1936) began a series based on the author's training at Massachusetts General Hospital that is still attracting readers. The most

popular series set in New England is Ann M. Martin's "Baby-Sitters Club," which began with *Kristy's Great Idea* (1986) and features a group of preteen girls who run a baby-sitting service in Stoneybrook, Conn.

Adolescent literature is a post–World War II development. Like his character Holden Caulfield, who longed to escape the phoniness of New York City for the isolation of a cabin in Vermont, J. D. Salinger has lived in relative seclusion in Cornish, N.H., since 1953 after publishing *The Catcher in the Rye* (1951), which is considered one of the key novels of adolescent literature. Thornton Wilder's play *Our Town* (1938), the drama of adolescent love and loss set in Grovers Corner, N.H., remains a popular production in high schools. Robert Cormier's grim and violent fiction has helped establish new realism in adolescent literature with novels such as *The Chocolate War* (1974) and *I Am the Cheese* (1977), set in the fictional New England city of Monument, loosely based on Cormier's hometown of Leominster, Mass.

Given the concentration of children's authors and illustrators living in New England, as well as the region's rich history, children's and adolescent books featuring New England geography or characters remain an important part of children's literature.

Gillian Avery, *Behold the Child: American Children and Their Books 1621–1922* (1994); Barbara Bader, *American Picturebooks from Noah's Ark to the Beast Within* (1976); Jerry Griswold, *Audacious Kids: Coming of Age in America's Classic Children's Books* (1992); Alethea K. Helbig and Agnes Regan Perkins, *Dictionary of American Children's Fiction, 1859–1959* (1985); Helbig and Perkins, *Dictionary of American Children's Fiction, 1960–1984* (1986); Mary H. Lystad, *From Dr. Mather to Dr. Seuss: 200 Years of American Books for Children* (1980); Anne Scott MacLeod, *American Childhood: Essays on Children's Literature of the 19th and 20th Centuries* (1994); Elfrieda McCauley, *Reading for Young People: New England* (1985).

Jan Susina

Contemporary Literature

Contemporary literature generally refers to writing after 1945 and is often divided into modernist and postmodernist eras. In literature, modernism is known for its experiments in form, allied with a self-consciousness that foregrounds the artistic process, and for its challenge to national, middle-class taste and cultural authority. Postmodernism emerged in the 1970s. It shares with modernism self-consciousness and cultural fragmentation, but it challenges the capacity of literature or any artistic form to represent stable identities or cultural forms. New England writers after 1945 participated in national literary trends, but they also continued regional affinities for styles and themes harking back to the Transcendentalists and to

the high modernism of the 1920s and 1930s of T. S. Eliot and Wallace Stevens rather than more radical experimentation of later decades. Compared with writers from other regions, New Englanders are less occupied by themes of race and ethnicity and perhaps more so by philosophical and formal literary trends and by issues of gender and sexuality. Their literature is distinctive for the way the authors transform traditional Romantic themes into postmodern ones, such as Robert Lowell's examination of the fragmentation of his New England identity and intellectual heritage in *Life Studies* (1959) and *For the Union Dead* (1964). The postmodern suspicion of all truths save the particular and the local is manifested in contemporary New England writing, but with a simultaneous if contradictory affirmation of the Emersonian belief that the individual and the particular represent the universal. This paradox of competing claims for individualism distinguishes markedly postmodern, but not all contemporary, New England literature.

A distinctive feature of contemporary New England writing after World War II is the influence of the writers of the Beat generation. In his fiction, poetry, and essays the canonical Beat author Jack Kerouac eulogizes prewar New England and his hometown, Lowell, Mass. Anticipating national literary trends, his stories challenge the centrality of white masculine identity with the postwar rise of women and people of color. His innovative writing was characterized by uncensored confession, spontaneous composition, and the breakdown of distinctions among forms of writing, such as poetry, prose, fiction, and autobiography. Kerouac's *On the Road* (1957) is a postwar American tribute to the individual spiritual quest reminiscent of Ralph Waldo Emerson, Herman Melville, and Henry David Thoreau.

Other Beat writers also cultivated New England backgrounds and literary legacies in producing early postmodern texts. The work of John Clellon Holmes, author of the first Beat novel *Go* (1952), is modified by his self-consciousness of his Anglo-Saxon New England connections. Elaborating states of madness in his poetry, John Wieners sees this confessional, autobiographical work as a map of regional manners and occasions. The title of his highly personal collection reads as if it is a government document: *Cultural Affairs in Boston: Poetry and Prose 1956–1985* (1988). Legendary hipster Herbert Huncke of Greenfield, Mass., who gave the term "beat" to Kerouac and morphine to William S. Burroughs, adds to transcendental-confessional Beat discourse with sketches of the drug underworld in *The Evening Sky Turned Crimson* (1980) and his

Carolyn Chute with her husband, Michael, ca. 1985

autobiography of addiction, *Guilty of Everything* (1990).

Associated with Black Mountain College, but also connected to the Beats, poet Robert Creeley retains elements of his New England upbringing in his economy of speech and Puritan rigor. The poems in Creeley's volume *Words* (1967) confront strictures of his New England background, depicting a struggle between the self-conscious mind and the instinctual body. With Allen Ginsberg, Creeley edited the historic seventh issue of *Black Mountain Review* (1957), which published Beat and Black Mountain poets, joining two influential postwar literary movements formed by and around New England writers.

The preeminent New England poet linking the Beats to Black Mountain is Charles Olson, who influenced Wieners (*A Letter to Charles Olson* [1968]) and had a close friendship with Creeley. Olson memorialized his region and home, the North Shore fishing town of Gloucester, Mass., in *The Maximus Poems*, which he dedicated to Creeley. The first poem, "I, Maximus of Gloucester, to You," fuses New England to the poet's voice and perception as it projects the social, historical, and geographical presence of the town. Olson's regional commitments are also evident in *Call Me Ishmael*, his famous work on Melville and *Moby-Dick*, a fervently personal, unorthodox literary study. Olson was the first writer to use the term *postmodern*. Nonetheless recalling New England Transcendentalism, his poetics emphasize action over description, the dispersal of distinctions between the ego and the natural world, and the belief in "language as the act of the instant."

In his initial, modernist poetry collections *Lord Weary's Castle* (1946) and *The Mills of the Kavanaughs* (1951), Robert Lowell confronted the social, moral, and spiritual decline of his New England background and Episcopalian Brahmin ancestry. With his breakthrough collection of confessional poems, *Life Studies* (1959), Lowell entered the Beat worldview, loosening his verse with personal emotion and unlocked forms. Lowell influenced two other important confessional poets, New Englanders Sylvia Plath and Anne Sexton, who studied with him in his celebrated poetry workshop at Boston University during the 1960s. Sexton's *To Bedlam and Part Way Back* (1960) was written under Lowell's encouragement. Her Pulitzer Prize–winning volume *To Live or Die* (1966) and Plath's posthumous volume *Ariel* (1965) typify confessional poetry's display of the individual conscious and unconscious mind. This literature fits with the postmodern preference for the local over the universal but also exemplifies traditional regional thought, the way "the inmost . . . becomes the outmost," as Emerson proclaimed in "Self-Reliance." Other contemporary New England poets, such as Donald Hall, Maxine Kumin, Stanley Kunitz, and John Ciardi, are formalists who blend modernist themes with new poetic styles and new ways of presenting their lives and consciousness as New England literary subjects.

The Beat and confessional emphasis on personal literary vision and voice was embraced in the countercultural postmodern 1960s. This era's anti-establishment individuality is a New England tradition: Emerson's charge to "do your thing. . . . Your conformity

explains nothing" and Thoreau's counsel to simplify and to resist civil government foreshadowed the ethics of the hippies, communards, and politicos of postmodern U.S. culture. Yippie Abbie Hoffman's influential and acclaimed *Revolution for the Hell of It* (1968) and *Steal This Book* (1971) shape essentially Romantic styles of individuality and political and moral dissent through sixties Marxist ideologies. Raymond Mungo, of French Canadian New England descent like Kerouac, memorializes New Left media from his gay hippie perspective in *Famous Long Ago: My Life and Hard Times with Liberation News Service* (1970). His *Total Loss Farm* (1971) relates affairs on a Vermont commune. The ironic title hails and recycles this book's antecedents in Brook Farm, the experimental collective in Concord, Mass., that Nathaniel Hawthorne explored in *The Blithedale Romance* (1852).

Another distinguishing feature of contemporary New England literature is the continuing focus on the New England town in the domestic novel produced by both popular and serious contemporary regional writers. New Hampshire native Grace Metalious exposed the bigotry, hypocrisy, and narrow-mindedness of a puritanical New England small town in her 1956 bestseller *Peyton Place*. Her tale is the dark, albeit sensationalized side of the decorous, repressed accounts of suburban wars between the sexes in the New England fiction of John Updike, especially in *Couples* (1968), and in the work of John Cheever in *The Wapshot Chronicle* (1957) and his acclaimed short stories. Updike's and Cheever's refined, highly finished tales of discontented, affluent suburbanites epitomize high-culture art and angstridden Hawthornian Puritanism. Succeeding women writers combine both the popular- and high-culture approaches of their predecessors in their versions of the regional domestic novel. Carolyn Chute's *The Beans of Egypt, Maine* (1985) depicts rural poverty, incest, and family violence, while Sue Miller's *The Good Mother* (1986) focuses on the wrenching dilemmas of a single mother in Cambridge, Mass., during the sexual revolution.

As the demographics of New England have shifted away from the Yankee, the location of the Yankee New England town has drifted northward in fiction. A number of writers have blended mythic images of upcountry New England with the hardscrabble realities of lives confronted by a changing society. Ernest Hebert's trilogy of novels set in and around Keene, N.H., probe the dislocation of identities for natives and newcomers alike. Russell Banks explores with chilling beauty the psychological costs, particularly for men, in the new tourist economy of northern New England in *Trailerpark* (1981) and *Affliction*

(1989). Howard Frank Mosher has made Vermont's Northeast Kingdom the setting for mythic characters and stories embodying the deep appeal of the landscape.

The presentation of the white female, proto-feminist subject in a confessional style in New England women's postwar writing coincides with the growing women's movement of the postmodern mid-1960s. For example, poet Elizabeth Bishop's last books, *Questions of Travel* (1965) and *Geography III* (1976); Adrienne Rich's landmark poems of women's and lesbian liberation in *Snapshots of a Daughter-in-Law* (1963) and *Diving into the Wreck* (1973); and May Sarton's novel about a lesbian artist, *Mrs. Stevens Hears the Mermaids Singing* (1965), emphasize gender and sexual orientation, establishing New England in the advent of gay and lesbian literature. Born and raised in Massachusetts, Paul Monette is an important post-Stonewall writer whose poetry and fiction, memoir and autobiography depict the gay male subject and gay liberation; his novel *Afterlife* (1990) amplifies his historical account in *Borrowed Time: An AIDS Memoir* (1988). Monette's narratives of affluent gay life in suburban Los Angeles expand on Updike's stories of prosperous New England enclaves and exalt homoerotic desires repressed in Cheever. The use of the memoir as an exemplary or cautionary tale in gay and feminist literature reflects an important regional tendency also found in the writing of John Preston.

New England's contemporary writers also use a variety of popular forms to present regional themes and places. One of the most famous is Stephen King, whose science fiction and horror stories are often deeply based in the region's history. Mystery writers Robert Parker, Dennis Lehane, Brendan DuBois, and Barbara Neely, in two of her "Blanche" books, reveal aspects of New England's ethnic and racial communities ignored by other works.

Susan Cheever, daughter of John Cheever, has produced two memoirs about her family and illustrious New England origins, *Home before Dark* (1984) and *Treetops* (1991). Turning from her work in fiction, Susanna Kaysen recounts in *Girl, Interrupted* (1993) her confinement at McLean, a famous Massachusetts mental hospital. Caroline Knapp's *Drinking: A Love Story* (1996) chronicles the writer's decline into and recovery from alcoholism in Cambridge. Kaysen and Knapp are upper-middle-class white daughters of wealthy families connected to Harvard University; their memoirs, like those of Susan Cheever, confess hidden costs and debits of this privileged New England status in polished prose reminiscent of Cheever and Updike, who, in contrast, tend to veil the painful material these women writers expose. In the emphasis on and evolution of confessional forms into the 21st century, contemporary New England writing expresses its postmodern time and continues to reflect its modernist and American Romantic regional heritage.

Henry Abelove, ed., *The Lesbian and Gay Studies Reader* (1993); John Barth, "The Literature of Replenishment," in *The Friday Book: Essays and Other Nonfiction* (1984); Hal Foster, ed., *The Anti-Aesthetic: Essays on Postmodern Culture* (1983); Phillip Brian Harper, *Framing the Margins: The Social Logic of Postmodern Culture* (1994); Ihab Hassan, *The Postmodern Turn* (1987); Linda Hutcheon, *A Poetics of Postmodernism: History, Theory, Fiction* (1988); Linda Nicholson, ed., *Feminism/Postmodernism* (1990); Robert von Hallberg, *American Poetry and Culture, 1945–1980* (1985).

Ronna C. Johnson

cummings, e. e. (1894–1962) Poet, painter, novelist, and playwright. Edward Estlin Cummings was born in Cambridge, Mass., the son of the Reverend Edward Cummings, a Harvard lecturer and Unitarian minister (and a talented artist, photographer, and actor), and Rebecca Haswell Clarke Cummings. He attended public schools and later enrolled at Harvard University, earning an A.B. (1915) and an M.A. in English and classical studies (1916). A few months after his graduation, cummings went to serve as a volunteer ambulance driver in France, where he was later interned on suspicion of treason for a minor military offense. After the war he returned to France to study art in Paris. By the time he returned to the United States in 1924, he had become celebrated for both *The Enormous Room* (1922), an autobiographical novel based on his internment, and his first book of poems, *Tulips and Chimneys* (1923). During the next 40 years cummings would publish 20 collections of poems and receive many honors and awards, including the Shelley Memorial Award, the Bollingen Prize, and a National Book Award Special Citation. His reputation as a major poet was firmly established by the time of his death at North Conway, N.H.

As a poet cummings thumbed his nose at New England tradition while remaining very much a part of it. The spiritual descendant of Ralph Waldo Emerson, cummings inherited the mantle of New England Transcendentalism. Like that of Emerson, his work is marked by a view of nature as a state of becoming rather than of being and by a belief that through imagination the individual can see beyond the confines of the familiar, the material, and the accepted. His poems celebrate the profoundly moral nature of the individual, the "I" and the "you," while condemning through ridicule the cruel stupidity of the conventional world of "manunkind," the "mobs" and "gangs" that try to stifle individuality. Also like Emerson, he chose to flout convention by exercising the freedom that has always been a hallmark of the New England mind.

Nowhere can cummings's rejection of convention be seen more clearly than in his poetic style. While his sensibility may have its roots in New England tradition, in style and form his poems reflect the modernist spirit that swept the United States after World War I. In response to this atmosphere of change, cummings developed a distinctly unorthodox poetic style that initially resulted in unfavorable critical response and skepticism. His typographical and stylistic innovations—in capitalization and punctuation, grammar and syntax, spelling and word coinages (for example, "anyone lived in a pretty how town" and "pity this poor monster,manunkind")—were not merely assertions of individuality or idiosyncratic pranks. They were, rather, cummings's way of altering perception by altering language—transforming the world by transforming the word—and in so doing, confronting reality with a new sense of surprise and wonder.

Cummings's irrepressible style and vision mark him as a true New England original and a figure whose experimentation influenced the evolution of free verse style in American poetry.

e. e. cummings, *Complete Poems, 1913–1962* (1972); Norman Friedman, ed., *e. e. cummings: A Collection of Critical Essays* (1972); Richard S. Kennedy, *Dreams in the Mirror: A Biography of e. e. cummings* (1980); Guy L. Rotella, ed., *Critical Essays on e. e. cummings* (1984).

David Bradt

Dialect Writing Dialect writing, the imitation of the patterns of vernacular speech in print, often for humorous or satirical effect, reached its high-water mark in New England in the mid-19th century. Although dialect writing has declined in popularity since then, a respectable company of 20th-century writers have continued to draw on this tradition.

Like their counterparts in other parts of the country, such as the frontier humorists of the old Southwest, the early dialect writers in New England reflected an emerging sense of nationalism, a delight in things local and American. As James Russell Lowell wrote in his introduction to the second series of the *Biglow Papers* (1867), "our popular idiom is racy with life and vigor and originality, buxsome . . . to our new occasions." Although the bizarre spellings, eccentric characters, and low comedy favored by the dialect writers often have not weathered well with age, the reception of their works at the time is of continuing interest, and many pieces have genuine merit as comic literature.

Among the leading dialect writers is Seba Smith, who in 1830 was casting about for ways to make his newspaper, the *Portland Courier*, profitable, when he hit upon the idea of publishing humorous sketches by "Major Jack Downing," a down east Yankee who combined rustic speech with cracker-barrel wit. Received well in Maine and beyond, the Downing letters were collected in several books. Thomas Chandler Halliburton, a Canadian by birth, achieved wide popularity through the creation of Sam Slick, an archetypal Yankee trader of clocks, tinware, and notions, whose shrewdness was displayed in a series of books and sketches published between 1836 and 1860. James Russell Lowell, strongly opposed to the war with Mexico in 1846 and its expansion of slavery, created Hosea Biglow, an illiterate bumpkin who was nonetheless capable of satirizing U.S. foreign policy in homespun verse:

> Them thet rule us, them slave-traders,
>   Haint they cut a thunderin' swarth
> (Helped by Yankee renegaders)
>   Thru the vartu o' the North!
> We begin to think it's nater
>   To take the sarse an' not be riled;—
> Who'd expect to see a tater
>   All on eend ar bein' biled?

Biglow's musings were published first in the *Boston Courier* and then collectively as the *Biglow Papers* (1848). Lowell resurrected his character to support the northern cause in the Civil War in a new series of verses. Other dialect writers, immensely popular in their day, include Frances M. Whitcher, Benjamin P. Shillaber, Charles Farrar Brown ("Artemas Ward"), and Henry Wheeler Shaw ("Josh Billings").

Although many 19th-century writers used dialect for broad comic effect, a few relied on the vernacular to achieve other literary ends. Harriet Beecher Stowe, for example, drew upon a knowledge of New England speechways in her pursuit of a realistic delineation of life and character. Works such as *The Minister's Wooing* (1859), *The Pearl of Orr's Island* (1862), *Oldtown Folks* (1869), and *Poganuc People* (1878) reflect Stowe's professed attempt to get at "the whole spirit and body of New England," and one means to that end was representing the speech of ordinary people. Perhaps most successful in using dialect as an element of literary art was Sarah Orne Jewett. In her sketches and stories of Maine life, Jewett created characters who are more than simply quaint or representative types. In Jewett's hands, dialect is seldom pursued for its own sake but unobtrusively woven into the larger purposes of the narrative. In numerous magazine stories and published collections, from *Deephaven* (1877) to *The Country of the Pointed Firs* (1896), Jewett achieved a depth and precision that few dialect writers before or since have matched.

While the high tide of dialect writing receded with the onset of the 20th century, one can point to traces of its influence in writers as diverse as Robert Frost, Thornton Wilder, and John Cheever. Frost in particular had a great gift for depicting the common speech of New England. Especially in his dramatic monologues and narratives, Frost took ordinary subjects and events and transformed them through the medium of poetry. In his hands, a vernacular word or phrase—such as "Good fences make good neighbors," from "Mending Wall"—was more than simply a window on a region: it pointed toward universal themes as well.

Contemporary writers have continued to follow both the comic and realistic traditions of dialect writing. John Gould, for example, has used dialect for humorous effect in numerous books of personal essays and reminiscences. *Maine Lingo: Boiled Owls, Billdads, and Wazzats* (1975) distills Gould's lifelong fascination with the speech of his native state. Native materials are put to different uses in Carolyn Chute's novel *The Beans of Egypt, Maine* (1985), in which she has given a voice to the victims of working-class poverty. The ever-changing stream of dialect that continues to flow through New England provides rich material for regional writers, even in an age of homogeneity.

Walter Blair, *Native American Humor* (1960 [1937]); Josephine Donovan, *New England Local Color Literature: A Woman's Tradition* (1983); John C. Kemp, *Robert Frost and New England: The Poet as Regionalist* (1979); Cameron C. Nickels, *New England Humor: From the Revolutionary War to the Civil War* (1993).

Russell L. Martin III

Dickinson, Emily (1830–86) Poet.

In our time, Emily Elizabeth Dickinson is acknowledged as one of America's greatest poets for her brilliant, enigmatic investigations of love, death, madness, nature, and eternity. In her own time, she was known as Squire Dickinson's eccentric daughter, a recluse who sent cakes, flowers, and odd little verses to friends and neighbors and who dispatched puzzling letters and verses to eminent men. Both representations are accurate. Dickinson claimed that she saw the world "New Englandly," and indeed her New England Puritan heritage is attested to by the lifelong quarrel with God she carried on in her poems. But her life and her work were also very much influenced by the culture and opportunities of prosperous, progressive, small-town New England life.

Emily Dickinson was born into a prominent Amherst, Mass., family, whose comfortable circumstances allowed her to remain at home. Her grandfather, father, and brother were attorneys and civic activists. Dickinson's paternal grandfather was one of the founders of Amherst College, and her father, Edward, served as a U.S. representative from 1853 to 1855. Dickinson was educated at the local school, at Amherst Academy, and at nearby Mount Holyoke Female Seminary. But like her mother Emily (Norcross) Dickinson and sister Lavinia, the poet was a domestic woman. Although she rarely traveled far from the family's Main Street home, Dickinson was surprisingly well connected to the publishing community through her family and social network. Influential writers and editors such as Samuel Bowles, Josiah G. Holland, and Helen Hunt Jackson (also born in Amherst in 1830) visited Emily Dickinson's home and corresponded with her. In 1862 Dickinson initiated an epistolary relationship that was of major importance to her with the Massachusetts writer, clergyman, and social activist Thomas Wentworth Higginson. Although Higginson advised her to "delay to publish" her unconventional poems, it was most likely her own reticence combined with prevailing notions of proper female behavior that encouraged Dickinson to keep her poetry private. Only 10 poems are known to have been published during her lifetime.

Despite her isolation from the professional literary world, Dickinson wrote copiously. Poems inscribed on such mundane household materials as a baking-chocolate wrapper and the back of a set of instructions for cleaning kerosene lamps indicate that Dickinson integrated her poetry into her domestic routine. After Dickinson's death, her sister Lavinia found more than 1,700 of her poems and determined to have them published. *Poems*, edited by Higginson and Mabel Loomis Todd, appeared in 1890, followed by *Poems: Second Series* (1891), and *Poems: Third Series* (1896). Reviews were either bemused or enthusiastic, but when additional poems appeared in editions between 1914 and 1945, Dickinson's place in the canon of American literature was assured. Dickinson's letters, edited by Thomas H. Johnson and Theodora Ward in 1958, are significant for their insight into the poet's intense friendships, meditations on the nature of art and eternity, and intensely poetic prose style.

When Emily Dickinson died in 1886 at the age of 55, her death certificate, in the space for occupation, read "At Home." The imaginative power of her poetry, contrasted with her seemingly uneventful everyday existence, has led to much scholarly speculation about her inner life. Dickinson herself assessed that life in a characteristically playful and enigmatic way when she wrote,

> For Occupation—This—
> The spreading wide my narrow Hands
> To gather Paradise—.

Joanne Dobson, *Dickinson and the Strategies of Reticence: The Woman Writer in 19th-Century America* (1989); R. W. Franklin, ed., *The Manuscript Books of Emily Dickinson*, 2 vols. (1981); Thomas H. Johnson, ed., *The Complete Poems of Emily Dickinson* (1955); Richard B. Sewall, *The Life of Emily Dickinson* (1974); Robert Weisbuch, *Emily Dickinson's Poetry* (1975).

Joanne Dobson

Didactic and Instructional Literature

New England didactic and instructional literature has shaped an understanding of regional identity and a historical tendency to see its culture as a stand-in for national identity. More specifically, the genre's depictions of gendered social roles; childhood, domestic, and school-centered educational practices; and regional histories have been crucial to national community building. This functional and often moral literature may have reached the zenith of its social power during the 19th century, when mass-market publishing gained New England writers wider access to middle-class readers, but its national influence is still evident today. New England writers have taken the lead in a number of reform movements, and part of the literary image of the region remains that of the author/activist who harkens back to a long tradition of saints, rebels, and reformers.

Contemporary divisions between "aesthetic" and "didactic" elements in literature are largely inventions of the modern era. Nineteenth-century audiences would have been less likely to distinguish between the kinds of literary texts that taught life lessons with their plots and characterizations and texts that are now considered purely functional or instructional, such as schoolbooks or guides to home decorating. From the perspective of earlier audiences and literary arbiters, the instructive force of Susanna Rowson's early-19th-century prefaces in *Charlotte Temple* (1808, 1813, 1815) and, conversely, 1850s critics' condemnation of Herman Melville's *Pierre* on moral grounds, clearly descend from the Puritan insistence that all writing and reading be instructive. Similarly, we can accept the ease with which many pre-20th-century writers moved between what is today considered "juvenile literature" and serious or adult literature. The "literary" elements in texts such as Lydia Sigourney's *Letters to My Pupils* (1856), which blends personal reminiscence with tractlike instruction, are more obvious, as are the pedagogical impulses in novels such as Catharine Maria Sedgwick's *The Boy of Mount Rhigi*

(1848), which integrates valuable lessons on being kind to the less fortunate with pictures of idealized republican village life.

The interplay between men's and women's overtly instructional printed texts further reveals how instructional literature can help "make" culture. Sarah Josepha Hale's support for women's education in myriad *Godey's Lady's Book* articles during her multidecade reign as editor actually built upon arguments made nearly a century earlier by Dr. Benjamin Rush in his *Thoughts upon Female Education* (1787), as well as complementary ones being circulated in Hale's own era by William Russell in *The Education of Females* (1843). Similarly, published booklets describing courses at Catharine Beecher's Hartford Seminary insisted on the school's ties to a masculine New England scholarly rigor associated with men's colleges such as Harvard and Yale. But they also drew upon a tradition of printed justification for distinctive women's curricula in their own educational institutions, such as Susanna Rowson's *A Present for Young Ladies; Containing Poems, Dialogues, Addresses, &c. as Recited by the Pupils of Mrs. Rowson's Academy at the Annual Exhibitions* (1811).

A related line of influence is traceable in the writing associated with New Englanders' commitment to literacy development at home. Puritan school alphabet books, Webster's blueback speller, and his equally influential dictionary all exemplify a recurring pattern of regional school teaching materials becoming national, partly because of the sophisticated production and transportation networks that developed in the Northeast when the U.S. publishing industry shifted from a local to a national model beginning at the turn of the 19th century. Another important way that publishers, booksellers, and writers contributed to the making of culture was in the multitude of books marketed for the much smaller home-based "dame" schools, run by women for young children, and for individual mothers to teach their children to read while impressing upon them the gendered ideology of middle-class social relations. These texts appeared at first in the form of straight reprints (often pirated editions) of English books by Maria Edgeworth, Hannah More, and Anna Barbauld. But they were quickly transformed—via strategies ranging from simply adding illustrations to making extensive changes to the printed text—to appeal to the distinctive New England audience. Soon, Lydia Maria Child and others (Sigourney and Sedgwick, for example) were producing original publications for domestic teaching, frequently idealizing the New England–style home and village as representative of what America should be. Meanwhile, specific homemaking directions

were also widely circulated by these busy New England writers, as in Child's *The Frugal Housewife* (1829).

If New England's own brand of practical domesticity has been repeatedly represented in instructional packages for the nation, so too New Englanders have eagerly turned themselves into traveling representatives of their culture, often writing didactic texts about the very process of teaching others the values of the region. Along those lines, Catharine Beecher's portrayal in *Educational Reminiscences* (1874) of her famous family's migration to the West and her establishment of a women's seminary in Cincinnati echoes Puritan historians' depictions of their righteous creation of New England and thereby indirectly justifies continued westward expansion of her regional heritage, both literally and symbolically. Similarly, stories, satires, and poems in *The Semicolon* (1845), a Cincinnati-published anthology of contributions to the literary club in which the Beechers were all active members, frequently depict the pervasive influence of New England on the West. For instance, one didactic tale about an Ohio rose garden planted with seeds carried from a New England home equates the resulting hearty-yet-lovely flowers with transplanted morality and civic virtue.

Formal histories written by New Englanders have also created links between regional and national culture. Key figures include John Gorham Palfrey (*History of New England*, 1858) and George Bancroft, whose national history, published over several decades through the mid- to late 1800s, was the most popular of the 19th century. Despite notable differences, these histories share the strategy of building a powerful mythology grounded in the New England colonial experience. These pioneering male historians marketed individual New Englanders as idealized role models. Women writers enthusiastically used this technique as well. Popular New England autobiographers included Catharine Sedgwick and Lucy Larcom. Sedgwick demonstrated a sense of New England noblesse oblige in her 1853 autobiography, purportedly written with her niece as the primary audience. Larcom's class identity was less stable, but she shared Sedgwick's confidence in the regional aspects of her identity and its potential social force, especially for young girls.

Along with autobiographies, the region's women writers circulated instructive personal histories of others. Biographies of famous leaders from the past (such as Benjamin Franklin) were anthologized along with depictions of less illustrious figures whose New England–style virtues were offered for readers to emulate. For instance, in *Examples of Life* and Death (1851), Sigourney included portraits of Ann Elliot and Mary Lloyd, early New England settlers whose work as maternal teachers she touted as models. Recent print biographies of New England women such as Carolyn Karcher's *The First Woman in the Republic: A Cultural Biography of Lydia Maria Child* (1994) and Joan Hedrick's *Harriet Beecher Stowe: A Life* (1994) have reemphasized a continuing interest in the region's notable individuals. These new texts have in common with their New England ancestors a conviction that one way to understand the nation is through personal histories set in the region's culture.

Many of New England's best-known teaching texts caused complex controversies during their time. For instance, the calm arguments of Child's *An Appeal in Favor of That Class of Americans Called Africans* (1836) exacted a high price from its author, including the failure of her children's magazine and the loss of her membership in the Boston Athenaeum.

Some of the African American New England women who wrote instructional texts about 19th-century experiences reached relatively limited audiences in their day but can nonetheless be crucial to our understanding of the interplay among regional, class, and racial identities in this literature. Susie King Taylor, a longtime Boston resident, self-published a memoir in 1902 (*A Black Woman's Civil War Memoirs)*, to teach northerners about her life as an African American teacher in Savannah, Ga., and a nurse for "colored" troops during the war. Decades earlier, as editor Lois Brown notes, Susan Paul had tried to persuade the American Sunday School Union to publish *Memoir of James Jackson,* about a young student in her Boston school. When they rejected her manuscript, she was unable to reach the broad national audience to which she had aspired, but supporters of the Massachusetts antislavery movement did disseminate the biography through their more specialized venues. Frances E. W. Harper, meanwhile, wrote didactic works such as her postbellum serial novels (for example, *Minnie's Sacrifice* and *Trial and Triumph*) for middle-class African American readers but reached even broader, mixed audiences with her poetry and speeches.

The tradition of didactic and instructional literature has had a lingering effect on regional and national culture, especially as seen in seemingly homogenized contemporary versions such as Martha Stewart's guides to refined homemaking, the popular television series *This Old House,* Julia Child's cookbooks, and high school American literature anthologies emphasizing simplified versions of New England history over the roles of other regions in creating national culture.

Gillian Avery, *Behold the Child: American Children and Their Books, 1621–1922* (1994); Sacvan Bercovitch and Myra Jehlen, eds., *Ideology and Classic American Literature* (1986); Richard H. Brodhead, *Cultures of Letters: Scenes of Reading and Writing in 19th-Century America* (1993); Cathy N. Davidson, *Revolution and the Word: The Rise of the Novel in America* (1986); Mary Kelley, ed., *The Power of Her Sympathy: The Autobiography and Journal of Catharine Maria Sedgwick* (1993); Linda Kerber, "Separate Spheres, Female Worlds, Woman's Place: The Rhetoric of Woman's History," *Journal of American History* 75 (1988); Michael Kraus, *The Writing of American History* (1953); Lucy Larcom, *A New England Girlhood: Outlined from Memory* (1986 [1889]).

Sarah Robbins

Early National Identity

When J. Hector St. John de Crèvecoeur, author of *Letters from an American Farmer* (1782), asked, "What is an American?" he was posing a question that was at the center of public and private debates about the nature of the newly formed United States. Crèvecoeur and his New England contemporaries recognized that concepts of national identity depended on international distinctions but also on local and regional ideas. His question reflects a moment of national self-examination during a period that evoked not only political and cultural crises but a crisis of authority as well. Although the United States had been established as a republic, its citizens clung to democratic ideals as guideposts for the new republic. Federalism, the new political order, was a government system in which power was centrally located; yet in the early years of the new nation, democratic ideals were realized to the extent that people from all political factions, from all classes, and of both sexes sought inclusion in the construction of the new national identity.

In a country that demanded that "American" be contrasted to all things English and European and be exclusively aligned with the United States, the development of an American literature was a primary force in the construction of national identity, and no region so strongly influenced this body of literature as did New England. During the revolutionary era, Mercy Otis Warren produced several plays that supported the American cause. *The Group* (1775), for instance, argued for the moral righteousness of the colonial soldiers, who often were poor and bedraggled, against the moral corruptness of the well-supported English soldiers. *The Group* was written in resistance to the Massachusetts Government Act of 1774, which transferred control of major political appointments from local colonists to the king of England. Warren's play emphasized the ability of locals to represent themselves. Warren's plays, like Thomas Paine's series of 13 tracts, *The Crisis* (1776–83), were significant

influences in gaining support for the revolutionary cause.

Royall Tyler, also a playwright and chief justice of the Supreme Court of Vermont (1807–13), recognized that class was an element of identity. Tyler's plays helped to establish the commonplace Yankee character that became a touchstone of mainstream New England identity. Jonathan, a character in Tyler's *The Contrast* (1790), is one of the early portraits of the humble but noble Yankee, a country bumpkin who is depicted as being far superior to hypocritical aristocratic Europeans.

Despite the popularity of such characters, national identity was a site of conflict that was ardently defended and not easily negotiated. The Yankee figure was typically male, often socially inept, and usually outside the main circles of political influence. John Adams, one of the leaders of the Revolution and second president of the United States, was an ardent Federalist who believed in an elite system of representation. When a colleague suggested that men without property should have the right to vote, Adams dissented, arguing that such a decision would "confound all distinctions and prostrate all ranks to one common level." Republicanism itself was a contested idea, even among its supporters. Abigail Adams represented many women when she demanded that her spouse and his colleagues at the Continental Congress "Remember the Ladies" when they were crafting the "new Code of Laws." Her remark reflects an awareness that national identity was inseparable from legal and political questions. As more and more citizens—and individuals who were denied the status of citizen—entered the debate on American identity, the law played a crucial role. The petition, for instance, was a legal instrument that many enslaved African Americans used to seek personal freedom and to expose the inequities of slavery—and of the Constitution, which classified each African American as three-fifths of a person. Such legal maneuverings, often unsuccessful on a personal basis, were powerful means of inserting race into the national debate on identity.

Several New England writers raised the issue of racial inclusiveness in the national consciousness, arguing for truly democratic values in the new republic. As a slave, Phillis Wheatley was unable to express open resistance to slavery and racism. But in poems such as "On Imagination" (1773) and "Liberty and Peace" (1785), she raised the banner of national liberty as emblematic of personal freedom. In "A Short Narrative of My Life" (1768) and other writings, Samson Occom, a Christianized Mohegan, recounted the complexities of being a person of color in a white-dominated society. As a missionary to other Native

Americans, Occom both acculturated native people to Christian and western values and at the same time resisted the erasure of Native Americans from the national consciousness.

If Occom was a negotiator of dual cultures, Lydia Sigourney's writings also suggest the complex ways in which conservative writers tried to present a complex sense of national identity. In *Sketch of Connecticut* (1824), Sigourney depicted the local community as a diverse microcosm of the nation. By returning to the Puritan past, Sigourney was able to trace the means by which national identity eliminated Native Americans and European American women from its scope.

Wit and satire were also effective means of advocating particular attitudes about national identity. Like Warren and Tyler, the Connecticut Wits were consciously trying to create a national literature, especially in the "high culture" mode. The Wits—John Trumbull, Joel Barlow, Timothy Dwight, and David Humphreys—were all Yale graduates who collaborated in the 1770s and 1780s, but their own diversities of class and vision uniquely capture the complex nature of national identity during the early Federal period. Their collaboration on *The Anarchiad* (1786–87), for instance, produced a pro-Federalist text that was a powerful dystopian satire decrying civil disorder. While many of the Wits retained their conservative, elite visions of national identity, Barlow diverged in the most radical ways. Unlike most of the Wits who were from privileged backgrounds, Barlow was a farmer's son and he broke with the others in politics, religion, and literary focus. His later anti-establishment views did not preclude a utopian vision, and in *The Columbiad* (1807), Barlow created a powerful myth of progress that would remain a key element of U.S. nationalism.

Federalists in Boston founded the *Monthly Anthology and Boston Review* (1803–11) to promote political, social, and aesthetic principles. It featured essays and poetry by John Quincy Adams, John Sylvester, John Gardiner, William Emerson (father of Ralph Waldo Emerson), and Joseph Stevens Buckminster, to name a few conservative literary lights. The politically influenced debates over a New England aesthetic and subject to serve as models for America emerged in the works of New England novelists. Tales of seduction by Susanna Rowson (*Charlotte Temple* [1794]), Hannah Webster Foster (*The Coquette* [1797]), and William Hill Brown (*The Power of Sympathy* [1789]) illuminated issues of authority and gender relations in the new republic. Tabitha Gilman Tenney of Exeter, N.H., satirized the influence of European romantic conventions on American women in *Female Quixotism*

(1801). These works established a women's literary tradition in the novel for a later generation of New England writers.

Many women believed, however, that progress was relative and that the United States must be founded upon the ideal of gender inclusiveness. In crafting a national identity in the early years of the Revolution and the new republic, most political leaders presented a decidedly masculine vision of the new "American" and the next generation of citizens. Crèvecoeur looked to his son as the next "American Farmer"; Benjamin Franklin penned his autobiography to his son only as the heir to his political and cultural achievements; Thomas Paine presented the good parent of the new nation as the father willing to sacrifice now so his progeny could live in peace. It is little wonder that Abigail Adams felt it necessary to remind her spouse that "Ladies" sought representation as well.

In contrast to Abigail Adams's private reminders, a few women spoke publicly about their concerns. Like the Connecticut Wits, Judith Sargent Murray understood the power of satire as a political and cultural vehicle of change. In "On the Equality of the Sexes" (1790), she satirized educational, religious, and cultural inequalities. In later essays, including the four-part "Observations on Female Abilities" (1798), Murray wrote women back into international history, suggesting that all national identities must be reconsidered in light of women's long-standing contributions.

While not all individuals or groups in the early nationalist period succeeded in their claims to be represented in the configuration of an "American," their recognition of the importance of literature in establishing such an identity is a significant legacy. New England writers set the stage for subsequent generations of writers who understood that political equality was intimately related to the ability to represent one's own views by gaining a literary voice.

Lawrence Buell, *New England Literary Culture: From Revolution through Renaissance* (1986); L. H. Butterfield, ed., *Adams Family Correspondence* (1963); Cathy N. Davidson, *Revolution and the Word: The Rise of the Novel in America* (1986); Sharon M. Harris, ed., *American Women Writers to 1800* (1995); Dana D. Nelson, *The Word in Black and White: Reading 'Race' in American Literature 1638–1867* (1993); Jeffrey H. Richards, *Mercy Otis Warren* (1995); Frank Shuffleton, ed., *A Mixed Race: Ethnicity in Early America* (1993); Sandra A. Zagarell, "Expanding 'America': Lydia Sigourney's *Sketch of Connecticut*, Catharine Sedgwick's *Hope Leslie*," *Tulsa Studies in Women's Literature* 6 (1987).

Sharon M. Harris

Emerson, Ralph Waldo (1803–82) Lecturer, essayist, and poet. Ralph Waldo Emerson was born in Boston, lived most of his adult

life in nearby Concord, and, as the primary exponent on American Transcendentalism, figured prominently in what has been called the flowering of New England culture in the 19th century. He received his degree from Harvard in 1821, taught briefly at his brother William's school for girls in Boston, and then returned to Harvard Divinity School, subsequently preaching from the same pulpit his father had occupied at First Church in Boston. Later he took a position at Second Church, but resigned in 1832 after becoming uncomfortable with administering the rite of the Lord's Supper and eventually transferred his powers of oration to secular platforms. Emerson endured several tragedies in early adulthood, including the deaths of his first wife, Ellen; his two younger brothers, Edward and Charles; and little Waldo, the five-year-old son of Emerson and his second wife, Lidia. Despite these losses, he pressed on, believing that one must try to alleviate worldly suffering through patience, persistence, insight, and principled action. He died in Concord, where he had established himself as one of the region's best-loved (if frequently misunderstood) thinkers, and is buried in Sleepy Hollow cemetery.

With the exception of several voyages abroad (including an important visit to England in 1833, during which he became a friend to Thomas Carlyle), speaking tours in the Midwest, and a journey to California, Emerson was a constant and influential figure in the New England cultural scene. He lectured prolifically on a wide variety of topics, helped edit the Transcendentalist journal *The Dial*, was a member of several intellectual clubs, and attracted many visitors to his home. An early influence on Henry David Thoreau's philosophy and longtime supporter of Margaret Fuller's work, Emerson inspired (as well as irritated) countless other literary figures, from poets (for example, Emily Dickinson and Walt Whitman) to self-help writers (Ralph Waldo Trine and Norman Vincent Peale) to novelists (Nathaniel Hawthorne and Herman Melville) to nature essayists (John Burroughs and John Muir). He confronted his audience with challenging ideas on a wide range of subjects: scathing criticism of Unitarian complacency, Boston materialism, and philosophical empiricism; advocacy of abolition; and the need for personal improvement and spiritual growth through reliance on the Over-Soul (a divine force circulating through everyone). Emerson thus drew from and added to strong currents running through the New England skepticism of doctrine and institutions, belief in the importance of religious inquiry and in the value of the lessons of nature, and encouragement of social reform through individual responsibility.

Emerson lectured and published exten-

Ralph Waldo Emerson, ca. 1870

sively on New England subjects, including his sharp analysis of the psychology of reformers in "New England Reformers" (1844); his historical essays *A Historical Discourse, Delivered before the Citizens of Concord, 12th September 1835. On the Second Centennial Anniversary of the Incorporation of the Town* (1835) and "Historic Notes of Life and Letters in New England"; biographical sketches of Theodore Parker and Henry David Thoreau; and the oft-quoted "Concord Hymn," celebrating the "shot heard round the world."

Emerson enjoyed great success as a lecturer, but the ideas he expressed were frequently lost in the elegance of his presentation so that the lectures both thrilled and puzzled his audiences. To some extent, similar conditions surround his writing; his complex prose and diverse sources (including Samuel Taylor Coleridge, William Wordsworth, Emanuel Swedenborg, Carlyle, and Montaigne) make for often difficult reading that can be variously interpreted. An essay such as "Self-Reliance" (1841), for example, has been interpreted as both a call for personal financial success through individualism and a strong work ethic and an attack on consistent individual identity and corporate capitalism. In any case, from early works of idealism such as *Nature* (1836), to such provocative orations as "The American Scholar" (1837) and "The Divinity School Address" (1838); from the difficult philosophical essay "Experience" (1844) and the biographical *Representative Men* (1850), to the later and more pragmatic *Conduct of Life* (1860), Emerson's writings dazzle, confuse, enlighten, irk, and urge readers to rethink the nature of the self and its place in the world.

Although he became known in his own lifetime as the "Sage of Concord" for countless epigrammatic phrases that seem to provide remedies to life's challenges, Emerson ever cautioned against the acceptance of pat answers. Instead, he preferred that each person take responsibility for thoroughly engaging philosophical questions, an ongoing exploration summarized in his poem "The Sphinx":

> So take thy quest through nature,
> It through thousand natures ply:
> Ask on, thou clothed eternity;
> Time is the false reply.

In his published writings and in his multivolume *Journal*, Emerson left a legacy of New England self-scrutiny, self-improvement, and social progress that extends well beyond the geographic region and historical context from which his thoughts emerged.

Edward Waldo Emerson, ed., *The Complete Works of Ralph Waldo Emerson*, 12 vols. (1903–04); Alfred R. Ferguson, Robert E. Spiller, and Jean Ferguson Carr, eds., *The Collected Works of Ralph Waldo Emerson* (1971); Maurice Gonnaud, *An Uneasy Solitude: Individual and Society in the Work of Ralph Waldo Emerson*, tr. Lawrence Rosenwald (1999); Robert D. Richardson, Jr., *Emerson: The Mind on Fire: A Biography* (1995).

T. S. McMillin

Epitaphs, Elegies, and Gravestones

The American gravestone is a significant, distinctive art form, a great historic resource, and a New England invention. There is beautiful carving on some European monuments, but the artistic combining of literary epitaph and carved icon begins in eastern Massachusetts. Perhaps because of the Second Commandment's prohibition of graven images, sculpture was slow to develop in New England except in the burying ground.

The earliest stones were either richly sculpted or unadorned and had little or no epitaph material—just names, dates, and perhaps relationships, such as "wife to." In the 18th century, with the rapid spread of the icon of the winged skull, came the fashion to include more verbal material, though most stones still had little or none; and most dead had no stone or epitaph at all. Epitaphs are among the oldest forms of the art of language, often comprising little more than identification of the dead, as on Egyptian steles. They are often simple and unsophisticated, though not necessarily artless. One particularly moving example is found in Truro, Mass.:

> Mary dr to
> Ira Atkins
> Har 14 days
> 1744

That is, "Here lies the body of Mary Atkins, daughter to Ira Atkins, who lived (was 'har') 14 days in 1744." The stone next to it is simply incised "I. A."

Epitaphs may also be poems or parts of poems, typically some form of this memento mori, which appears in hundreds of variants:

> Stranger, stop and cast an eye,
> As you are now, so once was I,
> As I am now, so shall you be,
> Prepare for death and follow me.

This little quatrain in common meter is no masterpiece, but its popularity is entirely deserved as it fulfills every requirement of the good epitaph: it is terse, rhythmic, tonally powerful, and connects the living and the dead through "direct address," reminding the living that death is always near. Another popular early epitaph marked as a New England classic for its laconic brevity and theme is

> Death's a debt to nature due
> Which I have paid and so must you.

More elegant literary variants, from sources such as Isaac Watts's Horae Lyricae or the "graveyard school" of English poets, appear on some stones. For example, the elegy of Benjamin Bangs in Brewster, Mass., reads

> Some Hearty friend may drop his tear
> On my dry bones and say
> These once were strong as mine appear,
> And mine shall be as they
> So shall our mouldering members teach
> What now our senses learn;

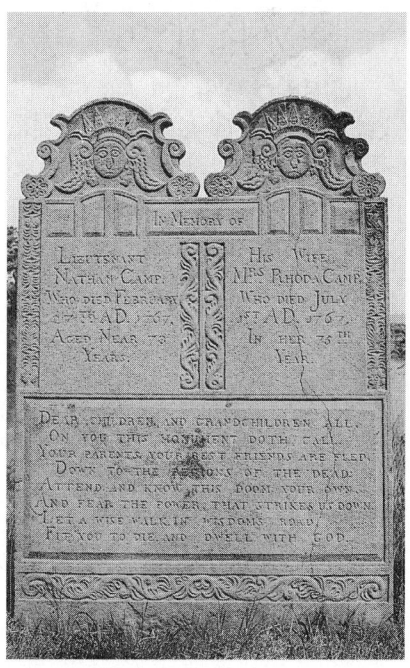

The Nathan and Rhoda Camp stone, 1767, Durham, Conn.

For dust and ashes loudest preach
Man's infinite concern [from Isaac Watts]

New England epitaphs may be more personal and individual. These may take the form
of brief statements that purport to capture
something of the nature of the deceased, as of
a wife who "hath done what she could" or who
"meddled not in the affairs of others." Rarer
still are long elegiac statements by a mourner
about the deceased. These can be fairly conventional, too, or simply lists of titles, civic positions, or relationships. At their best they are
stunning, as in this, probably written by a
Brewster, Mass., Congregationalist minister
for his son and namesake, dead in 1799, aged
two years and one month:

Lovely in life,
Pleasant in death,
Reader:
Let this stone, erected over the grave,
Of one who was once, the florid picture
    of health,
but rapidly changed, into the pale image
    of death,
Remind thee
That God "destroyeth the hope of man."

The quote, from Job 14:26, is a poignant attempt to find meaning or consolation in the
sorrows of a biblical father whose children
died. Direct quotations from the Bible are surprisingly rare, reminding us that the funeral
and the burying ground were regarded as essentially secular institutions.

New England epitaphs communicate theological and moral sentiments, but they also defined social roles, and, on occasion, provided
an opportunity for last words to right wrongs
or challenge social structures by means of the
authority of a voice from beyond the grave.
One of New England's most famous epitaphs,
for John Jack, of Concord, Mass., points to the
hypocrisy of slavery in the cradle of the American Revolution:

God wills us free—Man wills us slaves
I will as God wills: Gods will be done.
Here lies the body of
John Jack
A native of Africa who died
March 1773, aged about sixty years.
Tho born in the land of slavery
He was born free:
Tho he lived in a land of liberty
He lived a slave
Till by his honest tho stolen labours
He acquired the source of slavery
Which gave him his freedom:
Tho not long before
Death the great Tyrant
Gave him his final emancipation
And put him on a footing with kings.

Tho a slave to vice
He practiced those virtues
Without which kings are but slaves.

Elegies are a much more sophisticated literary genre, not originally devoted to memorialization or mourning; the elegies of the Roman
poet Propertius, for example, dealt with erotic
love. In New England they were the grand and
formal counterpart of the epitaph, often composed quickly after the death of a renowned
man, both to capitalize on the event and to
suggest suitable responses for public mourning, and were very popular. They often imitate
the stiff, pompous diction of fashionable English poetry of the age. They were not intended to be, nor were they, incised on any but
the largest of gravestones; sadly, they often
lacked the wit that the brevity of epitaphs can
confer. Formal elegies printed as broadsides
functioned in the elaborate social and religious
rituals of late 17th- and 18th-century New England. Like the accompanying funeral sermon, elegies not only commemorated the
dead but also set forth a broad vision of social
order. The elegy was the most popular form of
early New England poetry, with numerous examples by Edward Johnson, John Fiske, Edward Taylor, Anne Bradstreet, John Danforth,
and Cotton Mather. The exemplary elegy
from the Puritan era is Urian Oakes's elegy for
his brother, Thomas Shepard, who died in
1677. Over some 52 stanzas, Oakes enumerates
the individuals, churches, and communities
mourning the loss of Shepard, and he introduces the jeremiadic theme that Shepard's
death is a punishment for the sins of New England, whose status as a new Israel is threatened by such sins and by the loss of such a
leader.

By the early 18th century, such formal productions, and the notion of New England's
mission that inspired them, had become shop-
worn. Benjamin Franklin, writing as Silence
Dogood, published a spoof formula for elegy
writing in 1722. In the 19th century, elegies remained a popular New England genre, most
notably in the work of Lydia Sigourney, but
the tradition was ripe for parody. For instance,
Mark Twain lambasted the form in Emmeline
Grangerford's "Ode on the Death of Stephen
Dowling Botts, Deceased" from *Huckleberry
Finn.*

Nineteenth-century memorial fashion replaced dark slate with white marble, skull and
cherub with urn and willow, and terse epitaphs
with longer elegies, usually demonstrating
very ordinary Victorian parlor taste in poetry.
Because marble weathers poorly, those that
remain are often nearly impossible to read,
unlike the briefer verses on older slates.

But surely the finest flowering of the New

England epitaph and elegy is in poems that
are neither—particularly those of Emily
Dickinson, so often bereft by death, or preparing for another funeral, or anticipating her
own death, or feeling the weight of death in
the room, or going for "that last ride with our
boy Death," Anne Sexton's witty and predictive note to Sylvia Plath on Dickinson's best-
known poem. As Dickinson learned her poetic form chiefly from the hymnal, so she may
have learned much of her power and many of
her ideas from the burying ground.

Indeed, Emily Dickinson's body lies in the
family plot in Amherst, Mass. Her stone is
graced by the briefest of epitaphs, the entire
body of the last letter she wrote her cousins the
day before she died, a fine memorial for the
most terse and most epigrammatic of New
England poets: "Called back."

Diana Hume George and Malcolm A. Nelson, *Epi-
taph and Icon: A Field Guide to the Old Burying
Grounds of Cape Cod, Martha's Vineyard, and Nan-
tucket* (1983); Andrew Kull, *New England Cemeteries:
A Collector's Guide* (1975); Thomas C. Mann and Janet
Greene, *Sudden and Awful: American Epitaphs and the
Finger of God* (1968); Charles L. Wallis, *American
Epitaphs, Grave and Humorous* (1973).

Malcolm A. Nelson

Fisher, Dorothy Canfield (1879–1958)

Writer. Dorothy (originally Dorothea) Frances Canfield Fisher was born in Lawrence,
Kan., but like Robert Frost, who was once her
neighbor, she was a New Englander by choice
and temperament. Fisher spent her childhood
summers in Arlington, Vt., and when she
married John Fisher in 1907 she became a
year-round resident. Working at home while
rearing two children, Fisher became a prolific
writer and influential public figure. Like another neighbor, the illustrator Norman Rockwell, she was often inspired by the Vermont
landscape and the character of its people.

Fisher graduated from Ohio State University in 1899, studied briefly at the Sorbonne in
Paris, and earned a Ph.D. from Columbia
University in 1904. In her varied career she
wrote novels and short story collections, most
under her family name Dorothy Canfield. Her
nonfiction works, most published under her
full name, consist of general sociological studies of contemporary educational trends, popular histories of Vermont, and biographies of
American heroes. A perceptive commentator
on the shifts and movements of modern life,
Fisher also wrote numerous articles on marriage, the family, and women's issues.

Eleanor Roosevelt once ranked Fisher—a
popular lecturer and recipient of several honorary degrees—among the 10 most influential
women in America. Trained as a teacher,
Fisher served on many state and national

boards dedicated to education and the arts. She was an enthusiastic advocate of the teaching methods of Maria Montessori and the first woman to serve on the Vermont State Board of Education. As one of America's foremost women of letters, Fisher acted as a panel judge for the Book-of-the-Month Club for 25 years and was elected to the National Institute of Arts and Letters.

Fisher, however, most wanted to be remembered for her fiction. Like Mary E. Wilkins Freeman, Sarah Orne Jewett, and Louisa May Alcott, Fisher wrote about the weave of country village life. Her short story collections, such as *Hillsboro People* (1915) and *Raw Material* (1923), show stoic characters of Puritan stock confronting the harsh New England elements and cultivating rich communities out of its unpromising soil. In her longer works, such as *The Brimming Cup* (1921), *Bonfire* (1933), and *Seasoned Timber* (1939), Fisher records the rhythms of rural domesticity at a time when it was unfashionable to do so. Although Fisher's New Englanders struggle with modern problems of adultery, psychological angst, and anti-Semitism, their strength lies in their ability to weather social change. In the depressed economic climate of the 1920s and 1930s, much of Fisher's appeal must have stemmed from her steadfast optimism.

Perhaps her classic young-adult novel, *Understood Betsy* (1917), shows best what Fisher found most valuable and enduring about New England. The young protagonist, Elizabeth Ann, leaves a suffocating upper-middle-class city life to live on a Vermont farm with her Putney cousins. There the child's formerly idle and largely decorative life is transformed by the realities of farm life: tending to animals, making butter, and walking to school by herself. The once pale and prissy Elizabeth Ann becomes the independent, self-sufficient Betsy, and Fisher celebrates a New England rural life shaped by industriousness and moral fortitude.

Fisher died of a stroke in Arlington in 1958, and her work gradually went out of print, probably because the moral messages of her fiction seemed old-fashioned in the turbulence of the 1960s and 1970s. A new generation of critics and readers has recently rediscovered the enduring traits of her work: her fine ear for rural New England dialect and her talent for storytelling.

Dorothy Canfield Fisher, *The Bedquilt and Other Stories*, ed. Mark J. Madigan (1997); Mark J. Madigan, ed., *Keeping Fires Night and Day: Selected Letters of Dorothy Canfield Fisher* (1993); Joan Shelley Rubin, *The Making of Middlebrow Culture* (1992); Ida H. Washington, *Dorothy Canfield Fisher: A Biography* (1982).

Anne M. Downey

Francis, Robert

Francis, Robert (1901–87) Poet. Robert Francis was born in Pennsylvania and "became a New Englander" in 1910; his life and poems reflect the region. Francis grew up in West Medford, Mass., graduated from Harvard in 1923, and taught for a year in Beirut. He returned to Harvard, taking his M.Ed. in 1926, and then moved to Amherst, Mass., where he lived until his death. Francis rarely did regular work: he briefly taught school and music, served as a conscientious objector during World War II, wrote newspaper columns, and occasionally gave poetry readings and taught at writers' conferences. From 1940 he kept a small house called Fort Juniper where he satisfied his needs for solitude and a life among plain people, wrote his poems, and practiced Thoreau-inspired principles of diet and economy, an intense form of making do and doing without. Francis's autobiography recounts his slow growth from duty-bound timidity to self-reliant achievement and explains his happy, atheistic pessimism; it also reveals his homosexuality (consummated in late midlife) and his dislike for most poetry.

Francis's first three books were published by Macmillan, but he remained a marginal literary figure, with no publisher between 1944 and 1960, although one volume, *The Face against the Glass*, was privately printed in 1950. In 1960 Wesleyan University Press published *The Orb Weaver*, and beginning in 1965 the University of Massachusetts Press brought out several volumes of poetry and prose, including a memoir of Robert Frost. In those years, Francis went from being unknown to being known for being unknown (Frost, a friend and strong influence, called him "our best neglected poet"), and Francis's intensely calm and crafted poems (written outside literary fashion and debate) found an admiring audience, as did his independent, frugal style of living. His honors include selection as Phi Beta Kappa poet at Tufts and Harvard, the Shelley Memorial Award, and travel fellowships to Italy.

Francis's poems developed from coolly quiet to warm and occasionally frisky (in late work he experimented with word count and fragmentation), but his best poems remain intensely observed portraits of local places, people, activities, and things. Typically, those portraits both honor their subjects (praising the marginal and small) and interpret them, discovering or locating broader implications within what they describe. The poems are reasoned and reflect formal and intellectual wit, but they distrust generalization, prefer paradox, and often demonstrate that multiple shadings convey reality more accurately than polar oppositions. "Pitcher" is Francis's best-known poem; its baseball metaphor illustrates his poetics: "How not to hit the mark he seems to aim at." Putting the reader off stride by changing up or tossing curves at expectations is Francis's style (like Emily Dickinson's telling things "slant"). This trips us into reconsideration, producing modest revelations of clarity, opacity, and their overlappings. Some charge that Francis is too decorously mild, but his refusal of excess is thoroughgoing; it tracks the folly of certitude in philosophy, poetry, and politics. Like his personal economics, Francis's poems exemplify his New Englander's delight that "thrifty" means frugal and fruitful alike.

Robert Francis, *Collected Poems: 1936–1976* (1976); Francis, *Pot Shots at Poetry* (1980); Francis, *The Trouble with Francis: An Autobiography* (1971); Howard Nelson, "Moving Unnoticed: Notes on Robert Francis's Poetry," *The Hollins Critic* 14 (1977).

Guy Rotella

Franco-American Literature

Franco-American Literature A body of Franco-American literature began to take shape in New England during the last quarter of the 19th century. Written in either French or English by French Canadian immigrants and their descendants, it drew on the cultures of both Quebec and the United States. Early authors were members of the Francophone elite of New England's mill towns, whose written work found a forum in the press. Many poems, short stories, and novels were first printed in newspapers—from 1868, New England witnessed the founding and closing of some 330 Franco-American newspapers— and were penned by doctors, lawyers, and journalists who wanted both to entertain and to teach their readers. Trained in Quebec, these individuals were heavily influenced by French literary trends, notably Romanticism. These early Franco-American writers imitated the French masters, sometimes nearly copying them outright.

While poetry addressed patriotic, social, and personal themes, the seven known novels published in French between 1878 and 1936 all had a documentary character and often a didactic purpose. (This is less the case for later novels such as *Sanatorium* by Paul Dufault [1938], a Quebecois who settled in Rutland, Mass., and *Les Enfances de Fanny* [Fanny] [1951] by Louis Dantin, who immigrated to Roxbury, Mass.) Franco-American fiction, like Franco-American nonfiction, was first and foremost utilitarian, the goal being to instill in the reader a particular viewpoint. In *Jeanne la fileuse* [Joan the spinner] (1878), for example, Honoré Beaugrand of Lowell, Mass., used his pen to defend the immigrants against critics within Quebec who spoke out against the exodus toward the United States, while in *La Jeune Franco-Américaine* [Franco-American girl] (1933) Alberte Gastonguay emphasized the importance of maintaining ancestral traditions.

Thus there was tension in Franco-American literary works between what was perceived as French Canadian reality and American reality, the old and the new. With the passage of time, novelists and poets became more influenced by their country of adoption and its literature. This was notably true for Louis Dantin, a poet, novelist, and critic who interpreted American literature for Quebec's cultural elites, and the Nashua, N.H., poet Rosaire Dion-Lévesque, who translated Walt Whitman into French, calling him "a new Christ."

The publication in 1939 of *The Delusson Family* by Jacques Ducharme, a native of Holyoke, Mass., inaugurated Franco-American literature in English and reflected the reality of linguistic assimilation. Here, as in the novels of the Auburn, Maine, resident Gérard Robichaud, such as *Papa Martel* (1961) and *The Apple of His Eye* (1965), the transition from French Canadian traditional life to modern American life is painted positively. However, the tensions between the two worlds are central in the lives and works of Jean-Louis "Jack" Kerouac of Lowell, Mass., and, to a lesser extent, Manchester, N.H., native Grace Metalious. Metalious wrote the huge best-seller *Peyton Place* (1956), revealing a scandalous netherworld beneath the prim and proper surface of a thinly veiled Gilmanton, N.H., and *No Adam in Eden* (1963). A leader of the Beat poets, Kerouac is best known for the anti-establishment novel *On the Road* (1957). After the publication of his first novel, *The Town and the City* (1950), Kerouac wrote that "all my knowledge rests in my 'French Canadianness' and nowhere else." Since then several Anglophone writers and poets have made rich use of their "Franco-Americanness," the most celebrated being David Plante, whose series of novels about the Francoeur family are set in the Providence Catholic parish of his boyhood.

The rebel Kerouac greatly influenced the young Franco-American writers who participated in the ethnic renaissance of the 1970s, such as the playwright Grégoire Chabot of Waterville, Maine, author of *Un Jacques Cartier errant* [Jacques Cartier discovers North America] (1977) and *Chère maman* [Mama, dear] (1979). In 1983 another Manchester, N.H., native, Robert Perreault, tried to reawaken the ancestral spirit with the publication of *L'Héritage*, the first New England novel written in French since 1951. But this ethnic renaissance was short-lived and all indications are that Franco-American literature will be written in English in the future.

Gerard J. Brault, *The French-Canadian Heritage in New England* (1986); Armand B. Chartier, *The Franco-Americans of New England: A History* (1999); Claire Quintal, ed., *Steeples and Smokestacks: The Franco-American Experience in New England* (1996).

Yves Frenette

Freeman, Mary E. Wilkins (1852–1930)

Short story writer and novelist. Mary Eleanor Wilkins Freeman, whose work set the stage for 20th-century women's psychological fiction, was born in Randolph, Mass. The daughter of orthodox Congregationalists, Wilkins grew up in a repressive environment and was expected to conform to traditional standards of female passivity. As a youth she listened to the stories women told one another in family kitchens and thereby learned to value, and later depict, the subtle forms of rebellion that New England women used to appropriate power within the domestic realm.

At the age of 15 Wilkins moved to Brattleboro, Vt., with her family. After graduating from high school in 1870, she attended Mount Holyoke Female Seminary. Like Emily Dickinson, she lasted there for only one year. Wilkins disliked the school's restrictive rules and longed for the privacy that would enable her to write.

Back in Brattleboro Wilkins began writing in earnest, viewing her work as a way to achieve financial stability and independence. In 1883 she returned to her Massachusetts birthplace to spend the 20 most productive years of her literary career sharing a home with her lifelong friend Mary Wales. Wilkins resisted the pressure to wed through her childbearing years but finally married Dr. Charles Freeman in 1902 and moved to Metuchen, N.J. The marriage dissolved in 1921 largely because of Charles's decline into alcoholism and drug addiction. Although she wrote to a friend in 1910 that she had "not a blessed thing to write about" there, Freeman remained in Metuchen until her death at age 78.

Freeman is best known for the short stories she published in *Harper's Bazaar* before her unhappy marriage. Her writing explores a wide range of conflicts related to 19th-century patriarchal strictures on women: submission and autonomy, heterosexuality and lesbianism, the nurturing of others and self-nurturing, to name a few. Freeman depicted rebellious though often ambivalent heroines struggling toward self-realization and empowerment. In the 1891 story "The Revolt of 'Mother,'" for example, a farm wife moves her family into the new barn her husband has built instead of a long-promised new house. In "A New England Nun," from the same year, Freeman examines the price of autonomy for a woman who, after years of waiting for her fiancé to return from the sea, decides to reject marriage.

Freeman was among the first American women writers to explore openly the complexity of female sexuality, the role of work in women's lives, the experience and stigma of spinsterhood, and the unique relationships that women of her era formed outside of marriage. Her finest work reflects her experience as a single woman struggling both with and against the 19th century's ideology of womanhood. While her short stories are her most frequently anthologized and widely read works, Freeman also wrote 14 novels—*Pembroke* (1894) is the best known—250 short stories, 15 short story collections, several plays, children's stories, and essays. She was the first recipient, in 1926, of the William Dean Howells Medal for Distinction in Fiction from the American Academy of Arts and Letters, and the bronze doors of the academy still carry the inscription "Dedicated to the Memory of Mary E. Wilkins Freeman and the Women Writers of America."

Leah Blatt Glasser, *In a Closet Hidden: The Life and Work of Mary E. Wilkins Freeman* (1996); Brent L. Kendrick, ed., *The Infant Sphinx: Collected Letters of Mary E. Wilkins Freeman* (1985); Shirley Marchalonis, ed., *Critical Essays on Mary Wilkins Freeman* (1991); Marjorie Pryse, ed., *Selected Stories of Mary E. Wilkins Freeman* (1983).

Leah Blatt Glasser

Frost, Robert (1874–1963)

Poet. Robert Lee Frost was born in San Francisco, Calif., the son of William Prescott Frost, Jr., of New England ancestry, and Isabelle (Moodie) Frost, a schoolteacher from Scotland. Frost's father died in 1885 and his mother moved the family to Lawrence, Mass., to live with her husband's parents.

Robert Frost declared himself a poet while still in high school and served as editor of his school newspaper. He and his future wife, Elinor Miriam White, were covaledictorians of the Lawrence High School class of 1892. Frost attended Dartmouth College briefly, returning home to write poetry and work at a number of jobs. After their marriage in 1895 Robert and Elinor Frost spent the next few years helping Robert's mother run a private school in Salem, N.H. Frost continued to write; a few of his poems were published in the New York *Independent* and other journals. He entered Harvard College in 1897 but withdrew in 1899 because of the need to support his wife and son Elliott (born 1896).

By 1900 the Frosts had settled on a farm near Derry, N.H. Elliott died shortly before the move, a loss expressed in Frost's poem

"Home Burial." Although Frost tried to work the farm, by 1906 he had started teaching at nearby Pinkerton Academy, moving his family, which now included four children, into Derry Village in 1909. Frost later proclaimed that the core of his writing was produced during the "free years" (1900–1905) he had on the Derry farm. He went on to teach for one year (1911–12) at Plymouth Normal School but found teaching to be a serious distraction from his writing. Frost sold the Derry farm, and he and his family traveled to England in 1912. There he met Ezra Pound, William Butler Yeats, and the so-called Georgian poets Lascelles Abercrombie and W. W. Gibson and formed a lifelong friendship with the journalist-critic Edward Thomas. His first two volumes of verse—*A Boy's Will* (1913) and *North of Boston* (1914)—were published in London by David Nutt to critical acclaim on both sides of the Atlantic.

With the outbreak of war in Europe, the Frosts returned to the United States and settled in Franconia, N.H. In 1916 Frost began his lifetime association with Amherst College, where he served as professor of English and poet-in-residence (1917–20, 1923–25, 1927–38, 1948–63). During his career he also held teaching positions at the University of Michigan (1921–23, 1925–26), Harvard University (1939–43), and Dartmouth College (1943–48). Other volumes of verse published over his lifetime include *Mountain Interval* (1916), *New Hampshire* (1923), *West-Running Brook* (1928), *A Further Range* (1936), *A Witness Tree* (1942), *A Masque of Reason* (1945), *A Masque of Mercy* (1947), *Steeple Bush* (1947), and *In the Clearing* (1962). He was awarded the Pulitzer Prize four times and received more than 50 honorary degrees. Frost was consultant in poetry to the Library of Congress, received the congressional gold medal, became poet laureate of Vermont, and participated in President John F. Kennedy's inauguration.

Beginning in 1921 Frost spent summers at his home in South Shaftsbury, Vt., where he began his 40-year association with the Bread Loaf School of English in nearby Ripton, Vt., and helped found the Bread Loaf Writers' Conference, which began in 1926. In the years following his wife's death in 1938, he maintained homes in Ripton and in Cambridge, Mass. Beginning in 1954, when he was already 80 years old, Frost carried out numerous goodwill missions to foreign countries on behalf of the United States, including one to Russia to meet with Premier Nikita Khrushchev in 1962.

Frost took seriously his role as the voice of New England. In a 1937 lecture titled "What Became of New England?" Frost expressed his view that "The thing New England gave most to America was . . . a stubborn clinging to meaning,—to purify words until they meant again what they should mean." Frost's nature poetry celebrated the beauty and virtues of the New England landscape in the tradition of Ralph Waldo Emerson, Henry David Thoreau, and Emily Dickinson, yet poems such as "The Oven Bird" and "Ghost House" acknowledge New England's worn-out landscape and the harsh views of nature presented by Charles Darwin, William James, and Henri Bergson. Frost's Yankee characters in the dramatic monologues and dialogues of *North of Boston* blend a lingering Puritan sense of the tragedy of life with ironic wit and self-deprecation. Van Wyck Brooks acknowledged in *New England: Indian Summer* (1940) that "the region was born again" in Frost's poetry and that it was Frost's "function to mediate between New England and the mind of the rest of the nation."

Robert Frost is one of America's most beloved writers, and his poetry has had a profound and lasting effect on American literature. In poems such as "The Death of the Hired Man," "Mending Wall," "Birches," and "Stopping by Woods on a Snowy Evening," Frost captured the themes and rhythms of New England speech, its "sound of sense," using common images to make profound statements. Four of Frost's homes are preserved and open to the public: the Frost Farm in Derry, Frost Place in Franconia, the "stone cottage" in Shaftbury, and his cabin near Ripton, owned by Middlebury College.

Lesley Lee Francis, *The Frost Family's Adventure in Poetry: Sheer Morning Gladness at the Brim* (1994); Robert Frost, *Collected Poems of Robert Frost* (1996); Lawrance Thompson, *Robert Frost: The Early Years, 1874–1915* (1966); Thompson, *Robert Frost: The Years of Triumph, 1915–1938* (1970); Lawrance Thompson and R. H. Winnick, *Robert Frost: The Later Years, 1938–1963* (1976).

Lesley Lee Francis

Fuller, Margaret

Fuller, Margaret (1810–50) Writer, feminist educator, and social reformer. In *Making the American Self* (1997), Daniel Walker Howe called Margaret Fuller "the most formidably learned New Englander since Cotton Mather." Fuller was a citizen of the world who brought European literary culture to New England, a Boston Transcendentalist who carried her belief in human potential to the prisons of New York and the prairies of the Midwest, a prophet of gender liberation, and an American abroad who saw her country's democratic principles come alive in the European revolutions of 1848.

Sarah Margaret Fuller was born in Cambridgeport, Mass., the first child of Margaret and Timothy Fuller. A child prodigy tutored by her Harvard-educated father, a lawyer and legislator, she established lifelong habits of study and self-improvement. In successive schools and in the elite circles of Cambridge and Boston, her flamboyance, wit, and "gladiatorial disposition" set her apart but also gained her the confidence and friendship of intellectuals and reformers.

A self-taught authority on Goethe and German culture, Fuller championed their cause in critical essays and translations, passionately attracted to ideas and experiences denied in repressed New England. In 1836 she began a mutually influential friendship with Ralph Waldo Emerson, becoming a force in the emerging Transcendentalist movement and the first editor of its journal, *The Dial*, to which she also contributed important work of her own.

After her father's death in 1835, which traumatized her, Fuller helped support her mother and siblings, first by teaching school and then by conducting a series of "Conversations" for women in Boston (1839–44) that encouraged participants to think independently. A trip to the Midwest in 1843 resulted in *Summer on the Lakes* (1844) and led Horace Greeley to ask Fuller to write literary criticism and social reportage for his *New York Tribune;* when she left for Europe in 1846, she became the paper's foreign correspondent—and the nation's first female to occupy that position.

After travels in Britain, France, Switzerland, and Italy, Fuller settled in Rome in 1847. Within two dramatic years she became the lover of young Marchese Giovanni Angelo d'Ossoli, a supporter and defender (with Ossoli) of the Roman revolution of 1848–49, and the mother of Angelo Ossoli. She directed a hospital, wrote impassioned dispatches for the *Tribune*, and, as a refugee in Florence, penned a history of the Roman revolution. That manuscript was lost when Fuller perished, with Giovanni and Angelo, in a shipwreck off the New York shore on July 19, 1850.

Fuller left a lasting impression on the generation that knew her, and the long-term influence of her life and work is still felt to this day. Her cosmopolitan outlook set new standards in literary and cultural criticism; in her journalism and travel writing, she directed attention to the lives of the urban poor, displaced Native Americans and transplanted women in frontier settlements, and oppressed populations in Europe, eventually embracing radical democratic ideas to address the social problems of her age.

Through her conversations and her best-known book, *Woman in the Nineteenth Century*

Margaret Fuller, 1840s

(1845), Fuller influenced the emerging movement for women's rights. *Woman* analyzes gender as a set of historically evolving social relationships, opening up opportunities for both women and men: "the development of the one cannot be effected without that of the other." In their wide range and intellectual sophistication, Fuller's writings continue to inspire feminist theory and cultural critique today.

Charles Capper, *Margaret Fuller: An American Romantic Life* (1992); Bell Gale Chevigny, *The Woman and the Myth: Margaret Fuller's Life and Writings*, rev. ed. (1994); Daniel Walker Howe, *Making the American Self: Jonathan Edwards to Abraham Lincoln* (1997); Robert N. Hudspeth, ed., *The Letters of Margaret Fuller*, 6 vols. (1983–94).

Fritz Fleischmann

Gay, Lesbian, and Bisexual Writers

While benefiting from New England's tradition of personal privacy, lesbians and gay men have also suffered the censorship and persecution inherent in the Puritan heritage. As early as 1641 the Reverend Thomas Shepard found within his Cambridge, Mass., congregation a "foul sink of all atheism, sodomy, blasphemy, murder, whoredom, adultery, witchcraft, buggery." Colonial Massachusetts and Connecticut long maintained the death penalty for the "abominable and detestable crime against nature."

Censorship has created many problems for gay, lesbian, bisexual, transvestite, and transgender writings. Boston, for example, banned the 1882 edition of *Leaves of Grass* by Walt Whitman, the 1913 translation of Petronius's comic novel *Satyricon* (more for its homosexual content than its vulgarity), and Radclyffe Hall's pioneering British lesbian novel *The Well of Loneliness* (1928). In December 1973 Governor Meldrim Thompson threatened to close the University of New Hampshire after a student group sponsored a performance there of Jonathan Katz's work in progress *Coming Out* (1975). Beyond mere censorship, in 1998 the AIDS activist, writer, and wealthy alumnus of Yale University Larry Kramer denounced his alma mater after school officials rejected his offer to fund a gay studies professorship on campus, challenging the field's legitimacy.

Gay and lesbian writers have often been subject to editorial cutting. The publisher of Beat movement leader Jack Kerouac, from Lowell, Mass., removed homoerotic passages from *On the Road* (1957). Many writers disguise queer slants in the hope of reaching sympathetic ears and avoiding such editing. Recent interpretation identifies homoeroticism in the life and writings of Margaret Fuller, Nathaniel Hawthorne, Herman Melville, Henry James, Emily Dickinson, Thornton Wilder, Horatio Alger, and others. These writers often manifest queerness by sly indirection. After reading page proofs of Whitman's "Calamus" poems evoking what seems to be a homosexual love affair and on the day

Whitman left Boston for New York City, Henry David Thoreau wrote a long botanical entry on the phallic calamus flower in his *Journal* (May 23, 1860).

A Yankee ancestral heritage has given some writers the freedom to speak with a discreetly queer voice. Amy Lowell, among the prominent Lowells of Boston, wrote what has been called the literature of lesbian encoding, in which an unknowing reader might assume love poems are addressed to a male, when she wrote her exquisite poems for Ada Russell: "You are ice and fire, / The touch of you burns my hands like snow." Amy's distant cousin Robert Lowell had three wives and few male friends, but his confessional verse offered lesbian and gay poets a means of expressing their love because of his own allusive style of making deeply personal and erotic encounters available as the subject of poetry. Of his friend Elizabeth Bishop, Lowell wrote that her poetry opens "the classical serenity of a new country," referring at once to her sexuality and to her move to the freer social space of Brazil, where Bishop felt safer to live openly with Lota de Macedo Soares. Adrienne Rich, a student of Lowell's, flowered as a writer speaking from her lesbian identity only with the Civil Rights and women's movements. Lowell's literary executor, Frank Bidart, an award-winning poet in his own right, has extended the Yankee spirit to include gay love and in turn has integrated the two, thereby encouraging such poets as Lloyd Schwartz and Rudy Kikel.

Gay writers from immigrant families have often had to face both homophobia and xenophobia or religious discrimination. May Sarton spent decades looking for a congenial home; the poet had fled Belgium with her parents during World War I but felt out of place and constricted in Cambridge and New York. She found a home in Nelson, N.H., and then York, Maine, where her writing only hinted at the difficulties her love affairs caused. Only late in her career did she include explicitly lesbian characters in her books. The homosexuality of John Horne Burns was no more acceptable to his Irish family than to the Yankees. His finest novel, *The Gallery* (1947), takes place in Italy. Quite consciously, the Boston College graduate John Wieners contrasts himself with Robert Lowell in *Behind the State Capitol* (1975), a title evoking the back side of Beacon Hill, a neighborhood once a haven for queers and African Americans, as opposed to Lowell's address, 91 Revere Street, an address on the front side of Beacon Hill described in Lowell's autobiographical *Life Studies* (1959). Wieners's "Children of the Working Class" evokes another aspect of the city:

I am witness
not to Whitman's vision, but instead the
poorhouses, the mad city asylums.

Born in Malden, Mass., John Gilgun effectively captures the double outcast life as chore boy and choirboy in his appropriately titled short story "Boats against the Current" (1999), published in the online *Blithe House Quarterly*.

Some authors wrestled with multiple identities in their lives and works, and sometimes suffered personal and literary consequences. The Lebanese mystic Khalil Gibran first posed for Boston photographer Fred Holland Day and gained an early following among Boston's gay circles. Beirut censors publicly burned his *Spirits Rebellious* (1901; translated 1948), and Gibran later married and settled in Manhattan. Steven Jonas identified himself as Portuguese, thus distancing himself from New England's tendency to classify Portuguese-speaking natives of Cape Verde and the Azores as Negroes, and as a disciple of Ezra Pound but avoided African or homosexual labels. In the last poem he wrote before his death Jonas nonetheless links the two oppressions:

When God created
the world he stood
on the Negro . . .
thereafter
sex and the single man.

The Boston-based black gay performance artist Craig Hickman, by contrast, embraces his various identities; he has become a slam, or competitive performance, poetry champion and is the author of *Rituals* (1994). Freddie Greenfield, a native of Chelsea, Mass., championed his street life as an outlaw, Jew, and queer in *Were You Always a Criminal?* (1989). On the faculty of Harvard Medical School and the staff of Beth Israel Deaconess Hospital, the Cuban exile Rafael Campo captures the anguish of multiple identities in *The Other Man Was Me: A Voyage to the New World* (1994):

My country, in the end, unfortunate
In being not an island nor a continent,
In being gay and full of immigrants,
Is vanishing where seas and mountains
meet.

Some homosexuals have fled New England. Raised in Worcester, Mass., and educated at Harvard University, Frank O'Hara, like his Harvard classmate and fellow poet John Ashbery, thrived in Manhattan, although the flippancy and wit for which both writers are known first developed in New England. Carl Morse, born in Showhegan, Maine, is likewise best known as a New York poet. David Plante, born in Providence of

French Canadian and Indian ancestry, has followed Henry James into English exile. Stephen Riel, on the other hand, has successfully combined his French Canadian, New England, and gay identities in the remarkable volume of poetry *How to Dream* (1992).

By moving from one place to another, lesbians and gay men seek an ever-elusive freedom for their lives and art. Some have found that freedom in the same New England that others have fled. Federico García Lorca wrote moving poems in Vermont, where the landscape and the death of a child awakened memories of his youth in Andalusia. Harvey Fierstein, author of the Broadway hit *Torch Song Trilogy*, like the lesbian novelist Bertha Harris, moved to Connecticut, where Harris was able to employ "magic, / fantasy, play, sex" to elude what she called in the semi-autobiographical poem "Saradove" "warped rituals / of love and hate." The New York City–born poet James Merrill wove metaphors of sex and the deep sea from the Greek Islands through Key West to his Stonington, Conn., home in *The Changing Light at Sandover* (1982).

New England's seaside communities have offered lesbian and gay writers both inspiration and relief. While living in Ellsworth, Maine, the painter Marsden Hartley wrote *Sea Burial* (1941), a collection of poems memorializing his fisherman-lover lost at sea. Gerrit Lansing, in *Heavenly Tree, Soluble Forest* (1995), said of Cape Ann, in Massachusetts, that "Urban hells seem fictive here, / Where . . . the Gloucester buoys dip." Provincetown, a gay and lesbian mecca at the tip of Cape Cod, attracts artists of all stripes year-round. The very southern Broadway playwright Tennessee Williams summered in Provincetown and Nantucket, Mass. The Provincetown Poets Series often provides financial support for poetry readings on Cape Cod. Provincetown's Mark Doty bestows a new dimension on both poetry and understanding AIDS in *My Alexandria* (1993), *Atlantis* (1995), and his memoir *Heaven's Coast* (1996). Michael Klein, also active in Provincetown AIDS work, edited *Poets for Life: Seventy-six Poets Respond to AIDS* (1992). Born in Greece, the poet Olga Broumas has carried some of the Aegean into Provincetown Harbor. In "Lullaby," she sings,

You leaned
into me like a ship embracing
the water.

Homosexual students and teachers have often been attracted to New England's educational institutions. Gertrude Stein developed her ideas while at Radcliffe College studying psychology with William James. Her paper "Cultivated Motor Automatism: A Study of Character in Relation to Attention" (1896)

provides clues to her later style. At Wellesley, Katherine Lee Bates wrote the hymn "America the Beautiful," became chair of the English department, and lived happily with her lover, the economist Katherine Coleman. The black activist and novelist James Baldwin taught before his death at Hampshire College, whose Amherst, Mass., campus he found confining. The African American novelist Samuel R. Delany, by contrast, a professor of comparative literature since 1988 at the University of Massachusetts, has enjoyed living in that same campus town.

New England homosexuals have organized several literary circles. Douglass Shand-Tucci's *Boston Bohemia* (1995) identifies Boston groups that admired the work of Walt Whitman, Oscar Wilde, Sappho, Aubrey Beardsley, and others. Antonio Alfredo Giarraputo served as founding editor of the *Homophile Union of Boston* magazine and organized the Calamus Poets. Boston's Good Gay Poets took its name from the expression "good gray poets," used to describe Henry Wadsworth Longfellow, James Russell Lowell, and John Greenleaf Whittier. In 1972 the group published a gay liberation broadside by Aaron Shurin entitled *Exorcism of the Straight Man Demon* (1972). It has since issued more than a dozen titles from writers including Salvatore Farinella (*The Orange Telephone* [1975]), Stephanie Byrd (*25 Years of Malcontent* [1976]), Maurice Kenny (*Only as Far as Brooklyn* [1979]), Pat Kuras (*The Pinball Player* [1982]), David Eberly (*What Has Been Lost* [1982]), and Walta Borawski (*Sexually Dangerous Poet* [1984]). An organizer of the Good Gay Poets and himself the author of seven books of poetry, the Boston professor and poet Ron Schreiber has inspired the next generation of lesbian and gay writers.

Lesbian feminist circles have flourished in the Connecticut River valley from northern New Hampshire to Long Island Sound. The valley's rural setting has provided sanctuary to writers Adrienne Rich, Jewelle Gomez, and Jill Johnson. Cherríe Moraga worked with Persephone Press in Watertown, Mass., where she edited the pathbreaking *This Bridge Called My Back: Writings by Radical Women of Color* (1981). The book takes its title from a poem by Kate Rushin, a Boston-area activist and poet whose powerful voice has inspired participants at many gatherings. She delivered the Audre Lorde Memorial Lecture in 1993 for Outwrite, a yearly gathering of lesbian and gay writers sponsored by Boston's *Gay Community News*.

Regional, ethnic, literary, and sexual identifications carry varying weights for different writers. Published by Zoland Books of Cambridge, Kim Vaeth reveals herself to be a poet of deep and tonic lyricism in *Her Yes* (1994). Speaking of the need to resist the denial or silencing of queer expression, she proclaims in that collection,

> It's not that a place
> belongs to us
> but that we
> resist the right things.

Sarah Orne Jewett followed her own path with more discretion but plenty of intensity in South Berwick, Maine, where she was born and died. She lived for many years with Annie Fields in a so-called Boston marriage as she developed her vision of rural New England. Resisting his New England birthplace, John Preston traveled to Los Angeles to become a gay liberationist but came back east to Portland, Maine, where he wrote *Winter's Light: Reflections of a Yankee Queer* (1995) in his final years. Preston celebrates New England bondage, discipline, and queerness while seeking to resolve "the permanent mystery of how to fit in."

Eve Kosofsky Sedgwick, *The Epistemology of the Closet* (1990); Douglass Shand-Tucci, *The Crimson Letter: Harvard, Homosexuality, and the Shaping of American Culture* (2003); Claude J. Summers, ed., *Gay and Lesbian Literary Heritage: A Reader's Companion to the Writers and Their Works, from Antiquity to the Present* (2002).

Charley Shively

Hall, Donald (1928–) Poet.

Donald Andrew Hall, Jr., was born in New Haven, Conn. Throughout his childhood, Hall spent summers at his maternal grandparents' farm on Eagle Pond in Wilmot, N.H. This summer retreat influenced his life and poetry, infusing it with the rural New England quality it has retained throughout his career. While still a student at Phillips Exeter Academy, Hall attended the Bread Loaf Writers' Conference; there, the 16-year-old poet met Robert Frost. In his prose memoir *Remembering Poets* (1978), Hall describes the public Frost as "rustic, witty, avuncular," three qualities that Hall would later apply to his own work. Hall was graduated in 1951 from Harvard University, where he met poet Dylan Thomas and interviewed T. S. Eliot, an experience he also recalled in *Remembering Poets*. Hall studied at Oxford (B.Litt. 1953) and was a Harvard Junior Fellow (1954–57); in 1955 his first collection of poems, *Exiles and Marriages*, won the Lamont Poetry Prize. Not yet 30, Hall edited, with Robert Pack and Louis Simpson, *New Poets of England and America* (1957), an anthology praised for introducing W. D. Snodgrass, Adrienne Rich, Denise Levertov, and W. S. Merwin and vilified for excluding Allen Ginsberg and others of the Beat and Black Mountain schools.

Donald Hall, Wilmont, N.H., 1987

Though known widely as a poet, Hall has produced a prolific body of prose, ranging from a book-length profile of the sculptor Henry Moore (1966) to a sports biography, *Dock Ellis in the Country of Baseball* (1976). His beautifully illustrated children's book *Ox-Cart Man* (1979) won the prestigious Caldecott Medal in 1980 and is still popular. He has also edited and contributed to several major textbooks on the teaching of poetry and fiction writing and is editor of the influential composition textbook *Writing Well*, first published in 1973.

Life in New England, however, is the subject of Hall's best-known work. In his first memoir, *String Too Short to Be Saved* (1961), he recounts his grandparents' stories of the New England countryside surrounding the ancestral Eagle Pond Farm and clearly places New England at the center of the reader's imagination. The importance of storytelling and the rural values of thrift and hard work often surface in Hall's writing. In his second memoir, *Seasons at Eagle Pond* (1987), Hall circles back to the themes of his first, underlining the importance of cycles (seasons), memory (family stories), and the vanishing rural life. Like Robert Frost, Donald Hall finds solace in the traditions and imagination of his native New England.

Hall's literary life was marked from the beginning by accelerating professional success, including a distinguished teaching career at the University of Michigan (1957–75). In 1972 Hall married the poet Jane Kenyon (his second marriage). Hall and Kenyon left Michigan in 1975 and moved to Eagle Pond Farm, where they lived and worked together as poets. Hall's poetry, once quite formal, became primarily free verse, concerned largely with memory and reminiscence. "He carried the pails of sap, sixteen-quart / buckets, dangling from each end / of a wooden yoke," Hall writes of his grandfather in "Maple Syrup," a poem in the highly acclaimed *Kicking the Leaves* (1978). *The Happy Man* (1986), which was awarded the Lenore Marshall Prize in 1987, followed, and in 1988 *The One Day, A Poem in Three Parts,* won the National Book Critics Circle Award.

In the 1990s Hall published prose books, numerous children's books, and several poetry collections, including *Old and New Poems* (1990), *The Museum of Clear Ideas* (1993), *The Old Life* (1996), and *Without* (1998). Hall has twice battled cancer (an experience he describes in his 1993 memoir, *Life Work*) and continues to live at Eagle Pond. Jane Kenyon died of leukemia in 1995, the same year she was named New Hampshire's poet laureate.

Hall's lifelong commitment to poetry, place, and the literary life has led to dozens of prizes, countless readings at colleges and universities, appointments as poet laureate of New Hampshire (1984–89), and, like Robert Frost earlier in the century, international prominence as a man of letters.

Liam Rector, ed. *The Day I Was Older: On the Poetry of Donald Hall* (1989); *Tennessee Poetry Journal,* special Donald Hall issue (Winter 1971).

John Edward Lane

Hawthorne, Nathaniel (1804–64)

Writer. Nathaniel Hawthorne was born in Salem, Mass., the second child of a Salem ship's captain and a direct descendant of Puritan worthies including a judge in Salem's witch trials. Hawthorne spent most of his life in New England, and the region's historical and legendary past permeates his fiction.

After his father died at sea in 1808, Hawthorne moved with his mother and sisters into the home of his mother's large family, the Mannings. A bookish boy dependent on the Mannings's bounty, Hawthorne felt liberated only when he lived with his mother and sisters for extended periods in Raymond, Maine, on Lake Sebago. Summoned back to Salem to prepare for college, he worked part time in the Mannings's stagecoach office and sadly concluded, "No Man can be a Poet and a Book-Keeper at the same time."

Hawthorne graduated from Bowdoin College in 1825, 18th in a class of 35 that included Henry Wadsworth Longfellow and Franklin Pierce. He then spent "twelve lonely years" in the Mannings's "chamber under the eaves," trying to establish himself as a writer. In 1828 he published at his own expense the slender novel *Fanshawe* (1828), drawn from his college experience, but never acknowledged writing it. Disappointed by a publisher's unenthusiastic response to his proposed collection, *Seven Tales of My Native Land,* Hawthorne burned most of the manuscript and failed to secure publication of two subsequent collections. But in 1830 Hawthorne's tales began appearing regularly in periodicals and literary annuals, among them such challenging fictional interrogations of the New England past as "Young Goodman Brown," "My Kinsman, Major Molineux," "Roger Malvin's Burial," and "The Gentle Boy."

Hawthorne's career was furthered considerably in 1837 when *Twice-Told Tales* was published. This collection of 18 previously published stories won Hawthorne warm praise from distinguished critics such as Longfellow. *Twice-Told Tales* was more than a literary milestone for Hawthorne; by 1839 he was secretly engaged to Sophia Peabody, a frail amateur artist who was also from Salem.

To supplement the income he earned as a writer, Hawthorne accepted an appointment as measurer in the Boston Custom House in January 1839 but quit after a year. That year he produced only three children's books—*Grandfather's Chair, Famous Old People,* and *Liberty Tree.* In April 1841 he joined the Brook Farm experimental commune in West Roxbury, Mass. Although skeptical about the community's Transcendentalist beliefs in individual and social perfectibility, Hawthorne hoped to build a home there for himself and Sophia. But the burdens of farm work left him too tired to write, and he returned to Salem in November.

Nathaniel Hawthorne, ca. 1860

An expanded version of *Twice-Told Tales* appeared in 1842. That year Hawthorne and Sophia were married and moved into the Old Manse, Ralph Waldo Emerson's ancestral home in Concord, Mass. A typical day for Hawthorne included swimming, rowing, gardening, and conversing with Henry David Thoreau and Emerson. He produced nearly two dozen stories and sketches, including "The Birth-mark" and "Rappaccini's Daughter," but could not earn enough as a writer to support his family, particularly after the birth of his daughter Una in 1844.

In April 1846 Hawthorne became surveyor of the Salem Custom House. In June, *Mosses from an Old Manse,* a collection of short stories that included "Young Goodman Brown," "The Artist of the Beautiful," and "The Birth-mark," was published and the Hawthornes' son Julian was born. Hawthorne was dismissed from the Custom House by the victorious Whigs in 1849 and became anguished that summer when his mother died. He began writing a fictional indictment of patriarchal tyranny in Puritan New England; in March 1850 *The Scarlet Letter* was published by Boston's major literary house, Ticknor and Fields, securing Hawthorne's reputation as a major writer. Its prefatory essay, "The Custom-House," gibes the officials who connived his dismissal and defines his prerequisites for writing fiction: "a neutral territory, somewhere between the real world and fairy-land, where the Actual and the Imaginary may meet, and each imbue itself with the nature of the other." Although the novel itself excited controversy

as a story of adultery, it was widely praised for its profound originality and tight artistic control.

Hawthorne next moved to Lenox, Mass., where he wrote *The House of the Seven Gables* (1851), a novel about a Salem family burdened by ancestral guilt; retold Greek myths for children in *A Wonder-Book for Girls and Boys* (1851); assembled *The Snow-Image and Other Twice-Told Tales* (1852); and drew on his experiences at Brook Farm for his third major novel, *The Blithedale Romance* (1852). His daughter Rose was born in 1851. This was also the period of his close friendship with the much younger Herman Melville, whose unsigned essay "Hawthorne and His Mosses" praised Hawthorne's "power of blackness." Melville dedicated *Moby-Dick* (1851) to Hawthorne with "admiration for his genius."

In 1852 Hawthorne bought a house in Concord that he named Wayside; it was the only house he ever owned. He wrote a campaign biography for Franklin Pierce, which resulted in his third political appointment—as American Consul at Liverpool—in 1853. Until his term ended in 1857, Hawthorne completed no other literary works. During a year and a half sojourn in Italy, he began *The Marble Faun,* the last novel he would complete.

Hawthorne returned to Concord in 1860 and then worked abortively on three other romances; except for a wry report on his visit to wartime Washington, he published only a series of sketches drawn from his English notebooks. His health had seriously deteriorated, and in 1864 Hawthorne died in his sleep in Plymouth, N.H., while on a trip with Pierce.

Despite changes in critical climate, Hawthorne has been recognized for more than a century as one of the most important American writers. His writing influenced later writers such as Henry James, Edith Wharton, and John Updike. Hawthorne's works explore the enduring features of the New England psyche—its Puritan introspection and guilt, its reformist impulse, and its ambivalent attitudes about nature as either paradisiacal or fallen and sinful.

Nina Baym, *The Shape of Hawthorne's Career* (1976); Nathaniel Hawthorne, *The Centenary Edition of the Works of Nathaniel Hawthorne,* 23 vols., ed. William Charvat et al. (1962–97); Terence Martin, *Nathaniel Hawthorne* (1983); James Mellow, *Nathaniel Hawthorne in His Times* (1980); Arlin Turner, *Nathaniel Hawthorne: A Biography* (1980); Brenda Wineapple, *Hawthorne: A Life* (2003).

Rita K. Gollin

Historical Fiction There can be little doubt that Nathaniel Hawthorne's *The Scarlet Letter* (1850) has significantly contributed to the national (and perhaps international) image of New England. Generations of high school students have read about the trials of Hester Prynne and her guilt-ridden lover, absorbing Hawthorne's portrayals of stern Puritan elders, shadowy Native Americans, and supernatural phenomena, all of which have been perennially and problematically associated with the region. Several strains emerged during this period and remain popular: a focus on the Puritans; a questioning of the truth of the official historical record; an emphasis on New England's revolutionary era to promote the region's national significance or to criticize current policy; and a nostalgia for New England's past.

At the time of its emergence in the United States in the 1820s, historical fiction was sometimes virtually indistinguishable from other forms of historical narrative, from popular biography and schoolbooks to academic histories that combined documentary evidence with local lore. Given the blending of fact and fiction in these genres, writers of historical fiction played an important role in creating a repository of images and stories about New England's past and the role of that past in the founding of a nation. Historical fiction may perpetuate the idea that New England exists as a distinct, homogenous community, but it also poses alternative histories of the region as a culturally diverse society troubled by religious and racial conflict. Moreover, as Philip Gould notes, the accuracy of historical fiction's presentation of the past is dubious, so these works need to be seen as a commentary as much on the era of their publication as on the region's past. Twentieth-century historical fiction furthers the genre's examination of New England's regional identity, demonstrating both nostalgia for a bygone order and discomfort over the colonial legacy.

Coming to vogue as it does during the early national period, historical fiction often seeks to bolster the endangered reputation of the Puritan colonists. John Lothrop Motley's *Merry-Mount; A Romance of the Massachusetts Colony* (1849), for instance, was written to awaken "a spark of sympathy for the heroic souls, who . . . laid the foundation of this fair inheritance of ours." In detailing the 1627 incident, however, in which Thomas Morton observed May Day by setting up a maypole, an Anglican custom, at Merry Mount (present-day Quincy, Mass.), Motley necessarily raises the issue of Puritan religious intolerance, a theme addressed by many writers of the genre. In Eliza Buckminster Lee's *Naomi; or, Boston 200 Years Ago* (1848), a young woman is banished from the Massachusetts Bay Colony on the charge of helping a convicted Quaker to escape. Linking the execution of a Quaker woman in the mid-1600s with the witch trials

at the end of the century, John Neal's *Rachel Dyer* (1828) suggests the ramifications of Puritan fanaticism. The title character of Hawthorne's "Young Goodman Brown" (1835) witnesses the Puritan "saints" attending the witches' Sabbath, an incident that not only suggests the hypocrisy of the Puritan elders but also challenges the objectivity of historical documents, such as Cotton Mather's *The Wonders of the Invisible World* (1692). At the end of the 19th century, Mary E. Wilkins Freeman's "The Little Maid at the Door" (1892) suggests an even more uncanny uncertainty about Salem history. The tale, based on the "Records of Salem Witchcraft" (1864), evokes the ghost of a child left to starve at the Proctor house after her family's arrest, a child visible only to Ann, wife of Joseph Bayley, who testified against Elizabeth Proctor in 1692. The continuing value of the Puritan era to historical fiction is seen in recent works, such as John Updike's retelling of *The Scarlet Letter* in his novel *S.* (1988) and Maryse Condé's *I, Tituba, Black Witch of Salem* (1992); these works tend to evoke the Puritan past in order to undermine its sexual and racial order.

Questioning New England's historical record provides much of historical fiction's driving force in the early 19th century. James Fenimore Cooper's *The Wept of Wish-Ton-Wish* (1829), a retelling of King Philip's War (1675–76), challenges contemporary justifications for Puritan greed, indicting historians and contemporary New England political attitudes as well as the Puritan settlers. Catharine Sedgwick's *Hope Leslie* (1827) allows Magawisca, daughter of a Pequot chief, to recite the 1637 Pequot War from a Native American viewpoint, emphasizing that the Indians were slaughtered, driven into exile, sold into slavery in the West Indies, and forced into servitude in Puritan homes. Presenting an alternative to race war, Lydia Maria Child's *Hobomok* (1824) envisions a marriage between the Native American Hobomok and Mary Conant, daughter of a Puritan colonist. They produce a child, but when Mary's former lover, thought lost at sea, returns to claim her, Hobomok steps aside without protest, and his son, "Little Hobomok," is raised as a white man, attending university and studying in England. "His father was seldom spoken of," Child's narrator notes, "and by degrees his Indian appellation was silently omitted." As Nina Baym has observed, these fictions, while criticizing the Puritan treatment of the Native American, nevertheless legitimate the inevitability of Indian removal.

As much as New England historical fiction is a genre of place, then, it is equally a genre of displacement, a theme that explores and criticizes the region's complicity in the slave trade.

Lydia Huntley Sigourney, eventually a noted supporter of the Liberia colonization scheme, depicts in *Sketch of Connecticut, Forty Years Since* (1824) an aged African named Primus, torn from his native land to be made a slave in Connecticut. Several novels contest the accepted image of the antislavery North. In *The Minister's Wooing* (1859), set in slave-trading Newport, R.I., in the 1790s, Harriet Beecher Stowe calls on Candace, a slave, to challenge the morality of the American republic. "When Gineral Washington was here," Candace testifies, "I hearn 'em read de Declaration ob Independence and Bill o' Rights; an' I tole Cato den, says I, 'Ef dat ar' true, you an' I are as free as anybody.'" Truman John Nelson's *The Sin of the Prophet* explores in 1952 the case of Anthony Burns, an escaped slave who was captured and returned to slavery from Boston in 1854 under the Fugitive Slave Law of 1850, a compromise on the part of the North to preserve the Union.

The patriotism of the New Englanders who fought to establish that union in 1776 is a subject on which writers of historical fiction have relied to promote the region's significance to the national identity. Child's *The Rebels; or, Boston before the Revolution* (1825) and Ann Sophia Stephens's *Sir Henry's Ward: A Tale of the Revolution* (1846) honor the achievement of the early patriots, as do F. Van Wyck Mason's *Eagle in the Sky* (1948) and Howard Fast's *April Morning* (1961) more than 100 years later. Herman Melville's *Israel Potter* (1855), however, is not so unequivocally nationalist. Potter fights at Bunker Hill, only to spend the ensuing 50 years in England as prisoner or pauper. When he returns to his native New England, he is nearly killed by a float in a Fourth of July parade, a satirical comment on the ideals of the Revolution.

Sarah Orne Jewett's *The Tory Lover* (1901) also acknowledges ambiguities in the revolutionary project, exploring the troubling dual allegiance of the British loyalists. The Maine author Kenneth Roberts claims that "the intellectual cream of America" during the revolutionary era were the Tories, which provides the foundation for *Oliver Wiswell* (1940). The best-selling novel, which portrays the events of the Revolution from the loyalist standpoint and includes inflammatory attacks on the Declaration of Independence, earned Roberts a firestorm of criticism (from New England and beyond) that considered the novel one-sided and antipatriotic. Although it finds problems with the received history of the region, Roberts's novel nevertheless emphasizes the American patriotism of the alienated loyalists, expressing nostalgia for the civilized sentiments of the "intellectual" British sympathizers. Esther Forbes wrote a series of popular books that evoked the colonial past and its corrective values during a time of economic depression and war. Her books continue a long New England tradition of historical works for children and adults alike, with her *Johnny Tremain* (1943) and *A Mirror for Witches* (1928). Other best-sellers evoking the revolutionary era were Kenneth Roberts's *Rabble in Arms* (1933) and *Lydia Bailey* (1947), and Daniel P. Thompson's *The Green Mountain Boys* (1839).

A similar nostalgia marks Stephen Vincent Benét's classic "The Devil and Daniel Webster" (1937), a humorous tale in which the famed orator and statesman argues for the soul of one Jabez Stone, an "ordinary" New Hampshire man, before a jury that includes King Philip (Metacom), Thomas Morton, Blackbeard, and nine others from "the fires of hell," who all "played a part in America." The trial is conducted by Justice Hathorne, who presided over the Salem witch trials, bequeathing to Nathaniel Hawthorne the writer's famed ancestral guilt. Webster invokes "the things that make a country a country, and a man a man. . . . He talked of the early days of America and the men who made those days. . . . [H]e showed how, out of the wrong and the right, the suffering and the starvations, something new had come. . . . And his words came back at the end to New Hampshire ground, and the one spot of land that each man loves and clings to. He painted a picture of that, and to each one of that jury he spoke of things long forgotten." As Benét represents it, making a country, making history, is man's work, not woman's, and (the notable exception of King Philip notwithstanding) it is apparently white man's work. The ownership of land, additionally, is deemed essential to manhood.

Not surprisingly, the effects on New England of this patriarchal point of view are suggested in late-20th-century historical fiction. E. Annie Proulx's *Postcards* (1991), set in post–World War II Vermont, chronicles the disintegration of the Blood family and their small farm, out of step with the industrial postwar economy. In this unexpectedly optimistic exploration of recent New England history, the genre frees itself of the burden of historical responsibility but retains the legacy of New England character, demonstrating the unflagging resilience of the region's inhabitants in the face of a radically changed world.

Nina Baym, *American Women Writers and the Work of History, 1790–1860* (1995); Michael Davitt Bell, *Hawthorne and the Historical Romance of New England* (1971); Lawrence Buell, *New England Literary Culture: From Revolution through Renaissance* (1986); Philip Gould, *Covenant and Republic: Historical Romance and the Politics of Puritanism* (1996).

Victoria Clements and Etsuko Taketani

Hopkins, Pauline Elizabeth (1859–1930)

Novelist, editor, journalist, playwright, performer, biographer. Born in Portland, Maine, and reared in Boston, Pauline Elizabeth Hopkins published mainly in the Boston-based *Colored American Magazine,* the first major journal owned and operated by African Americans. She spent most of her life in the Boston area, devoting her career to the cause of "Negro Uplift"—the social, economic, and political betterment of African American people. In both fiction and journalism, Hopkins celebrated family and community and explored racism, miscegenation, and the role of women in the rising black middle class. Plot-driven and drawing on conventions of both sentimental and protest fiction, her novels were written to mobilize her readership by appealing to what she saw as the specifically New England values of liberty, justice, and radical political action.

The daughter of Northrup Hopkins of Virginia and Sarah (Allen) Hopkins of Exeter, N.H., Pauline Hopkins was descended on her mother's side from the New Hampshire African American poet and activist James M. Whitfield (1822–71) and from Nathaniel and Thomas Paul, founders of Boston's Saint Paul Baptist Church. Before graduating from Boston's Girls High School, 15-year-old Hopkins won an essay contest sponsored by William Wells Brown and the Congregational Publishing Society of Boston with her essay "Evils of Intemperance and Their Remedy," initiating her lifelong interest in social and political issues. Her *Slaves' Escape; or, The Underground Railroad* (1879), the first known play by an African American woman, was retitled and performed the following year in Boston as *Peculiar Sam; or, The Underground Railroad* with Hopkins in the starring role. She continued singing and acting until the early 1890s with her family's troupe, the Hopkins' Colored Troubadours. During this period she also lectured in Boston, wrote a second play—*One Scene from the Drama of Early Days*—and began working as a stenographer, an occupation she would return to off and on throughout her life.

In 1900 Hopkins joined the board of the newly formed *Colored American Magazine.* She served as editor of the Women's Department from 1901 to 1903, literary editor from 1903 to 1904, and unacknowledged editor-in-chief for an unknown period of time. In these capacities Hopkins showcased African American cultural achievements and offered revisionist accounts of African American history. She published her own works of fiction and nonfiction in the magazine, including three serialized novels (*Hagar's Daughter: A Story of Southern Caste Prejudice* [1901–02]; *Winona: A Tale of Negro Life in the South and Southwest* [1902]; and *Of One Blood; or, The Hidden Self* [1902–03]). Her best-known novel, *Contending Forces: A Romance Illustrative of Negro Life North and South* (1900), examines the legacy of slavery in a middle-class Boston African American family. In 1904 Fred R. Moore, a supporter of Booker T. Washington's conciliatory racial politics, purchased *Colored American Magazine,* and Hopkins, who adhered to W. E. B. Du Bois's more assertive politics, was forced to resign. Two of her articles—"The New York Subway" (1904) and "The Dark Races of the 20th Century" (1905)—appeared in *Voice of the Negro,* and in 1916 she founded and edited the short-lived *New Era* magazine, in which she serially published her novella *Topsy Templeton* (1916). Little is known of her life after this. Hopkins had been working as a stenographer at the Massachusetts Institute of Technology when she died in an accidental fire in her home in Cambridge, Mass. With the republication of her work in the Schomburg Library of African American Women Writers and in numerous anthologies, and with increased critical attention paid to her work over the past decade, Hopkins's reputation has grown steadily.

Hazel V. Carby, *Reconstructing Womanhood: The Emergence of the Afro-American Woman Novelist* (1987); John Cullen Gruesser, ed., *The Unruly Voice: Rediscovering Pauline Elizabeth Hopkins* (1996); Claudia Tate, *Domestic Allegories of Political Desire: The Black Heroine's Text at the Turn of the Century* (1992).

Kate McCullough

Howells, William Dean (1837–1920)

Writer and editor. William Dean Howells, one of America's most prolific and influential novelists, was born in Martinsville (now Martin's Ferry), Ohio, the son of William Cooper Howells and Mary (Dean) Howells. Although he identified himself as a "westerner" and had an ambiguous relation with New England culture, Howells lived most of his life in Boston, where he became editor of the *Atlantic Monthly,* and New York, where he wrote "The Editor's Study" and later "The Editor's Easy Chair" for *Harpers' Monthly.* In his 60-year career, he produced nearly 100 books, including novels, plays, reminiscences, travel books, criticism, poetry, and campaign biographies, as well as voluminous book reviews and editorial columns. He was an early advocate of American realism—the accurate portrayal of contemporary social life—and was generous and effective in promoting the careers of two generations of realists, including his closest friends, Mark Twain and Henry James.

As a largely self-educated Ohio reporter aspiring to be a Romantic poet, Howells made a

William Dean Howells, ca. 1870

pilgrimage to New England in 1860 that confirmed his commitment to a literary vocation. He was warmly received by James Russell Lowell, then editor of the *Atlantic*, who introduced him to the luminaries of literary Boston, including Nathaniel Hawthorne, Ralph Waldo Emerson, Oliver Wendell Holmes, Sr., C. E. Norton, and the new owner of the *Atlantic*, James T. Fields. In 1866 Fields hired him as assistant editor at the *Atlantic*, and in 1871 he succeeded Fields as editor-in-chief, a position he held until 1881. While continuing to publish New England writers, Howells gave the *Atlantic* a fully national scope by publishing postwar regional writing from the South and West and by promoting the beginnings of a more modern realism.

Many of Howells's works describe New England settings, characters, and culture and reflect his complex ambivalence toward the New England cultural elite that had enthusiastically embraced him. In several of his early novels these conflicting feelings are embodied in clever, independent, middle-class, midwestern or small-town girls who demonstrate their intellectual and moral superiority to effete, Europeanized, antidemocratic Brahmins. Two of Howells's best novels, *A Modern Instance* (1882) and *The Rise of Silas Lapham* (1885), are also set in New England and deal with issues of social class and the ethics of business and of divorce.

In 1888 Howells moved from Boston to New York—reflecting a shift in the national center of literature and publishing from Boston to Manhattan—and lived there until his death. He was strongly influenced first by the depth psychology of Ivan Turgenev and later, after a mental breakdown at the height of his success and prosperity, by the aesthetic and ethical example of Lev Tolstoy. Increasingly politically liberal and pro-labor, he petitioned for the pardon of the anarchists convicted of inciting violence in Chicago's Haymarket labor riots of 1886, joined Mark Twain in opposing American imperialism, and became a founding sponsor of the National Association for the Advancement of Colored People (NAACP). While middle-class domestic life remained his essential subject, later novels (most notably *A Hazard of New Fortunes* [1890]) focused on contemporary social issues such as the corrosive effects of poverty and excessive wealth, religious demagoguery, and class conflict, belying modernists' dismissal of Howells as treating only "the smiling aspects" of American life. Writers whom he influenced and to whom he gave important critical and personal support include Twain, John William DeForest, Charles Chesnutt, Henry Fuller, Hamlin Garland, Stephen Crane, and New Englanders Mary E. Wilkins Freeman and Sarah Orne Jewett.

George Arms and Christopher Lohman, eds., *Selected Letters of William Dean Howells* (1979–83); June Howard, *Publishing the Family* (2001); Clara M. Kirk and Rudolph Kirk, *William Dean Howells* (1962); Kenneth S. Lynn, *William Dean Howells: An American Life* (1971); Elizabeth Stevens Prioleau, *The Circle of Eros: Sexuality in the Work of William Dean Howells* (1983).

Ellery Sedgwick

Humorists to 1900

The phrase "New England humor" evokes images of Yankee peddlers, tricksters, and swains spinning yarns in dialect and eventually evolving into the character of Uncle Sam. It also recalls "crackerbarrel philosophers," whose correspondence enlivened newspapers across the country with down east critiques of national politics and culture. But the story of New England humor is more various, encompassing attempts at moral reform, political satire, oral history, and even the betterment of women's education.

The earliest voices from pulpit, press, and stage belonged mainly to the literate elite, chiefly from Massachusetts, who wanted to reform through ridicule. The Puritan preacher Nathaniel Ward, assuming a rustic persona in *The Simple Cobler of Aggawam in America* (1647), defended Congregational orthodoxy and attacked women's fashions. Nathaniel Ames, in his *Astronomical Diary and Almanack* (1726), included shrewd observations and homely advice to fops, flirts, and scamps.

Late in the 18th century, John Trumbull, one of the Connecticut Wits, penned the satiric *Progress of Dulness* (1772) and the mock epic *M'Fingal* (1776, 1782). Satiric playwrights included the Tory Jonathan Sewall, who ridiculed the Continental Congress in *The Americans Roused, in a Cure for the Spleen* (1775), and the patriot Mercy Otis Warren, who exposed British/Tory ineptitude and praised Yankee ingenuity in *The Group* (1775) and *The Blockheads* (1776). Royall Tyler, in his comedy *The Contrast* (1790), created the comic servant Jonathan, the epitome of "Yankee Doodle," who is socially ignorant but shrewd.

After the War of 1812, New England humorists emphasized vernacular expressions—characteristic sayings and vocabulary—instead of trying to re-create a complete dialect. In 1832 actor George Handel "Yankee" Hill brought Jonathan Ploughboy to life in Samuel Woodworth's *The Forest Rose* (1825) and in 1833 hit his stride as Jedediah Homebred in Joseph Jones's *The Green Mountain Boy*.

The 1830s initiated the "naive" political correspondent. In his *Portland Courier* (1830), Seba Smith introduced the prototype Jack Downing, who subsequently reported on his escapades from the Maine statehouse to the national capital; Ann Sophia Stephens's Jonathan Slick of Wethersfield, Conn., wrote home in *High Life in New York* (1843, 1873); and James Russell Lowell traced Hosea Biglow's saga in *The Biglow Papers* (1848, 1867), which satirically represented northerners' opposition to the war with Mexico, suggesting that the real purpose of the war was to expand slavery.

Other humorists whose alter egos became national personalities included New Hampshire's Benjamin Penhallow Shillaber, whose Mrs. Partington never allowed malapropisms to obscure her Yankee wisdom; James M. Bailey, whose Danbury News Man became a kind of regional historian; Henry Wheeler Shaw, whose Josh Billings uttered aphorisms that earned national usage; and Maine's Charles Farrar Browne, who, as garrulous showman Artemas Ward, lectured in this country and abroad.

" Stop Major ! I'll give you a ride."—
" Cant stop ; got an express for the Gineral."

Seba Smith's Jack Downing, 1833

A parallel tradition of humor by women countered the sexist strain that ran through men's humor. Poet Anne Bradstreet (*The Tenth Muse* [1650]) and essayist and playwright Judith Sargent Murray (*Virtue Triumphant* [1798]) used witty devices such as the ironic "apology" to address the plight of creative and intellectual women. Illustrating the evils that accrue to women who read only frivolous works that nurture romantic expectations, the New Hampshire satirist Tabitha Gilman Tenney, in *Female Quixotism* (1801), pleaded indirectly for better education for girls.

Other New England women spoke out more directly. Publishing weekly columns from 1851 to 1872 (primarily in the *New York Ledger*) under the pseudonym Fanny Fern, Sara Willis Parton caustically criticized society's double standard. Abby Morton Diaz in *The Schoolmaster's Trunk* (1874) strongly advocated women's education and cultural development, but in her *William Henry Letters* (1870) she voiced a gentler rural spirit.

Carl Holliday, *The Wit and Humor of Colonial Days, 1607–1800* (1912); Cameron C. Nickels, *New England Humor: From the Revolutionary War to the Civil War* (1993); Jennette Tandy, *Crackerbox Philosophers in American Humor and Satire* (1925); Nancy Walker and Zita Dresner, eds., *Redressing the Balance: American Women's Literary Humor from Colonial Times to the 1980s* (1988).

Lucy M. Freibert

Humorists, 1900 to the Present

Twentieth-century New England humor continued the late-19th-century tradition of Rowland Robinson, who described his stories of Uncle Lisha and Sam Lovel as portraying characters, customs, and speech "fortified against the march of improvement." In the first half of the century, writers such as Sarah Pratt McClean Greene, George S. Wasson, Walter Hard, and Holman Day recounted stories of preindustrial New England folkways from farm, village, lumber camp, and the sea, often rooted in both folk and literary humor. Greene's regionalist novels, including *Cape Cod Folks* (1881), *Vesty of the Basins* (1892), *Flood-tide* (1901), and *Winslow Plain* (1902), typically feature a cosmopolitan narrator or other city dweller living with more rough-hewn characters from the shores and backcountry of New England, often with predictably comic results. In Wasson's *Cap'n Simeon's Store* (1903) retired skippers gather regularly at Simeon's in Killick Cove, Maine, a once-prosperous seaport, to swap stories of the old days and to complain about "rusticators" (later, "summer people" or "those from away") and newfangled ways generally in a local dialect salted with seafaring slang. "A set-fired sight less of bookin' of it, and consid'ble

more hoss sense is jest what the world is fairly achin' for now'days!" says Asa Fairway. *The Outlook* called Day's first book of verse, *Up in Maine* (1900), a "delicious adjunct" to James Russell Lowell's *Biglow Papers,* no doubt in reference to Day's own skillful rendering of New England folk speech into formal rhyme and rhythm. Hard, on the other hand, in books such as *Salt of Vermont* (1931) and *Vermont Valley* (1933), wrote in a free verse that he called "a kind of Vermont rhythm" so that "people will read it more as I mean it." Hard often ended his compact vignettes of local character with italicized dialect as a kind of comic punch line, but sometimes as the terse, understated commentary on life often called typically New England.

The "humor" of New England humor in the second half of the century, roughly speaking, lies not so much in recollections of the past but in the contrasts between native New England ways of life and the changes represented by government regulations, industrialism, and the inroads into a region attractive to people identified as "those from away," "summer people," or "flatlanders." John Gould's work over many years, particularly his "Dispatches from the Farm" in the *Christian Science Monitor* beginning in 1942 and his many books—from *Farmer Takes a Wife* (1945) to *It Is Not Now* (1993)—are written in that spirit. Although firmly centered in Maine, Gould's stories addressed a national audience that could identify with people who preserved a sense of local individuality and protested the various powers that be.

The most identifiable and distinguishing feature of New England humor in the 20th century may well be the effort to capture native pronunciations and expressions that are themselves humorous but that also implicitly affirm and preserve ways of life eroded by the inevitable uniformity of a mass culture and a national economy. As the century ended, New England humor enjoyed a renaissance that made good use of electronic media that preserve regional speech and, because aural, make it more accessible than print can. That began in 1958 with Robert Bryan's and Marshall Dodge's best-selling recording *Bert and I and Other Stories from Down East;* Vermonter Francis A. Colburn's *A Commencement Address,* of about the same time; and Norman Lewis's 1962 appearance as Danny Gore, perennial candidate for governor of Vermont for 34 years. A syndicated columnist from 1974 to 1990, Robert Skoglund, "The Humble Farmer," holds forth today on local television and Maine Public Radio and can be found on "The Internet Home for Maine Humor," along with Joe Perham, Kendall Morse, and others whose work is available on audio

recordings. So, too, is the work of a new generation of Vermont storytellers and humorists, Mac Parker and Tom Weakley.

New England humor today often portrays native New Englanders and their ways of life as comically backward but inherently superior to outsiders with pretensions to adopting a native identity. Ironically, although the butt of such humor, New Englanders are often the market for it. Offered as "an indispensable guide to Real Vermonters and Flatlanders alike," *Real Vermonters Don't Milk Goats* (1983), by Frank Bryan and William Mares, takes that stance, as do many of the cartoons of Don Bousquet. Appearing regularly in the *Providence Journal, Yankee* magazine, and other publications, Bousquet's work also pokes good fun at contemporary Rhode Islanders and New Englanders generally. Jeff Danziger, now political cartoonist for the *Los Angeles Times* syndicate, began his career in the late 1970s by delineating the waning of Vermont farm life in "The Teeds, Tales of Agriculture for Young and Old," a comic strip that still appears in the *Rutland (Vt.) Herald.* The work of Jack Maxson recalls an earlier, literary tradition of New England humor. His "Fenwick Snade" column began in the Keene, N.H., *Sentinel* in 1985, and with his creation of the fictional town of Piddlington and Fenwick's commentary on regional and national matters, Maxson is something of a latter-day Seba Smith.

The most visible New England humorist today is Tim Sample, whose "Postcards from Maine" have been featured on *CBS Sunday Morning* since 1993. (The political cartoonist Garry Trudeau cannot be considered a regional humorist, although his comic strip, *Doonesbury,* contains frequent allusions to his alma mater, Yale University, and to New Haven, Conn.) Sample began his career performing with Marshall Dodge in 1980, and through his illustrations, books, and audio and video recordings, he shows that New England humor is alive and well.

Jim Brunelle, ed., *Over to Home and from Away* (1980); Richard Dorson, *Jonathan Draws the Longbow* (1959); Patrick Flynn, "The Wicked Good Sense of Humor Down East," *Washington Post,* July 31, 1988; Judson Hale, "The Search for New England's Humor," *Yankee* 41 (1987); Alan J. Keays, "Funny Bones: What Makes Vermont Humor Work," *Vermont Magazine,* August 24, 1977.

Cameron C. Nickels

Images of Native Americans

In 1611 a Wampanoag named Epenowe was captured on Martha's Vineyard and taken to England, where he was displayed to curious eyes as "a wonder." Sir Ferdinando Gorges, who later purchased Epenowe, provides a typical pre-*Mayflower* description of New England natives, viewed as taller and healthier looking than the English, quick to learn their way around a new culture, and largely useless: "He was a goodly man," Gorges writes, "of a brave aspect, stout and sober in his demeanor, and had learned so much English as to bid those that wondered at him 'Welcome! Welcome!,' this being the last and best use they could make of him." There were more than a few captive New England natives in Europe at this time, among them Tisquantum, better known as Squanto. In that same year of 1611 Shakespeare's Trinculo in *The Tempest* expresses disgust for voyeurs who will "not give a doit to relieve a lame beggar, but will lay out ten to see a dead Indian." London quickly tired of the spectacle, and Epenowe tricked Gorges into taking him home with the promise that New England was full of gold.

Echoes of Epenowe's welcoming cry, along with the ghost of Shakespeare's dead Indian, pervade nonnative representations of aboriginal New England. "That welcome," Lydia Sigourney wrote in 1835, "was a blast and ban / Upon thy race unborn" ("The Indian's Welcome to the Pilgrim Fathers"). Ever since Abraham Lincoln made Thanksgiving a national holiday, children in feathers have brought popcorn to children with buckles pasted on their shoes, enacting a pageant of national origin that celebrates the generosity of native New Englanders. Meanwhile, the Abenaki, Pequot, Mohegan, Narragansett, and Penobscot, to name only a few of New England's native peoples, have struggled to gain and maintain recognition in the face of the widely held belief that all New England native people died or disappeared after King Philip's War (1675–76). The changing image of the Native American in white New England literature has constantly tried to negotiate the distance between these two poles. Friendly, good-looking Indians with "welcome" on their lips have contrasted with a huge number of dead ones whose demise is perceived as tragic but ultimately necessary. New England came to be viewed as a white homeland in part as a result of what inventive white writers did to steer their way between the violence of native-white conflict and the fact of native presence and persistence despite it.

Although Roger Williams and his followers in Providence sought to treat native peoples as equals, they were a rare exception to the rule. From the beginning English settlers saw Indians sometimes as innocents, more often as devil worshipers. Early colonists did not, however, see natives as a separate race. They generally thought that indigenous populations were a lost tribe of Israel and were white; conversion efforts operated side by side with warfare throughout the 17th century. The anti-

Puritan, free-living Thomas Morton, whose fraternization with native people did not endear him to his more pious neighbors, wrote in *New English Canaan* (1637) that native babies were "of complexion as white as our nations"; adults had a "tawny" appearance only because of exposure to the sun and the use of dyes. Initially, prejudice against native New Englanders arose from a belief not that they were racial others but that they were heathens and savages. Not until the late 18th century did scientific racism begin to supplant the early settlers' understanding of native origins.

Before they started leaning on the crutch of racial superiority, Europeans based disdain for indigenous people partly on the difference between native and white gender roles. Mary Rowlandson, who recounted her captivity experience in *The Soveraignty and Goodness of GOD . . . a Narrative of the Captivity and Restauration of Mrs. Mary Rowlandson* (1682), could not respect her captor, the powerful female sachem Weetamoo, because she could not comprehend female power operating so far outside the domestic sphere. Instead, Rowlandson portrayed Weetamoo, an important ally of Metacom (King Philip), as a domineering shrew who used makeup because she wasn't chaste. Edward Winslow had described native gender roles as corrupt in *Good Newes from New England* (1624), creating an image that became ubiquitous: "The men employ their time wholly in hunting [a leisure activity among the English gentry] and other exercises of the bow. The women live a most slavish life: they carry all the burdens, set and dress their corn, gather it in, and seek out much of their food." A common argument justifying European acquisition of native land was that European men labored to "improve" land by farming it, while native men idled their time away hunting; the fact that farming was women's work in native cultures did little to counter this argument for white sovereignty.

Two hundred years later Henry David Thoreau, who had exhaustive knowledge of native histories and culture, admitted that male natives farmed as well as hunted when he wanted to establish an unbroken lineage between native owners of New England soil and himself. He wrote in *Walden* (1854): "This generation is very sure to plant corn and beans each new year precisely as the Indians did centuries ago and taught the first settlers to do, as if there were a fate in it." In the 1862 essay "Walking," however, Thoreau used farming to assert his own right to the land, invoking farming as a masculine task performed on a feminine soil: "It is said to be the task of the American 'to work the virgin soil.' . . . I think that the farmer displaces the Indian even because he redeems the meadow, and so makes

himself stronger and in some respects more natural."

The saying "The Puritans fell first on their knees and then on the aborigines" has been attributed to several full- and part-time New Englanders, including Oliver Wendell Holmes and Mark Twain. Its dreadful irony sits uncomfortably alongside the magnitude of native suffering after 1620 but goes straight to the heart of colonist-native relations. The settlers were hard put to reconcile their desire to establish a blameless society with escalating violence between European immigrants and natives. William Bradford, Plymouth's second governor, repeatedly tried to navigate those dangerous waters. His painfully detailed account of the end of the Pequot War (1636–37) in *Of Plymouth Plantation* (1630–50) acknowledges the slaughter of the native population as horrifying even as the colonists thanked God for it: "It was a fearful sight to see them thus frying in the fire and the streams of blood quenching the same, and horrible was the stink and scent thereof; but the victory seemed a sweet sacrifice, and they [the colonists] gave the praise thereof to God, who had wrought so wonderfully for them."

The violence of early native-white relations continued to be a moral problem in the captivity narrative, a genre that dominated New England representations of native people during most of the 18th century. After the Revolution, however, a large body of sentimental literature emerged in which the question of native disappearance in the 17th century became a subject of shame and mourning. Writers in this genre reworked early atrocities out of a conviction that Indian policy in their own times was unfair and unnecessarily brutal. Some, like John Augustus Stone, whose 1828 play *Metamora; or, The Last of the Wampanoags* was hugely and unexpectedly popular, represented the violence of dispossession. A dramatization of King Philip's War, the play ends with Metamora cursing the Puritans as he dies of gunshot wounds: "My curses on you, white men! May the Great Spirit curse you when he speaks in his war voice from the clouds! Murderers!" It was far more common for writers to resolve their stories of native-white conflict in the quiet disappearance of the native hero or heroine, thus supplying a more or less comfortable rationale for white entitlement. Sarah Wentworth Morton's 1790 poem "Ouabi; or, The Virtues of Nature" is typical of the effort to both romanticize and eulogize the vanished native. Lydia Maria Child followed in 1824 with *Hobomok*, a work revolutionary for its depiction of interracial marriage but that nonetheless closes with a vanishing native. Uncas, James Fenimore Cooper's young native warrior who dies without leaving a son in *The Last* of the Mohicans (1826), takes his name from a Connecticut Mahican sachem who sided with the English during the Pequot War. New England's "good" Indians, Cooper implies, sadly faded before the advancing white man. Catharine Sedgwick's 1827 Hope Leslie continues the theme. The poetry of William Cullen Bryant and Lydia Sigourney similarly eulogized and utilized the disappearing native, and the argument reached an international audience with the 1855 publication of Henry Wadsworth Longfellow's Song of Hiawatha, the world's best-selling poem.

The literary tendency to romanticize the vanished New England native declined sharply in the second half of the 19th century, as Indian-white conflict in the West caught the nation's attention. After the Indian Removal Act, a policy effected in the 1830s and 1840s that relocated eastern native nations west of the Mississippi, and the Civil War, the imperative that white New Englanders justify their historical treatment of natives diminished. In the white American imagination the Indian had became a feathered, horseback-riding Plains chief. New England writers might still use the conceit of vanished natives, but indigenous New England was no longer a central ideological focus for the late-19th-century white writers of the region. In Sarah Orne Jewett's novel Country of the Pointed Firs (1896), for example, a character speaks of an island once inhabited by Indians: "I've heard myself 'twas one o' their cannibal places, but I never could believe it. There never was no cannibals on the coast o' Maine. All the Indians o' these regions are tame-looking folks." Jewett is able to depict Maine's coastal natives as absent culturally (no one can tell what their cultural practices were) but not physically (there are Indians in Maine). With the necessity to justify Puritan atrocities no longer in the forefront, Jewett can acknowledge a contemporary native presence, albeit "tame" and emptied of cultural efficacy.

Twentieth-century white writers found even fewer reasons to invoke New England's indigenous past, much less its present. Nevertheless, in 1923 Robert Frost brought the violence of Indian dispossession back to the myth of the disappearing native in his ironically titled "The Vanishing Red." The poem, which chronicles the demise of "the last Red Man / in Acton," hints that the Indian in question did not fade away but was murdered. But Frost declined to judge the murderer, claiming that

you can't go back and see it as he [the
    murderer] saw it. . . .
You'd have to have been there and lived it.
Then you wouldn't have looked on it as
    just a matter
Of who began it between the two races.

Frost's reluctance to analyze the history of native-white conflict in New England characterizes 20th-century white representations of native New Englanders. Disenchanted modernists did not fail to see how brutally New England's native peoples had been treated, but for 20th-century white writers, revealing the power of the myth that had obscured that brutality held more interest than the history itself. Robert Lowell's essay "New England and Further" (1977) mocks the myth's simplicity: "And the bad Indians—their extermination as crisp, bracing, and colorful as a pheasant shooting. . . . All gone." With respect to Thanksgiving he speaks of "the chorus of Indians, painted like women, and yet to the Pilgrims like Saint Bernards in a time of dearth." Lowell's Indians and their sufferings render ridiculous the solemn pageantry of Puritan historiography.

Native writers and speakers who used the English language to resist the power of white New Englanders' narratives of native devilry, unworthiness, and disappearance struggled against difficult odds. Indian writing and speech were often lost or ignored. John Eliot, known as the Apostle to the Indians, eventually learned enough Massachusett to be able to preach, but he relied on interpreters named Cockenoe and Job Nesutan, whose help he barely acknowledged though they "could oftentimes express our minds more distinctly than any of us could." Because efforts to teach native New Englanders English were most often undertaken by missionaries, most of the region's early indigenous writers were Christians. Ironically, that fact, along with the reading and writing they had learned from white teachers, tended to divest Christian Indians of authenticity in the eyes of white readers and listeners. Samson Occom, a Mohegan missionary writing home in 1765 from a fund-raising trip to England, puts his finger on the problems New England natives faced trying to represent themselves to European—or white American—audiences. White people "think it is nothing but a Shame to send me over the great Water. They say it is to impose upon the good People [of England]. They further affirm I was bro't up Regularly and a Christian all my Days. Some say I can't talk Indian. Others say I can't read." A Christian unable to "talk Indian," Occom was seen as an inauthentic native too far removed from the fantasy of the naked heathen in the woods. If he could not read, he was a poor representative of a people successfully Christianized. Either way, the result was rejection.

A generation later the Pequot minister William Apess penned a critique of New England Christian practice in which he struggled to articulate native equality and defend native sovereignty. His 1831 biography, A Son of the Forest, was written at the height of white writers' attempts to solidify the belief that New England was entirely empty of Indians. Insisting that the region's native peoples not only existed but had rights, Apess's powerful Eulogy on King Philip (1836) asks that "every man of color wrap himself in mourning, for the 22nd of December [the day the Pilgrims landed at Plymouth] and the 4th of July are days of mourning and not of joy. Let them rather fast and pray to the Great Spirit, the Indian's God, who deals out mercy to his red children, and not destruction." Here Apess stretches his own Christianity to the limit, almost claiming status as a heathen; it was a desperate rhetorical move made at a desperate historical juncture. Apess's voice rang out strongly affirming indigenous presence when almost every other writer on the subject was maintaining that native New Englanders had disappeared 200 years earlier.

If native people had not vanished by 1836, neither have they done so since that time, as a few nonnative writers have acknowledged. In Moby-Dick (1851), for example, Herman Melville's Stubbs, first mate of the significantly named Pequod, urges the Gay Head Wampanoag harpooner Tashtego to kill whales "for Old Gay head," acknowledging that nation's unbroken sovereignty there. Shortly after the turn of the 20th century, the black sociologist and protest leader W. E. B. Du Bois clearly perceived that black and native New Englanders confronted similar obstacles in their struggles for equality. Describing the first time he realized that his skin color differentiated him from his classmates in Souls of Black Folk (1903), Du Bois remembers "when the shadow swept across me. I was a little thing, away up in the hills of New England, where the dark Housatonic winds between Hoosac and Taghkanic to the sea." No sentimental user of native place-names to signify a sad but unavoidable disappearance of indigenous populations, Du Bois chooses Indian words instead of English ones to locate himself, a black man, as a New Englander. He thus inaugurates a policy of acknowledging native presence on the land and native dispossession that he maintains throughout his discourse on black history and identity in the United States.

During the 1920s New England native nations that had existed in self-protective obscurity began holding powwows and launched the endeavor of reclaiming both cultural and legal sovereignty. Contemporary New England native writers such as Abenaki poet Cheryl Savageau, Micmac poet Rita Joe, Penobscot novelist Ssipsis, Sokoki poet Robert Chute, and prolific Abenaki writer and editor Joseph Bruchac focus on the vital project of cultural recovery and preservation. They continue to engage the difficulties of representing oneself as a member of a particular native nation, as an American Indian, and as a native New Englander, with all the cultural and historical ramifications the name New England carries.

Robert F. Berkhofer, Jr., *The White Man's Indian* (1978); Helen Carr, *Inventing the American Primitive: Politics, Gender, and the Representation of Native American Literary Traditions, 1789–1936* (1996); Jill Lepore, *The Name of War: King Philip's War and the Origins of American Identity* (1998); Richard Slotkin, *Regeneration through Violence: The Mythology of the American Frontier, 1600–1860* (2000); Alden T. Vaughan, *New England Frontier: Puritans and Indians, 1620–1675* (1965).

Bethany Schneider

Immigrant Literature

Immigrant Literature Henry James begins his remarkable reflections on the state of American culture in *The American Scene* (1905) with a telling anecdote. Walking alone in a New Hampshire wood, he comes upon a decidedly foreign-looking, dark-complexioned working man. He tries some French on him, then a little Italian, getting only a puzzled look in return. "What are you?" he finally asks with exasperation. "Why, an Armenian," comes the reply, as if, James muses, that were "the most natural thing in the world." Indeed, it was then and still is now entirely natural for New England to display a rich and varied ethnicity, and for James the key to American culture lay precisely in its response to "the great ethnic question."

The native peoples of New England greeted or resisted the first immigrants, and immigrants have peopled New England since. Not all, like William Bradford, left a written or literary record such as the Mayflower Compact (1620) or *Of Plymouth Plantation* (1630–50), but the contributions to New England culture made by Irish, Italian, Jewish , Polish, Greek, Armenian, French Canadian, Portuguese, Cape Verdean, and, most recently, Asian immigrants comprise a rich lode.

Broadly speaking, most early Puritan literature was written by immigrants. After Bradford, we should note Anne Bradstreet, who wrote movingly in poems about the lot of women accommodating themselves to uprootedness, and Mother Ann Lee, a visionary who came over from England and began setting up Shaker communities in New England by the end of the 18th century. Narrowing our focus to immigration that occurred after statistics began to be kept in 1820, we can properly appreciate the fact that almost a third of all immigrants to America arrived between 1901 and 1910, 73 percent of them from southern and eastern Europe. An enormous immigration of Irish had occurred after the famine

in 1844, but this was the era of the great influx of Jews, Italians, Poles and other Slavic peoples, Greeks, and Armenians (quite likely including the woodsman whom James encountered). Cape Verdeans and Portuguese had been settling in New Bedford, Mass., and other whaling centers from the mid-19th century onward. West Indians came in a trickle that subsequently swelled, as did Puerto Ricans (properly speaking not immigrants, because they are American citizens at birth), other Hispanics, and Asians. The Chinese have a long history in and around Boston, but most Chinese, and Japanese, have settled in and around San Francisco, New York, and Los Angeles. French Canadians have been a vital presence since the late 19th century; the Catholic mass is still conducted in French in one Holyoke, Mass., church; Jack Kerouac made his home in Lowell, Mass.; and Paul Theroux settled in Medford, Mass. An early work on immigrant themes is *The Delusson Family* (1939) by Jacque Ducharme.

Longtime residents of New England or so-called older stock of British descent wrote about later immigrants in works typically dealing with the themes of accommodating to or deploring the arrival of the various nationalities who came to labor in New England's fields, factories, mills, or homes. Frances Bainbridge Colby's *The Black Winds Blow* (1940), for example, depicts the conflict between an Irish bride and her husband's upper-class Boston family, a theme that reappears in Mary Doyle Curran's *The Parish and the Hill* (1948). Curran was the daughter and granddaughter of immigrants, and her poignant tale of three generations of Irish Americans in Holyoke, Mass., presents a perspective markedly different from Colby's. One could also cite the racist depiction of the Portuguese in Joseph C. Lincoln's *The Portygee* (1920), written in an era grossly unsympathetic to new immigrants. Ruth Chatterton writes well in *Homeward Borne* (1950) about what happens when a Jewish refugee child is taken into a "regular" New Englander's home. More complex work from a different point of view can be found in *Between Wars and Other Poems* (1965) and *The Bearded Mother* (1979) by the German Jewish refugee poet and fiction writer Anne Halley, educated and long resident in Massachusetts.

A prolific strain of writing on immigrants concerns the Poles, who began entering New England, especially western Massachusetts and parts of Connecticut and Maine, during the late 19th century. Stereotype-infected works include Edith Miniter's *Our Natupski Neighbors* (1916) and Gladys Hasty Carroll's *As the Earth Turns* (1933); the best and least stereotypical of such novels is Mary Ellen Chase's *A Journey to Boston* (1965). Recent nov-

els by Polish Americans include Suzanne Strempek Shea's *Selling the Lite of Heaven* (1994), *Hoopi Shoopi Donna* (1996), and *Lily of the Valley* (1999).

Distinguished works by near descendants of immigrants, typically dealing with economic and social struggle, accommodation, the loss or survival of tradition, defeats, and occasional triumphs, include the brilliant Franconia trilogy by David Lodge about a large French Canadian family based in Providence; Harry Barba's novel about Armenian acculturation patterns, *For the Grape Seasons* (1960); and Ben Field's *The Outside Leaf* (1943), about Jewish farmers and Lithuanian and Polish workers in the Connecticut River valley tobacco industry.

Jewish immigrants to New England, along with the Irish, have produced a noteworthy literature. Mary Antin's *The Promised Land* (1912), a memoir about the author's departure from a narrow life in an East European shtetl and her rebirth as an American of transcendent vision, has been derided in the era of ethnic revivalism as part of a "cult of gratitude." It is a classic story, however, beautifully written, and a permanent addition to American literature. Another immigrant, Ezra Brudno, tells the story of an immigrant Jewish boy struggling to get an education (he goes to Boston Latin School and then enters Harvard) in *The Tether* (1908). The art critic Bernard Berenson had gone that route, too, a decade earlier. Charles Angoff, a prolific novelist over a long career, wrote *When I Was a Boy in Boston* (1947), as well as a trilogy about a Jewish immigrant family set in that city.

The heartrending masterpiece of Italian immigrant literature remains the 1920s jailhouse correspondence between the two anarchists Nicola Sacco and Bartolomeo Vanzetti, who were executed on August 23, 1927, after being convicted of murder by a Boston jury in what many have viewed as an unfair trial. Arturo Giovannitti wrote his collected poems, *Arrows in the Gale* (1914), while imprisoned for organizing the great textile mill strike of 1912 in Lawrence, Mass. Armand Peretto's *Take a Number* (1957) celebrates Italian immigrant life and community. Mari Tomasi's *Like Lesser Gods* (1988) depicts the life of Italian stoneworkers in Vermont.

Lesser-known contributions to New England literature include a novel about Armenian life by Richard Hagopian, *Faraway the Spring* (1952); stories about Greek Americans by H. L. Mountzoures, *The Empire of Things, and Other Stories* (1968); and two novels about Irish American immigrant life by Edward McSorley, *Our Own Kind* (1946) and *Kitty, I Hardly Knew You* (1959). The brilliant *Typical American* (1991), by Gish Jen, portrays a post-

World War II Chinese immigrant family very much like the author's that has long lived in Massachusetts.

Not all literature by immigrant New Englanders takes life in the region as its subject, of course. The luminous poems by the northern Irish immigrant, Nobel Prize winner, and Harvard professor Seamus Heaney are not really about a group's experience in the United States any more than are the masterful tales of the Korean War by Korean American Massachusetts resident Richard Kim, *The Martyred* (1964) and *The Innocent* (1968). West Indian immigrants have been producing memorable work since William Stanley Braithwaite's *The House of Falling Leaves and Other Poems* (1908). Among others from Trinidad, Tobago, Jamaica, and other Anglophone West Indies, we can name the Nobel Prize–winning poet Derek Walcott and novelists Caryl Phillips and Michael Thelwell, all teaching in regional colleges. Cape Verdeans have been actively telling their stories in films and documentaries. George Santayana, born in Spain, was reared and educated in Boston and Cambridge, where he taught philosophy; his *The Last Puritan: A Memoir in the Form of a Novel* (1936), has received near universal acclaim. Writers will no doubt continue to grapple creatively with the problems and hopes of immigrating to New England as long as the promised land retains its lure and keeps at least some of its promises.

Babette F. Inglehart and Anthony R. Mangione, eds., *The Image of Pluralism in American Literature: An Annotated Bibliography on the American Experience of European Ethnic Groups* (1974); Wayne Charles Miller, ed., *A Comprehensive Bibliography for the Study of American Minorities* (1976); Werner Sollers, ed., *Multilingual America: Transnationalism, Ethnicity, and the Languages of American Literature* (1998); Stephan Thernstrom, Ann Orlov, and Oscar Handlin, eds., *The Harvard Encyclopedia of American Ethnic Groups* (1980).

Jules Chametzky

Irving, John (1942–) Writer.

Born in Exeter, N.H., and permitted an education at Phillips Exeter Academy as a faculty member's son, John Winslow Irving emerged in 1961 from his prep school experience with two abiding passions: wrestling and writing. In part to satisfy the former he briefly attended the University of Pittsburgh but, finding himself an average athlete at best, left for Europe to attend the University of Vienna. Irving returned to the United States in 1964 and received his bachelor's degree the following year from the University of New Hampshire; in 1967 he received a master of fine arts degree from the University of Iowa, where he studied under Kurt Vonnegut. The experiences and images from his time abroad—touring the

John Irving, 1980

countryside by motorcycle, seeing a trained bear act on a city street, responding to the beguiling nature of a place so foreign—jostle with those of Irving's New England home in his subsequent writings.

His first novel, *Setting Free the Bears*, was published in 1968, the same year Irving settled in Vermont for a one-year teaching assignment at Windham College. A three-year return to Vienna followed as he worked on a film version of this book, a project that eventually fizzled. Upon his return to the United States in 1972, Irving won a Rockefeller Foundation Grant; this financial windfall allowed him to complete his second novel, *The Water-Method Man* (1972). Shortly after that book's publication, Irving became the writer-in-residence at the University of Iowa. During his three years in the Midwest he finished his third book, *The 158-Pound Marriage* (1974). Although critically successful, Irving's first three novels failed to find an audience, and it was a restless and frustrated writer who returned to New England in 1975 to fill a teaching position at Mount Holyoke College. In 1978 a new publisher, E. P. Dutton, brought out *The World According to Garp*, an astounding critical, popular, and financial success that allowed Irving to leave academia and concentrate his energies on writing.

Since the late 1970s Irving's popularity has been enhanced by the appearance of several additional books: the novels *The Hotel New Hampshire* (1981), *The Cider House Rules* (1985), *A Prayer for Owen Meany* (1989), *A Son of the Circus* (1994), *A Widow for One Year* (1998), and *The Fourth Hand* (2001); a volume of essays, memoirs, and short fiction titled *Trying to Save Piggy Sneed* (1996); a memoir, *My Movie Business* (1999); and a children's book, *A Sound*

Like Someone Trying Not to Make a Sound (2004). Three of the novels—*Garp*, *The Hotel New Hampshire*, and *The Cider House Rules*—were made into films.

To charges that his books portray bizarre characters living through incredible experiences, Irving responds that the authors of such comments fail to observe closely the society in which they live. He maintains that rather than invent bizarre circumstances or characters, he notices instead how commonplace the bizarre is. Many of Irving's novels are set in the coastal regions of New Hampshire and Maine, with Boston making repeated appearances. Irving's parodic portraits of regional preparatory schools in *Garp*, *The Hotel New Hampshire*, and *A Prayer for Owen Meany* contradict the traditional darker treatments of this New England institution by J. D. Salinger and John Knowles. Often the tension in his work arises from both subtle and blunt explorations of sexuality in a region of lingering puritanical prudishness. Irving's local settings, provocative themes, and unforgettable eccentric characters lend a distinctive New England flavor to his works.

Carol C. Harter and James R. Thompson, *John Irving* (1986); John Irving, *My Movie Business: A Memoir* (1999); Gabriel Miller, *John Irving* (1982); Edward C. Reilly, *Understanding John Irving* (1991).

Paul D. Nygard

Jewett, Sarah Orne (1849–1909) Writer.

The regional fiction writer Sarah Orne Jewett was born into a privileged South Berwick, Maine, family. Her grandfather was a prosperous shipowner, her father the town physician. Accompanying Dr. Jewett on his rounds, the young writer became closely acquainted with her working-class neighbors, men and women whose lives and stories her father taught her to respect. Jewett's *Country of the Pointed Firs* (1896) provides an enduring portrait of the rural Maine coast. Its focus is on preindustrial life: face-to-face relationships, homely rituals, quiet interactions that ease connections and manage conflict. Attentive to everyday detail and dialect speech, Jewett's writing is at once grounded in the American regional tradition represented by Harriet Beecher Stowe and Mark Twain and disciplined by the realist aesthetic practiced by Henry James, Gustave Flaubert, and William Dean Howells.

The United States during Jewett's time was increasingly diverse; its growing cities were marked by industrial strikes and anxieties over immigration. Her sketches and stories tended to avoid this turmoil and offered themselves as a kind of antidote, "a gift of the past," to an increasingly complex American present. Jewett's two best-known books dealt not with ethnic or racial conflict but with overcoming divi-

Sarah Orne Jewett, ca. 1885

sions between New England's elite tourists and its native villagers. In *Deephaven* (1877), two young women from Boston spend a summer in a fictional seacoast town whose quiet, old-fashioned ways, "not in the least American," they come to appreciate. In *Pointed Firs* an anonymous writer summering in Maine acquires a healing wisdom from her landlady and the rural community. This representation of coastal New England as pastoral retreat was partly fictionalized; Jewett quietly erased from her sketches evidence of the region's industrialization, highlighting instead its "ancient" qualities, just as coastal New England was promoting itself as a destination for tourists seeking respite from the rigors of modern life.

A more troubling side of the region's appeal was its supposed ethnic homogeneity. Jewett herself was proud of her family's "Norman" roots, and her stories often stressed New Englanders' links to English culture. This construction of the region as the Anglo-Norman cradle of American civilization came disturbingly close to the xenophobia that led to the period's immigration restrictions and racial segregation. Jewett seemed less concerned with preserving some spurious ethnic purity, however, than with delineating a romantic (and perhaps sentimentalized) folk culture "rooted" in the land and steeped in long-standing tradition. Although the Irish and French Canadians, devalued as industrial and domestic workers, were the most recent immigrants to her own region, Jewett treated

both groups sympathetically in stories such as "Bold Words at the Bridge" (1899), "The Gray Mills of Farley" (1898), and "Where's Nora?" (1898).

Moreover, in "The Foreigner" (1900), one of the Dunnet Landing stories, Jewett dealt with ethnic difference directly. In the tale of Mrs. Tolland, a French-speaking Catholic woman marooned far from her Caribbean home, Jewett explored rural attitudes toward the outsider, which ranged from distrust and outright rejection to compassion and halting understanding. Although one character denounces Mrs. Tolland's unorthodox behavior, another lectures her daughter on her duty to "neighbor" with the stranger: "Think if it was you in a foreign land!" Thus while the narrator of *Pointed Firs* enjoys Dunnet Landing's sense of "being the centre of civilization," she also recognizes it as a "childish" belief. One character, voicing Jewett's own view, recommends the cultivation of "a sense of proportion" and notes that in the glory days of the shipping trade, Maine's seafaring men and women saw their home in relation to a larger world. They knew, as the minister says at "the foreigner's" funeral, that "there might be roads leadin' up to the New Jerusalem from various points."

This sense of proportion, Jewett felt, was important to the artist as well as the citizen. Her own background and travels provided her with some multiple perspectives. Although raised in rural Maine, she gained early access to elite Boston society through her publication in the *Atlantic Monthly*. That connection led to her friendship with Annie Fields, the widow of James T. Fields, who published Nathaniel Hawthorne and John Greenleaf Whittier. An author in her own right and an important force in Boston charitable work, Fields partnered with Jewett in a romantic friendship that lasted until Jewett's death in 1909. The two women traveled to Europe several times and belonged to a large circle of intellectuals and artists, including Celia Thaxter, Sarah Wyman Whitman, and Harriet Prescott Spofford. Her "delight and dependence" on these friends and family inform Jewett's best writing.

South Berwick's Hamilton House, setting of *The Tory Lover* (1901), and the Jewett family home are both owned and operated by the preservationist group Historic New England, and both are open to the public.

Paula Blanchard, *Sarah Orne Jewett: Her World and Her Work* (1994); Karen L. Kilcup and Thomas S. Edwards, eds., *Jewett and Her Contemporaries: Reshaping the Canon* (1999); June Howard, *New Essays on The Country of the Pointed Firs* (1994); Sarah Way Sherman, *Sarah Orne Jewett: An American Persephone* (1989).

Sarah Way Sherman

Kerouac, Jack (1922–69) Poet and novelist. Born in Lowell, Mass., to French Canadian parents, Jean-Louis "Jack" Kerouac was a leader of the Beat movement of the 1950s and 1960s. Known for his unconventional literary style, Kerouac wrote extensively about his New England upbringing. Throughout his life he retained a special affection for his hometown, and he is memorialized there in a monument on Bridge Street in what is unofficially known as Kerouac Park. His words of homage to the city are engraved on a series of marble sculptures by Ben Woitena.

Kerouac attended local Catholic grammar schools and graduated from Lowell High School, where he was a varsity athlete in football and track. He dropped out of Columbia College to join the navy and served in the U.S. Merchant Marine during World War II. After the war he returned to New York City; there, he became close friends with Allen Ginsberg and William Burroughs, who, like Sebastian Sampas, his boyhood friend in Lowell, encouraged him to become a writer. Kerouac's first published novel, *The Town and the City* (1950), which he later dismissed as too conventional, was modeled on Thomas Wolfe's literary style and is a fictionalized account of his memories of growing up in New England.

In April 1951 Kerouac spent three weeks writing an autobiographical narrative about cross-country trips he had taken with his Denver friend Neal Cassady. Written on a 120-foot roll of paper, this novel would be published seven years later as *On the Road* (1957), Kerouac's most successful book. Dissatisfied with his writing, Kerouac discovered what he called sketching, or "spontaneous prose," a method of writing without revision inspired by his love for bebop jazz improvisation. Between 1951 and 1956 he wrote several books that were too stylistically innovative to attract publishers and earned his living by working a series of jobs, including stints as a railroad brakeman and a fire lookout. Kerouac traveled between the East and West coasts but saved enough money to live with his widowed mother for long periods while he wrote what he conceived of as his life's work, the autobiographical novels of "The Legend of Duluoz" (Duluoz was his fictional name for himself). Several of these—*Visions of Gerard* (1963), *Doctor Sax* (1959), *Maggie Cassidy* (1959), and *Vanity of Duluoz* (1968)—deal extensively with his boyhood experiences in Lowell.

When *On the Road* was finally published in 1957, it catapulted Kerouac to literary fame. Controversy over this best-selling novel continued after the publication of *The Dharma Bums* (1958) and *The Subterraneans* (1958), books celebrating an impulsive, unrestrained, and spontaneous lifestyle that most critics feared would encourage antisocial behavior among the restless young. Kerouac came to be regarded as the public spokesperson for the Beat Generation, a role he detested. Although he spent the last decade of his life in a losing battle with alcoholism, he continued to write. Shortly before his death in Saint Petersburg, Fla., he published his "Bippie in the Middle" article, defining what he saw as his unpopular position between political conservatives of his generation and political radicals like his former friend Ginsberg.

Perhaps because of the attention paid to Kerouac as a Beat writer, critics have been slow to recognize the merit of his books about the French Canadian community in Lowell that are the cornerstones of his Duluoz legend. These books dramatize events from his childhood and adolescence and celebrate his love for his family, his ethnic heritage, and his boyhood home. Kerouac is buried in Edson Cemetery in Lowell; his hometown hosts an annual Kerouac Festival during the first weekend of October.

Ann Charters, *Kerouac: A Biography* (1973); Charters, *Jack Kerouac: Selected Letters, 1940–1956* (1995); Clark Coolidge, Michael Gizzi, and John Yau, *Lowell Connector: Lines and Shots from Kerouac's Town* (1993); Tim Hunt, *Kerouac's Crooked Road: Development of a Fiction* (1996).

Ann Charters

King, Stephen (1947–) Writer. Stephen Edwin King is one of the most prolific and best-selling novelists of the last quarter of the 20th century and the beginning of the 21st. Between 1973 and 2004 King published 64 books. His works have been translated into more than 30 languages and made into feature films and television movies. A division of the Book-of-the-Month Club, the Stephen King Book Club, is solely devoted to selling his fiction.

King was born in Portland, Maine, to Donald Edwin King and Nellie Ruth Pillsbury King. King's father deserted the family, which by then included Stephen's adopted brother, David, and was never heard from again. From 1949 to 1958 the family lived in Fort Wayne, Ind., and Stratford, Conn., though they frequently returned to Maine and Massachusetts to visit Nellie King's family during the summers. In 1958 the family moved to Durham, Maine. King graduated from the University of Maine at Orono in 1970 with a bachelor's degree in English. While in college he was active in the antiwar movement and as a student writer; King published his first commercial story, "The Glass Floor," in *Startling Mystery Stories* in 1967.

In 1971 King married Tabitha Spruce, a writer and photographer. From 1971 to 1973 he

Stephen King leads the Rock Bottom Remainders in Cambridge, Mass., 1993

taught English at Hampden Academy in Hampden, Maine. In 1974 Doubleday published *Carrie*, which became a best-seller and was adapted into a successful movie in 1976. In 1978 King spent a year as writer-in-residence at the University of Maine at Orono. Except for a year in England, King has lived in Maine ever since, settling in Bangor in 1980, where in addition to writing he hosts a weekly radio show.

Best known as a writer of horror and fantasy fiction, King is also identified as a Maine writer, one whose fiction probes the dark underside of New England society. Although some of his major works (for instance, *The Shining* [1977] and *The Stand* [1978 and 1990]) have only a peripheral relation to New England, a number of his novels are set in the fictional town of Castle Rock, Maine. King published "the last Castle Rock story," *Needful Things,* in 1991. Other Castle Rock stories include "The Body" (published in the collection *Different Seasons* [1982]), *The Dark Half* (1989), and "Sun Dog" (published in the collection *Four Past Midnight* [1990]). The latter two works, along with *Needful Things,* form what King calls the "Castle Rock Trilogy." He has also set novels in other fictional Maine locations, such as Jerusalem's Lot (*Salem's Lot* [1975]) and Derry (*It* [1986]). Other novels with Maine settings include *Pet Sematary* (1983), *The Tommyknockers* (1987), *Gerald's Game* (1992), *Dolores Claiborne* (1993), *Insom-*

nia (1994), *Bag of Bones* (1998), *Hearts in Atlantis* (1999), and *Dreamcatcher* (2001).

King's novels often combine gothic/horror stories with acutely remembered and observed evocations of small-town Maine; *Gerald's Game* and *Dolores Claiborne* have virtually no supernatural or horror elements. The more realistic side of King's work attends to the lives of children, class conflicts, the nature of masculinity, and the condition of the writer, especially in an impoverished regional environment. King's portrayal of rural Maine is often harsh, focusing on the domestic violence, bullying, and pettiness of the small-town world. But he is also aware of the diversity and complexity of such settings and how they can nourish as well as harm people.

King's books have sold more than 100 million copies to date, including novels written under his pseudonym, Richard Bachman. Known also for his philanthropic activities, King's recent bequests include major gifts to the University of Maine at Orono, Milton Academy, and the city of Bangor. King's papers, including some unpublished material, are located in the Special Collections of the University of Maine at Orono Library. In 2003 King was awarded the National Book Foundation Medal for distinguished contribution to American letters.

Michael R. Collings, *The Work of Stephen King: An Annotated Bibliography and Guide* (1996); Stephen King, *Danse Macabre* (1981); King, *On Writing: A*

Memoir of the Craft (2000); Stephen Spignesi, *The Shape under the Sheet: The Complete Stephen King Encyclopedia* (1991); Douglas E. Winter, *Stephen King: The Art of Darkness* (1984).

William Patrick Day

Kumin, Maxine (1925–) Writer. Maxine Kumin (née Winokur) was born in Germantown, Pa., a suburb of Philadelphia. She was reared in a Jewish family, the youngest of four children. In 1946 she married the engineer Victor Kumin, and the couple bought a 200-acre farm in Warner, N.H., in 1963 as a weekend retreat; they have lived there year-round since 1976. Much of Kumin's work is influenced by the geography of central New Hampshire.

While her work spans several genres, including fiction, essays, criticism, and children's books, Kumin is best known as a formal poet. Secondary school teachers inspired in her a love of metrics and form. She studied literature and history at Radcliffe College, where she earned her bachelor's and master's degrees. As a burgeoning poet, she patterned her poems after those of W. H. Auden, which provided her with a model for integrity of line, rhyme, and metaphor.

The realities of New England farm life have inspired Maxine Kumin for more than 30 years. Her poetry and prose reveal intense relationships with the land and with family (which encompasses relatives, friends, poets, farmers, and wild and domestic animals). Kumin's essays on rural living are contemplative and explicit. For example, *Women, Animals, and Vegetables* (1994) contains exquisite details on buying and caring for horses, differentiating edible mushrooms from poisonous ones, and mulching a garden using the *New York Times*.

In her poems, creatures become humans and vice versa. A case in point is the opening lines of "The Retrieval System," where affection for father and dog are evoked through a merging of their characteristics:

> It begins with my dog, now dead, who all
>   his long life
> carried about in his head the brown eyes
>   of my father,
> keen, loving, accepting, sorrowful,
>   whatever.

Kumin has been compared to Robert Frost and Henry David Thoreau because of the bucolic sensibilities of her work. "Without religious faith and without the sense of primal certitude that faith brings," she has written, "I must take my only comfort from the natural order of things." Her pastorals use intimacy with the natural world as a means for exploring global issues, particularly the problematic relationship between humans and nature.

Since the publication of her first book of poems, *Halfway* (1961), Kumin has received several honors as a poet, including the 1973 Pulitzer Prize for Poetry (for *Up Country: Poems of New England* [1972]), The Poets Prize (1993), and the Aiken Taylor Poetry Prize (1995). She was consultant in poetry to the Library of Congress (1981–82) and poet laureate of New Hampshire (1989–95). She became a chancellor of the Academy of American Poets in 1995. Among her latest works are *Inside the Halo and Beyond: The Anatomy of a Recovery* (2000); *Always Beginning: Essays on a Life in Poetry* (2000), *Long Marriage* (2001), and *Bringing Together: Uncollected Early Poems, 1958–1988* (2003).

Emily Grosholz, ed., *Telling the Barn Swallow: Poets on the Poetry of Maxine Kumin* (1997); Maxine Kumin, *In Deep: Country Essays* (1987); Kumin, *Selected Poems 1960–1990* (1997); Enid Shomer, "An Interview with Maxine Kumin," *The Massachusetts Review* 37 (1997).

Ruth Farmer

Literary Boston Boston first took shape in the mind's eye of John Winthrop in 1630, when he and his Puritan followers set sail for the "New World" on what Perry Miller, historian of the New England mind, called their "errand into the wilderness." Winthrop's "A Modell of Christian Charity" articulated his vision of "a city upon a hill." Thus Boston was evoked as an image before it was realized as a fact. Boston was founded to fulfill an ideal— "an ideal not merely religious, though permeated by religion; an ideal of transmitted civilization," as Samuel Eliot Morison, historian and Bostonian, wrote. Henry Adams, a descendant of one of Boston's first families, praised Boston in more ironic terms: "Boston had solved the problem of the universe; or had offered and realized the best solution yet tried."

Boston became the self-appointed conscience of the nation during the colonial and revolutionary eras; it solidified its position as the country's center of cultural and intellectual influence in the mid-19th century, when Dr. Oliver Wendell Holmes playfully claimed that the "Boston State-House is the hub of the solar system." That center held for decades, before and after the Civil War, an encompassing geographic and imaginative territory that radiated from the Boston office of Ticknor and Fields, publisher of Nathaniel Hawthorne, Henry Wadsworth Longfellow, Ralph Waldo Emerson, Harriet Beecher Stowe, and other inventors of American literature. In nearby Cambridge, Harvard—that "first flower" of Puritan planting—shaped the minds that shaped the nation.

Ralph Waldo Emerson centered his life in Concord, west of Boston, where he inspired a generation of writers known as Transcendentalists, most notably Henry David Thoreau, to live more thoughtfully. Led by Emerson, Margaret Fuller edited the Transcendentalist journal *The Dial*, wrote *Woman in the Nineteenth Century* (1845), and helped to establish Boston as a feminist center. Thus Greater Boston became the hub of the nation's moral, political, and literary idealism.

Literary Boston's "refulgent summer," as Emerson had called it, turned, after the Civil War, in the words of the literary historian Van Wyck Brooks, into an "Indian Summer"— still splendid but waning. Through Boston's finest literary and cultural journal, the *Atlantic,* notably under the editorship of William Dean Howells, and through Houghton Mifflin, the city's enterprising and influential publishing house, the work of Boston's writers reached all parts of the republic; the center of publishing and culture, however, soon shifted to New York City. Many notable works set in Boston—Henry Adams's *Education of Henry Adams* (1918), George Santayana's *The Last Puritan* (1935), John P. Marquand's *The Late George Apley* (1937), and Edwin O'Connor's *The Last Hurrah* (1956), for example—convey a note of nostalgia and depletion at the same time they reinvent the city in original imaginative designs.

Like Henry Adams before him, Robert Lowell was born "under the shadow" of the Boston State House and spent his life coming to terms with his family's and his city's heritage. In his poem "For the Union Dead" (1960), Lowell celebrates a Boston hero, Colonel Robert Gould Shaw, who was killed while leading the 54th Massachusetts Regiment, composed of African American soldiers, in the Civil War; but Lowell excoriates Boston for failing to live up to its own ideals, for trading polity and purpose for commerce. Lowell's Boston has compromised its "old Faith"—"the old Faith was something of mind," something of conscience—yet his poem renews the covenant of purpose, piety, and passionate expression that has characterized Boston literature.

Though seen as the center of the Yankee-Brahmin world, literary Boston has been enriched by many other voices and cultures. From Phillis Wheatley's poetry in the 18th century through Frederick Douglass's abolitionist autobiography in the 19th century to Malcolm X's coming-of-age memoir in the 20th, Boston has been a center of African American expression. John Boyle O'Reilly, poet and patriot, helped reconcile Irish and Yankee tensions late in the 19th century when Irish Americans took political power in Boston. Jewish American and Italian American writers likewise vividly reflected their communities' cultural perspectives; thus Boston continues to evolve as it is successively reimagined by its articulate and diverse citizenry.

In the late 1950s Boston was the site of poetic energies stirred by Robert Lowell, Sylvia Plath, Anne Sexton, Maxine Kumin, and many others. Literary Boston at the end of the 20th century and the beginning of the 21st is characterized by a flourishing artistic community. Poets in particular thrive, drawn to Boston by its many great universities, publishers, and bookshops, its frequent poetry readings, and its exemplary poets in residence, including the Irish poet Seamus Heaney, a Nobel laureate who teaches at Harvard.

Boston did not solve the problems of the universe, but its writers did erect an impressive city of words. Robert Frost, author of *North of Boston* (1914), found in the New England heritage, originating in Boston, a determination "to purify words until they meant again what they should mean." Boston, then, was born in imagery and realized in fact, but it has been perfected in language.

Van Wyck Brooks, *The Flowering of New England, 1815–1865* (1936); Brooks, *New England Indian Summer* (1965); Samuel Eliot Morison, *Builders of the Bay Colony* (1930); Shaun O'Connell, *Imagining Boston: A Literary Landscape* (1990).

Shaun O'Connell

Literary Culture to 1900 Centers of literary culture took many forms in New England before 1900. From Boston to Hartford, from Concord to the Berkshires, New Englanders exchanged ideas in person and in print, informally and in more institutionalized settings. In a region where learning was held in high regard, men and women of letters came together both to defend and to oppose the dominant ideas of their times. A survey of New England's literary communities reveals the rich legacy and limits of its intellectual heritage and culture.

The community of scholars at Harvard College in Cambridge, Mass., occupied from the college's beginnings in 1636 with its mission to train young men for the ministry, generally complied with the Puritan practice of unadorned plainness in writing. Interest in imaginative literature occurred only in student societies such as the Institute of 1770, Phi Beta Kappa (1781), the Porcellian Club (1791), and the Hasty Pudding Club (1795). In these self-governing associations, students learned about the latest intellectual developments in Europe, participated in literary contests, operated libraries, and even conferred awards. Similar societies at Yale, Dartmouth, and most other New England colleges by the mid-

John Greenleaf Whittier, ca. 1870

19th century could be more vital sources of learning than the formal curriculum taught by their professors.

In the life of the early republic, it initially appeared that Connecticut might emerge as the center of New England literary culture. The political prominence and literary nationalism of John Trumbull, Joel Barlow, Timothy Dwight, and David Humphreys helped secure the fame of these Connecticut Wits during the 1770s and 1780s. They had a Yale education and Hartford Federalism in common, but their literary efforts were independent. Connecticut's writers did not develop the kind of cohesiveness of Boston's writing community until almost a century later, when Harriet Beecher Stowe, Mark Twain, and Charles Dudley Warner formed a closely knit group in the exclusive neighborhood of Nook Farm in Hartford. These were highly sociable and productive years for Stowe (1863–96) and Twain (1874–91). From within the tranquil environment of Nook Farm, Stowe noted her dissatisfaction with contemporary manners in urban America, while Twain presented a more profoundly unsettling portrait of the United States during the Gilded Age.

The tradition of belles lettres—the pursuit of friendship, refined conversation, and correct taste—found a more congenial home in cosmopolitan Boston. The intellectual worlds of Cambridge and Boston began to coalesce, however, in the pages of the *Monthly Anthology and Boston Review* (1803–11) and in the weekly dinner meetings of the Anthology Society. This group of Harvard-trained lawyers, doctors, business leaders, and ministers published reviews and notices on science, theology, literature, and history and helped to transform the pursuit of letters from an exclu-

sively private realm of face-to-face communication to public oratory and printed discourse. Joseph Stevens Buckminster, one of the more influential members, helped the Unitarians wrest control of Harvard away from the Calvinists by the 1820s, opening higher learning to greater literary influences in the process. The Anthologists' reading room became the Boston Athenaeum in 1807 and went on to serve as an exclusive but indispensable library for several generations of New England literati. Elitist in spirit, staunchly Federalist in politics, and generally supportive of neoclassical critical doctrines, with occasional nods to Romantic ideas, Unitarian men of letters set an enduring tone in Boston and Cambridge.

The founding of The Saturday Club (1855) and publication of the *Atlantic Monthly* (1857) marked the high tide of literary Boston in the 19th century. The new journal secured the bulk of its articles and many of its editors from the group that assembled at the Parker House on the last Saturday of every month. Ralph Waldo Emerson, James Russell Lowell, Henry Wadsworth Longfellow, Oliver Wendell Holmes, Sr., John Greenleaf Whittier, and Nathaniel Hawthorne joined the club early on. Later members included William Dean Howells and Henry James. During the colonial era, women had been excluded from such literary activities as a way to preserve moderate sociability and avoid distracting passions. The Saturday Club excluded women in part to protect their activities from feminine associations in an era when a majority of successful fiction writers and their readers were women. The club also provided members with a safe haven from the mercenary spirit of a burgeoning capitalist society. Yet the Boston Brahmins, as they came to be known, were neither as conservative nor as long lasting as their modern critics have argued or their own pronouncements would suggest. Holmes only half-jokingly referred to the Boston statehouse as "the Hub of the Solar System" (in *The Autocrat of the Breakfast-Table*). Still, members of this circle of Boston writers and editors earned New England writers a national audience. They not only transformed literature into high culture, they also came to personify the plainspoken wisdom and irreverent wit of the Yankee persona. By the mid-19th century, Boston and Cambridge gave high praise to their literary intellectuals, leaving them prone to conservatism and a sense of self-importance.

The power of Boston's writers was strengthened by their loyalty to Boston publishers. The offices of Ticknor and Fields served as a meeting place for an impressive stable of writers that included Emerson, Hawthorne, Holmes, Longfellow, Lowell, Julia Ward Howe, and Stowe. The contacts of Boston's literary elite extended beyond the limits of the city. The friendship of Hawthorne and Herman Melville was inaugurated at a gathering in the Berkshires that also included part-time and permanent residents Holmes and writer Catharine Maria Sedgwick. This same environment inspired the poetry of William Cullen Bryant. New England writers often supplemented their rather meager literary earnings by giving public lectures. Most New England towns of any size had a lyceum or similar institution in place by the 1830s. The increased contact they afforded between lecturer and audience supported a more familiar and simplistic style in New England literature.

While publishing and lecturing remained a male preserve, the rise of the novel during the early 1800s generated new kinds of communities dominated by women writers and readers. The works of Sedgwick, Lydia Maria Child, Stowe, and Maria Cummins provoked common emotional responses in their readers that were routinely shared in conversation and written correspondence. Similarly, the regional realism of Rose Terry Cooke, Sarah Orne Jewett, and Mary E. Wilkins Freeman captured finely drawn portraits of rural New England left behind in the rush of industrialization and western migration. Women's fiction created intimate communities in print that defied the obstacles of great distances. By the end of the century, women such as Annie Fields and her companion Jewett formed the center of a circle of literary and artistic women that included Celia Thaxter. Thaxter herself was the center of a network of writers and artists, such as Childe Hassam, who gathered at her family's hotel on Appledore Island, off the coast of New Hampshire. The developing women's club movement, led by the New England Women's Club, also provided a venue for women to discuss books and hear lectures by writers and scholars.

The philosophical, religious, and literary movement known as Transcendentalism resists any narrow definition but was grounded in a definite place: Concord. Emerson moved to the village of his ancestors in 1835, where he explored the full meaning of self-culture and his belief in the spark of divinity in every person. Transcendentalism drew its energy from the conversations of the remarkable circle of friends he attracted to Concord. Unlike the formal sermon, lecture, or essay, the conversations that Emerson and his circle prized were highly aphoristic, improvisational, and mutually stimulating. Most of all, they were serious. Henry David Thoreau and Margaret Fuller, in particular, found the amiable soirees of the Boston literary scene contemptible. The

founding of the Transcendental Club (1836) led to the appearance of *The Dial* (1840–44), a quarterly edited in turn by Fuller and Emerson. Although the journal attracted few readers and much ridicule, its pages captured the extraordinary range of the club's discussions. The intellectual stimulation they provided made its way into Emerson's notebook entries, lectures, and published works.

Fuller opened a series of formal "Conversations" in the Boston bookshop of fellow Transcendentalist Elizabeth Palmer Peabody in 1839. She was motivated by her pressing financial situation as well as her desire to offer women the kind of systematic education and intellectual exertion they were routinely denied. Fuller's program proved popular; more than 100 women enrolled in her conversation groups over the next five years. Of all Transcendentalist works, however, those of Thoreau are most closely identified with Concord, the place of his birth. His jaunts in and around Concord formed the basis for a parallel series of literary excursions in *A Week on the Concord and Merrimack Rivers* (1849) and *Walden* (1854).

Louisa May Alcott and Hawthorne also made Concord the home of literature. Alcott grew up in Concord and based many of the characters, scenes, and episodes in *Little Women* (1868–69) on her experiences there. Her father, Amos Bronson Alcott, developed his own circle of writers and philosophers at the Concord School of Philosophy. His ill-fated attempt to establish a community of writers and philosophers at Fruitlands in Harvard, Mass., is lampooned in Louisa May Alcott's *Transcendental Wild Oats* (1873). Hawthorne lived in Emerson's former home, Old Manse, and provided a sketch of Concord in an introduction to *Mosses from an Old Manse* (1846), a collection of tales he wrote while he lived there. Brook Farm, an experimental community located 9 miles from Boston in West Roxbury, Mass., had ties to the Transcendentalists in Concord. Hawthorne invested in the project and briefly lived there; the experience provided material for *The Blithedale Romance* (1852). Other visitors to Brook Farm included Emerson, Fuller, and Peabody. There were many other centers of literary culture throughout New England where writers found good libraries, educational institutions, and a publisher. Portland, Maine; Portsmouth, N.H.; Salem and Springfield, Mass.; Providence and Newport, R.I.; and New Haven, Conn., could all boast local literary lights.

The locations and places of literary New England derive their significance as sites of stimulating and productive associations and friendships. The conversations of the Parker House, Peabody's bookshop, the Old Manse

of Emerson and Hawthorne, and the Berkshire retreats of Melville and Holmes continue to resonate in the culture of the region and the nation.

Kenneth R. Andrews, *Nook Farm: Mark Twain's Hartford Circle* (1950); Richard D. Birdsall, *Berkshire County: A Cultural History* (1959); Richard H. Brodhead, *Cultures of Letters: Scenes of Reading and Writing in 19th-Century America* (1993); Van Wyck Brooks, *The Flowering of New England, 1815–1865* (1936); Brooks, *New England: Indian Summer, 1865–1915* (1940); Lawrence Buell, *New England Literary Culture from Revolution through Renaissance* (1986); Joseph A. Conforti, *Imagining New England: Explorations of Regional Identity from the Pilgrims to the Mid-20th Century* (2001); Josephine Donovan, *New England Local Color Literature: A Women's Tradition* (1983); Leon Howard, *The Connecticut Wits* (1943); Perry D. Westbrook, *The New England Town in Fact and Fiction* (1982).

Timothy P. Duffy

Literature of Industrialism

Despite the association of New England literature with scenes of village life and natural beauty, the region was the first in America to become thoroughly industrialized, whether in small mills or in large urban complexes. Industrialization brought a new subject to literature, and, some would argue, a new style of realism, but it also brought new means of literary production and distribution and a larger reading public.

Many writers were ambivalent about the effect of industrialization. Henry David Thoreau at Walden Pond speculated on the effect of the "machine in the garden," to use critic Leo Marx's term, and he noted sardonically the cost in human labor, primarily Irish immigrants, in its construction. Many Transcendentalist writers were attracted to reformers who would harness industrialization to utopian schemes, such as the Hopedale Community in Hopedale, Mass., but others were skeptical. Nathaniel Hawthorne spoofed beliefs in improvements in human society and human nature through technology in "The Celestial Railroad" (1843), and Herman Melville depicted the degradation of female factory operatives in "The Paradise of Bachelors and the Tartarus of Maids" (1855).

While writers such as Melville, Ralph Waldo Emerson, and Thoreau addressed the subject of industrialism during the 19th century, the female textile factory workers of Massachusetts and southeastern New Hampshire issued a body of literature in the periodicals *The Lowell Offering* (1840–45), the *New England Offering* (1847–50), and the *Voice of Industry* (1845–47) as well as in such miscellanies as the *Factory Girl and Ladies Garland* (1842), *Mind Amongst the Spindles* (1845), and the *Factory Girls Album and Operatives Advo-*

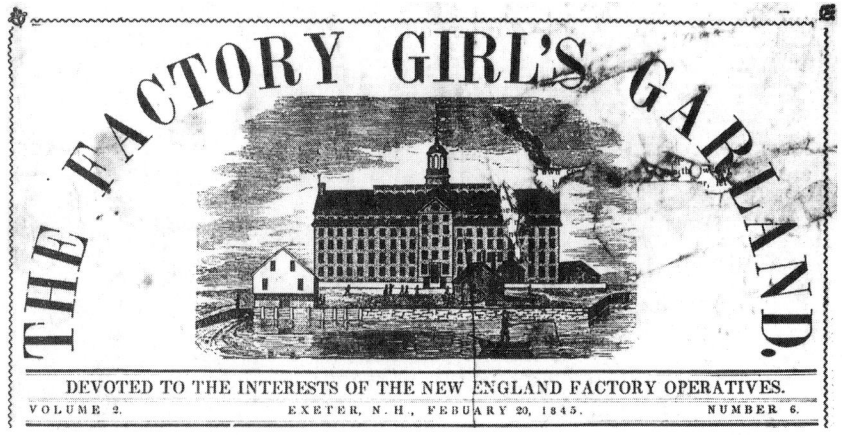

Banner head from the February 20, 1845, edition of The Factory Girl's Garland, *Exeter, N.H.*

cate (1846). Some of this literary production was concerned with temperance, the abolition of slavery, labor, and labor reform. Most of the writing by these mill girls, though, reflects the tastes and talents of the culturally dominant code of true womanhood. The subjects of nature, spirituality, longing for family and home, idealized motherhood, and sick or dying children are found in works of various genres.

No doubt—in places such as the shoe shops of Lynn, Mass.; the textile factories of Fall River, Mass.; the glass factories of Keene, N.H.; and the wool and cotton factories of Manchester, N.H.—female and male workers wrote about their experiences and their hopes. Little of this writing remains. In contrast to the factory towns in England and in the United States, Lowell, Mass., was established as a capitalist utopian experiment yielding industrial productivity in a climate of intellectual and moral enterprise. The Lowell working-class literary periodicals, like those of many middle-class women's magazines, were meant to showcase the moral fiber, intellect, and talent of U.S. factory workers. Editorials, short fiction, spiritual autobiography, personal narratives, and poetry are the genres represented in these literary magazines.

In keeping with the code of true womanhood, most working-class women writers of the literary periodical *The Lowell Offering* published pseudonymously so as to retain their privacy when they returned to the domestic sphere. A few women wrote under their own names. Among the most notable self-identified writers are *Offering* editor Harriet Farley, Lucy Larcom, Harriet Hanson Robinson, and Sarah Bagley. *The Lowell Offering,* which eventually became the *New England Offering,* was solely conducted by mill girls and was funded by the factory owners, the Boston Associates. In the issues of *The Lowell Offering* and the *New England Offering,* contributions in different genres are

evenly balanced. Mill girl poets employ a range of recognized poetic styles, from the sonnet to the lyric in free verse.

Labor unrest and disagreements about the appropriate response by women workers to this strife split the writers of *The Lowell Offering.* Bagley, other members of the Lowell Female Labor Reform Association, and their male counterparts began publishing the *Voice of Industry,* a weekly newspaper concerned with the state of the New England industrial worker. Under Bagley's editorial direction, the *Voice of Industry* included a poetry column on the first page. Original submissions from male and female workers were often published pseudonymously, as many writers feared job-related reprisals for their poetic critique of the working conditions in textile mills and the hypocrisy of the Lowell experiment. Some poets, however, signed their own names to works on temperance and the abolition of slavery. In contrast to *The Lowell Offering,* the poetic form of the ballad dominated the poetry in the *Voice of Industry.* The column also contained reprinted material from British labor poets and radical poetry by Percy Bysshe Shelley. Few of the same poetic subjects are shared by the *Voice of Industry* and *The Lowell Offering;* short fiction, spiritual autobiography, and personal narratives are rare in this labor newspaper.

After 1850, few female factory workers continued to write and to publish. By 1850, most of the writers who had contributed to *The Lowell Offering, New England Offering,* and the *Voice of Industry* had left the factories to return to their rural northern New England homes or to go west seeking better opportunities. Sarah Bagley, after testifying at the First Official Investigation into Labor Conditions by the Massachusetts Legislature (1845), went on to serve in various leadership positions in the new labor unions. Of those early industrial worker writers, only Harriet Hanson Robin-

son and Lucy Larcom retrospectively documented their experiences in the mills. Robinson's *Loom and Spindle* (1898) and Larcom's autobiography, *A New England Girlhood* (1889), are idealistic narratives that recall, in Robinson's terms, the "mill girls alma mater." Larcom's autobiography follows the 19th-century literary pattern of a spiritual journey, representing her life in the Lowell factories as a time of intellectual, spiritual, and artistic growth.

Of all contributors to these antebellum working-class periodicals, only Larcom managed to construct a literary career for herself. Although she needed to financially support herself through teaching at Wheaton and Bradford (Massachusetts) seminaries for women and through editorial work at Ticknor and Fields, she took her place among the late-19th-century New England literati of John Greenleaf Whittier, James T. Fields, Henry Wadsworth Longfellow, and Oliver Wendell Holmes. Over the course of her life Larcom published seven volumes of poetry, including the Houghton Mifflin Household Edition of *Poetical Works* (1884). Many 20th-century literary critics consider Larcom's *Wild Roses of Cape Ann and Other Poems* (1880) her best volume for it contains topographical New England poetry similar to the best of Celia Thaxter, Longfellow, and Whittier. Larcom's life and career exemplify the conflicted status of the individually celebrated working-class woman poet who negotiated her publishing success to enter and be accepted by the middle class.

The influence of industrial means of production and finance on traditional New England trades is a subtext of such works as Melville's *Moby-Dick* (1851) and Richard Henry Dana, Jr.'s *Two Years before the Mast* (1840). As these traditional employments declined or were transformed, writers turned in the second half of the 19th century and in the 20th century, as they did elsewhere in America, to the growth of industrial cities and their attendant conditions for laborers and their families. Elizabeth Stuart Phelps's *The Silent Partner* (1871) presented life in textile factories, and Winston Churchill's *The Dwelling Place of Light* (1917) casts a jaundiced eye on the transformation of Manchester, N.H., by the Amoskeag mills and their polyglot workforce. The fear that New England's Yankee values would be lost is featured in William Dean Howells's *The Rise of Silas Lapham* (1885), and the suspicion that New England values contributed to industrial tyranny is explored in Mark Twain's *A Connecticut Yankee in King Arthur's Court* (1889). After World War I, the literature of industrialization in New England was less distinctively a regional literature.

There were literature-inspiring events associated with the region, such as the 1912 Bread and Roses strike in Lawrence, Mass.; the trial of Sacco and Vanzetti; and, more recently, the literary and cinematic explorations of industrial pollution in Jonathan Harr's *A Civil Action* (1995) and commercial fishing in Sebastian Junger's *The Perfect Storm: A True Story of Men against the Sea* (1997).

Susan Alves, "Intruding upon the Poet's Art: Considering the Poetic Production of 19th-Century Female Factory Workers," *Over Here* 17, no. 2 (Winter 1997); Benita Eisler, *The Lowell Offering* (1998); Laura Hapke, "Proletarians or True Women?: The Female Working-Class Experience and 19th-Century U.S. Labor Authors," *Over Here* 17, no. 2 (Winter 1997); Marie Jean Lutes, "Cultivating Domesticity: Labor Reform and the Literary Culture of the Lowell Mill Girls," *Works and Days* 11, no. 2 (Fall 1993).

Susan Alves

Lowell, Amy (1874–1925) Literary critic, lecturer, and poet. Amy Lowell was born in Brookline, Mass., the daughter of Augustus Lowell and Katharine (Lawrence) Lowell, both of whom belonged to wealthy and prominent New England families. The industrial towns of Lowell and Lawrence, Mass., were founded, respectively, by her paternal and maternal ascendants. Her cousin James Russell Lowell was a leading poet of his era and the first editor of the *Atlantic Monthly;* her brother Lawrence was a president of Harvard. As both a female and an upper-class New Englander of her era, Lowell had to defy convention to achieve prominence in her own right.

Privately educated and well traveled, Lowell did not begin writing seriously until 1902, when she was 28 years old. She claimed that it was watching the tragedian Eleonora Duse perform onstage in Boston that "loosed a bolt in [her] brain," revealing "where [her] true function lay." Not until 10 years later did Lowell's first book of poems, *A Dome of Many-Coloured Glass* (1912), make its way into print.

Her defiance of contemporary convention is noteworthy. She lived as a lesbian with a degree of openness surprising for a woman of her position at a time when so-called Boston marriages, or two women living in domestic partnership, had already fallen from fashion. She loved to irritate middle-class sensibilities by smoking cigars in public. She was bumptious and combative at a time when women of her social standing and region were supposed to be genteel and even passive.

In 1913 Lowell discovered the Anglo-American school of Imagism, founded by Ezra Pound the year before with the goal of promoting a style of poetry that employed common but precise language from which

vagueness and superfluous adornment were banned. She immediately identified herself as an Imagist and traveled to England specifically to meet Pound. Predictably, the two dominant personalities clashed. Lowell initiated her career as entrepreneur and patron of the arts by publishing three anthologies titled *Some Imagist Poets* (1915–17), which included the work of H.D. (Hilda Doolittle), John Gould Fletcher, D. H. Lawrence, and others. Pound disassociated himself from her efforts and scoffingly called Lowell's brand of Imagism "Amygism."

Although she lived for only 13 years after her first book appeared, Lowell became a prolific writer. She published a book of poems every year or two until 1925, and two more poetry collections were published posthumously, *East Wind* (1926) and *Ballads for Sale* (1927). She also published several volumes of prose, including *Six French Poets: Studies in Contemporary Literature* (1915), *Tendencies in Modern American Poetry* (1917), and the two-volume biography *John Keats* (1925). In addition, Lowell was highly successful as a public reader of dramatic monologues, among them her most famous poem, "Patterns," first published in the August 1915 issue of the *Little Review.* Lowell died at her home in Brookline at the age of 51. She was posthumously awarded a Pulitzer Prize in 1926 for her poetry collection *What's o'Clock* (1925).

With the exception of the much anthologized "Patterns," Lowell's work fell into oblivion soon after her death when it was no longer supported by the force of her personality both on stage and off. Most of Lowell's sentimental monologues deserve oblivion, but many of her lyric poems are still remarkable today and have justly enjoyed a recent revival of interest. The most notable of these is a series of lesbian love poems from *Pictures of the Floating World* (1919), "Two Speak Together," reflecting her relationship with the actress Ada Dwyer Russell, with whom Lowell lived on her Brookline estate from 1912 until her death.

Richard Benvenuto, *Amy Lowell* (1985); S. Foster Damon, *Amy Lowell: A Chronicle, with Extracts from Her Correspondence* (1935); Jean Gould, *Amy: The World of Amy Lowell and the Imagist Movement* (1975); Adrienne Munich and Melissa Bradshaw, eds., *Amy Lowell, American Modern* (2004); Glenn Richard Ruihley, *The Thorn of a Rose: Amy Lowell Reconsidered* (1975).

Lillian Faderman

Lowell, Robert (1917–77) Poet, translator, and dramatist. Born in Boston, Robert Traill Spence Lowell, Jr., was named for his grandfather, the 19th-century poet, educator, and Episcopal clergyman. His prominent family also included the poets James Russell Lowell and Amy Lowell. Lowell was known

Robert Lowell reads his work at Harvard University, 1977

for his allusive, intellectual, and formal early verse and for his later innovative and confessional personal poetry. When he died in New York in 1977, many considered Lowell to be the most important and influential poet of his generation.

Lowell was a student of the poet Richard Eberhart at Saint Mark's School; he also attended Harvard College for two years. He then attended Kenyon College in Ohio, where he studied with the poet and critic John Crowe Ransom, graduating as valedictorian of the class of 1940. He later studied with the writers Cleanth Brooks and Robert Penn Warren—leading proponents of the New Criticism—at Louisiana State University. Brooks and Warren praised Lowell's early poetry, which exemplified their formalist theories.

In 1940 Lowell converted to Catholicism and married the writer Jean Stafford; they remained married until 1948. From 1949 to 1972 he was married to the novelist Elizabeth Hardwick; from 1972 until his death he was married to Lady Caroline Blackwood. During his marriage to Blackwood, he divided his time between England and periods of teaching at Harvard. Like many of his relationships, these emotionally charged marriages intensified his volatile mental condition and stimulated his writing.

Lowell's first poetry collection, *Land of Unlikeness* (1944), depicts a longing for New England tradition amid the modern world's corruption and chaos. The poems of *Lord Weary's Castle* (1946), which won a Pulitzer Prize in 1947, employ Catholic symbols and ethos and voice Lowell's antagonism to his Protestant mercantile roots. In the dramatic monologues of *The Mills of the Kavanaughs* (1951), Lowell portrays the social, moral, and spiritual decay of his New England heritage in dense, allusive language.

Lowell's most famous book, *Life Studies* (1959), contains 15 poems of self-revelation inspired by the Beat poet Allen Ginsberg as well as an autobiographical essay entitled "91 Revere Street." Lowell wrote of his mental breakdowns and hospitalizations in a self-disclosing discourse that influenced the poets Anne Sexton and Sylvia Plath, who met one another while participating in the celebrated poetry workshops Lowell taught at Boston University during the 1960s. Lowell's breakthrough writing marked the advent of a school of confessional poetry characterized by autobiographical verse and poetic language that is open, direct, and accessible.

Various eclectic works followed. *Imitations* (1961) contains verse adaptations of foreign poems; *Phaedra* (1961) is a free translation of the play by Jean Racine; *Prometheus Bound* (1969) is a prose work derived from Aeschylus. Preoccupied with his New England literary precursors, Lowell based the three one-act plays in *The Old Glory* (1965) on stories by Herman Melville and Nathaniel Hawthorne. After *Notebook 1967–1968* (1969), he earned another Pulitzer Prize for *The Dolphin* (1973), a sonnet cycle; his final book of poetry was *Day by Day* (1977). *The Collected Prose* of Lowell was issued in 1987.

For some, Robert Lowell stands at the center of his literary era, and in many ways his life and art trace the distinctive turns of the period 1940 to 1977. Lowell was jailed as a conscientious objector during World War II, an experience that inspired his poem "Memories of West Street and Lepke." A well-known activist, he boycotted a 1965 White House Fine Arts Festival in protest against U.S. foreign policy, and in 1967 he was arrested during an anti–Vietnam War march on the Pentagon. Recounting the march in *The Armies of the Night* (1968), Norman Mailer captured Lowell's Thoreauvian indignation and donnish Boston Brahmin bearing, memorializing the poet's New England eminence and stature in the civic, intellectual, and literary circles of his time, a time that has been called the Age of Lowell.

Ian Hamilton, *Robert Lowell: A Biography* (1982); Henry Hart, *Robert Lowell and the Sublime* (1995); Jeffrey Meyers, *Manic Power: Robert Lowell and His Circle* (1987); Marjorie Perloff, *The Poetic Art of Robert Lowell* (1973).

Ronna C. Johnson

Maritime Literature

Long before New England was either new or English, its indigenous inhabitants and first seafaring explorers from Europe spun stories about the sea. Algonquian oral traditions include the earth's creation from ocean waters, a great wind-bird who fans the sea into waves with its wings, a giant hunter who spears whales, a trickster-hero who rescues beached whales and gives them pipes to smoke, and flying canoes that carry men across the ocean.

The Vinland sagas of the Vikings set down in the *Skalholtsbók* (ca. 1334) and the *Flateyjarbók* (1385) arguably constitute the region's first written literature of the sea. Storms, feats of seamanship, strange new shores, and battles with aboriginal "Skraelings" fill Norse sagas recounting voyages to North America led by Leif Ericsson and others around A.D. 1000.

Five centuries later, as European nations competed to dominate newly discovered shores, Richard Hakluyt launched a maritime publishing project to buttress England's hegemony in America. His compilations of mariners' journals, *Diverse Voyages* (1582) and *Principal Navigations* (1589), popularized the nonfiction "voyage of discovery." Intended to promote colonization and trade, such "voyages" downplayed the rigors of the crossing to describe America as a land of opportunity. New England examples include John Brereton's *Brief and True Relation* (1602) and James Rosier's *True Relation of the Most Prosperous Voyage* (1605), as well as Captain John Smith's *General History of . . . New England . . .* (1624) and *True Travels . . .* (1630). Smith also created the earliest handbooks for mariners in English—*Pathway to Experience for all Young Sea-Men* (1626) and *A Sea Grammar* (1627).

An actual 17th- or 18th-century North Atlantic crossing was a long, terrifying ordeal by seasickness, foul and insufficient rations, and the real possibility of shipwreck. The Puritans abandoned the colonialist "voyage" in favor of the sea-deliverance narrative, reinventing the passage as a spiritual pilgrimage. Richard Mather, in his *Journal* (1635); Increase Mather, in *Illustrious Providences* (1684); and Cotton Mather, in *Magnalia Christi Americana* (1702) used stories of deliverance from shipwreck, storm, and starvation at sea to illustrate American exceptionalism and the Puritans' special covenant with God.

Booksellers as well as ministers grasped the potential of "true adventure" cloaked as spiritual autobiography. *Ashton's Memorial* (1725) combines a fisherman's capture by pirates with reflections on providence. A London edition influenced Daniel Defoe, demonstrating the early novel's indebtedness to the sea-deliverance genre. Briton Hammon's *Narrative of the Uncommon Sufferings and Surprising Deliverance* (1760), the first voyage account by an African American, ponders the spiritual meaning of his shipwreck, Indian captivity, enslavement, and Royal Navy service.

Two wars made America a growing maritime power. New England figures in James Fenimore Cooper's sea novels about the Revolution. In *The Pilot* (1824), Nantucket whaleman Long Tom Coffin wields his harpoon against the British, while in *The Red Rover* (1827), pirates and revolutionaries sail from Newport, R.I. The War of 1812 produced *The Female Marine* (1815), probably by Nathaniel Coverly, but published under various female pseudonyms. This fictitious "narrative" treats cross-dressing Lucy Brewer's heroic naval service on the USS *Constitution*.

A new, American age of discovery began as early 19th-century New England mariners pressed around Cape Horn. Whalers, sealers, and explorers discovered Antarctica, untold Pacific islands, exotic peoples, and worlds of flora and fauna unknown to science. The public relished firsthand accounts of new oceanic frontiers by New England mariners. Captain Amasa Delano's *Narrative* (1817) as well as Edmund Fanning's *Voyages Round the World* (1833) and *Voyages to the South Seas* (1838) are archetypal "voyages of discovery."

Pulp sea fiction involving everything from sea serpents to pirates' daughters flourished under pseudonyms such as Harry Halyard. Joseph C. Hart produced *Miriam Coffin; or, The Whale-Fisherman* (1834), a minor novel that influenced Edgar Allan Poe and Herman Melville. But on the whole, readers preferred true stories of mutiny, hostile natives, shipwrecks, starvation, and cannibalism, with or without reflections on providence. Connecticut printers pirated Archibald Duncan's *A Mariner's Chronicle* (1804), a British compendium of disasters at sea, and added more disasters, from polar bear attacks to steamboat explosions. Nantucket whalemen, among the earliest Americans to experience the Pacific frontier, wrote especially popular disaster narratives. Owen Chase's *Narrative of the Shipwreck of the Whale-ship "Essex" of Nantucket* (1821), a source for *Moby-Dick*, describes the sinking of a ship by an enraged whale. William Lay and Cyrus Hussey's *Narrative of the Mutiny on Board the Whaleship "Globe" of Nantucket* (1828) was also widely read. Edgar Allan Poe's only novel, *The Narrative of Arthur Gordon Pym of Nantucket* (1838), is a lively parody of the popular disaster, deliverance, and discovery genres.

New Englanders created a uniquely American type of sea narrative—accounts by educated young gentlemen who made the democratic experiment of joining the maritime proletariat. Nathaniel Ames, who left Harvard for the forecastle, wrote *A Mariner's Sketches* (1830) and *Nautical Reminiscences*

(1832) attacking the romanticism of Cooper's sea novels while realistically describing actual seafaring life. Inspired by Ames, Richard Henry Dana, Jr., left Harvard on a ship bound to California for leather hides. *Two Years before the Mast* (1840) chronicles the brutal realities of labor at sea and Dana's growth to manhood. He also wrote *The Seaman's Friend* (1841), a handbook of nautical vocabulary and procedures, and in his later career as a lawyer championed the rights of sailors. In the 1840s, Dana's success encouraged many other literary young gentlemen to go to sea and write about their adventures.

Herman Melville sailed before the mast as a matter of financial necessity. Four of his first five novels—*Typee* (1846), *Omoo* (1847), *Redburn* (1849), and *White-Jacket* (1850)—are thinly disguised accounts of his own voyages on whaleships, a merchant vessel, and a U.S. Navy frigate. The narratives canvass the hypocrisy of missionaries, the plight of immigrants, the working conditions of sailors, and the practice of flogging. Adhering to Dana's sea formula, they were Melville's most successful novels during his lifetime. *Moby-Dick* (1851) broke the mold. Melville's novel is a spiritual allegory of leviathanic proportions, a voyage into the riddles of creation. *Moby-Dick*'s beautiful, dense, and mysterious prose includes all of New England's sea genres, and more. Native American legend, expansionist rhetoric, sermon, hymn, sea-deliverance narrative, voyage of discovery, marine natural history, nautical glossary, maritime technical manual, African American humor and song, dime novel, disaster narrative, sea chantey, and "before the mast" democratic experiment combine to make *Moby-Dick* America's greatest contribution to literature of the sea.

Among 19th-century poets, Oliver Wendell Holmes helped save the *Constitution* from the scrap yard with "Old Ironsides" (1830) and made "The Chambered Nautilus" (1858) a metaphor for spiritual growth. Henry Wadsworth Longfellow revisited the Viking tradition in "The Skeleton in Armor" (1841); but "The Wreck of the *Hesperus*" (1841), recounting the demise of a Gloucester schooner, and "The Phantom Ship" (1858), a ghostly sea story borrowed from Cotton Mather, were his most popular efforts. John Greenleaf Whittier also found inspiration in Vikings ("The Norsemen," 1841) and phantom ships ("The Dead Ship of Harpswell," 1866, and "The Palatine," 1867), as did James Russell Lowell in "Voyage to Vinland" (1868) and "The Flying Dutchman" (1869).

New England's literature of the sea faltered as the 19th century advanced. The transcontinental railroad made voyages around Cape Horn obsolete, while steam-powered, iron-clad vessels replaced wooden sailing ships. Maritime enterprise shifted to large urban ports such as New York and San Francisco. Literature of the sea became nostalgic. Henry David Thoreau walked almost entirely around Cape Cod, recording a vanishing way of life in magazine pieces (*Cape Cod*, 1865). Celia Thaxter did the same for island folkways and history (*Among the Isles of Shoals*, 1873). Harriet Beecher Stowe, in *The Pearl of Orr's Island* (1862), and Sarah Orne Jewett, in *The Country of the Pointed Firs* (1896), produced domestic fictions foregrounding the resourceful men and women of Maine's fading maritime communities.

Writers turned to the fishing port of Gloucester for New England's remaining authentic seafaring enterprise. Rudyard Kipling's novel *Captains Courageous* (1897) tells the story of Harvey Cheyne, a selfish, pampered teenager who falls off a passenger liner and is picked up by a Gloucester schooner. The rough tutelage of Captain Disko Troop, the hard labor of fishing, and tragedy at sea forge Harvey into a man of moral and physical courage. As the 20th century began, novelists James Brendan Connolly and Edmund Gilligan mourned the demise of Gloucester's all-sail fishing fleet. Today's motor fleet, still fishing supremely dangerous North Atlantic waters, also has its literature, including the poetry of Vincent Ferrini (*Know Fish*, 1979) and Charles Olson (*The Maximus Poems*, 1983). Sebastian Junger's *The Perfect Storm* (1997), a disaster narrative about the loss of the fishing vessel *Andrea Gail*, and Linda Greenlaw's *The Hungry Ocean* (1999), a firsthand account of commercial longlining, became bestsellers.

The age of sail may have ended, but 20th-century New England authors continued to seek adventure under sail. Joshua Slocum's classic, *Sailing Alone around the World* (1900), recounted his solo circumnavigation in the refitted oyster sloop *Spray*. Artist Rockwell Kent had success with *N by E* (1930), describing his disastrous voyage to Greenland. Irving Johnson circumnavigated the globe four times in sailing ships; *Westward Bound in the Schooner Yankee* (1936) is the best-known of his many narratives. Sterling Hayden's *Wanderer* (1963) narrates a solo voyage to Tahiti, while Harvey Oxenhorn's *Tuning the Rig* (1990) recounts an Arctic sailing expedition to observe whales. In *The Happy Isles of Oceania* (1992), Paul Theroux undertakes a more primitive form of voyaging, kayaking from New Zealand to Hawaii.

Maritime historians too enjoyed popular success. Henry Beetle Hough wrote memorable books about Martha's Vineyard and whaling. Edward Rowe Snow worked the disaster vein, producing 97 books with titles such as *Great Storms and Famous Shipwrecks of the New England Coast* (1943). Nathaniel Philbrick's more scholarly *In the Heart of the Sea* (2000) revisited the *Essex* disaster. John Stilgoe's *Alongshore* (1996) and Mark Kurlansky's *Cod* (1997) introduced a new field, maritime environmental history, to a wide audience.

New England's 20th-century sea fiction includes John Hersey's *Blues* (1987), a fictional meditation (with poetry and recipes) on fishing for bluefish off Martha's Vineyard. John Casey's *Spartina* (1989) is set among Rhode Island's contemporary fishermen. Most of the era's maritime fiction, however, is notably historical. Kenneth Roberts's *The Lively Lady* (1931), *Captain Caution* (1934), *Lydia Bailey* (1947), and *Boon Island* (1956) embrace seafaring romance and adventure. Joseph C. Lincoln, "the literary dean of Cape Cod," and F. Van Wyck Mason produced a cornucopia of salty novels. William Martin's sagas, *Back Bay* (1980) and *Cape Cod* (1991), connect New England's maritime past and present, while Anita Shreve's *The Weight of Water* (1997) revisits a brutal 1873 murder on Smuttynose Island.

Some of American literature's strongest 20th-century poets have incorporated New England seascapes into their best work. T. S. Eliot found the imagery for his redemptive poem "The Dry Salvages" (1941) in boyhood summers sailing off Cape Ann. Robert Lowell's "The Quaker Graveyard at Nantucket" (1946) memorializes a cousin lost at sea during World War II. *Near the Ocean* (1967) and *The Dolphin* (1973) collect poems involving the sea near Lowell's summer home in Castine, Maine. Elizabeth Bishop's opus is rich in sea imagery from many shores; "At the Fishhouses" (1955) is a fine example.

The Nobel prize–winning playwright Eugene O'Neill also contributed to New England's 20th-century literature of the sea. Childhood summers in New London, Conn., inspired the young O'Neill to ship out on windjammers and steamships, earning the rank of able-bodied seaman. The Provincetown Players produced his first play, *Bound East for Cardiff* (1916). Together with three additional one-act plays, it forms the *S.S. Glencairn* cycle, drawing on O'Neill's experience of forecastle life. Among many O'Neill plays inspired by the sea, *Ile* (1919) and *The Hairy Ape* (1922) have special importance.

Today, New England's coast is largely suburbanized, its once-rich fisheries depleted, its only economically vigorous maritime enterprise issuing from industrial container ports. For most residents, life on the water means summer recreation. Whether 21st-century literature of the sea will continue looking backward to a romantic past or will address present realities remains to be seen. One thing is certain, as Melville reminds us: "Meditation and water are wedded forever."

Jill B. Gidmark, ed., *American Literature of the Sea and Great Lakes* (2001); Peter Kemp, ed., *The Oxford Companion to Ships and the Sea* (1988); Benjamin W. Labaree, William M. Fowler, Jr., John B. Hattendorf, Jeffrey Sanford, Edward W. Sloan, and Andrew W. German, *America and the Sea: A Maritime History* (1998); Charles G. Leland, *The Algonquin Legends of New England, or Myths and Folk Lore of the Micmac, Passamaquoddy, and Penobscot Tribes* (1884); Samuel Eliot Morison, *Maritime History of Massachusetts, 1783–1863* (1921); Frederick J. Pohl, *The Viking Settlements of North America* (1972); Haskell Springer, ed., *America and the Sea: A Literary History* (1995); Colin Woodard, *The Lobster Coast: Rebels, Rusticators, and the Struggle for a Forgotten Frontier* (2004).

Susan F. Beegel

Mather, Cotton

Mather, Cotton (1663–1728) Minister, theologian, writer, and scientist. Considered to be the quintessential New England Puritan, Cotton Mather was the oldest son of the Boston minister Increase Mather and Maria (Cotton) Mather and grandson of ministers Richard Mather and John Cotton. Cotton Mather graduated from Harvard College in 1678 and attained a master's degree in 1681. He was a melancholy child and suffered from a stammer that initially kept him out of the pulpit; in 1685, his speech impediment largely conquered, he was finally ordained as his father's colleague at Boston's Second, or Old North, Church, where he served until his death. His personal and religious anxieties, his egotism, and his defense of the New England way, science, and the Salem witchcraft trials have made his name a byword for those who attack or praise New England's Puritan past.

Cotton Mather lived a full and varied intellectual life, both as a scientist (he was elected a fellow of the Royal Society of London in 1713) and as a prominent theologian, and he strongly influenced events of his own day. His efforts to cure two children through fasting and prayer whom he believed to be bewitched resulted in *Memorable Providences, Relating to Witchcrafts and Possessions* (1689), a work that may have helped ignite the Salem witchcraft hysteria of 1692. Mather's warnings (and those of his father) that prosecutions should not be based on testimony concerning the acts of disembodied spirits, known as spectral evidence, actually helped bring the episode to an end, but history has since associated him with the tragedy of the witchcraft trials. In 1721 and 1722 Mather again found himself in the midst of intense controversy when he advocated inoculation against smallpox, but on this question history has proved him to have been ahead of his time.

Mather's most prominent writings include *The Wonders of the Invisible World* (1692), a chronicle and vindication of some of the Salem witchcraft trials; *Magnalia Christi Americana* (1702); *Bonifacius: An Essay upon the Good* (1710); *The Christian Philosopher: A Collection of the Best Discoveries in Nature, with Religious Improvements* (1721); *The Angel of Bethesda, Visiting the Invalids of a Miserable World* (1722); *Manuductio ad Ministerium: Directions for a Candidate of the Ministry* (1726); and his *Diary*, a huge work that was not published until 1911–12. These works demonstrate the extraordinary range of Mather's intellect, which in the colonies was unsurpassed before the career of Thomas Jefferson. *The Christian Philosopher*, Mather's most important scientific work, exhibits the beginnings of American scientific and philosophical inquiry and established Mather as a leading philosopher of science. Based on close observation of the natural world, the first 11 essays of *The Christian Philosopher* organize the physical sciences and are predominantly astronomical, and the later section is essentially a treatise on the biological sciences. His great ecclesiastical history of New England, the *Magnalia Christi Americana*, portrays the Puritans in England as analogous to the Israelites enslaved in Egypt. Liberated by Moses (William Bradford and John Winthrop) and led into the Promised Land (New England), they create a model society under God's watchful protection. The *Magnalia*'s 60 detailed biographical sketches of eminent people add to Mather's message and serve to reinforce the moral value of New England's divine calling. His many sermons generally follow the basic pattern of the Puritan sermon form but offer a more intense and personal treatment of the theme of "divine mission" than his histories.

A tragic figure in many ways, he buried two wives and lost another to insanity. Of his 15 children, nine died young, and only two survived him. He was a fellow and overseer of Harvard College, but its presidency eluded him. He was often tormented by doubts about his soul and questions about his ability to carry on the traditions of his illustrious family. In many respects he lived his entire life in the shadow of his public and powerful father, whom he survived by only five years.

Sacvan Bercovitch, *The Puritan Origins of the American Self* (1975); Mitchell Robert Breitweiser, *Cotton Mather and Benjamin Franklin: The Price of Representative Personality* (1984); Robert Middlekauff, *The Mathers: Three Generations of Puritan Intellectuals, 1596–1728* (1971); Kenneth Silverman, *The Life and Times of Cotton Mather* (1984).

Mason I. Lowance, Jr.

Melville, Herman

Melville, Herman (1819–91) Writer. The biggest shock for many upon hearing of Herman Melville's death in 1891 was that he had still been alive despite many years of absence from the public eye; "even his own generation has long thought him dead," noted one obituary. Now revered as a great American author, Melville initially gained fame as a writer of popular South Seas adventure novels. When he tired of his reputation as the "man who lived among the cannibals," he set out to create more ambitious literary works. But by doing so, he lost most of his readership. His desire to join the literary aristocracy and yet appeal to a democratic audience mostly went unrealized.

Such conflicts marked Melville's life and career: he was an adventurous soul, yet plagued by poor physical and mental health; he was surrounded by wealth, yet often in debt; he was skeptical of reform movements, yet engaged with major political and social problems of his day, including slavery, industrialization, and imperialism. Although he had personal ties to New England, Melville was never quite part of the literary circle that included Nathaniel Hawthorne, Ralph Waldo Emerson, and Henry David Thoreau. Indeed, many of his works contain critiques of traditional New England values such as Calvinism and transcendentalism, and parodies of figures such as Emerson and Ben Franklin.

Born in New York City to Allan Melvill and Maria Gansevoort, Melville (the final "e" may have been added by Melville's brother Gansevoort as an aristocratic affectation, but is most likely a common variant spelling) was descended from patrician Boston and New York families. His paternal grandfather participated in the Boston Tea Party, and his maternal grandfather served heroically in the American Revolution. In 1830, after his father's business failed, the family moved to Albany, N.Y. Two years later, Allan Melvill died, deep in debt. During his school years, Melville worked as a bank clerk, farmhand, and bookkeeper. After considering careers as a school teacher and surveyor, he embarked on four years (1839–44) of travel and adventure, including trips to Liverpool and down the Mississippi River, a brief stint in the navy, and work on whale ships in the Pacific. In 1847 Melville married Elizabeth Shaw, daughter of the chief justice of the Massachusetts Supreme Judicial Court. With their four children, Melville and his wife lived in New York and at Arrowhead—their farm in Pittsfield, Mass.—where Melville wrote part of *Moby-Dick* (1851) and cultivated a friendship with Nathaniel Hawthorne.

Inspired by his travels, Melville began writing semi-autobiographical accounts of his South Seas adventures. His first two novels—*Typee* (1846) and *Omoo* (1847)—were commercially and critically successful and established his reputation as a popular writer. Melville's experimentation with style and philosophical speculation in *Mardi* (1849) disappointed his readers, and the book failed. Already in debt, he quickly produced two more popular novels—*Redburn* (1849) and *White-Jacket* (1850)—to shore up his reputation and income. Influenced by the literary success of Hawthorne, Melville decided to make *Moby-Dick* a different kind of book—one that would combine the popular appeal of his earlier novels with the seriousness of purpose he found in writers such as Shakespeare and Dante. The lukewarm reception of his masterwork left Melville intensely disappointed. Failing physically, mentally, and fiscally, he wrote three more novels—*Pierre* (1852), *Israel Potter* (1855), and *The Confidence-Man* (1857)—and a series of shorter works including "Benito Cereno" and "Bartleby, the Scrivener." After 10 productive years, he stopped writing novels.

Starting in 1866, Melville served as a customs inspector in New York. He continued writing, mostly poetry on topics such as the Civil War and his journey to the Holy Land. In 1885, thanks in part to generous inheritances, he retired, finally out of debt and largely out of print. The posthumous publication of *Billy Budd* in 1924 revived an interest in Melville's works that has continued unabated for more than 80 years. A New Yorker by birth and a world traveler at heart, Melville nevertheless remained deeply invested in New England culture as the origin, for better and for worse, of the defining traits of both his family and his nation.

Andrew Delbanco, *Herman Melville: His World and Work* (2005); Harrison Hayford, Hershel Parker, and G. Thomas Tanselle, eds., *The Writings of Herman Melville* (1968); Jay Leyda, *The Melville Log: A Documentary Life of Herman Melville, 1819–1891* (1969); Hershel Parker, *Herman Melville: A Biography,* 2 vols (1996, 2002).

Michael Kaufmann

Millay, Edna St. Vincent (1892–1950)

Poet. Edna St. Vincent Millay, known familiarly as "Vincent," was born in Rockland, Maine, the first child of Henry and Cora Millay. The Millays divorced when Edna was eight, and Cora moved with her three daughters to Rockport and Newburyport, Mass., then to Camden, Maine, keeping the girls in books and music lessons by working as a private practical nurse and economizing. The title poem of Millay's Pulitzer Prize–winning *Harp-Weaver and Other Poems* (1923) features a self-sacrificing artistic mother whose playing and singing magically clothe her cold and hungry child—a son in the poem—though they extinguish the mother's own life. In an-

other, untitled poem, Millay eulogizes her mother:

> The courage that my mother had
> Went with her, and is with her still
> Rock from New England quarried;
> Now granite in a granite hill.

As a young girl Millay published poems in the children's magazine *St. Nicholas,* edited and composed poems and essays for her high school magazine, and wrote and performed in plays for her class. At age 19 Millay received acclaim for her poems, especially "Renascence," which appeared in the anthology *The Lyric Year* in November 1912. A long and serious poem, "Renascence" takes its inspiration from Transcendental and Romantic poets but is also homegrown, revealing both Millay's penchant for life's larger questions and her attention to a sense of place—specifically, the coast of Maine. The poem presents a view from a mountain overlooking Camden and is today inscribed on a monument to Millay there.

The story of the poem's reception is also legendary; Millay's public reading at the Whitehall Inn in Camden so impressed Caroline Dow, executive secretary of the national training school of the Young Women's Christian Association (YWCA) in New York, that she helped Millay obtain a scholarship to attend a women's college.

From 1913 to 1917 Millay attended Vassar College in Poughkeepsie, N.Y., and then lived in Greenwich Village through 1920; during this period she also appeared as an actress at the Provincetown Playhouse. She traveled abroad from 1921 to 1923 and brought her mother to join her for several months. In 1923 Millay was the first woman to win the Pulitzer Prize for poetry. In that year she also married Eugen Boissevain, a Dutch importer and the widower of feminist activist Inez Milholland.

Millay left New York City to live with her husband in Austerlitz, N.Y., at Steepletop, a 700-acre farm they had purchased, but the couple spent most summers in Millay's beloved Maine, on Ragged Island.

Although Millay is seen less as a regional writer, much of her work is filled with and informed by the imagery of the New England coast and countryside. Millay donated the proceeds from her poem "Justice Denied in Massachusetts" to the defense of Sacco and Vanzetti in 1927 and personally appealed to the governor to spare their lives. Over the years Millay has been variously reviewed as a sentimental lyricist at the rearguard of high modernism, a femme fatale, and a "new woman" with modern ideas about love. Her poetic themes include mortality, grief, beauty, the

natural world in peril, poetic form, womanhood, and relations between the sexes. Millay's reputation as a poet of direct emotion was aided by her early figure as performer—beautiful, ethereal, she gave her dramatic readings in flowing ball gowns. Her sonnets were appreciated for their careful craft and seductively provocative attitudes, revealed in such direct statements as "I shall forget you presently, my dear" and "Oh, think not I am faithful to a vow!"—about a woman's right to sexual and personal freedom.

In 1949 Boissevain died, followed by Millay herself in October 1950 at Steepletop. Although she had published nothing after 1943, she had been working on another book of poems, which was published posthumously as *Mine the Harvest* (1954). The publication of collected and selected poems and of her letters followed; a volume of her uncollected prose is under preparation.

The volumes published during Millay's lifetime include the poems for which she is most well-known, verse drama, pseudonymous fiction, a collection of translations, and an opera libretto.

Norma Brittin, *Edna St. Vincent Millay* (1982); Diane P. Freedman, ed., *Millay at 100: A Critical Reappraisal* (1995); Nancy Milford, *Savage Beauty: The Life of Edna St. Vincent Millay* (2001); Edna St. Vincent Millay, *Collected Poems* (1956); William Thesing, ed., *Critical Essays on Edna St. Vincent Millay* (1993).

Diane P. Freedman

Native American Literature

New England's Native American literature covers a wider area than the six New England states. Because the borders of the states artificially divide tribal homelands, "New England Native Americans" therefore include Micmac and Abenaki living in Canada, as well as Nipmucks, Pequots, and others who have groups in more than one state. Outside the region, only a small number of published writers from these groups seem widely known. Nevertheless, they belong to a long and rich literary history, encompassing not only novels, poetry, and memoirs, but also hymnals, dictionaries, political documents, oral performances, diaries, newspapers, and Web sites.

Indigenous people have always produced oral literature; some may also have practiced forms of writing before contact with Europeans. The Micmac, for example, created hieroglyphic prayers out of their own writing systems. The added presence of Christian missionaries, who wanted to teach Indians to read the Bible, led many more native people to write, in more forms. Soon they began using writing to underscore their cultural and political status. During the 1700s, for example, Wabanaki leaders supplemented their oratory by writing petitions to French and British officials in which they forcefully asserted their nations' claim to their lands.

One of the best and earliest known New England native writers is the Mohegan minister Samson Occom. Born in 1723 in Connecticut, he converted to Christianity in his teens and preached in various native settlements, including the Montauk community at Long Island, about which he wrote a tribal history. Occom also wrote a short narrative in 1768, though not for publication, that details his experiences as a minister and teacher and his frustrations at the racism he encountered among his white colleagues. In 1772, he published an execution sermon for a convicted murderer and fellow Mohegan, Moses Paul, and in 1774 he issued a hymnal. Occom is renowned today as the Indian pupil who traveled to England to help raise money for Dartmouth College, but equally important is his commitment to indigenous land claims and self-governance—ends he saw ministry and literacy as serving, not obliterating.

Other native people who had converted to Christianity, attended European American schools, or both produced letters, diaries, and other documents, many of them now held in historical archives and personal collections. An exception is William Apess, whose work is now back in print. In 1829 Apess garnered attention with what is possibly the first published, full-length Native American autobiography, *A Son of the Forest*. In this, he blended some of the conventions of Christian conversion narrative with rhetorically canny attacks on Christian racism and hypocrisy. Apess was ordained as a Methodist preacher and traveled, among other places, to Mashpee, then the largest Indian town in Massachusetts. There, he helped lead the struggle against the commonwealth for Mashpee self-government, a process he describes in "Indian Nullification" (1835).

The publication of northeastern native writing increased dramatically during the late 19th and early 20th centuries. Some people published for mainly tribal purposes. In 1884, for example, Abenaki Chief Joseph Laurent produced an Abenaki primer that is still an important linguistic resource. Henry Lorne Masta, another Abenaki chief, followed with *Abenaki Indian Legends, Grammar, and Place Names* in 1932. The first Penobscot book may have been Joseph Nicolar's *Life and Traditions of the Red Man* (1893), a compendium of Wabanaki history and spiritual tradition. Nicolar's daughter, Florence Nicola Shay, was also a tribal historian, issuing a short pamphlet in the 1940s titled "History of the Penobscot

Tribe of Indians." Other native writers, meanwhile, sought wider audiences. Betsey Guppy Chamberlain, a woman of either Narragansett or Abenaki heritage, found a venue in *The Lowell Offering*, a newspaper published in the Massachusetts textile mill where she worked. Chamberlain also wrote some radically pro-Indian fiction, including "A Fire-Side Scene" (1842), a scathingly ironic story in which a young boy prompts his uncle to recount his participation in a 1794 massacre of Miami Indians.

In southern New England, from 1935 to 1936, the Narragansetts produced the magazine *Narragansett Dawn*, edited by the celebrated writer and storyteller Princess Red Wing. Native women were some of the most active writers in other Indian groups as well. Among the Mohegans, Emma Baker created tribal documents about language, genealogy, and burial desecration. Fidelia Fielding, a medicine woman who worked with the anthropologist Frank Speck to produce texts on Mohegan language and tradition, also kept her own diaries, which Speck published in the prestigious Bureau of American Ethnology (BAE) annual reports in 1928. Later, another revered Mohegan culture-keeper, Gladys Tantaquidgeon, went to study with Speck at the University of Pennsylvania, finally publishing her own fieldwork as *Folk Medicine of the Delaware and Related Algonkian Indians* (1972).

Writing and publication never replaced indigenous oral tradition but actively helped continue it. Ethnographers such as Speck, eager to record Indian traditions and stories, helped create new opportunities for native literary production. Many of these transcribed oral performances found their way into academic journals, such as the BAE reports; others were worked into books purporting to represent a given native group or region, such as Charles Godfrey Leland's tome, *Algonquin Legends of New England* (1884). Another important oral history was produced in 1939 when an interviewer for the Federal Writers' Project recorded conversations with Henry Mitchell, a Penobscot man who had been laid off by the Old Town Canoe Company during the Depression. In some cases, the people who dictated these oral texts, like Fidelia Fielding, produced writing of their own, either after working with ethnographers or even before meeting such people. In Maine, for example, Passamaquoddy scholar Lewis Mitchell had recorded traditional narratives and wampum records, in Passamaquoddy, decades before being invited to redictate the texts in the 1920s.

In the late 20th century New England native literature began to explode. The Abenaki

writer Joseph Bruchac is the most visible, having produced a steady stream of novels, poetry, books for children and young adults, collections of oral traditions, tape recordings, and a memoir about growing up with his Abenaki grandfather, *Bowman's Store: A Journey to Myself* (2001). Bruchac's family has been active in promoting Abenaki tradition not only through writing (his sister Marge has written many essays as well as *1621: A New Look at Thanksgiving* [2001]) but also as oral storytellers. Moreover, they have been instrumental in promoting other indigenous writers and artists. In *Returning the Gift* (1994), Bruchac included several northeastern writers often overlooked in such anthologies.

The Abenaki have produced some of the region's most prolific writers. Cheryl Savageau and Suzanne Rancourt have won acclaim for their poetry; Trudy Ann Parker has written fiction as well as a book about a relative, *Aunt Sarah: Woman of the Dawnland* (1994); visual artists Gerard and Yolaikia Tsonakwa collaborated on *Seven Eyes, Seven Legs: Supernatural Stories of the Abenaki* (2001); and archaeologist Frederick Matthew Wiseman has issued a groundbreaking prosovereignty book, *Voice of the Dawn: An Autohistory of the Abenaki Nation* (2001). The Micmac also boast a number of successful writers, including two highly esteemed poets: Gail Tremblay, writer of *Indian Singing* (1998); and Rita Joe, who received the Order of Canada on the strength of her verse and later wrote a widely read autobiography, *Song of Rita Joe* (1996).

Each of the two Wampanoag communities—Mashpee (Cape Cod) and Aquinnah (Martha's Vineyard)—maintains its own vibrant sense of literary history. At Mashpee, tribal council president Russell Peters wrote several books, including *Clambake: A Wampanoag Tradition*, before his death in 2002. At Aquinnah, Helen Attaquin, who became the first tribal member to earn a Ph.D., wrote a Wampanoag history; and Marie Vanderhoop and June Manning wrote a series of newspaper articles. In 2001, the elder and educator Helen Manning published *Moshup's Footsteps*, a collection of personal reminiscences, oral traditions, photographs, and recipes.

In blending the personal with the tribal, these writers follow in the footsteps of many cultural heroes—sacred, historical, and familial. *Molly Molasses and Me* (1988), the title of a wildly funny collection of female escapades by Penobscot storyteller Ssipsis, pays tribute both to the writer's close friend and to a respected 19th-century Penobscot shamaness. Stephen Laurent honored his father Joseph by publishing an extended Abenaki dictionary in 1995. And Melissa Fawcett has written *Medi-*

cine Trail (2000) about her great-great-aunt Gladys Tantaquidgeon. Fawcett is also the author of a brilliant history, *The Lasting of the Mohegans* (1995), as well as a novel.

Many native writers shift constantly from fiction to nonfiction to storytelling to activism. Narragansett writer Paula Dove Jennings has spoken eloquently about this shifting. She is justly proud of her book *Strawberry Thanksgivings* (1992), published by the Boston Children's Museum. Yet after seeing how writers lose control over editing and distribution, she decided that the stories weren't hers alone to tell; today, she prefers oral storytelling. For many native writers, oral performance is an equal, sometimes even a greater, form of literature. Books such as *The Wabanakis of Maine and the Maritimes* (1989) and other new media such as the Passamaquoddy CD-ROM *Maliyan* preserve and extend oral art not only by reproducing it, but also by presenting authorship itself as a collective, rather than an individual, enterprise.

Colin Calloway, ed., *After King Philip's War: Presence and Persistence in Indian New England* (1997); Helen Jaskoski, ed., *Early Native American Writing: New Critical Essays* (1996); Barry O'Connell, ed., *On Our Own Ground: The Complete Writings of William Apess, a Pequot* (1992); Will and Rudi Ottery, *A Man Called Sampson 1580–1989* (1989); A. LaVonne Brown Ruoff, *American Indian Literatures* (1990); William Simmons, *Spirit of the New England Tribes* (1986); Jace Weaver, *That the People Might Live: Native American Literatures and Native American Community* (1997); Ron Welburn, *Roanoke and Wampum: Topics in Native American Heritage and Literatures* (2001).

Siobhan Senier

Nature Writing

"The land was ours before we were the land's," writes Robert Frost, revealing a historic task of New England nature writing: to know a dangerous but marvelous new land so that it could become a familiar home. The long process of understanding the land has become entwined with the process of learning how to live rightly on it. In response to these needs, the nature writing created in New England has had a widespread and lasting influence, not only because of its depiction of natural beauty but also because of its conscientious exploration of humanity's relationships with the earth.

Early settlers in New England from Europe saw nature simultaneously as malevolently wild and marvelously useful, a dichotomy that emerged respectively from Puritan theology and from the Renaissance preoccupation with power. The Puritans sought to create a garden for the chosen people out of "a waste and howling wilderness / Where none inhabited / But hellish fiends," as poet Michael Wigglesworth put it. The dynamic of Puritan

saints redeeming a fallen world is not without exception: in Jonathan Edwards's spiritual autobiography "Personal Narrative" (ca. 1739), for example, the famous minister often tells of realizing God's grace while walking through Connecticut's wild beauty of forest and field. But it fell to a later generation of visionaries, the Transcendentalists, to turn wholeheartedly to the holiness of creation. Their principal spokesman, Ralph Waldo Emerson (1803–82), asserts in the essay "Nature" (1836) that through the physical harmony of nature humans can perceive a deeper, transcendent reality akin to divine glory.

The Transcendentalist predisposition for finding profound meaning in natural phenomena had roots in British Romanticism and bore magnificent progeny in the highly realistic poetry of Robert Frost (1874–1963). His nature poetry achieves distinction as the most important in the New England tradition. Frost's place is "North of Boston," and knowledge of it in his poems often draws upon the region's mundane rural occupations. In lyrics and narratives about picking apples, repairing a stone fence, splitting cord wood, watching a snowstorm arrive, he transforms minute natural details into thoughtful emblems of human value. His profoundly deep themes and rich details helped earn Frost four Pulitzer Prizes for poetry.

Long before his time, however, the need to "know the place" engendered a rich tradition of local description, a celebration of the familiar that extended from down east Maine to the Connecticut River valley. One of the most famous texts is *Walden* (1854) by Henry David Thoreau (1817–62), whose significance is discussed below. The Berkshires of western Massachusetts provide William Cullen Bryant (1794–1878) with the setting for reverent poems infused with a deistic sense of holiness. Cape Cod has inspired a host of nature writers, chief among them Henry Beston, whose *The Outermost House* (1928) remains a world classic. Describing his year's experience at Nauset, Beston exquisitely conveys the beach's raw beauty and articulates a famous regret that we denizens of the modern age may be "sick to death for lack of elemental things." *The Outermost House* and Thoreau's *Cape Cod* (1865) influenced later Cape writers John Hay and Robert Finch. Hay's extensive expertise in natural history informs *The Run* (1959), *Nature's Year: The Seasons of Cape Cod* (1961), and *The Great Beach* (1963). Finch's *The Primal Place* (1983) and *Outlands* (1986) feature personal essays about coming to know "the particular neighborhood in which I lived."

In a starker seascape, the rocky Isles of Shoals off the coast of New Hampshire, Celia Thaxter (1835–94) gained literary renown for

her autobiographical nature essays. *Among the Isles of Shoals* (1873) and *An Island Garden* (1894) integrated the wild North Atlantic, the barren, rockbound islands, and her gardens into a portrait of a spiritual home. The relationships necessary to create a home are a major concern of Maine's Sarah Orne Jewett (1849–1909), whose complex communities include not only humans, but also land, plants, and animals. The sea itself is exquisitely depicted by Rachel Carson (1907–64): *The Sea around Us* (1951) and *The Edge of the Sea* (1953) combine scientific competence and reverent affection. Finally, a glimpse toward the future of local description is offered by John Elder in *Reading the Mountains of Home* (1998). Using tools drawn from literature, science, and personal observation, he contemplates Vermont's Green Mountains, interpreting vestiges of old settlement and envisioning new, healthier relationships with the land.

Thoreau's *Walden* is a masterpiece not merely in its description of a real locality. In it Thoreau poses fundamental questions about how to live and for answers looks to direct, intimate experience of the natural world. In *Walden* and in his extensive *Journals* he connects himself to the facts of natural history by what he called "direct intercourse and sympathy," evidenced in his observations of pickerel and woodchuck, seed and bean row. Moreover, Thoreau articulates profound environmental concerns. He asks how we should spend our time, and how much material wealth we need to be happy, questions of extraordinary contemporary relevance. His answer remains equally relevant: "a man is rich in proportion to the number of things he can afford to let alone." The idea of letting wild things alone is key to much of Thoreau's thinking, from his diatribe against the industrial destruction of the great northern forest in *The Maine Woods* (1864) to his prescription that "each Town should have a park, or rather a primitive forest . . . Where a stick should never be cut . . . but stand and decay for higher uses—a common possession forever for instruction and recreation." Thus does Thoreau lay foundation stones for the modern conservation movement even while composing its anthem: "In wildness is the preservation of the world." When he asks the value of a fine house if one has not a decent world on which to place it, his question resonates through generations of environmentalists down to the current hour.

A conscience-driven critique of human consumption has long been present in New England nature writing. Sarah Orne Jewett's short story "A White Heron" (1886) gently but profoundly dramatizes the dilemma of using living creatures to advance scientific curiosity and material gain. The first systematic documentation of historical and global environmental degradation, accompanied by spirited advocacy against it, comes from Vermont's scholar, statesman, and congressman George Perkins Marsh (1801–82) in *The Earth as Modified by Human Action* (1874). The most influential critique of technological arrogance, however, comes from Rachel Carson. In *Silent Spring* (1962) she demonstrates the harmful consequences of pesticide use so effectively that a single book initiated major change in public policy and brought about the birth of our contemporary environmental sensibility.

The scholarly interpretation of nature literature has been especially advanced by two New Englanders who have helped guide the new study of "ecocriticism": John Elder of Middlebury College and Lawrence Buell of Harvard University. Buell uses Thoreau and Thoreau's influence in *The Environmental Imagination* (1995) as reference to explore the intellectual consequences of American nature literature. His goal is to "imagine a more ecocentric way of being." In *Imagining the Earth: Poetry and the Vision of Nature* (1985) Elder begins an ambitious and sorely needed task: resolving the seeming opposition between contemporary environmental sensibility and the tradition of Western civilization. Through a close examination of writers such as William Wordsworth and Alfred North Whitehead, juxtaposed with a close reading of contemporary environmental poets, Elder "discovers grounds for reconciliation in the inextricable wholeness of the world."

Robert J. Begiebing and Owen Grumbling, eds., *The Literature of Nature: The British and American Traditions* (1990); Lawrence Buell, *The Environmental Imagination: Thoreau, Nature Writing, and the Formation of American Culture* (1995); John Elder and Robert Finch, eds., *The Norton Book of Nature Writing* (1990); Thomas J. Lyon, ed., *This Incomperable Lande: A Book of American Nature Writing* (1989).

Owen Grumbling

Oliver, Mary (1935–) Poet.

Mary Oliver was born in Ohio. She attended Ohio State University for a year and then Vassar College. But she left college before completing her degree in order to pursue a career in writing. She is the author of more than a dozen volumes of poetry, including *New and Selected Poems* (1992), which won the National Book Award, and *House of Light* (1990), which won the Christopher Award and the L. L. Winship/PEN New England Award. The *Boston Globe* established this award in 1975 for the best book by a New England author or with a New England topic or setting. In 1983 her book *American Primitive* won the Pulitzer Prize. She has been selected for inclusion in *The Best American Poetry* on several occasions. She also has published books of prose, essays, and handbooks about the craft of writing.

Oliver lives in Provincetown, Mass., and Bennington, Vt., and her time in New England firmly locates her poetry and prose in the geography that surrounds her. Her work resonates with the tradition of Robert Frost in her choice of subject matter in the New England landscape as well as her lyric voice. Simply reading the table of contents in her books of poems is enough to surmise that this poet has a creative and deep relationship to the landscape and seasons, particularly those of Cape Cod, which is a primary location for much of her poetry. A strong sense of place, and of identity in relation to it, is central to her writing. Realities of swamp, pond, woods, and shore lead to moments of transcendence. She has been compared to Emily Dickinson for these assertions as well as her desire for seclusion. Oliver protects her private and professional lives and often fends off interviews and media proposals in order to stay grounded in the solitary nature of her craft.

Her poems of 30 years disclose a style and vocabulary driven by visionary conviction in a mode analogous to her claimed influences, William Blake and Walt Whitman. Like Thoreau, another New Englander, she takes frequent walks in the settings that envelop her to gain inspiration for the poetry she writes. She keeps a notebook with her at all times to capture the fragments and thoughts that arise. She often titles her poems with one or two words and then launches into a meditation that immerses the reader into the life and habits of the animate creatures in the outside world. Her poems follow the cycles of the seasons and she observes and notes the constancy of loss and renewal in nature. This is exemplified in "Wild Geese," one of her most well-known and quoted poems, which draws deeply on New England traditions of poetry:

> Meanwhile the wild geese, high in the
>   clean blue air,
> are heading home again.
> Whoever you are, no matter how lonely,
> the world offers itself to your imagination,
> calls to you like the wild geese, harsh and
>   exciting—
> over and over announcing your place
> in the family of things.

Oliver's honors are many, and she has received fellowships from the Guggenheim Foundation and the National Endowment for the Arts. After holding a variety of positions she became the Banister Writer-in-Residence at Sweet Briar College in Virginia for several years. She also holds the Catharine Osgood Foster Chair for Distinguished Teaching at Bennington College.

Janet McNew, "Mary Oliver and the Tradition of Romantic Nature Poetry," *Contemporary Literature* 30, no. 1 (1989); Steve Ratiner, *Giving Their Word* (2002); Robin Riley Fast, "The Native American Presence in Mary Oliver's Poetry," *Kentucky Review* 12 (autumn 1993).

Dianne Bilyak

Parker, Robert B. (1932–) Writer.

Robert B. Parker, author of the Spenser series of detective novels, is considered by many to be the foremost interpreter of the tradition of detective fiction created by Raymond Chandler and Dashiell Hammett. A native of Springfield, Mass., Parker graduated from Colby College in 1954 and served in the Korean War. Before earning his doctoral degree in English in 1971 from Boston University, where the topic of his dissertation was the hard-boiled detective tradition in American literature, he alternated between teaching and freelancing as an advertising copywriter. Parker joined the faculty of Northeastern University and in 1973 published the first of his Spenser novels, *The Godwulf Manuscript*. In 1976 Parker's fourth novel, *Promised Land*, won the Mystery Writers of America's Edgar Allan Poe Award for best novel. In 1982 his *Valediction* appeared on the *New York Times* national best-seller list, and his titles have appeared there every year since. Notably, Parker completed Raymond Chandler's unfinished Marlowe novel, *The Poodle Springs Story*, and subsequently ghostwrote a sequel to Chandler's *The Big Sleep*, titled *Perchance to Dream*.

When *The Godwulf Manuscript* was published, critics hailed it as a fresh reinvention of the hard-boiled detective genre. In his novels, Parker has made Boston and its suburbs into a setting for crime that rivals that of Los Angeles, New York, or Miami. Spenser, a self-described "literate thug," is a bright figure who seems to be sustained by a constant optimism, in contrast to the darker Philip Marlowes and Sam Spades that have frequented American mystery fiction since the 1930s. When not preparing meals for his amour, psychologist Susan Silverman, Spenser triumphs with gun or fist over any opposition. He insults his betters with impunity and leaves a trail of bodies that the Boston Police Department seems content merely to tally. Spenser's friend Hawk, who typifies the streetwise black gangster, often comes to his aid when the going gets tough. The Spenser novels were adapted into a popular television series on ABC starring Robert Urich (who became as strongly identified with Spenser as Chester Morris did with Boston Blackie and Raymond Burr with Perry Mason) that aired from 1985 to 1988, as well as several television movies.

In addition to their intriguing plots and likable characters, Parker's stories often include detailed descriptions of New England settings and the cultural clashes therein. *Walking Shadow* (1994), for instance, is set in a small coastal town modeled on New Bedford, Mass., where cultural and racial divides are played out against a richly textured backdrop of societal unrest and murder. Parker's handful of nonmystery novels, including *Wilderness* (1979), about a murder witness who is stalked by the killer, and *All Our Yesterdays* (1994), an homage to Parker's Irish ancestry, are also set in New England.

Parker's recent projects include a new series based on Jesse Stone, a worn-out Los Angeles detective who becomes police chief of a small, troubled Massachusetts town. Parker also created a series featuring Boston private investigator Sunny Randall. Parker has two sons, David and Daniel, with his wife, Joan, whom he married in 1956. He lives in Cambridge and Concord, Mass., and is founder, along with his wife, of Pearl Productions, an independent film company.

David Geherin, *Sons of Sam Spade: The Private-Eye Novel in the 70s: Robert B. Parker, Roger L. Simon, Andrew Bergman* (1980); Robert B. Parker, *The Private Eye in Hammett and Chandler* (1984); Parker and Kasho Kumagai (photographer), *Spenser's Boston* (1994).

Scott E. Green

Petry, Ann Lane (1908–97) Novelist and writer of short stories and books for children. Ann Petry, one of New England's most important writers, explored in her fiction the psychological and social contexts of a racially and geographically diverse cast of characters. Because much of her work is set in New England, it resembles that of other New England writers just as much as it resembles that of African American writers who were her contemporaries, such as Richard Wright and Gwendolyn Brooks.

Petry was born in Old Saybrook, Conn. Her father was one of the first black pharmacists in the state, and she followed him into the profession, earning a Ph.G. at the University of Connecticut in 1931. Petry worked as a druggist until her marriage to George Petry in 1938. The couple moved to New York later that year, and Petry began working for the *Amsterdam News* and *People's Voice*, two Harlem-based newspapers. During this time she also published several short stories, including "On Saturday the Siren Sounds at Noon" (1943), and enrolled in writing classes at Columbia University. In 1945 Petry received the Houghton Mifflin Literary Fellowship in fiction, which allowed her to complete work on her first and best-known novel, *The Street* (1946).

The story of a young black woman's experience as a working-class single mother dealing with poverty and sexual harassment, *The Street* was the first novel by an African American woman to sell more than 1 million copies.

By 1948 the Petrys had returned to Old Saybrook. Her early life in Old Saybrook and her family's pharmacy provide the basis for much of her fiction, including *Country Place* (1947), *The Narrows* (1953), the short story "Miss Muriel" (1971), and the children's book *The Drugstore Cat* (1949). *Country Place* is set in the fictional New England town of Lennox and features no major black characters. The focus instead is on gender conflict and the relations between the small town's inhabitants. *The Narrows*, by contrast, Petry's second New England novel, deals with interracial relations in the fictional Monmouth, Conn. The most significant of Petry's New England writings, *The Narrows* takes the illicit interracial affairs, the false accusations of rape, and the lynchings that are familiar topics in southern novels and short stories and sets them in New England. It also portrays characters that rarely appear in American fiction, especially so-called black Yankees, descendants of the earliest black New Englanders. The critic Sybil Weir places *The Narrows* in a tradition of domestic feminism and realism "created primarily by New England women writers." In addition to her adult novels, Petry also wrote several works for children. In this she resembles other African American writers, such as W. E. B. Du Bois and Langston Hughes, who deemed it important to write nonracist, historically accurate literature for black children.

Reviewers and literary critics have devoted less attention to Petry's New England novels than to *The Street* because those works cannot easily be categorized as sociological treatments of black urban life. Both *Country Place* and *The Narrows*, as well as many of Petry's short stories, challenge the notion of a racially and culturally coherent New England or of a coherent black racial identity. Furthermore, Petry's fiction is not based on the tradition of black women's writing shaped by folk-inspired fictions such as those found in Zora Neale Hurston and Alice Walker. Finally, Petry's intentional exploration of New England as a black landscape upsets usual understandings of black culture as specifically southern or migrant.

During the 1980s and 1990s Ann Petry finally achieved recognition as an important New England writer, receiving numerous citations, awards, honorary degrees, and tributes from the region's colleges and universities. Her works are enduring testaments to American life, and they have influenced a generation

of African American women writers, including Toni Morrison, Toni Cade Bambara, and Gloria Naylor.

Farah Jasmine Griffin

Phelps, Elizabeth Stuart (1844–1911) Writer. Elizabeth Stuart Phelps's life was shaped by two New England cultural movements that were essentially oppositional: Calvinism, the conservative and patriarchal Protestantism that the Puritans brought with them to America, and the 19th-century women's movement, a revolution that sought political and social freedom for women. Perhaps it was this tension, so evident in the lives of many 19th-century New England women writers, that inspired Phelps to write, as her female protagonists most often wrestle with traditional women's roles that they find contrary to their natures.

Born in Boston to Elizabeth Stuart Phelps, a writer, and Austin Phelps, a minister, the young Elizabeth (christened Mary Gray) grew up in devoutly religious surroundings, first in the parsonage of Boston's Pine Street Congregational Church and then in Andover, Mass., where Austin Phelps taught at the Andover Theological Seminary. While her father immersed himself in his profession, Elizabeth watched her mother strive to realize her literary ambitions while performing her duties as a minister's wife and a mother to three children. Phelps's mother's death in 1852 affected her profoundly; she may have taken her mother's name, Elizabeth, in memoriam. She wrote in her autobiography, *Chapters from a Life* (1896), that her mother's "struggle" to be writer, minister's wife, and mother "killed her." This early sense of the difficulties for women of combining a career with marriage and motherhood informs the plots of many of Phelps's best novels, notably *The Silent Partner* (1871), *The Story of Avis* (1877), and *Doctor Zay* (1882).

Like her mother's fiction, Phelps's early stories, such as her *Tiny* series and her *Gypsy* books, are Christian morality tales for children. Her first novel, *The Gates Ajar* (1868), was an immensely popular depiction of a utopian heaven that closely resembled a New England village; the book offers sentimental consolation to a young woman who grieves for her brother. In a transformation of Calvinism of the sort offered by Harriet Beecher Stowe and other women writers of the Civil War era, heaven is a refuge even for those who may not have experienced the sort of dramatic conversion expected of orthodox believers. Years later, she would publish two more *Gates* books, *Beyond the Gates* (1883) and *The Gates Between* (1887). In the meantime, Phelps became interested in the social and political position of women and wrote feminist articles for the popular press. She also began to consider social problems in her fiction. In *The Silent Partner*, for example, she examines the plight of New England mill workers along with the problems that her female protagonist, Perley Kelso, inherits with the mill. Perley's desire to be a business partner is thwarted by the male power structure at the mill, and Phelps criticizes social constraints that interfere with women's career ambitions.

While the quality of her fiction is uneven, Phelps's best novel, *The Story of Avis*, successfully balances social criticism with artistic merit. Her protagonist, Avis Dobell, is torn between her commitment to her career as a painter and her love for Philip Ostrander, a Latin professor. Phelps's depiction of their marriage and Avis's lack of fulfillment in it is unsentimental and moving. The novel, set in the fictional seaport community of Harmouth, a university town based on Phelps's homes in Andover and Gloucester, Mass., is also distinguished by its fine depictions of the New England landscape.

Lori D. Kelly, *Life and Works of Elizabeth Stuart Phelps, Victorian Feminist Writer* (1983); Carol Farley Kessler, *Elizabeth Stuart Phelps* (1982); Ronna Coffey Privett, *A Comprehensive Study of American Writer Elizabeth Stuart Phelps, 1844–1911: Art for Truth's Sake* (2003).

Anne M. Downey

Piercy, Marge (1936–) Novelist and poet. Born in Detroit, Mich., to working-class parents of Welsh English Protestant and Russian Lithuanian Jewish descent, Marge Piercy settled in the Cape Cod town of Wellfleet, Mass., in 1971 to make her living as a novelist, poet, essayist, reviewer, lecturer, and occasional writer-in-residence. She has published more than a dozen volumes of poetry and as many novels. Although she claims Emily Dickinson as an important early influence, she can also be linked to Charlotte Perkins Gilman, Rebecca Harding Davis, and Anzia Yezierska, as well as to Audre Lorde, June Jordan, and Adrienne Rich in her intense awareness of the effects of gender norms, race, class, sexual preference, and social displacement on the lives of women. Whether the setting is the landscape of Cape Cod; the cities of Boston, Chicago, or Paris; or a fictional utopia, Piercy's great subject is the struggle of women "to be of use" as fully developed, interdependent people in a world that must continue to change in order to become just. A realist in her observation of natural and social phenomena, Piercy nonetheless challenges conventional constructions of reality with her intricate narratives and bold images. Unlike many of her literary precur-

Marge Piercy, ca. 1979

sors, she remains optimistic about the ability of human beings to understand and reconstruct their social world.

The Longings of Women (1994), for example, is set in Boston and told from the perspectives of three women, each grappling with displacement from her home. The oldest, Mary, divorced and homeless, narrowly escapes death with help from an employer, Leila. The youngest, Becky, murders her husband to avoid losing their condominium—her toehold in respectability. Leila chooses divorce. In a thorough reversal of traditional narrative expectations, all three women survive without marriage and look forward to new challenges, in Becky's case, from prison.

Piercy developed her unusual ability to sustain a positive view of change in the face of negative circumstances in Detroit, Chicago, and New York, where she faced many personal challenges, including performing her own abortion, experiencing prejudice as a Jewish female and as a feminist writer, and losing her health in the movements for civil rights, for choice, and against the war in Vietnam. The move to Cape Cod literally saved her life by providing the retreat that New England has offered other writers, but it also gave her a base near Boston from which to observe and research late-20th- and early-21st-century social problems, to search out the roots of democracy, and to envision other social orders. Her poems, though no less politically concerned than her novels, have become more autobiographical and meditative since her move, extending Henry David Thoreau's famous chapter of *Walden*, "Where I Lived, and What I Lived For," which inaugurated a New England tradition of presenting a writer's life as a series of ethical choices, and revealing her passionate hope for ethical relationships based on love, justice, and respect for all forms of life.

Pat Doherty, *Marge Piercy: An Annotated Bibliography* (1997); Marge Piercy, *Parti-Colored Blocks for a Quilt* (1982); Kerstin W. Shands, *The Repair of the World* (1994); Sue Walker and Eugenie Hamner, *Ways of Knowing: Essays on Marge Piercy* (1991).

Estella Lauter

Plath, Sylvia (1932–63) Poet and novelist. Born in Jamaica Plain, Mass., Sylvia Plath wrote more than 300 poems, a radio play, a novel, 70 short stories (mostly unpublished), and a children's book during her brief career. Her *Collected Poems* (1981) earned the Pulitzer Prize in 1982. Although her work was not available to readers in its entirety until nearly two decades after her death, Plath's *Ariel* poems were immediately recognized as a breakthrough in contemporary poetry and as a fountainhead for women's writing in their stark imagery, acerbic personae, and unabashed use of autobiographical material.

Raised by her mother, Aurelia Schober Plath, after the early death of her father, Otto, in 1940, Plath was educated in public schools in the affluent suburb of Wellesley, Mass. Plath's ambition to be a famous writer was spurred by early publication and prizes, confirmed by a scholarship to Smith College and crowned by her summer as a college editor at *Mademoiselle* magazine in 1953. After a suicide attempt and hospitalization at McLean Hospital in the fall of that same year, Plath returned to Smith and graduated with honors in 1955.

While a Fulbright scholar at Cambridge University, Plath met English poet Ted Hughes. They married in June 1956 and returned to the United States in 1957. Plath taught at Smith College before moving to Boston to write in 1958. She met the poet Anne Sexton while auditing Robert Lowell's poetry workshop. Although Plath's circle of acquaintances included Philip Booth, Peter Davison, Elizabeth Hardwick (then Lowell's wife), W. S. Merwin, John Sweeney, and George Starbuck, Plath viewed other writers chiefly as rivals and measured her achievements jealously against her female contemporaries, especially Adrienne Rich. After spending the fall as a fellow at Yaddo, an artists' colony in Saratoga Springs, N.Y., Plath and Hughes moved to England, where their children Frieda (1960) and Nicholas (1962) were born. Plath and Hughes separated in the summer of 1962. Over the following six months the rupture produced more than a third of the poems that Plath wrote during the last decade of her life, searing accounts of loss, reprisal, and attempted rebirth. In December Plath moved to London, renting a house that once had been occupied by William Butler Yeats;

she committed suicide there on February 11, 1963, at the age of 30.

Hughes, whom Plath idealized as mentor and muse, figures often in her writing as a rival, critic, and censor. As her posthumous editor, Hughes controlled publication and access to Plath's writing. His decision to exclude many poems from her plan for *Ariel* (1965), to change the order of poems in the volume, and to destroy journals from her most productive years (1961 and 1962) encourages a misreading of her late poems, which appear to chart an inevitable trajectory toward suicide. Preoccupation with Plath's autobiography has persistently shadowed critical estimation of her poetry.

Although the poems that made Plath famous were written in England, she always considered herself an American writer. Her writing is marked by the aspirations and disappointments of middle-class postwar culture. Although *Letters Home* (1975) and *Journals* (1982) reveal her psychic investment in the ideals of companionate marriage and sexual and maternal fulfillment, her mature work critiques traditional gender roles. Her novel *The Bell Jar* (1963) satirizes the cultural forces of 1950s America that teach the heroine femininity, police her sexuality, and eventually precipitate her hospitalization for depression. Plath's first volume of poetry, *Colossus and Other Poems* (1962), was allusive and formally constrained. It includes meditations on Massachusetts landscapes and seascapes that are superseded in the later poems by interior psychological landscapes. Initially labeled a confessional or extremist poet and compared to Robert Lowell, John Berryman, and Ann Sexton, Plath was later praised by feminist critics for using her art to fiercely avenge her victimization by patriarchal villains. Manuscripts for Plath's poetry (housed in the Lilly Library at Indiana University and at Smith College) prove that Plath revised carefully to recast autobiographical material into larger, often mythic narratives with optimistic if apocalyptic endings.

Steven Axelrod, *Sylvia Plath: The Wound and the Cure of Words* (1990); Jacqueline Rose, *The Haunting of Sylvia Plath* (1991); Susan R. Van Dyne, *Revising Life: Sylvia Plath's Ariel Poems* (1993); Linda W. Wagner, *Sylvia Plath: The Critical Heritage* (1988).
Susan R. Van Dyne

Preston, John (1945–94)

Writer and activist. Raised in Medfield, Mass., John Preston published more than 30 books of fiction and nonfiction on topics related to gay life. In later essays, Preston explored his complex connections to conservative New England and his exile from his hometown and was a pioneer advocate of safe sex during the early days of AIDS awareness. Preston helped found the Maine Health Foundation and was president of the AIDS Project of Portland, Maine.

Educated at Lake Forest College in Chicago and the University of Minnesota Medical School, Preston became certified as a sexual health consultant and during the early 1970s founded two of Minneapolis's first organizations to serve the gay community. After editing a newsletter produced by the Sex Education Council of the United States in New York City, Preston moved to San Francisco in 1975 to become editor of *The Advocate*, "the best gay job in America at the time," but resigned the position after one year and returned to New York City.

While doing temp work, Preston wrote a 20-page story for *Drummer* magazine that, at the suggestion of editor John Embry, was expanded into the novel *Mr. Benson* in 1978. This "SM cult classic" initiated Preston's career as a writer of porn and a sadomasochist cult hero. In 1979 Preston left New York City and moved to Portland, Maine, where he wrote *Franny, the Queen of Provincetown* (1983). To support himself, Preston wrote adventure novels celebrating gay superhero Alex Kane. In response to the AIDS epidemic, he edited *Hot Living: Erotic Stories about Safer Sex* (1985) and published *Safe Sex: The Ultimate Erotic Guide* (1987) with Glenn Swann. After his own HIV diagnosis in 1987, he published *Personal Dispatches: Writers Confront AIDS* (1989).

Preston wrote for various audiences, including mainstream readers. *Hometowns: Gay Men Write about Where They Belong* (1991) and *The Big Gay Book: A Man's Survival Guide for the Nineties* (1991) were selected by the Book-of-the-Month Club. A successful anthologist, he edited *A Member of the Family: Gay Men Write about Their Families* (1992) and *Friends and Lovers: Gay Men Write about the Families They Create* (1995), among other collections.

Preston emphasized his lifelong connection with New England in essays such as "Medfield, Massachusetts" and "Portland, Maine: Life's Good Here" published in *Winter's Light: Reflections of a Yankee Queer* (1995). The first documents his love for his hometown—its history, its traditions, its Yankee insularity. The second celebrates his return to New England after years of exile from his hometown, where his ancestors date back to the town's 17th-century origins. Preston laments: "I was being taken away from Medfield and everything it stood for. I was the one who should have gotten a law degree and come home to settle into comfortable Charles River Valley politics—perhaps with a seat in the Great and General Court. . . . But I was no longer one of them. I had become too different."

Preston eventually found a new home in Maine, where he continued chronicling contemporary issues of gay life and working as advocate for the gay community until his death in 1994 due to complications from AIDS. Preston's papers are currently held in the John Hay Library at Brown University.

Jane L. Troxell, "John Preston (1945–)," in *Contemporary Gay American Novelists: A Bio-Bibliographical Critical Sourcebook*, ed. Emmanuel S. Nelson (1993).
John Gilgun

Profession of Writing to 1900

In the United States, the profession of writing, both as a way of making a living and as an acknowledged cultural identity, emerged during the 19th century. From its tentative beginnings in the early national period, professional authorship became a middle-class vocation in the antebellum period and even, for some writers, a profitable undertaking. By the 19th century's end, as the publishing industry became more specialized, systems of marketing and distribution became more fully developed, and the number of periodicals and newspapers increased dramatically, writing became the full-time occupation of thousands. The beginning of this historical development coincides roughly with the passage of the first national copyright law in 1790. As William Charvat once said of this law, "No literary profession was possible until law had given products of the mind the status of *property*."

In New England the history of professional writing was further shaped by several distinctive conditions. A high rate of literacy sustained a system of local publishing that lingered longer than in other areas of the country and that delayed Boston's emergence as a regional and national publishing center until the 1840s. This delay led to the regional loss of many writers, who moved to New York or Philadelphia in pursuit of a literary career, but this exodus also extended New England's influence into the national culture. Another characteristic was the persistence of a traditional, elite ideal of the function of literature: to guide the nation.

Writers after the Revolution conceived of writing for publication in ways markedly different from writers after 1820. They defined writing as a civic act, part of the public sphere of discourse, and best carried out by elites who wrote not for profit but for the good of the republic, that is, in order to diffuse knowledge among "the people" and to influence political and social debate. This republican vision of authorship, with its reliance on stable social hierarchies and communal values, was exemplified in the 1780s and 1790s by a group of poets known as the Connecticut Wits; this group included Yale president and staunch Federalist

Timothy Dwight, whose poems celebrated both the American Revolution and the agrarian and deferential order of New England communities. The republicanism and conservatism of the Wits were further embodied in the "Society of Gentlemen" who edited and wrote for the *Monthly Anthology and Boston Review* (1803–11); this group saw their periodical as a bulwark against the increasing social mobility and commercialism of American culture. Neither the Wits nor the "Anthology men" needed what little, if any, income they derived from their literary work. And they tended to combat lower-class assumptions of the privilege of authorship; when the shoemaker David Hitchcock began to publish poetry, he was pilloried, although not silenced, by the *Monthly Anthology*. On the other hand, they were suspicious of writing as a reputable primary occupation, a suspicion confirmed by the career of the Brahmin poet Robert Treat Paine, Jr., who, despite patronage by his class, fell into a bohemian existence.

Although such republican and amateur ideas of authorship hindered the professionalization of writing, they also coexisted with and even unwittingly furthered the process. Late-18th-century proto-professional writers exemplify these tensions and the movement toward the liberal model of authorship characteristic of the 19th century. As editor of and a writer for one of the best magazines in New England—the *Farmer's Weekly Museum* (1796–1801), published in Walpole, N.H.—Joseph Dennie, as Michael Gilmore has pointed out, at once embodied the antidemocratic, amateur position and was an early literary entrepreneur who marketed his paper to a democratic readership. He published such Federalist "gentlemen" writers as Royall Tyler but also depended on his literary labor for his livelihood and made polite letters an object of popular consumption. Dennie's tactics, together with his move to Philadelphia, helped to put periodical publishing on a financially stable footing and secured the longevity of his later magazine, the *Port Folio* (1801–27).

The careers of other proto-professional writers reveal the shifting grounds not only of class but also of race, gender, and genre as writing became a profession. The republican ideal of a meritocracy invited writers other than privileged Anglo-American males into authorship, even as those same males often policed the borders of polite letters against such encroachers. Examples include one of the Connecticut Wits, the farmer's son Joel Barlow, and Phillis Wheatley, an African American slave who in 1773 published a book of poetry in England and then sold it by subscription to members of Boston's upper class. Susanna Rowson may be the best example of

this kind of early writer; she supported herself by a mix of professions, including acting, writing, and teaching. Her popular novel *Charlotte Temple* (1791) earned her little because it was originally published in England before her emigration (and so was unprotected by American copyright), but it gained her a wide audience and empowered women readers despite patrician warnings that novels threatened the social order. Indeed, novelists and magazine editors catered to a growing female readership by supporting women's education, a stance that encouraged women writers to enter the profession during the 19th century, often in the emerging field of fiction.

The 19th-century formation of professional authorship developed together with the shift from republican values to Jacksonian ideologies of individualism and marketplace competition. In 1820, with the financially successful publication of New York author Washington Irving's *Sketch Book*, writing became more of a commodity, a process supported by increasingly efficient forms of book manufacturing and distribution and by the growth of capital in the book trade. The shift is evident in the career of Hartford poet and teacher Lydia Sigourney, who began publishing during the 1810s in the amateur tradition but who, after her husband suffered financial setbacks, went on to publish substantial amounts of poetry during the 1830s and to earn money doing it. During the 1820s a number of influential New England writers who would derive much of their livelihood through writing, or by editing journals, published their first books: William Cullen Bryant (*Poems* [1821]), Catharine Maria Sedgwick (*A New England Tale* [1822] and *Hope Leslie* [1827]), Lydia Maria Child (*Hobomok* [1824]), and Sarah Josepha Hale (*Northwood* [1827]). These writers' careers were typical of broader patterns in New England; three of them combined writing with editing to forge careers as literary professionals, and all either left New England for New York or Philadelphia to edit journals or published their works in these other cities in order to gain a national hearing. Two became profoundly influential voices in American culture because of their editorships; Hale, who left New Hampshire for Philadelphia to edit *Godey's Lady's Book* (1837–77), was a pervasive presence in antebellum women's culture, and Bryant, as editor of the *New York Evening Post* (1829–78), shaped the course of national debates on political, social, and literary issues.

Midcentury New England saw writing flourish even as it also saw the professionalization of the publishing industry and the consolidation of Boston as a literary center for both the region and the nation. Writers continued to support themselves by combining

literary with related occupations but now made careers in which writing was increasingly central. Margaret Fuller moved from teaching in New England to becoming a full-time writer for Horace Greeley's *New York Tribune*. Nathaniel Hawthorne followed a typical pattern for male writers by alternating between full-time authorship and government appointments, while Ralph Waldo Emerson followed another pattern: supplementing his earnings as a writer with income from lecture tours. Henry Wadsworth Longfellow gradually developed a broad market for his poetry while teaching modern languages at Harvard until commercial success allowed him to retire from academia and write full time.

A number of writers followed a different route to professional authorship; Mary Kelley has called them "literary domestics"—white middle-class women who wrote in the "private sphere" of their homes. Women continued to find fiction one of the genres most open to them and by midcentury became the main producers of novels for the market. Several New England literary domestics were best-selling writers: Maria Susanna Cummins (*The Lamplighter* [1854]), Fanny Fern (*Ruth Hall* [1854]), and Harriet Beecher Stowe (*Uncle Tom's Cabin* [1852]). This form of authorship, however, was not readily available to African American women writers. Harriet Wilson, who wrote her autobiographical novel *Our Nig* (1859) in order to support herself and her child, did not enjoy the same success as Fern, who wrote her autobiographical novel for the same reason. Both the literary domestics and most of their successful male counterparts combined a traditional New England understanding of writing as a medium of national guidance, reform, and moral uplift with a professional accommodation to the democratic marketplace and its popular genres: newspaper columns, narrative poetry, lectures, and fiction.

Boston emerged at midcentury as a major publishing center; the book trade in New England became centralized there, the railroad connected it to a national market, effective literary institutions developed, and the publishing house of Ticknor and Fields courted many of the best New England writers. One of the institutions that defined literature from the 1850s to the end of the century was the new periodical the *Atlantic Monthly*, owned by Ticknor and Fields and quickly established as the preeminent literary journal in the United States. The *Atlantic*, especially under the editorship (1871–81) of William Dean Howells, set a new standard for literary excellence and, in doing so, furthered a post–Civil War stratification of publishing into "high" and popular literature, a new variation on the class issues connected with writing in a market society. The journal published writers from different class, ethnic, or regional origins (including Mark Twain and the Sioux writer Zitkala-Sa), published both women (Harriet Prescott Spofford, Elizabeth Stuart Phelps) and men, and paid well enough so that it was finally possible for a writer to derive a middle-class income from writing for periodicals. It was also one of the institutions that centralized literary power in the hands of a small, white, male elite; this Boston-based elite defined the first nationally recognized canon of American literature (largely composed of New England writers) through editing such magazines as the *Atlantic,* overseeing the writing of textbooks for schools, and setting policies for the growing public libraries of the period.

The centralization of publishing actually may have helped white middle-class women writers; the paternal ideal of the "gentleman publisher," as Susan Coultrap-McQuin has argued, which emphasized personal relationships with writers and "noncommercial aims, and moral guardianship" and which was embodied by such Boston publishers as James Fields and Henry Houghton, allowed many women to create a concept of authorship that did not conflict radically with 19th-century definitions of womanhood. This centralization also meant that writers no longer had to be near urban centers to publish successfully; regionalist writers, including Sarah Orne Jewett (*The Country of the Pointed Firs* [1896]) and Rose Terry Cooke, published in such magazines as the *Atlantic* and had professional ties to Boston even as they depicted the New England hinterland. Indeed, the consolidation of the publishing industry and its associated literary institutions helped to foster markets for and commodify regionalist writings; just as the *Atlantic* offered its readers Charles Chesnutt's stories of southern African American folk traditions, so *Harper's Bazar* [*sic*] in New York found a national market for Mary E. Wilkins Freeman's tales of New England rural life.

As Richard Brodhead has argued, the late 19th century saw the establishment of several audiences and literary "zones." The novels of the literary domestics, not defined as "high" literature, continued to be the best-selling fiction nationally, while new mass-market forms such as the dime novel came into being; the first dime novel (*Malaeska* [1860]) was a reissue of a novel by a Portland and New York writer, Ann Sophia Stephens. The most famous of these mass-market novelists, Horatio Alger, Jr., was an ex-clergyman from Massachusetts whose books (for example, *Ragged Dick* [1868]) about boys who climb from the street into middle-class respectability sold millions well into the 20th century.

By 1900 various models of professional authorship were available in New England, from the nationally acclaimed writer who found writing lucrative (Stowe and Twain both built expensive houses in Hartford) to what Brodhead calls the "industrial hand," grinding out standardized products for the publishers of story papers and dime novels. Writers sometimes moved among these models; Louisa May Alcott wrote potboilers for story papers at the same time that she wrote "literature" for the *Atlantic Monthly.* African American writers developed literary careers and publishing institutions with more success; Pauline Hopkins published her novel *Contending Forces* (1900) with the Colored Cooperative Publishing Company and edited *The Colored American Magazine* in Boston, while William Monroe Trotter founded the *Boston Guardian* in 1901. New trends in publishing emerged that would shape the profession of writing in the 20th century: the increasing commercialization and "masculinization" of the publishing business and the emergence of the new "art" magazine, addressed to a small audience of cultural initiates and the forerunner of the "little magazines" of the modernist writers. In 1900, just as printed matter virtually saturated New England society, writing was a more viable career than it had ever been before and the field of work more diversified.

Richard H. Brodhead, *Cultures of Letters: Scenes of Reading and Writing in 19th-Century America* (1993); Lawrence Buell, *New England Literary Culture: From Revolution through Renaissance* (1986); William Charvat, *The Profession of Authorship in America, 1800–1870,* ed. Matthew J. Bruccoli (1992); Susan Coultrap-McQuin, *Doing Literary Business: American Women Writers in the 19th Century* (1990); Michael T. Gilmore, "The Literature of the Revolutionary and Early National Periods," in *The Cambridge History of American Literature,* vol. I, ed. Sacvan Bercovitch (1994); Mary Kelley, *Private Woman, Public Stage: Literary Domesticity in 19th-Century America* (1984); Michael Warner, *The Letters of the Republic: Publication and the Public Sphere in 18th-Century America* (1990); Michael Winship, *American Literary Publishing in the Mid-19th Century: The Business of Ticknor and Fields* (1995).

Brigitte Bailey

Puritan Literature   The term *Puritan* is loosely applied to radical individuals of the English Protestant Reformation who were inspired by the writings of the French theologian John Calvin. In colonial New England, the literature of the Puritans flourished in published and manuscript form from the settlement of the Plymouth Colony in 1620 and the Massachusetts Bay Colony in 1630 through the gradual demise of the theocracy in the early 18th century. As a whole, Puritan literature tries to articulate the New Testament image of a "city upon a hill," used to construct the New England Puritan identity as a chosen people. As it attempts to perform this task, the literature becomes characterized by the clash between ideals and reality, by tensions rising out of historical circumstance and the desire for ideological control. Puritan writing often features a "plain style" in characteristic genres such as sermons, biographies, autobiographies, histories, and poetry.

The Puritans are best understood as a people in a wilderness, that is, an intellectual civilization with the now characteristic New England willingness to confront unknown nature. This confrontation was possible only because the Bible depicts in the Hebrews a God-favored wilderness people whom the Puritans could use as a model. For Puritans, biblical text had to define their ideology, their identity, and the scope of their literature. Fortunately, the nature of the Bible made it possible for the Puritan production of new texts to be both contained and liberated; for example, the psalms in New England's first book, the *Bay Psalm Book* (1640), were both faithful to the original text of the psalms and singable.

New England Puritan writing contains an odd mix of imagistic awareness of the wilderness condition and biblical insistence on the spiritual dimension of that plight. Metaphors of planting and cultivation abound in the literature, as in John Cotton's migration sermon, "God's Promise to His Plantations" (1630), and Samuel Danforth's later jeremiad "A Brief Recognition of New England's Errand into the Wilderness" (1670). The contradictory views contained in this imagery exemplify the dialectical nature of Puritan literature; the wildness of New England nature is at once a gift from God meant to be cultivated as a showcase for his goodness and, at the same time, a trick of the devil or even a sign that God is punishing the settlers for their misdeeds. The Puritans also show this vacillation in their contradictory views of the Native Americans, whom they represent in literature as either God's purpose for their settlement or Satan's protest against their presence in New England, and sometimes as both. This ambivalence toward nature becomes characteristic of New England literature, exemplified in the writings of Nathaniel Hawthorne, Robert Frost, and John Cheever.

This ambivalence parallels the many tensions in the spiritual life of Puritan colonists that inform their literature in both content and structure. Early writing by community spiritual leaders such as John Winthrop, the first Massachusetts Bay Colony governor, and John Cotton articulates a recurring conflict between community solidarity and individual salvation that later erupts into the Antinomian Controversy, which came to a head in 1637. This confrontation between what the

Puritans called the covenant of grace and the covenant of works (simply put, whether salvation is a free and private gift of God or must be earned by a person's obedience to his word and allegiance to his ordinances) reveals the clash between the ideal of a solid Christian community and the reality of trying to carve the perfect theocracy out of a colony in the New England wilderness.

Related to this conflict is the Puritan attitude about hierarchy, which begins as a belief that each individual Puritan congregation should be theologically independent, with no central control, and gradually evolves into an insistence on orthodoxy that subordinates the individual search for salvation to the good of the community and the ministers and magistrates who run it. John Winthrop's evolution from the imagery of the naturally binding power of love in his sermon "A Modell of Christian Charity" (1630) to that of separation and surveillance in "Defense of an Order of Court" (1637) demonstrates this shift from trust of the private quest for grace to suspicion of anything unorthodox.

A balance between orthodoxy and conformity on one hand and sympathy for the oppressed and the desire for individual freedom on the other also marks Puritan literature. Anti-hierarchical texts in the colony, such as the court document of Anne Hutchinson's trial for heresy (1637) and Roger Williams's protest literature in his 1635–37 debate with Cotton, go hand in hand with tolerance for the marginalized. Even community leader and judge Samuel Sewall's 1700 antislavery document *The Selling of Joseph* was written after Sewall recanted his role in the abortive Salem witch trials of the decade before. This balance is part of the New England literary heritage, manifested in the 20th century perhaps most poignantly by Edith Wharton's tormented title character of *Ethan Frome* (1911). More recently, New Englander Shirley Jackson created a similarly fragmented individual in the character of Eleanor Vance in *The Haunting of Hill House* (1959), who is torn between the conformity of her lonely life and the romantic individualism of her paranormal abilities.

Contradiction, ambivalence, and debate always empower literature with the spirit of imagination. Together with the Puritan belief in typology, that is, a way of seeing Old Testament figures, events, and objects as analogies for the reality of Christ, theological differences invested the Puritan way of knowing with a linguistic structure akin to metaphor: the view of reality as analogy, which finds signs of the spiritual in the natural and physical. One can easily see how this orthodox Puritan linguistic practice evolves into the Romantic nature theory of Ralph Waldo Emerson and Henry David Thoreau, following its quasi-Puritan evolution in the works of Jonathan Edwards.

The sermon and religious treatise-polemic are by far the most prevalent forms of writing to come out of the colonies, as the early New Englanders considered the textual construction of the theocracy most worthy of publication. Thus, most sermons and treatises—couched in biblical metaphor and often using such biblical imagery as lightness and darkness—deal with the theological arguments in the colony. For example, Edward Taylor uses his 1679 Foundation Day Sermon and its revision to defend his belief in closing the sacrament of communion to all but converted Christians. Most sermons—election day, execution day, errand, and jeremiad among them—try to promote a theological position in the evolution of the Puritan theocracy. The jeremiad, named for its imitation of the prophet Jeremiah's castigation of the chosen people of Israel for falling away from a supposed earlier golden era of piety and obedience, became a powerful theological and political tool. Its images of threatened punishment sparked the imagination, and its excessive evocation of deceased exemplary leaders, as well as its elevation of the preacher himself, influenced later writers and politicians. The jeremiad was popular in times of crisis, such as drought, Indian warfare, witchcraft trials, and political controversies with London authorities. To study Puritan sermon literature, then, is to study the religious history of the colonies.

Puritan history writing, on the other hand, becomes an exercise in mythmaking. Along with the migration literature—a group of essays and sermons meant to attract people to join the errand into the wilderness—Puritan histories such as William Bradford's *Of Plymouth Plantation* (1630–50), Edward Johnson's *Wonder-working Providence of Sions Saviour in New-England* (1654), and Cotton Mather's *Magnalia Christi Americana* (1702) tend to present the Puritan vision as though it were actual. These histories, then, render the early New England experience according to biblical models, so that a colonial leader becomes a New World Moses, a colonial writer becomes a new David, and New England itself becomes a land of refuge, the New Israel. As a result, Puritan history becomes a chronicle of desire.

A related genre is the narrative, which for the Puritans becomes evidence of God's presence in their lives. The Puritan narrative comes in two major categories: the personal and spiritual narrative and the captivity narrative. Because of the regularity of their structures and the archetypes they use—spiritual death and rebirth, captivity and release—Puritan narratives were precursors for the flowering of fiction in New England in the 19th century and beyond, informing such works as Harriet Beecher Stowe's *The Minister's Wooing* (1859), John Cheever's *The Wapshot Chronicle* (1957), and Carolyn Chute's *The Beans of Egypt, Maine* (1985). Puritan narratives also began the work of morally fictionalized autobiography that continued in the writings of Jonathan Edwards and Benjamin Franklin. Puritan spiritual narratives, most often in the form of transcribed conversion narratives delivered by Puritans seeking church membership, were largely oral but exist for 20th-century readers in unearthed church records and ministerial journals. Captivity narratives, the most famous being Mary Rowlandson's *The Soveraignty and Goodness of GOD . . . a Narrative of the Captivity and Restauration of Mrs. Mary Rowlandson* (1682), were often published because of a Puritan belief in their ability to edify through the literal experience of captivity and restoration. Like earlier texts, these captivity narratives also showed Native Americans in a negative light to help further the spiritual goals of the Puritan colony.

Much poetry also came out of Puritan New England, beginning a heritage of devotional verse with deep roots in the English Renaissance and the meditative tradition of 16th- and 17th-century England. The individualizing impulse mixed with the more orthodox modeling of verse image and technique on the Bible found in the work of such Puritan poets as Edward Taylor, Anne Bradstreet, and Michael Wigglesworth (although Wigglesworth tended more to adopt the tradition of theological debate from Puritan sermon literature) continued later in the personal and spiritual poetry of New Englanders Emerson, Emily Dickinson, Robert Frost, and Robert Lowell. Even the unearthing of personal demons in Sylvia Plath's poetry has similarities to Edward Taylor's more self-deprecating work: "My Sin! my Sin, My God, these Cursed Dregs, / Green, Yellow, Blew streakt Poyson hellish, ranck." This self-deprecation, common in Renaissance writing, is a legacy from the Book of Psalms, in which the writer often expresses the inferiority of his ability to write praises to God. Other features of Puritan poetry include the attempt to make God understandable by representing him, his attributes, and his ordinances with earthly metaphors like Edward Taylor's spinner in "Huswifery" (ca. 1682–83) and the use of elaborate metaphors drawn from biblical images, a technique also used in sermons. Unless Puritans wrote poetry for public occasions, such as their ubiquitous funeral elegies, publication was sought only if they or someone close to them possessed a sincere belief in the ability of the verse to instruct. The exception was Wigglesworth's *The Day of Doom* (1662), a poetic jeremiad that became America's first best-seller. Most poetry existed as private meditative exercise, although poems such as Anne Bradstreet's "Quarternions" and "The Four Monarchies" (1650) and Taylor's "Verses on Pope Joan" (ca. 1723) showed a sophisticated knowledge of the world beyond Puritan New England.

The earliest New England literature in English, then, invested colonial beginnings with an essence of spirituality and intellect. The conflict between the desire for a uniform community and the reality of clashing individual views created a climate in the wilderness fraught with imaginative interplay that continues to characterize New England literary culture into the 21st century.

Sacvan Bercovitch, *The American Jeremiad* (1978); Bercovitch, *The Puritan Origins of the American Self* (1975); Patricia Caldwell, *The Puritan Conversion Narrative: The Beginnings of American Expression* (1983); Charles L. Cohen, *God's Caress: The Psychology of Puritan Religious Experience* (1986); Kathryn Zabelle Derounian-Stodola and James A. Levernier, *The Indian Captivity Narrative, 1550–1900* (1993); Jeffrey A. Hammond, *Sinful Self, Saintly Self: The Puritan Experience of Poetry* (1993); William J. Scheick, *Design in Puritan American Literature* (1992); Teresa Toulouse, *The Art of Prophesying: New England Sermons and the Shaping of Belief* (1987).

Rosemary Fithian Guruswamy

Reform Literature Reform was almost synonymous with literature for the Puritans, New England's first writers, who used writing to advocate for the establishment of New England as a place to reform religious and civil society, if not humanity itself. This impulse, with its moralistic core, in increasingly secular form, characterized New England literature through the revolutionary era and beyond. Nineteenth-century New England culture reflects an almost seamless connection between literature and social reform issues. In the 20th century, however, writers have contested this connection between literature and social reform, just as they have contested the identity of New England. Although many writers have been committed to reform movements, fewer can be as clearly identified with New England as a discrete region in cultural or political terms. Greater geographical mobility and the region's decline as a national center have contributed to the increasing difficulty of identifying a specifically "New England" literature of social reform.

The Progressive Era of political reform did not produce major works of literature from New England to rival those from Chicago or New York. Articles critical of child labor in New England mills accompanied Lewis Hines's photographic expose in 1911–12. Winston Churchill's *Coniston* (1906) exposed the corrupt influence of the Boston and Maine Railroad in New Hampshire politics, and it contributed to making that state a bastion of reform. Two events from the first third of the century, however, the strike in the mills of Lawrence, Mass., and the Boston-area judicial murder of Nicola Sacco and Bartolomeo Vanzetti, typify the early-20th-century relation between literature and social reform, as each inspired a wave of imaginative literature in its own day and in the following decades. Representing the years from the 1930s through the end of the century, the career of poet Robert Lowell, the 1971 labor novel *Between the Hills and the Sea* by K. B. Gilden, and the 1985 nonfiction document *Common Ground* by J. Anthony Lukas reflect the continued intimate connection between the regional voice and social engagement.

The 1912 strike in the Lawrence woolen and worsted mills involved not only the thousands of male and female workers, but also the town's women and children. By instituting mass picketing and making use of women's neighborhood support networks within and across the ethnic groups that constituted the Lawrence working class, the Industrial Workers of the World (IWW) helped create a militant and eventually victorious force of strikers from a huge range of immigrant groups. (In addition to native-born workers, there were immigrants from England and Ireland, as well as Italians, Jews, French Canadians, Franco-Belgians, Poles, Syrians, Germans, Russians, Turks, Austrians, Armenians, Chinese, Portuguese, Lithuanians, and others.) The effect of what she witnessed in Lawrence as she covered the strike for *Harpers* turned genteel Boston novelist Mary Heaton Vorse into a labor journalist, a calling she followed for the rest of her career. Others who provided firsthand reportage of conditions in Lawrence included birth-control activist Margaret Sanger; Walter Weyl, cofounder of the *New Republic;* and liberal clergyman Harry Emerson Fosdick.

But beyond what might be called the official record, the Lawrence strike left its mark on New England through the literary voices of its participants. Arturo Giovannitti, an Italian poet in charge of strike relief and one of the leaders falsely accused of being an accessory to the murder of a woman striker, wrote prison poetry that contemporaries compared to Oscar Wilde's "Ballad of Reading Gaol," as well as other poems crying out for social justice. The IWW newspaper, *Solidarity,* published the militant and satirical songs chorused on the picket lines of Lawrence. And IWW songwriter extraordinaire Joe Hill ironically chose a hymn tune for a lyric attack on business unionism at Lawrence.

The handmade banner carried by a group of women strikers, "We want bread and roses too," inspired a poem by James Oppenheim that, set to music, is considered the anthem of 20th-century American feminism. Giovannitti, also moved by that slogan, wrote an Italian song titled "Pane e Rose" that was long popular with Italian immigrant garment workers. The dramatic exodus in which the children of Lawrence were sent out of the embattled town to live with sympathetic families around the Northeast figures not only in contemporary journalism, but in much later fiction, including novels otherwise as different as Laura Z. Hobson's *First Papers* (1964) and E. L. Doctorow's *Ragtime* (1975). Protest against working conditions among New England's ethnic minorities continued in Mari Tomasi's *Like Lesser Gods* (1949), about silicosis among Vermont's Italian granite carvers, and, to a lesser degree, in Mildred Savage's *Parrish* (1958), set in the tobacco fields of Connecticut.

The case of Sacco and Vanzetti, Italian anarchists falsely accused in a 1920 Braintree, Mass., payroll robbery and murder, and executed in 1927 over the protests of an international support movement, also served as the focus for poetry, drama, fiction, and literary journalism by New Englanders and others. Edna St. Vincent Millay's poem "Justice Denied in Massachusetts" is joined in her works by a number of more symbolic poems about the betrayal of justice, including a pair of sonnets explicitly dedicated to the two political martyrs. The Sacco-Vanzetti case is the subject of Maxwell Anderson's play *Winterset* (1936), as well as of Jeannette Marks's memoir *Thirteen Days* (1929), Upton Sinclair's *Boston: A Novel* (1930), James T. Farrell's *Bernard Clare* (1946), Howard Fast's *The Passion of Sacco and Vanzetti* (1953), and Katherine Anne Porter's *The Never-Ending Wrong* (1977). The case also figures in John Dos Passos's 1930s trilogy *USA* in the volume titled *The Big Money.*

Vanzetti's prison letters and the last words attributed to him have also become literary artifacts. The latter are the basis for a famous pair of 1958 silk-screen prints and a 1962 poster by the artist Ben Shahn, who, nearly three decades earlier, had painted a series of 23 Sacco-Vanzetti gouaches. Vanzetti's letters are also the source of the lyrics to a song recorded by Joan Baez in 1979 in connection with an Italian film about the case. *The Male Animal,* a 1940 play by James Thurber and Elliott Nugent, uses controversy over an English professor's right to read Vanzetti's final speech to his class as the springboard for its defense of academic freedom.

In both of these historical events involving working-class movements, the traditional New England tones—principled, privileged, and Anglo-Saxon—joined a "new New England" chorus of ethnic immigrant and working-class voices to describe oppressive conditions and call for social reform. In the last seven decades of the century, the personalities and works identified as typifying the later social reform literature share that ethnic polyphony. Literature addressing reform—political, economic, legal, or moral—sometimes sets an idealistic Yankee, in the person of a newspaper reporter or lawyer, in New England's complex ethnic mix, and this results in a reevaluation of naive ideals. Edwin O'Connor's *The Last Hurrah* (1956), Geoffrey Wolff's *Providence* (1986), and Carolyn Chute's *Snow Man* (1999) are but three examples.

Robert Lowell, one of the major American poets of the second half of the 20th century and a member of an old Massachusetts ruling-class family, was a distant cousin of poets James Russell Lowell and Amy Lowell and of Harvard President Lawrence Lowell, one of the "villains" of Sacco-Vanzetti literature. His imaginative writing includes "For the Union Dead," title poem of a 1964 collection, in which he memorializes Colonel Robert Shaw, the white Boston patrician who led the first black Civil War unit into combat and died with his men. Although Lowell may be said to have turned his back on his Harvard and Brahmin heritage when he chose to live and study with poets associated with the southern agrarian movement of the 1930s, this poem challenges Allen Tate's "Ode to the Confederate Dead" through its assertion of the poet's own regional tradition as one historically concerned with racial justice. As an antiwar poet, Lowell wrote about such topics as his prison experience while incarcerated for draft refusal in 1943, the anniversary of the annihilation of Hiroshima, the 1967 march on the Pentagon, and his admiration for antiwar presidential aspirant Eugene McCarthy. In 1965, he wrote *The Old Glory*, a play based on dramatizations of Nathaniel Hawthorne and Herman Melville and emphasizing, at a time of national crisis over race relations and war, the progressive, "reform" dimension of classic 19th-century New England literature. Lowell's prose writings include letters to Presidents Franklin Roosevelt and Lyndon Johnson about the wars that marked their respective administrations, as well as a call for a day of mourning for all "the people we have sent into misery . . . that we have sent out of life." Marge Piercy (1936–) joined anti–Vietnam War protest and feminism in her literary works and life. Piercy was active in Students for a Democratic Society (SDS) and the women's movement in Michigan and New York City before moving to Cape Cod in 1971. Her New England works established her as an important voice for change. Her novel *Small Changes* (1973), which takes place in the vicinity of Boston and Cam-

bridge, and a volume of her poetry, *The Moon Is Always Female* (1980), are considered important works in their exploration of feminist themes.

Another side of New England is reflected in *Between the Hills and the Sea* (1971) in which New England–born and educated novelists Katya and Bert Gilden, collaborating under the pseudonym K. B. Gilden, describe working conditions and labor struggles in a fictionalized version of the United Electrical Workers local at General Electric's plant in Bridgeport, Conn. The novel, which takes place in the years between 1946 and 1956, focuses on the deteriorating influence of the labor movement during an era of political repression. There are even fewer workers of old American stock in the Gildens's cast of characters than there were at Lawrence; rather, the ethnic mix includes Italian, Jewish, Russian, French Canadian, and black workers, supported by one old WASP family whose history embraces all the progressive causes of the 19th and 20th centuries. *Between the Hills and the Sea* also foreshadows concerns of the 1970s and beyond, raising environmental, feminist, and gay issues in the context of postwar multiethnic working-class life.

Although many tensions existed in 20th-century social reform movements between older Americans and ethnic immigrants, as well as among the various ethnic and racial groups, the literature cited here has tended to emphasize moments of cooperation and mutual support. By contrast, J. Anthony Lukas's *Common Ground* (1985), a work of creative nonfiction based on sensitive oral histories, takes precisely those conflicts as its subject; the common ground is the ground of racial conflict. Lukas traces the attitudes, histories, and actions of three Boston-area families from the murder of Martin Luther King, Jr., through the school-integration conflicts of the 1970s and 1980s, allowing their own voices to tell the respective stories of professional-class WASP integrationists, poor black community activists, and working-class Irish busing foes. What is perhaps most salient in this document from the penultimate decade of the century is not only that justice, in Millay's words, was still being denied in Massachusetts, but that the collective New England voice, with its range of class and ethnic registers, told of the shared perception that both power and justice lay—perhaps permanently—elsewhere.

David Felix, *Protest: Sacco-Vanzetti and the Intellectuals* (1965); Robert Lowell, *Collected Poems* (1987); Lowell, *Collected Prose* (1987); Edna St. Vincent Millay, *Collected Poems* (1956); Donald E. Winterson, Jr., *The Soul of the Workers: The IWW, Religion, and American Culture in the Progressive Era* (1985).

Lillian S. Robinson

Regionalism

The evolution of a literary genre rooted in the New England village emerged within the overall development of American regional writing during the latter half of the 19th century. Regional literature—emerging likewise from the Midwest and the South—stressed the idiosyncrasies of geography, community, speech, dress, and manner that differentiated a particular region from mainstream society. Although New England in fact shared much with the rapidly modernizing American nation, writers seeking a specific cultural identity emphasized values traditionally associated with the village community of the region's preindustrial past. In numerous stories, poems, and novels, New England was portrayed as a bastion of rural simplicity, sturdy individualism, and an endearing predictability in day-to-day life. Not surprisingly, the popularization of such an image helped to attract legions of white-collar professionals and their families seeking refuge from the tumult of their mechanized, urban lives. This symbolic village had an equally dramatic effect on literature, for numerous writers—whether as enthusiasts or critics—have reflected on the nature and consequence of the New England ideal.

Although such antebellum writers as Nathaniel Hawthorne and Lydia Maria Child were no doubt influential, the boundaries of New England regionalist writing were initially drawn by those once known as "local color" writers. Harriet Beecher Stowe (1811–96) in many ways set the standard with such novels as *The Minister's Wooing* (1859) and *The Pearl of Orr's Island* (1862). The first explored the lingering effects of Puritanism on what was essentially a preindustrial New England Arcadia, while the second examined the ways of life created by geography and a changing economy in a coastal Maine fishing village. Many subsequent writers drew inspiration from Stowe, including Connecticut native Rose Terry Cooke (1827–92) who wrote short fiction that—after initially appearing in a popular magazine—was published in such volumes as *Root-Bound and Other Sketches* (1885) and *Huckleberries Gathered from New England Hills* (1891). Although far from reticent about writing of the frequent narrowness of village life, she presented her characters in a spirit of both optimism and good humor. In young adulthood, Boston-born Elizabeth Stuart Phelps (1844–1911) achieved the status of a best-selling writer with *The Gates Ajar* (1868), a somber novel about the effects of the Civil War on a small New England town. Phelps wrote numerous books, including two novels—*The Madonna of the Tubs* (1886) and *Jack, the Fisherman* (1887)—based on her observations of the grim lives endured by local fishers and their families in the village of East Gloucester, Mass.

Around the turn of the century Mary E. Wilkins Freeman (1852–1930) became perhaps the best-known interpreter of rural New England life, writing most effectively about the people who inhabited the countryside around her Randolph, Mass., home. Her short stories, gathered in *A Humble Romance* (1887), *A New England Nun and Other Stories* (1891), and other volumes, offered characters whose austere circumstances were redeemed by what Freeman believed was the inherent dignity of the rural New Englander. Also popular were the writings of Alice Brown (1857–1948), who gained a national audience with her *Meadow-Grass: Tales of New England Life* (1895) and *Tiverton Tales* (1899). Although Brown wrote poetry, biography, and drama, her most significant literary efforts were these fictional sketches of life in Tiverton, a small farming community based on her hometown of Hampton Falls, N.H. Sarah Orne Jewett (1849–1909), born and raised in South Berwick, Maine, was at one time considered a local colorist, though her best work transcends the quaintness and other limitations that often characterized this genre. Jewett's *The Country of the Pointed Firs* (1896) simply and movingly described a rural hamlet not only in retreat from past glories but nearly bereft of the young who were either taken by the war or lured away by economic opportunities elsewhere.

Each of these writers enjoyed a significant readership, a popularity that other chroniclers of the New England village came to share. Newspaper illustrator Rowland Evans Robinson, who began writing late in life, found in his native Vermont countryside the basis for several essays, travelogues, and novels. One of his fictional works—*Uncle Lisha's Shop: Life in a Corner of Yankeedom* (1887)—remained in print until the 1930s. In rural Vermont, Dorothy Canfield Fisher (1879–1958) found inspiration for her poetry and patriotic essays, as well as settings for much of her fiction, most notably her early collections of short stories—*Hillsboro People* (1915) and *The Real Motive* (1916)—and her novel *Seasoned Timber* (1939), among others.

Significant poetry also found a focus in the rural villages of New England. In the 1890s Edwin Arlington Robinson (1869–1935) privately published two books of his own verse—*The Torrent and the Night Before* (1896) and *Children of the Night* (1897)—that included "Richard Cory," "The Clerks," and "Cliff Klingenhagen." Tilbury Town, the fictional setting for these portrait poems, bore no small resemblance to his boyhood home of Gardiner, Maine. Despite achieving popular success in the 1920s with his long Arthurian epics,

Robinson's most moving work remains his quiet musings on Reuben Bright, Miniver Cheevy, and Mr. Flood. Maine was also the birthplace of two poets who found their subjects among the coastal communities of that state. Wilbert Snow (1884–1977), in such books as *Maine Coast* (1923), *Down East* (1932), and *Spruce Head* (1959), used both short lyrics and long narrative poems to convey the beauty and vitality of the world he knew as a child in Spruce Head Village. Much of the poetry by Robert P. Tristram Coffin (1892–1955) found a similar inspiration in his boyhood on a saltwater farm near Brunswick, Maine. The tone of such volumes as *Strange Holiness* (1935) and *Saltwater Farm* (1937) is celebratory, though one of Coffin's last books—*One Horse Farm* (1949)—betrays the sadness he felt in seeing the young abandon the region's small farms and traditional ways. Such details of rural life appeared frequently in the work of Robert Frost (1874–1963), who often used his poetry to explore metaphorically the New England landscape. A poem from Frost's *New Hampshire* (1923)—"The Census Taker"—describes how

> The melancholy of having to count souls
> Where they grow fewer every year
> Is extreme where they shrink to none
>   at all.

The great loneliness Robinson often expressed in his poetry as well as the dark psychological portraits found in a Frost volume such as *North of Boston* (1914) were part of a reaction against the image of the village cultivated since the end of the Civil War. Rural New England continued to capture the interest of American writers in the 20th century as a literary countercurrent emerged that focused on the entrapment of people within that landscape. In 1911 Edith Wharton (1862–1937), best known for her New York stories, published *Ethan Frome*, a short novel in which the benign literary landscape of rural New England was supplanted by a bleaker version, one that reflected the spirits of its inhabitants. Wharton returned to a similar landscape in *Summer* (1917), a novel about the hopeless existence of those trapped in a stultifying rural backwater. "Things don't change at North Dormer," a local advises a visitor, "people just get used to them."

This darkly interpreted image of the New England village appeared in other forms, as well. The fictional Grovers Corners, N.H., was created by playwright Thornton Wilder (1897–1975) for *Our Town* (1938), an innovative theatrical rendering of small-town American life. Although depicted onstage by folding chairs and stepladders, the accouterments of the New England village maintain an undeni-

able presence as Wilder portrays a community where life is neither simple nor predictable. Similar backdrops made effective and unsettling appearances in several works by Shirley Jackson (1919–65), most notably in a short story first published in 1948, "The Lottery." Jackson's tale of a ritualized killing was all the more horrific for its setting of white clapboard houses, village greens, and church steeples. Grace Metalious (1924–64), the wife of a school principal in Gilmanton, N.H., gave the New England village an even more notorious treatment in her best-selling novel *Peyton Place* (1956). The popular appeal of Metalious's book, set in a seemingly well-ordered, churchgoing community, no doubt rested on the contradictory public and private behavior of her characters.

Recent times have brought unremitting change to New England life, but many writers continue to follow the examples of Jewett, Wharton, and Robinson by examining the regional image in their work. Louisiana native Andre Dubus (1936–99), who lived in Haverhill, Mass., for years, found in his adopted home a setting for much of his fiction. His novel *Voices from the Moon* (1984) and several of the short stories collected in *Finding a Girl in America* (1980) and *Dancing after Hours: Stories* (1996) are clearly rooted in the economically depressed blue-collar communities northeast of Boston. In 1985 Carolyn Chute (1947–) published *The Beans of Egypt, Maine*, a powerful and unsettling novel about the rural poor of northern New England. Set at a small crossroads settlement in Maine, this ultimately compassionate story is told through the voices of children who see all, understand much, and vividly report on everything that touches their lives. Chute subsequently returned to the same landscape for her novels *Letourneau's Used Auto Parts* (1988) and *Merry Men* (1994). Although social dislocation and poverty are far from unique to New England, the works of Dubus and Chute demonstrate that the small town and rural community remain central to the region's cultural identity and at the heart of a thriving literary tradition.

Dona Brown, ed., *A Tourist's New England: Travel Fiction, 1820–1920* (1999); Brown, *Inventing New England: Regional Tourism in the 19th Century* (1995); Josephine Donovan, *New England Local Color Literature: A Women's Tradition* (1983); Robert Frost, *New Hampshire: A Poem with Notes and Grace Notes* (1923); Thomas E. Kennedy, *Andre Dubus: A Study in Short Fiction* (1988); Robert A. Lecker and Kathleen R. Brown, *An Anthology of Maine Literature* (1982); Charles and Samuella Shain, *The Maine Reader: The Down East Experience, 1614 to the Present* (1991).

Paul D. Nygard

Rich, Adrienne (1929–) Poet. Adrienne Cecile Rich was born in Baltimore, Md., to

Adrienne Rich, 1993

Arnold Rich, an eminent physician, and his wife, Helen. Rich attended Radcliffe College from 1947 to 1951. In 1951 she won the Yale Younger Poets Award for her first volume, *A Change of World.* The regional poet Robert Lowell was among Rich's earliest mentors. Like many of her New England contemporaries, Rich was schooled in the intellectual formalism of post–World War II poetry, but like Lowell, Anne Sexton, and others, she found poetic and personal liberation in free verse and themes that were at once confessional and political. Her identity and destiny as a writer and political dissident are intertwined with New England's heritage.

Defying her parents, Rich married the Harvard economist Alfred H. Conrad in 1953 and fell into the genteel life of academic wife and mother to three sons, who were born too swiftly—1955, 1957, and 1959—causing Rich to be ambivalent about her role as a mother. Her controversial critique of motherhood, *Of Woman Born* (1976), mingles scholarship with personal testimony about her conflicted feelings of anger and tenderness toward her children.

Rich's practice of dating each of her poems and essays began in 1963 with *Snapshots of a Daughter-in-Law.* The publication of *Necessities of Life* (1966), *Leaflets* (1969), and *The Will to Change* (1971) coincided with the Civil Rights movement and the Vietnam War, historical upheavals that shaped Rich's poetic identity even while new political allegiances transformed her personal life. After her husband's suicide in 1970, Rich embraced a lesbian and radical feminist identity. In her most militantly feminist volume, *Diving into the Wreck* (1973), Rich mourns her old life yet celebrates a new identity as the androgyne who condemns Western culture as patriarchal and

deadening. *Diving into the Wreck* won the National Book Award, but Rich rejected the honor in solidarity with sister poets and women of color, Alice Walker and Audre Lorde, who, in her view, had not received adequate recognition.

For the next 10 years, Rich's writing focused on the female body as its point of departure. The poems in *The Dream of a Common Language* (1978) idealize the maternal and lesbian bodies and express the desire for a community of ordinary and woman-identified women. Many of her finest lyrics from this period are meditations situated in a New England pastoral locale reverberating with the voices of American women brought to America both willingly and as slaves. Essays in *On Lies, Secrets, and Silence* (1979) and poems in *A Wild Patience Has Taken Me This Far* (1981) consolidate Rich's place in the women's movement.

In the late 1980s and 1990s the women's movement was cracked by emerging American ethnic voices, representative of identity politics. Correspondingly, Rich's voice was complicated by two realizations: first, that no single woman could speak for all women, and second, that she had ignored her own ethnic heritage as a Jew. The poems in *Your Native Land, Your Life* and the essays in *Blood, Bread, and Poetry*, together with a new edition of *Of Woman Born* (all published in 1986), acknowledge the potential arrogance of speaking on behalf of all women and reflect a more inclusive American feminism.

Rich's writing continues to evolve and to revise her identity as an American woman and poet. After *Time's Power* (1989), Rich assumed the role of historical remembering and adopted Walt Whitman's lengthy lines to catalog American woes and dreams of renewal in *An Atlas of the Difficult World* (1991) and *Dark Fields of the Republic* (1995). Her most recent volumes of poetry are *Fox: Poems, 1998–2000* (2001) and *Fact of a Doorframe: Selected Poems, 1950–2001* (2002), *School among the Ruins: Poems, 2000–2004* (2004). In her collection of essays *What Is Found There* (1993), Rich traced her allegiances to America's "beginners," including reclusive Emily Dickinson of Amherst, Mass.; the expansive lover and everyman, Whitman; and Muriel Rukeyser—the Jew, the lover of women, and the poet remembered by a poetic daughter. Like her New England predecessors, Rich understands herself as a pilgrim with a destiny.

Paula Bennett, *My Life, a Loaded Gun: Female Creativity and Feminist Poetics* (1986); Jane Roberta Cooper, ed., *Reading Adrienne Rich: Reviews and Revisions, 1951–81* (1984); Barbara Charlesworth Gelpi and Albert Gelpi, eds., *Adrienne Rich's Poetry and Prose: A Norton Critical Edition* (1993); Adrienne Rich, *Arts of the Possible: Essays and Conversations* (2001); Alice Templeton, *The Dream and the Dialogue: Adrienne Rich's Feminist Poetics* (1994).

Lynda K. Bundtzen

Robinson, Edwin Arlington (1869–1935)

Poet. Best remembered for his fictional "Tilbury Town," which included such resonant portraits as "Richard Cory" and "Miniver Cheevy," Edwin Arlington Robinson was the first poet to be awarded the Pulitzer Prize. Robinson's poetry was prolific and wide ranging and engaged a number of formal traditions; he mastered complex verse forms as well as book-length blank verse narratives, monologues, and dialogues.

Born in 1869 in Head Tide, Maine, to Edward and Mary Palmer Robinson, "Win," as he was known, claimed a distant relation on his mother's side to the early American poet Anne Bradstreet. Robinson and his two older brothers were reared according to the New England reticence of their father, a prosperous merchant. Robinson attended Harvard between 1891 and 1893. The years between 1890 and 1896 were characterized by profound loss: both of Robinson's parents died, the 1893 recession claimed his family's fortune, one brother died—presumably by suicide—and the other brother married Robinson's sweetheart. Robinson himself never married.

Influenced by a neighbor who counseled him to study verse, Robinson mastered poetic form early in his career, as evidenced in his self-published first volume, *The Torrent and the Night Before* (1896), which appeared soon after his mother's death. This collection introduces Tilbury Town, which, modeled on the town he grew up in, Gardiner, Maine, would frame a number of his collections. The seeming simplicity of these early poems not only belies their complex structure but also conveys the values of Robinson's New England upbringing as he uses an economical, unpretentious style to depict austere subjects.

In 1897 Robinson moved to New York and in 1902 published "Captain Craig," an experimental long narrative poem that was poorly received. For several years, Robinson struggled economically and drank heavily until his work came to the attention of Theodore Roosevelt, whose son Kermit had admired *The Children of the Night* (1897). Roosevelt appointed the poet to a post in the New York Custom House, a service that Robinson noted when he dedicated *The Town Down the River* (1910) to the former president.

Robinson spent the summer of 1911 at the artistic community of MacDowell Colony in Peterborough, N.H.; he returned there every summer until his death. Throughout his career, Robinson questioned New England's spiritual and climatic influence. His early poem "Boston" imagines an alternative to the city's "living nearness, noise, and common speech," and in his later "New England," the poet notes that "Joy shivers in the corner where she knits / And Conscience always has the rocking-chair." Robinson drew on local color to create his settings and characters but probed beyond sentimental imagery or stock New England eccentricity to examine the lingering psychological effects of Puritan influence in the region and the cost of living in a rural backwater during modern times. In addition to the Tilbury Town poems, Robinson was also known for several blank verse narratives that recount Arthurian legends, and four book-length narrative poems. Robinson was thrice awarded the Pulitzer Prize: in 1922 for his *Collected Poems*, in 1925 for *The Man Who Died Twice*, and in 1928 for *Tristram*. He was twice awarded an honorary doctorate: from Yale in 1922 and from Bowdoin in 1925.

Robinson was a dedicated writer and wrote more than 20 volumes of poetry, two plays, and several prose pieces during his lifetime. He edited his final work, "King Jasper," while on his hospital deathbed with cancer; it was published posthumously and included an oft-cited introductory essay by Robert Frost.

Jeanetta Boswell, *Edwin Arlington Robinson and the Critics: A Bibliography of Secondary Sources with Selective Annotations* (1988); Louis O. Coxe, *Edwin Arlington Robinson: The Life of Poetry* (1969); Hermann Hagedorn, *Edwin Arlington Robinson: A Biography* (1938); W. R. Robinson, "E. A. Robinson's Yankee Conscience," in *Appreciation of Edwin Arlington Robinson: 28 Interpretive Essays*, ed. Richard Cary (1969).

Kathleen Pfeiffer

Sarton, May (1912–95) Writer. May Sarton, poet, novelist, and author of autobiographical journals, lived most of her life in New England. Born in Belgium, Sarton, who was an only child, fled Europe with her parents, George and Eleanor Mabel Sarton, in 1916. After first immigrating to Washington, D.C., the family moved to Cambridge, Mass., when her father accepted a position at Harvard. The family lived in Cambridge where Sarton attended the Shady Hill School. At age 17, Sarton left Cambridge to study acting in New York City with Eve Le Gallienne. She later founded an acting company that drew favorable attention but did not succeed financially. Returning to New England, Sarton settled again in Cambridge where she lived with her lover, Judith Matlack. During this period, Sarton began publishing poetry and novels and giving public readings; she also was employed as a writing instructor at Harvard and then at Wellesley College.

With her writing providing financial stabil-

May Sarton at home in York, Maine, 1992, beneath a portrait of her at age 25

ity, Sarton moved alone to the village of Nelson, N.H., in 1958, thus entering a new stage of her life. Although she remained dedicated to Matlack, Sarton sought the solitude she needed for her writing. In 1973, she relocated to a home on the ocean at York, Maine.

With the publication of *Mrs. Stevens Hears the Mermaids Singing* (1965), Sarton came out as a lesbian. Still, it was many years before she accepted the political and social importance of being known as a lesbian writer. In 1989 Sarton told National Public Radio interviewer Terry Gross that she was "embarrassed that it has taken me so long" to publicly embrace the lesbian writer distinction. Her last novel, *The Education of Harriet Hatfield* (1989), deals with homophobia in a small New England town and may be Sarton's attempt to acknowledge the importance of coming out and of addressing bigotry directly. When Sarton died in York, Maine, on July 16, 1995, she had written 19 novels, 14 nonfiction works including her journals, 14 books of poetry, and four retrospective collections of her writing.

Most of Sarton's writing is marked by her affinity for the geography and attitudes of 20th-century New England. In journals such as *Journal of a Solitude* (1973) and *The House by the Sea* (1977), Sarton details the daily rituals of her inner life, which is shaped by the rugged mountains and shoreline of New England as well as by the rhythm of the four seasons. In these, as in her other journals and novels, Sarton explores such themes as the passage of time, silence, solitude, work, independence, interdependence, and aging. Various elements

of the changing seasons in New England such as the brilliant colors of trees in the fall, the frozen whiteness of a lake in winter, and the heaviness of a humid summer's afternoon can be found in the images, metaphors, and similes of Sarton's poetry. Sarton uses these literary elements to refract, illuminate, and explore the prisms of emotion, of relationship, and of aging.

Constance Hunting, ed., *A Celebration for May Sarton* (1993); Marilyn Kallet, ed., *A House of Gathering: Poets on May Sarton's Poetry* (1993); Margot Peters, *May Sarton: A Biography* (1997); Susan Swartzlander and Marilyn R. Mumford, ed., *That Great Sanity: Critical Essays on May Sarton* (1992).

Susan Alves

Schoolroom Poets

Thy task is done: the bond are free.
We bear thee to an honored grave,
Whose proudest monument shall be
The broken fetters of the slave.
—from "Lincoln," by William Cullen
Bryant (1794–1878)

Life is real! Life is earnest!
And the grave is not its goal;
Dust thou art, to dust returnest
Was not spoken of the soul.
—from "The Psalm of Life," by Henry
Wadsworth Longfellow (1807–82)

"Shoot, if you must, this old gray head,
But spare your country's flag," she said.
—from "Barbara Frietchie," by John
Greenleaf Whittier (1807–92)

Ef you take a sword an' dror it,
An' go stick a feller thru,
Guv'ment ain't to answer for it,
God'll send the bill to you.
—from *The Biglow Papers*, by James
Russell Lowell (1819–91)

Nail to the mast her holy flag,
Set every threadbare sail,
And give her to the god of storms,
The lightning and the gale!
—from "Old Ironsides," by Oliver
Wendell Holmes (1809–94)

If to some 20th-century readers the verses above seem too familiar to be stimulating—brain-numbing jingles better parodied than sung—it is because they were, in the moment of their conception, that difficult wonder that Maya Angelou has called the hard writing that makes easy reading. The writers of these lyrics are lumped together as "the schoolroom poets" because several generations of Americans (including poets and critics whose careers as realists and modernists would repudiate these poets' art) grew up reciting their verses out of McGuffey readers in late-19th- and early-20th-century elementary schools, where the models that these "poets of the hearth" offered of New England and U.S. history, democratic individualist ideals, and simple, perfectly lucid English were deemed essential for the primary education and indoctrination of American schoolchildren.

The label has been the kiss of death to the poets as subjects of critical study in the 20th century, in which the modernist values such as formal innovation, ambiguity, and inwardness make the smooth regularity of 19th-century versification seem monotonous. Furthermore, the realities of industrial transformation and world warfare make this poetry's liberal humanist optimism and simple sentiment seem at best bland and naive and at worst vapid and phony—the self-congratulatory mythology of an educated elite. But American culture has not left this poetry behind, and will not, as long as the ballad form and its variations continue to be used as tools for the expression of political concern; indeed, the lyrics of many 20th-century popular songwriters tell the news in much the same way, for similar reasons.

All except Whittier were highly educated men who influenced New England culture not only through their poetry but through their careers as editors (Bryant with the *New York Post,* Lowell with the *Atlantic Monthly*) and college professors (Longfellow, Lowell, and Holmes); in these capacities they became major arbiters of literary taste in the United States throughout the 19th century. Their work expressed the advantages and limitations of their privileges as Anglo-American males of educated middle-class families. In their efforts to forge a hybrid literature that brought the best elements of European tradition to bear upon themes uniquely North American, they were trying to share the fruits of their privileged education with an audience much less advantaged than themselves. The project inevitably enthroned, as "the" American voice, however, a model presupposing the supremacy of Anglo-European culture (and the ancestry of Anglo-European Americans) over world cultures—and peoples—from which other Americans descended.

But the 20th-century tendency to dismiss these poets as the elite literary "Brahmins" of a self-proclaimed New England aristocracy neglects the sincerity of their commitment to democratic ideals and to the development of a national culture dedicated to those ideals. Bryant was among the first of Anglo-American poets to conceive a variant of the emerging European Romanticism that was uniquely American in its emphasis on the wilderness of North American nature confronted, in poems such as "The Prairies," by the relentless

transforming activity of European American settlement. Holmes composed ballad upon ballad of occasional verse discussing contemporary events of regional or national importance, and his satirical verse, like that of Lowell, skewers whatever he deemed pretentious in himself as well as in his fellow Americans. Longfellow's famous narrative poetry tried to celebrate with equal respect and accuracy both the histories of New England pilgrims and patriots (*The Courtship of Miles Standish,* "Paul Revere's Ride") and the oral traditions of northeastern Native Americans *(The Song of Hiawatha),* and his "The Jewish Cemetery at Newport" offers a poignant condemnation of anti-Semitism in Europe and the United States. Whittier, raised with little formal education on the small farm of a large, poor Quaker family, devoted the most productive years of his life entirely to the cause of abolition and wrote a torrent of fiercely impassioned ballads designed to arouse the consciences of his compatriots against the enslavement of their fellow men and women. In honor of Whittier's tireless activism in the cause of African American liberty, Frederick Douglass called him "the slaves' poet." Longfellow published a volume of poetry devoted entirely to the subject of slavery, and Bryant and Lowell also expressed abolitionist sentiments in their verse.

The long careers of these men, in the eye of a growing popular audience, almost inevitably led, however, to bodies of work that were uneven in quality. But the liberal humanitarianism that, to a significant degree, they all shared, moved these writers to use the privilege of their rich literary education not to impress one another with their formal virtuosity nor even to devote their energies to the discipline of art for art's sake, but to create poetry in a public voice on subjects of regional and national relevance crafted to appeal to the broadest audience they could imagine, with considerable respect for the consciousness and tastes of that audience. Their poetry was designed to be easily committed to memory, so that people who had limited access to print materials could bring the verses to mind while walking behind a plow or sitting around a fireside, and the ideals and landmarks of a shared democratic tradition—and shared outrage when those ideals were violated—could be passed from voice to voice across the barriers of class, race, and locale. It should come as no surprise to find their closest artistic descendants not among the gifted innovators of modern poetry but within the Anglo-American branch of 20th-century popular singer-songwriters, from Woody Guthrie to Bob Dylan to Bruce Springsteen and beyond.

Michael Bell, "'The Only True Folk Songs We Have in English': J. R. Lowell and the Politics of the Nation," *Journal of American Folklore* 108, no. 428 (1995); Stanley Brodwin, ed., *William Cullen Bryant and His America: Centennial Conference Proceedings 1878–1978* (1983); Dana Gioia, "Longfellow in the Aftermath of Modernism," in *Columbia Literary History of the United States,* ed. Emory Elliott (1987); Len Gougeon, "Holmes' Emerson and the Conservative Critique of Realism," *South Atlantic Review* 59, no. 1 (1994); James H. Justus, "The Fireside Poets: Hearthside Values and the Language of Care," in *Nineteenth Century American Poetry,* ed. A. Robert Lee (1985); Jayne K. Kribbs, ed., *Critical Essays on John Greenleaf Whittier* (1980); Timothy Morris, "Bryant and the American Poetic Tradition," *American Transcendental Quarterly* 8, no. 1 (1994).

Elaine Apthorp

Science Fiction and Fantasy Science fiction and fantasy literature have always found a warm home in New England; currently more than 100 professional writers of science fiction live and work in the region, many in the greater Boston area. New England is fertile ground for professional activity in these genres for several reasons. One is the New England literary ancestor of the genres, Nathaniel Hawthorne, considered by many to be, along with Edgar Allan Poe, a father of modern American science fiction and fantasy. Hawthorne's stories of mad scientists, "The Birth-Mark" (1843) and "Rappacini's Garden" (1844), combined the scientific thought of his contemporaries with his deep Puritanic probing of guilt, power, and sexual obsession. The work of Massachusetts native Edward Bellamy likewise may have influenced generations of science fiction and fantasy writers; his utopian novel *Looking Backward, 2000–1887* (1888) was set in Boston and depicted an ideal United States in the year 2000. The rich academic environments of Boston; Cambridge, Mass.; Providence; and New Haven, Conn., are draws for established professionals in the field as well as breeding grounds for new science fiction and fantasy writers. The same academic environments also sustain the large "fannish" community that generates the conventions, amateur publications (known as fanzines), and other community activities that have become associated with the science fiction and fantasy genres.

The major science fiction and fantasy writers currently working in New England include Jane Yolen, who lives outside of Amherst, Mass., and has been a pioneering writer of the genre in the children's and young adult markets. Donald M. Grant of Rhode Island works as an independent publisher; he published the work of Robert E. Howard during the 1950s when there was little public interest in heroic fantasy. Robert A. W. Lowndes published and edited a series of minor magazines that kept alive the dark fantasy and horror genre of stories popular in *Weird Tales*, the leading pulp magazine published from 1923 to 1954, and provided a publishing home for new horror writers in the early 1960s, including Stephen King and Thomas A. Easton of Maine. Easton may be unknown to many readers, but he influences the careers of other writers in this genre as book critic for *Analog*, which is still the leading science fiction magazine in the field. Samuel R. Delany, highly acclaimed African American science fiction novelist and critic, has been professor of comparative literature at the University of Massachusetts at Amherst since the late 1980s; Fred Lerner of Vermont was one of the pioneers of academic research in science fiction and fantasy; James Patrick Kelly has made a futuristic version of his hometown of Portsmouth, N.H., an essential part of his Nebula and Hugo Award–winning short fiction; and Ron Goulart of Connecticut is master of a sharp-witted style of science fiction and fantasy.

Regional institutions have contributed to the flourishing of science fiction and fantasy in New England. Since its founding after World War II, Greenwood Press of Westport, Conn., the largest publisher of reference books on science fiction and fantasy, has played a role in the establishment of high literary standards for the genre. New England academic institutions, though less active than those of the Midwest or the Pacific Northwest, have also played a role. The University of Rhode Island is home to the Council for the Literature of the Fantastic, which publishes a newsletter and supports publications to promote the fantastic in literary expression. The Department of Special Collections at Boston University's Mugar Memorial Library is a major repository for the papers of prominent professionals in the genre, including Isaac Asimov, who played a leading role in persuading his colleagues to donate their papers to Boston University. Major fan organizations, too, have emerged in New England. The headquarters of the New England Science Fiction Association, one of the nation's largest fan organizations, are in located Boston. The association sponsors the Boston Science Fiction Convention (known as Boskone) and has an extensive publication program that often includes anthologies of the works of the convention's guests of honor. The Massachusetts Institute of Technology Science Fiction Society has one of the nation's largest English-language collections of science fiction and fantasy books and periodicals. The New England Regional Conference on Horror, one of the nation's few annual conventions dedicated to this genre, takes place in Rhode Island. The conference

organizers also established the World Fantasy Convention, first held in 1975 in Providence.

Science fiction is typically nonregionalist, but the work of some writers does reflect a New England quality. The dark fantasies of H. P. Lovecraft are obsessively concerned with two themes: the demise of traditional New England Anglo-Saxon culture attendant on increased immigration to the region, and the concurrent degeneration of Yankee stock. The latter, a vestige of the theme of the degeneration of prominent families that appears in the work of Hawthorne and other New England writers, is also evident in the dark fantasy writing of Maine writer Stephen King. Unconcerned with such fears of decline, the work of Harry Stubbs, whose pseudonym is Hal Clement, democratically features diverse heroes—both human and alien—who combine courage and practical knowledge to overcome great odds.

Despite the fact that the genres of science fiction and fantasy support work detached from realistic, regional writing, New Englanders have long incorporated local themes and places. While many New England writers participate in the contemporary popular culture in which regional emphases may play a regional role, leading authors, such as King and Kelly, have used New England's traditions and its traditional images to create a tension between such materials and the imaginative reach of their narratives.

Brian W. Aldiss, *Billion Year Spree: The True History of Science Fiction* (1973); James Gunn, ed., *The New Encyclopedia of Science Fiction* (1988); John J. Pierce, *Foundations of Science Fiction: A Study in Imagination and Evolution* (1987); Curtis C. Smith, *Twentieth-Century Science-Fiction Writers*, 2d ed. (1986).

Scott E. Green

Seuss, Dr. (Theodor Seuss Geisel)

(1904–91) Children's author and illustrator. Theodor Seuss Geisel grew up in Springfield, Mass. His father, Theodor Robert Geisel, was a brewer; his mother, Henrietta Seuss, was the daughter of a baker. As Ted Geisel remembered, his mother chanting the names of pies inspired "the rhythms in which I write and the urgency with which I do it." On childhood trips to Springfield's zoo, Geisel drew somewhat cockeyed versions of the animals—probably inspiring his book *If I Ran the Zoo* (1950), in which a boy gathers fantastic creatures for his zoo. References to Springfield appear throughout his books: the Once-ler's factory in *The Lorax* (1971) recalls the Springfield Gas Company; the red motorcycles in *And to Think That I Saw It on Mulberry Street* (1937) resemble Springfield's Indian Motorcycles.

Mulberry Street—named for a Springfield street—launched Dr. Seuss as an author-illus-

trator of children's books, but he adopted his famous pseudonym as a Dartmouth senior in 1925. When Geisel was caught drinking, the dean barred him from contributing to the campus humor magazine. Evading punishment, Geisel signed his work using aliases, including "Seuss." As a magazine cartoonist, he adopted the mock-scholarly "Dr. Theophrastus Seuss" in 1927, shortening it to "Dr. Seuss" in 1928. That year he created "Quick, Henry, the Flit!" Designed to sell Flit insect repellent, the slogan caught on and made Dr. Seuss a successful advertising man.

Between 1937 and 1940, he published four children's books, including *The 500 Hats of Bartholomew Cubbins* (1938) and *Horton Hatches the Egg* (1940). Anxious that the United States would be drawn into World War II, he became a political cartoonist for *PM* in April 1941. Attacking isolationists, criticizing anti-Semitism, and advocating civil rights for African Americans, his cartoons inspired the postwar parables *Yertle the Turtle* (1958), loosely based on the rise of Hitler, and *The Sneetches* (1961), inspired by his opposition to anti-Semitism. In 1943, Geisel moved to California and enlisted in the U.S. Army's Information and Education Division, where he made animated and documentary films for U.S. troops.

Remaining in California after the war, Dr. Seuss resumed creating children's books. *The Cat in the Hat* and *How the Grinch Stole Christmas!* (both 1957) made him a household name. Convinced that the boring *Dick and Jane* books were a deterrent to literacy, Seuss created the Cat and launched Random House's "Beginner Books" series to give children enjoyable reading primers. *Green Eggs and Ham* (1960), *The Cat in the Hat, One fish two fish red fish blue fish* (1960), *Hop on Pop* (1963)—all Beginner Books—remain his best-selling titles today.

Key to Seuss's success was respect for his audience. As he said, "I don't write for children. I write for people." The rhythm of his verse, the energetic cartoon surrealism of his pictures, and the humorous wisdom of his books appeal to all ages. When asked why he and his first wife, Helen Palmer, had no children of their own, Geisel liked to reply, "You make 'em. I'll amuse 'em." And he did. The 43 books Dr. Seuss wrote and illustrated encourage readers to think and to imagine. As *Oh, the Thinks You Can Think!* (1975) says,

> Think left and think right
> and think low and think high
> Oh, the THINKS you can think up
> if only you try!

Charles D. Cohen, *The Seuss, the Whole Seuss, and Nothing but the Seuss: A Visual Biography of Theodor Seuss Geisel* (2004); Richard Minear, *Dr. Seuss Goes to*

War: The World War II Editorial Cartoons of Theodor Seuss Geisel (1999); Judith and Neil Morgan, *Dr. Seuss and Mr. Geisel: A Biography* (1995); Philip Nel, *Dr. Seuss: American Icon* (2004).

Philip Nel

Sexton, Anne (1928–74) Poet. Anne Sexton was born Anne Gray Harvey, November 9, 1928, in Newton, Mass., and committed suicide October 4, 1974, one month before her 45th birthday. Sexton, who lived in New England most of her life, was the youngest in a family of three daughters born to wealth and privilege. Her father, Ralph Churchill Harvey, was a wool trader when New England fortunes could still be made in textiles, and her mother, Mary Gray Staples, was the only child of wealthy Maine aristocrats known for newspaper journalism and politics. Sexton would later work through her emotionally charged childhood in the psychoanalytic therapy that became a permanent part of her life after her first breakdown and suicide attempt in 1956. The same intimate and familial terrain would also be the subject of her poetic revelation and confession.

The writing that began as therapy to bolster her self-esteem eventually turned into poetic gold and a career as a poet. Against the wishes of her husband "Kayo" Sexton, a wool trader who wanted his wife at home with their daughters Linda and Joy while he traveled, Sexton attended poetry workshops in Boston between 1957 and 1960 (often followed by sessions with her psychiatrist), taught by John Holmes and Robert Lowell, and a summer writing workshop with W. D. Snodgrass. With their mentoring, she found her poetic vocation—indeed felt herself reborn into a new identity at the age of 29—and made friends with her peers Sylvia Plath, George Starbuck, and especially Maxine Kumin. Kumin was also a housewife, mother, and poet living in the Boston suburbs and was Sexton's lifelong confidante and occasional collaborator on children's books.

Sexton's poetic flowering occurred in the company of like-minded poets based in Cambridge, Mass. An intensely intellectual and introspective group, they wrestled with New England issues of class and prestige (often a conservative force), even as they drew on traditional New England themes of and concerns with the interior life. To the "School of Anguish," as Elizabeth Bishop called the confessional poets (Lowell, Plath, Snodgrass, and John Berryman), Sexton would eventually contribute 10 volumes of poetry and one play. With the publication of her first volume, *To Bedlam and Part Way Back* (1960), she immediately pushed the boundaries of the confessional style. She invariably began her famous public readings with the poem about witchcraft, "Her Kind," and mesmerized audiences with her charismatic presence: part sexy exhibitionist, part emotionally vulnerable woman-child. Despite her meager education at Garland, a Boston "finishing school," Sexton would win every available award and accolade for a poet in her time. The fact that Sexton felt she didn't "fit" with America's norms for women in the 1950s—early marriage and motherhood—contributed to her recurring bouts of suicidal depression. As Sexton put it, "I live the wrong life for the person I am," but she found cathartic expression in writing poetry.

Sexton's publications include *All My Pretty Ones* (1962), awarded *Poetry* magazine's Levinson Prize; *Live or Die* (1966), awarded both the Shelley Award by the Poetry Society of America and the Pulitzer Prize; *Love Poems* (1969); *Transformations* (1971); *The Book of Folly* (1972); and *The Death Notebooks* (1974). Three volumes were published posthumously: *The Awful Rowing toward God* (1975), *45 Mercy Street* (1976), and *Words for Dr. Y.* (1978). Sexton's reputation is still being shaped and her poetry still being evaluated, but her image as the eloquent if mad housewife of 1950s America persists.

Diana Hume George, ed., *Sexton: Selected Criticism* (1988); Diane Wood Middlebrook, *Anne Sexton: A Biography* (1991); Linda Gray Sexton, *Searching for Mercy Street: My Journey Back to My Mother, Anne Sexton* (1994); Anne Sexton, *Anne Sexton: A Self-Portrait in Letters,* ed. Linda Gray Sexton and Lois Ames (1977).

Lynda K. Bundtzen

Standish, Burt L. (George William "Gilbert" Patten) (ca. 1866–1945) Dime novelist. Burt L. Standish was the pen name for dime novelist George William "Gilbert" Patten, author of the most popular pulp fiction series from the turn of the century until the eve of World War I. Patten was born in Corinna, Maine, in 1866 and lived much of his life in Corinna and later Camden, Maine. His best-selling Merriwell series featured juvenile fiction hero and athlete extraordinaire Frank Merriwell, and later brother Dick, young men who excelled at sports of all kinds while maintaining high standards of fair play and morally upright behavior.

Patten wrote the Merriwell saga for publishing house Smith and Street's *Tip Top Weekly* for a total of 17 years beginning in 1896, at an average of 20,000 words a week. At the height of their popularity, the Merriwell stories reached an estimated national audience of 500,000. Although the stories earned a fortune for Smith and Street, Patten himself was paid a modest salary under contract and received no royalties. He retired from writing the Merriwell series in 1913 although he continued writing for Smith and Street's *Top-Notch* magazine for many years. He died in Vista, Calif., in 1945.

Anne Sexton and family, Newton Lower Falls, Mass., 1961

As a boy growing up in Corinna, the awkward young Patten frequently took refuge in the heroic antics of dime novel pirates and adventurers. His particular idol was the writer Colonel Prentiss Ingraham, of Buffalo Bill fame. Although his mother hoped he would become a preacher, at age 16 Patten published his first two stories with the publishing house of Beadle and Adams. The $50 he received for a longer story soon after cemented his commitment to a writing career. By 1894 Patten had published a total of 27 Western and detective tales with Beadle and Adams under the pen names of William G. Patten, Wyoming Will, and William West Wilder.

In an attempt to corner the juvenile market and revive flagging dime novel sales, Smith and Street approached Patten in 1895 to discuss a new series for boys. The stories were to feature the adventures of a "thoroughly up to date" young athlete hero enrolled in a New England military academy and later Yale University. Patten accepted the project enthusiastically. He conceived Frank Merriwell as the manly ideal. At a time when middle-class men were increasingly concerned with physical displays of manliness and the value of competitive sports in the education of American boys, Frank combined athletic prowess and physical strength with the traditional bourgeois values of self-discipline and moral authority. Although he didn't smoke, drink, or swear, his athletic abilities ensured that Frank could never be considered a "sissy." Frank was best known on the baseball diamond and football field for his trademark execution of dramatic winning plays in the final seconds of a game. The Merriwell series ran through 1916 and was revived in comic strip form and on radio broadcasts in the 1930s.

John Cutler, *Gilbert Patten and His Frank Merriwell Saga* (1934); William R. Gowen, "Gilbert Patten: A Look beyond the Merriwells," *Newsboy* 32, no. 5 (1994); Gilbert Patten, "Dime-Novel Days," *Saturday Evening Post*, February 1931; Patten, *Frank Merriwell's "Father"* (1964).

Jonna Eagle

Stevens, Wallace (1879–1955) Poet. Highly respected as a Pulitzer Prize–winning poet whose work questioned the relation between abstract ideas and the concrete world, Wallace Stevens is also remembered for his prosaic professional life. Although he dedicated his life to poetry, he simultaneously worked—until well past retirement age—as an insurance attorney, eventually serving as the vice president of the Hartford Accident and Indemnity Company.

Born in Reading, Penn., Stevens was the second of five children in a family that valued the sober and industrious Puritan work ethic.

Stevens claimed to have inherited imagination from his mother, Margaretha Catharine Zeller (known as Kate), and practicality from his father, Garrett Barcalow Stevens. Stevens published his first poetry while a student at Harvard University, which he attended between 1897 and 1900. He then worked as a reporter for the *New York Tribune* before attending the New York Law School, from which he received an LL.B. in 1903. In 1909 he married Elsie Viola Kachel, his sweetheart from Reading, and worked at several law firms and insurance companies before moving to Hartford in 1916. His only daughter, Holly Bright Stevens, was born in 1924.

Although Stevens gave up writing poetry when he entered law school, he returned to it nearly a decade later and began publishing verse in 1914. His poems appeared regularly in literary journals, but when *Harmonium*, his first collection, appeared in 1923, it was largely unnoticed. Stevens gave up writing poetry for another decade and devoted himself to his insurance work. In 1933 he published his second collection, *Ideas of Order;* a year later he was named vice president of his company. Stevens continued to write and publish poetry that not only challenged the meaning of poetry but also the relation between chaos and order, between ideas and things.

Particularly in his later collections, Stevens figured Connecticut into his work, not only as landscape, but as concept. "An Ordinary Evening in New Haven" tries to present, in the poet's words, "plain reality." Likewise, "The River of Rivers in Connecticut" conveys the austerity of New England, where "The river is fateful" and reflects "the seasons, the folk-lore / Of each of the senses."

Stevens was elected to the National Institute of Arts and Letters in 1946 and was awarded the D.Litt. several times. In 1951 *Auroras of Autumn* won the National Book Award; in 1955 *The Collected Poems of Wallace Stevens* was awarded both the National Book Award and the Pulitzer Prize. He declined Harvard's invitation to occupy the Charles Eliot Norton chair that same year, preferring to maintain privacy in his executive position at an office where his identity as a poet was little noted. He is buried in Hartford's Cedar Hill Cemetery.

William Doreski, "Wallace Stevens in Connecticut," *Twentieth Century Literature* 39, no. 2 (1993); James Longenbach, *Wallace Stevens: The Plain Sense of Things* (1991); Joan Richardson, *Wallace Stevens* (1986–88); Helen Vendler, *Wallace Stevens: Words Chosen Out of Desire* (1984).

Kathleen Pfeiffer

Stoddard, Elizabeth (1823–1902) Fiction writer. Elizabeth Drew Barstow Stod- dard was born in Mattapoisett, Mass., at the base of Cape Cod. Her shipbuilding father was Mattapoisett's wealthiest man, though his success was punctuated by periodic bankruptcies. Elizabeth was educated at a local grammar school and attended Wheaton Seminary for two semesters. Although a recalcitrant student, she was an avid reader and made good use of a local clergyman's extensive library. Even as a young girl she was skeptical, outspoken, iconoclastic, and sometimes brusque (her father once said that she had the greatest "talent for the disagreeable" of anyone he knew), all of which underwrote her dissatisfaction with the provincialism of Mattapoisett life as she matured and propelled her to travel.

On a visit to New York in 1851 she met a number of literati, among them poet Richard Henry Stoddard. Marrying Stoddard in 1853, she moved to New York, which was henceforth her home, though she made long visits to Mattapoisett until the 1890s. Richard's commitment to a literary career and his support of her inspired Elizabeth to write poetry and sketches. In 1854 she served as the "Lady Correspondent" of a San Francisco newspaper, the California *Alta.* The 75 columns she wrote allowed her to experiment with voice and subject matter and encouraged her to pitch depictions of life in New York and Massachusetts to readers elsewhere whose lives differed greatly from those she portrayed.

When Stoddard turned to short fiction and novels set in New England in about 1860 she accentuated this perspective, highlighting the peculiarities of the region and its inhabitants. Her New England, in contrast to that of contemporaries such as Harriet Beecher Stowe or even Rose Terry Cooke and more like that of her distant cousin Nathaniel Hawthorne, is an exotic region. Protagonists such as Cassandra Morgeson of *The Morgesons* (1862) engage in psychosexual dramas while struggling with the internal and external constraints of a Puritan heritage. Like the male protagonists of her other novels, *Two Men* (1865) and *Temple House* (1867), the unconventional Cassandra is intensely individualistic, resists the strictures of conventional gender, and is embroiled in tangled family dynamics. In all three novels, moreover, vernacular-speaking secondary characters embody the more everyday elements and smaller-scale peculiarities of the local culture with harsh charm. While Stoddard's more conventional short fiction was written for magazine sale, even the best of that work—"Lemorne *vs.* Huell" (*Harper's*, 1863; mainly set in Newport, R.I.), "The Chimneys" (*Harper's*, 1865; set in rural Massachusetts)—also variously blends characters' intense emotion with sharp descriptions of local customs.

The unorthodox character of Stoddard's New England was matched by a terse, indirect style; emphasis on dialogue; and sparing use of commentary. Although her contemporaries often recognized the power of her writing, her novels, in particular, baffled them, and she never attained the success she felt was her due. Richard's very conventional writing also failed to sell; literary hackwork and editing, as well as several government appointments, provided his income, and financial hardship always plagued the Stoddards. So did tragedy: two of their children died in childhood, and the third, Lorimer, died in 1901, just as Richard's playwriting career was taking off.

Although Stoddard's fiction confounded her contemporaries, its powerful originality is the source of her recognition today. She would have seen the irony in this situation. She also would have felt the justness of current estimations of her artistry.

Stacy Alaimo, "Elizabeth Stoddard's *The Morgesons*: A Feminist Dialogics of Bildung and Descent," *Legacy* 8 (1991); Lawrence Buell, *New England Literary Culture* (1986); Lawrence Buell and Sandra A. Zagarell, eds., *The Morgesons and Other Writings by Elizabeth Stoddard* (1984); Sandra A. Zagarell, "Legacy Profile: Elizabeth Drew Barstow Stoddard: 1823–1902" *Legacy* 8 (1991).

Sandra A. Zagarell

Stowe, Harriet Beecher (1811–96)

Writer. Born in Litchfield, Conn., Harriet Beecher Stowe, the best-selling novelist of 19th-century America, merged a millennial vision for the nation with a commitment to social activism. Like her father, evangelical preacher Lyman Beecher; her sister, women's educational reformer Catharine Beecher; and her grand-niece, writer Charlotte Perkins Gilman, Stowe sought to influence Americans "to feel right" through her remarkably varied writings, which included historical romances, novels of manners, regional sketches, poetry, hymns, and essays on politics, the "woman question," home decorating, and religion. Beecher became so widely known that Abraham Lincoln, upon meeting her in 1863, reportedly stated "so you're the little woman who started this great war."

Lincoln referred to Stowe's most famous and controversial work, *Uncle Tom's Cabin* (1852), written in Brunswick, Maine, and drawn from Stowe's experiences in Cincinnati during the late 1830s and 1840s. Translated into several languages, embraced by abolitionists, reviled by slaveholders, and equivocally received by African American audiences, the novel galvanized the growing antebellum crisis over slavery. That crisis spoke as well to the constitution of a distinctively American cultural identity that Stowe believed to be rooted in New England, "the seed-bed of this great American Republic." She explored its religious, political, and social institutions forged in the early years of the republic in her critically acclaimed historical fiction (*The Minister's Wooing* [1859], *The Pearl of Orr's Island* [1862], and *Oldtown Folks* [1869]) and her regional sketches. But Stowe's New England contrasted sharply with that of her contemporary, Nathaniel Hawthorne. Hers was a sunnier, more tolerant, and altogether gentler location, moving toward an egalitarian future in which men and women from different classes and racial and ethnic backgrounds would live and work harmoniously—albeit with clear social hierarchies that privileged the values of white and middle-class New Englanders.

Despite her sense of class, racial, and regional superiority, she nonetheless was a progressive in subtle but important ways. She celebrated sensible Yankee women blessed with domestic "faculty" over upper-class belles; she advocated an interracial sisterhood based on common maternal experiences; she preached thrift, education, and self-sufficiency; and she challenged the harsh Calvinism associated with Hawthorne's Puritans, emphasizing Christ's love over God's judgment and human experience over logic. The values she claimed for New England became associated not only with the region's but with the nation's identity throughout the 19th century.

As a writer rather than a moralist, she excelled at capturing physical descriptions of rural landscapes and seascapes, assessing the effect of the region's varied climate and rugged features on its people, who, she argued, absorbed both the austerity and the startling natural beauty. She recorded distinctive regional voices, capturing dialect and bits of local slang; and she chronicled disappearing local customs (the wood spell, the quilting) and mythologized local figures (the widow, the town parson, the independent farmer). Stowe's craft and her interpretation of region influenced a generation of regional writers, including Mary E. Wilkins Freeman, Rose Terry Cooke, and Sarah Orne Jewett.

Joan D. Hedrick, *Harriet Beecher Stowe: A Life* (1994); Ellen Moers, *Harriet Beecher Stowe and American Literature* (1978); Robert Forrest Wilson, *Crusader in Crinoline: The Life of Harriet Beecher Stowe* (1941).

Lisa MacFarlane

Suburban Realists

Several generations of writers who chronicle middle- to upper-class American life during the period after World War II are collectively known as suburban realists. The genre owes much to the postwar conversion from a wartime economy in which the housing boom caused a migration from the cities to the suburbs and countryside. Suburban realism is known by its polished narratives and generally objective and naturalistic tone. Its style is typified by an insistence on descriptive detail; an almost formulaic use of consumer references, lifestyle minutiae, and triviality; and a detached, rather succinct manner. The white and relatively affluent characters and their situations descend ethnically and culturally from the refined spirit of 19th-century Concord, Mass., one of America's first suburbs.

Suburban realism is a national style, but some of its most notable practitioners are from New England. The publication of many stories in this genre in the *New Yorker* magazine meant a prevalence of depictions of Westchester County and Connecticut. The themes of loss of identity and community play out especially well in New England, long identified with strong community values and a sense of place.

The first generation of suburban realists are the well-known *New Yorker* writers John Cheever (1912–82) and John Updike (1932–). Their seriocomic tales of New England suburban life reveal that prosperity and security are not necessarily synonymous with happiness or insulation from harm. With a genteel veneer, Cheever and Updike scrupulously render the upper- and middle-class life of small-town America's rural villages and complacent suburbs but burst the bubble of the postwar dream of nuclear familial bliss based on material plenty. Cheever has been praised as writing realistic portraits of suburban manners and morals. His cool characters, pampered in decorator houses, suffer from their own excesses, the superficiality of their lives, and sexual repression. Cheever's suburbs range from Boston's South Shore suburbs of *The Wapshot Chronicle* (1957) and *The Wapshot Scandal* (1964) to the New Haven Railroad corridor along Connecticut's Long Island Sound. The elegant blandness of Updike's prose barely masks the mess of the carefully built, pious, suburban existence; his stories depict young couples who, to all outward appearances, are secure but who in fact are teetering on the brink of catastrophe. Updike's New England stories are set in the North Shore suburbs of Boston. Updike has used the conventions of suburban realism to address broader themes of sexual politics and future social decline in *The Witches of Eastwick* (1984) and *Toward the End of Time* (1997). The close focus of both Cheever and Updike on a relatively circumscribed region fits their chronicles of suburbanites who watch their lives crumble along with the hopes and ambitions they brought to the suburbs.

A second generation of suburban realists is represented by Ann Beattie (1947–), who, working a next generation of suburban conventions and characters, develops the vein of the absurd in her predecessors Cheever and Updike. Beattie's works, set in Cheever country in Connecticut and in Vermont, where suburbanites and urbanites flee, depict fears that plague baby boomers such as unrequited or failed love, manic lovers, and lost or unworkable jobs. Her stories, most notably in *Chilly Scenes of Winter* (1976), and her novel *Falling in Place* (1980) explore problems so absurd that the reader questions the validity of the complaints as well as the degree of the characters' suffering. The subject matter of New England suburban realists moves with the suburbs, often into unlikely places. Some writers explore the clash between rural locals and those who would bring suburban development and attitudes to these places. Paul Theroux's books present Cape Cod; David Plante depicts the Franco-American neighborhoods of Rhode Island; and Ernest Hebert chronicles the tensions of newcomers and old-timers around Keene, N.H., in a series of novels.

A third generation of suburban realists is marked by Marian Thurm (1950–), whose work moves between New England and Florida and evokes a minimal style reminiscent of that of Beattie and Updike. Susan Minot's *Monkeys* (1986) chronicles the destruction of illusions about family values in 1980s North Shore towns.

While many writers largely have abandoned the conventions of realism since Cheever's day, the persistence of suburban realism in New England writing reflects demographic trends of movement to the suburbs and the region's preoccupation with the meanings of those trends.

Robert A. Beuka, *SuburbiaNation: Reading Suburban Landscape in 20th-Century American Fiction and Film* (2004); John Cheever, *The Stories of John Cheever* (1978); Scott Donaldson, *John Cheever: A Biography* (1988); Larry E. Taylor, *Pastoral and Anti-Pastoral Patterns in John Updike's Fiction* (2002); John Updike, *Couples* (1968).

Ronna C. Johnson

Taylor, Edward (ca. 1642–1729) Congregational minister, poet, and writer.

Although virtually none of the works of Edward Taylor were printed during his lifetime, since the 1930s, when scholars first discovered his writings, Edward Taylor has been regarded as one of New England's most remarkable 17th- and early-18th-century writers. The Puritan minister of the First Congregational Church in Westfield, Mass., from 1671 until his death, Taylor is now celebrated as colonial New England's most prolific and imaginative poet.

Born in the vicinity of Coventry or Sketchley in central England, Taylor probably studied briefly at Cambridge University before emigrating to Massachusetts. As his *Diary* (written 1668–71; published 1964) recounts, Taylor arrived in Boston on July 5, 1668, filled with a missionary zeal to establish the true church of elect saints in the wilderness of this "New Israel." He finished his education at Harvard College, graduating with the class of 1671, and accepted a pastoral call to Westfield, a frontier outpost in the Connecticut River valley, but King Philip's War delayed the church's formal founding and Taylor's ordination until August 1679. *Edward Taylor's "Church Records" and Related Sermons* (1679–1725; 1981) records his 50 years as Westfield's spiritual guide, biblical exegete, country physician, and historian.

Married in 1674 to Elizabeth Fitch, daughter of clergyman James Fitch of Norwich, Conn., Taylor wrote love poems, including an elaborate acrostic and "Were but my Muse an Huswife Good," to his beloved "Dove"; reflections "Upon Wedlock, and Death of Children" (five of their eight children died in infancy); and "A Funerall Poem" filled with "Gusts of Sorrows groan" upon his wife's death in 1689, at age 39. In 1692 he took a second wife, Ruth Wyllys of Hartford, with whom he had six more children.

Although Taylor never published his numerous writings, his carefully revised and copied manuscripts were preserved by family descendants and in various regional libraries. Discovered by Thomas H. Johnson at a time that coincided with the scholarly revival of Puritan history and culture spearheaded by Perry Miller, Taylor's poetry and prose radically altered the critical appraisal of Puritan literature. Johnson collected the sequence of 35 poems titled *Gods Determinations* and 31 selected sacramental meditations into the first published volume of his writings, *The Poetical Works of Edward Taylor*, in 1939, but the complete 217 poems from the *Preparatory Meditations* (1682–1725) did not appear until 1960 in Donald E. Stanford's edition, *The Poems of Edward Taylor*. Dubbed initially a metaphysical devotionalist in the manner of George Herbert, Taylor is now heralded as a New England original—an inventive poet whose witty wordplays and bold metaphors transform scriptural explication into spiritual psalms. His introspective meditations vacillate between scatological self-abasements and ecstatic exaltations of Christ's radiant glory, relentless doubt and uplifting faith, earthbound sensuality and near mystical illuminations of a nuptial consummation with Christ. By disrupting earlier stereotypes of a Puritan "plain style" of moral instruction, Taylor's work testifies to an intensely affective poetic imagination at work vitalizing the austere intellectualism of orthodox Calvinism.

Since their discovery, Taylor's voluminous works have appeared in a number of editions. *Edward Taylor's Minor Poetry* (1981) includes political satires, elegies memorializing prominent secular and religious leaders, verse declamations, anagrams and chronograms, acrostics, love missives, and occasional (1674–83) and allegorical lyrics ("Huswifery"); metrical paraphrases of Psalms and Job (1674/75–1700); and his late valedictions and memento mori, written in the 1720s as he anticipated his own death.

Taylor's skillful explanation of biblical texts and staunchly conservative Puritan theology are revealed in sermons from the *Treatise Concerning the Lord's Supper* (1693–94; 1965), the *Christographia* (1701–3; 1962), and *Upon the Types of the Old Testament* (1693–1706; 1989). Scrupulous expositions of Christian martyrdoms and teachings abound in a 20,000-line *Metrical History of Christianity* (ca. 1692–1710; 1962) and in the four-volume *Harmony of the Gospels* (mid-1680s–1710; 1983). The controversial letters and refutations collected in *Edward Taylor vs. Solomon Stoddard* (1687/88–1711; 1981) reflect how bitterly Taylor feuded with Stoddard, the pastor of the Northampton church, who believed in admitting his whole congregations to the Lord's Supper, even those who had not made a confession of saving faith. Taylor vigorously defended the Lord's Supper as a "sealing" ordinance, strictly limited to communicants who had publicly related their conversion and become full church members.

Gods Determinations touching his Elect (ca. 1679–81/82; 1939), in which Christ wars with Satan for the "ranks" of elect saints "in their Conversion," and the *Preparatory Meditations*, in which Taylor confessionally renounces his foul sinfulness in order to receive Christ's sanctifying grace, are the poet's finest verses on religious themes. In the *Meditations* Taylor not only examines his soul before administering the Lord's Supper and preaching God's Word but also records his lifelong journey toward Heaven's "Wedden feast," which will celebrate his eternal union with the divine bridegroom, Christ. Although he is inspired primarily by biblical images drawn from Old Testament types, New Testament Christology, and the allegorical Song of Solomon, Taylor nevertheless condemns the fallenness of human language, seeking always to perfect both his faith and the aesthetics of a divinely "Transcendent style."

In a 1767 memoir Taylor's grandson Ezra Stiles, president of Yale College from 1778 to 1795, lauded his grandfather as "a Man . . . of quick Passions—yet serious and grave," as "a vigorous Advocate of Oliver Cromwell, civil and religious Liberty," and as "Examplary in Piety, and for a very sacred Observa[nce] of the Lord's Day." Many scholars had viewed such a stringently pious Puritanism as antithetical to poetry; however, the discovery of Taylor's writings showed how an integrated poetics and theology reflected the Puritan emphasis on language, specifically on God's Word in the Bible, to be interpreted through the merely proximate human rhetoric of sermon oratory, scriptural interpretation, *and* poetic art. In Taylor's writings modern readers still hear the Puritan preacher's and poet's voice echoing forth from New England's cultural past.

Thomas M. Davis, *A Reading of Edward Taylor* (1992); Norman S. Grabo, *Edward Taylor*, rev. ed. (1988); Jeffrey A. Hammond, *Sinful Self, Saintly Self: The Puritan Experience of Poetry* (1993); Karen E. Rowe, *Saint and Singer: Edward Taylor's Typology and the Poetics of Meditation* (1986).

Karen E. Rowe

Thaxter, Celia (1835–94) Poet, writer, artist, gardener. Celia (Laighton) Thaxter, born in Portsmouth, N.H., and reared on the isolated, ruggedly beautiful Isles of Shoals, became one of the most popular New England poets of the late 19th century. In addition, she was a prolific writer, talented painter, and creative gardener. That she overcame the vicissitudes of a troubled marriage, the pain of caring for her physically and emotionally disabled oldest child, and the demands of an overly dependent mother is a compelling story. Each summer she reigned over a distinguished island artistic and literary salon. Her circle of friends included some of the best-known men and women in the literary, artistic, and musical worlds. James Russell Lowell, John Greenleaf Whittier, Annie and James T. Fields, Harriet Prescott Spofford, and Sarah Orne Jewett were among the authors who journeyed regularly to Appledore House, her family's hotel. Childe Hassam, John Appleton Brown, and William Morris were the resident artists; Ole Bull, Julius Eichberg, William Mason, and John Knowles Paine provided the music.

Thomas Laighton took his young family to tiny White Island in the Isles of Shoals in 1839 when he became the lighthouse keeper. The Isles of Shoals, a group of nine islands, lie off the coasts of Maine and New Hampshire. Many assumed Laighton made this move because of political disappointments, but in reality it was a financial decision. He was able to buy many of the islands and soon established a thriving resort hotel on Appledore Island. In *Among the Isles of Shoals* (1873), Thaxter describes the idyllic childhood she shared with

her close-knit family; living so intimately with nature affected her entire life.

In 1851 Celia married Levi Thaxter; she was 16 and he 27. A Harvard graduate and scion of a prosperous New England family, Levi became Thomas Laighton's partner, helping to finance the building of Appledore House. He was hired as a tutor for the children and fell in love with Celia. After their marriage they moved to the mainland and a home in Newtonville, Mass., where Levi was unable to decide upon an occupation. With three young sons and no source of income, the family faced a financial crisis. When Celia's first poem, "Landlocked," was published in the *Atlantic Monthly* in 1861, she began to contribute to the family income. "Sandpiper," her most anthologized poem, appeared the next year, and Celia Thaxter's life-changing career was launched. She soon became part of Annie Fields's circle of Boston's most popular literati. Her poems and children's stories were published widely; *An Island Garden* (1894), illustrated by Childe Hassam, is still popular, and her watercolors, illustrated books, and painted china were displayed at an exhibition, *One Woman's Work*, in 2001.

As Thaxter's horizons broadened, she embraced the intellectual currents of her time. Her art, garden, and parlor reflect her enchantment with the Aesthetic Movement. Spiritualism enhanced her unconventional approach to religion; a love of nature led to her activist involvement in the Audubon Society. In 1880 she and Levi Thaxter separated, ending a marriage that was unhappy for both. This decision defied 19th-century norms and was a daring act of independence on her part.

When Celia Thaxter died at her island home, Sarah Orne Jewett wrote: "She was made of that very dust, and set about with that sea, islanded indeed in the reserves of her lonely nature, with its storms and calmness of high tides."

Norma H. Mandel, *Beyond the Garden Gate* (2004); *The Poems of Celia Thaxter*, ed. Sarah Orne Jewett (1896).

Norma H. Mandel

Thoreau, Henry David (1817–62) Lecturer, writer, and naturalist. "I have traveled a good deal in Concord," Henry David Thoreau wrote in *Walden* (1854), his most famous work, "and everywhere, in shops, and offices, and fields, the inhabitants have appeared to me to be doing penance in a thousand remarkable ways." Thoreau began and ended his life in that Massachusetts village made famous by the presence of Ralph Waldo Emerson (in whose home he lived for a time and on whose property he built his hut at Walden Pond). Excepting infrequent excursions, Thoreau re-

mained in Concord yet traveled a good deal indeed, recording his observations of natural phenomena in the surrounding landscape and making challenges to the traditions and institutions that governed the unnecessary "penance" of his fellow citizens.

An ardent agitator for abolition and a supporter of the abolitionist John Brown, a wide-ranging rambler and naturalist, and an uncompromising critic of economic policies and social customs that hinder rather than enhance life, Thoreau is often unfairly remembered as something of a crank and an outcast. He did spend ample time alone, walking and thinking and writing, and he did not withhold his opinions on what he thought to be the "quiet desperation" that marked the lives of those around him. But he was also remembered by his sister Sophia as a loving brother and by the poet William Ellery Channing as a steadfast friend and favorite with children. In any case, Thoreau was an undeniably talented man who, failing to earn much for his writing in his own day, made his way by admirably performing myriad jobs. Gardener, house-painter, teacher, surveyor, pencil maker, and, as he puts it, "self-appointed inspector of snowstorms and rainstorms," Thoreau was nevertheless always a writer. Among his chief works, *Walden, A Week on the Concord and Merrimack Rivers* (1849), which described an 1839 trip with his beloved brother John, and "Civil Disobedience" (1849), one must include the expansive, astonishingly insightful, and intellectually provocative 14-volume *Journal*.

Thoreau used the journal to note his detailed examinations and richly poetic visions of the New England countryside and drew from it to produce a wide array of texts, from "A Natural History of Massachusetts" (1842) to the posthumously published *Maine Woods* (1864) and *Cape Cod* (1865). It is *Walden*, however, on which Thoreau's reputation as a writer primarily rests. A meditative and imaginative rendering of his removal to the woods alongside Walden Pond (1845–47), *Walden* searches the intersections where literature connects with politics, work with life, nature with philosophy, seeing with being, and each with each. Intricately tied to the context of the changing seasons of New England, *Walden* provides an unflinching critique of the economies—fiscal, social, metaphysical—in which Thoreau's fellow citizens make their livings and serves as a persistent reminder that we are prone to falling into devastatingly somnambulant routine and resignation. In *Walden*, the writer returns from the woods for the same reasons he escaped there: to deliberately discern, through physical and metaphorical movement, the essentials of life, as well as the obstacles that prevent humans from living

Henry David Thoreau's gravestone, Authors Ridge, Sleepy Hollow Cemetery, Concord, Mass.

truthfully; and to brashly report his findings and awaken his sleeping neighbors.

More than a century later, Thoreau's works have earned him a reputation as a careful and masterful literary ecologist, and his study of New England nature, shown throughout his work, makes him one of the nation's first and foremost nature writers. But it would be a mistake to see this concern with place as any sort of provincialism. Indeed, Thoreau's methods for understanding the relations between humans and nature in the effort to illuminate political and philosophical questions continue to inspire and instruct contemporary thinkers, political activists, naturalists, poets, and essayists. His belief that individuals have the right and the responsibility to resist improper governmental policies—demonstrated by his protests against slavery and the Mexican War (for which he was jailed in 1845) and most clearly expressed in "Civil Disobedience"—had a profound effect on the ideas and strategies of Mahatma Gandhi and Martin Luther King, Jr. Thus, while his shrewd eye, ingenuity, and pluck make him an emblem of Yankee simplicity and resourcefulness, his work carries the mark of a complex, broadminded truth seeker who well knew that "the universe is wider than our views of it."

Carl Bode, ed., *The Portable Thoreau* (1977); Stanley Cavell, *The Senses of Walden: An Expanded Edition* (1992); William Ellery Channing, *Thoreau: The Poet-Naturalist* (1873); Walter Harding and Michael Meyer, *The New Thoreau Handbook* (1980).

T. S. McMillin

Transcendentalist Writers Two basic premises underlie most Transcendentalist writing. First, divinity is inherent in the human soul, and the individual's own perceptions and intuition, therefore, offer access to knowledge of the divine and are the only path to religious truth and the only basis for moral judgment. Second, a spiritual correspondence exists between human beings and nature. But individual Transcendentalists, for whom consistency was not a virtue, emphasize different aspects of these principles and use them for varying purposes. The result is a certain vagueness that was a hallmark of the movement even in its heyday during the three decades before the Civil War. Charles Dickens, after traveling through the United States in 1842, wrote satirically that he "was given to understand that whatever was unintelligible would be certainly transcendental." The comment is representative of a widespread bewilderment at the often deliberately imprecise utterances of Transcendentalist writers and thinkers.

The Transcendentalist movement arose in opposition to the rationalist theology of conservative Unitarians, which Ralph Waldo Emerson, Transcendentalism's chief spokesperson, described as "corpse-cold." The Transcendentalists, many of whom were actually liberal Unitarian ministers, found support for their beliefs in a wide variety of sources. The term "transcendental" comes from German philosopher Immanuel Kant. Responding to 17th-century English philosopher John Locke, who believed that all knowledge or understanding is acquired through sensory experience, Kant argued that certain concepts such as space and time, which he called "transcendental," are innate categories of the mind and are known intuitively. While most Transcendentalists did not encounter Kant directly, they were introduced to German philosophy through the work of British writers Samuel Taylor Coleridge and Thomas Carlyle, the latter a lifelong correspondent of Emerson. The Transcendentalists also drew on idealist Platonic and Neoplatonic philosophy, on Hindu religious texts such as the Upanishads and the *Bhagavad Gita*, and on the works of Swedish mystic Emanuel Swedenborg and French philosopher Victor Cousin. These varied sources, however, were filtered through a distinctively New England sensibility rooted in the region's Puritan past.

Primarily located in or near Boston, the adherents of Transcendentalism established a number of forums for the exchange of ideas and enjoyed a lively intellectual community. In 1836 the Transcendental Club met for the first time to discuss theology and philosophy. At first composed primarily of liberal Unitarian ministers such as George Ripley, Orestes Brownson, Frederic Henry Hedge, and James Freeman Clarke (Emerson, who helped organize the meeting, had already resigned from the pulpit), membership in the loosely organized group soon expanded. Over the course of the next four years, meetings were attended by nearly every prominent figure associated with the Transcendentalist movement, including Henry David Thoreau, Margaret Fuller, educator and philosopher Bronson Alcott, minister and antislavery activist Theodore Parker, and historian George Bancroft.

From 1839 to 1844 Fuller held a series of "Conversations" at the West Street Bookshop run by Elizabeth Peabody, another major female Transcendentalist. Unlike meetings of the Transcendental Club, which were attended primarily by professional intellectuals, these discussions—on topics ranging from Greek mythology to contemporary European literature—were attended by well-to-do women who paid for the rare opportunity to participate in intellectually challenging debate. Thus they were not only an important vehicle for the development of Fuller's thought, but also a means by which Transcendentalist ideas were disseminated to a wider audience.

The most important periodical of the Transcendentalist movement was *The Dial*, which featured essays on literature, social issues, philosophy, and religion. This eclectic journal was edited by Fuller from 1840 to 1842 and then by Emerson until its demise in 1844. No other Transcendentalist journal had the scope or influence of *The Dial*, but two others deserve mention. *The Western Messenger* was published in Louisville, Ky., and Cincinnati, Ohio, by transplanted New Englanders James Freeman Clarke, Christopher Pearse Cranch, and William Henry Channing. At first devoted primarily to religious issues, it soon adopted a more literary program. It is perhaps most notable for Clarke's publication of Jones Very's poetry. Very, an intensely spiritual and intermittently mentally unstable man who favored the Shakespearean sonnet form, is often considered to be the Transcendentalist movement's best poet. *Aesthetic Papers,* edited by Elizabeth Peabody, was intended to be a successor to *The Dial* but failed after the publication of only one issue in 1849. That one issue was a remarkable achievement, however, containing a number of significant works, including Thoreau's essay "Resistance to Civil Government" (retitled "Civil Disobedience" after Thoreau's death).

The ideas that circulated in these gatherings and journals inspired intriguing endeavors in a variety of fields. Bronson Alcott, for example, set out to apply Transcendentalist theories in the field of education. In his Temple School, young children were encouraged to learn through discussion and to respond freely to the Bible. George Ripley tried to put Transcendentalist ideas into action by establishing the utopian community Brook Farm.

It was through literary channels, however, that Transcendentalism most significantly affected American culture. Transcendentalist writers shared a number of concerns, most notably an interest in nature and a belief in the primacy of the individual (expounded most powerfully by Emerson in "Divinity School Address" and his essays "The American Scholar" and "Self-Reliance"). Another characteristic of Transcendentalist writing is its rather disjointed style, largely due to the high value that the Transcendentalists placed on inspiration. They wanted their writings to suggest an oracular spontaneity, and in many cases they carefully avoided the imposition of a more rigid structure. Transcendentalist literary style also owes something to the writers' method of composition. Both Emerson and Thoreau kept copious journals and mined them for passages that could be expanded, refined, and then combined to create essays or books. Although some readers, accustomed to more explicit connections between the parts of a literary whole, have occasionally found this quality frustrating, it also accounts for the visceral, imagistic power of much Transcendentalist writing. The Transcendentalists' writing process resulted in the production of texts that sought to engage readers in creating meaning and that would consequently inspire them to process similarly the world in which they lived.

Within the range of their shared interests, each of the major Transcendentalists developed unique preoccupations and priorities. For example, Emerson's *Nature* (1836)—the lyrical treatise that galvanized the Transcendentalist movement—is a relatively straightforward exposition of the theory of correspondence between human beings and nature: because human beings and the physical world are both creations of the divine spirit that Emerson calls the "Over-Soul," nature is composed of spiritually significant symbols. (It is the poet's special task to interpret the natural world.) Thoreau's writings, on the other hand, reveal a productive tension between his belief in the theory of correspondence and his naturalist's eye for detail and interest in the thing itself, nature for its own sake.

The stress that Transcendentalist thought placed on the individual also bore substantially different fruit in the various writings of the Transcendentalists. Emerson urged individuals to rely on their own intuitions rather than on tradition and inherited cultural forms. In so doing, he played a crucial role in the development of American cultural autonomy. Fuller, in her most famous work, *Woman in the Nineteenth Century* (1845), applied Emersonian precepts of self-reliance to the problem of women's subordinate status in society, arguing that women must achieve "self-dependence, and a greater simplicity and fulness of being." Thoreau's essay "Resistance to Civil Government," a major contribution to political theory, argued that the individual has the right to oppose the state on moral grounds. Like Emerson's essays, Thoreau's *Walden* (1854) urged individuals to develop what Emerson called "an original relation to the universe." But *Walden* is unique among Transcendentalist writings in its sustained critique of commercialism and greed.

Precisely because it was so multifaceted, Transcendentalist writing has powerfully influenced other writers and thinkers. Walt Whitman acknowledged his debt to Emerson in typically exuberant fashion: "I was simmering, simmering, simmering; Emerson brought me to a boil." Both Nathaniel Hawthorne and Herman Melville had deep misgivings about the radical individualism expressed in Emerson's writings and felt that Transcendentalism as a whole was dangerously blind to the darker side of human nature. Their misgivings, however, shaped their own writing in vital ways. Emerson's work profoundly influenced the poetry of Emily Dickinson, who transformed many Transcendentalist beliefs into an intensely personal philosophy and poetic practice.

The influence of Fuller and Thoreau has been felt more significantly by later generations. Fuller is widely regarded as one of the founders of American feminism. Thoreau, thanks to *Walden,* has become the elder statesman of American nature writing and the environmental movement. His "Resistance to Civil Government" has also inspired political activists such as Mahatma Gandhi and Martin Luther King, Jr. The Transcendentalist writers' appeal to nature and to organic form in the arts inspired later figures such as architect Louis Sullivan, composer Charles Ives, and philosophers William James and John Dewey, as well as a host of writers from Robert Frost to Donald Hall.

Brian M. Barbour, ed., *American Transcendentalism: An Anthology of Criticism* (1973); Lawrence Buell, *Literary Transcendentalism: Style and Vision in the American Renaissance* (1973); Octavius B. Frothingham, *Transcendentalism in New England: A History* (1876); Donald N. Koster, *Transcendentalism in America* (1975); Louis Menand, *The Metaphysical Club: A Story of Ideas in America* (2001); Perry Miller, ed., *The Transcendentalists: An Anthology* (1950); Robert D. Richardson, *Emerson: The Mind on Fire: A Biography* (1995).

Anne Baker

Twain, Mark (Samuel L. Clemens)

(1835–1910) Writer. Mark Twain, born Samuel Langhorne Clemens in Florida, Mo., did not arrive in New England until 1871. Between 1871 and 1874 Clemens and his wife, Olivia Langdon, rented a house in Hartford from John Hooker and Isabella Beecher Hooker while building a home of their own in a Hartford neighborhood known as Nook Farm. Among their close neighbors were Susan and Charles Dudley Warner and Calvin and Harriet Beecher Stowe. These Nook Farm neighbors formed a supportive literary community for Twain, who experienced his most productive years there. He wrote *The Gilded Age: A Tale of Today* (1873) with Warner and wrote or finished such classics as *The Adventures of Tom Sawyer* (1876) and *Adventures of Huckleberry Finn* (1885).

Although Twain is best known for writings that recall antebellum life in Mississippi river towns, he also produced literature that reflected New England life and mores, most notably *A Connecticut Yankee in King Arthur's Court* (1889) and "The Facts Concerning the Recent Carnival of Crime in Connecticut" (1876). One might also argue that *Date, 1601: Conversation, as It Was by the Social Fireside, in the Time of the Tudors* (written 1876; published privately 1880), his scatological sketch featuring Elizabeth I, Shakespeare, and sundry other Renaissance notables discussing flatulence and sexual intercourse, was produced in response to the dull respectability of Hartford society. That Twain had studied New Englanders and their values is clear in his portrayal of Hank Morgan, the protagonist of *A Connecticut Yankee;* introducing his character as "a Yankee of the Yankees," Twain achieves his humorous effects by milking the contrast between Hank's dry practicality and the magical worldview of the sixth century. While *A Connecticut Yankee* focuses on the New England mentality, "The Facts Concerning the Recent Carnival of Crime in Connecticut" responds to it more obliquely, featuring a first-person narrator who, confronted and taunted by the physical manifestation of his shriveled Conscience, kills it, freeing himself for a blissful lifetime of mayhem and murder. Both "Facts Concerning" and *Date 1601* challenge New England pieties. He also criticized and lampooned the new religion of Christian Science, founded in New England, in *Christian Science: With Notes Containing Corrections to Date* (1907).

The Clemens family lived in the Hartford house for 17 years, leaving it in 1891 when they could no longer afford their lifestyle and selling it in 1901. In 1908, four years after his wife's death, Twain built a house in Redding, Conn., which he called Stormfield, where he died in 1910. Twain had spent 40 years living, lecturing, and socializing in New England. Although he may have had his own reservations about New Englanders, they found him attractive, inviting him to speak at celebrations for John Greenleaf Whittier, reading his contributions to the *Atlantic Monthly,* and responding to him as to one of their own. "It is most curious and interesting to watch this growing man of 40—to see how he studies and how high his aims are," wrote Boston blue blood Annie Adams Fields after visiting the Clemenses in April 1876. "His conversation is always earnest and careful, though full of fun." Associated in the popular mind with Mississippi or the West, Twain was also an acute observer of, and participant in, New England culture.

Kenneth R. Andrews, *Nook Farm: Mark Twain's Hartford Circle* (1950); Gregg Camfield, *The Oxford Companion to Mark Twain* (2003); Susan K. Harris, *The Courtship of Olivia Langdon and Mark Twain* (1996); J. R. LeMaster and James D. Wilson, eds., *The Mark Twain Encyclopedia* (1993).

Susan K. Harris

Updike, John (1932–) Writer. John Hoyer Updike was born in Shillington, Penn., the son of Linda Grace (Hoyer) Updike, an aspiring writer, and Wesley Russell Updike, a mathematics schoolteacher. He entered Harvard University in 1950 and soon began drawing and writing for the *Harvard Lampoon,* of which he became editor in 1953. He graduated from Harvard summa cum laude in 1954, with a major in English literature. That same year, he sold his first short story, "Friends from Philadelphia," to the *New Yorker* magazine.

The turning point in Updike's career came in 1957 when, determined to become a full-time writer, he quit a staff position at the *New Yorker* and moved from Manhattan to Ipswich, Mass. "If Shillington gave me life," Updike would write years later in *Self-Consciousness,* "Ipswich was where I took possession of it." Updike retained his connection to the *New Yorker* as a regular contributor of reviews, essays, and stories, now collected in several volumes. He was instrumental in establishing a certain *New Yorker* style and culture that has influenced upper-middle-class writing and sensibility in the United States.

The decision to move to Ipswich paid off: within a year his first novel, *The Poorhouse Fair* (1958), was on its way to press. Other novels, poems, and short stories followed with impressive speed, as well as a large collection of essays, reviews, and literary criticism.

Updike's most widely acclaimed body of work is the Rabbit tetralogy: *Rabbit, Run* (1960), *Rabbit Redux* (1971), *Rabbit Is Rich* (1981), and *Rabbit at Rest* (1990). These novels portray the life of white, Anglo-Saxon, Protestant Harry (Rabbit) Angstrom during the 1950s, 1960s, 1970s, and 1980s, respectively. Rabbit is revisited at the end of each decade as Updike leads him to confront the major issues of his day and place. Although at times shockingly honest and highly sensitive and human, Rabbit is not always a likable character. His treatment of communists, foreigners, blacks, women, and homosexuals often brings him close to the belligerent anticommunist, the angry nationalist, and the phallocentric racist. It is, however, precisely Rabbit's ambiguity, combined with Updike's stylistic virtuosity and masterful depiction of everyday life, that has been the object of continuous admiration of readers and critics alike.

New England's influence can be felt throughout Updike's works. Many of his short stories and novels have New England settings or show the strong influence of its people, culture, and literary tradition. Novels such as *Couples* (1968), *Marry Me* (1976), *The Witches of Eastwick* (1984), and *Memories of the Ford Administration* (1992) are set in New England towns. *A Month of Sundays* (1975), *Roger's Version* (1986), and *S.* (1988), on the other hand, are Updike's public tribute to one of New England's and America's greatest writers, Nathaniel Hawthorne. *S.,* for example, retells the story of *The Scarlet Letter* from Hester Prynne's point of view. Like Hawthorne, Updike is interested in the conjunction and disjunction of the past, so powerfully present in New England, and the social mores of the times, particularly of middle-class life. He also has a great appreciation of local nature and culture, expressed in his various autobiographical writings, essays (including writing on golf), and short stories. His 1997 novel *Toward the End of Time* envisions the breakdown of the New England social contract envisioned by the Puritan founders but is filtered through a distinctly modern consciousness forged by other New Englanders such as Henry James and Henry Adams.

Recognition of Updike's talent came as early as 1959 when "A Gift from the City" was included in *Best American Short Stories.* In the years that followed, he has won the National Book Award, the American Book Award, two Pulitzer Prizes, the National Medal of the Arts, and the Edward MacDowell Medal. In 1997 the French honored him with the title Commandeur de l'Ordre des Arts et des Lettres, very appropriately expressing the commanding role Updike has played in the literary world during the past five decades.

Robert Detweiler, *John Updike* (1972); Donald J. Greiner, *John Updike's Novels* (1984); Dilvo I. Ristoff, *Updike's America: The Presence of Contemporary American History in John Updike's Rabbit Trilogy* (1988); Suzanne Henning Uphaus, *John Updike* (1980).

Dilvo I. Ristoff

Utopias and Dystopias One could say that New England began as a utopian idea, most famously articulated by John Winthrop in 1630 when he admonished his shipload of Puritan saints onboard the *Arbella* that their new colony should be "a city upon a hill," with the world's eyes judging whether they lived up to their ideals of Christian community. Winthrop's command is a sterner, more immediate echo of Captain John Smith's 1616 published appeal for those Londoners who "have but a taste of virtue and magnanimitie" to transplant themselves in New England and in doing so "recreate themselves before their owne doores, in their owne boates upon the sea." From its earliest articulation to its later incarnations as part of 19th-century reform efforts, New England utopianism demonstrated the tensions that lie at the heart of most utopian endeavors: to model a new world order or to withdraw behind boundaries that admit only the true believer; to celebrate personal rights and development or to subordinate the individual to the community; to share wealth and power or to rely on the profit motive and strong leadership. The image of New England as a literary landscape upon which fantastic utopias flourish and frightful dystopias unfold has remained potent over the ensuing four centuries of literary activity. From Smith and the Puritans to Transcendentalists, abolitionists, suffragists, and socialists, all the way up to contemporary writers as diverse as Canadian-born Margaret Atwood and Maine's resident horror writer Stephen King, the Northeast has been the setting for communal bliss, cynical parody, and hallucinatory social disintegration.

New England utopian communities reached their peak during the 1840s and were created in response to serious economic and social crises that led to a broad range of religious and secular movements: evangelical religion, abolition, temperance, progressive education, peace, workers' and women's rights. The most famous of the several utopian experimental communities in 19th-century New England were those influenced by Transcendentalism. Brook Farm (1841–46) was founded by Unitarian minister George Ripley at West Roxbury, Mass. Ripley was interested in integrating intellectual and physical labor in a cooperative venture that would help to prepare a society of liberally educated people who would live a more simple, wholesome, and harmonious life. Many literary and other notables visited it, including Margaret Fuller, Ralph Waldo Emerson, and Elizabeth Peabody. Newspaper editor Charles Dana and Nathaniel Hawthorne joined the community, and Hawthorne satirized it in *The Blithedale Romance* (1852).

Fruitlands (1843–45) was founded by Bronson Alcott and Charles Lane in Harvard, Mass., as a primitive agricultural community, to the immense discomfort and exasperation of Alcott's wife and his daughter Louisa May, who satirized the brief life of the colony in her witty memoir *Transcendental Wild Oats* (1873). A few miles down the road was the most solitary of utopian enterprises—Henry David Thoreau's Walden experiment (1845–47) in Concord, "which carried to a logical extreme the utopian promise of America to grant every single individual the right and opportunity to pursue his own vision, however idiosyncratic, of the good life."

Two of the most interesting industrial reform utopias were Hopedale (1842–56), founded by Adin Ballou, a Universalist minister and Christian Socialist, at Milford, Mass., and the Northampton Association of Education and Industry (1842–46), whose chief architects were radical communitarians David Mack, Samuel Hill, and George Benson. Hopedale was a cooperative experiment in applied Christianity that attracted activists involved in the temperance, peace, and antislavery movements. Northampton, founded on the values of racial equality, women's rights, and religious tolerance, sought to reform the industrial system by combining work, domestic life, and education. Black activists Sojourner Truth and David Ruggles lived there, and visitor Frederick Douglass remarked that it was the most democratic place he had seen.

The utopian promise of a progressive society blending New England values and technological advance finds its classic expression in Edward Bellamy's *Looking Backward* (1888), which imagines Boston as a late-20th-century socialist utopia. A strong tradition of dystopian literature, however, questions such optimism. If utopian literature develops imaginatively social and economic tendencies and the values upon which they are based, then dystopian literature creates a fictive world in which repressed or unintended features of those same items are revealed. In New England literature, dystopian fiction often alludes to the darker side of Puritanism, and it also probes the social and environmental consequences of the Yankee character. These features have combined in classic texts such as Herman Melville's "The Paradise of Bachelors and the Tartarus of Maids" (1855). This story presents female workers in a western Massachusetts paper mill as if they are slaves to the biological machinery of reproduction, while the mill itself is owned by wealthy bachelors far removed from such working conditions. Margaret Atwood's *The Handmaid's Tale* (1986) is set in a future Cambridge, Mass., where a patriarchal society with Puritan undertones kidnaps and trains young fertile women to reproduce in a society beset with infertility caused by chemical pollution. Charlotte Perkins Gilman's depictions of feminist utopias and patriarchal dystopias in such works as *Herland* (1915) present her reflections on women's status in New England and across the United States in the late 19th century. Mark Twain's *A Connecticut Yankee in King Arthur's Court* (1889) transports a Colt factory foreman to medieval times where technological innovations meant to improve humankind lead to a massacre.

New England dystopian writings may criticize corrupted regional values but they also, in the tradition of the Puritan jeremiad, can issue a conservative call for a return to these same values in purer form. For example, Shirley Jackson's "The Lottery" (1948) parodies New England's community ritual of the town meeting where one townsperson is selected to be sacrificed each year; but the effect of the story is to call for resistance to community conformity, the sort of individualism identified with early New England. Brendan DuBois's *Resurrection Day* (1999) imagines a revolt from a military dictatorship set up after a nuclear exchange in 1962. The book questions the values of John F. Kennedy's "New Frontier" and presents a depressed, shabby Boston not unlike parts of the city during the 1970s. But the hero is a newspaper reporter who reasserts freedom of the press to resurrect democracy in America. The sense that ecological disaster might also challenge New England values plays out in the science fiction stories of New Hampshire's James Patrick Kelly. Most notable among dystopian writers, though some would place his New England works in the horror category, is Maine's Stephen King, whose *Salem's Lot* (1975) and *The Stand* (1978), to name just two, feature New England scenes and social conflicts emergent in the region.

Robert Fogarty, *Dictionary of American Communal and Utopian History* (1980); Carol Kessler, ed., *Daring to Dream: Utopian Stories by United States Women: 1836–1919* (1984); Krishan Kumar, *Utopia and Anti-Utopia in Modern Times* (1987); John L. Thomas, *Alternative America* (1983).

Lois Rudnick

West, Dorothy (1907–98) Writer.

Dorothy West was the youngest participant in the flowering of African American literature and arts known as the Harlem Renaissance and an insightful writer, but her literary contributions were nearly forgotten until her neighbor, Jacqueline Kennedy Onassis, encouraged her to finish *The Wedding*. This 1995 novel's rare insights into the upper-class black community at Oak Bluffs on Martha's Vineyard brought West popular success and critical acclaim and prompted renewed interest in her earlier writings.

West was born in Boston, the only child of Rachel Pease Benson and Isaac Christopher West, a former slave from Virginia whose business acumen as a produce wholesaler earned him the title of Boston's "Black Banana King." An intelligent child, West received two years of private tutoring from Bessie Trotter, the sister of *Boston Guardian* editor William Monroe Trotter, and was admitted to the second grade of the Farragut School at age four. She also attended the Martin School on Mission Hill and the Girls' Latin School.

Even as a child West wanted to be a writer; she began composing stories at age seven, eventually sending them to the *Boston Post* and receiving $10 prizes for her work. At age 18 she submitted her short story "The Typewriter" to a contest sponsored by *Opportunity* magazine and persuaded her protective parents to allow her and her cousin, poet Helene Johnson, to attend the New York awards ceremony. West shared the second-place prize with Zora Neale Hurston and remained in New York, thereby becoming a part of the Harlem Renaissance. West continued to write—though her efforts to publish were generally frustrated—and she also studied journalism and philosophy at Columbia. In 1932 she traveled to Russia in the company of many notable American communists and African American intellectuals, including Langston Hughes, to participate in a film on racial discrimination in the United States. Although it had come to an end during her absence, West's contributions to the Harlem Renaissance were many and

Dorothy West, 1989

varied. She founded and edited the short-lived literary journal *Challenge* and was editor of its attempted revival, *New Challenge*, with collaborator Richard Wright.

In 1945 West took up permanent residence on Martha's Vineyard, where she continued writing and completed her novel *The Living Is Easy* (1948). This semi-autobiographical tale examines the inadvertent emotional havoc wrought by the ambitious Cleo Judson (based on West's own mother) whose desire to join Boston's black elite destroys her family. West wrote stories and occasional pieces for the *Vineyard Gazette* and the *New York Daily News*. Her work enjoyed renewed critical interest during the 1980s when she was interviewed by Mary Helen Washington for the Bunting Library Oral History project. West donated her extensive papers to that library, providing materials for scholarly work on her career. In the late 1980s she returned to *The Wedding* (1995), which she had begun writing in the 1930s. The novel explores class and color consciousness among the Oak Bluffs aristocracy in the face of an interracial marriage. The novel is dedicated to Onassis and was made into a television movie by Oprah Winfrey. *The Wedding* was followed by a collection of short stories, *The Richer, the Poorer: Stories, Sketches, and Reminiscences* (1995). West's style is characterized by deftly ironic twists, particularly in matters of race and racial hypocrisy; she was particularly talented at subtle and rich character portraits.

West never married and had no children.

Katrine Dalsgard, "Alive and Well and Living on the Island of Martha's Vineyard: An Interview with Dorothy West," *Langston Hughes Review* 12 (1993); SallyAnn H. Ferguson, "Dorothy West," *Dictionary of Literary Biography* 76 (1988); Deborah McDowell, "Conversations with Dorothy West," in *The Harlem Renaissance Re-Examined*, ed. Victor A. Kramer (1987); Mary Helen Washington, "I Sign My Mother's Name," in *Mothering the Mind: Twelve Studies of Writers and Their Silent Partners*, ed. Ruth Perry and Martine Watson Brownley (1984).

Kathleen Pfeiffer

Wharton, Edith (1862–1937) Writer.

Edith Newbold (Jones) Wharton, novelist, short story writer, essayist, and travel writer, was born to George Frederic Jones and Lucretia Rhinelander Jones and grew up as a member of a wealthy and socially elite family in New York. From early childhood, she inhabited a cosmopolitan culture in which she moved frequently among Europe, New York, and summer homes in New England; she spent her last 30 years as an expatriate in France. Wharton is known for her critical, even anthropological analyses of New York society in such novels as *The House of Mirth* (1905) and *The Age of Innocence* (1920). But some of her best works, especially the short novels *Ethan Frome* (1911) and *Summer* (1917), focus on New England.

Wharton married within her social class, but her 1885 union with Edward Wharton of Boston was marked by incompatibility from the start and ended in divorce in 1913. Her most sustained intimate relationship was with Walter Berry, a lawyer with whom she shared a lifelong, probably platonic friendship. The first decade of her married life resulted both in severe bouts of depression and in the beginning of her professional writing career. After a few short poems and stories, she collaborated with Ogden Codman, an architect and interior decorator who worked on her homes in Newport and New York, to write *The Decoration of Houses* (1897). This interest led to her first major New England work: her country house, the Mount, in Lenox, Mass., which she helped to design and which, along with its gardens, was now being restored. Always concerned with shaping her own environment, Wharton was practically engaged with and wrote about architecture, landscape architecture, and gardening for much of her life.

Wharton's New England works span her career, up through her last story, "All Souls'" (1937). In addition to *Ethan Frome* and *Summer*, New England was the setting for a longer novel, *The Fruit of the Tree* (1907), and 21 short stories. These works fuse her observations of New England landscape and culture with the concerns she brought to the scenes. In *Ethan Frome* Wharton explored issues central to her work—sexual repression, gender relations, cultural starvation—in terms of rural life. Her fiction also includes analyses of the cultural past and its relation to the present: Transcendentalism ("The Angel at the Grave" [1901]); academic communities and sexual and intellectual aridity ("The Pretext" [1908] and "Xingu" [1911]); country houses and elite avarice ("The Triumph of Night" [1914]); and mill towns and progressive reform (*The Fruit of the Tree*). In *Summer*, what Wharton called her "hot Ethan," she revisited the Berkshires landscape of her earlier novel, but instead of using a winter setting to record a diminished life, she used the passage of a summer season to record an adolescent girl's coming to sexual maturity. *Summer*, however, signifies not only sexuality and fertility but also the tourist season and thus the (sexual) politics of interactions between local inhabitants and elite visitors drawn to the image of rural New England elaborated by the turn-of-the-century Colonial Revival and "Old Home Day" movements.

In 1907 Wharton moved to Paris, which became her base for the next 10 years. Her circle of friends included the writers Henry James, Paul Bourget, and Vernon Lee (Violet Paget); the art historian Bernard Berenson; and the journalist Morton Fullerton, with whom she had an affair (1908–9). During World War I she worked extensively on behalf of war refugees, efforts for which the French government made her a Chevalier of the Legion of Honor. *The Age of Innocence* earned her the Pulitzer Prize in 1921. She died in her home in Saint Brice-sous-Fôret, near Paris.

Millicent Bell, ed., *The Cambridge Companion to Edith Wharton* (1995); R. W. B. Lewis, *Edith Wharton: A Biography* (1975); R. W. B. Lewis and Nancy Lewis, eds., *The Letters of Edith Wharton* (1988); Barbara A. White, ed., *Wharton's New England: Seven Stories and Ethan Frome* (1995).

Brigitte Bailey

Wheatley, Phillis (1753–84) Poet.

A Revolutionary War–era poet and the first African American writer to publish a book, Phillis Wheatley was probably the best, and certainly the most celebrated, poet in Boston in the 1770s, even as she wrote most of her poetry as a slave. Living at a time of debate over concepts of freedom and with a Congregationalist family who had ties to an international Methodist evangelical movement, Wheatley wrote poetry that exemplified the era's politics and piety but that also emphasized her African persona. In doing so, she claimed liberty, Christianity, and the public forum of print culture for African Americans.

Born in West Africa and shipped to Boston in 1761, Wheatley was bought by a well-to-do and pious merchant, John Wheatley, and his wife, Susanna Wheatley, as a companion for Susanna. Sensing her intelligence, Susanna

Phillis Wheatley, from the frontispiece to her first published volume (1773), engraved from a painting by Wheatley's friend Scipio Moorhead

and her daughter tutored Wheatley in English literature, Latin, classical literature, and the Bible. Susanna exempted Phillis from most household labor and actively promoted her writing.

After publishing some poems in newspapers and as broadsides—including her first internationally famous poem, an elegy on the evangelical preacher George Whitefield—and unable to find a Boston publisher, Wheatley published *Poems on Various Subjects, Religious and Moral* (1773) in London. The book was sponsored by a wealthy patron, the Countess of Huntingdon, and, to counter the widely spread belief that blacks were incapable of literary expression, was prefaced by a statement of authenticity signed by the most prominent men in Boston. The Wheatleys freed Phillis in 1773, but she continued to live with them until 1778. After the deaths of Susanna and John, she married a free black man, John Peters, whose fortunes shifted between middle-class prosperity and poverty. After trying unsuccessfully to publish a second volume of poetry, Wheatley died, along with the last of her three children, in poverty in Boston.

Wheatley composed neoclassical verse, often in heroic couplets, with allusions to classical myths and personifications of abstractions ("Freedom") and national identities ("Columbia"). Her strongest literary influences were Alexander Pope and John Milton. Her poetry includes philosophical meditations ("On Recollection"), biblical narratives ("Goliath of Gath"), religious instruction ("An Address to the Atheist"), addresses to public figures (such as George III and George Washington), and poems on public events (such as one on the

Boston Massacre, now lost). But her largest group of poems participates in a long-standing New England tradition: the elegy or funeral poem, written to commemorate the piety of the dead and to exhort the living toward greater faith. Wheatley was aware of the complexity of her position as a protégée of an evangelical, white elite in a racist society, as such poems as "On Being Brought from Africa to America" show. Although black writers have always been aware of her, and her poems were in fact reissued in the 1830s to further the cause of abolition, academic study of the poetry of this first significant African American writer has begun in earnest only during the past 30 years.

Frances Smith Foster, *Written by Herself: Literary Production by African American Women, 1746–1892* (1993); William H. Robinson, *Phillis Wheatley and Her Writings* (1984); Phillis Wheatley, *The Collected Works of Phillis Wheatley,* ed. John Shields (1988); Wheatley, *The Poems of Phillis Wheatley,* ed. Julian D. Mason, Jr. (1989).

Brigitte Bailey

White, E. B., and Katharine (1899–1985 and 1893–1977) Writers.

Elwyn Brooks White and Katharine Sergeant Angell met in 1927 when E.B. joined the staff of the *New Yorker* magazine, where Katharine was the magazine's first fiction editor. They married in 1929 and left Manhattan in 1938 for their salt marsh farm in North Brooklin, Maine. They stayed in Maine full time for five years, returning to New York part time in 1943 to be closer to the magazine. The Whites traveled down east frequently and continued this commute until E.B. retired from the *New Yorker* in 1957. He remained on the farm until his death in 1985. In a letter written to a friend toward the end of his life, he explains with his signature simplicity the metaphysical balm offered by Maine life: "There is a certain serenity here that heals my spirit, and I can still buy Moxie in a tiny supermarket six miles away. Moxie contains gentian root, which is the path to the good life. This was known in the second century before Christ, and it is a boon to me today."

Katharine Sergeant was born in Boston to an affluent Brahmin family and was an alumna of Miss Winsor's School and Bryn Mawr. When she met White, she was a recently divorced mother of two and was six years his senior; together they had a son, Joel, born in 1930. After the family moved to Maine, Katharine continued working from there for the *New Yorker* until she retired in 1959; she has been described as the *New Yorker*'s "intellectual soul." Over time, she took on the role of agent for her increasingly famous and widely sought-after husband. In

1941, she and E.B. coedited *A Subtreasury of American Humor,* and in 2002 her correspondence with Elizabeth Lawrence was published under the title *Two Gardeners: A Friendship in Letters.* She was as passionate about gardening as she was about her own writing and her lifelong collaborations with and encouragement of gifted, unknown writers. Katharine died of congestive heart failure in 1977.

E.B., known as Andy to his friends, craved a life of simplicity and physical labor. By profession he was a writer, but by temperament he was a keeper of small livestock: in particular, geese, chickens, sheep, and the occasional annual pig. He was born in Mount Vernon, N.Y., and graduated from Cornell University in 1921. He began his career at the *New Yorker* by contributing verse and other short pieces but quickly became a regular staff writer and continued to contribute to the magazine throughout his career. From 1938 to 1943, he wrote a monthly column for *Harper's* magazine under the title "One Man's Meat." These essays were collected and published in a volume with the same title in 1942 and again in 1944.

E.B.'s devotion to rural Maine life started in 1904, the first year that his family made what would become a yearly annual pilgrimage during the month of August to Bert Mosher's Camps, Great Pond. He often delighted his readers with tales of his animals and the everyday adventures of farm life in essays such as "Death of a Pig" (1947), in which the "antique pattern," a "tragedy enacted on most farms with perfect fidelity to the original script," of purchasing a young pig in the spring and fattening it for winter slaughter goes awry. He also made famous the idiosyncratic sounds, cadences, and images of his daily conversations in "Maine Speech" (1940): "The most difficult sound is the 'a.' I've been in Maine, off and on, all my life, but I still have to pause sometimes when somebody asks me something with an 'a' in it. The other day a friend met me in front of the store, and asked, 'How's the famine comin' along?' I had to think fast before I got the word 'farming' out of his famine."

White's devotion to syntactic clarity and semantic simplicity has been immortalized in *The Elements of Style,* a manual originally written and published privately in 1919 by his late Cornell professor William Strunk. In 1959, at the request of Macmillan publishers, White revised and expanded Strunk's original 43-page pamphlet, adding examples, new material, and a 3,500-word introductory essay titled "An Approach to Style." White also edited the 1972 edition; the 1999 edition is edited by White's stepson, Roger Angell.

E.B.'s greatest fame has derived from his

three children's books: *Stuart Little* (1945), *Charlotte's Web* (1952), and *The Trumpet of the Swan* (1970). In the fictional world White created, fantasy mingles with a realism based in the most mundane aspects of daily life to create a lulling plausibility about the beauty of the world and the common bond among all creatures. *Stuart Little* is set primarily in New York City, but White's next children's books depend on their New England settings for their scenery, characters, and mood. Charlotte, of *Charlotte's Web*, is an articulate and artistically inclined spider who saves the life of Wilbur the pig by writing "Some Pig!" and "Terrific!" in her web, thus stunning the humans who plan to butcher him for a winter of bacon, ham, and pork chops into preserving his life. Louis, the mute trumpeter swan protagonist of *The Trumpet of the Swan*, hopes to pay for the trumpet his father stole for him from a music store in Billings, Mont., and finds musical fame playing for the crowds in the Boston Public Garden and takes a room at the Ritz Carlton Hotel.

Just as Louis finds early fame in Boston, the tales of Stuart Little and Wilbur also evoke, though less specifically, an idyllic New England. Stuart travels from Manhattan to Ames Crossing, "the loveliest town of all," and then continues northward explaining to a likeminded friend, "I rather expect that I will be traveling north until the end of my days." The Zuckerman Farm, where Wilbur and Charlotte live, is an homage to the joys and difficulties White discovered on his own farm in North Brooklin, rendered by peering into the microcosm of the barn and the society of the creatures living there.

E.B. was presented with a number of honors, including the Presidential Medal of Freedom (1963), the Laura Ingalls Wilder Award (1970), the National Medal for Literature (1971), the gold medal for essays and criticism of the American Academy of Arts and Letters (1973), and a Pulitzer Prize (1978). He also received several honorary degrees.

In the years after Katharine's death, E.B. spent his time netting turtles in Allen Cove, canoeing on Great Pond, observing his geese for comic relief, editing collections of his own essays and letters, distributing Katharine's papers to libraries, and overseeing the publication of a collection of her *New Yorker* pieces on gardening, *Onward and Upward in the Garden* (1979). In the introduction to *Onward and Upward*, White wrote of his life as a widower, "Life without Katharine is no good for me." The Friend Memorial Library in Brooklin, Maine, houses a collection of the works of Katharine and E. B. White.

Scott Elledge, *E. B. White: A Biography* (1984); Dorothy Lobrano Guth, *Letters of E. B. White* (1976); Isabel Russell, *Katharine and E. B. White: An Affec-* *tionate Memoir* (1988); E. B. White, *Essays of E. B. White* (1977).

Jennifer Beard

Wilbur, Richard (1921–) Poet and translator. Born in New York City to Marylander Helen Purdy Wilbur and Lawrence Wilbur, a native Nebraskan, Richard Wilbur was raised in North Caldwell, N.J., and has lived in New England since entering college. Wilbur's ancestors were among the earliest settlers of Massachusetts and Rhode Island, and the region has played a pivotal if subtle role in his long literary career. Some of Wilbur's lyric poems, such as "Fern-Beds in Hampshire County" from the 1969 collection *Waking to Sleep* and "The Puritans" from the 1950 volume *Ceremony and Other Poems*, evoke New England's natural landscapes or analyze aspects of its cultural history. Even poems that do not explore regional topics or themes express a pragmatic philosophical outlook in a reticent poetic voice that reflects the influence of regional styles of thought and verbal communication.

Throughout his career Wilbur has demonstrated a facility with poetic form and language. Writing verses from an early age, Wilbur grew fascinated with modernist poetry as a teenager, especially the work of Hart Crane, T. S. Eliot, the dadaists, and the surrealists. He attended Amherst College, taking English courses there and editing the school newspaper. After graduating in 1942, he married Bostonian Charlotte Hayes Ward and then joined the U.S. Army.

To cope with the horrors he witnessed during World War II, Wilbur wrote poems. By using traditional forms, regular meters and rhyme schemes, and a controlled, emotionally restrained tone, the distraught poet found he could establish psychic order amid destruction and fear. After the war, while his contemporaries across the nation were favoring free verse, Wilbur continued to utilize formal versification, believing it to be a means of balancing the dynamic, potentially overwhelming forces of the modern world.

Over the years Wilbur's work has found its most enthusiastic support within New England, no doubt in part because of the poet's longtime affiliation with the region's academic community. Earning a master's degree at Harvard University in 1947, Wilbur taught at that institution until 1955, when he accepted a position at Wellesley College. In 1957 he joined the faculty at Wesleyan University, where he remained until 1977. From that year until he retired from academia in 1986, Wilbur was writer-in-residence at Smith College.

Beyond his regional loyalties Wilbur has a national, even international, reputation. He has served as poet laureate of the United States and consultant in poetry to the Library of Congress (1987–88); he has received two Guggenheim Fellowships, numerous honorary degrees from national colleges and universities, and major literary awards, including two Pulitzer Prizes, the National Book Award, and the Bollingen Prize. Collections of Wilbur's poetry include *The Beautiful Changes and Other Poems* (1947), *Things of This World* (1956), and *New and Collected Poems* (1988). He also wrote *Responses, Prose Pieces: 1953–1976* (1976), the children's book *Loudmouse* (1963), and the lyrics for *Candide: A Comic Operetta Based on Voltaire's Satire* (1957), with book by Lillian Hellman and music by Leonard Bernstein.

Wilbur has won wide acclaim and several prestigious awards as a translator. Although he has rendered lyric poetry by French, Spanish, and Russian poets into English, he is better known for his English translations of a number of 17th-century French dramatic works, such as Molière's *The Misanthrope* (Wilbur's version appeared in 1955) and *Tartuffe* (1963) and Racine's *Andromaque* (1982) and *Phaedra* (1986).

Frances Bixler, *Richard Wilbur: A Reference Guide* (1991); William Butts, ed., *Conversations with Richard Wilbur* (1990); Donald Louis Hill, *Richard Wilbur* (1967); Wendy Salinger, ed., *Richard Wilbur's Creation* (1983).

Ted Olson

Wilson, Harriet (ca. 1828–ca. 1863) Writer. The first African American woman known to have published a novel in English, Harriet E. (Adams) Wilson set her fictionalized autobiography *Our Nig* (1859) in Milford, N.H., where she grew up. The book is significant not only because of its status as a first but also because it treats racism in New England at a time when most attention was directed toward southern slavery. Wilson subtitled her narrative *Sketches from the Life of a Free Black, in a Two-Story White House, North, Showing That Slavery's Shadows Fall Even There*.

Very little is known about Wilson's life. Apparently she was born in 1827 or 1828 in New Hampshire, perhaps to a black father who died young and a white mother who abandoned her, as described in *Our Nig*. She became indentured as a child to the family of Nehemiah Hayward and in 1840 was the only "colored female" enumerated in the Milford census.

By the time Wilson left the Haywards at age 18, her health had so deteriorated that she could not consistently support herself; in 1850 she was listed among the town poor. According to her friend "Allida," whose testimonial is appended to *Our Nig*, she then moved to "W" (probably Worcester, Mass.) and made straw hats for a living. Late in 1851 she returned to

Milford to marry Thomas Wilson, a professed fugitive slave who turned out to be a fake and left her just before she gave birth to a son, George Mason Wilson, in 1852 at the local poorhouse. Leaving her son with white foster parents, Harriet Wilson sought work in Boston and eventually wrote *Our Nig* in the hope of making enough money to support him. In the preface to her narrative Wilson explains that "deserted by kindred, disabled by failing health, I am forced to some experiment which shall aid me in maintaining myself and child without extinguishing this feeble life."

Wilson's narrative highlights her years as a servant. The protagonist, Frado, is a lively six-year-old girl when left at the Bellmonts' farm. While some members of the family befriend her, Mrs. Bellmont, a blatantly racist "she-devil," regards Frado as "our nig" and overworks and beats her. Wilson enlivens this grim story with wit and irony and borrows from a number of genres familiar to her, including the slave narrative, sentimental novel, Gothic novel, autobiography, and satire. No one form served Wilson's purposes completely. For example, Wilson followed the model of the slave narrative in having Frado overcome her oppressor's attempts to keep her illiterate and learn to assert herself: "Stop!" shouted Frado, "strike me, and I'll never work a mite more for you." But she cannot move from slavery to freedom because she is supposedly already free, and "slavery's shadows" in New England perpetuate her economic dependence.

At times Wilson's narrator remarks bitterly on the hypocrisy of abolitionists (perhaps because Milford was an abolitionist stronghold and Mrs. Nehemiah Hayward, on whom Mrs. Bellmont was based, had abolitionist connections). Those comments cost the author a crucial source of support for her narrative. Ironically, after Wilson self-published *Our Nig* in 1859, her son died of a fever, and the book fell into obscurity. Harriet Wilson disappears from public records in 1863; the date and place of her death are unknown. Not until 1983 was *Our Nig* rediscovered by the Harvard professor Henry Louis Gates, Jr., as part of the current recovery of African American texts. Initially, some critics viewed the narrative as relatively unsophisticated, but *Our Nig* is now regarded as a complex and original precursor to the African American women's literary tradition.

David Ames Curtis and Henry Louis Gates, Jr., "Establishing the Identity of the Author of *Our Nig*," in *Wild Women in the Whirlwind: Afra-American Culture and the Contemporary Literary Renaissance,* ed. Joanne M. Braxton and Andrée Nicola McLaughlin (1990); Henry Louis Gates Jr., Introduction to *Our Nig,* by Harriet E. Wilson (1983); Carla L. Peterson, *Doers of the Word: African-American Women Speakers and Writers in the North (1830–1880)* (1995); Barbara A. White, "'Our Nig' and the She-Devil: New Information about Harriet Wilson and the 'Bellmont' Family," *American Literature* 65 (1993).

Barbara A. White

Maritime
New England

W. Jeffrey Bolster, Section Editor

INTRODUCTION

S hipping and commercial fishing have fallen on hard times in New England today, but no region remains so thoroughly associated with the sea. Old piers have collapsed into murky green waters, ignored unless condominiums or marinas rise in their stead. But New Bedford whaleships are eternal thanks to *Moby-Dick,* and the monumental clipper ship *Flying Cloud* remains in the record books thanks to the genius of a Boston shipwright named Donald McKay. Like roof walks atop Nantucket houses, those icons speak to a Yankee people defined by seafaring. So does contemporary culture: Sebastian Junger's *Perfect Storm* (1997) became a best-seller and later a Hollywood blockbuster (2000). The chilling account of the loss of a Cape Ann, Mass., swordfishing boat in 1991, it capitalized on Gloucester's centuries of intimacy with the cruelly indifferent sea.

Centuries ago profits from fish and ships were the sheet anchor of New England society, the salvation of a folk whose stony soil and utopian Puritan faith were insufficient to support them. Today every coastal town boasts sites or shops that evoke historic seafaring. Replica ships are all the rage. A version of John Paul Jones's sloop *Providence* (made of fiberglass) sails from the city of that name. Mystic Seaport in Connecticut launched the "Freedom Schooner" *Amistad* in 2000, celebrating African Americans' liberation struggle. Tall ship festivals like Sail Boston 1992 and Sail Boston 2000 attract hundreds of thousands of visitors. Maritime museums are thriving in New England, if shipping companies are not, and maritime legacies clearly grip modern imaginations.

The historic Yankees (white, black, and Native American) who made their living in the sea's embrace, alternating between fear and boredom, might be puzzled by this shift from maritime work to maritime memories. The 17th-, 18th-, and early-19th-century cultures to which they belonged had less room for openly commercial celebrations of heritage. Yet it was the toil of those seafarers that laid the foundation for a myth of maritime New England that would endure long beyond the age of sail. Since 1925 a bronze helmsman in oilskins has gazed stoically from a Gloucester pedestal inscribed, "They that go down to the sea in ships." The statue, a memorial to fishermen lost at sea, is a testament to centuries of New Englanders' seafaring and to the cultivation of certain memories (at the expense of others) about the past and the place.

Maritime New England thus means many things. It is certainly a definable coastal region, a geographic place that looks and feels like no other. For a handful of people it still describes occupation and locale, as it once did for many. Maritime New England is also a mythic ideal, a nostalgic form of historical thinking that selectively imagines the past. That myth began as a challenge to modernism and a signature of New England's historical uniqueness. It persists today as a marker of localism and a commodity for sale in many forms. Television programs about lighthouses, for instance, emphasize sturdy self-reliance and timeless simplicity, as do Maine tourism brochures advertising Camden's vacation cruise schooners. Residents and visitors alike have trafficked for generations in representations of pipe-smoking old salts and serenely enduring fishing villages. Such images have become staples of New England's tourist industry. Found in expensive art galleries and on restaurant placemats, they now smack of the quintessential Yankee, and more than one lobsterman, harbor pilot, or fair-weather yachtsman has styled himself in response to those cues.

Of course, the image of stalwart sailors sells precisely because there is truth at its core. Consumers recognize that all mariners, whether historic or contemporary, faced elemental challenges. Relying on strength and skill to return safely from the hostile environment beyond the horizon, they become larger than life, no matter how their particular seafaring experience was socially constructed with class or race, and regardless of whether they sailed in clipper ships or tugboats.

To understand maritime New England one needs to know something of the actual history of ships, seaport families, and sailors, including contemporary ones. But it also requires comprehending the refashioning of maritime culture that began more than a century ago in response to modernism's discontents. Genteel preservationists and tourist promoters asserted that New England had a "rich maritime heritage." Sometimes that became a code for suspending attention to complicated and contested histories, reducing them instead to simple essences. Today many historians and curators are actively working to present a more inclusive rendition of the maritime past, recognizing that it is an extraordinarily bold canvas, with room for the contradictions and internal tensions that define any epic story.

New England is not essentially a maritime society anymore, even though small ports like New Haven, Conn., and Portsmouth, N.H., still handle some cargo. Portland, Maine, was the most active port in New England in 2000, but in terms of tonnage handled, it ranked only 25th in the nation. Boston ranked 35th that year, sinking dramatically from its second place in 1900. Tractor-trailer trucks using the federal highway system and the port of New York turned Boston into a backwater. Ironically, active vessel operations do not matter to maritime heritage advocates. As cultural homogeneity threatens local distinctiveness nationwide, New Englanders and visitors alike hang on to the region's maritime heritage as a marker of place, a symbol of accomplishment, and a bulwark against the tides of change.

REGIONALISM

From the spruce-clad islands and granite headlands of Passamaquoddy Bay, where the borders of Maine and New Brunswick converge on the Bay of Fundy, the coast of New England trends west–southwest to the New York state border. Bisected by Cape Cod's bold flexed arm, the New England coast actually has at least three distinctive shorelines.

Cartouche from an 1802 map of Maine

From Quoddy Head to Cape Elizabeth (near Portland) stretches the serrated edge of Maine, whose rockbound peninsulas and spruce-studded islands are jewels in a cold gray sea. It is a spectacular and somber seascape at the dawnland of America, a place of unforgiving ledges and racing tides, where the living still comes hard and where, east of Schoodic Point, gannets, terns, and seals outnumber people. An active lobster fishery still thrives along that coast.

From Cape Elizabeth westward to Cape Cod and Nantucket, Mass., the coast is lower, flatter, sandier, and more populated. The mile-thick glacier that sculpted the Maine coast and the interior of New Hampshire and Massachusetts began to melt 13,000 years ago, depositing a terminal moraine of sand that became Georges Bank, Cape Cod, and Long Island. The Cape's sands can be more forgiving to errant mariners than Maine's rocks, but the currents are less predictable, and the fog just as thick. Thousands of ships have perished on that great sandy elbow and its off-lying shoals, including the *Argo Merchant,* a Liberian tanker whose 7.5 million gallons of oil created ecological havoc during the winter of 1976–77. The Cape is a bold marker in other ways, too. Ocean water is noticeably warmer south of Cape Cod and home to different species of fish and birds.

From Westerly, R.I., to Greenwich, Conn., the coast of New England changes yet again, becoming protected from the ocean's fury. Connecticut's shoreline is entirely within Long Island Sound, an inland arm of the sea more than 100 miles long. Home of the Electric Boat submarine construction facility in Groton, Conn., the Sound has long provided an inland passage for coasters navigating to and from New York City. The sheltered nature of the Sound means that its currents are often gentler, its tides are less extreme, and pollution is more concentrated. Nearly one of every 10 Americans lives within 50 miles of the Sound, and it has borne the brunt of overdevelopment and estuarine loss. Until quite recently, Long Island Sound boasted a productive lobster fishery. But in 1999 the lobster population crashed catastrophically, possibly from the pesticides used to kill mosquitoes carrying the West Nile virus. This is only the latest in a long series of environmental problems. Soundkeeper and other conservation groups are increasingly active, and environmentally friendly legislation has begun to stem Long Island Sound's degradation. Ironically, the recreational boaters for whom clean waters are so important have a noticeable impact on the Sound, for one of the largest pleasure fleets in the nation cruises its summer waters.

Maritime New England obviously encompasses a wide range of ecosystems and communities. Norwalk, Conn., is a far cry culturally (and several days' sail) from Jonesport, Maine. As a result of this physical and cultural variation, place has always mattered a great deal in how New Englanders have used the sea, thought about it, and imagined themselves in relation to it. Before the age of automobiles these variations were accentuated. Long Island Sound oystermen, Nantucket whalemen, Boston steamboat captains, and shipbuilders in Bath, Maine, all spoke a language of the sea, but with different vernaculars. They lived and worked in worlds apart, with different tools, assumptions, rhythms, and skills. Cultural homogeneity is more the norm today, even if some people in Jonesport retain locally based customs and aspirations that vary considerably from those of Norwalkers.

Jonesporters, all 1,500 of them, work on the water or know people who do, and proudly bill their town as home of "The World's Fastest Lobsterboat Races." Norwalk, in the vanguard of the maritime heritage movement, sports the Norwalk Seaport Association and its annual Oyster Festival, as well as the Maritime Aquarium. Yet its 80,000 residents are much less personally involved in making a living on the water than citizens in Jonesport. Over the centuries maritime New England spawned not only hundreds of indigenous small craft—including Friendship sloops, Cape Cod catboats, Piscataqua gundalows, and Swampscott dories—but a host of ways of making a living from the sea that varied with time and place.

THE GENESIS OF A MARITIME CULTURE

In the beginning, there were fish. The apparently limitless timber and innumerable fine harbors were a secondary blessing. Cod lured 17th-century men to New England as surely as gold later lured forty-niners to California. For centuries cod were so abundant that it seemed incomprehensible that they could ever be exhausted. Easy to catch, and easy to preserve in an age that knew no refrigeration, cod became a staple, a commodity, and a way of life. Cod made untold fortunes and innumerable widows, and it shaped regional cuisines in New England, the West Indies, and Iberia. For centuries codfishing was the mainstay of maritime New England. Long after whalers, clipper ships, and night-boat steamers had come and gone from the waterfront, codfishing remained, a changing same. Yet by the 1990s a combination of pinpoint navigational precision, wide-mouthed polyester nets, and politicians' mismanagement had spelled doom for both fish and fishermen. The destruction of the New England fisheries was an ecological disaster and a cultural tragedy of the first magnitude.

The fishery began briskly, but Europeans were by no means the first mariners on the coast. Giovanni da Verrazano commented in 1524 that native people in Narragansett Bay "make their barges from the trunk of a single tree hollowed out in which 14–15 men will go comfortably." Natives routinely traveled to islands 10 or more miles offshore, such as Block Island or Monhegan Island, where they fished or harpooned whales. This clearly required sea sense. English mariners marveled at some native craft for their extraordinarily light construction and versatility. "Their boats," wrote Martin Pring in 1603, "were in proportion like a Wherrie of the River Thames, seventeen foot long and foure foot broad, and made of the Barke of a Birch-tree . . . almost incredible in regard of the largeness and capacitie thereof."

Although they lacked the tools and skills to build plank-on-frame vessels, native fishers appropriated European fishermen's boats almost from the first moment of contact and quickly learned to operate them. In the spring of 1602, long before permanent English settlement in New England, John Brereton and his shipmates "came to an anker" in southern Maine, "where six Indians, in a Baske-shallop with mast and saile, an iron grapple, and a kettle of copper, came boldly aboord us." The last significant marine attack by natives against the English in southern New England occurred in 1634, a few years before the Pequot War (1636–37), but eastern natives in Maine, New Brunswick, and Nova Scotia successfully harassed coasters and fishermen until the 1720s. Long before "cowboys and Indians" came to define the American West, "fishermen and Indians" were the norm on the coast of New England.

The first European fishermen in the region established seasonal outposts on Damariscove Island, Monhegan, and the Isles of Shoals. By 1650, however, newly settled merchants had organized labor for a successful resident fishery. By 1675 there were reportedly 440 boats and at least 1,000 men fishing the coast between Boston and the Kennebec River, producing 6 million pounds of dried salt cod annually. The best fish went to Catholic markets in Europe. The lowest grade, "refuse fish," went to Caribbean sugar islands as food for slaves. Their descendants still savor it. Harry Belafonte invoked Jamaicans' enduring taste for salt cod when he sang "Ackee rice, salt fish are nice" in his platinum hit "Banana Boat," known as "Day-O."

For two centuries New England fishermen jigged for cod with handlines. They split and salted the fish, later air-drying it ashore before export. The drying racks, called fish flakes, occupied a prominent place in every coastal town. Acres of white fish distinguished the landscape of New Castle, N.H., Marblehead, Mass., and Gloucester, just as ripening cotton defined the Mississippi Delta.

Men initially fished in locally built Chebacco boats and pinky schooners, and shipbuilding developed alongside fishing as a premier regional industry. Until the age of iron and steel ships, New England had extraordinary advantages in ship construction. Oak for framing, white pine for spars, and other ship timber was abundant, as were sites with gently sloping beaches and deep water—ideal for wooden ship construction. Shipwrights in Bath, Portsmouth, Boston, Mystic, and many other towns built wooden ships from the mid-1600s to the early 1900s. South Berwick, Maine, for instance, once launched mighty square-riggers that roamed the world. Today it is a tiny town at the head of the Salmon Falls River. Salmon no longer run to the falls, and the river has silted from erosion so that now only outboard motorboats can navigate it. Moreover, a low highway bridge blocks access to the sea. Nothing remains there or in a host of other shipbuilding towns that reveals them as the Silicon Valley of their age. But they were. Inexpensive ships were the backbone of a mighty merchant marine, and New England vessels made shipping a leading sector of the American economy from the colonial era to the 1850s.

The myth of maritime New England thus rests on indisputable foundations. Shipping was king. Along with land sales, customs duties provided the federal government's chief revenue source in the early republic, from 1790 to the 1830s. America's first millionaire, Elias Haskett Derby (1739–99) of Salem, Mass., accrued his fortune in the East Indian spice trade. In many ways, the wooden ships and iron men from that era have every right to grab modern imaginations. They represent technological innovation, first-class entrepreneurship, and persistence in the face of adversity. And maritime work employed more New England men than any other occupation except farming well into the 19th century.

Yankee seamen in the 18th and 19th centuries were also the most cosmopolitan people in America, despite New Englanders' reputations as stiff and unbending descendants of the Puritans. Sailors flew their flags in China, the Indonesian Spice Islands, and throughout the South Pacific. They sailed so regularly to places like the Canadian Maritimes (Nova Scotia, New Brunswick, and Newfoundland) and to the Cape Verde Islands off Africa that many Cape Verdeans and "provincials" (as the Canadians were then called) became New Englanders. Thousands of Yankee mariners redefined "home" against the places they had been and decorated their homes with exotic souvenirs. Merchants and captains, like those who founded Salem's East India Marine Society in 1797 (today, the Peabody Essex Museum), cultivated reputations based on seafaring's mystique, as did ordinary seamen. Voyaging's psychological impact was profound, both for men who went to sea and for women who remained at home. The whaling wives of Nantucket and New Bedford, Mass., whose husbands left for years, coped in a variety of ways. Some developed habits of initiative and self-reliance; others developed a habit for laudanum.

Antiquarians' and preservationists' version of New England's maritime past, however, long misrepresented much of the story. Not only did these advocates suspend attention to their conscious refashioning of history as a commodity, but they ignored essential themes and participants. For instance, nearly one-fifth of the sailors aboard New England cargo ships in the early 19th century were black men. Black hands sheeted home white sails from the beginning of settlement to the 20th century. On the eve of the War of 1812, black New Englanders were seven times as likely to go to sea as white New Englanders (on a per capita basis), because shipping was one of the few occupations open to them. Every black family in the region had friends or kin who followed the sea. And although New England may have become a hotbed of abolitionism during the generation before the Civil War, maritime New England long maintained a marriage of convenience with slavery. Captains and merchants profited handsomely by transporting sugar, tobacco, rice, and cotton produced by slaves. Many old seaports' colonial and Federal mansions preserved today were built from profits earned in this marriage of shipping and slavery.

Late-19th- and early-20th-century maritime preservationists, for the most part, were genteel whites from "leading families" who emphasized financially successful shipowners, dashing captains, and improvements in ship design. Yankee seafaring in the age of sail provided marvelous raw material for refashioning as heritage. Its elemental struggle with nature, its distance from hearth and home, and its possibilities for Olympian profiteering all contributed to a compelling myth carefully pruned of competing narratives. Yet sea life was rampant with inequities and physical brutality. Differences abounded among sailors supposedly "all in the same boat." That metaphor tidily ignored the strains of class, gender, and race that actually defined seafaring.

REFASHIONING MARITIME CULTURE

By the middle of the 19th century ambitious fishermen were tempting fate offshore on Georges Bank. A nursery for fish, its unpredictable nor'easters and shoals made it a graveyard for sailors. And from about 1845 to 1880, New England fishing schooners lacked the stability of earlier—and later—models. Fatalities soared. In 1862, 162 Gloucester fishermen drowned; in 1873, 181 men; in 1879, 249 men. For fishing village families, maritime culture was a culture of grief, characterized by prolonged absences, untimely deaths, loneliness, and poverty.

Most fishermen before 1900 were American-born, although Irishmen swelled their ranks during the 19th century, as did "provincials" from the Canadian Maritime Provinces. Around 1900 Italian fishermen became a presence in the Boston fisheries. Several immigrant groups, each with a long fishing heritage, became established locally throughout the 20th century: Portuguese in New Bedford and Cape Cod's Provincetown, Newfoundlanders in Boston, Italians in Gloucester, and Scandinavians in New Bedford.

Most fishermen, like gamblers, found occasionally heady paydays chronically offset by instability and poverty. And fishermen's situations worsened with time. Eighteenth-century fishermen in Essex County owned some land and livestock. By the mid-19th century, however, fishermen there owned little but their fishing gear. By 1840 only 3 percent of Gloucester fishermen even owned the boats they sailed. Many Yankee fishermen had become proletarians.

During the Colonial Revival, which swept New England from the 1870s to about 1930, artists and writers reinvented fishermen. Many middle-class whites of Anglo-Saxon descent were uncomfortable with American society after the Civil War. Belching smokestacks, clattering factories, and Catholic immigrants besieged their world. If Bridgeport, Conn., Lowell, Mass., and Providence were already lost to this assault (which, of course, middle-class New Englanders had helped to create) life down east promised redemption. "Down east" meant the coast of Maine, which sailors knew was east from Boston, not north, and which, as every sailor also knew, was downwind with the prevailing westerlies. There, along the primeval coast, a race of hardy Anglo-Saxons apparently still followed the sea under sail, earning their bread as had their fathers. During the 1880s Winslow Homer began to produce influential watercolors evoking what "summer people" felt about fishermen. Homer envisioned maritime New England as a heroic environment, emphasizing the masculine pioneering virtues of trial by nature.

Writers and painters in artists' colonies from Rocky Neck, Mass., to Monhegan Island ignored the poverty and tenuousness of fisherfolk's lives and the sordid aspects of deep-sea sail. Harvard historian Samuel Eliot Morison capitalized on this romanticism in 1921 when he published *The Maritime History of Massachusetts.* Morison wistfully ascribed Massachusetts's "moods" to "rugged faith" and to a struggle with "the ocean [which] knows no favorites"; and he claimed that those moods could be "traced in the national character of America." This sentiment bolstered a regional maritime preservation movement during the Great Depression. Connecticut's Marine Historical Association (later renamed Mystic Seaport) was founded in 1929, the Salem (Mass.) Maritime National Historic Site in 1938, and Maine's Kennebec Marine Museum in 1936. They all provided a priceless service by saving vessels and objects from New England's maritime past.

For the most part, however, the inspiration behind those institutions was blind to class strife, race, and environmental degradation. Yet large-scale capitalistic enterprise came to the maritime industries at precisely the time that sentimental artists were redefining the image of Yankee mariners. Fish dealers in Boston, who understood the benefits of vertical integration, formed the New England Fish Exchange in 1898 to control vessels, piers, and marketing, thus "stabilizing" the business. Fishermen saw "stabilization" as price control. To this day fishermen do not earn a wage but rather a share of the catch. And for more than a century they have complained of bribery, pilferage, and price-fixing that defraud them of their hard-won earnings. "Fishing is the rottenest goddam business in the world," is how one union man on the Boston waterfront put it in the 1970s; "everybody's out to screw you." Etching that sentiment next to the scriptural verse on the base of the Gloucester fishermen's memorial might have been blasphemous, but it would have balanced an appreciation of the awesomeness of the sea with a critique of capitalism's excesses. Fishermen lived with both.

New England's coastwise trade boomed between the Civil War and World War I. The era of the Colonial Revival, this was also an era of great economic expansion and inequality known as the Gilded Age. A growing population and industrializing economy demanded more shipping, and every harbor bristled with schooners' masts and steamers' stacks. Federal law had barred foreign competition in the coastwise trade since 1817, so all were American ships operated by American sailors. In the year 1835, for example, 3,879 coasting vessels arrived in Boston; by 1900 the number (including tugs and barges) had risen to 10,436. The queens of this fleet were unquestionably the white passenger steamers that ran down east from Boston to ports in Maine. A similar fleet, dominated by the famous Fall River Line, ran between New York City and ports in Connecticut and Rhode Island. Although the Fall River Line was notable for its regularity, safety, and elegance, the steamboating era was marred by several notorious catastrophes. A famous November storm in 1898 became known as "the *Portland* storm" after the steamer *Portland* sank, taking all 176 passengers and crew to the bottom.

The whaleship Charles W. Morgan *in 1934 during Harry Neyland and Colonel Edward H. R. Greene's operation of it as a museum in South Dartmouth, Mass.*

Jaunty coastal steamers, whose black stacks and belching coal smoke contrasted so sharply with glistening white hulls and superstructures, allowed New Englanders to travel comfortably between Maine and New York, and on to such distant destinations as Philadelphia, Baltimore, and Savannah, Ga. They also had the potential for vast profits in an era whose hallmarks were trusts and tycoons. In 1901 Charles Morse, a native of Bath, combined the Portland Steam Packet Company with several other Boston-based steamboat lines to form the Eastern Steamship Company. Morse was not content to dominate New England shipping: he sought to control coastal shipping from Maine to Texas, and for a time he was referred to as "the Admiral of the Atlantic Coast." Steamboats were big business.

But these same flamboyant years were a dark age for American shipping overall. American shipbuilders never competed successfully in the construction of steam-powered metal ships for international commerce, and the New England shipping industry began a precipitous downward slide after the Civil War. Only the sailing coasters hung on. Big specialized multimasted schooners were built for the coal trade, running from Chesapeake Bay and Delaware Bay to New England ports. Four-masters, five-masters, and six-masters, like those of the famous Palmer fleet, remained a common sight through the 1930s. Carrying energy, they were analogous to the oil tankers frequenting New England ports today. But the future of shipping was not with sail.

Tramp steamers with foreign flags dominated New England seaports' international commerce at this time. During the several decades before World War I, tramps brought raw wool from Australia and England for the textile mills of Massachusetts, and wool became Boston's largest import. Cotton also arrived by ship, as did hides and animal skins for Massachusetts tanneries. Meanwhile, a steady stream of immigrants arrived by sea. During the last decades of the 19th century, 30,000 to 50,000 arrived in Boston each year, with the greatest number—more than 100,000 annually—arriving on the eve of World War I. Many of the region's future citizens got their first glimpse of New England from the waterfront.

Until the late 20th century, life aboard ship (except for passenger vessels) was almost entirely a man's world. Wives of coasting captains, however, sometimes moved aboard ship with their husbands, as did adventurous whaling wives. Dorothea Balano's diary, published in 1979 as *The Log of the Skipper's Wife,* reveals one brilliant, earthy, and independent woman's struggle to cope with a hidebound masculine society. "I can't turn to anyone for understanding, let alone help," she wrote after one run-in with her husband aboard the four-masted schooner *R. W. Hopkins,* "because all the creatures on board are completely and absolutely in his power." The experiences of seafaring women have recently received considerable attention from scholars, as has the study of gender as a fundamental component of seafaring. Such work suggests that there is still much to learn about New England's maritime past, and that our understanding of it has the potential to be refashioned yet again.

CONTEMPORARY MARITIME CULTURE

Coastal shipping companies faced serious problems when they attempted to resume operations after World War II, and they never recovered from the competition with newly empowered truckers. During the second half of the 20th century the interstate highway system's cars and trucks dominated New England as surely as had steamboats and schooners in a previous age. A handful of tugs and coastal tankers are all that remain of a once-vast coastal fleet. International shipping in American vessels, despite a brief rebound after each World War, is virtually moribund. Once-busy harbors are ghostly.

Modern ships from abroad arrive at highly automated terminals like the container port in Charlestown, Mass., or the oil terminal in Searsport, Maine. Port calls are fleeting. Cargo handling is containerized, and no longer tinged with exotic hints, as when off-loaded casks and bales were piled on piers. Understated as modern maritime activity is, it remains central to New England's economy. Yet none of the ships that arrive with bananas in Bridgeport, road salt in Portsmouth, or automobiles in Boston are manned by New Englanders or fly the American flag. American merchant ships carry only a fraction of the United States trade, and most graduates from the state maritime academies in Castine, Maine, and Wareham, Mass., do not find seafaring jobs.

Shipyards are defunct, too. The only large ships still built in New England in 2003 were naval vessels: destroyers at Bath Iron Works and submarines at Electric Boat. Smaller commercial vessels such as tugs and ferries used in American waters (which by federal law must be American built) are still constructed in small numbers at a few yards like Washburn and Dougherty in East Boothbay, Maine. Even yacht building is not nearly as prominent as it once was, although firms like Shannon Yachts in

Bristol, R. I., maintain that tradition. Many of the mass-produced fiberglass boats found in New England marinas today were manufactured elsewhere and delivered by truck. While a few builders like Hinckley Yachts in Southwest Harbor, Maine, successfully shifted from building wooden yachts to producing fiberglass ones, most of New England's eminent wooden yacht construction yards failed during the 20th century.

Recreational boating is nevertheless expanding. The percentage of sailboats continues to decrease, perhaps a reflection of Americans' fast-paced lifestyle. Pearson Yachts in Warren, R. I., long known for building quality sailboats, now builds and sells only a fast, 38-foot power cruiser. Meanwhile, luxury yachts are on the rise, as are easy-to-purchase and easy-to-operate boats like sea kayaks and outboards. Other changes loom. As recently as 40 years ago recreational boating was securely in the hands of enthusiasts who looked to tradition as their guide. They shared with commercial seafarers the idea, and some of the skills, of "the lore of the sea." Humility and time-honored practice were at the heart of good seamanship. Boaters today are not nearly as enamored of tradition. Raised with global positioning navigation systems and a sense of entitlement from horsepower to spare, most contemporary boaters do not see themselves as part of an ongoing maritime tradition.

One maritime tradition that ended abruptly in New England in 1983 was the America's Cup races that had been held off Newport, R.I., for more than half a century. The America's Cup, first awarded in 1851, is the oldest trophy in international sporting and is considered by sailors to be the holy grail of sailboat racing. Named for the rakish schooner yacht *America,* which sailed across the Atlantic and beat 15 of Britain's finest racers in 1851, the race and its ornate silver cup have inspired a century and a half of intense competition and technological refinement.

Perhaps no single family has played a more important role in the America's Cup than the Herreshoffs from Bristol. Nathanael Greene Herreshoff, the "Wizard of Bristol," built several Cup defenders, including *Reliance,* a monstrous sloop that carried 16,160 square feet of sail, and *Resolute,* which defeated Sir Thomas Lipton's *Shamrock IV* in 1914. During the 1930s, 1940s, and early 1950s, J-boats like *Endeavor* competed for the Cup. Huge and expensive, the J-class was replaced in 1958 with 12-meter yachts, whose teams nevertheless spend tens of millions of dollars either to defend or to challenge for the Cup. The New York Yacht Club successfully defended the Cup 24 times over a span of 132 years, much of that time on racecourses off Newport. But in 1983 the unthinkable happened: an Australian challenger, *Australia II,* defeated the American defender, *Liberty.* Since then the America's Cup has been held by an Australian syndicate, by a New Zealand syndicate, by the San Diego Yacht Club, and most recently by the Swiss syndicate that campaigned *Alinghi* to victory in 2003. For New Englanders, who had come to associate its defense with the Newport yachting scene, the change of venue meant the end of a long tradition.

Other changes have been even more catastrophic for the coast of New England. After factory trawlers from the Soviet Union, the United Kingdom, and elsewhere had precipitously overfished New England waters during the 1960s and 1970s, Congress passed the Magnuson Act in 1976. Guaranteeing Americans sovereignty up to

200 miles offshore, it drove away foreign fishing vessels. Then, in a classic case of setting the fox to guard the henhouse, the federal government allowed the fishing industry to regulate harvests of cod, haddock, scallops, yellowtail flounder, and other valuable species. The American fleet increased exponentially—and the end came quickly. In 1993, after almost two decades of colossal mismanagement, the New England Regional Fishery Management Council was forced to close most of Georges Bank to commercial fishing. Later, sections of the Gulf of Maine were closed. By the mid-1990s New England, once synonymous with America's best fishing, was the poster child for its most ineffective fisheries management. A 500-year run was over on what should have been an eternally renewable resource. An ecosystem, an economy, and a way of life were in tatters.

The mythical image of the fisherman, however, appears more resilient. During the 1990s, as New England fishing staggered on the verge of collapse and as fishermen were scandalously discarding tons of "by-catch" (less valuable species), AT&T, Rite Aid, and the makers of TheraFlu cough suppressant all ran television advertising that featured fishermen as heroic, vigorous, and dependable—the sort of people one could trust when deciding which products to purchase. In some ways, Madison Avenue's image of fishermen had become more valuable than fish.

Maritime New England is not all history. Despite the litany of decline, shipbuilders, ship operators, and fishermen continue to innovate, restricted as they are to niche markets. Hodgson Brothers in East Boothbay, a town with centuries of shipbuilding history, built several of the world's largest and most luxurious WEST SYSTEM (wood epoxy saturation technique) yachts during the late 1990s. They have orders for more. The Mashantucket Pequot reservation in Connecticut, best known for Foxwoods Casino, built a high-speed passenger catamaran in the 1990s to carry gamblers from New York City to Foxwoods, a route formerly popularized by

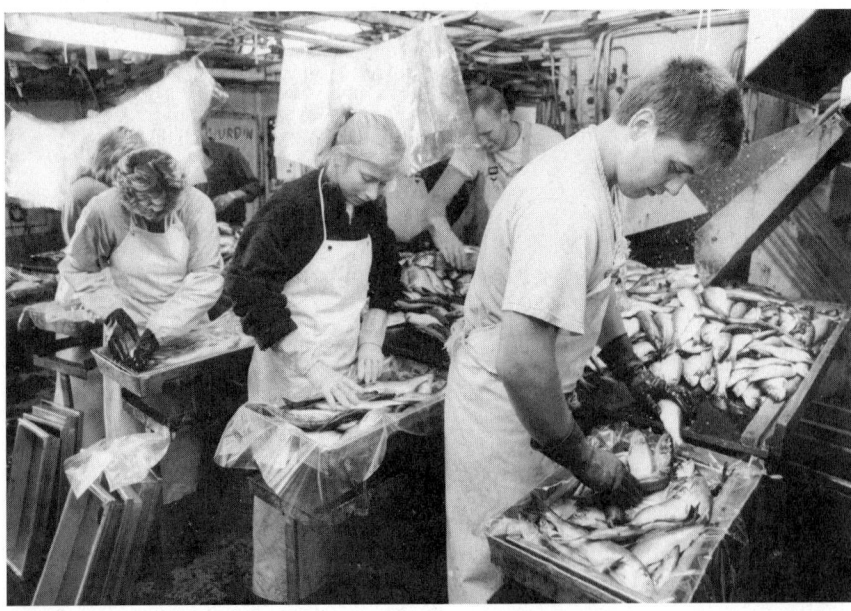

Factory workers putting fish away, 1977

Fall River Line steamboats. Commercial fishermen, meanwhile, targeted "under-utilized" species in the 1990s, pioneering sea urchin and slime eel fisheries for Asian markets.

Traditional and modern maritime skills are alive. Tall ship sailors today have genuine skills, even though they sail on replica vessels. Expert wooden boatbuilders and sailmakers still ply their craft, as attested by the classified advertising in every issue of *WoodenBoat* magazine, published in Brooklin, Maine. These workers are not curiosities or recluses from modernity but craftspeople making a living in New England's contemporary economy. The fishery as a whole may be dying, but every fisher who unties his or her boat confronts the sea's challenge, even though modern technology has reduced some of the risk. People today could do much worse than look for role models among long-gone and present-day mariners, even as they cultivate awareness of how certain myths regarding maritime New England were constructed.

THE PAST, PRESENT, AND FUTURE OF MARITIME NEW ENGLAND

New Bedford combines the past, present, and future of maritime New England as well as any place. It was once the nation's preeminent whaling port, and later one of the top three fishing ports. New Bedford's waterfront is not nearly as busy today. Even the Seafarers International Union, the largest North American union representing unlicensed American mariners, moved its only union hall in New England from a tiny storefront in New Bedford to Boston in 2004. Nevertheless, the Waterfront Historic Area League, whose acronym is WHALE, had a much larger presence than the SIU. Today in New Bedford the sale of associations with whaling overshadows possibilities for making a living aboard ship. Heritage tourism prevails.

New Bedford is distinct in other ways. Whaleships brought numerous Cape Verdeans to the region, and "ownership" of the maritime past is shared between descendants of old-time white Yankees, whose preservationist ancestors founded the New Bedford Whaling Museum, and black Americans, many of whom are of Cape Verdean descent. In 1915 city fathers commissioned a bronze statue of a whaleman to ornament City Hall. Bela Pratt, the sculptor, asked for introductions to harpooners who might model for him. The city was full of men who had darted whales, but most were of African descent. Pratt rejected all of them, wanting, he said, an "Ahab type." Pratt got his man, and the city got its statue, which still stands. That racially selective vision of the maritime past endured until 1987, when advocates of a multicultural approach to public history demanded an alternative monument. A statue of Lewis Temple, the 19th-century African American shipsmith from New Bedford whose Temple toggle-iron harpoon revolutionized hand whaling, now stands in bronze next to Pratt's harpooner.

No port in New England has done more to promote its maritime heritage than New Bedford. The Whaling Museum supports modern scholarship and encourages accessibility to its fabulous collections. New Bedford's historic tall ship is the *Ernestina,* ex-*Effie M. Morrissey,* whose unique history connects with many constituencies. Built at Essex, Mass., in 1894, *Ernestina* is the oldest remaining Grand Banks fishing schooner. It also carried freight in Newfoundland, explored the Arctic for the Museum of Natural History, and, as a Cape Verdean packet, was the last sailing ship to bring immigrants to America. Truly an anachronism, the ship made its last transatlantic voyage under sail (without an engine) carrying immigrants in 1964. Now owned by the Commonwealth of Massachusetts, *Ernestina* is a Sailing School Vessel actively operated to expose students to traditional seamanship and to the multicultural nature of New England's shipping. Long may it sail!

In ways now unimaginable, ships and harbors once dominated virtually every coastal New England town's economy, imagination, and sense of place. Robert Salmon's bold oil painting *Boston Harbor from Castle Island* (1839) and Fitz Hugh Lane's luminous *Gloucester Harbor* (1848) convey something of that lost world.

Sea-gazing Yankees today use the coasts more for leisure than work, and they regard coastal environments with an unprecedented ethic of conservation. As the population grows, however, the volume of cargo moving through New England's ports will increase, including the oil that threatens the environment with every shipwreck. Meanwhile, the number of workers per capita directly involved in marine transportation will decline because of automation. Future New Englanders may see a rejuvenated fishery, in which habitat-damaging otter trawls have been outlawed and in which individual fishers (or companies) manage specific fishery zones. This would end the free-for-all approach to seafood resources that characterized fishing for too long with disastrous results.

For centuries the sea symbolized timelessness and a threat to the humans who ventured there. Today the tables are turned. The sea appears fragile and vulnerable in the face of human arrogance. It is still a frontier for science, profit, and individual development, but it is also a trust calling for stewardship. New Englanders were once at the forefront of fishing, shipping, shipbuilding, and maritime preservation. Today the region's oceanographers, artists, activists, and mariners are leading the crusade to save our seas.

Robert G. Albion, William A. Baker, and Benjamin W. Labaree, *New England and the Sea* (1972); Tom Andersen, *This Fine Piece of Water: An Environmental History of Long Island Sound* (2002); James W. Balano, ed., *The Log of the Skipper's Wife* (1979); Horace P. Beck, *The American Indian as a Sea Fighter in Colonial Times* (1959); David Boeri and James Gibson, *"Tell It Good-Bye, Kiddo": The Decline of the New England Offshore Fishery* (1976); W. Jeffrey Bolster, *Black Jacks: African American Seamen in the Age of Sail* (1997); W. H. Bunting, *Portrait of a Port: Boston, 1852–1914* (1971); Howard I. Chapelle, *The American Fishing Schooners, 1825–1935* (1973); Philip W. Conkling, *Islands in Time: A Natural and Cultural History of the Islands of the Gulf of Maine* (1999); Margaret S. Creighton, *Rites and Passages: The Experience of American Whaling, 1830–1870* (1995); Carl C. Cutler, *Greyhounds of the Sea: The Story of the American Clipper Ship* (1930); Lance E. Davis, Robert E. Gallman, and Karin Gleiter, *In Pursuit of Leviathan: Technology, Institutions, Productivity, and Profits in American Whaling, 1816–1906* (1997); David Dobbs, *The Great Gulf: Fishermen, Scientists, and the Struggle to Revive the World's Greatest Fishery* (2000); Roger F. Duncan, *Coastal Maine* (1992); Andrew W. German, *Down on T Wharf: The Boston Fisheries as Seen through the Photographs of Henry D. Fisher* (1982); Federal Writers' Project, *Boston Looks Seaward: The Story of the Port, 1630–1940* (1941); Lloyd Goodrich, *Homer and the Sea* (1964); Government Printing Office, *The U.S. Waterway System Facts* (1995); Linda Greenlaw, *The Hungry Ocean: A Swordboat Captain's Journey* (1999); Alfred T. Hill, *Voyages* (1977); John G. B. Hutchins, *The American Maritime Industries and Public Policy* (1941); Sebastian Junger, *The Perfect Storm: A True Story of Men against the Sea* (1997); Edward

Chase Kirkland, *Men, Cities and Transportation: A Study in New England History, 1820–1900*, 2 vols. (1948); Mark Kurlansky, *Cod: A Biography of the Fish That Changed the World* (1997); John F. Leavitt, *Wake of the Coasters* (1970); Michael Jay Mjelde, *Glory of the Seas* (1970); Samuel Eliot Morison, *The Maritime History of Massachusetts, 1783–1860* (1921); Lisa Norling, *Captain Ahab Had a Wife: New England Women and the Whalefishery, 1720–1870* (2000); Wayne M. O'Leary, *Maine Sea Fisheries: The Rise and Fall of a Native Industry, 1830–1890* (1996); Bruce Robertson, "Perils of the Sea," in *Picturing Old New England: Image and Memory*, ed. William H. Truettner and Roger B. Stein (1999); Carl Safina, *Song for the Blue Ocean* (1997); Edward W. Smith, Jr., *Workaday Schooners: The Edward W. Smith Photographs* (1975); Charles Tyng, *Before the Wind: The Memoir of an American Sea Captain, 1808–1833* (1999); Daniel Vickers, *Farmers and Fishermen: Two Centuries of Work in Essex County, Massachusetts, 1630–1850* (1994); John Wilmerding, *A History of American Marine Painting* (1968).

W. Jeffrey Bolster

Atlantic Slave Trade

Rhode Island's "Guinea trade" in African slaves dominated New England's slave trading during most of the 18th century. In relation to that of Britain, France, or Portugal, Rhode Island's trade in slaves was small, both in terms of the number of voyages and the size of slave ships. From 1725 to 1808, when the trade was abolished, Rhode Island merchants had bought an estimated 106,000 slaves, while traders in Great Britain, for example, had purchased approximately 2.5 million slaves. The smaller size of Rhode Island's ships made both buying and selling slaves easier on the open market (while making the "middle passage" even more miserable for the slaves than it was on European ships), and the high demand for New England rum made for a successful slave-trading operation for much of the 18th century.

Established in the first decades of the 18th century, the Rhode Island slave trade immediately conformed to a classic triangle of trade. Ships left New England bound for West Africa to trade cargoes of rum for slaves, whom they traded in the Caribbean for molasses, which was then delivered to Newport and Bristol and distilled into rum. The difficulties of farming along the coast of southeastern New England made for few resources to trade, but molasses from the Caribbean trade, distilled into rum, gave Rhode Island merchants a valuable commodity. The triangle trade was the most lucrative option for Rhode Island merchants. "Viewed from this perspective," writes historian Jay Coughtry, "the slave trade was simply the most profitable method of selling rum, Rhode Island's most important export." It has been estimated that by 1750, 90 distilleries were in operation in Massachusetts and Rhode Island. Whereas European ships frequently carried cargoes of cloth, guns, and iron to trade for slaves, Rhode Island's "rummen" displaced French brandy and held a monopoly on spirits in the West African trade.

Even as they traded in slaves and alcohol, New Englanders who pursued this trade spread to Africa and the Caribbean the reputation of the taciturn and sober Yankee. European slave traders saw New England slaveship captains as "an industrious honest people, who despise the gaudy toys of the foolish for things more substantial and necessary for the life of man."

Most slaves in New England labored as domestic help, and the historian Joanne Pope Melish argues that such labor allowed white males to leave home and farm duties and enter mercantile and professional occupations, contributing to the transition from a household-based living to a market economy. Of these slaves, a few prospered under tremendous handicaps. John Quamino, who was brought to Rhode Island from the Gold Coast in 1754, became a prominent member of the colony's black community and purchased his freedom in 1774 with lottery winnings. To buy his wife out of slavery, Quamino shipped on a privateer during the American Revolution. He was killed in its first battle.

Newport had been the leader in American slave trading during the first half of the 1700s, but the British occupation during the Revolutionary War ruined many of its merchants, and the center of slave trading moved to Bristol, where it flourished for the rest of the century. Rhode Island had turned toward the slave trade after 1725 as the colony moved away from agriculture. The illegal trade that developed once the slave trade was abolished in 1808 formed in centers far south of Bristol. By then, Rhode Island's economy had begun to turn back to the land, toward the factory, fitfully exchanging the profits of manufacturing for those of trade in slaves.

Jay Coughtry, *The Notorious Triangle: Rhode Island and the African Slave Trade, 1700–1807* (1981); Philip Curtin, *The Atlantic Slave Trade: A Census* (1969); Joanne Pope Melish, *Disowning Slavery* (1998); James Pope-Hennessy, *Sins of the Fathers: A Study of the Atlantic Slave Traders, 1441–1807* (1968).

Louis Mazzari

Bowditch, Nathaniel

(1773–1838) Mathematician, astronomer, mariner. Nathaniel Bowditch belonged to the generation of American Enlightenment thinkers who established the scientific and philosophical reputation of the new republic as, led by homegrown New England inventors and entrepreneurs, the United States entered the Industrial Revolution.

Born to a coaster captain and his wife in a rented house in Salem, Mass., Bowditch moved to nearby Danvers after his father's schooner foundered in the Caribbean. In a Danvers dame school he received his first formal instruction in reading, writing, and possibly arithmetic. In 1779 the family returned to Salem, and his father became a cooper. There Nathaniel entered Master Watson's school, where he confounded the teacher by solving a problem put before him for the purpose of proving that he was too young to study math. Bowditch left his studies in 1783 to help in the cooperage, his father having developed a strong affection for another famous product of New England, rum. While working for his father, Bowditch studied bookkeeping and was then apprenticed in 1785 to a succession of ship chandlers. Although his apprenticeships ended with his majority in 1794, Bowditch spent these years educating himself at the local philosophical library, which thanks to a public-minded Yankee privateer contained the *Philosophical Transactions* of the Royal Society of

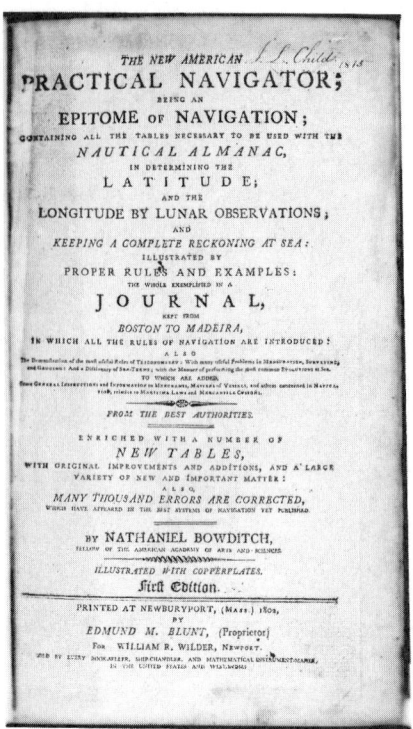

Title page, Nathaniel Bowditch, The New American Practical Navigator *(1802)*

London, one of Europe's oldest scientific organizations. Here Bowditch taught himself enough Latin to read Sir Isaac Newton's *Principia*, in which he found an error. He also acquired reading knowledge of Greek, French, Spanish, Portuguese, and German and began to read European scientific literature. Using knowledge thus gleaned, he compiled in 1788 an almanac for the year 1790 and created various scientific instruments for his own amusement. In 1794, at age 21, he began working as an assistant surveyor, taking over the business three years later.

Meanwhile, Bowditch had begun the voyages that would establish his fame. Five times between 1795 and 1803 he sailed to Europe and the West Indies—first as clerk, then as supercargo, and finally as master and supercargo. His interest in navigation derived from his mathematical work rather than vice versa, and on his fifth voyage he apparently left most navigation to his mate. In 1799 he began editing John Hamilton Moore's popular *New Practical Navigator* (1794), in which he eventually found more than 8,000 errors. That same year he was elected to the American Academy of Arts and Sciences in recognition of his mathematical work. By 1802 he had published his own *New American Practical Navigator*, which was endorsed by the East India Marine Society of Salem. That August, Harvard College recognized his work by giving him an honorary master's degree. Later he became a

Harvard overseer and fellow of the Harvard Corporation. In 1800 Bowditch acquired a copy of Pierre Laplace's *Mécanique céleste* and began an annotated translation of the four volumes then extant, a project that occupied him almost until his death. His added notes doubled the size of the original work.

Returning from his fifth voyage on Christmas Day 1803, Bowditch sailed his ship into fogbound Salem Harbor at night. This feat earned him a place among the heroes of the early republic. Previously known to philosophers, he now was famous among mariners; having studied under him made a sailor's career.

Bowditch spent the following years publishing aids to navigation. He surveyed the harbors of Salem, Beverly, and Manchester, Mass., from 1804 to 1806 and then brought out sailing directions for entering those harbors and Marblehead. A frequent contributor to the *Memoirs of the American Academy of Arts and Sciences,* he also published papers on astronomy and methods of measuring.

Soon after coming ashore, he became president of the Essex Fire and Marine Insurance Company. In 1823 he accepted positions as actuary of the Massachusetts Hospital Life Insurance Company and president of the Commercial Insurance Company in Boston, where he moved in 1826. Although a man of the Enlightenment, he was also a man of his time. He refused mortgage applications from women on the grounds that he could never foreclose on them. He also refused to possess the works of Lord Byron because of their immorality. Physically, he was also a man of his time: Bowditch suffered from tuberculosis.

Bowditch died in 1838 at home in Boston. By then his *New American Practical Navigator* had become so universally popular that on news of his death some European vessels lowered their flags along with the Americans. His *Navigator* remains the vade mecum of mariners and is still used in instruction at the U.S. Naval Academy and the U.S. Coast Guard Academy.

Harold Bowditch, *Nathaniel Bowditch* (1945); Nathaniel I. Bowditch, *Memoir of Nathaniel Bowditch,* 3d ed. (1884).

William B. Leavenworth

Cape Cod Canal

The Cape Cod Canal is one of New England's best-known landmarks thanks to both its distinctive design and its status as the gateway to Cape Cod. As early as 1623, Governor William Bradford of Plymouth Colony and Myles Standish, his military leader, proposed that a watercourse be dug across the upper Cape from Cape Cod Bay to Buzzards Bay. A succession of committees studied the idea for almost 300 years.

Many groups were granted charters for construction, but no canal materialized until the 20th century.

During the last decade of the 19th century about 30,000 vessels, ranging in size from small fishing boats to battleships, rounded Cape Cod. Fog, shallow water, riptides, swift currents, and ice made the passage particularly hazardous. In fact, between 1875 and 1914 some 750 vessels were wrecked and more than 150 lives and countless dollars lost in the ocean graveyard off Cape Cod. At the turn of the 20th century one magazine writer described the area as "the most dangerous coast in winter to be found on the map of the United States."

The canal remained for decades only an idea because its reason for being was not to make money but to save lives. Washington began to show interest in the project in 1881, however, when military officials began to believe that a canal would be useful in time of war. Government money funded a number of starts, all of which were subsequently abandoned. A serious effort began in March 1884, and about 7,000 feet were dug before the project languished again. In 1909 construction recommenced under the auspices of the Boston, Cape Cod and New York Canal Company, with workers this time carving channels from the eastern and western ends of the isthmus. By 1910–11 they had completed a railroad bridge and two highway bridges over the canal site. The presence of many large glacial boulders, which had to be broken up with dynamite, slowed their progress, however. Finally, with great fanfare, the Cape Cod Canal opened to one-way traffic in a 15-foot-deep channel on July 29, 1914.

It was evident even on opening day that the canal needed substantial improvement. The depth of the channel was soon augmented to 25 feet, after which traffic increased steadily. The U.S. government took over canal operations in 1918, after a German U-boat sank a coal barge in nearby waters. In 1928 the canal was entrusted to the U.S. Army Corps of Engineers, who have remained in charge to this day.

The 1930s brought more improvements. The highway and railroad bridges over the canal were replaced. The design of the new railroad bridge reflected a prevailing belief among bridge builders at the time that one could improve on the stark ugliness of naked beams. Thus the new design featured two towers capped by steel abstractions meant to represent lighthouses. The bridge, known as a vertical-lift type, was completed in 1935. At that time the channel was widened to 500 feet, thus becoming the world's widest artificial waterway; it was also further deepened to 32 feet, which allowed two-way traffic. Once the approaches were dredged, the total waterway attained its present length of 17.5 miles.

All of this work was completed just as World War II broke out. By the peak war year of 1944 almost 19 million tons of cargo were passing through Cape Cod Canal. Fifty years later slightly more than 6,000 vessels, two-thirds of them tugs and barges, were using the canal to carry almost 14 million tons of cargo through the canal annually, proof of the waterway's continuing commercial value in peacetime. Since the 2001 terrorist attacks information on canal traffic has been classified.

For the thousands of yearly visitors to the Cape, the canal is more than a commercial waterway. Its bridges mean that one has arrived. The twin towers of each highway bridge can be seen long before the canal comes into view, and children vie to be the one who spots them first. Few drivers look forward to the legendary traffic jams leading to the bridges with the same sense of anticipation, however.

At summer's start the canal serves as both the real and the symbolic divide between the workaday world and Cape days by the sea, where mornings slip into lunch, beach clothes are the norm, and nights are for relaxing. At summer's end the bridges and canal signal time's rapid passage and something that is coming to a close, as carloads of summer folk toss pennies in the water below for good luck.

Robert H. Farson, *The Cape Cod Canal* (1977); U.S. Army Corps of Engineers, *Waterborne Commerce of the United States,* pt. 1: *Waterways and Harbors: Atlantic Coast, 1994* (1995).

Thomas R. Lewis

Charles W. Morgan

The most tangible piece of New England's whaling heritage is preserved in Mystic, Conn. Nearly 500,000 visitors each year walk the decks of the *Charles W. Morgan,* the last surviving American whaleship. Visitors to the old vessel contemplate the exploitation of human beings and other living creatures, the challenge and promise of cultural diversity, the value of preserving our natural resources, and the shared human experience at sea and ashore that the *Charles W. Morgan* evokes.

Though an icon from New England's maritime past, the *Morgan* is very much alive in the present. Whaling during the 19th century was a distinctly Yankee venture, and whaleships from Yankee ports sought their prey on all the oceans of the world. At the height of the industry's success in 1846, there were 737 American whaling vessels, only two of which did not hail from southern New England or the adjacent waters of Long Island Sound. Whaling under sail was almost exclusively a New England industry, for the fleets of foreign nations were paltry by comparison.

One of the many images mythologized in New England's popular culture is that of the sturdy whaleman. For many Americans in the mid-20th century, a Gregory Peck–like Ahab became the model of a Yankee skipper. Whaling itself is also closely linked to the character of place often ascribed to New England. As brutal and exploitative as the whaling industry may have been, whalemen from ports like New Bedford and Nantucket, Mass.—and their enterprising wives—are still admired for tenacity and self-reliance.

Visitors to Mystic Seaport may view the quarters that the captain's wife and children inhabited, compare those accommodations to the common sailor's forecastle, and clamber down into the hold, where thousands of barrels of oil were stowed over the years. Schoolchildren and adults alike may grasp the ship's wheel and help hoist a sail. They come face to face with whaleboats, tryworks, harpoons, and barrels, all implements from an era in which whales were flensed and processed for their oil and baleen aboard floating factories like the *Morgan*.

The *Morgan* was built in 1841 in New Bedford, whaling capital of the world (and the *Morgan's* homeport for most of its active career). Generations of expertise had gone into the vessel's design and construction. It worked the seas for 80 years, until 1921. The ship's career ended only a few short years before traditional whaling was abandoned altogether. For thousands of whalemen it had been at once workplace, home, jail, and ticket to adventure. For hundreds of investors it had been a profitable capital asset.

The whaling industry always recruited crews from varied racial and ethnic groups. American Indians and African Americans worked shoulder to shoulder with white Yankees and men from abroad. In many cases foreign workers arrived in southern New England aboard whaleships, having joined the crews in their native land. On reaching Massachusetts, Connecticut, and Rhode Island, these newcomers created communities alongside those of the established residents. The diversity of New England's populace was enriched throughout the 19th century as Azorean and Cape Verdean whalemen, and eventually their families, arrived in ports all along the region's southern coast. The *Charles W. Morgan* is material evidence of how a preeminent New England industry used (and abused) a very mixed workforce and changed the ethnic makeup of New England forever.

Initially, there was nothing particularly unusual about the ship: the *Charles W. Morgan* was a quintessential Yankee whaler built as the industry approached its zenith. What is unique about the vessel, however, is its second career, whose length will soon exceed its first. The *Morgan's* second lease on life began in South Dartmouth, Mass., in 1925, when New Bedford artist Harry Neyland and Colonel Edward H. R. Greene, a wealthy whaling heir, first turned the old whaler into a museum ship. They wished to celebrate New England's maritime heritage, then seen as slipping away in the face of industrialization and urbanization. For men like Neyland and Greene, and many of their contemporaries, the Yankee character consisted of such admirable elements as courage, fortitude, and self-reliance, all represented by sailing whaleships. Traits such as these were understood as having helped the Pilgrims make a home for themselves in a forbidding wilderness, bolstering the patriots of 1776, and sustaining Yankee farming and mill families thereafter. At the beginning of the *Morgan's* life as a museum, those aspects of whaling received more emphasis in the ship's interpretation than did the ecological, multicultural, and exploitative aspects of whaling.

Over time the representation of New England has evolved. Changing perceptions of the region and of America's place in a rapidly changing world have been mirrored in the role played by the old whaleship as a tourist attraction and educational resource.

The *Morgan* was moved to Mystic Seaport in November 1941. During the 1950s and 1960s Mystic Seaport expanded rapidly, as hundreds of thousands of visitors each year sought out the ship and the village museum that had grown around it. At the height of the Cold War era, schoolchildren were shown a film entitled *Origins of Freedom*. Within the cabins and forecastle of the *Morgan,* the film said, could be found one of the seedbeds of American independence, for it was on Yankee-built and Yankee-run ships like it that our forebears discovered the meaning of freedom. Built to withstand the sea, capture whales, and make a profit, the *Morgan,* like many other patriotic icons during those uncertain years, mirrored the politics of the day.

By the late 1960s the old whaler was in need of extensive restoration. The *Morgan* had been embedded in gravel and sand since its arrival in Mystic. In 1941 its long-term survival had already been in question. Wooden ships need to float to breathe. In 1970 the museum devised a plan to ensure the vessel's future, a plan that changed the character of the old whaler. To meet the needs of the *Charles W. Morgan* and the other ships in its fleet, Mystic Seaport built its own preservation shipyard. This yard, the only one of its kind in the world today, established Mystic Seaport as a world leader in maritime historic preservation. In the decades since the *Morgan's* restoration in the new shipyard, scores of other museums have sought out Mystic Seaport for guidance concerning historic preservation, interpretation, and programming. Designated a National Historic Landmark in 1977, the old whaleship has served as the catalyst for maritime preservation efforts both at home and abroad.

Richard Ellis, *Men and Whales* (1991); John F. Leavitt, *The Charles W. Morgan* (1973).

Glenn Gordinier

Clamming and Oystering Since prehistoric times people around the world have enjoyed the gastronomic delights of oysters and clams. In New England alone, for a century or more clamming and oystering have been a multimillion dollar industry. These tasty, highly nutritious shellfish possess qualities—perhaps exaggerated—expressed by the catch phrase "Eat clams, live longer; eat oysters, love longer." Clams themselves can live between 25 and 30 years in the sandy or muddy areas between high- and low-water marks and in shallow waters beyond, either on or, more usually, several inches below the mud or sand; oysters, which live on the surface of the bottom, have a life expectancy of up to 46 years. Under ideal conditions, such as in a hatchery, oysters and clams during their spawning periods can produce larvae offspring numbering in the millions.

A relatively small number of oyster species exist worldwide, though only one species is commercially harvested in New England, the *Crassostrea virginica,* or Atlantic oyster. There are about 12,000 clam species known around the world, although only four grow and are consumed in New England. These are commonly called the hard clam (quahog), soft clam (steamer), surf clam, and razor clam; the razor is not generally harvested in New England while the surf clam is more popular in New York and the South.

Native Americans used hard clams for food and bartering. During the colonial period the purple area on the inside shell of the hard clam was fashioned into beads called wampum, or "Indian money." From this use scientists gave the hard clam the Latin name *mercenaria* ("money," in rather free translation). Other, more descriptive words for the hard clam refer to its size. From largest to the smallest they are the quahog or chowder clam ($3^3/_4$ in. or larger), the cherrystone ($2^3/_8$ in. to 3 in.), the topneck ($2^2/_3$ in.), and the little neck ($1^7/_8$ in. to 2 in.). The last three are usually eaten raw on the half shell.

Although oysters and clams today can be eaten fried, steamed, or incorporated into stews and chowders, or gussied up with toppings to make clams casino and oysters Rockefeller, one of the most popular ways to eat them is still the way the Native Americans probably ate them—raw. Oysters and clams "on the half shell" require nothing more than a knife (or rock) to prepare, although many people add cocktail sauce, whose basic ingredients are ketchup, horseradish, and lemon juice.

The history of the oyster and clam fisheries follows a similar path in each of the coastal New England states, although in each state the industries retained distinct characteristics. The Indians and early settlers considered clams and oysters a limitless bounty; in some communities oysters and other seafood were a staple. Local inhabitants simply had to wade out into the shallows and pick up the clams and oysters as easily as they might pick wildflowers or berries in the fields.

As the coastal and inland populations increased, so did the demand for these shellfish. At this point watermen began to specialize in harvesting and selling clams and oysters to those near the shore and farther inland. By the mid-1700s it had become apparent that the oyster and clam beds were nearing extinction, and state and local authorities passed laws and restrictions on the harvest of the shellfish.

Many of these early shellfish laws remain essentially the same today with variations to fit local conditions. Most common are the closed season, daily catch limits, and town residence restrictions. The closed season law prohibits oystering, and in some places clamming, during the warm spawning months. From this law came the dictum that oysters should not be eaten in a month with the letter *r* in it. But even these and other laws were inadequate to maintain a good supply of shellfish, and shellfishermen began importing oysters and even clams. Oystermen in the 19th century imported oysters from Virginia to New Haven, Conn., and Wellfleet, Mass. But it was shellfish farming, cultivation, and, in the 20th century, hatcheries in which seed oysters and clams were reared for transplantation to their natural habitat that saved the industry.

Until the early 20th century, shellfish laws and regulations were imposed to maintain a supply of shellfish to meet the demand—to protect the oyster and clam from the consumer. Little was done to protect the consumer from the shellfish. Outbreaks of typhoid fever and gastrointestinal disorders brought on by eating bad shellfish appeared at Wesleyan University in 1894, in Atlantic City, N.J., in 1902, and elsewhere in 1924 and 1925. These outbreaks led to efforts by federal, state, and local authorities, scientists, and the fishermen themselves to find a way to make shellfish safer.

Practically every facet of shellfish production, from the beds to the consumer, is now controlled by federal, state, and local laws.

The National Shellfish Sanitation Program (NSSP) was established in 1925 to ensure that shellfish harvested in or imported to the United States were safe for human consumption. The NSSP is now administered by the Food and Drug Administration, which annually evaluates the states' shellfish programs to make sure they comply with the NSSP Model Ordinance. For example, all shellfish waters are frequently tested for purity. In fact, the federal regulations require higher purity standards of harvesting waters for oysters and clams for human consumption than are the standard for swimming areas.

Clams and oysters can be found in suitable ground near all the New England coastal states, but they are not equally viable commercially in these states. Maine had high oyster populations before and during the colonial period at Damariscotta, for instance, where the famous oyster-shell midden left by the Indians enabled archaeologists to explore the living habits of these early inhabitants. But there is little commercial harvesting of oysters in Maine today. The state now specializes in the mussel and soft-shell fisheries. Maine is ranked first in the nation in marine aquaculture production, which includes haddock, halibut, cod, salmon, scallops, mussels, clams, and oysters, but the last two represent a small percentage of the total.

New Hampshire's short (about 18 miles long) coastline is not conducive to a major commercial clam or oyster industry, although such fisheries did exist in the 1800s. Still, residents in Portsmouth and elsewhere can obtain clam and oyster licenses that allow them to harvest a designated amount of these shellfish in their own waters for their own use as well as to sell them to local restaurants.

Massachusetts, particularly Cape Cod, was known as a producer of oysters in the early 1900s and even before. During the decades since then, oystering has had its ups and downs, and today the fishery is not what it was in its heyday. Nevertheless, oysters are still harvested in Wellfleet and Barnstable. Quahogs are now the principal shellfish crop of Massachusetts, and Chatham and Wellfleet are the largest producers. Quahogs are also harvested in Martha's Vineyard, Nantucket Sound, and Buzzards Bay. Many of these quahogs come from hatchery seed. Several of the Massachusetts coastline towns north of Cape Cod produce soft-shell clams rather than quahogs. Recreational and commercial clammers in Ipswich, among other towns, harvest soft-shell clams for family use or sell them locally. The only soft-shell company in Ipswich sells its catch to a wider market. The sea or surf clam fishery was viable up to the 1990s, but currently these clams are not being harvested.

For 100 years the oyster was king in Rhode Island. Huge oyster companies with their big steamers and gasoline-powered boats dominated the industry. The peak year of Rhode Island's oyster production was 1910; after that set failures, hurricanes, and other factors put the industry into a dramatic decline from which it never recovered. (Oyster populations followed a similar decline in Massachusetts and Connecticut.) The oyster industry in Rhode Island picked up a little around 2000, but it is essentially small, as is the soft-shell clamming industry. Today the only significant commercial shell fishery in Rhode Island is hard-shell or quahog clamming. The clammers are independent fishers who work on the "free bottom" throughout Narragansett Bay. No companies are involved in the fishery for, with the exception of a few leases for aquaculture, there is no leasing of clam beds in the state. There is also a certain amount of surf clamming near the mouth of the Narragansett Bay.

Connecticut has been for more than 100 years the foremost oyster producer in New England. According to the National Marine Fisheries Service, Connecticut has ranked first, second, or third in the United States from about 1988 to 1996 as the producer of the most oysters; it is always ranked first for the most valuable oysters measured in dollar value per bushel. The oyster business, however, has suffered crop failures in the last few years due mostly to the oyster diseases MSX and Dermo. Most of the shellfish companies have started to increase their clamming fisheries, previously only a supplement to their oyster business. Clamming was so successful that in 2001 Connecticut harvested more hard clams than any other state on the East Coast. In 2004 the prospects for the future looked promising.

Over the centuries a number of methods for harvesting clams and oysters have been tried. Among the methods used to harvest quahogs commercially and recreationally in New England are treading (practiced by the Indians and still in use recreationally), forks, raking (using short rakes, bull rakes, or the now-obsolete basket rakes), tongs, sail dredges, scuba divers, and rocking chair dredges (first developed for use in Narragansett Bay in 1945–46 and then employed in Massachusetts and Connecticut) and their replacement, hydraulic dredges, which are used commercially today. A variety of oar- or sail-powered boats were used; today clammers also use trailerable motor boats and larger diesel-powered craft. Like clams, oysters were harvested with tongs, rakes, and dredges. Oyster boats have ranged from early dugout canoes, simple rowboats, sailing sharpies, catboats, sloops, schooners, steamboats, to today's powered scows and large diesel-powered boats.

Throughout the centuries clams and oysters have held an important place in the culture of New England, especially in the form of the clambake and clam chowder, part of the New England heritage from the time of the Indians. Ernest Ingersoll's 1887 words still hold true for New Englanders: "A 'clam-bake' expresses the sum of all human happiness to the Rhode Islander, and to gather all his relatives and friends on the sea-shore, bake the roistering clam in dried seaweed, and eat it with other good things, fills his cup of joy!"

D. C. Belding, *A Report upon the Quahaug and Oyster Fisheries of Massachusetts . . .* (1912); George Brown Goode, *The Fisheries and Fishery Industries of the United State* (1887); Ernest Ingersoll, *The History and Present Conditions of the Fishery Industries* (1881); John M. Kochiss, *Oystering from New York to Boston* (1974); Clyde L. MacKenzie, Jr., Allan Morrison, David L. Taylor, Victor G. Burrell, Jr., William S. Arnold, Armando T. Wakida-Kusunoki, "Quahogs in Eastern North America: Part 1, Biology, Ecology, and Historical Uses" *Marine Fisheries Review* 64, no. 2 (2002); MacKenzie, Morrison, Taylor, Burrell, Arnold, Wakida-Kusunoki, "Quahogs in Eastern North America: Part 2, History by Province and State," *Marine Fisheries Review* 64, no. 3 (2002).

John M. Kochiss

Clipper Ships and the China Trade

In 1786 the Salem ship *Grand Turk* arrived at Canton (Guangzhou), introducing New England to a trade that would be integral to its economy for the next 100 years. The legacy of this trade survives in the commercial adroitness, technological ingenuity, and international perspective so central to New England culture. With the dissolution of the land-based Silk Route across Asia, European mariners rounded the Cape of Good Hope to trade directly with merchants in South and East Asia. The trade was driven primarily by Western demand for Chinese tea, silk, and porcelain. In 1757 the Chinese restricted foreign traders to an enclave outside the city of Guangzhou on the Pearl River.

The Chinese desired few commodities from the United States. Thus in the early 19th century New England mariners favored the route around Cape Horn and across the Pacific Ocean, which allowed them to acquire such natural products as Hawaiian and Marquesas Islands sandalwood, sea otter pelts from the northwest coast of North America, and sea cucumber from the Fiji Islands, all of which the Chinese desired. With many New England trading stations established at the sources of these natural resources, the China trade became the initial impetus for much of the strong American influence in Pacific regions that lasted well into the 20th century. As many Pacific trade resources became depleted, Americans followed the European practice of

The clipper ship John Cushing *in Hong Kong harbor, ca. 1860*

importing opium illegally. In an alternative to the trans-Pacific route, Americans purchased opium in Turkey and sold it illicitly along the coast outside Guangzhou. A British war with China from 1839 to 1842 resulted in the opening of several other ports to facilitate export of increasing quantities of tea.

The perishability of tea and the traders' desire to avoid shipping during monsoon season promoted the development of swift ships, or "clippers," designed to carry their cargo to market with the greatest possible speed. In its generic form, the word *clipper* describes ships that were designed for maximum speed rather than for cargo capacity. The 19th-century full-rigged merchant ships that became known as true clippers had visually distinctive attributes such as a sharply raked stem, aft-raking masts, and a narrow bow that expanded outward above the water line. The sloping counter-stern extended over the water to increase capacity. Boston and other New England shipwrights excelled at constructing these graceful vessels, which carried such expressive names as *Romance of the Seas* and *Meteor.*

The demand for fast clippers increased with the repeal of the British Navigation Acts in 1849; American ships could now import tea directly to England. Gold rushes in California (1849) and Australia (1850) and the transatlantic packet lines all increased demands for fast ships capable of carrying people and cargo in quantity. The short life spans and high operating costs of these ships, however, permitted their use only for highly lucrative cargo. True clipper ships were an ephemeral phenomenon: none were built after 1855. But long after the decline in importance of America's

China trade, Chinese export goods continue to adorn the homes of wealthy New Englanders.

Dorothy Schurman Hawes, *To the Farthest Gulf: The Story of the American China Trade* (1990); Phyllis Forbes Kerr, *Letters from China: The Canton-Boston Correspondence of Robert Bennet Forbes, 1838–1840* (1996); David MacGregor, *British and American Clippers: A Comparison of Their Design, Construction and Performance in the 1850s* (1993); Ernest R. May and John K. Fairbank, eds., *America's China Trade in Historical Perspective: The Chinese and American Performance* (1986).

Daniel Finamore

Coastal Defense

New Englanders have always played a major role in determining the coastal defense policies of the United States, and antiquated forts are still visible in many of the region's harbors. The British blockade during the War of 1812 was particularly disabling to New England's merchants. It was largely through their influence that the U.S. Navy included battleships of the sailing era in its pre–Civil War budgets. American naval doctrine, however, shortsightedly perceived these behemoths mainly as blockade busters: the big ships would sally from blockaded ports to disperse enemy squadrons at the doorstep. Rarely used, these wooden giants were kept in a state of permanent storage, available for duty but not consuming scarce navy funds. The ships of the line were often used as floating barracks and training ships, and they also served as prestigious commands for very senior captains. After the Civil War, the vessels were quickly converted into floating warehouses. The last of these relics, the USS *New*

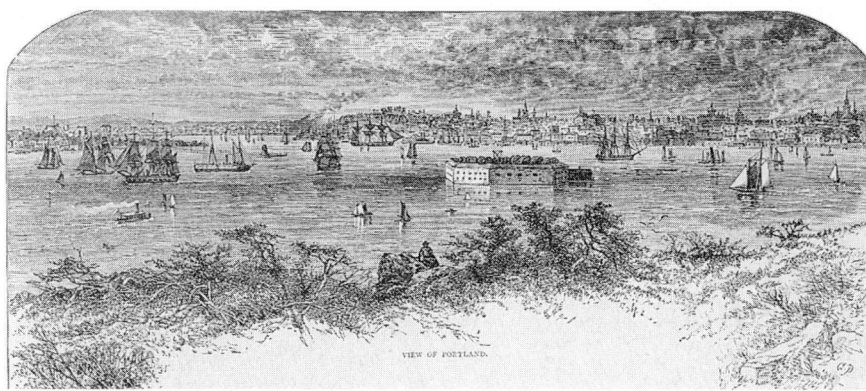

Fortifications in Portland, Maine, 1881

Hampshire, was scrapped in 1898 after serving many years at Portsmouth (N.H.) Navy Yard under the name *Granite State.*

Unlike many countries, the United States has relied equally for coastal defense upon the army, which was responsible for the country's land-based defenses of maritime frontiers. Although coastal defense forts and batteries were a constant part of American military budgets, they were generally kept in active storage, rather than fully manned, until after the Spanish-American War, when the United States began to maintain full-time coastal defense. For the first time, state militias (now known as the National Guard) had a specific role to play. Guard units were trained and equipped as coastal artillery units and were expected to expand regular garrisons in times of war. Often, they were assigned to patrol unfortified stretches of the coast. The pre-World War II New Hampshire, Maine, and Rhode Island National Guards were essentially coastal artillery brigades.

Before World War II, New England coastal artillery fortifications were concentrated at Portland, Maine; Portsmouth, N.H.; Boston and New Bedford, Mass.; and Narragansett Bay, R.I. Antisubmarine nets, mines, and patrols were concentrated in Portland, base of the North Atlantic navy operations, and in Portsmouth, home of the Portsmouth Navy Yard (renamed in 1945 the Portsmouth Naval Shipyard). When it became obvious during and after World War II that American coasts needed to be defended by shore-based patrol aircraft and warships, soldiers were stripped from coastal artillery garrisons and converted to either field or anti-aircraft artillery. Fort Constitution in Portsmouth Harbor, no longer the modern symbol of coastal defense, was replaced by the Brunswick (Maine) Naval Air Station, with its complement of Cold War naval antisubmarine-warfare aircraft squadrons. Substantial World War II artillery bunkers remain off the coast of Portland on the

Casco Bay Islands and near the outlet of the Piscataqua River below Portsmouth.

Although coastal defense is commonly perceived as a national responsibility, some states have attempted to maintain coastal defense capabilities on their own. During the Civil War, Massachusetts (along with New York and Pennsylvania) set up autonomous artillery and infantry forces for coastal defense. These were quickly absorbed, however, into the Union Army. In the later 19th century, several states, including Massachusetts, Connecticut, Rhode Island, and Maine, maintained naval militias. The high cost of maintaining old, obsolete, and worn-out warships, however, soon ended that practice.

The realities of World War II coastal defense had faded from the public mind by the 1960s when a popular Hollywood film, Norman Jewison's *The Russians Are Coming! The Russians Are Coming!* (1966), presented comic New Englanders responding to a supposed invasion when a Russian submarine is grounded off the coast of a small Maine island. Today, many historic coastal defense fortifications, whether from the 19th or the early 20th century, have been converted into parks for public seaside access, and the real job of coastal defense rests with satellites and aircraft far beyond the horizon.

Raymond A. Brighton, *They Came to Fish: A Brief Look at Portsmouth's 350 Years of History* (1994); Howard I. Chapelle, *The History of the American Sailing Navy* (1949); Fred T. Jane, *Jane's Fighting Ships, 1914* (1969); New Hampshire Department of Resources and Economic Development, *State Coastal Properties* (1983).

Scott E. Green

Cod Of the many natural resources that define New England, few have been as prominent as the North Atlantic cod. From the Massachusetts cape that bears its name to the coastal communities built upon its bounty, cod (*Gadus morhua*) has provided New England

with prosperity, notoriety, and sustenance. On Georges Bank, the Grand Banks, and many other smaller banks in the Gulf of Maine, codfish inhabited marine communities rich in nutrients, zooplankton, and phytoplankton. A large, predatory groundfish, cod thrived in these productive waters, once numbering in the millions and dominating fish stocks in the Northwest Atlantic for centuries. Native Americans pursued inshore fisheries with bone hooks, and shell middens from 5,000 to 400 years ago furnish evidence that cod once averaged greater than 3 feet in length and were the most dominant species caught by coastal inhabitants.

Beginning in the 16th century, Europeans were drawn to the massive cod populations in New England's coastal waters. In 1616 Captain John Smith's *Description of New England* portrayed an abundance of cod in the region such that "a man may take with a hooke or line what he will." Indeed, the development of cod fisheries in New England was one of the many great promises the region held for settlers. In the 17th century cod caught with hooks and lines from small inshore vessels were dried, salted, and then exported across the Atlantic to markets throughout Europe. As systems of capital and markets grew, so, too, did New England fisheries. By the end of the American colonial era, large oceangoing schooners were landing more and more cod for a well-established international market. By 1775, with a workforce of 4,000 men, Massachusetts alone was producing more than 250,000 barrels of fish yearly. As evidence of the economic preeminence and sacred nature of the cod in Massachusetts, a gilded wooden carving of the fish was hung in the old statehouse in 1784 and was later moved to the new statehouse on Beacon Hill.

In the 19th century rail transportation enabled the development of domestic markets for fresh fish, transforming the New England fisheries economy. Shifting from handlines to longlines set by men in dories, the fisheries of the mid-19th century focused on cod and other groundfish to supply these markets. Technological advances in the early 20th century produced the otter trawl, and the ecological impacts on cod populations escalated exponentially. Otter trawls allowed cod and other species of all sizes and ages to be caught and landed or discarded as by-catch. In the 1920s came the first drastic decrease in cod size and breeding stock, an event whose impact continued to ripple through the Northwest Atlantic's marine ecosystems for the rest of the 20th century.

International fleets of factory trawlers began fishing the Northwest Atlantic in the 1950s, not just for cod but for any species worth catching. The production capacity and

A cod has hung in the Massachusetts State House since 1784

trawling capability of these industrial trawlers was unprecedented. In 1976 the Magnuson Fishery Conservation and Management Act redefined the mission of the National Marine Fisheries Service and created a conservation zone extending 200 miles off the U.S. coast that excluded all foreign fishing vessels. Instead of managing and protecting fish stocks, however, the act allowed domestic fishing vessels to complete the overfishing that foreign vessels had begun. When Georges Bank and the Grand Banks were closed to commercial fishing in the early 1990s, cod were greatly depleted. With biomass levels well below what they had been 100 years or even 50 years earlier, cod were unable to perform their roles in ecosystems. The fate of cod in New England's waters thus remains tenuous at best. Although reports have indicated an increase in the number and size of codfish in the region, it is readily apparent that cod may never again support fisheries like those that brought New England so much economic and cultural wealth.

Harold A. Innis, *The Cod Fisheries: The History of an International Economy* (1978); Mark Kurlansky, *Cod: A Biography of the Fish That Changed the World* (1997); Robert S. Steneck and James T. Carlton, "Human Alterations in Marine Communities: Students Beware!" in *Marine Community Ecology,* ed. Mark D. Bertness, Steven D. Gaines, and Mark E. Hay (2001); Daniel Vickers, *Farmers and Fishermen: Two Centuries of Work in Essex County, Massachusetts, 1630–1850* (1994).

Andrew N. Case

Cuffe, Paul (1759–1817) Sea captain and entrepreneur.

Paul Cuffe, son of a former slave, Coffe Slocum from Akan-speaking West Africa, and Ruth Moses from a local Wampanoag community, was born on Cuttyhunk Island in Buzzards Bay within the Massachusetts Bay Colony. Within a few years the family settled among the native community in the town of Chilmark on Martha's Vineyard. Cuffe later pointedly described living apart "from the main," suggesting dimensions of the family's initial separation from New England's mainstream colonial Anglo-Puritan culture.

The family moved in 1766 to the mainland, where Cuffe found ready employment in the lucrative and culturally encompassing whaling industry of Dartmouth, Mass. Subsequent struggles for the intrepid mariner during the Revolution originated both from dangerous encounters at sea and from threatening social forces ashore. The former included imprisonment with his Yankee crew by the British in New York as well as repeated setbacks and beatings by reputed pirates as he dodged the British blockade on commercial runs from the mainland to Nantucket Island. He was also incarcerated with his brother John for tax eva-

sion after the two and other "Poor Despised blacks" had twice petitioned the Massachusetts General Court on grounds of taxation without representation.

Whether as a disruptive political activist or as a perpetual social outsider, Cuffe survived profitably among the homogeneous white community of Westport, Mass. He owned 200 acres of land, including his farm and a shipyard, where he constructed seven oceangoing vessels in partnership with his Native American brother-in-law Michael Wainer and two sons-in-law who were former slaves. Over opposition he built Cuff's [*sic*] School, the town's first community school. He joined the Westport Meeting of the Society of Friends in 1808 and, within the year, established Cuffe and Howards, a New Bedford, Mass., mercantile enterprise. Always identified in the media as a captain of black crews, he commanded or ordered vessels into coastal trade from Maine to Louisiana, transatlantic commerce from Portugal to the Baltic Sea, and whaling off Africa and South America.

This black merchant who navigated from Anglocentric New England repeatedly exceeded and astonished competitors. Cuffe reaped large profits over the objections of recalcitrant residents of Vienna, Md., an eastern-shore slaveholding community, and survived months awaiting departure for the Baltic from the Southern slaving entrepôt of Savannah, Ga. Despite approaching British-American hostilities, Cuffe embarked in 1811 for Britain's West African colony of Sierra Leone and then for England, but his Federalist leanings had their price. To extricate an inbound British cargo from customs, he had to call on President James Madison; during the War of 1812 the Republican-dominated Congress denied the Yankee Cuffe a trading license to Sierra Leone.

Precautions against America's malignant racism and institutionalized slavery shaped Cuffe's decision making to the very end. Life in the New Bedford maritime community seemed more accommodating to people of color than it was elsewhere, but social ostracism plagued Cuffe there, as it would Frederick Douglass years later. Identification as an African, prospects of legitimate commerce, and antislavery motives drew him to focus on Sierra Leone, the sole West African asylum for freed slaves and disenchanted African Americans inclined to emigrate. As a pioneering Pan-African, Cuffe envisioned a triangular commercial scheme linking three continents. In 1816 he embarked with 38 passengers and a cargo of $5,000, only to lose it and more upon arrival.

Notwithstanding the costly philanthropy of underwriting emigration, Cuffe concluded that blacks might better "rise to be a people" in Africa than in white slaveholding America. Even local Friends, although opponents of slaveholding, interred the black Friend apart from his white coreligionists on his death in September 1817—or, more accurately, apart from regional as well as national mainstream culture.

Arthur Diamond, *Paul Cuffe, Merchant and Abolitionist* (1989); Sheldon H. Harris, *Paul Cuffe: Black America and the African Return* (1972); George Arnold Salvador, *Paul Cuffe, the Black Yankee, 1759–1817* (1969); Lamont D. Thomas, *Rise to Be a People: A Biography of Paul Cuffe* (1986), retitled *Paul Cuffe: Black Entrepreneur and Pan-Africanist* (1988).

Lamont D. Thomas

Dana, Richard Henry, Jr. (1815–82)

Author and lawyer. Richard Henry Dana, Jr., was the son of the poet and editor Richard Henry Dana, whose interests in law and literature he inherited. Whether his skill in writing was hereditary or learned, his *Two Years before the Mast* (1840) is remarkable chiefly for the style through which the point of view of a "common sailor" is presented. No common sailor himself, Dana was a rusticated Brahmin who shipped as a green hand on the *Pilgrim* in 1834, bound for California. He returned on the *Alert* in 1836 to continue his studies, interrupted initially by illness, at Harvard College.

The appearance of *Two Years before the Mast* made Dana known outside Boston and Cambridge, where he was already recognized as the promising scion of a solid if somewhat romantic lineage. He bolstered his incipient law practice the following year by publishing *The Seaman's Friend,* a manual of the rights and duties of merchant sailors, mates, and masters. Despite the publication of numerous other books, a distinguished legal career, and various political endeavors, Dana is remembered chiefly for *Two Years before the Mast,* which has never been out of print.

This classic narrative provides gripping depictions of storms at sea, of the hard labor of sailors loading hides in California for use in New England's shoe industry, and of the mixed society of Americans, Russians, Spaniards, and Indians in frontier California. But towering above all else is the figure of Frank Thompson, the monomaniacal captain who bullies and flogs his crew. (Thompson was the inspiration for Herman Melville's Captain Ahab.) Through Thompson's floggings and unquestioned power, Dana linked the plight of the common sailor to that of the slave. Even as the life of the sea receded in importance to New England's economy by 1900, *Two Years before the Mast* remained a popular means of identifying New Englanders' heritage as a seafaring people. When Dana added an appendix

to the work recounting changes that had taken place in California, such as the establishment of the thriving city of San Francisco where there had been only a trading post in 1834, he captured the nostalgia of New Englanders and Americans for an era of seafaring adventure gone by.

Dana aptly embodies the struggle in the New England mind between the conservative desire for order and the liberal championing of the disadvantaged. Passages in *Two Years before the Mast* that reflect the horror and indignity of flogging are balanced by the coolness of the discussion of punishment in *The Seaman's Friend.* In 1851, when the latter work was revised after the abolition of flogging, Dana specifically defended the use of force "to secure the instant performance of duty." Perhaps the change (if it is one) in Dana is best illustrated by his response to the *Somers* affair in 1842. Called upon to comment on the justice or injustice of Alexander Slidell Mackenzie's action in hanging of three of his men for intended mutiny, Dana sided firmly and vociferously with the commander. Perhaps ironically, the Boston conservative William Sturgis became the most articulate of Mackenzie's attackers in New England, and the exchange of letters between the two disputants (published in the *Boston Courier* in 1843) marked the complexity of the Brahmin Dana's response to the tragedy.

The heart of Dana's philosophy seems to be the importance of law to the preservation and advance of civilization. Ridiculed by D. H. Lawrence for his attempt to idealize brute labor, Dana emerges consistently as a champion not of individual classes but of civilization itself—in its highest New England form. Thus his reproof of flogging in *Two Years before the Mast,* along with his later aggressive support of abolition and his defense of the runaway slave Anthony Burns, emanated from the sensibilities that rendered him fit to be a member of Boston society. Those same sensibilities warned Dana that were he further brutalized on the coast of California, he would have no choice but to be, in his terms, "a sailor for the rest of my days."

Charles Francis Adams, *Richard Henry Dana: A Biography* (1968 [1890]); D. H. Lawrence, *Studies in Classic American Literature* (1977 [1923]); Robert F. Lucid, ed., *The Journal of Richard Henry Dana, Jr.* (1968); Philip McFarland, *Sea Dangers: The Affair of the "Somers"* (1985).

Robert Durwood Madison

Disasters

The New England coast is renowned for its natural beauty, and the adjacent cruising grounds enjoy a worldwide reputation among sailors. Unfortunately, the same geographic features that attract tourists and

amateur sailors in summer make New England waters very dangerous for shipping. From Cape Cod south, the inshore waters are shoal, with shifting sandbars. North of Cape Cod, and increasing with the latitude, are thousands of ledges and half-tide rocks. Around all these bars and ledges sweep tidal currents that vary constantly, some of them at times strong enough to pull navigational buoys out of sight under the surface. Combined with the treacherous waters are weather conditions that in an hour may vary from flat calm to a gale, and from miles of clear visibility to a horizon of less than 100 feet in fog. It is not surprising, therefore, that maritime disasters have claimed thousands of vessels and tens of thousands of lives since the first European explorers coasted the shore in the 16th century.

The Pilgrims who settled Plymouth found the grave of a shipwrecked European among Native American habitations. English fishermen who frequented the Maine coast in the first decades of the 17th century rescued survivors of a French shipwreck. Death in a maritime disaster was as common an occurrence in New England's age of sail as is death in a plane or car crash today. Many maritime disasters profoundly affected the vessel's and crew's community of origin, as well as the merchants who had financed the voyage. Early in the 17th century the new settlement at New Haven, Conn., shipped an entire year's product in a vessel that was never heard from again; the city never became a significant port. Disasters also affected the communities where the wreckage and bodies came ashore; in the older cemeteries of nearly every coastal community in New England is at least one monument marking the common grave of unidentified, unclaimed shipwreck victims. In particularly treacherous areas, salvage constituted an important part of the local economy.

Perhaps the earliest recorded New England shipwreck was that of the *Angel Gabriel* in a 1635 hurricane; this ship had just arrived at Pemaquid, Maine, when it sank in the harbor. In the 18th and 19th centuries, disasters were carefully recorded in local newspapers and, with the advent of mariners' societies such as the Seamen's Bethel, were compiled and recorded monthly. *The Sailor's Magazine* of March 1842 has nearly three pages of such losses, including this typical example: "Schooner *Azora,* Lemont, of Bath, Maine, for Edgartown, endeavouring to make the mouth of the Kennebec, evening of 1st Jan. wind fresh, struck on the Whale's Back, near Pond Island, whence she drifted onto Salter's Island, and went to pieces. Capt. L. and crew were all lost, excepting two men—one coloured."

With the advent of the U.S. Lifesaving Service, authorized by Congress in 1878, and of a well-maintained system of navigational aids (buoys and lights), the number of shipwrecks decreased dramatically. It was reduced further by the advent of steam power in the 19th century and reliable diesel power and electronic communications in the 20th century. Modern navigation and communication, however, did not prevent the loss of the Italian luxury liner *Andrea Doria* in a collision with the Swedish-American liner *Stockholm* in heavy fog off Nantucket, Mass., on July 25, 1956. This was, in fact, a classic case of "radar assisted collision"; the incident was still being taught in merchant marine academies' collision avoidance courses as recently as 2002. When the *Andrea Doria* collided with the *Stockholm*, all 52 fatalities resulted from the impact of the collision—not drowning—and the survivors were successfully transferred to the *Isle de France,* another liner that happened to be nearby at the time.

Thankfully, the era of great maritime disasters with substantial loss of life is probably behind us, although during the late 20th century the government abandoned selected buoys and electronic navigational aids in a cost-cutting program. Vessels still sink, and several mariners—mostly fishermen—are lost in New England waters almost every year. New England is not likely to experience again the disappearance in a storm of a fully laden passenger ferry like the *City of Portland,* which sank on Stellwagen Bank on November 26, 1898, or the sinking of a ferry loaded with circus animals, as in Penobscot Bay in the 19th century.

Today's maritime disasters cause more harm to the environment than to sailors or passengers. For instance, when the Norwegian tanker *Tamano* grounded near Hussey Shoal in Portland, Maine, in the summer of 1972, 100,000 gallons of heavy petroleum spilled into the waters of Portland harbor. When the Liberian tanker *Argo Merchant* ran aground southeast of Nantucket in 1976, the resulting oil slick spread for almost 100 miles. Since the Oil Pollution Act of 1990, Congress has required all ports handling oil to have the necessary equipment and plans to mitigate spills, and in certain locales, such as the Piscataqua River, local partnerships of oil-handling facilities have created spill-response teams. Still, the threat of oil spills in harbors and on exposed beaches and ledges is daunting. New Englanders today know that when a vessel founders or runs onto a ledge, the crew is likely to be saved, and the victims will be the flora and fauna destroyed by leaking oil or other toxic chemicals, giving a whole new meaning to the term "maritime disaster."

John Perry Fish, *Unfinished Voyages: A Chronology of Shipwrecks in the Northeastern United States* (1989);

The Mariner's Chronicle, Containing Narratives of the Most Remarkable Disasters at Sea (1834); William P. Quinn, *Shipwrecks around Maine* (1983); Quinn, *Shipwrecks around New England* (1979).

William B. Leavenworth

Fishing Fish have fascinated the inhabitants of North America's eastern corner since long before European explorers first spotted teeming multitudes of cod in the cold waters off Newfoundland. Coastal people along the Gulf of Maine and Bay of Fundy are believed to have practiced a marine subsistence strategy as long ago as 9500–6000 B.C. Swordfish remains and other artifacts found in sites associated with the Red Paint people suggest that fishing was one aspect of the Maritime Archaic Tradition. Changes in sea level over the centuries have hampered a full investigation, because many of the suspected sites are currently submerged; scallop draggers, divers, and marine scientists, however, have uncovered numerous artifacts.

Reports of the remarkable abundance of fish identified in 1497 during John Cabot's voyage drew fishermen from Portugal, Spain, the Basque country, France, and England's West Country to fish the Grand Banks during the next 10 years. John Smith wrote in 1614 that fewer than two dozen men were able to hook 60,000 fish in a month off the Isles of Shoals. Not until 1621, however, was a permanent fishing settlement founded on the Avalon Peninsula of Newfoundland.

Gloucester, Mass., was settled in 1625 when rival fishing companies from Dorchester and Gloucester, England, sent crew, salt makers, and shipbuilders to compete for coastal, Georges Bank, and Grand Banks fish. As fishermen explored the region, they soon found a variety of rich grounds; Browns Bank, Stellwagen Bank, Jefferies Ledge, Cashes Ledge, and other areas were swimming with mackerel, herring, redfish, cod, halibut, haddock, and lobsters, not to mention a bounty of whales.

Marblehead, Mass., founded a few years later, became North America's largest fishing port by the mid-18th century, but by the 1840s Gloucester had become New England's leading fishing port. Renowned for its beautiful two-masted schooners, Gloucester and its fishing industry were immortalized in such books as James Connolly's *Gloucestermen* (1930), revealed in stories about legendary figures such as Howard Blackburn, and depicted in the oil paintings of Fitz Hugh Lane. Before the Civil War, Newfoundlanders, Danes, Swedes, and Portuguese were active in the Gloucester fisheries. By the early 1900s Italian fishermen had joined the fleet, and Sicilian fishermen arrived later. Finns first came to quarry granite, but stayed for lobstering.

For the first several centuries of New England fishing, most fish were salted and dried for long shelf life. During the 1920s, however, a Gloucester native, Clarence Birdseye, developed a "quick freezing" technique to freeze fish for home storage, eventually helping the Gorton Company develop the frozen fish products so popular today. Despite difficulties associated with strict regulations and recent downturns in the stocks of cod, haddock, and yellowtail flounder, Gloucester remains an active port. Its trawler-fleet crews are predominantly Sicilian American, while gillnetters and hook fishermen tend to be of mixed "Yankee" stock.

Boston was built on a maritime economy that included fishing, shipbuilding, and commerce. During the colonial era, fish were among the four most valuable exports from the British American colonies, and Boston was the heart of New England's commercial network. Boston pioneered in later years, as well; early in the 1900s the Italian fishing fleet of Boston adopted the new otter and beam trawls towed by powered vessels. Ultimately this technology would revolutionize the fishery. Onshore processors filleted the fresh fish for consumers and demand increased. The fresh fish business peaked in Boston during the 1930s, when 300 million pounds were landed annually at the Fish Pier.

New Bedford, Mass., was founded in 1652 when 36 settlers purchased land from the Wampanoag Indians, though it was almost destroyed 23 years later during King Philip's War (1675–76). In the 19th century, New Bedford became the whaling capital of the world. As late as 1857 there were 429 registered whaling vessels in New Bedford and only 271 registered elsewhere in the United States. But the discovery of petroleum in 1859 replaced the demand for sperm oil, and whaling quickly declined. After an interlude of about 40 years when the textile industry dominated in New Bedford, maritime interests returned to the fore. With its catch of deep sea scallops and yellowtail flounder, New Bedford generally ranks among the top 10 ports in the nation for the value of its landed seafood. In 2002 the value of landings was $169 million, first in the nation. Although participants in the harvesting sector of New Bedford's fishing industry include immigrants from Norway, Sweden, Portugal, Poland, Newfoundland, Cambodia, and Vietnam, Norwegians have traditionally dominated the ownership of scallop vessels, whereas Portuguese have dominated the trawl fleet.

Portland, Maine, is a more recent entry on the rolls of New England's significant fishing ports. Though Portland, originally named Falmouth, was settled less than a decade after Gloucester in 1632, it was destroyed in an at-

Weighing and stacking fish in Gloucester, Mass., 1991

tack by French and Indian forces in 1703 and again by the British in 1775. Reestablished as Portland, its shipping grew rapidly after the Revolutionary War. Fishing has long been a part of Portland's economic diversity, and the city has been an important transshipment point for fish and lobster from elsewhere in Maine. Portland made an immense contribution to New England's fishing industry in 1986 by introducing the first display auction on the East Coast. Before this, New England's fishing industry had relied on a dealer-driven, sight unseen, daily auction of fish. For years, Boston's Fish Exchange set the prices for the whole region. The system favored dealers and resulted in abuse of fair trading practices. The success of Portland's display auction has led to efforts to replicate it in Gloucester and New Bedford.

Rhode Island's economy was never dominated by fishing. Nevertheless, a commercial fishery out of Newport and Sakonnet Point originated in the 17th century. Indeed, Sakonnet Point still has a fish trap that is said to have been in continuous operation for 300 years. The Upper Narragansett Bay ports of Warren and Bristol hosted an important oyster fishery until the 1940s, and the shellfish industry remains actively engaged in clam fishing in the bay. As Newport became more fashionable and the waterfront turned to supporting recreational pursuits, Point Judith (Galilee) became the center of oceanic fishing. Point Judith benefits from its geographic location at the nexus of northern and southern fish

species. Groundfish, bluefish, scup, squid, butterfish, mackerel, and herring are all sought by local fishermen. A fishermen's cooperative at Point Judith has been a highly successful marketing platform from its founding in 1948. The town remains a significant port in the region, with landings by value ranking it 16th in the nation in 2003.

The old dory fishermen working hooks and lines from sailing vessels and romanticized in books and film have been replaced by fishermen wielding polyester nets or longlines a mile in length. Armed with hydraulics and high-tech electronics, they pursue fish on diesel-powered boats built of steel or fiberglass. Changes in technology, gear, prey, markets, and costs have all been faced with varying degrees of success. Nevertheless, some aspects of the fishing life have changed little.

New England's fishing fleet is predominantly owner-operated. Until recently, fishing was a family tradition with fathers and sons or uncles and nephews often fishing together. Women commonly served as "shore captains," performing a variety of essential jobs such as bookkeeping, ordering supplies, contacting gear manufacturers, and lobbying for improvements in fisheries management, in addition to running their household and rearing children. While today many fishing families are encouraging children to stay in school to increase their opportunities for alternative career choices, some have found that their children return to fishing after trying different jobs. Though the practice is still relatively rare,

more and more women fish and refer to themselves as fishermen. Regardless of their position, whether owner, captain, or crewmember, most fishermen love the work and value their independence.

The typical 20th-century pattern for vessels that fished offshore, on Georges Bank, for example, was to take seven- to 14-day trips, then stay home for three or four days to unload, make repairs, mend nets, resupply, and see families before departing for another trip. The size of the crews varied from an ideal six on the average offshore groundfish boat to 10 or 11 on scallop boats. Day boats, typically with a four-man crew, would leave the dock at 4:30 or 5:00 A.M. and return anywhere from 2:30 to 7:00 P.M.

Although the largest fishing vessels tend to congregate in ports that have the infrastructure to support high volumes of fish, New England's small ports are critical components of the industry. New Hampshire's few miles of shoreline, combined with the Piscataqua River, support a small but active fishing fleet in Portsmouth, Seabrook, Rye, and Newington. The rocky coast of Maine east of Portland supports hundreds of lobster fishermen as well as groundfishermen, herring fishermen, and shrimp fishermen. Cape Cod, from Sandwich to Provincetown, boasts a wealth of fishing communities that contribute to the regional economy and attract visitors with their working waterfronts.

In 1976, U.S. sovereignty was extended from the traditional 12 miles from shore to 200 miles. Until then, the distant water fleets of modern factory trawlers belonging to Poland, the Soviet Union, Germany, Spain, and several other countries plied the rich fishing grounds of the Northwest Atlantic, dwarfing American fishermen's vessels and catch. With the passage of the Fisheries Conservation and Management Act of 1976, commonly known as the Magnuson Act, eight regional fisheries management councils were established and given the responsibility of managing U.S. fisheries for sustainability and economic value. With the oversight of the secretary of commerce and the National Marine Fisheries Service, and with advice from scientists and industry participants, the councils have designed fishery management plans for more than a quarter of a century.

During the early flush of enthusiasm for the takeover of fishing by domestic boats, Congress created programs that provided incentives for investment in the industry. A capital construction fund and loan guarantee program have since been criticized as having enabled the domestic harvesting sector to overcapitalize, and thus overfish, stocks that were already vulnerable from years of heavy fishing by foreign boats.

The first efforts of the New England Regional Fishery Management Council to control fishing were quotas imposed in 1977. Serious problems with enforcement ensued, and the next plan instituted larger minimum mesh sizes and closed areas, among other restrictions. A blow to the industry came in 1984 when the International Court of Justice resolved a boundary dispute between the United States and Canada. That decision placed the haddock- and scallop-rich portion of Georges Bank's northeast peak in Canadian waters. Various management plans have struggled ineffectively to conserve fish without ruining the industry. After years of strict regulations, however, the fishing industry may begin to reap the benefits of its sacrifice. Collaborative research projects are drawing on fishermen's broad ecological knowledge and regional scientific expertise. The ultimate goal, of course, is sustainable and economically viable fisheries.

Margaret E. Dewar, *Industry in Trouble: The Federal Government and the New England Fisheries* (1983); Sebastian Junger, *The Perfect Storm: A True Story of Men against the Sea* (1997); Mark Kurlansky, *Cod: A Biography of the Fish That Changed the World* (1997); Raymond McFarland, *A History of the New England Fisheries, with Maps* (1911).

Madeleine Hall-Arber

Fishing Schooners

For more than 250 years schooner-rigged watercraft fished from New England ports. In spite of their common name, fishing schooners have displayed as many differences as similarities, whether regarding their size, their configuration, the uses to which they were put, or their place in popular culture. The principal similarity was in the rigging. No matter what the shape of the hull, any vessel used for fishing that had two (or, rarely, three) masts and sails fore and aft, the larger one located on the after (main) mast, was called a fishing schooner.

In New England the fishing schooner gained prominence early in the 18th century, with the move from alongshore to more distant-water fishing. Small fore-and-aft-rigged vessels collectively known as shallops were superseded in the developing Massachusetts fishing ports of Marblehead and Gloucester by oceangoing vessels that could frequent the fishing grounds as far east as Newfoundland. The large Marblehead fishing schooners of the 18th and early 19th centuries, with their raised quarterdecks, looked much like North American and northern European cargo schooners of the times and frequently served that purpose, carrying processed fish to the Caribbean or Europe in winter. More economical and easier to manage than a square-rigged vessel, the fore-and-aft-rigged schooner was particularly suitable

for sailing home from the fishing grounds against the prevailing westerly winds.

After the New England fishing fleet was decimated during the American Revolution, a second tradition of boat design emerged in the area of Essex County and Gloucester, Mass. There the small, schooner-rigged Chebacco boat, or "dog-body," carved out a niche for itself fishing the nearer grounds. For ease of construction and safety in "following seas"— that is, traveling in the same direction as the waves—the Chebacco boat had a sharp stern rather than the usual wide-transom stern. This seaworthy style of hull was retained in the larger pinky schooner that became typical for the coastal region from Massachusetts up into Maine through the 1830s.

Although Massachusetts designs have been considered most characteristic of the New England fishing schooner, Connecticut and Maine had their own distinct traditions. The small, fine-lined, seaworthy schooners of eastern Connecticut frequently featured water-filled wet wells in which fishermen kept their catch alive and commonly sailed as far south as Havana, Cuba, in winter to serve urban markets. Maine fishing schooners often carried cargo in winter, so they tended to be larger and more full-bodied than their typical Massachusetts counterparts.

Through the 19th century Massachusetts designers responded to outside influences. With the expansion of the mackerel and halibut fisheries in the 1840s, a new class of New England fishing schooner with a wide deck, shallow hull, and tall, raked masts was derived from Chesapeake Bay models. Noted for their speed but unstable in extreme conditions, these so-called sharpshooter and larger clipper schooners prevailed through the 1870s, even as schooners began to carry dories for the newly adopted trawl-line method of fishing.

The need for stable, seaworthy fishing schooners became more apparent as crews began to fish for cod and haddock year-round to meet market demands for fresh fish in the 1870s. Appalling losses among the shallow-draft vessels, with 29 ships and 249 New England fishermen lost in 1879 alone, proclaimed the need for craft better suited to winter conditions in the North Atlantic.

Immigrant Irish fishermen in Boston established a contrasting tradition in the 1850s, bringing their deep-draft, schooner-rigged Galway hookers to New England waters. The speed and stability of these vessels began to influence fishing-schooner design in the region in the 1880s; yacht designers, too, had an impact, including Edward Burgess in the 1880s and 1890s and Bowdoin B. Crowninshield early in the 20th century.

As the offshore fishing industry became

concentrated in a few large ports, a syndicated form of schooner ownership superseded the earlier communal approach. At the same time, fishermen increasingly became migrant, and were often immigrant laborers. As in the earliest ventures, Massachusetts fishermen were paid a share of the proceeds of the voyage rather than a wage. Under these conditions the reputation of a schooner and its captain became increasingly important in attracting competent crews. Rudyard Kipling's novel *Captains Courageous* (1896) and the stories of James B. Connolly suggest the emotional attachment of fishermen to their vessels as both home and workplace. These stories have also contributed to the popular impression that fishing schooners were characteristic of New England.

Among the shipbuilders, fishing captains, and professional naval architects who created influential fishing-schooner designs, the most prolific was the Boston fish dealer Thomas F. McManus, son of an immigrant Irish sailmaker. Between 1892 and the mid-1920s, more than 400 New England and Canadian fishing schooners were built to McManus designs. In his search to combine speed, capacity, stability, and safety, McManus altered the profile of fishing schooners and even eliminated the bowsprit from the so-called knockabout model, so that fishermen would not have to work on an exposed spar to take in sail during stormy weather.

With the adoption of auxiliary motor power after 1900, then the introduction of otter-trawl (net) fishing after 1905, the schooner, with its many-hooked longline trawls set from dories, was facing extinction just as the vessel's design was reaching its apex. By 1920, when most working schooners had been equipped with engines and were using smaller sails, New England and Canadian fishing ports had begun to celebrate their traditional skills, which were becoming obsolete. The *Halifax Herald* North Atlantic Fishermen's International Trophy lent a formal, nationalistic aura to the schooner racing that fishermen had long enjoyed. Competitors first sailed in conventional schooners, but the races soon spawned the construction of exaggerated models, culminating in the Canadian *Bluenose* and American *Gertrude L. Thebaud*, which came to symbolize fishing schooners in the popular imagination.

Even as these schooners built for speed were attracting international attention, the shift to power and small, compact schooner-rigged draggers proclaimed the end of the conventional fishing schooner. The subsequent eastern rig dragger was configured much like a schooner and carried a small rig despite its engine and fishing net. Although the last New England fishing schooner ceased working in the early 1950s, the eastern rig dragger carried the tradition through the 1970s, when it, too, was superseded by a new type of vessel, the stern trawler.

William A. Baker, "Fishing under Sail in the North Atlantic," in *The Atlantic World of Robert G. Albion*, ed. Benjamin W. Labaree (1975); Howard I. Chapelle, *The American Fishing Schooners, 1825–1935* (1973); W. M. P. Dunne, *Thomas F. McManus and the American Fishing Schooners: An Irish-American Success Story* (1994); Wayne M. O'Leary, "The Antebellum Maine Fishing Schooner and the Factors Influencing Its Design and Construction," *American Neptune* 44 (1984); Dana A. Story, *The Shipbuilders of Essex: A Chronicle of Yankee Endeavor* (1995).

Andrew W. German

Friendship Sloops

For more than a century the gracefully distinctive sailboats known as Friendship sloops have been a common sight along the coast of Maine. While many wooden Friendships, some more than half a century old, still proudly ply the seas, today's models are usually made of fiberglass. Operated by recreational sailors rather than lobstermen, the sloops provide an evocative link to Maine's maritime past.

Designed to be sailed by one person, the all-purpose sloops got their name from the village of Friendship, Maine, about 75 miles northeast of Portland on Muscongus Bay, whose inhabitants have been fishing and lobstering for more than two centuries. According to the noted naval architect and marine historian Howard Chapelle, the Friendship sloop resembles the centerboard sloops of the 1850s known as Muscongus Bay boats. Most early Friendship sloops were 26 feet long with an 8-foot beam and, if centerboard, a $2\frac{1}{4}$-foot draft when the board was raised. The sloops were usually gaff-rigged with a single headsail and featured a 26-foot mast and boom, a 15-foot gaff, and an 8-foot bowsprit.

A deep-keel version of these clipper-bowed sloops later became popular, its design chiefly influenced by the boatbuilding Morse family in Friendship and later Thomaston, Maine. These vessels were so well balanced that they could be used year-round for both fishing and lobstering.

Wilbur Morse created an offshore version of the Friendship sloop around 1890. With gravel and stones located lower in the hull for ballast, it became an even more seaworthy craft than its forebear. Chapelle wrote that Morse designed the sloops with "great beam, rather flat floors, hard bilges and wide heavy quarters," which enabled them to sail well in heavy weather under mainsail alone.

A forward cuddy, or small cabin, provided a compact but comfortable space for a shipmate cookstove. The boat had an ample tumblehome, or curvature, and an elliptical transom.

The most distinctive features of the Friendship sloop are its graceful clipper bow and cutwater, the forepart of a ship's stem, and its handsomely carved trail boards, on which the builder stamps his name.

During the 20th century Friendship sloops became popular with recreational sailors, and builders like Jarvis Newman of Southwest Harbor, Maine, began to make them out of fiberglass. Equipped with an ample cockpit and improved, larger cabin, the new boats are comfortable cruisers. Friendship sloop owners congregate annually for a cruise from Friendship south to Merrymeeting Bay and back on up the coast to Rockland, Maine. As of 2000 the Friendship Sloop Society, founded in 1961, had 268 known sloops in its registry. The group publishes an annual yearbook, *Friendship Sloop Days*.

One of the finest examples of a restored Friendship sloop is the *Estella A*, which can be viewed at southern Connecticut's Mystic Seaport. Antique Friendship sloops are also on display at the Maine Watercraft Museum in Thomaston.

Howard I. Chapelle, *American Sailing Craft* (1936); Roger F. Duncan, *Eastward: A Marine Cruise in a Friendship Sloop* (1995 [1976]); Herald A. Jones, ed., *It's a Friendship* (1965); Hope Herman Wurmfeld, *Boatbuilder* (1988).

Renny A. Stackpole

Herreshoff Brothers

The Herreshoff name has been connected with yachting for so many years that it is impossible to think of the sport without considering the enduring influence of the boats and yachting products that were built at the Herreshoff Manufacturing Company of Bristol, R.I. The Herreshoff brothers and their successors revolutionized yacht design and led the way to better and faster craft during the years of the company's existence, from 1863 to 1945. Always leaders in yachting, the two brothers, John Brown Herreshoff (1841–1915) and Nathanael Greene Herreshoff (1848–1938), combined Yankee genius and ingenuity to make theirs one of America's foremost yacht and boatbuilding businesses.

John B. Herreshoff, born with defective eyesight, became totally blind at age 15 as the result of an accident. His strong will and determination to continue working despite the handicap ultimately led to his interest in building small craft. During the Civil War, John established a boat construction business employing several workmen, and soon gained a reputation for fast and excellent craft. John relied on his younger brother, Nathanael, to design the vessels. From a preliminary sketch, Nat would fashion a half-model from soft pine using innate technical skill and infallible

Nathanael Greene Herreshoff, 1899

engineering insight. Offsets were then taken from the model using an instrument of his own invention. From these offsets, the yachts were built. In 1878 John prevailed on Nathanael, who had studied engineering at the Massachusetts Institute of Technology, to leave his employment at the Corliss Steam Engine Company in Providence and join him as a partner in the Herreshoff Manufacturing Company.

With John as president and Nathanael as designer and superintendent, the boatyard prospered. More buildings were constructed, and the mostly open-air shipyard was transformed into a first-class manufacturing facility where the work of building boats was accomplished both efficiently and well. In addition to the waterfront construction shops, the complex included buildings where boilers, steam engines, castings and forgings, and even sails and upholstery were produced.

Before the 1890s, the Herreshoff brothers concentrated mainly on power craft, especially fine yachts, and naval torpedo boats. Construction of sailing yachts began with the success of *Gloriana* in the 46-Footer Class in 1891 and subsequent orders for yachts built to defend the America's Cup, yachting's most coveted prize. The Herreshoff Company defended the America's Cup six times with yachts designed by Nathanael G. Herreshoff (*Vigilant*, 1893; *Defender*, 1895; *Columbia*, 1899 and 1901; *Reliance*, 1903; *Resolute*, 1920). After Nathanael's retirement, the company built the next two defenders: *Enterprise*, 1930, and *Rainbow*, 1934.

The death of John Herreshoff in 1915 signaled a new era for the business. Unable to find a suitable replacement for his brother, and under pressure from the trustees of John's estate to liquidate their holdings in the company, Nathanael decided to sell his stock in the company in 1917. The holdings sold quickly, most of it bought by a group of yachtsmen connected with the Cup defender *Resolute*. In 1919 the company gained considerable fame as the builders of the flying ship NC-4, the first plane to fly the Atlantic Ocean.

In 1924 the company was put up for auction, with most of the holdings going to Rudolf F. Haffenreffer and his sons, Carl W. Haffenreffer and Rudolf F. Haffenreffer III. The company was improved and the yard remained in business for over 20 additional years. During World War II, 100 wooden vessels were built for the military (two 130-foot YMS minesweepers, eight 71-foot Vosper PT boats, four 97-foot minesweepers, 22 103-foot coastal transports, 20 71-foot U.S. Navy PT boats, eight 85-foot U.S. Army Air Force Rescue boats, and 36 63-foot army-navy rescue boats). With the completion of the war contracts, the company was closed in 1945.

Among the many accomplishments of the Herreshoff Manufacturing Company have been the profound effect of Nathanael Herreshoff's talent and creativity on the development of yacht design and construction. Some of his accomplishments that are still in use include light wooden-hull construction, the web frame and longitudinal system of framing a metal vessel, the crosscut sail, light hollow-steel spars with scientific rigging, and overhangs on sailing yachts to allow longer lines and greater stability. He designed the first full-size successful fin-keel yacht and was one of the principal developers of the bulb keel. The type of sail track and sail slides in common use today were his invention, and he introduced into this country screw fastenings for planking wooden hulls. Herreshoff designs of cleats, winches, anchors, and propellers established new and higher standards still evident today in the marine industry. Modern yachting sustains the traditions of excellence embodied in the design, construction, and performance of the yachts of the Herreshoff brothers and those who succeeded them.

Maynard Bray and Carlton J. Pinheiro, *Herreshoff of Bristol* (1989); Constance Buel Burnett, *Let the Best Boat Win: The Story of America's Greatest Yacht Designer* (1957); L. Francis Herreshoff, *Capt. Nat Herreshoff: The Wizard of Bristol* (1953).

Carlton J. Pinheiro

Lake Champlain

Located primarily in the northeastern United States, the nearly 500-square-mile Lake Champlain extends southward from lower Quebec Province in Canada, forming part of the Vermont–New York border, to present-day Whitehall, N.Y.

Samuel de Champlain, explorer of New France (present-day Canada), came to see the "large lake filled with beautiful islands" that his Algonquian friends had described to him. The lake was in the land of their enemy, the Iroquois. He arrived there in July 1609 with 60 fighters traveling in 24 canoes. Meeting the Iroquois for traditional battle, Champlain introduced them to the deadly ways of gunpowder, explosively inflicting his culture upon theirs. It was the beginning of a century and a half of European battles for control of the valley that now carries Champlain's name.

As New France and New England encroached on each other, Lake Champlain's strategic importance increased. Forts sprang up. Violent raids were launched. Armies composed of Europeans, provincials, and Native Americans fought to gain control of the waterway, a contest ultimately won by the British, who built important fortifications at Crown Point and Fort Ticonderoga near the southern end of the lake. Ethan Allen's surprise capture of Fort Ticonderoga on May 10, 1775, provided cannons for George Washington's assault on British troops occupying Boston. Control of the strategic lake was an early focus of the American Revolution during the days when Benedict Arnold was the best field commander of the American forces. It was also the focus during the War of 1812, when Lieutenant Thomas Macdonough became commodore of a fleet that defeated the British navy at the Battle of Plattsburg. The lake's military significance then diminished, while its importance as a shipping channel rose.

After the Revolution the Champlain Valley experienced a rapid annual increase in migration from southern New England to Vermont. As the years passed the New York territory, less hospitable to farmers but boasting large deposits of iron ore and thick forests of timber, also attracted settlers. Lake Champlain provided immigrating travelers with a highway into the region. Later, when connected to other great inland water systems by canal, the lake served as a conduit to the West. As the 19th century advanced, it was also a means of access for French Canadian and Irish immigrants entering the United States via Montreal. Some stayed in the Champlain Valley, while others passed through on their way to more distant destinations.

Steamboats, sailboats, canal boats with whole families living on board, schooner-rigged scows, sail- and horse-powered ferryboats, breakwaters, and lighthouses all added to the richness of maritime life. The lake connected Vermont and New York communities facing one another across the water, whose members frequently attended church together and in many cases chose marriage partners from the opposite shore. Railroads and automobiles transformed the lake again, this time recreationally, into a place where people went to escape the heat of the city, to fish, to explore historic sites, and to bask in the lake's natural grandeur.

Strikingly beautiful, rich in natural and historic resources, Lake Champlain and the surrounding valley are a complex and fascinating area. Aware that they collectively share the Lake Champlain basin, Vermont, New York, and Quebec work to coordinate regional idiosyncrasies with a view to preserving the lake for future generations. Since the 1980s it has come to light that Lake Champlain contains beneath its surface the best-preserved collection of wooden shipwrecks in North America. Exciting archaeological discoveries such as these open a window onto past economies, technology, and human activities.

Russell P. Bellico, *Sails and Steam in the Mountains* (1992); Harrison Bird, *Navies in the Mountains: The Battles on the Waters of Lake Champlain and Lake George, 1609–1814* (1962); Walter Hill Crockett, *A History of Lake Champlain: The Record of Three Centuries, 1609–1909* (1909); Ralph Nading Hill, *Lake Champlain: Key to Liberty* (1995 [1976]).

Arthur B. Cohn

Lifesaving Service

The Lifesaving Service grew out of private organizations and salvagers that helped mariners in trouble at sea. But these ad hoc wreckers and privately funded lifesaving organizations provided limited and often treacherous service. Mariners knew that they needed professionally trained and equipped lifesavers who would be available when emergencies came. In 1807 the Massachusetts Humane Society, the most important private lifesaving organization in New England, erected a hut in Cohassett to provide lifesaving services for Cape Cod. From this hut grew a system of houses of refuge—buildings with supplies for shipwreck victims such as food, blankets, medical supplies, and firewood—and lifeboat stations. At the same time, revenue cutters—part of the U.S. Customs Official, of the Treasury Department—began patrolling the ocean in the winter months, searching for vessels in distress. In 1848 Congress passed the Newell Act, authorizing $10,000 to build and equip stations along the New Jersey coast. By 1854 there were 137 lifeboat stations stretching from Cape Cod down Long Island and the coast of New Jersey to the Outer Banks of North Carolina. The act also authorized houses of refuge and trained lifesavers. Small boat stations or lifesaving stations provided with rescue equipment and trained personnel were put on the alert to perform rescues.

The Point Allerton (Mass.) Lifesaving Station was founded in 1889 with the legendary lifesaver Joshua James as keeper. Although at 63 James was 18 years over the service age limit, the restriction was waived in view of his unparalleled record. James served as keeper for 13 years; he and his crew saved 540 lives, losing none of their own. Today the restored station houses the Hull Lifesaving Museum.

In 1871 the Treasury Department hired a civilian, Sumner Kimball of Maine, to run the Revenue Marine. As bureau chief Kimball worked at developing the lifesaving service. In 1878 Congress created the U.S. Lifesaving Service (USLSS) as a separate bureau within the Treasury Department, and Kimball moved over to run it. In 1915 Congress merged the USLSS with the Revenue Cutter Service (as the Revenue Marine was now called) to create the U.S. Coast Guard. Kimball, who had built the USLSS into one of the most efficient agencies in the government, retired after the merger.

During his tenure with the USLSS, Kimball had involved architects in the design of boathouses, stables for the horses who pulled the lifesaving boats from the station to the water, and living quarters that were functional, comfortable, and distinctive. Boat designers developed self-righting, self-bailing lifeboats. An army ordnance officer, David Lyle, developed a gun that could fire the line for the breeches buoy, used to get passengers off foundering ships: after the surfmen and the shipwreck victims had rigged the breeches buoy, a canvas seat was attached to a pulley by which the victims rode ashore to safety. Kimball's bureau published first-aid manuals and manuals for training lifesaving crews. Newspapers and magazines began publishing accounts of the exploits of the "storm warriors," whose motto was "You have to go out, but you don't have to come back," and Congress authorized two medals, the gold and silver lifesaving medals.

In 1890 the government maintained 11 lifesaving stations in Maine, 21 stations in Massachusetts, and 38 stations in Rhode Island and Long Island, the barrier island for Connecticut. These 70 stations were part of a national system of 233 lifesaving stations. In the three New England districts, the lifesavers responded to 132 disasters, involving 1,214 people, of whom only seven were lost, and preserved more than $1.2 million in vessels and cargo. Also in 1890 the stations on Cape Cod received telephone service, connecting the 10 stations between Race Point (near Provincetown) and Monomoy Island, off the elbow, and allowing the stations to call on one another for reinforcements.

By 1920 the U.S. Coast Guard operated 58 stations on the New England coast. In addition the service began experimenting with using aircraft for search-and-rescue missions, and in 1927 the Coast Guard established an air station on Ten Pound Island off Gloucester, Mass. In 1935 the air station moved to Salem, Mass. At both locations the crews learned to perform search-and-rescue operations with amphibious aircraft and flying boats. They experimented with radio communication systems, for ocean rescue depended on the newly invented wireless. In addition, the amphibian airplane opened a new aspect of rescue: transporting ill or injured merchant mariners from ship to hospital. In 1933 the Coast Guard maintained 240 Coast Guard or lifesaving stations and the secretary of the treasury awarded 5 gold and 16 silver lifesaving medals.

In the 1940s the Coast Guard Aviation branch begin experimenting with helicopters, first produced by Sikorsky Aircraft in Stratford, Conn., under the direction of the inventor Igor Sikorsky. The helicopter changed search-and-rescue operations. Rescue crews no longer needed to send a boat to people in distress. Instead, a cutter could act as a platform from which helicopters took off and returned; people at sea could be rescued directly by the hovering aircraft. Today three classes of Coast Guard cutters carry helicopters: the 378-foot high-endurance cutter, the 270-foot medium-endurance cutter, and the 210-foot medium-endurance cutter. New England, known to the Coast Guard as First District, has five 270-foot cutters and one 210-foot cutter, whose home port is Boston. The Coast Guard station still provides immediate response to emergencies, and the Coast Guard maintains more than 20 small-boat stations and crews in New England. The station crews use various small boats, including the new 47-foot patrol boats. Often an 87-foot patrol boat is nearby to assist; in addition, five 110-foot patrol boats work the waters off New England. The Coast Guard Air Station near Woods Hole, Mass., provides HU-25 Falcon Jets and HU-60J Jayhawk helicopters. If more aircraft are needed the Coast Guard can call on the Air Station at Brooklyn, N.Y. Every day the U.S. Coast Guard receives more than 100 distress calls. Every day, it lives up to its motto, "Semper Paratus" (Always Ready). The distinctive red roof of the stations and the orange racing stripe on the boats and cutters bring comfort to mariners and recreational boaters alike.

Annual Report of the Operations of the United States Life-Saving Service for the Fiscal Year Ending June 30, 1890 (1892); "The Life-Savers of America and England," *Harper's Weekly* (January 21, 1888); Arthur Pearcy, *U.S. Coast Guard Aircraft since 1916* (1991); "The Storm Fighters," *Coast Guard Magazine* (February 1932).

Cindee Herrick

Lighthouses New England lighthouses have served as essential aids to navigation since Boston Light, the first permanent lighthouse in North America, was completed on Brewster's Island in 1716. Seven of the 12 colonial lighthouses guarded New England harbors and shoals, as did 10 of the first 14 built by the new republic. Although lighthouses were constructed on the initiative of local communities, responsibility for staffing and maintaining them transferred to the U.S. Lighthouse Establishment in 1789. Lighthouses tamed rugged coastlines, signifying the human triumph over treacherous seas. Between 1838 and 1851 the Maine Lighthouse Establishment engineer Alexander Parris erected six

Nubble Light House, Cape Neddick, York, Maine, 1989

new granite towers along that state's coast, proclaiming Maine's increasing commercial maturity, growing population, and eagerness to assume its share of responsibility for maritime traffic.

By 1850, however, complaints about the condition, reliability, and visibility of New England lighthouses warranted congressional investigation. The Brant Point Light on Nantucket Island, Mass., for example, had long been nicknamed the "bug light" by seamen, because it burned so dimly. Control passed to the U.S. Lighthouse Board, which moved to adopt modern equipment, including the Fresnel lens; standardize building practices; professionalize personnel; and coordinate the nation's 345 lighthouses and other navigational aids. This change coincided with the heyday of the clipper ship and golden age of American sail.

The self-sufficient lighthouses occupied isolated promontories, fingerlike peninsulas, barren islands, and submerged rocks generally removed from other habitations. Although some combined tower and dwelling, many others rose above a small complex of buildings. The keeper's residence stood apart from the lighthouse or connected to it via a passageway like those that often linked farm buildings in rural New England; bell houses, boathouses, fog-signal buildings, oil-storage sheds, cisterns, and barns were erected where land permitted. Families often accompanied the lighthouse keeper on station and frequently shared in the chores. Isolation was particularly hard on wives. Schooling children was also a problem, yet many learned to read and write. Abbie Burgess, for example, one of 10 children of a 19th-century Maine lighthouse keeper at Matinicus Rock, was home-schooled and tended lights herself for nearly 40 years.

The keeper maintained the light, the fog-signal apparatus, and the building complex. Danger seldom punctuated daily loneliness and monotony. Yet during severe storms some lighthouse keepers, such as Marcus Hanna of the Cape Elizabeth Light in Maine and Ida Lewis Wilson of Lime Rock Light in Newport Harbor, R.I., performed daring rescues of

shipwrecked seamen, earning the whole service a reputation for bravery. Minot's Ledge Light outside Boston Harbor, a wooden platform precariously set atop wrought-iron stilts rising almost directly out of the sea, washed away with its two male keepers in the Great Storm of 1851.

In July 1939 the U.S. Lighthouse Service merged with the U.S. Coast Guard. Electricity allowed for more thorough automation. The introduction of electronic navigation signals in 1940 gradually diminished the importance of visual aids, and, one by one, New England's lighthouses were automated. In 1989 Boston Light became—and thanks to legislation sponsored by Senator Edward Kennedy will forever remain—the only lighthouse in the country still manned, by a Coast Guard keeper. Today many of the surviving stations fall under the jurisdiction of the National Park Service.

The lighthouse has become a symbol of New England, appearing on license plates in Massachusetts and Connecticut, on restaurant facades, salt and pepper shakers, and innumerable souvenir items. Preservation efforts are under way in several states to save Fresnel lenses and other artifacts in museums, and the Southeast Light on Block Island, R.I., was moved 245 feet inland in 1994 to save it from toppling into the sea. New England's strong traditional connections to the sea long manifest in shipbuilding, trade, and fishing still seem tangible in these tall sentinels fixed on the littoral boundary between a safe haven and the wild sea.

Sarah C. Gleason, *Kindly Lights: A History of the Lighthouses of Southern New England* (1991); Bruce Roberts, *New England Lighthouses: Bay of Fundy to Long Island Sound* (1996); Constance Covill Small, *Lighthouse Keeper's Wife* (1986); Courtney Thompson, *Massachusetts Lighthouses: A Pictorial Guide* (1998).

Karen Alexander

Lobstering In the language of a lobsterman, "short" does not mean the sudden discovery that one is cash poor, though many are. The price of a decent lobster boat these days runs about $75,000, and 1,000 traps cost an-

other $30,000. Then the lobsterman must find a place to put them. Even if a young person entering the lobster industry can swing the cash, nearly every inch of fishable bottom already has a trap on it. Along New England's coast in 2003 there were more than 3.5 million traps, and strong territorial claims among established lobstermen to the best ocean bottom. The lobster industry does not exactly welcome newcomers, unless they come from lobstering families or have put in their time on an established boat.

New England lobstermen covet the life, of course—one of the few occupations, said New Hampshire lobsterman Ed Heaphy of Dover Point, "in which you can still control your own destiny." But these days that freedom is measured in very practical terms: Can a lobsterman set a line of traps without getting it tangled up in someone else's?

Ask longtime lobstermen like Heaphy, who has fished out of Dover Point for decades, what has changed most since they entered the business, and they will say that synthetics have made the lines, warp, and heads (netting on traps) last longer than the old sisal and manila. Then they will add that the proliferation of traps has changed the way they fish, forcing them to set more traps, since overcrowding means each one is set less strategically. It was not unusual in the late 1990s for a full-time lobsterman, a "highliner," to set more than 1,000 traps, each of which had to be hauled every other day and rebaited. Ten years earlier, half that many was the average. Trap limits, popular among fishermen, may or may not curtail this fishery's version of the arms race. Biologists don't think so.

Consider things from the lobster's perspective. Researchers say a just-legal-sized lobster living in coastal waters has a 90 percent chance of walking into a trap and ending up on someone's dinner table. And most of these lobsters have never had the opportunity to reproduce. "The real enigma of all this from a biological point of view," said one biologist, "is how the devil does the resource maintain itself?" The best way of protecting the species, say the scientists, is to increase the lobsters' reproductive potential by increasing the minimum size they must attain before they're taken.

That doesn't sit well with lobstermen, whose traps are already filled with so-called shorts. One New Hampshire study reported that lobstermen are forced to throw back as many as 80 percent of the lobsters they catch because they are below the legal minimum. Resistance to raising the minimum size stiffened even further in the face of record landings in the late 1990s, which made the dire warnings of biologists about the collapse of the fishery seem rather flimsy.

Might the New England lobster prove more resilient than the cod, that other symbol of the region's fishing tradition? The debate has persisted since at least 1880, when one prominent observer predicted the lobster's extermination because of overfishing. Like much else in New England, it's an argument with a long history. A lobster shortage would be hard for the coastal region's native peoples to imagine; apparently the creatures were so abundant in the precolonial period that one could pick them right up off the beach or simply wade a few feet into the surf and pluck them from the ocean floor.

The early European settlers thought the idea of eating lobsters distasteful and often used the crustaceans as fertilizer. It wasn't until well into the 18th century that New Yorkers, Bostonians, and other urbanites developed a fondness for lobster, a passion that led to the first reports of scarcity in the waters of New York Harbor. That situation was blamed not on overfishing but on the "incessant cannonading" of the Revolutionary War. As demand increased, the industry extended its reach up the coast to Connecticut, where lobster smacks, or wooden boats with large fish wells, brought live lobsters to urban markets. A 3-pounder sold for about three cents.

But the lobster industry's boom can be attributed to an unlikely cause: the invention of canned foods. The Scottish pioneered the technology of sealing foods in tin cans, and in 1842 the first cannery in the United States was established in Eastport, Maine. Lobster was one of the first foods canned in America. In 1843 a 1-pound tin, containing the meat from 3½ pounds of live lobster, sold for as little as five cents. The appetite for canned lobster grew to the point that by 1880 Maine alone was home to 23 canneries.

The canneries' demand for fresh lobster seriously stressed the fishery. One factory, for instance, might require the services of 50 to 60 lobstermen. The first laws regulating the lobster fishery were a direct result of the canneries' overexploitation of the resource. Some of the first lobster laws imposed a closed season, but today's regulations focus on promoting lobster reproduction. Do they work? If the success of fisheries regulation is measured by landings, then the industry seems healthy indeed. Lobster landings increased steadily in the last decade of the 20th century, though more efficient fishing practices may account for the rise. Biologists and some lobstermen still believe the fishery is overexploited, however. Landings have plummeted in Connecticut since 1999 and in southern Massachusetts and Rhode Island since 2000, although they have remained high in Maine, with a record 63.6 million pounds in 2002.

Lobster laws protecting undersized lobsters offer no solace to really big lobsters, most of which inhabit deep water at the continental shelf. How big is really big? Big George, who may have been the largest lobster ever caught, weighed in at 37½ pounds and spent the last six months of his life in a tank at Captain Scott's Fish Market in Sandwich, Mass. Big George was a popular local attraction, though he apparently hated men. "The only ones who could feed him were females," said Scott. "He especially liked my wife and daughters." After Big George died, Captain Scott donated the lobster to the Massachusetts Lobsterman Association, where he now travels to meetings mounted on a wooden plaque for all to see and marvel at, no matter their sex.

Bruce Ballenger, *The Lobster Almanac* (1988); Mike Brown, *The Great Lobster Chase: The Real Story of Maine Lobsters and the Men Who Catch Them* (1985); J. Stanley Cobb and Bruce F. Phillips, eds., *The Biology and Management of Lobsters*, 2 vols. (1980); Francis Hobart Herrick, *Natural History of the American Lobster* (1977 [1911]).

Bruce Ballenger

Malaga Island

"Of old, muskets drove the Abenakis off the coast of Maine. Today money is driving away another race," observed the author and filmmaker Holman Day in the September 1909 issue of *Harper's Monthly*. At the turn of the 20th century, Day's was one of the few voices raised against the increasingly high-handed treatment of Maine's coastal poor, a group caught between the pressures of tourist development, well-intentioned social reformers, and society's growing belief that crime and poverty emanated from so-called retrograde families.

Day's worst fears were realized on July 1, 1912, when the governor and council of Maine ordered the destruction of the mixed-race settlement of Malaga Island, a political "no-man's-land" off Phippsburg, in Casco Bay

near the mouth of the New Meadows River. The 40 to 45 inhabitants were rounded up; a few were allowed to raft their dwellings to the mainland, while others were ordered to their town of origin and a number were sent to the new Maine School for the Feeble-Minded (now Pineland Hospital) in West Pownal. In a macabre effort to extinguish the colony for all time, the remaining buildings were torn down and burned, and the bones of the dead exhumed, placed in "five large caskets," and reburied at West Pownal.

Malaga was only one of the "pockets of social indigents" broken up by the state of Maine. However, the African roots of Malaga's inhabitants brought its story considerable publicity. Casco Bay had long been home to African settlers, including William Black, whose family pioneered Bailey (formerly Will's) Island in the 1720s. Indeed, the passage between Bailey and Orr's Island is still called Will's Gut. On July 6, 1794, Benjamin Darling, a former slave, bought Horse (now Harbor) Island. Located just below Malaga, Horse remained Darling family property until 1847. About this time, some Darlings became squatters on Malaga, a low-lying island measuring a half-mile long and a quarter-mile wide. Eventually, they were joined by families and individuals of Irish, Scotch-Irish, Portuguese, Yankee, and African background.

Probably never numbering more than 45, the islanders lived a quiet, hardscrabble existence as fisherfolk and subsistence farmers. It was on these people, and their kin on other islands, that Elijah Kellogg, the author of a number of popular books for boys, modeled his black characters in *The Young Deliverers of Pleasant Cove* (1871) and *The Cruise of the Casco* (1872). A rare glimpse inside the "colony of colored men" in the *Portland Daily Press* of July 18, 1862, reported that all the "hearty, healthy and intelligent" young men on the island were trying to enlist in the Union Army.

Boston Post-Card Company image of Malaga Island, Maine, ca. 1910

At least one islander, William Johnson, eventually served in the valorous 54th Massachusetts Regiment.

After the war, life on Malaga proceeded undisturbed until the 1890s. In that decade, the town of Phippsburg briefly assumed control of the island's "pauper families," and newspapers began to publish feature articles about the "degenerate colony" in the midst of a rapidly developing region. The reformer George Lane built a schoolhouse in 1903, and a Malaga Settlement Association was formed. Phippsburg eventually tried to claim that the town of Harpswell owned Malaga. In 1904 the state of Maine spent $48 on Malaga. The following year the state assumed control of the island, which Phippsburg had abandoned, and by 1910 was spending $1,170 annually to maintain it.

Donations of goods and money from civic groups served, in the course of time, to undermine the lean but functional fishing economy of Malaga. In the eyes of educators and officials the signs of poverty remained, and the state felt growing pressure to take action. The press had a field day, pejoratively identifying island resident and spokesman James McKenney, and later his son-in-law John "Jerry" Murphy, as "King of Malaga." Reformers came to believe that the children and some older people would be better off institutionalized. Many mainlanders simply wanted the aesthetic embarrassment of the poverty-stricken island erased, and politicians wanted the matter resolved quickly.

In 1911 tests for retardation were given, and an entire family along with one single woman were sent to the School for the Feeble-Minded. The state also found the legal absentee owner, bought the island, and placed it within the town of Phippsburg. Whatever the motives had been, the result was the complete destruction of the settlement. Some islanders were confined at West Pownal and one at the Soldier's Home in Togus. Others successfully transplanted themselves to the mainland, and one family, with no place to land their dwelling, tied it up to Bushy Island. Their misfortune and the death of one displaced woman in late 1914 finally led the press to question the entire relocation episode, but by then it was too late. Summer cottages, resorts, and marinas burgeoned throughout the area. Ironically, though, no one has ever built or lived on the island that the state forcibly depopulated. The only memorial to the generations of African American Malaga Islanders is a row of numbered white grave markers on the slope of a grassy hill in West Pownal.

William David Barry, "The Shameful Story of Malaga Island," *Down East* 27 (November 1980).

William David Barry

Marine Policy   The story of marine policy in New England is inextricably bound to the region's history of economic development. Codfishing played an important role in the economic life of colonial New England, and salt cod became an important export. Codfishing remained important to some New Englanders well into the 20th century, and the 1994 closure of Georges Bank to commercial fishing had a devastating impact on many coastal communities. In Massachusetts, the wealth created by the famous whaling ships of Nantucket and New Bedford later financed the development of the great mills of New Bedford and Fall River. The development of the mill system, in turn, destroyed the habitat of the once-great Atlantic salmon, whose journey up New England's many rivers was fatally interrupted by the dams and turbines constructed to power the mills.

Before the development of regional road and rail systems, coastwise trade created the need for many small ports, typically located at the mouth of navigable rivers. Those desirable port locations became the development core of New England's largest cities and towns. The expanding population drawn to growing port regions in turn created the need for more land, resulting in massive land filling of harbor areas, particularly in Boston. The filling was done in what were known as "mosquito-ridden swamps" or "waste-lands"; today we call them wetlands and recognize their enormous role in the primary productivity of the coastal zone.

The population expansion in coastal communities created another problem: waste disposal. Historically, the easiest and most common solution was to send the waste to sea. Rivers took on new colors and smells as the great textile and paper mills dumped their waste products directly into the streams. When that water reached the coast, it was joined by the sewage effluent pumped into harbors and bays by expanding coastal communities.

Not surprisingly, coastal marine resources declined. The shellfish populations that remained in those developed areas became too polluted to harvest. With the growth of other forms of transportation, cities began to turn their backs on the sea, and the destruction of coastal waters was even easier to ignore.

Ironically, the latest economic engine to drive the New England economy—tourism and marine recreation—has created the stimulus to clean up the waterways and reorient coastal communities to the marine environment. The tremendous growth in recreational boating and fishing after World War II created a constituency that demanded better stewardship of the region's coastal resources.

The federal Clean Water Act in 1970 began a process of cleanup that culminated in one of the region's largest construction projects ever: a state-of-the-art sewage treatment system for all of metropolitan Boston.

With water quality improving, the region's cities have reversed course and redeveloped decaying urban waterfronts into magnets for populations eager to "reconnect" to their maritime heritage. The supreme courts of Massachusetts, Vermont, and Rhode Island have all considered cases about the public's right to coastal lands—now filled—that no longer serve their intended purpose of enhancing maritime trade. The result is most dramatically seen in Boston, where the state coastal management agency requires that the first floor of buildings built on filled harbor-front lands must be used for "facilities of public accommodation." In Providence, the city's rivers (once covered by the world's widest bridge) have been reopened for public use, and its historic core has been marked by the development of Waterplace Park. Where the river once flowed red from the local slaughterhouses, canoes and kayaks can be rented to paddle past happily feeding ducks.

The marine policy of New England can thus be characterized roughly as the sum total of all the laws and practices affecting human interactions with the marine and coastal environment. In the colonial era, fishing, shipping, and defense drove the policy agenda. The industrial era of the 19th century added waste disposal as an important use, despite the rather obvious effect on fishing. Most recently, pressures on coastal waters have come from coastal land development, marine recreation, and the emerging aquaculture industry.

Even though all of the above uses frequently interact in the same small area (Narragansett Bay, for example), no single regulatory authority has jurisdiction over those activities. Instead, a bewildering array of local, state, and federal authorities act with often conflicting objectives.

A classic example is the subject of harbor management. The tremendous growth in the popularity of recreational boating in the 1980s placed an unprecedented strain on the capacity of many of New England's small harbors. Besides the obvious space shortage, negative environmental impacts and conflicts with other user groups were also frequently a problem. The policy "solution" was to develop a harbor management plan for each locale. Although the state owns all of the submerged lands within its harbor areas, it was willing to cede control and management authority to the local community if certain statewide standards were met. Simple in theory, harbor management plans and ordinances have been hotly contested from Maine to Connecticut.

What are some of the problems that have been experienced? The local community faces spatial limits for the number of moorings it can license. Local political pressure mandates that the town reserve as many spots as possible for local residents. The state government, however, which must approve the program, will reject the proposal if sufficient access is not made available to residents of other communities. The federal government, through the Army Corps of Engineers, is concerned with the availability of safe anchorage for all vessels, foreign or domestic, making use of "federally navigable" waters. The appropriate balance is always difficult to achieve.

When a harbor is adjacent to a shellfish management area, other problems arise. The state Department of Health, which is charged with enforcing interstate shellfish sanitation standards, may restrict the density of boats moored nearby and require the installation of an expensive pump-out facility to empty ships' holding tanks.

Paying for this—in addition to a harbormaster to manage all the details—requires harbor management fees placed on all users. Although, once again, local communities are tempted to charge exorbitant rates to nonresident mooring holders, both the state and federal governments prohibit such a move. The net result is a program that blends the interests of all three levels of government in an integrated harbor management policy.

In spite of the relative success of marine policy close to shore, the news has been less positive on the famed offshore fishing ground of Georges Bank. In December 1994, the National Marine Fisheries Service closed more than 6,000 square miles of prime offshore fishing area off the coast of Massachusetts after chronic overfishing depleted fish populations.

How could a policy failure of this magnitude have occurred? The law that established U.S. jurisdiction over the region's fishing resources to 200 miles offshore—the Magnuson Act of 1976—delegated the management of fish stocks in the region to the newly created New England Regional Fishery Management Council. Two flaws in the drafting of that law made its failure almost inevitable. First, the biological management standard of maximum sustainable yield was abandoned in favor of a new standard called "optimum yield." This new standard was initially based on maximum sustainable yield but then could be modified by "any relevant, social, economic, or ecological factor." The second flaw in the law was closely tied to the first. Management decisions were to be made by the fisheries council composed of individuals "knowledgeable and experienced in the fishing industry." By design, the New England Council came to be dominated by the leaders of the New England fishing industry who were unable to make the hard, long-term decisions to limit fishing effectively—until the fishery virtually collapsed. The Magnuson Act was updated in 1996 by the Sustainable Fisheries Act, which addressed both of those problems and placed a new emphasis on conservation issues. Congress also provided millions of dollars to buy back fishing vessels and remove them from the fishery. With fewer vessels fishing a total of only a few months a year, stocks on Georges Bank have begun to recover. The area nevertheless remains years away from a full recovery. If and when that occurs, it seems likely that the fishing industry of tomorrow will be composed of a far smaller fleet of highly efficient vessels that have the ability to harvest a variety of species. By all accounts, the collapse of the New England fishery was a major policy failure made all the more depressing because the outcome was predicted for many years but ignored until it was too late.

The evolution of marine resources use has had an indelible impact on the culture of coastal New England. With hindsight, we can see that many historic policy choices were shortsighted and have had long-term negative effects. We cannot, however, judge the decisions of the past based on criteria we take for granted today. The history of New England's marine policy merely reflects the complex, evolving relationship of its people to the sea. As the region's economy grows from exploitative to information-based, respect for the marine environment will likewise evolve.

Darlene Boyle, *Weighing the Options: Identifying Harbour Use Goals* (1990); Peter Doeringer, Philip Moss, and David Terkla, *The New England Fishing Economy* (1986); Elmer Keen, *Ownership and Productivity of Marine Fishery Resources* (1988); Marine Law Institute, *Managing the Shoreline for Water Dependent Uses* (1988); Dennis W. Nixon, *Marine and Coastal Law* (1994).

Dennis W. Nixon

Maritime Past in the Present New England's maritime past is the story of its people fishing the rich marine resources off the region's shores, using the raw materials of its forests to build ships, and crewing the ships that carried trade goods to and from its ports where these industries flourished. This past lives on in fewer than two dozen preserved vessels and in a scattering of fine maritime museums that dot New England's villages and port cities.

Gloucester (Mass.) fishermen's memorial (1925)

Eighteenth-century maritime New England grew around the nationally important fishing, lumbering, and shipbuilding industries. In the 19th century—as New England became more industrialized and as local resources of fish and lumber and distant ocean resources of whales became less profitable—maritime industries, with the exception of shipbuilding, became only regionally important. As the industrial age waned in New England during the last half of the 20th century, tourism became increasingly important, and the maritime past became a marketable economic asset. As we ask what remains of New England's maritime past, we might also ask how that past has been changed to preserve, present, and market it.

Half a dozen wooden commercial sailing vessels remain from the waning years of the 19th century and the first years of the 20th century. The *Charles W. Morgan*, which was sent in search of whale oil from 1841 to 1921, is the oldest wooden sailing commercial vessel still floating—though not sailing—in New England. It lies at Mystic Seaport, in Mystic, Conn. The one-time fishing vessel and later packet vessel *Ernestina*, built in 1894 as the *Effie M. Morrissey*, still sails out of New Bedford, Mass. The late-19th-century vessel the *Stephen Taber* still sails along the New England coast, carrying summer passengers in sheltered Maine waters. Three 20th-century fishing vessels remain on display—the *L. A. Dunton* (1921) at Mystic Seaport; the *Adventure* (1926), still sailing out of Gloucester, Mass.; and the *Sherman Zwicker* (1942), a Grand Banks schooner owned by the Grand Banks Schooner Museum and on display in summer at Bath's Maine Maritime Museum. The former Maine coastal passenger and freight steamboat *Sabino* (1908) still steams out of Mystic Seaport. Maritime enthusiasts can view three replicas of earlier wooden sailing vessels: the *Mayflower II* at Plimoth Plantation in Plymouth, Mass.; the topsail sloop *Providence,* the first vessel commissioned into the U.S. Navy, sailing out of Providence; and the 18th-century replica of the British frigate HMS *Rose,* sailing out of Bridgeport, Conn.

Ten naval vessels on exhibit today are reminders that New England shipbuilders made a major contribution to America's naval, as well as mercantile, past. The vessels, all but one of which were built in New England, include the 18th-century frigate USS *Constitution* at the Charlestown Navy Yard (Boston) and seven warships of World War II vintage: the battleship *Massachusetts,* the destroyer *Joseph P. Kennedy, Jr.,* a submarine, and a patrol torpedo boat at the USS *Massachusetts* Memorial Commission, in Fall River, Mass.; a second destroyer, the *Cassin Young,* also at the Charlestown Navy Yard; and the cruiser *Salem* and diesel-powered submarine *Sailfish* at the Quincy, Mass., yard where they were built. The world's first nuclear-powered submarine, the *Nautilus,* built in Groton, Conn., in 1954 and now moored at the Nautilus Memorial and Submarine Force Museum in Groton, and the USS *Albacore,* a submarine with a radical new underwater body, built in the Portsmouth Naval Shipyard, now on view in Portsmouth, N.H., are reminders that New England shipbuilders remained on the cutting edge of technology in naval architecture and engineering well into the 20th century. New England ports also have been home to many naval vessels from the days of sail to the present.

Although most vessels of the past have been destroyed and the waterfronts at which they tied up have been filled in, the towns and cities where they were built, and from which people went to sea in them, remain. The syllables "port" or "haven" in the names of those places continue to evoke the region's maritime past: Bucksport, Searsport, Portland, Newburyport, Kennebunkport, Bridgeport, Vinalhaven, New Haven, and Fairhaven. So, too, many streets were named for their approximation to (Front, Fore, Commercial) or distance from (High, Pleasant, Church) the waterfront, the center of commerce at that time. The architecture of many homes in these ports attests to the wealth that their owners accumulated from mercantile and shipbuilding pursuits in an earlier era. Some of these "period" buildings now house fine maritime museums, and a few larger maritime museums have collections of fine "period" buildings.

Mystic Seaport is the most inclusive repository of New England's maritime past. The Dartmouth and Nantucket, Mass., Whaling Museums specialize in whaling history; the New Bedford Museum houses memorabilia of Long Island steamboats; the collections of the USS *Massachusetts* Memorial Commission, in Fall River and Quincy and the Charlestown Navy Yard appeal to the U.S. Navy World War II buff. The Maine Maritime Museum, the Penobscot Marine Museum in Bucksport, Maine, the Peabody Essex Museum of Salem, Mass., and the Lake Champlain Maritime Museum at Basin Harbor, Vt., concentrate on the maritime past of their respective locales.

Many maritime museums have come a long way in recent years, from offering fine artifacts and paintings of vessels behind glass in poorly lit display cases to providing the opportunity to board vessels of the past and stride their decks while listening to chantey men sing of seafarers' complaints and joys. Visitors can now meet and talk with role players in period costume. This "living" experience offers insight into the lives of the people who made America's maritime past. Some museums are also home to educational programs: Mystic Seaport has the Williams College–Mystic Seaport Program in Maritime Studies, for example. Others feature training in historical maritime skills that have been adapted to the present, such as boatbuilding and rigging.

The United States is not a consciously maritime-oriented nation. Few educational institutions support an interest in, or study of, the maritime past. No university in the United States grants a doctorate in maritime history or maritime literature. Nevertheless, museum curators and individual faculty members in a few universities have helped recover, preserve, and reinterpret its maritime past. Knowledge of New England's maritime culture has been informed in recent years by their research. Using new information and new sources, and treating previous sources differently, scholars and curators have shown the region's maritime past "from the bottom up"—from the worker's view as well as from management's view. They have revealed that African Americans and men from the Azores and Cape Verde Islands contributed greatly to past maritime activity. Many women's journals and diaries have been uncovered and published, revealing the significant role of women in the maritime community. Some of the maritime museums reflect this new information and interpretation.

New England's maritime past also lives in the present, outside the universities and museums, in its icons. The three most visible images of New England's maritime past are the Portland Head Light, the statue of the Gloucester fisherman, and the *Charles W. Morgan.* Maine's Portland Head Light stands as a bold symbol of security and stability. The statue of the Gloucester fisherman stands as a symbol of seafaring and of endurance and steadfastness against adversity. The *Charles W. Morgan,* around which Mystic Seaport was literally built, has come to stand for the past of seafaring men and women who went down to the sea in ships. These icons (along with other lighthouses, weather-beaten faces of salty mariners, and images of sailing vessels) grace calendars, note cards, and postcards. Billboards, television commercials, and other advertising media have also reproduced images of New England's maritime past to attract tourists and sell products. The *Charles W. Morgan,* for example, although used to advertise the principles of "strength, courage, . . . and the burning light of freedom," has also been used to advertise Hit Parade and Colony Hundreds cigarettes, State Line potato chips, and gasoline products for Mobile, Esso, and Atlantic Richfield. Portland Head light, too, has appeared in banking advertisements and ads for Kool cigarettes and gasoline. Commercialization and tourism clearly profit from associations with New England's maritime past.

What is preserved is often an "accident" of history. The *Sabino* still steams, primarily because in its last days as a working steamboat in a fleet of diesel-powered passenger vessels it was slow and small and hardly used, and, when used, not used hard. Such artifacts reveal the interests of the preserver and the presenter more than an authentic past. A clean look back to the past is often clouded by wishful thinking, sometimes by family interests, sometimes by artistic interests, sometimes by the interests of an entrepreneur or of a director or a board of trustees. Artifacts out of context do more to evoke a wistful sense of maritime heritage than provide an accurate sense of life in the past.

Editors of family memoirs have been known to use a "judicious" pen when presenting the diaries or letters of an ancestor for publication. Sometimes this is merely a matter of cleaning up language or editing out a family scandal, but sometimes the changes are more significant. Many authors have romanticized New England maritime life in their work, and not always with the reality of the times in mind. When we hear seafarers' songs sung by present-day chantey men, we are actually hearing a beat that once beat men to exhaustion. When the exhibit of an individual marine artist is introduced by the words, "His work captured the majesty of the square-rigged sailing ship," we must remember that the word *majesty* is an owner's word, not a word spoken by a forecastle hand.

Museums have found it difficult to represent the past "as it was." Old vessels are often converted into tourist attractions by the addition of electric lighting and air conditioning. Visitors, therefore, find it difficult to imagine life in the forecastle of the *L. A. Dunton,* for instance. Today tourists see the varnished wood of a restored forecastle gleaming in electric lights. Yet the men who fished the boat remember a smoky, poorly lit, and poorly ventilated bunkroom, kitchen, and recreation room—a cramped space for a dozen men. The steamer *Sabino,* once a grimy working vessel covered with many layers of sooty, scaly, peeling white paint, has also been restored and is now immaculately clean, well varnished, and highly polished.

In the early 21st century, New England retains a connection with the sea. That connection is manifest in the fishing vessels that sail from Gloucester, New Bedford, Portland, Provincetown, Rockland, Maine; Point Judith, R.I.; and many smaller harbors. More and more, however, docks are being filled with pleasure boats. On adjacent piers, condominiums are replacing warehouses, fish-processing plants, and piles of fishing gear. Some working sail still remains; a summertime "dude schooner fleet" consisting of new and rebuilt vessels operates in the sailing cruise trade in Maine and Massachusetts waters. The only year-round vessels other than fishing vessels are ferries serving the islands of Maine, Massachusetts, and Rhode Island and crossing from Connecticut to Long Island. The two international ferries serving Maine and Nova Scotia operate only during the summer; many other New England ferries are seasonal as well.

A number of fine small shipyards launch excellent fishing vessels, ferries, and excursion boats, and other yards build yachts and pleasure boats. The discretionary dollar keeps a number of commercial vessels alive in recreational fishing and whale watching. Whales, once considered a natural resource, are now viewed as a natural wonder, and whale watching adds considerable tourist dollars annually to the local summer economies of New England. Many recreational beaches remain, and lobstermen continue to catch one of the few remaining natural resources in New England's inshore waters. Their boats still moor picturesquely in many coves and harbors now guarded by automated lighthouses.

The maritime past exists all around New Englanders. Their character has been formed at the intersection of that past and by continuing reactions to the sea at their doorstep. The maritime present, on the noisy truck- and drug-infested waterfront, will tomorrow become the maritime past. The rust-streaked tanker that brought oil from Texas may turn into a well-loved vessel in a maritime museum of the future. For who in the 19th century would have thought that the *Charles W. Morgan,* an old whaling vessel—the equivalent of a present-day cross between an oil rig and the butchering floor at the Chicago Stock Yard—would end up as the most visited commercial vessel in a museum in the United States?

Robert G. Albion, William A. Baker, and Benjamin W. Labaree, *New England and the Sea* (1972); W. H. Bunting, *Portrait of a Port: Boston, 1852–1914* (1971); Jerry Morris, *New England under Sail: A Guide to Sailing Ships, Ferries and Historic Vessels* (1993); Joseph M. Stanford, ed., *Sea History's Guide to American and Canadian Maritime Museums* (1990).

James F. Millinger

Moby-Dick

Moby-Dick *Moby-Dick,* Herman Melville's greatest work, was published in 1851. Melville had risen to prominence as a writer of adventure tales based on his own experiences at sea. In January 1841 he left Fairhaven, Mass., on the maiden voyage of the whaleship *Acushnet.* He deserted at Nuka Hiva in the Marquesas Islands, then joined the Australian whaleship *Lucy Ann.* After a bloodless mutiny the vessel returned to Tahiti. Melville made his way to the neighboring island of Eimeo (present-day Moorea), where he joined his third whaler, the *Charles and Henry* of Nantucket, Mass.

Melville's sixth book, originally titled *The Whale,* began as an adventure story drawing on both the author's whaling experiences and the real-life sinking of the whaleship *Essex* by a sperm whale. Although Melville generally wrote very quickly—*Redburn* (1849) and *White-Jacket* (1850) together were written in four months—*Moby-Dick* took him almost a year and a half to complete. As he wrote, Melville struggled to include an increasingly complex body of ideas that evolved during his new friendships with Nathaniel Hawthorne, to whom *Moby-Dick* is dedicated, and a circle of New England literati. These influences, and his rereading of Shakespeare, transformed the book from a whaling adventure into a story of the search for truth. What had begun as a relation of Captain Ahab's hunt for the white whale became in the writing a masterpiece salted with brilliantly drawn characters and inimitable wry humor that blends detailed accounts of whaling with Melville's quest for the limits of human understanding. Ahab posits in Moby Dick all that is unknowable and inscrutable, declaring, "To me, the white whale is that wall [the bounds of human knowledge], shoved near to me." Ahab believes that if he can strike through the wall, he will attain truth. The attempt drives Ahab to madness and, in the end, to the destruction of his vessel and every member of his crew except the narrator, Ishmael.

Many scholars have studied the genesis of *Moby-Dick.* Harrison Hayford noticed a curious pattern of "unnecessary" duplicates and theorized that the novel was written in several stages. In the earliest of these Queequeg was an ordinary seaman and Peleg was the one-legged Quaker captain. Ahab did not appear until late in the game. Melville went back, rewrote some passages, and inserted others, leaving vestiges of earlier writing.

Melville represents conventions of New England culture with Starbuck, the conscience-stricken Puritan; Stubb, the pragmatic, cynical Yankee; Flask, the plodder, bereft of imagination; and Ahab, the seeker consumed by his obsession. The four harpooners represent other ethnic groups commonly found on whaleships: Queequeg is a South Sea Islander, Tashtego a Native American from Gay Head on Martha's Vineyard, Mass., Daggoo an African, and the hidden, mysterious Fedallah is Asian. All these characters serve as foils for Melville's musings on humanity's place in the universe and the mechanisms of human society.

Only the first English and first American editions of *Moby-Dick* were printed during Melville's lifetime. Not until the 1920s was Melville rediscovered and *Moby-Dick* recognized as perhaps the greatest American novel. The first cinematic adaptation of the text was the silent film *The Sea Beast* (1926), which was followed by a sound version called *Moby Dick* (1930). Both movies featured John Barrymore as Ahab, who, in a drastic departure from the book, survives and returns to marry the girl he left behind. The 1956 motion picture, also called *Moby Dick,* was written by Ray Bradbury and directed by John Huston; it starred Gregory Peck as Ahab. A 1998 television adaptation of Melville's tale featured Patrick Stewart as Ahab and Gregory Peck as Father Mapple. The film *Jaws* (1975), based on the 1974 novel by Peter Benchley, is a latter-day version of *Moby-Dick.*

As can be seen in countless cartoons, notably in the *New Yorker* and Gary Larson's Far Side series, *Moby-Dick* has assumed a prominent place in American popular culture. Indeed, many seafood restaurants bear the name Moby Dick. Even the Starbucks coffee chain was named after the first mate of the *Pequod. Moby-Dick* has become an integral part of New England culture. Those who have not read the book still know of crazy Ahab and his monomaniacal pursuit of the great white whale.

Mary K. Bercaw, *Melville's Sources* (1987); Harrison Hayford, "Unnecessary Duplicates: A Key to the Writing of *Moby-Dick*," in *New Perspectives on Melville*, ed. Faith Pullin (1978); Elizabeth A. Schultz, *Unpainted to the Last: "Moby-Dick" and 20th-Century American Art* (1995); Haskell Springer and Douglas Robillard, "Herman Melville," in *America and the Sea: A Literary History,* ed. Haskell Springer (1995).

Mary K. Bercaw Edwards

Monhegan Island Located some 11 miles off midcoast Maine in Muscongus Bay, Monhegan was first sighted by Europeans during the exploratory voyage of Giovanni da Verrazano in 1524. When Captain John Smith sojourned on "Monahigan" in 1614, he praised its convenient harbor, buffered from open winds by the tiny isle of "Monanis" (Manana), and its abundant ocean harvests. Many other early adventurers also noted this 2-square-mile island in the Gulf of Maine. They traded there with Native Americans, who camped seasonally to fish, and later established fishing stations. English cod fleets quartered at Monhegan helped sustain the fledgling colony established at Plymouth in 1620.

Permanent settlement began shortly after 1777, the year Henry Trefethren of Kittery purchased Monhegan and its outlying islands for £300 and three of his married children moved there to farm and fish. When Monhegan was incorporated as a plantation in 1839, it had 100 residents, numerous dwellings, a schoolhouse, a church, and well-fenced fields and pastures. During the second half of the 19th century fishing eclipsed farming, and Monhegan experienced the beginnings of tourism. Although the island remained isolated and insular into the 20th century, as early as the 1870s cottagers and boarders began summering there. A reporter for the *Boothbay Register* explained in 1907, "The artists followed the fishermen, literary men came next, then people of wealth and refinement." The island's exquisite landscape makes it a summer haven for artists, nature lovers, and those seeking respite from the world. Artists found the island particularly appealing. Encouraged by his teacher, Robert Henri, the painter Rockwell Kent worked as an artist and a carpenter on Monhegan during extended stays between 1905 and 1911. He was followed in 1911 by George Bellows and by many other artists since that time. Their paintings of the stark meeting of land, sea, and sky and of the fishermen and other island folk who toil on Monhegan have contributed to an image of the island as a place embodying core Yankee values.

Monhegan's year-round population has ebbed and flowed over time. Well into the 19th century descendants of original settlers predominated. New families arrived in the 1850s, increasing the population to a high of 195 in 1860. That number had declined by more than half by 1900. In 1940 population reached a 20th-century peak of 150, owing to natural increase and newcomers. With the outbreak of World War II, the island's young men all enlisted and then returned to shape the community for the next quarter century. As they matured and their children moved off-island, the year-round population dropped below 50. In 1964 the one-room school closed. During the 1960s and 1970s young people—many of them children and grandchildren of cottagers—began moving to Monhegan to live, work, and raise families in the relative safety and isolation of the island community. Since the mid-1970s the year-round population has hovered between 70 and 100, and in 1972 the school reopened permanently.

Monhegan lacks many commonplace amenities and is not always accessible in winter, when the mail boat runs three times a week, weather permitting. The town, a cluster of wooden structures built mostly along the island's few dirt roadways, covers barely a third of the island's surface. There are no cars on Monhegan, though the island is home to a number of rusted-out pickups; modest wooden signs mark commercial establishments; doors can still be left unlocked; daily interactions are face to face. Most of the island is owned by Monhegan Associates, organized in 1954 to "preserve for posterity the natural wild beauty" of the headlands and forests.

Monhegan has for generations been home to a working year-round community whose economic mainstay is lobstering. This community defines the character and culture of the island. Since 1909, under a state law imposed by the islanders themselves, the lobster season has been restricted to six months of the year in order to maintain a plentiful supply in a protected 2-mile zone around Monhegan's shores. The 2-mile zone was customary until 1998, when challenges from inshore fishermen brought the matter into the courts, where it was codified into law. At the beginning of the off-season, which coincides with the arrival of summer sojourners and day-trippers, lobster traps are stacked along roadways, and many of their owners join the island's full-time tradespeople in tourist-related occupations.

Islanders generally share a desire to preserve Monhegan roughly as it is. Some changes have nonetheless occurred. In the 1980s electricity replaced kerosene and gas lamps in many houses and businesses, and regular phone service was installed. The number of summer boat crossings has also increased. As islanders look toward the future, they worry about the delicate balance between the quality of the natural environment and tourism, about the economic and cultural costs of modernization, and about protecting the viability of their way of life.

Ted Bernard and Jora Young, *The Ecology of Hope: Communities Collaborate for Sustainability* (1997); Ruth Grant Faller, *Monhegan: Her Houses and Her People, 1780–1970* (1995); Charles B. McLane, *Islands of the Mid-Maine Coast*, vol. 3: *Muscongus Bay and Monhegan Island*, rev. ed. (1997); Ida Sedgwick Proper, *Monhegan: The Cradle of New England* (1930).

Holly V. Izard

Morison, Samuel Eliot (1887–1976) Historian. Rarely has a professional historian attained the level of public recognition enjoyed by Samuel Eliot Morison. A remarkably skilled writer, this Harvard College professor at-

Monhegan Island, 1973

Unveiling of the Samuel Eliot Morison monument, Boston, 1982

tracted a wide audience for his books, which were both scholarly and accessible to the general reader. Many had maritime themes, and two won the Pulitzer Prize. Morison established a lasting reputation as a self-professed sailor-historian with his masterful biography of Christopher Columbus, *Admiral of the Ocean Sea* (1942), for which he retraced Columbus's route and probable landfall in the Bahamas. Throughout Morison's life, recreational sailing remained important to him.

Morison was born into a distinguished Boston family and recalled in later years a childhood often spent in the company of his grandfather and namesake, the historian Samuel Eliot. In 1904 he enrolled at Harvard and by his sophomore year had resolved to study history, a decision further inspired by the presence at Harvard of an extraordinary group of historians, including Frederick Jackson Turner. After graduating in 1908, Morison studied in France for a year before returning to Harvard for graduate work. After receiving his doctorate, he taught at Berkeley but returned to Harvard in 1915 for an appointment to the history faculty. With the exception of three years at Oxford in the 1920s, he remained at Harvard until his retirement in 1955.

The prolific Morison wrote history as the story of individuals and their strivings, and did so in a highly effective and approachable manner. Early publications included *The Maritime History of Massachusetts, 1783–1860* (1921), *The Oxford History of the United States, 1783–1917*

(1927), and *The Growth of the American Republic* (1930), a popular textbook co-written with Henry Steele Commager. Morison's work consistently touched on the American promise of opportunity and individual liberty, with a clear emphasis on a foundation of social order. Never shy professionally, Morison advocated and then undertook the writing of the three-volume *Tercentennial History of Harvard College* (1935–36). During World War II he used political connections to become the U.S. Navy's semiofficial wartime chronicler, receiving a commission as a lieutenant commander and serving on several warships in the process. The payoff in terms of scholarship was the 15-volume *History of United States Naval Operations in World War II* (1947–62).

As the postwar decades unfolded, Morison continued to produce significant work, including *John Paul Jones: A Sailor's Biography* (1959) and the two volumes of *The European Discovery of America: The Northern Voyages* (1971) and *The Southern Voyages* (1974). During his retirement years Morison also maintained an extensive schedule of public lectures, further enhancing his popularity. Morison died in Boston in 1976; in 1982 the city recognized the life and achievements of Samuel Eliot Morison by erecting a monument in his honor on the Commonwealth Mall.

William Bentinck-Smith, "Samuel Eliot Morison," *Proceedings of the Massachusetts Historical Society* 88 (1976); Samuel Eliot Morison, *One Boy's Boston, 1887–1901* (1962); George M. Pfitzer, *Samuel Eliot Morison's*

Historical World (1991); Wilcomb E. Washburn, "Samuel Eliot Morison, Historian," *William and Mary Quarterly*, 3d ser., 36 (July 1979).

Paul D. Nygard

Museums Much of New England's maritime past is being extraordinarily well preserved in museums. The focus of these museums' collections varies widely, including naval architecture, yachting, whaling, 19th-century maritime life, and submarines. Because of the complex technology of the maritime world, curators and historians have difficulty explaining maritime events without devoting concentrated study to ship construction, nautical language, sail handling, navigation, and naval tactics, among other subjects. This necessary specialization, in addition to New England's rich seafaring heritage, explains the existence of so many fine maritime museums in the region.

The Peabody Essex Museum of Salem, Mass., which began in 1799 as the Salem East India Marine Society, was initially a professional organization for ship captains and supercargoes. Established to promote knowledge of trade to the East Indies and to create a museum of curiosities, it also assisted widows and orphans of deceased members of the society. Although its founders did not intend to create one of the nation's preeminent maritime museums, the staff in later decades would recognize the need to preserve the art and artifacts of Salem's dying maritime trades. By 1889 the Peabody had acquired enough material to designate a special maritime collection; today the Peabody Essex Museum is one of the largest museums in New England and its holdings have grown to include collections of decorative arts, architecture, and cultural artifacts.

The Peabody remained the region's sole maritime museum until the New Bedford (Mass.) Whaling Museum was established in 1903; in 1922 the Hart Nautical Collection was established at the MIT Museum in Cambridge, Mass. Maritime museums did not evolve in the era when museums as a whole consisted of difficult-to-access collections of esoteric objects intended only for the use of scholars. Instead, they emphasized the preservation of New England's seafaring heritage. And when the family car made it possible for American families to vacation in coastal towns, maritime museums blossomed. During the 1920s and 1930s, several influential maritime museums were created, including the Marine Historical Association, now Mystic Seaport (1929), the Nantucket Whaling Museum (1930), and the Penobscot Marine Museum (1936). All were inspired by awareness that New England's maritime industries were

Visitors at Maine Maritime Museum, Bath

in steep decline. By the 1920s sailing ships were disappearing, and mariners who had sailed during the glory days of clipper ships and whaling fleets were dying out. Growing public interest in "the old days" led to the establishment of these museums. Preservationists celebrated Yankee sailors' hardiness and ingenuity and acknowledged shipping as the mainstay of many regional fortunes.

The most spectacular period of growth for maritime museums occurred during the 1960s and 1970s. Fully half of New England's maritime museums were established between 1962 and 1978. This growth was part of a national trend; a boom in the creation of new museums resulted from, among other things, renewed public interest in the past, growth in the tourist industry, and new interest in traditional folkways such as wooden boatbuilding. Museum professionals reacted to new potential audiences by changing exhibit styles. Rather than simply displaying everything in their collections, curators created elaborate thematic exhibits that reflected concern for the education and interests of all visitors.

Every New England state (even landlocked Vermont) has had at least one maritime museum; most are located in Massachusetts and Maine. More than 60 institutions in New England have important maritime collections. About half of these have mission statements that emphasize maritime history entirely or significantly, and about one-quarter of them are active in the Council of American Maritime Museums.

Most maritime museums today exhibit nautical artifacts, including ship models, ship portraits, fishing and whaling implements, nautical gear, naval weaponry, small craft, and historic memorabilia. Some museums possess large historic vessels, and some museums *are*

historic vessels, such as *Battleship Massachusetts*, nicknamed "Big Mamie," located at Battleship Cove in Fall River, Mass. The best museums emphasize public education through guided tours, onsite interpreters, lectures and other public events, publications (print, Internet, and video), internships, school programs, sail training, traveling exhibits, and research libraries. Museums often occupy a maritime site such as a wharf or shipyard. Those fortunate enough to have a waterfront site with a view of passing vessels offer visitors yet another dimension of New England's seafaring heritage.

Edward P. Alexander, *Museums in Motion: An Introduction to the History and Functions of Museums* (1979); American Association of Museums, *Museums for a New Century* (1984); American Association of Museums, *The Official Museum Directory* (1997).

Nathan R. Lipfert

Pirates, Privateers, and Smugglers

Pirates, privateers, and smugglers have plied the coasts and borders of New England and captured the attention of its residents for centuries. During the 16th and 17th centuries, descendants of the Puritans illegally conveyed various goods, including molasses, distilled into rum, to avoid acts of the British Parliament. From 1919 to 1933, New Englanders smuggled liquor by boat and across the Canadian border to thwart Prohibition. In the 21st century smugglers bring illegal drugs and immigrants, automatic weapons, and bootleg cigarettes in and out of New England.

A pirate is someone who robs at sea. Although pirates still operate in Asian and Caribbean seas, piracy had ended in New England waters by 1720, especially after the British government stepped up its efforts against piracy in 1700. Deceived by Lord Bellomont, Captain Kidd found himself in a Boston jail in 1699. In 1704 authorities executed six pirates in Boston after exhortations from the Reverend Cotton Mather. Another 26 pirates died by hanging in Newport, R.I., in 1723. In some areas, pirates' corpses were coated with tar and displayed publicly as a warning to others.

The end of widespread piracy coincided with the expansion of privateering. Considered little more than legalized piracy by many, it only took a license or a "letter of marque and reprisal" from the government to convert a private armed vessel into a privateer.

Privateers performed an important role in America's early wars. During the War of Austrian Succession (1740–48) American privateers played the leading role in America's war effort and significantly assisted England by impeding Spanish and French shipping. At least 230 privateers, carrying more than 5,000

men, sailed from New York City, Newport, and Boston during the French and Indian War (1754–63). Over the course of the Revolutionary War, there were between 2,000 and 3,000 American privateer attacks on British shipping. Although Rhode Island, Connecticut, and New Hampshire all commissioned privateers, no state sent more privateers to sea than Massachusetts between the Revolution and the War of 1812. In the latter conflict 515 American privateers captured 1,345 British vessels.

After the war years, the expiration of letters of marque led some privateers into piracy. A more diverse and realistic portrait of the people who sailed on privateers and pirate ships—long considered nothing more than "all kinds of flotsam and jetsam"—has emerged. David Cordingly argues that pirates practiced egalitarianism and democracy. In addition to electing their captains and relying on profit sharing, pirates voted on other matters affecting their vessels and resolved disputes through arbitration. Displaced workers and family members often sailed on privateers, as did African Americans, who frequently sailed on privateers based in northern seaports.

Smuggling was a violation of the law but occurred regularly and became an economic necessity for many New Englanders. Opportunities for smuggling African slaves, European manufactures, rum, sugar, and sugar products abounded in colonial America. England's economic policies and lax enforcement, moreover, encouraged American smuggling with the Dutch, the French, and the Spanish West Indies. America's trading with the enemy during the French and Indian War infuriated the British. Intended to discourage smuggling and curb the legitimate trade of the colonies with continental Europe, the American Revenue Act (generally known as the Sugar Act) of 1764 hit New England particularly hard. John Tyler argues that smuggling played a larger role in the Tea Act, the Boston Tea Party, and the interests of the Boston merchants and America's revolutionary leaders than generally realized.

Although only a small portion of New England mariners engaged in piracy, and the impact of smuggling and privateering far exceeded piracy's impact on the region, pirates dominate tales of seafarers. Whether they emerge as ruthless, as in Robert Louis Stevenson's *Treasure Island,* as entertaining caricatures in a Gilbert and Sullivan opera, or as peg-legged Lego pirates, pirates continue to capture the imagination.

The 1984 discovery near Cape Cod of the *Whydah,* the only pirate shipwreck ever found, galvanized the interest of the public, treasure hunters, and maritime archaeologists. Seeking recruits and supplies in New England, the

Whydah got caught in a storm in 1717 and joined the 3,000 other sunken vessels along the 40 miles of shoals beyond the Cape's outer beach. The ship, which had captured more than 50 merchant vessels, seemed destined to reemerge as a theme park and museum in the Charlestown Navy Yard; controversy surrounding its early history as a slave galley, however, prompted developers to seek a final home for the proposed *Whydah* attraction elsewhere. A Cape Cod museum devoted to the *Whydah*'s continued excavation is open to the public and offers information about conservation of the ship's artifacts.

David Cordingly, *Under the Black Flag: The Romance and Reality of Life among the Pirates* (1997); Simon Smith, "Piracy in Early British America," *History Today* 47 (May 1996); John Stilgoe, *Alongshore* (1994); John Tyler, *Smugglers and Patriots: Boston Merchants and the Advent of the American Revolution* (1986).

William A. Baller

Ports In 1916 Hildegarde Hawthorne published a travel book entitled *Old Seaport Towns of New England,* in which she described the scenery and history of towns from Portland, Maine, to New Haven, Conn. She tried to capture the charm of these seaport towns for readers who had never visited New England. Hawthorne lamented the disappearance of the traditional maritime trades and crafts, the rotting wharves and dilapidated shipbuilding yards. All of the cities, New London, Conn., especially, had shifted their emphasis toward manufacturing.

Many characteristics that made New England's seaports "maritime" cities have been disappearing for some time. Traditional maritime industries have fallen victim to a variety of economic and political factors over the past 150 years. At the turn of the 19th century at least 10 percent of New Englanders made their living from the sea. Commercial use of the coast is still evident today by the sight of fishing trawlers in nearly every New England port and lobster boats off the coast of central and northern Maine, but government regulations on the fishing industry and technological improvements (containerized cargo, for instance) have made it increasingly difficult for New Englanders to make a living from the sea.

After the Civil War, environmental, economic, and political factors forced much of the region's shipbuilding to move to Maine. The introduction of iron and steel to ship construction in the latter part of the 19th century, however, made it hard for Maine builders to compete in the world market. Shipbuilding is now confined to a few coastal cities such as Bath, Maine, and Groton, Conn.; these cities are so dependent on navy contracts, however, that their future is uncertain in a post–Cold War America. Most vessels built in New England now serve either as military or as pleasure boats.

Another important task of coastal cities is to serve as an entrepôt for goods moving into the interior hinterland. The transshipment of goods largely shifted to New York and New Jersey early in the 20th century, but by the end of the century Boston was making efforts to improve its position in international trade. The introduction of containerized cargo in the early 1960s, however, drastically reduced the need for dockworkers.

Today, only a few remaining New England ports can still service large, oceangoing vessels, and the commercial use of space on the waterfront is being replaced with recreation and leisure industries. Many high-paying manufacturing jobs have been replaced by lower-paying service jobs. A marina that services large pleasure yachts has replaced the navy yard in Newport, R.I. Commercial wharves are being converted into "dockominiums." The gentrification of the waterfront has caused property values to soar and has driven working-class neighborhoods inland.

Tourism is now actively promoted in New England's coastal cities. Massport's Cruiseport has seen a dramatic increase in cruise ship passengers since 1995, when 42 ships carried 59,720 passengers; in 2004, 96 ships carried 199,453 passengers. Senator Edward Kennedy of Massachusetts worked for and passed federal legislation in the 1980s to help preserve America's historic ships. Some cities, like Fall River, Mass., have invested in maritime museums and waterfront redevelopment projects using private and state dollars. New England states now promote their waterfronts with everything from license plates to television advertisements. As coastal cities continue to promote the recreational uses of the sea, they face the challenge of providing a clean and safe aquatic environment.

But New England's ports have not merely become amusement parks and weekend playgrounds. Massport's Conley Terminal moved 51,770 containers in 1998, importing more than 500,000 tons and exporting nearly 190,000 tons. The Massport Marine Facilities also moved more than 40,000 automobiles, plus petroleum products, salt, liquefied natural gas, gypsum, cement, and scrap metal. Connecticut's three deep-water ports, Bridgeport, New Haven, and New London, specialize in cargo markets that overlap in some respects with Boston. These ports also transship forest products, produce, chemicals, metals, and waste papers. The port of Portland handled more than 650,000 tons of dry cargo in 1997, putting it in the same league with Boston in terms of tonnage. Portland likewise handles forest products, scrap metal, coal, salt, tapioca, and fertilizer.

New England's port facilities today represent a variety of public-private ownership arrangements. For instance, Merrill's Marine Terminal in Portland (built in 1982) is privately owned, whereas port facilities in Portsmouth are run by the New Hampshire State Port Authority (created by the state legislature in 1957), an independent agency superintended by a board of directors appointed by the governor and executive council. But although some New England coastal cities and towns are recovering the historic charm that Hildegarde Hawthorne described, it is unlikely that many will reindustrialize with those traditional maritime industries she described.

Robert G. Albion, William A. Baker, and Benjamin W. Labaree, *New England and the Sea* (1972); Elaine Forman Crane, *Ebb Tide in New England: Women, Seaports, and Social Change, 1630–1800* (1998); William L. Taylor, *A Productive Monopoly: The Effect of Railroad Control on New England Coastal Steamship Lines, 1870–1916* (1970).

Steven H. Park

Sea Chanteys Chanteys (also *chanties* or *shanties*) are shipboard work songs used informally to coordinate rhythms when hoisting sail, weighing anchor, loading cargo, and, occasionally, furling sail, hauling nets, and rowing. Chanteying was initially a phenomenon of the American and British merchant marine and the songs themselves descended directly from West African work songs. The practice in Scandinavian, French, German, and other European vessels derived from the Anglo-American example in an international shipboard labor pool. Unaccountably, the term almost certainly derives from the French *chanter* (to sing) or its command form, *chantez* (you, sing). Whatever the spelling, it is properly pronounced *shanty*, and it refers as much to the specific occupational use of such songs as to the songs themselves.

Shipboard chanteying arose largely as a generalized phenomenon in the years following the Napoleonic Wars, occasioned by sailors' exposure to the traditional call-and-response work songs of African slave laborers loading cargo in the Gulf Coast and Caribbean ports. Singing at work was inherently infectious, and on shipboard it proved effective in allaying boredom, increasing efficiency, and elevating crew morale in an era when merchant ships tended to be chronically undermanned. Meanwhile, increasing numbers of slaves and free blacks were serving in the crews of merchant vessels, bringing their songs and age-old African singing traditions with them. These became intermingled with Anglo-Scots-Irish genres, popular songs, and various other European and American influences, resulting in a distinctive occupational type. Typically, chanteys were sung by that portion of a ship's crew at work on a given task, unaccompanied by musical instruments. They were led by a so-called chanteyman, who was formally or informally selected from the crew.

Regarding their origins, chanteys can be organized into four groups: songs and chants adopted directly from the African American stevedores, of which few survive in their original forms; chanteys indigenous to the merchant service—the characteristic body of songs made up by sailors for the performance of specific shipboard tasks; songs imported intact from the general culture and turned to the purpose of accompanying shipboard tasks; and various hybrids, mostly adaptations and derivations from popular culture ashore. Like any folk process of oral tradition, as the songs were passed from ship to ship they were expanded and improvised upon until they became inextricably intermixed and the distinctions obscure.

Chanteys are classified into three main types, distinguished primarily by function and by rhythm and structure. The first type, the hauling chantey, includes three species: long-drag or long-haul halyard chanteys were used for hoisting topsails, for other types of heavy hauling, and occasionally (though not customarily) for rowing and other rhythmic chores of long duration. They are typified by a call-and-response format, with a single line sung as a solo, followed by a one-line chorus joined by all hands. The crew would haul on the accentuated downbeats of the chorus:

SOLO: As I was a-walking down Paradise Street
CHORUS: To me WAY, aye, blow the man DOWN!
SOLO : A pretty young damsel I chanced for to meet
CHORUS : GIVE me some time to BLOW the man down!

Short-drag or short-haul chanteys were for working topgallants, royals, and the other smaller sails, and for working sheets, clews, bunts, and braces to position square sails:

SOLO : Boney was a warrior
CHORUS : Away ay-YAH!!
SOLO : A harrier and a terrier
CHORUS : John Fran-SWAH!

A small family of chanteys was intended for furling sail aloft, which requires a unified haul among several hands to gather, fold, and tuck the bunt. The structure of these chanteys is unique, the important feature being a recognizable burden (sung as a solo or in unison) leading up to a final syllable that was the signal to haul:

To me way, hey, yah! We'll pay Paddy Doyle for his BOOTS!
To me way, hey, yah! We'll all throw much at the COOK!

Or:

SOLO : Oh do, my Johnny Boker, come rock and roll me over;
CHORUS : Do, my Johnny Boker, DO!

Technically, these are short-haul types intended for a special purpose, as are the sweating-up and hand-over-hand chanteys, used for setting jibs, staysails, and the smaller square sails high aloft. Although almost any halyard chantey might do, one that was particularly associated with hand-over-hand work is nowadays probably the most famous chantey of all:

SOLO : What shall we do with a drunken sailor?
CHORUS : What shall we do with a drunken sailor?
What shall we do with a drunken sailor?
Early in the morning.

The second type, heaving chanteys, are those used for working the capstan, brake windlass, and pumps—thus for weighing anchor, cutting-in whales, loading cargo, and pumping ship. These may be generally (but not rigidly) subdivided by rhythm and structure. Capstan chanteys are suited to walking around the capstan in waltz or march time. Often they are structured like halyard chanteys, the distinction being more one of customary usage than of rhythm or format:

SOLO : Oh the times are hard and the wages low.
CHORUS : Amelia, where you bound to?
SOLO : The Rocky Mountains is my home.
CHORUS : Across the Western Ocean.

They frequently have a longer solo followed by a chorus of two or more lines, however, and because of the long duration of the tasks for which they are intended, the lyrics are often ballad-like narratives:

SOLO : From the West Indies docks I bid adieu
To lovely Sal, and charming Sue;
Our ship's unmoored, our sails unfurled,
We are bound to plow the watery world.
CHORUS : For we are outward bound;
Hurrah! we are outward bound!

The stroke required to work the seesaw-like "jiggity-jig" brake windlass apparatus has a more staccato rhythm than capstan work. Many of the same chanteys were also used to operate the bilge pumps, which entailed a similar up-and-down motion. The extent to which chanteys were interchangeable among capstan, windlass, and pumps seems to have

been a matter of individual preference among chanteymen and crews. Halyard chanteys and capstan chanteys were converted for walka-way, a method of hoisting a sail by walking along the deck with the halyard, rather than hauling it in place. Similarly, halyard chanteys were sometimes recruited for use at the windlass and pumps. Often, shore songs were employed; others were hybridized, such as "Banks of the Sacramento," a ubiquitous derivative of Stephen Foster's "Camptown Races."

Finally, a few ceremonial and occasional chanteys were reserved for special occasions during a voyage. The "Salt Horse Chantey" or "Poor Old Man," though unrelated to the practical heaving-and-hauling required in the sailors' regular work, has ritual significance as an ironic tribute to the sailors' paying off their advances after a month or two at sea. "Homeward bound" songs for the capstan and windlass are specific chanteys (or variants of chanteys) purported to have been sung only at the conclusion of a voyage, when the bowsprit was pointed home.

Chanteys were occupational work songs, seldom if ever sung on shipboard for any purpose not connected with actual work. As early as the 1870s they were popularized and romanticized in arrangements for the parlor, glee clubs, and schools. Meanwhile, as steam propulsion gradually supplanted commercial sail, chanteying aboard ship declined and by 1930 had become extinct. In his play *Moon of the Caribbees*, written around the time of World War I, Eugene O'Neill employs chanteys as a point of pride symbolic of "real" deepwater sailors, as distinguished from the newer breed of steamship men who—like the Hairy Ape—work inside a machine and therefore never had use for chanteys.

Joanna C. Colcord, *Songs of the American Sailormen* (1938); Stuart M. Frank, *The Book of Pirate Songs* (1998); Frederick Pease Harlow, *Chanteying aboard American Ships* (1962); Stan Hugill, *Shanties from the Seven Seas* (1961).

Stuart M. Frank

Seamen   During the colonial and Federalist eras, many coastal New Englanders worked as mariners. Seaborne commerce, fishing, and whaling expanded rapidly from the 1600s through the early 1800s. New England's maritime industries declined steadily after the Civil War; consequently the numbers of employed seamen declined as well. In the 17th and 18th centuries, seamen brought cultural diversity to New England's coastal cities and towns with their travels and experiences; in the 19th century, with their ethnic and regional backgrounds; and in the 20th century, with their traditions and history.

White seamen in colonial New England

shipped out with slaves, free blacks, and Native Americans. In 1742, 8 percent of Boston's population of 16,400 was enslaved, and most slaves worked in some maritime capacity; one-fifth were owned by mariners. Early Nantucket, Mass., settlers may have learned whaling from the local Gay Head Indians, and New Bedford, Mass., New London, Conn., and several other ports took up whaling soon after the Revolutionary War. Whalers from most Massachusetts ports employed Native Americans well into the 19th century. Nantucket whalers recruited seamen from the Massachusetts mainland, and many African Americans accepted the invitation and settled on the island with their families.

Merchant trade with the West Indies and with the other American colonies began in the mid-17th century. "Coasting" (seaborne trade along the American coast) allowed towns and small coastal settlements to exchange farm and forest products for British manufactured goods, providing both agricultural profits and a higher rural standard of living. Port cities, especially Boston, prospered as commercial centers. In 1698 there were 171 merchant vessels registered in Massachusetts, and Boston had 194 ships engaged in merchant trade, and for the rest of the colonial era maritime commerce employed a quarter or more of Boston's male residents.

New England had an early tradition of community participation in maritime commerce. By 1740, New Englanders owned some 1,500 merchant vessels. In ports such as Boston, New London, and Salem, Mass., merchants built and financed ships and hired their captains; frequently the merchant owners were retired captains themselves. In many small communities, the ships were built and financed as communal ventures, with local captains, most of the crew, and a good percentage of the populace sharing in the profits. The captains hired the mates (officers) and sailors. In the smaller ports, the majority of the crews were local men, neighbors, and often relatives.

Slavery ended in all the New England states shortly after the Revolutionary War, and New England's black population increased steadily. The federal Seamen's Act of 1790 mandated contracts for seamen that stipulated employment and wages regardless of race, and New England blacks hired on as seamen in large numbers. For the most part, African American seamen were career mariners with homes and families in port towns. The 1830 city directory for Portland, Maine, listed 33 African American seamen who were also homeowners. Approximately one-fifth of the sailors from Newport, R.I., Providence, Boston, and Nantucket were African American; the majority of them were residents. In 1832, 25 percent of Providence's African American heads of household were mariners. From 1803 to 1860, some 3,000 African Americans shipped aboard New Bedford vessels; that city had the highest percentage of black population of any in New England, at nearly 7 percent in 1838.

After the Revolutionary War, New England's maritime industries expanded rapidly, with the encouragement and support of the new federal government. Jobs for seamen multiplied until there was virtually a berth for any American who wanted to go to sea, from masters (captains) to green hands (new sailors). New England boys from ports and fishing villages followed their fathers and brothers to sea, along with thousands of others who left farms and small towns to go "before the mast," as they referred to it.

The resident population of seamen brought a certain sophistication to coastal New England, from Boston to the smallest Maine port. Souvenirs and consumer goods from all over the world were displayed in homes and sold in shops. Geography and navigation were taught in public schools along with the "three Rs," and some seaports that traded with Latin America also offered Spanish in their schools. Young men and women alike studied this relatively cosmopolitan curriculum, thus enriching the culture of the entire community.

Although seafaring jobs continued to increase, the percentage of American-born seamen declined sharply after 1830. Merchant and whaling vessel owners began to emphasize greater speed and larger cargoes, and voyages became more difficult and more dangerous. Captains turned the hiring of crews over to recruiting agents who rounded up the cheapest white laborers they could find, often shutting out experienced sailors. There were also new opportunities ashore by 1850, and fewer American-born young men went to sea. Eager to take their place, laborers from abroad signed on.

Portuguese sailors joined New England crews relatively early, first from the Azores and later from Cape Verde. In the 1780s whaling ships had begun stopping at both archipelagoes, first to take on salt and later expressly to hire crews. The Portuguese were regarded as good sailors and hard workers, and by the 1860s well over 25 percent of New England's whaling crews were Portuguese. The majority of Azorean sailors settled in New England, primarily in New Bedford and New London. Initially most Cape Verdean sailors left their families behind on the islands and returned when they could, but in the decades after the Civil War they began establishing homes and families in New Bedford and Providence.

Boston received 311,000 European immi-

Seamen's Bethel, 1872

grants in its harbor from 1820 to 1855, more than half of them Irish. Of the Irish who stayed in Boston, most found jobs ashore and only a few went to sea. Many Irish immigrants went to Provincetown and Gloucester, Mass., and to Portland looking for other employment and became seamen in those ports. The same process held for other immigrant groups, and by midcentury a great many of Boston's seamen were transients. Sailors went to Boston for a berth but no longer for a home. The welfare of mariners had concerned New England's clergy and social reformers since colonial times, and in 1833 the Boston Port Society opened a boardinghouse and the Seamen's Bethel, a church for mariners, "to improve the moral, religious and general condition of seamen and their families." The mission continues to this day in Boston's North End.

The fishing fleets of Massachusetts were slower to hire foreign-born seamen than were the merchants and whalers. Fishing boats went on shorter trips and fishermen were paid by a percentage of the catch, so their shoreside lives were relatively stable and their pay remained competitive. Nevertheless, by the 19th century, fishing ports began attracting foreign-born seamen to their wharves. Irish laborers came to Provincetown and Gloucester in midcentury to work in the shipyards and went fishing instead. Significant numbers of Azorean Portuguese left New Bedford and whaling for Gloucester and Provincetown and fishing. Gloucester's population grew by more than 10,000 between 1840 and 1875, making it not only New England's busiest fishing port but also its most diverse city. Along with the Portuguese and Irish, Italians, Nova Scotians, and Scandinavians came to Gloucester.

The percentage of Maine's seamen who were foreign-born did not increase to the same degree as it did elsewhere. Maine's maritime commerce flourished in relatively independent community ports, with predominantly local captains and crews. Maine was home to half of the entire U.S. Atlantic fishery in the 1820s, with small fleets employing 2,600 men out of 70 harbors. Many of those men fished in the summer and farmed or built ships for the rest of the year. Maine's merchant vessels were also relatively small and often a community or even family venture, with the captain owning a controlling interest. Seafaring was the center of Maine's coastal life, and its communal structure was its strength. Independence and a strong sense of community still characterize Maine's coastal towns.

During the Civil War, the Union's merchant marine fleet was decimated; half of New England's vessels were lost. Neither American nor New England shipping ever recovered. Merchant vessels built in Maine and captained by Maine masters continued trading in the decades after the Civil War. Elsewhere, New England's presence in maritime commerce steadily declined, from carrying one-third of U.S. merchant trade in 1880 to only 4 percent in 1950. The whaling industry, too, collapsed after the Civil War. Azoreans and Cape Verdeans in New Bedford dominated what remained of the industry, but after the 1880s few vessels were still whaling.

New England's fishing industry remained viable and economically important. By the end of the 19th century, the fishing fleets were manned primarily by Portuguese, Nova Scotian, and Scandinavian seamen. By 1880 New Bedford's fishermen were almost entirely Azorean and Cape Verdean, and Provincetown's population was more than one-third Portuguese. From that time on, Italians, mainland Portuguese, Swedes, and Norwegians began coming to Boston to fish. Most moved north to the ports of Gloucester and Portland or south to the fishing towns of Rhode Island.

Today, New Bedford, Gloucester, and Provincetown still have fleets of offshore fishing boats, but the rest of New England's fishing industry is inshore and small-boat. Meanwhile, ferries, other passenger vessels, workboats, tugs, and recreational vessels continue to employ mariners, some of whom are trained at Maine Maritime Academy or at the Massachusetts Maritime Academy. Seafaring as a way of life is still compelling to a few people in New England. But while the region may always have busy ports such as Boston and Portland, its prominent role in merchant shipping is in the past.

Richard Henry Dana, Jr., *Two Years before the Mast* (1840); Sebastian Junger, *The Perfect Storm: A True Story of Men against the Sea* (1997); Rudyard Kipling, *Captains Courageous* (1897); Samuel Eliot Morison, *The Maritime History of Massachusetts* (1961); Charles Nordhoff, *Whaling and Fishing* (1856); William Hutchinson Rowe, *The Maritime History of Maine* (1948); Walter Teller, ed., *Five Sea Captains: Their Own Accounts of Voyages under Sail* (1960).

Wendy Knickerbocker

Shipbuilding

"Build me straight, O worthy Master," wrote the New England poet Henry Wadsworth Longfellow in "The Building of the Ship," aptly choosing a theme close to his New England heart as a metaphor for the state. For until the Civil War nearly wrecked Longfellow's ship of state and decimated the American merchant marine, New England shipbuilders were producing at least half the ships that floated the nation's ocean-going commerce. During the entire era of wooden ships, from the 1620s to the 1920s, New England ships and shipbuilding were defining elements of the region.

New England shipbuilding in fact predates permanent settlement in the region. The short-lived Popham Colony at the mouth of Maine's Kennebec River constructed the pinnace *Virginia* in 1607, considered to be the first ship built in North America. Massachusetts launched its first vessel, the *Blessing of the Bay*, in 1631, and the other colonies followed suit shortly after settlement.

Shipbuilding became a characteristic New England industry for several reasons. North of Cape Cod, especially, agricultural opportunities were limited, whereas one of the world's richest fishing grounds lay just offshore. Colonists required ships to engage in fishing and to transport the surplus catch, along with surplus agricultural produce and wood, to distant markets in exchange for manufactured goods and produce unavailable at home. Even within New England, waterborne transportation was more efficient than land transport until the development of the railroad in the second quarter of the 19th century. Coastal New Englanders became mariners to provide for their economic needs and increasingly to take advantage of the transportation needs of other regions.

The need to build ships was served by New England's natural features. The coast's many estuaries and rivers provided sheltered shoreline close to deep water where vessels might be constructed and launched. And New England forests contained the most desirable mix of woods for shipbuilding: white oak preferred for ship frames and planking, white pine for deck planking and spars, hackmatack (larch) for strengthening knees, and a variety of hard-

woods that could be used with or in place of oak.

The beginning of New England shipbuilding was an extension of the trade in old England. For 300 years the industry retained the craft organization that was established in England by the end of the 16th century. A "master" builder headed a shipyard, having earned his title through a formal or informal apprenticeship of up to seven years with an older master. The master builder was experienced in all aspects of ship construction, from design through framing, planking, caulking, rigging, and management of the shipbuilding crew. In a colonial era shipyard, a crew might consist of as few as three to five men. Some might be journeymen who had completed an apprenticeship and were gaining further experience in the trade before establishing their own yards. At least one might be a specialized craftsman, especially a caulker, who drove tarred hemp fibers called oakum into the seams between the ship's hull and deck plans to strengthen and seal the hull. Most of the labor was supplied by general ship carpenters, who used broad ax and adze to shape timbers, sawed out the planks, bored the holes for wooden treenail fastenings, and put the vessel together, working alongside the master builder. The completion of this collective effort was commonly celebrated in a launching ceremony, sometimes including much of the local community along with shipbuilders and owners. In the larger shipbuilding communities, such ancillary tradesmen as sparmakers, riggers, shipcarvers (who carved the decorative work for vessels), ship painters, pump and block makers, boatbuilders, and sailmakers worked on contract to complete a vessel after launch.

New England shipyards operated on two models. The most common approach through the mid-19th century was the "contract" yard, which produced vessels on demand from merchant shipowners, occasionally building on speculation to keep the shipyard crew together in slack times. Contract yards ranged from the smallest operation, producing only one or two vessels on a tidal creek, to the noted East Boston yards of Paul Curtis and Donald McKay that produced world-renowned clipper ships in the 1850s.

In the second approach, sometimes called the "captive" yard, the builder was also the shipowner. In these yards, which became a larger segment of the New England industry around the mid-19th century, the vessels were designed and built specifically for the yard owner's personal shipping activities. Captain Paul Cuffe of Westport, Mass., whose father was African and whose mother was Wampanoag, operated such a yard between 1790 and 1810. In the 19th century, some or all of the ships built by such noted yards as the Skolfield yard in Brunswick, Maine, the Thatcher Magoun yard at Medford, Mass., and the Arthur Sewall yard of Bath, Maine, were operated by the yard owners. The naval shipyards at Boston and Portsmouth, N.H., which produced government vessels, were specialized forms of the captive yard.

Some shipbuilding communities, such as Greenmanville at Mystic, Conn., were the maritime equivalent of mill villages. In the paternalistic structure of a wooden shipyard, shipwrights supplied their own tools and claimed certain perquisites. Workmen routinely took chips—scrap wood—as fuel until the second quarter of the 19th century, when some owners began to sell chips. In many shipyards, a twice-a-day rum ration was replaced by a coffee break as the temperance movement grew in the 1830s and 1840s. Store pay, in which credit at the yard owner's store was issued in lieu of cash wages, survived into the 1880s in some areas. Beginning around 1840, ship carpenters used labor actions to reduce the working day from a sunup-to-sundown schedule to 10 hours, and later to seek higher wages. Craft associations for ship carpenters existed in the larger shipbuilding communities, and the Knights of Labor had some success in negotiating for ship carpenters in the larger yards in the 1880s, but organized labor was not a major force in New England's wooden shipyards.

By the middle of the 1850s, when the United States merchant marine surpassed Great Britain's as the largest oceangoing fleet in the world, New England–built ships were among the most prominent. New England and shipbuilding were synonymous, and the shipbuilding industry prospered. The merchant marine was crippled by economic contraction after 1857, and by the effects of the Civil War; thereafter, New England ships were increasingly designed for bulk cargo carriage in the coastal trades, which were protected from foreign competition. Continuing to build large sailing ships when other regions were shifting to steam-powered vessels, New England yards produced large square-rigged freighters often termed "down easters" (because so many were built "down east" in Maine) to carry bulk cargo to and from the West Coast, and increasingly large fore-and-aft-rigged schooners for carrying bulk cargo—principally coal for steam and electric power—from Middle Atlantic ports to New England.

New England wooden shipbuilding experienced increasing consolidation during the 19th century. As local timber supplies were de-

pleted; as average vessel size exceeded the capacity of the smaller estuaries; as maritime trade became increasingly centralized in the largest ports; and as the demand for ships became more sporadic, the industry abandoned many of the smaller and more remote building sites. A few survived owing to specialization, such as Essex, Mass., whose marginal location on a narrow tidal river was overcome by the proximity of Gloucester and the local specialization in building fishing vessels for the Gloucester, Boston, and Provincetown fishing fleets. In both large and small ports, the surviving yards became reliant on outside timber sources, obtaining oak in the Middle Atlantic and southern states and mast timber in the Midwest and eventually the Pacific Northwest.

As shipbuilding became less a small local industry and more a consolidated one, the shipwright's trade became a more specialized and transient one. In the larger yards, which might employ as many as 100 men, the tasks and skills were divided among sawyers, framers, plankers, caulkers, and joiners. In the largest shipbuilding communities, such as Bath, independent contractors operated crews of plankers and caulkers who moved from shipyard to shipyard as their skills were required. Itinerant shipwrights also moved from region to region. Ship carpenters from New Brunswick and Nova Scotia sought work in New England yards as the Canadian industry shrank, and New England ship carpenters migrated between centers in response to economic shifts. As an extreme example, Donald McKay, New England's best-known shipbuilder, was born in Nova Scotia and learned the shipwright's trade in New York before setting up his yards in Massachusetts. The characteristic wooden shipbuilding industry survived longest in Maine, where skill and low wages kept wooden shipyards viable until the end of the World War I. Scattered small yards, which produced either large boats or small ships, survived into the 1980s building wooden fishing and recreational vessels.

After the colonial era, New England shipyards were extremely homogeneous. The former slave Frederick Douglass's inability to find work as a caulker in the prosperous and diverse whaling port of New Bedford, Mass., in 1839 underscores the lack of diversity. Despite the captive yard operated by Paul Cuffe and the contract yard co-owned by African American shipbuilder John Mashow in South Dartmouth, Mass., the vast majority of New England wooden shipwrights were of northern European extraction and New England, New York, or Maritime Canada nativity. Women might operate boardinghouses or

stores that served shipwrights, but they did not work in the yards.

Beyond a few isolated cases, iron and steel shipbuilding was not introduced in New England until the 1890s, more than two decades after its establishment in New York and along the Delaware River. But with the creation of iron and steel shipyards at Bath in the 1890s and at Quincy, Mass., and Groton, Conn., in 1900, the complexion of New England shipbuilding changed. A steel shipyard is the maritime equivalent of a factory, with the capability to assemble identical vessels from preformed parts. Builders of metal ships operate cutting, bending, and punching machines for metal plates, riveting or welding tools to construct the hulls, and pipefitting and other metalworking tools to complete the vessel. Relatively few ship carpenters seem to have acquired the metalworking skills necessary in the new yards, so there was little continuity between the new and old yards.

Like the wooden shipyards, the steel shipyards flourished intermittently, building many vessels during times of war, very few during economic contractions. With corporate ownership to capitalize the mechanized facilities, with heavy unionization, with a diverse workforce that included women—especially during World War II—these yards resembled steel shipyards elsewhere in the United States more than they did their precursors in New England. With little demand for merchant ships, modern steel shipyards in the United States have been increasingly dependent on naval contracts to survive. The Fore River Shipyard in Quincy, Mass., for instance, was unable to compete economically even though it built very sophisticated LNG (liquefied natural gas) ships during the 1970s. The two large yards in Bath and in Groton carry on the process of shipbuilding in New England through the construction of naval surface ships and submarines. A few smaller yards, like Washburn and Dougherty, in East Boothbay, Maine, still build ferries, research vessels, and tugs.

In his gloss of the shipbuilding process, Longfellow captured the sense that a wooden shipyard produced an organic being, an animate object almost imbued with a soul by the hands that shaped it. It is the wooden vessel, however obsolete, that relates most closely to the popular notion of the New England character. Yards that built wooden ships were organized as paternalistic communities that used resources at hand to produce practical, yet aesthetically pleasing and complex products cheaply and efficiently. The idealized wooden shipyard thus represents the imagined resourcefulness and strength of character associated with New England. Like New England itself, modern steel ships are large and complex. Modern steel ships are shaped and assembled in corporate, departmentalized, unionized shipyards largely dependent upon federal contracts for their work. Both surviving large yards in New England stress their innovative approach to construction and the quality of their vessels. Modern New England shipwrights may identify more strongly with their trade union than their shipyard, but few can resist the emotional bond to their product, a vast structure that seems to come to life once it is delivered into the sea.

Robert G. Albion, William A. Baker, and Benjamin W. Labaree, *New England and the Sea* (1972); William A. Baker, *A Maritime History of Bath, Maine, and the Kennebec River Region,* 2 vols. (1973); Joseph A. Goldenberg, *Shipbuilding in Colonial America* (1976); Henry Hall, *Report on the Ship-Building Industry of the United States* (1884); John G. B. Hutchins, *The American Maritime Industries and Public Policy, 1789–1914* (1941); William N. Peterson, *"Mystic Built": Ships and Shipyards of the Mystic River, Connecticut, 1784–1919* (1989); Ralph L. Snow, *Bath Iron Works: The First 100 Years* (1987); Dana A. Story, *Growing up in a Shipyard: Reminiscences of a Shipbuilding Life in Essex, Massachusetts* (1991).

Andrew W. German

Ships and Boats

Given New England's long coastline, ample timber resources, and the early orientation of its settlers to the sea, it is not surprising that numerous characteristic watercraft were developed in this region. Although most have become obsolete and have disappeared from the contemporary waterfront, distinctive traditional vessels such as Friendship sloops, Marshall catboats, and Long Island Sound oyster dredges still ply New England waters. Meanwhile, regional yacht builders produce fiberglass pleasure boats. Shipbuilders turn out fishing boats, ferries, Aegis-class destroyers, and submarines that carry the American flag around the world. Yankee clipper ships may have gone the way of the dinosaurs, but New Englanders still go "down to the sea in ships," as the fishermen's bronze memorial in Gloucester, Mass., proclaims.

Gloucester's "ships" were in fact fishing schooners that, in various shapes and sizes, pursued the natural riches of the banks just offshore. Built with a convex bow, gracefully curved sheer lines, and lofty rig, the "Gloucester" fishing schooner evolved over 200 years, and in its final early-20th-century form displayed a distinctive profile. This schooner is perhaps the most recognizable New England vessel type and was portrayed in the classic 1937 film adaptation of Rudyard Kipling's novel *Captains Courageous,* starring Spencer Tracy, Lionel Barrymore, and Freddie Bar-

Gloucester schooners in harbor, 1881

tholomew. Perhaps no image of a sailing vessel so evokes the idea of a New England "ship" more than the Gloucester fishing schooner. And perhaps no boat evokes New England small craft as readily as the flat-bottomed Banks fishing dory. Carried aboard the Gloucester schooners, dories were cheap and easy to build, in part because of their distinctive narrow triangular stern. Today they are almost as common at seafood restaurants or on postcards as they once were in the harbors of Gloucester, Boston, and Rockland, Maine.

The bluff-bowed whaleship, with its ungainly but utilitarian lines, is another classic New England vessel. Whaleships were often bark-rigged, and commonly were reconditioned packet vessels. The old packets were chosen for their full-bodied cargo holds, capable of storing hundreds of barrels of oil and tons of whalebone. Originally built in New Bedford, Mass., in 1832, the ship *Gen. Washington* of New London, Conn., was just such a vessel and at 606 tons was considered one of the largest of its breed. Like Herman Melville's *Pequod* in the novel *Moby-Dick,* these vessels were sometimes built specifically for whaling. Whaleships were often constructed near their port of sail, particularly during the first half of the 19th century, the "golden era" of American whaling. The last surviving example of this type is the bark *Charles W. Morgan,* now berthed at Mystic Seaport in Mystic, Conn. It was built at New Bedford in 1841 and sailed most of its profitable career out of that port, which for most of the 19th century was

the whaling center of the United States. Toward the end of the century many local shipyards closed owing to the general demise of wooden shipbuilding in the United States and the decline of whale fishery. Wooden shipbuilding, except for the construction of yachts and fishing vessels, remained primarily on the Maine coast.

The smaller, double-ended whaleboats carried on board the larger ships were actually used to "catch" the whale. Whaleboats had European origins but tended to be identified with New England boatbuilders—particularly those builders working in New Bedford, New London, and Nantucket, Mass.—who brought them to a high state of refinement. New Bedford specialized in constructing a modified Arctic whaleboat, used both for whaling and for exploration in icy waters. Whaleboats were also adapted as seine boats, from which fishermen set large fishnets for menhaden and mackerel.

New England's changing coastline frequently influenced the design of local vessels. The work they engaged in as well as the commodities they carried were also factored into their construction and appearance. The rocky, indented coast of Maine with its dramatic tides contrasts sharply with the sandy shores of Cape Cod, for instance, and with the marshy, low-sloping lands of the southern Connecticut coast. As the eminent historian of American small craft John Gardner pointed out, the sailing dory of Swampscott, Mass., is illustrative of regional and local factors; it was designed with a round bottom "yet with enough flat to sit upright on the beach when it grounds out . . . the outer layer of which is easily renewed when it wears thin from dragging over rocks." The Piscataqua River wherry was designed with a low freeboard to allow for free and easy rowing, since the current of that river was very strong, particularly near Eliot, Maine, where it was principally built.

One of the most remarkable indigenous watercraft to evolve in New England was the Piscataqua River gundalow, a flat-bottomed sailing barge designed to take advantage of the Piscataqua's fierce currents. Gundalows had an extraordinarily short mast, on which a long pivoting-yard with a lateen sail could be raised or lowered. This unique rig allowed them to pass under the low fixed bridges common in the region. Watermen abandoned the last working gundalow in 1920, but today a reproduction named *Captain Edward H. Adams,* launched at Portsmouth, N.H., in 1982, plies the Piscataqua estuary on educational missions.

Small craft in particular came to be associated with the town or region in which they were developed. The Block Island "cow horn," the "Yarmouth" pinky, the Connecticut River shad boat, the Rhode Island hook boat, the New Haven sharpie, or the Maine "reach boat" are among the numerous examples. The general characteristics of many of these boats often took on subtle local variations and evolved as they were adapted or designed for particular uses most commonly associated with the various New England fisheries. Any resident of Savannah, Ga., or Key West, Fla., in the 1850s, for instance, would have recognized the Connecticut fishing smack even though it was built in New London, Waterford, or Noank, Conn. These 10- to 40-ton sloops and schooners were particularly known as products of southeastern Connecticut shipyards and were designed to spend the winter months fishing in southern waters. They were also designed with wet wells, allowing fishermen to keep fish alive in the hold of the vessel for delivery to market. In Maine, where the 20th-century lobster fishery spawned a number of local types, the open Hampton boat came to have discernible local variations. Compare the slightly sharper-bowed boats built at Orr's Island with those from Boothbay Harbor or elsewhere in the state. The Hampton boat may have evolved into a larger version, which is the typical Maine lobster boat of today. Early versions of this boat tended to be narrower than the more modern types, such as the "Beal's Island boat" with its covered wheelhouse.

The menhaden fishery, which harvested great quantities of menhaden for bait, oil, and fertilizer, was first started commercially in New England during the mid-19th century.

The necessary inshore seining produced singular fishing-boat designs such as the beamy "carryaway" boats and the heavily planked seine boats. Later the more efficient and at one time ubiquitous menhaden steamer, first developed in Bristol, R.I., became a well-recognized type on the East Coast. It sported a distinctive profile characterized by a tall wheelhouse constructed over a forward deck cabin. A second long deckhouse aft, which contained a hoisting engine, was punctuated by a tall engine-stack. This general deck layout worked so well that modern vessels in this fishery have retained it.

During New England's early colonial period, small shallops (a type of open-decked, two-masted fishing vessel) and single-masted sloops were the most common fishing and coastal trading vessels. Pinnaces, somewhat larger vessels that were often described as small ships, were also common in 17th-century transatlantic trades and coastal work. Indeed, the pinnace *Virginia,* launched in 1607 at what is today the town of Popham, Maine, located at the mouth of the Kennebec River, was the first vessel launched in British North America. In the 18th century, larger sloops, brigs, and scows, as well as ships of 400 tons' burthen, were the common carriers of the period. Many were constructed specifically for the important West Indies trade. Often referred to as "horse jockeys," they were specially fitted with high-railed decks for carrying the horses, mules, and cattle that were among New England's principal exports.

As the 19th century dawned, so did the great era of shipbuilding in New England. It was an industry that increasingly became tied to southern cotton. Vessels of a special form were constructed to transport this commercially important crop to markets in New York, New England, and Europe. Southern ports tended to be relatively shallow, so vessels were designed with flatter floors or bottoms rather than the more traditional "V" shape that had characterized earlier ships. In some instances, vessels with particularly shallow drafts were built in New England for specific southern ports or coasts, such as those that existed along the Gulf of Mexico. Shipyards in Maine and Connecticut were particularly favored in this regard by the New York merchants who dominated this trade. These schooners, brigs, and small barks were also frequently designed with centerboards that could be retracted, allowing them to pass along the shallow Texas coast and the notorious sandbars that guarded such ports as Galveston and Lavaca. At the same time these vessels were seaworthy and thus favored for the often-dangerous coastal passage between cotton ports and New York or Boston.

With the opening of more European and Asian markets to trade in the 1840s and the discovery of gold in California, the era of the clipper ship was born. New York City was the homeport for most of these distinctively handsome ships. They were lofty, heavily sparred, and characterized in popular vision by a graceful concave bow and stern. These large ships were also constructed with considerable deadrise that contributed to their speed but constrained their cargo capacity. More often than not clipper ships were the products of New England shipyards. Vessels such as Donald McKay's *Flying Cloud* launched at East Boston, or Irons and Grinnell's *Andrew Jackson,* a product of Mystic, were touted in their time as being the fastest sailing ships in the world. The *Andrew Jackson,* in fact, was a "medium clipper," meaning that it had a fuller body allowing greater carrying capacity. It also sported a distinctively graceful round stern that came to be associated with so many large sailing vessels built at Mystic. Other New England ports such as Medford, Mass., and Portsmouth, N.H., also produced their share of these "greyhounds of the sea," ships with metaphorical names such as *Atmosphere, Winged Arrow,* and *Whirlwind.*

As the 19th century drew to a close, Yankee shipwrights developed another type of large commercial vessel for the American grain trades; the fabled "down-easters" were principally built in Maine. These large ship-rigged vessels were designed for maximum carrying capacity, while retaining some of the speed and appearance of medium clippers. One of the last to survive was the Bath-built *Benjamin F. Packard,* which ended its life as a tourist attraction at Playland Amusement Park in Rye, N.Y., during the 1930s.

The era of the great coastal schooners began at roughly the same time, but extended well into the 20th century. These were very large vessels designed to carry huge quantities of such bulk cargoes as grain, timber, oil, ice, and coal. These four-, five-, and six-masted schooners came to be generally identified with the wooden shipbuilding yards in Maine. Typical of these vessels were the five-master *Rebecca Palmer,* launched at Rockland, and the six-master *Eleanor A. Percy* and flush-decked four-master *Annie C. Ross,* both products of Bath. By the end of the century, Bath led the nation in building wooden ships.

Yacht builders also added their special touch to designs developed in New England. Examples include George F. Lawley and Sons of South Boston, whose designs and shipyard influenced all late-19th-century racing yachts. David O. Richmond of Mystic, a lesser-known builder, did much to perfect the lines of the colorful "sandbagger" sloop. The most renowned of the New England builders was the Herreshoff Manufacturing Company of Bristol, R.I. This firm was well known for its "fin-keeled" racing sloops such as *Gloriana* (1891), as well as for its sharp "clipper-bowed" steam yachts like *Eugenia* (1899). Nathanael Greene Herreshoff's most celebrated creations were the America's Cup sloops *Columbia, Constitution, Reliance,* and *Resolute.* Writing of *Columbia* in *Rudder Magazine* in 1899, editor W. E. Robinson expounded, "Nothing so handsome in naval architecture was ever seen."

Large navy ships are still built in Bath, but these destroyers and guided-missile frigates lack distinctive regional characteristics. During World War II the "fleet"-style submarine came to be closely associated with the Electric Boat Company of Groton, Conn., as did the large nuclear-powered Polaris and Trident "missile boats" and 688-class Fast Attack submarines of recent decades. Certainly Groton, located across the Thames River from New London, has the right to call itself the "submarine capital of the world."

Commercial ships and boats are much less common than they once were in New England's harbors because trucks, not coasters, carry freight today. Nevertheless, freight, fish, and fun will inspire future New Englanders to build ships and boats as they have done for centuries.

William A. Baker, *Colonial Vessels: Some 17th-Century Sailing Craft Ship Designs* (1962); Baker, *Sloops and Shallops* (1966); Howard I. Chapelle, *The American Fishing Schooners, 1825–1935* (1973); Albert Cook Church, *Whale Ships and Whaling* (1978); John Gardner, *Building Classic Small Craft,* vol. 1 (1977); Kenneth R. Martin and Nathan R. Lipfert, *Lobstering and the Maine Coast* (1985); William N. Peterson, *"Mystic Built": Ships and Shipyards of the Mystic River, Connecticut, 1789–1919* (1989); Dana A. Story, *The Shipbuilders of Essex* (1995).

William N. Peterson

Slocum, Joshua (1844–1909) Sailor and author. Joshua Slocum, arguably New England's most famous sailor, was not a native New Englander. Born in Nova Scotia, where loyalist ancestors had emigrated, he made his way to Massachusetts, his family's former home, and between voyages lived with relatives near Boston. Having chosen a career in the merchant marine in the twilight of the age of sail, he quickly rose to command and ownership. In 1871 he married Virginia Albertina Walker, a New Yorker then resident in Sydney, Australia, who went to sea with him until her death, in the merchant ship *Aquidneck* at anchor off Buenos Aires, in 1884. Slocum married Henrietta Elliott in Boston in 1886: she was 24; he was 42. After a disastrous honeymoon voyage, in which the *Aquidneck* was wrecked in South America and the family re-turned in the 35-foot canoe *Liberdade,* Hettie never sailed again.

Having experienced all the vicissitudes of the merchant sailor, Slocum was now back where he started—lacking funds, a ship, and a soul mate. He turned to writing but had little success with his first book, *The Voyage of the "Liberdade"* (1890).

Slocum's old friend Captain Eben Pierce, a retired whaleman, ought to go down in history among New England's greatest practical psychologists. He knew Slocum's past and present predicament, and when the two met again in 1892, Pierce provided Slocum with precisely the therapy he needed: "Come to Fairhaven," he casually offered, "and I'll give you a ship." The ship in question turned out to be the hulk of a sloop propped up in a pasture. Named *Spray,* the 36-foot, 9-inch vessel wasn't even near the water.

What happened next goes beyond Yankee self-reliance or ingenuity. Slocum undertook the reconstruction of the boat, and although interrupted by an 1893 voyage on the *Destroyer,* which became the basis of his second book, in 13 months he completely rebuilt the *Spray.* After a brief spell of charter fishing, in April 1895 the 51-year-old Slocum left Boston in the *Spray* on a 46,000-mile trip that would make him the first man to sail around the world alone. His voyage took him to Gloucester, Mass., Nova Scotia, the Azores, Gibraltar, South America, Samoa, Australia, South Africa, and the West Indies before he returned to New England, arriving in Newport, R.I., in June 1898. Soon thereafter, on July 3, Slocum went back to Fairhaven and dropped anchor not far from where he had rebuilt the *Spray.* His cargo hold was brimming with curiosities acquired during his voyage, among them a stick of bamboo grown by the late Robert Louis Stevenson, a gift of the Scottish poet and novelist's widow, along with several of Stevenson's books.

The voyage, remarkable in itself, was made even more so by the book that Slocum wrote about it. Although he was not exactly a celebrity when he arrived in Newport in the summer of 1898, amid the hubbub of the Spanish-American War, he soon arranged with the Century Company to serialize his account and publish the book version of *Sailing Alone around the World,* which appeared in 1900. Often regarded as a nautical equivalent of Henry David Thoreau's *Walden,* the work is less a study of philosophy or nature than a straightforward account, powerful and charming, of a Rooseveltian man of action, and it is no surprise that the rough-riding hero of San Juan Hill and the captain of the *Spray* met and enjoyed each other's company. The influence of Theodore Roosevelt can be seen in the *Spray*'s final cargoes: orchids for the summer White House, Sagamore Hill, in Oyster Bay, N.Y., in 1906 and a 2-ton block of coral for the American Museum of Natural History in 1908.

As early as 1898 Slocum had also toyed with the idea of creating a sailing school, an idea that may have come to fruition, with Slocum's literary friend Clifton Johnson serving as an intermediary, in the voyages of three vessels named *Yankee*—a schooner, a brigantine, and a ketch—under the command of Irving and Electa Johnson. With Gloucester, as their homeport, the Johnsons circumnavigated the globe seven times with a handpicked crew of amateur sailors eager to learn. Their teaching voyages were the forebear of today's proliferation of sail-training programs, to which Slocum's own book serves as an inevitable and always welcome addition.

On November 14, 1909, Slocum set sail in the *Spray* from Vineyard Haven, Mass., and was never heard from again.

Kenneth E. Slack, *In the Wake of the "Spray"* (1966); Victor Slocum, *Capt. Joshua Slocum: The Life and Voyages of America's Best Known Sailor* (1950); Walter Magnes Teller, *The Search for Captain Slocum: A Biography* (1956); Teller, ed., *The Voyages of Joshua Slocum* (1985 [1958]).

Robert Durwood Madison

Submarines For more than two centuries the submarine has played a significant role in New England history, firing the imaginations of Yankee inventors, contractors, entrepreneurs, politicians, and naval personnel. New England remains the hub of American submarine design, technology, construction, repair, training, and even tourism for both practical and historical reasons: port facilities, sufficient capital, a skilled workforce, and long-standing naval and maritime traditions.

In 1775 at Saybrook, Conn., David Bushnell built a human-propelled submarine and subjected it to sea trials on Long Island Sound. Called the *Turtle,* Bushnell's craft became the first combat submersible when it attempted to blow up a British warship during the American Revolution.

Subsequent efforts to increase submarine viability succeeded when John P. Holland sold his New Jersey–built sub to the U.S. Navy on April 11, 1900, a date now observed as the official birthday of the Submarine Force. Thereafter most submarine construction shifted to New England's private yards, Electric Boat in Groton, Conn., and Lake Torpedo Boat Company in Bridgeport, Conn. In 1914 the Portsmouth Navy Yard (now the Portsmouth Naval Shipyard), at the mouth of the Piscataqua River between New Hampshire and Maine, secured the first contract for a submarine built in a government yard.

Submarine construction, Portsmouth Navy Yard, New Hampshire, ca. 1944

July 29, 1995, commissioning of the Trident-class USS *Maine* at the Portsmouth yard sparked a half dozen organizations, including Greenpeace, to demonstrate in large numbers against the sub's nuclear armament.

There is no doubt, however, that David Bushnell's rudimentary submersible has transformed the history of New England, the United States, and indeed the world. In the future, submarines will continue to serve as mighty deterrents to war and to become increasingly sophisticated devices for peaceful pursuits. Along with submersibles, their peaceful counterparts, submarines contribute to scientific discoveries and human betterment, mapping the ocean floor, recovering lost nuclear bombs, and providing disabled subs with advanced rescue capabilities that can save the lives of trapped crew members. The underwater voyages of Electric Boat's USS *Skate* and Portsmouth's *Seadragon* in largely inaccessible Arctic waters have yielded previously unobtainable oceanographic and geographic data.

John D. Alden, *The Fleet Submarine in the U.S. Navy: A Design and Construction History* (1979); Norman Polmar, *The American Submarine* (1981); Gary E. Weir, *Forged in War: The Naval-Industrial Complex and American Submarine Construction, 1940–1961* (1993); Richard E. Winslow III, *Portsmouth-Built: Submarines of the Portsmouth Naval Shipyard* (1985).

Richard E. Winslow III

World War I spurred production of diesel-powered submarines. Upstream from Electric Boat on Connecticut's Thames River a New London navy yard evolved into the country's first submarine base. A training school was established there after the war.

During the 1920s and 1930s Electric Boat and Portsmouth Navy Yard continued to deliver improved subs for the so-called silent service. In World War II, Portsmouth (with 79 subs) and Electric Boat (with 78) supplied the vast majority of U.S. combat submarines. Led by Medal of Honor skippers Dick O'Kane of Durham, N.H., and Red Ramage of Monroe Bridge, Mass., American submariners sank 5.5 million tons of Japanese shipping.

With the onset of the Cold War, New England–built submarines incorporated the latest technological advances. In 1955 Electric Boat's *Nautilus* sent the historic message "Under way on nuclear power," inaugurating a new era in maritime propulsion. Five years later Portsmouth Naval Shipyard's *Seadragon* surfaced through an opening in the ice at the North Pole. Portsmouth's *Albacore*, with its experimental whale shape for maximum speed, revolutionized hull design worldwide. On July 27, 1996, the 18th and last Trident-class submarine, Electric Boat's *Louisiana*, was commissioned. These subs carry 24 nuclear-tipped missiles and can individually deliver more firepower than was expended in World War II. Electric Boat has built two Seawolf-class submarines, the first of which was commissioned

in July 1997. The company delivered the first Virginia-class sub in 2004.

New England has actively promoted its historic ties to submarines. Visitors can tour several decommissioned subs in the region: the USS *Lionfish* in Fall River, Mass.; the USS *Croaker* and *Nautilus,* in Groton, Conn.; and the USS *Albacore* in Portsmouth, N.H. They can also view the conning tower and bridge superstructures of the USS *Flasher* in Groton, Conn., and the USS *Sailfish* at the Portsmouth Naval Shipyard. Since the end of the Cold War the U.S. Navy has loosened security restrictions and invited the public aboard active boats.

In addition to its purely military importance, the submarine industry in New England continues to have major politico-economic ramifications. Buoyed by trillions of dollars in defense appropriations over the years, congressional representatives from navy-yard districts vigorously seek government funds to maintain adequate workloads for their constituents.

Despite the successes, the modern submarine era has been the site of human sacrifice and controversy. In 1963 the Portsmouth Naval Shipyard's *Thresher,* a nuclear-attack submarine launched in 1960, sank some 200 miles off Cape Cod, Mass., killing everyone on board. Antiwar and antinuclear protests were commonplace at Groton and Portsmouth during and after the Cold War whenever a launching or commissioning ceremony took place. The

Tall Ship Festivals During the final quarter of the 20th century tall ships came back to New England with a vengeance. Shipwrights in Maine, Massachusetts, and Connecticut launched new schooners, and New England's fabled coast attracted sail-training vessels from around the world.

Although the real work of those vessels takes place below the horizon, between the stars and the loneliness of the sea, waterfront festivals featuring tall ships have become a staple of summertime popular culture in New England. Saluting the past by invoking an era of "wooden ships and iron men," those festivals nevertheless are resolutely forward-looking. Corporate sponsorship and appearance fees are important for the vessels. Meanwhile, city planners and business groups look to the ships as key players in the revitalization of urban waterfronts. "Almost every community wants to be part of a tall ships visit," said Vice Admiral Tom Weschler, coordinator of Newport Salute 2000. "It's a perfectly natural inclination to follow a winner."

The tall ships' visit to Boston for the Millennium Celebration—called Sail Boston 2000—drew more than a million spectators and generated hundreds of millions of dollars in revenue. That summer, an alternative convocation of sailing ships gathered in New

London and Mystic, Conn. Those events followed earlier successful ones, such as Sail Boston 1992 and a similar gathering in Newport, R.I., in 1986. Newport had hosted its last America's Cup race in 1983, and this new infusion of cash and maritime activity was especially welcome. Smaller-scale events, such as the various oyster festivals in Norwalk, Conn., continuously nurture public interest in the ships themselves, and provide social events for the crews during years in which no major festivals are planned. Norwalk's shallow harbor can only accommodate small vessels, unlike deepwater ports that can host Europe's finest Class A tall ships. In general, tall ship festivals attract regionally based vessels such as R/V *Corwith Cramer* from Woods Hole, Mass., and vacation cruise schooners from Maine and Mystic, in addition to ships from abroad. Some are spanking new, built for sail training, while others, like *Ernestina* of New Bedford, Mass., are noteworthy historic ships.

This renaissance of sail was unimaginable earlier in the 20th century. By the 1930s, commercial sail appeared to be dead, and the arrival in Boston or Portland of a rust-streaked schooner or a Spanish square-rigger laden with salt always attracted people who imagined they were seeing the last of a dying breed. It would have taken a visionary then to predict that sail training and vacations under sail would become a growth industry in the late 20th century, making an aesthetic mark and an economic impact that could not be ignored. But following the success of President John F. Kennedy's invitation to foreign tall ships to congregate at the New York World's Fair in 1964, and the even more spectacular success of Operation Sail in New York during the nation's Bicentennial in 1976, promoters and public officials capitalized on resurgent interest in sailing ships. Today there is intense competition to lure the best ships for each event.

Sailing technology has not been used effectively for modern cargo ships or tankers, despite fervent dreams and valiant attempts by both romantics and engineers (especially during the OPEC oil crisis in the 1970s). But sailing ships have a powerful grip on the imagination of educators and entrepreneurs. Writing in 1840 in *Two Years before the Mast,* Richard Henry Dana rightly observed, "There is a witchery in the sea, its songs and stories, and in the mere sight of a ship, and the sailors' dress, especially to a young mind, which has done more to man navies, and fill merchantmen, than all the press gangs of Europe."

Captain Daniel D. Moreland, who grew up in Connecticut and is one of the most respected sailing shipmasters working today, has participated in many recent tall ship festivals.

He understands the primal attraction of these apparently obsolete vessels both to committed trainees and to casual visitors. "These ships connect us in time to our rich past," he noted in his address to the Admiral's Ball in Halifax, Nova Scotia, in April 2000. "As they sail over the horizon bound we know not where, they sail with our imaginations in tow into the unknown of the future."

It is unlikely that tall ship festivals will endure forever, even if auxiliary sailing ships continue to operate. But for the time being, these gatherings of majestic ships, so rooted in the past and so forward-looking, are a fundamental part of maritime New England's contemporary culture.

Julie Michaels, ed., *Tall Ships: Supplement to the Boston Globe Associated with Sail Boston 2000* (July 11–21, 2000); *Sail Tall Ships: A Directory of Sail Training and Adventure at Sea* (2001).

W. Jeffrey Bolster

USS *Constitution* The 204-foot, 44-gun frigate *Constitution,* undefeated in battle and captor of more than 30 enemy vessels, was built in Boston's North End in the Edmund Hartt shipyard during 1795–97 and was the largest ship built in Boston to that time. Beginning its service in 1798, it was active in the West Indies during the Quasi-War with France (1798–1801) and then in the Barbary War (1803–7). During the latter conflict, *Constitution* was flagship of the Mediterranean Squadron under Commodore Edward Preble and led several attacks against Tripoli, contributing significantly to the conclusion of a peace treaty.

At the outset of the War of 1812, *Constitution* was one of only 17 units in the entire U.S. Navy and faced a Royal Navy numbering nearly 1,000. In a duel with HMS *Guerrière* on August 19, 1812, Captain Isaac Hull led the ship to an unexpected and most welcome victory. The success rallied American morale, and from it the ship gained the nickname "Old Ironsides" in recognition of the imperviousness of its stout wooden hull to enemy shot. When the news reached England, an article in

USS Constitution *at Charlestown Navy Yard, Boston, 1970s*

the December 28, 1812, edition of the *London Times* observed that "such an unexpected triumph" could give "tone and character to the war. Never before in the history of the world did an English frigate strike to an American." On December 29, 1812, Commodore William Bainbridge led Old Ironsides to a second victory, over HMS *Java*. On being informed, the British admiralty forbade any further one-on-one duels with big American frigates; henceforth, they were to be engaged only when in squadron strength.

Following an overhaul and a period blockaded in Boston, the ship sailed on two more war cruises. In the second, Captain Charles Stewart led it in a textbook action against the combined force of HMS *Cyane* and HMS *Levant* on February 20, 1815. First dividing his foes, he then defeated them in detail. By the time the ship returned to the United States in May 1815, the war over, it clearly had become the focal point of American pride, representing in its perfect record the successful defense of their independence by a federation of often contentious states that hitherto had put local interests first, and the recognition that to America now belonged their principal allegiance. An article in the May 23, 1815, edition of the *National Intelligencer* expressed that *Constitution* had become "a Nation's Ship, and should be preserved. Not as 'sheer hulk' . . . but, in honorable pomp, as a glorious Monument of her own."

The ship continued active in regular service until 1881, even circling the globe in 1844–46. Following a period as a receiving ship and a longer period of neglect, *Constitution* was restored during the late 1920s with the help of pennies collected and donated by children from all over the country and has since served as a patriotic symbol and source of civic inspiration. In celebration of the 200th anniversary of its launching, *Constitution* underwent further restoration to make it seaworthy and on July 21, 1997, made a brief cruise under sail for the first time in 116 years. By congressional directive, the ship is maintained in the city of its birth and each year is visited at the Charlestown Navy Yard by approximately a million people from all over the world.

Tyrone G. Martin, "*Constitution's*" *Finest Fight* (2000); Martin, *Creating a Legend* (1997); Martin, *A Most Fortunate Ship* (1997); Martin, *Undefeated* (1996).

Tyrone G. Martin

USS *Thresher*

On April 10, 1963, the nation mourned the loss of 129 sailors and civilians in one of the worst naval tragedies in American history. The world's most advanced nuclear-attack submarine, the USS *Thresher*, imploded at a depth of about 1,000 feet 220 miles off the New England coast, killing everyone aboard. Among the survivors left behind by the crew were 187 children.

The *Thresher* was built at the Portsmouth Naval Shipyard at the mouth of the Piscataqua River between New Hampshire and Maine. Shipyard officials were strongly encouraged to complete work on the ship with all due speed. The international climate, heavily accented by the Cold War, contributed to a pervasive sense of urgency.

The *Thresher* was launched in July 1960. It was commissioned in August 1961, about one year before Soviet nuclear missiles aimed at the United States were detected in Cuba and six years after the formation of the Warsaw Pact. British warships, Revolutionary War frigates, Civil War ironclads, and submarines for World Wars I and II had been built at the Portsmouth yard. The *Thresher* was the first of a new class of search-and-destroy submarines, one of many firsts for a shipyard with a sterling reputation for quality that traces its formal establishment to 1800.

The motto "Silent Strength" suggested a virtual invincibility ensured by the ship's speed, maneuverability, and near invisibility to predators. Despite the advantages supplied by highly sophisticated engineering, the *Thresher* spent 406 days undergoing repairs or overhauls before its final voyage. Safety, according to some critics, placed second to expedience in this process.

On April 9, 1963, the submarine departed Portsmouth Harbor for test dives. The next day, off the Massachusetts coast shortly after 9:00 A.M., the *Thresher* reported "minor difficulties." The *Skylark*, a surface ship accompanying the submarine, lost contact with the vessel about three minutes later.

At or near test depth a packing gland may have broken, creating a mist that probably caused the electrical system to fail and the engine to stop. Total darkness blanketed the people on board before emergency batteries restored a small amount of light. In this circumstance it would have taken approximately seven minutes for the vessel's nuclear reactor to generate sufficient energy to get the *Thresher* moving again. Leaks probably occurred throughout the submarine, causing the sub to sink slowly deeper.

Soon the ocean's power broke through the *Thresher's* hull, instantly killing the sailors nearby. Theoretically, the force of compressed air would have killed people in other parts of the vessel almost immediately as well. Because diesel fuel is pressure sensitive, what was left of the submarine exploded.

Several months later parts of the vessel were found scattered over a wide area at a depth of 8,400 feet by the *Trieste*, a research ship capable of very deep dives. An observer on the research craft called the area a "junkyard."

The loss of the *Thresher* and its crew has been commemorated every April 10 since 1964 in Portsmouth, N.H., and Kittery, Maine. The annual ceremony serves as a painful reminder of the tensions of the Cold War era and a salute to the Portsmouth Naval Shipyard's contribution to national defense.

John Bentley, *The "Thresher" Disaster: The Most Tragic Dive in Submarine History* (1975); Robert F. Burgess, *Ships beneath the Sea: A History of Subs and Submersibles* (1975); Norman Polmar, *Death of the "Thresher"* (1964); U.S. Navy, *United States Ship "Thresher" (SSN 593): In Memoriam, April 10, 1963* (1964).

Paul Peter Jesep

Vacation Cruise Schooners

Penobscot Bay serves as the locus for a fleet of 15 working schooners currently carrying passengers on six-day cruises among the islands of Maine. No other state can boast such a concentration of historic schooners in one area.

During the late 1930s Frank Swift of Camden, Maine, outfitted the former two-masted cargo-carrying schooners *Mabel*, *Mattie*, and *Mercantile* to entice vacationers to experience life on a coasting schooner. Until World War I, these vessels and thousands like them had carried lumber, lime, granite, and other cargoes while also serving as freight and mail boats for Maine's remote islands. Following World War II, Maine's windjammer fleet was expanded with the addition of veteran schooners *Alice Wentworth*, *Victory Chimes*, and *Adventure*. Beginning in 1962 a series of vacation sailing schooners—the *Shenandoah*, the *Bill of Rights*, the *Harvey Gamage*, and the *Mary Day*—were constructed for both southeastern New England and Maine waters at the shipyard of Harvey Gamage at South Bristol, Maine.

Presently, Rockland, Maine, is home to a fleet of historic schooners involved in the vacation cruise business, including the *Mary Day* (constructed in 1962) the *J&E Riggin*, a former oyster dredger (1927); the *Isaac Evans*, also an oyster schooner (1886); and three former fishing schooners: the *Lewis R. French* (1871), the *Nathaniel Bowditch* (1922), and the *American Eagle* (1930). The former brick schooner *Stephen Taber* (1871), the venerable three-masted "ram" schooner *Victory Chimes* (1900), and the *Summertime* (1986) complete this fleet of schooners, most of which are listed on the National Register of Historic Places. In 1983 Captains Douglas and Linda Lee built the *Heritage*, based on the lines of a traditional Maine coaster.

Less than 10 miles north of Rockland, the picturesque town of Camden is home to four wooden schooners—*Roseway* (1935), a former Boston pilot vessel; *Mercantile* (1916); *Grace Bailey* (1882); and *Mistress* (1960)—and a steel ketch, *Angélique* (1980). Nearby Rockport is home to the pilot schooner *Timberwind* (1931). The average length of these vacation "windjammers" is 75–80 feet on deck. Accommodations are provided in small staterooms with two, three, or four bunks.

Cruises traditionally run Monday through Saturday, from early June to late September. Destinations depend on wind, tide, and other weather considerations. Life aboard is relaxing but also affords guests the opportunity to participate by raising or furling sails. Most schooners have no engine but are assisted by a yawl boat (an auxiliary power launch) used while leaving or entering port. The paid crew and cook handle skilled tasks under the watchful eye of the captain, who must be licensed by the U.S. Coast Guard. The food, always bountiful, is served up family style, and coffee is always ready for early risers. Each year the Maine schooners provide thousands of vacationers a taste of life in the age of sail and a tangible connection to one aspect of New England's maritime heritage.

John F. Leavitt, *Wake of the Coasters* (1970); Edward W. Smith, Jr., *Workaday Schooners* (1975); Harry W. Smith, *Windjammers of the Maine Coast* (1983); Peter H. Spectre, *A Passage in Time: Along the Coast of Maine by Schooner* (1991).

Renny A. Stackpole

Waterfronts Many of New England's historically important landscape features are found where land and water meet. Waterfronts conjure up romantic images of the past: of iron men and wooden ships, of fishing shacks, ship launchings, and homecomings. As New Englanders turned to the waterfront for their livelihood, sail lofts, chandleries, counting houses, West India shops, and other businesses jammed busy lanes and alleys. Wharves and warehouses multiplied, reaching ever deeper into harbors. When space was no longer available, new land was created.

Change has always been characteristic of New England's waterfronts. The wealth accumulated by merchants trading with Europe and the Caribbean from 1650 was invested in the industrial transformation that was taking place there. As a consequence of the wealth accumulated, seats of art, learning, and worship were funded, as were scores of magnificent "sea captains'" homes that still dot the genteel landscape of coastal towns and cities. Among the best known of these places is Strawbery Banke in Portsmouth, N.H. Others include Salem, Newburyport, and Nantucket, Mass.; Stonington and New London, Conn.; and Kennebunkport and Portland, Maine, to name just a few.

The Industrial Revolution changed the character of New England's waterfront cities. After 1830 the thrust of urban growth shifted from the wharf to inland waterfalls. Waterfront cities continued to grow because they were the entry places for the raw materials and finished products of the interior. The first places in New England to reach a population of 100,000 were waterfront cities: Boston in 1850, Providence in 1880, Fall River, Mass., and New Haven, Conn., by 1900.

Before the mid-19th century, manufacturing was clustered along the waterfront, as were warehouses, wharves, and docks. As railroad terminals grew, they accommodated the warehousing and other storage and distribution facilities, and thus some waterfront buildings were abandoned; wharves crumbled and marine-related functions suffered. Later, the advent of the motor truck brought further change; this flexible and faster mode of moving bulk goods short distances reduced the disadvantage of locating away from rail sites and piers at harborside. Waterfront space often became derelict space.

The recreational waterfront landscape has also changed. Newport, R.I., was a summer resort for wealthy planters as early as the 1720s. The American Revolution interrupted that trend, but by 1830 its popularity had rebounded. Other elegant retreats grew along the shores of nearby Narragansett Bay and also at Bar Harbor, Maine; Watch Hill, R.I.; and in Stonington, Groton, Saybrook, and Bridgeport, Conn. This prompted Noah Webster to tab Long Island Sound an "American Mediterranean."

Immigrants accounted for much of the late-19th-century urban growth. These newcomers' ideas about Sunday leisure added to the increasing tendency of New Englanders to forsake the traditional observance of the Sabbath in favor of a day of play. The growth of the recreational waterfront was stimulated by the expanding trolley, railroad, and steamboat network. A strong aspect of waterfront resorts was the great variety of attractions they offered. Some were quiet, family-oriented places with strict temperance observances, a few private and selective; some were religious enclaves; while at others nude bathing was allowed. Most, however, catered to the average person. Often the beach was part of an amusement park, and popular places they were! By 1900, as many as 50,000 people a day traveled by steamboat down the Providence River to the Narragansett Bay waterfront resorts.

After 1900 the nature of waterfront recreational land use changed. The expanding trolley lines allowed greater numbers of working-class tourists to frequent the shore, causing the social elite to find it a less desirable place to spend time. A few of the most expensive spots, such as Bar Harbor and Newport, hung on. By the late 19th century, seasonal blue-collar cottage colonies had become popular because they allowed people greater control over their leisure environment. As cottages grew, the older hotels, gardens, and amusement parks gave way to make room for them. Cottages rapidly dominated the waterfront. Because many of the older resorts were in need of renovation, their owners often found it more convenient to encourage cottage development or other types of land subdivision and sale. In addition, after 1918, expanding military waterfront uses contributed to erasing much of the older social landscape. The Hurricane of 1938 further devastated some of the older resorts. Those hotels that remained functioned as retreats for people of ordinary means rather than as gathering places for the very wealthy.

More recently, many former summer resorts have been occupied year-round thanks to improvements in highway transportation. Accordingly, throughout New England, shoreline towns have experienced great population growth. Once-sleepy little villages are now busy places. Tony shops now cater to visiting city dwellers, no longer to those who go to sea. In old, weathered waterfront buildings, and newer ones made to look old, quaint boutiques and shops offer jewelry, arts and crafts, and gourmet food. "Nautical" antiques such as divers' helmets, weather instruments, and binnacles can be found. Shop windows promote chamber music concerts, holistic medicine lectures, and old house tours. Increasingly the old resort hotels have been converted to condominiums and apartments. Their users frequent restaurants that no longer require jackets and ties for dinner. Nearby yacht clubs have had to relax not only dress codes but also membership requirements in response to a growing public perception that exclusivity is no longer de rigeur.

Yet New England's waterfronts remain centers of commerce. All types of ships and barges, with the exception of supertankers, call. They transport commodities such as lumber and stone, chemicals, scrap iron, gypsum, lime, wood, pulp and paper, rubber and auto parts, other manufactured items, tar, asphalt, and food. In the summer, cruise ships, large and small, call at some ports. Bulk fuels such as coal and oil make up the greatest tonnage. New England relies heavily on oil for its energy needs, so oil-tank farms take up much space along the region's waterfronts. In Connecticut, for example, there are more than 1,000 coastal tanks with a combined capacity of 14 million barrels of oil. The tonnage of oil arriving and the size of the vessels that bring it continue to increase.

New England's waters have always been dangerous for navigators, especially in the winter. Rocks, shoal water, narrow passages

Ship in a lightbulb, by Winson Morill of South Hamilton, Mass., 1978

and channels, fog and high winds, treacherous currents, and tides are hazards. In the past few years the number of oil spills has increased, resulting in damage to waterfront property, beaches, and wildlife. In the winter of 1996 an oil barge went aground at the southwestern end of Narragansett Bay during a raging storm, spilling about 850,000 gallons of its 4-million-gallon cargo of heating oil. Some of the spill was carried to Block Island, 12 miles south and near the eastern end of Long Island Sound. This, the largest such incident in Rhode Island history, closed shellfish beds, stopped commercial fishing and lobstering, and killed or injured hundreds of shorebirds. As the possibility of such large accidents has increased, so has public and private concern.

As the number of recreational boaters has increased, more small spills are occurring. As a result, water-oriented businesses such as boatyards, repair shops, marinas, and yacht clubs have put pollution-control devices and action plans into place in response to state and federal regulations. The presence of fuel-containment booms at such facilities is increasingly common, as is prominent signage outlining correct refueling procedure. A waste-oil facility is common and the use of environmentally friendly boat paints and solvents is encouraged, if not required.

The landscape of boatyards has changed in other ways. In 2004 more than 110,000 recreational boats were registered in Connecticut alone. All over New England marina owners have had to accommodate the needs of weekend captains, their mates, and guests—needs far different from those who made a living at sea. Copious parking space is provided. In addition, showers and toilets, playscapes for children, and sometimes swimming pools and tennis courts are in evidence as well as a restaurant and snack bar. There may be 20, 200, or 2,000 slips. Mooring space is more and more difficult to find and the waiting lists are longer. Space for dinghies is also at a premium. Weekend sailors must spend valuable

sailing time trying to get to and launch them. The need for storage space has made vertical structures for tenders and other small craft an increasingly common waterfront land use.

The technology of hauling and repairing boats has also changed. The marine railway that once hugged the water's edge is now a relic. The ever-present mobile travel-lift has allowed boats to be stored away from the water well above the tide line, causing a type of "mari-urban" sprawl. Many boatyard owners and managers, frustrated by the stress of demands made upon them and by increasing government regulations, insist they will sell as soon as they are able. As the quest for coastal living space increases, boatyards are increasingly seen as potential condominium developments.

In some yards, however, the past is still present. At the Lowell Boat Shop in Amesbury, Mass., founded in 1793, one can visit the oldest boatshop in the United States—the birthplace of the dory. Two hundred thousand such vessels were built there. The Crosby Boat Yard in Osterville, Mass., on Cape Cod, carries on a 150-year-old tradition of boatbuilding, but now incorporates state-of-the-art materials and computer-aided design. Other such places include the Palmer and Latham Yard in Noank, Conn.; nearby, the old Latham Chester Store, a focus of mercantile activity for almost 90 years, was recently saved from demolition and restored.

Preservationists have become increasingly concerned about the future of historically significant waterfront structures. The National Trust for Historic Preservation launched a program in 1977 aimed at preserving America's maritime heritage. Historic waterfront properties are increasingly threatened by renewal and development. The same accessibility that allowed the growth of suburban waterfront boating facilities helped render the old, multistoried downtown waterfront properties obsolete. Much waterfront space lies in limbo in the older portions of New England's cities, increasingly threatened by the wrecker's ball.

The interest in waterfront preservation comes at a time when urban policymakers are recognizing that cities that cut themselves off from rivers and waterfronts suffered a loss of vitality. The success of Boston's Quincy Market, the harbor fronts of Norwalk, Conn., and Salem, and the renewed wharves of Portland show that waterfront festival marketplaces can be a focus of retail activity for the city. Boston and Hartford are tearing down highways that hinder access to the waterfront. Housing along waterfronts, as in Boston, Newport, Stamford, Conn., and Portland, has become a growing trend. Theme parks, science museums, and marinas are also replacing derelict waterfront space. In the future, New England's waterfront will be characterized less by walls and fences, vista-obstructing tall buildings, and unsafe, windswept space. Waterfronts will be people-oriented, incorporating parks, pathways, and green spaces. Historic landmarks and vistas will help remind visitors where the city's past began.

Ralph H. Brown, *Historical Geography of the United States* (1948); Thomas R. Lewis and John Harmon, *Connecticut: A Geography* (1986); D. W. Meinig, *The Shaping of America*, vol. 1: *Atlantic America, 1482–1800* (1986); John R. Stilgoe, *Alongshore* (1994); James Vance, *This Scene of Man* (1977); Robert Wenkam, *New England* (1974).

Thomas R. Lewis

Whaling Few occupations are as closely tied economically and symbolically to New England as whaling. To many, whaling conjures up images of hardy seamen engaged in a pursuit that could either cost their lives or make their fortunes. A touch of romance lingers in the fictional and the factual accounts of New England's whaling days. Both chronicle the drama of men who pit their lives, skills, and luck against the mighty whale, demonstrating something essential about the American character. Yet to others, the history of whaling in New England is a tale of systematic slaughter for profit when times were good and then of port towns in decline, having cast their fate with a way of life that was doomed to become obsolete. Today, thanks to conservation groups and whale-watching tours, the great mammals remain an important part of New England's identity and economy.

Europeans followed the whale to the east coast of North America in the 16th and 17th centuries, and like the Algonquian inhabitants of the region, they attempted to drive the right and sperm whales into shore by harpooning them and wearing them down. Once killed, whales were butchered and try-pots were set up on beaches to render the oil from their blubber. Whereas Indians used whales for bone, food, and oil, Europeans were primarily interested in the oil for lubrication and illumination. The advent of permanent English settlements in the early 17th century established land-based whaling as one of the region's first commercial enterprises. Nantucket's early Quaker settlement took advantage of the island's proximity to a whale-migration path, became experts at the hunt, and quickly established Nantucket as the center for British colonial production of spermaceti candles and lubricating oil. A booming market led to technological improvements that changed the nature of whaling and its geographic base in the late 18th century.

Whaling became an increasingly important source of New England's wealth as demand for whale products rose and shipowners sought new ways to extend the range of ships, lengthen the time spent in hunting grounds, and increase the yield of their hunt. The development of on-board tryworks, which allowed crews to render whale blubber in iron pots on deck, turned ships into floating factories. After the Revolution, New London, Conn., and New Bedford, Mass., replaced Nantucket as the nation's whaling centers. By 1830 whaling was firmly established in New Bedford, spurring the growth of ancillary businesses that ranged from ships' suppliers to shipbuilding and banking.

The middle decades of the 19th century were the zenith of American whaling. Up to 700 ships were in service, and as many as 70,000 people were employed in the industry by 1850. The continued demand for oil and improvements in ship design prompted owners to expand their hunting range first into the eastern Atlantic and then around Cape Horn into the Pacific Ocean. Rounding the Horn and sailing into dangerous Arctic and Antarctic waters had long been avoided, but heightened competition forced whalers to increase both their range and the length of their voyages; hunts could last for up to four years.

An additional impetus to Pacific voyages was the discovery of petroleum deposits in 1859 in Pennsylvania, which brought a flood of kerosene onto the home-illumination oil market. The whaling industry responded by trying to find more oil at lower cost and by creating other markets for whale products. Baleen, the material that forms a straining filter in the mouths of baleen whales such as the Arctic bowhead, was processed to provide ribs for umbrellas and corsets or worked into hoops, combs, shoehorns, and whips. The high prices commanded by these items provided the incentive for extended Pacific voyages. These voyages in turn would provide a setting for literary depictions of the men who pursued the great whale.

Seafaring had always been an occupation

"A Dead Whale or a Stove Boat"; Bela Pratt's controversial 1915 whaling monument at New Bedford, Mass., depicts an atypically "Yankee" harpooner

that defined what it meant to be a man. New England whaling men confronted not only all the dangers of the sea but the largest living creature on earth. He who battled both and won was a man among men. Individual skill, courage, and strength were greatly prized but ultimately had to be put to a communal purpose if the hunt was to succeed. Fraternity was central to the cohesion of crew members who depended on each other during critical moments of the voyage and the kill. Whaleships were some of the most diverse workplaces in 19th-century American society. Atlantic and Pacific islanders were often recruited for American ships, joining crews of Yankee, black, and Native American seamen. The Cape Verde Islands and the Azores contributed many competent crewmen who quickly learned the skills required for whaling.

Whalers shared many of the eternal customs of men at sea, as well as some peculiar to their own specialized pursuits. Long stretches of idle time were spent creating scrimshaw, an art form unique to whaling ships and now prized by collectors. Whaling's exotic and intensely masculine culture caught the imagination of writers, artists, and balladeers. A primary work in the American literary canon, Herman Melville's *Moby-Dick* (1851), used a Pacific whaling voyage out of New Bedford to explore the theme of man and his eternal struggle with nature and self. An existential novel written long before the coining of the term, *Moby-Dick* works at many levels of meaning. The persistent themes of trial, redemption, and regeneration in New England and American culture no doubt account in part for the continued popu-

larity of the novel throughout the 20th century and into the 21st. *Moby-Dick* has generated four popular films from the silent-movie era to the present. While each adds plot elements for contemporary markets, the essential symbols remain the same.

As the 19th century closed, whaling began to take on a role that was more symbolic than vital within New England's society and economy. The Civil War disrupted the industry and destroyed ships. Changing postbellum fashions and emerging technologies doomed whaling, as petroleum refineries provided cheap illuminating and lubricating oils and light steel replaced whalebone in many popular products. The transcontinental railroad lowered the cost of shipping whale products to the East and caused a shift in the base of operations from New England to the West Coast. The last wooden whaling ship, the New Bedford–built *Charles W. Morgan*, was retired from duty in 1921, more a relic than part of a vital industry. By the 1960s most countries had called a halt to commercial whaling in recognition of drastically declining whale populations. Iceland, Japan, and Norway were still hunting whales at the beginning of the 21st century.

Ironically, the same forces that contributed to the demise of New England whaling provided the means by which the old whaling towns revived their economies. As "save the whales" became one of the main slogans of the ecology movement in the 1970s and 1980s, the once-feared whale became a benign symbol of the need to conserve the earth's resources. In the 1980s and 1990s movies portrayed whales as victims of humans' rapacious attitudes toward nature, and television audiences were riveted by efforts to save whales that had washed up on beaches or been trapped in ice floes. Whaling was reinvented, as boatloads of tourists armed with cameras instead of harpoons sailed out to Stellwagen Bank, a national marine sanctuary at the mouth of Massachusetts Bay, and other spots where the great mammals congregate.

The interpretation of the whaling past has long been a central feature of tourist attractions and museums in the southern New England towns of Nantucket and New Bedford, Mass., and Mystic, Conn. Whaling thus remains part of the regional economy. But today's cultural sensibilities make it hard to imagine someone hefting a razor-sharp harpoon and shouting, "A dead whale or a stove boat!"

Margaret S. Creighton, *Rites and Passages: The Experience of American Whaling, 1830–1870* (1995); Lance E. Davis, Robert E. Gallman, and Karin Gleiter, *In Pursuit of the Leviathan: Technology, Institutions, Productivity, and Profits in American Whaling, 1816–1906* (1997); Elmo P. Hohman, *The American Whaleman: A Study of Life and Labor in the Whaling Industry* (1928).

Gretchen A. Adams

Women Seafaring is among the most male-dominated occupations in Western civilization, a strikingly marked division of labor to which Margaret Fuller famously made reference in her 1845 appeal to expand opportunities for women, "Let them be sea captains if they will." New England's ships and boats were crewed almost exclusively by men, while coastal villages and seaports were disproportionately female throughout the centuries in which maritime commerce dominated the region. Since relatively few women have gone to sea, it has been harder to identify maritime women than to see sailors or fishermen themselves. Most did not walk with a rolling gait, their faces were not unusually weather-beaten, nor did they dress distinctively or flaunt tattoos. To the amusement of nonmaritime observers, their speech might be salted with nautical terms, but in general these women displayed the particular characteristics of their locality, socioeconomic status, and ethnicity. What unites the disparate group of New England maritime women is that their lives were and are largely defined by the rhythms and risks of men's maritime enterprise.

Before the first English settlers arrived, indigenous coastal peoples of both sexes exploited the abundant inshore marine resources. Algonquian women fished with line or net, dove for lobsters, and harvested clams, oysters, and scallops, processing their catch for food or fertilizer to be used on the corn and squash fields for which they were primarily responsible. During the 17th and 18th centuries, Native Americans were dispossessed of their lands and displaced by English colonizers up and down the New England coast. Indigenous ways of life were supplanted by the European gendered patterns that assigned the sea to men and the land to women in maritime communities ranging from primitive fishing outposts to bustling, cosmopolitan port towns.

As sailors' kith and kin, as providers of all sorts of services (licit and illicit) to seamen on shore leave, European American and African American women on land have played mediating roles in maritime culture, maintaining and renewing family, community, and the local economy during and in between men's repeated absences at sea. Like the shore where sea and land meet, New England maritime women have served both as substance and symbol of crucial connections between men at sea and society on land.

The earliest settlers of the Massachusetts Bay Colony established fishing outposts on the coast north of Boston to exploit the wealth of cod and other fish on the offshore banks. These settlements differed from the unusually stable villages of the interior: women and men were equally notably irreverent, violent, and hostile to authority. The early New England fishing industry apparently did not employ women directly, as did, for instance, the Newfoundland fishery, where women worked on shore processing fish. New England women seem to have participated only occasionally in drying and curing the catch, which primarily occurred in men's seasonal camps nearer the fishing grounds. Wives and other women provided room, board, laundry, and other domestic services for both single and married fishermen; they also made and mended seines, nets, and lines. Wives also regularly represented their husbands' interests onshore, occasionally even marketing their shares of the catch, and most often in performing the wide range of tasks necessary to sustain family and homestead during men's absences. The extreme risks of the fishing industry were reflected in the high percentage of widows; the exploitative credit relations of the fishery were reflected in those widows' poverty.

Fishing villages remained on the margins of colonial and early national New England society, but the bustling seaports—Boston, Newport, R.I., Salem, Mass., and a host of smaller towns—were at its heart. As in other urban centers throughout the Atlantic world, women were integrated throughout the local economies that thrived on seaborne commerce. Many women onshore contributed to maritime enterprise directly by boarding and feeding, sewing and mending, and washing and ironing for sailors and other travelers. Women baked ships' bread and preserved meat and fruit for voyages. A few women even worked as shipwrights, helping build the vessels on which men sailed.

Many more serviced seamen sexually, drifting in and out of prostitution as poverty demanded and opportunity dictated. For instance, Mahala Green was cited twice in two years by the sheriff in Providence for keeping "a house of ill-fame and disorder" during the early 1830s. In New London, Conn., a black madam named Mary Craig Lopez ran the favorite brothel of African American whalemen before she was jailed in the 1840s. Beginning in the early 19th century, other women from the middling and elite classes worked energetically to eradicate this sort of activity. They strove to assist "deserving" seamen's wives and children, and to reform sailors and maritime culture more generally through their activities in religiously inspired seamen's aid organizations and port societies. In Boston, Sarah Josepha Hale, a prominent editor whose brother had been lost at sea, founded the Seamen's Aid Society.

Such efforts notwithstanding, sailors' wives sustained their families partially on advances from their husbands' employers and partially on barter and cash-producing activities in their own right. Alongside other seaport women, maritime wives and widows also ran boardinghouses; sold dry goods, groceries, and other sundries; operated taverns; leased land, buildings, and wharf space; taught school; and even participated in small-scale trading ventures on the voyages their husbands sailed or financed. Wives often settled their husbands' accounts and paid their taxes while men were at sea. The range and extent of maritime women's activities ebbed and flowed with the industries and commerce on which the seaport economy was based, but many of these forms of female participation persisted well into the 20th century.

Radically new technological developments and consequent economic restructuring fundamentally altered New England maritime women's relationship to the sea in the mid- and late 19th century. The numbers of maritime women diminished overall in traditional ports such as Salem, Boston, and Providence, as the center of deepwater shipping shifted "down east" to Maine. For those women who remained connected to the sea, new roles were introduced while older ones persisted. The fisheries declined with worldwide shifts in demand and supply at the same time as New England industrialized, drawing both men and women away from the sea. Women in fishing communities continued to fill traditional support functions. They also took on new kinds of work created by new methods of processing, preserving, and marketing fish; for example, by 1886, fully a third of the cannery workers in Maine were female.

New technologies (most important, the shift from sail to steam) and global economic forces in merchant shipping similarly affected women onshore. Fewer New England women found themselves connected to sailors, their lives dictated by the rhythms of seafaring, as American shipowners found foreign labor cheaper and more tractable. But by the middle of the 19th century, a surprising number of women actually went to sea themselves, not as crewmembers, but as family. At least several hundred wives and daughters went along to provide the domestic trappings of family life for captain husbands or fathers on long international voyages. Mary Chipman Lawrence, for instance, spent three and a half years aboard the whaler *Addison* during the 1850s; her journal was later published as *The Captain's Best Mate*. This sort of voyaging was a paradoxical consequence of the middle-class Victorian notions of companionate marriage and of work as public, stressful, and male, necessarily complemented by a home that was private, nurturing, and female.

Other women embarked on shorter local trips, cooking and cleaning for fathers, brothers, or husbands on smaller coasting vessels in a floating version of a family economy. In the post–Civil War period, some women found employment as stewardesses on large passenger steamships that featured an elaborate hierarchy of labor organized by gender and race, as well as by skill. Some of those stewardesses were married to male crew members; others were single.

The effects of 20th-century trends on women and gender roles in New England maritime communities are even less well understood. Economic competition and federal regulation of the fisheries may have reshaped gender roles as onshore wives expanded their support by developing marketing strategies and negotiating government bureaucracy. In the 1930s and 1940s, some legislation even encouraged fishermen to carry their wives to sea in an effort to double the catch they were allowed. As maritime leisure industries expanded dramatically beginning in the late 19th century, women figured prominently as entrepreneurs catering to seaside tourists, rather than sailors, and also as consumers themselves. More recently, small numbers of women have begun to enter previously male-dominated occupations, finding jobs as licensed merchant marine officers, marine scientists, and lobstermen.

Our understanding of women's contributions to New England maritime enterprise over four centuries remains uneven. Much is yet unexamined, reflecting the persistence of strongly gendered symbolism that has pervaded both high and popular culture. Maritime culture has been and still is replete with myths, and nowhere is this more the case than in its gender stereotyping. Visual and literary imagery from the colonial period perpetuated the association of land, solid and reassuringly stationary, with women, while the sea, wide open and turbulent, but also the route to adventure and wealth, was associated with men. Cross-dressing, seagoing, working-class heroines of ballads and broadsides ultimately reinforced the dichotomy by stressing the exceptional qualities of such "Female Sailors Bold." In the late 18th and early 19th centuries, Romantic artists and writers exaggerated the division, juxtaposing their vision of the ocean as sublime masculine space, immeasurably vast and uncontrollable, with a feminized world of land that was enclosed, gentle, nurturing, and knowable. The ocean's force was underscored in part by characterizing maritime women, especially wives and widows and their orphaned children, as long-suffering, poignant reminders of the mortal risks with high costs of seafaring.

Throughout the 19th century, these images and themes were embellished and sentimentalized in the literary productions of such popular writers as Harriet Beecher Stowe and Lydia Sigourney, as well as in vernacular forms ranging from quilt designs to Currier and Ives lithographs, from temperance tracts to sea chanteys. Writers more commonly associated with the sea (James Fenimore Cooper, Richard Henry Dana, Herman Melville, Joseph Conrad, and Jack London) drew on gender conventions in counterposing a claustrophobic femininity on land to a muscular fraternity redemptively forged at sea. In the post–Civil War period, images of strong, stoic, and sometimes independent maritime women also emerged, reflecting the power of the sea more directly, though still from shore, in regionalist literature and art (notably associated with Sarah Orne Jewett and Winslow Homer) and in popular culture (such as the late-19th-century acclaim of the Newport harbor lighthouse keeper's daughter, Ida Lewis, the "Heroine of Lime Rock").

Even as New England's relation to the sea has shifted to predominantly recreational use shared by women and men, the dichotomized gender stereotyping in maritime culture remains potent in many forms, from movies to museum exhibits to perennially popular sea fiction and nonfiction. Only recently have nautical enthusiasts been joined by gender studies scholars who have begun to disentangle the symbol from the substance of New England women's engagement with the sea.

W. Jeffrey Bolster, *Black Jacks: African American Seamen in the Age of Sail* (1997); Margaret S. Creighton and Lisa Norling, eds., *Iron Men, Wooden Women: Gender and Seafaring in the Atlantic World, 1700–1920* (1996); Linda Greenlaw, *The Hungry Ocean: A Swordboat Captain's Journey* (1999); Benjamin W. Labaree, *America and the Sea: A Maritime History* (1998); Mary Chipman Lawrence, *The Captain's Best Mate: The Journal of Mary Chipman Lawrence on the Whaler "Addison," 1856–1860*, ed. Stanton Garner (1966); Lisa Norling, *Captain Ahab Had a Wife: New England Women and the Whalefishery, 1720–1870* (2000); Haskell Springer, ed., *America and the Sea: A Literary History* (1995); Roger B. Stein, *Seascape and the American Imagination* (1975).

Lisa Norling

Wooden Boat Revival

Wooden Boat Revival The wooden boat revival, the worldwide repopularization of wooden watercraft, is a movement that began in the early 1970s. Much of the activity associated with the wooden boat revival occurred in and around New England.

Until World War II, most boats were constructed from wood. These boats were built in both large and small shops, and required the personal attention of skilled craftsmen. In the 1950s, fiberglass was introduced as a boat-building material. It made forming hulls in a mold relatively fast and inexpensive, and the new material also promised a low-maintenance boat. Given these economies, fiberglass boats quickly displaced wooden ones.

During the fiberglass revolution, wooden boats were still built and used, but the reputation of wood as a construction material had been diminished by the marketing efforts of fiberglass boat companies. In the early 1970s, a movement to revive wooden boats and wooden boat craftsmanship came to a head. The movement was spurred by a deep sense of impending loss—both of the craft and a way of life—as well as by a growing recognition that wood has structural and aesthetic qualities that are superior to those of fiberglass. Today, wooden boats enjoy a wide following, and wood is often used in ways that earlier traditional builders would not recognize—in combination with modern materials like epoxy adhesives and fiberglass.

The wooden boat revival originated in a number of places around the world. In New England, several notable people and institutions were influential, including John Gardner, the curator of small craft at Mystic Seaport in Mystic, Conn. Gardner originated the concept of teaching traditional small-craft construction in the museum's classes. He also published several books and articles on the

New Hampshire boatbuilder, 1999

topic, including important articles in the *National Fisherman.* Captain R. D. "Pete" Culler, a designer and builder from Hyannis, Mass., also published several books and articles on wooden boats. His influence on the aesthetics of traditional boats remains strong.

Information dissemination and education were critical to the movement's success. The Apprenticeshop figured prominently in this regard. This program was founded by Lance Lee in Bath, Maine, in 1972, and is modeled after the famous Outward Bound outdoor experiential education courses. Apprentices attending Lee's program typically sign on for a two-year apprenticeship and come away with a solid foundation in traditional boatbuilding. The operation is located today in Rockland, Maine. The Landing School in Kennebunkport, Maine, was founded in 1978, and has grown to be crucial to the boatbuilding industry in general. Students learn the fundamentals of classic boatbuilding and can apply these skills in careers using modern techniques and materials.

WoodenBoat magazine, founded in 1974 by boatbuilder Jonathan Wilson, serves as a mode of communication for the wooden boat industry. Founded in Brooksville, Maine, and now published in Brooklin, Maine, the magazine provides information for boatbuilders as well as for owners and designers and serves as a marketplace for boatbuilders and vendors of boat-related items. The company also publishes books on wooden boat construction. Similarly, International Marine Publishing Company of Camden, Maine, has published numerous books on wooden boats and related topics, and a group called the Traditional Small Craft Association, dedicated to the survival of traditional watercraft, publishes a newsletter called the *Ash Breeze.* Many other wooden

boat publications are collected at maritime museum libraries, and at the WoodenBoat Library, located at the magazine's Brooklin headquarters.

John Gardner, *Building Classic Small Craft* (1977); Gardner, *Building Classic Small Craft,* vol. 2 (1984); David C. "Bud" McIntosh, *How to Build a Wooden Boat* (1987); Peter Spectre, *Different Waterfront: Stories from the Wooden Boat Revival* (1989).

Matthew P. Murphy

Yachting and Recreational Boating

Recreational boating is big business in contemporary New England, and is likely to continue expanding in the foreseeable future. This is quite a change from the colonial era, when common wisdom held that "those who would go to sea for pleasure would go to hell for a pastime." Today coastal New Englanders are more likely to share the sentiments expressed by Rat in Kenneth Grahame's *Wind in the Willows:* "Believe me, my young friend, there is *nothing*—absolutely nothing—half so much worth doing as simply messing about in boats."

Roger F. Duncan and John P. Ware, authors of the best-selling *Cruising Guide to the New England Coast* (1979), noted there the "tremendous changes in the coastal communities and in the yachts and yachtsmen who visit them" compared to just 40 years earlier:

In the thirties we saw commercial sailing vessels on the coast still carrying cargoes more or less profitably and the few yachts we saw were usually over 30 feet and often much bigger. The 100-foot schooner *Constellation,* carrying main and fore gaff topsails, sparkling in brass, varnish, and black paint, passed us off Rockland, her paid crew standing by in the lee of the foresail. Today our harbors are crowded with scores of cruising boats under 30 feet, requiring the construction of marinas and stimulating a tremendous service industry.

The democratization of yachting has expanded even more since Duncan and Ware wrote in 1979, as has its contribution to the regional economy. The Massachusetts Marine Trade Association proudly noted that in 2001 there were more than 146,000 boats in that state alone, not counting canoes, kayaks, and rowboats, which do not require registration. Thirty-five thousand of those recreational vessels were sufficiently large to be kept in moorings, marinas, or docks along the coast of the commonwealth; the rest were in lakes, or went to the water sporadically on boat trailers or car tops. Boaters in Massachusetts alone spent more than $192 million in 2000 on new boats, engines, and equipment, and contributed more than $297 million to the state economy in peripheral spending for repairs, insurance, supplies, and groceries. The other New England states could tell a similar story. In Rhode Island, for example, Newport no longer hosts the America's Cup race, but it continues to sponsor yacht races and regattas for recreational boaters of all abilities, while the Museum of Yachting is a popular tourist attraction. Recreational boating thus ranges from multimillion-dollar sailing yachts to modest fiberglass runabouts, to kayaks and aluminum johnboats. Today almost anyone who desires to "mess about in boats" can afford to do so. As a result, the cultural values and meanings associated with boating in contemporary New England vary widely.

Members of the Eastern Yacht Club in Marblehead, Mass., a town sometimes described as "the yachting capital of the world," are serious sailboat racers and long-distance cruisers. They include Olympic sailing competitors, America's Cup defenders, and noted yacht designers. Founded in 1870, the Eastern is a venerable club steeped in tradition, and its elegant building is full of trophies and memorabilia from generations of yachting. The culture of boating as practiced at the Eastern Yacht Club is significantly different from that of the Great Bay Yacht Club, in Dover, N.H. Initially home to the locally built Merrimack class of racing dinghies, the Great Bay Yacht Club is less august and less competitive than the Eastern. It has no clubhouse, and the organization itself, which is much more middle class, is only about 30 years old. The South Norwalk Boat Club, in Connecticut, exemplifies yet another variant of recreational boating. It consists primarily of powerboat enthusiasts and sport fishermen, and its members' interests vary significantly from those of sailors. In fact, sailors and powerboaters often maintain a rivalry, sometimes good-natured, sometimes not.

This wide array of interests and values among recreational boaters is mirrored by a

Columbia, *the 1899 and 1901 America's Cup defender*

ing has changed during the past century and a half, one needs only to pick up a copy of *Carter's Coast of New England,* first published in 1864 as *A Summer Cruise on the Coast of New England.* Robert Carter and three friends, in the company of two professionals they dubbed the Pilot and the Skipper, sailed from Boston to Provincetown, then along the short New Hampshire coast, and ultimately down east to Bar Harbor, Maine, in a 30-foot fishing smack. The boat itself, its spartan lack of amenities, the presence of the professional crew, and the frighteningly small number of other recreational boaters they encountered suggest that the world of yachting has been revolutionized since the Civil War.

Fiberglass hulls, inboard engines, and navigational electronics reflect that change. So does the emphasis on leisure in modern society and the availability of discretionary income. The glossy magazines and spic-and-span marinas that define boating today signal a cultural shift of great magnitude. More people than ever before can experience the challenge of tacking a sloop to windward or the sense of adventure that accompanies any voyage, no matter how brief. But as all yachtsmen and women worth their salt know, some things never change. The east wind still bodes ill, the summer fog remains unsettling, and half-tide ledges lurk nonchalantly, as they always have, for unwary mariners.

Robert Carter, *Carter's Coast of New England,* ed. Daniel Ford (1977); Roger F. Duncan and John P. Ware, *A Cruising Guide to the New England Coast* (1979).

W. Jeffrey Bolster

spectrum of niche publications, many of which are based in New England. *SAIL,* which describes itself as the "world's leading sailing magazine," is published in Boston. *Messing about in Boats,* a bible for "backyard Noahs," and an inspiration for individuals

with a modest budget who yearn to get afloat, is published in Wenham, Mass. *WoodenBoat* magazine, the baby-boomer generation's primer for the wooden boat revival, is produced in Brooklin, Maine.

To get an idea of how New England yacht-

Media

Susan Smulyan, Section Editor
Mark Herlihy, Consulting Editor

INTRODUCTION

S ome would call New England the birthplace of American media. Certainly the region has long been widely known as a repository and producer of print culture, as a place that defined freedom of the press, and as an influential originator of such media forms as newspapers, almanacs, and political pamphlets. The American Antiquarian Society of Worcester, Mass., founded in 1812 and now perhaps the nation's most important center for the study of early materials printed in the United States, bears active witness to New England's contribution to media history. The society's founder, Isaiah Thomas, a printer, newspaper publisher, bookseller, Revolutionary War patriot, and historian, believed that a historical collection of printed material could be used to "aid the progress of science, to perpetuate the history of moral and political events, and to improve and interest posterity." The Antiquarian Society continues to pursue its mission today with a planned five-volume work of collaborative scholarship under the editorship of the historian David Hall of Harvard University entitled *A History of the Book in America* (2000–). Yet, even as the Antiquarian Society records the role New England has played for more than 300 years in both communications and the preservation of its history, the society's work tells a national story as well as a regional one. Its Web site boasts that the "AAS is the third oldest historical society in this country and the first to be national rather than regional in its purpose and in the scope of its collections." Any study of regional media, at any time in the nation's history, will inevitably tell a national story.

The predominant movement in the history of communications media has been from local to regional to national, and in the 21st-century United States, the media are national entities. Local outlets may support or resist their national counterparts, but they always exist in relation to them. No examination of telecommunications media can ignore the way their economic and social organization structure media content. Although it is possible to study representations of New England, say, on television, one would probably learn more about how that medium is financed than about New England itself. The concept of New England held by scholars and the general public differs significantly from the market picture seen and acted on by advertisers and media moguls.

The media have always recycled clichés about regions, groups, and the history of different places and peoples. Contributors to this section of the *Encyclopedia of New England* cover national media enterprises that were first launched in New England, New England media outlets and personalities, media productions with New England settings or content, and prominent figures in the national media who came from the region.

We have chosen to examine newspapers, magazines, film, radio, television, advertising, and the new digital media, particularly the World Wide Web. These forms have much in common. Each began as a means of communicating facts, although most made the shift to both nonfictional and fictional content. Each can be thought of as public rather than private. And each is a form of broadcasting, in which one person or entity addresses many people or entities, as opposed to what radio pioneers called narrowcasting. So, for example, the entries will not address point-to-point communications such as letters, telegrams, telephone calls, or e-mail messages, although most of these were at least somewhat public early on and could have been included. Most important, all the media examined here are commercial, in that advertising provides their primary funding rather than subscriptions. We include advertising in our list of media because of its importance as a form but also because it has become a constitutive element of all other media.

Newspapers, magazines, film, radio, television, advertising, and the World Wide Web are often referred to as "mass" media. We have avoided that word for two reasons. First, what does *mass* mean in the regional context? Certainly the population of New England is large enough to be called a public, but does it qualify as a mass audience? In general scholarly usage, the word *mass* has referred to a homogeneous national audience. It is this concept that our essays and entries interrogate. Second, the notion of mass media itself comes from a 1950s critique of the conformity generated by media. Scholars saw mass media as something unthinkingly accepted by those it addressed, as a form that both influenced and satisfied audiences who had no knowledge of its workings. Mass media kept people from engaging with, or posing questions about, the important issues that confronted them. This version has been challenged by more recent scholarship that shows audience members actively engaging with media content and using it for their own purposes.

The term "mass media" can be questioned in other ways as well. Many contemporary print outlets and most television broadcasting, film production, and advertising aim at a national market; radio stations and newspapers are owned by national conglomerates; and the World Wide Web is increasingly international in scope. But it is also true that local or regional racial, ethnic, religious, and labor groups have sponsored and supported various media throughout their history. Many have founded and run newspapers, magazines, radio stations, cable television stations, or Web sites; some have created and distributed feature or documentary films. Because these groups—joined in recent decades by lesbian and gay organizations, women's groups, and other special interests—exist at both the regional and the national level, they challenge the idea of any media audience as an undifferentiated mass.

The media on which the contributors to this section focus have a range of similarities, but the differences among them also help illuminate the contours of regional media. The federal government oversees some forms of communication, such as radio and television; others, such as newspapers and magazines, are staunchly unregulated. At important historical moments both film and advertising have practiced self-regulation to deflect government interference. The World Wide Web remains largely unfettered for the time being, but powerful commercial interests have already won court cases that place limits on what can and what cannot be done online.

The differences between communication technologies, in how content is delivered, have helped shape varying degrees of government involvement. Neither radio nor television can be locally contained; broadcasting waves pay no heed to state or regional boundaries. Future delivery of radio and television by wire may well alter who regulates media because cable companies have traditionally remained within the bailiwick of local governments. Still, media monopolies remain an important federal and local concern, as technological and economic changes make it easier for large national companies to own and control all kinds of media outlets.

One example may serve to demonstrate the constantly shifting balance between local and national control of media concerns. David Pearlman, a former radio station manager, founded a radio empire with the purchase of one station in Hartford in 1990. Pearlman told the *Hartford Courant* that he sought to buy a local station in a place where he could live with his family and that he planned to start a chain. Once he had procured that station, WZMX, Pearlman used audience research, advertising, promotion, and community involvement to capture a top spot in the Hartford market. Merging with other companies, and taking advantage of new rules issued by the Federal Communications Commission (FCC) that allowed companies to own more than one station in a market, Pearlman in 1992 began to build a Boston-based company, American Radio Systems (ARS). In 1998, ARS, then the fifth-largest radio broadcasting company in the United States, with 98 radio stations located in 19 markets, was purchased by Westinghouse CBS. A New England–based company controlling radio stations across the country was now owned by one of the largest national broadcasting networks. It remains to be seen how much local programming Hartford's WZMX will continue to do.

In a 1999 article in the journal *Media, Culture, and Society,* Charles Fairchild wrote that the Telecommunications Act of 1996 "served to 'deterritorialize' radio, that is, remove any necessary connection between a radio station and its local community, a remarkable achievement given radio's long-standing status as a uniquely local medium." Fairchild contends that the deregulation of broadcasting has removed restrictions on ownership limits as well as content regulations and restrictions. Because it is no longer necessary at license-renewal time to prove that a station has served the local community, and because large companies can purchase radio stations across the country, programming now originates from a central location. Fairchild concludes that deregulation has consolidated the industry and created "companies whose power to dominate local markets is unprecedented." Even before the ARS sale, in 1997, the Boston radio consultant and Emerson College instructor Donna Halper told the *Boston Globe,* "I see large companies cutting out the connection with local listeners and programming, and that worries me. Radio stations could become something that looks good on a balance sheet, rather than performing a service for a community."

The *Globe* article also warned that radio mergers could lead to the decline of foreign-language and ethnic radio stations, such as the Massachusetts-based WRCA in Waltham, which broadcasts programming in Spanish and Haitian Creole, and WLYN, an ethnically diverse station in Lynn, Mass. By 1997, 83 percent of all advertising dollars in Portland, Maine, were going to two radio companies, while in Providence one firm owned three of the four top-rated stations. The Massachusetts congressman Edward Markey, an important contributor to telecommunications legislation, called Portland and Providence "canaries in the mineshaft" that will demonstrate the effects of consolidation on communities.

Radio broadcasting began locally and then was taken over by national networks. After World War II, when television replaced radio as the primary medium of news and entertainment, radio reinvented itself as a local medium. In the 1990s radio lost its local flavor once again, as it fell under the control of national broadcasting conglomerates. Over the past two centuries every U.S. broadcasting medium has repeated this swing between local and national control. The prospect of nationalization and the tendency for stations to nationalize always influence local media variants. But do periods of local control also influence the national media? The relation between these two entities can best be explored with an examination of their history, beginning with the Industrial Revolution and the changes in economics, politics, and social structure that accompanied it. Precursors of some media forms existed before the early 19th century, but the Industrial Revolution transformed them. Because the American Industrial Revolution began in New England, its impact on the media can be seen clearly in this region.

Newspapers provide the best example of the changes brought by industrialization. The entry "Colonial Printers" describes newspapers in preindustrial New England. Printing shops published weekly newspapers containing primarily classified advertisements, public notices, and partisan editorials or letters. As the Industrial Revolution unfolded in New England in the 1820s and 1830s, newspapers began to take on a different role. Historians have long argued about the reasons for the change. Often-cited factors include new printing technologies, the rise of the market economy, improved modes of transportation (and later communication), an increase in literacy rates, and a growing involvement of working people in the political process.

The historian Michael Schudson points out that one can roughly trace the transformation through the names of the newspapers. Hoping to attract readers from commercial elites, early newspapers used names like those of Boston's two leading papers of the 1820s, the *Boston Daily Advertiser* and the *Boston Patriot and Daily Mercantile Advertiser*. In the 1830s new, less expensive dailies appeared, whose titles showed that they reflected an editor's ideas. Sold in the street, these large-circulation "penny papers" focused on general news rather than detailed descriptions of commercial transactions. The *Boston Daily Times*, for example, began publication in February 1836 and quickly became the city's largest paper, claiming a circulation of 8,000 by mid-March.

Then came the invention and development of electric telegraphy. As the historian Daniel Czitrom has noted, the decoupling of transportation and communication had a large impact on media. Before the telegraph, communication and transporta-

A man reads Boston's Vietnamese newspaper, 1992

tion were tightly linked. If you wanted to communicate with someone, either individually or by means of a newspaper, your written message had to be transported from one place to another. The telegraph sent news over wires, making national—and, in the late 19th century, international—communication much faster and easier. Several important New England newspapers date from this era, known as the Second Industrial Revolution. Whereas the *Boston Globe* (1872) and Manchester, N.H., *Union Leader* (founded as the *Manchester Leader* in 1912) were aimed at local and regional audiences, Boston church leaders launched the *Christian Science Monitor* (1908) to serve a national audience. With the telegraph bringing news quickly to New England and a coast-to-coast railway system to deliver the newspapers, nationwide publication and distribution were now possible.

The development of a national market for goods, and of advertising to serve the new large-scale manufacturers, also had a profound effect on communications media. The rise of national advertising for branded products changed both the advertising industry and the media funded by advertising revenue. Early advertising agencies sold space in newspapers and magazines to companies who wanted to advertise nationally but did not know how to contact local publications. Advertisers worried that the agencies really worked for the publishers because only by doing favors for the publishers could the agencies get space cheaply. The agency N. W. Ayer and Son, founded in 1869 by Francis Wayland Ayer, a native of Lee, Mass., became the first to advocate an "open contract," whereby the agency promised to work for the advertiser. The younger Ayer's 1890 move to make advertising agents more than space jobbers pointed to the future, earning him a reputation among many as the father of modern advertising.

The early film industry was also putting down important New England roots at about the same time. In 1907 Louis B. Mayer, a 22-year-old Jewish immigrant, opened a movie theater in Haverhill, Mass. Known as the Queen Slipper City for its quality footwear, Haverhill already had several theaters and a range of other attractions, mostly of the traveling variety. Mayer opened Haverhill's third movie house, and it proved so successful after a few setbacks that he moved to an even bigger venue, the Colonial. The historian Diana Altman reports that a local newspaper described the Colonial, opened in 1911, as an "amusement palace." Having learned about the movie business on the local level, Mayer moved to Boston and went into film distribution.

Buying exclusive New England rights to the racist but highly popular and cinematically groundbreaking *Birth of a Nation*, Mayer made enough money to become a movie producer. His first film, *Virtuous Wives*, starring Anita Stewart, premiered in New York in December 1918. Joining the migration of the film industry from the East Coast to the West, Mayer quickly moved to California and set up a studio there. Through mergers and alliances with William Randolph Hearst, Mayer soon became a principal in one of the biggest of the early studios, Metro-Goldwyn-Mayer. Mayer's evolution from local theater owner to regional film distributor to national film producer and studio head exemplifies the way in which the media in general developed in the early 20th century.

Combining the importance of advertising with the nationwide distribution of films, the beginning of radio broadcasting reflects the pressure for 20th-century media to provide a national service. The entry "Radio" reports that the first broadcast radio station in New England, WNBR, went on the air on May 21, 1921, in New Bedford, Mass. Over the next year most other New England states also acquired radio stations, although Maine had to wait until 1924, when WABI in Bangor began broadcasting. Early stations programmed haphazardly, putting anyone willing to perform on the air. Often owned by local enterprises such as newspapers, feed stores, municipalities, colleges, and radio-equipment manufacturers, stations existed either as publicity for their owners or as a way for the local communities (extended somewhat by the range of the transmitter) to speak to one another.

But listeners, some of whom had earlier operated ham radios, quickly began to search for distant stations. They sought out programs from farflung places as a way to connect to other parts of the country, to be reminded of family and culture left behind, to hear accurate city-market prices for farm products, or even to follow favorite sports teams. One eccentric part-time New Englander, the railroad capitalist known as Colonel Edward Green, made an early attempt to link radio stations together because he wanted to hear programs aired by New York's WEAF from his home in South Dartmouth, Mass. Soon Colonel Green was using wires to connect his station, WMAF, to both WEAF in New York and WJAR in Providence in what was probably the first broadcasting network.

Colonel Green's network presaged radio's new scope. Wired networks soon connected stations across the country. Programming was often a creative or financial challenge for early radio stations, and wired networks stepped in to provide programs of interest from cultural centers such as New York or Chicago. The wired system avoided the appearance of a radio monopoly, because the stations that were broadcasting national programs were all local. But network radio carried with it expensive wire-line charges; the previous system, in which radio manufacturers, newspapers, and various other enterprises supported radio stations as a cost of doing business or a way to publicize their products, was no longer adequate. By the mid-1920s radio stations in large cities were selling time for commercial messages or accepting free programs provided by commercial enterprises in order to raise money and cut programming costs. Because radio came to be financed through the sale of time, broadcasting became a way to gather audiences for national advertisers rather than a means of communication for local or regional groups. After World War II television would go down a similar path.

Television quickly took over from radio the central place in New Englanders' living rooms, presenting news, entertainment, and educational programs for largely white middle-class families who watched together in the evening, and airing programs aimed at women and children in specialized time slots. Television's structure was based on that of radio, with local radio stations or national broadcasters founding early television stations and each new station adopting a network affiliation. Local radio station owners started the first television station in New England, WNHC in New Haven, Conn., closely followed by Boston's WBZ and WNAC, owned by Westinghouse and RKO. Like network radio, network television did only as much local programming as it had to do to meet FCC requirements. As the historian J. Fred MacDonald has noted, "At every step television served interests seeking to amalgamate Americans. Audiences were to be as large as possible, shows as popular as possible, and program content was to be as common as necessary to attract viewers. . . . National TV offered the same products to everyone everywhere: everything worked, looked, and tasted the same. The United States may have been the most pluralistic civilization on Earth, but network monopolistic practices confined the population to sameness." In other words, American broadcasting has worked against regional identity in every possible way.

Radio, with its programming usurped by television, reinvented itself after the war as a commercialized music box programmed for particular audience segments. While its commercial structure limited programming options, postwar radio became more locally and regionally oriented than it had been in its network heyday. Local radio personalities came to have particular meaning for New Englanders' everyday lives. Rhode Island's Salty Brine, who entered radio in 1942, and Hartford's Bob Steele, who began his morning show in 1943, both had long and illustrious careers broadcasting New England news, talk shows, commercials, and community events.

Local disk jockeys also became an important part of the New England scene, although few lasted as long as Brine or Steele. In response to television's popularity, radio stations adopted a strategy they once had rejected: specialization. Many African Americans, uninterested in television and in some cases unable to afford the new sets, turned to radio. Hoping for a new audience to replace those listeners lost to TV, a few radio stations responded by playing recordings made for black audiences, so-called race records. "Negro radio" had important implications for broadcasting. The first specialized radio stations, programmed for African American listeners, attracted another audience as well. White teenagers found the music they heard on such stations so compelling in its content and form that they spent more and more time tuned in. Postwar broadcast radio had found its best audience: teenagers.

Teenage interest in radio was boosted by a technological change, the invention of the transistor in 1947. The transistor allowed radios to be cheaper, smaller, and more durable than their prewar counterparts. With transistor radios, broadcast listening became a personal, solitary experience and thus helped radio compete with television. A teenager could listen alone in her bedroom or car to programs the whole family might not enjoy or even condone. Radio became the medium of those marginalized by society. Much of the recent history of radio reflects these continued trends, with local stations programming mostly music and talk for audiences ignored by television. Yet even radio stations did not remain local for long. Particularly in the 1990s, national companies such as American Radio Systems bought groups of stations and centralized programming. Salty Brine left his longtime station, WPRO, in 1993 when it was bought by Tele-Media Corporation of Philadelphia.

For a while, with the introduction of cable and satellite television, it seemed that national television broadcasting might give way to regional and local cable systems that would provide "community access" and allow television to appeal to more diverse audiences. In some respects cable television has delivered more local and regional programming than did network broadcasting. The New England Cable News network, founded in 1992 as a local version of CNN, has grown, according to the company's Web site, to become the largest regional cable news network in the country, serving, in 2004, 2.85 million homes in 930 communities throughout New England. Still, cable companies set aside only a few stations for local use. Owned by national media giants, cable systems filled their lineups with high-paying national stations and objected even to carrying local over-the-air stations, let alone nurturing new local outlets. In 1995 Cablevision of Boston tried to substitute the New England Cable News Network for Channel 30, Cuencavision, a 24-hour-a-day television station broadcasting primarily in Spanish. Channel 30 also offered local programming for the Haitian, Jamaican, Cape Verdean, and Brazilian communities and had an estimated 100,000 viewers in Boston who received its broadcasts via cable. No matter how large their audience (Latinos are the largest minority in Massachusetts), cable operators have limited space for local stations in their lineup. A community protest prevented Cablevision from cutting the Spanish-language station, which remained in the lineup when AT&T began servicing Boston's cable customers in 1997. Unlike broadcast networks or national media companies, cable companies are subject to local regulation, which can sometimes make them more sensitive to audience concerns.

American newspapers, film, radio, and television all began in New England, have important New England roots, and continue to have local outlets. But the history of their development, and their resulting economic structure, has meant that most of these media outlets are controlled, both financially and ideologically, by national companies. At certain times in the development of these media, local operations have come to the fore, but almost as quickly as the local variants appear, they are swallowed by national concerns. What chance does a regional identity or a regional audience have in the face of such an unrelenting national focus?

The *Media Guidebook*, edited by Maria Silva and published quarterly by the Boston University Office of Public Information, provides a good overview of contemporary New England media. According to the fall 2004 issue of the guidebook, New England has 350 local radio stations, 80 cable television systems, 45 television stations, 110 magazines, 85 daily newspapers, and about 475 weekly newspapers. Massachusetts has the largest number of media outlets. Using the media directory launched by Francis Ayer, which was published until 1982, we can chart the way these numbers have evolved, with the biggest change coming in a decline in the number of daily newspapers. (Weekly newspapers, which also seemed to decline steadily, have recently risen in number.) *N. W. Ayer and Son's American Newspaper Annual and Directory* of 1917 lists 177 daily newspapers in New England and 755 weeklies. In 1937 those numbers stood at 144 and 463, respectively. By 1957 the number of dailies had dropped further, to 119, and the weeklies to 370. Twenty years later, in 1977, there were 113 dailies and 350 weeklies.

New England's media outlets exist today in a national context. Most contemporary newspapers, broadcast stations, and magazines are owned by, and incorporated into, national media companies. Advertising agencies, media buyers, and networks see New England as several distinct markets rather than as a single region. The *Broadcasting and Cable Yearbook, 1999* lists eight designated market areas (DMAs) in New England. Five of them (Portland-Auburn, Burlington-Plattsburgh, Springfield-Holyoke, Bangor, and Presque Isle) cover less than 10 percent each of the territory, and only one (Boston) is in the top ten DMAs in the United States. The *Yearbook* offers New England as an example of how advertisers might use DMAs, noting that if "the national media is not delivering sufficient advertising weight in New England, the planner will find that three TV markets (Boston, Hartford–New Haven, and Providence) cover 75 percent of New England territory households."

In this book we may set New England apart from the rest of the country in cultural and social terms, but the commercial media see things differently. For the modern media regions exist first and foremost as markets, and secondarily as repositories of meaning. Media content works to make us believe that regions are more than just a way to rationalize the sale and purchase of space and time. When media planners use New England as a concept, however, it is often for reasons destructive of regional identity.

We have seen that several forms of media had early manifestations in New England, including film production and distribution, the modern advertising agency, and network radio. Sometimes these early media also expressed New England ideals while paving the way for new forms. As Russell Martin notes in his entry "Almanacs," these publications have a long history in the region and continue to encapsulate New England's essence for many Americans. In Dublin, N.H., Yankee Publishing still puts out *The Old Farmer's Almanac*, launched in 1792 and the oldest continuously published periodical in North America. The most recent incarnation of the *Almanac*, its Web site, lays claim to the New England identity embodied in a publication still guided by its founder's words: "Our main endeavour is to be useful, but with a pleasant degree of humour." In her entry on the *Atlantic Monthly*, Amy Blair writes that a historian of the magazine (founded in 1857) called it "as much an organ for the export of New England conscience as for New England literary culture." By the time radio appeared on the scene, the idea of New England had definite contours, and *America's Town Meeting of the Air,* as described in the entry by Jason Loviglio, presented New England's small-town, participatory democracy to the nation. In essence, the radio show helped revive the town meeting tradition in New England.

Many of the articles in this section explore the use of New England settings and symbols to invoke a set of meanings. Kent Ryden's "Regional Identity" offers an insightful view of how this works. Ryden uses concepts developed by geographers D. W. Meinig (symbolic landscape) and Wilbur Zelinsky (vernacular region) to discuss the contrasting ideas of places whose meanings are imposed on them by others and places defined by their inhabitants. We can add to these distinctions the importance of the medium within which such ideas are expressed.

One example of how New England identity is constructed in media is the Public Broadcasting System (PBS) programs produced by Boston's WGBH. In his entry on the television station, Louis Mazzari explains that PBS depends on local stations to produce all its programming, with WGBH creating more of public television's primetime lineup than any other single source. The early, classic programs, including Julia Child's cooking shows, *The Victory Garden,* and perhaps especially *This Old House,* come from people who live in New England and thus, in some small way, are a vernacular expression of the region. Although they surely invoke New England stereotypes (symbolic landscapes) to seem more authentic, their existence owes itself to the national structure of public television. As Carolyn Goldstein perceptively notes in her entry on *This Old House,* "the program drew on New England historicity and thriftiness and Yankee ingenuity to attract a national audience."

Many of the entries in this section treat prominent New Englanders in the national media. In his entry on "Stars and Personalities," Daniel Cavicchi usefully notes that "mass culture may not have erased the importance of local and regional identity but rather provided a new forum for such an identity. . . . In many ways stars and personalities embody the tensions between mass culture and local culture in the modern United States." Documentary filmmakers straddle the boundaries of symbolic landscapes, vernacular regions, and structural imperatives. Operating outside the commercialized film industry, documentarians have a long history in New England, as outlined in Charles Warren's entry "Documentaries." Warren asserts that New England has a tradition of nonfiction filmmakers, including Ken Burns and Henry Hampton, and continues, "New England has asserted itself as a center for nonfiction filmmakers and filmmaking. And the audience for this medium has grown and become solid. Like a Renaissance city-state with its special mode of art, New England expects documentary filmmakers to be part of its culture as they pursue their work of finding subject matter and experimenting in observation and understanding." While perhaps not as well known as New Englanders Katharine Hepburn or Jay Leno, the region's documentary filmmakers actually work in New England and, with more control over their output than commercial stars, might be said to produce materials with a New England sensibility.

Having examined the past and present relations between local and national media, we might now ask whether the future will place New England media on an international stage, raising further questions about the nature of regional identity. Rounder Records, which the *New York Times* has called "America's most prominent independent roots-oriented label," was founded in Boston in 1970 by three college students who shared a love of folk music. They first released a recording of a banjo player, quickly followed by one featuring a Cambridge string band. Over time the tensions explicit in the fact that Rounder Records was made up of New England lovers of traditional music, much of which originated in the South, who published records for a national audience, were overshadowed by the expanding definition of "roots" music. Today, in addition to a series called North American Traditions, Rounder Records has series in zydeco, Celtic, reggae, Tex-Mex, Afro-Caribbean, and Cuban and Mexican music, in addition to a large world-music catalog. Following the "roots" of New England and and the larger American culture quickly led beyond the borders of both.

Writing about music and the idea of place, the cultural historian George Lipsitz notes that "recorded music travels from place to place, transcending physical and temporal barriers. It alters our understanding of the local and the immediate, making it possible for us to experience close contact with cultures far away. Yet, precisely because music travels, it also augments our appreciation of place. Commercial popular music demonstrates and dramatizes contrasts between places by calling attention to how people from different places create culture in different ways." Will the future internationalization of media lead to a new appreciation of New England as a place?

Evolving alongside and crucially connected to the internationalization of the media are the new Internet-related technologies. Media historians today find it fascinating to watch the World Wide Web develop. It is like living through the era when radio broadcasting was born. But the older media began locally, with ties to particular communities, and quickly became national. The new media seem to have begun with no geographic ties. The metaphors used to describe the World Wide Web are based on place—"sites," "home pages," "neighborhoods"—but the people who use these online spaces are not tied to any particular locality. Will the new digital media move beyond the national to the global, in the same way that broadcasting moved from the local to the national? *Convergence* is the word that comes up most often in discussions of new media. Those who look ahead believe that the different media forms will become more intertwined. Will they then become so big that no one region, or nation, can contain them? Will future advances in technology cause place to matter less than access, as national borders grow more porous?

New Englanders may be the first to learn the answers to these questions. The Massachusetts Institute of Technology's Media Laboratory, as described in the entry by Madeline Bodin, is leading the way into the media future. The Media Lab joins high-tech industries throughout the region to ensure that no matter how intense the pressure toward nationalization and internationalization, New England will continue to be a home for media innovation.

Diana Altman, *Hollywood East: Louis B. Mayer and the Origins of the Studio System* (1992); American Antiquarian Society, *Under Its Generous Dome: The Collection and Programs of the*

American Antiquarian Society, 2d ed., rev. (1992); Stewart Brand, *The Media Lab: Inventing the Future at M.I.T.* (1987); *Broadcasting and Cable Yearbook* (annual, 1993–); Daniel J. Czitrom, *Media and the American Mind: From Morse to McLuhan* (1982); Susan Douglas, *Listening In: Radio and the American Imagination, from Amos 'n' Andy and Edward R. Murrow to Wolfman Jack and Howard Stern* (1999); Ralph Engelman, *Public Radio and Television in America: A Political History* (1996); Charles Fairchild, "Deterritorializing Radio: Deregulation and the Continuing Triumph of the Corporatist Perspective in the USA," *Media, Culture, and Society* 21 (1999); Gary Ferris, *Media Guidebook* (quarterly, 1984–); Michele Hilmes, *Radio Voices: American Broadcasting, 1922–1952* (1997); Bill Keveney, "Radio High Flier: From Social Single Station Rises Major Media Player," *Hartford Courant,* September 29, 1995; Mark Landler, "Westinghouse to Acquire 98 Radio Stations," *New York Times,* September 20, 1997; George Lipsitz, *Dangerous Crossroads: Popular Music, Postmodernism, and the Poetics of Place* (1994); J. Fred MacDonald, *One Nation under Television: The Rise and Decline of Network Television* (1990); Daniel Pope, *The Making of Modern Advertising* (1983); Ann Powers, "Showing Their Roots and Proud of It," *New York Times,* October 10, 2000; Michael Schudson, *Discovering the News: A Social History of American Newspapers* (1978); Ellery Sedgwick, *The "Atlantic Monthly," 1857– 1909: Yankee Humanism at High Tide and Ebb* (1994); Robert Sklar, *Movie-Made America: A Cultural History of American Movies* (1994); Susan Smulyan, *Selling Radio: The Commercialization of American Broadcasting, 1920–1934* (1994); Lynn Spigel, *Make Room for TV: Television and the Family Ideal in Postwar America* (1992); Susan Strasser, *Satisfaction Guaranteed: The Making of the American Mass Market* (1989); Alisa Valdes, "Latinos Protest Plan to Cut Cable Channel," *Boston Globe,* November 17, 1995; Aaron Zitner, "Who Calls Tune?" *Boston Globe,* September 7, 1997.

Susan Smulyan

Almanacs *An Almanack for New England for the Year 1639*, printed by Stephen Daye in Cambridge, Mass., has the distinction of being the first in a long line of almanacs "adapted to the longitude and latitude" of the New England states. From Daye's imprint (no copy of which survives) to the most recent *Old Farmer's Almanac*, published in Dublin, N.H., by Yankee Publishing Inc., almanacs have amused and instructed generations of loyal readers, providing them with an annual calendar and many other kinds of information as well.

Although nostalgia helps explain the popularity of almanacs today, earlier examples of this genre were necessities used by individuals from all walks of life. In addition to monthly calendars and tables of astronomical events, almanacs included advice for farmers; cures for ailments; tips on managing home and family; lists of roads; anecdotes; puzzles; proverbs; essays; and poems. In an era before the widespread circulation of newspapers, almanacs provided essential information on markets, courts, stage routes, and college graduations, and they offered commentary on events of the past year in introductory essays. In all its diversity, however, the almanac had one great theme: time itself. As Nathaniel Ames expressed it in his almanac for 1744, published in Boston:

This little book serves well to help you date
And settle many petty worldly Things,
Think on the Day writ in the Book of Fate,
Which your own final dissolution brings.

Unlike their British counterparts, which often emphasized astrology and necromancy, the earliest almanacs in New England stressed practical instruction and wholesome entertainment, partly because of the Puritans (17th-century Harvard students, most of them destined for the ministry, were some of the earliest compilers) and partly because of the almanac's proliferation during the more enlightened 18th century.

Massachusetts alone accounted for 645 surviving imprints, or 52 percent of New England's almanacs, through 1800, with other states' shares as follows: Connecticut, 291 imprints (24 percent); Rhode Island, 142 (12 percent); New Hampshire, 96 (8 percent); Vermont, 30 (2 percent); and Maine, 17 (1 percent). Edition sizes varied, but even the most mediocre almanacs were printed in press runs of 1,000 to 2,000 copies, while successful series, such as that of Ames, were printed in editions of 50,000 to 60,000 copies. From 1801 to 1850, the last period for which reliable numbers are available, Massachusetts continued to lead in the overall production of almanacs, but the Bay State's share of the region's output declined to 35 percent of the total (836 imprints), with Connecticut (710 imprints, 30 percent) again in second place. New Hampshire (314, 13 percent), Vermont (245, 10 percent), and Maine (190, 8 percent) showed gains, but the number of Rhode Island's imprints fell (92, 4 percent). One can only guess at the figures from 1851 to the beginning of the 21st century, but doubtless they would exhibit a steady decline as New England's population grew more urban and as other media absorbed many of the almanac's functions.

For understanding New England's rural and maritime past, however, the almanac is an especially rich source. In 1728 James Franklin ("Poor Robin") issued his first *Rhode-Island Almanack,* characterized by the same wit displayed in younger brother Benjamin's *Poor Richard* series. Nathan Daboll published the *Connecticut Almanack* in 1771, and for more than 100 years the Daboll family was associated with almanacs that guided New Englanders on land and at sea. Robert Bailey Thomas of West Boylston, Mass., established his *Farmer's Almanac* with the edition for 1793; by the mid-19th century, sales were estimated at 225,000 copies. Thousands of readers used the works of other compilers to regulate their lives, among them Dudley Leavitt's variously titled *New England Farmers' Almanac* (New Hampshire, 1797), Truman Abell's *New England Farmer's Diary and Almanac* (Vermont, 1816), and Moses Springer's *Maine Farmers' Almanac* (1818). Nineteenth-century almanacs were also issued under the banner of numerous special interests and causes, including temperance, abolitionism, health, politics, and Christianity. "It is the age itself that writes newspapers and almanacs," wrote Nathaniel Hawthorne, "which, therefore have a distinct purpose and meaning at the time, and a kind of intelligible truth for all times." To find the meaning of the almanac in our time, one would have to look to the World Wide Web, where resides the durable *Old Farmer's Almanac,* "fitted for Boston and the New England states, with special corrections and calculations to answer for all the United States," at www.almanac.com.

Milton Drake, *Almanacs of the United States* (1962); George Lyman Kittredge, *The Old Farmer and His Almanack: Being Some Observations on Life and Manners in New England a Hundred Years Ago: Suggested by Reading the Earlier Numbers of Mr. Robert B. Thomas's "Farmers Almanack": Together with Extracts Curious, Instructive, and Entertaining, as Well as a Variety of Miscellaneous Matter* (1904); Robb Sagendorph, *America and Her Almanacs: Wit, Wisdom, and Weather, 1639–1970* (1970); Marion Barber Stowell, *Early American Almanacs: The Colonial Weekday Bible* (1977).

Russell L. Martin III

America's Town Meeting of the Air *America's Town Meeting of the Air* was one of the first and most successful of the public-forum radio broadcasts to originate in the mid-1930s. It ran for 21 years, from 1935 to 1956, addressing the major political and social issues of the day from the New Deal to the Cold War. The weekly show took its inspiration from the ideal of small-town, participatory democracy associated with the colonial New England town meeting. It was one of several efforts to identify the origins of American democratic institutions with New England's common folk as a means of countering claims of communism and fascism. Norman Rockwell epitomized this appropriation of a local New England practice for national political purposes in the famous image of a town meeting that was part of his *Four Freedoms* series of paintings.

America's Town Meeting of the Air began with a town crier in colonial garb ringing a bell and calling the meeting to order before a live audience. It typically featured several guest speakers representing different positions on a contemporary political or social question. The debut program, on May 30, 1935, was titled "Which Way America—Fascism, Communism, Socialism, or Democracy?" a question taken up by representatives of the four ideological positions: Lawrence Dennis, A. J. Muste, Norman Thomas, and Raymond Moley. Over the course of its 21 years *America's Town Meeting of the Air* came to be regarded as an important forum for political debate, attracting such speakers as Eleanor Roosevelt, Reinhold Niebuhr, Dean Acheson, and Fiorello La Guardia.

One of the show's unique contributions to the public-forum format was the role it gave members of the studio audience, who questioned featured speakers on the air. The boisterous debates that ensued became a trademark of the program. The interactive nature of *America's Town Meeting of the Air* soon proved to be its most compelling feature. Across the country listeners organized over 1,000 *America's Town Meeting* discussion groups, gathering in schools, clubs, and homes to listen to the broadcast and then continue debating the issues on their own.

The idea for *America's Town Meeting of the Air* grew out of the educational and political activity of New York City's Town Hall, a West 43rd Street auditorium that had served as an important forum for public debate since 1921. The League for Political Education , an organization that had been working for woman suffrage since 1894, established the Town Hall to foster adult education and democratic values. In 1935 associate director George V. Denny, Jr., conceived of broadcasting from

Town Hall, creating a national forum for public debate. *America's Town Meeting of the Air* aired on NBC's Blue Network from 1935 to 1941 and then on ABC until 1956.

Through a series of stunts and innovations, the show linked the ideal of participatory democracy to developments in the technology of communication and transportation. By 1936 network lines enabled the program to field questions from audiences in auditoriums in cities across the country. In 1941 it became the first radio forum to be televised. Another first occurred in 1943, when the show aired from two sides of the Atlantic. In 1947 *America's Town Meeting of the Air* was broadcast simultaneously from Radio City Music Hall in New York and from a DC-9 flying above Hollywood, Calif. Two years later it traveled the world, transmitting from 14 different cities. In 1950 and 1954 the show received the George Peabody Institute award, the radio equivalent of the Oscar.

Though based in New York City, *America's Town Meeting of the Air* contributed to the revival of the town meeting in New England after years of decline. By the 1960s New England town meetings had become a vehicle for debating national issues such as the Vietnam War and nuclear power.

Erik Barnouw, *A History of Broadcasting in the United States*, vol. 2, *The Golden Web, 1933 to 1953* (1968); Harry A. Overstreet and Bonaro W. Overstreet, *Town Meeting Comes to Town* (1938); Town Hall, *500 Hours Old: Being the Record of the First 500 Broadcasts of "America's Town Meeting of the Air," 1935–1948* (1948) and *"Good Evening Neighbors": The Story of an American Institution; 15 Years of "America's Town Meeting of the Air,"* with a Glance Ahead (1950).

Jason Loviglio

Atlantic Monthly The inaugural issue of the *Atlantic Monthly* in November 1857 bore the manifesto "In Politics, the Atlantic will be the organ of no party or clique, but will honestly endeavor to be the exponent of what its conductors believe to be the American idea." This American idea was the didactic mission of its illustrious group of founders. James Russell Lowell, Ralph Waldo Emerson, Henry Wadsworth Longfellow, Oliver Wendell Holmes, Francis H. Underwood, John Lothrop Motley, James Eliot Cabot, and Moses Dresser Phillips felt that America needed to get out from under Europe's long cultural shadow by adapting Western intellectual traditions to the unique history and institutions of the United States. While these men expounded a national culture, in practice the new magazine was often regional in flavor; opening manifesto aside, from its antislavery politics to its Puritan-inspired moral conscience, the young *Atlantic* was, as Ellery

Sedgwick has written, "For better or worse, as much an organ for the export of New England conscience as for New England literary culture." James Russell Lowell served as editor-in-chief from 1857 to 1861. Lowell's magazine was primarily literary, emphasizing realistic, ethically concerned fiction. But the literary bent did not preclude active political engagement: with essays from Emerson, Holmes, and others, the *Atlantic* proved itself a formidable voice in politics and philosophy. An example of the journal's commitment to knowledge was its publication in 1860 of Asa Gray's three-part defense of Darwin's theories of evolution and natural selection.

The magazine's patronage of New England local-color realism expanded during James T. Fields's editorial tenure (1861–71). Fields replaced Lowell when his publishing company, Ticknor and Fields, purchased the *Atlantic Monthly*. Fields brought business savvy to the job, founding the "cult of New England letters" by promoting an "*Atlantic* group" of authors that included Nathaniel Hawthorne, Thomas Wentworth Higginson, and Charles W. Eliot. But after this period of prosperity, during which circulation reached 50,000, the *Atlantic*'s fortunes foundered. Though the critical essays of William Dean Howells, editor from 1871 to 1881, helped define a new era of literary realism, and Howells's tenure saw the magazine embracing new writers and subscribers from west of the Mississippi, the post–Civil War explosion of a New York–based mass market created heavy competition for the middle-class readership Howells wanted to reach. To the distress of new publisher Henry O. Houghton (whose firms published the *Atlantic* from 1873 to 1908), circulation dropped, despite the serialization of three of Henry James's novels and the frequent contributions of Mark Twain.

Howells resigned just as Henry D. Lloyd's early muckraking exposé of Standard Oil, "Story of a Great Monopoly," was published, and his successors, Thomas Bailey Aldrich (1881–90) and Horace Elisha Scudder (1890–98), steered the magazine in a more belletristic direction. Aldrich's old-style humanistic sensibilities were battered by the industrialization of American life, and his magazine reflected this anxiety in its political disengagement. Scudder brought back current affairs reporting, but he, too, was most interested in preserving the liberalism of Emerson and Holmes. Houghton hired Walter Hines Page as assistant editor in 1895 and gave him the express mission of revitalizing the magazine, a task with which Page carried on during his brief stint as editor-in-chief (1898–99).

Page modernized the *Atlantic Monthly* by shifting the editorial focus from literature to current affairs, cutting the length of essays, and increasing the advertising content. He solicited pieces with broad social import such as Lafcadio Hearn's reflections on Japan, Jacob Riis's account of New York slums, and Jane Addams's "The Subtle Problems of Charity." Abraham Cahan and W. E. B. Du Bois wrote for the *Atlantic Monthly*, and while fiction had a lower priority during his tenure, Page championed the work of adventure writers Jack London and Stephen Crane. Circulation and revenues rose, and they continued to do so, though at a slower rate, under the more conservative Bliss Perry (1899–1909).

Houghton Mifflin had been fending off bids to buy the *Atlantic Monthly* for years, but when Ellery Sedgwick proposed to found the Atlantic Monthly Company in 1908, Houghton Mifflin accepted, in hopes of keeping the magazine as a feeder for its book-publishing operation. Sedgwick proceeded to set up the Atlantic Monthly Press for precisely that purpose, however. Sedgwick served as editor of the *Atlantic Monthly* from 1908 to 1938, during which time he returned to Page's strategies for cultivating a mass audience while preserving the magazine's traditional readership. Circulation increased from 17,000 to 135,000 during his editorship and continued to grow under that of Edward Weeks (1938–66), whose Under Thirty column profiled the young Joseph P. Kennedy and David Riesman, Jr., and whose excellent New York connections garnered regular contributions from Walter Lippmann, Archibald MacLeish, and Edmund Wilson.

When Robert Manning took the editorial helm in 1966, Americans were becoming voracious nonfiction readers, and book publishers began to woo reporters away from magazines. The *Atlantic Monthly* adapted, excerpting James D. Watson's groundbreaking study of DNA, *The Double Helix*, and the memoirs of Joseph Stalin's daughter, among other works. The long-standing *Atlantic Monthly* tradition of reading all unsolicited manuscripts continued, and the slush pile yielded such fiction writers as Joyce Carol Oates, Ann Beattie, and Bobbie Ann Mason. Under Peter Davison's poetry editorship, the magazine published verse by every major 20th-century poet, and C. Michael Curtis oversaw an impressive list of short fiction from the likes of John Updike, John Barth, Jorge Luis Borges, and Philip Roth. In 1980 the *Atlantic Monthly* was sold, amid some controversy, to real estate developer Mortimer Zuckerman. Zuckerman hired William Whitworth as editor-in-chief, and the magazine continued to prosper, with circulation topping 450,000 in 1998. In September 1999 the magazine was purchased again, by David G. Bradley, chairman of the National

Journal Group. Bradley replaced Whitworth with Michael Kelly, the former editor-in-chief of *National Journal.*

In 2002 Kelly opted to become an editor-at-large for the *Atlantic.* In April 2003, Kelly was killed during the U.S. war against Iraq, the first embedded U.S. reporter to die in the conflict. Kelly's replacement, managing editor Cullen Murphy, is presently the magazine's de facto editor-in-chief. The *Atlantic* is still known for intellectual rigor, innovative fiction, and lead stories that tackle complex issues in demographics, the environment, and U.S. history.

Philip B. Eppard and George Monteiro, *A Guide to the "Atlantic Monthly" Contributors' Club* (1983); Frank Luther Mott, *A History of American Magazines* (1938–68); Ellery Sedgwick, *The "Atlantic Monthly," 1857–1909: Yankee Humanism at High Tide and Ebb* (1994).

Amy L. Blair

Morning with the Boston Globe, *1976*

Boston Globe The *Boston Globe* is "an institution rooted in New England," writes Louis Lyons, chronicler of the newspaper's first century. The *Globe's* pages "have mirrored the life of its region and have both influenced and reflected its condition through these hundred years."

For most of the 20th century the *Globe* was owned and run by the Taylor family, who provided an extraordinary measure of continuity and established the paper as a community voice. Founded in 1872, the *Globe* struggled at first, until Charles H. Taylor, a veteran journalist at 27, was hired to develop a broader readership, to include a new generation of immigrants, women, and children. Taylor changed the daily's political slant from Republican to Democratic, advocating woman suffrage, a shorter workday, and tariff reductions.

By 1886 the *Globe* was the largest circulation newspaper in the country outside New York. Taylor ran it personally for the next half century. His sons assumed control in the 1930s, managing the daily through intense competition during the Depression, when Boston had more newspapers than any other city in America.

Through much of its early history the *Globe* combined an often folksy style with liberal and humane values. For 75 years the *Globe's* "Uncle Dudley" editorials inspired sermons all over New England. Lyons wrote in 1971 of the 100-year-old broadsheet: "The wit and whimsy of 'Editorial Points' and 'Weather Ears,' its household recipes, and its remarkable club of women letter-writers in 'Confidential Chat' have made it a household [name] familiar down the years." It was also first in the newspaper industry to establish an in-house photoengraving department. The *Globe's* nationally renowned sports section dates back to the 1880s.

By the early 1930s, the *Globe* had lost circulation to the *Boston Herald-Traveler*, which had moved into newer facilities and updated its typography, adopting a metropolitan look, while the *Globe* stuck with its old-fashioned presses and appearance. Finally, in 1958, after 86 years on Boston's downtown Newspaper Row, the Globe moved to its present facilities on Morrissey Boulevard along the Southeast Expressway.

During the 1950s the *Globe* reached into suburban areas, covering civic affairs and public issues more aggressively. A liberal voice on civic policy, the *Globe* was solidly behind urban renewal plans to reshape Boston in the early 1960s. In the last year of that decade the *Globe* became the first U.S. newspaper to call for unilateral withdrawal of American troops in Vietnam, and it was one of three American dailies, with the *New York Times* and the *Washington Post*, to fight the Nixon administration for the right to publish secret Pentagon studies on America's involvement in Vietnam. In the 1970s the *Globe* urged support of the Equal Rights Amendment and advocated the integration of Boston's public schools, although its stance alienated a substantial portion of its readership.

The *Globe* won its first Pulitzer Prize in 1966, and by 2003 it had won a total of 17 Pulitzers, for editorial cartooning, commentary and criticism, photography, national and local reporting, public service, and investigative reporting. Among its prize-winning columnists have been Ellen Goodman, David Nyhan, Eileen McNamara, and sportswriter Will McDonough. Prize-winning photographers on staff have included Stan Grossfeld, Bill Greene, and Janet Knott.

Like most of the nation's largest newspapers, the *Globe* slowly lost readership over the last decade of the 20th century, with daily circulation declining from 519,000 in 1991 to 466,000 in 2001. Its Sunday edition readership also dropped in the same period, from 795,000 to 716,000. The *Globe* now considers its regional focus to include area politics, high technology, and local environmental issues. Its weekly zoned editions, part of the *Boston Sunday Globe,* provide increased local coverage throughout New England.

In 1993 the New York Times Company purchased the *Globe* for $1.1 billion in the single largest newspaper merger and acquisition in U.S. history. The sale marked the end of more than 120 years of the Taylors' local ownership. According to the terms of the transaction, the *Globe* maintained its editorial independence.

Under its new owners, the *Globe* has continued to garner national attention and awards while serving the New England region, especially eastern Massachusetts. In 1998 the paper made news by forcing the resignation of columnists Mike Barnicle and Patricia Smith for breaches of journalistic ethics. The *Globe* has also attracted notice for its aggressive reporting of the sex-abuse scandal in the Catholic Church. The paper's sustained focus on the handling of the abuse cases in the Boston Archdiocese led to the resignation of Bernard Cardinal Law in 2002, prompted investigations in other dioceses throughout the country, and earned the paper a Pulitzer Prize in 2003.

Jane T. Harrigan, *Read All about It! A Day in the Life of a Metropolitan Newspaper* (1987); Louis M. Lyons, *Newspaper Story: One Hundred Years of the* Boston

Globe (1971); James Morgan, *Charles H. Taylor, Builder of the "Boston Globe"* (1923).

Louis Mazzari

Boston in Film Boston's rich history and distinctive character have attracted filmmakers since the earliest days of the cinema. *Boston's Subway* (1897), probably the first movie filmed on location in the city, showed an entrance to Boston's subway and emerging trolley cars. The film was manufactured by American Mutoscope and Biograph, which shot a number of other Boston subjects, including *During the Blizzard* (1898); *Boston Navy Yard* (1898); and *Bathing in the Ice at the L Street Bath, Boston* (1905), in which the L Street Brownies cavorted, as they still do every January 1, in subfreezing temperatures before a New Year's Day dive into the icy waters of Boston Harbor. The Edison Company made several one- and two-scene short films in the city, including *The Boston Horseless Fire Department* (1899), *Admiral Dewey at State House* (1899), and *Canoeing on the Charles River* (1904).

Boston's key role in the country's colonial and revolutionary history was recalled in Edison's one-reel *The Boston Tea Party* (1908), D. W. Griffith's *America* (1924), and Cosmopolitan Pictures' *Janice Meredith* (1924), which dramatized the Tea Party, Paul Revere's ride, and the Battle of Lexington. Nineteenth-century Boston has also served as the setting for movies ranging from the low-budget PRC (Producers Releasing Corporation) adaptation of Louisa May Alcott's *An Old-Fashioned Girl* (1949) to the highbrow Merchant Ivory adaptation of Henry James's *The Bostonians* (1984). The invention of the telephone and anesthesia in Boston were chronicled in *The Story of Alexander Graham Bell* (1939) and *The Great Moment* (1944). Even in early films not set in Boston's past, Hollywood tended to equate Bostonians with another age, characterizing them as wealthy blue bloods or snobs in dramas such as *The Liar* (1918), *Small Town Girl* (1936), and *Private Affairs* (1940) and in comedies like *Getting Mary Married* (1919), *A Kiss in Time* (1921), and *The Late George Apley* (1947). The hillbilly Kettle clan was forced to contend with snooty in-laws from Boston in *Ma and Pa Kettle Back on the Farm* (1951). A different view of Boston society as a place of well-intentioned but often racist Brahmins and various communities of "Black Yankees" emerges from Oscar Micheaux's masterpiece *Within Our Gates* (1919), the earliest surviving feature film directed by an African American.

What New York is to Broadway or Pittsburgh is to steel in the national memory, Boston is to higher education and medicine.

Selig Polyscope's *Brown of Harvard* (1918)—remade by MGM in 1926—contained some scenes shot on the Cambridge campus, and both Harvard and Radcliffe served as the backdrop for Erich Segal's popular *Love Story* (1970). Harvard has served as the archetypal college of the nation in such films as *Dealing, or The Berkeley-to-Boston Forty-Brick Lost-Bag Blues* (1972), *The Paper Chase* (1973), *A Small Circle of Friends* (1980), and *With Honors* (1994), while in *Good Will Hunting* (1997) a rebellious South Boston math whiz is discovered working as a janitor in the halls of MIT. Boston's renown as a center of medical research made it the setting for *Charly* (1968), about an operation that turns a retarded man into a genius, and *Coma* (1978), a thriller set in the fictional Boston Memorial Hospital. Another fictional hospital—actually the Massachusetts State House—figures prominently in *The Verdict* (1982). In that film Paul Newman played the down-and-out lawyer Frank Galvin, who attempts to resurrect his career by taking a malpractice suit to trial. David Mamet's screenplay subtly reveals many of the tensions that are part of life in Boston: Irish Catholic versus Protestant establishment, black versus white, working-class versus wealthy.

Blown Away (1994) is one of a long list of crime films set in Boston. In that movie a crazed IRA bomber targets numerous landmarks, including MIT, Copley Square, and sites in nearby Charlestown, Mass. The film's climax revolves around the annual Independence Day celebration on the Charles River Esplanade. The city's infamous armored car robbery of 1950 served as the basis for several movies, including *Blueprint for Robbery* (1961), *Six Bridges to Cross* (1955), and *The Brink's Job* (1978), the last two of which were shot on location. Scenes of Boston became more familiar to audiences after World War II, when Hollywood moved off the back lots and began filming on location. *Mystery Street* (1950) found Ricardo Montalban investigating a murder with the help of a Harvard scientist and hunting for leads in the seedy boarding houses of postwar Beacon Hill. In the fact-based *Walk East on Beacon* (1952) a communist spy ring operated in the shadow of the state house, and *The Boston Strangler* (1968) starred Tony Curtis as the title character in the true story of the area's most famous murderer. Fictional Boston criminals on film have ranged from Steve McQueen's millionaire bank robber in *The Thomas Crown Affair* (1968) to Robert Mitchum's low-rent hood marked for murder in *The Friends of Eddie Coyle* (1973) to the basketball fans-turned-kidnappers in *Celtic Pride* (1996). *Mystic River* (2003), the film adaptation of Boston native Dennis Lehane's novel of the same title, earned critical acclaim for its portrayal of crime and community identity in the city.

If Hollywood has tended to focus on Boston's Brahmins and Irish Americans, the small independent productions shot in Boston have increasingly centered on a broader range of the city's constituent groups: the working class of *Mission Hill* (1982), the Jewish community of turn-of-the-20th-century Boston in *The Imported Bridegroom* (1990), Italian Americans from the North End in *The Blinking Madonna* (1995) and *The North End* (1998), the South End's gay community in *All the Rage* (1998), and disaffected 30-somethings in *Next Stop, Wonderland* (1998). *Squeeze* (1997), set in the Field's Corner neighborhood, follows a multiethnic trio of young men who must choose between the straight and narrow, in the context of a community youth center, and the easy money of drug dealing. *Southie* (1998) and *Monument Ave.* (1998) explore the legacy of criminal influences on South Boston and Charlestown respectively. Along with its historical significance, the city's growing diversity will continue to make Boston a favored location for filmmakers.

American Film Institute, *The American Film Institute Catalog of Feature Films,* 6 vols. (1988, 1993, 1995, 1997, 1998, 1999); Charles Musser, *History of the American Cinema,* vol. 1, *The Emergence of Cinema: The American Screen to 1907* (1990).

Eric Schaefer

Brine, Walter "Salty" (1918–) Radio and television personality. Familiar as the rocky coastline and reliable as New England's winter storms, the Rhode Island media legend Walter "Salty" Brine was born in Boston and raised in Arlington, Mass. At the age of nine he lost a leg attempting to hop a freight train. Ineligible for military service because of this injury, Brine went to the former Staley College of the Spoken Word in Brookline, originally planning to become a court stenographer.

He began his broadcast career in 1942. After a brief stint at Boston's WHDH-AM, he left for WPRO-AM, a Providence radio station featuring news, talk, and sports. For 51 years he dominated the morning airwaves there. From 1958 until 1968 he also hosted the hit children's television program *Salty Brine's Shack* on Channel 12.

Commuting more than 40 miles from his home in Narragansett before dawn to be on air at 5:30 A.M., Brine was the bell that woke many from their slumber, and he came to occupy a comfortable spot alongside the milk and cereal at breakfast tables across Rhode Island. Potent as a steaming cup of coffee, this folksy radio personality and cornball humorist gave listeners the get up and go with which to start the workday. Storm cancellations were a popular feature of his show, and "No school today in Foster-Glocester" (a northwest portion of the state that often gets buried when other areas are just dodging flurries) quickly became Salty's trademark line.

In 1993 WPRO was bought by Tele-Media Corporation of Pennsylvania, and Salty did not find the new owners to his liking. Along with his wife, Mickey, whom he called his "silent radio partner," Brine decided that April 28 would mark his final broadcast with the station. On that bittersweet day for Salty and his audience, the *Providence Journal* columnist John Martin remarked that in Rhode Island, "We've got cabinets and bubblers and stuffies and coffee syrup. And an old character with a name like Salty Brine on the radio every morning who would have been put in mothballs years ago anywhere else in the country. . . . Howard Stern? Salty Brine has socks older than Howard Stern." The studio was packed with well-wishers poised for a powerful moment in Rhode Island's broadcast history. Saying goodbye to his fans, Brine reflected: "To all of you folks listening, this is my state. I love everybody in it. From the time they are born through the time they get through school and college, I think I've lived through about four generations."

Salty's parting with WPRO was cordial, but he refused to settle for retirement at age 75, noting that he and Mickey would consider "another position in broadcasting, perhaps sales or public service." The state's media mascot was true to his word. He appeared in television commercials for Cardi's Furniture and took several roles in theater productions before the debut of his television feature, *Salty's Southern New England*, on WJAR Channel 10 in September 1993. Although this hometown segment lasted only a few episodes, Brine's popularity never waned; a year later WHJJ-AM began broadcasting one-minute *Salty Tales* each day at 6:22 and 7:22 A.M.

Described as warm and caring by admirers, Salty has supported charities throughout his life, frequently hosting telethons and gala fund-raising events. He has garnered many awards and accolades, among them the renaming of a Narragansett beach in his honor. In remarks made at the dedication ceremony, Governor Edward DiPrete placed Brine among distinguished company, noting with pride that "we have Roger Williams, the *Independent Man* and Salty Brine."

Gerald S. Goldstein, "Salty Brine Brightens Ceremony to Rename Beach in His Honor," *Providence Journal*, June 24, 1990; John Martin, "A Rhode Island Institution," *Providence Journal*, April 28, 1993, and "Words Fail," *Providence Journal*, April 29, 1993.

Tracy Manforte Sweet

Burns, Ken (1953–) Documentary filmmaker. The New Hampshire–based filmmaker Kenneth Lauren Burns is famous for using old photographs and drawings, vintage film footage, interviews with well-known scholars, voice-over narration, evocative music, and voices representing participants in historical events to bring history to life. His most acclaimed work, the 11-hour *The Civil War,* was broadcast in 1990 to one of the largest public television audiences ever. A strong advocate of government funding for the arts and humanities, Burns has also come into the public eye as a supporter of the National Endowment for the Humanities (NEH) and the Public Broadcasting System (PBS)

Born in Brooklyn, N.Y., Burns was raised in academic communities in Delaware and Michigan. His father, a professor of anthropology, fostered his sons' interest in photography, and the youthful Burns and his brother Ric (co-producer of *The Civil War*) developed a love of film. Burns attended Hampshire College in Amherst, Mass., where he enrolled in the photography and filmmaking program under the guidance of photographer Jerome Liebling. His senior thesis film on daily life in early New England was shot at Old Stur-

bridge Village, Mass. Upon graduation in 1975, Burns originally established Florentine Films in western Massachusetts, then moved to Walpole, N.H., in 1979. With a mix of capitalist enterprise, a sense of mission about educating people, and a love for history, Burns, along with fellow Hampshire alumni, sought to create documentaries that would appeal to a mass audience.

Burns's first success came with *The Brooklyn Bridge,* the story of the bridge's conception and construction, which PBS broadcast in 1982. During the next three years Burns turned out three major films, which his first wife, Amy Stechler, edited: *The Shakers: Hands to Work, Hearts to God* (PBS, 1985), *The Statue of Liberty* (debut, French Embassy in Washington, 1985; PBS, 1985), and *Huey Long* (debut, Louisiana State Capitol, 1985; PBS, 1986). *The Shakers,* inspired by a restored Shaker barn in western Massachusetts, explores the communitarian sect that played an important role in 19th-century New England life.

The first of Burns's multipart documentaries, *The Civil War* was a five-and-a-half-year undertaking that received major funding from the NEH and turned him into a national celebrity. The film combines descriptions of

Ken Burns sitting in a replica of Thomas Jefferson's garden tower, Walpole, N.H., 1994

complex military campaigns, fascinating photographs and songs from the period, and readings from letters and memoirs including those of the commander of the 20th Maine Regiment (and later Maine governor and Bowdoin college president) Joshua Lawrence Chamberlain. As a result, the film provides a strong sense of the feelings of common soldiers, officers, and the families they left behind. Historian and writer Shelby Foote, a major presence in the film, offers an intriguing and personal perspective on the war. Although *The Civil War* has been criticized for leaving important depths unplumbed, it has had a significant impact on the popular view of the conflict.

Burns's even longer series, *Baseball,* a history of the game with a focus on the racial divide, appeared in 1994. *Thomas Jefferson* (1997) initiated a series of documentary portraits of important figures in American history. The 19-hour *Jazz* (2001), a social and artistic history of jazz music in America, is one of Burns's most widely viewed films. *Unforgiveable Blackness: The Rise and Fall of Jack Johnson* (2005) continues Burns's nuanced explorations of race relations in America. Burns has also produced the work of other directors, such as Steven Ives's *The West* (1996).

Like Alain Resnais before him in *Night and Fog* (1956), Burns has discovered the emotional power of using still photographs and old film footage in a newly structured presentation with contemporary commentary and period music. His films have shaped the historical documentary decisively, making it accessible to a large audience.

Thomas Cripps, "Historical Truth: An Interview with Ken Burns," *American Historical Review* 100 (1995); Gary R. Edgerton, *Ken Burns's America: Packaging the Past for Television* (2001); Brian Henderson, "The Civil War: 'Did It Not Seem Real?'" *Film Quarterly* 44 (1991); David Thelen, "The Movie Maker as Historian: Conversations with Ken Burns," *Journal of American History* 81 (1994).

Charles Warren

Car Talk   *Car Talk,* heard nationally over the Public Broadcasting System (PBS), is a radio call-in show that mixes humor and irreverence with sound advice for callers with troubles or questions about their cars and trucks. The show was founded in 1977 by hosts Tom and Ray Magliozzi, aka Click and Clack, the Tappet Brothers. The Magliozzis are natives of East Cambridge, Mass., and lifelong New Englanders. The show originates from WBUR, Boston University's public radio station.

The Magliozzis' humorous approach to auto mechanics led to the show's popularity, and eventually to its syndication through PBS. Knowledgeable mechanics who have

Ray and Tom Magliozzi (Click and Clack), the hosts of Car Talk, *at their garage in Cambridge, Mass., 1983*

operated their own garage for more than 20 years, the brothers demystify the subject of car repair. Their lighthearted attitude draws a wide audience that includes many women and extends well beyond car aficionados and the mechanically inclined.

From their irreverence, self-deprecating humor, and thick Boston accents to their education and technical expertise to their ethnic heritage, the Magliozzis represent the region's urban culture. Both grew up loving to "take things apart and put them back together again." Both graduated from the Massachusetts Institute of Technology. Tom Magliozzi went on to receive an MBA and worked in the semiconductor industry, while Ray joined the Volunteers in Service to America (VISTA) program, then taught science in Bennington, Vt., before the brothers decided to start a do-it-yourself garage, Hacker's Haven, in Cambridge, Mass. The shop is now called the Good News Garage.

Soon after the brothers opened their garage, WBUR invited them, in 1977, to take part in a panel broadcast of local automotive experts. According to Tom Magliozzi, *Car Talk* was born when the other experts failed to show up. "The early days of *Car Talk,*" he explains, "was a time when dinosaurs roamed the earth and people actually worked on their own cars."

Car Talk was broadcast on WBUR for 10 years when National Public Radio (NPR) picked it up in 1987 to run as a featured segment on *Sunday Weekend Edition* with Susan

Stamberg. Nine months later, the show received its own NPR slot. By the mid-1990s, *Car Talk* was carried on more than 370 stations and had earned a weekly listenership of over 2 million people.

"How we ended up going national is somewhat a matter of contention," according to Tom Magliozzi. "Robert Seigel, one of NPR's hosts of *All Things Considered,* claims credit. He says that one day when he was on vacation here in Massachusetts, he was surfing the dial and heard the show—and somehow decided that we were national material. Jay Kernis, the original producer of NPR's *Morning Edition,* tells a similar story. NPR field producer Gary Covino says the same damn thing."

In 1989 the Magliozzis introduced a twice-weekly newspaper column, "Click and Clack Talk Cars," which runs in 200 papers across the country. "The column is a lot like the radio show," explains Tom Magliozzi, "meaning we take questions and espouse all kinds of solutions—a small fraction of which may actually be correct." In recent years, the Magliozzis have also introduced an extensive and popular Web site as well as *Car Talk* audio repair books, tapes, and compact disks.

National recognition for *Car Talk* has come in the form of a Peabody Award in 1992 and appearances on the *Tonight Show, CBS Evening News, The Today Show, 60 Minutes,* and *Late Night with David Letterman.*

Tom Magliozzi and Ray Magliozzi, *Car Talk* (1991); Magliozzi and Magliozzi, *The Best of "Car Talk": With Click and Clack, the Tappet Brothers* [sound recording] (1995); Magliozzi and Magliozzi, *The Second Best of "Car Talk": More Used Calls from Click and Clack* [sound recording] (1997); Magliozzi and Magliozzi, *"Car Talk": Men Are from GM, Women Are from Ford* [sound recording] (1997).

Louis Mazzari

Christian Science Monitor and Monitor Broadcasting   One of America's most prestigious newspapers, the *Christian Science Monitor* was founded in 1908 by the 87-year-old Christian Science head Mary Baker Eddy, a New England native, as a nondenominational effort of her church. With experienced editorial and publishing experts from around the country lending a hand, the first edition appeared just 100 days after Eddy first suggested it. According to Eddy's editorial in that first issue, the paper intended "to injure no man, but to bless all mankind."

The *Monitor* was to be a general-interest newspaper, rather than a self-serving or doctrinal house organ. In an age of yellow journalism (from which Eddy herself had suffered severely), monopolies, insufficient freedom, and dangerous unrest among nations, Eddy wanted the *Monitor* to "lighten mankind," perhaps the best explanation for its founding. Democracy, in a context of religious freedom, depends on enlightened public opinion. Eddy was convinced that matters of the spirit could be translated into justice and freedom on the human scene. For a religious institution without clergy, parsonages, schools, missions, or hospitals, underwriting the *Monitor* would become by far the Christian Science church's largest charitable undertaking—and an affordable one. Eddy viewed the publication as the culmination of her lifework.

Over the course of the *Monitor*'s first decade its readership grew to 120,000. Erwin D. Canham served as managing editor and editor of the paper from 1940 until 1964, during which period *Monitor* journalism gained a worldwide reputation for quality. Published Monday through Friday, the *Monitor* relies more heavily on its own reporters than on the wire-service stories—distributed, for instance, by the Associated Press or Reuters—from which most American dailies get their news. Those reporters are based in 11 bureaus around the United States and 10 other locations around the world.

For most of its nearly 100-year history, the *Monitor* has not shied away from covering vital world issues and has shown strong support for home and family. It has gained an international reputation for fairness, accuracy, dignity, and usefulness among educators, legislators, clergy, and members of the general public. To readers around the country, and even around the globe, *Monitor* names such as Roscoe Drummond, Richard L. Strout, Joseph C. Harsch, and Erwin D. Canham have become synonymous with quality reporting and commentary. The paper has won countless awards, including several Pulitzer Prizes.

In the mid-1980s, however, with the paper steadily losing money, significant changes were made. Business-oriented new members of the *Monitor*'s management team—almost entirely from outside the *Monitor* family if not new to the communications field altogether—believed that the paper's reputation could profitably be applied to a wide range of highly expensive electronic and publishing ventures. The church had accumulated large financial reserves, primarily through well-invested legacies, and the entrepreneurial new management executives won church directors over to the daring concept of creating a vast communications empire. Management would tack the name "Monitor" (minus "Christian Science") onto every new venture, thus exploiting the paper's well-earned reputation. In only a few years more than half a billion dollars was lost, and many on the *Monitor*'s staff resigned, retired early, or were fired.

In a flurry of activity, elaborate state-of-the-art television and radio studios were built and equipped. Programming was created and staff hired to establish public Monitor Radio and shortwave broadcasting. A sophisticated nightly television news program was produced for the Discovery Channel. Original, though generally rather mundane, programming was aired on a new Monitor cable-television channel. The company also bought Channel 68, a Boston television station, and part of a communications satellite. To reach the world, it built two costly shortwave stations, in Maine and South Carolina, and purchased another on the Pacific island of Saipan. The monthly magazine *World Monitor* emerged, along with television tie-ins to schools. The dignified Monitor logo began to appear on pins, shirts, and umbrellas.

But by late 1991 the media empire was rapidly bankrupting the church, causing it to dip secretly into restricted endowments, including its pension fund. As quickly and dramatically as the empire had formed, its parts were disassembled or sold off. Television operations suddenly folded in the spring of 1992, and several members of the church's and *Monitor*'s senior management went with them on golden parachutes. Not long afterward the magazine shut down. Finally, in the spring of 1997, the church announced it would discontinue its news-radio efforts and seek to sell or lease the shortwave stations.

At the same time the church reinforced its commitment to the print *Monitor*, as well as to a World Wide Web site, but most of the paper's leading writers and editors were not invited back. The personnel trained and inspired under Eddy's implied mandate, people dedicated to that balanced entity called "*Monitor* journalism," were largely gone. Some in management had hard feelings toward members of the former staff, whom they blamed for the failure of the ill-fated media explosion.

It remains to be seen whether the *Christian Science Monitor* can recapture in the 21st century the reputation for trustworthiness, depth, dignity, and usefulness it once had and whether the church can reconstruct the paper and its staff.

Erwin D. Canham, *Commitment to Freedom: The Story of the "Christian Science Monitor"* (1958); Robert Peel, *Mary Baker Eddy*, 3 vols. (1966–77).

J. Denis Glover

Colonial Printers The craft of printing came to New England long before it appeared anywhere else in British America, and for most of the 17th and 18th centuries Boston was the printing capital of the colonies. Printing had a significant history in nearby Cambridge,

however, beginning in 1639. Stephen Daye published the first New England book, *The Whole Booke of Psalmes,* there in 1640, and Marmaduke Johnson printed John Eliot's famous Indian Bible in 1663. Not until 1675 did one of the two presses in Cambridge move to Boston.

The printer's occupation in the 18th century became far more complex than that of simple craftsman. Printing was a handicraft, of course, one that demanded both manual dexterity and physical strength. A future printer served a long apprenticeship like that of his counterparts in England or that of other tradesmen on both sides of the Atlantic. On gaining his freedom, he could hire himself out as a journeyman to work under the guidance of a master craftsman. In most cases the journeyman eventually became a master printer with a press and shop of his own, often in partnership with and sometimes under the sponsorship of another printer. Printing was also of necessity the most literate of trades and thus tended to attract bookish young men to its ranks. Benjamin Franklin, the most famous of all the Boston printing apprentices, got a start on his writing and printing career while under the supervision of his older brother James.

The printing office—and in Boston there were six of them by 1740, operated by 10 master printers—was much more than just an artisan's shop. Printers sold books, stationery supplies, and a surprising variety of other goods; sometimes functioned as brokers of real estate, indentures, and slaves; trained apprentices and hired journeymen; and published some of the more significant products of their presses on their own account. They also carried on a job-printing business, with patrons paying for printed pieces that ranged from lottery tickets to business and legal forms to broadside proclamations and ballads to pamphlets and small books.

At least one printer in each provincial capital held the government printing contract, and from about midcentury on, the local postmaster in any sizable seaport town was likely to be a printer—Boston was the exception in this respect. Most printers published an annual almanac, and nearly all of them put out a weekly newspaper. It was especially the latter activity, combined in most places with the post office, that gave the printing office its distinctive public character. Merchants and shopkeepers came in with advertisements, town and province officials with public announcements, others with letters and essays of opinion, busybodies of all description with fragments of news and tidbits of gossip—and the hope of hearing more.

Before the Revolution, limited supplies of type and equipment prevented the colonial production of many large books. Most such volumes were imported from England. Colonial presses issued pamphlets in great variety, however. In New England the most characteristic publication of this sort was the printed sermon, but as the Revolution approached, the proportion of religious works declined in relation to political pamphlets.

Printing spread from Boston to New London, Conn., in 1709; Newport, R.I., in 1732; Portsmouth, N.H., in 1756; and Salem, Mass., in 1768. A press was established in New Haven, Conn., in 1754, but it was part of Franklin's widespread Philadelphia-based printing network and had no Boston connections. By 1775 printers were located in 14 New England cities and towns including Newburyport, Chelmsford, Watertown, and Worcester, Mass.; Hartford and Norwich, Conn.; Providence, R.I.; and Exeter, N.H.

Charles E. Clark, "The Colonial Press," in *Intellect, Technology, the Arts, Education, Religion, Independence,* vol. 3 of *Encyclopedia of the North American Colonies,* ed. Jacob Ernest Cook (1993); Isaiah Thomas, *The History of Printing in America, with a Biography of Printers and an Account of Newspapers,* 2d ed. (1874; reprint edited by Marcus A. McCorison, 1970); Lawrence C. Wroth, *The Colonial Printer,* 2d ed. (1964 [1938]).

Charles E. Clark

Documentaries Since the late 1950s, New England has been a great center for documentary filmmaking, with Boston serving as a hub of activity through its filmmaking schools, production companies, and many resident filmmakers. The story begins with a connection to Robert Flaherty, the midwesterner whose *Nanook of the North* (1922), *Moana* (1926), and *Man of Aran* (1934) are among the first nonfiction films to be considered works of art. In 1955 Flaherty's widow and erstwhile collaborator, Frances Hubbard Flaherty, began the Flaherty Seminars at her farm in Vermont. Nonfiction filmmakers met there, screened films for one another, and discussed their ambitions and the potential of the medium.

At the end of the 1950s, the development of lighter camera equipment with synchronized sound recording capability made possible the worldwide movement known as *cinéma vérité.* The new technology allowed a two-person crew or even a solitary filmmaker to move about freely in the world, simultaneously filming and recording sound. Most American practitioners of cinéma vérité worked in a way that suited Frances Flaherty's advice in the Vermont seminars: do not set out to make an instructional film about something you presume to understand in advance. Rather, film without preconceptions, observe and follow, let the film be shaped by what is discovered.

Harvard University's Peabody Museum of Archaeology and Ethnology played an important early role in fostering freely structured observational cinema. John Marshall, working out of the museum with Robert Gardner, won wide acclaim, including the Robert Flaherty Award, for *The Hunters* (1958), about the !Kung people of the Kalahari desert in southern Africa. Based in Boston, Marshall has dedicated his work to documenting the !Kung and advocating for their way of life. Gardner, scion of an old Boston family, initiated the teaching of filmmaking at Harvard in the early 1960s and taught there until 1998. He has won many awards and been given retrospectives in many countries for a series of poetic documentaries including *Dead Birds* (1964), about warring tribes in central New Guinea; *Rivers of Sand* (1974), about abuse of women among the Hamar people of southwestern Ethiopia; and *Forest of Bliss* (1986), about care for the dying and disposal of the dead in Benares, India, presenting images and sounds of the place with no spoken commentary.

British-born and Harvard-educated Richard Leacock worked as Flaherty's cameraman on *Louisiana Story* (1948), and a decade later he became a leading light of the American cinéma vérité movement, often called "direct cinema." Leacock was part of the New York–based Drew Associates in the early 1960s, working with D. A. Pennebaker and others on films about American life for television broadcast, such as *Primary* (1960), winner of the Robert Flaherty Award, about the Kennedy versus Humphrey presidential campaign, and *A Happy Mother's Day* (1963), about a South Dakota family with newborn quintuplets. In the 1970s Leacock taught at the Massachu-

setts Institute of Technology. Also associated with the Drew group were Boston-born Albert and David Maysles, whose direct cinema landmark *Salesman* (1969) follows the lives of four Massachusetts door-to-door Bible salesmen as they work their Florida territory.

Frederick Wiseman has developed his own kind of cinéma vérité, which he likes to call "reality fiction." Working with John Marshall as cameraman, he began with *Titicut Follies* in 1967, a scandal-causing look at the Bridgewater, Mass., prison for the criminally insane. Through his Boston-based company, Zipporah Films, Wiseman has now made a distinguished series of more than 30 documentaries about American institutions, organizations, and services, including *High School* (1968), *Basic Training* (1971), *Welfare* (1975), *Near Death* (1980) (about a Boston hospital's intensive care ward for the terminally ill), *Zoo* (1993), and *Ballet* (1995). *Belfast, Maine* (2000) is a four-hour study of that town, taking the viewer into its schools, cafes, and factories, and following social workers as they visit town residents. Wiseman's style is one of silent, unflinching observation of daily life, without explanation or commentary, creating connections and ironies through his editing strategies.

Edward Pincus gave a new personal direction to documentary film through his teaching at MIT in the 1970s, and by making himself and his family the subject of the monumental *Diaries (1971–1976)* (1980), set in Cambridge and Vermont. Pincus and Steven Ascher, who also taught at MIT, co-wrote the classic *Filmmaker's Handbook,* originally published in 1984. Ascher and his wife, Jeanne Jordan, both based in Boston, made the widely seen *Troublesome Creek: A Midwestern* (1995), about Jor-

Documentary filmmaker Frederick Wiseman, 1969

dan's family's tribulations while trying to hold on to their small working farm. Prominent New England filmmakers who studied at MIT include Vermont-based David Parry, who made *Yukon Journal* in the 1980s, and Harvard faculty members Rob Moss and Ross McElwee. Moss made the autobiographical *River Dogs* (1978) and *The Tourist* (1992), and McElwee, a transplanted southerner, created a series of rich, ironic films about his own life, including *Sherman's March* (1986), *Time Indefinite* (1992), and *Six o'Clock News* (1997), which were distributed widely among theater and television outlets.

The filmmaking faculty at Harvard includes Alfred Guzzetti; Richard Rogers was also a faculty member until his death in 2001. Guzzetti and Rogers made numerous experimental and documentary films, such as Guzzetti's *Family Portrait Sittings* (1976), about his family background, and Rogers's *Quarry* (1970), about a working-class swimming hole in Quincy, Mass. The two worked together with still photographer Susan Meiselas on *Pictures from a Revolution* (1992), a devastating portrait of Nicaragua's decline because of outside pressures in the decade following the Sandanista revolution. Mira Nair studied filmmaking at Harvard and made two fine documentaries, *So Far from India* (1982) and *India Cabaret* (1985), and then used her documentary skills and style to create her successful fictional feature film *Salaam Bombay* (1987).

Michael Roemer's many years of teaching at Yale University forged another important link between New England's academic institutions and its active filmmaking community. With Robert M. Young, Roemer made *Cortile Cascino* (1962), a powerful study of a Palermo slum; and the fictional *Nothing But a Man* (1964), about southern racism from a black perspective, shot in the style of documentary realism. Roemer also made the moving documentary *Dying* (1976), about terminally ill cancer patients.

Creative arts–oriented Hampshire College, in Amherst, Mass., began to promote documentary filmmaking in the 1970s under the guidance of photographer Jerome Liebling. New Hampshire–based filmmaker Ken Burns, a student there during this period, went on to make *The Brooklyn Bridge* (1982), *The Civil War* (1990), *Baseball* (1994), *Jazz* (2001), and other acclaimed films and series. New Hampshire native Tom Joslin taught and made films at Hampshire in the 1970s. He is best known for his posthumously released film, *Silverlake Life* (1993), which he and his lover, Mark Massi, made about their life together. The viewer sees the pair living with AIDS and witnesses Joslin's decline and death. Abraham Ravett, the primary film teacher at Hampshire, has pushed the documentary medium in an avant-garde direction in his own work by experimenting with editing and printing techniques.

Experimental documentary in New England goes back decades with the work of Maine resident Abbott Meader, who examines his own locale in films such as *Shadows from the Western Wall* (1974), *Deep Trout* (1979–80), *South Slope* (1980), and *Winter Fence* (1986). Meader also collaborated with his former student, Maine-based filmmaker Huey (James Coleman), on a large-scale project, *Wilderness and Spirit: A Mountain Called Katahdin* (2002). Some of Meader's work is preserved at Northeast Historic Film in Bucksport, Maine, a valuable archive and screening center for films about northern New England. Theodore Lyman, who teaches at the University of Vermont, takes the autobiographical film in an experimental direction. And Mark Lapore, who teaches at Boston's Massachusetts College of Art, pushes the documentary about foreign cultures toward the personal and experimental with work such as *The Sleepers* (1989), linking life in Sudan to the way either a westerner or a Chinese individual forms impressions and remembers. Lapore meditates on recent experiences in Sri Lanka and India in *A Depression in the Bay of Bengal* (1996) and *The Five Bad Elements* (1997).

The Boston area boasts many independent documentary filmmakers, drawn in part by the technical and commercial work available and in part by the opportunity to function within a community of filmmakers and enthusiasts. Boston's public television station, WGBH, provides much technical work and has produced and commissioned numerous investigative and educational films, notably for *Frontline* and *Nova*. The station commissioned the Civil Rights movement epic *Eyes on the Prize* (1987) and its 1990 sequel, produced by Henry Hampton's Boston company, Blackside Films. The Boston Film and Video Foundation sponsors documentary filmmaking and holds an annual New England Film Festival, with awards. Documentaries are regularly screened by the Boston Museum of Fine Arts, the Harvard Film Archive, and the Coolidge Corner and Brattle theaters.

Boston independent filmmakers include Errol Morris, who has made bizarre and fantastical films such as *Gates of Heaven* (1978), about a pet cemetery; *Vernon, Florida* (1981), about inhabitants of a strange community; *The Thin Blue Line* (1988), about coercive police procedures in Texas; *A Brief History of Time* (1990), about Stephen Hawking; and *Mr. Death* (2000), about a Massachusetts designer of execution equipment and Holocaust denier. Another remarkable Boston filmmaker is David Sutherland, whose *Out of Sight* (1993) presents the romantic and work life of a blind woman who is a cowgirl in the West. Sutherland's widely seen and acclaimed *The Farmer's Wife* (1998) studies the life and trials of a young farm family in intimate detail over a period of years. Richard Gordon and Carma Hinton's *Gate of Heavenly Peace* (1995), an exhaustive study of the Tiananmen Square protest and massacre, has been widely screened for educational purposes. Michal Goldman makes films about music and musicians and their ethnic significance, such as the popular *Umm Kulthum: A Voice Like Egypt* (1997).

The tradition of socially conscious documentary-making among Boston independents goes back to Richard Broadman's *Mission Hill and the Miracle of Boston* (1978). Jane Gillooly's *Leonie's Sister Gerri* (1994) uncovers the life of a woman killed by an illegal abortion before the *Roe v. Wade* decision. Mark Lipman and Leah Mahan's *Holding Ground: The Life and Death of Dudley Street* (1996) follows a Roxbury community project, and Joshua Feftel's *Taking on the Kennedys* (1997) offers a shrewd study of a political campaign in Rhode Island. The best-known of these socially conscious films is Margaret Lazarus and Renner Wunderlich's *Defending Our Lives,* which won an Oscar in 1994, chronicling the lives of battered women.

From the Flaherty seminars in the 1950s and the cinéma vérité innovations of the 1960s, up to the present with its rich and varied field of filmmakers, New England has asserted itself as a center for nonfiction filmmakers and filmmaking. And the audience for this medium has grown and become solid. Like a Renaissance city-state with its special mode of art, New England expects documentary filmmakers to be part of its culture as they pursue their work of finding subject matter and experimenting in observation and understanding.

Erik Barnouw, *Documentary: A History of the Non-Fiction Film,* 2d ed. (1993); Richard Meran Barsam, *Non-Fiction Film: A Critical History* (1992); Barry Keith Grant, *Voyages of Discovery: The Cinema of Frederick Wiseman* (1992); G. Roy Levin, *Documentary Explorations: Fifteen Interviews with Film Makers* (1971); Stephen Mamber, *Cinéma Vérité in America* (1974); William Rothman, *Documentary Film Classics* (1997); Charles Warren, ed., *Beyond Document: Essays on Nonfiction Film* (1996).

Charles Warren

ESPN ESPN, the Entertainment and Sports Programming Network, was founded in Bristol, Conn., in 1979. The brainchild of Bill Rasmussen, the first 24-hour sports network began as a channel for broadcasting sports events at the University of Connecticut and locally. Since then, it has grown into the leading multinational, multimedia sports entertainment company in the country, made up of seven domestic television networks, plus ESPN HD (a high-definition simulcast service), ESPN Radio, ESPN.com, ESPN *The Magazine,* SportsTicker, sports-themed restaurants (ESPN Zones), and other businesses. Its technical innovations and flagship program *SportsCenter,* watched by up to 18 million people a day, have changed the way sports is broadcast in America.

ESPN was launched from a plot of redevelopment land measuring less than an acre that Rasmussen bought sight unseen in Bristol. Learning that emerging satellite technology could provide coast-to-coast distribution for his network, Rasmussen developed his channel into a national service, covering sports across the country. Although the idea of a 24-hour sports network seemed risky, it soon became clear that viewers were responding to the constant accessibility of a wide variety of sports coverage. Today ESPN offers coverage of 65 sports, and its 65-acre campus contains 27 satellite dishes taking in more than 40,000 feeds a year and recording approximately 200 hours of highlights and program content each day. *SportsCenter* has become the definitive national sports news show, combining highlights, analysis, and features, often presented with a humorous touch. The information provided is voluminous; each edition includes an average of 95 insert graphics and 14 animation elements.

ESPN is committed to development and innovation and has been a leader in sports television production trends, such as the "electronic cut-in," which is used to cut away from game action to provide live and taped coverage of other games. In 2003, ESPN HD launched a high-definition simulcast of ESPN designed for the clarity and widescreen format of high-definition television. The network's technical innovations have brought ESPN a number of awards.

ESPN now includes six other television networks, among them ESPN2 and ESPN Classic, which telecasts great moments in the history of sports. In 1992 ESPN started ESPN Radio, now the country's largest sports radio network, with more than 700 affiliates. ESPN entered the Internet world in 1995 with the creation of ESPN.com, which has grown into the leading sports Web site, averaging more than 16 million unique users per month. In 1996 ESPNEWS, the only 24-hour sports news network, was launched. ESPN *The Magazine* debuted in 1998; it is now an award-winning periodical. Still located in Connecticut, where its Bristol campus employs 2,600 Connecticut residents, who work out of

700,000 square feet of buildings, including a 120,000-square-foot digital television center that opened in 2004, ESPN has become part of national as well as New England culture.

Mark Gentzkow, *25 Years of Excellence,* ESPN publication (2004); Dave Larson, *Quick Facts,* ESPN publication (2004).

Colleen Davidson

Film Festivals *Independent* is the word that seems to best define the focus of the film festivals held in New England, a term consistent with the region's traditional character. Not for New England, the glitz and excesses of Hollywood. Indeed, "Hollywood film" has become synonymous with huge budgets, temperamental stars, and the commercialism that is at the heart of the American feature-film industry. Independent films, those produced outside the Hollywood system, require the kind of individual strength, even stoicism, for which New England has long been known.

Area film festivals are often associated with academic, educational, and cultural institutions. The New England Film and Video Festival, launched in 1976, is the region's premier showcase for independent film. It was run until 1996 by the Arts Extension Service of the University of Massachusetts, Amherst, and the Boston Film and Video Foundation (BFVF), a nonprofit organization founded to support independent productions by New England–based artists at all stages in their careers. In 1996 BFVF became sole organizer of the event, held every spring. Screenings take place at Boston's Museum of Fine Arts and the Coolidge Corner Theatre in nearby Brookline, Mass.

Boston's Museum of Fine Arts has one of the most active and exciting film programs in the region, hosting festivals that showcase everything from the avant-garde films of Peter Greenaway to the latest in cinema from China and Korea. Far from being the rather dusty conservative institution of the not too distant past, the museum, together with the Harvard Film Archive, has played host to the Boston Gay and Lesbian Film/Video Festival, founded in 1985, and often takes advocacy positions by presenting documentary films that focus on such themes as human rights and global politics. In April 1993 the first annual Boston International Festival of Women's Cinema was held at the Brattle Theatre in nearby Cambridge. The New England chapter of Women in Film and Video, based in Watertown, Mass., takes advantage of that event to sponsor screenings of films and videos produced or directed by women from New England. The Center for Children's Media of Medford, Mass., organizes another yearly cinematic happening in Boston, the

New England Children's Film and Video Festival.

Although much of New England's film festival activity is centered in or near the Massachusetts capital, other regions also are worthy of mention. Northampton, Mass., is developing a reputation as a regional center for film and media. Area colleges have added majors in film and media studies. The Northampton Film Festival, organized by the nonprofit Northampton Film Associates and held each year in early November since 1995, showcases independent short and feature films from around the United States. The Northampton Film Expo, occurring in conjunction with the film and video festival, features products and services of interest to film and video makers as well as members of the general public. The Berkshire Film Festival in Great Barrington, Mass., and the Nantucket Film Festival, held on the island of Nantucket off the Massachusetts coast, both take advantage of their attractive geographic locations to draw an audience. The Nantucket event takes the unique approach of honoring screenplays and adaptations in addition to offering a full schedule of entertainment that includes staged readings of screenplays, screenings of documentaries, short and feature-length films, and panel discussions.

The Vermont International Film Foundation has sponsored a festival in Burlington since 1990. The Maine International Film Festival, created by the Friends of Art and Film in Central Maine and held yearly in midsummer at Waterville's Railroad Square Cinema, began in 1998 and features a variety of foreign, American independent, and Maine-made films. In 1986 Bill Pence, cofounder of the famed Telluride (Colo.) Film Festival and director of the Hopkins Center film program at Dartmouth College, began screening a selection of Telluride's most promising offerings from around the world at Dartmouth in Hanover, N.H. Cinema lovers on the seacoast in that state were treated to the same slate of independent movies from Telluride for the first time at Portsmouth's Music Hall in September 1999. Although not technically full-fledged film festivals, the Telluride screenings quickly became much-anticipated annual events in both New Hampshire locations.

The Rhode Island International Film Festival, established in 1997, is centered in Providence but also features venues in other communities, such as Woonsocket and Middletown; many of its nearly 200 films are East Coast or New England premieres. Connecticut's Film Fest New Haven, which debuted in 1996, screens films and videos, shorts and features, comedy, drama, documentary, and "works that defy classification." The Connecticut Gay and Lesbian Film Festival, featuring local filmmakers as well as works from around the globe, began in 1988 and is held every June in Hartford. Film festivals are clearly a form of entertainment whose star is on the rise in New England.

Michael Blowen, "Festival Shows Off Talented New England Filmmakers," *Boston Globe,* June 14, 1984; Loren King, "Film Festivals Offer Fun, Sun, Screenings" *Boston Globe,* May 19, 2002.

Cynthia Close

Hampton, Henry (1940–98) Documentary filmmaker, author, executive. One of America's leading documentary filmmakers, Henry Hampton was born in Saint Louis, Mo., and graduated from Washington University in 1961. He was best known as the creator and executive producer of *Eyes on the Prize,* the award-winning 14-hour PBS film series on America's Civil Rights movement. As president of Blackside, Inc., the minority-owned independent documentary film company he founded in Boston in 1968, Hampton was responsible for the production of a number of celebrated film series examining the nature of democracy, leadership, poverty, and the dynamics of social change.

Eyes I (1987), the first six hours of the *Eyes on the Prize* series, became one of the most highly acclaimed programs in television history. It traces the development of the Civil Rights movement from 1954 to 1965, from the murder of black high school student Emmett Till to the signing of the Voting Rights Act in 1965. *Eyes II* (1990) chronicles the civil rights struggle through the mid-1980s, examining the rise of Malcolm X and the Black Panthers, as well as the Boston busing crisis of the 1970s. The *Eyes* series has been broadcast in more than a dozen countries and is used in secondary schools and colleges throughout the United States. Hampton also co-wrote a companion book to the series, *Voices of Freedom: An Oral History of the Civil Rights Movement from the 1950s through the 1980s* (1990).

For Hampton, who grew up in an upper-middle-class black family in Saint Louis and was stricken with polio at age 15, the idea of making a film about the Civil Rights movement came in 1965 when he was in Selma, Ala., to join a march on the city led by Martin Luther King, Jr. At the time, Hampton was director of broadcasting and information for the Boston-based Unitarian Universalist Association, and part of a delegation the association sent to the South after James Reeb, a Unitarian civil rights worker from Boston, was killed in Selma. Recalling confrontations between demonstrators and police that he witnessed, Hampton told an interviewer, "It was like a circus. It was theatrical. I was thinking, 'This is terrific film.'"

While giving due attention to the role of government officials and movement leaders in influencing the course of events, Hampton's films focus on documenting the role ordinary people play in shaping history. Often combining compelling archival footage and testimony from eyewitnesses to events, Hampton's films have been acclaimed for their sense of drama and relevance to contemporary social and political issues.

Despite difficulty obtaining funding for his company's projects, Hampton also served as executive producer for *The Great Depression* (1993); *Malcolm X: Make It Plain* (1994); *America's War on Poverty* (1995); and *Breakthrough: The Changing Face of Science in America* (1996), his first fully funded project. Blackside documentaries that Hampton helped launch but aired after his death in 1998 include *I'll Make Me a World,* a 100-year retrospective of African American arts, which premiered on PBS in February 1999; *Hopes on the Horizon,* about prodemocracy movements in Africa in the 1990s (2001); and *This Far by Faith: African-American Spiritual Journeys* (2003), co-produced by the Faith Project.

Hampton made Blackside a training ground for more than 200 minority producers, technicians, and researchers. In addition, the filmmaker was active in the Boston community. As chair of the board of directors of the Museum of Afro American History from the late 1960s through 1990, he led the museum's campaign to acquire and restore Boston's African Meetinghouse, the oldest black church in America. He also served on numerous community boards and won dozens of awards and fellowships.

Bill Barol, "A Struggle for the Prize," *Newsweek* (August 22, 1988); Norman Boucher, "Eyes on Henry Hampton," *Boston Globe Magazine* (June 12, 1988); Wil Haygood, "Hampton: Back from Hard Times," *Boston Globe,* October 29, 1993; K. Anthony Norris, "Blackside's Henry Hampton: Telling and Selling the Truth," *American Visions* 9 (February-March 1994).

Mark Herlihy

Henry Hampton in his South End office, Boston, 1989

Hartford Courant The *Hartford Courant* is Connecticut's leading news medium and the oldest continuously published newspaper in America. It dates its birth to October 29, 1764, when printer Thomas Green published a four-page prospectus for a weekly he called the *Connecticut Courant.* Official publication began the next month, never to cease except for a few issues that were canceled by the British Stamp Act and a Revolutionary War paper shortage. In its almost 250-year history the *Courant* has won two Pulitzer Prizes (1992 and 1999) and earned a reputation as one of the nation's best-designed newspapers.

Soon after he began publication Green sold

the paper to Ebenezer Watson, who died early in the Revolutionary War, leaving the paper in the hands of his widow, Hannah Watson, and an apprentice, George Goodwin. The two printed as many as 8,000 copies a week, making the *Courant,* a patriot publication, one of the most important newspapers during the Revolution. As a female publisher during the war, Watson acquired legendary status. Goodwin, who had been apprenticed to the paper since the age of nine and whom Watson made a partner before he was 21, earned his own place as a legend by his longevity. Goodwin essentially ran the paper until his death in 1836, the year before the *Courant* began daily publication.

The *Courant* entered its Gilded Age, along with Hartford and the rest of the nation, after the Civil War, when its chief owners were General Joseph Hawley and Charles Dudley Warner. While copresident of the paper, Hawley served four terms as U.S. senator. Warner, a celebrated essayist, lived in the same Nook Farm neighborhood as his friend and fellow newspaperman Mark Twain, and in 1873 Warner and Twain collaborated on *The Gilded Age,* a novel that satirized postwar greed and corruption.

As each became more famous, Hawley and Warner gradually ceded control of the paper to Charles Hopkins Clark, their managing editor, who at his death in 1926 had become a co-owner and a confidant of U.S. presidents. After Clark's death the *Courant* would no longer be linked as closely with individual owners. The *Courant* continued as a respected, if somewhat staid paper until it was overtaken by fortune after World War II. The movement of readers to the suburbs favored morning papers like the *Courant.* In 1964, the year of its 200th anniversary, the paper's circulation reached 130,000 and began to pull away from that of its cross-town afternoon rival, the *Hartford Times.* When the *Times* ceased publication in 1976, the still independently owned *Courant* suddenly became a prize sought after by national newspaper chains.

In 1979 the *Courant* was bought by the Times Mirror Company and added to a newspaper group that included the Los Angeles *Times,* Long Island's *Newsday,* and the Stamford *Advocate,* among other papers. In 2000 the Times Mirror chain was itself bought by the Tribune Company of Chicago. In addition to the print version of the paper, the *Courant* produces a Web site, ctnow.com.

Joel Lang, "From Thomas Green to Times Mirror," *Hartford Courant,* November 4, 1990; J. Bard McNulty, *Older Than the Nation: The Story of the "Hartford Courant"* (1964); J. Eugene Smith, *One Hundred Years of Hartford's "Courant"* (1949).

Joel Lang

Harvard Lampoon   America's oldest college humor magazine, the Harvard *Lampoon* was founded in 1876 when a student flicked a note to a friend during a boring lecture, urging that they devote their resources to a more worthwhile enterprise. As that note sailed across the room, a tradition of irreverence began that continues to the present, with *Lampoon* graduates distributed throughout the upper echelons of the media and entertainment industries.

In its early years, the *Lampoon* mirrored the elitist culture of Harvard. The magazine's humor depended painfully on words like *Egad* and *Pshaw,* alongside comments on the gaucheries of social inferiors. It more or less echoed the style of *Punch,* the magazine's English inspiration. Prominent early members included philosopher George Santayana and newspaper magnate William Randolph Hearst (before his expulsion from Harvard for giving his professors chamber pots with their pictures on them).

As the *Lampoon* crept into the 20th century it became a more serious organization. A remarkable mock-Flemish edifice was built in 1909 to house the magazine. Designed by Edmund March Wheelwright, one of the *Lampoon*'s founders, and funded by arts patron Isabella Stewart Gardner and by Hearst and other graduates, the Lampoon Castle is one of the most eccentric buildings in the United States. Like a sphinx, it peers over Freedom Square in Cambridge, smiling at secrets it dare not divulge.

The *Lampoon* editors in the early century included writer Robert Benchley and cartoonist Gluyas Williams; both became active in New York journalism, helping to found the original *Life* magazine and the *New Yorker.* Benchley was also a moving spirit behind New York's famed "Algonquin set," along with Robert Sherwood, another *Lampoon* graduate. John Reed, chronicler of the Russian Revolution, was another prominent alumnus.

In the 1940s and 1950s several *Lampoon* graduates became serious writers, including William Gaddis, John Updike, and George Plimpton. Other graduates earned distinction in different ways, including Elliot Richardson, the hero of Richard Nixon's "Saturday Night Massacre," and Fred Gwynne, star of the television series *The Munsters.*

The *Lampoon* evolved yet again in the 1960s. The magazine had always performed pranks and issued parodies, but this was usually confined to a small, local audience of amused bystanders and befuddled police officers. In the 1960s and 1970s, ambitious editors issued several successful national magazine parodies, including *Sports Illustrated, Playboy,* and *Cosmopolitan* (featuring a nude centerfold

of Henry Kissinger). The annual ranking of Hollywood's worst movies also made waves, and several stars came to receive their insulting awards in person. In addition the *Lampoon* offers honorary memberships to distinguished persons and other celebrities. When John Wayne was made an honorary member in 1975 he drove up to the Castle in a tank.

In 1969, three former *Harvard Lampoon* editors, Henry Beard, Doug Kenney, and Rob Hoffman, founded the *National Lampoon,* whose first issue was published in April 1970. Doug Kenney became a screenwriter, writing the scripts for *Animal House* and *Caddyshack.* This dispersion of former *Lampoon* editors was arguably the beginning of a humor revolution, ultimately penetrating the farthest reaches of film and television but traceable to a small castle outside Harvard Square. Since then, *Lampoon* alumni have more or less eschewed literature to work on projects from *Saturday Night Live* to *Seinfeld,* from *The Simpsons* to *The Larry Sanders Show,* as well as the Comedy Central television network. Massachusetts native and national talk-show host Conan O'Brien is also a *Lampoon* alumnus. The *Harvard Lampoon,* which is staffed strictly by undergraduates, is published five times a year.

Tony Hendra, *Going Too Far* (1987); Martin Kaplan, *The "Harvard Lampoon" Centennial Celebration, 1876–1973* (1973); *The "Harvard Lampoon" Hundredth Anniversary, 1876–1976* (1976).

Ted Widmer

Manchester Union Leader   The *Manchester Union Leader,* now known as the *Union Leader,* is the most widely circulated daily newspaper in New Hampshire, with a weekday circulation in 2004 of approximately 62,000 and 83,000 for the Sunday edition. Begun under the auspices of William Franklin Knox in 1913, the newspaper today is nationally recognized for its controversial right-wing political and social views, which often are expressed on the front page, and for its wideranging impact on state and national politics.

The immediate roots of the *Union Leader* can be traced to 1912, when Progressives in New Hampshire's Republican Party invited Knox and John Muehling, two Michigan newspapermen, to establish a newspaper in Manchester. Thanks in part to financing arranged by then Governor Robert P. Bass, the duo introduced the *Evening Leader* to compete with two established Manchester newspapers, the *Morning Union,* founded in 1851, and the *Manchester Mirror,* established in 1850. Although Knox disappointed his Progressive backers by supporting more conservative elements of the Republican Party, his newspaper proved successful. Knox purchased the *Morn-*

ing Union in 1913, and formed the Union-Leader Publishing Company shortly thereafter. By 1924, Knox also had purchased the *Mirror.*

With no statewide competition, Knox's newly named *Manchester Union* and *Manchester Leader* became the most read newspapers in New Hampshire. Knox's success caught the attention of publishing mogul William Randolph Hearst, who hired the Manchester publisher in the 1920s and 1930s to oversee newspapers in Boston and Washington, D.C. Knox also used his position as a springboard into politics, unsuccessfully running for the governor of New Hampshire as a Republican in 1924 and for vice president in 1936, before becoming secretary of the navy under Franklin D. Roosevelt in 1940.

In 1946, two years after Knox's death, Vermont newspaper publisher William Loeb purchased the Union-Leader Publishing Company and, in 1948, the fledgling *New Hampshire Sunday News.* His beliefs in moral absolutes, individual rights, and conservative values permeated the papers, and often were expressed in front-page editorials that became Loeb's trademark. In his editorials Loeb railed against feminism, labor unions, and a variety of other liberal issues. He was not afraid to attack religious leaders, academic institutions, politicians, and even politicians' families to support his causes, regardless of whether his views—or the people whom he attacked—were popular. By the late 1950s, the *Union Leader* clearly influenced state elections, and

by the 1960s the paper even affected the outcome of New Hampshire's first-in-the-nation presidential primary. In particular, the newspaper is acknowledged for helping spoil Maine Senator Edmund Muskie's presidential bid in 1972, an effort that brought national attention to the *Union Leader.*

Following Loeb's death in 1981, the *Union Leader* was published by his widow, Nackey Scripps Loeb, until 1999. Under her successor, Joseph McQuaid, conservative issues have continued to dominate the newspaper. Its editors routinely attack liberal issues and have been vocal critics of Democrats and moderate Republicans. The newspaper's support of conservative presidential candidate Patrick Buchanan, for example, was credited with helping to derail the campaigns of Republicans George Bush and Robert Dole in the 1992 and 1996 presidential elections, respectively.

Grace Holbrook Blood, *Manchester on the Merrimack,* rev. ed. (1975); Kevin Cash, *Who the Hell Is William Loeb?* (1975); G. H. Waldham, "A Conversation with Nackey Loeb," *New Hampshire Profiles* 35 (1986); James Wright, *The Progressive Yankees: Republican Reformers in New Hampshire, 1906–1916* (1987).
Scott Roper

MIT Media Laboratory

The MIT Media Laboratory in Cambridge, Mass., is part degree-granting academic department, part research facility, part think tank, and part evangelical pulpit from which to preach a vision of the digital future. The Media Lab employs about 40 faculty members and senior researchers; some 85 support personnel assist with research, facilities, and administration. The lab's 133 graduate students are master's and doctoral candidates in almost equal numbers. Approximately 200 undergraduates at the Massachusetts Institute of Technology also work in the Media Lab each year.

Jerome Wiesner and Nicholas Negroponte founded the Media Lab in 1980. Wiesner, who died in 1994, was an MIT president, a science adviser to Presidents John F. Kennedy and Lyndon Johnson, and an esteemed physicist. Negroponte, trained as an architect, had headed MIT's Architecture Machine Group, a university department that studied the human interface with computers, from which the Media Lab evolved. Negroponte continues to personify the essence of the Media Lab, as its founding chairman and most vocal exponent.

That the Media Lab would play many sometimes divergent roles was guaranteed from the beginning; when bringing together disparate media and concepts, it is impossible to travel a single path. The vision behind the Media Lab is a convergence, today expressed as a convergence between perceptual comput-

ing, information and entertainment, and learning and common sense. Previously, the Media Lab saw itself at the convergence of the computer industry, the print and publishing industry, and the broadcast and motion picture industry. Although the concepts have broadened, the essential philosophy remains the same, centering on the multiple ways that computing touches people. Researchers at the Media Lab are currently engaged in a wide variety of projects. The Lab's Web site lists a project exploring how to build robots that "people can physically interact with, communicate with, understand, and teach in human terms"; a project concerned with improving "online environments and interfaces for human communication"; and a project investigating how to enhance storytelling "using new computational approaches for the creator and user of media such as video, cinema, and photography."

In 1985 the Media Lab moved into the $45 million Wiesner Building, designed by I. M. Pei. This sleek, four-story structure plays a vital role in the Media Lab's identity. The building's architecture sets it apart from the rest of the MIT campus. Its entryway and atrium mural, created by the artist Kenneth Noland and often described as Mondrian-like, provides a motif that is used in the Media Lab's marketing materials. Plans for an expansion of the Lab's facilities that will double its present size are under way.

The desired outcome of a successful Media Lab project is not a published journal article but a commercially polished demonstration illustrating the concept at issue. Elsewhere in the academy the mandate is "Publish or perish"; at the Media Lab the slogan is "Demo or die."

Although the Media Lab seems to have perfected the art of the computer demo, the nature of its demonstrations has opened it up to criticism from the computer industry. In industry, a demo must be quickly followed by a commercial product; otherwise it is viewed as mere marketing hype. The Media Lab's demos have a different purpose, illustrating a research finding that may not make its way into a commercial product for decades, causing confusion and perhaps disappointment. Other criticisms of the Media Lab focus on the opinions of its outspoken director, Negroponte.

Even its critics agree, however, that the MIT Media Laboratory is one of the nation's leading research facilities for new information technologies. When people as diverse as journalists, science fiction writers, and executives from the computer, publishing, and broadcast industries want a peek at the future or a well-informed opinion on a current computing

William Loeb, longtime editor of the Manchester Union Leader, *1975*

trend, time and again they turn to the Media Lab.

Stewart Brand, *The Media Lab: Inventing the Future at MIT* (1987); Nicholas Negroponte, *Being Digital* (1995).

Madeline Bodin

Morning Pro Musica *Morning pro musica,* the popular and innovative classical-music radio program of the 1970s and 1980s hosted by Robert J. Lurtsema, played an important role in enlarging New England audiences for public radio. It also drew many people to classical music for the first time and broadened the appreciation of those already familiar with the repertory.

From 1971 to 1993 the deep-voiced, slow-talking Lurtsema (known to everyone, on air and off, as "Robert J.") broadcast *Morning pro musica* for five hours a day, seven days a week, from the studios of WGBH radio in Boston. The program was carried by a network of stations that stretched from Maine to western New York State, and because of this regional exposure the successful mixture of classical music and morning radio guided by Lurtsema's strong personality became one of the flagship programs for National Public Radio (NPR) in the Northeast. The large, loyal, and diverse audience listened regularly, talked a lot about Robert J. (not only *what* he said, but *how* he said it), and gave donations generously during the fund-raising drives of local stations. Indeed, before the rise in popularity of NPR's news programs, *Morning pro musica* probably brought New England public radio stations more new listeners and more financial support than any other program.

The success of *Morning pro musica* depended not only on Lurtsema's distinctive voice (resonant, organlike, with a touch of authoritative "gravel," and laced with his trademark pauses) but also on the skill with which he programmed each show. He always chose his music three months in advance, so that local stations could list the performances in their program guides. Lurtsema fit his selections to what his audience was doing at the time; before 8 A.M. he played only early or baroque music, while for breakfast and the drive to work, he scheduled familiar classical composers like Mozart or Beethoven. As lunchtime approached, he offered longer and more challenging pieces, such as complete symphonies by Mahler or Bruckner; and during the last hour of the program he often broadcast live performances and interviews. His guest list ranged from local concert artists to renowned performers such as Isaac Stern, Victor Borge, and Marcel Marceau. He also liked to create unusual commemorative broadcasts: on Bastille Day he might play a full morning

of uninterrupted (and unidentified) French music.

Lurtsema's habits and eccentricities were legendary and could both charm and irritate his legions of listeners. Every program would start with three or four minutes of unaccompanied bird songs—probably the most famous wake-up music ever broadcast on New England radio. Following this Lurtsema would fade in orchestral music through the birds, a different theme tune for each day in the week (another characteristic touch). Following this long prelude he would finally speak his first words of the day, a surprisingly light-toned "Good morning," after which he settled his voice down among those "pedal tones" that were particularly effective during the first hours of the program.

A critic in *The New York Times* once described the Lurtsema voice as sounding like "thick fudge." Certainly there were times when it flowed no faster—especially during his newscasts ("edited and reported by your *Morning pro musica* host, Robert J. Lurtsema"), when he seemed to extemporize revisions of newswire copy and sounded as though he were thinking about each word before he spoke it. His long regional weather forecasts were also famous, as Lurtsema made his own summaries of the official text, dividing the forecasts by the sections of New England that heard his program.

The undertone of informality in Lurtsema's on-air personality sometimes took surprising forms, as when he might start to play the wrong side of a record, stop, apologize, and (sometimes noisily) cue up the correct selection. Such clumsy moments only added to the persona that Lurtsema wanted to project—that of a devoted amateur, rather than a hidebound expert. Lurtsema often spoke about how his life had been transformed by his first exposure to classical music; one of the purposes behind his radio program was to share the thrill of his discoveries with his audience. Thus, when he scheduled his musical series—such as the complete cantatas of Bach or all 104 Symphonies of Haydn—Lurtsema communicated to his listeners that he was not going to pontificate about the music but was learning about it along with his audience.

As *Morning pro musica* grew in popularity and significance, Lurtsema became an important figure in New England cultural life, serving on the boards of many artistic institutions and performing (as a reader) at many symphony concerts. He also pursued studies in art and musical composition; part of a bassoon quartet he composed became the basis for the theme music of Julia Child's cooking show on PBS. Such a status as a New England cultural icon could hardly have been predicted for the

young Robert John Lurtsema, who was born in Cambridge, Mass., in 1931 and spent his early years neither in privilege nor conventionality. He served four years with the navy before attending Boston University (he graduated in 1957) and then worked at a wide range of jobs, from lumberjack to trapeze artist to encyclopedia salesman. For five years he hosted a folk music radio program. He was working as a painter in Boston in 1971 when he landed the job of classical-music announcer at WGBH.

By the 1990s, with the rise of NPR's *Morning Edition* and a general change in the listening habits of the public radio audience, *Morning pro musica* often became a point of controversy at local stations, many of whose managers felt that they could better serve their local audiences (and raise more money) if they carried news in the early morning and then aired local music programs that played shorter, less demanding works. Lurtsema himself was also getting tired, and in 1993 he bowed out of the daily broadcast, appearing only on weekends. That effectively marked the end of the New England–wide broadcasts of *Morning pro musica.* When Lurtsema died in 2000, at the age of 69, the early era of public radio broadcasting in New England effectively came to a close.

Thomas Looker, *The Sound and the Story: NPR and the Art of Radio* (1995).

Thomas Looker

Movie Palaces Movie palaces were an architectural and cultural presence in New England's large and medium-sized cities for much of the 20th century and some continue on into the 21st. Many began their life as music halls. B. F. Keith, often called the founder of American vaudeville, may also be considered the grandfather of the movie palace.

Keith came to Boston in the 1880s and was soon producing scrupulously clean entertainment suitable for Victorian families. His success is credited to two key concepts: continuous performances and unusually elegant theaters. Keith's New Theatre opened in 1894 on Boston's Washington Street. Noted especially for its so-called crystal subway, a luxurious underground lobby extending to Tremont Street, it remained the flagship venue of an expanding entertainment empire even after the 1913 opening of Keith's Palace Theatre in New York City.

A little over a decade after its construction, Keith's New Theatre was combined with the 3,000-seat Boston Theatre (1854), the city's opera house during the 19th century, to form a huge theatrical complex. Keith first began to show moving pictures there between stage shows during the 1890s to clear the house. Be-

Loews State Theatre, Boston, 1959

fore long, of course, those movies stole the show, and Keith's elaborate place of amusement became the prototype of the early-20th-century movie palace.

Downtown movie houses had their heyday throughout New England in the 1920s and 1930s. As the century wore on, many fell into disrepair. They reached their nadir when modern multiplex cinemas located in strip malls spread through the region during the 1960s and 1970s. Untold numbers of vintage movie houses were transformed into paint stores, condominiums, or parking lots. But through the efforts of arts-conscious, civic-minded citizens and corporations, many also were eventually rescued. Boston's Metropolitan Theater of 1925, modeled after the Palace of Versailles and the Paris Opera House by renowned architect Clarence Blackall, was beautifully restored in 1991 and is now the Wang Center for the Performing Arts. The 1929 State Theatre on Congress Street in Portland, Maine—a pornographic movie house at one point in its history—was saved by volunteer efforts in 1993 and is now a thriving venue for comedy, dance, and performances of rock, folk, blues, big-band, and alternative music. The 1928 Loews State Theatre in Providence, once reduced to showing 99-cent films to a dwindling number of patrons, barely escaped demolition in 1977. On October 7 the following year, a freshly refurbished theater, renamed the Providence Performing Arts Center, opened to Ethel Merman belting out show tunes. It has flourished ever since. Similar successes have occurred in smaller cities from New London, Conn., to Portsmouth, N.H.

After B. F. Keith died, his firm tore down the old Boston Theatre and replaced it with an opera house designed by Thomas Lamb as a memorial to the renowned impresario. It is arguably the most refined example in America of a building type that could sometimes be quite vulgar and ostentatious. There can be no doubt, however, that the grandeur of ornate movie palaces made an important contribution to the magic and romance of going to the movies.

Ben M. Hall, *The Best Remaining Seats: The Golden Age of the Movie Palace* (1975 [1961]); John Margolies and Emily Gwathmey, *Ticket to Paradise: American Movie Theaters and How We Had Fun* (1991).

Douglass Shand-Tucci

New England in Feature Film From the early days of projected motion pictures, representations of New England appeared on screens wherever movies were seen. Despite limited literature defining and analyzing "New England film," recognizable character types, situations, and uses of landscape are rooted in the region's literature, traditions of 19th-century stage melodrama, and now a century of film conventions.

Although similar thematic constructs may be found in other regional bodies of film, those cited here are central to perceptions of New England. Five themes serve to organize a discussion of New England in feature films: development of Yankee characters, small-town life contrasted with city values, seafaring tales, family secrets, and haunted New England.

Nineteenth-century stage traditions and literature from Nathaniel Hawthorne to Car-

olyn Chute have served as sources for film narrative. Films draw heavily on the regional literary tradition: once a title proves commercially successful it may be remade many times, emphasizing and reinterpreting New England characters and landscape. *The Scarlet Letter,* first produced in 1909, was remade numerous times—most recently in 1995 with Demi Moore as Hester Prynne—and at least two versions have aired on television, including one produced by Boston's WGBH in 1979.

Novels featuring wholesome women in New England settings by writers like Kate Douglas Wiggin and Louisa May Alcott are perennial favorites for film treatments, establishing a framework for later characterizations of New England women. Wiggins's *Mother Carey's Chickens* was filmed in 1938 with Fay Bainter, Anne Shirley, and Ruby Keeler and adapted by Disney for Hayley Mills as *Summer Magic* in 1963. Katharine Hepburn's appearance in *Little Women* (1933), based on Alcott's novel, established her androgynous independent character, Jo March, with the protest, "I loathe elegant society." Hepburn's voice and posture may be the most widely known representation of the New England female, encompassing roles from ingénues to the aging heroin addict Mary Tyrone in Eugene O'Neill's *Long Day's Journey into Night* (1962).

Other literary sources for film include Edith Wharton's *Ethan Frome* (1993) and Henry James's *The Bostonians* (1984). Contemporary literature has been the source for a number of films, including *The Cider House Rules* (1999) from John Irving's novel, and Carolyn Chute's *The Beans of Egypt, Maine* (1994), released on videotape as *Forbidden Choices.*

Early stage melodramas introduced a character, a rube or rustic often called "Uncle Josh," and a situation, the city's siren call to country folks, that are both present in many New England films. An early surviving example is *Uncle Josh at the Moving Picture Show* (1902), in which a naive farmer goes to the movies and tries to interact with the projected entertainment. This plot device repeats that of the first American play to present a "stage Yankee," Royall Tyler's *The Contrast* (1787). *The Old Homestead* (1915) was produced by Famous Players from Denman Thompson's popular 19th-century play about Joshua Whitcomb set in West Swanzey, N.H., and New York City. The film pits the civility and safety of the old homestead against such hazards of city life as gangs and strong drink.

Many theatrical films with New England themes helped solidify notions of Yankeeness to a broad audience. Radio personality Phillips Lord developed the male Yankee rustic

New England Feature Filmography

The Actress, 1953
Affliction, 1997
Ah, Wilderness! 1935
Alex and Emma, 2003
Alice's Restaurant, 1969
All That Heaven Allows, 1955
All That Money Can Buy, 1941
All the Brothers Were Valiant, 1953
All the Rage, 1998
America, 1924
American Buffalo, 1996
And Now Tomorrow, 1944
As the Earth Turns, 1934
Autumn Heart, 1998
Baby Boom, 1987
Backbone, 1923
Back to the Woods, 1918
Banjo, 1947
The Beans of Egypt, Maine, 1994
Bed and Breakfast, 1992
Beetlejuice, 1988
Before and After, 1996
Behind Masks, 1921
Behind the Door, 1919
Belfast, Maine, 1999
Between the Lines, 1977
Biography of a Bachelor Girl, 1935
The Blinking Madonna, 1995
Blown Away, 1994
Blueprint for Robbery, 1961
Boomerang, 1947
The Bostonians, 1984
The Boston Strangler, 1968
The Bride Goes Wild, 1948
Bringing Up Baby, 1938
The Brinks Job, 1978
Brown of Harvard, 1918, 1926
Cappy Ricks, 1921
Captain January, 1924, 1936
Captain Salvation, 1927
Captains Courageous, 1937
Carnal Knowledge, 1971
Carousel, 1956
Casper, 1995
Celtic Pride, 1996
Charlotte's Web, 1973
Charly, 1968
Christmas in Connecticut, 1945
The Cider House Rules, 1999
The City of the Dead, 1960
A Civil Action, 1998
The Coast Patrol, 1925
Coma, 1978
The Come-back, 1916
Come to the Stable, 1949
The Conflict, 1921
The Courtship of Miles Standish, 1923
Crash Dive, 1943

Creepshow 2, 1987
The Crucible, 1996
Darkness Falls, 2003
Dark Victory, 1939
A Daughter of the Sea, 1915
David Harum, 1934
Dead Men Tell No Tales, 1920
Dead Poets Society, 1989
Dealing; or, The Berkeley-to-Boston Forty-Brick Lost-Bag-Blues, 1972
Deep Waters, 1947
A Delicate Balance, 1973
Desire under the Elms, 1958
The Devil and Daniel Webster, 1941
Disappearances, 2004
Doctor Bull, 1933
Dolores Claiborne, 1995
Down to the Sea in Ships, 1922
Dreamcatcher, 2003
Eadie Was a Lady, 1945
Ethan Frome, 1993
Ever in My Heart, 1933
The Face in the Sky, 1933
Far from Heaven, 2002
Fear Strikes Out, 1957
Federal Hill, 1995
Feed, 1992
The Firm, 1993
Flames of the Flesh, 1920
The Flaming Sword, 1915
Floating, 1997
Follow the Band, 1943
The Friends of Eddie Coyle, 1973
Funny Farm, 1988
The Gazebo, 1959
Get Going, 1943
Get Hep to Love, 1942
Getting Mary Married, 1919
Girl Loves Boy, 1937
The Good Mother, 1988
The Good Son, 1993
Good Will Hunting, 1997
Graveyard Shift, 1990
The Great John L., 1945
The Great Moment, 1944
Greater Southbridge, 2003
The Haunting, 1963
Head above Water, 1996
Hearts of Oak, 1924
Here Comes the Groom, 1951
H. M. Pulham, Esq., 1941
Holiday Inn, 1942
Home before Dark, 1958, 1996
The Hotel New Hampshire, 1984
The House of the Seven Gables, 1910, 1940
House Sitter, 1992
Huddle, 1932
The Human Stain, 2003

Hush, 1921
I Am the Cheese, 1983
Icebound, 1924
Ice Capades Revue, 1942
The Ice Storm, 1997
I Married a Witch, 1942
The Imported Bridegroom, 1989
In Dreams, 1998
The Inkwell, 1994
The Inside Story, 1947
In the Bedroom, 2001
The Iron Giant, 1999
It Happened to Jane, 1959
Jacqueline, or Blazing Barriers, 1922
Janice Meredith, 1924
Jaws, 1975
Jazz on a Summer's Day, 1959
Joe and Joe, 1996
Johnny Tremain, 1957
The Judge Steps Out, 1949
Jumanji, 1996
Key to the City, 1950
Kissing Jessica Stein, 2001
A Kiss in Time, 1921
The Last Hurrah, 1958
The Late George Apley, 1947
Leave Her to Heaven, 1945
Legally Blonde, 2001
Lemony Snicket's A Series of Unfortunate Events, 2004
The Liar, 1918
The Lighthouse by the Sea, 1924
Little Black Book, 2004
Little Men, 1934, 1940, 1997
Little Women, 1919, 1933, 1949, 1994
Lonesome Corners, 1922
Long Day's Journey into Night, 1962
Lost Boundaries, 1949
The Love Nest, 1922
Love Story, 1970
Lydia, 1941
Maid of Salem, 1937
Make a Wish, 1937
Malice, 1993
The Man in the Net, 1959
Man with a Plan, 1995
The Man without a Face, 1993
Marriage Is a Private Affair, 1944
The Matchmaker, 1997
Me, Myself, and Irene, 2000
Mermaids, 1990
Message in a Bottle, 1999
A Midwife's Tale, 1994
A Mighty Wind, 2003
The Miracle Man, 1919, 1932
Mission Hill, 1982
Moby Dick, 1930, 1956
Mona Lisa Smile, 2003

(continued)

New England Feature Filmography (continued)

Moonlight in Vermont, 1943
Moonlight Mile, 2002
Mother Carey's Chickens, 1938
Mourning Becomes Electra, 1947
Mr. and Mrs. North, 1942
Mr. Barrington, 2003
Mr. Deeds, 2002
Mr. North, 1988
Mrs. Winterbourne, 1996
The Mudge Boy, 2003
My Architect, a Son's Journey, 2003
My Kingdom for a Cook, 1943
Mystery Street, 1950
Mystic Pizza, 1988
Mystic River, 2003
The Myth of Fingerprints, 1997
The Nature Man, 1915
Never Met Picasso, 1996
A New Leaf, 1971
Next Stop, Wonderland, 1998
The North End, 1998
The Offenders, 1924
An Old-Fashioned Girl, 1949
The Old Homestead, 1915, 1922, 1942
Old School, 2003
Oleanna, 1994
One Crazy Summer, 1986
One Man's Journey, 1933
On Golden Pond, 1981
Other People's Money, 1991
Our Hearts Were Growing Up, 1946
Our Town, 1940
Outside Providence, 1999
The Paper Chase, 1973
The Parent Trap, 1961, 1998
Parrish, 1961
The Pearl of Love, 1925
The Perfect Storm, 2000
Pete's Dragon, 1977
Pet Sematary, 1989
Peyton Place, 1957
Pied Piper Malone, 1924
Portrait of Jennie, 1948
Practical Magic, 1996
The President's Mystery, 1936
Pretty Poison, 1968
The Price of Success, 1925
Private Affairs, 1940
Private Number, 1936
Prophecy, 1979
Puritan Passions, 1923
Queen of the Sea, 1918
Quincy Adams Sawyer, 1912, 1922
Rachel, Rachel, 1968
The Raid, 1954
Ready for Love, 1934

Rebecca of Sunnybrook Farm, 1917, 1932, 1938
Reckless, 1995
The Ref, 1994
The Reincarnation of Peter Proud, 1975
The Resurrected, 1992
Return of the Secaucus Seven, 1980
Reversal of Fortune, 1990
Revolution, 1985
Rich and Famous, 1981
Riddle: The Woman, 1920
The Rider of the King Log, 1921
Route One/USA, 1989
*The Russians Are Coming! The Russians Are
   Coming! 1966*
Ruthless, 1948
The Sainted Sisters, 1948
Same Difference, 1999
The Scarlet Letter, 1917, 1926, 1934, 1995
Scattergood [series], 1941
Scenes from a Mall, 1991
School Ties, 1992
Sci-fighters, 1996
The Sea Beast, 1926
Second Sight, 1989
A Separate Peace, 1972
The Seventh Day, 1922
Shadows, 1922
The Shocking Miss Pilgrim, 1947
The Shuttered Room, 1967
Signs of Life, 1989
Simon Birch, 1998
The Singing Kid, 1936
Six Bridges to Cross, 1955
The Skulls, 2000
A Small Circle of Friends, 1980
Small Town Girl, 1936
Snitch, 1998
Song of Surrender, 1948
Southie, 1998
The Spitfire Grill, 1996
Splash, 1984
Squanto: A Warrior's Tale, 1994
Squeeze, 1996
State and Main, 2000
Stella Dallas, 1925, 1937
The Stepford Wives, 1975, 2004
A Stolen Life, 1946
The Story of Alexander Graham Bell, 1939
The Strange Affair of Uncle Harry, 1945
Strange Interlude, 1932
The Stranger, 1946
A Stranger in the Kingdom, 1997
The Strange Woman, 1946
Summer Holiday, 1948
Summer Magic, 1963
A Summer Place, 1959

Summer Stock, 1950
Sunrise at Campobello, 1960
The Swimmer, 1968
Tarnished, 1950
That Certain Age, 1938
That Darn Cat, 1997
That's My Boy, 1932
Theodora Goes Wild, 1936
The Thomas Crown Affair, 1968
Those Calloways, 1965
The Time of Their Lives, 1946
Time out of Mind, 1947
Timothy's Quest, 1921, 1936
Titicut Follies, 1967
To Die For, 1995
Together Again, 1944
To Gillian on Her 37th Birthday, 1996
Too Young to Kiss, 1951
The Trail of the Law, 1924
The Trouble with Harry, 1955
Two Sisters from Boston, 1946
Uncle Tom's Cabin, 1918
The Unseen, 1945
The Verdict, 1982
Vermont Is for Lovers, 1992
A Vermont Romance, 1916
Voice of the Whistler, 1945
Wake, 2003
A Wake in Providence, 1999
Walk East on Beacon, 1952
Warlock, 1989
Way Back Home, 1931
Way Down East, 1920, 1935
The Weight of Water, 2000
Welcome Stranger, 1947
The Whales of August, 1987
What about Bob? 1991
What Lies Beneath, 2000
Where Are the Children? 1986
Where the Rivers Flow North, 1992
Whispering Winds, 1929
Whistle at Eaton Falls, 1951
White Christmas, 1954
Who's Afraid of Virginia Woolf? 1966
Winter Carnival, 1939
The Witches of Eastwick, 1987
With Honors, 1994
Within Our Gates, 1919
The Wizard of Loneliness, 1988
The Woman, 1915
The Working Man, 1933
The World According to Garp, 1982
Wreck of the "Hesperus," 1948
The Yankee Clipper, 1927
The Yankee Way, 1917
Young People, 1940

Thanks to these contributors: AFI catalogs, Margie Compton, Philip Carli, Paul Frobose, Chris Haskell, Jan-Christopher Horak, Rob Edelman, Kathryn Fuller, Saul Fussiner, Eithne Johnson, Audrey Kupferberg, John Lowe, Mac McKinley, BJ Roche, Donna Ross, Eric Schaefer, John Skillin

character with the preacher Seth Parker in *Way Back Home* (1931). Hayseed men ranged from squire to bumpkin; women's roles encompassed the town gossip, the stalwart farm mother, and the wronged virgin, all on view in *Way Down East* (1920), with Vivia Ogden, Kate Bruce, and Lillian Gish in the respective roles.

In the first half of the 20th century the shorthand for expressing the peculiarities of a region excluded many complications of regional heritage. Films for the most part avoided New England's urban communities and varied ancestral origins. While serious dramas seldom portrayed New England's French Canadian culture or the region's Native Americans, the latter half of the century was characterized by a broadening of the definition of screen New Englander. In the independent feature film set in 1927 rural Vermont, *Where the Rivers Flow North* (1992), the leading female role is played by Tantoo Cardinal, a Native American. Films with New England themes have included Jewish, Italian, Portuguese, and African American main characters, and more than a few feature Irish protagonists. *Mermaids* (1990) stars Cher and Bob Hoskins as Jews in a coastal Massachusetts town. The character delineations in the comedy allow explorations of religious and cultural differences. Cher's older daughter has an affinity for Catholicism, promoted by their proximity to a convent and tested by her attraction to an Italian Catholic handyman. *Mermaids* plays with nationally recognized iconography born of New England origins. Rural Massachusetts in 1963 is conveyed through a variety of textual means: a classroom instructional film on the first Thanksgiving; the Kennedy assassination in television footage and a tableau vivant of the town as people stop to absorb the news; the young handyman's recollection of his mother's death, with the lament, "I didn't care about anything any more, not even the Red Sox."

The Inkwell (1994), directed by Matty Rich, is a coming-of-age film set in the African American summer community on Martha's Vineyard. *Same Difference* (1999), written by Rhode Island filmmaker Don Mays and co-directed by Mays and Roderick Giles, explores gang violence in the African American community and AIDS and HIV in the gay community. Mays's latest film is *The First*, portraying a black regiment from Rhode Island that fought in the Revolution. The Portuguese fisherman played by Spencer Tracy in *Captains Courageous* (1937); the Portuguese American families in Mystic, Conn., in *Mystic Pizza* (1988); and Ali MacGraw's Italian character in *Love Story* (1970) are other film roles representing New Englanders with ancestry

other than British. *The Last Hurrah* (1958), directed by John Ford and starring Spencer Tracy, broadly sketched urban Boston Irish and other immigrant groups in a political melodrama. Urban dramas on film have drawn increasingly large audiences and now involve more diverse populations, both behind and in front of the camera.

Depictions of a character's ancestry may be either supported or undermined by casting. Spencer Tracy in *Captains Courageous*, Sophia Loren in *Desire under the Elms* (1958), and Donald Woods as Stan Janowski in *As the Earth Turns* (1934), from a Gladys Hasty Carroll novel about rural Yankee and Polish families, may all be described as dissonant portrayals. The actors' failure to mimic New England regional voice patterns undermines their characters' authenticity.

In early film, rural landscapes were used for a pragmatic reason: in the prefeature era, before air conditioning made cities more bearable in the summer, major film companies including Vitagraph, Edison, and Lubin took working vacations in New England seaside towns and other resorts. *Message in a Bottle* (1999), *Me, Myself and Irene* (2000), and *In the Bedroom* (2001) are contemporary examples of productions shot on location in New England. David Mamet's *State and Main* (2000), with Massachusetts location photography, spoofs what happens when Hollywood comes to town. To the dismay of New England film commissions, nowadays Canadian locations often stand in for the New England landscape, as in *Dolores Claiborne* (1995), *Affliction* (1997), and *The Weight of Water* (2000).

Directors employ production designers, carpenters, costumers, cinematographers, and lighting directors to create "New England" under the constraints of period conventions and studio or independent budgets. Filmmakers evoke and represent New England by using real and constructed places—wooden sets, paint on glass, and digitally created streetscapes and vistas like those used in *Jumanji* (1996). A shoe factory shown in *Jumanji* is notable because relatively few films depict New England's industrial heritage. Prominent exceptions to this tendency include *Whistle at Eaton Falls* (1951), a didactic film about labor issues in a New Hampshire mill, the comedy *Other People's Money* (1991), and the courtroom ecodrama *A Civil Action* (1998).

Before virtually all production decamped to California in the early 20th century, numerous film companies were based in New England, among them Rhode Island's Eastern Film Corporation, the Commonwealth Photoplay Corporation in Massachusetts, and Maine's Dirigo Pictures and Pine Tree Pictures. These companies made many two-reel films and a few features, but little of their output survives.

Irving Berlin's *White Christmas* (1954) typifies Hollywood's representation of bucolic New England, created, with no verisimilitude intended, entirely on a set. Bing Crosby and Danny Kaye put on a show at an inn in Pine Tree, Vt.; the housekeeper, a "Yankee gossip," says of the inn's proprietor, "He sunk everything—his pension, his life savings—into remodeling this place. Used to be a grist mill and a barn. Now it's a Tyrolean haunted house." Other New England musicals include *Welcome*

Location shot for Where the Rivers Flow North, *1992*

Stranger (1947), with Bing Crosby as a singing doctor, and Henry King's *Carousel* (1956), shot in Camden, Maine. The fantasy New England setting is played for laughs in *Christmas in Connecticut* (1945), starring Barbara Stanwyck as a hard-bitten New York food writer who must create an ideal New England Christmas for G.I. Dennis Morgan. The movie was re-made for television in 1992 with Dyan Cannon and Kris Kristofferson.

The contrast between city and country life drives the storyline of many feature films. Exposition often includes the disappearance of a family member into the maw of a city, which is sometimes Boston, as in *Way Down East,* but more often New York. *Theodora Goes Wild* (1936) is a screwball comedy set in Lynnfield, Conn., in which small-town moral strictures are contrasted with those of decadent New York. The protagonist, played by Irene Dunne, is Theodora Lynn or Caroline Adams, depending on where she is and whom she's with. The film includes motifs representative of New England film traditions, among them town gossip and scandal, fear of outsiders, the small-town newspaper, and the dilemma of an unmarried women with a child. Movie depictions of small-town mores are typified by *Peyton Place* (1957), adapted from Grace Metalious's novel, and *Our Town* (1940), based on Thornton Wilder's play set in Grovers Corners, N.H., probably the best-known fictional New England town.

The Seventh Day (1921) begins at a New York City club and takes a yacht full of Prohibition-averse New Yorkers to a coastal Maine village where they find romance and encounter the local people's traditional ways, such as observing the Sabbath and dressing conservatively. Richard Barthelmess plays a sea captain as romantic lead in the role that followed his success in *Way Down East.* Common to many later New England–themed films is the idealization of isolated small-town life as a refuge from urban trouble. In *House-Sitter* (1992), Goldie Hawn says, "I just wanted to see what it would be like to live in that picture," to explain why she fled her job in Boston to experience life in a village.

The salty sea captain, like the hick farmer, was a stock character from 19th-century melodrama still found in *The Perfect Storm* (2000), adapted from Sebastian Junger's book and starring George Clooney. *The Lighthouse by the Sea* (1924) stars dog hero Rin-Tin-Tin foiling bootleggers off the coast of Maine. *Down to the Sea in Ships* (1922), *The Coast Patrol* (1925), *Old Ironsides* (1926), *The Yankee Clipper* (1927), and *The Wreck of the "Hesperus"* (1927) all take the Yankee, or Yankee ship, to sea. *Captain Salvation* (1927) concerns a seagoing seminary graduate, "a youth in a narrow

little New England sea town," reported *Variety.*

Other New England seafaring films include *Moby Dick,* which made it to the big screen in 1926 as *The Sea Beast,* in 1930, and then in 1956, directed by John Huston and starring Gregory Peck as Captain Ahab. In *The Sea Beast,* starring John Barrymore as Ahab, the filmmakers added romance. According to the *American Film Institute Catalog of Motion Pictures* summary, "Ahab returns to New Bedford and, his obsession gone, settles down with Esther," a minister's beautiful daughter. The 1930 *Moby-Dick* also starred John Barrymore, but this time the romance is with "Faith Mapple." This Vitaphone sound film was also produced in a German-language version. *Jaws* (1975) is *Moby Dick'*s most successful sea-creature descendant, with its own multiple sequels.

Shadows (1922) features an Asian character prevailing over an evil Yankee. When a New England captain is lost at sea, his wife, Sympathy, marries a young minister. Lon Chaney plays the couple's Chinese friend, Yen Sin, whose advantageous connection with another Chinese launderer allows him to reveal the duplicity of the minister's jealous Yankee rival, Nate Snow.

Many films set in New England portray the dysfunction and pain that can mark family life. *Reversal of Fortune* (1990) focuses on poisoned family life in Newport, R.I., as it dramatizes the real-life relationship between Claus and Sunny von Bülow. *The Ice Storm* (1997), set in Connecticut, depicts the jaded, upwardly mobile social sensibilities and desperate isolation of wealthy white suburbia during the 1970s. *Far from Heaven* (2002) challenges idealized notions of 1950s family life when a Hartford housewife discovers that her husband has a secret homosexual life.

Eugene O'Neill's plays translated to film are linchpins in the definition of screen New England and have stimulated some of the few scholarly works on New England film and literature. These films also examine family dynamics. *Long Day's Journey into Night* (1962) features a drug-addicted mother, an alcoholic father, and an emotionally unstable son. A dysfunctional 19th-century rural family appears in *Desire under the Elms* (1958). O'Neill could offer levity as well, however, as the film adaptation of *Ah, Wilderness!* (1935) presents the comic side of family life in rural New England in the early 20th century.

Dolores Claiborne (1995), a suspense drama directed by Taylor Hackford, is thick with New England themes including an isolated setting on a Maine island, class conflict, family secrets, city-country contrast, a monochromatic present, and an intensely polychromatic if traumatic past. The film is carried by strong

women, notably Kathy Bates, who as a hardy survivor declares, "Sometimes being a bitch is the only thing a woman has to hold on to," and Judy Parfitt, as an upper-class crone.

The imagined heritage of Salem, Mass., in *I Married a Witch* (1942), and *Maid of Salem* (1937), along with the regional presence of Stephen King lend energy to Gothic New England in such movies as *Pet Sematary* (1989), *Casper* (1995), and *What Lies Beneath* (2000). "Haunted houses aren't easy to come by," is the theme of *Beetlejuice* (1988), a film that takes place in a Connecticut house whose value as real estate is contested by the protagonists, Alec Baldwin and Geena Davis, as house-haunters in conflict with a family from New York. The comedy uses the trendy new owner, Catherine O'Hara, to deride country life: "I can't believe we're eating Cantonese. Is there no Szechuan up here?" She prepares a dinner for "The few hip people I can get to set foot in this part of Connecticut." Her urban interior designer, horrified by the house's hick decor, wails, "Deliver me from L.L. Bean!"

The Faust theme of selling oneself to the devil underlies a number of these films, from *The Devil and Daniel Webster* (1941) to *The Witches of Eastwick* (1987), adapted from the novel by John Updike, with the establishing shot of a New England green and church. Jack Nicholson, as Daryl Van Horne, dominates the enormous house of the devil, conjured up by three women—blonde, redheaded, and dark-haired, their superficial ethnic differentiation overshadowed by Hollywood glamour—in an exchange of souls for thrills. *Uncle Josh in a Spooky Hotel* (1900) may be the grand-daddy of these films, placing the rube in the haunted house.

North Woods dramas were once a popular subgenre of adventure film. In the 1910s and 1920s loggers, timber barons, hunters and hunting guides, French Canadian trappers, and Mounties populated "snow pictures" set in a mythic North that conflated northern New England with Canada (especially the Yukon) and Alaska. A number of these films featured heroic female stars shooting, riding, and river-driving. One of these is the lumber-country melodrama *The Conflict* (1921). The interchangeable nature of location shooting is exemplified by *The Girl from Porcupine* (1921), a James Oliver Curwood story, shot in South Portland, Maine, but representing the Yukon. Both the comedy *A New Leaf* (1971), directed by Elaine May, and the strange horror film *Prophecy* (1979), directed by John Frankenheimer, are later mutations of the North Woods genre.

The Paper Chase (1973), set at Harvard Law School, and *Love Story* (1970), which also had a Harvard background, were based on and perpetuated Ivy League mythology. In 1994 Harvard graduate Alek Keshishian made a campus drama, *With Honors,* starring Joe Pesci and Brendan Fraser. A New England college is the setting for *Who's Afraid of Virginia Woolf?* (1966), an adaptation of Edward Albee's play directed by Mike Nichols, starring Elizabeth Taylor and Richard Burton. *Carnal Knowledge* (1971) includes a collegiate setting and was partially shot on location in New England. Boys' prep schools are the setting for *A Separate Peace* (1972) and *Dead Poets Society* (1989).

Feature films by important directors have used conventions of setting, character, and social issues closely tied to New England. Alfred Hitchcock's dry comedy *The Trouble with Harry* (1955) is set in a tiny Vermont village in which natives interact with new residents who are glad to have escaped the city. Sam Marlowe, played by John Forsythe, puts down Fifth Avenue's "little people with hats on." Mildred Natwick's observation about her husband's demise, "He was caught in a threshing machine," is delivered for laughs, capturing the irony of violence in peaceful rural surroundings. Orson Welles's *The Stranger* (1946) centers on a Nazi living in a Connecticut town. In addition to directing *Whistle at Eaton Falls,* the New Hampshire resident Louis de Rochemont produced *Lost Boundaries* (1949), directed by Alfred L. Werker, a film about a black family facing racial bigotry in a small New England town. And Oscar Micheaux's *Within Our Gates* (1919) portrays African American professionals living in Boston.

An understanding of New England in film may be enriched by delving into these themes and others. One might examine Troy Donahue's roles in *Parrish* (1961), set on a Connecticut tobacco farm, and *A Summer Place* (1959), set on a Maine island, both directed by Delmer Daves. Or one might wish to view the late-20th-century explorations of urban New England in films such as *Monument Ave.,* also known as *Snitch* (1998); *Southie* (1998); and *Outside Providence* (1999) side by side with screen representations of the region's smaller communities, such as Jay Craven's *A Stranger in the Kingdom* (1997) and Frederick Wiseman's documentary *Belfast, Maine* (1999).

Denis Gifford, *Books and Plays in Films 1896–1915* (1991); Kemp R. Niver, *Early Motion Pictures: The Paper Print Collections in the Library of Congress* (1985); Elias Savada, comp., *The American Film Institute Catalog of Feature Films: Film Beginnings, 1893–1910* (1995).

Karan Sheldon

Northeast Historic Film

Northeast Historic Film (NHF), founded in 1986, is an independent nonprofit organization that collects, preserves, and makes accessible motion picture film and videotape relating to northern New England. NHF also acquires technology for recording and playing back images and sound and maintains a growing research library. Holdings focus on Maine, Massachusetts, New Hampshire, and Vermont. The archives employ a professional staff, assisted by volunteers and student interns. Policies are set with guidance from a board of directors and an advisory board made up of experts in the fields of media history, audiovisual production, technology, and broadcasting.

The organization preserves 16-millimeter broadcast news film, videotaped television programs, home movies, dramatic and industrial films, and the works of independent film and video artists linked to northern New England by their setting, subject, creator, or source—if not all four. More than 5 million feet of film and 2,000 hours of videotape document everyday life as seen on television news programs from the 1950s to the 1970s—changing practices in the region's fisheries, transformations undergone by some of northern New England's small towns, and many other facets of life in the region. Works in the NHF archives were created by itinerant producers, Hollywood crews seeking rustic locations, newsreel stringers, and ordinary people. Scholars have noted, for instance, that many home movies were shot by women who wished to record their environment, family, and friends, perhaps much as their 19th-century counterparts kept journals and scrapbooks. These films provide a record of daily life as well as ceremonial occasions.

The collections prioritize material that is unique or hard to find and that would likely be lost in the absence of a preservation effort. The curatorial staff seeks to procure copies that are as close as possible to the initial film or tape generation, such as original elements, master copies, or unique prints. NHF also gathers explanatory notes and other documentary materials, which often help explain the significance of a moving-image collection.

In 1992 the organization purchased the derelict Alamo Theatre, a 1916 cinema in Bucksport, Maine, and began creating a research center, a 125-seat theater for film and community events, and a climate-controlled audiovisual storage repository. From that location Northeast Historic Film promotes the use of archival moving images in education and public history that are local, regional, and national in scope. It is one of the largest repositories of amateur film in North America, with approximately 200 individual collections of edited and unedited home movies from 1916 to the present, including the films of Hiram Maxim (1869–1936), who in 1926 founded the Amateur Cinema League, an international organization of nonprofessional movie makers.

Among the works available through NHF, as rights allow, are titles in the *Reflets et Lumière* series (1979–81), a Maine Public Broadcasting Network production on the Franco-American experience; *Maine's TV Time Machine,* a 1960s compilation from WABI-TV in Bangor; and a number of independently produced videos, whose creators share in all revenue earned by their films, such as *From Stump to Ship: A 1930 Logging Film,* about long-log lumbering; *Dead River Rough Cut,* about trappers; and *Anchor of the Soul,* about a New England African American community.

Members of the Association of Moving Image Archivists, a professional organization fostering cooperation regarding the collection, preservation, and use of moving images, launched an interest group for regional archives in 1998. Although NHF has been virtually the only independent regional archive, other geographically focused moving-image collections do exist within U.S. parent institutions, including those of Hawaii's Bishop Museum, the Minnesota Historical Society, the Mississippi Department of Archives and History, and the West Virginia Division of Culture and History. These institutions offer outreach programs of various kinds, ranging from making footage available for reuse in broadcast documentaries to traveling film programs and lunchtime screenings.

In 1999 the National Endowment for the Humanities helped underwrite the NHF exhibit *Going to the Movies: A Century of Motion Picture Audiences in Northern New England.* Two years later, the NEH awarded the organization a major grant to aid in the construction of a three-story film conservation center and to support educational programming.

Northeast Historic Film's holdings continue to grow thanks to public donations and connections with other public archives in the United States and Canada. The access that NHF collections provide to a century of moving images, whether for academic study or personal enjoyment, should prove an increasingly valuable cultural resource as the history of northern New England continues to unfold in the third millennium.

Patricia Burdick, Crystal Hall Cole, Karan Sheldon, *Collections Guide: Moving Image Collections of Northeast Historic Film* (1995); *Moving Image Review* (1988–present); Karan Sheldon, "Northeast Historic Film," *Historical Journal of Film, Radio, and Television* (March 1996).

Karan Sheldon

On Golden Pond

Set in the still unspoiled, idyllic sylvan environment of New Hampshire's Squam Lakes, the movie *On Golden Pond* captured national attention when it was released in 1981, winning several Academy Awards and breaking box-office records. Based on Ernest Thompson's Broadway play, produced by Bruce Gilbert, and directed by Mark Rydell, this charming film brought together for the first and last time two venerable veterans of stage and screen, Henry Fonda and Katharine Hepburn. It featured Norman Thayer, Jr., an irascible, witty retired professor, played by Fonda, and his adoring, imperturbable wife, Ethel, played by Hepburn, on vacation at their New England lakeside summer cottage. Appearing in the principal supporting role of the Thayers' disaffected and elusive divorced daughter Chelsea is Fonda's daughter, Jane. Fraught with symbolism, much of it related to the breathtaking natural scenery of a mythical Loon Lake, this memorable motion picture examines family relationships, the perils of old age, failures in communication, conflict, and reconciliation. At a deeper level it concerns lifelong love, devotion, a child's longing for parental affection and commitment, unshakable Yankee pride and strength, and the transitory cycles of life.

On Golden Pond eloquently celebrates the beauty, peace, and simplicity of the natural world, which it contrasts with the sordidness, complexities, and rapid pace of urban life. Much of the film is staged at the Thayers' rusticated turn-of-the-century wooden cottage, itself a direct reflection of the back-to-nature movement that captivated late-Victorian America. This movement encouraged people to seek forms of escape in retreatlike vacation environments that it associated with authenticity, ruggedness, religious spirituality, healthfulness, outdoor recreation, athleticism, and the picturesque. The cottage also embodies the basic principles of the arts-and-crafts, or craftsman, architectural idiom, which strongly influenced American architecture and decorative arts from the 1890s until World War II. Its primary features are the natural wood siding, diagonal roof-gable brackets, exposed roof rafters, and unfinished porch-support posts and balustrades. The porch and interior rooms are furnished with rusticated wooden, wicker-backed rockers and straight-back chairs, as well as other naturalistic pieces. Constructed with hand tools, utilizing traditional methods of artisanship, the Thayer cottage seems to have been conceived for another place in another time as a response to the advancing American machine age. As such, the cottage and the lake's scenery create a film image of timeless New England values, which serve as a context for the family's struggles.

The filming of *On Golden Pond* on Squam and Little Squam Lakes has had a lingering impact on the immediate region. Still evident today are the aftereffects, some quite pronounced, that are the not uncommon result of on-site production of popular, award-winning cinema. The shooting of scenes for the movie

and the presence of its high-profile cast members were a constant attraction to year-round residents, summer-cottage occupants, and the visiting public. In the years since the film's release the two lakes have grown more and more popular, as evidenced by an increased demand for real estate and summer rentals, pressure for public boating access, spiraling local tax rates, and the inauguration of narrated water tours in pontooned, canopy-covered motorized party boats. On the northwest side of Little Squam Lake overlooking the main highway that links the towns of Holderness and Ashland is a large, plain, pitched-roof white farmhouse with a sign in front announcing "The Inn on Golden Pond." Pointedly named, this unpretentious, attractive hostelry provides commercial proof of the movie's enduring legacy.

Film Review Annual, 1982 (1983); Jay Robert Nash and Stanley Ralph Ross, *The Motion Picture Guide,* vol. 6 (1986); Lois R. Shea, "A Lesson in Black History: Unusual Beginning for a Squam Camp," *Boston Globe,* August 17, 1997; Bryant F. Tolles, Jr., "Comfortable and Practical Rustic: The Architecture of Rockywold-Deephaven Camps," in *Roots and Recollections: A Century of Rockywold-Deephaven Camps,* ed. Megan Thorn (1997).

Bryant F. Tolles, Jr.

Photojournalism Photojournalism, which relies on both pictures and words to tell a story, has been a popular form of news reportage for the national media in the 20th century owing to photographers' abilities to portray domestic and international social conflicts, and the public's desire to visualize these situations through photographs. New England photojournalism developed in dialogue with these national trends. Thus, photojournalists working for the region's newspapers and magazines capture daily events and social issues using techniques established in the national media.

At the turn of the 20th century, new printing technologies enabled publishers to reproduce half-tone photographs in print. Not all magazines and newspapers, however, welcomed these innovations. The *Boston Transcript,* a daily newspaper, refused to publish photographs because its editors believed that readers would never accept their "truthfulness." Overcoming such fears by the 1910s, newspapers routinely published photographs as they competed for the growing market of urban readers. Tabloids in the 1920s experimented with various techniques, such as hidden cameras, in search of sensational images to capture their readers' interests. By the 1930s, even the government turned to photographs to report on national and regional issues. Photographers of the Farm Security Administration (FSA), for example, depicted the agricultural crisis during the Great Depression but also photographed regions like New England

to show the agency's successful programs. Photojournalists Jack Delano and John Collier, Jr., traveled from Connecticut to Maine in 1940, photographing farms run by proud men whose wives prepared harvest meals for the workers. These images of agrarian self-sufficiency, however, ignored cultural differences in the region, so that French Canadian farmers in Acadia, Maine, looked remarkably similar to Polish tobacco farmers in Connecticut. Such pictures demonstrated how the cultural assumptions of national photographers overlooked New England's diverse populations.

During World War II, *Life* magazine secured photojournalism's preeminence by providing readers with a weekly abundance of photographs of this global conflict. *Life,* under the leadership of Henry Luce, also established the importance of the photoessay as a narrative vehicle to represent the news. Local newspapers like the *Hartford Courant* and the *Providence Journal-Bulletin* followed these national conventions, using photoessays to depict local events. Increasingly since the postwar period, regional photojournalists have used their cameras to depict urban crises, such as crime and economic devastation, in vivid contrast to the picturesque tradition of idyllic New England coastlines and rural farms.

Beginning in the 1960s, the cultural significance of national magazines began to decline. As a result regional newspapers have used staff photojournalists to report on international events. In 1987, for instance, the *Boston Globe* published "The People of Flight," a series of photoessays on refugees from Africa, Guatemala, and Pakistan. In this way, regional newspapers have become important national outlets for photojournalists' work. At the same time, a tradition of photographing social change in New England is today being revitalized. The Salt Center for Documentary Field Studies, founded in 1973 in Portland, Maine, continues the tradition established by photographers like Lewis Hine who used their cameras to record the effects of industrialism in cities like Manchester, N.H. Hine, a recognized pioneer in photojournalism, focused his work specifically on child labor, traveling up and down the eastern seaboard to record the plight of working children. Continuing in this tradition, students at Salt learn documentary techniques as they explore Maine's urban and rural cultures through photographs of migrant labor, racial conflicts, and industrial decline. Thus, even as New England photojournalists increasingly participate in the culture of the national media, local photojournalists continue to focus their cameras on the diversity of the region.

Hugh T. French, ed., *Maine, A Peopled Landscape: Salt Documentary Photography, 1978 to 1995* (1995); Marianne Fulton, *Eyes of Time: Photojournalism in America* (1988); James Guimond, *American Photogra-*

Regional Journals of New England

Connecticut

Connecticut Magazine
Published: Trumbull
Established: October 1971
Circulation: 89,645

Discover Connecticut
Published: Colchester
Circulation: 6,000

Maine

Down East Magazine
Published: Camden
Established: 1954
Circulation: 110,832

Portland
Published: Portland
Established: March 1956
Circulation: 50,000

Massachusetts

Art New England
Published: Brighton
Established: 1979
Circulation: 35,000

Boston Magazine
Published: Boston
Established: 1961
Circulation: 125,000

Cape Cod Life
Published: Hyannis
Established: 1979
Circulation: 34,059

Matha's Vineyard Magazine
Published: Edgartown
Established: 1985
Circulatio: 12,000

Nantucket Magazine
Published: Nantucket
Circulation: 8,000

New England Antiques Journal
Published: Palmer
Established: 1982
Circulation: 25,000

New England Quarterly
Published: Boston
Established: 1928
Circulation: 2,400

New England Travel and Life
Published: Boston
Established: 1991
Circulation: 201,000

Provincetown Magazine
Published: Provincetown
Established: 1970
Circulation: 50,000 (summer)

Worcester Magazine
Published: Worcester
Established: 1976
Circulation: 40,000

New Hampshire

Northen New Hampshire Magazine
Published: Colebrook
Established: 1993
Circulation: 12,000

Yankee
Published: Dublin
Established: September 1935
Circulation: 500,000

Rhode Island

Newport Life
Published: Newport
Established: 1993
Circulation: 12,000

Rhode Island Monthly
Published: Providence
Established: May 1988
Circulation: 42,000

Vermont

Vermont Life
Published: Montpelier
Established: September 1946
Circulation: 75,550

Vermont Magazine
Published: Middlebury
Established: September 1989
Circulation: 23,000

Source: Carolyn A. Fischer, ed. *Gale Directory of Publications and Broadcast Media*, 131st ed. (Detroit: Gale, 1998); James L. Hayes, ed. *Burrelle's Media Directory: New England, 1998* (Livingston, N.J.: Burrelle's, 1997); Web sites, 2004.

---

phy and the American Dream (1991); Richard Lacayo and George Russell, *Eyewitness: 150 Years of Photojournalism* (1990).

Wendy Kozol

Publishing New England has a long, rich history as a publishing center. The first press in British North America was established in Cambridge, in the Massachusetts Bay Colony, in late 1638. The Cambridge Press published *The Whole Book of Psalmes* in 1640 and *The Eliot Indian Bible*—the first Bible published in the colonies—in 1663. In addition to religious works, the Cambridge Press also pub-

lished legal and political writings and Harvard College theses. When it was dissolved in 1692, it had already established the importance of print to the culture of New England.

During the 18th century Boston became a publishing center, even as presses were established in other parts of New England. The first newspaper published in the colonies, *The Boston News-Letter*, was founded in 1704; its was followed by a number of other important colonial papers, including Daniel Fowle's *New Hampshire Gazette* (1756); James Parker's *Connecticut Gazette* (1757); and Ann and James Franklin, Jr.'s *Newport Mercury* (1758). The

Hartford Courant, the oldest continuously published newspaper in the country, was founded in 1764. At the same time, independent presses were established in Providence, Hanover, N.H., and Falmouth, Maine. During the Revolutionary War, the Tory government tried to suppress Isaiah Thomas's publication of *The Massachusetts Spy*, an anti-British Boston weekly. Thomas moved his presses to Worcester, Mass., where he continued to publish *The Spy* and founded the American Antiquarian Society. He also published *The Farmer's Museum* in Walpole, N.H. As a master printer who believed in including

Connecticut

1. *The Hartford Courant*
   Published: Hartford
   Established: October 29, 1764
   Circulation: Monday–Friday 191,500
                Saturday 204,664
                Sunday 281,714

2. *New Haven Register*
   Published: New Haven
   Established: December 1812
   Circulation: Monday–Saturday 92,098
                Sunday 100,177

3. *Connecticut Post*
   Published: Bridgeport
   Circulation: Monday–Saturday 76,283
                Sunday 88,331

4. *The Waterbury Republican-American*
   Published: Waterbury
   Established: 1844
   Circulation: Monday–Saturday 54,584
                Sunday 64,784

5. *The Advocate*
   Published: Stamford
   Established: 1829
   Circulation: Monday–Friday 28,357
                Saturday 27,054
                Sunday 39,445

Maine

1. *Bangor Daily News*
   Published: Bangor
   Established: 1834
   Circulation: Monday–Friday 62,640
                Saturday–Sunday 74,753

2. *Portland Press Herald*
   Published: Portland
   Established: 1862
   Circulation: Monday–Saturday 77,788

3. *Maine Sunday Telegram*
   Published: Portland
   Established: 1887
   Circulation: 125,858

4. *Lewiston Sun Journal*
   Published: Lewiston
   Established: 1893
   Circulation: Monday–Saturday 34,035
                Sunday 34,808

5. *Kennebec Journal*
   Published: Augusta
   Established: 1825
   Circulation: Monday–Saturday 15,167
                Sunday 14,422

Massachusetts

1. *The Boston Globe*
   Published: Boston
   Established: 1872
   Circulation: Monday–Friday 451,471
                Saturday 423,632
                Sunday 707,813

2. *Boston Herald*
   Published: Boston
   Established: 1982
   Circulation: Monday–Friday 240,759
                Saturday 181,018
                Sunday 152,813

3. *Telegram and Gazette*
   Published: Worcester
   Established: 1866
   Circulation: Monday–Saturday 103,113
                Sunday 121,437

4. *Union-News and Sunday Republican*
   Published: Springfield
   Established: 1824
   Circulation: Monday–Saturday 85,745
                Sunday 128,627

5. *The Patriot Ledger*
   Published: Quincy
   Established: January 7, 1837
   Circulation: Monday–Friday 57,676
                Saturday–Sunday 70,703

New Hampshire

1. *The Union Leader*
   Published: Manchester
   Established: 1863
   Circulation: Monday–Friday 59,384
                Saturday 57,754
                Sunday 81,144

2. *The Telegraph*
   Published: Nashua
   Established: 1832
   Circulation: Monday–Saturday 26,566
                Sunday 32,672

3. *Foster's Democrat*
   Published: Dover
   Established: 1873
   Circulation: Monday–Saturday 22,720
                Sunday 27,728

4. *Portsmouth Herald*
   Published: Portsmouth
   Established: 1886
   Circulation: Monday–Saturday 14,380
                Sunday 19,968

5. *Eagle Times*
   Published: Claremont
   Established: 1835

Circulation: Monday–Friday 8,821
             Sunday 9,298

Rhode Island

1. *The Providence Journal-Bulletin*
   Published: Providence
   Established: 1863
   Circulation: Monday–Saturday 168,021
                Sunday 236,476

2. *The Newport Daily News*
   Published: Newport
   Established: 1846
   Circulation: Monday–Saturday 14,550

3. *The Call*
   Published: Woonsocket
   Established: 1892
   Circulation: Monday–Saturday 11,984
                Sunday 17,638

4. *The Times*
   Published: Pawtucket
   Established: April 30, 1885
   Circulation: Monday–Saturday 11,104

5. *The Westerly Sun*
   Published: Westerly
   Established: August 7, 1893
   Circulation: Monday–Saturday 9,421
                Sunday 9,978

Vermont

1. *The Burlington Free Press*
   Published: Burlington
   Established: 1827
   Circulation: Monday–Saturday 48,524
                Sunday 56,850

2. *Rutland Herald*
   Published: Rutland
   Established: 1794
   Circulation: Monday–Saturday 20,833
                Sunday 20,953

3. *The Times-Argus*
   Published: Barre
   Established: 1897
   Circulation: Monday–Saturday 10,343
                Sunday 11,228

4. *Caledonian-Record*
   Published: St. Johnsbury
   Established: 1837
   Circulation: Monday–Saturday 10,094

5. *Brattleboro Reformer*
   Published: Brattleboro
   Established: 1913
   Circulation: Monday–Friday 10,003
                Saturday–Sunday 11,453

Source: Carolyn A. Fischer, ed. *Gale Directory of Publications and Broadcast Media* 131st ed. (Detroit: Gale, 1998); Audit Bureau of Circulations FAS-FAX Report, September 30, 2004; John S. and James L. Knight Foundation, report, May 2004.

fine engravings in his publications, Thomas was a pivotal figure in the development of fine art and music publishing.

During the period 1820–52, there were 147 different publishers operating in Boston alone, working primarily on a regional basis. After 1850 Boston became, along with Philadelphia and New York, one of the publishing centers, centralizing American publishing and supporting the rise of a few major publishers. This move toward centralization was aided by the expansion of railroads and technological advances in type-casting and setting, papermaking, and press building, including the development of the cylinder press. One of the keys to this centralization was the rise of magazines with national circulations, many of which were founded in Boston: *The North American Review* (1815); Joseph Buckingham's *New England Magazine* (1825); Sarah J. Hale's *Ladies' Magazine* (later *Godey's Lady's Book*) (1828); William Lloyd Garrison's *Liberator*, published by the New England Anti-Slavery Society (1832); and the *Atlantic Monthly* (1857). In addition, New England intellectuals began a nationalistic push to promote a distinctively American literature.

In 1859 the *Atlantic Monthly* was acquired by the Boston company Ticknor and Fields, arguably the most prestigious publishing house in the United States during the 19th century. Other leading Boston publishers, such as Little, Brown, tended to publish only a few American authors, focusing instead on reprints and translations of foreign authors. In 1853, for instance, Little, Brown launched a series of the works of British poets, from Chaucer to Wordsworth. Ticknor and Fields, by contrast, actively recruited and supported American authors. They developed a house style, which made their books uniform and collectible. They also established patterns for book promotion that helped make authors such as Nathaniel Hawthorne and Henry Wadsworth Longfellow into literary celebrities.

After the Civil War and a series of short-lived partnerships, the Ticknor and Fields imprint merged into Houghton, Mifflin and Company. Oscar Houghton, a working-class native of Vermont, teamed with George Mifflin, an upper-class Bostonian, to continue to reprint the works of many of the best-known authors from the Ticknor and Fields list. At the same time, Houghton, Mifflin began what would in the 20th century be a staple of New England publishing: production of textbooks and literary readers. In 1882 the firm began publishing the Riverside Editions, a literature series that still continues today.

Two other major 19th-century Boston publishing houses, Lee and Shepard (1862–1904)

and D. Lothrop and Company (1868–95), were particularly successful in publishing children's books. Lee and Shepard was best known for its publication of the Oliver Optic series and of an early American edition of Lewis Carroll's *Alice's Adventures in Wonderland* (1869), while D. Lothrop (purchased by Lee and Shepard in 1895) published Margaret Sidney's *Five Little Peppers and How They Grew* (1881) as well as two important children's magazines, *Pansy* and *Wide Awake*. Lee and Shepard moved their operations to New York City at the end of the 19th century.

Lee and Shepard's move was indicative of a general consolidation that made New York the publishing center of the United States. Although Boston was still home to a number of publishing companies, in the 20th century they tended increasingly to publish for niche rather than general markets. Houghton Mifflin continued to publish a number of works by important American authors, including John Dos Passos, Carson McCullers, and Raymond Chandler, but the company also became known for children's books (especially the *Curious George* and *Paddington Bear* series) and for Roger Tory Peterson's series of birding field guides. In 1979 Ticknor and Fields was revived in New Haven, Conn.

The niche publishing that continued in New England included a number of important university presses, including Yale University Press (founded in 1908 by George Parmly Day), Harvard University Press (founded in 1913 by C. C. Lane), and Brown University Press, which began in 1932 and joined with the University Press of New England in 1980. Major textbook publishers with New England roots include Silver Burdett/Ginn; Allyn and Bacon; and Bedford/St. Martin's. Springfield, Mass., is the home of *Webster's New Collegiate Dictionary*. New England has also remained a magnet for independent and alternative publishers. In Massachusetts, James Laughlin established New Directions press in 1936 in Cambridge, Norfolk, and Boston in order to encourage experimental poetry and fiction; the Branden Press was established in Boston in 1965 to promote poetry, music, and art; and David Godine began publishing art books in 1969 from a letter press in Boston and Brookline, signaling a return to New England's roots as a center for excellence in printing.

Paul Brooks, *Two Park Street: A Publishing Memoir* (1986); William Charvat, *Literary Publishing in America, 1790–1850* (1959); Peter Dzwonkoski, ed., *American Literary Publishing Houses, 1638–1899* (1986); Dzwonkoski, ed., *American Literary Publishing Houses, 1900–1980: Trade and Paperback* (1986); Hellmut Lehmann-Haupt, *The Book in America* (1952); John Tebbel, *The American Magazine: A Compact History* (1969); Michael Winship, *American Literary Publish-

ing in the Mid-19th Century: The Business of Ticknor and Fields (1995).

Susan S. Williams

Radio Initially conceived as a method of point-to-point communication, radio has a long history in New England. During its very early development Cape Cod, Mass., served as a site for experimentation and commerce in the industry. In an era when ships were unable to communicate with land after they sailed over the horizon, the Cape was seen as an advantageous location from which to make contact with vessels arriving from Europe or communicate with sites across the Atlantic. In 1901, before voice transmission became possible, Guglielmo Marconi established a station in Wellfleet, Mass. He found the area was not without peril, however, when a storm leveled the operation, causing him to relocate in Newfoundland. Experiments conducted by Reginald Fessenden at his station in Brant Rock, Mass., just south of Plymouth, played a significant role in the development of continuous-wave technology. A continuous wave was essential to moving radio transmission from Morse code to speech. The first voice and music program was broadcast to sailors on Christmas Eve 1906 from Brant Rock. John S. Stone, another inventor, chose Massachusetts as the site for his laboratory. Stone was based in Cambridge and regularly conducted experiments along the Charles River and in Lynn.

New England's radio stations were among the first in the nation to air regularly scheduled commercial broadcasts. The first to be licensed in the region was WNBR in New Bedford, Mass., which went on the air on May 21, 1921. WSKO in Providence began broadcasting on June 2, 1922. Vermont, New Hampshire, and Connecticut also got their first stations in 1922, with, respectively, WVMT in Burlington beginning operations on May 20, WEZS in Laconia on August 22, and WDRC in Hartford (WPAJ until 1925) on December 10. Maine had to wait until WABI in Bangor went on the air in 1924. As stations grew more numerous, they often linked up to broadcast programming from other states or regions. WNAC in Boston and WEAF in New York made the first such connection via telephone on January 24, 1923. The first permanent cable hookup linked WEAF and WMAF of South Dartmouth, Mass. WMAF was owned by Colonel Edward Green, who personally paid the $60,000 annual line charges. He also paid a flat fee for unsponsored programs and got sponsored programs for free. Taking advantage of a signal already running through Providence, American Telephone and Telegraph offered to provide programming to WJAR, a

Broadcasting from the WEEI radio studio, Boston, 1927

Providence station already licensed by the company. WEAF received the right to sell time on WJAR. In return for each hour of sponsored programming, WEAF would give WJAR two hours of unsponsored programming. With few modifications this arrangement has governed relations between networks and affiliates until the present.

From the late 1920s through the 1940s, while CBS and NBC-Red or NBC-Blue focused on nationwide broadcasting, smaller regional networks also played a significant role in the development of radio. They organized regional advertising packages for sponsors and provided programming options to smaller stations unaffiliated with national chains. In 1941 there were 20 regional networks, although 14 of them operated in only one state (Massachusetts). One of the largest and most enduring of the regional networks during this era was the New England–based Yankee network. Managed by John Shepard III, the Yankee network began with 10 associated stations in 1936. Its largest affiliate was WNAC in Boston, which Shepard owned. By 1938 Yankee consisted of 17 stations, 20 by 1943. The Yankee network also maintained close ties with the Colonial network, another New England chain. Colonial was affiliated with many of the same stations, and the two chains shared cable lines. Smaller than Yankee, Colonial was affiliated with 13 stations clustered around WAAB in Boston. Both networks were affiliated with the Mutual Broadcasting System, a loose conglomeration of small regional stations across the country.

New England was again a site of radio experimentation during the 1930s, when the inventor Edwin Armstrong laid the groundwork for FM broadcasting. Although Armstrong's station, W2XMN, was based in Alpine, N.J., the inventor used stations in New England to conduct experiments with range and relay broadcasting. Relay broadcasting was a process whereby signals could be sent from one location to another and then rebroadcast. With AM signals, interference caused the signal to degrade, but FM allowed retransmission with no loss of sound quality. Not surprisingly, regional networks were interested in Armstrong's discoveries, as relay broadcasting would spare them the high cost of AT&T line charges. The Yankee network played a central role in supporting Armstrong's experiments with FM. In spring 1937 it sought approval from the Federal Radio Commission to build an experimental FM station in Paxton, Mass. By mid-1939 the network was broadcasting over two FM stations as well as its AM stations.

The full possibilities of FM rebroadcasting were realized on January 5, 1940, when five stations relayed a signal around New England. The signal originated at W2XMN and was sent to W1XPW, an experimental station owned by Yale University professor Frank Doolittle and located on West Rock in Meriden, Conn. From Connecticut the signal was forwarded to WSRS-FM, the Yankee affiliate outside Worcester, Mass., then relayed to an experimental station on Mount Washington. Finally the signal was sent to Boston, where it was converted to AM and broadcast one last time. FM broadcasting flourished in New England and elsewhere until the Federal Com-

munications Commission reallocated its frequency range upward in 1947.

Connecticut became the first New England state to have a regularly operating FM station when WDRC in Hartford went on the air in 1936. Massachusetts was next, with WSRS-FM in Worcester beginning June 17, 1940. Maine's first FM station, WCYI in Lewiston, went on the air February 29, 1948. WLWI began broadcasting on July 11 of that same year, becoming the first FM station in Rhode Island. Two FM stations went on the air in New Hampshire in 1948, WZID in Manchester and WTSV in Claremont. Vermont was the last New England state to have an FM station when WRMC began broadcasting in Middlebury in May 1949.

In the 1950s New England stations began broadcasting more musical programming instead of network fare and turned to local advertising. While the Yankee network lasted until 1967 and numerous other stations desperately tried to retain listeners, most stations broadcast locally based shows. As of 2002 there were 611 radio stations licensed to New England states. Of these, 455 were commercial and 156 noncommercial. Massachusetts had the most, with 188 (128 commercial, 60 noncommercial). Maine followed, with 121 stations (97, 24). Connecticut was served by 103 stations (72, 31). There were 86 stations (71, 15) in New Hampshire and 76 (58, 18) in Vermont. The smallest state, Rhode Island, also had the fewest stations, with 37 (29, 8). Boston was the largest radio market, ranked ninth in the nation, with more than 50 stations serving a metropolitan-area population of more than 3.8 million. Adult contemporary music and news/talk were the most popular formats.

The structure of regional broadcasting will change significantly in the near future. Although stations continue to seek local audiences, increasingly they are owned by national networks. The Telecommunications Act of 1996 relaxed restrictions on the number of stations a single entity could own within the same media market. Whether stations will retain a local or regional orientation remains to be seen. Moreover, technology is also changing what it means to be a radio station. Satellite radio providers like Sirius and XM and "Webcasting" over the Internet challenge the ideals of localism that have governed broadcasting policy and practice in the United States, leaving the future of regional radio identity uncertain.

Erik Barnouw, *A History of Broadcasting in the United States,* 3 vols. (1966–70); *Broadcasting and Cable Yearbook, 2002–3* (2002); Susan J. Douglas, *Inventing American Broadcasting, 1899–1922* (1987); Tom Lewis, *Empire of the Air: The Men Who Made Radio* (1991); Lawrence Lichty and Malachi C. Topping, *American*

Broadcasting: A Source Book on the History of Radio and Television (1975); Christopher H. Sterling and John M. Kittross, *Stay Tuned: A Concise History of American Broadcasting* (1978).

Alexander Russo

Regional Identity

At first blush the media of mass communication may seem to be inimical to, if not actively destructive of, any notion of regional identity, be it that of New England or any other. The argument is well known: mass culture as disseminated through modern communications media has largely displaced the sorts of localized vernacular cultures that typically show strong regional and spatial variations, obscuring or erasing differences between one part of the country and another; the cultural life and experience of Taunton, Mass., differs little from that of Tucson, Ariz.; Bostonian joins Houstonian in pledging primary allegiance to a single, national, media-borne sense of cultural identity.

To accept this indictment wholesale, however, is to ignore the many complex ways in which media on different scales, from national to local, are deeply intertwined with notions of New England's identity as seen from both within the region and without. By and large the national media, while smoothing over many regional differences, also draw on and perpetuate popular conceptions of New England—conceptions that privilege certain aspects of regional experience—imprinting a specific definition of New England on the mental maps of a national audience. Media of mass communication, however, are not inherently hostile to the local and regional; to attack particular media themselves for eroding regional identity is to shoot the messenger. What matters is the scale of distribution, the common denominators catered to; producers can conceive of audiences on local as well as national scales. Also, those audiences do not passively absorb media messages but actively interpret the materials they encounter, placing them within the context of their own lives and experiences.

Although national media must attract as large an audience as possible in order to be economically viable, many New England media outlets have appealed to smaller and more localized audiences in the service of identities that lie at least to some extent within New England or within particular cities or states in the region. These media draw on and reflect distinguishing aspects of regional and subregional life, helping local audiences construct a sense of identity from within—an identity drawn from a variety of aspects of regional experience rather than imposed monolithically by a national culture.

The geographer D. W. Meinig has called the traditional New England village, with its steepled churches, village greens, and white clapboard houses occupied by crusty, independent Yankees, a "symbolic landscape." This image has come to stand in many individuals' minds, and in popular culture in general, as an idealized image of community, a symbol with powerful positive connotations. It is this interpretation of regional identity—New England as symbol, not as experiential reality—that the national media have seized on most readily, perpetuating it for a mass audience in a variety of productions, taking advantage of its ready-made meanings and strong idealized associations in an attempt to gain market popularity.

To take television as a prominent example, two highly popular series in the 1980s and 1990s were set in small-town New England, the situation comedy *Newhart* and the whodunit *Murder, She Wrote.* These programs were set, respectively, in the fictional villages of Stratford, Vt., and Cabot Cove, Maine, places whose beauty and charm are established by a montage of images that accompanies the opening credits. Aside from their settings, however, neither program made much of an attempt to engage with the nature of New England village life; both located standard situation-comedy and murder-mystery plots in a New England setting rather than told stories of New England origin. Even if their settings had been changed, the shows' episodes would have played out identically, as regional verisimilitude was largely limited to the occasional character's having a vaguely New England accent or the sporadic and incidental use of a stereotypically regional plot device such as a town meeting.

The long-running comedy hit *Cheers* maintained a similarly tenuous relation to the city of Boston, confining itself to references to Boston-area sports teams and universities and using one overtly Italian American character to reflect Boston's ethnic diversity. In a case of life imitating art, however, the Boston tavern that inspired *Cheers* started aggressively marketing that connection, offering itself as a tourist destination for visitors wishing to experience the Boston they had seen on television.

In all these instances, the mass-media, popular-culture version of New England obscured any sense of authentic regional identity that might be felt by Vermonters, coastal Mainers, or Bostonians, and it is this version—New England as a national symbol—that producers take advantage of in crafting what they hope will be marketable products. Even the best-selling novel *Peyton Place* (1956), by Grace Metalious (and the 1960s television series based on it), draws on this phenomenon in an ironic way, attracting readers through the symbolic power of small-town New England only to subvert the symbol's meanings and associations.

In contrast to Meinig's notion of symbolic landscapes, places whose meanings are imposed on them from without, geographer Wilbur Zelinsky has discussed the phenomenon of the vernacular region, the region whose existence, extent, and uniquely distinguishing characteristics are perceived and defined from within, by the residents of the region themselves. Unlike the fare broadcast by the national media, a large variety of media content produced and distributed within New England may be seen as both reflecting and creating a sense of vernacular regional identity—providing images and references for the use of specifically local audiences that grow out of or communicate an understanding of various New Englanders' cultural distinctiveness or both. Frequently these productions focus on specific areas within New England, such as particular states or cities, demonstrating or helping to develop vernacular subregions within the New England whole.

To look at television broadcasting again: although television stations air many hours of network and nationally syndicated programming, and although many New Englanders have ample access to national cable channels, local-origin programs focusing on life in a station's immediate vicinity form an important part of regional broadcasting. Network affiliates carry up to three hours of local news each day, not only informing viewers of current events in their areas but also including feature stories on aspects of local life and culture, stories deemed likely to appeal to a local audience. On a state-by-state basis, public television stations produce many hours of programming devoted to state politics, arts, traditions, and current issues, taking it as part of their mission to inform their audience about the unique qualities and textures of life in their particular part of New England.

Television and radio broadcasts of Boston Red Sox, Celtics, and Bruins games throughout New England may contribute to a shared sense of cultural identity and belonging, at least for sports fans. Local and regional publishing also plays an important part in reflecting and promoting a sense of regional or subregional identity. Magazines such as *Vermont Life, Yankee,* and *Down East,* while admittedly attempting to put the best face on their target markets and catering at least in part to potential visitors, also owe their existence and continued publication to local readers' sense that their states, and the region within which they are nestled, are distinctive and worthy of media attention. Many individual cities within New England not only are homes to glossy magazines but also harbor so-called alternative weeklies—for example, the *Boston Phoenix,* Providence's *NewPaper,* and Portland, Maine's *Casco Bay Weekly*—which provide a knowing but less reverent view of local culture and events.

Most products of mass communications media do not engage in objective ethnography. Media are driven by economics as well as vision and thus must be made congenial to a particular audience. Nor do they necessarily recognize either New England's racial, ethnic, and socioeconomic complexity or the urban-industrial character of much of the region. Once a media production is put into distribution, however, the audience begins its work, interpreting the media text according to its own needs, perspectives, and experiences. As consumers of national mass media, New Englanders are largely construed to be just another part of a national audience possessing uniform tastes, an audience that would likely not appreciate distinctively, authentically regional materials. And many of these media productions present New England in stereotyped, symbolic ways, responding to the imagined region rather than the region itself. Still, media productions have been and continue to be crafted within New England, providing images and ideas for audiences to select and interpret as they create and express their own sense of regional identity, be those audiences New Englanders as a whole or members of particular social, cultural, or subregional groups within New England. These media help to express and create a sense that their viewers, readers, and listeners, far from simply being interchangeable pieces within the national whole, possess identities that are uniquely theirs. In their production and consumption, New England's media indicate the persistent presence of a vernacular distinctiveness.

Charles Hamm, "The Media, Politics, and Regionalism," in *Regional Studies: The Interplay of Land and People,* ed. Glen E. Lich (1992); D. W. Meinig, "Symbolic Landscapes: Some Idealizations of American Communities," in *The Interpretation of Ordinary Landscapes: Geographical Essays,* ed. D. W. Meinig (1979); Wilbur Zelinsky, "North America's Vernacular Regions," *Annals of the Association of American Geographers* 70 (1980).

Kent C. Ryden

Salt *Salt* magazine was launched at Kennebunk (Maine) High School in 1973 as an alternative to outdated textbooks in a folklore class. The Salt educational program, which takes a collaborative, experiential approach to learning, was founded by educator Pamela H. Wood to engage students in the study of the culture of their region. Wishing to bring a real-world dimension to the classroom, Wood got her students to interview their parents, grandparents, and neighbors about their lives and traditional ways of doing things. At its heart *Salt* became a way of giving back to the

people whose stories it tells. Through nonfiction writing and documentary photography, the magazine now focuses not just on the seacoast but on contemporary Maine and the changes and traditions at play in the state.

The students chose the name "Salt" for its multiple associations with the Kennebunk region where the project was founded, a region boasting salty people, saltwater, salt marshes, salt of the earth. The magazine, like the educational program, has been described as a mix of literary journalism, documentary photography, and ethnography. The lack of a clear descriptive name led Wood to coin the phrase "cultural journalism" in the early 1970s. Although the magazine is a noncommercial venture, *Salt* has always sought to meet the highest professional standards in design and content.

Soon after the program's founding, a loose association developed between Salt and the Foxfire project of Georgia, begun several years earlier. Although similarities existed between the two projects and their periodicals, *Salt* magazine maintained its distinct identity and independence. Before long, two compilations of *Salt* magazine articles were published in book form—*The Salt Book* in 1977 and *Salt 2* in 1980—by Anchor/Doubleday. Between them they have sold more than 100,000 copies.

Since its early days *Salt* magazine has evolved in a manner that reflects ongoing shifts within the Salt educational program. By 1980 educational retrenchment at the coastal Maine high school and funding cutbacks within state and federal government programs that had encouraged Salt's growth forced the program to refocus. Abandoning its involvement with secondary education, Salt launched a semester-length off-campus field studies program for undergraduate college students in 1982. By 1989 the program had outgrown its Kennebunk location and moved to the more urban area of Portland. There it developed the Salt Center for Documentary Field Studies, where undergraduate and graduate students in residence concentrate on either documentary photography or nonfiction writing. The Salt Center also hosts an archive that serves as a repository for tape-recorded interviews, transcripts, photographic negatives, and prints.

While remaining true to its original, collaborative educational practices whereby students learn by doing, the Salt program was embraced as a field studies option for college and university students within a more traditional, campus-based curriculum. In turn, *Salt* magazine broadened its subject matter to include the entire state of Maine and a much wider range of topics and perspectives. Published quarterly for most of its history, the magazine is now published annually. In 1995 a third book, *Maine: A Peopled Landscape,* a compilation of

photography, was published to coincide with the opening of a major Salt photographic exhibit at the Portland Museum of Art. Students no longer come exclusively from the Kennebunk area or even Maine—more than three-quarters now hail from outside the state, drawn by the nature of the documentary work and the emphasis on regional perspectives.

Hugh French, *Maine, a Peopled Landscape: Salt Documentary Photography, 1978–1995* (1995); Pamela Wood, *You and Aunt Arie: A Guide to Cultural Journalism Based on Foxfire and Its Descendants* (1975); Pamela Wood, ed., *The Salt Book: Lobstering, Sea Moss Pudding, Stone Walls, Rum Running, Maple Syrup, Snowshoes, and Other Yankee Doings* (1977); Wood, ed., *Salt 2: Boatbuilding, Sailmaking, Island People, River Driving, Bean Hole Beans, Wooden Paddles, and More Yankee Doings* (1980).

Hugh T. French

Sports Broadcasters Despite the presence of some outstanding college athletic programs, New England's primary media focus has been on the region's professional sports teams. Using Boston flag stations as the hub for a galaxy of satellite affiliates, announcers of all four major sports have broadcast events to every corner of New England. Radio, particularly, with its capacity to permeate daily life—be it at the beach, the dentist's office, or a restaurant—unites the region, and it is primarily through this medium that the region's distinctive broadcasters are known.

Longevity is among the distinguishing traits of New England's sports broadcasters. Ned Martin, for example, broadcast Red Sox games for 32 years; Bob Wilson and Fred Cusick, combined, spent approximately 70 years behind the Boston Bruins microphone; Johnny Most called Celtics games "high above courtside" for almost 40 years. In general, New England sports broadcasters have emphasized an objective rendering of the game rather than their own personalities. Cusick's ecstatic "He scores!" enhanced the excitement of the moment, but his sense of detail and matter-of-factness marked him as a true professional. Red Sox broadcasters such as Jim Britt, Curt Gowdy, Ned Martin, Ken Coleman, Joe Castiglione, and Sean McDonough have been low-key, reportorial, and literate, respectful of the summer game's slower rhythm yet alert for its big moments. Ned Martin's 1967 call of Rico Petrocelli's pennant-clinching grab of a pop-up serves as example: "The pitch . . . is looped towards shortstop, Petrocelli's back, he's got it! The Red Sox win! And there's pandemonium on the field! Listen!" Television critic Jack Craig consistently praised Martin's vocabulary, particularly his use of action verbs. Martin's calls were characterized by restrained excitement and the modesty to step back and let the action reveal itself. (Audiences appreciate "color men" in a somewhat different way, yet even here the cult of the "the Rem Dog," baseball color analyst Jerry Remy, celebrates a plainspoken, undemonstrative man.)

Another regional sportscasting characteristic is candor. From wry observations such as Martin's "If you just tuned in, welcome to the debacle" to Remy and Sean McDonough's understated critiques of managerial strategy to Bob Cousy's observations on the need for the extra pass, New England broadcasters have not spared the local team. This trait is particularly noticeable among sportscasters who were former athletes: commentators who, in many markets, tend to be "homers." The evolution of former Red Sox catcher Bob Montgomery and Patriot wide receiver Gino Cappelletti from organizational loyalists to independent observers shows this tendency even as the transformation of former outfielder Ken Harrelson from rigorous Red Sox analyst to partisan White Sox broadcaster reveals his awareness of regional media differences.

As the case of Johnny Most demonstrates, those differences are not absolute. That gravel-voiced announcer shamelessly praised the Celtics, humorously denounced opponents with nicknames such as "McFilthy" and "McNasty," and provided the region's most famous broadcasting moment with his delirious: "Havlicek stole the ball! Havlicek stole the ball! It's all over! It's all over!" at the conclusion of the 1965 NBA Eastern Finals. Unlike other play by play announcers, Most became a celebrity in his own right, inspiring Johnny Most sound-alike contests throughout the Boston area. At the same time, Most also had a deep knowledge of the game; a practicing poet capable of describing "pirouettes" in the lane or "rainbow jumpers," he simultaneously tapped into a passionate parochialism and the basketball junkie's need for inside information.

New England broadcasters, with their universal love of language, detailed reporting, and general recourse to candor and humor, reveal something of the audience that embraces them. Literate and passionate, ironic true believers, New England audiences have made allegiance to the messenger as traditional as allegiance to the sport itself.

Jack Craig, "Fred Cusick" *Boston Globe*, April 16, 1997; Craig, "Johnny Most," *Boston Globe*, September 15, 1989; Dan Shaughnessy, *Ever Green: The Boston Celtics* (1990); Curt Smith, *Voices of the Game: The First Full-Scale Overview of Baseball Broadcasting, 1921 to Present* (1987).

Christopher A. Fahy

Stars and Personalities Stars and personalities are people who have achieved widespread celebrity through significant exposure in the mass media and who are identified publicly with certain personal qualities, talents, or achievements. They are typically performers from realms of popular entertainment such as theater, comedy, sports, film, television, or popular music, but public figures from politics, education, or the fine arts may also attain such status.

The terms *star* and *personality* are often used interchangeably, but they actually have slightly different origins and meanings. The use of *star* to refer to a well-known public figure can be traced back to Greek myths in which illustrious persons, after their deaths, often became constellations. Usually the modern-day star is internationally famous, a larger-than-life figure whose image and lifestyle remove him or her from ordinary, localized existence. A *personality* is someone who is simply well known for being him-or herself. Unlike stars, personalities are not considered above the ordinary, although they may appear in advertisements or the media more often than other people.

Although region has not been a particularly prominent issue in the study of celebrity—in part because of the homogenizing influence of national mass media—ideas about place and its influence on the quality of social relations underlie several approaches to the topic. Criticism of celebrity is often tied to a distrust of mass culture, particularly of the ways it usurps traditional face-to-face social relations, encouraging a sense of identity based not on values arising from a shared way of life in a particular locality but on participation in an ever-expanding national consumer market. Yet mass culture may not have erased the importance of local and regional identity but rather provided a new forum for such an identity. Stars and personalities may in fact represent or reinforce ideas of regional culture.

In many ways stars and personalities embody the tensions between mass culture and local culture in the modern United States. Even though stars exist primarily as images reproduced nationwide in the mass media and are fascinating because of their unattainability, they nevertheless engender feelings of intimacy in their audiences similar to those that would result from face-to-face interaction. People behave toward stars as they might toward close friends, identifying with them, picking up on their mannerisms and habits, or referring to them by their first names only.

Conversely, people tend to regard personalities as regular folks simply enjoying their modest allotment of fame. "Where are they now?" features in newspapers or on television hold appeal because they satisfyingly bring personalities from the netherworld of the media back into ordinary, actual localities. Yet at the same time, meeting a personality is often an extraordinary social moment in which common modes of interaction are abandoned and the personality becomes a famous outsider: people are apt to fawn, ask for an autograph, and talk about the encounter proudly later to friends.

Likewise, even though stars may gain near universal fame, leaving behind their ordinary existence in a specific region, they often symbolize a regional identity. Indeed, New England magazines, newspapers, and television shows regularly feature stories on stars' affiliations with the region. New England's home-grown stars include the black nationalist leader Malcolm X, the comedian Jay Leno, and the film actress Geena Davis, who were all born or raised in Massachusetts.

Sometimes the connection is established when a star moves to the region as an adult. Thus New Englanders may feel a special bond with such transplanted celebrities as suspense author Stephen King of Maine, movie actors Paul Newman and Joanne Woodward of Connecticut, or singer-songwriter James Taylor of Massachusetts. Some affiliations are more tenuous, based only on time spent in the region. Babe Ruth once played for the Boston Red Sox, for example; film star Faye Dunaway attended Boston University; and folk singer Tracy Chapman got her start in Cambridge, Mass., coffeehouses. Many famous artists and writers have moved to or summered in Maine, attracted by the rugged beauty of that state's long coastline; they include the painter Andrew Wyeth, the environmentalist author Rachel Carson, and the novelist Harriet Beecher Stowe, who became a star without the benefit of today's broadcast media. Provincetown, Mass., at the tip of Cape Cod, has been another New England star magnet, attracting celebrities ranging from the poet and philosopher Henry David Thoreau to the playwright Eugene O'Neill to the novelist Norman Mailer. Especially important in all these affiliations is a sense of pride that New England could have produced, or attracted, such public figures. Even though stars are members of a much wider realm of renown, local admirers hope they will remember how the region contributed to their success and somehow represent a bit of what New England is about for non–New Englanders.

Certain stars are more closely identified with New England, shaping the image of the region at the same time they are shaped by it. President John Fitzgerald Kennedy, born into a powerful Boston Irish family, was one such. A war hero and a graduate of Harvard University, Kennedy spoke with an unmistakable Boston accent and embodied a kind of idealism that has long been perceived as a constitutive element of New England's political character. The actress Katharine Hepburn, born in Hartford, is another. From a socially prominent Connecticut family, Hepburn, whose accent is more Brahmin than Boston, has represented New England refinement on stage and screen since her career began in the early 1930s. The 1981 film *On Golden Pond,* which earned Hepburn her fourth Academy Award as best actress, was filmed on New Hampshire's Squam Lakes and shows Hepburn at her New England flintiest.

Skowhegan, Maine's Margaret Chase Smith, a U.S. representative, senator, and recipient of the Presidential Medal of Freedom, was one of the first public figures to speak out, on the floor of the Senate, against fellow Republican Joseph McCarthy's Communist witch hunt. Smith's 1950 "declaration of conscience" brought the first-term senator to national prominence and helped build Maine's reputation for independent-minded politicians of integrity whom many continue to associate with the likes of Edmund S. Muskie, George Mitchell, William S. Cohen, and Olympia Snow.

Because personalities, for their part, usually have not attained fame in the mythical movement from the local to the universal but instead have become well known simply for being themselves, they generally do not inspire the same claims for regional identity. In many cases, however, personalities have relied on local and regional affiliations to attain mass appeal. Local radio and television personalities often come to represent their hometowns or cities. Boston's longtime husband-and-wife television news team Chet Curtis and Natalie Jacobson, for example, became important figures in the promotion of community events and charities in that city, although their professional partnership ended in 2000 and their divorce became final the following year. Other personalities are known for personal characteristics commonly identified with various localities in New England. Thus, for example, Vincent "Buddy" Cianci, Jr., the former mayor of Providence, epitomizes the street-smart, tough but affable Italian politicians for which that city is known; Mike Barnicle, a longtime columnist for the *Boston Globe,* now employed elsewhere and still in the public eye, represents the no-nonsense skepticism of working-class Irish Boston; transplanted New Yorkers Ben Cohen and Jerry Greenfield, founders of Ben and Jerry's ice cream company, symbolize the socially conscious, liberal sensibility that many associate with Vermont.

The role regional connections play in the lives of modern stars and personalities, like the extent to which celebrities incarnate traits associated with their regional connections, ultimately varies from one person to the next. But celebrities clearly have power, whether it be used to attract ever larger audiences to national media or to draw attention to more localized concerns. Above all, they mark the dramatic impact of mass communications technology on people's lives over the past century and are integral to understanding the current nature of social relations and identity throughout the United States.

Daniel J. Boorstin, "From Hero to Celebrity: The Human Pseudo-Event," in *The Image: A Guide to Pseudo-Events in America* (1992 [1961]); Leo Braudy, *Frenzy of Renown: Fame and Its History* (1997 [1986]); John L. Caughey, *Imaginary Social Worlds: A Cultural Approach* (1984); Richard Dyer, *Stars* (1979; new ed., 1998); Jib Fowles, *Starstruck: Celebrity Performers and the American Public* (1992); Christine Gledhill, ed., *Stardom: Industry of Desire* (1991); Richard Schickel, *Intimate Strangers: The Culture of Celebrity* (1985); Warren Susman, "Personality and the Making of 20th-Century Culture," in *Culture as History: The Transformation of American Society in the Twentieth Century* (1984).

Daniel Cavicchi

Steele, Bob (Robert L.) (1911–2002)

Radio broadcaster. Described by colleagues as the "great one in radio," Bob Steele broadcast from WTIC-AM in Hartford from 1936 to 1991, and commanded the largest share of a local market nationwide. Thousands of southern New Englanders woke up each weekday to Steele's theme music, "A Hunt in the Black Forest," and awaited his popular segments: his word of the day, corny jokes, and the daily Birthday Club. Steele's large audience remained loyal throughout his 55-year radio career.

Despite his long tenure at WTIC, Steele did not begin his career in radio or in New England. Born in Kansas City, Mo., Steele migrated to Connecticut in 1936, when he left his job with the Works Progress Administration in California to announce motorcycle races in Hartford. His desire was to work in radio when the racing season ended, although he had no broadcasting experience. After two Connecticut radio stations rejected him, Steele successfully auditioned for WTIC and began his long relation with the station.

Steele began his radio career doing station breaks, commercials, and sportscasting. Even after he started his morning show in 1943, Steele, a former boxer, continued to announce events and interview notable sports personalities, such as Satchel Paige, Babe Ruth, Jack Dempsey, and Muhammad Ali. His influence on and participation in the southern New England sports scene was acknowledged in 1993, when he was inducted into the Connecticut Sports Museum and Hall of Fame.

Once his career as a morning show host began, Steele developed a loyal following who appreciated his unique style and regular segments. Even his musical selections of marches, polkas, and swing tunes were distinctive. Each day, Steele gave weather forecasts from around the world, defined a word of the day, and predicted winners for various sporting events. Although his definitions were always correct, his sports picks rarely were accurate. At nine o'clock each morning, Steele announced new members of the Birthday Club, consisting of fans who were celebrating their 80th birthdays or beyond. He became a member of his famed club a few months before he retired in 1991.

Listeners also enjoyed Steele's casual, sincere on-air demeanor and his sense of humor, which he often displayed through self-deprecating stories. He was so comfortable with his audience that he involved them in his struggle to keep his weight under 200 pounds by weighing in on the air every Friday. He held his audience captive with his ability to tell good jokes and bad puns. For example, he created a cast of fictitious family members, playing on the homonym of Steele, including Uncle Corrugated, Aunt Bessemer, and Uncle Stainless.

Steele's fans responded to his consistency, sincerity, and wit with devotion and thousands of letters of appreciation. After retiring from broadcasting, Steele appeared in commercials and at local events in the Hartford area.

"Fare Thee Well, Bob Steele," *Hartford Courant,* October 3, 1991; Jon Lender, "Bob Steele Throws Last Punch Line 'Sayonara, Adios' after 55 Years of Radio Wizardry," *Hartford Courant,* October 1, 1991; Jane Moskowitz and Jane Gillard, *Bob Steele's 50th Anniversary: An Affectionate Memoir* (1986); Spoonwood Press, ed., *Bob Steele: A Man and His Humor* (1980).

Sheila A. Brennan

Television

New England's first television station, WNHC-TV, began broadcasting from Gaylord Mountain in Hamden, Conn., at 11:30 P.M. on June 2, 1948. The station was owned by Elm City Broadcasting, a partnership of six New Haven entrepreneurs: Aldo Domenicis, Michael Goode, Patrick Goode, Vincent DeLaurentis, Garo Ray, and David Harris. Like many early television broadcasters, the Elm City group also owned local radio stations, in this case WNHC-AM and WNHC-FM. Other New England outlets, such as Boston's WBZ-TV and WNAC-TV, were owned by national corporations (Westinghouse and RKO Television, respectively). The New Haven ownership of WNHC-TV brought a local orientation to the station's programming choices, particularly in its first five years of operation.

As the only station operating in Connecticut until 1953, WNHC-TV had tremendous programming latitude during its early years. Although ostensibly affiliated with the Du-Mont network, WNHC took shows from NBC, CBS, and ABC. Programming choices were made with local preferences in mind. Like most early television stations, WNHC also produced a significant amount of its own programming, including local news broadcasts, several cooking shows, a craft-oriented interview show, contemporary-issues programs, and a teen-oriented *American Bandstand*–type program. It also covered area elections and broadcast special events such as Yale College football games and local beauty pageants.

After the Federal Communications Commission (FCC) lifted its license freeze in 1952, WNHC programming choices were limited by the appearance of new Connecticut network affiliates. The NBC subsidiary WNBC-TV, Channel 30, in New Britain took to the air in 1953; CBS-owned WHCT-TV, Channel 18, in Hartford began broadcasting in 1956; Traveler's Insurance Company started WTIC-TV, Channel 3, in Hartford, also in 1956. WNHC-TV, now Channel 8, could no longer choose its programming from all the networks and found its options further limited when the DuMont network ceased operations in the summer of 1955.

Perhaps in response to this new competition and the narrowing of programming options, in 1956 Elm City Broadcasting sold WNHC-TV to Philadelphia-based Triangle Publications, owned by Walter Annenberg, which published the *Philadelphia Inquirer* and *TV Guide*. While WNHC continued to produce a few local shows, the national outlook of absentee owners dramatically altered the station's programming philosophy. Triangle urged the station to concentrate on programs that would be suitable for national syndication

and affiliated the station with the ABC network. In 1971 WNHC was sold again, becoming part of the Capital Cities group and changing its call letters to WTNH. This final sale permanently wed the station to a nationally oriented corporate philosophy.

Other New England stations were also among television's pioneers. WBZ-TV, Channel 4, in Boston began broadcasting on June 9, 1948. Also in Boston, WHDH-TV, Channel 42, went on the air later that same month, on June 21. Just over a year later, on July 10, 1949, WJAR, Channel 10, in Providence began operations. These four stations were the only television outlets in New England until the end of the FCC's license freeze in 1952, when numerous stations began broadcasting. Maine got its first station, WABI-TV, Channel 5, in Bangor, on January 25, 1953. WMUR-TV, Channel 9, in Manchester, N.H., was that state's first station. Vermont was the last New England state to claim a television station of its own when WCAX-TV, Channel 3, in Burlington went on the air on September 26, 1954. In 2002 there were 86 FCC-licensed television stations in New England, although not all had begun broadcasting at that time. Massachusetts had the largest number, with 29. Maine followed, with 17, while Connecticut had 15, Vermont and New Hampshire each had 9, and Rhode Island had 7. In 2001 Boston was the largest market area, with 29 stations serving more than 2.3 million television households. Additionally, a growing number of stations in New England have been licensed to transmit digital television signals.

If New England can lay claim to a central role within U.S. television history, it is in the realm of public broadcasting. All six New England states possess strong public broadcasting networks. Connecticut Public Broadcasting operates three stations; WGBH-TV

(Boston) Educational Foundation, five; Maine Public Broadcasting and Vermont ETV, four each; and the University of New Hampshire, three. Of these, Massachusetts-based WGBH, Channels 2 and 44 in Boston and Channel 57 in Springfield, has a national scope and has played a crucial role in the history of public broadcasting in the United States. WGBH began airing educational programs in May 1955 as part of an FCC-mandated frequency allocation for noncommercial educational stations issued in 1952.

WGBH served as a source of educational television programming from the outset. As part of a regionally based production network, the station provided tapes of concerts by the Boston Symphony Orchestra and language instruction with *French on TV*, as well as such programs as *Of Science and Scientists* and *The Constitution and Human Rights*. These were sent to the National Educational Television and Radio Center in Ann Arbor, Mich. This center, which later became the National Educational Television Center (NET), was the chief location for the reproduction and national distribution of educational television programming.

As educational television became public television, it retained its regional production philosophy, with WGBH continuing to serve as a primary supplier of programming. Regional suppliers are essential to public television, because the Corporation for Public Broadcasting (CPB) cannot distribute programming. Legislators who feared that public television would become a fourth network dominated by Eastern liberals worked to make sure programming decisions remained decentralized, even as they created the CPB through the Public Broadcasting Act of 1967. Their preventive efforts were not entirely successful. While other production centers do exist, such as WQED in Pittsburgh, WTTW in Chicago, and KQED in San Francisco and KCET in Los Angeles, nearly half the programming on public television continues to emanate from WGBH in Boston and WNET in New York.

As one of the largest producers of public television programming, WGBH-TV has a significant impact on the schedule of public television stations across the United States. Shows such as *Antiques Roadshow, Nova, The Victory Garden, Mystery!* and *Sister Wendy's American Collection*, as well as the documentaries of *Frontline* and *American Experience* are all products of WGBH. The station also serves as the American distribution center for the *Masterpiece Theatre* productions of the British Broadcasting Company. Critical successes in this series have included *Elizabeth R, The Six Wives of Henry VIII, Upstairs, Down-*

Al Benjamin interviews Massachusetts Attorney General Edward Brooke on the Yankee Network, 1964

stairs, and *Pride and Prejudice.* WGBH was also one of the first stations to approach corporations for sponsorship of specific programs. Thus, even as individual public television station managers retain control over which shows they air, the origin of much of public television programming continues to lie in New England.

Nonetheless, relatively few television shows, whether public or commercial, depict New England in an accurate or realistic way. In an effort to appeal to the largest possible audience, commercial television makes broadly based national appeals. With the exception of *Spenser: For Hire,* which was shot on location in Boston, New England tends only to be a source of local color for most shows that use the region as a backdrop: *St. Elsewhere* and *Ally McBeal,* also set in Boston, *Dawson's Creek,* set on Cape Cod, and *Providence,* set in Rhode Island, are examples of this trend. One recurring location type is the small New England town. Peyton Place, N.H., in the serial drama *Peyton Place;* Cabot Cove, Maine, in *Murder, She Wrote;* and Stratford, Vt., in *Newhart* all added to their respective shows' appeal but did not play a central role in character development.

Another significant example is *Cheers,* an extremely popular program during its 11-year run. *Cheers* revolved around the antics of the employees and patrons of a Boston bar where, according to the show's theme song, "everybody knows your name." Yet while the show made frequent reference to nationally recognizable Bean Town sports teams such as the Red Sox, Celtics, and Bruins or to the Boston-area universities attended by graduate student Diane, it could easily have been set in a bar in another metropolitan area. Indeed, *Cheers* failed to draw explicitly on West End Irish types, as the less successful *Costello* on the Fox cable network did, or on the kind of student life featured in NBC's *Boston Common.* The lower ratings garnered by these shows may be due in part to their regionalism, commercial mass media perhaps continuing to demand mass recognition. The superficiality of the New England component of *Cheers,* for example, is clearly demonstrated by the existence of Cheers bars in major airports throughout the United States. Situated in the ultimate nonlocation, the Cheers franchise may evoke the aura of a neighborhood bar, but the bars are anything but a place where "everybody knows your name."

Broadcasting and Cable Yearbook, 2002–3 (2002); Carnegie Commission on Educational Television, *Public Television: A Program for Action* (1967); James Day, *The Vanishing Vision: The Inside Story of Public Television* (1995); Ralph Engelman, *Public Radio and Television in America: A Political History* (1996);

Douglas Gomery, "Rethinking TV History," *Journalism and Mass Communication Quarterly* 3 (1997); Michael Murray and Donald Godfrey, *Television in America: Local Station History from Across the Nation* (1997); Christopher Sterling and John Kittross, *Stay Tuned: A Concise History of American Broadcasting* (1978).

Alexander Russo

This Old House *This Old House* is a weekly half-hour television program about home renovation, produced for public television by WGBH Boston. Created in 1979 in response to growing interest in antique homes and historic preservation, the program drew on New England historicity and thriftiness and Yankee ingenuity to attract a national audience.

Executive producer Russell Morash conceived the program while remodeling his 19th-century farmhouse in Lexington, Mass. Morash had studied theater direction at Boston University and in 1957 joined WGBH, where he eventually introduced cookbook author Julia Child to American television audiences and launched *Crockett's Victory Garden* (later *The Victory Garden*) in 1975. With *This Old House,* Morash continued his pioneering work with "how-to" television programming by placing local building experts at center stage. Serving as the program's master carpenter, Norm Abram is a key figure on the show as well as on *The New Yankee Workshop,* which debuted in 1989. General contractor Tom Silva and heating and plumbing contractor Richard Trethewey are among the many other Boston-area locals who make regular appearances on the show. *This Old House* was originally hosted

by developer Bob Vila; he was replaced in 1989 by sailor and author Steve Thomas, followed by Kevin O'Connor in 2003.

Focusing on two houses per television season, *This Old House* shows how dilapidated old structures can be transformed in ways that are sensitive to their historic integrity. The first 13-week episode, broadcast locally in Boston on WGBH, featured the renovation of a Victorian house in Dorchester, Mass. Subsequent seasons reached a national audience and highlighted a range of domestic structures in and around Boston, including an 18th-century farmhouse, a 19th-century New England barn converted into a timberframe home, a "three-decker" (apartment house), and a post–World War II suburban ranch house. In 1985 the program began venturing outside New England to explore renovation challenges presented by house types in other regions of the United States. The program has remained tied, nevertheless, to New England with season episodes alternating between a house in the Boston area and one in a more distant location.

By providing detailed, step-by-step explanations of renovation processes, *This Old House* gives many viewers the confidence with which to undertake their own home improvement projects. At the same time, the show fosters an interest in regional and historic house styles and promotes an appreciation for architectural crafts among viewers who never intend to take up a hammer. The program thus serves as much to inspire viewers and guide them in the savvy consumption of contracting services as to instruct them in remodeling methods. Most episodes document the expe-

Master carpenter Norm Abram and homeowner Terry Maitlan at a This Old House *project, Acton, Mass., 1994*

riences of real homeowners as they renovate their dwellings with the assistance of professional contractors and the show's staff. The program also regularly features trips to factories and specialty workshops to show the variety of skills involved in restoring historic structures. Initially, the program focused on small-scale, relatively affordable projects to which homeowners contributed "sweat equity" to keep costs down. In recent years, the program's producers have highlighted more elaborate, big-budget renovations. The program does not adhere to a single definition of restoration but instead celebrates old and new renovation techniques with equal enthusiasm.

Although some preservationists complain that renovation projects on the program often fail to conform to the strictest of preservation guidelines, *This Old House* is the most popular home improvement program on television today. While making its hosts national celebrities, the program has been so successful that its creators launched a spin-off commercial magazine in 1995, have published several tie-in books, and created a new series, *Ask This Old House*, which premiered in 2002 and features regular program specialists making "House Calls" to address renovation and remodeling questions posed by viewers. The fact that the program has inspired similar television programs to emulate its format and the launching of the television situation comedy *Home Improvement* suggest its importance as a focal point for the strong interest in both restoration and renovation throughout the 1980s and 1990s, and now into the 21st century. In the process, *This Old House* has helped solidify New England's central place in popular ideas about the American past.

Bill Ervolino, "PBS Hit Continues to Bring Down the House," *The Hackensack* (N.J.) *Record*, September 27, 1998; Alan J. Heavens, "Tune In, Fix Up: Some of Today's Hottest TV Shows Give Tips on Building and Remodeling," *Philadelphia Inquirer*, March 1, 1996; Bill Sharpsteen, "If I Were a Carpenter," *Los Angeles Times Magazine*, June 22, 1997.

Carolyn M. Goldstein

WGBH WGBH, Boston's public broadcaster, is one of the nation's leading producers of programming for public television and radio and a pioneer in educational and access technologies. Founded in 1951 and officially named the WGBH Educational Foundation, the organization encompasses New England's most powerful radio station at 89.7 FM, and three television stations, Channels 2 and 44 in Boston and Channel 57 in Springfield. A number of national, award-winning productions, among them, *Nova, This Old House, Masterpiece Theatre, Frontline, Mystery!* and *The World*, are created by WGBH. In fact, WGBH produces more of public television's primetime lineup than any other single PBS program source.

With radio and television signals that extend throughout most of New England, WGBH attracts a weekly audience of more than 2 million viewers and 375,000 listeners. The station's roots actually go back to 1836 and a bequest by John Lowell, Jr., whose family founded the New England textile industry. The bequest called for the creation of the Lowell Institute to provide free public lectures on philosophy, natural history, and the arts and sciences for the citizens of Boston.

In the mid-1940s, Harvard University President James B. Conant suggested that the Lowell Institute consider expanding its audience by broadcasting lectures over the radio. Difficulty in obtaining reliable air time, coupled with a rise in popular interest, prompted the fledgling Lowell Institute Cooperative Broadcasting Council to obtain its own station. In 1950 the Federal Communications Commission granted the council permission to operate WGBH, the call letters of which stand for Great Blue Hill, in Milton, where the station's transmitter was located.

Through the 1950s, the radio station carried programming that ranged from live concerts by the Boston Symphony Orchestra to the WGBH-produced *Prospects of Mankind*, for which Eleanor Roosevelt interviewed world leaders. WBGH radio is a charter member of National Public Radio (NPR). Channel 2 debuted in 1955, with modest offerings of concerts, lectures, children's programs, and live news, but in 1962, educational television's first star was born when Julia Child began broadcasting programs on French cooking. In 1968 WGBH began airing *Say Brother*, one of the nation's longest-running programs for African Americans. In 1970 *Evening at Pops* debuted, with Arthur Fiedler conducting the Boston Pops Orchestra. In 1971 WGBH first aired *Masterpiece Theatre*, on which host Alistair Cooke introduced American audiences to television adaptations of British classics, and *Morning pro musica*, a classical-music radio program hosted by Robert J. Lurtsema. WGBH pioneered captioning for deaf and hard-of-hearing viewers in 1972. *This Old House*, which began on WGBH in 1979, became public television's most watched half-hour series.

Over the years, WGBH television has specialized in the production of science and technology series, including *Nova, Race to Save the Planet*, and *The Secret of Life*, among others. More recently the station has produced programs focusing on history, including *Columbus and the Age of Discovery, War and Peace in the Nuclear Age, Vietnam: A Television History*, and *The American Experience*.

WGBH has also produced many television shows for children and teenagers, including *Zoom, Degrassi Junior High, Arthur*, and *Where in Time Is Carmen Sandiego?* In fact, the organization considers itself a resource for educators, as well as parents, and offers teacher's guides, interactive software, on-line services for teachers, and special versions of programs tailored to classroom curricula. College students view many WGBH television productions for credit. *Visions of America* is one of a growing series of WGBH multimedia learning tools combining a textbook, videotapes, videodiscs, and multimedia software.

WGBH radio distributes broadcasts to more than 350 noncommercial stations in the United States. Programs range from a daily news magazine, "The World," to historic recordings on Ray Smith's "The Jazz Decades" to music analysis on "A Note to You," produced in conjunction with Northeastern University. Through such popular, long-running broadcasts as *Morning pro musica* and *Jazz with Eric in the Evening*, hosted by Eric Jackson, WGBH radio continues to emphasize live performances and music that reflects the region's vibrant musical community.

Sandra Hackman, *The NOVA Reader: Science at the Turn of the Millennium* (1999); Ithiel de Sola Pool and Barbara Adler, *The Out-of-Classroom Audience of WGBH: A Study of Motivation in Viewing* (1963); Christopher Pullman, *WGBH, Boston: A Design Anatomy* (1981).

Louis Mazzari

Music and the
Performing Arts

Barbara L. Tischler, Section Editor

INTRODUCTION

The creation of a distinctive New England cultural aesthetic and the extent to which a distinctive New England style exists are subjects of much debate. But clearly many varieties of music and dance, from the most structured concert performances to the least formal everyday activity, have grown and thrived throughout the region. The history of music and dance in what is now New England does not begin, of course, with the Europeanization of the New World but rather with native forms. Native music in New England is best understood in context. Music, in the form of chanting, drumming, and rhythmic bell ringing, was an integral part of religious rituals and community ceremonies, as was dancing. Most music was monophonic, that is, without harmony; men and women often sang the same melodies an octave apart. Music of the Iroquois of upstate New York and northern Vermont and New Hampshire that accompanied work or religious observance was often antiphonal, with the same melodies sung as if in conversation by groups situated near each other.

The musicologist Bruno Nettl analyzed Native American music of the eastern region, extending from Labrador to the border of Florida. He observed that the music of the eastern tribes included short, undulating phrases, asymmetrical rhythmic patterns, and repetition of musical phrases. The average range of the songs Nettl described was about one octave, and many are preceded and followed by shouts and yells, often associated with religious rituals or preparation for battle.

Captain John Smith observed the musical activity of the natives he encountered in Virginia, which was similar to that of the northern Indian nations. He heard drumming, the playing of a pipe that sounded like a recorder, and rattles made of gourds and pumpkin shells in various pitch ranges. Describing the communal singing and chanting, Smith noted that the rattles, mingled with voices "sometimes 20 or 30 together, make such a terrible noise as would rather affright than delight any men." Similarly, ceremonies that chronicled the cycles of individual lives (births, marriages, deaths) or events in the life of the village (such as a good harvest) often featured dances and dramatic events, many of which had a specifically religious emphasis.

European settlers who came to New England in the 1620s brought with them definite ideas about the role of music in religious life. Opposed to opulent "popish" influences in worship that included complex polyphonous church music, the Puritan settlers relied on the simple chanting of the psalms from the *Ainsworth Psalter,* published in 1612 in Amsterdam. Such melodies as "Old Hundredth," still a part of the Protestant doxology, were simple and unornamented in order to highlight the devotional texts. Indeed, according to the preface to *The Whole Book of Psalmes Faithfully*

Translated into English Meter, commonly known as the *Bay Psalm Book* (1640), the early Congregationalists did not need fancy musical accompaniments to worship, as "God's altar needs not our polishings."

Because the Puritans valued sincerity of worship more than elegance of singing style, they did not feel it necessary to learn to read musical notation. Over several generations, as worshipers sang their individual, often embellished, versions of traditional psalm tunes, hymn singing in the meetinghouse became a cacophonous undertaking. The practice of "lining out" the melody or "setting the key" by a member of the congregation often led to unsingable results. Judge Samuel Sewall, better known for his standing in the community and his famous diary than for his musical ability, wrote, when charged with setting the key for the psalm one evening, "I knew not that I had the tune till I got to the 2d line . . . and the tune I guess'd at, was in so high a Key that I could not reach it." This, of course, was worship to the tune of a cappella singing only—musical instruments were not present in the meetinghouse, nor were any forms of dancing or other expressions of religious enthusiasm permitted.

Similarly, New England in general and Boston in particular were known for their hostility to drama and actors, who were not regarded as respectable citizens. In 1687 John Wing tried to establish a theater in his Boston tavern. The venture drew the disapprobation of such notables as the Reverend Increase Mather and Judge Sewall. As late as 1750, an attempt to perform Thomas Otway's *The Orphan* in Boston inspired not only a riot but also a local law prohibiting the staging of plays, which, according to the Boston selectmen, tended to "increase immorality, impiety and a contempt for religion." The law only heightened tensions between the citizens of Boston and occupying British troops, who occasionally staged plays for their own amusement. The soldiery contended that the English Licensing Act of 1737 took precedence over any colonial legal enactment and thus sanctioned their dramatic productions. In 1793 the legislative leaders of Boston repealed the law. By this time New Englanders were learning the latest steps of what came to be called contra dances from itinerant dancing masters. As hostility to theater, musical instruments, and various forms of dancing subsided, New England joined other regions of the country in welcoming actors from England, along with native-born performers and playwrights.

A century after the initial Puritan settlements in New England, a battle raged in the Congregational meetinghouse over the purity of worship versus the purity of congregational singing. In the 1720s many ministers joined the crusade for Regular Singing, in which worshipers learned the rudiments of note reading so that they could sing approximately the same tunes at the same time. Opponents of this innovation argued that Usual Singing could not be altered, no matter how much the resulting clamor assaulted the ear. To achieve the desired musical result of returning to the melodic purity of the original psalm chanters, proponents of Regular Singing advocated the formation of singing schools to teach congregants how to read music. Ironically, the call for a return to basic Puritan values supported a musical innovation that the founding settlers could not have anticipated and of which they probably would not have approved.

The singing schools of 18th-century New England were run by part-time singing masters who conducted classes that often evolved into recreational choruses. These groups sang new compositions created by the singing masters, who often used their musical craft to express religious and, by the 1770s, political sentiments relating to New England's revolutionary cause. One of the best-known singing masters was William Billings, a tanner by trade, who wrote a significant body of religious music in a style barely influenced by the European styles of his day. Billings was fiercely independent of prevailing musical styles and practices, declaring in *The New England Psalm-Singer* (1770) that "it is best for every composer to be his own Carver." Billings's contribution to the revolutionary effort included his famous anthem "Chester":

> Let Tyrants shake their iron rods,
> And slavery clank her galling chains.
> We fear them not, we trust in God,
> New England's God forever reigns.

The revolutionary cause also inspired numerous political satires and farces, most of which did not survive their cultural moment. The plays of Mercy Otis Warren (*The Adulateur*, 1773; *The Group*, 1775; *The Blockheads; or, The Affrighted Officers*, 1776; *The Motley Assembly*, 1779) and Hugh Henry Brackenridge (*The Battle of Bunkers-Hill*, 1776, and *The Death of General Montgomery*, 1777) presented the colonial perspective on the conflict with England with irony and wit. Similarly, loyalist satirists lost few opportunities to ridicule the colonists and cast aspersions on their desire for independence. The first known comedy written by an American and performed by a professional company was *The Contrast* (1787), by the Harvard graduate and Continental Army major Royall Tyler. After the play's premiere at New York's John Street Theatre, Tyler returned to the army to serve at the time of Shays's Rebellion. He later served as a justice on Vermont's supreme court.

The period immediately following the Revolution produced many assertions of American cultural exceptionalism, although the Americans who asserted most strongly the need for a unique American culture often claimed that the mechanism for achieving this goal lay in imitating European cultural models. American cities, including Boston, welcomed the efforts of immigrants to teach instrumental and vocal music, publish sheet music, import scores from Europe, and establish cultural institutions. Johann Christian Gottlieb Graupner came to Boston in 1797 to perform as an oboist at the Federal Street Theatre. He founded the American Conservatorio as a publishing venture in 1801. Oliver Ditson, one of the most famous New England music publishers, purchased some of the plates of this company. In 1809 Graupner also helped to found Boston's Philo-Harmonic Society dedicated to the study and performance of symphonies by Haydn and others and, in 1815, the Handel and Haydn Society for the performance of choral music.

Educated native-born composers also contributed to the development of an American musical aesthetic after the Revolution, but they generally did so in opposition to earlier models from composers like Billings, whose work they regarded as crude and unrefined. Andrew Law, Oliver Holden, and Samuel Holyoke, all New Englanders, advocated dignity in religious expression. They used the melodies of Handel, Haydn, and Mozart rather than the music of their self-taught American colleagues for the setting of devotional texts.

Law called American musical expression faulty. These men contributed important hymn collections to the American repertory, but they utilized the music of European masters rather than American imitators. John Hubbard, a professor of mathematics and moral philosophy at Dartmouth College, had no praise at all for the fuguing tunes and psalm settings of Billings's generation, and his *Thirty Anthems*, compiled in 1814 for use at Harvard College, included music by Handel, Henry Purcell, and William Byrd. For Hubbard, American music was not yet worthy of the attention of American scholars.

Secular music thrived in New England in the form of folk music in the hinterlands and small communities and a more formal and professional concert life in Boston. Graupner's additions to musical life in the city were followed by the founding of the Boston Academy of Music by George James Webb in 1833. This organization premiered seven of Beethoven's symphonies in Boston and presented concerts featuring the diverse musical talents of Ole Bull and Henri Vieuxtemps. The academy was succeeded in 1847 by the Musical Fund Society, also conducted by Webb, which, like the New York Philharmonic Society founded a few years earlier in 1844, was a musicians' cooperative.

By the 1820s theatergoers could attend productions at Boston's Tremont and Federal Theaters. Although New England's best-known playwrights, including Nathaniel Parker Willis and Epes Sargent, relocated to New York, stage plays no longer attracted the public antipathy they had in the pre–Revolutionary War years. One of the most popular character types of the early 19th century was the Yankee, the purveyor of homespun wisdom. Cornelius Logan's *The Wag of Maine* (1834) and *The Vermont Wool Dealer* (1838) showcased the wit and wisdom of a Yankee character unafraid to speak his mind on politics and social mores.

In music, Berlin's Germania Society first performed in Boston in 1849 and made the city its U.S. headquarters until the orchestra disbanded in 1854. A Germania flutist, Carl Zerrahn, remained in Boston and started his own concert series in 1857, which continued until 1863. The Civil War did not interrupt concert performances in Boston for long, with the founding in 1865 of a new orchestra, also conducted by Zerrahn, under the auspices of the Harvard Musical Association. This group performed concerts of serious symphonic music, eschewing the lighter touch of touring orchestras like that of Louis Antoine Jullien or the brass bands that contributed more to a wartime patriotic spirit than to the elevation of musical taste. The Harvard Musical Association concerts continued until 1882, when Major Henry Lee Higginson's Boston Symphony Orchestra became the predominant symphonic organization in the city.

One of the most important American advocates of high culture and good taste in music rather than native-born musical enthusiasm was John Sullivan Dwight, whose *Dwight's Journal of Music* emanated from Boston from 1852 to 1881. Dwight belonged to the generation of Bostonians that identified with Transcendentalism, Fourierism, and other reform causes. He wrote for the *Dial*, spent time at the utopian experiment Brook Farm, and published articles on culture in the *Harbinger*. Dwight believed in the transformative power of good music, by which he meant the symphonic music of acknowledged European masters. He hoped that the salutary effects of good music would reach the masses, who would then abandon their popular entertainments and "sounding demonstrations" in favor of the more elevating offerings of the concert hall.

Dwight did not get his wish. He criticized the patriotic excesses of the Mexican War and, on the Fourth of July in 1856, decried the "ringing of bells, the thunder of big cannons, the petulant plague of petty fire-crackers, the blare of numberless brass bands, and all the confusing patriotic noises that make up the celebrations of the nation's birth-day." Nevertheless, Americans, including proper Bostonians, liked patriotic displays, and it was the enormous orchestras and brass bands of Patrick Sarsfield Gilmore that captured the popular spirit in the post–Civil War period. On June 15–19, 1869, Gilmore produced the Great National Peace Jubilee and Music Festival "in Honor of the Restoration of Peace and Union throughout the Land." This event was sponsored by private and business donations and necessitated the construction of a 50,000-seat coliseum for performances by a 1,000-member orchestra, conducted by Ole Bull, and a chorus of 10,000. The event attracted President Ulysses S. Grant and members of his cabinet. A second World Peace Jubilee and International Music Festival in 1871, organized to mark the end of the Franco-Prussian War, was larger in scope, with an orchestra of 2,000 and a chorus of 20,000. But European wars proved less compelling to Bostonians, and the event did not attract the attendance or the enthusiasm of Gilmore's first venture. The festival did, however, include significant musical contributions from New Englanders. In addition to a full complement of national airs and novelty pieces, Gilmore programmed hymns by Lowell Mason, a "Festival Hymn" by Dudley Buck, and a chorus from "St. Peter," an oratorio by John Knowles Paine.

In the 19th century, theatrical performances thrived at the Boston Museum and the Boston Theatre, and the city had become a favored stop of American, English, and continental artists on tour. The city was also home to popular variety performances at Bowen's Columbian Museum and the Howard Athenaeum, which was the site of the first human fly act in 1868. By 1883 the Gaiety Museum had become home to variety acts as vaudeville took hold of the popular imagination. By the second decade of the 20th century, theater operators faced the threat of serious local censorship, first from the Watch and Ward Society and later by an official of the theater licensing division, giving rise to the popular phrase "banned in Boston."

Immigrant groups, from Germans to Irish to French Canadian, Greek, and Armenian, have contributed to the musical life of New England. By the middle of the 19th century, Irish communities were an important locus of musical activity. Some

Catholic parishes in Boston sponsored bands, either as recreational activities or as organizations that performed at temperance rallies and other community events. Gilmore's Boston Brass Band and Boston Brigade Band were known for their appearances at parades, where they performed "the soul-stirring airs of Old Ireland." Professional singers performed Irish songs before paying audiences, and Irish music was often employed to remind immigrants of their homeland and to inspire Irish patriotism (and anti-British feeling) in the United States.

Italian immigrant musicians contributed to a national craze for the operas of Gaetano Donizetti, Vincenzo Bellini, and Gioacchino Rossini in the years following the Civil War. Indeed, Italian, or Italianate, music (excerpts from Italian operas, selections sung in English, and new pieces composed in the Italian bel canto style) held sway in Boston's immigrant communities just as German romantic symphonies established their dominance in concert halls in Boston and throughout the country. In high culture, American composers eager to establish themselves as serious musicians preferred the German symphonic style.

The career of John Knowles Paine is important to the development of music in New England because he was the first professor of music at an American university and is identified as the primary representative of the Second New England School of so-called academic composers. Paine began his academic career as an unpaid lecturer at Harvard University in 1862. He developed a series of University Lectures in music and performed on the organ at Harvard's Appleton Chapel. Paine's appointment as a full professor of music at Harvard came in 1876, and he helped to ensure that music would have a secure place in the liberal arts curriculum. Paine performed organ recitals and composed music for events at the university throughout his Harvard career of 43 years. He also taught at Boston University, sat on the board of the New England Conservatory, and advised Major Higginson when he founded the Boston Symphony Orchestra. His music, like that of a number of his New England colleagues, was regarded as correct in terms of its adherence to the stylistic tenets of the European, specifically Germanic, 19th-century romantic style. John Sullivan Dwight wrote approvingly of Paine's contribution to American musical life, and Paine's students in both composition and music history continued the academic tradition he helped to establish in late-19th-century Cambridge. Other members of this New England school of composers were Amy Beach, George Whitefield Chadwick, Edward MacDowell, Horatio Parker, and Arthur Foote. Parker's most famous student, Charles Ives, made New England an integral part of his musical aesthetic—he identified with the New England Transcendentalists and set many of his works in New England towns.

The academic environment was also fertile ground for theater in New England, and the work of George Pierce Baker of Harvard University was instrumental in bringing drama into the halls of academe. Baker developed a graduate English composition course called "The Technique of Drama," whose students included Eugene O'Neill and Sidney Howard. Unable to persuade Harvard administrators of the validity of theater as a field of study, Baker left Cambridge in 1924 to help found the Yale School of Drama. Along with university theater, small-scale community theater

Amy Beach, ca. 1927

that eschewed the commercialism of Broadway but established professionalism as one of its goals emerged in venues all over the United States, including Boston's Toy Theatre and at the home of the Provincetown Players, established in 1915. After its first season on Cape Cod, the Provincetown Players moved to New York's Greenwich Village in 1916.

The establishment of the Boston Symphony Orchestra (BSO) in 1881 and the Boston Opera Company in 1909 demonstrated the influence of wealthy businessmen whose conservative tastes dictated performance style and choice of repertory in the early decades of the 20th century. Major Henry Lee Higginson was a member of a well-known banking family whose taste in music did not extend beyond the standard symphonic repertory. Higginson believed that good music and gifted musicians came from Germany. Rehearsals were conducted in German, and BSO programs typically included symphonies, overtures, concerti, and opera excerpts by composers whose origins and cultural aesthetic were German. In spite of his aspirations to the highest standards of culture, however, Higginson occasionally approved the inclusion of lighter music on BSO programs, and he made it a practice to make reduced price tickets available to students and working people.

That aesthetic was challenged in 1917 when the BSO, under the direction of Karl Muck, did not perform the "Star Spangled Banner" at a concert in Providence. The women of the local Chaminade Club launched a campaign against Muck, accusing him of undermining the American war effort, of expressing the high-handed, anti-American notion that the song (which did not become the national anthem until 1931) was not good music, and of declaring that the public had no business meddling in the orchestra's programming choices. Muck was arrested as an "enemy alien" and deported to Germany in 1919, and Higginson withdrew his support from the orchestra. In the post-Muck era Henri Rabaud was appointed principal conductor; more modern French and Russian music began to appear on the programs, along with an occasional piece written by an American.

The Boston Opera Company was established in 1909 through the financial auspices of the department store owner Eben D. Jordan, whose father had been one of Gilmore's major backers for the Peace Jubilees. Jordan poured more than $1 million of his own money into the construction of a 2,700-seat opera house built by the designer of Symphony Hall, Wallace Clement Sabine, a Harvard architect. Jordan guaranteed the company's deficit for its first three years of operation, and the Opera House became the home of standard repertory and a stopping ground for established stars, including Nellie Melba, Luisa Tetrazzini, and Leo Slezak. After Jordan's departure, poor management—including an expensive season in Paris in the spring of 1914—led to the company's bankruptcy in 1915. In 1916 and 1917, the Boston Grand Opera Company emerged to produce limited seasons. From 1917 to 1932, the Chicago Lyric Opera performed regularly in the Opera House, which was used as a theater and then demolished in 1958.

Starting in the 1920s, as American composers and artists pursued their study of modern music in Paris and Berlin, New England became a locus of modernist creative activity, particularly in dance. The Bennington School of the Dance was founded in 1934, only two years after the establishment of the progressive and experimental college in Bennington, Vt. The school helped to promote modern dance as an art and a form of aesthetic expression rather than as an aspect of physical education. Martha Graham, Hanya Holm, Doris Humphrey, and Charles Weidman—the Big Four of early modern dance—all put on important early work at Bennington. As modern dance matured, centers for study expanded, particularly during the summer months. The Connecticut College summer sessions in dance became another important site for dance creativity starting in 1948 and ending with the closing of the program in 1977. From its founding in 1981 until its demise in 2001, Dance Umbrella of Boston was well known for its modern dance performances as well as for its experiments in presenting dances in which able-bodied and disabled performers integrated movement and participated equally in the creative process.

Performances of new operas and experiments with new staging techniques often come from conservatory workshops and smaller opera companies. In 1942 Boris Goldovsky began staging unusual productions at the New England Conservatory Opera Workshop. Many of these productions were sung in English, and most focused on the ensemble rather than particular stars. In 1946 the New England Opera Theater emerged out of this educational and artistic experiment. In 1958 Sarah Caldwell, James Stagliano, and Linda Cabot Black formed the Boston Opera Company, which later changed its name to the Opera Company of Boston. This company presented many American premieres and gave rise to Opera New England, a touring company that presents opera throughout the region.

In 1976 the Boston Lyric Opera was founded principally to provide performance venues for singers who had been trained in New England. Starting in 1989, the company established its performances at Emerson College's Majestic Theatre; since 1998 it has performed at the Shubert Theatre on Tremont Street. Opera North, founded in 1981 in Hanover, N.H., serves as a training company and a venue for professional performances in northern New England. The company includes a Young Artist Program for singer-actors and a Production Intern Program. The Boston Early Music Festival includes performances of early opera in its repertory.

At the dawn of the 21st century, orchestral music can be found all across the region, not just in Boston, including orchestras in Waltham (the Brandeis University Orchestra), Brockton, Gloucester (the Cape Ann Symphony), Worcester (the Central Massachusetts Symphony), Concord, Littleton (Indian Hill Symphony), Jamaica Plain, Melrose, New Bedford, Wakefield (New England String Ensemble), Newton, Greenfield (Pioneer Valley Symphony), Plymouth, Wollaston (Quincy Symphony), Northampton (Smith College Student Orchestra), Springfield (Springfield Symphony and Western Massachusetts Young People's Symphony and Philharmonia), Salem (Symphony by the Sea), Hudson (Symphony Pro Musica), South Lancaster (Thayer Symphony Orchestra), and Amherst (University of Massachusetts Symphony Orchestra), Mass. Simmons College in Boston is the home of the New England Philharmonic, originally founded as the Mystic Valley Chamber Orchestra in 1976. The philharmonic is known for its performance of new music, its composer-in-residence program, and its Call for Scores competition, which encourages both established and new composers.

Contemporary concert life in New England has been marked by a decentralization of orchestral, choral, and operatic performances, as local communities have produced the talent and provided the resources for performing groups in smaller cities and towns. The BSO continued its dominant presence in the region with the inauguration of the Boston Pops and the summer season at Tanglewood, Mass., which offered a home to such American musical luminaries as Aaron Copland, Leonard Bernstein, and Seiji Ozawa, as well as to countless young musicians who received orchestral training there. Tanglewood also became a popular venue for folk and popular music concerts that drew large crowds to the pavilion and grounds in the Berkshires.

The Hartford Civic Concert Orchestra was organized in 1934 with funding from the Federal Emergency Relief Administration. This group did not perform during World War II, but the orchestra's administrative structure remained in place, and the renamed Hartford Symphony Orchestra (HSO) resumed a regular concert season in 1947. Arthur Winograd, the founding cellist of the Juilliard String Quartet, became the HSO's music director in 1965, serving in that capacity for 20 years, during which the orchestra instituted a Pops series, engaged internationally known soloists, and performed in Carnegie Hall in New York City. The HSO also performed with the Hartford Chorale, the Hartford Ballet, and the Connecticut Opera Company. Financial difficulties have plagued the HSO, but cooperation among local banks and insurance companies, the orchestra's board, and musicians has resulted in a workable structure in which musicians can continue to grow with the organization, both musically and professionally.

Music lovers looking for symphonic music outside of the state capital can find a variety of orchestras in Connecticut, ranging from ensembles that offer full-time employment for professional musicians to groups comprised of local musicians, teachers, and students. Connecticut symphonic organizations include Greater Bridgeport Symphony, Connecticut Chamber Orchestra (New Haven), Connecticut Philharmonic (Greenwich), Connecticut Youth Symphony (West Hartford), Eastern Connecticut Symphony and Youth Orchestra (New London), Fairfield Orchestra, Greenwich Symphony, Hartt Symphony Orchestra (Hartt School of Music), Meriden Symphony, Greater New Britain Symphony, New Haven Symphony, Norwalk Symphony and Youth Symphony, Orchestra New England (West Haven), Ridgefield Symphony, Stamford Symphony, Symphony on the Sound (Greenwich), Wallingford Symphony, Waterbury Symphony, Willimantic Orchestra, and Yale Philharmonic (New Haven).

Throughout New England, local orchestras offer entertainment and educational programs to enthusiastic audiences. The Portland (Maine) Symphony Orchestra, for example, offers monthly programs organized around a theme, ranging from celebrations of George Gershwin's birthday in 1998 to tributes to Duke Ellington, "A Symphonic Night at the Movies," and "Around the World in 80 Days" featuring music from the film of the same name along with other light pieces that evoked scenes from Australia, Romania, and Greece, and a *Mostly Mozart* program. Augusta and Bangor also have orchestras. Orchestras provide local programming in Nashua, Gilford, and Manchester, N.H.; Shaftsbury, Montpelier, and Burlington, Vt.; and Kingston and Providence, R.I.

Bands play an important part of local musical life in New England. Most high schools have bands that perform at sporting events and in concert, and highly skilled high school players can compete for places in All-State Bands. The New England Music Festival Association, founded in 1928, offers opportunities for young musicians to audition for places in a wind ensemble, orchestra, and concert chorus. The selected singers and players gather in a different New England city each spring, are housed in local homes, and spend several days rehearsing and performing. The festival attracts accomplished high school musicians and offers an opportunity for high-level performance under renowned conductors.

Many local communities have summer bands that play old-fashioned outdoor concerts for the public on summer nights. In Concord, Mass., the Concord Band has been in residence for 40 years, offering a regular concert season, competitions for young artists who perform with the band, and an annual winter festival. In addition, the Concord Band participates in the Boston Band Festival each spring. This all-day event is held at Boston's Faneuil Hall and showcases adult bands in New England. Music festivals abound in New England, including the Connecticut Early Music Festival held at Connecticut College in New London; the Arcady Music Festival in Bar Harbor, Maine, and the Bowdoin Summer Music Festival in Brunswick, Maine; the Cape and Islands Chamber Music Festival in Orleans, Mass., and the South Mountain Concerts in Pittsfield, Mass.; the Apple Hill Center for Chamber Music in East Sullivan, N.H.; Concerts by the Bay in Bristol, R.I.; and the Marlboro (Vt.) Music Festival and the Discover Jazz Festival in Burlington, Vt.

Contemporary theater and dance in New England take on both classic and experimental forms. In New Haven's Meat and Produce Terminal, the Long Wharf Theatre has been presenting performances in two intimate settings since 1965. Many of the Long Wharf Theatre's productions have staged successful runs on Broadway. Also in New Haven is Yale Repertory Theatre, created in 1966 as a professional theater connected to the Yale School of Drama. The Rep produces both classic and original works, presenting world premieres by August Wilson and Athol Fugard, among others. The Hartford Stage, located in what had been a supermarket building, has offered high-quality regional theater since 1964. The Boston Ballet, founded in 1958 as the New England Civic Ballet, grew out of E. Virginia Williams's ballet school in Malden, Mass., and was the first American ballet company to perform in China, traveling there in 1980. Local summer theater thrives at Theatre-by-the-Sea, located in Matunuck, R.I. The International Festival of Arts and Ideas in New Haven has been bringing cutting-edge performing arts groups to the area from around the world since 1996.

In the 1980s, Harvard and Boston Universities established theater companies. Harvard's American Repertory Company was founded in 1980 and performs in a technologically advanced space. Productions at the Huntington Theater, founded in 1982 by Boston University, place a special emphasis on adhering to original dramatic texts.

In the contemporary world, Native Americans have created and recorded music and performed dances from a variety of traditions and, in some cases, have created new works in a fusion process of interaction with European styles, blues, and even rock. The popularity of the traditional music and dance performances of the North Dakota–based Makoche festival in Somerville, Mass., attests to contemporary interest in modern music by Native Americans.

Since the early 1970s, Water Music/Mainstage has produced jazz concerts in Boston. Among its main booking venues is the Regattabar, which produces an an-

Emily Sailers and Amy Ray perform at the Newport Folk Festival, 1990

nual jazz festival. The most famous New England jazz venue is the Newport Jazz Festival, founded in Rhode Island in the summer of 1953. (The Newport Folk Festival followed in 1959.) Jazz performances take place at Tanglewood, and myriad local radio stations devote considerable amounts of programming time to many varieties of jazz.

Peter and Jane Benes, *New England Music: The Public Sphere, 1600–1900* (1998); Henry Cowell and Sidney Robertson, *Charles Ives and His Music* (1955); Charles Hamm, *Music in the New World* (1983); M. A. DeWolfe Howe, *The Boston Symphony Orchestra, 1881–1931* (1931); Charles Ives, *Essays Before a Sonata* (1961); Walter J. Meserve, *An Outline History of American Drama;* Frank Rossiter, *Charles Ives and His Music* (1975); Earl L. Stewart, *African-American Music, An Introduction* (1998); Barbara L. Tischler, *An American Music: The Search for an American Musical Identity* (1986); Barbara Ann Zuck, *A History of Musical Americanism* (1980).

Barbara L. Tischler

African American Music

West African music was highly developed when Portuguese navigators first made contact in the 15th century. Music, an important element of West African culture, was performed by professionals who held high standing in the community and whose play marked all aspects of life. In the colonies, slaves used their African traditions to create the work songs of the field and hearth. During the 18th century, as New England's slaves became integrated into the English communities in which they toiled, their skills as musicians broadened and diversified. In the small towns of colonial New England, the favorite form of social entertainment was dancing, and the most popular instrument was the violin, which was played by both black and white fiddlers. Black musicians provided much of the dance music for colonists of all classes; they played for country dances, balls in the towns, and frequently for dancing schools.

For black New Englanders, as for whites, singing became part of daily life in the 18th century and later, from work songs to tavern ballads to children's tunes to psalm singing at weddings and funerals. Black servants in New England often became part of the musical rituals of English families. Black musicians were mostly self-taught, but slaveholders also engaged slave musicians to teach their slaves and white servants a variety of instruments. Boston newspapers published listings of slaves for hire, many including references to slaves' highly sought-after musical abilities.

One of the best-known fiddlers in New England was named Sampson, slave of Colonel Archelaus Moore. For many years Sampson "afforded fine fun for frolicsome fellows in Concord (N.H.) with his fiddle on Election Days." Polydor Gardiner of Narragansett was a fiddler in great demand for parties and dances, as were Caesar, a slave fiddler of East Guilford, and Barzillai (Zelah) Lew, a fiddler of Groton, Conn. In Wallingford, Conn., Colonel Barker's slave Cato "ranked high as a fiddler in the community," noted the musicologist Eileen Southern, and provided music "for balls on the nights preceding the annual Thanksgiving and other occasions when dancing was expected. Most of the colonial villages and towns had access to some fiddler on whom they could rely to furnish music for their dances, and very often that fiddler was a black man, slave or free."

Unlike white southerners, English New Englanders allowed slaves their own festivals, the most important and raucous being 'Lection Day, a carnival originating in Connecticut around 1750 and lasting in some New England towns until the 1850s. These festivities included fifes, fiddles, clarinets, and drums, along with singing and dancing. Minstrel shows were established in New England by the 1840s. Minstrels popularized a rich vein of black music and developed a new approach to song and dance that influenced all aspects of American music in the next century. By the 1820s, African Americans in New England had not only adapted the hymns of the Anglican church but were prominent in the more boisterous religious revivals and Methodist camp meetings around the region.

In the years immediately following the Civil War, black spirituals became a highly developed and popular form in New England, as elsewhere, and later, in the 1890s, ragtime changed the dance habits of the world. The foxtrot, with its faster rhythm, replaced the waltz as the favorite ballroom dance, and the cakewalk, which developed from the old minstrel shows, became popular entertainment among whites everywhere. New England abolitionists played a significant role in making the nation aware of black song traditions, particularly in an influential collection, *Slave Songs of the United States* (1867).

According to the musicologist Thomas Hennessey, black music from 1890 to 1935 was not a revolution against the values of mainstream America but one of the few ways in which African Americans could receive recognition and be economically successful. Regional jazz "territory bands" appeared around the country, most with distinctive sounds, from New Orleans and Kansas City to Chicago and New York. Only New England lacked the sustained tradition to develop its own brand of black jazz, and throughout the swing era the region's contributions followed the so-called East Coast sound developed in New York and Philadelphia. And as national touring bands began to gain prominence on the radio, New England was most affected by New York's dominance of all the territories. The best black players moved to New York, and New England's regional style became, in fact, the New York style.

Although New England is not strongly associated with African American music, most of its forms are present in the region's black communities, including blues, gospel, and rhythm and blues. In the 20th century, individual performers captured national attention—Donna Summer, of Dorchester, Mass., for example, was an international disco star in the 1970s—and New England remains a viable market for jazz and black popular music. But the region's distinctive contributions to African American music have long been subsumed by the rise of the national media.

Thomas J. Hennessey, *From Jazz to Swing: African-American Jazz Musicians and Their Music, 1890–1935* (1994); John Rublowsky, *Black Music in America* (1971); Eileen Southern, *The Music of Black Americans: A History* (1997).

Louis Mazzari

Avedis Zildjian Company

The Avedis Zildjian (pronounced ZILL-jun) Company, with international headquarters in Norwell, Mass., is the world's preeminent manufacturer of cymbals. The company was founded in Turkey about 1623 by Avedis Zildjian I, a metalworker of considerable skill who discovered the process of treating copper, tin, and silver alloys to produce cymbals with superior sound qualities. The process remained a closely guarded family secret; the name Zildjian literally means "cymbal maker" in Turkish. The story of how the company came to New England centers on Avedis Zildjian III.

Born in 1889 near Constantinople (now Istanbul), Avedis Zildjian III arrived in Boston in 1908 and established a successful confectionery firm. His firm prospered, he married Alice "Sally" Goodale of Dorchester, Mass., and he became a U.S. citizen. He was therefore reluctant to uproot his life when, in 1927, his uncle Aram wrote from Constantinople to inform him that "except for me, you are the oldest living male member of the Zildjian family. As such, you are the next in line to become heir to the family's secret formula. It now becomes your responsibility to take over the secret that is your heritage."

A savvy businessman, Avedis realized that it made little sense to return to Turkey when most of the company's cymbals were, owing to the growth of jazz, destined for the American market. Avedis suggested that Aram undertake a journey to America, pass on the secret formula to him, and train him in the art of making cymbals. Aram agreed, and in 1929, Avedis and Aram established the Avedis Zildjian Company at 39 Fayette Street, Norfolk Downs, Mass.

Aram died shortly after returning to Turkey in 1930, but family members continued to operate the company's foundry in Constantinople until the American company acquired all international trademarks in 1983. In 1939 a fire destroyed the Norfolk Downs building and the company moved to North Quincy, Mass. A second factory opened in Meductic, New Brunswick, Canada, in 1968 under the name Azco Ltd.

In 1972 the main plant relocated to a state-of-the-art, 10-acre facility in Norwell, just in time for the company's 350th anniversary. Avedis Zildjian died in 1979, and his two sons, Armand and Robert, took over operation of the company. Within two years, however, the two parted ways, Armand retaining control of the Avedis Zildjian Company, and Robert gaining proprietorship of the Azco factory,

The original Zildjian factory, Norfolk Downs, Mass., with Avedis (front row, third from left) and Aram (front row, second from left), 1930s

which he renamed SABIAN—a composite of the names of his three children, Sally, Billy, and Andy.

Today, the Avedis Zildjian Company remains a family business, with Armand at its head and his two daughters, Craigie and Debbie, the 14th generation of Zildjians to manufacture cymbals, serving as executives. The company also has offices in the Los Angeles area and in Windsor, England, and manufactures drumsticks in an Alabama factory. With annual sales of more than $30 million, Zildjian employs 150 people worldwide and distributes its products to 110 foreign countries.

The Avedis Zildjian Memorial Scholarship program, established in 1979, includes support for students at such noted music schools as Juilliard, the Curtis Institute of Music, Oberlin Conservatory, Eastman School of Music, and the New England Conservatory. The company also annually provides educational clinics free of charge to thousands of students. In musical circles, the name Zildjian is synonymous with superior cymbals and represents a continuing family tradition of craftsmanship.

Avedis Zildjian Company, *The Avedis Zildjian Story* (1996); Thomas R. Navin, "World's Leading Cymbal Maker: Avedis Zildjian Company," *Bulletin of the Business Historical Society* (December 1949); Hugo Pinksterboer, *The Cymbal Book* (1993); Pars Tuaeglac, *Turkish Bands of Past and Present* (1986).

James A. Strain

Baker, George Pierce (1866–1935) Theater educator. Arguably the strongest individual influence on American theater in the first half of the 20th century, George Pierce Baker was born in Providence and graduated from Harvard in 1887. He joined the Harvard faculty the following year and remained until 1925, when he left to start the Yale School of Drama. Interested in the drama throughout his youth, Baker was active in undergraduate theater and drew inspiration from university president Charles W. Eliot's encouragement of the arts. Harvard's limited support for theater, however, frustrated Baker for decades. Although he became Harvard's first professor of dramatic literature, Baker was never able to realize his dream of having a fully equipped university theater there, although he was able to persuade the university to create the Harvard Theatre Collection in 1901.

Throughout his academic career Baker produced plays and pageants (most notably the extraordinary pageant *The Pilgrim Spirit*, commemorating the tercentenary of the Plymouth landing, which he wrote and directed in 1921). He even acted in Tavern Club theatricals in Boston and played the title role in *Marlowe*, by Josephine Preston Peabody, a former student. This play, which he also produced, inaugurated the auditorium of Radcliffe's Agassiz House in 1905. In that year he started the playwriting course at Radcliffe that would lead to his great achievements. The following year

he offered the course at Harvard; it would develop into the famous "47 Workshop," which became a laboratory for the staging of plays written by his students. Baker's methods brought immediate success; in 1906 Mrs. Fiske (Minnie Maddern Fiske) agreed to star in *Salvation Nell*, written by Baker's student Edward Sheldon. The play became a national sensation, and the Baker legend was born.

Eugene O'Neill was the only undeniably great dramatist to take Baker's course, and although O'Neill rejected the idea that Baker taught him anything, he nonetheless used Baker's method of constructing a detailed scenario for each play that he wrote. Among other playwrights who attended Baker's special courses were Sidney Howard, Philip Barry, S. N. Behrman, George Abbott, and Hung Shen (who took Baker's methods to China). John Mason Brown was inspired by Baker to give up on playwriting and become a critic—as was Heywood Broun. Thomas Wolfe, another failed playwright, caricatured Baker in his novel *Of Time and the River* (1935). Baker admitted only 12 students per year (the famous Baker's dozen), based on plays they submitted to him. His students were not only playwrights: Robert Edmond Jones, Donald Oenslager, and Lee Simonson are among the great designers he taught.

Baker's influence can be seen in such disparate endeavors as the American art theater movement, the Theatre Guild, the Group Theatre, and the Actors' Studio; many of his students, including Winthrop Ames, Theresa Helburn, Kenneth Macgowan, and Elia Kazan were involved in these important ventures. Recognized by 1925 as the most important force in the development of American drama, Baker gave up trying to persuade Harvard to build a theater and decamped to Yale, where Edward Harkness had endowed a university theater. There he served as head of its department of drama until his retirement in 1933. Baker wrote *The Development of Shakespeare as a Dramatist* (1907) and *Dramatic Technique* (1919) and edited various Renaissance, Restoration, and modern plays, collections of plays by his students, and unpublished letters by the 18th-century British theatrical actor-manager David Garrick (1907).

Baker was an inspiring mentor who gained satisfaction through the achievements of his students. His aesthetics were Emersonian; Baker once wrote, "Beauty may and must be combined with utility and power." Yet he countered this philosophy with a thorough knowledge of theater history and practice. A major criticism of Baker was his emphasis on technique, yet he clearly encouraged his students to do more than craft box office successes. While hagiographies of Baker have not served him well, his impact may be even greater than his contemporary admirers would have us believe, for Baker influenced the entire American theater and created the means and methods of teaching drama and theater in the United States.

John Mason Brown, *A Memorial* (1939); Wisner Payne Kinne, *George Pierce Baker and the American Theatre* (1954, repr. 1968); Stanley McCandless, "A Map of these United States Showing the Influence of George Pierce Baker," *Theatre Arts Monthly* 9 (1925).

Thomas F. Connolly

Beach, Amy (1867–1944) Composer, pianist.

Amy Beach was born Amy Marcy Cheney in West Henniker, N.H., the only child of parents with roots in colonial New England. She became the first woman in the United States to succeed as the creator of large-scale art music, earning an international reputation.

Beach began piano studies in 1873 with her mother, the amateur musician Clara Imogene Marcy Cheney. In 1875 Beach and her parents moved to Boston, where local musicians quickly recognized her gifts. At the age of seven, she played a solo by Chopin and her own "Mamma's Waltz" at a private recital, but when her performance was reviewed in the newspapers, her mother prohibited her from playing in public again. She thought it was unseemly for a young girl to be in the public eye. Beach continued her studies, however, and her later teachers Ernst Perabo and Carl Baermann, believing her to be a young second Mozart, encouraged her career aspirations.

In spite of her mother's objections, in 1883, at the age of 16, Beach made her formal piano debut with a Boston orchestra. Reviewers predicted she would have a stellar career as a concert artist, and for the next two years she played on the Boston concert circuit, making her debut with the Boston Symphony Orchestra (BSO) in 1885.

That same year her career took an abrupt turn: she married Henry Harris Aubrey Beach, a 43-year-old physician at the Massachusetts General Hospital, instructor at Harvard Medical School, and amateur musician. At the insistence of her socially prominent husband, she limited her performances to one or two benefit concerts a year, thus maintaining her status as a society matron. Dr. Beach relished his role as patron and mentor of his young wife, and although he declared that her future lay in composition he rejected the idea that she have a composition teacher; she spent the next 10 years teaching herself composition and orchestration by studying the old masters. During this time she regularly turned out new works, all issued by Arthur P. Schmidt, a pioneer publisher of music by composers of the Second New England School.

Boston's musical institutions were quick to feature Beach's work. Her soaring musical lines and sensitive matching of word to tone made her songs favorites of singers. Her first major work, however, was the Grand Mass, op. 5, for soloists, chorus, orchestra, and organ, which was produced to acclaim by Boston's Handel and Haydn Society in 1892. The BSO gave the premieres of her Symphony in E minor, "Gaelic," op. 32 (1896), and of her Piano Concerto, op. 45, with the composer at the piano (1900); the Kneisel Quartet gave the premiere and successive presentations of her Sonata for Violin and Piano, op. 34 (1897).

After her husband's death in 1910, Beach reestablished her career as a pianist with a grand European tour (1911–14). Her homecoming recital in Boston, attended by musical luminaries, was well received by critics. In 1916 and 1917 she traveled with the Kneisel Quartet, playing a repertoire that featured her Quintet for Piano and Strings, op. 67. Beach spent the second half of her professional life on tour, keeping homes in Hillsborough, N.H. (1916–44), on Cape Cod (1894–1944), and in New York (1930–44). She also returned annually to Boston to perform and to the MacDowell Colony (1921–41) in Peterborough, N.H., to compose. She died of heart disease in New York City and is buried in Forest Hills Cemetery, Boston.

Amy Beach became the flashpoint for the critical controversy over women as composers that began in 1880 and regularly flared up in newspapers and music journals between women's supporters and detractors. Beach composed more than 300 works, many written in the woods of New England, her favorite venue for creative work; indeed, nature itself is the subject of many of her compositions. Her reputation reached its peak between 1914 and 1918. Thereafter, in spite of her mainly unrecognized exploration of modernist musical techniques, she was increasingly perceived as an old-fashioned composer. Although mainstream support declined, women's and music clubs, colleges, and churches nationwide continued to present her music. The recent neoromantic movement has inspired a renewed appreciation of Beach as a composer of music of lyricism, harmonic richness, and emotional intensity.

Adrienne Fried Block, *Amy Beach, Passionate Victorian: The Life and Work of the American Composer (1867–1944)* (1998); Block, "A Veritable Autobiography? Amy Beach's Piano Concerto in C-sharp Minor, op. 45," *Musical Quarterly* 78 (1994); Block, *The New Grove Dictionary of Women Composers*, s.v. "Amy Marcy Beach" (1995); Block, "Why Amy Beach Succeeded as a Composer: The Early Years," *Current Musicology* 36 (1983).

Adrienne Fried Block

Berklee College of Music

The Berklee College of Music in Boston was founded in 1945 by Lawrence Berk, a graduate of the Massachusetts Institute of Technology, a musician, and a student of the music theorist Joseph Schillinger. The president until 2004 was Lee Eliot Berk, son of the school's founder, who headed the school since 1979. The current president is Roger H. Brown. Focused entirely on contemporary music, Berklee offers majors in performance, composition, music production and engineering, film scoring, music business and management, music synthesis, music education, and music therapy. In addition to offering the first major in songwriting and film scoring, Berklee considers itself the first school of music to wed a rigorous conservatory approach to the idiom of popular music, specifically jazz, which historically has had no systematized pedagogy.

The school's commitment to keeping up with musical technology—especially as that technology relates to music as a vocation—is reflected in its facilities, which include 11 recording studios, six film and video scoring and editing laboratories, six music synthesis studios, a computerized learning center that includes more than 100 computerized workstations and synthesizers, and a 1,200-seat performance center. Prominent alumni of Berklee include Quincy Jones, Melissa Etheridge, Alan Silvestri, and Branford Marsalis. Its current endowment is $67 million.

The Berklee College of Music is a pioneer school. Founded immediately after World War II, it attracted returning servicemen, many of whom comprised the 50-member student body in 1946. To date it has attracted students from more than 70 countries, and they make up 37 percent of its student body. Its mission, somewhat different from that of other conservatories, has remained unchanged since the beginning, emphasizing the popular and commercial aspects of the music field. The school is committed to producing graduates who can adapt to a career that is subject to evolving public tastes. Berklee currently offers a Master of Music in Jazz in collaboration with Boston Conservatory of Music, which incorporates several fields of study, including Jazz performance, Jazz Composition, and Jazz Pedagogy.

Nancy Uscher, *The Schirmer Guide to Schools of Music and Conservatories Throughout the World* (1988).

Helen M. Greenwald

Bernstein, Leonard (1918–90) Conductor, composer, pianist, educator.

Leonard Bernstein was born in Lawrence, Mass., to a family of Russian Jewish immigrants and grew up in Boston. He began private piano studies in 1928, was accepted by the Boston Latin

Leonard Bernstein chats with school students visiting Tanglewood, 1975

School in 1929, and enrolled at Harvard in 1935. Bernstein's musical experiences as an undergraduate foreshadowed the diversity of his later career; in addition to meeting the conductor Dimitri Mitropoulos and the composer Aaron Copland, Bernstein composed incidental music, directed musical theater, and contributed essays to the *Harvard Advocate*. Outside the university Bernstein continued his piano studies with Heinrich Gebhard and made his first professional appearance as a solo pianist.

In 1939 Bernstein graduated from Harvard and entered the Curtis Institute of Music in Philadelphia, graduating in 1941. Bernstein also received summer training at the Berkshire (now Tanglewood) Music Center (1940–41), where he studied with the conductor Serge Koussevitzky and nurtured his relationship with Aaron Copland. Within three summers the student became a teacher, and virtually every summer for 50 years Bernstein returned to Tanglewood to, as he said, "replenish my soul." Tanglewood reciprocated the affection by honoring Bernstein with elaborate birthday celebrations in his later years and with the dedication of the Leonard Bernstein campus in 1994.

In 1943 Bernstein became assistant conductor of the New York Philharmonic Orchestra. November 14 of that year proved to be one of the most auspicious moments of his career. With less than a day's notice, Bernstein was called upon to substitute for the ailing Bruno

Walter in a performance that was broadcast nationwide; his unqualified success as a conductor was hailed across the country.

In 1958 Bernstein became the first American-born music director of the New York Philharmonic (1958–69). Bernstein's conducting also took him to the preeminent opera stages of the world, and in 1953 he became the first American conductor to lead a regular performance at La Scala, in Milan.

As a composer Bernstein achieved the pinnacle of his critical and popular success with his musical *West Side Story* (1957). In other compositions for the theater, Bernstein worked within established genres such as ballet (*Fancy Free*, 1944) and opera (*A Quiet Place*, 1983), while also crafting such innovative works as *Candide* (1956) and *Mass* (1971). In his symphonic and chamber works Bernstein drew inspiration from literature, popular music, and his Jewish heritage to create compositions of spiritual urgency and physical vitality.

Through his televised *Young People's Concerts* (1958–73), Bernstein harnessed the medium of television to introduce a generation of Americans to classical music. In these broadcasts and a companion publication, *Young People's Concerts for Reading and Listening* (1962; rev. ed. 1970), he explained such topics as opera and modern music to his audience with the adroitness of a master teacher. Although Bernstein's international reputation reached its apex during the 1950s and 1960s, he remained a public figure. In 1972–73 he delivered

the Charles Eliot Norton lectures at Harvard (published as *The Unanswered Question: Six Talks at Harvard*) and in 1989 joined the international celebration of the demolition of the Berlin Wall with widely broadcast performances of Beethoven's Ninth Symphony in both East and West Berlin.

Bernstein gave his final concert in August 1990 with the Boston Symphony at Tanglewood. Within two months, at the age of 72, he died in New York City of a heart attack. Bernstein's achievements stand as monuments to the humanist impulse within American music.

Humphrey Burton, *Leonard Bernstein* (1994); David Schiff, "Re-Hearing Bernstein," *Atlantic Monthly* (June 1993); Nicolas Slonimsky, *Baker's Biographical Dictionary of Musicians* (7th ed.), s.v. "Bernstein, Leonard" (1984); *Bernstein: A Portrait* [sound recording] (Sony Classical, 1991).

G. Anthony Harne

Boston Pops   The Boston Pops Orchestra, which performs light classical and popular music in May and June, consists of the Boston Symphony Orchestra (BSO) minus the first-desk players. In addition to its Symphony Hall performances, the Boston Pops performs free concerts on the Esplanade—most notably, the nationally televised Fourth of July concert. It also performs a program of holiday concerts in the winter.

Precedents in other cities included free or popularly priced concerts in 19th-century New York and Chicago, London's Promenade (Proms) Concerts, and the various waltz band establishments of Vienna and Paris. When Henry Lee Higginson founded the BSO in 1881, he long insisted that his musicians play nothing but the finest works and under conditions conducive to attentive listening. In 1885, after three BSO seasons, Higginson yielded, and the concerts immediately attracted a wide audience, from women of Boston's elite families to sometimes rowdy Harvard boys.

In its early years, the Boston Pops had a succession of conductors, most of them European-born and many drawn from the Boston Symphony: the violist Max Zach, the violinist Gustav Strube, the violinist Timothée Adamowski. When Alfredo Casella resigned in 1929, Arthur Fiedler, a Boston-born violist in the symphony, offered his services. Fiedler had already established his conducting credentials and his appeal to audiences with two orchestral series he had founded: the Boston Sinfonietta, which toured throughout New England, and the Esplanade Concerts, held on the banks of the Charles River. Fiedler led most of the Pops' concerts, at home and on tour, for the next 47 years. Assistant Conductor Harry Ellis Dickson also led a significant

Arthur Fiedler conducting the Boston Pops, 1971

number of concerts, beginning in 1955. After Fiedler's death in 1979, the coveted position of conductor went to John Williams, the famed composer of award-winning musical scores for such movies as the *Stars Wars* trilogy and *Schindler's List*. In 1993 Williams became conductor laureate, and Keith Lockhart was named conductor in 1995.

Fiedler made the Boston Pops a regional and national institution through a relaxed atmosphere, a varied repertoire, canny public relations, and solid performances. The orchestra has made numerous fine recordings under Fiedler and later conductors. From 1953 Fiedler toured the United States with a separate Boston Pops Tour Orchestra. In 1938 Fiedler's Esplanade series became an official extension of the Pops' Symphony Hall season, and in 1939–40 the city constructed the Hatch Memorial Shell for the Boston Pops out of New Hampshire granite with a teak interior. Today, the Boston Pops Esplanade Orchestra includes few BSO musicians because most of the Esplanade season overlaps with the BSO's summer season at the Tanglewood Festival in Lenox, Mass. As of 1995, some 900,000 people per year attend the Pops and Esplanade concerts, and some 40 million viewers watch the telecasts, "Evening at Pops."

The format of a Boston Pops concert was successfully standardized under Fiedler into three segments separated by intermissions: lighter classical items for orchestra (such as an opera overture, ballet excerpts, a Liszt Hungarian Rhapsody); then a concerto (sometimes performed by a young local musician or

a member of an ethnic, professional, or alumni group that has bought a block of tickets for that performance); and finally a selection of short, popular orchestral items, such as Tchaikovsky's "None But the Lonely Heart," show tune medleys, or Beatles hits. Noted arrangers and composers of "novelty pieces" for the Boston Pops include Leroy Anderson, Peter Bodge, Morton Gould, Richard Hayman, and Jack Mason.

Over the years, works by such composers as Dimitri Kabalevsky, Benjamin Britten, Jean Françaix, and Aram Khachaturian have made their American premieres at Boston Pops concerts. Composers who have written pieces for the orchestra include Peter Maxwell Davies, William Bolcom, and John Corigliano. In recent years, a number of concerts have featured a segment with pop musicians like Judy Collins and Bonnie Raitt and celebrity narrators such as Julia Child and William F. Buckley.

Harry Ellis Dickson, *Arthur Fiedler and the Boston Pops* (1981); Johanna Fiedler, *Arthur Fiedler: Papa, the Pops, and Me* (1994); M. A. DeWolfe Howe, *The Boston Symphony Orchestra, 1881–1931* (1931); Carol Green Wilson, *Arthur Fiedler: Music for the Millions* (1968).

Ralph P. Locke

Boston Symphony Orchestra Founded in 1881 by Major Henry Lee Higginson, a Civil War veteran and member of a prominent Boston banking family, the Boston Symphony Orchestra (BSO) was one of the nation's first permanent resident symphony orchestras. As

a music student in Vienna, Higginson heard the symphonies of Mozart, Schubert, and Beethoven performed. Returning to Boston, he devoted the remainder of his life, and much of his fortune, to building an orchestra equal to Europe's finest—one dedicated to providing a considerable number of concert tickets at affordable prices. The first concert, conducted by Georg Henschel, was held in Boston's Music Hall on October 22, 1881. The inaugural season of 20 concerts was a huge success; within a few years, the BSO was recognized as a first-rank American orchestra. With its move into the newly constructed Symphony Hall in 1900, the BSO was hailed as one of the finest in the world. By offering lighter concerts (and later, *Young People's Concerts*), broadcasting, and recording, as well as through its notable association with the Tanglewood Festival and Berkshire Music Center, the orchestra became a leading force in democratizing the consumption of concert music in both the community and nation.

Until the end of World War I, the orchestra was led by a number of conductors schooled in the German tradition who engaged players from Europe, predominantly Germany. The repertoire drew from the widely accepted canon of the 18th and 19th centuries, although some of the early conductors bravely introduced unfamiliar music, to which audiences proved unreceptive. At the end of the 1884–85 season, Wilhelm Gericke, the second principal conductor of the BSO, instituted a summer season of lighter music. These Promenade Concerts, first conducted by Adolf Neuendorff, evolved into the ever-popular Boston Pops by 1900. With Arthur Fiedler at the helm beginning in 1930, the Pops would become a national institution and the most-recorded orchestra in the world. Its special Bicentennial concert (the Esplanade Concerts have been held annually on every Fourth of July since 1929 under the Boston Symphony's auspices) attracted 400,000 people to the east bank of the Charles River in 1976—the largest audience in the history of orchestral concerts. After Fiedler's death in 1979, his longtime associate conductor, Harry Ellis Dickson, who had also been directing the BSO's Young People's Concerts for 20 years, took over as interim leader for a very brief period. John Williams, the award-winning film composer, was appointed conductor in 1980, to be followed by the Pops' current director, Keith Lockhart, in 1994.

Among the conductors who led the BSO during its first few decades, Karl Muck came with the soundest reputation. With the rise of anti-German hysteria during World War I, however, Muck's eight glorious seasons came to an abrupt halt when his arrest as an "enemy alien" forced his resignation in 1918 along with two dozen German orchestra members.

The end of World War I marked the end of an era, and when Major Higginson felt he could no longer financially sustain the orchestra, he entrusted this responsibility to a board of trustees made up of nine prominent local citizens. Incorporated in the spring of 1918, the board took as its first responsibility the rebuilding of the orchestra's damaged musical structure. With the appointments of the French conductors Henri Rabaud and, a year later, Pierre Monteux, a French influence was felt in both the sound and repertoire of the orchestra. Monteux began to rebuild the orchestra to its former greatness. More native talent joined the orchestra as America became a more musically proficient country. Roland Hayes, the leading African American concert singer of the day, crossed the color line when he made his appearance with the orchestra on November 15, 1923. As the first African American to sing with a major American orchestra, he opened the doors to Paul Robeson, Marian Anderson, and others. Bostonians were introduced to the new music of Stravinsky and Ravel, as Monteux cultivated a new receptiveness among traditionally conservative Boston audiences.

Such innovative programming would continue when Serge Koussevitzky became principal conductor in 1924. Over the next 25 years, while Arturo Toscanini presided in New York and Leopold Stokowski conducted the Philadelphia Orchestra, Koussevitzky led the BSO to greater virtuosity while also championing new works, especially those of the American composers Aaron Copland, Howard Hanson, Roy Harris, Walter Piston, Samuel Barber, William Schuman, and Leonard Bernstein. Koussevitzky's orchestra became a workshop for what would become America's two most important generations of composers. In 1937, when the BSO took up its annual summer residence at Tanglewood, Koussevitzky assumed control of the Berkshire Music Center and transformed it into a school for young musicians. As the orchestra celebrated its fiftieth anniversary in 1931, it commissioned many noteworthy world premieres, among them Paul Hindemith's Konzertmusik for String and Brass Instruments (April 3, 1931), Sergey Prokofiev's Symphony No. 4 (November 14, 1930), Albert Roussel's Symphony No. 3 in G Minor (October 24, 1930), and Igor Stravinsky's *Symphonie de Psaumes* for orchestra with chorus (December 19, 1930).

During Charles Münch's tenure (1949–62), the season expanded greatly, and the orchestra made its first European tours, becoming the first American orchestra to play in the Soviet Union. Seventy-fifth Anniversary Commissions, under Münch, would produce the world premieres of some of America's best symphonic works by Piston, Schuman, and Sessions. The Boston Symphony Chamber Players, established in 1964 under the next music director, Erich Leinsdorf, is today the world's only permanent chamber ensemble composed of a major orchestra's principal players. Seiji Ozawa was the first Berkshire Music Center alumnus to lead the orchestra. Under his leadership, the orchestra increased its commission of new works, which included such important world premieres as Leonard Bernstein's Divertimento for Orchestra (September 25, 1980), Roger Sessions's Concerto for Orchestra (October 23, 1981), and Michael Tippett's *The Mask of Time* (April 5, 1984). Maestro Ozawa retired after the 2001–2 season, thereby making his tenure of 27 years with the orchestra the longest in its history. In 2002 James Levine took over as conductor.

The Boston Symphony Orchestra continues to be a source of civic achievement and national pride. The duration and diversity of its season and its property holdings in both Boston and Tanglewood make its budget larger than that of any other American orchestra. The realization of Major Higginson's dream of bringing quality classical and contemporary music to diverse audiences has led the federal government to designate the venerable Boston Symphony Orchestra a national treasure.

Janet Baker-Carr, *Evening at Symphony: A Portrait of the Boston Symphony Orchestra* (1977); M. A. DeWolfe Howe, *The Boston Symphony Orchestra 1881–1931* (1931); H. E. Johnson, *Symphony Hall, Boston* (1950); Louis Snyder, *Community of Sound: Boston Symphony and its World of Players* (1979).

Geoffrey S. Cahn

Bread and Puppet Theater
The Bread and Puppet Theater flourishes on a former dairy farm in the foothills of Vermont's Green Mountains. Founded by the German-born sculptor Peter Schumann in 1963, the Bread and Puppet Theater's unique visual and performance style has various influences: puppet traditions and other popular performance forms from around the world; political theater in its numerous varieties; and avant-garde theater techniques from Europe and America. Schumann has eschewed the commercial theater world by bringing his art directly to ordinary people in the streets of small towns and cities in the Americas, Europe, North Africa, Asia, and Australia; and by welcoming audiences to the outdoor and indoor performing spaces at Bread and Puppet's farm in Glover, Vt.

Bread and Puppet's various shows include small-scale street performances, indoor proscenium-arch productions, giant indoor and outdoor spectacles incorporating local volunteers, and street processions and parades. Bread and Puppet audiences often do not pay to see a performance, but are instead drawn to it by happenstance. A first experience of Bread and Puppet may be a parade in which hundreds of puppeteers dressed in white fill the streets waving brightly colored banners and cavorting in large animal masks. Schumann typically presides on 12-foot stilts as Uncle Sam. Gigantic puppets made of papier-mâché, cloth, and wood sway high above spectators' heads. Accompanied by the rhythm of handmade instruments and a brass band, a succession of symbolic dramas unfolds. At most Bread and Puppet performances, sourdough rye bread baked by Schumann is broken and shared. For Schumann, the sharing of bread is both a communal ritual with spiritual resonance and a reminder that things as simple as bread and puppet theater are essential.

During the 1960s, Schumann and his friends made puppet shows and parades about life on the Lower East Side of Manhattan. At that time, important social issues for the Bread and Puppet Theater were housing, rent strikes, voter registration, and the Vietnam War. Schumann started his artistic activities by studying dance in the burgeoning performance scene at Judson Memorial Church on Washington Square, but felt compelled to leave the insular world of high art and perform his puppet and mask shows in the streets. Bread and Puppet began to use oversized puppets in protest parades, vigils, and street shows. In 1970 Schumann, his wife Elka, their five children, and his core company moved to Vermont, first as artists-in-residence at Goddard College in Plainfield and then to the theater's present home in the Northeast Kingdom. Rural living and the Vermont landscape itself have shaped the themes and imagery of Bread and Puppet performances, while political topics from the war in Bosnia to the World Bank to New York City's community gardens are common themes.

From 1971 through 1998, the central focus of the Bread and Puppet year was *Our Domestic Resurrection Circus*, an annual outdoor spectacle performed for two days in August on the Bread and Puppet Farm. Each performance drew an audience of 20,000 to 30,000. The *Circus* began, in Schumann's words, as "an effort to find a new way of doing circus that is more human, . . . not merely a collection of extraordinary feats arbitrarily mixed together, but something that becomes a story of the world circus." Beginning at noon and continuing until 10 P.M., the *Domestic Resurrection Circus* presented audiences with abundant puppet shows, from solo performances during

Giant Washerwomen and Garbagemen at Bread and Puppet Theater's Our Domestic Resurrection Circus, *Glover, Vt., 1980s*

the sideshow period to giant pageants incorporating hundreds of audience volunteers. Visitors toured the Bread and Puppet Museum, a 19th-century barn filled from floor to rafters with tableaux of veteran puppets, or wandered into the pine forest to see sideshows. In the late afternoon, the audience gathered in the natural amphitheater as brightly painted school buses with puppeteers on top waving celebratory banners came over the hill. The quiet landscape filled with the jazzy sound and action of a three-ring circus of puppets. Recognizable characters played year to year, reconstructing their past lives in new incarnations; after 30 years, the washerwomen and garbagemen had become archetypal figures. The pageant unfolded at twilight and ended with the burning of a gigantic puppet against the night sky.

The enormous popularity of the *Circus* proved to be its undoing, as the annual influx of thousands of spectators put a strain on the resources of Bread and Puppet and the Glover community. Bread and Puppet ceased performing the event in 1998, but since then it has been performing smaller *Circus* events on Sundays in the summer. These continue the intense creativity of Schumann and his Bread and Puppet colleagues and have helped the theater find new audiences.

Bread and Puppet's influence reaches far beyond the community that gathers to make and share in its ritual celebrations. Hundreds of puppeteers and puppet theaters have been inspired by Bread and Puppet's embrace of a simple, inexpensive, and direct theater that responds to immediate global and community concerns. Schumann's Bread and Puppet The-

ater evocatively challenges American and international theater with the power of visual imagery, gesture, and sound to reflect on important social and political issues of the past and present.

John Bell, *Landscape and Desire: Bread and Puppet Pageants in the 1990s* (1997); Stefan Brecht, *Peter Schumann's Bread and Puppet Theater*, 2 vols. (1988); Susan Green, *Bread and Puppet: Stories of Struggle and Faith from Central America* (1985); Peter Schumann, *The Radicality of the Puppet Theater* (1990).

F. Elaine Williams and John Bell

Caldwell, Sarah (1924–) Conductor, producer. Best known as the founder of the Opera Company of Boston (OCB), Sarah Caldwell was born in Maryville, Mo., and at-

tended the University of Arkansas. She studied violin with Richard Burgin and viola with Georges Fourel at the New England Conservatory in Boston, graduating in 1946. While she was a fellowship student at Tanglewood, the Boston Symphony Orchestra conductor Serge Koussevitzky inspired her to conduct, and in 1947 Caldwell became chief assistant to the conductor and opera producer Boris Goldovsky at the New England Conservatory. Caldwell led the Boston University Opera Workshop from 1952 to 1960 and founded the Boston Opera Group in 1957. Renamed the Opera Company of Boston in 1965, the group was housed (beginning in 1978), in the B. F. Keith Memorial Theater on Washington Street.

Caldwell has conducted in major cities around the world. In January 1976, she was the first woman to conduct New York's Metropolitan Opera, leading the company in a performance of Giuseppe Verdi's *La Traviata*, and in 1975 she became the second woman to conduct the New York Philharmonic. Caldwell also has led the Pittsburgh Symphony Orchestra, the Indianapolis Symphony Orchestra, and the Boston Symphony Orchestra. Her participation in the Soviet-American festival "Making Music Together" (1988) resulted in her appointment as principal guest conductor of the Ural Philharmonic in Yekaterinburg and marked the beginning of her ongoing relationship with Russia. Caldwell has made it her mission to bring American music to this once closed city, and in 1994 she led the orchestra before a Moscow audience that included Boris Yeltsin and Bill Clinton.

In November 1975, *Time* magazine dubbed Caldwell "Music's Wonder Woman." Described variously as creative, innovative, controversial, impulsive, and driven, she is noted

Sarah Caldwell conducting a rehearsal, 1977

for the intensity of her vision. In preparation for the 1971 premiere of Roger Sessions's *Montezuma*, for instance, Caldwell traveled to Mexico in search of authentic models for such production details as Montezuma's throne and the proper Aztec "whoop." Caldwell has always dealt creatively with adverse conditions, perhaps most notably when, forced to stage Gaetano Donizetti's *La fille du régiment* in an athletic facility at Tufts University, she engaged the bleachered audience in the event by having them display, on cue, the French *tricouleur* on large colored cards. In Boston, Caldwell has overseen premieres of Sergey Prokofiev's *War and Peace* and Arnold Schoenberg's *Moses und Aron* as well as the original versions of Modest Mussorgsky's *Boris Godunov* and Verdi's *Don Carlos*.

Caldwell's dynamism has drawn many of the world's greatest singers to perform for the OCB, including Marilyn Horne, Placido Domingo, Beverly Sills, and Joan Sutherland. Although she had established the OCB on a shoestring budget, inadequate financial support for artistic needs and insufficient funding for building maintenance eventually took their toll; in 1990 the Opera House on Washington Street closed; it reopened in 2004.

Sarah Caldwell remains an important figure in the performing arts, especially through her successful efforts to rehabilitate Boston's Opera House. Her current activities include working with the Library of Congress to restore and preserve on colored microfilm precious documents such as the Schoenberg manuscripts and the Prokofiev archives in England and Russia. In January 1997, in recognition of her lifetime achievements, President Bill Clinton and First Lady Hillary Rodham Clinton awarded Sarah Caldwell the National Medal of the Arts.

Sandra Burton, "Music's Wonder Woman," *Time* (November 10, 1975); Susan Larson, "Homeless in Boston," *Opera News* (September 1996); *The New Grove Dictionary of Opera*, s.v. "Sarah Caldwell" (1992).

Helen M. Greenwald

Choral Societies New England's choral societies originated in the late 18th century. Some emanated from the singing school movement, but singing schools were usually connected with churches and intended to help improve church music. The choral society was a group of amateurs, usually unconnected to any organization, who gathered to rehearse and publicly perform choral music.

Two of New England's oldest choral societies, however, are examples of groups that did have their genesis in singing schools. The Stoughton Musical Society (now known as the Old Stoughton Musical Society), founded in Stoughton, Mass., in 1786, owes its beginnings to singing schools led by the composer and teacher William Billings, as did a shorter-lived Musical Society in Concord, N.H., that was incorporated in 1799. At first, much of Stoughton's repertoire came from the singing school tradition. Even in the second half of the 19th century the society was known as a leader in the revival of this "ancient music," performing it at such venues as the 1893 World's Columbian Exposition in Chicago. By this time, however, the more standard repertoire of the Stoughton Musical Society included, as it does today, European music and works by contemporary American composers.

By the late 18th century, immigrant musicians like William Selby of Boston began introducing American audiences to the choral music of European composers. Interest in this repertoire flourished in the cosmopolitan atmosphere of postrevolutionary Boston, where the Handel and Haydn Society was formed in 1815. The society's first concert featured excerpts from oratorios by George Frideric Handel and Franz Joseph Haydn, but the society soon began to perform entire works by its signature composers. In 1818 the society gave the first complete performance of Handel's *Messiah* for an American audience and presented Haydn's *Creation* in 1819. Subsequent concerts included oratorios and selections by various composers; Wolfgang Amadeus Mozart entered the repertoire in the 1820s, Ludwig van Beethoven in the 1830s, Felix Mendelssohn and Ludwig (Louis) Spohr in the 1840s, but no works by Johann Sebastian Bach were performed until the 1870s.

Boston was not the only New England community attracted to concert music. As early as 1807 undergraduates at Dartmouth College in Hanover, N.H., formed a Handel Society Chorus under the direction of Professor John Hubbard. Incorporated in 1816, the Psallonian Society of Providence, founded by the composer, teacher, and singer Oliver Shaw, gave concerts of the music of Handel and others until its dissolution in 1833. The popularity of various composers is reflected in the names of many early choral societies. Bath, Maine, had a Handel Society in 1821, and Portland had a Handel and Haydn Society from 1828 to 1831. A Beethoven Society was founded in Portland in 1819 and lasted until 1826, and its first concert included works by Handel, Mozart, Vicenzo Pucitta, and, of course, Beethoven. Beethoven Societies could be found in Taunton, Mass. (founded 1821), Providence (founded 1846), Hartford (founded 1857), and at Yale University in New Haven, Conn. (founded 1847). The leading choral group in Worcester, Mass., for some years was the Mozart Society, founded in 1858 by the singer and music teacher Edward B. Hamilton. It merged with the Beethoven Choral Union to form the Worcester Choral Union in 1871; its present-day successor is the Worcester Chorus.

From 1850 to the present, choral societies have proliferated in New England's cities and towns. In northwestern Connecticut several such choruses, founded in the 1870s and 1880s, merged in 1899 to form the Litchfield County Choral Union, which has presented a number of large-scale choral works. The Oratorio Society of Concord, N.H., held the first of several annual festivals in 1901. In New Haven, Conn., an Oratorio Society, directed for several years by Horatio Parker, was formed in the early 1900s, and in 1918 Professor David Stanley Smith of Yale University founded the city's Choral Art Society and became its long-time director. Men's choruses became popular in the latter part of the century and included the Apollo Club of Boston (founded 1868), the Orpheus Club of Springfield, Mass. (founded 1874), and the Choral Club of Hartford (founded 1907).

Many choruses were short-lived, but in Boston present-day survivors include the Cecilia Society, founded in 1874 by Benjamin J. Lang, and the Apollo Club, although the emphasis of the latter has shifted from classical to more light and popular repertoire, while the former now leans in the direction of early music. The Handel and Haydn Society, directed by Christopher Hogwood since 1986 and pared down to a select professional chorus and orchestra, likewise leans toward the baroque period, although its repertoire includes romantic and contemporary works.

The Boston area today boasts many small and often specialized choruses, most founded within the past 30 years. Norumbega Harmony (founded 1976) is devoted solely to the performance of singing school and "Sacred Harp" music. A few choruses, such as Youth Pro Musica and the Treble Chorus, are expressly for children. One of Boston's larger choral groups is the Boston Gay Men's Chorus (founded 1982), which has commissioned many new works for male voices.

One of the newer and more visible groups in Connecticut is Concora (founded 1980), a regional chorus based in the Hartford area. The Rockingham Choral Society has been active since 1957 in the Portsmouth, N.H., area, and the Newburyport Choral Society, founded in 1935, is a large regional chorus in Essex County, Mass., as is Chorus North Shore (founded 1931 as the Rockport Community Chorus). The 200-member Community Chorus in Westerly, R.I., founded in 1959 by director George Kent, boasts its own building, a summer camp in New Hampshire, and a repertoire ranging from Renaissance to contemporary, including several premiere performances. It began touring abroad in 1981 and, unlike most other choruses of its size, welcomes children into its membership.

Choral music has been a part of New England life for more than two centuries, and today's societies usually represent a cultural cross section of the communities in which they are located.

George T. Edwards, *Music and Musicians of Maine* (1928); Louis C. Elson, *The History of American Music* (1904); Frances Hall Johnson, *Musical Memories of Hartford* (1931); Lemuel W. Standish, *The Old Stoughton Musical Society* (1928).

Barbara Owen

Classical Music In the 1830s and 1840s, the notion spread from Europe that some music had a special spiritual capacity to uplift audiences. The music of a few European composers was considered sacred because of its abstract and lofty quality; such music was called classical and encompassed at first the instrumental works of Haydn, Mozart, and Beethoven. Soon the music of many other composers was included.

The Boston Academy of Music was the instrument of change in New England attitudes. It was founded originally as an institution to improve the quality of music in Boston churches, and Samuel Atkins Eliot, later mayor of Boston, transformed it when he became its president in 1835. He disbanded the choir, established an orchestra, and lobbied for a higher status for abstract music. The Boston academy introduced many in New England to symphonic music. Eliot's efforts were furthered by John S. Dwight, who argued the importance of instrumental music first in the *Dial* and the *Harbinger* and then in his own *Dwight's Journal of Music*.

Before the rise of a shared concept of classical music in the 1830s, various singing societies presented elaborate choral programs, including Handel's *Messiah* and Haydn's *Creation*. The Boston Handel and Haydn Society, the most important of those groups, is still active today. Johann Gottlieb Graupner, one of several immigrant musicians to settle in Boston after theaters were allowed in 1792, helped found the Philo-Harmonic in 1809. It began to give public concerts in 1819, seeking to create a serious atmosphere for instrumental music, but remained active only until 1824. Opera, frowned upon in New England because its Puritan heritage led it to associate opera with carnal themes and Catholic churches, had little importance prior to the Civil War.

Contributing to the rise of classical music was the appearance of many touring European virtuosi in the 1840s, in particular the violinists Ole Bull and Henri Vieuxtemps and the cellist George Knoop. Before their arrival, few in America were aware of the potential of these instruments. Public chamber music concerts began at this time; the first string quartet performances occurred in 1844 under the direction of the Harvard Musical Association. Other chamber groups soon followed, the most important being the Mendelssohn Quintet, founded in 1849.

The success of the orchestra of the Boston Academy of Music fostered rival organizations. The Boston Philharmonic Society was founded in 1843, and the Musical Fund Society in 1847. In 1849, the Germania Musical Society, a German instrumental ensemble that toured throughout the United States, appeared. Boston became its unofficial headquarters, and when it disbanded in 1854 many musicians remained. Carl Zerrahn, its flutist, started an orchestral series in 1857, and in 1865 the Harvard Musical Association began to sponsor orchestral concerts.

By 1880 earlier orchestras appeared stale and moribund. Their concerts were irregular, their personnel unsteady, and their performances uninspired. Henry Lee Higginson, a member of a wealthy Boston family, was passionately interested in music, but his position precluded a musical career. Seeing the need for a "full and permanent orchestra," he established the Boston Symphony Orchestra (BSO) in 1881. It gave its first concert on October 22, 1881, under Georg Henschel, who served as BSO conductor until 1883. Higginson personally underwrote the expenses of the orchestra and from 1881 until he retired in 1918 retained autocratic control over it. He personally managed even the minutest details. He chose personnel and demanded that they sign exclusive contracts promising to perform in no other ensemble. He expected long rehearsal time. The effort paid off, and the BSO today remains one of the country's premier ensembles. Recent conductors have included Pierre Monteux (1919–24), Serge Koussevitzky (1924–49), Charles Münch (1949–62), Erich Leinsdorf (1962–69), William Steinberg (1969–72), Seiji Ozawa (1972–2002), and James Levine (2002–).

In 1909 Eben D. Jordan, Jr., attempted to duplicate Higginson's feat in opera. With Henry Russell he founded the Boston Opera Company, built a 2,700-seat opera house, and underwrote productions. The company lasted only five years, and after that there was no permanent opera company in Boston until the Opera Company of Boston, originally called the Boston Opera Group, was formed in 1958.

New England has been fertile ground for composers, and historians identify a First and Second New England School. The first school consisted of late 18th-century "tunesmiths" who composed almost exclusively vocal music for church and singing schools. By far the most important was William Billings, who also wrote music celebrating the patriot revolutionary cause.

The Second New England School consisted mostly of academics who lived in Boston in the late 19th century. John Knowles Paine was the acknowledged dean of this group. Other members were Arthur Foote, George Whitefield Chadwick, Amy Beach, Horatio Parker, and Daniel Gregory Mason. Chadwick's and Beach's music in particular stand out. Beach had an unusual career; an exceptional pianist and one of the few outstanding women composers in 19th-century America, she curtailed her musical activities when she married in 1885 but resumed them fully after the death of her husband in 1910.

Although not usually labeled as such, a third New England school—modernists who wrote in a highly experimental, dissonant style—appeared in the early 20th century. Charles Ives, Carl Ruggles, and Charles Seeger were pioneering New England avant-garde composers, although Seeger was more important as a theorist of modernism. Ives, from Danbury, Conn., was arguably the most significant composer in American musical history. He earned his living as a highly successful insurance agent and until 1921, when his compositional career was virtually over, seldom attempted to put his music before the public.

The close ties between the composers of the Second New England School and educational institutions reflect the importance of education in the cultural life of New England. The Harvard Musical Association, founded in 1837, grew out of an undergraduate musical society, the Pierian Sodality, although the association soon severed its ties with Harvard because music was not considered a legitimate subject of study. That soon changed, and in 1862 Harvard began to offer instruction in music, and this was followed by the appointment of John Knowles Paine to the first professorship in music in the United States in 1875. In 1867 the New England Conservatory was founded. Today, musical offerings at several colleges and universities contribute significantly to the high level of musical activity in Boston.

Two centers of musical activity outside of Boston were Hartford and New Haven, Conn. Educational institutions assumed leading roles in the musical activities of both cities. The Hartford Conservatory, originally the Hartford School of Music, was founded in 1890, and the Hartt School of Music, now part of the University of Hartford, in 1920. The Yale

School of Music was created in New Haven in 1894, although a musical society existed at Yale from 1812. Horatio Parker was the first professor and dean at the Yale School of Music; its later faculty included the refugee German composer Paul Hindemith (1940–53).

Located halfway between Boston and New York, Hartford attracted many virtuosi and traveling orchestras in the 19th century. Its first major orchestra, the Hartford Philharmonic (1899–1924), was followed by the Hartford Symphony Orchestra in 1934. Prominent musical activity in New Haven began when Gustave J. Stockel founded the Mendelssohn Society in 1858. Morris Steinert, after failing to establish a permanent orchestra in 1867, established the New Haven Symphony Orchestra in 1894, which is still active.

Summer music festivals have been important to New England since the early 19th century. The earliest festival, the Promenade and Concert performances at the Exchange Coffee House in Boston in 1810, followed the 18th-century European model of garden concerts and entertainment. The first modern festival to survive was the Worcester (Mass.) Music Festival, established in 1858, featuring choral music. In 1899 the Norfolk (Conn.) Festival was founded, and today is part of Yale University. Jacob's Pillow, featuring modern dance, was founded in 1930.

The largest summer festival today is Tanglewood, which began in 1934 as the Berkshire Festival. In 1936 the Boston Symphony Orchestra became the resident orchestra, and in 1945, following lean years because of the war and conflict between the Berkshire Festival and BSO trustees, the Berkshire Festival turned all rights and assets over to the orchestra. Today, Tanglewood, which features an array of educational programs as well as a concert series, is the summer home of the BSO.

Michael Broyles *"Music of the Highest Class": Elitism and Populism in Antebellum Boston* (1992); John S. Dwight, "The History of Music in Boston," in *The Memorial History of Boston*, ed. Justin Winsor (1881); M. A. DeWolfe Howe, *The Boston Symphony Orchestra: An Historical Sketch* (rev. ed. 1978); Herbert Kupferberg, *Tanglewood* (1976); Luther Noss, *A History of the Yale School of Music, 1848–1970* (1984); Charles R. Nutter, *The Harvard Musical Association 1837–1937* (1937); Nicholas Tawa, *The Coming of Age of American Art Music: New England's Classical Romanticists* (1991).

Michael E. Broyles

Conservatories

New England hosts several major schools of music and a number of smaller conservatories and schools devoted to the education and development of musicians as performing artists, teachers, and scholars. New England's growing support for orchestral music in the second half of the 19th century led to the establishment of important conservatories; the region's distinguished educational institutions also contributed to this trend. The conservatories have attracted a distinguished music faculty and performers, and their graduates influence music beyond the region.

Many New England conservatories enjoy international reputations and boast long traditions. Of them, the Boston Conservatory, founded in 1867 by Julius Eichberg, is among the oldest. Although founded in the same year as the New England Conservatory, which was incorporated in 1870 under the laws of the Commonwealth of Massachusetts, the Boston Conservatory was not incorporated until 1896. The Boston Conservatory, like the Juilliard School in New York, also supports programs in dance and drama. Eben Tourjée, the founder of the New England Conservatory, was also the first dean of Boston University's School of Music and was responsible for codifying that institution's goals in 1873. In Connecticut, the Hartt School of Music, established in 1920, offers undergraduate and graduate degrees in performance, composition, dance, jazz, music history, music management, and production and technology of music. Since 1948 it has housed the Institute of Contemporary American Music. The Yale School of Music, in New Haven, Conn., distinguished from its academic counterpart, the Yale Department of Music, was established in 1894 by Samuel Simons Sanford. Its first dean was the renowned composer Horatio Parker; among his students was the unique New Englander Charles Ives. Known for its graduate programs in music performance, the Yale School of Music has produced a number of distinguished graduates, including the current president of Juilliard, Joseph Polisi, the internationally acclaimed guitarist Eliot Fisk (currently on the faculty of the New England Conservatory), the clarinetist Richard Stoltzman (a frequent guest artist in Boston), and Mel Powell, composer and founder of the California Institute of the Arts. In 1973 the Institute of Sacred Music was founded at Yale for the purpose of integrating liturgical music and the arts.

Programs specializing in performance, many of which are part of larger university systems and are members of the National Association of Schools of Music, include the Hartt School and the Hartt Community School of the University of Hartford, the University of Connecticut at Storrs, and the Yale School of Music, all in Connecticut; the University of Maine at Orono and the University of Southern Maine at Gorham in Maine; the New England Conservatory of Music, Berklee College of Music, the Boston Conservatory of Music, Boston University—including the Tanglewood Institute—and the Longy School of Music, all in Massachusetts. Massachusetts schools servicing younger students and the community at large include the New England Conservatory Preparatory School and School of Continuing Education, All Newton Music School, the Boston University Tanglewood Institute, Brookline Music School, Cape Cod Conservatory of Music and Arts, Community Music Center of Boston, Longy School of Music, University of Lowell College of Music, and the University of Massachusetts at Amherst. New Hampshire schools of music include the Apple Hill Center for Chamber Music, Manchester Community Music School, and the University of New Hampshire at Durham; Rhode Island's include the University of Rhode Island at Kingston, Providence College, and Rhode Island College; and Vermont is home to the University of Vermont at Burlington, Kinhaven Music School, and the Music School of Brattleboro Music Center.

Therese Schneider, ed., *Musical America, 1996: International Directory of the Performing Arts* (1996); Nancy Uscher, *The Schirmer Guide to Schools of Music and Conservatories Throughout the World* (1988).

Helen M. Greenwald

The Crucible

The Crucible (1953), by Arthur Miller, is a historical play that dramatizes the Salem, Mass., witchcraft trials of 1692, trials that resulted in the execution of 19 men and women by the Massachusetts Bay Colony. As even a brief summary of the play will suggest, Miller uses the trials as the basis for his powerful, if melodramatic, representation of a community in crisis.

The play opens when Abigail Williams and her friends, fearing punishment for misbehavior, claim to have been manipulated by witches. The resulting furor creates a situation wherein virtually anyone in the community can invoke the threat of witchcraft whenever they want to eliminate social pariahs or do away with a rival. For Abigail, the charge of witchcraft allows her to indict Elizabeth Proctor as a witch in a vain attempt to possess John, Proctor's husband and Abigail's former lover. John Proctor spurns Abigail, however, and soon he, his wife, and some of his closest friends find themselves awaiting hanging on charges of witchcraft. Offered a last chance to save himself if he indicts other alleged witches in the community, Proctor at first accepts and then in a heroic moment refuses the offer and dies at the gallows. His wife and Abigail survive, the latter having fled Salem long before.

Miller was not the first American dramatist to use the witch trials as a source of material. They had provoked the interest of American playwrights as far back as 1846 (Cornelius Matthews's *Witchcraft; or, The Martyrs of Salem*) and as recently as 1952 (Florence Stevenson's *Child Play*). Yet of all the dramatic and narrative representations of the Salem trials in American cultural history, only *The Crucible* has succeeded in stimulating enormous popular interest in these historical events.

The popularity of the play for American audiences has a great deal to do with Miller's deliberate parallel of the trials with the hearings conducted by the House Committee on Un-American Activities (HUAC) during the late 1940s and 1950s. In his introduction and notes to the play, Miller explains that he understands both the trials of 1692 and the hearings of the post–World War II era as occasions in which the state unjustly decreed the accused guilty until proven innocent. John Proctor's ethical predicament—having to choose between his own survival and the survival of a communitarian ideal—no doubt struck a powerful chord with American theatergoers confronted by the spectacle of HUAC witnesses agonizing over whether or not they would give the committee the names of suspected communists.

If audiences from the 1950s to the present have followed Miller in understanding the play as an allegory about the abuse of state power, in recent years critics have focused on how the romantic triangle of Abigail, John, and Elizabeth destabilizes gender relations as well. *The Crucible* is a play in which a woman decides to fulfill her desire regardless of the consequences. For feminist viewers of the play, Miller's political limitations no doubt emerge in his inability to imagine Abigail as anything other than a femme fatale irrelevant to the ethical issues that occupy the last third of the play. In his recent screenplay for the film version of *The Crucible* (1996), however, Miller devotes more attention to Abigail's desire and personality and even adds a scene in which the wayward teenager pleads with John to flee the town with her. Although Abigail may represent a somewhat two-dimensional female villain in the play, in the recent film she appears as a considerably more complex figure. While hardly a feminist paradigm, Miller's new characterization of Abigail reminds us of the writer's sensitivity to historical change—in this case the extraordinary impact of the women's movement on American society. For all its identification with Puritan New England and the Red Scare of the 1950s, *The Crucible* signifies powerfully in a wide range of historical registers. The popularity of the play,

combined with the marketing of Salem as a tourist destination and a site of witchcraft past and present, has served to promote an identification of early New England, and Puritanism itself, with the witch trials of 1692.

E. Miller Budick, "History and Other Spectres in Arthur Miller's *The Crucible*," *Modern Drama* 4 (1985); James J. Martine, *The Crucible: Politics, Property, and Pretense* (1993).

Harry Stecopoulos

Dance Umbrella Founded in 1981 in Cambridge, Mass., by Jeremy Alliger, Dance Umbrella was for 20 years New England's leading year-round presenter of contemporary and culturally diverse dance. Based in Boston, Dance Umbrella saw its mission to inspire, educate, entertain, and empower audiences by presenting dance performance groups from around the world. The organization nurtured artists, commissioned new work, and created educational programs and opportunities to promote cultural understanding and acceptance. During its tenure, Dance Umbrella presented more than 300 dance companies to Boston audiences, including world premieres by such internationally acclaimed artists as Bill T. Jones, Mark Morris, and Mikhail Baryshnikov and the White Oak Dance Project.

Dance Umbrella historically reached out to traditionally underserved Boston populations through free community and youth education activities, discount tickets, and a range of programming. Its outreach programs linked professional performances with Boston-area school and community activities. Its annual *Dancing in Our Seats* matinee performance series enabled more than 3,000 students and teachers to attend professional dance performances at a reduced or fully subsidized cost.

Dance Umbrella was an international advocate of mixed-ability dance (a developing movement form that integrates both disabled and fully abled dancers) and offered innovative programs to promote the attributes of this dance form. Such programs included presentations of companies with disabled dancers, and accessible programs that specifically targeted children and adults in the disability community. Dance Umbrella regularly provided both sign language interpretation and large-print programs at its performances. In 1997 Dance Umbrella produced and presented the first International Festival of Wheelchair Dance, a 10-day gathering of more than a dozen mixed-ability national and international dance companies.

Dance Umbrella has collaborated with other institutions like the Women's Project, which provided dance therapy for abused and

homeless women, women living with cancer, women with drug dependencies, and teenage girls. Dance Umbrella organized its Dance in the Classroom education initiative in partnership with the Boston public schools.

Recognized nationally for its long-term commitment to the contemporary urban dance forms of jazz tap and hip-hop, Dance Umbrella presented its first jazz tap festival in 1987, bringing together the tap legends Charles "Honi" Coles, the Nicholas Brothers, Steve Condos, Gregory Hines, and others in the largest tap gathering ever produced. This festival developed—with the participation of other New England partners, including the Bates Dance Festival, the Flynn Theatre, and Jacob's Pillow Dance Festival—into *Fascinatin' Rhythms: A Celebration of Jazz Tap* and visited 14 New England cities as a touring project of New England Presenters. *Fascinatin' Rhythms* included the first commission for the 11-year-old Savion Glover, who developed a performance using 20 young Boston-area tappers during an extended Boston residency. Other Dance Umbrella jazz tap and hip-hop presentations included *Hip-Hop Boston*, a showcase for Boston-based dancers, and *Cool Heat Urban Beat*, which toured internationally. Dance Umbrella also increased the visibility of underrepresented dance forms and cultures through special project presentations, including Native American powwows, Asian and Indonesian dance festivals, and an Israeli Jewish American festival.

Despite its leading role in the research and advocacy of emerging dance groups and original dance forms and its commitment to personal and political empowerment, cultural expression, and community development, Dance Umbrella ceased operations in 2001, shortly after Alliger left the company.

Theodore Bale, "Dance Umbrella Bows Out," *Boston Herald*, April 6, 2001; Theodore Bale, "Sean Curran Company Gives Dance Umbrella a Fine Sendoff," *Boston Herald*, April 30, 2001; Maureen Dezell, "After 20 Years, the Curtain Closes on Dance Umbrella," *Boston Globe*, April 6, 2001.

Susan Scott

Davis, Bette (1908–89) Actress. Bette Davis was born Ruth Elizabeth Davis in Lowell, Mass., to Ruth Favor and Harlow Davis. She graduated from Cushing Academy in Ashburnham, Mass., in 1925, and after a brief time with the Provincetown Players she landed a Broadway debut in *Broken Dishes*, which opened in November 1929. She changed her name from Betty to Bette (after the heroine of Balzac's *La Cousine Bette*) and thus remade herself from New England mill town girl into Hollywood royalty.

Bette Davis and Gary Merrill in Boston, 1959

It was primarily in her affinity for ripping away the polished Hollywood veneer to expose haggard biological truths and frayed nerves that Davis came close to conjuring overt New England associations. If Katharine Hepburn was the quintessential Yankee blue blood, then Bette Davis was ripe for immolation at the Salem stake, a quality noted by E. Arnot Robinson as early as 1935 in a review of *Dangerous*, in which he declared his contentious admiration: "I think that Bette Davis would probably be burned as a witch if she had lived two or three hundred years ago. She gives the curious feeling of being charged with power which can find no ordinary outlet."

Although Davis's star persona was more witch than Daughter of the American Revolution, she did maintain close ties to her New England roots throughout much of her life. Based on her Massachusetts origins, she demanded and won the role of Charlotte Vale in *Now, Voyager* (1942). In 1939 she met and began an affair with Arthur Farnsworth ("Farney"), the manager of Peckett's Inn in Sugar Hill, N.H., her beloved retreat from the Warner Brothers' lot. Shortly afterward, Davis purchased a 90-acre farm and farmhouse in Sugar Hill, named it Butternut, and planned to divide her time and identity between her two dissimilar realities: leading lady and flannel-clad homesteader. Though Butternut and New Hampshire remained an important balm for Davis's increasingly hectic life, her relationship with Farney soon soured, and their rustic hideaway in equal measures mocked and soothed their domestic turmoil. Davis married Farney in 1940, in her own words because he embodied the non-Hollywood side of her personality: "I was not violently in love with Farney. I loved his loving me, and our mutual love of the New England way of life was the tie that finally bound."

Their battles eventually became physical and arguably resulted in injuries to Farnsworth's skull. These fractures, found at his autopsy, were ultimately designated as the cause of his premature and mysterious death. The degree to which Warner Brothers was or was not involved in a legal cover-up of the case and of Davis's role in it are points of some contention.

In 1945 Davis married William Grant Sherry. The two maintained a dual residence in California and Butternut, and in 1947 Davis gave birth to their daughter, Barbara Davis Sherry. Then in 1950, Davis married her *All about Eve* costar, Gary Merrill, a Connecticut native deeply invested in New England politics. They moved to a house Davis named WitchWay on Zeb Cove, Cape Elizabeth, Maine, and during that period Merrill was instrumental in the election of the Democratic candidate Edmund Muskie as state governor. After her marriage to Merrill disintegrated, Davis seems to have given up on trying to enact her sentimental visions of cozy New England domesticity.

Though Davis made more than 80 films, the sweetly or tearfully ingenuous heroine was never an automatic fit for her. In her most memorable roles, she is starkly manipulative. Her portrayal of cold-blooded Mildred Rogers opposite a cowering Leslie Howard in *Of Human Bondage* (1934) is more memorable than her dewy-but-doomed rich girl of *Dark Victory* (1939). David Thomson describes her mystique: "Davis's unexpectedness began with the implausibility of a far-from-pretty girl becoming a movie star. At once hysterically mortified and daring us to admit that she was not attractive, how could the lady with pulsing eyes succeed unless she was a serious actress?" In 1962 she commanded a new kind of attention by perfecting the glamour-queen-turned-gargoyle in *What Ever Happened to Baby Jane?* Throughout her career, Davis was frequently honored for her ability to rivet audience attention. She won Academy Awards for *Dangerous* in 1935 and *Jezebel* in 1938, and over the course of her career received a total of 10 nominations. For her testy portrayal of Margo Channing in *All about Eve*, Davis was awarded the 1950 New York Film Critics Award for Best Actress. In 1977 she was the first woman to be honored with an American Film Institute Life Achievement Award.

Davis made a symbolic return to the Maine coast at the end of her life as part of the ensemble cast of her penultimate film, *The Whales of August* (1987), a story about two sisters (played by Davis and Lillian Gish) who share a summer cottage on a small island in Casco Bay. True to type, Davis's character is domineeringly scathing, opposite Gish's gen-

tle determination. Davis died in France, far from her New England roots, in 1989.

Jeanine Basinger, *A Woman's View: How Hollywood Spoke to Women, 1930–1960* (1995); Bette Davis and Michael Herskovitz, *This 'n That* (1987); James Spada, *More than a Woman: An Intimate Biography of Bette Davis* (1993); Whitney Stine and Bette Davis, *Mother Goddam* (1974).

Jennifer Beard

Dwight, John Sullivan (1813–93)

Music critic and writer. The first important American-born critic of art music, John Sullivan Dwight is best remembered as founder, editor, and primary author of the influential *Dwight's Journal of Music*, published in Boston from 1852 to 1881. Dwight encouraged his readers to become musically informed listeners, and he fostered the creation of a substantive critical tradition for music in America. His pragmatic educative goals were to guide public taste, inspire performing artists, and encourage respect for music as a profession.

Born in Boston, Dwight graduated from Boston Latin School in 1828 and Harvard College in 1832. He excelled in the study of classics and modern languages and literature, especially German, during his undergraduate years. Although Harvard did not yet include music in its formal curriculum, Dwight played clarinet with a group of student instrumentalists in the Pierian Sodality during his senior year. Having received piano instruction from his father, a Harvard-educated freethinker who became a physician after rejecting the ministry, Dwight possessed sufficient keyboard skill by 1832 to study Beethoven's piano sonatas at a time when they were little known in America. Upon graduation from Harvard Divinity School in 1836, Dwight supplied several pulpits and published a respected translation, with notes, of the poems of Johann Wolfgang von Goethe and Friedrich Schiller (1839). A liberal Unitarian, Dwight served for only one year as pastor of the Second Congregational Church in Northampton, Mass., before leaving the ministry in 1841.

An idealist and nonconformist in his early years, Dwight had participated since 1836 in Transcendentalist meetings led by Ralph Waldo Emerson and George Ripley. In 1841 he joined the experimental utopian community at Brook Farm, in West Roxbury, Mass., residing there until its closing in 1847. There he taught music and Latin, organized musical celebrations, directed the school program, and wrote, translated, and assisted Ripley with editorial responsibilities for *The Harbinger* (1845–49), a reform periodical originally published at Brook Farm. Although he contributed noteworthy articles to such journals as *The Pioneer*, *The Dial*, and the *United States*

Magazine, and Democratic Review, it was his essays in *The Harbinger* that were particularly important in establishing the significance of art music for American readers who were musically unsophisticated. One of his fundamental early accomplishments was to describe the humanistic significance and large-scale structures of Beethoven's complete symphonies during the 1840s at a time when these compositions were first being included in regular public orchestral performances in Boston and New York.

Dwight continued his support for art music in *Dwight's Journal,* an invaluable primary source chronicling the development of concert activity in America and championing the music of many European composers through original and contributed essays, translations, reprints, and reports from domestic and foreign correspondents. He himself commented perceptively on European compositions, including Handel's oratorios; orchestral works by Franz Joseph Haydn, Wolfgang Amadeus Mozart, Beethoven, Franz Schubert, and Robert Schumann; operas by Mozart, Carl Maria von Weber, and Vincenzo Bellini; and art songs by Schubert. Dwight acknowledged the legitimacy of solo virtuosic music by Franz Liszt and Frédéric Chopin, furthered public performances of chamber music, and supported certain American composers, including the Bostonians James C. D. Parker and John Knowles Paine. Dwight encouraged early orchestras in Boston before the establishment of the permanent Boston Symphony Orchestra and championed music as a field of learning indispensable to general education. He was one of the leaders of the Harvard Musical Association and fought, together with his fellow members, for the inclusion of music in the college curriculum.

In his later decades Dwight was increasingly resistant to much new music and found it difficult to accept the divergent programmatic approaches manifested in varied genres, including symphonic poems. Among his last writings is "The History of Music in Boston" in Justin Winsor's *The Memorial History of Boston* (1881). Dwight died in Boston in 1893.

George Willis Cooke, *John Sullivan Dwight: Brook-Farmer, Editor, and Critic of Music; A Biography* (1898); Irving Sablosky, *What They Heard: Music in America, 1852–1881, from the Pages of "Dwight's Journal of Music"* (1986); Ora Frishberg Saloman, *Beethoven's Symphonies and J. S. Dwight: The Birth of American Music Criticism* (1995).

Ora Frishberg Saloman

Ethnic Music Ethnic music traditions—other than those practiced by Native Americans and early English settlers—emerged as a presence in New England in the mid-19th century. Ethnic music traditions continued to build throughout the 20th century and remained most active in urban centers, especially with the steady influx of immigrants within a given ethnic community or where there is frequent travel back and forth between New England and the native country. This is particularly true of Canadians (French and Scottish), Greeks, Irish, and Portuguese. Urban centers have also tended to attract larger ethnic populations and therefore provide more opportunities for ethnic musicians to perform and, in some cases, to earn a living as professional musicians.

Instrumental traditions have been more likely to survive over time within a given ethnic community, while singing traditions are inevitably tied to language; when a community's language begins to die out, so too does its song literature. The rare exception is religious settings, in which liturgical music continues to be performed in the native language even after it ceases to be spoken in the community.

In some respects, the ethnic music communities of New England resemble those found in New York City. Many of the same ethnic groups who settled in New York in the past 100 to 150 years (Irish, Italian, Hispanic, Jewish, African American, East European, and others) can be found in smaller numbers in the larger New England cities. The proximity to New York has also led to the gradual migration of former New York–based communities to southwestern Connecticut and has served to bolster the musical careers of many New England ethnic band leaders and recording artists. The New England ethnic musical landscape is nevertheless unique, thanks, in part, to the influx of Scots and especially French Canadian immigrants from Quebec and the Maritime Provinces. Their song and dance music traditions are an essential element of Franco-American social gatherings and are integrated into the larger musical lexicon of rural New England. Other ethnic groups, such as the Portuguese, Cape Verdeans, and Syrian-Lebanese immigrants, established their first and largest communities in New England. As a result, the community infrastructure that supports ongoing cultural activities is much older and stronger in New England than in other areas of the country.

The first ethnic music communities in New England were Native American: Wabanaki, Wampanoag, Paugusset, and Iroquois confederacies, and other Rhode Island and Connecticut–based tribes such as the Pequot, Mohegan, and Narragansett. The world's first musical recording was of Native Americans in New England. In March 1890 the Harvard University anthropologist Jesse Walter Fewkes used an Edison cylinder to record songs of Passamaquoddy Indians in Calais, Maine. Since Fewkes's landmark recording, Native American music and dance traditions in the region have continued to be documented by anthropologists and ethnomusicologists, and more recently by tribal members themselves. Collections of their recordings are held in the Archive of Folk Culture, Library of Congress, Washington, D.C., and other ethnomusicology archives in Canada and the United States.

Many Native Americans in northern New England converted to Catholicism during the 17th and 18th centuries; as a result, native music in religious ceremonies was often replaced by Christian hymnody. The traditions of magical, ceremonial, greeting, "chief-making," corn harvest, wedding, funeral, and dance songs remain active, however, and in some cases have been revived, particularly among the Wabanaki. The regional singing style is characteristically open and resonant, with little of the tension associated with the more widely known Plains Indian singing. Songs for social dancing are often antiphonal, a call-and-response form of lead singer alternating with a chorus. Musical instruments have historically included handheld drums, rattles, and flutes. Similarly portable instruments like fiddles and guitars that were introduced by European settlers have been adopted over the course of the past century and are now an active element of many Native American secular musical events.

Irish folk ballads and dance music have had a profound influence on the development of American popular music. The "stage" Irish music and vaudeville of mid- to late-19th-century America had evolved from the folk idiom. George M. Cohan, a Providence native, is among the best-known Irish musicians, actors, and producers. By the early 20th century, Irish traditional music competitions and dances, with talented *ceilidh* bands, were established in Boston and Providence. Among the most extensively recorded was Dan Sullivan's Shamrock Band, which is credited with having a profound and lasting influence on Irish traditional music both in America and in Ireland. The band was established by the son of the revered Boston fiddler Dan Sullivan and included piano, *uillean* pipes, flute, and the fiddle playing of one of Boston's most celebrated Irish musicians, Michael Hanafin. When the Boston Comhaltas Ceoltoiri Eireann (Musicians' association of Ireland) was established in 1975, it was named the Hanafin-Cooley branch, in honor of Hanafin and the accordion player Joseph Cooley.

Deacon Hall in South Boston and Hibernian Hall in Roxbury, Mass., were regular dance venues in the 1930s and 1940s, and Irish music was broadcast live on radio stations in Boston and Providence. By the 1940s, the major recording companies were no longer producing Irish ethnic recordings. The O'Byrne DeWitt family responded by introducing their own label and founded the Copley Record Company in Boston in the late 1940s. They went on to record many of New England's most talented Irish musicians of the time, such as the Kerry fiddler Paddy Cronin and the button accordion player Joe Derrane. During the 1990s, New England's Irish community created an impressive infrastructure for its traditional music. Concert presenters and local Celtic music radio programs feature regional and touring artists, and the Stonehill College Irish Festival has become an annual event. Several New England–based record labels have specialized in Irish music since the 1970s, among them Philo in Vermont, Rex in western Massachusetts, and Innisfree/Green Linnet in Connecticut. Owing in part to the efforts of the Boston Comhaltas group and the fiddler Seamus Connolly, Boston College has added a musical component to its Irish studies program.

Since the early 19th century, Italian immigrants have had a notable influence on the development of concert bands and band repertory in the region; this is still evident today in southern New England, where many prominent concert band musicians, conductors, and educators are Italian. Large Italian communities in Boston and Rhode Island have for decades continued the tradition of the *festa*, or saint's festival, featuring the music of local bands. The repertory of many of these bands was typified by a Portsmouth, N.H., band (1839) with a mix of patriotic American songs and Italian opera. Opera has for nearly 200 years functioned as a kind of vernacular music for Italian Americans, uniting immigrants from northern and southern regions of Italy across class lines.

Italian-born Loreto Marsella was one of the better-known organizers and conductors of Italian community bands at the turn of the 20th century. He is credited with establishing the Crescent Park Concert Orchestra and the Duke of Abruzzi Band in Providence. The piano accordion could be found in many Italian American social and musical settings such as restaurants, community picnics, and family gatherings. Two generations of the Gulietti family operated an accordion manufacturing and retail business in Springfield, Mass., for most of the 20th century; Gulietti accordions were sought by Italian musicians in New England and beyond. The Calabrians are a southern Italian group whose traditional polkas, tarantellas, stornelli, cantastoria, and serenades are accompanied by concertina, guitar,

and tambourine. The folklorist Anna Chairetakis has documented the unique musical traditions and repertory of a Calabrian community in Westerly, R.I.

From the 1910s through the late 1950s and 1960s, the Finn Temperance and Socialist Halls of the Cape Ann and Fitchburg areas of Massachusetts and southern New Hampshire were vibrant social and cultural centers that hosted plays and dances and supported brass bands. The horn player George E. Wahlstrom became known as the Father of Finnish-American Bands and directed such major ensembles as the Imatra Band of Maynard, Mass., founded in 1903, which played for civic and ethnic functions. Their largely Finnish repertory also included Western classical and American popular pieces. Two Cape Ann musicians of the Vainola Temperance Society brass band became important recording artists in the 1920s and 1930s. Antti Syrjaniemi was a popular singer who performed in Finnish halls throughout Massachusetts and was known for his topical and satirical songs. In 1929 he recorded five titles for Victor's Finnish catalog in New York and remained an active musician in the Finnish community until his death in 1962. Syrjaniemi's fellow band member the cornetist Sylvester Ahola became a professional musician, playing with many important dance orchestras in the Northeast and in Europe. Ahola left a prolific career as a studio and recording artist in New York to return to Gloucester, Mass., in 1940 to perform the local music of his Finnish heritage.

The highest concentration of Swedes in New England is found in the greater Boston area and in Worcester. Swedish populations are also found in Vermont, New Hampshire, and Maine. Social dancing was an active part of Swedish community life, and the repertory of dance forms included waltzes, polkas, and schottisches. The fiddle was the most common accompaniment to Swedish dances. Vocal music in the community received support from religious institutions such as the Lutheran church, and older traditional ballads were sometimes set to familiar hymn tunes. The Reverend J. A. Hultman of Worcester (1861–1942) was an important Swedish songwriter whose *solskenssanger* (sunshine songs) were widely available to Swedish Americans in both book and recorded form. Partly because of the relative age of Scandinavian communities, assimilation, and lack of recent immigration, less ethnic music is performed today than in the early 20th century.

Latvian, Estonian, and Lithuanian immigrants were drawn to the textile industry centers of New England in the late 19th century and later in the 20th century as political exiles after World War II. The largest of these

communities were Lithuanian. Folk dance and instrumental music have been an essential element of their ethnic musical life, but Lithuanians are distinct in their emphasis on vocal traditions. Song festivals and church-based choral groups continue into the 21st century. In 1949–50, the Lithuanian community scholar and folklorist Jonas Balys recorded more than 1,000 traditional songs from Lithuanians, many of them from communities in South Boston, Brockton, and Worcester, Mass. Selections from his impressive collection were released, with annotations, by Folkways Records in New York in 1955 and 1962. In contrast to West European music, Lithuanian folk songs are characterized by a unique rhythmic and harmonic structure. In addition to other Lithuanian song literature, the contemporary Boston-based group Sodauto has revived the art of *sutartine,* two-part singing in alternating meters and intervals of a second.

Most Polish immigrants arrived in New England in the late 19th and early 20th centuries and settled in the factory and industrial towns of Connecticut, Rhode Island, western Massachusetts, and southern New Hampshire. Those who wanted to continue farming as they had in rural Poland were drawn to the Connecticut River valley and to small towns in Vermont, New Hampshire, and Maine. The popular folk dances of 19th-century Central and Eastern Europe were the polka and the waltz; polka was common in German and Scandinavian communities but was destined to become one of America's most popular ethnic musical forms of the 20th century. Before the 1920s, *wiejska* (village style) music, which was derived from folk music, was performed in the Polish fraternal halls. The Dom Polski (Polish National Homes) held regular social dances accompanied by string ensembles that featured violin and bass. After the depression, a new type of Polish dance orchestra developed what came to be known as eastern style polka. New England polka bands gained great national popularity from the 1930s through the 1950s.

A number of regional Polish band leaders were proponents of this new style. Ed Kroklikowski, Walt Solek, and Frank Wojnarowski from Connecticut and Jozef Lazarz and Jan Robak from Chicopee, Mass., all established well-known eastern-style polka bands that were in great demand locally and beyond New England. They began to expand their orchestras to play larger dance halls and ballrooms, changing the instrumentation from strings to brass, accordion, and drums to add volume to their sound. Many who sought to appeal to wider, non-Polish audiences added English songs to their repertory and incorporated some swing and big band sounds during the

1930s and 1940s. Kroklikowski of Bridgeport, Conn., labeled "the Polish Paul Whiteman," made effective use of the media by performing on live weekly radio programs. Others followed his example. Many of the most popular polka bands made recordings with major record labels of that era, including Victor, Columbia, Standard International, and Dana.

Large ballrooms opened throughout southern New England and New York, and polka bands were regularly booked at the famous Ritz ballroom in Bridgeport, Pleasure Park, White City in Worcester, and others. The golden age of eastern-style polka has passed, but Polish polka bands still play for dances throughout New England. With the introduction of new popular dance forms, polka has lost some of its earlier broad appeal and is once again a predominantly Polish ethnic music, performed largely for an older generation. Paying homage to this ethnic art form, the annual Pillar Polkabration was established in Preston, Conn., in 1965; it is the longest running polka festival in America. Polish vocal traditions have not fared as well. As the language disappears, so too does evidence of a folk song repertory. Some uniquely Polish carols and religious songs are still part of community celebrations of Christmas and Easter. Several traditional Polish and Russian folk songs have been preserved as part of the Helen Hartness Flanders Ballad Collection at Middlebury College, recorded by Flanders in Springfield, Vt., in the late 1940s.

Portuguese and Cape Verdeans are among the earliest immigrants to New England, their first settlements dating back nearly 200 years. The Portuguese host annual festivals honoring their patron saints, such as the widely celebrated Feast of San João Baptista (Saint John the Baptist) and the Procession of Santo Christo held the fifth Sunday after Easter. Portuguese communities also support local concert bands that march in procession behind the statues of the saints. The musical function of these bands is both sacred and secular; they play for religious holidays and events, community concerts, and dancing. Many south European cultures have a tradition of a progressive musical serenade associated with the Christmas season in which a group of musicians wander from house to house, singing the songs of the season. For the Portuguese, this tradition is *Janeiras* (January festival), celebrated on the New Year to commemorate the visit of the three wise men to the infant Jesus.

Song and dance traditions remain strong in New England Portuguese communities, largely because of frequent travel back and forth to Portugal. Songs that accompany dance, such as *carrasquinha* and *chamarrita*, are performed for annual country festivals. Dances from the Azores are usually accompanied by the guitar; those of mainland Portugal are accompanied by accordion, tambourine, drum, and castinets. *Fado* is an urban folk tradition that originated in the waterfront nightclubs and restaurants of Lisbon. In New England it can be heard in Portuguese restaurants and clubs. The lyrics have historically been about *saudade* (longing and nostalgia). Fado songs are performed by a solo vocalist who is accompanied by two to four string players on the *guitarra* (Portuguese guitar) and *viola* (Spanish guitar).

Immigrants from the Cape Verde Islands, formerly a Portuguese colony, are of mixed African and south European heritage. They have settled into the same towns in Massachusetts, Rhode Island, and Connecticut as the Portuguese, sharing a language and culture. Their musical traditions, however, while influenced by Portugal, have evolved into performance styles and forms that are uniquely Cape Verdean. Cape Verdeans celebrate many of the same saints' festivals and religious holidays as the Portuguese, but the prominent musical activity in their communities is social dancing. Cape Verdean social clubs, dance halls, and nightclubs offer social dancing to live music three and four nights a week. As a general rule, older community members dance to the Portuguese-influenced musical forms of *morna* and *coladeira,* while younger Cape Verdeans are drawn to the more African-influenced dance music, *funana* and *batuque.*

Cape Verdean music has a Latin flavor, with rhythms similar to the Brazilian samba, Dominican merengue, and Columbian *cumbia.* The older dance bands feature guitar and violin or trumpet as lead instruments, backed up by bass and percussion. The lead instruments trade phrases and often improvise, in a manner similar to a jazz band. The younger bands are much more rock-influenced and tend to perform on electric guitar, bass, and keyboards, with percussion. Brazilian music and dance forms most frequently performed in New England, largely in the Boston area and southern Connecticut, are samba and the Afro-Brazilian music, dance, and martial art form, *capoeira.*

New England is home to some of the largest Greek, Albanian, Armenian, and Syrian/Lebanese communities in the United States, with high concentrations in Boston and Worcester. Many came to work in the textile and shoe factories at the turn of the 20th century in Lowell and Lawrence, Mass.; Manchester and Dover, N.H.; Rutland and Burlington, Vt.; and Saco and Biddeford, Maine. Some moved north and east from New York to settle in other industrial centers in Connecticut and Rhode Island. Early Leb-

anese settlements were established as far north as Eastport and Van Buren, Maine. While each of these communities maintains its own distinct language and identity, they are also linked to one another by cultural similarities, including music. Their shared experience as 20th-century immigrants to New England has strengthened this bond. As Nicholas Tawa notes in his book *Sound of Strangers: Musical Culture, Acculturation, and Post–Civil War Ethnic America,* "All first-generation Americans from the entire eastern rim of the Mediterranean, from Albania to Palestine, enjoyed similar compositions."

The stylistic similarities among Albanian, Greek, Armenian, and Syrian/Lebanese musical traditions are extensive melodic ornamentation, heterophonic texture, the use of compound and irregular meters, chromatic as well as pentatonic and diatonic scales, microtones and Arabic modes (*maqam*), and improvisation. A common family of musical instruments includes a reed aerophone (usually a clarinet), a bowed lute (usually a violin in U.S. ensembles), a plucked lute (such as the Greek *lauto,* the *oud,* or, in more contemporary ensembles, the bouzouki), and percussion (tambourine and goblet drums such as *darabuke*).

Through various forms of patronage New England's Balkan and Middle Eastern communities have supported ensembles of talented professional and semiprofessional musicians. Musical performances are an integral part of church-sponsored social events such as parties (*glendi*), festivals (*paniyiri*) and community picnics. The Lebanese communities established large three-day outdoor summer events known as *maharajan* that always include food, music, and dancing and the somewhat more formal *haflah,* an evening party or concert at which couples reserve tables and are served snacks (*mazza*) and alcoholic beverages. The Boston-based Syrian musician Russell Bunai had both an interest in hearing and performing the Middle Eastern classical repertoire. Bunai organized many local haflah and also home parties and coffeehouse gatherings in more intimate musical settings. These audiences of *sammi'ah* (music connoisseurs) were usually men; informal musical performance alternated with card playing and conversation.

Recording opportunities lured many professional Greek, Armenian, and Arab musicians from New England to New York. Such artists as the Armenian oud player Marko Melkon, who influenced many younger players in New England, recorded with New York–based labels that specialized in Middle Eastern music. Columbia began producing some of these recordings in the early 1920s and was soon replaced by Kaliphon, Balkan, and

Panhellion, labels that were owned and run by Balkan immigrants. By the 1960s a new venue had emerged: musicians were performing regularly in restaurants and nightclubs, touring New England, New York, and the Midwest, and musical ensembles were increasingly polyethnic in membership. During this period, which the musicologist Anne Rasmussen describes as "innovative assimilation," Balkan and Middle Eastern artists accompanied solo belly dancing, experimented with the use of Western popular instruments such as guitars, keyboards, and drum sets, and attempted to "create a product that was palatable and yet intriguing for mixed audiences." The violinist Fred Elias is a well-known New Hampshire–based Lebanese artist who has been an active musician for years on the New England nightclub scene. Elias's composition "Dance of Contessa" has become a standard in the repertory of Balkan and Middle Eastern club musicians and is an example of the kind of "palatable exoticism" that would accompany dance performance.

Church music has always remained a separate but significant element of community life. Armenian, Albanian, Greek Orthodox, and Eastern-rite church choirs perform Christian hymns and liturgical chants that are unique to central and eastern Europe and the Adriatic coast. The Greek Orthodox Church maintains a cantorial tradition including musical notation that dates back to the Byzantine. The continuous influx of Greek and Albanian immigrants to New England helps to keep their musical traditions vibrant. Younger players, instrument builders, and the recently established Greek Music Society of Boston support and develop existing musical infrastructure.

New England's ethnic diversity has expanded dramatically over the past 30 years. Puerto Ricans, once the region's largest Hispanic community, have been joined in recent years by Dominicans and Central and South Americans. While each has unique musical traditions, together they combine forces to perform a broadly pan-Latin repertory that includes Caribbean dance forms like merengue, *son,* salsa, Columbian cumbia, Venezuelan *joropo,* Brazilian samba, and Argentinean tango. New England's urban centers have become home to numerous Latin dance clubs, classes, and cultural organizations. The audiences reflect the diverse and growing Hispanic communities, but also draw from the larger population. Clubs and organizations target specific Hispanic populations such as those interested in folkloric traditions or the Dominican dance clubs in Rhode Island and eastern Massachusetts. They have at times made use of an infrastructure established by earlier ethnic groups, such as the Polish American Hall in Nashua, N.H., which is now a venue for Mexican community social dances.

At the end of the Vietnam War, large Southeast Asian refugee populations of Cambodians, Vietnamese, Laotian, and Hmong people were resettled in New England. Unlike Hispanic groups, who have a common language and religion and who easily exchange the latest popular dance rhythms, the various Southeast Asian cultures and music are more distinct.

The Vietnamese from lowland Vietnam are influenced by Chinese culture and predictably have settled, in some cases, in New England's old Chinese communities such as Boston's Chinatown. Their music ranges from solo contemplative traditions performed on such instruments as the *dan tranh* (plucked zither), to ensemble accompaniment for dance and opera or musical theater, to drum and cymbal accompaniment for a New Year's lion dance.

Cambodians, Laotians, and Hmong also use music to celebrate the important New Year holiday. Skilled local musicians are employed to perform the very specific repertory of wedding music for each of these communities. Weddings are often a three- to four-day sequence of rituals, with music an integral part of the event. For Cambodians, the term *phleng kar* refers to both the ensemble and the repertory associated with weddings. Hmong wedding rituals are conducted in part by designated wedding singers, though the Hmong regard their performance as a form of poetry rather than music. Immigrant Cambodians consider folk and classical dance to be among the most significant artistic expressions of their culture. As a result they have invested much time and energy in establishing and maintaining the Lowell-based Angkor Dance Troupe. Talented musicians are drawn from Cambodian communities in Rhode Island and Massachusetts to provide a *mohori* ensemble to accompany the troupe in performance.

A similar emphasis on dance is found in New England's South Asian communities, the largest of which are Gujarati. Classical and folk dance schools have been established in Connecticut, western and northeastern Massachusetts, and southern New Hampshire, though it is rare to see them perform to live music. East Asian immigrants in New England tend to be highly educated professionals who work largely in medicine and technology. Their musical interests often include the Indian classical traditions, and community-based cultural organizations often sponsor concert series that present touring Indian classical artists, especially in the Boston area.

Other large refugee populations that have resettled in New England urban centers include Haitians and East Africans (Ethiopians, Somalians, Eritreans). Musical and cultural events in these communities often serve as a means to bolster morale under trying circumstances, and are organized by local leaders to help create a more cohesive sense of community. Younger Haitian *compas* bands have taken advantage of recent interest in Afro-pop and perform in urban dance clubs.

Berklee School of Music has played a significant role in drawing many foreign musicians to the greater Boston area to study jazz and rock traditions. As a result, many talented Caribbean and Central and South American musicians are shaping the Boston music scene, often blending their traditional ethnic musics with jazz and other more established American musical forms. Over the past 20 years, an emphasis on multicultural education and programming, the development of government-based public folklore programs, and the availability of public funding to support such programs have brought many local ethnic musics to the attention of a much larger population. Many events, such as the Lowell Folk Festival, have become annual venues for traditional music in the region. The popularization of "world music" has contributed to the development of regional presenters of ethnic music, more radio programming, and more opportunities to perform outside of ethnic community settings.

Maud Cuney-Hare, "Portuguese Folk Songs from Provincetown (Cape Cod, MA)," *Musical Quarterly* 14 (1928); Jesse Walter Fewkes, "A Contribution to Passamaquoddy Folklore," *Journal of American Folklore* 3 (1890); Victor Greene, *A Passion for Polka: Old Time Ethnic Music in America* (1992); Kip Lornell, *Introducing American Folk Music* (1992); Judith McCulloh, ed., *Ethnic Recordings in America: A Neglected Heritage* (1982); Anne Rasmussen, "The Music of Arab Americans: Performance Contexts and Musical Transformation," *Pacific Review of Ethnomusicology* 5 (1989); Nicholas Tawa, *Sound of Strangers: Musical Culture, Acculturation and Post–Civil War Ethnic America* (1982); Paul Vernon, *Ethnic and Vernacular Music, 1989–1960: A Resource and Guide to Recordings* (1995).

Discography: Armenians on 8th Avenue, notes by Harold G. Hagopian (Traditional Crossroads CD 4279, 1996); *Calabria Bella, Dove T'hai Lasciate?* notes and recording by Anna L. Chairetakis (Folkways FES 34042, 1979); *Dan Sullivan's Shamrock Band,* notes by Mick Maloney and Leo Sullivan (Topic, 1979); *Joe Derrane: Irish Accordion,* notes by Phillipe Varlet (Copley, 1993); *Joe Lazarz and His International Orchestra,* notes by Bill Czupta (Polka Music Hall of Fame, Chicago Polkas Collectors Series LP 4102); *Lithuanian Folk Songs in the United States,* notes and recording by Jonas Balys (Folkways FM 4009, 1955, 1962); *Traditional Music of Maine,*

Vols. I–IV, notes and recordings by Jeff McKeen and Ernie Freeberg (Northeast Archives of Folklore and Oral History, 1988); *We're Irish Still* (Comhaltas Ceoltoiri Eireann, Hanafin-Cooley Branch, Boston, 1979).

Jill I. Linzee

Experimental Music since World War II

In the latter half of the 20th century, many American composers have sought to extend the boundaries of the Western classical tradition by employing alternative technical and conceptual approaches to composition and performance. Their most radical innovations have challenged the traditional roles of composer, performer, and audience. Such innovations include aleatoric composition, in which musical events are determined by chance, and collaborative performances that involve the players or the audience in the creative act. Postwar experimentalists have also examined the potential of sound material itself by devising new tuning systems, exploring the acoustical potential of objects and performance spaces, and engaging electroacoustic and computer resources.

Among the experimentalists active in New England was John Cage, a pioneer of chance music who profoundly influenced musical life in the United States and abroad. While primarily associated with New York, Cage periodically visited New England and was in residence at Wesleyan University (in Connecticut) and Harvard. A prominent associate of Cage, Christian Wolff (Dartmouth University), has explored methods for bringing chance into performance. In his *Duo for Pianists II* (1958) the performers choose their material in response to cues they receive from one another.

Alvin Lucier at Wesleyan is a composer who combines an aleatoric approach with technological resources. Lucier explores the potential of sound in performance by constructing installations in which electronics interact with objects or people. In his first experimental work, *Music for Solo Performer* (1965), he calls for a performer to generate alpha brain waves by entering a meditative state. The electronics amplify the brain waves to resonate with percussion instruments.

New musical applications for electronics have been developed in the Media Lab at the Massachusetts Institute of Technology. Barry Vercoe, co-founder of the laboratory, has invented languages for digital audio processing, as well as "cpmusic," a system in which a computer responds to a performer in real time. Tod Machover has designed "Hyperinstruments," interactive musical devices for virtuosic performers and the general public. In his

Brain Opera (1996), the audience collectively shapes the work within the performance space and through the Internet. Aside from MIT, there are centers for electronic and computer-assisted composition at Dartmouth, Harvard, Yale, and many other institutions.

Henry Brant, formerly at Bennington College in Vermont, has explored the potential of spatial composition. His pieces use physical separation and contrast to achieve polyphonic complexity and are often designed for specific performance spaces. The compositions of Joseph Celli of Hartford involve improvisation and extended instrumental techniques. Boston's Ezra Sims has created works that are based on a microtonal scale derived from a 72-note division of the octave.

The abundance and high quality of musical activity in New England continue to provide fertile ground for innovation. In addition to the academic institutions that support composition and performance, many independent organizations sponsor new music. Groups in Boston include Dinosaur Annex, Boston Musica Viva, Composers in Red Sneakers, Collage New Music, NuClassix, and Phantom Arts; in Maine, Portland Performing Arts; in Burlington, Vt., the Flynn Theatre for the Performing Arts; and in Hartford, Real Art Ways.

Christopher Ballantine, "An Aesthetic of Experimental Music," *Music and Its Social Meanings* (1984); John Cage, *Silence: Lectures and Writings* (1961); Alvin Lucier, *Reflections: Interviews, Scores, Writings* (1995); Michael Nyman, *Experimental Music: Cage and Beyond* (1974).

Roberta Lukes

Fiddling and Fiddlers

Fiddlers have furnished dance music for people at all levels of New England society from perhaps as early as the 1660s. Fiddlers provided music for the fashionable country dances brought to the region by British colonists in the 17th century and, as new dance forms and tune types were introduced, continued to play for both high society events and impromptu affairs in taverns and bawdy houses into the 19th century. When dance fashions changed during the 19th century and urban socialites left fiddle music behind, fiddlers continued to hold forth at dances in rural community halls, sometimes in bands with woodwind and brass instruments, other times by themselves in informal "junkets," "rackets," and "tunks" in wintertime farmhouse kitchens.

As the ethnic makeup of New England's population diversified, so did that of the area's fiddlers. We know of African American fiddlers in New England as early as 1734, and throughout the 18th and early 19th centuries

Fiddler Willie Beaudoin and his son Roger in Burlington, Vt., 2001

the role of village fiddler was often filled by a black man. The influx of Irish and French Canadian immigrants in the 19th century brought related, but distinct, repertories and styles to New England's industrial cities. Later, people of Scottish heritage from Cape Breton, Nova Scotia, brought fiddling with strong roots in old Scottish highland musical culture to Boston. More recently, professional fiddling from Canada and Nashville has had a potent impact on fiddling in New England, with younger musicians often striving to emulate Graham Townsend or Vassar Clements rather than older traditional players in their communities.

Fiddling in New England has never been strictly an oral/aural tradition. Manuscript tunebooks from the 18th century onward provide documentation of repertoire and an indication of musical literacy. In the 19th century, printed tunebooks, especially those of the Boston publisher Elias Howe, both reflected traditional repertoire and influenced it. Howe's most remarkable and influential publication was *Ryan's Mammoth Collection* (1883), compiled by William Bradbury Ryan, which remains in print in modified form as *One Thousand Fiddle Tunes* (1940) and in a 1995 reprint as *Mel Bay Presents Ryan's Mammoth Collection* (although this, too, is incomplete). Evidence suggests that Ryan gathered the diverse contents from working musicians in the region.

The New England fiddler's repertoire consists largely of the same types of fast, duple-meter, 16- or 32-bar tunes that are common in fiddling traditions throughout North America, the British Isles, and Ireland. Reels and hornpipes in $\frac{2}{4}$ or $\frac{4}{4}$ time and jigs in $\frac{6}{8}$ and, infrequently, $\frac{9}{8}$ time are the most prevalent and are the tune types that have been used historically to accompany contra dances and sometimes square dances. Hornpipes traditionally differ from reels by featuring a pattern of dotted-8th notes followed by 16th notes (thus emphasizing the first and third notes of each group of four), whereas reels consist primarily of continuous groups of 16th notes. This distinction is often lost in Yankee and French Canadian practice, however, but is maintained by the Irish and Cape Breton players in the region. Reels, hornpipes, and jigs share a common melodic structure, typically consisting of two 8-bar melodic sections, each of which is played twice to yield one rendering of the tune. This AABB structure is repeated as many times as the player wishes in an informal or listening situation, but might be repeated a prescribed number of times in order to fulfill the requirements of a dance. Tunes for couple dances, such as waltzes (slower tunes in $\frac{3}{4}$ time) and polkas (fast, two-beat tunes) are also popular. In contest play fiddlers typically are required to play a hoe-down (reel or hornpipe), a waltz, and a tune of choice, often a jig.

By the turn of the 20th century rural Yankee fiddling traditions were in decline, but an awareness of the cultural importance of folk traditions and an urge to preserve them emerged early in the century. Elizabeth Burchenal, Helen Hartness Flanders, and Eloise Hubbard Linscott recorded and published materials gathered from fiddlers and other folk musicians. New Englanders were largely overlooked by the commercial record companies that began exploiting the market for southeastern and urban ethnic traditional music in the 1920s. A small handful of Yankee fiddlers made records in 1926 as a result of Henry Ford's promotion of old-time fiddling and dancing. Many fiddle contests were staged throughout New England, and the fiddlers Mellie Dunham of Maine, John Wilder of Vermont, and Joe Shippee of Connecticut made a few 78 rpm recordings.

Fiddle music nevertheless flourished in New England's Irish, French Canadian, and Cape Breton communities, especially in Boston, where there were many active dance halls in the 1930s, 1940s, and 1950s. A few Irish and Cape Breton fiddlers recorded for Canadian and U.S. labels, and the Copley label, established in Boston in the late 1940s, recorded local musicians.

The folk revival of the 1950s and 1960s generated new interest in New England's fiddling and dance traditions. The Northeast Fiddlers' Association was formed in northern Vermont in 1965 and instituted regular gatherings of fiddlers and an annual regional contest. Many other contests followed, with interest spurred by the back-to-the-land movement and the national Bicentennial. Fiddlers from various New England traditions came to prominence in the 1970s, appearing at folk festivals outside the region and making recordings. These included the Yankee fiddlers Clem Myers, Ron West, and Neal Converse; the French Canadians Louis Beaudoin, the Riendeau Family, Wilfred Guillette, and Gerry Robichaud; and the Cape Breton–style players Joe Cormier, John Campbell, and Jerry Holland.

Dudley Laufman and Corinne Nash, *Dick Richardson, Old Time New Hampshire Fiddler* [sound recording] (1992); Eloise Hubbard Linscott, *Folk Songs of Old New England* (1939 [1962]); Patrick Sky, ed., *Mel Bay Presents Ryan's Mammoth Collection* (1995 [1883]); Paul F. Wells, *New England Traditional Fiddling* [sound recording] (1978).

Paul F. Wells

Fife and Drum Music

Fife and drum music in New England originated in Anglo-American military music practices of the mid-18th century. The music and parades with fife and drums also characterized 18th-century African American election ceremonies and Pinkster celebrations of minstrelsy. The music was revived in towns along the lower Connecticut River valley in the 20th century. Colloquially termed "ancient" to distinguish it from concurrent fife, drum, and bugle traditions, these relatively small marching bands (corps) are composed generally of self-taught musicians who play deep, wooden, rope-tension snare and bass drums and simple-system wooden fifes. Ancients combine rote, aural, and, more recently, note-reading practices to assimilate a repertory composed mostly of quicksteps and marches dating from the mid-18th, 19th, and early 20th centuries, but also include Irish fiddle tunes, composed melodies, and patriotic airs. Both snare and bass drummers employ a defined system of rudiments to accompany the fifers, who apply the "Connecticut tongue" to achieve "slur-to-staccato" performance style. Corps are led by a color guard and utilize a quasi-military system of dress and drill when participating in parades, historical pageants, competitions, and musters.

The first modern muster was held in 1953 in Deep River, Conn., to promote fellowship among ancient corps (and to heal old wounds fostered by the highly competitive field days). Musters begin with a parade through town and end with "the circle of friendship" and an informal but enthusiastic jam session ("jollification") lasting well into the night. At musters, musicians eagerly take in the performance of their fellow ancients, and when playing informally gather in a circle, facing inward. Beer is the preferred refreshment, the bonding tonic of all "regular guys." Although in the past women were rare participants, they fill all roles today.

Minutemen reenactors play fifes, Concord, Mass., 1992

While a separate Pennsylvania tradition and an imitation of the Connecticut ancients in New York existed as early as the 1930s, it was the bicentennial of the American Revolution that spawned formation of new corps, most notably in Massachusetts but also in Vermont, Rhode Island, New Jersey, Maryland, Michigan, Virginia, and Connecticut itself. These corps combined ancient practices with historical interpretations to present a recreation of American field music of the Revolutionary and Civil Wars, using an expanded traditional repertory that included newly discovered examples of 18th- and early-19th-century fife and flute tunes.

Meanwhile, an interest in the Swiss Basel tradition introduced new rudiments to ancient drumming, and participation in field days and musters led to further changes in performance practice. The repertory was promoted increasingly through publications and less so by ear, heralding a sharp decline of the Connecticut tongue. The emphasis on musical literacy, which began even before the Bicentennial, led to tonal improvements in the fife, resulting in the development of tunable, conical bore models of 10 and 11 holes that compete for predominance with the traditional six-hole, straight-bore instrument still in use today.

In 1965 the Company of Fifers and Drummers was formed in Ivoryton, Conn., to preserve the ancient tradition through its Museum of Fife and Drum. The museum preserves the colonial-era history of military strategy as well as the musical traditions of the fife and drum. The company also houses a meeting hall for its 100-plus member corps and promotes interest in ancient and related traditions through its library, archives, participation in musical events, and scholarly affiliations.

Bob Castillo and Susan Cifaldi, *Benjamin Clark's Drum Book 1797* (1989); Susan Cifaldi, "Henry Blake, A New Hampshire Fifer in the Revolutionary War," *The Sonneck Society for American Music Bulletin* 14 (1988); Cifaldi, "The Company of Fifers and Drummers: Preserving the Music of the Ancient Fifes and Drums," *The Sonneck Society for American Music Bulletin* 16 (1990); William D. Piersen, *Black Yankees: The Development of an Afro-American Subculture in 18th-Century New England* (1988).

Susan Cifaldi

Folk Revival The folk revival of the late 1950s and 1960s was a brief cultural phenomenon. For approximately a decade, relatively affluent, well-educated, middle-class youth reinterpreted such traditional music forms as ballads, blues, country and bluegrass, and old-time string bands to create a new popular music genre that was an alternative to mass entertainment. New England was at the center of the folk revival, in part because of its many colleges and universities, which attracted young people and hangers-on, along with the surrounding coffeehouses, folksong societies, contra dance groups, and music stores with instruments and recordings. Two Amherst College students, Bill Keith and Jim Rooney, and a University of Massachusetts student, Taj Mahal, organized the Pioneer Valley Folklore Society in the late 1950s to put on concerts by popular folksingers, an activity repeated on other campuses and by folksong societies throughout the region. Soon they themselves became popular performers. Other groups formed at the same time, such as the Folk Song Society of Greater Boston, reflected the politics and social activism of earlier revivalists, particularly those in New York in the 1940s.

Part of the uniqueness of the New England folk song revival was that music and musicianship, rather than political activism, were firmly at its hub. Epicenters were venues in Boston like the Golden Vanity and Café Yana, and in Cambridge, Mass., Club 47, in addition to the annual Newport Folk Festival in Rhode Island. Club 47, a cultural icon and one of the most important revival venues in the country, started as a jazz club in 1958 but soon joined the folk music boom. It launched such regional performers as the folksinger Joan Baez; the Charles River Valley Boys, one of the first urban bluegrass groups to combine traditional musicians and revivalists; Tom Rush, a Harvard student from New Hampshire whose eclectic repertoire came in part from 19th- and early-20th-century academic song collections; Jackie Washington and Taj Mahal, who drew on their families' Puerto Rican, Caribbean, and African American traditions; Arlo Guthrie, whose "Alice's Restaurant" chronicled a Thanksgiving in the Berkshires along with commentary on Vietnam-era draft resistance; and the Jim Kweskin Jug Band, which took the revival into folk-rock and psychedelia before it ended. All of them played the Newport festivals and toured nationally. In addition, Club 47 and Newport worked together to introduce revivalists to earlier generations of recorded southern roots artists from the 1920s and 1930s, including Maybelle Carter, Mississippi John Hurt, Bill Monroe, and Muddy Waters.

Directly and indirectly, the folk revival was part of a long tradition in New England of interest in folk music, both inside and outside the academic milieu. The American Folklore Society (AFS) was founded in 1888 at Harvard. Many of its founders were independent scholars and antiquarians, particularly folk song collectors, such as Francis James Child, a medievalist at Harvard and first president of the AFS. Child's six-volume *English and Scottish Popular Ballads,* published between 1882 and 1898, provided texts for songs that revivalists sang half a century later at coffeehouses, festivals, concerts, and on recordings.

Country music also influenced the later revival. A decade before the coffeehouse boom, the radio show *Hillbilly at Harvard* began as *Barn Howl* in 1948, a closed-circuit country music broadcast to the college community that began transmitting publicly in 1957 and continues today. Commercial shows such as Boston WCOP's *Hayloft Jamboree* began broadcasting in the early 1950s and also organized Opry-like revues at Symphony Hall with touring country acts. Such bars as the Hillbilly Ranch in Park Square and nearby Mohawk Ranch catered to the thriving live country music scene supported by military personnel stationed nearby and the many Southerners who had come north to work or study. Groups like the Lilly Brothers from West Virginia included the banjo whiz Don Stover and the fiddler Tex Logan, whom many local musicians credit as major influences. Moreover, Everett Lilly had recorded with Flatt and Scruggs, and his son Everett Alan contributed traditional music-making credentials to the Charles River Valley Boys.

All of these artists, venues, and activities influenced revivalists who went on to become performers, record company and festival producers, agents and managers, and fans. Rounder Records was founded by several music enthusiasts in 1970 as a direct result of the revival and continues to record roots musicians from many traditions. Passim, the successor to Club 47, persevered during the lean years of the music business in the 1970s and 1980s and was a major player in developing and supporting the singer-songwriter phenomenon that contributed to the region's rich community-based coffeehouse tradition today and which combines traditional/roots and multicultural performers with newer contemporary genres The Newport Folk Festival, which paralleled all of these developments, ran from 1959 to 1969 and was revived in the mid-1980s and continues today.

By 1969, with the last Newport festival and the first Woodstock event in nearby New York, the revival was in decline. Fans and scholars have attributed the beginning of the end to Bob Dylan going electric at Newport in July 1965, although he was not the first to do so. A new generation of performers and genres was attracting their own followings.

The folk music revival of the late 1950s and 1960s left an important legacy in the region. The cultural connections inspired by the music made in coffeehouses and at festivals literally changed individual lives, public policy, and the course of American history in the second half of the 20th century. The revival helped to change notions of whom collective culture belongs to, and it helped create new models of social and political interaction in which the prevailing ethos was inspired and united by music. Today's popular culture regularly calls upon elders from the 1960s for its roots and continuity, and those who once sat at the feet of their heroes during the revival are now the ones at whose feet new generations are sitting. In its way, the folk revival lives on to influence new generations shaping the region's culture in the 21st century.

David Gahr and Robert Shelton, *The Face of Folk Music* (1968); Millie Rahn, "The Folk Revival: Beyond Child's Collecting and Sharp's Song Catching," in Rachel Rubin and Jeffrey Melnick, eds., *American Popular Music* (2001); Neil Rosenberg, ed., *Transforming Tradition: Folk Music Revivals Examined* (1993); Eric von Schmidt and Jim Rooney, *Baby, Let Me Follow You Down: The Illustrated Story of the Cambridge Folk Years* (1979).

Millie Rahn

Franco-American Music Franco-American music is rooted in the social experience of French-speaking immigrants who left Quebec and the Maritime Provinces between roughly 1850 and 1950 to seek jobs in New England's burgeoning textile, manufacturing, and forestry industries and to farm small plots of land in the northern border regions. Living largely in Francophone enclaves but exposed to a broad range of folk and popular music that circulated in New England, Franco-Americans developed an eclectic musical tradition that joined genres and performance styles imported from Francophone Canada with local musical influences. As Franco-Americans appropriated local music, they left their mark on it. For example, the present-day tune repertory of New England square and contra dancing includes many melodies commonly played in French Canada, including "St. Anne's Reel," "Reel de Tadoussac" ("Glise à Sherbrooke"), and "Reel des Moissonneurs" ("Irish-American Reel"). As the primacy of the French language has receded among the descendants of immigrants, and neighborhood enclaves have given way to assimilation and intermingling, Franco-American music has assumed new social roles. Identified less with an ethnic group bound together by shared language, culture, and territory than with an ethnically heterogeneous community united by common musical interests, Franco-American music has become one among many elements of New England's folk music culture. At the same time, it has provided an expressive outlet for a small but active group of younger Franco-American artists who are striving to

Ben Guillemette performs at La Kermesse, a Franco-American festival, Biddeford, Maine, 1985

revive and reimagine a sense of Franco-American identity in the face of diaspora, assimilation, and language loss.

Franco-American music includes both vocal and instrumental genres. Instrumental music consists of reels and, to a lesser extent, waltzes, and jigs in $\frac{6}{8}$ time, performed on the violin, harmonica, or, more rarely, accordion and typically accompanied on piano or guitar. A distinctive feature of such dance music is the rhythmic foot clogging with which players of melody instruments typically accompany themselves—the vestige of a rural Quebec performance tradition that arose at a time when pianos and guitars were rarely available. These days, the Franco-American tune repertory includes not only tunes indigenous to Quebec and the Maritimes—many with the characteristic Quebecois "crooked" meter (*air crôche* or *air tordu*) in which one or more melodic phrases are expanded or contracted through the addition of an extra, and unanticipated, metrical beat—but tunes whose origins are linked to New England or to the southern Appalachian region. Southern tunes became popular in Quebec and the Maritimes and subsequently among Franco-American musicians through the influence of recordings, radio and television and, for the past 30 to 40 years, fiddle contests.

Vocal genres include strophic songs (*chanson*) traditionally sung a cappella by a single singer, "response songs" (*chanson à répondre*), in which a group of singers (*répondeurs*) antiphonally repeats the refrain and last line or couplet of a strophe sung by a soloist, and "mouth music" (*turlutte*)—lilting to fast dance tunes. Macaronic French-English texts have long been a presence in the song repertory. The traditional venue for chanson singing is the *soirée* or *veillé*—a social evening of participatory music making centered on extended family members and friends. Singers often compile their own handwritten collections of song texts. Published chanson collections from Quebec are also in circulation, but no

single publication has emerged as an authoritative representation of Franco-American song repertory, which includes pre-19th-century French songs, 19th- and 20th-century popular songs, and local compositions.

As fluency in French has waned among younger generations of Franco-Americans, the soirée or veillé as a venue of egalitarian and participatory music making has all but been replaced by contemporary forms of musical commodification. Franco-American musicians, often performing in small ensembles, entertain audiences at regional folk and folk heritage festivals, record and distribute their own compact discs and cassettes, and play for community events and at clubs and cafes that feature traditional folk music. Among the best-known annual folk festivals that focus on or include Franco-American music are the Champlain Valley Folk Festival in Burlington, Vt.; the New World Festival in Randolph, Vt.; the Festival de la joie in Lewiston, Maine; Festival La Kermesse in Biddeford, Maine; Festival acadien in Madawaska, Maine; Le Jubile in Woonsocket, R.I.; and La semaine franco-américaine in Lowell, Mass. A rising generation of Franco-American singer-songwriters continues to add to the chanson repertory, turning out compositions that often dwell reflexively on the experience of being Franco-American in an Anglophone society. Writing in a mixture of French and English, such performers as Michèle Choinière, Donna Hébert, Lillian Labbé, Lucie Therrien, and Josée Vachon have helped the new Franco-American chanson to enter the mainstream of the New England folk revival.

Brigitte Marie Lane, *Franco-American Folk Traditions and Popular Culture in a Former Milltown: Aspects of Ethnic Urban Folklore and the Dynamics of Folklore Change in Lowell, Massachusetts* (1990); Genevive Massignon, *Trésors de la chanson populaire française: autour de cinquante chansons recueillies en Acadie*, 2 vols. (1994); Eusbe Viau and Ernest Philie, *Chants populaires des Franco-Américains*, 12 vols. (1929); *Franco-America: French Music from the New England Borderlands* [sound recording] (1998), Smithsonian Folkways.

Theodore Levin

Gardner, Newport (ca. 1746–1826) Composer. Born Occramer Marycoo, Newport Gardner was an African slave in colonial Rhode Island who showed conspicuous talent as a music composer; most of his music is now unfortunately lost. In 1760, Captain Caleb Gardner, a prominent merchant of Newport, R.I., purchased the 14-year-old slave, who had just arrived from Africa, and renamed him Newport. The Gardners quickly recognized his intelligence; he was taught to speak and read English and quickly became proficient in music. By age 18, he was composing church music. He also had a strong singing voice and gave music lessons to men and women in his community.

Gardner studied music under Andrew Law, a well-known itinerant Congregationalist composer. Other prominent composers living in Newport in the late colonial period were William Selby, Josiah Flagg, and W. S. Morgan, all briefly organists at Trinity Episcopal Church, and Gardner could easily have studied with any or all of them before they returned to Boston. Gardner's piety and zeal as a Christian prompted the abolitionist minister the Reverend Dr. Samuel Hopkins to appoint him the sexton of his First Congregational Church and to give him private lessons in theology. Hopkins, one of the first clergymen to denounce slavery publicly, hoped to buy Gardner's freedom and send him to Africa as a missionary, but the American Revolution intervened.

Gardner and his wife and children were not granted their freedom until 1791; in that year Gardner established a school on High Street in Newport to teach reading, writing, music, and country dance. One of his first music students at the school was the wife of his former master. Gardner wrote at least one lengthy church anthem, "Promise," the text of which (based loosely on a passage from Jeremiah) survives, although the music has been lost. "Crook'd Shanks," a country dance tune, was published in 1803 under Gardner's name but was published twice previously in Britain under the names "The Seaside" (Bride, 1768) and "Bill of Rights" (Thompson, 1776). Undoubtedly, Caleb Gardner was so impressed by these country dances written by a young African man so recently introduced to Western music and dance forms that he sent them to London to be published—but neglected to see that the composer's identity was revealed. Although Newport Gardner was known to have composed many melodies, his name is no longer connected with any specific music other than these few.

Gardner founded the Free African Union Society in 1780, which was essentially the first black self-help society in America. The organization eventually evolved into the African Benevolent Society and in 1808 opened a school thought to be the country's first to be financed and run entirely by blacks. Gardner was among the school's first teachers. In 1824, he founded the Colored Union Church in Newport. A leader of the back-to-Africa movement in the United States, Gardner persisted in his lifelong desire to return to his native country. In 1826 Gardner (then about 80) and Solmar Nubia, both deacons, led 32 black colonists aboard the brig *Vine,* sailing from Boston to Liberia. Gardner stated that he was embarking on such a perilous undertaking at his great age in order to encourage younger people to return to Africa. Within six months of their arrival in Africa, however, both leaders and many other group members died, as they had no immunity to West African diseases.

John F. Millar, *Country Dances in Colonial America* (1990); Eileen Southern, "On Composers: Newport Gardner," *The Black Perspective in Music* (July 1976).

John F. Millar

Gray, Spalding (1941–2004)

Actor, writer. Born in Barrington, R.I., the actor Spalding Gray made a career of intense self-examination with demandingly autobiographical works that plumb his family and experience, laying bare his innermost life and its intersection with his times. Raised in a quintessential suburban neighborhood, Gray probed the anxieties behind the calm exterior of 1950s life. As a New Englander who grew up in an increasingly complex and multiethnic, though highly parochial state, Gray presented with irony, wit, and considerable affection the secrets of his family life.

Gray began acting in 1965 after earning a B.A. degree from Emerson College in Boston. In 1970 he joined the Performance Group, an avant-garde environmental theater project operating out of a garage on Wooster Street in New York's Soho section, the center of the emerging "downtown scene." The group, an important influence on Gray, featured him in such roles as Hoss in Sam Shepard's *The Tooth of Crime* (1974), Swiss Cheese in Bertolt Brecht's *Mother Courage and Her Children* (1975 and 1977), and the Bishop in Jean Genet's *The Balcony* (1979).

Gray's downtown period also saw his emergence as an autobiographical performance artist with his *Three Places in Rhode Island* (1975–78) trilogy (*Sakonnet Point, Rumstick Road,* and *Nayatt School*), which he developed in collaboration with fellow group member Elizabeth LeCompte. Works assuming a regional slant are his play *Point Judith: An Epilog* (Performing Garage, 1979) and the monologue *Travels through New England* (Brattle Theatre, Cambridge, Mass., 1984). Although he worked mostly on the off- and off-off-Broadway stage, he made a critically acclaimed Broadway debut in 1988 as the Stage Manager in Thornton Wilder's *Our Town.*

The most important of Gray's many film appearances involved his own unflinching yet comic-neurotic self-reflections. He starred in three films based on his monologues: *Swimming to Cambodia* (1987), *Monster in a Box* (1992), and *Gray's Anatomy* (1996); the last two were autobiographical books as well. In *Gray's Anatomy,* directed by Steven Soderbergh, Gray, who was raised a Christian Scientist, learns he has a rare eye disease and, with a tragicomic desperation, explores the gamut of alternative treatments. As in his other monologue films, his self-examination is never mere self-indulgence. While a kind of talk therapy for his own fears and ambivalence, the monologues are also meditations on our troubled times. Gray structured them around a seated-at-a-desk direct address he developed on stage in the early 1980s as he grew uneasy portraying others' emotions and sought simpler, more direct audience contact. The handful of films based on Gray's monologues place him in the company of director Louis Malle and others who have cultivated a tiny, divergent niche known as talk movies.

Acting in a diverse set of potboilers since 1970, Gray played a variety of roles. More recently his screen persona leaned toward "bow tie type"—stiff, patrician New Englander roles: the formal, refined, reserved official; the well-educated professional; a member of the power elite. Among them are his U.S. consul in *The Killing Fields* (1984), his clergymen in *Stars and Bars* (1988) and *Twenty Bucks* (1993), his doctors in *Seven Minutes in Heaven* (1986), *Beaches* (1988), *Straight Talk* (1992), and *The Pickle* (1993), and his newspaper editor in Ron Howard's *The Paper* (1994). In January 2004 Gray disappeared; his body was discovered two months later, an apparent suicide.

Spalding Gray, *Gray's Anatomy* (1994); Gray, *Monster in a Box* (1992); Gray, *Sex and Death to Age 14* (1986); Gray, *Swimming to Cambodia* (1985).

Wayne Munson

Hepburn, Katharine (1907–2003)

Actress. Born in Hartford, Katharine Hepburn had a distinguished career on stage and screen and is the only woman to have won the Best Actress Oscar four times—for *Morning Glory* (1933), *Guess Who's Coming to Dinner?* (1967), *The Lion in Winter* (1968), and *On Golden Pond* (1981). From her accent to her independent spirit, Hepburn's distinctive combination of on-screen qualities projected a New England persona. She was assertive yet sacrificially loyal, playful and adventurous yet proper, idealistic yet businesslike. Hepburn epitomized such qualities in her most quintessentially Yankee roles: Ethel Thayer in *On Golden Pond* and Jo March in *Little Women* (1933).

The product of a progressive, affluent upbringing—her mother was a birth control and women's rights advocate, her father a surgeon—Hepburn began a stage career in 1928, soon after graduating from Bryn Mawr College. Her first film, David O. Selznick's version of *A Bill of Divorcement* (1932), was directed by George Cukor and released by RKO. The film was Hepburn's breakthrough and the beginning of a longtime association with Cukor, with whom she worked on eight feature films and two made-for-TV movies.

Hepburn's early success with RKO faded by the mid-1930s, as seven consecutive box office failures turned her into "box office poison." She rejected the B-film roles RKO offered her and returned to the stage—a response consistent with her firm, secure, upper-crust independence. In 1938 her appearances with Cary Grant in *Holiday* and *Bringing Up Baby* rehabilitated her movie career. The film version of *The Philadelphia Story* (1940), in which she also starred opposite Grant, was written for the stage by Phillip Barry specifically for Hepburn. Hepburn bought the film rights to the play and made any film version conditional upon her playing the lead and George Cukor directing. The film's success earned her a long-term MGM contract.

Woman of the Year (1942) began her 25-year collaboration and love affair with Spencer Tracy. This film was another instance in which Hepburn sold film rights to a studio and selected her costar. She and Tracy made 10 films together; nine were MGM comedies. Cukor directed three: *Keeper of the Flame* (1942), *Adam's Rib* (1949), and *Pat and Mike* (1952). Cukor was best at creating the "loving competition" (in the film historian Janine Basinger's words) that would become the Tracy-Hepburn comic trademark. The high-mindedness of Hepburn's characters collided with the down-to-earth practicality of Tracy's, their emotional interdependence growing even as each remained strong-willed. By the 1950s, Hepburn took the part of formidable spinsters forced by circumstances to become involved with swaggering men in *The African Queen* (1951), costarring Humphrey Bogart, and *The Rainmaker* (1956), costarring Burt Lancaster. Throughout her career, Hepburn was cast in roles reflecting her New England roots; she represented the stable traditions of American morality and character.

Although she appeared rarely on the screen after the 1980s, she wrote two memoirs, *The Making of "The African Queen"* (1987) and *Me: Stories of My Life* (1991). She retired to her family's seaside home, Fenwick, in Old Saybrook, Conn., where she died in 2003 after a long illness.

Anne Edwards, *A Remarkable Woman: A Biography of Katharine Hepburn* (1985); Garson Kanin, *Tracy and Hepburn: An Intimate Memoir* (1971).

Wayne Munson

Hutchinson Family Singers (fl. 1840–90)

Popular singers and social reformers. The Hutchinson Family Singers were perhaps America's best-known popular singers of the 19th century. The group originated when the four youngest children of a large Milford,

N.H., family—Judson (1817–59), John (1821–1908), Asa (1823–84), and Abigail ("Abby," 1829–92)—fashioned themselves into a quartet after being inspired by the example of the Rainer Family, a Tyrolian group that made an extensive tour of the United States between 1839 and 1843. Like many New Englanders of the antebellum period, the Hutchinsons learned basic skills in singing school and developed their talents further through church and family singing. The group's popularity reached its peak in the mid-1840s after successful concerts throughout New England in late 1842 and in New York in May 1843. In 1845 and 1846 they toured Great Britain and Ireland, where they sang to adoring audiences that often numbered in the thousands.

At first the Hutchinsons sang popular and religious songs that did not reveal their commitment to social and political reform. By late 1843, however, their concerts included songs that championed the rights of disadvantaged groups such as American Indians, women, the sick, the insane, and the poor and promoted causes like temperance, communitarianism, and, most explosively, abolitionism. Although the music they performed was often composed by others, they also set topical texts of their own creation to tunes in the popular domain and claimed the songs as their own. Two of their best-known songs are of this type: "The Old Granite State" (1843), the Hutchinsons's signature song with verses that changed according to audience and circumstance, was set to a Millerite hymn tune; "Get Off the Track" (1844), one of their most powerful statements supporting William Lloyd Garrison's theme of immediate emancipation, was set, ironically, to "Old Dan Tucker," a tune from the blackface minstrel tradition.

Although they were mainly singers, the Hutchinsons often accompanied themselves with violins (probably played like fiddles), cello, harmonium, and, later, guitar. Their sound was unique for its sweet quality (unlike the harsh, nasal sound that was then prevalent), which they achieved through a seamless blending of their rich, flexible voices. They eschewed singing styles associated with European classical training and aimed rather for a natural, informal tone.

By singing reform music that was accessible and charming, the Hutchinson Family Singers proved especially attractive to an important segment of the period's new audience for concerts: those committed to family-based society, middle-class respectability, and the reformation of social mores. After Abby's marriage broke up the original quartet in 1849, the Hutchinson brothers sang together as the Tribe of Jesse (a tribute to their father) and then established touring and performing "tribes" of

their own family members. By so doing, the Hutchinson Family Singers remained a force in popular music until near the end of the century. Their commitment to social reform never wavered in any of the group's incarnations. The most important contribution the Hutchinson family made to American music was to fashion a popular, commercially successful means for white, middle-class tastes and values—many of which originated in New England—to find powerful expression through music.

Carol Ryrie Brink, *Harps in the Wind: The Story of the Singing Hutchinsons* (1947); Dale Cockrell, ed., *Excelsior: Journals of the Hutchinson Family Singers, 1842–1846* (1989); John W. Hutchinson, *Story of the Hutchinsons (Tribe of Jesse)*, 2 vols. (1896); Philip D. Jordan, *Singin' Yankees* (1946).

Dale Cockrell

Irish Music

Irish music has been popular in New England since the 1840s, when emigrants fleeing the Great Famine arrived in local ports. Musicians provided a salve during this period; as one newspaper noted, "Any person who can play violin, flute (or) pipe becomes of interest . . . and is kept in constant requisition."

A central part of Ireland's folk culture for many centuries, Irish music was transferred to urban enclaves in Boston, New Haven, Portland, and Providence, where it resides today. These cities, along with Hartford, Lawrence, Cape Cod, southern Vermont, and central and seacoast New Hampshire, form a well-traveled circuit for touring Irish bands performing at concert halls, dances, festivals, and parades.

Irish music ranges from songs (in English and Irish) and slow airs to dance music such as jigs, reels, hornpipes, and waltzes, typically played on acoustic instruments. Irish music blends readily with other regional genres like contra dance, maritime, folk, and popular music, while keeping its distinct sound. Of late, Irish tunes have turned up in New Age and World Music. Over time, the American influence has created a hybrid of popular Irish drinking songs, vaudeville jingles, and sentimental ballads. Traditional music is increasingly popular in pubs hosting nightly music sessions, particularly in Boston.

One reason Irish music has retained much of its vitality for a century and a half is that the Irish continue to immigrate here. Over roughly the past 80 years, Patsy Touhey, the Hanafin brothers, Dan Sullivan, Ann "Ma" McNulty, Larry Reynolds, Tommy Makem, and Paddy Keenan have all had a major impact on the region's Irish scene.

The high point of Irish music in this century may have been the 1950s, when Boston's Dudley Street boasted five dance halls featuring Irish, Scottish, and Canadian musicians and drawing people from the region. The combination of American-born musicians like Joe Derrane, Billy Caples, and Myles O'Malley with immigrants like Martin Flaherty, Paddy Cronin, and Matty Toohey created a high-caliber music scene, and interactions among musicians from various regional traditions encouraged considerable creativity. Irish set dancing was fashionable during this decade and has again been revived since the late 1980s by a new generation of dancers. Indeed, Irish music is currently very popular in many parts of North America and Europe, and this transnational Celtic revival has merged with the older New England scene, bringing new audiences, not necessarily Irish, to the music. Green Linnet, a record label in Danbury, Conn., has been influential in that revival.

Local chapters of Comhaltas Ceoltoiri Eireann (Musicians' association of Ireland) teach music to children and encourage non-Irish participation. Many Comhaltas musicians compete in the National Championships held in Ireland each summer.

Irish music now enjoys an academic distinction. Since 1992 Boston College's Irish studies program has featured the formal study of Irish music and dance. The program, headed by the acclaimed fiddler Seamus Connolly, offers student instruction during the year and hosts musical gatherings with local Irish musicians. Each June, numerous musicians from around the world convene on campus for a week of workshops and formal concerts. The John J. Burns Library at Boston College has a music archive that collects recordings and sheet music related to Irish music in North America.

The famed music collector Francis O'Neill's observations on the local Irish music scene in 1907 can be readily applied to New England today: "There is no danger that Irish music will be forgotten in Boston or its environs in the near future."

Francis O'Neill, *Irish Minstrels and Musicians: The Story of Irish Music* (1987); Deborah L. Schaeffer, *Irish Folk Music: A Selected Discography* (1989); William H. A. Williams, *'Twas Only an Irishman's Dream* (1996).
Michael P. Quinlin

Ives, Charles Edward (1874–1954)

Composer. The creative life of Charles Edward Ives, composer and businessman, bridged two centuries. Rooted in postbellum, 19th-century America, most of the works for which he is known were composed after the turn of the century. Distinctly modernist in style and avant-garde in its time, Ives's music is frequently based on the hymn tunes, college songs, sentimental parlor ballads, and the patriotic and military music characteristic of the second half of the 19th century. Indeed, the distinctive amalgamation of the old within the new that marks his style often evokes a sense of nostalgia for earlier times.

Ives was born in rural Connecticut and eventually settled on a farm in the Connecticut countryside at West Redding, near his Danbury birthplace. Other New England places, including Concord, Mass., became sacred to him. Ives embraced two careers, the second that of businessman, in which he was comparably creative, instituting such innovations in the insurance industry as estate planning that are still in practice. Adding to the complexity of man and artist, through his business career Ives achieved a degree of wealth rarely found in a composer.

Charles Ives was born of forebears whose varied and contrasting accomplishments foreshadow the unique integration of the diverse talents that characterize Ives's life and work. His father, George Edward Ives, was the village bandmaster in Danbury and, later in life, a clerk in a local bank founded by his own father. During the Civil War, George, at the age of 19, had served as bandmaster in the Union Army. He was a hero in the eyes of young Charlie, who would later, in his prose writings, create a highly idealized legend of his father, an inventive musician well trained in the Germanic tradition. Ives's mother, Mary Elizabeth Parmelee Ives, came from a modest working-class background in nearby Bethel. The Ives clan had distinguished itself in Danbury in many major civic accomplishments and commercial enterprises. Ives's father had eschewed such endeavors in favor of music only to turn to them later in order to earn an adequate living and send his sons to school. A further strong influence on the young Ives was a patrician maternal aunt, Amelia Ives Brewster, and her distinguished husband, Judge Lyman Brewster; they paved the way for Ives to attend Yale University, his uncle's alma mater.

If his father was, as Ives said, the Union's youngest bandmaster, Charlie, at the age of 15, was the youngest professional church organist in the state. He had already begun to compose with his father, who had considerable knowledge of traditional musical practice. Charlie's anticipated entry into Yale tempered the intense collaborative relationship between father and son. His father's death during Ives's first year at Yale proved to be a loss that he mourned in varied ways for the rest of his life. Some of his finest works—especially his Civil War pieces—are, in effect, memorials to his father, notably the "Decoration Day" movement of his *New England Holidays* symphony (1904–13) and the "The St. Gaudens in Boston Common" movement of his *Three Places in New England* (1903–14). "Thoreau," the final movement of his masterpiece, Piano Sonata No. 2, subtitled "Concord, Mass., 1840–1860" (1909–15), also falls into this category, the flute-playing Thoreau conflated with George Ives, the sound of his instrument wafting over the pond.

While at Yale, Ives studied with the exemplary American musician and composer-cum-teacher Horatio Parker, under whose influence he wrote his First Symphony (completed 1898) and portions of the Second (1897–1902). Parker served as a model for Ives and educated him further in the styles and genres of European classical tradition to which his father had introduced him. He also began composing in the three traditions that have been said to characterize Ives's work: American popular music, Protestant church music, and European classical music—all in addition to Ives's own developing experimental tendencies.

Following graduation from Yale in 1898, Ives worked in New York as an insurance clerk and part-time organist. In 1907 he founded the insurance company Ives and Myrick. Ives meanwhile entered his most innovative and experimental period, an interval of a half dozen years during which he composed evenings and weekends while working days in his Wall Street office. In effect, as his first biographers put it, he was writing "his father's music," replete with musical and literary allusions that related to the life of George Ives and his times. Ives's distinctive stylistic habit of musical quotation and the numerous innovative techniques and radical departures tinged frequently with humor were characteristic of the musical "stunts" and experimentation of his bandmaster father.

At Yale he had already experimented with such pieces as the *Fugue in Four Keys* (1897) and the markedly dissonant *Three Harvest Home Chorales* (1898–1901). Such works as *Halloween* (1906) and the string Trio (1904–11) with its humorous scherzo entitled "TSIAJ" (This scherzo is a joke) were produced during this innovative period

Also characteristic of this uniquely concentrated creative period is what has come to be Ives's signature piece, *The Unanswered Question* (1906), with its layering of diverse musical elements. There are two sections: I "A Contemplation of a Serious Matter" or "The Unanswered Perennial Question" and II "A Contemplation of Nothing Serious" or "Central Park in the Dark in 'The Good Old Summertime.'" In these pieces one encounters the intense spirituality characteristic of Ives's music. The spirituality of his Pulitzer Prize–winning Third Symphony, subtitled "The Camp Meeting" (1904–11), is of a homespun, conventional, and quotidian nature, distinctly

19th century and American in spirit. In contrast, the Fourth Symphony (1909–16) invokes a mystical eschatology of considerable emotional depth in its incorporation of the hymn "Watchman, Tell Us of the Night." Ives's spiritual apogee in a conceptualized *Universe Symphony* remained only in the composer's sketch and marginalia. Unrealized during Ives's lifetime, it may indeed be unrealizable as living music and perhaps an intentionally uncompletable aspiration.

Ives's marriage in 1908 to Harmony Twichell, daughter of the Reverend Joseph Twichell of Hartford, and adoption of daughter Edith brought not only a period of stability and happiness but another profound personal and artistic influence. Accordingly, it ushered in the most creative period of Ives's life. During this productive decade Ives completed his greatest works, including his *New England Holidays* symphony (an American "four seasons" consisting of "Washington's Birthday," "The Fourth of July," "Decoration Day," and "Thanksgiving and Forefathers' Day"), the *Three Places in New England* (namely, "The 'St. Gaudens' in Boston Common," "Putnam's Camp," and "The Housatonic at Stockbridge"), and the Piano Sonata No. 2. In conjunction with this last, also known as the *Concord Sonata*, Ives wrote his prose *Essays before a Sonata*. They constitute Ives's unique musical and verbal encomium for the New England Transcendentalists: Emerson, Hawthorne, Alcott, and Thoreau. In the sonata, they are together beside their final resting place in Sleepy Hollow Cemetery in Concord, Mass., one of the places in New England that Ives and Harmony visited on their honeymoon.

In 1922 Ives published the sonata and its *Essays* along with his *114 Songs,* a culminating compilation consisting of a significant portion of characteristic and quasi-autobiographical songs. Published without copyright, he distributed this final trilogy freely. He was by then aware of an ebbing creative flow, and although he lived until nearly 80, he stopped composing around the time he reached the age at which his father had died: 49.

The creative mind of Charles Ives was imbued with a profound sense of person, time, and place. Deeply attached to the people he loved, he achieved a unique integration of contrasting influences, "a union of diversities" that, in turn, is discernible in his music. The *114 Songs* reveal the man as if autobiography; the *Holidays* creates a temporal context within which the 19th and 20th centuries converge in a musical amalgam of past and present; and finally, the *Places* fixes Ives and his music in what was for him the center of his personal universe: New England.

J. Peter Burkholder, *Charles Ives: The Ideas behind the Music* (1985); Henry Cowell and Sidney Cowell, *Charles Ives and His Music* (1955); Stuart Feder, *Charles Ives, "My Father's Song": A Psychoanalytic Biography* (1992); Feder, *The Life of Charles Ives* (1999); Charles Ives, *Essays before a Sonata,* ed., Howard Boatwright (1970); Ives, *Memos,* ed., John Kirkpatrick (1972); Vivian Perlis, *Charles Ives Remembered: An Oral History* (1974); Larry Starr, *A Union of Diversities: Style in the Music of Charles Ives* (1992).

Stuart Feder

Jacob's Pillow Tucked off U.S. 20 as it winds through Massachusetts's Berkshire hills lies America's premier summer dance festival and school. Originally a farm owned by the Carter family, Jacob's Pillow was named in 1790 to complement the stage route connecting Boston and Albany, called Jacob's Ladder for its many switchbacks. In 1930 the modern dancer Ted Shawn, a former divinity student, bought the property, where he founded a summer dance retreat in 1933. Set on 150 bucolic acres, Jacob's Pillow has long been a center of intense creative activity. Here young dancers train in a wide variety of dance forms; renowned artists and choreographers perfect pieces, create new works, and share ideas with other artists; and the public enjoys formal performances as well as staged works-in-progress.

Shawn, who began dance as an adult, chose not to be constrained by balletic traditions. Rather, he folded diverse ethnic forms into his dance performances, as theatrical as they were graceful. As his style matured, his openness became a guiding principle: "Every way that any human being of any race or nationality, at any period of human history, has moved rhythmically to express himself, belongs to the dance." Shawn sought to systemize the basic elements of dance, and in 1915, with his wife, the dancer Ruth St. Denis, he opened the Denishawn School in Los Angeles, where a number of emerging modern dance artists trained. When the couple separated, Shawn launched a project to convince the American public that dance was an acceptable, indeed quintessentially masculine, career for men.

At Jacob's Pillow, Shawn founded his touring group of Men Dancers, including college athletes. There they trained, communed, and built housing and studio space. In July 1933 Shawn and the Men Dancers began offering promotional *Tea Lecture Demonstrations* at the Pillow. The Men Dancers disbanded in 1940 after seven highly successful years of performing throughout the United States, to join the armed forces. Mary Washington Ball, a dance educator, leased the Pillow and diversified the instructional and performance programs. The following year the British ballet stars Alicia Markova and Anton Dolin leased Jacob's Pillow and inaugurated an International Dance Festival that drew wide attention.

By 1941 all the building blocks of Jacob's Pillow Dance Festival were in place; local supporters incorporated the institution and hired Shawn to lead it. In 1942 a 514-seat (since expanded to 619) theater bearing Shawn's name, the first in the United States designed exclusively for dance, was erected. Shawn continued to direct Jacob's Pillow until his death in 1972.

The mission of Jacob's Pillow has remained firm as subsequent executive directors have broadened its offerings. Students and masters of ballet, modern, jazz, folk, and ethnic dance share studio space and perform on the three separate stages, one of which is set in the open air against a beautiful Berkshire backdrop. Each summer more than 50,000 visitors peek into studios, picnic on the Pillow's sprawling grounds, and attend lectures, exhibits, and performances.

One of the Berkshires' gems, Jacob's Pillow has been praised as the "hub and mecca of dance." Drawn across cultures and geographic boundaries, all who make the pilgrimage to its grounds experience the joys and transcendent rewards of the universalizing power of dance.

Norton Owen, *A Certain Place: The Jacob's Pillow Story* (1997); Thea Singer, "Context and Content," *Boston Globe,* July 5, 1998; *The Story of Jacob's Pillow* (n.d.); Walter Terry, *Ted Shawn: Father of American Dance* (1976).

Linda Smith Rhoads

Jewish Music The first Jewish music heard on New England shores was brought over by members of the Sephardic (Spanish- or Portuguese-rooted) Jewish community who came from New Amsterdam (New York) to Newport, R.I., in 1658, and New England has been the home of countless Jewish musicians since, supporting not only cantors and synagogue performers but also folksingers, Yiddish actors, composers, art singers, and instrumentalists performing in a wide variety of styles.

In the 1800s Jewish immigrants from Germany began to arrive in New England and quickly established communities in Boston, Providence, New Haven and Hartford, Conn., Manchester, N.H., and many smaller towns. They brought with them the classically influenced music of European cantors and church-influenced German Jewish hymn tunes. Unlike the unaccompanied chants of the Sephardim who preceded them, their religious music was often performed by mixed choirs with organ accompaniment.

During the last quarter of the 19th century a

large influx of East European Jewish immigrants arrived, settling in every major New England city. The Yiddish theater arrived in Boston shortly after 1900, first appearing at the South End's Grand Opera House and later at Roxbury's Franklin Park Theater. Ben Gailing, a mainstay of Boston's Yiddish music scene since 1931, kept traditional Yiddish theater music alive in that city well into the 1970s, bringing talent from New York on many occasions. Boston also spawned its fair share of popular Yiddish singers, including Dinah Goldberg, Annie Lubin, Irving Grossman, and Miriam Kressyn. Yiddish vaudeville traveled to and played in theaters all over New England through the 1930s.

Another cornerstone of New England's Jewish music scene was the New England Jewish Music Forum. Founded in 1958 by Herbert Fromm, the cantor Alex Zimmer, the composer Minuetta Kessler, and the vocalist-educator-impresario Mary Wolfman Epstein, the forum presented the best in local and internationally acclaimed Jewish talent in a low-priced subscription series and commissioned new works. The forum was dissolved in 1990, its records becoming part of the collection of the American Jewish Historical Society.

New England has also produced several important composers of Jewish concert music, including Leonard Bernstein, born in Lawrence, Mass.; Reuven Kosakoff, from New Haven, Conn.; and Herbert Fromm, who settled in Boston after emigrating from Germany in 1937.

New England's klezmer (East European Jewish instrumental) tradition centered in Boston and Providence. Most of Boston's klezmorim came from the same musical dynasty, which emanated from Iazaslav in the Ukraine. Although the area's original klezmer scene has virtually disappeared, a new tradition introduced in the 1980s by Boston's Klezmer Conservatory Band now flourishes. Other prominent New England groups include the Shirim Klezmer Orchestra and the Wholesale Klezmer Band and Klezamir of Massachusetts, Vermont's Nisht Geferlekh, the Casco Bay Tummlers of southern Maine, Connecticut's Yale Klezmer Band and Hartford Klezmer Ensemble, and the East Side Klezmer Band of Providence.

New England boasts a proud heritage of Jewish choral societies. The region's best-known Jewish chorus is the Zamir Chorale of Boston, an early offshoot of New York's Zamir Chorale. Founded and directed by the Northeastern University professor Joshua Jacobson in 1969, the group performs a full Jewish liturgical and secular repertoire and has initiated many creative collaborative presentations.

New England's Hasidic music centers are Boston (home of the Bostoner and Talner dynasties) and Providence (headquarters of the Zhviller Rebe). The region has a proud cantorial tradition and one of the most active chapters of the Jewish Ministers Cantors Association of America. The rich Sephardic heritage of Ladino folk song has been revived by the early music scholar Judith Wachs, who founded the pioneering Boston-based ensemble Voice of the Turtle in 1978. Recent Russian immigrants have had a profound impact on New England's Jewish music, as have the many Israeli musicians who have settled in the region. Locally based rock groups such as Safam have attracted a young audience to Jewish music. With courses in Jewish music now being offered by several area colleges and universities, New England has become well established as a center of Jewish musical creativity and talent.

Irene Heskes, *Passport to Jewish Music: Its History, Traditions, and Culture* (1994); Neil Levin, *Songs of the American Jewish Experience* (1976); Rosie Rosenzweig, ed., *The Jewish Guide to Boston and New England* (1995).

Hankus Netsky

Koussevitzky, Serge (Sergey Aleksandrovich Kusevitsky) (1874–1951)

Conductor, musician. Born in Russia, Serge Koussevitzky, the conductor of the Boston Symphony Orchestra (BSO) from 1924 to 1949, was a colorful and imposing figure. During his tenure, the BSO became one of the finest orchestras in the United States. His dedication to young composers and performers led him to found the Berkshire (now Tanglewood) Music Center and the Koussevitzky foundation, which has had a lasting impact on American music.

At the age of 14 Serge Koussevitzky received a scholarship to study the double-bass with Joseph Rambousek at the School of the Moscow Philharmonic Society. In 1894 he joined the Bolshoi Theater Orchestra and succeeded his teacher as principal double-bass in 1901. In 1905, he and his bride, the wealthy Natalie Ushkov, moved to Berlin, where he learned to conduct by observing the great Arthur Nikisch and others in performance. Koussevitzky hired the Berlin Philharmonic for his conducting debut. Returning to Moscow in 1909, he established a music publishing house and formed an orchestra to disseminate the European repertory and perform contemporary Russian works published by his company. After the Bolshevik Revolution, he was director of the State Symphony Orchestra (formerly the Imperial Orchestra) in Petrograd, but in 1920 he and his wife left Russia

Serge Koussevitzky, 1933

for Paris because of political differences. Forming his own orchestra in Paris, he organized the Concerts Symphoniques Koussevitzky, quickly establishing himself as a premier interpreter of French works and an advocate of new music. After turning down offers from other American orchestras, he accepted an appointment with the Boston Symphony Orchestra in 1924. He became an American citizen in 1941.

Under Koussevitzky, the BSO was known for its colorful and emotionally charged performances. He actively championed new music, and BSO performances helped establish the reputations of many young American composers, including Samuel Barber, Aaron Copland, Howard Hanson, David Diamond, Roy Harris, William Howard Schuman, and Walter Piston. For the BSO's 50th anniversary in 1931, Koussevitzky commissioned 10 new masterworks, most notably Igor Stravinsky's *Symphony of Psalms*. Leonard Bernstein became Koussevitzky's protégé after participating in conducting classes at Tanglewood in the summer of 1940.

In 1940 Koussevitzky founded the Berkshire (now Tanglewood) Music Center as a training ground for professional musicians, and in 1942, in his wife's memory, he created the Koussevitzky Music Foundation to encourage composition of new music. The Koussevitzky Music Foundation continues to support musical causes and organizations. In 1949, through an endowment from the original foundation, the commissioning and dissemination of new works was transferred to the Serge Koussevitzky Music Foundation at the Library of Congress. Koussevitzky retired from the BSO in 1949 and died in Boston two years later.

Dr. Koussevitzky, as he was known, was a charismatic figure on the podium. Comparisons to his contemporaries Leopold Stokowski in Philadelphia and Arturo Toscanini in New York are inevitable. While his conducting technique did not match theirs, his musical conception and command of his musicians produced highly scintillating, dramatic performances. Emphasizing nuance, color, and musical line, he was a preeminent interpreter of Russian music and the 20th-century French school. His enthusiasm and conviction in performance could persuade both orchestra and audience of the value of unfamiliar works. Because of the numbers of orchestral musicians trained at Tanglewood, as well as the BSO's reputation during his tenure as perhaps the best orchestra in America, Koussevitzky is often credited with creating the American symphonic school.

Elliott W. Galkin, *A History of Orchestral Conducting in Theory and Practice* (1988); Koussevitzky Music Foundation, *Catalog of Works Commissioned by the Koussevitzky Music Foundation* (1958); Arthur Lourié, *Serge Koussevitzky and His Epoch: A Biographical Chronicle* (1931); Moses Smith, *Koussevitzky* (1947).

Nancy Eagle Lindley

MacDowell Colony

The MacDowell Colony was founded in Peterborough, N.H., in 1907. Its mission is to provide creative artists with a supportive environment in which to pursue their work. The land was originally the property of the American composer Edward Alexander MacDowell and wife, Marian, who purchased a 65-acre farm in the spring of 1896, expanding the original structure in subsequent years. The couple eventually bought up surrounding properties and built other structures.

As the first professor of music at Columbia University (1896–1904), MacDowell often had to defend its position among the other arts and humanities, and in the winter of 1904–5, he decided to benefit musicians and other creative artists by leaving the Peterborough property for their use after his and his wife's deaths.

In May 1905 the MacDowell Club of New York was founded to honor the composer and to perpetuate his ideals. This club and another like it, founded in 1896 by MacDowell's students, became models for burgeoning arts organizations in numerous other American cities, many of which were also called MacDowell Clubs. The Mendelssohn Glee Club, a men's chorus MacDowell had directed from 1896 to 1898, organized the MacDowell Fund in the spring of 1906; within weeks the fund had contacted more than 40,000 persons across the country, including Grover Cleveland, Andrew Carnegie, and J. Pierpont Morgan, to raise money through concerts and

Edward MacDowell, ca. 1900

other efforts for the ailing composer's medical aid. On March 22, 1907, Marian deeded the Peterborough property, with a lifetime occupancy privilege, to the Edward MacDowell Memorial Association, a two-day-old organization incorporated for its acceptance, and in June the MacDowell Colony welcomed its first two colonists: Helen Farnsworth Mears, a sculptor who had studied with Augustus Saint-Gaudens, and her sister Mary, a writer. They stayed in Bark (now Schelling) Studio, the first of the colony's 32 studios.

Edward MacDowell died in New York on January 23, 1908. When the MacDowell Fund was terminated two months later, the sizable balance remaining from the almost $40,000 raised by worldwide contributions was turned over to the memorial association for endowment of the colony and realization of MacDowell's dream. For the next 38 years, Marian MacDowell dedicated her efforts to the colony; many of its artists' studios were built under her direction. As both its manager and primary fund-raiser, she made countless speeches and gave hundreds of piano recitals of MacDowell's music throughout the United States. She continued to raise funds until her death in 1956 at age 99. The 450-acre colony has survived in large part because of Marian's determination to realize and perpetuate Edward MacDowell's dream.

The colony has hosted more than 4,500 artists, composers, musicians, and writers, including such notable New Englanders as Edwin Arlington Robinson, John Updike, and Leonard Bernstein. Aaron Copland composed parts of *Appalachian Spring* there, and Thornton Wilder wrote *Our Town* there, basing its setting on nearby Peterborough. The Edward MacDowell Medal has been awarded annually since 1960 to honor outstanding contributions to the arts.

MacDowell Colony, *The MacDowell Colony: A History of Its Development and Architecture* (1981); New Hampshire Historical Society, *A House of Dreams Untold: The Story of the MacDowell Colony* (1996); New Hampshire Public Television, *MacDowell: An American Artists' Colony* [videorecording] (1996); Opal Wheeler and Sybil Deucher, *Edward MacDowell and His Cabin in the Pines* (1940).

Margery Morgan Lowens

Marlboro Music

In the early 1950s a small group of distinguished musicians were invited to make a summer home at Marlboro College in Marlboro, Vt. The result, known as Marlboro Music, has been nothing short of musical legend. Among the thousands of summer music programs now in existence nationwide, Marlboro Music, founded in 1951, retains its place at the top. And it has sustained its founders' vibrant spirit.

As both a festival and a school, Marlboro draws about 80 participants each summer, most from the upper reaches of elite-level professional chamber musicians. A number of talented up-and-coming musicians participate as well, and it is one of Marlboro's distinguishing features that these younger players are treated as colleagues, rather than students, of the more seasoned musicians.

Participants were friends and relatives: the violinist Adolf Busch and his brother Herman Busch, the flautist Marcel Moyse, his son Louis, and Louis's wife, Blanche Moyse. The pianist Rudolf Serkin (Adolf Busch's son-inlaw) was Marlboro's artistic director from its inception until his death in 1991, and his son, the pianist Peter Serkin, has also been a participant.

The long list of distinguished alumni at Marlboro includes such well-known soloists as Pablo Casals, Joshua Bell, Paula Robison, and Richard Stoltzman. The Guarneri and Vermeer string quartets were formed at Marlboro, and the festival has had an influence on virtually every major American chamber ensemble, including the Cleveland and Emerson quartets and the Beaux Arts Trio. Members of the Budapest Quartet also spent time at Marlboro. The group's second violinist, Alexander Schneider, was there for 20 years, during which time he was instrumental in the recruitment of Pablo Casals, who in turn gave 13 years to the festival as conductor and cellist.

Marlboro's setting is rustic and its style unpretentious. The college's old white buildings dot green hills nestled in southern Vermont's Green Mountains. Musicians bring their families and live a simple, informal life, taking turns serving meals, even occasionally cooking for one another.

Although the concerts, which take place from mid-July to mid-August, sell out long in advance, the music continues throughout the year via recordings (more than 40 are available on the Sony Classical label) and the Musicians from Marlboro Touring Program, which since its creation in 1964 has brought Marlboro ensembles to more than 350 cities throughout North America. The pianists Richard Goode and Mitsuku Uchida now direct the festival.

Marlboro Music, *Complete Marlboro Programs* (2001); Marlboro Music, *Marlboro Music School and Festival* (1992).

Gwendolyn Freed

Mason, Lowell (1792–1872) Hymn composer, music publisher, teacher. Born in Medfield, Mass., Lowell Mason significantly contributed to Boston's development as a center of musical culture and was instrumental in securing a place for music in the city's public school curriculum. He obtained his early music education in singing schools, first studying with Amos Albee and later with Oliver Shaw. He learned to play clarinet, violin, cello, flute, piano, and organ in his teens.

In 1813 Mason left Boston for Savannah, Ga., where he became active in the Presbyterian Church. Superintendent of a Sunday school, he worked as a bank teller, led singing schools, and took other odd jobs. He continued his musical studies under Frederick L. Abel and served as organist and choirmaster at the Independent Presbyterian Church.

In 1821, while on a trip north to seek a publisher for a collection of sacred music he had compiled, Mason met with members of Boston's Handel and Haydn Society, and they agreed to print his book as *The Boston Handel and Haydn Society Collection of Church Music* (1822). The book was a hit and aroused great interest in Mason and his work in Boston. In 1827 the society, along with four Boston churches, asked Mason to become president and musical director of the Handel and Haydn Society (1827–32) and music director for three of the four congregations (Hanover Street, Essex Street, and Park Street).

Mason developed a reputation as an outstanding teacher, musician, and conductor. As professor at the Boston Academy of Music from 1833 to 1844, he trained church choir directors and music teachers and published his most famous work, the *Manual of the Boston Academy of Music* (1834). His classes were extremely popular, and he offered short courses throughout New England as well as in various cities in New York, New Jersey, Ohio, Missouri, Kentucky, and Illinois. From 1832 to 1836 he also taught music at the Perkins School for the Blind in Boston.

Working in conjunction with the Boston Academy of Music, educators in public schools and colleges, and civic leaders from lo-cal government and business, Mason successfully spearheaded the campaign to establish music as part of Boston's public school curriculum. In 1837 Mason convinced the Boston School Committee to accept his ideas and voluntarily taught without pay for a year. He quickly demonstrated that he could teach children, even children with no prior experience, to read music and to sing. The committee responded by hiring Mason and five assistants to teach music in Boston's grammar schools in 1838. Soon other New England cities followed suit; within 25 years, the practice had spread across the nation.

A prolific composer, arranger, and compiler of sacred music, Mason began publishing his own and others' works after 1822 and became increasingly involved in marketing. His own works include 38 books of church music, 14 children's music books, 13 other choral collections, 19 compilations of song texts, and 28 individual compositions in sheet music form. Some of his best-known hymns include "Nearer My God to Thee," "Blest Be the Tie That Binds," and "Joy to the World!"

Mason moved to New York City in 1851 to pursue his publishing business with his sons Daniel, Lowell, and Timothy. He died at home in East Orange, N.J., in 1872. More than 10,000 items from Mason's personal library are now housed at Yale University.

George N. Heller, *Historical Research in Music Education: A Bibliography* (1995); Carol Pemberton, *Lowell Mason: A Bio-Bibliography* (1988); Pemberton, *Lowell Mason: His Life and Work* (1985 [1971]); Special issue, "Lowell Mason," *The Quarterly Journal of Music Teaching and Learning* (Fall 1992).

George N. Heller

Modern Dance In 1930s America modern dance was a revolutionary art. With roots going back to the late 19th century, it emerged in part as a protest against the style of movement associated with classical ballet. More a concept than a fixed art form, modern dance can be defined as a search for new ways of moving that aim to express feelings and ideas. Historians vary over the precise beginnings of modern dance. Some claim it was born when the pioneers Ruth St. Denis and Ted Shawn founded the Denishawn School in Los Angeles in 1915; others cite the year 1926, when Martha Graham gave her first solo concert. There can be no doubt, however, that several schools in New England played a major role in the evolution of this new form of expression.

First among them was Vermont's Bennington College, which opened its doors in 1932 at the foot of gently sloping hills in the Green Mountains. Two years later that progressive college became home to the Bennington School of Dance, a summer program for artists, composers, critics, and lighting designers who wished to explore and define modern dance in America. At a time when dance was often no more than a facet of the physical education program, Bennington honored it as an equal among the other arts. Students could obtain a bachelor's degree with a concentration in dance, and in 1936 dance became a separate academic division.

Founded and directed by Martha Hill and Mary Josephine Shelly, the summer dance festival attracted more than 100 students during its first six-week session. The program remained in Bennington through 1942, with the exception of 1939, when it traveled to Mills College in Oakland, Calif. During those early years, hundreds of students and teachers gathered to experiment, argue, choreograph, and perform on the campus of Bennington College.

The choreographers Martha Graham, Doris Humphrey, Hanya Holm, and Charles Weidman; the critics Walter Terry and John Martin; the composers John Cage, Henry Cowell, Wallingford Riegger; the stage designer Arch Lauterer—these are just a few of the artists who came together during Bennington's eight summer sessions. Their collaborations and experiments would influence dance in America for decades. Teachers who took classes at the Bennington festivals brought what they learned into universities, colleges, high schools, and elementary schools throughout the country. Young choreographers watching premieres of Humphrey's *New Dance* (1934), Weidman's *Quest* (1936), Holm's *Trend* (1937), and Graham's *American Document* (1938) witnessed and absorbed hitherto unimagined mergers of movement, form, and content, learning bold new dance vocabularies.

World War II curtailed dance activities at Bennington, and in 1948 the program moved to Connecticut College for Women in New London. Renamed the American Dance Festival (ADF), it remained in New London through 1977. Summer sessions there showcased the 1930s pioneers and cultivated the new talents of the 1960s and 1970s. While Bennington had been founded when modern dance was in its infancy, the Connecticut program began when the art was a mature, established form. Bennington College was located in a remote small town on the site of what had once been a 140-acre farm, and festival activities were housed in old, somewhat ramshackle buildings. New London was a city with easy access to New York, Boston, and Hartford, and Connecticut College had a modern 1,300-seat theater, along with new studios. Whereas rural Vermont had lent its sturdy sense of independent self-sufficiency to the early ADF, Connecticut College, with its picture-perfect traditional campus on a hill and the bustling port of New London nearby, opened onto a wider world.

The first decade of summer programs and courses at Connecticut College in the late 1940s and early 1950s featured primarily works composed by first- and second-generation modern dancers. The emphasis for these artists was on the abstraction of intense emotional experiences, often embodied in archetypal heroes and heroines. Concerts showcased choreography by Graham and Humphrey as well as by their students and company members, including Sophie Maslow, José Limón, Pauline Koner, Lucas Hoving, and Ruth Currier.

In 1956 there was a hint of something new. Alwin Nikolais's company performed *Kaleidoscope*, emphasizing the nonemotional use of shapes and props, and Margaret Dietz came from Germany to teach a style of modern dance unfamiliar to many in America. Two years later Merce Cunningham performed at the ADF at Connecticut College for the first time, and many had trouble accepting his experiments with abstraction, chance, and nonlinear juxtapositions of movement and sound. In 1969 Martha Myers was named dean of the ADF, a position she held in both New London and Durham, N.C., until her retirement in 2000.

By the early 1970s postmodern dance choreographers were challenging ideas developed by their predecessors in the thirties and forties. Artists dressed in jeans and sneakers experimented with site-specific dances around the campus set to popular music and incorporating the flow of passersby. Students now came to Connecticut College in the summer to study classical modern dance as well as to join in the experiments of Meredith Monk, Twyla Tharp, Laura Dean, Trisha Brown, Paul Taylor, Yvonne Rainer, Anna Halprin, and Erick Hawkins. African American choreographers including Alvin Ailey and Donald McKayle joined the faculty, performing and teaching. Ballet and Indian dance were added to the menu of course and performance offerings. Connecticut College, with its hot summer days and cool evening breezes, had helped hundreds of eager novices and seasoned professionals share both new and old ideas by the time the ADF left for North Carolina in 1977.

Into the 21st century, summer sessions in New England have continued to bring together American creators, teachers, performers, and students of modern dance, disseminating knowledge of the art to surrounding communities. In 1973 the philosopher Nelson Goodman, a professor at Harvard University, helped Martha Armstrong Gray establish the Harvard Summer Dance Center. Goodman believed that living artists could flourish on a university campus, and through 1995 over 200 students and numerous choreographers came together to study the past and redefine the art form for the future. After 1977, under the direction of then–Harvard faculty member Iris Fanger, numerous concerts featured new commissioned works and choreography in repertory.

In 1982 Bates College in Lewiston, Maine, became the home of a multifaceted summer program that continues to flourish. Under the leadership of Laura Faure, it boasts 50 artist teachers and more than 250 students from all over the world, attracting audiences of more than 35,000 from across the state and region. The Bates Dance Festival aims to give everyone a taste of modern dance, regardless of age, income, physical limitations, or experience. A Youth Arts Program provides free intensive dance and music training for underserved youth between the ages of six and 17 from the Lewiston-Auburn community. The Community Dance Project is a multigenerational program for nondancers from 16 to 80 years old, who collaborate with festival students and choreographers. Two artists are chosen every summer to create new work as part of the Emerging Choreographers' Program. The National High School Scholarship Program offers full scholarships to gifted high school dancers of color; the Environmental Performance Project is designed to support the creation of dances in natural settings; and the International Visiting Artist Program brings accomplished performers to campus from outside the United States.

In 1979 a smaller, highly focused summer program began in New Hampshire's White Mountains. Directed by the modern dancer Laura Glenn, the White Mountain Summer Dance Festival moved to Springfield College of Massachusetts in 1999. Some 40 students are usually enrolled, and the emphasis is on student choreography and repertory rather than new works. At the core of White Mountain's philosophy is the importance of the mind-body connection and education of the entire body through yoga, kinesiology, anatomy, and various body therapies.

Academic programs during the school year also play a role in New England's modern dance life. In the 1970s, the Five College Dance Department was created in western Massachusetts to serve the needs of Amherst, Hampshire, Mount Holyoke, and Smith Colleges and the main campus of the University of Massachusetts. A shuttle bus takes students from school to school, with each one contributing curriculum options that together form a unified undergraduate dance major. A graduate degree, offered by Smith College, is also available. The proximity of the small towns and schools, the distinct and independent character of each institution, the pride in a long tradition of excellence of the four older schools—Hampshire is the newest—and perhaps the New England habit of coming together for town meetings and sharing ideas make this a successful and distinctive program.

In 1971 two Dartmouth College undergraduates, Moses Pendleton and Jonathan Wolken, established a dance company they called Pilobolus as a collaborative enterprise based on work they were doing at school with their teacher Alison Chase. Their first dance, *Pilobolus*, premiered in 1971 at Dartmouth with original music by Jim Ruben and a revised score by Jim Appleton. During the next two years they performed at Hampshire College, Colby Junior College, and Putney School, and Pilobolus has since gone on to become a major professional company, performing nationally and internationally.

Boston Conservatory has a well-established, professionally oriented dance program with a large undergraduate enrollment. Through the 1950s the major influence there was Jan Veen, a modern dancer who emigrated from Germany, bringing with him a German Expressionist outlook on both teaching and choreography. Connecticut College for Women has an extensive dance program that focuses on dance within the context of the liberal arts. The Walnut Hill School of Natick, Mass., distinguishes itself as a residential academic and professional facility for talented high school students, and the dance department there prepares young people for both college and career.

The professional world of modern dance in New England is probably most extensive in Boston. The Boston Ballet, founded in 1963 by E. Virginia Williams, has been a showcase for modern dance choreographers from the beginning. Under the strong leadership of Bruce Marks, a ballet dancer whose early experience was in modern dance, such choreographers as Merce Cunningham and Twyla Tharp have contributed work to the repertory. The Concert Dance Company, now defunct, was for many years a major presence on Boston's modern dance scene. Prometheus Dance, founded in 1986 by Diane and codirected since 1997 by Arvanites-Noya and Tommy Neblett, has gained increasing prominence. Beth Soll and Susan Rose were important Boston choreographers for many years, and Marcus Schulkind, Caitlin Corbett, and Nicola Hawkins are artists of note. Outside Boston, probably the best-known groups are the Ram Island Dance Company in Portland, Maine, and the Island Moving Company of Newport, R.I.

Modern dance is alive and well in New England. Choreographers and teachers in all six states carry on traditions of innovation, excellence, and solid training. With many active in educational and community outreach, modern dance will continue to flourish in the region.

Jack Anderson, *The American Dance Festival* (1987); Sali Ann Kriegsman, *Modern Dance in America: The Bennington Years* (1981); Naima Prevots, *American Pageantry: A Movement for Art and Democracy* (1990).
Naima Prevots

Musical Instruments and Manufacturers

Before the Revolutionary War, musical instrument making in New England was sporadic, isolated, and usually done by nonprofessionals. By the 1790s, however, the number, quality, and diversity of products began a steady increase that peaked in the second half of the 19th century. Boston was the center of instrument-making activity, but manufacture also took place in smaller cities and towns, and handicrafts such as violin making were practiced throughout the region. Although American makers always faced considerable competition from imports, in the early 1800s enterprising New England craftsmen began developing instruments that successfully rivaled those manufactured abroad. But by the second quarter of the 20th century, many of the area's firms had failed or had been taken over by other companies and, in some cases, relocated. At present, only a handful of New England companies make musical instruments on a large commercial scale, but in the 1960s, reproduction of historic instruments such as recorders and harpsichords emerged as an important cottage industry.

Until the late 19th century, military drums dominated New England's output of percussion instruments, the Militia Act of 1792 and the Civil War both sparking demand. Extant 18th-century snare and bass drums often appear to have been homemade, but many finely built 19th-century drums survive from workshops of professionals such as Abner Stevens in Pittsfield, Mass., and members of the family of Eli Brown in Windsor and Bloomfield, Conn. The Avedis Zildjian Company, one of the world's leading manufacturers of cymbals for both classical and popular music, has been located in Norwell, Mass., since 1929.

In the early 19th century, New England's wood turners produced a considerable number of fifes, flutes, clarinets, oboes, and bassoons, the best of these on a par with ones of equivalent cost made in Europe. Working in a small factory in Winchester, N.H., Samuel Graves was the first American woodwind maker to use water-powered machinery, with which he and several workmen produced many fine flutes and clarinets. Other important woodwind makers of Graves's period include William Callender and Walter Crosby in Boston, and George Catlin in Hartford. Much later, William S. Haynes and his former apprentice, Verne Q. Powell, established separate firms in Boston and earned international acclaim for their silver flutes.

The earliest American bands combined woodwinds and brasses, but by the mid-1830s, especially in the Northeast, interest in all-brass bands began to grow. Commercial production of brasses flourished in New England after about 1837, when James Keat, an experienced craftsman from London, joined the firm of Graves and Company in Winchester, N.H. During the 1840s, Graves and Company was one of a handful of American makers specializing in such newfangled instruments as keyed bugles and ophicleides, and after the firm relocated to Boston in 1850 they focused exclusively on brasses. The Civil War fueled the brass band movement; henceforth, many of the country's best bugles, cornets, horns, trombones, and tubas came from New England. Besides Graves, noteworthy brass instrument makers in Boston were Elbridge G. Wright and J. Lathrop Allen. In Pawtucket, R.I., Thomas Dudley Paine developed a rotary valve with string linkage that was widely copied and remains in use on modern French horns. Isaac Fiske began business in 1842 in Worcester, Mass., where he built a large factory that produced all sorts of brass instruments; Fiske received five patents pertaining to their manufacture.

Apparently, New England's musicians demanded fewer locally made violins than larger, cello-size instruments called bass viols, which were widely played to accompany congregational singing in churches that could not afford an organ. In the late 18th century Benjamin Crehore of Milton, Mass., was the first maker to produce a significant number of bass viols, but Abraham Prescott, working in Deerfield and later in Concord, N.H., is more closely identified with their manufacture; his shop turned out several hundred bass viols between about 1820 and 1840. Many New England towns boasted a local violin maker, usually a self-taught amateur, but violins were not made here commercially before the 1840s. Serious professional violin making is considered to have begun in Boston about 1850, when Ira J. White and his brother Asa W. White set up their shop. Boston continued to be New England's only center for artistic violin making, and two of the more prolific makers of the generation after the Whites were Walter Solon Goss and Jerome Bonaparte Squire.

Toward the end of the 19th century, the banjo experienced a tremendous surge of popularity in America. The great demand was met by makers in Boston such as Albert C. Fairbanks, William A. Cole, and Lincoln B. Gatcomb, who produced banjos of various sizes ranging from basic and inexpensive models to fancy ones with elaborate carving and decorative inlay. New England did not produce any guitar makers of lasting repute before the 20th century, but between the 1930s and 1950s, Elmer Stromberg of Boston handcrafted a variety of high quality arch-top guitars favored by jazz performers. Ovation Instruments in New Hartford, Conn. (founded in 1966 and currently one of the country's largest supplier of acoustic guitars), produces an instrument with a unique arched back made of a fiberglass reinforced composite material.

The manufacture of pianos was arguably New England's premier musical instrument industry throughout the 19th century. Piano production centered almost exclusively in Boston, where it employed hundreds of craftsmen and laborers. As early as the 1790s, Benjamin Crehore, working alone in nearby Milton, was building modest "square" pianos based on English models. Two of his protégés, Alpheus Babcock and John Osborne, went on to produce instruments of exceptional quality and sophistication that challenged prevailing trends of piano manufacture in London and New York. Babcock is best known for his 1825 patent for a one-piece cast-iron frame (a concept eventually adopted by all piano makers), while Osborne is remembered for having trained Boston's most successful piano maker, Jonas Chickering. From modest beginnings in 1823, Chickering's firm had by midcentury gained worldwide distribution and recognition, and in 1853 they constructed a huge, steam-powered factory that annually produced hundreds of pianos in various models. Renamed Chickering and Sons in the 1850s, the company prospered into the 20th century; it was purchased by the American Piano Company in 1908 and relocated to New York State in 1927. Other leading Boston piano manufacturers in the 19th century included the brothers Timothy Gilbert and Lemuel Gilbert, and the firm of Hallet, Davis and Company (active 1844–90).

New England overcame early religious conservatism to become very progressive in the building of pipe organs. Boston and environs produced some of the country's most prominent 19th-century builders, including the brothers William Goodrich and Eben Goodrich, Thomas Appleton, and the firm of E. and G. G. Hook (founded 1827). Many organs by these and other local builders remain in use throughout the eastern United States. The 20th century has also brought national recognition to such leading builders as Charles

Brenton Fisk in Gloucester, Mass. and Fritz Noack in Georgetown, Mass. Smaller and less expensive reed organs, most popular in homes and small churches, were first produced in the 1840s, and their manufacture permeated virtually every corner of New England. Throughout the mid–19th century, Concord, N.H., was an especially active center for reed organ making; the families of Abraham Prescott and Charles Austin were among the town's chief manufacturers. By the 1860s, the Boston firm of Mason and Hamlin (active 1854–1911) was producing a quarter of all American reed organs. The Estey Organ Company (active 1846 to 1956) in Brattleboro, Vt., operated a large factory that employed up to 700 workers and averaged 10,000 instruments per year between 1880 and 1900; in 1901 Estey opened a pipe organ department.

Many fine New England–made instruments are housed in regional collections, such as the Yale University Collection of Musical Instruments, the Museum of Fine Arts, Boston, and at Old Sturbridge Village.

Christine Merrick Ayars, *Contributions to the Art of Music in America by the Music Industries of Boston, 1640 to 1936* (1937); William Copeley, "Musical Instrument Makers of New England, 1800–1960," *Historical New Hampshire* 46, no. 4 (Winter 1991); Robert E. Eliason, *Early American Brass Makers* (1981); H. E. Johnson, *Musical Interludes in Boston, 1795–1830* (1943); Darcy Kuronen, "Early Violin Making in New England," *Journal of the American Musical Instrument Society* 27 (2001); Barbara Owen, *The Organ in New England* (1979); Daniel Spillane, *History of the American Pianoforte* (1969 [1890]); Edward Wall, "Abraham Prescott: Bass Viol Maker of Deerfield and Concord," *Historical New Hampshire* 42, no. 2 (Summer 1987).

Darcy Kuronen

Music Education

Music education in New England dates to the native Abenaki, Mohegan, Maliseet, Massachusett, Narragansett, Passamaquoddy, Penobscot, Pequot, Wappinger, and many other groups who taught music to their children in domestic life and according to their priestly traditions. Indigenous peoples in New England encountered French Recollect Fathers and Jesuits who moved into the area from the north in the late 16th century. They also came into contact with various British Protestants who taught music as part of their missionary activities early in the 17th century.

Psalmody was an important feature of early religious life in New England; indeed, the first book printed in the colonies was the *Bay Psalm Book* (text, 1640; text and music, 1698). This fundamental interest in singing the psalms combined with an early interest in public education, leading to the formation of singing schools. Early in the 17th century, clergy members called for a reform of congregational singing. The Reverend Thomas Symmes published *The Reasonableness of Regular Singing, or Singing by Note* (1720) criticizing congregational singing and calling for the teaching of note reading. Responding to this and other calls for reform, two Boston clerics, the Reverend John Tufts and the Reverend Thomas Walter, each produced manuals in 1721 to help students read music. Their books contained theoretical introductions on the rudiments of music followed by several psalm tunes for the students to perform. Thus began the so-called regular singing movement, which advocated learning music by note instead of the old style or rote method of learning by lining out and setting the tune.

Most of the early leaders such as Tufts and Walter relied heavily on European—mainly British—composers for their music. While singing schools spread well beyond the bounds of New England in the 18th century, many of their greatest practitioners came from the region. Among these were William Billings of Boston, Andrew Law of Connecticut, Samuel A. Holyoke of Massachusetts and New Hampshire, and Supply Belcher, the so-called Handel of Maine. An unlikely member of this elite fraternity was Newport Gardner, a slave in Newport, R.I., who was a student of Andrew Law; Gardner became a composer as well as a singing school teacher. Like Gardner, many of these instructors composed music; they also compiled tunebooks and set out across the country to teach young Americans to read music and to sing their plain tunes, fuging tunes, set pieces, and anthems. Holyoke even wrote an instruction book for teaching instrumental music using the format of the singing school.

Increased immigration in the early 19th century coincided with a rapidly escalating interest in public education. William Channing Woodbridge of Boston and Hartford argued for inclusion of music in public education. He encouraged Elam Ives, Jr., to experiment with teaching music according to the Swiss Pestalozzian approach in Hartford schools in 1829–30. This experiment did not last long, but Lowell Mason began using Pestalozzian ideas, at first in private singing schools, then in the Boston Academy, and finally, in 1838, in the Boston public schools. Many regard this as the inception of public school music education in America.

Mason had many close friends and supporters who worked with him in Boston and elsewhere, such as William Batchelder Bradbury, Isaac Baker Woodbury, and George F. Root. Mason and his followers abandoned the work of Billings and his colleagues in favor of music that was more akin to European music of the late 18th and early 19th centuries. One noteworthy application of Mason's Pestalozzian approach was in his own work at the Perkins School for the Blind in Boston (1832–36). William Wolcott Turner and David Ely Bartlett also taught music at the New England School for the Deaf in Hartford from 1844 to 1872. Mason, Bradbury, and Root were all active in offering music teacher training at institutes that grew out of Mason's work at the Boston Academy, beginning in 1834. Music education was part of the curriculum at the Massachusetts State Normal School in Lexington in 1839 and continued in similar institutions until their absorption into state teachers' colleges in the 20th century.

Music conservatories have existed in New England since just after the Civil War. Founded in 1867, the New England Conservatory was one of the first of its kind, and many others soon followed its example. Music as part of a liberal arts higher education began at Harvard in the 17th century, first as an extracurricular activity and after 1862 as a subject of serious study with the appointment of John Knowles Paine as the nation's first professor of music. Students at Yale attended singing schools held on campus in the 18th century and later were able to study the history and theory of music there. Music education became increasingly common as the 19th century progressed, and extracurricular music performance activities (choirs, orchestras, and eventually bands) joined course offerings in colleges and universities during the 20th century. Composers often found occupations in teaching music theory at various colleges and universities. Important music educators included Eben Tourjée at the New England Conservatory, Paine at Harvard, Horatio Parker at Yale, and Thomas Whitney Surette at the Concord (Massachusetts) Summer School of Music.

Several New England music educators made significant contributions to the development of classroom music education. Luther Whiting Mason initiated music instruction in the primary grades in Boston in 1864 and published an important elementary general classroom series of music textbooks (*The National Music Course*) in 1870. Two Boston music educators, John Wheeler Tufts and Hosea E. Holt, also published a series titled *The Normal Music Course* in 1883. Mason (no relation to Lowell) also taught public school music at the New England Conservatory. There he met Japanese music educators who persuaded him to spend two years in Japan (1880–82) helping implement a Boston-style system of teaching music in that country.

Other noteworthy music educators of this period included Julius Eichberg of Boston; Benjamin Jepson of New Haven, Conn.; Samuel Winckley Cole of Brookline, Mass.; Sterrie A. Weaver of Westfield, Mass.; Francis E. Howard of Bridgeport, Conn.; and Osbourne McConathy of Chelsea, Mass. McConathy's work in developing a course of study in music appreciation, music theory, and applied music for students in the Chelsea schools was especially important. Many of these leaders were influential in establishing music teacher associations, such as the New England Public School Music Teachers Association and the Normal Music Teachers Association (both founded in Boston in 1885). Several held leadership positions in national music education organizations as well.

New Englanders also played important roles in the development of instrumental music in American music education. The effort began in the early 19th century with Samuel Holyoke and his instrumental method books, *The Instrumental Assistant* (2 vols., 1800, 1807). School orchestras, loosely organized string-wind-percussion ensembles, began with Mason's ensemble at the Perkins Schools (1832–36). The Boston Farm and Trade School had a student instrumental group in 1857, as did schools in Providence and Boston. The Nathan Hale School in New London, Conn., started an orchestra in 1896. Albert G. Mitchell introduced class instruction in instrumental music in the Boston schools in 1911. He based his approach on the English Maidstone movement and wrote *The Public School Class Method for Violin* (1912–16) and *The Class Method for Violin* (1918).

In the 20th century, New Englanders continue to be leaders in music education. The Eastern Music Supervisors Conference, founded in Boston in 1918, was an outgrowth of the Boston Pulse Club. The organization met annually from 1918 to 1927 and published the *Eastern School Music Herald.* That conference became the Eastern Division of the Music Supervisors National Conference in 1927. Now part of the Music Educators National Conference, the division includes the states of New England along with Delaware, Maryland, New Jersey, New York, Pennsylvania, and the District of Columbia. Founded in 1945 by Lawrence Berk, a graduate of MIT, a musician, and a student of the music theorist Joseph Schillinger, the Berklee School of Music in Boston was the first in the nation dedicated to teaching jazz and commercial music.

Several noteworthy gatherings of music educators took place in New England during the 1960s. The Yale Seminar (New Haven, 1963) initiated an important discussion about the kind of music taught in schools and the emphasis on performance at the expense of understanding and appreciation. The Tanglewood Symposium (Lenox, Mass., 1967) examined the role of music education in contemporary society with special emphasis on technology and cultural diversity. Ideas developed at these two conferences continue to influence music education practices and programs across the nation.

The New England tradition of music education is one of universal inclusion and diverse appeal. From precolonial times to the present, music educators in New England have sought to provide music instruction to as many students as possible, especially to children, regardless of ability or social status.

Edward Bailey Birge, *History of Public School Music in the United States* (1937); Allen P. Britton, "Music in Early American Public Education: A Historical Critique," in *Basic Concepts in Music Education*, ed. Nelson B. Henry (1958); Britton, "Musical Education in the United States of America," *Bulletin of Historical Research in Music Education* 3 (July 1982); George N. Heller, *Historical Research in Music Education: A Bibliography* (1995); James A. Keene, *A History of Music Education in the United States* (1982); Michael L. Mark and Charles L. Gary, *A History of American Music Education* (1992); A. Theodore Tellstrom, *Music in American Education: Past and Present* (1971).

George N. Heller

Music in Religious Life, 1820 to the Present

Since 1820 distinctive religious music traditions in New England include the development of choral music with instrumental accompaniment and the rise of regional composers and practitioners. The primary story concerns mainline Protestant and Catholic churches, but New England does offer examples of musical traditions whose origins and practice are more commonly identified with other regions, such as African American and Jewish music. After the War of 1812, settlement in northern rural areas and continued urban growth meant the establishment of new churches. Many of these sprang from the old Puritan roots, but often with a more liberal theological outlook; by 1820 there were 120 Unitarian churches in eastern Massachusetts alone, and a growing number of Universalist churches.

One of the most telling indicators of change was the departure from the old Puritan prohibition on instrumental music in worship. During the last decades of the 18th century, a few nonliturgical churches had acquired small organs, while others began using the three-stringed "church bass" or amateur instrumental groups. By 1820 the demand for organs was sufficient to support Boston's pioneer organ builder, William Goodrich. Within a decade several builders who had trained in his workshop had opened their own workshops, establishing New England as a center for organ building.

The singing school movement had been active since the days of William Billings (1746–1800), but some new and influential music masters radically changed the face of church music. Lowell Mason's *Boston Handel and Haydn Society Collection of Church Music* first appeared in 1821, at least in urban areas, and replaced the repertory of the homegrown singing masters with selections from the English and continental repertory. By the mid–19th century, nearly every nonliturgical church in New England had the largest choir and the largest organ they could afford.

The liturgical churches (primarily Episcopalian at this time in New England) had a long tradition of organs and choirs, and despite their break with the Church of England after the Revolution, increasingly sought their musical inspiration from the British Isles. Trinity Church not only imported a new organ from London in 1837, but the following year hired A. U. Hayter, a former organist and choirmaster of Hereford Cathedral, to play it.

Foreign-born church musicians were highly regarded in New England cities in this period. They included Lowell Mason's English-born collaborator George J. Webb, and the German-born composer Charles Zeuner, who served as organist of Boston's Park Street Church for 15 years. Hermann Kotzschmar, also German-born, served as organist of the First Parish Church of Portland for 47 years, beginning in 1851, and was an important force in the musical life of that city.

By the mid–19th century, Catholics began to make their mark in the cities and mill towns of New England. Saint Augustine's Church in South Boston boasted a large choir school in the 1860s, directed by Irish-born Joseph G. Lennon, and at the Feast of the Assumption in 1875, 50 vested choirboys sang the mass at Boston's Immaculate Conception Church. The organ of Boston's Holy Cross Cathedral, built by Hook and Hastings in 1875, was for several years the largest organ in New England. Toward the end of the 19th century, and before the *Motu Proprio* of Pope Pius X (1903) put a damper on extravagant church music, "concert masses," featuring choral music of Haydn, Schubert, and various operatic composers, drew large congregations to urban Catholic churches in Boston and elsewhere.

During the first half of the 19th century New England's church musicians were either self-taught or learned their trade as an apprentice to an older musician. George F. Root, in his autobiography, describes his own apprenticeship with A. N. Johnson of Boston, around 1840. He took piano and singing lessons and sang in choruses but soon was given responsibilities for accompanying hymns at prayer meetings and teaching beginning piano students, learning many skills (including, apparently, organ playing and choir directing) by the "sink or swim" method. In rural New England, traditional shape-note singing continued in evangelical churches, and the Shakers produced an astonishing repertoire of thousands of songs and tunes at their villages, especially during a revival in the decades prior to the Civil War.

By the 1850s and 1860s, young organists such as Portland's John Knowles Paine and Hartford's Dudley Buck studied abroad, where they learned sophisticated organ technique and repertoire and were exposed to cathedral choirs, symphony orchestras, and opera. They returned not only to propagate a more classical type of church music, but to establish a tradition of organ recitals, to compose church music of their own, and, eventually, to teach the next generation at one of the newly established conservatories. These so-called New England classicists—Paine, Buck, George Chadwick, Horatio Parker, Arthur Foote, Arthur Whiting, Samuel B. Whitney, Margaret Ruthven Lang, and Charles Ives—wrote church music and were at some point in their careers church musicians; Foote was organist of Boston's First Church for 32 years, and Whitney was at Church of the Advent for 37 years.

In Mason's heyday, large, well-rehearsed volunteer mixed choirs had been the musical glory of many Protestant churches, but increasingly after the 1860s churches employed paid quartets. Most quartets were mixed, but some consisted of male voices; King's Chapel in Boston had a mixed quartet directed by B. J. Lang in the 1890s, but by the 1920s it had become a male quartet. The principal advantage of the professional quartet was that it could perform elaborate (and frequently operatically inspired) contemporary anthems and service. When this music went out of fashion, so, in most cases, did the quartets. In 1933 Harvard's Archibald T. Davison referred to them disparagingly as "hired minstrels."

New England's Episcopal churches initially took a "low church" approach to their liturgy and music, and their choirs, quartets, and repertoire were little different from those in nonliturgical churches. As the liturgical concepts of the "high church" Oxford Movement began to spread to America after the middle of the 19th century, however, some churches began to model their music on Anglican lines. Boston's Church of the Advent was in 1852 the first in New England to employ boy choristers and, shortly after, to have a vested choir. This men-and-boys choir achieved some prominence under English-trained S. H. Cutler, followed by another Englishman, Henry Carter. In the 1870s Carter founded a similar choir at Saint Stephen's Church in Providence, but Saint Andrew's Church in that city had had a boys' choir since 1858, being the second New England church to do so.

By the 1880s the boychoir movement had gained momentum, with choirs being established in Saint Paul's, Emmanuel, and Church of the Messiah in Boston, and Saint James's, Cambridge. It quickly spread to Connecticut, with Trinity Church's men-and-boys choir directed by Warren Hedden in New Haven in 1885. Boychoirs were established in Trinity Church, Middletown, and Christ Church, Hartford.

By the turn of the century a wide variety of church music could be found in New England. Some rural choirs still sang from the old "oblong" tunebooks of the 19th century, while some urban quartets were singing anthems and cantatas in a floridly operatic style by such composers as Buck, Shelley, Schnecker, Charles Gounod, and Stainer, occasionally interspersed with oratorio choruses from Handel, Haydn, or Mendelssohn. In a few high church Episcopal and Catholic churches, plainchant and Palestrina might even be heard. Church soloists abounded everywhere; a rather astonishing number ran illustrated advertisements in the *Boston Church and Musical Directory* for 1907. Another influential element of the period was the rousing gospel songs and sentimental solos of the Moody and Sankey revival movement.

The papal *Motu Proprio* of 1903 revolutionized music in Catholic churches, where plainchant was reintroduced, a fact that profoundly affected a Boston Irish lad who would later become well known as Father Finn, director of Chicago's men-and-boys Paulist Choristers. After World War I, British influence was again felt in Episcopal churches. In New York City, T. Tertius Noble, formerly organist of York Minster, established a choir school at fashionable Saint Thomas's Church to which New England churches sent promising boys. In 1910, Everett Titcomb, a champion of plainchant and Renaissance polyphony, began a more than 50 year tenure as choirmaster of Boston's Church of Saint John the Evangelist.

Another influence on early-20th-century church music came from New England's colleges and conservatories, where budding organists and choir directors were exposed to a broad spectrum of the best classical and contemporary music taught by professors who often were distinguished church musicians themselves. Among these were Wallace Goodrich of New England Conservatory, organist of Boston's Trinity Church 1902–10, and William Churchill Hammond of Smith and Mount Holyoke Colleges, organist of the Second Congregational Church of Holyoke, Mass., from 1885 to 1949.

Before World War II, the multiple-choir movement began. By 1931 Plymouth Congregational Church in New Haven boasted a quartet, a mixed adult choir, and youth choirs for boys and girls. In 1960 the Hancock Congregational Church of Lexington, Mass., had five choirs totaling 250 members, beginning at the preschool level. Lutheran churches are relative newcomers in New England, but in 1952 Trinity Lutheran Church of Worcester, one of the largest, also had five choirs totaling 250, plus an instrumental group.

Economic and demographic factors caused the downsizing of many church music programs during the last three decades of the 20th century. Thanks to several prestigious New England music schools, the area is well supplied with professionally trained musicians. The latter-day dean of Boston composers is probably Daniel Pinkham, who, like many of his predecessors, is a part-time church musician, having served King's Chapel in that capacity since 1958. Another nationally known Boston composer who has written choral, organ, and liturgical music is Herbert Fromm, music director of Temple Israel for over 30 years. New England temples also feature a distinguished tradition of cantors. Among the younger generation of church music composers are Vermont's Charles Callahan, New Hampshire's Robin Dinda, Boston's James Woodman, and Paul Hamill of Great Barrington.

Music still plays an important role in the religious life of New England at the start of the 21st century. The fine pipe organs, professional-quality choirs, and conservatory-trained music directors of many urban churches enhance both the worship and concert life of the cities. White Protestant churches of a more evangelical or charismatic bent frequently rely heavily on the so-called contemporary type of music, tending to overtly secular influences, with piano or synthesizer accompaniment. And in African American and multiracial churches there has been a flowering of gospel music.

The musical impact of recent immigrant groups such as Hispanics and Asians is only beginning to be felt in church music, and some interesting mixes of musical styles are appearing in multiethnic urban churches. Catholic churches cover a broad spectrum, some having well-trained choirs and tasteful liturgical music (Saint Paul's in Cambridge still maintains a distinguished choir school), while others rely on amateur cantors and microphones. In some religious traditions, however, perhaps most notably the Jewish and Eastern Orthodox, a more conservative norm prevails, with heavy reliance on traditional repertory and style. As at the end of the 19th century, New England's church music today is a continually evolving cultural and stylistic mixture.

G. Huntington Byles, *The Organs and Music of Trinity Church, New Haven* (1952); Archibald T. Davison, *Protestant Church Music in America* (1933); William Dinneen, *Music at the Meeting House 1775–1958* (1953); Leonard Ellinwood, *The History of American Church Music* (1958); William J. Finn, *Sharps and Flats in Five Decades* (1947); Howard Hagan and Frank V. Brown, *A History of the Choir and Music of All Saints' Memorial Church, Providence* (1942); Barbara Owen, *The Organs and Music of King's Chapel, 1713–1991* (1993); Robert Stevenson, *Protestant Church Music in America* (1966).

Barbara Owen

Music Libraries

The latest directory of music libraries in New England cites 89 collections of music in 77 different institutions. These collections may be distinguished from those in other regions by their density, diversity, and a highly developed spirit of cooperation in formal and informal consortia.

Among the large research libraries, the music collections at the two largest universities, Harvard and Yale, have the greatest depth and breadth of both general and special collections. The collections at the Boston Public Library have grown chiefly from an endowed private collection but have nevertheless suffered from periodic (political) fluctuations in public support.

A number of colleges and universities have notable music collections, some with particular strengths built around their curricula or faculty. The Werner Josten Library at Smith College is by far the largest of the college libraries. There are strong collections at such doctoral degree–granting institutions as Boston University and Brandeis University. In addition the Massachusetts Institute of Technology, whose music faculty is active in composition and performance nationally, has a large collection of contemporary music. The music libraries at Brown University, Dartmouth College, Williams College, Trinity College, Tufts University, and the University of Connecticut (Storrs) have been amassed in support of strong curricula and enhanced by primary sources of American music elsewhere in their library system. A major collection of Anglo-American folk music is separately maintained at Middlebury College, as are the Archives of World Music at Wesleyan University. The University of New Hampshire houses the Amy Cheney Beach Collection, the New Hampshire Library of Traditional Jazz, and the New Hampshire Library of Traditional Music and Dance, including the Ralph Page Collection and the archives of the Country Dance and Song Society.

In addition to the School of Music at Yale University, the region supports four independent conservatories of music, each of which has its own music library. The largest and most comprehensive is that of the New England Conservatory of Music, with its separate libraries for the general, large ensemble, and recorded music collections, each with notable rare materials. The good-sized collection at the Hartt School of the University of Hartford has acquired some musicians' libraries, but the much older Boston Conservatory is more limited. Berklee College focuses on teaching jazz and commercial music; thus its ample library collects popular culture not otherwise represented in the region.

There are a large number of small- and medium-sized public libraries throughout the region with active circulating collections of chamber and piano ensemble music for amateur musicians, as well as audio and video recordings for the general public, thus fostering older traditions of musical literacy and enjoyment at home. Notable among these are the Forbes Library in Northampton, Mass., the Manchester City Library in New Hampshire, the Providence Public Library (scores only), the Springfield (Mass.) City Library, and several suburban libraries around Boston, including those in Arlington, Brookline, Medford, Newton, and Quincy.

State and local historical societies typically hold musical papers and correspondence. In recent years college and university archives have become more serious about collecting their institutional papers, including those of their music faculty and concert programs. Occasionally, as in the case of the Goodspeed Opera House (East Haddam, Conn.), and the Boston Symphony Orchestra, a musical organization has created significant archives of its own history.

Two unique private music libraries have played significant roles in the character of New England's music. The earliest extant independent music library in the United States, the Harvard Musical Association, was established in 1837 by Harvard graduates unhappy that their alma mater had no interest in musical performance. In a relatively short time, the Bagaduce Music Lending Library in Blue Hill, Maine, has amassed the largest circulating collection of scores in the nation (approximately 6,000), entirely by gift, maintained chiefly by volunteers.

Carol June Bradley, *Music Collections in American Libraries: A Chronology* (1981); *Directory of Music Libraries and Collections in New England*, 9th ed. (1994); *The New Grove Dictionary of American Music* (1986), s.v. "Libraries and Collections"; *Resources of American Music History: A Directory of Source Materials from Colonial Times to World War II* (1981).

Mary Wallace Davidson

Music Publishing

New England was the birthplace of the publishing industry in the United States, and Boston was the center of American music publishing until the beginning of the 20th century. The first book printed in the English-speaking colonies was *The Whole Booke of Psalmes Faithfully Translated into English Metre* (better known as the *Bay Psalm Book*), issued in 1640 at Cambridge. The first music publication, a supplement of tunes for the ninth edition of the *Bay Psalm Book*, appeared in Boston in 1698.

Congregational singing was the primary musical activity in the New England colonies. Consequently, most music published during the 18th century took the form of psalm tune collections and instruction books for singing schools. The first of these appeared in Boston in 1721: John Tufts's *A Very Plain and Easy Introduction to the Singing of Psalm Tunes*, and the Reverend Thomas Walter's *Grounds and Rules of Musick Explained*.

Early tunebooks were often published by booksellers and engraved by silversmiths. Paul Revere had a hand in engraving two of the most important books of early American music: Josiah Flagg's *A Collection of the Best Psalm Tunes* (Boston, 1764), the first music printed on American-made paper, and William Billings's *New England Psalm-Singer* (Boston, 1770), the first tunebook wholly composed by an American. Most publishers at this time were men of many trades, like Thomas Johnston of Boston, an organ builder and engraver who was the first to become actively involved in music publishing. Other engraver-publishers in the late 18th century included John Ward Gilman of Exeter, N.H., Joel Knott Allen of Middletown, Conn., and the father-son team of John and William Norman of Boston; musician-publishers included Daniel Bayley of Newburyport, Mass., and Daniel Read, Timothy Swan, and Oliver Brownson of Connecticut.

Connecticut was especially active in psalm tune publication. The first collection to designate pieces by American composers was *The Chorister's Companion*, published in 1782 in New Haven by the silversmith Amos Doolittle and the clockmaker Simeon Jocelyn. Doolittle also published, with the composer Daniel Read, the first musical periodical in America, the *American Musical Magazine* (1786–87). Andrew Law, a prolific composer, tunebook compiler, and itinerant singing master, whose brother William printed his works in Cheshire, Conn., was one of the first citizens to be granted legal copyright in the United States; this was issued in 1781 for his *Select Harmony,* Connecticut's first tunebook.

Technological change reached New England in the 1750s with the introduction of movable type by Isaiah Thomas of Worcester, Mass. Thomas, founder of the American Antiquarian Society, was the leading American printer and publisher of the period and the first to achieve success in music publishing. His *Worcester Collection of Sacred Harmony* (1786) became a best-seller, running through eight editions. Thomas's chief competitor was Henry Ranlet of Exeter, N.H., who, like Thomas, was a newspaper publisher.

Following the Revolutionary War and the lifting of the Continental Congress's ban on theatrical activities in 1789, entertainment music assumed a more prominent role in American life. Secular pieces first appeared in journals like Thomas's *Massachusetts Magazine,* a literary-political journal issued from 1789 to 1795. The growing demand for music in the 19th century spurred the establishment of new firms, notably Andrew Wright (Northampton, Mass.), Herman Mann (Dedham, Mass., and Providence), Joshua Cushing (Salem, Mass.), and Manning and Loring, J. T. Buckingham, and William P. Blake (Boston). They published not only tunebooks and popular songs, but instrumental music and dance tunes as well. Important early instrumental method books were Samuel Holyoke's *Instrumental Assistant* (Exeter, 1800) and *For the Gentlemen,* a compilation of marches, airs, and minuets by Oliver Shaw of Providence (1807). As contra dancing became more popular, collections of dance figures and tunes were published, such as those by Elias Howe of Boston, whose *Musician's Companion* of 1844 also included brass band pieces.

The first music store in Boston was opened in 1798 by Peter Albrecht von Hagen, a theater musician who issued sheet music for the burgeoning home market. Boston's leading music publisher and dealer in the early 19th century was Johann Gottlieb Graupner, whose catalog was later acquired by Oliver Ditson, one of the most important American music publishers. Ditson published two items of particular interest in New England history: songs of the Hutchinson Family Singers and *Dwight's Journal of Music,* a key source of information on musical activities in the second half of the 19th century.

After the Civil War, music publishing in Boston expanded greatly. One of the most important firms was that of Arthur P. Schmidt, who, although a German immigrant, demonstrated an unusual commitment to serious American music. Often referred to as "the pioneer publisher of American music," he was the first to win international recognition for

such American composers as Amy Beach and Edward MacDowell. Other specialist houses were Silver Burdett, Boston Music Company, B. F. Wood, and C. C. Birchard (educational music); White-Smith (parlor songs); Mason Bros. and McLaughlin and Reilly (sacred music); E. C. Schirmer (choral music); and Cundy-Bettoney (band music). Art music found its champions in smaller presses, such as Wa-Wan Press, founded by the composer Arthur Farwell (Newton Centre, Mass.); Smith College Press (Northampton, Mass.); and Margun Music and GunMar Music, founded by Gunther Schuller.

In the 20th century the center of American music publishing shifted from Boston to New York, as Tin Pan Alley came to dominate the popular music scene and firms succumbed to mergers and acquisitions. By the 1950s the golden age of music publishing in New England was over.

Christine Ayars, *Contributions to the Art of Music in America by the Music Industries of Boston, 1640–1936* (1937); Richard Crawford, *American Sacred Music Imprints 1698–1910: A Bibliography* (1990); Richard Crawford and D. W. Krummel, "Early American Music Printing and Publishing," in *Printing and Society in Early America* (1983); W. A. Fisher, *One Hundred and Fifty Years of Music Publishing in the United States* (1977 [1933]).

Wilma Reid Cipolla

National Center of Afro-American Artists

The National Center of Afro-American Artists (NCAAA) is a private, not-for-profit institution committed to preserving and fostering the cultural arts heritage of black peoples worldwide through arts teaching and the presentation of professional works in all fine arts disciplines. Located in Boston, it was founded by a national group of African American artists, including Dr. Elma Lewis, who was artistic director until her death in 2004.

The founding of the NCAAA and its incorporation in 1968 grew out of a confluence of powerful forces. In the mid-1960s, cultural and political nationalism, along with urban unrest and racial turmoil, were sweeping the nation. Black issues dominated the country's domestic agenda and were at the center of African American intracultural discussion. In this context, Columbia College in Chicago convened a conference of black creative intellectuals that eventually included such notables as John O. Killens, Charles White, Woodie King, Robert Hooks, Elma Lewis, and Jeff Donaldson. Attending scholars and artists lamented the absence of a genuinely national, multidisciplinary organization that could serve as the institutional platform and patron for black creativity. They came away resolved to address this need.

Museum director Edmund Barry Gaither (left) with Barnet Rubenstein at the Museum of the National Center of Afro-American Artists, 1970

Under Lewis's direction, the Elma Lewis School of Fine Arts (ELSFA) in Roxbury, Mass., had offered high quality training to black youth since 1950. A graduate of Emerson College (B.A.) and Boston University (M.A.), Lewis opened the school against all odds because of her belief in the power of arts knowledge and the importance of cultural self-knowledge in maximizing the realization of human potential. By the late sixties, many of Lewis's students—particularly those in dance—were enjoying careers in theater in New York. Her concerns then included how to bring greater stability to the careers of black artists, and she perceived that an institutional platform and patron could be helpful.

Addressing this need for stabilization as well as the concerns expressed by the Columbia College conference, Lewis conceived the NCAAA. Her vision for the NCAAA was expansive. It would subsume the ELSFA, thus creating a teaching, performing, and exhibiting institution that would emphasize both artistic excellence and the contribution of the arts to wholesome human development. It would be active on local, national, and international stages, seeking to bring to black heritage the respect and praise it deserved. This majestic concept and its implementation would later bring the NCAAA a National Medal of Art, citation by the National Bicentennial Commission, and to its founder a John D. and Catherine MacArthur Prize.

Late in 1968 the ELSFA acquired a former grand synagogue and Yeshiva school in Roxbury, now a predominately black section of Boston. The old synagogue was to become the home for the NCAAA's professional performing companies and museum, as well as a presentation venue for other productions. This goal, however, was never achieved. The old Yeshiva building, renovated at a cost of three-quarters of a million dollars between 1968 and 1971, served as the ELSFA and housed professional programs of the NCAAA throughout the next two decades.

With the acquisition of the aforementioned properties, the NCAAA/ELSFA greatly expanded their programs in 1969. In order to help get them started at an appropriately professional level, Lewis sought the help of older cultural institutions and foundations. The Museum of Fine Arts, under the directorship of Perry Rathbone and the chairmanship of George Seybolt, assisted with the development of NCAAA's museum. The New England Conservatory of Music participated in the very early launching of the music division. Both the Ford and Rockefeller Foundations were early supporters.

By the early 1970s, the NCAAA/ELSFA was offering professional and teaching programs in dance, music, theater, visual arts, sewing and costuming, and technical theater, as well as continuing the operation of the Elma Lewis Playhouse in the Park, which had started in 1967. By the mid-1970s, in addition to serving more than 400 six- to 12-year-old students and 100 teen and adult students, the NCAAA/ELSFA taught an additional 100 students from community schools and nearly as many prisoners in Norfolk Correctional Institution, a middle-security state prison. *Who Took the Weight?* (1972), a book of writings published by Little, Brown, was a product of the NCAAA/ELSFA's teaching program at Norfolk. Serving these students was a staff of more than 125 full and part-time teachers, including such distinguished artists as Michael Olatunji, Talley Beatty, Billy Wilson, and A. B. Spellman.

The ELSFA required that all students under age 12 take its full spectrum of graded arts courses. For older students, specialization was encouraged and performance or exhibition required. Because of the school's philosophy, its students enjoyed numerous opportunities to work directly with professional artists and to sometimes appear in professional performances. This tradition has been continued in the NCAAA's production of Langston Hughes's song-play *Black Nativity,* which has been presented annually since 1970. Other vehicles for integrating teaching and performance within the ELSFA included its youth

singing groups: the Black Persuasion, the Children of the Black Persuasion, and the Children's Theater Company.

Reclaiming the site of an abandoned firehouse in Boston's Franklin Park, the NCAA/ELSFA produced free nightly performances from the Fourth of July through Labor Day from 1967 through 1978. Traditionally, Michael Olatunji, the noted Nigerian drummer, opened the season. Each year, Duke Ellington was featured. Other greats presented over the years include Max Roach, Billy Taylor, Odetta, and the Boston Pops Orchestra. Myriad local groups also performed. The model of the Elma Lewis Playhouse in the Park inspired the city of Boston to begin its popular outdoor performance series dubbed Summerthing.

The NCAAA maintained professional companies in several disciplines. The NCAAA Dance Company, initially under the director of Talley Beatty, came into its own under artistic director Billy Wilson, who later created Broadway's *Bubbling Brown Sugar.* This company performed locally, nationally, and internationally until it was disbanded for replacement by the International Dance Forum. Headed by John A. Ross, Black Musical Productions, the NCAAA's music division, featured a big band directed by Jaki Byard, an adult chorus, and several chamber music ensembles. Additionally, the NCAAA, in association with the Boston Pops Orchestra, commissioned several new works for full orchestra and small jazz ensemble, including *Primal Rites* by Noel da Costa. The theater division of the NCAAA was directed by Vernon A. Blackman and consisted of a mime company, a writer's workshop conducted by A. B. Spellman, and an adult company. Among its most outstanding productions were *Kismet* and *Ballard Caribe.* All of the performing arts presentations involved multidisciplinary collaborations supported by the NCAAA's departments of sewing and costuming under the leadership of Augustus Bowen and Lucy Cordice, and technical theater directed by Larry Blumsack.

Beginning in 1971 the NCAAA presented *Celebrate!*—an annual spring extravaganza. Consisting of an art exhibition in City Hall, an original show of music, dance, and theater at the Music Hall (now the Wang Center), and a cabaret in its own facilities, Celebrate! events focused on aspects of black cultural and social history combining teaching, entertainment, and fund raising into one dynamic program series. *Celebrate!* brought many great cultural and artistic figures to Boston, including Mary Lou Williams, Eubie Blake, Muhammad Ali, Thomas Dorsey, Vinette Carroll, and Bea Richards.

The Museum of the NCAAA was developed in close cooperation with the Museum of Fine Arts (MFA), Boston, and, in addition to presentations in its own space, has co-presented nine exhibitions with the MFA. Prominent among these were *Afro-American Artists: New York and Boston* (1970); *Reflective Moments: Lois Mailou Jones* (1973); *Afro-American Artists on Afro-America* (1975); *Contemporary Art of Senegal* (1980); *Dialogue: John Wilson/Joseph Norman* (1994), and *The Art of John Biggers: View from the Upper Room* (1997).

The museum, which relocated to its own building in 1980, has organized and presented a rich schedule of exhibitions since 1969, including several that have toured nationally, including *Our Commonwealth: Our Collections/Works from Historically Black Colleges and Universities.* Other shows, such as *Invisible Man: Blacks in Post Colonial Europe* traveled internationally. In 1995 the museum opened *Aspelta: A Nubian King's Burial Chamber* featuring the world's only scale recreation of a Nubian tomb interior supported by more than 50 objects that are 2,600 years old. The museum's collection includes a 17th-century illuminated Ethiopian manuscript of the *Miracles of Mary* as well as art by Charles White, Romare Bearden, Elizabeth Catlett, and Jacob Lawrence. In addition to its continuous schedule of exhibitions, the museum has pioneered a remarkable series of multivisit educational programs that have drawn significant critical praise.

In the late seventies, the ELSFA underwent a period of great financial stress resulting in staff and service reductions and a transfer of facilities ownership from the ELSFA to the NCAAA. Compounding the problems was a fire that interrupted operations in 1980. Use of the school building ended altogether after a second fire in 1984. Nevertheless, the museum and Black Musical Productions remain vital divisions and are at the heart of a new plan to fully restore the NCAAA building on its original mission. In this endeavor, it has retained old partnerships such as that with the Museum of Fine Arts, Boston, while entering new ones with other institutions such as Northeastern University, which holds the papers of the NCAAA, donated by Elma Lewis in 1997.

The NCAAA remains the largest and most important black cultural arts institution in New England, maintaining an unbroken record of public celebration of the world heritage of black people for 30 years. A commitment to excellence in the arts and wholesome cultural development remain its hallmarks.

Ruth Edmonds Hill, "Elma Lewis," in *Epic Lives: One Hundred Black Women Who Made a Difference,* ed. Jessie Carney Smith (1993); Elma Lewis, ed., *Who Took the Weight? Black Voices from Norfolk Prison*

(1972); Sara Rimer, "An Arts Leader for Whom 'Anything Is Possible,'" *New York Times,* December 29, 1998; Dick Russell, *Black Genius and the American Experience* (1998).

Edmund Barry Gaither

New England Conservatory of Music

Founded in 1867 by Eben Tourjée, the New England Conservatory of Music in Boston is the oldest independent school of music in the United States and the only school of music to be designated a National Historic Landmark. Tourjée, who wished to establish a European-style conservatory in the United States, founded the Musical Institute of Rhode Island in 1853. This institution, enlarged and renamed the Providence Conservatory of Music, eventually moved to Boston and was reincarnated as the New England Conservatory of Music. Tourjée's model for the conservatory was Mendelssohn's Leipzig Conservatorium.

The young conservatory quickly outgrew its space in the Boston Music Hall and moved into the Saint James Hotel before its present home at 290 Huntington Avenue was built in 1902 with donations from trustee Eben Jordan. The main building now houses Jordan Hall, which was opened in 1903 under then-president, the composer George Chadwick. Jordan Hall is significant not only in the history of Boston, but in the musical life of New England and the United States. Its numerous free concerts make it an extraordinary public service institution, while the world's great artists and ensembles—among them Yo-Yo Ma, the Handel and Haydn Society, Boston Baroque, and Boston Cecilia—find it to be among the most inviting houses in which to perform and a favorable recording venue as well.

The New England Conservatory of Music has influenced the development of classical music, opera, and jazz in Boston and throughout the region. When Henry Higginson founded the Boston Symphony Orchestra in 1881, he chose 19 section leaders from among the conservatory faculty; today, 44 percent of the Boston Symphony Orchestra is made up of conservatory faculty and alumni. Graduates and faculty of the conservatory have variously served as players, musicians, and directors in Boston's intermittent experiments with opera companies. A fully accredited jazz performance program was established in 1969, the first of its kind among major music conservatories in America.

Among the successful graduates of the New England Conservatory are the soprano Lillian Nordica (1876), the Metropolitan Opera star Eleanor Steber (1936), the conductor and impresario Sarah Caldwell (1946), the jazz pianist, composer, and MacArthur fellow Cecil Taylor (1951), the bass baritone Justino Diaz (1963), the New York Philharmonic managing director Deborah Borda (1967), the concert pianist Christopher O'Riley (1981), the jazz clarinetist Don Byron (1984), the jazz clarinetist, mezzo-soprano, and Metropolitan Opera star Denyce Graves (1988), and the concert pianist and 1994 Tchaikovsky Competition finalist HaeSun Paik (1992).

The New England Conservatory employs a faculty of more than 360 in both the college and extension divisions, three of whom have been MacArthur fellows: Ran Blake, George Russell, and Gunther Schuller. More than 700 graduate and undergraduate students from, on average, 43 states and 33 countries enroll in the conservatory each year, while the extension division serves some 1,200 children, teenagers, and adults. The college offers 36 majors, including theory, musicology, and performance; 70 ensembles; and more than 450 concerts each year. In 1995 the former president Laurence Lesser successfully completed a $26 million capital campaign, $8 million of which was used to restore the centerpiece of the school, Jordan Hall, which was also named a National Historic Landmark.

Robert Freeman, director for 24 years of the Eastman School of Music in Rochester, N.Y., became president of the conservatory on January 1, 1997. The conservatory has been linked to prestigious local institutions, including Harvard University, Boston University, and Boston Conservatory and is currently affiliated with Tufts University through a joint degree program. New England Conservatory is housed in three buildings bounded by Huntington Avenue, Gainsborough Street, and Saint Botolph Street, adjacent to Northeastern University and diagonally across from historic Symphony Hall.

Robert Freeman, *The Orchestra and the University: A Tale of Two Organizations* (1998); Bruce McPherson and James Klein, *Measure by Measure: A History of New England Conservatory from 1867* (1995); Eleanor L. Miller, *The History and Development of the New England Conservatory of Music* (1991); Leo Eben Tourjée, *For God and Music: The Life Story of Eben Tourjée, Father of the American Conservatory* (1960).

Helen M. Greenwald

New England Schools of Composers

New England of the late 18th and 19th centuries spawned two important groups of composers of American music. Separated by roughly a century, these groups are commonly referred to as the First New England School and the Second New England School. Both sets of composers were tied together not only because of their historical and geographic proximity, which led to a flurry of musical activity, but also by shared outlooks on musical style, which created identifiable common approaches to composition.

The composers of the First New England School were active in the late 18th and early 19th centuries and hailed chiefly from Massachusetts and Connecticut. The group's principal members were William Billings (1746–1800), Justin Morgan (1747–98), Andrew Law (1748–1821), Supply Belcher (1751–1836), Jacob French (1754–1817), Daniel Read (1757–1836), Timothy Swan (1758–1842), Jacob Kimball (1761–1826), Samuel Holyoke (1762–1820), Jeremiah Ingalls (1764–1828), and Oliver Holden (1765–1844). Often referred to as the Yankee tunesmiths, these composers compiled collections of sacred music—songs, hymns, anthems, and fuging tunes. While earlier collections had been composed of European music, the collections of these New Englanders included their own works. By the end of the 18th century, the increase in works by American composers included in tunebooks was steadily rising, and the First New England School was born.

The activities of the Yankee tunesmiths were intimately tied to the singing school movement of the 18th century. The singing schools, which were ostensibly convened to improve congregational singing, became important social outlets and popular meeting grounds for rural New England communities. Most of the Yankee tunesmiths were also singing school masters who moved from town to town conducting schools in which their students learned and practiced the skill of sight-reading music. The need for tunebooks for singing schools prompted these singing masters to compile their own collections of music and to include their own works. The singing schools, therefore, provided a venue for the works of these early American composers as well as a mechanism for the dissemination of their compositions.

The most outstanding figure of the group was William Billings, whose first tunebook—*The New England Psalm-Singer; or, American Chorister* of 1770—was a landmark in American music, as its 127 tunes, all written by Billings, represented the most significant number of tunes published by a composer of the United States. Billings also stands out as the only one of the group to pursue music as his sole profession. Most of the other tunesmiths were amateur musical artisans who were employed in other trades. For example, Timothy Swan was also a hatter and merchant, Supply Belcher was originally a tavernkeeper, Justin Morgan—chiefly remembered as a breeder of the Morgan horse—was also a schoolmaster and tavernkeeper, and Andrew Law was a minister. Nonetheless, they all compiled tunebook collections including their own compositions and conducted singing schools throughout New England.

The tunes of Billings and his colleagues appealed to a significant number of New Englanders, as they incorporated two subjects close to their hearts: religion and patriotism. The most popular musical form was the fuging tune: a composition that begins in the manner of a choral hymn and then shifts to a fuging section in which the voices enter in staggered succession. Their other types of works were also important: many of the hymns that are standard in the United States today were written by these men. The works of these composers, however, are relatively homogeneous stylistically. The harmonic features of their music—parallel fifths and octaves, open fifths and somewhat surprising dissonances—created a distinctive and characteristically American sound associated with these works. The New England style, however, did not suit the tastes of postcolonial Americans, who were influenced by a new wave of immigrants with old world attitudes about music. Held up to foreign standards, the rugged, rough-hewn tunes of New England were awkward and archaic. Consequently European works were reintegrated into American tunebooks as a means of cultural improvement. By 1810 this "improvement" was in full swing, and the native tradition established by the Yankee tunesmiths was submerged in the re-Europeanization of American sacred music.

The Second New England School of composers was active in the late 19th century. In the time between the two schools a cultural transformation had taken place: the vernacular tradition (utilitarian and entertainment music) and the cultivated tradition (art music influenced by artistic, moral, and cultural idealism) gradually diverged. The ideal of an American art music tradition based on European models resulted in trained professional composers as well as new institutions and patronage, and the course of so-called serious composition in the United States was directed toward the imitation of foreign exemplars. By the end of the century, therefore, a second New England school appeared that was radically different from the first school: it was firmly rooted in the European tradition of art music composition and the cultural ideals of high art.

The Second New England School included John Knowles Paine (1839–1906), Arthur Foote (1853–1937), George Chadwick (1854–1931), Arthur Whiting (1861–1936), Horatio Parker (1863–1919), Amy Beach (1867–1944), Margaret Ruthven Lang (1867–1972), and Daniel Gregory Mason (1873–1953). Sometimes referred to as the Boston group, the New

England Academics, Boston classicists and New England Classical Romanticists, the Second New England School, unlike the Yankee tunesmiths, was urban and fundamentally influenced by European art music. The composers of this group were trained musicians who were talented and idealistic. All lived and worked as professional musicians primarily in Boston, which, as a musical and intellectual center of the later 19th century, provided an eager musical public, performance opportunities, educational institutions, and a social network that strongly supported art music. The city, therefore, supplied an atmosphere of support and collegiality among its composers as well as cultural validation of the pursuit of an American art music tradition.

Almost all of these composers were educated in Germany in the classical-Romantic tradition. As such, they attempted to write in the forms of their European model: symphonies, chamber works, cantatas, oratorios, and songs. Most notably their large-form works, especially the symphonies and other orchestral works, were among the first attempts at establishing an American orchestral tradition. In general, the style of their works draws largely on the Romanticism of 19th-century Europe but is infused with a somewhat characteristically American sentimentality. While all of these composers maintained a conservative, German-influenced musical style, each displayed individuality in approaching the model. As such, the works themselves reveal a broad range of musical styles within the confines of the fundamental ideal that the composers strove to realize.

John Knowles Paine, the oldest of the group, was the first to favor adherence to the forms of the European masters. His music is thus conservative, falling generally within the stylistic realm of the German romantics. Paine's emulation of European works and the attempt to establish an American cultivated tradition that it represented was passed along to the younger members of the group, many of whom were his students. The younger generation continued the task of advancing art music composition in the United States. Among them, George Chadwick and Horatio Parker stand out as the most talented. Parker was the more conservative of the two. His works, the majority of which are choral pieces, are all quite serious and deeply influenced by German romantic models. Chadwick was a prolific composer whose works reflect American Romanticism but also reveal more versatility than those of his colleagues, as his music often incorporates strains of the American vernacular tradition and humor. Of the remaining members of the group, Foote and Beach also deserve mention. Both were educated exclu-

sively in the United States but were skilled craftspeople in European musical forms. The works of all of the Boston composers, however, were critically acclaimed and frequently performed both regionally and across the country.

The members of the second New England group also hold an important place in American music history because of their ancillary activities and achievements. Paine, for example, became the first music professor at Harvard University, thus establishing the study of music in academia. Chadwick became the president of the New England Conservatory of Music, transforming it into one of the premier institutions for training professional musicians. Parker founded the music department at Yale University and was later the teacher of Charles Ives. The first performances of orchestral works by American women also arose from this group with Margaret Lang's *Dramatic* Overture in 1893 and Amy Beach's *Gaelic* Symphony in 1896.

The composers of the Second New England School by virtue of their musical output, their ideology, and their other activities formed a vital group that was integral to the establishment of an art music tradition in the United States. In attitude and purpose, they differed significantly from the First New England School, which responded to the needs and desires of communities. While the second school was cultivated and urban, the first was rural and utilitarian. The composers of the first group were amateur and untrained, while those of the second were professional and educated. Representing seemingly opposite traditions, the two New England schools of composers in fact embody the dynamic forces that have shaped American musical culture: the constant intersection of the amateur and the professional, the native and the foreign, the vernacular and the cultivated.

Gilbert Chase, *America's Music from the Pilgrims to the Present* (1987); Richard Crawford, *The American Musical Landscape* (1993); Charles Hamm, *Music in the New World* (1983); H. Wiley Hitchcock, *Music in the United States: A Historical Introduction* (1988); John Tasker Howard, *Our American Music: Three Hundred Years of It* (1939); John Warthen Struble, *The History of American Classical Music: MacDowell through Minimalism* (1995); Nicholas E. Tawa, *The Coming of Age of American Art Music: New England's Classical Romanticists* (1991).

Laurie K. Blunsom

Newport Folk Festival The Newport Folk Festival was the most important popular folk festival in America between 1959 and 1969. Held each July in the elite summer resort town of Newport, R.I., Newport, as the festival was popularly known, influenced and was influenced by the folk music revival of the late

1950s and 1960s, and audiences were a regional microcosm of the nationwide subculture.

From the beginning, the festival propelled—or reintroduced—many performers into the commercial music industry. Through informal workshops and formal concerts, Newport introduced audiences to tradition-bearers whose performance genres were juxtaposed with familiar citybillies, the term used for young musicians appropriating repertoires and styles from many folk traditions.

By 1963 Newport was an event that had become the annual gathering of revivalists principally from New York's Greenwich Village and from coffeehouses on both sides of the Charles River. No single venue contributed as much to Newport in terms of performers, board members, fieldworkers, producers, volunteers, and audiences as the contemporaneous Club 47 (now Club Passim) in Cambridge, Mass., an epicenter of the revival.

The festivals of 1959 and 1960 were organized by George Wein, a Boston nightclub impresario who began producing the Newport Jazz Festival in the early 1950s, and Albert Grossman, who ran Chicago's Gate of Horn and was soon to become a rock music promoter. The festival was suspended for two years because of financial losses and other problems and returned in 1963, reorganized under the aegis of the nonprofit Newport Folk Foundation. Until its demise, the event was nominally run by a board of directors.

The first Newport Folk Festival in 1959 is best known for launching a little-known and unbilled performer from Club 47, Joan Baez, who was invited on stage by the Chicago singer Bob Gibson. The eclectic genres that year included the old-time string band revivalists the New Lost City Ramblers, Ireland's Clancy Brothers, the bluegrass banjoist Earl Scruggs with country singers Hylo Brown and the Timberlines, the bluesman Reverend Gary Davis, and the wildly popular Kingston Trio.

When the festival returned in 1963 only weeks before the March on Washington, it was dedicated to civil rights. The final concert featured the Student Nonviolent Coordinating Committee's Freedom Singers, captured in an iconic photograph linking arms with the revival's reigning stars, Peter, Paul, and Mary, Joan Baez, Bob Dylan, and Pete Seeger. The 1964 theme was country blues and showcased southern African American artists who had recorded in the 1920s and 1930s and were "rediscovered" by young white revivalists and brought to the Northeast. The 1965 festival is noted for Bob Dylan's "going electric," abandoning his acoustic guitar and political commentary for an electric instrument and introspective lyrics. The ubiquity of the Dylan-Newport '65 legend suggests more about the course of the revival itself, which saw older, more liberal folk aficionados—many of whom sat on the Newport board—part company with younger, more roots-oriented and less overtly political folkies, who had already been exposed to electric music at earlier festivals. Newport in the late 1960s presented new genres such as folk-rock, featuring groups like Janis Joplin's Big Brother and the Holding Company, and new singer-songwriters like James Taylor.

The Newport Folk Festival was revived in 1985 and for many years was partially underwritten by Ben and Jerry's, the Vermont-based ice cream company, and renamed Ben and Jerry's Folk Festival–Newport. In 2000 the Newport Creamery, a Rhode Island–based ice cream company, became the festival's major sponsor for a year and restored the festival's name; however, it has since been renamed the Apple and Eve Newport Folk Festival after its current sponsor.

David Gahr and Robert Shelton, *The Face of Folk Music* (1968); Murray Lerner, *Festival!* [film] (1967); Neil Rosenberg, ed., *Transforming Tradition: Folk Music Revivals Examined* (1993); Eric von Schmidt and Jim Rooney, *Baby, Let Me Follow You Down: The Illustrated Story of the Cambridge Folk Years* (1994).

Millie Rahn

Newport Jazz Festival

The Newport Jazz Festival was conceived during the summer of 1953 by Louis and Elaine Lorillard, who were dissatisfied with two unsuccessful New York Philharmonic concerts at the Newport Casino in Rhode Island. Searching for summer entertainment that was unusual and attractive to a reasonably large audience, the Lorillards sought the advice of John Hammond, a jazz expert, Columbia Records executive, and member of the Vanderbilt family. Together, they selected George Wein, a jazz pianist and manager of a Boston jazz club called Storyville, to organize a jazz festival. Once a charter was drawn up, a nonprofit corporation established, and sponsors and a board of directors selected, Wein scheduled the musicians and attended to publicity and logistics. The jazz festival opened in 1954 on the grounds of the Newport Casino. The purpose, as published in the festival's first program book, was "to encourage America's enjoyment of jazz and to sponsor the study of our country's only original art form."

The first Newport Jazz Festival lasted only two days, but the lineup was impressive and included leading jazz musicians of the day. Eddie Condon, Dizzy Gillespie, the Modern Jazz Quartet, Horace Silver, Gerry Mulligan, Oscar Peterson, Lennie Tristano, Lee Konitz, Ella Fitzgerald, Billie Holiday, and Lester

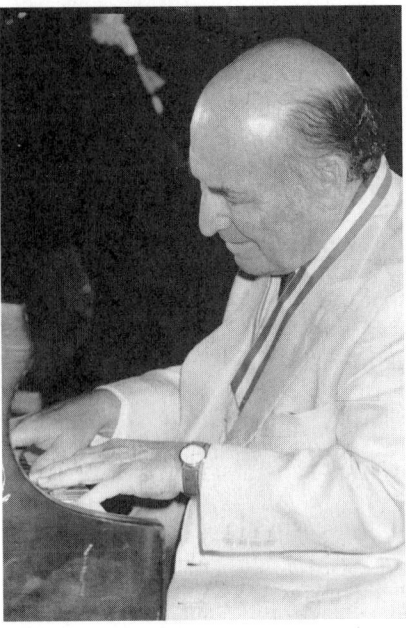

Founder George Wein opens the Newport Jazz Festival at the keyboard, 1989

Young were among the artists to appear. Several influential music industry figures, including the record producer George Avakian, the critic and disc jockey Nat Hentoff, and the scholar Marshall Stearns were also in attendance; their assessment and devotion to the festival helped secure its future.

Over the next five years the festival's program and audience expanded, but almost immediately the musicians and many of the wealthy sponsors were at odds. In 1955 the Newport Casino board voted against holding future festivals on their property, so the Newport Jazz Festival moved to Freebody Park, a municipally owned sports field in Newport. In 1958 the photographer Bert Stern made a stylish documentary film, *Jazz on a Summer's Day*, capturing the scope of the festival production, the diversity and relaxed attitude of the audience, and the musicians' seriousness of intent on stage and in rehearsal. Over the years, veterans of the original Newport Jazz Festival returned and new faces were added, including Louis Armstrong, Woody Herman, Duke Ellington, Clifford Brown, Miles Davis, Dave Brubeck, Teo Macero, Cecil Taylor, Mary Lou Williams, Carmen McCrae, Anita O'Day, Benny Goodman, Thelonius Monk, Stan Kenton, John Coltrane, Roy Eldridge, Nina Simone, and George Shearing.

In subsequent years, the tension between the residents of Newport and both audience and musicians continued. Crowds became larger and more unruly, beer cans littered the streets, drugs and whiskey were common, and teenagers and college students began arriving in droves. In 1961 the Newport City Council canceled the festival. Wein responded by changing the organization from a nonprofit festival to an incorporated business venture, renting his sites, billing it "Newport '62," and continuing full speed ahead. That same year he organized the Newport Jazz Festival in Europe, which toured 11 countries. To help pay the bills, such popular entertainers as Chuck Berry, Ray Charles, and Blood, Sweat, and Tears were added to the programs. The festival continued in Newport until 1971, when, after a riot in which an angry mob of drunken youths crashed the gate of the festival grounds, the city finally closed down the event.

The festival moved to New York and is now part of an international jazz festival program sponsored by JVC. The JVC Newport Jazz Festival appears each August at Fort Adams State Park, a breathtaking site located on Narragansett Bay near the famed Newport mansions. The opening night of the festival is typically held at the Newport Casino, location of the first festival. The festival has continued without interruption to the present day.

Anthony J. Agostinelli, ed., *The Newport Jazz Festival, Rhode Island, 1954–1971: A Bibliography, Discography, and Filmography* (1977); Burt Goldblatt, *Newport Jazz Festival: The Illustrated History* (1977).

Frank Tirro

The Old Homestead

Denman Thompson's play *The Old Homestead* (1886) is one of the great stage successes of the late-19th-century American theater, and its main character, Joshua, or Josh, Whitcomb (performed by Thompson himself from 1887 to 1911), was the last significant stage Yankee. *The Old Homestead* is largely responsible for reviving an interest in old-time New England culture and is popularly associated with the rise of Old Home Week celebrations.

After a triumphant run at the Boston Museum, the play opened in New York on January 10, 1887, at the 14th Street Theater, where it played for 20 weeks. It was the third version of what had been a vaudeville sketch, "Joshua Whitcomb," first performed in 1875. George W. Ryer was the unacknowledged coauthor. Earning its star more than $3 million over the years, it was associated with Thompson until his death in 1911.

The Old Homestead was taken seriously in its time. In the July 1889 issue of *Harper's Monthly*, William Dean Howells wrote, "On a wider plane than anyone else has yet attempted, Mr. Thompson gives us in this piece a representation of American life. [Even] at its sketchiest, it is true . . . the simpler phases of our life still make the strongest appeal to all."

Thompson saw to it that audiences could immediately recognize the play's New England location. The script establishes Josh's

humor and wisdom, while minor roles convey local ambience. There is a conventional greenhorn Irish servant, Maggie, and four musicians appear as characters in the play to provide "natural" music, singing for their supper. In keeping with Thompson's awareness of his audience, Happy Jack's tippling underscores the play's muted temperance theme.

The plot is simple: the noble farmer Joshua Whitcomb must save his son, Reuben, from the evils of big city living. The son had run off to New York after being accused of a crime. Following Reuben to the city, Whitcomb rescues his son, and the prodigal returns. Josh has restored order to the old homestead.

In contrast to the dialect of its New Hampshire characters, the play's New York City characters hardly ever use contractions. Certain phrases used in the play add to its authentic New England atmosphere: "Martin gills," for example, refers to the martingale on a harness that keeps a horse from tossing back its head; the "watch-meeting" is the traditional New Year's Eve service at the meetinghouse; "Scarlet Runners" are flowering bean plants.

Even though the play is mainly concerned with humorously detailing the perils of New York City, it was its function as an emblem of old New England that kept audiences flocking to it. Thompson seized on the archetypal Wise Old Man aspects of Josh Whitcomb and took to playing the role in real life, in effect becoming Josh Whitcomb, the living embodiment of the play's virtues and values.

The play is periodically revived in a community summer theater production in West Swanzey, N.H.

Denman Thompson, *The Old Homestead*, in *S.R.O.: The Most Successful Plays*, ed. Bennett Cerf and Van H. Cartmell (1944); William H. Walsh, *Historical and Personal Reminiscences of Denman Thompson* (ca. 1910).

Thomas F. Connolly

O'Neill, Eugene Gladstone

(1888–1953) Playwright. Eugene O'Neill was born in New York City to Mary Ellen Quinlan and James O'Neill, an Irish immigrant and professional actor. The author of more than 50 published plays, O'Neill was the recipient of four Pulitzer Prizes, for *Beyond the Horizon* (1920), *Anna Christie* (1922), *Strange Interlude* (1928), and *Long Day's Journey into Night* (1957). In 1936 he was awarded the Nobel Prize for Literature in recognition of his long trilogy *Mourning Becomes Electra* (1931). He spent more than 25 summers at his family home (the Monte Cristo Cottage) in New London, Conn., and continued to visit the cottage until its sale in 1919.

O'Neill studied under the great theater scholar George Pierce Baker at Harvard. His

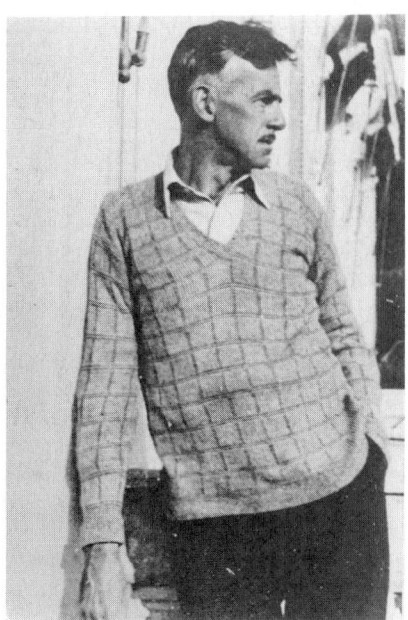

Eugene O'Neill, 1933

career began in 1916 when he joined the playwrights George Cram Cook and Susan Glaspell at the fledgling Wharf Theatre in Provincetown, Mass. In the fall of 1916 the Provincetown Players, for whom O'Neill served as dramatist and manager, moved to New York City, and American realism was born.

O'Neill's most significant work reflects his love of the sea and his ties to New England Puritanism. In his first three-act drama, *Beyond the Horizon*, the Mayo brothers vie for the same woman in bleak isolation on a New England farm, and in *Desire under the Elms* (1924), a similar cruel, yet seductive, landscape informs the lives of the Cabot family. The survivors of both plays are left alone to farm the unforgiving New England land. *Mourning Becomes Electra* takes place at the end of the Civil War in an austere New England seaport modeled on New London, Conn. In this play, the Mannon family is haunted by Puritan ancestors whose ghosts provoke the crimes of incest, greed, and murder.

In 1937 O'Neill and his third wife, Carlotta Monterey, built Tao House, a mansion nestled in the hills of Danville, Calif. For the next six years, the playwright worked concurrently on several projects: his projected cycle of 11 plays about American greed and opportunism, titled *A Tale of Possessors Self-Dispossessed* (1932–43); *The Iceman Cometh* (1940); *Long Day's Journey into Night* (1941); *Hughie* (1942); and *A Moon for the Misbegotten* (1943). Of the cycle plays, two were published after his death: *A Touch of the Poet* (1957) and *More Stately Mansions* (1964). With the exception of *Iceman* and *Hughie,* all of these plays focus on the conflict between Irish Catholic immigrants and the white, Anglo-Saxon, Protestant establishment in New England.

Two autobiographical plays, *Long Day's Journey into Night* and *A Moon for the Misbegotten,* are also set in New London. In these plays, the Tyrones (O'Neills) are virtually excluded from New London society; in isolation they battle the demons of drugs, alcohol, and guilt. Like O'Neill himself, the characters long to be accepted by the Protestant elite but are irresistibly drawn to their Irish Catholic roots. This pervasive tension makes O'Neill's plays culturally realistic and theatrically compelling.

From 1948 to 1951 O'Neill and Monterey resided in Marblehead, Mass., and from 1951 to 1953 they lived in a Boston hotel, where O'Neill died of a form of Parkinson's disease. Most of O'Neill's papers are housed at the Beinecke Library at Yale University.

Stephen A. Black, *Eugene O'Neill: Beyond Mourning and Tragedy* (1999); Martha Gilman Bower, *Eugene O'Neill's Unfinished Threnody and Process of Invention in Four Cycle Plays* (1992); Marc Maufort, *Eugene O'Neill and the Emergence of American Drama* (1989); Eugene O'Neill, *Complete Plays,* 3 vols. (1988); Louis Sheaffer, *O'Neill: Son and Playwright* (1968); Sheaffer, *O'Neill: Son and Artist* (1973).

Martha Gilman Bower

Opera During the period that the Venetians opened the first public opera house, San Cassiano, Harvard College was founded in Cambridge, Mass., to train ministers. Musical institutions, however, were slower to develop in New England. Once English opera gained a toehold in the turbulent revolutionary days and the colonial antitheater ordinance was rescinded, opera increased in popularity, primarily by means of touring English opera groups. Foreign-language opera became even more strongly entrenched in New England, particularly in Boston, than English opera. As early as 1797, Gretry's *Richard the Lion Heart,* a French opera, played in Boston and became John Quincy Adams's favorite opera. English-language performances of operas by Philidor and Rousseau also played in Boston, but performances of French and Italian operas in their original language were infrequent until the late 1840s.

Eben Jordan, a prominent New England merchant, transformed Boston's operatic situation; in early 1908, he announced plans to fully finance and build an opera house on his own Huntington Avenue site. He selected the Boston architectural firm Wheelwright and Haven, with Parkman B. Haven in charge of the project. The architects set off on a tour of European opera houses while Jordan organized an opera company that would be a permanent Boston resident. He proposed stock offerings that entitled each buyer to one ticket before the public sale; the opera house boxes sold at $2,000 a year for three years. Jordan, meanwhile, would guarantee the deficit, if any, for three years. The response to the stock and box offering was so enthusiastic that the house was enlarged to seat 2,700. Ground was broken in July 1908, and on November 30, "lovers of music, songbirds of the stage, and patrons of the arts" gathered for the laying of the cornerstone. Jordan chose as his general manager Henry Russell, who brought new European and American talent, including Enrico Caruso, to Boston in an effort to undermine the star system. A Boston opera school was formed within the New England Conservatory and six scholarships set up. Experienced singers, such as the tenor Florencio Constantino, the sopranos Alice Nielsen, Maria Gay, and Lydia Lipkowska, the baritone George Baklanoff, and the bass José Mardones, were recruited. But these were not stars, and Russell reversed his original decision by arranging with the New York Metropolitan Opera to borrow famous singers.

The Boston Opera House opened on November 8, 1909, in the fashionable Fenway Park section. Its exterior was made of subdued red brick, gray limestone, and white terracotta, with four massive pillars dominating the facade. Under the main cornice, glazed and colored bas-relief by Bela L. Pratt, a local sculptor, symbolized Music, Dancing, and Drama. The opening gala, *La Gioconda,* served as a homecoming for three singers, Lillian Nordica, Louise Homer, and Constantino, who were not members of the regular company but had New England antecedents and associations. The first season demonstrated the difficulty of creating a loyal audience. The older traditional repertory, including *La Traviata* and *Faust,* filled the boxes but emptied the upper tiers. The boxes, by contrast, did not seem interested in modern Italian opera, which packed the gallery and balcony. A "very Italianate assembly" came to *Madama Butterfly.* The second season was shortened, and a more innovative repertory was cautiously embarked upon, but the 1910–11 season ended with a deficit larger than Jordan had anticipated. Opera lovers had come faithfully to the balcony and gallery. Galvanized by the conductor Felix Weingartner and the designer Joseph Urban, the Boston Opera began a two-year period of remarkable achievement and sustained excitement.

In spring 1912, Jordan reaffirmed that he would not guarantee deficits beyond the three years originally stipulated. Mayor John G. "Honey Fitz" Fitzgerald tried to exempt the company from taxes. A Boston legislator introduced a bill to provide money for the city to purchase the opera house. Neither of these approaches was successful. After some financial manipulations, Russell was reengaged for another three-year period and went ahead with the fourth and fifth seasons. With the approach of World War I, the Boston Opera season ended when the company went bankrupt in April 1915 as ticket sales declined, but performances continued sporadically through the Depression and during World War II. By the 1950s and 1960s, opera appealed to different audiences, including those at major opera houses who preferred companies defined as major by the size of their budgets and their use of international singing stars; regional companies that emphasized lively interpretations and offbeat repertories; and those built on local foundations that emphasized community effort, often through amateur performance. Something of this audience was represented by the Goodspeed Opera House in East Haddam, Conn., which, restored to its 1870s glory, revived the popular American works of the 1910s, 1920s, and 1930s, such as John Philip Sousa's *El Capitan* and George M. Cohan's *Little Johnny Jones.* A younger operatic audience, nourished on rock, jazz, non-Western music, and multimedia shows, found its home in colleges and universities.

A revival began in 1957 when a new company, the Opera Company of Boston, aimed to attract a new audience by emphasizing an unusual repertory. Its inspiration was Sarah Caldwell, Boston's "prima dynamo." At the Berkshire Music Center in 1947, Caldwell staged Vaughan Williams's *Riders to the Sea.* From 1952 to 1960, she was head of the Boston University Opera Workshop, where she began to produce opera with lively ideas and little money. In 1957 she founded the Boston Opera Group, later the Opera Company of Boston, where she attracted international attention with her innovative stagings of both new and standard works. In Boston, Caldwell found an audience that had grown up in the city since World War II—a large college population, educated middle-class professionals, intellectuals, people in the arts, and journalists. During the 1960s and 1970s, Caldwell made her company a dynamic voice in opera with an impressive number of firsts to its credit. In 1968 her production of Berg's *Lulu* was the first use of film on the operatic stage in the United States, a technique she also employed two years later for Kurka's *The Good Soldier Schweik.* Her interest in class and political conflicts was evident in the American premiere of Luigi Nono's *Intolleranza* (1965), which used television images on the operatic stage for the first time.

From the beginning, the Opera Company of Boston suffered from having no home. The season took the form of three or four operas, performed two or three times. It moved from theater to theater, often playing in old movie houses. An abandoned synagogue doubled as rehearsal hall and workshop, but the constant peregrinations and the improvised conditions added a sense of adventure to the company's productions. Competition for Caldwell came from the Boston Lyric Opera New England (BLO), founded in 1976 and considered one of North America's fastest growing opera companies. Along with its productions of varied repertoire with young, world-class singers, its educational and community programs presented specialized events for children and adults. In 1982 the BLO performed Wagner's *Ring* cycle on four successive Sundays in Alumni Auditorium of Northeastern University, Boston. Today, performances are held in the Shubert Theater on Tremont Street, only a few blocks from the site of Sarah Caldwell's opera house.

Although most of the major operatic activity in New England is centered in Boston, other areas of the region have begun or attempted opera performance. In 1918 Elizabeth Sprague Coolidge opened the Berkshire Music Center on her estate in Pittsfield, Mass., for concerts that would feature classical and modern American and European music. BLO's 2001 spring tour of New England with Mozart's *Die Zauberflöte* included cities and towns throughout New England; performance venues included high schools, cultural centers, local auditoriums, and movie theaters; indeed, none of these touring performances of Mozart's fantasy opera were given in standard opera houses. The Sudbury (Mass.) Opera Lovers Group, numbering about 75, meets monthly to hear educational programs presented by its members. The New England Opera Club, made up of about 300 active members, also meets monthly to hear invited speakers.

Also in Massachusetts, opera is performed in such venues as the College Light Opera in Falmouth, and in Castle Hill, a Georgian mansion overlooking Massachusetts Bay and home to the Castle Hill Festival in the summer. Simsbury Light Opera Company performs the works of Gilbert and Sullivan at the Simsbury High School, while the Connecticut Opera Association performs in Bushnell Memorial Hall next to the state capitol building in Hartford. The American Shakespeare Theatre, Connecticut Center for the Performing Arts, Stratford, has been the setting for ballet, symphonic music, and pops as well as opera. The Barre Opera Company, with its opera house near Montpelier, Vt., has become an important landmark that, in conjunction with the Onion Rivers Council of Montpelier, provides opera and other musical genres.

Maine has the Portland Opera Repertory Theatre and the Rockport Opera House, which is popular with the summer crowd. In Providence, the American Opera Company stages productions, as do Brown University, Providence College, and the state university in Westerly. In New Hampshire, Opera North in Hanover performs summertime opera, combining performance with education. The now-defunct New England Marionette Opera in Peterborough, N.H., used recorded music and marionettes in its operatic performances in the elegant Marionette Theatre, considered one of the most elemental in New England. A fire destroyed the church-turned-theater and 200 marionettes in 1999.

John L. DiGaetani, *An Invitation to the Opera* (1986); John Dizikes, *Opera in America: A Cultural History* (1993); Andrew H. Drummond, *American Opera Librettos* (1973); Quaintance Eaton, *Boston Opera Company* (1965); Lynne Gusikoff, *Guide to Musical America* (1984); Katherine K. Preston, *Opera on the Road: Traveling Opera Troupes in the United States, 1825–60* (1993).

Martin J. Manning

Oratory

Oratory From Daniel Webster to John F. Kennedy, prominent New Englanders have used oratory as a means to articulate and elaborate ideas about the principles, purpose, and future of the community and nation. Oratory, the art of persuasive public speech (with secular forms derived from classical traditions), can be divided into three categories: legal, political, or deliberative; ceremonial; and religious, including variations suited to church doctrine and ritual. New England oratory is best characterized by diversity, both in style and in the types of orators who shaped public speech—a diversity that helped define a regional ethic even as those orators sought to shape the nation as a whole.

Much surviving colonial oratory is theological in nature, reflecting the character of the era's print culture as much as the importance of religion to colonial New Englanders. These sermons substantively reflect on the condition and meaning of social relations. In "A Modell of Christian Charity" (1630), for example, Massachusetts governor John Winthrop idealized a hierarchical social order, "a city upon a hill," that would guide the rest of the Christian world to redemption. After 1650 ministers increasingly used the jeremiad style of sermon to reprove their congregations for falling away from the religious purity of the founding generation; this sense of declension marked New England literature for a century.

Since their founding, elite institutions like Harvard and Yale have promoted an oratorical

"The attitude in which a boy should always place himself when he begins to speak," from William Scott, Lessons in Elocution; or, A Selection of Pieces in Prose and Verse, for the Improvement of Youth in Reading and Speaking *(Concord, N.H., 1820)*

culture by preparing prospective ministers, lawyers, and statesmen with extensive training in rhetoric and "pulpit eloquence." Oratory was thus identified with status and authority. Yet by the mid–18th century, antiauthoritarianism also infused public speech. The Great Awakening and subsequent revivals fortified the power of oratory, as itinerant preachers such as George Whitefield, Eleazar Wheelock, and James Davenport preached hundreds of sermons a year to attentive throngs, and Jonathan Edwards reached rhetorical heights with his "Sinners in the Hands of an Angry God" (1741) sermon. As early as the 1740s the Great Awakening fostered a revitalized anticlerical movement. Later, rebellious sentiments fueled anti-British protest, beginning with the Stamp Act Crisis (1765–66) and the Boston Massacre (1770); inspired by Samuel Adams's incendiary words, a Boston crowd dumped highly taxed British tea into the harbor in 1773.

Oratory played an important role in fostering early nationalism; to contemporaries, the pre–Civil War era was known as "the golden age of oratory." Such renowned speakers as Edward Everett, Daniel Webster, and Charles Sumner helped define national identity as well as a pro-union position strongly identified with New England. Webster, an outstanding orator, argued more than 150 cases before the U.S. Supreme Court, debated important historical issues in the U.S. Senate, made famous addresses at the Pilgrim bicentennial in 1820 and the dedication of the Bunker Hill Monument in 1825, and eulogized Thomas Jefferson and John Adams at Faneuil Hall in 1826.

New kinds of public speakers emerged during this period as well, in part because of the pervasive pedagogical practice of gaining literacy by reading aloud from "readers" of reprinted speeches, stories, and poetry. This gave New Englanders the opportunity to practice their own oratorical skills by using the words of religious and political leaders. Frederick Douglass, for example, rose to the New England abolitionist stage after learning his craft from the Boston-printed *Columbian Orator* (1798). Local lyceums, the crusade against slavery, and other movements also brought women, workingmen, and Native Americans to the stage in unprecedented numbers, especially in New England. The black abolitionist Maria Stewart, for instance, was the first woman to give a public address in antebellum New England, and such women as Mary Baker Eddy, Ann Lee, and Jemima Wilkinson inspired religious movements through their powerful oral testimonies. These new speakers changed the style and content of public discourse and helped define American culture by its diversity.

After the Civil War, the importance of public speech in American culture waned, as other modes of persuasion—print, advertising, and visual images—became more ubiquitous. New England orators in particular lost their standing, as orators from other regions of the country gained in prominence. Senator Margaret Chase Smith of Maine, however, gained fame for her Senate speech "A Declaration of Conscience" (1950), which condemned unscrupulous McCarthy-era tactics. President John F. Kennedy of Massachusetts is, of course, another notable exception. Combining long-standing oratorical themes of nationalism, democracy, and censure, his inaugural address of 1961, which contained the phrase, "Ask not what your country can do for you, ask what you can do for your country," sought to move the nation toward a New Frontier, a new beginning. Vietnam War protests also revitalized the art of oratory through great speakers and preachers such as the Reverend William Sloane Coffin. The region's political culture continues to produce memorable oratorical moments in local and regional broadcast debates. Boston's Faneuil Hall remains a symbolically appropriate forum for such events.

Barnet Baskerville, *The People's Voice: The Orator in American Society* (1979); Robert T. Oliver, *History of Public Speaking in America* (1965).

Carolyn Eastman

Our Town Thornton Wilder's *Our Town*, produced and directed by Jed Harris, opened in New York on February 4, 1938. The play is set in Grover's Corners, a fictional town inspired by Peterborough, N.H., home of the MacDowell Colony, where, from 1924 on, Wilder had frequently been a resident. In 1938 *Our Town* was awarded the Pulitzer Prize for Drama.

Critics praised the play's modernistic stagecraft—no curtain and no scenery were used—and Wilder's use of a character, the Stage Manager, as the chorus, the property man, and the actor who takes on minor roles. Wilder, who also won the Pulitzer Prize for his earlier novel *The Bridge of San Luis Rey* (1928) and for his later play *The Skin of Our Teeth* (1943), played this role on Broadway for two weeks in September 1938 and later in summer stock theaters in Pennsylvania and New England. A 1940 film version of *Our Town,* produced by Sol Lesser, directed by Sam Wood, and with music by Wilder's fellow MacDowell colonist Aaron Copland, was nominated for an Academy Award for Best Picture.

Centered around two families and the friendship and marriage of their children Emily Webb and George Gibbs between 1901 and 1913, the play depicts family life, love and marriage, and the afterlife. Emily, who has died in childbirth, asks to relive her twelfth birthday; in so doing she realizes that the most insignificant events of daily life pale against the immensity of the universe, but ultimately make up the whole of human experience. Simon Stimson, the town drunk and also one of the dead, comments on her anguish: "Now you know! That's what it was to be alive. To spend and waste time as though you had a million years. To be always at the mercy of one self-centered passion, or another."

The play is filled with poignant moments: Dr. Gibbs gently scolding his son for neglecting to chop firewood for his mother; Emily's plaintive question to her mother, "Am I pretty enough . . . to get anybody?"; and the shyness of George and Emily when they realize they love each other. But, as Wilder wrote, his play was not intended as "a sentimental picture of life in a New Hampshire village," or as speculation on life after death. Rather, he considered it "an attempt to find a value above all price for the smallest events of our daily life."

The cozy world of Grover's Corners is contrasted throughout with the immense universe—most notably when George's sister Rebecca recalls a minister's address that evolves from the nearest reference point, "June Croft, the Croft Farm, Grover's Corners, Sultan County, New Hampshire" to "the Universe; the Mind of God." This address recalls traditional sampler and schoolbook inscriptions and locates a very New England place at the center of an expanding universe. The play has endured as an iconic presentation of New England and all small-town American life in an era of profound change. In this, Wilder joined Robert Frost and Norman Rockwell in the revitalization of the New England image as the repository of traditional values and as counterpoint to the world crises of the Depression and the rise of fascism and communism. The play endures as a staple of summer stock and high school drama.

Jackson R. Bryer, ed., *Conversations with Thornton Wilder* (1992); Edward M. Burns and Ulla E. Dydo, eds., *The Letters of Gertrude Stein and Thornton Wilder* (1997); Paul Lifton, *"Vast Encyclopedia": The Theatre of Thornton Wilder* (1995); Charlotte Walsh, compiler, *Thornton Wilder: A Reference Guide, 1926–1990* (1993); Thornton Wilder, *Three Plays* (1998).

Edward M. Burns

Patronage Most forms of music in New England have been noncommercial but financially self-supporting (much folk music), commercially supported (Broadway musicals; Big Band music, dance bands, Folksong Revival, jazz, and rock music), or supported by a nonmusical organization (religious music). In contrast, Western classical or concert music, including orchestral concerts, opera, chamber music, solo recitals, and large choral works outside of a liturgical context, has, in New England and throughout the world, been unable to support itself by box office revenues alone. In the mid–19th century, musical organizations such as the orchestra of the Harvard Musical Association often combined overworked and underpaid professionals with amateur performers.

By the 1880s, Boston was the site of some of the nation's earliest efforts at private musical patronage, most strikingly the philanthropist Henry Lee Higginson's decision to found, shape, and support the Boston Symphony Orchestra. Other musical institutions were supported not by one wealthy citizen but by a board of a dozen or more who would persuade their friends to attend and subscribe and who, as "guarantors," could be counted on to supply any funds still needed to replenish the coffers at season's end. Around the turn of the 20th century active patrons of music included, among others, Isabella Stewart and John A. Gardner, Jr., and Mr. and Mrs. J. Montgomery Sears. Some gave additional support to individual musicians by hiring them to play recitals for their guests; the Gardners and Searses, among others, had substantial concert spaces in their homes. Music lovers in Boston were also active in encouraging professional-quality concerts for children as well as musical activities in colleges, conservatories, public schools, settlement houses, public libraries, and music libraries.

In other New England cities, a few wealthy

individuals established concert series, funded college departments of music, and otherwise patronized the musical arts. The South Mountain Chamber Music Festival was established in Pittsfield, Mass., by Elizabeth Sprague Coolidge; Carl and Ellen Battell Stoeckel helped establish the Norfolk Music Festival and the Litchfield Choral Union in Connecticut. Arthur Fiedler relied on individual donors when creating the Esplanade concerts in 1929, though these concerts were eventually absorbed by the Boston Pops Orchestra and supported by the city of Boston.

In more recent years, fund-raising committees everywhere in the region (and throughout the United States) have had to emphasize more grassroots approaches, such as gathering smaller donations from large numbers of supporters and seeking funding from federal, state, and city governments. Still, in New England as throughout the nation, major capital expenses continue to require large infusions from a few wealthy donors who are generally rewarded with invitations to social events or engraved wall plaques.

Richard Crawford, *The American Musical Landscape* (1993); Paul J. DiMaggio, "Cultural Entrepreneurship in 19th-Century Boston," *Media, Culture, and Society* 4 (1982); Ralph P. Locke, "Music Lovers, Patrons, and the 'Sacralization' of Culture in America," *Nineteenth-Century Music* 17 and 18 (1992–93); Ralph P. Locke and Cyrilla Barr, eds., *Cultivating Music in America: Women Patrons and Activists since 1860* (1997).

Ralph P. Locke

Provincetown Players

The "little theater" movement that spread throughout the United States between 1900 and 1920 was inspired by alternative theaters in France, Germany, England, and Russia that were committed to social realism and experimentation and to unification of all the elements of a play—text, production, stagecraft—in order to effect greater authenticity and expressiveness. Those who formed the Provincetown Players were powerfully influenced by the Irish Abbey Players' U.S. tour in 1911–12, as well as by the Jewish, Italian, German, and Chinese ethnic theaters of New York City.

The small group of Greenwich Village journalists, painters, and writers who began to summer in Provincetown between 1907 and 1915 formed the core of the Provincetown Players during their first and only two seasons in Provincetown (1915–16), Mass., where they performed in a renovated fish-house at the end of a wharf. Provincetown offered this rebel group a relaxed atmosphere, cheap rentals, and the tolerant atmosphere of a Portuguese community not unlike their Italian neighborhood in the Village.

George Cram "Jig" Cook, Susan Glaspell,

Neith Boyce, Hutchins Hapgood, Robert Edmond Jones, Wilbur Daniel Steele, Eugene O'Neill, Floyd Dell, John Reed, Louise Bryant, and Marguerite and William Zorach were in the vanguard of those who hoped to forge a national culture that would reflect the new spirit that was part of the ferment of the 1910s. Their concept of total theater was the basis of innovative collaborations that reflected the social problems, politics, art, and sexual mores of their time, often in plays that included healthy doses of self-parody.

Cook, their mastermind and first president, dreamed of reviving the spiritual origins of Greek theater in modern forms that would embrace actors, playwrights, set designers, directors, and producers. The Provincetown Players were unique in their commitment to produce plays written only by American writers. Their productions were to be judged as experiments, not for their commercial value, with support provided by a subscription audience.

Over the six years of their existence, the Provincetown Players provided a venue for 93 new plays by 47 American writers and nurtured the talents of two of the country's most important 20th-century playwrights: Glaspell and O'Neill. In fall 1916 they moved the theater to MacDougal Street in the Village, where they had six seasons. Cook left for Greece in the spring of 1922 when he felt the group was on the verge of becoming commercially successful; he died there in 1924.

The Provincetown Players also performed the works of Alfred Kreymborg, Djuna Barnes, Michael Gold, Edna St. Vincent Millay, Wallace Stevens, Theodore Dreiser, and Edmund Wilson. In their short but intensely creative lifespan, the Provincetown Players helped to lay the groundwork for a continuing tradition of experimental American theater.

Leona Rust Egan, *Provincetown as a Stage: Provincetown, the Provincetown Players, and the Discovery of Eugene O'Neill* (1994); Adele Heller and Lois Rudnick, eds., *1915, The Cultural Moment: The New Politics, the New Woman, the New Psychology, the New Art, and the New Theatre in America* (1991); Barbara Ozieblo, ed., *The Provincetown Players: A Choice of the Shorter Works* (1994); Robert K. Sarlos, *Jig Cook and the Provincetown Players: Theatre in Ferment* (1982).

Lois Rudnick

Recording Companies

Historically, New Englanders have made vast contributions to a wide range of musical genres, but with the exception of the American Graphophone Company, founded in Bridgeport, Conn., in 1886, which merged with Columbia and moved to New York in 1897, the region has only recently developed indigenous recording companies that release material by local as well as national and international performers.

For many, New England's prominence as a recording center began in 1967, when the independent producer Alan Lorber observed that Boston had a local rock scene equal to that of any other major city. He convinced MGM Records of that proposition and recorded three groups for the label: Beacon Street Union, Orpheus, and Ultimate Spinach. Only the last was commercially successful, but a backlash against the overaggressive marketing of the Boss-Town Sound broke it down, and a year later all three groups were dropped by MGM.

At the same time, small, entrepreneur-driven labels sprang up and dissolved, often virtually overnight. They recorded music by local musicians and appealed to audiences untapped by national companies. Any number of regional rock and roll bands were signed by small independents like Sam Lembo's Cupid Records and Al Hawkes's Event label. Performers who signed with these companies hoped for some measure of national exposure but more often merely achieved a greater degree of local notoriety. Other companies were founded by record store owners. Among the most notable were the labels organized by the long-time Boston merchant Skippy White. On his Ditto and Stop label, he recorded rhythm and blues groups, while his Bluestown line featured blues musicians and Silver Cross Records featured black gospel performers. One of the most significant artists White signed was Alvin "Guitar Nubbit" Hankerson, so named because part of his right thumb was missing. His "Georgia Chain Gang" (1962) is felt to be one of the greatest country blues recorded in the postwar era.

In the postpunk world of the 1980s, Boston gained recognition once again as individuals rejected the need for major labels and adopted instead a do-it-yourself approach to recording. Numerous independent labels sprang up; two of the most prominent were Taang!, which includes the popular Lemonheads, and Ace of Hearts, which released recordings by the retro-garage band the Lyres and the deliberately abrasive Mission of Burma.

Folk music has long been a New England staple, beginning with the folk revival of the 1950s. Much regional folk music activity centered on Cambridge's Club 47 and the annual Newport Folk Festival, held in Rhode Island. Several New England folk musicians gained national exposure and recording contracts with major labels and small-scale, genre-specific companies, beginning in 1962 when the producer Paul Rothchild first heard the bluegrass ensemble the Charles River Valley Boys at Club 47 and proposed a record label, MTA 47. Rothchild went on to record many of the prominent members of the New England folk community for the Prestige and Elektra labels, including Tom Rush, Eric von Schmidt and Jim Rooney, and Bill Keith. When the commercial bottom fell out of acoustic-folk music and the major labels largely abandoned the field, a number of individuals—Tom Rush and Arlo Guthrie among them—began record companies. They manufactured and distributed their own recordings and, in Guthrie's case, bought back the master tapes of material they produced for major labels.

While New England lacks sufficient visibility as a home for jazz performers, many of its most successful practitioners trained at Boston's Berklee School of Music and the New England Conservatory of Music. Small jazz labels do not abound in the region, but two current companies stand out. Arabesque Records, owned and operated by members of the avant-garde big band the Either-Orchestra, releases a wide range of high-quality music. The Connecticut-based Mosaic Records focuses on reissues of significant portions of the jazz repertoire, largely but not exclusively drawn from the vaults of Blue Note Records. Their limited pressings in both vinyl and CD are tailored for the connoisseur and keep the jazz tradition alive and available.

Two of the most enduring and successful regional independent labels are the Massachusetts-based Rounder and Rykodisc. The latter was one of the first record companies to exclusively produce and manufacture compact discs and has notably released elaborate repackagings of the catalogs of such major artists as David Bowie, Frank Zappa, and Elvis Costello. The output of Rounder Records reflects remarkable diversity, ranging from blues to bluegrass, jazz to reggae, rock to rhythm and blues. Rounder's noteworthy role in the independent record business is measured by outstanding sales, critical acclaim, and the diversity of its catalog. Several successful mainstream careers owe their start to Rounder, including the blues guitarist George Thorogood and the bluegrass vocalist Alison Krauss. The company's recent twenty-fifth anniversary crowns the notable achievements of one of New England's most laudable contributors to music in America.

Colin Larkin, ed., *The Guinness Encyclopedia of Popular Music* (1995); Alan Lorber, *Bosstown Sound 1968 The Music and The Time* [sound recording] (1996); Brett Milano, *DIY. Mass. Ave. The Boston Scene (1975–83)* [sound recording] (1993); Billy Miller and Jack Warner, *The Raging Teens: Wild New England Rock N' Roll*, vols. 1–3 [sound recordings] (1992); Eric von Schmidt and Jim Rooney, *Baby, Let Me Follow You Down: The Illustrated Story of the Cambridge Folk Years* (1994).

David Sanjek

Rock Music Despite its reputation for highbrow cultural preferences, New England has offered the world some of the most primi-

The J. Geils Band at Boston Garden, ca. 1980

tive and exciting rock and roll ever recorded. While the region basks in the glory of its scholars and statesmen, it is also a place like many others in America, where people work hard for a living and teenagers dream of forbidden pleasures and aimless rebellions. Ergo, rock and roll.

It is difficult to know where and when the rock tradition began in New England. Boston has long been home to a thriving African American musical scene, as any reader of *The Autobiography of Malcolm X* will recall. Chuck Berry had an early local following, and to repay his supporters he enshrined Boston in the first line of one of his greatest songs, "Sweet Little Sixteen" (1958) ("They're really rocking in Boston!"). Because so many performers in rock and roll history, including the Beatles and the Beach Boys, have covered this song, Berry gave Boston a permanent place in the repertoire of rock.

The rock and roll explosion of the mid-1950s hit Boston hard. A notable event was the riot that erupted in 1958 when Alan Freed, the deejay who likely coined the term *rock and roll*, brought his traveling show of black and white entertainers to the Boston Arena. Freed was arrested by the unsympathetic Boston police, and local authorities indicted him for inciting the riot, but the charges were eventually dropped.

Like every major American city, Boston had its rock and roll deejays and radio stations (notably, Arnie "Woo Woo" Ginsburg at WMEX). It also had a few minor stars, such as Freddy "Boom Boom" Cannon, born in Lynn, Mass. Cannon belted out a regional hit, "Boston, My Home Town," but most of his hits were about other cities. One local rhythm and blues singer was to become Minister Louis Farrakhan, head of the Nation of Islam.

In the 1960s, an important folk music scene began in Harvard Square, particularly at Club 47, where Joan Baez emerged and performers ranging from Bob Dylan to Muddy Waters played regularly. From the mid-1950s through the 1960s, the Newport Jazz and Folk Festivals hosted electrifying performances by a wide range of artists. Famously, Bob Dylan began to play an electric guitar at the 1965 folk festival, but relented when the crowd turned against him. Less well known is the fact that bands like Led Zeppelin played the festival in the late 1960s. A riveting performance by Chuck Berry from the 1958 jazz festival is captured in the 1959 film *Jazz on a Summer's Day*.

Another important scene formed around the Boston Tea Party, a club in the Back Bay. Opened in 1967, the club catered to the rapidly evolving market for countercultural rock in the late 1960s. Boston nurtured a thriving rock scene in those years, aided by such progressive FM radio stations as WBCN, and newspapers such as the *Boston Phoenix, Boston after Dark,* and the *Real Paper.* WBCN deejay Peter Wolf went on to sing for the J. Geils Band. Possibly the best-known song ever recorded about Boston was "Dirty Water" by the California band the Standells (1966), with its unforgettable riff and lyrics about bugs and frustrated women ("Aww, Boston you're my home!").

But if the Standells were ersatz New Englanders, there was no shortage of the real thing. Hundreds of bands formed in garages around New England, most of their careers short-lived. But a few survived briefly. The Remains were a brilliant band that never really scored a hit, but backed up the Beatles on their 1965 tour. The Beatles themselves played at Suffolk Downs in 1964, adding to the local rock and roll fervor. The Barbarians were led by their drummer, Moulty, who had lost a hand and instead had a large hook at the end of his arm. They had a minor hit, "Are You a Boy or Are You a Girl?" In Rhode Island, the Tradewinds sang "New York's a Lonely Town," about a surfer boy stranded in Manhattan during the winter.

There was also a thriving rhythm and blues scene throughout the 1960s and well into the 1970s. The music historian Peter Guralnick recounted the thrill of following local soul music, abetted by record stores like Skippy White's. One of the most stirring nights in New England musical history occurred on April 4, 1968, the day the Reverend Martin Luther King, Jr., was killed. James Brown was scheduled to play Boston Garden; fearful of rioting, city authorities decided to air the concert live on WGBH-TV. Brown's conciliatory remarks greatly helped to defuse the potential crisis. Another crisis of sorts occurred in New Haven, Conn., in 1967, when Jim Morrison of the Doors was arrested onstage for remarks he made that incited a riot (needless to say, the group's popularity skyrocketed).

A brief, embarrassing episode in the region's musical history was the excitement over "the Bosstown Sound." Following San Francisco's emergence as the rock capital in 1967, executives assumed Boston would soon follow. They were mistaken, and none of the local bands they signed hit the big time.

But other Boston bands became extremely popular. Aerosmith, "the bad boys from Boston," eschewed by the rock establishment at first, had working-class appeal. They began gigging around Sunapee, N.H., in 1969 but soon brought their hard rocking, bluesy sound to Boston. In their early incarnation, they were considered a kind of lowbrow Rolling Stones, but their songs have stood up well over the years, and they helped a rising generation of young heavy-metal musicians define themselves. Equally durable, Boston's J. Geils Band began to strike pay dirt in the late 1970s and became very popular in the 1980s.

James Taylor, though hardly a rock and roller, was also an enormous success and brought a thrill of recognition when he sang about the turnpike from Stockbridge to Boston (later folkies Tracy Chapman and Mary Chapin Carpenter also had New England connections). In the early 1970s, hardly a teenage girl in the region did not own his album "Sweet Baby James." Bonnie Raitt also earned a local following in the 1970s for her bluesy ballads. Finally, no discussion of 1970s rock would be complete without mentioning Boston, an eclectic group led by the MIT graduate Tom Scholz. Their first album, *Boston* (1977), remains one of the top-selling records of all time (the song "Rock and Roll Band" has some regional references).

New England also provided two stars of the disco era. Tavares, from New Bedford, Mass., scored several giant hits and played on the soundtrack to *Saturday Night Fever* (their original name was Chubby and the Turnpikes). And the diva Donna Summer is from Roxbury, Mass. In 1975 her mock-orgasmic "Love to Love You Baby" shot to number one on the charts, beginning a long string of monster hits.

While all these hits were being recorded, usually in other regions, a subterranean music scene was developing beneath the noses of oblivious record executives. Out of Natick, Mass., came the unlikely troubadour figure of Jonathan Richman. Richman was influenced by the Velvet Underground during their forays into the Boston Tea Party, and he formed his own band, the Modern Lovers, in the early 1970s. Their "Roadrunner" was arguably the greatest rock song ever recorded in New England. It not only satisfies musically with its churning rhythm and irresistible chorus, but also intersperses lyrics about driving along Route 128 listening to AM radio. Later, when the Sex Pistols covered the song, listeners were treated to Johnny Rotten singing about Stop and Shop, a local supermarket chain. Richman has returned to New England for subject matter many times ("Government Center," "Old New England").

Willie Alexander, a veteran of the 1960s garage scene, made many records filled with local detail, such as "Mass. Ave." The Cars, featuring Ric Ocasek, broke through to big-time success, combining elements of mainstream rock with the "new wave" beginning to spread throughout the region. In Providence, Talking Heads formed while attending the Rhode Island School of Design. Once again, a rock and roll revolution seemed to be happening, and Boston welcomed a thriving new musical scene. This scene, which coalesced in the late 1970s with notable avant-rockers Mission of Burma, has never really subsided and continues to change and take form.

New England still furnishes the occasional rock star or two. In the mid-1980s, the smooth stylings of New Edition and New Kids on the Block were all the rage. Aerosmith achieved a miraculous resurgence that returned it to the top of the industry charts (far higher than the band had ever been). In 1986 University of Massachusetts dropout Charles Thompson (aka Black Francis) moved to Boston to form the seminal band the Pixies. Although they had only a brief career (they reunited for a few shows in 2004), the Pixies are said to be pioneers of alternative music, a genre that reached its peak in the early 1990s. Nirvana's Kurt Cobain cited them as a major influence. When the Vermont group Phish formed in 1988 many of the band's fans called it the leading "jam band" in America, heir to the Grateful Dead's improvisational approach to concerts. But Phish did not match the Dead's longevity, giving its farewell performance in 2004. Staind, from Springfield, Mass., achieved national prominence with the release of the band's third album, *Break the Cycle*, in 2001. Each year exciting new bands emerge, unsurprising in a region that welcomes hundreds of thousands of young people to college every year.

Robert Cantwell, *When We Were Good: The Folk Revival* (1996); Fred Goodman, *The Mansion on the Hill: Dylan, Young, Geffen, Springsteen, and the Head-On Collision of Rock and Commerce* (1997); Peter Guralnick, *Sweet Soul Music: Rhythm and Blues and the Southern Dream of Freedom* (1986); *Mass. Ave.: The Boston Scene (1975–1983)* (sound recording, Rhino 71179); Barry Tashian, *A Ticket to Ride: An Extraordinary Diary of the Beatles' Last Tour* (1996).

Ted Widmer

Sacred Music One of New England's most substantive contributions to American culture has been an enormous number of choral settings of religious poetry created in the late 18th and early 19th centuries for use in Protestant congregational churches. In the late 20th century this music was heard with increasing frequency at "shape-note" singings as well as in concerts and church services, thereby constituting a living part of the region's culture.

The very existence of this huge musical repertory is something of an irony. The first book published in New England, in 1640, was a book of psalms commonly known as the *Bay Psalm Book*, but its translation aimed at being as faithful as possible to the original Hebrew, with less regard for easy singing. Moreover, the Puritan practice of "deaconing" a psalm, whereby each line was sung first by a deacon and then by the congregation, did not encourage musical ability or vocal regularity. Puritans also rejected instrumental accompaniment in church singing. In the early 1720s, Boston ministers, alarmed at the disintegration of congregational singing in their parishes, began to preach in favor of something they called regular singing—that is, singing by the rules inherent in musical notation. The goal was to improve the quality of that part of worship in which the entire flock sang a psalm text set to music; at the time, some two dozen tunes, almost all European in origin, had been approved by the various churches. The method was to have some parishioners attend singing schools a couple of times a week for a period, then bring their newly acquired skills back to the meetinghouse on the Sabbath. There was no notion, at the start, that singing schools might lead to anything more than this; certainly not that the musical part of worship would become an opportunity for artistic display by a select group rather than a participatory activity shared by all.

What the singing school led to, however, was church choirs, an explosion of the tune repertory, the advent of the American composer, and, eventually, a distinctively American system of music education. Singing school graduates—many of them in their teens—agitated for the right to sit together in the meetinghouse, rather than in their respective family pews, arguing that they could lead the singing better as a group than if they were dispersed throughout the assembly. Eventually, in town after town, particularly in the decade of the 1760s, this right was granted, and the stage was set for independent choral performance in New England's meetinghouses. The choristers' acquisition of musical proficiency led to a desire for more music—and more challenging music—to sing. When the supply of recently written anthems and "fuging tunes" (psalm or hymn settings including some contrapuntal writing) in imported English tunebooks ran low, New England's singing school teachers started to compose. By 1770 as many as 40 American-made sacred compositions had been published. While the earliest of these, "Southwel New Tune" and "100 Psalm Tune New," had appeared in Boston collections of the 1720s, most had made their printed debuts in 1760s tunebooks published outside of New England. But then in the fall of 1770 William Billings, a young Boston tanner acquainted and allied with some of the city's most prominent Sons of Liberty, published a collection titled *The New-England Psalm-Singer* containing 127 original psalm tunes, anthems, and canons. Six years before the Declaration of Independence, the American composer had become a presence on the cultural scene.

Billings's example proved irresistible to church musicians of his generation, the so-called First New England School of composers. After four of his collections were published, Daniel Read in New Haven put out an all-original *American Singing Book* in 1785; Jacob French of Medway, Mass., and Abraham Wood of Northboro, Mass., also published all-original tunebooks (*New American Melody* and *Divine Songs*, both 1789). And Connecticut compilers such as Andrew Law, Simeon Jocelyn, and Oliver Brownson, and the publisher Isaiah Thomas in Worcester, Mass., introduced dozens more New England composers—men with names like Alexander Gillet, Lewis Edson, Asahel Benham, and Elias Mann. These tunesmiths seem to have followed Billings's injunction (in *The New-England Psalm-Singer*) for "every *Composer* to be his own *Carver*," finding their way to compositional proficiency, tunefulness, and in several cases a somewhat distinctive individual style on the strength of no more musical education than several months' study in a singing school, where they had learned the rudiments of musical notation and how to sing in time and in tune.

In the four decades following Billings's audacious debut, almost five thousand musical compositions by some 260 Americans—the vast majority of them New Englanders—were published in American sacred tunebooks. As in any repertory, much of this music is of unexceptional quality. But much of it is good—including not only the output of composers relatively well known today (Billings, Read, Timothy Swan, Justin Morgan), but music by figures of such obscurity that frequently their full names are not known (M. Kyes, John Bushnell, J. P. Storm). That New England's early sacred music has started to receive serious and sustained attention from scholars and performers is evident from the fact that all eight of the composers named in the preceding paragraph have received complete works editions in recent years—two of these with extensive scholarly apparatus.

With the arrival of increasing numbers of European musical immigrants at the end of the 18th century and the beginning of the 19th, awareness of the glories of Handel and Haydn (evidenced in the founding of several Handel and Haydn Societies; Boston's dates from 1815) and a corresponding distaste for the lowly little fuging tune increased in New England. The balance of American and European repertory in American tunebooks changed sharply in favor of European in the middle of the new century's first decade, and by 1810 very little original church music that was not derivative of the European classical style was being composed on these shores. The expressive, unsophisticated music of Billings and his contemporaries was crowded out of New England's tunebooks, only to find enthusiastic reception among singers in the Middle Atlantic States, the Midwest, and the South. Although the musical tastes of such educator-reformers as Lowell Mason and Thomas Hastings predominated in New England's cities during the 19th century, there is considerable evidence—in the pages of rural musical periodicals such as *The World of Music* (Bellows Falls and Chester, Vt., and Claremont, N.H., 1840–48), in retrospective collections such as *Ancient Harmony Revived* (Hallowell, Maine, 1847; at least five later editions), in the "Old Folks' Concerts" of "Father" Robert Kemp and others in the 1850s through the 1880s—that a taste for the older music was still very much alive.

Nevertheless, the first half of the 20th century seems to have been a dry period in the publication and performance of early New England sacred music. A doctoral dissertation by Allen Perdue Britton, "Theoretical Introductions in American Tune-books to 1800" (1949), inaugurated the present era of serious scholarly inquiry into the topic. (Britton's dissertation would become the nucleus of a monumental bibliography of early American tunebooks, completed by Richard Crawford and published in 1990.) Theses devoted to the lives and works of several tunebook composers and compilers appeared through the 1950s and 1960s. Then, as the nation's Bicentennial approached, interest in its musical forefathers increased markedly. A major biography of William Billings was published in 1975; this was followed two years later by the first volume of Billings's complete works in a scholarly edition sponsored by the American Musicological Society (the first such edition for an American composer). In New England the early 1970s were marked by increasing awareness and appreciation of the living southern traditions of singing early American sacred music from such books as *The Sacred Harp* (first published by two Georgia singing masters in 1844 and never out of print since; its note-heads are printed with different shapes to enable sight reading). In the Bicentennial year Massachusetts singers' enthusiasm for shape-note music led to the founding of a *Sacred Harp* singing group, Norumbega Harmony, under the leadership of Stephen A. Marini of Wellesley College. That same year, the first New England Sacred Harp Singing Convention was held; it became an annual event. Both institutions, along with the Word of Mouth Chorus and other singing groups led by Larry Gordon in Vermont from the early 1970s on, have continued to play vital roles in the steadily expanding renaissance of early New England's sacred music in the region where it was born. This renaissance has been marked by the publication of a new tunebook, *Northern Harmony*, now in its third edition; by a proliferation of shape-note singing groups; and by hundreds of new compositions written in the early style—many of them the work of teenagers who are the 21st-century counterparts of the first singing school students.

Allen Perdue Britton, Irving Lowens, and Richard Crawford, *American Sacred Music Imprints 1698–1810: A Bibliography* (1990); Buell E. Cobb, Jr., *The Sacred Harp: A Tradition and Its Music* (1978); Richard Crawford, "'Ancient Music' and the Europeanizing of American Psalmody, 1800–1810," in *A Celebration of American Music: Words and Music in Honor of H. Wiley Hitchcock*, ed. Richard Crawford, R. Allen Lott, and Carol J. Oja (1990); Karl Kroeger, ed., *Music of the New American Nation: Sacred Music from 1780 to 1820*, 15 vols. (1995–); David P. McKay and Richard Crawford, *William Billings of Boston: 18th-Century Composer* (1975); Hans Nathan and Karl Kroeger, eds., *The Complete Works of William Billings*, 4 vols. (1977–90); Judith T. Steinberg, "Old Folks' Concerts and the Revival of New England Psalmody," *Musical Quarterly* 59, no. 4 (October 1973); Nicholas Temperley, "First Forty: The Earliest American Compositions," *American Music* 15, no. 1 (Spring 1997).

Nym Cooke

Schuller, Gunther (1925–) Composer, conductor, author. One of America's finest composers, Gunther Schuller has also distinguished himself as a visionary music educator, a leading historian and analytical theorist of jazz, an orchestral conductor and teacher of conducting, a performer on the French horn, a music publisher, and a spokesperson and champion of American music of all styles and historical periods.

Schuller was reared in New York City. His father, a member of the New York Philharmonic Orchestra, sent him to Saint Thomas Choir School and arranged private instruction in theory, flute, and French horn. In 1943, while still a teenager, Schuller was appointed principal horn of the Cincinnati Orchestra; two years later he returned to New York to accept the post of principal horn with the Metropolitan Opera Orchestra. He taught at the Manhattan School of Music from 1950 to 1963 and made a significant career decision in 1959 when he gave up performing to devote himself to composition.

In 1964 Schuller was appointed professor of composition at the Yale University School of Music, and in 1967 he moved to the Boston area to become president of the New England Conservatory. Three years later he assumed the duties of artistic director of the Berkshire Music Center and Summer Festival at Tanglewood. In these positions he distinguished himself as a visionary leader and a champion of American music, both contemporary and historic, classical and jazz. Largely through his

Gunther Schuller at home, Newton Centre, Mass., 1981

efforts, the music of the 19th-century composers John Knowles Paine and Louis Moreau Gottschalk gained renewed public interest; the orchestral music of Charles Ives was given additional credibility; and the ragtime music of Scott Joplin was uncovered and validated. Schuller's recording of Joplin's *The Red Back Book* won a Grammy in 1973. The young, late-20th-century composers who are indebted to Schuller's teaching, advocacy, performance, and recording are too numerous to list.

As a composer, Schuller is prolific and a meticulous craftsman. In 1994 he received the Pulitzer Prize for his work "Of Reminiscences and Reflections," a musical reaction to the death of his wife, Marjorie. Since the 1950s, the quality and effectiveness of his compositions have been consistent; his Woodwind Quintet of 1958 is brilliant, and his *Transformations* of the same period became the hallmark of a new style that he coined Third Stream Jazz. His two operas, *The Visitation* (1966) and *The Fisherman and His Wife* (1970), are fine, if underappreciated, works. Over the years, Schuller has amassed numerous honorary degrees and awards for his composition.

Schuller's career as an author and historian of jazz is no less significant; his *Early Jazz: Its Roots and Development* (1968) and *The Swing Era: The Development of Jazz 1930–1945* (1989) are among the best analytical studies of the subjects published and are the definitive works to date. His *Musings: The Musical Worlds of Gunther Schuller* (1986) is both autobiographical and philosophical and pulls no punches in damning those who do not meet Schuller's high musical tastes and standards. And his *Compleat Conductor* (1997) illuminates his work as conductor of most of the leading orchestras of the world and as a teacher of conducting at his Summer Festival at Sandpoint, Idaho. Among the notable concerts he has conducted, the *Twentieth Century Innovations* concerts in Carnegie Hall in 1962–65 have perhaps been the most influential. The repertoire he conducts is encyclopedic, from Wagner's *Parsifal* to Joplin's *Treemonisha*.

Schuller bases his worldwide activities at his longtime residence in Newton Centre, Mass., where he continues to compose, write, and run Margun Music, his music publishing company. The quantity and scope of Schuller's activities are so great that one tongue-in-cheek critic identified him as a one-man musical monopoly.

Norbert Carnovale, *Gunther Schuller: A Bio-Bibliography* (1987).

Frank Tirro

Summer Stock Summer stock theater is not an exclusively New England phenomenon, but the majority of theaters during its

golden age from the 1920s through 1960s were located there. The term *summer stock* refers to a particular type of summertime entertainment that evolved in the northeastern United States during the 1920s and 1930s. It is an umbrella term for independent theaters with a resident company presenting a number of different plays in weekly or biweekly repertory, either in a permanent house or on tour, between the months of June and September. The theaters were established in attractive rural environments near the new resorts developed for middle- and working-class clientele who, thanks to advances in corporate management and federal legislation, now enjoyed annual paid vacations. Wherever city dwellers fled to escape the summer heat at sylvan lakes, beaches, and mountainsides, a summer stock theater was likely to appear to provide nightly entertainment.

The first summer stock theaters—Elitch's Gardens, founded in Denver, Colo., in 1890, and Maine's Lakewood Theater, located five miles north of Skowhegan, which opened in 1898 but did not begin offering regular summer stock seasons until 1901—were actually late-19th-century stock theaters that happened to establish themselves as summertime ventures. Summer stock as we know it didn't evolve until the establishment of three prominent theaters which are still extant: the Manhattan Theatre Colony, which first opened in 1927 at Mariarden outside of Peterborough, N.H., and then moved to its current home in Ogunquit, Maine; the Cape Playhouse, which acquired its permanent home in Dennis, Mass., in the middle of Cape Cod, in 1927; and the Berkshire Playhouse, now known as the Berkshire Theatre Festival, which opened in Stockbridge, Mass., in 1928. Other notable, still-active playhouses which debuted shortly thereafter include the Dorset Players (now Dorset Theatre Festival) in Dorset, Vt. (1927); the Barnstormers in Tamworth, N.H. (1931); Ivoryton Playhouse in Ivoryton, Conn. (1931); the Westport Country Playhouse in Westport, Conn. (1931); New London Barn Players in New London, N.H. (1933); the Peterborough Players in Peterborough (1933); and Theatre-by-the-Sea in Matunuck, R.I. (1931). In the 1930s successful theaters also opened in Guilford, Conn.; Bar Harbor, Boothbay Harbor, and Surrey, Maine; Cohasset and Fitchburg, Mass.; Newport, R.I.; and Weston, Vt. What became known as the straw hat circuit of summer stock theaters also extended into New York, Pennsylvania, Maryland, Virginia, and other East Coast and Middle Atlantic states.

Summer stock is popularly associated with barns because these tall, commodious, solidly built wooden structures became the venue of choice for entrepreneurs looking for an inexpensive means of opening their theaters. New

England-style barns were especially adaptable to easy conversion into playhouses since they tended to have wide, open floor spaces without vertical support beams that would impede audience sightlines. They also had high ceilings, sturdy cross beams that could be used for hanging scenery and lights, and haylofts that could be converted into balconies. Since most of the New England vacationlands where the new theaters emerged had recently been farm country, there were plenty of barns that could be purchased or rented at reasonable prices and moved, if necessary, to the most propitious site for a playhouse.

What is arguably the most famous summer theater, erroneously called the Provincetown Playhouse in Provincetown, Mass., was not a summer stock theater, although it was an important precursor to the theaters that would develop in the following decade. The theater that introduced the plays of the Nobel laureate Eugene O'Neill to the world was actually the Wharf Theatre, a shack on the end of Mary Heaton Vorse's wharf in Provincetown Harbor, which had been crudely converted into a makeshift theater by a group of intellectual theater enthusiasts who summered there in the 1910s. These devoted amateurs offered their first season of plays during the summer of 1915, but it wasn't until 1916 that they premiered two one-acts by O'Neill, *Bound East for Cardiff* and *Thirst*. At the end of the 1916 season, they officially organized as the Provincetown Players and promptly left Cape Cod for their winter homes in New York's Greenwich Village to open the Provincetown Playhouse on MacDougal Street. Thanks to O'Neill, however, their humble Massachusetts theater has attained an honored place in the annals of theater history.

Summer stock continues to be a vital force in the American theater. From the 1930s through the 1960s, summer stock was the leading employer of theater professionals in the United States. More actors, directors, designers, and technicians worked in legitimate theater during the summer months than at any other time of the year. It also has provided a place for young theater artists to garner their first professional credentials and to learn their craft. It is still true that most theater professionals have worked at some time during their careers in summer stock.

Although the golden age of summer stock theater is over, there are still more than 50 active venues operating throughout New England in the 21st century. Some are offering proper stock seasons, while others host a variety of live entertainments, from legitimate theater through Renaissance fairs through rock concerts, in locales that include old barns seating a few hundred patrons, large arenas holding thousands of theatergoers, and everything in between.

Anne Goodrich, *Enjoying the Summer Theatres of New England: A Guide* (1954); Charlotte Harmon and Rosemary Taylor, *Broadway in a Barn* (1957); Martha Schmoyer LoMonaco, *Summer Stock! An American Theatrical Phenomenon* (2004).

Martha Schmoyer LoMonaco

Symphonic Orchestras In New England, symphonic orchestras developed initially in Boston and a few other sites along the route between Boston and New York during the 19th century and were established in other urban New England areas during the 20th century. Found in every New England state, orchestras are today most numerous in southern New England, particularly in Massachusetts, where the Boston Symphony Orchestra (BSO) is among the foremost in the nation.

Symphonic orchestras were created as economic and social conditions emerged to foster the development of European refinements. In postrevolutionary times, commerce created enough prosperity to support cultural institutions, and attitudes permitted and even encouraged the patronage of the arts as a pleasure, ornament, and benefit to society. With a public affluent and interested enough to create an audience, the influx of European immigrants to fill the majority of American orchestral positions, and an educational system to train musicians and cultivate music appreciation, New England's orchestral history began.

The development of concert music, including orchestras, was, for the most part, led by immigrant European musicians. Many professional musicians, particularly Germans, wishing to flee political turmoil in Europe such as the revolutions of 1848, were attracted by American prosperity. Many came to Boston (among other American cities), where they found work as conductors, performers, and teachers, and promoted European methods and repertory.

Boston's orchestral history began around the turn of the 19th century. Its earliest orchestras included ad hoc ensembles, theater orchestras, and various societies of mixed amateur and professional musicians who performed only occasionally in public. Following the Civil War, the Harvard Musical Association formed a fairly stable and competent orchestra. The goal of establishing a world-class professional resident orchestra to rival those of Europe, however, was not met until the formation of the Boston Symphony Orchestra in 1881 by Major Henry Lee Higginson.

Some organizations, such as Providence's Beethoven Society of the 1840s and Springfield's Orchestral Club of 1875, preceded the resident orchestras of the next century. Several 19th-century New England cities experienced symphonic music only through touring orchestras like the Theodore Thomas Orchestra, whose itinerary included Hartford and New Haven, Conn., Providence, and Worcester and Springfield, Mass., each of which later developed its own orchestra.

The example of the BSO, which also toured, encouraged further orchestral development in Boston itself and in other cities. Each New England state eventually formed resident orchestras. Most are in Massachusetts, followed by Connecticut, whose New Haven orchestra, founded in 1894 by Morris Steinert, is currently the highest ranked regional orchestra next to Boston's. Hartford has had two major orchestras: the Hartford Philharmonic Orchestra (1899–1924) and the Hartford Symphony Orchestra, founded in 1934. Other orchestras in Massachusetts include the Worcester Orchestra, founded by Harry Levenson in 1947; the New Bedford Symphony Orchestra Association, founded in 1957; and the Springfield Symphony Orchestra, which gave its first concert in 1944. In Providence, a Beethoven Society performed during the 1840s; Fairman's Orchestra gave concerts during the 1920s; and in 1932, Wassili Leps founded the Providence Symphony Orchestra. The Rhode Island Philharmonic Orchestra was established in 1945.

North of Massachusetts, orchestral sites include Nashua, Manchester, and Concord, N.H.; Portland and Bangor, Maine; and Burlington, Vt. Throughout the region there are also community, festival, university, and youth orchestras. In addition to offering concerts, some orchestras have associated programs such as the composer-in-residence and call-for-scores programs of the New England Philharmonic, founded in 1976. The New Haven Symphony Orchestra commissions a major orchestral work each season. Past commissions have gone to Quincy Porter, Luigi Dallapiccola, and Mel Powell.

Over time, the original immigrant character of orchestral personnel changed; the Germanic core of works promoted by the orchestra's creators has nevertheless remained standard, though the repertoire has broadened internationally. Avid interest during the 19th century in creating an American music led to acceptance of the works of American composers, but, with little exception, American composition continued European traditions. Increased late-20th-century attention to historical performance practices—influencing the formation of some specialty orchestras such as Boston Baroque and the Boston Classical Orchestra—further perpetuated European art forms. Though accommodating regional expressions and interpreters, the orchestra as a vehicle for local culture never superseded its role as importer of European refinement to America.

M. A. De Wolfe Howe, *The Boston Symphony Orchestra, 1881–1931* (1931); Hugo Leichtentritt, *Serge Koussevitzky, Boston Symphony, and the New American Music* (1946); George Seltzer, *The Professional Symphony Orchestra in the United States* (1975).

Ellen Knight

Taj Mahal (1942–) Musician. Taj Mahal, whose dozens of acclaimed albums and musical projects over the past three decades have reflected the many sounds of the African diaspora found in the Western Hemisphere, including reggae, ragtime, country and urban blues, jazz, rhythm and blues, and rock and roll, began his musical career in New England. Taj Mahal was born Henry Saint Claire Fredericks in New York City; his family moved to Springfield, Mass., while he was still an infant. Raised in a rich musical environment, Taj was surrounded by sounds from the American South (his mother, a pianist and gospel singer, was from Cheraw, N.C.) and from the West Indies (his father, a composer and avid jazz fan, hailed from Saint Kitts).

Springfield provided Taj Mahal with a musical education that reinforced the lessons he learned at home. He was influenced by local musicians, including the Perry family, originally from North Carolina, and the Nichols family from Mississippi. This neighborhood musical education was expanded by countless hours spent listening to the radio and playing his father's large record collection.

New England offered Taj Mahal yet another important musical experience: the folk revival. While attending college at the University of Massachusetts, Amherst, he took advantage of the offerings of the Connecticut Valley Folksong Society. At the Salladin, a coffeehouse in Amherst, he played and listened to other revivalist musicians. Taj Mahal also frequented the famous Club 47 in Cambridge, Mass., where he was further inspired by the 1960s folk renaissance. After graduating in 1964, he cofounded the musical group the Rising Sons with the guitarist Ry Cooder.

From his musical origins in New England, Taj Mahal launched a performing career that has included almost four dozen albums on which he sings and plays guitar, mandolin, banjo, piano, harmonica, and various other instruments. He is respected as both a solo performer and an ensemble player whose collaborators have included Eric Clapton, Bonnie Raitt, B. B. King, John Lee Hooker, Miles Davis, Jimi Hendrix, Bob Dylan, Sheryl Crow, and the international musicians V. M. Bhatt and Ali Farka Toure. His music includes adaptations of American roots music and

Taj Mahal in performance, 1968

more exotic sounds from the Caribbean and Africa. Taj Mahal often mixes these genres, adding West Indies spice to country blues, for instance. He has written scores for films, including *Sounder* (1972), *The Mighty Quinn* (1989), and *Phenomenon* (1996), and the score for the Broadway production *Mule Bone* (1991). His music also enriched the NEH-funded television adaptation of Richard Wright's short story "Almost a Man." Taj Mahal has recorded several albums of children's music and won Grammy awards for his albums *Señor Blues* (1997) and *Shoutin' in Key* (2000). He published his autobiography, *Taj Mahal: Autobiography of a Bluesman*, in 2001.

Fred Metting, *The Unbroken Circle: Tradition and Innovation in the Music of Ry Cooder and Taj Mahal* (2001); Taj Mahal with Stephen Foehr: *Taj Mahal: Autobiography of a Bluesman* (2001); Eric von Schmidt and Jim Rooney, *Baby, Let Me Follow You Down: The Illustrated Story of the Cambridge Folk Years* (1979); Josef Woodard. "Taj Mahal: Giant Steps Backward and Forward," *Down Beat* (February 1991).

Fred Metting

Tanglewood Founded in 1937 by Serge Koussevitzky, Tanglewood, in Lenox, Mass., is the summer home of the Boston Symphony Orchestra (BSO) and the seat of the Tanglewood Music Center, an academy for advanced training in composition and ensemble performance. The 10 weeks of festival concerts attract more than 300,000 listeners each year. Set on 330 acres in the scenic Berkshires of western Massachusetts, Tanglewood is the largest music festival in New England and an international tourism attraction. Nathaniel

Hawthorne lived on the grounds in 1850 and 1851, and a replica of his cottage is open to visitors in the summer.

Under such noted conductors as Seiji Ozawa (the orchestra's music director from 1973 to 2002), Bernard Haitink, and Simon Rattle, the BSO and guest artists, including orchestras from the United States and Europe, perform eight weekends of concerts. A chamber music weekend opens the season and a jazz weekend closes it; there is also a weeknight chamber and recital series presenting well-known ensembles and artists. Student groups, including the impressive Tanglewood Music Center Orchestra, give an additional five to seven concerts each week. A weeklong Festival of Contemporary Music, presented mainly by student and guest ensembles, is the leading new music festival on the East Coast. Most Tanglewood concerts, however, are oriented toward vacationers and others seeking the standard repertoire, from Haydn through Stravinsky, with a leavening of American music and nonstandard works from the past.

Tanglewood came into being in the midst of the Depression through the organizing efforts of well-to-do residents of the Berkshire resort community. The first season, 1937, consisted of two weekends of BSO concerts conducted in a tent by Koussevitzky, the orchestra's director from 1924 to 1949. In 1938 the Music Shed opened for orchestral concerts; a 5,000-seat pavilion noted for its good acoustics, it remains in use today. In 1940 Koussevitzky founded the Berkshire (now Tanglewood) Music Center to provide training for young musicians just embarking on professional careers. The school offers tuition-free study each summer to approximately 150 conductors, composers, instrumentalists, singers, and vocal coaches. Aaron Copland was the first faculty chairman; Leonard Bernstein was in the first class of students. Other leading conductor-graduates include Ozawa, Zubin Mehta, Claudio Abbado, Lorin Maazel, and Michael Tilson Thomas. About 20 percent of the players in the nation's principal symphony orchestras have emerged from the Music Center. A student opera program, mainly directed by Boris Goldovsky, put on many pioneering productions from 1940 to 1962. A revival of the opera program is in progress. Leading figures from the United States and Europe serve as composers in residence. The Boston University Tanglewood Institute offers a separate program of studies for high school–aged instrumentalists and singers.

In 1994 Tanglewood inaugurated Seiji Ozawa Hall, a 1,200-seat facility for student and chamber concerts. Widely praised for its comfort, attractiveness, and acoustics, it freed the original Theater-Concert Hall (opened in

1941) for restoration and use as a theater in the revived opera program.

Tanglewood has an informal air that makes it inviting for neophytes as well as experienced concertgoers. Adding to the informality are such popular events as the Boston Pops, a Fourth of July celebration, and Tanglewood on Parade, a gala benefit for the Music Center. Many concertgoers enjoy picnicking while listening to the music on the extensive lawns, which command a fine view of a nearby lake and hills.

Herbert Kupferberg, *Tanglewood* (1976); Andrew L. Pincus, *Scenes from Tanglewood* (1989); Pincus, *Tanglewood: The Clash between Tradition and Change* (1998); Meryle Secrest, *Leonard Bernstein* (1994).

Andrew L. Pincus

Taylor, James (1948–) Singer and songwriter. James (Vernon) Taylor, along with the singer-songwriters Paul Simon, Joni Mitchell, Jackson Browne, and Laura Nyro, founded the confessional soft-rock style that dominated American popular music in the early 1970s. Distinguished by the artful angst of songs like "Fire and Rain," Taylor became a spokesman for the times. Taylor was among the pioneers of his generation, and his music has changed the least; his acerbic yet tender Appalachian-flavored style is as immediately recognizable today as it was almost 30 years ago.

Born in Boston, Taylor, along with his three brothers, including the singer-songwriter Livingston Taylor, and one sister, the singer Kate Taylor, spent his childhood between Chapel Hill, near the campus of the University of North Carolina, where his father, who came from an affluent southern family, was a faculty member and later dean of the medical school, and another huge house near the white beaches of Martha's Vineyard, in Massachusetts. Taylor remembers the thriving folk scene during the summers he spent on the island and recalls winning a hootenanny concert there at age 15. Taylor, who now owns his own home on Martha's Vineyard, frequently returns to the Vineyard and often gives benefit concerts for island charities.

Taylor first studied the cello but later was introduced by his brother Alex to the acoustic guitar. The first songs he played were hymns and carols from the Protestant hymnal used at the Massachusetts boarding school he attended, Milton Academy. He built his exceptional finger-picking technique around the harmonic structure of these hymns. Taylor found formal schooling trying and left Milton for a term to join Alex's rock band in North Carolina. Returning to school at age 17, he grew increasingly despondent and committed himself for nine months to McLean Psychi-

James Taylor performing, 1990

atric Hospital. His experiences there are implicit in the song "Knockin' Round the Zoo," which was recorded in 1966 with his friend Danny Kortchmar's New York band, the Flying Machine. While living in New York, the 18-year-old experimented with drugs; in an effort to break his habit, he traveled to London. With the help of Peter Asher, who became his producer and manager, and Paul McCartney, he cut his first album, *James Taylor,* for Apple Records in 1968. Though it did not sell well, Taylor's debut album contained the song "Carolina in My Mind," which later became a hit.

Taylor performed at the Newport Folk Festival in 1969, then recorded another album that launched not only his career but a new era in rock. Both the album, *Sweet Baby James* (1970), and one of its cuts, "Fire and Rain," became huge commercial successes. Critics acclaimed Taylor's sensitive and introverted artistry as guiding rock music away from its current frenzied pitch. Soon Taylor played to standing-room audiences throughout the nation while his recording career continued to produce a number of hits. *Mud Slide Slim and the Blue Horizon,* for example, went beyond the gold record milestone in 1971 and also included a version of Carole King's "You've Got

a Friend," which became the number one song that year.

Taylor married the singer Carly Simon in 1972 and the couple had two children. Although domestic life removed the anguished edge from many of his songs, he continued to produce a string of hits, including "Handy Man," "How Sweet It Is," "Her Town Too," and the cheerful song he wrote for his daughter, "Your Smiling Face." Taylor, however, did not abandon the concerns of his generation, performing at a series of antinuclear concerts, including the "No Nukes" concert at Madison Square Garden.

In the 1980s Taylor's life and career epitomized the cultural shifts of his generation. With the breakup of his 10-year marriage and the sagging sales of his albums, Taylor's bouts with drugs and alcohol returned. Several albums that he recorded at this time, such as *Dad Loves His Work* (1981), reflect his personal struggles.

After the deaths of his brother Alex, his father, his producer and friend Don Grolnick, and the breakup of his second marriage, Taylor produced his critically acclaimed album *Hourglass* (1997), recorded on Martha's Vineyard, which is anything but mournful. Many of its songs reflect an aging baby-boomer's peaceful acceptance of life's inevitable changes. In 2001, he married Caroline "Kim" Smedvig, a Boston Symphony Orchestra executive. Taylor remains a perennial favorite; his much-imitated acoustic guitar and vocal style influenced the direction of the New Folk movement of the 1990s, largely centered in Boston.

Peter Herbst, "Interview: James Taylor," *Rolling Stone*, September 6, 1979; Stephen Holden, "A Troubadour from the 70's in Search of Serenity," *New York Times*, May 18, 1997; Irwin Stambler, *Encyclopedia of Pop, Rock and Soul* (1977); Timothy White, *Rock Lives: Profiles and Interviews* (1990).

Geoffrey S. Cahn

Theater in Boston The legacy of Puritanism is not the only reason that theater in Boston has had such a fitful history; narrow-minded patriots kept alive the strictures of their forebears by opposing British attempts to circumvent colonial prohibitions on the theater. In 1687, when John Wing tried to set up a theater in his tavern, he incurred the wrath of Increase Mather and Judge Samuel Sewall, who immediately stifled his attempt. The next theatrical venture was an abortive production of Thomas Otway's *The Orphan* (1750) by two English amateurs and sundry locals at the Coffee House on King (now State) Street. The performance was broken up by a crush of would-be spectators, and the ensuing melee caused the General Court to proscribe stage plays. This law exacerbated tensions between the colonists and the troops quartered in the city for the next 25 years for the military, eager for dramatic diversions, claimed that the English Licensing Act of 1737 overruled provincial provisions.

In 1769, the rumor that the garrison was contemplating a performance caused local unrest. After the Revolution broke out, sometime playwright General Burgoyne organized several performances for the benefit of his soldiers' widows and children. One of these, *The Blockade of Boston* (1775) at Faneuil Hall, was terminated by news of the Battle of Bunker Hill. *The New England Chronicle* trumpeted a report of the ill-starred performance by labeling its audience "deluded wretches." After the war, attempts were made to overturn the theater ban, and in 1792, speaking in the legislature, John Gardiner made the first recorded American defense of the theater. Later that year Joseph Harper opened the New Exhibition Room on Board Alley (near present-day Hawley Street). Boston's first theater had a capacity of 500 and was probably little more than a refurbished stable, featuring rope dancing, singing, recitation, and ballet in its opening performances. Plays masquerading as "moral lectures" came afterward; Garrick's *Lethe* and

Otway's *Venice Preserved* were the first plays presented.

Five months after the New Exhibition Room opened, public agitation arose over its allegedly foreign (most of the actors were English) and antidemocratic (most of the characters were lords and ladies) predisposition. Because the theater ban was still on the books, the sheriff was dispatched to close the room. His arrival during a performance of *The School for Scandal* caused an uproar: the audience tore down both Governor John Hancock's portrait and the Seal of the Commonwealth from the walls. The performance was stopped, but the law was never enforced again. It was finally repealed in 1797. The Board Alley Theater's brief success encouraged the construction of a permanent theater, and in 1794 the Federal Street Theater, an elegantly appointed house seating approximately 1,000, opened. The following year this theater presented the first professional production of a play by an American woman, *The Medium* by Judith Sargent Murray.

A second, much larger, theater, the Haymarket, opened in 1797 near the heart of today's theater district, at the corner of Boylston and Tremont Streets. The Haymarket barely survived the turn of the century, but during the next 100 years a building boom produced 21 new theaters. The Tremont (1827) was the next significant theater built; it hoped to cater to fashionable patrons who were unsatisfied by the program of only one theater. The growing sophistication of the Boston audience encouraged the proliferation, if not the success, of a variety of theatrical enterprises.

The rivalry between the Federal Street and Tremont theaters was so intense that both closed by midcentury. The city's two most important theaters in the 19th century were the Boston Museum and the Boston Theatre. The former housed the best American stock company through the century's middle decades and was the home of William Warren, the greatest American comic actor, and the beloved Mrs. J. R. Vincent. The enormous Boston Theatre presented stock, opera, and variety performances as well as touring stars. The city had become a regular stopping place for English, American, and European tours early in the century—George Frederick Cooke first played Boston in 1811. Ten years later, on his mistimed second visit, Edmund Kean, chagrined by a poor turnout, arrogantly refused to go on. Bostonians repaid the insult four years later by running Kean out of town before he could even open. Other performers fared better. Boston was William Charles Macready's favorite American city.

Variety acts were popular from the first. A

"learned pig" is reported to have entertained Bostonians at Bowen's Columbian Museum (1798), and 70 years later the ceiling of the Howard Athenaeum was the setting for the first human fly act. The Viennoise Children, the Ravels, and performers of lesser quality held the stage for so much of the time that in 1853 William W. Clapp complained of "Thespis and Melpomene weeping over the tomb of legitimate drama" in Boston. Variety's ascendancy caused him to demand a new theater that would present drama exclusively; his call went unheeded.

When Keith and Albee began their dime "show-store" (1883) at the Gaiety Museum, local stock had largely succumbed to the touring combination companies. By 1894, when they opened the Colonial, the first all-vaudeville theater, variety seemed triumphant. Nonetheless, the Broadway tryout system, pioneered at the Boston Theatre by the playwright Charles H. Hoyt for *A Trip to Chinatown* (1891), reinvigorated the city's legitimate theater for most of the following century.

The Shuberts gained a monopoly on the downtown houses by 1934, and anything playing in them was either headed for Broadway or on tour from it. The Shuberts had to contend with the strictest local censorship in the country, which was no longer solely in the hands of the amateur Watch and Ward Society but was now enforced by "the chief of the city's licensing division" (there never was an official city censor). "Banned in Boston" became the playwright's bane and the press agent's boon. From 1915 through 1965, when ACLU pressure overturned it, a secret rider was attached to every theatrical contract signed by producers and managers that prohibited everything from lascivious language to "all forms of muscle dancing by either sex." *Strange Interlude*'s consignment to nearby Quincy (1929) was the most notorious banning incident. The system's hypocrisy was transparent: at the "Old" Howard theater, strippers muscle danced with impunity.

In the meantime, the "little theater" movement made its impact on the city. A combination of forces from Mrs. Lyman Gale's Toy Theatre (1912) and the failed Castle Square Theater, which had presented George Pierce Baker's Harvard prize plays (1911–17), were marshaled by the Australian actor Henry Jewett and his wife, Frances, to form a resident company. They managed to construct the Repertory Theatre of Boston (1925), but his death (1930) ended this endeavor.

Through the Depression and war years, the New England Repertory and the Tributary Theatre of Boston struggled to keep local theatrics alive, and Jerome Kilty's Brattle Theater

Company briefly vitalized the local scene (1947–52). The Boston Players, a significant black company founded in 1930, was taken over by the actor Ralf Coleman later in the decade. After the demise of the local Federal Theatre Project Negro Unit, he gathered several of its veterans and founded the Boston Negro Theatre, which was active through the 1940s. In 1957 Michael Murray's Charles Playhouse troupe created the first new legitimate performance space in Boston since Jewett's when they converted an old church into their own theater (1957). They remained 13 years. The 1960s found Harvard a proving ground for local artistry: the student productions of Thomas Babe and the late Timothy Mayer set standards that laid the groundwork for the careers of the director Peter Sellars, Stockard Channing, and many others. Across the river, David Wheeler's Theatre Company of Boston gave the American premiere of Pinter's *The Dwarfs* (1966) and presented Al Pacino in *Richard III* (1973).

The 1970s was a transitional decade—by its end the tryout system was virtually dead. There were still artistically successful small theaters, most notably the Cambridge Ensemble, but many of the efforts of other experimental groups seemed forced. Encouraged by grants from a new state arts council, dozens of fringe companies indulged themselves until the Commonwealth's fiscal collapse in 1989. One tiny theater that managed to survive and prosper through these years was the Lyric Stage, which celebrated its 17th season by moving to a large new theater (1991). There continue to be some 50 companies operating in and around Boston. The climax of the postwar era was the almost simultaneous arrival in town of two resident companies: the American Repertory Company (1980) and the Huntington Theatre (1982), sponsored, respectively, by Harvard and Boston University. The ART is a technically dazzling director's theater; the Huntington reverences the dramatic text above all else.

Boston's theater critics have been a significant part of 20th-century theatrical life. The legendarily Waspish H. T. Parker, known as H.T.P., served the *Boston Evening Transcript* from 1903 to 1934. Well known in London and New York theater circles, he was Brooks Atkinson's mentor. Elliot Norton wrote for several major dailies from 1934 to 1982 and became one of the most influential critics in American theater history. Numerous producers and directors believed that Norton's taste was an infallible guide to the public's, so they frequently revised plays according to his reviews or even consulted with him during Boston tryouts. Norton was also a fixture on public television, hosting his own program,

"Elliot Norton Reviews." Norton's successor at the *Herald*, Arthur Friedman, had been proclaimed the "guru of Harvard theatre" in the 1960s and had gone on to write for several alternative weeklies. Friedman maintained the highest standards of integrity and was highly respected by both readers and performers. He consistently challenged Boston's theater community and his fellow critics to do better.

The enduring legacy of Boston's critics was solemnized with the creation of the annual Elliot Norton Awards (1982). These prizes, bestowed by a committee of leading local critics, were as much a tribute to the dean of American drama critics as a reflection of Boston's sudden rebirth as a center of regional theater.

W. Ball, "The Old Federal St. Theatre," *Bostonian Society Publications* 8 (1911); William W. Clapp, *W. W. Record of the Boston Stage*, Boston (1853); D. King, "Historical Survey of the Theatre in Boston," *Marquee* 4, no. 3 (1974); Brooks McNamara, *The American Playhouse in the 18th Century* (1969); Elliot Norton, *Broadway Down East* (1978); Eugene Tompkins, *The History of the Boston Theatre 1854–1901* (1908).

Thomas F. Connolly

Theater in New Haven Yale University has always played a crucial role in the development of theater in New Haven. In the first references to theatrical activity in New Haven, in 1755 Yale students flouted a Yale College rule of 1726 prohibiting the "wearing of women's apparel and playing at swords, files, and cudgels," and surreptitiously put on plays only to find themselves censured by the president and tutors. Eventually the college tolerated some amateur performances. By 1767, Yale literary societies were putting on annual exhibitions of tragedies, comedies, and farces. These performances were enhanced by an increasingly elaborate use of costume and scenery.

New Haven's first professional performance was probably an evening of "theatrical entertainments" in 1800 featuring patriotic songs and monodies, short plays, and a diorama. That year Connecticut passed a law prohibiting theatrical shows and exhibitions by professional performers. Amateur theater persisted, however. In 1831 children in the elocution classes of the Lancastorian School, the forerunner of public education in New Haven, began presenting short plays. These annual productions were lavishly costumed and attended by a broader range of public than attended the plays put on by the college literary societies. That same year New Haven's first Lyceum was built as a venue for lectures, but it ultimately was used for the presentations of dialogues, recitations of Shakespeare, ventriloquists, magicians, and other theatrical fare.

During the 1840s visits from Christy's Min-

strels and Campbell's Ethiopian Serenaders helped to make minstrelsy one of New Haven's favorite forms of entertainment. In 1843 the elocution class of the Young Men's Institute, originally founded as a self-improvement group, the Apprentices' Literary Association in 1826, branched into amateur theatricals. Under the leadership of Elisha F. Homan and his family, the group became New Haven's first amateur repertory company.

In 1852 the Connecticut General Assembly repealed the 1800 antitheater law and granted individual towns the authority to authorize and regulate theater themselves. Within a year Homan opened Homan's Athenaeum, New Haven's first professional resident stock company, and George H. Wyatt's touring company began to present plays regularly, beginning with *Uncle Tom's Cabin*. Owing in part to the competition from Wyatt's touring company, Homan's Athenaeum folded in 1854. All other attempts at establishing a resident theater in New Haven had also failed by 1861.

After the Civil War the road show became the usual source of theatrical entertainment in the United States. The Music Hall, New Haven's first major auditorium, opened in 1860. Remodeled to accommodate scenery in 1869, it helped to make New Haven a major stop for theatrical companies on the road between New York and Boston. Soon other theaters were erected. The Hyperion Theater (1880) was New Haven's principal venue for legitimate theater before the opening of the Shubert Theater. Sylvester Poli began business at his Palace Theater in 1906, and the Paramount followed in 1913. Both were important vaudeville houses.

The Shubert Theater opened in 1914 and quickly became the country's most important "try-out house" for Broadway-bound shows. For the next 72 years the best theater in America passed through New Haven. The Shubert closed in 1976 but reopened in 1983 as the Shubert Performing Arts Center.

Even as commercial theater thrived, so did amateur theater, owing in large part to Yale and its extended community. In 1921 New Haven's Little Theater opened, organized primarily by Yale associates. The Little Theater served as home to the New Haven Theater Guild, part of America's Little Theater movement. When Yale's Department of Drama, founded in 1924, began presenting plays at the University Theater free to the public, the prominence of the Theater Guild began to diminish.

The Little Theater was home not only to the Theater Guild but also to the Yale Playcraftsmen, an antecedent to the Yale Dramat, a Works Progress Administration Federal Theatre Project during the 1930s, and an in-

Playbill (left) and official guide, International Festival of Arts and Ideas, New Haven, Conn., 2003

creasing number of community theaters, including the Dixwell Community House Players. Today the Little Theater is the home of the theater program of the Educational Center for the Arts.

The advent of radio and talking movies in combination with the Depression and World War II hurt live theater in New Haven. By 1930 Poli's Palace had become a glamorous movie theater; by 1945 the Little Theater, renamed the Lincoln, had become an art-movie theater, and in 1952 the Paramount presented its last live stage show. The Shubert Theater and Yale's Drama Department, reorganized in 1955 as the Yale School of Drama, remained.

In 1965 John Jory and Harlen Kleiman, both graduates of the Yale School of Drama, founded the Long Wharf Theatre. Long Wharf is a nonprofit theater, which features a thrust stage and specializes in well-cast productions of classics and contemporary American plays. Over the years, many of Long Wharf's productions have transferred to Broadway and off-Broadway.

Yale Repertory Theatre was established in 1966, creating a symbiotic relationship between the School of Drama and a professional theater. Under the artistic direction of Robert Brustein, the Rep presented significant contemporary plays of the world theater repertoire as well as classics. Brustein also introduced New Haven to important experimental theater, such as the work of the Living Theater and Andre Serban. Under the direction of Lloyd Richards, the Rep presented the works of August Wilson and Athol Fugard. Its current director is James Bundy.

During the 1980s there was a surge of local theater activity. International Performance Actions, under the leadership of Jeff and Nicola Burnett, produced site-specific, highly visual experimental work; the Performance Studio presented cabaret, improv-comedy, and Free Shakespeare on the Green; and Art-Space provided a venue for an annual Little Theater Festival on Audubon Street. The audience for Elm City Shakespeare, founded in 1995 as a professional multicultural company that presents free performances at Edgerton Park, has grown to 30,000 since the company's first production in 1996.

Today, New Haven has Long Wharf, the Yale Rep, the University Theater of the School of Drama (where students perform mostly classics), the Shubert Theater, a range of community theater, and the International Festival of Arts and Ideas. Every June, this festival, which began in 1996, has brought to New Haven classical and experimental theater from around the world, including England's Royal Shakespeare Company, Ireland's Abbey Theatre, Russia's Taganka Theatre, and Singapore's TheatreWorks.

Gerald M. Berkowitz, *New Broadways: Theater across America as the Millennium Approaches* (1997); Arthur W. Bloom, "History of the Theatre in New Haven, Connecticut, before 1860" (Ph.D. diss., 1966); Committee to Save the Lincoln Theatre, "History and Background of the Little Theatre Guild, Its Founders and the Building They Built (1982); WPA

Research Project on the History of the Theater in New Haven, Conn.

Robert Bresnik

Women Composers Music by women composers began to surface in the late 18th and early 19th centuries—roughly the time that secular music began to be published in significant quantity in the United States. The main difference between men and women as classes of composers, apart from their numbers, is the absence of women as composers of church hymns and psalms; this important indigenous style of the New England singing school passed them by. Songs and piano music dominated their output until the 20th century. In the 1880s and 1890s a generation of female Boston composers rose to prominence, ushering in an era that celebrated compositions by women, and Boston emerged as a center for women composers. Amy Beach (1867–1944), who led this group of pioneering women, was the first American woman to compose a symphony (Gaelic Symphony in E Minor, op. 32) performed in the United States (1896, Boston Symphony Orchestra).

Throughout the 19th century the role of women in American musical life was associated with the tradition of music as a feminine "accomplishment." Women learned to play the piano or guitar as a social skill to provide entertainment in the home. Because musical training was a conventional component of genteel education, the first conservatory in the United States was a seminary for women, the Music Vale Academy or Salem Normal School in Salem, Conn., founded in 1835. Among the small number of women composers in the 18th and early 19th centuries, Elisabeth Von Hagen was the most important; she was the best-known member of a prominent family of Boston musicians.

The transition from parlor to professional activity took place during the middle decades of the 19th century. New England supported a few women composers, among them Abby Hutchinson (1829–92), the sole female member of a famous politically active singing family, and Marion Dix Sullivan, who composed "The Blue Juniata" (1844), one of the most popular parlor songs of the 19th century and the first composition by an American woman to become a commercial hit song.

At the turn of the 20th century a generation of renowned female composers marked the arrival of the professional woman composer. This Boston group included Beach, one of the major composers of the Second New England School; Margaret Ruthven Lang (1867–1972); Helen Hopekirk (1856–1945); and Clara Kathleen Rogers (1844–1931), with Mabel Daniels (1877–1971) representing the next generation.

Various all-women performing ensembles, such as the Fadette Women's Orchestra of Boston (founded in 1888), the Boston Women's Symphony Orchestra (founded in 1927), and the Women's Symphony of Boston (founded 1939), supported the work of female composers.

Nevertheless, this trend in Boston at the turn of the past century did not endure. With the decline of Boston as a center of classical composition in the early 20th century and persistent discrimination against women in the academy, only a few women composers joined the composition faculties of the conservatories and universities that are so important to New England's cultural life. These include Vivian Fine (b. 1913) at Bennington College, Vt., from 1964 to 1988; Joyce Mekeel (b. 1931) at Boston University; Pozzi Escot (b. 1933), director of the electronic music studio at Wheaton College, Norton, Mass.; Arlene Zallman (b. 1934) at Wellesley College in Massachusetts; and Marilyn Ziffrin (b. 1926) at New England College, Henniker, N.H.

Renewed interest in works composed by women, however, began in the 1970s, with the formation of the Massachusetts chapter of American Women Composers. Some Boston classical composers of note emerged from this milieu, among them Ruth Lomon (b. 1930), Dianne Goolkasian Rahbee (b. 1938), and Elizabeth Vercoe (b. 1941), who directed the Women's Music Festival/85 in Boston. New England's long-standing cultural intersect with musical composition is likewise evident in the numerous women singer-songwriters to emerged from the Cambridge coffeehouse circuit of the 1960s and the New Folk movement of the 1990s.

Christine Ammer, *Unsung: A History of Women in American Music* (1980); Adrienne Fried Block and Carol Neuls-Bates, *Women in American Music: A Bibliography of Music and Literature* (1979); Julie Ann Sadie and Rhian Samuel, eds., *The New Grove Dictionary of Women Composers* (1994); Judith Tick, *American Women Composers before 1870*, 2d ed. (1993).

Judith Tick

Politics

Maureen F. Moakley, Section Editor

William E. Hudson, Consulting Editor

INTRODUCTION

The cultural distinctiveness of New England, readily seen in its lifestyles, literature, architecture, geography, and landscape, is also apparent in the character and patterns of contemporary politics. The six New England states form a distinctive political region. Although variations exist among the states and changes have occurred over time, a common political culture and heritage remain and can be seen in the structure of contemporary political institutions; patterns of political support and social interaction among citizens; the style, interests, and activities of elected politicians; and the character of substantive public policies within the states.

Political culture has been broadly defined as the attitudes, feelings, and expectations that citizens and political elites have toward government and the public order. Academic studies and intuitive understandings of the character of U.S. government and politics usually focus on a unique American political culture with broad commonalties in the orientations and political expectations of Americans. A more careful view, however, reveals distinct ideas about politics that are nonetheless integral to that common political tradition. Those who take a communitarian perspective see politics and the public order contributing toward a political community in which all citizens have an obligation to promote the mutual interests of the commonwealth and create a just, democratic society. Those favoring individualism, on the other hand, see the public order as secular and neutral, supporting interested individuals or groups who wish to compete and bargain to promote private or group interests.

These two attitudes stem from and reflect an evolving pattern. After the lofty ideals expressed in the Declaration of Independence that stressed equality and common purpose, the founding fathers retreated to a more utilitarian view of politics, expressed in the Constitution and the *Federalist Papers* (1778). This perspective is synonymous with a traditional interest in group politics that James Madison articulated in his classic statement of the purpose of politics, developed in conjunction with the ratification of the Constitution. Madison noted that "a landed interest, a manufacturing interest, a mercantile interest, a moneyed interest, with many lesser interests, grow up of necessity in civilized nations, and divide them into different classes actuated by different sentiments and views. The regulation of these various and interfering interests forms the principal task of modern legislation, and involves the spirit of party and faction in the necessary and ordinary operations of the government."

The political culture of the United States essentially derives from these two visions of the public order. How they developed and evolved—as a result of the distinctive life experiences, physical environment, and belief systems of the settlers of various regions—provides us with core definitions of regional political subcultures and offers insights into how these enduring visions of politics mutated and matured into distinct cultural variations.

By the time of the Revolution, the distinctiveness of New England's political culture, as well as that of other regions in the emerging country, was obvious. This distinctiveness is wonderfully illustrated by Garry Wills's discussion of the various delegates convening in Philadelphia in 1776 to draft and sign the Declaration of Independence. Although they all held similar ideas about representation and private property, they came from very different worlds and were, in many ways, "strangers." John Adams and his cousin Samuel were fairly representative of the delegation from New England. Both were born and reared in the predictable, established, and homogeneous world of Yankee New England, were educated at Harvard, and took their place in public life as part of the expectations of public service created by the generations who went before them. Shrewd and taciturn participants at the convention, they worked, often behind the scenes, to understand the motives and connections of other delegates in order to protect and promote the interests of the commonwealth of Massachusetts.

John Adams, in his observations about the other delegates to the convention, noted with some amazement and concern that they were indeed "strangers" and that the "diversity of religions, educations, manners, and interests" of the various delegations might make one concerted effort for independence all but impossible. In Adams's writing about the delegates we find glimpses of three subcultures. Adams noted, in contrast to life in New England, the raucous character of Philadelphia, a city in the mid-Atlantic region with a heterogeneous population and heavy commercial activity. There, Quakers and Catholics intermingled and prospered along with Protestants of many denominations, exchanges that would have been unthinkable in Massachusetts at the time. And he, like other delegates, was stunned by the flamboyant arrival of the Virginia delegation. As Wills notes, these tall, stately outdoorsmen, riding splendid horses and attended by slaves, "clattered into Philadelphia with the glitter, almost, of Magi."

In an imaginative and pathbreaking study, Daniel Elazar took these descriptive and intuitive observations about regional differences and in 1966 identified three distinct political subcultures that had evolved in various regions in the country: the moralistic, individualistic, and traditionalistic traditions. The moralistic political culture, based on ideas of a commonwealth, dominated in New England. An individualistic political subculture, such as that which emerged in the mid-Atlantic states, views politics as a utilitarian marketplace where groups compete to promote secular ends. This ethic does not preclude the idea that individuals, driven by goals to promote the good society, will participate in politics, but its dominant pattern is one of interest-group politics. The traditionalistic political culture, which evolved in the hierarchical plantation structure of the South, developed a paternalistic concept of politics wherein an established elite assumed decision-making responsibility in order to preserve the status quo.

Elazar then traced patterns of migrations from these original regions whereby migrant groups took aspects of these basic ideas about politics and subsequent variations to all regions of the country. Although these variations represent ideal types that have been melded over the years, it is remarkable that despite the passage of time, enduring aspects of these subcultures remain.

In order to understand political culture, we need to look to the past and discuss early colonial settlement in the region. In New England, the roots of the moralistic political culture are found in the life experiences, physical environment, and belief systems of the Puritan settlers. The Mayflower Compact, signed before the Pilgrims landed and settled in New England in 1620, provides the basis of one of the critical and enduring visions of the region's culture. As Carey McWilliams notes, this document articulates the communitarian alternative to individualism. The compact, along with the writings of such Puritan leaders as John Winthrop and Cotton Mather, emphasizes the idea that settlements in New England and political activities there should be based on positive moral obligations and reflect the community's moral values. So strong was this commitment that the early Puritan leaders rejected the idea of religious self-determination somewhat implicit in Protestantism and insisted on the intimate link between religion and state, initially establishing a crude form of theocracy. Their mandates resulted in the banishment of religious dissidents to Rhode Island, where Roger Williams and Anne Hutchinson founded a somewhat more tolerant and heterogeneous colony in which, therefore, strains of individualism flourished earlier on.

These early religious beginnings were eventually muted by the impulse toward self-determination and individualism inherent in a community of believers wherein all recognized members of a congregation were equal and obligated to participate in community and church affairs. This pattern quickly evolved into a highly participatory representative system of government in which authority emanated from the people (who held property) at the community level and ultimately manifested itself in the direct democracy of the town meeting, for which New England was renowned. The Puritan ethic was also modified by notions of what McWilliams calls the "special providence" of individual actions and efforts to accumulate wealth and power, which came to be perceived as a "sign" of salvation and God's grace. These ideas evolved into the Yankee culture of white Anglo-Saxon Protestants who worked to accumulate wealth and property but retained a strong commitment to public service, good government, and the well-being of the commonwealth, an ethic that remains evident in New England today.

EVOLVING PATTERNS OF POLITICAL CULTURE

The rocky New England soil was never especially hospitable to farming, and during the colonial era extensive shipping industries and merchant trade developed and flourished in the shore colonies. Boston and Newport, R.I., were the premier ports in the region. Boston lost preeminence to New York after the opening of the Erie Canal in 1825 denied New England access to the widening markets of America's westward expansion, and the port of Newport never recovered from the British occupation during the Revolutionary War. The China trade, whaling, and lingering vestiges of the slave trade continued, but it was the Industrial Revolution in America, launched in New England, that produced the economic growth and profound social and demographic changes that altered the political culture of the region.

As a result of labor demands associated with industrialization, as well as events in Europe, during the first half of the 19th century more than 5 million immigrants came to New England from northern and western Europe. They were followed by a second wave of immigrants from southern and eastern Europe. Most of these immigrants settled in Massachusetts, Rhode Island, and Connecticut. A contingent of French Canadians made northern New England their home.

For the most part, these new groups were vastly different from the Yankee population; they were poorer, less educated, and mostly Catholic. By necessity, most of them settled in expanding urban centers, creating a much more heterogeneous demographic and social order, and creating as well—as Duane Lockard noted—"two New Englands," a northern and a southern tier. While the northern states of New Hampshire, Maine, and Vermont retained much of the distinctive Yankee character, the southern states of Rhode Island, Massachusetts, and Connecticut developed a distinct individualistic dimension in their politics.

PARTISAN POLITICS

This shifting demographic and social picture altered the political culture of the New England states. Most immigrant groups, particularly those that come in large numbers, face a discriminatory environment in which the established elite class tries to retain power and restrict the economic and political influence of newer groups. This was certainly the case in New England, where in response to discrimination, the newer groups eventually mobilized and accessed the political system to improve their economic and political status. Contrary to the ideals of the Puritans, the main goal of such New England immigrant groups was not to promote the Yankee concept of good government but rather to use politics for the utilitarian purpose of gaining political and economic power. As a result, a rough interest-group politics emerged in various forms of political organizations in Connecticut, Massachusetts, and Rhode Island, where after the Depression immigrant groups eventually took over the political system, mobilizing primarily around the Democratic Party. During those years, the union movement and the 1928 presidential candidacy of the Democrat Al Smith, an ethnic Catholic from the Northeast, had a stunning effect on enrollment in the Democratic Party. Smith may have been a weak national candidate, but his impact on the political mobilization of the working classes was critical to the formation of emerging Democratic majorities in the southern-tier states.

To this day, the southern-tier states remain more Democratic and unionized than the rest of New England. Indeed, after World War II, while the general orientation of the region reflected a more liberal, progressive tradition evident in both parties, there was a sharp demarcation between these two tiers in the partisan loyalties of

ELEPHANT

This is the Republican Elephant.
Why is the Elephant Republican?
Because it stands for Intelligence,
Solidity and Strength.

DONKEY

This is the Democratic Donkey.
Why is the Donkey Democratic?
Because it kicks much and accomplishes nothing.

Republican elephant and Democratic donkey, from
The New England Republican Primer, *1905*

voters. The northern-tier states remained staunchly Republican, Connecticut became competitive, and the Democrats dominated Rhode Island and Massachusetts. In the 21st century, a curious new pattern has emerged. The older partisan loyalties have become blurred—and to some extent less significant—while regional commonalties across party lines have become more important and continue to define the enduring political culture of the region.

POLITICS AND CULTURE IN THE 21ST CENTURY

In terms of partisan loyalties, the most significant change in New England has been the recent decline of the Republican Party (GOP), especially in the three northern-tier states. This decline is partly a result of an enduring legacy based on tolerant and progressive attitudes in the local GOP, rooted in the moralistic political subculture, that are no longer in sync with those of the national party. While the Republican Party always had and continues to display strong ties to business interests, it also was characterized by a liberal and progressive ideology; it was, after all, the party of abolition and civil rights, voting rights for women, the Equal Rights Amendment, separation of church and state, and other tolerant ideals about civic society. The ascendancy of Ronald Reagan in the 1980s marked a seismic shift in the GOP toward a more conservative, less progressive base centered in the South and Southwest. During the 1980s, for example, the GOP removed its long-standing support for the Equal Rights Amendment from its party platform, endorsed a prolife-antichoice policy with regard to abortion, and promoted a more prominent state role for religion, which was closely tied to Christian fundamentalist leanings. As a result, many New Englanders abandoned the Republican Party. Vermont swung toward the Democratic Party, Maine became increasingly independent, and even more-conservative New Hampshire became more competitive.

These shifts reflect continuing ideals of a more liberal and tolerant culture that no longer resonates within the mainstream of the GOP. One can now argue that New England is becoming Democratic territory. During the 1990s and in 2004, all New England states supported the Democratic candidate; in the 2000 election, only New Hampshire supported the Republican. These shifts are evident at the congressional level as well. In races for the U.S. House of Representatives in 1900, the New England delegation consisted of 24 Republicans and three Democrats. In 2005, the delegation consisted of 16 Democrats, 5 Republicans, and one independent—Bernie

Sanders of Vermont, who usually votes with the Democrats but is officially a socialist. A similar picture emerges in the U.S. Senate. In 1900 all 12 senators were Republican; by 2005 the delegation consisted of six Democrats, five Republicans, and one independent—James Jeffords of Vermont, whose defection from the Republican Party is symptomatic of the changing politics of the region. The 2000 election gave the GOP a majority in both the House and the Senate. Shortly thereafter, Jeffords, a longtime Republican who felt increasingly alienated from the rigid and dogmatic GOP leadership in Congress, left the party and became an independent, but he voted with the Democrats to give them the majority until the 2002 and 2004 elections, when the Republicans reclaimed their lead.

Moreover, even among the remaining Republicans in the New England delegation, the partisan fit for most of them remains uneasy, as they tend to represent the liberal wing of the GOP and often vote against the party leadership. Indeed, there was a marked confluence of partisan ideals at the beginning of the new century in New England. In tandem with shifts in the GOP, the Democrats abandoned some of the more radical aspects of their platform and programs and moved more toward the center of the political spectrum. Although variations between the two parties remain, in New England most of their differences exist on the margins, leaving a substantial common ground that reflects a core set of basic values.

Although the defection of Jeffords represented a significant event in national politics—because it resulted in the Republicans temporarily losing control of the Senate—in general, the influence of New England in national politics is mixed. Certainly, compared with the prominence of the region in national affairs at the dawn of the republic, its position is diminished. New England is now a relatively small region in a much larger nation. In 1790 the New England delegation constituted about 30 percent of the membership of the House of Representatives; by 2005 it was only about 6 percent. Nor does New England any longer provide the congressional leadership it did when the likes of Joseph Martin, Tip O'Neill, George Mitchell, John McCormack, John Pastore, and Claiborne Pell held sway. Of course, much of this decline is related to the shift of control of Congress to the Republican Party, whose leadership is drawn mainly from the South and Southwest. Even those New England legislators who remain prominent in the Democratic leadership of the Congress, such as Ted Kennedy, John Kerry, and Christopher Dodd, have much less clout during an era of Republican congressional control.

In presidential politics, however, New England still seems an important player. The continued significance of the New Hampshire primary in the selection of nominees in both parties means that the concerns of New Englanders influence who becomes president. And New England continues to produce major contenders for the Democratic Party nomination, as it did in 1988 and 2004 with the nominations of Michael Dukakis and John Kerry of Massachusetts and in 2004 with the influential Democratic primary campaign of former Vermont governor Howard Dean. Because New England voters decisively support the Democratic Party in national politics, the region's national influence seems closely tied to the overall success or failure of the Democrats.

STRUCTURE OF CONTEMPORARY
POLITICAL INSTITUTIONS

The distinctiveness of New England politics is also rooted in state constitutions, which directly reflect the values of the times in which they were drafted. With the exception of Connecticut's constitution, the existing New England state constitutions are among the oldest in the country, with the Massachusetts Constitution, written by John Adams and adopted in 1780, the oldest. Vermont (1793) and New Hampshire (1784) also still operate under 18th-century documents, and the Rhode Island (1842) and Maine (1819) Constitutions were drafted and adopted during the first half of the 19th century. As a result, these states retain a balance of institutional power that reflects historical doubt about executive authority and have governors with weak institutional powers. Only Connecticut has a revised constitution, drafted in 1965, that makes Connecticut's governor one of the strongest in the country, reflecting more modern notions of strong executive authority.

Other contemporary New England governors are constricted in their constitutional and statutory authority. Most have limited appointment power; two, in New Hampshire and Vermont, still have two-year terms. Most governors must run and manage the government in cooperation with a number of other elected statewide officers with power and turf of their own, as well as work with limited veto power and budgetary authority. In fact, in all rankings of gubernatorial authority, New England governors, with the exception of Connecticut's, are considered among the weakest in the country. Although many are successful at using their bully pulpit in a media age to enhance their stature and clout, in the end they must work with strong legislative bodies that are usually run by powerful legislative leaders. Legislative power is also enhanced by the relative size of the region's state legislatures.

New England states tend to have large legislative bodies based on a broad representative system, reflecting older traditions of direct representation by citizen legislators. All New England states have legislatures with numbers of representatives well above the national average. And these bodies are especially large in relation to the relative population; New Hampshire is the most notable in this regard, with 400 representatives in the lower House, which serves a population of just over 1 million. This also tends to reinforce the power of many legislative leaders because the rule of thumb in representative politics is the larger the body the more powerful the leadership. Moreover, in keeping with the "amateur tradition" of citizen legislators, the New England states have resisted trends toward professionalization by paying state legislators salaries well below the national average, requiring most representatives to pursue other forms of employment. Only Connecticut and Massachusetts have recently revised compensation packages so that they are more consistent with those of the rest of the country. Large amateur representative bodies also tend to develop strong leadership systems, producing in New England legendary legislative leaders who manage the legislative process with considerable autonomy and authority and usually represent the most powerful individuals in the state.

Another result of the older constitutions and the political traditions that emanate

Demonstrators against the Vietnam War, Boston Common, early 1970s

from them is that the early 20th century's Progressive movement, which brought voter initiative, recall, and referendum to newer states, particularly in the West, tended to bypass New England. These processes, where they existed at all, were severely limited and restricted. The more recent initiative movement of the 1980s, which gained momentum across the country, had only a minor effect in the New England states. In other parts of the country it has spawned tax revolts, policymaking by ballot box, and legislative term limits, which many regard as detrimental to the representative process. In New England only Maine has term limits, and the movement, as well as the whole initiative movement, appears to be on the wane. This is regarded as a happy circumstance by most political scientists, who note that these activities tend to create instability in the political and policymaking process and a lack of the institutional memory necessary to sustain the vitality of representative institutions.

In New England citizens still participate the old-fashioned way. Although the traditional New England town meeting is on the wane, voting turnout percentages (except in New Hampshire) are in the top third of states in the country. The gap between New England and the rest of the country was wider in the past, but as voting restrictions were eliminated and minority participation increased, turnout in other states, particularly in the South, increased significantly. Nonetheless, the "responsibility" of participation, which has long been a part of the region's political culture, keeps the New England states in the top tiers of voter turnout rankings.

POLITICAL CULTURE AND PUBLIC POLICY

The late 18th and early 19th centuries were a period of blatant economic discrimination, especially against new immigrant groups. By the mid-20th century, these groups not only had been acculturated into the system, but in many instances—through the Democratic Party—had taken over politics and proceeded to enact progressive legislation that extended the franchise of and established social and economic protections to expanding poor, working-class, and middle-class constituencies. This pattern continues today. It is striking to note that on any range of indices of monthly welfare payments, state social security supplements, and state and local welfare spending as a percentage of all general revenue spending, all the New England states, regardless of relative wealth in terms of per capita income, consistently fall in the top 10 or 15 of the 50 states. The original impetus for this might have been partisan in nature, but on a number of public policy choices there is a distinct tradition of responsibility for the well-being of all members of the community that reflects earlier ideals.

The New England states also always rank far above all other regions in terms of the overall welfare of children. In studies from various child advocacy groups, New England is always in the top tier of states in terms of policies having to do with child health, school dropout rates, juvenile arrests, teen births, child poverty, infant mortality rates, state preventive and insurance programs that support children's health, immunization rates, reports of child abuse, prenatal care, and divorce rates. In a ranking by the Children's Rights Council of Washington, D.C., that examined a mix of these measures in 1999, five of the New England states were rated as the top five spots in the country for children, with Rhode Island coming in 12th.

Related to children's interests and consistent with rich historical and intellectual traditions is the central role that education plays in the policy focus of the New England states. Although the region is renowned for an array of illustrious and outstanding private schools that traditionally serve a national and international elite, public education at the primary and secondary levels is an important priority in all New England states. Spending per pupil and student-teacher ratios are—even in states where per capita income is low—in the top third of the states in the country. And public library holdings per capita are in the top 10 of all the states.

When it comes to higher education, however, the educational traditions of an array of elite private institutions, deeply rooted in the culture of the region, appear to have worked against policies that promote public higher education. The presence of Harvard, the Massachusetts Institute of Technology, Yale, and Brown, as well as of a string of illustrious small liberal arts colleges, creates a situation whereby public higher education in the region usually gets short shrift. New Englanders continue to identify with these elite private institutions, regardless of the fact that they are difficult to get into, are prohibitively expensive, and, as institutions of national and international recognition, do not serve the state populations. Americans from the South, Midwest, and West are routinely surprised at the relative standing, public support, and public recognition afforded to state university systems in the region. These schools are not cherished as a source of pride and identification the way they are in other regions of the country, and they clearly are not a policy priority for state governments. Indeed, as a portion of states' operating budgets, spending for public higher education routinely puts New England among the bottom 10 states.

The paucity of support for public higher education notwithstanding, the progressive priorities and policies of the region are expensive, and the New England states tend to be high tax territory. One commonly used overall indicator, "State and Local Tax Effort," which examines the relative burden of state and local taxes, finds that with the exception of New Hampshire, the New England states consistently fall in the top half of all states in terms of the effort they make, relative to wealth, to collect revenues. Again exempting New Hampshire, which principally relies on the property tax, the New England states have tax systems that are decidedly progressive, in that their state and local taxes per capita, individual income taxes per capita, and high-end personal income tax rates are all in the top half of the 50 states. Conversely, New England's sales tax revenues, which are generally considered regressive because they place a greater burden on low-end wage earners, are in the bottom third of the 50 states. And though New Hampshire, as one might expect, ranks at the top if measures of property tax as a portion of personal income and on a per capita basis are taken into account, the other New England states fall in the top quarter as well. In short, New Englanders pay dearly for a tradition of services and progressiveness that is part of the political culture.

A more modern translation of progressive tradition is a ranking of "cultural liberalism," often used in conjunction with charting the ideological leanings of the states. One significant factor appears to be the relative lack of fundamentalist Protestant denominations. These groups are fairly small in New England and the Northeast generally. Whereas this tradition is especially strong and significantly influences the contemporary culture and politics in the South and the West, fundamentalist Protestants average less than 5 percent of the population in New England.

Along with some other progressive states, the entire region has strict hate crime laws that increase penalties for crimes motivated by racial, religious, or ethnic prejudice; New England states also have laws that offer protection for and recognition of the rights of homosexual groups. Vermont passed the most progressive legislation in the nation in recognizing same-sex civil unions in 2001, but that legislation apparently pushed voters a bit too far, and they expressed their displeasure by giving back control of the legislature to the Republicans and starting a "Take Back Vermont" movement. Whatever the tolerant leanings of New Englanders toward minorities, it is worth noting that minority populations are relatively small in New England. The New England states rank in the bottom half all states in total black population, with African Americans accounting for less than 1 percent of the population in Maine, New Hampshire, and Vermont. In Rhode Island, Connecticut, and Massachusetts the Hispanic population will probably grow to almost 10 percent over the next two decades, while in the northern-tier states Hispanics constitute approximately 2 percent of the population.

Civility manifests itself in another interesting way: the distinct lack of crime that has long characterized New England. Many argue that violence is as "American as apple pie," but this is not true in New England. Surveying a range of indices, we can see a distinct pattern that makes New England clearly the lowest in terms of regional crime rates. More specifically, the New England states cluster among the bottom 10 in all indices of overall rates of crime, violent crime, murder and rape, and property crime. This in turn creates a relatively small regional prison population. Capital punishment is uncommon. Of the six New England states, only Connecticut and New Hampshire have provisions for the death penalty, but they have not used it since 1960 and 1939, respectively.

In the early 21st century, the class, labor, and ethnic divisions that characterized interest-group politics, especially in southern New England during the early 20th century, appear to have been muted. Although hardball, self-interested, and sometimes corrupt politics can still be found in the region, and many groups still harbor intolerance, bias, and a complete lack of public regard, New England remains true to a moralistic culture that in many ways reflects its founding ideals. In an intensely individualistic and modern society, glimpses of the gentler communitarian legacy forged so long ago can still be observed in the politics of New England.

Kristi Anderson, *The Creation of a Democratic Majority, 1928–1936* (1979); Lawrence Becker, "New England as a Region," *Polity* 30 (1997); Daniel J. Elazar, *American Federalism: A View from the States* (1966); Steven P. Erie, *Rainbow's End: Irish-Americans and the Dilemmas of Urban Machine Politics, 1840–1985* (1988); Robert S. Erikson, Gerald C. Wright, and John P. McIver, *Statehouse Democracy: Public Opinion and Policy in the American States* (1993); James Garand, "Partisan Change and Shifting Expenditure Priorities in the American States," *American Politics Quarterly* 13 (1985); Virginia Gray, Russell L. Hanson, and Herbert Jacob, eds., *Politics in the American States: A Comparative Analysis,* 7th ed. (1999); Kendra A. Hovey and Harold A. Hovey, *CQ's State Fact Finder: Rankings across America* (2002); Everett Carll Ladd, Jr., and Charles D. Hadley, *Transformations of the American Party System: Political Coalitions from the New Deal to the 1970s,* 2d ed. (1978); Duane Lockard, *New England State Politics* (1959); Wilson Carey McWilliams, *The Idea of Fraternity in America* (1973); Jerome M. Mileur, ed., *Parties and Politics in the New England States* (1997); Perry Miller, *Orthodoxy in Massachusetts: 1630–1650* (1970 [1933]); Maureen Moakley, *Rhode Island Politics and Government* (2001); Edmund S. Morgan, *Roger Williams: The Church and State* (1967); James A. Morone, *The Democratic Wish: Popular Participation and the Limits of American Government* (1990); Samuel C. Patterson, "The Political Cultures of the American States," *Journal of Politics* 30 (1968); Walter A. Rosenbaum, *Political Culture* (1975); Ira Sharkansky, "The Utility of Elazar's Political Culture," *Polity* 2 (1969); Garry Wills, *Inventing America: Jefferson's Declaration of Independence* (1978); Gordon S. Wood, *The Radicalism of the American Revolution* (1991).

Maureen F. Moakley

Aldrich, Nelson W. (1841–1915) Politician, financier, U.S. representative, and U.S. senator. Nelson Wilmarth Aldrich, one of the most powerful Republican senators of the late 19th and early 20th centuries, was born on a farm in Foster, R.I. He augmented his basic common-school education with energetic activity in fraternal societies, debating clubs, and lyceums. As a teenager, Aldrich mastered parliamentary law and the major points in the raging debates between the proponents of free trade, protectionism, and currency reform. After serving briefly in the Civil War, he worked his way into a management position at a local wholesale grocery and in 1866 married Abby Chapman. Their daughter Abby married John D. Rockefeller, Jr., amassed a significant collection of American folk art, and was the grandmother of Nelson Aldrich Rockefeller, U.S. vice president from 1974 to 1977.

Aldrich's engaging personality and financial expertise earned him a seat on the Providence City Council in 1869 and the presidency of that body in 1871. He became a state representative in 1875 and Speaker of the Rhode Island House of Representatives a year later. Under the guidance of U.S. senator Henry Bowen Anthony, the local Republican Party groomed Aldrich for higher office: the House in 1879 and the Senate in 1881. His Washington career lasted more than 30 years and elevated him to the powerful chairmanship of the Senate Finance Committee (1899–1911). Unofficially dubbed general manager of the United States, Aldrich became a close confidant to several Republican presidents and the leading member of a powerful GOP legislative coterie. He wrote most of the protectionist tariffs, ushered into law the Gold Standard Act of 1900, chaired the National Monetary Commission in 1908, and, after retiring in 1911, helped institute the Federal Reserve System, which went into effect in 1913.

Throughout his career Aldrich promoted tariffs and conservative monetary policies to protect northeastern business interests, especially the New England textile industry, from foreign competition. He championed many national trusts, personally seeking a commercial peace amid cutthroat competition, and advocated lower duties on imported raw materials such as wool, lead, hides, and sugar for American processors while simultaneously crafting legislation to increase the tariff on finished foreign products. In 1890 his duty on processed sugar produced windfall earnings of $35 million for the American Sugar Refining Company of New York City. In grateful appreciation, the firm advanced Aldrich $1.5 million to purchase and electrify the Union Horse Railroad in Providence. The *New York*

Times revealed the transaction and hinted at bribery in June 1894, but the allegations never significantly affected Aldrich's career.

Aldrich ordinarily stood aloof from Rhode Island politics, leaving everyday matters to the legendary Republican boss Charles Brayton, who managed the corrupt political machine that kept Aldrich in office. Before the passage of the 17th Amendment in 1913, the Rhode Island General Assembly chose the state's U.S. senators and essentially bestowed Aldrich with a lifetime appointment. His congressional seniority and financial wizardry made him a target for progressive Republicans and the era's muckrakers, as did his opposition to popular measures such as the income tax, the Pure Food Act, and the inheritance tax. Despite his humble beginnings, Aldrich presented himself as a natural aristocrat "who refused to play to the crowd."

During his years in office, Aldrich slowly amassed a significant fortune and in 1907 sold his interest in the Providence street railway to J. P. Morgan for a price that allegedly made the latter gasp. Aldrich retired to his magnificent estate in Warwick, R.I., in 1911. He died in New York City in 1915.

Nelson W. Aldrich, *Nelson W. Aldrich: A Register and Index of His Papers in the Library of Congress*, (1973); Nathaniel Stephenson, *Nelson W. Aldrich: A Leader in American Politics* (1930); Jerome Sternstein, "Corruption in the Gilded Age Senate: Nelson W. Aldrich and the Sugar Trust," *Capitol Studies* 6 (1978).

Scott Molloy

Bailey, John M. (1904–75) Politician and Democratic Party leader. John Moran Bailey was born into a prominent Irish Catholic family in Hartford. Educated at Catholic University and Harvard Law School, he was admitted to the bar in both Connecticut and Massachusetts in 1929. While pursuing an independent legal practice in Hartford, he began a singularly successful career as a party organizer in local, state, and eventually national politics.

Bailey began his political career in Hartford ward politics. He joined the Democratic machine of city boss Thomas Spellacy as an errand runner in 1930 and quickly moved up the ranks, becoming a member of the Democratic state committee in 1932. In 1938 Bailey turned against Spellacy and successfully placed his own candidates on the ballot at Hartford's Democratic caucus. One of these was the upstart politician Abraham Ribicoff, with whose fortunes Bailey's political success later become intertwined.

Bailey reached the top of the Connecticut Democratic Party in 1946 when he orchestrated the gubernatorial nomination of Wilbur Snow over heavily favored Chester Bowles

at the statewide convention. As a reward for his support, Snow nominated Bailey for the position of Democratic state chairman. Snow was soundly defeated in the general election of 1946, but Bailey was elected head of the Democratic Party. From this behind-the-scenes position Bailey would decisively change the fortunes of that party in Connecticut.

As Democratic state chairman, Bailey took advantage of new electoral demographics resulting from an influx of Irish, Italian, and Polish immigrants after the turn of the century that would make Connecticut firmly Democratic by 1958. He assisted in electing Governors Chester Bowles, Abraham Ribicoff, John Dempsey, and Ella Grasso and Senators Thomas Dodd and Abraham Ribicoff. He also consistently raised Democratic Party representation at the state level, an effort crowned by the Democratic sweep of both houses in 1958.

In 1956 Bailey backed Senator John F. Kennedy's bid for the vice presidential nomination and after Kennedy's defeat immediately began working toward his presidential nomination in 1960. After Kennedy's election Bailey was appointed chair of the Democratic National Committee. Although Bailey retained that position after Kennedy's assassination in 1963, President Lyndon B. Johnson relegated him to a minor role in the 1964 presidential election. In 1966, with Bailey still at its head, the Democratic National Committee was not adequately funded, and Democrats made a poor showing in that year's midterm elections. After Johnson's withdrawal from the presidential race and Hubert Humphrey's defeat in 1968, Bailey returned to Connecticut and held the position of Democratic state chair until his death in 1975.

Although he was known as Boss Bailey throughout his long career, Bailey could hardly be characterized as a typical party machine boss. Rather, he oversaw the most sweeping political reforms in Connecticut history, including the creation of a state primary (1955), reform of the local court system (1959), reorganization of county government (1959), and the drawing of a new and more representative electoral map (1965). In effect, Bailey presided over the dismantling of Connecticut's political parties as they had previously been known, removed many avenues of patronage through organizational reform, and substantially weakened the party chair's position by allowing for primaries. Similarly, his choice of candidates for the state's highest offices—particularly the liberal Bowles, the reformer Ribicoff, and the "good government" leader Grasso—could hardly be considered typical of a party hack. Faced with a Connecticut electorate of which fully one-third were reform-minded independents, John Bailey fashioned a Democratic Party that could win those independent votes but in the long term, ironically, this weakened the party organization that had made reform possible.

Joseph I. Lieberman, *The Power Broker: A Biography of John M. Bailey, Modern Political Boss* (1966); Duane Lockard, *New England State Politics* (1959).

Patrick J. Deneen

Boston City Government

The current structure of Boston's city government is the product of old ethnic suspicions and more recent ethnic and racial tensions that affect public functions. Boston is unusual in the amount of state oversight it must endure, a legacy of early-20th century Brahmin distrust concerning the capability and integrity of the new wave of Irish public officials. Within Boston officials' sphere of control, the mayor is a powerful figure and the city council is relatively weak. The city charter has grown piecemeal over time. Reforms since the 1980s have been aimed at both increasing government efficiency and fostering diversity in governmental bodies—but these two goals have sometimes clashed.

Boston's city government is subject to substantial interference from the state legislature. Most ordinances passed by the city council must be forwarded to the legislature in the form of a home rule petition, that is, a request to be free of direct state legislative control on a particular issue. These petitions are necessary because of the legal doctrine that municipalities are the creations of the state legislature without autonomy over their own affairs. Such submissions may be as crucial to government functioning as a tax increase or as minor as a measure to require the licensing of bicycle messengers. Much to the frustration of local leaders, the state legislature is under no obligation to deal with Boston's home rule petitions quickly. It may delay action, reject a petition, or amend it into something the city council finds unacceptable. For example, in 1995 the council passed an ordinance that would extend insurance coverage to the partners of gay and lesbian city workers. The ordinance required legislative approval and arrived at the State House in 1996, where it languished for two years, reportedly because of the opposition of the Speaker of the House. When the legislation finally passed, a governor who had long supported the bill vetoed it in an effort to shore up his conservative support.

State officials seem unable to resist tinkering with Boston's governmental initiatives. A proposal to develop and improve the bleak plaza in front of City Hall was halted by the state's attorney general, who ruled that any change to open space is subject to a two-thirds vote by the legislature, a decision that enraged the mayor. In 1997, acting at the behest of police unions, the legislature stripped the city's police commissioner of the power to make personnel changes without union approval. Boston was not even allowed to appoint its own police commissioner for most of the 20th century; this responsibility was restored by the legislature only in 1962.

Early in the century, with ethnic and class tensions smoldering, the Brahmin-controlled state legislature began to rein in the growing power of the Boston Irish. The administration of Mayor John F. "Honey Fitz" Fitzgerald (grandfather of President John F. Kennedy) was so plagued by corruption that Fitzgerald was forced to accept oversight of city spending by a finance commission appointed by the legislature. The Boston Finance Commission, now appointed by the governor but paid for by the city, still exists to look over the mayor's shoulder and monitor local spending programs. The governor also controls appointments to local licensing boards, such as those that regulate liquor. Nonpartisan elections are another of the city's legacies. The Brahmins saw that white ethnic groups, especially the Irish, were flocking to the Democratic Party, endangering any hopes of a Republican gaining an electoral post. The strategy worked for some time, though Boston city government has not seen a Republican elected official for years.

Within the city itself, government power is configured in the form of a strong mayor and a weak city council. With rare exceptions, the mayor enjoys autonomy to make appointments to high government positions without the approval of the city council. The mayor's sweeping control over city jobs also places the executive in a strong political position relative to the councillors. The mayor is usually the only local politician with an effective citywide political organization (consisting mostly of city workers), an asset that can be used to assist councillors who curry the executive's favor or to bedevil those who get out of line. The mayoral position comes up for election every four years, though in contrast to the past, now spirited contests occur only when the seat is open. The councillors must run every two years, giving the mayor added freedom to mold a malleable council.

The mayor also enjoys a strong position on budgetary matters. The executive sends the council a proposed budget, and the council may cut particular spending items but may not increase spending on any item. The mayor does not have a line item veto, so if the council has tinkered too extensively with departmental cuts, the mayor must sign the budget as returned or decline to sign. If this happens, the city will continue to function on a one-twelfth budget based on the spending plan of the previous fiscal year. But such procedures are brief because the interim spending plans often fail to meet collective bargaining agreements, and the preponderance of power in the executive seat puts the mayor in a strong position to enforce spending priorities. The council may override mayoral vetoes of ordinances.

The passage in 1980 of the statewide ballot initiative Proposition 2½ has substantially affected Boston's spending. The proposition limits the growth of the property tax in the state's municipalities and has been effective in keeping tax rates relatively stable. Before passage, it was not unknown for Boston's incumbent mayors to increase spending significantly in reelection years. This practice has been restrained. Some sidestepped Proposition 2½ by overriding the tax limit at the polls, a tactic that Boston's leaders disliked. While most of Boston's residents are now relatively young and new to the city, most of its voters are older, longtime residents who are reluctant to authorize new taxes.

In 1981 Boston's voters approved a plan to restructure the membership of the elected city council and school committee. For 30 years, the city had elected nine councillors and five committee members at large. The plan imposed a new structure: each body would elect four members citywide, and another nine members would be elected from newly created districts. Reform backers believed the plan would bring elected officials closer to their constituents, promote electoral competition, and foster recognition of the city's growing minority communities. The effort to promote competition has floundered; incumbents dominate the at-large and district positions. Critics also argue that the district councillors have adopted a shortsighted concern for constituent services over policy. The measure has helped promote minority officeholding, though Boston's conservative white voting base continues to make it difficult for minority office seekers to win citywide.

Racial and ethnic concerns seem never far from conflicts over the structure of city government. In 1983 the first election to be held under the new form was briefly halted when minority plaintiffs convinced a federal judge that the district plan passed by the council was based on an out-of-date census that disadvantaged minority citizens. A new plan was hastily drawn up and approved by the court, which found it to be fair to the minority population. The courts have also become involved over the years in reforming minority hiring programs in some city departments.

The restructuring of the school committee,

however, was found to be unsatisfactory. Elected committee members had long since earned the reputation of placing patronage concerns over educational issues. Several members—particularly during Boston's busing crisis in the mid-1970s—had also become notorious for racist comments, corruption, and general buffoonery. At the urging of Mayor Raymond L. Flynn, the council passed a home rule petition abolishing the elected school committee, which was to be replaced with a seven-member committee appointed by the mayor. As the petition wended its way through the legislature, it attracted the opposition of many of Boston's minority leaders, including elected officials. They argued that the elected committee provided an opportunity for increasing the number of minority elected officials as Boston's demographics changed, and that an appointed board could harm the relationship between the committee and the city's large minority- student population. The council fumed that the school committee might spend the city into bankruptcy while the legislation was pending. Finally, recognizing that the school system was "in desperate need of fundamental change," the governor signed the petition passed by the legislature. Still, the outgoing committee managed to hire a new school superintendent against the mayor's wishes. A 1996 effort to reinstate the elected school committee failed at the polls as Mayor Thomas M. Menino mobilized in opposition. Mayor Menino has adopted educational progress as a touchstone and appointed his own superintendent, and some progress has been evident in Boston's public schools.

Boston generally has enjoyed effective local government. Despite the conflicts that play out in the city, residents have regarded Mayors Flynn and Menino as providing sincere and effective efforts.

Matthew Brelis, "State to Boston: 'Beg,'" *The Boston Globe*, July 5, 1998; James J. Connolly, *The Triumph of Ethnic Progressivism: Urban Political Culture in Boston, 1900–1925* (1998); John H. Mollenkopf, *The Contested City* (1983); Eric A. Nordlinger, *Decentralizing the City: A Study of Boston's Little City Halls* (1972); Thomas H. O'Connor, *The Boston Irish: A Political History* (1995); O'Connor, *Building a New Boston: Politics and Urban Renewal, 1950–1970* (1993).

Maurice Cunningham

Brahmins and Yankees New England's first European settlers were predominantly English Puritans who proclaimed themselves a chosen people, destined to establish a pious commonwealth unprecedented in its fusion of church, community, and state. By the 18th century, the term *Yankee* was particularly applied to descendants of these early Puritans.

Senators Henry Cabot Lodge, Jr., and Leverett Saltonstall with performing elephants, Topsfield, Mass., 1951

But New Englanders were so prominent in the American Revolution that the British generally identified all citizens of the new United States as Yankees. At the time of the nation's founding, New England Yankees made up roughly half the white population and had a commonality of religion and culture not found in other regions of the country. Yankees celebrated Boston as the capital of New England, hailed by one observer as blessed by "more strictly one people, with one common center and capital, than any other equal amount of the population of the United States." Such homogeneity led the revolutionary firebrand Samuel Adams to envision no less than a "Christian Sparta" emerging in late-18th-century Massachusetts. The original Calvinist theology that inspired Puritan settlers would be refashioned for later generations by a series of fiery preachers, from Lyman Beecher to Washington Gladden, unifying Yankees around the Congregational Church and its Unitarian and Universalist offshoots.

Whereas most New England Yankees lived humbly as farmers, sailors, fishers, artisans, and industrial workers, others saw themselves as select gentry called upon to serve as stewards of American civilization. This would-be Yankee aristocracy, later described by Oliver Wendell Holmes as "the Brahmin caste of New England," was composed of descendants of an old Puritan elite, as well as of farmers and merchants who amassed impressive fortunes after the Revolution. As much as Puritan leaders considered their settlement a shin-

ing "city upon a hill" inspired by God for others to emulate, New England Brahmins believed they represented the nation's intellectual, spiritual, and political lifeblood. Before 1800, members of Boston's Federalist gentry stood confidently at the forefront of American political affairs. Yet the ascendance of Thomas Jefferson and his Democratic-Republican supporters in the election of 1800 not only marked the demise of John Adams and the Federalists, but also signaled the waning influence of New England in national affairs.

Adjusting to the new world produced by the dislocations of Jeffersonianism, Unitarianism, and industrialism, a new generation of Brahmin Federalists such as Harrison Gray Otis and Josiah Quincy aggressively fought to retain control of New England politics and to uphold Boston in particular as a model of the virtuous community. This younger breed of Brahmins reluctantly accepted the inevitability of such democratic developments as universal manhood suffrage and party politics. Throwing themselves into the rough-and-tumble of political campaigning, new Brahmin leaders persuaded working-class voters of Boston to empower the "happy and respectable classes" to protect "the less prosperous portions of the community." With a sense of noblesse oblige, Quincy served six terms as an energetic mayor of Boston, rallying fellow conservatives to revitalize the city's physical, social, and economic conditions during the 1820s and 1830s. Proper New Englanders became heavily involved in a rich variety of humanitarian and educational undertakings during the first decades of the 19th century, promoting public education, temperance, humane prisons, urban renewal, pollution control, and other causes. They also gave generously to Harvard and Yale, historical and genealogical societies, and the arts and for construction of patriotic monuments and parks. While control of national politics remained at best elusive for proper New Englanders during the Jacksonian era, they took great solace in the fact that voters of their own region, and of the city of Boston especially, had the good judgment to entrust government to "the wise, the well-born, and the good."

The antebellum years of the 1840s and 1850s were a time of upheaval for upper-class New Englanders, as younger notables who embraced more radical social-reform movements, new religious beliefs, and utopian notions of community challenged the Brahmin establishment. "We are a little wild here with numberless projects of social reform," an exuberant Ralph Waldo Emerson wrote the English historian Thomas Carlyle in 1840. "Not a reading man but has a draft of a new Community in his waistcoat pocket." Highly educated, fervently religious, and stridently idealistic, young Brahmins crusaded for social reforms that many of their elders deemed too radical—including pacifism, women's rights, and the abolition of slavery. Younger members of New England's social aristocracy believed they stood in the moral vanguard of the country, expressing an impulse for human perfectibility reminiscent of earlier Puritan yearnings.

Brahmin political influence steadily eroded over the course of the late 19th and 20th centuries, as new ethnic groups, especially Irish newcomers joined by Italians, Jews, and others, ascended to important positions of power. In the Brahmin mind, new immigration was to be blamed for a host of disquieting social and economic problems associated with industrialization and urbanization at the turn of the 20th century. New England's original Yankee stock, they feared, was under siege from an inferior foreign population lacking in virtue and hereditary vitality. During the Progressive Era, young people from prominent Brahmin families, educated at Harvard and keenly troubled by the demographic changes occurring in their region, formed the nativist Immigration Restriction League. They vigorously renounced the egalitarian idealism expressed by Yankee opinion leaders before the Civil War and celebrated Anglo-Saxonism with social notables across the country. But even as such prominent Brahmins as Harvard president A. Lawrence Lowell and Senator Henry Cabot Lodge spoke of "the need for homogeneity in democracy," they were acutely

aware that political control was slipping from their grasp. Some Brahmins, however, embraced aspects of the reform movement led by the so-called mugwumps: direct election of senators, woman suffrage, electoral reform, and civil service exams. Republican reformers like the New Hampshire governor Robert P. Bass carried the Progressive cause to victory.

To the chagrin of Republican Brahmins, the Irish and other new ethnic groups recast political affairs in New England by breathing life into the region's Democratic Party organizations and electing Democratic candidates. Boston, the city that Yankees claimed as their capital, became an important hub of ethnic political ascendancy at the turn of the 20th century. Boston's first Irish mayors, Hugh O'Brien and Patrick Collins, were virtually indistinguishable from their Yankee predecessors in their fidelity to low tax rates, aesthetic improvements of the city, and efficient administration. But Irish party machines devoted to the Democratic Party had taken root in local neighborhoods across Boston. While highly competitive with one another, Irish ward bosses commonly saw politics as a means of assisting their own people, who encountered daunting economic and social barriers imposed by the Yankee establishment. "The great mass of people are interested in only three things—food, clothing, and shelter," the ward boss Martin Lomasney reflected. "A politician in a district such as mine sees to it that his people get these things."

For several years, Progressive Era Yankees found consolation in the fact that rivalries between Irish ward bosses saved the Bay State from the sort of omnipotent Tammany machine that dominated New York politics. Yet Brahmin Republicans were shaken to their core in 1905 when the brash North End boss John "Honey Fitz" Fitzgerald won the mayoral race and effectively centralized control of Boston's Democratic machine. Rallying to save their city from unseemly machine politics, proper Yankees formed a Good Government Association that successfully championed a watchdog agency to monitor government finances, nonpartisan elections, and civil service requirements for city employees. Despite such efforts, Fitzgerald easily defeated candidates endorsed by Brahmin reformers, calling on ethnic supporters to defy the Yankee merchants' undue influence with the battle cry "Manhood against Money."

Another charismatic Irish politician, James Michael Curley, transformed Boston politics when Fitzgerald retired in 1914. Curley transcended the city's existing power structure, using his ample skills as a fiery public speaker to win election as mayor of Boston without the support of either Irish ward bosses or Brahmin

elites. Using city hall to build a formidable personal constituency, offering jobs to loyalists and public assistance to needy voters, Curley dominated political life in Boston until after World War II. When construction projects drained the city's coffers, Curley used whatever pressure was necessary to obtain loans from the Brahmin bankers of Boston, including threats that city inspectors might need to close certain banks for improper wiring or plumbing. During campaigns, Curley delighted in mocking proper Yankees who opposed his administrations. He once characterized Boston's Brahmin elites as little more than "clubs of female faddists, old gentlemen with disordered livers, or pessimists croaking over imaginary good old days and ignoring the sunlit present." Curley also playfully proposed selling Boston's Public Gardens and constructing a water-pumping station under the Boston Common, provoking outraged protests from frustrated Yankees.

Such tactics intensified the political gulf between Yankees and other ethnic groups not only within Boston, but also in state politics. Indeed, the "Curley machine" and Irish Democrats often found themselves at odds with Yankee Republicans, who tended to control the state legislature. Similar political cleavages developed in Connecticut and Rhode Island state politics, where various ethnic groups aligned with the Democratic Party and eventually overwhelmed an old-guard Yankee Republican elite.

The steady political decline over the past century and a half of the once preeminent Brahmin establishment has taken much of the edge off past rivalries. Yet as late as 1987 the legendary former House Speaker Thomas "Tip" O'Neill, Jr., railed against "confident Ivy League Yankees who had everything handed to them in life." Evoking sentiments expressed by Irish ward bosses decades earlier, O'Neill wrote that he "dreamed of bringing my own people—and *all* Americans who weren't born to wealth or advantage—into the great American tent of opportunity." Long after Yankee families of substance have lost their hold on civic affairs, images of Brahmin privilege have staying power in New England politics.

Henry Adams, *The Education of Henry Adams* (1918); James Michael Curley, *I'd Do It Again: A Record of All My Uproarious Years* (1957); Oscar Handlin, *Boston's Immigrants, 1790–1880* (1959); Laurence Lader, *The Bold Brahmins: New England's War against Slavery* (1961); Samuel Eliot Morison, *Harrison Gray Otis: Urbane Federalist* (1969); Thomas H. O'Connor, *Bibles, Brahmins, and Bosses: A Short History of Boston* (1984); Thomas P. O'Neill, *Man of the House: The Life and Political Memoirs of Speaker Tip O'Neill* (1987); Barbara Miller Solomon, *Ancestors and Immigrants: A Changing New England Tradition* (1956).

Daniel J. Tichenor

Brooke, Edward W. III (1919–) U.S.

senator. In 1966 Edward William Brooke III, a Republican from Massachusetts, became the first African American from any state elected to the U.S. Senate since the end of Reconstruction.

Born to Helen (Seldon) and Edward Brooke, Jr., young Ed Brooke grew up in an integrated, middle-class neighborhood in Washington, D.C. "I was a happy child," he later recalled. "I grew up segregated, but there was not much feeling of being shut out of anything." Brooke's father, a graduate of Howard University Law School, worked as an attorney for the Veterans Administration, and his commitment to public service made a strong impression on his only son. Brooke attended the prestigious Dunbar High School in Washington before going on to Howard University, where he received his bachelor of science degree in 1941.

During World War II Brooke served in the 366th Combat Infantry Regiment—an all-black unit—in North Africa and Italy, where he rose from the rank of second lieutenant to captain, won a Bronze Star, and met his future wife, Remigia Ferrari-Scacco. After the war ended, Brooke entered law school at Boston University in 1946. There, in his final year, Brooke edited the school's law review. In 1948 he passed the Massachusetts bar examination.

The move to Boston proved significant in that it also led to a political career that might not have been possible in Washington, where during the 1950s African Americans still were prohibited from voting. After three unsuccessful bids for public office, Brooke won election as attorney general of the commonwealth of Massachusetts in 1962, making him the first African American in the country to be elected

to a major statewide office in almost a century. As attorney general, Brooke earned a reputation as a gradualist when he helped defuse a school boycott planned by the black community in protest of de facto segregation in Boston schools.

Such pragmatism helped get him elected to two terms in the U.S. Senate beginning in 1967. As a senator, Brooke quickly made a name for himself as an advocate of public housing, affirmative action, and school integration. Following urban riots in the summer of 1967, President Lyndon Johnson appointed Brooke to the President's Commission on Civil Disorders. That same year, despite campaigning as a peace candidate, Brooke traveled to Vietnam and returned a supporter of Johnson's policies there. His concomitant criticism of Martin Luther King's heightened opposition to the war as harmful to the Civil Rights movement alienated him from other civil rights leaders.

In 1968 and 1972 Brooke supported Richard Nixon in the presidential elections but became the first Republican to call for Nixon's resignation as the Watergate scandal unfolded. Brooke lost his Senate seat to Paul Tsongas in 1978 and soon after returned to private practice in Washington. He became chairman of the National Low-Income Housing Coalition in 1979. In 1992 a former aide implicated Brooke in an influence-peddling scandal centered in the Department of Housing and Urban Development during the Reagan administration, but he was never indicted.

Edward Brooke, *The Challenge of Change: Crisis in Our Two-Party System* (1966); John Henry Cutler, *Ed Brooke: Biography of a Senator* (1972).

Michael S. Foley

Buckley Family The Buckleys are one of

the most distinguished political families of the latter half of the 20th century. William F. Buckley, Sr. (1881–1958), and particularly his two most prominent children—the politician and onetime U.S. senator from New York, James (1923–), and the writer, editor, and journalist, William Jr. (1925–)—have played an important role in developing a respectable conservative philosophy and establishing the conservative political movement in the United States. A wealthy oilman, William F. Buckley, Sr., raised his family in Connecticut; most of his children attended prestigious prep schools, and his sons went to Yale. William Sr.'s conservatism, reflected in the work of his children, can be seen as a reaction against the liberal tendencies of late-20th-century New England politics. The family's efforts, however, have mainly been focused on reshaping national politics. Their endeavors reveal the difficulty of merging a cultural conservatism that values tradition and Christian morality with the individualism of classic liberalism and the dynamic and transformative power of capitalism.

William F. Buckley, Jr., has dealt with this problem in his numerous books—most notably *God and Man at Yale* (1951) and *Up from Liberalism* (1959)—and in his bimonthly magazine, the *National Review*. Founded in 1955, this magazine was William Jr.'s first foray into national political affairs and has served as a literary home to many conservative writers. William Jr.'s fame was enhanced by the weekly television series *Firing Line*, on which he debated with many of the most significant political players and thinkers of the day. In these and other television appearances, the erudite Buckley spoke on numerous topics in an admittedly upper-class accent that solidified his reputation as a member of the New England elite, despite his Catholic background.

The Buckleys sought to create a powerful conservative movement that would harmonize all voices on the political right. Forged in opposition to the activist government liberalism of the Democratic Party, this conservatism also coalesced during the 1950s around a hatred of the atheistic communism of the Soviet Union. William Jr. achieved this synthesis at a time when anti-Semitism and unthinking isolationism still clouded much of what passed for conservatism.

In the 1960s the Buckleys played a key role in founding New York state's Conservative Party and in creating the conservative youth group Young Americans for Freedom. In 1965 William Jr. ran for mayor of New York City on the Conservative Party ticket and gained more than 13 percent of the vote; in 1970 James Buckley won the Senate race in New York as a

Senator Edward W. Brooke III (waving) with civil rights activist Henry Hampton (left), and Roxbury (Boston) community leaders, 1972

William F. Buckley, Jr., speaks at the Young Americans for Freedom convention, Boston, 1981

Conservative. While in the Senate, James Buckley established himself as a consistent opponent of big government and a believer in individual freedom. Although James lost his reelection bid in 1976, the Conservative Party has lived on in New York. After leaving the Senate, James Buckley became a federal judge on the U.S. Court of Appeals.

In recent years, the limitations of the alliance between libertarianism and cultural conservatism have come to the fore. As the threat of Soviet communism receded, the coalition that the Buckleys had worked so hard to create—never particularly stable—began to show signs of dividing along the expected fault lines. It is not surprising, then, that William F. Buckley, Jr., now devotes most of his time to writing spy novels and that the best-known Buckley of the baby-boomer generation is the wickedly satirical novelist Christopher Buckley (born in 1952, son of William Jr.), whose works include *Thank You for Smoking* (1994). When the conservative movement was young, the Buckleys wrote with urgency and justified their cause. As the movement has aged, their commentary has become laced with humor and irony.

L. Clayton Dubois, "The First Family of Conservatism," *New York Times Magazine,* August 9, 1970; Charles Lam Markmann, *The Buckleys: A Family Examined* (1973); Mitchell S. Ross, *The Literary Politicians* (1978); Mark Royden Winchell, *William F. Buckley, Jr.* (1984).

Joseph Romance

Bulger, William (1934–) Politician, president of the Massachusetts Senate, and president of the University of Massachusetts, Boston. William Michael Bulger, long-time

president of the Massachusetts Senate, was born in Boston and moved with his family to the Old Harbor Village housing project in South Boston when he was four years old; he has lived in the neighborhood ever since. Bulger is a "Triple Eagle"—a graduate of Boston College High School, Boston College (1958), and Boston College Law School (1961)—as well as an army veteran. He married Mary Foley in 1960; they have nine children.

Elected to represent South Boston in the Massachusetts House of Representatives in 1960, Bulger won a seat in the state senate in 1970 and became president of the senate in 1978. He held the post until 1996, when he resigned to become president of the University of Massachusetts, Boston. A Democrat, Bulger's political career has combined a traditional "lunch-bucket" liberalism, providing generous government benefits to his constituents, with a devotion to his home neighborhood, which is largely Catholic and socially conservative. One of few recent Massachusetts politicians to have allies in both conservative and liberal camps, Bulger has joined with liberal social-service advocates to support public housing and generous welfare benefits, while combining with conservatives to oppose abortion and court-ordered busing to achieve racial integration. A fierce defender of the prerogatives of the state legislature, Bulger opposes term limits and believes that the legislature should write its own rules of procedure.

In his 17 years as senate president, Bulger established a leadership style that his critics labeled "iron-fisted" and his defenders described as "firm." He rewarded his allies by elevating them to positions of leadership, and expected loyalty in return. A seeker of consen-

sus, Bulger and his committee chairs often mapped out senate proceedings in advance. This style promoted a sense of collective responsibility that gave members some degree of protection on controversial votes. His successor, Thomas Birmingham, sought to continue Bulger's leadership style.

Bulger consistently defended South Boston's interests and rewarded his loyal neighbors with patronage positions in the government and court system. In the early 1970s, Bulger led the fight against a school desegregation plan that bused black students to South Boston High School and white students from "Southie" to schools outside the neighborhood. Bulger attacked busing as "social engineering" and argued that it imposed huge burdens on urban, working-class white and black families, while leaving suburban liberals untouched.

During this controversial period, Bulger's relationship with the local media soured. At times the vilification of Bulger in the *Boston Globe* and the *Boston Herald* has been extraordinary, with one columnist referring to him continually as the "corrupt Midget" and others hinting at a link between the senator's business and the activities of his older brother, James "Whitey" Bulger, a reputed Boston gangland figure who was recently identified as a long-time FBI informant. Boston's newspapers have not escaped Bulger's wit, however; on several occasions he has described the *Boston Globe,* the more "upscale" of the two, as the "*Boston Herald* with verbs."

Bulger is famous for his annual Saint Patrick's Day breakfasts, at which thousands of guests enjoy corned beef and cabbage while governors, mayors, legislators, and even judges rise to the podium and compete with Bulger's jests and songs. A lover of Irish music, Bulger kept a fiddler on his staff for years, and one of his sons enjoys local renown as a master of the Irish fiddle. Bulger published *While the Music Lasts: My Life in Politics* in 1996.

As president of the University of Massachusetts, Boston, Bulger was a traditionalist who was educated under the old Jesuit curriculum. Appointed to bring a fresh approach to the problems of the state's higher-education system, Bulger pledged to stabilize the university's finances, to raise admission standards, and to reestablish the public's respect for public higher education—difficult challenges to meet in a state with chronic budget problems and an abundance of prestigious private colleges and universities. In June 2003 Bulger testified about his brother's activities before the U.S. House Government Reform Committee. Charging that Bulger's "evasive" testimony made him "unfit" to be president of the university, Massachusetts governor Mitt

Romney called for Bulger's resignation—a move that was derailed by the Board of Trustees, who gave him a vote of confidence in late June. Following months of controversy, Bulger resigned, on August 6, 2003.

Richard Brookhiser, "Dancing with the Girl That Brung Him," *The New Yorker,* October 28, 1991; William H. Honan, "An Icon of State Politics Is Picked to Lead U. Mass.," *New York Times,* November 29, 1995.

Dennis B. Hale

Bush Family The Bush family has had a long and prominent presence in New England, especially Connecticut and Maine. Prescott Sheldon Bush (1895–1972) was born in Columbus, Ohio; he attended school in Newport, R.I. (1908–13), and graduated from Yale University (1913–17). A member of the Connecticut National Guard, he later served with the Army Expeditionary Forces during World War I. On his return he entered the banking business, commuting to New York City from his home in Greenwich, Conn. He became involved in local politics as moderator of the Representative Town Meeting, the 148-member governing body in Greenwich (1940–52) before serving as a U.S. senator from Connecticut (1953–62). A strong advocate for fiscal responsibility in government, Bush served on the Senate Committee on Banking and Currency, sponsoring a price-stability amendment to the Employment Act of 1946. New England issues that concerned him included urban renewal legislation and tidal flooding; he sponsored the Bush Hurricane Survey Act, under which army engineers could prepare a community protection program against flooding, and the Bush-McCormack Act (with Congressman John W. McCormack) to facilitate construction of flood-protection works. Choosing not to run for reelection in 1962, Bush returned to the banking business; he died in New York City.

Prescott Bush's son George H. W. Bush was born in Milton, Mass., in 1924 and spent most of his childhood in Greenwich. After graduating from Phillips Academy in Andover, Mass., in 1942, Bush joined the navy, where he was the youngest commissioned pilot and won the Distinguished Flying Cross for courageous service as a bomber pilot in the Pacific. After his discharge he attended Yale University (1944–48), graduating with a degree in economics. Bush married Barbara Pierce in 1945 and subsequently moved to Texas, where he cofounded the Zapata Petroleum Corporation.

In Texas, after losing several attempts at local and national election, Bush retired from electoral politics and took a series of federal administrative appointments, including am-

President George H. W. Bush gives pep talk at Raytheon, Andover, Mass., 1991

bassador to the United Nations (1971–73); chief liaison officer in Beijing (1974–75), and director of the Central Intelligence Agency (1976–77). In 1980 Bush sought the presidency. Although he won all the New England primaries except New Hampshire's, Bush lost the nomination to Ronald Reagan; however, Reagan named Bush his vice presidential running mate. After serving as vice president from 1980 to 1988, Bush ran for president, becoming the first incumbent vice president since Martin Van Buren to be elected president in his own right.

George H. W. Bush's most important accomplishments as president came in foreign affairs: imprisoning the Panamanian dictator Manuel Noriega on drug and racketeering charges (1989) and rallying a coalition of Middle Eastern countries and Western nations to liberate Kuwait in the Persian Gulf War (1991). Bush also presided over the end of the Cold War, as communist rule of the Soviet Union collapsed in December 1991.

On the domestic side, having repeatedly pledged that he would impose no new taxes, Bush compromised with the Democrat-controlled Congress in 1989 on a tax hike. The end of the Cold War meant that thousands of defense workers lost their jobs. These economic problems had their effect: Bush lost his reelection bid to Democrat Bill Clinton. Since leaving the White House in 1993, George H. W. Bush has devoted his attention to building his presidential library, which opened in November 1997 on the campus of Texas A&M University in College Station.

George H. W. Bush's son George W. Bush was born in New Haven, Conn., in 1946. Shortly afterward, the family moved to Midland, Texas, where the younger Bush spent his childhood years. He returned to New England to attend Phillips Academy (1961–65), Yale University (1965–68), and Harvard University (1973–75), from which he earned a master's degree in business administration. Although George W. Bush spent nearly 14 years attending some of New England's most prestigious schools, he never became part of the region's culture. After receiving his MBA, he moved back to the place he considered home: Midland, where he met and married a Texan, Laura Welch, in 1977.

After losing his bid for a congressional seat in the district that included Midland in 1978, Bush concentrated on his business ventures, returning to politics in 1994, when he won election for governor against the incumbent, Ann Richards. As governor, Bush pursued an agenda of reducing taxes, improving education, instituting tort reform, and initiating a number of programs that allowed private agencies (many of them faith-based) to receive state funding for social work. In 1998 Bush became the first Republican governor in Texas history to win reelection.

In 2000 Bush entered the presidential race, running into trouble in his native New England, where he lost five of the six New England states to Arizona senator John McCain. Bush won only in Maine, the site of the family's summer vacation home at Walker's Point in Kennebunkport. Bush recouped, however, and won the Republican nomination, facing Vice President Al Gore. Although Gore defeated Bush in the popular vote, Bush won the electoral vote—the first time since 1876 that the winner of the popular vote had not won the presidency. The outcome of the 2000 election was controversial, especially in Florida, where just 537 votes separated Bush and Gore in the official statewide tally. The U.S. Supreme Court, in *Bush v. Gore*, awarded the state, and the presidency, to George W. Bush by a five-to-four vote.

As president, Bush's first goal was reform of the nation's education system. He won congressional passage of the "No Child Left Behind" Act (2001), which mandated federal testing in the public schools at specified grade levels. Bush also won a $1.35 trillion reduction in federal tax rates. A second tax cut ($350 billion) was enacted in 2003.

But after the al Qaeda terrorist attacks on New York City and Washington, D.C., on September 11, 2001, Bush turned his attention to fighting terrorism. He ordered an attack against Afghanistan in October, seeking to destroy the al Qaeda training camps, which were supported by Afghanistan's Taliban-controlled government. Although the government was quickly toppled, the effort to root out al Qaeda moved more slowly.

In 2002, over Bush's initial objections, Congress passed legislation to create a new Department of Homeland Security. The institution of the cabinet-level department in 2003 marked the most important government reorganization since the Department of Defense was created in 1947. Also in 2002, the Bush administration won authorization from Congress to wage a "preemptive" war against the government of Iraq led by President Saddam Hussein, maintaining that the dictatorship posed a threat to U.S. security. The war, codenamed Operation Iraqi Freedom, began on March 19, 2003. Hussein's government quickly fell, and a U.S.-led occupation force ruled the country until June 28, 2004, when an interim Iraqi government was given sovereignty. While the Iraqis moved to create a government of their own, the U.S.-led coalition ran into increased opposition and mounting casualties. By September 2004, 1,000 U.S. soldiers had been killed in Iraq.

Faced with growing opposition at home to the war and a languishing economy, Bush ran for reelection in 2004 against John Kerry, Democratic senator from Massachusetts. After a close contest—though not as close as the election of 2000—President Bush was reelected.

Frank Bruni, *Ambling into History: The Unlikely Odyssey of George W. Bush* (2002); George Bush and Brent Scrowcroft, *A World Transformed* (1998); George W. Bush, *A Charge to Keep: My Journey to the White House* (1999); Michael Duffy and Dan Goodgame, *Marching in Place: The Status-Quo Presidency of George Bush* (1992); David Frum, *The Right Man: The Surprise Presidency of George W. Bush* (2003); David Mervin, *George Bush and the Guardianship Presidency* (1996); Kevin Phillips, *American Dynasty: Aristocracy, Fortune, and the Politics of Deceit in the House of Bush* (2004); Steven Schier, ed., *High Risk and Big Ambition: The Presidency of George W. Bush* (2004).

John Kenneth White

Cianci, Vincent A. "Buddy," Jr. (1941–)

Politician. One hundred sixty thousand people live in Providence, many of them in ethnic neighborhoods: Italian, Portuguese, Irish, and, more recently, Hispanic and Southeast Asian. Mayor Vincent A. "Buddy" Cianci knows not only the neighborhoods but most of the people who live in them. He remembers the names of their children and their grandchildren, who needs a job, whose kid just won the Little League championship, whose kid is in trouble with the police. They call him Buddy or His Honor, never Vinny. Cianci has been their mayor since 1974 (not counting five years off for bad behavior) and has presided over the transformation of Providence from a fading factory town to an urban-renewal success story. His strategy: strengthen the neighborhoods to stem the exodus of people to the suburbs (and thereby retain his power base), and turn the downtown center city into a dazzling European-style capital.

Cianci's physical presence may not be imposing—he is short, stocky, and perpetually overweight—but his persona is thoroughly

Mayor Vincent "Buddy" Cianci speaks in Pawtucket, R.I., 1978

distinctive. He sports a hairpiece, wears makeup, and is seldom seen without an attractive woman by his side. Larger than life, a whirlwind of energy who seems to be everywhere at once and an accomplished standup comic, Cianci is a charismatic and controversial leader whose failings have been forgiven by his supporters but not forgotten by his critics.

Born and reared in the Italian American Silver Lake neighborhood of Providence, the son of a doctor, Cianci was educated at Moses Brown, a private boys' school on the Yankee-dominated East Side of the city. A graduate of Fairfield University and Marquette University Law School, Cianci served in the U.S. Army and began his legal career as a special assistant in the Rhode Island attorney general's office, where he was later a prosecutor. At age 33 he became the youngest mayor Providence had ever elected, the first Italian American to serve in the post, and the first Republican to hold the office in 34 years. His rise to power symbolized the changing demographics of a city long ruled by Irish Democratic machine politics. Increasingly prosperous, the Irish fled to the suburbs during the early 1970s, leaving behind an organization that collapsed, a victim of internal bickering.

During Cianci's first two terms (1975–82) hundreds of millions of federal, state, and private dollars poured into the center city and the neighborhoods. The Biltmore Hotel, a long-vacant eyesore, reopened after extensive renovations; historic buildings were brought back to life; an old movie theater was transformed into a performing arts center; and two major office buildings were constructed. Neighborhood parks were created or restored; home-renovation projects were completed; and $8 million was spent on the Roger Williams Park, whose zoo, once nearly closed by the U.S. Department of Agriculture, was rated best in New England in 1982 by the Humane Society of the United States.

Then came the troubles, both inevitable and self-created: inflation, mismanagement, historic tax increases, falling bond ratings, administrative corruption, and Cianci's unsuccessful 1980 bid for governor. After squeaking through a three-way race for mayor in 1982, running as an independent, Cianci was indicted for assaulting his estranged wife's lover. He survived a recall attempt but pled guilty to the charge of assault, received a five-year suspended sentence, and resigned from office ("the most painful thing I've ever done") in 1984.

Six years later Cianci was reelected mayor by a slim margin in another three-way race. During his five-year forced hiatus from office, he had kept in touch with his supporters by hosting a popular radio talk show and making various appearances as a TV commentator on the local political scene. "I never stopped loving Providence," he declared in his reelection campaign. Enough voters apparently believed him.

Cianci's fourth and fifth terms (1991–98) brought further improvements to downtown Providence: a convention center, an upscale mall, an outdoor skating rink, an arts and entertainment district with tax incentives to encourage a residential artistic community, and a dramatic waterfront park that features walkways and bridges and even an Italian gondolier. They also brought a more politically secure but no less flamboyant mayor. Running as an independent since 1982, Cianci has built a strong personal political organization that transcends traditional political parties. He was elected to a sixth term as mayor in 1998, running without opposition.

Faced in 1999 with a tax base that was 50 percent nonprofit and a tax structure dependent on the property tax, a growing immigrant population straining the resources of the school system, a declining manufacturing base, and a federal investigation into alleged corruption at Providence City Hall, Buddy Cianci nonetheless appeared undaunted as he looked toward the 21st century. He professed to have no other political ambition than to keep on being mayor. His Mayor's Own Marinara Sauce, with profits going to a scholarship fund for low-income Providence students, did so well that he subsequently branched out into olive oil. For this resourceful politician, the future seemed full of possibilities.

On June 24, 2002, however, Mayor Cianci was convicted on a charge of racketeering conspiracy and sentenced to a term in federal prison. Although his political career seems at an end, his legacy remains alive in the form of a revitalized Providence, where debates over Cianci's politics and personality will doubtless continue for many years to come.

Dick Lehr, "The Buddy Show," *Boston Globe*, September 3, 1996; Franklin S. Prosnitz, "Vincent A. Cianci, Jr.: Optimistic Mayor Foresees a Revitalized City," *Providence Business News*, December 12, 1994; Mike Swift, "Can Providence, with Its Revitalized Downtown, Show Hartford the Way? The Art of a City," *Hartford Courant*, May 4, 1997.

Sarah T. Dowling

Cohen, William S. (1940–) U.S. representative, senator, and secretary of defense. A widely respected member of the U.S. House and Senate since 1973, William Cohen became secretary of state under President Bill Clinton in 1997. He was the first Republican named to a senior post in a Democratic cabinet since the 1960s.

Born in Bangor, Maine, Cohen was the son of a baker. He graduated from Bowdoin College and received his law degree from Boston University Law School in 1965. In his first foray into local politics, he was elected to Bangor's city council in 1968 and soon became mayor of that city.

One of the first politicians in his state to appreciate the techniques of modern campaigning, Cohen easily won election to Congress in 1972. Outgoing and telegenic, he used television to great effect in his subsequent electoral campaigns. Nor did it hurt to be a basketball star—Cohen was inducted into the New England Basketball All-Star Hall of Fame in 1962—in basketball-crazy Maine. At a time when that state's once invulnerable Republican Party began losing ground to the Democrats, Cohen also benefited from the political independence that media electioneering made possible. Never beholden to politicos within his party, Cohen demonstrated an independent voting record in Congress, gaining national recognition as one of the few Republicans to vote for impeachment hearings against Richard Nixon in 1974.

Appealing to a broad constituency of Republicans, independents, and moderate Democrats, Cohen moved to the Senate with an impressive margin of victory in 1978, when he took 56.6 percent of the two-party vote. He easily won reelection in 1984 and again in 1990, with the help of an impressive personal machine of professional consultants and media experts. As senator, Cohen impressed home voters as a voice of moderation on most issues. Fiscally conservative yet generally supportive of defense spending, he nevertheless maintained liberal positions on most social and environmental issues, a perfect blend for Maine's libertarian electorate. As a leading member of the Senate Armed Services Committee, Cohen raised eyebrows among his Senate colleagues and at the Pentagon with his dogged criticism of fiscal mismanagement in the Defense Department. He also played a peripheral role in the START I Arms Control Treaty of 1980 and led Republican critics of the Reagan administration's actions during the Iran-Contra scandal of 1987.

Seemingly at the height of his popularity in 1996, Cohen made the surprising decision to retire from the Senate, an action that many attributed to his recent marriage to a local television-news reporter. In December 1996, as part of his campaign commitment to appoint at least one Republican to his cabinet in a display of bipartisanship, President Clinton appointed Cohen secretary of defense. Although the popular former senator was unanimously confirmed, many voices in the media and military quietly questioned the choice. Without managerial experience or any military service

record, some wondered how Cohen could direct the largest agency of the federal government. Questions were also raised as to whether the solidly pragmatic Cohen, renowned for his ability to compromise, possessed the theoretical and strategic vision to overhaul the Cold War–era military establishment for the requirements of 21st-century theater warfare.

In keeping with the middle-of-the road approach he had honed as a senator, Cohen endorsed limited reforms in the armed services. He supported bureaucratic personnel cuts inside the Pentagon along with more rounds of base closings. He held fast, however, against major changes in the existing force structure, such as abandoning the long-held two-front combat-readiness strategy (the capacity for U.S. forces to fight and win two regional wars simultaneously). Nevertheless, limited budgetary cutbacks may have alienated segments of the military hierarchy, as the highly publicized complaints from the Joint Chiefs of Staff before Congress in 1998 seemed to indicate.

Cohen's strategic vision for U.S. foreign policy objectives proved difficult to isolate. A firm believer in the need for and advisability of U.S. global leadership throughout the Cold War, Cohen grew less enthusiastic about prolonged U.S. engagements in international crises after his cabinet appointment. His public support for an early U.S. troop withdrawal from Bosnia, begun as part of the U.S.-brokered Dayton Agreement that brought about a truce in 1996, directly contradicted official administration policy and drew the ire of Secretary of State Madeleine Albright. Cohen's support for NATO expansion into former Warsaw Pact nations, however, was more consistent with his internationalist foreign policy background, as was his endorsement in 1999 of NATO air strikes against Serbian military targets after Serbian president Slobodan Milosevic's crackdown on Albanian secessionists in Kosovo province.

Cohen is the author or coauthor of nine books, including the mystery novel *The Double Man* (1985), with Democratic senator Gary Hart; the poetry collection *A Baker's Nickel* (1986); and *Men of Zeal: A Candid Inside Story of the Iran-Contra Hearings* (1988), with his fellow senator, and former Democratic Senate majority leader, George J. Mitchell.

Charles Lane, "The Double Man: The Secretary of Defense, Forever Becoming," *New Republic* 217, no. 4 (1997); Jerome M. Mileur, ed., *Parties and Politics in the New England States* (1997); Pat Towell, "Cohen's National Security Record Stresses Toughness, Consensus," *Congressional Quarterly Weekly Report* 55, no. 3 (1997).

Scott Harris

Congress Sectional interests have played themselves out in the U.S. Congress since the establishment of that body in 1789. During the second half of the 20th century, for example, southern members of Congress, benefiting from an absence of two-party competition at home, high reelection rates, and a strong seniority system, pursued regional policies through the standing-committee system. Representatives and senators from New England have traditionally focused more of their energy on party-leadership positions. In fact, the topic of New England in Congress immediately summons visions of the many giants of legislative leadership who have hailed from the region.

Of the 51 Speakers of the House who served between 1789 and 2005, 11 represented states in the region, including four since 1919. During the 19th century powerful Republican Speakers such as James G. Blaine (1869–75) and Thomas Brackett Reed (1889–91, 1895–99) of Maine set the standard by which other strong speakers would be judged. Blaine's willingness to use the Speaker's power of recognition more aggressively than his predecessors allowed that House leader to shape the legislative agenda in ways few others had. On occasion Blaine used the power of recognition to thwart Reconstruction legislation proposed by other members from the North. Reed is credited, similarly, with a number of measures that further strengthened party leadership in the House of Representatives. He is best known for ending the practice of the "disappearing quorum" and other delaying tactics commonly used by members of the minority party during his era. This practice, the precedents for which could be traced back to the 1830s, dictated that nonvoting members could not be counted for the purposes of establishing a quorum. The Reed Rules, enacted in February 1890, reduced the number necessary for a quorum in the committee of the whole from 165 to 100 and established that nonvoting members would be counted as present during quorum calls.

In the 20th century what came to be known as the Austin-Boston Axis emerged. A disproportionate number of Speakers represented districts in Texas and Massachusetts, beginning with Frederick H. Gillett (R-Mass., 1919–25) and including Joseph W. Martin, Jr. (R-Mass., 1947–48, 1953–54), and John W. McCormack (D-Mass., 1961–71). More recently Thomas P. "Tip" O'Neill (D-Mass., 1977–87) revitalized the modern speakership, setting the stage for the more centralized but short-lived leadership organizations of Democrat Jim Wright of Texas (1987–90) and Republican Newt Gingrich of Georgia (1995–98). As Speaker, O'Neill was the Democratic Party's leading policy spokesman between 1981 and 1986, during which time the Republicans

U.S. Senators from New England in 1965 included (standing, from left) Claiborne Pell (D-R.I.), Edward Kennedy (D-Mass.), Edmund S. Muskie (D-Maine), and Thomas Dodd (D-Conn., far right); (seated, left) Leverett Saltonstall (R-Mass.), and (seated, right), John O. Pastore (D-R.I.)

controlled both the White House and the Senate.

The Senate, too, has looked to New Englanders for leadership throughout its existence. New Englanders dominated the leadership of that body's Republican caucus between the 1860s and the 1950s, a period highlighted by the forceful presence of Finance Committee member Nelson Aldrich of Rhode Island in the 1890s and 1900s and that of Massachusetts senator Henry Cabot Lodge, who served as floor leader from 1918 until 1924. Aldrich was the first of the modern party leaders in the Senate, and, like the powerful speakers of the House who were his contemporaries, he remains arguably the strongest party leader the chamber has ever seen. Lodge is best known for leading what President Woodrow Wilson called the "little group of willful men" in a successful effort to defeat the League of Nations in 1919. Wallace White (R-Maine, minority leader, 1945–47; majority leader, 1947–49) and Styles Bridges (R-N.H., minority leader, 1952–53) also led their party in the Senate, but no New Englander of either party did so between 1953 and 1989. George Mitchell of Maine put an end to that drought in 1989, when he became Democratic majority leader. Serving in that post until 1995, Mitchell established himself as one of the most universally respected leaders in the modern Senate.

While New England's history of leadership on Capitol Hill remains impressive, the region is fighting an uphill battle for representation in the House. Demographic trends dictated that New England's percentage of the entire

House of Representatives declined from 23.6 percent at the turn of the 19th century to 7.6 percent at the turn of the 20th to just 5.3 percent at the turn of the 21st. Continued outmigration is expected to perpetuate this downward trend.

The most glaring tendency involving the region's congressional delegation over the course of the 20th century was the dramatic shift away from Republican to Democratic dominance. In describing this transition, we can break the century into three distinct periods. The first third of the century was characterized by Republican dominance. Between 1900 and 1930 Republicans held a majority of New England's House seats in 15 of 16 Congresses, or 94 percent of the time. On average, Republicans held a five-to-one advantage over Democrats in the region's House delegation and never held fewer than 10 of the region's 12 Senate seats. From 1932 to 1960 the Republican Party retained its majority status in the region's congressional delegation, but the Democratic Party became much more competitive. Republicans held a majority of New England's House seats in 12 of 14 Congresses (85.7 percent), with the 1960 election producing a split delegation at 14 members each. However, on average the Republican-to-Democratic ratio was closer to three to two. In the Senate Democratic progress came more slowly. Democrats made inroads in Connecticut, Massachusetts, and Rhode Island, but as a rule Republicans still held more than eight of the region's 12 Senate seats between 1932 and 1960. Since 1960 the story has been altogether different.

Between 1962 and 2000 Democrats retained a two-to-one ratio over Republicans in the New England House delegation, constituting a majority of the delegation in all 19 Congresses. In the Senate the post-1960 delegation has remained largely split, with ratios of seven to five and six to six the norm, although Democrats captured as many as nine of the region's 12 Senate seats in the mid-1970s in the wake of the Watergate scandal.

One implication of this partisan transition has been the increasing loyalty of New England congressional Democrats to their party. In the 1950s that group voted with a majority of their party about as often as the average Democrat. Since the early 1960s, however, party loyalty among New England congressional Democrats has consistently stayed well above the national average. Conversely, as the national Republican Party has moved to the right, the remaining New England Republicans, usually more moderate on social issues than their counterparts from other regions, have become their party's least reliable regional base of support in the House and Senate.

Aggregate trends in the partisan breakdown of the region's congressional delegation mask the central role played by Massachusetts's transition from a predominantly Republican state to a predominantly Democratic one in determining the partisan makeup of the region's House delegation. Traditionally, Massachusetts has held approximately half of the region's House seats. While Democrats slightly dominated the state's House delegation between 1948 and 1970, Republicans held the vast majority of its seats before 1948. Since 1970 the Democrats have controlled the Massachusetts delegation.

Until the 1992 election of Carol Moseley-Braun (D-Ill.), it appeared that Massachusetts senator Edward Brooke III would be the only African American to serve in the U.S. Senate during the 20th century. The Republican Brooke served from 1967 to 1979. Despite Brooke's long tenure in the Senate, the region did not send an African American representative to the House until 1990, when Republican Gary Franks was elected to represent Connecticut's Fifth Congressional District. At the time, Franks was the only African American in Congress who represented a majority white district. New England has a long-standing tradition of sending women to Congress as well. Massachusetts representative Edith Nourse Rogers served in the U.S. House from 1925 to 1960, overlapping with other prominent female New England members of Congress: Margaret Chase Smith (R-Maine, 1940–49), Clare Boothe Luce (R-Conn., 1943–47), and Chase Woodhouse (D-Conn., 1945–47). In

fact, as of 2004 both senators from Maine, Republicans Olympia J. Snowe and Susan Collins, were women.

In 1990 Vermont sent former Burlington mayor Bernie Sanders to Congress. While he caucused with the Democrats, Sanders stood out as Congress's lone independent member until fellow New Englander Bob Smith of New Hampshire declared his political independence, leaving the Republican Party in July 1999 (Smith returned to the Republican Party later that year). At first glance Sanders, who as mayor of Burlington was an avowed socialist, would appear out of place as Vermont's sole representative in the House. Vermont voters supported every Republican presidential nominee from 1856 through 1988 with the single exception of Barry Goldwater in 1964. However, Sanders appeared to be ahead of the trend: Democrat Bill Clinton's victories in the state in 1992 and 1996 and John Kerry's in 2004 revealed a move away from the Republican Party in Vermont.

Unlike their counterparts in the South, members of the New England congressional delegation spent the 1950s, 1960s, and 1970s underrepresented in the ranks of standing-committee chairs in the House and Senate. Between 1955 and 1977, the period in the century when committees were the strongest, New Englanders chaired no standing committees in the House. Only five different representatives from the region chaired standing committees at some point between 1977 and 1998, and just two—Robert N. Giaimo (D-Conn.), who chaired the House Budget Committee from 1977 to 1981, and John Joseph Moakley (D-Mass.), who chaired the Rules Committee from 1989 to 1995—headed relatively prestigious panels. In 1955 and 1965, by comparison, though they made up less than 30 percent of the chamber, representatives from the 11 states of the former Confederacy constituted 63 percent and 65 percent of all standing-committee chairs, respectively. New England's minor presence in the House committee system is further illustrated by the fact that at no time since the passage of the Legislative Reorganization Act of 1946 have members from the region chaired the two premier House committees, Appropriations and Ways and Means.

Because of the relatively small size of the region and all but one of its states, the Senate would be the more likely place to find New England pursuing sectional interests within the committee system. In that body the region's record of committee leadership since World War II is stronger than in the House but is still lacking in some ways. Since 1946 New England senators have chaired standing committees 22 times. However, of the four tra-

ditional major committees in the Senate—Appropriations, Armed Services, Finance, and Foreign Relations—only Foreign Relations has been chaired by a senator from New England in recent years (Claiborne Pell, D-R.I., 1987–95). Of the remaining three none has been chaired by a New Englander since 1955. Also surprising is the fact that despite the region's strong labor union presence (four of the six states have union membership percentages above the national average), it was not until 1987 that a senator from New England, Edward Kennedy (D-Mass.), chaired the Labor and Human Resources Committee, a post he held until 1995. In 1997 Vermont's James Jeffords, arguably the most liberal Republican in the Senate (now an independent), took over the labor panel.

Sectional interests have traditionally been pursued in Congress. During the mid-20th century the race issue brought southern Democrats together on Capitol Hill in the same way that southern Republicans coalesced around issues of social conservatism during the 1980s and 1990s. Natural resources policy has served to unite western envoys to Washington. In fact, as the mountain West became more solidly Republican, cooperation between members of Congress from that region increased. Despite its small size, the New England congressional delegation continues to exhibit deeply rooted diversity in the areas of economic and social welfare policy. The domestic agenda items that would likely unite the region's delegation—moral and cultural issues such as abortion rights and school prayer—tend to play themselves out not in the halls of Congress but in the courts. As a consequence, during the second half of the 20th century the region's influence on Congress, and in turn on public policy, tended to be more the result of dynamic leaders and policy advocates than of the kinds of concerted regional strategies used by members from the South and West.

De Alva Stanwood Alexander, *History and Procedure of the House of Representatives* (1970 [1916]); Richard A. Baker and Roger H. Davidson, eds., *First among Equals: Outstanding Senate Leaders of the 20th Century* (1991); Richard B. Cheney and Lynne V. Cheney, *Kings of the Hill: Power and Personality in the House of Representatives* (1996); *Congressional Quarterly's Guide to Congress*, 4th ed. (1991); Jerome M. Mileur, ed., *Parties and Politics in the New England States* (1997); Neal R. Peirce, ed., *The New England States: People, Politics, and Power in the Six New England States* (1976).

Vincent G. Moscardelli

Curley, James Michael (1874–1958) Politician, mayor of Boston, and Democratic Party leader. Boston's most colorful, memorable, and talented mayor, James Michael

Curley, was born in a working-class neighborhood in Roxbury, Mass., to parents from Galway, Ireland. Curley left public school at age 16 to work in local shops and as a traveling salesman before allying with the Roxbury ward boss, P. J. Maguire. Self-educated in the public library, Curley served on the Boston Common Council in 1900 and 1901 and in the state legislature from 1902 to 1903. In 1904 he was elected to the office of city alderman (which he held until 1909) while serving a 60-day jail sentence for taking a civil service examination for one of his campaign workers.

After a year on the new Boston City Council (1910–11), Curley won a seat in Congress (1912–14), resigning when he was elected mayor of Boston in 1914. Curley ran for mayor 10 times and served four terms (1914–18, 1922–26, 1930–34, 1946–50). He boasted that he was not a ward politician; his powerful, personal, citywide machine was a multiethnic, biracial network of allies, admirers, and friends. His genius for coalition building was legendary, and his oratorical skills and genteel style made him a formidable opponent in debate or on the campaign trail. Denied a seat at the 1932 Democratic National Convention in Chicago, the irrepressible Curley appeared as a delegate from Puerto Rico to cast his vote for Franklin D. Roosevelt.

Curley supported Roosevelt early and campaigned for him nationally, but when FDR did not appoint Curley to a cabinet post, the two became enemies. Curley's revenge was to become Massachusetts's governor in 1934. During his term (1935–37), Curley undertook large-scale public works projects that foreshadowed the New Deal.

Curley was defeated in his bid for a U.S. Senate seat in 1936 but served in the House of Representatives from 1942 to 1946 before voters returned him to the mayor's office. During his fourth term as mayor, he was convicted of mail fraud (as a director of a construction firm seeking federal contracts) by a jury in Washington, D.C. After six months in federal prison, Curley was paroled and later pardoned by President Harry Truman and then finished his term as mayor. He ran for mayor again in 1950 and 1954, but these campaigns were largely symbolic efforts to restore his political war chest. Although his personal fortune was never large, he spent liberally, and the favor-seekers outside his Jamaicaway home and at his City Hall office were never disappointed. Accused of wholesale graft, charges he denied and delighted in, Curley was generous to his impoverished supporters.

Edwin O'Connor's best-selling novel *The Last Hurrah* (1956) and John Ford's 1958 film by the same title are fictional but evocative accounts of Curley's life. Although he threatened to sue, Curley enjoyed these portrayals of him as a kindhearted rogue. His autobiography, *I'd Do It Again* (1957), underscored this public image. At the time of his death in 1958 at the Boston City Hospital he had built for his needy constituents, the city was in sad disrepair and its future dim. His critics have attributed the city's decline to Curley's divisive politics, but this view overlooks his role as a hero to the poor and the friendless. He was a larger-than-life figure whose career symbolized ethnic politics, public service, and showmanship of a type now obsolete. Curley's legacy to New England and to the nation endures, however, with government concern for the average citizen now an intrinsic feature of U.S. political life.

Jack Beatty, *The Rascal King: The Life and Times of James Michael Curley, 1874–1958* (1992); Joseph F. Dinneen, *The Purple Shamrock* (1949); Edwin O'Connor, *The Last Hurrah* (1956).

Peter C. Holloran

Dodd Family A U.S. senator from Connecticut, Thomas J. Dodd (1907–71) was an early Cold Warrior and an advocate for minority rights. His influence ended in 1967 when he was censured for financial misconduct. Dodd's eldest son, Thomas J. Dodd, Jr. (1935–), was ambassador first to Uruguay and then to Costa Rica during the Clinton administration, and his fifth son, Christopher J. Dodd (1944–), also became a senator. The fortunes of this political family illustrate the troubled legacy of the Cold War and the changing outlook for Irish Americans in politics.

Dodd Sr. was a devout Catholic and a more devout New Dealer. Unlike early Irish American politicians, who entered politics through the urban machines, he began as a prosecutor and civil servant. After graduating from Yale Law School in 1933, he worked in the Federal Bureau of Investigation, the Works Progress Administration, and then in the South as a civil rights prosecutor for the Justice Department. In 1945 he became Justice Robert Jackson's top assistant at the Nuremberg war crimes trials. After winning the Medal of Freedom in 1947, Dodd decided to run for governor in Connecticut as an anticommunist Democrat.

In 1948 Dodd's anticommunism was a constant source of tension in party chairman John Bailey's state organization. To pacify the left, Bailey abandoned Dodd and supported New Dealer Chester Bowles. In 1950 Bailey asked Dodd to defend the patriotism of Senator Brien McMahon against McCarthyist attacks and in 1952 rewarded him with Abraham Ribicoff's vacated House seat. Dodd failed to defeat Senator Prescott Bush in 1956 but won against Senator William Purtell two years later.

Senator Dodd preached against the Soviet Union, racism, television violence, handguns, and juvenile delinquency. These moral crusades brought him praise but met with little legislative success. His influence was strongest in civil rights and foreign policy. He ardently supported both the 1964 Civil Rights Act and the U.S. presence in Vietnam. He nearly became President Lyndon Johnson's 1964 running mate.

Dodd's crusader image was punctured when the Senate censured him in 1967 for diverting $116,000 in campaign donations to his personal use. Indignantly refusing to resign, he lost the 1970 Democratic senatorial nomination to Joseph Duffey and then ran as an independent. He split the Democratic vote, and Republican Lowell Weicker won the election. Dodd died of a heart attack six months later.

Dodd's sons tried to both vindicate their father and step out of his shadow. Thomas Dodd, Jr., became a diplomat and an expert on Central America. He was a professor at Georgetown University in 1993 when he was named ambassador to Uruguay; in the fall of 1997 he became ambassador to Costa Rica. Christopher Dodd followed his father into politics but was far more liberal. At age 30 the younger Dodd was elected to the House in the post-Watergate class of 1974. In 1980, after six undistinguished years in the House, he won election to the Senate and almost overnight became that body's most articulate critic of President Ronald Reagan's foreign policy. Although he protected funding for the *Seawolf* submarine in New London, Conn., he condemned Reagan's support of the authoritarian regime in El Salvador, opposed the MX missile, and attacked the U.S. military backing of the Nicaraguan Contra rebels. Dodd was an advocate for working women and families. He sponsored expanded health-care coverage for women, including abortion funding. In 1993 he engineered passage of the Family and Medical Leave Act.

In 1995 Christopher Dodd was nearly chosen to be Senate minority leader and ended up becoming general chairman of the Democratic National Committee. In the 1996 campaign Dodd superbly defended the policies of President Bill Clinton. As Clinton's impeachment trial began in 1999, Dodd made an inspiring plea to his fellow senators for civility. While condemning the president's misconduct, he ultimately voted for acquittal. Dodd's current committee assignments reflect his continued interest in issues of health care, family issues, and foreign affairs.

James Boyd, *Above the Law* (1968); Thomas J. Dodd, *Freedom and Foreign Policy* (1962); Thomas J. Dodd

[Jr.], *Managing Democracy in Central America: A Case Study, United States Election Supervision in Nicaragua, 1927–1933* (1992).

Scott L. McLean

Dukakis, Michael (1933–) Politician and Massachusetts governor. Michael Stanley Dukakis was born in the Boston suburb of Brookline, Mass., a son of Greek immigrants, Panos and Euterpe (Boukis) Dukakis, who personified the American dream. From humble beginnings, his father went to Harvard Medical School to become the first American-trained, Greek-speaking doctor in metropolitan Boston; his mother, a teacher, was one of the first Greek women in New England to go to college (at Bates, in Maine). His parents often told Dukakis that "much has been given to you and much is expected," and he took those words to heart, working as a reformer and becoming a three-term governor of Massachusetts and the 1988 Democratic Party candidate for president of the United States.

Designated "most brilliant" senior by his Brookline High School classmates, Dukakis showed his leadership early, becoming an Eagle Scout, president of the student council, and winner of three athletic letters. At the age of 17 he ran the Boston Marathon, finishing a respectable 57th out of 191 entrants. He went on to graduate from Swarthmore College (1955) and Harvard Law School (1960). Between college and law school he served for two years in the U.S. Army, 16 months of it in Korea. Upon admission to the Massachusetts bar,

he joined the Boston law firm of Hill and Barlow and specialized in housing law. In 1963 he married Kitty Dickson, daughter of Harry Ellis Dickson, associate conductor of the Boston Pops Orchestra.

In 1959 Dukakis's political career began with his election as a Brookline Town Meeting member. In 1960 he was elected chairman of Brookline's Democratic organization and by 1962 had won a seat in the Massachusetts House of Representatives. Dukakis served for four terms as a legislator, winning each reelection by increasingly large margins. In 1970 he ran for lieutenant governor with the Democratic gubernatorial candidate (and Boston mayor) Kevin White, but lost.

In 1974 Dukakis became his party's nominee for governor and defeated Republican Governor Francis Sargent in the fall election. Dukakis inherited a record deficit and high unemployment and found himself in the unenviable position of having to cut services and raise taxes during his early months in office. Those unpopular actions led to Dukakis's defeat by Edward King in the 1978 Democratic primary. In 1982, after a teaching stint at Harvard's John F. Kennedy School of Government, Dukakis came back to defeat King and was subsequently reelected to an unprecedented third four-year term in 1986 by one of the largest margins in Massachusetts history. In 1986 the National Governors Association voted Dukakis the nation's most effective governor. As governor he accomplished welfare reform, universal health care, environmental

protection, and the first comprehensive state urban policy in the country.

Dukakis won the Democratic nomination for president in 1988. He highlighted in his campaign the strength of Massachusetts's economic turnaround, known as the "Massachusetts Miracle," as he described it in his book *Creating the Future* (1988). Despite his enormous popularity during the Democratic primary campaign, Dukakis encountered difficulties leading up to the fall election. Especially harmful to his candidacy were attack ads from his Republican opponent, George H. W. Bush, on crime, race, and defense issues.

After his loss, Dukakis announced that he would not run for reelection as governor. Since 1991 he has been a distinguished professor in the Political Science Department at Northeastern University.

Dukakis will be remembered as a reformer with integrity who worked to improve the quality of government in Massachusetts. According to the *Boston Globe,* as governor he "set standards of probity in office against which all public figures will be measured in the years to come."

Michael Dukakis with Rosabeth Moss Kanter, *Creating the Future: The Massachusetts Comeback and Its Promise for America* (1988); Richard Gaines and Michael Segal, *Dukakis and the Reform Impulse* (1987); Charles Kenney and Robert L. Turner, *Dukakis: An American Odyssey* (1988); Richard A. Loverd, "Michael S. Dukakis: Blending Principle with Politics in Leading State Government from 'Duke I' to 'Duke II,'" in *Leadership for the Public Service: Power and Policy in Action,* ed. Richard A. Loverd (1997).

Richard A. Loverd

Flanders, Ralph (1880–1970) Draftsman, writer, businessman, and U.S. senator. A true Yankee not only by temperament but also by birth and upbringing, Ralph Flanders was born in Vermont and spent most of his early years in Rhode Island. His family's relative poverty and a limited formal education led Flanders to choose a working-class career, and at the age of 17 he became an apprentice mechanic and draftsman at the Brown and Sharpe Manufacturing Company of Providence. In 1903 he moved to Nashua, N.H., to become a designer for the International Paper Box Machinery Company, and from 1905 to 1910 he wrote for the magazine *Machinery* in New York City. He returned to the world of business in 1910 to take an engineering job at the Fellows Gear Shaper Company of Springfield, Vt. He left this post in 1912 to serve as a manager with the Jones and Lamson Machine Company, also of Springfield; in 1933 he became that company's president. His prominence in Vermont business circles and his articles on public affairs drew Flanders into

Michael Dukakis on the presidential campaign trail in Nashua, N.H., 1988

politics: from 1946 to 1959 Flanders was one of Vermont's U.S. senators. Although a Republican, he rose to distinction for publicly attacking Senator Joseph McCarthy and contributed to the New England tradition of independent-thinking Republicans in the Senate. He died in Springfield, Vt., in February 1970.

With the coming of the Great Depression, Flanders's political interest focused on the problem of employment. He was a member of several state and national business commissions during the 1930s and worked with the Roosevelt administration in that capacity. Although he recognized the need for federal action of some kind to fight the Depression, Flanders was one of the first to criticize the National Recovery Administration and Roosevelt's move toward "too much government planning." Flanders was a lifelong conservative, but his conservatism was tempered by his working-class roots and his immense respect for the human dignity found through work. Elected to the Senate in 1946 (he had run and lost in the Republican primary of 1940), Flanders established himself as a moderate Republican with ties to the international wing of the party. He was an early and enthusiastic supporter of the Marshall Plan and a backer of public housing.

A firm believer in Christianity and capitalism, Flanders was resolutely anticommunist. However, he believed the external threat posed by communism to be considerably greater than the internal danger. For Flanders the harm done by McCarthy's politics of fear far outweighed any good that the Wisconsin crusader could have hoped to achieve. Flanders's most illustrious moment came when he chastised the anticommunist senator. Despite hostility from some Republican colleagues, Flanders continued to make speeches against McCarthy, and he was the one who introduced the first motion to censure him.

Senator Flanders counted his opposition to McCarthy as one of three shining instances of personal bravery in his life. The first occurred when, as a young worker, he demanded time off on a Saturday, thus striking a blow against management. The second took place when Flanders challenged Franklin D. Roosevelt over certain provisions of his economic recovery program, thus standing up to management again. In all his actions Flanders revealed himself to be a man of character in the old Yankee sense. He was a conservative in business, a resolute Christian, and a supporter of any program that would help individuals work harder and better. In this sense Flanders was a believer in the power of human reason and the individual will to overcome life's challenges.

Robert Griffith, *The Politics of Fear: Joseph R. McCarthy and the Senate,* 2d ed. (1987); Ben Pearse, "The Case of the Unexpected Senator," *Saturday Evening Post,* July 31, 1954.

Joseph Romance

Frank, Barney (1940–) Politician and U.S. representative. In 2002 Barney Frank was elected to his 12th term as a Democratic representative from Massachusetts's Fourth Congressional District. Known for his keen intellect, biting humor, and adroit debating style, Frank was the senior ranking Democrat on the House Financial Services Committee and is a member of the Select Committee on Homeland Security. His legislative successes include creating housing programs for low-income groups, preventing cutbacks in immigration and immigrant services, and protecting people with HIV from discrimination.

Born and raised in Bayonne, N.J., Frank went to Massachusetts to attend Harvard, graduating in 1962. In 1967 he began his political career as executive assistant to the newly elected mayor of Boston, Kevin White. After serving for a year as administrative assistant to U.S. Representative Michael Harrington (D-Mass.), Frank was elected to the Massachusetts House in 1972 and served for the next eight years in the state legislature. During his tenure in state government, he earned a law degree from Harvard (1977) and a reputation as an independent and critical voice within his own party.

In 1980 Frank moved his home to Brookline, Mass., to run for the congressional seat vacated by retiring Democrat Robert Drinan

Representative Barney Frank speaks in Fall River, Mass., 1989

in a district known for its liberal constituency. Frank won the election but faced an uphill re-election battle when, after the 1980 census cost Massachusetts a House seat, his district was combined with that of a popular moderate Republican, Margaret Heckler. With the country in the grips of a recession, the 1982 race became a referendum on President Ronald Reagan's economic policies, and Frank was the unexpected victor. He has won reelection by wide margins ever since.

Frank publicly announced his homosexuality in 1987. He has fought discrimination against those infected with HIV and has suggested that homosexuals in the military be allowed an openly gay lifestyle when not on duty. In 1989 allegations that one of Frank's former employees was running a prostitution business out of the congressman's Washington apartment prompted calls for Frank's resignation. Although an Ethics Committee investigation cleared him of all but two minor charges, Frank was reprimanded by the House in 1990. In an article in the *Boston Globe Magazine* (May 21, 1995) that charted his remarkable comeback after this low point in his career, Frank said, "I think members will agree that I have always had a reputation for honesty, not always tact or tolerance."

In his book *Speaking Frankly: What's Wrong with the Democrats and How to Fix It* (1992), Frank warned that Democrats would not succeed in advancing their mainstream commitments to economic fairness and social justice by denigrating basic values held by the majority of voters. He also proposed that the United States declare a post–Cold War victory dividend, cut its defense budget, and ask its allies to share the costs of stationing U.S. troops abroad.

After Democrats lost their House majority in 1994, party leaders asked Frank to spearhead criticism of the Republican leadership and its programs. Frank assumed that role, energetically fighting budget cuts in domestic programs. A fierce critic of George W. Bush's administration, Frank opposed the president's tax cuts and his decision to invade Iraq. He was the subject of a 2003 documentary, *Let's Get Frank.* The passion and pragmatism with which Frank has upheld the ideals of Massachusetts liberalism have led even his foes to admit that he has been one of the most effective members in Congress at the end of the 20th century and into the 21st.

Michael Barone, Grant Ujifusa, and Douglas Matthews, comps., *The Almanac of American Politics, 1998* (1997); Chris Black, "Feisty Siblings Fight on Clinton's Side: Barney Frank, Ann Lewis Won Spurs Long Ago in Liberal Causes," *Boston Globe Magazine,* March 29, 1998; David Grann, "Barney Rumbles," *New Republic* 219, no. 1 (1998); Bob Hohler,

"Brawler on the Hill in a Remarkable Comeback,"
Boston Globe Magazine, May 21, 1995.

*Christine B. Williams and
William Clayton Kimball*

Governors New Englanders have never treated politics casually. From the region's earliest colonial beginnings, a political ideology embracing local participatory government has been a central pillar of New England's cultural identity. The Puritan founders were keenly interested in questions of political authority, having fled England in part to escape what they regarded as persecution at the hands of the Crown. Contemptuous of hierarchical institutions associated with papism and fearing the potential for abuse inherent in centralized authority, Puritan New England consciously avoided endowing executive agents of the Crown with political prerogatives. Real authority outside cuhrch leadership rested in localized assemblies, the forerunners of New England's famous town meetings. Although granted by the English Crown, all charters empowered elected legislatures to manage a colony's affairs; most important was control over taxation. At the pinnacle of each colony's social elite were governors who presided over their respective colonies, but for the most part they played only a peripheral role in governing. There were some bold exceptions to this rule, such as Sir Edmund Andros, colonial governor in the American Northeast during the three-year reign of James II (1685–88). Andros consolidated regional administration in the Dominion of New England, which he ruled by executive fiat. However, the public resisted experiments like this one; Andros was deposed by a town militia and returned to England in chains.

By the time of the American Revolution public participation in political decision making had taken permanent root in the minds of New Englanders as a moral and civic obligation. Once the struggle for freedom from Britain had been won and religious authority disestablished, democracy became akin to a secular religion. By the 19th century a typical governor's duties consisted of little more than helping manage his party's patronage system and ceremonially officiating at public affairs. Most issues of public policy remained under the jurisdiction of state legislatures.

There were many structural barriers to gubernatorial leadership. In most New England states governor's councils survived from the colonial era to supervise and regulate the highly limited gubernatorial prerogatives that existed. As defined in state constitutions, these councils were part of the executive branch yet were elected separately and were wholly independent from the governor. These

bodies possessed a veto over many gubernatorial actions and in practice amounted to a second, competing branch of the executive.

Governors also lacked the unilateral authority to appoint members to New England's numerous state boards and commissions, perfect vehicles for rewarding party patronage. From supreme court justices to minor bureaucrats, state legislatures dictated appointments, relying on pliant governors to rubber-stamp their choices, and state budgets were never created under gubernatorial direction.

This system was ideally suited for localized, relatively independent communities with homogeneous interests. By the turn of the 20th century, however, New England clearly was no longer such a society—if indeed it ever was. Industrialization had created complicated economic networks that cut across local and state boundaries, requiring management and oversight for which localized bodies were not suited. Urbanization and the growth of working classes also called for greater centralized planning and statewide initiatives. State legislatures hampered by the laws of collective action were not capable of leading aggressively on many of these issues, with which state government had never been expected to deal in the past.

New England also experienced rapid demographic shifts in the ethnic makeup of its citizenry. Until the late 19th century much of New England's Puritan Yankee population remained homogeneous, permitting an easy transmission of traditional political values that had changed little since the Revolution. New waves of immigrants, however, especially from Ireland, southern Europe, and French Canada, had no history in their own native political cultures of weak executive authority and little respect for such beliefs. Composing mostly the urban working classes, especially in Rhode Island, Connecticut, and Massachusetts, these new groups were particularly in need of centralized initiatives to meet 20th-century problems, and they helped transform the political culture of the states in which they settled.

Conditions were in place for expanding the responsibilities and power of New England governors. The first great impetus came with the Depression, when, following national trends, state legislatures delegated crisis-management responsibility to their formerly symbolic executives. Many state boards and commissions were consolidated under gubernatorial control. After World War II gubernatorial authority continued to be strengthened, albeit in fits and starts unique to each individual state.

Of all the New England states, Connecticut has undergone the most dramatic reorganization of its executive branch. Unique in this

respect for the region, Connecticut operates under the authority of a modern state constitution devised to meet 20th-century political needs and ratified in 1965. No other New England state constitution was ratified after 1842.

Connecticut's new constitution substantially enhanced the governor's political role. Among other things, it accorded the governor full responsibility over state budgets, without legislative revision. It also instituted a two-thirds majority rather than the previous simple majority to override gubernatorial vetoes and created new boards and commissions under gubernatorial oversight. Today, most observers recognize Connecticut governors as among the most powerful in the country, their institutional authority easily outdistancing that of all of their New England counterparts.

Massachusetts, operating under the oldest state constitution in the country, has embraced fewer changes and retained a more traditional New England preference for legislative leadership than Connecticut has. Nonetheless, a similar pattern of executive reorganization has taken place, to a lesser degree, over the past several decades, principally through statutory reforms.

In 1964 Massachusetts voters approved a public referendum extending the length of gubernatorial terms to four years. The same vote stripped the state's governor's council—a refuge of political cronyism that had recently been exposed as riotously corrupt—of all but ceremonial powers, finally consolidating the state's executive authority in the person of the governor. Over the next decade 10 cabinet-level departments were created under the direct control of the governor, a process that combined and redefined more than 300 previously independent state agencies of questionable accountability.

Gubernatorial reforms have had less effect in Rhode Island, the smallest state in both New England and the country. Like its neighbors, Rhode Island underwent a period of departmental consolidation and an expansion of gubernatorial authority after the Democrats took control of state government in 1935. New executive agencies were created in the decades after the war, and the governor was granted substantial budgetary authority. These statutory reforms had limited effect, however, and it was not until 1992 that the constitution was amended to give the governor a four-year term.

Farther north, in Vermont and New Hampshire, social conditions have changed less dramatically than in the states of southern New England. Consequently, there has been less need and desire for the executive reorganizations typical in more urban Connecticut, Massachusetts, and Rhode Island. The political culture of Vermont remains traditionally Yankee in its appreciation of localized politics and legislative ascendancy. Along with New Hampshire, Vermont is one of the few states in the country whose governors serve two-year terms. New Hampshire, historically one of the most conservative states in the nation, has similarly avoided any dramatic transferals of power to its executive branch. In fact, New Hampshire is alone among New England states in retaining a colonial-era governor's council with authority to frustrate gubernatorial appointments and contracts.

In a bow to the inescapable pressures of modernization, however, various executive agencies have been introduced in Vermont and New Hampshire over recent decades. The creation of these agencies has undoubtedly elevated gubernatorial responsibilities somewhat, but neither of these two northern New England states seems poised to alter its traditional arrangements in the foreseeable future.

Maine, the physically largest and northernmost New England state, has also embraced only limited reforms, maintaining legislative supremacy over politics and policy. Recent election trends have set the stage for greater gubernatorial intervention in state policy, however; over the last three decades of the 20th century Maine elected two independent candidates to office, James B. Longley in 1974 and Angus King in 1994 and 1998. Lacking the support of political parties, these governors have hinged their success on maintaining highly outspoken, media-friendly administrations. The tactic has provided them with a degree of political leverage in areas of public policy in the absence of substantial statutory or constitutional reforms.

While economic and demographic trends prompted the first increase in gubernatorial responsibility throughout New England, the more recent national move toward passing policy responsibilities from the federal government to the states seems likely to further the process. Greater responsibility at the state level will require greater executive managerial authority. As the most visible spokespersons of state government, governors will likely be called on to assume that authority. In 1996, for example, when states had to implement their own welfare programs, five of the six states in New England formulated them under executive supervision.

New England nonetheless continues to distinguish itself for its relative lack of gubernatorial authority. According to a respected social-science indicator, *CQ's State Fact Finder*, all New England governors except Connecticut's rank at the low end of a gubernatorial power-ranking scale. With a score of one being most powerful, Massachusetts and New Hampshire are tied for 32d place; Maine is 38th, Rhode Island 41st, and Vermont 48th. Since the pattern of constrained executive authority reflects a cultural legacy dating back three centuries, one would be hard-pressed to predict that the current air of neo-Federalism will decisively alter the dynamics of New England's gubernatorial institutions.

Michael Barone, Grant Ujifusa, and Richard E. Cohen, comps., *The Almanac of American Politics, 1998: The Senators, the Representatives, and the Governors* (1997); Council of State Governments, *The Book of the States 32* (1998); Kendra A. Hovey and Harold A. Hovey, *CQ's State Fact Finder, 1998: Rankings across America* (1998); Massachusetts General Court, *A Manual for the Use of the General Court, 1997–1998* (1997); Jerome M. Mileur, ed., *Parties and Politics in the New England States* (1997); Neal R. Peirce, *The New England States: People, Politics, and Power in the Six New England States* (1976); *Register and Manual: State of Connecticut* (1997).

Scott Harris

Grasso, Ella T. (1919–81) Politician, U.S. representative, governor of Connecticut. Ella (Tambussi) Grasso was born in Windsor Locks, Conn., where her parents' bakery served the town's large Italian American community. Educated at Mount Holyoke College, from which she earned both a bachelor's and a master's degree, Grasso became active in local and state civic organizations during World War II. Grasso received the Windsor Locks Democratic Town Committee's backing for a seat in the state assembly and was elected in 1952. Serving from 1952 until 1956, she quickly gained a reputation as a proponent of good government by supporting workmen's compensation reform, advocating the elimination of the county governmental structure, and assisting education groups, the disabled, and

Governor Ella Grasso, 1978

consumers. At the same time, she attracted the attention of Democratic state chairman John Bailey, who assisted her in her ascent to the upper ranks of Connecticut's Democratic leadership.

In 1958 Grasso ran for her first statewide position as secretary of state and won the office in a Democratic landslide led by Governor Abraham Ribicoff. From the unofficial command post in her office during the next two years Grasso, Bailey, and other Democratic leaders guided the legislative session that passed court reform and abolished county government. In 1960, following Bailey's appointment as chairman of the Democratic National Committee, Grasso became Bailey's first lieutenant in Connecticut. She also gained national prominence by serving as a member of the platform committee at the 1960 Democratic National Convention. Reelected secretary of state in 1962 and 1966 by large pluralities, Grasso served in that position longer than anyone else in Connecticut history. In 1970 she was elected U.S. representative for Connecticut's Sixth Congressional District. Although Grasso did not achieve the quick success and prominence in Washington, D.C., that she had in Connecticut, she was reelected in 1972 despite Richard Nixon's Republican landslide. Her victory fueled speculation that she might be able to capture the Connecticut governorship in 1974.

With Bailey's assistance Grasso was unanimously chosen the Democratic Party's gubernatorial candidate. She defeated her opponent by more than 200,000 votes in the general election, becoming the nation's first female governor to be elected without having been preceded by her husband.

Immediately following her election she was confronted with major budget shortfalls. Although Grasso had built a reputation as a reformer and supporter of social causes throughout her political career, she proceeded to alienate liberal groups by instituting an aggressive austerity program. Despite her growing unpopularity in the state, Democratic leaders considered her for the 1976 presidential and vice presidential nominations. She sought neither but served as cochair of the Democratic National Convention. By 1976 the state budget situation had markedly improved, and Grasso began repairing ties to her traditional constituents in addition to building support within the Connecticut business community. In 1978 Grasso effectively used the media to guide the state through a devastating blizzard and, after overcoming a primary challenge from her lieutenant governor, was overwhelmingly reelected.

During her second term Grasso led the state through an energy crisis and recovery from a violent tornado that devastated parts of Windsor Locks and Windsor in 1979. Her calmness and sympathy during these and previous crises gained her a reputation as Connecticut's caring "mother." In 1980, at the peak of her power and popularity, Grasso was diagnosed with cancer and, in failing health, resigned as governor on December 31, 1980. She died on February 5, 1981, in Windsor Locks.

Ella Grasso spent three decades in public life and never lost an election. Neither a feminist nor a liberal, Grasso was a consummate Connecticut moderate, concerned with social causes but unwilling to force change. This attribute, which served her so well in her bids for elective office, was also the source of some criticism, as Grasso—like the popular Governor Ribicoff before her, following the precepts of party boss Bailey—refused to consider a progressive state income tax. To maintain her popularity among state moderates, she, ironically, supported the heavy taxation—Connecticut had the highest sales tax in the nation—of people with lower incomes, the very constituency whose support had launched her career.

Susan Bysiewicz, *Ella: A Biography of Governor Ella Grasso* (1984); Joseph I. Lieberman, *The Legacy: Connecticut Politics, 1930–1980* (1981).

Patrick J. Deneen

Green, Theodore Francis (1867–1966)

Politician, governor of Rhode Island, and U.S. senator. Theodore Francis Green was born in 1867 into a family that was part of a rich tradition of patrician involvement in public affairs. He graduated from Brown University with both bachelor's and master's degrees and lived throughout his life in the large Green family home on the genteel East Side of Providence. People like Green became the urban, middle-class leaders of the Progressive movement that dominated American political life from 1900 to the end of World War I. During his political career Green succeeded in changing the political landscape of Rhode Island, and his legacy still resonates in the public life of his native state.

After studying law at Harvard University, Green was admitted to the Rhode Island bar in 1892. He then furthered his studies at the universities of Bonn and Berlin in Germany. In 1894 Green began teaching Roman law at Brown University and went into practice with his father the same year. The Spanish-American War (1898) brought Green a commission as second lieutenant. After his father died in 1903, Green spent 20 years practicing law, first on his own and then as a member of several different firms. He also held positions on the boards of numerous Providence companies. Green began his political career in 1906, just as the Progressives were coming to power nationally, when he was elected to the Rhode Island House of Representatives. A Democrat, he did not hold a major statewide office until 1932 because Rhode Island politics was dominated by Republicans who kept their party in power by limiting the right to vote. Nonetheless, Green honed his skills as a politician by staying involved in the complicated political affairs of his home state. By the end of the 1920s he and others had fashioned an urban, working-class political machine. By 1932 Green was in a position to take advantage of the political revolution that occurred with the onset of the Great Depression and the election of Franklin D. Roosevelt to the presidency.

Rhode Island was deeply in need of reform. Heavily industrialized since the mid-19th century, the state had a significant working-class population of European immigrants who were all but disfranchised by archaic political practices that still operated in the Ocean State. Green was elected to his first term as governor in 1932 and was reelected two years later. In 1935, after Green and his supporters had gained full control of the Rhode Island legislature, Democrats succeeded in taking patronage away from the upper house of the legislature and placing it for the first time in the hands of the governor, thereby establishing a Democratic dominance in the state that in many ways remains today.

In 1936, at the age of 69, Green won election to the U.S. Senate. Over the next 24 years (1937–61) he was a model of personal integrity, service to the state of Rhode Island, and national involvement in New Deal liberalism. His close personal ties to President Roosevelt were of considerable help in enabling Rhode Island to become home to major U.S. naval installations at Newport and Quonset Point. He was a consistent defender of New Deal domestic social programs throughout his career. In the 1950s Green was also one of the few politicians whom Joseph McCarthy hesitated to attack. He strongly opposed McCarthy and voted for his censure when the Senate finally decided to discipline the Wisconsinite. Green also took great interest in foreign policy matters, was a member of the Senate Foreign Relations Committee for most of his senatorial career, and became chairman of that powerful committee in the late 1950s. He retired from the Senate in January 1961 at the age of 93 and died in Providence five years later.

James Findlay, "The Great Textile Strike of 1934: Illuminating Rhode Island History in the Thirties," *Rhode Island History* 42 (1983); Erwin L. Levine, *Theodore Francis Green: The Rhode Island Years, 1906–1936* (1963); Levine, *Theodore Francis Green: The Washington Years, 1937–1960* (1971).

James Findlay

John F. Kennedy School of Government

The John F. Kennedy School of Government was dedicated in 1978, following a decision to combine Harvard University's existing Master in Public Administration Program, Master in Public Policy Program, and Institute of Politics. Harvard and Kennedy family members and friends had established the Institute of Politics in 1966, as a living memorial to the late president, to connect the study of government with the practice of politics. The Kennedy School of Government has since grown to include many research, executive, and professional programs.

The school has long had an image in the public mind of liberal activism, dating from the 1936 inception of the Harvard University Graduate School of Public Administration during the New Deal. In the late 1960s and 1970s, many of its faculty members were associated with the Kennedy administration and its policies, establishing a "brain trust" with a distinctly liberal bent. The Kennedy School conducted orientation programs for newly elected members of Congress until the Republican Party took control in 1994. In recent years, however, the image of the school has changed with the inclusion of noted conservatives such as the former Republican senator from Wyoming Alan Simpson, the former congressman from Oklahoma Mickey Edwards, and the former mayor from Indianapolis Stephen Goldsmith.

The Kennedy School of Government prepares its students for public service by emphasizing research and experience and by fostering the collaborative efforts of scholars, public officials, and others concerned with the public good. The Kennedy School's more than 15,000 graduates from nearly 120 countries have led governments on five continents. Alumni of the school and its predecessors have held cabinet-level positions and served as senior advisers to every U.S. president since Franklin D. Roosevelt. Graduates currently serve in both houses of Congress. Other alumni play important roles in state and local government, while still others guide the activities of private and nonprofit organizations. The school's international students often assume critical positions in their countries of origin at all levels of government. Many more shape important public policies and direct institutional research.

The Kennedy School attracts a perpetual stream of activists, theorists, and politicians. Students participate in events and discussions with members of Congress, state legislators, world leaders, political pollsters, candidates, campaign managers, policymakers, community activists, public interest group leaders, and others. The Institute of Politics sponsors the ARCO Forum of Public Affairs, considered a center of political discourse in New England and the nation. The ARCO Forum has held public events featuring notable figures from around the world; recent ARCO Forum speakers have included the Dalai Lama, Yasser Arafat, Bob Dole, Lech Walesa, George H. W. Bush, Hillary Rodham Clinton, and Pakistan's Benazir Bhutto.

Each year, approximately 800 full-time students, 37 percent of whom are international students, are enrolled in the school's degree programs, which include the Master in Public Policy, Master in Public Policy and Urban Planning, Mid-Career Master in Public Administration, and the two-year Master in Public Administration programs, and doctoral programs. A Master in Public Administration in International Development was recently added. The school also offers nondegree executive programs for administrators from public and nonprofit organizations.

The Kennedy School has more than 100 full-time faculty representing 15 academic disciplines, including economics, political science, sociology, law, public policy, and history. Additionally, the school's faculty includes former elected officials from international, national, and state governments, as well as officials from the nonprofit and private sectors. Actively engaged in world affairs, faculty at the Kennedy School shape public policy, advise governments, and help run major institutions in the United States and abroad.

Morton Keller and Phyllis Keller, *Making Harvard Modern: The Rise of America's University* (2001).

Adrianne Kaufmann

Kennedy Family The Kennedy family's attainment of social status and political ascendancy reflects the ethnic, cultural, and religious transformation of New England society and politics between 1850 and 1900. After her husband, Patrick (1823–58), died, Bridget (Murphy) Kennedy (1821–88) was left with four children to rear on her own. Like thousands of Irish Catholic immigrants to Massachusetts in the second quarter of the 19th century, she worked to overcome poverty and prejudice. She eventually scraped together the money to buy a small notions shop in East Boston. Her son, Patrick Joseph (1858–1929), assisted by her savings, opened a tavern in 1882.

Like many tavern keepers of the time, Kennedy found his tavern clientele to be the basis for a political career. Elected to the state legislature at the age of 28, Patrick Joseph Kennedy was already a political force in Boston when he clashed with the Massachusetts congressman John Francis "Honey Fitz" Fitzgerald over their party's choice for mayor

Joseph P. Kennedy and family, 1930s

of Boston in 1905. The rivalry finally ended in 1914, when Kennedy's son, Joseph Patrick (1888–1969), who had graduated from Harvard in 1912, and the mayor's daughter, Rose Elizabeth Fitzgerald (1890–1995), were married.

Over the next two decades, Rose (Fitzgerald) Kennedy raised five daughters (Rosemary [1918–2005], Kathleen [1920–48], Eunice [1921–], Patricia [1924–], and Jean [1928–]) and four sons (Joseph Jr. [1915–44], John (Jack) [1917–63], Robert [1925–68], and Edward (Ted) [1932–]) while her husband sought wealth, social acceptance, and political influence. Despite Joseph's prolonged absences from home and apparent infidelities, the couple remained bound together by genuine affection, their Roman Catholic faith, and a fierce commitment to the future of their children. By the 1930s Kennedy had made a fortune in the stock market and real estate, in Hollywood films, and by importing liquor after the repeal of Prohibition.

In 1932 Joseph Kennedy supported Franklin D. Roosevelt for president, hoping to fill an important post in a Democratic administration. FDR made Kennedy chair of the new Securities and Exchange Commission even though several of his advisers opposed Kennedy, calling him an unscrupulous Wall Street operator. Kennedy developed an uneasy working relationship with Roosevelt and used his skill for self-promotion to become one of the most quoted members of the administration. Kennedy contributed time, money, and a ghostwritten book, *I'm for Roosevelt*, to the president's 1936 reelection campaign in the hope of becoming secretary of the treasury.

FDR made him chair of the Maritime Commission in 1937 and in December of that year appointed him ambassador to Great Britain, the most coveted American diplomatic post.

The attractive Kennedy family was soon front-page news as Rose and the children became instant celebrities in British high society in 1938. The new ambassador delighted the press with his contempt for social protocol and angered the State Department with his disdain for the diplomatic establishment. Kennedy was drawn into the circle around Prime Minister Neville Chamberlain and supported efforts to appease Nazi Germany, believing that the 1938 Munich Pact would satisfy Adolf Hitler. If he could help to keep the United States out of war, Kennedy reasoned, he might emerge as a credible successor to FDR in 1940. Instead, he became anathema to Chamberlain's successor, Winston Churchill, nearly broke with FDR over the president's support of Churchill's fight against Nazi aggression, and was fatally identified with the collapse of appeasement. His political hopes shattered, Joseph P. Kennedy returned to business pursuits and became determined to promote the political career of his son Joseph Jr.

In the 1940s a series of tragedies transformed the Kennedy family. In 1941, without consulting his wife, the ambassador arranged for a risky lobotomy for their eldest daughter, Rosemary, whose behavior had become increasingly erratic and unmanageable. The operation failed and the 23-year-old had to be institutionalized. In 1944 Joseph Jr. was killed when his plane exploded during a bombing mission over Europe. In 1948 daughter Kathleen died in a plane crash in France.

Both parents expected their sons to go to the best prep schools and colleges to prepare for careers in business, law, and politics. Their daughters attended parochial schools. John Fitzgerald Kennedy, despite a sickly childhood and adolescence, entered Harvard in 1936 and published, with his father's help, a revision of his senior thesis, *Why England Slept*, in 1940. Three years later, after leading his crew through a weeklong ordeal after the sinking of their patrol boat by a Japanese destroyer off the Solomon Islands, Jack Kennedy became a decorated war hero.

In 1946, already ill with Addison's disease, a debilitating hormonal imbalance, the 29-year-old JFK was elected to Congress from Massachusetts. Joseph Kennedy financed the campaign but, in a pattern repeated throughout his son's career, remained discreetly in the background. After three terms in the House, JFK ran for the U.S. Senate against the popular Republican incumbent Henry Cabot Lodge, Jr., in 1952. Rose Kennedy and her daughters organized a series of teas to bring women to the polls, helping JFK win despite a Republican presidential landslide. In 1953 the freshman senator married the socialite Jacqueline Lee Bouvier (1929–94) in a highly publicized wedding in Newport, R.I. The press began to speculate that JFK had his sights on the White House.

Kennedy survived nearly fatal spinal surgery in 1954. During his convalescence, with the aid of his wife and several associates, he wrote *Profiles in Courage* (1956), which won the Pulitzer Prize for biography in 1957. Reelected to the Senate in 1958 with 74 percent of the vote, Kennedy announced his bid for the presidency early in 1960. In response to concerns about his youth and Catholic religion, JFK entered primaries in West Virginia and Wisconsin to prove he could win in states with Protestant majorities. The strategy worked; he captured the nomination on the first ballot. Trailing in the polls, Kennedy challenged his Republican rival, Vice President Richard Nixon, to a series of live television debates that helped to mute the religious issue and erode the public perception that JFK was too young and inexperienced to be president. The election was very close; Kennedy's popular vote margin was less than 119,000 out of the 69 million votes cast.

The Kennedys and their small children (Caroline [1957–] and John Jr. [1960–99]) captivated the public. JFK's 34-month presidency was marked by confrontations with the Soviet Union over Berlin and Cuba, acceleration of the nuclear arms race, and escalation of the U.S. military presence in South Vietnam. Kennedy was slow to act on civil rights but in

1963 became the first president to declare racial equality a moral issue and submit comprehensive legislation to Congress to end racial segregation. Later that year he also signed the first arms control agreement of the Cold War, the Limited Test Ban Treaty.

With the president's brother Robert serving as attorney general, his brother-in-law Sargent Shriver serving as head of the Peace Corps, and his youngest brother, Ted, elected to JFK's Senate seat in 1962, commentators talked of a Kennedy dynasty. The press delighted in covering family touch-football games at the Kennedys' Hyannisport, Mass., home, and satirists mimicked the president's Boston accent. Disabled by a stroke in late 1961 and unable to speak, Joseph Kennedy remained in the background while Rose Kennedy presided as matriarch over her famous clan. The Kennedy ascendancy ended, however, when the 46-year-old JFK was shot and killed in Dallas, Tex., on November 22, 1963.

Although Robert Kennedy was shattered by his brother's death, he left the Justice Department in 1964 and ran successfully for a U.S. Senate seat in New York. During the next four years he became a champion of economic and racial justice and an outspoken opponent of the war in Vietnam, which he had once supported. In 1968 he entered the presidential race but was assassinated in Los Angeles after winning the California primary. A year later, Edward Kennedy withstood pressure to resign from the Senate after a young woman passenger drowned when he drove his car off a bridge on Martha's Vineyard. Joseph Kennedy died late in 1969, a mute and helpless witness to the tragedies that had engulfed his family and his ambitions.

Despite a failed challenge to President Jimmy Carter for the 1980 presidential nomination, Ted Kennedy was reelected to the Senate in 1982, and became one of the most influential senators of the 20th century. His son Patrick (1967–) was elected to the Rhode Island legislature in 1988 and won a seat in Congress in 1994. Two of Robert Kennedy's children have also entered politics: Joseph P. Kennedy II (1952–) became a U.S. congressman from Massachusetts in 1986, and Kathleen Kennedy Townsend (1951–) became the first Kennedy woman to hold public office when she was elected lieutenant governor of Maryland in 1994; she failed, however, to be elected governor in 2002.

Jacqueline Bouvier Kennedy married the shipping tycoon Aristotle Onassis in 1968. After his death, she became a successful editor; she died in New York in 1994. Caroline (Kennedy) Schlossberg earned a law degree and has written several books on constitu-

tional issues. John F. Kennedy, Jr., completed law school and became a magazine editor before his death in a private plane crash in 1999.

The Kennedys have long been known for their social activism. Eunice (Kennedy) Shriver began the organization that has grown into the Special Olympics, and other family members have become environmental activists and advocates of low-cost energy for the poor. The Kennedys have remained, whether in triumph or tragedy, one of the most interesting and enduring public families in American history.

Peter Collier and David Horowitz, *The Kennedys: An American Drama* (1984); Doris Kearns Goodwin, *The Fitzgeralds and the Kennedys* (1987); Nigel Hamilton, *JFK: Reckless Youth* (1992); Rose Kennedy, *Times to Remember* (1974); David E. Koskoff, *Joseph P. Kennedy: A Life and Times* (1974); Laurence Leamer, *The Kennedy Women: The Saga of an American Family* (1994); Herbert Parmet, *Jack: The Struggles of John F. Kennedy* (1980); Garry Wills, *The Kennedy Imprisonment: A Meditation on Power* (1982).

Sheldon M. Stern

Kerry, John (Forbes) (1943–) U.S. senator, Democratic candidate for president.

John Kerry decided early in life that he shared the politics and ambition of another man from Massachusetts with the same initials, John F. Kennedy. Kerry was born in Denver, Colo., but grew up in locations around the country and in Europe depending on the postings of his father, Richard Kerry, a foreign service officer. John Kerry attended a series of boarding schools, including the exclusive Saint Paul's School in Concord, N.H., before following in his father's footsteps to Yale. Kerry fared well, becoming a leader in the debate club and the Yale political union, and he joked that he "majored in flying" his senior year, often going on aerial jaunts. Upon graduation in 1966, Kerry joined the navy, serving in Vietnam, where he earned three purple hearts, a Bronze Star, and a Silver Star.

While in Vietnam, Kerry began to question the conduct and purpose of the war. After obtaining an early release from active naval service to seek a state house seat in Massachusetts (unsuccessfully), Kerry became active in the group Vietnam Veterans against the War. By 1971, Kerry had become a leader of the group, testifying before the Senate Foreign Relations Committee about stories of atrocities allegedly committed by U.S. soldiers and asking, "How do you ask a man to be the last man to die for a mistake?" In secretly recorded tapes, President Richard Nixon noted that Kerry was "extremely effective," but also wondered whether he was sincere.

After failing in a 1972 bid for Congress,

Kerry attended law school, then worked as a prosecutor, and in 1982 successfully ran for lieutenant governor of Massachusetts. He won a U.S. Senate seat in 1984, quickly using his talent as a prosecutor to launch a series of investigations, starting with a probe into the Iran-Contra affair. Kerry's voting record was often rated liberal, but he noted that he also backed more conservative legislation, such as a deficit-reduction bill.

Kerry and his first wife, Julia Thorne (with whom he had two daughters, Alexandra and Vanessa), were divorced in 1988. He met his second wife, Teresa Heinz, at the 1992 Earth Summit in Brazil. Heinz, the Mozambique-born widow of the late Pennsylvania Republican senator John Heinz, had taken over running his family's ketchup business. Heinz and Kerry were married in 1995, and she became an outspoken advocate for her husband on the campaign trail.

In 2004, Kerry received the Democratic nomination for president, running against fellow Yale alumnus President George W. Bush. Kerry lost the close race, although he retains his Senate seat.

Michael Kranish, Brian C. Mooney, and Nina Easton, *John F. Kerry: The Complete Biography by the Boston Globe Reporters Who Know Him Best* (2004).
Michael Kranish

Kunin, Madeleine M. (1933–) Governor of Vermont and U.S. ambassador to Switzerland. One of the first female governors in the United States, Madeleine Kunin was born Madeleine May in Zurich, Switzerland. After service in the Vermont legislature and two terms as lieutenant governor, she was elected as Vermont's first female governor in 1984 and served three terms (1984–90). After her Vermont political career, Kunin served on President Bill Clinton's 1992 transition team, as deputy secretary of education (1993–96), and then as U.S. ambassador to Switzerland and Liechtenstein (1996–99).

Like many Vermonters, Kunin is an immigrant to the state, having arrived in the United States in 1940 with her mother and brother as refugees from the Nazi onslaught in Europe. With a bachelor's degree in history from the University of Massachusetts (1956) and a master's from Columbia's prestigious School of Journalism (1957), her first reporting job took her to Vermont, where she met and married Dr. Arthur Kunin in 1959. While raising four children during the 1960s, she was actively involved in the League of Women Voters and community affairs, also earning a master's degree in English literature from the University of Vermont (1967).

Kunin's political interests and abilities

Vermont state legislator (later governor) Madeleine Kunin, 1976

quickly expanded when she ran for the Vermont House in 1972. During her legislative years (1972–78), she became the first woman in Vermont to hold legislative leadership posts, as Democratic House minority whip and as the first female chair of the House Appropriations Committee. Her subsequent election and tenure as Vermont's second female lieutenant governor (1978–82) was marked by frequent policy splits with Republican governor Richard Snelling, and her first effort to rise to the governorship ended in a close loss to Snelling in 1982.

Kunin's tenure as governor was notable for its focus on promoting women leaders. Following in the footsteps of Connecticut governor Ella Grasso (the first woman elected governor without having been preceded by her husband), Kunin appointed women to key positions, including the first woman on the Vermont Supreme Court, the first female director of forests and parks in the United States, and numerous female cabinet secretaries. Her many policy initiatives included establishment of a family court, expansion of programs for children, improvement of community mental health services, establishment of property tax relief, and institution of landmark land use legislation (Act 200).

Kunin's administration also reflected changes in the political culture of Vermont and New England. An influx since the 1960s of people with different political orientations resulted in

a string of governors who (like Kunin) were born outside Vermont, as well as a shift to Democratic Party dominance in the state. These "new Vermonters" were concerned about economic, environmental, and educational issues that set much of the agenda for Kunin and her successor, Howard Dean. Her political legacy to this "new Vermont" is twofold: promotion of a pathbreaking generation of women leaders, and nationally recognized achievement in education, environmental, and mental health policies.

After leaving the governor's office, Kunin founded the Institute of Sustainable Communities, a nonprofit organization dedicated to helping communities in democracies and emerging democracies solve problems by offering training, technical assistance, and grants. She is currently distinguished visiting professor at the University of Vermont and Saint Michael's College.

Michael Barone and Grant Ujifusa, "Vermont," in *Almanac of American Politics 1990* (1990); Madeleine Kunin, *Living a Political Life* (1994); Garrison Nelson, "Vermont's Politics Transformed: 'How Come It Got Fixed When It Warn't Broke?'" *Polity Supplement* (1997); Joe Sherman, *Fast Lane on a Dirt Road: Vermont Transformed, 1945–1990* (1991).
Paul R. Petterson

League of Women Voters The League of Women Voters is a significant nonpartisan force in New England, working through state

and local chapters to promote active, informed participation in electoral politics and government; to help citizens better understand public policy issues; and to improve the health, education, and welfare of the region's inhabitants.

On February 14, 1920, with the 19th Amendment to the Constitution on its way to ratification, Carrie Chapman Catt (1859–1947) transformed the National American Woman Suffrage Association (NAWSA) into the National League of Women Voters (later League of Women Voters of the United States) at the NAWSA convention in Chicago. Chapters of the league, open to both women and men, had formed in every New England state by 1921.

From the outset the New England affiliates have made important contributions to the national organization. A Maine resident, Maud Wood Park, served as the league's first president from 1920 to 1924. Dorothy Brown, president of the Massachusetts chapter of the league from 1939 to 1942, served as child welfare chair while the league worked toward passage of the Sheppard-Towner Act, coordinating state and federal aid to mothers and children, in 1921. Katharine Ludington, founder of Connecticut's chapter of the league, became national treasurer during the pioneering years of the organization (1922–27). Percy Lee, a former Connecticut president, led the national organization from 1950 until 1958, a period during which the league dropped its opposition to the Equal Rights Amendment (1954) and is credited with updating its initiatives.

All New England affiliates campaigned jointly for legislation such as the Clean Air Act of 1990, the passage of which capped a 10-year league effort, and the "motor voter" provision of the National Voter Registration Act of 1993, which enables citizens to register to vote at the same time as they apply for a driver's license.

New England league chapters have also enthusiastically adopted programs to address educational concerns and political challenges in their respective states. In 1997, for example, the Massachusetts league undertook a two-year study to determine how funds for special education could be distributed more equitably and led the campaign to limit the terms of elected officials in that state. The Connecticut affiliate, along with the *Hartford Courant*, has sponsored student-parent mock elections to encourage young people to become engaged in the political process and regularly publishes nonpartisan citizen-education materials, including *Voting in Connecticut* and *Connecticut: A Guide to State Government*. In 1997 the Maine branch began conducting an in-depth

study of the University of Maine system in response to budgetary problems and low enrollment. The chapter also sponsored candidate-training workshops to encourage women and minorities to run for elective public offices. Representative Jane Saxl of Bangor, Maine, a former league president, credited the league with providing the on-the-job training that led her to make a bid for public office. The Rhode Island chapter's Internet Mentoring Project has coordinated funding and technical support that allows public school students in Providence to access the Internet and has lobbied against legislative appointments to public boards and commissions, which the organization views as a commingling of executive and legislative powers. Vermont's affiliate, though New England's smallest, joins with other civic-minded organizations to sponsor forums on public policy issues affecting the residents of that state.

For more than eight decades the League of Women Voters has pursued the organization's founding objectives of education and advocacy, and the New England chapters have made significant contributions to advancing those goals.

Louise M. Young, *In the Public Interest: The League of Women Voters, 1920–1970* (1989).

Julieanne Phillips

Lieberman, Joe (Joseph Isadore)

(1942–) U.S. senator, attorney general of Connecticut, Democratic nominee for vice president. Joe Lieberman, the son of two first-generation Americans, was born in Stamford, Conn. The first member of his family to attend college, he graduated from Yale College (1964) and Yale Law School (1967). An impassioned advocate of the importance of public service, Lieberman acknowledges the strong influence that President John Kennedy of Massachusetts and longtime Connecticut state Democratic chairman John Bailey have had on his political ideals. In the 1960s he participated in the 1963 March on Washington and went south to register black voters in Mississippi.

Throughout his political career Lieberman has maintained a reputation for civility and allegiance to principle. Though he demonstrates loyalty to the Democratic Party, he has proven to be a legislator who tries to find bipartisan solutions. From an early age he was willing to challenge the political status quo. He helped establish a reform and antiwar caucus of Connecticut Democrats, and in 1970 he defeated the state senate majority leader in a primary. Lieberman spent 10 years in the state senate, the last six as majority leader.

In 1980 he ran for an open U.S. House seat but he lost the general election. Two years later

he was elected Connecticut's attorney general. During his six-year tenure he focused on fathers who reneged on child-support payments, polluters, and corporate fraud. In 1988 Lieberman narrowly defeated three-term incumbent Lowell Weicker in the U.S. Senate race. He has subsequently been reelected to the Senate twice by overwhelming margins.

During his Senate years Lieberman has served as both chairman and ranking member of the Senate Governmental Affairs Committee and was an influential chair of the Democratic Leadership Council, although he stood apart from most members of the Senate Democratic caucus when he criticized President Clinton's behavior in the Monica Lewinsky scandal. He has been a strong advocate for a cleaner environment and campaign finance reform. In foreign policy he has supported the use of U.S. military power, including the Gulf War (1991), ground troops in Kosovo (1998), and the invasions of Afghanistan (2001) and Iraq (2004). Lieberman also helped persuade President George W. Bush to support the creation of a Department of Homeland Security.

In the summer of 2000, Lieberman was chosen as Al Gore's vice presidential running mate—the first Jew to receive a place on a major party presidential ticket. The choice catapulted Lieberman into the national spotlight. He refused to campaign on the Jewish Sabbath or on religious holidays, and his deeply held faith became the central focus of his early campaign. Yet despite the emphasis on his religion, there is no evidence that it hurt the Democratic ticket; most analysts have argued that Lieberman was a positive factor for the Democrats.

After the contested 2000 election was decided by the Supreme Court, Lieberman resumed his duties in the Senate. He pledged not to run for president in 2004 if Al Gore decided to run, a promise he kept, though perhaps to his political detriment. Lieberman's late start in 2004 was clearly a factor (along with his hawkish foreign policy stance) in his failure to capture the Democratic nomination.

Michael Barone and Richard E. Cohen, *The Almanac of American Politics, 2004* (2003); Joseph I. Lieberman, *In Praise of Public Life* (2000).

Ira Forman

Lodge Family

In the annals of New England political families the Lodges rank close to the Adamses and Kennedys in their commitment and contributions to this nation's history. As ambassadors, senators and congressmen, presidential troubleshooters, governor, vice presidential nominee, and recipients of distinguished foreign awards and high academic degrees, the Lodges have earned their lofty status. These formidable achievements define three Lodges: Henry Cabot Lodge (1850–1924) and his grandsons, Henry Cabot Lodge, Jr. (1902–85) and John Davis Lodge (1903–85).

The union of the Cabots and the Lodges began with the marriage in the early 1830s between Anna Cabot and John Ellerton Lodge. The bride's family was a century-long member of Boston's elite; the groom was the son of Giles Lodge, the first Lodge to arrive in America, in 1791. Their son was Henry Cabot Lodge, Harvard professor and leader of the U.S. Senate's successful opposition to President Woodrow Wilson's effort to bring the United States into the League of Nations. The motivation for this extraordinary trio's record of public service might have originated with George Cabot (1751–1823), an influential figure in American politics after the Revolutionary War. He was a Massachusetts federal senator, titular head of the Federalist Party after Alexander Hamilton's death, and the elected president of the Hartford Convention. Its report, written partly by him, rejected secession owing to his commanding influence. Henry Cabot Lodge, a biographer of George Washington, Hamilton, and Daniel Webster, author of other scholarly works, and the preeminent model of the scholar in politics, was elected to the U.S. Senate in 1893 following several terms in the Massachusetts House. As a member and later chairman of the Senate's Foreign Relations Committee, he was instrumental in resolving the dispute over the Alaskan boundary and bringing about immigration reform (which included verbal skirmishing with a Bostonian from a different Boston, Congressman James Michael Curley). He supported Theodore Roosevelt's maneuverings to build the Panama Canal, Admiral Thomas Mahan's arguments for a strong navy, and the nation's imperialism that arose out of the Spanish American War. He opposed the populist movement in general and free silver in particular, woman suffrage, prohibition, direct election of senators, and international arbitration. Henry Cabot Lodge's son, George Cabot "Bay" Lodge (1873–1909), had not the slightest interest in politics. He was a published poet with a good working knowledge of ancient Egyptian and French and Italian Renaissance literature, but he died at age 36 of acute appendicitis.

Henry Cabot Lodge, Jr., and John Davis Lodge shared an inspiring, humanities-tempered political inheritance. Henry Cabot was the model Republican liberal; John Davis was the model Republican conservative. After two terms in the Massachusetts House, Henry Cabot was elected to the U.S. Senate in 1936, where he would remain, with the interruption of wartime service in the army, until his loss to

John F. Kennedy in 1952. He was appointed ambassador to the United Nations in the same year. His seven well-televised years gave him national status, leading to his selection as Richard Nixon's vice presidential nominee in 1960. He was appointed ambassador to Vietnam by President Kennedy, the first of several appointments, where he was in effect a troubleshooter and often at odds with generals and upper-level politicians, both Vietnamese and American. He ended his political career with an unsuccessful bid for the 1964 Republican Party presidential nomination, a brief tenure as ambassador to the German Federal Republic, and as chief negotiator at the 1969 Paris Peace Talks.

To many Americans of the 1930s and early 1940s, John Davis was likely better known than his brother. He was a popular Hollywood star who appeared often with box office idols. After wartime service with the navy, he served two terms in Congress, where he caused headline controversy at home and in Europe during a trip to Russian satellite countries by proposing to honor their anticommunist heroes. He was elected governor of Connecticut in 1950 but lost his bid for a second term to Abraham Ribicoff in 1954. John Davis is best remembered in Connecticut for his building of the Connecticut Thruway, overcoming strong opposition from immensely wealthy Fairfield County Republicans. He ended his political career as ambassador to Spain and, briefly, to Argentina.

Alden Hatch, *The Lodges of Massachusetts* (1973); Henry Cabot Lodge, Jr., *As It Was: An Insider's View of Politics and Power in the '50s and '60s* (1976); William J. Miller, *Henry Cabot Lodge: A Biography* (1967); William C. Widenor, *Henry Cabot Lodge and the Search for an American Foreign Policy* (1980).

Edmund B. Sullivan

Martin, Joseph W., Jr. (1884–1968)

U.S. representative and Speaker of the House. Born in North Attleboro, Mass., Joseph W. Martin, Jr., spent most of his life in public service. During the 1940s and 1950s he was the Republican leader in the U.S. House of Representatives and symbolized the compromise-oriented conservatism that dominated the GOP during that era. A pragmatic conservative from a traditionally Republican district, Martin relied on hard work, loyalty, compromise, and sociability to lead the party through a Democrat-dominated era.

Martin was educated in local public schools and chose a career in journalism over college. Initially a newspaper reporter, he eventually became owner and publisher of the *Evening Chronicle* (North Attleboro), which loyally served GOP interests until his death. Martin was elected to the Massachusetts House of

Representatives in 1911. In 1924 he won the U.S. House seat that he was to hold for the next 42 years. He entered the national political scene in 1936, when he managed Alf Landon's presidential campaign on the East Coast. He later managed Wendell Willkie's 1940 presidential campaign. These posts gave Martin the opportunity to forge national political connections and push his own brand of conservatism.

In 1939 Martin was elected Republican minority leader of the House, a position he held until 1959. He also served as Speaker of the House in 1947–48 and 1953–54, periods during which Republicans constituted a majority in that body. In 1940 he presided over the first of five consecutive Republican national conventions, more than have been chaired by any other American in history. In these positions he was noted for his evenhandedness and willingness to compromise to preserve party unity.

Throughout his legislative career Martin upheld his core ideals of limited government and checks on the growth of presidential power. More important than conservative ideology, though, was his loyalty to the GOP and the House, which Martin saw as embodiments of the national interest. Martin always supported compromises that made government work better. During an era when the Republican Party was often divided by internal conflicts, Martin played an important role in maintaining party solidarity.

Always opposed to the expansion of the federal government inherent in the New Deal and the Fair Deal, Martin nevertheless voted in favor of Social Security and the minimum wage. Although he was reluctant to drag the nation into World War II, Martin became a strong supporter of the Cold War, particularly during the Korean War. Although he often used his personal charisma to entice Democrats to join his voting coalitions, Martin rarely took the lead on an issue. Instead, he waited for Republican committee members to recommend a policy and then supported that policy out of party loyalty. Martin felt more comfortable in the role of minority leader in a House controlled by Democrats than he did as Speaker for a Republican majority. He had a close personal relationship with the Democratic Speaker Sam Rayburn, who served during periods of Democratic ascendancy during the 1940s and 1950s, and liked being free to force Democrats to make prudent compromises.

Martin was always attentive to his constituents, attending weddings and club meetings in his district and making appearances at local post offices. Although he opposed the creation of new federal programs, once a program was passed Martin made sure that its funding flowed into his district. Martin's autobiography, *My First Fifty Years in Politics,* appeared in 1960. He left the House on January 3, 1967, after more than 50 years of service to the people of southeastern Massachusetts. Martin died while vacationing in Florida in 1968.

Michael L. Magoon

Mayflower Compact Signed by the Pilgrims before they disembarked at Plymouth on November 21 (November 11 in the old date style), 1620, the Mayflower Compact bound the British colonists to "covenant and combine" themselves into a "civill body politick" promising "just and equall lawes" for the "better ordering and preservation" of the community, the glory of God, the advancement of the Christian faith, and the honor of king and country.

According to William Bradford's history of Plymouth, the compact was deemed necessary because some discontented "strangers" (that is, people not belonging to the Pilgrims' church) had declared their intention to "use their own liberty" when ashore because the royal patent for the colony applied only to Virginia. John Robinson's farewell letters, written in July 1620, had nonetheless already declared that the colonists "are become a body politic" characterized by equality and destined to choose their own rulers. In other words, the Mayflower Compact reflected well-established doctrine among the colonists regarding the nature and purpose of government in church and civil society. Unlike the Fundamental Orders of Connecticut (1639), however, the Mayflower Compact is not a written constitution because it does not ordain specific institutions. It does not frame a government; it proclaims a political community.

In American political culture the Mayflower Compact articulates a communitarian alternative to individualism; historically, its importance grew with perceptions of social fragmentation and disorder. The compact received relatively little attention even in New England until the Jeffersonian era, when New England leaders following the example of John Quincy Adams began to celebrate it as a founding document with claims to rivaling the Declaration of Independence. By the late 19th century the compact was widely incorporated in the curriculum of civic education, especially outside the South.

The Mayflower Compact is still valued because it models a fundamentally democratic polity that in its first principles appeals to the laws of God and nature rather than English common law and hence is not narrowly Anglo-Saxon. Conservative interpreters, however, are apt to stress the compact's concern for social order and discipline: while many com-

mentators have treated the compact as an approximation of social-contract theory, it makes no mention, unlike the Declaration of Independence, of rights or liberties and commits its signatories to "due submission and obedience." Moreover, the compact furnishes support for the argument that American political culture rests on broadly Protestant foundations. (At the same time, since the Pilgrims are less closely associated with repression than are the Puritans, the compact is more easily assimilated to ideas of religious toleration.) More radical thinkers, on the other hand, find something to cherish in the compact's implied precept that individual rights, and especially the right to property, should be subordinated to the common good.

In the 20th century, the Mayflower Compact gradually declined as a civic text. Educators and political leaders today are apt to regard it as too regional, too religious, and too unfriendly to individual liberty, preferring to direct students and citizens to the Declaration of Independence and the Constitution. Still, the Mayflower Compact, a symbol of America's beginnings, upholds—if only in whispers—the dignity of community and public life.

William Bradford, *Of Plymouth Plantation, 1620–1647,* ed. Samuel Eliot Morison (1952); J. Mark Jacobson, *Development of American Political Thought, a Documentary History* (1932); Michael Kammen, *Mystic Chords of Memory: The Transformation of Tradition in American Culture* (1991); Mark L. Sargent, "The Conservative Covenant: The Rise of the Mayflower Compact in American Myth," *New England Quarterly* 61 (1988).

Wilson Carey McWilliams

McCormack, John W. (1891–1980) Politician, U.S. representative, and Speaker of the House. John William McCormack was born in the working-class Irish Catholic neighborhood of South Boston, Mass. His father abandoned the family when John was 13, and the young man dropped out of school in the eighth grade to help support his mother and two younger brothers. He delivered newspapers, served as a messenger for a brokerage house, and worked as an office boy for the attorney William T. Way. Way encouraged McCormack to read law, and in 1913 McCormack passed the Massachusetts bar examination. By the time he was 25, he had embarked on the political career that would take him to Washington, D.C.

McCormack's first bid for public office—to become a delegate to the 1917–18 Massachusetts Constitutional Convention—was successful. World War I soon intervened, however, and he left politics to enlist in the army, rising to the highest noncommissioned rank, sergeant major. After returning from military service, McCormack was elected to the Massachusetts House of Representatives and served from 1920 to 1922. In 1923 he moved on to the state senate for four years, attaining the position of minority leader.

Building on his success at the state level, McCormack decided to go into national politics. His first attempt to gain the 12th Congressional District seat failed, but when he ran again in 1928, he won the seat that he would hold for the next 42 years. Once in Washington, McCormack became acquainted with two Texas Democrats who helped further his rise to power: John Nance Garner, later Franklin D. Roosevelt's vice president, and Sam Rayburn, later Speaker of the House. With the help of these powerful allies, McCormack was appointed to the House Ways and

Former Speaker of the House John McCormack welcomes Tip O'Neill and Paul Tsongas to his office, 1978

Means Committee after only two terms in office.

In the years that followed, McCormack held a series of leadership posts. From 1940 until 1961, depending on which party controlled the House, he served alternately as majority floor leader and minority whip. In late 1961 he was appointed Speaker of the House pro tempore to fill the vacancy caused by Sam Rayburn's death. He was then elected to the post on January 10, 1962, when the 87th Congress reconvened. Interestingly, McCormack, the first Roman Catholic to hold that position, was chosen to be Speaker during the term of the country's first Roman Catholic president, John F. Kennedy.

During his years in Congress, McCormack was an ardent advocate of social welfare programs at home and a strong defense position abroad. He promoted New Deal and Great Society programs, helped keep the Selective Service Act in place before World War II, and assisted in hiding appropriations for the Manhattan Project and the atomic bomb during that war. During the Cold War he promoted science and technology legislation to keep the United States ahead of its adversaries and sponsored the bill that created the National Aeronautics and Space Administration.

McCormack had a reputation as an effective negotiator who knew the art of compromise, believed in the exchange of favors, took care of constituents in his district and in the House, and enjoyed cigars and a good game of poker. In 1971, at the age of 79, McCormack stepped down as Speaker and returned to Boston. He died in his sleep on November 22, 1980.

Ronald M. Peters, Jr., *The American Speakership: The Office in Historical Perspective,* 2d ed. (1997).

Richard A. Loverd

Media and Politics

Considered the birthplace of American journalism, New England at the beginning of the 21st century is home to nearly 100 daily and more than 400 weekly newspapers, more than 500 radio stations, and 63 actively broadcasting television stations.

From the criticism of colonial policy toward Native Americans published in Boston's short-lived *Publick Occurrences* (its first issue, in September 1690, was also its last) to the role played by the *Providence Journal-Bulletin* in forcing two chief justices of the Rhode Island Supreme Court to resign, New England print media have often used their front pages to expose government abuses and have raised passionate editorial voices to guard against continued offenses. Of the four key organizations supporting print journalism in the six-state region, the New England Society of Newspaper

Editors has focused considerable energy on promoting international editorial exchanges, particularly between the United States and the former Soviet Union. The Soviet editorial exchange program, involving more than 60 journalists, began in 1982 and spanned 12 years. According to participants, the exchange contributed significantly to glasnost and to critical change in the politics of the former Soviet regime. Despite the growing influence of television, the print media remain a dominant political force in New England, with major newspapers in all six states significantly shaping and defining the political agenda.

Talk radio also has strong roots in New England. The first broadcast of WBZ in Boston on September 19, 1921, aired speeches delivered by the governors of Massachusetts and Connecticut at the opening of the Eastern States Exposition in Springfield, Mass. Since then, talk radio has taken on a life of its own, and Boston has produced powerful talk-show hosts who have spurred the discussion of topics ranging from affirmative action to school prayer. Jerry Williams, credited with starting two-way telephone talk radio in 1957, is best known for assembling a network of talk-show hosts to oppose the congressional pay raise of 1978. Paul Benzaquin, a former *Boston Globe* reporter turned talk-show host, was so influential in Boston politics that former governor John Volpe was known to call Benzaquin's show from his limousine to set the record straight. Throughout New England, talk shows feature a broad range of political programming, from daily call-in broadcasts that focus on local political issues and debates to more in-depth discussion of political events on an extensive network of public-broadcasting affiliates.

Boston is home to the *Christian Science Monitor,* which has been one of the region's, and the country's, most renowned newspapers. Established as a daily newspaper in 1908 by Mary Baker Eddy, the founder of Christian Science, the original mission of the *Monitor* was to promote economic liberalism and thwart "insufficient freedoms" such as the lack of workers' rights and lack of honest business competition. The winner of seven Pulitzer Prizes—three for international reporting, two for national reporting, one for editorial cartooning, and a special citation—the *Monitor* has taken an editorial stand on such political events as expansion of the British Empire, major 20th-century wars, and woman suffrage. The *Monitor* does not hide the fact that it reports conservatively on medical news because of the position Christian Scientists take on spiritual healing.

The *Boston Globe* flexes the biggest political muscle in the Northeast when it comes to

state and national issues. Established in 1872, the *Globe* boasts 17 Pulitzer Prizes, many of them earned in the 1970s and 1980s for national and local political reporting, distinguished commentary, and political cartoons. The *Globe* employs an award-winning investigative "spotlight team," which diligently reports on state and local governmental abuses. Now owned by the New York Times Corporation, the paper is home to several nationally syndicated columnists, including Ellen Goodman, David Shribman, and David Nyhan. In the Boston political arena, however, the *Globe* shares coverage with Rupert Murdoch's *Boston Herald.*

In broadcasting, the state has 19 television stations, including three public-broadcasting stations owned by the WGBH Educational Foundation. Approximately 166 radio stations, including about 40 with talk or public-affairs programming, share the state's airwaves. *Talkers* magazine, the only trade publication devoted entirely to the talk-radio format, is based in Massachusetts.

The *Hartford Courant,* considered the nation's oldest continuously operating newspaper, wields the most political clout in Connecticut. From its staunch criticisms of Thomas Jefferson's Louisiana Purchase to its fight to access police records involving Governor John G. Rowland, the *Courant* keeps its finger on the political pulse of the state. Today the paper is owned and operated by the Times Mirror Company. The second most influential newspaper group in Connecticut is the Journal Register Company of Trenton, N.J., whose *New Haven Register* is the flagship paper of a string of five dailies. In total, Connecticut is home to 20 daily and approximately 75 weekly newspapers.

Of Connecticut's 12 television stations, three are owned by Connecticut Public Broadcasting and feature forums on the press and on politics such as *Connecticut Lawmakers* and *The Fourth Estate.* Of the state's 91 radio stations, approximately 25 feature talk-radio programming.

Of the eight daily and approximately 20 weekly newspapers that circulate in Rhode Island, the *Providence Journal-Bulletin* undeniably sets the political agenda. The only daily with a statewide distribution, the *Providence Journal-Bulletin,* has been the recipient of four Pulitzer Prizes, including one in 1974 for reporting on President Richard Nixon's income tax filings. The paper's 1994 Pulitzer Prize was awarded for a series of articles that exposed cronyism and abuses within the state court system, eventually forcing the resignation of the chief justice of the Rhode Island Supreme Court. The weekly alternative paper the *Providence Phoenix* provides irreverent, pointed commentary on the state's political affairs—and on the coverage of those affairs in the *Providence Journal-Bulletin.*

Rhode Island is also home to one public-broadcasting station and three network television stations, including WLNE-TV, which has earned both praise and criticism for its award-winning show *You Paid for It*, a periodic news segment that exposes government waste. Nine of the state's 34 radio stations include talk-radio formats. Rhode Island politics has a distinctly colorful cast and is something of a spectator sport; radio and television talk shows are often hosted by former officeholders, among them Providence mayor Vincent A. Cianci (between mayoral terms) and former state attorney general Arlene Violet.

Under the leadership of William Loeb (1946–81), the *Union Leader* of Manchester, N.H., was known for its fiery and often venomous front-page editorials, which did not shrink, for example, from calling President Gerald Ford "Jerry the Jerk," Secretary of State Henry Kissinger "Kissinger the Kike," and Secretary of State John Foster Dulles "Dulles, Duller and Dullest." The son of Teddy Roosevelt's executive secretary, Loeb proudly flaunted his reputation as a king-maker and is best remembered as "the man who made [Maine senator Edmund] Muskie cry." Under the auspices of its current publisher, Joseph McQuaid, the paper today continues to wield enormous political influence in the state. For example, although the *Union Leader* was the only New Hampshire daily to endorse the conservative candidate Pat Buchanan in the 1996 Republican presidential primary, Buchanan carried the state.

New Hampshire is also home to approximately 40 weeklies and 12 other daily newspapers, including the *Concord Monitor* and the *Nashua Telegraph*, which were among the first newspapers in the country to establish a site on the World Wide Web to disseminate news relating to the 1996 presidential primary.

Three of the state's six television stations are owned and operated by the University of New Hampshire and produce such public-affairs programming as *New Hampshire Round-table* and *Hitting Home.* The state has about 65 radio stations, with at least 18 offering talk-radio broadcasts.

Located in central Maine, the *Bangor Daily News* is distributed throughout 68 percent of the state and boasts the largest circulation of Maine's seven daily newspapers. The *Portland Press Herald*, the flagship paper in the Blethen Maine Newspapers group, wields enormous political influence in southern Maine, along with two of its sister papers, the *Kennebec Journal* in Augusta and the *Central Maine Morn-ing Sentinel* in Waterville. Maine is also home to more than 56 weekly newspapers.

Five of the 13 television stations in Maine are owned by Maine Public Broadcasting Corporation. Of the 96 radio stations in the Pine Tree State, about 17 offer some form of talk radio.

Vermont's eight daily and approximately 35 weekly newspapers are the major suppliers of the state's in-depth printed political news. None of the dailies blankets the state, but the two largest ones, the more conservative *Burlington Free Press*, owned by the Gannett Company of Arlington, Va., and the more liberal, family-owned, 200-year-old *Rutland Herald*, have the largest effect. The *Free Press*, which subscribes to the Associated Press and the Gannett News Service, dominates central Vermont's most populous areas with its local, state, and national news. Although the *Free Press* long maintained a policy of initialing editorials, allowing the paper to present conflicting political viewpoints, that practice was eventually abandoned.

Of nine television stations in Vermont, four are publicly owned by Vermont ETV and produce such political programs as *Vermont This Week* and *Call the Governor. In the Public Interest*, a grant-funded special program aimed at exploring legislative issues, is broadcast several times a year. Of Vermont's 63 radio stations, 11 feature talk-radio formats.

Garrett D. Byrnes and Charles H. Spilman, *The Providence Journal: 150 Years* (1980); Erwin D. Canham, *Commitment to Freedom: The Story of the Christian Science Monitor* (1958); Kevin Cash, *Who the Hell Is William Loeb?* (1975); *Editor and Publisher International Year Book* (1999); Michael Emery and Edwin Emery, *The Press and America* (1996); Ralph Engelman, *Public Radio and Television in America: A Political History* (1996); Loren Ghiglione, *Evaluating the Press* (1973); James L. Hayes, *Burrelle's Media Directory* (1999); Peter Laufer, *Inside Talk Radio: America's Voice or Just Hot Air?* (1995); Louis M. Lyons, *Newspaper Story: 100 Years of the Boston Globe* (1971); Hilly Rose, *But, That's Not What I Called About* (1978); James Eugene Smith, *100 Years of Hartford's Courant: From Colonial Times through the Civil War* (1970 [1949]).

Karen A. Bordeleau

Mitchell, George J. (1933–) Politician, lawyer, and U.S. senator.

George John Mitchell represented Maine in the U.S. Senate from 1980 until January 1995, serving as Democratic majority leader of that body throughout his final term. Like his mentor, the legendary Maine senator Edmund S. Muskie, Mitchell played a key role in developing national environmental legislation.

Born and reared in Waterville, Maine, the son of poor parents of Lebanese and Irish descent, Mitchell graduated from Bowdoin Col-

Senator George Mitchell, ca. 1990

lege in 1954 and, after serving for two years as an officer in the U.S. Army, earned a law degree from Georgetown University in 1960. Mitchell worked for several years in Washington, D.C., first as a trial lawyer in the Antitrust Division of the Justice Department and then as executive assistant to Senator Muskie, before returning to Maine to practice law and enter politics. Mitchell was chair of the Maine Democratic Party from 1966 to 1968 and Maine's Democratic national committeeman between 1969 and 1977. After serving as deputy director of the Muskie vice presidential and presidential campaigns in 1968 and 1972, Mitchell in 1974 was the unsuccessful Democratic candidate for governor of Maine. After Jimmy Carter's election as president in 1976, Mitchell was appointed Maine's U.S. attorney; two years later he was named to a federal district court judgeship.

Mitchell's career took an unexpected turn in 1980 when Senator Muskie resigned to become secretary of state. At Muskie's urging, Governor Joseph Brennan offered Mitchell Muskie's Senate seat for the remaining two and a half years of Muskie's term. Generally regarded as a poor bet to keep the seat in 1982, Mitchell capitalized on Maine voters' disenchantment with Reaganomics and won a victory with 61 percent of the vote.

In 1984 Mitchell became head of the Democratic senatorial campaign committee, and his tactical know-how helped engineer the Democrats' surprising takeover of the Senate two years later. After grateful Democratic colleagues elected him to the largely ceremonial post of deputy president pro tempore of the Senate, Mitchell achieved national prominence in 1987 as a member of the Select Committee on the Iran-Contra Affair when he sternly reminded National Security Council staff member Lieutenant Colonel Oliver

North during televised hearings that "God does not take sides in American politics." With his colleague from Maine, William S. Cohen, Mitchell wrote *Men of Zeal: A Candid Inside Story of the Iran-Contra Hearings,* published in 1988. When Robert Byrd stepped down as majority leader of the Senate in 1989, Mitchell, freshly reelected with an all-time Maine record of 81 percent of the vote, easily won the post.

As Senate majority leader during the George H. W. Bush administration, Mitchell effectively brokered compromises with the president on the reauthorization of the 1990 Clean Air Act and on an amendment to the 1964 Civil Rights Act providing damages for victims of unlawful discrimination. Mitchell also produced an 11th-hour defeat of Bush's 1989 capital gains tax cut. After Bill Clinton was elected in 1992, however, Mitchell was unable, despite Herculean efforts, to deliver the votes to pass Clinton's ambitious universal health care plan.

Early in 1994 Mitchell stunned political observers by announcing that he would not seek reelection to the Senate in November. Several months later he again surprised both press and public by turning down Clinton's offer of a Supreme Court nomination. In 1995 President Clinton made Mitchell his special adviser on Northern Ireland, where the skilled and patient negotiator mediated talks between representatives of the Catholic and Protestant parties in the long-standing conflict. Those negotiations were crowned by the signing on April 12, 1998, of the historic Good Friday peace accord.

Mitchell has also again turned his hand to writing. *Not for America Alone: The Triumph of Democracy and the Fall of Communism* appeared in 1997. *Making Peace,* in which Mitchell relates his experience in Northern Ireland, came out in 1999 (rev. 2000). Mitchell's personal papers are housed at his Maine alma mater, Bowdoin College.

Sidney Blumenthal, "The Wisdom of George Mitchell," *New Yorker* 70, no. 10 (1994); Alberta Gould, *George Mitchell: In Search of Peace* (1996).

Richard J. Maiman

Muskie, Edmund S. (1914–96) Governor of Maine, U.S. senator, and U.S. secretary of state. Edmund Sixtus Muskie was born in Rumford, Maine, the son of Polish immigrants (the family name, Marciszewski, was simplified to Muskie). He attended public schools, graduated from Bates College (1936) and the Cornell University School of Law (1939), and began practicing law in Waterville, Maine, in 1940. Muskie served in the navy during World War II, achieving the rank of lieutenant by the time of his discharge in 1945.

Edmund Muskie on the presidential campaign trail in Quincy, Mass., 1972

After the war he became a prominent force in Maine politics, reviving the state's Democratic Party. On the national level Muskie is best known for his pioneering environmental legislation.

Muskie's political career began when he was elected to the Maine House of Representatives in 1946. He became Democratic floor leader in 1948, leaving in 1951 to become director of the federal Office of Price Stabilization in Maine. The next year Muskie became Maine's Democratic national committeeman and began reorganizing the state's tiny, highly factional Democratic Party. Drafted to run for governor in 1954, Muskie conducted a vigorous grassroots campaign that attracted considerable Republican support. During two terms as governor Muskie broadened Maine's efforts to develop economically, seeking to reduce the state's dependence on power companies and the pulp and paper industry. He also initiated the state's first environmental protection laws.

In 1958 Muskie became Maine's first popularly elected Democratic U.S. senator. He served on the Senate committees on Governmental Operations, Banking and Currency, and Intergovernmental Relations. As chair of the Senate's Subcommittee on Environmental Protection, Muskie became the chief architect of the earliest and arguably most successful pieces of major pollution-control legislation, the Clean Air Act of 1963 and the Water Quality Act of 1965. Muskie was also instru-

mental in the passage of the Model Cities Act of 1966.

In 1968 Hubert Humphrey, the Democratic presidential candidate, selected Muskie as his running mate. Muskie's calm, thoughtful demeanor won him favorable press coverage, and when the Humphrey-Muskie ticket narrowly lost the election to Republicans Richard Nixon and Spiro Agnew, Muskie immediately became a leading contender for his party's 1972 presidential nomination. On the eve of the congressional elections in November 1970, he solidified his standing with a well-received speech that was broadcast on national television. Muskie's front-runner status barely lasted into the 1972 presidential primaries, however. The defining moment in that campaign occurred during the New Hampshire primary, when Muskie held a news conference outside the offices of the archconservative *Manchester Union Leader* to denounce two stories it had published, one based on an untrue allegation made by the Nixon campaign and the other an unflattering article about Muskie's wife. According to some reporters, in the middle of his statement Muskie began to cry. Widespread coverage of the story destroyed Muskie's statesmanlike public image. Some believe the incident doomed the Muskie presidential campaign; others claim that Muskie's defeat was due to the superior mobilization of grassroots support by the anti–Vietnam War senator George McGovern in that year's greatly expanded number of primaries and caucuses.

His presidential ambitions thwarted, Muskie resumed his senatorial duties, leading the effort to reform the congressional budget-making process. As chair of the newly established Senate Budget Committee, Muskie was critical of his colleagues' inability to trim spending programs to fit available revenues. He described the typical senatorial strategy as "Talk like Scrooge on the campaign trail. Vote like Santa Claus on the Senate floor." In 1980 President Jimmy Carter appointed Muskie to replace Cyrus Vance as secretary of state. After Carter's defeat by Ronald Reagan in 1980, Muskie practiced law in Washington, D.C., where he died in 1996.

Bernard Asbell, *The Senate Nobody Knows* (1978); Theo Lippman, Jr., and Donald C. Hansen, *Muskie* (1971); David Nevin, *Muskie of Maine* (1972).

Richard J. Maiman

New Hampshire Presidential Primary

Every four years political activists and observers around the world focus their attention on New Hampshire, site of the first-in-the-nation U.S. presidential primary. Relative to the number of votes cast, the primary has become the world's most extensively covered election. The state's fairly small geographic area and low population give lesser-known candidates with limited budgets a chance to practice the face-to-face campaigning known as "retail politics" with hopes of gaining a popular following and notice from the national media. The tiny northern towns of Dixville Notch and Hart's Location (with 26 and 31 registered voters, respectively, in 2004) have for decades garnered their own disproportionate share of the quadrennial media spotlight, casting their ballots virtually at the stroke of midnight on primary day.

Historically, the New Hampshire presidential primary has proved to be a reliable indicator of popular sentiment nationwide. Until the election of Arkansas governor Bill Clinton to the presidency in 1992, no candidate in 40 years had captured the White House without first having won his party's preference poll in the Granite State. Lackluster showings by two sitting presidents—Harry Truman in 1952 and Lyndon Johnson in 1968—prompted both men to withdraw from contention for their party's nomination shortly after the New Hampshire primary.

Although 1952 is widely regarded as the first year of the New Hampshire primary, the modern electoral event evolved from earlier political traditions in the state. Until 1878 New Hampshire's state elections coincided with its annual Town Meeting Day, held the second Tuesday of March. Because these returns were the first partisan votes of the year's election season, the national press closely monitored the results as a probable index of popular sentiment. In 1910 New Hampshire reformed the nomination process for statewide office, selecting candidates by popular vote rather than at nominating conventions. By opening up the state primary system, these reforms loosened the grip of the Boston and Maine Railroad on the state's Republican Party nomination process, which had allowed for proxy votes that were often bartered or purchased. The changes made at the state level, however, did not extend to the selection of candidates for national office, who were chosen, between 1916 and 1948, by elected delegates to the national conventions whose candidate preferences were not necessarily known to New Hampshire voters. It was in 1916, for reasons of convenience and Yankee frugality, that the national primary was scheduled for the same March Tuesday on which state ballots were cast. That year the New Hampshire primary coincided with Minnesota's and followed Indiana's by a week, but since 1920 it has preceded all others.

It was not until the mid-20th century, however, that New Hampshire could boast the most celebrated national primary in the country. In 1949 a New Hampshire law was passed that provided for the direct election of presidential candidates. A so-called beauty-contest provision in the statute allowed candidates or hopefuls, for the first time, to add their names to the ballot if they were able to gather a specified number of voter signatures. This new exercise in American democracy was first tested in 1952. On the primary ballot that year were President Harry S. Truman, General Dwight D. Eisenhower, and Senators Henry Cabot Lodge, Estes Kefauver, and Robert A. Taft. In a stunning result, the relatively unknown Kefauver beat Truman by 10 points, and Eisenhower bested Taft by a similar margin.

Since that first contest of the modern era, the New Hampshire primary has produced quite a number of legendary moments: Edmund Muskie breaking into tears before the national press corps on the steps of the *Manchester Union Leader* building in 1972; Ronald Reagan's "I paid for that microphone," in a Nashua dispute over candidate participation in the 1980 Republican primary debate; Gary Hart's surprise victory in 1984, which propelled future governor Jeanne Shaheen into prominence; and Bill Clinton's promise to work his heart out for New Hampshire voters "until the last dog dies" in a speech on February 12, 1992, at the Dover Elks Club.

Despite the primary's high public profile and impressive record of predicting future presidents, the contest continues to receive criticism. Above all, detractors charge that this small, rural, overwhelmingly white, and generally conservative state does not represent the nation's population. Many candidates complain of the extraordinary influence of New Hampshire's major newspaper, the ultraconservative *Manchester Union Leader*. New Hampshire law currently requires that the state's primary election be held at least a full week before any other similar contest, but new nationwide rules may jeopardize the state's long-cherished primacy. Moreover, the powerful influence of national media and the attention given to the Iowa caucuses, which precede the New Hampshire primary, have slightly diminished the importance of this key electoral event. It remains to be seen how it will fare through the 21st century.

Charles Brereton, *First in the Nation: New Hampshire and the Premier Presidential Primary* (1987); William Mayer, ed., *In Pursuit of the White House: How We Choose Our Presidential Nominees* (1996).

Mari Boor Tonn

O'Neill, Thomas P. "Tip," Jr.

(1912–94) Politician, U.S. representative, and Speaker of the House. Thomas Phillip O'Neill, Jr., known as Tip, was born in Cambridge, Mass., to Thomas Phillip and Rose Ann (Tolan) O'Neill. Thomas Sr., son of an immigrant bricklayer from County Cork, Ireland, won election to the Cambridge City Council in 1900 and subsequently became a sewer commissioner in Cambridge. In both positions the elder O'Neill controlled patronage jobs that he used to serve the community while building political support. Thomas Jr. observed his father closely and learned much that would later be of use in his own political career.

Thomas O'Neill, Jr., attended parochial schools, graduating from Saint John's High School in 1931 and Boston College in 1936. A lover of sports, he acquired the nickname Tip when friends equated his tenaciousness with the baseball player James Edward O'Neill's habit of hitting foul tips until the pitcher walked him.

While still a senior at Boston College, O'Neill ran for the Cambridge City Council. He lost the election but learned the enduring lesson that "all politics is local," a phrase he featured in the title of his political primer *All Politics Is Local, and Other Rules of the Game* (1994) and emphasized in his memoirs, *Man of the House* (1987). O'Neill gave the needs of his constituents top priority and believed he should not assume that his friends would vote for him simply because they knew him; he had to ask them personally. A "work and wages" New Deal liberal, O'Neill sought and won election to the Massachusetts House of Representatives in 1936. He served for eight terms, rising to the position of minority leader in 1947. After engineering a Democratic majority in 1949, he became the first Democratic Speaker in Massachusetts history.

When John F. Kennedy moved on to the Senate in 1952, O'Neill was elected by voters of the Eighth Congressional District to take his seat in the U.S. House of Representatives, a seat that had also once been held by the legendary Boston politician James Michael Curley. As a congressman, O'Neill once again rose to prominence. With the help of fellow Bostonian and Democratic whip John McCormack (who later became Speaker), O'Neill learned how to attend to the needs of key players in the back rooms of Congress, much as he had in the Massachusetts House. Soon becoming the consummate Washington insider, O'Neill, with his quick wit and omnipresent cigar, won a coveted seat on the House Rules Committee in his second term. In 1967 O'Neill became one of the first political leaders to denounce U.S. involvement in the Vietnam War. It was an uncharacteristic break from the ranks for O'Neill, an act of conscience that required a great deal of explaining to his working-class constituents in Cambridge. Continuing to lead, he was appointed majority whip in 1971, elected majority leader in 1973, and made Speaker of the House by acclamation in 1976. By the time he left his post in January 1987, he had served the longest continuous term of any speaker since the start of the republic. O'Neill received the Presidential Medal of Freedom in 1991. On January 5, 1994, at the age of 81, he died in Boston of cardiac arrest.

In his memoirs O'Neill described himself as a "bread and butter liberal who believes that every family deserves the opportunity to earn an income, own a home, educate their children and afford medical care." This was his American dream, one that he believed required the active participation of the federal government through a host of social programs, even as such programs fell out of favor during the 1980s and 1990s.

Paul Clancy and Shirley Elder, *Tip: A Biography of Thomas P. O'Neill, Speaker of the House* (1980); Richard A. Loverd, "Michael S. Dukakis: Blending Principle with Politics in Leading State Government from 'Duke I' to 'Duke II,'" in *Leadership for the Public Service: Power and Policy in Action,* ed. Richard A. Loverd (1997); Ronald M. Peters, Jr., *The American Speakership: The Office in Historical Perspective,* 2d ed. (1997).

Richard A. Loverd

Organized Crime Organized crime, especially in its guise as the Mafia, La Cosa Nostra, the "syndicate," or the "Mob," has entered American legend. Movies from *Scarface* to *The Godfather* trilogy have glamorized the violence and the criminal code of conduct that governs members of organized crime.

The Mafia possibly existed as early as the 13th century as a secret guerrilla organization resisting French oppression in Sicily. The Mafia clans of Sicily had an organizational structure and a close-knit, ruthless culture that were ideally suited to organized crime in 19th-century America. The Mafia traditions—and a willingness to kill to enforce these traditions—were imported to the criminal gangs of low-income Italian neighborhoods in the United States and disciplined fledgling criminal organizations, hindering effective law enforcement.

The Mafia in New England and elsewhere was organized into five major "families" with similar formal structures controlled by a "boss" of the family. The families warred with each other for decades over territory and control of the various illegal schemes, or "rackets," and enforced internal discipline through beatings and murders.

During Prohibition, organized crime expanded in the United States as the vast industry of liquor production and consumption went underground. Gangsters gained wealth and prominence during Prohibition well beyond what they could have achieved through traditional rackets such as gambling, extortion, loan-sharking, prostitution, and sometimes narcotics trafficking, and Mafia families became wealthy enough to spread the traditional rackets, particularly gambling, to Cuba and the American West.

Organized crime used its enormous profits to corrupt local governments and infiltrated legitimate businesses and labor unions nationwide. The extent of its reach attracted the attention of Congress, which through the 1950s and 1960s held repeated hearings exposing the scope and influence of racketeering. The Department of Justice, most notably under Attorney General Robert F. Kennedy, attacked the racketeers and mobsters by forming a series of organized-crime strike forces, as well as pushing for and enforcing the antiracketeering provisions included in the Organized Crime Control Act of 1970. This concentrated law enforcement effort led by the federal government has decimated the traditional Mafia in most areas.

The New England branch of the Mafia formed in Boston at the turn of the 20th century. Although the first New England Mafia gangs were dangerous and violent, they were confined to a few distinct areas of New England until the 1950s. The first boss of the Boston family was Gaspare Messina, who started the family in 1916 and died in 1924. Phil Buccola succeeded him and acquired wealth and power for the family through loan-sharking, gambling, and bootlegging. Buccola retired in 1954 and was succeeded by Raymond

L. S. Patriarca (1908–84), and a rapid consolidation of the New England Mafia began. From a small vending machine company in the Federal Hill section of Providence, Patriarca consolidated and came to control the Mafia throughout New England. In the mid-1960s, annoyed by hoodlum violence in Boston, Patriarca stated his ability "to declare martial law up there."

Under Patriarca's rule, the Mafia gained strength, power, and influence in New England, and it was not unusual for politicians at all levels of government to pay calls on him. Indeed, when the Gorham silver service of the USS *Rhode Island* was stolen from its display case in the Rhode Island State House, a call to Patriarca is believed to have prompted its immediate return. The most public connection between mob and government in Rhode Island came in 1986 when the chief justice of the Rhode Island Supreme Court—a former speaker of the Rhode Island House of Representatives—resigned during impeachment hearings investigating his contacts with figures associated with the Mafia.

Patriarca was eventually tried and convicted of conspiring to commit murder. After his 1975 release from an Atlanta prison, he was hauled into court time and again; in 1980 he was indicted for labor racketeering and in 1981 for ordering the execution of two mobsters. He died of a heart attack in 1984 and lies in a massive gray marble crypt in the Gate of Heaven Cemetery in East Providence. Some mourned his passing: one local politician noted, "Federal Hill was safe because he was there."

Patriarca's son Raymond (known as Junior) then took over the family, but he did not have his father's skills. The release of a secret Mafia induction ceremony tape that the FBI had recorded in Medford, Mass., in 1989 embarrassed Junior and weakened him as the New England Mafia boss. This was the first released recording of such a ceremony, and graphically demonstrated that the Mafia was no figment of prosecutors' imaginations. Junior was arrested shortly thereafter and pled guilty to federal racketeering charges in 1991. He was briefly succeeded by Nicholas Bianco, who was also convicted on federal charges in 1991. Francis "Cadillac Frank" Salemme, the next boss, fled upon his indictment in 1994 on federal racketeering charges. Salemme was captured in Florida in August 1995.

For decades, James "Whitey" Bulger (brother of the former president of the University of Massachusetts, Boston, William Bulger) and Stephen "The Rifleman" Flemmi were leaders of Boston's Irish gangsters known as the Winter Hill Gang and were also FBI informants against Italian American gangsters from the North End. The FBI allegedly gave Bulger and Flemmi, who were indicted and arrested along with Salemme, virtual license to steal in return for their information. Bulger, who was tipped about the 1995 indictment, has been in hiding ever since and was last spotted in Manchester, England, in 2003.

Although the structure of New England's organized crime has been disassembled by aggressive state and federal prosecutions, crimes such as gambling, prostitution, extortion, and loan-sharking remain lucrative. Low-level criminals will continue to participate in these rackets, and the most enterprising and ruthless will seek to control them. New waves of immigrants from South America, the Caribbean, and Southeast Asia have produced organized criminal activity in these populations, and the cycle of criminal organization continues. Moreover, the crippled leadership of New England's organized crime groups presents an opportunity for other, more powerful criminal families. But the heyday of the New England Mafia, when it could boast of relative immunity from the law and wide influence in state and local governments, is now over.

Diego Gambetta, *The Sicilian Mafia: The Business of Private Protection* (1996); James B. Jacobs, Christopher Panarella, and Jay Worthington, *Busting the Mob: United States v. Cosa Nostra* (1994); Carl Sifakis, *Mafia Encyclopedia* (1987); Vincent Teresa, *My Life in the Mafia* (1973).

Sheldon Whitehouse

Pell, Claiborne (de Borda) (1918–)

U.S. senator. Born in New York City, Claiborne de Borda Pell is the son of former congressman Herbert Claiborne Pell, Jr., and part of an old line of aristocratic families from Newport society that had deep roots in Rhode Island. Pell graduated from Princeton in 1940 and earned a master's degree from Columbia in 1946. After serving with distinction in World War II, he pursued a career in the foreign service, mostly in the European area, where he established himself as an expert on international affairs. He returned to Rhode Island, and in 1960, at the age of 41, in his first try for public office, ran for a seat in the U.S. Senate. His securing of the Democratic nomination for this office signaled the end of an era in Rhode Island politics. He ran against three former governors and was the first Democrat in the state's history to win the nomination without the endorsement of the Democratic Party. He went on to win easily in the general election. His dignified presence and social status played extremely well in what was then a working-class state, and he faced little competition in subsequent races.

During his 36 years in the Senate, Pell became one of the most influential and respected members of that body, and his national and in-

Senator Claiborne Pell, 1972

ternational efforts created an impressive legacy. Regarded as one of the deans of the New England delegation, he remains something of an icon in his own state of Rhode Island. In late 1960, as senator-elect, he traveled to Cuba to meet with Fidel Castro, who had installed himself as head of state. Upon his return, he warned the director of the CIA against trying to overturn Castro because Cubans would not support such action; the warning was ignored and the Bay of Pigs fiasco followed. When President Kennedy reprimanded Pell for not coming to him directly, Pell noted that he felt "too low down on the totem pole to bother the President." That position, however, did not last long. He was one of the leaders of efforts to enhance international security and a main actor in ratification of the arms control treaties. He went on to become chair of the Senate Foreign Relations Committee. In 1997 he was appointed U.S. delegate to the United Nations.

Pell's initiatives in domestic policies form the core of his legacy. His legislation creating the Pell Federal Student Financial Aid and Grant Program has become a cornerstone of access to higher education for well over 80 million U.S. students. During his tenure he also founded the National Endowment for the Arts and the National Endowment for the Humanities, which—despite periodic conservative efforts to dismantle them—are likely to remain lasting public commitments to the arts and humanities in this country.

He did not neglect his state and region. Pell was instrumental in the electrification of rail

lines in the northeast corridor and sent considerable federal government benefits to his state. His long-standing interest in the sea led to the establishment of numerous programs related to marine environmental protection and security, which generated considerable largesse for projects in Rhode Island (the Ocean State). He retired in 1996 for health reasons but remains a revered presence in Rhode Island. Indeed, the state has many programs, awards, and sites named in his honor, including a bridge and public and college buildings.

Richard Fenno, Jr., *Senators on the Campaign Trail: The Politics of Representation* (1992); Claiborne Pell, "Federal Support for the Arts Has a Future," *Annals of the American Academy of Social and Political Science* 471 (January 1984); Pell, *Power and Policy: America's Role in World Affairs* (1972); Claiborne Pell and Harold Leland Goodwin, *Challenge of the Seven Seas* (1986).

Bruce Sundlun

Political Machines

Political machines—referring mostly to tightly organized, highly disciplined party organizations grounded in patronage and ethnicity, controlling both access to public office and the content of public policy—date from the earliest years of nationhood and flourished in an older America. They were typically headed by a "boss" who had gone up through the ranks and was at the pinnacle of a hierarchical structure that rose organizationally from precinct or township to a peak at the city, county, or sometimes state level of government.

The bosses were a primary target of Progressive reformers in the late 19th and early 20th centuries, and their political reforms—civil service, ballot laws, and the direct primary—led to the decline of the machine. Most of the once great party machines have disappeared, and the terms "machine" and "boss" are today more pejorative than descriptive of American politics. They conjure images of party organizations, mainly Democratic but often Republican, in the nation's major cities of the mid-Atlantic states—New York City, Jersey City, Philadelphia, Pittsburgh—and those of the lower Midwest—Chicago, Cincinnati, Kansas City, and Memphis. Of these, only the Chicago Democratic organization survives.

Party machines in New England prospered from the Civil War through World War II, but they for the most part disappeared during the second half of the 20th century. Contrary to the familiar image of the party machine, the earliest and most powerful in the New England states were rural and Republican. The GOP dominated politics in the region from the late 19th well into the 20th century, and a strong Republican Party organization, grounded in patronage and allied with business interests, governed in each of the six states.

Democratic Party machines existed in many of the region's cities during this era and grew in strength with the growing number of immigrants arriving in New England in the decades around the turn of the 20th century. From the 1880s, they had success in mayoral and other local elections but rarely statewide until the 1928 Democratic presidential nomination of Al Smith, when the party became more competitive in the southern New England states. In his study of the region's politics, Duane Lockard notes that there are "two New Englands"—the northern and the southern tier of states—which have differed in their political development since the heyday of Republican dominance.

In the northern New England states—Maine, New Hampshire, and Vermont—Republican Party machines were undermined by the 1912 national party split into Progressive and Old Guard factions, as well as by direct primary and other electoral reforms that made insurgent challenges to the party organizations easier. A system of bifactional Republican politics emerged in each of the states, displacing the primacy of the machines and becoming the norm until yielding in the 1960s to a more candidate-centered politics.

There were no noteworthy Democratic Party machines in these states, and indeed the party enjoyed few successes in any of them until the 1950s. During that decade, Democrats in Maine began to organize more aggressively and, led by Edmund Muskie, became more competitive with the GOP. The Democratic organization put in place then has survived, outliving its founders, and continues to have successes, but it never approximated a machine. During the 1960s, Democrats began to win occasional statewide and national offices in Vermont, owing less, however, to their party organization than to the more independent, candidate-centered politics that has developed there over the past four decades. Democrats have enjoyed less success in New Hampshire, where party factionalism and the state's conservative politics have worked regularly to the advantage of the GOP.

It is a different story in the southern New England states, where industrialization and immigration combined to produce Democratic Party machines in many of the cities of Connecticut, Massachusetts, and Rhode Island. Al Smith's presidential bid in 1928 together with the onset of the Depression in 1929 made these urban Democratic machines increasingly competitive with their rural Republican counterparts, which until then had dominated state and national politics in these three states as

GOP organizations had in the northern New England states.

During the early decades of the 20th century Connecticut, Massachusetts, and Rhode Island had strong Republican Party organizations built on the support of rural and small-town voters. In Massachusetts, the GOP leadership did not center on a single boss, but did, through its party "elevator," effectively prepare candidates for statewide office and control their advancement. In Connecticut, there was a Republican boss, J. Henry Rorabeck, who doubled as state party chair and national committeeman and exercised near absolute rule over GOP officeholders at both levels. Lockard describes Rorabeck's tightly knit, highly disciplined, very conservative command of the state GOP as "virtually a benevolent dictatorship."

Some of the best examples of local political machines in New England, all of them Democratic, were to be found in the Connecticut cities of New Haven, New London, Bridgeport, and Waterbury. There was no Democratic counterpart to Rorabeck, though for two decades beginning in the late 1940s, John Bailey was clearly the most powerful Democrat in the state. Never seriously challenged as state party chair, Bailey was more accommodating and less ideological than Rorabeck in his leadership style, but his control of patronage and influence over legislation provided the power needed to sustain his position. Bailey went on to chair the Democratic National Committee in the 1960s but even then did not relinquish his control of the state party. Since Bailey, there has been no statewide party leader of comparable stature in Connecticut. Lowell Weicker had a large and loyal following that enabled him to win election to the U.S. Senate three times as a Republican and then the governorship on a third-party ticket. But his organization was entirely personal, and he was unable to transfer support to other candidates.

Like Connecticut in the early decades of the 20th century, Rhode Island had Republican bosses who ran the state party machine, the best known of whom was General Charles Brayton. Supported by corporate interests and with a disciplined organization, Brayton maintained tight control over officeholding and legislation. As in Connecticut, Democratic Party machines developed in the major cities of Rhode Island, and although the Democrats never produced a leader like Brayton, Dennis J. Roberts, boss of the Providence organization and later governor, did emerge as the effective leader of the state party for a decade from the mid-1940s to the mid-1950s. But as in Connecticut and also Massachusetts, the state Democratic Party organization in Rhode

Island was for the most part a coalition of local party machines whose jealousies and ethnic differences often led to factional fights that frustrated the party's statewide ambitions. As in Massachusetts, although not so much in Connecticut, leaders of the state party were usually elected officials—governors, U.S. senators, and mayors.

Massachusetts has not known any statewide political boss like Rorabeck in Connecticut or Brayton in Rhode Island, nor for that matter a strong party leader such as Bailey in Connecticut. Local Democratic machines thrived in cities across the commonwealth and dominated party politics into the 1960s. In Boston, however, politics resided in the neighborhoods and, early in the century, produced powerful ward bosses like Martin Lomasney in the West End and John F. Fitzgerald in the North End. Of these factional leaders, none is better known than James Michael Curley, the Robin Hood–like champion of the "newer races" who parlayed charm and guile into four terms as mayor, four as congressman, one as governor, and two in state prison. Curley dominated Boston politics for four decades, fighting with Brahmin Republicans and Democratic ward bosses alike. But Curley was not a boss in the usual sense; his appeal and power were charismatic, not organizational, and he made no effort to build political machinery that might be transferable to someone else.

In the 1980s, another Boston mayor, Kevin White, did try to construct a political organization along the lines of the Democratic machine in Chicago. Through a network of little city halls spread across the city, White sought to build a party structure from the top down to the precinct and neighborhood, but the organization did not survive his tenure as the city's chief executive. Similarly, in the 1980s, Governor Michael Dukakis dominated the state Democratic Party, leaving behind a more active and stronger organization that nonetheless reverted to legislative control when he left office.

More than in any of the other New England states, great family organizations have decorated the political history of Massachusetts. From the Adamses in the first half of the 19th century through the Lodges in the first half of the 20th to the Kennedys in the second half of the 20th, these families, while not machines in the usual sense, have attracted devoted followings and sustained political prominence and influence beyond one generation. None, however, has been successful in transferring its power to any outside the family.

Party organizations remain prominent in the politics of the New England states, and from time to time there are echoes of the old machine politics in the southern tier of states.

But electoral politics in all of these states is now characterized by self-selected candidates and candidate-centered campaign organizations, and while the political cultures and styles of the six states may still differ, their history of political development and machine politics is similar.

Edward Banfield and James Q. Wilson, *City Politics* (1963); J. Joseph Huthmacher, *Massachusetts People and Politics* (1959); Duane Lockard, *New England State Politics* (1959); Josephine F. Milburn and William Doyle, eds., *New England Political Parties* (1983); Thomas H. O'Connor, *The Boston Irish* (1995); Gary L. Rose, *Connecticut at the Crossroads* (1992); Alfred Steinberg, *The Bosses* (1972).

Jerome M. Mileur

Political Parties In his 1959 study of New England state politics, Duane Lockard identified "two New Englands," arguing that different patterns of social and economic development in northern and southern New England had produced distinctly different political environments. Although the clarity of the distinction has waned over the decades since Lockard's book came out, important economic and demographic differences between the southern-tier states (Connecticut, Rhode Island, and Massachusetts) and the northern-tier states (Vermont, New Hampshire, and Maine) persist. Those differences have created conditions more hospitable to the Democratic Party in southern New England and to the Republican Party in the north.

Perhaps the most important demographic disparity between northern and southern New England involves population density. Less than 23 percent of New England's population lives in the northern-tier states, yet together these states account for more than 76 percent of the total geographic area of the region. As a result, while in 1997 Rhode Island, Massachusetts, and Connecticut ranked second, third, and fourth among all states in terms of population density, New Hampshire, Vermont, and Maine ranked 20th, 30th, and 38th, respectively. The more urban character of southern New England is also underscored by the fact that with the exception of Manchester, N.H., all of New England's cities with a population over 100,000 are in one of the three southern-tier states. Less than 20 percent of the population of the southern-tier states is found in nonmetropolitan areas, while well over 50 percent of the population of northern New England is located in nonmetropolitan areas.

In addition to its more urban character, southern New England also differs greatly from northern New England in its social, religious, ethnic, and racial composition. Each of the southern New England states has a higher

percentage of unionized workers than any of the northern New England states. In northern New England, 79 percent of the population is categorized as Christian, and there are approximately four Protestants for every three Catholics; in the south 81 percent of the population is categorized as Christian, and Catholics outnumber Protestants four to three. As a percentage of total state population, the Jewish communities in the southern-tier states are also far larger than in the northern-tier states. Similarly, the ethnic and racial makeup of the southern-tier states is far more diverse, with a higher percentage of Hispanics and blacks living there.

Given the sharp demographic contrasts between southern and northern New England, it is not surprising that the Democratic Party fares far better today in Massachusetts, Rhode Island, and Connecticut than it does in Maine, New Hampshire, and Vermont. Urban citizens, union members, Catholics, Jews, blacks, and Hispanics all tend to vote Democratic, and their influence is clearly felt in the politics of southern New England. Electoral trends at virtually every level testify to the difference between the two New Englands.

New England's historical status as a Republican stronghold goes back to before the Civil War. Vermont, for example, gave its electoral votes to the Republican presidential candidate 27 consecutive times from 1856 through 1960; in 1964 Barry Goldwater became the first Republican nominee ever to lose in that state. Since the start of the New Deal, however, Democratic nominees for president have dominated in Massachusetts and Rhode Island and have been competitive in Connecticut while continuing to lose regularly in northern New England. In the 15 presidential elections from 1932 through 1988, the Democratic nominee won only four times in New Hampshire, twice in Maine, and once in Vermont. Since 1992, however, the Democratic candidate has carried every New England state except in 2000, when Al Gore won all New England states except New Hampshire.

In Senate races between 1968 and 1996, Democrats had far more success in southern New England than they did in the north, winning nine, seven, and six elections out of 10 in Massachusetts, Connecticut, and Rhode Island, respectively; and five, four, and only two in Maine, Vermont, and New Hampshire. Elections for representatives in Congress have displayed a similar pattern. From 1968 to 1996, Republican candidates won 18 House elections out of 30 in Maine, 23 of 30 in New Hampshire, and 11 of 15 in Vermont. During the same period in southern New England Republicans won only 29 of 169 elections in

Massachusetts, eight of 30 in Rhode Island, and 36 of 90 in Connecticut. As at the presidential level, however, there has been a noticeable recent shift away from the Republican Party in northern New England. In Maine Democrats have filled both congressional seats since 1996. In 1996 in New Hampshire both Republican candidates won by no more than 7 percent, though in the elections since 2000 the Republican candidates have reasserted the party's dominance. In 2002, former governor and Democratic candidate Jeanne Shaheen came within four percentage points of beating Republican John Sununu despite the national Republican trend that year. Given the influx of more independent and Democratic voters into southern New Hampshire, Democratic prospects for breaking the Republican dominance of the New Hampshire congressional delegation in the early twenty-first century look good. Finally, Vermont, the former bastion of Republican rule, has elected the independent but self-proclaimed socialist Bernie Sanders to the U.S. House of Representatives eight consecutive times. With the shift of Senator Jim Jeffords from Republican to independent in 2000, both Vermont senators (Democrat Patrick Leahy won reelection easily in 2004) are effectively Democrats as Jeffords votes and caucuses with the Democrats.

At the gubernatorial level cracks in the Republican armor in northern New England become even more apparent. Between 1968 and 1998 New Hampshire Republicans won 12 of 16 gubernatorial elections but lost in 1996 by nearly 18 percentage points to Democrat Jeanne Shaheen. Shaheen's victory began a streak of four Democratic wins in five gubernatorial elections. Maine hasn't had a Republican governor since the independent Angus King was elected in 1994. In Vermont Democratic candidates lost every gubernatorial election between 1855 and 1962, but beginning in 1984 the Democrats Madeleine Kunin and Howard Dean gave their party an almost unbroken 18-year stay in the govenor's office until Republican Jim Douglas was elected in 2002. Strangely, in southern New England, it is Republicans that have been breaking through at the gubernatorial level. Massachusetts, Rhode Island, and Connecticut have all had Republican governors since 1994, if not earlier.

In state legislative races Democrats in northern New England have had a great deal more success than when running for other offices. But a difference still remains between northern and southern New England. In 1996 Democrats regained control of both houses of Maine's state legislature, and they maintained that edge in 2004. In New Hampshire Republicans maintained control of both houses in 2004, though Democrats had begun to make significant gains in the house of representatives and had even held the state senate briefly for the first time since 1912. In Vermont Democrats controlled both houses after the 2004 election, but the Republicans had held a majority in the house of representatives for the previous four years. In southern New England, by contrast, since the late 1960s the Democratic Party has controlled both houses of each state legislature with only a few exceptional years in Connecticut.

The picture that emerges from the history of party politics in New England is one of a region still split between north and south but also one of a region in transition. While New England was consistently Federalist, Whig, and then Republican during the 19th century, the political picture in the region was much more complicated and bipartisan during the 20th century. In the south Democrats emerged as a competitive force by the 1930s and became the majority party in the 1950s, with near one-party rule in Massachusetts and Rhode Island. In the north Republicans continued to dominate until roughly the mid-1960s. Since then the Democratic Party has become an equal competitor in Maine and Vermont and has made significant gains even in New Hampshire.

Given the regional success of Democrats in presidential elections since 1992, their continued dominance in congressional races in southern New England, and their gains in the northern New England states, the region is becoming one of the most Democratic in the nation. In response, New England Republicans have had to adapt to their minority status. The Republicanism of New England no longer resembles the Republicanism of the party's national leadership. The most successful Republicans in New England, former governor William Weld of Massachusetts, Senator Warren Rudman of New Hampshire, Senator James Jeffords of Vermont, the late Senator John Chafee of Rhode Island, and former Senator and Secretary of Defense William Cohen of Maine, were not in any way associated with the vanguard of the so-called Republican revolution of the mid-1990s, led by Speaker of the House Newt Gingrich, in Washington, D.C. In fact, so disaffected was Jeffords with the new trend of the Republican Party that in 2000 he became an independent, temporarily throwing control of the Senate to the Democrats. He now tends to vote organizationally with the Democrats. Among current Senate Republicans, Senators Susan Collins and Olympia Snowe of Maine and Senator Lincoln Chafee of Rhode Island are more and more isolated as the last of the "moderate" Republicans. Christopher Caldwell was correct to assert in 1998 that the militant conservatism of national Republicans has undermined their party in New England.

After the redistricting in 2000, there is little reason to think that northern New England's drift toward the Democratic Party will be arrested. Given the Democratic dominance of southern New England, it is possible for the first time to imagine that New England could become for the Democratic Party in the 21st century what it was for the Republican Party in the 19th.

John F. Bibby and Thomas M. Holbrook, "Parties and Elections," in *Politics in the American States: A Comparative Analysis*, ed. Virginia Gray and Herbert Jacob, 6th ed. (1996); Christopher Caldwell, "The Southern Captivity of the GOP," *Atlantic Monthly*, June 1998; Duane Lockard, *New England State Politics* (1959); Garrison Nelson, "Vermont's Politics Transformed: 'How Come It Got Fixed When It Warn't Broke?'" in *Parties and Politics in the New England States*, ed. Jerome M. Mileur (1997); Austin Ranney, "Parties in State Politics," in *Politics in the American States: A Comparative Analysis*, ed. Herbert Jacob and Kenneth A. Vines, 3d ed. (1976); U.S. Bureau of the Census, *Statistical Abstract of the United States, 1997*, CD-ROM (1998).

Lawrence Becker

Political Protest Given New England's long-standing reputation for moralistic politics, a detailed survey of political protests in the region could be extensive. Three protest movements that occurred in the latter decades of the 20th century—against the Vietnam War, court-ordered busing, and nuclear power—can serve, however, to illustrate the ways in which local and regional issues of concern to New Englanders have interacted with larger national and international crosscurrents.

As elsewhere across the country, New England college campuses were radicalized by the U.S. government's Vietnam War policy. As early as the day before the off-year election in November 1966, protesters at Harvard University confronted and shouted down Secretary of Defense Robert McNamara. For many years after that, McNamara did not speak publicly about the war again, except before Congress.

Antiwar demonstrations continued throughout the late sixties and early seventies. In 1967 protesters gathered at the Arlington Street Church in Boston to burn their draft cards. The same church established a sanctuary for draft resisters in 1968, a practice that spread across the country. Senator Edward M. Kennedy was raucously booed in that same year as he tried to introduce Vice President Hubert H. Humphrey at a downtown election rally.

In early April 1969 Harvard activists took

Representative Tip O'Neill with protesters of Logan Airport expansion, East Boston, 1969

over the university's administration building. Authorities called in more than 400 police, who entered the building and dislodged the students in a violent melee. Nearly 200 protesters were arrested and 48 sustained injuries, including fractured skulls, broken legs, and smashed kneecaps.

The largest antiwar demonstration in New England occurred on October 15, 1969. Moratorium Day—during which participants nationwide were to challenge Vietnam policy by taking the day off from work—was the brainchild of Massachusetts antiwar activist Jerome Grossman. More than 100,000 people gathered on Boston Common to hear Senator George McGovern and other speakers denounce the war. The *Boston Globe* dubbed the peaceful gathering a "political Woodstock on the Common."

In 1970 the Massachusetts legislature passed and Governor Francis Sargent signed a primarily symbolic bill that tried to protect any Massachusetts citizen who refused to serve in a war that had not been declared by Congress. Unfortunately, the movement itself did not remain nonviolent. On April 15, 1970, 75,000 protesters gathered on Boston Common, and rioting militants trashed stores in Harvard Square. Police battled into the night with some 2,000 to 3,000 youths; 200 were injured and 35 were arrested.

The violence did not stop there. An angry crowd gathered on the Common after the invasion of Laos in 1971. Some crowd members broke away and marched down Huntington Avenue burning flags, tangling traffic, and spray-painting antiwar slogans on public and private property. In April 1972 protesters again smashed store windows in Harvard Square, chanting "How are the nation's elite?" in the direction of the Harvard dorms. Also that month a young member of Vietnam Veterans against the War, Lieutenant Junior Grade John Forbes Kerry (later a Massachusetts senator), appeared before the Senate Foreign Relations Committee and posed the question "How do you ask a man to be the last man to die for a mistake?"

Protests continued at a lower level of intensity until the war ended in 1975. Twenty years later Robert McNamara again came to Harvard to speak about the war. In a marketing tour for his memoir *In Retrospect: The Tragedy and Lessons of Vietnam* (1995), he was silenced again, not by aspiring radicals this time but by the aggrieved widow of a serviceman killed in Vietnam.

Similarly long-lived was the controversy over school desegregation in Boston. In June 1974 U.S. District Court Judge W. Arthur Garrity, Jr., handed down a verdict in the case of *Morgan v. Hennigan* in which he found that the Boston School Committee had intentionally created a segregated school system. In that ruling Garrity ordered that thousands of students be bused to schools outside their communities as a remedy. Thus began an experiment that led to protests of unmatched intensity in the region. Emotions grew most virulent not between black and white Bostonians—though feelings did intensify, engendering violence and threats—but between the "Irish who had made it and the Irish who hadn't." Judge Garrity was a "two-toilet" Irishman who had moved from downtown to the wealthy suburb of Wellesley. Many of those who were to bear the consequences of his decision were working-class Irish lacking the means to leave the city.

The first phase of busing began in September 1974 and involved transporting students between predominantly Irish South Boston and mostly African American Roxbury. South Boston residents saw their community schools as fundamental to control of their children's upbringing and essential to their cultural integrity. They regarded the massive police presence when school opened that fall as a hostile force of occupation. Some South Bostonians conducted themselves egregiously. Black students being bused were met on the first day of class with cries of "Niggers, go home," and the buses were pelted with eggs and rocks.

The schism in the Irish community was apparent even before the opening of school. City Councillor Louise Day Hicks, champion of the "little guy," had formed a protest group called Restore Our Alienated Rights (ROAR). In August Senator Edward M. Kennedy tried to speak at a ROAR rally at City Hall Plaza.

He was shouted down by a crowd of 8,000, which then turned away from him and toward the federal building named for his late brother, President John F. Kennedy. Angry crowd members chased the senator as he left for the sanctuary of his office. The white working class came to feel similarly estranged from such former favorites as Mayor Kevin H. White, Congressman Thomas P. "Tip" O'Neill, and leaders of the Catholic Church, whom the residents perceived as abandoning them in their hour of need.

In certain protests women played a notable role, fighting to control their children's educational destiny. Around South Boston and Charlestown High Schools, one commonly saw groups of mothers, some with strollers, advancing on lines of police while chanting and singing patriotic slogans and songs. Often they would seek to engage the police in prayer. These protests were among the more dignified moments of the tumultuous busing years.

One of the most horrific incidents occurred in April 1976. A large group of antibusing protesters had congregated on City Hall Plaza. A small splinter group spotted Ted Landsmark, a black attorney, crossing the plaza and set upon him angrily. Perhaps the most searing image of the racial turmoil in Boston was captured in a photographer's shot of the besieged Landsmark as an assailant tried to spear him with a staff bearing the American flag.

The fury abated but the controversy lived on. Ruth Batson, an original busing plaintiff, praised Judge Garrity 20 years later for opening up the Boston school system. South Boston's champion, senate president William Bulger, by contrast, reviled Garrity for destroying everything Bostonians held dear.

During the early years of court-ordered busing in Boston, trouble was brewing as well to the north over nuclear power. Seabrook, N.H., has been described as the "birthplace" of the American antinuclear movement. When the Public Service Company of New Hampshire (PSNH) decided to revive its plans to build a nuclear power station in the seacoast town of Seabrook, its only organized opposition consisted of a ragtag band of volunteers from the Seacoast Anti-Pollution League (SAPL) made up mostly of amateur lobbyists and lobster fishers. By 1975 SAPL was nearly exhausted, physically and financially, from battles with PSNH over regulatory matters. SAPL's new, more confrontational leader, Guy Chichester, soon alienated the more traditional environmentalist members of the league with his intense suspicion of regulators and his attempts to broaden the conflict over Seabrook. Within a year Chichester left SAPL for the Clamshell Alliance, a group more open to other forms of protest.

The alliance favored civil disobedience. Often members of the Woodstock generation, the young, colorful, disorganized, and intensely committed Clams were devoted to democratic principles and opposed to centralized control. On August 1, 1976, 600 Clamshell protesters sought to seize the Seabrook construction site; 18 of them were arrested. Three weeks later 180 were taken into custody at another Clamshell protest.

In April 1977 the Clams tried to occupy the Seabrook construction site. New Hampshire governor Meldrim Thompson, who tended to overreact, ordered the arrest of more than 1,400 protesters. When most of them could not post the $1,500 bail (suspected to have been set at the urging of Governor Thompson), they remained in jail, draining the state's scarce resources, until their eventual release two weeks later. Most of the cases were dismissed, but the alliance was disappointed that its sacrifice garnered little mass response.

By the time of a planned protest in 1978 New Hampshire officials had changed their tactics, and Clamshell leaders, aware that at least some of the 1977 protesters had received jail sentences, opted for a less confrontational rally with speeches and exhibits. That time New Hampshire and PSNH cooperated with the Clams. However, this compromise split the alliance between those who favored less confrontation and those who preferred direct action. The organization never regained its momentum.

SAPL and the alliance continued to oppose Seabrook, joined by allies ranging from local gadflies to Massachusetts governor Michael Dukakis, who refused to permit the filing of a necessary emergency plan for nearby Massachusetts communities. Legal challenges dragged on, but eventually Seabrook was built and brought online. The battles were not without result, however. PSNH, a model of mismanagement, eventually filed for bankruptcy and was reorganized. The Seabrook plant continues to provide some of the most expensive power in New England.

Citizen protests against Seabrook Station and the movement opposing the Vietnam War are prime examples of a moralistic strain in New England politics that goes back to the region's first dissident settlers. But the riots associated with court-ordered busing in Boston reveal tensions between the region's deep-rooted sentiments of social justice and the more individualistic perspectives of working-class ethnic communities trying to preserve local interests and political control. Some of the same tensions surfaced again in the battles that waged over education funding in several New England legislatures in the latter 1990s. It remains to be seen which forces will prevail in those conflicts.

Henry F. Bedford, *Seabrook Station: Citizen Politics and Nuclear Power* (1990); William M. Bulger, *While the Music Lasts: My Life in Politics* (1996); Charles DeBenedetti and Charles Chatfield, *An American Ordeal: The Antiwar Movement of the Vietnam Era* (1990); Ronald P. Formisano, *Boston against Busing: Race, Class, and Ethnicity in the 1960s and 1970s* (1991); Joel Garreau, *The Nine Nations of North America* (1981); J. Anthony Lukas, *Common Ground: A Turbulent Decade in the Lives of Three American Families* (1985); Tom Wells, *The War Within: America's Battle over Vietnam* (1994); Nancy Zaroulis and Gerald Sullivan, *Who Spoke Up? American Protest against the War in Vietnam, 1963–1975* (1984).

Maurice Cunningham

Race and Ethnicity

Race and ethnicity have played differing roles in the politics of each New England state. Generally speaking, Connecticut, Rhode Island, and Massachusetts have seen more ethnic and racial conflict than have Vermont, New Hampshire, and Maine. Each state bears the imprint, however, of its specific racial and ethnic mix.

Large numbers of Irish immigrants began to arrive in Connecticut around the time of the Great Potato Famine in the mid-1840s. Germans also migrated to the state in the mid-19th century, followed by Scandinavians after 1870, Italians from 1900 to 1915, and in later years Lithuanians and Czechoslovakians. Polish immigration was especially heavy; municipal directives printed in Polish can still be found in cities such as New Britain. Official texts issued in Spanish recognize a more recent immigrant population. In 1920 almost 70 percent of Connecticut residents were foreign born or children of foreign-born parents—the third highest percentage in the nation behind only Rhode Island and Massachusetts. Sizable black migrations occurred after 1870 and after World War II. At the time of the 2000 census Connecticut was 82.0 percent white, 9.1 percent black, 9.4 percent Hispanic, and 2.4 percent Asian.

Early in the 20th century Yankee Republicans dominated Connecticut politics. Immigrants congregated in the Democratic Party, which broke through as a political power in 1928, when Alfred "Al" Smith, the first Roman Catholic candidate for president, ignited political fervor in ethnic cities.

Ethnic politics was the name of the game. With John Bailey as party chair from 1946 to 1975, the Democrats paid assiduous attention to ethnic balance on their tickets. Bailey was instrumental in the election of the first Irish Catholic president, John F. Kennedy; helped Connecticut elect a Jewish senator, Abraham Ribicoff, and an Italian woman governor, Ella Grasso; found congressional seats for Polish candidates; and elevated blacks to statewide office. Republicans discovered the value of placing members of ethnic groups on their tickets and in 1970 managed to elect Thomas Meskill, of Irish lineage, as governor.

From 1976 to 1990 Democrats won every election for governor or U.S. senator save those contested by Lowell Weicker, Jr. The maverick Weicker won three terms as a Republican senator and one term as governor as the head of his own Connecticut Party. Connecticut's uniqueness was evident in another regard: in 1990 the Fifth Congressional District elected Gary Franks, the first black Republican congressman since 1932. Franks was defeated in 1996 by the Irish American Democrat James Maloney. Racial conflict in the 1990s was evident in a school-desegregation suit brought by a black parent in Hartford and Voting Rights Act litigation pursued by black and Hispanic citizens in Bridgeport.

Rhode Island, too, saw ethnic struggle. Irish, French Canadian, and Italian immigrants have traditionally been the most prominent ethnic groups, along with lesser numbers of Germans, Armenians, Greeks, Lithuanians, Finns, and Syrians. In 2000 the state's population was 85.0 percent white, 8.7 percent Hispanic, and 4.5 percent black.

In the 19th century members of white ethnic groups harbored an especially virulent hatred of the upper-class Yankee Republican mill owners on account of poor working conditions, low pay, and political oppression linked to severe limitations of the franchise. This animosity was a prime motivating factor in Rhode Island politics into the 1950s and, in some instances, beyond. As in Connecticut, the presidential candidacy of Al Smith energized ethnic Catholics in 1928. Union membership also tied them into a Democratic voting bloc.

One of Rhode Island's most significant and colorful episodes of ethnic conflict occurred in January 1935 when Democrats staged a political coup against the long-dominant Republicans in the general assembly. Holding the governorship and House of Representatives but facing a two-seat Republican majority in the Senate, the Democratic lieutenant governor, Robert E. Quinn, refused to swear in two Republicans from contested races. The Senate formed a committee to review the elections and, with Quinn serving as tiebreaker, seated Democrats in the contested districts. The Democrats thereupon vacated the all-Republican supreme court, abolished the boards controlling Democratic cities, reorganized the government, granted new powers to the Democratic governor, and evicted Republican officials from their state jobs.

Rhode Island Democrats proved adept at presenting ethnically balanced tickets. Republicans acquired the same skill, electing John Pastore as the state's first governor of Italian heritage in the 1940s and later sending him to the U.S. Senate. For most of the last quarter of the century this most Democratic and Catholic state in the union sent two white Anglo-Saxon Protestants, Democrat Claiborne Pell and Republican John Chafee, to the U.S. Senate.

Irish immigrants poured into Massachusetts during and after the famine, with Italians, Poles, Lithuanians, and French Canadians, among others, arriving in their wake. These ethnic constituencies threatened Anglo-Yankee hegemony. In the latter half of the 20th century Massachusetts also had growing populations of African Americans, Hispanics, and Asians. The 2000 census showed a population base that was approximately 84.5 percent white, 5.4 percent black, 6.8 percent Hispanic, and 3.8 percent Asian. Hispanic and Asian populations were especially fast growing and concentrated in the cities.

In Massachusetts, where the Irish suffered severe mistreatment at the hands of Boston Brahmins, ethnic hatreds were particularly bitter. The legendary Irish politico James Michael Curley, a dominating figure in Boston throughout most of the first half of the 20th century, practiced an incendiary form of patronage politics that aimed to satisfy his various class and ethnic constituencies. The 1928 Smith candidacy and Franklin Roosevelt's presidency were boosts to Massachusetts's Democratic Party, which was controlled by the Irish. Irish domination led some Italian politicians, among them Governor John Volpe, to depart for the Republican Party. The political prominence of Irish Democrats did not shut out Yankee Republicans altogether, however. A small number, such as Senator Henry Cabot Lodge, Jr., Senator Leverett Saltonstall, and Governor William Weld, managed to win office more than once in Massachusetts over the course of the 20th century.

The nature of ethnic politics in Massachusetts changed after World War II, as the career and character of John F. Kennedy exemplify. Kennedy appealed to a more self-assured Irish population, one whose members felt they had finally "made it" as Americans. They still appreciated politics as theater, but they wanted less Curley-style skullduggery and more dignity. The sophisticated JFK and such managerial politicians as Boston Mayor John Collins gave it to them.

Massachusetts also sent the first black U.S. senator since Reconstruction to Washington, Republican Edward Brooke. Yet racial animosities still played a substantial role in Massachusetts politics, especially in white-ethnic cities in transition. Mel King, an African American, made it into the final round of

Boston's mayoral election in 1983, but few candidates of color have succeeded in state- or citywide races. Hispanics, consisting mostly of young, dispersed urban populations, had succeeded at electing only one state lawmaker until three Hispanic candidates, from Cambridge, Lawrence, and Springfield, won seats in the state legislature in 1998. Battles have been waged in several Massachusetts cities over redistricting plans that might enhance electoral opportunities for minority citizens.

Racial and ethnic politics have played a less dominant but still not inconsequential role in Vermont, New Hampshire, and Maine. Each of these more northerly New England states remained at least 96 percent white in the 2000 census. Vermont was an Anglo-Yankee stronghold throughout much of the 20th century. Irish, Italians, Poles, Finns, and French Canadians emigrated to that destination, but Vermont's foreign-born population never exceeded 15 percent. One measure of Yankee dominance can be seen in the fact that in 1936 Vermont and Maine were the only states in the union that voted for Republican Alfred Landon over President Franklin Roosevelt. The Yankee-dominated Republican Party was aided by Vermont's small-town rural character; the state's small number of cities gave working-class Democratic ethnic constituencies few places to take root. Moreover, although immigrants faced prejudice in Vermont, the state proved assimilative. Real two-party politics took hold only during the 1960s, owing not to racial or ethnic matters but to the migration of socially liberal and environmentally conscious residents.

Ethnic divisions in New Hampshire can be noted in the topography of the state's two congressional districts. Their composition has remained substantially the same since 1881, when Manchester and Nashua were separated in order to split the Roman Catholic vote. Such motives were long forgotten during most of the 20th century, however, with the two cities repeatedly voting Republican. Not until 1996, when both supported Democrat Jeanne Shaheen over Republican Ovide Lamontagne in the gubernatorial election and Bill Clinton over Bob Dole in the presidential race, did that pattern change. New Hampshire has become the home of Irish, Polish, Scandinavian, Italian, Greek, and, especially, French Canadian residents. Ronald Reagan found a strong base among conservative French Canadian workers, many of whom were once Democratic but, like many New Hampshire residents, are tax phobic. Since the 1960s migrants into New Hampshire have been a hodgepodge, driven more by the appeal of the state's low taxes than by other forces.

Between 1900 and 1960 Italians, Poles, Greeks, Albanians, and other ethnic groups migrated to Maine but in numbers too small to change the state's unique character. The tradition-minded nature of Mainers kept the state Republican long after the New Deal realigned much of the rest of New England. However, white Anglo-Saxon Protestant dominance was disturbed in 1948 when Margaret Chase Smith, whose mother was Franco-American, defeated two former Yankee governors for the Republican nomination to the U.S. Senate. The state has subsequently been represented in the Senate by Edmund Muskie, of Polish heritage; George Mitchell, of Lebanese and Irish descent; and Olympia Snowe, whose family background is Greek. But members of ethnic groups have not so much taken over Maine politics as they have adopted Maine folkways and the sense of Maine as a unique place.

One small group that has had a large effect is Maine's Native American population. Two of Maine's remaining groups of native peoples, the Passamaquoddy and the Penobscot, sued the state in the 1970s for the restitution of 12.5 million acres of land that they declared had been stolen from them and succeeded in securing restitution amounting to more than $80 million from the federal government.

Michael Barone and Grant Ujifusa, *The Almanac of American Politics* (1996); Jerry Hagstrom, *Beyond Reagan: The New Landscape of American Politics* (1988); James Jennings and Suzanne M. Baker, *Blacks, Latinos, and Asians in Massachusetts: A Statistical Socio-Demographic Profile, 1990* (1992); Duane Lockard, *New England State Politics* (1959); Kenneth T. Palmer, G. Thomas Taylor, and Marcus A. LiBrizzi, *Maine Politics and Government* (1992); Neal R. Peirce, *The New England States: People, Politics, and Power in the Six New England States* (1976).

Maurice Cunningham

Ribicoff, Abraham (1910–98) Connecticut governor and U.S. senator. Born in New Britain, Conn., Abraham Alexander Ribicoff, the son of Polish immigrants, emerged from a working-class background to gain prominence as governor of Connecticut, cabinet secretary in the Kennedy administration, and U.S. senator.

Ribicoff attended public schools in New Britain before studying at New York University and the University of Chicago. In 1933 he received his law degree from Chicago and was admitted to the Connecticut bar. He began his political career in 1938, when, as a Democrat, he was elected to the Connecticut General Assembly. Ten years later, voters in the First Congressional District elected Ribicoff to the U.S. House of Representatives; they reelected him in 1950. Two years later, however, he suffered his first political defeat when he lost

Secretary of Health, Education, and Welfare Abraham Ribicoff and Richard Cardinal Cushing, 1961

an election for the U.S. Senate by 29,000 votes to Prescott Bush, father of future president George H. W. Bush.

In 1954 Ribicoff recovered politically, becoming the first Jewish governor of the state of Connecticut. He was the only successful Democrat on his ticket that year and in 1958 was reelected with the largest margin of victory in the state's history. As governor, Ribicoff expanded programs for education and welfare, created a commission on the problems of aging, established a State Board of Mental Health, abolished county government, and took strong measures to improve highway safety, including the suspension of every convicted speeder's operating license.

When John F. Kennedy won the 1960 presidential election he asked Ribicoff to join his cabinet as attorney general, but Ribicoff declined. The president-elect persisted, however, and persuaded Ribicoff to resign as governor and accept the position of secretary of health, education, and welfare. In that job he advocated an early version of what later became known as Medicare, sought to improve teacher education programs, and proposed various welfare reforms, including the tracking of parents who desert their children.

Ribicoff left the cabinet in 1962 to run again for the Senate. This time he won. During 18 years in the Senate he continued to promote programs for education, Medicare, and automobile safety. Ribicoff's most visible public moment came at the Democratic National Convention in 1968 when, after seeing footage of Chicago police beating antiwar demonstrators on Michigan Avenue, he rose to nominate George McGovern as the party's candidate for president. Directing his stare at Chicago mayor Richard M. Daley, Ribicoff said, "With George McGovern, we wouldn't have Gestapo tactics on the streets of Chicago." When Daley erupted with a flurry of profanity and anti-Semitic epithets, Ribicoff calmly responded, "How hard it is to accept the truth. How hard it is."

In 1981 Ribicoff retired from the Senate and joined the New York law firm of Kaye, Scholer, Fierman, Hays, and Handler. He died after a lengthy bout with Alzheimer's disease in Riverdale, N.Y.

Abraham Ribicoff, *America Can Make It!* (1972); Abraham Ribicoff and Jon O. Newman, *Politics: The American Way* (1967).

Michael S. Foley

Roman Catholics and Politics
The stature of the Roman Catholic Church in New England has undergone a remarkable transformation since colonial times. New England's Protestant settlers regarded the Catholic Church with intense hostility, and its political influence was nonexistent. Following great waves of immigration in the 19th and 20th centuries, however, the power of the church increased dramatically, so by the end of World War II, the Catholic Church was a prominent political force in New England. During the 1960s, a decade that brought many Catholics into mainstream American society, the church lost ground. Today, though more than 40 percent of New Englanders are baptized Catholics, little is distinctively Catholic about New England politics.

New England's British settlers generally belonged to a reformed Protestant denomination. The late-17th-century *New-England Primer,* the only elementary textbook used in the colonies for decades, was referring to the Catholic Church when it spoke of the "arrant whore of Rome and all her blasphemies." The practice of the faith was largely proscribed by law. The Massachusetts Bay Colony forbade any Catholic priest to enter its territory under pain of life imprisonment. Religious tests often prohibited Catholics from holding public office. Only the colony of Providence Plantation, subsequently Rhode Island, provided for freedom of conscience and worship in its charter of 1663. Still, few Catholics chose to live in any part of New England. Some Jesuit missionaries remained in remote northern reaches of the region, but colonial wars against the French and their Indian allies inflamed passions against them. Father Sébastien Râle, for example, founder of the first school in what is now Maine, was killed by Massachusetts militia at war with the Abenaki in 1724. Even if we count the handful of Acadians driven south by the British and a few indentured servants from

Archbishop Richard Cushing with Monsignor Wright, Rose Fitzgerald Kennedy, John F. Kennedy, Mother Emile Ange, and Sister Herbert at a shrine, Orient Heights, Boston, 1946

Ireland, the Catholic presence in early New England remains minuscule. The first American bishop, John Carroll, made no mention of Catholics living in the region when he sent his report on the state of the American church to the Vatican in 1785.

The Revolutionary War enhanced the image of Catholicism somewhat, as the war was supported by prominent American Catholics such as Charles Carroll as well as by non-American Catholics such as the Marquis de Lafayette, Casimir Pulaski, and Tadeusz Kosciuszko. Although religious tests for public office remained widespread for another half century, Catholics were allowed to practice their faith in public. In 1788 the first public mass was celebrated in Boston, and in 1808 a diocese, encompassing all of New England, was established there. Nonetheless, the Catholic presence grew slowly. By 1820 there were still fewer than 4,000 Catholics in all of New England.

Immigration in the mid-19th century changed the situation radically. Catholics from Ireland were the first to arrive in large numbers. Driven from their homeland by famine and oppression, they poured into Boston during the 1840s. Many remained there, rapidly becoming the dominant political force. Others, especially those involved with building the railroads and canals, dispersed throughout New England. The 1855 Massachusetts census reported that, counting the children of foreign-born parents as aliens, 62 percent of the residents of Boston were foreigners. In Lawrence, 72 percent of the population was foreign born; in Fall River, 60 percent; and in Lowell,

54 percent. According to the same counting method, the 1865 Rhode Island census reported that the population of Providence was 44 percent foreign.

The Irish were followed by German immigrants during the 1850s, French Canadians after the Civil War, and southern and eastern Europeans around the turn of the 20th century. Between 1890 and 1920 the number of Italian immigrants in southern New England increased from about 16,000 to 229,000; the number of Poles rose from slightly more than 5,000 to 124,000; and the number of Russian-born immigrants grew from 11,000 to 150,000. By the time federal legislation in the 1920s stopped the flood of immigration, the ethnic and religious makeup of New England had been fundamentally altered. In 1920 first- or second-generation immigrants, largely Catholics, made up more than two-thirds of the populations of Connecticut, Rhode Island, and Massachusetts; half the population of New Hampshire; and one-third of the populations of Maine and Vermont.

With the increasing numbers of Catholics in New England came an increasing Catholic presence at all levels of government. Bloc voting by these new citizens allowed Catholic politicians, especially Irish Catholics, to rise to power in the cities, where immigrants tended to cluster. Highly effective political machines catapulted Catholics into city halls, Congress, and eventually even statehouses. Their growing strength generated fear and hostility among the native Protestants, who had previously enjoyed undisputed hegemony in the region. In 1854, for example, Protestant militants destroyed a Catholic church in Boston with gunpowder, and during the 1850s the anti-immigrant, anti-Catholic Know-Nothing Party enjoyed great success. The Know-Nothings captured all statewide offices in Massachusetts in 1854, garnering significant support in Rhode Island and Connecticut as well. If the largely Protestant Republican Party proved able to retain political dominance well into the 20th century, it did so by way of voting restrictions and gerrymandering.

Catholic political strength continued to grow in New England and, with it, the influence of the Catholic Church. William Cardinal O'Connell, the archbishop of Boston from 1907 until 1944, had a registered lobbyist in the Massachusetts legislature who frequently communicated the church's position on matters such as birth control, gambling, and child labor to its members. Both Catholic voters and Catholic politicians retained close ties to the church. Many immigrants had brought with them from their homelands a deep commitment to the Catholic faith. They believed that the church had been established by Christ and accepted its authority as legitimate, treating the opinions of church leaders with deference and respect. These bonds were reinforced by the mediating role the church played in many aspects of its members' lives. A wide-ranging web of church-sponsored institutions—schools, hospitals, professional associations, and social groups—provided Catholics with support and leadership in a society that often seemed hostile. The educational system erected by the church was especially helpful to lower-class and immigrant Catholics. With schools at the elementary, secondary, and university levels, it offered Catholics a stepping-stone into the professions and the middle class while simultaneously delivering instruction in the Catholic moral and religious worldview. Many Catholic politicians were products of this system, which helped facilitate cooperation with the church hierarchy.

Since the 1960s assimilation into the mainstream has become more the rule than the exception, and the political strength of the Catholic Church in New England has diminished significantly. With no major new influxes of immigrants between the world wars, the percentage of foreign-born Catholics plummeted. Increasingly, the church was composed of third- and fourth-generation Americans rather than recent immigrants and their children. Moreover, after World War II many Catholic veterans went to college on the G.I. Bill and embarked on professional careers. The rising affluence of Catholics led many to abandon the close-knit ethnic communities of the cities in favor of the suburbs, where they were often isolated from their coreligionists. Increasingly, too, Catholicism began to be perceived as an acceptable form of religious worship rather than a threat to U.S. democratic institutions. The most telling evidence of this new acceptance was the 1960 election of John F. Kennedy, a Catholic senator from Massachusetts, as president of the United States. Kennedy's public campaign pledge not to let his faith interfere with his constitutional duties suggests that some were still wary of Catholicism at that time. Nonetheless, Kennedy's election was widely viewed as a sign that Catholics had ceased to be a marginalized and somewhat mistrusted minority group. In this changed environment, Catholics no longer felt the need to be protected by the church from the wider society; rather, they sought to become part of it. Rising educational levels among Catholics meant that laypeople could look beyond the clergy for educated leaders.

In addition, life as a member of the Catholic faith was dramatically changed for Americans by the Second Vatican Council, convened in 1962. Although the documents produced by the council were thoroughly orthodox, they were issued at a time of social turmoil in the United States and caused substantial confusion for laity and clergy alike. Radical, often unauthorized changes were made to the sacramental and liturgical practices of many Catholics. Thousands of priests and religious left their vocations. Many laypeople stopped attending mass or left the church altogether. More remained in the church but rejected the authority of its teachings, especially in the area of sexual morality. The weakening of the legitimacy of the church's authority in the eyes of its members translated into a decline in its political influence. This decline was especially evident in New England, where Catholic politicians began to run on platforms that were directly opposed to church teachings and received strong support from Catholic voters.

The church has remained involved in New England politics, albeit with mixed results. In 1974, for example, a federal judge declared Boston's public schools unconstitutionally segregated and mandated student busing to achieve integration. Many white Bostonians—including large numbers of Catholics with children in the public schools—vehemently opposed the plan as a violation of parental control over their children's education. Boston's archbishop, Humberto Sousa Cardinal Medeiros, generally supported the court order, however, and refused to condone its defiance. Many Catholics resented his position, and tensions over busing remained high for many years. Although Cardinal Medeiros's stance apparently helped minimize overt acts of resistance to court-ordered busing, the subsequent "white flight" from Boston to the suburbs undermined the court's efforts to integrate Boston's public schools.

More recent areas of political involvement by church leaders in New England have included vocal advocacy against abortion, euthanasia, same-sex marriage, embryonic stem cell research, and human cloning. Yet the church has had mixed success in advancing these views as New England voters and political leaders, including Catholics, have frequently taken the opposite position. In the late 1990s, for example, senior Catholic prelates in New England and across America gave undivided, vocal support to a federal bill to ban partial-birth abortion. Still, in a 1997 congressional vote on the bill, only six of 14 Catholic representatives and two of the seven Catholic senators from New England voted for it.

The political influence of the Catholic Church was further eroded by the shocking details of a sex-abuse scandal that erupted in 2002. The scandal initially revolved around two Boston priests, John Geoghan and Paul Shanley, who had sexually abused many boys during their clerical careers. Further revelations indicated that such clerical abuse had occurred across the country and had often been covered up by church leaders. Although the American Catholic bishops instituted policies in 2003 to prevent such abuse from happening again, the scandal will undoubtedly undermine the moral authority and the political influence of the church for years to come.

Still, church leaders have shown no signs of backing away from promoting the policies they believe will be most conducive to the common good of society and the happiness of individuals. Members of the Catholic hierarchy became unusually involved in the 2004 presidential campaign after Senator John Kerry, a Catholic politician from Massachusetts, was selected as the Democratic nominee for president. Although Kerry is the first Catholic nominated by a major party for the presidency since John Kennedy, his candidacy immediately drew fire from church leaders in large part because of his stand in favor of abortion rights; it also set off a vigorous debate among Catholic prelates and laypeople over how the church should respond to politicians who assert that they hold the Catholic faith while simultaneously rejecting central church teachings. The archbishop of Saint Louis publicly announced that he would deny communion to Senator Kerry while he was campaigning in the city, while the archbishop of

Boston issued a statement saying that Catholic voters and politicians who favored abortion rights ought voluntarily to refrain from receiving communion. While there is an ongoing debate within the church as to the appropriateness of these actions, the Kerry nomination may well have transformed the way in which church leaders interact with Catholics in the political realm.

Catholic University of America, comp., *New Catholic Encyclopedia* (1967); Thomas H. O'Connor, *Boston Catholics: A History of the Church and Its People* (1998); Neal R. Peirce, *The New England States: People, Politics, and Power in the Six New England States* (1976); Edward L. Queen II, ed., *Encyclopedia of American Religious History* (1996); Thomas Sowell, *Ethnic America: A History* (1981); John Kenneth White, *The Fractured Electorate: Political Parties and Social Change in Southern New England* (1983).

Lawrence J. Kapp

Sanders, Bernie (Bernard) (1941–)

Mayor of Burlington, Vt., and U.S. representative. The two-party monopoly of the U.S. House of Representatives was upset in 1990 with the election of a socialist-leaning independent from Vermont, Bernie Sanders. Sanders became the first non-major-party candidate to win a House seat from New England since 1878. But Sanders was used to making history.

The most intriguing political development of the 1980s in Vermont was the electoral takeover of Burlington, the state's largest city, by Sanders, a native of Brooklyn, N.Y., and an independent filmmaker educated at the University of Chicago. Sanders was one of many countercultural activists who moved to Vermont during the late 1960s and 1970s. After a number of quixotic statewide races, Sanders stunned Vermonters and Americans everywhere in March 1981—weeks after the nation had inaugurated Ronald Reagan, its most conservative president in 60 years—when he was elected mayor of Burlington by a scant 10 votes over Gordon Paquette, a five-term Democratic incumbent. Sanders was helped by a huge turnout among the city's renters, squeezed by landlords eager to replace young families with affluent out-of-state college students attending the University of Vermont.

Burlington, with its mix of Irish and French Canadian families, had long been the bastion of the state's Democratic Party, even during bad times. Although its initial takeover by his Progressive Coalition—the "Sanderistas"—was thought to be a fluke, Sanders went on to victories in 1983, 1985, and 1987 and was succeeded in 1989 by the development director of his administration, Peter Clavelle.

During his eight years in office, Sanders did a lot to limit in Burlington the kind of "Yup-

pification" and gentrification that had taken place in other small New England cities. As the 1980s economic boom ripped through New England, wealthy young urban professionals pushed lower-income residents out of many communities into substandard housing in less scenic towns. Sanders put a stop to that by pushing for "inclusionary zoning" to guarantee a class-mixed city population. In addition, Burlington's city council developed its own foreign policy, regularly debating stands on Latin America and criticizing the Reagan administration's involvement in Nicaragua and El Salvador, apartheid in South Africa, and British occupation in Northern Ireland.

Sanders's initial efforts to take his mayoral message statewide were less successful. He suffered a bad loss in the 1986 governor's race, finishing third, with 14.6 percent of the vote, behind the incumbent Democratic governor, Madeleine Kunin, and the Republican lieutenant governor, Peter P. Smith. Two years later he fared better in the contest for the state's lone seat in the U.S. House, which had been vacated by Jim Jeffords's departure for the Senate. Sanders finished a surprisingly close second in that race, with 37.5 percent of the vote, trailing the winner, Peter Smith, by only 8,911 votes and 3.7 points and outpolling the Democratic candidate, House floor leader Paul Poirier.

In the 1990 Smith-Sanders rematch, Smith seemed to have no clear ideological focus, lurching toward opponents of assault weapons and antagonizing his supporters in the National Rifle Association, then supporting and rejecting President George H. W. Bush's tax increases. Distrusted in the windup by all factions, Smith was the most decisively defeated House incumbent in 1990, gaining only 39.5 percent of the vote. Thus did Vermont, long the nation's most Republican state, send to the House of Representatives Bernie Sanders, the first true independent since Frazier Reams of Ohio (1951–55), and the first House member identified with socialist politics since New York's Vito Marcantonio.

Congressman Sanders went on to win reelection to the House in every election since 1992. Initially, he was rebuffed by conservative southern Democrats in the Democratic Caucus. However, conservative Republican successes in the South during the 1990s eliminated many of those opposing Sanders from that body. Also, his consistently high level of support for Democratic Party positions endeared him to key House Democratic leaders such as David Bonior of Michigan and David Obey of Wisconsin. Sanders created the House Progressive Caucus early in his congressional career, and it rapidly grew to almost

60 members—more than one-fourth of the House's Democratic leadership. Even though Representative Sanders continues to campaign in Vermont as an independent, his Washington career is now entwined with those of liberal Democrats in the House.

W. J. Conroy, *Challenging the Boundaries of Reform: Socialism in Burlington* (1990); Greg Guma, *The People's Republic: Vermont and the Sanders Revolution* (1989); Steven Rosenfeld, *Making History in Vermont: The Election of a Socialist to Congress* (1992); Bernard Sanders and Huck Gutman, *Outsider in the House* (1997).

Garrison Nelson

Smith, Margaret Chase (1897–1995)

U.S. representative and senator. Despite her strong support for U.S. Cold War defense policies and her sponsorship of legislation to ban the American Communist Party, Margaret Chase Smith is probably best known for the "declaration of conscience" she delivered in the Senate on June 1, 1950, attacking the tactics of "trial by accusation" and "character prosecution" used by her fellow Republican Joseph McCarthy. The speech, one of the first public denunciations of McCarthyism, made Smith a national figure and one of the most prominent female politicians of her era. In 1964 Smith's name was placed in nomination for president at the Republican National Convention; she was the first woman so honored by a major party.

Born in Skowhegan, Maine, Smith came from a mixed background: Franco-American on her mother's side (the family name had been changed from Morin to Murray), Yankee on her father's. After completing high school, she worked as a teacher, a switchboard operator, and a newspaper office manager while becoming increasingly active in state Republican Party circles. At the age of 32 she married Clyde Smith, who was elected to Congress in 1937. Three years later Clyde Smith suffered a heart attack and asked voters to let his wife succeed him in office. Maine voters complied, electing Margaret Chase Smith to four terms in the U.S. House of Representatives. In 1948 Smith easily defeated two former Republican governors for her party's U.S. Senate nomination and went on to win the general election with more than 70 percent of the vote.

Throughout her career Smith skillfully identified herself with a set of qualities—frugality, hard work, independence, and plainspokenness—popularly associated with Maine and New England. Smith was famous for running shoestring campaigns that relied exclusively on volunteers and for refusing to accept unsolicited campaign contributions. Between 1955 and 1968 Smith answered a record 2,941

Former senator Margaret Chase Smith, 1991

consecutive Senate roll calls. Another noteworthy aspect of Smith's voting was her refusal to announce her position publicly before important votes. This habit, along with her occasional well-publicized departures from Republican orthodoxy—she voted against funding for the Safeguard missile in 1968 and opposed the Supreme Court nominations of Clement Haynsworth and G. Harold Carswell—earned Smith a reputation as something of a party maverick. In fact, she took pains to support presidents, whether Republican or Democratic, on important matters whenever possible.

Seeking reelection to a fifth Senate term in 1972, Smith found that the campaign tactics that had served her well in the past were no longer effective. Accustomed to highly positive media coverage, Smith resisted buying television time to sell herself to the voters. After defeating a challenger in the primary (her first nomination fight since 1940), Smith declined a campaign gift from the Maine Republican Party, stating that she was opposed to "buying" elections. Smith's Democratic opponent, Congressman William Hathaway, outspent her on campaign advertising by a margin of more than 15 to 1 and won the election by a margin of 53 to 47 percent.

Among the many accolades and awards Smith received in her more than two decades of retirement was the Presidential Medal of Freedom, conferred by President George H. W. Bush in 1989. She died in Skowhegan at the age of 97.

Frank Graham, *Margaret Chase Smith: Woman of Courage* (1964); Patricia L. Schmidt, *Margaret Chase Smith: Beyond Convention* (1996); Marlene Boyd Vallin, *Margaret Chase Smith: Model Public Servant* (1998); Patricia Ward Wallace, *Politics of Conscience: A Biography of Margaret Chase Smith* (1995).

Richard J. Maiman

State Legislatures As a region, New England has the country's most diverse population patterns. Legislators in the six states represent large districts that are urban, districts that are predominately rural, cities that have high proportions of immigrants and poor citizens, and towns that have per capita incomes that are among the highest in the country. Demographic factors influence both the substance and style of politics and, when combined with legislative rules and norms, produce different methods of campaigning and governing in the six states.

Despite these variations, legislative politics exhibit common characteristics: the historic rise and continued success of Democratic legislators; enduring styles of representation; and, most recently, the emergence of split-ticket voting leading to governors and legislatures controlled by different political parties. This last feature underscores the increasingly complex political environment that was the hallmark of legislative politics at the turn of the 21st century.

Writing in 1959, Duane Lockard found it expedient to describe "two New Englands," dividing the region at the northern Massachusetts border. The three northern states he considered to be one-party systems, with Republicans dominating the legislatures and other state political offices. The southern states, in contrast, had somewhat competitive parties and legislatures.

In more than 40 years much has changed. Until the 1960s Republicans controlled the legislatures of Vermont, New Hampshire, and Maine. Changing demographic patterns, however, left an imprint on the political culture of these states. Younger families and professionals began moving north, bringing with them more liberal attitudes and a predilection for Democratic candidates. In addition, Democratic officials in these states reorganized the parties and began to recruit candidates for areas previously uncontested.

These developments have reversed party fortunes in Maine and Vermont. With few exceptions, Democrats have controlled legislatures in these states in recent years. New Hampshire, with its more homogeneous population, remained the "triumph of conservatism" and was least affected by these changes until the election of 1998, when, led by incumbent Democratic governor Jeanne Shaheen, Democrats captured control of the senate for the first time since 1912. Nevertheless, observers of New Hampshire politics note that the success of Democratic candidates for the legislature represents a shift in political culture similar to, though not as profound as, that found in Vermont and Maine.

Democrats in the southern states have increased their presence in state legislatures, enhancing what has been a dominant position for decades. The party has generally received strong support from the densely populated, ethnic, and urban centers. Rhode Island continues to be the least competitive state in New England, routinely having four times as many Democrats as Republicans in the legislature. Since winning both houses in Massachusetts in 1958, the Democrats have, with few exceptions, maintained majorities of at least three to one in both chambers. Although the margins of victory are considerably less, Connecticut voters have consistently placed Democratic majorities in the legislature.

Lockard's regional divide was also designed to differentiate qualities of representation; the "friend and neighbors" approach of northern legislatures from the less personal politics of the southern states. Other scholars have likewise separated the region based on orientations to governing. Daniel Elazar, for instance, argues that citizens in the northern states have a "moralistic culture" that prizes a communitarian approach to politics and views legislative service as a civic obligation. Moralistic attitudes are also present in southern New England states, but to a lesser degree; there, they are countered by "individualistic" values that dampen citizen involvement and give rise to a more careerist class of politicians. While these categories contain exceptions, they nonetheless illuminate persistent styles of representation in the six states.

In the northern states, a localistic culture born of the town meeting remains strong, and personal politics are both expected and rewarded. These orientations are reinforced by small constituencies. In Vermont, the average House member serves only 7,500 people; the average senator has 32,000 constituents. The New Hampshire House, which has 400 members, is the largest state legislative body in the country. Although Maine has one-third the population of Connecticut, it has the same number of legislators. In addition, parties do less recruiting and funding of candidates in the north, forcing legislators to cultivate a style that reinforces community ties.

A low cost of campaigning eases the entry into politics, but limited pay makes exit more likely as well. With low salaries, legislative service has a voluntary and sporadic quality. In New Hampshire, for instance, legislators receive $100 for a legislative session of 45 days. In recent years, salaries in Maine and Vermont have increased substantially, but political life is still generally pursued as an avocation and perceived as a civic obligation. Without large material benefits, legislative turnover has been consistently high, sometimes approaching 30 percent in each chamber in all three states.

Of the southern-tier states, the Rhode Island legislature comes closest to resembling its northern counterparts. Small districts encourage the face-to-face campaigning and "retail politicking" found in the northern states. Moreover, half-year sessions and a history of minimal pay have precluded politics as a profession. Despite low barriers to the legislature, however, turnover is smaller and legislative service is more continuous. Only recently have many legislators had to face primary opponents. The small size of the state contributes to a "politics of intimacy," but legislative bargaining is typically done between leaders with long political backgrounds.

In Connecticut, legislative duties require a more full-time commitment. Although the Connecticut legislature meets for approximately half the year, special sessions are common, thereby expanding the duties of members. Compensation reflects these work requirements; Connecticut members have the second highest salaries and number of staff in the region. Large districts contribute to impersonal politics and raise campaign costs. Since political parties defray these campaign costs, challenges from political amateurs are discouraged.

With year-round sessions, full-time staff, and salaries competitive with other professions, the Massachusetts legislature is different from the others in New England. For many members, politics is their sole occupation. High election costs and substantial pay make both entry and exit from the legislature less inviting. With the assistance of election staff and other services provided by the parties, the power of incumbency is strong. Legislative turnover is consistently the lowest in the region, further contributing to an elite and specialized class of politicians.

During the 1980s and 1990s, elections in the region produced legislatures and governorships controlled by different parties. In 1998, with the exception of Vermont, no party controlled both branches of government. Although individual states have often had divided government, the prevalence of split-ticket voting is an unusual development. Under these conditions, legislative politics has become filled with more conflict and legislative outcomes have become less certain.

The emergence of split-ticket voting has enabled recent governors to influence public policy, despite their party's weaker positions in the legislature. Particularly in Massachusetts and Connecticut, strong governors have been able to set the political agenda that legislators have followed. Generally, legislators in states with divided government have had significantly less control over the content of legislation.

In the past, political scholars have viewed such divided government as a manifestation of "split-level bipartyism," in which parties are competitive for high offices but are less strong in local races. Recent evidence, however, suggests that the parties are becoming more com-

petitive even at the legislative level. Although legislatures in Massachusetts, Rhode Island, and New Hampshire have traditions of party dominance, more minority party candidates are making bids for legislative office, and these races have become closer.

The presence of split-ticket voting also underscores shifting voter orientations within the states. In Connecticut, for instance, the gap between registered Democrats and Republicans has narrowed at the same time that the number of voters without a party affiliation has risen. This pattern has also occurred in Rhode Island: an increase in both registered Republicans and those declaring no affiliation. There is a growing proportion of independents in Massachusetts. These "swing voters" in Massachusetts often decide elections, and many of them have supported moderate Republicans. New Hampshire voters have been willing to elect more Democratic legislative candidates, especially those who appear moderate. These shifting attitudes have yet to translate into widespread legislative changes, but individual legislators are encountering more volatile constituencies.

As states gain more responsibility for governing, the qualities that define New England legislative politics—localism, volunteerism, amateurism—become more precarious. Around the country, states have responded to waves of devolution of federal government power and have become more professionalized by increasing pay and adding legislative staff. New England states, particularly Rhode Island, Maine, and Vermont, have taken similar steps to cope with increasing responsibilities. Only New Hampshire, which prides itself on its civic legislature, has remained unaffected. Whether the increasing stakes of politics produce a new kind of legislative politician remains to be seen, but entrenched styles of representation stand as barriers.

In an increasingly complex political environment, the context of legislative decision-making remains less certain. The political cultures of states continue to fluctuate, and changing attitudes about parties have produced surprising combinations of elected officials in states with histories of one-party dominance. Already diverse, campaigning for and governing in state legislatures is becoming more complicated.

Andrew M. Appleton and Daniel S. Ward, eds., *State Party Profiles: A 50-State Guide to Development, Organization, and Resources* (1997); Council of State Governments, *The Book of the States* (1996–97); Council of State Governments, *State Leadership Directory: Legislative Leadership, Committees, and Staff* (1996); Daniel J. Elazar, *American Federalism: A View from the States* (1972); Ronald J. Hrebenar and Clive S. Thomas, *Interest Group Politics in the Northeastern*

States* (1993); Duane Lockard, *New England State Politics* (1959); Josephine F. Milburn and William Doyle, eds., *New England Political Parties* (1983); Alan Rosenthal and Maureen Moakley, eds., *The Political Life of the American States* (1984).

Richard M. Francis

Taxes and Spending

Taxes and Spending Throughout the United States the main sources of public revenue for state and local governments, other than federal aid, are taxes on personal and corporate incomes, sales taxes, property taxes, and special fees and user charges. With some exceptions, all of them outside New England, income and sales taxes are collected by state governments, while property taxes are the preserve of cities and towns.

Public-finance systems in New England are generally similar to those of other states but differ in three important respects: local governments have broader authority and wider jurisdictions than local governments in other regions; local governments rely much more heavily on property taxes than do their counterparts elsewhere; and the region as a whole taxes and spends at rates well above the national average.

Because of decisions made during the 17th century about how local political life should be organized, the New England states show a marked preference for general-purpose governments with wide-ranging responsibilities rather than special-district governments with narrow jurisdictions. A general-purpose city or town government usually has primary authority over all public functions within its geographic boundaries. Decisions about all public services are made by the same governing body, whether it is a town meeting, a board of selectmen, or a mayor and council. One local tax rate generates the bulk of local tax revenue, and one budget encompasses all local services. A special-district government, by contrast, has jurisdiction over only one function. In many parts of the United States special school districts run the schools, library districts administer the libraries, sanitation districts oversee garbage disposal, and so on. Special-district governments do exist in New England, to be sure; but most of the local authority to tax and spend is concentrated in the hands of cities and towns, which are responsible for education, public safety, public health and sanitation, environmental regulation, building permits, and much more.

Where voters are faced with several special-district governments, each with its own tax rate, they may lose track of the real size of their tax burden (especially their local tax burden), just as they may lose sight of which administrative unit is responsible for which services. Where general-purpose governments are charged with a wide array of public functions, a single city election or town meeting can have much higher visibility and relevance than multiple elections for the independent boards and commissions that run school, sanitation, and library districts. In fact, supporters of special-district governments often argue precisely that the operations of those bodies are less political—that is, less connected to the existing social, economic, and political conflicts in the community—and more professional than the operations of councils and town meetings.

A related peculiarity is that while county governments are important administrative and judicial units in most states, they play a very small role in New England. In general, what counties do in other states, cities and towns do in New England, or the state does so directly—a legacy of the time when towns were controlled by voters and counties were controlled by magistrates and commissioners appointed by the Crown. Two states, Connecticut and Rhode Island, do not even have counties in the conventional sense, and Massachusetts has embarked on a project to abolish county government. The 14 original Massachusetts counties, which were never more than regional administrative districts (with some responsibility for record keeping, jails, road maintenance, and courts) are being phased out, although voters have the option of transforming their own county into a regional government. Barnstable County, encompassing the communities of Cape Cod, has chosen that option, while Middlesex County has been eliminated. When a county is abolished, the commonwealth assumes its administrative functions although the county continues to be used as a geographic division. County government was abolished in Connecticut in 1960, and the counties remain only as geographic subdivisions of the state. Tiny Rhode Island has always relied on the simple division of responsibilities between the state government in Providence on the one hand and the cities and towns on the other. As in Connecticut and some parts of Massachusetts, Rhode Island counties are geographic divisions only and do not identify actual governments.

Despite broad responsibilities and wide jurisdictions, local governments in New England must rely on a very limited tax base to fund their operations. No New England state permits its local governments to collect income or sales taxes, and most New England states show a marked preference for taxes over fees and service charges as a way of financing public goods. This leaves the municipal property tax as the chief—virtually the sole—source of own-source revenue at the local level. In the United States as a whole local property tax revenue constitutes about 18 per-

cent of general revenue (that is, revenue from all sources, including all taxes, fees, and intergovernmental transfers); in New England the average is 25 percent. The difference is even more striking if one measures tax revenue only, excluding fees, service charges, and transfers. Nationally, property taxes supply about 75 percent of the tax revenues collected by local governments; in New England the average is 99 percent. Consequently, the average local share of state and local revenue is lower in New England (at 37.1 percent) than it is nationwide (44.6 percent), as is the average local share of state and local expenditures (59.9 percent nationally but only 46.1 percent in New England).

This pattern has been the subject of criticism and complaint for many years. Critics argue that New England's local governments cannot adequately discharge their responsibilities without being granted wider tax bases—or substantially more state aid. New England's heavy reliance on the property tax for local own-source revenue has also been condemned on the grounds that property taxes tend to be inflexible and regressive. Despite these criticisms, which not all economists accept, property-tax burdens in New England remain among the highest in the country. New Hampshire, which has neither a state sales tax nor a state income tax, has the highest property tax burden in the country, at $59 per $1,000 in personal income.

Complaints about high property taxes, and requests for more state aid to local governments, are perennial features of state and local politics in New England. In Massachusetts they led to the 1980 passage of Proposition 2½, an initiative petition that limits a municipality's property-tax levy to 2.5 percent of the town's or city's total assessed value and forbids increasing the tax rate by more than 2.5 percent per year without special voter approval. Proposition 2½ was bitterly contested by municipal officials, public-employee unions, and advocates for local services and programs, who correctly predicted that deep reductions in property-tax revenues would require deep reductions in local services, especially in education. During the first year after the law was enacted, cities and towns had to cut nearly half a billion dollars from their local budgets, recovering only about half of that amount in increased state aid. Nearly 8,000 school employees lost their jobs, and 230 schools were closed. Cuts were equally severe in other areas: during the first year after Proposition 2½ took effect, 550 firefighters and 360 police officers also had to be let go.

Beginning in 1983, in response to concerns about declining public services, the Massachusetts legislature made the first of a series of

important amendments to Proposition 2½, rendering tax-levy increases somewhat easier. State aid to cities and towns—which had been below the national average before 1980—increased steadily thereafter until 1992, when a state budget crisis and a fiscally conservative Republican administration forced the first reduction in the state aid account in several years. Between the various amendments to Proposition 2½ and more generous state aid, municipal spending in Massachusetts increased by 1.8 percent annually from 1981 to 1991 after declining (in real terms) during the late 1970s—an ironic footnote to the hopes of the conservative tax reformers who first championed tax limits in 1980.

In New Hampshire tax issues came to a head in 1996, when the supreme court ruled unconstitutional the use of local property taxes to fund education in the state. Three years later Democratic governor Jeanne Shaheen signed a controversial statewide property tax into law, raising rates precipitously in so-called donor towns while lowering them in more property-poor receiver communities. A coalition of cities and towns hardest hit by the tax quickly formed, vowing to take the state to court. Vermont's 1997 Act 60 has met with similar resistance. That state's Coalition of Municipalities, having failed to get the law declared unconstitutional, brought suit in late 1999 against the Vermont Tax Department on the grounds that the statewide tax-equalization formula distributes the tax burden unfairly. Battles in both states are ongoing.

While Massachusetts, New Hampshire, and Vermont have experienced the severest clashes over property taxes, no New England state has completely escaped tax and budget conflicts in recent years. With the sole exception of tax-averse New Hampshire, per capita tax burdens and spending exceed the national average in New England, with fiscal patterns in the region closely resembling those in highly urbanized states along the Boston-to-Washington corridor. State general revenues averaged $2,534 per capita in the United States in 1993; in New England that average was $2,933. Per capita state expenditures averaged $2,506 nationwide in the same year; New England's average was $2,978, and only New Hampshire (again) fell below the national average. Governors and state legislatures have thus engaged in many an acrimonious debate over how to balance state budgets without sacrificing services or raising taxes.

Budget shortfalls have prompted a search for new sources of state revenue, among them legalized casino gambling. But New England's tax and budget crises have often been linked to slow rates of economic growth (around 1 percent per year, for example, between 1988 and 1992, with a 2 percent reduction in nonfarm employment), especially when compared with the more robust growth rates in the Sunbelt (nearly 7 percent per year for the same period). State governments have therefore turned their attention to making the region more hospitable to business, with fewer regulations, easier permit processes, lower business taxes, and more investment in the kinds of infrastructure improvements that buttress the regional economy.

Dennis Hale, "Proposition 2¹/₂ a Decade Later: The Ambiguous Legacy of Tax Reform in Massachusetts," *State and Local Government Review* 25 (1993); Ronald John Hy and William L. Waugh, Jr., *State and Local Tax Policies: A Comparative Handbook* (1995); Helen F. Ladd and Nicolaus Tideman, *Tax and Expenditure Limitations* (1981); Dick Netzer, *Economics of the Property Tax* (1966); Diane B. Paul, *The Politics of the Property Tax* (1975); U.S. Bureau of the Census, *Census of Governments*, vol. 4, no. 5: *Compendium of Government Finances* (1987).

Dennis B. Hale

Third Parties Despite its leading role as a cauldron of radical ideas and readiness to initiate them in its early history, New England has never been especially receptive to third parties in national elections. Along with the South, New England was the only other region of the country totally resistant to Theodore Roosevelt's Progressive American, or "Bull Moose," Party, the only third party (with the exception of Ralph Nader's Green Party in 2000) to make a difference in a presidential election. But third-party activity in New England at the state and community levels has always been a significant factor in the region's politics and is equally indicative of the strain of contrariness that runs deep in its political life.

During the 19th century, slavery, the heavy influx of Irish immigrants coupled with xenophobic nationalism, temperance-prohibition, and the shift from craft to factory economy were the motivations for the existence of the Anti-Slavery Party and the Native American or Know-Nothing Party, for various temperance societies eventually merging into the Prohibition Party, and for early workingman associations evolving into socialist parties. In the 20th century, the Great Depression and wars abroad stimulated the rise of the American Communist Party and various peace parties while the Prohibition Party and socialist parties have continued, ineffectually, into the present. Most of these parties have been varyingly successful over the years in electing their members to local and state offices and in effecting legislation at both levels. During the 1850s, the Know-Nothing Party elected governors in Maine and Connecticut; dominated the Massachusetts, Rhode Island, and Con-

necticut legislatures; elected several members of Congress; and enjoyed some success at the local community level. The Prohibition Party originated in Maine with Portland mayor Neal Dow as its first presidential nominee in 1872, and it has been running White House candidates ever since. From the 1890s to the 1950s, several small industrial cities elected socialist mayors, most notably Jasper McLevy, mayor of Bridgeport, Conn., from 1938 to 1953 and now something of a legend in that state's political history.

In modern times neither the various peace parties nor the American Communist Party have had much luck in New England, though not from lack of candidates or effort. The wealthy communist Otis Hood campaigned frequently for high office in Massachusetts during the 1940s and early 1950s, and Florence Luscomb was just one of several antiwar activists who have enjoyed sporadic success, usually in college towns and districts, since the end of World War II. In 1990 former Republican U.S. senator Lowell P. Weicker, Jr., candidate of A Connecticut Party, won the Connecticut governorship. Maine's Independent Party (always a handy designation when would-be candidates lack or reject major party support) brought nominees James Longley (1975–79) and Angus King (1995–2002) the governorship. But the political career of Vermont congressman and independent (originally socialist) Bernie Sanders is the resounding third-party success story in New England: he is the sole independent in the U.S. Congress (1990–) and still the only independent in the House. In 2000, Senator James Jeffords of Vermont left the Republican Party to become an independent; like Sanders, he tends to vote organizationally with the Democrats. The influence, generally unmeasurable, of such national third-party luminaries (at least to their admirers) as Eugene V. Debs, George Wallace, Henry Wallace, and Ross Perot has forced the major parties to rethink their state-by-state strategy. In New England, the political contrariness of its citizens is assured for the future.

Henry F. Bedford, *Socialism and the Workers in Massachusetts, 1886–1912* (1966); David H. Bennett, *The Party of Fear* (1988); John R. Mulkern, *The Know-Nothing Party in Massachusetts* (1990).

Edmund B. Sullivan

Town Meeting The town meeting is one of New England's most important governmental institutions. The region contains approximately 1,370 incorporated towns, and all but a few conduct much of their public business in these meetings.

Town meetings regionwide have common elements. Items for consideration are placed

on a town warrant, and copies are sent to all eligible voters before the meeting. An elected moderator systematically reviews the warrant until business has been completed; often this takes more than a single session. The votes taken bind the entire community to the items that have been approved.

Despite these similarities, individual town meetings vary widely in procedures, content, and style. Many large towns use a "representative" system in which only elected neighborhood delegates—usually between 50 and 100—can vote, although all citizens have the right to participate in the discussion. In most communities various elected or appointed school, finance, and planning boards hold hearings and make recommendations long before the town formally meets; when this happens the town meeting's function is to reject, amend, or ratify policy. Secret ballots, voice votes, and hand votes are used, sometimes all three at the same meeting. In some towns attendance at the meeting is necessary if residents want to vote; at others the polls are open before and after meetings for selected warrant items. Because state governments determine the general ground rules for permissible meeting procedures, some variations stem from differences in state laws.

The first New England town meeting convened in Massachusetts soon after John Winthrop and his associates settled in the Massachusetts Bay area in the 17th century. A natural extension of congregationalism—the belief that the members of a church should determine policy and chose their own minister—the institution quickly became the primary instrument of local governance, not just in Massachusetts, but also in neighboring jurisdictions inhabited by Bay Colony émigrés. Town meetings functioned to preserve local independence up to the Revolution; their image was later used during the Depression and World War II to symbolize democracy. Town meetings also served as forums for protest during the Vietnam War, the McCarthy era, and the nuclear freeze campaign. Commitment to the institution remained powerful despite modernization. Towns can petition state legislatures for special charters eliminating town meetings and adopt a municipal government based on a city council or alderman model. Only about 110 former towns now function under such city charters.

Periodically, town meetings come under attack as antiquated, subject to manipulation, and irrelevant to the needs of a rapidly changing world. The attacks never last long, however, as town meetings provide a powerful example of democracy in practice. Their existence has attracted a new batch of regional immigrants—counterculture types, retirees, and high-tech operatives—now moving into rural New England. As the United States as a whole moves, however tentatively, toward governmental decentralization, town meetings are becoming an even stronger symbol for citizen participation in governmental affairs. The flexibility of the institution all but guarantees its continued use and popularity. New England town meetings have lasted nearly 400 years; they're apt to last another 400.

Austin De Wolf, *The Town Meeting: A Manual of Massachusetts Law* (1890); Joseph Francis Zimmerman, *The New England Town Meeting: Democracy in Action* (1999).

Jere Daniell

Voting and Participation

From the beginnings of European settlement in the 17th century, the area that became New England has been known for its participatory political culture. Growing out of congregational church governance, the New England town meeting became a national and international symbol of local self-government. The historical and modern reality is a bit more complex, however. Where voter turnout, the town meeting, local control, and direct-democracy devices such as the initiative and referendum are concerned, New England's democratic record is mixed.

The most basic right of democratic participation open to citizens is voting. Historically, while Vermont guaranteed universal manhood suffrage in its constitution of 1777, the other New England states maintained a variety of religious and property qualifications for voting into the early 19th century. In Rhode Island property qualifications for some local elections persisted until 1928. Moreover, with the exception of presidential suffrage, granted earlier in Rhode Island (1917) and Maine (1919), New England women did not gain the right to vote until 1920. Since the 1920s that right has been effectively universal for all citizens of New England, with 18- to 21-year-olds gaining the privilege in 1970.

Exercising the right to vote is as important as the right itself. Modern turnout trends in New England show voting rates that compare well with other regions of the United States. In recent election years all six states have ranked in the first or second quintile of states in the percentage of the voting-age population who actually register and cast ballots, with Maine and Vermont often being among the top 10 states in turnout. On average, 55 to 65 percent of New England voters cast ballots in presidential election years, a figure that falls to between 45 and 55 percent in nonpresidential years. Thus, while a full third of New England's eligible voters may stay away from the polls, enough do come to maintain the region's reputation as having a participatory political culture.

New England residents also raise their political voices at town meetings. In contrast to voting, however, this tradition has been subject to various challenges in the modern era. While town meetings continue to be held in all of the New England states except Rhode Island (where meetings are nonetheless still held to discuss financial issues), they are often as symbolic as they are substantive. Since the expansion of national government involvement in state affairs that began with the New Deal, more and more policymaking has been centralized at the state or federal level, leaving few policy areas for town meetings to control. Social changes, furthermore, have made families more mobile and more pressed for free time, with some communities adopting representational forms of government. It is therefore not surprising that town meetings no longer play the central role they once did in the democratic life of most New Englanders.

Change has affected each state differently, however. Particularly in Vermont and Massachusetts, town meetings have in a sense been reinvented—often by a new generation of participants—as forums of protest and action on state, national, and even international issues. In 1982, for example, many towns in Vermont passed nuclear-freeze resolutions; although they had little legal effect, the resolutions fueled a national freeze movement. Recent efforts aimed at devolving power from the government back to individual states and localities also theoretically offer some hope for renewing the town meeting, but most of the real policy authority is likely to remain in the hands of trained policy specialists at the state level.

The waning influence of town meetings has also given rise to a concern for so-called local control. New England, to a greater degree than the rest of the United States, has a strong tradition of home rule and local independence. Until the forced legislative reapportionments of the 1960s, legislatures overrepresented small rural towns, allowing them to protect their parochial interests against much larger (but underrepresented) urban areas. New Hampshire continues to honor the principle of local representation by maintaining the nation's largest state legislature, with a 400-member house and a 24-member senate.

Even though legislative representation has now been equalized by population, New England's smaller communities continue to fight to maintain their local authority. Heated legal or legislative debates over education funding and educational equity in Connecticut, Vermont, New Hampshire, and Maine, raising the specter of regional or statewide school policies and control, exemplify New Englanders' continuing belief that they should be in charge of their own local affairs, particularly in sensitive areas such as education. While proponents of local control may seem to be fighting a losing battle in an era of centralized government, the fact that suburban and rural residents continue to vote more regularly than urban voters has given their cause significant support among state officials eager for their votes. The idea of local control is a still potent force in New England politics.

While many of the ways in which New Englanders can take part in the democratic process are exclusively local, the citizen initiative and referendum offer voters a chance to make or unmake statewide as well as local laws. Voter access to these devices in the New England states has, however, been limited. Vermont, New Hampshire, Rhode Island, and Connecticut have all chosen not to adopt either device, leaving constitutional revision and lawmaking to their legislatures. Even Maine and Massachusetts allow their legislatures to control the placement of citizen initiatives on the ballot. Despite this limitation, the citizens of both states have used both the initiative and the referendum to make major policy changes in recent decades. In 1980 Massachusetts passed Proposition 2½, which placed a significant limitation on governmental growth by capping the property-tax rate. In 1998 citizens in Maine used the referendum to overturn that state's gay-rights law, passed and signed into law by the governor the previous year. Although both devices appear alive and well in Maine and Massachusetts, the other New England states show no signs of being poised to adopt them, preferring a blend of local and representative democratic institutions.

On the whole, New England politics continues to merit its participatory image. A 1997 survey carried out by Tom Rice and Alexander Sumberg found that all of the New England states rank high on measures of "civic culture." The dark side of the picture is that many New Englanders, particularly urban residents and people of color, continue to register, vote, and participate in politics at lower rates than other citizens do. From that perspective local control can be a double-edged sword, with local interests often prevailing at the expense of disadvantaged constituencies in each state. It is this conflict between local control, town meeting–style democracy, and statewide, collective democracy that will shape voting and participation patterns and representative institutions in New England in the years to come.

Kimball W. Brace, ed., *The Election Data Book: A Statistical Portrait of Voting in America, 1992* (1993); George Goodwin, Jr., and Victoria Schuck, eds., *Party Politics in the New England States* (1968);

Josephine F. Milburn and Victoria Schuck, eds., *New England Politics* (1981); Jerome M. Mileur, ed., *Parties and Politics in the New England States* (1997); Tom W. Rice and Alexander F. Sumberg, "Civic Culture and Government Performance," *Publius* 27, no. 1 (1997); Carl E. Van Horn, ed., *The State of the States*, 2d ed. (1993).

Paul R. Petterson

Weicker, Lowell P., Jr. (1931–) U.S.
representative and senator, governor of Connecticut. Lowell Palmer Weicker, Jr., served in most of the important posts in Connecticut politics—state representative, U.S. representative and senator, and governor. Nominally a member of the Republican Party for most of his career, Weicker often broke ranks with his Republican colleagues. His fierce independence earned him the nickname "Maverick," which became the title of his 1995 political autobiography and aptly captures his willingness to pursue "good government" policies regardless of their electoral implications.

Weicker entered the army after graduating from Yale and then went on to law school at the University of Virginia. Admitted to the Connecticut bar in 1960, Weicker began his career as an attorney in Greenwich, Conn. He lost the Republican primary for state representative that same year but won the nomination and election in 1962. In 1968 Weicker was elected U.S. representative from Connecticut's Fourth Congressional District after a tireless campaign against the hawkish incumbent, Donald J. Irwin. A traditional Republican at this point in his development, Weicker criticized President Lyndon Johnson's handling of the Vietnam War, supported an amendment to the Constitution allowing school prayer, and proposed the impeachment of the liberal Supreme Court justice William O. Douglas. Weicker's career would eventually be marked, however, by his fierce opposition to school prayer and consistent defense of the Supreme Court's independence.

In 1970 the Republican gubernatorial candidate Thomas Meskill asked Weicker to run for the U.S. Senate. That race pitted antiwar Democrat Joseph Duffey against former Democratic senator Thomas Dodd, who was running as an independent. Weicker benefited from this Democratic split and was elected with 42 percent of the vote. Once in office, he vigorously advocated better funding for public transportation and for the National Aeronautics and Space Administration; he also introduced legislation to help journalists keep their sources confidential, to reform campaign practices, and to restrict campaign contributions.

As a member of the Republican Senatorial Campaign Committee, Weicker was shocked

Governor Lowell Weicker receiving the Profiles in Courage Award from John F. Kennedy, Jr., and Caroline Kennedy, 1992

by the practices of Richard Nixon's Committee to Reelect the President during the 1972 election. When Congress formed the seven-member Select Committee on Presidential Campaign Activities to investigate the Watergate burglary in 1973, Weicker was chosen as one of the committee's junior members. He was promptly denounced by his own party—and praised by Democrats and independents. Weicker's persistent criticism of the administration rocketed the young senator to national prominence and helped bring about Nixon's resignation in 1974.

During his three terms in the Senate, Weicker continued to depart from Republican Party positions, supporting a variety of purportedly liberal causes such as environmental protection (particularly, oceanic preservation), assistance to the disabled, funding for AIDS research, and the normalization of relations with Cuba. He actively opposed conservative Republicans such as Jesse Helms by supporting the Supreme Court's decisions on school prayer as well as abortion rights and busing to achieve racial integration. As a member of the Labor and Human Resources and Appropriations Committees and as chair of the Appropriations Subcommittee on Labor, Health and Human Services, and Education, Weicker prevented the full implementation of budgetary cuts to human services and poverty programs during the presidency of Ronald Reagan.

In 1988 Weicker lost his first general election, to Democrat Joseph I. Lieberman. He had battled active opposition from conserva-

tive Republicans led by William F. Buckley, Jr., who professed a preference for a real Democratic senator rather than a Democrat posing as a Republican. Two years later Weicker stunned Democrats and Republicans alike when he declared his independent candidacy for the Connecticut governorship under the banner of his own Connecticut Party. Running at a time of growing disillusionment with the major parties and inestimably aided by his statewide fame, Weicker was elected by a 41 percent plurality. He served only one term as governor but instituted a reform that changed the state's political landscape. In 1991 Weicker proposed a progressive state income tax to make up a projected $250 million budget deficit. Passed primarily with the support of Democratic legislators, the measure resulted in violent protests in front of the state's capitol, and Weicker's popularity plunged. Yet within a year Connecticut was operating with a budget surplus and for the first time in decades was able to rely on a steady source of revenue achieved with more fairness than had prevailed when the state had the nation's highest sales tax. Frequently mentioned as a possible independent contender for the presidency, Weicker has devoted his postpolitical career to health-related causes.

Sam J. Ervin, Jr., *The Whole Truth: The Watergate Conspiracy* (1980); Barry Sussman, *The Great Coverup: Nixon and the Scandal of Watergate*, 3d ed. (1992).

Patrick J. Deneen

Religion

Louise A. Breen, Section Editor

Elizabeth C. Nordbeck, Consulting Editor

INTRODUCTION

The regional culture of New England has been profoundly influenced by the Puritanism to which its earliest colonists subscribed, and yet the Puritan legacy is highly ambiguous. Depending on who is doing the telling, the Puritans can be portrayed as grim persecutors of Quakers and witches or as hardworking men and women with a strong communalistic ethos whose example instilled in future generations a work ethic, a will to reform society, and a sense of America as a "chosen nation." Colonists themselves scoured their own recent past in the 17th century in an effort to discern God's providential plan, and the nature of the Puritan legacy has been hotly contested by every subsequent generation of scholars. Especially since the 19th century, when the face of New England was transformed by immigration and economic change, it would be more appropriate, in the apt words of the historian Joseph A. Conforti, to describe the region as an "ethnic city by the mill" than a "Puritan-Yankee city on a hill." Yet Puritan-related tales and symbols inhabit the minds of schoolchildren, having taken on secular or broadly cultural connotations rather than religious ones.

In the 17th century, English Puritanism was the dominant religious force shaping the southern New England colonies of Massachusetts, Connecticut, Plymouth, and New Haven. The first Puritans to arrive in New England settled in Plymouth in 1620. These were Separatists who made the radical decision to cut their ties with England's Anglican Church. Having initially left England in the face of persecution, they relocated first to the Netherlands and then to America, where they could practice their religion and retain their English culture. Although these Pilgrims, and their "first Thanksgiving," command center stage in the popular iconography of early New England, a more numerous and historically significant group of Puritan colonists, some 20,000 strong, settled in Massachusetts during the so-called Great Migration, which took place roughly between 1630 and 1642 (an advance group under John Endecott arrived at Salem in 1628). Puritans then spread into Connecticut, as well as organizing towns in New Hampshire and the region that eventually became Maine.

Compared with fellow Englishmen who migrated to the tobacco colony of Virginia in the same period, Puritans, while not unmindful of the importance of making a living, behaved in ways that suggest they were motivated more by religious than by economic goals. Typically drawn from the "middling" social ranks in England, they came to America primarily in family units rather than as young men on the make. Their migration came to a virtual standstill in the early 1640s, when the English Civil

War opened up the possibility for Puritans to remake church and society in a godly image at home.

The term *Puritan* began as an epithet hurled at church reformers whom others perceived as annoyingly precise, exacting, and meddlesome in the practice of their faith. Although such people tended to think of themselves simply as "the godly," the name Puritan stuck. Puritans were predestinarian Calvinists dedicated to living according to "primitive" scriptural rules. They believed that England's established religion, Anglicanism, had retained too many characteristics of Catholicism, and during the 1620s they deplored the rise among high-ranking church authorities of theological Arminianism, which emphasized human effort rather than divine predestination as the key to salvation. Placing great value upon laboriously constructed sermons preached by highly educated ministers who could persuade listeners of humankind's utter depravity and total reliance on God for salvation, Puritans denounced as "dumb dogs" those Anglican clergymen who emphasized the liturgy over sermons and primarily read from the Book of Common Prayer on Sabbath days instead of putting forth the effort to produce the types of sermons that Puritans prized.

Puritans were also disaffected by Stuart England's foreign policy, which appeared to give short shrift to the Protestant struggle on the Continent while aligning England with Catholic powers. They came to believe that if England and its Anglican Church continued to move in the direction it was headed during the reigns of James I (1603–25) and Charles I (1625–49), then God would bring divine vengeance down upon the land. The creation of religiously inspired colonies in America, some held, might help ensure that a "saving remnant" would survive God's wrath and help rebuild the Church of England. John Winthrop, who served many times as governor of the Massachusetts Bay Colony, told colonists while they were en route to New England in 1630 that, should they succeed in setting up a godly commonwealth, their colony might someday emerge as a "city upon a hill," or a model of right religion for Englishmen at home to follow.

Participants in the Great Migration tended to see themselves as exiles seeking sanctuary from an absolutist government and an increasingly anti-Calvinist church, their most ambitious hope being that their example might inspire the Church of England to reform. The second generation of Puritan expositors, however, including the influential Increase Mather, identified New England with the biblical Israel, recast the founders as having gone forth on an "errand into the wilderness," and reconceptualized New England as a chosen nation with a pivotal role to play in world redemption and the unfolding of God's providential scheme. Although this language of world-redemptive mission had to be suppressed in the early 18th century as the region was drawn deeper into the imperial web, it reemerged during the revolutionary and early national periods, when it was transferred to the new nation as a whole.

The belief that the region had a special destiny relevant to the uplift of all humankind allowed New Englanders long to claim a special place within the nation, their redemptive zeal coming to the fore especially during the 19th century, when the region launched reform movements designed to transform and uplift less enlightened areas and people. Subsequently, the idea that the United States was a chosen nation was used to justify conquest of the continent (manifest destiny), as well as later attempts to remake other parts of the world in the American image, by force if necessary.

Puritans in early-17th-century Massachusetts rejected the episcopal order—a hierarchy including bishops—of the Catholic Church and the Church of England, and preferred a congregational polity, in which church members chose their own minister and had a voice in a wide range of matters in their congregations. Men and women received membership in these congregations only after they presented an acceptable conversion narrative, not simply because they were born in a particular locality. Although Puritans held that humans could never be certain about who was among the elect, they wanted to be reasonably sure that those with whom they communed in the churches were likely to have been saved. With church membership, or "visible sainthood," came the right to have one's children baptized. Male church members additionally had the right to vote in colony-wide elections and in matters pertaining to the governance of their own congregations, such as the hiring of ministers or the disciplining of fellow saints.

The congregational structure thus conferred a certain degree of power on the laity. Congregations sometimes experienced lay-clerical tensions, and in cases where they were unable to settle their own conflicts church councils consisting of neighboring ministers, lay elders, and magistrates were brought in to help resolve matters. Although Puritan practices in Massachusetts were very different from those of the Church of England, the colonists' stated goal was to reform the church from within, not to separate from it. Unlike those who settled at Plymouth, they were "nonseparating congregationalists."

The Puritans migrated to America so that they could organize their churches as they saw fit, but they did not confer that right on those who differed from them in religious judgment. Baptists—with the exception of General Baptists, who lived mostly in Rhode Island and denied predestinarian doctrine—held much theological ground in common with Congregationalists, but their belief that infant baptism was not warranted in Scripture and that only adult regenerate believers should receive the ordinance represented a threat to family religion and the survival of a religiously inspired community. Baptist worship was therefore proscribed. If parents could not use baptism to bring their children under church watch and guidance, then the ability to inculcate right religion into future generations might be compromised.

Quakers, who failed to observe proper social deference, such as "hat honor," and who condoned and sponsored disorderly female exhorters, were seen as far more dangerous than Baptists, primarily because the Quakers used their own "inner light," not just scriptural rule, to guide their beliefs and behavior. While Quakers were welcome in none of the Puritan colonies, Massachusetts took the most severe measures, executing four Quakers between 1659 and 1661 for returning to proselytize in the colony after they had been banished.

Ministers with Presbyterian leanings, such as Thomas Parker and James Noyes of Newbury, Mass., and Peter Hobart of Hingham, Mass., also came in for public scrutiny. These clergymen wished to open the church ordinances of baptism and the

Lord's Supper to all reasonably upstanding Christian believers, not just visible saints, while at the same time curbing lay influence over church affairs. In 1646 a group of merchants, inspired by Presbyterian ideas, petitioned the Massachusetts General Court, criticizing the practice of making the voting franchise conditional on church membership and denouncing the way the colony's exclusionary gathered churches denied believers who were living overtly moral lives the comfort of access to the Lord's Supper and baptism for their children. The so-called Remonstrants were fined heavily because they threatened to bring their grievances before Parliament, effectively appealing above the heads of the Bay Colony magistrates.

Puritan New England's most aggressive treatment of dissenters from the dominant orthodoxy came at times when the region felt threatened. The banishment of Anne Hutchinson and Roger Williams, arguably the Massachusetts colony's best-known dissidents, came during the 1630s, when the colony felt itself to be in danger of losing its charter from the home government under Charles I and was engaged in a war against the Pequot Indians.

Once the English Civil War was under way in the 1640s, New England Puritans, struggling to maintain a "middle way" between sectarian radicalism and Presbyterianism, took heart whenever the Independents, who supported congregationalism, got the upper hand. Radical groups, such as the Quakers, arose out of the religious ferment in England and attempted to spread their message and gain converts in the colonies. At the other end of the spectrum, Presbyterian tendencies were to be feared, for if Presbyterians were to win control over Parliament, they might establish a state church to which New Englanders would be compelled to conform.

Despite Puritan dominance, New England was by no means monolithic in its religiosity. Fishing villages along the "eastern frontier" (New Hampshire and Maine) contained Anglicans as well as unchurched people, and the more populous Puritan towns also contained people who did not wish to be active in their churches. The colony of Connecticut, under its longtime governor John Winthrop, Jr., tended to be less harsh toward dissenters than the Bay Colony. The exiled Roger Williams, who subscribed briefly to the Baptist faith but then became a Seeker—one who believed that the church had fallen into such corruption after the apostolic age that humans could not revive the true church and must await its restoration by divine intervention—introduced the principle of liberty of conscience into Rhode Island, which became a refuge for those banished during the antinomian controversy of 1636–38, and later for Quakers.

In 1658 a small group of Sephardic Jews, probably from Curaçao in the West Indies, settled in Newport, R.I. The small Jewish community worshiped in private homes until 1763, when they completed the famous Touro Synagogue, which housed the congregation Yeshuat Israel. George Washington addressed a town meeting held in the synagogue during a 1781 visit to Newport, and proclaimed in a 1790 letter to the congregation that the new United States would give "to bigotry no sanction, to persecution no assistance."

Diversity in the 17th century could also be found within Puritanism itself. Puritans did not all agree with one another on all matters. Shades of religious difference were tolerated as long as they seemed to pose no danger to the community as a whole. In addition, folk traditions, such as astrological beliefs, fortune telling, and divination, persisted despite the warnings of ministers. Even when communities became caught up in prosecuting a reputed witch, elites and ordinary folk had different concerns: ministers were most interested to learn whether the accused person had made a covenant with Satan, while the average townsfolk worried about the "harms" the witch might have inflicted on livestock, children, and the health of anyone who had been cursed.

Just as Puritan leaders were motivated to eradicate the "dark corners" of English superstition, so too did they attempt to Christianize the indigenous peoples of New England. The Puritans condemned as devil worship the native peoples' efforts to maintain, through the performance of rituals, balanced and reciprocal relationships with various forces and "other-than-human" beings. Yet some clergymen, such as John Eliot of Roxbury, Mass., believed that the Indians were the 10 lost tribes of Israel and that their conversion to Christianity was one of the necessary precursors to the millennium.

In the 1640s Eliot translated the Bible and other devotional literature into the Massachusett language and began the work of converting Indians to the Puritan faith, believing that they must be "civilized" before they could become Christian. Under Eliot's system, proselytes would have to give up their semisedentary way of life, fix themselves to a particular locality, and farm in the English manner, with men responsible for agriculture and women responsible for the household—a division of labor that altered Indians' traditional gender roles, where women farmed and men hunted. At midcentury, Eliot was instrumental in setting up 14 "praying" towns for Christian Indians, where those who wished to convert lived under Bay Colony rule, with local leaders drawn in part from their own ranks. Another major missionary effort was undertaken by the clergyman Thomas Mayhew on Martha's Vineyard.

It was difficult for Puritans to propagate their version of Christianity among native peoples. Unlike the Jesuit missionaries in French Canada whose methods garnered considerable success, Puritans did not offer elaborate rituals and symbols with which prospective converts could identify, and Puritan ministers did not go out to live in Indian villages. Indians also had difficulty constructing the sorts of conversion narratives that Puritans found convincing. Such narratives needed to reflect not only a sense of having sinned but also the recognition that humans could do nothing to earn their own salvation, since faith was imparted to them by God. The notion of a deity who gave the gift of salvation out of eternity, before the establishment of a relationship involving set forms of mutual gift giving, was alien to native peoples, who thought in terms of maintaining a favorable relationship with powerful other-than-human beings though propitiatory rituals.

Indians were ambivalent in their response to Christian missions. Those whose villages had become depopulated by the deadly virgin soil epidemics that ravaged the native population in the pre- and early contact periods were the most susceptible to missionary overtures. Strong sachems such as Uncas of the Mohegans and Metacom

(King Philip) of the Wampanoags might participate in trade and diplomatic and military alliances with English colonists, but such leaders resisted the call to Christ, both because they feared that the Christianization of their people would undercut the power of the traditional leadership and because the demands of missionaries were disruptive to indigenous cultural patterns, requiring that even the most intimate bonds between wives and husbands, children and parents be reconfigured. Peoples who were in a more weakened position, on the other hand, might see "praying to God" as a viable option, allowing them to retain some sort of communal presence in an increasingly dangerous colonial world. The "praying towns" offered space where members of decimated villages could reconstitute their families and establish distinctive Indian communities. They could reasonably expect that their lands would be protected, at least for a time, from land-hungry English colonists, and they gained some degree of spiritual succor from the Christian message. As Indians themselves pointed out, however, English Christians rarely lived up to the values they professed when dealing with native peoples.

Despite the teachings of English missionaries, Indians understood and practiced Christianity in their own style, and for their own reasons, emphasizing communal relationships and the collective and personal relationship with God over formal points of theology. Words from a conversion narrative related by a man at Natick, Mass., the preeminent "praying" town, poignantly express this dedication to place and community: "When I heard the Word I did not like of it but thought of running away, because I loved sin, but I loved the place of my dwelling, and therefore I thought I will rather pray to God, and began to do it."

Missionary work among the Indians remained vital until King Philip's War (1675–76), a conflict that pitted most of New England's native peoples against the English colonies. Ordinary folk, including Mary Rowlandson, who wrote a narrative about her captivity among hostile Indians, expressed doubts that Christian Indians could be trusted as English allies. At the height of the war, in 1676, the "praying" Indians were interned on an island in Boston Harbor, where they nearly starved to death. The magistrate and militia officer Daniel Gookin, who had worked with John Eliot and served as the colony's superintendent over the Christian Indians, was openly threatened with assassination because he had attested to the loyalty of the converts and advocated employing them in the war effort. In the wake of King Philip's War, missionary efforts among the Indians did not cease, but they declined precipitously as distrustful colonists multiplied and placed increasing pressure on the land. Whereas colonists had once valued Indians as trading partners and allies, they increasingly became interested in sweeping Indians off the land so that Englishmen could occupy it.

In the late 17th century, New Englanders adapted to political changes in England and a perceived decline in piety among themselves. The Restoration of the Stuart monarchy in 1660, soon after the death of Oliver Cromwell, meant that England would not be remodeled in a Puritan image. A series of disasters, including the devastation of King Philip's War , the loss of the Massachusetts charter in 1684, a generalized sense that colonists were becoming too focused on material ambitions, and the witchcraft delusion at Salem, shook Massachusetts to its core, generating fear that the region had incurred the wrath of God.

In 1662 a synod was called in Massachusetts to deal with an internal crisis in the churches: second-generation Puritan colonists had shown themselves unwilling or unable to produce the conversion narratives necessary to gain church membership. If allowed to continue, this situation might conceivably lead to the demise of Puritan culture, leaving the infant seed of the second generation cut off from baptism at a time when hope for the creation of a Puritan state in England was dead. The solution devised by the Halfway Synod, as it came to be called, introduced an attenuated form of membership that allowed the adult children of regenerate parents to have their children baptized but did not give halfway members access to the Lord's Supper, thereby ensuring the purity of the churches (by excluding the unregenerate from the Lord's Supper), while still increasing the number of baptized children over whom the churches could claim some degree of authority.

A minority of clergymen, including New Haven's John Davenport, and, in many congregations, members of the laity, resisted the use of this halfway covenant, both because they still feared for the purity of the churches and because the synod had recommended that ministers exert more power through consociations of clergymen that might erode the congregational autonomy on which lay authority was based. In the long run, however, this adjustment in Congregationalism was a boon to families who wanted to pass their religion on to their children. Women in particular took advantage of halfway status, choosing to "own" a church covenant around the time they married so that they would be able to have their infants baptized.

The last decades of the 17th century found Massachusetts Puritans adjusting to a diminished place in the transatlantic world. The danger of Stuart monarchy ended in 1688, when William and Mary succeeded James II in a bloodless coup orchestrated by the English Parliament. Yet although the new monarchs granted Massachusetts a second provincial charter in 1691, its provisions were less satisfactory than those of the original Bay Colony charter. Under the terms of the new charter, colonists were no longer allowed to elect their own governor but were to receive an appointed royal governor instead; they were forbidden to make church membership a prerequisite for exercising the franchise; and the Act of Toleration (1689) enjoined them to countenance other Protestant groups they had formerly persecuted.

The stresses of the late 17th century formed the context for one of the great tragedies of Puritan New England: the needless executions of 19 innocent people and the death of one man under torture during the Salem witch hunts of 1692. Puritan clergymen and magistrates, desperate to find an explanation for the problems that stalked New England—ongoing Indian warfare in Maine, charter troubles, the tyrannical rule of royally appointed Governor Edmund Andros, and the pernicious effects of materialism—gave credence to the claims of adolescent girls in Salem village that they were being attacked by the "specters" of witches who tortured them in hopes of getting them to sign the devil's book. The judges who heard the witchcraft cases convicted people on the basis of "spectral" evidence, a controversial move against which some ministers cautioned, given that only the "afflicted" girls could "see" their invisible assailants. As the trials progressed, the lives of people who confessed and named other "witches" were spared, while those who refused to admit falsely to such a reprehensible crime—or to implicate others—went to the gallows. As dozens of accused persons sat in jail, the new governor, William Phips, put an end to the trials, in part because people too far up the social hierarchy were being cried down as witches.

The notion that the devil walked among them was attractive to Massachusetts Puritans in the last decade of the 17th century because they wanted some explanation as to why so many unfortunate things seemed to be happening to their colony. It was easier to believe that misfortune came because traitors in their midst plotted against godly society with the devil than to conclude that God was angry or that leaders were ineffective. People who were designated witches came, in many instances, from families that were perceived as having too many profitable connections with transatlantic or frontier trade. The witchcraft trials allowed the drift toward materialism, and possible instances of collusion with the enemy in frontier trading houses, to be attributed to a satanic plot, as opposed to failings within godly society as a whole. There is some indication, too, that witchcraft accusations were used as a way to police those suspected of religious imposture at a time when the Bay Colony was no longer permitted to persecute dissent.

To their credit, most New Englanders came to understand that what had happened at Salem was wrong. Samuel Sewall, who served as one of the judges in the witchcraft trials, became so convinced that God was punishing him for the role he had played in putting innocent people to death that he composed a confession and apology for his actions during the trials and had his pastor read it publicly on a Sabbath day before his congregation while Sewall stood in the midst of his fellow worshipers. While Puritans did not give up their belief in witchcraft as a result of the trials, they began to move toward the opinion that it was impossible for human beings to discern who among them was a witch. The devil was a master of deceit and trickery and would use those powers, they came to believe, to cause the godly to turn against one another.

In the aftermath of the witchcraft trials, it became necessary to rehabilitate the Puritan image in the transatlantic world. The Congregational minister Cotton Mather, son of Increase Mather and pastor of the Old North Church, wrote his *Magnalia Christi Americana* (1702), a seven-volume ecclesiastical history of Puritan settlement, at a time when critics on both sides of the Atlantic decried Puritan leaders for harboring the credulous views that led to disaster at Salem. In presenting the history of settlement in New England, Mather argued that Puritan religion was reasonable rather than fanatical or sectarian and stressed John Eliot's accomplishments in proselytizing Indians, suggesting to readers that New England was a valuable part of the empire—a beachhead of English civilization in the wilderness. Knowing that he must come to terms with a more assertive imperial presence, Mather was determined to cultivate ties with sympathetic figures in the metropolis who might intercede when necessary to prevent further erosion of the colony's rights and reputation within the empire. Advocating ecumenical ties with English Nonconformists and Scottish Presbyterians, and cordial relations with Anglican latitudinarians, Mather endeavored to solidify valuable ecumenical support in the transatlantic world but continued to maintain that congregational practices were appropriate for New Englanders.

Other competing ministerial voices, however, offered different ways to revitalize the religious culture of New England. Solomon Stoddard, in Northampton, Mass., opened up church membership and access to the sacraments (baptism and the Lord's Supper) to all Christian believers, regardless of whether a parent had been in covenant, a liberalization that went far beyond the reforms of the halfway covenant.

In Boston, a group of liberal, or "catholick," clergymen, including Benjamin Colman, Thomas Foxcroft, Nathaniel Appleton, and William Brattle, modeled themselves on the latitudinarianism of English Anglicans like John Tillotson, who sought to counteract the violent passions that had characterized the English Civil War years by cautioning against sectarian animosity, discouraging inflammatory rhetoric, and emphasizing the common beliefs that Anglicans, Congregationalists, Presbyterians, and Baptists shared, rather than the differences that drove them apart. The "liberals" attacked the more traditional position staked out by the Mathers, and attempted to undercut Increase Mather's presidency at Harvard College. In 1698 Benjamin Colman, who had been educated in Massachusetts but ordained as a Presbyterian in England, was hired to be the first pastor of the Brattle Street Church, a new congregation formed by Boston merchants, many of whom resented the influence of the traditionalists. In his congregation, Colman, like Stoddard, eliminated restrictions on membership, made the sacraments widely accessible, and used "set forms" of prayer that sermon-oriented Puritans had traditionally deplored. Cotton Mather, meanwhile, continued to insist that his and his father's congregationalism was the most appropriate religion for New England because of its deep historical roots there. He described attempts to introduce liberal reforms into Massachusetts as "Rigid and High-Flown" and portrayed himself as being "crusht" between "Violent Persons on both Extreams [liberal and sectarian]."

Throughout the 18th century, the religious concerns of ordinary New Englanders continued to revolve around their families, their communities, and the hard business of coming into and leaving this world. An energetic laity, in subtle and more dramatic ways, sometimes adopted beliefs and behaviors that contradicted the teachings of ministers. Parents cleaved to the notion that baptism conferred on their children real rather than just symbolic protection from damnation. Participants in the Lord's Supper looked forward to the camaraderie they would enjoy in sharing the ordinance with a community of fellow saints, while ministers emphasized the solitary introspection with which one was to prepare for the Supper. Dying words, including those uttered by women, took on magnified importance, with observers tending to believe, contrary to their ministers' teachings, that a good deathbed performance indicated that the dying person had achieved salvation. Women fared differently in the religious culture in the sense that they were more likely than men to be criticized for excessive mourning of deceased loved ones or excessive emotionalism in times of revival. Laypeople in general evinced far less interest in the onset of the millennium than did clergymen.

Despite rivalry and conflicts among ministers, and differences of opinion between ministers and their flocks, the 18th century was a time of religious growth in New England. Churches that made membership and access to the sacraments more open were popular among mercantile families who financially supported their congregations' efforts in catechizing the young and reaching out to christianize the dark corners of New England. Well-funded congregations were able to beautify their churches inside and out, acquiring such luxuries as communion silver, in keeping with growing participation in the consumer revolution and the "empire of goods." Rather than reflecting a decline from the original purity of the founders, as some contemporaries feared, this material largesse enriched worship for some people and allowed the churches to engage in outreach activities.

Anglicanism too made inroads into New England during this period. Christ Church, with its impressive 200-foot spire, was built in Boston in 1723, soon followed by Trinity Church in Newport. Far more shocking to Puritans was the news—announced at Yale College's 1722 commencement—that seven of its ministers and tutors were converting to Anglicanism and seeking ordination in London (though some soon changed their minds). Also distressing was the establishment in London in 1701 of the Society for the Propagation of the Gospel in Foreign Parts (SPG), an Anglican missionary organization whose activities in New England were perceived as an unfriendly intrusion. The SPG aimed to attract not only Indians and enslaved Africans in British North America but also colonists of English descent, including Puritans and unchurched people in the outlying settlements of New England. In addition, it competed with the Society for the Propagation of the Gospel in New England (the New England Company), which had been established by Parliament in 1649—and then rechartered during the Restoration—to raise funds for missionary efforts among the indigenous peoples of Massachusetts.

The rivalry between the SPG and the New England Company came vividly to life one night in Boston in 1714 when the Anglican Sir Charles Hobby, Lieutenant Governor of Massachusetts, banged on the door of local Indian commissioner Samuel Sewall demanding to see documents pertaining to the New England Company's authorization to operate in the colony—thus disappointing the hope that the pursuit of lofty goals would cause Englishmen of various Protestant temperaments to forget their differences and work together to impart the general principles of Christianity to Indians. Cotton Mather meanwhile complained regularly to English correspondents about how the "new society" poached on outlying Puritan communities rather than focusing on the real "pagans" among Native Americans, Africans, and unchurched English colonists to the south. Despite the dramatic events associated with the Yale defections and the SPG, however, Anglicanism won few converts among New England Puritans.

What appealed to the ordinary folk of New England far more than Anglicanism or the liberal theology of the port towns was the revivalism of what has come to be known as the Great Awakening. This was a series of revivals that coursed through New England during the period 1720–50, peaking in the early 1740s in the wake of a preaching tour by the charismatic English evangelist George Whitefield. The leading theological light of the awakening was the New England–based Jonathan Edwards, who inspired a revival in his Northampton, Mass., church in 1734–35. Although Edwards was dismissed from his pastorate in 1750 when he introduced measures that would limit access to the Lord's Supper, he gained lasting fame as a theologian who integrated Calvinist ideas with Newtonian physics and Lockean psychology. In the context of the revivals, he strove to affect the emotions and senses of believers, and wrote influential works defending the awakening from those who criticized it as imposture.

The itinerant ministers who spread revival downplayed denominational differences. They deliberately preached so as to affect their hearers on an emotional level, and they emphasized the experience of the "new birth," which all converted people shared. Critics complained about the dangers that might ensue from appealing to the passions, as opposed to the rationality, of ordinary people. While the awakening had the effect of swelling church membership in the congregations of ministers who supported evangelicalism, the revivals also sparked controversy. Traveling preachers encouraged listeners to pay heed only to those ministers they considered to be "converted," a practice that could easily compromise the authority of established local ministers and lead to conflicts and separations between New Lights (supporters of revival) and Old Lights (opponents of revival). The notion that one could question the authority of one's preacher undermined the deference that was supposed to be exhibited toward people higher than oneself in the social hierarchy and may have given colonists the confidence to similarly question the authority of their political leaders and, eventually, of British rule over the colonies.

The "heart religion" of the Great Awakening, with its prioritization of spiritual gifts over formal training, held special appeal to marginalized groups like women, blacks, and Indians, who were excluded from educational opportunities and could not claim an authoritative religious voice on that basis. Women, both as church members and as exhorters, seized upon the opportunities presented by the awakening. Phillis Wheatley, a Boston poet from Africa who began writing while enslaved, and Lemuel Haynes, a mulatto who began life as an indentured servant and became the minister of a congregation in Rutland, Vt., both used evangelical religion as a vantage point from which to criticize the institution of slavery. Haynes clashed with white colleagues in speaking out against a prevailing notion that slavery, while evil in itself, could be looked upon as fortunate in the long term because it exposed Africans to the benefits of Christianity. The Mohegan Indian Samson Occom was sufficiently touched by revivalism to convert to Christianity during the awakening and become a minister, but he was highly critical of the way New Englanders had dispossessed the indigenous peoples of the region and disillusioned by the manner in which the proceeds of a speaking tour he undertook in England for the benefit of an Indian school in Connecticut were diverted to support the education of white students when the school was reconstituted as Dartmouth College. Revival religion inspired people from a wide range of perspectives and backgrounds to question the social order in new ways.

Although those who participated in the awakening aimed to revive the vital piety that some felt had been lost in the secularizing world of the 18th century, we can also look at the series of revivals as part of a modernizing trend. The explosion of print that occurred as revival groups in different parts of the transatlantic world broadcast news of their successes to faraway confederates had the effect of broadening peoples' horizons, inspiring them to conceptualize themselves as part of a larger world than that of their own town or province. The marketing of religious books and news, as well as the revivalists' advance notices of their travel routes, represented the transformation of religion into a commodity, drawing spiritual expression and events into the ever expanding empire of goods. Finally, the awakening was an important factor in the erosion of traditional social deference.

Whatever the complex relation may have been between the religious Great Awakening and the secular American Revolution, Congregational ministers overwhelmingly supported independence and were known as the region's "black regiment." In the postwar period, however, the Congregationalists and Presbyterians who had dominated the colonial era declined in popularity in comparison with Methodists and Baptists, and old religious ways were challenged on numerous fronts. In rural New England many people embraced Universalism, which held that all, not just the predestined few, would be saved. Ethan Allen, of revolutionary fame, became a deist, denying Christian claims to possess a special biblical revelation. Free Will Baptists meanwhile rejected predestination, and Shakers, following the revelations of Ann Lee as an alternative to Calvinist doctrine, organized themselves into separate communities. Anglicanism had been wildly unpopular during the Revolution because of its ties to the English government and its close association with royalist officialdom, but in the postrevolutionary period Anglicans reconstituted themselves as Episcopalians, and Samuel Seabury of Connecticut was consecrated a bishop in 1784.

The Congregationalist heirs of the Puritans adapted to the sensibilities of the new democratic age with renewals and revivals, endeavoring to maintain a central place in the spiritual life of New England. In Connecticut during the late 18th and early 19th centuries, Timothy Dwight, the president of Yale College, and his students Lyman Beecher and Nathaniel William Taylor labored to revitalize Congregationalism by counteracting the influence of Episcopalians and Methodists, groups that favored the curtailment of government financial support for religion (because they did not benefit from it). These Congregationalists aimed to defend a Calvinist position while emphasizing the importance of moral action, human capabilities, benevolence, and participation in voluntary associations in an effort to reach out to converts during a time of intense denominational competition.

Also at odds with the interpretation of the Puritan legacy put forward by Dwight, Beecher, and Taylor were the Unitarians, whose most prominent spokesmen were Henry Ware, Hollis Professor of Divinity at Harvard College, and William Ellery Channing, the pastor of the Federal Street Church in Boston from 1803 until his death in 1845. Unitarians put forward a vision of God as benevolent rather than judg-

Brother Irving Greenwood, Sister Aida Elam, and Sister Evelyn Polsey of the Shaker community in Canterbury Village, N.H., ca. 1932

mental, rejected the doctrine of the trinity as irrational, and heralded the perfectibility of human beings rather than the fallen nature of humankind. Unitarianism descended from the tradition of the earlier catholick ministers of New England, with expositors expanding on earlier inclinations toward Enlightenment rationalism and moderation. They drew their constituency from genteel folk in eastern New England. Unitarians were elitist rather than populist, but Channing proclaimed that his denomination, in keeping with the republican spirit of the age, had eschewed a vision of a tyrannical God. The Unitarians' religious sensibility was therefore synchronous with the spirit of the newly independent United States. Congregationalists felt so threatened by this new denomination that Lyman Beecher, who served in both Congregational and Presbyterian churches, relocated from Connecticut to Boston so that he could more effectively challenge the Unitarian menace.

The early national period was difficult for New Englanders because the region's Federalist leaders could not hold their own against the southern Jeffersonians, whose republican ideals were more secular and less deferential than those of New England. Ever since the time of the Puritans, New Englanders had believed in the superiority of their religious and cultural mores, and had wanted to impose their vision on, or at least be a model to, others. The Federalists and Whigs who followed them in the late 18th and early 19th centuries were no less didactic than their ancestors, but the new nation's territorial expansion, the Jeffersonians' and Jacksonians' rise to political power, and the disgrace that accrued to New England for its failure to support the War of 1812, all threatened to diminish the region's ability to influence the national culture. During the antebellum period, as the market revolution transformed the region, old-stock New Englanders also had to contend with what they regarded as the undesirable changes wrought by industrialization, urbanization, and immigration, all of which made them fearful of losing their grasp over their own increasingly diverse region. The assertion of cultural predominance, however, could be supported by harking back to the early religious history of New England. The Plymouth "Pilgrims," for example, were rescued from historical obscurity and promoted as harbingers of America's religious and political liberty; their Mayflower Compact was said to prefigure the principles of representative self-government that became enshrined in the U.S. Constitution.

The Second Great Awakening, lasting roughly from the late 18th century through the antebellum period, affected most regions of the United States but had special resonance in New England, easing the tensions associated with the market revolution and serving also as a vehicle for the spread of New England ways into other regions, particularly the frontier areas of upstate New York, the old Northwest, and parts of the Midwest. It was during this period too that missions were launched to other parts of the world. The prominent New England Congregationalist Lyman Beecher at first took exception to the methods of the preeminent evangelist of the period, Charles G. Finney, a Connecticut-born Presbyterian who incorporated Methodist techniques into his revivals and experienced great success in the canal towns of New York. The enthusiastic shows of emotion that Finney permitted in his revivals, and his use of the "anxious bench" for putting on display those who felt themselves close to conversion, appeared unseemly to the more decorous Beecher, yet a meeting of minds was reached at a gathering of about 20 ministers from New York and New England held in 1827 in New Lebanon, N.Y. Just four years later the New Englander participated in inviting Finney to preach in a Boston church served by one of Beecher's sons. As New England–born migrants and exhorters moved out of the region and settled in the Northwest in the postrevolutionary decades, they brought with them cultural memories of New England, as well as the habit, begun with the Puritans, of using religion to reform self and society.

The Second Great Awakening had a broader influence than its antecedent because of its explicit attention not only to personal salvation but to the reform of society. Through interdenominational cooperation among Protestant evangelicals, a plethora of voluntary societies and reform organizations were created. Voluntary societies spread the Protestant message by performing such tasks as the dissemination of religious literature, for example, while reform groups attempted to fight social ills such as drunkenness.

Elite New Englanders were especially aware of the need for societal reform because the market revolution was transforming life both in the new mill towns that sprouted up along waterways and in the countryside, where farm families began participating more widely in the home manufacture of consumer goods. The evangelical religion of the early 19th century emphasized the ability of humans to lay hold to grace so long as they exerted the effort, and comported well with notions of the "self-made" economic man. Workers as well as employers no doubt experienced real comfort from this evangelical message, but some historians have emphasized how managers and business owners may have coercively encouraged workers to participate in revivals and go to church because such practices ensured a hard-working and respectful labor force. Working-class people and their middle-class bosses increasingly lived in separate neighborhoods, rather than cohabiting in artisan shops or farms, as had been the case traditionally. The middle class was therefore inclined to perceive the new working class as alien and potentially disorderly. When the reform societies, which set out to combat social ills, denounced working-class amusements and forms of male sociability, such as drinking, the working class sometimes perceived them as overbearing and invasive. Of course, the reformation of self along evangelical lines could help working-class people gain a sense of control and self-worth in an unstable world, and many working-class people responded to the evangelical call genuinely but on their own terms.

Voluntary associations and reform movements also gave new scope to the energies of middle-class women. Women had long played an important role in religion. Beginning in the late 17th century, they had made up a majority of church members, and during the revolutionary period women had been explicitly recognized as "Republican Mothers," capable of instilling political and religious virtue in their offspring. In the early 19th century, as the workplace for middle-class men moved from the home-based family farm or artisan shop to the outside factory or office, women took charge of the domestic sphere, asserting that their active participation in various voluntary or reform associations was necessary in order to provide better communities in which to rear their children. In some cases women, like the Free Will Baptist Nancy Towle, emerged in preaching roles during the ferment of the Second Great Awakening, while Mary Baker Eddy founded the Christian Science movement after the Civil War. If women were primarily expected to play a supportive role in good evangelical households during the 19th century, their forays into reform movements could inspire them to begin advocating for the rights of women, as was particularly the case with many of the women who participated in the abolitionist societies.

Abolitionism, which pushed for the immediate eradication of slavery, was the most controversial of the reform movements whose impetus was evangelical in nature. The best-known of the New England abolitionists, William Lloyd Garrison, had been influenced by the Quaker faith (like many other activists in the cause) in his youth, and he thundered forth against intemperance and slavery in an evangelical style. His opponents' insistence that parts of the Bible sanctioned slavery led Garrison to deny that all parts of the Bible were to be believed literally, a position that placed him into conflict with clergymen who were against slavery but did not want to give up the idea of a divinely inspired and literally true Bible. The concentration of abolitionist and reformist energies in New England, meanwhile, was highly offensive to southerners, who viewed abolitionists as irrational zealots out to overturn the proper social order, fully living up to the example of their fanatical Puritan ancestors.

The didactic nature of reforms and revivals alienated non-Protestant immigrants even more than southerners and the native-born working class. The potato famines of the 1840s in Ireland brought large numbers of Catholics to New England, and their presence was galling both to social elites, who feared the destruction of New England's cultural integrity, and to workers, who resented competing for jobs with these new immigrants. For generations New Englanders had regarded the Catholic religion with horror and disdain. The memory of the 17th-century Stuart kings of England, who had favored Catholicism and absolutism and persecuted Puritans, conditioned the Yankee descendants of the Puritans to associate Protestantism with liberty and Catholicism with tyranny. During the 18th century, the region had fought a series of wars against the Catholic French Canadians and their Indian allies, many of whom had been converted by Jesuits whose missionary efforts were more success-

Father Robert F. Drinan and Rabbi Samuel Chiel, 1980

ful than those of the Puritans. Protestant Americans in the 19th century believed that Catholics could never be "real" Americans because of their loyalty to the pope. In this era, nativist political parties, such as the American Party (referred to also as the Know-Nothing Party), were strong in New England. Nativist political parties worked to delay citizenship, circumscribe the voting rights of immigrants, and render them a permanent underclass. Evangelicals in Boston sponsored publication of the derogatory tract *Six Months in a Convent* in 1835, just one year after a mob burned the Ursuline Convent in Charlestown (now Somerville), Mass. In 1855 the Massachusetts legislature set up a Nunnery Committee to investigate the abuses that many erroneously believed were occurring in convents. The committee carried out several inspections of convents and schools—highly offensive and humiliating to the Catholic community—before its activities were curtailed.

Although Catholic immigrants began their lives in America in extreme poverty and faced considerable prejudice, they built effective parishes that helped immigrants cope with their new lives. In the late antebellum period, Boston's Bishop John Fitzpatrick, a native New Englander who gained the respect of Protestant civic leaders, encouraged Catholics to fight nativist influence by exercising the right to vote, but he cautioned them to refrain from the use of violence. Riotous behavior, he warned, would serve only to reinforce the negative stereotype of the brawling Irishman. Parish clergy effectively drove this message home and in some cases policed their parishioners to ensure orderliness. The reputation of Catholics began gradually to improve during the Civil War, as Catholic soldiers—despite their antipathy toward the Emancipation Proclamation—distinguished themselves on the battlefield, and nuns from numerous religious orders stepped forward to perform valuable nursing services. The social and economic capital gained both from military service and employment in wartime industries allowed Catholics to assert themselves in new ways.

Catholics had long resented the public schools because the curricula, intended to acculturate immigrants into Yankee ways, were infused with Protestant ideas and concepts. Before the Civil War, Bishop Fitzpatrick had encouraged Catholics to keep their children in the public schools as a symbol of their willingness to assimilate. But in the latter half of the 19th century, Boston's archbishop John Williams, less fearful of being perceived as separatist, embarked on the creation of an impressive parochial-school system as well as a web of Catholic social agencies, hospitals, and orphanages staffed largely by nuns. Catholic fraternal organizations mirroring the voluntary associations popular in the broader culture were also established. The Knights of Columbus, for example, began in New Haven, Conn., in 1882.

The early 20th century found Catholics even more confident, given their ever increasing numbers, upward mobility, and growing political influence. In this changed atmosphere, Boston's archbishop William Henry O'Connell rejected the accommodationist practices of the past and urged Catholics to celebrate their own history and avoid contact with non-Catholic churches and organizations. Catholics, he directed, were not to venture into non-Catholic churches, even for weddings or funerals, and children were to join the CYO (Catholic Youth Organization) rather than the Boy Scouts or Girl Scouts. At a sermon celebrating the centennial of the Boston archdiocese in 1908, O'Connell proclaimed, "The Puritan has passed; the Catholic remains." Catholics gained a powerful sense of community and yet were insulated from the broader society, as families immersed themselves in the devotional life of their parishes.

The immigration of Catholics from southern and eastern Europe in the late 19th and early 20th centuries created new challenges for the Catholic Church. German, Portuguese, Italian, and Polish immigrants resented a New England church hierarchy that was dominated by the Irish, and tensions arose because Catholics of different nationalities had different ways of celebrating their faith. The Catholic hierarchy was motivated to respond to the needs of new parishioners, however, because unresolved tensions could lead to schism, as was the case in 1901 when four Polish parishes in Boston, Cambridge, Lynn, and Lawrence separated from the Boston archdiocese. In most cases, the church accommodated diversity by providing priests who could say mass and hear confessions in the immigrants' native languages, and by opening churches in ethnically defined neighborhoods that would serve the specific needs of residents. As subsequent waves of immigration in the 1970s and 1980s brought Hispanic, West Indian, and Asian Catholics to New England, the church worked to fill their needs as well.

In the latter part of the 20th century, the Catholic Church continued to confront new challenges, particularly in the form of internal disagreements concerning how the church should adapt to modernity. The Second Vatican Council, held in the 1960s, liberalized Catholic practices. Among other changes, Vatican II allowed mass to be celebrated in the vernacular, lifted the proscription against eating meat on Fridays, gave greater scope for lay involvement in parish matters, and permitted new liturgies and modern music to be introduced into religious worship. Conflicts ensued in numerous parishes over the speed and implementation of the changes recommended by Vatican II, as some parishioners resisted alterations in the mass and obligatory rituals of the church while others embraced them.

Catholics were divided too over the Civil Rights movement, particularly the attempt in 1974 to end racial segregation in the Boston schools by busing white students into predominantly black schools and vice versa. Working-class Catholics, whose children would be most affected by policies to integrate the schools, felt betrayed by the tendency of church leaders and members of the lay Catholic elite, such as Senator Ted Kennedy and Congressman Tip O'Neill, to support busing. Traditionally, the Catholic Church had defended the right of families to make decisions about their children without government interference and had opposed what they regarded as high-handed, intrusive social-reform movements. Although Humberto Sousa Cardinal Medeiros of Boston did not specifically endorse any particular plan for desegregation, both he and his predecessor, Richard Cardinal Cushing, favored racial justice. (Cushing had earlier fought against anti-Semitism among Catholics in Boston, working to dispel the myth that Jews were responsible for the death of Christ.) The Catholic community, divided along class and generational lines, no longer spoke with a single voice.

In recent years, the Catholic church has suffered from a decline in vocations, and members of the laity, in keeping with the spirit of Vatican II, have stepped in to perform a number of church functions formerly reserved to the clergy. Recent scandals involving priests found guilty of pedophilia after having been shielded for long periods of time by the church have damaged its reputation, and compelled the 2002 resignation of Bernard Cardinal Law as archbishop of Boston.

Although some Catholics remain faithful to the traditional teachings of the church, others question church policies on such matters as birth control, abortion, divorce, clerical celibacy, and the ordination of women, essentially choosing which doctrines they are willing to accept. In doing so, they participate in a broader trend that finds believers taking from their respective religious traditions only what they find most meaningful to their individual lives, or trying out several denominations before finding a congenial spiritual home.

The religious landscape of New England has been remade in the 20th and early 21st centuries. Churches of the United Church of Christ (the result of a 1959 merger between Congregationalists and the Evangelical and Reformed Church) still dominate the landscape of many New England towns, and other old-line Protestant denominations are far from dead in the region. Harvard Divinity School, Yale Divininty School, and the School of Theology of Boston University are leading ecumenical Protestant theological seminaries. But Catholics vastly outnumber Protestants, and the region is home to thriving Jewish and Muslim communities and to practitioners of Asian religions such as Buddhism, Hinduism, Sikhism, Confucianism, and Daoism. Newcomers have turned to religion for both social and spiritual support in what was, more often than not, forbidding terrain for immigrants. Faith communities provided, and continue to provide, a means for newcomers to gain a voice and carve out social space for themselves. Just as the Puritan colonists

Religious Identification in New England

	Connecticut (%)[a]	Maine (%)[a]	Massachusetts (%)[a]	New Hampshire (%)[a]	Rhode Island (%)[a]	Vermont (%)[a]
Catholic	36	25	50	39	55	43
Baptist	11	15	5	6	7	4
No Religion	14	17	18	19	17	24
Christian	7	8	4	5	4	4
Methodist	5	10	3	4	1	6
Lutheran	4	4	1	1	0	0
Presbyterian	1	1	1	1	1	0
Protestant	5	7	4	11	1	2
Pentecostal	1	2	2	1	1	0
Episcopalian	7	1	4	4	8	5
Jewish[b]	1	0	2	1	0	0
Mormon	2	3	0	0	0	1
Churches of Christ	1	2	1	0	0	0
Nondenominational	1	1	0	0	0	1
Congregational/UCC	3	2	4	7	1	6
Jehovah's Witness	0	0	0	0	2	0
Assemblies of God	1	0	0	0	0	1
Muslim	2	0	1	0	0	0
Buddhist	0	0	1	1	1	1
Evangelical	0	1	0	0	0	1
Church of God	0	1	0	0	0	0
Seventh Day Adventists	0	0	0	0	0	2

[a]Percentage of survey respondents.
[b]Only Jews by religion are included in this tabulation. The category represents only 53 percent of the total population of American adults who may regard themselves as Jewish by virtue of parentage, upbringing, or self-identification.
Source: Graduate Center of the City University of New York, *American Religious Identification Survey, 2001* (New York: Graduate Center of the City University of New York, 2001)

turned to religion to help them confront a new world, so too have numerous generations of immigrants made sense of their experiences through religious mediation.

Virginia DeJohn Anderson, *New England's Generation: The Great Migration and the Formation of Society and Culture in The Seventeenth Century* (1991); Paul Boyer and Stephen Nissenbaum, *Salem Possessed: The Social Origins of Witchcraft* (1974); Theodore Dwight Bozeman, *To Live Ancient Lives: The Primitivist Dimension in Puritanism* (1988); Louise A. Breen, *Transgressing the Bounds: Subversive Enterprises among the Puritan Elite in Massachusetts, 1630–92* (2001); Catherine A. Brekus, *Strangers and Pilgrims: Female Preaching in America, 1740–1845* (1998); Francis J. Bremer, *Congregational Communion: Clerical Friendship in the Anglo-American Puritan Community, 1610–1692* (1994); Richard Bushman, *From Puritan to Yankee: Character and Social Order in Connecticut, 1690–1765* (1967); Jon Butler, *Awash in a Sea of Faith: Christianizing the American People* (1990); Colin G. Calloway, ed., *After King Philip's War: Presence and Persistence in Indian New England* (1997); Richard W. Cogley, *John Eliot's Mission to the Indians before King Philip's War* (1999); Francis D. Cogliano, *No King, No Popery: Anti-Catholicism in Revolutionary New England* (1995); Charles L. Cohen, *God's Caress: The Psychology of Puritan Religious Experience* (1986); Joseph A. Conforti, *Imagining New England: Explorations of Regional Identity from the Pilgrims to the Mid-Twentieth Century* (2001); James F. Cooper, *Tenacious of their Liberties: The Congregationalists in Colonial Massachusetts* (1999); John Corrigan, *The Prism of Piety: Catholick Congregational Clergy at the Beginning of the Enlightenment* (1991); Stephen Foster, *The Long Argument: English Puritanism and the Shaping of New England Culture, 1570–1700* (1991); Richard P. Gildrie, *The Profane, the Civil and the Godly: The Reformation of Manners in Orthodox New England, 1679–1749* (1994); Richard Godbeer, *The Devil's Dominion: Magic and Religion in Early New England* (1992); Philip F. Gura, *A Glimpse of Sion's Glory:*

Puritan Radicalism in New England, 1620–1660 (1984); David D. Hall, *Worlds of Wonder, Days of Judgment: Popular Religious Belief in Early New England* (1989); Timothy D. Hall, *Contested Boundaries: Itinerary and the Reshaping of the Colonial American Religious World* (1994); Charles E. Hambrick-Stowe, *The Practice of Piety: Puritan Devotional Disciplines in Seventeenth-Century New England* (1982); Barry Hankins, *The Second Great Awakening and the Transcendentalists* (2004); Christine Leigh Heyrman, *Commerce and Culture: The Maritime Communities of Massachusetts, 1690–1750* (1984); E. Brooks Holifield, *The Covenant Sealed: The Development of Puritan Sacramental Theology in Old and New England, 1570–1720* (1974); E. Brooks Holifield, *Theology in America: Christian Thought from the Age of the Puritans to the Civil War* (2003); Noel Ignatiev, *How the Irish Became White* (1994); Paul E. Johnson, "The Modernization of Mayo Greenleaf Patch: Land, Family and Marginality in New England, 1766–1818," *New England Quarterly* 55 (1982): 488–516; Susan Juster, *Disorderly Women: Sexual Politics and Evangelicalism in Revolutionary New England* (1994); Jane Kamensky, *Governing the Tongue: The Politics of Speech in Early New England* (1997); Janice Knight, *Orthodoxies in Massachusetts: Rereading American Puritanism* (1994); Bernard Kusinitz, "The Contribution of Newport's Colonial Jews to the American Way of Life," *Rhode Island Jewish Historical Notes* 2 (1992); Frank Lambert, *Pedlar in Divinity: George Whitefield and the Transatlantic Revivals, 1737–1770* (1994); Ned C. Landsman, *From Colonials to Provincials: American Thought and Culture, 1680–1760* (1997); Jama Lazerow, *Religion and the Working Class in Antebellum America* (1995); Jill Lepore, *The Name of War: King Philip's War and the Origins of American Identity* (1998); Theodore Lewis, "Touro Synagogue, Newport Rhode Island," *Newport History* 48 (1975): 281–320; Mark A. Noll, *America's God: From Jonathan Edwards to Abraham Lincoln* (2002); Mark A. Noll, *The Old Religion in a New World: The History of North American Christianity* (2002); Mary Beth Norton, *In the Devil's Snare: The Salem Witchcraft Crisis of 1692* (2002); Michael Oberg, *Uncas: First of the Mohegans* (2003); Jean M. O'Brien, *Dispossession by Degrees: Indian Land and Identity in Natick, Massachusetts, 1650–1790* (1997); Thomas H. O'Connor, *Boston Catholics: A History of the Church and Its People* (1998); Carla Gardina Pestana, *Quakers and Baptists in Colonial Massachusetts* (1991); Mark A. Peterson, *The Price of Redemption: The Spiritual Economy of Puritan New England* (1997); Mark A. Peterson, "Puritans and Refinement in Early New England: Reflections on Communion Silver," *William and Mary Quarterly* 58 (April 2001); Ann Marie Plane, *Colonial Intimacies: Indian Marriage in Early New England* (2000); Amanda Porterfield, *Female Piety in Puritan New England: The Emergence of Religious Humanism* (1992); Daniel K. Richter, *Facing East from Indian Country: A Native History of Early America* (2001); James R. Rohrer, *Keepers of the Covenant: Frontier Missions and the Decline of Congregationalism, 1774–1818* (1995); Neal Salisbury, *Manitou and Providence: Indians, Europeans and the Making of New England, 1500–1643* (1982); Erik R. Seeman, *Pious Persuasions: Laity and Clergy in Eighteenth-Century New England* (1999); Harry S. Stout, *The New England Soul: Preaching and Religious Culture in Colonial New England* (1986); Michael P. Winship, *Making Heretics: Militant Protestantism and Free Grace in Massachusetts, 1636–1641* (2002); Conrad Wright, *Congregational Polity: A Historical Survey of Unitarian Universalist Practice* (1997).

Louise A. Breen

Apess, William (1798–1839) Historian, clergyman, political activist. William Apess presented himself to the world as a Pequot Indian at a time when most historians, following Increase Mather and other Puritan writers, insisted that the Pequots had disappeared after their war with the colonists in 1636–37. In five books published over seven years, Apess insisted that New England Indians had not disappeared, and he denounced white racism, describing the ways it justified political oppression and psychologically damaged both whites and native peoples. He demanded recognition of Native Americans' equal humanity and political rights.

After a peripatetic adolescence and young adulthood, Apess became by the 1820s an itinerant Methodist minister in New England and New York, preaching to mixed congregations about the evils of white racism as well as the salvation of Christianity. His first book, the autobiography *A Son of the Forest* (1829; rev. 1831), fuses the story of his struggle to become a Christian with his developing analysis of the racism of white Christians. In 1832 he joined Edward Everett, Lyman Beecher, and Elias Boudinot at William Ellery Channing's Federal Street Church in Boston in an evening of oratory on behalf of the Cherokees. As a result, he gained the favorable notice of William Lloyd Garrison and the support of the antislavery community, made up of both whites and African Americans. He also became acquainted with the Cape Cod Mashpees, who had been battling their plantation's white administrators for years. They invited Apess to their community to orchestrate their fight for self-rule against the commonwealth and Harvard University; Apess chronicled the "Mashpee Revolt" in *Indian Nullification of the Unconstitutional Laws of Massachusetts; or, the Pretended Riot Explained* (1835), which received favorable notice in Boston. While the Mashpees succeeded in obtaining some concessions on self-government, Apess himself mysteriously fell out of favor with the group around the time of the publication of his book.

His last appearance as a public figure occurred in January 1836, when he gave the oration *Eulogy on King Philip* in Boston. Pointedly first given on a day associated with Andrew Jackson only a month after the Cherokees were forced into a removal treaty, the *Eulogy* attacked New England historians, politicians, and missionaries who dehumanized Indian people in order, Apess maintained, to justify their theft of Indian land, making pious New Englanders no better than Jackson himself. Unlike his previous activities, neither the oration nor the book received public comment. Indians no longer interested Boston's elites; this apathy as well as the Panic

of 1837 may have sent Apess to New York City to improve his always-precarious fortunes. He died there in May 1839 of a cerebral hemorrhage.

Relentlessly skewering the hypocrisy and willful misrepresentations of the intellectuals who were reinventing New England as the virtuous birthplace of the republic, Apess produced a sustained critique of the spread of European imperialism and its continuity in the politics and culture of the United States. Although he remained virtually unknown for 150 years after his death, his writing is a profound contribution to the history of Native American letters in English and a testament to the struggles of native peoples in New England.

William Apess, *On Our Own Ground: The Collected Writings of William Apess, a Pequot*, ed. Barry O'Connell (1992); Maureen Konkle, *Writing Indian Nations: Native Intellectuals and the Politics of Historiography, 1827–63* (2004); Barry O'Connell, "'Once More Let Us Consider': William Apess in the Writing of New England Native American History," in *After King Philip's War: Presence and Persistence in Indian New England*, ed. Colin G. Calloway (1997); Scott Manning Stevens, "William Apess's Historical Self," *Northwest Review* 35, no. 3 (1997).

Maureen Konkle

Asian Religions An old saying has it that Unitarians profess "the fatherhood of God, the brotherhood of man, and the neighborhood of Boston." But Unitarians long ago lost their stranglehold on Boston, which is now home not only to Catholics and Jews but also to practitioners of Buddhism, Hinduism, Sikhism, Confucianism, Daoism, and other religions of Asian origin.

When it comes to religion, New England is far from homogeneous. At the Insight Meditation Center in Barre, Mass., Joseph Goldstein and Sharon Salzburg—both Jewish converts to Buddhism—teach Vipassana-style meditation in a Theravada Buddhist retreat that, in a previous incarnation, served as a Catholic seminary. Members of the Jain Center of Greater Boston worship in a former Swedish Lutheran church in Norwood, Mass. The New England Sikh Study Circle meets in a former Kingdom Hall of Jehovah's Witnesses in Milford, Mass. And Boston-area Hindu immigrants worship at the Sri Lakshmi Temple, a structure they built in the South Indian style, in Ashland.

New England's pilgrimage from provincialism to cosmopolitanism in religious matters is typically traced to the arrival of an English translation of the Hindu scripture the *Bhagavad Gita* in Concord, Mass., in the 1840s. But the region's encounter with Asian religions actually began in the 18th rather than the 19th century, with Salem ship captains, not Transcendentalist writers. The United States

opened trade with China and India in 1784, and shortly thereafter New England ships began sailing for ports from Canton to Pondicherry. New Englanders discovered Asia, therefore, not through books or gurus but through artifacts: japanned highboys, Madras cottons, and bone-china teacups.

Protestant missionaries also encountered Asian religions decades before the Transcendentalists. The American Board of Commissioners for Foreign Missionaries (ABCFM), top-heavy with Massachusetts Congregationalists, was founded in 1810. It dispatched the first generation of American missionaries—virtually all of them New Englanders—to mission fields in South Asia beginning in 1812 and China beginning in 1830. Unlike other New Englanders of their time, these missionaries encountered Asian religions face to face. Still, the reports they sent home were for the most part scathing critiques of "heathen" religions.

The first New Englanders to find truth in Asian religions were Deists and Unitarians. New England's Transcendentalists were, however, the first group of American intellectuals to ascribe wholeheartedly to the truth and beauty of Asian scriptures. In his youth Transcendentalist Ralph Waldo Emerson complained about the "cruelty and sensuality" of Hinduism but later came to see the *Bhagavad Gita* as "the first of books." Emerson's poem "Brahma" (1857) and his essay "Plato" (1850) also drew deeply from Asian sources, as did Henry David Thoreau's *Walden* (1854). Thoreau scandalized New England readers when, in *A Week on the Concord and Merrimack Rivers* (1849), he referred to "My Buddha." In an oft-quoted 1849 letter he wrote, "To some extent, and at rare intervals, even I am a yogi."

The American Oriental Society promoted a more scholarly understanding of Asian religions; established in Boston in 1842, this organization was as rife with New Englanders as the ABCFM. Edward Salisbury of Boston became America's first professional Orientalist when he joined the faculty at Yale (his alma mater) in 1843. He would later serve as the president of the American Oriental Society, as would his student and successor at Yale, William Dwight Whitney of Northampton, Mass.

Thanks to the pioneering work of Unitarians and Transcendentalists, the Buddhist translations of American Oriental Society members, and the opening of Japan to trade in 1853–54 by Commodore Matthew C. Perry of Newport, R.I., Buddhism enjoyed a vogue among New England intellectuals at the end of the 19th century. In 1883 Phillips Brooks of Boston's Trinity Church joked that "a large part of Boston prefers to consider itself Bud-

A family honors ancestors during Phum-Ben, at the Cambodian Buddhist Center, Lynn, Mass., September 1989

dhist rather than Christian." In 1895 Henry King of the First Baptist Church of Providence rhetorically asked, "Shall we all become Buddhists?" Buddhism had made inroads into New England's high society in the half century since Emerson and Thoreau published the first American translation of a Buddhist scripture in *The Dial* in 1844. "Boston Brahmins" were becoming "Boston Buddhists."

In 1885 William Sturgis Bigelow and Ernest Fenollosa—both Harvard graduates from prominent New England families—formally converted to Tendai Buddhism in Japan. Like other Boston Buddhists, both were attracted to the religion for aesthetic rather than philosophical reasons. And both were collectors of Japanese Buddhist art. Fenollosa would later serve as curator of the Department of Oriental Art at Boston's Museum of Fine Arts—a major conduit for *japonisme* in the late 19th century and beyond.

Following the World's Parliament of Religions, held in conjunction with the Chicago World's Columbian Exposition of 1893, Hinduism became institutionalized in New England. Swami Vivekananda, the first Hindu missionary to the West and the most popular Asian to speak at the parliament, toured the country after the exposition ended. He lectured at Harvard, Radcliffe, and Smith, and was a regular attraction at Greenacre, a summer conference begun in Eliot, Maine, in 1896 in an effort to spread the parliament's mandate for interreligious dialogue among New England's religious liberals.

Vivekananda's Vedanta Society set up shop in New England in 1907. That year Sara Bull, a Massachusetts woman of means and refinement who ran a European-style salon out of her Cambridge home, persuaded Swami Paramananda to establish the Boston Vedanta Centre, which quickly became the most vibrant Vedantist organization in early-20th-century America. In 1910 Swami Abhedananda broke away from mainstream Vedanta to found a Hindu ashram in West Cornwall, Conn. Two years later, Paramananda's Boston branch began publishing *The Message of the East*, a journal the group continued to produce until 1962.

The popularity of Vedanta among high-society women produced the first Asian religious scandal in New England. After Sara Bull died in 1911, the Vedantists were poised, in keeping with the provisions of her will, to collect several hundred thousand dollars from her estate. But Bull's daughter, believing that her mother had been brainwashed, took the case to court. Boston newspapers gloried in the scandal, which concluded when the court decided that Bull's Hindu devotions were evidence of mental incapacity. Her considerable fortune reverted to her daughter.

Following the passage in 1924 of the Asian Exclusion Act, which severely restricted immigration from Asia for more than four decades, Asian religions went into a period of decline. But they were not entirely quiescent. In 1928 a Vedanta society opened in Providence, and a year later Swami Paramananda

established a Hindu ashram in the woods of Cohasset, Mass. In the early thirties Dwight Goddard, a Hartford Theological Seminary graduate who had converted to Buddhism while serving as a Baptist missionary to China, established a monastic group called the American Buddhist Brotherhood. His dream of a bicoastal contingent of wandering monks who would spend half the year in a Vermont retreat and the other half in California was never realized. But in the 1950s the Beat Generation picked up Goddard's *Buddhist Bible* (1932); led by Jack Kerouac of Lowell, Mass., they started a "rucksack revolution" that turned on American youth not only to drugs but also to Buddhism. In the late 1950s and early 1960s, Zen centers sprang up around the country. One of the most important—the Cambridge Buddhist Association—was started in 1959 by Zen popularizer D. T. Suzuki.

Also gaining a foothold in pre-1960s New England was the Self-Realization Fellowship of Hindu guru Swami Paramahansa Yogananda, whose *Autobiography of a Yogi* (1946) was destined to become a countercultural classic. Yogananda, who came to America as a delegate to the International Congress of Religious Liberals held in Boston in 1920, established his first U.S. society in the Massachusetts capital.

A major change in U.S. law in 1965 prompted a new wave of immigration from Asia, along with a national boom in Asian religions. Gurus and Zen masters received most of the early press, but the big story was the transplantation, via laypeople, of virtually every form of Asian religion to America. Beginning in the 1970s Asian immigrants began to build Hindu, Buddhist, and Sikh temples across the country. While most of these new immigrants flocked to the West Coast (most notably, California), New England was also a popular destination. According to the U.S. census, 2.1 percent of all Asian Americans lived in Massachusetts in 1990. Northeastern states were the top destination for South Asian immigrants. In 1990, 35 percent of Asian Indians lived in the Northeast. Thanks to this new Asian immigration, Lowell now boasts the largest Cambodian community east of the Mississippi, as well as one of the nation's most intriguing complexes of Cambodian and Laotian Buddhist temples.

But Asian religions aren't just for immigrants. Many native-born New Englanders have converted to Hinduism or Buddhism, and a variety of convert-oriented groups (most visibly the Hare Krishnas) are active in the region. Moreover, some converts have gone on to become gurus themselves. Former Harvard faculty member Richard Alpert, for example, now teaches a mixture of Asian truths and practices under the name Ram Dass. Many New Englanders who do not identify themselves as Buddhists or Hindus practice some form of yoga or meditation. Martial arts centers are located within easy reach of virtually every New England town. New England remains a remarkably diverse region, its culture indelibly marked by the influence of Asian religions.

Diana Eck, *On Common Ground: World Religions in America* [CD-Rom] (1997); Rick Fields, *How the Swans Came to the Lake: A Narrative History of Buddhism in America* (1992); Carl T. Jackson, *The Oriental Religions and American Thought: Nineteenth-Century Explorations* (1981); Jackson, *Vedanta for the West: The Ramakrishna Movement in the United States* (1994); Carole Tonkinson, ed., *Big Sky Mind: Buddhism and the Beat Generation* (1995); Thomas A. Tweed, *The American Encounter with Buddhism, 1844–1912: Victorian Culture and the Limits of Dissent* (1992); Arthur Versluis, *American Transcendentalism and Asian Religions* (1993); Raymond Brady Williams, *Religions of Immigrants from India and Pakistan: New Threads in the American Tapestry* (1988).

Stephen Prothero

Baptists Baptists, the group of Protestant Christians who rejected infant baptism and insisted on the absolute autonomy of congregations, were few and scattered in early New England. Puritan authorities associated them with the religious radicalism and social disruption of 16th-century Anabaptists in Europe; as Urian Oakes, president of Harvard College, commented in 1672, "Anabaptism we shall find hath ever been look't at by the Godly Leaders of this people as a Scab to be contended against." His attitude prevailed throughout the 17th century in New England.

The earliest haven for dissenters in New England was established when Roger Williams, who championed complete religious liberty, was expelled by the Puritans from the Massachusetts Bay Colony for his radical views. Williams founded Providence Plantations (now the state of Rhode Island), where he helped form the first Baptist church in America in early 1639. John Clarke founded the second Baptist church in Newport, R.I., no later than 1644 and possibly earlier. Together, Williams and Clarke obtained a charter for the colony of Rhode Island in 1663.

Baptists continued to arrive from England and Wales, where the movement was well established. John Myles, the founder of the first Baptist church in Wales, arrived in America in 1663 and founded a church in Rehoboth, Mass., that eventually moved to Swansea, Mass. What would eventually become the First Baptist Church of Boston was founded in the home of Thomas Gould of Charlestown, Mass., in 1655. For several years the church endured persistent persecution; Gould was sentenced to exile but refused to leave and was imprisoned. In 1679 the congregation built its first building, but civic authorities nailed the doors shut and passed a law declaring that "no person should erect or make use of a house for public worship, without license from the authorities." William Screven was ordained by the First Baptist Church of Boston to form another church in Kittery, Maine, in 1682. Screven later led a migration of members of the Kittery church to South Carolina, where they founded the First Baptist Church of Charleston in 1684.

The period of greatest growth among Baptists in New England occurred in the 18th century during the Great Awakening. Baptists had little to do with initiating the religious revivals, but they benefited from them nonetheless. Although early Baptist theology was largely influenced by Calvinism, the revival movements tempered this position. Those who supported revivalism came to be known as Separate Baptists, or "New Lights," and over a hundred New Light Congregational churches eventually became Baptist. In this way Baptists gained talented new leadership, including the preacher and historian Isaac Backus, who led his Congregational church in Middleborough, Mass., to become Baptist in 1756. In 1764 Backus helped found Rhode Island College (later Brown University) in Warren, R.I.; it moved in 1770 to Providence. The college inaugurated a new idea in America: education without theological constraints. No religious tests of any kind were required of students.

Thus Baptists established themselves as leaders in the American idea of complete religious freedom and the separation of church and state. The General Convention, a centralized Baptist organization formed in 1814, eventually divided over the issue of slavery; the resulting schism produced the Southern Baptist Convention in 1845. The Northern Baptist Convention, now the American Baptist Churches, was established in 1907. Each group espouses distinct theological, ecumenical, and worship practices. Most contemporary Baptists in New England are American Baptists, who believe in the local congregation's absolute autonomy.

C. C. Goen, *Revivalism and Separatism in New England, 1740–1800: Strict Congregationalists and Separate Baptists in the Great Awakening* (1962); Susan Juster, *Disorderly Women: Sexual Politics and Evangelicalism in Revolutionary New England* (1994); H. Leon McBeth, *The Baptist Heritage: Four Centuries of Baptist Witness* (1987); William G. McLoughlin, *New England Dissent, 1630–1833* (1971); Carla Pestana, *Quakers and Baptists in Colonial Massachusetts* (1991); Robert G. Torbet, *A History of the Baptists* (1963).

Thomas R. McKibbens

Brooks, Phillips (1835–93) Episcopal clergyman. Phillips Brooks was born in Boston; his parents, Arthur Brooks and Mary Ann Phillips, both came from established New England families. Though his father was of Unitarian background, the Brooks family became members of the solidly evangelical Saint Paul's Episcopal Church on Tremont Street. Phillips Brooks graduated from Harvard College in 1855. After a brief and difficult stint as an instructor at Boston Latin School, Brooks decided to train for the Episcopal ministry at Virginia Theological Seminary in Alexandria. Although his feeling softened as time passed, the young Brooks disliked the seminary and was intolerant of the sort of evangelical piety characteristic of much of the student body. Finding many of his classes unchallenging, he read widely in the early Church Fathers and contemporary English Romantic literature. Among his most obvious influences were Samuel Taylor Coleridge and the American Romantic evangelical Horace Bushnell. From these and other thinkers, Brooks acquired an aversion to abstract doctrinal systems and a belief in ethical behavior as the essence of authentic Christianity.

Upon graduating from seminary in 1859, Brooks was assigned to parishes in Philadelphia, where he gained a reputation as a gifted young preacher. (It was during his years in Philadelphia that he wrote the popular Christmas carol "O Little Town of Bethlehem.") In 1869 Brooks accepted an appointment to Trinity Church in Copley Square, Boston. Although he had moved in low-church circles in Philadelphia, soon after his move back to Boston he became increasingly identified with the liberal, or Broad Church, wing of Episcopalianism, which embraced higher critical approaches to the Bible, tended to be looser about certain doctrinal strictures and emphasized the humanity of Jesus more than his divinity. He delivered the prestigious Yale "Lectures on Preaching" in 1877 and the Bohlen Lectures (published later as *The Influence of Jesus*) in Philadelphia in 1879. In the Yale lectures, Brooks defined preaching as "the bringing of truth through personality." Under its young rector, Trinity Church became Boston's preeminent preaching station and Brooks became the most popular preacher of Gilded Age Boston. In 1891 Brooks accepted election as bishop of Massachusetts. He served less than two years in this position before his sudden death in Boston in 1893.

Brooks was a central figure in the religious and intellectual life of late-19th-century New England. His sermons (several volumes of which appeared during his lifetime) were enormously popular and evince a warm, Christ-centered liberal Protestantism. Although Brooks's

The Phillips Brooks monument outside Trinity Church, Boston, was conceived by Augustus Saint-Gaudens and completed by Frances Grimes, Elsie Ward, and Henry Hering (1896–1907)

Christianity was pragmatic and nonconfessional (traits that earned him the opposition of orthodox high churchmen when he was elected bishop), his traditional religious vocabulary and irenic manner won him a wide audience.

Raymond Wolf Albright, *Focus on Infinity: A Life of Phillips Brooks* (1961); Alexander V. G. Allen, *Life and Letters of Phillips Brooks* (1901); Gillis J. Harp, "The Young Phillips Brooks: A Reassessment and the Shaping of a Liberal Protestant," *Journal of Ecclesiastical History* 49 (1998); John Frederick Woolverton, *The Education of Phillips Brooks* (1995).

Gillis J. Harp

Bushnell, Horace (1802–76) Congregational minister, theologian, civic pioneer. Horace Bushnell was born in the Litchfield hills of Connecticut, in Bantam, and after a rigorous farm upbringing graduated from Yale in 1827. He experimented with various careers—teaching, journalism, and law—before entering Yale Divinity School, and in 1833 he became pastor of the North Congregational Church in Hartford. During his 26-year tenure Bushnell developed into an exceptional preacher, less popular than his friendly rival Henry Ward Beecher but more original.

Out of his pastoral experience Bushnell developed a fresh body of Christian thought, not liberal in the modern sense but more in tune with prevailing ideas of his time than was dogmatic New England orthodoxy. Bushnell, who upset the establishment by emphasizing God's merciful qualities, became embroiled in a theological battle that nearly cost him his ministerial standing but survived the controversy. His advanced views, set forth in such books as *God in Christ* (1849), *Sermons for the New Life* (1858), and *The Vicarious Sacrifice* (1866), began to change the face of American Protestantism and also attracted a British following.

Bushnell had a broad range of secular interests. He was a ready commentator on current events, and Hartford businessmen turned to him for advice in hard times. Bushnell also possessed native talent as a civil engineer. He did most of the political lobbying, as well as the legal and real estate work, that against heavy odds during the 1850s turned the Hartford city dump into scenic Bushnell Park, the country's first municipally financed urban preserve.

In education Bushnell labored with Henry Barnard to reform Connecticut's public schools. While in California seeking improved health in 1856, he played a supportive role in establishing the University of California and was urged (in vain) to become its first president. His most enduring contribution to education, however, was *Christian Nurture* (1847), which challenged the existing emphasis on dramatic religious conversion and instead proposed that children grow in grace through exposure to religion from earliest childhood, their faith taking shape under the care of home, school, and church.

A student of language, Bushnell challenged the Calvinist notion that words are rigidly precise, arguing that meanings have changed over time and that language is essentially suggestive and poetic. Along with Ralph Waldo Emerson and Mark Twain, he championed a distinctively American literature, and in a succession of addresses—most notably, his 1848 Phi Beta Kappa lecture at Harvard, "Work and Play," and his famous "Age of Homespun," delivered at the 1851 Litchfield County centennial—he carved a niche for himself as a social historian and man of letters.

Bushnell was an outspoken critic of slavery but did not agree with abolitionist demands for immediate emancipation. Initially skeptical, he eventually supported African American civil rights, although he opposed woman suffrage. He did believe, however, that women should have equal standing with men before the law and favored the admission of women to a broad range of business and professional occupations.

In spite of his liberalizing creativity, Bushnell's unchanging belief in the sovereignty of God and his focus on Christ as the ultimate answer for stumbling humanity made him something of a latter-day Puritan. He dreamed of a time when the New England model of society, based on education and intelligent Christianity, would be adopted by the entire nation.

Mary Bushnell Cheney, *Life and Letters of Horace Bushnell* (1880); Conrad Cherry, ed., *Horace Bushnell: Sermons* (1985); Robert L. Edwards, *Of Singular Genius, of Singular Grace: A Biography of Horace Bushnell* (1992); H. Shelton Smith, ed., *Horace Bushnell: Twelve Selections* (1965).

Robert L. Edwards

Camp Meeting Grounds

Camp meeting grounds are a unique part of the American religious experience and have had a tremendous impact on religious life in New England. At various times, New England's camp meeting grounds have served as settings for revivalism, church planting, missions, Christian education, national reform, and political action.

The first camp meeting in the United States was held in southwestern Kentucky in 1799 as part of a sacramental service conducted by the Presbyterian minister James McGready. Before McGready, there had been Methodist revivals in Georgia and the Carolinas as well as similar services held by Baptists in Virginia in 1769 and—in New England—the outdoor services conducted by followers of the English revivalist George Whitefield and the Wesleys.

Camp meetings are characterized by four basic features: outdoor religious exercises; camping on the grounds; food and accommodations provided by the campers; and a standardized camp meeting "method." While the earliest services in Kentucky emphasized the sacraments, preaching and revival were central to New England services.

The first documented camp meeting in New England took place in Haddam, Conn., in 1802, shortly after the Kentucky revivals. Participants of a revival held in Monmouth, Maine, in 1809, established a camp meeting ground in Hebron, Conn., the following year. People came to the Hebron camp meeting from as far as 50 miles away, and 500 people were said to have been "felled" or "slain in the spirit" during a single evening's service.

Camp meeting grounds can be found throughout New England. A large number were established in the mid-1800s, and many of these are still in operation. In the 20th century, however, a number of meeting grounds—such as the Willimantic, Conn., camp meeting—broadened their theology to incorporate Spiritualism and various New Age beliefs. Some of the oldest and best-attended camp meetings are located in Connecticut, Vermont, New Hampshire, and Massachusetts. Prominent Connecticut camp meeting grounds include Southington, New Preston, Ashford, Canaan, Bristol, Plainville, New Britain, and Willimantic. In Massachusetts, meeting grounds are located in South Hamilton, Wareham, Hamilton, North Redding, Douglas, Groton, Northampton, Martha's Vineyard, Conway, Tewksbury, New Bedford, South Lancaster, and Yarmouth.

Perhaps the best-known camp meeting ground in New England is Wesleyan Grove on Martha's Vineyard. Wesleyan Grove was featured on the television series *Restoring America*, as master carpenter Bob Villa restored one of the cottages. Jeremiah Pease founded the 34-acre camp meeting ground in 1835, originally intending his meetings for local (island) Methodists, but services began attracting outsiders as well—including members of other Protestant denominations and some Roman Catholics. By the late 1850s, off-island attendees had replaced their tents with the elaborately decorated Gothic cottages for which Wesleyan Grove has become internationally famous. Although the Wesleyan Grove site is bigger, more elaborate, and better preserved than most New England camp meeting grounds, the description given by Ellen Weiss in *City in the Woods* (1987) gives a feel for a typical New England camp meeting ground. She reports considerable variation in building styles and construction techniques, even within the same compound. Most buildings at Wesleyan Grove—as elsewhere—are narrow, cramped, two-story cottages (similar to the one restored by Bob Vila). Units were constructed on tiny lots and allowed their occupants little privacy. On the other hand, there are also a number of large, ornate structures situated on much larger lots. What is most significant about the Martha's Vineyard grounds is that of the 500 buildings recorded on the site in the late 19th century, 300 are still extant.

Doug Adams, *Meeting Houses to Camp Meetings: Toward a History of American Free Church Worship from 1620 to 1835* (1981); Kenneth O. Brown, *Holy Ground: A Study of the American Camp Meeting* (1992); Dickson Bruce, *And They All Sang Hallelujah: Plain Folk Camp Meeting Religion, 1800–1845* (1974); Ellen Weiss, *City in the Woods: The Life and Design of an American Camp Meeting on Martha's Vineyard* (1987).

Stephen D. Glazier

Channing, William Ellery (1780–1842)

Clergyman and author. William Ellery Channing was a leader in shaping Unitarian Christianity in antebellum New England. A mentor to many writers of the American Renaissance, Channing was an early and influential champion of the causes of American literature, social reform, and abolition.

Channing was born to an established Newport, R.I., family. At age 14 he entered Harvard, where he encountered the writings of the Scottish Enlightenment. Reared with Calvinism's more pessimistic view of human nature, Channing was deeply moved by Francis Hutcheson's argument that God endows the human soul with a natural sympathy toward the good. He vowed then to pursue a life worthy of this principle of "benevolence."

In 1803 Channing accepted a call to become pastor of Boston's Federal Street Church at a time of great conflict among Massachusetts Congregational churches. Calvinists felt that the ministry was being betrayed by liberals who rejected the orthodox doctrines of original sin and predestination and the evangelical faith in conversions. This decades-old conflict peaked in 1805, when Harvard granted a theological professorship, and then the presidency, to men in the liberal camp. The orthodox believers revolted, forming their own seminary and launching a pamphlet campaign against those whom they believed were building "a half-way house to infidelity."

At first Channing urged both sides to reconcile, keeping controversy out of the pulpit. But his greatest contribution to the liberal cause came in 1819, when he delivered his sermon "Unitarian Christianity" at the ordination of Jared Sparks, the minister for a new liberal congregation in Baltimore. Although liberals had previously shunned the Unitarian label, Channing embraced the doctrine of the unity of God, rejecting Trinitarianism as a superstition unsupported by Scripture. Further, he argued that reason should guide the interpretation of all Scripture. "The Bible is a book written for men, in the language of men," he explained, and reason should be used to sift human error from God's truth. The greatest superstitions of his day, he went on, were the Calvinist ideas that humans are born sinful and that God predestines many to eternal damnation. Channing's sermon was widely reprinted, scandalizing orthodox believers but inspiring liberals to finalize their divorce from Calvinist churches by establishing the Unitarian Christian denomination. Channing convened a conference of liberal Congregationalist ministers in 1820; the gathering became known as the American Unitarian Association in 1825.

While continuing to promote Unitarian Christianity, Channing branched out in the 1820s, writing essays on literary criticism and social reform, and calling for Americans to establish their own literary tradition. These essays won him an international reputation as one of the most important American writers of his day. Channing was best known, however, as a pulpit speaker. Distinguished visitors to Boston considered a Sabbath visit at the Federal Street Church an important stop on their tours. Even though the young Ralph Waldo Emerson found most Unitarian preaching too "corpse-cold" and rational for his taste, he walked many miles each Sunday to hear Channing preach.

In the early 1830s, at the height of his fame, Channing alienated many members of his wealthy congregation when he called for the abolition of slavery. Paradoxically, the more radical Garrisonian abolitionists also denounced him for moving too slowly. While Channing's support added invaluable prestige to the fledgling movement, he refused to condone Garrison's verbal violence against the South. The "moral power" of example and persuasion, he insisted, was the only Christian way to fight slavery.

Channing gave his final address in August 1842 to an abolitionist audience in Lenox, Mass. Never in full health, the minister was exhausted by the journey and died on the return trip. He was buried in Mount Auburn Cemetery in Cambridge, Mass. Today Channing's reputation is overshadowed by some who were once his disciples, but a generation of distinguished writers and reformers—including Dorothea Dix, Horace Mann, Elizabeth Peabody, and Theodore Parker—paid tribute to Channing as their mentor.

Arthur W. Brown, *William Ellery Channing* (1961); Andrew Delbanco, *William Ellery Channing: An Essay on the Liberal Spirit in America* (1981); Jack Mendelsohn, *Channing: The Reluctant Radical: A Biography* (1980 [1971]); Conrad Wright, ed., *Three Prophets of Religious Liberalism: Channing, Emerson, Parker* (1961).

Ernest Freeberg

Christian Science Organized in 1879, the Christian Science Church (officially, the Church of Christ, Scientist)—representing one of the few indigenous American religions with worldwide recognition—has its roots in New England. Its New Hampshire–born founder, Mary Baker Eddy, a former Congregationalist, lived her entire life in New England, including an active period of preaching and teaching in Boston in the 1880s. Eddy studied the fashionable theories of her day, including homeopathy and Quimbyism (a method of healing devised by the mesmerist Phineas Parkhurst Quimby), but eventually she rejected each and ultimately described her Scripture-centered religion as "hopelessly original," deriving its theological origins from a combination of biblical study and what she considered direct spiritual inspiration, as well as from practical application through Christian prayer.

Eddy did not conceive of Christian Science as a denomination or an institution but viewed it as a practical Christian theology that could be useful to adherents of all religions. She defined Christian Science as "the law of God, the

First Church of Christ, Scientist (1879), Christian Science Center, Boston, 1972

law of good, interpreting and demonstrating the divine Principle and rule of universal harmony." Its first tenet reads, "As adherents of Truth, we take the inspired Word of the Bible as our sufficient guide to eternal Life." The Bible is the Christian Scientist's primary text, with denominational writings taking an ancillary place. Eddy's major work, *Science and Health with Key to the Scriptures* (1875), contains the full statement of her teachings.

The concept "inspired Word" is important to Christian Scientists. Even though Christian Science accepts the words and works of Jesus as savior, it does not accept as literal truth all biblical statements, especially certain Old Testament passages, but stresses the need to search out and pray for underlying spiritual meaning. Christian Science takes the Bible literally, however, in its emphasis on Jesus' requirement to overcome sin and heal sickness through spiritual means alone—love, faith, prayer, reform, spiritual understanding, and the graces of the Holy Spirit.

Christian Science has extensive commonalties with generally accepted Christian theology, as well as insights concerning a less ritualistic or creedal approach to religion. Like other Christian religions, Christian Science accepts Jesus as the son of God. However, adherents perceive Jesus not as God or as part of the Trinity but as the most spiritual, perfect individual who ever lived; his title "Christ" represents his "divineness," in the sense that he was divinely conceived, inspired, and animated, but does not indicate that he was the deity or part of the godhead. Christian Sci-

ence, therefore, is unitarian, rather than Trinitarian, although its adherents do not generally use either term. Christian Scientists do believe, however, that the same Christliness that Jesus exemplified lives still and continues to inspire, heal, save, and animate humankind.

Christian Science theology is commonly known for its emphasis on spiritual healing of physical ills, and a Christian Scientist sees that practice as an integral part of Christianity. However, a believer's decision to rely upon a spiritual method of healing is an individual choice, not a coercive denominational requirement. And while Christian Scientists maintain a corps of nonmedical nurses and home aides for those who request practical nursing care, they point to a substantial body of information on successful Christian Science healing over the past 100 years.

Christian Science is most visibly represented by its Christian Science Reading Rooms, located throughout the region, and by the international mother church in Boston, the First Church of Christ, Scientist (established 1879), the centerpiece of the massive Christian Science Center complex in the Back Bay district. Behind the church structure stretches a block-long publishing house where the *Christian Science Monitor,* the *Christian Science Journal,* and other denominational literature are published and visitors can walk through the Mapparium—a stained-glass model of the world. Even more dramatic than the extension and publishing house is the colossal 1970s addition to the site designed by I. M. Pei.

Although semi-independent, all other Christian Science churches are considered branches of the mother church. They govern themselves democratically and generally manage their own affairs. Sunday services worldwide include alternate readings of the Bible and the Christian Science denominational textbook. Churches also hold Wednesday-evening meetings, at which readers share inspirational citations and open the floor for comments, including testimonies of Christian healing. Christian Scientists may hold membership in the mother church, a branch church, or both.

In recent years, the church has encountered controversy because of its publication of an adulatory volume on Mary Baker Eddy; its abortive and expensive venture into television broadcasting; the question of eligibility of Christian Science nurses (who engage in a form of low-level practical nursing) and practical-care centers for health-insurance reimbursement; and occasional instances in which Christian Science parents turned exclusively to spiritual means to heal their children.

Although membership figures in the church are not given out and are not large, Christian Science has had a marked influence not only on New England culture but also on thought centers around the world. This influence may result in part from its Pulitzer Prize-winning newspaper and in part from the Christian Science intention to reinstate what it views as Christianity's lost element of healing and the effect that intention has had upon religious and therapeutic trends worldwide.

Gillian Gill, *Mary Baker Eddy* (1998); Stephen Gottschalk, *The Emergence of Christian Science in American Religious Life* (1973); Robert Peel, *Christian Science: Its Encounter with American Culture* (1958).

J. Denis Glover

Coffin, William Sloane, Jr. (1924–)

Protestant minister and political activist. The Reverend William Sloane Coffin, Jr., has been one of the nation's most influential and controversial ministers since the early 1960s. An army and CIA veteran, flamboyant civil rights, anti–Vietnam War, and disarmament activist, Coffin was until the mid-1990s the most visible northern exponent of liberal Protestantism since Reinhold Niebuhr. From the end of World War II, few figures outside established positions of power (Martin Luther King, Jr., Michael Harrington, Allard Lowenstein, Jesse Jackson) have so vigorously engaged in so many political and moral issues.

Born into New York City's liberal Republican elite, the Yale-educated Coffin inherited his family's deep involvement in public and religious affairs. His uncle, the eminent Presbyterian divine Henry Sloane Coffin, served as

William Sloane Coffin, Jr., speaking at Radcliffe College commencement, Cambridge, Mass., June 1969

president of Union Theological Seminary for decades.

Coffin learned a visceral anticommunism (never understood by his critics) at the end of World War II when he participated as a translator in the bloody repatriation of anti-Soviet Russian soldiers in 1946. Partly to atone for his role in that debacle, Coffin joined the CIA when the Korean War broke out, and spent three years trying to place agents in the Soviet Union—to little avail.

At Yale Divinity School (1953–56), Coffin's magnetic personality, quick wit, musical talent, and imposing physical presence captivated his fellow students and teachers. Just two years after his ordination, in 1958, he was hired as university chaplain, a post he held for the next 18 years. With a powerful preaching style that made liberal use of quotable epigrams that became known as "Coffinisms," an instinct for controversy, and a knack for attracting the limelight (and followers), Coffin transformed his genteel pulpit into one with a national influence.

Angry at the injustice tolerated by his class, beginning with quotas on Jewish admissions at Yale, which he helped lift, Coffin began preaching and publishing well-received criticisms of American social inequality and spiri-

tual vacuity. He first turned against the U.S. government during the Civil Rights movement when, in May 1961, against the advice of the Kennedy administration, he organized a perilous Freedom Ride, an act that thrust him into a position of national celebrity and religious leadership.

By 1967 Coffin—who has always had sensitive antennae for shifts in the current of public life—had become *the* outstanding religious voice opposing the war in Vietnam and the driving force within the group that became Clergy and Laity Concerned. Indicted in 1968 (along with Dr. Benjamin Spock and three others) by the U.S. government and convicted, in a high-profile Boston trial, of conspiracy to aid and abet draft resistance, Coffin avoided prison when his conviction was overturned on appeal, and the government decided not to retry the case. In 1971 Garry Trudeau used Coffin as the basis for the Reverend Scot Sloan, "the fighting young priest who can talk to the young," an ongoing character in his political comic strip *Doonesbury*.

Called as minister of New York City's Riverside Church in 1977, Coffin quickly moved the country's premier mainline Protestant pulpit to the center of national antinuclear-war organizing. After a decade at Riverside, Coffin spent three years, from 1987 to 1990, as president of the antinuclear group SANE/FREEZE. His public career effectively concluded with the end of the Cold War, and he retired to Strafford, Vt.

William Sloane Coffin, Jr., *Once to Every Man: A Memoir* (1977); Warren Goldstein, *William Sloane Coffin, Jr.: A Holy Impatience* (2004); Jessica Mitford, *The Trial of Dr. Spock, the Rev. William Sloane Coffin, Jr., Michael Ferber, Mitchell Goodman, and Marcus Raskin* (1969).

Warren Goldstein

Communes

Communes—experimental and alternative communities that seek to provide either an ideal society withdrawn from the world or a model for radical change in society at large—have a long history in America and have played a significant role in both religious and secular life. The first American communes were formed by German pietists in the middle colonies, but after the Revolution they began to appear in New England as well. Communes have existed in the region ever since, although historians note periods when they were more prevalent: the late 18th century, the 1840s, around 1900, and the 1960s and after. In the first two of these phases, New England and areas of Yankee frontier settlement played a leading national role in communal movements. Subsequently, the focus shifted westward. But even though California has long been the preeminent center of communal activity, parts of New England remain strong in several of these movements.

Alternative communities have never been numerically large in relation to the general population, and most have been short-lived. Communities founded in the 1840s lasted an average of just over two years; more than half of those listed in the 1991 *Directory of Intentional Communities* had been around for only six years or fewer. Nevertheless, their existence, their characteristics, and their connections to wider social and religious movements provide evidence about more general hopes for a better society and beliefs in the future. Establishing or living in a commune has usually required a greater degree of commitment to a vision of social or spiritual progress than participation in other, less all-embracing organizations.

For two centuries New England communities have displayed a wide variety of patterns and beliefs. They have been religious and secular, adopted communal or individual property ownership and forms of economic organization, and retained or rejected conventional assumptions and arrangements about gender roles, marriage, the family, and sexuality. But most have claimed to create equality and harmony and have sought to overcome social inequalities, injustices, and conflicts. In addition, whatever their precise religious origins or inspiration, most have emphasized their spiritual role or the ability of a holistic alternative to mainstream society to provide their members with something more or better than the outer world's materialism and greed.

Late-18th-century New England communities were outgrowths of the religious radicalism that flourished during the American Revolution and in the attacks on Calvinism that followed. Millennarian sects both large and small arose, some claiming that it was possible to create a perfect life on earth. Some of these sects created communities in which they gathered members together, often rejecting private property or marriage or both. Most notable of such groups were the Shakers, established in America in 1774 by an Englishwoman named Ann Lee and organized after her death in 1784 into a remarkable series of communal villages. Believing in a dual godhead (of which Lee herself was the female counterpart and "second appearing" of the male Christ), Shakers practiced strict celibacy, confession of sins, and community of goods. Eleven Shaker communities had been founded in rural New England and eastern New York by 1794. The peak Shaker membership seems to have been around 4,600 in 1840, of whom some 2,700 lived in the eastern communities. A long decline followed, although one small community of Shakers still continues at Sabbathday Lake, Maine.

After their early missionary efforts, Shakers largely abandoned active recruiting, and their communities became examples of shelters withdrawn from society. After 1945 nostalgia and an increasingly active market in antique furniture have turned the group into a popularly recognized symbol of timelessness and perfection. In fact, early-19th-century Shaker documents attest to the variety, volatility, and changeability of Shaker life during its period of growth. Since the Shakers' prime, however, other community founders have taken their very existence as proof of the feasibility of communal ventures.

Economic depression, religious change, and social-reform movements produced a new upsurge in such efforts after 1840, in which New England—particularly Massachusetts—played a leading role. With the exception of Bronson Alcott's Fruitlands community (1843), which sought spiritual uplift through the renunciation of worldly practices, these movements aimed to be models of reform for an unequal, competitive society. Though differing in organization and religious practice, all three Massachusetts communities—Brook Farm (1841–47), Hopedale (1841–56), and Northampton (1842–46)—attempted to apply Christian principles to practical social arrangements. "The true followers of Jesus," wrote Brook Farm's founder, George Ripley, in 1840, "are a band of brothers; they compose one family." Each attempted cooperative forms of work and maintained close involvement with other movements, including abolitionism, nonresistance (the belief that Christians should take no part in bloodshed or violence), temperance, and dietary and medical reform. The Transcendentalist Brook Farm attached itself in 1844 to the Fourierist movement, which advocated the reorganization of society into small, self-sufficient communities and was setting up two dozen such communities in the Mid-Atlantic region and the Midwest. Brook Farm became one of Fourierism's intellectual centers and published the movement's journal, *The Harbinger*.

Though they adjusted their economic arrangements, none of these Massachusetts communities adopted communal property or rejected conventional marriage and family ties. Coupled with practical difficulties, this may actually have been a reason for their collapse. By contrast, the perfectionist John Humphrey Noyes established a community at Putney, Vt., around 1840 that adopted both communal property and a system of "complex marriage" that opponents denounced as "free love." Though forced to flee the state in 1848 to avoid charges of adultery, Noyes and his followers reestablished themselves at Oneida, N.Y., in a community that lasted another 30 years, while the other New England communities of the 1840s, more socially conventional and with strong ties to other movements, paradoxically declined as the revived economy, together with political and religious shifts, drew away their support and reinforced skepticism as to the value of communitarian solutions to social ills.

This skepticism shaped New England attitudes to communities for the rest of the 19th century. To reformers the increasing scale of American society and the triumph over slavery brought about by the Civil War confirmed the irrelevance of communities to social improvement. The few groups founded in Massachusetts and Vermont in the 1860s and 1870s were inward-looking. When utopian visions again attracted notice in the 1880s and 1890s, they took literary form, inspired above all by Edward Bellamy's novel *Looking Backward* (1888).

According to some historians, literary utopias supplanted real-life communities. But it was not as simple as this. Literary utopias helped fuel movements that themselves attempted community efforts. Craft and farm communities, such as Edward P. Pressy's New Clairvaux at Montague, Mass., and others near Boston in the early-20th century, reacted against the scale and impersonality of industrial society, while several "single-tax" communities in Massachusetts and Maine sought to test the ideas of the reformer Henry George. However, none of these communities expressed the confidence of their 1840s predecessors that they were creating a social revolution. Defensive or accommodating to capitalism, they served more as retreats from modern society than as visions of the future. At most, they sought to revivify spiritual life through work and proximity to the land.

By the turn of the 20th century New England was no longer central to American community movements; the region took little or no part, for instance, in New Deal–era communes. The communal revivals of the 1960s counterculture and its successors have, however, been significant, and communes have sprung up in hundreds of rural and urban locations across the region. By the early 1990s the annual *Directory of Intentional Communities* was listing two dozen or so in Massachusetts, Vermont, and New Hampshire, clustered particularly in the Boston area, the Connecticut River valley, and the Berkshires; this did not include religious sects. These communities represent a movement on a scale larger than at any time since the early 1840s, one that is being constantly reshaped and renewed.

Since the 1960s a whole range of social developments, from New Age religions to feminism and environmentalism, have spawned efforts at communal living, and the movement is more varied in character than it has ever been. On one hand, this variety evokes the fragmentation and social cooptation that overtook the 1840s communities; in the diverse 21st-century world, alternative communities can be treated not as a threat but as a "lifestyle choice." On the other, advocates of communal life are extending a tradition with a long history, one that still addresses the impoverishment of modern societies and their lack of harmony, equality, and spiritual sustenance. The golden age of New England communities may yet lie in the future.

Brian J. L. Berry, *America's Utopian Experiments: Communal Havens from Long-Wave Crises* (1992); Christopher Clark, *The Communitarian Moment: The Radical Challenge of the Northampton Association* (1995); Carl J. Guarneri, *The Utopian Alternative: Fourierism in Nineteenth-Century America* (1991); Stephen A. Marini, *Radical Sects of Revolutionary New England* (1982); Donald E. Pitzer, ed., *America's Communal Utopias* (1997); Anne E. Rose, *Transcendentalism as a Social Movement* (1981); Edward K. Spann, *Hopedale: From Commune to Company Town, 1840–1920* (1992); Stephen J. Stein, *The Shaker Experience in America: A History of the United Society of Believers* (1992).

Christopher Clark

Congregationalism

The Congregational movement, which eventually became a mainline American denomination, took its name from the form of church government advocated by its leaders, English Puritan Calvinists who migrated to New England early in the 17th century because they despaired of reforming the Church of England in the direction and to the degree required by their literal reading of the Bible. Rejecting rule over local churches by bishops (as in Episcopalianism) or by representative church courts (as in Presbyterianism, the polity preferred by the majority of Puritans), Congregationalists identified the true visible church with the particular local congregation. Membership in such churches, they soon decided, should be restricted to Christians deemed by their peers to be intellectually, morally, and experientially identifiable (as far as fallible human judgment could determine) as being among God's predestined elect. Constituted by the covenanting together of such "visible saints," each local church was understood to be empowered by Christ to accomplish without any external supervision all acts needful and proper to church estate. Those acts, however, did include fel-

Congregational Church (1764), Wethersfield, Conn.

lowship ("communion") for moral support and consultation with other similarly constituted local congregations.

Congregational churches dominated New England's religious landscape (except for Rhode Island) well into the 18th century, remaining in later years a cultural force, albeit with a steadily shrinking sphere of influence in politics and social life. Shorn of any claim to hegemony by the mandate of toleration for religious dissenters provided in the new Massachusetts charter of 1692, and with its mandatory tax support eliminated throughout the region by 1834, Congregationalism nonetheless managed to change, to survive, and in some areas to flourish. Following a synod in 1662, many churches adopted a "halfway covenant" that allowed baptized but unconverted persons to baptize their children into the congregation, a right originally reserved for converted adult saints. Other churches demurred, however, and their "pure church" ideal was resoundingly affirmed by the Great Awakening of the 1730s and 1740s.

The development of Congregationalism involved an ongoing creative tension between its two polestars: the freedom of each local church and the Congregational Church's call to fellowship with other Christian bodies. Congregational leaders wanted more collegial control of ministerial standards and oversight of the health of the churches, giving rise in

Massachusetts to ministerial associations (from 1692), while in parts of Connecticut consociations of clergy and laity became legally mandated judicatories over the churches in those areas (from 1708). At the beginning of the 19th century, statewide "general associations" or "conferences" were convened annually to assess the condition of religion in their areas. But more representative policy-framing bodies for Congregationalism were yet to be born; having ceased to be an establishment, the church became more of a regionally defined movement.

Following the Revolution, new fields of service arose to help break Congregationalism out of its New England mold. Beyond the Hudson River to the west, frontiers were expanding with explosive speed, and although the Congregationalists' success in moving into these areas was limited by their misgivings about the suitability of their forms to pioneer conditions, exponents of this New England church managed to plant outposts in upstate New York and the northern Midwest. No less challenging was missionary work to foreign lands. These enterprises required structure, and voluntary lay associations were created for that purpose. At the same time, a number of other reform organizations sprang up to do battle with a host of social evils—among them war, intemperance, and slavery—and to provide orthodox ministers and missionaries for the many good works at hand. Congregationalism expanded nationally, despite the loss of its liberal theological wing to what became Unitarianism. It eventually became a modern mainstream denomination, deeply involved in the 20th-century ecumenical movement.

Each chapter of Congregationalism's history has a New England component. Today the Congregational tradition is claimed by not one but three denominations, each with a fifth to a quarter of its national membership living in New England. Those denominations—the United Church of Christ, the National Association of Congregational Christian Churches, and the Conservative Congregational Christian Conference—number 1,331 congregations in New England, composing 86.4 percent, 8.7 percent, and 4.9 percent, respectively, of the total number of churches of this tradition in the region today.

Congregationalism has contributed many influential figures to the cultural history of New England and beyond, most notably William Bradford, John Winthrop, John Cotton, Thomas Hooker, Increase and Cotton Mather, Jonathan Edwards, Lyman Beecher, Washington Gladden, Mary Lyon, and Harriet Beecher Stowe. Scores of parish ministers and educators, domestic and foreign missionaries, and laymen and women supported the many endeavors for social betterment that have been Congregationalism's trademark. Congregationalists initiated or cultivated many American institutions—government by consent of the governed, the town meeting, public schools, and higher education among them. They were among the first to admit women to the fully ordained pastoral ministry (1853). Still, any reference to "the New England town" invariably calls up a nostalgic image of a village green surrounded by modest clapboard houses and fronted by a white-steepled Congregational meetinghouse. But these meetinghouses can by no means claim anything like a majority of the populace of their towns. Those who attend are Christians, most of whom neither are required to have undergone nor claim to have had a born-again conversion experience; they are a middle-class constituency whose ethnic and religious roots are as varied as the general population of the region.

James F. Cooper, *Tenacious of Their Liberties: The Congregationalists in Colonial Massachusetts* (1998); Horton Davies, *The Worship of American Puritans, 1629–1730* (1990); Harry S. Stout, *The New England Soul: Preaching and Religious Culture in Colonial New England* (1986); John Von Rohr, *The Shaping of American Congregationalism, 1620–1957* (1992); Williston Walker, *The Creeds and Platforms of Congregationalism* (1991 [1893]).

Harold F. Worthley

Cushing, Richard Cardinal (1895–1970) Roman Catholic cardinal.

Richard James Cushing, born in South Boston, Mass., was the son of an Irish immigrant blacksmith, Patrick Cushing, and his wife, Mary Dahill Cushing. He was educated in Boston public schools, Boston College High School, and Boston College before entering Saint John's Seminary in Brighton, Mass., to study for the priesthood. There he became president of the Mission Academia, the student society promoting missionary activity, and he was ordained in Boston in 1921. After brief assignment to parish work, he asked to be sent to the missions but was instead assigned to the Boston office of the Society for the Propagation of the Faith. He became director of the society in 1928, was made auxiliary bishop of Boston in 1939, and was created archbishop in 1944 on the death of William Cardinal O'Connell.

As leader of the archdiocese of Boston, Cushing employed his considerable energies and fundraising abilities to build more than 50 schools, 80 churches, and six hospitals; to welcome more than 60 religious orders to participate in the work of the archdiocese; and to develop a radio and television apostolate. A

Richard Cardinal Cushing with parishioners, South Boston, 1968

special interest in Latin America led him to establish the Missionary Society of Saint James the Apostle, which conducted missions in Peru, Bolivia, and Ecuador and raised $1 million to ransom prisoners taken in the failed Bay of Pigs invasion. His commitment to ecumenism was genuine, and his blunt, gregarious manner made him fast friends among the leaders and the rank and file of other denominations. At the Second Vatican Council he supported statements on ecumenism and religious liberty, and in domestic politics he weighed in on the side of independence of politicians from church control and in favor of the barriers separating church and state.

The early years of Cushing's archbishopric were agitated by the so-called Boston heresy, the contention of a group led by the Reverend Leonard Feeney, S.J., that non-Catholics could not achieve eternal salvation. Questions as to whether he was forceful enough in dealing with the situation delayed his elevation to cardinal until 1958, a slight he felt keenly. In his later years he had to cope with an array of physical ills while dealing with the financial consequences of archdiocesan overexpansion.

John Henry Cutler, *Cardinal Cushing of Boston* (1970); John Tracy Ellis, *Catholic Bishops: A Memoir* (1983); Lawrence H. Fuchs, *John F. Kennedy and American Catholicism* (1967); Thomas H. O'Connor, *Boston Catholics: A History of the Church and Its People* (1998).

Joseph M. McCarthy

Eastern Orthodoxy

In 330 the Roman emperor Constantine relocated the capital city of the empire from Rome to New Rome—Constantinople—on the site of Byzantium, an old Greek colony on the Bosporus. Constantinople became a Christian city, the center

of the new Christian commonwealth that flourished for more than 1,100 years. An extraordinary civilization was created, in which many different races and peoples were incorporated into the life of the church, and all shared a common Christian faith. These included Romans, Greeks, Arabs, Syrians, and later Bulgarians, Serbians, Romanians, Albanians, and Russians. Their religion, Eastern Orthodoxy, represents an extraordinary achievement of unity in diversity and reflects a partial but telling correspondence to the political unity within the ethnic and cultural diversity of the United States today.

In the United States alone there are approximately 5 million Eastern Orthodox Christians, organized under several ecclesiastical jurisdictions with more than 2,160 parishes, 177 of which are located in the New England states and range from huge conclaves with thousands of members to small mission communities. These Orthodox Christians can be distinguished not only by their domed churches, which dot the New England landscape from Stamford, Conn., to Bangor, Maine, and from New Bedford, Mass., to Berlin, N.H., but, more importantly, by their community life, which is centered on the church and provides a strong, distinctive spiritual and cultural contribution to the fabric of New England society.

The Orthodox Christian faith was brought to North America by the tens of thousands of immigrants from the Middle East, the countries of eastern Europe (especially Greece), and Russia after the revolution of 1917. These immigrants were attracted not only to the large cities of New York and Chicago but also to the mill towns of New England, such as Lowell, Mass., and Manchester, N.H., where they found work in the textile and shoe factories at the end of 19th and beginning of the 20th centuries. These immigrants established communities and parishes and built churches and schools. Some of the earliest parishes began as communities containing immigrants from various ethnic backgrounds who shared the same Christian faith. As the numbers of Eastern Orthodox immigrants increased during successive waves, the parishes began to serve particular ethnic groups. Most of these earlier parishes were founded and developed without hierarchical supervision, a fact that bears testimony to the determination and independent spirit of these early pioneers.

As more and more Eastern Orthodox came and settled in the various areas of North America, the autocephalous churches of the old world began to establish jurisdictions in the United States to serve their own faithful and to provide leadership and organization for them. After World War II, Eastern Orthodox

Christians from various jurisdictions began to establish ways of cooperation, and this led to the formation of the Standing Conference of Canonical Orthodox Bishops in America in 1960, with 11 participating jurisdictions. The largest and most well organized is the Greek Orthodox Archdiocese of America, headquartered in New York City. In 1970 the Church of Russia granted self-governing status to its jurisdiction in the United States, which became known as the Orthodox Church in America, based in Syosset, N.Y. In the 1980s many thousands of Evangelical Christians joined the Orthodox Church and came under the jurisdiction of the Antiochian Archdiocese.

In New England, Orthodox leadership is provided by Metropolitan Methodios of the Greek Orthodox Diocese of Boston, with parishes in major cities such as Lowell, Springfield, Worcester, Peabody, and Lynn, Mass., Cranston, R.I., and Manchester, but also in smaller towns throughout New England. Holy Cross Greek Orthodox School of Theology and Hellenic College in Brookline, Mass., is a beacon of Orthodox theological education and priestly formation for the New England area (as well as the entire country). Today the fall of communism in several of the countries of the former Soviet Union has opened up tremendous opportunities for millions of Orthodox Christians and the possibility of a revitalized Eastern Orthodoxy. Significant numbers of new immigrants come to the New England area from these countries. Indeed, immigrants from Romania founded the newest Orthodox parish in New England recently in Manchester.

Anthony M. Coniaris, *Introducing the Orthodox Church: Its Faith and Life* (1982); Georges Florovsky, *Bible, Church, Tradition: An Eastern Orthodox View* (1972); Stanley S. Harakas, *The Orthodox Church: 455 Questions and Answers* (1987); Thomas Hopko, *The Orthodox Faith*, vols. 1–4 (1979); Fotios K. Litsas, ed., *A Companion to the Greek Orthodox Church* (1984); Vladimir Lossky, *The Mystical Theology of the Eastern Church* (1976); Alexander Schmemann, *The Historical Road of Eastern Orthodoxy* (1963); Timothy Kallistos Ware, *The Orthodox Church* (1993).

Peter A. Chamberas

Eddy, Mary Baker (1821–1910) Founder of the Christian Science Church. One of six children, Mary Baker was reared in a New England saltbox house on a small, picturesque homestead in the Bow Hills of New Hampshire and died in one of the two rooms she occupied by choice in a stone mansion in Chestnut Hill, Mass. Although she was virtually unknown well into middle age, in her final years Eddy was recognized internationally as the founder of the Christian Science Church.

Eddy was educated in rural New Hampshire schools and at home, where she practiced daily oral reading and exposition of the Bible. She observed household debates on major issues and spent endless hours in church. Eddy's brother Albert, a graduate of Dartmouth College and associate of Franklin Pierce, was her educational mentor.

Eddy had an innate interest in religion and in relieving human suffering, of which she experienced much: the early and tragic death of her beloved first husband, the loss of custody of her son, her persistent undiagnosed ill health, destitution, and divorce from an unfaithful second husband. Seeking healing from physical, financial, and familial hardship, Eddy turned variously to homeopathy, hydropathy, Quimbyism (a system of healing devised by the mesmerist Phineas Parkhurst Quimby), and spiritualism before discarding them all in favor of the conviction that help could come only from spirituality. In early 1866, after a severe fall had compounded her problems, Eddy turned to the Bible for inspiration. In three days she found herself healed; although she suffered a temporary relapse, she became convinced of God's healing power. She then began her most serious and methodical study of the Bible.

Eddy eventually named the healing insight into spirituality she had glimpsed Christian Science and in 1872 began writing her major work, *Science and Health with Key to the Scriptures* (1875), which eventually became a religious best-seller. Today the Bible and *Science and Health* not only constitute the Christian Scientists' only textbooks, they are also the Scientists' only "pastor." Selections from these books serve as the only sermons in Christian Science churches.

Eddy began expanding her spiritual viewpoint through what she called "reason, revelation, and demonstration." She began actively teaching Christian healing to others and in 1877 married her student Asa Gilbert Eddy. In 1879 Mary Baker Eddy founded what became the worldwide Church of Christ, Scientist, headquartered in Boston. The church grew rapidly after a somewhat fitful start; in the early 20th century it represented one of the fastest-growing denominations in the country. In 1881 Eddy founded the Massachusetts Metaphysical College. Her husband died shortly after their move to Boston in 1882.

From 1883 on, Eddy established five periodicals: the monthly *Christian Science Journal,* the weekly *Christian Science Sentinel,* a *Quarterly* of Bible lessons, the foreign-language *Herald,* and the international *Christian Science Monitor,* a nondenominational newspaper. All except the *Quarterly* and *Monitor* include testimonies of spiritual healing. Eddy required

Christian Science churches to maintain free public reading rooms for the study of the Bible and Christian Science writings. She also set up a board of Christian Science teachers and an international board of lectureship to present Christian healing to the public.

In 1889, in order to forward her own spiritual growth and serve effectively as church leader at the same time, Mary Baker Eddy withdrew from public life to devote herself to prayer, Bible study, writing, organizing, counseling, and, on rare occasions, speaking and teaching. She lived quietly in Concord, N.H., until 1908, when she moved to Chestnut Hill, where she died in 1910. She is buried in Mount Auburn Cemetery in Cambridge, Mass. The central message of Eddy's life is summarized in *Science and Health,* "The spiritual reality is the scientific fact in all things," and in her final written words, which she inscribed on a pad: "God is my life."

Mary Baker Eddy, *Miscellaneous Writings* (1896); Gillian Gill, *Mary Baker Eddy* (1998); Robert David Thomas, *"With Bleeding Footsteps": Mary Baker Eddy's Path to Religious Leadership* (1994); Robert Peel, *Mary Baker Eddy,* 3 vols. (1972–77).

J. Denis Glover

Edwards, Jonathan (1703–58) Congregational minister and theologian. Born in East Windsor, Conn., Jonathan Edwards was the only son of Timothy Edwards and Esther Stoddard in a family of 11 children. He rose to regional prominence in Northampton, Mass., as the most sophisticated defender of the religious revivals of the 1730s and 1740s and to international fame as colonial America's most articulate advocate for evangelical religion. His religious and cultural legacy endures.

Schooled by his minister father at home, Edwards subsequently attended Yale College (B.A., 1720; M.A., 1723). He served briefly as a supply minister in New York City and Bolton, Conn., before becoming a tutor at Yale for two years. In 1727 he joined his maternal grandfather, Solomon Stoddard, as associate minister in Northampton. That year he married Sarah Pierpont of New Haven, Conn.; they had 11 children. In 1729 he assumed full ministerial responsibilities following Stoddard's death.

In Northampton, Edwards followed a regimen of private study that informed his preaching and writing. He gained attention throughout America and in Great Britain with his account of the 1734–35 revival in his congregation, *A Faithful Narrative of the Surprizing Work of God* (1737). Beginning in the fall of 1740 New England was the scene for widespread religious revivals known later as the Great Awakening. Edwards supported this movement both as a revivalist and as a writer. In July 1741 he preached his most fa-

Jonathan Edwards, ca. 1750s

mous sermon, "Sinners in the Hands of an Angry God," which compared the human condition to that of a spider suspended over a fire. In September he delivered the Yale commencement address. His most significant work, *A Treatise Concerning Religious Affections* (1746), is a sustained defense of evangelical religion.

When Edwards began demanding stricter standards for admission to communion in his congregation the ensuing struggle led to his dismissal from Northampton in 1750. The next year he accepted a position as missionary to the Housatonic Indians at Stockbridge, Mass. There he labored on several major projects, including the works published as *Freedom of the Will* (1754), *Original Sin* (1758), and *The Nature of True Virtue* (1765). In 1757 the trustees of the College of New Jersey (later Princeton University) invited him to become the president, a position he held for less than three months before he died as a result of complications from a smallpox inoculation.

Edwards was America's leading Protestant theologian in the 18th century. He represents the transition between the Puritanism of early New England and subsequent forms of evangelical Congregationalism. His disciples and admirers—the Edwardseans—republished his writings during the 19th century. In the 20th century a renaissance of interest in his work has brought him acclaim as America's premier philosopher-theologian. Jonathan Edwards College at Yale was named in his honor; Yale University Press is publishing a new critical edition of his writings; and Northampton now contains monuments to his memory. He has been the subject of scholarly literature, poetry, and drama. The figure of Edwards has become the embodiment of New England Protestantism, an icon in contemporary evangelical circles, and the subject of intense scholarly interest.

Joseph A. Conforti, *Jonathan Edwards, Religious Tradition, and American Culture* (1995); Nathan O. Hatch and Harry S. Stout, eds., *Jonathan Edwards and the American Experience* (1988); George M. Marsden, *Jonathan Edwards: A Life* (2003); John E. Smith, Harry S. Stout, and Kenneth P. Minkema, eds., *A Jonathan Edwards Reader* (1995); Stephen J. Stein, ed., *Jonathan Edwards's Writings: Text, Context, Interpretation* (1996).

Stephen J. Stein

Episcopalianism The Episcopal Church is part of the worldwide Anglican communion representing some 29 autonomous churches spread across 160 countries with a total membership of more than 70 million Anglicans. As stated in the preface to the Book of Common Prayer, the Episcopal Church is "indebted, under God [to the Church of England], for her first foundation and long continuance of nursing care and protection."

King's Chapel in Boston, the first Episcopal Church in New England, was opened in 1689; in 1698 a church was established at Newport, R.I. In New Hampshire religion was so dominated by the Puritans of the Bay Colony that the only Anglican minister to serve there in the 17th century returned to England. The church in Connecticut began its growth slowly, culminating with the first Anglican parish organized at Stratford in 1707. By 1742 there were 14 churches served by seven clergymen. In 1784 Dr. Samuel Seabury of Connecticut became the first New England bishop.

The shaky beginnings of Anglicanism in New England can be attributed to its identification and organic relation with the Church of England and the English government. The American Revolution devastated the Anglican Church in New England; only four Anglican clergymen remained in Massachusetts, one in New Hampshire, and none in Rhode Island at the conclusion of the war.

Revival for the Episcopal Church came with William White's pamphlet *The Case for the Episcopal Churches in the United States Considered*, written in 1782. This plea for unity and reorganization served as an impetus for the adoption of a new name, the Protestant (as distinguished from the Church of Rome) Episcopal (as distinguished from Presbyterians and Congregationalists) Church. In 1789 the Constitution of the Protestant Episcopal Church was adopted in Philadelphia, and the Book of Common Prayer was revised for American use as the church became an independent, self-governing body representing Anglicanism in the United States.

The Episcopal Church in New England is referred to as Province I and has a total of 661 parishes in New England and 232,000 members in dioceses throughout the region. Barbara Harris of the Massachusetts diocese, an African American, became the first female bishop in 1989; in Vermont, Mary McLeod became the first female bishop to lead a diocese in 1993; and in New Hampshire, Gene Robinson became the first openly gay bishop in 2003.

As a "bridge" between the Roman Catholic and Protestant churches, the Episcopal Church subscribes to what has been termed the Anglican "three-legged stool" of Scripture, tradition, and reason, undergirded by the lived experience of the church as foundational and authoritative for ministry. Bishops, priests, and deacons work closely with lay persons in carrying out the church's mission to "follow Christ; to come together weekly for corporate worship; and to work, pray, and give for the spread of the Kingdom of God" (from the Catechism of the Book of Common Prayer).

The term *Episcopalianism* can best be understood by noting that the 2.5 million Episcopalians making up 7,500 parish churches in the United States pledge loyalty to the doctrine, discipline, and worship of the one holy catholic and apostolic church in all essentials but allow great liberty in nonessentials. Liberals and conservatives; modernists, postmodernists, and fundamentalists; high church and low; Anglo-Catholics and Evangelicals; all find common ground for worship in the Book of Common Prayer.

A signature church of Episcopalians in New England is the Trinity Church in Boston's Copley Square, designed by Henry Hobson Richardson (1872–77). Many other Episcopal churches have become familiar elements of New England's architectural landscape. The Episcopal Church has had a profound influence on a number of educational institutions, and one of New England's best preparatory schools, Saint Paul's, is affiliated with it.

James Thayer Addison, *The Episcopal Church in the United States, 1789–1931* (1951); Catherine M. Prelinger, ed., *Episcopal Women: Gender, Spirituality, and Commitment in an American Mainline Denomination* (1992); Origen Storrs Seymour, *The Beginnings of the Episcopal Church in Connecticut* (1934); John Wallace Suter and George Julius Cleaveland, *The American Book of Common Prayer: Its Origin and Development* (1949).

Craig B. Anderson

Evangelicalism Evangelicalism emphasizes the sole authority of the Bible and teaches that Jesus is the sole means of salvation. Its roots run deep in New England's his-

Walter White's evangelical mission shelter, Brattleboro, Vt., 1986

tory. From Jonathan Edwards's Northampton, Mass., revivals (1734–35) to the contemporary revival of urban evangelicalism spurred by institutions such as Gordon-Conwell Theological Seminary, evangelicals have attempted to shape the political, social, and religious lives of New Englanders.

The evangelicalism pronounced from the pulpits of colonial and early-republic New England became the foundation for America's emerging national identity of individualism, laissez-faire business practices, constitutional democracy, the Protestant work ethic, and the hope of a unified European American Protestant America. Called the Great Awakening, it consisted of local revivals like Edwards's and region-wide revivals led by itinerants like the visiting Englishman George Whitefield in the 1740s. By the early 1800s Yale president Timothy Dwight hoped that evangelicalism would serve as a viable alternative to disunity between the Protestant establishment and dissenters like the Unitarians.

Dwight wanted a full-scale revival of American society and acquiescence from those who had yet to accept Protestantism. To Dwight pluralism signified sinfulness and disunity. But as much as evangelicals saw evangelicalism as a unifying bond between New England's European American communities, contentious divisions often resulted. The Great Awakening produced more than 200 schismatic congregations that split from established New England denominations. Presbyterians and Congregationalists split into the Old Lights (anti-revivalists) and the New Lights (revivalists), and new groups like the Baptists and the Methodists emerged.

The evangelical emphasis on "heart" religion was conducive to inclusiveness and egalitarianism. Marginalized groups, including women and people of color, were sometimes permitted to share in church governance and

to exhort. In most cases, however, gains for such groups proved elusive and short-lived. By the end of the 18th century, for example, the Rhode Island Baptist community had curtailed the liberty women once enjoyed within the denomination.

Meanwhile, Dwight's students Nathaniel Taylor and Lyman Beecher took his legacy in a different direction. Gradually, to the dismay of Calvinist critics, they joined forces with the Second Great Awakening's preeminent revivalist, Charles Finney. In the Second Great Awakening, which took place between the late-18th and the mid-19th centuries in New York and New England, Finney changed the focus of evangelicalism from Calvinist predestination to a moral decision to choose God. Additionally, Finney shifted the evangelical impulse toward social-reform movements like abolition and temperance. By the end of the 19th century, the debates within evangelicalism produced more schisms—Social Gospel advocates emphasized curing social ills, and Holiness advocates stressed pious, sanctified living through an experience of the Holy Spirit.

By the 20th century evangelicalism's New England roots had been replanted in the West. Harold Ockenga, the former pastor of Boston's Park Street Congregational Church and the founder of the National Association of Evangelicals (1942), became the founding president of Fuller Theological Seminary in California (1947). In 1969 Ockenga returned to New England to become president of Gordon-Conwell Theological Seminary.

Today, with some exceptions, such as urban evangelical revivalism, evangelicals like the Southern Baptists are finding New England a tough mission field. Gordon-Conwell, with its emphasis on urban mission, has played a crucial role in the growth of evangelical revivals in Massachusetts, particularly among

African Americans and Hispanics. The new multicultural component to New England evangelicalism may signal not only the restructuring of society but a reorganization of evangelicalism as well.

Stephen E. Berk, *Calvinism versus Democracy: Timothy Dwight and the Origins of American Evangelical Orthodoxy* (1974); Catherine A. Brekus, *Strangers and Pilgrims: Female Preaching in American, 1740–1845* (1998); Richard Carwardine, *Transatlantic Revivalism: Popular Evangelicalism in Britain and America, 1790–1865* (1978); Timothy D. Hall, *Contested Boundaries: Itineracy and the Reshaping of the Colonial American Religious World* (1994); Susan Juster, *Disorderly Women: Sexual Politics and Evangelicalism in Revolutionary New England* (1994); William G. McLoughlin, ed., *The American Evangelicals, 1800–1900: An Anthology* (1968); Harry S. Stout, *Divine Dramatist: George Whitefield and the Rise of Modern Evangelicalism* (1990).

Arlene M. Sánchez Walsh

Free Will Baptists There were two major branches of the Free Will Baptist movement: northern and southern. The southern branch was founded in Chowan, N.C., in 1727 by Paul Palmer. The northern branch was formed in 1780 in New Durham, N.H., by Benjamin Randall. Randall, who was converted in one of the English evangelical George Whitefield's revivals, had undergone many religious transformations. He began his ministry as a Congregationalist and later became a Regular Baptist but parted company with them over Calvin's doctrine of predestination. As might be expected, Free Will Baptists emphasize free will and free grace. Baptists do not subscribe to the doctrine of election, whereby a select group has been prechosen by God to be saved. According to Free Will Baptists, Christ sacrificed himself so that everyone could be saved. Free Will Baptists also stress a literal interpretation of the Bible, baptism by full immersion, washing of the feet, evangelism, and open communion.

Free Will Baptist churches experienced considerable growth in New England throughout the 19th century. In addition to founding new congregations, they began to incorporate other established churches into their organization; for example, the Free Communion Baptists of Central New York joined them in 1841, and later the Six Principle Baptists of Rhode Island affiliated with them. A General New England Conference was established in 1827, and the Free Will Baptist Foreign Mission Society was organized in 1833; India was a major mission field. Under the leadership of Silas Curtis of Concord, N.H., the Free Will Baptist Home Mission Society carried out notable charity work among blacks in the rural South. The denomination was also instrumental in establishing

Bates College in Maine. By 1880 the northern branch, which included Michigan and Ohio, had 77,641 members, 1,440 churches, 1,280 ordained ministers, and two colleges. New England churches also organized successful missions to the western and southwestern United States, where a number of churches were established.

In 1910 the majority of the Free Will Baptist churches in New England merged with the Northern Baptist Convention, taking 857 of the 1,100 churches, all the denominational properties, and Bates College. In 1916 the remaining churches of the Randall movement were organized into the Cooperative General Association of Free Will Baptists, and in 1935 the remaining New England churches merged with the southern General Conference to form a single, unified denomination known as the National Association of Free Will Baptists. At the time of the merger, the denomination claimed 243,00 members in 40 states and 2,500 churches. Membership has remained stable. Then as now, the majority of members and churches are in the South and West. In matters of church governance, Free Will Baptists remain strictly congregational, but they hold quarterly and yearly meetings and General Conferences; the denominational headquarters is located in Nashville, Tenn. The 2004 *Free Will Baptist Yearbook* lists 12 Free Will Baptists churches in New England and 1,037 members in the region. Active New England churches include First Free Will Baptist Church in New Durham, N.H. (the mother church, pastored by Jim Nason); Heritage Free Will Baptist Church in Laconia, N.H.; Linneus Free Will Baptist Church in Houlton, Maine; and Free Will Baptist Church in Manomet, Mass. Joel Nason (Jim's son) is spokesman for the Northeast Association. The Home Missions department in Nashville regularly conducts "heritage tours" to New England churches.

William F. Davidson, *The Free Will Baptists in America, 1927–1984* (1985); William G. McLoughlin, *Soul Liberty: The Baptists' Struggle in New England* (1991); Robert E. Picirilli, ed., *History of Free Will Baptist State Associations* (1976).

Stephen D. Glazier

Great Awakening

Between 1720 and 1750 New England experienced a religious revival movement that came to be known as the Great Awakening. Reflecting a resurgence of evangelical pietism within Protestantism, the Great Awakening began with isolated and sporadic revivals in towns of the Connecticut River valley under the leadership of Solomon Stoddard, a minister in Northampton, Mass. Stoddard professed religious conversion to be a manifest emotional experience that was

achievable only with the guidance of ministers who themselves had been converted. He held that before people were ready to seize the Gospel's offer of free grace, they had to be awakened to the dangers of damnation and to their inability to save themselves. The movement in the Connecticut River valley reached a climax in 1734–35, as numerous towns underwent revivals at nearly the same time. Stoddard's grandson Jonathan Edwards, who assumed the ministry at Northampton after his grandfather's death, brought international attention to this remarkable concurrence with the publication in 1737 of *A Faithful Narrative of the Surprizing Work of God*. Through such works as this and *Some Thoughts Concerning the Present Revival of Religion* (1742), Edwards was to become the leading apologist for orthodox revivalism.

A more intense period of revivals, affecting a much larger area of New England, followed the first New England preaching tour of George Whitefield in September and October 1740. An Anglican priest and Calvinist Methodist, the British Whitefield denounced the cold moralism of his own Church of England and gave passionate and soul-searching sermons on the necessity of the New Birth. For a year and a half following Whitefield's visit, local religious revivals swept across New England.

A reinvigorated Calvinism characterized the Great Awakening. Edwards's sermon "Sinners in the Hands of an Angry God" (1741) typifies the revivalists' preaching on the horrors of eternal damnation that awaited the unconverted. New traditions were introduced into religious practice as well: the singing of hymns became part of Congregational worship, and a new religious literary genre evolved, the revival narrative, which traced the progress of a special dispensation of grace as it transformed a town into a holy community. Some evangelicals believed that Christ's millennial kingdom would begin in New England through this spreading revival of religion.

The Great Awakening loosened traditional restraints on females speaking in churches, as women felt the motions of the Holy Spirit and exhorted in private religious meetings or even publicly in the meetinghouses. A few revivalists continued to endorse religious leadership roles for women well after the revivals subsided. Several New Light preachers, believing that the time when God would pour out his Spirit on all nations was at hand, reinvigorated the missionary movement among Native Americans. Their most famous convert, the Connecticut Mohegan Samson Occom, became New England's first ordained Native American missionary.

The source of religious authority appeared to shift from the formal office of the ministry to the spiritual gifts, particularly the power to awaken consciences, that clerics exercised. People dissatisfied with their ministers turned to other, more powerful preachers, lay revivalists developed followings of their own, itinerants preached uninvited in established churches, and many converts separated from established churches to form new ones with stricter membership requirements. Charles Chauncy, an antirevivalist minister from Boston, condemned such activities as well as the faintings and visions of the subjects as proof of the base origins of the awakening. Other opponents criticized the orthodox doctrines of predestination and original sin. In 1742 Connecticut's General Assembly passed laws against itinerancy and lay exhorting. Separates in both Connecticut and Massachusetts could be fined or put in jail for refusing to pay taxes in support of established ministers.

The Great Awakening led to the temporary emergence of two new denominations, the Strict Separates and the Separate Baptists. By the end of the eighteenth century the Strict Separates had either merged with the Baptists or rejoined the Congregational churches, and the Separate Baptists had merged with the Particular (Calvinist) Baptist churches. Attempts by colonial governments to keep ecclesiastical order resulted in growing sentiment for the separation of church and state. The Great Awakening helped strengthen Anglicanism, as persons disgusted by the revivals or excluded by the renewed requirement of a conversion experience found welcome in the Church of England. The movement also planted the seeds of a new, permanent denomination, Unitarianism, as those who were attracted by Enlightenment ideas and repulsed by the uncompromising Calvinism of the revivals formulated a more congenial creed.

Richard Lyman Bushman, *From Puritan to Yankee: Character and the Social Order in Connecticut, 1690–1765* (1967); Michael J. Crawford, *Seasons of Grace: Colonial New England's Revival Tradition in Its British Context* (1991); Edwin S. Gaustad, *The Great Awakening in New England* (1957); C. C. Goen, *Revivalism and Separatism in New England, 1740–1800: Strict Congregationalists and Separate Baptists in the Great Awakening* (1987 [1962]).

Michael J. Crawford

Haynes, Lemuel

(1753–1833) Minister and writer. Lemuel Haynes was considered one of the more controversial and prolific African American authors before 1845. The son of a black man who was abandoned in Connecticut by his white mother, Haynes matured as an indentured servant in a Massachusetts household. He served briefly as a minuteman and soldier in the War for Independence. After the war, Haynes bartered labor for tutorials in theology, became a Congregational minister in 1785, and accepted a pulpit in rural Rutland, Vt., in 1788. Dismissed by his congregation in 1818, he spent his last 15 years preaching in various pulpits. Reflecting on his dismissal, Haynes was reported to say, "'He lived with the people of Rutland thirty years, and they were so sagacious that at the end of the time they found out that he was a *nigger*, and so turned him away.'" His writings, some of which were uncovered only in the late 20th century, include a 1776 abolitionist essay, addresses on politics, sermons in defense of New England Calvinism, and a small book on two Vermonters mistakenly convicted of murder. He died in New York.

Haynes united some of the prominent threads of 18th-century New England religion, politics, and race relations. In *Liberty Further Extended* (1776), he argued that slavery is immoral because it violates both a natural right to liberty and the sentiments of affection and benevolence that should unite humankind in harmony. Slavery and the slave trade, by contrast, rest on degradation, violence, and destruction of societies, he noted. In his political essays, he argued for "true republicanism," a New Englander's mix of revolutionary rights and small-town order. In theology, he was a Calvinistic New Divinity man, self-professedly a "Hopkintonian," heir of Jonathan Edwards, Joseph Bellamy, and Samuel Hopkins. His last major work, *Mystery Developed* (1820), idealized a New England town in which two men mistakenly convicted of murder (one reprieved shortly before execution) were joyfully reintegrated into the social fabric once their innocence was revealed. Blacks, also wrongly condemned, he suggested, could be joyfully integrated into society once slavery was extirpated.

Politics and theology led Haynes into the Federalist Party as well as to Jonathan Edwards's former pulpit at Yale College, where Haynes preached in 1814. Increasingly offended by Haynes's outmoded views, his congregation dismissed him in 1818, ostensibly because of his vocal opposition to the War of 1812. Many Federalists opposed the war, but for Haynes's congregation his antiwar sentiment was probably the last straw.

The mix of abolitionism and persistent New England traditions in politics and religion made Haynes's career possible and made it polemical. In Europe and most of North America in the late 18th century and early 19th century, abolitionism was a liberal cause, linked to free-will religion, atomistic and individualist views of humankind, and the virtues of the marketplace. As an abolitionist scourge

of liberalism, Haynes was inevitably controversial. He believed that only the cohesive, ordered, protected society idealized in federalism and the New Divinity could provide dignity, equality, and freedom for blacks. He scorned a commercial, individualistic society for its instability and deleterious effects on church and family. Blacks, he believed, should ascend from slavery and oppression into a strong social order.

It is probable that Haynes could have thrived only in rural New England during the revolutionary era. There he found a world where 17th-century traditions in religion coexisted with 18th-century and early-19th-century politics and abolitionism, in relative isolation from the liberal commercialism of the larger Atlantic circuit. In this setting, Haynes produced the strongest critique of slavery of the revolutionary era.

Timothy Mather Cooley, *Sketches of the Life and Character of Rev. Lemuel Haynes* (1837); Richard Newman, ed., *Black Preacher to White America: The Collected Writings of Lemuel Haynes, 1774–1833* (1990); Rita Roberts, "Patriotism and Political Criticism: The Evolution of Political Consciousness in the Mind of a Black Revolutionary Soldier," *18th-Century Studies* 27 (1994); John Saillant, "Lemuel Haynes's Black Republicanism and the American Republican Tradition, 1775–1820," *Journal of the Early Republic* 14 (1994).

John Saillant

Healy, James Augustine (1830–1900)

Roman Catholic bishop. Although he was reared in the rural South and came to maturity during the years of struggle over slavery in the United States, James Healy overcame these obstacles to become the first African American to hold the office of bishop in the American Roman Catholic church. Healy was born in 1830 in a log cabin on a rural plantation in Macon, Ga., where his father, Michael Morris Healy, an Irish immigrant, had settled in 1818. Michael Healy eventually acquired a large estate of more than 1,300 acres in the land lotteries of 1823, and in 1829 he purchased a 16-year-old female slave for his plantation named Mary Elisa, who bore him 10 children, including James and two other boys who later became priests. According to Georgia statute at the time, however, the Healy children were slaves. Michael Healy therefore arranged in 1837 for his children to be placed in a Quaker academy in Flushing, N.Y. More Quaker education followed in New Jersey for Healy, who eventually attended Holy Cross College in Worcester, Mass., along with his brothers.

At Holy Cross the Healy brothers converted to Catholicism. James graduated at the top of his class in 1849, a member of the first group to complete the full academic course at

the college. Following graduation, Healy went on to pursue his religious training at the Sulpician Seminary in Montreal and later at the Sulpician Seminary in Paris, where he again distinguished himself as a brilliant student, and was ordained on June 10, 1854.

Healy took up a post in Boston, where he became noted as a gifted preacher and a priest who worked tirelessly administering the Catholic sacraments among disfranchised immigrants and the urban poor. He was named the first chancellor of the Boston diocese in 1855, handling most of the routine business as a close associate of Bishop John Fitzpatrick. Active in numerous social causes, Healy was also instrumental in establishing the Home for Destitute Catholic Children and the House of the Good Shepherd, a shelter for girls, among many other benevolent institutions.

Healy was named second bishop of Portland, Maine, in 1875. As bishop, Healy was responsible for creating missions and new parishes in remote rural towns where Roman Catholicism was not yet well established. He helped found the Healy Asylum in Lewiston, Maine, as well as Saint Joseph's Academy in Deering (now part of Portland), Saint Elizabeth's Orphan Asylum, the Sacred Heart School for Boys, and a home for elderly women, all in Portland. Healy died in 1900, a well-loved and respected orator, scholar, and priest.

Albert S. Foley, *Bishop Healy: Beloved Outcaste* (1969).

James Emmett Ryan

Herald of Gospel Liberty

Widely recognized as the first religious newspaper in the world, the *Herald of Gospel Liberty* began publication in Portsmouth, N.H., on September 1, 1808. Its founder, Elias Smith (1769–1846), was a lifelong religious seeker who at age 21 rejected the Calvinism of his Connecticut and Vermont Baptist upbringing. Thereafter he vacillated between the Christian Connection (a postrevolutionary movement of popular Christian piety with separate origins in New England, Virginia, and Kentucky) and Universalism, periodically renouncing one to take up the other.

Elias Smith founded the *Herald* primarily to promote his own passionate and iconoclastic views about civil and religious liberty. Like other "come-outers" of his generation who were disaffected with conventional religious practice, Smith believed that liberty was no less essential in the church than in the state. In the pages of the *Herald* he used his considerable intelligence and acerbic pen to condemn all things that in his view contravened liberty, including "hireling ministers," creeds, titles, the various trappings of ecclesiastical privilege, and above all "partyism"—the denominations' competitive emphasis on their own sectarian particularities. But the *Herald* soon became significant in ways Smith himself did not anticipate.

Most obviously, the newspaper propelled the parochial, rural Christian Connection into a national movement. Published weekly, the paper was filled with accounts of local revivals, church plantings, and practical "religious intelligence." Within months of the first edition, supporters of the Christian movement far from New England had begun to correspond regularly with one another in its pages. Itinerant evangelists wrote in to report on their whereabouts and the successes (or failures) of their endeavors; thus the *Herald* swiftly became the connective tissue that bound together one of America's first indigenous religious movements. With the Christian Connection's separate and geographically dispersed centers of activity, the members might eventually have hardened into three distinct and largely unrelated sects without the *Herald's* stabilizing influence. Smith's innovative newspaper also spawned imitation. By midcentury, a handful of regional variants, in locations ranging from upstate New York to Ohio, Kentucky, and the South, were providing news and theological conversation to members of the Christian Connection throughout the country.

Like its theologically peripatetic founder, the *Herald* underwent numerous changes of venue and editorial commitment during more than a century of publication. Elias Smith himself gave up the paper in 1817—having moved its headquarters from Portsmouth to Boston, Portland, Philadelphia, and back again—during one of his periodic flirtations with Universalism. Sold to layman Robert Foster, the *Herald of Gospel Liberty* became the *Christian Herald* and continued to print correspondence and religious news but without the controversial spirit that had characterized it under Smith's editorship. The paper merged finally with the *Congregationalist* when members of the Christian Connection, who were still calling themselves simply "Christians," merged with Congregationalists in 1931. Both Elias Smith and his newspaper are remembered, however, as pioneers in the establishment of a genre of publication that continues to have profound influence in the 21st century.

J. Pressley Barrett, *The Centennial of Religious Journalism* (1908); Milo True Morrill, *A History of the Christian Denomination in America, 1794–1911* (1912).
Elizabeth C. Nordbeck

Huguenots Between the 1680s and the 1740s a small number of Protestant refugees from France—Huguenots—settled in New England. In a region famous for religion, these exiles made their mark through assimilation and economic success rather than persistence as a distinct religious group.

New England's Huguenot settlers represented one small thread of a double exile from France and Europe. In 1685 Louis XIV capped France's decade-long anti-Protestant campaign by revoking the Edict of Nantes, which had guaranteed limited Protestant worship since 1598. More than 150,000 Protestants fled to Protestant areas of modern Germany, the Netherlands, and England in response. Many of these refugees experienced exceptional poverty, and in London, for example, aid committees regularly distributed clothing and blankets and occasionally sent refugees to America to assist both the city and the Huguenot refugee families.

Most of the approximately 2,000 refugee Huguenots who came to Britain's North American mainland colonies between 1680 and 1700 settled in New York and South Carolina. Perhaps 150 Huguenot families settled in New England in agricultural settlements in the Narragansett area of Rhode Island and Oxford, Mass., as well as in Boston. Legal problems at Narragansett and unfulfilled promises at Oxford quickly doomed both settlements. In 1685 the Reverend Ezechiel Carré organized Huguenot refugees in London to purchase land at Narragansett from Rhode Island's Atherton Company. Unknown to Carré, the Atherton land claims had long been disputed, and when the crown voided them in 1688 the Narragansett Huguenots became squatters competing with English settlers to control the property. Meanwhile, Huguenot church elders squabbled with the laity about illicit card playing and baptismal ritual, and then berated the congregation's "ill will and rebellion" in carping about Carré's salary. The disputes persisted, and Carré moved to Boston in 1689; the settlement disbanded in 1691.

Economic problems and Indian disputes doomed the Oxford settlement. Gabriel Bernon, a French Protestant merchant who had been active in Canada, purchased land at Oxford in 1686–87 to settle Huguenot refugees. But only 15 families ever arrived, and Bernon's expansive plans for a grist mill and grape arbors proved unrealistic. In 1691 the Reverend Daniel Bondet reported that Oxford's Huguenots were trading alcohol with nearby Nipmuck Indians, and when Indian resentment led to the murder of the English husband and children of the refugee Susanne Sigourney in 1696, the Oxford Huguenots fled to Boston, never to return.

In Boston, town ministers condemned what Cotton Mather termed "the sore persecution of the Saints in France" in the 1680s, prompted by the scattered arrival of Huguenots from London as well as from Narragansett and Oxford. By 1695 Boston probably held more than 30 Huguenot families, with perhaps 50 or more by 1705. A small refugee church, formed in Boston by the mid-1680s, also managed to survive three short-lived ministries—the irritating Laurent Van Den Bosch (1685–87), who angered Boston officials by covertly marrying English residents using Church of England liturgy; Narragansett's Ezechiel Carré, who left for England in 1691 after two years; and Daniel Bondet, who ministered jointly at Oxford and Boston between 1691 and 1694, then moved to the Huguenot settlement of New Rochelle in New York in 1696 after only two years in Boston. The ministries of the pious Pierre Daillé (1696–1715) and the studious if aloof André le Mercier (1716–48) could have stabilized the Huguenot community in Boston. But economic success, cultural acceptance, and increasing departures to English congregations doomed Boston's tiny French Church, and it closed in 1748.

The Faneuils quickly became Boston's most affluent Huguenots. André Faneuil of Boston and his brother Benjamin of New York built an exceptionally large trading business that courted the new refugee Huguenot merchant communities outside France. When Benjamin Faneuil died in 1719, André Faneuil concentrated their business in Boston. The gift of Faneuil Hall in 1742 by André Faneuil's son Peter symbolized the family's extraordinary wealth in Britain's mid-18th-century mainland colonies.

Other Huguenot refugees also experienced economic success in Boston. The European-trained silversmiths René Grignon and Peter Feurt produced exceptional crafts in early 18th-century Boston, and James Bowdoin, Stephen Boutineau, and Daniel Johonot enjoyed success as merchants and Boston office holders. Paul Revere, on the other hand, had little connection to Boston's Huguenot refugee community. His father, Apollos Rivoire, arrived directly from France about 1715, married a Massachusetts woman, apprenticed with the English silversmith John Coney, and appears to have had no connection to Boston's French Church.

Social and religious assimilation paralleled the Huguenots' economic success. In the 1690s crusty Judge Samuel Sewall carped about the Huguenots' too festive celebration of Christ's birth, "Christmas-day, as they abusively call it." But other Bostonians hardly noticed. Boston's many Congregational, Presbyterian, and Church of England congregations regularly received Huguenots as members, and Huguenots quickly found non-French spouses. Between 1700 and 1720 Boston's English ministers performed four-fifths of all marriages involving Huguenots, most of whom married non-Huguenots, and even half of the few Huguenots the Reverend Pierre Daillé married took English spouses.

By the 1740s Boston's French Church had become an empty shell, its minister's salary paid as a charity by Huguenots who had joined other congregations and most often married outside the Huguenot community. When the congregation disbanded in 1748, le Mercier demurred that young Huguenots were "altogether Educated in the English Tongue [and] frequent and belong to the English Churches," while the elders retorted that le Mercier had "driven all our Young People to other Churches." Their quarrel obscured a larger point: that the Huguenots' experience in Boston demonstrated their remarkable assimilation in a town and region not well known for their prediction of a more open, modern America.

Charles Washington Baird, *History of the Huguenot Emigration to America* (1885); J. F. Bosher, "Huguenot Merchants and the Protestant International in the Seventeenth Century," *William and Mary Quarterly,* 3d ser., 52 (1995): 77–103; Jon Butler, "The Huguenots and the American Immigrant Experience," in *Memory and Identity: The Huguenots in France and the Atlantic Diaspora,* ed. Bertrand van Ruymbeke (2003); Butler, *The Huguenots in America: A Refugee People in New World Society* (1983); Paula Wheeler Carlo, "The Huguenots of Colonial New Paltz and New Rochelle: A Social and Religious History" (Ph.D. diss., 2001); Arthur Henry Hirsch, *The Huguenots of Colonial South Carolina* (1928); Andrew le Mercier, *The Church History of Geneva* (1732).

Jon Butler

Hutchinson, Anne (1591–1643) Religious dissenter.

Anne Hutchinson was born Anne Marbury in Alford, England, the daughter of the Reverend Francis Marbury and his wife, Bridget Dryden. In 1612 she married William Hutchinson, a prosperous farmer and wool merchant, with whom she had 15 children. During her years in Alford, Hutchinson was influenced by the preaching of John Cotton, a brilliant Puritan theologian. In 1634, Hutchinson, her husband, and their 11 surviving children followed Cotton to Boston in the Massachusetts Bay Colony, seeking religious freedom. Hutchinson's midwifery and nursing skills quickly established her as a valued and respected member of the community, but her outspoken theological criticisms of the fledgling colony's most prominent religious leaders soon got her into trouble. Her brother-in-law the Reverend John Wheelwright joined her in this criticism of colonial civil and ecclesiastical authorities. Within a short time, Hutchinson had a strong following, and when religious dissension erupted into serious fac-

The statue of Anne Hutchinson by Cyrus Dallin (1922) stands outside the State House, Boston

tional strife, spurred in particular by the Cambridge minister Thomas Shepard, the civil and religious authorities took measures to bring the Hutchinsonians under control. In a civil trial in November 1637, Hutchinson and many of her followers were banished from the colony. She spent the winter of 1637–38 under house arrest and, after a religious trial in the spring of 1638, was excommunicated from the church. She left immediately for Rhode Island, accompanied by her husband and several other family members. In 1642, she moved with six of her children to a Dutch settlement on Long Island where she and all but one daughter were murdered by Native Americans in August 1643.

Although the Antinomian Controversy, as it came to be called, had many dimensions, Hutchinson's original complaint—which she believed she shared with her mentor, John Cotton—was that many of the ministers were teaching a "covenant of works," or that obedience to God's laws could be taken as evidence that a person was saved. Hutchinson held that only the experience of Christ's saving grace (the "covenant of grace") could give a sinner the assurance that he or she was "justified," or saved from eternal damnation. Believing that any hypocrite could mimic righteous actions, Hutchinson did not see an inevitable connection between good behavior and salvation. Furthermore, whereas the ministers taught that assurance of salvation was a lifelong struggle, Hutchinson believed that once people had experienced Christ's grace they never again had to doubt that they were among the saved.

The crisis precipitated by the Antinomian Controversy had a profound effect on the development of religious ideas in New England, as ministers moved away from Calvin's harsh predestinarianism, as propounded by the Hutchinson faction, to a theology that emphasized the efficacy of human action in the process of salvation. Additionally, Hutchinson's belief that an individual's assurance of Christ's saving grace did not require the mediation of a minister was to be reflected in the growing influence of Quaker beliefs later in the century. (Mary Dyer, who left the church when Hutchinson was excommunicated, was also banished from the colony in 1637; she later returned as a Quaker and was hanged for her beliefs on the Boston Common in 1659.) John Winthrop, Hutchinson's most powerful adversary and governor of the Massachusetts Bay Colony during her civil and ecclesiastical trials, wrote an account of the controversy, *A Short Story,* in which he condemned Hutchinson's theological views.

Emory Battis, *Saints and Sectaries: Anne Hutchinson and the Antinomian Controversy in the Massachusetts Bay Colony* (1692); Jean Cameron, *Anne Hutchinson, Guilty or Not?: A Closer Look at Her Trials* (1994); David D. Hall, ed., *The Antinomian Controversy, 1636–1638: A Documentary History,* 2d ed. (1990); Janice Knight, *Orthodoxies in Massachusetts: Rereading American Puritanism* (1994); Amy Schrager Lang, *Prophetic Woman: Anne Hutchinson and the Problem of Dissent in the Literature of New England* (1987); Michael P. Winship, *Making Heretics: Protestantism and Free Grace in Massachusetts* (2002).

Darcy Sweeney

Islam

National survey estimates suggest a population of nearly 80,000 Muslims in New England, making up at least 1 percent of total religious adherents in Massachusetts and Connecticut. More than 70 mosques, at least nine Islamic schools, 18 Muslim student associations, and seven regional Muslim organizations attest to New England's active Islamic community from diverse ethnic backgrounds. Islam is a rapidly growing feature of the urban, suburban, and academic landscape in New England.

Muslims in the United States trace their roots along two general lines. The African American "indigenous" Islamic tradition reclaims the suppressed Islamic identity of African ancestors brought to this country as slaves. Sectarian movements like the Nation of Islam, founded by Elijah Muhammad in the 1930s, "rediscovered" elements of this Islamic heritage. Malcolm X and Louis Farrakhan both served Temple 11 in Dorchester, Mass., and the Nation formed an important part of urban communities in New England. After Elijah Muhammad died in 1975, his son Warith Deen Muhammad led the majority of his followers away from the founder's separatism toward unity with traditional Sunni Muslims. Many congregations embraced a Sunni identity while maintaining a network of African American Muslims with a shared history.

The second line is the "immigrant" Islamic tradition. Muslim immigrants came from Syria and Lebanon in the late 19th century, settling in New England cities. Early groups formed cultural and social organizations. In the 1960s, however, when the region experienced a great influx of students and educated professionals from Muslim countries in Asia, the Middle East, and Africa, overtly Islamic institutions began to form. The Harvard Islamic Society was inaugurated in 1958, and today most universities have a Muslim student association. Students joined with older immigrant groups to provide Islamic education for the second generation. Education was the primary impulse for founding dozens of Islamic centers, mosques, and charitable organizations in New England in the 1970s and 1980s. Though Sunni (followers of the Qur'an and traditions of Muhammad) and Shi'i Muslims (who follow supplementary traditions of charismatic descendants of Muhammad) often worship together, small Shi'i centers have developed, and at least three Sufi orders (mystical fraternities who follow the teachings of a spiritual master) operate in the region.

A growing number of Anglo and Hispanic converts participate in New England's Islamic centers. It was a New England convert, Mohammed Russell Alexander Webb, who addressed Chicago's 1893 World's Parliament of Religions regarding Islam. On feast days the Islamic communities display their multicultural tapestry in large shared celebrations in Bridgeport and Hartford, Conn.; Providence, R.I.; and Boston, Worcester, and Springfield, Mass.

Regional networks developed in the 1980s. Since 1984 the Islamic Council of New England has sponsored conferences and interfaith events, youth programs, camps, and sports leagues, and developed resources for Islamic schools. Councils of imams decide matters of Islamic law for various mosque associations. The New England Muslim Sisters Association organizes women's conferences and provides information on Islam and Islamic rights for women for local groups. The Tablighi Jamaat, a movement that propagates Islam, maintains a network throughout New England. These and other organizations bridge cultural gaps between Muslims and represent diverse Muslim interests to fellow New Englanders.

Since the 2001 terrorist attacks on New York and Washington, government scrutiny and hate crimes against Muslims have risen, but so have conversions to Islam and attendance at Islamic schools, mosques, and public events, necessitating new building programs and expansion of services. While some have withdrawn from public view, many centers now organize educational events for non-Muslims and have developed grassroots interfaith alliances with Jewish and Christian neighbors. The influx of Muslim refugees from Somalia and Bosnia has exposed both prejudice and support for Muslims and religious diversity in places like Holyoke, Mass., and Lewiston and Portland, Maine, while a Muslim graduation speech at Harvard touched off a national debate.

Diana Eck, *On Common Ground: World Religions in America* [CD-ROM] (1997); Yvonne Yazbeck Haddad, ed., *The Muslims of America* (1991); Yvonne Yazbeck Haddad and Jane Idleman Smith, *Muslim Communities in North America* (1994); C. Eric Lincoln, *The Black Muslims in America* (1994).

Lance D. Laird

Judaism The approximately 300,000 Jews of New England represent, in the patterns of their religious life, a microcosm of Jewish religious life nationally. Jews first settled in Newport, R.I., in 1658; Newport's Touro Synagogue is the oldest extant synagogue in North America. Following the national pattern, during the 1950s and 1960s substantial growth and development of synagogues took place, principally in urban centers and their suburban peripheries. Major synagogue centers were built primarily by Conservative and Reform congregations, which represent at least 85 percent of Jews affiliated with synagogues. Most others are affiliated with Orthodox congregations. A small number belong to the recently established Reconstructionist movement, a humanist religious movement established in the 1930s by the American rabbi and theologian Mordecai M. Kaplan.

In addition to Boston, which boasts the highest concentration of Jews and the largest number of synagogues in New England, other major Jewish centers include Providence; Hartford, New Haven, Bridgeport, and Stamford, Conn.; Worcester, Mass.; Portland, Maine; and Manchester, N.H. Synagogues and synagogue centers exist and flourish in several smaller cities in New England, and associations of Jews to further Jewish education, religion, and spirituality have been formed in rural New England, specifically Maine, Vermont, and New Hampshire.

For Jews, religious behavior is closely associated with broader issues of Jewish identity. Though Jews are best understood as a "people" (that is, members of a group that defies the usual sociodemographic classifications of nationality, ethnic group, religion, and cultural group), in New England as elsewhere religious affiliation is crucial to Jewish identity. Because religion is the starting point and core of all Jewish identity, and because the synagogue is the principal instrument of Jewish affiliation and engagement, the development of major synagogue centers represents both a religious and a sociodemographic phenomenon, involving the establishment of diverse Jewish communities around synagogue centers that were nominally religious institutions but in reality were as much communal as religious in their functions.

The dominant characteristic of Jewish religious life in New England is its diversity. Synagogues cover the entire range of denominational and ideological groups in Jewish life, and practices vary substantially within these groups. In the Reform community, a number of "classical" Reform congregations still function. Services are generally formal, although much of the liturgy is read in English rather than Hebrew, and the atmosphere may be described as "high church." More recently, a more informal but also more traditional style of worship has entered many Reform congregations. Increasing portions of the liturgy are read in Hebrew, and a higher level of congregational participation coincides with a greater degree of informality.

In the Conservative movement, a similar process has taken place. Shaped to a considerable degree by the experience of participants in Jewish summer camps, many of them sponsored by the National Camp Ramah Commission (the national camping movement of the Conservative movement), informal, participatory *havurot* (egalitarian fellowships) have developed. The prayer groups tend to function without professional clergy; they are traditional in usage and ritual but highly egalitarian, departing from Orthodox patterns of separate seating for men and women in the synagogue and clear differentiation of roles with minimum participation by women in synagogue rituals.

The greatest diversity in style and practice exists in the smallest of the denominational groups: Orthodox Jews. Most New England cities with substantial Jewish populations have at least one modern Orthodox congregation whose members are generally observant of Jewish practice but participate fully in the life of the larger community. Other Orthodox groups, including Hasidic groups clustered around such figures as the Bostoner Rebbe in Brookline, adopt a more separatist way of life, participating less extensively in the larger

Lighting the Hanukkah menorah, Temple Israel, Brookline, Mass., 1989

community. A remarkable figure of New England Jewry combined in a single personality two dimensions of New England: Rabbi Isadore Twersky (1930–97) headed a Hasidic dynasty as the Tallner Rebbe and served as professor of Jewish studies at Harvard University, leading its Center for Jewish Studies for many years. Rabbi Ira Korff, heir of several generations of Zhviller Hasidim, is owner and publisher of New England's largest Jewish newspaper, Boston's *Jewish Advocate*, and is an attorney and businessman. The Lubavitcher Hasidic movement, the most prominent Orthodox movement in outreach efforts to the larger Jewish community, is active in Boston and on several college campuses in New England.

As a center of academic life generally, New England is a major arena for Jewish student life. Hillel foundations, the central address for Jewish religious and cultural life on campus, are active at most colleges and universities. Notable among them are the Hillel at Harvard—housed in a building designed by internationally renowned architect Moshe Safdie—and those at Yale, Tufts, Boston University, Brown, and Dartmouth. Among campuses where Jewish religious life flourishes, special mention should be made of Brandeis University, in Waltham, Mass., founded by the Jewish community in 1948. Brandeis is a nonsectarian university with special interests in Jewish life and Jewish studies. Its department of Near Eastern and Jewish Studies has served as a major center of Jewish scholarship since its founding and its Hornstein Program trains students for a variety of professional and educational positions in the Jewish community. Hebrew College, established in Brookline, Mass., in 1922, is another center of Jewish scholarship and research, academic and community teaching, and professional training. In the fall of 2001, Hebrew College moved from Brookline to a new location contiguous to the Andover Newton Theological School campus in Newton Centre, Mass. The two schools have implemented a range of cooperative programs and activities.

Secondary-level Jewish religious education is provided in both supplemental programs to general high schools and in a number of parochial schools in several cities. Notable among these are the Maimonides School in Brookline, an elite elementary and high school under Orthodox auspices, and Hebrew College's Prozdor, a supplementary high school. The New Jewish High School of Greater Boston, a non-Orthodox parochial high school in Waltham, accepted its first students in the fall of 1997.

A recent development in religious education is the proliferation of Jewish day schools on the primary school level. Once exclusively under Orthodox auspices, many Solomon Schechter Day Schools of the Conservative movement have opened in recent years throughout the United States and New England, and a number of day schools under Reform auspices have now been established and are flourishing. Nonformal Jewish religious and cultural education take place in a network of Jewish summer camps, including the Cohen Foundation Camps in Pembroke, Mass., Hampstead, N.H., and Brookline, N.H.; Camp Ramah in Needham Heights, Mass.; and Camp Yavneh in West Nottingham, N.H., organized under Hebrew College's auspices. Youth activities are conducted under the auspices of the three major national denominational groups: National Conference of Synagogue Youth (Orthodox), United Synagogue Youth (Conservative), and National Federation of Temple Youth (Reform).

In addition to synagogues and campus-based Jewish programs, central institutions provide forums for professional groups and services for those in need of religious supervision of various kinds. These include the interdenominational Synagogue Council of Massachusetts, boards of rabbis in Massachusetts and other states, bureaus of Jewish education in Boston, New Haven, Hartford, Providence, and several smaller cities, entities to provide supervision of meats and other foods for compliance with the Jewish dietary laws, educational programs for potential converts to Judaism, and traditional Jewish law courts to handle matters of divorce and conversion.

Concern for the future vitality of Jewish life, popularly known as the "Jewish continuity" agenda, has created new alliances between the religious components of the Jewish community and the more secularly oriented "organized" Jewish community embodied in Jewish federations. Once preoccupied with issues of political action, support for Israel, and opposition to anti-Semitism, Jewish federations have now become major players in efforts to stem the inroads of intermarriage into the life of the Jewish community and to enhance and strengthen the programs of synagogues and religious educational enterprises. In Boston, under the leadership of a dynamic president, the Combined Jewish Philanthropies in collaboration with the synagogue movements and other institutions has established the Commission on Jewish Continuity to nurture initiatives in Jewish family education, universal Jewish literacy for adults, and programs for teens. Boston's federation, the oldest in the country, celebrated its centennial in 1996. Its efforts are emulated by those of other cities in New England and throughout the country. Federations throughout New England have attempted to expand the resources available for religious schools and to fund traditional and innovative programs providing access to

Jewish learning and participation to groups of all ages.

Two parallel trends characterize the religious condition of New England Jewry for the new millennium: on one hand, the community seeks to stem the assimilation of Jews into the larger society now that they have been accepted into social and professional circles once closed to them. This may be viewed as a defensive stand. On the other hand, there is a widespread sense of religious and spiritual awakening and searching on the part of a small but significant and growing number of Jews, especially young adults. Religious, educational, cultural, and communal organizations have been attempting to respond creatively and imaginatively to this movement. The impact and direction of these trends will emerge only through historical perspective several decades into the new century.

Arthur Hertzberg, *The Jews in America: Four Centuries of an Uneasy Encounter* (1997); Howard Morley Sachar, *The Course of Modern Jewish History* (1990); Sachar, *A History of the Jews in America* (1992); Ruth R. Seldin and David Singer, eds., *The American Jewish Yearbook* (1998); Jack Wertheimer, *A People Divided: Judaism in Contemporary America* (1997); Jonathan S. Woocher, *Sacred Survival: The Civil Religion of American Jews* (1986).

David Gordis

Missionary Activities Missionaries have been part of New England's religious life since the arrival of Europeans in the 16th century. The obligation to bring Christianity to the region's inhabitants was entangled with other motives in the commissions, charters, publications, and actions of French and English explorers, entrepreneurs, and colonists. A famous Massachusetts Bay Colony emblem crowned the image of a Native American with the biblical plea, "Come over and help us."

Although Puritan missions—many of them supported by the London-based Society for the Propagation of the Gospel—were in fact limited and produced minimal results, early missionaries have inspired three centuries of imitation, admiration, and condemnation. In the 17th century the Mayhew family proslytized on Martha's Vineyard and Richard Bourne labored in Mashpee, Mass. John Eliot translated the Bible into Massachusett and was the motive force in the establishment of 14 towns for "praying Indians" throughout the colony. In Rhode Island, Roger Williams studied native languages and criticized the land-grabbing of European settlers. John Sargent and Jonathan Edwards in Stockbridge, Mass., followed in the 18th century, as did Eleazar Wheelock, who founded a New Hampshire Indian missionary school, which

later became Dartmouth College. Wheelock's protégé, the Mohegan Samson Occom, was an important missionary who broke with Wheelock over Dartmouth's failure to serve Native American youth.

The most enduring Christian legacy from New England's colonial-era missions, however, has been the Catholicism of Maine's Abenaki. This was the outgrowth of a persistent missionary presence that began in 1611. Sébastien Râle is the best known of the Jesuits whose dedication and respect for native culture nurtured in the Abenaki a commitment to the church that survived his death in 1724 at the hands of Massachusetts militiamen; the triumph of the English over the French; American independence from England; and centuries of Protestant missionary efforts.

The Protestant foreign-mission movement in the United States was born in New England in the early 19th century, a product of the same evangelical activism that produced a host of voluntary societies promoting education, home missions, and a variety of social and moral reforms. The missionary vows of a group of young men at Williams College led to the creation of the American Board of Commissioners for Foreign Missions in 1810. Supported by Congregationalist, Presbyterian, and Reformed churches, the board had its offices in Boston until the mid-20th century. Its most successful and controversial mission was the one to Hawaii, begun in 1820 and described in James Michener's popular novel *Hawaii* (1959; made into a motion picture in 1966). In 1993 the United Church of Christ, denominational descendant of Congregationalism and inheritor of the American Board, formally apologized to Hawaiians for the involvement of the descendants of New England missionaries in the forcible annexation of the islands by the United States in the 1890s.

Meanwhile, Boston also became the home of the Baptist mission board, formed after three of the first American Board missionaries, including the famous Adoniram and Ann Judson, became Baptists while on their way to India. Even the Unitarians of New England caught the spirit; the American Unitarian Association supported Charles H. A. Dall's liberal Christian mission in Calcutta from 1855 to 1886. During and after the Civil War, educational missionary activities were common among communities of freed slaves, such as those in Port-Royal on the Sea Islands of South Carolina, chronicled in the journals of educator and abolitionist Charlotte Forten Grimké.

The influential Student Volunteer Movement for Foreign Missions grew out of confer-

ences held by the revivalist Dwight L. Moody in Mount Hermon (near Northfield), Mass., in the summer of 1886. Among the college students recruited for foreign missions were several who became prominent ecumenical leaders, including John R. Mott, Robert P. Wilder, G. Sherwood Eddy, and Robert E. Speer. When conservative Protestants developed their own educational system in a network of bible colleges and missionary training institutes, prominent among them were the Boston Missionary Training School (founded 1889, now Gordon College in Wenham, Mass.) and the Boston Bible School (founded 1897, now Berkshire Christian College in Lenox, Mass.).

Traditional Protestantism's heritage of reaching out from New England has been counterbalanced since the end of the 19th century by the missionary activity of other religious traditions. Among the most visible and controversial groups has been the Rev. Sun Myung Moon's Unification Church, which attracted attention in the late 1970s when it purchased a fishing fleet in Gloucester, Mass., and again in the early 1990s when the church-supported Professors World Peace Academy invested heavily in the financially ailing University of Bridgeport in Connecticut.

John A. Andrew III, *Rebuilding the Christian Commonwealth: New England Congregationalists and Foreign Missions, 1800–1830* (1976); Virginia Lieson Brereton, *Training God's Army: The American Bible School, 1880–1940* (1990); Richard W. Cogley, *John Eliot's Mission to the Indians before King Philip's War* (1999); William R. Hutchison, *Errand to the World: American Protestant Thought and Foreign Missions* (1987); Jean M. O'Brien, *Dispossession by Degrees: Indian Land and Identity in Natick, Massachusetts, 1650–1790* (1997); George E. Tinker, *Missionary Conquest: The Gospel and Native American Cultural Genocide* (1993).

Robert A. Schneider

Moravians The Moravian Church was one of the most dynamic and controversial bodies within the transatlantic pietist movement—a renewal movement that began within German Lutheranism and stressed religious experience and social improvement—of the 18th century. Though the church originated during the Hussite movement in 15th-century Bohemia and Moravia, it was transformed into a German pietist community by Nikolaus Ludwig von Zinzendorf in the 1720s and 1730s. Zinzendorf promoted a nonrational approach to Christianity that influenced Friedrich Schleiermacher, but his views often met with strong opposition in the 18th century. Moravian refugees founded a village named Herrnhut on Zinzendorf's estate in Saxony in 1722, and five years later the residents signed a "Brotherly Agreement" that established Herrnhut as a religious community with a planned economy and unique social structure. Doctrinal disputes, concerning such issues as predestination and the nature of the Eucharist, were intentionally put aside in favor of intense devotion to Christ and love for one another. These became the main themes of Moravian preaching and hymnody and formed the basis of the Moravian mission effort that took them to five continents before 1760.

The Moravians were attracted to British North America for several reasons. They hoped to work among the native peoples, organize an ecumenical church, evangelize among the German immigrants, establish communal Christian societies, and provide a place of refuge if they were expelled from Germany. They first tried to build a settlement in Savannah, Ga., but the only lasting result of that venture was the conversion of John Wesley. In 1741 they established a permanent base of operations at Bethlehem, Pa., north of Philadelphia. The first large group of colonists for Bethlehem, known as the First Sea Congregation, landed in New Haven, Conn., in the spring of 1742.

The earliest Moravian work in Connecticut was connected to their mission to the Indians. Missionaries Christian Henry Rauch and John Martin Mack established a base at Shekomeko, N.Y., just south of the Connecticut border, in 1739, from which they ministered to the Indians of Connecticut. Count Zinzendorf visited this village in 1742, and for years it was the site for Moravian regional conferences. Other mission stations included Sichem and Patchgatgoch on the modern-day Scaticoke Reservation near Kent, Conn. The last missionaries to the Indians in New England, though, were withdrawn in 1770 since the native peoples had been forced to relocate to the West. Some of the Moravian converts from New England tribes eventually wound up in Fairfield, Canada, following the massacre of the Moravian community at Gnaddenhutten, Ohio.

The Moravians pioneered culturally sensitive missions that attempted to preserve the language, economy, and mores of native cultures while introducing individuals to the idea of the redemptive blood and wounds of Jesus. They also described the Holy Spirit as the divine mother who is always present with those who love Christ. Unlike many Christian missionaries, the Moravians assumed that Indians were as moral, religious, and intelligent as other people but like all people needed to experience salvation through Christ. It was reported that the Moravian missionaries were sometimes mistaken for Native Americans

when traveling. Accounts written by Moravian missionaries were a strong influence on James Fennimore Cooper's *Leatherstocking Tales*.

Though there was some Moravian work among the European immigrants during New England's Great Awakening of the 1730s, the first systematic effort in New England was led by Georg Soelle, who was sent from Pennsylvania to be an itinerant preacher in 1758. Soelle had been ordained into the Danish Lutheran Church in 1741, but united with the Moravians in 1748; he arrived in America in 1753. According to his commission, he was to be "like a peddler who always keeps on traveling. . . . It may be that there is some one, now here, now there, who longs for peace in his heart and who will be for him a welcome messenger." Soelle's travels included Boston, Litchfield, Conn.; Broad Bay (now Waldoboro), Maine; Newport, R.I.; Shekomeko; and Philadelphia.

Soelle's most effective work was among a community of German immigrants who had settled in Broad Bay. He found the people were very poor and not well accepted by the English population, but he managed to establish a vibrant Moravian congregation. His efforts to introduce Moravian piety and discipline in the region, though, led to violent opposition from the local Lutheran minister, Martin Schäffer, who arranged for a band of armed men to jail Soelle in 1763. The authorities released him the next day, but the incident did little to endear the Moravians to New England. By 1770 most of the Broad Bay community gave up trying to farm the poor soil and immigrated to the Moravian colony of Wachovia in North Carolina.

The most successful New England Moravian congregation was in New London, Conn., which was usually served by Moravian pastors from England. Jacob Rogers, a deacon in the Anglican Church, arrived in 1758, and often preached in the local Anglican Church building. Until the Moravian chapel was built in 1767, services were held in "a room where there is a bed and perhaps some disorderly people" or at a fisherman's house in a room with "tubs, lobster pots, kettles, bedstead." In 1767 the congregation numbered about 75 men, women, and children with 13 communicants. As with the Broad Bay congregation, they were mainly laborers, carpenters, joiners, smiths, tailors, and sailors. Ezra Stiles, the future president of Yale College, was friends with the pastor, Albert Ludolph Ruszmeyer, in the 1770s and regularly attended Christmas and Easter services. The last Moravian congregation in New England was established in Newport, R.I., and survived until the mid-19th century.

Craig D. Atwood, *Community of the Cross: Moravian Piety in Colonial Bethlehem* (2004); J. Taylor Hamilton and Kenneth G. Hamilton, *History of the Moravian Church: The Renewed Unitas Fratrum, 1722–1957* (1967); Helmut T. Lehmann, "Moravian Missionaries in Colonial New England," *Transactions of the Moravian Historical Society* 25 (1988); A. W. Wallace, ed., *The Travels of John Heckewelder in Frontier America* (1985); C. A. Weslager, *The Delaware Indians: A History* (1972); Karl W. Westmeier, "Out of a Distant Past: A Challenge for Modern Missions from a Diary of Colonial New York (Shekomeko, 1744)," *Transactions of the Moravian Historical Society* 27 (1992); Rachel Wheeler, "Women and Christian Practice in a Mahican Village," *Religion and American Culture* 13 (2003).

Craig D. Atwood

Mormonism Joseph Smith, the founder of the Church of Jesus Christ of Latter-day Saints, was born in Sharon, Vt., in 1805, a descendant on both sides of New England families. Smith's first American ancestor, Robert Smith, arrived in Massachusetts in 1638 and eventually settled in Topsfield, Mass., 8 miles north of Salem, where the Smiths had achieved success as one of the town's notable families. The family remained in New England until 1816, when they moved to Palmyra, N.Y. Smith is noted for his authorship—or "translation," as he termed it—of the Book of Mormon from gold plates discovered in a hill near his home in Manchester, N.Y. The preeminent visionary in an age of visionary religions, Smith was regarded by his followers as a prophet in the tradition of the Old Testament. They considered his works—the Book of Mormon (a religious history of Israelites in ancient America) and his collected revelations, known as the Doctrine and Covenants—Holy Scripture. Smith's works instructed believers to gather into a "City of Zion," build a temple, and prepare for the coming of Christ. In addition, they restored priesthood on an Old Testament model and reinstituted plural marriage. One of the more controversial Morman tenets, plural marriage was abandoned in 1890, but Mormons still believe in continuing revelation and emphasize close community cooperation. After visiting Utah, where the Mormons eventually settled, Ralph Waldo Emerson described Mormonism as an "afterclap" of Puritanism.

In search of the City of Zion, the Latter-day Saints moved westward, away from New England, but the church remained connected to New England through Joseph Smith, Brigham Young, and other early leaders who were born in the region, as well as through thousands of New England converts. Young was born in 1801 in Whitingham, Vt., where his father had moved from Hopkinton, Mass.

Young's ancestors on both his mother's and his father's sides—Treadways, Howes, and Goddards as well as Youngs—had lived in Hopkinton for generations, and his father, John, had farmed and done millwork in the town before the move to Vermont. John Young left his rocky Whitingham farm in 1804 for central New York, moving many times in search of work and better land. Brigham and other Young family members learned of Mormonism soon after the church was organized in 1830 and were baptized in 1832.

Other prominent early Mormons, including Wilford Woodruff, later a church president, and Heber C. Kimball, a counselor to President Brigham Young, came from New England. The New England connection continued even after the westward move as Mormon missionaries returned to their former towns to recruit new members; in addition, meetings were held in Boston and other New England cities in the 1840s. Young and many of the church's 12 Apostles were proselytizing in New England when news of Joseph Smith's murder reached them in July 1844. Through the missionaries' efforts, a steady stream of New England converts flowed into Mormonism, though the number of Mormons in the region increased very little. The missionaries instructed converts to "gather" to Mormon centers in Ohio, Missouri, Illinois, and eventually Utah, draining off new members as fast as they joined. In 1842 more than half the adults in the Mormon settlement at Nauvoo, Ill., were New Englanders.

Until the 20th century, Mormonism left few traces on the New England landscape. At the turn of that century, as part of an effort to recover its history, the church purchased the farm where Joseph Smith was born and in 1905 erected a monument to commemorate his birth. Subsequently, an information center and chapel were constructed, and tourists are now invited to visit the farm. Proselytizing in New England came under the supervision of the Eastern States Mission, headquartered in New York City until 1937, when a New England Mission was established in Cambridge, Mass.

After World War II, the eastward migration of Mormons for school and work brought Latter-day Saints back to the region, and their numbers increased. Experienced families from the Mormon heartland in the West stabilized little congregations meeting in rented halls and schools. The first Mormon chapel built by the church was constructed in West Hartford, Conn., in 1952, and in 1959 a chapel building was finished on Brattle Street in Cambridge. Mormon chapels have multiplied ever since. The first stake (roughly equivalent to a diocese) was organized in Cambridge in 1962, a sign of the maturing church organization. By 1977 at least one stake existed in every New England state. As of 2004 New England was home to approximately 56,000 Mormons. A temple, the structure used by Latter-day Saints for marriages and other ordinances, was constructed in Belmont, Mass., in 2000.

Richard L. Anderson, *Joseph Smith's New England Heritage* (1971); Richard Lyman Bushman, *Joseph Smith and the Beginnings of Mormonism* (1984); David Brion Davis, "The New England Origins of Mormonism," *New England Quarterly* 27 (June 1953); Richard Neitzel Holzapfel and T. Jeffrey Cottle, *Old Mormon Palmyra and New England: Historic Photographs and Guide* (1991).

Richard Lyman Bushman

Occom, Samson

Occom, Samson (1723–92) Presbyterian minister, Native American leader, author, missionary. During an era of rapid decline for many New England Indian communities, the Mohegan Samson Occom developed an indigenous brand of Christianity which promoted American Indian political independence and spiritual vitality.

Born to a traditional Mohegan family near what is now Uncasville, Conn., Occom converted to Christianity during the Great Awakening. At the age of 20 he sought out the Reverend Eleazar Wheelock of Lebanon Crank, Conn., who gave him training in Scripture and ancient languages. Occom moved to Long Island in 1749 to serve the Montauk as a schoolteacher and minister. He married Mary Fowler, a Montauk, in 1751; the couple had 10 children.

After his ordination by the Long Island Presbytery in 1756, Occom traveled extensively throughout the Northeast, especially among the nations of the Iroquois Confederacy. From 1765 to 1768, he traveled throughout England as a fundraising emissary for Wheelock's Moor's Indian Charity School (now Dartmouth College), delivering sermons and visiting nobles and religious figures, including the celebrated preacher George Whitefield. Occom raised more than £13,000 for the school. Upon his return from England, however, he cut ties with Wheelock when he discovered that his former teacher planned to relocate the school to Hanover, N.H., and phase out enrollments of American Indians in favor of whites.

Occom was the first Native American to write and publish in English. In 1771 he delivered an execution sermon at the invitation of Moses Paul, a fellow Mohegan and an accused murderer. *A Sermon at the Execution of Moses Paul*, published in 1772, generated significant attention for its appeal to Native Americans to reject the evils—including alcohol and violence—introduced to tribal communities by Anglo-American colonialism. The sermon was republished more than 20 times. Occom responded to a strong culture of hymn-singing among revivalist New England "New Light" Congregationalists and Christian Indians by compiling and publishing one of the first interdenominational American hymnals, *A Collection of Hymns and Sacred Songs* (1774), which featured his own original hymn-texts. His manuscript archive of letters, sermons, petitions, autobiographies, ethnographies, hymns, and journals constitutes the largest extant single-author body of early American Indian literature.

Frustrated by continuing colonial incursions into New England Indian lands and outsiders' attempts to control Indian governments and churches, Occom founded an intertribal movement away from New England in 1774. Occom, his son-in-law Joseph Johnson (a Mohegan), and several other Native American missionaries and tribal leaders gathered Christian members of seven southern New England and Long Island groups—Mohegan, Pequot, Narragansett, Montauk, Niantic, Farmington, and Stockbridge—to establish Brotherton, an intertribal settlement on Iroquois lands in upstate New York. Delayed by the American War of Independence, Occom did not move to Brotherton until 1785; he lived the rest of his life there as one of the community's political and religious elders.

Harold Blodgett, *Samson Occom* (1935); William DeLoss Love, *Samson Occom and the Christian Indians of New England* (2000 [1899]); Bernd Peyer, *The Tutor'd Mind: Indian Missionary Writers in Antebellum America* (1997); Hilary Wyss, *Writing Indians: Literacy, Christianity, and Native Community in Early America* (2000).

Joanna Brooks

Osborn, Sarah

Osborn, Sarah (1714–96) Religious leader. Sarah Osborn was a well-known 18th-century evangelist and schoolteacher in Newport, R.I. Born Sarah Haggar in London, she was reared as a dissenter, heir to the 17th-century British Puritans who had wanted to purify the Church of England. In 1723 she moved to Boston with her family, and in 1729 they settled in Newport, where she lived for the rest of her life.

As Osborn recorded in her memoir, which she wrote at the age of 30, she had a tumultuous childhood and adolescence. She had a difficult relationship with her parents, who were strict, and soon after arriving in Newport, she contemplated suicide. In 1731 when she was only 17, she married Samuel Wheaten, a sailor, against her parent's wishes. Her son

Samuel was born a year later. When her husband died at sea in 1733, Sarah became a teacher to support herself and her son.

She then married Henry Osborn, a tailor, in 1742, perhaps hoping to find greater financial security, but soon after their marriage, Henry suffered either a physical or psychological breakdown that left him unable to work. They had to sell all their possessions to pay their debts, and Sarah became responsible for supporting Henry and his three sons. In 1744, Samuel, Sarah's only child, died of an illness. Sarah herself suffered from a recurring illness.

Osborn turned to evangelism during the Great Awakening of the 1730s and 1740s, inspired by the preaching of the ministers George Whitefield, Gilbert Tennent, and Eleazar Wheelock, and for the rest of her life she devoted herself to spreading the gospel. As early as 1741 she had begun holding prayer meetings for women, and during the 1760s others began flock to her house as well. Between 1765 and 1767, their numbers increased so rapidly that she began holding separate meetings every night of the week for young men, young women, African Americans of both sexes, adult white men, and adult white women. At the height of the revival, as many as 525 people would crowd into her house each week. Newport was a major slavetrading port, and Osborn's prayer meetings with slaves were controversial, but she insisted that she was obeying God's call in ministering to all.

Osborn was a prolific writer as well as a charismatic evangelist. Besides publishing an anonymous tract, *The Nature, Certainty, and Evidence of True Christianity* (1755), she wrote hundreds of letters, more than 25 volumes of diaries, and a memoir. Although she spent her last 20 years confined to her house, unable to walk and nearly blind, she remained an influential figure among evangelicals in 18th-century America.

Charles E. Hambrick-Stowe, "The Spiritual Pilgrimage of Sarah Osborn (1714–1796)," *Church History* 61 (December 1992); Samuel Hopkins, *Familiar Letters, Written by Mrs. Sarah Osborn and Miss Susanna Anthony* (1807); Hopkins, *Memoirs of the Life of Mrs. Sarah Osborn* (1799); Mary Beth Norton, ed., "'My Resting Reaping Times': Sarah Osborn's Defense of Her 'Unfeminine Activities,'" *Signs* 2 (1976).
Catherine A. Brekus

Presbyterianism A Protestant denomination that favors Calvinistic theology, Presbyterianism is noted for the practice of a distinct form of hierarchical church government. Unlike their Congregationalist counterparts in New England, who consider each parish church autonomous, Presbyterians allow higher governing bodies to exert binding

Presbyterian minister and benefactor of Harvard College John Harvard, sculpted by Daniel Chester French (1884), Harvard Yard, Cambridge, Mass.

power over particular congregations. Individual churches are presided over by a board of elected elders from the congregation and its ministers called a session or consistory. A higher governing body, a presbytery—which exerts authority over an entire geographical region—is elected by these sessions and from a body of continuing member ministers. Above even these regional presbyteries are synods and a general assembly or general synod, elected by the presbyteries to preside over an entire nation. With ordained and lay elders elected at all levels, Presbyterianism is a representative form of ecclesiastical polity that seeks to ensure uniformity in church theology and administration.

Rooted in the Protestant Reformation of Europe, Presbyterianism experienced sporadic growth and popularity in 16th- and 17th-century England while finding a long-lasting home in Scotland, owing in part to the Scottish reformer John Knox. As a Presbyterian, Knox studied Calvinistic theology in Geneva before returning to Scotland to support Protestants during the reign of the Catholic monarch Mary Queen of Scots. His influence compelled the Scottish Parliament to adopt a Calvinistic confession of faith by 1560 and to set up a Presbyterian system of church govern-

ment and worship throughout the entire country. Just over 80 years later, Knox's Scottish disciples and numerous English divines, in an effort to attain ecclesiastical unity between Scotland and England, outlined a Presbyterian form of church government for the kingdom. This Westminster Confession (1646) which received universal approval from Congregationalists, Baptists, and Presbyterians alike, remains a significant doctrinal and governmental statement for Presbyterians throughout the world.

Despite the popularity of Presbyterianism in England and Scotland and the overwhelming success of the 1646 confession, America's New English settlements seemed little affected by the growth of Presbyterianism and the momentous conclusions of the Westminster assembly during the early 17th century. Several years before the confession, thousands of Congregationalists had flocked from England during the great migration of the 1630s in an effort to practice their localized form of church polity. Their early dominance of New England's religious culture and extreme intolerance toward all other forms of ecclesiastical government allowed little room for Presbyterian polity to develop in the region. The history of New English Presbyterianism, then, became strongly tied to Congregational developments.

With the exception of a small number of French Huguenots who settled in Rhode Island, a colony of Irish Presbyterians in Londonderry, N.H., and a handful of Scottish and Irish immigrants in Worcester, Mass., the earliest Presbyterians in the northeastern colonies were sprinkled among the Congregational churches. These few ministers and lay members who preferred to adhere to Presbyterian polity often found themselves at odds with their Congregational counterparts. Although theologically similar to the Congregationalists, New England's Presbyterians often emphasized the governmental differences in their various churches, arguing that higher binding councils be implemented over the churches, more lenient membership requirements be practiced in individual congregations, and ministerial power be increased. In the middle of the 17th century one such minister, Thomas Parker of Newbury, Mass., attempted to implement certain of these Presbyterian-leaning governmental policies in his rigid Congregational church. His endeavors caused a quarter century of conflict in the church. With support of the colony's political and religious leaders, the majority of the Newbury congregation, which Congregational rule granted ultimate control over the church, forced Parker to cease practicing his Presbyterian-like government and compelled his assistant, Timothy Woodbridge, to resign from office. Other Presbyterian-leaning clergymen, such as Peter Hobart of Hingham, Mass., met similar fates in their attempts to implement Presbyterian governance in eastern New England.

Notwithstanding the failures of early East Coast Presbyterians, subsequent adherents found some successes in western New England. Connecticut and western Massachusetts had been largely settled by freethinking Congregationalists who often preferred Presbyterian policies. In true Presbyterian fashion, the minister at Northampton, Mass., Solomon Stoddard, a disciple of the Scottish Presbyterian Samuel Rutherford, successfully increased his clerical authority while easing admission requirements. In late 1714 he also established a Presbyterian-like council of ministers called the Hampshire Association, whose decisions he considered binding over the churches represented. Numerous ministers in Connecticut reached similar conclusions in 1708 when they resolved to create a consociation of ministers and churches resembling a presbytery. Their Saybrook Platform (1708) revealed the continual attraction many New England Puritans felt for Presbyterian polity and linked these ministers and their churches to the numerous Presbyterians of New York and Pennsylvania who had only two years earlier formed the first American presbytery in Philadelphia.

This first presbytery, established as a response to a demand from the large population of Scottish and Irish Presbyterians living in the middle colonies, found many supporters in New England. Various Presbyterian-leaning Congregational ministers, mostly from southern New England, attended the councils that formed the first presbytery, making it resemble a Congregationalist ministerial association as much as a true presbytery. Their support also led to the creation of the first American synod in 1716 and the first general assembly in 1789. The tensions between Congregationalists and Presbyterians had eased in the later 17th century with the signing of the "Heads of Agreement" in London, which created a union between the two parties. Because the Presbyterians and Congregationalists maintained such close ties in New England, the lines between them often became blurred. In the middle of the 18th century, for example, Congregationally trained ministers from Connecticut like Jonathan Edwards and Jonathan Dickinson served as presidents of the College of New Jersey (later Princeton), which had been established as an unofficial Presbyterian school.

The great strides made between the two denominations during the 18th and 19th centuries permitted the church to grow tremendously in New England. A number of clergymen and congregations throughout the region organized themselves into New England's first presbytery in 1745. Just under 30 years later, in 1774, the Boston presbytery became the first formal synod of New England, presiding over three regional presbyteries, not including the two independent presbyteries of Boothbay, Maine, and Grafton, N.H.

Boundaries between Presbyterians and Congregationalists became further obscured in the 1790s when representatives from each denomination were allowed to speak and vote in each other's deliberations. The 1801 "Plan of Union," which created an alliance between the two groups in an effort to cultivate the rich western missionary field, coupled with various subsequent cooperative organizations such as the American Bible Society and the American Home Missionary Society, allowed Presbyterianism to flourish in the West and to become more acceptable in New England.

The vast growth of Presbyterianism in New England and elsewhere also brought numerous divisions within the denomination. Since most Presbyterians had supported the American Revolution, the first general synod, formed in 1789, pledged its loyalty and support to the new government. Large numbers of Scots and Scots-Irish Presbyterians in the middle colonies, however, refused to pledge their loyalty or vote in presidential elections. These "covenanters" as they became known, did not join the general synod and, unlike most Presbyterian churches of New England, did not practice open communion. Most of these covenanters eventually formed the United Presbyterian Church of North America, while most New England Presbyterians became part of the Presbyterian Church in the U.S.A. The denomination further split with the coming of the Civil War as theologically conservative "old school" Presbyterians opposed the 1801 Plan of Union and any pronouncement on slavery. "New schoolers," which made up a majority of New England's Presbyterians, however, maintained close bonds to other Christian denominations including the Congregationalists, supporting temperance movements and opposing slavery. Following the war, the old and new schools in the North united as the Presbyterian Church in the U.S.A., while southerners formed the Presbyterian Church in the United States. After various shifts in the late 19th and early 20th centuries, the two estranged groups reunited as the Presbyterian Church in the U.S.A. in 1982.

Although the Presbyterian denomination continues to have splinter groups and is divided over such issues as same-sex marriage, it remains focused on the Bible and its traditional confessions. Ranging from strictly liturgical to informal and free, the diverse Presbyterian churches of New England have, as a general rule, become less restrictive over time. Turning away from such doctrines as predestination, Presbyterians now emphasize the fundamental need for Christ's atonement, the reality of bodily resurrection, Christ's virgin birth, his ability to perform miracles, and the inerrant nature of Scripture. Many of New England's Presbyterians are also deeply involved in political events such as civil rights and feminist movements, often encouraging women within their own denomination to enter the ministry.

Sydney E. Ahlstrom, *A Religious History of the American People* (1972); Alexander Blaikie, *A History of Presbyterianism in New England* (1881); Robert Ellis Thompson, *A History of the Presbyterian Churches in the United States* (1895); Leonard J. Trinterud, *The Forming of an American Tradition: A Re-examination of Colonial Presbyterianism* (1949); Williston Walker, *Creeds and Platforms of Congregationalism* (1893).

Aaron F. Christensen

Protestantism *Protestantism* refers to all the Christian denominations, now numbering in the hundreds, that trace their roots to the Reformation, a cluster of religious and social protests that radically reshaped the culture of Western Europe in the 16th century. The majority of Americans who claim religious affiliation identify themselves as Protestant, although the proportion of Protestants in New England is likely to be somewhat lower because of the region's comparatively large populations of Roman Catholics and Jews. There is no single religion known as Protestantism, and Protestant denominations differ widely in doctrine, practice, and demographics. Nevertheless, American Protestantism is characterized by a broad cohesiveness among those who so identify themselves, and perhaps nowhere more than in New England.

The term *Protestant* was first used in 1529 by German princes who sought autonomy from Roman Catholic rulers. The history of Christian resistance to centralized authority is complex, but credit for the decisive splitting away of much of Christian Europe from the Roman Catholic Church goes to Martin Luther, who nailed his 95 theses against papal authority on a church door in Wittenberg, Germany, in 1517. Luther's most startling and enduring theological innovations were two. First, he was convinced that divine authority is present only in the Bible (*sola scriptura*), which individual believers could read for themselves, and not in the priests, bishops, popes, and magistrates who appeared to stand between them and God. Second, he promulgated the doctrine of justification by grace though faith. This meant that only God's grace saves believers from damnation; salvation is merited only through faith in Christ, not through good works or actions prescribed by the church.

The Swiss theologian John Calvin, who, following Luther, broke with Catholicism in the 1530s, added to Luther's theology the doctrine of predestination. According to Calvin, God had predestined the fate of every soul—to be saved or damned—and alone knew who had been "elected" to receive the grace of salvation. Further, while the elect would inevitably lead holy lives, piety was not necessarily a sign of saving grace. Sinful, unrepentant behavior, however, was almost surely a sign of damnation.

From colonial days New England Protestantism has had a strong Calvinist cast, owing to its English roots. The Protestant Reformation in England was launched by Henry VIII, who broke from the Catholic Church in a political dispute over his right to divorce. When Henry's daughter Mary Tudor attempted to restore Catholicism to England, refugees from the ensuing violence fled to Geneva, where Calvin's reforms had taken hold, and England became more Calvinist upon their return. Henry VIII had made himself—rather than the pope—the head of the Church of En-

gland, and the first British Protestants to settle in New England's scattered fishing villages were Anglicans who accepted the monarch as head of the church. They were followed by the more stringently Calvinist Puritans, who sought even greater autonomy from both church and civil hierarchy, even as they recognized in name the authority of the Anglican Church. Separatists, such as Plymouth's Pilgrims, broke entirely with Anglican authority.

The peculiar, relentlessly enforced precariousness of Puritan spiritual life, where backsliding signaled damnation and even pious lives were subject to routine public and private scrutiny, proved predictably useful for securing public order in the wilds of North America. It also created enormous pressures, however, both psychic and social, that led to the gradual splintering of Protestant congregations in the 17th century and culminated in the shattering, if energizing, impact of the revival movements of the 18th century. The dominant Protestant church in the colonial period was what we now call the Congregational Church. There were also Baptist and Presbyterian churches in the region, and scattered Quakers. After the Great Awakening of the 1740s and the religious revivals of the Second Great Awakening in the late 18th and early 19th centuries, many other Protestant denominations appeared, including Methodism, Universalism, and Unitarianism.

The groundwork for New England Protestantism's burgeoning doctrinal diversity since the 18th century had been prepared, however, by the strict congregationalism of the Puritans and their commitment to the value of the individual conscience. Moreover, if New England Protestant churches were eventually divided by the divergent experiences of their congregations, they remained united in the conviction (again, soundly Puritan in its origins) that the world, like the individual, could be transformed and redeemed by grace, however various its legitimate modes of working.

An enduring legacy of New England Protestantism has been the enormous value it places on education and the written word. New England boasts some of the nation's finest schools—Harvard, Yale, Phillips Exeter and Andover academies, Boston Latin and Cambridge Latin Schools—as well as the highest proportion of college students of any region in the country. Literacy was especially widespread in colonial New England because private Bible reading was required for both religious discussions and individual understanding and appreciation of sermons. The Protestant conviction of a "priesthood of all believers" placed restrictions on the role of the clergy and authorized private judgment in scriptural interpretation. This encouraged not

only literacy, therefore, but interpretive competence, which empowered lay persons to make sense of their own inner and outer worlds. Much of the literature to come out of New England—works by Harriet Beecher Stowe, William Dean Howells, Henry James, Robert Frost, John Updike, and others—represents a dialogue, often dissenting, with Protestantism.

When Robert Frost said that New England's gift to American letters was "a stubborn clinging to meaning—to purify words until they mean again what they should mean," he identified another Protestant legacy to New England: its aesthetic of spareness. The "plain style" of Protestant sermons and the spiritual horror of hypocrisy (or showiness) led to a culture of understatement. The Protestant aesthetic of spareness is evident in a wide variety of cultural forms, ranging from the lean cadences of Frost or Emily Dickinson to the vernacular architecture of New England churches ("God's altar needs not our polishing") to the conservative, functional clothing styles of Talbot's and L.L. Bean.

The material spareness of New England Protestantism, however, was very different from material poverty. For Puritans, the absence of guarantees to salvation acted as a constant, anxious prod to work. Material success in this life became an unofficial addition to the list of signs of the workings of grace on individual souls; poverty, as many Puritans saw it, was a reflection of sin. The aesthetic of plainness that characterizes much of New England culture reflects what Max Weber described as the Protestant ethic. According to Weber, the Protestant ethic was defined by an ambivalent asceticism that encouraged material success and the laying-by of surplus (thrift) alongside a spiritual detachment from the things of the world.

New England Protestantism is often credited with encouraging the growth of democracy through its attachment of value not to money or birth but to spiritual election. The experience of grace was theoretically open to all, regardless of sex, social standing, or race. The veneration of Scripture meant independence from the earthly powers of pope and king; Calvinism had in fact been viewed by European monarchs as a system of insubordination and dissent. The hospitality of New England Protestantism to democratizing currents in American Life is clear from its central role in the abolitionist and women's movements of the 19th century.

At the same time, the annals of New England Protestantism are not lacking in defenses of the status quo and the relatively privileged position of white Protestants. The establishment clause of the First Amendment

"Christmas Eve," from Youth's Keepsake: A Christmas and New Year's Gift for Young People *(Boston, 1836), illustrates the increasing emphasis 19th-century Protestants put on the celebration of Christmas as a family holiday*

to the Constitution—"Congress shall make no law respecting the establishment of religion, or prohibiting the free exercise thereof"—was understood to preclude disestablishment as well, and Protestant establishment in fact survived in Vermont, Connecticut, New Hampshire, and Massachusetts until the early 19th century. In 1780 Massachusetts permitted Catholics to hold high office only if they publicly rejected papal authority in all civil, spiritual, and ecclesiastical matters. Jews remained ineligible for high office in Rhode Island until 1843; Catholics remained ineligible in New Hampshire until 1877. Moreover, the Protestant values of education, industry, and internalized authority easily converted themselves into ways of perceiving and enforcing social differences. Leaders of the common-school movement of the mid-19th century drew up curricula to instill punctuality, discipline, and thrift in the children of immigrant workers, whom they viewed as lacking the graces conferred by the Puritan heritage.

For their part, Puritans had perceived the objects of their own fear and wrath—for example, Roman Catholics, Quakers, and other "heretics"—as favorites of the devil who were to be vigilantly guarded against. During the witch trials of the 17th century, Cotton Mather claimed that an allegedly bewitched girl who could not read Scripture could easily read a "Quaker or a Popish book." Massachusetts Bay hanged four Quakers between 1658 and 1661, and in 1647 prescribed "perpetual imprisonment" for any Catholic priest who was unlikely and unfortunate enough to enter the colony. The French and Indian Wars of 1754–

63 fostered Protestant militancy against both Catholics and Native Americans. Both the anti-immigrant Know-Nothing movement of the 1850s and the Ku Klux Klan revivals in the 1920s represented themselves as carrying forward the redemptive mission of New England Puritanism.

The habit of equating the traditional Protestant values (individualism, rationalism, freedom of expression, prosperity) with distinctly American liberties also points to the success with which Protestantism has survived secularization; indeed, Protestant values have dominated American public life, heavily influencing even those Americans who are not churchgoers. The legacy of New England Protestantism is visible today in both the rise of evangelicalism, with its designs on the moral and political life of the nation, and the zealous guarding of secular freedoms, two poles that have kept Protestant values in productive tension.

Sacvan Bercovitch, *The Puritan Origins of the American Self* (1975); Francis J. Bremer, *Congregational Communion: Clerical Friendship in the Anglo-American Puritan Community, 1610–1692* (1994); James F. Cooper, *Tenacious of Their Liberties: The Congregationalists in Colonial Massachusetts* (1998); Stephen Foster, *The Long Argument: English Puritanism and the Shaping of New England Culture, 1570–1700* (1991); Martin E. Marty, *Protestantism* (1972); Perry Miller, *The New England Mind*, 2 vols. (1939 and 1953); Edmund S. Morgan, *Visible Saints: The History of a Puritan Idea* (1963); Harry S. Stout, *The New England Soul: Preaching and Religious Culture in Colonial New England* (1986).

Tracy Fessenden

Puritanism *Puritan New England* is a term that signifies the union of a 17th-century cultural movement with a geographical place. Puritanism was a religious stance that began in England and was carried to America by John Winthrop and his fellow colonists in 1630. Originally signifying the identification of the settlers with those they left behind, it eventually became a badge of the region's distinctiveness.

The English religious reformation of Henry VIII (r. 1509–47), was an imperfect one in the eyes of many, denying the Roman Catholic pope's authority in England while doing little to modify church doctrine and practice. From the time of that first reform, "Protestants of the hotter sort" as they have been designated by some historians, the "godly" in their self-identification, struggled to purify the English church. During the reigns of Elizabeth I (1553–1603), James I (1603–25), and Charles I (1625–49), this reform movement became stigmatized by its opponents as Puritanism. It is a movement that English historians have found difficult to

define because its reformers had no institutional identity. They remained members of the Church of England and were distinguished from their neighbors only by their more intense piety and their dislike of forms and practices, many of which they nevertheless complied with as the price of their membership in the national church. This stance of moderate nonconformity distinguished them from the Separatists, who, beginning in the latter decades of the 16th century, refused all compromise, abandoned the church, and established their own congregations, first in England and then, following persecution, in exile. One such group of pilgrims journeyed to the Netherlands in 1607 and then to Plymouth, Mass., in 1620 in search of freedom to practice their faith.

When, during the reign of Charles I, pressure for complete conformity increased, "Catholic" innovations were introduced by the bishops, and the Calvinistic creedal foundations of the English church were called into question, some Puritans organized the Massachusetts Bay Company as a means whereby a model Puritan society might be established in the colonies. In addressing his fellow emigrants in 1630, Winthrop spoke of the colonists' covenant with God and one another to establish a "city upon a hill" that would be a model for all in England and elsewhere who still needed evidence that the Puritan way was God's way. That covenant demanded that the colonists identify and establish God's wishes; there was to be no toleration of those who offered alternative visions of the truth. This "new" England was not originally envisioned as the only remaining hope for English reform, and colonial clerical leaders maintained close contact with friends abroad who shared their zeal. New Englanders rejoiced in the Puritan Revolution in England (1642–49) and saw hope in the regime established by Oliver Cromwell in the 1650s. Common Puritan hopes united colonial culture with that of the motherland at midcentury, and many colonists returned home to play roles in the religious and political reform of England. Only with the fall of the Puritan regime there and the restoration of the Stuart monarchy in 1660 did New Englanders begin to feel separate from the flow of English history. As England changed, the Puritanism that originally united New Englanders with the culture of their homeland came to be a mark of distinction, leading to a redefinition of purpose that emphasized American uniqueness.

The way of life that New Englanders first offered for adoption by the English—and which they eventually came to regard as their unique heritage—was permeated by Puritanism. Coming to New England in the 1630s, the Puritans had the opportunity to create congregations of the godly. Freed from the close supervision of unsympathetic ecclesiastical superiors, they erected simple wooden meetinghouses without the statuary, crucifixes, stained glass, and religious paintings that adorned the masonry parish churches of old England; they believed such ornamentation distracted from proper devotion and promoted saint-worshiping idolatry. Surviving examples include the Old Ship Meeting House in Hingham, Mass., and the Old South Meeting House in Boston. Deliberately rejecting the rich church music tradition of William Byrd, they insisted that only the psalms—Scripture songs—be sung in worship and without instrumental accompaniment. Altars were replaced with communion tables, and a set liturgy of prescribed prayer was replaced with services emphasizing powerful sermons and extempore prayer. An aesthetic preference for the simple over the ornate would come to characterize secular art and entertainment as well. This aesthetic, called the plain style, came to define many New England vernacular traditions in material culture.

A restructuring of church polity accompanied this transformation of worship. There was no place for bishops in New England. Each member of the communion of saints was called in his or her way to build the new Jerusalem and preserve it in a way that promoted democratic forms. Congregations were self-generated; esteemed saints in a community came together to draft and sign a church covenant, invited all who were similarly born again to join them, and then the congregation chose and ordained its own pastor and church officers. Regional unity was maintained by informal consociation of clergy and formal assemblies and synods that advised but could not coerce the constituent congregations. The safety of the whole was preserved against heresy by the protecting arm of the magistrate.

Just as this congregational system placed responsibility for its operation upon the community of saints, so too each saint was made to feel responsibility for his or her own salvation. New England Puritan doctrine was a variant of Calvinist teachings. Puritans believed themselves to have been born tainted by original sin, which made their violation of God's covenant inevitable. They accepted responsibility for their transgressions and believed that they deserved damnation. No work or will of the individual could affect this; only God's election to offer one the covenant of grace could transform the sinner into a saint. This rebirth was marked by the infusion of a divine and supernatural light that enabled one to lead life in closer accordance with God's law.

Good works were the fruit of salvation and, together with a sense that the individual had indeed received God's caress, were evidence that one was saved. Searching for such evidence in their hearts and deeds led Puritans to become masters of introspection, leading to the habit of diary keeping and a literature of self-examination. The journals of John Winthrop and the diaries of Michael Wigglesworth, Samuel Sewall, and Cotton Mather reveal an introspection at times obsessive. They also show a Puritan search for God's providences; when a snake enters a meetinghouse, for instance, a child dies, and witchcraft besets Salem.

Though denying that works alone were efficacious, the Puritans believed they were bound by the covenant of works and by their own special communal covenant with God to bring Christian belief into everyday practice. Thus, religion came to permeate all aspects of Puritan culture. Because Puritanism was centered on the individual's confrontation with the God of the Scriptures, it was essential that believers know how to read, and Puritanism thus became a driving force in making colonial New England one of the most literate societies in the world at that time. Harvard College was founded in 1636 in Cambridge, Mass. Parents were legally charged with teaching their children to read and to aid them against the "old deluder Satan"; by a Massachusetts statute of 1642, towns were required to make schools available. The Bible was the most widely owned, but not the only, reading material available. Colonial sermons were printed in England and in Massachusetts for distribution within the wider Puritan community; historians like Edward Johnson and Winthrop chronicled the region's special relation with God; and such poets as Anne Bradstreet used verse to meditate on the mysteries of existence in God's world. Widespread literacy led to the use of the printing press, and from the 1640s some religious literature was printed in the colonies, including the *Bay Psalm Book* and the Indian Bible.

The congregational meetinghouse was the center of town society, and Puritanism determined the patterns of everyday life for the townspeople. The Sabbath was strictly observed from sundown on Saturday to sundown on Sunday. No work was to be performed, and all were to devote themselves to attendance at services and to family scripture reading and religious discussion. A reformed calendar allowed no celebration of annual feasts or holidays, not even Christmas. Special days of fast were designed to focus the community on prayers of petition to God, while special days of thanksgiving were observed with prayer and feasting to thank God for petitions answered. The laws of England were transferred to the colonies but interpreted with scriptural glosses. Colonists saw themselves as their brothers' keepers and sought to shame and correct those who strayed from the path of righteousness. While some diversions, such as theater, were proscribed in their colonies, New Englanders drank alcoholic beverages, engaged in loving marital sex, made music, and engaged in sports—but as Puritans they did so in proper contexts and proper proportion, struggling to avoid the overdoing that was the most common way of sinning.

Evidence of Puritanism in New England remained long after church reform in England. Puritanism became a byword for intrusive, self-righteous moralizing, excessive introspection, and governmental intrusion on individual liberties in the aftermath of the Salem witchcraft trials. By the time of his death in 1728, Cotton Mather had come to symbolize this negative Puritan spirit, and the hellfire preaching of Jonathan Edwards, while reviving certain Puritan doctrines, served further to cement an identification of excessive religious zeal with New England Puritans. In the 19th century, such writers as Nathaniel Hawthorne, Harriet Beecher Stowe, and Catharine Sedgwick participated in a revival of interest in Puritan New England, even as they criticized its spirit. In the twentieth century, periodic waves of interest in Puritan history and literature, in antique collecting, early gravestone art, museum exhibits, architectural style, and living history sites at Salem and Plymouth were offset by the easy use of *Cotton Mather* and *Puritan* as derogatory epithets. Although later generations would blame Winthrop's generation for much that they found distasteful in New England, it is to those Puritans that credit is due for the concern for community over self, the high regard for education, and the moral stance toward political life that have been identified with New England culture long after that culture ceased to be called Puritan.

Francis J. Bremer, *The Puritan Experiment: New England Society from Bradford to Edwards*, rev. ed. (1995); Bruce C. Daniels, *Puritans at Play: Leisure and Recreation in Colonial New England* (1995); Jonathan Fairbanks, ed., *New England Begins: The 17th Century*, 3 vols. (1982); Stephen Foster, *The Long Argument: English Puritanism and the Shaping of New England Culture, 1570–1700* (1991); David D. Hall, *Worlds of Wonder, Days of Judgment: Popular Religious Belief in Early New England* (1989); Harry S. Stout, *The New England Soul: Preaching and Religious Culture in Colonial New England* (1986).

Francis J. Bremer

Quakers The Religious Society of Friends, commonly known as the Quakers, is a denomination of Protestant origin whose distinctive belief is that direct communion between the believer and the Holy Spirit is both available and necessary. The Society rejects sacraments and affirms ethical "testimonies" against bearing arms and for simplicity and human equality. Quaker polity is congregational. Local bodies, called Monthly Meetings, may include one or several worship groups. Monthly Meetings are affiliated in larger Quarterly and Yearly Meetings. Since the late 19th century, most Yearly Meetings have been organized into conferences. All these bodies make decisions by spiritually based consensus.

Quakerism emerged from the religious ferment of radical Puritanism in 17th-century England. It shared the "radical Reformation's" emphases on the gathered or believers' church, the primacy of the Holy Spirit in interpreting Scripture, and the relative unimportance of clergy, sacraments, and institutional structures. George Fox (1624–91), an itinerant visionary of working-class background, began to preach in 1647 and generated a strong and well-organized following. Fox's message was that the inner struggles common to many religious seekers of the period could be resolved by direct experience of the "light" of Christ. This inward revelation was available to all and, moreover, signified the beginning of the reign of Christ on earth. Thus early Quakerism—so nicknamed because believers trembled under the work of the Spirit—was a spiritist, apocalyptic, and missionary movement with radical social and political implications.

The first Quakers in New England arrived in the Massachusetts Bay Colony in 1656. Their claim to spiritual authority, disregard of social and political convention, and confrontational manner were taken as a threat to a colony already chastened by the Antinomian Controversy of 1636–37. A series of laws levied harsh punishments on Quaker preachers and their supporters: fines, whipping, physical mutilation, and banishment on pain of death. Between 1659 and 1661 four Quakers were hanged on Boston Common for repeatedly entering the colony. Persecution also occurred in Connecticut and in scattered locations elsewhere. Executions ceased by royal order after the restoration of Charles II.

Quakers settled and flourished in outlying areas: Salem and Plymouth Colony, Mass., Rhode Island, and what is now southern Maine. The southeast coastal areas were the center of New England Quakerism through the mid-19th century. Fox organized the annual "general meetings" of New England Friends, held in Newport, R.I., into a Yearly Meeting in 1672, at which time Quakers dominated Rhode Island's government. On Nantucket, under the influence of Quaker visitors, a majority of the population became Friends between 1698 and 1704. Beyond religious conviction, they may have been motivated by the prospect of withholding taxes from the Massachusetts Standing Order.

Quakerism reflected wider currents in American religion while maintaining distinctive beliefs and practices. As toleration increased, Quaker numbers grew—by conversions north of Boston and by natural increase to the south—until about 1770. At that time, coincident with the awakenings of the mid-18th century, a reform movement initiated in the powerful Yearly Meetings of London and Philadelphia led to more stringent standards of membership and discipline. The movement also addressed social issues; New England Yearly Meeting banned slaveholding in 1770, three years before Philadelphia. Quaker spiritual practice in the course of the 18th century turned to quietism: submission to the will of God through complete stilling of the self. Worship was largely silent; speech "led by the Spirit" was spontaneous but used ritualized mannerisms.

Friends also reflected currents of renewal in the early 19th century. David Sands's itinerant preaching helped to spread an evangelical form of Quakerism through the northern backcountry. In the well-established meetings of Lynn and New Bedford, Mass., "New Light" Quakers challenged theological and institutional authority; many in New Bedford eventually joined the Unitarian Church. Issues of renewal and authority also contributed to schisms in 1827–29, known as the Orthodox-Hicksite separations, which affected most of American Quakerism. New England Yearly Meeting remained united and formally recognized the Orthodox factions.

However, the Gurneyite-Wilburite schism of 1845, which concerned the relation of Quakerism to the evangelical mainstream, began in New England. Joseph John Gurney, an English Friend, and his supporters emphasized the Quakers' biblical heritage, restated their theology in evangelical terms, and promoted cooperation with other Protestants on social reforms. John Wilbur of Rhode Island represented the minority position, advocating quietism, Quaker distinctiveness, and the authority of early Quaker writings. After the separation in New England, other Orthodox Yearly Meetings addressed the same issues, with most adopting the Gurneyite position. Many, including New England, eventually introduced pastors and "programmed" worship similar to Protestant church services.

In confronting modernism during the late 19th and the 20th centuries, Quakers began to rediscover the spiritist and quietist aspects of their heritage. Instrumental in this process was the New England Quaker Rufus M. Jones, later professor of philosophy at Haverford College in Pennsylvania. Reared in a rural Maine meeting, converted by a traveling revivalist, Jones's faith was shaken by encounters with science and history in early adulthood. His eventual rethinking of Quakerism, in company with several English Friends, emphasized its evolutionary and mystical potential through "progressive" or "continuing" revelation and the primacy of the Inner Light. Jones integrated this theology with social action: he was among the founders of the American Friends Service Committee and worked to obtain government recognition of conscientious objection to military service.

Throughout the southeast coastal region of New England, Quakers, notably the Starbuck, Rotch, and Coffin families, were prominent in whaling, shipping, and overseas trade until the middle of the 19th century. Paul Cuffe (1759–1817), born near New Bedford to a former slave and a Wampanoag Indian, made a maritime fortune and worked for abolition, resettlement of former slaves in Africa, and voting rights for men of color. He joined the Society of Friends in 1808 after long contact. Quaker dominance of Nantucket was well known. John Woolman, the Quaker "saint" and reformer, recorded his 1760 visit to the island, and Hector St. John de Crèvecoeur described the "frugal, sober, orderly" life of Nantucket Friends in 1782.

Later New England literature and thought also reflects the Quaker presence. Ralph Waldo Emerson's admiration of Quaker antiformalism and inwardness influenced his Transcendentalist views. The poet and abolitionist John Greenleaf Whittier was the best-known Friend of his day. In Moby-Dick, Herman Melville commented at length on the Quaker whalers of New Bedford and Nantucket. Nathaniel Hawthorne reflected on the era of persecutions in his tale "The Gentle Boy" (1832), in which a Quaker child loses his father to hanging and his mother to uncompromising religion and is rejected by the Puritan community. In the 20th century, New England Quakerism has appeared in notable children's literature, including Elizabeth George Speare's The Witch of Blackbird Pond (Newbery Medal, 1959), about the early persecutions, and Brinton Turkle's Thy Friend, Obadiah (Caldecott Honor, 1970), one of a series about a Nantucket boy.

A number of Quakers participated in the antislavery, women's rights, and temperance movements. Among the most important were Lucretia Coffin Mott, the abolitionist and Seneca Falls Convention organizer, who was born on Nantucket; and Susan B. Anthony, the suffragist leader, who was born in western Massachusetts to a Quaker father and a Baptist mother. These and other activists credited the egalitarianism of their Quaker backgrounds but were often at odds with official Quakerism. Maria Mitchell, the astronomer and women's educator, was reared as a Nantucket Friend but left the Society in early adulthood.

A few Friends' meetinghouses are historically significant. The oldest surviving in New England is the Great Friends Meeting House at Newport, probably begun in 1699 and the site of the Yearly Meeting gathering until 1905. It seats some 2,000 people and is maintained by its current owner, the Newport Historical Society. Vernacular 18th-century meetinghouses survive in numerous locations along the coast; several in Rhode Island and one at North Pembroke, Mass., date from near 1700. All but one of the historic meetinghouses on Nantucket are gone or in private hands, but the large central meetinghouse in New Bedford is in active use by Friends. The Dover, N.H., meetinghouse (1768) is connected with the Whittier family, and the meetinghouse in Adams, Mass. (1782), is associated with Clara Barton and Susan B. Anthony. A memorial at the Westport, Mass., meetinghouse commemorates the African American merchant Paul Cuffe, who was a member. A statue of Mary Dyer, the only Quaker woman executed in Boston, stands on the Massachusetts State House lawn.

Modernist Quakerism's fusion of mysticism and social activism took hold gradually in New England. Although there was little increase in Yearly Meeting membership during the 20th century (except during the 1970s), the character of worship began to change around 1930. Meetings practicing silent worship without pastors were founded in college towns and suburbs and by rural homesteaders. Gurneyites and Wilburites reunited in 1945, but a few years later Newport withdrew from the Yearly Meeting to join a more conservative Holiness body of Friends, which later became the Evangelical Friends Church—Eastern Region. By 1980 liberal unprogrammed meetings outnumbered older pastoral ones, though some of the latter still thrive. The Yearly Meeting maintains membership in both the Gurneyite-descended Friends United Meeting and the Hicksite-descended Friends General Conference.

In 2002 New England Yearly Meeting counted 4,271 members constituting 66 Monthly Meetings and 30 smaller Preparative Meetings and worship groups, most of them affiliated with Monthly Meetings. Outside New England Yearly Meeting, three Evangelical Friends Churches, one of them Latino, related to the older Newport meeting claim 224 attenders. Small independent groups, often transient, also form occasionally. Within the Yearly Meeting, issues under discussion in recent years have included same-sex marriage and the tension between a Christcentric and a universalistic identity. At the start of the 21st century, New England Quakers are visible in peace, social-action, antinuclear, and environmental movements.

Margery Post Abbott, Mary Ellen Chijioke, Pink Dandelion, John William Oliver, *Historical Dictionary of the Friends (Quakers)* (2003); Hugh Barbour and J. William Frost, *The Quakers* (1988); Jonathan M. Chu, *Neighbors, Friends, or Madmen: The Puritan Adjustment to Quakerism in the 17th Century* (1985); Thomas D. Hamm, *The Quakers in America* (2003); Hamm, *The Transformation of American Quakerism: Orthodox Friends, 1800–1907* (1988); Carla Pestana, *Quakers and Baptists in Colonial Massachusetts* (1991); Frederick B. Tolles, "The New-Light Quakers of Lynn and New Bedford," *New England Quarterly* 32 (1959); Meredith Baldwin Weddle, *Walking in the Way of Peace: Quaker Reform in the 17th Century* (2001); Arthur J. Worrall, *Quakers in the Colonial Northeast* (1980)

Patricia Appelbaum

Religion in Hispanic Culture

Nationwide, 35 million people of Hispanic origin live in the United States, and estimates suggest that by the year 2050 one in four Americans will be Hispanic. Hispanics constituted 5 percent of New England's population in 2000 and are projected to make up 8 percent in 2025. Given these figures and the fact that the median age for Hispanics is 24 (compared to 35 for Caucasians), it is not surprising that Hispanics are making their cultural presence felt both nationally and in New England. An integral part of this presence is religion, which takes an array of institutional and quotidian forms. While most Hispanics are Roman Catholic, Hispanic Protestants are significant in number, increasing at both the national and regional level.

In the United States today, 67 percent of all Hispanics are Catholic, and Hispanic Catholics will soon account for half of all Catholics in the United States. Though the number of Hispanic Catholics in New England is not as large as in other areas of the country, this group is gaining prominence in the region, especially in the states of Connecticut, Massachusetts, and Rhode Island. Half a million Hispanic Catholics, for instance, live in the Boston archdiocese alone, accounting for 25 percent of its total Catholic population. Historically speaking, Hispanics in New England represent the "third wave" of immigration to the area, after the Irish and continental Europeans.

In 1976 the Northeast Hispanic Catholic Center, located in New York City, was established to minister to the needs of Catholics from Maine to Virginia. On the national ecclesiastical level, the National Conference of Catholic Bishops further declared its solidarity with Hispanic Catholics in two pastoral documents, *Hispanic Presence: Challenge and Commitment* (1983) and *National Pastoral Plan for Hispanic Ministry* (1987).

Unlike the Southwest, where Mexican Catholics predated the arrival of the Pilgrims, migrants to the Northeast, including New England, are more recent arrivals, among them migrants from the Caribbean, particularly Puerto Rico and the Dominican Republic. Today an increasing number of immigrants are also arriving from Mexico and Central America, most notably Guatemala.

Hispanic Catholics bring to New England strong religious practices and long-held expressions of faith. Many Catholic Hispanic parishioners, like certain other ethnic Catholics in New England (Italians, Irish, Polish), have continued such traditional popular religious practices as observing the feast days of saints, praying the rosary, and paying daily adoration to the Blessed Sacrament. However, Hispanic Catholics in New England have also introduced such traditional Latin American practices as *quinceañeras* ("coming of age" celebrations for young women) and the celebration of Día de los Muertos (a syncretic Aztec-Christian practice that honors the memory of lost loved ones). These practices have gained some prominence in New England. Salem, Mass., known for its infamous witch trials, is now host to one of the most elaborate Day of the Dead altars in the Northeast.

In addition, in recent years there have been a proliferation of *iglesias domesticas* in Northeast and, increasingly, New England. These "home churches," led by lay people, serve as prayer and bible study groups and offer more intimate settings for reflection. The charismatic movement among New England Hispanic Catholics is also strong. As with Hispanic devotion in general, Catholics in the area continue to express their faith in community. Though not endorsed by the Catholic Church, the African Cuban practice of Santería has gained some visibility in New England. A combination of African Yoruba religion and Spanish Catholicism, Santería originated in Cuba when Yoruba slaves used the names and faces of Catholic saints to pray to their *orishas*, Yoruba ancestor gods. In spite of a relatively small Cuban community in New England (yet in line with the growing Puerto

Santería shrine in Dorchester, Mass., 1994

Rican and Dominican population), it is estimated that well over 100 Santería paraphernalia shops, or *botánicas,* exist in the Northeast, many of them in New England towns and cities such as Boston, Hartford, Providence, and Lawrence, Mass.

Studies by the Emmanuel Gospel Center in Boston suggest that there are roughly 300 Spanish-speaking churches in New England. Of these, many are Protestant and, in particular, Pentecostal churches. Of some 60 Hispanic Protestant churches in Boston, for example, only 13 are associated with mainline Protestant denominations (Baptist, Episcopal, Congregational, Methodist, and Presbyterian). Almost all the remaining are Hispanic Pentecostal churches, a subset of the fastest-growing Christian movement worldwide. Both the mainline Protestant and Pentecostal Hispanic congregations are active, and the Pentecostal churches, in particular, often hold worship and prayer services three or four times a week. Pentecostal churches tend to draw from the poorer communities among Hispanics, and, correlatively, Pentecostal leaders, who often do not hold advanced professional degrees, tend to be close to their congregations in socioeconomic status. Over the years New England Hispanic Protestant churches have produced a noteworthy cadre of grassroots leaders who have helped preserve and pass on cultural traditions, language, and community-development initiatives.

One of the unique features of New England Hispanic Protestantism has been its creative use of physical space. Hispanic churches affiliated with mainline Protestant denominations have often been founded and maintained by sharing space with non-Hispanic congregations. Sometimes in transitional communities, especially in the inner cities of New England, the Spanish-speaking congregations have inherited or purchased the church buildings of "dying" congregations. Hispanic Pentecostals, in particular, are well known for renting low-cost storefront properties in communities long abandoned by others in order to create new churches that can serve their poorest members.

Music and worship in almost all Hispanic Protestant congregations, both mainline and Pentecostal, tend to be free in style and to incorporate significant participation from the laity, in the form of leading worship, special music performances, personal testimony, and even preaching. Such occasions encourage grassroots leadership and community involvement at large. Furthermore, New England is home to some of the most dynamic and historically significant Latina pastors, including the Reverend Julie Ramirez, the founding pastor of what was at one point the largest Hispanic Protestant church in all New England, Templo Fe in Hartford.

While it is clear that Hispanic Protestant and Hispanic Roman Catholic churches alike have supported and sustained first-generation Hispanics through a period of migratory transition, an ongoing challenge for both groups will be to minister successfully to Hispanic youth. As Hispanic young people grow up in cities like Boston, Hartford, Providence, and Bridgeport, Conn., with values and ideas different from those of their immigrant parents,

the Hispanic churches will have to keep their language and worship approaches in step with the new generations of New England Hispanics.

Emmanual Gospel Center, *Boston Church Directory* (1995); National Conference of Catholic Bishops, *Hispanic Ministry at the Turn of the Millennium* (1999); National Conference of Catholic Bishops, *Hispanic Presence: Challenge and Commitment* (1983); Earl Shorris, *Latinos: A Biography of a People* (1992); Marcelo Suárez-Orozco and Mariela Páez, eds., *Latinos: Remaking America* (2002); Eldin Villafañe, *The Liberating Spirit: Toward a Hispanic Pentecostal Social Ethic* (1993).

Efrain Agosto and Christopher Tirres

Roman Catholicism Roman Catholicism has been an aspect of New England culture since the 17th century, long before significant numbers of Catholics settled in the region. The stories of English Catholic plots and papal conspiracies were fresh in the minds of the Puritans who established the Massachusetts Bay Colony in 1629. Colonial printers produced newspapers and pamphlets that told of the horrors of the "popish faith" and warned colonists to be vigilant. Given this climate of hostility, Catholicism did not become truly established in New England until the 19th century.

The fear of Catholicism was fueled, in part, by the presence of Catholic missionaries in the northern reaches of the colony. Jesuit priests had migrated down from New France to preach to Abenaki Indians. In response, the Massachusetts General Court passed an act in 1700 expelling all priests from the province. Although many priests did leave, the response was not unanimous. One, Father Sébastien Râle, defied the act and refused to abandon his missions. Râle managed to evade capture by colonial authorities for more than two decades but was finally killed in 1724 by militiamen in retaliation for Indian attacks he supposedly led on Maine settlements. Although Massachusetts Bay was rid of a pesky priest, Râle became a martyr among the Abenaki, and his story lived on for generations.

Attitudes began to shift during the American Revolution. The newly independent colonies allied themselves with Catholic France in 1778, and Catholics living in New England were guaranteed religious freedom in the new state constitutions of Massachusetts, Rhode Island, and Vermont. Other Catholic liberties were slow to emerge, however; although many states gave Catholics full civic rights soon after the war started, vestiges of anti-Catholicism remained well into the 19th century. Aside from one parish in Boston and a few Catholic missionaries in isolated pockets of the region, the Catholic population remained

High mass at the Cathedral of the Holy Cross, Boston, 1960

low until the 1820s. Nevertheless, in 1808 the Vatican designated all New England as the Diocese of Boston and selected French missionary Jean Cheverus as its first bishop.

Cheverus's charm won over even the most anti-Catholic of Boston's leaders. He enjoyed popularity among Protestants and a rapid increase in the Catholic population of his diocese through the immigration of tens of thousands of Catholics from Ireland. Cheverus left Boston in 1826; the new bishop, John Fitzpatrick, lacked the charm of his predecessor. Fitzpatrick was overwhelmed by the rapid increase in the Irish Catholic population and unable to meet the growing demand for more churches and priests.

Protestants became uneasy about the growing Catholic population and on the evening of August 11, 1834, vented their rage by vandalizing and setting fire to the Ursuline Convent school that had been established for girls in Charlestown, Mass., in 1818. Under Cheverus the institution had been viewed as a finishing school, but by 1836 Protestant ministers saw it as a symbol of rising Catholic power, despite the fact that the daughters of some Boston's most elite Protestant families attended. The trial of the arsonists was a mockery of justice, and the accused were carried out of the courtroom as heroes. Over the next 20 years, anti-Catholicism arose in Dorchester and Law-

rence, Mass.; in Manchester, N.H.; and in Bath and Ellsworth, Maine, where Catholic churches were destroyed. Even in Rhode Island, where a large Catholic population offered some measure of protection, nativists threatened to storm a Catholic convent.

But this hostile climate seemed to have little impact on the decision of Catholic immigrants to settle in the region. In truth, poor Catholics from Ireland may have arrived at Boston with no funds to migrate farther. By 1850 the two New England Catholic archdioceses—Boston and Hartford—reported a combined Catholic population of 170,000, but it is likely that the actual count exceeded 200,000. In 1853 two more New England dioceses were established—at Portland, Maine, and Burlington, Vt.—further evidence of the growing Catholic population. By 1860 Catholicism was the largest single denomination in the region.

The Catholic population in New England grew in proportion to the general population over the next 30 years. By 1884 new dioceses had been established at Springfield, Mass., Providence, and Manchester. Despite this expansion, the majority of Catholics in New England lived in the Boston area. Between 1880 and 1900 the number of Catholics quadrupled, while the general population of the region only doubled. By 1885 Boston had elected

Hugh O'Brien as its first Catholic mayor, a reflection of the growing Catholic political power in that city.

The majority of 19th-century New England Catholics were Irish. But beginning in the 1870s, large numbers of French Canadian Catholics began moving into the Springfield area, attracted by work in the mills. In the 1880s a new wave of Catholic immigration to New England began; while the Irish continued to immigrate in the largest numbers, Italians, Hungarians, Portuguese, and Poles also became part of the mix. Polish Catholic immigrants stand out because of their enthusiasm for establishing new parishes almost from the time of their arrival. Their motives were not strictly religious; they, like the French Canadian immigrants before them, viewed new parishes as an opportunity to preserve their language and culture as well as their faith. Many Italian immigrants, on the other hand, were ambivalent about their religion, and this indifference was reflected in the structure of the parishes they established in New England. Some Italian parishes had elaborate church buildings, often constructed by the parishioners themselves, but few schools or other social institutions. Other Italians attended Irish Catholic churches or didn't attend at all.

Catholic European immigrants continued to arrive in New England in large numbers during the first three decades of the 20th century, settling in ethnic neighborhoods across an increasing urbanized region. Migration in the 1920s took on a distinctly French cast when more than 500,000 Quebecois Catholics fled an economic depression in Canada and migrated across the border seeking employment. The influence of these French Canadian Catholics grew as they settled in a cross section of New England communities, particularly the mill centers of New Hampshire and Maine. With the substantial increase in Catholic immigrants after 1880 came a revival of anti-Catholicism, particularly in Boston, where the so-called Committee of One Hundred formed. The committee distributed widely its scurrilous newspaper, *The Menace*, which accused Catholics of heinous crimes.

Immigration to the United States declined after 1930, and the issues facing Catholicism shifted from a concern with Americanization to a concern about preserving the faith in children. Many dioceses reorganized their parish school systems, established boards of education, and appointed superintendents. In an effort to meet the increasing demand for teachers, women who entered religious orders in New England were given little choice but to become teachers. This concern about children expanded in the 1950s to include a preoccupation with a perceived decline in morals and an increase in secular values. The Legion of Decency, which evaluated and rated popular films, was active in the region during these years. The Catholic Church continued to grow in the 1950s, and the Vatican established new dioceses in Worcester, Mass., and in Norwich and Bridgeport, Conn.

A less-visible change took place in New England Catholicism in the 1950s, when Catholics from Boston and the other major cities of the region began moving to the suburbs. Leaving the comfortable and intimate ethnic neighborhoods of their parents, young Catholics set out to build new lives for themselves in multifaith communities. The result was a decrease in ethnic Catholicism and an increase in mixed marriages. The election of John F. Kennedy as the first Catholic president of the United States in 1960 was an important historical moment for the region's Catholics.

The image of Catholicism in the past half-century was largely shaped by the three cardinal archbishops of Boston during those years. Richard Cushing was a garrulous Irishman who represented the church triumphant in the years from the end of World War II to the Vatican Council. Cushing was succeeded by the saintly Humberto Medeiros, who led a conflicted church through the late 1960s and 1970s. Finally, Bernard Law was the controversial conservative spokesman for the authority of the church in the last decades of the 20th century and into the 21st. Sexual scandals involving Boston priests, however, compelled Law to resign in 2002; he was replaced by Sean Patrick O'Malley.

Conflict emerged within New England Catholicism over the changes called for by the Second Vatican Council (Vatican II), held in Rome from 1962 to 1965. Younger Catholics in the suburbs of Boston, Providence, and Hartford welcomed the changes that modernized the liturgy and made Catholicism less defensive and more ecumenical. But older Catholics, especially those living in smaller cities with strong ethnic neighborhoods, saw the decrees as weakening their religious practices. Over the past 30 years, Catholicism in New England has struggled with a number of challenges, including a decline in religious vocations, the closure of parishes, and ethnic and racial tensions.

Yet for all of its challenges, Catholicism has fared better in New England than in most regions of the country. In the 20 years after Vatican II, the Catholic population grew significantly in every New England diocese except Springfield; the number of parishes increased in every diocese; and the decline in religious vocations was smaller than in other regions of the country. At the turn of the 21st century, New England had 11 Catholic dioceses and 1,644 parishes in the six-state region. In 2000, Massachusetts reported the region's highest number of practicing Catholics, at 2,962,776; Connecticut followed with 1,331,222; Rhode Island's Catholic parishes had 635,590 practitioners; New Hampshire was home to 342,662 Catholics; Maine to 215,007; and Vermont to 148,246. Such major Catholic institutions of higher education as Boston and Providence Colleges have had considerable influence on the political culture of their respective states.

Catholics have likewise made their mark on the artistic and literary culture of the region; popular writers whose Roman Catholic roots influence their work, for instance, include Bridgeport's Maureen Howard, Rhode Island writer David Plante, and Boston's Edwin O'Connor and James Carroll.

Ray Allen Billington, *The Protestant Crusade, 1800–1860: A Study of the Origins of Nativism* (1938); Joseph J. Casino, "From Sanctuary to Involvement: A History of the Catholic Parish in the Northeast," in Jay P. Dolan, ed., *The American Catholic Parish*, 2 vols. (1987); Paula Kane, *Separatism and Subculture: Boston Catholicism, 1900–1920* (1994); Robert H. Lord, John E. Sexton, and Edward T. Harrington, *A History of the Archdiocese of Boston, 1643–1943*, 3 vols. (1944); James M. O'Toole, *Militant and Triumphant: William Henry O'Connell and the Catholic Church in Boston, 1859–1944* (1992); Arthur Riley, *Catholicism in New England to 1788* (1936); Robert E. Sullivan and James M. O'Toole, eds., *Catholic Boston: Studies in Religion and Community, 1870–1970* (1985); Timothy Walch, *Parish School: American Catholic Parochial Education from Colonial Times to the Present* (1996).

Timothy Walch

Second Great Awakening

The Second Great Awakening is the term used to describe the great burst of evangelical fervor that swept across the United States in the first three decades of the 19th century and peaked in the 1820s and early 1830s. Unlike the First Great Awakening of the 1730s, the Second Great Awakening was not confined to New England, although it began there and took strong hold in the region. The revival transformed American culture, politics, and religion. It made evangelical Protestantism the dominant faith, inspired a great wave of social reforms, and fostered the abolitionist movement.

The Second Great Awakening took different forms in different regions. In New England, men like Lyman Beecher and Yale University president Timothy Dwight challenged the old Puritan notion that God had preordained salvation or perdition and individuals could do nothing to change that predetermination. Now the revivalists preached that everyone could win heaven if they embraced God's grace. The churches launched organizations to fight sin and convert the nation—indeed, the world. Their benevolent empire fought liquor (the American Temperance Society was formed in Boston in 1826), handed out moralizing pamphlets (the New England Tract Society), distributed Bibles (the American Bible Society), organized Sunday schools (the American Sunday School Union), and sent missionaries far and wide. The church leaders and their organizations raised funds, signed petitions, held rallies, and indefatigably organized still more uplift societies.

In the West, the revivals took on a more raucous and ecstatic spirit marked by wild preaching and enormous revival meetings. The most famous meeting drew a crowd of between 10,000 and 25,000 to Cane Ridge, Ky., in the summer of 1801. The born-again frenzy lasted almost a week. One preacher, James Finley, described the tumult in his autobiography: "The noise was like the roar of Niagara. I counted seven ministers, all preaching at one time, some on stumps, others in wagons. . . . People were singing, others praying, some crying for mercy in the most piteous accents while others were shouting most vociferously. . . . A strange supernatural power seemed to pervade the entire mass. . . . At one time I saw at least five hundred swept down in a moment, as if a battery of a thousand guns had been opened upon them, and then immediately followed shrieks and shouts that rent the very heavens." Itinerant preachers in the South and West organized a kind of people's church. They preached, gathered new congregations, and enlisted local lay leaders. Then they moved on, while their recruits continued preaching. The yield was stunning: 14,000 American Methodists in 1784 grew to 250,000 by 1820 and more than 1 million by 1844. Baptists organized their own popular church (they were even more democratic, thanks to an emphasis on congregational autonomy) and almost kept pace with the Methodists. Anyone who heard the call could get a license and begin saving the neighbors. The loose organizational form made it easier to spread the word to the slave quarters in the South and the frontier settlements in the West. The evangelical message blazed across America.

The frenzied western itinerants and the grave Yale divines were unwitting partners in a grand American project: they brought individualism to the nation's religious life. Together, the revivalists introduced four great changes. First, they threw aside Calvinism. The preachers rejected the notion that anybody was predestined for hell. In Boston, Lyman Beecher condemned the idea as "odious," and "twisted." The colorful western Methodist Lorenzo Dow put it more pointedly: "Christ gave himself for ALL ... and A-double-L does not spell SOME nor FEW but ... ALL." When a heckler challenged Dow to explain Calvin's doctrine, the preacher shot back with a sarcastic rendition of the old faith:

You can and you can't ...
You will and you won't ...
You will be damned if you do
And you will be damned if you don't.

Second, people were considered responsible for their own souls. No frowning clergyman could render judgments about God's intentions. Now the clerics scrambled for business against a swarm of new competitors. In *The Radicalism of the American Revolution*, historian Gordon S. Wood illustrates the explosion of sects by simply drawing up an inventory of Baptist factions: General Baptists, Regular Baptists, Free Will Baptists, Separate Baptists, Dutch River Baptists, Permanent Baptists, and Two-Seed-in-the-Spirit Baptists—and all before nine southern states bolted and formed the proslavery Southern Baptist Convention in 1845. Other denominations splintered into similar factions. Religious choices fell, willy nilly, to the customer.

Third, the Second Great Awakening pushed religion into the popular vernacular. Rousing gospel songs thrust aside formal church music. Western revivalists scorned the "dry science" in the boring, Latinate sermons—"all hic haec hoc and no God in it," scoffed Charles Finney. Finney led a roaring evangelical revival in Rochester, N.Y., where he prayed for the conversion of the damned by name. He set aside an "anxious bench" for people wrestling with conversion. He pioneered that revival classic, testimony from sinners who had seen the light. However, the heart of Finney's technique lay in his simple sermons and common prayers—"anything but dry science."

Finally, the revivalists emphasized personal discipline—sobriety, piety, and hard work. This focus came just in time to help the United States negotiate the transition to industrial capitalism, a shift that was largely centered in the New England states. Inculcating personal virtues helped break the inefficient habits of an artisan and farm economy—no more lunchtime rum or spontaneous afternoons off. Christian discipline would bend the workers to the regulated, clock-driven monotony of mill and factory. Entrepreneurs and ambitious young professional men eagerly signed up for what would later be dubbed a "shopkeepers' millennium." Urban workers often resisted, cursing the elite meddling in their private lives. European revivals had protected the old social order; in contrast, American revivals promoted a new economic attitude. Faith prepared the way for an Industrial Revolution—although this ultimately served stability and reinforced the emerging industrial powers.

In short, the Second Great Awakening fostered a new American spirit. Individuals would make their own spiritual way without waiting on ministers or church elders or the inscrutable motion of the Holy Spirit. Religion reorganized American morals for a new era of broad markets and mass democracy. One final twist gave the Second Great Awakening its extraordinary force. Many Americans saw the revival as a millennial sign that the United States would redeem the biblical Book of Revelation and usher in the second coming of Jesus. Lorenzo Dow parsed Revelation, verse by verse, and concluded, "the prophesies were ... perfectly fulfilled under American government." Charles Finney challenged his listeners to come forward, dedicate their lives to Jesus, and bring on the millennium right then and there in Rochester.

The millennial drama came from the way evangelicals read a key passage in Revelation: "And they lived and reigned with Christ a thousand years." A premillennial reading (popular today) expects Christ to abruptly return bringing his thousand years of peace and justice. In contrast, most 19th-century revivalists were postmillennialists: for them Jesus would appear only after humanity had achieved the thousand years of peace and justice. Men and women would be the central agents in the cosmic pageant. The millennial visions reflected the rest of the Second Great Awakening: destiny had passed from divine volition to the people's free will.

The preachers recast history and prophesy into a distinctly American idiom. A great teleological arc ran from 1517 (Martin Luther) to 1642 (Oliver Cromwell) to 1688 (the Glorious Revolution) and soared toward its millennial culmination with the American Revolution of 1776. Fulfilling the Scriptures required spreading three reforms around the world. First, those who tilled the soil must own it. Second, representative government must triumph over kings and tyrants. Third, the rights of conscience must prevail over religious despotism. For guidance in all these matters, the world had only to study the United States. However, if America was going to reform the world, Americans had to prove themselves worthy exemplars. The second coming waited for Americans' social vices to "abate their violence," preached the Boston Methodist Gilbert Haven. The "graces of Christianity" would have to replace "intemperance, Sabbath breaking and infidelity."

All the high moralizing and millennial hopes eventually forced the issue of American slavery. Was this not a sin? How could Americans offer humankind a vision of liberty—universal land reform, no less—when they held 2 million humans (almost one in six Americans) in bondage? As the Second Great Awakening rushed toward its peak, millennial dreams began turning into antislavery jeremiads, particularly in New England, where abolitionist fervor was especially strong. In the moral hothouse of antebellum America, a righteous blow against slavery began to attract believers.

In short, the millennial search for God changed American society in two very different ways. On the one hand, the revival fostered individualism. It seized moral authority from the pulpit and invested it in ordinary men and women. On the other, the revival kindled a passion for reforming the community. Sin was collective, retribution would be shared, and redemption must include everyone. If Americans were going to fulfill the Bible prophesies sinners had to be converted. By the 1830s, slavery began to eclipse all of Satan's works. For the next three decades, Americans broadcast millennial dreams and blasted jeremiad warnings at one another with more gusto than they had ever worked up before—or would ever muster again.

Robert Abzug, *Cosmos Crumbling: American Reform and the Religious Imagination* (1994); Sydney E. Ahlstrom, *A Religious History of the American People* (1972); Lorenzo Dow, *History of Cosmopolite: The Four Volumes of Lorenzo Dow's Journal* (1848); Nathan O. Hatch, *The Democratization of American Christianity* (1989); James Morone, *Hellfire Nation: The Politics of Sin in American History* (2003).

James A. Morone

Shakers The Shakers are the members of a religious community, formally named the United Society of Believers in Christ's Second Appearing, with a history of more than 200 years. The American branch was founded in 1774 by Ann Lee (ca. 1736–84), an unlettered English visionary, who transplanted the movement of "Shaking Quakers" (as they were called) from England, where its members had been persecuted because they condemned the established churches, proclaimed impending judgment, and engaged in ecstatic worship. In America, Lee and her followers eventually located in New Lebanon, N.Y., outside Albany. Beginning in 1781 she and several disciples traveled for more than two years throughout eastern New York and New England, winning converts to their cause. The movement expanded from a handful of Believers in the 1770s to a national organization with 4,500 members in villages located from the East

Shaker Villages in New England

Location	Years	Peak Size (est.)
Alfred, Maine	1793–1931	158
Canterbury, N.H.	1792–1992	260
Enfield, Conn.	1790–1917	213
Enfield, N.H.	1793–1923	297
Hancock, Mass.	1790–1960	338
Harvard, Mass.	1791–1918	178
Shirley, Mass.	1793–1908	84
Sabbathday Lake, Maine	1794–present	139
Tyringham, Mass.	1792–1875	93

Coast to the Ohio River valley by the 1840s. Although New Lebanon remained the headquarters of the society for most of its history, New England also played a central role in the story of Shakerism.

The Shakers challenged their hearers to pursue a righteous life by confessing their sins and accepting Lee's authority. She associated sin with sexual intercourse and called for her followers to flee procreation in favor of a regenerate life and celibacy. On several occasions opponents physically abused the Shakers, yet the journey was successful in numerous towns in Massachusetts and Connecticut. The group of traveling Believers centered their activities for a time in Harvard, Mass., where they drew converts from among the disciples of another visionary, Shadrach Ireland.

Lee's successors in the ministry gathered the converts scattered across New England into communities, assigned leaders from the most faithful, and supervised the building of villages. By the beginning of the 19th century there were nine major villages in New England, each with its own ministry of elders and eldresses. Each also attempted to establish economic independence. The Shakers were generally successful with their communal enterprises, from farm products to pharmaceuticals, furniture to fancy goods. The Canterbury, N.H., village, for example, prospered because of its successful seed industry and the production of textiles and herbal medicines. The Hancock, Mass., village was noted for its dairy herds. The Harvard village had a mill that produced a variety of wooden products for sale. The society espoused a vigorous work ethic, and at all sites members were expected to contribute their labor for the common good. Tradition ascribes to Ann Lee the saying, "Hands to work, and hearts to God." The Believers established the principle of joint ownership in the society, which meant an end to private property. Individual needs were met from the common store.

Religiously, the Believers everywhere were united in joint commitment to celibacy, confession, and obedience to the ministry. Among the Shakers' most distinctive religious ideas was the notion of the dual nature of God as Father and Mother, reflecting both the power and wisdom of the deity. The Shakers also drew parallels between Ann Lee and Jesus of Nazareth, declaring that both shared in the redemptive process. In that frame of reference, Lee was declared by some of her followers to be a second Christ. The Shakers created a rich repertoire of worship forms, including dances, rituals, and songs, all believed to be products of divine inspiration. Their meetinghouses were designed to accommodate religious exercises by community members. The decades of the 1830s and 1840s were an especially rich period for innovation in Shaker worship. In those years there was an outpouring of spiritual gifts throughout the society. Elaborate rituals, lively dances and marches, spirit visitations—these were manifestations of the Shaker revival known as "Mother Ann's Work." The most famous musical product of the period is the hymn "'Tis the Gift to Be Simple," often attributed to Joseph Brackett of the Alfred, Maine, community.

As the 19th century wore on, the Shakers experienced numerical decline. They proved unable to attract sufficient young converts and to retain male members. They also engaged in risky business ventures that cost the society dearly. In 1875 the Tyringham, Mass., village closed—a pattern repeated numerous times over the next century. When the headquarters at New Lebanon closed in 1947, Canterbury became the site of the Central Ministry. By 1962 the society consisted of a small group of aging sisters at two villages. At the same time, the Shakers attracted new attention from collectors and historians. Surging interest in material culture created a wave of enthusiasm for Shaker objects; even their religious ideas attracted positive commentary. The Shakers became synonymous in popular culture with the virtues associated with simplicity, hard work, and an agrarian lifestyle. Today one remaining village—Sabbathday Lake, Maine—carries forward the living tradition of Shaker religion and culture.

Edward Deming Andrews, *The People Called Shakers: A Search for the Perfect Society* (1953); Priscilla J. Brewer, *Shaker Community, Shaker Lives* (1986); Stephen J. Stein, *The Shaker Experience in America: A History of the United Society of Believers* (1992); Gerard C. Wertkin, *The Four Seasons of Shaker Life: An Intimate Portrait of the Community at Sabbathday Lake* (1986).

Stephen J. Stein

Spiritualism Spiritualism is a religious movement that appeared in New England and other parts of the northeastern United States in the mid-19th century as a reflection of and response to religious, social, and cultural developments that were profoundly transforming the region. Spiritualism originated in an area of western New York that had been heavily populated by New England out-migration and strongly influenced by New England cultural currents. Sisters Margaret (1833–93), Catharine (1839–82), and Leah Fox (1818–90) claimed to be able to communicate with the spirit world and became founders and leaders of American Spiritualism, a movement that found thousands of adherents in New England within a few years of its appearance. Boston in particular became an important center of Spiritualist activity and remained so for the rest of the 19th century.

Spiritualists believe that they can contact the spirits of the dead through "mediums" and achieve harmony with the spiritual forces governing their universe. They understand spirits as essential mediators between themselves and a deity who was rendered uncomfortably abstract and impersonal by liberal Protestant theologies that emanated from New England's intellectual centers in the 19th century. Like some Universalists, Unitarians, and Transcendentalists—many of whom became Spiritualism's earliest adherents—they denied the existence of hell, downplayed the reality of evil, and emphasized the inner divine potential of each individual. Although Spiritualists joined religious liberals in questioning the revival techniques that were gaining increasing prominence in regional and national religious culture, their concern to achieve direct personal experience of a supramundane reality was as much akin to revivalism as it was to liberal notions of inward spirituality.

Spiritualism has been shaped as much by secular forces as by religious currents. Fear of bewildering social and economic change and scientific materialism have underlain Spiritualist beliefs that the spirit world is an idealized version of earthly society, that spirits use their influence to impose order and harmony on a chaotic world, that the séance is a needed source of spiritual renewal, that the spirit is a form of matter subject to natural law and amenable to scientific analysis, and that Spiritualists have successfully grounded religious faith in scientific proof of human immortality.

Spiritualism emerged as part of the larger middle-class reform impulse that had become an integral part of 19th-century New England life. It was attractive to activists in abolitionism and especially women's rights, and became closely intertwined with these movements as they rose to cultural prominence during the second half of the 19th century. Among the reform-minded New Englanders interested in Spiritualism were William Lloyd Garrison and Harriet Beecher Stowe. Spiritualists also allied themselves with various movements in medical reform, seeking spiritual and other heterodox methods of healing. Even earlier, an informal spiritualism was evident when Shakers in New England and elsewhere welcomed spirits of departed community members as well as political leaders, Indians, and African Americans into meetings during revivals in the 1830s and 1840s.

Spiritualism not only continues to appeal to Americans seeking cosmic connection but decisively influenced religious and scientific currents that spread from New England origins to national cultural appeal. Phineas P. Quimby, whose ideas were developed by Mary Baker Eddy into the doctrines of Christian Science, was strongly influenced by Spiritualist writings, and Eddy herself sought adherents for her new religion by advertising in the long-running Boston Spiritualist periodical *Banner of Light*. Boston remains the international headquarters for Christian Science. Harvard psychologist William James, meanwhile, was moved by his scientific interest in mediumship and other paranormal phenomena to establish the American Society for Psychical Research in 1885. Spiritualism figured prominently in New England fiction, including Nathaniel Hawthorne's *The Blithedale Romance*, Henry James's *The Bostonians*, and William Dean Howell's *The Undiscovered Country*. Spiritualism's popularity and influence in New England typifies the region's enduring fascination with the possibility of hidden spiritual realities.

Ann Braude, *Radical Spirits: Spiritualism and Women's Rights in 19th-Century America* (1989); Bret E. Carroll, *Spiritualism in Antebellum America* (1997); R. Laurence Moore, *In Search of White Crows: Spiritualism, Parapsychology, and American Culture* (1977).

Bret E. Carroll

Theological Education

New England has had a profound influence on theological education from the earliest days of English settlement. Its colleges and seminaries provided ministers for important Protestant denominations in the region and beyond, and many missionaries took their New England brand of faith westward with the frontier. In 1636 New England Puritans founded Harvard College to continue the pattern of clerical education many had experienced at the University of Cambridge, especially Christ College. The English college did more than train clergy; since the young men who attended lived under the supervision of tutors and ate with the Fellows, the schools provided opportunities for the transmission of piety.

Fears that Harvard was moving away from its ancient Calvinist heritage (as well as Connecticut local pride) led to the formation of Yale in 1701. By the mid-1700s both colleges provided an opportunity for students to read theology under a professor of divinity in the period between receiving their bachelor of arts degree and their call to the ministry. After the Great Awakening, the followers of Jonathan Edwards also invited recent graduates to read divinity with them. These Edwardsean programs were more popular than those that were college based.

Theological controversy sparked the next developments in the training of ministers in New England. When Harvard appointed Unitarian Henry Ware as Hollis Professor of Divinity in 1805, more orthodox Calvinists banded together to establish Andover Theological Seminary, which opened in 1808. Andover was a new departure in theological education. Students were to study for three years under professors who would devote their lives to a specific theological discipline. Thus, the new program improved the quantity and length of postgraduate theological education. Other schools on this new model quickly appeared while Harvard and Yale were taking the first steps toward creating full divinity schools or departments at this time. The Maine Charity School, founded in 1814 to train ministers for northern New England, followed the newer model of training after 1819. Theological conservatives founded the Theological Institute of Connecticut, later Hartford Seminary, in 1833 in reaction to the allegedly false doctrines taught at Andover and Yale. Other denominations quickly followed. Baptists established Newton Theological Institution in 1825, and Methodists opened the country's first Methodist seminary in Newbury, Vt., in 1839. This seminary was moved to Concord, N.H., in 1847, then reopened in Boston in 1867 as the Boston Theological Seminary; in 1869 it would become Boston University. By the Civil War, New England had proportionately more seminaries than any other region of the country.

After the war, New England theological schools took the lead in the development of a new style of ministerial preparation. New directions in biblical study, often pioneered in Germany, led instructors to take a more comprehensive view of biblical history. Since this new view was less dependent on Hebrew and Greek, more time was available for students to explore different areas. Almost all New England schools had adopted a modified elective system before World War I. At Andover Seminary, William Jewett Tucker experimented with field education, while Boston University became known for its pioneering work in social ethics and religious education. Hartford Theological Seminary experimented with other models and tried becoming a theological university with separate "schools" of religious education, missions, and theology.

In the 20th century New England's theological schools took the lead in experimenting with the idea of consolidation. Andover Seminary originally united with Harvard in 1908, but the courts set aside that alliance, so it merged with Newton Theological Institution in 1931. Andover-Newton developed the nation's first program in Clinical Pastoral Education. Harold John Ockenga, pastor of Boston's Park Street Church, led the 1969 merger of Boston's Gordon Divinity School with Philadelphia's Conwell School of Theology, which was affiliated with Temple University. The Boston Theological Institute, formed in the 1960s, allows students in the participating institutions to enroll in classes on the different campuses and provides common access to the school's libraries.

E. Brooks Holifield, *A History of Pastoral Care in America: From Salvation to Self-Realization* (1983); Charles Lippy and Peter Williams, eds., *The Encyclopedia of the American Religious Experience*, s.v. "Christian Theological Education" (1988); Glenn T. Miller, *Piety and Intellect: The Aims and Purposes of Ante-Bellum Theological Education* (1990).

Glenn T. Miller

Unification Church

The Unification Church was one of several new religious movements that became prominent in New England and elsewhere during the 1970s. Founded in Korea in 1954 by the Rev. Sun Myung Moon (1920–), it began mission activity in America later that decade. The Unification movement proposes to unite all branches of Christianity into a single body, emphasizing strict family values and communal and devotional discipline. Unificationists believe that the crucifixion of Jesus prevented God's efforts to establish divine rule on earth, but the completion of this work has been conferred on Rev. Moon and his wife, who represent the ideal family.

Members in front of the Unification church, Beacon Street, Boston, 1978

During the 1970s the Unification Church sparked controversy because of its proselytization of white, middle-class youth and alleged disruption of families. In New England, several high-profile cases led three state legislatures to undertake investigations, and "anticult" sentiment eventually led to the establishment of organizations opposing the Unification Church and other groups believed to practice "mind control."

The Unification Church had minimal impact in New England during the 1960s. However, it began actively proselytizing on college campuses and in urban settings during the early 1970s. The church also set up workshop sites in New York to which it invited guests from neighboring states. In 1974 Wendy Helander, then 18, dropped out of the University of New Hampshire to join and became the New England's best-known convert. Twice "rescued" by her parents and subjected to "deprogramming," her later lawsuit against them and her deprogrammers was trumpeted in the press. Vermont, Connecticut, and Massachusetts held public hearings on the church that, while inconclusive, helped galvanize "anticult" sentiment. The Lexington, Mass.–based American Family Foundation (est. 1979) exerted influence nationally, setting up a Center on Destructive Cults and publishing *Cultic Studies Journal.* Still, there were discordant voices. Harvard Divinity School theologian Harvey Cox, for example, attended a Unification Church weekend workshop and wrote that "the attraction of the Moon movement" was "not the result of sinister brainwashing but an inevitable consequence of the utter vacuum on what might be called the 'Christian left.'"

Between 1978 and 1980 Unification Church–related corporations purchased property worth approximately $2 million in Gloucester, Mass., while also building up a commercial tuna-fishing fleet. The same corporations sponsored a World Tuna Tournament with total prize money of $100,000, dwarfing the amounts offered in local, established tournaments. The Unification Church's stated intention was to revive the fishing industry and educate people about the ocean as a food source. However, its initiatives were greeted with angry responses ranging from attempts to block property sales and refusal to accept advertising or service boat engines to boycotts, protest gatherings, and threats. Still, fears that children would be "stolen" or the town economy taken over did not materialize as the church adhered to a policy of no recruitment, and although Unification Church sea captains, including Rev. Moon, harvested unprecedented numbers of tuna, its Gloucester operations were only moderately successful.

In 1992 another controversy broke out when the Professors World Peace Academy (PWPA), an organization which received 90 percent of its funding from the Unification Church, gained a controlling interest in the University of Bridgeport. The university had fallen on hard times marked by declining enrollment, being placed on probation by regional accreditors, and a devastating faculty strike. Nevertheless, several prominent trustees and townspeople preferred closing the university to accepting the terms of PWPA's bailout: $68 million in forgivable loans in exchange for control of 60 percent of the board and the right to approve the university president. Unification Church spokespersons emphasized a vision of peace and a world university network appropriate to an emerging global culture. However, a vociferous Coalition of Concerned Citizens labeled the Unification Church a cult that practices deception and mind control, accused the university of betraying its nonsectarian charter, and charged that the school afforded the church a way to bring in money, gain access to academics, and win respectability. New England regional accreditors disagreed that the school's program had been compromised and in March 1996 restored the university's full academic accreditation, lifting the probationary status that had been in effect for six years. Whether the Unification Church and its related institutions will have a transient or permanent place in New England culture, however, remains uncertain.

George D. Chryssides, *The Advent of Sun Myung Moon* (1991); Harvey Cox, "The Real Threat of the Moonies," *Christianity and Crisis* 37 (1977); Scott Cranmer, "Why 'Moonies' Catch More Tuna," *Yankee* 44 (1980); Michael L. Mickler, *Forty Years in America: An Intimate History of the Unification Movement, 1959–1999* (2000).

Michael L. Mickler

Unitarianism As its name suggests, Unitarianism differs in important ways from Trinitarianism, or the Christian belief in a tripartite God consisting of Father, Son, and Holy Spirit. Most Unitarians advocated the idea that Trinitarianism was not supported by Scripture, and that Christ himself, while indeed a higher being, was not actually part of the Godhead. Moreover, unlike the more conservative Calvinist Protestants who taught that humans were innately sinful and unable to influence their own religious salvation, Unitarians generally followed the doctrine called Arminianism, which held that humans have the capacity for both good and evil and that salvation can be achieved through human actions combined with religious understanding. Linked to the Unitarian idea that religious salvation could be achieved by moral actions and faith, a theological position called "supernatural rationalism" formed another crucial tenet of Unitarianism. Distinct from evangelical groups that promoted a highly emotional version of Christianity, Unitarians influenced by the theory of supernatural rationalism believed that divine revelation through the study of Scripture must be combined with the careful and sophisticated application of human reason. For Unitarians, reason alone could establish the basic rules of "natural religion," whereas the influence of divine revelation could make those religious findings of reason clearer and more profound.

A Protestant denomination of singular importance in the development of New England religious and secular thought, especially in the 19th century, Unitarianism traces its earliest American appearance to the 1787 ordination of James Freeman, a Harvard graduate with liberal religious views, as senior warden at the previously Episcopalian King's Chapel in Boston. One of Freeman's early projects was to produce an edited edition of the Book of Common Prayer that removed all Trinitarian references. By 1805 Henry Ware had become the first Unitarian professor of divinity at Harvard University, an appointment that eventually led to the founding of Harvard Divinity School—the nation's first nondenominational seminary—in 1816. Soon after, in 1825, the church formally organized itself into the American Unitarian Association, which would become the dominant Unitarian group in the United States for more than a century.

A liberalizing force within New England Protestantism more broadly, the Unitarian movement drew its strength from both the increasingly latitudinarian Anglican churches in England and the steadily declining influence of the conservative New England Congregational churches, with their Calvinistic emphasis on innately sinful humans ruled by a fearsome and wrathful God. By contrast, Unitarians came to believe that human nature was essentially good (and certainly improvable), and that benevolence was the primary trait of the Christian God. At the same time, however, Unitarians firmly opposed the far more popular evangelical Christian movements that had been sweeping the United States since the middle of the 18th century. Whereas evangelical groups such as Methodists and Baptists often favored large, enthusiastic revival meetings led by charismatic preachers and fervently emotional conversion experiences, Unitarians preferred that religious experiences be built primarily upon rationality and biblical exegesis. And like the 18th-century Scottish "commonsense" philosophers who influenced them, Unitarians established theological positions that attempted to reconcile the intellectual and scientific discoveries of the Enlightenment with a belief in a supernatural God. In this way, Unitarianism could strike a religious balance between two extremes: the atheism suggested by certain advocates of science and rationality, and what was perceived as the excessive emotionalism of some Protestant denominations.

The significance of Unitarianism in New England proved to be far broader than its theological dissent from both evangelical and Calvinistic Christianity. Because of its popularity among the elite of New England culture during the 19th century, including its wealthiest citizens and most accomplished intellectuals affiliated with Harvard University, Unitarianism also became a major factor in the development of modern New England morals, literature, and society. Despite its importance for 19th-century New England, however, Unitarianism has always been a relatively small denomination. Indeed, its failure to become a widely popular religion in the United States, along with its parochialism and solid ties to New England, led to the witticism that Unitarianism's preaching was restricted to "the fatherhood of God, the brotherhood of man, and the neighborhood of Boston."

By the early years of the 19th century, Harvard University, previously a bastion of conservative Congregational theology, had begun its long period of control by liberal thinkers and administrators who sided with the Unitarian movement. Harvard Divinity School became a de facto Unitarian school and remained aligned with Unitarianism for most of the 19th century, largely through the efforts of faculty members such as the eminent Unitarian theologian and biblical scholar Andrews Norton. Most Harvard students and faculty during the 19th century were themselves Unitarians, as were the university administrators. The Harvard curriculum likewise reflected the values of Unitarianism, and thus the university as a whole served as a major force in instilling Unitarian thinking among several generations of the most influential groups of educated men in Massachusetts. Following these developments, many of the previously conservative religious congregations of Massachusetts began gradually to reshape themselves according to the more liberal values of Unitarian theology.

The first half of the 19th century was a particularly active period in the development of American Unitarian thought by theologians and other writers affiliated with Harvard. The 1810 election of John Thornton Kirkland to the Harvard presidency marked the academic transition to Unitarian dominance in Boston, while William Ellery Channing set the theological tone for Unitarianism with his controversial 1819 manifesto "Unitarian Christianity," delivered as a sermon in Baltimore at the ordination of Jared Sparks. Channing himself became an enduringly popular figure in New England Unitarianism, serving for 40 years at the epicenter of Boston Unitarianism: the Federal Street Church. His assertion that Christianity, modernized according to Unitarian principles, "should be comprehended as having but one purpose, the perfection of human nature, the elevation of men into nobler beings," encapsulates much of the Unitarian insistence on a benevolent God and a perfectible human nature.

The emergence of New England Transcendentalism, the intellectual and literary movement centered in Massachusetts and spearheaded by Ralph Waldo Emerson, has long been associated with developments in Unitarian religion. Many of the leading Transcendentalists—writers like Orestes Brownson, Margaret Fuller, Henry David Thoreau, Bronson Alcott, and George Ripley—either were Unitarians themselves or were affected profoundly by the Unitarian intellectual environment of antebellum Massachusetts. Emerson, who studied at Harvard College and Harvard Divinity School, was himself an ordained Unitarian minister, although he resigned his ministry because of disagreements related to Unitarian theology. Some historians and literary critics have even argued that Transcendentalism, with its gospel of spiritual self-sufficiency and its radical questioning of all religious traditions, should be considered an extension of ideas generated years earlier within Unitarianism.

Aside from the writers associated with the Transcendentalist circle, much of the most important literary production of 19th-century New England can be attributed to writers influenced heavily by the values of Unitarianism. The most prominent and influential American Unitarian journal, the *North American Review* (founded 1815 and published in Boston), served as a forum for many of these writers, and its editors included such notables as Edward Everett, William Emerson (father of Ralph Waldo), George Ticknor, Jared Sparks, Richard Henry Dana, Henry Adams, James Russell Lowell, and Edward Everett Hale. In addition, the popular writers William Cullen Bryant, Henry Wadsworth Longfellow, and Oliver Wendell Holmes were also products of the Harvard Unitarian establishment.

The religious principles of Unitarianism, translated from theology into practical action in New England society, provided much of the impetus and moral force to the numerous social-reform movements of the period such as abolitionism, temperance, and women's

Unitarian Universalist church, Portsmouth, N.H., 1986

rights. In fact, along with its significance as a key force in liberal Christianity in the United States, the most durable legacy of New England Unitarianism may be found in the establishment and support by its members of a broad range of philanthropic organizations and activities. Many of the major charitable institutions in Boston—such as Massachusetts General Hospital, McLean Asylum for the Insane, Perkins School for the Blind, and the Female Orphan Asylum—were organized by prominent Unitarians during the early decades of the 19th century. The American Society for the Prevention of Cruelty to Animals, which was begun after the Civil War by New York Unitarians, had by 1868 opened its Massachusetts chapter under the leadership of the Unitarian George T. Angell. Other early New England efforts at social change that received significant Unitarian leadership included educational missions abroad and to Native Americans and African Americans, as well as the common-school movement (the latter spearheaded by the Massachusetts Unitarian educator Horace Mann). For the late 19th and 20th centuries, Unitarianism has been especially notable for the degree to which it has generally recognized women as vital contributors to education, literature, the professions, and in the management of church affairs.

Unitarianism, which in its earliest phases in New England had resisted the enthusiasm of evangelical Christian groups in favor of a more rationalistic and humanistic religious view, continued in the 20th century to promote the ideas of nonsectarian worship with no formal creed, the autonomy of local congregations, and broad support for social justice and world peace. Twentieth-century Unitarians have lent their support to a wide array of causes such as the American Civil Liberties Union, the War Resisters League, nuclear dis-

armament, the Civil Rights Movement, and gay and lesbian rights. By the 1930s, though, the divide within Unitarianism between those who viewed themselves as humanists and those who still held theistic beliefs had grown, leading to a denominational split in 1945. The theist wing of the church separated from the humanistic American Unitarian Association, naming themselves the Unitarian Christian Church, with headquarters in Boston. The larger American Unitarian Association continued as the primary Unitarian group until 1961, when the decision was made to merge with the Universalist Church, creating the Unitarian Universalist Association, which continues to this day as the leading American Unitarian group, with approximately 52,000 members in 243 churches throughout New England.

Conrad Wright, *The Beginnings of Unitarianism in America* (1955); Conrad Edick Wright, ed., *American Unitarianism, 1805–1865* (1989); Daniel Walker Howe, *The Unitarian Conscience: Harvard Moral Philosophy, 1805–1861* (1970).

James Emmett Ryan

Unitarian Universalist Association

The Unitarian Universalist Association was formed in 1961 from a merger of the American Unitarian Association and the Universalist Church of America. Both Unitarianism and Universalism had emerged in New England in the late 1700s in reaction to the Calvinist theology of the New England Puritans. The new movements represented different liberal alternatives to both Calvinism and the evangelical revivalism of the early 1800s; their eventual merger in the 20th century thus represented the institutional consolidation of two of America's most liberal denominations.

Although Unitarianism and Universalism shared an aversion to Calvinism and agreed on

certain basic theological principles, their early institutional histories are quite distinct. Unitarianism developed largely within the Churches of the Standing Order in Massachusetts and was based in Boston. Charles Chauncy, minister of the First Church in Boston, mounted an attack on the emotional excesses of the revivals of the Great Awakening in the 1740s, offering intellectual leadership to a group of Boston-area ministers who found themselves in increasing opposition to the Calvinist doctrines of innate depravity and election to grace. Open controversy between liberals and the orthodox Calvinists erupted in 1805 over the election of the liberal Henry Ware as Hollis Professor of Divinity at Harvard. William Ellery Channing, the most important early Unitarian leader, accepted the inevitability of the separation of the liberals from the Calvinists in his 1819 sermon "Unitarian Christianity" and articulated a liberal theology that stressed the benevolence of God and the centrality of self-culture to the religious life. The American Unitarian Association was formed in 1825, and many of the original Puritan churches in Boston and eastern Massachusetts declared themselves Unitarian. The efforts of Henry Whitney Bellows to organize the National Conference of Unitarian Churches in 1865 added further institutional stability to the Unitarian movement.

Universalism in America began with the preaching of John Murray, who came to New Jersey from England in 1770 and founded a church on Universalist principles in Gloucester, Mass., in 1779. The Universalists stressed belief in a loving God who offered universal salvation, a doctrine that was preached most persuasively in the 19th century by Hosea Ballou, the longtime minister of the Second Universalist Society of Boston and author of *A Treatise on Atonement* (1805), the *summa theologica* of early Universalist thinking. The Winchester Profession, a summary of early Universalist theological principles, was adopted in 1803 at a meeting of the New England Convention of Universalists, and in 1865 Universalists formed the Universalist General Convention, the institutional focus for their national movement.

Unitarianism, centered at Harvard and in the more established churches of eastern Massachusetts, remained the more intellectually vital of the two denominations, internally generating a series of tense but productive challenges to its hardly settled theology: Transcendentalism in the 1830s and 1840s, the Free Religion movement in the 1860s and 1870s, and the Humanist movement in the 1920s and 1930s. The Universalists, with a less affluent and more rural constituency than the Unitarians, gradually evolved from their original focus on universal salvation to progressive political causes, their universalism coming to mean an inclusive social justice. Since the merger in 1961, Unitarian Universalism has been characterized by a creedless openness to a variety of religious opinion and a commitment to progressive social causes. The recent emphases of Unitarian Universalism include new attention to feminist theologies, concern over issues of racial injustice and excessive military armament, and efforts to discover or revive new forms and expressions of spirituality. In 1998 approximately 52,000 New Englanders were members in 243 Unitarian Universalist churches throughout the region.

Russell E. Miller, *The Larger Hope: The First Century of the Universalist Church in America, 1770–1870* (1979); Russell E. Miller, *The Larger Hope: The Second Century of the Universalist Church in America, 1870–1970* (1985); David Robinson, *The Unitarians and the Universalists* (1985); Conrad Wright, ed., *A Stream of Light: A Sesquicentennial History of American Unitarianism* (1975).

David M. Robinson

Ursuline Convent School Fire

New England's first convent school was founded in 1820 by the Roman Catholic Ursuline sisters in Boston, but it quickly outgrew its original location. In 1826 the Catholics purchased several acres on Ploughed Hill, a former Revolutionary fortification in Charlestown (now Somerville), Mass., and renamed it Mount Benedict in honor of their bishop, Benedict Fenwick. At the summit the Ursulines built a magnificent girls' boarding school. With its elaborate three-story brick building, tasteful furnishings, and terraced gardens, the school enrolled the daughters not only of Catholics but of some Boston's most elite Protestant families. (Tuition was expensive and only a few of the pupils were Catholic.) With its solid curriculum, including courses in both arts and sciences, the academy flourished under the able leadership of Mother Superior Mary Edmond St. George. But on the night of August 11, 1834, a group of men gathered at the convent gates and began shouting anti-Catholic slogans. When they broke through the front doors, the terrified nuns and nightgown-clad pupils escaped to the home of a neighbor. At midnight, after vandalizing the property and desecrating the corpses of nuns in the convent's mausoleum, the rioters set the school ablaze. Two thousand onlookers, including members of local fire companies who had answered the alarm, did nothing to intervene as the convent burned to the ground. (There were no fatalities.)

The causes of this riot are complex and overlapping, but they include anti-Catholic sentiment exacerbated by the increasing numbers of Irish Catholic immigrants settling in Boston; warnings by prominent Protestant clergy, including the strict Calvinist Lyman Beecher, about the dangers of educating Protestant children in Catholic institutions; resentment fueled by the financial success of a female-run institution; and the appeal of a popular literary genre—the convent captivity narrative, which provided titillating stories of women imprisoned in convent dungeons. Rebecca Reed, a charity pupil who claimed to have escaped the Charlestown convent in 1832, spread rumors about cruelties she suffered there. Her narrative, *Six Months in a Convent* (1835), sold more than 200,000 copies. When one of the Ursuline nuns suffered a breakdown in 1834, fled the convent, and was returned by the bishop, local newspapers hinted that she might be murdered. This volatile combination of causes led to the convent's destruction.

Following an emergency meeting in Boston on the day after the riot, an investigating committee of leading citizens was formed, and many upper-class Protestants publicly denounced the violence. Armed militia patrolled the streets of Boston for several nights. Twelve rioters were arrested and brought to trial, but most were acquitted and all were eventually released. Several unsuccessful petitions to reimburse the convent's diocese for its losses, estimated at $50,000 to $100,000, were brought before the Massachusetts legislature. The ruins of the Ursuline convent stood until the late 1880s, becoming a popular tourist attraction, before much of the hill was razed for landfill. Today only a small section of Mount Benedict remains in Somerville in the neighborhood known as the Nunnery Grounds. The Ursuline sisters waited for more than a century before reopening their academy in Boston. Today their school, Ursuline Academy, and convent is located in Dedham, Mass.

David Grimsted, *American Mobbing, 1828–1861: Toward Civil War* (1998): Mary Anne Ursula Moffatt, *An Answer to Six Months in a Convent, Exposing Its False-hoods and Manifold Absurdities* (1835); Rebecca Theresa Reed, *Six Months in a Convent, or The Narrative of Rebecca Theresa Reed* (1835); Nancy Lusignan Schultz, *Fire and Roses: The Burning of the Charlestown Convent, 1834* (2000); Nancy Lusignan Schultz, ed., *Veil of Fear: Nineteenth-Century Convent Tales by Rebecca Reed and Maria Monk* (1999).

Nancy Lusignan Schultz

Science and Medicine

Russell M. Lawson and Richard A. Meckel, Section Editors

Wright, Chauncey

Zakrzewska, Marie Elizabeth

At the same time that Captain John Smith christened *New* England in 1614, he set the course for New England science. Smith was a practical thinker who directed his observations toward the problem of adapting to a wilderness environment, and New England science never lost this pragmatic bent. Puritan clergymen were the leading scientists of colonial New England, as well as practical moralists committed to reforming the parishioners under their charge. Cotton Mather, for example, risked the disapproval of the Boston medical community in 1721 when he advocated smallpox inoculation in that city, disarming his critics with the simple evidence of its unqualified success. New Hampshire's natural historian the Reverend Jeremy Belknap and his friends and Congregationalist colleagues Jedidiah Morse and Manasseh Cutler sought to inform their fellow citizens of the infant country's geographic, meteorological, and botanical riches. These scientific pioneers felt deeply the spirit of Renaissance and Enlightenment inquiry, fueled in part by the initial discovery and ongoing exploration of the New World, America.

New Englanders who believed that the new republic required organizations to promote applied knowledge founded the American Academy of Arts and Sciences in 1780 and the Massachusetts Historical Society in 1791. The 19th-century observations of astronomers such as Maria Mitchell, the first woman elected to the American Academy of Arts and Sciences, supported New England's maritime economy. Meanwhile, Harvard College psychologists like William James provided a pragmatic approach to everyday life. During the 20th century B. F. Skinner eschewed metaphysics to argue for a controlled community environment, and Robert Goddard took the first steps toward landing a man on the moon with down-to-earth experiments on liquid-fueled rockets. Even such philosophers of science as Thomas Kuhn embraced institutions over ideas.

The social and biological sciences were the first important objects of scientific inquiry in colonial New England simply out of the need to build thriving communities. The first significant geographers, cartographers, and ethnographers were explorers of the New England coast, including such late-16th- and early-17th-century figures as Bartholomew Gosnold, Martin Pring, Samuel de Champlain, and John Smith. Smith's *Description of New England* (1616) is a superb account of the landscape, resources, and cultures of the Atlantic coast from Maine's Penobscot Bay to Cape Cod. Smith painted a sensitive portrait of Native American culture even as he made plans for English conquest.

The Puritans in general welcomed the new science arriving across the Atlantic from the minds of Newton, Galileo, Robert Boyle, and Johannes Kepler. Indeed, the greatest explicators of the ideas of invisible corpuscles, elliptical orbits, distant galaxies, and constant motion occupied the Congregational pulpit, from which Harvard- and Yale-educated clergymen expounded philosophy alongside theology. The Reverend Isaac Greenwood, the first Hollis Professor of Divinity at Harvard, taught Newtonian physics from the *Compendium Physicae* (1687) of Charles Morton, who wrote that "though Man can't fully know what God hath done, yet 'tis his duty still to think thereon." Jeremy Belknap wrote volumes on human and natural history to help New Englanders recognize and utilize God's hints for successful living in a wilderness environment. Daniel Little of Maine, another man of the cloth, analyzed the society and culture of the Penobscot Indians. The Connecticut-born Reverend Manasseh Cutler climbed mountains for the sake of botany. His fellow Yale alumnus Jedidiah Morse traveled throughout the new and varied United States to create a collage of the assorted natural and human productions of North America. It was to this end of creating theologians who were also naturalists that Harvard, upon the death of the Boston lawyer Paul Dudley in 1751, endowed the annual Dudleian Lectures on religion.

Scientists who were not clergymen held similar views. As late as the mid-19th century the New England geologist Benjamin Silliman, a native of North Stratford, Conn., argued that Genesis and modern geology could be reconciled; science was a tool of faith. The Swiss-born U.S. naturalist Louis Agassiz, a Harvard professor of zoology, responded angrily to Darwin's evolutionary theories, which implied a distant creation and a distant God. Agassiz did not believe in a singular creation, seeing differences among separate species as resulting from multiple creative acts of God.

The greatest naturalist of the young republic, Thomas Nuttall, illustrated the extensive scientific reach of the New England intellectual. Nuttall was at once an explorer, a discoverer, a botanist, a historian, a writer, an ornithologist, and an ethnologist. A native Englishman, Nuttall botanized his way down the Ohio and Mississippi Rivers and up the Missouri and Arkansas Rivers on foot and by boat in three long, dangerous journeys between 1808 and 1835. Under the patronage of the Philadelphian Benjamin Smith Barton, the young Nuttall followed in the wake of Lewis and Clark, exploring the Missouri River from 1810 to 1812. Ten years later, under the auspices of the American Philosophical Society, Nuttall journeyed to the Arkansas River, through present-day Arkansas and Oklahoma, and into Indian Territory. He sought to discover the varied species of flora of the trans-Mississippi prairies as well as the source of the Arkansas River in the Rocky Mountains. Nuttall recorded his adventures and scientific discoveries in *A Journal of Travels into the Arkansa Territory, during the Year 1819* (1821). Returning to New England in 1820, Nuttall became a lecturer on natural history at Harvard, where for the next two decades he produced fundamental treatises on American ornithology and plant life. Like other New England scientists, Nuttall believed that the study of natural history was a way to discover universal moral and religious standards. Truth was reflected in nature.

Harvard College took the lead in the study of nature, at the macroscopic and microscopic levels. The earliest American astronomers were Harvard alumni such as

Increase Mather and his son Cotton, who formed a short-lived scientific society with Boston colleagues in 1683. The Mathers used a telescope that John Winthrop, Jr., had donated to Harvard to study Halley's Comet. The ubiquitous New England almanacs spread knowledge of solar eclipses, transits of Venus and Mercury, phases of the moon, and astrological data as well. Over the years Harvard developed a sophisticated curriculum that included the study of physics and astronomy. John Winthrop IV, the Hollis Professor from 1738 to 1779, taught a generation of New England intellectuals the latest in natural science in his "experimental philosophy" course.

The most famous 18th-century empiricist produced by New England was Benjamin Thompson, a Tory who fled to Europe during the American Revolution, where in time he became Count Rumford. In 1796 he published a volume in which he discussed principles of heat, motion, and friction as well as many ideas for the application of science, ranging from the most effective fireplace to the method for brewing the best cup of coffee. The count from Woburn, Mass., never forgot his pragmatic New England roots.

Over the centuries since that era, scientists of every stripe, in association with various New England institutions, have contributed to astronomy, embryology, mathematics, biology, sociobiology, chemistry, and linguistics. Ernest Everett Just, a graduate of Dartmouth College, gained renown for his discoveries in marine and cell biology, many of them made while he was working at the Woods Hole Marine Biological Laboratory in Massachusetts. The research chemist James Bryant Conant, elected president of Harvard in 1933, made a name for himself not only in scientific circles but in political and diplomatic ones as well. Having helped develop the atomic bomb, Conant became U.S. high commissioner for West Germany after World War II. Norbert Wiener of the Massachusetts Institute of Technology added to our understanding of probability and randomness in mathematics and the universe; he also wrote a fascinating autobiography. The English-born astronomer Cecilia Helena Payne-Gaposchkin took a fellowship at Harvard Observatory and published groundbreaking research in the early 1930s on the makeup and evolution of stars. Her conclusions, which contradicted the prevailing theories of the time, were dismissed as "impossible" by prominent astronomers, but they soon proved to be right.

The biologist Rachel Carson, like Ernest Everett Just, performed marine research at Woods Hole. In 1962 she almost single-handedly launched the modern environmental movement with her best-selling book *Silent Spring,* which revealed the damage being done to nature by the overuse of chemical pesticides. Carson's sense of wonder in the face of the world's beauty makes her a direct spiritual descendant of New England's Puritan settlers and of the 19th century's Transcendentalist writers and philosophers. The biologist Ruth Hubbard earned her doctorate from Radcliffe College in 1950 and received a Guggenheim fellowship two years later. Hubbard began her scientific career researching the chemistry of vision; in the 1970s she turned her attention to the sociobiology of science, critiquing the gender-based orientation of much scientific research and publishing in the field of women's health. She is one of several Harvard scientists who have raised ethical questions about human gene research and the purposes to which it is put. The Harvard entomologist and two-time Pulitzer Prize winner Edward O. Wilson founded his career on the study of ants and has since gained renown for his pioneering work in the field of evolutionary biology. His book *The Future of Life* (2002) cautions that the living world will die unless we stop destroying the natural environment and protect the earth's remaining biodiversity. The paleontologist Stephen Jay Gould, also from Harvard, popularized natural science and evolution in a series of elegantly literary, best-selling books. MIT's linguist Noam Chomsky has been a staunch critic of both B. F. Skinner's philosophy of behaviorism, particularly as it relates to language acquisition, and, since the Vietnam War, U.S. foreign policy.

One of the great recent accomplishments in applied science relied largely on research carried out by New England engineers before, during, and after World War II. In 1930 the MIT electrical engineer Vannevar Bush invented a "general-purpose automatic analog computer," a high-speed calculating device, to assist in the solution of difficult engineering problems. A decade later Harvard's Howard Aiken, assisted by the mathematician Grace Murray Hopper, developed an elaborate "digital computer" called Mark I. Hopper went on to become a rear admiral in the U.S. Navy, specializing in naval applications for COBOL (common business-oriented language); in 1991 she received the National Medal of Technology. It was left to MIT engineer Jay Forrester to create Whirlwind, one of the world's first successful computer operating systems. Whirlwind was unique in that it used a "magnetic core memory" pushed along in the age before transistors by thousands of vacuum tubes (which failed at an alarming rate). Whirlwind, renamed SAGE, in time became the basis of the tracking systems used by the U.S. Air Force.

From John Smith to Jay Forrester, from the 17th century to the present, New England scientists, many of them immigrants or descendants of immigrants, have responded to the practical challenges posed by a beautiful but difficult region scarred by the natural movements of the past. They have built institutions to preserve their accomplishments and pass their knowledge on to future generations: Harvard (1636) and Yale (1701) Universities, Dartmouth College (1769), the American Academy of Arts and Sciences (1780), the Massachusetts Historical Society (1791), Boston University (1839), the Massachusetts Institute of Technology (1861), Worcester (Mass.) Polytechnic University (1865), Clark University (1887; also in Worcester), and the many smaller liberal arts colleges and state universities. How such institutions acquired and disseminated knowledge was the focus of Thomas Kuhn's scholarly life.

Kuhn, who taught at Harvard and MIT, gained fame for his works on the history of science, in particular *The Structure of Scientific Revolutions,* published in 1962. Kuhn challenged the traditional view that the methods of science are strictly objective, that science is progressive, that accumulated knowledge, generation upon generation, will yield absolute insights, and—mirroring Newton's assumptions—that organized knowledge is linear and constant in time and space. Rather, Kuhn argued that the organization and methods of science are subjective. The acquisition of scientific knowledge is shifting and relative. Scientists are conservative puzzle solvers

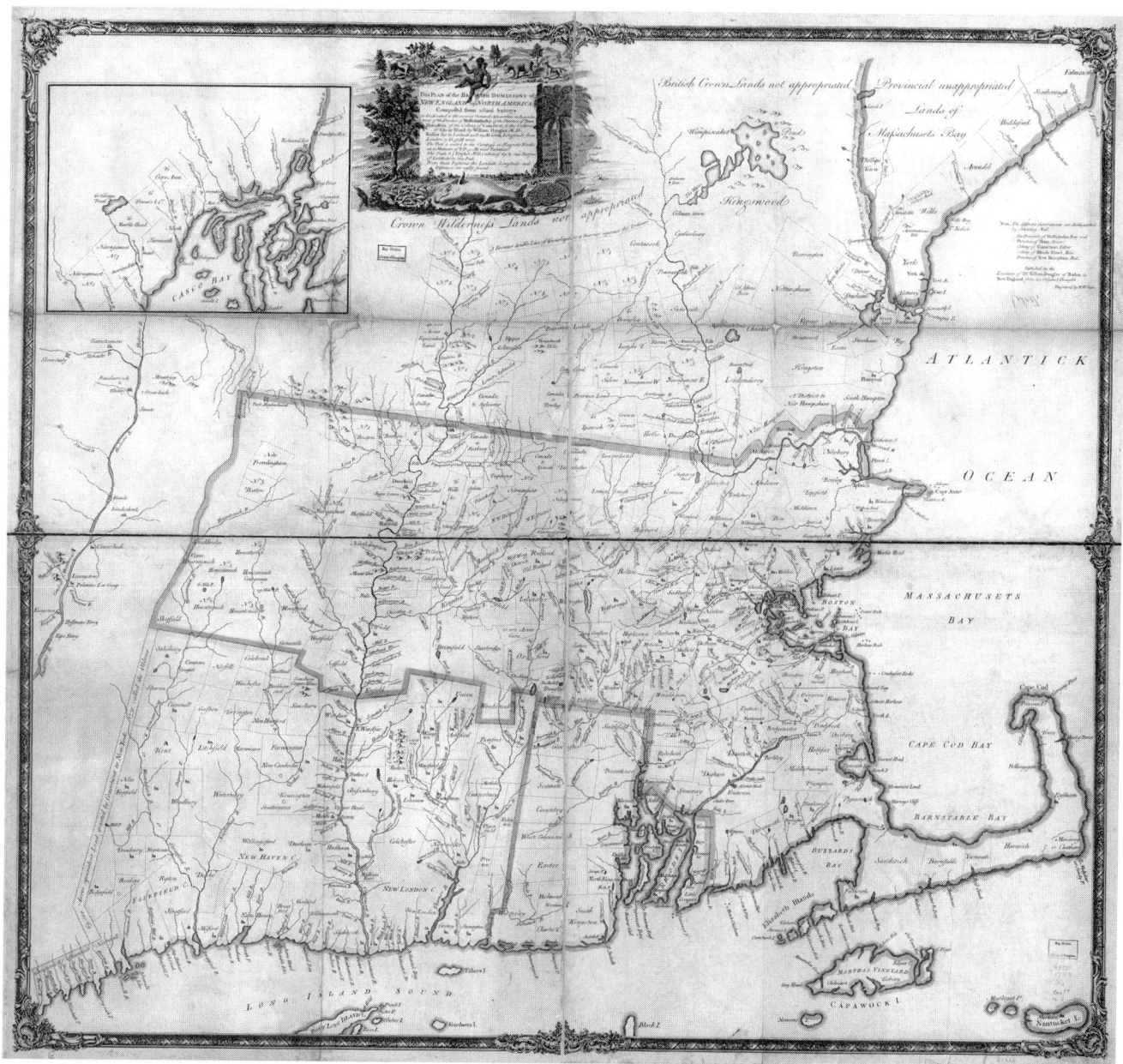

A Scottish immigrant, the physician William Douglass settled in Boston and pursued a number of interests: natural history, geography, economics, and politics (he paid to have a township in Massachusetts named after himself). Douglass published an almanac, A Summary, Historical and Political, . . . of the British Settlements in North-America *(1747–52), and a treatise on smallpox, about which he engaged in acrimonious debate with Cotton Mather, who supported inoculation, which Douglass opposed. Douglass's map, posthumously published as* This Plan of the British Dominions of New England *(1753?), was unusual because it was based on surveyed "plans" of towns compiled into a regional map rather than on standard mapping sources.*

oriented to preserving the past rather than conquering the future. Kuhn believed that paradigms, "a set of . . . principles that have proven their ability to order the experiences of a given social constituency," orient the methods and structures of science. Each generation of scientists places its faith in certain fundamental assumptions and theories that order their work and their world. Isaac Newton's way of explaining natural phenomena organized the worldview of early American scientists, just as Einstein's theory of relativity unites modern scientists under a common paradigm.

Kuhn's theory of paradigmatic science, a practical rather than a metaphysical approach to explaining the acquisition of knowledge, illustrates the characteristics of science in New England since the beginning. All along, the paradigm of New England science has been a devotion to common sense, applied knowledge, and discovering concrete solutions to life's perplexities, especially those unique to the six states in North America known as New England.

Martha J. Bailey, *American Women in Science: A Biographical Dictionary* (1994); Bailey, *American Women in Science, 1950 to the Present: A Biographical Dictionary* (1998); Daniel J. Boorstin, *The Americans: The Colonial Experience* (1958); George H. Daniels, *Science in American Society: A Social History* (1971); Charles Flowers, *A Science Odyssey: 100 Years of Discovery* (1998); Owen Gingerich, *The Physical Sciences in the 20th Century* (1989); Jeannette E. Graustein, *Thomas Nuttall, Naturalist: Explorations in America, 1808–1841* (1967); John C. Greene, *American Science in the Age of Jefferson* (1984); Brooke Hindle, *The Pursuit of Science in Revolutionary America, 1735–1789* (1956); Russell M. Lawson, *The American Plutarch: Jeremy Belknap and the Historian's Dialogue with the Past* (1998); Lawson, "Science and Medicine," in *The Colonial Era, 1600–1754*, vol. 2 of *American Eras*, ed. Jessica Kross (1998); Margaret W. Rossiter, *Women Scientists in America: Before Affirmative Action, 1940–1972* (1995); Rossiter, *Women Scientists in America: Struggles and Strategies to 1940* (1982); Cynthia Eagle Russett, *Darwin in America: The Intellectual Response, 1865–1912* (1976); Raymond Stearns, *Science in the British Colonies of America* (1970).

Russell M. Lawson

Over the centuries there has been an increasingly synergistic relation between science and medicine. Cotton Mather, Manasseh Cutler, and Ruth Hubbard may be seen as incarnating the intersection between the two in New England at various historical moments between 1600 and 2000. Cutler, for example, was a botanist as well as a physician. During the colonial period in particular, physicians had to be good botanists if they were to acquire the necessary medicines with which to treat their patients. Early members of the clergy were trained as physicians of the body as well as of the soul. Colonial medicine, however, bore little resemblance to the sophisticated system that exists today. It involved a variety of practitioners and therapies patterned largely after English traditions, particularly those of the East Anglia region. There were no general hospitals, no anesthesia, no antibiotics, no sterilization of medical instruments, and little understanding of the causes of infection. This began to change in the decades following the founding of the republic.

Although republican sentiment often inspired New Englanders in the late 18th and early 19th centuries to boast that America in general and their region in particular were salubrious and healthful, the reality was considerably different. Although it was lucky enough to escape the yellow fever epidemic of the 1820s, New England was ravaged by at least three major incursions of pandemic cholera between 1832 and 1866. Typhus and typhoid epidemics were frequent, especially where people were crowded together and sanitation was poor. Smallpox, though largely controllable through vaccination, also continued to make regular visits. Less terrifying but considerably more deadly were a host of endemic diseases. Gastroenteric disorders in the summer and respiratory diseases in the winter carried off thousands of New England infants each year. Measles, scarlet fever, diphtheria, and other childhood diseases were a deadly scourge among the young. Indeed, a conservative estimate would be that 20 percent of New England's youth never reached adulthood. Moreover, those who did faced a significant risk of developing and dying from tuberculosis, the greatest killer of the century and a disease so prevalent that it permeates 19th-century Romantic imagery. Against these diseases, regular, irregular, folk, and popular therapeutics remained largely ineffective. Thus the story of medicine between the Revolutionary and Civil Wars is one not of conquering disease but of competition between various therapeutic strategies.

During the last quarter of the 18th century and the first decade of the 19th, elite physicians in New England tried in various ways to impose some degree of order on medical training and practice. They founded professional societies dedicated to raising standards and combating quackery, lobbied for licensing laws, established medical schools at Harvard (1782) and Yale (1810), and promoted a university education as a prerequisite to medical training. Nevertheless, New England medicine entered the 19th century only slightly more organized, regulated, and respected than it had been during the colonial era. Moreover, what little progress toward coherence may have been made in the latter part of the 18th century was largely reversed in the early 19th, as the profession fractured into competing sects; proprietary medical schools proliferated, vastly increasing the number of barely trained physicians; and New Englanders from all classes and all corners of the region registered their low opinion of orthodox medicine by embracing a wide variety of popular health and self-treatment regimens.

In the first third of the 19th century the already disparate universe of medical caregivers fragmented even further, with the emergence of a number of sects whose practitioners promoted a variety of new hygienic philosophies, special therapies, and medical systems as a challenge to orthodox medicine, which since the late 18th century had attracted increasing public disfavor by its liberal use of such "heroic" therapies as cathartics and purgatives along with copious bleeding of patients to achieve systemic balance. Contending that the "regulars" did more harm than good, the sectarians, the most prominent of whom were botanics, homeopaths, hydropaths, and eclectics, made the New England medical marketplace intensely competitive and gave 19th-century New Englanders a variety of medical choices.

Of all the sects, the botanic system known as Thomsonianism was most closely associated with New England. Developed in the first decade of the century by Samuel Thomson, a New Hampshire farmer, Thomsonianism was an amalgam of Anglo-American rural folk herbalism and botanic emetics and cathartic practices long used by New England's native peoples. Intuitively sensing the commercial possibilities occasioned by the popular resentment of physicians, Thomson obtained a patent for his system and sold the rights to it to families so that they could avoid orthodox practitioners and treat themselves. Especially popular in rural areas, Thomsonianism attracted tens of thousands of adherents; by 1840, close to 100,000 families had purchased the rights to the system.

Various forms of faith and spiritual healing also attracted 19th-century New Englanders. Most prominent among these was Christian Science, which originated in New England in the 1870s, when Mary Baker Eddy published *Science and Health* and began to organize congregations. By 1900, more than 500 congregations had been founded. For urban and small-town New Englanders, particularly those in the emerging middle class, homeopathy was usually the alternative medical system of choice, in large part because it eschewed heroic therapies while mimicking orthodox medicine's stress on science, education, and professional organization. Middle-class New Englanders, caught in the powerful currents of antebellum religious and moral perfectionism, also embraced and reinvigorated the age-old idea that living temperately and hygienically was the key to improving and maintaining personal health.

In doing so, they were guided and encouraged by a large and varied collection of popular health reformers, many of whom were from the region. Among the more prominent of these were the dietary reformer Sylvester Graham, the temperance advocate Mary Hunt, and the writer of popular health manuals William Alcott. Less prominent though more prevalent were numerous quacks and charlatans, who marketed a wide variety of pseudoscientific therapies and patent medicines, often profiting considerably from New Englanders' continuing devotion to self-dosage and self-treatment. Among the most popular and pervasive of these patent medicines was a vegetable and alcohol compound based on the home remedy devised by Lydia Estes Pinkham of Lynn, Mass.

The middle-class conviction that hygiene was both moral and healthy was also at the core of the sanitary-reform movement, which began developing around mid-century in response to growing fears that urban growth led to declining personal and environmental hygiene and rising morbidity and mortality. To document such fears and to encourage public action, American sanitarians, like Boston's Lemuel Shattuck, conducted sanitary surveys of their cities, thereby laying the foundation for subsequent initiation of systematic health-data collection. In the decades after the Civil War, New England municipalities and states established health departments and granted them police powers to control communicable diseases and clean up environmental filth.

Religious and moral perfectionism, along with increasing urbanization, also spurred an effort to provide more orderly and humane lodging than the almshouse for the infirm in mind and body. Small general hospitals such as Boston's Massachusetts General, which dates back to 1811, were established in major cities. Asylums and schools for the blind and for the deaf and mute were constructed. Among these were the Perkins School for the Blind in Watertown, Mass., which received its first students in 1832, and the American School for the Deaf in Hartford, which opened in 1817. In addition to serving a charitable purpose, the new hospitals and asylums provided some physicians with clinical training not yet available as part of formal medical education. This was one of the principal functions of the New England Hospital for Women and Children, founded in 1862 by Marie Zakrzewska as a women's hospital and a site at which female physicians could obtain clinical training.

Orthodox physicians reacted to the proliferation of sectarians and popular health schemes in a variety of ways. Many, perhaps most, were vigorously defensive of their therapeutics. Along with the American Medical Association, which was organized in 1847, they labeled all alternatives to heroic medicine as quackery and sought, albeit unsuccessfully, to limit access to the medical marketplace. Others, by contrast, lessened their reliance on depletion, promoted moderate diet and hygienic living, and raised serious questions about the effectiveness and scientific validity of orthodox therapeutics. Indeed, while being perhaps somewhat extreme, Oliver Wendell Holmes, Sr., New England's popular literary physician, suggested that throwing the entire orthodox materia medica into the sea would harm no one but the unsuspecting fish.

The last two decades of the 19th century marked a turning point for U.S. and New England medicine, as a science, as a practice, and as an institution. Between 1880 and 1940 a series of factors altered medicine dramatically: radical reform of the education and training of health-care professionals, the increasing importance of the hospital as a primary treatment and teaching site, the reorganization of the profession into specialties and allied professions such as nursing and dentistry, the amalgamation of organized orthodox practitioners into a politically and economically powerful force, and, perhaps most of all, a revolution in the biochemical sciences, in clinical techniques, and in medical technology that provided the foundation for the ultimate development of what physicians and other medical practitioners had previously lacked: a demonstrably effective medical, surgical, and chemotherapeutical armamentarium with which to prevent, manage, and combat disease and correct other health problems. New England's role in this transformation was important but not distinct.

At the end of the 19th and the beginning of the 20th centuries many new hospitals were constructed. In 1873 there were 178 medical and mental hospitals in the nation; by 1923 there were 6,830. In New England, hospitals were built in every major city and in some of the larger towns. Like their antebellum predecessors, the hospitals built after the Civil War initially were charitable enterprises, the majority of whose patients were poor. By the 1920s, however, hospitals were attracting increasingly large numbers of middle-class patients by offering services performed by technically proficient physicians, especially obstetrical deliveries, appendectomies, and tonsillectomies.

Attending the proliferation of hospitals was the transformation of nursing into a professional service. Before the 1870s no nurses had formal training, and hospital nurses were accorded less respect than charwomen. By 1923 there were 1,700 nursing schools, most of them attached to hospitals. Indeed, in New England nursing programs were established not only at major hospitals such as Massachusetts General, Boston City, Rhode Island Hospital, New Haven Hospital in Connecticut, Worcester Memorial, and Elliot Hospital in Keene, N.H., but also at approximately 25 percent of the other hospitals. Many nurses who graduated from these programs worked in hospitals. Some went to work for health and school departments, charities, and visiting-nurse associations, however, becoming the ground troops in the early-20th-century public-health battle to improve the health of schoolchildren, reduce infant mortality, and combat tuberculosis and other widespread communicable diseases.

Physician training was also undergoing reform. At the end of the Civil War virtually all medical schools in New England and the nation were proprietary schools; that is, they were largely independent institutions run by faculty who collected fees directly from their students and split what was left after expenses. Easy to establish and relatively cheap to operate, proprietary medical schools proliferated in 19th-century America and competed for students by maintaining minimal entrance requirements, keeping the course of study short, and making degrees easy to obtain. Even at Harvard, considered one of the best schools in the nation, a college degree was not a prerequisite for admission; the program consisted of two four-month courses of study, with no laboratory work in the basic sciences or clinical training required; and students only had to pass a majority of their courses to graduate.

The reform of medical education did not come overnight, but by 1920 most

American medical schools were part of universities and featured an extended course of study requiring lab work and clinical training. Johns Hopkins provided the model of the new medical school, but Harvard pioneered it in the 1870s, when the university brought its medical school under university control and extended and reformed its curriculum. To a certain extent the reform of medical education was prompted by ever stricter licensing laws that states began adopting at the end of the century. And to a certain extent it was part of the maturation of American universities into institutions of research and postgraduate training. But both these developments reflected a larger revolution in biomedical science that by 1940 had transformed medical research from the spare-time activity of a few physician-scientists to a huge enterprise involving thousands of highly trained researchers.

For most of the 19th century, little medical research—either in the basic biomedical sciences or in the clinical sciences—was done in the United States. Nineteenth-century American physicians with an interest in science had to travel to Europe, initially to France and then to Germany and Austria, for training. One of these itinerants, Henry Pickering Bowditch, returned to Boston in 1871 to set up the nation's first physiology lab and help train such late-19th-century New England medical luminaries as Walter B. Cannon and the pioneering psychologists William James and G. Stanley Hall.

It was not until the turn of the century, however, when medical schools and university science departments began establishing research and training relationships with major hospitals and wealthy philanthropists and foundations began funding research and research institutes, that medical research began developing into the huge biomedical enterprise that it would be by 1940. Again, Boston and Harvard were at the center of these developments in New England, although by the 1920s Worcester and New Haven were also becoming biomedical research centers. One critical step in the emergence of Boston as a biomedical research center came in the first two decades of the 20th century, when Harvard, with the help of Rockefeller funds, created a medical-school complex in Roxbury and built as part of it the state-of-the-art Brigham Hospital. Covering more than 250 acres, the new complex united basic science and clinical research with classroom and clinical training.

This biomedical scientific revolution—during which scientists between 1880 and 1900 identified 21 microorganisms as specific causes of disease—also helped define the methods and goals of the wide-ranging public-health movement. Armed with the new science of bacteriology and working out of newly created laboratories, New England state and municipal health-department scientists were increasingly able to identify, track, and control the pathogenic pollution of food and water, and thus prevent diseases like typhoid, and to positively identify those infected with diphtheria, tuberculosis, and a host of other infectious diseases. Especially prominent among these public-health reformers was Providence Superintendent of Health Charles Chapin, who achieved an international reputation for innovative expertise in municipal sanitation and the control of infectious disease.

Attending the emergence of modern medicine was a decline of mortality rates in New England and a change in the most prevalent causes of death. At the beginning of the 20th century, life in New England was still precarious. Life expectancy at birth was less than 50 years. Tuberculosis and typhoid still ravaged the population, killing thousands. Pneumonia struck down thousands more, especially the old and very young. The great epidemics of the previous century—smallpox and cholera—had receded as threats, but fatal epidemics had not become a thing of the past. In 1918 pandemic influenza struck, killing tens of thousands of New Englanders and more than a half million Americans nationwide. Polio was a growing peril, killing or crippling thousands of New Englanders, many of them children, during a 1916 epidemic outbreak. Diarrhea and enteritis were still endemic, regularly incapacitating adults and older children and cutting a deadly swath through the infant population, especially during the hot summer months. More than 10 percent of all New Englanders failed to survive the first year of life, some 18 percent never reached the age of five, and close to 23 percent died before age 20. Adulthood was safer, but not safe. Women still died frequently in childbirth, and extraordinary numbers of both sexes succumbed to tuberculosis and other diseases.

Just three decades later, life expectancy at birth had risen to about 60 years; typhoid had all but disappeared as a major threat, with tuberculosis fast receding; infant mortality had been cut in half; deaths from the major childhood diseases had declined some 60 percent; and maternal mortality, while still high, had begun to fall. After 300 years infectious disease was relinquishing its status as death's most familiar handmaiden in New England. In 1930 four of the five leading causes of death were chronic and degenerative diseases.

How important a role medicine played in the decline of mortality from infectious disease has long been a subject of debate. Some argue that its role was relatively small, that medicine had no curative armamentarium before the 1940s, and that the chief causes of the decline were rising living standards, better nutrition, and a consequent increase in resistance to disease. Others, while acknowledging that effective drug therapies did not exist in the first third of the century, argue that late-19th- and early-20th-century biomedical research, especially in bacteriology, epidemiology, serology, and nutrition, had a significant impact on lowering the prevalence of pathogens and controlling their transmission.

At the beginning of World War II biomedical research, health care, and their allied industries were a growing but still relatively minor segment of American society and the U.S. economy. Fifty years later they had become a major force, gobbling up more than 10 percent of the gross national product and employing millions of Americans. World War II was a major catalyst in the phenomenal growth of the biomedical enterprise that occurred after 1945. In addition to introducing new drugs (most notably, penicillin), prompting improvements in hospital management and care, and vastly enlarging the pharmaceutical and medical-supply industry, the war initiated massive federal spending on research, training, and facilities. The continuation and growth of this spending after the war helped make the quality of American medical training, research, practice, and facilities the envy of the world and helped turn New England cities like Boston and New Haven into international medical centers that attract large numbers of foreign students, practitioners, and researchers.

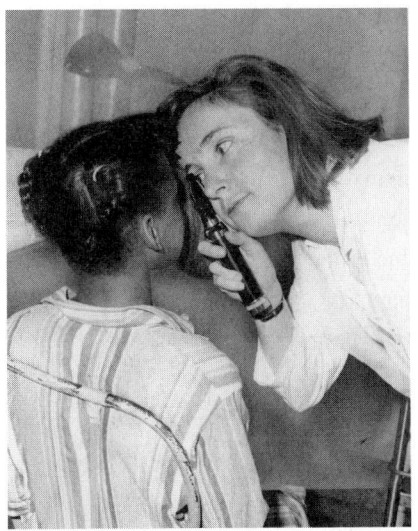

Boston University pediatrics intern checks a child's eyes, 1965

The remarkable postwar growth of the American biomedical enterprise has been accompanied by an unprecedented expansion of the concepts of health and disease to include a vast array of human experiences, conditions, and behaviors and by the spectacular success orthodox medicine has had in managing and curing certain age-old diseases and health problems. Since World War II, and especially since 1960, infant and particularly neonatal mortality in New England has plummeted. So, too, has that of middle-aged men and of the population between the ages of 65 and 75. Maternal mortality, which had remained high into the 1930s, has become exceedingly rare.

If medicine has become increasingly effective in the past several decades, it has also become increasingly expensive and, in the eyes of some, increasingly inhumane and intrusive. Indeed, since World War II those two issues have dominated sociopolitical discussions of medicine. The postwar development of private, employer-provided health insurance and the 1960s creation of the federally funded Medicaid and Medicare programs have significantly, if inequitably, helped offset for many the increasing cost of medical care, but they have also helped fuel rising costs. As a consequence, since the 1970s a number of health-delivery schemes have been developed to bring various economies to medicine. One of these, the health maintenance organization, was pioneered in New England by Harvard Health.

The popularity of unorthodox health-care strategies and opposition to orthodox medicine did not diminish in the postwar era. Indeed, especially since 1970, alternative medicine and medical nihilism have flourished in New England and the nation. Like the mid-19th-century subscribers to Samuel Thomson's botanic cures, tens of thousands of modern-day New Englanders have sought natural herbal remedies for everything from depression to cancer. Millions of others have sought to prevent disease and degeneration and improve health by modifying their diets and engaging in physical exercise.

Like the heroic medicine of the past, contemporary scientific medicine has attracted its share of critics, especially for the way it has transformed two ostensibly natural processes: birth and death. Both the right-to-die and the hospice movement have sprung from widespread revulsion over the dehumanizing character of dying in the modern hospital. Similarly, while acknowledging that scientific obstetrics has helped make birth far less dangerous, women in New England and elsewhere have increasingly charged that it has transformed birth into an experience characterized by subjugation, alienation, and indignity. Since at least the 1960s there has been a fairly influential feminist revolt against scientific medicine. Among the more important early moments of that revolt was the 1970 publication of a preliminary version of *Our Bodies, Ourselves* by the Boston Women's Health Book Collective.

Like the much-respected *New England Journal of Medicine,* many fine research hospitals and medical schools located in the region are nominally identified with New England. But from the distinctively regional character it once had, New England medicine has become thoroughly national and international. New England nonetheless continues to exercise considerable influence in shaping the future of American medicine. That the region, and specifically the greater Boston area, currently hosts the world's highest concentration of biotechnology firms suggests that its medical research and educational and clinical facilities continue to act as powerful magnets for those charting new directions in medical science, training, and practice.

Daniel J. Boorstin, *The Americans: The Colonial Experience* (1958); James Cassedy, *Charles V. Chapin and the Public Health Movement* (1962); Norman Gevitz, ed., *Other Healers: Unorthodox Medicine in America* (1988); Lawrence B. Goodheart, *Mad Yankees: The Hartford Retreat for the Insane and 19th-Century Psychiatry* (2003); Gerald N. Grob, *Edward Jarvis and the Medical World of 19th-Century America* (1978); Grob, *The Mad among Us: A History of the Care of America's Mentally Ill* (1994); Russell M. Lawson, "Science and Medicine," in *The Colonial Era, 1600–1754,* vol. 2 of *American Eras,* ed. Jessica Kross (1998); Kenneth M. Ludmerer, *Learning to Heal: The Development of American Medical Education* (1985); Ludmerer, *Time to Heal: American Medical Education from the Turn of the Century to the Era of Managed Care* (1999); Richard A. Meckel, *Save the Babies: American Public Health Reform and the Prevention of Infant Mortality, 1850–1929* (1998 [1990]); Regina Markell Morantz-Sanchez, *Sympathy and Science: Women Physicians in American Medicine* (1985); Ellen S. More, *Restoring the Balance: Women Physicians and the Profession of Medicine, 1850–1995* (1999); Ronald L. Numbers, ed., *Medicine in the New World: New Spain, New France, and New England* (1987); Heather Munro Prescott, *A Doctor of Their Own: A History of Adolescent Medicine* (1998); Susan Reverby, *Ordered to Care: The Dilemma of American Nursing, 1850–1945* (1987); Barbara Gutman Rosenkrantz, *Public Health and the State: Changing Views in Massachusetts, 1842–1936* (1972); Paul Starr, *The Social Transformation of American Medicine* (1987); Martha Verbrugge, *Able-Bodied Womanhood: Personal Health and Social Change in 19th-Century Boston* (1988); James C. Whorton, *Crusaders for Fitness: The History of American Health Reformers* (1982).

Richard A. Meckel

Agassiz, (Jean) Louis (Rodolphe)

(1807–73) Geologist, paleontologist, and ichthyologist. The prominent 19th-century naturalist Louis Agassiz made fundamental contributions to the fields of geology, paleontology, ichthyology, and embryology at a time when those areas were in their infancy. An enthusiastic teacher of natural science, initially in Europe and then in the United States, the Swiss-born Agassiz throughout his life undertook extensive research, publishing, and institution-building projects. His son, Alexander, a famous naturalist in his own right and a wealthy New England entrepreneur, described his father's urge "to capture the animal kingdom all at once," feeling it was impossible to stop this "steam engine," Louis Agassiz, from his insatiable quest to dominate the field, especially in the United States. Despite the opinion of some colleagues that Agassiz's inability to husband his resources and his penchant for popular instruction made his research less significant in his later years, he was to many a "prince of naturalists" and a "pied piper of science," enticing many to follow in his footsteps.

Educated at the universities of Zurich, Erlangen, Heidelberg, and Berlin, Agassiz at an early age determined to become "the first naturalist of his time." In 1832 Baron Georges Cuvier, the noted French ichthyologist, granted Agassiz permission to study his collections and those at the Jardin des Plantes in Paris; Cuvier's unfinished work became Agassiz's province as he inherited the mantle of his famous supporter. Agassiz's first monograph, a study of Brazilian fishes (1829), won him immediate recognition from the doyens of natural science. The research and publication of his multivolume work on paleoichthyology (*Recherches sur les poissons fossiles* [1833–43]) secured financial support for future projects. The geographer Alexander von Humboldt recognized Agassiz's genius and obtained a teaching position for him at the College de Neuchâtel in Switzerland.

During this time, Agassiz advanced the "glacial theory," wherein he held that a vast ice age had covered Europe in the immediate past. Subsequently, he successfully extended the glacial hypothesis to North America.

Agassiz's reputation was such that John Amory Lowell invited him to deliver a course of lectures at Boston's Lowell Institute; his success resulted in lecture appearances throughout New England. Agassiz was offered a professorship at the newly established Lawrence Scientific School of Harvard University (his salary underwritten by cotton magnate Abbott Lawrence). Enamored of the promise of American science, the optimism of its people, and its support of research, he vowed to remain in the United States. Soon after the death of his first wife in 1848, Agassiz married Elizabeth Cabot Cary, daughter of a wealthy Boston family and a founder of Radcliffe College. In Cambridge, the couple welcomed Henry Wadsworth Longfellow, James Russell Lowell, Benjamin Pierce, and other literati as close friends and neighbors. Agassiz's favorite pastime was presiding, with Oliver Wendell Holmes, at meetings of the Saturday Club.

By the mid-1850s Agassiz had achieved nationwide status as a preeminent naturalist. Such colleagues as Harvard botanist Asa Gray, Yale geologist James Dwight Dana, and Dana's father-in-law, Benjamin Silliman, all marveled at their good fortune in claiming Agassiz as their own. In turn, Agassiz rewarded his adopted country with research, teaching, and books that he hoped would put American science on par with Europe. From 1855 to 1862, for example, Agassiz began a study of North American fishes, undertook research resulting in the multivolume *Contributions to the Natural History of the United States,* and raised nearly $1 million for the establishment of the Museum of Comparative Zoology at Harvard College. Government aid and private philanthropy helped Agassiz found the first summer school for natural history teachers on Penikese Island, Mass., in 1872–73.

During the 1860s, however, American naturalists, notably Gray and Dana, became increasingly displeased with what they perceived to be Agassiz's denial of the validity of Darwin's evolution theory. Agassiz believed in the separate, special creation of species, unchanging over time, as willed by an all-powerful deity. Further, his detractors chafed at his attempts to dominate the political character of national science when Agassiz and some close associates convinced the government in 1863 to create the National Academy of Sciences with 50 hand-picked charter members.

The concerns of his critics notwithstanding, Agassiz's impact on American culture and intellectual life was profound and long lasting. In his attempt to elevate American scientific standards, Agassiz was notably involved in establishing and directing such venerable institutions as the American Association for the Advancement of Science, the Smithsonian Institution, and the Harvard Museum. At once dogmatic, romantic, and ambitious beyond his means, Agassiz's spirit infused 19th-century scientific study and laid the groundwork for private and public philanthropic support for the sciences.

Elizabeth Cary Agassiz, ed., *Louis Agassiz: His Life and Correspondence,* 2 vols. (1885); Edward Lurie, *Louis Agassiz: A Life in Science,* rev. ed. (1988).

Edward Lurie

AIDS Action Committee of Massachusetts

Organized in 1983 by a small group of volunteers, the community-based AIDS Action Committee of Massachusetts is New England's oldest and largest AIDS organization. Its professional staff numbers more than 70 and coordinates the efforts of several thousand volunteers. AIDS Action provides support services to 2,500 men, women, and children living with AIDS and HIV. It also educates the public and health-care professionals about HIV and advocates for fair and effective AIDS policy on the city, state, and federal levels. The organization has served as a model for other AIDS-action groups from the AIDS Project of Portland, Maine, to New Hampshire's AIDS Response Seacoast to AIDS Support of New Haven, Conn., to name only a few.

By January 1983, 11 cases of AIDS had been reported in Massachusetts. That month a

AIDS Action Committee of Massachusetts contingent in annual Gay Pride Parade, Boston, 1998

group of lesbians and gay men met in the basement of the Fenway Community Health Center to organize a group to support those who were ill and educate the community. Initially, AIDS Action was housed in that same basement, which served as command central for volunteers and as a drop-in center for people with AIDS. AIDS Action soon outgrew that space, however, and moved into its own offices in Boston's Back Bay.

AIDS Action's early volunteers responded to the hysterical atmosphere that surrounded the epidemic in the early years with a heroic display of respect, compassion, empowerment, and love. They hand-delivered trays of food that had been left outside hospital doors. They comforted the sick and the dying. They confronted landlords and raised their voices until politicians, legislators, and other government officials started listening. They set an example of sensitivity and decency that helped health-care workers and others to overcome irrational fears and abandon their prejudices against people with AIDS.

In the absence of leadership, the AIDS Action Committee became a national player, pleading with federal officials for increased AIDS funding and speaking out against irrational public policy. Among other high-profile fund-raising events, an AIDS walk has been held every year since 1985, raising millions of dollars for AIDS Action and other AIDS service providers.

In 1984 those involved in AIDS Action believed that a cure for AIDS would be found within five years and expected to close the agency's doors. Instead, the ever-increasing scope of the AIDS epidemic has compelled the organization to expand its services, increase staffing levels, and redouble its volunteer and fund-raising efforts. Its announced agenda for 2004 includes lobbying state health officials to establish statewide clean syringe access policy and working to ensure a more efficient and effective service delivery system.

Peter Erbland

Alchemy Alchemy, a secretive spiritual and scientific pursuit among New England Puritan intellectuals, was based on a belief that God sometimes revealed to spiritually worthy investigators two extraordinary secrets: transmutation—how to turn base metals into gold—and how to make the Alkahest—a chemical elixir that cured all diseases. God intended alchemical knowledge for the betterment of society, not mere personal gain. Alchemical practitioners, therefore, maintained strict secrecy to protect their discoveries from misuse.

John Winthrop, Jr., governor of Connecticut and son of the Massachusetts governor, was Puritan New England's first resident al-

chemist and remained the most important one in British America until his death in 1676. A member of England's Royal Society, Winthrop employed alchemically derived knowledge in many projects: establishing New England's first ironworks, developing potential silver mines, initiating Connecticut plantations, promoting salt and saltpeter production, and practicing medicine. Winthrop was New England's most sought-after physician, largely because of the reputation enjoyed by his alchemical medicines. More powerful and mysterious than traditional herbal remedies, alchemical curatives gained large followings for the practitioners who administered them. George Starkey, whose alchemical texts influenced Isaac Newton, was remarkably successful as a young Boston physician. Gershom Bulkeley of Connecticut left the ministry to pursue a successful alchemical medical practice. The Puritan minister-physicians Michael Wigglesworth and Edward Taylor blended prayers for the sick with alchemical prescriptions. Taylor's poetry, like that of Andover poet Anne Bradstreet, incorporates rich alchemical imagery.

Harvard students displayed early interest in the subject. George Starkey shared alchemical pursuits with Harvard classmates in the 1640s. Elnathan Chauncy, son of the college's president, transcribed alchemical notes while a Harvard student in the 1650s. Alchemy formally entered Harvard textbooks during the 1680s, in Nathaniel Morton's *Compendium Physicae.*

New Englanders' enthusiasm for alchemy continued into the 1700s, despite increasing skepticism about its legitimacy. Massachusetts Judge Samuel Danforth offered to send a dubious Benjamin Franklin his experimentally obtained Alkahest in 1773. Ezra Stiles, Yale's president from 1778 to 1795, was believed by many to have achieved transmutation. Nevertheless, alchemy was almost fully discredited among intellectuals by the early 1800s. Alchemical doctrines, however, filtered into popular culture, where they helped provide the cosmological foundations of the Mormonism espoused by Vermont native Joseph Smith in the 1830s and 1840s.

Robert C. Black, *The Younger John Winthrop* (1966); John L. Brooke, *The Refiner's Fire: The Making of Mormon Cosmology, 1644–1844* (1994); William R. Newman, *Gehennical Fire: The Lives of George Starkey, an American Alchemist in the Scientific Revolution* (1994); Ronald S. Wilkinson, "New England's Last Alchemists," *Ambix* 10 (1962).

Walter W. Woodward

American Academy of Arts and Sciences The American Academy of Arts and Sciences is a learned society that promotes the study of social and intellectual issues. Begun in

1780, the academy sought, according to its original charter, "to cultivate every art and science which may tend to advance the interest, honor, dignity, and happiness of a free, independent, and virtuous people." Its function today is twofold: it honors achievements in the arts, sciences, and public affairs, and it runs programs that reflect its members' wide range of intellectual interests.

The American Academy of Arts and Sciences emerged as a Boston organization primarily to share information with fellow scholars and to disseminate useful knowledge for the public's benefit. Its founder, John Adams, wanted to create a society that would rival the clubs of Europe, such as the Académie des Sciences in Paris and the Royal Society of London. More important, Adams hoped to form a society that was comparable to the much-heralded Philadelphia-based American Philosophical Society. The Massachusetts legislature quickly passed an act incorporating the academy in 1780. The academy began its first year with 60 resident members, drawn mostly from Harvard, including notable New Englanders James Bowdoin, Samuel Cooper, and Joseph Willard. The group met four times annually, and all fellows had to be elected by a council member and approved by the whole society. Throughout the 18th century, the society elected many political and civic leaders, and also managed to attract several nonresident European scientists, including Joseph Priestley and Richard Price.

The academy's mission was to support North American agriculture, manufacturing, and commerce. Attempting to bolster America's position as an independent nation, the members wrote and published papers on scientific topics that benefited American production and increased North American prominence internationally. Most of the early scientific pursuits centered on astronomy, natural philosophy, and medicine. Many experiments focused on agricultural improvements and the development of better medicinal treatments. During the 1780s, for instance, academy members collected and compiled data on diseases that flourished in the New England region in an attempt to lower incidents of early death.

The American Academy of Arts and Sciences is still an active organization. Based in Cambridge, Mass., it now boasts 4,000 fellows (and 600 foreign honorary members). The academy continues to emphasize interdisciplinary study of current intellectual and social issues and publishes a quarterly journal, *Daedalus.*

Brooke Hindle, *The Pursuit of Science in Revolutionary America, 1735–1789* (1956); Henry F. May, *The Enlightenment in America* (1976).

Leslee K. Gilbert

Astronomy Since the colonial period New England scientists have found in the study of astronomy an intellectual pursuit at the same time practical and sublime. New England Puritans believed the heavens revealed the glory of God and perhaps—with comets, eclipses, and other providential signs—his will. But astronomical information was also important for navigation, agriculture, and medicine. The sextant, theodolite, quadrant, mariner's compass, and telescope were useful tools for surveyors, navigators, merchants, road-builders, and farmers. Almost from the beginning of settlement in the 17th century, amateur astronomers such as Samuel Danforth and Zechariah Brigden published almanacs that included precise calendars, phases of the moon, dates of eclipses, the position of constellations, and weather predictions. Brigden's almanac of 1659 included the first explication in the colonies of the new science of Copernicus, Boyle, Galileo, and Kepler. Even so, early American almanacs were still beholden to astrological assumptions, integrating heavenly and human affairs, calculating the impact of the zodiac on human behavior and personality.

The first center of astronomical observation was at Harvard College. John Winthrop, Jr., wanting to support empirical observation of the heavens, donated one of his two telescopes to Harvard in 1672. Thomas Brattle, Increase Mather, and his son Cotton Mather used the telescope to observe planets and comets, and formed a "philosophical club" around their new interest. Cotton Mather speculated about extraterrestrial life. Eighteenth-century Harvard graduates and professors such as Thomas Robie examined and tried to explain the aurora borealis, the transits of the paths of Mercury and Venus across the sun's disk, the nature of comets, and planetary distances. John Winthrop IV studied sunspots and journeyed

OBSERVATORY YALE COLLEGE.

Observatory, Yale College, 1860

to Newfoundland to observe the transit of Venus in 1769. Nineteenth-century New England astronomers such as James Coffin and John Farrar published treatises on "nautical astronomy" and solar and lunar eclipses, including "the method of calculating them according to the theory of astronomy, as taught in New England colleges." Indeed, by the mid-19th century the *Annals of the Astronomical Observatory of Harvard College* became essential for the study of astronomy in general as well as for the particular needs of the New England cartographer, surveyor, and navigator. William Bond was the catalyst in the opening of the Harvard Observatory (1839), which housed chronometers, telescopes, quadrants, sextants, and "an astronomical clock."

One of the most proficient 19th-century American astronomers was Maria Mitchell. A native of Nantucket, Mass., Mitchell gained fame for discovering a "telescopic" comet in 1847, after which she lectured to groups about astronomy, attended scientific meetings, and joined the American Academy of Arts and Sciences and the American Philosophical Society. In 1865 Mitchell became the first female professor of astronomy, at Vassar College, where she directed the astronomical observatory at the new women's school. Mitchell was a pioneer in the study of sunspots and wrote extensively on solar eclipses.

Equally successful was Cecilia Payne-Gaposchkin, a native of England who studied under Ernst Rutherford at Cambridge University. The work of the Harvard Observatory attracted her to New England, where she earned Harvard's first doctorate in astronomy in 1925. A highly decorated scientist who published numerous books on stellar phenomena, she later became full professor and chair of Harvard's astronomy department.

The typical New England astronomer, however, was not a Harvard intellectual with the latest telescopic technology, but an amateur thinker concerned with nature, society, and human behavior. Manasseh Cutler, the late-18th-century clergyman of Hamilton, Mass., exemplified the New England astronomer. A jack-of-all-trades scientist, Cutler was also a physician, botanist, chaplain, lawyer, clergyman, land speculator, explorer—and astronomer. His daily journal reveals that Cutler always found time to stargaze, to examine Jupiter's moons, to trace the transit of Venus, or to spend an afternoon or evening studying an eclipse. For what purpose? Simply to know better God and His works. Cutler believed that knowledge—any knowledge—contributed to successful community building in New England.

I. B. Cohen, ed., *Aspects of Astronomy in America in the 19th Century* (1980); Russell Lawson, "Science and

Medicine," in *American Eras*, vol. 2, *The Colonial Era, 1600–1754*, ed. Jessica Kross (1998).

Russell M. Lawson

Bentley, Wilson Alwyn "Snowflake"
(1865–1931) Amateur scientist and meteorological enthusiast. "Snowflake" Bentley was a lifetime resident of Jericho, Vt. An amateur scientist, Bentley was the first person to photograph snow crystals. He also performed important meteorological research.

Bentley was educated at home; his primary occupation was farming. At the age of 15, Bentley became enamored with viewing snow crystals, the individual building blocks of snowflakes, under a microscope. After first sketching snow crystals, Bentley began experimenting with photomicrography in 1883. He took his first successful photograph of a snow crystal in 1885. Refining his technique, Bentley continued to photograph snow crystals in anonymity until 1898, five years after the first academic paper on snow crystal photomicrography was published in Europe. In that year, he made his research known to George Henry Perkins, a professor of natural sciences at the University of Vermont. Perkins arranged for a selection of Bentley's photographs to be sold to the Harvard University Mineralogical Museum, where they were displayed. In 1898 Bentley and Perkins were coauthors of a paper on Bentley's research, which was published in *Appleton's Popular Science Monthly*. Bentley achieved a measure of fame for his statement in that article that no two snow crystals are alike.

In the decade that followed, Bentley wrote a number of important articles, based on both experiments and speculation, about a variety of atmospheric phenomena. He identified many of the factors that influence the form and size of snow crystals. He was the first scientist to measure the size of various types of raindrops and the first to identify that rain had a dual origin in both frozen and nonfrozen forms. Bentley's articles appeared both in specialized academic and professional journals and in such widely circulated magazines as *Harper's Weekly*.

Bentley wrote only two short articles on meteorology between 1910 and 1921. His meteorological research during the 1920s, however, allowed him to emerge from temporary obscurity. His fame can be attributed both to the significance of his meteorological research and to the appeal of his homespun story in a decade of adjustment to rapid modernization. Bentley lectured widely in the 1920s and was among the first group of scientists elected a fellow of the American Meteorological Society. His only book, *Snow Crystals*, co-written with W. J. Humphreys, was published shortly before his death.

Bentley remains an icon in Vermont, purportedly representative of Yankee ingenuity and persistence. There is a permanent exhibit on his life and work in his hometown of Jericho. In 1999, a children's book on the life of Bentley, written by Jacqueline Briggs Martin and illustrated by Mary Azarian, won the Caldecott Award.

W. A. Bentley and W. J. Humphreys, *Snow Crystals* (1931); Duane C. Blanchard, *The Snowflake Man: A Biography of Wilson A. Bentley* (1998); Jacqueline Briggs Martin, *Snowflake Bentley* (1998); Gloria May Stoddard, *Snowflake Bentley: Man of Science, Man of God* (1979).

Paul Searls

Chapin, Charles Value (1856–1941)

Physician, public health movement leader. One of the preeminent figures in the late 19th and early 20th century American public health movement, Charles V. Chapin was born and died in Providence. Chapin graduated from Brown University and apprenticed with his father, a physician, before attending New York's Bellevue Hospital Medical College, where he studied microscopic pathology and bacteriology with the young William H. Welch, the future dean of the Johns Hopkins School of Medicine. Following a year interning at Bellevue Hospital, Chapin returned to Providence in 1880 and quickly became an influential member of the city's medical community. After only two years in private practice, he was appointed attending physician at the Providence Dispensary, lecturer on anatomy and staff pathologist at Rhode Island Hospital, and instructor of physiology at Brown University, a position he held for 13 years, eventually rising to the rank of professor.

In 1884 Chapin was elected Providence's superintendent of health. Remaining in the post for close to a half century, Chapin became a leader of the American movement to create a public health model based on scientific epidemiology and bacteriology and codified into a set of standards and procedures that could be applied by most municipal health departments. Indeed, Chapin's influence was so great in part because his innovations were both scientific and administrative.

Along with Herman Biggs of New York City, Chapin led the charge to move public health work beyond general sanitation and toward fighting specific diseases based on what was known about their causes and modes of transmission. Establishing the first municipal bacteriological laboratory (1888), Chapin was a dedicated scientific researcher of communicable diseases and a tireless proponent of the contact theory of disease transmission. His greatest achievement was *The Sources and Modes of Infection* (1910), which became the

bible of the New Public Health. This exhaustive examination of extant theories on communicable diseases in the light of recent findings by bacteriologists and epidemiologists demolished the filth theory of disease, disproved the existence of fomites, and questioned the effectiveness of accepted ventilation and disinfection practices.

Responsible for supervising the public health work of a midsize city, Chapin developed a set of principles and procedures that were both scientifically justified and practical for the health departments of the typical American city. Promoted in both the "Municipal Sanitation" column he wrote for the *Journal of the American Public Health Association* and his *Municipal Sanitation in the United States* (1901), these principles and procedures guided state and local health departments for over three decades.

A giant among a generation of American public health officials who, through the preventive control of disease, saved or extended the lives of thousands of Americans, Charles Chapin retired in 1932 at the age of 76. His last official act was to have himself revaccinated.

James H. Cassedy, *Charles V. Chapin and the Public Health Movement* (1962); John Duffy, *The Sanitarians: A History of American Public Health* (1990); George Rosen, *Preventive Medicine in the United States, 1900–1975: Trends and Interpretation* (1975).

Richard A. Meckel

Child Health

"A dead child is no more rare than a broken pitcher," lamented Cotton Mather, and indeed, the health of children in early New England was a precarious situation, considered subject to the severest judgment of God and the passing whim of chance. Nearly 10 percent of New England's children died during infancy in Puritan times. Today fewer than 1 percent of American children do not survive.

In 17th-century New England, as throughout the rest of colonial America, the child's primary physician was usually a family member, most often the mother. She was typically assisted by other female relatives, midwives, and wet nurses, and by clergymen and town elders. Physicians and other medical practitioners were seldom involved, and based on infant and maternal mortality rates, at least some New England midwives were as skilled and successful as more formally trained colonial physicians.

Children's most common ailments during this period were worms, teething, and convulsions. Along with prayer, young and old alike fought sickness with concoctions of herbs and other vegetable and animal matter and by alternately dieting and bleeding, purging and sweating. Smallpox was the worst terror, but

diphtheria and yellow fever were also epidemic. New England's first significant medical advance—inoculation against smallpox—was introduced in 1721, when, at Cotton Mather's suggestion, Zabdiel Boylston inoculated his son.

New England often took the lead in developing a scientific approach to the study of children's health. The first dedicated and systematic course in childhood diseases was offered at Yale Medical School by Dr. Eli Ives (1778–1861). Children's Hospital in Boston was established in 1869 to advance scientific practices, and in 1903 formed a partnership with Harvard Medical School, thereafter becoming a teaching hospital. And in 1888 Harvard established a professorship in pediatrics.

The Industrial Revolution pushed New Englanders from farms to cities, where they encountered bacteriological diseases borne of crowding and unsanitary living. Like New York City, Boston had a high infant mortality rate. In 1865, for instance, 276 of every 1,000 live-born infants died within the year. Nevertheless, during the first half of the 19th century, unprecedented attention was placed on hygiene and the medical care of children. In the 19th century, children began to be seen as innocent souls requiring nurture, and New England mothers increasingly assumed the role of guardians for the moral development of their children, caring for their mental and moral as well as physical health.

By the early 20th century, New England's social reformers, pediatricians, and public health officials had promulgated a public sense of responsibility for mothers and children. Government and academic officials joined forces with social progressives to bring a new level of organized public oversight to New England's child medicine. In 1909 Thomas M. Rotch, Harvard Medical School's first chair of pediatrics, complimented his allies: "The large body of women who are connected with the Child Labor Movement has added greatly to the accomplishment of markedly successful results."

Since the mid-1900s, New England has been identified as a leader in child health and care. In 1946 the Connecticut-born physician Benjamin Spock published *Baby and Child Care*, which originally sold for 25 cents, making it widely available. Young parents found great appeal in Spock's thesis that parenting is a matter of common sense and love, rather than strict feeding timetables and disciplinary regimens. Numerous New England agencies, foundations, and institutions carry on the legacy of child health advocacy pioneered by Cotton Mather, Zabdiel Boylston, and Benjamin Spock. The Brazelton Foundation, established by pediatrician T. Berry Brazelton in

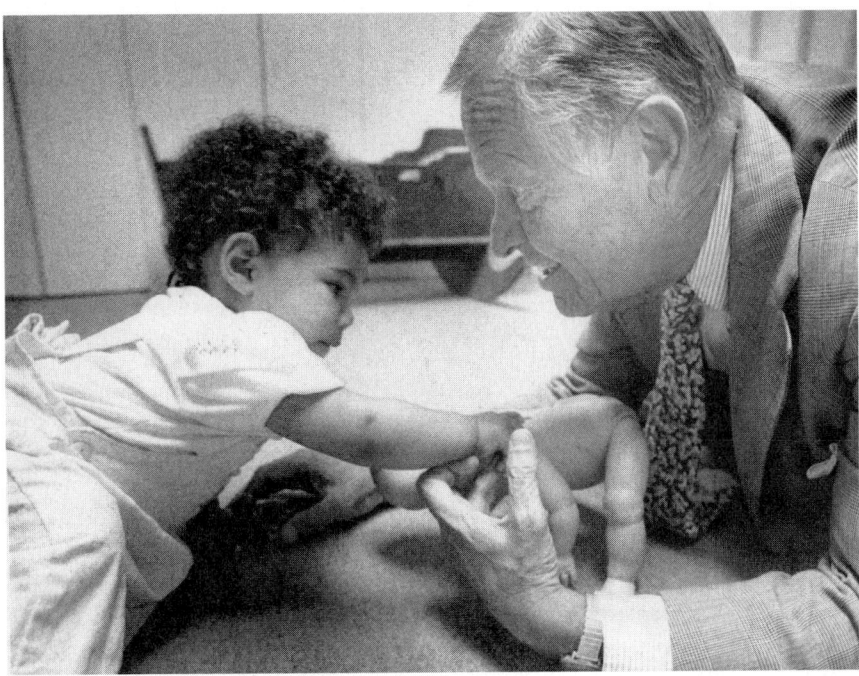

Dr. T. Berry Brazelton with a nine-month-old, Cambridge, Mass., 1991

Boston, is at the forefront of advocacy for the emotional and social health of children through the promotion of positive relationships in a child's daily life at home, at school, and in the community. Boston's Dana-Farber Cancer Institute is home to the Jimmy Fund, a major fund-raising organization that supports childhood cancer research and treatment efforts.

Environmental factors contributing to childhood illness and mortality in New England today include lead poisoning, a risk associated with residences and schools in old buildings that contain chipped lead paint and paint dust. Childhood lead poisoning prevention has become a primary focus of EPA-New England. The danger to children of overexposure to the sun has also received special attention in New England; indeed, Boston is one of three national cities to pilot a new EPA environmental and public health education program for elementary school children. Other pioneering programs throughout the region include the Manchester Child Health Champion Project in New Hampshire, one of 11 such pilot community projects, dedicated to reducing environmental health risks to children.

Vince L. Hutchins, "A History of Child Health and Pediatrics in the United States," in *Health Care for Children: What's Right, What's Wrong, What's Next*, ed. Ruth E. K. Stein (1997); Charles R. King, *Children's Health in America: A History* (1993); Benjamin Spock, *Baby and Child Care* (1992); Laurel Thatcher Ulrich, *A Midwife's Tale: The Life of Martha Ballard, Based on Her Diary, 1785–1812* (1990).

Louis Mazzari

Chomsky, (Avram) Noam (1928–)

Linguist. Noam Chomsky is recognized as the foremost figure in modern linguistics and for his contributions to philosophy and the cognitive sciences. Beginning his formal study of language as an undergraduate at the University of Pennsylvania, Chomsky was named to the Society of Fellows at Harvard University in 1951, received his Ph.D. from the University of Pennsylvania in 1955, and became an associate professor at the Massachusetts Institute of Technology in 1957.

Chomsky's research at MIT, an international center of cognitive and linguistic research, revolutionized the field of linguistics by demonstrating an innate basis for the structure of language, reflected by an abstract "universal grammar" that establishes the parameters within which language acquisition and use occur. Chomsky provided scientific proof for his claim with a descriptive system known as transformational-generative grammar. Chomsky's findings had significant implications for philosophy, providing empirical support for the rationalist philosophers who argued against the empiricist contention that human thought is solely the product of experience.

Chomsky's study of language led him to develop a penetrating critique of radical behaviorism, a school of thought in the social sciences that claimed human behavior is exclusively the product of external conditioning. Rejecting its scientific credibility and findings, Chomsky argued that behaviorism supported a view of humans as objects to be manipulated, rather than inherently creative and autonomous beings.

Chomsky became a public figure in the 1960s, gaining notoriety as an early and radical critic of the war in Vietnam. His interest in politics began when he closely followed the debates of the leftist and radical immigrant communities of his youth. Chomsky's political philosophy, libertarian socialism, argues that most forms of authority are illegitimate, as they are constructed to further the interests of privileged social groups.

Chomsky's major linguistic works include *Syntactic Structures* (1957), which presented his theory of transformational-generative gram-

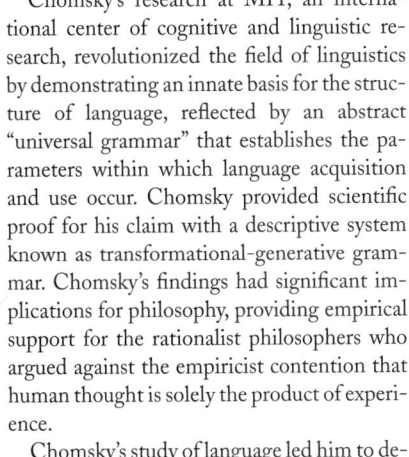

Noam Chomsky, 1989

mar; *Aspects of the Theory of Syntax* (1965); and *Language and Mind* (1968, rev. 1972). More recent refinements of his theory of an innate language capacity are presented in *Knowledge of Language* (1986) and *The Minimalist Program* (1995). Influential political works include *American Power and the New Mandarins* (1969), a caustic critique of American involvement in the Vietnam War; *Manufacturing Consent: The Politics of the Mass Media* (1988) with Edward Herman, and *Necessary Illusions: Thought Control in Democratic Societies* (1989), studies of how the mass media function as organs of government propaganda; *Deterring Democracy* (1991); and *World Orders, Old and New* (1994). *Powers and Prospects: Reflections on Human Nature and the Social Order* (1996) is a collection of essays on linguistics, philosophy, ethics, and international affairs.

Chomsky's political criticism has appeared in dozens of books and hundreds of articles, in film, and in thousands of lectures delivered throughout the world. It has included detailed criticism of American foreign policy in Southeast Asia, the Middle East, and Latin America, focusing on the role of the United States government as an imperial power working to protect and advance American commercial interests. His detailed studies of the American media centered on a "propaganda model" reveal how the media manipulates public opinion on behalf of powerful interests. Chomsky is recognized as one of the foremost intellectuals of the 20th century, and is one of the 10 most cited authors of all time. He is the recipient of numerous awards and honorary degrees, including the 1988 Kyoto Prize for his contributions to science. Since 1975 he has been an Institute Professor at MIT.

Robert F. Barsky, *Noam Chomsky: A Life of Dissent* (1997); James Peck, ed., *The Chomsky Reader* (1987).
                                   Robert G. Goodby

Cleanliness and Personal Hygiene

Today, cleanliness is central to American middle-class identity, but it was not always so. Events from 1820 to 1920, beginning in New England, helped clean up Americans.

Like their European contemporaries, the Puritans were hardly pure. An abstract link between cleanliness and godliness discouraged clutter and disorder but excused dirt. Large families crowded into tiny houses, unfazed by spitting, flatulence, fleas, and lice; they filled chamber pots or visited the smelly privy. They changed clothes every few days, and laundered monthly or quarterly. Very few families owned a bath-sized washtub. Over the next two centuries, as commercial wealth grew, even privileged New Englanders remained largely casual about cleanliness.

Bit by bit, standards began to change. In the late 18th century, Benjamin Franklin included cleanliness with the precept "Tolerate no Uncleanness in Body, Cloaths or Habitation" in his *Autobiography*'s plan for moral perfection. Industrialization after about 1820 brought material improvements, first to the northern urban middle and upper classes. Wash basins for the face, then large washtubs, became common. More people wore underwear, now made of cheap, washable cotton in New England's new mills. Rich families installed indoor bathrooms. Boston's Tremont House opened in 1829 with eight water closets and eight bathtubs, becoming the nation's best-plumbed hotel. The city's water system upgrade in the 1840s made clean water more available.

At the same time a flurry of new books tutored Americans in propriety. Etiquette guides directed readers to spit discreetly and scratch in private. Medical advice manuals and hygiene textbooks explained the health benefits of changing clothes, washing all over, and brushing the teeth. New England health reformers Sylvester Graham and William Alcott publicized the message further in books and lectures. The water cure movement showed the medical potency of baths and showers. Most people managed to wash their hands and faces daily, bathe on Saturday nights, and launder on Mondays. Catharine Beecher's popular *Treatise on Domestic Economy* (1841) detailed systematic ways to keep house and clothing clean. The orderly New England housewife was a familiar character in novels and tidiness became part of the region's image. The Shakers took literally the assertion of founder Ann Lee that there is no dirt in heaven, and their spotless villages became famous models of cleanliness and health in the eyes of 19th-century visitors. Paternalistic mill owners in Lowell and other emerging industrial centers established rules for cleanliness in their boardinghouses and mill complexes.

During the next decades other Americans caught up with New Englanders, raising personal cleanliness to a national fetish. Cholera epidemics in 1832, 1849, and 1866 demonstrated the tragic consequences of poor urban sanitation. The Civil War also provided a vast, high-stakes hygiene lesson. When the Union Army's nursing corps (headed by Massachusetts native Dorothea Dix) cleaned up hospitals and patients, statistics proved that their scrubbing saved lives. Once-unkempt soldiers learned hygienic ways through Sanitary Commission inspections.

After the war, as cities swelled with immigrants, municipal governments struggled to improve public works, realizing that better drainage curbed the spread of illness. But by the 1890s, the new germ theory of disease implied that personal cleanliness must complete the chain of germ control. Providence public health commissioner Charles V. Chapin took the lead in this "new public health" crusade. Social workers in Boston, as elsewhere, taught immigrant mothers that becoming American meant practicing hygiene. Led by MIT chemistry graduate Ellen Swallow Richards and the Boston School of Housekeeping, the domestic science movement developed the idea scientifically: clean persons, clothes, and houses were a moral, medical, even patriotic duty. By the 1960s indoor plumbing and laundry facilities came to seem as necessary to housekeeping and personal cleanliness as they do today.

Barbara Ehrenreich and Deirdre English, *For Her Own Good: 150 Years of the Experts' Advice to Women* (1978); Suellen Hoy, *Chasing Dirt: The American Pursuit of Cleanliness* (1995); John F. Kasson, *Rudeness and Civility: Manners in 19th-Century Urban America* (1990).

                                   Rebecca R. Noel

Cogswell, Mason Fitch (1761–1830)

Physician and author. Mason Fitch Cogswell was born in Canterbury, Conn., son of James Mason, a minister, and Alice Fitch Cogswell. When Cogswell's mother died in 1772, his father moved to Windham, Conn., and sent him to live with his stepsister and her husband, Samuel Huntington, later president of the Continental Congress and governor of Connecticut. Cogswell graduated from Yale in 1780, then studied surgery and medicine with his brother James, a surgeon in the Revolutionary army.

Cogswell spent several years in Stamford, Conn., and in 1784 moved to New York, where he trained in surgery at the Soldier's Hospital and entered a medical practice with his brother in 1787. In the late 1780s he married Mary Austin Ledyard, with whom he had five children. The family settled in Hartford, and by December 1799, Cogswell's work had become so well known that he was elected to the Connecticut Academy of Arts and Sciences and, a year later, to the Academy of Medicine of Philadelphia. In 1810 Cogswell was given an honorary M.D. from the Connecticut Medical Society; he then served 10 consecutive terms as its president. Among his accomplishments, Cogswell introduced surgical methods for removing cataracts from the eye and tying the carotid artery, both in 1803. Cogswell was also one of the founders of the Connecticut Retreat for the Insane, in Hartford (later the Hartford Retreat).

Although he was offered a professorship in obstetrics and surgery at Yale's new medical school, he turned it down to help find a better method of deaf education in the United States. Because his daughter Alice was deaf,

Cogswell began a campaign to start a school for the deaf in Connecticut. He first approached Thomas Braidwood, who taught deaf students to speak and sign at his school in Edinburgh, Scotland, but when Braidwood declined, Cogswell turned to his neighbor, Thomas Gallaudet. Gallaudet traveled to Europe in 1815 to learn the latest methods of deaf education and returned to Hartford along with Laurent Clerc, who was deaf, to establish the Connecticut Asylum for the Education and Instruction of Deaf and Dumb Persons (now the American School for the Deaf) in April 1817. Alice Cogswell was the school's first student.

In his literary endeavors, Cogswell was one of the Connecticut (or Hartford) Wits, a group of authors centered around Yale graduates and including such poets as Timothy Dwight, Jonathan Trumbull, and Joel Barlow, who wanted a strong central government, flourishing trade and commerce, and a well-ordered society. Cogswell contributed to the Wits' serial publication, "The Echo" (1791–98), which started as a satire of literary pedantry, bombast, and bad taste but soon became a political diatribe against American Republicans (called Jacobins, Democrats, or Republicans) and the French Revolution, and a forum for criticism of individuals such as Samuel Adams, John Hancock, and Thomas Jefferson. Cogswell died in Hartford in 1830.

Harlan Lane, *When the Mind Hears: A History of the Deaf* (1984); Grace Cogswell Root, *Father and Daughter: A Collection of Cogswell Family Letters and Diaries, 1772–1830* (1924); Edward L. Scouten, *Turning Points in the Education of Deaf People* (1984).

Martin J. Manning

Colonial Medicine Contemporary accounts of 17th-century New England are fairly uniform in their depiction of the region as thoroughly unwholesome, a place where the climate was so severe, where disease and debility were so rife, and where fearsome epidemics were so common that survival was always in doubt. More recently, however, demographic historians have shown that early colonial New England was a relatively healthy place, at least when compared to the European continent, to England, and to the other English colonies in North America.

Although death and disease were less frequent visitors to New England than to other parts of the Americas, they were no strangers to the region's inhabitants, nor were their visits predictable or evenly distributed. When diphtheria or scarlet fever arrived in a town or village, it was likely that some families would lose all of their children. The experience of the Reverend Samuel Danforth was typical; in 1659 he penned a short entry in his church's records noting that in less than a fortnight, all three of his previously healthy children had come down with a strange disorder of the throat, from which they all died. Through the early part of the 18th century, such occurrences—and their frequency—did much to reinforce a Calvinist-inspired worldview in which life and human happiness were always at risk.

Early colonial New Englanders, however, were not always fatalistic in the face of death and disease. As numerous surviving diaries show, they prayed, pleaded, and occasionally bargained with God, dosed themselves and their children with folk and family medications, and sometimes called in a local medical practitioner. Rarely a trained physician, that individual might be a clergyman with a smattering of medical knowledge, a self-taught healer, an apothecary or barber-surgeon, or any of a wide variety of other healers who composed the unstructured universe of early colonial medical practitioners.

The organization and practice of medicine and the healing arts in colonial New England had certain regionally distinctive characteristics. Unlike in New Spain and New France, where formal European medical institutions such as schools, hospitals, regulatory agencies, and hierarchically ordered systems of specialties were early transplanted, medicine in New England remained without institutional support, more or less unregulated, and informally organized through the entire colonial period. Not until 1783 did Harvard establish the region's first medical school, and not until after the turn of the century did New England's first general hospital open. Moreover, although as early as the 1720s Boston's elite practitioners organized a medical society to establish standards and oppose quackery, there was little or no regulation. Indeed, in Europe, New France, and New Spain, the duties, training, and titles of the major branches of medical practice—physicians, barber-surgeons, midwives, and apothecaries—were well defined and governed. In New England, in contrast, a wide variety of practitioners ranging from the self-taught to the formally trained assumed the title of physician or doctor and often offered the complete panoply of medical services: diagnosis and therapeutics, surgery and bone setting, midwifery, and the preparation of drugs.

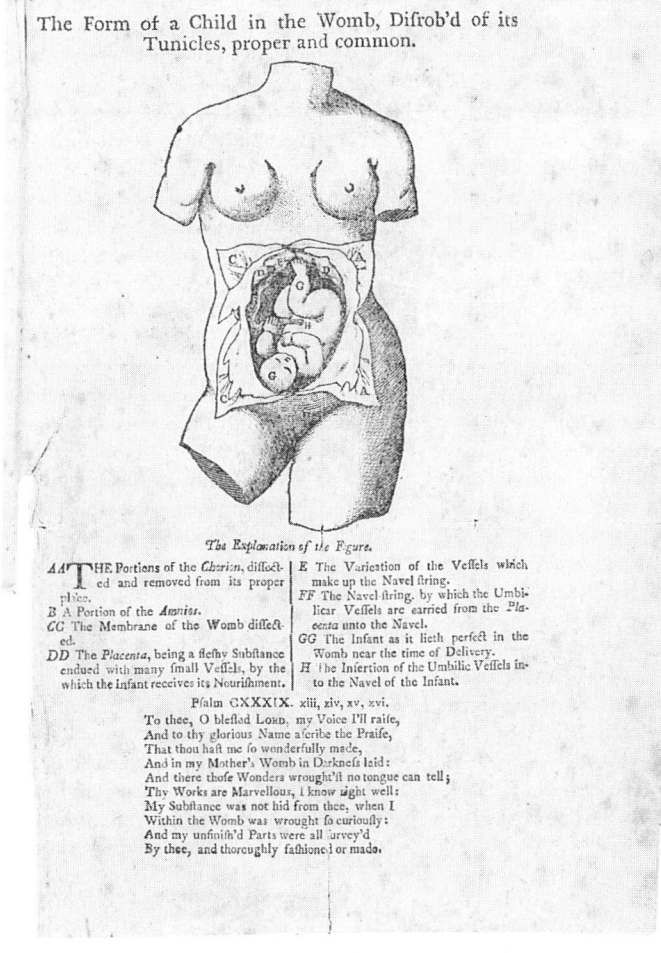

"The form of a child in the womb," from The Works of Aristotle, in Four Parts *(Worcester, Mass., 1792)*

The heterogeneity of practitioners and the blurring of medical functions, titles, and distinctions between them seem to have been common to the villages and rural areas of East Anglia from which so many 17th-century migrants to New England came. Actual medical thought and practice were also imported from provincial England. Although New Englanders adopted and used indigenous plants and Native American folk remedies, their understanding of health and sickness and the therapies they employed were quite similar to those of their homeland. New England practitioners who had read about traditional medicine probably combined knowledge gained from practical experience with a general subscription to Galenic humoralism (the tradition that health required a balance between the four bodily humors) and thus dealt with nontraumatic illness with techniques designed to restore humoral balance. These techniques sometimes included much-reviled measures such as bleeding and purging. Yet contrary to what contemporary and 19th-century critics charged, the use of heroic measures by colonial New England physicians seems to have been the exception rather than the rule.

Beyond what passed as formal medical knowledge and practice was a varied mixture of practical experience and learned skills, folklore, family remedies, and traditional treatments, shared to a lesser or greater extent by most of the adult population of New England. This is not to say, however, that all adults were equally knowledgeable or skilled. Every community had a small number of individuals who were recognized as talented healers. The local midwife or clergyman would often be among these, but so too would others. During the many years he served as governor in mid-17th-century Connecticut, John Winthrop, Jr., became well known throughout the colony as a talented healer. Winthrop was, in fact, the center of a network of physicians and minister-physicians who corresponded about traditional medicine as well as the newest treatments and theories in medical care. Cotton Mather, minister of Boston's Old North Church, learned of inoculation for smallpox from his African slave, and Boston physician Zabdiel Boylston performed the first inoculation in America in 1721. About 1720, Mather wrote a massive compendium of medical theory and treatments, *The Angel of Bethesda: An Essay Upon the Common Maladies of Mankind.* Historian Laurel Thatcher Ulrich has written of midwives, such as Maine's Martha Ballard, who performed important medical services by the end of the colonial era.

Whitfield J. Bell, *The Colonial Physician and Other Essays* (1975); Philip Cash, Eric Christianson, and J. Worth Estes, eds., *Medicine in Colonial Massachu-setts, 1620–1820* (1980); John Duffy, *Epidemics in Colonial America* (1953); Ronald Numbers, ed., *Medicine in the New World: New Spain, New France, and New England* (1987); Laurel Thatcher Ulrich, *A Midwife's Tale: The Life of Martha Ballard, Based on Her Diary, 1785–1812* (1990); Patricia Watson, *The Angelical Connection: The Preacher-Physician in Colonial New England* (1991).

Richard A. Meckel

Colonial Science Science in colonial New England began with the first voyages of discovery along the New England coast. The unknown forests and rivers of New England demanded active explorers seeking to comprehend a new and hitherto unknown wilderness. Science demanded a pursuit for practical knowledge with which to survive and to thrive in a primitive environment of uncertain topography, strange peoples, and new (and sometimes exotic) species of flora and fauna. Colonial New England scientists, who were amateurs rather than professionals, and often clergymen, were less apt to study the hard sciences, such as mathematics, astronomy, and physics, and more apt to study geography, cartography, botany, zoology, demography, history, and government.

Science was conceived broadly as any empirical study that relied less on theory than on the accumulation and classification of data. Colonial scientists used the scientific models provided by the great European scientists and philosophers Nicolaus Copernicus, Galileo Galilei, Robert Boyle, Isaac Newton, and Carolus Linnaeus. But the demands of the American environment required the collection of usable data to help in building successful communities. Colonial scientists were naturalists who focused on applied knowledge. Colonial naturalists were little different from Native American naturalists, particularly those who practiced medicine, who acquired information on the natural environment and applied it to particular problems. These Native American scientists were never recognized as such. Nevertheless, Native American understanding of New England native flora, fauna, and ecology, however, was an invaluable resource. Their healers had extensive knowledge of medicinal herbs that they shared with Europeans; some of these traditions continue today. And Indians also instructed Europeans in the agricultural and other uses of native plants, trees, and dyestuffs.

Captain John Smith was the typical ad hoc colonial scientist. Smith is remembered as a soldier, colonizer, and promoter of English colonization, but over four months during the summer of 1614 he accompanied a whaling expedition to the waters off the coast of Maine. Whales were not forthcoming, so Smith sailed a small boat down the coast from Penobscot Bay to Cape Cod. Along the way he described plant and animal life, the coastal landscape, rivers and mountains, and the climate. He observed and conversed with the native Algonquians to acquire information about their customs, institutions, and government as well as about the inland landscape. Perhaps his greatest achievement was the creation of the most precise map of the coast of his time. Smith provided original names for islands, mountains, rivers, and capes. Few of his names survived time, save his designation for the region as a whole—New England.

A more purposeful and erudite explorer-scientist was the Englishman John Josselyn, who journeyed to New England twice, briefly in 1638 and more extensively from 1663 to 1671. Josselyn was a botanist who sought to create a materia medica from the plants and animals of New England. Josselyn's *New England's Rarities Discovered* (1672) and *An Account of Two Voyages to New-England* (1674) provided an extensive natural history. His focus was on those herbs, barks, plants, and such that were useful remedies for common ailments such as the cold, influenza, gout, and toothache. Josselyn was so indefatigable in his botanizing that he ascended New England's tallest mountain, Mount Washington. From its summit, Josselyn wrote in *New England's Rarities Discovered*, "you may see the whole country round about: it is far above the lower clouds, and from hence we beheld a vapour (like a great pillar) drawn up by the sunbeams out of a great lake or pond into the air, where it was formed into a cloud."

The pamphlets and books based on the travel notes of a Josselyn or a Smith found an audience among colonial promoters, would-be colonists, naturalists, and perhaps the random literate homesteader. Another, more popular source of scientific information in colonial New England was the almanac. Particularly after 1700, New England almanacs provided a cornucopia of weather forecasts, home remedies, agronomical techniques, descriptions of remarkable occurrences, commonsense advice, astrological tables, and astronomical data. The amateur New England astronomer found information on the phases of the moon, eclipses, planetary transits of the sun, and random speculations about comets and other extraterrestrial phenomena.

Most New Englanders were apathetic about astronomy. Yet there were a few scientists who, in the latter half of the 17th century, advanced beyond the typical stargazer to make the empirical study of comets, the aurora borealis, the transits of Venus or Mercury, and lunar and solar eclipses. Increase Mather and his son Cotton were noteworthy in this regard, as was John Winthrop, Jr., Thomas Brattle, and Samuel Sewall. Harvard College was the premier center of the hard sciences. Professors such as Thomas Robie, Isaac Greenwood, and Charles Morton taught the mathematical foundations of planetary motions. In the process such scientists informed New Englanders of the "new science" of Copernicus, Johannes Kepler, Galileo, and Newton and the ideas of a heliocentric, boundless universe that operates according to constant laws of motion.

Surprisingly, many of the leading exponents of the "new science" were clergymen. Harvard was largely a seminary where the prospective Congregational clergyman read the works of Isaac Watts, John Calvin, and Jonathan Edwards, but also Charles Morton's *Compendium of Physics*. In addition to the standard courses in theology the student would be taught "Experimental Philosophy" by John Winthrop IV, a Harvard professor from 1738 to 1779. Cotton Mather was the finest example of the "Christian Philosopher," the title of his book of 1721 that outlined his idea of the marriage of religion and science. Mather believed in witches and the manifold miracles of God, yet he was the leading advocate of smallpox inoculation at a time when his opponents, such as William Douglass, the physician and author of *A Summary, Historical and Political, of the First Planting, Progressive Improvements, and Present State of the British Settlements in North America* (1749–52), argued that inoculation was in direct contradiction to God's providence. Mather used reason, common sense, and empirical data when confronting disease, the motions of the planets, botany, and zoology.

Cotton Mather was one among many New England thinkers who believed that the scientist and the theologian worked for the same goal. "The book of Nature and the book of Scripture," wrote the clergyman and scientist Jeremy Belknap, "are open to the inspection of all men, and our business is to search them, and learn what we can of them." Belknap referred to the natural environment as "elder Scripture, writ by God's own hand." The logic of the natural theologian was that God's creation—natural and human history—constantly reflects the handwriting of the great "Author." One must read the past of human events and the past of natural occurrences to obtain insights into the divine ways to supplement God's scriptural revelation, the New Testament. Piety was not an unworthy characteristic of the New England scientist.

Science at the end of the colonial period became allied to politics. New England scientists wanted to show that America was a land of great plenty, diversity, and uniqueness that at the same time had mountains, rivers, and animal species as grand as if not grander than European phenomena. Free scientific inquiry correlated with political and social freedom. Science complemented republicanism by helping Americans discover the variety and usefulness of the natural productions of the North American continent.

Manasseh Cutler, a scientist and clergyman from Massachusetts, studied botany and zoology for scientific as well as patriotic reasons, believing that a successful American republic depended upon reliable knowledge of plant and animal life. Born in Connecticut and a Yale graduate, Cutler wore many hats during his life: clergyman, chaplain, physician, Massachusetts congressman. Cutler was an amateur astronomer who observed comets, traced Jupiter's moons, tracked the transit of planets, and studied sunspots. In 1779 he repeated Franklin's experiments in electricity. He taught himself the use of the microscope, the quadrant, the sextant, and the barometer, employing the latter to perform meteorological observations. In 1784 he scaled Mount Washington to ascertain its height, but broken instruments and cloud cover prevented accurate measurements. Dissatisfied with his estimate that the altitude of the mountain was 9,000–10,000 feet, Cutler returned 20 years later and achieved more accurate results. He was the first to understand Mount Washington's alpine environment.

Cutler's companion on the first scientific expedition to the White Mountains in 1784, Jeremy Belknap, was late-18th-century New England's chief student of natural history. Belknap refused to separate human from natural history. The third and final volume of his *History of New-Hampshire* was a complete discussion of New Hampshire's plant and animal life, topography, and climate to which he added a discussion of the human dimension of natural history: agricultural practices; social, religious, and legal institutions; community life; the agrarian basis of the economy. Uninterested in providing a detached, objective study of New Hampshire's political and natural history, Belknap used his historical and scientific analysis to create a pastoral vision of New Hampshire's future.

There was very little that separated Jeremy Belknap from John Smith, John Josselyn, and Cotton Mather. From John Smith's voyage in 1614 to Manasseh Cutler's second ascent of Mount Washington in 1804, New England scientists accumulated a variety of geographic, climatic, botanic, and zoological data as scientific explorers penetrated the frontiers of Maine, New Hampshire, Massachusetts, Connecticut, Rhode Island, and Vermont. What remained the same were the assumptions of these early American scientists. They saw nature as the product of a benevolent creation: science involved a pious response. Living and surviving in the New World was the primary objective: there was no room for the metaphysician and theorist. Students of nature with a practical bent constantly searched for the "hints" of nature that could result in more productive, harmonious lives. Scientific inquiry was the essential means of community building.

Jeremy Belknap, *The History of New-Hampshire*, 3 vols. (1784, 1791, 1792); William and Julia Cutler, eds., *Life, Journals, and Correspondence of Rev. Manasseh Cutler*, 2 vols. (1888); John C. Greene, *American Science in the Age of Jefferson* (1984); Brooke Hindle, *The Pursuit of Science in Revolutionary America, 1735–1789* (1956); Russell M. Lawson, *The American Plutarch: Jeremy Belknap and the Historian's Dialogue with the Past* (1998); Lawson, *Passaconaway's Realm: Captain John Evans and the Exploration of Mount Washington* (2002); John Smith, *The Complete Works of Captain John Smith*, ed. Philip Barbour, 3 vols. (1986); Raymond P. Stearns, *Science in the British Colonies of North America* (1970).

Russell M. Lawson

Conant, James Bryant (1893–1978) Scientist, educator, diplomat.

James Bryant Conant, chemist, Harvard University president, diplomat, and educational reformer, was at the center of national and international affairs for several decades. Although both of his parents came from old New England families, he grew up in modest circumstances in Dorchester, Mass., a working-class Boston suburb. His proficiency in chemistry manifested itself well before 1910, when he entered Harvard. Graduating in just three years, he received a Ph.D. in 1916 with a double dissertation in inorganic and organic chemistry. After unsuccessfully attempting to manufacture chemicals, he served in the U.S. Army during World War I, helping to develop poison gases. Conant returned to Harvard in 1919 as assistant professor. He married and had two children with Grace Richards, daughter of his Harvard mentor.

By the time Conant accepted the Harvard presidency in 1933 upon the retirement of A. Lawrence Lowell, he was chair of the Harvard chemistry department and among America's most distinguished chemists. In 1922 he voted in the minority for a Lowell-backed faculty resolution establishing explicit quotas limiting the number of Jews admitted to Harvard. Yet as president he instituted national scholarships to recruit talented (male) undergraduates from beyond the New England elite, regardless of their religious, ethnic, and social (if not racial) backgrounds. Years later, Conant defended academic freedom at Harvard from the specter of McCarthyism; meanwhile, he not only dismissed some avowed leftist in-

James Bryant Conant, 1942

structors but also opposed hiring Communists and sympathizers in any educational enterprise.

Conant was nonetheless a successful president whose commitment to a meritocracy for the gifted—faculty and students alike—strengthened Harvard. So, too, did his promotion of Harvard's General Education undergraduate core curriculum and the admission of Radcliffe students to Harvard courses.

Harvard, however, took second place to international affairs as World War II began. Conant became a prominent interventionist and, in 1940, a member and then head of the National Defense Research Committee. Leaving Harvard's daily administration to Provost Paul Buck, Conant recruited civilian scientists for the development of synthetic rubber, bombs, fuels, gases, chemical weapons, radar, and atomic energy. As an administrator and scientist, he worked on the secret Manhattan Project and was influential in the decision to use the atomic bomb against Japan and specifically on Hiroshima.

Conant believed that modern total war precluded conventional moral restraints, especially if powerful weapons ended conflicts sooner and therefore saved lives. As an official adviser to the postwar Atomic Energy Commission, however, Conant both supported stationing atomic nuclear warheads in Western Europe and opposed the hydrogen bomb as too dangerous. Conant even opposed atomic power plants and the potential peaceful uses of

atomic energy as not worth the risks. In the style of American establishment insiders, he rarely dissented in public, leaving his reputation as a typical cold war warrior intact and his prophetic warnings neglected.

In 1953 Conant left Harvard to become American High Commissioner for Germany, and, when West Germany became a sovereign state two years later, its first American ambassador. Less successful in diplomacy than in other endeavors, he resigned in 1957 and turned instead to public education. With Carnegie Corporation funding, Conant investigated economic, social, and racial inequalities in public schooling and wrote the influential *Slums and Suburbs* (1961). It highlighted his lifelong commitment to public education as the key to a classless society. To be sure, this work, like his *Education and Liberty* (1953), which opposed expanding private secondary schools, did not quite extend to elitist private universities.

In his autobiography, *My Several Lives: Memoirs of a Social Inventor* (1970), Conant was reticent about revealing his inner feelings. His Puritan rectitude and reserve never faded. Yet in old age he confided to a few his sense of having failed in all of his "lives"—parenthood included—except as a chemist. He also acknowledged his greatly diminished faith in pure quantitative science as social panacea.

James G. Hershberg, *James B. Conant: Harvard to Hiroshima and the Making of the Nuclear Age* (1993).

Howard P. Segal

Dix, Dorothea Lynde (1802–87) Social

reformer and humanitarian. "I come to present the strong claims of suffering humanity. I come to place before the Legislature of Massachusetts the condition of the miserable, the desolate, the outcast. I come as the advocate of helpless, forgotten, insane and idiotic men and women." With these stirring words from her 1843 *Memorial,* Dorothea Lynde Dix launched a 50-year crusade to promote proper care for the mentally ill. Before 1840 only a dozen mental asylums existed in the United States. From 1841 to 1880, Dix exposed the abuses that the insane received in prisons, workhouses, and private homes by visiting these institutions one by one and recording the horrors she found there. Christian charity, she argued, demanded that humane asylums for the insane be readily available and publicly funded. By 1880, Dix was responsible for founding 32 state mental hospitals throughout the United States and Canada.

Born in Hampden, in the District of Maine, Dix had an unhappy and deprived childhood, which helped her identify with the plight of the indigent insane. As a young child, she abandoned her parents' home to live

with well-to-do relatives in Worcester and Boston, where she later established schools for young girls and published several inspirational books. Her active intellect and concern with social reform brought her into the elite Unitarian circles in Boston, which gave her the opportunity to tutor the children of the influential minister and writer William Ellery Channing. Illness and uncertainty about her ability to continue teaching led her to spend 18 months in England during the mid-1830s at the estate of William Rathbone, a friend of Channing's. There she met many of England's social activists and learned firsthand about the asylum movement.

After her return to the United States, Dix gradually concluded that the indigent insane in prisons would be better off in hospitals. Encouraged by Horace Mann and Samuel Gridley Howe, both advocates of the new asylums, she began in 1841 to systematically investigate institutions throughout Massachusetts, which resulted in the successful petition of the state legislature two years later. Over the next decade, she employed the same procedure with remarkable success over much of the eastern half of North America from Canada to the Deep South. She traveled extensively, and usually alone, to gather documentation of sordid abuses, enlist prominent spokesmen, effectively employ the press, and garner political majorities in favor of her cause: to build public asylums. Yet she cultivated the image of a dignified and demure Victorian lady, a necessary accommodation in an age that celebrated feminine domesticity.

In the years prior to the Civil War, not even her political acumen and dogged persistence could overcome the limited conceptions of federalism, especially at a time of growing sectional contention. After six years of struggle, her visionary proposal to fund state hospitals through a federal land grant of 10 million acres passed Congress only to die in 1854 with Franklin Pierce's veto. The president thought charity belonged at home, with the states, not the federal government. Disheartened, Dix traveled to Europe that year and, in a whirlwind of activity, spurred a government probe of the conditions for the insane in Scotland, founded asylums on the island of Jersey and in Rome, and investigated hospitals from Paris to Istanbul. With the outbreak of the Civil War, she secured in 1861 the unpaid position of superintendent of women nurses. She soon found, however, that her new career was undercut by the male bias of the military and her own lack of administrative experience.

After the war, Dix continued to aid public asylums until her retirement in 1881 to the New Jersey State Hospital in Trenton, where she died in 1887. Despite an extraordinary record of accomplishment at a time when few women held public careers, her opposition to abolitionism and women's rights set her outside the mainstream of 19th-century liberalism. With so much invested in the institutionalization of the insane, she failed to appreciate the tragic irony that by midcentury public mental hospitals were becoming more like warehouses, overflowing with chronic cases without the possibility of cure.

David Gollaher, *Voice for the Mad: The Life of Dorothea Dix* (1995); Gerald N. Grob, *The Mad among Us: A History of the Care of America's Mentally Ill* (1994).
Lawrence B. Goodheart

Drugs Physicians trained in Britain brought their own materia medica across the Atlantic. Colonial midwives, domestic or folk healers, apothecaries, and prominent ministers of New England also used some combination of mineral, chemical, and vegetable herbs and botanicals. The Salem, Mass., apothecary Bartholomew Browne was dispensing mostly chemical medicines in 1698. Martha Moore Ballard, an 18th-century midwife who practiced in Massachusetts and Maine, relied on herbal remedies listed in Culpeper's *London Dispensatory* (the first complete medical book and first pharmacopoeial text published in North America, in Boston, 1720) or in E. Smith's widely used *The Compleat Housewife; or, Accomplish'd Gentlewoman's Companion*. Most of the ingredients Ballard incorporated in her "simples," remedies administered in small doses both internally and externally, were herbs grown in her own garden. The simples ranged in form from teas, syrups, and vapors to poultices, baths, and salves. A few of Ballard's mineral or chemical medicines were purchased from local physicians, who usually got them from England.

Additional remedies that Ballard and her contemporaries used came from knowledge that Native American healers had obtained through trading with native peoples within and outside New England or through their own collecting, growing, and administering in various preparations. New England health practitioners, especially the British-trained physicians, were more reluctant to rely on local Indian healers for medicinal knowledge because of cultural and religious prejudices categorizing Indian remedies as medically inferior or the work of the devil. Nevertheless, this knowledge was gathered and incorporated into almanacs, newspapers, domestic health handbooks, and, eventually, the first *U.S. Pharmacopoeia*, published in 1820. The prominent New England ministers John Winthrop and Cotton Mather acknowledged the virtues of local Native American remedies such as teas brewed with sassafras and smoking and chewing tobacco, as well as the curative properties of substances obtained through trade with Latin America, especially cocoa, cinchona or Peruvian bark (quinine), and ipecac.

When a smallpox epidemic struck Boston in 1721, the Reverend Mather first learned of the benefits of inoculation (more technically, variolation) from his African American slave Onesimus. Despite stormy debate, Mather supported the physician Zabdiel Boylston, who inoculated members of Mather's family and others in the Boston community. Although opposed by another respected Boston physician, William Douglass, who declared inoculation a dangerous practice "learnt from the Heathens," Mather pleaded publicly that inoculation be adopted as routine prophylaxis, concluding that "experience has declared, that there never was a more unfailing Remedy employed among the Children of Men." By the mid-18th century, administration of smallpox inoculation in such isolation hospitals as those found on the Boston Harbor Islands was common throughout most of the American colonies.

After the American Revolution medical practice divided into two groups. Conventional physicians, known as regulars, sought an identity as learned men, followed the advancement of medical knowledge from Europe, and organized through medical societies. The so-called irregulars fell into a variety of medical sects. Although often accused of "heroic" prescribing (excessively administering purgatives, for example), trained physicians employed flexible therapeutic measures in everyday practice. Their treatments led to recovery often enough that patients returned to them for care. In addition to bloodletting, they administered an elaborate array of local and imported medicinal products, generally more mineral than botanic. Through tonics, stimulants, sedatives, cathartics, diaphoretics, emetics, and diuretics, they balanced "humors" or "fibers" in the context of the second-century physician Galen's theory of the four humors. Nonetheless, in pursuit of health New Englanders also embraced patent medicines and sought medicinal relief from a variety of sectarians.

In early 1800 the New Hampshire farmer Samuel Thomson, drawing on both local folk-healing practice and his own interpretation of Galen's theory, developed a system of vegetable remedies relying heavily on lobelia, cayenne pepper, and a "steaming" technique Thomson borrowed from Indian practices. In the 1820s and 1830s Thomsonianism challenged the elitism of conventional doctors with the notion that "each man should be his own physician," establishing a strong following in New England and beyond. After Thomson obtained a government patent, followers purchased "family rights" to his "system," which included a copy of the domestic handbook *New Guide to Health; or, Botanic Family Physician* (1822) and life membership in the Friendly Botanic Society. Thomsonians held conventions, published drug circulars and periodicals, and founded medical societies, pharmacies, and infirmaries.

The wide popularity of Thomson's focus on vegetable rather than mineral preparations contributed to New England's high concentration of proprietary medicine manufacturers in the 19th century, an era during which the Shaker villages of Harvard and Shirley, Mass., and Canterbury, N.H., were also significant centers for the manufacture of herbal remedies. New England was also home to several firsts: the first printing in the colonies of a patent-medicine advertisement, for Daffy's Elixir Salutis in 1708, in the *Boston News-Letter;* and the first U.S. medicinal patent, in 1796, to Samuel Lee, Jr., of Windham, Conn., for his Bilious Pills. New England proprietary medicine manufacturers and distributors, from Boston, Lowell, and Lynn, Mass., to New Haven, Conn., and Providence, made magical self-improvement pitches and reported record profits throughout the 19th century. Their botanical nostrums promoted the cure of individual ailments and claimed multipurpose "tonic" properties that strengthened the body; New England used the term *tonic* to refer to soft drinks until well into the 20th century. From Lowell, James C. Ayer marketed Ayer's Sarsaparilla with the slogan "Makes the Weak Strong," and Charles Ira Hood promoted Hood's Sarsaparilla as a blood-purifying tonic.

The Connecticut-based Kickapoo Medicine Company, in its *Kickapoo Almanac*, reinterpreted the relationship between early New England settlers and Native Americans, inventing the Noble Savage and Little Bright Eye, the Indian princess. These new Native American "trademarks" were designed to appeal to Jacksonian Democrats, who mistrusted the professional medical elite. The company established the "tribal" traveling show to publicize Kickapoo Indian Oil and Kickapoo Indian Sagwa, claiming Native American botanical origins.

Manufacturers of "bitters," remedies originally known for their high alcohol content, included H. S. Flint of Providence, who capitalized on the reputation of the integrity of the Society of Friends when he patented Quaker Bitters in 1872. At the turn of the century Quaker Bitters trade cards warned the public to "obey implicitly the laws of health" and promised, "Give nature a chance and you may dispense with a Doctor almost entirely, at the small cost of a few bottles of QUAKER BITTERS, the STANDARD FAMILY MEDICINE of New England for the past 25 years." Perry Davis's Vegetable Pain Killer, an analgesic sold as a remedy for nearly every illness, including cholera, was manufactured with opium and alcohol in Providence.

The most widely known of the proprietary medicines of the late 19th and early 20th centuries was Lydia E. Pinkham's Vegetable Compound. Pinkham, an antislavery and women's rights advocate from Lynn, was also a domestic healer who mixed the recipe for the vegetable compound on her kitchen stove. Originally dispensing it to family and neighbors, she and her sons began marketing the compound when they fell upon adverse financial circumstances in 1875. In 1879, with a new trademark featuring Lydia's grandmotherly face on each bottle, the compound (suspended in 18 percent alcohol) was presented as both a botanical remedy and a scientific cure that allowed women to avoid doctors and pursue good health "in harmony with the laws of nature." Over time, its properties claimed to relieve the popularly defined symptoms and complaints of "female weakness," including painful menstruation, prolapsed uterus, uterine tumors, diseases of the ovaries, nervousness, faintness, sleeplessness, and irritability. Product users were offered Pinkham's pamphlet, "A Woman's Guide to Health," and in the 1890s the company received testimonials from not only the expected white consumers but also from "colored women." One component of the compound, black cohosh, has been demonstrated to produce effects similar to estrogen and to suppress hot flashes when taken in sufficient amounts, helping to account for the patent medicine's continued popularity. Lydia Pinkham Herbal Tablets are still available and contain black cohosh, six additional natural herbs, and other vitamins and minerals. The label promises "nutritional support to help you feel better during menstruation and menopause."

Although New England featured prominently in the narrative of the 19th- and early-20th-century patent-medicine industry, it has also played a smaller but still prominent role in the illicit drug culture, particularly where the synthesized drug LSD (lysergic acid diethylamide) is concerned and, at turn of the 21st century, in efforts to legalize the medical use of marijuana.

In 1959 Timothy Leary, a clinical psychologist at Harvard University, began a research project with Richard Alpert on the hallucinogenic drug psilocybin, which they obtained from Sandoz Pharmaceuticals. The two researchers, later joined by Aldous Huxley (at the time a visiting lecturer at the Massachu-

setts Institute of Technology), experimented with the hallucinogenic themselves. More formal experiments were conducted with prison inmates to determine whether the drug would lower recidivism rates, and with theology students and professors to determine whether there were similarities between the psychedelic experience of taking psilocybin and mystical religious experiences. Leary went beyond academic studies to hold experimental sessions in his home in Newton, Mass., with the writers Allen Ginsberg and William Burroughs and began to shift his intellectual focus on the drug from whether it could solve human psychological problems to whether it could take the human mind to higher levels of consciousness and enlightenment. Offered the chance in early 1961 to take the chemical hallucinogenic drug Delysid or LSD-25 (lysergic acid diethylamide-25), Leary was converted to its use, establishing the International Foundation for Internal Freedom to establish the use of psychedelics as a "basic human right." With his declaration to Harvard colleagues that he was "through with playing the science game" and growing rumors in the popular press of "acid parties" with college students, Leary was fired in the spring of 1963. He established a center in Millbrook, N.Y., to study the psychedelic experience and quickly became a media celebrity. By the end of the 1960s, Leary's advocacy of "turn on, tune in, drop out" mind expansion was resonating less strongly among American youth, although the use of hallucinogenics was on the rise again near the end of the 20th century with the widespread popularity among youth of such new drugs as ecstasy.

New England played a part in the American narrative of marijuana use when Maine entered the fray over legalization of the drug for medicinal purposes. In 1999 Maine's voters, despite the opposition of local police, some sheriffs' associations, and the Maine Medical Association, passed a citizen initiative sponsored by the Mainers for Medical Rights "to allow patients with specific illnesses to grow and use small amounts of marijuana for treatment, as long as such use is approved by a doctor." Such illnesses as AIDS, cancer, glaucoma, epilepsy, and multiple sclerosis qualified as diseases whose complications could be treated by marijuana. As in Alaska and several western states with similar laws, patients are exempt from legal prosecution at the state level but remain subject to federal prosecution.

New England has provided several distinguishing contributions to the development of medical therapeutics and technology, the first being the breakthrough in treating pain during surgery. In 1844 the Hartford dentist Ho-

race Wells attended a "grand exhibition" in which volunteers inhaled nitrous oxide. The next day, using the anesthesia, he underwent a painless wisdom tooth extraction. Invited to John C. Warren's medical class in Boston in 1845, Wells squandered his opportunity for immediate celebrity when he administered insufficient nitrous oxide, causing his patient to cry out at the procedure's conclusion. The following year, William T. G. Morton, Wells's former dental partner, successfully administered ether anesthesia in an operation performed by Warren at Massachusetts General Hospital.

In initially responding to ether anesthesia, practitioners outside New England labeled William Morton's entrepreneurial promotion of his inhalation ether, dubbed Letheon gas, "quackery" and mere Yankee "cleverness." In Jacksonian America this kind of commercialism threatened physicians' images as professional gentlemen, although Wells and the Jefferson, Ga., physician Crawford Williamson Long made counterclaims to the patent rights and discovery credit. Massachusetts eagerly incorporated the new drug technology, with Massachusetts General surgeons administering ether more often than surgeons at rival medical-school clinics outside New England until the 1870s, when its use became more commonplace. Robert C. Hinckley commemorated Morton's successful administration of ether during surgery in a painting completed in 1894, *First Operation under Ether,* which was later hung in the entry hall of Harvard Medical School's Countway Library. The Ether Dome amphitheater where the surgery was conducted at the Massachusetts General Hospital is designated a historic landmark.

Several New England figures played important roles in the 20th-century advancement of the contraceptive most commonly known as "the pill": John Rock, a Roman Catholic and Harvard Medical School obstetrician-gynecologist; Gregory Pincus, the cofounder of the Worcester Foundation for Experimental Biology; and Katherine McCormick, a biologist and Boston philanthropist who financed the research in hopes that technology would provide better birth-control choices for women. Rock and Pincus completed animal research trials in Massachusetts in 1956 and recruited medical and public health professionals in Puerto Rico to conduct controversial clinical field trials with poor, illiterate women volunteers. In 1960 the Food and Drug Administration approved the pharmaceutical company G. D. Searle's application to market the contraceptive pill Enovid, a combination of synthetic progesterone and estrogen, as a prescription drug available only through consultation with a physician.

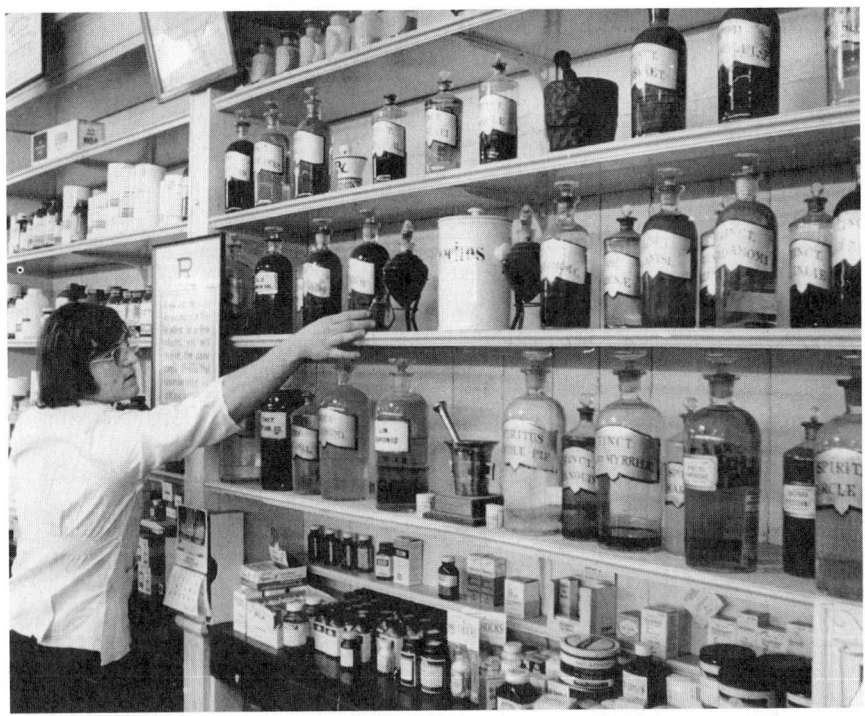

Pharmacist's supplies, old and new, 1971

Later in that decade, despite opposition from the pharmaceutical industry and the medical profession, safety issues ignored in the pill trials were successfully raised by the new consumer and women's movements, including founders of the Boston Women's Health Book Collective. Movement advocacy helped lead to a safer and more effective dose and to the FDA's ruling that patient package inserts containing information about drug indications, contraindications, efficacy, and side effects be provided for all prescription drugs.

New England is at the center of 21st-century biotechnology ventures in genome-based drug research using receptor geometry, biophysics, molecular biology, and computer technology to develop new diagnostic tests, medical devices, and "blockbuster" drugs that attack an underlying disease rather than its symptoms. New England firms have been conducting research and generating products in such areas as biomaterials, oncology, diabetes, anemia, cardiovascular disorders, and infectious diseases since the early 1980s. Drawn by local research universities, young science-graduate talent, and numerous medical centers, global pharmaceutical companies such as Pfizer, Novartis, and Merck have established and expanded research facilities in the Boston-Cambridge area. Although most firms have not located manufacturing plants in the region, Massachusetts Bay at the dawn of the 21st century lays claim to the world's largest concentration of biotechnology firms.

John B. Blake, "The Inoculation Controversy in Boston, 1721–1722," *New England Quarterly* 25 (1952); Colin G. Calloway, *New Worlds for All: Indians, Europeans, and the Remaking of Early America* (1997); J. Worth Estes and David M. Goodman, *The Changing Humors of Portsmouth: The Medical Biography of an American Town, 1623–1983* (1986); Jill Jonnes, *Hep-Cats, Narcs, and Pipe Dreams: A History of America's Romance with Illegal Drugs* (1996); Martin S. Pernick, *A Calculus of Suffering: Pain, Professionalism, and Anesthesia in 19th-Century America* (1985); Sarah Stage, *Female Complaints: Lydia Pinkham and the Business of Women's Medicine* (1979); Laurel Thatcher Ulrich, *A Midwife's Tale: The Life of Martha Ballard, Based on Her Diary, 1785–1812* (1990); Elizabeth Siegel Watkins, *On the Pill: A Social History of Oral Contraceptives, 1950–1970* (1998).

Jennifer Tebbe-Grossman

Earth Sciences Contributions to the earth sciences in New England are strongly linked to its centers of higher education. Instruction in mineralogy began in 1805 at Maine's Bowdoin College under Parker Cleaveland, who wrote the earliest American textbook on the subject in 1816. Connecticut's Yale College offered similar instruction in 1806 under Benjamin Silliman, who founded the *American Journal of Science* in 1818. It rapidly became an important outlet for research by American geologists, and continues to be so today. In Massachusetts, Williams College brought geology into its curriculum in 1818, and Amos Eaton dedicated the first guidebook on New England geology to its

students. At Harvard, the Lawrence Scientific School was founded in 1847, with the Swiss geologist Louis Agassiz as its first professor. Yale's Sheffield Scientific School followed in 1861, with Benjamin Silliman, Jr., on its staff. The Massachusetts Institute of Technology, which opened its doors in 1865, had the geologist William Rogers as its first president. Together with MIT, the Yale and Harvard schools grew to become prominent sources of graduates holding advanced degrees in geology during the latter part of the 19th century.

New England's state geological surveys also advanced basic research in the earth sciences. Although their early focus was on natural resources, details regarding the region's geological history accrued through systematic mapping. In 1830, Massachusetts became the first state in New England to support a survey through state revenues, and Edward Hitchcock of Amherst College was named state geologist. In 1858 he described fossil trackways from the Connecticut River valley, and interpreted more than 80 species of extinct giant birds and lizards. These trackways are now understood to belong to a diverse group of Triassic and Jurassic dinosaurs.

After these early endeavors, the next major contribution of the earth sciences came in the 1960s, when the plate-tectonics revolution changed the way geologists viewed the region. Geologists were puzzled about why Cambrian trilobites, for example, occur as identical species in eastern Massachusetts and across the Atlantic in Wales. Such fossils were attributed to the so-called Atlantic realm. Equally difficult to explain was why other Cambrian trilobites were more widespread in North America, but also appear in Scotland and coastal Norway. Those fossils were attributed to the so-called Pacific realm. In 1966, J. Tuzo Wilson proposed that a proto-Atlantic ocean existed during the early Paleozoic. Parts of New England and the Canadian Maritimes were suspected to have belonged originally to Europe on the opposite side of this ocean; Scotland and coastal Norway were considered to have been part of North America. Wilson disposed of the awkward fossil realms by arguing that closure of the proto-Atlantic ocean formed a single Euramerican continent in mid-Paleozoic time. He interpreted a line of faults running through Connecticut, Massachusetts, and southeastern New Hampshire as a suture zone where the two paleocontinents joined together. The Taconic and Acadian orogenies are regional mountain-building events related to ocean closure and continental collision. When the ocean reopened during Mesozoic time, bits from the European side were left behind and pieces from the North American side were torn away and carried off on the European side. The Connecticut River valley is now reinterpreted as a rift zone where the Atlantic initiated but failed to fully open. The environment in which the New England dinosaurs left their tracks is compared to the present lakeshores lining the East African rift valley. Renewed mapping by survey geologists and their associates from the region's many colleges and universities continues to refine and expand the complex geological history of New England.

Parker Cleaveland, *Elementary Treatise on Mineralogy and Geology* (1806); Amos Eaton, *An Index to the Geology of the Northern States* (1818); Edward Hitchcock, *Ichnology of New England: A Report on the Sandstone of the Connecticut Valley, Especially Its Fossil Footmarks* (1858); J. Tuzo Wilson, "Did the Atlantic Close and Then Re-open?" *Nature* 211 (1966).

Markes E. Johnson

Evolution The concept of organic evolution, as set forth by Charles Darwin in *On the Origin of Species* (1859), was among the most dynamic ideas of the 19th century. Earlier theories of animal and plant development were vague and speculative; the views propounded by Aristotle and 18th-century naturalists held sway. Darwin's work was unique in that it proposed a cogent rationale for the origin of species and their preservation in nature through a struggle for existence that favored those best equipped to survive. Evolution and change were constant; species were mere artificial categories; and naturalists could trace species' origins to a common center and a single pair. Drawing upon the research of botanists, geologists, paleontologists, and zoologists, Darwin presented an argument that, while lacking much factual support, was far superior to the work of former development advocates.

It was inevitable that the Darwinian worldview would clash with that of special creationism, the doctrine that God created the universe essentially in its present form, at one time. In the United States the most informed advocates of each position were active scientists living, working, and teaching at New England universities, primarily in the Boston and Cambridge area. Darwin's supporters—Harvard botanist Asa Gray, Boston geologist William Barton Rogers, and Yale geologist James Dwight Dana—were all familiar with Darwin's work and had furnished him with factual evidence for his "big book." Dana and Gray were not staunch evolutionists, but their knowledge of geology and geographical distribution persuaded them that Darwin's theory needed serious investigation. Louis Agassiz, Lawrence Professor of Zoology and Geology at Harvard, was also familiar with Darwin's thesis and believed that change took place

within fixed limits and toward determined ends.

In initial debates over Darwin's book, from 1858 until 1862, the principal antagonists were Asa Gray and Louis Agassiz. Gray's knowledge of geographical distribution, his work on flora of North America and Japan, and his interchanges with Darwin made him especially suited to see that Darwin received a fair hearing among scientists and his worldwide network of friends. But since 1846, when both Gray and Agassiz had joined in condemning the vague and unsubstantiated claims of creation theory proffered by Robert Chambers in his *Vestiges of the Natural History of Creation,* Gray had been moving more and more toward views that admitted the possibility of descent with modification. The publication of Darwin's *Origin of Species* convinced Gray that there was another way of understanding natural processes than relying on the fixity of species and operations of a deity. Still, he maintained some doubts until much later on in life by trying to bridge the gap between science and religion while keeping the issue of evolution in the forefront. As a disciple of the eminent French zoologist Georges Cuvier, Agassiz was, in contrast, firmly wedded to the view of creation that saw species as permanent signposts of God's plan for nature. In 1857 Agassiz published *An Essay on Classification,* in which he applied special creationist ideas to every branch of the animal kingdom, putting forth his own taxonomy that reified the truths he had upheld. Agassiz stood behind the doctrine of separate and special creations, even though Gray offered geological arguments supporting the continuity and evolution of species over time. The most important aspect of the evolution debates between 1858 and 1862 was that Gray, who was supported by both Rogers and Dana with their geological findings, had succeeded in introducing Darwin to America in such a way that completely altered the course of future discussion.

Before and during the Civil War, Agassiz put forth his view of separate creationism as a concept of the separate and special creation of mankind. This view led him to assert that there were physical and intellectual differences between blacks and whites that denied any concept of racial equality. Southern slavery apologists used these arguments to buttress their case, and Agassiz's popularity in the South cast doubt on his science in the North. Liberal theologians nonetheless defended his right to interpret the Bible in the way he did. Beginning in 1862, Agassiz stated again and again in the public press his unalterable opposition to the theory of evolution. New England audiences read in Agassiz's well-written and reasoned articles for the *Atlantic Monthly*

how the facts of geology and the power of theology and zoology made Darwin merely speculative and untrue to the facts. The *Atlantic* articles appeared in book form in 1863 and again in 1868, with the latter volume appearing in 18 editions. Meanwhile, Dana, Gray, and Rogers had become increasingly distrustful of Agassiz in his research and in his professional life, particularly in the formation of the National Academy of Sciences in 1863, which was undertaken in secret by a group of Agassiz supporters. Resentments emerged, so much so that Agassiz's power was severely damaged in the Academy and in scientific politics by an alliance of Gray and Dana. The efforts of these men around issues of science and academic politics played a significant role in drawing the scientific community into the Darwinian debate.

From 1867 on, American naturalists undertook research and publication that showed them in the forefront of evolution. Benjamin D. Walsh, an entomologist from Illinois, and Jeffries Wyman, an anatomist at Harvard, illustrated variation in species. The latter's study of the anatomy of the gorilla was a pathbreaking work in this regard. In 1866 Alpheus Hyatt, a paleontologist at the Massachusetts Institute of Technology and former student of Louis Agassiz, applied evolutionary principles to the classification of shellfish, showing how the doctrine could be employed in his master's own field. In 1867 Dana's student Othniel Charles Marsh began doing fundamental work in the fossil beds of the far West, making discovery after discovery until his death in 1899. Marsh's discoveries made up a vast body of work that earned him Darwin's high admiration and esteem. Marsh had done, according to Darwin, more than anyone to prove evolutionary theory with regard to paleontology and geology, where his discoveries of serial development of the horse from a small doglike creature to a modern type answered Agassiz's insistence on the absence of connections in the geological record. The paleontologist Edward Drinker Cope was a brilliant investigator whose discoveries and reconstructions of fossils rank as perhaps the most important American contributions to paleontology in the 19th century. Fielding Bradford Meek, a paleontologist at the Smithsonian Institution, and Henry Fairfield Osborn, a paleontologist at the American Museum of Natural History, added still further evidence and interpretation from zoology and paleontology in these years, so that by the early 1880s, American scientists had done a good deal to support the Darwinian hypothesis.

In 1872 Asa Gray publicly announced his support of the doctrine of evolution in his presidential address at the American Association for the Advancement of Science, but he rejected the concept of natural selection as the mode of transmission of variation. He held that the natural world was shaped by design and not by chance, and that evolution could not account for the origin of man. He closed the circle in identifying religion with evolutionary science.

James Dwight Dana had similar views. In his fifth and final edition of *Manual of Geology* (1894), Dana took a positive stand for evolution, but still reserved the origin and nature of humans for a higher power. Significantly, most of evolution's early American opponents and proponents of note were educated, taught, and worked in New England.

A. Hunter Dupree, *Asa Gray: 1810–1888* (1959); Edward Lurie, *Louis Agassiz: A Life in Science* (1960); Edward J. Pfeifer, "United States," in Thomas F. Glick, ed., *The Comparative Reception of Darwinism* (1972).

Edward Lurie

Geological Surveys

New England state governments were among the first to recognize the importance of geological surveying within their boundaries, and all states currently maintain offices through which such research is conducted. Geological mapping brings predictability to the search for natural resources, which are essential to a strong regional economy. Resulting commercial products range from building stone and road aggregate to minerals and fossil fuels. Aquifers that control local groundwater vary under different geological circumstances. Geological surveys were inspired, in part, by the region's drive to harness natural resources to support growing industries. But for some geologists, such as Amherst College professor Edward Hitchcock (1793–1864), geological surveys provided, in pre-Darwinian days, extensive evidence of God's hand in creation.

Although the earliest geological maps were produced privately in France in 1810 and England in 1815, it was within the young American republic that individual states first supported geological surveys through public taxation. State legislatures in the Carolinas approved surveys during the 1820s, but Massachusetts sponsored the first adequately financed state geological survey in 1830 with Hitchcock serving as director from 1830 to 1833 and 1837 to 1839. Connecticut formed a survey under James G. Percival, a Yale-trained geologist, in office from 1835 to 1842. Charles T. Jackson, a Harvard-trained medical doctor, became the first state geologist of Maine (1836–38), New Hampshire (1839–44), and Rhode Island (1839–40). Charles B. Adams, an Amherst graduate, was appointed the first state geologist of Vermont (1844–48).

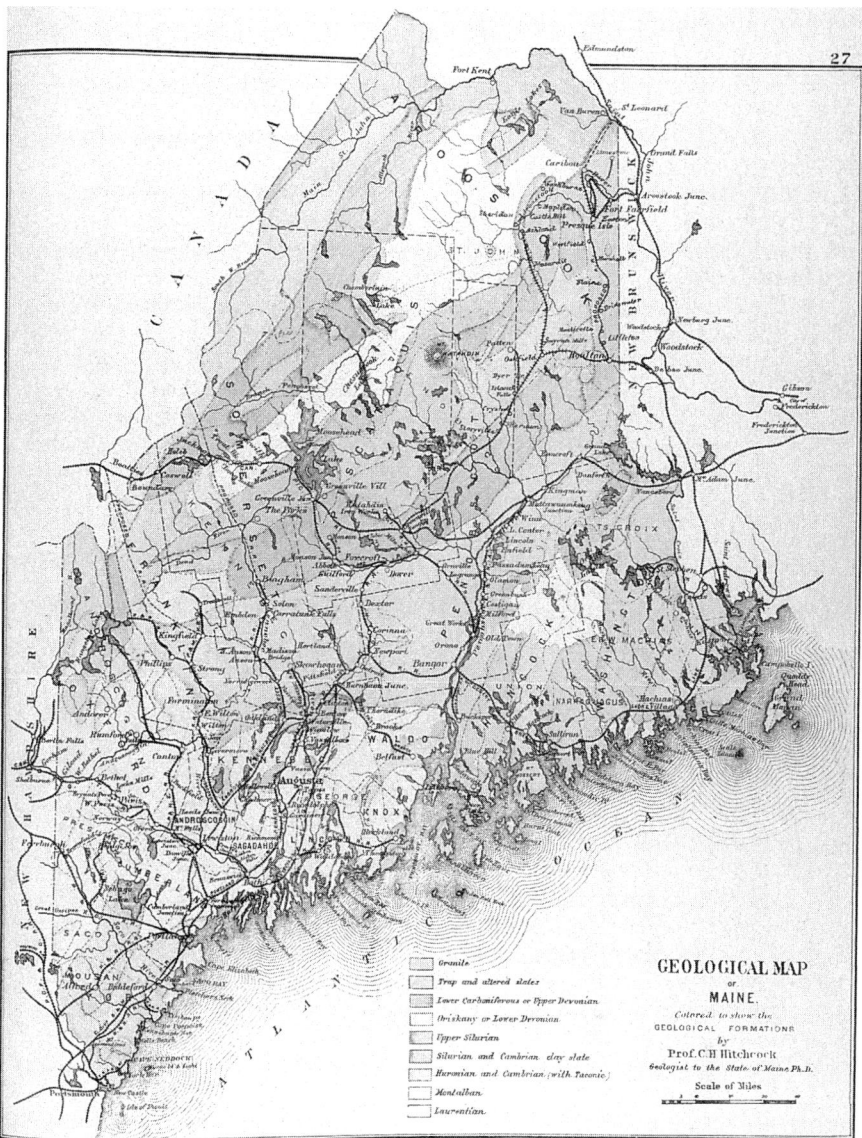

Geological map of Maine, 1901

Now collector's items, the early New England state-survey volumes are often well illustrated with drawings of natural rock formations at waterfalls or scenic cliffs, lithographic plates that depict fossil discoveries, and colored foldouts that interpret bedrock geology in map view and by means of cross sections. Hitchcock's *Final Report on the Geology of Massachusetts* (1841), for example, fills 831 octavo pages, including views from vantage points such as Mount Holyoke and illustrations of fossil footprints made by dinosaurs in the Connecticut River valley.

None of the early surveys were considered permanent operations, as legislators failed to grasp either the complex evolution of the geological sciences or changes in the needs and welfare of their electorate. All New England states today employ a chief state geologist, although some states maintain larger operational staffs and facilities than others. Vermont has the longest history of a survey in continuous operation (1853 to present). Maine and Connecticut support the largest staffs, with active divisions that include marine geology. Groundwater, waste disposal (including radioactive waste management), and the maintenance of geographic information systems (topographic base maps and aerial photography), have become increasingly important.

George P. Merrill, *The First 100 Years of American Geology* (1924); Martin Rudwick, "Cuvier and Brongniart, William Smith, and the Reconstruction of Geohistory," *Earth Sciences History* 5 (1996); Arthur A. Socolow, ed., *The State Geological Surveys: A History* (1988).

Markes E. Johnson

Gesell, Arnold

Gesell, Arnold (1880–1961) Child psychologist. Founding the Yale Clinic of Child Development in 1911 and serving as its director for 37 years, Arnold Gesell was among the most influential of those American physicians and psychologists who in the first half of the 20th century established infant and child development as a research field in both psychology and pediatrics. During his tenure, Gesell made New Haven, Conn., a mecca for the study of child development, training dozens of future child psychologists and pediatricians, and becoming the nation's leading exponent of the theory that infants, children, and adolescents develop according to chartable and orderly internal schedules.

Gesell originally intended to be a teacher, but became interested in psychology while attending Stevens Point Normal School and the University of Wisconsin. In 1904 he accepted a tuition scholarship to study psychology at Clark University in Worcester, Mass., under G. Stanley Hall and was awarded a Ph.D. two years later. Following graduation, he took a position teaching psychology at Los Angeles State Normal School.

In the summer of 1909 Gesell took a trip back East, studying the work being done by Lightner Witmer and Henry H. Goddard in their training schools for "feeble-minded children." The trip convinced Gesell that he wanted to work on what were then called backward and defective children but also convinced him that he would need medical training to do so. Two years later he was given a chance to do both when he was offered an assistant professorship in the education department at Yale and was accepted as a student in the university's medical department. Within a few months of arriving in New Haven, Gesell had established a psychoclinic for children.

Initially concerned with mentally retarded children, the clinic's work gradually expanded as Gesell became convinced that understanding normal development was essential to understanding abnormal development. Organized around the extensive and ongoing observation of a small number of children in a variety of situations, the research done by Gesell and his staff resulted in a set of standardized test schedules that could be used to gauge a child's developmental status according to motor, adoptive, language, and personal-social behavior criteria. The clinic also pioneered the use of one-way mirrors, photography, and filming as research tools.

By midcentury Gesell had become perhaps the nation's most widely recognized authority on infant and child development, publishing such best-selling books as *Infant and Child in the Culture Today* (1943) and *The Child from 5 to 10* (1946). However, within a few years of his death in 1961, his influence began to wane as the science of child development swayed to new theories identifying social and cultural environmental determinants as equally or more important than internal ones. Although it continued to be accorded respect as important pioneering work in the field, Gesell's research has increasingly been questioned for its focus on a relatively small group of white, middle-class children from a single city.

Louise Bates Ames, *Arnold Gesell: Themes of His Work* (1989); "Arnold Gesell," *Gale Encyclopedia of Psychology*, 2d ed. (2001); Walter R. Miles, "Arnold Lucius Gesell," *Biographical Memoirs of the National Academy of Medicine* 37 (1964): 55–96.

Richard A. Meckel

Gibbs, Josiah Willard

Gibbs, Josiah Willard (1839–1903) Mathematician and physicist. Born in New Haven, Conn., Josiah Willard Gibbs was the son of Josiah Willar Gibbs, a professor of sacred literature in Yale Divinity School, and Mary Anna Van Cleve. He graduated from Yale College in 1858, was awarded a Ph.D. from Yale in 1863, then continued as a tutor in the college, where he taught Latin for two years and natural philosophy for a third year. Between 1866 and 1869 Gibbs studied in Paris, Berlin, and Heidelberg, then returned to New Haven to take up the post of professor of mathematical physics at Yale in 1871. He remained at Yale until his death, declining offers of professorships at Bowdoin College (1873) and at the newly established Johns Hopkins University (1884).

Gibbs devoted himself to the development and presentation of his theory of thermodynamics. His first two scientific papers appeared in *Transactions of the Connecticut Academy Arts and Sciences* (1873): "Graphical Methods in the Thermodynamics of Fluids" and "A Method of Geometrical Representation of the Thermodynamic Properties of Substances by Means of Surfaces," which attracted the attention of England's leading physicist, J. C. Maxwell. Maxwell constructed three three-dimensional models illustrating a portion of this work and sent a plaster cast of one of them to Gibbs.

In 1876 the first half of Gibbs's great "On the Equilibrium of Heterogeneous Substances" appeared in the *Transactions of the Connecticut Academy of Arts and Sciences*, followed in 1878 by the second half in the same journal and a lengthy abstract in the more widely read *American Journal of Science*. His papers and theories made difficult reading, and it was not until 1892, when Wilhelm Oswald translated Gibbs's work into German and published it in the journal *Zeitschrift für physikalische Chemie*, that its impact was strongly felt; a French translation appeared in 1899.

In 1879 Gibbs formulated the fundamental principles of dynamics and the vapor densities of a number of substances in several short papers. From 1880 to 1884, he modified the work of Sir William Rowan Hamilton in quaternions, and of Hermann Grassmann on geometric algebra, into a system of vector analysis; later he became involved in a controversy in the journal *Nature* (1891–93) over the merits and priority of the two related systems of mathematical representation. Gibbs published four articles on the role of quaternions and vector analysis and, in his 1881–84 lectures, distributed printed copies of the calculation procedure to his physics students. These notes, greatly expanded, were published, with Gibbs's permission, by his student Edwin B. Wilson as *Vector Analysis* in 1901.

From 1882 to 1889, Gibbs developed his theories of optics and set them forth in articles he contributed to the *American Journal of Science* on the electromagnetic theory of light. His last major work, *Elementary Principles in Statistical Mechanics* (1902), was based on his lectures, although he had read parts of it as a paper as early as 1884.

Gibbs received honorary degrees from Williams College and Princeton, Erlangen, and Christiania Universities. The American Academy (Boston) awarded him its Rumford Medal (1881) and the Royal Society of London elected him a foreign honorary member and gave him its Copley Medal in 1901. He was a member of the National Academy of Sciences, the American Association for the Advancement of Science, and the American Philosophical Society. Gibbs died in New Haven, where there is a bronze bas-relief of his likeness at the J. Willard Gibbs Laboratory, Yale University.

Lynde Phelps Wheeler, *Josiah Willard Gibbs: The History of a Great Mind* (1951); J. Willard Gibbs, *The Collected Works of J. Willard Gibbs* (1928); Gibbs, *The Scientific Papers of J. Willard Gibbs* (1906).

Martin J. Manning

Goddard, Robert Hutchings

Goddard, Robert Hutchings (1882–1945) Rocket scientist. Robert Hutchings Goddard was a pioneer in the science of rocketry. He was among the first to establish the theory of rocket propulsion and turned theory into reality through years of dedicated experimentation. He was born in Worcester, Mass., an industrial city with an economy fueled by the application of new ideas in many fields. This milieu encouraged Goddard to pursue his experiments and to be more concerned with patenting his ideas than publishing them. Goddard's 214 patents cover many components of modern rockets.

As a young man Goddard was captivated by science fiction, especially the writings of H. G. Wells, and dreamed of creating rockets that would explore space. He received a B.S. from Worcester Polytechnic Institute (1908), followed by a Ph.D. in physics from Clark University (1911) in Worcester, Mass., both of which helped him overcome the theoretical obstacles to realizing his dream. In 1914, the same year he joined the faculty at Clark, Goddard received patents for two inventions that made space flight possible: the liquid-propellant rocket and the multistage rocket.

A modest grant from the Smithsonian Institution led to the publication in 1919 of "A Method of Reaching Extreme Altitudes," a fundamental treatise on the principles of rocketry that influenced future researchers in America and Europe. The popular press emphasized his suggestion that rockets might one day reach the moon, and Goddard was frequently ridiculed as an eccentric dreamer.

Virtually alone and with minimal financial backing, Goddard showed great determination in working through the practical problems of building and launching a liquid-fuel rocket. He successfully launched the first such rocket on March 16, 1926, in Auburn, Mass. Three years later the noise and fire associated with his experiments drew unwanted attention, and he was forced to discontinue his launches in the Worcester area.

In 1929 pioneer aviator Charles Lindbergh, excited by the potential of Goddard's work, helped him win financial support from the Guggenheim Foundation. Goddard moved his laboratory to Roswell, N.Mex., to take advantage of the clear, dry climate and open spaces. Throughout the 1930s his experimentation led to important new developments, such as an effective method for cooling the combustion chamber of liquid-fuel rockets and for controlling and stabilizing rocket flight.

Goddard's preference for working alone and in secret prevented a full appreciation of his accomplishments and limited his influence. During World War II, the U.S. military rejected his arguments for the importance of liquid-fuel rockets. His inventions, however, did influence the design of the German V-2 rockets fired at Allied targets during the last months of the war.

After his death in 1945 in Baltimore, Md., Goddard's creativity and leadership in the field of rocketry were more widely recognized as the U.S. government sought the use of his patents. NASA named its major space science laboratory, which opened in 1959 in Greenbelt, Md., after Goddard. Clark University's Goddard Memorial Library holds most of the scientist's personal and professional papers

and many parts of rockets and related hardware, much of which is on permanent display.

Robert H. Goddard, *The Papers of Robert H. Goddard*, 3 vols., ed. Esther C. Goddard and G. Edward Pendray (1970); Milton Lehman, *This High Man: The Life of Robert H. Goddard* (1963).

J. Michael Moore

Gould, Stephen Jay (1941–2002) Evolutionary biologist.

A distinguished Harvard zoologist, Stephen Jay Gould was also a prolific science writer whose best-selling books and monthly magazine columns have enthralled students, scholars, and lay readers alike. Gould marveled at life's essential diversity and relished the contingent nature of history. Few other authors or public speakers possessed his extraordinary ability to remain succinct and engaging, whether describing complex scientific processes, challenging deeply held cultural beliefs in objectivity and progress, or illuminating consistent patterns in the shrinking size of chocolate bars.

Born into a working-class family in New York City, Gould graduated from Antioch College in 1963 and received his Ph.D. in paleontology from Columbia University in 1967. Immediately thereafter, he was appointed to the Harvard faculty and gained widespread recognition five years later with the publication of an article advancing the theory of "punctuated equilibria." Influenced by Thomas S. Kuhn's *Structure of Scientific Revolutions* (1962), Gould and coauthor Niles Eldredge dissented from the gradualist beliefs of most Darwinists to assert that temporal change was

best understood in terms of long periods of static continuity followed by sudden, unpredictable flurries of activity. This dissension carried on a long tradition of debate over Darwinism that has been centered at Harvard since the time of the 19th-century naturalist Louis Agassiz. With *The Mismeasure of Man* (1981), a landmark study exposing the racist ideological assumptions behind the advent of intelligence testing, Gould captured the popular imagination for his critique of genetic determinism and reductionist patterns of evolutionary development; it also earned him one of the first MacArthur Foundation "genius grants."

Though his writings emphasized the role of culture in structuring human perceptions, Gould was no moral relativist. "Creation science," in his judgment, deserves to be debunked, while certain historical and biological facts such as the natural equality of the races defy all contradiction. Gould was author of several hundred scholarly articles and more than a dozen books, including the National Book Award winner *The Panda's Thumb* (1980) and the Pulitzer Prize finalist *Wonderful Life* (1989). In *Full House: The Spread of Excellence from Plato to Darwin* (1996), Gould related his personal experiences battling abdominal mesothelioma, a rare and often fatal form of cancer, as a means of demonstrating the principle of variation within systems. His message is liberating: individuals must not complacently accept common tendencies as the likely outcome of their lives. Yet it is also humbling, for, having recognized that evolution does not

Stephen Jay Gould in 1981, shortly after publication of The Panda's Thumb

naturally result in complexity, humans can no longer fashion themselves as select rulers of the Earth. We are rather one small point along the wide arch of biological diversity.

In *Full House,* as in many of his writings, Gould drew on his great love of baseball to illustrate the central tenets of his philosophy. The cyclical and linear nature of time seem evident to him in the sport's rich history and long seasons. Likewise, Joe DiMaggio's 56-game hitting streak reveals that the improbable can still happen, just as the disappearance of .400 hitters demonstrates how extremes decrease as diversity within systems declines. Even the pace of the game, with its sudden outbursts of scoring over the course of nine innings, provides a striking example of punctuated equilibria at work.

John Horgan, "Escaping in a Cloud of Ink," *Scientific American* 273 (1995); Louis P. Masur, "Stephen Jay Gould's Vision of History," *Massachusetts Review* 30 (1989); Jack Selzer, ed., *Understanding Scientific Prose* (1993); John Tierney, "Stephen Jay Gould," *Rolling Stone,* January 15, 1987.

Eric Robert Papenfuse

Gray, Asa (1810–88) Botanist. Asa Gray was professor of botany at Harvard University for 30 years, from 1842 to 1873. He was best known for his classification of North American plants and his work on plant geography; for his friendship with Charles Darwin and his reconciliation of Darwin's evolutionary theory with a belief in God; and for his debates over Darwinism with his Harvard colleague Louis Agassiz.

Born in Sauquoit, N.Y., the oldest child of Moses Gray, a tanner and farmer, and Roxanna Howard Gray, Asa Gray trained as a medical doctor at Fairfield's College of Physicians and Surgeons in western New York state. He received an M.D. in 1831 and practiced medicine briefly in Bridgewater, N.Y., but by 1832 he had begun to collaborate with John Torrey, a leading American botanist based in New York, and spent the next six years remaking himself as a botanist. Supporting himself by part-time teaching and library positions, Gray collaborated with Torrey on *The Flora of North America;* Gray also published his own first textbook, *Elements of Botany,* in 1836. In 1838 he joined the faculty of the University of Michigan; his appointment entailed a yearlong sojourn in Europe (1838–39), where he briefly met Charles Darwin and associated with William and Joseph Hooker, the father-and-son British botanist team. Upon his return, Gray continued his work with Torrey, but he never took up the job at Michigan. Instead, in 1842 he was appointed Fisher Professor of Natural History at Harvard, becoming the first American professor to specialize in botany.

Gray was the premier American botanical taxonomist and nomenclaturist in the 19th century, classifying plants in dozens of reports according to the "natural" system of A. P. de Candolle, in which the entire plant was considered in its classification rather than only certain selected parts, as in the older system of Linnaeus. Gray maintained a nationwide network of plant collectors and amateur botanists who sent him specimens from all over the northern hemisphere, especially from botanical explorations resulting from the westward expansion. Gray also maintained his network, and his place at the center of American botany, by writing series of textbooks, among them *Botanical Textbook* (1845), and *Manual of the Botany of the Northern United States* (1846–47), as well as more elementary texts, *First Lessons in Botany and Vegetable Physiology* (1857) and *How Plants Grow* (1858). These went through numerous editions and some were in use well into the 20th century. In 1848 he also published the first volume of *Genera of the Plants of the United States.* That same year he married Jane Lathrop Loring; the couple had no children.

In 1851, while on a trip to Europe, Gray again met Darwin. They began a correspondence in 1855, when Darwin asked Gray to analyze the geographical distribution of a species of plants, an analysis Darwin used to support his theory of evolution by natural selection. Darwin told Gray of his theory in 1857, making Gray the first American scientist to be so privileged. Influenced by Darwin's ideas, Gray observed similarities between plant species in Japan and the eastern United States and became convinced that they were descendants of a common ancestral form. Along with Joseph Hooker and geologist Charles Lyell, Gray was a member of Darwin's inner circle in the years leading up to the 1859 publication of *On the Origin of Species.*

Gray's sympathy with Darwinian ideas led him into the controversy with Harvard zoologist Louis Agassiz. Influenced by the French anatomist Georges Cuvier and German idealistic philosophy, Agassiz held that species were static forms, separately and specially created by God, each one based on an unchanging ideal type. Darwinian notions of change in a species over time and of descent from a common ancestor were entirely foreign to him; he and Gray clashed on these issues as well as on the issue of slavery. Agassiz believed that black and white races had been separately created and did not share a common ancestor—an argument he turned to proslavery purposes. Gray, believing that all the human races constituted a single species, opposed slavery and firmly supported Lincoln and the Union Army during the Civil War. Gray managed to

refute Agassiz's positions in the 1858–59 debates, during which Gray introduced Darwin's theory to an American audience.

Gray continued his friendship with Darwin after 1859 and was responsible for seeing the American editions of *Origin* through publication. An orthodox Presbyterian his whole life, Gray could never accept the materialistic and atheistic implications that were supposed to accompany the theory of natural selection. Rather, for Gray, Darwinian evolution was always completely compatible with the so-called argument from design. This idea, that a beneficent Creator must be responsible for the marvelous adaptations observable in nature, derived from the natural theology of William Paley. In 1860 Gray wrote a pamphlet entitled "Natural Selection not Inconsistent with Natural Theology"; his writings on religion and evolution were also collected in *Darwiniana* (1876) and *Natural Science and Religion* (1881).

Gray established the Gray Herbarium and Botanic Garden, which he ultimately bequeathed to Harvard and which continues to be part of his legacy. He retired from teaching in 1873, but remained in his house in the botanic garden until his death in 1888. Gray is buried in Mount Auburn Cemetery in Cambridge, Mass.

Hunter Dupree, *Asa Gray, 1810–1888* (1959); Dupree, *Asa Gray, American Botanist, Friend of Darwin* (1988).

Nadine Weidman

Hall, G. Stanley (1844–1924) Psychologist. Granville Stanley Hall pioneered some of the most significant scientific and cultural developments shaping turn-of-the-20th-century American life. One of the founders of academic psychology in the United States, Hall made enduring contributions to both the institutional organization and the popularization of his discipline.

Born in Ashfield, Mass., Hall was an ambitious youth who set his sights early on a life beyond the farming community of his childhood. He made his way first to Williams College and then to Union Theological Seminary in New York City, where he readied himself for a career in the ministry. He quickly abandoned the clerical profession, however, for pursuits that would better satisfy his broad philosophical concerns and his growing interest in natural science.

In the late 19th century, such a concert of philosophy and biology was just beginning to be realized in the new field of scientific psychology. For Hall, this meant a resumption of his education, now at Harvard, where he studied under the direction of William James. From this initial formal foray into the new psychology, Hall's professional career was marked by a number of notable firsts in the field. He graduated from Harvard in 1878 with the first doctorate in psychology awarded by an American university. He then traveled to Germany for further study, where he became the first American to work in Wilhelm Wundt's prototypical psychological laboratory. Upon returning to the United States, Hall assumed the country's first chair position in the new psychology at Johns Hopkins University. While at Hopkins, he established the nation's first formal psychological laboratory and served as the founding editor of the *American Journal of Psychology*.

In 1888 Hall returned to Massachusetts to become the founding president of Clark University in Worcester, a position he held until his retirement in 1920. Although falling short of Hall's dream of a university that would be the flagship for graduate studies in the sciences, Clark nonetheless came to offer an influential model for emerging programs of advanced education in America, achieving particular preeminence in the field of psychology. In 1892 Hall held the preliminary meeting of the American Psychological Association at Clark and was elected by his colleagues to serve as its first president. The university also became the site of Sigmund Freud's first visit to the United States in 1909, when Hall organized a conference that offered the first academic recognition of psychoanalysis anywhere in the world.

In addition to his formidable efforts at institution-building, Hall helped to inaugurate one of psychology's most prominent subfields, the study of the child development. During the 1890s he led the popular child study movement, convincing an audience of parents, pedagogues, and fellow psychologists of the importance of bringing a scientific psychology to bear on the practical art of child rearing. Hall wrote that movement's most important work, a two-volume text entitled *Adolescence* (1904), in which he offered the first modern synthesis of the adolescent stage of development. His primary imperative, that education should follow the nature of the child, garnered its main inspiration from the framework of evolutionary science. The child, Hall argued, passed through the same stages of development as the human race, and each therefore offered important insight into the understanding of the other. Recapitulation theory, as this idea was known, was widely discredited during the early years of the 20th century. Nonetheless, Hall's genetic psychology drew significant attention to such areas as the emotional development and the physical health of the child that would have lasting impact on the future direction of developmental psychology. In addition, even as the child study movement lost momentum, Hall's influence reverberated

through a network of students trained at Clark who went on to careers in such newly emerging specialties as clinical psychology and mental testing.

A man poised between two centuries, Hall built his career by maintaining a firm foothold in tradition even as he blazed trails into modernity. Thus, his study of psychology preserved a devotion to religious themes, while also confidently asserting the authority of science. Likewise, Hall at once reinforced notions of racial hierarchy and essential gender difference that were mainstays of 19th-century evolutionary science, even as he waxed poetic about the untapped powers of the "primitive" and feminine psyches. And in matters concerning child rearing, he at once managed to extol the older virtues of self-control, hard work, and obedience, while also convincingly advocating that self-expression, play, and rebellion were essential for optimum development.

In 1924, Hall was bestowed the rare honor of being elected president of the American Psychological Association for the second time. He died that same year, willing most of his substantial estate to Clark University. His bequest established a professorship in genetic psychology, thus perpetuating his foundational contributions to the scientific study of development.

Gail Bederman, "'Teaching Our Sons to Do What We Have Been Teaching the Savages to Avoid': G. Stanley Hall, Racial Recapitulation, and the Neurasthenic Paradox," in *Manliness and Civilization: A Cultural History of Gender and Race in the United States, 1880–1917*, ed. Gail Bederman (1995); G. Stanley Hall, *Life and Confessions of a Psychologist* (1923); Dorothy Ross, *G. Stanley Hall: The Psychologist as Prophet* (1972).

Crista DeLuzio

Hamilton, Alice (1869–1970) Pathologist and public health reformer. Alice Hamilton was a physician and activist who studied and challenged poor working conditions that were found to cause industrial diseases. The sister of the author and educator Edith Hamilton, Alice was born in New York City and grew up in Fort Wayne, Indiana. A career in medical research promised to satisfy her wishes for professional independence and travel. In 1897, following extensive postgraduate work, she settled at Jane Addams's Chicago settlement house, Hull House, and began a career as a pathologist. Her work, however, did not fulfill the goal nurtured at Hull House to be of service to others. Hamilton resolved this conflict when, in her forties, she creatively combined research and service to study the health risks faced by industrial workers.

Her pioneering work in "industrial hy-

giene" studies, some for the federal government, led to the recognition of many industrial diseases and to the abatement of conditions that caused them. Hamilton's works, *Industrial Toxicology* (1934) and *Exploring the Dangerous Trades* (1943), helped to promote safer conditions for industrial workers. After studying conditions in factories and mines both at home and overseas, she contributed to the establishment of workers' compensation laws in the United States. In 1919 Hamilton became the first female professor at Harvard Medical School.

Hamilton had few New England connections before she moved to Boston. She had studied at Miss Porter's School in Farmington, Conn., before earning her medical degree at the University of Michigan and studying pathology in Germany and at Johns Hopkins University. A nine-month internship at the New England Hospital for Women and Children introduced her to Boston. She returned there after graduation with some trepidation because of a self-defined "midwestern" notion that its residents were "aloof, indifferent to outsiders, self-contained, [and] quite devoid of the warm, easy cordiality of Chicago." Instead she was met with "warm kindness" and "more of the old American respect for individual's rights, more willingness to go against the stream" than in Chicago. She especially appreciated what she perceived as a traditional Massachusetts "respect for free speech." She also found, however, that to more conservative Bostonians her labor sympathies were indistinguishable from "Bolshevism" and that, although she considered Boston the "home of Progressive Movements," this "enlightened city . . . opposed woman suffrage long after Chicagoans had won it."

Hamilton was also a pioneering international peace worker and opposed World War I. With Jane Addams, she was present at the founding of the Women's International League for Peace and Freedom (WILPF) in 1915 and then traveled to European capitals attempting to convince political leaders to mediate their differences rather than use military action. After the war, shocked by stories of the starvation deliberately imposed by the Allies' postwar blockade of Germany, Austria, Hungary, and Russia, Addams and Hamilton toured Germany to investigate the pitiful condition of children there. American Quakers soon began relief efforts for which Hamilton raised funds upon her return to the United States. Like several of her counterparts in the WILPF, Hamilton's pacifism was challenged by German expansionist nationalism and the Nazi oppression of Jews, and she supported American military efforts in Europe during World War II.

After World War II, Hamilton criticized both American foreign policy for its obsession with anticommunism and American domestic policies for endangering free speech and other civil rights at home. She was active in the National Consumers' League throughout her life and served as its president between 1944 and 1949. Hamilton withdrew objections to the Equal Rights Amendment in 1952, and she called for an end to the Vietnam War in 1963. Her progressive faith never flagged; she unfailingly insisted that scientific research and industrial reform had improved workers' health: "As I look back . . . I can see an advance that is truly amazing. . . . The reforms already great are continuing." In her retirement, Hamilton continued her professional and political life from Hadlyme, Conn., until her death in 1970.

Claudia Clark, *Radium Girls: Women and Industrial Health Reform, 1910–1935* (1997); Christopher Sellers, *Hazards of the Job: From Industrial Disease to Environmental Health Science* (1997); Barbara Sicherman, *Alice Hamilton: A Life in Letters* (1984).

Claudia Clark

Health-Care Providers

Colonial New England, like Great Britain, was served by a variety of medical providers, physicians, and surgeons, as well as ministers, midwives, nurses, grocers, traveling mountebanks, and patients themselves who prescribed their own cures from apothecaries. And on both sides of the Atlantic, the practice of 17th-century physicians differed little from that of physicians in ancient Greece and Rome.

Deacon Samuel Fuller, ship's surgeon on the *Mayflower* and New England's first medical practitioner, became the model for the region's early doctors. A clergyman-physician, Fuller practiced the public-health aspects of medicine, circulating information on health through pamphlets, treating deficiency diseases such as scurvy, and establishing quarantines during epidemics. Like many early colonial doctors, Fuller believed that internal medicine was sacrilegious because it risked tampering with the length of life that had been predetermined for each individual.

Early New England, along with all of colonial America, quickly became a melting pot of diseases. Natives suffered most, contracting smallpox and diphtheria borne by European settlers and African slaves. In the winter, English colonists died of respiratory diseases and malnutrition; in the summer, gastroenteritis and malaria were common. Although surgery and obstetrics were developed in Europe during the course of the 17th century, these medical practices were little known in rural New England. Instead, cures were sought through bleeding and purging, ridding the body of excess or impure fluids. Surgery was limited to fractures, amputations, and tooth extractions, as well as skin conditions.

Unlike Spain, Britain did not sponsor a code of medicine to be followed by colonies, regarding licensing, ethics, and costs. Therefore, through much of its early history, New England had no medical schools, societies, or hospitals. Most routine care was based on folk remedies, including knowledge of treatment gained from the Indians. By using a technique gleaned from folk medicine, the Reverend Cotton Mather developed the first successful use of a preventive medicine by introducing inoculation against smallpox in the Boston epidemic of 1721.

Men and women alike practiced medicine, often in the absence of any formal education, but through 1750 midwives were the main providers of health care in New England. Before apprenticeships and university-trained physicians increased in numbers and began to consolidate their authority during the decades surrounding the American Revolution, women were prominent members of the medical community. Responsibility for health care largely fell within the family unit, most often to the mother. When families could not treat their own medical problems, they called in a neighbor or sought the advice of local persons reputed to have medical expertise: grocers, booksellers, midwives, nurses, bone setters, and ministers, as well as apothecaries, surgeons, and physicians.

Analyses of more than 7,000 patient visits made by five apprentice-trained New England doctors from 1770 to 1795—three of whom practiced in New Hampshire and two in the Boston area—show that almost 70 percent of prescriptions were for botanical medications, some of which were made from native plants. At least a dozen apothecary shops in early-18th-century Boston supplied herbs and medicines to physicians, but some medical practitioners prepared their own prescriptions and remedies.

Only after 1720 did a few New England colonists begin to travel to England and Europe for formal medical training. While physicians from Philadelphia, New York, and Virginia traveled to Europe throughout the 18th century to gain medical degrees, most New England doctors stayed home and pursued local opportunities, particularly apprenticeships. In contrast with England, where medical apprentices were required to serve up to seven years, New England's apprenticeships often lasted only a year or more. Massachusetts doctors traveled to Britain for training, often studying midwifery and surgery. Not until the 1780s did Harvard establish a medical school; Dartmouth followed in 1797. The New England Medical College, founded in Boston in 1848, was the first medical school in the world exclusively for women. In the 1800s, instruction in health was considered especially critical for women. Because women most often oversaw the health of their families, reformers contended that the hygienic and moral influence of women permeated society as a whole. Therefore, women's involvement was viewed as a vital component of personal health reform during the mid-1800s.

By 1820, with diseases declining and malaria eradicated from the region, New England's doctors and facilities were comparable to Europe's. Physicians began to downplay information about treatment, stressing instead facts about disease prevention in an effort to ease New Englanders away from treating their own diseases. Among the most prolific advocates of healthy living were hydropathists, homoeopathists, and a variety of female practitioners. Through the middle of the 19th century, licensed physicians were eventually perceived as the sole purveyors of disease management, replacing traditional home remedies, although not without some resistance. The licensing authority that doctors secured often had little more than honorific value, though, and many state legislatures voted to do away with medical licensure. Oliver Wendell Holmes, Sr., told the graduating class at Harvard in 1844 that the profession was not being allowed "to be the best judge of its own men and doctrines." Lay practitioners using native herbs and folk remedies continued to flourish in New England's rural villages and towns, claiming that the practice of medicine was an inalienable liberty, comparable to religious freedom. In addition, many leading physicians also questioned the effectiveness of professional medicine.

The most successful alternative to the medical profession emerged in the radical movement of botanic medicine led by the New Englander Samuel Thomson. Thomson, who had no formal education, began practicing in the years after 1800. He managed to obtain a patent from the federal government for his system of botanic medicine, enabling him to sell the rights for use of his methods and to claim official endorsement. His followers, mostly rural, spread from New England through the Mohawk Valley to western New York, following the same route as a wave of religious enthusiasm. By 1839 Thomson claimed to have sold 100,000 families rights to his system.

Because there were few restrictions on who could practice, physicians were available to the most remote New England towns, but the competition was often cutthroat. In 1836, for example, a young Vermont doctor thinking of settling in Georgia was told that the "only way to get practice would be to underbid those already practicing." Medical practice offered too small a financial return for many doctors to invest in a lengthy professional education, and poverty encouraged most families to care for themselves. As the nation became industrialized, the economic opportunities of the medical profession expanded dramatically.

The tremendous scientific and technological advances of the 19th century shaped the practice of medicine in New England. In 1846, at the Massachusetts General Hospital, William Thomas Green Morton, a Boston dentist, looking for a way to ease the pulling of teeth, administered ether to a patient, which virtually created the field of surgery. From the 1870s on, the telephone made it less costly to reach a physician by greatly reducing the time formerly spent tracking down practitioners on foot or horseback. The first rudimentary telephone exchange on record, in 1877, connected the Capital Avenue Drugstore in Hartford with 21 local doctors. As automobiles became more reliable after the turn of the century, they further reduced time lost in travel. Doctors were often among the earliest members of a community to buy cars.

As part of the growth of hospitals in expanding urban areas after the Civil War, the professionalization of nursing began with the establishment in 1873 of training schools in New York, New Haven, and Boston. Even more than nursing, surgery enjoyed a spectacular rise in prestige and accomplishment in the late 1800s. After W. T. Morton's demonstration of ether at Massachusetts General Hospital in 1846, anesthesia came quickly into use, making possible slower and more careful operations once antiseptic surgery was introduced. Children's Hospital in Boston was founded in 1869 not only to cure the city's poor children but also "to bring them under the influence of order, purity and kindness." By 1883 moral uplift of the poor had disappeared from statements of the hospital's objectives, while the treatment of disease and injury became paramount.

The professionalization of New England medical education began around 1870. As American medical education became increasingly dominated by scientists and researchers, doctors came to be trained according to the values and standards of academic specialists. Such reform-minded educators as Harvard president Charles Eliot felt that medicine epitomized both the backward state of higher education and the degraded state of the professions in America. Previously, candidates without high school diplomas could easily find admission to study medicine at any school in the country. To graduate from Harvard

Medical School, students needed only to pass half their examinations, even if they failed the rest. The reforms at Harvard initially caused a sharp decrease in enrollment, but the faculty held firm through a few difficult years, and medical schools around the country began to follow Harvard's lead. When the more progressive schools formed a national association in 1890—now the Association of American Medical Colleges (AAMC)—they set a three-year standard for member institutions and required laboratory work in histology, chemistry, and pathology. Most New Englanders finally began to consider their physician as their primary health-care practitioner. Muckraking revelations about the danger of patent medicines may also have stimulated reliance on professional opinion. *Ladies' Home Journal* and other domestic magazines warned women about the risks of self-medication and recommended doctor visits instead. The American Medical Association institutionalized the work of the muckrakers by pursuing fraudulent drug purveyors. This brought doctors more firmly into the role of sole health-care provider.

Soon the medical profession, including leaders among New England's institutions, came to consider almost every aspect of life within its jurisdiction. In 1920 Charles-Edward Amory Winslow, professor of public health at Yale, defined public health not only as "the science and art of preventing disease, and prolonging life," but as everything from social engineering to the machinery of proper sanitation.

At the same time, midwives remained the chief health practitioners through much of rural New England, traveling the local neighborhood and administering to the sick, as well as birthing children. In many communities this pattern continued into the 20th century. Midwives were considered "experienced," while physicians were "learned." Into the 20th century, the Abenaki played an important role in the practice of Vermont folk medicine. Many of Vermont's early midwives were Native American or part Native American.

Harvey Cushing, the pioneering brain surgeon, was perhaps New England's most renowned medical practitioner in the 20th century. Cushing, a Yale undergraduate, pursued cranial research at Harvard Medical School in the 1890s, where he literally redrew diagrams of the brain, revising knowledge of the various motor areas. After graduation, Cushing served as a house pupil at Mass General where he helped launch the clinical use of X-rays in 1896. He began work at Johns Hopkins, where he was drawn into neurology and disorders of the central nervous system. Between 1900 and 1908 Cushing made brain

surgery a recognized specialty. Returning to Harvard in 1911, he became the first surgeon to devote himself to problems of the nervous system. He trained surgeons from around the world, carried out research on intracranial tumors and many other problems, and introduced a number of revolutionary surgical procedures.

New England also can claim several nursing pioneers, including Dorothea Dix, who, in the era before professional nursing, advocated treatment reform for the mentally ill. Mary Eliza Mahoney (1845–1926) of Roxbury, Mass., was the first professional African American nurse in America, graduating from the New England Hospital for Women and Children Training School for Nurses in 1879. The Lucy Lincoln Drown Nursing History Society is named for a nursing pioneer who led the Boston City Hospital School of Nursing from 1885 to 1910. The Massachusetts Nursing Association was founded in 1903, and Boston University holds the History of Nursing Archives, containing collections from many early schools of nursing and professional associations founded in New England. The history of nursing in Connecticut is part of the archives at the University of Connecticut School of Nursing, assembled by its first nursing professor, Josephine A. Dolan.

By the 1930s New England's private physicians were worried about the corporatization of medicine, while reformers, including New Deal officials, saw organized health services as the wave of a more efficient profession. During the Depression, empty waiting rooms and unpaid bills convinced doctors to consider engaging in some form of health insurance, moving toward a more corporate means of practicing medicine. In 1958 Aime Forand, a congressman from Rhode Island, introduced the legislation for Medicare, a new and modest proposal covering hospital costs for the elderly on Social Security.

The hegemony of the medical establishment was challenged once again in the 1960s, this time over the issues of access and equity, and the solutions were seen in terms of new, neighborhood-targeted services, expanded governmental benefits, institutional reform, and citizen participation and control. A second challenge emerged from the women's movement, which criticized professional male authority over women's lives and simultaneously raised the issue of overmedicalization.

By the 1980s health-care corporations had become a central element in the region's medical system. Arnold S. Relman, editor of the *New England Journal of Medicine,* wrote about the rise of a "new medical-industrial complex," distinguishing between the growing businesses that sell health services to patients for a profit—chain hospitals, walk-in clinics, dialysis centers, home-care companies, and the like—from traditional medical firms that sold drugs, equipment, and insurance to individual doctors. Dozens of other related health-care businesses now extend across the region, covering dental care, optical services, weight control, rehabilitation, CAT scanning, and various kinds of laboratory services. Typical, and perhaps most important, are urgent care centers—also called minor emergency centers, convenience clinics, or walk-in clinics. Often located in shopping centers, they provide immediate treatment for many medical problems, generally without an appointment.

The Internet has also helped to create a hybrid health-care provider, continuing in a new way to reflect the tension between a medical establishment and forms of alternative and self-administered medicine, and combining elements of both. Author Tom Ferguson, for example, president of an organization called Self-Care Productions, is a Yale-trained physician and senior associate at Harvard Medical School's Center for Clinical Computing. Claiming he "wants to get people away from the medical establishment and back to taking care of their own health," Ferguson advocates an approach in the 21st century that would not have been unfamiliar to New Englanders of the 18th or 19th centuries.

Jane C. Beck, "Traditional Folk Medicine in Vermont," in *Medicine and Healing,* ed. Peter Benes and Jane Montague Benes (1992); Geoffrey Marks and William K. Beatty, *The Story of Medicine in America* (1973); Lamar Riley Murphy, *Enter the Physician: The Transformation of Domestic Medicine, 1760–1860* (1991); Jeanne C. Ryer, *HealthNet: Your Essential Resource for the Most Up-to-Date Medical Information Online* (1997); Richard Harrison Shryock, *Medicine in America: Historical Essays* (1966); Paul Starr, *The Social Transformation of American Medicine* (1982); Laurel Thatcher Ulrich, *A Midwife's Tale: The Life of Martha Ballard, Based on Her Diary, 1785–1812* (1990); Patricia A. Watson, "The 'Hidden Ones': Women and Healing in Colonial New England," in *Medicine and Healing,* ed. Peter Benes and Jane Montague Benes (1992).

Louis Mazzari

Holmes, Oliver Wendell, Sr. (1809–94)

Physician and man of letters. Among the most popular American writers of the mid- and late 19th century, Oliver Wendell Holmes was also a surgeon and Harvard professor of anatomy who carved an enduring place for himself in American medical history with his biting critiques of medical fashion and fad and his courageous and prescient insistence that physicians played a significant role in the spread of puerperal fever.

Born in Cambridge, where his father was a clergyman and professor, Holmes graduated from Harvard in 1829 and studied law for a year before abandoning it for medicine. In 1836, after study in Cambridge, Paris, and Edinburgh, Holmes was granted a medical degree by Harvard and took up practice in Boston. His interest, however, was less in treating patients than in research and writing, and essays he wrote on intermittent fever, neuralgia, and diagnostic techniques won prestigious Boylston prizes in 1836 and 1837.

In 1838 Holmes accepted a professorship of anatomy and physiology at Dartmouth but resigned after a little more than a year and returned to Boston, where he married Amelia Lee Jackson and again took up writing and research while attending to a practice and teaching part-time at the Tremont Street Medical College. It was during this time that Holmes began to establish himself as a medical academic and an informed and acerbic critic of both regular and irregular medical practice. In 1842 he published two lectures on "Homeopathy and Its Kindred Delusions" in which he mocked popular alternative treatments as little more than senseless fads. The following year he publicly read and had an essay published which anticipated by over a decade the contention of Ignaz Philipp Semmelweis that puerperal, or childbed, fever was contagious and was often spread from by physicians who failed to clean their hands or instruments after doing autopsies or attending other infected patients.

Although, or perhaps because, he succeeded in outraging many practicing physicians with his comments, Holmes was in 1847 appointed professor of anatomy at Harvard, a position he retained until 1882. For a decade, Holmes devoted himself to teaching, medical writing, and serving as dean of the medical school, but in 1857 he revived an early passion for literature and embarked on a complementary career as poet, novelist, and essayist. Accepting an invitation from James Russell Lowell to become an essayist for the newly launched *Atlantic Monthly,* Holmes began contributing witty, erudite, and conversationally but elegantly written "Breakfast Table" pieces, later collected and published as *The Autocrat of the Breakfast Table* (1858), *The Professor at the Breakfast Table* (1860), and *The Poet at the Breakfast Table* (1872). He also penned several poems, the most popular of which may be "The Chambered Nautilus" (1858), and wrote a controversial and widely read psychological novel, *Elsie Venner* (1861). Continuing to write even as he grew elderly, Holmes published his last collection of essays, *Over the Teacups,* only three years before his death in 1894 at the age of 85. Holmes was the father of the celebrated jurist Oliver Wendell Holmes, Jr.

J. H. Mason Knox, "The Medical Life of Oliver Wendell Holmes," *Johns Hopkins Hospital Bulletin* 18 (1907): 45–51; Miriam Rossiter Small, *Oliver Wendell Holmes* (1962); Eleanor M. Tilton, *The Amiable Autocrat: A Biography of Oliver Wendell Holmes* (1947).

Richard A. Meckel

Hospitals and Clinics

The history of hospitals in New England reflects the urban and rural nature of the region, from cottage hospitals run by local physicians in small villages to the development of large urban medical centers. Common to both, however, is the charitable nature of hospitals since their inception in colonial times.

New Englanders erected military hospitals during the Revolutionary War, but the earliest permanent hospital facility was the almshouse familiar to both urban dwellers and farmers. Dedicated to care of the poor, care of the sick at these facilities was incidental. Almshouses that were near medical schools received free services from students, but those beyond the reach of Harvard Medical School or Dartmouth, both founded before 1800, relied on the paid services of practicing physicians.

When contagious diseases such as smallpox swept through coastal regions, towns hastily constructed quarantine hospitals, sometimes known as pesthouses, usually on outlying islands. Town officials in Newport, R.I., authorized a quarantine hospital on Coaster's Harbor Island in 1716, while Boston's quarantine hospital was located first on Spectacle Island and later on Rainsford Island. Pesthouses continued to operate into the 20th century on islands as well as in mainland communities. For patients with communicable diseases such as scarlet fever, the pesthouse in Rockland, Maine, was situated on top of Dodge's Mountain, and patients there generally provided their own care unless they could find a nurse who had had the disease and was immune.

New England's first permanent hospitals were established to treat the work-related illnesses and injuries of sailors. The Boston Marine Society petitioned Congress for funds to build a hospital and opened a temporary building for sailors on Castle Island in 1799. A permanent facility was built in 1804. Marine hospitals were funded through a compulsory tax on seamen's wages, and shipmasters were charged with collecting the money through payroll deductions. Portsmouth, N.H., established a variety of health-care centers for seamen, including a combination temperance house and hospital in 1835. Local physicians were awarded government contracts to care for seamen at home or elsewhere in town until after the Civil War, when ill sailors were routinely sent to Boston.

The specific needs of city and village

dwellers determined the basis of funding for other hospital facilities. For instance, the 19th-century growth of New England cities increasingly meant that hospitals were funded by manufacturers for the care of injured workers. Lowell, Mass., textile corporations created such an institution in 1839. Even in rural areas, employers were persuaded to support hospital facilities; the president of a local logging company, for instance, built a hospital in Greenville Junction, Maine, in 1911.

Massachusetts General Hospital was founded in Boston in 1811. Like hospitals elsewhere during this period, MGH was supported by the city's elite families, and its admissions criteria excluded those with chronic or contagious diseases or questionable morals. Hospital administrators distinguished their institutions from almshouses or insane asylums, which quickly became repositories for those with chronic illnesses. Despite admissions standards, hospital care was inferior to private care. Hospitals were the medical treatment of last resort; poverty, rather than medical condition, sent patients to the hospital.

Before the Civil War, nearly every state had at least one public asylum for the insane and several had private asylums as well. The Maine Insane Hospital (Augusta Mental Health Institute) opened in 1840 and was in many ways typical of public asylums in its source of funding, the expectations of its directors, and its treatment of patients. State funding opened the facility but directors expected patients to pay for their care. Believing that mental illnesses were caused by adverse environmental

conditions, towns paid for their poorer residents' care with the expectation that they would be cured and become self-supporting in a short time. This seldom happened, and most insane asylums were overcrowded from the start. Increased asylum populations also reflected broader societal changes within families. Families were becoming smaller, and some family members spent significant amounts of time away from home, making it more difficult to care for chronically and mentally ill family members. Changes in middle-class families, especially in urban areas, made the hospital the more logical if not more medically sound choice for medical care.

In the urban centers of New England, especially Boston, medical schools created and maintained ties with hospitals, resulting in a somewhat mutually comfortable exchange of clinical experience and scientific expertise. In some cases, hospitals also provided training for African Americans and women who wanted to become physicians but had little access to the traditional hospital system. In Boston, the New England Hospital for Women and Children opened in 1862 and provided women physicians with much-needed clinical training and allowed poor women to receive medical, surgical, and obstetrical services. Many of these facilities declined and closed in the early years of the 20th century.

An influential report by Abraham Flexner appeared in 1910, criticizing medical school graduates' lack of appropriate clinical training in hospitals. If hospitals and medical schools could not reorient their work, they closed.

Medical colleges also closed, although in New England, rural areas had already felt the lack of clinical opportunities in their neighborhoods. The Medical School of Maine was established in 1820 at Bowdoin College in Brunswick, but the lack of a hospital there continually limited the school's ability to attract students until it closed in 1921. Similarly, hospitals in rural areas, like the Rumford (Maine) Community Hospital, which suffered from the lack of adequately trained physicians, had to rely on other institutions, often sending patients far from home for specialized treatment.

The rural character of New England has consistently and uniquely shaped its history of medicine. Physicians recommended the tranquil, clean, and bucolic characteristics of the country for their tubercular patients, and many moved to these regions to take advantage of the services provided there. Sanitariums transformed many small farming communities, which profited by providing workers and agricultural products for the institution. Like the sanitarium, other rural medical institutions stressed the health advantages of the countryside. Even in growing cities like Portland, Maine, the Maine General Hospital (Maine Medical Center) spent as much time describing its beautiful grounds as it did its medical facilities. Similarly, the Eastern Branch of the National Home for Disabled Volunteer Soldiers (Veterans Administration Hospital at Togus) developed its grounds in keeping with the rural origins of many of its residents, incorporating flower gardens, farms, and horse stables into the landscape.

Medical facilities in rural New England also demonstrated a commitment to modern scientific methods. Annual reports addressed to supporters proudly described new (and healthful) ventilation systems and sanitary kitchen and dining facilities that were separate from the wards. Poor hygiene in the early 20th century still plagued these health-care institutions, which therefore needed to emphasize their homey appearance and scientific accouterments in order to attract patients. Finally, small communities established "cottage hospitals," often in a physician's home. The Portsmouth Cottage Hospital (Portsmouth Hospital), supported by local churches, opened in 1884 in a 100-year-old building and was staffed by a family who lived there rent-free in exchange for care of any patients. This arrangement proved unreliable, but the home-like atmosphere endured. The live-in matron not only attended to physical needs, but also became the patients' companion, playing cards with them, taking them to church, or reading to them. A physician and a single mother working as a private-duty nurse

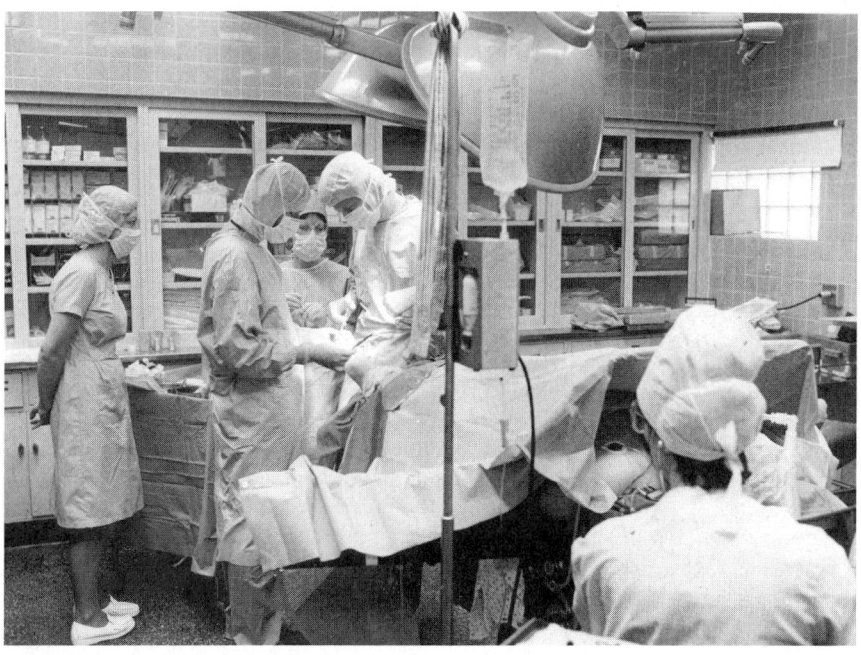

Worcester Memorial Hospital operating room, Worcester, Mass., 1985

opened the Cottage Hospital in Whitefield, Maine, in 1923. The hospital admitted war veterans, injured workers from local sawmills, and pregnant women, among others; its letterhead advertised that it specialized in "chronics and incurables." While more serious cases were sent to the hospital in nearby Lewiston, the physician and the nurse performed minor surgery and obstetric care. Like other cottage hospitals, this closed when its principal providers died or moved elsewhere, but facilities like these have left an enduring mark on the New England landscape.

In the 20th century, New England's teaching hospitals associated with medical schools, including those at Harvard, Yale, Brown, and Dartmouth, developed a reputation for research and medical education. Harvard Medical School opened its Quadrangle on Longwood Avenue in Boston in 1906, and the area now hosts a complex of hospitals and clinics.

Virginia G. Drachman, *Hospital with a Heart: Women Doctors and the Paradox of Separatism at the New England Hospital, 1862–1969* (1984); Leonard K. Eaton, *New England Hospitals, 1790–1833* (1957); Gerald N. Grob, *From Asylum to Community: Mental Health Policy in Modern America*, (1991); Charles E. Rosenberg, *The Care of Strangers: The Rise of America's Hospital System* (1987); David J. Rothman, *The Discovery of the Asylum: Social Order and Disorder in the New Republic* (1971); Sheila M. Rothman, *Living in the Shadow of Death: Tuberculosis and the Social Experience of Illness in American History* (1994); Morris J. Vogel, *The Invention of the Modern Hospital: Boston, 1870–1930* (1980).

Allison L. Hepler

Hubbard, Ruth (1924–) Scientist and feminist.

Born on March 3, 1924, Ruth Hubbard escaped from her native Vienna, Austria, with her family during Nazi occupation in 1938. She received a doctorate in biology from Radcliffe College in 1950, where she worked with Harvard professor George Wald on the chemistry and photochemistry of visual pigments in the retina. Biochemist Jeffries Wyman also had an important influence on her scientific development. Now professor emerita of biology at Harvard University, Hubbard has not only made important contributions to our understanding of the chemistry of vision and the synthesis of visual pigments but also pioneered, in the early 1970s, feminist critiques of science, especially women's biology and health. Her work on the political nature of science and health and her activism for responsible science, particularly in genetics, have influenced many scientists and feminists.

In 1958 Hubbard married Wald (later to share the Nobel Prize in Medicine for his discovery of the function of vitamin A in maintaining vision) with whom she had two children—a daughter, Deborah, and a son, the musician and writer Elijah Wald. Hubbard conducted most of her scientific research at Harvard in nontenured positions, which in the 1950s and 1960s were typically held by productive female scientists supported by their own research grants. At that time most colleges and universities awarded few women tenure, particularly in the sciences. Hubbard received recognition for her scientific work in 1952 in the form of a prestigious Guggenheim Fellowship, which she used to work at the Carlsberg Laboratory in Copenhagen. In 1967 she and Wald shared the Paul Karrer Medal from the Swiss Chemical Society. Hubbard began teaching biology courses at Harvard as a lecturer and in 1972 was a visiting professor at the Massachusetts Institute of Technology.

As the second wave of the women's movement grew during the 1960s and 1970s, Hubbard became active in promoting the status of women in academe. In 1973, when elite schools like Harvard were threatened with funding cuts and, in some cases, class-action lawsuits because of discriminatory hiring, Hubbard was appointed professor of biology at Harvard, becoming the first woman to be tenured in its biology department.

In 1975 Hubbard began to teach the seminar Biology and Women's Issues in which she and her students elaborated on the dearth of information about women's biology and discussed an agenda for action. As a result of that seminar, she and two of her students edited a collection of essays and created an extensive annotated bibliography. Published in 1979, *Women Look at Biology Looking at Women* (updated in 1982 as *Biological Woman: The Convenient Myth*) was one of the first publications of its kind. It included Hubbard's essay "Have

Ruth Hubbard at home in Cambridge, Mass., ca. 1990

Only Men Evolved?" which quickly became a classic in feminist science studies. In this essay she showed how Darwin's work was shaped by his time and culture, including the prevailing Victorian views about behavior appropriate for women and men.

Throughout the 1980s and 1990s, Hubbard lectured widely and published on such topics as genetic testing, assisted reproduction, and the importance of political action and education about health for nonprofessionals. She has been active in major social movements for peace and justice, and helped found the Council for Responsible Genetics. In the wake of the recombinant DNA revolution, the Boston-based national organization has formulated ethical guidelines for the use of the powerful tools of molecular genetics.

Hubbard's gift for writing and speaking clearly, accessibly, and accurately about the limitations of science has made her a popular and effective spokeswoman for feminist approaches to science, including the ways that cultural beliefs about sex and gender affect the natural sciences. A photograph of her lifting weights appears in the *Our Bodies, Ourselves* chapter "Women Growing Older." She continues to reside in Cambridge and in Woods Hole, Mass., where she has been a member of the corporation and a trustee of the Marine Biological Laboratory.

Lynda Birke and Ruth Hubbard, eds., *Reinventing Biology: Respect for Life and the Creation of Knowledge* (1995); Ruth Hubbard, *The Politics of Women's Biology* (1990); Hubbard, *Profitable Promises: Essays on Women, Science and Health* (1995); Ruth Hubbard and Elijah Wald, *Exploding the Gene Myth: How Genetic Information Is Produced and Manipulated by Scientists, Physicians, Employers, Insurance Companies, Educators, and Law Enforcers* (1999).

Bonnie B. Spanier

Jackson Laboratory The Jackson Laboratory

in Bar Harbor, Maine, is one of New England's top institutions for the support of research into biomedicine and genetics. Founded in 1929 by C. C. Little, the Jackson Lab is a nonprofit institution principally involved in the development of different strains of genetically altered mice. Research laboratories around the world request shipment of laboratory mice from the Jackson Lab; these mice are helping scientists discover genetic information about human diseases, particularly cancer.

The idea of using laboratory mice for research and experimentation was popularized in New England first by Abbie Lathrop, who had a poultry farm at Granby, Mass. After the turn of the 20th century, she traded poultry for mice in response to a rage among wealthy Victorians for "fancy mice"—mice with coats of various colors or other distinct physical characteristics. Lathrop bred the rodents to meet the growing demand for ornamental mice. One of her customers, however, was interested in something different. Professor William Castle of Harvard purchased mice from Lathrop for scientific research, performing genetic experiments on them. Several years later one of his students, Clarence C. Little, bred sibling mice repeatedly to produce a strain of mice that were almost identical (genetically as well as in appearance). Little left Harvard and, after years of research, in 1929 he founded the Roscoe Jackson Laboratory at Bar Harbor with the help of financing from Roscoe Jackson of the Hudson Motorcar Company and Edsel Ford of the Ford Motor Company. The connection between the Jackson Laboratory and mice research had begun.

As New England scientists increasingly recognized the value of mice for study that would benefit humans, the Jackson Lab under Little's tenure became the premier scientific institution for developing genetic strains of mice and mutants for research. Genetically altered strains of mice soon numbered in the hundreds. Some strains are still identifiable as the originals of Abbie Lathrop and Clarence Little: C57BL is derived from Lathrop's work; DBA/2 is derived from Little's experiments. As a graduate student Little himself had studied the relation between various tumors and mice. The Jackson Lab subsequently became well known as a cancer-research institution. Over the years the lab diversified into other research fields in which the study and use of mice are key. During World War II, Jackson scientists used mice to study encephalitis and the effects of poison gases. The lab became an important research center in immunology, neurology, and comparative biomedicine. In 1980 George D. Snell won the Nobel Prize for Medicine and Physiology because of work he did as a staff scientist at the lab. In 2003 the lab joined with the University of Maine and Maine Medical Center Research Institute to launch the university's Institute for Molecular Biophysics.

Jackson Laboratory Oral History Collection, American Philosophical Society (1986); Karen Rader, *Making Mice: Standardizing Animals for American Biomedical Research, 1900–1955* (2004); Michael Stroh, "From Pests to Pets to Tests," *Baltimore Sun*, December 5, 2002.

Russell M. Lawson

James, William (1842–1910) Philosopher and psychologist. The oldest son of the idiosyncratic Swedenborgian Henry James, and the brother of the novelist Henry James and the diarist Alice James, William James trained as a physician at Harvard Medical School and began his career as an experimental psychologist by creating the country's first experimental psychology laboratory at Harvard. He was among the founders of what has come to be called the "classic period"—from the end of the Civil War to the beginning of World War II—in American philosophy. His seminal text, *Principles of Psychology* (1890), occasioned new respect for the psychological research being carried out in the United States.

Schooled in New York, Boulogne, and Geneva, James was largely influenced by the rigorous intellectual atmosphere in his father's house, where he learned to debate philosophical questions and defend his views. In adulthood, influenced by the work of lifelong friend Charles Sanders Peirce, James extended the scope of the distinctly American philosophy of pragmatism beyond Peirce's theory of meaning. James's version of the theory of pragmatism was more appealing to the characteristic individualism of New Englanders; he used pragmatism to criticize what he took to be empty metaphysics, particularly European absolute idealism.

James served as a founder and president of the American Society for Psychical Research, a group that investigated paranormal psychological and physical phenomena. He also investigated the psychology of religious experience and published his results in *The Varieties of Religious Experience* (1902). In this classic volume, he argued that the personal benefits of religious experiences are far more important than their relation to a supreme being.

James opposed militarism and researched the psychology of war in an effort to find an alternative to warfare. He lived his philosophical opposition to war on moral grounds and entered into passionate public debates on ethical and political controversies. He carried on a public exchange of letters to the Harvard *Crimson* with his former student, Theodore Roosevelt, over the Spanish-American War. James opposed the war as a member of the Anti-Imperialist League during a period when Congress openly defended colonial expansion as justified by national "Manifest Destiny" to liberate Puerto Rico, Cuba, and the Philippines from Spain.

James suffered from vague illnesses and neurasthenia throughout his early life, but his marriage to Alice H. Gibbens of Cambridge, Mass., in 1878 and his study of the Kantian Charles Renouvier's writings on free will heralded a period of improved health and increased productivity. By the time of his death in 1910, James had become the dean of American philosophy. Though he left few definitive answers to the philosophical questions he raised, his vitality and creativity served as a model and pointed to fruitful lines of philosophical development for John Dewey, Alfred North Whitehead, and other successors throughout the 20th century.

William James, *The Works of William James*, 19 vols. (1975–); John McDermott, ed., *The Writings of William James* (1967); Gerald E. Myers, *William James: His Life and Thought* (1986).

Willard M. Miller

Just, Ernest Everett (1883–1941) Embryologist. Ernest Everett Just was born in Charleston, S.C. After completing a teaching certificate at the state industrial school in Orangeburg as a teenager, the African American Just desired a better education and enrolled at Kimball Union Academy, a college preparatory school in Meriden, N.H., in 1900. Although New England customs contrasted sharply with those of the South, Just thrived from the encouragement he received from students, teachers, and the community. He participated in extracurricular activities, editing the school newspaper and joining the debating society. Just graduated with honors and earned a scholarship to Dartmouth College in Hanover, N.H. His education at Dartmouth inspired his interest in biological research, a field in which he achieved international fame while working at the Woods Hole Marine Biological Laboratory in Massachusetts.

Just had considered quitting Dartmouth because he was disappointed by its obsession with football and frustrated by the lack of intellectual stimulation in his classes. A biology course taught by William Patten, however, changed his mind. Just immersed himself in biological research, studying the development of animal eggs. He changed his major to zoology, was named a Rufus Choate Scholar, was elected to Phi Beta Kappa, and graduated in 1907 with high honors.

After seven years in New England, Just felt "hemmed in" by New Hampshire's granite hills and was homesick for the South. He accepted a position at Howard University in Washington, D.C., where he began teaching biology in 1910 and directed the department of zoology from 1912 to 1941. He also received a joint appointment at Howard's medical school as head of the physiology department. Just helped students found the fraternity Omega Psi Phi. In 1912 he married Ethel Highwarden, a German teacher.

In response to Just's inquiry about graduate programs, Patten suggested that Just contact Dr. Frank R. Lillie, a University of Chicago professor who was director of the Marine Biological Laboratory at Woods Hole. Lillie warned Just that he would be denied access to many research laboratories because of his race but offered to assist him to get a position at Woods Hole. Just began graduate studies in 1909 and also enrolled in a doctoral program at the University of Chicago. He conducted cell biology research every summer at Woods Hole, publishing numerous journal articles, beginning with "The Relation of the First Cleavage Plane to the Entrance Point of the Sperm" (1912).

In 1915 Just received the first Spingarn Medal presented by the National Association for the Advancement of Colored People. He completed his doctorate in 1916 and gained renown for his understanding of cell reproduction and for presenting new theories of cell structures. Just also explored how magnetism affected cell division after fertilization, a problem examined in late-20th-century space research.

Frustrated by inadequate facilities at Howard and racism at Woods Hole, Just discouraged African American students from research careers, urging them to attend medical school instead. By the 1930s he had exiled himself to European laboratories, where he was well received. He was the first American invited to do research at the Kaiser Wilhelm Institut für Biologie at Berlin. During this time, Just divorced his wife; he married the scientist Hedwig Schnetzler in 1939. When laboratories were closed to him during World War II, Just returned to Washington, D.C., where he died of pancreatic cancer in 1941.

During his lifetime, Just wrote 60 papers and two books, *Basic Methods for Experiments on Eggs of Marine Animals* (1939) and *The Biology of the Cell Surface* (1939). He served on the editorial boards of several scientific journals, was elected to membership in the New York Academy of Sciences, was vice president of the American Society of Zoologists, and was named a fellow of the American Association for the Advancement of Science. A conference on developmental biology honored the centennial of his birth and the importance of the basic principles he illuminated, which remain viable decades later, even with the advancement of modern biological research tools such as electron microscopes and molecular probes. In 1996 a U.S. postage stamp was issued in Just's honor as part of the series on African American leaders.

Kenneth R. Manning, *Black Apollo of Science: The Life of Ernest Everett Just* (1983); Roger H. Sawyer and Richard M. Showman, eds., *The Cellular and Molecular Biology of Invertebrate Development* (1985).

Elizabeth D. Schafer

Lyme Disease

Lyme Disease Lyme disease is the leading vector-borne illness in the United States, occurring when the *Borrelia burgdorferi* (Bb) spirochete is inadvertently transmitted to humans from the blood of mice, deer, or domestic pets via blacklegged deer ticks. The spirochete was named for Willy Burgdorfer, the National Institutes of Health scientist who pinpointed it as the bacterium directly responsible for Lyme infection in 1981. The *Ixodes scapularis* nymph ticks carrying the spirochete are endemic to New England and Middle Atlantic states, where almost 1,500 Lyme disease cases are reported annually. Humans are increasingly subject to infection where suburbs have extended into wooded areas. Dogs are also vulnerable to the spirochete and display similar symptoms of infection. Of the New England states, Connecticut, Massachusetts, and Rhode Island are high-risk areas. Maine, New Hampshire, and Vermont are listed by the Centers for Disease Control as moderate risk areas.

The disease began making headlines in the 1970s when an unprecedented number of related cases of skin rash followed by headache, listlessness, and often acute rheumatoid arthritis clustered in Old Lyme, Conn., caught the attention of Alan Steere and his colleagues at Yale University. Steere and his research team began their epidemiological investigation along the Connecticut River, and eventually focused on four country roads where one in 10 children displayed symptoms. The source was still not definitively determined, but Steere deducted that the distinctive skin lesion resembled a tick bite, and that the outbreaks were most prevalent in summer months. Steere published his findings in 1977, and continued to study symptom patterns and possible cures.

In 1984 the Bb pathogen was isolated in the blood of those displaying symptoms of the bull's-eye Lyme disease rash, erythema migrans (EM). What has made the vector-borne illness so elusive (and its diagnosis and cure subject to controversy) is its ability to mask itself as a variety of acute ailments with no clear source, conditions often dismissed as psychosomatic, ranging from general malaise to cardiac and neurological symptoms.

Because of this vagueness, statistics for reported cases are subject to contention. New England state health departments, striving to be conservative because of the potential for blanket diagnosis, and using a definition created by the CDC, reported approximately 40,000 cases between 1990 and 2001. According to patient advocacy groups, however, Lyme diagnoses have been notoriously difficult for mystified and desperate patients to receive. As a result, activist groups and sympathetic community doctors claim a staggeringly higher statistic of approximately 2 million cases.

Since the 1980s, doctors have relied on antibiotic treatment to arrest symptoms, and scientists have attempted to refine a precise blood test that can detect the disease in the earliest stages of infection, when blood tests often come back negative. In 1990 a preventive vaccination was licensed for veterinary purposes, and in 1999 a vaccine for adults and minors 15 years of age and older was made available.

The most recent cause taken up by patient advocacy groups is the expansion of the CDC's narrowly defined criteria to include the late-stage neurological symptoms of what is often referred to as chronic Lyme disease. Although many patients respond rapidly to short-term antibiotic therapy when their symptoms are acute and in the earliest stages, others suffer from cognitive dysfunction, most commonly from encephalopathy, and find it difficult to get the long-term intravenous antibiotic therapy that allays their symptoms. Conservative doctors and researchers follow the CDC's relatively narrow surveillance case definition and are wary of the health risks of long-term antibiotic therapy. Physicians who accept a more inclusive definition treat patients with "probable Lyme disease," believing that the antibiotic-related risks of treating those not suffering from the disease are outweighed by the physical, cognitive, and functional disability suffered by those who do.

The Lyme Disease Foundation, based in Hartford, was established in 1988 by Karen Vanderhoof-Forschner and Thomas Forschner; Willy Burgdorfer is a member of the board of directors. The foundation publishes the *Journal of Spirochetal and Tick-Borne Diseases*, a peer-reviewed journal founded in 1994.

Willy Burgdorfer, Alan G. Barbour, Stanley F. Hayes, Jorge L. Benach, Edgar Grunwaldt, and Jeffrey P. Davis, "Lyme Disease: A Tick-Borne Spirochetosis?" *Science* 216 (1982); Jonathan A. Edlow, *Bull's Eye: Unraveling the Medical Mystery of Lyme Disease* (2003); David Grann, "Stalking Dr. Steere," *New York Times Magazine* (June 17, 2001); A. C. Steere, S. E. Malawista, D. R. Snydman, R. E. Shope, W. A. Andiman, M. R. Ross, F. M. Steele, "Lyme Arthritis: An Epidemic of Oligoarticular Arthritis in Children and Adults in Three Connecticut Communities," *Arthritis and Rheumatism* 20 (1977); Karen Vanderhoof-Forschner, *Everything You Need to Know about Lyme Disease and Other Tick-Borne Disorders* (1997).

Jennifer Beard

Mathematics

Mathematics New England has produced many important mathematicians who have made noteworthy contributions to the field. Nathaniel Bowditch, a seaman born in Salem, Mass., in 1773 who taught himself the science of navigation, was among the earliest. Others were educated at or affiliated with prestigious universities such as Harvard and the Massachusetts Institute of Technology in Cambridge, Mass. Mathematics has been taught at Brown University in Providence since its founding in 1764; the university has one of the oldest and strongest applied mathematics departments in the country, established in 1941 and led by the noted German applied mathematician William Prager.

The study of mathematics in New England began in the 17th century at Harvard College, where gifted students were assigned the task of creating astronomical tables for New England almanacs. This early interest was both scientific and religious, and great attention was paid to eclipses and comets. The study of optics was also part of the early Harvard curriculum. Outside the academy, navigational skills were essential for the region's sea captains, and merchants needed increasingly sophisticated mathematical skills as commerce developed. The popularity of the word *calculate* in early New England dialect signals that a familiarity with mathematical skills was an attribute of a sharp Yankee. In later centuries, the presence of leading educational, scientific, and astronomical observatories created fertile ground for the work of notable mathematicians.

Several New Englanders made important contributions to math and science in the 19th century. Salem-born Benjamin Pierce graduated from Harvard University, joined its faculty in 1833, and later established the observatory there. His significant contributions to astronomy include using mathematics to study Neptune's orbit and its effect on the orbits of other planets. The crater Pierce on the moon is named for him. Pierce also published *Linear Associative Algebra* (1870), which classified complex associative algebras of dimensions less than seven.

The Harvard graduate and professor Maxime Böcher was born in Boston in 1867. His prolific publications include *Introduction to Higher Algebra* (1907), *Introduction to the Study of Integral Equations* (1909), and elementary texts on analytic geometry and trigonometry. He also published more than 100 papers on differential equations, series, and algebra and became the first editor-in-chief of the journal *Transactions of the American Mathematical Society*. He gave the first series of colloquium lectures for the American Mathematical Society, which later created a prize in his honor.

In 1953 the American Mathematical Society awarded the Böcher Prize to mathematician Norman Levinson, who was born in Boston in 1912, received his Ph.D. from MIT in 1935, and began a lifelong career there in 1937. Levinson's research in time series applied to seismic activity led to improved methods of oil exploration. He also worked in the fields of differential equations, probability, quantum mechanics, and number theory.

Daniel Gorenstein, a mathematician whose work gained international recognition, taught himself calculus at the age of 12. Born in Boston in 1923, Gorenstein studied at Harvard where he wrote his doctoral thesis on algebraic geometry. The Gorenstein rings were named in his honor. Gorenstein's major achievement, with the help of mathematicians from around the world, was the classification of finite simple groups. He taught at Clark University in Worcester, Mass., from 1951 until 1964 and at Northeastern University in Boston from 1964 until 1969.

Today, New England continues its long tradition of innovation in mathematics with work by eminent mathematicians such as Robert L. Devaney of Boston University, who researches chaos theory. The region's prominent educational institutions and distinguished mathematicians ensure that New England will be a leader in mathematics well into the 21st century.

Samuel Eliot Morison, *Harvard College in the 17th Century* (1936); Marion Barber Stowell, *Early American Almanacs: The Colonial Weekday Bible* (1976).

Joyce A. Cryan

Medical Education New England's nine medical schools, most founded before the 20th century, include some of the nation's finest. Boston's three medical schools have multiple hospital affiliations and pursue world-renowned scientific research. Dozens of schools train nurses and more than a dozen produce physical therapists. Four schools train pharmacists. Facilities for educating alternative practitioners, however, are less common. The region features a few schools for physician's assistant training; two undergraduate schools and one graduate school of optometry; and one school each for graduate training in osteopathy, chiropractic, and naturopathic medicine, and acupuncture. New England's medical education landscape bears the imprint of two centuries of change and development.

Medical schools reached New England belatedly, a century and a half after settlement. Colonial medical education took other forms. When English settlers arrived in the early 17th century, the region's Native Americans used a system of medical practices involving plants, steam baths, and religious observances. European colonists unknowingly brought with them new pathogens that wiped out thousands of Native Americans. In peaceful times, Indians instructed the newcomers in indigenous botanic medicine, while colonial physicians treated native neighbors with simple surgery. Some settlers even became practitioners of "Indian medicine." Meanwhile, as in Europe, older women learned midwifery on the job, handled other common complaints, and cultivated and gathered medicinal plants.

A handful of New Englanders, mostly Puritan clergymen, journeyed to European medical schools, but most American-born colonial physicians gained their education through the preceptorial system. Would-be doctors paid a practicing physician to be their "preceptor." For several years, the apprentice performed his preceptor's menial chores such as mixing medicines and hand-rolling pills, later dressing wounds and bleeding patients. Using the preceptor's personal library, the student studied and memorized book knowledge. But the quality of this education varied widely depending on the preceptor. Most students never witnessed an autopsy; some preceptors owned no books, heard no recitations, and pocketed the cash. Two preceptor-trained sisters, Harriot and Sarah Hunt, practiced botanic medicine in Boston beginning in 1835, but most physicians were men.

The medical crisis of the Revolutionary War highlighted the need for more and better-educated physicians and surgeons. In 1783, noting the inefficiency of one-on-one education, a society of Cambridge physicians founded a medical school at Harvard with three professors. Thus was finally born the first New England medical school, just as the colonial period ended. (Columbia University and the University of Pennsylvania had founded medical schools in the 1760s.) After medical schools began to appear, they augmented rather than replaced the preceptor system. Two or three years of preceptor training plus two three-month "years" of lectures at a medical school—the identical course repeated—earned one a medical degree. Early medical schools were generally proprietary—the faculty owned the school, profiting directly from enrollment—creating every incentive to keep standards low and admissions high. Dozens of such short-lived medical schools churned out low-skilled doctors.

In 1797 Dartmouth founded the second New England medical school in one cramped room. The school moved in 1811 to the nation's first building designed for educating physicians, complete with a chemistry laboratory. In that year Brown established a medical school that lasted only 16 years (but was revived in 1973). Yale's medical school opened in 1813 and Bowdoin's in 1821, just after Maine became a state. Vermont boasted three medical schools; the Castleton Medical Academy (later College) was the largest medical school in New England during the 1820s. Its impressive 1821 building featured a museum, dissecting chamber, amphitheater for lectures, and chemical laboratory. The University of Vermont's medical department struggled from its 1822 start until Castleton closed in 1862. At Woodstock, the Clinical School of Medicine (later the Vermont Medical College) opened

The New Research Building at Harvard Medical School, 2003

in 1827 and featured a free public infirmary, but vanished by 1860. In Massachusetts, the Berkshire Medical College in Pittsfield was briefly one of New England's largest, lasting from 1822 to 1869. Boston's Tremont Street School opened in 1838, and semiofficially served as a summer school for Harvard. It offered further instruction and clinical opportunities, which tacitly admitted Harvard's gaps. Boston's ephemeral but innovative Boylston Medical School specified three terms of graded instruction, rather than a repeated course.

All early medical schools faced a problem of finding "clinical material"—living and not—with which to train aspiring doctors. Public disapproval of autopsy persisted in New England, as residents of New Haven discovered. In 1824 the fresh corpse of 19-year-old Bathsheba Smith disappeared from its grave and then turned up in a basement at Yale Medical School, apparently awaiting dissection. During the ensuing riot, windows were smashed, the militia was called in, and two suspected students hotfooted it out of state. An anatomy teaching assistant—nearly tarred and feathered—was later sentenced to jail and a fine. Connecticut speedily passed a law regulating procurement of cadavers that quieted public fears and enabled anatomy teaching to proceed. Massachusetts General Hospital, founded in 1821, provided patients for Harvard students to observe, though not to treat.

The training of so-called regular physicians is only part of the story of medical education. New Hampshire farmer Samuel Thomson learned about medicinal plants from a local female healer. By 1805 he was treating patients with packaged herbal concoctions and steam baths. Thomson's self-education system of books, kits, and study groups became especially popular in the Midwest. New Englander Wooster Beach developed a revised version called "eclectic" medicine with a medical college at Worcester, Mass., from 1846 to 1859.

Beginning in the late 18th century, male physicians had begun to serve as "men-midwives" to better-off families for even ordinary deliveries. The proliferation of medical schools sped up this trend, and many midwives hung up their aprons. But concern for delicacy suggested the importance of educated female caregivers. This impulse led in two directions: the training of female physicians and the establishment of nursing as a profession.

In 1848 Samuel Gregory founded in Boston the world's first medical school for women. The New England Female Medical College secured state authorization to grant the M.D. degree in 1856; Rebecca Lee, an 1864 graduate, was the nation's first formally trained African American physician. In 1873 the impoverished school merged with Boston University, which offered training in homeopathic medicine and remained coeducational.

Nursing as a skilled profession had just begun to develop before the Civil War. Gregory's institution served as the nation's second nursing school. But the Civil War most glaringly proved the value of skilled nursing care. Dorothea Dix of Massachusetts recruited and trained over 3,200 Union Army nursing volunteers, whose lives Louisa May Alcott depicted in *Hospital Sketches*. Boston's New England Hospital for Women and Children (which graduated the first African American nurse, Mary Eliza Mahoney, in 1879), Massachusetts General Hospital, the New Haven State Hospital, and Boston City Hospital instituted nurse-training programs in the postwar years.

The Civil War also exposed the need for better-educated physicians. Competition among schools had kept academic standards soft. Professors also maintained their own clinical practices, devoting insufficient time to teaching. Medicine and science operated separately; a medical student might never use a microscope, for instance. And, perhaps worst of all, only a few students practiced treating or operating on patients. Unlucky wounded soldiers provided many doctors with their first crack at surgery.

Harvard pioneered in correcting these nationwide problems. In 1869 new university president Charles Eliot seized control of the Boston-based medical school. He raised admission standards (noting that perhaps half of the medical students could not even write), and put the professors on salary. He created a logically graded three-year curriculum of nine months per year, and added laboratory instruction in basic sciences. In 1880 an optional fourth year was added, and then made mandatory in 1892. In 1900 a college degree became an admission requirement. Harvard's reforms spread to other medical schools around the country.

This reform drive snuffed out many marginal medical schools even before its most famous product, the 1910 Flexner Report. Abraham Flexner visited every medical, homeopathic, eclectic, and osteopathic school in the country. His report lambasted most schools for low academic standards and lack of clinical and scientific facilities; standards were shored up all over as a result.

Boston University survived this shakedown but elected an orthodox orientation in 1918. Medical coeducation became a Boston specialty as most of the city's schools admitted women. Women made up 42 percent of Tufts graduates by 1900. Then a drop-off occurred: by 1919 only 2 percent of Tufts medical graduates were women. Coeducational medical schools' admission of women continued to wax and wane. When World War I exerted temporary pressure for more doctors, Yale and other schools admitted a few women beginning in 1917. World War II gave an even greater, but also short-lived, boost to medical coeducation. Boston University's female enrollment rose from 1 percent to 19 percent during the war years; the surge at Tufts was almost as great. Starved for students, Harvard Medical School first admitted women starting in 1945. Massachusetts General Hospital trained more female interns (nine) during the war than in its previous 130 years. After the war, female enrollment dropped again to 5 percent. Recently more women and minorities have sought medical education of various kinds; currently about 48 percent of students enrolled in medical schools are women and 18 percent are minorities. New England's currently fine facilities for medical education reflect what Flexner would have hoped.

Barbara Barzansky and Norman Gevitz, eds., *Beyond Flexner: Medical Education in the 20th Century* (1992); James H. Cassedy, *Medicine in America: A Short History* (1991); Norman Gevitz, ed., *Other Healers: Unorthodox Medicine in America* (1988); Kenneth M. Ludmerer, *Learning to Heal: The Development of American Medical Education* (1985); Regina Markell Morantz-Sanchez, *Sympathy and Science: Women Physicians in American Medicine* (1985); Susan Reverby, *Ordered to Care: The Dilemma of American Nursing, 1850–1945* (1987); William F. Norwood, *Medical Education in the United States before the Civil War* (1944); Mary Roth Walsh, *"Doctors Wanted: No Women Need Apply": Sexual Barriers in the Medical Profession, 1835–1975* (1977).

Rebecca R. Noel

Medical Publishing The early presence of medical education at Harvard University and other institutions and the presence of influential physicians and scientists in colonial New England, combined with an extensive network of early printers, made the region a center of the medical press. This tradition continues today with outstanding publishers and leading medical and public health journals.

The first medical publication in the American colonies was *A Brief Rule to Guide the Common-People of New-England, How to Order Themselves and Theirs in the Small Pocks, or Measles*, issued in 1677 by Thomas Thatcher, a minister at the Old South Meeting House in Boston. The greatest New England medical treatise of the colonial era, Cotton Mather's *Angel of Bethesda* (ca. 1724), was unpublished, but by the 19th century, medical writers found printers throughout New England. Boston was the center of printing activity, and produced notable works including Samuel D. Gross's *Elements of Pathological Anatomy* (1839), the first treatment of the subject in English. Boston publishers included W. D. Ticknor, whose *Catalogue of Medical Books* (1847) is ample testimony to the wide range of medical literature that was available, and the Massachusetts Medical Society, which published the respected *Library of Practical Medicine* (22 vols., 1831–38). Ticknor, in addition to its prominence in belle-lettres, published Oliver Wendell Holmes's *Homoeopathy and Its Kindred Delusions* (1842).

The Massachusetts Medical Society, incorporated in 1781, was established, among other purposes, to disseminate current medical information through the publication and distribution of journals and periodicals. The *New England Journal of Medicine and Surgery and the Collateral Branches of Science* was first published in January 1812, and then merged in 1828 with the *Medical Intelligencer* (1823), becoming the weekly *Boston Medical and Surgical Journal*. This periodical became the official publication of the Massachusetts Medical Society in 1914, and its name was changed in 1928 to the *New England Journal of Medicine*. Now the world's premier medical journal, the venerable *Journal* continues to be published in Boston.

An extraordinary number of other leading medical journals have been published in New England. Among them are *New England Medical Review and Journal* (1827). *New England Quarterly Journal of Medicine and Surgery* (1842), *New England Botanic, Medical, and Surgical Journal* (1847), *Boston Domestic Journal of Medicine* (1852), *Journal of the Gynecological Society of Boston* (1869), *Transactions of the Gynecological Society of the Medical Sciences* (1896), *Apothecary and New England Druggist* (1903), *Boston Dispensary Quarterly* (1912), *Boston Tuberculosis Association Bulletin* (1929), and *Transactions of the New England Surgical Society* (1916).

Although Boston continued to be New England's publishing center, medical publishing was largely concentrated in New York City and Philadelphia by the turn of the 20th century. Today, New England's remaining medical publishers include Little, Brown, MIT Press, Harvard University Press, Yale University Press, and Blackwell.

Francesco Cordasco, *Medical Publishing in 19th-Century America* (1990); Francis A. Countway Library of Medicine, Boston, *Author-Title Catalog of the Francis A. Countway Library of Medicine for Imprints through 1959*, 10 vols. (1973).

Francesco Cordasco

Mental Health Colonial New England's Puritan belief system shaped early American attitudes toward the mentally ill. Settlers linked madness to supernatural actors, which reduced the mystery of deviant behavior, placing it within a divine scheme that fostered charitable attitudes toward the insane. Intimate colonial communities, where the mad person was a neighbor and where friends were familiar with lifelong patterns of conduct, encouraged tolerance and supported the belief that madness was periodic rather than permanent. Confinement was rare, and never constant, occurring only when an afflicted person had destroyed property or harmed others.

By the late 18th century the First Great Awakening had provoked a new religious responsibility; the Enlightenment had undermined belief in supernatural forces; economic changes and population pressures had shattered family and community ties; and the new republican ideology, relying on the capacity of individuals to act responsibly, had given irrationality a new and threatening meaning. As the supernatural lost its cultural hold, a medical model of insanity developed emphasizing the individual's control over his or her own health. The mad were now perceived not only as diseased but as having brought on their own madness, and they were increasingly isolated from the rest of society. Families sometimes simply kept their intractable members in a locked room or outside shelter, while some communities paid for the support of their insane in the almshouses or jails of larger towns such as Salem, Danvers, and Boston, Mass. By the beginning of the 19th century, the mad in New England and elsewhere faced confinement as a way of life.

Confinement often led to abuse, and a Massachusetts survey of the mad in 1830 revealed much inhumane treatment. The Second Great Awakening, begun before the turn of the century, called for moral and social reform, and many New Englanders responded with fervor. Some joined sabbatarian and moral-reform societies, taught Sunday school, campaigned for prison reform, or crusaded against intemperance, capitalism, or slavery; others, among them Horace Mann, Louis Dwight, Eli Todd, Samuel Woodward, Rufus Wyman, and in the 1840s Dorothea Dix, sought to alleviate the sufferings of the insane. Their solution still entailed confinement, but in specialized asylums where patients could receive therapy informed by the latest medical thought.

Neither the asylum nor the new moral regimen of treatment, based on educational, recreational, religious, and occupational activities, began in New England, but New Englanders shaped therapeutic practices in ways that would significantly affect the mentally ill across the nation for the next century and a half. Philippe Pinel in France and William Tuke in England, who pioneered humane treatment of the mentally ill, influenced the American founders of the Friends Asylum, a private Quaker hospital established in Philadelphia in 1817, which became the prototype for the McLean Asylum (1818) in Boston and later Belmont, Mass., and the Hartford (Conn.) Retreat (1824). McLean and Hartford in turn became training grounds for New Englanders who would propel the asylum to the forefront among American methods of treating the insane. Their enthusiastic claims of curability made possible by moral treatment intrigued those who understood the state's increasing responsibility for all its citizens.

In 1833 the Massachusetts legislature fully

recognized that madness was a social problem requiring the state to invest public funds in the construction of the Worcester Asylum. Within a decade most states had followed Massachusetts's lead, acclaiming the commonwealth as a national leader in treating the insane. Samuel Woodward, a cofounder of the Hartford Retreat and the first medical superintendent at Worcester, demonstrated that patients receiving medical and moral treatment could be cured. But his success led to larger asylums, whose size undermined the effectiveness of moral treatment. The burgeoning numbers and increasing diversity of patients, often poor and chronically ill, fueled yet another set of trends that once again showed up first in New England. In Massachusetts, for instance, indigent immigrant patients, many of them Irish, were discharged to make room for paying clients; black patients for the most part were not admitted in the first place. Massachusetts later became the first state to establish a Board of State Charities to oversee all of its responsibilities for the indigent, an action that reversed the inappropriate discharge of patients but reinforced the custodial aspect of care in the state-supported asylum. By the 1890s asylums built for hundreds of patients were housing thousands, most therapy had disappeared, and even attempts at decent custodial care were failing.

It was in the 19th century as well that gender emerged as a focus of diagnosis and treatment. While gynecological surgery to cure mental illness briefly raged in the 1860s, neurasthenia, or nervous exhaustion, was the preferred diagnosis later in the century. George M. Beard of Connecticut named it but was quickly overshadowed by S. Weir Mitchell and his so-called rest cure. Mitchell's prescription of complete bed rest for Charlotte Perkins Gilman, another Connecticut native, drove Gilman to write *The Yellow Wallpaper* (1892), a scathing denouncement of Mitchell's—and late-19th-century America's—attitude toward women. Though not unique to New England, and despite Gilman's protest, gender-specific diagnoses continued to prevail: men's mental illnesses were seen as arising from overwork, sexual disabilities, and alcoholism; women's from reproductive-system malfunctions or family troubles.

At the dawn of the 20th century asylum doctors, even those in Massachusetts and elsewhere in New England, were no longer in the vanguard and found themselves increasingly isolated from the rest of the medical and psychiatric profession. Yet New England had not lost its grip on innovation. In 1908 Clifford Beers, a native of Connecticut and a graduate of Yale, not only published a description of his experiences as a patient at the Hartford Re-

treat and the Connecticut Hospital for the Insane in *A Mind That Found Itself* but also created the Connecticut Society for Mental Hygiene to address institutional defects. The following year Beers joined with the prominent psychodynamic psychiatrist Adolf Meyer, who had served as medical superintendent at the Worcester Asylum in the 1890s, to found the National Committee for Mental Hygiene. That group's stress on preventive measures significantly shifted the focus of treatment from mental illness to mental health.

Psychodynamic psychiatry heralded yet another a change in which New England institutions played a prominent role. Clark University in Worcester invited Sigmund Freud to deliver a series of lectures in 1909, an event that eventually led to a broadened pool of patients and an emphasis on private practice. The Boston Psychoanalytical Society also had considerable influence in spreading Freud's doctrine of psychoanalysis in the United States.

The 1890s had seen the emergence of the psychopathic hospital, which offered local treatment to patients in the early stage of mental illness and connected the process to a research center. These facilities altered the environment and breadth of psychiatric practice. The Boston Psychopathic Hospital (1912), one of the first, had a staff of somaticists who explored chemical imbalances, endocrine systems, and other physiological factors. Their work led to experiments with insulin coma, Metrazol convulsion, and electroshock therapies as well as psychosurgery, all of them cutting-edge methods of treating mental illness

in the 1930s. Boston Psychopathic, under the leadership of E. E. Southard and Mary Jarrett, had also played a prominent role in establishing the field of psychiatric social work in the 1920s. Whatever the attitude toward the institutionalized insane, New England, with Massachusetts in the lead, still spent the most per capita on its patients in the mid-20th century.

After World War II, shifting intellectual and social arguments resulted in mass deinstitutionalization. Psychodynamic therapies, community-based treatment centers, prevention-oriented clinics, and the advent of psychotropic drugs all played a role. The National Mental Health Act in 1946, the 1961 recommendation of the Joint Commission on Mental Illness and Health that large state mental hospitals be dismantled, and the Community Mental Health Centers Act of 1963 moved the process further along. In part, support for emptying the asylums marked a change in popular attitudes, one encouraged by the candor of people such as Jimmy Piersall of the Boston Red Sox, who was willing to talk publicly about his mental illness. The publication of *Fear Strikes Out* (1955) and the Hollywood film version of Piersall's struggle (1957) put a human face on mental illness in the 1950s, much as Pearl S. Buck, Dale Evans Rogers, and later the Kennedys did for those afflicted with mental retardation. Deinstitutionalization was equally aided by civil rights defenders, antipsychiatry intellectuals, and patient advocates. Indeed, it was once again in New England that the patient's right to treatment was first recognized, in a 1968 decision of

The Retreat, a sanitarium in Brattleboro, Vt., 1934

the Massachusetts Supreme Court. And as the population of asylums plummeted, states scurried for the federal funds to support their community mental-health centers.

Ironically, it was these federal funds that returned the treatment of the mentally ill to local communities. When the Vermont Longitudinal Research Project provided evidence in the 1960s that even people with severe mental illness could live outside institutions, the Green Mountain State became the national model for community mental-health care. In 1966 Vermont began discharging patients from its state hospital and providing for their care and treatment in 10 community mental-health centers across the state. The system worked, and even in the late 1980s, when patient advocates still criticized the pared-down state hospital, no one attacked the community mental-health system. The state of Maine, by contrast, was placed under court order in 1990 to vastly improve care at the Augusta Mental Health Institute, housed in an obsolete mid-19th-century facility, as well as outpatient housing and treatment. As a result, it is currently building a 92-bed forensic psychiatric treatment center.

At the beginning of the 21st century, inadequate resources and therapeutic failures continue to plague both hospitalized and deinstitutionalized recipients of mental-health care. New England for the most part, like other regions of the country, still has not found a way to combine humane treatment for the chronically ill with readily available therapeutic services for the less seriously stricken.

Norman Dain, *Concepts of Insanity in the United States, 1789–1865* (1964); Gerald N. Grob, *From Asylum to Community: Mental Health Policy in Modern America* (1991); Grob, *Mental Illness and American Society, 1875–1940* (1983); Grob, *Mental Institutions in America: Social Policy to 1875* (1973); Grob, *The State and the Mentally Ill: A History of Worcester State Hospital in Massachusetts, 1830–1920* (1966); Mary Ann Jimenez, *Changing Faces of Madness: Early American Attitudes and Treatment of the Insane* (1987); Constance M. McGovern, *Masters of Madness: Social Origins of the American Psychiatric Profession* (1985); and David J. Rothman, *The Discovery of the Asylum: Social Order and Disorder in the New Republic* (1971).

Constance M. McGovern

Meteorology In the 17th and 18th centuries New Englanders worried about the weather and what its changes portended. Cotton Mather believed his fellows were changing the climate. "Our cold is much moderated since the opening and clearing of our woods, and the winds do not blow roughly as in the days of our fathers." Benjamin Franklin agreed that "cleared land absorbs more heat and melts snow quicker." At Harvard, Hugh Williamson found the winters becoming

milder, too, and felt the cleared fields ameliorated the northwest winds.

By the mid-18th century, James MacSparran had been a missionary to Rhode Island for more than 30 years, and he wanted his own misery to serve as a warning to those back home in England. His 1753 book told them everything they needed to know about New England's weather before they read even one page: *America Dissected, Being a Full and True Account of All the American Colonies, Shewing the Intemperance of the Climates, Excessive Heat and Cold, and Sudden Violent Changes of Weather, Terrible and Mischievous Thunder and Lightning, Bad and Unwholesome Air, Destructive to Human Bodies, etc.*

Throughout colonial America, as in New England, the science of meteorology had consisted of isolated diarists carefully recording local weather and climate, without reliable instruments, sponsoring institutions, or instruction. In the mid-18th century Dr. Edward Holyoke, a promoter of medical education in Massachusetts, began compiling monthly data on the weather, observations on the prevailing diseases, and, in 1786, death statistics for the town of Salem. Prevailing science linked weather and illness, exemplified by Noah Webster's theory that weather, comets and meteors, volcanic eruptions, and earthquakes were all pestilential epidemics.

Early in the 19th century the editors of medical and literary journals in New England began working within an atmosphere of scientific inquiry supported by the administration

of Thomas Jefferson, president of the nation's leading scientific societies. New England's greatest contribution to meteorology lies perhaps in the efforts of its colleges to standardize meteorological observations. Middlebury, Williams, Yale, Harvard, and Bowdoin colleges synchronized their observations under the leadership of Fredrick Hall, editor of the *Literary and Philosophical Repertory* and professor of natural history at Middlebury, where he published records that led to the analysis of large-scale weather patterns. In 1817 Jacob Bigelow, a Harvard botanist, corresponded with observers all along the Atlantic coast about the blooming of peach trees, thus entering into the study of seasonal change. Williams College founded the country's first meteorological association in 1838; Harvard soon followed suit, and Yale began offering lectures on meteorology as part of its curriculum in natural philosophy.

By the mid-19th century, national institutions and advanced technology had pushed further in developing large-scale weather observations, with the Smithsonian taking the lead. By 1861 observers at 600 telegraph stations across the continent were transmitting standardized data to Washington, D.C. The National Weather Service was established by President Ulysses S. Grant in 1870 under the auspices of the U.S. Army Signal Service.

Using family resources amassed in the New Bedford whaling industry, Abbott Lawrence Rotch established the Blue Hill Meteorological Observatory in Milton, Mass., the highest

Morse Hall at the Institute for the Study of Earth, Oceans, and Space, University of New Hampshire, Durham

point within 10 miles of the coast to be found south of Maine. Beginning in 1885 Blue Hill provided the United States with a major advance in facilities for weather research. Because of its many landscapes and altitudes, and its long and varied seacoast, meteorologists now consider New England as consisting of numerous microclimates, some bearing surprisingly little relationship to those nearby. The summer fogs of coastal Maine are legendary, for example, while inland areas are seldom obscured. For this reason, in recent years New England meteorologists have advocated the construction of a network of transmitters, set 50 miles apart throughout the region, to chart the course of weather events as they move through each particular weather pocket. The meteorological station at the summit of Mount Washington records extremes of cold and wind. Research on climate change in New England is centered at the Institute for the Study of Earth, Oceans, and Space, established at the University of New Hampshire in 1985.

New Englanders' concern for meteorological forecasting has been fostered by the proverbial variability of the weather in the region and by natural disasters caused by storms that many believed the weather service should have predicted. Most notable were the hurricane of 1938, which caused massive loss of life and property, the blizzard of 1978, which brought New England to a standstill, and the storm of 1998, which disabled the power grids of northern New England, upstate New York, and Canada for more than two weeks. A freak meeting of three storm systems off the New England coast in late October 1991 destroyed the Gloucester, Mass., swordfish boat *Andrea Gale* and its six crew members, leaving almost no trace of the 70-foot ship in its wake. A Boston meteorologist dubbed this event "the perfect storm"—that is, a storm that could not possibly have been worse—and Sebastian Junger, a Massachusetts native, used the phrase as the title of his best-selling book (1997) about the deadly episode.

Charles Franklin Brooks, *Why the Weather?* (1935); James Rodger Fleming, *Meteorology in America, 1800–1870* (1990); William A. Koelsch, "Ben Franklin's Heir: Alexander McAdie and the Experimental Analysis and Forecasting of New England Storms, 1884–1892," *New England Quarterly* 59 (1986); Eric Pinder, *Tying Down the Wind: Adventures in the Worst Weather on Earth* (2000).

Louis Mazzari

Mitchell, Maria

Mitchell, Maria (1818–89) Astronomer and educator. Considered the first American female astronomer, Maria Mitchell was born on the island of Nantucket, Mass., to Quaker parents, William and Lydia (Coleman) Mitch-

Maria Mitchell, ca. 1865

ell. She assisted her father with astronomical observations that were crucial for the livelihoods of the island's whaling community. Each night Maria gathered data for her father and recorded it in logbooks. From the rooftops she counted the seconds during eclipses on a chronometer and assessed celestial phenomena.

At age 16, Mitchell began teaching school, first as the assistant to the Reverend Cyrus Peirce in his school for "Young Ladies," and later on her own at the Franklin School House. When her funds were depleted, she began a 20-year career as librarian of the Nantucket Atheneum, reading scientific tomes every afternoon and scanning the sky each evening. She helped her father with astronomical work for the U.S. Coast Survey. On October 1, 1847, during her routine observations, Mitchell saw a comet and calculated its coordinates. Her father notified William Bond of the Harvard College Observatory who verified her sighting. Despite controversial claims by others reporting the same comet, the king of Denmark awarded Mitchell with a gold medal for finding the first comet discovered solely with a telescope.

Following this achievement, Mitchell became famous. Tourists traveled to Nantucket to see her, and she was invited to speak at scientific meetings. She was the first woman elected to the American Academy of Arts and Sciences (1848; as an honorary member), the American Association for the Advancement of Science (1850), and the American Philosophical Society (1869). Mitchell received honorary degrees, probably the first given to a woman by American colleges, and was presented with a state-of-the-art telescope by a group of well-known women of the time, among them Elizabeth Peabody, a Transcendentalist, publisher, and reformer.

Beginning in 1849, Mitchell was a part-time computer for *The American Ephemeris and Nautical Almanac;* her computations were applied to navigational directions for sailors. In 1857 Mitchell agreed to accompany a young woman traveling to Europe, where she visited notable observatories and astronomers. After her mother's death in 1861, Mitchell and her father moved to Lynn, Mass., where she wrote articles about her astronomical activities.

In 1865 Mitchell accepted a position as professor of astronomy and observatory director at newly established Vassar College for women. The first female astronomy professor, Mitchell inspired her students with her lectures during meteor showers and other celestial events. She encouraged her students to assist her in the observatory (which had the third-largest telescope in the United States at that time), photographing sunspots and describing changes on Jupiter and Saturn, her primary areas of study. Many of her protégées, such as Mary Whitney, became proficient astronomers, teaching Mitchell's methods to new generations of students.

Despite wage discrimination, which she protested, Mitchell remained at Vassar and promoted women's rights in education. She was a founder and served as president of the American Association for the Advancement of Women in 1875 and 1876, speaking in favor of women's opportunities to reach their full potential professionally. She traveled abroad and in the United States, reading feminist and scientific papers and conducting astronomical observations.

Mitchell retired from Vassar in 1888 and died in Lynn, Mass. A moon crater was named in her honor, and both Nantucket and Vassar established Maria Mitchell Observatories. On Nantucket, the Maria Mitchell Association opened a museum at Mitchell's childhood home on Vestal Street; today the association sponsors a scientific library that preserves her archival records, a full-time astronomer, and a department of natural science.

Henry Albers, ed., *Maria Mitchell: A Life in Journals and Letters* (2001); Thomas E. Drake, *A Scientific Outpost: The First Half Century of the Nantucket Maria Mitchell Association* (1968); Phebe Mitchell Kendall, *Maria Mitchell: Life, Letters and Journals* (1896); Sally Gregory Kohlstedt, "Maria Mitchell and the Advancement of Women in Science," in *Uneasy Careers and Intimate Lives: Women in Science, 1789–1979*, ed. Pnina G. Abir-Am and Dorinda Outram (1987); Helen Wright, *Sweeper in the Sky: The Life of Maria Mitchell, First Woman Astronomer in America* (1949).

Elizabeth D. Schafer

Morse, Jedidiah

Morse, Jedidiah (1761–1826) Geographer. Jedidiah Morse, American geographer and clergyman, was born in Woodstock, Conn. Upon graduating from Yale College in 1785 he worked as a teacher and itinerant preacher until appointed to the First Parish of Charlestown, Mass. In 1789 he married Elisabeth Ann Breese, granddaughter of Samuel Finley, the president of Princeton College. They had 11 children, one of whom was Samuel Finley Breese Morse, the inventor of the telegraph.

Morse was a studious, sometimes controversial man. In 1788 American historian Ebenezer Hazard described the young Morse as a strict Calvinist, who was "judicious and sensible, decent and modest in his deportment, a chearful companion, who prettily supports the dignity of the clergyman in the midst of friendly affability." Morse was a staunch Federalist who was equally suspicious of the French, Jefferson-Republicans, southerners, and Unitarians. He feared liberal religion that focused less on the drama of sin and predestination and more on God's benevolence and universal salvation.

Morse put more of his energy into studying geography than theology; in fact, he failed to acquire one clerical position because of his fondness for geographical research. When he was a young teacher, the lack of available material on American geography inspired Morse to write *Geography Made Easy* (1784), which became a widely used textbook. In 1789, the same year he was installed as a preacher in Charlestown, he published the first of numerous editions of *The American Geography*, an encyclopedic compilation describing the flora, fauna, landscapes, and history of the United States. Morse pored over books and maps to compile the volume. He used information provided by correspondents throughout the United States, including Ebenezer Hazard of New York and Jeremy Belknap of New Hampshire. During the next three decades Morse produced subsequent editions of the book, later known as *The American Universal Geography*, adding information gleaned from his study of new sources of information such as Lewis and Clark's journey up the Missouri River.

Morse's fascination with American geography and natural history occasionally led to journeys of discovery into the American interior. In 1796 Morse and his fellow clergyman and geographer Jeremy Belknap traveled to upstate New York as missionaries for the Society in Scotland for the Propagating of Christian Knowledge. Their goal was to investigate the progress toward civilization of the Oneida and Mohekunuh Indians. They reported on Native American beliefs and agricultural practices as well as how the American Revolution had been detrimental to ordered native society.

In 1820, commissioned by Secretary of War John C. Calhoun to investigate the Indians of North America, Morse ventured much farther west, traveling with his son Richard Morse by stage and boat to Lake Michigan. A year later Morse journeyed to Niagara Falls and Canada for the same purpose. His efforts resulted in *A Report to the Secretary of War of the United States, on Indian Affairs* (1822), a compilation of facts, statistics, letters, journals, and reports covering the various Native American groups of North America.

Jedidiah Morse continued to publish revised editions of his works until his death in 1826 in New Haven, Conn. Although Morse's geographical work was often erroneous and based on hearsay, his great contribution was in conceiving of North America as a single geographical unit for systematic study. Like Noah Webster in the field of language, Morse believed his publications would strengthen the new American republic by providing resources that emphasized the distinctive features of the newly independent land.

John C. Greene, *American Science in the Age of Jefferson* (1984); James King Morse, *Jedidiah Morse: A Champion of New England Orthodoxy* (1939); Richard J. Moss, *The Life of Jedidiah Morse: A Station of Peculiar Exposure* (1995); Joseph W. Phillips, *Jedidiah Morse and New England Congregationalism* (1983).

Russell M. Lawson

Museums of Science

New England's science museums have evolved greatly since Dr. Walter Channing and five other men established the Boston Society of Natural History in 1830 to study local flora and fauna. The scope of science museums and the breadth of subjects they address, the mission of informal science education, and the approach to exhibits and programs have all changed significantly since that time. New England's science museums now range from planetariums to aquariums and zoos; from children's discovery centers to thematic museums such as the National Plastics Center and Museum; from a computer museum to general science centers that feature hands-on activities in an ever-changing array of scientific fields. Often originating with a fairly narrow field of interest, many science museums have been moving toward widening the scope of their collections. The myriad dynamic changes continue today as the region's science museums strive to increase their role in contributing to the public's understanding of science and technology.

Every state in New England has member institutions in the Association of Science and Technology Centers (ASTC), a national umbrella organization for science museums in all fields. Several states also have private science museums. Many colleges and universities have exceptional museums that are open to the public, such as Harvard University's Museum of Natural History with its exquisite collection of more than 3,000 glass flowers in its botanical museum. In Maine, Bowdoin College's Peary-MacMillan Arctic Museum contains navigational instruments from Peary's expedition to the North Pole in 1909, and the Mount Desert Oceanarium provides exhibits and interpretation of marine life at three locations. The Haffenreffer Museum of Anthropology in Bristol, R.I., contains internationally renowned collections on the native peoples of the world, with particularly strong holdings in New England and Plains Indians. It is located on Mount Hope, once the domain of King Philip (Metacom). The EcoTarium in Worcester, Mass., offers exhibits on nature and science, nature trails for personal discovery, and a planetarium.

When the Boston Society of Natural History was founded, there was not a single museum of natural history, or journal on the subject, in all of New England. While the initial impetus of the society's members was to collect and discuss local plant and animal specimens among themselves, the scope of their endeavor quickly expanded to include public education. The society offered a public lecture series on various topics, and in 1837 conducted the first complete "scientific survey" for the Commonwealth of Massachusetts. The group became the New England Museum of Natural History when its new building was completed in 1864. Now known as the Boston Museum of Science, it is located in a sprawling seven-story facility that opened in 1950 on the site of the original Charles River Dam and is the largest institution of its kind in New England.

Today, the museum—while maintaining as part of its mission the study of natural history—also includes a planetarium, an Omni Theater, and exhibits on such diverse areas of science and technology as space exploration, biotechnology, the human body, remote sensing, dinosaurs, mathematics, optics, and tropical rainforests. The museum also features a live animal center with about 75 species, including alligators, a gray-headed flying fox, a great-horned owl, and boa constrictors; a computer discovery space; a working greenhouse for growing plants and conducting experiments on them; a theater of electricity that houses the world's largest Van de Graaff generator; two theaters for lectures and demonstrations; several laboratories and classrooms; and a library.

The museum's public and school programs have likewise broadened their appeal. Today's educational programs run the gamut from daily presentations on lightning, live animals, and science "magic"; films on topics of current controversy or interest in the sciences such as the Human Genome Project; DNA laboratory programs for high school students; overnight camp-ins for children, complete with directed science activities; a discovery room for preschoolers; science kit rentals on a wide variety of topics; teacher workshops and sabbaticals; and museum vans that travel to schools, libraries, and community events with an inflatable planetarium and artifacts from the museum. In 1989 the museum began the implementation of a new exhibit plan called *Science Is an Activity;* it will construct six large-scale, permanent activity centers over 20 years featuring exhibits based on various aspects of the scientific process in which visitors practice scientific thinking skills. The museum recently established a Current Science and Technology center, where visitors can learn about technological advances—some of them controversial—in medical research, telecommunications, and biotechnology.

Other museums of science in New England have similar histories of change as they have broadened their subject matter and widened their appeal. The Science Center of Connecticut in West Hartford was originally established in 1927 as the one-room Children's Museum of Hartford. This museum now includes an aquarium, a mini-zoo, a planetarium, and a 125-acre nature center in nearby Canton. The Mount Washington Museum, at the summit of Mount Washington in New Hampshire, was founded in 1973 as an offshoot of the Mount Washington Observatory, which conducts meteorological observations and scientific research. The Mount Washington Museum includes exhibits on history, geology, biology, and other fields, and serves as a repository for artifacts from the entire White Mountains area.

The Montshire Museum of Science in Norwich, Vt., began in 1974 in a former bowling alley in Hanover, N.H., as a natural history museum. This museum was established to house the 100,000 specimens that Dartmouth College's Museum of Natural Science was no longer able to hold. The original Montshire Museum contained fossils, shells, mounted mammal skins, birds, and insects. The current museum, in a building constructed in 1989, exemplifies the participatory approach to diverse exhibits and programs that engage visitors and school groups to learn science in a friendly, informal environment. A glass elevator shaft, a do-it-yourself physics of bubbles exhibit, challenging rope puzzles, and hands-on exhibits on more traditional subjects like gravity, electricity, and biology are among the museum's attractions.

The Yale Peabody Museum, in New Haven, Conn., has been one of New En-

Wetu (Algonquian word for summer dwelling) at Brown University's Haffenreffer Museum of Anthropology, Bristol, R.I.

gland's premier venues for natural history research and exhibits since its inception in 1866. The museum was founded with a $150,000 gift from the wealthy international financier George Peabody, who was persuaded to build the museum by his nephew O. C. Marsh, professor of paleontology at Yale University. Marsh also led a number of excavations in the western United States that brought important collections of fossils to the museum. Later expeditions by other scientists added the Peabody's collection of dinosaur and Mesozoic mammal fossils. The original building was demolished in 1917 to make way for Yale dormitories, and the collections remained in storage until the present site of the Peabody Museum was opened to the public in 1925. The museum is best known for its collection of vertebrate fossils, which consists of some 70,000 specimens, including the 1985 addition of the Princeton University collection. Favorite permanent features of the museum include the wildlife dioramas with backgrounds painted by J. Perry Wilson and F. Lee Jaques, the "Brontosaurus" (Apatosaurus), completed in 1931 (a new, correct, head was added in 1981), the 110-foot-long mural, *The Age of Reptiles,* painted by Rudolph F. Zallinger in 1947, and exhibits on Connecticut birds. The Peabody hosts a number of educational and family programs, including its annual *Dino-Snore,* in which families camp overnight in the Great Hall of Dinosaurs. The museum also recently added an Environmental Science Center.

With the proliferation of community exhibits throughout the region and an emphasis

on experiential learning, New England's science museums have attracted more and more visitors over the past 20 years. These leading institutions have become an important component in the national effort to increase scientific literacy in an age when scientific knowledge and technological advances are progressing at breakneck speed. Whether in the field of biotechnology, environmental awareness, space exploration, or advances in computer technology, New England's science museums offer education and stimulation to visitors of diverse ages and interests in a friendly and informal atmosphere.

Stella V. F. Butler, *Science and Technology Museums* (1992); Victor J. Danilov, *Science and Technology Centers* (1982); Peter Davis, *Museums and the Natural Environment: The Role of Natural History Museums in Biological Conservation* (1996).

Ben Brooks and David W. Ellis

New England Journal of Medicine

The *New England Journal of Medicine* is the oldest continuously published medical periodical in the world. In January 1812 John Collins Warren, a Boston physician and scholar, and his colleague James Jackson launched the first medical journal in New England. The *New England Journal of Medicine and Surgery, and the Collateral Branches of Science,* as it was called, was published quarterly, and subscriptions cost two dollars a year. Several other prominent Boston physicians were brought on board, meeting monthly to review submissions. In 1823 another journal, the *Boston Medical Intelligencer,* arrived on the scene, in response to the need among the growing Boston medical community for a weekly publication. The *Intelligencer* soon ran into financial troubles, and Warren and Jackson purchased the journal in 1828 for $600. The publications merged to form the weekly *Boston Medical and Surgical Journal.*

In 1921 the Massachusetts Medical Society purchased the *Boston Medical and Surgical Journal* for a dollar, and in 1928 it was renamed the *New England Journal of Medicine;* it remains a weekly publication. In the 20th century the *Journal's* influence began to reach far beyond New England. The *Journal* documented the first public demonstration of ether anesthesia in 1846, the first full description of a spinal-disk rupture in 1934, and the first comprehensive study of early childhood leukemia in 1948. In 1981 a phone call to the editorial office about a possible epidemic among homosexual men led to rapid publication in *Morbidity and Mortality Weekly Report,* followed by peer-reviewed publication in the *Journal,* of the first reports on a disease that later became known as AIDS. In 2003 the *Journal* editors solicited and published papers in a matter of days on the first cases of severe acute respiratory syndrome (SARS) and the identification of the SARS-associated coronavirus, playing a major role in informing physicians worldwide about the rapid spread of a highly infectious disease.

True to its historical roots, the modern *Journal* aims to be a comprehensive publication on innovations in health care, covering a wide range of topics including novel approaches to medical and surgical therapy, the biology and epidemiology of emerging diseases, public and global health, health policy and economics, and biomedical ethics. It is published in print and electronic formats and influences medical practice and the delivery of health care around the world through its readership of physicians, allied health-care professionals, policymakers, and opinion leaders.

Editors of the New England
Journal of Medicine

Payne-Gaposchkin, Cecilia Helena

(1900–1979) Astronomer. Born Cecilia Helena Payne in Wendover, Buckinghamshire, England, Cecilia Payne-Gaposchkin decided that she wanted to be an astronomer while watching a meteor at the age of five and went on to have a distinguished career in astronomy. Payne-Gaposchkin received many awards and honors, including the distinction of being the first woman at Harvard University to achieve the rank of professor.

In 1918 Payne chose to read botany when she matriculated at Cambridge University's Newnham College. Inspired by the lectures of prominent physicists such as Ernest Rutherford and Niels Bohr, she began telescope observations in the Cambridge astronomy department. Payne published a scholarly paper and was elected to the Royal Astronomical Society. She met Harlow Shapley, director of the Harvard College Observatory, when he visited Cambridge, and she decided to study at Harvard after receiving her undergraduate degree in 1923.

Funded by the Pickering fellowship, Payne began postgraduate research at the Harvard College Observatory. She later reminisced in her autobiography that the "climate of the New England fall was so stimulating that I found I could work prodigiously long hours" and that "in the heady atmosphere of New England in October, nothing seemed impossible." Payne focused on stellar atmospheres, analyzing hundreds of the observatory's photographic plates of constellations. Her dissertation discussed the temperatures and chemical compositions of stars and was published as *Stellar Atmospheres: A Contribution to the Observational Study of Matter at High Temperatures* (1925).

Payne received the first astronomy doctorate granted to a Harvard College Observatory student from Harvard's sister college, Radcliffe, in 1925. She had been elected to membership in the American Astronomical Society in 1924, and secured a National Research Council Fellowship from 1925 to 1927 to finance her work at the observatory until she was employed as an astronomer.

She continued her research to develop a method using photographic plates to determine stellar magnitudes and distances as well as to examine galactic structures and novae. Payne's most significant work revealed that bodies in the universe consist of primarily hydrogen and helium. Noting that differing spectra indicated celestial surface temperatures, Payne's classification of stars with regard to variable brightness helped astronomers studying stellar evolution.

Payne secured American citizenship in 1931. In 1933 she met the political refugee and astronomer Sergei Gaposchkin in Germany and sponsored his immigration to the United States. The couple married in 1934 and became scholarly collaborators. They had three children.

Tolerating minimal pay, support, and recognition at Harvard, Payne-Gaposchkin received her first academic appointment in the 1930s. By the 1940s she had applied atomic theory to variable stars, measuring distances as great as 30 million light-years. Payne-Gaposchkin was given the title Phillips Astronomer in 1938, and in 1956 she received the rank of professor and was named chair of the department. She retired in 1965 and was on the staff of the Smithsonian Astrophysical Observatory from 1967 to 1979.

Payne-Gaposchkin was awarded numerous honors during her career, including election to the National Academy of Sciences. She won the first Annie J. Cannon Prize presented by the American Astronomical Society in 1934 and was the first woman to receive the society's Henry Norris Russell Prize for lifetime achievement in 1976. Payne-Gaposchkin wrote numerous papers and books, including *Variable Stars* (1938), *Stars in the Making* (1952), *Introduction to Astronomy,* with daughter Katherine Haramundanis (1954), *The Galactic Novae* (1957), and *Stars and Clusters* (1979).

Katherine Haramundanis, ed., *Cecilia Payne-Gaposchkin: An Autobiography and Other Recollections* (1996); Bessie Zaban Jones and Lyle Gifford Boyd, *The Harvard College Observatory: The First Four Directorships, 1839–1919* (1971); Peggy A. Kidwell, "Cecilia Payne-Gaposchkin: Astronomy in the Family," in *Uneasy Careers and Intimate Lives: Women in Science, 1789–1979,* ed. Pnina G. Abir-Am and Dorinda Outram (1987); Margaret W. Rossiter, *Women Scientists in America: Struggles and Strategies to 1940* (1982).

Elizabeth D. Schafer

Peirce, Charles Sanders (1839–1914)

Philosopher and scientist. Charles Sanders Peirce, a logician of great creativity who developed the truth table, graphical logic, and multivalue logic systems, was a philosopher and historian of science, as well as a working scientist. One of the first experimental psychologists, Peirce broke ground with his work in subliminal perception. He made significant contributions to spectroscopic analysis in astronomy, designed improved instruments for determining the earth's gravitational constant, and invented the quincuncial map projection of the world. Peirce is most widely known as the founder of pragmatism, though his close friend William James is often mistakenly given the credit. Pragmatism, the theory that the meaning of an idea consists in all possible consequences that idea could have for the future experience of the continuing community of inquiry, was later popularized by James—to Peirce's considerable distress—as a theory of truth.

Born in Cambridge, Mass., Peirce grew up among the Brahmins and intelligentsia of Boston, surrounded by luminaries such as Ralph Waldo Emerson, Oliver Wendell Holmes, and Chauncey Wright. Peirce's father, Benjamin, a mathematician at Harvard, challenged his son Charles to intellectual competitions. Peirce graduated from Harvard, but enmity with President Charles W. Eliot blocked his appointment at the university.

Peirce, both a philosopher and practitioner of science, worked at laboratory research, instrument design, and fieldwork in physics and geodesy. Much of his early astronomical work was done at the Harvard Observatory. He was among the first to conceive of science as a process through which successive working theories are displaced as new evidence and the range of our experience require it, as opposed to the traditional view of science as a body of finished, systematic knowledge. This commitment to truth as a collaborative long-term process is central to Peirce's view that logic is ultimately based on the ethics of membership in a community of inquiry.

Peirce was an unpredictable genius, difficult even for his friends, always eccentric, and for the last years of his life a recluse. Peirce's lifelong affliction with episodes of an extremely painful neurological disorder not only hampered his immense productivity but also produced occasional outbursts of bad temper—made more puzzling by his concealment of his illness and his otherwise pleasant and engaging manner. He was a lecturer in logic at Johns Hopkins University from 1879 to 1884, only to lose his position when the department was restructured and his lectureship eliminated. His exclusion from the academy may have resulted from his interdisciplinary work that made him seem either threatening or unprofessional to the conservative universities of his time. While hoping all his life for an academic position, he worked for 30 years (1861–1891) for the U.S. Coastal and Geodetic Survey as a physical scientist and special assistant in gravity research. His work with the survey led him to experiment with the swinging pendulum as a tool for measuring the force of gravity.

Peirce's closest friends were Josiah Royce and William James. After William James died in 1910, Peirce changed his own name to Charles Sanders Santiago (St. James) Peirce to honor James. Ironically, Peirce wrote volumes of unpublished works for a future community of inquirers whose criticisms and suggestions he would not live to hear. If Royce, at Harvard, had not rescued Peirce's papers from an uncertain future after his death, his work might never have had an audience.

Peirce is also considered the modern founder of semiotics—the study of language as a general theory of signs. In 1976 Noam Chomsky said, "In relation to the questions [on the philosophy of language] we have just been discussing, the philosopher to whom I feel closest and whom I am almost paraphrasing is Charles Sanders Peirce."

Joseph Brent, *Charles Sanders Peirce: A Life* (1993); Max H. Fisch, *Peirce, Semiotic, and Pragmatism: Essays,* ed. K. L. Ketner and C. J. W. Kloesel (1986); Fisch, ed., *The Writings of Charles S. Peirce: A Chronological Edition* (1982–); Charles S. Peirce, *Collected Papers of Charles Sanders Peirce,* vols. 1–6, ed. Charles Hartshorne and Paul Weiss (1931–35), and vols. 7–8, ed. Arthur Burks (1958).

Willard M. Miller

Pinkham, Lydia E. (1819–83) Medical entrepreneur. Lydia Estes Pinkham was born on a farm in Lynn, Mass., to socially progressive parents; she combined a lifelong interest in women's rights, temperance, abolition of slavery, suffrage, and a distinct distrust of the male medical model to create the most successful proprietary medical company of the late 19th century. An educated schoolteacher, she formed the Freeman's Institute in 1842, a radical debating society whose membership not only included both men and women but also welcomed people of color and members of any religious belief. Its first president was Frederick Douglass, whose wife learned to read from Pinkham personally. One of the society's recurring themes was "Is the rightful prerogative of man to exercise control over woman?" Pinkham would fight this notion her entire life.

Through the debating society she met and married Isaac Pinkham, an enterprising but ultimately unfocused businessman. During the first years of their marriage, Lydia—who had an interest in natural medicine—tinkered with creating a botanical mixture for the relief of various female ailments. She gave small bottles of her tonic to neighbors and friends alike. The recipe contained black cohosh and pleurisy root, both of which were later revealed to have estrogenlike substances that acted in combination as both a uterine tonic and a uterine sedative. In addition, her home remedy contained alcohol, making it addictive in nature as with other home remedies that were alcohol- or opium-based.

When the Panic of 1873 wiped out the Pinkham family financially, Lydia and her children decided to try their hand at marketing and selling her locally popular tonic, known as Lydia E. Pinkham's Vegetable Compound. They revolutionized the advertising industry by using Pinkham's portrait, the first-ever appearance of a woman's photo in an ad, to sell the compound. More than half of the company's early revenues were spent to have her face and product information printed on the front page of large daily newspapers, including the *Boston Herald.* Within a few years, only Queen Victoria's face was better known. Tapping on women's concerns of the era, "Only a woman knows a woman," the appeal of homespun New England products, and testimonials from a devoted clientele, the compound enjoyed a steady climb in popularity and demand.

Pinkham also used the company as a platform for disseminating her progressive views on public health. Along with the widespread diffusion of her views through daily newspaper advertisements, she penned *Lydia E. Pinkham's Guide to Health: A Private Textbook* (n.d.), which served as the first primer of its kind on hygiene, conception, birth, and menopause. Viewed as both realistic and lucid, the *Guide* sold millions of copies and was distributed for free across the world, which lent the book greater influence than any American novel written in Pinkham's time. Prior to World War I, women still wrote the company and requested copies of the book. Although Pinkham died on May 17, 1883, in Lynn, the company she founded in her small kitchen grossed nearly $4 million by 1925, and her compound was sold to millions worldwide until 1979. A modified version, containing black cohosh and a mixture of natural herbs, vitamins, and minerals, is currently marketed under the label Lydia Pinkham Herbal Tablets.

Jean Burton, *Lydia Pinkham Is Her Name* (1949); Dona L. Davis, "George Beard and Lydia Pinkham: Gender, Class, and Nerves in Late-19th-Century America," *Health Care for Women International* 10 (1989); Donald Dale Jackson, "If Women Needed a Quick Pick-Me-Up, Lydia Provided One," *Smithsonian* 15 (1984); Sarah Stage, *Female Complaints: Lydia Pinkham and the Business of Women's Medicine* (1979).

Susan J. Warner

Public Health Public health in New England has a long history grounded in the region's medical, social, and moral traditions. Public health legislation began in New England in July 1701 with the passing of the Massachusetts Quarantine Act. In 1784 Massachusetts passed the first American pure-food law, and in 1797 the Health Act was passed, answering in a preliminary fashion the need for local boards of health. The Massachusetts Humane Society, established in 1786, focused on rescuing people who were drowning, and in 1788 the temperance movement—begun by Dr. Benjamin Rush in Philadelphia—gained momentum in the Northeast when Rush's "Enquiry into the Effects of Spiritous Liquors upon the Human Body" was printed by the *Massachusetts Sentinel.* In 1799 the Boston Board of Health was established, under president Paul Revere, with the expressed intent of enforcing quarantine regulations and mitigating the spread of infectious diseases, which had ravaged the American colonies from the earliest days of settlement.

For the Puritan colonists, smallpox epidemics were a constant reminder of human vulnerability in the face of a fiercely unpredictable deity. The first medical publication in the American colonies was *A Brief Rule to*

Guide the Common-People of New-England, How to Order Themselves and Theirs in the Small Pocks, or Measles, issued in 1677 by Thomas Thatcher, a minister at the Old South Meeting House in Boston. The connection between religion and medicine in early colonial New England history is a constant refrain, repeated more recently in the fervent, if secularized, tones of contemporary public health as being, in the words of Wilson Smillie, nothing short of a vocation for "service to mankind to which one dedicates his life."

The Pilgrims chose New England over a more mild southerly location in the hope of avoiding malaria. As admirable as this forethought might have been, it did not protect the colonists from malaria or a host of other infectious diseases. Contagion in colonial New England abounded in a variety of forms from yellow fever to diphtheria, dysentery, measles, and the lethal combination of influenza and pneumonia. The greatest epidemic challenge for both European settlers and Native Americans was smallpox.

For the century prior to the arrival of the Pilgrims in Plymouth, indigenous North American populations had been grappling with plagues delivered to them by the Spanish in the early 16th century. Smallpox was introduced in Mexico in 1520, where it killed one-half of the population. It did not end there, spreading with fatal results across the continent and decimating families, communities, and cultures. In 1618, just as the Pilgrims were sailing from England, native populations were hit anew with a "pestilential putrid fever," the likes of which they had not experienced before. There has been great debate over the centuries about what so depleted the Abenaki and Wampanoag peoples; historically, smallpox has been pinpointed as the culprit. But the natives were adamant that this epidemic was not smallpox, the symptoms of which they knew well. This has left posterity with an epidemiological mystery.

Approximately 70 years before Edward Jenner introduced the cowpox vaccine in England, inoculation against smallpox was being promoted in the North American colonies by Cotton Mather and other colonists watching their communities suffer from a disease that spread itself anew every couple of years. Mather began exploring the prospect of inoculation as early as 1706 when his slave Onesimus told him of an "operation" he had undergone in his African homeland, "which had given him something of ye *Small-Pox,* and would forever Praeserve him from it." It was not until 1721, however, that the first official inoculations were given in the Massachusetts Bay Colony by Zabdiel Boylston, a physician

who continued with this controversial though generally effective practice through 1764, when the Bay Colony made the legality of inoculation dependent upon permission from individual town selectmen.

Jenner's vaccine made its way to the New World in 1800 via Harvard Medical School professor Benjamin Waterhouse, who received a dried specimen that he used to inoculate his young son. In 1802 Waterhouse and colleagues conducted an experiment on 11 boys that proved the effectiveness of the cowpox vaccine against smallpox, and in 1809 the first official vaccination clinic in North America was established in Milton, Mass.

Over the course of the 18th and 19th centuries came an ideological shift from early Puritan acceptance of scourge, to a national mythos that North Americans were inherently healthier and stronger than the denizens of other, less bountiful lands. This attitude gained strength silently until the 1840s; it then found a xenophobic voice when rapid urbanization, industrialization, and a steady influx of European laborers living in crowded conditions created newly fertile breeding grounds for infection.

With increased populations and increased infectious disease outbreaks came theories of sanitation and ventilation. The standard medical opinion of the day was that disease was spread by noxious odors produced by the putrefaction of organic matter. Ventilation as a way of defusing the foul miasmas was the focus of public health discussions. Leading the way in this movement was Lemuel Shattuck, a self-educated Massachusetts schoolteacher and community activist who was deeply influenced by social and sanitation reforms in England stimulated by Edwin Chadwick's *General Report on the Sanitary Condition of the Laboring Population of Great Britain* (1842).

Shattuck was the single nonmedical member of the Committee on Medical Nomenclature, which called for the general adoption of disease categories and names created by William Farr, who in 1841 in England had begun compiling annual epidemiological reports. The 1847 National Medical Convention at which this call was presented went on to request that all doctors begin to use recognized disease names and to register disease diagnoses and morbidity rates.

Shattuck was instrumental in establishing the Massachusetts Sanitary Commission in 1848 to monitor noxious fumes in urban homes and public buildings and improve ventilation, and he is the primary author of the *Report of the Sanitary Commission of Massachusetts, 1850,* in which a direct correlation is drawn among disease, poverty, and unhygienic living conditions. Shattuck called for American adoption

of a sanitary movement similar to that begun a decade earlier in Great Britain, a formal medical training for women "to be nurses of the sick," and for "sanitary professorships" to be established at universities where "the science of preserving health and preventing disease should be taught as one of the most important sciences."

In 1869 Henry I. Bowditch established and headed the Massachusetts State Board of Health. Almost immediately upon its formation, the seven members of the board set out to study pollution, and by the mid-1870s the board was already focusing its efforts on prevention. New Englanders were becoming conscious of the fact that polluted water and air are not limited to the immediate environs of the polluting community. No matter what legislation the board succeeded in passing in Massachusetts, the pollution drifting downstream and downwind from New Hampshire mills could not be avoided. New Hampshire did not establish a state board of health until 1881.

Lowell, Mass., was hit with a typhoid epidemic in 1890, and in the next two months its downstream neighbor, Lawrence, also began to report an epidemic number of typhoid cases. Tellingly, these cities were the only two in Massachusetts that took their drinking water from the Merrimack River at points less than 20 miles below toxic dumping points. Hiram Mills, a civil engineer, noticed that the water taken from points on the river where infection rates were highest did not have a higher level of impurity than in half of the Massachusetts water supply. Mills and his colleagues hypothesized a crucial distinction, that chemical analysis was not detecting the deadly microorganisms responsible for the disease clustering along the Merrimack and Connecticut Rivers where the sewage was most concentrated: in the environs of Holyoke, Lawrence, Lowell, and Chicopee.

Biologist William T. Sedgwick, associated with the Lawrence Experimental Station, confirmed that the Merrimack had become a giant conduit delivering *Salmonella typhi* directly from privies into the water supply. With this epidemiological hypothesis eventually proven many times over by meticulous case studies focusing on outbreak and drinking water pathways, Mills, Sedgwick, and colleagues successfully experimented with sand filtration systems for sewage-contaminated water that became a model for similar projects around the country. Thus ended the powerfully misguided and overly permissive ecomyth that rivers are self-purifying, natural sewers ready to carry away and dissipate all the toxins thrown into them from their industrialized shores.

The bacteriological era, spanning the last quarter of the 19th century and the first 20 years of the 20th century, marks the important shift from public health's preoccupation with foul miasmas and sanitation to the science of epidemiology. The difference between theories of ventilation and etiologies of pathogens is that while the former were empirically unprovable, epidemiologists were producing factual data about the newly unveiled world of microorganisms.

This epistemological shift is most evident in the career of Charles V. Chapin, who pioneered the move in New England public health research and administration away from sanitation and into bacteriological analysis. In *Municipal Sanitation in the United States* (1901), Chapin provided elaborate instructions for fumigating a household with formaldehyde generators and giant pressurized steam disinfectors. By 1906, however, he reported to a stunned audience at the public health meeting of the American Medical Society that the elaborate and wealthy industry that had built up around the theory of fumigation and ventilation was futile. Chapin's illusion-shattering hypothesis was published in the *Journal of the American Medical Association* that same year under a title bound to anger his colleagues, "The Fetish of Disinfection." By the end of the decade, however, many of Chapin's contemporaries had been won over to the bacteriological theory of disease, a science Chapin instituted even more fully in 1912 with his influential report *Sources and Modes of Infection*.

Between 1890 and 1980, infectious disease in North America and Europe came under control and attention was refocused on chronic diseases such as cancer, diabetes, and heart disease. One particularly noteworthy but often overlooked public health pioneer is William Augustus Hinton, M.D., who in 1913 became the first African American professor at Harvard Medical School. He is best known for developing the Hinton test for syphilis, which was adopted by the U.S. Public Health Service after being extensively and successfully used by the army during World War II.

In 1948 an epidemiological study of heart disease was launched in Framingham, Mass.; 5,000 healthy people were examined and tracked for the rest of their lives. Their offspring are now being tracked in an extended cross-generational study. Safety and substance addiction and rehabilitation also increasingly claimed a great deal of public health attention throughout the past century. In the early 1980s infectious disease began to demand attention again with the rapid spread of HIV/AIDS, new outbreaks of tuberculosis and cholera, the controversies sparked by Lyme disease, discovery of West Nile virus in birds, and fears of

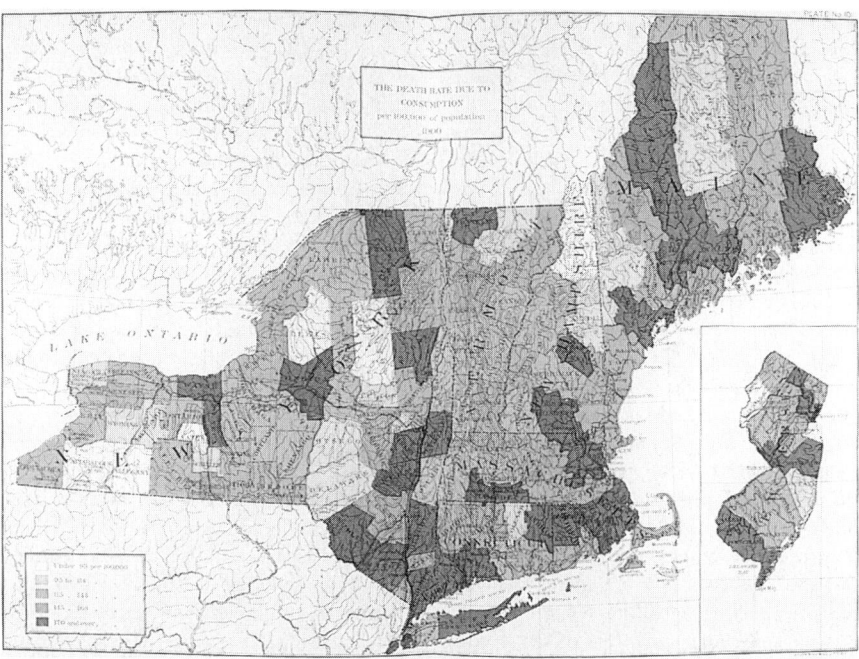

Map showing the consumption (tuberculosis) death rate in 1900

biological warfare conducted with weapons-grade anthrax and smallpox.

The American Public Health Association was founded in 1872, and by the end of 1873 the number of state boards of health had increased from four to about a dozen. Today, each New England state relies on a sprawling network of both governmental and nongovernmental public health agencies. There are four schools of public health associated with major universities in the region: Boston University School of Public Health (1976), the Harvard School of Public Health (1922), the University of Massachusetts School of Public Health and Health Sciences (accredited 1970), and the Yale University School of Public Health (1915). The University of New Hampshire School of Health and Human Services offers the only Master's degree in public health in northern New England.

The Public Health Museum in Tewksbury, Mass. (located in the Old Administration Building of the Tewksbury Hospital), was established in 1994, and houses exhibits of the early epidemic history of the region and pays homage to public health pioneers, their battles, and their breakthroughs. The museum also holds histories of dental health, the tuberculosis campaign, state laboratories, mental health, nursing, and patent medicine.

John B. Blake, *Public Health and the Town of Boston* (1959); Lloyd Novick and Glen P. Mays, *Public Health Administration: Principles for Population-Based Management* (2001); Barbara Gutman Rosenkrantz, *Public Health and the State: Changing Views in Massachusetts, 1842–1936* (1972); Mary-Jane Schneider, *Introduction to Public Health* (2000); Wilson G. Smillie, *Public Health: Its Promise for the Future* (1955); Theodore Steinberg, *Nature Incorporated: Industrialization and the Waters of New England* (1991); Laurel Thatcher Ulrich, *A Midwife's Tale: The Life of Martha Ballard, Based on Her Diary, 1785–1812* (1990).

Jennifer Beard

Rotch, Thomas Morgan (1849–1914)

Pediatrician. Thomas Morgan Rotch was born in Philadelphia but descended from an established New Bedford, Mass., whaling and shipping family. Rotch received both his undergraduate and medical degrees from Harvard University (1870 and 1874, respectively) and served as a medical house officer at the Massachusetts General Hospital (1873–74). After the customary two years abroad, he spent his entire medical career at Boston hospitals and became one of the first academic pediatricians in the United States. Rotch was appointed "professor of diseases of children" at Harvard Medical School in 1893; his title was changed to professor of pediatrics in 1903. In 1888, he became a founding member of the American Pediatric Society and served as its third president in 1891. Rotch was also the first president of the New England Pediatric Society. The Thomas Morgan Rotch Professorship, the senior chair in pediatrics at Harvard Medical School and Children's Hospital of Boston, was established in 1924 in his honor.

Rotch published on a wide variety of pediatric topics, but historians of pediatrics recognize him primarily for his extensive writing and teaching on infant feeding practices.

One-fourth of the first edition of his 1,100-page textbook *Pediatrics: The Hygienic and Medical Treatment of Children* (1895) was devoted to infant feeding.

In the late 19th century, breastfeeding was generally recommended, although a significant number of infants were "artificially" fed. The best of these alternatives were made up of cow's milk and/or cereal. Rotch taught that cow's milk was relatively indigestible by human infants and had to be diluted before feeding. Because dilution reduced fat and carbohydrate content, cream and sugar had to be added to provide calories and simulate human milk. This scientifically sound and surprisingly modern theory became rather unwieldy when carried out as Rotch directed. He called for minute variations in the composition of the formula, on a daily basis, according to the age and condition of the infant. Subsequent chemical analyses showed that most of Rotch's assumptions about the content of milk, as well as the measurements of his ingredients, were highly inaccurate.

Rotch practiced in an era when infectious disease was rampant, and infant mortality was high. Infants fed according to Rotch's precepts fared better than those fed by other methods. His clinical success has been attributed to the fact that he insisted on clean, fresh milk. In addition, the formula was often prepared in commercial milk laboratories, where conditions were better than in most homes or hospitals. Rotch's "percentage method" of feeding became known as the "American method," a reflection of its widespread acceptance in the United States though not in Europe.

Rotch also wrote the first textbook of pediatric radiology, *The Roentgen Method in Pediatrics* (1910). Although he made a number of technical errors, Rotch was one of the first physicians to recognize the diagnostic value, as well as the limitations, of radiology for pediatric practice. His interest, combined with his influence as physician-in-chief at Children's Hospital, is credited for the fact that radiology there was at least 20 years ahead of pediatric radiology in the rest of the country.

Rotch had a particular interest in the health of children from birth to age two. He served as the director of the Infants' Hospital across town from the Harvard Medical School as well as physician-in-chief at the Children's Hospital near the medical school. After the turn of the century, Rotch devoted a great deal of effort to designing, financing, and building a hospital for infants at the Harvard Medical School campus. It was to be named for his only child, Thomas Morgan Rotch, Jr., who had died in 1902. Rotch himself died in Boston on March 9, 1914, days before the planned opening of the new hospital. The first

official ceremony in the new building was thus the funeral for the man whose vision had led to its construction. Although many of his theories were later disproven, Rotch is remembered as an important figure in American pediatrics and as a tireless advocate for infants and children, for improved public health, and for the specialty of pediatrics.

John Caffey, "The First 60 Years of Pediatric Roentgenology in the United States—1896 to 1956," *American Journal of Roentgenology* 76 (1956); Thomas E. Cone, Jr., *History of American Pediatrics* (1979); Howard A. Pearson, "Pediatrics in the United States," in *History of Pediatrics, 1850–1950*, ed. Buford L. Nichols, Jr., Angel Ballabriga, and Norman Kretchmer (1991); Clement A. Smith, *The Children's Hospital of Boston* (1983).

Alix Handelsman

Sheffield Scientific School

Sheffield Scientific School Originally known as the Yale Scientific School, the Sheffield Scientific School of New Haven, Conn., was a premier engineering school until it closed its doors in 1956. Sheffield graduates and teachers were leaders in many fields of science and technology, including transportation, health care, biotechnology, and electronics. The school was founded in 1846 in a modest frame house, where it had no formal curriculum, no awarding of degrees, and only 11 students. Had not two dedicated scientists, Benjamin Silliman, Jr., and his pupil John Pitkin Norton, devoted themselves to the enterprise, the school might have closed. Appointed professors of practical and agricultural chemistry, respectively, in 1846, Silliman and Norton financed the early school from their own resources and what fees they could collect. Indeed, Norton died from overwork at the age of 30.

Although Yale Scientific School continued to expand, its future was far from assured when the New Haven industrialist Joseph E. Sheffield created an endowment fund and purchased the first of several buildings in which the school operated. Sheffield had constructed the railroads between Chicago and Rock Island, Ill., between New York and New Haven, and between New Haven and Northampton, Mass. He saw the importance of science for U.S. development and wanted the school to serve as a link between education, government, and industry. His contributions to the school totaled more than $100,000, and in recognition of his generosity, Yale renamed the institute the Sheffield Scientific School in 1861.

As more gifts came in, the school created new professorships, introduced admissions requirements, expanded the curriculum, and began to award the bachelor's degree in civil engineering. After much struggle Daniel Cady

Eaton, a botanist with the largest herbarium in the United States and an extraordinary collection of rare books on plants, was appointed professor of botany. In 1861 the school awarded a doctorate to Josiah Willard Gibbs, the first Ph.D. degree granted on American soil. After Congress passed the Morrill Act in 1862, allowing states to use public lands to provide agricultural courses at colleges, the Sheffield School became Connecticut's only beneficiary and expanded its agricultural course offerings. William Henry Brewer, who helped complete the first geological survey of California, was appointed professor of agriculture.

The connection between the Sheffield Scientific School and government was a strong one. In the 19th century Addison E. Verrill, a professor of zoology, worked with the U.S. Commission of Fish and Fisheries to dredge the American coastlines. Othniel C. Marsh, a paleontology professor, organized expeditions to the Northwest Territories. Guarded by soldiers, his team collected fossils that became part of the collection of the Peabody Museum of Archaeology in Andover, Mass. The Connecticut State Board of Agriculture held its meetings at the Sheffield School.

The school also made an effort to reach out to the public. In 1866 professors began giving a series of talks on scientific principles called Public Lectures to Mechanics, which later became known as the Sheffield Lectures. A great success, the lectures served to educate the public and spread scientific knowledge.

The Sheffield School continues to be remembered in the Yale School of Engineering's Sheffield Fellowship, which brings in leaders in science, engineering, business, and government to give a public lecture.

George Alfred Baitsell, *The Centennial of the Sheffield Scientific School* (1950); Russell H. Chittenden, *History of the Sheffield Scientific School of Yale University, 1846–1922* (1928); Richard Shelton Kirby, *Inventors and Engineers of Old New Haven: A Series of Six Lectures Given in 1938 Under the Auspices of the School of Engineering, Yale University* (1939).

Suzanna Nyberg

Silliman, Benjamin, Sr.

Silliman, Benjamin, Sr. (1779–1864) Scientist and educator. Born in Trumbull, Conn., and educated at Yale College, where he served on the faculty for more than 50 years, Benjamin Silliman, Sr., was one of the most influential scientists of the early republic. A pioneering chemist and mineralogist, a founder of the Yale Medical School, and the first editor of the *American Journal of Science and Arts* (1818), Silliman is best remembered as an inspiring teacher who trained many of the 19th century's foremost geologists. He also successfully made science a popular subject with his standing-room-only public lectures that captivated diverse audiences in nearly every major American city and earned him international acclaim. Whether one chooses to emphasize a young man's struggle to preserve a traditional way of life in the face of unprecedented social change, or the professional accomplishments of a gifted Yale scholar, Silliman's writings and travels mark him as an exemplary ambassador of New England culture.

Shortly after the Revolutionary War, Benjamin's father, General Gold Selleck Silliman, was accused of misappropriating public funds, a charge that stripped the family of its savings and left the proud veteran greatly disillusioned. Benjamin's mother, Mary, assumed much of the responsibility for raising her son and sent him to college at the age of 13. Though prone to repeated fits of melancholia and forced to go "quite shoeless" in order to afford expensive textbooks like *The American Geography* (1789) by Jedidiah Morse, Benjamin graduated with distinction in 1796. That year, he discovered in the religious conservatism and strident federalism of Yale's president, Timothy Dwight, an ideological assurance that bolstered his spirits and provided comfort during the tumultuous decades surrounding the presidential election of 1800. A strong sense of filial duty, an inherent predilection for order, as well as an abiding need for financial security help explain his initial choice of a legal career. Yet far more satisfying for Silliman than his admission to the bar in 1802 was the public's enthusiastic reception of his anonymously penned *Letters of Shahcoolen, a Hindu Philosopher* (1802), which condemned the social degeneracy accompanying unbridled democratic thought.

Owing largely to Silliman's acceptable political views, rather than his academic credentials, Dwight offered the new lawyer a job teaching chemistry and natural history in September 1802. To increase his knowledge of science, Silliman journeyed to Europe, where he studied with many of the era's most eminent professors. His memoirs of this trip were published in 1810 as *A Journal of Travels in England, Holland and Scotland*, the first of three popular travel narratives that he wrote during his lifetime. Over the course of a long and distinguished professional career, Silliman contributed numerous scholarly articles on subjects such as New Haven's geology and the 1807 Weston meteor, edited several popular textbooks, and assisted in a wide array of scientific innovations.

On November 24, 1864, having dedicated the final years of his life to the eradication of slavery and the success of the Republican Party, he died at his Connecticut home. Today,

Silliman's personal and scientific legacy is most visible at Yale University, where paintings and a life-size statue perpetuate his image and the largest of 12 undergraduate residential colleges bears his name.

Chandos Michael Brown, *Benjamin Silliman: A Life in the Young Republic* (1989); Joy Day Buel and Richard Buel, Jr., *The Way of Duty: A Woman and Her Family in Revolutionary America* (1984); George Park Fisher, *Life of Benjamin Silliman, M.D., LLD, Late Professor of Chemistry, Mineralogy, and Geology in Yale College*, 2 vols. (1866); Leonard G. Wilson, ed., *Benjamin Silliman and His Circle: Studies on the Influence of Benjamin Silliman on Science in America* (1979).

Eric Robert Papenfuse

Skinner, B. F. (Burrhus Frederic)

(1904–90) Behavioral psychologist. B. F. Skinner, the foremost champion of behaviorist psychology in the 20th century, was born in Susquehanna, Penn. In an imaginative range of technical experiments and in a prodigious outpouring of monographs and books, including works aimed at a general audience, Skinner sought to demonstrate that behavior is influenced far more by environment than by native endowment or personal motivation. Through his work, he determined that outside stimuli rather than conscious agency best account for the vagaries of human conduct, and that conditions can be rationally altered according to scientific principles for the sake of social betterment.

Skinner's lifetime association with Harvard University began in 1928 with his graduate study and continued until his retirement as the Edgar Pierce Professor of Psychology in 1974. After attempting to forge a literary career, Skinner was inspired to explore behaviorism upon reading the work of its American pioneer, John B. Watson. Skinner soon gained

recognition through his ingenious laboratory experiments that showed that other species can be "conditioned" through either positive or averse stimuli; actions can be determined by making their consequences apparent. He taught pigeons to play ping-pong, to dance with each other, and, during World War II, to control guided missiles by pecking at a screen (that experiment, however, was never tested under actual military conditions). Skinner applied such techniques to human beings as well; his most famous, in 1945, involved placing his younger daughter Deborah in an insulated "air crib." Inevitably, the device was nicknamed an "Heir Conditioner." The Harvard professor also constructed teaching machines, among them the "Skinner Box," that offered rewards for correct answers. Beginning in the 1950s, such programmed instruction was implemented in classrooms.

In his novel *Walden Two* (1948), Skinner conceived a perfected community organized according to behaviorist techniques, so that asocial conduct could be eliminated with the help of healthy and peaceful stimuli. Human nature, Skinner suggested, is plastic, and a "designed culture" can eliminate the evil of which previous utopian theorists—bereft of expertise in operant conditioning—could only dream. Sales of *Walden Two* did not soar until the 1960s, when social and political dissatisfaction with the postwar status quo peaked, as did Skinner's own prestige. In 1970 the journal *American Psychologist* ranked him the century's most influential psychologist after Sigmund Freud.

Skinner's most controversial volume, *Beyond Freedom and Dignity*, was released in 1971. In it, he denied autonomy and agency (or the religious belief in an innate "soul") and dismissed any hope of eluding the social forces

B. F. Skinner and daughter Deborah at home in Cambridge, Mass., 1979

that determine consciousness. The book, and indeed the philosophy that permeated Skinner's collective works, were attacked by critics as dehumanizing, nihilistic, and as an utterly inadequate account of how humans act. Critics deemed the stimulus-response model as particularly weak in explaining language capacity. The quandary is not between determinism and free will, Skinner rebutted, but between which pressures mold the citizenry—political propaganda and commercial manipulation, or effective rational control through collective ideals. Skinner asserted that psychology validates itself as a science by examining what is observable and by testing what is predictable.

B. F. Skinner died in Cambridge, Mass., in 1990. In refusing to flinch from the unsentimental implications of his research, Skinner bequeathed a legacy that poses disturbing, fundamental questions of human character and conduct.

Daniel W. Bjork, *B. F. Skinner: A Life* (1993); B. F. Skinner, *Science and Human Behavior* (1953).

Stephen J. Whitfield

Spock, Benjamin (McLane) (1903–98)

Pediatrician and peace activist. Benjamin Spock was born in New Haven, Conn., to Benjamin Ives Spock, a railroad lawyer, and Mildred (Stoughton) Spock. He was the oldest of six children, all of whom were delivered at home. His mother's stringent, puritanical child-rearing methods, including year-round outdoor schooling, were the opposite of those for which he would later become famous. Something remained of them, however, in her son's upright manner, capacity for moral indignation, and three-piece suits, which stood out amid the more casual style of his fellow antiwar activists in the 1960s and 1970s.

The young Spock attended Phillips Academy in Andover, Mass., and graduated from Yale University with a B.A. in English in 1925. In 1929 he took his M.D. degree from the College of Physicians and Surgeons at Columbia University. While in college, Spock rowed on the Yale crew team that won a gold medal in the 1924 Olympics at Paris. He was a passionate sailor throughout his life, spending many summers after his retirement aboard a 23-foot sloop moored at Camden, Maine, where his family had summered when Spock was a child.

Early in his career Spock practiced pediatrics and taught medical students in New York, Rochester, Minn., Pittsburgh, and Cleveland. In 1927 he married Jane Cheney, with whom he had two sons, Michael, who for 22 years served as director of the Boston Children's Museum; and John, a partner in a West Coast construction firm. From 1944 until 1946 Spock served in the navy. During his pediatric

Benjamin Spock with granddaughter, 1969

residency he decided to train in psychiatry as well and became one of the first to combine the fields. For that reason Pocket Books approached him to write a popular book for parents that would sell for a quarter. The result was *Baby and Child Care* (1946), which sold three-quarters of a million copies in its first year and made Dr. Spock a household name. The book has remained in print to the present, with revised editions in 1957, 1968, 1976, 1985, and 1992. The paperback version of the seventh edition, written with the Boston pediatrician Stephen J. Parker, appeared on what would have been Spock's 95th birthday in 1998. The book has now sold more than 55 million copies, making it the second-best-selling publication of all time, behind the Bible. Spock also wrote several other books on babies and children, a book addressed to teenagers, and one on Vietnam.

The famous opening sentences of *Baby and Child Care*—"Trust yourself. You know more than you think you do."—set the tone for a book that departed from the orthodox doctor-sanctioned rules for feeding, sleeping, bathing, and so on and appealed instead to the common sense of loving parents. Infants may be fed when they are hungry, for example, and ought not be awakened in order to eat. As the Spock revolution in child care spread, its originator was wrongly accused of permissiveness. Vice President Spiro Agnew, among others, blamed Spock's child-rearing methods for creating a generation of unruly children, the rebels and hippies of the 1960s, although Spock's sons describe him as a strict father.

Spock was not much involved in political causes until atmospheric nuclear testing led him to appear in a 1962 *New York Times* advertisement for the nuclear-disarmament group

Committee for a Sane Nuclear Policy (SANE): "Dr. Spock is worried." In 1964 he publicly supported Lyndon Johnson on the strength of his promise to keep America out of war, but within a year Spock felt betrayed and joined the anti–Vietnam War movement. In 1967 he helped lead a march on the Pentagon. His support for young men who were returning their draft cards to the government and refusing induction caused Spock to be indicted for conspiracy in 1968, along with the Reverend William Sloane Coffin, Jr., Mitchell Goodman, Marcus Raskin, and Michael Ferber. All but Raskin were convicted by a Boston jury that same year but acquitted on appeal in 1969. In 1972 Spock was the left-wing People's Party candidate for president.

Spock and his first wife divorced after nearly 50 years of marriage in 1976. Later that year he married Mary Morgan Wright, 40 years his junior. He continued to write and give speeches well into his nineties. Spock donated much of the money earned from his popular books to antiwar and civil rights groups and spent large amounts on legal fees. He died in La Jolla, Calif., at the age of 94.

Lynn Z. Bloom, *Doctor Spock: Biography of a Conservative Radical* (1972); Thomas Maier, *Dr. Spock: An American Life* (1998); Jessica Mitford, *The Trial of Dr. Spock, the Rev. William Sloane Coffin Jr., Michael Ferber, Mitchell Goodman, and Marcus Raskin* (1969); Benjamin Spock and Mary Morgan, *Spock on Spock: A Memoir of Growing Up with the Century* (1989).

Michael Ferber

Temperance

More than any other social reform, temperance galvanized New England's 19th-century medical profession. Americans drank heavily during the colonial and early national periods, probably at the rate they do today. By the 1830s, however, physicians were urging New Englanders to limit their intake of alcohol. Joining hands with ministers and merchants, doctors campaigned for measures to regulate or prohibit its sale. Some physicians stressed the dangers of excessive drinking to the heart, liver, and stomach. Others emphasized its social effects, linking alcohol consumption to poverty, disease, and domestic abuse. Struggling to define their new profession, doctors also increasingly repudiated the therapeutic use of alcohol. In 1832, for example, more than 90 percent of Boston's physicians signed a declaration condemning "ardent spirits" as a medicine. This move helped distinguish the "regular" doctors from folk practitioners, who prescribed alcoholic drinks for a wide variety of ailments.

New England physicians were also pioneers in the diagnosis and treatment of alcohol addiction. Superintendents of insane asylums took the lead, describing "inebriety" as a dis-

ADVERTISEMENT
OF AN
HONEST RUMSELLER
AS IT SHOULD BE!

FRIENDS AND NEIGHBORS: Having just opened a commodious shop for the sale of "Liquid Fire," I embrace this early opportunity of informing you that, on Saturday next, I shall commence the business of making drunkards, paupers, and beggars, for the sober, industrious, and respectable portion of the community to support.

I shall deal in "familiar spirits" which will excite men to deeds of riot, robbery, and blood; and, by so doing, diminish the comforts, augment the expenses and ENDANGER THE WELFARE of the community.

I will undertake, at a short notice, for a small sum, and with great expedition, to rescue victims for the Asylums, the Poor-Houses, the Prisons, and the Gallows.

I will furnish an article which will increase the amount of fatal accidents, multiply the number of distressing diseases, and render those which are harmless incurable.

I shall deal in drugs, which will deprive some of life, many of reason, most of property, and all of peace; which will cause the fathers to become fiends, wives widows, children orphans, and all mendicants.

I will cause many of the rising generation to grow up in ignorance, and prove a burden and nuisance to the nation.

I will cause mothers to forget their offspring, and cruelty to take the place of love.

I will sometimes even corrupt the ministers of religion, obstruct the progress of the Gospel, defile the purity of the church, and cause temporal, spiritual, and eternal death; and, if any should be so impertinent as to ask why I have the audacity to bring such accumulated misery upon a comparatively happy people, my honest reply is, MONEY.

The Spirit Trade is lucrative, and some professing Christians give it their cheerful countenance.

I have a License; and, if I do not bring these evils upon you, somebody else will.

I live in a Land of Liberty.

I have purchased the RIGHT to DEMOLISH the character, destroy the health, shorten the lives, and ruin the souls of those who choose to honor me with their custom.

I pledge myself to do all I have herein promised. Those who wish any of the evils above specified, brought upon themselves or their dearest friends, are requested to meet me at my Bar, where I will, for a few cents, furnish them with the certain means of doing so.

"Advertisement of an Honest Rumseller as It Should Be!" temperance poster, Boston, ca. 1850

tinct disease and demanding separate institutions for its victims. Because all six states in the region banned alcohol for parts of the 19th century—Maine being the first state to effectively enact a prohibition law in 1851—legislators were loath to furnish violators with special facilities. So private "inebriety asylums" sprang up, starting with the Boston Washingtonian Home in 1857. These early asylums stressed the moral and spiritual poverty of the drunkard, whose cure hinged upon his own cooperation. By the 1880s, a new generation of neurologists began to describe inebriety as a biological and often hereditary affliction, controllable only through physical coercion. Led by Thomas D. Crothers, superintendent of the Walnut Lodge Hospital in Hartford, these "inebriests" continued to press for state aid. Due to lobbying by physicians, Massachusetts opened the nation's first public inebriate facility in Foxboro in 1893.

Still, physicians were hardly united on the subject of alcohol. Many doctors continued to prescribe it, since its effects were so much milder than bloodletting, purging, and the other "heroic" techniques of 19th-century medicine. With the rise of laboratory science in the 1890s, meanwhile, doctors began to question earlier claims about the physiological

dangers of drink. Publicity focused on the experiments of Wesleyan University chemist Wilbur O. Atwater, whose shimmering "calorimeter" seemed to show that alcohol was digested like a food. Here Atwater ran afoul of Massachusetts native Mary Hanchett Hunt, who had spearheaded a national drive to teach schoolchildren that alcohol was a "poison." Recruiting inebriests like Crothers, Hunt and her assistants in the Woman's Christian Temperance Union (founded in 1874 in Cleveland, Ohio) maintained their curriculum in local classrooms. Yet the tide of medical opinion was clearly turning against them and toward a more open-ended view of alcohol.

The advent of national Prohibition in 1919 hastened the death of the Foxboro asylum and other early efforts to address inebriety. After the repeal of Prohibition in 1933, however, New England physicians rediscovered the disease under a different name: alcoholism. At Yale, a new Center of Alcohol Studies promoted the concept of alcoholism through journals, summer teaching sessions, and outpatient clinics. It also helped establish the nation's first state alcohol program. In conjunction with Alcoholics Anonymous, the center helped bring *alcoholism* into America's popular and scientific lexicon.

Jack S. Blocker, Jr., *American Temperance Movements: Cycles of Reform* (1989); James H. Cassedy, "An Early American Hangover: The Medical Profession and Intemperance, 1800–1860," *Bulletin of the History of Medicine* 50 (1976); Jonathan Zimmerman, *Distilling Democracy: Alcohol Education in American Public Schools, 1880–1925* (1999).

Jonathan Zimmerman

Thompson, Benjamin, Count Rumford (1753–1814) Scientist and inventor. Benjamin Thompson, the physicist, inventor, and government administrator, was born on a farmstead in North Woburn, Mass. He founded the Royal Institution of Great Britain, established the Rumford Professorship at Harvard, and invented the Rumford fireplace, which many New Englanders used to heat their homes in winter. While working as an apprentice to Dr. John Hay of Woburn during the turbulent 1760s, he showed an interest in and aptitude for mathematics and science. At age 18 he studied medicine and contrived to attend John Winthrop IV's physics lectures at Harvard. He taught grammar school in Bradford, Mass., then in Rumford (now Concord), N.H., where he married Sarah Walker Rolfe, a wealthy widow, in 1772.

Thompson was quickly introduced into New Hampshire society, and Governor John Wentworth offered him a commission as a major in the New Hampshire militia. During the next few years Thompson earned the wrath of the rebelling colonists for his apparent Tory sympathies. Specifically, he was thought to have been the courier for Dr. Benjamin Church, Jr., who directed British espionage rings in and around Boston at the start of the Revolutionary War. At the same time Rumford allegedly helped General George Washington move books from Harvard's library to safety. When the British retreated from Boston, Rumford was among them; abandoning his wife and daughter, he departed for England in 1776 and served the British as a lieutenant colonel. He was knighted in 1784 by George III, and then became police minister and lord chamberlain to the duke of Bavaria, eventually being named a count of the Holy Roman Empire in 1791. Something of an eccentric, he chose the name Rumford for the town in New England where he had made his first fortune. While in Bavaria, he experimented with and introduced various social reforms and inventions for improving the population's standard of living, including establishing free schools for the poor and public gardens.

In 1796 Thompson published *Essays, Political, Economical, and Philosophical,* an encyclopedic work. Thompson's philanthropic mind constantly sought ways to use scientific knowledge to serve the whole of humankind. Believing that rooms poorly heated or too smoky because of inefficient fireplaces caused disease and death in thousands every year, Thompson determined to bring his knowledge on the nature of heat to bear on the problem of creating the most efficient fireplace. He designed the Rumford fireplace, a shallow chamber with a narrow throat through which smoke and gases pass up the chimney. Its narrow, sloping fireback made of smooth materials help to radiate heat into the room, and it had a high, wide opening, and slanting sides. A small shelf in the smoke chamber creates a draft of exiting hot air and entering cool air. He also described a do-it-yourself drip coffee machine that could make a delightful cup of coffee with added cream and sugar.

Thompson established a chair in chemistry at Harvard; its holder later founded the Rumford Chemical Works of East Providence, R.I., makers of the popular Rumford Baking Powder. Benjamin Thompson combined the best of European scientific thought with Yankee technical know-how to develop theories that yielded practical, beneficial results.

Sanborn C. Brown, *Benjamin Thompson, Count Rumford* (1979); Sanborn C. Brown, ed., *Collected Works of Count Rumford* (1970); Egon Larsen, *An American in Europe: The Life of Benjamin Thompson, Count Rumford* (1953); Vrest Orton, *The Forgotten Art of Building a Good Fireplace: The Story of Sir Benjamin Thompson, Count Rumford, an American Genius, and His Principles of Fireplace Designs which have Remained Unchanged for 174 Years* (1974).

Russell M. Lawson

Waterhouse, Benjamin (1754–1846)

Physician, scientist, and writer. Born in Newport, R.I., and a first cousin to John Fothergill, the noted London physician and philanthropist, Benjamin Waterhouse is best known as the first professor of medicine at Harvard Medical School (1782–1812) and for his pivotal role in the introduction and dissemination of Jennerian vaccination in America, a technique for smallpox immunization that was developed in England by the physician Edward Jenner. In this endeavor he enjoyed the support and friendship of President Thomas Jefferson. He also developed and taught the first course given in natural history (biology and mineralogy) at the College of Rhode Island (now Brown University) in 1786 and at Harvard from 1788 to 1809. In addition, he did much to raise interest in the subject of natural history in the Boston area.

A popular writer, Waterhouse served as a penman for the Massachusetts Democratic-Republicans. Two of his major literary works have a New England connection: the highly successful *Journal of A Young Man from Massa-*

chusetts (1816), based on a true narrative of the experience of a Massachusetts surgeon, Dr. Amos Babcock of the privateer *Enterprise*, captured by the British during the War of 1812; and *Oregon: A Short History of a Long Journey from the Atlantic Ocean to the Region of the Pacific by Land* (1833), based on the written and verbal account of John B. Wyeth, a member of the Boston-based 1832 expedition to the Oregon country. Both of these works were originally published anonymously.

While a youth in Newport, Waterhouse became a close friend of the portrait artist Gilbert Stuart. After attending the Anglican Charity School, reading widely in the Redwood library, and studying medicine with physician John Halliburton, Waterhouse left Newport in March 1775 for six years of medical and scientific study in London, Edinburgh, and Leiden. While in Leiden, he finished his medical degree and lived for a time in the same house as John Adams and his sons, Charles and John Quincy. This led to a lifelong friendship with the Adams family.

When Waterhouse returned to Newport in June 1782, he was considered the best-educated physician in New England and had unmatched medical and scientific contacts in Great Britain. He was named to the original faculty of the Harvard Medical School, but his appointment aroused great opposition, especially within Boston's medical community. His detractors questioned his loyalty to the new republic, complaining of his Quaker background and that he was neither a Massachusetts native nor a graduate of Harvard. In 1787 he left Boston for the more hospitable Cambridge, Mass.

In 1807 Jefferson rewarded Waterhouse for his work on the smallpox vaccination by appointing him head physician to the Boston Marine Hospital in Charlestown, Mass. Despite making improvements there, he was dismissed in 1809 on charges of nepotism and petty graft. His removal seems to have been the result of arrogance, political naivete, and the machinations of his medical and political enemies. In 1812 he was dismissed from his professorship at Harvard because of his incompatibility with the rest of the medical faculty and for his role in the failed attempt to establish a new medical society, which would presumably lead to the founding of a new medical school.

In 1813 Waterhouse was appointed hospital surgeon to the First Medical District as a reward for his services to the Democratic-Republican Party. Between 1818 and 1821 he served as medical superintendent of the military posts in New England. The remaining years of his life were devoted to literary pursuits, serving as a spokesman for vaccination,

and championing the medical maverick Samuel Thomson. He died in Cambridge, Mass., on October 2, 1846.

John B. Blake, *Benjamin Waterhouse and the Introduction of Vaccination: A Reappraisal* (1957); Philip Cash, "Setting the Stage: Dr. Benjamin Waterhouse's Reception in Boston, 1782–1788," *Journal of the History of Medicine* 47 (1992); I. B. Cohen, ed., *The Life and Scientific and Medical Career of Benjamin Waterhouse: With Some Account of the Introduction of Vaccination in America*, reprint ed., 2 vols. (1980); Josiah Charles Trent, "The London Years of Benjamin Waterhouse," *Journal of the History of Medicine* 1 (1946).

Philip Cash

Wiener, Norbert (1894–1964)

Mathematician. Norbert Wiener ranks among the first great American mathematicians. As a member of the Massachusetts Institute of Technology faculty from 1919 to 1960, he made major contributions to pure mathematics in the field of analysis, influenced the development of probability theory, and established the science of cybernetics. His theoretical work characteristically modeled real-world phenomena and is therefore widely applicable to science, engineering, and beyond. Wiener recognized the underlying role of irregularity in the physical universe, and the notion of random behavior permeates his work.

Norbert Wiener was born in Columbia, Mo., to Leo Wiener and Bertha Kahn, who moved to Massachusetts shortly after their son's birth. Under the careful tutelage of his father, who became a professor of language and literature at Harvard University, Norbert took to his studies from an early age. Recognized as a child prodigy, he graduated from Tufts College at age 14, and earned a Ph.D. in philosophy from Harvard in 1913. During a semester of postdoctoral study in Cambridge, England, in 1913, Wiener was introduced to Lebesgue integration by prominent analyst Godfrey H. Hardy, and to Brownian motion by his mentor Bertrand Russell. In 1926 he married a college teacher, Margaret Engemann, and together they raised two daughters.

Wiener joined the MIT faculty in 1919, at a time when the institute was just beginning to establish itself as a national center for science and technology. By 1932 he had made three major contributions to pure mathematics. First, out of his research on Lebesgue integration, Wiener constructed a rigorous mathematical model of Brownian motion. In the spirit of Josiah Willard Gibbs's statistical approach to physics, Wiener described the behavior of a single Brownian particle by considering a statistical assemblage of paths. For this, he constructed a measure, now called the Wiener measure, which would later give rise to the theory of stochastic processes and in turn to modern probability theory.

His second contribution was in the area of potential theory. Wiener gave a generalized solution of the Dirichlet problem—the obstacle to solving a partial differential equation that arises in the study of electrostatic potential and in the study of the flow of heat and electricity—and introduced the basic concepts of modern potential theory.

Finally, in order to explain phenomena such as white light, Wiener developed his theory of generalized harmonic analysis, in which he studied a class of functions too irregular for treatment by existing classical methods. For these achievements, Wiener was promoted to the rank of full professor at MIT in 1932 and in 1933 was awarded the Böcher Prize in analysis by the American Mathematical Society.

In the early 1930s, Wiener worked productively with mathematicians Eberhard Hopf and Raymond E. A. C. Paley. His interest in the processes of communication and control common to both humans and machines was nourished by neurophysiologist Arturo Rosenblueth. Wiener named the study of such processes *cybernetics,* and he is publicly recognized as its founder.

Following the outbreak of World War II, Wiener turned to the problem of the control of anti-aircraft fire. Thus began his work on prediction theory and filters, which he accomplished between 1940 and 1959.

Norbert Wiener retired from MIT in 1960. His intellectual mastery and interdisciplinary approach had enriched the entire institute and played a major role in its achievement of world-class status as a research-oriented educational institution. He died in Stockholm, Sweden, at the age of 69.

"Norbert Wiener, 1894–1964," *Bulletin of the American Mathematical Society* 72 (1966); V. Mandrekar, "Mathematical Work of Norbert Wiener," *Notices of the American Mathematical Society* 42 (1995); Pesi R. Masani, ed., *Norbert Wiener: Collected Works,* 4 vols. (1976, 1979, 1981, 1984); Susan Williamson, "Norbert Wiener," in *American National Biography,* ed. John A. Garraty and Mark C. Carnes (1999).

Susan Williamson

Wilson, Edward Osborne (1929–)

Biologist. Although he has devoted much of his career to studying ants, Edward O. Wilson is inextricably associated with the field of sociobiology and with the outburst of controversy that followed his publication of *Sociobiology: The New Synthesis* in 1975. Born in Birmingham, Ala., Wilson obtained undergraduate and master's degrees from the University of Alabama and a doctorate from Harvard University, where he worked on a thorough taxonomic analysis of the ant genus

Lasius; later he would design the taxon cycle of classification while working with ants in the South Pacific. In 1956 he joined the biology faculty of Harvard. Among his most important contributions was the discovery that ants communicate primarily through the transmission of pheromones. His first book, *The Insect Societies,* was published in 1971 to moderate scientific interest. With the publication of *Sociobiology,* however, Wilson became one of the country's most notorious biologists.

Animal behavior, Wilson argued, is subject to the forces of natural selection. To understand behavior, therefore, we must understand its biological grounding in evolution and genetics. Most of *Sociobiology* was a detailed survey of behavioral research on nonhuman animals, but Wilson also argued that sociobiological principles can and should be applied to human beings. His first chapter, "The Morality of the Gene," suggested that even ethics is a product of natural selection, while the final chapter, "Man: From Sociobiology to Sociology," outlined sociobiology's contributions to understanding individual and social behavior, culture, ethics, and cultural change.

The book was at first warmly received, but soon a group of Boston area biologists, medical doctors, students, and educators—including Wilson's Harvard colleagues Stephen Jay Gould, Ruth Hubbard, and Richard Lewontin—published a scathing critique of its extension of sociobiology to human beings. Sociobiology, they insisted, is a politically reactionary revival of biological determinism based on faulty biological assumptions, inappropriate use of metaphors, speculative reconstructions of human prehistory, and the circular logic that what exists is adaptive, what is adaptive is good, so what exists is good. It serves, they concluded, to justify the status quo and to reinforce existing hierarchies of race, sex, and class.

Wilson insisted that his book had been misrepresented and accused his critics of judging scientific arguments by political, not scientific, criteria. Supporters came to his defense, sometimes taking stands that were significantly more extreme than his. Wilson's own views often became obscured in the claims and counterclaims that filled both scientific and popular periodicals. Depending on who was writing, sociobiology could be the long-awaited key for understanding all human relations, or an insidious throwback to the age of eugenics, rampant racism and sexism, and even Nazism.

The controversy prompted Wilson to refine his application of population biology and evolutionary theory to human beings, and in 1978 he published his Pulitzer Prize–winning *On Human Nature.* In the 1980s his interests

turned more toward ecology and environmental conservation, as he published three books on biological diversity and for 11 years served on the board of directors of the World Wildlife Fund. His sixth book, *The Ants* (1990), synthesized his work on the remarkable animal societies that had first attracted his attention and won him a second Pulitzer Prize. In *Consilience* (1998), Wilson returned to the thesis on which *Sociobiology* had been based—that all fields of human knowledge will ultimately be reduced to a few fundamental natural laws.

Arthur L. Caplan, ed., *The Sociobiology Debate: Readings on Ethical and Scientific Issues* (1978); Carl N. Degler, *In Search of Human Nature: The Decline and Revival of Darwinism in American Social Thought* (1991); Edward O. Wilson, *Naturalist* (1994).

Lori Kenschaft

Wilson, William Griffith ("Bill W.")

(1895–1971) Cofounder of Alcoholics Anonymous. William G. Wilson, better known as "Bill W." to members of Alcoholics Anonymous, was born at the Wilson House Inn, owned by his family in East Dorset, Vt. Bill's father left the family to work the quarries in Canada when Bill was 10 years old; his mother obtained a divorce and moved to Boston to become an osteopathic physician, leaving Bill and his sister Dorothy in the care of their maternal grandparents. Wilson attended Burr and Burton Academy in Manchester, Vt., where, as a senior, he suffered emotional trauma following the death of the girl he loved. He studied engineering at Norwich University, a military academy in Northfield, Vt., then enlisted and was accepted at officer training school when the United States entered World War I.

Wilson's first experience with alcohol came at a reception given by society women in New Bedford, Mass. Initially shy, he remembered that his first drink brought feelings of completeness and invulnerability; Wilson spent a lifetime trying to recapture that sensation. After marrying Lois Burnham and a brief army stint, Wilson became an investigative analyst on Wall Street. With the 1929 stock market crash, his alcohol-fueled dreams of wealth became a nightmare of drinking to numb the pain of his failure. Treated three times at New York's Towns Hospital, Wilson learned from Dr. William D. Silkworth that his alcoholism was a physical and psychological malady involving obsession and compulsion, and that it could be arrested, but not cured.

This knowledge made little difference in Wilson's life until December 1934, when former drinking buddy Ebby T. told him about the Oxford Group, a nonsectarian attempt to recapture primitive Christianity, which, Ebby claimed, had helped him become sober. Despite participation in the Oxford Group, Wilson was again admitted to Towns Hospital, where he experienced a profound "spiritual awakening" characterized by the vision of a bright light, the sound of rushing wind, and an overwhelming feeling of peace. Encouraged by Silkworth to regard the experience as real rather than hallucinatory, Wilson returned to the Oxford Group, achieved sobriety, and, according to group practice, tried to carry his experience to others.

Wilson found none willing to follow him until May 1935 when, on a business trip to Akron, Ohio, he was attacked by a craving for alcohol for the first time since his spiritual experience. He contacted an Akron minister who put him in touch with local Oxford Group members through whom he met an alcoholic surgeon, Dr. Robert Holbrook Smith. With Wilson's help, Smith attained sobriety on June 10, 1935, and he and Wilson became cofounders of the group that would become Alcoholics Anonymous. This new fellowship slowly grew within the Oxford Group, and then branched out in 1939. The Alcoholics Anonymous *Big Book* was published the same year, its text largely drafted by Wilson.

A more outgoing personality with the advantages of location (New York) and longevity (Smith died in 1950), Wilson, or "Bill W.," emerged as coordinator of the fellowship and chief interpreter of its 12-step program. Mindful of the rebelliousness character of A.A.'s alcoholic members, Wilson guided rather than governed, enshrining in A.A.'s Twelve Traditions a singleness of purpose and respect for the "group conscience." Under Wilson's guidance, Alcoholics Anonymous spread worldwide, gaining the respect of professionals, as well as broad social acceptance. Bill W. attempted to retire from Alcoholics Anonymous leadership several times but kept being pulled back into his role until his death from pneumonia on January 24, 1971.

Bill Wilson's body was buried in a hillside cemetery overlooking East Dorset, where the Wilson House Inn is now a nonprofit, volunteer-run organization that hosts A.A. meetings every day of the week. Though his memory remains honored within A.A., Wilson's reputation has come under scrutiny in recent years. His interest in vitamin therapy and experimentation with LSD have drawn prurient interest, as has his "womanizing." Wilson did have a mistress, to whom he seems to have been faithful, even providing for her in his will. Wilson was also unable to overcome his addiction to nicotine despite suffering from emphysema. But as he wrote in the A.A. *Big Book*, "We are not saints. . . . We claim spiritual progress rather than spiritual perfection."

Ernest Kurtz, *Not-God: A History of Alcoholics Anonymous* (1979); *"Pass It On": The Story of Bill Wilson and How the A.A. Message Reached the World* (1984); Robert Thomsen, *Bill W.* (1975); Bill W., *Alcoholics Anonymous: The Story of How Many Thousands of Men and Women Have Recovered from Alcoholism* (1976).

Ernest Kurtz

Winternitz, Milton Charles (1885–1959) Pathologist and medical school dean.

As its dean from 1920 to 1935, Milton C. Winternitz helped transform the Yale Medical School from an underfunded, weak institution with a handful of students into one of the nation's leading centers for medical education, training, and research. Admired by some of his colleagues for being bold and visionary and hated by others as a martinet and a bully, Winternitz integrated the medical school with the graduate school by forcing his faculty to meet the university's academic standards, raised millions of dollars to build buildings, improve facilities, strengthen departments, and hire outstanding faculty, implemented a full-time system of teaching in the clinical departments, designed and pushed through what came to be known as the Yale system of medical education, and founded the controversial Institute for Human Relations. His accomplishments have had a lasting effect on medical education and practice.

Born in Baltimore, the son of an immigrant Czech Jewish physician, Winternitz received an M.D. from Johns Hopkins in 1907 and stayed on to work under the school's eminent pathologist and founding dean, William Welch. Ten years later, disappointed in his hope to succeed Welch, he left Hopkins to take a professorship in the pathology department of Yale Medical School. Three years later he was elected dean.

The school Winternitz took over was in trouble. Although it had improved some since Abraham Flexner judged it weak but worth saving, it remained underfunded and fundamentally outside the university, and had recently experienced the resignation or retirement of many of its most respected professors. Winternitz immediately set about building up the faculty, by hiring full-time clinical professors while demoting several local practitioners and by raising the money to endow chairs in pediatrics, internal medicine, surgery, and other departments. He also convinced the Yale Corporation to build the school a new home, Sterling Hall of Medicine, completed in 1925. Most important, perhaps, he designed and implemented the Yale system of medical education, which eliminated course examinations, made the curriculum more flexible, encouraged original thesis research and the taking of electives, and, in general, treated medical students like graduate students.

Along with transforming the way medical students were taught, Winternitz also hoped to transform the way they practiced medicine. Influenced by the currents of social and psychosomatic medicine then coursing though the medical world, Winternitz promoted the idea that medicine was a social science and sought to persuade present and future physicians to deal with the psychological and social as well as the physical patient and to promote health by embracing preventive as well as corrective medicine. To realize his hope, he joined with Yale President James Angell and the law school dean, Robert Hutchins, to found the Institute of Human Relations as a center for interdisciplinary research.

Winternitz's ideas on medical education and practice were controversial, but not nearly so controversial as he. In his time as dean, he succeeded in dividing the faculty into a small faction who admired his energy and drive and a larger faction who despised his autocratic ways and his refusal, despite being Yale's first Jewish medical professor and dean, to challenge quotas limiting the acceptance of Jewish medical school applicants. In 1935, bowing to pressure from the larger faction, Winternitz resigned as dean and returned to the pathology department, which he chaired until his retirement in 1950.

John Paul, "Dean Winternitz and the Rebirth of Yale Medical School in the 1920s," *Yale Journal of Biology and Medicine* 43 (1970).

Richard A. Meckel

Winthrop, John, Jr. (1606–76) Colonial

leader, alchemist, and physician. Born in Groton, England, John Winthrop, Jr., was a renowned alchemist and physician, and a founding member of England's scientific Royal Society. In New England, Winthrop represented a tolerant Puritanism much different from the restrictive faith of his celebrated father. Although writers from Hawthorne to Mencken have depicted Puritanism as synonymous with the older Winthrop's intolerance, the ecumenical John Winthrop, Jr., exemplifies a substantial countervailing tendency in colonial New England culture. Winthrop was a political leader in New England from his 1631 arrival in Massachusetts until his death in 1676. He was governor of Connecticut for 19 years (1657, 1659–76), and founded three towns (Ipswich, Mass., 1633; Saybrook, Conn., 1636; New London, Conn., 1646). He was an able Indian negotiator, military engineer, industrial entrepreneur, and ambassador to the court of Charles II.

Winthrop's religious tolerance and entrepreneurial activities were closely related to his scientific and religious beliefs. Winthrop identified with the Universalist principles of the natural philosophers John Dee, Paracelsus, the Rosicrucians, and the London Puritan Samuel Hartlib, who held that God was literally the source of all knowledge, and that humans only imperfectly understood divine truth, whether in religion or in science. Actively seeking unification of Christian sects in anticipation of Christ's second coming, they maintained that religious tolerance, within reason, was necessary for all Christians. Unlike his prosecutorial father, Winthrop absented himself from the trial of the religious radical Anne Hutchinson. He befriended the exiled Roger Williams and, as Connecticut's governor, interceded with Massachusetts in an unsuccessful attempt to save condemned Quakers. Winthrop's theosophy gave him a tolerance for religious diversity.

Winthrop's theosophic pursuits found practical application through alchemy and alchemical medicine, early forms of chemistry incorporating science, spiritualism, and natural magic. Believing God might grant control over the natural world to worthy experimenters, Winthrop made New England a utilitarian laboratory, where spiritual scientific pursuits and practical development projects intertwined.

Winthrop's alchemical knowledge helped attract investors for ironworks at Saugus, Mass., and New Haven, Conn., and strengthened proposals for saltpeter and potash manufacture, and for salt works and mining projects. Alchemy figured importantly in the founding of New London, intended as an ironworks site, alchemical research center, and transshipment port for silver-bearing lead ore from a mine near present-day Sturbridge, Mass. Although such development projects achieved only minimal success, Winthrop's medical practice made his alchemical knowledge invaluable. Winthrop was New England's most sought-after physician, largely for his powerful, mysterious alchemical medicines.

Winthrop's principles of tolerance helped him establish particularly harmonious relationships with Native Americans. At New London, he became patron to the remaining members of the nearly vanquished Pequot nation, vigorously defending their interests against unremitting colonial hostility. Tolerance also boosted Winthrop's effectiveness in England. His reputation for religious ecumenism and alchemical expertise provided him connections that helped secure the royal charter incorporating New Haven Colony into Connecticut in 1663. The 70-year-old Winthrop died in Boston, where he had been urging moderation in colonial prosecution of King Philip's War.

Robert C. Black, *The Younger John Winthrop* (1966); Richard S. Dunn, *Puritans and Yankees: The Winthrop Dynasty of New England, 1630–1717* (1962); Samuel Eliot Morison, *Builders of the Bay Colony* (1981 [1930]); Ronald Sterne Wilkinson, "Hermes Christianus: John Winthrop, Jr. and Chemical Medicine in 17th-Century New England," in *Science, Medicine and Society in the Renaissance: Essays to Honor Walter Pagel*, ed. Allen G. Debus (1972).

Walter W. Woodward

Wright, Chauncey (1830–75) Philosopher.

America's most influential mid-19th-century philosopher, Chauncey Wright is remembered less for his writings than for the deep impression his ideas and personality left on illustrious others: Charles Darwin; Henry James, Sr., Henry James, and William James; Oliver Wendell Holmes, Jr.; and Charles Sanders Peirce. Wright, a lifelong resident of Massachusetts, was born in Northampton and remained in Cambridge after graduating from Harvard in 1852. Calm, gentle, solitary, melancholic, and "somewhat insolent," according to his friend William James, Wright lived alone and supported himself as a human "computer" for *The American Ephemeris and Nautical Almanac.* Two courses he taught at Harvard on psychology and on mathematical physics were pedagogical failures.

Darwin's *Origin of Species* (1859) provoked questions about science and religion that dominated Cambridge intellectual discussion for more than a decade. Wright sided with Darwin and Darwin's foremost American proponent, Harvard botanist Asa Gray, against the relentless opposition of Harvard zoologist Louis Agassiz. Darwin, whom Wright visited in 1872, published at his own expense Wright's careful defense of natural selection against critics who accepted evolutionary change but rejected Darwin's proposed mechanism. With its conscientious, abstract assessment of Darwin's evolutionary hypotheses and its comparisons with Isaac Newton's theory of gravitation, Wright's "Genesis of Species" is a sophisticated essay in the philosophy of science.

Wright was deeply influenced by British empiricism, particularly John Stuart Mill's views on scientific method and associational psychology. Wright extended the caution, skepticism, and rigor he appreciated among scientists to questions of metaphysics, morality, psychology, and religion. A defense of a physical origin of the mind is the main topic of his "Evolution of Self-Consciousness." He endorsed utilitarian ethics, progressive (even socialist) politics, and religious agnosticism.

The Metaphysical Club, a discussion group that sometimes met at Wright's quarters in the early 1870s, originated the philosophy known as American pragmatism. Other members of the club included James, Peirce, and Holmes. The ramifications of Darwin's evolutionary theory were a prime concern. Peirce described Wright as the club's intellectual "boxing master." The pragmatist school, led by William James and John Dewey, became America's most influential philosophy during the first quarter of the 20th century.

Wright died of a stroke at age 45. After his death, Charles Eliot Norton, editor of the *North American Review,* printed a volume of Wright's collected papers: *Philosophical Discussions* (1877). William James wrote of his friend in an obituary for the *Nation:* "Of the two motives to which philosophic systems owe their being, the craving for consistency or unity in thought, and the desire for a solid outward warrant for our emotional ends, his mind was dominated only by the former. Never in a human head was contemplation more separated from desire." Amazed and repelled by the purity of Wright's scientific and theoretical temperament, James was fundamentally unable to accept the equanimity with which Wright described events as resulting from chance, mere "cosmic weather," and with which he withheld judgment on issues of the deepest import—immortality, free will, and God's existence. James's essay "The Will to Believe," which champions the legitimacy of belief on limited evidence when a decision is "forced, living and momentous," is an extended reply to Wright.

Edward H. Madden, *Chauncey Wright and the Foundations of Pragmatism* (1963); Madden, ed., *The Philosophical Writings of Chauncey Wright: Representative Selections* (1958); Chauncey Wright, *Philosophical Discussions* (1971).

Drew Christie

Zakrzewska, Marie Elizabeth (1829–1902) Midwife and physician.

Marie Elizabeth Zakrzewska (pronounced Zak-shef´-ska) was born in Berlin, Germany, and trained there as a midwife before immigrating to America in 1853 to study medicine, believing her mentor's claim that "only in a republic can it be proved that science has no sex." Most of her subsequent experiences convinced her that America was not yet so advanced, although she did earn her M.D. from Western Reserve College in Cleveland, Ohio. Thereafter she spent three years in New York City, helping to establish the New York Infirmary for Indigent Women and Children. In March 1859 she left for Boston, accepting a position as professor of obstetrics and director of a new clinical department at the New England Female Medical College. She made this career change, she explained, in order to help advance "the cause of the medical education of women."

The Zakrzewska Building of the Dimock Community Health Care Complex, Roxbury, Mass., which was founded by Marie Zakrzewska in 1862 as the New England Hospital for Women and Children

with its founder, Samuel Gregory, who resisted her efforts to introduce instruction in microscopy, thermometry, and dissection into the curriculum. She also left because she had the opportunity to start her own hospital. In 1862, with the support of several of Boston's leading liberal reformers, including Edna Cheney, Caroline Severance, and William Lloyd Garrison, Zakrzewska founded the New England Hospital for Women and Children, one of a small number of medical institutions which offered clinical training to women at midcentury. For all intents and purposes Zakrzewska ran the hospital until her retirement in 1899. Dedicated, ambitious, and proud of her independence, she won the respect of her colleagues, male and female alike.

Zakrzewska stood out among her contemporaries for her unusual stance on scientific medicine. At a time when most women physicians promoted an image of themselves as caring and sympathetic, she insisted that nothing was more important than developing scientific acumen. For her strong views, and for the large number of women who trained in her hospital, Zakrzewska earned a reputation as one of the most prominent female physicians in 19th-century America.

Virginia G. Drachman, *Hospital with a Heart: Women Doctors and the Paradox of Separatism at the New England Hospital, 1862–1969* (1984); New England Hospital for Women and Children, *Marie Elizabeth Zakrzewska: A Memoir* (1903); R. L. Numbers and J. W. Leavitt, ed., *Sickness and Health in America*, 2d ed. (1985); Agnes Vietor, *A Woman's Quest: The Life of Marie E. Zakrzewska, M.D.* (1972 [1924]).

Arleen Marcia Tuchman

Much later in life Zakrzewska claimed that another reason she moved was to follow a close friend, the German political émigré Karl Heinzen, who had recently settled in Boston with his wife and child. For Zakrzewska, their friendship was "based not simply on affinity by nature but also on principle," which included a commitment to abolition, women's rights, and radical democracy. Zakrzewska shared her home in Roxbury with Heinzen and his family for 20 years. This unusual living arrangement also included Julia A. Sprague, a founding member of the New England Women's Club and Zakrzewska's companion for more than 40 years. In Boston, Zakrzewska supported several political causes, but her most important work was in the education of women physicians.

Zakrzewska soon left the New England Female Medical College over disagreements

Sports and Recreation

Warren Goldstein, Section Editor

INTRODUCTION

New England's sports and recreation activities have been and are still shaped by five principal factors: the region's deep Puritan religious heritage, its powerful tradition of higher education, its large number of immigrants, its peculiar geography and distinct seasonal cycle, and the centrality of Boston, the dominant commercial, population, and cultural center of the region.

Even before its European history, New England supported a recreational life among its Native Americans, who staged footraces and wrestling contests and played a version of the game now known as lacrosse. But though Indians and European settlers played some similar games, their cultures differed so vastly that there does not appear to have been much borrowing of recreational pursuits between them. Most English settlers were frightened of the wilderness and repelled by what they thought of as Native American "paganism," so the shape and content of the Puritans' recreational lives were much more powerfully influenced by English roots.

Historians long ago put to rest the stereotyped image of Puritans as gray, somber, sober, and humorless sourpusses, but the Puritans nonetheless carried a deep suspicion of traditional English recreational life, with its intense merrymaking on saints' days; its fondness for free-flowing drink, dancing, general carousing, and blood sports such as bull- and bearbaiting; and its occasional sexual wantonness. Disgusted by what struck them as "Romish" holidays and often blasphemous merrymaking, Puritans not only reserved the Sabbath for worship (and early on prohibited sports and drinking on Saturday night as well), they subordinated all things playful to their commitments to God and work. Not that they shunned the pleasures of palate or body; they insisted, on the contrary, that recreation—like all things—be taken in moderation. John Winthrop, the first governor of the Massachusetts Bay Colony, initially worried that play could sap his energy. "I examined my heart," he concluded, "and findinge it needfull to recreate my minde with some outward recreation, I yielded unto it, and by a moderate exercise herein was much refreshed." Increase Mather condemned gambling but also noted, "For a Christian to use Recreation is very lawful, and in some cases a great Duty." According to the historians Elliott Gorn and Warren Goldstein, "Drink was from God, Puritans believed, but drunkenness from the devil; sex was one of the delights of marriage, adultery one of the most heinous sins."

Faced with a belief in divinely ordained predestination, Puritans scrutinized their souls and their lives for evidence that they were among the elect. Capacity to work and worship might offer a clue, so when these early New Englanders thought about recreation, they meant it literally as re-creating oneself for the important work of life.

Play, therefore, they tended to view with a certain mistrust, except when it accompanied more useful activities, such as barn raisings, harvest times, ordinations, elections, and other occasions in the religious, civic, or farming calendar. At such gatherings men engaged in footraces, shooting, wrestling, sword-fighting contests, and other English sports.

Throughout the colonies—even Virginia, where planters raised leisure to a high art—women had considerably less recreational latitude. In Puritan New England, though women could occasionally dance or play games such as cards and backgammon in their own homes, in public they were expected to limit themselves to more proper pursuits, such as cornhusking or quilting.

Despite a widespread social consensus about the virtues of moderation, town elders often enough found themselves in struggles with energetic youth or the less devout over proper observance of the Sabbath or play that seemed to take on a life of its own. But as Puritan society expanded demographically and geographically, the restraints on organized play began to weaken, particularly in the port cities, where merchants, immigrants, and sailors gathered, often far from the supervision of church or state. As coffeehouse and tavern life grew through the 18th century, the range of acceptable recreations—including horse racing, cardplaying, dancing, and bowling—widened as well.

Nineteenth-century recreational life in New England followed the ebb and flow of religious revivals and population growth. The intense piety aroused by the Second Great Awakening invited converts to imagine themselves infinitely perfectible in the image of God. Rough sports of the working class and seaport roustabouts stood as a rebuke to such godly intentions, and evangelical ministers and voluntary societies did their best to put blood sports (like cockfighting) and gambling games out of business. In fact, although New England has surely been shaped by its Puritan origins, the crusading zeal of antebellum evangelicals actually accounted for far more of the image of dour churchgoers banning leisure pursuits on behalf of Christian piety.

The Victorian interest in health reform, spearheaded in large part by New England physicians and educators, surfaced during the 1820s and 1830s and offered a new religious and moral impetus to physical exercise for both men and women. Mount Holyoke College founder Mary Lyon argued that "those who enjoy bodily idleness enjoy sin"; Catharine Beecher, the Connecticut-based preeminent female architect of Victorian domesticity, published *Course of Female Calisthenics* (1832); Horace Mann, secretary of the Massachusetts State Board of Education, as well as Presidents Mark Hopkins of Williams College and Francis Wayland of Brown University, promoted physical education as morally uplifting.

Midcentury brought further changes as New England embraced the new ideology of "muscular Christianity," which linked male bodily vigor with Christian mission. A dramatically different way of conceptualizing the flesh, muscular Christianity solved the mind-body conflict for Christian men by inviting them to keep their bodies healthy and pure (rather than dissipated, debauched, or degenerate) in the service of godliness. It also dealt practically with the increasingly sedentary life of commercial and managerial middle-class office workers who labored more and more indoors.

Once its male residents received genuine religious encouragement to engage in physical activity, New England underwent a sports boom, partly centered in its colleges and universities. Students at Yale and Harvard, among others, were happy to focus more of their energies away from the classroom and on newer extracurricular activities in the late 19th century. Chief among these nonacademic and in some cases anti-academic pursuits was the sport of football, which was invented in its modern form by Walter Camp at Yale in the 1880s. As Michael Oriard points out, the Big Three of early college football (Yale, Harvard, and Princeton), through their battles over recruiting, professionalism, and violence, "taught the rest of the country's colleges not just the rules of the game but also how to break them, not only the game's virtues but also its problems and excesses, not only how to play football but also how to stage and promote it." And for years during the late 19th century, the big game between Harvard and Yale—preceded by a parade up Fifth Avenue and attended by as many as 100,000—served as a key event in New York's fall social season.

In fact, New England colleges provided national leadership in a variety of athletic undertakings, ranging from the first intercollegiate baseball and ice hockey games (1859 and 1895), crew regatta (1852), tennis match (1883), and gymnastics competition (1899), to early associations for football and track and field. Yale and Harvard dominated college football until World War I. Field hockey began at private girls' schools and women's colleges in New England during the early years of the 20th century. And the Harvard educator and gymnasium director Dudley Sargent, according to Harvey Green, "trained generations of physical education instructors."

New England shared in the changing demographics of 19th- and early 20th-century America caused by immigration. Rather than bringing distinctive recreational forms across the Atlantic, however, most immigrants to New England engaged in previously established activities, such as boxing and baseball. The single most popular sports hero of the late 19th century was the son of an Irish immigrant. John L. Sullivan, known as the Boston Strong Boy, after winning the heavyweight championship in 1882 went on to become, according to Elliott Gorn, "one of the best-known public figures in the world, and the most idolized athlete of the entire nineteenth century." He was also a hero to Irish Americans at a time when Yankee discrimination flourished.

Basketball, born in Springfield, Mass., at the Young Men's Christian Association (YMCA) training college, exemplified the marriage of Christianity and physical and moral uplift that characterized religious Progressivism in the late 19th and early 20th centuries. It also proved adaptable to new directions in women's collegiate athletics at the turn of the century, as "women's rules" made the game more "cooperative" and less individualistically competitive than the men's game. Both these innovations—men's basketball and its women's variant—despite being taken up around the country, had quintessentially New England origins. While New York City and Chicago soon became the centers of the Social Gospel, the settlement house movement, and the YMCA, the peculiar combination of body and spirit, and the conviction that the two were connected morally, breathed an updated spirit of New England reform: grounded in Christianity, eminently practical, containing a whiff of the crusading temper.

As "new women" of the 1890s and the turn of the 20th century headed outdoors on their bicycles along with millions of men who felt similar urges, and tens of millions of immigrants from southern and eastern Europe flooded into American cities, two contradictory developments in New Englanders' recreational lives were soon under way.

First, by 1900 almost everyone in American society manifested a new interest in recreation in general, and outdoor recreation in particular. As working people successfully struggled to reduce the length of the working day and workweek, more people had more time to devote to leisure pursuits. Furthermore, with the end of the severe depression of 1893–98, the economy entered a modestly prosperous time, and Americans had more disposable income to spend on such pursuits. While cities transformed their nighttime streets from menacing, gaslit warrens to electrically floodlit downtowns, entrepreneurs showed extraordinary imagination in turning technological innovations in transportation and electricity into forms of commercialized amusement.

These were the decades of the rise of Coney Island in New York and a spate of similar attractions throughout New England, many of them modeled on Coney Island, such as Wonderland at Revere Beach in Massachusetts, Luna Park in Hartford, and Paragon Park at Nantasket Beach in Hull, Mass. For working-class immigrant New Englanders, along with many of their middle-class counterparts, the early 20th century brought home the reality of mass culture by attracting masses of people to particular locales in search of active recreation.

Second, while this movement affected nearly all New Englanders, indeed all Americans, they participated in it in different ways depending on their class status.

Street hockey, Boston, 1975

The well-to-do (and those who catered to their wishes) began to construct recreational institutions separate from the crush and smell—but above all, the presence—of the immigrants swelling the U.S. population during these years. They founded the Country Club in Brookline, Mass., for example, to escape Boston's crowds and air. And even farther from the city, the rich created the exclusive resorts of Bar Harbor, Maine, as well as the Ponham Club, Squantum, and the Rhode Island Yacht Club on Narragansett Bay.

The combination of improved transportation and the population concentration in Boston provided the underpinnings of New England's rich traditions in professional sports. Boston's hockey, football, basketball, and baseball teams have played key roles in the historical development of their respective sports, not least by providing sports homes to such great and admired players as Bobby Orr, Doug Flutie, Larry Bird, and Carl Yastrzemski. Even though Harry Wright's Boston Red Stockings (ancestors of the Braves) dominated the first professional league from 1871 to 1875, New England's most storied sports franchise team remains the long-suffering—but ultimately victorious—Boston Red Sox.

One of the true baseball powerhouses of the early 20th century, the Red Sox won American League pennants six times and the World Series five times between 1903 and 1918. But since 1918, the Red Sox and their fans endured the longest drought in baseball history until their World Series triumph in 2004. No team, however, and no ballpark has ever attracted the talents of more writers and intellectuals—among them Roger Angell, John Updike, and A. Bartlett Giamatti—compelled by the regular hopes and agonizing disappointments generated by the Sox.

Top 100 New England Athletes

1. Ted Williams–Baseball
2. Bill Russell–Basketball
3. Bobby Orr–Hockey
4. Larry Bird–Basketball
5. Rocky Marciano–Boxing
6. Eddie Shore–Baseball
7. Ray Bourque–Hockey
8. Bob Cousy–Basketball
9. Red Auerbach–Basketball
10. Carl Yastrzemski–Baseball
11. John Havlicek–Basketball
12. John Hannah–Football
13. Roger Clemens–Baseball
14. Doug Flutie–Football
15. Milt Schmidt–Hockey
16. Phil Esposito–Hockey
17. Babe Ruth–Baseball
18. 1980 Olympic hockey team
19. Marvin Hagler–Boxing
20. Bill Rodgers–Running
21. Kevin McHale–Basketball
22. Jim Rice–Baseball
23. Cam Neely–Hockey
24. Robert Parish–Basketball
25. Carlton Fisk–Baseball
26. Joan Benoit–Running
27. Harry Agganis–Baseball
28. Dave Cowens–Basketball
29. Drew Bledsoe–Football
30. Tom Yawkey–Baseball
31. Nomar Garciaparra–Baseball
32. Tony Conigliaro–Baseball
33. Johnny Bucyk–Hockey
34. Pedro Martinez–Baseball
35. Billy Sullivan–Baseball
36. Luis Tiant–Baseball
37. Bill Parcells–Football
38. Jimmie Foxx–Baseball
39. Dorothy Hamill–Figure skating
40. Steve Grogan–Football
41. Cy Young–Baseball
42. Bobby Doerr–Baseball
43. Gino Cappelletti–Football
44. Francis Ouimet–Golf
45. Tommy Heinsohn–Basketball
46. Mike Haynes–Football
47. Gerry Cheevers–Hockey
48. Ben Coates–Football
49. Patrick Ewing–Basketball
50. Joe Cronin–Baseball
51. Wade Boggs–Baseball
52. Jim Nance–Football
53. Sam Jones–Basketball
54. Harry Sinden–Golf
55. Walter Brown–Hockey
56. Chris McCarron–Horseracing
57. Johnny Kelley–Running
58. K. C. Jones–Basketball
59. Tom Glavine–Baseball
60. Jenny Thompson–Swimming
61. Steve Nelson–Football
62. Tony Plansky–Football
63. Pat Bradley–Golf
64. Robbie Ftorek–Hockey
65. Lynn Jennings–Running
66. Mickey Cochrane–Baseball
67. Willie Pep–Boxing
68. Bill Cleary–Hockey
69. Mo Vaughn–Baseball
70. Clarence DeMar–Running
71. Jimmy Walker–Basketball
72. Jeff Bagwell–Baseball
73. Stanley Morgan–Football
74. Reggie Lewis–Basketball
75. Joe Bellino–Football
76. Rebecca Lobo–Basketball
77. Napoleon Lajoie–Baseball
78. Julius Boros–Golf
79. Andrea Lawrence–Skiing
80. Pie Traynor–Baseball
81. Snooks Kelley–Hockey
82. Johnny Pesky–Baseball
83. Ernie DiGregorio–Basketball
84. Fred Lynn–Baseball
85. Hazel Wightman–Golf
86. Don Cherry–Hockey
87. Gabby Hartnett–Baseball
88. Stasia Czernicki–Candlepin bowling
89. Bobby Carpenter–Hockey
90. Art Ross–Hockey
91. U.S. women's college hockey teams
92. Frankie Brimsek–Hockey
93. John Thomas–Track and field
94. Tris Speaker–Baseball
95. Dennis Johnson–Basketball
96. Bruce Armstrong–Football
97. Jim Lonborg–Baseball
98. Tenley Albright–Figure skating
99. Rico Petrocelli–Baseball
100. Warren Spahn–Baseball

Although like other franchises Boston baseball teams absorbed Irish, Italian, and Polish immigrants as such players entered the major leagues, the Red Sox became the last team in major league baseball to hire an African American ballplayer—in 1959. Boston had also been one of the few major American cities without a Negro League franchise in the days of baseball segregation. The genuine historical "curse" facing the Red Sox is less that occasioned by selling Babe Ruth to the New York Yankees in 1919—the most shortsighted deal in the history of the game—than Boston's failure to take advantage of the flood of talented African American ballplayers who entered major league baseball in the 1940s and 1950s. Only the current owners of the Red Sox have finally undertaken to bridge the enormous rift between Boston's African American community and the team.

No other U.S. region boasts such intense geographical contrasts in such a compact area, and only the Midwest experiences all four seasons as distinctively as New England. Three of the four seasons have given rise to separate recreational traditions, most of which have parallels in other parts of the country, but none of which are practiced alongside each other in such a small region. New Englanders have perhaps shown their greatest resourcefulness in converting their harsh, punishing winters into economically successful recreational environments. Since the arrival of Scandinavian immigrants in the 1870s, skiing has had a growing role in winter recreational and tourist life and continues as a mainstay of the region's winter economy, supplemented by snowboarding and snowmobiling.

As Dona Brown points out in her book on New England tourism, residents have also been inventive in converting the beauties of autumn foliage in the mountains into a multimillion-dollar tourist activity known as leaf-peeping. Summer camps for children and families have transformed the shores of hundreds of New England lakes into commercial propositions offering a comfortable experience of "nature" not too distant from "civilization." And for those who prefer the shore, New England's Atlantic coastline boasts an extraordinary variety of beaches featuring chilly water and brisk winds ideal for sailing.

Partly because of the commercial intensity of its ports and cities, partly because of its rich history of manufacturing, New England played a pioneering role in the development of new forms of transportation in the 19th and early 20th centuries. Advances in transportation, in turn, encouraged new or expanded recreational activities, from railroad excursions before the Civil War to snowmobiling and skiing in the 1930s, to automobile racing since the 1890s. From Frank and Charles Duryea in 1896 to Mike Stefanik in 1997, New Englanders, their cars, and their speedways have played important roles in the development of the nation's most popular spectator sport.

An occasionally quirky feel remains to the recreational lives of New Englanders, apparently born of Yankee flintiness; an often harsh, demanding environment; the peculiar pessimism of the Puritan legacy; a nearly four-century-old European history; the arrival of immigrants first at the middle of the 19th century and then at the turn of the 20th century; and powerful traditions in higher education. The exploits of Harvard and Yale sports teams, for example, continue to be followed by millions who have never set foot on either campus. In a world speeding up by the month, in the middle of winter many thousands of New Englanders head for frozen lakes to take up ice fishing in huts (perhaps the single least efficient manner of obtaining a fish), warming themselves with comradeship and alcohol.

Despite their vigorous commercialization of recreation since the early 19th century, New Englanders at play retain a pessimistic outlook on the world that long preceded the cheerful Transcendentalists and lives long after them. Those with fishing poles in the water, after all, rarely catch many fish and sailors must beware the treacherously rocky coastlines. Although Massachusetts voters repealed one of the last "blue laws" prohibiting the sale of package liquor on Sundays, the New England Sabbath endures in Connecticut, where stores are still closed. Among the most rabid sports fans in America, boasting successful traditions in basketball, football, and hockey, Bostonians—along with most New Englanders—remained committed to the Red Sox through 86 years of defeat.

E. John B. Allen, *From Skisport to Skiing: One Hundred Years of an American Sport, 1840–1940* (1993); Cleveland Amory, *The Last Resorts* (1952); Roger Angell, *Five Seasons: A Baseball Companion* (1977); Angell, *Late Innings: A Baseball Companion* (1982); Angell, *The Summer Game* (1972); Albert G. Applin II, *From Muscular Christianity to the Marketplace: The History of Men's and Boy's Basketball in the United States, 1891–1957* (1982); Thomas G. Bergin, *The Game: The Harvard-Yale Football Rivalry, 1875–1983* (1984); Dona Brown, *Inventing New England: Regional Tourism in the 19th Century* (1995); Bruce C. Daniels, *Puritans at Play: Leisure and Recreation in Colonial New England* (1995); Tom Derderian, *The Boston Marathon: The History of the World's Premier Running Event* (1994); Stan Fischler, *Bobby Orr and the Big, Bad Bruins* (1969); Elliott Gorn, *The Manly Art: Bare-Knuckle Prize Fighting in America* (1986); Elliott Gorn and Warren Goldstein, *A Brief History of American Sports* (1993); Harvey Green, *Fit for America: Health, Fitness, Sport, and American Society* (1986); Michael Isenberg, *John L. Sullivan and His America* (1998); John Kasson, *Amusing the Million: Coney Island at the Turn of the Century* (1978); Alan B. Newman, ed., *New England Reflections, 1882–1907* (1981); Michael Oriard, *Reading Football: How the Popular Press Created an American Sporting Spectacle* (1993); Bob Ryan and Dick Raphael, *The Boston Celtics: The History, Legends, and Images of America's Most Celebrated Team* (1989); Dan Shaughnessy, *At Fenway: Dispatches from Red Sox Nation* (1996); Ronald A. Smith, *Sports and Freedom: The Rise of Big-Time College Athletics* (1988); Nancy Struna, "Puritans and Sport: The Irretrievable Tide of Change," *Journal of Sport History* 4 (Spring 1977); John Updike, "Hub Fans Bid Kid Adieu," in *Assorted Prose* (1965); Kathleen D. Valenzi and Michael W. Hopp, *Champion of Sport: The Life of Walter Camp, 1859–1925* (1990).
Warren Goldstein

Amusement and Theme Parks Although only a few amusement parks remain, New England at various times has been home to an estimated 170 or more. In the late 1800s, as New Englanders gained more leisure time, rail and transit companies created recreation areas, casinos, and picnic groves known as "trolley parks." Notable examples included Burgett Park, near Dover, N.H.; Crystal Lake Park in Gardner, Mass.; Lincoln Park, in North Dartmouth, Mass.; and Lake Kenosia at Danbury, Conn. Originally built to generate weekend ridership, trolley parks led to the development of the region's first amusement parks and fairyland-style resorts such as Ridge Hill Farms in Wellesley, Mass. (ca. 1870).

By the early 1900s, many of these parks had dance pavilions, bandstands, swimming, boating, roller skating, and stage performances. But the most popular attractions were usually the game arcades and rides, some of which were hand- or mule-powered. The Philadelphia Toboggan Company (PTC) designed and built many of the area's carousels; with their hard-carved flying horses and wooden roller coasters, they were a dips-and-thrills offshoot of scenic railway rides.

The new mobility afforded by automobiles encouraged parks to compete with one another by installing bigger and better coasters, and soon New England boasted more of these "white knuckle rides" than any other region. With the addition of Ferris wheels, "dodge 'em" cars, airplane swings, "whips," miniature trains, shooting galleries, and fun houses, amusement parks enjoyed a golden age.

The lavish, short-lived Vanity Fair, near Providence, was an early precursor of Disneyland-style theme parks, as was Wonderland, the elaborate oceanside site at Revere Beach in Massachusetts. Regarded as the amusement capital of New England for nearly 75 years, Revere Beach was from 1906 to 1911 a collection of independently owned amusements and arcades. The area was home to a large pier, four roller coasters, several carousels, fun houses, diving horses, circus acts, the spectacular "Fighting the Flames" reenactment show, and the Virginia Reel, "the most sensational ride in the world."

Equally elaborate was Paragon Park at Nantasket Beach, in Hull, Mass., with its 110-foot tower decorated with 100,000 lights. Other notable sites included Hartford's Luna Park; Merrimack Park in Methuen, Mass.; Rocky Point and Newport Beach, R.I.; Maine's Old Orchard Beach; Pleasure Beach in Bridgeport, Conn.; the White City parks at Worcester, Mass.; and Savin Rock, the famed seaside resort in West Haven, Conn.

Band concerts were a popular draw; John Philip Sousa drew up to 15,000 fans at concerts on his 1897 tour of New England. Music and ballroom dancing helped many parks through the Depression and World War II as they presented the big bands of Rudy Vallee, Benny Goodman, the Dorsey Brothers, and later, rock 'n' rollers.

But in the 1950s, families increasingly loaded into their cars for distant vacations rather than local amusement parks. By the 1970s, a combination of fire, floods, high maintenance costs, neglect, and changing real estate values and entertainment preferences had wiped out all but a few of New England's amusement parks and classic roller coasters.

Once glorious parks often became shabby and crumbling in their final years. Massachusetts's Acushnet Park in New Bedford, Mass., and Lakeview Park, in Dracut, Mass., lasted into the 1950s. Pleasure Beach in Bridgeport went bankrupt in 1960. All traces of Savin Rock had disappeared by 1967, while Crescent Park at Riverside, R.I., limped through until the 1970s. In 1959, Pleasure Island in Wakefield, Mass., tried to imitate Disney's theme park concept. Although this was a good idea, it was poorly executed: ownership changed hands several times before the park folded in 1969.

Revere Beach's 1927 Cyclone, the last of its 10 coasters, was razed in 1974, leaving only a grand ballroom as a clue that the park was once the Coney Island of Boston. Salisbury Beach's 1927 Comet came down that same year. Mountain Park in Holyoke, Mass., and its 1929 Mountain Flyer were torn down in 1987.

Traditional amusement parks—particularly their vintage roller coasters—enjoyed a revival beginning in the mid-1980s. But that wasn't enough to save Paragon Park, which was torn down in 1985 for condominiums and a gambling casino that was never constructed. Paragon's classic 1928 PTC carousel still stands. Its 1917 roller coaster, The Giant, a favorite of Judy Garland, Ted Williams, and Cardinal Cushing (who celebrated his birthday each year with a ride), was auctioned off for a reported $26,000. Using old photos and postcards as a guide, a double-helix curve destroyed in a 1963 fire was rebuilt when The Giant was relocated to Adventure World near Washington, D.C.

Still standing, but out of service, and the subject of an ongoing preservation effort, is the twisting 1946 Comet coaster at Lincoln Park, which closed in 1987. The restored carousel at Oak Bluffs, Martha's Vineyard, still stands. Rocky Point, which sold off many attractions, has a limited number of rides.

Two former lakeside trolley parks—Canobie Lake Park, which opened in 1902 in Salem N.H., and Whalom Park, founded in 1893 in Lunenburg, Mass.—were top examples of New England's classic, family-oriented amusement parks. Tree-lined Canobie Lake Park, continuing to operate and named one of the most beautiful amusement parks in the country in *Amusement Park Guidebook*, offers a

The carousel at Rocky Point Amusement Park, Warwick, R.I., 1981

varied collection of traditional kiddie and adult rides. Its PTC coaster, the Yankee Cannonball, was relocated in 1936 from Lakewood Park in Waterbury, Conn. Attractions at Whalom, closed since 2000, included a classic carousel, the Tumblebug ride, kiddie rides, a country dance hall, and the midsized 1940 Flyer Comet, fashioned after a 1939 New York World's Fair roller coaster.

New England's largest amusement park is Six Flags New England, formerly Riverside, founded in 1912 at a picnic grove in Agawam, Mass., near Springfield. Attendance figures reaching up to 900,000 per season rank it as one of the top 50 amusement parks in the world. The 150-foot Colossus Ferris wheel is one of the tallest structures in western Massachusetts. Its top-rated $2.3 million wooden coaster, Cyclone, was erected in 1983. Lake Compounce in Bristol, Conn., is America's oldest amusement park, though its operating schedules were spotty in the early 1990s. Compounce's attractions include a grand ballroom, a classic merry-go-round, and New England's oldest operating roller coaster, the twisting 1927 Wildcat. Smaller parks, designed for families with children of mixed ages, include Quassy Amusement Park's lakeside setting in Middlebury, Conn., and York's Wild Kingdom in York Beach, Maine. New Hampshire has Santa's Village in Jefferson, and Storyland, the perennial family favorite in Glen.

In 1996 there was considerable activity on the amusement park front by many outside concerns who viewed New England as ripe for theme park development. In April of that year, Pittsburgh's Kennywood Entertainment bought Lake Compounce with plans to rehabilitate the park after years of neglect. In December 1999 Riverside Park became Six Flags New England, and the newly refurbished park features two huge roller coasters and Island Kingdom. Whalom Park closed in 2000 and its famous carousel was sold at auction. The ballroom that once hosted Duke Ellington burned on March 2, 2002, but local park supporters are trying to save the rest of the site from development.

Bob Goldsack, *A Century of Fun: A Pictorial History of New England Amusement Parks* (1993); *Guide to Ride 2000: A Guidebook to the Roller Coasters of North America* (2000); Edward and Frank Nazzaro, *Revere Beach's Wonderland: Mystic City by the Sea* (1990); Mark Wyatt, *White Knuckle Ride* (1996).

Tristram Lozaw

Auerbach, Arnold "Red" (1917–) Bas-
ketball coach and executive. Born in Brooklyn, N.Y., Arnold "Red" Auerbach helped his father, a Russian Jewish immigrant, with his laundry business and never seemed to lack an odd job. Auerbach starred on his high school basketball team and accepted a partial scholarship to Seth Low Junior College in New York City where he played basketball and studied to be a teacher. When Seth Low shut down, he transferred to George Washington University in Washington, D.C. There, Auerbach learned "fast break" basketball from his coach, Bill Reinhart, as well as lessons about managing people as a counselor in youth programs.

In 1941 Auerbach earned a master's degree in education from George Washington, coached basketball at a private high school, and married Dorothy Lewis, whom he had met while both were students. After a stint teaching physical education and coaching basketball at a public school, Auerbach joined the navy and spent three years stateside primarily coordinating a recreational program. In 1946 he contracted to coach the Washington Capitals, a professional team in the newly formed Basketball Association of America (BAA). Auerbach's team—composed mainly of players he knew from the navy—compiled the best record over the next three years by emphasizing team play. Unable to secure a three-year contract, Auerbach accepted a position at Duke University but soon left to coach the TriCities Blackhawks, a professional team in the National Basketball Association (NBA), successor to the BAA. A dispute with the owner prompted his resignation after one winning season.

The woeful Boston Celtics franchise turned to Auerbach in 1950, and he immediately made the team competitive. Auerbach developed an excellent relationship with club owner Walter Brown and tirelessly promoted basketball throughout New England by playing exhibitions, giving clinics, and speaking seemingly everywhere. A high profile gained through his animated coaching style and often gruff remarks to the press became larger than life when he acquired star center Bill Russell and won nine league championships over his last 10 years as a coach. When Auerbach retired from coaching in 1966, his 938 wins were a record, and his notorious victory cigars and perceived arrogance left both enduring loyalties and enemies. He was inducted into the Basketball Hall of Fame in 1969.

Auerbach's legend grew over the next two decades as his shrewd moves as general manager—especially drafting Larry Bird a year before he would turn professional—brought the Celtics seven more championships and financial prosperity. Auerbach alone provided continuity during stretches of inept ownership. He became a Boston icon, honored with a life-sized statue and many other recognitions. The NBA named their annual coaching award for him. Auerbach remains Celtics president but has taken an increasingly less active role in the daily operations of the franchise since the late 1980s, a time of tragic misfortunes and frustrating competitive decline. Auerbach laments many of the changes that have complicated the business of basketball, but his career achievements remain benchmarks of excellence.

Arnold "Red" Auerbach, *Basketball for the Player, the Fan and the Coach* (1952); Auerbach and Joe Fitzgerald, *Red Auerbach: An Autobiography* (1977); Dan Shaughnessy, *Seeing Red: The Red Auerbach Story* (1994).

William M. Ferraro

Automobile Racing   New England's long
history of automobile manufacture, its infrastructure of small machine shops and liveries, and its extensive road systems have bound New Englanders closely to the automobile industry and auto ownership. A long-standing regional interest in speed and racing as well as technological innovation have furthered New England's ties to automobile competition, which date back to November 1895 when Frank and Charles Duryea of Springfield, Mass., won the Chicago *Times-Herald* race, considered the first official automobile race in America. In 1896 the Duryea brothers were the first Americans to take an automobile— one they designed and built—overseas for racing purposes. The Duryeas competed in the London-to-Brighton Liberty Day Run, marking America's entry into international motor sports.

Brothers Francis and Freelan Stanley of Newton, Mass., followed the Duryeas into racing by setting a world land speed record with a car of their own design called The Rocket. The Stanleys' steam-powered car was driven at Daytona Beach, Fla., by Fred Marriott to a record of 127.66 mph in 1906. The Stanleys made another record attempt in 1907, but Marriott crashed and destroyed The Rocket at a speed estimated by witnesses to be more than 150 mph.

In 1908 drivers George Robertson and Joe Florida finished first and third for the Locomobile Company of America in Bridgeport, Conn., in the fourth Vanderbilt Cup race. Robertson turned the event's fastest lap, covering the 23.46-mile circuit at an average speed of 69.4 mph. Robertson's winning Locomobile had also been the fastest car in the 1906 Vanderbilt Cup races, where it turned a lap at more than 67 mph and finished 10th.

New England has continued to produce outstanding race cars and drivers over the past 90 years. Lime Rock Park, a 1.53-mile road course in Lakeville, Conn., is home to several national racing divisions, including the International Motor Sports Group, the Sports Car Club of America, and the National Asso-

Kart auto racing at Lime Rock Park, Lakeville, Conn., 1992

ciation for Stock Car Automobile Racing (NASCAR) Busch Grand National North series. New England is also home to New Hampshire International Speedway in Loudon, which hosts two NASCAR Winston Cup races each year, in addition to Busch Grand National races, the Indy Racing League, the NASCAR Featherlite Modified Tour, and the NASCAR Craftsman Truck Series. The international speedway is known for breaking the long-standing record for the most fans at a New England sporting event held since the early 1900s by the Yale Bowl.

Automobile racing in New England has shaped the careers of many nationally recognized drivers, including NASCAR Winston Cup driver Ricky Craven, two-time NASCAR Busch Grand National champion Randy LaJoie, and 1970 Daytona 500 winner Pete Hamilton. Famous sports car racers from New England include Bob Sharp and his son, Scott; Sam Posey; and actor-turned-driver Paul Newman. Another New England native to gain national recognition was Mike Stefanik from Coventry, R.I., who was the first driver to win two NASCAR championships in one season. Stefanik won the 1997 Busch Grand National North and Featherlite Modified titles.

New England's role in automobile racing has been solidified by its attention to local racing competition. The New England region contains numerous small speedways where relationships have been fostered between regional drivers and their loyal fans. Such tracks as Thunder Valley International Speedbowl in Gardiner, Maine, and Stafford Motor Speedway in Stafford Springs, Conn., are central el-

ements of the culture, history, and tradition that have made automobile racing America's most popular spectator sport.

Christopher Finch, *Highways to Heaven: The Auto Biography of America* (1992); Peter Golenbock and Greg Fielden, *The Stock Car Racing Encyclopedia: The Complete Record of America's Most Popular Sport* (1997); Peter Helck, *The Checkered Flag* (1961); Mark D. Howell, *From Moonshine to Madison Avenue: A Cultural History of the NASCAR Winston Cup Series* (1997).

Mark D. Howell

Baseball Versions of baseball, a game in which players use a bat to try to hit a small hard ball thrown by a pitcher and then proceed around a series of bases to score points, have been part of New England's culture and recreational life since before the Revolutionary War.

Baseball developed from rounders, a game played by English children. In mid-19th-century New England, a game called "base" or "base ball" was played in a square, under what were known as "Massachusetts rules." Batters stood halfway between first base and home base, a single "out" retired the side, and runners could be put out by being hit with the thrown ball (which, at that time, was larger and softer than a traditional baseball). Teams varied in numbers of players.

A similar game played on a diamond-shaped field flourished in New York. By the mid-1850s, both games were being played in New England. By the early 1860s, however, New England clubs had switched to the more exciting—and more widespread—New York game. Junior players, up to age 18 (some

sources say 16) competed for trophies and championships; senior teams also competed for trophies and championships and often for purses offered in "match" games. Massachusetts clubs held state championship competitions from 1855 to 1870. In the late 1860s, Dirigo, a junior team in Augusta, Maine, won the New England championship and in 1871 competed for the national championship. The first intercollegiate game took place in 1859, between Amherst and Williams College (Amherst won, 73 to 32).

The first Boston Red Stockings, led by legendary player-manager Harry Wright, dominated the brief life of the first professional baseball league, the National Association of Professional Base Ball Players (1871–75). The Red Stockings, staffed mainly with players from the pioneering Cincinnati Red Stockings of 1869–70, won four of the league's five pennants.

In 1876 the National League of Professional Base Ball Clubs was formed, including teams from Hartford and Boston. The league controlled play, set the rules, determined the championships, and increasingly controlled the players themselves. Other professional leagues formed as well during this time, including the Eastern League and the New England League. Semiprofessional teams existed in virtually every town, with many teams in larger cities. From the late 19th century, New England has supported numerous local professional minor league teams. The Nashua Dodgers, in fact, contributed to the racial integration of professional baseball in 1946 by playing new Brooklyn minor leaguers Roy Campanella and Don Newcombe.

The Boston Red Sox remain New England's preeminent major league team, but the Boston Braves, the lineal descendants of the old Boston Red Stockings, were a National League franchise until 1961. New England has produced its share of well-known players, from Robert "Red" Rolfe to Bob Tewksbury and Carlton Fisk. New England's baseball story also includes the manufacture of equipment. The Draper-Maynard Company of Plymouth, N.H., was the foremost maker of gloves in the early decades of the 20th century. Baseball writing, especially about the trials and tribulations of the Boston Red Sox, has established a place for the sport in New England and national culture. Classic stories include John Updike's account of Ted Williams's last game in 1960, "Hub Fans Bid Kid Adieu," and Roger Angell's "The Web of the Game," a 1981 *New Yorker* article that surveyed New England pitchers from the 1912 World Series to future New York Mets star pitcher Ron Darling's games as a Yale University student. Poet Robert Frost was an avid baseball fan, as is

Donald Hall, author of *Fathers Playing Catch with Sons* (1985) and the nine-part poem "Baseball." Another side of baseball is presented in Jimmy Piersall's autobiography *Fear Strikes Out* (1955), which chronicles his experiences from his early days of playing baseball in Waterbury, Conn., to his playing for the Boston Red Sox when he suffered a nervous breakdown. The book has been adapted to the screen twice.

Women are drawn to the great American pastime, as well, as both spectators and players. In 1999 the Women's New England Baseball League was founded in Massachusetts by Chris Lindeborg and Jerry Dawson. The league originally started with four teams and continues to expand.

Warren Goldstein, *Playing for Keeps: A History of Early Baseball* (1989); Troy Soos, *Before the Curse: The Glory Days of New England Baseball, 1858–1918* (1997); Glenn Stout and Richard A. Johnson, *Red Sox Century* (2001).

David C. Smith

Basketball Basketball, one of the world's most widely played sports, originated at the Young Men's Christian Association (YMCA) Training School in Springfield, Mass. In 1891 Luther Halsey Gulick, the institution's director of physical training, asked James Naismith, one of his instructors, to develop a vigorous indoor game to replace the gymnastic exercises routinely practiced during the harsh New England winters. Naismith experimented with various games until he observed a group of rugby players throwing balls to each other and tossing them into boxes. This observation led him to develop a game in which two teams passed, and later bounced, a ball the length of the YMCA gymnasium and scored points by tossing the ball into a goal suspended above the floor. Naismith fashioned the goals from bottomless peach baskets and hung them 10 feet above the floor at opposite ends of the YMCA gymnasium. He also developed 13 rules for the game, most of which were aimed at promoting sportsmanship and precluding unnecessarily rough play. Players sat out fouls on the sideline, and three fouls in a row resulted in a goal for the opposing team. Although each team consisted of five players initially, the first game, played in December 1891, was between two nine-man teams because Naismith's class had 18 students. By the time he had introduced the game to his class, they had grown tired of their teacher's experimentation with new games, but "after the ball was thrown up," he recalled, "there was no need for furthering coaxing." Enthusiastic about the game, his students wanted to name it Naismith-Ball, but settled on Basket-Ball as recommended by their reserved coach.

Basketball quickly spread throughout the YMCAs of New England, becoming the cornerstone of the institution's movement to promote Christianity through sport. "Muscular Christianity," as the movement became known in the late 19th century, reflected a broader effort by religious leaders, progressive reformers, physical educators, and physicians toward promoting physical fitness in public schools, colleges and universities, and urban playgrounds. YMCAs also used basketball as a lure to increase membership and encourage athletic competition between locations.

Competition between YMCAs became so intense, however, that basketball threatened the organization's mission to promote spiritual growth. The YMCAs tried to regulate competition through the establishment of separate basketball leagues, but professionalism—that is, paying for better players—soon undermined these organizations. The rise of professionalism within YMCA basketball leagues, according to Gulick, resulted from "men of lower character going into the game." In 1896 the YMCA turned to the Amateur Athletic Union (AAU) for assistance in regulating its basketball leagues. The AAU reasserted the amateur ethic by exercising editorial control over the official rules, which had been published by the A. G. Spalding and Brothers Company since 1894. Moreover, the organization established uniform play according to those rules; established municipal and regional leagues; sponsored municipal, regional, and national championship tournaments; and required players and teams to register with and pay dues to the AAU. In 1897 the AAU held its first national championship tournaments.

Colleges and universities throughout New England, the Midwest, and the West quickly embraced basketball. In addition to the positioning of YMCAs on many college campuses, the diffusion of physical educators trained by Naismith accounted for the rapid spread of basketball from Springfield. The Minnesota School of Agriculture and Mining College defeated Hamline College, 9 to 3, in the first men's intercollegiate game in 1895. This game, however, was played between nine-man teams; a month later, the University of Chicago defeated the University of Iowa, 15 to 12, in the first men's intercollegiate game between five-man teams.

In 1900, Columbia, Cornell, Harvard, Princeton, and Yale established the Eastern League, the first intercollegiate basketball league. The AAU opposed the formation of the Eastern League because the conduct of Yale and Harvard, particularly in hiring coaches, bordered on professionalism. The University of Pennsylvania joined the Eastern

League in 1905, despite threats from the AAU to ban it from amateur play. Representatives of the Eastern League and the Western League, led by the University of Chicago, exerted their autonomy against the AAU by drafting their own rules in 1905. The National Collegiate Athletic Association (NCAA), organized in 1906, allegedly to reform college football, took over control of men's college basketball in 1915 when the AAU and YMCA joined the NCAA in a basketball rules committee that guided the sport for much of the 20th century. The first intercollegiate championship playoff series, the National Invitation Tournament (NIT), occurred in 1938. The NCAA held its first national basketball championship in 1939, but the NIT overshadowed the NCAA tournament until 1951, when scandals rocked the older contest. In 1942 Dartmouth College lost the NCAA championship to Stanford University. Holy Cross became New England's first NCAA basketball champion in 1947. Providence College finished fourth in the tournament in 1973 and 1987. The University of Connecticut, in 1999, defeated Duke University for the NCAA championship and in 2004 made college basketball history when its men's and women's team won the NCAA championship in the same year.

Within a year of the invention of basketball at the Springfield YMCA in 1891, Senda Berenson, the director of physical training at nearby Smith College in Northampton, Mass., introduced the game to women. She modified Naismith's rules, however, to reduce vigorous play and emphasize cooperation over competition. Berenson divided the court into three rather than two sections, with two players from each six-woman team in each section. Only the players in the immediate vicinity of the basket could score. As a result of these modifications a distinct brand of basketball developed for women, and not until the 1960s did women widely begin playing the men's version of the game.

In 1899 Berenson and representatives of Radcliffe, Oberlin, and the Boston Normal School of Gymnastics formed the Women's Basketball Rules Committee, which codified women's basketball rules and had them published by the A. G. Spalding Company. In the first intercollegiate women's basketball game in 1901, Smith defeated Bryn Mawr, 4 to 3. As women's intercollegiate basketball developed and spread nationwide, the game became increasingly competitive and strenuous, with men often coaching women's teams. The nation's leading female physical educators objected to this evolution and abolished intercollegiate play in the late 1920s. Women's basketball became part of the general play-day motif in women's sport, one of several games contested by teams of women from several schools. By emphasizing greater student participation in physical training and stressing social and cooperative rather than competitive aspects of the game, women's basketball thrived in this context until the late 1960s, when it became a varsity sport once again. After the 1972 passage of Title IX, which prohibited sex discrimination at educational institutions receiving federal funds, women embraced the men's game, and in the early 1980s the NCAA took control of women's intercollegiate basketball. The University of Connecticut has been the most successful New England team in the women's NCAA basketball championship, in recent years earning semifinal finishes in 1991 and 1996 and championships in 1995, 2000, 2002, 2003, and 2004.

In the late 1890s, professional basketball developed as independent teams fiercely resisted the control of the AAU. In 1949, the National Basketball Association (NBA) was formed from teams belonging to the National Basketball League (organized in 1937) and the Basketball Association of America (organized in 1946). The American Basketball Association, a rival professional league, organized in 1967 but collapsed in 1976, with four of its teams joining the NBA. The Boston Celtics reached the NBA championship finals 19 times since 1957, when the team won its first of 16 NBA championships. Led by the scoring of Bob Cousy and the defensive prowess of Bill Russell, the Celtics won 10 straight titles from 1959 to 1969. John Havlicek led Boston to titles in 1974 and 1976, and Larry Bird rallied the Celtics to titles in 1981, 1984, and 1986.

Like Naismith's students who spread the gospel of basketball throughout U.S. colleges and universities, YMCA missionaries spread the game globally. By 1930, 50 nations had embraced the sport. In 1932 representatives of amateur basketball organizations from Africa, Asia, Australia, Europe, and North and South America formed the International Federation of Amateur Basketball (FIBA). At the 1936 Olympic Games in Berlin, Germany, basketball was first contested as an Olympic sport. Introduced to the University of Berlin in the mid-1930s, the Nazis denied the game's New England origins, claiming that the sport demonstrated the speed, strength, and stamina of Aryan superiority. Despite the Nazi claims, the United States won the gold medal, their first of 11 Olympic gold medals in basketball. At the 1972 Olympic Games in Munich, Germany, the former USSR defeated the United States in a game marred by controversy over the last few seconds of the game. At the 1980 Olympic Games in Moscow, Russia, which the United States boycotted, the former

Yugoslavia garnered the gold medal. Basketball became an Olympic sport for women in 1976. In 1992, 1996, 2000, and 2004 one or the other U.S. "Dream Teams" of professional men's and women's basketball players has won the Olympic gold medal. American professionals were permitted to compete in the Olympic Games by FIBA and the International Olympic Committee because most of the best players of many nations were professionals playing in the NBA.

Stephen Fox, *Big Leagues: Professional Baseball, Football, and Basketball in National Memory* (1994); Joan S. Hult and Marianna Trekel, eds., *A Century of Women's Basketball: From Frailty to the Final Four* (1991); Neil D. Isaacs, *All the Moves: A History of College Basketball* (1975); Robert W. Peterson, *Cages to Jump Shots: Pro Basketball's Early Years* (1990).

Adam R. Hornbuckle

Bird, Larry (1956–) Basketball player. Larry Bird, one of the most popular players in the history of the National Basketball Association (NBA), led the Boston Celtics to three NBA championships during the 1980s. Born in French Lick, Ind., Larry Joe Bird started playing basketball as a high school sophomore. He entered Indiana University to play under the legendary coach Bobby Knight but left the school during the 1975 fall semester and briefly attended Northwood Institute, a junior college. Enrolling at Indiana State University in 1975, he sat on the bench for one season before emerging to become one of college basketball's greatest players, posting a career average of 30.3 points per game. In 1979 Bird led Indiana State to the National Collegiate Athletic Association (NCAA) championship final, only to lose to Michigan State University and its 6-foot-9-inch guard, Earvin "Magic" Johnson.

After graduating in 1979, Bird signed a five-year contract with the Boston Celtics for $3.25 million, making him the highest paid rookie in NBA history. Selected Rookie of the Year in 1980, he averaged 21.3 points and 10.9 rebounds per game. Under Bird's leadership, the Celtics posted a 61–21 record, winning 32 more games than the previous season. He played for the Celtics 13 years, leading the club to NBA titles in 1981, 1984, and 1986. Bird, who played in 10 All-Star Games from 1980 to 1990, captured the first of three consecutive Most Valuable Player titles in 1984. Co-captain of the "Dream Team," he won an Olympic gold medal in 1992.

Bird retired from the NBA in 1992 and became head coach of the Indiana Pacers in 1997. As a player, he not only rejuvenated basketball in Boston but, together with Magic Johnson of the Los Angeles Lakers, breathed new life into the entire sport. The rivalry between Bird

and Magic, which started in the 1979 NCAA championship game, continued throughout their professional careers.

Clifton Brown, "Bird Bows to Bad Back and Calls It a Career," *New York Times Biographical Service,* August 1992; Frederick L. Corn, *Basketball's Magnificent Bird: The Larry Bird Story* (1982); Bruce Weber, *Magic Johnson . . . Larry Bird* (1986).

Adam R. Hornbuckle

Boston Braves The Boston Braves baseball team played in the National League from 1876 to 1952. The Braves were one of the eight original teams in the National League and were known also as the Bees and the Beaneaters. From 1876 until 1901, the Braves were the only major league team in Boston and were one of the finest teams in professional baseball, winning eight National League pennants. With the arrival of the American League and the Boston Red Sox in 1901, Boston had an entry in both major leagues, similar to New York, Philadelphia, Saint Louis, and Chicago. From 1901 until 1952, the Braves only won two pennants in Boston and lost the attention and devotion of Boston's baseball fans to the American League Red Sox.

When the National League was formed in 1876, many of the players from Boston's National Association team, the Red Stockings, moved to the Braves. The Red Stockings were the best team in the National Association between 1872 and 1875, winning four straight championships while compiling a 205–50 record (including 71–8 in 1875). The Red Stockings were led by Harry Wright, one of professional baseball's earliest stars and a member of the first professional team, the 1869 Cincinnati Red Stockings. The key players for those championship teams were George Wright (Harry's brother) and pitcher Albert Spalding. Before the 1876 season, however, the Chicago White Stockings lured away Spalding and three teammates. The Red Stockings name would be adapted by the American League entry in Boston (Red Sox) the same way that the White Stockings name would be carried forward by the Chicago White Sox.

With the loss of the players to the Chicago White Stockings, the Boston Braves fell to fourth place during the initial National League season. They rebounded in 1877, winning their first of three consecutive National League pennants. The team also won three straight pennants from 1891 to 1893 and back-to-back pennants in 1897 and 1898. Changes took place in the 1880s, when former player John Morrill became the manager of the club and the Braves saw the rise to fame of one of baseball's earliest superstars, King Kelly, who played for Boston between 1887 and 1889 and

1891 and 1892. The other future Hall-of-Famers who played for the Braves during the 19th century include pitcher "Kid" Nichols, who won 330 games between 1890 and 1901, Dan Brouthers (1889–91), and John Clarkson (1888–92). Through the end of the 19th century, the Braves remained one of baseball's dominant teams.

With the arrival of the 20th century, the Braves' fortunes on the field and at the gate slipped. The Boston Red Sox had immediate success in the new American League and won over Boston's baseball fans. The Red Sox won the first modern World Series over the highly favored Pittsburgh Pirates and took four more titles before 1918. The Braves, however, finished no higher than fifth for 11 consecutive years until their miracle season of 1914. During that season, the Braves were in last place in July but made a tremendous comeback to win the National League pennant. In the 1914 World Series, the Braves swept the powerful Philadelphia Athletics. After a second- and third-place finish the following two years, the Braves fell back in the standings and did not compete for the pennant again until after World War II. They later won the 1957 World Series in Milwaukee, Wis., and the 1995 World Series in Atlanta, Ga., marking the only franchise to win three World Series crowns for three different cities.

After World War II, team president and part owner Lou Perini poured a great deal of money into the Braves to improve their fortunes on the field. Perini improved the lighting at Braves Field, expanded the minor league system that brought young players to the team, and spent time and money promoting the team. In 1948, Braves pitchers Warren Spahn and Johnny Sain led the team to the National League pennant and the World Series (a six-game loss to the Cleveland Indians). The lack of depth on the pitching staff during those years brought about the well-known baseball saying "Spahn and Sain, and pray for rain." Despite moderate success on the field in the ensuing years, the Braves continued to lose the devotion of Boston baseball fans. The team averaged fewer than 400,000 fans a year in 1951 and 1952, far below the major league average.

In the spring of 1953, Perini surprised the baseball world by moving the Braves to Milwaukee, the site of their American Association minor league affiliate. The Braves' move was the first of many franchise shifts that took place during the 1950s. Despite being one of the smallest cities in the major leagues, Milwaukee embraced the Braves, moving them from the bottom to the top of major league attendance. The Braves went on to win the World Series in 1957 and the pennant in 1958

with the nucleus of players from the Boston team. In 1966, the Braves left Milwaukee and moved to Atlanta.

Atlanta Braves, *1990 Media Guide* (1990); Gary Caruso, *The Braves Encyclopedia* (1995); Harold Kaese and R. G. Lynch, *The Milwaukee Braves* (1954).

Corey Seeman

Boston Bruins For more than 60 years the Boston Bruins have offered ice hockey fans an entertaining style featuring hard-hitting physical play, high-scoring offenses, and tenacious goaltending. Although they lack the numerous championships claimed by the Boston Celtics, their co-tenants in both the Boston Garden and the Fleet Center, the Bruins proudly boast their own tradition of excellence, capped by five Stanley Cup championships. Bruins fans, in turn, are passionate about their team even as they demand and expect much from it.

The first National Hockey League franchise based in the United States, the Bruins were formed in 1924 by Charles F. Adams—a local grocer who possessed as good a Boston name as one could have. The team's debut during the 1924–25 season was inauspicious, as it won only six of 30 games. Within a few years, however, the Bruins became highly competitive, and in the 1928–29 season the team claimed its first Stanley Cup championship. During the 1930s the Bruins proved a dominant team in the regular season, led by goaltenders Tiny Thompson and Frank Brimsek, defenseman Eddie Shore, and a collection of forwards led by Milt Schmidt, Dit Clapper, Woody Dumart, and Bobby Bauer, all under the nearly continuous supervision of coach Art Ross. However, the Bruins could manage only two more Stanley Cup championships (1939 and 1941), and then several key players left to serve in the armed forces during World War II.

After the war the Bruins could not recapture their former level of achievement. Throughout the 1950s the team consistently struggled to make the playoffs, although it managed to reach the finals three times; it opened the 1960s by missing the postseason playoffs for eight consecutive years, with only winger John Bucyk providing consistently good play. Slowly, however, general managers Hap Emms and Schmidt began building a powerhouse team. The signing of rookie defenseman sensation Bobby Orr in 1966 and a major trade that brought center Phil Esposito and two other forwards to Boston in 1967 proved pivotal to the team's rebirth. Coach Harry Sinden forged a team that punished foes with hard hitting and intimidation tactics as well as an explosive attack; the team deserved its nickname, the Big Bad Bruins. Sin-

den's efforts culminated in the 1969–70 season, as the Bruins battled past the New York Rangers, the Chicago Black Hawks, and the St. Louis Blues to win their first Stanley Cup Championship in nearly 30 years when Orr scored in overtime to win the clinching contest at Boston Garden.

The following season proved bittersweet. The Bruins dominated the regular season, setting several league scoring records; Esposito led the way with a record-shattering 76 goals and 152 points, while Orr had 102 assists and 139 points, amazing totals for a defenseman. However, the Montreal Canadiens dethroned the defending champions in a grueling first-round playoff series. It would not be until the next year that the Bruins would reclaim the Stanley Cup by beating their bitter rivals, the Rangers, with Orr and Esposito once again leading the way. All the pieces seemed to be in place for the team to maintain its level of excellence, but a combination of player defections to the upstart World Hockey Association, the erosion of player skills, and Orr's recurring injury problems meant that, aside from an appearance in the 1974 finals, the Bruins would henceforth be very good, not great. Sinden, now general manager, traded Esposito to the Rangers in 1975; the following year Orr left for Chicago. Goalie Gerry Cheevers's return and the combined efforts of defenseman Brad Park and forwards Jean Ratelle, Terry O'Reilly, and Rick Middleton helped the team to two more appearances in the playoff finals during the 1970s, but it never quite regained its former dominance. The arrival of defenseman Ray Bourque in 1979 offered new hope, for Bourque's offensive skills, if not Orr-like, were remarkable enough; but the Bruins had to settle for solid seasons and two more unsuccessful appearances in the playoff finals. By the middle of the 1990s the team was once again struggling; during 1996–97 it failed to qualify for the playoffs for the first time since Orr's rookie season. That the team now played at the Fleet Center, a new facility with the same address as the old Boston Garden, did not soften the sting of defeat.

The Bruins have not enjoyed the level of success achieved by the Celtics, but the team has an equal claim on the hearts of Bostonians and New Englanders. Even the team crest, a B serving as the hub of a wheel, reminds fans of its hometown's self-professed location in the universe. Moreover, the Bruins' success during the 1970s and 1980s, televised as it was throughout the region, encouraged a growing number of boys to take up ice hockey. Today, several of the game's leading stars, including Keith Tkachuk, Jeremy Roenick, and John LeClair, hail from New England, testifying to the team's role in the influx of American-born players to a sport once dominated by Canadians.

Dan Diamond, ed., *The Official National Hockey League 75th Anniversary Commemorative Book* (1991); Douglas Hunter, *Champions: The Illustrated History of Hockey's Greatest Dynasties* (1997); Harry Sinden, *The Picture History of the Boston Bruins: From Shore to Orr and the Years Between* (1976).

Brooks D. Simpson

Boston Celtics The Boston Celtics are generally viewed either as the most revered franchise in professional basketball or the most obnoxious. Founded in 1946 by Walter Brown, a likable sports impresario, the Celtics initially endured lean years. Hiring Arnold "Red" Auerbach as coach in 1950 changed fortunes. Bringing an unrivaled commitment to winning, confidence bordering on arrogance, a gruff—sometimes tactless—manner, and a notorious cigar, Auerbach had an unbroken connection with the Celtics that has stamped his name indelibly on team history.

Under Auerbach's direction, ballhandling innovator Bob Cousy made Boston exciting, but not until the coming of revolutionary defensive center Bill Russell in 1956 did the team reach championship caliber. The Celtics dominated the National Basketball Association (NBA) from 1957 to 1969, winning 11 titles during that time. Despite unparalleled success on the court, the team faltered at the gate, averaging only 8,000 spectators per game, roughly 5,000 less than capacity at Boston Garden. Brown's death in 1964 led to several changes in ownership over the next decades as the team struggled to remain solvent.

When Red Auerbach retired after the 1965–66 season, he named Russell player-coach. Russell, the NBA's first black coach, retired at the end of the 1968–69 season and former Celtics star Tom Heinsohn assumed coaching duties. Led by holdover swingman John Havlicek and newcomers Dave Cowens at center and Jo Jo White at guard, the Celtics won titles in 1974 and 1976 before a steep decline. Managerial shrewdness and luck brought college sensation Larry Bird in 1979 and front court teammates Kevin McHale and Robert Parish in 1980 to the Celtics, propelling the team—first under Bill Fitch as coach and then K. C. Jones—to titles in 1981, 1984, and 1986. Celtic playoff series with Bird against the Los Angeles Lakers with Earvin "Magic" Johnson became legendary, eclipsing even the storied duels between Bill Russell and Wilt Chamberlain.

Age and improbable tragedies ended this glorious run and tarnished what had become known as the Celtic mystique. In 1986 Len Bias died from cocaine use a few days after being drafted second overall; in 1993, team captain Reggie Lewis died from a heart abnor-

Celtics raise the championship banner, 1986

mality. Celtic management proved less than adept in negotiating within a new world of player agents, global competition, and waning team loyalty. Problematic treatment of black players on the part of both management and fans—cloaked by success through the years—created additional concerns.

Dismal years through the 1990s finally gave way to renewed hope and better teams in the early 21st century. The venerable Boston Garden, where hyperbolic announcer Johnny Most rasped memorable calls like "Havlicek stole the ball!" and opposing players suffered physical and competitive indignities, has been demolished and no longer holds the 16 championship banners or echoes with the bellows of overheated fans. The Celtics, whose lasting status as an institution is reflected by a statue of Red Auerbach in Boston, face the future with an undeniable legacy of achievement.

Harvey Araton and Filip Bondy, *The Selling of the Green: The Financial Rise and Moral Decline of the Boston Celtics* (1992); Joe Fitzgerald, *That Championship Feeling: The Story of the Boston Celtics* (1975); Bob Ryan and Dick Raphael, *The Boston Celtics: The History, Legends, and Images of America's Most Celebrated Team* (1989); Dan Shaughnessy, *Seeing Red: The Red Auerbach Story* (1994).

William M. Ferraro

Boston Garden   Dedicated on November 14, 1928, when President Calvin Coolidge switched on the lights from the White House, the Boston Garden, located at 150 Causeway Street, was originally built by Madison Square Garden president Tex Rickard to host boxing matches. But it earned its great fame as the home of the Boston Celtics and Boston Bruins and became an important part of the social fabric of New England. Mystery surrounded the old edifice, including legends of leprechaun sightings and dead spots on the floor. It became known fondly to Boston fans as the "the Gah-den."

The Boston Garden's famed parquet floor originated in 1946 when Celtics president Walter Brown arranged to have a basketball floor built in the Boston Arena, where the team occasionally played. Because of postwar lumber shortages, the floor had to be constructed from small pieces of wood fitted together in the parquet style. The floor was made of 247 panels held together by brass screws and 988 bolts and was moved to the Boston Garden in 1952. The custom of hanging banners from the Garden's rafters began when the Bruins first won the Stanley Cup in 1929. Numerous championship banners and the numbers of retired players hanging from the rafters attested to the Garden's long history of hosting successful teams.

The Bruins began playing there in 1928 and won the first of five Stanley Cup championships in 1929. Through the years the fans, or "Gallery Gods," spurred on their beloved Bruins. Great Bruins players who skated on the Garden's small ice surface include Phil Esposito, John Bucyk, Eddie Shore, and Bobby Orr, who scored the winning goal in May 1970 to give the Bruins their first Stanley Cup win in 29 years.

The Boston Celtics began to play at the Garden in 1946 and went on to win 16 National Basketball Association (NBA) championships. Players who starred in Celtic Green include Bob Cousy, Sam Jones, K. C. Jones, Bill Russell, John Havlicek, Larry Bird, Robert Parish, and Kevin McHale. In Game seven of the 1965 NBA Eastern finals, Havlicek deflected an inbounds pass, making for a Celtic victory in the final seconds of the game, resulting in Johnny Most's famed exclamation, "Havlicek stole the ball!"

Amateur sport competition formed a large part of the Garden's history. Two well-known events were the Beanpot Hockey Tournament, involving Boston University, Boston College, Northeastern University, and Harvard; and the Tech Tourney, which was a competition to determine the best high school basketball team in New England.

The Garden was also much more than a sports arena; Elvis Presley, the Beatles, the Grateful Dead, and the Rolling Stones performed there, as did almost every pop act of the 1960s, 1970s, and 1980s. It hosted ice skating shows, the Ringling Brothers and Barnum and Bailey Circus, the Harlem Globetrotters, roller derbies, rodeos, bird shows, horse shows, even indoor ski jumping. The Garden also hosted political rallies for Franklin D. Roosevelt, Harry Truman, and Winston Churchill. John F. Kennedy, on the eve of his election as president, spoke to a standing-room-only crowd.

Lacking air-conditioning, the Garden closed every July and August. When the Bruins and Celtics extended their seasons, the lack of climate control created problems; the temperature inside the arena soared to 100 degrees during the 1984 NBA finals. During the 1988 Stanley Cup finals, the fog rising from the ice was so thick that the game had to be stopped. Players then skated around to break up the fog.

The old Boston Garden closed on September 29, 1995, and was demolished two years later. Today, the Garden's 67-year storied existence survives in memory only—the championship banners of the Bruins and Celtics hanging from the rafters, Red Auerbach lighting up the victory cigars after the Celtic wins. But the Garden's parquet floor survives as part of the new Fleet Center, which stands less than a foot away from the site of the old Boston Garden.

Faye Bowers, "Last Hurrah for the Storied Boston Garden," *Christian Science Monitor*, May 5, 1995; Bill Bradley, "Always a Lively Place, Dead Spots and All," *New York Times*, April 16, 1995; Jack Cavanaugh, "The Last Days of a Garden Where Memories Grew," *New York Times*, April 16, 1995; Kevin Paul Dupont, "A Rollicking Ride at the Station: Boston Garden Special," *Boston Globe*, April 30, 1995.

Harvey Frommer

Boston Marathon   On Patriot's Day, April 19, 1897, 15 men ran the first Boston Athletic Association (BAA) Marathon of 24.5 miles. In 1996, steeped in prestige and tradition as the oldest annual marathon and the largest single-day sporting event in New England, the BAA celebration of the 100th running of the Boston Marathon included 38,708 official entrants from 84 countries.

The Boston Marathon began as the brainchild of the patrician BAA, the original organizers and designers of the long-distance course. For 10 years before the running of the first Boston Marathon, the BAA, whose members descended from monied Yankee trader families, had supported physical fitness and athletics through its exclusive Back Bay clubhouse. Six BAA members brought home gold medals from the first modern Olympic games held in Athens, Greece, in 1896. Close in configuration to the Athens route, the present 26.2-mile course passes through the eight Massachusetts cities and towns of Hopkinton, Ashland, Framingham, Natick, Wellesley, Newton, Brookline, and Boston.

Ten of the 15 starters finished the first Boston Marathon; the winner was John J. McDermott of New York, who finished the course in 2:55:10. Clarence DeMar of Melrose, Mass., had by 1930 won seven Boston Marathons, including three straight wins in 1922, 1923, and 1924. The 1928 marathon marked the debut of Boston favorite John A. Kelley, who twice won the marathon—in 1935 and 1945—and finished in the top five 15 times; Kelley holds the record for starting 61 Boston Marathons and finishing 58. In 1992, at the age of 84, Kelley ran his last Boston Marathon; he was the official Grand Marshall of the event through 2004, the year he died. The grueling Heartbreak Hill in Newton was named with Kelley in mind, and the base of it is marked by a statue erected in his honor.

Although the women's division of the Boston Marathon did not become official until 1972, a few determined women during the 1960s would not be denied a place in the marathon or in history. Roberta Gibb, in 1966, was the first woman to cross the Boston Marathon finish line, placing 126th overall in 3:21:40, and was also the unofficial women's winner in 1967 and 1968. In 1967 Katharine Switzer, registered as K. V. Switzer on her race application, was the first official female entrant. BAA coach and trainer Jock Semple and BAA president Will Cloney tried to physically remove Switzer's official entry number 261 from her jersey when they discovered the ruse during the race. Associated Press photographs of Semple pursuing Switzer and being pushed away by her boyfriend ran worldwide. Notable female runners such as Sara Mae Berman, who finished first in 1969, 1970, and 1971; Nina Kuscsik, who in 1972 was the first to "officially" win the women's division in 3:10:26; and Jacqueline Hansen, who won the following year in 3:05:59, together with Switzer, were in the forefront of the movement to bring a women's marathon to the 1984 Olympics.

Bill Rodgers, another Massachusetts resident, local favorite, and marathon legend, won his first of four Boston Marathons in 1975, and Maine's Joan Benoit Samuelson won her second Boston Marathon in 1983; her time of 2:22:43 was a course, national, and world record. One of the marathon's most infamous episodes was the crowning of Rosie Ruiz as the women's winner in 1980. Ruiz, wearing number W50, ran onto the race course from Kenmore Square with the men and was the first woman across the finish line. No official checkpoint had recorded the passage of W50, however, and the characteristic pattern of sweat on her clothing and the distinctive tautness of leg muscles after a long run were missing. BAA officials investigated the incident and disqualified her as the women's winner.

In 1970 Boston became the first major marathon to hold a wheelchair competition and in 1984 wheelchair entries became an official BAA division. Most notably, Jean Driscoll of Illinois won seven successive wheelchair races between 1990 and 1997, tying Clarence DeMar's record of seven titles. Also in the 1970s, the BAA imposed a standard qualifying time to limit the size of the running field and to attract the most prestigious runners. Today, proof of qualification on a certified course in another sanctioned USA Track and Field or foreign equivalent is necessary to enter the Boston Marathon.

From the mid-1930s to the late 1970s, the Boston Marathon was supported by benefactors such as the Prudential Life Insurance Company. In order to continue as a world-recognized race, the marathon became a fully professional event in the 1980s. Sponsorship in 1986 by the John Hancock Financial Services attracted elite runners from all over the world; runners from Africa came to run the Boston Marathon for the first time in 1988. Kenyan Ibrahim Hussein won the 1988 race, and Kenyan runners have won all but three of the races since then. In 2004 both the men's (Timothy Cherigat) and women's (Catherine Ndereba) champions were Kenyan. The historical Boston Marathon, one of the most high-profile athletic events in the world, continues to signify the pursuit of athletic perfection and personal bests for those who seek to gain entry.

Boston Athletic Association, *The Official Map of the Boston Marathon* (1997); Tom Derderian, *The Boston Marathon: The History of the World's Premier Running Event* (1994); Hal Higdon, *Boston: A Century of Running* (1995).

Donna Jean Zane

Boston Red Sox World Series champions. It took 86 years, but in 2004 the Boston Red Sox finally were able to claim the title again, for the first time since 1918. That long drought came to define the team, much of its history being synonymous with a deep sense of pessimism. The Red Sox ruled baseball in the early 1900s and personified defeat for the rest of the century. They won the first World Series, in 1903, and their fifth title in 1918. But in 1919 they sold Babe Ruth, who went on to become the greatest player in the history of the game, to their nemesis, the New York Yankees. The worst blunder in sports history became central to the mythology of baseball, creating the sport's greatest dynasty in the Yankees and consigning the Red Sox to a series of tumbles, broken promises, and near misses. All their lives New Englanders had to watch as the Yankees won title after title, 26 in all, while their beloved Sox endured defeat and what came to be called the Curse of the Bambino.

For most of the 20th century, the Sox were linked in baseball minds with the Chicago Cubs, baseball's other perennial loser playing in a quaint old ballpark. But the Cubs were usually good-natured also-rans, shuffling off to another sixth-place finish. Red Sox history was a recurring dream of glory that always crashed in flames at the last possible moment. Four times since the sale of Ruth—in 1946, 1967, 1975, and 1986—the Sox made it to the World Series. Each time, they lost in the seventh game, twice in unbearable fashion. There have been three one-game playoffs in American League history; the Sox have been in two of them, in 1948 and 1978, and suffered close, crushing losses in both.

The Red Sox were also on the brink of the pennant several times, only to fold in the end. In 1949 they finished the season with two games in New York, needing to win only one to clinch the pennant. The Yankees beat them in both. In 1972 the Sox lost the title at the end of the season on a base-running mistake. In 1974 they blew a seven-and-a-half game lead in the season's final month. In 1978 the Sox led the Yankees by 14 games on July 20 and then staggered through one of the game's most spectacular collapses before losing a one-game playoff when the Yankees' light-hitting shortstop, Bucky Dent, popped a three-run homer to shallow left to seal their fate. His name is still reviled throughout New England. The Sox lost the 1986 World Series against the New York Mets in horrifying fashion, after being one strike away from the championship in the sixth game before they imploded in a series of miscues culminating in an easy grounder that dribbled through Bill Buckner's legs—the most infamous error in World Series history—giving the Mets an impossible victory. Over the next decade, the Sox became the only major league team ever to lose 13 consecutive postseason games. In 2003 the Yankees left another indelible stain on the psyche of New England when, five outs away from victory in the seventh game of the American League championship series, Sox manager Grady Little stuck with his obviously tiring ace pitcher, Pedro Martinez, and Boston fans watched in agony once again as New York methodically rallied from a three-run deficit to claim yet another pennant.

In the dark shadow of this dismal defeat, team management wasted little time in firing Little and pursuing more pitchers, landing star closer Keith Foulke and another ace, Curt Schilling, now paired with Martinez, to go with their explosive offense. The result was victory at last in 2004, ringing as loudly in Sox history as the taunt of 1918 had signaled its heartbreak.

Through mid-season, the team of stars was slowly sinking into the familiar mire of another second-place finish when general manager Theo Epstein engineered an audacious move, trading away the team's icon, shortstop Nomar Garciaparra, to improve its defense and speed. Garciaparra's departure immediately sparked the players, and the Sox became baseball's hottest team, combining relentless hitting with clutch defense and superb pitching. They entered the 2004 playoffs in top form, swept the Anaheim Angels in the first round, and set the stage for a drama that would captivate the nation.

In the championship series, the Yankees quickly took a disturbing 3–0 lead in games. But the Sox pulled out a dramatic victory in the 12th inning of game four, and then a second win in the 14th inning the next night, on the strength of extraordinary pitching and slugger David Ortiz's clutch hitting. Then Schilling, in a performance that reached for the mythological, pitched through the pain of an injured and bleeding ankle to tie the series. When the Sox routed New York in the deciding game and players tumbled in celebration across the infield of Yankee Stadium, all of Red Sox Nation drank deeply from the glass of redemption. It was the greatest comeback in the history of sports, and fittingly it happened against the Yankees, finally breaking the tradition of suffering that had shaped the memories of Sox fans for generations. Boston then hammered the point home with a crushing sweep of the powerful St. Louis Cardinals in the World Series, and the effect on New England was surreal.

The team was formally established in 1901 as a charter member of the American League and went through a handful of nicknames, including the Americans, the Pilgrims, and the Puritans, before settling on the Red Sox in 1907. They won five of the first 15 World Series—in 1903, the first ever, and again in 1912, 1915, 1916, and 1918—with a team that included some of the giants of the game: Tris

Speaker, "Smoky" Joe Wood, Cy Young, and of course Babe Ruth. Ruth not only became baseball's greatest hitter, but while playing for the Red Sox he was one of his era's best pitchers as well. But in 1919 owner Harry Frazee, a New York theater producer, began selling off one player after another, including Ruth, to finance a series of Broadway plays. After he made the deal for Ruth, Frazee said of the Yankees, "I do not mind saying I think they are taking a gamble."

In the 1920s, furnished with Ruth and other former Red Sox stars, the Yankees reenergized and modernized the game, becoming the dominant sports team of the century. The Red Sox, conversely, slumped for years, finishing last in the league six years in a row and nine years out of 11 through 1932, when they lost 111 games and ended up 64 games out of first. They finally emerged in the mid-1930s under new owner Tom Yawkey, whose free spending attracted a solid group of stars, including Jimmie Foxx, Joe Cronin, and Ted Williams, a brilliant hitter who characterized the potential and the pain of the Red Sox for 23 years. Williams's relations with the press and fans were often stormy, but he remained the team's best player and a wonderfully gifted batter—still the last man to hit better than .400 for a season, in 1941.

Williams's Sox were among the game's best teams in the late 1940s—with Bobby Doerr, Dom DiMaggio, Johnny Pesky, and pitchers Mel Parnell and Ellis Kinder—but a series of cruel losses led to a decline that persisted through the 1950s and beyond. From 1951 through 1966 they finished far from first place, including the 1954 season when they were 42 games back; for the seven seasons beginning in 1960, the best they could manage was sixth in the league. Through the 1940s and 1950s, when baseball was integrating and hiring players from the Negro Leagues, the Red Sox held the color line; they were the last team to have an African American on the roster, and they were similarly slow to sign Hispanic players later.

Ted Williams retired in 1960, as the team struggled, but his position in left field was taken over by Carl Yastrzemski, and in 1967 the Sox broke through again when Yaz won the Triple Crown—a baseball feat that has not been achieved since—and led the Sox to the American League pennant. Their Impossible Dream season was capped with a trip to the World Series, but the hope was snuffed out in the end when the St. Louis Cardinals won it in seven games. Yaz was the team's captain through its succession of near misses in the 1970s, with a lineup that included stars like Fred Lynn and Jim Rice. The drama they provided, particularly in the 1975 series against the Cincinnati Reds, perhaps the greatest World Series ever,

spurred a resurgence of interest in baseball. The game-winning home run in the 12th inning of game six by the Vermont native Carlton Fisk remains perhaps the single greatest moment in Red Sox history, but then Cincinnati came back to win the deciding seventh game.

Such a rich history created a unique base of fans who are knowledgeable, skeptical, and intensely loyal. The Boston media, like the fans, have a reputation for being competitive, cynical, intelligent, and sometimes cruel. The Red Sox play on baseball's oldest field, Fenway Park, celebrated for its character and intimacy that make fans feel like participants. John Updike described Fenway as "a lyric little bandbox of a ballpark. Everything is painted green and seems in curiously sharp focus, like the inside of an old-fashioned peeping-type Easter egg. It was built in 1912 and rebuilt in 1934, and offers, as do most Boston artifacts, a compromise between Man's Euclidean determinations and Nature's beguiling irregularities."

There is little parking at Fenway. Its old wooden seats are cramped, and many are behind poles. "Comfort is not the index people use to measure a day at Fenway," writes columnist Mike Barnicle. From the street it looks like a brick warehouse; only inside does it reveal itself as a ballpark. What strikes a fan first upon emerging from the narrow, crowded tunnels beneath Fenway, out into the open expanse of grass and sky, is the looming presence of the Green Monster, the 37-foot-high wall in left field, only 310 feet from home plate—the shortest distance in the big leagues—daring right-handed hitters to try to poke one over. That tantalizing wall—with its promise of easy success running so counter to the New England temperament—proved Boston's downfall for decades. Year after year, the Sox built teams loaded with right-handed power hitters, expected to tattoo the wall, at the expense of the game's other fundamentals—pitching, speed, and defense. In recent years, to increase revenues from the smallest ballpark in the majors, seats have been added on the field, along the right-field grandstands, and most strikingly, atop the Green Monster.

In 2000 the Yawkey family trust announced that it would sell the club after 70 years of ownership, spurring more spending on star players and culminating in a huge contract for slugger Manny Ramirez. In January 2002 a group led by futures investor John Henry and television producer Tom Werner bought the Sox in a record-setting sale, which included New England's cable television sports network, ensuring that the team would remain among the richest in baseball. The Sox payroll became one of the game's highest—behind only the Yankees—and the team drew record numbers of fans, night after night, to sold-out

Fenway. Directed by Epstein, the youngest general manager in the history of baseball, and veteran executive Larry Lucchino, the Sox combined the benefits of an exorbitant payroll with a quantitative, statistics-based approach to player selection and a new emphasis on pitching and defense. The team has joined the trend of signing an increasing number of players from Latin America and Asia, and fans have embraced new stars like Garciaparra, Martinez, and Ortiz as local heroes. When Epstein and Lucchino allowed the legendary Martinez, a former Cy Young award winner, to defect to the Mets following the World Series victory, it was a sign that the team had dropped its tradition of keeping aging stars, just as it had broken the habit of building teams around big, slow sluggers. With a new ownership and management style, the Red Sox began to write a new ending to a suddenly old story.

Bruce Chadwick and David M. Spindel, *The Boston Red Sox: Memories and Mementos of New England's Team* (1992); David Halberstam, "The Fan Divided," *Boston Globe*, October 6, 1986; Halberstam, *The Summer of '49* (1989); Donald Hall, *Fathers Playing Catch with Sons* (1985); Dan Shaughnessy, *At Fenway: Dispatches from Red Sox Nation* (1996); Shaughnessy, *Curse of the Bambino* (1990); Mike Sowell, *One Pitch Away: The Players' Stories of the 1986 League Championships and World Series* (1995); John Updike, "Hub Fans Bid Kid Adieu," in *Assorted Prose* (1965); Updike, "Rapt by the Radio," *Boston Globe*, October 6, 1986.

Louis Mazzari

Boxing Boxing, one of the world's oldest and most violent sports, has been a part of New England culture since the early 19th century. Introduced into New England in the late 1830s as bare-knuckle prizefighting, boxing's popularity expanded throughout the region during the 1840s, particularly in Boston, where scores of recently arrived Irish immigrants had settled. In 1849, Massachusetts passed legislation prohibiting bare-knuckle prizefighting, imposing severe prison sentences and steep fines on combatants, promoters, and other ring attendants. Despite these penalties, Boston permitted bare-knuckle prizefighting exhibitions in theaters, saloons, and show halls. Boston's Irish American males highly esteemed the manly prowess expressed by prizefighting. The sport, moreover, provided Irish American men, many of whom were denied access to legitimate avenues of economic and social opportunities, alternate means to material success. Later, in the 20th century, boxing would afford similar gains to other disadvantaged ethnic and racial groups in New England, including Italians and African Americans.

In 1890 New Orleans legalized boxing under the Queensberry rules, which limited rounds to three minutes each, classified boxers by weight, and required them to wear gloves and fight in an upright position. In the first official world heavyweight championship contested under these rules, James J. Corbett defeated John L. Sullivan of Roxbury, Mass., in 1892. Sullivan, known throughout New England and the world as the "Boston Strong Boy," was the last world heavyweight champion prizefighter of the bare-knuckle era, claiming the title in 1882 by knocking out Paddy Ryan. As the champion, Sullivan promoted the Queensberry rules in his exhibitions against all-comers. In 1920, New York, through passage of the Walker Law, became one of the first states to legalize public prizefighting. In the same year Massachusetts, over the protest of religious leaders, passed similar legislation, and shortly thereafter other New England states enacted laws legalizing boxing. Throughout the 20th century, however, New England state legislatures periodically introduced bills to ban professional boxing because of the corruption, injury, and death associated with the sport. In 1965 Connecticut banned the sport but lifted the ban in 1974.

Since Sullivan, New England has been home to several boxing champions and the site of dozens of championship bouts. The graceful Willie Pep, of Hartford, Conn., known as the "Will o' the Wisp," won his first 63 fights after turning pro in 1940 and held the featherweight title from 1942 to 1948 and again from 1949 to 1950. From 1947 to 1956 Rocky Marciano of Brockton, Mass., won 49 consecutive heavyweight bouts, including 43 knockouts. In 1952 "The Brockton Blockbuster" won the world heavyweight title, knocking out Jersey Joe Walcott in a 13-round bout in Philadelphia. Marciano, who defended the title six times, retired as heavyweight champion in 1956. Paul Pender of Brookline, Mass., who captured the New England middleweight championship in 1959, defeated Sugar Ray Robinson in a 15-round bout in 1960. One of the more recent boxing champions hailing from New England is Marvelous Marvin Hagler, also from Brockton. Hagler, who turned professional after gaining the Amateur Athletic Union middleweight championship in 1973, compiled a record of 61 wins, three losses, and two draws. Hagler won the world middleweight title in 1980 by knocking out Alan Minter in three rounds in London. He then successfully defended his title 12 times over the next six years. In 1987 Sugar Ray Leonard defeated Hagler for the world middleweight title in a controversial 12-round split decision in Las Vegas.

Important championship fights that have taken place in New England include Joe Louis's defeat of Al McCoy for the world heavyweight title at the Boston Garden on December 16, 1940, and Muhammad Ali's defeat of Sonny Liston for the heavyweight title in Lewiston, Maine, on May 25, 1965. Sam Silverman stands as one of the region's top boxing promoters. Club boxing continues in New England, and the Mashantucket Pequot Foxwoods Resort in Mashantucket, Conn., has become a major venue for championship boxing.

Herbert G. Goldman, ed., *The Ring: 1985 Record Book and Boxing Encyclopedia* (1985); Elliot J. Gorn, *The Manly Art: Bare-Knuckle Prize Fighting in America* (1986); Michael T. Isenberg, *John L. Sullivan and His America* (1988); Jeffery T. Sammons, *Beyond the Ring: The Role of Boxing in American Society* (1988).

Adam R. Hornbuckle

Camping New England's varied landscape has long provided camping opportunities for the recreational enthusiast. From seacoast camping along Cape Cod's beaches or Maine's rocky coastline, to backcountry destinations deep in the mountains of New Hampshire, Maine, and Vermont, the Northeast's state parks, national forests, and national parks offer accessible facilities for diverse roadside and backcountry camping.

Like much outdoor recreation, camping has its origins in the transformation of the New England frontier landscape to a settled environment that began to attract visitors interested in escaping growing urban populations. Recreational camping began with the first innkeepers and guides in the White Mountains who accompanied their guests on hunting, and later, hiking trips. Abel and Ethan Crawford, having cut the first footpath to the summit of Mount Washington in 1819, began a steady business of guiding climbers to its peak, often making a necessary stop for the night in a makeshift lean-to of fir boughs and bark. The construction of these three-sided shelters was commonplace among guides and their clients throughout the 19th century.

Popular regional guidebooks such as Theodore Dwight's *Northern Traveler* (1825), Thomas Starr King's *The White Hills* (1859), and Julius Ward's *The White Mountains* (1890) wrote into the New England landscape a romantic tradition of the sublime. With such sentiment to inspire them, campers were drawn to participate in a prescribed vision of the mountains wherein, as Ward suggests, "the sublime and the grand and the awful and the terrible are all wrought up to a fearful intensity at the same moment." In the last quarter of the century, however, the public began to place greater emphasis on experiential recreation; many New Englanders associated hiking and camping with the notion of uplifting physical health promoted by the "muscular Christianity" movement. Late-19th-century guides such as John Gould's *How to Camp Out* (1877) covered every topic from packing provisions to building tents to walking efficiently.

As the popularity of New England's larger resort hotels began to wane and travel became more efficient and more accessible during the first decades of the 20th century, tourists began to escape urban areas for more remote destinations. Many middle- and upper-class visitors to northern New England began to view camping as an extended pursuit and were drawn to steadily growing numbers of established shelters, lean-tos, hunting camps, and mountain huts. Children's summer camps, too, were proliferating in the backwoods of New Hampshire, Vermont, and Maine. Maine alone was home to 230 separate camps by 1920. After World War II, family camping grew in popularity as the automobile made state and national parks in northern New England more accessible and sporting goods companies such as L. L. Bean and Old Town Canoe promoted camping equipment.

With the growth of camping as recreation in the second half of the 20th century, New England's hiking and camping organizations began to identify the growing problem of overuse in more popular camping destinations. The variety of shelters built by these groups, reaching a high during the 1950s and 1960s, were designed and built for concentrated use. Unprecedented numbers of shelters were constructed along the Appalachian Trail throughout New England. These shelters, combined with the prevalence of automobile travel, allowed a new group of working-class campers to reach ever farther into the backcountry. In the years following this boom, however, public opinion began simultaneously to value conservation and to strive for an even more remote wilderness experience. As a result of this ideological transformation, groups such as the Appalachian Mountain Club began to remove many of the shelters, emphasize camper education, and limit the once concentrated use that shelters had promoted.

The forests of northern and western New England continue to be popular destinations for backcountry campers who are often outfitted with the latest equipment and educated about the techniques of making a minimal impact on the wilderness. Camping has become a significant industry in New England and continues to support a variety of niche industries, from equipment manufacturing and sales, to guiding and education, to outdoor clubs. Although the northern states remain the most popular camping destinations, Connecticut, Rhode Island, and Massachusetts also draw about 1 million camping enthusiasts each year. As a result of this increase in recreational use, many industry professionals support an economy of backcountry use that minimizes impact and maximizes comfort through innovations in equipment. As it competes with a variety of outdoor activities in the Northeast's limited backwoods resources, camping is increasingly becoming an act of negotiation between the ideals of recreation and preservation.

Dona Brown, *Inventing New England: Regional Tourism in the 19th Century* (1995); Laura and Guy Waterman, *Forest and Crag: A History of Hiking, Trail Blazing, and Adventure in the Northeast Mountains* (1989).

Pavel Cenkl

Candlepin Bowling

Centuries from now, despite historical New England legacies such as Puritanism and Transcendentalism, the most enduring remnant of New England culture may prove to be candlepin bowling—a game played with small balls and tall, thin pins. The balls and pins, most of which are made locally, are so durable that surely a few shaky pins will remain standing somewhere in northern Maine after whatever disasters may ravage the region.

Candlepin bowling is a distinctly regional pastime, enjoyed in very specific locations: Massachusetts, New Hampshire, Maine, New Brunswick, and Nova Scotia (but not in Rhode Island and Connecticut, where duckpins are preferred; Vermont has a few candlepin lanes). Massachusetts, where the sport was invented, in Worcester, is the heart of this confederation and has the most candlepin alleys of all the states and provinces. It is also the home of Paramount Industries in Medway, purveyors of candlepin accessories.

The sport was invented around 1880 by Justin P. White of Jamaica, Vt., who was experimenting with new types of bowling at the Worcester bowling alley he owned. White developed the "Worcester pin," which was 12 inches tall and 2 inches wide at the center, tapering to 1 inch at each end; later, the taller and wider "Boston pin" was eventually standardized. In 1893 White's protégé, Jack Monsey, standardized the rules; the standard ball size became 4.5 inches, and the playing of deadwood, or knocked-over pins, which previously could be played or removed at the bowler's discretion, was required.

As candlepin bowling gained popularity throughout the region, it attracted women as well as men (the balls are light, weighing roughly 2 lb., 4 oz.) and was one of the few recreational activities that became permissible to play on the Sabbath early in the 20th century. The new game challenged bowlers who were tired of tenpins (candlepin scores are lower, and no one has ever come close to bowling a perfect game).

Lucky Strike Candlepin Bowling Lanes, Dorchester, Mass., 1976

During the early century the game was primarily urban, popular around Worcester, Boston, and Portland, Maine. The problem of hiring people who were willing to set pins was solved when, in 1947, attorneys Howard Dowd and Lionel Barrow invented the "Bowl-Mor" automatic pinsetter, which allowed pins to be set up exactly the same way for every frame. In 1949 the "Bowl-Mor" pinsetter was installed at Whalom Park in Lunenburg, Mass. In Newburyport, Mass., Paul Tedford built a 12-lane bowling "center" and roller-skating rink, where in 1953 the Bowl-Mor corporation sponsored the first automatic lanes. Soon, modern establishments with pinsetters were dotting the region's highway landscape.

In 1958 Boston's Channel 5 began its televised bowling shows, and there are few New Englanders of a certain generation who have not watched "Candlepins for Cash" at some point in their lives. The future of candlepin bowling is uncertain because it is unlikely to move west of the Hudson, or for that matter, anywhere. But as long as there are adventurous New Englanders who love the thrill of healthy athletic competition, the candlepins will continue to fall like so many autumn leaves.

Jim Fairhurst, *Candlepin Bowling: The Light Side* (1985); Florence E. Greenleaf, *The Game of Candlepin Bowling* (1981).

Ted Widmer

Canoeing

The canoe is an icon of North American culture and a symbol of human endeavor in harmony with nature. Developed in the Saint Lawrence River valley by native peoples, canoes had long been the primary mode of transportation in eastern Canada and throughout New England long before European exploration. When the French and English arrived, they quickly adopted the natives' useful boat. Whenever Native Americans and Europeans met to trade, talk, or fight, canoes were present, and perhaps no single object did more to mix the two cultures. A pre-Columbian example of the dugout canoe is held at the New Hampshire Historical Society.

By the early 19th century, the natives' bark canoe had become impractical to Americans who needed to transport freight and goods. Canvas sheathing was introduced, and then cedar-strip planking. The canoe's use for transport declined through the 19th century with the introduction of roads, rail, schooners, and then steamships. By the end of the century, however, the public was gripped by a great popular enthusiasm for canoeing. Late in the 1800s, rail and roads gave easier access to the wilderness areas of northern New England. Resort living and cottaging became a lifestyle for the wealthy, and canoeing became a major part of summer leisure living. Enthusiasts who began using canoes for recreation brought about the biggest changes in canoe use, design, and construction. The nation's oldest canoeing group, the American Canoe Association (ACA), was formed in 1898. The Old Town Canoe Company, founded on the Penobscot River in northern Maine, began selling canoes built for recreation in 1898. Many Penobscots from nearby Indian Island worked at the factory during its early years, and some continue to do so today. Competitive racing became popular, along with large-scale organized canoeing. At the turn of the 20th century, though, group canoeing quickly lost its participants to bicycling, and the remaining enthusiasts split into two camps: canoeing for the cottage experience or for the racecourse. The middle ground of multipurpose boats upon which the ACA had been founded was largely abandoned.

After World War II, aluminum became the material of choice in building aircraft, and it was soon adopted for use in canoes. Fiberglass followed, which allowed canoe designers great freedom of shape at a reasonable price. Fiberglass and aluminum types are now the most common recreational canoes. In the past 20 years, the growth of canoeing and kayaking in New England has mirrored its growth around the world, and today, canoeing and kayaking associations exist in all six New England states.

Canoeing has always been viewed as more than simple recreation and has often been imbued with a sense of spiritual or moral purpose. For instance, in recent years the ACA has become involved in efforts to reduce water pollution, and the United States Canoe Association, formed in 1968, promotes "conservation, safety, fitness, good mental health, and participation in family and community life to the fullest extent possible."

The popular image of a wilderness experience with canoe and guide began with Henry David Thoreau's *The Maine Woods* (1864), which included his description of travel by canoe with an Indian guide. The image grew during the late 19th century, including Lucius Lee Hubbard's *Woods and Lakes of Maine: A Trip from Moosehead Lake to New Brunswick in a Birch-Bark Canoe, to which are added some Indian Place-Names and the Meanings* (1884). Sports enthusiasts and tourists could purchase Indian-made birch-bark canoes on Mount Desert Island when it became a fashionable summer destination at the end of the 19th century. Miniature birch-bark canoes have been a staple Native American souvenir item for sale to tourists for more than a century. Henri Vaillaincourt, a notable birch-bark canoe maker, was profiled by John McPhee in *The Survival of the Bark Canoe* (1975).

While Old Town is the most representative of New England's old-line canoe manufacturers, Mad River Canoes might best represent the newer generation of canoe makers. In 1971, Jim Henry, a geophysicist and weekend paddler from New York City, moved to Vermont and built a handmade fiberglass canoe. After winning the Whitewater National Championships, he began reproducing his design for sale. Now, Mad River markets nationwide through such firms as L. L. Bean and Eastern Mountain Sports. Since the 1980s, with canoeing's growing popularity, the industry has experienced significant growth, with many new models and an emphasis on high-tech materials.

Maine is probably the best organized of New England's states in terms of delineating canoe routes and organizing guides and campsites. The most popular trip is the Allagash Lake route from Northeast Carry or Chesuncook Dam and return after 90 miles of tumbling water, heavy timber, portages, and trout fishing. The East Branch of the Penobscot River, racing for 118 miles, takes the canoeist through some typical Maine wilderness experiences. The Grand Lake–Machias River trip, 75 miles from Princeton to Whitneyville, includes travel through excellent fishing waters. The longest and most difficult route is the 201-mile trip on the Saint John River from Northeast Carry to Fort Kent.

Canoeing is available throughout the region, though, mostly on such amiable waters as the Connecticut River. This "historic, venerable, and austere" river, writes naturalist John Malo, "threading from Canada between New Hampshire and Vermont offers the canoeist, in its four hundred miles, an insight into the past and the beauty of the present. The peacefulness enjoyed by our ancestors seems to rub off onto the modern canoeist who plies the picturesque, wide, and meandering river. The river's short stretches of wilderness are broken up by New Hampshire's majestic pine hills, and Vermont's farm lands, apple orchards, and historic churches."

Appalachian Mountain Club, *River Guide* (1991); Marialisa Calta, "Mad River Canoe: Paddling a Trend-Setter into the Mainstream," *Vermont Life* (Spring 1988); John W. Malo, *Complete Guide to Canoeing and Canoe-Camping* (1969); John Summers, "Toward a Material History of Watercraft," *Material History Review* (Fall 1994).

Louis Mazzari

Class and Recreation New England is nationally known for its wealth of recreational activities; consequently, class differences in leisure patterns within the region are often obscured. The relation between social class and leisure in New England is, in fact, influenced by the region's potential as a vacation destination. The popularity of the mountains as winter wonderlands and wooded retreats at the turn of the 20th century, for example, made northern New England symbolic of the natural world to be explored by enterprising visitors. This popularity persists today as tour buses full of "leaf peepers" continue to drive through the countryside each fall to witness nature's splendor. During the 19th century, however, this fascination with the natural world was a luxury of the upper class. It was only as transportation conveniences increased and the industrial era created more leisure time and resources that tourism and travel became possible for the general public. Recreation in New England, therefore, is characterized by the gradual convergence of activities once exclusive to the very rich with those of the general public.

Before the 1900s, the leisure markets of the "wilderness" regions of New England catered primarily to the upper class. The camps of the Adirondacks, summer "cottages" of coastal resorts, and lakeside estates were built for the wealthy families of New York, Boston, Philadelphia, and Pittsburgh and maintained by local craftspeople and service providers. Shelburne Farms, for example, the estate of William Seward and Lila Vanderbilt Webb on the shores of Lake Champlain, included a model farm as well as ornate gardens and stunning views of the Adirondack and Green Mountains for the amusement of its guests. This quest for "back-to-nature" experiences was inspired by Victorian naturalists in England, the fashionable ideas and images of writers and artists such as Ralph Waldo Emerson and John Ruskin, and, later, the public efforts of Theodore Roosevelt to bring national attention to the outdoors.

Carriage Weekend at the Elms, Newport, R.I., 1989

Playing bocce in Boston's North End, 1970s

Even within metropolitan areas, the ideal of pastoral recreation appealed to established elites as a setting for exclusive recreation and social life. New England, for example, can claim to be the home of the nation's first "country club": Brookline's aptly named Country Club, founded in Massachusetts in 1882, was long regarded as one of the most exclusive institutions in matters of race, religion, ethnicity, and income. Exclusion by Anglo-Protestants, however, fostered a pattern in which some barred groups built their own recreational enclaves, such as the affluent Jewish resort community of Bethlehem, N.H.

Despite the exclusive nature of most clubs and resort communities, the rise of the middle class resulted in an increase in public participation in previously stratified activities because of expanded access by rail and steam to rural and coastal resort areas and media popularization of the "sporting life" of the leisure class. The decline in working hours during the 20th century also contributed to this increase. Organized sports played a role, too, as high school and community leagues appropriated popular college sports. Public interest in basketball and football crossed class lines. Overall, however, educational levels and social status remained important in determining patterns of recreation activities and leisure interests. Intercollegiate sports, even when diffused among old and new institutions, retained strong elements of social class pride. At the prestigious Protestant institutions, college sports were invoked as a means of building character and ratifying existing social status. In contrast, a victory over Harvard or Yale by a Catholic college or land-grant institution, for

example, had symbolic importance as a sign of upward social mobility.

In the early 20th century, towns across New England participated in the growing leisure market by developing recreation facilities closer to home. Building programs of the Works Progress Administration during the 1930s and postwar interest in community development resulted in a variety of accessible and affordable recreation sites for the general public. Town beaches, state parks, and "camps" became the playgrounds of the rising middle class, again appropriating some examples set by the very rich but in much more democratic ways: they were more accessible in terms of transportation, they were cheaper, and they were not as isolated.

Middle-class families also began to travel to their own vacation destinations. An interesting example of this phenomenon is the town of Oak Bluffs on the island of Martha's Vineyard. Originally the site of an annual Methodist revival, participating families over the years constructed small vacation homes where they had once pitched tents, and the town grew into a middle-class resort despite the reputation of "the Vineyard" as an exclusive, upper-class destination. Throughout New England, the middle class built vacation cottages, cabins, and camps and joined outing clubs and athletic organizations.

Tourism, however, has remained separate from community-based activities in rural areas of the region. Skiing, for example, has only recently become an activity in which the working class or rural population of northern New England might take part; local residents were much more likely to work at a local ski

resort than to enjoy the slopes. Traditionally more popular activities such as snowmobiling, ice fishing, and community hockey leagues have become thriving leisure markets in themselves as the resources of the working class have increased. The fishing market, for example, now offers specialized equipment, and leisure dollars are often spent on boats and other gear. In addition, national competition for tourism dollars has resulted in competitive marketing of leisure activities in New England to the "public" (especially the young) rather than depending on the affluent tourist. As a result, the class division between "tourist" and "local" has also decreased as local residents have started to participate in "tourism" activities such as skiing or sailing. Recent examples of this can be found in locally based marketing campaigns such as reduced-rate "bash-badges" for ski lift tickets and in community-based recreation facilities such as public golf courses and marinas.

Urban residents, especially those who could not or would not travel, often found entertainment in spectator sports and neighborhood activities. In the early part of the 20th century, neighborhood teams sponsored by local fraternal lodges or factory clubs competed in fierce rivalries across urban boundaries. With the development of the radio in the 1920s and then television, neighborhood rivalries merged into city contests and later regional ones. An interesting sign of regional identity came about in the 1970s when the Boston Patriots professional football team changed its name to the New England Patriots, indicative of the widespread following that transcended city and state boundaries. Similar progressions from community to regional competitions could also be found in youth organizations of Little League baseball, Pee Wee hockey, and youth soccer.

While the differences in recreation patterns within urban areas tend to follow class lines, researchers in leisure studies increasingly view these patterns of certain groups through the lenses of ethnicity, race, and gender. Although both white and black members of middle-class communities, for example, are likely to share leisure interests, the recreation patterns of low-income communities often diverge along racial and ethnic lines. Overall, low-income neighborhoods tend to have more locally based activities centered on opportunities found in the streets, local parks, and playgrounds than their suburban and upper-class counterparts. For example, in urban Rhode Island, the popularity of bocce, an Italian game similar to lawn bowling, reflects the strong presence of southern European immigrants in the state, while horseshoes or bowling might be more popular in other working-class areas.

As the economy has shifted in New England away from industry to service- and knowledge-based enterprises, middle- and upper-class patterns of recreation have also shifted. In a service economy, the very rich are a global elite rather than the sons and daughters of a particular regional aristocracy, such as the so-called Boston Brahmins. Members of the global elite are more likely to be heli-skiing in the Bugaboos than standing in line at the ski lifts in Stowe, Vt., or hiking in Patagonia than climbing Mount Washington. In many ways the overlap of upper- and middle-class leisure activities in New England has resulted in a desire to marry work and recreation, what Robert Frost once described as combining one's vocation and avocation. In other words, it is now possible, for some, to live in the winter wonderlands of northern New England or the ocean playgrounds of the coastal resorts and telecommute to work in the city or run small businesses with international clients.

While the recreational activities of the middle and upper classes have increasingly converged, this movement is not complete. For example, yachting is still the province of the rich. Tennis, one of the identifying sports of the wealthy and prominent, particularly in Newport, R.I., is dominated even today by those who can afford the expensive tennis camps, lessons, equipment, and court time. The middle class does, however, engage in less expensive versions of what used to be exclusively upper-class pastimes. As the effects of the globalization of the world's economy and the deindustrialization of North America become well understood, we may find the social stratification of recreation patterns increasing. In many ways, it was the industrial era that made the convergence of affluent and popular recreation activities possible. With the decline of that industrial base, resources to support those activities may be hard to sustain. Overall, economic changes in New England's social structure may produce increasing stratification between those who have the resources to access the region's "playgrounds" and those who do not.

E. Digby Baltzell, *The Protestant Establishment: Aristocracy and Caste in America* (1964); Dona Brown, *Inventing New England: Regional Tourism in the 19th Century* (1995); Foster Rhea Dulles, *America Learns to Play: A History of Popular Recreation* (1940); Christopher Lasch, "The Moral and Intellectual Rehabilitation of the Ruling Class," in *The World of Nations: Reflections on American History, Politics, and Culture* (1973); Dean MacCannell, *The Tourist: A New Theory of the Leisure Class* (1976); Alan B. Newman, ed., *New England Reflections: 1882–1907* (1981); Kimberly J. Shinew, Myron R. Floyd, and Francis A. McGuire, "Class Popularization and Leisure Activity Preferences of African Americans: Intragroup Compar-

isons," *Journal of Leisure Research* 28 (1996); *The WPA Guide to Massachusetts: The Federal Writers' Project Guide to 1930s Massachusetts* (1983 [1937]).

Jane McEldowney Jensen

College Sports Before 1850, intercollegiate sports were marginal in New England's collegiate life. If there was a need for physical activity in the student regimen, college presidents and deans thought manual labor in the form of farming or clearing boulders from college lands was both economical and expedient. Students were unconvinced by this logic, however, and devised their own elaborate (and often brutal) intramural contests known as "class rushes"—usually a combination of ritualized initiation and hazing, pitting freshmen against sophomores. Despite college officials' attempts to curb these activities, they persisted and eventually became organized events in which a team representing one institution competed against its counterpart from another. But from 1850 to about 1920, colleges and universities in New England were both pioneering and powerful in their contribution to intercollegiate athletics in the United States. After 1920 their innovations and examples continued to be emulated elsewhere.

The outstanding feature of the New England contribution to college sports in the late 19th and early 20th centuries was its pervasiveness and diversity across institutions. Although the oldest and largest institutions—Harvard and Yale—justifiably gained most attention in newspaper coverage, numerous other campuses made significant contributions. In 1891 James Naismith developed basketball at the Young Men's Christian Association (YMCA) Training School in Springfield, Mass., later known as Springfield College. Amherst College initiated both varsity baseball and the incorporation of calisthenics and physical fitness into the collegiate curriculum. By 1900 Wellesley College had acquired renown for having developed a distinctive approach to women's athletics in such sports as crew and basketball. Examples of New England's innovations in U.S. college sports include the following:

- First intercollegiate crew regatta (Harvard versus Yale), 1852
- First college baseball game (Williams versus Amherst), 1859
- First intercollegiate track and field association (Intercollegiate Association of Amateur Athletes of America, IC 4-A), 1875
- First intercollegiate tennis championship (Trinity College, Hartford), 1883
- Creation of and first play of modern basketball, 1891 (Naismith in Springfield)

- Women's basketball, a modified version of men's, introduced, Smith College, 1892
- First intercollegiate ice hockey game (Harvard versus Brown), 1895
- First intercollegiate gymnastics competition, 1899

Not only were the varsity teams from New England colleges innovative, they were successful and prominent. Yale dominated intercollegiate football and also came to be known as the "cradle of coaches" as it spread the Yale football gospel of well-organized training and strategy across the nation. By 1910 Harvard adopted Yale's system and asserted itself as a national champion in football and numerous other sports. Harvard also set the pace in terms of spectator sports facilities with construction in 1903 of Soldiers Field—considered the finest, largest example of reinforced concrete architecture of the period. This elite competition for architectural and spectator expansion continued when the Yale Bowl opened in 1914 with a grand design and seating capacity of more than 70,000.

New England colleges also played a crucial role in the evolution of administration and control of college sports. Harvard's hiring of Bill Reid in 1905 represented a major escalation of professionalizing college coaches, including paying them a high salary—a practice soon emulated throughout the nation. At Yale, Walter Camp's long tenure as athletics director perfected the financial and political control of an entire athletics program that had little accountability to students, faculty, or academic administration. It was an organizational scheme that tended to give disproportionate and enduring support to a select few spectator sports—in particular, football—with relatively few resources dedicated to the numerous other varsity squads. In fact, athletic associations run by alumni became the wedge by which alumni gained overall control of universities that had been governed mostly by the faculty.

Between World War I and World War II, New England's dominance of college sports changed. The June 1937 issue of *Life* magazine devoted to higher education included a feature article titled "Sports Records Move West." The emergence of top-caliber intercollegiate teams in the Midwest and on the Pacific Coast "left Eastern collegians clinging to a steadily dwindling share of athletic supremacy." A good illustration of this parity across regions after World War II took place in 1948 when the National Collegiate Athletic Association (NCAA) sponsored the first College World Series, during which the University of California, Berkeley, defeated the Yale squad for the national championship.

But if New England's historic domination

over college athletics had waned, it hardly meant a loss of excellence in or commitment to sports by the region's colleges. Athletes and teams continued to be a significant presence in national-level competition in all sports. One finds over the past half century representation and achievement by many New England colleges—whether it be the powerful swimmers from Yale, particularly during the 1940s and 1950s, the 1980s NCAA men's hockey championship squads from Harvard or Boston University, or the men's and women's basketball teams at the University of Connecticut, which in 2004 became the first school to both win NCAA championships in the same year. Other illustrations include Doug Flutie's "Hail Mary" pass, which won the Orange Bowl for Boston College in 1984, and the University of Massachusetts's football team victory in the NCAA Division I-AA football championship in 1999. Whatever advantages college baseball teams from the Sun Belt gained from mild climates made little difference to the University of Maine, whose teams were perennial finalists in the NCAA College World Series. Once again, a salient characteristic of New England college sports is that success is distributed among a range of institutions—including, for example, NCAA Division III championship teams in cross-country from Brandeis University, the success of Providence College's basketball team in qualifying for the NCAA's Final Four, and, on an individual level, Bowdoin's Joan Benoit, who gained fame in women's distance running as an Olympic champion in 1984 and a winner of the Boston Marathon—even though her varsity letter was awarded for field hockey.

The New England commitment to collegiate sports has remained strong. In the early 1970s, *Sports Illustrated* saluted the Massachusetts Institute of Technology's comprehensive intercollegiate athletics program in an article that gave well-deserved praise for the most number of varsity sports offered by any college in the nation. By 1996 Harvard would claim the honor of offering the most varsity sports.

College sports often became a symbolic litmus test of regional and ethnic pride and assimilation. For example, the Jesuit Boston College gained national visibility and became a rallying point for local Catholic pride in 1940 with its undefeated football team, including a victory in the Sugar Bowl. Four decades later, Boston College football thrilled the region with championship seasons, a Heisman Trophy winner, and a victory over Notre Dame. In the governance and administration of college sports, a good indicator of regional contribution was the creation of the postwar Yankee Conference, whose members included the state universities of the six New England states.

The New England collegiate legacy in race relations as part of athletics is distinctive yet limited. On one hand, some African American student-athletes were included relatively early in the late 19th and early 20th centuries. At the highest levels of athletic fame, this included the achievements of Fritz Pollard of Brown University, who was an All-American in football in 1916 and the first African American to play in the Rose Bowl. William H. Lewis, who played football for Harvard in 1892 and 1893, served as Harvard's assistant football coach in 1902 and 1903. Later into the 20th century, Levi Jackson was the first African American captain of the Yale football team in 1949. On the other hand, much of this racial integration was marginal, and hence exceptional, well after World War II; so although New England avoided the blatant racial segregation associated with college sports contests in the South, substantial desegregation remained an unfulfilled goal by the start of the 21st century.

During the 1996–97 academic year, Williams College continued the pioneering tradition of New England college sports: it was the first college in the nation to have a female varsity wrestler in intercollegiate competition. But women had been becoming more and more involved in athletic competition through the 1970s and 1980s. The inclusion of women as bona fide participants in varsity athletes invigorated the national championship presence of New England institutions—as indicated by the five NCAA championships by the University of Connecticut's women's basketball team in 1995, 2000, 2002, 2003, and 2004. This record extended to other sports, such as in crew by Brown, in hockey by Northeastern and Brown, and in skiing by the Universities of Vermont and New Hampshire, Dartmouth, and Middlebury College. In a variety of sports—such as soccer, field hockey, lacrosse, and track and field—women athletes from New England colleges were repeatedly conspicuous in national competition and championships.

The popularity and prevalence of intercollegiate athletics in New England institutions of all sizes created by the year 2000 a paradox of success: New England colleges, for example, had come to dominate the NCAA's Division III (small college) national championship competition in so many sports that faculty at such academically strong institutions as Amherst and Williams expressed concerns about student-athletes being absent from classes. Coaches and athletic directors at Harvard contended that recruiting student-athletes to the Ivy League was more demanding than, for instance, at the Big Ten and Pacific Ten conferences because the Ivy League imposed the multiple burden of competing for students who were excellent in academics and athletics—and in a conference that prohibited athletic scholarships.

New England's colleges continue to be integrally involved in pioneering the expansion and diversification of college sports—in the courtroom as well as on campus playing fields. In 1997 the Supreme Court upheld lower court rulings requiring Brown University to comply with Title IX guidelines. This decision gave new, rigorous interpretation of guidelines for compliance with the 1972 Title IX legislation that provided for equal opportunities for women and girls in school sports. Its implications are far-reaching and now prompt academic leaders and athletic directors to review the intercollegiate athletic enterprise to assure that women are acknowledged, supported, and funded as athletes.

Joe Bertagna, *Crimson in Triumph: A Pictorial History of Harvard Athletics, 1852–1985* (1986); Elliot Gorn and Warren Goldstein, *A Brief History of American Sports* (1993); Craig Lambert, "Superstars and Sponsors: The Professionalization of Ivy League Sports," *Harvard Magazine* 100, no. 1 (1997); Douglas Looney, "Pure and Simple: In the New England Small College Athletic Conference, Players Compete for Love of Sport," *Sports Illustrated* (October 31, 1994); Frederick Rudolph, "The Rise of Football," in *The American College and University: A History* (1962); Ronald A. Smith, *Sports and Freedom: The Rise of Big-Time College Athletics* (1988); Murray Sperber, *Onward to Victory: The Crises That Shaped College Sports* (1999); John R. Thelin, *Games Colleges Play: Scandal and Reform in Intercollegiate Athletics* (1994).

John R. Thelin

Contra Dance Contra dancing is a social dance form that has been part of New England's culture since the 17th century. In contemporary usage, the term refers both to the dance form and to the dance event that features contra dancing. Contra dances are part of a larger genre of figure dances called country dance—a generic term for group mixed-sex dances in line, square, or circle formation. Contras fall into the first category: they are danced in two opposing lines in which the dancers face each other. Each grouping of two lines on the dance floor is called a set. As in other types of country dance, dancers interact both with their partners and with other members of their set. Individual dances consist of several figures combined from a stock vocabulary, such as "circle four," "star right," and "balance and swing." During each contra, partners perform the same sequence of figures over and over, but each time with new neighbors. Contras are called "progressive" because traditionally, couples move or progress one place up or down the contra line during each repetition of the dance sequence. In other contras, partners

Contra dancing with Dudley Laufman, fiddler and caller, New Hampshire, 1999

progress directly from the top to the bottom of the set. The steps and figures of the dance are closely wedded to the form and rhythm of the accompanying music. Dances are choreographed to fit into 32 bars of music—the standard length of a fiddle tune.

Extant sources show that country dance originated in England before the 16th century. Indeed, the first anthology of country dances with accompanying tunes was published by John Playford, a London music publisher, in 1651. Exported to America, as well as France, Germany, Holland, and Spain, country dance later became the most popular social dance genre of the 18th century. By the mid-18th century the terms "country dance" and "progressive longways formation" or "longways for as many as will" became synonymous, as the circle and square formations dropped out of fashion. By the 1780s Americans began to call these line dances contras, although both terms, country and contra, were used throughout the 19th century.

In New England, dances took place regularly at balls, assemblies, private parties, and taverns. Because dancing was regarded as an essential social skill, itinerant dancing masters set up schools in which to teach deportment, the latest steps, and new dances. In 1788, John Griffiths, a dancing master who taught throughout New England during the 1780s and 1790s, was the first to publish a collection of country dances in America.

From the mid- to late-19th century in New England, French country dances in square formation known as quadrilles, and couple dances, such as the waltz and polka, became the more fashionable social dances of the period. Contras were considered old-fashioned, but extant tune books, dance manuals, and dance cards indicate that they did continue to be danced as part of public dance events and for home entertainment. Since many such events in New England consisted of a variety of dance types, one or two contras were often included in the evening's entertainment. A static core repertory emerged at this time—each dance associated with a tune by the same name.

This core repertory and the role of the contra dance as a traditional or novelty item continued through several revivals of square dance during the 20th century. It was not until the pioneering work of Ralph Page (1903–85), a square dance caller from New Hampshire, that contras were popularized as a New England dance form throughout the United States, Europe, and Japan. Page, who published a small dance magazine called *Northern Junket*, also had considerable influence on the next generation of New England callers who further revitalized the tradition. The Ralph Page collection—papers, publications, and recordings—is housed in at the University of New Hampshire's special collections.

By the late 1960s, contra dance emerged as a genre in its own right, separate from the square dance world. It was at this time that dance events began to be called contra dances rather than square dances. Dudley Laufman, a dance caller and musician originally from Massachusetts and now a longtime resident of New Hampshire, was a key individual at the center of this resurgence, which dovetailed with the folk music revival. He acted as a catalyst for what is now a nationwide grassroots network of dancers, callers, and musicians. During the past 30 years, the tradition has been transformed by the inclusion of thousands of new dances and new tunes, and by changes in performance style. Participants in the contra dance world are also part of a larger network that includes many other traditional dance and music genres.

Public dances take place regularly at specified venues, including libraries, town halls, grange halls, and churches throughout New England. Each dance event features a caller and a live band consisting of at least two players, with fiddle and piano as the core instruments. Dances are open to the public at a nominal fee. All contra dances are called so that both newcomers and experienced dancers can be guided through the figures. Unlike square dance callers, however, the contra caller stops calling when he or she feels that the dancers have mastered the dance sequence. The dancers perform most of the repetitions without prompting, guided solely by the form and rhythm of the music.

The current contra dance music repertoire is a blend of dance tune traditions. Many tunes are of Irish, Scottish, English, French Canadian, and Cape Breton origin, including some that date back to 18th-century sources. Tunes such as "Hull's Victory," "Money Musk," and "Patronella" became New England standards by the end of the 19th century and are still associated with contra dances of the same names. Bands often use a mix of old and new tunes, but most conform to the standard fiddle tune structure of 32 bars of music. New England contra dance has inspired dancers across the country and seems on its way to becoming a national form.

Choose Your Partners! Contra Dance and Square Dance Music of New Hampshire [sound recording] (Smithsonian Folkways, 1999); Dorothea Hast, "Performance, Transformation, and Community: Contra Dance in New England," *Dance Research Journal* 25, no. 1 (1993); Beth Tolman and Ralph Page, *The Country Dance Book* (1980); Kate Van Winkle Keller and Ralph Sweet, *A Choice Selection of American Country Dances of the Revolutionary Era 1775–1795* (1975).

Dorothea Hast

Cousy, Bob (Robert Joseph) (1928–)

Basketball player, coach, and broadcaster. Robert Joseph "Bob" Cousy was born on Manhattan's depressed East Side, the only son of recent French immigrants. He did not play basketball until the age of 13, by which time his family had moved to Long Island. Cousy learned fundamentals from a friendly playground manager and honed his skills through endless practice. Cut as a high school freshman because of his small size, Cousy persisted with his practice and gained a spot on the junior varsity team midway through his sophomore year. A failing grade delayed his varsity debut the next year, but 28 points in his first game made headlines. As a senior, Cousy led the city in scoring. He then fulfilled a promise to his grandmother and parents and entered the Catholic college Holy Cross.

With wartime regulations still in effect when Cousy went to college, Cousy played varsity as a freshman at Holy Cross and was an important reserve on the 1947 NCAA tournament championship team. Upset with his coach, Cousy considered transferring to Saint John's University on Long Island. The Saint John's coach sternly advised that he remain at Holy Cross, and Cousy heeded the advice. He enjoyed a successful sophomore year on the court and then flourished as an upperclassman under new coach Lester "Buster" Sheary. Cousy's exciting Holy Cross teams compiled long winning streaks, and he earned All-American honors.

Cousy hoped to play professionally for the Boston Celtics, and his wish came true after convoluted personnel maneuvers ended with Celtics owner Walter Brown pulling the guard's name from a hat. Cousy's scoring and ball-handling wizardry, keen court sense, and competitive drive earned almost instant acclaim. He made the All NBA First Team in 1952 and won this honor each year through 1961. After the arrival of center Bill Russell, Cousy's Celtics won NBA titles in six of his final seven years. His statistics remained remarkably consistent throughout his 13-year career, which ended in 1963. Cousy credited his coach Arnold "Red" Auerbach with giving him freedom to make the most of his talents.

Cousy was inducted into the Basketball Hall of Fame in 1971 and named one of the NBA's 50 greatest players in 1996. Widely recognized for his play, it is less known that Cousy organized the NBA Players Union in 1953. Seeking modest goals such as restrictions on fines, limits on exhibition games, and an arbitration process for disputes, he felt immense satisfaction when the owners recognized the union in 1957.

Cousy successfully coached Boston College (1963–69) and then fared less well as coach of the NBA franchise that moved from Cincinnati to Kansas City–Omaha (1969–74). He reflected on these years in *The Killer Instinct* (1975). Subsequently, Cousy has shared his basketball insights and blunt observations on the state of the game as a Celtics broadcaster. In 2003, the Basketball Hall of Fame again honored Cousy by instituting the "Bob Cousy Collegiate Point Guard Award" to recognize the point guard who contributed the most to his team's success.

Bob Cousy, *Cousy on the Celtic Mystique* (1988); Cousy and Al Hirshberg, *Basketball Is My Life* (1957); Cousy and Ed Linn, *The Last Loud Roar* (1964).

William M. Ferraro

Field Hockey Although field hockey is played in schools, clubs, and national as well as Olympic competitions, the sport is historically (like lacrosse) aligned in New England with the prestige of private education. The modern game of field hockey evolved in 19th-century England and spread throughout the British empire. The game eventually became popular among women active in sport, and the first women's hockey club was organized in England in 1887. It reached the United States in 1901 when Constance Applebee, a British physical education instructor, staged an exhibition game at a Harvard gathering. Physical education programs at the time typically argued for fitness benefits that prepared women for healthy childbearing while carefully differentiating women's programs from the vices of men's sports, such as the excessive violence and corruption that prompted the 1906 creation of the National Collegiate Athletic Association.

Field hockey is typically played outdoors on a rectangular field (100 yards long and 60 yards wide) by two teams of 11 players each. Players use the flat side of a curved stick to hit a small hard ball in the opposing team's goal, as in ice hockey. As an import of the British model of sport and education, field hockey was not exclusively a women's game but was the same game played by men all over the colonial empire. Lacrosse, on the other hand, which became field hockey's spring companion sport for women in the United States, had already been modified in Britain to be played almost exclusively by women, whereas in the United States the game historically attracted men. Because private schools in New England were segregated by sex, field hockey took on an appropriateness to girls and women in its exclusivity. Contradictions in appeal and appropriateness were apparent in rules of sport: field hockey, for example, demanded that women run the length of the field repeatedly, while the same athletes playing basketball were restricted to fractions of the court for the sake of their health. The sport nevertheless became a stronghold for 20th-century women athletes, coaches, and administrators. Field hockey retains something of its Victorian origins, however, in the persistence of skirts as the sport's uniform.

In 1993 the United States Field Hockey Association, which had overseen the women's sport since 1922, became the single governing body of men and women's field hockey, merging with the Field Hockey Association of America, which governed the men's sport since 1933. With the merger and federal legislation to ensure equal opportunities in education for women in sports (Title IX, 1972), field hockey lost its exclusiveness to women. High school programs in Massachusetts were chal-

lenged in the 1990s by male students who wanted to play on girls' teams, in the same manner that girls have challenged single-sex team restrictions from Little League to college wrestling. Despite these changes, field hockey remains overwhelmingly a women's sport and now competes in the fall with soccer programs expanded to accommodate women. Collegiate field hockey in the United States continues to be played mainly in the Northeast, and New England colleges consistently turn out All-American Team collegiate field hockey players.

Anne Lee Delano, *Field Hockey* (1966); Helen T. Mackey, *Field Hockey: An International Team Sport* (1963); Harriet Stewart, ed., *Selected Field Hockey and Lacrosse Articles* (1971).

Roseanne V. Camacho

Fitness Fitness of the body became important to New Englanders by the 1850s. Like the temperance movement, abolitionism, and insane-asylum reform, efforts to improve bodily health were part of a larger impetus to reform and improve American society. Before the Civil War, New England's most important advocate of fitness was Catharine Beecher. Her *Physiology and Calisthenics* (1856) was a standard work of advice and criticism for those inclined to physical regeneration. In it Beecher criticized Americans' fondness for tobacco ("the weed is a rank poison"), alcohol, and spicy, fatty, fried foods; she also offered all sorts of exercises for sedentary adults and schoolchildren.

The fitness movement gained momentum in 1862 with the publication of Dioclesian Lewis's *New Gymnastics for Men, Women, and Children*. Lewis conducted exhibitions and exercise classes throughout New England, spreading the gospel of health as defined by groups such as the Young Men's Christian Association (YMCA), which had been established in 1858. The YMCA—and related religious and fitness organizations—stressed the importance of what reformers called "muscular Christianity."

New England was home to many innovations in physical fitness and training. In 1891 in Springfield, Mass., YMCA director Luther Gulick commissioned James Naismith to devise an indoor game for the winter months; the result was basketball. Harvard educator Dudley Sargent trained generations of physical education instructors, and by the 1920s nearly every school that could afford them had regular classes. Weight lifter George Windship ("The Roxbury Hercules") became famous for his great feats of strength and weight training regimen. Yale football coach Walter Camp headed the Navy's Commission on Training Camp Activities during World War I.

University of New Hampshire students exercising, ca. 1920

Fitness crusades in New England often were tinged with religious and social righteousness. By 1900 fitness was part of the psychological protective armor old New England families used to distinguish themselves from new waves of urban immigrants. This strategy ignored the fact that many immigrant groups—the Germans and central Europeans especially—brought to America long-established social and fitness organizations, such as the *Turnverein* (Turners), dedicated to physical fitness, education, and social activities.

Intimately tied to these activities were the various organized sports that grew in participation and spectator interest after 1880. Collegiate and school football gained favor in New England; many commentators thought its players "better fitted for the stern work of life that assails us all at some time." A great wave of stadium building also occurred after 1900, first in the colleges and then in high schools throughout the region.

Interest in fitness waned during the Depression, World War II, and the immediate postwar era. But by the early 1960s, with the vigorous and seemingly fit John F. Kennedy as president, Cold War fears of Russian aggression, and a widespread conviction that Americans had "gone soft," another fitness revival ensued. Gyms filled again, old YMCAs were replaced or refurbished, and criticism of American children as laggards surfaced in the mass media. The youth of that era—the baby boomers—interpreted the fitness calling differently as they aged, worrying more about their attractiveness than fighting the Communists. The new fitness "boom" is now an integral part of a consumer culture rather than a crusade to save souls or societies.

Harvey Green, *Fit for America: Health, Fitness, Sport, and American Society, 1830–1940* (1986); Donald J. Mrozek, *Sport and American Mentality, 1880–1910*

(1983); James C. Whorton, *Crusaders for Fitness: The History of American Health Reformers* (1982).

Harvey Green

Football Like much else in American culture, football as we know it was created in New England (and the greater Northeast—including New York, New Jersey, and Pennsylvania), whence it spread to other regions. American football was developed and institutionalized on college campuses, chief among them—as in many areas of higher education—Harvard, Princeton, and particularly Yale. Professional football was not organized until the 1920s—mostly in small industrial towns in the Midwest and later in the major metropolitan areas of the North and East—and New England's contribution was minimal.

A simple kind of football had been played since the 17th century in New England as a folk game that had been carried across the Atlantic with the rest of the colonists' cultural heritage. By the 19th century, students at colleges in New England and elsewhere in the Northeast were playing football as part of a student culture generally at odds with the authority of faculty and administrators. Within this local student culture intercollegiate competition was inaugurated on November 6, 1869, by teams representing Princeton and Rutgers playing a version of soccer. After several years of sporadically arranged games among a handful of northeastern colleges, representatives from Harvard, Yale, Princeton, and Columbia met in 1876 to form the Intercollegiate Football Association and adopt a common code of rules. Harvard and Yale prevailed in advocating a rugby-type game.

The transformation of the sport from a form of rugby to American football was led by Walter Camp, who as Yale's representative to the all-important rules committee beginning

in 1877 (and continuing until his death in 1925) proposed the early rule changes that created the distinctive American game of offense and defense. Camp was the game's first great organizer and strategist; the system he inaugurated at Yale became the model for colleges throughout the country (many of them initially with Yale graduates as coaches). Camp was also football's first great publicist. Through his books, his numerous articles in newspapers and popular periodicals, and his selection of All-American teams beginning in 1889, he fed the popular enthusiasm that made football by the 1890s not just the premier intercollegiate sport but also a great popular spectacle.

Harvard, Yale, and Princeton remained the Big Three of intercollegiate football through the 1940s, although their football prowess had not matched their prestige since the 1920s. The Big Three inaugurated the Thanksgiving Day game and the more general Big Game between traditional rivals. Harvard and Yale built the first huge football stadiums—Harvard's in 1903, Yale's in 1914—that came to dominate college campuses around the country. The Big Three also battled off the field in the 1880s and 1890s over players' eligibility; "professionalism," that is, paying players and coaches; and excessive violence. In short, the Big Three taught the rest of the country's colleges not just the rules of the game but also how to break them; not only the game's virtues but also its problems and excesses; not only how to play football but also how to stage it and promote it. They created "big-time" college football. But when Harvard, Yale, and Princeton, along with Cornell, Dartmouth, Brown, Columbia, and Penn officially formed the Ivy League in 1956, they also offered a model for "deemphasized" football that was not adopted elsewhere. The Big Game remains a major social event throughout the Ivy League, but college football's importance in New England is today more local than national.

New England football traditions extend, of course, beyond the Ivy League, when teams attract a following beyond their campuses and alumni. Doug Flutie's famous 48-yard "Hail Mary" pass with no time remaining gave the Boston College Eagles an Orange Bowl victory over the Miami Hurricanes in 1984. Boston College's games against rival Notre Dame attract large audiences. Professional football arrived in New England when William H. "Billy" Sullivan and a group of partners received a franchise for the American Football League. The team was renamed the New England Patriots when they moved to a new stadium in Foxboro, Mass., in 1971. The New England Patriots won the Super Bowl in 2002, 2004, and 2005.

Mark F. Bernstein, *Football: The Ivy League Origins of an American Obsession* (2001); Michael Oriard, *Reading Football: How the Popular Press Created an American Spectacle* (1993); Ronald A. Smith, *Sports and Freedom: The Rise of Big-Time College Athletics* (1988); John Sayle Watterson, *College Football: History, Spectacle, Controversy* (2000).

Michael Oriard

Gardening Tradition, moral inclinations, and the desire to expand knowledge have always characterized New England gardening. Institutions such as the Arnold Arboretum and the Massachusetts Horticultural Society, founded and supported by regional gardeners, attest to New Englanders' passionate commitment to the advancement of horticulture.

Far from being the more recreational pursuit it is today, gardening in colonial New England was a necessary way of life as early colonists wrested a living from the soil. Early gardens reflected Puritan beliefs of austerity and usefulness. Vegetables, herbs, and flowers were utilitarian; only the rose was grown for beauty. Colonists to Plymouth, the first permanent settlement, brought their own seeds from England. They organized the land into house plots where they grew smaller crops, and exchanged their seeds or saved them for the next year. Many of the transported seeds did not take, however, and eventually native corn, pumpkins, and squash saved the colonists from famine. The house garden was the woman's responsibility, and she used its produce to make medicine, freshen the air, brew, bake, and dye cloth.

Puritan garden customs gave way by the end of the 18th century, and people began to garden for pleasure. The typical flower garden, in front of the house under the parlor windows, was enclosed by a fence and divided by a central walk leading from the door to the road. For the housewife with more leisure, this garden, situated along the village street, was less utilitarian than its predecessors; it had more shrubs, a more elaborate design, and greater variety.

After the Revolution, the affluent maintained gardens to display their wealth and good taste, with the English manor garden providing the model. Joseph Breck in Boston was one of many to establish a seed house, and for the first time gardeners could choose from a greater variety of plants, particularly exotics. C. M. Hovey of Cambridge, Mass., carried stocks from China. Andrew Faneuil had the first greenhouse in Boston, and by 1800, these greenhouses were common on the estates of the wealthy.

By the middle of the 1800s, Boston, crowded with urban gardens, saw a rise in commercial nurseries that carried a wide range of stock; the city itself became a center of horticultural experimentation. By 1850 the affluent were using box edgings and gravel walks to create colorful ornamental gardens, or parterres. Lawns, too, became popular, although not as the open stretches we have today. As an open space along a forest, lawns were sprinkled with shrubs and trees.

Bostonians discovered Newport, R.I., during this era, and the great estates that grew up in that area's vicinity included Vaucluse. Samuel Elam purchased the property in 1785 and turned it into a pleasure garden with shaded serpentine walks, a boxwood maze, and marble nymphs. Thomas Hazard increased the property's size by purchasing the farm of Metcalf Bowler, the man who introduced the Rhode Island Greening apple. Like so many gardens, however, this one eventually passed into oblivion.

As gardeners continued to import exotic plants, their gardens became more ornamental, and gardening styles turned once more to form. Italian gardens, replete with statuary, terraces, and topiary, the art of clipping trees, had little relationship to their settings but spread from Cornish, N.H., to Greenwich, Conn. Gardeners on Hollis Hunnewell's estate in Wellesley, Mass., clipped his larch, hemlock, and arborvitae into cones and pyramids. Pinetums, vast numbers of cone-bearing evergreens, were also found on large estates, and landowners collected trees to create private arboretums. Although never completed, an arboretum of only Vermont trees at Shelburne Farms on Lake Champlain contained oak, willow, hemlock, American chestnut, and hickory. Designed by the eminent landscape architect Frederick Law Olmsted, the grounds included many plants native to the American wild. Olmsted was far ahead of his time in his desire to reproduce a region's diversity in a landscape he designed rather than decorate with plants from other areas, or even other countries.

During the Victorian era, not only the great estates but also the average home had its own garden, one appropriate to the plot of land and structure on it. The rise and growth of the suburb turned the garden into a vehicle to enhance the home, and gardening became a favorite hobby of the middle class. As in colonial times, the garden maintained its connection with the suburban home. Immigration was high during this time, and all immigrants to New England had to adapt either to the harsh countryside or to compact urban spaces. Urban immigrants continued to garden by need, not choice; cramming a tremendous variety of vegetables and flowers into small spaces, they created gardens that resembled their European cousins with one exception: no empty spaces. These efforts helped to found the urban gardening movement.

The English garden and the Arts and Crafts movement influenced late-19th-century gardens, generating an interest in old-fashioned flowers and design. The poet Celia

Deadheading roses in a New England variant of the English cottage garden, Nantucket, Mass., 1986

Thaxter's garden on Appledore Island off the southern coast of Maine had no exotic ornamentals but instead clematis, wild cucumber, hollyhocks, sweet peas, hop, and poppies, her favorite flower.

As property in the United States was not automatically inherited by the eldest son, estates and their gardens often passed to new owners after the master's death, so during the 20th century much land was subdivided into residential housing developments. John Perkins Cushing's Bellmont in Watertown, Mass., exemplifies the rise and fall of a tremendous garden as well as a family. Cushing, a prosperous merchant, purchased plants from around the world, and his conservatory and adjacent greenhouses incorporated the latest horticultural techniques. His sons, however, took no interest in their father's pursuits and sold the property when he died. The Hunnewell estate in Wellesley, Mass., is one of the few gardens to have passed from generation to generation.

In the early 20th century, interest grew in native wildflowers, but this movement was put on hold with the many changes after World War II. People no longer relied on gardens for food, and the commuter lifestyle cut down on leisure time. Gardens began to fade from the New England landscape. Heavily fertilized lawns took the place of herbaceous borders or annual beds as people found the ways of their ancestors too expensive and time-consuming. In the 1980s, however, interest in gardening revived, with a renewed emphasis on native plants. Many New England towns offer contests for those who beautify their homes through gardening. Yet the average New England garden still has not recovered its old beauty and use, and it will be a while before flowers and vegetables, and not lawns, become the stars of our landscape again.

To that end, many gardeners are looking to revive the past with antique and heirloom seeds. The first commercial New England nursery was Fenwicks in Saybrook, Conn. Numerous seed companies arose during the 20th century. The Cook's Garden Seed Company in Burlington, Vt., began as an organic market and in 1983 began selling seeds. The company promises to preserve and promote heirloom vegetables and flowers and has signed the Safe Seed Pledge, refusing to support the development of genetically engineered seeds. Other New England seed companies include Johnny's Selected Seeds in Albion and Winslow, Maine, New England Seed Company in Hartford, and Sheperd's Seeds in Torrington, Conn.

Tourists today can visit many historic estates and gardens throughout New England. Harriet Beecher Stowe's garden in the Nook Farm development in Hartford still has

groups of trees with flower beds cut into the lawn. The writer Adelma Simmons owned Caprilands, a 100-acre herb farm in Coventry, Conn. She and her parents bought the land and the 18th-century farmhouse in 1929; Caprilands now has 30 gardens, and its farmhouse serves food made with ingredients grown in the garden. In Rhode Island, Hammersmith Farm, once the summer home of Jacqueline Kennedy, still bears the structures of its creator, Frederick Law Olmsted.

Visitors will also find some fine examples of topiary, a practice that peaked during the Victorian era. The Green Animals Topiary Gardens in Portsmouth, R.I., is the oldest and most northern topiary in the United States. Thomas Brayton purchased the 7 acres in the late 19th century, and his daughter, Alice, made it her permanent home in 1940. She left the estate to the Preservation Society of Newport County. The estate has 80 pieces of topiary, including 21 animals and birds made from California privet and yew, as well as ornamental designs in California privet and English boxwood and numerous geometric figures.

Priscilla Dunhill and Sue Freedman, *Glorious Gardens to Visit* (1989); Walter Prichard Eaton, *Wild Gardens of New England* (1936); Alan Emmet, *So Fine a Prospect: Historic New England Gardens* (1996); Ann Leighton, *American Gardens in the 18th Century* (1976); Leighton, *American Gardens in the 19th Century* (1978); Michael Weishan, *The New Traditional Garden: A Practical Guide to Creating and Restoring Authentic American Gardens for Homes of All Ages* (1999).

Suzanna Nyberg

Harvard-Yale Football Game

Known simply as "The Game," the annual football game between Harvard and Yale is one of the nation's oldest college football rivalries. First played in 1875, The Game brings together two of America's oldest college football teams in a contest that may, during an exceptionally good year for both teams, decide the Ivy League champion, but more often only affords one bragging rights for the following year. Yale leads the series, winning 64 of the 120 contests. Eight games have ended in ties. Because Harvard and Yale played such instrumental roles in the development of American football during the late 19th and early 20th centuries, The Game carries significance not only for New England but also for the nation as a whole.

The first game played between Harvard and Yale on November 13, 1875, is significant for setting the course for the development of American football. For the previous five years, Yale, Harvard, Rutgers, Princeton, Columbia, and other schools disagreed over whether football should be played mostly as a soccer game (in which players kick the ball) or with

Harvard-Yale game at New Haven, Conn., 1995

elements from rugby (in which players can run with the ball). Although Harvard was the principal holdout for the rugby style, it was able to persuade Yale to play according to a modified version of the Harvard rules in the first meeting of the two teams. In a game that resembled rugby more than soccer, Harvard not only defeated Yale 4–0 but also converted its rival permanently to the rugby style of play.

Although Harvard won the first game between the schools, Yale dominated the series until 1907; out of 28 games, Yale won 20, Harvard won four, and four games resulted in scoreless ties.

The driving force behind Yale's success was Walter Camp, who played football as an undergraduate from 1876 to 1880 and as a medical student from 1881 to 1882. After coaching the team in 1878 and 1879 and from 1888 to 1892, Camp served as an adviser to the team until 1910. Most notably, he transformed rugby into American football through several fundamental rule changes. In 1880 Camp introduced the scrimmage, which gave one team undisputed possession of the ball, and replaced the chance possession found in the rugby scrum. In 1882 he proposed the system of downs, in which the offensive team had three possessions to advance the ball 5 yards before relinquishing it to the opposing team. Harvard's contribution to game tactics during the Camp era was the "flying wedge" in 1892. In the formation, players linked arms, forming an angle to protect the ball carrier. Conceived by Lorin Deland, a chess expert, the flying wedge led to serious injuries and the suspension of the game in 1895 and 1896.

From 1908 to 1930, Harvard dominated the series, winning 12 of 21 contests. Of the remaining contests, Yale won six, and three ended in scoreless ties. In 1915 Harvard defeated Yale by the score of 41–0, its largest margin of victory over its rival.

Harvard's three national titles in 1910, 1912, and 1913 were largely owing to Percy Haughton, who coached the team from 1908 to 1916. Harvard's first paid coach, Haughton imitated Camp's organization and emphasized skill and intelligence over brute force, introducing the single wing offense, running pass, and trap play. Defensively, he instituted the roving middle linebacker and the five-man line buffered by linebackers. In a direct challenge to Camp, he pushed through adoption of four downs to make 10 yards before relinquishing the ball to the opposing team, implementation of the forward pass, and limits upon the use of substitutes.

Although today the Harvard-Yale rivalry does not carry the same national significance as it did in the late 19th and early 20th centuries, it has often served as the linchpin in determining the Ivy League champion. Since the formal establishment of the Ivy League in 1956, the outcome of the Harvard-Yale game has had a direct effect on deciding the league champion 20 times. Yale, which has won 23 games since 1956, has garnered six sole Ivy League titles and shared five with teams other than Harvard. Harvard, which has won 25 games, has garnered three league championships and shared four with teams other than Yale. Although the game has ended in a tie only once since 1956, Harvard and Yale have tied twice for the Ivy League championship. The tie, which came in 1968, is one of the rivalry's most memorable games. Harvard scored 16 points in the last 16 seconds to preserve an undefeated 8–0–1 season.

Thomas G. Bergin, *The Game: The Harvard-Yale Football Rivalry, 1875–1983* (1984); Elliot Gorn and Warren Goldstein, *A Brief History of American Sports* (1993); *Harvard Football Media Guide* (2000); Ronald A. Smith, *Sports and Freedom: The Rise of Big-Time College Athletics* (1988); *Yale Football Media Guide* (2000).

Adam R. Hornbuckle

Head of the Charles Regatta

Although no one knew it at the time, a New England institution was born on October 16, 1965. Rowing had long been popular at New England's colleges, preparatory schools, and boat clubs, and the Charles River was the site of many races hosted by Harvard, the Massachusetts Institute of Technology, Boston University, and the Cambridge Boat Club. But on that day, the club held its first "head" race—or race in which rowers compete against the clock rather than against each other. They called it the Globe-Cambridge Boat House

Head of the River Rowing Regatta on the Charles. The 3-mile race has grown in size and popularity over the years and is now known as the Head of the Charles Regatta. With 5,400 competitors from across the United States and 14 countries around the world, the Head of the Charles has become the largest rowing competition in the world, holding the same honor and status for the rowing community that the Boston Marathon holds for runners.

The worldwide prestige of the Head of the Charles was an unexpected surprise for its founders, including Harvard University sculling instructor Ernest Arlett, who had originally proposed the head race. In 1965 the Cambridge Boat Club had to hunt down the 87 boats for those they had persuaded to enter the race. The regatta continued to grow from this inauspicious beginning, and by the 1970s, celebrating race day along the banks of the river had become a favorite autumn event for fraternity crowds. The cost of the race increased with the size of the crowd, and organizers were forced to look for corporate sponsors, an idea that did not sit well with the founders, who had hoped to keep the race from becoming commercial. For the first three

Head of the Charles Regatta, Cambridge, Mass., 1979

years, the *Boston Globe* was the only sponsor, enabling the regatta to stay focused on the sport of rowing. Today, sponsors such as BankBoston, J. Crew, AT&T, and others set up large tents, giving the regatta an added dimension of commercialism and the appearance of a festival.

The regatta has seen dramatic changes in recent years. In 1996 it was canceled for the first time in its history because of a freak hurricane that swept through New England, disappointing both fans and competitors who had traveled from around the world to participate in the race. While rowers are accustomed to competing in cold, wet conditions, winds were so high and the rain so cold that it would have been extremely dangerous for crews to negotiate the course. The storm of 1996 and the rising number of applicants persuaded organizers to extend the regatta to two days instead of one. Holding the event over two days decreased the chances that weather would force a cancellation and allowed up to 80 percent of applicants to enter. This arrangement also improved the safety of the racers by allowing more time between the 19 events. These changes have increased the race's popularity and enabled the Head of the Charles Regatta to remain a leader in the rowing world and an important Boston institution.

Tony Chamberlain, "It's a River Rage," *Boston Globe,* October 17, 1997; Jody Feinberg, "Charging up the Charles," *The Patriot Ledger,* October 11/12, 1997; Michael O'Connor, "They're on a Row," *Boston Herald,* October 18, 1997; Sara Rimer, "For Rowers, It's Getting There, First or Not," *The New York Times,* October 20, 1997.

Beth A. Kaputa

Hiking, Rock Climbing, and Mountaineering

Hiking has evolved into one of the most common forms of recreation in New England, as throughout North America, providing a way for enthusiasts of all ages to explore nature, exercise, and relax.

New England's earliest recorded hiking exploit was the ascent of Mount Washington by Darby Field in 1642. Ethan Allen Crawford, who ran a tavern in Crawford Notch, N.H., guided a scientific expedition to the peak in 1794 and gained legendary stature as a guide; he cut the first path up the mountain and led countless parties of hikers. Writers such as Nathaniel Hawthorne popularized Crawford's inn and the surrounding area, especially after the dramatic death of the Willey family in an 1826 landslide in the Notch.

Before the Civil War, White Mountain artists and writers popularized hiking and mountain climbing as spiritually beneficial. Thomas Starr King's *The White Hills: Their Legends, Landscape and Poetry* (1859) was a favorite guidebook to the mountains, combining hiking routes, poetry, and engravings. It and other guidebooks, as well as the development of great hotels connected by railroad to Boston and New York, helped promote mountain recreation. A concurrent interest in wilderness experience and more strenuous mountain climbing focused on Maine's Mount Katahdin. Henry David Thoreau's *The Maine Woods* (1864) chronicled his two trips to the region and his experience with Indian guides. Similar interest in hiking in other states centered on ascents of the highest peaks, such as Vermont's Mount Mansfield or Massachusetts's Mount Greylock, the latter famous in literature for the ascent made by a party that included writers Herman Melville and Nathaniel Hawthorne and editor Evert Duyckinck. The popularity of certain peaks, celebrated in 19th-century literature, continues today with hikers who have ascended all the 4,000-foot peaks in the White Mountains. The smaller Mount Monadnock, Camel's Hump, and Mount Chocorua are popular family hiking destinations. Many New England peaks feature summits above tree line, usually due to logging or fire, offering an unusual environment and splendid views.

One of the most famous and frequented hiking areas in New England is the northern portion of the Appalachian Trail, which includes areas in the western mountains of Connecticut and Massachusetts, the Green Mountains of Vermont, the White Mountains of New Hampshire, and the central mountains of Maine. The entire length of the Appalachian Trail, which extends from Springer Mountain in Georgia to Mount Katahdin in Maine, covers approximately 2,160 miles. It is second only to the more recently developed Pacific Crest Trail as the longest hiking path in North America. The idea of the Appalachian Trail was conceived in the early 1900s by Benton MacKaye, a Harvard graduate who was a forester in Massachusetts. He viewed the trail as the perfect escape for people in the large cities of the East, with wilderness areas serving as a source for studying nature and experiencing much needed respite. Trailblazing for the Appalachian Trail began in 1922 and was completed by a group of trail workers from the Civilian Conservation Corps on the western slope of Sugarloaf Mountain in Maine on August 14, 1937. After moderate use, Earl Schaffer, a navy sailor from Pennsylvania, became the first person to complete the hike in 1948. By 1995, more than 3,500 hikers had completed the trek, with 90 percent of them beginning in Georgia and hiking north to Maine. The trials and tribulations of trail hikers on the Maine section of the trail, with its difficult culmination at Mount Katahdin, are legendary.

Recent technological changes have made hiking and backpacking easier, more enjoyable, and more popular; therefore, issues concerning access, human effects on wilderness areas, and safety have arisen. The resolution of such issues will be critical to the continued success of hiking and backpacking as recreational outlets.

Two of the fastest emerging outdoor recreational pursuits in New England are rock climbing and mountaineering. While often grouped under the term "climbing," and seen as quite similar because they use many of the same techniques and types of equipment, these pursuits can be quite different in application.

Rock climbing is generally seen as a subset of mountaineering, in which the climber focuses on scaling steep rock faces ranging in height from boulders to rock faces well over several thousand feet. In the United States, rock climbs are rated by class (the type of climbing required) and grade (the amount of time the climb generally takes to complete). Most rock climbers focus on fifth-class climbing in which a rope, climbing equipment, and methods of placing protection are used to keep climbers safe should they fall. The most well-known rock climbing areas of New England include Cannon, Whitehorse, and Cathedral ledges near North Conway, N.H.; Acadia National Park and Baxter State Park in Maine; and the Ragged Mountain area in Connecticut. Rock climbing has also appeared indoors with the establishment of indoor climbing walls throughout New England.

Mountaineering is generally seen as requiring a combination of outdoor skills, including rock climbing, snow and ice climbing, and wilderness travel skills. While lacking the height often found in mountains in the western United States, several areas in New England can produce some of the harshest mountaineering conditions found in the continent. More than 120 climbers have died on New Hampshire's Mount Washington alone from mountaineering-related accidents. Favorite mountaineering areas in New England include the White Mountains of New Hampshire, Baxter State Park in Maine, and the ice cliffs of Smuggler's Notch in Vermont.

Access has become a prominent concern for climbers. Many climbing areas are on private land and are therefore subject to closing by landowners. Other areas located on state and federal land are subject to regulation and closings as well, often because of real and perceived safety concerns, misuse by some climbers, and the sheer volume of participants. New England climbers, with the support of the Access Fund organization located in Boulder, Co., continue to work to ensure access for climbers throughout the region.

Bill Bryson, *A Walk in the Woods: Rediscovering America on the Appalachian Trail* (1997); Jerry Cinnamon, *Climbing Rock and Ice* (1994); Lucy Crawford, *History of the White Mountains, from the First Settlement of Upper Coos and Pequaket* (1846); James M. and Hertha Flack, *Ambling and Scrambling on the Appalachian Trail* (1981); Don Graydon, *Mountaineering: The Freedom of the Hills* (1992); John Hart, *Walking Softly in the Wilderness: The Sierra Club Guide to Backpacking* (1977); National Outdoor Leadership School, *Soft Paths* (1992); Eric Seaborg and Ellen Dudley, *Hiking and Backpacking* (1994).

Michael Gass

Ice Fishing Ice fishing is a common outdoor recreational activity in New England and a regular feature of the region's wintertime landscape. Structures of various shapes and sizes, known in the local vernacular as "bob houses," "ice shacks," or "ice shanties," gather into small villages on frozen rivers and lakes; most resemble small huts built on runners. These homemade, typically wooden, huts provide shelter from the winter elements. Often creative in design and unique in construction, some include kitchen stoves, fold-down bunk beds, and tables and chairs.

Ice fishing begins with the simple task of cutting a hole in ice. Either a hand or gas-powered ice auger is handy for the job, although some fishers have been known to wield an ax. Fish are typically caught in one of two ways: through the use of "tip-ups" (known in some localities as "tilts"), or by "jigging." Tip-ups, which rest on four outstretched wooden legs, release a brightly colored flag when a fish pulls on the line, signaling a bite. Jigging fishers drop a line from a short fishing rod that is gently rocked up and down, keeping the bait moving enticingly beneath the ice. Freshwater ice fishers in New England use a wide selection of bait, including live minnows and shiners, rainbow smelt, and larval varieties such as maggots, mousies, and mealworms. Artificial lures, including such exotically named favorites as Swedish Pimple, Daredevil, and Jigging Rampala, offer fishers speed and convenience, though not necessarily luck or success.

Ice fishers in New England pursue a number of species in both freshwater and saltwater. Underwater features such as edges, drop-offs, points, and weed beds are all good places to find fish. Some freshwater species such as the cusk, togue, and white perch are found low in the stratigraphic layering of a lake and can be caught with traps that support a deep line weighted with a sinker. Others, such as pickerel; yellow perch; and calico, large-, and small-mouth bass, prefer the warmer waters of shallow, weedy areas and often are caught closer to shore. Rainbow, lake, and brown trout enjoy water of more moderate depth and colder temperature. They are especially popu-

Ice fishing shacks on Lake Winnipesaukee, Meredith, N.H., 1971

lar on the larger and deeper lakes throughout New England.

Fishers along the coast of New Hampshire and Maine pursue the small but bountiful saltwater smelt, a species that follows the ocean tide as it swells inland through the region's many brackish streams, rivers, and inlets. Local fishing lore informs New Englanders of the patterns the smelt trace under the ice during their annual runs upstream; smelt fishers try to position their holes over such lines of travel. Some ice smelters set as many as a dozen "hand lines" with multiple hooks baited with worms, while others jig for their quarry. Numerous commercially run camps in Maine cater to recreational ice smelters, providing them with a bob house, bait, electricity, and a wooden stove.

New England's ice fishing derbies, like the one held each February on Lake Winnipesaukee in Meredith, N.H., have a carnival-like atmosphere. Contest officials carefully inspect the length and weight of each fish submitted by fishers, who compete for gifts and prize money. As the contest unfolds, crowds of fishers and onlookers gather to view the Fish Board, where the largest specimens are hung for display.

Researchers have noted that relative to the amount of time spent on the ice, ice fishers catch few fish. Nevertheless, ice fishing, a tradition passed on to and shared liberally among neighbors, friends, and relatives, endures as a popular feature of New England life.

Ernest Stanley Didge, "Unchanging Ways," *Old Time New England* (Winter 1952); Stephen O. Muskie, "When the Smelt are Running," *Yankee Magazine* (January 1982).

Simon Hart Phillips

Ice Hockey
New England and Minnesota are the only indigenous hotbeds of ice hockey in the United States. The sport has drama-

tized New England's distinctive history and evolving culture for 150 years, particularly the region's manufacturing past, its recent chapters in urban renewal, its educational institutions, and its perennially fickle weather.

The forerunners of ice hockey included hurley, shinny, and bandy; all were simple field games—whacking a ball with a stick toward a goal—brought to the ice. Native Americans had their own versions, though probably without skates. An 1855 lithograph by Currier and Ives, *Winter Pastime,* depicts how New England's frozen waterways lent themselves to these games, which required little equipment. Well into the 1880s, New Englanders such as John Perry of New Ipswich, N.H., were still making their own skates by mounting metal runners on hand-turned wood blocks. They whacked at balls, rocks, or wood pucks with "hockeys" made of fresh-cut ash.

After the Civil War, New England's dominant place in manufacturing and education influenced the future of ice hockey. Although skate factories in Worcester, Mass., and Torrington, Conn., had produced ready-made skates before the war, competition grew after 1865, and ice skating enjoyed a boom. Hockey followed skating, especially at places such as Saint Paul's School in Concord, N.H., where schoolboys played several forms of hockey before codifying their rules in 1883; these were probably the first distinct ice hockey rules published in the United States. In the mid-1890s, players from Saint Paul's, Yale, and Brown were central to the U.S. embrace of the "modern" Canadian game.

New England colleges and schools have promoted the sport ever since. Their matches and tournaments have linked backwoods to big city, public to private, Yankee to immigrant. The long hockey traditions for men at Harvard, Dartmouth, and Bowdoin have been matched by recent dynasties at Boston Uni-

versity, Middlebury, and the University of Maine. Boston's Beanpot Tournament (Harvard, Boston University, Boston College, and Northeastern) began quietly in 1952 in the shadow of college basketball; it now puts college hockey at center stage of Boston sports for the first two Mondays in February. New England college coaches have influenced the game's growth as tacticians, promoters, and rule makers. Hall-of-Fame coaches include Ralph Winsor and Cooney Weiland (Harvard), John "Snooks" Kelley and Len Ceglarski (Boston College), Jim Fullerton (Brown), Eddie Jeremiah (Dartmouth), Jack Kelly (Boston University), Charlie Holt (University of New Hampshire), Sid Watson (Bowdoin), and Fernie Flaman (Northeastern).

Women organized hockey teams at Mount Holyoke and Smith a century ago. In the past two decades, New England institutions drove the rapid national growth of women's hockey, highlighted by New Hampshire's victory in the first women's national championship, held at Boston's Fleet Center in 1998, and Harvard's victory in 1999. New England college players, male and female, have led the most prominent U.S. Olympic gold medal teams— the Cleary brothers (Harvard) and Dick Rodenheiser (Boston University) in 1960; Mike Eruzione, Jim Craig, and Jack O'Callahan (Boston University) in 1980; and Karyn Bye and Colleen Coyne (New Hampshire), Cammi Granato (Providence), Shelly Looney (Northeastern), and A. J. Mleczko (Harvard) in 1998.

By the 1930s, the early dominance of preparatory schools such as Saint Paul's and Phillips Andover Academy fell to public school programs in Melrose, Mass.; Hamden, Conn.; and Burrillville, R.I. By the 1940s, three Francophone high schools were New England powerhouses: Saint Doms of Lewiston, Maine; Mount Saint Charles of Woonsocket, R.I.; and Notre Dame of Berlin, N.H. Hockey has enjoyed a resurgence of popularity at the secondary school level, largely because many prep schools own indoor rinks.

New England towns and cities have promoted teams, leagues, and tournaments at all levels. Pee-wees and old-timers alike have graced frozen ponds and indoor rinks, often in emulation of their professional heroes. The Boston Bruins, the first U.S. team to join the National Hockey League (NHL) in 1924, is the most famous professional team, with a long list of Hall-of-Famers that includes Art Ross, Eddie Shore, and Bobby Orr. One level below the NHL, the American Hockey League (AHL) included franchises in Providence; New Haven, Conn.; and Springfield, Mass., at its birth in 1936–37. The AHL, headquartered in Springfield, now has additional franchises in Worcester, Mass.; Portland, Maine; Hartford; Lowell, Mass; and Manchester, N.H.

New England winters—with alternating blizzards, thaws, drizzles, and arctic blasts—have never favored a sustained outdoor hockey season. But Yankee ingenuity spawned an assortment of techniques and devices for building and maintaining smooth, hard ice on outdoor rinks. Removable boards or light reflectors on exposed north and west sides minimized melting in the February sun; oil drums pulled by student crews served as proto-Zambonis. But in the long run, indoor rinks were the keys to growth. One of the earliest indoor ice rinks was Rinkle Rink (1896) at Mount Holyoke College, where the women played "ice polo." The Boston Arena was New England's first major indoor, artificial ice venue (1910), followed by Tex Rickard's Boston Garden (1928), and later by major facilities in Springfield and Providence. College (and some school) rinks sprouted in the 1950s. Urban renewal programs in the 1970s, 1980s, and 1990s included new facilities (and teams) in Portland, Providence, Hartford, Springfield, Worcester, Lowell, and (to come full historical circle) Boston. Civic boosters in cities and university towns built hockey rinks as new anchors of prosperity. In one sense, these rinks became sporting analogues to 19th-century textile mills—symbols of competitiveness and community. To succeed, the arenas have had to weather more than economic maelstroms. Heavy blizzards in 1969 and 1978 crushed the roofs at several facilities, including Alfond Arena in Waterville, Maine, and the Hartford Civic Center. Because of gritty New England determination, new roofs went up, and the games went on.

Gai Berlage, "The Development of Intercollegiate Women's Ice Hockey in the United States," *Colby Quarterly* (March 1996); Dan Diamond, James Duplacey, and Igor Kuperman, eds., *Total Hockey: The Official Encyclopedia of the National Hockey League* (1998); Jack Grinold, "Nine Decades of Arena History," in *Northeastern University Hockey Guide* (1996); Stephen Hardy, "Performance, Memory and History: The Making of American Ice Hockey at St. Paul's School, 1860–1915," *International Journal of the History of Sport* (April 1997); Luna Lambert, "The American Skating Mania," *Journal of American Culture* 1, no. 4 (1978); Joseph Oxendine, *American Indian Sports Heritage* (1988); Richard Sorrell, "Sports and Franco-Americans in Woonsocket, 1870–1930," *Rhode Island History* (Fall 1972); David Tirrell, "The Outdoor Rink," in *NCAA Ice Hockey Guide* (1945).

Stephen Hardy

Laconia Motorcycle Rally and Race Week

The Laconia Motorcycle Rally and Race Week is the oldest rally—and one of the largest—of its kind in the world and one of New England's largest recreational events. In 1916 a group of approximately 300 motorcyclists, organized by the Bay State Cycle Club, spent several days at Weirs Beach in Laconia,

N.H., enjoying the sights of Lake Winnipesaukee and the White Mountains. In 1917 the first Gypsy Tour (a road ride to a scenic or recreational locale) sanctioned by the Federation of American Motorcyclists was held in Laconia. Hill climbs were held on Tower Hill Street, while other events took place anywhere they could be held. The event gained popularity and continued through the 1920s and into the 1930s.

A motorcycle hill climber named Fritzie Baer was instrumental in bringing road races to Belknap Recreation Area (now called Gunstock) near Laconia in 1938. For the next 30 years Baer and his supporters, called The Red Hat Brigade, worked hard to keep the Laconia Motorcycle Rally at full steam.

The 1960s were a time of upheaval for motorcycle events around the country. In 1960 the name Gypsy Tour was no longer used by the American Motorcycle Association (AMA), and the weeklong rally was referred to only as Motorcycle Week or Laconia. In 1962 the last hill climbs were held at Belknap, and the last road races were held in 1963. In 1964 the races were moved to the New Hampshire International Speedway in Loudon, 15 miles south of Laconia, and the event was renamed the Laconia Classic. Relations between visiting motorcyclists and the Weirs Beach police chief had been strained, and many motorcyclists no longer felt welcome. Trouble broke out between some motorcyclists and the large police and National Guard force. As a result, Motorcycle Week became Motorcycle Weekend in 1965, as all events except for the races in Loudon were canceled. By the late 1970s, the event was renamed the Loudon Classic.

During the 1980s, the other two national motorcycle rallies, Sturgis and Daytona, were growing in size and popularity. In 1990, on the 50th anniversary of Sturgis, 400,000 motorcyclists attended the 10-day event. The *Boston Sunday Globe* covered the Sturgis rally that year, comparing it to bygone years in Laconia. Bob Lawton, a local businessperson from Weirs Beach, contacted the local AMA motorcycle club—the Lakeside Sharks—about bringing the rally back to the area. A Motorcycle Week Association was formed, and in 1991 the event returned to Laconia and a rally headquarters was set up at Weirs Beach. In 1992 the AMA brought back the Gypsy Tour, and the hill climbs returned to Gunstock in 1993.

Thanks to the efforts of the Laconia Motorcycle Rally and Race Week Association, composed of state, local, and private interests, the event has regained its popularity and status in the world of motorcycling. In recent years, an estimated 320,000 motorcyclists attended the nine-day rally.

Annamarie Timmons, "Hats Off to a Bike Week Legend: Baer's Passion Led to Event's Creation," *Concord Monitor*, June 12, 1999; Paula Tracy, "Cycle Weekend Fun for 50, 000," *The Union Leader,* June 14, 1990.

Charlie St. Clair

Lacrosse Lacrosse, a field game played with a webbed stick and ball by both men and women, evokes the playing fields of New England's elite educational institutions, where the game enjoys a long history. The sport is currently played in schools, clubs, and national and international competitions. Although played in other parts of the country, lacrosse remains closely linked with New England in most people's minds, perhaps because of the region's association with prestigious private education. This traditional regional connection is in fact more recognizable than the game's historical connection to its Native American origins. Recent developments in national legislation, however, such as the passage of Title IX in 1972 and the National Collegiate Athletic Association's (NCAA) management of athletics by stratifying schools into regulated divisions in 1973, now allow administrative decisions to influence the status and future of collegiate sports. The desire for national sports contests and competition among institutions for the best athletes may eventually either obscure the regional character of lacrosse or continue to prove that its association with New England will not be overshadowed by the specific conditions of play that might contradict that image.

Europeans' attraction to lacrosse, played by the Six Nations of Iroquois as early as the 17th century, is evident in its French name, reportedly signifying the Catholic bishop's crosier, a symbolic shepherd's staff that resembles a lacrosse stick. By the 19th century Canadians made lacrosse their official national sport and played it by the rules of ice hockey. Lacrosse became popular in New England, particularly among women, as much through English influence on American education in the late 19th century as through French Canadian or Native American cultural influence. New England's private institutions added lacrosse to college and preparatory school curricula in the late 19th and early 20th centuries—the era of the modern Olympic movement and the first wave of women's struggle for equality in all aspects of educational experience. Yale and Harvard adopted the sport in the 1880s.

Although men's and women's lacrosse are very different games in play, both trace their origins to the same North American Indian competition, "Baggataway," or "little brother of war." This roaming game without boundaries and an unlimited number of participants,

Lacrosse player at Phillips Exeter Academy, 1970s

in which both ball and stick were used as weapons, was considered good preparation for war. Contemporary men's lacrosse, an aggressive game of body-checking and hitting, is readily comparable to the original warlike play. Women's lacrosse by contrast is often called "purer" and closer to the Native American game in its lack of outer boundaries and use of the more "natural" wooden crafted stick, although many women players now prefer plastic. Women players originally wore long skirts and high collars; this attire has been replaced by the traditional women's lacrosse uniform of short skirts. The current discussion about introducing helmets for women challenges the preservation of the no-contact rules and the distinctive pace of the women's game. After 100 years of close association with traditional New England institutions, men's and women's lacrosse, like all paired sports, continues to spark debate about sport itself and appropriate sex separations.

The United States Intercollegiate Lacrosse League was formed in 1906 and then reorganized in 1926 as the United States Intercollegiate Lacrosse Association. In 1931, the United States Women's Lacrosse Association was formed. New England Lacrosse, the local chapter of U.S. Lacrosse, is dedicated to promoting the sport throughout the region. Lacrosse was adopted by the NCAA in 1970. Postcollegiate clubs such as the New England Club Lacrosse League offer opportunities for lacrosse players to continue participating in the sport after college.

William Kelso Morrill, *Lacrosse* (1966); Thomas Vennum, Jr., *American Indian Lacrosse: Little Brother of War* (1994); Alexander M. Weyand and Milton R. Roberts, *The Lacrosse Story* (1965).

Roseanne V. Camacho

Minor League Baseball
Since 1877 New England cities have actively hosted teams in baseball's minor leagues. *Minor league baseball* is the term given to professional baseball leagues not at the major league, or highest, level (currently National League and Ameri-

can League). Despite their name, these organizations have been a vital component of professional baseball since its inception. The minor leagues should not be confused with amateur and semi-pro leagues in the region. In addition, numerous summer collegiate leagues have been formed for college players while still enrolled in school; the Cape Cod League is the most prominent of these leagues and is often mistaken for a minor league.

Almost 70 New England communities have hosted teams in all minor league classifications, from the Class AAA International League to the Class D New York–Penn League. Of the first three minor leagues formed in 1877, two had numerous teams in New England. The International Association had seven teams, including Lynn, Mass., and other cities in the northeastern United States and Canada. The Lynn team featured Hall-of-Fame pitcher Candy Cummings, who is attributed with inventing the curveball. The other initial league with a strong New England connection was the aptly named New England League (NEL).

The NEL, which included teams in nearly every New England community, operated sporadically between 1877 and 1949. The modern incarnation of the league was founded in 1902 and operated from 1902 to 1915, in 1919, from 1926 to 1930, in 1933, and from 1946 to 1949. The gaps in operation during these years were very common throughout the minor leagues, as most of them responded both to economic downturns and to the two world wars. The NEL included 26 teams in Massachusetts, Rhode Island, New Hampshire, and Maine. During the Great Depression, the NEL reorganized as the Class A Northeastern League, but that lasted only for the 1934 season. The NEL was reorganized after World War II when the minor leagues blossomed in nearly every corner of the country.

The NEL also played an important role in the early years of integration of professional baseball. Brooklyn Dodgers' president Branch Rickey sent African American baseball players to northern teams in his minor league systems, which were established during the 1930s and remain to this day. This centralized the player transactions from a team-by-team basis, in which one minor league team could trade a player to any other, to one in which the players followed a specific path to reach the major leagues. Rickey felt that the African American baseball players would be better accepted in the northern leagues and placed his leading prospects, including Jackie Robinson, at Montreal of the International League. The Nashua (N.H.) Dodgers were also stocked with stars from the Negro leagues and quickly became one of the NEL's best teams. Winners

of three straight league championships between 1946 and 1948, the Nashua Dodgers were led by Roy Campanella (1946), Don Newcombe (1947), and Dan Bankhead (1948), three African Americans who would make tremendous contributions to the Brooklyn Dodgers. While the Dodgers had great success on the field, the NEL's fortunes were waning, like those of most minor leagues, under the competitive pressure of televised baseball. Midway through the 1949 season, four teams folded, leaving only four teams to finish the season. The NEL folded at the end of the season.

Another prominent minor league in New England was the Connecticut State League (1899–1912), which consisted of teams in the larger industrial cities such as Bridgeport, Hartford, Meriden, New Britain, New Haven, New London, and Waterbury. The league was one of the more stable minor leagues and existed for 14 consecutive seasons. Many of the teams in the league's larger cities moved to the Eastern Association in 1913 and then to the Eastern League in 1916. One of the leading operators of minor league baseball in the state was New Haven's George Weiss, a National Baseball Hall-of-Famer who would later serve as general manager and president for New York's Yankees and Mets, respectively. The Eastern League, which continues to this day, has traditionally been well represented by New England teams, especially the Connecticut cities of New Haven, New Britain, and Norwich.

Other leagues that operated in the Northeast that included numerous cities in New England include the International League, the New York–Penn League, and the Independent Northeast League (which has since merged with the Northern League). The International League is one of baseball's oldest, tracing its history back to 1884. Also known between 1902 and 1911 as the Eastern League, New England has been represented by Pawtucket (1973–present), Old Orchard Beach (Maine) (1984–88), and Providence (1902–17). The New York–Penn League also had a strong presence in New England, with teams in Pittsfield and Lowell, Mass., and Montpelier, Vt.

In many of New England's smaller cities, minor league teams assumed a special role in a community's popular culture, becoming a source of local pride. Besides providing a recreational activity that was often embraced by civic boosters, the teams also provided national recognition as their scores were broadcast in newspapers across the country. Even cities that today are considered part of suburban areas had teams that helped promote their civic pride. The Lowell Spinners, located only 27 miles northeast of Boston, draw upon the history of their community with their team name and benefit from their close proximity to a major league market. During the 1999 and 2000 seasons, they averaged more than 5,000 fans a night, exceeding their capacity for 50 straight games. In Bridgeport, Conn., the Bluefish were charter members of the independent Atlantic League in 1998 and served as a visible urban renewal plan for that city. As with teams throughout the country in the 1990s, New England communities sought minor league teams as a recognized form of recreation and entertainment and, in many cases, a visible reminder of the economic rebirth of a community.

The continued success of minor league baseball in New England can be attributed to numerous factors, most importantly, the close proximity of New England's communities. The location of teams in New England has allowed leagues to develop rivalries between close-in cities, thereby reducing transportation costs and forgoing the added financial burden of hotel accommodations for team road trips.

Another reason for the original success of minor league baseball in New England is the development of the Boston Red Sox and Boston Braves minor league farm system, whereby major league teams had agreements with a group of minor league teams at different levels, all of which were engaged in developing players for the "parent" team. As they developed during the 1930s, Boston major league teams generally included local teams in their farm systems. Boston teams signed working agreements with New England minor league teams for two primary reasons. First, the players would be training physically close to Boston, allowing the team to move them quickly to the parent club should the need arise. This proximity allowed the team to scout more easily the players in their system and, to a lesser degree, get the players acclimated to New England weather (especially for early-season games). Second, the New England affiliates with the Red Sox and Braves would help promote fan interest in the Boston major league clubs. Since 1967, the Boston Red Sox's highest affiliate in the minor leagues has been the Pawtucket (R.I.) International League team. Located approximately one hour from Boston, the fans of Pawtucket help broaden the Red Sox's marketing area. In 2004 the Red Sox farm system included teams in Portland, Maine, and Lowell.

Will Anderson, *Was Baseball Really Invented in Maine?* (1992); Lloyd Johnson, *Encyclopedia of Minor League Baseball* (1997); Robert Obojski, *Bush League: A History of Minor League Baseball* (1975).

Corey Seeman

Naismith Memorial Basketball Hall of Fame Founded in 1959, even before it was a physical reality, the Naismith Memorial Basketball Hall of Fame in Springfield, Mass., pays tribute to Dr. James Naismith, the game's founder, and to those individuals and teams who have made significant contributions to the game's past, present, and future. The history of the Basketball Hall of Fame dates back to 1936 when the National Association of Basketball Coaches (NABC) took Naismith to the Berlin Olympics, where basketball was making its Olympic debut. During the games, the NABC was impressed by both the sport's popularity and Naismith's reception from the international community. Legend has it that when the Olympics ended, Naismith told the NABC to use his extra spending money to build a memorial to the game of basketball. Embracing the idea, the NABC decided that Springfield College, the birthplace of the sport, should be the new home for the Hall of Fame and that the memorial should be named after Naismith himself.

While the Hall of Fame began inducting heroes of the sport in 1959, it opened its doors in 1968 on the campus of Springfield College. In 1985 it opened a new, larger facility on the banks of the Connecticut River and finished redesigning a dramatic new facility that opened in 2004. The new museum features a full-length basketball court, more than 33,000 square feet of exhibition space (with an additional 9,500 square feet of expansion space), a gift shop, a restaurant, and a theater.

Through exhibits, educational programs, publications, and promotional ventures, the Hall of Fame documents the growth of the game of basketball for men and women on the high school, college, amateur, professional, and international levels from 1891 to the present. The museum's collection consists of uniforms, trophies, basketballs, medals, archival and library material, photographs, film and video, oral histories, and professional and college team information. The museum's collection is particularly strong in New England high school, club, and college photographs from the first two decades of the 20th century.

Since 1959, the Basketball Hall of Fame has elected a new class of Hall-of-Famers each year. Presently, 246 individuals and five teams are enshrined in the museum. Eligible candidates include players, coaches, referees, and contributors. Individuals must receive 18 of 24 votes from the Honors Committee to be elected. The enshrinement ceremony is held annually in late September or early October.

Albert G. Applin II, *From Muscular Christianity to the Marketplace: The History of Men's and Boy's Basketball in the United States, 1891–1957* (1982); James Naismith, *Basketball: Its Origin and Development* (1996); Bernice Larson Webb, *The Basketball Man* (1973).

Doug Stark

New England Patriots The New England Patriots were one of the eight original American Football League (AFL) teams. In 1959 the AFL awarded the franchise, then called the Boston Patriots, to a group of New

Naismith Memorial Basketball Hall of Fame, Springfield, Mass., 2004

England businessmen led by William H. Sullivan, Jr., who became the club's president. The team's name resulted from a contest sponsored by a Boston newspaper. Although Boston lost to the Denver Broncos in the first regular season AFL game on September 9, 1960, the team won its next game against the New York Titans (now Jets) and finished its first season with a record of 5–9.

In 1961 Boston acquired Vito "Babe" Parilli, an experienced quarterback, from the Oakland Raiders; with wide receiver/placekicker Gino Cappelletti, the team's leading scorer during the 1960s, Parilli lifted Boston's offensive play to a championship level. After finishing with records of 9–4–1 in 1961 and 1962, the Patriots defeated the Buffalo Bills for the Eastern Division title in 1963 but lost the AFL title game against the Western Division champion San Diego Chargers. Boston drafted Jim Nance, a powerful fullback from Syracuse University, in 1965. On the strength of Nance's AFL rushing record of 1,458 yards, the Patriots finished the 1966 season with a record of 8–4–2 but lost the Eastern Division title to the New York Jets.

Winning seasons eluded the Patriots from 1967 to 1975. Poor trades and injured and aging players contributed to the team's decline. In 1966, civic leaders and professional sports magnates proposed an all-season urban sports complex to house the Patriots, but an unresolved debate over how to finance the $80 million project thwarted its construction. In 1970 team officials selected Foxboro, a town south of Boston, as the site for a permanent stadium. The Patriots, now part of the American Football Conference (AFC) of the newly reorganized National Football League (NFL)—resulting from the merger of the old AFL and NFL—began playing in Schaefer Stadium in 1971. Before moving to Foxboro, the team had played home games at Boston University (1960–62), Fenway Park (1963–68), Boston College (1969), and Harvard University (1970). No longer representing solely Boston, the team changed its name to the New England Patriots in 1971 to reflect a larger geographical representation.

The Patriots rebuilt in the early 1970s, drafting Jim Plunkett, the Heisman Trophy winner from Stanford University, in 1971 and hiring Chuck Fairbanks of the University of Oklahoma as coach in 1973. New England made key rookie acquisitions in fullback Sam Cunningham, wide receiver Darryl Stingley, and guard John Hannah in 1973. The selection of quarterback Steve Grogan in the 1975 college draft led to a rivalry with Plunkett over the starting quarterback position. After trading Plunkett to the San Francisco 49ers in

1976, the Patriots won 11 of 14 games but lost to the Oakland Raiders 24–21 in the playoffs. Despite losing Stingley to a paralyzing tackle by Oakland's Jack Tatum in the 1978 preseason, New England posted an 11–5 record and captured the Eastern Division title in 1978. Controversy enveloped the team when Fairbanks announced before the season finale that he would become head coach at the University of Colorado the following year. Sullivan barred Fairbanks from coaching the team through its final game against the Cincinnati Bengals but permitted him to rejoin the team for its playoff game against the Houston Oilers. New England lost both games 24–3 and 31–14, respectively.

After six unaccomplished seasons, New England enjoyed one of its most memorable in 1985, winning the AFC championship after qualifying for the playoffs as a wild card team—that is, the second-place team with the best record in the conference. In addition to the leadership provided by head coach Raymond Berry, a Hall-of-Fame wide receiver for the Baltimore Colts, the Patriots' resurgence came from precision play by quarterbacks Grogan and Tony Eason, all-pro guard Hannah, running back Craig James, wide receiver Irving Friar, and placekicker Tony Franklin. After clinching the wild card berth by defeating Cincinnati 34–23, New England defeated New York and the Los Angeles Raiders, thus setting the AFC title match against the Miami Dolphins. The Patriots defeated Miami 31–14 for their first AFC championship but lost to the National Football Conference (NFC) champion Chicago Bears 46–10 in Super Bowl XX. In 1986 the Patriots, with an 11–5 record, won the Eastern Division but lost to Denver 22–17 in the playoffs.

The Sullivan family sold the club to Victor Kiam in 1988, and after four mediocre years, James B. Orthwein bought controlling interest in the team. Hannah, who retired after Super Bowl XX, became the first Patriot elected to the Professional Football Hall of Fame in 1991. Orthwein hired Bill Parcells, who had coached the New York Giants to Super Bowl victories in 1984 and 1985, as coach in 1992. Determined to rebuild the team, Parcells made quarterback Drew Bledsoe of Washington State University New England's first-round draft pick in 1993. Purchased by Robert Kraft in 1994, the Patriots won 10 of 16 games, earned a wild-card playoff berth, but lost to the Cleveland Browns 20–13. Parcells continued to rebuild, selecting talented rookies such as Curtis Martin, who rushed 1,487 yards and garnered the Rookie-of-the-Year title in 1995. Terry Glenn, who established an NFL rookie record of 90 receptions, led New England to

an 11–5 record in 1996. The Patriots defeated the Jacksonville Jaguars 20–6 for the AFC championship that year but lost to the NFC champion Green Bay Packers 35–21 in Super Bowl XXXI.

In 1997 New England hired Pete Carroll when Parcells left to become the head coach of the New York Jets. In Carroll's first year, the Patriots defended their Eastern Division championship title, winning 10 of 16 games. In 1998 New England finished the season with a record of 9–7 and qualified for the playoffs for a third consecutive year. The desire for a new stadium led Kraft to court Hartford, Conn., as a new home for the team. In 1998, the Connecticut legislature approved a $375 million referendum to build a stadium as part of a massive urban renewal program for Hartford. In May 1999, however, Kraft terminated the deal and announced that the Patriots would remain in Massachusetts. Within a year, the team unveiled plans for a new, 68,000-seat Foxboro stadium. In 2000 New England hired Bill Belichick, who had served as a New England assistant head coach in 1996, as head coach. The New England Patriots won the Super Bowl in 2002, 2004, and 2005.

Bob Carroll, Michael Gershman, David Neft, and John Thorn, *Total Football: The Official Encyclopedia of the National Football League* (1997).

Adam R. Hornbuckle

New England Sabbath   In the Judeo-Christian tradition, the Sabbath is a day of rest and worship, but it is also understood as a set of laws, practices, and rituals that came to be associated with Sundays in the New England region. During the colonial period, New England's Sabbath laws prohibited many activities, including recreation; these laws were replicated throughout the colonies, and few challenged the primacy of the New England Sabbath.

The New England Sabbath became a symbol of repressive and joyless Puritanism that stuck in the American cultural imagination. This symbolism surfaces in parodies; in references to the "dour New England Sabbath" that dot political, religious, and social commentary through the mid-20th century; and in several canonical American poems, most notably Emily Dickinson's "Some Keep the Sabbath Going to Church"; Wallace Stevens's "Sunday Morning"; and Robert Lowell's "Waking Sunday Morning." Thomas Bailey Aldrich's *The Story of a Bad Boy* (1869) presented a satiric, though affectionate, view of the Sabbath-day sufferings of boys in the old families of Portsmouth, N.H.

That the New England Sabbath seized the American imagination as a symbol of repression and antipathy toward recreation both healthy and "unhealthy" is no surprise. New Englanders were loath to introduce anything but the strictest religious observances to the day, fearful that should the Sabbath go, so would the health of the individual, community, and nation. Divines such as Lyman Beecher predicted that if the Sabbath should become "a mere holiday" (as it was in continental Europe) it would exert "a most terrific demoralizing influence." Paired with these fears were concerns about preserving it as a day of rest, although few could agree on what constituted rest. While some found churchgoing restful, many laborers found recreation or pure relaxation most restorative. The challenge to traditional Sabbath observance was fueled in antebellum New England by the presence of large populations of immigrants, such as the Irish, whose six days of labor in the mills left little time for recreation other than on Sunday.

For women, the day of rest was yet another affair. Many were responsible for running households in such a way that all members, including servants, could obtain an optimal amount of rest. Women who worked for wages found in Sunday the time for household chores, not rest. Despite gender and class differences that determined how much and what style of rest one might enjoy, a widespread allegiance to rest sustained Sunday codes and laws, however convoluted they might have been.

By the end of the 19th century industrialization, demographic change, and urbanization resulted in new styles of Sunday observance. A Sabbath spent at church and in prayer was one of many regulations meant to keep New England's antebellum textile workers sober, industrious, and pious. In the same mill towns where Yankee farm girls were required to attend church, however, Irish day laborers were known to be under orders to dig ditches, repair machinery, and haul goods seven days a week. Such inconsistency severely compromised Sunday's status as a day of rest, let alone as the Sabbath. As the region continued to industrialize, Sunday labor increased.

The development of an extensive transportation network connecting small and large communities further eroded the foundations of the traditional New England Sabbath, enabling a new style of Sunday observance involving "innocent" (and not so innocent) recreation to flourish. As early as the 1840s local trains were running between city and country, enabling Sunday excursions. "Milk trains," which brought fresh milk to the city early Sunday mornings, often dropped off carloads of country people seeking diversion in the city and returned packed with city people

seeking a day in the country. Despite resistance, by the late 1870s trains and ferries transported goods and people seven days a week. Middle-class men and women who caught the bicycle craze debated the propriety of Sunday cycling during the 1880s, but by the mid-1890s some ministers were cycling to church and even leading their congregations on Sunday-afternoon spins. Within the first three decades of the 20th century, the Sunday drive became part of the New England Sabbath, commemorated in the building of Memorial Drive, in Cambridge, Mass., meant specifically to accommodate Sunday drivers. In sum, the extension of commercial and private transportation networks across New England at once eroded the traditional New England Sabbath and at the same time enhanced the potential for Sunday to become a delight.

The establishment and growth of urban institutions, such as the public library, the public park, and the professional baseball team, further altered the New England Sabbath. Since the work week extended through Saturday, Sunday was the obvious time for visits to the library, strolls in the park, and excitement in the ballpark. But this incursion of the worldly into sacred time worried religious and civil leaders who resisted Sunday opening with varying degrees of success. For instance, a controversy concerning the opening of the Boston Public Library extended nearly a decade before the city council resolved in 1873 to open the reading room each Sunday afternoon. Worcester, Mass., opened its public library the same year, and by the 1890s public libraries in New England's small towns opened only once a week—on Sundays during the hours immediately after church. A discourse focused on moral and spiritual uplift pervaded other controversies about Sunday openings, particularly among museums and galleries.

Diversion in the library or at the museum was close enough to spiritual exercise that disapproval of Sunday opening evaporated by the turn of the century; other forms of recreation, however, faced a great deal of resistance when their proponents tried to initiate them on Sunday. Laws, arrests, even riots marked efforts to hold baseball games on Sundays, to open saloons, to run rides at amusement parks, to screen movies, and to provide other diversions for New England's heterogeneous population. It was believed that such activities desecrated the Sabbath and demoralized the working classes, who needed rest and spiritual sustenance. Nevertheless, working people (and others) sought amusement and recreation in saloons, on the shores of lakes, and on promenades through town each Sunday. Irish Catholics' perfunctory Sunday observance—mass in the morning, revelry in the after-

noon—at first horrified, but eventually seduced, some Protestants, such as the minister Washington Gladden, who began to see in the world of amusements the potential for uplift. Gladden and others incorporated worldly activities, such as attending a play or walking in a park, into the realm of the sacred, thereby expanding the sphere of acceptable Sunday activities. In reaction, religious conservatives resisted the insinuation of the worldly. Some joined associations such as the New England Lord's Day Alliance; others in the late 1880s and early 1890s sent petitions to the nation's capitol in support of New Hampshire Senator Henry Blair's bill to set Sunday aside as a national holiday; and still others engaged in efforts to keep the 1893 Columbian Exposition (held in Chicago) closed on Sunday. Nevertheless, by the early 20th century a critical mass of religious and cultural leaders agreed with psychologist G. Stanley Hall that "true rest" was possible through "healthful" recreation, which would not contravene the religious purposes of the day. But some still criticized the commercial nature of many recreational activities, which they claimed turned "the day of rest into a day of gain."

The trend toward commercialization of Sunday characterizes the 20th and early 21st centuries' New England Sabbath. In 1994 Massachusetts residents voted to repeal laws that prohibited the selling of package liquor on Sundays and the opening of large retail establishments on Sunday mornings. This repeal of the "blue laws" effectively severed legislative continuity with New England's Sabbath laws that the Puritans brought to America. Nevertheless, the spirit of the New England Sabbath continues to pervade Sundays across the region and the nation, when church bells still often ring in the morning, and fewer people rush about the streets.

Bruce C. Daniels, *Puritans at Play: Leisure and Recreation in Colonial New England* (1995); Alice Morse Earle, *The Sabbath in Puritan New England* (1891); Richard John, "Taking Sabbatarianism Seriously," *Journal of the Early Republic* 10 (1990); Massachusetts Council of Churches, *Sunday Closing Laws Revisited* (1993); Alexis McCrossen, *Holy Day, Holiday: The American Sunday* (1998); Daniel T. Rodgers, *The Work Ethic in Industrial America, 1850–1920* (1978); Winton U. Solberg, *Redeem the Time: The Puritan Sabbath in Early America* (1977); Harriet Beecher Stowe, *Old Town Folks* (1869); Carroll D. Wright, *Sunday Labor* (1885).

Alexis McCrossen

Orr, Bobby (Robert Gordon) (1948–)

Ice hockey player. Born in Parry Sound, Ontario, Robert Gordon "Bobby" Orr demonstrated the talent and ability to excel at ice hockey from an early age. By the time he joined the Oshawa Generals, a junior team, at

Legendary hockey player Francis M. "King" Clancy congratulates Bobby Orr, April 1972

age 14, several National Hockey League (NHL) teams were eagerly awaiting his arrival—none more so than the success-starved Boston Bruins, who had placed Orr on their "protected list" when he was only 12 years old. Instead of passively accepting an opportunity to play in the NHL, Orr hired an agent, Alan Eagleson, to negotiate his first contract with the Bruins for the then-unheard-of sum rumored to be in the neighborhood of $150,000 for two years. Orr thus helped lay the foundation for the establishment of a player's union, the National Hockey League Players Association.

The investment paid off for the Bruins, who had languished for several years among teams that aspired to mediocrity. In his rookie season (1966–67), Orr won the Calder Trophy as the NHL's rookie of the year, the first of many individual trophies. The following season the Bruins, strengthened by the acquisition of high-scoring center Phil Esposito and the maturation of several other players, made the playoffs for the first time in nine years. Esposito and Orr were the cornerstones of a team that combined offensive firepower and bruising physical play to claim the Stanley Cup at the end of the 1969–70 and 1971–72 seasons. Both times, Orr was named winner of the Conn Smythe Trophy as the most valuable postseason player. Awarded the Hart Trophy as the league's most valuable player in three consecutive seasons (1969 through 1972), Orr also won the James Norris Trophy as the league's best defenseman for eight consecutive

seasons (1967 through 1975). Twice he claimed the Art Ross Trophy as the NHL's leading scorer (for the 1969–70 and 1974–75 seasons), an accomplishment all the more remarkable because he played defense. During his career he established season and career marks for goals, assists, and points by a defenseman, finishing with 270 goals, 645 assists, and 915 points; he still holds the single-season marks for assists (102) and points (139) by a defenseman.

Orr's style of play and his accomplishments fired the imaginations of fans and aspiring hockey players. His patented end-to-end rushes, in which he wheeled out of his own zone and smoothly wove his way between opposing players, brought spectators to their feet; youngsters on many a neighborhood rink emulated his style, shouting, "Goal by Number 4, Bobby Orr!" For many Bruins fans (and hockey fans in general), his championship-winning goal in overtime of game four of the 1970 Stanley Cup Finals remains vividly etched in the mind, with an open-mouthed Orr, horizontal in mid-flight (the result of a belated attempt to upend him), celebrating ultimate victory. Orr revolutionized the way the game was played with his offensive skills, particularly his ability to move the puck to open teammates, a style many defensemen favor today.

Injuries, rather than opposing players, caught up with Orr. Persistent knee problems plagued him throughout his career, and in the 1975–76 season he played only 10 games. At

the end of that season he became a free agent and signed with the Chicago Black Hawks, for whom he played only 26 games over the next two seasons before retiring on November 9, 1978. He remained involved in the game, eventually becoming an agent. Waiving its customary three-year waiting period, the Hockey Hall of Fame inducted him in 1979. When the *Boston Globe* conducted a survey to determine Boston's most popular sports figure, the winner was not Ted Williams, Carl Yastrzemski, Bill Russell, or Bob Cousy, but Bobby Orr.

Stan Fischler, *Bobby Orr and the Big, Bad Bruins* (1969); Bobby Orr, *My Game* (1974).

Brooks D. Simpson

Ouimet, Francis (1893–1967) Amateur golfer. Francis Ouimet's victory in the 1913 United States Open golf championship over the British professional golfers Harry Vardon and Ted Ray heralded the ascendancy of American golf and sparked an explosion of public interest in the sport.

Golf in the United States was only a few years older than Ouimet, the first permanent club having been established in Yonkers, N.Y., in 1888. Although by the turn of the century several cities had opened municipal courses, the game was played primarily by wealthy Americans who belonged to private clubs. In 1892 the Country Club in Brookline, Mass., was one of the first two clubs in New England (the other was in Newport, R.I.) to build a golf course, and there Ouimet was introduced to the game—though not as a member. Ouimet's working-class family lived in a small house on Clyde Street, across from the club, and Francis and his older brother, Wilfred, caddied there. Ouimet learned golf by watching some of the best players of the era in tournaments at The Country Club and by practicing his swing with a borrowed club on a makeshift course that Wilfred had laid out in a pasture by their house. In 1909 Ouimet won the Boston Interscholastic Championship, and the next year he began to compete in national tournaments.

In 1913 Harry Vardon, regarded as the finest golfer in the world, was making his second American tour, accompanied by another leading British professional, Edward "Ted" Ray. Vardon was expected to cap the tour—as he had his first—with a victory in the United States Open at The Country Club in September. Vardon took the lead in the first of the tournament's four rounds, but by the end of the third round he had been caught by Ray and a 20-year-old local, Francis Ouimet, who had captured attention earlier in the summer by winning the Massachusetts State Amateur and playing well in the U.S. Amateur. In the final round Ouimet was expected to fade: no amateur—let alone a "schoolboy," as the newspapers called him—had ever won the Open, and no American was thought capable of besting Vardon. In a steady rain, and after a shaky start, Ouimet played the final six holes in two strokes under par to keep up with Vardon and Ray and force an extra round the next day. In the playoff Ouimet took the lead on the 10th hole and never relinquished it. The decisive victory was touted as akin to David's slaying of Goliath. "Great British Golfers Defeated by Massachusetts Boy," read the headline in the *New York Times*. One British writer pronounced Ouimet's triumph "the greatest shock ever experienced in the British Isles."

Ouimet was embraced by the American public as the boy next door, whom fame could not rob of a natural modesty and gentleness. Ouimet was not in the game for the money: when jubilant spectators at the 1913 Open tried to stuff cash in his hands after the victory, the young man let it fall to the ground, lest he jeopardize his status as an amateur. In 1917 Ouimet opened a sporting goods store in Brookline. The United States Golf Association, ruling that any profit from sports constituted a professional interest, stripped him of amateur status, but after a public outcry it rescinded its decision.

In 1914 Ouimet won the U.S. Amateur championship—a prize he valued above the Open title—and the French Amateur, and won a second U.S. Amateur in 1931. He played on the U.S. team in the semi-annual Walker Cup competition against Great Britain from 1922 through 1934 and was nonplaying captain of the squad from 1936 through 1949. In 1951 he became the first non-Briton to be elected captain of the Royal and Ancient Golf Club of St. Andrews.

Ouimet's accomplishments on the golf course were soon eclipsed by those of Walter Hagen and Robert Trent "Bobby" Jones, but he retains pride of place as the first native-born American to succeed in golf against the best international competition.

Robert Sommers, *The U.S. Open* (1996); Herbert Warren Wind, *The Story of American Golf* (1956).

Richard Miller

Racquetball Joe Sobek, a former tennis and squash instructor, invented racquetball in Greenwich, Conn., in 1949. Sobek left his instructor's job at the Greenwich Country Club, and while working as an executive at a rubber manufacturing plant, searched for a new form of exercise. He rejected handball and paddleball but felt that the latter game could be improved if a stringed racket replaced the wooden paddle. Sobek originally used a plat-

form tennis paddle altered with strings. He found a proper ball, modified the rules of squash and paddleball, and then began playing the new game at the paddleball court of the Greenwich Young Men's Christian Association (YMCA). Unfortunately, the children's balls best suited for racquetball were out of production, and the new supply from the A. G. Spalding Company proved too lively, but with the aid of the Seamless Rubber Company in New Haven, Conn., Sobek designed a new ball that became the standard for paddlerackets, his name for the game.

Between 1949 and 1959, Sobek sent rackets and balls to the national YMCA and asked them to try the game, which helped spread racquetball. The game offered a fast-paced, strenuous workout but required less ability and experience than similar games. It also provided lower construction expense for courts and year-round indoor exercise, which was ideal for the Northeast during the winter.

From its New England origins, the game spread to the Midwest, which became the focal point of the game during the 1960s. In 1968, delegates met at a tournament in Milwaukee, Wis., formalized the rules, and changed the sport's name to racquetball. They also formed the International Racquetball Association (IRA) and held the first national championships in 1969. The IRA sought Olympic recognition for the sport and gained it in 1985. In 1997, the organization became the U.S. Racquetball Association (USRA) and remains the game's primary regulatory body.

Racquetball's popularity rocketed in the late 1970s and early 1980s as part of the fitness boom that swept the United States. During that time, it was one of the fastest growing American sports. In 1980, eight to 10 million Americans played the game, up from only 50,000 in 1970; and in 1981, the first world championships were held in Santa Clara, Calif. Since that time, however, the market has become saturated, and many racquetball courts have either closed or been converted to fitness centers to take advantage of rapid growth in that industry. After its peak popularity in the mid-1980s, player numbers dropped but have since stabilized at around five million in the United States.

In New England, competition from squash, paddleball, and handball hindered racquetball's early growth, and today the sport faces a dwindling number of courts along with an aging participant base. Worldwide, the game achieved recognized sport status from the International Olympic Committee and is a full medal sport at the Pan-American Games. Racquetball is now played in more than 90 countries, and world championships are held

biannually. Professional racquetball tours exist for both men and women in the United States and internationally, as well as intercollegiate championships sponsored by the USRA.

Thomas T. Fancher, "A History of Racquetball" (M.S. thesis, 1975); Carol Morgenstern, *Playing the Rackets: The Complete Guide to the Basics of Tennis, Squash, Racquetball, Paddle Tennis, Platform Tennis, One- and Four-Wall Paddleball* (1980).

Russ Crawford

Reenactments Reenactments of historical events, from military battles to the landing at Plymouth Rock, are popular pastimes that link modern Americans to a sense of New England's past. New Englanders participated in "sham battles" and in re-creations of Pilgrim history as early as 1801. These original reenactments shared with their modern counterparts the desire of people to celebrate New England's mythical past as the basis for civic or regional identity. Recently, reenactors have also turned their attention to minute historically accurate detail in an attempt to educate the public.

One of the first military reenactments in New England took place in 1822, when surviving members of the Lexington militia re-created their part in the Battle of Lexington. Occasional sham battles followed throughout the century, though they did not necessarily strive for historical accuracy.

By the mid-20th century, New Englanders had joined the growing national movement of battle reenactors who began to wear authentic uniforms and to value historical detail. Modern reenactors form themselves into companies based on military organization, and most spend a great amount of time researching the individuals they portray.

Battle reenactments connect New Englanders to their military heritage and most carry overtones of patriotism. For more than 40 years, the largest reenactment in New England has taken place on Patriot's Day, when hundreds of people re-create Paul Revere's ride and the battles of Lexington and Concord in real time. Other reenactors portray smaller New England skirmishes of the American Revolution, such as the burning of a replica of the ship *Gaspee* in Warwick, R.I. In the 1970s, the Bicentennial celebration spawned the formation of many "minute man" and militia groups, with thousands of members marching in local parades and gathering in Concord on Patriot's Day. Many New Englanders are involved in Civil War reenactments; notably, since 1989, a group has portrayed the Massachusetts 54th Regiment of African American soldiers.

The Pilgrims have long been popular sub-

Minutemen cross the Old North Bridge for the Bicentennial celebration at Concord, Mass., April 19, 1975

jects of historical reenactment in New England. The first reenactment of the landing at Plymouth Rock took place on Forefathers Day in December 1801. Throughout the 19th century, residents of Plymouth occasionally re-created public scenes or tableaux of Pilgrim life, culminating in one of the largest commemorative pageants in American history, "The Pilgrim Spirit," which was staged in 1921 for the Plymouth Tercentenary.

Beginning in 1945, reenactments were staged at a re-creation of the Pilgrim Village in Plymouth. By 1969 the Pilgrim Village had become Plimoth Plantation, a "living history" museum dedicated to representing Pilgrim life in the year 1627. Museum workers assume the identity of individual Pilgrims and reenact the minute details of their daily lives. The plantation added an Indian village in 1973. The museum also sponsors an annual reenactment and public Thanksgiving dinner and has re-created authentic fishing voyages. Reenactors in Provincetown, Mass., the original landing point of the Pilgrims, have challenged Plymouth's primacy and accuracy over the years and have sponsored their own re-creations of Pilgrim landings.

Although many reenactments in the late 20th and early 21st century have shied away from the tone of a kind of ancestor worship prevalent in earlier historical re-creations, they nonetheless help to create a sense of New England's uniqueness and pride of place.

Edward Tabor Linenthal, *Sacred Ground: Americans and Their Battlefields* (1993); William G. Schofield, "The Man Who Bombed Plymouth Rock," *Yankee Magazine* 57 (1993); John Skow, "Bang, Bang! You're History, Buddy," *Time Magazine,* August 11, 1986; Stephen E. Snow, *Performing the Pilgrims: A Study in Ethnohistorical Role-Playing at Plimoth Plantation* (1993).

Sarah J. Purcell

Russell, Bill (William Felton) (1934–)

Basketball player. With the arrival of Bill Russell in 1956, the Boston Celtics of the National Basketball Association (NBA) acquired the defensive muscle required to become a championship team. William Felton Russell, born in Monroe, La., was raised by his father in Oakland, Calif. He began playing basketball in junior high school and earned an athletic scholarship to the University of San Francisco in 1952. Reviving San Francisco's basketball program, Russell and teammate K. C. Jones led their team to 55 straight victories and two National Collegiate Athletic Association championships from 1954 to 1956. Before joining the Celtics, Russell led the U.S. Olympic basketball team to a gold medal in 1956.

Before Russell's arrival in Boston, the Celtics ranked as one of the NBA's most talented offensive teams with the scoring and ball-handling skills of Bob Cousy and others. With Russell's superb shot blocking and rebounding, Boston overwhelmed opponents both offensively and defensively. In his rookie year, 1956–57, Russell led the Celtics to an NBA title, the first of 11 from 1956 to 1969. From 1966 to 1969, he served as a player-coach, appointed by Red Auerbach, who retired as coach to become the general manager of the Celtics in 1966. Russell was the first African American to coach an NBA club. Moreover, those years featured a thrilling rivalry between Russell and 7-foot Wilt Chamberlain of the Philadelphia 76ers. In 142 matchups, Chamberlain av-

eraged 28.7 points and 28.7 rebounds, while Russell averaged 14.5 points and 23.7 rebounds; but Russell led his team to 85 wins and only 57 losses against Chamberlain's teams. When Chamberlain signed a $100,000 contract with the San Francisco Warriors in 1965, Russell renegotiated his own contract with the Celtics to be paid $100,001.

Russell retired from the Celtics in 1969 and was elected to the National Basketball Hall of Fame in 1974. During his career, Russell made more than 21,000 rebounds, scored more than 14,000 points, and was voted NBA Most Valuable Player in 1958, 1961, 1962, 1963, and 1965. Named the "Greatest Player in the History of the NBA" by the Professional Basketball Writers Association in 1980, Russell became a sports commentator, an actor, and an author. He used his prestige as an athlete to become an outspoken proponent for civil rights and social justice. He coached the Seattle Supersonics (1983–87) and the Sacramento Kings (1987–88), before becoming the vice president of the Kings in 1988.

Bill Russell dunks the ball, 1969

Bill Russell (as told to William McSweeny), *Go up for Glory* (1966); Bill Russell and Taylor Branch, *Second Wind: Memoirs of an Opinionated Man* (1979).

Adam R. Hornbuckle

Seashore The New England seashore, winding its way from southeastern Connecticut to the Maine-Canada border, has played a crucial role in the development of the region's history, economy, and identity. Over time New England's seashore has served as the site of Native American summer encampments, Revolutionary War battles, shipyards, and fisheries. Since the late 19th century, however, it has been closely identified as a prime recreation area and tourist destination. Today, millions flock to New England's shores each summer to swim, sunbathe, sail, fish, or enjoy that quintessential regional ritual, the clambake.

Just as the physical characteristics of the region's shores—sandy, smooth, or marshy in some spots, rocky and treacherous in others—differ considerably, the uses and meanings of the seashore throughout New England's history have varied. In different eras and locations, the seashore has been home to exclusive, fashionable resorts and elegant hotels, but also to cottages and pitched tents. It has been sought by people desiring a second home, by those interested in renting a cottage for a week or two, and by day-trippers seeking temporary relief from the summer heat.

The ebb and flow of the tide lends a timeless quality to the seashore, but the relationship of New Englanders and tourists to the region's shores has been shaped by technological, economic, and cultural developments over time. Before the Civil War, only the wealthy had the time and money to summer at the ocean. From colonial days, Newport, R.I., was a haven for the well-to-do, attracting visitors from throughout the Northeast and from as far away as South Carolina. The coastal town of Nahant, Mass., was another early exclusive resort area, whose development in the mid-1820s marked the beginning of the transformation of Boston's North Shore into a summer refuge. Mid-19th-century visitors to these and other resorts usually found accommodations in grand hotels that represented the "conspicuous consumption" of the wealthy.

After the Civil War, and steadily throughout the late 19th and early 20th centuries, the seashore became democratized, and resort areas proliferated along the New England coast. The shift was measurable in the number of middle- and working-class people heading to the shore but also in the spread of cottages they came to occupy. Gradually replacing the grand hotels, cottages signaled a more informal, family-oriented approach to summering by the sea.

The reasons for the growing popularity of the seashore as a recreational area are varied. In general, as labor groups led successful campaigns to shorten the workday and paid vacations were introduced, people were able to devote more time to leisure. They could also spend more money on leisure activities, with real wages increasing. Furthermore, attitudes toward leisure changed during this period as an ethic of indulgence—an acceptance of fun for its own sake—gradually replaced older, more puritanical views.

As urban areas became increasingly congested at the turn of the century, the seashore came to be considered an important recreation space. Recognizing its value, Boston reformers during the late 19th century campaigned to save the seashore from encroachments by commercial and residential development. With the establishment of the Metropolitan Park Commission in 1893, they were able to achieve their goal; within a decade, the commission, armed with powers of eminent domain, acquired and improved Nantasket Beach, Revere Beach, and four other shore "reservations" near Boston.

Expanded rail service throughout the region, especially the completion of the eastern branch of the Boston and Maine Railroad in 1873, and improvements in mass transportation made the shore more accessible just as the automobile and the extension of coastal roads—especially Routes 1 and 1A, and along Cape Cod, Routes 6 and 28—did later.

Finally, travelogue literature in the late 19th and early 20th centuries extolled the charm and quaintness of the New England seashore; advertising in the form of innumerable picture postcards also helped promote and romanticize life by the sea.

These converging factors led to a sharp rise in the number of resorts throughout New England during this period, many of which became distinguished by the presence of subgroups that claimed them as their own. For example, in Rhode Island's upper Narragansett Bay, according to J. Stanley Lemons, "more than thirty shore resorts, campgrounds, parks, and recreation areas flourished in the years between 1865 and 1925. Some were public beaches, like Kirwin's Beach, that swarmed with the urban masses; others were exclusively for the rich, such as the Ponham Club, Squantum, and the Rhode Island Yacht Club."

Janet Schulte, in her analysis of summer vacation communities in northern New England between 1880 and 1940 has argued that residents of seaside cottage villages segregated themselves by ethnicity, class, and occupation and used the vacation experience to reinforce their identities in a world that was becoming more racially and ethnically diverse. Such groups ensured the homogeneity of their communities either formally through deed restrictions on their shorefront property or informally by inviting only relatives and approved newcomers to join the community.

Class continued to determine the reputation of seaside resort communities. Toward the end of the 19th century, Bar Harbor, Maine, emerged as an enclave of the rich. Salisbury Beach in Massachusetts, however, attracted the families of factory workers from Lawrence, Lowell, and Haverhill, many of whom created ethnically segregated cottage communities close to the shore.

Several seashore resorts began with a strong religious identification. Buttonwoods in Warwick, R.I., founded in 1871, and Ocean Park in Maine, founded a decade later, served as summer retreats for Baptists; Methodists favored Oak Bluffs on Martha's Vineyard. Other coastal towns, notably Old Lyme, Conn.; Rockport, Mass.; and Ogunquit, Maine, have traditionally been popular among artists.

The increasing popularity of the New England seashore as a recreational area did not necessarily signal an embrace of the seashore as an antidote to city life. For features of a burgeoning commercial leisure industry transformed the seashore experience in many spots along the coast. At Savin Rock in Connecticut, Hampton Beach in New Hampshire, York Beach and Old Orchard Beach in Maine, and at many other spots, amusement venues sprang up near the shore or were built on piers extending into the water. At such locales, a stroll along the row of restaurants, hotels, arcades, theaters, clubs, candy stores, souvenir shops, and dance halls, or a turn on a mechanical ride, transformed a day at the beach and extended the seashore experience into the evening. Where boulevards passed between the beach and the commercial strip, automobile cruising became a popular pastime. Where commercial development could not occur opposite the beach, it often appeared inland, as on Cape Cod. Some shore resorts, such as Crescent Park and Rocky Point Park in Rhode Island, evolved into full-fledged amusement parks, although the latter spot was most famous for its shore dinners.

Beaches, occupying space between culture (in the form of shore development) and nature, have served as sites where social conventions have been flaunted and new manners and morals have been introduced. The anonymity afforded by New England's crowded beaches, for example, has emboldened visitors to engage in brazen, public displays of intimacy. Pondering this phenomenon, a Boston journalist once asked, "Why do the young people . . . become familiar and permit impossible liberties . . . when they are

*At the seashore,
Ogunquit, Maine,
1990*

within sight of the 'sad seas waves'?" Though many such encounters were surely fleeting, the reportedly high number of married people who met for trysts at the region's beaches has secured for the seashore a reputation as a place for romantic liaisons.

The two most popular beach activities, swimming and sunbathing, have undergone considerable change over time. Until the first decade of the 20th century, beachgoers took a dip in the ocean primarily for medicinal purposes, and the activity was known as seabathing. Swimming, as a sport and term, did not attain popularity until after 1910. Before the 1920s, in the eyes of the middle and upper class, a deep tan marked someone of lower status who engaged in outdoor, physical labor. During the 1920s and beyond, however, tans came to signify health and one's membership in the leisure class.

The emergence of swimming and sunbathing as forms of recreation led to changes in swimwear, especially for women. Heavy beach attire considered proper for women at the start of the 20th century—a bathing dress with skirt (some with weights sewn in the hem), stockings, and shoes—was impractical for female swimmers and certainly didn't con-

tribute toward a tan. Consequently, new fashions—ranging over time from form-fitting one-piece body suits to bikinis—were introduced and, after considerable controversy, ultimately accepted.

Aside from seaside resorts and beaches, areas along the New England coast that once served as important centers of shipbuilding, such as Mystic, Conn.; and whaling, such as New Bedford, Mass., have been developed into popular tourist attractions.

Given the importance of seaside recreation in New England, the issue of public access to the region's shores has been and remains a heated issue. Much of the New England shoreline has been privatized, and access to it is limited. Although state control of portions of the shore—at Hammonasset Beach State Park and Rocky Neck State Park in Connecticut, and at beaches in Rhode Island such as Misquamicut, Scarborough, and Wheeler—have made the seashore accessible to more people, significant stretches of it remain off-limits to the public.

Throughout its history, the New England seashore has also been threatened with erosion, and more recently, uncontrolled development. Environmental groups and local, state,

and federal authorities have made efforts to protect the region's shores. The establishment in 1919 of Acadia National Park in Maine and in 1961 of the Cape Cod National Seashore represents the most notable results of such efforts. Through the control of these and other areas, a balance between human and natural needs is sought so that the New England seashore can continue to function as a vital recreation space yet survive ecologically.

Cleveland Amory, *The Last Resorts* (1952); Richmond Barrett, *Good Old Summer Days* (1941); Joseph E. Garland, *Boston's Gold Coast: The North Shore, 1890–1929* (1981); Jewelle Gomez, "A Swimming Lesson," in *Forty-three Septembers* (1993); Kathy Neustadt, *Clambake: A History and Celebration of an American Tradition* (1992); Rhode Island Historical Society, *What a Difference a Bay Makes* (1993); John R. Stilgoe, *Alongshore* (1994).

Mark Herlihy

Skiing The sport of skiing provides employment and recreation in many of New England's mountain regions, and the resulting tax revenues are a major part of the winter budget in Vermont, New Hampshire, Maine, and Massachusetts. It was not always that way, however. Although the use of snowshoes for utilitarian purposes and social outings increased during the latter part of the 19th century, skiing did not begin until Scandinavian immigrants arrived in the 1870s. In a 1910 Boston *Sunday Herald* interview, Dr. Andreas Christian, a Norwegian immigrant, rejoiced at the hundreds of skiers in Massachusetts swarming over the Newtons and Brooklines, Middlesex Falls, and Blue Hills. Skis were readily available in Boston shops, and he believed that the New Hampshire countryside 50 miles to the north was perfect for skiing across field and dale; nor were the Berkshires to be belittled. The article, with eight large instructional photographs, included many asides on the sport's affordability, its appeal to children, and the benefits for the physical and mental health of men. For women, Dr. Christian assured his readers, skiing was also "a great antidote for corsets."

Dr. Christian's assessment, especially of the number of participants and the availability of equipment, was overdrawn. But the *Herald* article does indicate what was important to those who skied before the advent of steel edges, ski lifts, and ski areas. Norwegians had brought the culture of *skiidraet* with them to America—an ideal of all-around expertise in nature's outdoors that would engender sound body and mind and would benefit not only the individual but also society as a whole. Until the downhill *Schuss* from the Alps challenged it in the 1920s and 1930s, *skiidraet* was the way skiing was thought of and practiced.

Skiing at Pico Peak in Vermont, 1994

The organization of skiing as a sport, paralleled by a growth of interest among the middle class, began at schools and colleges, especially Dartmouth College in New Hampshire. Founded by Fred Harris in 1909, the Outing Club sponsored the Winter Carnival, and other New England universities soon offered skiing competition, with Canadians from Montreal adding an international touch. The high point of the competitions was always the jump. Jumps appeared in every village where skiing became popular, with the largest ones attracting a national and even international roster. Brattleboro, Vt., saw the national championships in 1924, and Nansen in Berlin, N.H., became the East's premier jump in 1938, the year of its construction.

Graduates returned home to found or join similar outing clubs. Prominent in promoting skiing was the Boston-based Appalachian Mountain Club. During the 1920s skiing became a bourgeois sport to be enjoyed along a logging road with a glide or two down a sloping meadow. Country inns stayed open for winter sporting from Poland Spring in Maine to Northfield Inn in Massachusetts, their reputations resting sometimes on a resident Norwegian instructor, such as Strand Mikkelsen at the Weldon Inn in Greenfield, Mass.

The well-to-do of Europe, however, were taken with alpine skiing. Austrian Hannes Schneider had developed his Arlberg technique for skiing downhill, which he also taught to increasing numbers of wealthy Americans who journeyed to St. Anton to learn the sport. They re-created the Arlberg in New England by bringing Austrians to the White Mountains of New Hampshire and the Green Mountains of Vermont, such as Sepp Ruschp at Stowe, Vt. Dartmouth acquired Otto Schniebs as coach for the 1929–30 sea-

son. Under his direction, Dartmouth teams in downhill, slalom, cross-country, and jumping provided the mark against which all others were measured. Four students represented the United States in the Winter Olympics in Garmisch-Partenkirchen in 1936, with Dick Durrance placing eighth and 11th in the slalom and downhill. New England continues to provide the venues for early training of Olympic racers, such as Maine's John Bower, the only American to win the King's Cup at Norway's Holmenkollen. And men and women from Dartmouth continue to represent the United States.

The problem of getting to the top of a hill for alpine skiing had been solved in Europe with cog railways and aerial tramways. Based on a Canadian model, rope tows appeared on hills first in Vermont and then spread quickly throughout New England. J-bars and T-bars followed in the 1930s, and the second chairlift appeared in the United States at New Hampshire's Belknap Recreation Area in 1938; that same year New Hampshire's Cannon Tram promised "the sky route to ski fun" at 60 cents a ride. These permanent lifts made the creation of trails necessary. The ski center took shape during the depression years, helped along by the Civilian Conservation Corps, which participated in trail cutting.

The glacial cirque on New England's highest mountain remained untouched by industrial modernization. Mount Washington had first been climbed on skis in 1899, and after 1926 winter visits became regular. The attraction, towering 900 feet, was the Headwall, a 50-degree steep first climbed and descended on skis in 1931 by Olympians John Carleton (1924) and Charles Proctor (1928). The first to schuss the Headwall was a Norwegian, Sigmund Ruud. Tuckerman Ravine became a

place of pilgrimage for the skier during the 1930s. The Inferno races, modeled on a madcap, down-mountain dash of the English at Mürren, were first run in April 1932. The 1939 Inferno, in which Toni Matt from Austria schussed the Headwall, has added to the Tuckerman lore and mystique.

During the economically difficult times of the 1930s, skiing received a boost from the snow trains, which ran first out of Boston in 1931 mostly to New Hampshire and then also from Grand Central Station in New York to Connecticut, Massachusetts, and Vermont. The trains brought a new clientele (Boston and Maine Railroad figures show 10,314 passengers in 1931, and 24,290 in 1936): the shop boss, secretary, and floor salesman or -woman who set out to enjoy a good "Sun-day," people rather different from the youthful, wealthy collegians.

The business infrastructure of skiing spread through New England with emporia from Burlington, Vt., to Portland, Maine, and in Massachusetts with Boston as the hub. Ski schools, virtually all boasting a resident Austrian, taught the Arlberg technique to weekenders in brightly fashioned ski togs for a day of sun and snow in the hilly north country. New England, in the years before World War II, set the skiing pace and style for the North American continent: Cannon Mountain with its Tram and Taft Racing trail, Greylock's Thunderbolt in Massachusetts, Woodstock's first rope tow, and Mount Washington Valley's "American Branch of the Hannes Schneider Ski School." All made New England the center of American alpine skiing.

The war put the development of skiing on hold. But wartime experiments with over-the-snow vehicles; light and durable metals; warm, strong, and elastic fabrics; even snowmaking boosted skiing after the war in New England. It seemed that the region would continue its premier place in the United States as it hosted the National Championships in 1946. An immense amount of capital was invested—helicopters hovered with steel lift pilings for area development. Stowe became the premier venue to ski during the 1950s and 1960s; there was "always snow in Stowe."

Ski development in New England seemed to have limitless possibilities. But the oil embargo of 1973 put an end to the manic rate of expansion. The ski area was becoming one of four-season real estate investment in which skiing was but one of the sports, occupations, and entertainments offered. No new ski area has been built in New England since the early 1970s, and many small ones have folded. The ones that continue, not always financially secure, have turned themselves into condominium havens with conference facilities.

They survive by supplying the captive population with recreation throughout the year that includes hiking, fishing, and tennis. Skiing is merely one part of the leisure menu.

Ski lifts of increasing efficiency whisk, at $40 to $56 a day, an expensively accoutered skier up to the top of a mountain. All leading ski areas have over 2,000-foot verticals. The trails are groomed to carpet smoothness and patrolled by employees who often have the unenviable task of policing the slopes for reckless skiers. For some years snowboarding, which combines a surfing and skiing background with a youth cult image, appeared to be on a collision course with skiers and ski management. An uneasy relation was worked out, and snowboarding today is seen as an economic lift to what has become a "no growth" industry.

Cross-country skiing, which never disappeared entirely, became part of the regular ski scene during the 1970s as America took to its fitness fad. With increasing costs of lift skiing and the boost received from Bill Koch's silver medal in the 30-kilometer event at the Innsbruck Olympics in 1976, ski areas began to provide groomed trails for cross-country enthusiasts. The national forests also marked trails for winter enjoyment.

For more than 100 years, New Englanders have been on skis. Today's snow is guaranteed by vast machines: Maine's Sunday River boasts 1,500 snow guns, while Loon in New Hampshire covers 98 percent of its terrain using 160 million gallons of water. Mechanization and business have standardized styles, equipment, and terrain, yet the attraction remains the same: the thrill of a rush down a hill or, out in the woods, the magic of gliding through snow-laden firs. Both provide an antidote to our urbanized lifestyles.

E. John B. Allen, "The Development of New Hampshire Skiing: 1870s–1940," *Historical New Hampshire* 36 (1981); Allen, *New England Skiing 1870–1940* (1997); Allen, *From Skisport to Skiing: One Hundred Years of an American Sport, 1840–1940* (1993); Glenn Parkinson, *First Tracks: Stories from Maine's Skiing Heritage* (1995); Ronald Story, ed., *Sports in Massachusetts: Historical Essays* (1991).

E. John B. Allen

Snowboarding

Snowboarding Snowboarding, the mountain snow sport characterized by a sideways stance on a single board, has roots in both the United States and Europe in the late 1960s. While rudimentary snowboards popped up all over America (the most successful of which is the Snurfer, introduced by Sherman Poppen in the Midwest in 1965), one of the "fathers of snowboarding," Jake Burton Carpenter, made his name in New England. Snowboarding's legendary entrepreneur, Carpenter founded a business called Burton Snowboards in Londonderry, Vt., in the late 1970s, producing 350 boards in 1978 alone, which he sold for $80 apiece. Today Burton Snowboards, located in Burlington, Vt., is the premier producer of snowboards and a sponsor of the U.S. Open Snowboarding Championship.

The first national snowboarding competition was held on a hill called Suicide Six outside Woodstock, Vt., in 1982; the next year, renamed the U.S. Open Snowboarding Championship, it moved to Snow Valley, Vt. Since 1985 the Open has been held in Stratton, Vt.; in 2004 it drew 566 snowboarders from more than 18 countries.

In its early years snowboarding offered a cool mix of cultures, which helps account for the speed with which it took off. A little bit dangerous, a little bit punk rock, a little bit hip-hop, snowboarding draws its tricks, a series of jumps and slides on metal rails, from skateboarding. Also derived from skateboarding is the halfpipe, which enables riders to launch into the air. Snowboarding's equipment technology, on the other hand, with its combination of wood, plastic, and resin boards with metal edges, owes more to skiing. And many claim that the soul of snowboarding, its basic tie to nature's power, comes straight from surfing.

Snowboarding, however, is much easier to learn than skateboarding, skiing, or surfing. The sport's accessibility also explains why in just a few years it achieved a popularity that the other sports took decades to build up. And because snowboarding demands special clothes and equipment in addition to a mountain and a lift, entrepreneurs have been able to build the industry. In fact, snowboarding is said to have saved the ski and mountain resort industry from near demise during the recession of the early 1990s.

But as often happens in popular culture, saturation has led to homogenization. In the late 1990s, ski companies absorbed snowboarding into their industry; for many, snowboarding has now become just another mainstream sport, no longer a cultural phenomenon. Snowboarders have become more athletic, equipment is more finely tuned. By 1998 snowboarding was ready for the Olympics. The first U.S. medal in snowboarding, a bronze, was won by Vermonter Ross Powers, who went on to win the gold in the men's halfpipe in 2002, along with his fellow Vermonter Kelly Clark (born in Newport, R.I.), who also struck gold, winning the women's halfpipe. With its smallish hills New England doesn't offer much scope for other rides, but New Englanders get a lot of practice in halfpipes, as the Olympic results attest.

Susanna Howe

Snowmobiling

Snowmobiling The term *snowmobile* was coined in 1913 by Virgil White, an automobile dealer from West Ossipee, N.H., who made a motor vehicle capable of traversing snow. But White was not the first New Hampshirite to do so. In 1908 George Brewster of Wolfeboro converted a Crestmobile—an early, buggylike automobile—into a vehicle able to make its way over snow-covered terrain. In the years between the two world wars inventors from New England and the Midwest, mostly in Wisconsin, were developing and selling these converted vehicles by the thousands to rural letter carriers, country doctors, utility companies, winter resorts, and anyone else who might need transportation over snowy terrain.

In 1930 White's Snowmobile Company was acquired by B. F. Arps of New Holstein, Wis., who had distributed snowmobiles made by that firm since the late 1920s. Arps, a farm-implement manufacturer, then started building his own version of a snowmobile, the Snow Bird, which, like its predecessors, combined a snow-traversing system with a Ford motor vehicle. After acquiring another competitor, Snow Flyer, Arps merged all operations into his Snow Bird Company. Snow Bird operated until the beginning of World War II when Arps closed it down for three reasons: defense contracts were more profitable, the new generation of cars and light trucks were too wide to accommodate the snow-traversing systems, and rural letter carriers were no longer required to deliver the mail in treacherous weather conditions.

In the mid-1950s two small firms in the Midwest (later named Polaris and Arctic Cat) and Bombardier in Quebec realized that there was a market among farmers, trappers, and law-enforcement officers, among others, for a small, light one- or two-person vehicle for moving over snow. These and other companies brought small snow vehicles to market, where they became commonly known as snowmobiles.

Initially, public agencies in New England and New York were the principal buyers of snowmobiles. Soon enough, however, snowmobiles were being ridden not only by those whose livelihoods required them but also by thousands of people who wanted recreational access to New England's woods and fields.

In response to the growing use of snowmobiles, by 1967 New Hampshire was creating legislation to regulate and license snowmobile operators. That state's laws became a model for legislation passed elsewhere in New England and in the Midwest. Still, controversies have arisen over the environmental and social impact of snowmobiles.

Scores of snowmobile clubs have been created with a view to both defending the rights of their members in the political arena and preventing environmental abuses on the trails. This network of clubs, whose membership is mostly local, has helped create a positive political atmosphere in which the sport can thrive; the New Hampshire Snowmobile Association and its affiliates throughout the state, for example, engage in community-action projects and fund-raising for hometown charities. The users of trail bikes, all-terrain vehicles, and jet skis, by contrast, have faced restriction if not outright prohibition of their activities, in large part because most of them are out-of-state tourists who have not always respected the rights of local property owners.

Paul T. Doherty, *Smoke from a Thousand Campfires* (1994); Robert L. Horney, *Snowmobiling*, ed. Judith E. Goldstein (1970); Sally Wimer, *The Snowmobiler's Companion* (1973).

Scott E. Green

Soccer

Soccer When the first European settlers arrived in Massachusetts, they discovered local natives playing a game called Pasuckquakkohowog, which they translated into "They gather to play football," making soccer, or something similar, one of New England's oldest sports. The game was most often played on beaches near present-day Lynn, Revere, or Cape Cod, Mass., and involved maneuvering a deerskin ball, about the size of a handball and stuffed with deer hair, across the opponent's goal. The game pitted teams from rival villages against one another, and tribal land often changed hands as result of wagering on matches.

Arguably the first regular soccer team in the United States began play in 1862, when Gerrit Smith Miller, a student at the Sargent Dixiwell Private Latin School in Boston, formed the Oneida Football Club, which went undefeated and unscored upon between 1862 and 1865. In 1925 a statue to Miller was erected near the Spruce Street Gate on Boston Common. The game, with regularized rules brought by British immigrants who arrived to work in the textile mills in the 1870s and 1880s, spread to other New England towns including Quincy, Fall River, and Lawrence, Mass., and Pawtucket and Providence, R.I., all of which became soccer hotbeds in the late 19th century. Between 1894 and 1899 the American Football Association (AFA) spread the sport's popularity, but labor unrest in Fall River deprived the association of many of its best players and teams, and it folded.

One of the first professional soccer games took place in New England, when the Boston Beaneaters defeated the Brooklyn (N.Y.) Superbas 3–2 at Boston's South End Grounds in 1894. The first professional soccer league lasted only one season, but fans continued to support matches of locals against touring international teams. The Fall River Rovers, which had survived the collapse of the AFA, scored a famous upset by defeating the Corinthians, a powerful English professional team that traveled the Northeast in 1906, then went on to win three consecutive U.S. Open cups (1916–18) playing in the Southern New England Soccer League. The American national team, coached and managed by George Matthew Collins, the soccer editor of the *Boston Daily Globe*, competed in the 1924 Olympics in Paris, winning its first game before losing to the eventual champion, Uruguay.

Despite enjoying a brief golden age in the 1920s, soccer struggled for popularity through much of the 20th century. The sport gained momentum in 1964, when American Youth Soccer began promoting the game for young players. In 1974, with Boston Celtics and Holy Cross legend Bob Cousy as commissioner of the North American Soccer League, professional soccer expanded to the West Coast. The signing of the legendary Pelé and other international stars also gave the sport a boost, but professional soccer still failed to hold public interest, though the popularity of youth and collegiate play increased dramatically. Soccer's visibility increased in 1994, when Los Angeles hosted the World Cup, giving the men's national team an automatic berth; the team's strong showing boosted soccer awareness among Americans.

Today soccer's popularity is growing among American youth, especially girls. The women's national team's victories at the Olympics in Atlanta (1996) and Athens (2004), along with their victory in the World Cup in 1999, fueled this surge. There are outdoor men's and women's professional leagues, and an indoor men's league. There are more than 700 men's collegiate programs, more than 600 women's programs, and over 8 million children playing in youth leagues.

Harry Blauvelt, "Girls' Soccer Is Sport on the Move," *USA Today*, September 10, 2003; Corey Bray, *Sports Sponsorship and Participation Rates Report* (2003); Sam Foulds and Paul Harris, *America's Soccer Heritage*, (1979); Jerry Langdon, "Soccer's Popularity Continues to Soar," *Gannett News Service*, October 16, 1998.

Russ Crawford

Sockalexis, Louis Francis "Chief"

Sockalexis, Louis Francis "Chief" (1871–1913) Baseball player. Louis Francis Sockalexis, a Penobscot Indian from Indian Island in Old Town, Maine, was the first Native American to play baseball at the major league level. His spectacular play earned him the nicknames "Deerfoot of the Diamond" and "Chief Sock-Em." He was the cousin of Andrew Sockalexis, a marathon runner and medal winner for the United States in the 1912 Olympics. Despite a brief career plagued by alcoholism and injuries, Sockalexis inspired a series of popular children's books, *Frank Merriwell Stories for Boys*, as well as the name of a major league baseball team.

As a teenager in Maine, Sockalexis attended Saint Anne's Convent School where he participated in track, football, and baseball. In the summer, he played amateur and semiprofessional baseball. Reputedly, he could throw a baseball 414 feet in a line, run 100 yards in 10 seconds, and hit towering home runs. His talent impressed Gilbert Patten, the manager of an opposing team in the Knox County League, who, under the pseudonym Burt L. Standish, created the character of consummate sports hero "Frank Merriwell."

In 1894, after attending Ricker Classical Institute in Houlton, Maine, Sockalexis entered the College of the Holy Cross in Worcester, Mass. Although the Maine native awed the city with his football abilities, he was best known for his superior baseball talent. After two seasons in which he had batting averages of .436 and .444, respectively, he transferred to Notre Dame in South Bend, Indiana. In March 1897, Sockalexis was asked to leave the school because of an alcohol-related incident, so he accepted the offer of Patsy Tebeau, manager of the Cleveland Spiders, to join that National League club as an outfielder.

Sockalexis's arrival in the major leagues initially was met with derision by opposing fans because he was the first Native American to play at that level. Still, he established himself by hitting a home run in his first at-bat and by compiling an average of approximately .400 within months; he quickly became a fan favorite. However, a worsening alcohol problem and a foot injury hampered him after July. Throughout that first season, he hit .338 and stole 16 bases in 66 games. His alcohol problem limited him to 21 games and a .224 average in 1898; after seven games in 1899, Cleveland released Sockalexis. The former star unsuccessfully tried comebacks with minor league teams in Lowell, Mass., and Hartford and Waterbury-Bristol, Conn.

Sockalexis eventually returned to Old Town, Maine, after several years of vagrancy. He occasionally umpired baseball games in the area and worked at times as a ferryman and a lumberjack; it was while working at a lumber camp in Burlington, Maine, that Sockalexis died of a heart attack. However, he was not forgotten. In 1915, when a Cleveland newspaper held a contest to rename the city's American League baseball team, a fan submitted the name "Cleveland Indians" to honor the man who some believed could have become the greatest baseball player in major league history.

Will Anderson, *Was Baseball Really Invented in Maine?* (1992); Troy Soos, *Before the Curse: The Glory Days of New England Baseball, 1858–1918* (1997); Geoffrey C. Ward and Ken Burns, *Baseball: An Illustrated History* (1994).

Scott Roper

Sullivan, John L. (1858–1918) Prize-

fighter. John Lawrence Sullivan, the last world heavyweight prizefighting champion of the bare-knuckle era, was one of America's, and particularly New England's, first sporting heroes. Born in Roxbury, Mass., he was the son of Irish immigrants Michael and Catherine Sullivan. A powerfully built youth, Sullivan worked at various trades and, at times, supplemented his income by playing semiprofessional baseball, earning as much as $25 per game. His baseball skills reportedly earned him a $1,300 contract with the Cincinnati Red Stockings. Shunning baseball as a profession, Sullivan began fighting in exhibitions held in Boston theaters and music halls. In 1878 he registered his first knockout against Johnny "Cockey" Woods, and within the next year, he began to support himself solely as a prizefighter. In 1880 Sullivan defeated John Donaldson, the "champion of the West," in a 10-round bout in the back room of a Cincinnati saloon. Brimming with confidence after that triumph, the "Boston Strong Boy" issued a challenge to all boxers, but especially to the existing heavyweight champion, Paddy Ryan, to meet him in the ring.

Ryan snubbed Sullivan's challenge for two years, recommending that the young pugilist establish a reputation. In the meantime, Sullivan offered $50 to any man who could fight him for four complete rounds under the Queensberry rules, which outlawed wrestling holds and required the fighters to wear gloves. Veteran fighters such as Steve Taylor accepted the challenge but lasted only a couple of rounds with Sullivan. Managed by Billy Madden, a former fighter, Sullivan boxed the Northeast and Midwest, earning $150 a week, roughly 10 times the average laborer's wage at that time. In 1881 he won $1,000 by knocking out John Flood in a bare-knuckle battle on a barge in the Hudson River off Manhattan. In 1882 Ryan accepted Sullivan's challenge and lost the world heavyweight title to the Boston parvenu in a brutal nine-round battle in Mississippi City. Sullivan's triumph galvanized civic pride, as Bostonians put aside social class and ethnic differences to celebrate their hometown hero. Nationally, Sullivan became a household name as the sporting presses throughout the Northeast and Midwest hailed his triumph.

Sullivan did not defend his title until 1888

Chalkware folk sculpture of John L. Sullivan, ca. 1890

when he defeated Charley Mitchell, the British heavyweight champion, in Chantilly, France, after a 39-round draw. Before that fight, however, Sullivan toured much of the nation, fighting all-comers with or without gloves in exhibition bouts. Sullivan preferred to fight with gloves rather than violate local ordinances against bare-knuckle fist fighting. During a 20-week road trip in 1882 he earned up to $500 per night. From 1883 to 1884, Sullivan garnered $80,000, mostly from exhibitions in which veteran boxers simply endured four punishing rounds in the ring with him. In the late 1880s he toured England and Australia with a circus troupe, earning more than a quarter of a million dollars. During this time, Sullivan adopted many techniques used by circus, vaudeville, and theater promoters to transform boxing into a legitimate form of entertainment. Moreover, his insistence on challenging all-comers in fights governed by the Queensberry rules encouraged the transition from bare-knuckle free-for-alls to ordered bouts. On July 8, 1889, Sullivan won the last world heavyweight bare-knuckle championship by defeating Jake Kilrain in 15 rounds in Richburg, Miss. On September 7, 1892, in the first heavyweight world championship match governed by the Queensberry rules, he lost the world heavyweight championship to James J. "Gentleman Jim" Corbett.

Elliott J. Gorn, *The Manly Art: Bare-Knuckle Prize Fighting in America* (1986); Michael T. Isenberg, *John L. Sullivan and His America* (1988).

Adam R. Hornbuckle

Summer Camp From the 1880s through

the 1930s, the children's "resident" or sleep-away summer camp retextured the New England landscape, evolved into a national movement, and emerged as an icon of American democracy and community. These developments occurred within the context of a nationwide reform movement called Progressivism based on the idea that life would be improved through pragmatic reforms. Leaders of the movement tried to improve children's lives by testing novel ideas about education and leisure within the isolated world of the resident camp, where boys and girls lived for two weeks to two months. From the turn of the 19th century onward, camp advocates persuaded parents to send their sons and daughters to camp by describing it as a "worthy use of leisure." While its location within the countryside provided a safe and healthy space for children to play and rest, daily activities developed physical fitness, character, and patriotism. Beyond just a place for play, the summer camp was a means for developing manners and talents. More generally, the axiom that the health of the nation was located in the fitness of the child fueled the summer camp movement throughout the 20th century.

The children's summer camp took root and thrived in the New England woods. George Bird Grinnell and Dr. Eugene L. Swan, editors of the 1911 edition of *Harper's Camping and Scouting: An Outdoor Guide for American Boys,* attributed this regional summer camp phenomenon to nature. They wrote that the "long line of lakes extending through the heart of New Hampshire," "the green hills of Vermont," and the "splendid winding coast line, noble rivers and countless lakes of Maine, exerted a lure that few could resist who loved the open country."

That New England was a center of Progressivism further explains why the summer camp spread through the region. Influenced by new ideas about childhood development from the Progressive philosopher John Dewey, psychologist G. Stanley Hall, and YMCA leader Luther Gulick, summer camp activists hoped to dramatically improve children's lives through programs of play and education. Four theories were particularly important for the summer camp movement. First, children learned through "direct experiences," exploring and discovering for themselves. Second, they learned while at play. Third, physical fitness was linked to good mental health. Fourth, a "good" education developed the "total child," simultaneously strengthening his or her body, mind, and soul.

Another strand in the summer camp movement adopted "Indian" skills and rituals. The juxtaposition of the primitive with the modern crystallized in a camping trend that pledged to civilize boys by turning them into "Indian" scouts. Scouting camps such as the Woodcraft Indians in Connecticut (1902) were forerunners of the Boy Scouts of America (1910).

Organizers of different types of boys' camps conjured a mythical Indian from America's colonial past that was noble, strong, and skillful. They appropriated Indian names, songs, and rituals, some of which were taken from real Native American groups, to structure daily life. Counselors urged campers to mimic the "noble savage's" character in daily life, as well as during special activities such as the camp fire, the real and symbolic centerpiece of summer camp life. Young "warriors" displayed their Indian morality, strength, and skills at the camp fire by solemnly challenging each other to wrestling matches and other competitive sports, through storytelling, and by leading fire lighting and "peace pipe" ceremonies.

Girls also mimicked the noble Indian at summer camp. In 1902, teacher Laura Matton led an expedition of eight into the New Hampshire wilderness and founded one of the earliest camps for girls named Camp Kehonka. The group's practical clothing, Indian existence, and "strenuous life" were ridiculed by local villagers who deemed their behavior and attire unfeminine. But the young campers found the "freedom from the restraints of fashion and iron bound convention" appealing. Kehonka became a yearly tradition, and its establishment marks a milestone in the history of camping for girls.

By 1910, when Luther Gulick and his wife Charlotte founded the Camp Fire Girls, there were already 41 organized camps for girls. Their first camp, WoHeLo, was named by taking the first letters of the words *work, health,* and *love.* The Camp Fire Girls was the first nonsectarian organization for girls, and its pledge to "serve family, community, and nation" suggests that camping for girls developed within both a traditionally feminine and a patriotic context.

Whereas most of these camps catered to children from middle-class and upper-middle-class homes, the turn-of-the-century urbanization of America inspired a Fresh Air movement aimed at boys and girls from lower-class homes. Its founders hoped to promote good health by taking children out of urban centers and placing them at camps in the countryside during the hot summer months. Children's Country Week in Massachusetts (1877) and Incarnation Camp (1886) and Life Camps (1887) in Connecticut were expressions of this quest.

The need for "constructive leisure" and rest also inspired Young Men's and Young Wom-

en's Christian Associations (YMCA and YWCA) to establish summer camps. Camp Seaside in Rhode Island (1870) was founded under YWCA auspices, for instance, to give "taxed young working women of the city . . . a happy and healthful vacation from toil." Camps established by the YMCA were intent on providing "healthful recreation without temptation" that would foster a "manly Christian character." By 1940, an estimated 1,425,230 boys and 262,694 girls attended YMCA and YWCA camps across the country, most of them clustered within Connecticut, New Hampshire, Vermont, Massachusetts, and Rhode Island.

Concern with physical and moral fitness focused Progressive attention on the 27 million eastern European people who migrated to American cities at the turn of the century. Many reformers perceived summer camp as an excellent site of Americanization because it provided immigrant children with healthy vacations while familiarizing them with U.S. customs and values. Camps including Tent Camp (1906) for boys and Camp Content (1908) for girls, both established in Maine, and Camp Dorchester founded in Massachusetts (ca. 1920), transmitted "American" culture to boys and girls through lessons on diet and hygiene and songs praising loyalty to the nation, bravery, obedience, and cheerfulness.

World War I marked a turning point in camp history. After the war, the popularity of camps grew tremendously, and the series of private camp initiatives cohered into a national movement. Fueled by xenophobia and nativist claims that eastern European immigrants were causing a nationwide moral and physical decline, some immigrant groups responded by using camps to prove that they were valuable U.S. citizens. For example, camps such as Kennebec, a Jewish camp in Maine, responded to the piercing cry for "100 percent Americanism" that resonated throughout the 1920s by pledging to perpetuate "American Anglo-Saxon Civilization." By the same token, however, Kennebec directors bolstered ethnic pride by cultivating a "muscular Judaism" that paralleled the "muscular Christianity" movement developed at YMCA camps.

Nondenominational, as well as ethnic and Christian, camping grew after World War I. By 1930, approximately 5 million children attended 24,000 summer camps nationwide. In short, children were socialized into 20th-century urban life within a camp environment premised on the values and sensibilities associated with preindustrial, even pre-European, America. Summer camp customs countered urban isolation with a communal existence in nature. They also reinvented the Indian as the personification of the natural.

Summer camp owners and activists began

to standardize the summer camp during the 1920s. As a result, summer camps with different political and religious orientations began to look, sound, and feel more alike. Cabins with screened outer walls and buildings with wraparound porches, drawn from the design of turn-of-the-century tuberculosis sanatoriums, became a hallmark of the children's camp; the sound of reveille signaled that a camp was nearby; outfits such as bloomers and middies were increasingly uniform; and professional training, such as that offered by the Girl Scouts National Training Camp in Massachusetts (founded in 1923), became a requirement for work at many summer camps.

The end of World War II marked a second turning point in summer camp history. Displaced children, the G.I. bill, the formation of a Jewish state, McCarthyism, civil rights, and new prosperity redefined the nation's identity and its cultural landscape. Americans living in the 1950s defined excellence as the axis of their new society. The quest for excellence was reflected in the special focus camp, a trend that dominated the children's summer camp scene during the second half of the 20th century.

The special focus camp took a variety of religious, political, artistic, and therapeutic forms. Quakerism, for instance, was the focus at the Friends Camp founded in Maine in 1953, where campers could partake in daily ecumenical Quaker meeting for worship as well as programs in crafts, pottery, drama, nature study, and noncompetitive sports. Camp Tel Noar in New Hampshire (1952), on the other hand, focused on promoting Zionist sentiments. Camp Belvoir Terrace in Lenox, Mass. (1954), developed campers' skills and interests in the performing arts such as dance, drama, and music.

Other camps were created to help children suffering from a range of physical, intellectual, and social disorders become productive members of society. Some, like Camp Thorpe in Goshen, Vt. (1927), had been established before World War II and were expanded in its aftermath. Thorpe catered to girls and boys with cerebral palsy, mental retardation, spina bifida, epilepsy, muscular dystrophy, histories of being abused, and attention deficit disorder. Adventurelore, founded in Maine in 1982, was established for children with diabetes.

Fashions of the times informed camp trends. Camp Kingsmont, a "slim down camp for girls and trim down camps for boys," organized in West Stockbridge, Mass., in 1971, for example, was one of a spate of camps devoted to helping children achieve and maintain an ideal body weight. Other types of specialty camps included Dunkley's Gymnastic Camp, founded in South Hero, Vt., in 1973. The camp trends of the 1970s continued into the 1980s, a decade marked by the advent of the "computer camp." Circus Smirkus Summer Camp, a co-ed camp founded in Greensboro, Vt., in 1987, was among the "circus camps" that provided professional training in acrobatics, juggling, clowning, trapeze, and tightrope.

The 1990s witnessed the continued success and discovery of new categories of special focus camps and new ways to advertise summer camps. In the 1940s, directors such as Elsie Reich of Berkshire Hills Camp advertised her camp and recruited campers by visiting parents in their homes. Today, the Internet enables thousands of camp owners and directors to bring their summer camps into the homes of perspective campers without leaving their desks. Web sites combine image with sound, providing a virtual sense of the summer camp, an American cultural tradition that continues to thrive in the New England woods.

Eleanor Eells, *History of Organized Camping: The First 100 Years* (1986); Elizabeth Frazer, "Young America Takes to the Wilds," *The Saturday Evening Post* (1926); H. W. Gibson, "The History of Organized Camping," *Camping Magazine* (1936); Harvey J. Graff, *Conflicting Paths: Growing up in America* (1995); David I. Macleod, *Building Character in the American Boy: The Boy Scouts, YMCA, and Their Forerunners, 1870–1920* (1983); Lloyd Burgess Sharp, *Education and the Summer Camp: An Experiment* (1930); John P. Sprague, "The Essence of Camping," *Red Book Magazine* (1928).

Nancy Mykoff

Tennis Although no one can be certain where tennis was first played in the United States, 1874 was the year, and New England was the fountainhead of the American game, particularly in Massachusetts and Rhode Island. Tennis sightings were reported throughout the country in 1874: at Camp Apache, Ariz., Philadelphia, Newport, R.I., New York, New Orleans, and Nahant, Mass., among other places. However, the most influential claimant to the title of birthplace of American tennis was the seaside resort of Nahant, where two Bostonians batted balls: Fred Sears and Dr. James Dwight, a Harvard-trained physician who would become known as the father of American tennis. The following year Dwight organized the initial tennis tournament, a sociable round-robin at Nahant.

Six years later Dwight helped plan the original U.S. Championships (for men only) on the grass courts of the Newport Casino. Built in 1880 by James Gordon Bennett, publisher of the New York *Herald,* the Newport Casino is the world's oldest active tennis ground. Dick Sears, a 19-year-old Harvard student, was the first U.S. champion in 1881 and continued as champion through 1887, winning the doubles title with Dwight five times. A Yale man, Henry Slocum, followed Sears as U.S. cham-

pion in 1888–89. But only a few other New Englanders have won the U.S. singles title: Fred Hovey (1895), Beals Wright (1905), Evelyn Sears (1907), Hazel Hotchkiss Wightman (1909–11, 1919), and Sarah Palfrey Cooke (1941, 1945).

In 1915 the U.S. Championships moved to New York, but Newport remained a prominent stop on the international men's circuit, a tradition that continues today with a professional event, the Jimmy Van Alen Cup, on the American Tennis Professionals (ATP) Tour. The event is named for the energetic innovator who in 1954 founded the International Tennis Hall of Fame at the Newport Casino, where he presided for many years. Van Alen also bankrolled Newport's first professional tourney in 1965, at which he unveiled his suggested scoring alteration, the tie-breaker. Adopted in 1970, the tie-breaker is the only significant rule change since the earliest days of the sport.

Longwood Cricket Club, formed in Boston in 1877, soon became a tennis bastion, a site for important international tourneys from 1891 through 1999. In 1900 a 21-year-old member, Harvardian Dwight Davis, donated a large sterling silver punchbowl for what he called the International Lawn Tennis Challenge Trophy: a proposed team championship tournament among nations that would be overseen by James Dwight. The first year only one other country, Britain, competed, and the British team was defeated at Longwood 3–0 by the U.S. team. Since then the competition that eventually became known as the Davis Cup has grown into a truly international event: 137 countries competed in 2004. Another Longwood member, Hazel Hotchkiss Wightman, inspired women's team competition by presenting a prize she called the Wightman Cup in 1923 for a tournament between Britain and the United States. Running through 1989, the Wightman Cup was abandoned when the British were no longer able to be competitive, but it was the impetus for today's international Federation Cup.

Various national and international championships were contested at Longwood, including the Longwood Bowl Championships (1891–1916, 1919–39, 1942), the U.S. Doubles Championships (1917–67, except 1934, 1942–45), the U.S. Amateur Championships (1968–69), the U.S. Pro Championships (1964–99), the Davis Cup final (1903) and nine Davis Cup early-round series, the Wightman Cup (1951, 1973), and a Federation Cup series (1997). Neighboring Longwood Covered Courts was the site of the U.S. Women's Indoor Championships (1921–33, 1941–46, 1954–66). The tournament was later held in Winchester, Mass. (1967–70).

Among the most successful of the other professional tournaments in New England was the Volvo International, held at Bretton Woods, N.H. (1973–74), North Conway, N.H. (1975–84), Stratton Mountain, Vt. (1985–89), and New Haven, Conn. (1990–95), on the Yale campus. A women's professional tournament has been held at Yale since 1998.

Bud Collins

Volleyball In 1895, William G. Morgan invented volleyball while serving as an instructor at the International Young Men's Christian Association (YMCA) Training School in Springfield, Mass. Morgan sought a new game that would require the same degree of physical activity found in basketball but would eliminate the rough contact of that sport. It was designed to be a game that middle-class businessmen would find less challenging to learn and play, thereby increasing their physical and, under the YMCA's philosophy, moral fitness. Designing the ball was the first task Morgan tackled, and he and the A. G. Spalding Brothers Company developed one that remains essentially the same today.

The new game debuted at the physical directors' conference of the eastern section of the YMCA during the week of July 7–16, 1896, at Springfield College, as the training school later became known. J. J. Curran and John Lynch, the mayor and the chief of the fire department of Holyoke, Mass., captained one of the teams that played the inaugural match before an audience of physical educators. During the demonstration, Dr. T. A. Halstead, a Springfield physical education instructor, observed that perhaps the game's name should be changed from *mintonette* to *volleyball* because it involved volleying a ball over the net—and so volleyball was born.

Descriptions of the new game first appeared in print in the handbook of the Athletic League of the YMCAs of North America in 1897, and it spread worldwide rapidly through the efforts of people who supported the YMCA's mission of blending Protestantism and physical fitness. Although volleyball's popularity lagged in America, the two world wars helped spread knowledge of, and appreciation for, the game. During World War I alone, more than 16,000 volleyballs were distributed to the American Expeditionary Force. With action that could fit in a hangar deck or jungle clearing, volleyball's popularity spread again during World War II.

In the early 1900s rule changes set the modern shape of the game. In 1922 the YMCA introduced the three-hit rule for returning the ball over the net; it also held its first national championship tournament that year. In 1923 the official size of the court was set at 30 by

60 feet, and the first international championship was held. The YMCA's control over the game ended at the Amateur Athletic Union's 1937 convention in Boston when the U.S. Volleyball Association became the sport's governing body.

After World War II, beach volleyball became a popular sport in California, and the International Volleyball Federation, formed in Paris in 1947, held the first non-YMCA world championship in Prague in 1949. Volleyball became an Olympic sport at the Tokyo Olympics in 1964, and the exposure, plus a new style of play called "power volleyball," increased the sport's popularity in the United States and worldwide. Today, volleyball is played by 603 women's teams and 63 men's teams in colleges and universities; more than 400,000 girls and boys play the sport in American high schools; and it is estimated that more than 800 million play the game worldwide, placing volleyball among the world's most popular sports.

Corey Bray, "NCAA Year by Year Sports Participation, 1981–82 to 2001–02" (2003); J. Tilman Hall, ed., "Volleyball," Goodyear Physical Education Series (1970); Elmer L. Johnson, *The History of YMCA Physical Education* (1979).

Russ Crawford

Wiffle Ball The wiffle ball was invented in 1952 in Fairfield, Conn., when David Nelson Mullany, seeking an alternative to a golf- or baseball for his son David's backyard games, cut eight oblong holes into one hemisphere of a plastic ball used as packing material for Coty perfume. The game of wiffle ball, which now boasts adult tournaments and a national association, evolved from the rules Mullany created for his son's informal contests. Mullany's game could be played with only a few players, and the plastic ball eliminated the broken windows common to backyard baseball. The wild curves a pitcher could accomplish with the ball led young David to name it "whiffle," a modification of the slang term for a strikeout, "whiff." David reportedly shortened the spelling to "wiff," so that when the company his father organized to produce and sell the balls erected a sign, it could pay the sign painter for one less character.

Mullany began manufacturing wiffle balls in Fairfield in 1953, and the game spread from there to become popular in the Northeast. A cut-off broomstick originally served as the bat, but in 1954 the company began producing a bat called the "Official Wiffle King" at its new factory site in Shelton, Conn. In 1959 the familiar yellow plastic bat, dubbed the "Official Wiffle Bat," replaced the wooden model; it served as standard equipment until 1999. Since then wiffle ball, like the older games of baseball and softball, has succumbed to technological advances, and the serious wiffle player now uses an aluminum bat (the "Wiffle Pro") or similar models.

And there *are* serious wiffle ball players. In 2001, six players met in Baltimore to create the U.S. Perforated Plastic Baseball Association (USPPBA), which standardized rules for the game and sponsored post-season playoffs leading to an annual national championship. Teams consist of three players, and USPPBA, located in Rehoboth, Mass., sponsors 20 regional tournaments from Florida to Alaska, each typically drawing more than 100 teams. One of the top teams in the nation, In the Box, hails from New England and is led by pitcher Bruce Chrystie of Rehoboth, who also serves as the executive director of USPPBA. The official version of the game features six-inning games, an abbreviated field, and no base running. Typical ground rules award one base for a ball that lands safely in the outfield and counts a ground ball fielded while in motion as an out. The aerodynamic qualities provided by the perforations give the pitcher a distinct advantage, and pitches can break between 4 to 6 feet from the pitcher's mound to home plate 42 feet away.

Wiffle Ball is still a family company located in Shelton; of the millions of balls and bats it sells annually, most are still used by children.

Joe Capozzi, "Serious about Wiffle Ball," *Palm Beach Post*, November 15, 2002; Lee Green, "The Wiffle Effect: Wiffle Ball Goes Big Time—Well, Not So Big," *Atlantic Monthly* (June 2002).

Russ Crawford

Williams, Ted (1918–2002) Baseball player. From 1939 to 1960, the monumental talent and monumental temper of Theodore Samuel Williams stirred Boston Red Sox fans in ways unmatched by any other ballplayer in the past half century. Among the two or three greatest pure power hitters ever to play the game, Williams achieved a .344 lifetime batting average; hit a total of 521 home runs; and led the American League in batting six times, in home runs four times, and in runs batted in four times. He was the last major leaguer to hit over .400 in a season (.406 in 1941).

Born in San Diego, Calif., Williams, a right-handed pitcher and left-handed hitter, was a standout at San Diego's Hoover High. He signed with the minor league San Diego Padres of the Pacific Coast League in 1936 and played for Boston's top farm club, the Minneapolis Millers, in 1938. Williams broke in with the Red Sox as the team's right fielder in 1939, hitting .327, with 31 home runs and 145 runs batted in.

Local fans and sportswriters quickly dubbed the gregarious rookie Baby Ruth, the Splen-

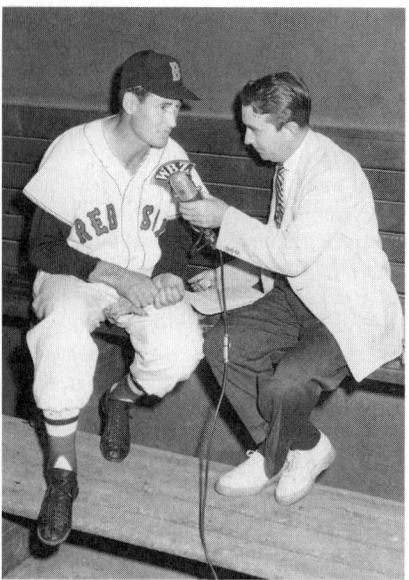

Ted Williams interviewed by Leo Egan, 1953

did Splinter, and the Kid. The gangly Williams, who had a deadly accurate right arm, moved to Fenway Park's tricky left field for the 1940 season, and his legendary troubles began. Occasionally lackadaisical on the field, Williams also suffered a midseason power slump. Raucous left-field fans and Boston's ornery reporters reacted, and Williams, in turn, lambasted everything from New England's weather to Boston's drivers. The most notorious incident of his career came in August 1956 when he spat in the direction of jeering fans at Fenway after dropping an easy Mickey Mantle fly ball in left. At times petulant and at times tempestuous, Williams over the years directed his ire at Red Sox management, at the Selective Service for redrafting him as an aging pilot during the Korean War (where he landed his reconnaissance jet in a ball of flame after it was hit by enemy gunfire), and at Fenway's "wolf-pack" of fans. But the madder Williams got, the better he hit. Fans and writers loved to hate him and hated to love him. Williams remains so much a part of Boston's psyche that in 1995 the city officially named one of its principal traffic arteries the Ted Williams Tunnel.

Williams's achievements were stunning, especially considering that he lost almost four prime years to military service in two wars and nearly another year to injuries. He is perhaps best remembered for his .406 batting average in 1941, capped by a legendary performance in a doubleheader against the Philadelphia Athletics. Williams could have sustained his average at a statistically rounded .400 by sitting out the last games of the season but insisted on playing. With six hits in eight at-bats—including a smash off one of the overhanging loudspeakers at Shibe Park—he raised his average six points.

Williams's career highlights included a dramatic ninth-inning home run off the facade of the right-field roof at Detroit's Briggs Stadium to win the 1941 All-Star game for the American League; another All-Star-game home run off Rip Sewell's famous blooper pitch (the "eephus") in 1946; a .388 batting average at the age of 39 in 1957; and a home run at Fenway Park on the very last at-bat of his career in 1960, a moment chronicled by John Updike in his feature story "Hub Fans Bid Kid Adieu."

Williams won the American League's Triple Crown (leading the league in batting average, home runs, and runs batted in) twice (1942 and 1947) and its Most Valuable Player award twice (1946 and 1949). He also might have won the most valuable player award in his triple crown years had not key Boston sportswriters placed him low on their ballots. Williams's most disappointing performance came during his only World Series in 1946. Nagged by an elbow injury sustained in a postseason practice game, and baffled by Harry "the Cat" Brecheen's pitching, Williams barely hit .200 in the Red Sox's series loss to the St. Louis Cardinals. The Cardinals used a version of the famous Williams shift in which the majority of fielders moved to the right side of the diamond to plug the gaps in Williams's power alleys. Nonetheless, Williams insisted on hitting directly into the right field shift, believing it folly to alter the natural arc of his swing. In *My Turn at Bat* (1969) and *The Science of Hitting* (1971), two minor baseball classics, Williams explains his theories of hitting.

When he was inducted into the National Baseball Hall of Fame in 1966, Williams gave a moving speech in which he praised baseball for altering its policies on racial segregation, although everyone knew that Boston had been slow to integrate its roster. In 1969 he managed the Washington Senators; he stayed with the club through 1972 in its new incarnation as the Texas Rangers.

In his retirement Williams pursued freshwater and saltwater sports fishing, directed hitting camps for New England's young ballplayers, and raised money for Boston's Jimmy Fund to help fight childhood cancer. In

1994 the Ted Williams Museum opened in Hernando, Fla., and Williams made his last public appearance at his induction into the Hitters Hall of Fame in February 2002. Ted Williams died in Iverness, Fla., having suffered the effects of a series of strokes and congestive heart failure.

Ed Linn, *Hitter: Life and Turmoils of Ted Williams* (1993); Michael Seidel, *Ted Williams: A Baseball Life* (1991); John Updike, "Hub Fans Bid Kid Adieu," *The New Yorker,* October 22, 1960; Ted Williams, *My Turn at Bat: The Story of My Life* (1969).

Michael A. Seidel

Yastrzemski, Carl (1939–) Baseball player. One of baseball's greatest fielders and hitters, Carl Michael Yastrzemski started with the Boston Red Sox in 1961 and led the club to the American League (AL) pennant, its first in 21 years, in 1967. Born in Southampton, N.Y., he impressed major league scouts as a high schooler but played a season at Notre Dame before signing with Boston in 1958. After two years in the minor leagues, Yastrzemski replaced the venerable Ted Williams, who retired in 1960, in left field. Part of Yastrzemski's appeal to Boston fans was the way he met the challenge of replacing a legend. He embodied a work ethic, a spirit of teamwork, and a dedication to the fans throughout his career, becoming a bulwark of consistency even as the team's fortunes and its management were unstable. By 1963 he had played in the first of 18 All-Star games, won the first of six Golden Gloves, and won the first of three AL batting titles.

Yastrzemski's best season came in 1967, the year of the "Impossible Dream," when, in taking Boston from last place in 1966 to the pennant, he led the AL with a .326 batting average, 121 runs batted in, 44 home runs, 189 hits, and 112 runs. In the World Series against the St. Louis Cardinals, which Boston lost in seven games, Yastrzemski batted .400 and hit three home runs. Selected as the AL's Most Valuable Player in 1967, he missed a unanimous election by one vote. Yastrzemski, who reached a career high batting average of .329 in 1970, helped Boston reach the World Series again in 1975, only to lose to the Cincinnati Reds in seven games.

When Yastrzemski retired from baseball in

Carl Yastrzemski, 1983

1983, he ranked first in career games (3,308), third in at-bats (11,988) and walks (1,845), sixth in total bases (5,539), seventh in hits (3,419) and doubles (646), and ninth in runs batted in (1,844). He is the only AL player with more than 3,000 hits and 400 home runs. "Yaz" was honored by the fans at his last home game appearance on October 1, as he circled the field to the cheers and tears of the crowd. He was elected to the Baseball Hall of Fame in 1989. A song was recorded about his 1967 exploits, and a local bakery marketed "Big Yaz Bread." Yastrzemski's accomplishments came during troubled times both in the Red Sox clubhouse and in the streets of Boston itself, and he was truly a hero for his times.

Mike Shatzkin, ed., *The Ballplayers: Baseball's Ultimate Biographical Reference* (1990); John Thorn, Pete Palmer, Michael Gershman, and David Pietrusza, eds., *Total Baseball: The Official Encyclopedia of Major League Baseball* (1997).

Adam R. Hornbuckle

Tourism

Dona Brown, Section Editor

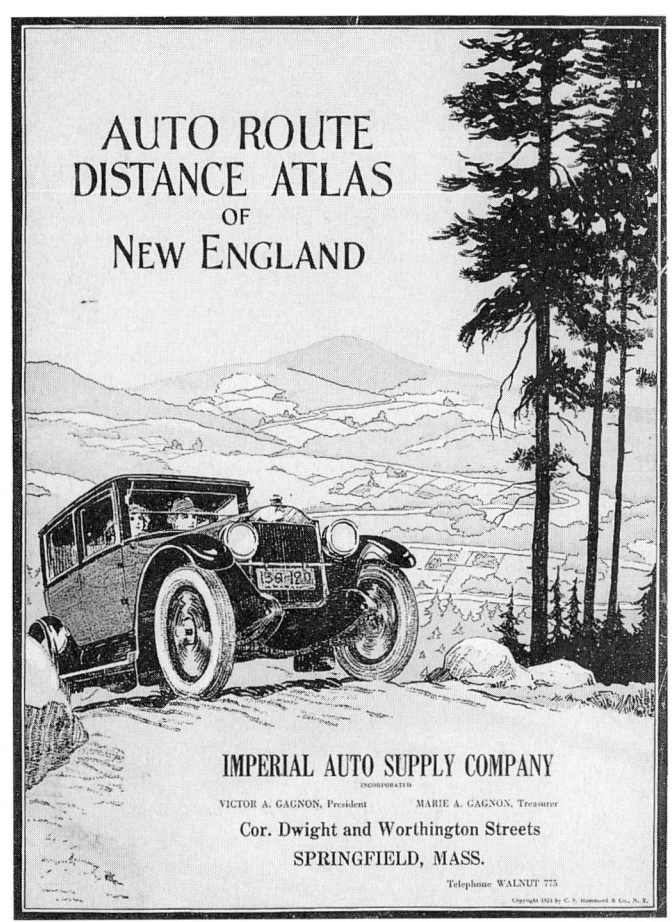

INTRODUCTION

The tourist industry in New England today is both extensive and diverse. It plays a key role in all six states, dominating the economy and landscape of many parts of the region. All New England states report that tourism is either the second biggest industry (Vermont, Rhode Island, Maine, New Hampshire) or the third (Massachusetts and Connecticut). But the impact of tourism is not spread evenly throughout the region. Massachusetts received 28 million visitors in 2002; Vermont, with a year-round population of a little over 600,000, hosted just a million and a half visitors—but nearly 15 percent of Vermont's economy and more than 20 percent of the state's jobs depend on tourism.

It is not easy to characterize exactly what draws tourists to New England today, partly because New England is diverse and partly because tourists themselves are a diverse lot. A New Yorker might praise the small towns of Vermont as the last bastion of old-fashioned ways of life, while a European walking the Freedom Trail in Boston might see the region as the home of one of the great 18th-century political revolutions. Travelers along Interstate 95 North could include Californians in search of quaint seaports and antiques or Bostonians bent on mountain climbing or skiing.

The majority of visitors to the New England states, however, are themselves New Englanders; most of the rest are from the nearby Middle Atlantic states. Nearly 90 percent come from the United States, although the state industries are working to increase their share of international tourists. Most tourists travel in the summer, but the fall foliage season attracts nearly a quarter of the three northern states' visitors within two or three weeks. Winter sports also play a key role in Vermont, New Hampshire, and Maine. In New England as a whole, tourists are drawn to natural attractions and cultural attractions in roughly equal numbers.

Tourism is one of New England's oldest industries, dating back to the beginnings of the Industrial Revolution. In the early 1800s, while the mills of Lowell, Mass., and the workshops of the Blackstone River valley were being built, the business of tourism began to take shape. The earliest visitors were especially intrigued by what might be called the cultural tour of the region. This experience had its roots in the European Grand Tour, a voyage taken by elite English travelers to view the ancient monuments and great art treasures of Italy and, along the way, to assess the political and social institutions found in other European countries. In America similarly educated and well-to-do travelers visited political landmarks like Faneuil Hall in Boston, where the sparks that lit the blaze of the American Revolution flew.

But they were also likely to visit certain sites that rarely attract the modern traveler. Captain Basil Hall, according to his *Travels in North America* (1830), made a round of visits in Boston that included "houses of correction—prisons—hospitals—penitentiaries—schools—almshouses—Navy and building yards." Travelers of Captain Hall's ilk called on the president of Harvard for private tours of the college. They flocked to hear William Ellery Channing preach radical Unitarianism in Boston. They made the rounds of such innovative institutions as Hartford's American Asylum for the Deaf. And they took side trips to visit such experimental communities as the Shaker village near Harvard, Mass., and the equally intriguing new city of Lowell, where they might judge for themselves whether the famous "mill girls" were mistreated or coddled.

Today's travelers still visit a few such spots. Although they no longer expect the president of the college to serve as their guide, groups of tourists still wander around Harvard Yard posing for photographs. Indeed, the Greater Boston area is still the single most popular travel destination in New England. But tourists today rarely seek out state prisons or modern factories or think of New England, as they once did, as the place to look for radical innovation and experimentation.

By the 1820s some travelers were beginning to seek out experiences that would seem more familiar to contemporary tourists. Fashionable travelers began to show an interest in seeing the American equivalent of the wild, romantic scenery that was luring European travelers to Switzerland, Wales, and the Lake District of England. Entrepreneurs all over the rural Northeast recognized the vast potential for profit in the new fad for scenery and moved quickly to capitalize on it. In the 1820s, Ethan Allen Crawford and his family built a series of inns in the primitive, half-settled region of New Hampshire's White Mountains that now bears their name, Crawford Notch. At about the same time in western Massachusetts a group of small-town businessmen constructed a hotel atop Mount Holyoke, providing an extensive view of the Connecticut River valley. And in 1820 Cornelius Coolidge, the speculator and architect who had designed Boston's popular Beacon Hill townhouses, bought and developed cottage lots on the Massachusetts peninsula of Nahant, hoping to lure the same Bostonians to his summer resort.

Wild scenery appealed to an educated and sophisticated clientele. They were looking for a romantic experience, a vision of nature shaped by Byron, Coleridge, and Wordsworth. Scenic tourists were attracted especially by visions of the Romantic sublime—the wild crashing of the ocean waves at Nahant, the terrifying grandeur of Niagara Falls, the dizzying heights of New Hampshire's White Mountains. Scenic attractions like these brought visitors into entirely new situations, far from urban centers and their everyday world, into places where ordinary life, ordinary farms and towns, and ordinary names were replaced by romantic names, by tourist businesses, and by signposts that showed them where to look.

By the mid-19th century the scenic tourist trade had come to dominate certain parts of New England. The White Mountains were the nation's preeminent scenic attraction, but Newport, R.I., and the Isles of Shoals off Portsmouth, N.H., also had well-developed scenic industries. By midcentury such places were growing and changing, too. The handful of romantic nomads who had visited the scenic regions in the 1820s and 1830s had been joined by thousands of travelers less interested in a sublime experience than in getting out of the growing northeastern cities for the summer. By then the guidebook, the railroad, and the summer hotel had taken on paramount importance.

The generation of New Englanders that came of age after the Civil War could choose from a wide array of tourist experiences. Grand hotels dominated the landscape of the White Mountains and the coast of New England from Rhode Island's Narragansett Bay to Connecticut's Long Island Sound and from Martha's Vineyard, Mass., to Bar Harbor, Maine. If these seemed too public or formal, as by then many people were complaining they were, vacationers could buy or rent their own cottages in resort communities. These abodes ranged in price and style from the great palaces of Newport's robber barons to the modest Carpenter Gothic structures of Oak Bluffs on Martha's Vineyard. For even less money vacationers could stay in a boardinghouse in the country or on a farm—an option considered both healthy and economical for a family with small children. Increasingly, too, resort communities catered to working-class vacationers with only a Sunday afternoon to spare. Tired factory workers could take a trolley car to the beach and enjoy a day's entertainment and relaxation for a minimal outlay of cash. Revere Beach was developed by Boston investors as just such an inexpensive day-trippers' resort in 1872.

Coastal resorts were highly diverse, catering to fine distinctions of wealth, class, religion, and ethnicity. Wealthy families selected their vacation spot with some anxiety because that choice, much like other major expenditures, was a matter of extremely conspicuous consumption. At Bar Harbor outdoorsy types played tennis and rowed. Nahant, out of fashion for almost everyone else, was still frequented by the oldest of Boston's Back Bay families. The premier African American summer resort was at Oak Bluffs on Martha's Vineyard. The resort town of Old Orchard Beach, Maine, testified to just how clearly these lines in the sand could be drawn. Each of its summer cottage neighborhoods catered to its own entirely separate group: Jewish families from Boston and Montreal in Butlerville, Irish politicians in Camp Comfort, and college professors in Ocean Park.

By the last quarter of the 19th century, much of coastal and mountain New England depended in small or large part on the tourist trade. But as resorts filled up those areas, a new kind of tourist trade was once again emerging. Summer vacation spots like Old Orchard Beach and Martha's Vineyard were not usually seen as distinctively regional—and they were not. Vacationers could look south to Long Branch, N.J., Far Rockaway, N.Y., and White Sulphur Springs, Va., to find the non–New England counterparts of these resorts. But the post–Civil War generation began to develop a new interest in visiting New England, based on a fresh perception of the region's distinctiveness. Increasingly, New England was seen as a kind of museum, a storehouse for a collection of old-fashioned values and beliefs. In a general sense tourists began to expect—and guidebooks to promise—that people would experience the good old days when they visited New England.

Historical tourist attractions had thrived earlier, of course: Faneuil Hall and the Bunker Hill Monument had always commanded their fair share of interest. But something different was happening now. In the late 19th century New England was

Revere Beach in Massachusetts, 1971

in many ways the most modern part of the country. It was highly urbanized, an industrial giant, and much more ethnically diverse than most places in America. But as massive brick factories were taking over the New England landscape and the immigrants who worked in them were coming to dominate the region's population, the tourist's vision of New England was taking a turn in the opposite direction. Tourists in the late 19th century sought out a New England that was anything but urban, complex, and modern. They wanted a New England that was Yankee, rural, simple, and unchanging.

There are several ways of explaining this shift. One side effect of New England's rapid urbanization and industrialization in the second half of the 19th century was the deindustrialization of smaller cities and towns and the more remote parts of the region. New England's massive industrial and urban growth left depopulated backwaters in its wake. Small-town manufacturers could not keep pace with their larger urban counterparts; old harbors were too shallow for the new ships; upcountry farmers competed unsuccessfully with western grain and foreign wool; young people grew up and moved away.

To some people, tourism seemed the perfect solution. One of the most dramatic transformations of this kind took place on the Massachusetts island of Nantucket. The whaling industry had made the small city of Nantucket rich, ambitious, and crowded, but the industry collapsed in midcentury, leaving the island depressed and depopulated. Despite vigorous efforts to find alternative sources of income—textile mills like New Bedford, Mass., or cod fishing like Gloucester, Mass.—the island grew quiet and empty. In time, discriminating tourists were drawn precisely to that quiet emptiness. Once visitors to Nantucket had remarked on its urban bustle; now the island offered an escape from urban stress.

Many of New England's most enduring and popular tourist attractions owe their existence to this late-19th-century transformation. Residents of Deerfield, Mass., responded to the loss of their competitive edge in agriculture and manufacturing by transforming their village into a living memorial to the bloody, tragic battles with Native Americans that lay in Deerfield's past. In Litchfield, Conn., wealthy summer residents transformed the streetscape into a model New England village, a project that took generations to complete and culminated in 1913 in an all-out drive to "colonialize" the entire town. In the early 20th century the picturesque fishing village of Provincetown, Mass., drew painters, writers, and actors to its own old-fashioned charms.

In rural and northern New England a similar phenomenon helped transform the countryside near the turn of the 20th century. In 1899 the governor of New Hampshire, Frank Rollins, issued a decree creating Old Home Week, a program designed to bring former residents "back home" to the rural North for a week during the summer. Rollins's idea grew into several state-sponsored programs in northern New England. These programs, sponsored by the boards of agriculture in Vermont, New Hampshire, and Maine, were pioneering efforts by state governments to promote tourism as an economic strategy. From the turn of the century onward, state governments in New England would play increasingly active roles in supporting tourist industries in the region.

New England tourist destinations promised the visitor an escape from the most difficult problems facing contemporary America. Tourists in the late 19th century turned their backs on the factories of Lowell, the immigrants of Manchester, N.H., and the ostentatious Gilded Age mansions of Boston's Back Bay and went in search of pastoral countryside, historic houses, and the simplicity of a former time. As a consequence the tourist industry, once confined to clearly defined districts along the coast and in the mountains, began to spread throughout the New England countryside. By the 1880s, railroad brochures sported titles such as *By-Ways of Central Vermont, Here and There in New England,* and *Down-East Latch Strings.* Anywhere along these byways, it seemed, was now vacationland.

New England may have seemed especially old at the turn of the century. By then the railroads had made it possible for wealthy Americans to go beyond the familiar resorts and travel in luxury to the scenic wonders of the Far West. Next to competition of that kind, New England did indeed seem longer established and more historical (provided that Anglo-American history was the primary interest). The vast perspectives and amazing sights of the Yosemite Valley, the Grand Canyon, and Yellowstone National Park made New England seem smaller and older than it ever had before.

Nevertheless, New England did not escape the wilderness craze that swept the country in the late 19th and early 20th centuries. While some vacationers were searching out the old, the quaint, and the colonial, others were turning back to the wilderness for what was viewed as a more authentic experience of communion with nature. The wilderness movement had its roots in the Adirondack camping fad of the late 19th century and had deeper roots still in an older tradition of hunting and fishing. Wilderness enthusiasts rejected the practices of more sedentary nature lovers. A scenic tourist of the 1850s would have ascended New Hampshire's Mount Washington on horseback; at the top he or she would have viewed the scenery, recited poetry or sketched a panorama, and then dined at the hotel. The grandchild of that tourist might visit the same places but do very different things. The Appalachian Mountain Club (AMC) was organized in 1876 in Boston; its members actively promoted an alternative to the older forms of tourism by encouraging outdoor recreation and constructing hiking trails and shelters. In 1920 the AMC established a permanent base camp in Pinkham Notch at the foot of Mount Washington.

In the first decades of the 20th century, the craze for wilderness camping and hiking hit New England—especially northern New England. Between 1910 and 1928, the Green Mountain Club built the Long Trail across the ridgeline of that Vermont mountain range. The last section, in Maine, of the Appalachian Trail, which follows the Long Trail for some 100 miles, was completed in 1937. Both state and national governments set aside tracts of land for preservation and public enjoyment: Acadia National Park was founded in 1919, and in 1931 Maine created its own Baxter State Park to protect Mount Katahdin and the end of the Appalachian Trail.

In the meantime the Dartmouth Outing Club, founded in 1909, discovered its own use for the northern mountains: skiing. In the early years of the 20th century many Americans were looking for new kinds of physical exercise that would help create a tougher, more competitive society. Skiing was a perfect fit. Theodore Roosevelt's pronouncements on the "unhealthy softening and relaxation of fibre" among native-born Americans hit a raw nerve for some vacationers. Such cultural concerns led many Americans to embrace a wide range of activities designed to bring overcivilized men (and some women) back into contact with the "primitive."

Ironically, the demand for a wilderness experience was associated in the public mind with a fascinating new technology: the automobile. Soon after its creation in 1911, the White Mountain National Forest opened its first auto camp. The automobile was linked in the American imagination with new styles of "roughing it." Railroad travel was described as passive, unhealthily luxurious, regimented. Automobiles, by contrast, brought out the individualist in travelers. They provided a personal and physical challenge and a sense of adventure that were simply not available to those who traveled by rail.

Automobile touring was also closely associated with the new interest in the old. The grand hotels and their railroad links seemed preeminently modern, running on precise, mechanical timetables, employing the latest technologies to provide luxurious ease to their guests. Auto tourists, however, seemed to be in contact with all that was *not* modern. They could go camping in the wilderness and get in touch with primitive nature or they could discover a quaint hideaway in a country village off the beaten track, perhaps sleeping in an old colonial inn where George Washington had slept.

Auto touring helped create a demand for historic houses and inns located on the former coach roads, newly refurbished to accommodate automobiles. In West Brookfield, Conn., for example, along the old turnpike now turned into U.S. Route

7, an 18th-century tavern that had once hosted Washington and Lafayette became Ye Olde Tavern, a popular stop for auto tourists. Wallace Nutting's illustrated state guides, published between 1922 and 1924, offer a perfect example of the link between the fascination with old New England buildings and the means by which travelers explored them. In the handbook *Connecticut Beautiful* (1923), among others, Nutting combined commentary on the negative impact of modern auto culture with the recognition that his readers would need good roads for their tours of colonial houses and old-fashioned landscapes.

Early automobile travelers imagined themselves as creating an adventurous alternative to slow-paced Victorian routines. They idealized the speed and flexibility of automobile travel. They liked to explore back roads and towns off the beaten track, staying for only a night or two in any one place. Auto-oriented guidebooks encouraged that sense of freedom, nudging travelers to be more adventurous. "Why follow a tour, anyway?" asked the 1937 guide to Massachusetts composed by the Works Progress Administration (WPA). "Be your own gypsy"; "Abandon all rules and directions and make up your own tours." Vacationers who would once have spent their month's vacation at a single grand hotel might now wander through a whole series of towns and villages, including but not limiting themselves to traditional resort destinations.

All this enthusiasm did not spring up entirely uncultivated. New England state governments, and later the U.S. government, played a key role in encouraging auto touring at the expense, it turned out, of railroad touring. They were deeply involved in road development long before most vacationers even knew what cars were. (Frank Rollins, the progressive governor of New Hampshire who invented Old Home Week, also campaigned for better roads in that state, but he did so before automobiles were even invented, arguing that visitors would soon be touring New Hampshire by bicycle.) The first American automobile legislation (a speed limit) was passed in Hartford in 1901.

The New England states launched massive road-building programs at the turn of the century, hoping to improve the commercial prospects of New England farmers as well as to encourage tourism. Massachusetts created its first highway commission in 1893, and Connecticut followed suit in 1895. Highway commissions centralized control of highway expenditures once handled by towns and often built or improved the roads that tempted early tourists. The Mohawk Trail, a part of Route 2 from Boston to the Berkshires, opened in 1915. Cape Cod's old stagecoach roads were transformed into what the Porter Sargent *Handbook of New England* series called "splendid state Macadam, with red markers" as early as 1916. Only the most intrepid auto travelers braved the locally maintained dirt roads that had served most rural areas before the states stepped in.

Both state and federal governments worked to set up auto-related tourist services and businesses. As early as 1917 the White Mountain National Forest Service, then only six years old, opened its first campground for automobile travelers. By 1937 the WPA guide for New Hampshire credited that state with having 40 public campgrounds. Skiing in particular benefited from state and national government intervention on its behalf. In the 1920s, for example, the state of New Hampshire took responsibility for keeping the White Mountain notch roads open all winter long to facilitate travel for skiing, an effort that required a heavy investment in new plowing equipment.

By the time of the Great Depression, New Deal programs for employment fit conveniently with the Roosevelt administration's enthusiasm for parks and forestry: Civilian Conservation Corps (CCC) workers all over New England built parks, camping facilities, and ski lifts. New England reached the end of the Depression and World War II with a highly developed summer and winter tourist trade. The war did little to interfere with that trade, and in its wake tourism became ever more important to the economy of the region. In many ways the post–World War II boom in tourism built on the foundations the industry had established in earlier years. State governments involved themselves even more deeply in promoting tourism. Vermont entered a new age of state promotion with the publication of the glossy magazine *Vermont Life,* launched in 1947 with a cover that sported a glamorous woman in a diaphanous gown gamboling amid the fall foliage. In the post–World War II era, vacationing would be a growth industry.

One reason for that expansion was the full employment economy enjoyed by much of southern New England after the war. Fourth-generation immigrant families found themselves lifted out of their factory jobs into an increasingly white-collar and service-oriented economy. The ripples of that economic transformation were felt in the more marginal and rural parts of New England, too, as those regions were transformed into tourist destinations that could meet the demands of newly leisured workers. On Cape Cod, a postwar building boom catered to a new Boston market, families who had only recently acquired the prosperity and security to take a two-week vacation or buy a modest vacation home.

The end of the war also generated an explosion of interest in New England's historical attractions. Six major museum villages were founded in the postwar years, each inspired in part by two multimillion-dollar projects carried out before the war began: Henry Ford's Greenfield Village had opened in Dearborn, Mich., in 1933 and John D. Rockefeller's Colonial Williamsburg in Virginia in 1934. Old Sturbridge Village, a re-created New England village in Massachusetts, began receiving visitors in 1946. Also in Massachusetts, Plimoth Plantation, founded in 1947, was committed to representing the life of the first generation of Plymouth settlers, and Historic Deerfield opened in 1952, the same year Electra Havemeyer Webb's eccentric collection of buildings called the Shelburne Museum opened in northern Vermont. Strawbery Banke, an assemblage of colonial-era buildings in Portsmouth, N.H., welcomed its first visitors in 1958. Mystic Seaport, a re-created seafaring town in Connecticut, had actually opened on a small scale in 1930 but grew rapidly after the war.

At their inception the postwar village museums enshrined a vision of New England that had been forged in the 19th century. To visitors in the 1950s and 1960s, New England presented itself as a place populated by hardy sailors (Mystic Seaport), rugged pioneers (Historic Deerfield), self-reliant farmers (Old Sturbridge Village), elegant colonial gentry (Strawbery Banke), and pious Pilgrims (Plimoth Planta-

Children try out the pillory and stocks at Old Sturbridge Village, 1969

tion)—all with a penchant for old-fashioned spelling. The Old New England concept would have been familiar to 19th-century tourists, but it wore a somewhat different guise in the context of postwar international tensions. At one time New England villages had been held up as the counterforce to the advancing spread of urban industrial society and its immigrant masses; now those villages offered themselves as the last bastions against world communism.

New England's historical sense of itself did not remain stuck in the Cold War for long. In the 1960s and 1970s, these same museums were transformed by compelling revisionist discoveries about life in early New England. The commitment to accuracy placed mills in the rural landscape of Old Sturbridge Village and dirtied the hands of the Pilgrim Fathers. In the meantime, spurred in part by the attention (and funding) generated by the nation's Bicentennial celebration in 1976, social and labor historians finally brought New England's ethnic and industrial past to the tourist's attention. The Lowell National Historical Park was created in 1978 to celebrate and explore the history of the great industrial operations of that city. In the same year Massachusetts launched a series of heritage state parks, designed as a combined project of historic preservation and economic revitalization for the decaying industrial cities of Fall River, Holyoke, Lowell, North Adams, Gardner, Lawrence, Lynn, and Springfield. These new parks openly celebrated the heritage that had once been suppressed. One walking tour of Lawrence, for example, drew attention to the site of the great Lawrence textile strike of 1912. State governments under the inspiration of the Bicentennial funded other celebratory and popular historical experiences, among them Rhode Island's Tall Ship Festivals.

Continuing the trend established with the first automobile travelers, the tourist industries of the second half of the 20th century were inextricably linked with roads—not the old state highways of an earlier time but the Eisenhower-era super highways that now link New England's mostly urban tourists with its more or less rural tourist destinations. The attractions of the Connecticut and Massachusetts Berkshires and of western Vermont owe a great deal to the Northway, the superhighway linking Greater New York City with its northern playgrounds. Along that route a wide assortment of cultural attractions can be found, from the music of the Boston Symphony Orchestra at Tanglewood to the Norman Rockwell shrines in Great Barrington, Mass., and Bennington, Vt. Similarly, northbound Interstates 89, 91, and 95 have made the countryside and villages of New Hampshire, Vermont, and Maine ever more accessible to their urban visitors.

At the same time, the old roads of the early 20th century have become attractions in their own right, particularly during that odd period called foliage season. In September and October the Mohawk Trail (U.S. Route 2) competes with Vermont's Molly Stark Trail and U.S. Route 7 through the Connecticut and Massachusetts Berkshires for recognition as the best place from which to view peak foliage from an automobile. In the few weeks of foliage season, the natural beauty of New England's autumn leaves combines with farm stands selling cider, pumpkins, and shocks of corn to give leaf peepers a truly nostalgic experience.

History, nostalgia, and culture have survived into the 21st century as premier New England attractions, and so has the natural environment. The Cape Cod National Seashore was added to the list of the region's most appealing natural attractions in 1961 and is now a cornerstone of New England's huge and growing green tourist industry. Whale watches and Audubon tours have become key parts of the tourist industry in many places, and almost every historical village or museum has its own nature walk.

Perhaps at the other end of the tourist spectrum, the Mashantucket Pequot have created New England's most popular attraction today, the Foxwoods Resort Casino in Mashantucket, Conn., near Ledyard. L. L. Bean has become the symbol of a new trend toward "shopping tourism" that has transformed entire towns—Freeport, Maine; North Conway, N.H.; Manchester, Vt.—into shopping meccas distinguished by a pioneering style of architecture that combines the rambling sprawl of outlet malls with the white clapboards and shuttered windows of quaint New England.

One characteristic has stood the test of time: the desire of tourists and those who cater to them to organize resorts and vacation destinations along extremely fine lines of class, ethnicity, and personal identity. Although Jewish clients are no longer turned away from hotels in the White Mountains, New England's resorts are still segregated—these days by age, profession, and lifestyle. Provincetown's reputation as a gay and lesbian hotspot does not extend up the Cape to Hyannis, where college students tend bar by night and work on their tans by day, or to Wellfleet, the secluded second home of the psychiatric profession.

And a second tradition is still with us as the 21st century begins: the tendency to see tourism as an answer to economic problems great and small. As the industry grows ever more diverse and specialized, every part of the region has felt its impact. All six New England states operate ambitious tourist promotional campaigns. And as the new century begins, it is no longer only state governments that promote tourism: from the city officials of struggling mill towns to the directors of local historical societies, the curators of museums, and the trustees of universities, everyone wants a piece of the tourism pie.

Cindy Aron, *Working at Play: A History of Vacations in the United States* (1999); Warren Belasco, *Americans on the Road: From Autocamp to Motel, 1910–1945* (1979); Peter Benes, ed., *New England Prospect: Maps, Place Names, and the Historical Landscape* (1980); Dona Brown, *Inventing New England: Regional Tourism in the 19th Century* (1995); John Hope Franklin, *A Southern Odyssey: Travelers in the Antebellum North* (1976); John Jakle, *The Tourist: Travel in 20th-Century North America* (1985); Jane Louise Mesick, *The English Traveler in America, 1785–1835* (1970); James C. O'Connell, *Becoming Cape Cod: Creating a Seaside Resort* (2003); Bryant F. Tolles, Jr., *The Grand Resort Hotels of the White Mountains: A Vanishing Architectural Legacy* (1998).

Dona Brown

Acadian Village Since the late 18th century, the upper Saint John River valley, the boundary between northern Maine and northwest New Brunswick, has been the home of a French-speaking population of mixed Acadian and French Canadian (or Quebecois) origins. The Acadians, who had come from France in the 17th century and settled in what is now known as Nova Scotia, resettled in other parts of America after 1755, when British forces destroyed their settlements and deported many of them. Presently, the population residing on the Canadian side of the Saint John River refer to themselves as Acadian, and the term *Maine Acadians* has become the preferred name for the French-speaking settlers of the American Saint John valley. This Acadian heritage is celebrated today in the form of an open air museum, the Acadian Village, which can be found on U.S. Route 1 a few miles west of the town of Van Buren, Maine. It is sponsored and operated by a local cultural organization, the Historical Society of Living Heritage/La Société Historique–Héritage Vivant.

The Acadian Village was started in 1976 as a Bicentennial project and has since been listed on the National Register of Historic Places. It comprises a dozen structures: original buildings moved to the site, portions of buildings not preserved in their entirety, and reconstructions of old buildings. Among the original structures are a schoolhouse built in 1875, the workers' quarters from a 19th-century farm, an early-20th-century barbershop, part of a 1910 house, and a late-19th-century smithy. The Roy House, built between 1790 and 1820 and the village's oldest building, is a one-room hewn-log structure. The Acadian barn, dating from the early 1800s, is part of the Roy farmstead. Constructed in the late 1850s, the Levasseur House and the Morneault House are built of square hewn logs (*pièce sur pièce*) covered with clapboards and are representative of the Georgian massing architectural style common in the early 19th century. Completing the site are a house built from 19th-century lumber and the modern reconstruction of a general store.

Many of the buildings of the Acadian Village possess distinctive architectural features; among the most notable are "ship's knees" (braces made from a portion of the lower trunk and root system of a tree and thus naturally curved), symmetrically placed windows, and flax chinking of the buildings. The buildings also house a large collection of artifacts. Among them are an array of cupboards representing a wide variety of designs, a fine collection of locally made 19th-century chairs, some household weavings, and a sampling of *cata-*

lognes: bed-rugs made of cotton warp and wefts of thin strips of recycled fabric.

In addition to supporting the Acadian Village, residents of the Saint John valley take a lively interest in celebrating other aspects of their history. This interest manifests itself in a wide range of institutions, ranging from historical societies and museums to archives and documentation centers, on both sides of the river. One outcome has been the preservation of an important number of properties with historical and architectural significance throughout the Saint John valley. On the American side of the valley, several Maine Acadian properties and landmarks are listed on the National Register of Historic Places. Among them are the Fort Kent blockhouse (1838–39) and the church of Notre Dame du Mont Carmel in Lille, a high-vernacular style edifice built in 1909 and now the Musée et Centre Culturel du Mont Carmel. Other attractions include the Acadian Cross Historic Site (a complex in Saint David that includes a museum), a mid-19th-century homestead house, a one-room schoolhouse built in 1870, and a cross commemorating the landing of the first Acadian settlers in 1785. In addition, some significant buildings are still on their original sites and are in use, like the unique Madawaska twin barns in the Sainte Agatha area. The preservation efforts by those in the region reflect an ongoing interest in the language, culture, and heritage of the Acadian people.

Richard W. Judd, Edwin A. Churchill, and Joel W. Eastman, eds., *Maine: The Pine Tree State from Prehistory to the Present* (1995); Victor A. Konrad, "Against the Tide: French Canadian Barn Building Traditions in the St. John Valley of Maine," *American Review of Canadian Studies* 12 (1982); Gerald Ward, ed., *Perspectives on American Furniture* (1988).

Béatrice Craig

Architecture of Tourism Since the early 19th century, the growth of regional tourism has strongly influenced the evolution of several pronounced architectural forms throughout New England. Most notable among these are inns, taverns, and hotels. The consummate architectural expression of the influence of tourism between 1850 and 1930 is the grand resort hotel. The summer cottage, with its emphasis on privacy, flexibility, and family life, was a direct outgrowth of the grand hotel experience, whether in seacoast, mountain, or lake resort areas. Closely connected with the development of resort centers and profiting from a symbiotic relation with the hotels were the distinctive rural passenger and freight railroad stations and other service buildings. Many resorts featured such structures as theaters, libraries, clubhouses, and

churches that likewise owe their origins to tourism. In the 20th century came the advent of the automobile, the expansion and improvement of road systems, and the resultant creation of a highly functional architecture embodied in gas stations, dining facilities, campground buildings, cabins, motor courts, motels, and modern hotel complexes. Historically, tourism has left an indelible imprint on both New England's natural landscape and its built environment.

The first architectural manifestations of tourism in New England may be seen in the simple, modest-sized, vernacular roadside inns and taverns and in the town and village center hotels built between 1790 and 1860. This group of structures, many representative examples of which stand today, reveal the origins of the grand resort hotel concept in the region. As specimens of architecture, the hotels, built in the 1840s and 1850s, were virtually islands, organized to offer all that their clientele desired in a setting that emphasized comfort, efficiency, recreation, and aesthetic attractions.

Many of the grand resort hotels in New England were planned in intriguing, picturesque, eclectic styles borrowed from foreign cultures and intended to make distinct architectural statements. The hotels were designed in several revival styles (or combinations of styles), including Greek, Italian, and Gothic, or later Victorian idioms such as French Second Empire (Mansard), Stick, English Queen Anne, Italian Renaissance, Spanish Renaissance, and Colonial Revival. As conservatively run business enterprises, some grand resort hotels displayed simplified decorative elements derived from residential buildings, while others were pacesetting architectural and engineering marvels. The two best extant examples of the latter are the Mount Washington Hotel (Charles Alling Gifford, 1901–6) at Bretton Woods and Hampshire House (Chase R. Whitcher, 1916–18) at the Balsams in Dixville Notch, both in New Hampshire's White Mountains.

After the Civil War and the initial impact of industrialization, Americans sought pristine retreats from society's mounting pressures and gravitated to hotels conceived in styles that satisfied their desire for escape, nostalgia, and historicity. Well suited to this period was the American version of the English Queen Anne style, whose asymmetry and textural variety were represented in the third Mount Kineo House (Arthur H. Vinal, 1884–1911) on Moosehead Lake in Maine and in two additional White Mountain hostelries: Wentworth Hall and Cottages (William A. Bates, 1869–80s) in Jackson, N.H., and the second Glen House (Francis H. Fassett, 1885–87) at Pinkham Notch.

During the 1880s and 1890s, when the grand resort hotel phenomenon peaked in New England, the Queen Anne and older styles were abandoned for markedly new architectural vernaculars, some European-derived, others indigenous and inspired by America's colonial past. The highly flexible Shingle Style proved particularly adaptable to the hotel function, and many hotels were built in this idiom, including the Bay of Naples Inn (John Calvin Stevens, 1898–99) on Long Lake in Maine, the Hotel Thorndike (ca. 1885) at Jamestown, R.I., and the Ottawa House (Clarence Luce, 1887–88) on Cushing's Island, also in Maine. Many hotel owners embraced the Colonial Revival style with its fine proportions, charming domestic forms, and many integrally related classical elements. The giant New Ocean House (ca. 1883–84) in Swampscott, Mass., and the Waumbek Hotel (Carrère and Hastings, 1860–1901) in Jefferson and the Mount Pleasant House (John Calvin Stevens and Francis H. Fassett, 1875–95) at Bretton Woods, both in the White Mountains, were among New England's most renowned resort hotels, each refurbished and enlarged in the Colonial Revival vein. Arguably the greatest of them all, the Poland Spring House (George M. Coombs and John Calvin Stevens and Albert Winslow Cobb, 1876–1903) at Poland Spring, Maine, brought together in a single complex the features of four styles—Stick, Shingle, Queen Anne, and Colonial Revival—to create a provocative, eclectic medley. By the first decade of the 20th century, however, the grand resort hotel movement was in decline. The grandiose Spanish Renaissance Revival–style Mount Washington Hotel at Bretton Woods was one of the last of these sprawling and elaborate complexes to be built.

The summer cottage phenomenon, originating in the 1850s, was largely the outgrowth of hotel development. Many of the region's earliest cottage owners were former hotel guests who had stayed in cottages owned by the hotels. Perhaps New England's finest example of a resort hotel with related cottage community was the New Profile House, the second hotel of that name to occupy the spot (Sylvanus D. Morgan, 1905–6), at Franconia Notch in the White Mountains. In the early 1920s this complex included 20 cottages, one of which was a Colonial Revival replica of George Washington's home, Mount Vernon.

Cottages varied greatly in size, scale, architectural style, interior decor, physical setting, and landscaping. The largest, most lavish, and most ornately appointed of the region's cottages were those constructed at Newport, R.I., Manchester-by-the-Sea, Mass., the Berkshires of western Massachusetts, and Bar Harbor, Maine. More modest and more successfully linked with their environments, both aesthetically and functionally, were the cottages of Cape Cod, the remainder of the Massachusetts shoreline, the Champlain Valley of Vermont, the White Mountains, and the coastlines of southern Connecticut, western Rhode Island, New Hampshire, and Maine. The cottages along the Maine coast and on offshore islands were the product of an impressive group of eastern architects, including John Calvin Stevens of Portland, Maine; Bruce Price and Clarence Luce of New York City; and William Ralph Emerson and the firm of Peabody and Stearns of Boston. The Maine cottages, built largely of native materials, were a collective expression of American architectural styles, commencing with Stick and Queen Anne, peaking with Shingle and Colonial Revival, and culminating with Craftsman, English Tudor, and Spanish Renaissance revivals, along with other eclectic combinations.

Associated with the hotels and cottages of New England resort communities were fascinating and ingeniously designed structures serving recreational, social, entertainment, intellectual, and religious purposes. Those buildings or complexes erected before World War I were customarily planned in the Shingle or Colonial Revival styles, often but not always designed by major architects or architectural partnerships. Among the region's finest casinos, all still at least partially intact, are those at Newport (McKim, Mead and White, 1880–81) and Narragansett Pier, R.I. (McKim, Mead and White, 1884–86), and Bethlehem, N.H. (Edward Thornton Sanderson, ca. 1887). Modest-sized churches, chapels, and libraries, frequently architect-designed, sophisticated in their ornamentation, and financed by summer residents, still serve their original purposes in many vacation towns. Golf, tennis, and social clubhouses were another outgrowth of tourism, and several fine representative examples have survived.

The architecture of tourism in the 20th century was conceived to accommodate tourists' increased mobility resulting from the supplanting of railroads by the automobile as the principal means of land transportation. Unlike the railroads, road systems could reach virtually any location, and, as a consequence, tourists could move about freely, breaking traditional patterns of long visits in single locations and precipitating the decline of the grand resort hotel industry.

Cabins, motor courts, campgrounds, and gas stations of simple but varied design were constructed along major tourist routes in seacoast, mountain, and lake regions. Superb samplings of these structures, many worthy of cultural landmark designation, have survived, largely because of their location on secondary, rural roads bypassed by post–World War II interstate highway development. One may view excellent examples of such drive-in buildings along Route 1 on the Maine coast (York to Kennebunk), on Route 1A south of Boston, and in Woodstock, North Woodstock, Bethlehem, and North Conway in the White Mountains. Since World War II, motels, inns, and hotels of neocolonial or modernistic design have largely replaced older hostelries and may be seen on Cape Cod and along Route 1 on the Connecticut and Rhode Island shorelines. Highly functional but visually bland complexes housing restaurants, stores, and amusement attractions exist at seacoast tourist spots such as Revere Beach in Massachusetts, Hampton Beach in New Hampshire, and Old Orchard Beach in Maine. The architecture of tourism in New England, however, continues to undergo unceasing change in response to new economic and social demands. Hence, the preservation record will continue to be sporadic, and certain outmoded building forms linked with the age of the automobile face an uncertain future.

Warren J. Belasco, *Americans on the Road: From Autocamp to Motel, 1910–1945* (1979); Donna-Belle Garvin and James L. Garvin, *On the Road North of Boston: New Hampshire Taverns and Turnpikes, 1700–1900* (1988); G. W. Helfrich and Gladys O'Neil, *Lost Bar Harbor* (1982); Roger G. Reed, *A Delight to All Who Knew It: The Maine Summer Architecture of William R. Emerson* (1990); Vincent J. Scully, Jr., *The Architecture of the American Summer: The Flowering of the Shingle Style* (1989); Earle G. Shettleworth, *The Summer Cottages of Islesboro, 1890–1930* (1989); Bryant F. Tolles, Jr., *The Grand Resort Hotels of the White Mountains: A Vanishing Architectural Legacy* (1998); Tolles, *Summer Cottages in the White Mountains: The Architecture of Leisure and Recreation, 1870 to 1930* (2000).

Bryant F. Tolles, Jr.

Authors' Homes and Literary Sites

New England's many important literary sites reflect the region's deep interest in its cultural past. Authors whose homes have been preserved and converted to museums include the native New Englanders Nathaniel Hawthorne, Ralph Waldo Emerson, Emily Dickinson, and Harriet Beecher Stowe as well as writers who came to the region as adults, among them Edith Wharton, Herman Melville, Mark Twain, and Rudyard Kipling. Some writers, including Henry Wadsworth Longfellow and Robert Frost, have been memorialized at more than one New England home. While the styles and histories of the houses vary greatly, their continued popularity as tourist destinations reveals the extent to which literary and architectural history contribute to the region's identity.

Since the publication in 1853 of *Homes of American Authors,* a collection of essays, the residences of New England writers have been presented as places to visit and admire. With its engravings and descriptions of notable literary residences, the book simultaneously assumed and fueled an interest in the architectural manifestation of literary success. Although nominally devoted to authors from all parts of the United States, the book stressed New England's contributions to the nation's literary life: 11 of the 17 writers discussed hailed from New England. Nearly 50 years later, continued public interest in authorial homes led publishers to issue guidebooks with walking tours through New England's centers of literary activity. In *Literary Pilgrimages in New England* (1902), for example, Edwin M. Bacon adopted the rhetoric of popular travelogues by discussing the history and legends surrounding famous writers' homes. These books and the subsequent campaigns to save and restore literary sites underscore the popular idea that New England has produced an enduring literary culture.

The impetus to turn authors' homes into tourist sites frequently comes from the descendants of the writers. Longfellow's boyhood home in Portland, Maine, for example, remained in the family long after he settled in Cambridge, Mass., in the 1830s. Remaining in the house until her death in 1901, Anne Longfellow Pierce, the poet's sister, devoted the last years of her life to preparing the house as a monument to her brother's memory. Although Longfellow wrote only nine poems inside its walls, Anne left the house and its contents to the Maine Historical Society, thereby ensuring that Longfellow would always be associated with his boyhood home. The three-story brick house, which opened to the public within months of Anne's death, quickly became central to the city's efforts to siphon tourist trade away from the nearby resorts at Orchard Beach and York. In its use of a well-known structure from the past, Portland's campaign represents an early example of a city's effort to pursue revenue through tourism rather than through manufacturing and industry.

New England's literary shrines also emerged as tourist destinations through the efforts of disciples of dead authors. This approach has been particularly common for writers who had begun to fall from critical favor at the time their homes were preserved. John Greenleaf Whittier's home in Amesbury, Mass., for example, was purchased by the Whittier Home Association in 1918, at a time when American literary scholars were beginning to investigate writers they considered to be more serious than the fireside poets. Thomas Bailey Aldrich's boyhood home in Portsmouth, N.H., was similarly preserved by local boosters in 1908, even though Aldrich's critical reputation barely survived his death the previous year. In another example, Clara Endicott Sears purchased the farmhouse and surrounding farmland once belonging to Fruitlands, Amos Bronson Alcott's short-lived Transcendental community in Harvard, Mass. Sears, who believed Alcott represented the hardy independence of her own Puritan ancestors, opened the house and grounds to the public in 1914, nearly 70 years after Alcott's communitarian experiment failed. The site has been expanded considerably since its opening. Today, visitors can tour the Alcott farmhouse, a gallery of American art, separate museums devoted to Native Americans and the Shakers, and an important research library, all of which render Fruitlands the most elaborate of New England's surviving literary shrines.

Devotion to a particular author encouraged Harriet Lothrop to preserve the memory of Nathaniel Hawthorne at the Wayside in Concord, Mass., a house also once lived in by Bronson and Louisa May Alcott. Lothrop, who wrote popular children's books under the name Margaret Sidney, purchased the house in 1883 from Hawthorne's daughter Rose. Until her death in 1924 she assiduously collected Hawthorne memorabilia and vowed to preserve all traces of his presence in the house. Lothrop's daughter Margaret continued her mother's work until she eventually sold the property to the National Park Service in 1963, as part of the Minute Man National Park. Today, the Wayside offers an odd mixture of historical styles, reflecting its several well-known occupants and the quirks of the owner who first opened its doors to the public.

Literary sites have also been opened to the public after being acquired by preservation groups. Usually, these groups have aims that extend beyond the mere preservation of literary reputation. Of the 45 properties held by Historic New England, formerly the Society for the Preservation of New England Antiquities (SPNEA), only Sarah Orne Jewett's house in South Berwick, Maine, is popularly associated with a famous writer. When Jewett's nephew left the property to SPNEA in 1930, the organization was devoted to acquiring, preserving, and maintaining homes from New England's colonial past. Although Historic New England now promotes the house as a literary shrine, its appearance and presentation are best understood in light of the organization's early efforts to save structures of architectural rather than literary distinction. Another organization, the conservation-minded Trustees of Reservations, has helped preserve the boyhood home of William Cullen Bryant in Cummington, Mass., as well as the Old Manse in Concord, a house associated with Hawthorne and Emerson. Because the organization dedicates itself to the conservation of open space, the restored Bryant house and the Old Manse must be seen as part of the broader environmental preservation goals of the organization. Similarly, Kipling's residence Naulakha, just outside of Brattleboro, Vt., has been memorialized by Landmark Trust USA, a British organization devoted to preserving historic structures. Today, Naulakha, where Kipling wrote *The Jungle Books* (1894, 1895) during a four-year residence, can be rented for overnight stays, making it the only author's home in New England where one can sleep as well as visit.

Since the 1960s various government agencies have promoted the homes of authors as part of their tourism campaigns. Franconia, N.H., for example, purchased the house where Robert Frost lived from 1915 to 1923 to serve as a visitor center and meeting place for poets. New Hampshire established a state park at Robert Frost's farm in Derry in 1966, after purchasing the property from an automobile salvage company. With the help of the poet's daughter, the house has been restored to its turn-of-the-century appearance. Today, visitors can view the small house and wander through the landscape that inspired such poems as "Hyla Brook" and "Mending Wall." The state of Vermont adopted a similar literary and environmental approach at the Robert Frost Recreation Area around his small house in Ripton, where Frost spent a good deal of time from 1940 until his death in 1963. Frost actively lobbied friends in the Kennedy administration to have the land around his last house converted into a national park. Although Frost's efforts fell short in Vermont, the National Park Service does play a role in the restoration and presentation of New England authorial homes, including the Wayside in Concord, which had belonged to a soldier in the battles of Lexington and Concord before being inhabited by Hawthorne and the Alcotts, and Longfellow's house in Cambridge, where George Washington had his headquarters in the early days of the Revolutionary War. In both cases, literary and architectural fame is woven into the broader outlines of American history.

More recently, Hartford officials have used Mark Twain's 19-room Victorian mansion as part of their efforts to make the urban core attractive to tourists. Although not often associ-

Rudyard Kipling's house, Naulakha, in Dummerston, Vt.

ated with New England, Twain lived in Connecticut's capital for 17 years, and wrote *The Adventures of Tom Sawyer* (1876) and *The Prince and the Pauper* (1881) there. Today, political and business leaders use the house and the neighboring home of Harriet Beecher Stowe, the author of *Uncle Tom's Cabin* (1852), to help reinvigorate the downtown economy. With the homes of Twain and Stowe nearly adjacent to each other, Hartford rivals Concord in the importance of its literary memorials.

Not every literary shrine, however, depends upon its association with a single author. With its several sites, including the Authors Ridge in its burial ground, the town of Concord offers visitors a literary environment that depends more on the combined efforts of its famous residents than on any one of them in particular. Another example is Edith Wharton's house in the Berkshires, which was for many years the home of a theater company that leased the grounds from the Edith Wharton Restorations. Wharton's Mount has been the site of imaginative productions of Shakespeare, a fact that has sparked controversy over the proper use of the property. Hawthorne never lived in the House of the Seven Gables, yet the Salem, Mass., landmark remains one of the most popular visitor destinations in a city that also uses its history of witch trials to lure tourists. Similarly, Thoreau's cabin at Walden Pond was torn down shortly after he returned to Concord, but his two-year retreat to the Massachusetts woods transformed a rather ordinary New England pond into an essential stopping point for tourists hoping to rekindle Thoreau's iconoclastic vision. Yet another example is the small Stockbridge, Mass., house where Hawthorne lived in 1850 and 1851.

After burning to the ground in 1890, it was rebuilt 57 years later on the same site and is now used as a practice studio for the nearby Tanglewood Music Festival. Like the House of the Seven Gables and Walden Pond, Hawthorne's rebuilt red farmhouse functions as a physical reminder of literary accomplishment. Whether an actual authorial home remains at some of these sites, visitors continue to view these architectural spaces as reaffirming New England's literary past.

Robert H. Babcock, "The Rise and Fall of Portland's Waterfront, 1850–1920," *Maine Historical Society Quarterly* 22 (1982); William Corbett, *Literary New England: A History and Guide* (1993); Charles B. Hosmer, Jr., *The Presence of the Past: A History of the Preservation Movement in the United States before Williamsburg* (1965); Miriam Levine, *A Guide to Writers' Homes in New England* (1991); James M. Lindgren, *Preserving Historic New England: Preservation, Progressivism, and the Remaking of Memory* (1995); Jane H. Sciacca, *History Begins at Home: The Story of Margaret Lothrop and the Wayside* (1995); Thomas G. Smith, "Robert Frost, Stewart Udall, and the 'Last Go-Down,'" *New England Quarterly* (March 1997); Adam W. Sweeting, *Reading Houses and Building Books: Andrew Jackson Downing and the Architecture of Popular Antebellum Literature, 1835–1855* (1996).

Adam W. Sweeting

Berkshires One of the nation's oldest tourist destinations for the middle and upper classes, the Berkshire Hills are located in Berkshire County, Mass., and northern Litchfield County, Conn. A part of the Appalachian range, they are crossed by the Appalachian Trail and include among their summits Mount Greylock, the highest point in Massachusetts (3,491 ft.). This region of rolling, verdant hills has attracted some of the

wealthiest as well as the most artistic Americans of the past two centuries. Today the region appears at first glance to be a cultural and economic extension of the New York metropolitan area, a perception based on both its high real estate prices and the diversity of its cultural offerings.

But the Berkshires have long been at once a destination for pleasure-seekers and a seat of abject poverty. Indeed, Edith Wharton, one of the area's richest residents when she settled in Lenox, Mass., in 1899, based the scenes of crippling economic deprivation in *Ethan Frome* (1911) on sights she had seen in the countryside not far from her palatial home at the Mount. The Berkshires also encompass some of America's earliest industrial landscapes. During most of the 19th century and well into the 20th, Pittsfield and North Adams, Mass., and several other Berkshire towns and villages were bustling commercial and manufacturing centers. Today the Berkshires continue to offer a study in contrasts. In the less developed rural areas and the economically faltering industrial towns traces of an older, more spartan New England can still be seen, presenting a striking contrast to the popular tourist destinations.

In the early decades of the 18th century, the Berkshire region, midway between the thickly settled Connecticut and Hudson River valleys, was a place apart for both Native Americans and colonists. "Physically and socially," wrote the Great Barrington, Mass., native W. E. B. Du Bois in his *Autobiography* (1968), "our community belonged to the Dutch valley of the Hudson rather than to Puritan New England." Indeed, generations back, English Puritans, most of whom had made their way into the Berkshires from the Connecticut River valley settlement of Westfield, Mass., had lamented the less-than-Puritanical Dutch presence nearby. For their part, the English asserted their influence in the region by establishing a mission to the Housatonic Indians along the shores of the Stockbridge Bowl in 1734. This cross-cultural experiment was a prominent but temporary success. (Jonathan Edwards himself headed the mission from 1750 to 1757.) Like the native population throughout New England, the Housatonics—despite their service to the Patriot cause in the Revolution—experienced heavy attrition before the end of the century, and the group's remaining members moved west around 1800.

Immediately following the Revolutionary War, as the massive debts incurred during the war by the commonwealth of Massachusetts and the Continental government came due, the Berkshires became the scene of what may well have been the early republic's most portentous farmers' revolt: Shays's Rebellion. Desperate not to lose their small farms and livelihoods, the rebels, many of them unpaid veterans of the Revolution, closed down the debtors' courts in Northampton and Pittsfield, Mass., whose primary business was to collect the taxes that would fill the empty coffers in Boston. The national alarm was sounded, and military forces were assembled. The rebellion was put down with relative ease, but it served to support the cause of the advocates for a stronger national government who were assembling at what became the Constitutional Convention of 1787.

For most residents of the region, agriculture was rarely a road to prosperity. Beginning in the early decades of the 19th century, enterprising industrialists opened several textile factories, most of which relied on local labor. Up to World War II, textile and paper mills dominated the economic life of the region, supporting both rich and poor. In Pittsfield and North Adams, the principal manufacturing centers, millwork became a magnet for workers of various ethnic backgrounds. Indeed, the cultural diversity of the Berkshires today began with the massive influx of foreign mill workers in the 1840s. By the end of the 19th century, cities like North Adams had become composites of distinctly Irish, Franco-American, southern Italian, Tyrolese, and Jewish neighborhoods. Many descendants of those immigrants remain in the region, but most of the industries they once served ceased operation during the postwar period. In Pittsfield, a large General Electric plastics plant employs several thousand workers, but for the most part the Berkshires have been in the process of "going tourist" since before the Civil War.

"The cultural Berkshires" is the slogan upon which most residents pin their greatest hopes for economic prosperity. The Berkshires first entered the American imagination in the early decades of the 19th century with the local-color novels of Catherine Maria Sedgwick. In the years that followed, Nathaniel Hawthorne, Oliver Wendell Holmes, Herman Melville, and Edith Wharton took up residence within a 10-mile radius of the Stockbridge Bowl, which quickly became a fashionable summer resort. The proximity of extreme wealth to extreme poverty appeared in Melville's chilling contrast between the flowery sunlit meadows of the Glendinning estate and the dark, joyless home of the friendless Isabel in his novel *Pierre* (1852). Similarly, in Du Bois's formulation of the "double consciousness" metaphor for African American life, his experience of a borderland with contrasting landscapes and peoples casts an influential

shadow. In short, the Berkshires were culturally rich in the late 19th and early 20th centuries because they supplied artists with a varied palette.

During the Gilded Age, the once-secluded village of Lenox drew many of the nation's richest industrialists. Huge mansions were erected in the 1880s by the Vanderbilts, the Carnegies, and the Westinghouses, among others. While the mills of North Adams, a scant 20 miles to the north, were attracting emigrants from an increasingly forbidding Europe, the denizens of Lenox were building "an inland Newport." As these American elite discovered other playgrounds, many of their Victorian-era mansions were bought and converted into schools and museums. On the site of the old Carnegie estate, the Kripalu Center for Yoga and Health, a high-priced New Age healing center, contributes to the Berkshires' new image as a destination for spiritually inclined visitors who also happen to be very wealthy.

The Berkshires today are above all an arts-oriented tourist destination. In the years since the founding of Tanglewood as the summer home of the Boston Symphony Orchestra in 1937, the area around Stockbridge Bowl has been home not only to the Tanglewood Music Festival but also to the Jacob's Pillow Dance Festival, the Berkshire Theatre Festival, and Chesterwood, a sculpture museum situated on the former estate of the sculptor Daniel Chester French. Stockbridge, the home of the illustrator Norman Rockwell for the last 25 years of his life, now boasts the Norman Rockwell Museum (opened 1969), which houses the artist's personal collection of his works. Hancock Shaker Village, a popular tourist attraction near the New York border, pays curatorial homage to one of the 19th century's communal religious experiments and to the Shakers' heterodox legacy.

The arts are well served in the northern Berkshires as well. Williamstown, Mass., is the site not only of Williams College and the Williamstown Theatre Festival but also of two major art museums, the Sterling and Francine Clark Art Institute and the Williams College Museum of Art. In neighboring North Adams, the site of the now-defunct Sprague Electric plant has been converted into the Massachusetts Museum of Contemporary Art (MASS MoCA). Berkshire natives and outside developers alike are heavily invested in the notion of culture as an economic driving force, and to date—notwithstanding the recession of the 1980s and early 1990s, as well as the region's apparent predilection for remaining at the margins of the economic life of the nation—they have not been proven wrong.

Katherine Mixer Abbott, *Old Paths and Legends of New England* (1907); Joe Manning, *Steeples: Sketches of North Adams* (1997); Richard Nunley, ed., *The Berkshire Reader* (1992).

Michael Hoberman

Bethlehem, N.H.

Bethlehem, N.H., in Grafton County at the northwest entry to the White Mountain National Forest, is approximately 1,425 feet above sea level and claims to be the loftiest town east of the Rockies. Settled in 1787 but not incorporated until 1799, Bethlehem's population reached 1,267 in 1890 and 2,294 in 2003. From its origins as an agricultural community the town has evolved into a tourist community sustained by promotion of the surrounding landscape.

When Timothy Dwight traveled through the area in 1797, primitiveness and privation greeted him. During the early 19th century, the lure of unsettled farmland and the bounty of forest products brought settlers to Bethlehem. The town enjoyed a measure of prosperity when a stage route was established that passed through Bethlehem on its way to Portland, Maine. Railroads soon redirected commerce away from Bethlehem, however, arresting the town's development and laying the foundation for a new industry—tourism.

Writing in 1859, Thomas Starr King foreshadowed Bethlehem's future when he lamented that travelers did not stop and take in the grand panoramic views visible from the town. Nevertheless, it was not until 1863, when a runaway stage overturned on its descent from nearby Mount Agassiz, that the seeds were sown for Bethlehem to become a tourist destination. Henry Howard, one of several injured passengers from the stage wreck to recuperate in Bethlehem at the Sinclair House, attributed his family's rapid recovery to the healthfulness of the site and began turning local farmsteads into resorts. Other entrepreneurs followed. Soon Bethlehem boasted more than 30 boardinghouses, cottages, and hotels, the largest number in any White Mountain community.

In the early 20th century, guests at Bethlehem's palatial resorts, such as the Maplewood, spent the summer admiring scenery, playing golf, watching baseball, hiking mountain trails, attending concerts and balls, and feasting on farm-fresh food. Visitors to Bethlehem enjoyed promenading along the 3-mile boardwalk that lined Main Street, breathing the pure mountain air, and participating in the annual Gala Day celebration. Held in August from 1887 to 1935, Gala Day was highlighted by a coach parade featuring entries created by amusement committees at each hotel. The parade helped foster a sense of community at individual resorts as the status-conscious guests vied to see which establishment could present the most extravagantly decorated coach.

Because Bethlehem's elevation spares it from irritating pollens, it became home to a succession of hay fever relief associations. Among the urban health-seekers attracted by Bethlehem's reputation as a "Sneezer's Paradise" were a sizable number of Jewish families from New York City. By the mid-1930s Jewish guests predominated at most of the hotels in Bethlehem. During the 1940s and 1950s, the town even gained a reputation as a strictly Jewish resort. Since the 1960s it has served a more diverse clientele. Traditionally garbed Hasidic Jews now share the tourist landscape with more casually attired summer vacationers.

Although the grand hotels have long since disappeared, much of the local economy still caters to tourists. Inns, motels, restaurants, and antique shops are the most prevalent businesses. Two country clubs, one based in the historic Maplewood Casino, remain as vestigial attractions from the resort era. Remnants of Bethlehem's agricultural and tourist heritage merge at the Rocks Estate. Once the summer home of a wealthy Chicago family, the 1,300-acre tract is managed as a Christmas tree farm by the Society for the Protection of New Hampshire Forests.

Karl P. Abbott, *Open for the Season* (1950); Shirley Good Ramsey, ed., *The White Mountains: Place and Perceptions* (1980); Bryant F. Tolles, Jr., ed., "The Grand Resort Hotels and Tourism in the White Mountains," *Historical New Hampshire* 50 (1995); Tolles, *The Grand Resort Hotels of the White Mountains: A Vanishing Architectural Legacy* (1998); Gregory C. Wilson, ed., *Bethlehem, New Hampshire: A Bicentennial History* (1974).

David L. Richards

Black Heritage Trails

Black public history projects emerged in the late 20th century in response to changing cultural assumptions about New England's history and regional identity. Widespread interest in black heritage originated when mid-20th-century assumptions of a monolithic national culture were called into question. Study of African American heritage subsequently emerged as a means to understand cultural origins and personal identity in a modern context and was facilitated by research methods developed by social historians in the 1960s and 1970s.

New England's black heritage trails take varied forms. Boston's Black Heritage Trail is devoted to the city's 19th-century African American community, which, like the tour itself, was centered on Beacon Hill. Its 14 sites depict a variety of themes: African American military service in the Revolution and Civil War, trades, spiritual life, education, integration of schools and churches, black abolitionists, the Underground Railroad, and home and community building. The project was conceived by Sue Bailey Thurman, refined by J. Marcus and Gauzetta L. Mitchell, and researched by Byron Rushing; a publication of the project is edited by the staff of the Museum of Afro-American History and designed, printed, and issued by the Boston African American National Historic Site, a division of the National Park Service. The trail's walking-tour booklet includes essays on each of its sites.

The Connecticut Freedom Trail originated in a 1995 authorization by the Connecticut General Assembly to develop a trail linking sites associated with the movement toward freedom of its African American citizens in order to enhance public appreciation of their experience and contributions. A pamphlet describing the trail has short entries on notable African American people, events, and sites, linked together as a statewide driving tour. As its name implies, the trail is devoted mostly to slavery and abolition, although postemancipation and 20th-century sites are also included. Twenty-three sites are clustered into four regional tours representing southwest, northwest, central, and eastern Connecticut. Two essays and site lists emphasize special topics, including the Underground Railroad and the *Amistad* case.

The Portsmouth (N.H.) Black Heritage Trail was conceived in 1995 as a walking-tour brochure by Valerie Cunningham of the African American Resource Center and Mark J. Sammons of Strawbery Banke Museum. They developed a 300-page resource book from which community volunteers create custom tours and programs upon request for teachers, churches, and civic organizations. Copies are placed in Portsmouth public schools and libraries as well as in the city's seven historic house museums. Essays on 42 sites interpret slavery, resistance, institution building, Africanisms, trades, spiritual life, education, military service, marriage, family, women, black abolitionists, social clubs, and civil rights. Portsmouth black history is placed in regional and national context, and separate essays examine the impact of slavery on white society, law, and civil order. A pocket brochure abstract of 20 sites for self-guided walking tours is also available.

Many other institutions conduct research and provide public programing related to African American history in New England: the Rhode Island Black Heritage Society in Providence; the Prudence Crandall House, Harriet Beecher Stowe Center, and the *Amistad* project, all in Connecticut; two African Meeting House Museums (Boston and Nantucket) and Old Sturbridge Village, all in Massachusetts; Strawbery Banke Museum with the African American Resource Center in New Hampshire; the black history archives at Bowdoin College in Maine; and the Old Stone House Museum in Brownington, Vt. The Maine Historical Society in Portland offers public programs on black genealogy. Independent research is under way on Maine's prominent African American people and sites, and a historic Abyssinian Church in Portland that once sheltered escaping slaves is being restored.

Unlike the celebratory origins of white history narratives, black history necessarily highlights conflict, resistance, and tragedy as well as resourcefulness and triumph. Even when skirting difficult issues, black history projects almost inevitably raise provocative questions about the region's past and present. Lacking the South's large, clustered black populations, and accustomed to learning New England history in terms of white Protestant homogeneity, New Englanders often overlook the region's historical black presence. Black heritage trails have been important in redefining regional identity for New Englanders of all ethnic backgrounds.

Valerie Cunningham, "The First Blacks in Portsmouth," *Historical New Hampshire* (Winter 1989); Lorenzo Johnston Green, *The Negro in Colonial New England, 1620–1776* (1942); Sidney Kaplan, *The Black Presence in the Era of the American Revolution, 1770–1800* (1973); Jack Salzman, David Smith, and Cornel West, eds., *Encyclopedia of African-American Culture and History* (1996).

Mark J. Sammons

Block Island

Block Island is a popular New England summer resort, part of the state of Rhode Island and located 12 miles off its southern coast. Accessible only by boat or plane, the island was once a bustling tourist destination in the late 1880s and since the 1960s has again become a desirable vacation spot for tourists seeking a secluded, peaceful getaway. Year-round ferry service is available from Point Judith, R.I., and from New London, Conn., Montauk, N.Y., and Providence and Newport, R.I., during the summer months. Commercial, private, and charter flights bring tourists to the island from many points.

Originally populated by Narragansett Indians, Block Island was settled by Europeans in 1661. The original 16 English families of the island were searching for a haven of religious freedom, a quest typical of many of the early inhabitants of Rhode Island. A memorial to these people is located where they landed, at Settler's Rock in Cow Cove. Block Island's name was taken from Adriaen Block, a Dutch trader who landed there in 1614, and it was later christened the town of New Shoreham by the Rhode Island Assembly in 1672, a designation that lasted into the late 19th century.

Because of Block Island's isolation, small size (11 square miles), and lack of a good harbor, its population grew slowly. The first census in 1708 showed only 200 people. By the outbreak of the American Revolution, it had grown to 478 people and at the start of the Civil War to 1,350. The present year-round population is approximately 800 to 1,000, though thousands of tourists live temporarily on the island during the summer months.

Unlike so much of coastal New England, Block Island never evolved through the typical stages of regional economic growth. Apart from some early privateering, it did not play a role in maritime trade nor did it participate in either the cotton or woolen manufacturing boom of the mid- and late 19th century. In fact, it has never undergone any significant industrial growth during its history but has maintained an economy based primarily on fishing and farming and, today, on tourism.

Block Island, however, did follow another New England cultural initiative—the use of its natural beauty and seclusion to foster a tourist resort economy. In modern times islanders have capitalized on the island's landscape of steep coastal cliffs, rolling hills, and stone walls. It is studded with Victorian buildings, particularly in Old Harbor, and is watched over by two 19th-century lighthouses, South East Lighthouse and North Light. In addition, many tourists are drawn by the island's wildlife habitat, which is protected by the Nature Conservancy. It is home to a diverse array of habitats—beaches, maritime scrubland, salt and brackish ponds, and various freshwater wetland ecosystems—which support many species, including more than 40 that are considered rare or endangered. The island is also a stopover point for thousands of migratory birds each year, attracting many tourists who come to witness the event.

Block Island's environmental concerns have perhaps been best symbolized by its huge federally funded windmill, which was erected in the late 1970s to cut the island's enormously expensive energy bills. The 160-foot structure has a wingspan of 125 feet and uses the high winds of Block Island Sound to generate electricity. The windmill represents a partial response to the need for both environmental conservation and cheaper energy costs that are a concern throughout New England.

Block Island maintains its sense of uniqueness to satisfy both its full-time residents and its waves of summer visitors. For decades it has offered a quaint, quiet regional experience proclaimed by the promotional slogan, "New England as it was meant to be." From that comparative perspective the island stands in contrast to the entire region's rapid development during the 19th and 20th centuries.

Peter J. Coleman, *The Transformation of Rhode Island, 1790–1860* (1963); Joel Garreau, *The Nine Nations of North America* (1981); Rick Sylvain, "Timeless Isle," *Detroit Free Press,* May 15, 1994; Betsy Wittemann, "Cycling on Block Island," *Coastal Living,* July-August 1992.

Eric Jarvis

Boston Tourism

Every year the greater Boston area attracts millions of visitors. They come to peek into the cradle of the American Revolution, shop for colleges, and attend conventions, commencements, art exhibits, and sporting events. But much of Boston's appeal lies in its historical legacy.

Since 1974, 16 historic sites, largely from the Puritan and Federal periods, have been organized into a National Historic Park and can be visited by following a three-mile marked path called the Freedom Trail. Originating at the Boston Common, the Freedom Trail leads tourists through much of downtown on the old Boston peninsula, past cemeteries, churches, and meetinghouses to the North End, where Paul Revere lived, on to the Old North Church, whose lights in the belfry announced the approach of the British troops in 1775, and then to Copp's Hill, where, among other noted Bostonians, the Puritan Mather family lies buried. The trail ends at Bunker Hill in Charlestown, where, in June 1775, British troops achieved a Pyrrhic victory over the colonists.

On Boston Common, a 48-acre park owned by the people of Boston since 1634, visitors are only steps away from Beacon Hill, an enclave of Boston's most distinguished homes. The hill is topped by the classicist State House (1795–98) designed by Charles Bulfinch, the first professional architect in the United States. The building of the State House on John Hancock's pasture caused massive real estate speculation and triggered the residential development of Beacon Hill. By the mid-19th century the hill was densely covered with Federal-style mansions and elegant Greek Revival town houses displaying brick facades, pitched and dormered roof-lines, swelled and flat bays, and delicate wrought-iron balconies. On the hill's sunny southern slope lived Boston's social elite, its intellectuals, merchants, and politicians, at a time when wit was as important as a flamboyant display of money.

Approximately half the city's black population lived on the northern slope of Beacon Hill; their history is documented along the Black Heritage Trail beginning at the *Memorial to Robert Gould Shaw and the Massachusetts Fifty-fourth Regiment* relief located opposite the State House. The trail leads up the hill to Pinckney Street, the unofficial demarcation line between black and white in the early 19th century. The oldest structure on the hill, a modest clapboard house built in 1797, was once the home of George Middleton, leader of the Bucks of America, an all-black regiment during the American Revolution, and Louis Clapion, a hairdresser from the French West Indies. When Clapion married in 1792,

Trolley tour bus in Louisburg Square, Boston, 1992

they divided the house. Since Middleton never married and had his closest friends among men, the house has also become a marker in Boston's emerging gay and lesbian historiography. Further along the trail on Phillips Street, the house of Lewis and Harriet Hayden was an important stop on the Underground Railroad, sheltering slaves on their way to freedom, and the 1844 house of the black cloth merchant John P. Coburn served as a private retreat for games of chance and love. Some decades later, as Jewish immigrants pushed onto the hill and blacks moved to better quarters in Roxbury, the African Meeting House, the oldest extant black church in the country, was sold to the Jewish community and served as a synagogue; the building eventually changed hands again to reopen as the Museum of Afro-American History in 1972.

During the second half of the 19th century, when the mudflats along the Charles River had been transformed into habitable land and the ostentatious display of money became more fashionable, wealthy families moved into fancy Victorian houses in the Back Bay. In 1856 this residential area was laid out on a rectangular grid. Its seven avenues are dissected by streets named in alphabetical order from Arlington to Hereford, beginning at the Public Garden (1837) and ending at Massachusetts Avenue, which connects the heart of Boston with the heart of Cambridge. Back Bay's central axis, Commonwealth Avenue, a tree-lined mall 240 feet across, was planned in the 1860s as a grand boulevard with massive blocks of brownstone mansions to match those being built in Paris. Commonwealth Avenue connected the "emerald necklace," a 7-mile stretch of parks and parkways encircling Boston that was constructed between 1878 and 1895, to the existing Boston Common and Public Garden. Newbury Street, parallel to Commonwealth Avenue, developed into Boston's most expensive shopping street. Newbury Street separates the residential Back Bay to its north from the business district to its south and features many of Boston's largest hotels and public buildings.

Facing Boston Common today is the Bull and Finch Pub, "where everybody knows your name," as the theme song from the long-running television show *Cheers* claims. On the Common, tourists can view the Central Burying Ground, the resting place of Crispus Attucks and other victims of the Boston Massacre of 1773 and of many Bunker Hill battle casualties. Such famous colonial figures as Samuel Adams, Paul Revere, and, reputedly, Mother Goose are buried in the nearby Old Granary Burying Ground, and across the street in the King's Chapel Burying Ground

lie the graves of several founders, including John Winthrop. The Common features several notable sculptures, including Andrzej Pitynski's *The Partisans,* and in the adjacent Public Garden tourists can ride the famous Swan Boats and admire Nancy Schön's 1987 bronze sculptures commemorating Robert McCloskey's classic children's book *Make Way for Ducklings* (1941).

As Boston's leading families moved from the hill into the Back Bay, amassing ever-greater fortunes in commerce and industry, the undeveloped land to the south and west invited the construction of large projects for the public good. They included the Boston Public Library (founded in 1848, moved to Copley Square in 1895), the New England Conservatory of Music (1867), Symphony Hall (1900), and the Museum of Fine Arts (1909). The Romanesque Christian Science Mother Church (1894) and its byzantine extension (1906) jarred with the strict classicist lines of Boston's large public buildings. In the 1960s, however, Boston, which had never quite recovered from the Great Depression, embarked on a massive urban renewal. Whole sections of the city were razed, and modernist designs, particularly those of Boston's star architect I. M. Pei, replaced 19th-century structures (Government Center, 1964; Hancock Tower, 1972–75). In 1972 the firms of I. M. Pei and Partners and Cossutta and Ponte were called in to rethink the Christian Science complex. Their solution, an arrangement of old and modern buildings in clear lines around a body of water, is representative of Boston's architectural attempts to combine its past with a drive toward the future.

In recent years Boston has followed the example of New York in arranging megashows in its museums. In 1997 the Museum of Science's *Leonardo da Vinci* exhibit drew 400,000 visitors. Similar numbers turned out for *Monet in the 20th Century* (1998) at the Museum of Fine Arts. Such exhibits boosted museum attendance by more than 10 percent. In addition to the Museum of Fine Arts, the Museum of Science, and the Charles Hayden Planetarium, Boston's museums and attractions include the Isabella Stewart Gardner Museum, the Children's Museum, the Computer Museum, the Institute of Contemporary Art, the museum at the John Fitzgerald Kennedy Library, the New England Aquarium, and the Franklin Park Zoo. Many historic sites, such as the Bunker Hill Monument, the USS *Constitution,* and the Boston Tea Party Ship, have small museums attached.

The Boston Public Library has also functioned as an exhibition space, most notably in June 1996, when it hosted *Public Faces/Private Lives: Boston's Lesbian and Gay History,* compiled by the History Project. The book that grew out of the exhibit documented how the urban renewal of the 1960s affected the gay bar scene by destroying old neighborhoods whose nooks and crannies had sheltered alternative lifestyles.

There are many more museums in the Greater Boston area. The most significant of these are just across the Charles River in Cambridge, where tourists visit Harvard Square and Harvard Yard and the many museums at Harvard University. Harvard offers the Fogg Art Museum, which houses a superb collection of German expressionist art, the Arthur M. Sackler Museum, the Semitic Museum, and the Peabody Museum, which includes a unique collection of 19th-century glass flowers. Near Harvard Square is the Longfellow National Historic Site, one of the homes of Henry Wadsworth Longfellow. Tourists to Boston also visit the nearby historic community of Charlestown, the location of the Bunker Hill Monument and the Charlestown Navy Yard, which houses the USS *Constitution.*

Boston's nightlife is concentrated in a small theater district and in the bars and clubs on Lansdowne Street near the Fenway, at Faneuil Hall, and in the North End. The Faneuil Hall Marketplace includes Quincy Market, the massive granite market buildings designed in 1826 by Alexander Parris. Faneuil Hall attracts tourists and is still the scene of political debates and meetings. Nearby is the famous Union Oyster House, the oldest restaurant in Boston. Tourists can also visit Boston's North End, an Italian enclave. With the cleanup of Boston Harbor, the harbor islands are becoming popular tourist destinations. Georges Island is the site of Fort Warren, a Civil War-era prison and National Historic Landmark.

Boston restaurants venture far beyond traditional New England seafood fare, offering menus from all corners of the globe. Cajun, Chinese, Indian, Italian, Japanese, and Mexican cooking, in particular, have achieved top quality in Boston, reflecting not so much the demands of its international visitors as the exciting new ethnic mix of Boston's dynamic population.

Noelle Blackmer Beatty, *Literary Byways of Boston and Cambridge* (1991); Bainbridge Bunting, *Houses of Boston's Back Bay: An Architectural History, 1840–1917* (1967); Robert Campbell and Peter Vanderwarker, *Cityscapes of Boston: An American City through Time* (1992); Martin Green, *The Mount Vernon Street Warrens: A Boston Story, 1860–1910* (1989); *Improper Bostonians: Lesbian and Gay History from the Puritans to Playland,* comp. History Project (1998); A. C. Lyons, *Invitation to Boston: A Merry Guide to Her Past, Present, and Future* (1947); Thomas H. O'Connor, *Building a New Boston: Politics and Urban Renewal, 1950 to 1970* (1993); Mark R. Schneider, *Boston Confronts Jim*

Crow, 1890–1920 (1997); Cynthia Zaitzevsky, *Frederick Law Olmsted and the Boston Park System* (1982).

Susanne Klingenstein

Boston Women's Heritage Trail

In the tradition of Boston's Black Heritage Trail, itself modeled after the Freedom Trail, the Boston Women's Heritage Trail introduces its visitors to historical figures whose contribution to New England and American culture has too often been overlooked. There are important distinctions between the Boston Women's Heritage Trail and its predecessors. For one, the Boston Women's Heritage Trail covers more time and more ground. For another, it does not require that only original buildings be included in the walk, as do both the Freedom and Black Heritage Trails. Its sites include vacant lots with markers indicating what was once there. While the Boston Women's Heritage Trail shares sites with its predecessors, it tells a different story about them. Rather than heralding the Boston men who bravely fought the British during the American Revolution, for instance, this walk highlights the mothers, wives, and daughters who kept the city going while its men were on battlefields fighting the war or in Philadelphia building the new nation.

The Boston Women's Heritage Trail was conceived in 1989, when the public school administrator Meg Campbell proposed a writing project to Boston educators as a way of celebrating Women's History Month. Campbell was disturbed by the failure of the city's public monuments and of the history texts used in the schools to recognize the accomplishments of women. She originally planned to ask students in grades four through eight to research the lives of 12 female Bostonians and write about what they had learned. Students and teachers would then vote for their favorite heroines, and a guidebook to the trail would be based on the results. The enthusiasm that her idea generated among both teachers and students led to a much bigger project than Campbell had foreseen. The efforts of 17 schools, 42 teachers, and more than 1,000 students from all over Boston led to the nomination of 123 women for inclusion in the guidebook.

In the end students gathered so much information that it could not all be used in one tour; four walks were thus created, each one focusing on a different theme. The downtown walk, called "The Search for Equal Rights," focuses on women who fought for their rights and the rights of others over four centuries. It shares five of its 14 sites with the Freedom Trail. The North End walk, "A Diversity of Cultures," celebrates the lives of women from the various ethnic groups that have occupied Boston's North End from its Yankee beginnings through the waves of immigration of the 20th century. The Beacon Hill walk, "Writers, Artists, and Activists," focuses on women who worked for such causes as abolition and peace, highlighting the lives of more African American women than any of its counterparts. Women activists for social and economic change are the subjects of the South Cove/Chinatown walk, "Action for Economic and Social Justice." A fifth walk, through Back Bay, "Educators, Artists, and Social Reformers," became part of the trail in 1999.

The Boston Women's Heritage Trail continues to grow in popularity and scope. An expanded and updated guidebook came out in 1999, along with a Web site that offered a virtual tour of the downtown walk. The Women's Heritage Trail has inspired thousands who have walked it to look at Boston's history in a new way. Other organizations have adopted its goal and created similar walks in other areas or refocused existing trails to include women's history. The National Park Service, for example, now conducts a "Remember the Ladies" tour following the sites of the Freedom Trail on occasions of significance to women. Meg Campbell and the students of the Boston public schools have themselves made history by successfully recovering the lives of hundreds of women who worked to make Boston and the world a better place.

Boston Women's Heritage Trail: Four Centuries of Boston Women, a Guide to Five Walks: Downtown, North End, Beacon Hill, South Cove/Chinatown, Back Bay, 2d ed. (1999); Michael Kenney, "Trailing Women's History," *Boston Globe*, April 24, 1999; Bruce McCabe, "Women's History Gets Spotlight in March," *Boston Globe*, March 6, 1993; Susan Wilson, "Women's Heritage Trail," *Boston Globe*, March 19, 1992.

Beth A. Kaputa

Bunker Hill Monument

Bunker Hill Monument, completed in 1842 and dedicated on June 17, 1843, in a national ceremony, is now listed as a National Historic Landmark. Located on Breed's Hill (not Bunker Hill) in Charlestown, Mass., the 221-foot granite obelisk with a temple lodge commemorates the resistance of a united colonial army to the British siege of June 17, 1775. Nearby is William Wetmore Story's statue of Colonel William Prescott, who reportedly said to his troops, "Don't fire until you see the whites of their eyes." In this first major bloody battle of the Revolution, the Americans retreated after two assaults.

Although John Trumbull's painting *The Death of General Warren at the Battle of Bunker's Hill* (1786) kindled interest in the battle, the first memorial was not erected until 1794. Amidst intensifying partisanship between the Federalists and Democratic-Republicans, King Solomon's Lodge of Freemasons honored their colleague Joseph Warren and his compatriots with a small wooden column. Development later threatened the site. The Bunker Hill Monument Association (BHMA) was incorporated in 1823 and led by Daniel Webster and Edward Everett. It began fund-raising for a new monument before the 50th anniversary of the battle. Its design is credited to the engineer Loammi Baldwin. Some Yankees opposed the construction, however, instead demanding provisions for destitute veterans. While anti-Masonry sentiments were rising, the cornerstone was laid in Masonic fashion on June 17, 1825, in a grand celebration attended by the marquis de Lafayette.

Constructed intermittently between 1827 and 1842 under the architect Solomon Willard, the monument was composed of Quincy granite, hammered and dressed at the Charlestown prison. America's first railroad was constructed to haul the granite blocks from the Quincy quarries to the monument. The cost exceeded $150,000, an expense funded by a public subscription whose poor return necessitated selling the adjacent battlefield. In 1840 a weeklong Ladies' Fair raised more than $30,000 for the cause.

With President John Tyler and his cabinet in attendance, the monument was dedicated in 1843. A three-hour procession preceded an oration in which Daniel Webster praised America and posited that its ideals had been born in the Reformation and nurtured by the Pilgrims and Puritans. An editorial in the Catholic-affiliated *Boston Pilot*, however, called him a "pettifogger" for repeating those claims. Meanwhile, ethnic tensions were intensifying as Charlestown attracted Irish immigrants, and the once-patriotic symbolism of the monument became contested.

The BHMA's celebrations on June 17 gradually waned as the importance of the July 4 celebration waxed and the town's ethnicity shifted. The association did hold a grand centennial affair in 1875 that evoked the criticism of the feminist Lucy Stone, who claimed the monument "was made by men who refuse to women the rights for which men died on that memorable battlefield." The town's Irish majority remade the commemoration afterward. Mixing patriotism with street theater, their "morning carnival" drew immense crowds. With the onset of the depressed 1890s, the celebration lampooned Boston's rich and genteel. It began at midnight with drinking, fireworks, street fairs, and open-house parties.

The symbolic uses of the Bunker Hill Monument varied widely over time. Irish Americans often praised the monument and the

Bunker Hill Monument, with militia reenactment, Charlestown, Mass., 1973

Revolution it commemorated as a model for patriots in Ireland. Amidst the turmoil of industrialization, patriotic groups sometimes made the shrine a symbol of their Americanism. In 1899, the BHMA itself used the historical site to condemn American imperialism in the Spanish-American War. Yet in 1919 the neglected site was given to the state after the BHMA fell into bankruptcy while constructing its exhibit lodge.

Years later, the approach of America's Bicentennial refocused attention on the monument. Trumbull's painting appeared on postage stamps in 1968 and 1975. A nine-day celebration in 1975 included military reenactments and a diverse parade. Meanwhile, others used the monument to protest the Vietnam War and to resist school desegregation. Finally, Senator Edward Kennedy introduced legislation establishing the Boston National Historical Park, and the site was transferred to federal authorities in 1976. Since 1794 the monument has indeed been a contested symbol representing a changing nation.

Michael Kammen, *A Season of Youth: The American Revolution and the Historical Imagination* (1988); James M. Lindgren, *Preserving Historic New England: Preservation, Progressivism, and the Remaking of Memory* (1995); Michael Musuraca, "The 'Celebration Begins at Midnight': Irish Immigrants and the Celebration of Bunker Hill Day," *Labor's Heritage* 23 (1990); George Washington Warren, *The History of the Bunker Hill Monument Association during the First Century of the United States of America* (1877).

James M. Lindgren

Cape Cod It is difficult now to imagine a time when Cape Cod, in Massachusetts, was not a popular tourist destination. In the 19th century, though, the Cape was one of the regions of New England that was least likely to attract visitors. True, Henry David Thoreau wrote with great admiration of the landscape of the Cape after his walking tours there in the 1850s. But Thoreau's essays on Cape Cod describe a place very different from the Cape of today. Writing about what is now one of the region's most popular beaches, Thoreau described it as "a vast *morgue*, where famished dogs may range in packs—the most uninviting landscape on earth." Thoreau preferred the empty, forbidding coast of the Cape to the more civilized charms of heavily traveled regions such as the White Mountains of New Hampshire or Newport, R.I., but he knew that few of his contemporaries would agree with him. In fact, that was what he liked about Cape Cod: "I trust that for a long time [fashionable visitors] will be disappointed here." And for a long time, they were.

Twenty years after Thoreau made his famous tramp through the Cape, the situation had not changed much. National guidebooks gave Cape Cod very little attention. In *Appleton's Guide to American Resorts,* published in 1876, the whole region of the Cape rated only a one-page treatment. By contrast, the White Mountains received 14 pages of coverage. This obscurity was not caused by the Cape's isolation. By 1873 the Old Colony Railroad had reached the tip of the Cape in Provincetown, making all points on Cape Cod easily accessible by rail. Steamboats moved efficiently between Boston and Provincetown and between Fall River and the south-facing towns of Falmouth and Hyannis. In fact, the Cape was arguably more accessible to travelers in the late 19th century than it is today. But rather than bringing tourists in, the trains seem instead to have tempted Cape Codders to leave the poverty of their region and migrate to the cities or the West.

Between 1860 and 1920, the region of Cape Cod shared the economic dislocation of much of rural New England. Its population declined by 26 percent; its major industries, including coastal shipping, commercial fishing, whaling, salt making, and a variety of manufactures, all declined drastically. But while much of the rest of rural New England, under similar economic pressure, turned toward tourism, most Cape Codders held out, continuing to survive by fishing, farming, and foraging through the turn of the century.

By contrast, in the 20th century Cape Cod became nationally known for its great natural beauty, its quaint "Old New England" atmosphere, its variety of resorts—and eventually also for its crowds and traffic jams. But that did not begin to happen until the 1920s, when a technological breakthrough, the automobile, transformed the experience of tourism. Automobiles shaped a new kind of travel experience on Cape Cod and everywhere else.

Tourist industries that catered to the auto tourist, usually small-scale, informal, and relentlessly road-oriented, found a comfortable niche on Cape Cod. Within a few decades, they completely dominated the scene. A single summer Sunday in 1936 reportedly brought 55,000 "motor cars" over only one of the two canal bridges that separate the Cape from the rest of Massachusetts. Today, hundreds of thousands of automobiles come over the two bridges in July and August every year, causing world-class traffic jams and supporting the

Tourist accommodations, Cape Cod, Mass., 1990s

endless chain of roadside restaurants, souvenir shops, motels, and gas stations that line the major roads.

After World War II, Cape Cod became the vacation destination of choice for thousands of southern New Englanders who were reaping the benefits of a postwar economic boom. In the decades that followed, the Cape's summer and winter population exploded; between 1955 and 1980, the year-round population nearly tripled. The numbers reflect not only the exponential growth of the vacation industry but also a change in its direction. Those 25 years brought a massive influx of second-home buyers and retirees, whose impact on the region's population, economy, and environment has proven to be even more dramatic than that of more transient tourists. They have linked the tourist industry on the Cape ever more closely to the boom-bust cycle of the larger economy. The "Massachusetts miracle" of the mid-1980s fostered yet another wave of building expansion on the Cape, predictably jeopardized by the economic depression that followed.

As the popularity of Cape Cod has soared, the entire landscape has been carved up to fit the preferences of widely diverse vacationers. Summer resorts have a history of segregation along extremely fine lines of class, ethnicity, and religion; today on Cape Cod vacation communities are also divided by such social factors as age, profession, and lifestyle. At the very tip of the Cape lies perhaps the region's best-known example of such specialization. Provincetown has been many things: a whal-

ing port, a haven for Portuguese immigrants, a resort for 19th-century painters, and a center for modern drama. Today, though, it is best known as a resort for gay and lesbian tourists from across the Northeast.

The rest of the Cape is equally specialized. Sprawling, urban Hyannis provides the nightlife and bar scenes that attract college students from all over New England. Chatham, at the elbow of the Cape, is distinguished by its colony of wealthy, established summer folk living in rambling shingled cottages reminiscent of their exclusive neighbor, Nantucket, across Nantucket Sound. Along Route 6A, towns all the way from Sandwich to Orleans present the polished quaintness of preservation, with rose-covered cottages, inns named after ships' captains, and well-kept town greens. The bay towns attract retirees and also more than their share of exurbanites fleeing to the countryside to open art galleries, gourmet restaurants, and brokerages.

If there is anything that all these varied vacationers have in common, it is their increased fascination with Cape Cod's unique landscape over the past 35 years. Much of the recent attention to Cape Cod's environment has focused on the outer Cape—from Chatham to Provincetown, from the elbow to the fist of the Cape—where the Cape Cod National Seashore was created by Congress in 1961, preserving the longest unbroken and undeveloped stretch of beach in the Northeast. A cluster of publications by naturalists, geologists, and poets has helped to set the stage for a new appreciation of Cape Cod's rich and

fragile natural beauty. Perhaps the best advertisement for the National Seashore, however, came in the form of widely published photographs of glamorous Kennedys strolling the dunes of Cape Cod.

The sense of both the fragility and the value of the natural environment has grown since the 1960s. As housing tracts, malls, and hotels have advanced rapidly over the remaining open land, an uneasy sense overtook many regional enthusiasts that the Cape was being "loved to death." By the end of the building boom in the 1980s, that sense had become so urgent that a uniquely powerful Cape Cod Commission was empowered by referendum in 1990 to protect the dwindling natural resources of the Cape. Along with other groups like the Association for the Preservation of Cape Cod, the Massachusetts Audubon Society, and the Cape Cod Natural History Museum, the commission worked to balance the Cape's need for revenue with its need to protect limited resources.

In the 1990s, Cape residents (seasonal, temporary, and permanent) engaged in a great debate over the proper balance of those conflicting community needs, a debate that most often took the form of arguments over how the Cape Cod Commission should act. Many argued that the Cape is in danger of becoming a regional sacrifice area. Water resources were profoundly jeopardized by the uncontrolled growth of the 1980s. The regional economy since World War II has become heavily dependent on part-time, low-paying, dead-end jobs that ebb and flow with every season. Some social observers attribute equally serious social problems to the Cape's dominant industry, ranging from a general sense of alienation among long-term residents to epidemic alcoholism and its attendant medical and social ailments.

In many circles, support for the tourist industry has waned as its reputation as a clean industry suffered and as concern for the Cape's unique environment has grown. The Cape Cod Commission found in a 1991 survey that the great majority of Cape residents favored a limit to further growth in the tourist industries, preferring that the commission encourage the development of light industry instead. Protourist forces on the Cape vigorously counterattacked. All sides acknowledged, however, that for the foreseeable future, tourism would be the inescapable economic reality of Cape Cod. The difficulty would lie in balancing the requirements of that dominant industry with the need to protect community, environmental, and cultural resources. The way in which Cape residents resolve that dilemma will have a profound impact, not only on Cape Cod itself but also on many other tourist regions facing similar conflicts in the future.

Josef Berger, *Cape Cod Pilot: A WPA Guide* (1985 [1937]); Robert Finch, *Common Ground: A Naturalist's Cape Cod* (1981); Greg O'Brien, ed., *A Guide to Nature on Cape Cod and the Islands* (1990); James C. O'Connell, *Becoming Cape Cod: Creating a Seaside Resort* (2003); Henry David Thoreau, *Cape Cod* (1985 [1865]).

Dona Brown

Cape Cod Commission The Cape Cod Commission was created by an act of the Massachusetts General Court in 1990 and confirmed by a majority of Barnstable County voters. It evolved as an instrument to control the region's expansive development. Cape Cod's population grew from nearly 96,656 in 1970 to 229,545 in 2003, one of the fastest growth rates of any area within New England. The sprawling development of the 1980s generated a backlash, especially among retirees and other "wash-ashores" who had moved to the Cape for its rural seaside charm. On July 6, 1986, Alexander Theroux wrote in the *Boston Globe* that Cape Cod was "overrun, exploited, ripped up, bulldozed, and just about drained dry." The development of the commission and the controversy surrounding its role reflect a heated struggle between preservation and development interests over the character of the famed resort region.

The Cape Cod Commission's roots lay with the Cape Cod Planning and Economic Development Commission (CCPEDC), a strictly advisory regional planning agency established in 1965. During the late 1980s, CCPEDC's executive director, Armando Carbonell, initiated a strategic planning process, "Prospect Cape Cod," which called for the formation of a regional planning agency with strong land use and environmental protection authority. In 1988 former U.S. senator Paul Tsongas gave impetus to the Cape Cod Commission proposal when he advocated a complete moratorium on new construction, influencing Cape Codders to adopt the more moderate alternative of regional planning and regulation of large-scale development. The Association for the Preservation of Cape Cod also played a role in establishing the commission and was pivotal in educating the public about environmental degradation, particularly the need to protect the region's sole source aquifer from such threats as groundwater pollution at the Massachusetts Military Reservation. In a 1988 nonbinding referendum, 76 percent of the voters favored the proposal to establish a Cape Cod Commission. After a heated campaign, a binding referendum on a bill was passed by the state legislature, with 53 percent in favor, and approved by Governor Michael Dukakis in March 1990.

The Cape Cod Commission, part of Barnstable county government, has 19 appointed members and a professional staff. The commission reviews the regional impact of new commercial and residential developments, focusing on the effects that development has on water quality, wastewater, transportation, natural habitat, open space, and community character. The planning guidelines are embodied in the Regional Policy Plan, which was updated in 1996 and 2002. Elements of the plan address groundwater protection, affordable housing, open-space acquisition, sustainable economic development, and non-auto transportation alternatives like public transit and bikeways. The commission has also pioneered studies on the carrying capacity of the natural environment and infrastructure of Cape towns. The 2002 Regional Policy Plan included regulatory incentives for new, more concentrated development to be located in designated growth centers.

The commission's oversight of new development has generated controversy. Opponents of the commission have criticized its regulation for discouraging business development, while others have been wary of a regional approach to planning. In 1994 seven of Cape Cod's 15 towns voted on proposals to withdraw from the commission, but all seven elected to remain under the commission's jurisdiction. Since then, strong public concern for environmental protection and preservation of the region's sense of place has produced substantial support for the Cape Cod Commission.

Association for the Preservation of Cape Cod, *State of the Cape, 1994: Progress toward Preservation* (1994); Cape Cod Planning and Economic Development Commission, *Prospect Cape Cod* (1987); Cape Cod Commission, *Regional Policy Plan* (1991, 1996, 2002); Armando J. Carbonell and Daniel Hamilton, "Cape Cod Commission History," *State and Regional Initiatives for Managing Development Policy Issues and Practical Concerns* (1992); James C. O'Connell, *Becoming Cape Cod: Creating a Seaside Resort* (2003).

James C. O'Connell

Concord, Mass. A town of approximately 15,500 residents in 2002, Concord projects a powerful sense of place. The town's early incorporation and settlement, its influence as the seat of Middlesex County courts from the late 17th to the mid-19th century, its prominence at the outset of the American Revolution, and its significance as the home of Emerson, Thoreau, the Alcotts, and Hawthorne all contribute to Concord's role in national history and to its present importance to regional tourism.

Musketaquid, Concord's Native American name, was originally a village of the Massachusett tribe. The first inland English settlement in Massachusetts, Concord was established in 1635 by the Puritan minister Peter Bulkeley, the fur trader Simon Willard, and a group of 12 families. The land within its boundaries was purchased from the Native Americans after incorporation and settlement. Over time, parts of the original town broke off, forming Bedford, Acton, Lincoln, and Carlisle.

Concord is best known for historical events that occurred there in the 18th and 19th centuries. The battles of Lexington and Concord on April 19, 1775, marked the beginning of the American Revolution; Concord has since attracted tourists with anniversary celebrations of the day. The independent spirit that informed colonial opposition to British rule expressed itself once again during the 19th century in protest against government complicity in slavery (voiced in Thoreau's "Resistance to Civil Government") and in other reform efforts. Ralph Waldo Emerson, a descendant of Peter Bulkeley and of the revolutionary chaplain William Emerson, moved to Concord in 1834. His essay *Nature*, a systematic exposition of Transcendental philosophy, was published in 1836. Emerson's presence in Concord made the town a popular destination for visitors; his written and spoken appreciation of Concord's history and Thoreau's celebration of its natural attractions enhanced the town's appeal as a place of pilgrimage.

Concord tourism began in earnest around 1880, as people came in ever-greater numbers to see the homes and sites made famous by the Concord authors and to visit their resting places in Sleepy Hollow Cemetery. The 1875 Centennial celebration of the battles of Lexington and Concord, at which Daniel Chester French's *Minute Man* statue was unveiled beside the rebuilt North Bridge, generated fresh interest in revolutionary landmarks. The 1975 Bicentennial celebration of the battles featured an elaborate parade including re-created ceremonial minutemen and militia companies in 18th-century garb, a speech at the North Bridge by President Gerald Ford, and a protest organized by the People's Bicentennial Commission. A new surge of tourism followed.

Today hundreds of thousands of tourists visit a wide array of Concord attractions annually: the Concord Museum, established in 1886 as the Concord Antiquarian Society; Orchard House, operated by the Louisa May Alcott Memorial Association; the Emerson House, run by the Ralph Waldo Emerson Memorial Association; the Old Manse, deeded to the Trustees of Reservations in 1939; the Wayside, a home once lived in by Nathaniel Hawthorne, acquired by the Minute Man National Historical Park in 1965, and opened in 1971; the Walden Pond State Reservation, under the Massachusetts Department of Environmental Management; the Great Meadows National Wildlife Refuge, donated to the federal government in 1944; the Hill and Main Street Burying Grounds, both dating from the 17th century; the Sleepy Hollow Cemetery, dedicated in 1855; and the Concord Free Public Library, founded in 1873. The annual meeting of the Thoreau Society, established in 1941, draws members to Concord each July. The Thoreau Lyceum, once a popular tourist stop in Concord, contains the author's personal effects and memorabilia as well as a replica of his Walden Pond cabin. Other Thoreau effects, a reconstruction of Emerson's study, and extensive collections of Concord historical materials from the 17th century to the present are housed in the Concord Museum.

Concordians have long enjoyed a vigorous intellectual and cultural life. From the late 18th century, an unbroken succession of libraries led up to the founding in 1873 of the Concord Free Public Library. The Concord Lyceum was formed in December 1828. Several musical and dramatic organizations developed later in the 19th century. Today, performances by the Concord Orchestra and the Concord Players attract both residents and visitors. Bronson Alcott's Concord School of Philosophy (1879–88) was transformed in the 20th century into the Summer Conversational Series, held in the original School of Philosophy building. Programs and lectures on topics of broad interest are regularly offered by Concord institutions and organizations.

The town is governed by selectmen, a town manager, and an open town meeting. Numerous citizens' committees provide the opportunity for individual participation. In recent years, the struggle between historic preservation, land conservation, and environmental protection on the one side and development on the other has had a polarizing effect. By and large, however, residents trust in political processes. A shared sense of Concord as Thoreau's "most estimable place in all the world" motivates individuals to work toward resolution. The perception that the town is unique moves visitors who come to enrich their historical, literary, environmental, or genealogical understanding as strongly as it does local residents.

Anne McCarthy Forbes, *Narrative Histories of Concord and West Concord* (1995); Robert A. Gross, "Transcendentalism and Urbanism: Concord, Boston, and the Wider World," *Journal of American Studies* 18, no. 3 (1984); Edward Jarvis, *Traditions and Reminiscences of Concord, Massachusetts, 1779–1878*, ed. Sarah Chapin (1993); Lemuel Shattuck, *A History of the Town of Concord . . . from Its Earliest Settlement to 1832 . . .* (1835); Ruth R. Wheeler, *Concord: Climate for Freedom* (1967).

Leslie Perrin Wilson

Ecotourism Ecotourism is an ecologically sensitive or envirocentric form of travel that centers on caring for natural and cultural resources within a host community, region, or country. Whether an ecotourist prefers to engage in activities guaranteed to raise the pulse rate or elects to sit quietly for hours observing nature at work, New England offers a great variety of settings for the environmentally conscious visitor.

In New England, as in other areas, the revenue generated from visitors' expenditures can provide funds to purchase and improve or maintain natural areas. Protecting areas from the economic activities that exploit the environment will ensure that these lands will provide scenic and recreational experiences for future generations of visitors. Conservationists, however, also argue that tourism can compromise the quality of the environment if economic gain becomes the principal motivation of developers. Damage inevitably results when the demands of visitors exceed the carrying capacity of the host environment or community.

Although hardly a panacea, ecotourism may offer a solution to the conflict between the forces of economic development and those espousing biological conservation and cultural preservation. Ecotourists engage in activities that support, or are harmless to, the host environment or community. These activities may include environmental restoration efforts such as tree planting and area cleanup or environmentally supportive behavior such as avoiding forms of travel that require a large-scale transportation infrastructure and excessive services. Ecotourists hike only on marked paths while avoiding activities that may contribute to erosion or soil compaction; support only those travel businesses that adhere to the highest ecological standards; and observe local customs.

The two centerpieces of New England's ecotourism industry are its mountains and its coastline. The New England segment of the Appalachian Trail (A.T.) begins atop Maine's Mount Katahdin and extends through New Hampshire's White Mountains and Vermont's Green Mountains to Massachusetts's Berkshire Hills and Connecticut's Taconic Range. Established in 1951 and protected when the 1968 National Trails Systems Act made it the first linear national park, the A.T. is visited annually by thousands of hikers, backpackers, and nature lovers. Under the terms of its establishment, the A.T. conserves natural, scenic, historical, and cultural resources while protecting the trail environment from incompatible uses. Its attributes include weathered mountain peaks; clear lakes, ponds, and streams; wooded slopes and valleys; and

abandoned farmlands. The outstanding hiking areas in this system include Maine's Mount Katahdin, New Hampshire's Presidential Range and Franconia Notch, Vermont's Sherburne Pass, Massachusetts's Mount Greylock and Mount Everett, and Connecticut's Housatonic River valley.

Land-based ecotourism within New England is not limited to the Appalachian Trail. Vermont's Quechee Bog and Connecticut's Woodcock Nature Center each offer interesting and unusual natural outings. Agritourism is a variety of ecotourism that is growing in popularity among the region's rural and urban residents. In Massachusetts alone, there are more than 150 farms that offer activities ranging from helping with farm chores to fruit and berry picking.

Other forms of land-based ecotourism include rock climbing and horseback riding; the former qualifies because it has very little impact upon the region's hardened lithic environs, while the latter combines an element of agritourism with trail-based recreation. New England rock climbing activities range from alpine climbing to bouldering. Among the leading settings for this activity are Mount Desert, Barrett's Cove, and Rock-A-Dundee in Maine; Cathedral and White Horse Ledges and Franconia Notch's Cannon Cliff in New Hampshire; Branbury State Park and Deerleap in Vermont; the Great Barrington area in Massachusetts; Traprock and Pinnacle Rock in Connecticut; and Lincoln Woods State Park in Rhode Island. Horseback riding opportunities abound within New England; the trail systems within the national forest and state parks are popular.

Water-based ecotourism takes many forms, ranging from kayaking, canoeing, sailing, and rafting to whale watching, bird watching, and other forms of observation of natural processes. Sea and lake kayaking and canoeing afford sensual experiences similar to those of sailing but require greater physical exertion. White-water rafting provides perhaps the most action-filled form of water-based ecotourism. In this exciting activity, groups of people subject themselves to the turning, twisting, rising, and falling of some of New England's wildest rivers. White-water rafting can be enjoyed in all six New England states, but some of the most challenging white water is found on the Saco and the Androscoggin Rivers in New Hampshire and Maine, the West River in Vermont, and the Millers River in Massachusetts.

Coastal excursions offer opportunities to observe interactions among mammals, birds, and other ocean dwellers. Whale watching has long been a popular New England pastime. Numerous New England ports offer the opportunity to catch a sight of northern right or humpback whales migrating through the region's waters: Bar Harbor, Maine; Gloucester, Newburyport, Boston, and Provincetown, Mass.; Portsmouth and Rye, N.H.; and Galilee, R.I., among others. Two of New England's most popular sites for observing coastal wildlife are Acadia National Park on Mount Desert Island in Maine and the Stellwagen Bank National Marine Sanctuary, located off the coast of Massachusetts. Within each of these areas, ecotourists may observe whales, fish, birds of prey, ducks, geese, loons, moose, bears, and beavers. Coastal areas also allow visitors to investigate the activities of starfish, sea anemones, sea cucumbers, crabs, and lobsters. In addition, opportunities abound to examine the unique landforms created by the dynamic action of ocean water striking the land in its never-ending cycle.

The idea of ecotourism is perfectly expressed by the maxim "Take nothing but photographs, leave nothing but footprints." Whether ecotourists prefer to engage in active or passive experiences, New England offers myriad settings for this environmentally gentle alternative to traditional travel and recreation. These activities, in turn, provide economic gain for the tourism industry while causing minimal negative impact on the region's natural and human environs.

Louis D'Amore and Jafar Jafari, eds., *Tourism: A Vital Force for Peace* (1988); Alister Mathieson and Geoffrey Wall, *Tourism: Economic, Physical, and Social Impacts* (1986); Robert McIntosh, Charles Goeldner, and J. R. Brent Ritchie, *Tourism: Principles, Practices, and Philosophies* (1995); *Sierra Club Policy: Ecotourism* (1993).

Mark J. Okrant and Elisabeth D. Okrant

Freedom Trail Boston's Freedom Trail, recognized as a National Recreation Trail, is a 3-mile walking tour of 16 publicly and privately operated sites and structures of historic importance in downtown Boston and neighboring Charlestown. The sites along the Freedom Trail are loosely linked by a red brick (and occasionally red-painted) line that meanders through the center of Boston. The trail is one of the most popular tourist destinations in New England, attracting millions of visitors each year from all over the United States and the world.

Although many of the sites along the trail date to the era of the American Revolution, the trail itself is of more recent origin. In 1951 William Schofield, an editorial writer for the *Boston Herald-Traveler*, noted that many visitors to Boston became lost in the confusing maze of downtown streets while trying to locate important historic sites. As a remedy for this problem, Schofield suggested that a trail

Worker freshens up Freedom Trail stripe on Tremont Street, Boston, 1980s

be laid out with suitable markers to link the various historic sites. At first, the trail consisted of little more than a series of signs, but by 1958 a painted red line on the pavement appeared. The painted line was later converted in most places to a double row of red bricks.

The Freedom Trail begins at the Greater Boston Convention and Visitors' Bureau on Boston Common, the nation's oldest public park, then leads tourists up Beacon Hill to the building Bostonians still know as the "new" State House, which was designed by Charles Bulfinch and built in 1798 on land originally owned by the John Hancock family. The *Memorial to Robert Gould Shaw and the Massachusetts Fifty-fourth Regiment* is located opposite the State House; this is also the starting point of the Black Heritage Trail. Visitors then pass by the Park Street Church located on "Brimstone Corner"; built in 1809, the church is the site of William Lloyd Garrison's first antislavery speech. The adjacent Granary Burying Ground, one of Boston's oldest cemeteries, is the final resting place of several famous Bostonians, including John Hancock and Samuel Adams. King's Chapel and Burying Ground is the next stop along the trail. King's Chapel, founded in 1688, was the first Anglican church in Boston and, after the Revolution, became the nation's first Unitarian church. The present structure was completed in 1754. Governor John Winthrop and William Dawes, Jr., are interred in its adjacent burying ground. The trail then wends its way past the Franklin Statue, designed by Richard S. Greenough to commemorate Benjamin Franklin's career and contributions; this site also marks the location of the nation's first

public school, built in 1645. The nearby Old Corner Bookstore, built circa 1712, was the center of literary Boston in the 19th century.

The next site on the Freedom Trail is Boston's Old South Meeting House, built in 1729 as a Congregational church. Old South became famous on December 16, 1773, when angry colonists rallied at a mass town meeting to debate the new British tax on tea; this meeting led directly to the Boston Tea Party. The trail then proceeds north along Washington Street to the original, or "Old" State House, built in 1713, the seat of colonial government before the construction of the State House on Beacon Hill. A simple circle of cobblestones outside the Old State House marks the approximate site of the Boston Massacre, in which five American patriots were killed in a scuffle with British soldiers on March 5, 1770.

Faneuil Hall, built at the expense of the wealthy Boston merchant Peter Faneuil in 1742 and given to the town as a marketplace and meeting hall, is the next stop along the trail. The first floor of the hall has always been a market, and today it offers tourists an ever-expanding selection of foods. The meeting hall on Faneuil Hall's second floor has been dubbed the Cradle of Liberty because of the many protests against British rule that took place there; the third floor houses the museum and armory of the Ancient and Honorable Artillery Company of Massachusetts. The neighboring Quincy Market buildings were constructed in the 19th century to house Boston's wholesale food market. Faneuil Hall and Quincy Market were renovated in the 1970s; today they contain many fine shops and restaurants and are a favorite among tourists.

From here the trail winds through some of the oldest streets in Boston, passing into the North End, one of the city's oldest neighborhoods. The trail leads tourists to Paul Revere's House, built around 1680, where the famous silversmith and patriot lived at the time he made his midnight ride on April 18–19, 1775. Nearby is the city's oldest standing church, Christ Church, built in 1723 and popularly known as the Old North Church. In its belfry, two signal lanterns were hung on the night of Revere's ride to indicate that British troops were crossing the Charles River by boat before marching to Lexington and Concord. Originally the Freedom Trail ended at this point; since the 1970s, however, the trail has been extended down Copp's Hill and across the Charles River. Copp's Hill Burying Ground, dating to the 1660s, overlooks the Charles and is the final resting place of the Puritan intellectual Cotton Mather and Edmund Hartt, builder of the USS *Constitution*. Fondly known as Old Ironsides, the frigate *Constitution* was launched in Boston in 1797 and is now moored at a wharf in the Charlestown Navy Yard. The Navy Yard opened in 1800 and is also the home of a World War II destroyer, the USS *Cassin Young*. The Freedom Trail ends at the 221-foot granite obelisk constructed as a monument to the Battle of Bunker Hill, the first major battle of the American Revolution, which took place on June 17, 1775. Tourists may climb the Bunker Hill Monument's 294 steps for an impressive view of Boston.

Charles Bahne, *The Complete Guide to Boston's Freedom Trail*, 2d ed. (1998); Patrick M. Leehey, "Myths and Realities along Boston's Freedom Trail," *History Today* 44, no. 9 (1994); William Schofield, *Freedom by the Bay: The Boston Freedom Trail* (1988).

Patrick M. Leehey

Grand Resort Hotels

The grand resort hotels of New England, with their distinctive architecture, massive size, and devotion to leisure and recreation, were for nearly a century the primary reflection of and driving force behind tourism in the region. Originating as early as the 1850s, these attractive guest establishments initially achieved great popularity and success, peaking at the turn of the century, only to suffer a prolonged decline in the 20th century. Their almost total demise today is attributed to a number of factors: the deterioration of New England's railroad systems, the development of which had once helped to boost attendance at the hotels; growing operational expense; the advent of the automobile, which increased vacationing options; the dampening effects of the two world wars and the Depression; and competition from smaller hotels, inns, campgrounds, and motels. Today, only a half dozen of New England's approximately 50 grand resort hotels predating World War II survive. The most notable of these are located in New Hampshire's White Mountains: the Balsams at Dixville Notch, constructed from 1866 to 1918, and the Mount Washington Hotel at Bretton Woods, constructed from 1902 to 1906.

Because of their shared characteristics, tangible features, and traditions, New England's grand resort hotels form a clearly definable group. Having maximum capacities ranging from 200 to more than 600 guests, these great hostelries have long been a magnetic attraction to visitors and scholars alike. Exuding an aura of exclusiveness and an ambiance of romance, they provide a living example of an important segment of American social, cultural, economic, and architectural history.

As architectural complexes, the grand resort hotels were insular worlds unto themselves, intended to provide all the amenities that their guests could desire in rural, retreat-like surroundings. An emphasis was placed on comfort, variety of experience, novelty, fash-

Mount Washington Hotel (1902–6), Bretton Woods, N.H.

ion, aesthetics, and efficiency. In many instances, they were set amidst captivating natural surroundings, offering their guests the visual, spiritual, and physical benefits of the landscape. They were conceived in a variety of Victorian, eclectic, or more recent architectural styles, sometimes incorporating European or Asian-derived picturesque forms and conveying an impression of fantasy, escape, elegance, and material indulgence. As providers of summer social interaction, excellent food and drink, cultural and intellectual stimulation, and opportunities for rest and recreation, they were considered nonpareil by their patrons.

The hotels were frequented by world leaders, presidents, and celebrities as well as by a newly emerging middle class, which grew out of the Industrial Revolution. Not only were they sites of recreation and socializing, but they also served important roles in matters of diplomacy. In 1905 the Wentworth-by-the-Sea Hotel in New Castle, N.H., hosted delegates from Japan and Russia who came to negotiate the end of the Russo-Japanese War through the mediation of President Theodore Roosevelt. Another influential summit took place at the Mount Washington Hotel in 1944, called by President Franklin Roosevelt to establish the World Bank.

The largest and earliest concentration of grand resort hotels in New England was located in the White Mountains, beginning with the Glen, Crawford, and Profile Houses, which opened in the 1850s. Between 1850 and 1917, an impressive total of 30 of these expansive complexes were constructed in this district. Concurrently, grand resort hotels were built along the New England coast, from southern Connecticut to northeastern Maine. Among the primary examples were the Colo-

nial Arms (1903–4) in Gloucester, Mass., the Wentworth-by-the-Sea (1874) in New Castle, N.H., and the Samoset Hotel (1889) in Rockland, Maine. The interior areas of Maine once boasted several of these great hotels, including the Poland Spring House (1876) at Poland Spring, the third Kineo House (1844) on Moosehead Lake, and the Rangeley Lake House (1877) at Rangeley. These and their counterparts spoke eloquently of an era that has long since past. Those that have survived, the Balsams and the Mount Washington Hotel among them, can attribute their success to excellent management, interested ownership, elegant facilities, and beautiful settings. Others, such as Wentworth-by-the-Sea, continue to struggle. Closed in 1982 and designated one of America's eleven most endangered historic places by the National Trust for Historic Preservation in 1997, the Wentworth was extensively restored and expanded; it reopened in 2002.

Rod Fensom, *America's Grand Resort Hotels: Eighty Classic Resorts in the United States and Canada* (1985); Jeffrey Limerick, Nancy Ferguson, and Richard Oliver, *America's Grand Resort Hotels* (1979); Vincent Joseph Scully, *The Shingle Style and the Stick Style: Architectural Theory and Design from Richardson to the Origins of Wright* (1971); Bryant F. Tolles, Jr., *The Grand Resort Hotels of the White Mountains: A Vanishing Architectural Legacy* (1998).

Bryant F. Tolles, Jr.

Green Mountain Parkway

In 1933 Colonel William J. Wilgus, who had retired to Ascutney, Vt., proposed that the state seek federal funding for the construction of a Green Mountain Parkway, a limited-access scenic road to run the length of the western crest of the Green Mountains in Vermont from Massachusetts to Canada. The project was meant to capitalize on construction funds made available to the states through the New Deal's National Industrial Recovery Act (NIRA). Despite these projected benefits, the project engendered enormous controversy in Vermont during the three years it was debated. In attempting to understand this controversy, historians have identified several key individuals and organizations who, between them, articulated most of the major arguments for and against the project.

Nationally known as the former chief engineer of the New York Central Railroad and and the designer of New York's Grand Central Terminal, Wilgus believed that the road would create thousands of jobs for the unemployed, greatly increase tourism, and protect large areas of the Green Mountains from haphazard development. He argued that only a project of the scope of the proposed parkway would allow Vermont to gain its share of NIRA funds, which he estimated to be between $7 million and $10 million.

Working closely with Wilgus in promoting the parkway was James P. Taylor, the founder of the Green Mountain Club and the originator of the idea for the Long Trail. Taylor was the secretary of Vermont's Chamber of Commerce, an organization that would support the project from early in its inception. Both men were strongly influenced by the popular progressive faith in the ability of engineers and other professionals to solve intractable social problems and make life better for average people. Taylor believed that the parkway, like the Long Trail, would encourage Vermonters to travel to the tops of their mountains and thus overcome what he described as their "valley-mindedness"—a narrow and conservative view of the world.

Wilgus's Washington contacts, national reputation, and tireless campaigning convinced many members of Vermont's business community of the feasibility and desirability of the parkway project. Taylor worked behind the scenes, flooding organizations and individuals with promotional materials on the parkway and working with sympathetic newspapers, most notably the *Burlington Free Press*, to spread the parkway gospel. Despite their general opposition to New Deal programs, the editors of the *Free Press* believed that the parkway would be an economic boon to the city of Burlington.

The principal opponents of the parkway project were the Green Mountain Club and the anti–New Deal *Rutland Herald*. Although the Green Mountain Club's membership was split on the issue, its influential leadership was not. The trustees and their supporters feared that the Long Trail's wilderness value would be lost if the parkway were built and that the

trail would be flooded with hikers whose numbers and social inferiority would destroy the ambiance of the hiking experience for club members. The *Herald* believed the parkway to be a needless extravagance that would split the state down the middle, give huge amounts of land over to federal control, and siphon money away from Vermont's more pressing needs, particularly the reconstruction of valley roads and bridges wiped out by a devastating flood in 1927. The *Herald* went so far as to coordinate a huge petition drive to register opposition to the project and send the petition to Washington.

In 1935 the parkway project was hotly debated in the state legislature, where opponents voiced fears about the amount of land Vermont would lose to federal control should the road be built. Finally, in a March 1936 referendum, Vermonters rejected the parkway by a wide margin.

Some commentators cite the parkway episode as an early example of the conflict between economic need and environmental protection that has come to characterize contemporary debates on the efficacy and appropriateness of Vermont's land use control law, Act 250, and the projects it regulates. Others argue that the positions of the people on the two sides on the parkway issue reflect older, more human-centered responses to nature as well as political, social, and economic concerns that were firmly rooted in the state's past. On both sides the nagging question is asked: How can Vermont's landscape best be used to enrich its people without destroying rural life or relinquishing control of the state to outsiders?

Frank M. Bryan, *Yankee Politics in Rural Vermont* (1974); Hal Goldman, "'A Desirable Class of People': The Green Mountain Club and Social Exclusivity, 1920–1936," *Vermont History* 65 (Summer–Fall 1997); Goldman, "James Taylor's Progressive Vision: The Green Mountain Parkway," *Vermont History* 63 (Summer 1995); Hannah Silverstein, "No Parking: Vermont Rejects the Green Mountain Parkway," *Vermont History* 63 (Summer 1995).

Hal Goldman

Guidebooks The thousands of New England guidebooks published since the 1820s mirror the cyclical rise, fall, and resurgence of tourism in the region. While a number of gazetteers and geography texts provided information on New England places before that decade, the guidebook did not become a recognizable genre until the tourist industry developed in the region during the early decades of the 19th century. One important account of a tour through New England and a forerunner to the true guidebook, *Travels in New-England and New-York* (1821), identified New

England as a place worthy of touring by American and European gentry. It also laid out what would become popular routes and sites. Its author, Yale University president Timothy Dwight, identified New England as a unique region and its "Yankee" residents as a "distinct, recognizable people."

Guidebooks multiplied in number and variety over the first half of the 19th century with the revolution in canal, rail, and steamboat travel. Nineteenth-century guidebooks ranged from inexpensive pocket-sized editions to large, elegantly produced parlor table books. At one end of the spectrum, they were not much more than railroad timetables, reprinted yearly in cheap paperback editions. At the other end, guidebooks could be heavy, handsome, and very expensive, like Thomas Starr King's *The White Hills: Their Legends, Landscape and Poetry* (1859). King, a Unitarian minister who wrote regularly for the *Boston Transcript*, offered readers a collection of poetry and engravings designed to illuminate the experience of scenic travel.

Mid-19th-century guidebooks were often locally produced efforts like Alonzo Lewis's *Guide through Nahant* (1848), George C. Mason's *Newport Illustrated* (1854), John Eden's *Mount Holyoke Hand-Book* (1852), and Samuel C. Eastman's long-running *White Mountain Guide Book,* published every few years between 1858 and 1884. After the Civil War, summer tourism in New England boomed and guidebook publishing flourished; the number and variety of guidebooks produced during this period would remain unequaled until the 1980s. National publishing houses produced more standardized guidebooks like the series *Appletons' Hand-Book of American Travel,* published almost yearly from the 1850s to the 1880s. Perhaps the most typical of these new, more standardized guidebooks was Moses F. Sweetser's *New England: A Handbook for Travellers* (1880)—a compact but crowded volume featuring a paragraph on nearly every town in the region, with hotel prices and travel distances included.

Typically, railroads were the primary feeders for the great destination resorts of the Gilded Age. But with names like *By-Ways of the Central Vermont Railroad* (1894) and *Here and There in New England and Canada* (1889), railroad-sponsored guidebooks sometimes conveyed the impression that anywhere the train stopped was a suitable tourist destination. In keeping with new tastes among travelers, some guidebooks began to appear in the late 19th century that promised to guide tourists entirely off the beaten railroad track. Samuel Adams Drake's *Nooks and Corners of the New England Coast* (1876) was an early example, offering the discriminating traveler the chance to visit parts of New England that were far from the established summer resorts and their railroad connections. That trend continued into the early 20th century, as tourists began to seek out new kinds of experiences on foot, by bicycle, and finally by automobile. Early-20th-century tourists with a desire to rough it in the wilderness could turn to the Appalachian Mountain Club's *Guide to the Paths and Camps of the White Mountains* (1907), the first of many hiking and river guides that continue to be meticulously updated. By the 1920s auto-touring books began to appear.

Some automobile guides were practical attempts by the American Automobile Association (AAA) and local motor clubs to find the best "macadamized" roads. Others offered nostalgic trips on New England's back roads through forgotten villages, like Wallace Nutting's pictorial series *Maine Beautiful, New Hampshire Beautiful, Connecticut Beautiful, Vermont Beautiful,* and *Massachusetts Beautiful,* published in the 1920s and 1930s. Still others were highly personal travel accounts: *This Is Vermont* (1936), by Walter and Margaret Hard, made no attempt at comprehensive coverage, but provided a personal and idiosyncratic response to the state. Indirectly the new demand for automobile guides helped to redirect many guidebooks toward a nostalgic vision of the region, as authors followed the old stage routes now being transformed into automobile roads.

In the late 1930s the Federal Writers' Project of the Works Progress Administration (WPA) published guides to each of the New England states. The fruits of a New Deal project to employ writers and editors, these books combined the best features of the new automobile guides with a new perspective on the attractions of New England. They included general information on each state and detailed town-by-town descriptions, presented alphabetically. They provided equally detailed information on touring routes, mileage, and roads. Some included small literary masterpieces like the poet Conrad Aiken's sketch of Deerfield in the Massachusetts guide. All the New England guide writers attempted to define the spirit of the region, sometimes in spectacularly controversial ways: the Massachusetts guide, for example, came under fire after a reporter counted the number of lines in the book devoted to telling the story of Sacco and Vanzetti—42—and noted that only nine lines had been devoted to the Boston Tea Party.

After World War II, New England experienced a surge of family auto-based tourism. Old inns and summer hotels were abandoned for roadside cabins and motels, for which the *Mobil Guides* and *AAA Tour Books* became travel bibles. Gradually supplemented by national guidebook series like *Fodor's,* this dry, abbreviated form of guidebook was the norm until the 1970s, when two guidebooks, Norman T. Simpson's *Country Inns and Back Roads* and Elizabeth Squires's *Recommended Country Inns,* refocused interest on New England's forgotten inns and byways. This interest was fanned by the 1976 Bicentennial celebration, which inspired historical guides such as Christina Tree's *How New England Happened.*

In the 1980s New England guidebooks multiplied so quickly that bookstores began allotting them special sections. A spate of guides reflected the new interest in inns and bed-and-breakfast travel. Wood Pond Press began publishing a series of guidebooks dedicated to inns, most notably *Inn Spots and Special Places* by Nancy Webster and Richard Woodworth and *Bed and Breakfast in New England* by Bernice Chesler. The Explorers' Guides became the first to detail Massachusetts and each of the northern New England states region by region; several other guides, particularly the Off the Beaten Track series, focused on less traveled corners of the region.

Reflecting the proliferation of national and international guidebook series and the continued growth in tourism, New England guides multiplied during the 1990s and early 21st century. Each year they catered to more specialized demands: Michelin, the Smithsonian Institution, and the Compass Guides publish cultural guides and guides to antiquing, guides to dining and traveling with children and with pets, and guides to every kind of physical activity—sea kayaking, skiing, fishing, camping, biking, and sailing.

Samuel Adams Drake, *The Pine Tree Coast* (1988 [1891]); Timothy Dwight, *Travels in New England and New York* (1995 [1821]); Walter and Margaret Hard, *This Is Vermont* (1936); Thomas Starr King, *The White Hills, Their Legends, Landscape and Poetry* (1991 [1859]); Christina Tree, *How New England Happened: A Guide to New England through Its History* (1976).

Christina Tree

Historic Deerfield When Historic Deerfield was founded in 1952 as a museum of early New England history and life, it continued a long tradition of preservation, collecting, and tourism in the Connecticut River valley village of Deerfield, Mass. From early in the village's settlement, Deerfield was a place of allure and a destination for tourists. Conflict with Native Americans and their French allies made Deerfield's earliest history dramatic and well known throughout New England and beyond. The settlement was attacked first in a famous raid in 1675 during King Philip's War; it was abandoned, resettled, and devastated once again by a raid in 1704. In response, Deerfield's inhabitants became determined to remember their past and to share those memories with visitors.

The attack of 1704, in which the Reverend John Williams, his wife and five children, and more than half the town were either killed or captured, was forever memorialized in Williams's best-selling account, *The Redeemed Captive Returning to Zion* (1707). As early as 1728, a Harvard student noted in his diary, "I saw near the road the ruins of a monument built of brick and stone, in memory of a remarkable fight, called Muddy [*sic*] Brook Fight, being about fifty-two years ago last August, wherein about seventy English were killed." This commemoration of the Bloody Brook attack of 1675 is now recognized as the first historical marker in the United States. By the early 19th century, travelers arrived regularly at Deerfield to view "the old house that escaped the conflagration" of 1704. Its occupant, Colonel Elihu Hoyt, printed a booklet, *A Brief Sketch of the First Settlement of Deerfield, Mass.* (1833), apparently to meet the growing market of visitors who came to his door.

When the beef cattle industry that brought prosperity to Deerfield in the 18th century began to decline in the early 19th century, villagers turned to other livelihoods. By the end of the century it was clear tourism was the most viable alternative, and it seemed natural that tourism in Deerfield would highlight the village's past. In 1870 a group in Deerfield founded the Pocumtuck Valley Memorial Association (named for the Pocumtuck Indians, the town's first inhabitants) and opened its Memorial Hall Museum in 1880. At the same time, a network of women artists and educators began to buy picturesque old houses and to promote arts and crafts pursuits as employment for village women. They sold their wares to tourists arriving by train, then by rural trolley, and ultimately by automobile.

The Deerfield that was revived by antiquarian interests and the Arts and Crafts movement was attractive to many who sent their sons to Deerfield Academy, a college preparatory school founded in 1797. Among the academy's supporters were Henry Needham Flynt and Helen Geier Flynt of Greenwich, Conn., who in 1952 established the Heritage Foundation, a collection of old houses and early American decorative arts; in 1970 it was renamed Historic Deerfield. Fourteen historic houses open to the public through guided tours offer visitors a view of Deerfield's long history. They also display Deerfield's many collections: New England furniture; early American silver; American, English, and European textiles, needlework, and clothing; English and Asian export ceramics; and other household objects. In addition to the 14 house museums, Historic Deerfield includes the Deerfield Inn, a library, a silver shop and textile museum, and the Flynt Center for Early New England Life, which opened in September 1998. The open fields surrounding the village are still farmed, attesting to the agricultural fertility that has attracted Native Americans and Europeans for millennia, and providing visitors with the opportunity to see the buildings and collections not only in their economic and historical context but also in a setting of great natural beauty.

John Demos, *The Unredeemed Captive: A Family Story from Early America* (1994); Anne Digan Lanning and Marla R. Miller, "'Common Parlors': Women and the Recreation of Community Identity in Deerfield, Massachusetts, 1870–1920," *Gender and History* 6 (1994); Richard I. Melvoin, *New England Outpost: War and Society in Colonial Deerfield* (1989); Elizabeth Stillinger, *Historic Deerfield: A Portrait of Early America* (1992).

Donald R. Friary

The House of the Seven Gables, Salem, Mass.

Historic Houses

New England has a cornucopia of historic houses open to the public. Tradition-oriented Yankees began their preservation efforts in the late 19th century to honor their forebears, influence contemporaries, and remake the region's image. This once-limited focus has slowly diversified over time, centering now on preservation efforts and educational programs. House museums and re-created villages, most of which depict life before late-19th-century industrialism, are now generally held by local, ancestral, and patriotic organizations; Historic New England, for instance, owns and operates 45 historic properties. Often restored to their original period, these buildings have typically represented the past as more homogeneous, harmonious, and wholesome than the New England of today.

Beginning in the late 19th and early 20th centuries, and spurred by the region's changing ethnicity and class system, antiquarians created shrines to venerate heroes of the American Revolution and the new republic, among them the Paul Revere House (ca. 1680) in Boston and the homes of John and Abigail Adams (1681, 1731), both in Quincy (Braintree at that time), Mass. An interest in genealogy and memory also led to the preservation of many family homesteads, such as the Fairbanks House (ca. 1636) in Dedham, Mass. The Howland Society in Plymouth, Mass., the Ropes family in Salem, Mass., and the Robinson family in Ferrisburg, Vt., all established museums to commemorate their ancestors.

New Englanders have also honored their literary and artistic forebears by preserving their houses. In Concord, Mass., Orchard House (1690–1720) shows the inspiration for Louisa May Alcott's *Little Women* (1868–69), while the homes of numerous other authors commemorate their literary work: Henry Wadsworth Longfellow in both Cambridge, Mass., and Portland, Maine; Herman Melville and Edith Wharton in the Berkshires of Massachusetts; Emily Dickinson in Amherst, Mass.; Rudyard Kipling in Brattleboro, Vt.; Mark Twain and Harriet Beecher Stowe in Hartford, Conn.; Sarah Orne Jewett in South Berwick, Maine; Robert Frost in Ripton and Shaftsbury, Vt., and Franconia and Derry, N.H. Nathaniel Hawthorne's importance to the region has been commemorated by relocating the house of his birth next to the better-known House of the Seven Gables, christened by Hawthorne in a work of fiction of that name. The studio and home of the sculptors Daniel Chester French in Stockbridge, Mass., and Augustus Saint-Gaudens in Cornish, N.H., depict artists who helped to shape New England's memory.

The Colonial Revival movement of the late 19th and early 20th centuries encouraged a greater emphasis on architectural restoration in house museums. Buildings were restored to represent a bygone era, as is the case with the Whipple House (1640–55) in Ipswich, Mass., the Jackson House (1644) in Portsmouth, N.H., and the Hyde Log Cabin (ca. 1783) in Grand Isle, Vt. By the 1970s Historic New England had restored and sparsely furnished such colonial dwellings as the Arnold House (ca. 1687) in Lincoln, R.I., and the Browne House (1698) in Watertown, Mass., in order to display early construction techniques. Driven by the desire to re-create a colonial appearance and experience, the architect Joseph Everett Chandler restored both the House of the Seven Gables in Salem, Mass., and the Paul Revere House in Boston to their imagined 17th-century appearances. While the Salem site became a settlement house to acculturate immigrants, the Boston dwelling became a patriotic shrine to teach consensus politics.

The collector Wallace Nutting established a Colonial Chain of Picture Houses in 1915, purchasing five houses in Massachusetts, New Hampshire, and Connecticut and restoring them with what passed for authentic materials. Scorning foreign influences and industrial-made wares, Nutting wanted visitors to experience old-time Yankee values. His admission price of 25 cents could not offset the depressed wartime trade, however, and by 1918 his venture had failed.

House museums are slowly diversifing their focus. The Shapiro House (1795) in Portsmouth's Strawbery Banke interprets Jewish immigrant life in the early 20th century. Spencer-Peirce-Little Farm (ca. 1690) in Newbury, Mass., whose interpretation spans four centuries, remembers a Lithuanian tenant family. The Judith Sargent Murray House (1782) in Gloucester, Mass., honors an early feminist, while the Isaac Royal House (1732) in Medford, Mass., reportedly includes the North's only surviving slave quarters.

As architectural concerns reshaped the 20th-century preservation movement, more museums emphasized the decor and architectural style of houses. The brilliance of the Georgian period is shown at the Langdon House (1784) in Portsmouth, the Federal era at the Gardner-Pingree House (1804) in Salem, the Gothic Revival period at Roseland Cottage (1846) in Woodstock, Conn., and the Italian Villa style at the Morse-Libby House (1859) in Portland, Maine. The ostentation of the Gilded Age is conspicuous in the historic houses of Newport, R.I. Even such modern creations as Walter Gropius's Bauhaus home (1938) in Lincoln, Mass., and Frank Lloyd Wright's Zimmerman House (1952) in Manchester, N.H., are open to the public.

Federal Writers' Project, *Connecticut* (1938); Federal Writers' Project, *Maine* (1937); Federal Writers' Project, *Massachusetts* (1937); Federal Writers' Project, *New Hampshire* (1938); Federal Writers' Project, *Rhode Island* (1937); Federal Writers' Project, *Vermont* (1937); Mary Maynard, *Open Houses in New England* (1991); Nicholas Zook, *A Guide to Houses of New England Open to the Public* (1968).

James M. Lindgren

Historic New England

Historic New England, formerly the Society for the Preservation of New England Antiquities (SPNEA), is internationally renowned in the fields of historic preservation, building conservation, decorative arts, cultural history, and museum education. Founded in 1910 by William Sumner Appleton, Historic New England now owns 45 historic sites encompassing 120 buildings and 1,300 acres as well as a museum collection of more than 120,000 objects and library and archival holdings of more than 1 million photographs, architectural drawings, books, manuscripts, and ephemera. These collections focus on New England and cover the period from the early 17th century to the present.

Appleton was among the first to engage in a scientific method of building preservation, carefully photographing and documenting original features and subsequent alterations as well as all repair and restoration work. Historic New England's professional staff pioneered innovative techniques in preservation carpentry, paint research, and object conservation. Recognizing that photography offers the opportunity to record for posterity the appearance of endangered buildings, interiors, and landscapes that cannot be preserved, Historic New England commissions photographs and collects the negatives of professional photographers. Recognizing also that not all historic buildings deserve to be museums, and that the operation of house museums requires a sound financial base, Historic New England has developed reliable preservation restrictions for privately owned buildings. Through its Stewardship Program, more than 75 historic buildings throughout New England are protected in perpetuity. In 2004, to reflect its commitment to preserve and present New England's

Roseland Cottage, a Historic New England property on Woodstock Hill, Woodstock, Conn., 2002

heritage for 21st-century audiences, SPNEA changed its name to Historic New England.

The historic house museums owned by Historic New England represent the full range of architectural forms from 17th-century frame houses to the Bauhaus. The collection includes the work of such noted architects as Charles Bulfinch (Harrison Gray Otis House, Boston) and Walter Gropius (Gropius House, Lincoln, Mass.), as well as others that reflect the influences of Asher Benjamin, A. J. Downing, and vernacular styles. Many feature furnishings and accessories used by the last generation of family occupants; these furnishings often reflect many periods of ownership. The Sayward-Wheeler House at York, Maine; Coffin House in Newbury, Mass.; Rundlet-May House in Portsmouth, N.H.; Codman House and Gropius House in Lincoln; Bowen House in Woodstock, Conn.; and Castle Tucker in Wiscasset, Maine, are notable for their original furnishings and accessories. In South Berwick, Maine, Hamilton House epitomizes the Colonial Revival, while the Sarah Orne Jewett House presents the author's home as it was during her lifetime. In contrast, Beauport, in Gloucester, Mass., retains the furnishings and arrangements of the noted decorator Henry Davis Sleeper, while Cogswell's Grant at Essex, Mass., houses the famous folk art collections of former Historic New England director Bertram K. Little and his wife, Nina Fletcher Little.

Professional study of the historic landscapes associated with these properties has become a matter of scholarly focus in the past decade, with particular attention given to

the historic greenhouses of Lyman Estate in Waltham, Mass.; the gardens at the Codman Estate in Lincoln; the Rundlet-May and Langdon House Gardens in Portsmouth; and the Colonial Revival Gardens at the Hamilton House in South Berwick. Four large farms in Essex County, Mass., and South County, R.I., preserve 17th-century land grants while supporting sheep and cattle, crops of hay and flowers, and a community-funded agriculture program.

The Historic New England museum collections encompass the full range of decorative arts with exceptional strength in wallpaper, textiles and clothing, and New England furniture. These collections have been featured in exhibitions, catalogues, articles, lectures, and scholarly symposia sponsored by Historic New England as well as in loan exhibitions.

Historic New England shares the expertise of its staff with a broad public. Historic New England staff provide informal advice to individuals and groups as well as serving on the boards of local and national preservation organizations and museums. Former director Abbott Lowell Cummings was a founder of the American and New England Studies Program at Boston University, in which he and other staff members have taught courses. Many leaders in the preservation and museum fields today began their careers at Historic New England; although the society does not offer formal training programs, the informal apprenticeship and experiential learning that characterize Historic New England employment have had far-reaching influence in the profession. Through its extensive collections, reliable publications, and accumulated staff expertise, Historic New England continues the mission reflected in its new motto, "Defining the past, shaping the future."

Abbott Lowell Cummings, ed., *Bed Hangings* (1961); Brock Jobe and Myrna Kaye, *New England Furniture: The Colonial Era* (1984); Jane C. Nylander, *Windows on the Past: Four Centuries of New England Houses* (2000); Richard C. Nylander with Nancy Curtis, *Beauport: The Sleeper-McCann House* (1990); Richard C. Nylander, Elizabeth Redmond, and Penny J. Sander, *Wallpaper in New England* (1986), *Old Time New England* (1910–2001).

Jane C. Nylander

Historic Sites and Preservation Movements

New England's cultural image is much like a colonial cottage that has been expanded and remodeled with each generation. The region's historic sites reveal the patterns through which New Englanders have honored their ancestors, enlivened patriotism, and defined their identity over time.

New Englanders began to preserve and commemorate their past at a very early point in the region's history. New England's oldest continuously operating historical museum, the East India Marine Society (known today as the Peabody Essex Museum), was founded in 1799 in Salem, Mass. Established by the Reverend Dr. William Bentley, the museum collected everything from Native American artifacts to pieces of Plymouth Rock, but trophies from the Orient predominated. As Salem's hallmark, it taught innumerable visitors that New England and the world were linked.

On Forefathers' Day in 1801, New Englanders reenacted the *Mayflower* landing at Plymouth and, in 1820, established the Pilgrim Society. Those commemorations underscored New England's claim to national cultural and historical leadership at a time when many New Englanders feared they had entered a period of economic and political decline. The Bunker Hill Monument was erected between 1825 and 1843 as a shrine to the heroes of the Revolution; it adorned a prominent hilltop in Boston. The monument's meaning shifted as orators variously used it to question mass democracy and protest Irish immigration. Celebrations at the monument attracted throngs of visitors, as did festivities at a smaller obelisk at Concord, Mass., built in 1836.

By the mid-19th-century, however, awareness of the past was failing to save many historic spots from destruction; despite a preservation drive, the Old Indian House in Deerfield, Mass., fell in 1847, as did Boston's John Hancock House in 1863. Nevertheless, regional authors such as Nathaniel Hawthorne in *The House of the Seven Gables* (1851)

and Henry Wadsworth Longfellow in "Tales of a Wayside Inn" (1863) increasingly used historic buildings as backdrops to define New England identity in the national consciousness.

Beginning in the 1870s, the imminent national Centennial intensified interest in colonial history in New England as elsewhere. Crowds were drawn to view Daniel Chester French's *Minute Man* statue (1873) in Concord and to the myriad celebrations of the Centennial throughout New England in 1876. In Salem, the Essex Institute exhibited colonial artifacts. Boston's Old South Meeting House, however, stood fatefully before the wrecking ball in 1876. A preservation coalition spearheaded by women saved it; other Bostonians followed suit by restoring the Old State House in 1882 and fireproofing Faneuil Hall in 1898. Tradition-minded New Englanders had gradually come to regard such buildings as storehouses of memory.

In the wake of the Centennial, a boyish John Fitzgerald gave tours of Boston's North End with an Irish twist; as a congressman he brought the deteriorated USS *Constitution* to Boston as an attraction; as mayor he sponsored Old Home Week. In 1899, Bunker Hill reported 23,579 visitors, 75 percent of whom came from New England and New York.

But by the end of the century, preservation efforts were often spurred by a sense of malaise among Yankee New Englanders. Ancestral and patriotic societies like the Daughters of the American Revolution (1890) and the Society of Mayflower Descendants (1894) emerged. Familial associations formed as anxious New Englanders reclaimed their colonial roots. In 1902, the Fairbanks Family Association's reunion attracted 700 descendants to their ancestral hearth in Dedham, Mass.

At the turn of the century, regional museums began to show the impact of the Colonial Revival. At the Essex Institute, George Francis Dow began to experiment with period rooms in 1907. Soon after, he acquired, moved, and restored the John Ward House in Salem, where costumed guides acted as interpreters. Dow's lifelike exhibits persuaded Henry Watson Kent, who had moved to the Metropolitan Museum of New York from the Slater Memorial Museum in Norwich, Conn., to add Americana to his collections. In the 1920s, the Museum of Fine Arts in Boston followed suit, gradually acquiring the woodwork and furnishings for 10 New England period rooms.

In 1910, William Sumner Appleton, Jr., founded the Society for the Preservation of New England Antiquities (SPNEA). This organization, now Historic New England, reoriented the field of historic preservation and restoration by introducing new priorities such

as historical archaeology, architectural aesthetics, and business-minded management, including heritage tourism. At the high point of New England's industrial transformation, however, historical commemoration and preservation focused overwhelmingly on an imagined simple, homogeneous country life associated with New England's Yankee ancestors.

Twentieth-century developments revealed the inadequacy of this vision. With a few exceptions—notably the New Deal–sponsored Federal Writers' Project guides to the states that emerged in the 1930s—there were few voices encouraging New Englanders to view the history of urban, industrial immigrant New England as a heritage worth saving. Thus, there was little incentive to preserve urban neighborhoods (often including significant colonial-era structures) inhabited largely by Irish, Italian, and other European immigrants and their descendants. Even by mid-20th-century, there was little public sentiment for the preservation of urban neighborhoods when renewal projects and highway construction began in the 1950s and 1960s in Boston, Hartford, Providence, Springfield, Mass., and other cities. The tragic consequences became evident in Boston's West End.

Once a neighborhood of aspiring professionals in substantial townhouses, the West End of Boston had become home to a diverse, but poor, ethnic population. In 1958, the Boston Redevelopment Authority, revealing a sensibility rooted in a suburban, middle-class constituency, launched a project that was perversely called urban renewal. Leaving SPNEA's headquarters and the adjacent Old West Church intact, it erased the neighborhood around it. Critics of urban renewal, including Jane Jacobs and Herbert Gans, deplored the travesty and warned that such communities were necessary to the city's survival. It became evident that historic New England had been too narrowly defined, too focused on attractive houses, and too hostile to changes wrought by factories and immigrants. By the 1970s the face of New England's historic sites had begun to change. With the advent of the new social history and the passage of the Historic Preservation Act of 1966, new emphases on cultural diversity, community preservation, and "living" history emerged. A nascent generation of historians, curators, and preservationists wanted to present a more inclusive picture that reflected conflict, debate, and diversity.

The Bicentennial created such an opportunity. With the barrage of publicity, heritage tourism fostered patriotic extravaganzas and sentimentality. In stark contrast, the independent Peoples' Bicentennial Commission scorned such unthinking patriotism. Founded in the climate of Vietnam and Watergate, it sought a grassroots redefinition of the nation's history. It re-created the Boston Tea Party in 1973 by dumping empty oil barrels into Boston Harbor to protest profiteering by big oil companies. Repeatedly, it campaigned against "modern Tories."

Yet the ensuing reinterpretation of historic sites resulted largely from a recognition that New England's history had been more complex, heterogeneous, and acrimonious than earlier pictured. Plimoth Plantation in Massachusetts reflected this reinterpretation. When incorporated in 1947 as a memorial to the Pilgrim Fathers, it followed the precedent of Salem's Pioneer Village, the region's first outdoor museum, reconstructed in 1930 by George Francis Dow. Plimoth Plantation revised its presentation in the late 1970s with more authentic buildings, role-playing actors speaking in original dialects, and later a re-created Native American homesite.

Museums depicting native peoples today are quite different from earlier natural history displays, which customarily pictured them as savages and broke taboos by displaying human remains and burial artifacts. Since the late 1970s, mainstream museums have generally pictured Native Americans as dynamic people with strong traditions. Native Americans have themselves founded tribal museums, such as the Waponahki Museum established by the Passamaquoddy in 1987 in Perry, Maine, and the Mashantucket Pequot Museum and Research Center in Connecticut. They reject the biased image presented at older sites, as at the Hannah Duston Monument in Boscawen, N.H. Erected in 1874, this statue depicts Duston's massacre of 10 sleeping Indians who had captured her. She clutches a tomahawk in her right hand and a handful of scalps in her left. Native peoples call her a murderer and demand the statue's removal, but the ancestral association had refused.

Traditionally, the images of women presented at historical sites have not usually been so vivid. Women were either depicted as contented family members or overlooked entirely. The Sargent-Murray-Gilman House in Gloucester, Mass., however, offers a revised interpretation. Originally the house honored the founder of the Universalist Church, the Reverend John Murray. Today the house highlights his spouse, Judith Sargent Murray, a chief theorist of women's education and a leading feminist. In Hartford, the Harriet Beecher Stowe Museum credits the author of *Uncle Tom's Cabin* (1852) and focuses on race relations, women, and the decorative arts. Its restored kitchen shows the innovative housekeeping of *The American Woman's Home* (1869), written by Harriet Beecher Stowe and Cath-

arine Beecher. Still, house museums often overlook more ordinary women. Heritage trails like the one in Boston have been proposed to record their experiences.

Similarly, the lives of African Americans are increasingly represented at New England historical sites. In the mid-20th century, houses along the Underground Railroad were noted. In 1984 Connecticut established a museum at the Canterbury home of Prudence Crandall, a white woman persecuted for schooling black girls in 1833. This historical focus on whites assisting blacks has changed considerably, as at the Boston African American National Historic Site on Beacon Hill. New England's richest collection of antebellum black history is presented through the African Meeting House, built in 1806, and the Abiel Smith School of 1834. Monuments to the Civil War's 54th Massachusetts Regiment and to the victims of the Boston Massacre, including Crispus Attucks (an escaped Massachusetts slave of both African and Native American parentage), are situated for public display on the Boston Common. When erected, both memorials primarily honored whites, but their present interpretation is more inclusive. During the Bicentennial a Black Heritage Trail was designed for New Bedford, Mass., highlighting historically prominent African American figures, including the mariner Paul Cuffe and the reformer Frederick Douglass. New Bedford's Whaling Museum now includes Portuguese, Cape Verdean, and African American figures in its exhibits.

Other previously marginalized groups such as Irish and French Canadian people have also found a place, albeit small, at New England historic sites. In 1993 the Great Hunger Memorial was temporarily placed at Boston's Faneuil Hall, reportedly the first marker in the nation to commemorate the victims of the 1840s famine; a more impressive Irish Famine memorial replaced it in 1998 in downtown Boston. Nearby are two bronze statues of James Michael Curley, an Irish American politician who aroused the contempt of elite Yankees. In Newport, R.I., the National Recreation Trail that spotlights the ostentatious mansions of robber barons now also includes a humble monument to their Irish servants. "Little Canadas" can be found in older factory towns and at Acadian Village in Van Buren, Maine.

Perhaps the most significant immigrant presence is felt at historical sites in New England's industrial towns, such as Lowell, Mass., Waterbury, Conn., and Barre, Vt. Museums elsewhere in New England had historically accented industrial technology, progress, and traditional values, but Lowell changed that pattern. Epitomizing the evolution not

only from Yankee "mill girls" to a diverse proletariat but from prosperity to collapse, Lowell's landscape suffered further with urban renewal. Preservationists responded in the 1970s by creating state and national parks that reintroduce stories and themes of mill life, ethnically diverse neighborhoods, and workers' activism. In Connecticut's Brass Valley, the Mattatuck Museum in Waterbury similarly explores industrialism. In Barre, where heated battles occurred between skilled granite craftsmen and so-called scientific managers, the Old Labor Hall attracted the likes of Mother Jones and Eugene Debs. Nearby, Hope Cemetery brilliantly showcases the mostly Italian stonecutters' culture.

Increasingly, historical interpretation has emphasized diversity and community. Strawbery Banke Museum in Portsmouth, N.H., exemplifies this gradual change in interpretation. Originally organized in response to a threat of urban renewal in one of America's oldest neighborhoods, the 10-acre museum redeveloped the "slum's" oldest colonial buildings but allowed the demolition of older, Victorian-era buildings. Modeled initially on Colonial Williamsburg, which accented art and architecture, it first emphasized colonial crafts and architecture. Today Strawbery Banke showcases Portsmouth's community history from the 17th through the mid-20th centuries. The Drisco House interprets the home life of an Italian American shipyard worker in 1954, and World War II society is shown at Abbott's Little Corner Store, a mom-and-pop grocery that served ordinary people. Opened in 1997, the Shapiro House exhibits the lives of Jewish newcomers in 1919. The museum strives to "serve as a catalyst for frank discussions of immigration, tolerance and cultural differences." Other historical towns have challenged prejudice elsewhere. For the tercentenary of the Massachusetts witchcraft trials, Salem established a memorial park, while Danvers placed a marker to "remind us that we must forever confront intolerance and 'witch hunts' with integrity, clear vision, and courage."

While many cities gutted their downtowns and poor neighborhoods in the mid-20th century, small niches were preserved. By 1955 the first historic preservation districts in Massachusetts were created on Beacon Hill and Nantucket; in 1960 the College Hill District in Providence followed. City planners, however, usually neglected those who lived and worked in poorer neighborhoods. After a binge of demolition, Boston left standing an isolated Faneuil Hall and Quincy Market, which James Rouse developed in 1978 into a festival marketplace. Its success was widely imitated. New England's waterfront shifted from salty sailors to trendy boutiques, while country towns in every state created their own version with a prettified Main Street.

Heritage tourism has put dollars into remaking New England's landscape but has skewed its interpretation, at open-air museums that sentimentalize preindustrial life or heritage corridors that fail to separate commercial enterprises from real history. The public, which increasingly relies on such tourism for its learning, is often left with a muddled sense of its history, including the links between money, society, and politics. And as each generation rethinks its legacy, the region's image becomes an incongruous blend of older patterns and newer developments. The continuing development of historic sites, however, depends on the public's willingness to accept the past as complex, diverse, and often disordered.

Philip Burnham, *How the Other Half Lived: A People's Guide to American Historic Sites* (1995); Linda Cline and Robert C. Hayden, *A Cultural Guide to African-American Heritage in New England* (1992); Jane Holtz Kay, with Pauline Chase-Harrell, *Preserving New England* (1986); Charles B. Hosmer, Jr., *Presence of the Past: A History of the Preservation Movement in the United States before Williamsburg* (1965); Hosmer, *Preservation Comes of Age: From Williamsburg to the National Trust, 1926–1949* (1981); Michael Kammen, *Mystic Chords of Memory: The Transformation of Tradition in American Culture* (1991); Mark P. Leone and Neil Asher Silberman, *Invisible America: Unearthing Our Hidden History* (1995); James M. Lindgren, *Preserving Historic New England: Preservation, Progressivism, and the Remaking of Memory* (1995); Lynn Sherr and Jurate Kazickas, *Susan B. Anthony Slept Here: A Guide to American Women's Landmarks* (1994); Marion Tinling, *Women Remembered: A Guide to Landmarks of Women's History in the United States* (1986).

James M. Lindgren

Kennebunkport, Maine

This four-season resort in York County lies on the Atlantic coast, approximately 25 miles southwest of Portland, Maine. Founded in 1629, the original settlement was incorporated in 1653 and took the name Kennebunkport in 1821. Kennebunkport has four distinct neighborhoods. The main village is bordered by the tidal Kennebunk River, whose shipbuilding and shipping industries provided the town's initial prosperity. It is characterized by streets lined with closely packed 18th- and 19th-century homes, many of which have been turned into bed-and-breakfast lodgings and inns. The Cape Arundel settlement, located on the ocean bluffs of the town, is known for its high-style Victorian-era cottages, including Walker's Point, the summer home of former president and first lady George H. W. and Barbara (Pierce) Bush. The fishermen's village of Cape Porpoise, where Kennebunkport began as Cape Porpus, is the site of the town's active

harbor, complete with fishermen's pier and island lighthouse. Goose Rocks Beach, a former summer, now year-round colony of modest late 19th- and 20th-century homes, borders the 3-mile beach from which it takes its name.

In the 1870s, the first of many hotels, the Ocean Bluff, was built on Cape Arundel by the Boston and Kennebunkport Seashore Company (a consortium of Massachusetts and Kennebunkport entrepreneurs). Since then, tourism has had greater economic influence than Kennebunkport's traditional maritime enterprise. Vacationers at the turn of the 20th century valued the handsome river village, with its homes of local shipmasters and merchants, and enjoyed the area's "sea bathing," boating, and golf. When these visitors built summer homes, their wealth as well as their cultural and social expectations changed the town. Cape Arundel cottagers built Saint Ann's Church and the Kennebunk River Clubhouse (now on the National Register of Historic Places) and founded the Cape Arundel Golf Club. They wanted boardwalks, a cleaner and safer river, and a municipal water supply. Their presence brought Irish maids and gardeners, French photographers, African American cooks, and Native American entrepreneurs to the seaside resort. Artists and writers came to visit and, inspired by town life and local history, stayed. The Boston artist Abbott Fuller Graves posed local people for his genre paintings of country stores and captured Kennebunkport's houses and gardens in impressionistic landscapes. The writers Booth Tarkington, Margaret Deland, and the Kennebunkport-born novelist Kenneth Roberts all fictionalized local people and history.

Today a new generation of entrepreneurs has discovered Kennebunkport. They have turned private homes into inns and restaurants. Stores that sold groceries, fish, and hardware have become gift shops and art galleries. These in turn have brought day-trippers by car and bus. Bus trips alone carried more than 10,000 visitors to this village of 3,720 (2000) by the end of October of 2004. Marinas service the pleasure craft that crowd the river.

The merchants' annual Christmas Prelude weekend has attracted winter visitors since 1980. Christmas trees are decorated with lobster pots, and Santa comes by boat. Local organizations sponsor caroling, craft fairs, bean suppers, and historical pageants. The resort of Kennebunkport uses its heritage to preserve its contemporary vitality.

Charles Bradbury, *History of Kennebunk Port* (1967 [1837]); Joyce Butler, *A Kennebunkport Album* (1998); Butler, *Kennebunkport Scrapbook*, 2 vols. (1977, 1989, 1998).

Joyce Butler

Leaf-Peeping

New England is world renowned for its brilliant autumn foliage. Each year "leaf-peepers" descend upon the region in September and October to travel scenic routes, view historic points of interest, and experience rural hospitality and charm against the autumnal backdrop. This spectacular natural ritual is so closely associated with the image of New England today that it would be difficult to imagine New England without it. It is the forests that provide the display.

Most of the region is covered with hardword forests, made up of birches, American beech, and especially maples, which provide the brilliant reds. In the acidic soil and harsher climates above 2,500 feet, yellow and white birch and red spruce are found; evergreens such as red spruce and balsam fir prevail in the higher elevations. Peak color and leaf change cannot be predicted from season to season or place to place, but as fall approaches chlorophyll production diminishes according to changes in daylight and temperature, and the electric yellows, brilliant russet oranges, and fiery crimsons emerge. In general, leaves turn color first in the north, sweeping southward through New Hampshire, Vermont, Massachusetts, Rhode Island, and Connecticut from late September through October.

The practice of touring during the foliage season has its roots in the scenic touring practices associated with the grand resort hotels of the late 19th century, but it became truly popular with the rise of automobile touring in the mid-20th century. Especially after the post-World War II creation of the interstate highway system in New England, tourists found an autumn day trip or weekend getaway increasingly attractive. By then, foliage scenes had become part of the iconic image of New England through both art and photography. Nineteenth-century painters such as William Champney and other White Mountain School artists helped to popularize autumnal scenes. Inexpensive color prints and chromolithographs made such images accessible to a growing number of middle-class tourists. Later, with the advent of color film, tourists could capture the brilliant scenes with their own cameras.

Each of the New England states offers a unique panorama of fall colors. A must-see in Maine is the 35,000-acre Acadia National Park, located on Mount Desert Island, the largest rock island off the U.S. Atlantic coast. The 27-mile Park Loop Road leads through this national park, alternating spectacular ocean and foliage views.

New Hampshire's White Mountain National Forest offers many leaf-peeping attractions: the 34-mile Kancamagus Highway, designated a national scenic byway by the U.S.

Forest Service; the 8-mile Franconia Notch Parkway leading to a 6,440-acre state park; and the Crawford Notch Valley, filled with red maples and yellow birches on the hillsides.

The best fall foliage in Vermont runs along Interstate 91 from White River Junction to Newport and from the Connecticut River valley to the hills of the Northeast Kingdom. The splendor of Vermont's foliage can also be viewed from the Green Mountain Flyer, a vintage train that offers tourists a 26-mile ride from Burlington through central Vermont's countryside.

Throughout October, notable foliage trips through Massachusetts include Routes 2 and 4 from Boston to Lexington and Concord. Flaming, brilliant hillsides can be viewed from the observation towers at Mount Tom on U.S. Route 5 in Holyoke, and at Mount Sugarloaf off Route 116 near Amherst.

Rhode Island's Blackstone River valley presents a variety of activities for the avid leaf-peeper. One may choose to travel by car, airplane, or helicopter from North Central Airport, by train aboard the Providence and Worcester Railroad, by canoe along the Blackstone River, or by bicycle aboard the six-passenger Blackstone Valley Surrey.

Among the most popular drives in Connecticut are along U.S. Route 7 running south to north along the course of the Housatonic River and the approximately 20-mile drive off Interstate 84 through the lush Farmington Valley.

The phenomenon of leaf-peeping is an important part of New England's cultural and economic landscape. Each of the New England state tourism offices offers foliage hotlines during the season, furnishes maps for car touring, and provides assistance and information about tour packages and other sightseeing attractions allied to leaf-peeping. For example, leaf-peepers may enjoy carriage rides and hayrides on country lanes, sample the foods and crafts of harvest festivals, and, in short, experience the pleasures of a pared-down, rural lifestyle. Leaf-peeping is a seasonal pleasure that reflects a deeply felt connection between New England's past and present. It is also an important industry in all six states.

Anastasia Redmond Mills, ed., *Fodor's National Parks of the East: Plus Seashores, Forests and Wildlife Refuges*, 3d ed. (1998); Ogden Tanner and the editors of Time-Life Books, *New England Wilds* (1974); White Mountains Attractions Association, *Autumn in New Hampshire's White Mountains* (1994).

Donna Jean Zane

Lowell National and State Parks

Lowell National Historical Park offers tours and exhibits that interpret the pioneering role of the city of Lowell, Mass., in America's Industrial Revolution. The park also works with local government and the private sector to preserve historic structures, particularly the 5.6-mile power canal system, and 19th- and early-20th-century textile mills. The park's mission is to interpret themes related to industrialization, such as labor, immigration and ethnicity, technology, capital, urbanization, the environment, and industrial decline. Lowell Heritage State Park works cooperatively with the national park in historical interpretation and preservation, offers its own interpretive programs, and maintains three recreation areas in Lowell. Approximately 500,000 people visit Lowell National Historical Park each year; the majority of these visitors come during the summer months, when canal tours and other special events are offered.

Established by Congress in 1978, Lowell National Historical Park grew out of a local movement to build on Lowell's history and to revitalize the city after decades of industrial decline. Its significance long recognized by historians, Lowell may be considered America's first successful planned industrial city. Development for cotton textile manufacturing was undertaken in the 1820s by a group of Boston merchant-industrialists, later dubbed the Boston Associates. Their innovative practices in labor relations, industrial technology, and business organization earned them great renown and great fortunes. Lowell's early fame centered on its unique workforce of Yankee "mill girls": young women recruited from the farms of New England. Images of happy mill girls and benevolent paternalistic labor relations may belie the true experiences of Lowell's workers before the 1850s, when the arrival of immigrant workers and a series of strikes occurred. Nevertheless, the development of the mill girl system and other innovations in labor, technology, and capital support Lowell's claim to historical eminence.

The centerpiece of the national park is the Boott Cotton Mills Museum. It includes a re-created 1920s cotton mill weave room, with 88 operational power looms. The Working People Exhibit is dedicated to the social history of the workers, from the Yankee mill girls to later immigrant workers. The Suffolk Mill Turbine exhibit features a restored 19th-century turbine and power transmission system. Tours begin at the Visitor Center, which also screens an introductory video. The park's canal tours, offered during warm-weather months, take visitors by boat through parts of the extensive canal system. Re-created turn-of-the-century trolleys allow visitors to experience a historical mode of urban transportation. The park also sponsors a walking tour to view the bars, clubs, diners, and other favorite haunts of the Beat writer Jack Kerouac. An exhibit at the Boott Cotton Mills Museum called *A Time for Play* provides an opportunity to investigate the games of yesteryear. Another tour explores how the development of household technology affected the leisure time of housewives at the turn of the century.

Foremost among special programs is the Lowell Folk Festival, held on the last weekend of July. It is organized by the park in conjunction with community organizations. The Tsongas Industrial History Center, a joint venture between the park and the University of Massachusetts at Lowell, offers educational programs to school groups. In cooperation with the Sports Museum of New England, the Lowell National Historical Park also offers a series of baseball movies that complement the park's presentation of recreational activities in Lowell's history.

Lowell Heritage State Park was created in 1976 to interpret Lowell's industrial history, a role now performed largely by the national park. Today the state park maintains three recreational areas in Lowell, including Francis Gate Park, situated along the Pawtucket Canal, which is the site of a restored lock chamber and flood control gate complex. Along the Merrimack River, the Vandenburg Esplanade includes a concert pavilion, a bathhouse and beach, and the Bellegarde Boathouse. The Lowell-Dracut-Tyngsboro State Forest, encompassing 1,200 acres, offers trails for hiking and biking.

Robert F. Dalzell, Jr., *Enterprising Elite: The Boston Associates and the World They Made* (1987); Thomas Dublin, *Women at Work: The Transformation of Work and Community in Lowell, Massachusetts, 1826–1860* (1979); Thomas Dublin and Paul Marion, *Lowell: The Story of an Industrial City* (1992); National Park Foundation, *The Complete Guide to America's National Parks* (1996).

James Beauchesne

Martha's Vineyard

Reflecting on Martha's Vineyard, John Updike wrote, "When I think of the Vineyard, my ankles feel good— bare, airy, lean." Martha's Vineyard, an island 7 miles off the Cape Cod coast of Massachusetts, has been a vacation destination since the mid-19th century. The Vineyard, as it is popularly known, offers beaches as its primary attraction, as well as several outdoor activities, in a charming, picture-perfect setting.

Tourism is Martha's Vineyard's most important industry. The six-community, 100-square mile island's population swells from about 15,000 off-season to 102,000 during the summer. Tourism brings in millions of dollars a year. Summer visitors have included celebrities from Ulysses S. Grant to Bill Clinton. Although the Vineyard's popularity has brought profits, it has also brought crowding and damage to the delicate landscape.

Tourism began on the Vineyard in the mid-19th century. In 1835, in the midst of the religious revival known as the Second Great Awakening, island Methodists came together for a camp meeting near the town of Oak Bluffs. The campground came to be known as Wesleyan Grove and continued to be the site of revival meetings every August, each year growing larger and larger. By the mid-1850s, the congregation had swelled to 12,000 people, and some worshipers began to build summer cottages on the campground, returning year after year for vacations.

At the same time, the reputation of Martha's Vineyard as an ideal vacation spot was growing. Wesleyan Grove attracted increasing numbers of visitors who were interested in combining the religious climate of the campground with the attractions of a summer resort. Prayer meetings and preaching competed with more secular offerings, including ocean bathing, croquet, and berry picking. The communal tents erected by early worshipers were gradually replaced by cottages built by visitors from Providence and New Bedford and Fall River, Mass. These tiny, brightly painted Carpenter Gothic cottages are still in use on the grounds of the Martha's Vineyard Camp Meeting Association today; over 200 are listed on the National Register of Historic Places. By the late 19th century a full-scale resort surrounded the campground, complete with a grand hotel, elaborately decorated summer cottages, brass bands, a skating rink, and the Flying Horses Carousel, the oldest operating carousel in America.

Martha's Vineyard is notable because it has traditionally been an amenable vacation locale for African Americans, who were not welcomed at most resorts in the past. Blacks have lived on the Vineyard from as early as 1703, and African American visitors were recorded at Vineyard Grove, a Baptist camp meeting near the original Methodist campground, as early as the mid-19th century. Early in the 20th century, Martha's Vineyard began to attract well-established, affluent African Americans as vacationers. The town of Oak Bluffs, the historical center of the African American vacation community, continues to attract a sizable African American crowd.

Visitors come to Martha's Vineyard to enjoy its myriad activities, from hiking to boating and fishing. In addition to the premier attraction—its beaches—the Vineyard offers a many-faceted natural landscape, with woodlands and freshwater ponds as well as sand dunes. Among the Vineyard's most dramatic landmarks are the red clay cliffs at Gay Head, a National Historic Landmark and a site sacred to the Wampanoag people.

Visitors also enjoy the island's human environment—its architecture, summer theater, and museums. Martha's Vineyard is known for its famous residents—a wide variety of celebrities from popular musicians to political figures. A celebrity auction is held each year to support local charities. The fame of its well-known visitors has not always brought good publicity: the island made headlines after Senator Edward Kennedy's tragic 1969 accident at Chappaquiddick, a small island at the eastern end of Martha's Vineyard. Dyke Bridge, the site of the accident, has become a minor tourist destination in its own right.

But while the popularity of Martha's Vineyard has brought prosperity, it has led to environmental problems. For example, tourist traffic has contributed to the erosion of the cliffs at Gay Head. The Martha's Vineyard Commission was established in 1974 to preserve the island's fragile ecosystems. The commission helps to promote tourism, without which islanders would suffer severe economic hardship, but it does so with an eye toward protecting the natural beauty that attracts so many visitors. Those who love Martha's Vineyard seek to preserve its environment even as they welcome tourists. This formula ensures that tourism will continue to be the island's primary industry.

Cindy Aron, *Working at Play: A History of Vacations in the United States* (1999); Dona Brown, *Inventing New England: Regional Tourism in the 19th Century* (1995); Ellen Weiss, *City in the Woods: The Life and Design of an American Camp Meeting on Martha's Vineyard* (1998); Dorothy West, *The Wedding* (1996).

Rachelle Friedman

Mohawk Trail Identified on road maps as Route 2 and known by locals simply as the trail, the Mohawk Trail is one of the oldest continuously used roadways in New England. Between its eastern end at Greenfield, Mass., and its western terminus at Williamstown, Mass., the trail spans more than 50 miles of mountainous and scenic terrain and offers access to 50,000 acres of state parks and forests. It was the first toll-free interstate turnpike; constructed in 1786 and known as the Shunpike, it was used then primarily for transporting settlers and goods by oxcart. Since 1915, when it was rebuilt as the nation's first highway suitable for automobile tourists, the Mohawk Trail has been promoted as a symbol of New England's Native American legacy. The trail is said to be the main route by which the "warlike" Mohawks of northern and western New York raided the more peaceful Indians of what is now western Massachusetts.

The history of the Mohawk Trail is a factor of its varied topography. Like a miniature version of such overland routes as the Oregon Trail, the Mohawk Trail follows two river valleys—the Deerfield to the east and the Hoosac to the west—but also spans the foreboding terrain in between. The Mohawks had ample reason for traveling the trail's precipitous course. Near the eastern terminus of the trail lay two of New England's most important inland fishing sites—Salmon (now Shelburne) Falls on the Deerfield River and Peskeomskut (now Turners Falls, the site of Captain William Turner's infamous massacre of an encampment of Native Americans during King Philip's War) on the Connecticut River. Today, Turners Falls, Greenfield, and Shelburne Falls are significant population centers, and each town serves the area's mixed economic base. The central segment of the trail has in recent years become a focus for ecotourism; it runs parallel to the rapid course of the Deerfield River and attracts white-water and fly-fishing enthusiasts.

In the years of imperial conflict among rival European nations and their native allies, the Mohawk Trail was a route of war and captivity. Travelers along the Mohawk Trail today can see several stone monuments that mark the sites of prerevolutionary frontier garrisons ("the lines of forts") erected by the English to protect New England's northwestern extremity against threats posed by the French in Canada and their Mohawk and Abenaki allies.

These obscure markers rising from the overgrown grass stand in austere contrast to more recent and colorful displays. As the trail became a tourist route in the early 20th century, it sprouted a wide variety of attractions and facilities, from the Bridge of Flowers in Shelburne Falls to the mid-20th-century tourist cabins that line the road, now mostly in disrepair. Among the most interesting are the Indian Trading Posts, white-owned and operated establishments at which customers can purchase all manner of both genuine and spurious native memorabilia. Like the tourist image of the trail itself, the trading posts represent a national, as opposed to merely local, "Indian" mythology at work. Included among their displays are teepees, buffalo, and totem poles, all of which are associated with trans-Mississippi native cultures and Hollywood images. In a strange mix of fact and fantasy, one of the posts features the well-marked burial site of Elizabeth Nichols, "the first white woman killed on the Mohawk Trail." Ironically, this same trading post offers its grounds several times a year for use by an intertribal Native American powwow.

Douglas Edward Leach, *Flintlock and Tomahawk: New England in King Philip's War* (1958); Jill Lepore, *The Name of War: King Philip's War and the Origins of American Identity* (1998); Massachusetts Historical

Commission, *Historic and Archaeological Resources of the Connecticut Valley* (1984).

Michael Hoberman

Mystic, Conn., and Mystic Seaport

The historic resort village of Mystic, Conn., is located on the state's southeastern coast approximately 10 miles east of New London. The downtown area of Mystic—never a formally incorporated municipality—is divided by the Mystic River. The east side of the river, which includes major tourist attractions like the Seaport Museum, Mystic Aquarium, outlet malls, and the Olde Mistick Village shopping center, is part of the town of Stonington. The west side of the river is part of the town of Groton. Many businesses on the east side of the river were destroyed by fire in the 1950s and never rebuilt, while downtown buildings on the west side are much as they were in the 1920s and 1930s.

The first permanent British settlement of the area was established in 1654 at the head of the Mystic River in what is known today as Old Mystic. In May 1637 Captain John Mason led a surprise raid on the Pequot fort in the Mystic River valley. The Pequots were defeated, opening the way for further British settlement of the area. Over time, the original Pequot name for the area, "missi-tuk," was anglicized to Mystic. The Mystic River still posed a considerable barrier to settlement, and regular ferry service across it was not established until 1660. Mystic enjoyed its heyday between the Revolutionary War and the Civil War, a period during which the town prospered as a trading port and a center for shipbuilding. The shipyards of Mystic built many excellent vessels, most notably the clipper ships *David Crockett* (1853) and *Andrew Jackson* (1855).

Mystic's most famous attraction is the Marine Historical Association, or, as it is commonly known, Mystic Seaport, founded in 1929. Mystic Seaport is a nonprofit educational institution with more than 25,000 members from the 50 states and more than 30 countries worldwide. The 17-acre site is a center for the collection and preservation of historic ships, boats, maritime arts and records, and other maritime artifacts, including scrimshaw, figureheads, paintings, and ship models. Mystic Seaport's extensive collections include the whaling ship *Charles W. Morgan* (1841), the square-rigged ship *Joseph Conrad* (1882), and the Grand Banks schooner *L. A. Dunton* (1921). All three ships can be boarded. Mystic Seaport also features a number of restored historic homes, businesses, and other tourist attractions, including a cooperage, a ropewalk, a sail-making factory, a planetarium, an active shipyard (where a reconstruction of the slave ship *Amistad* was built), the Blunt White Library, and one of the largest maritime bookstores and art galleries in the world.

In addition to its museums, Mystic has many restored 19th-century homes. These homes are not open to the public, but tourists may visit the Denison Homestead on Pequotsepos Road next to the Pequotsepos Nature Center. Built in 1717, this historic homestead contains furnishings used by 11 generations of Denisons. Another popular attraction, the Mystic Aquarium, features more than 3,000 examples of marine life, including beluga whales, sea lions, bottlenose dolphins, a penguin exhibit, and an Open Sea exhibit with three species of sharks.

Mystic has become one of the most popular year-round tourist destinations in New England. Its proximity to Rhode Island and Connecticut beaches and to the Foxwoods Casino and Mashantucket Pequot Museum and Research Center, located in nearby Ledyard, Conn., contributes to its popularity as a tourist stop. Mystic attracts some 500,000 visitors a year.

Virginia B. Anderson, *Maritime Mystic* (1962); Carl C. Cutler, *Mystic: The Story of a Small New England Seaport* (1942); William N. Peterson, *Mystic Built: Ships and Shipyards of the Mystic River, Connecticut 1784–1919* (1989).

Stephen D. Glazier

Nantucket

For much of the year Nantucket slumbers peacefully under a heavy blanket of fog. Come Memorial Day, however, the increasing hum of planes and blast of ferry horns announces the start of the tourist season. Between June and September this small island, located 30 miles off the Cape Cod coast of Massachusetts, plays host to summer crowds who come to escape the pressures of life on the mainland. Shiny Range Rovers replace battered pickup trucks at the beaches, and sandy-footed tourists, many with children in tow, clog the bike paths and swarm to the ice cream shops of the main downtown area. During the summer Nantucket's population swells to more than 55,000 from its off-season low of around 10,500, and as a result the island's leisurely pace shifts into overdrive.

Nantucket measures roughly 14 miles from tip to tip and about 3 miles across at its widest point. The name, derived from a Native American word meaning "faraway island," suggests the remoteness of its early history. Populated by a small tribe of Wampanoag when it was first discovered and settled by the British in 1659, Nantucket reached its peak of influence in the early 1800s, when its status as a whaling capital made it the third most populous locale in Massachusetts, after Boston and Salem.

In 1846 fire decimated much of the town of Nantucket, including its wharves and commercial area, at roughly the same time the declining demand for whale oil and the increased difficulty of long whaling voyages plunged the island into an economic depression that lasted several decades. By the late 1880s, however, increased interest in tourism among wealthy New Englanders led to the "rediscovery" of Nantucket as an exclusive getaway, and its reputation as an elite island resort was born.

From the beginning, Nantucket's appeal to vacationers has rested on its ability to evoke misty images of a romantic past. The island's "quaint" image has been closely identified with its old, gray-shingled Quaker buildings, the remnants of its earlier whaling days. The Historic District Commission, established in 1955 to control the appearance and resultant feel of the island, today works with the Nantucket Chamber of Commerce, the island's board of selectmen, and various other committees and commissions to preserve the island's image as a charming, traditional, unspoiled place. The stated concern of these official bodies, to preserve what is both authentic and exclusive about Nantucket, is captured by the popular slogan, "It's nicer in Nantucket."

Nantucket is accessible by boat and air. Three ferry companies serve the island, offering both traditional and high-speed passage, and numerous small air operations plus several major carriers—enough planes to make Nantucket Airport the second busiest in Massachusetts—keep the skies filled with planes and the people of the island arguing over air routes and airplane noise. The island supports a fairly comprehensive shuttle bus service that connects the town of Nantucket to the other areas of the island, such as the village of Siasconset to the east; Dionis and Madaket to the west; and Surfside, Cisco, and Miacomet to the south. In addition, nearly all the major roads boast well-maintained bike paths. The Chamber of Commerce actively discourages visitors from bringing their cars. Indeed, increasingly clogged streets in recent years have prompted many Nantucketers to press for laws that would prohibit short-term visitors from ferrying their cars to the island; the mixed support from those whose livelihoods depend on tourism has thus far prevented such legislation from passing.

Indeed, with no real base other than that generated by tourism and the building and service trades it supports, Nantucket's economy is firmly tied up in the mechanisms of the industry. Of the nearly 9,000 year-round residents who make up the Nantucket workforce, a large number serve as manual laborers, holding jobs in technical, service, production, or repair-related fields. In 2002 the average annual household income on the island was $55,522 and the average earnings per job only $33,040. With the price of a single-family home costing on average almost $600,000, fewer and fewer year-round residents can afford to own their own home. In the case of land as well as supplies, crafts, and services, the monied status of most of Nantucket's summer visitors has driven up the cost of living on the island. The inequity in financial status between the year-rounders and the masses of tourists who flock to Nantucket has begun to attract increasing attention from the governing bodies of the island, and many Nantucketers have begun to demand intervention from the town.

For a quaint, serene island complete with tree-lined cobblestone streets and a strict conservation commission that protects wetlands and other natural preserves from human infringement, Nantucket possesses more than its share of conflicts. Most arise from the frenzied development and skyrocketing costs generated by tourism. The Nantucket Planning Board has in recent years been entrusted by residents to address the inherent conflicts between preservation and growth. Many hope this group will find a way to manage Nantucket's dependence on tourism without jeopardizing the tranquil way of life that endears the island to residents and tourists alike.

G. J. Ashworth and Brian Goodall, eds., *Marketing Tourism Places* (1990); Dona Brown, *Inventing New England: Regional Tourism in the 19th Century* (1995).
Diana B. Turk

Newport, R.I.

Newport was founded in 1639 by a group of colonists who fled Massachusetts in search of religious freedom. Because of its location at the southern tip of Rhode Island and its excellent harbor, Newport became a prosperous port. Newport merchants played a central role in the so-called triangle trade, shipping enslaved Africans to the Caribbean sugar plantations and slave-produced molasses to the rum manufactures of the northern British colonies. Following the Civil War, scenic Newport became an opulent summer resort for the very wealthy and has been in the limelight as a tourist destination since the mid-19th century. In 2000 Newport had a year-round population of roughly 26,000 residents. The city is home to the JVC Newport Jazz Festival, the Apple and Eve Newport Folk Festival, and the Newport Music Festival; it hosted the America's Cup yacht races until 1983 and now hosts many other regattas and boating events.

The city's visibility has created a succession of stereotypical images. The image of the city

Market Building (Peter Harrison, 1761–62), Newport, R.I.

as a summer playground for the rich, a city of mansions above a harbor full of yachts, however, is tempered by the reality of a much more complex and diverse community. As early as the 1840s, Newport was portrayed as a picturesque escape from America's burgeoning cities. Photographs of Newport began to appear in the pages of such national magazines as *Harper's Weekly* and *Frank Leslie's Illustrated* and helped to propel the city's status to that of Queen of Resorts. Through these images, Newport became a symbol of America's romantic ideals about itself. During the period before the Civil War there was some truth to those romantic images of the town. By the 1880s, however, Newport's summer colonists had replaced the sylvan landscape with palatial estates created by the country's finest architects and landscape designers. The city had become a place where summer colonists could play out their competitive rituals of conspicuous consumption. By the end of the Gilded Age, the nation gawked at the excesses portrayed by the popular press in increasingly satirical fashion.

By the late 19th century, Newport had become solely a resort for the wealthy, an image confirmed in the 1930s when the New York Yacht Club brought the America's Cup challenge races to Newport, and again in the 1960s when John F. Kennedy married the stepdaughter of the summer colonist Hugh D. Auchincloss and began to summer at the family's home at Hammersmith Farm. This image continues today as Newport is portrayed in the media as a slightly decadent playground for the yacht-owning jet set.

Most visitors to Newport today arrive with many preconceptions based on these and other images and head directly to the mansions of the Gilded Age, overlooking the rest of the city's rich historical landscape that first attracted summer visitors in the 19th century. The astute visitor, however, sees the Newport National Historic Landmark District, where more colonial buildings survive than in any other district in the country. The scattered houses of worship—including Touro Synagogue (1763), the oldest extant synagogue in North America—are testament to the religious diversity upon which the city was founded in the 1630s. The relatively modest cottages of the Kay–Catherine–Old Beach Road area recall the gatherings of Boston and Cambridge intellectuals in the 1870s to discuss scientific, literary, and artistic issues of the day. Behind the stereotypical image of Newport as a resort of the wealthy is the reality that Newport is, in fact, a complex and diverse city in a multilayered landscape.

Its mansions, many of which are open to the public, remain among Newport's most famous tourist attractions. The Preservation Society of Newport County maintains and operates many of these properties, formerly inhabited by the Astors, the Vanderbilts, and other millionaire American families. Among the most famous is the Breakers, a majestic building modeled after an Italian palazzo built for Cornelius Vanderbilt in 1895. Tourists can also visit Hammersmith Farm, Rosecliff, the Isaac Bell House, Chateau-Sur-Mer, and the Elms. Another popular tourist attraction is Newport's Cliff Walk. The 3.5-mile walk, designated a

National Recreation Trail in 1975, meanders over the dramatic rocky shoreline and past many of the spectacular mansions. Some of the steepest points along the walk are over 70 feet above the ocean. Maintenance of the Cliff Walk has been variously adopted and then abandoned by government and private groups but was most recently undertaken with the help of funds from the National Park Service and Water Conservation Fund. Newport's breathtaking scenery, temperate climate, historic sites, and contemporary events make it a perennially popular tourist destination.

Lucinda Brockway, "The Historic Designed Landscapes of Newport County," *Newport History* 64 (1991); Antoinette Downing and Vincent Scully, *The Architectural Heritage of Newport, Rhode Island, 1640–1915* (1979); C. P. B. Jefferys, *Newport: A Short History* (1992); Eileen Warburton, *In Living Memory: A Chronicle of Newport, Rhode Island, 1888–1988* (1988).

Daniel Snydacker, Jr.

Old Orchard Beach, Maine

Since 1837, when Ebenezer Staples opened his farmhouse to Canadian tourists, Old Orchard Beach (known as Old Orchard until 1929) has catered to summer visitors. Located 25 miles south of Portland, Maine, along the eastern seaboard, this small coastal community has a year-round population of 8,800 that grows to about 100,000 during the summer months. Attracted to the 7 mile sandy beach and its functions as promenade and playground, guests in Old Orchard Beach have typically sorted themselves into two groups. One group seeks out the cosmopolitan, adult-oriented experience offered by the hotels; the other is ensconced in family-oriented, often religiously affiliated cottage communities.

Transportation shaped Old Orchard's culture and the groups it attracted. The Boston and Maine (B&M) Railroad opened its Saco station in 1842, putting tourists a short wagon ride away from the hotels. The Grand Trunk Railroad of Montreal, completed in 1853, transported Canadians to Portland. Eventually, the B&M's eastern branch, which opened in 1873, dropped summer visitors in the heart of the hotel district. In 1880 a diminutive train called the Dummy was built to run from the downtown train station 3 miles eastward, passing through several middle-class summer vacation neighborhoods. The Biddeford-Saco Trolley brought factory workers and day-trippers to the beach from 1903 until 1938. As automobiles replaced the Pullman car, Maine established its first state highways in the 1920s. Route 5 from the north and Route 9 from the west intersect at Old Orchard Street and Grand Avenue in downtown Old Orchard Beach, bringing yet more tourists to the area. Old Orchard's so-called Plush and Velvet

Age (1873–1907) ended abruptly on August 15, 1907, when an overnight fire destroyed 17 waterfront hotels. The fire did not signal the resort's death, however, because other areas of Old Orchard were thriving. For each hotel guest who came to Old Orchard, four more people lived in the surrounding cottage communities. Individual cottages set side by side defined the family-oriented lifestyle in the neighborhoods, founded by such religious organizations as the Methodists' Old Orchard Beach Camp Meeting Association (1873), the Baptist-based Ocean Park Association (1881), and the Universalists' Ferry Beach Park Association (1901).

By the turn of the century the cottage culture had gained some ground as the most prominent form of tourism in Old Orchard. Astute investors began to build family-oriented attractions. The Old Orchard Pier (1898) soon housed ice cream and souvenir stands, bowling alleys, moving pictures, and a dance hall. By 1902 the Seaside Amusement Park boasted a Ferris wheel, merry-go-round, and roller coaster. In 1903 promotional materials advertised the beach as a safe playground for children. The town capitalized on its location and premier attraction in 1929, formally changing its name from Old Orchard to Old Orchard Beach.

Commercial, inexpensive forms of leisure also catered to working-class visitors from nearby factory towns and industrial centers only a few hours away. Day-trippers brought another dimension to the culture of the summer resort city—crowds and rowdiness. At-

tempting to experience leisure on a shortened schedule, these visitors welcomed the sense of freedom from their daily lives and from the heat, haze, and humidity of a New England summer day.

Hotels, cottages, and commercial attractions remain an integral part of Old Orchard Beach's culture. Today, the resort also features time-shares, condominiums, camping areas, and motels. The presence of different social groups, welcomed by resort owners eager to cater to a multitude of clients, makes Old Orchard Beach a fine example of the New England summer vacation place.

William David Barry and Debra Verrier, "Sun, Sand, Sea—and Neon: Old Orchard Beach Celebrates 100 Years of Summer Fun," *Down East* 29 (July 1983); Robert A. Dominique, *Greetings from Old Orchard, Maine: A Picture Post Card History* (1981); Roy P. Fairfield, *Sands, Spindles, and Steeples: A History of Saco, Maine* (1956); William H. Marnell, *Vacation Yesterdays of New England* (1975).

Janet E. Schulte

Old Sturbridge Village

Old Sturbridge Village is the largest outdoor living history museum in the Northeast. Located on 200 rural acres in Sturbridge, Mass., the village brings to life the rapidly changing world of the late 18th and early 19th centuries. Villagers in period costume emerge from more than 40 architecturally restored, reconstructed, and relocated buildings to greet museum guests. They demonstrate farming, food preparation, crafts, and other routine household tasks of the 1830s, and they re-create life-changing events

Costumed staff interpret rural New England of the 1830s at Old Sturbridge Village, in Massachusetts, 1980

such as weddings and funerals. Visitors are urged to make connections with their own daily lives, to remember their own ties to family, friends, and community; in this sense, the past is united with the present.

Old Sturbridge Village opened with a staff of 25 people on June 8, 1946, under the name Quinebaug Village. Its founders, the brothers Albert B. and Joel Cheney Wells, were successful local manufacturers who had become passionate collectors of traditional handicrafts. To house their increasingly large and complex collections, the Wells family eventually planned a living, or "open-air," museum based on European models and on the examples of other prominent American industrialists, particularly Henry Ford's Greenfield Village in Dearborn, Mich., and John D. Rockefeller's Colonial Williamsburg in Virginia. Using the waterpower of the Quinebaug River to operate three mills (carding, grist, and saw) on the grounds and to irrigate the farmlands, they envisioned a functioning village with a variety of traditional crafts activities taking place at the site.

Today, Old Sturbridge Village is divided into two main exhibit areas. The Countryside exhibits reflect the patterns of rural settlement: there are small family farms with a sawmill for cutting lumber, a gristmill for grinding grain, and a blacksmith shop to make and repair farm equipment. The Common and Center Village exhibits depict the movement from farm to center village: roads radiate out from a common area in the center of town to bring scattered homesteads into contact with the center meetinghouse and parsonage. In this setting, visitors see how families began to support themselves in businesses away from the farm and how cash transactions began to replace trade and exchange.

Since its opening year, when 5,172 visitors toured its two dozen exhibits, Old Sturbridge Village has experienced a number of changes. In the early 1970s, researchers made a series of revisions to the narrative interpretation of the village and refined many details related to period costume and furniture. Curatorial and research departments were established, with an emphasis on educational programs, workshops, publications, and special events demonstrations for visitors of all ages.

In 1972 the Asa Knight store moved to the Village Common; with an inventory reflecting the 1830s, it represents the most carefully researched and documented exhibit at Old Sturbridge Village. Today the village also portrays the women of early America as active contributors to the household income. In the Countryside exhibit area, for example, passages from Emerson Bixby's account book are on display; they indicate that the earnings of

his wife and daughters helped pay for the addition of a downstairs bedroom to their house.

Today, Old Sturbridge Village employs more than 350 full- and part-time workers, and its grounds offer lodging, food, recreation, and transportation services. Old Sturbridge Village continues to reach new audiences by providing sign language interpreters and wheelchair-accessible facilities and by implementing urban outreach programs.

Donna Jean Zane

Plimoth Plantation Plimoth Plantation is an open-air, living history museum located on Route 3A, 3 miles south of Plymouth, Mass. Its educational goal is to interpret the history of Plymouth Colony (1620–92) through re-creations of the 1627 Pilgrim Village, Hobbamock's (Wampanoag Indian) Homesite, and *Mayflower II,* as well as other exhibits and programs. Visiting Plimoth Plantation's Pilgrim Village today is like entering another country and experiencing life in a different culture. It presents a fresh, nontraditional analysis of the Pilgrim Fathers, in contrast to more mythic images of the past.

The museum was founded in 1947 through the efforts of the philanthropist and amateur achaeologist Harry Hornblower, who was searching for a way to communicate the Pilgrim story in a more active and compelling manner than existing monuments and relics could. The first re-created structures, designed by the architect Charles R. Strickland, were the First House (1948) and the Fort/Meetinghouse (1953), erected near Plymouth Rock to promote the proposed Pilgrim Village. Con-

struction began on the Pilgrim Village itself in 1957 and on an Indian Village in 1959, following a bequest of land from the Hornblower family. In 1958, Plimoth Plantation also assumed ownership of the *Mayflower II,* a reproduction of the Pilgrim vessel which had been built in England by Project Mayflower and had sailed to America the preceding year. During its early years the plantation followed the pattern of other restored villages in offering a view of Plymouth's colonial past shaped by patriotism and ancestor veneration. The plantation's exhibits employed the usual media of displays and antique and reproduction furnishings in the re-created houses and landscape.

From its inception, however, the plantation aimed at the greatest possible accuracy in its re-creations and historical interpretation. Lacking a collection of original structures or Pilgrim artifacts, the museum found educational legitimacy in the verisimilitude and quality of its program. In the mid-1960s a staff committee reexamined the plantation's original plan and proposed a number of changes. In 1969 the site was modified to improve its effectiveness as a living history exhibit. Static displays, mannequins, and antiques in the Pilgrim Village were replaced by consumable reproductions, kitchen gardens, and livestock. Until that time, demonstrations in the living village had been artificial and served mainly as a vehicle for lectures. For example, a single log might be sawn for an entire season. The new living history insisted on actual work and real production, which added greatly to the authenticity of the program.

By 1973 the unstaffed Indian Village had

Visitors in the reconstructed 1627 Pilgrim Village at Plimoth Plantation, in Massachusetts, 1982

been replaced by a mat-covered *wetu,* or Native American dwelling, staffed by members recruited from local native communities. In 1988 it became Hobbamock's Homesite, replicating the historically specific household of Wampanoag people who lived in close proximity to the Plymouth settlement in 1627. The Wampanoag Indian program today introduces visitors to the history, culture, traditions, and crafts of the indigenous southeastern New England people from a native viewpoint. The homesite includes two dwellings—a large, bark-covered *neesquttow* suitable for a native leader such as Hobbamock and a smaller, round, mat-covered *puttuckakuan*—a planting field for corn and other native crops, an arbor or shelter where open-air cooking takes place, and an area where *mishoon* (dugout canoes) were constructed. The staff manages the site by engaging in the same round of daily and seasonal work a native family would have observed 400 years ago.

Plimoth Plantation's best-known innovation was the introduction of first-person interpretation in 1978. Interpreters aboard *Mayflower II* and in the 1627 village portray known residents of the colony. Dressed in period attire and speaking in the appropriate English dialect for their place of origin, they pursue the daily and seasonal routines of 17th-century life, engaging visitors in discussions reflecting a 17th-century worldview of politics, economics, Calvinist theology, homemaking, and agriculture. Every effort is made to present an accurate picture of the diversity of life within two 17th-century cultures.

Jay Anderson, *Time Machines* (1984); James W. Baker, "Haunted by the Pilgrims," in Anne E. Yentch and Mary C. Beaudry, eds., *The Art and Mystery of Historical Archaeology* (1992); James Deetz, "A Sense of Another World," *Museum News* 58 (May–June 1980); Stephen E. Snow, *Performing the Pilgrims: A Study of Ethnohistorical Role Playing at Plimoth Plantation* (1993).

James W. Baker

Poland Spring

Poland Spring is a section of the town of Poland, Maine, but it has become better known as a mineral water and a tourist resort. Credit for developing the site goes to the Rickers family, who reluctantly traded for the property with the Shakers in 1793. By 1797 the family had opened its home to travelers journeying between Portland and northern New England. The coming of the Atlantic and St. Lawrence Railroad in 1849 initially drew traffic away from the family's inn. As the railroad replaced travelers with tourists, the Rickers transformed their farmstead into a leading Victorian vacation spot. It attracted urban patrons looking to escape the northeastern megalopolis for the nostalgia,

pastoralism, re-creation, healthfulness, and natural beauty of the Maine countryside. The resort grew into a community unto itself, featuring three hotels, nearly 100 support buildings, and 5,000 acres. A combination of factors sent the resort into decline by the 1930s: the popularity of the automobile, introduction of the federal income tax, overexpansion of the Ricker Hotel Company, and the problem of generational succession. The Depression ended the Ricker empire, although two sisters, Janette and Sarah, retained life tenancy after the property passed out of the family's control.

Until the 1960s, the resort went through several changes in ownership. Then in 1966, Saul Feldman stopped chasing bygone glories and leased the property to the Job Corps, which ran the site as a training center for young women. In 1972 Mel Robbins rescued the property from this Great Society experiment and re-created the site as a cut-rate resort appealing to an entirely different clientele from the millionaire leisure class. Gone are the Mansion and Poland Spring Houses, the latter to a towering inferno on July 3, 1975. The extant third historic hotel, the Riccar Inn, which has also served as the studio of WMTW-TV, has been renamed the Presidential Inn in tribute to previous prominent visitors to the resort. It joins two other hotels of more recent vintage as the Inns at Poland Spring. The site also still features one of the oldest golf courses in the country, dating back to 1896. The Poland Spring Preservation Society, formed in 1976, operates the Maine State Building, a transplant from the World's Columbian Exposition in Chicago (1893), and the All Soul's Chapel (1912), which is now a popular wedding location. Preservation Park is rounded out by the water company's restoration of the Spring House and Bottling Plant (1906) as a museum highlighting the geology of the region and history of the business.

Part of the uniqueness and allure of Poland Spring has been the "pure" water, although its history has become clouded over time. "From Maine since 1845" is now emblazoned across bottles of Poland Spring water. This claim differs from the family's account of the spring's discovery. While the patriarch of Poland Spring, Hiram Ricker, did claim cure by the water in 1845, he did not begin seriously marketing it until 1860. By the end of the century, Hiram Ricker and Sons were distributing Poland Spring water worldwide. Symbolic of the perceived purity, much of the water was sold in "Moses bottles"—bottles in the shape of the biblical prophet, who produced water in the wilderness by striking a rock with his staff. In contrast, Mae West served as a spokesperson for the company in the 20th century.

The therapeutic and commercial value of

Poland Spring water was rediscovered during the health craze of the 1970s. Today, the company is part of Nestlé Waters North America, a division of the Swiss conglomerate. The promotional power of this multinational corporation has driven Poland Spring to first place in spring water sales, and it trails only Pepsi's Aqua Fina and Coke's Dasani in the bottled water market. Poland Spring has seeped so deeply into popular culture that the television comedy *Seinfeld* once parodied it as Moland Spring, and it has become the official water of both Fenway Park and Yankee Stadium. Success, however, begets controversy. The company faces lawsuits disputing the water's purity, naturalness, and source. The crux of the matter is whether Poland Spring is principally a place or a brand. Can Poland Spring water come from Hollis, Maine, too? The current guardians believe so. For them, Poland Spring is more than a place; it is also "What it means to be from Maine." After more than two centuries of development, Poland Spring remains a symbol of nostalgia, nature, health, and purity.

Richard W. Judd, "Reshaping Maine's Landscape: Rural Culture, Tourism, and Conservation, 1890–1929," *Journal of Forest History* 32 (1988); Andy Opel, "Constructing Purity: Bottled Water and the Commodification of Nature," *Journal of American Culture* 22 (1999); *Poland Spring Centennial: A Souvenir* (1895); H. A. Poole and G. W. Poole, *History of Poland: Embracing a Period of over a Century* (1890); David L. Richards, "An Eden out of a Country Farm: Purity and Progress in the Landscapes of the Poland Spring Resort," *Maine Historical Society Quarterly* 34 (1994); George Ricker and Rose Ricker, eds., *Poland Spring Remembered: Recollections of Catharine Lewis Lennihan* (1988); Mel Robbins and Cyndi Robbins, *Poland Spring: Walk Hand in Hand with History, 1790s to Today* (2003).

David L. Richards

Postcards

Early in the 20th century postcards became an important element of the touring experience, as tourists sent postcards back home with "wishing you were here" greetings or purchased them as mementos for display in albums. Postcards enforced an image of New England as a tourist destination, depicting the many popular regional sites that reflected the developing tourism industry.

The United States first printed blank postal cards with a one-cent stamp in 1873. Private businesses began printing illustrated advertisements on the backs of these early cards, and other unmailable souvenir cards were available as early as 1876. The first mailable souvenir postcards were printed on U.S. government postal cards in 1893 commemorating the Columbian Exposition in Chicago. Subsequent postcard designs fall into historical periods determined by government regulations and technological innovations in color printing. *Pioneer Cards* (1893–98) are those printed on government one-cent postal cards. Some were printed privately on souvenir cards or mailcards requiring two cents postage. *Private Mailing Cards* (1898–1901) were privately printed. One side was used for the address only, while the other displayed a picture and message. On *Undivided Back Cards* (1901–7), only the address could be printed on the back, with the message and picture on the front. Black-and-white photographic cards became popular at this time. On *Divided Back Cards* (1907–15), the address appeared on the right side of the back of the card and the message on the left. On *White Border Cards* (1915–30), a white border was left around the picture. *Linen Cards* (1930–45) were postcards printed on a linenlike textured paper stock. *Modern Chrome Cards* (1939–present) display beautiful photochrome images first printed on regular size cards, now on the larger continental size.

Postcards were sent as a means of communication during the early 20th century much as the telephone and e-mail are used today. They were used for birth and wedding announcements and as invitations to social events. A card mailed on a Monday for an event the following weekend, for example, could easily receive a return postcard in proper time. Postcards sent during a short vacation would arrive before the vacationer returned home.

New England had many famous postcard publishers and distributors that were most active between 1900 and 1915, the golden age of postcards. The American Souvenir Company of Boston published the first and most popular pioneer series in New England in 1895, called Patriographic cards because of their images of historical buildings and places. Nearly every New England home had a postcard album on display containing cards of hometowns, family trips, and holiday greetings.

Each New England state had its most popular tourist spots and resultant souvenir postcards. Massachusetts cards featured views of the Berkshire Hills, the Mohawk Trail, Revere Beach, Plymouth, Cape Cod and the Islands, and, of course, Boston. Rhode Island cards displayed scenes of Newport and Narragansett Pier. Postcards from Vermont offered images of the Green Mountains, Lake Champlain, and general bucolic subjects. Connecticut postcards had views of Hartford, Mystic Seaport, Savin Rock Amusement Park, New London, New Haven, and Yale University. Postcards from Maine offered views of Old Orchard Beach, Boothbay Harbor, Acadia National Park, the Rangeley Lakes, Maine lighthouses, and the dramatic rocky coastline. Vacationers in New Hampshire could pur-chase postcards of Lake Winnipesaukee, the White Mountains, the Presidential Range, Mount Washington, and Bretton Woods.

Souvenir folders, which displayed 10 to 20 images of a specific tourist area, were also available. Coming before the advent of cheap photography and less expensive than buying a sketch or painting by an artist working at or near a tourist hotel, such sets provided a visual record, often idealized, of the vacation. These images were also cheaper than the sets of stereopticon cards that often depicted tourist destinations, historic sites, and scenery. Canterbury Shaker Village in New Hampshire produced card sets with staged groups of Shakers, putting forward the best image of the community, which was coming to depend on tourism as a source of income.

Although interest in postcards waned during and after World War I, it grew in the 1960s and has been accelerating ever since. Today, each New England state has active postcard clubs. More than a century after they were collected in family albums, the first pictorial cards are now being sought by collectors. Often the cards are the only old views of New England towns and cities and are used for historical research and to obtain information for historically accurate restorations.

Beverly H. Kallgren

Provincetown, Mass. Provincetown lies at the northern tip of Cape Cod, Mass., and is recognized as the first landing site of the *Mayflower*. The town, which was incorporated in 1727, has a year-round population of approximately 3,500 and a summer population that ranges between 20,000 and 50,000, with 250,000 annual visitors. Tourism is the main industry and the primary source of revenue, a fact that is reflected by Provincetown's more than 100 motels, inns, and guesthouses, nearly 50 restaurants, and more than 30 art galleries.

Provincetown was one of the last outposts of New England to be discovered as a vacation destination. Not until the turn of the 20th century did the town begin to attract tourists, after its role as an international port for fishing and whaling had gone into a serious decline. Tourism grew up first around the art colony founded by Charles Hawthorne. Hawthorne came to Provincetown in 1899, admiring its "primitive" qualities—including the "quaintness" of the Portuguese community that made up the majority of the town's residents—to establish the plein air (outdoor) Cape Cod School of Art. He was followed by other artists, traditional as well as modernist, many of whom joined the bohemian colony at the East End of Provincetown centered around the writer and journalist Mary Heaton Vorse and her Greenwich Village friends.

As early as the 1910s, artists and writers began converting the town's fishing shacks into artist studios and galleries, while restaurants appeared on the wharves, each with its barker calling out its specials to day-trippers. In 1915 the Provincetown Players opened a theater in

Commercial Street, Provincetown, Mass., 1989

a converted house on the wharf and began to stage the avant-garde works of Eugene O'Neill and others. By 1916 the *Boston Globe* was advertising Provincetown as the biggest art colony in the world. Writers, artists, and actors continued to flock to Provincetown as sojourners and settlers, establishing theaters and art schools from the 1920s through the present.

Tourism began to increase dramatically with the post–World War II economic boom that brought the Mid-Cape Highway to Provincetown, making access much easier for many New Englanders and New Yorkers. In the 1950s Provincetown began to be known as one of the primary gay and lesbian vacation sites in the United States. In 1978 the Provincetown Business Guild, made up of more than 200 gay-owned businesses, was founded to promote and support gay tourism. In the 1980s and 1990s came the "feminization of Provincetown," as lesbians moved in, bought businesses, and began to attract lesbian tourists.

With the establishment in 1961 of the Cape Cod National Seashore, which now makes up about 80 percent of the land of Provincetown, the environmental pleasures of nature walks and whale watching have become central to the tourist experience. The town has extended the traditional summer tourist season from early spring to late fall by continuing to develop events that draw on these elements of the town's historical and contemporary identity.

Today, dance bars and cabarets exist alongside fast food and family restaurants, fine arts galleries coexist with souvenir shops, and Fantasia Fair (a cross-dressers' festival), Carnival Week, and Women's Week compete with whale watching and the beach as tourist attractions. Provincetown continues to embrace both the traditional and the nontraditional as it wrestles with overdevelopment, a low-wage economy, and high unemployment rates, while trying to maintain its reputation as an all-purpose vacationers' paradise.

Dona Brown, *Inventing New England: Regional Tourism in the 19th Century* (1995); Gillian Drake, *The Complete Guide to Provincetown* (1992); Mary Heaton Vorse, *Time and the Town: A Provincetown Chronicle* (1991 [1942]).

Lois Rudnick

Salem, Mass. Best known for the witch trials of the 1690s and for being Nathaniel Hawthorne's native town, Salem was founded in 1626 by Roger Conant, who arrived with the town's first English settlers. Incorporated as a town in 1630, Salem stood for a short while as the first capital of the Massachusetts Bay Colony and had a thriving economic base of

Puritan monument and Salem Witch Museum, Salem, Mass., 1992

fishing and farming. This shifted during the 18th century to shipbuilding and privateering and, later, to a fortune-making trade with the Orient. The 19th century brought steam-run cotton mills, leather tanneries, and shoe factories to Salem. New England's 20th-century industrial decline left its mark on the urban landscape, yet today Salem flourishes as a major regional center of tourism, culture, and recreational activities.

Although the city has been a notable north-of-Boston tourist destination since Hawthorne's time, its renaissance in the 1990s is due to the fruitful collaboration of federal organizations, state agencies, local individuals, and institutions, all of whom have contributed millions of dollars to the expansion of Salem's public history initiatives. The National Park Service has built a Regional Visitors' Center that offers walking tours, exhibits, and films about Essex County's places of interest. Along the waterfront, the Salem Maritime National Historic Site re-creates life during the age of sail (1775–1820); its historical attractions include merchants' mansions, small homes, a shop, the Custom House (1819) where Hawthorne worked, and the new addition of a fully rigged, seaworthy replica of the sloop *Friendship* (1797), which traveled the world in search

of spices, sugar, coffee, and other goods for America.

Salem also boasts the nation's oldest continuously operating museum. Established in 1799 as the East India Marine Society and endowed by George Peabody in 1867, the museum features extensive collections of maritime history and paintings, Oriental art and export goods, and ethnological artifacts. The neighboring Essex Institute encompasses a research library, galleries of portraits, period furniture, decorative arts, and many impeccably restored historic homes. In 1992 the two museums merged to form the Peabody Essex Museum.

Although the great fire of 1914 destroyed some of the more industrialized quarters of the city, hundreds of colonial- and Federal-era residences remain. All of Chestnut Street, a tree-lined avenue of three-story brick mansions laid out in 1796, is a National Historic Landmark and a testament to the superior architectural design and woodcarving skills of the Salem native Samuel McIntire (1757–1811). Such streetscapes are a legacy of Salem's golden age, from 1790 to 1807, when it was one of America's most populous and prosperous seaports.

With a population of 40,407 according to

the 2000 census, the city has developed a thriving tourism-based commerce. The nation's oldest candy company still peddles the confections it has made since 1806. Shops with museum-quality antiques or fine reproductions are just steps away from co-ops packed with inexpensive curios and secondhand furniture. A used bookstore may feature scholarly and antiquarian books yet sell incense, essential oils, and tarot cards along the back wall—catering to the many tourists who associate Salem primarily with witches. The region's most visited spot remains the Salem Witch Museum, which features October's "haunted happenings," among other events. The home of the magistrate Jonathan Corwin has long been known as the Witch House and is open to the public today. In 1992 during the tercentenary, a memorial to the victims of the witch trials was dedicated near the Charter Street Old Burying Point. Other popular sites in Salem include the Pioneer Village, established in 1930 to depict the life of settlers in a 17th-century fishing village, and the House of Seven Gables museum, which commemorates the house that served as the backdrop for Hawthorne's famous novel. Since the tercentennial of the famed witch trials, these and other popular 17th-century sites like the Old Burying Ground and the Pickering House have been joined by wax, monster, and pirate museums, with interactive adventures to attract a new generation.

National Park Service, *Salem: Maritime Salem in the Age of Sail, Handbook 126* (1987); Bryant F. Tolles, Jr., with Carolyn K. Tolles, *Architecture in Salem: An Illustrated Guide* (1983).

Catherine Ann Lawrence

Shaker Villages Ever since the New England followers of Mother Ann Lee gathered into gospel order in the 1790s, the Shaker villages have attracted a host of visitors. There are nine major Shaker villages in New England: two in Maine (Alfred, est. 1793; Sabbathday Lake, est. 1794); two in New Hampshire (Canterbury, est. 1792; Enfield, est. 1793); four in Massachusetts (Hancock, est. 1790; Harvard, est. 1791; Tyringham, est. 1792; Shirley, est. 1793); and one in Connecticut (Enfield, est. 1790). The Shakers, members of the United Society of Believers in Christ's Second Appearing, also known as Believers, have offered a "kindly welcome" to "world's people" as disparate as James Monroe, Herman Melville, and members of Bob Dylan's Rolling Thunder tour.

The attraction of Shaker villages has varied over time. The literati who descended upon the Believers during the first half of the 19th century used Shaker communities as a standard by which to define a nascent national cultural identity. Such writers as James Fenimore

Draft horse hayride, Canterbury Shaker Village Harvest Day, Canterbury, N.H., 2001

Cooper, Ralph Waldo Emerson, and Nathaniel Hawthorne found much to commend about Shakerism—orderliness, cleanliness, industriousness, and craftsmanship. They also found much to condemn—celibacy, dullness, sublimation of self, and ecstatic worship.

As the nation's economy became more industrial and its society more urban after the Civil War, trends that took a toll on the membership of the United Society, Shaker villages attracted tourists seeking oases of reassuring nostalgia amid a landscape of unrestrained progress. The public, which had once vilified Believers and ridiculed their doctrines, now crowded into Shaker meetinghouses to experience worship services animated by testimonies and songs. Many Shaker villages catered to the visitors' expectations of quaintness by opening gift shops in which Sisters sold "poplarware" pin cushions, jewelry cases, sewing boxes, and quaint dolls dressed in traditional Shaker garb.

As the number of Shaker villages dwindled during the 20th century, preservationists worked to save remnants of the Shaker heritage. Clara Endicott Sears, for example, took up the cause in 1920; she moved the Trustees' Office, where the community transacted its business with the outside world, from its location at the former Harvard, Mass., Shaker community to the nearby Fruitlands Museum, also in Harvard. Among the fine pieces of Shaker furniture that Sears displayed at Fruitlands was a rocking chair associated with the religion's founder, Mother Ann Lee. Faith and Edward Deming Andrews, historians and collectors of Shaker objects, extended the

transformation from religious communities to cultural commodities after they stumbled on a treasure trove of antiques during a visit to the Hancock Shaker village near Pittsfield, Mass., in 1923. Thanks in part to the interest in the Shakers fostered by the couple's efforts, a group of local citizens purchased the Hancock property from the Shakers and in 1960 opened the site to the public as a museum.

Today, tourists can also visit Shaker museums in Enfield and Canterbury, N.H. Thousands of visitors come each year to tour the buildings, walk the grounds, participate in workshops, watch craft demonstrations, buy reproduction Shaker furniture, listen to Shaker music, eat Shaker meals, and perhaps even sleep in a Shaker dwelling. The attraction is not so much Shakerism as a religion but Shakerism as a reflection of a lost New England—quaint, simple, rural, pastoral, communal. World's people come for these same reasons to the Sabbathday Lake Shaker community of Maine, which is still home to a small but active group of Shakers. Here, however, visitors also have the opportunity to appreciate the site as a religious community inhabited by Believers who still practice the faith first brought to New England more than two centuries ago.

Flo Morse, *The Shakers and the World's People* (1980); Stuart Murray, *Shaker Heritage Guidebook: Exploring the Historic Sites, Museums and Collections* (1994); John F. Sears, *Sacred Places: American Tourist Attractions in the 19th Century* (1989); Stephen J. Stein, *The Shaker Experience in America: A History of the United Society of Believers* (1992).

David L. Richards

Shelburne Museum Shelburne Museum, located in Shelburne, Vt., presents early American life and culture in a distinctive way. A collection of historic houses, community buildings, and galleries illustrate many of the social and cultural developments of 19th-century America. At first glance, Shelburne Museum, founded in 1947, appears to be a well-preserved New England town. A covered bridge leads to a cluster of houses and barns, while nearby stand a schoolhouse, meetinghouse, blacksmith shop, and general store. But unlike other outdoor museums founded in the same era, Shelburne Museum features the juxtaposition of 19th-century architecture with 20th-century technology: an 1871 lighthouse on a lawn next to the 1906 steamboat *Ticonderoga;* an 1890 railroad depot near a 1920s carousel; and a round barn on a hill overlooking them all.

Electra Havemeyer Webb, the founder of Shelburne Museum, saw the beauty of the New England experience in the everyday forms of carriages, weathervanes, trade signs, salt-glazed jugs, dolls, scrimshaw, carousel animals, cigar store figures, and quilts. Webb lived during the 1920s and 1930s when public appreciation of American architecture and decorative arts was growing and when philanthropists were developing visitor parks dedicated to American heritage. Guided by the extensive fine art collecting of her parents, the sugar magnate Henry O. Havemeyer and his wife, Louisine, Electra Webb started her museum on 14 acres of unused farmland near the country estate of Dr. William Seward and Lila Vanderbilt Webb, whose son, James Watson, Webb married. Choosing to collect American folk art rather than European paintings as her parents had done, Webb considered folk art to be the "self-expression that has welled up from the hearts and hands of the people."

An eclectic arrangement of American architecture, art, and artifacts is exhibited throughout 45 acres of panoramic vistas and historic plantings. From the start, Shelburne Museum was assembled as a vast, three-dimensional collage of buildings and collections. Community buildings, farm structures, and village homes from throughout New England, including an 1840 horse and carriage stand from the Shaker community in Canterbury, N.H., were painstakingly moved to Shelburne and refurbished with exhibit galleries, historic interiors, or both. A Greek Revival farmhouse in Orwell, Vt., was reproduced on site in the 1960s to accommodate the replication of six rooms from the Webbs' Manhattan apartment. The interiors feature various impressionist paintings collected by Electra's parents as well as family memorabilia.

A collector's vision has become a nationally acclaimed institution with 80,000 examples of historic art, architecture, and artifacts that are interpretively combined into thematic guided tours, lecture programs, college courses, day camps, exhibits, workshops, and publications.

Eloise Beil, "The Shelburne Museum Story," *Quilts from the Shelburne Museum* (1996); Lauren B. Hewes and Celia Y. Oliver, *To Collect in Earnest: The Life and Work of Electra Havemeyer Webb* (1997).

Mimi Faulders Clark

Strawbery Banke Museum The Strawbery Banke Museum, in Portsmouth, N.H., is an outdoor history museum that occupies 10 acres and comprises more than 40 buildings. Opened to the public in 1965, it traces three centuries of cultural change in a continuously occupied neighborhood and is dedicated to studying the lives of ordinary people who left their mark on Portsmouth's history. The museum's curious name is a revival of the city's briefly used original name from the 1630s, derived from the profusion of wild berries found by early settlers on the banks of the adjacent Piscataqua River. The museum neighborhood itself was called Puddle Dock from the 18th through the 20th centuries, during which time it evolved from working waterfront to residential backwater.

The historic buildings of the museum are preserved and used in several ways. Ten have been restored and furnished as historic houses, portraying periods ranging from the revolutionary era to the Cold War. Others serve as topical galleries on such subjects as architectural structure, historic archaeology, and the "homefront battlefield" of World War II. A few buildings house demonstrations of traditional trades like boat building, pottery making, and coopering, while the balance accommodate staff offices, are rented, or await restoration. The restored yards and gardens surrounding the structures represent landscape design from 1720 to 1944.

In the 1950s Portsmouth's housing authority designated the blue-collar neighborhood of Puddle Dock as a slum and a target for urban renewal. When the original plans for redevelopment were abandoned, local preservationists came forward. Bolstered by the efforts of the Portsmouth librarian Dorothy Vaughan, who called attention to the rich history of the neighborhood, a new plan was adopted to make the area a historic museum. Professional consultants identified the surviving "slum" buildings as historic in themselves and in situ preservation was adopted as a goal. Consistent with the outlook of the era, only buildings built before 1850 were selected. The outdoor museum was envisioned as a northern Colonial Williamsburg, complete with costumed craftspeople.

When popular assumptions of a monolithic and shared national culture were challenged in the 1960s, historians responded by developing a new social history. Strawbery Banke in turn expanded its scope to encompass three centuries of tradition, addressing the roles that immigrants, widows, and laborers played in its development and history. During the American crafts revival of the 1970s, the museum's crafts demonstration program reached its peak, and during the 1980s the museum sponsored an annual women's history symposium. Amid rising national debate on the role and meaning of diversity in American culture, in the 1990s the museum cosponsored development of a black history trail, presented community forums on public issues including diversity, and opened the last of its 20th-century restorations, the Shapiro House, a Russian-Jewish immigrant family's home.

As the museum responded to the cultural forces around it, it also served as an example of preservation for the city of Portsmouth. When another urban renewal project swept away the North End of the city, a business partnership preserved a selection of historic buildings as an office enclave. Museum restoration inspired grassroots restoration in the adjacent South End, so that by 1970 the planned urban renewal demolition was irrelevant. The city of Portsmouth adopted an unusual historic district ordinance, which encompasses properties of all centuries and characters and illustrates the ways in which New Englanders perceive and preserve their history for the purposes of regional identity.

Raymond A. Brighton, *They Came to Fish: A Brief Look at Portsmouth's 350 Years of History* (1973); Richard M. Candee, *Building Portsmouth: The Neighborhoods and Architecture of New Hampshire's Oldest City* (1992); Valerie Cunningham and Mark Sammons, *Portsmouth Black Heritage Trail* (1996); John Mead Howells, *The Architectural Heritage of the Piscataqua: Houses and Gardens of the Portsmouth District of Maine and New Hampshire* (1965 [1937]).

Mark J. Sammons

Summer Resorts New England, perhaps the primary inheritor of the Puritan legacy, ironically also pioneered in creating places for summer resort and recreation. New England's Puritan forebears disapproved of many forms of amusement, setting their sights, rather, on the divine grace of God and the virtues of work. Many would doubtless have been horrified to see what was transpiring in Newport, R.I., and Nahant, Mass., by the early decades of the 19th century. New England was not the only region to sprout these early summer resorts, which typically hosted guests for extended stays from May through September and offered a wide range of indoor and outdoor activities for them. Saratoga Springs in New York and White Sulphur Springs in western Virginia were also beginning to draw visitors at that time. New England resorts, however, were among the first to offer the attractions of the seashore.

Many of those who visited places like Newport and Nahant in the early 19th century did so for their health. Some left homes made dangerous by summer heat and disease; others were following the advice of medical experts who believed that seawater could cure a variety of ailments and that a change of air could help restore health. Visiting a resort was, at that time, much like filling a doctor's prescription.

But the search for health proved only one motivation for visiting these resorts. Despite the misgivings of those who clung to Puritan ideals, amusement and recreation quickly became part of the picture. Invalids usually traveled in the company of family members who needed to be entertained, and most visitors were healthy enough to enjoy the amusements that resorts quickly began to provide. Bowling, billiards, and dances quickly became staples of resort life. Billiards was a game reserved exclusively for male guests, but women participated in most other forms of resort amusements.

For the most part, only wealthy people could afford to travel to a summer resort. Farmers could not abandon their farms, and artisans had neither the time nor the money for such a venture. Consequently, most early 19th-century resorts catered to the elite. Rich southern planters left their plantations in the hands of overseers as they packed up their families and headed for Newport. Members of Boston's literary and political elite, including the Quincy sisters (daughters of Harvard president Josiah Quincy), Charles Francis Adams (son of President John Quincy Adams), and the noted historian William Hickling Prescott, found their way to Nahant for extended periods during the summer.

By the middle of the 19th century, the face of New England's resorts was beginning to change. Mount Washington in the White Mountains of New Hampshire, for example, was touting tourist hotels by the 1840s. In 1848 guests started arriving at the Isles of Shoals, an archipelago 6 miles off the coast of Portsmouth, N.H., to visit such resorts as the Appledore House and to experience the lore of the islands' old fishing villages. The building of roads, canals, and, most important, railroads began to open up new areas for potential vacationers. The Civil War slowed the development of resorts somewhat, but in the postbellum years there was an explosion in the numbers of resorts and vacationers. In 1865 visitors to the Pequot Colony in New London

could enjoy the pleasures of the Connecticut shore. That year the *New York Times* explained that Brattleboro, Vt., had become "one of the most delightful of the smaller inland places of summer resort." Five years later, vacationers could choose hotels and boardinghouses along the entire Connecticut shoreline, from Greenwich to New London, where they would find "a fine combination of landscape scenery and water view . . . pure and invigorating atmosphere, and . . . all the pleasures of rural retreats and seacoast resorts at the same time." Not all descriptions of New England resorts were so complimentary. The *New York Times* reported in August 1880 that Bethlehem, N.H., was attracting "hay fever sufferers and exhausted brain workers" from Boston. The reporter admitted that Bethlehem "is not beautiful, nor is it a town. It is simply a long street leading from the White Mountains railroad depot." What Bethlehem did have to offer, however, was its location, situated both on a rail line and at "a central point from which to visit all the places of interest in the White and Franconia Mountains."

By the latter half of the 19th century, vacationing at summer resorts was no longer the preserve of the elite. Middle-class men and women increasingly found the time and resources for at least a week's respite from work and home during the summer months. Some professionals and small business owners managed to leave their practices or stores for a short period. Schoolteachers took advantage of the time between terms, and the increasing number of salaried, white-collar workers were granted a week's vacation.

Those who still harbored religious or ethical misgivings about the propriety of vacationing were heartened by the new ideas of some New England ministers. Once distrustful of nearly all forms of recreation, some religious men were beginning to recommend amusement to their parishioners. God, some argued, did not create people only for work and toil. Pleasure, too, was part of the divine plan. Recreation was also necessary to keep people fit for work; vacationers would return to their work restored and invigorated. Moreover, if innocent pleasures were not available, pleasure-starved people would, some feared, turn to the dangerous sorts of amusement that an increasingly urban, commercial culture was offering. A week in the country or by the seaside—time to reflect, heal, restore, and enjoy—was much preferable to the saloon, the theater, the circus, or, worse, the bawdy house. Some of New England's resorts grew out of Methodist camp meetings and catered specifically to a Christian clientele in search of healthful, innocent recreation. Others offered an array of activities—including tennis, golf, swimming, and bicycling—that reflected Americans' increasing interest in more vigorous and competitive physical activity.

Despite the growing numbers of resort communities that catered to a middle-class clientele, a small group of New England resorts continued to cater almost exclusively to people of great wealth. By the late 1800s, for example, the fabulously rich were congregating at Newport, where they built great mansions they referred to as cottages along the shoreline. In 1880 Newport opened its famous

Vacation cabins, Kittery, Maine, 2002

Casino, a private club where the elite could congregate and play. The Casino included not only clubrooms, private smoking and dining rooms, sitting rooms, and a restaurant but tennis courts, bowling alleys, and a ballroom. Between 1866 and 1872, Bar Harbor, Maine, grew from a field to a small, remote, low-key resort. Twenty years later, it was attracting the very wealthiest summer vacationers—people who built and patronized private boating, golf, and social clubs. Lenox, Mass., nestled in the Berkshires, also served as a favorite place of summer resort for elite New England families.

By 1900 many of New England's resorts were well established. In the early 20th century, however, some new resorts were established that served the needs of a new clientele. In 1908 Shearer Cottage in Oak Bluffs on Martha's Vineyard, for example, began welcoming African Americans who sought the pleasures of a summer resort. Middle-class black visitors came from New York, Boston, and Philadelphia to enjoy the cool weather, sea breezes, family-style meals, tennis courts, and front-porch views. The summer community of African Americans on Martha's Vineyard grew and prospered and remains today an important presence on the island.

By the 1920s, working-class white families were finding resorts along the New England shore that fit the limits of their pocketbooks. Since the late 1800s many had been making day excursions to places like Old Orchard Beach on the coast of Maine. While most still could not afford to stay in resort hotels or cottages, they could enjoy tenting at various campgrounds throughout New England. Libby's Oceanside Camp, between Long Sands Beach and York Harbor, Maine, for example, could accommodate hundreds of tents on its 4 acres of ocean frontage.

By World War II, summer resorts covered New England. The shore, the lakes, and the mountains received thousands of summer vacationers, representing all but the poorest of families. Although a few still remain active today, the majority have become defunct, as vacationers have shifted their funds and attention to personal summer cottages and condominium time-share accommodations.

Cindy Aron, *Working at Play: A History of Vacations in the United States* (1999); Dona Brown, *Inventing New England: Regional Tourism in the 19th Century* (1995); Adelaide M. Cromwell, "The History of Oak Bluffs as a Popular Resort for Blacks," *Dukes County Intelligencer* 26 (August 1984); Foster Rhea Dulles, *America Learns to Play: A History of Popular Recreation, 1607–1940* (1940); Richard Walden Hale, *The Story of Bar Harbor: An Informal History Recording 150 Years in the Life of a Community* (1949); Henry Beetle Hough, *Martha's Vineyard: Summer Resort, 1835–1935* (1936); Richard O'Connor, *The Golden Summers: An Antic*

History of Newport (1974); John F. Sears, *Sacred Places: American Tourist Attractions in the 19th Century* (1998).

Cindy Aron

Water Cures and Spas

New England plunged headfirst into the water cure vogue of the 1840s and 1850s. Two towns in particular—Brattleboro, Vt., and Northampton, Mass.—specialized in European-style hydropathy. Brattleboro's water cure opened in May 1845; by the following spring 400 patients jammed the town. Icy showers, group and solo baths under the trees and indoors, soaks, wraps, rubs, and drips made up the array of medically prescribed bath treatments. Simple food and beverages (no coffee, tea, alcohol, or tobacco) and miles of walking about the pretty town added to the rigorous regime. Patients also read, bowled, and played at billiards and charades; the cure even sponsored music lessons and formal balls, later adding a gymnasium. Boarding schools in town served the children of long-term patients.

Brattleboro's water cure, the nation's most posh, achieved nationwide fame as illustrious patients declared themselves healed of stubborn debilities. The poet Henry Wadsworth Longfellow, the editor Horace Greeley, the reformer Julia Ward Howe, and the novelist Fanny Fern became enthusiastic patrons. Like those who advanced other popular health reform movements, water cure enthusiasts tended to be involved in issues of social and political reform. Harriet Beecher Stowe stayed for almost a year, joined by her sister, the educator Catharine Beecher. Catharine Beecher also visited the Round Hill Water Cure located in Northampton, which opened in 1847 with facilities comparable to Brattleboro's. Another cure appeared in nearby Florence, Mass., run by David Ruggles, a blind African American abolitionist self-taught in medicine. The Ruggles Water Cure may have served as a stop on the Underground Railroad—Dr. Ruggles burned his papers to protect others' safety—but the Athol Water Cure was a known Underground Railroad sanctuary. When the Athol, Mass., cure's owner, the esteemed local physician and abolitionist Dr. George Hoyt, helped to free one young boy from slavery and then enrolled the lad in the local public school, the doctor faced such hostility that he traveled in town with a supply of rocks for self-defense.

Nearly 40 other water cures were scattered around New England. Massachusetts boasted additional cures at Sunderland, Lowell, Lynn (later moved to Waterford, Maine), Dracut, Boston, Westboro, Springfield, Easthampton, Harwichport, Fall River, Jamaica Plain, West Amesbury, North Adams, and East Medway.

Susan B. Anthony took the cure at Worcester, Mass., in the 1880s. In Vermont, Brattleboro's cure endured until 1871 along with cures at Manchester, Bennington, West Concord, West Randolph, and Clarendon Springs. In Rhode Island, water cures opened at Providence, Pawtucket, and Newport. Waterford, Maine; Meriden and New Haven, Conn.; and Concord, Franklin, Hill, and New Ipswich, N.H., all featured cures.

Orthodox medicine at the time specialized in harsh drugs, bloodletting, and blistering, which frequently did not lead to any improvement. Hydropathy, though sometimes bracing, offered a gentler alternative, as did movements like Thomsonian medicine, homeopathy, and Grahamism, all popular in antebellum New England. Women found relief at water cures from the lingering health effects of childbearing (and from new pregnancies, since they were often separated from their husbands), enjoyed more open relationships with their bodies and each other, and delivered babies more comfortably. Although today's medical standards throw doubt on the more drastic water treatments, sick women and men often recovered, perhaps from the wholesome food, cleanliness, relaxation, and exercise.

Most water cures survived a few years at best, but the meaning of the movement outlasted them. Antebellum Americans found their increasingly urban, industrialized society debilitating and longed for a romanticized agrarian past. Travel to pastoral New England for water cures inspired travel for pleasure alone. By 1852 the physician at Brattleboro had to advertise that his water cure was an infirmary, not just a fashionable resort. He had seen the future: water cures gave way to spas, which offered unique mineral properties and body treatments more for rejuvenation than for healing serious illnesses. Spas persisted into the 20th century, declined for several decades, then revived by century's end. Today New England's countryside hosts nearly two dozen spas, heirs of the curative pleasures of Brattleboro.

Susan E. Cayleff, *Wash and Be Healed: The Water-Cure Movement and Women's Health* (1987); Jane B. Donegan, *Hydropathic Highway to Health: Women and Water-Cure in Antebellum America* (1986); Kathryn Kish Sklar, "All Hail to Pure Cold Water!" *American Heritage* 26 (1974); Harry B. Weiss and Howard R. Kemble, *The Great American Water-Cure Craze: A History of Hydropathy in the United States* (1967).

Rebecca R. Noel

White Mountains Attractions

The White Mountains region has been a destination for summer visitors since the early 1800s and a winter resort since the 1930s. Today, people travel to the White Mountains during the summer and fall seasons for a variety of reasons, including day visits to 17 attractions promoted by the White Mountains Attractions Association. Each year, these White Mountains Attractions host approximately 2.2 million visitors between late June and the last vestiges of the fall foliage season. The 17 attractions can be grouped into four categories: family attractions, mountain rides, tours, and natural attractions.

The term *family attractions* refers to places where the majority of patrons are family parties including young children. Clark's Trading Post provides an opportunity to view trained bears as the sounds of antique music machines fill the air; Heritage New Hampshire allows visitors to experience 350 years of New Hampshire history in a climate-controlled setting; Santa's Village is a children's amusement park with numerous activities and exhibits with a Christmas theme; Six Gun City is a re-created western city with a water park; Story Land is a theme park with children's fairy tales as its focus; and Whale's Tale Water Park offers a wave pool, a lazy river, and waterslides.

The mountain rides offer visitors the opportunity to reach the top of several of the region's mountains quickly and effortlessly. From the summits, one can view the area's rugged landforms and diverse biotic life. The Cannon Mountain Aerial Tramway carries as many as 80 passengers to the summit of Cannon Mountain, 4,200 feet above sea level; the Attitash Bear Peak chairlift affords visitors an excellent view and the option of a ride on an alpine slide during the return trip; and the Mount Washington Cog Railway provides a steam engine–powered trip up the second-steepest railway track in the world. One can take the Mount Washington Auto Road in the family car or board a van to the summit of the Northeast's highest peak.

There are several tours available to visitors. On Lake Winnipesaukee one may tour the state's largest lake aboard the 230-foot M/S *Mount Washington* or one of its smaller sister vessels. Two railroad rides are also available: the Conway Scenic Railroad, offering views of the Intervale and spectacular Crawford Notch, and the Hobo Railroad, which travels along the Pemigewasset River.

Among the natural attractions are opportunities to view the workings of two of nature's most powerful landform sculpting agents: ice and water. In Lost River Gorge and the Polar Caves Park visitors can hike and crawl among huge boulders deposited by the same glaciers that shaped the topography of the northeastern states and southern Canada. The Flume Gorge provides visitors with a view of a spectacular chasm created by the erosive power of rushing water; beautiful waterfalls also await visitors to this attraction.

These and other natural and recreational attractions in the White Mountains region reflect the 20th-century shift in tourism from the grand hotels to middle-class auto touring and family entertainment. The White Mountain Attractions preserve a distinctive niche by capitalizing on spectacular settings that theme parks in urban or suburban settings cannot offer.

Frank Kenison and Sherman Adams, *The Enterprise of the North Country of New Hampshire* (1980); *The Official New Hampshire Guidebook* (1998); White Mountains Attractions Association, *The Official White Mountains Map and Guide* (1998).

Mark J. Okrant and Richard F. Hamilton

Woodstock, Vt. When people call to mind places that distill the essence of New England, Woodstock, Vt., usually ranks high on the list. This rural town in the foothills of the Green Mountains has a population of 4,798 (2000). Nestled in the Ottauquechee River valley in the east central part of the state, along U.S. Route 4, Woodstock has long been a magnet for tourists. Visitors flock to the area especially during fall foliage season, but also during other months, except for "mud season." With its splendid oval-shaped town green and architectural specimens ranging from the Romanesque Norman Williams Public Library to the classic Congregational church, Woodstock seems to embody a timeless ideal. Weary moderns regularly seek rest and relaxation in this enclave of bucolic beauty.

Much of the credit for this timeless quality is due to a few individuals who took steps to arrest unchecked development. In 1869 the railroad financier and lawyer Frederick Billings purchased the homestead of the noted ecologist and diplomat George Perkins Marsh and restored the farm and surrounding lands. Today Billings Farm and Museum is a living history agricultural museum. From the mid-1930s on, Laurance and Mary Rockefeller invested large sums of their oil and banking fortune in the Woodstock area, cushioning the impact of modern technology and contemporary styles on the village. From their own mansion on Elm Street to the impressive Woodstock Inn on the green to the Woodstock Country Club to the south, Woodstock bears the imprint of the Rockefellers' vision. Additionally, Harold and Elizabeth Connor founded the Ottauquechee River Restoration Fund in the mid-1980s to preserve the river and certain buildings in the village. For the most part, the town selectmen and zoning board have supported these philanthropic efforts.

Other sections of the town mirror the beauty of the central village. South Woodstock, in addition to being home to the Kedron Valley Inn, has hosted three important educational institutions. The Green Mountain Perkins Academy drew students in the last half of the 1800s; from 1955 until 1980 Woodstock Country School offered its students a rather unstructured format of academics and arts. On Church Hill Road southwest of the village stands the Vermont Institute of Natural Science with its renowned Raptor Center. Both West Woodstock and Taftsville, located to the east on Route 4, boast picturesque wooden covered bridges. Vermont's second-largest city, Rutland, lies 35 miles west and Hanover, N.H., the home of Dartmouth College, is 25 miles east.

For all of its idyllic qualities, however, disputes have plagued Woodstock over time. As in many New England towns, Woodstock settlers of 1761 contended over parcels of land, road repairs, and schooling responsibilities. By the 1790s, the town became a "shire town," or county seat, for Windsor County and eventually became the site of a correctional center. Throughout the 19th century, Woodstock was a bustling agricultural and commercial center and had the usual complement of Protestant denominations, a medical college, temperance and literary societies, and even a few spiritualists. In recent times the debates have centered on the development of condominiums to the east of the village, traffic congestion, and commercialization along Route 4. Still, many would agree with the 19th-century senator Jacob Collamer's remark, "The good people of Woodstock have less incentive than others to yearn for heaven."

Henry Swan Dana, *The History of Woodstock, Vermont, 1761–1886* (1980 [1889]); Peter S. Jennison, *The History of Woodstock, Vermont, 1890–1983* (1985); Marjorie Ryerson, "The Billings Farm and Museum," *Vermont Life* 38 (1984); Robin W. Winks, *Laurance S. Rockefeller, Catalyst for Conservation* (1997).

Thomas L. Altherr

CONTRIBUTORS

Gretchen A. Adams, Texas Tech University

Jay Adams, Old Fort Western

Efrain Agosto, Hartford Theological Seminary

Karin Aguilar-San Juan, MacAlester College

Janice M. Alberghene, Fitchburg State College

Karen Alexander, University of New Hampshire

E. John B. Allen, Plymouth State University

James P. Allen, California State University, Northridge

Onésimo T. Almeida, Brown University

Thomas L. Altherr, Metropolitan State College of Denver

Susan Alves, Rockport, Mass., High School

Angel Amy-Moreno, Roxbury Community College

Bishop Craig B. Anderson, Saint Paul's School

David Anderson, Society for the Protection of New Hampshire Forests

Virginia DeJohn Anderson, University of Colorado, Boulder

Joyce Antler, Brandeis University

Diane Apostolos-Cappadona, Georgetown University

Patricia Appelbaum, independent scholar

Deborah Applegate, Yale University

*deceased
**retired

Elaine Apthorp, Milton Academy

Arnold Arluke, Northeastern University

Dexter Arnold, New Hampshire AFL-CIO

Cindy Aron, University of Virginia

Robert Atkinson, University of Southern Maine

Craig D. Atwood, Home Moravian Church, Winston-Salem, N.C.

Charles Bahne, Boston Street Railway Association

Brigitte Bailey, University of New Hampshire

Anne Baker, North Carolina State University

James W. Baker, Alden House Historic Site

Bruce Ballenger, Boise State University

William A. Baller, Worcester Polytechnic Institute

Joan Bamberger, Wellesley College

Elliott R. Barkan, California State University, San Bernadino

Rebecca Barnes, Boston Redevelopment Authority

Hal S. Barron, Harvey Mudd College

William David Barry, Maine Historical Society

Robert Battistini, Franklin and Marshall College

Jennifer Beard, University of New Hampshire

Barbara Beatty, Wellesley College

James Beauchesne, Lawrence Heritage State Park

Horace P. Beck, Middlebury College*

Jane C. Beck, Vermont Folklife Center

Lawrence Becker, California State University, Northridge

Henry F. Bedford, independent scholar

Susan F. Beegel, Williams College–Mystic Seaport

Pamela J. Belanger, independent scholar

John Bell, Emerson College

Michael E. Bell, Rhode Island Folklife Project

Richard J. Bell, Harvard University

Ellen S. Bennett, Brookside Gardens

Christopher Berkeley, independent scholar

Dianne Bilyak, Yale University

Nancy Johnson Black, Metropolitan State University

Amy L. Blair, Marquette University

Karen J. Blair, Central Washington University

Michael D. Blanchard, Bingham McCutchen LLP

Stanislaus A. Blejwas, Central Connecticut State University**

Adrienne Fried Block, City University of New York

Laurie K. Blunsom, Minnesota State University, Moorhead

Madeline Bodin, independent scholar

Michele H. Bogart, Stony Brook University

W. Jeffrey Bolster, University of New Hampshire

Karen A. Bordeleau, University of Rhode Island

Harold W. Borns, Jr., University of Maine

Martha Gilman Bower, Indiana University of Pennsylvania

Trina Evarts Bowman, Wadsworth Atheneum

Jeanne Boydston, University of Wisconsin, Madison

Richard Bradley, Central Methodist University

David Bradt, New Hampshire College

Kathleen J. Bragdon, College of William and Mary

Gerard J. Brault, Pennsylvania State University

Louise A. Breen, Kansas State University

Kenneth A. Breisch, University of Southern California

Susan Roth Breitzer, University of Iowa

Catherine A. Brekus, University of Chicago

Francis J. Bremer, Millersville University

Sheila A. Brennan, George Mason University

Robert Bresnik, Azdak's Garden/Puppetsweat Theater

David Brody, West Chester University

John L. Brooke, Ohio State University

Ben Brooks, Emerson College

Joanna Brooks, University of Texas, Austin

Carrie Brown, independent scholar

Dona Brown, University of Vermont

Elspeth Brown, University of Toronto

Mary Ellen Brown, Indiana University

Alfred L. Brophy, University of Alabama School of Law

Michael E. Broyles, Pennsylvania State University

Cecelia Bucki, Fairfield University

Ann C. Bucklin, University of New Hampshire

Lynda K. Bundtzen, Williams College

Edward M. Burns, William Paterson University

Gerald T. Burns, Franklin Pierce College

Sarah Burns, Indiana University

Colin Burke, University of Maryland, Baltimore County**

Richard Lyman Bushman, Columbia University

Jon Butler, Yale University

Joyce Butler, independent scholar

Stephen L. Cabral, Bridgewater State College

Geoffrey S. Cahn, Yeshiva University High School, New York

Colin G. Calloway, Dartmouth College

Roseanne V. Camacho, Midway College

Ardis Cameron, University of Southern Maine

Thomas J. Campanella, University of North Carolina, Chapel Hill

Richard M. Candee, Boston University

Jane Caputi, Florida Atlantic University

Joseph M. Carlin, Food Heritage Press

Bret E. Carroll, California State University, Stanislaus

Charles F. Carroll, University of Massachusetts, Lowell

John E. Carroll, University of New Hampshire

Andrew N. Case, University of Wisconsin

Philip Cash, Emmanuel College

Donna M. Cassidy, University of Southern Maine

Daniel Cavicchi, Rhode Island School of Design

David A. Cecere, University of New Hampshire

Pavel Cenkl, Plymouth State University

Father Peter A. Chamberas, Holy Trinity Church, Concord, N.H.**

Lee Chambers-Schiller, University of Colorado, Boulder

Jules Chametzky, University of Massachusetts, Amherst

Michael P. Chaney, New Hampshire Political Library

Perry Chapman, Sasaki Associates

Ann Charters, University of Connecticut

Gabriel J. Chin, James E. Rogers School of Law, University of Arizona

Aaron F. Christensen, Oklahoma State University

Drew Christie, University of New Hampshire

Susan Cifaldi, The Company of Fifers and Drummers, Ivorytown, Conn.

Wilma Reid Cipolla, State University of New York, Buffalo

Gregory Clancey, National University of Singapore

Charles E. Clark, University of New Hampshire

Christopher Clark, University of Connecticut, Storrs

Claudia Clark, Central Michigan University*

Mimi Faulders Clark, Shelburne Museum

Victoria Clements, College of Southern Maryland

Cynthia Close, Documentary Educational Resources, Watertown, Mass.

Dale Cockrell, Vanderbilt University

Marion J. Coffey, Brown University

Tristram Potter Coffin, University of Pennsylvania

Bruce Cohen, Worcester State College

Jacob Cohen, Brandeis University

Joyce Cohen, Simmons College

Arthur B. Cohn, Lake Champlain Maritime Museum

Henry S. Cohn, Connecticut Superior Court

Donald B. Cole, Phillips Exeter Academy

Christopher Collier, University of Connecticut

Bud Collins, *Boston Globe*

Christine L. Compston, independent scholar

Rita F. Conant, Portsmouth Athenaeum

Joseph A. Conforti, University of Southern Maine

Patrick T. Conley, Conley and Conley

Michael J. Connolly, Saint Anselm College

Thomas F. Connolly, Suffolk University

James L. Conrad, Jr., Nichols College**

Drew Conroy, University of New Hampshire

Thomas E. Conroy, Stonehill College

J. North Conway, Taunton, Mass., District Court

Michael P. Conzen, University of Chicago

Stephen Cook, Mashantucket Pequot Museum and Research Center

Nym Cooke, Eagle Hill School

Francesco Cordasco, Montclair State University

Steven H. Corey, Worcester State College

James M. Cornelius, University of Illinois, Urbana

Grace George Corrigan, Christa Corrigan McAuliffe Center

Pattie Cowell, Colorado State University

Stephen L. Cox, Indiana Historical Society

Béatrice Craig, University of Ottawa

Ralph J. Crandall, New England Historic Genealogical Society

Michael J. Crawford, Naval Historical Center

Russ Crawford, University of Nebraska, Lincoln

Joyce A. Cryan, Salem State College**

John T. Cumbler, University of Louisville

Abbott Lowell Cummings, Historic New England**

Maurice Cunningham, University of Massachusetts, Boston

Laura Cuozzo, independent scholar

Paul Albert Cyr, New Bedford Free Library

Souad Dajani, independent development consultant, Boston

Paul S. D'Ambrosio, Fenimore Art Museum

Priscilla S. Dana, Kyiv International School, Quality Schools International

David Danbom, North Dakota State University

Donna A. Danielewski, independent scholar

Jere Daniell, Dartmouth College

Bruce Colin Daniels, Texas Tech University

Colleen Davidson, ESPN

Mary Wallace Davidson, Sibley Music Library

Allen F. Davis, Temple University

Gainor B. Davis, Vermont Historical Society

William Patrick Day, Oberlin College

David B. Dearinger, Boston Athenaeum

Richard M. DeGraaf, University of Massachusetts, Amherst

Crista DeLuzio, Southern Methodist University

David Demeritt, King's College, London

Todd A. DeMitchell, University of New Hampshire

George J. Demko, Dartmouth College

Claire W. Dempsey, Boston University

Patrick J. Deneen, Princeton University

Thomas Andrew Denenberg, Reynolds House Museum of American Art

Bert R. Denker, Winterthur Museum, Garden and Library

Jerry R. Desmond, Chattanooga Regional History Museum

James I. Deutsch, George Washington University

Elizabeth A. De Wolfe, University of New England

Mike Dickerman, Bondcliff Books

S. Lawrence Dingman, University of New Hampshire

Joanne Dobson, Fordham University

Maynard Weston Dow, Plymouth State University

Sarah T. Dowling, Adler Pollock and Sheehan P.C.

Anne M. Downey, independent scholar

Gregory K. Dreicer, Chicken and Egg Public Projects, Cambridge, Mass.

Martha Pellerin Drury, independent scholar*

Thomas Dublin, State University of New York, Binghamton

Timothy P. Duffy, Fredericksburg Academy

Cynthia Duncan, University of New Hampshire

*deceased
**retired

Sally Anne Duncan, Plymouth State University

Michael P. Dyer, New Bedford Whaling Museum

Jonna Eagle, Brown University

Steven C. Eames, Mount Ida College

Carolyn Eastman, University of Texas, Austin

John E. Ebel, Boston College

Susan Eckstein, Boston University

Editors of the *New England Journal of Medicine*

Matthew H. Edney, University of Southern Maine

Mary K. Bercaw Edwards, University of Connecticut

Robert L. Edwards, independent scholar

Linda Eisenmann, John Carroll University

Sarah S. Elkind, San Diego State University

David W. Ellis, Boston Museum of Science**

Jacqueline Ellis, Greenfield Community College

James W. Ely, Jr., Vanderbilt University

Robert P. Emlen, Brown University

Saul Engelbourg, Boston University

Peter Erbland, AIDS Action Committee, Boston

John Ernest, University of New Hampshire

Regina M. Faden, Saint Louis University

Lillian Faderman, California State University, Fresno

Christopher A. Fahy, Boston University

Ruth Farmer, Goddard College

Thomas J. Farnham, Southern Connecticut State University**

Patrick Feaster, Indiana University

Stuart Feder, Albert Einstein College of Medicine

Estelle F. Feinstein, University of Connecticut*

Burt Feintuch, University of New Hampshire

Michael Ferber, University of New Hampshire

William M. Ferraro, Southern Illinois University, Carbondale

Tracy Fessenden, Arizona State University

Peter S. Field, University of Canterbury, New Zealand

Daniel Finamore, Peabody Essex Museum

James Findlay, University of Rhode Island

Paul Finkelman, University of Tulsa College of Law

Fritz Fleischmann, Babson College

Margaret Henderson Floyd, Tufts University*

Michael S. Foley, College of Staten Island

Bonnie L. Ford, Sacramento City College

Ira Forman, National Jewish Democratic Council

Miriam Formanek-Brunell, University of Missouri, Kansas City

Ann Forsyth, University of Minnesota

William M. Fowler, Jr., Massachusetts Historical Society

John B. Fox, Jr., Harvard University

Lesley Lee Francis, independent scholar

Richard M. Francis, Brown University

Stuart M. Frank, Kendall Institute, New Bedford Whaling Museum

Paul B. Frederic, University of Maine, Farmington**

Ernest Freeberg, Colby-Sawyer College

Gwendolyn Freed, Greater Twin Cities Youth Symphonies

Diane P. Freedman, University of New Hampshire

William H. Freeman, Campbell University

Lucy M. Freibert, University of Louisville**

Hugh T. French, Tides Institute

Yves Frenette, York University

Donald R. Friary, Historic Deerfield

Rachelle Friedman, the Chapin School

Steve Frolking, University of New Hampshire

Harvey Frommer, Dartmouth College

Paul Gaffney, Landmark College

Robert B. Gagosian, Woods Hole Oceanographic Institution

Edmund Barry Gaither, Museum of the National Center of Afro-American Artists

Gregory J. Galer, Stonehill College

John S. Garner, University of Illinois, Urbana-Champaign

J. Ritchie Garrison, University of Delaware

James L. Garvin, New Hampshire Division of Historical Resources

Michael Gass, University of New Hampshire

Edith B. Gelles, Stanford University

Andrew W. German, Mystic Seaport Museum

Leslee K. Gilbert, Saint Mary's University of Minnesota

John Gilgun, Missouri Western State College**

Ross Gittell, University of New Hampshire

Leah Blatt Glasser, Mount Holyoke College

Stephen D. Glazier, University of Nebraska

J. Denis Glover, Bentley College

*deceased
**retired

Hal Goldman, University of Hartford

Larry Goldsmith, Hiram College

Carolyn M. Goldstein, Lowell National Historical Park

Lynda Goldstein, Pennsylvania State University

Warren Goldstein, University of Hartford

Rita K. Gollin, State University of New York, Geneseo

Robert G. Goodby, Franklin Pierce College

Lawrence B. Goodheart, University of Connecticut, Hartford

Glenn Gordinier, Mystic Seaport Museum

David Gordis, Hebrew College

Robert B. Gordon, Yale University

Joshua Goren, Columbia University

Trudie Grace, Putnam County Historical Society and Foundry School Museum, Fashion Institute of Technology

Nancy Price Graff, independent scholoar

Ellsworth S. Grant, independent scholar

Carol Hurd Green, Boston College

Harvey Green, Northeastern University

Scott E. Green, independent scholar

Steve Green, University of North Carolina, Chapel Hill

Briann G. Greenfield, Central Connecticut State University

Helen M. Greenwald, New England Conservatory of Music

Richard Greenwood, Rhode Island Historical Preservation and Heritage Commission

Farah Jasmine Griffin, Columbia University

*deceased
**retired

Jody Grimes, University of New Hampshire

Kali N. Gross, Drexel University

Laurence F. Gross, University of Massachusetts, Lowell

Kathryn Grover, independent scholar

Owen Grumbling, University of New England

Rosemary Fithian Guruswamy, Radford University

Melanie Gustafson, University of Vermont

Dennis B. Hale, Boston College

Judson D. Hale, Yankee Publishing

David Hall, Harvard Divinity School

Peter Dobkin Hall, Yale University

Robert L. Hall, Northeastern University

Madeleine Hall-Arber, Center for Marine Social Sciences, MIT Sea Grant College Program

Marilyn Halter, Boston University

Richard F. Hamilton, White Mountain Attraction Association

Scott Hancock, Gettysburg College

Samuel B. Hand, University of Vermont**

Alix Handelsman, River Road Pediatrics, Bedford, N.H.

James F. Haney, University of New Hampshire

James P. Hanlan, Worcester Polytechnic Institute

Roger D. Hardaway, Northwestern Oklahoma State University

M. Jeffrey Hardwick, Smithsonian Books

Stephen Hardy, University of New Hampshire

Tamara K. Hareven, University of Delaware*

Richard P. Harmond, independent scholar

G. Anthony Harne, Saint John's College

Gillis J. Harp, Grove City College

Judith E. Harper, independent scholar

Scott Harris, U.S. Department of State

Sharon M. Harris, Texas Christian University

Susan K. Harris, University of Kansas

Dorothea Hast, Southern Connecticut State University

Bernice L. Hausman, Virginia Polytechnic Institute

Janet A. Headley, Loyola College of Baltimore

Marlene Elizabeth Heck, Dartmouth College

Holly Heinzer, Yale University

George N. Heller, University of Kansas**

John B. Hench, American Antiquarian Society

James Henson, U.S. Department of Agriculture, Natural Resources Conservation Services

Allison L. Hepler, University of Maine, Farmington

Mark Herlihy, Endicott College

Katherine Hermes, Central Connecticut State University

Cindee Herrick, U.S. Coast Guard Museum

Erica E. Hirshler, Museum of Fine Arts, Boston

Michael Hoberman, Fitchburg State College

Peter C. Holloran, Worcester State College

Sally C. Hoople, Maine Maritime Academy**

Adam R. Hornbuckle, independent scholar

Stephen Hornsby, University of Maine

Herbert G. Houze, independent scholar

Angela M. Howard, University of Houston, Clear Lake

Joan E. Howard, Petite Plaisance

Susanna Howe, independent scholar

Mark D. Howell, Northwestern Michigan College

D. Roger Howlett, Childs Gallery

Nian-Sheng Huang, California State University, Channel Islands

Major Ralph J. Huber, New Hampshire State Armory

Thomas C. Hubka, University of Wisconsin, Milwaukee

William E. Hudson, Providence College

Tina Hummel, American University

Bradford Hunter, George Mason University

Susie Husted, Long Island Pine Barrens Society

Louisa Iarocci, University of British Columbia

Robert J. Imholt, Albertus Magnus College

Benjamin H. Irvin, McNeil Center for Early American Studies, University of Pennsylvania

Raymond D. Irwin, Kent State University

Holly V. Izard, Worcester Historical Museum

Diane Jacobsohn, independent scholar

Donald G. Janelle, University of California, Santa Barbara

Jennifer L. Jang, Brown University

Eric Jarvis, King's College, University of Western Ontario

Jane McEldowney Jensen, University of Kentucky

Paul Peter Jesep, independent scholar

Charles W. Johnson, Vermont State Naturalist**

Markes E. Johnson, Williams College

Niki Johnson, Boston University

Ronna C. Johnson, Tufts University

*deceased
**retired

Violet M. Johnson, Agnes Scott College

Richard W. Judd, University of Maine

Sara C. Junkin, independent scholar

Daniel L. Kahn, Rhode Island State Council on the Arts

Joseph P. Kahn, *Boston Globe*

Eugenia Kaledin, independent scholar

Beverly H. Kallgren, independent scholar

Pearl Rock Kane, Teachers College, Columbia University

Wendy Tarlow Kaplan, Brandeis University

Lawrence J. Kapp, Marymount University

Beth A. Kaputa, independent scholar

Ronald Dale Karr, University of Massachusetts, Lowell

Allen Kaufman, University of New Hampshire

Adrianne Kaufmann, Liberty Mutual

Michael Kaufmann, Temple University

Richard Kazarian, Richard Kazarian Antiques, Providence

Barry D. Keim, University of New Hampshire

Lori Kenschaft, Boston University

Louis J. Kern, Hofstra University

Andrea Moore Kerr, independent scholar

Amy Kesselman, State University of New York, New Paltz

Karen Chai Kim, Center for Immigration Research, University of Houston

Bruce A. Kimball, University of Rochester

William Clayton Kimball, Bentley College

Benjamin King, Hunter College, City University of New York

Rita M. Kissen, University of Southern Maine

Susanne Klingenstein, Massachusetts Institute of Technology

Wendy Knickerbocker, independent scholar

Ellen Knight, independent scholar

John M. Kochiss, Mystic Seaport Museum

David Thomas Konig, Washington University

Maureen Konkle, University of Missouri

Victor A. Konrad, Carleton University,

Elizabeth Mankin Kornhauser, Wadsworth Atheneum

Diana Korzenik, Massachusetts College of Art

Wendy Kozol, Oberlin College

Michael Kranish, *Boston Globe*

Shepard Krech III, Brown University

Arthur Krim, Boston Architectural Center

Gary Kulik, Winterthur Museum, Garden and Library

Karen Ordahl Kupperman, New York University

Darcy Kuronen, Museum of Fine Arts, Boston

Ernest Kurtz, University of Michigan Medical School

John F. LaBranche, independent scholar

Gary Laderman, Emory University

Dean Lahikainen, Peabody Essex Museum

Lance D. Laird, Boston University School of Medicine

David R. Lampe, Harvard University

Jane Lancaster, Brown University

Andrew Lane, independent scholar

John Edward Lane, Wofford College

Joel Lang, *Hartford Courant*

Shelley R. Langdale, Philadelphia Museum of Art

Christopher Lauricella, Brimmer and May School

Estella Lauter, University of Wisconsin

Paul Lauter, Trinity College

Lucianne Lavin, Institute for American Indian Studies

Catherine Ann Lawrence, MidtownScholar.com

Russell M. Lawson, Bacone College

Linda Lear, George Washington University

Thomas E. Leary, Youngstown State University

William B. Leavenworth, University of New Hampshire

Bryan F. Le Beau, University of Missouri, Kansas City

Patrick M. Leehey, Paul Revere House

David K. Leff, independent scholar

J. Stanley Lemons, Rhode Island College

Robin Lent, University of New Hampshire

Jill Lepore, Harvard University

Joan Lester, Tufts University

Ronald Lettieri, Mount Ida College*

Marya R. Levenson, Brandeis University

Seymour Leventman, Boston College

Theodore Levin, Dartmouth College

Peggy Levitt, Wellesley College

Louise Levy, Appalachian Mountain Club

Jan Leo Lewandoski, Restoration and Traditional Building, Vermont

Thomas R. Lewis, University of Connecticut, Storrs

James M. Lindgren, State University of New York, Plattsburgh

Nancy Eagle Lindley, Annapolis Opera

Jill I. Linzee, Northwest Folklife

*deceased
**retired

Nathan R. Lipfert, Maine Maritime Museum

Leah Lipton, Danforth Museum of Art

Garet D. Livermore, New York State Historical Association/The Farmers' Museum

Ralph P. Locke, Eastman School of Music, University of Rochester

Martha Schmoyer LoMonaco, Fairfield University

Thomas Looker, Amherst College

Judith Livingston Loto, Laconia Historical and Museum Societies

Richard A. Loverd, Northeastern University**

Jason Loviglio, University of Maryland, Baltimore County

Mason I. Lowance, Jr., University of Massachusetts, Amherst

Margery Morgan Lowens, Johns Hopkins University**

Tristram Lozaw, freelance journalist, *Boston Rock* magazine

Roberta Lukes, independent scholar

Edward Lurie, Arizona State University

Maura Lyons, Drake University

Christine Brooks Macdonald, University of Colorado, Boulder

Lisa MacFarlane, University of New Hampshire

Robert L. Macieski, University of New Hampshire

Edith Nye MacMullen, Yale University

Robert Durwood Madison, U.S. Naval Academy

Michael L. Magoon, Radionics, Burlington, Mass.

Richard J. Maiman, University of Southern Maine

Patrick M. Malone, Brown University

Norma H. Mandel, Barnard College

Richard Mandel, Babson College

Martin J. Manning, Bureau of International Information Programs, U.S. Department of State

Alexandra Maravel, Central Connecticut State University

Paul D. Marsella, Salem State College

Ana Cristina Braga Martes, School of Administration, Getulio Vargas Foundation, São Paulo

Donald B. Marti, Indiana University, South Bend**

Geoffrey J. Martin, Southern Connecticut State University**

Rebecca Martin, Litchfield Historical Society

Russell L. Martin III, DeGolyer Library

Tyrone G. Martin, USS *Constitution* Museum**

Mark A. Mastromarino, Duke University Press

Stephen Matchak, Salem State College

Stephen May, independent scholar

André Mayer, Associated Industries of Massachusetts

W. Barksdale Maynard, Johns Hopkins University

Marc F. Mazzarelli, independent scholar

Louis Mazzari, Fatih University, Istanbul

Robert P. McCaffery, University of New Hampshire

Joseph M. McCarthy, Suffolk University

Alexis McCrossen, Southern Methodist University

Kate McCullough, Cornell University

Sheila McDonald, Maine State Museum

Mary Drake McFeely, independent scholar

William S. McFeely, University of Georgia**

Cliff McGann, independent scholar

Constance M. McGovern, Frostburg State University

Barbara A. McGowan, Ripon College

Robert L. McGrath, Dartmouth College

Walter G. McIntire, University of Maine, Orono

Thomas R. McKibbens, First Baptist Church, Worcester, Mass.

Scott L. McLean, Quinnipiac University

Edgar J. McManus, Queens College, City University of New York

Ryan McMillen, University of Texas, Austin

T. S. McMillin, Oberlin College

Sally McMurry, Pennsylvania State University

Martha J. McNamara, University of Maine

Wilson Carey McWilliams, Rutgers University

Michael E. Meagher, University of Missouri, Rolla

Richard A. Meckel, Brown University

Jeffrey L. Meikle, University of Texas

Joanne Pope Melish, University of Kentucky

David Meschutt, New York State Office of Parks

Fred Metting, University of New Hampshire

David R. Meyer, Brown University

Michael L. Mickler, Unification Theological Seminary

Wolfgang Mieder, University of Vermont

Jeffrey Mifflin, Massachusetts Institute of Technology

Stephen Mihm, University of Georgia

Jerome M. Mileur, University of Massachusetts, Amherst

John F. Millar, independent scholar

Angela Miller, Washington University

David C. Miller, Allegheny College

Glenn T. Miller, Bangor Theological Seminary

John M. Miller, Johnson State College

Naomi Miller, Boston University

Richard Miller, independent scholar

Willard M. Miller, University of Vermont

James F. Millinger, independent scholar

Eugene S. Mills, Whittier College**

Paul J. Miranti, Jr., Rutgers University

Maureen F. Moakley, University of Rhode Island

Scott Molloy, University of Rhode Island

Sy Montgomery, independent scholar

J. Michael Moore, independent scholar

William D. Moore, University of North Carolina, Wilmington

Keith N. Morgan, Boston University

James A. Morone, Brown University

Dane Morrison, Salem State College

Vincent G. Moscardelli, University of Massachusetts, Amherst

Marina Moskowitz, University of Glasgow

Barry D. Mowell, Broward Community College

Mary M. Moynihan, University of New Hampshire

Wayne Munson, Fitchburg State College

Kevin D. Murphy, City University of New York

Martha W. Murphy, South County Hospital, Wakefield, R.I.

Matthew P. Murphy, *WoodenBoat* magazine

Nancy Mykoff, Roosevelt Academy, Middleburg, the Netherlands

Paul C. Nagel, University of Minnesota, Twin Cities

Philip Nel, Kansas State University

Garrison Nelson, University of Vermont

Malcolm A. Nelson, State University of New York, Fredonia

Stan Neptune, Eel Clan, Penobscot Nation

Hankus Netsky, New England Conservatory of Music

Kathy Neustadt, independent scholar

Thomas Newkirk, University of New Hampshire

Cameron C. Nickels, James Madison University

Jessica F. Nicoll, Portland Museum of Art

Jana Nidiffer, University of Michigan

Kenneth Nivison, University of Northern Colorado

Dennis W. Nixon, University of Rhode Island

Rebecca R. Noel, Plymouth State University

Elizabeth C. Nordbeck, Andover Newton Theological School

Lisa Norling, University of Minnesota, Twin Cities

Suzanna Nyberg, independent scholar

Paul D. Nygard, Saint Louis Community College

Jane C. Nylander, Historic New England**

Richard Ober, Monadnock Conservancy

Jeffrey Karl Ochsner, University of Washington

James C. O'Connell, National Park Service

Shaun O'Connell, University of Massachusetts, Boston

Richard S. Offenberg, Northeastern University*

*deceased
**retired

Elisabeth D. Okrant, New School University

Mark J. Okrant, Plymouth State University

Julien Olivier, independent scholar

Rodney D. Olsen, Temple University

Ted Olson, East Tennessee State University

Stephen C. O'Neill, Pilgrim Hall Museum

Michael Oriard, Oregon State University

Nancy Grey Osterud, Schlesinger Library, Radcliffe Institute for Advanced Study, Harvard University

Robin O'Sullivan, University of Texas, Austin

Eleanor Kokar Ott, independent scholar

Barbara Owen, Boston University

Eric Robert Papenfuse, MidtownScholar.com

Steven H. Park, University of Connecticut

Peyton Paxson, Middlesex Community College

Edwin J. Perkins, University of Southern California

Scott J. Peters, Cornell University

Kristen A. Petersen, Pine Manor College

Wayne R. Petersen, Swarovski Birding

William N. Peterson, Mystic Seaport Museum

Paul R. Petterson, Central Connecticut State University

Kathleen Pfeiffer, Oakland University

Allen K. Philbrick, University of Western Ontario**

Stephanie Philbrick, Maine Historical Society

Daniel J. Philippon, University of Minnesota, Twin Cities

Julieanne Phillips, Wright State University

Simon Hart Phillips, University of New Hampshire

William D. Piersen, Fisk University*

Andrew L. Pincus, independent scholar

Carlton J. Pinheiro, Herreshoff Marine Museum*

Gerald L. Pocius, Memorial University of Newfoundland

Marc R. Poirier, Seton Hall University School of Law

Anne Marie Pois, University of Colorado, Boulder

Amanda Porterfield, Florida State University

Naima Prevots, American University**

Laura Prieto, Simmons College

Stephen Prothero, Boston University

Lisa Purcell, Princeton University

Sarah J. Purcell, Grinnell College

Jack Quinan, State University of New York, Buffalo

Michael P. Quinlin, Boston Irish Tourism Association

Michael S. Raber, Raber Associates

Bruce Radde, San Jose State University**

Patrick Rael, Bowdoin College

Millie Rahn, Heritage Partnerships/ New England

Peter E. Randall, Portsmouth Marine Society

Krista Ratcliffe, Marquette University

Roger G. Reed, independent scholar

Carl Reidel, University of Vermont**

Akim D. Reinhardt, Towson State University

Shulamit Reinharz, Brandeis University

Benjamin Reiss, Tulane University

Linda Smith Rhoads, *New England Quarterly*

David L. Richards, Margaret Chase Smith Library, Northwood University

Cynthia Watkins Richardson, University of Maine

Marilyn Richardson, independent scholar

Milda B. Richardson, Brandeis University; Northeastern University

Thomas A. Rider, U.S. Military Academy

Faye Ringel, U.S. Coast Guard Academy

Dilvo I. Ristoff, Federal University of Santa Catarina, Florianópolis, Brazil

Sarah Robbins, Kennesaw State University

George Roberson, University of Massachusetts, Amherst

Paige W. Roberts, Springfield College

E. Bruce Robertson, University of California, Santa Barbara

David M. Robinson, Oregon State University

Lillian S. Robinson, Concordia University

Paul A. Robinson, Rhode Island Historic Preservation and Heritage Commission

Karen Rockow, independent scholar

Alfred B. Rollins, Jr., Old Dominion University**

Joseph Romance, Drew University

Adam W. Rome, Pennsylvania State University

George K. Romoser, University of New Hampshire

Bruce A. Ronda, Colorado State University

Sarah Rooker, The Flow of History

Scott Roper, West Texas A&M University

*deceased
**retired

Julia Rosenbaum, Bard College

Debra J. Rosenthal, John Carroll University

Roy Rosenzweig, George Mason University

Guy Rotella, Northeastern University

Randolph Roth, Ohio State University

Barbara Rotundo, State University of New York, Albany*

Karen E. Rowe, University of California, Los Angeles

Jeffrey T. Royal, University of California, Berkeley

Lois Rudnick, University of Massachusetts, Boston

Thomas A. Rumney, State University of New York, Plattsburgh

Alexander Russo, Catholic University of America

Paula C. Rodriguez Rust, Hamilton College

James Emmett Ryan, Auburn University

Kent C. Ryden, University of Southern Maine

Philip L. Safford, Kent State University**

John Saillant, Western Michigan University

Matt T. Salo, Gypsy Lore Society

Sheila M. Salo, Gypsy Lore Society

Ora Frishberg Saloman, Baruch College and the Graduate Center, City University of New York

John A. Saltmarsh, Brown University

Mark J. Sammons, Wentworth-Coolidge Museum

David Sanjek, BMI Archives

Eric Schaefer, Emerson College

Elizabeth D. Schafer, independent scholar

Leonard Schlup, independent scholar

Leigh E. Schmidt, Princeton University

Bethany Schneider, Bryn Mawr College

Mark R. Schneider, Massachusetts Bay Commuter Railroad Company

Rear Admiral Richard W. Schneider, Norwich University**

Robert A. Schneider, Middle States Commission on Higher Education

Janet E. Schulte, Lesley University

Nancy Lusignan Schultz, Salem State College

Susan Scott, Dance Umbrella

Alice Scourby, Long Island University

Judith Sealander, Bowling Green State University

Paul Searls, University of Vermont

Ellery Sedgwick, Longwood University

Corey Seeman, University of Toledo

Howard P. Segal, University of Maine

Michael A. Seidel, Columbia University

Christopher Sellers, State University of New York, Stony Brook

Paul E. Sendak, U.S. Department of Agriculture, Forest Service

Siobhan Senier, University of New Hampshire

Gene Sessions, Norwich University

Gilian Ford Shallcross, Museum of Fine Arts, Boston

Douglass Shand-Tucci, independent scholar

Gregory L. Sharrow, Vermont Folklife Center

Karan Sheldon, Northeast Historic Film

Nancy Sherman, National Yiddish Book Center

Sarah Way Sherman, University of New Hampshire

Charley Shively, University of Massachusetts, Boston**

Valerie Shrader, Appalachian Trail Conference

David Shuldiner, University of Connecticut*

David B. Sicilia, University of Maryland

Stephen A. Siegel, DePaul University

Susan J. Siggelakis, University of New Hampshire

Charles Simic, University of New Hampshire

Linda Simon, Skidmore College

Brooks D. Simpson, Arizona State University

Steve Siporin, Utah State University

Lisa Sisco, Johnson and Wales University

Sheila L. Skemp, University of Mississippi

Winthrop C. Skoglund, University of New Hampshire**

Caleb Slater, Massachusetts Division of Fisheries and Wildlife

Cheryl A. Smith, University of New Hampshire

David C. Smith, University of Maine**

David M. Smith, Yale University

Mark C. Smith, University of Texas, Austin

Robert Alexander Smith, Pickering Middle School, Lynn, Mass.

Virginia A. Smith, Pennsylvania State University

Nancy Smith-Hefner, Boston University

Susan Smulyan, Brown University

Dean R. Snow, Pennsylvania State University

Pamela Snow, University of Maine

Daniel Snydacker, Jr., Pequot Library

Holly Snyder, Brown University

Stacia A. Sower, University of New Hampshire

*deceased
**retired

Bonnie B. Spanier, State University of New York, Albany

Jay P. Spenser, Boeing Commercial Airplane Group

Ann Morrison Spinney, Boston Collge

Rajini Srikanth, University of Massachusetts, Boston

Renny A. Stackpole, Penobscot Marine Museum**

Doug Stark, Naismith Memorial Basketball Hall of Fame

Bruce M. Stave, University of Connecticut

Sondra Astor Stave, independent scholar

Charlie St. Clair, Laconia Motorcycle Rally and Race Week Association

Harry Stecopoulos, University of Iowa

Stephen J. Stein, Indiana University

Theodore L. Steinberg, Case Western Reserve University

Lisa Stepanski, Emmanuel College

Carlene E. Stephens, National Museum of American History

Sheldon M. Stern, John F. Kennedy Library**

Maggie Stier, The Fells

James A. Strain, Northern Michigan University

Edmund B. Sullivan, University of Hartford

Bruce Sundlun, University of Rhode Island

Jan Susina, Illinois State University

Scott T. Swank, Canterbury Shaker Village

Darcy Sweeney, Salem State College

Kevin M. Sweeney, Amherst College

Nancy F. Sweet, Columbia University

Tracy Manforte Sweet, Saint Anselm College

Adam W. Sweeting, Boston University

*deceased
**retired

Etsuko Taketani, Institute of Modern Languages, University of Tsukuba, Japan

Richard S. Taskin, solo legal practice in North Adams, Mass.

Jon C. Teaford, Purdue University

Jennifer Tebbe-Grossman, Massachusetts College of Pharmacy

Eleanor Hollis Tedesco, University of Maryland

Paul H. Tedesco, University of Maryland

Philip G. Terrie, Bowling Green State University

John R. Thelin, University of Kentucky

Lamont D. Thomas, University of Bridgeport

Douglas M. Thompson, Connecticut College

Tamara Plakins Thornton, State University of New York, Buffalo

Robert M. Thorson, University of Connecticut

Daniel J. Tichenor, Rutgers University

Judith Tick, Northeastern University

Christopher Tirres, Harvey Mudd College

Frank Tirro, Yale University

Barbara L. Tischler, Horace Mann School

Jeff Titon, Brown University

Bryant F. Tolles, Jr., University of Delaware

Edith A. Tonelli, independent scholar

Nicole Tonkovich, University of California, San Diego

Mari Boor Tonn, University of Maryland

Christina Tree, independent scholar

Michael Triff, Environmental Careers Organization

Elizabeth Trowbridge, Bangor Historical Society

Emery H. Trowbridge, Western Carolina University

Carol Troyen, Museum of Fine Arts, Boston

John R. Tschirch, Preservation Society of Newport County

Arleen Marcia Tuchman, Vanderbilt University

Louis Leonard Tucker, Massachusetts Historical Society

Diana B. Turk, University of Maryland, College Park

Diane D. Turner, University of South Florida

Reed Ueda, Tufts University

Andrius Valevicius, University of Sherbrooke

John Vickrey Van Cleve, Gallaudet University

Susan R. Van Dyne, Smith College

Cynthia J. Van Zandt, University of New Hampshire

Yvonne Vissing, Salem State College

Susanna L. von Oettingen, U.S. Fish and Wildlife Service

Eleanor Wachs, independent folklorist

Gary E. Wait, Connecticut Historical Society

Timothy Walch, Herbert Hoover Library

Nancy A. Walker, Vanderbilt University*

William H. Wallace, University of New Hampshire**

Alan Wallach, College of William and Mary

Arlene M. Sánchez Walsh, Claremont Graduate University

James Walsh, Central Connecticut State University

Jeff Wanser, Hiram College

Sally K. Ward, University of New Hampshire

Marc Warner, Warner Transportation Consulting

Susan J. Warner, Dartmouth College

Charles Warren, Boston University; Harvard University

Matthew Warshauer, Central Connecticut State University

David H. Watters, University of New Hampshire

Erika V. Wayne, Stanford Law School

Nadine Weidman, Harvard University

Ellen Weiss, Tulane University

Kimberly Charmaine Welch, Saint John's University

Paul F. Wells, Middle Tennessee State University

Scott C. Wells, Lev and Berlin, P.C.

Mark I. West, University of North Carolina, Charlotte

Nancy Wetzel, independent scholar

Barbara A. White, University of New Hampshire**

John Kenneth White, Catholic University of America

John S. Whitehead, University of Alaska, Fairbanks**

Sheldon Whitehouse, Edwards and Angell LLP

Stephen J. Whitfield, Brandeis University

Ted Widmer, Washington College

*deceased
**retired

Peter H. Wiebe, Woods Hole Oceanographic Institution

Elizabeth Otterson Wiley, George Washington University

Christine B. Williams, Bentley College

F. Elaine Williams, Bucknell University

Gerry Williams, Studio Potter Organization, Goffstown, N.H.

Susan S. Williams, Ohio State University

Susan Williamson, Regis College

Leslie Perrin Wilson, Concord, Mass., Free Public Library

Lauren Frances Winner, Columbia University

Richard E. Winslow III, Portsmouth Marine Society

John Fabian Witt, Yale University

Mara R. Witzling, University of New Hampshire

Suzanne L. Wones, Harvard University

K. Scott Wong, Williams College

Joseph S. Wood, George Mason University

Thomas A. Woods, Making Sense of Place

Susan K. Woodward, National Board for Professional Teaching Standards

Walter W. Woodward, University of Connecticut

William E. Worthington, Jr., National Museum of American History**

Harold F. Worthley, Congregational Library, Boston

Vicki C. Wright, University of New Hampshire

John R. Wunder, University of Nebraska, Lincoln

Susan Anderson Wunder, University of Nebraska, Lincoln

Margaret R. Yocom, George Mason University

Josiah Ulysses Young III, Wesley Theological Seminary

Sandra A. Zagarell, Oberlin College

Rosemarie Zagarri, George Mason University

Donna Jean Zane, independent scholar

Wilbur Zelinsky, Pennsylvania State University

Edward F. Zimmer, Lincoln, Nebraska, Planning Department

Jonathan Zimmerman, New York University

Philip D. Zimmerman, independent scholar

David A. Zonderman, North Carolina State University

Michael Zuckerman, University of Pennsylvania

PHOTOGRAPH CREDITS

300 Edward Hitchcock, *The Power of Christian Benevolence Illustrated in the Life and Labors of Mary Lyon* (Northampton, Mass.: Hopkins, Bridgman, 1852), courtesy of David H. Watters

303 Courtesy of Milne Special Collections and Archives Department, University of New Hampshire Library, Durham

306 Courtesy of Hopkins School Archives, New Haven, Conn.

314 Courtesy of the New Hampshire Historical Society, Concord

317 Photo by David H. Watters

320 Courtesy of Yale University

329 Lydia Marie Child, *An Appeal in Favor of That Class of Americans Called Africans* (Boston: Allen and Ticknor, 1833), courtesy of UNH Photographic Services, Dimond Library, University of New Hampshire, Durham

342 Photo by Eric White, courtesy of the SALT Center for Documentary Studies Archive, Portland, Maine

348 Courtesy of Milne Special Collections and Archives Department, University of New Hampshire Library, Durham

361 Courtesy of the Library of Congress, Washington, D.C.

380 Photo by Dr. Angel A. Amy-Moreno de Toro

385 Photo by Heather Goldman, courtesy of the SALT Center for Documentary Studies Archive, Portland, Maine

405 Courtesy of the New Hampshire Historical Society, Concord

418 Photo by Noreen Hogan, courtesy of the SALT Center for Documentary Studies Archive, Portland, Maine

422 Photo by David Gavril, courtesy of the SALT Center for Documentary Studies Archive, Portland, Maine

427 Photo by Gary Samson, Instructional Services, Dimond Library, University of New Hampshire, Durham

430 Photo by Gary Samson, Instructional Services, Dimond Library, University of New Hampshire, Durham

435 Photo by Gary Samson, Instructional Services, Dimond Library, University of New Hampshire, Durham

439 Courtesy of the Osher Map Library, University of Southern Maine, Portland

448 Courtesy of Canterbury Shaker Village, New Hampshire

458 Photo by Patricia Bashford, courtesy of the Newburyport Maritime Society

461 Sterling and Francine Clark Art Institute, Williamstown, Mass.

465 Photo by Gary Samson, Instructional Services, Dimond Library, University of New Hampshire, Durham, N.H.

473 Edward Hitchcock, *The Power of Christian Benevolence Illustrated in the Life and Labors of Mary Lyon* (Northampton, Mass., Hopkins, Bridgman, 1852), courtesy of David H. Watters

481 Photo by Erin Miller, courtesy of the SALT Center for Documentary Studies Archive, Portland, Maine

486 Catharine Beecher, *A Treatise on Domestic Economy for the Use of Young Ladies at Home and at School* (Boston: Allen and Ticknor, 1841). UNH Photographic Services, Dimond Library, University of New Hampshire, Durham

500 Courtesy of AP / Wide World Photos

504 Sarah Josepha Hale, *Northwood* (Boston: Bowles and Dearborn, 1827), courtesy of Milne Special Collections and Archives Department, University of New Hampshire Library, Durham

515 *Godey's Lady's Book*, May 1854, 390, courtesy of Milne Special Collections and Archives Department, University of New Hampshire Library, Durham

517 Photo by Julia Rodriguez, courtesy of the SALT Center for Documentary Studies Archive, Portland, Maine

546 Courtesy of Osher Map Library, University of Southern Maine, Portland

562 Courtesy of James P. Allen

574 Courtesy of the Osher Map Library, University of Southern Maine, Portland

575 Photo by Claire Sullivan, courtesy of the SALT Center for Documentary Studies Archive, Portland, Maine

584 Courtesy of the Osher Map Library, University of Southern Maine, Portland

587 Photo courtesy of Bruce Radde

605 Courtesy of the Osher Map Library, University of Southern Maine, Portland

610 Courtesy of the Osher Map Library, University of Southern Maine, Portland

619 Courtesy of the Library of Congress, Washington, D.C., Prints and Photographs Division, Detroit Publishing Company Photograph Collection

622 Photos by Jean Thomson Black

623 Courtesy of the Osher Map Library, University of Southern Maine, Portland

629 Photo by Burt Feintuch

638 Courtesy of the Osher Map Library, University of Southern Maine, Portland

656 Photo by David H. Watters

657 Courtesy of the Osher Map Library, University of Southern Maine, Portland

660 Courtesy of the Osher Map Library, University of Southern Maine, Portland

662 Courtesy of the Osher Map Library, University of Southern Maine, Portland

665 Courtesy of the Osher Map Library, University of Southern Maine, Portland

669 Courtesy of Milne Special Collections and Archives Department, University of New Hampshire Library, Durham

677 Della R. Prescott, *A Day in a Colonial Home* (Boston: Marshall Jones, 1929), courtesy of David H. Watters

679 Photo by David H. Watters

683 Courtesy of the Massachusetts Historical Society, Boston

684 Courtesy of the New Hampshire Historical Society, Concord

692 Courtesy of the Osher Map Library, University of Southern Maine, Portland

694 Courtesy of the Osher Map Library, University of Southern Maine, Portland

699 Courtesy of the Dartmouth College Library, Hanover, N.H.

701 (Pierce) Courtesy of Milne Special Collections and Archives Department, University of New Hampshire Library, Durham

701 Courtesy of the Osher Map Library, University of Southern Maine, Portland

705 Courtesy of the Osher Map Library, University of Southern Maine, Portland

709 Courtesy of the Peabody Essex Museum, Salem, Mass.

711 Courtesy of the Osher Map Library, University of Southern Maine, Portland

715 Courtesy of the Osher Map Library, University of Southern Maine, Portland

718 Courtesy of the New Hampshire Historical Society, Concord

730 Photo by Susan Laity

733 Photo by David H. Watters

735 Photo by Carol Traester

748 Photo by David H. Watters

753 (Covered bridge) Courtesy of the Library of Congress, Washngton, D.C., Prints and Photograph Division, Historic American Engineering Record

753 Photo by David Scott Allen, Kittery, Maine

758 Photo by David H. Watters

769 Photo by Donald Hoople

771 *Harper's School Geography* (New York: Harper and Brothers, 1881), courtesy of the Osher Map Library, University of Southern Maine, Portland

775 *The New-England Primer Improved for the More Easy Attaining the True Reading of English* (Boston: Edward Draper, 1777), courtesy of David H. Watters

782 (Nutting) Courtesy of the Archives of the Wadsworth Atheneum Museum of Art, Hartford

782 Robert B. Thomas, *The Farmer's Almanack, Calculated on a New and Improved Plan, for the Year of our Lord, 1823* (Boston: J. H. A. Frost, 1823), courtesy of David H. Watters

798 Dudley Leavitt, *Leavitt's Farmer's Almanac (Improved) 1898* (Concord, N.H.: Edson C. Eastman, 1898), courtesy of David H. Watters

802 Photo by David Scott Allen, Kittery, Maine

826 Courtesy of UNH Photographic Services, Dimond Library, University of New Hampshire, Durham

828 Courtesy of the Osher Map Library, University of Southern Maine, Portland

843 Photo by David H. Watters

851 Photo by David Scott Allen, Kittery, Maine

858 Wallace W. Atwood, *New Geography, Book One* (Boston: n.p., 1922), courtesy of the Osher Map Library, University of Southern Maine, Portland

860 Courtesy of the Osher Map Library, University of Southern Maine, Portland

862 Photo by David H. Watters

865 Courtesy of Milne Special Collections and Archives Department, University of New Hampshire Library, Durham

870 Courtesy of UNH Photographic Services, Dimond Library, University of New Hampshire, Durham

874 Photo by Matthew Zontine, courtesy of the SALT Center for Documentary Studies Archive, Portland, Maine

887 Photo by Harold Shapiro

906 Photo by Susan Laity

919 *Opinion of the Superior Court of the State of New-Hampshire, in the case of the Trustees of Dartmouth College, versus William H. Woodward, Esq.,* courtesy of Milne Special Collections and Archives Department, University of New Hampshire Library, Durham

924 Courtesy of Milne Special Collections and Archives Department, University of New Hampshire Library, Durham

938 Courtesy of the collection of the Litchfield Historical Society, Litchfield, Conn.

943 Harriet Beecher Stowe, *Uncle Tom's Cabin; or, Life Among the Lowly* (Boston: Houghton, Mifflin, 1892), courtesy of David H. Watters

967 Louisa May Alcott, *Little Women; or, Meg, Jo, Beth, and Amy* (Boston: Roberts Brothers, 1869), photo by David H. Watters

971 *A Narrative of the Captivity, Sufferings and Removes of Mrs. Mary Rowlandson* . . . (Haverhill, N.H.: Nathaniel Coverly and Son, 1796), courtesy of Milne Special Collections and Archives Department, University of New Hampshire Library, Durham

983 (Emerson) Courtesy of Milne Special Collections and Archives Department, University of New Hampshire Library, Durham

983 Photo by David H. Watters

991 Courtesy of Milne Special Collections and Archives Department, University of New Hampshire Library, Durham

994 (Howells) Courtesy of Milne Special Collections and Archives Department, University of New Hampshire Library, Durham

994 [Seba Smith], *The Life and Writings of Major Jack Downing of Downingville: Away Down East in the State of Maine* (Boston: Lilly, Wait, Colman and Holden, 1834), courtesy of Milne Special Collections and Archives Department, University of New Hampshire Library, Durham

1000 Courtesy of Milne Special Collections and Archives Department, University of New Hampshire Library, Durham

1003 Courtesy of UNH Photographic Services, Dimond Library, University of New Hampshire, Durham

1005 Courtesy of Milne Special Collections and Archives Department, University of New Hampshire Library, Durham

1037 Courtesy of Special Collections and Archives, W. E. B. Du Bois Library, University of Massachusetts, Amherst

1045 Courtesy of the Osher Map Library, University of Southern Maine, Portland

1058 Nathaniel Bowditch, *The New American Practical Navigator . . .* (Newburyport, Mass.: Edmund M. Blunt, 1802), courtesy of the Peabody Essex Museum, Salem, Mass.

1062 Photo by Patricia Bashford, courtesy of the Newburyport Maritime Society, Massachusetts

1063 Courtesy of the Osher Map Library, University of Southern Maine, Portland

1069 Courtesy of the Herreshoff Marine Museum, Bristol, R.I.

1071 Courtesy of the Collection of the Hull Lifesaving Station, Massachusetts

1073 Courtesy of W. D. Barry

1075 Courtesy of the Library of Congress Prints and Photographs Division, Washington, D.C., Farm Security Administration, Office of War Information Photograph Collection

1080 Photo by Paul Rocheleau, courtesy of the Maine Maritime Museum, Bath

1083 Gilbert Haven and Thomas Russell, *Father Taylor, the Sailor Preacher* (Boston: B. B. Russel, 1872), courtesy of David H. Watters

1086 Courtesy of the Osher Map Library, University of Southern Maine, Portland

1089 Courtesy of the Portsmouth Naval Shipyard Museum, New Hampshire

1093 Photo by Lynn Kippax, Jr., courtesy of the SALT Center for Documentary Studies Archive, Portland, Maine

1097 Photo by Gary Samson, courtesy of Instructional Services, Dimond Library, University of New Hampshire, Durham

1098 Courtesy of the Herreshoff Marine Museum, Bristol, R.I.

1099 Copyright © 2004, Hartford Courant, reprinted with permission

1130 Courtesy of Caledonia Pictures

1145 *Jacob's Pillow Dance Festival,* photo by Paul Rocheleau, courtesy of Jacob's Pillow Dance Festival

1153 Printed by permission of the MacDowell Colony, Peterborough, N.H., ca. 2002, the MacDowell Colony and Milne Special Collections and Archives Department, University of New Hampshire Library, Durham

1160 Courtesy of James A. Strain

1165 (Bread and Puppet Theater) Photo by Ron Simon, courtesy of Bread and Puppet Theater, Glover, Vt.

1175 Photo by Burt Feintuch

1178 Photo by Dana Gillian, courtesy of the SALT Center for Documentary Studies Archive, Portland, Maine

1184 Courtesy of University of New Hampshire

1199 William Scott, *Lessons in Elocution; or, A Selection of Pieces in Prose and Verse, for the Improvement of Youth in Reading and Speaking* (Concord, N.H.: Hill and Moore, 1820), courtesy of David H. Watters

1211 Courtesy of Cummings and Good, graphic design for the International Festival of Arts and Ideas, New Haven, Conn., 2003

1213 New Hampshire Historical Society, Concord

1219 *The New England Republican Primer; or, A Safe and Sound Guide to the Art of Voting Right, to which is added the Republican Catechism, Etc.* (Boston; Republican Club of Massachusetts, 1905), courtesy of David H. Watters

1271 Photo by Michael J. Kelly

1285 "Poplar Views," courtesy of Canterbury Shaker Village, Canterbury, N.H.

1301 Photo by David H. Watters

1304 Jonathan Edwards, *A Narrative of Many Surprising Conversions in Northampton and Vicinity* (Worcester, Mass.: Moses W. Grout, 1832), courtesy of David H. Watters

1318 *Youth's Keepsake: A Christmas and New Year's Gift for Young People* (Boston: William Crosby, 1841), courtesy of David H. Watters

1330 Photo by David H. Watters

1339 Courtesy of the Library of Congress, Washington, D.C.

1351 Courtesy of the Osher Map Library, University of Southern Maine, Portland

1355   *The Works of Aristotle, in Four Parts* (Worcester, Mass.: Isaiah Thomas, 1792), courtesy of David H. Watters

1363   Courtesy of the Osher Map Library, University of Southern Maine, Portland

1376   Courtesy of Harvard Medical School, Office of Public Affairs, Cambridge, Mass., by Stu Rosner

1379   Photo by Gary Samson, Instructional Services, Dimond Library, University of New Hampshire, Durham

1382   Courtesy of Haffenreffer Museum of Anthropology, Brown University, Providence

1386   Courtesy of the Osher Map Library, University of Southern Maine, Portland

1395   Courtesy of the Massachusetts Historical Commission, Office of the Secretary of the Commonwealth, Boston

1422   Photo by Gary Samson, Instructional Services, Dimond Library, University of New Hampshire, Durham

1424   Courtesy of UNH Photographic Services, Dimond Library, University of New Hampshire, Durham

1431   Courtesy of the Lotte Jacobi Collection, University of New Hampshire, Durham

1432   Courtesy of Naismith Memorial Basketball Hall of Fame, Springfield, Mass.

1449   *Auto Route Distance Atlas of New England* (Springfield, Mass: Imperial Auto Supply Company, 1924), courtesy of the Osher Map Library, University of Southern Maine, Portland

1479   Photo by David H. Watters

1480   Photo by David Scott Allen, Kittery, Maine

1487   Photo by David H. Watters

1489   Photo by David H. Watters

1491   Photo by David H. Watters

1495   Photo by David Scott Allen, Kittery, Maine

INDEX